AMERICAN ART DIRECTORY™
1997-98

56th EDITION

The 56th edition of the AMERICAN ART DIRECTORY
was prepared by R.R. Bowker's Database Publishing Group

Senior Staff of the Database Publishing Group includes:

Vice President, Database Publishing
Leigh C. Yuster-Freeman

Research Director
Judy Redel

Managing Editor, Editorial
Beverley McDonough

Managing Research Editor
Anila Rao Banerjee

Senior Editor, Editorial
Pete R. Palac

Associate Editors
Mary-Anne Lutter
Brian Pickton
Margaret A. Halpin-Williams

Assistant Editor
Betty Wilkerson

Senior Research Editor
Joyce A. Washington

Research Freelance Coordinator
Sharon O'Brien

Associate Research Editor
Kia Sipp

Director of Tampa Operations
Val Harris

Production Manager
Debbie Wilson

Project Coordinator
Carolyn Ollariu

Associate Coordinator
Jennifer Wincey

AMERICAN ART DIRECTORY™
1997-98

56th EDITION

R.R. Bowker
New Providence, New Jersey

Published by R.R. Bowker, a division of Reed Elsevier Inc.
Copyright © 1997 by Reed Elsevier Inc. All rights reserved.

Darryl Fisher - Chief Operating Officer, BIS
Andrew W. Meyer - Publisher

International Standard Book Number: 0-8352-3819-9
International Standard Serial Number: 0065-6968
Library of Congress Catalog Number: 99-1016
Printed and Bound in the United States of America.

ISBN 0 - 8352 - 3819 - 9

9 780835 238199

Contents

Preface

The *American Art Directory,* first published in 1898 as the American Art Annual, continues in its tradition of excellence with the 56th edition. The directory is a standard in the field of art, and an indispensable reference to art museums, libraries, organizations, schools and corporate art holdings.

The information for the directory is collected by means of direct communication whenever possible. Forms are sent to all entrants for corroboration and updating, and information submitted by entrants is included as completely as possible within the boundaries of editorial and space restrictions. Information is provided by new entrants in response to questionnaires. In those cases where no reply is received, data is obtained from secondary sources, and an asterisk (*) is shown to the right of the institutional name. Alphabetizing in the directory is strictly letter-by-letter. Those museums, libraries, associations and organizations which bear an individual's name are alphabetized by the last name of that individual. Colleges and universities are alphabetized by the first word of their name, whether or not it is named for an individual.

Section I contains both Alphabetical and Geographic indexes. The National and Regional Organizations indexes are arranged alphabetically and contain 140 organizations which administer and coordinate the arts within the United States and Canada. Included here are libraries affiliated with these organizations. The Museums, Libraries and Associations indexes are arranged geographically, and contain listings for 2,013 main museums, 289 main libraries, 614 area associations, and 110 corporations with art holdings. There are an additional 1,455 listings for galleries, museums and libraries affiliated with main entries.

A classification key is printed to the left of each entry to designate the type:

 A—Association
 C—Corporate Art
 L—Library
 M—Museum
 O—Organization

The key "M" is assigned to organizations whose primary function is gathering and preserving the visual arts.

The "O" designation is given to national and regional organizations supporting the arts through sponsorship of art activities. The "A" code is given to those supporting the arts on a more local level.

Section II lists detailed information on 1,816 art schools, and college and university departments of art, art history, and architecture in the United States and Canada.

Section III provides reference to art museums and schools abroad, state arts councils, directors and supervisors of art education, art magazines, newspapers and their art critics, art scholarships and fellowships, open exhibitions, and traveling exhibitions booking agencies.

Section IV is composed of three alphabetical indexes; organizational, personnel, and subject. The subject index includes general art subjects and specific collections, along with the name and location of the holding organization.

Every effort has been made to assure accurate reproduction of the material submitted. The publishers do not assume and hereby disclaim any liability to any party for any loss or damage caused by errors or omissions in the *American Art Directory,* whether such errors or omissions resulted from negligence, accident or any other cause. In the event of a publication error, the sole responsibility of the publisher will be the entry of corrected information in succeeding editions.

Please address any suggestions, comments or questions to The Editors, *American Art Directory*, R.R. Bowker, 121 Chanlon Road, New Providence, New Jersey 07974.

Beverley McDonough, *Managing Editor*

April, 1997

I ART ORGANIZATIONS

Arrangement and Abbreviations

National and Regional Organizations in the U.S.

Museums, Libraries and Associations in the U.S.

National and Regional Organizations in Canada

Museums, Libraries and Associations in Canada

ARRANGEMENT AND ABBREVIATIONS
KEY TO ART ORGANIZATIONS

ARRANGEMENT OF DATA

Name and address of institution; telephone number, including area code.

Names and titles of key personnel.

Hours open; admission fees; date established and purpose; average annual attendance; membership.

Annual figures on income and purchases.

Collections with enlarging collections indicated.

Exhibitions.

Activities sponsored, including classes for adults and children, dramatic programs and docent training; lectures, concerts, gallery talks and tours; competitions, awards, scholarships and fellowships; lending programs; museum or sales shops.

Libraries also list number of book volumes, periodical subscriptions, and audiovisual and micro holdings; subject covered by name of special collections

ABBREVIATIONS AND SYMBOLS

Acad—Academic
Admin—Administration, Administrative
Adminr—Administrator
Admis—Admission
A-tapes—Audio-tapes
Adv—Advisory
AM—Morning
Ann—Annual
Approx—Approximate, Approximately
Asn—Association
Assoc—Associate
Asst—Assistant
AV—Audiovisual
Ave—Avenue
Bldg—Building
Blvd—Boulevard
Bro—Brother
C—circa
Cert—Certificate
Chap—Chapter
Chmn—Chairman
Circ—Circulation
Cl—Closed
Col—College
Coll—Collection
Comt—Committee
Coordr—Coordinator
Corresp—Corresponding
Cr—Credit
Cur—Curator
D—Day
Den—Denominational
Dept—Department
Develop—Development
Dipl—Diploma
Dir—Director
Dist—District
Div—Division
Dorm—Dormitory
Dr—Doctor, Drive
E—East, Evening
Ed—Editor

Educ—Education
Elec Mail—Electronic Mail
Enrl—Enrollment
Ent—Entrance
Ent Req—Entrance Requirements
Est, Estab—Established
Exec—Executive
Exhib—Exhibition
Exten—Extension
Fel(s)—Fellowships
Fri—Friday
Fs—Filmstrips
Ft—Feet
FT—Full Time Instructor
GC—Graduate Course
Gen—General
Grad—Graduate
Hon—Honorary
Hr—Hour
HS—High School
Hwy—Highway
Inc—Incorporated
Incl—Including
Jr—Junior
Lect—Lecture(s)
Lectr—Lecturer
Librn—Librarian
M—Men
Maj—Major in Art
Mem—Membership
Mgr—Manager
Mon—Monday
Mss—Manuscripts
Mus—Museums
N—North
Nat—National
Nonres—Nonresident
Per subs—Periodical subscriptions
PM—Afternoon
Pres—President
Prin—Principal
Prof—Professor

Prog—Program
PT—Part Time Instructor
Pts—Points
Pub—Public
Publ—Publication
Pvt—Private
Qtr—Quarter
Rd—Road
Rec—Records
Reg—Registration
Req—Requirements
Res—Residence, Resident
S—South
Sat—Saturday
Schol—Scholarship
Secy—Secretary
Sem—Semester
Soc—Society
Sq—Square
Sr—Senior, Sister
St—Street
Ste—Suite
Sun—Sunday
Supt—Superintendent
Supv—Supervisor
Thurs—Thursday
Treas—Treasurer
Tues—Tuesday
Tui—Tuition
TV—Television
Undergrad—Undergraduate
Univ—University
Vis—Visiting
Vol—Volunteer
Vols—Volumes
VPres—Vice President
V-tapes—Videotapes
W—West, Women
Wed—Wednesday
Wk—Week
Yr—Year(s)

*   No response to questionnnaire
†   Denotes collection currently being enlarged
A   Association
C   Corporate Art Holding
L   Library
M   Museum
O   Organization

National and Regional Organizations In The United States

O **AFRICAN AMERICAN MUSEUMS ASSOCIATION,** PO Box 548, Wilberforce, OH 45384. Tel 937-376-4611; FAX 937-376-2007; *Pres* Juanita Moore
Open Mon - Fri 9 AM - 5 PM. Estab 1978 to represent black museums around the country. Offers consulting & networking services. Sponsors annual conferences. Mem: 496; dues institutional $100-$250
Publications: Profile of Black Museums - A Survey; biannual directory; quarterly newsletter scrip for mem only

O **THE ALLIED ARTISTS OF AMERICA, INC,** National Arts Club, 15 Gramercy Park S, New York, NY 10003. Tel 212-582-6411; *Pres* Gary Erbe; *VPres* Fay Moore
Open Nov - Dec daily Noon - 5 PM. Estab 1914, incorporated 1922, as a self-supporting exhibition cooperative, with juries elected each yr by the mem, to promote work by American artists. Mem: 3601; dues $20 & up; annual meeting in Apr
Income: Financed by memorial funds, dues & donations
Exhibitions: Members' Regional AAA exhibitions; annual exhibition in the winter; Annual held at National Arts Club; numerous awards & medals; prizes total $16,000 each year
Publications: Catalogs; newsletter
Activities: Lect open to public, 1-3 vis lectr per year; gallery talks; competitions with awards

O **AMERICAN ABSTRACT ARTISTS,** 470 W End Ave, Apt 9D, New York, NY 10024. Tel 212-874-0747; *Pres* Beatrice Riese; *Treas* Katinka Mann
Estab 1936, active 1937, to promote American abstract art; develop & educate through exhibitions & publications; to provide forums for the exchange of ideas among artists. Mem: 75; dues $25; bi-monthly meetings
Income: Financed by mem
Publications: Books and catalogs
Activities: Lect open to the public; gallery talks; individual and original objects of art lent to responsible galleries, museums and universities; originate traveling exhibitions

O **AMERICAN ACADEMY OF ARTS & LETTERS,** 633 W 155th St, New York, NY 10032-7599. Tel 212-368-5900; FAX 212-491-4615; *Exec Dir* Virginia Dajani
Open Tues - Sun 1 - 4 PM during exhibitions, by appointment other times. No admis fee. Estab 1898 as an honorary mem organization of artists, writers & composers whose function it is to foster, assist & sustain an interest in literature, music & the fine arts. Formed by 1976 merger of the American Academy of Arts & Letters & the National Institute of Arts & Letters. Maintains reference library of books & papers of members. Average Annual Attendance: 6000. Mem: 250; mem is by election; no dues; annual meeting May
Income: $1,400,000 (financed by endowment)
Purchases: $80,000-$90,000 Hassam Speicher Purchase Program
Collections: Works by members
Exhibitions: Exhibition of Candidates for Art Awards; Exhibition of Paintings Eligible for Hassam Fund Purchase; Newly Elected Members & Recipients of Honors & Awards Exhibitions, art, scores & manuscripts; Richard Rodgers Awards in Musical Theater (competition); Special Exhibitions
Publications: Proceedings, annual; exhibition catalogs
Activities: Awards given; individual paintings & original objects of art lent to major museums

O **AMERICAN ANTIQUARIAN SOCIETY,** 185 Salisbury St, Worcester, MA 01609. Tel 508-755-5221; FAX 508-753-3311; Elec Mail jdc@mark.mwa.org. *Pres* Ellen S Dunlap; *Cur Graphic Arts* Georgia B Barnhill
Open Mon - Fri 9 AM - 5 PM, cl Sat, Sun, holidays & Fri after Thanksgiving. No admis fee. Incorporated 1812 to collect, preserve & encourage serious study of the materials of American history & life through 1876. Mem: 600 honorary; meetings third Wed in Apr & Oct
Income: Financed by endowment, gifts & grants
Purchases: $165,000
Collections: Early American portraits; Staffordshire pottery; †bookplates, †prints, †lithographs, †cartoons, †engravings; Colonial furniture; †photographs
Exhibitions: Temporary exhibitions
Publications: Monographs; newsletters; Proceedings, semi-annually
Activities: Undergraduate seminar in American Studies; lect; scholarships & fels offered; sales shop sells books
L **Library,** 185 Salisbury St, Worcester, MA 01609-1634. Tel 508-755-5221; FAX 508-754-9069; *Librn* Nancy Burkett
For reference only
Library Holdings: Vols 670,000; Per subs 691; Micro — Cards, fiche, reels; AV — A-tapes, rec; Other — Exhibition catalogs, manuscripts, original art works, pamphlets, photographs, prints, sculpture
Special Subjects: Art Education, Cartoons, Decorative Arts, Etchings &

Engravings, Graphic Design, Illustration, Manuscripts, Maps, Miniatures, Painting - American, Photography, Portraits, Printmaking, Prints, Woodcuts
Collections: †750,000 titles dating before 1877, including early American books on art & 20th century books & periodicals relating to the history & culture of the United States
Activities: Lect; seminar; fels offered

O **AMERICAN ARTISTS PROFESSIONAL LEAGUE, INC,** 47 Fifth Ave, New York, NY 10003. Tel 212-645-1345; *Pres* Leo Yeni; *Recording Secy* Susanne Hurt
Estab 1928 to advance the cause of fine arts in America, through the promotion of high standards of beauty, integrity & craftsmanship in painting, sculpture & the graphic arts; to emphasize the importance of order & coherent communication as prime requisites of works of art through exhibitions & publications. Mem: 1000; annual meetings
Income: Financed by mem
Exhibitions: Annually
Publications: AAPL News Bulletin, annually
Activities: Art shows open to public; competitions with awards

O **AMERICAN ASSOCIATION OF MUSEUMS,** US National Committee of the International Council of Museums (AAM-ICOM), 1575 Eye St NW, Ste 400, Washington, DC 20005. Tel 202-289-1818; *Chair* Robert Bergman; *ViceChair* Peggy Loar; *Pres* Edward H Able; *Dir Mary Louise Wood; *VPres Finance & Admin* Ed Brenner; *VPres Policy & Progs* Patricia Williams
Open 9 AM - 5 PM. No admis fee. AAM estab 1906, affiliated with US-ICOM in 1973, represents international museum interests within the United States & American museum interests abroad through the AAM/ICOM office which disseminates information on international conferences, publications, travel & study grants & training programs in AAM's newsletter, AVISO. Mem: 1000; members must be museum professionals or institutions
Income: Financed by mem
Publications: International Column in Aviso, monthly; ICOM News, quarterly (from ICOM Secretariat in Paris)
Activities: Specialty committees; annual meeting; international meetings; professional exchanges; bookstore sells books, catalogue available

O **AMERICAN ASSOCIATION OF UNIVERSITY WOMEN,** 1111 16th St NW, Washington, DC 20036. Tel 202-785-7700; FAX 202-872-1425; *Exec Dir* Anne L Bryant
Estab 1881 to unite alumnae of different institutions for practical educational work; to further the advancement of women, lifelong learning, & responsibility to soc expressed through action, advocacy, research & enlightened leadership. Mem: 150,000; holds biennial conventions
Income: $14,000,000
Publications: Action Alert, biweekly; AAUW Outlook, quarterly; Leader in Action, quarterly; brochures; booklets; research studies; study guides
Activities: Associations local branches develop & maintain programs in the arts. AAUW Foundation funds first professional degree in architecture, doctoral/post doctoral candidates in the arts

O **AMERICAN CENTER FOR DESIGN,** 325 W Huron St, Ste 711, Chicago, IL 60610. Tel 312-787-2018; FAX 312-649-9518; Elec Mail acdchicago@megsinet.net. *Pres* Meredith Davis; *Exec Dir* Mary Davis
Open Mon - Fri 9 AM - 5 PM. Estab 1927 as a non-profit organization of design professionals, educators & students. Mem: 2000; dues $125, student $50
Publications: 100 Show Annual; annual membership directory; biannual journal; quarterly magazine; videos
Activities: Educ Foundation; design office visitation program; conferences; seminars; symposia; annual design awards program; lect open to public; tours; competitions; awards; scholarships; originate traveling exhibitions

O **AMERICAN CERAMIC SOCIETY,** 735 Ceramic Pl, Westerville, OH 43081-8720. Tel 614-890-4700; FAX 614-899-6109; *Exec Dir* W Paul Holbrook
Open Mon - Fri 8:30 AM - 5 PM. No admis fee. Estab 1899 to promote the arts, science & technology of ceramics. Mem: 10,050; dues $50; annual meeting in May
Income: $2,000,000 (financed by mem)
Publications: American Ceramic Society Journal, monthly; Ceramic Engineering & Science Proceedings, bi-monthly; Journal and Abstracts, bi-monthly

O **AMERICAN COLOR PRINT SOCIETY,** 4109 Locust St, Philadelphia, PA 19104. Tel 215-222-6195; *Pres* Michael Kuncevich; *VPres* Idaherma Williams; *Treas* Kay Grever Lichty
Estab 1939 to exhibit color prints. Mem: 75; dues $20
Income: Financed by mem
Activities: Sponsors annual national members exhibition of all media color prints; 6 annual prizes

O **AMERICAN CRAFT COUNCIL,** 72 Spring St, New York, NY 10012-4019. Tel 212-274-0630; FAX 212-274-0650; *Board Chmn* Robert E Libby; *Vice Chmn* Jane Sauer; *Exec Dir Council* Michael W Monroe; *Ed-in-Chief American Craft Magazine* Lois Moran
Estab 1943 by Aileen Osborn Webb. Council presents nine national juried craft fairs annually, offers educational workshops & seminars as services to professional craftspeople, maintains special library on 20th century craft.. Mem: 32,000; dues $40
Income: Financed by mem, private donations & government grants
Publications: American Craft Magazine (formerly Craft Horizons), bimonthly
L **Craft Information Center,** 72 Spring St, 10012-4019. Tel 212-274-0630; FAX 212-274-0650; Elec Mail amcraft@interramp.com.
Open to ACC members Mon - Fri 1 - 5 PM. For reference only
Library Holdings: Vols 8000; Per subs 132; Journals 110; AV — A-tapes, cassettes, fs, motion pictures, slides 40,000, v-tapes 85; Other — Clipping files, exhibition catalogs 7500, original art works, pamphlets, photographs
Special Subjects: Ceramics, Crafts, Decorative Arts, Enamels, Furniture, Glass, Goldsmithing, Jewelry, Metalwork, Porcelain, Pottery, Silversmithing, Stained Glass, Tapestries, Textiles
Collections: Artists Registry & Archives: files for over 2000 craftspeople working in all media containing biographical material, slides & photographs (computerized access to the files provides indexes by artist name, geographical location, medium, process & function); Slide Study Collection: slide sets from ACC's slide & film service; newsletters & catalogs of craft organizations & educational programs on national, regional & local levels (computerized access by name, medium, location & type of organization); Archives of the American Craft Council and American Craft Museum

O **THE AMERICAN FEDERATION OF ARTS,** 41 E 65th St, New York, NY 10021. Tel 212-988-7700; FAX 212-861-2487; *Chmn* Elizabeth Blake; *Pres* Robert M Meltzer; *VPres* David Supino; *VPres* Margot Linton; *VPres* Jan Mayer; *VPres* Stephanie French; *VPres* Tom L Freudenheim; *VPres* Gilbert H Kinney; *VPres* Hannelore Schulhof; *Treas-Secy* Richard Lane; *Dir* Serena Rattazzi; *Deputy Dir* Mark Gotlob; *Dir Exhib* Robert Workman; *Chief Develop Officer, Individual Giving* Rebecca Lubove; *Chief Develop Officer, Corporate Foundation & Government Giving* Cathy Shomstien; *Dir Pub Relations* Jillian Slonim
Estab 1909, a nonprofit visual arts museum, program & service that organizes traveling art, film & video exhibitions for art museums, art & media centers, university art galleries, schools & libraries. Mem: 1150; dues institutional members $220 - $500, individual $100 - $1,500
Income: Financed by government agencies, corporations, foundations & mem
Publications: ART: The Newsletter of the AFA, 3 per year; exhibition catalogs; Memo to Members, 6 per year for institutional members
Activities: Originate traveling exhibitions of fine arts & media arts

O **AMERICAN FINE ARTS SOCIETY,** 215 W 57th St, New York, NY 10019. Tel 212-247-4510; FAX 212-541-7024; *Admin Mgr* ira Goldberg
Open Sept - May, Mon - Fri 10 AM - 8 PM, Sat 10 AM - 4 PM. Inc 1889; provides facilities for art activities at the American Fine Arts Soc Building. Gallery used only for Art Student League Associations, associates & members. Average Annual Attendance: 8000 - 10,000. Mem: Annual meeting Jan
Activities: Sponsors lect by prominent persons in the art world, open to public

O **THE AMERICAN FOUNDATION FOR THE ARTS,** 3814 NE Miami Ct, Miami, FL 33137. Tel 305-576-0254; FAX 305-576-0259; *Dir* May Levine; *Pres* Richard Levine
Open Mon - Fri 10 AM - 4 PM. No admis fee. Estab 1974. Mem: Dues founder $25,000, trustee $10,000, life $5000, benefactor $1000, business $250, friend $100, sustaining $50, family $25, individual $15, student annual $5
Collections: Architecture; contemporary paintings; photography

O **AMERICAN INSTITUTE FOR CONSERVATION OF HISTORIC & ARTISTIC WORKS (AIC),** 1717 K St NW, Ste 301, Washington, DC 20006. Tel 202-452-9545; FAX 202-452-9328; Elec Mail jennaic@aol.com. *Pres* Debbie Hess Norris; *VPres* J Krueger; *Exec Dir* Sarah Z Rosenberg
Open 8 AM - 5 PM. Estab 1973 for professional organization of Conservators, people who take care of our cultural & historical patrimony. Mem: 3000; dues fellows, professional associates & associates $100, student $55; meetings in early June
Income: Financed by mem
Publications: Annual directory; bi-monthly newsletter; journal, 3 times per year
Activities: Educ Committee to keep abreast of all conservation educ facilities, programs; lect open to public; awards given

O **AMERICAN INSTITUTE OF ARCHITECTS,** 1735 New York Ave NW, Washington, DC 20006. Tel 202-626-7300; FAX 202-626-7420; *Exec VPres* Terrence M McDermoth
Open Mon - Fri 8:30 AM - 5 PM. Estab 1857 to organize & unite the architects of the United States & to promote the esthetic, scientific & practical efficiency of the profession
Income: Financed by members
Publications: AIA Memo (newsletter), monthly
Activities: Continuing educ program; awards given, Gold Medal, Kemper Award. Architectural Firm Award, R S Reynolds Memorial Award & Reynolds Aluminum Prize Citation of Honor, AIA Honor Awards, Institute Honors
L **AIA Library & Archives,** 1735 New York Ave NW, Washington, DC 20006. Tel 202-626-7492; FAX 202-626-7587; Elec Mail library@aia.org. *Sr Dir* Judy Marks
Open to the pub, lending provided for members only
Income: Financed by members
Library Holdings: Vols 32,000; Per subs 450; Micro — Fiche, reels; AV — A-tapes, cassettes, fs, Kodachromes, lantern slides, slides, v-tapes; Other — Clipping files, framed reproductions, manuscripts, memorabilia, original art works, photographs, sculpture
Special Subjects: Architecture, Architectural History, Landscape Architecture

O **AMERICAN INSTITUTE OF GRAPHIC ARTS,** 164 Fifth Ave, New York, NY 10010. Tel 212-807-1990; *Assoc Dir* Richard Groefe
Open Mon - Fri 9:30 AM - 4:45 PM. No admis fee. Estab 1914 as a national nonprofit educational organization devoted to raising standards in all branches of the graphic arts. Art gallery maintained for AI6A exhibitions resulting from design competitions; maintains library & slide archives. Mem: 5000; dues $125, junior $100, student $30
Income: Financed by mem
Exhibitions: Book Show; Communication Graphics
Publications: AIGA Graphic Design USA, hardbound annual; AIGA journal of Graphic Design, quarterly
Activities: Awards AIGA Medal for distinguished contributions to the graphic arts; originate traveling exhibitions
L **Library,** 164 Fifth Ave, 10010. Tel 212-807-1990
Open Mon - Fri 9:00 AM - 5:00 PM. For reference only. Art gallery maintained for AIGA exhibitions resulting from design competitions
Income: Financed by mem
Library Holdings: Vols 500; Per subs 25
Special Subjects: Aesthetics, Art Education, Art History, Commercial Art, Graphic Arts, Graphic Design, Illustration, Industrial Design, Posters

O **AMERICAN NUMISMATIC ASSOCIATION,** Museum, 818 N Cascade Ave, Colorado Springs, CO 80903. Tel 719-632-2646; FAX 719-634-4085; *Pres* Ken Bressett; *Museum Cur* Robert W Hoge
Open Tues - Sat 8:30 AM - 4 PM. No admis fee. Estab 1891 as an international organization to promote numismatics as a means of recording history. Maintains a mus & library; eight galleries display numismatic material from paper money through coins & art medals. Average Annual Attendance: 10,000. Mem: 40,000; to qualify for mem, a person must be at least 18 years of age & interested in coin collecting; dues $21 plus one-time initiation fee of $5; annual meeting held at National Conventions in Feb & Aug
Income: Financed by mem, endowment, donations & miscellaneous sources
Collections: Robert T Herdegen Memorial Collection of Coins of the World; Norman H Liebman Collection of Abraham Lincoln on Paper Money; Elliott Markoff Collection of Presidential Memorabilia; general and specialized collections from all other fields of numismatics
Exhibitions: Permanent galleries exhibiting coins of the American Colonial period, the United States 1792 to date and Modern Medallic Art from contemporary medals. Temporary exhibits on selected topics, including African Emblems of Wealth
Publications: The Numismatist, monthly
Activities: Classes for adults & children; annual seminar on campus of Colorado College, Colorado Springs; lect open to public, vis lectr; tours; sponsorship of National Coin Week third week in Apr (when members throughout the United States promote their avocations through exhibits in local areas); presentation of awards; scholarships offered; book traveling exhibitions; sales shop selling books, magazines, slides, medals & souvenir jewelry
L **Library,** 818 N Cascade Ave, Colorado Springs, CO 80903. Tel 719-632-2646; FAX 719-634-4085; *Librn* Lynn Chen
Open Mon - Fri 8:30 AM - 4 PM, summer Mon - Sat 8:30 AM - 4 PM. No admis fee. Estab 1891 to provide research materials to the members of the Assoc & the general pub. Open to the pub for reference; lending restricted to members. Circ 4500. Mem: 28,000; dues $32 first year, $26 to renew mem; meetings twice a year
Library Holdings: Vols 35,000; Per subs 110; Auction catalogs 20,000; Microfilm; Micro — Fiche; AV — Slides, v-tapes; Other — Pamphlets
Special Subjects: Coins & Medals
Collections: Arthur Braddan Coole Library on Oriental Numismatics; books, auction catalogs & periodicals, all on numismatics
Exhibitions: Annual Summer Conference
Activities: Classes for adults & children

O **AMERICAN NUMISMATIC SOCIETY,** Broadway at 155th St, New York, NY 10032. Tel 212-234-3130; FAX 212-234-3381; *Dir* Leslie A Elam; *Chief Cur* William E Metcalf; *Librn* Francis D Campbell
Open Tues - Sat 9 AM - 4:30 PM, Sun 1 - 4 PM, cl Mon. Estab 1858 as an international organization for the advancement of numismatic knowledge. Maintains mus & library; one exhibition hall, devoted to the World of Coins. Average Annual Attendance: 18,000. Mem: 2279; dues assoc $30; annual meeting second Sat in Oct
Income: Financed by endowment
Collections: Universal numismatics
Publications: American Journal of Numismatics, annual; Numismatic Literature, semi-annual
Activities: Lect open to public, 2 vis lectr per year; scholarships offered
L **Library,** Broadway at 155th St, New York, NY 10032. Tel 212-234-3130; *Librn* Francis D Campbell
For reference only
Library Holdings: Vols 100,000; Per subs 150; Auction catalogs; Micro — Reels 200; AV — Fs, slides; Other — Exhibition catalogs, manuscripts, pamphlets
Special Subjects: Coins & Medals
Collections: Auction catalogs

O **AMERICANS FOR THE ARTS,** One E 53rd St, New York, NY 10022-4210. Tel 212-223-2787, 800-321-4510 (Book orders only); FAX 212-223-4415; Elec Mail acatmn.com. *Communications Dir* Jennifer Neiman; *VPres Prog* Carole Sorell
Open by appointment. Estab 1960. Mem: 2500; dues organizations $150-$250, individual $30-$100
Publications: ACA Update, monthly newsletter of legislative & advocacy information available to members; books on arts policy, management, education & information for artists
L **Library,** One E 53rd St, New York, NY 10022-4210. Tel 212-223-2787, Ext 224; FAX 212-223-4415; WATS 800-232-2789 (Visual Artists Information Hotline, 2 - 5 PM). *Dir* David Bosca
Research collections available on an appointment only basis for a fee; information/referral service by phone, FAX & mail. Estab 1994. For reference

only
Library Holdings: Vols 7000; Per subs 300; Vertical files
Special Subjects: Art Education, Arts Advocacy, Arts Policy, Audience Surveys, Economic Impact Studies

O **AMERICANS FOR THE ARTS** (Formerly National Assembly of Local Arts Agencies), 927 15th St NW, 12th Flr, Washington, DC 20005. Tel 202-371-2830; FAX 202-371-0424;
Internet Home Page Address http://www.artsusa.org. *Pres & Chief Exec Officer* Robert L Lynch
Open Mon - Fri 9 AM - 5:30 PM. Estab to support the arts & culture through pub & private resource development, leadership development, pub policy development, information services, pub awareness & educ. Mem: 800; annual meeting June
Income: Financed by mem, foundations, corporations & government
Publications: Periodic journals; monthly newsletter
Activities: Annual convention; regional workshops; technical assistance

O **AMERICAN SOCIETY FOR AESTHETICS**, Cudahy Hall, Rm 404, Marquette Univ, PO Box 1881, Edmonton, AB 53051. Tel 414-288-7831; FAX 414-288-7889; Elec Mail asastcar@vms.csd.mu.edu. *Pres* Ted Cohen; *Journal Ed* Philip Alperson; *Secy-Treas* Curtis L Carter; *Bus Mgr* Susan Barnes
Estab 1942 for the advancement of philosophical & scientific study of the arts & related fields. Mem: 1050; dues $50
Income: Financed by mem, dues, subscriptions
Publications: Journal of Aesthetics & Art Criticism, quarterly; ASA Newsletter, 3 times per year

O **AMERICAN SOCIETY OF ARTISTS, INC**, PO Box 1326, Chicago, IL 60078. Tel 312-751-2500, 847-991-4748; *Pres* Nancy J Fregin; *VPres* Helen DelValle; *Dir Promotional Servs* Arnold Jackson; *American Artisans Dir* Judy A Edborg; *Dir Lecture & Demonstration Serv* Charles J Gruner; *Special Arts Servs Dir* Patricia E Nolan; *Dir Special Events* Marge Coughin; *Midwest Representative* Alajos Acs; *Chicago Representative* Donald Metcoff; *Southern Illinois Representative* Ann Childers
Estab 1972, mem organization of professional artists. Mem: Over 5000; qualifications for mem, must have work juried & pass jury to be accepted; dues $50, plus one initiation fee of $20; patronship, associateship & international mem also available
Income: Financed by mem
Collections: †Photographs & slides of members works
Exhibitions: Approximately 25 indoor & outdoor juried shows per year
Publications: Art Lovers' Art and Craft Fair Bulletin, quarterly; ASA Artisan, quarterly
Activities: Lect & demonstration service; assists members with various problems
L **Library Organization**, PO Box 1326, Palatine, IL 60078. Tel 312-751-2500, 708-991-4748; FAX 708-991-4748; *Librn* Donald Metcoff
Estab 1978 to provide reference material for member artists only
Income: Financed by dues & fees
Library Holdings: Per subs 8; AV — Lantern slides; Other — Photographs
Special Subjects: Art and craft supplies, exhibition and gallery information
Activities: Lect & demonstration service

O **AMERICAN SOCIETY OF BOOKPLATE COLLECTORS & DESIGNERS**, 605 N Stoneman Ave, No F, Alhambra, CA 91801. Tel 818-570-9404; *Dir & Ed* Audrey Spencer Arellanes
Estab 1922 as an international organization to foster an interest in the art of the bookplate through the publication of a YearBook & to encourage friendship & a greater knowledge of bookplates among members by an exchange membership list. Mem: 200 who are interested in bookplates as either a collector or artist, or just have an interest in bookplates & graphic arts; dues $60 which includes yearbook & quarterly newsletter
Income: Financed by members
Exhibitions: Bookplates, Prints in Miniature
Publications: Bookplates in the News, quarterly newsletter; YearBook, annually
Activities: Lect given upon request; contributes bookplates to the Prints & Photographs Division of the Library of Congress & furnishes them with copies of quarterly & YearBook; originate traveling exhibitions

O **AMERICAN SOCIETY OF CONTEMPORARY ARTISTS (ASCA)**, c/o 130 Gale Pl, No 9H, New York, NY 10463. Tel 718-548-6790; *Pres* Joseph V Lubrano
Estab 1917. Mem: 151 elected on basis of high level of professional distinction; dues $40; annual meeting May
Income: Financed by members
Exhibitions: (1997) Shelter Rock Art Gallery; Lever House Gallery
Activities: Educ dept; demonstrations in graphics, painting & sculpture; lect open to the public; awards; originate traveling exhibitions

O **AMERICAN SOCIETY OF PORTRAIT ARTISTS (ASOPA)**, 2781 Zelda Rd, Montgomery, AL 36106. Tel 334-270-1600; FAX 334-270-0150; WATS 800-235-6273. *Dir* Jennifer Frazer Williams; *Pres* Leon Loord; *VPres* Gordon Wetmore; *Treas* Joy Loord McRae
Estab 1989

O **AMERICAN WATERCOLOR SOCIETY**, 47 Fifth Ave, New York, NY 10003. Tel 212-206-8986; *Pres* Dale Meyers; *Treas* Joan Ashley Rothermel
Open daily 1 - 5 PM. Estab 1866 as a national organization to foster the advancement of the art of watercolor painting & to further the interests of painters in watercolor throughout the United States; occupies the galleries of the Salmagundi Club, 47 Fifth Ave, New York City for four weeks each yr for annual international exhibition. Average Annual Attendance: 4000-5000. Mem: 550 signature; to qualify for mem, an artist must exhibit in two annuals within past ten yrs, then submit application to mem chairman; dues $25; annual meeting in Apr
Income: Financed by mem & donations
Publications: AWS Newsletter, semi-annually; full color exhibition catalog
Activities: Lect open to the public; demonstrations during annual exhibitions; awards given at annual exhibitions; scholarships offered; originate traveling exhibitions

O **ARCHAEOLOGICAL INSTITUTE OF AMERICA**, 656 Beacon St, Boston, MA 02215-2010. Tel 617-353-9361; FAX 617-353-6550; Elec Mail aia@bu.edu. *Exec Dir* Mark J Meister
Estab 1879 as an international organization concerned with two major areas of responsibility: facilitating archaeological research & disseminating the results to the pub. Mem: 10,500 consisting of professionals & laypersons interested in archaeology; dues $56; annual meeting in Dec
Income: Financed by endowment & mem
Publications: Archaeology Magazine, bimonthly; Archaeological Fieldwork Opportunities Bulletin, annual; American Journal of Archaeology, quarterly
Activities: Lect open to public, 270 visiting lectr per year; awards given; one or more fellowships awarded for an academic year

O **ART DEALERS ASSOCIATION OF AMERICA, INC**, 575 Madison Ave, New York, NY 10022. Tel 212-940-8590; FAX 212-940-7013; Elec Mail artdeal@rosenman.com;
Internet Home Page Address http://www.artdealers.org. *Pres* James Goodman; *VPres* Ronald Feldman; *VPres* Mary-Anne Martin; *Secy & Treas* Lauren Brody; *Admin VPres & Counsel* Gilbert S Edelson; *Dir Admin* Donna Carlson
Estab 1962 as a national organization to improve the stature & status of the art-dealing profession. Mem: 145; mem by invitation
Income: Financed by mem
Exhibitions: The Art Show; annual group exhibition
Publications: Activities & Membership Roster; biannual newsletter for members
Activities: Sponsors lect series at Metropolitan Museum of Art; appraisal service for donors contributing works of art to nonprofit institutions

O **ART DIRECTORS CLUB, INC**, 250 Park Ave S, New York, NY 10003. Tel 212-674-0500; FAX 212-460-8506; *Pres* Carl Fischer; *VPres* Ruth Lubell; *Exec Dir* Myrna Davis; *Treas* Theodore Pettus
Open Mon - Fri 10 AM - 6 PM. No admis fee. Estab 1920 as an international organization to protect, promote & elevate the standards of practice of the profession of art directing. Owns gallery. Average Annual Attendance: 20,000. Mem: 850; criteria for regular mem: qualified art director, at least 21 years of age, of good character & at least two years of practical experience in creating & directing in the visual communication of graphic arts industry; dues $200, nonresident $165, young professional $75, student $35; annual meeting in June
Income: Financed by mem
Exhibitions: Art Directors' Annual Exhibition of National & International Advertising, Editorial & Television Art & Design & Now Media.. Bimonthly shows conceived to provide a showcase for works & ideas not readily viewed otherwise. They cover advertising & editiorial design & art education
Publications: The Art Directors Annual; bimonthly newsletter
Activities: Protfolio Review Programs; speaker events; seminars; lect open to public, 10-20 vis lectr per year; competitions with awards; scholarships offered; originate traveling exhibitions; Gallery sells books, tote bags, mouse pads, mugs, t-shirts, sweatshirts & videocassettes

O **ARTISTS' FELLOWSHIP, INC**, 47 Fifth Ave, New York, NY 10003. Tel 212-255-7740; *Pres* Marc Richard Mellon; *Treas* John R McCarthy; *Correspondence Secy* Robert J Riedinger; *Historian* Carl Thomson
Estab 1859, reorganized 1889 as Artists' Aid Society, then incorporated 1925 as Artists' Fellowship; to aid professional fine artists & their families in emergency situations including illness, disability & bereavement. Mem: 300; annual meeting in Dec
Publications: Quarterly newsletter
Activities: Awards the Gari Melchers Gold Medal for distinguished service to the arts, and Benjamin West Clinedinst Memorial Medal for outstanding achievement in the arts

O **ART LIBRARIES SOCIETY OF NORTH AMERICA**, 4101 Lake Boone Trail, Ste 201, Raleigh, NC 27607. Tel 919-787-5181; FAX 919-787-4916; Elec Mail pdepas@mercury.interpath.net. *Pres* Janis Ekdahl; *Exec Dir* Penney DePass, CAE
Open 8:45 AM - 4:45 PM, cl Sat & Sun. Estab 1972 to promote the profession of art librarianship & visual resources curatorship in North America. Mem: 1350; qualification for mem is an interest in art librarianship or related fields; dues institutional $75, individual $55; annual meeting Feb & Mar
Income: Financed by mem
Publications: Art Documentation, 4 per yr; Annual Handbook & List of Members; ARLIS/NA Update, 6 per yr; occasional papers; topical papers
Activities: Sponsors annual conference & educational programs; has 20 local chapters; Gerd Museum Award (for library school students); George Wittenborn Award (art publishing); Travel Awards (to attend annual conference); Research Fund (to assist members' research projects)

O **ART SERVICES INTERNATIONAL**, 700 N Fairfax St, Ste 220, Alexandria, VA 22314. Tel 703-548-4554; *Chief Exec Officer* Joseph Saunders; *Dir* Lynn K Rogerson
Nonprofit, educational institution which organizes & circulates fine arts exhibitions to museums & galleries in the US & abroad

O **ARTS EXTENSION SERVICE**, c/o Div·Continuing Educ, Univ of Mass, 602 Goodell Bldg, Amherst, MA 01003. Tel 413-545-2360; FAX 413-545-3351; Elec Mail aes@admin.umass.edu. *Dir* Craig Dreeszen; *Educ Coordr* Dyan Wiley; *Systems Coordr* Clare Wood
Open Mon - Fri 9 AM - 5 PM. No admis fee. Estab 1973 as a National arts service organization facilitating the continuing education of artists, arts organizations & community leaders. AES works for better access to the arts & integration of the arts in communities. AES is a nonprofit program of the Division of Continuing Education, University of Masachusetts at Amherst
Publications: Art Festival Work Kit; Artist in Business, 1996; Arts Management Bibliography & Publishers; Community Cultural Planning Work Kit; Education Collaborations; Fairs & Festivals 1997; Fundamentals of Local Arts Management; Going Public, A Field Guide to Development in Art in Public Places; Intersections, Community Arts & Education Collaborations
Activities: Professional level arts management workshops; consulting; retreats & conferences; exten dept serves civic sectors, community arts organizations

O **ASSOCIATION OF AMERICAN EDITORIAL CARTOONISTS**, 4101 Lake Boone Trail, Ste 201, Raleigh, NC 27607. Tel 919-787-5181; FAX 919-787-4916; *Pres* Milt Priggee; *Pres-Elect* Michael Ramirez; *General Mgr* Shannon Parham; *Membership Dir* Chris Adams
Estab 1957 as an international organization of professional editorial cartoonists for newspapers & newspaper syndicates. Mem: 300; to qualify for mem, editorial cartoonists must be primarily employed as a cartoonist & a resident of US, Canada or Mexico; dues $100
Income: Financed by mem
Publications: Best Editorial Cartoons of the Year; Notebook

O **ASSOCIATION OF ART MUSEUM DIRECTORS**, 41 E 65th St, New York, NY 10021. Tel 212-249-4423; FAX 212-535-5035; Elec Mail aamdny@aol.com. *Exec Dir* Millicent Hall Gaudieri
Estab 1916. Mem: 165; chief staff officers of major art museums
Income: Financed by mem dues
Publications: Conference Proceedings; Professional Practices in Art Museums; Annual Salary Survey

O **ASSOCIATION OF COLLEGIATE SCHOOLS OF ARCHITECTURE**, 1735 New York Ave NW, Washington, DC 20006. Tel 202-785-2324; FAX 202-628-0448; *Exec Dir* G Martin Moeller Jr
Open daily 9 AM - 5 PM. No admis fee. Estab 1912 as a non-profit, mem organization furthering the advancement of architectural educ. Mem: 3500 architecture faculty members; mem open to schools & their faculty as well as individuals; mem rates vary; annual meeting in Mar
Income: $1.4 million (financed by endowment, mem, state appropriation & grants)
Publications: ACSA News, 9 times per year; Journal of Architectural Education, quarterly; Annual Meeting Proceedings; Guide to Architecture Schools in North America, quadrennially; Architecture Off-Campus Study Programs; Abroad-US
Activities: Educational seminars; institutes; publications; services to membership; sponsor student design competitions with awards

O **ASSOCIATION OF INDEPENDENT COLLEGES OF ART & DESIGN**, 3957 22nd St, San Francisco, CA 94114-3205. Tel 415-642-8595; FAX 415-642-8590; Elec Mail bbaicad@best.com;
Internet Home Page Address http://www.aicad.org. *Exec Dir* William O Barrett
Open Mon - Fri 8 AM - 5 PM. Estab 1991 to improve quality of member colleges & provide information on art educ. Mem: 32; must be independent art college, fully accredited & grant BFA; dues $1000-$7000 depending on size; annual meeting in Oct
Income: $370,000 (financed by mem & occasional grants)
Publications: Newsletter
Activities: Lect open to members only, 3 vis lectr per year

O **ASSOCIATION OF MEDICAL ILLUSTRATORS**, 1819 Peachtree St NE, Ste 620, Atlanta, GA 30309. Tel 404-350-7900; Elec Mail assnhq@atl.mindspring.com. *Chmn* John Nyquist; *Pres* Diane Nelson; *Exec Dir* William Just
Estab 1945 as an international organization to encourage the advancement of medical illustration & allied fields of visual educ; to promote understanding & cooperation with the medical & related professions. Mem: 804; dues active $135; annual meeting in Aug
Exhibitions: Annual exhibition at national meeting
Publications: Journal of Biocommunications, 4 times per year; Medical Illustration, brochure; Newsletter, 6 times per year
Activities: Individual members throughout the world give lect on the profession; awards given for artistic achievements submitted to salon each year; originate traveling exhibitions; originate traveling exhibition

O **ATLATL**, PO Box 34090, Phoenix, AZ 85067-4090. Tel 602-277-3711; FAX 602-277-3690; Elec Mail atlatl@artswire.org. *Exec Dir* Carla A Roberts; *Prog Coordr* Patsy Phillips
Open 9 AM - 5 PM. No admis fee. Estab 1981 as a national service organization for Native American Art. Atlatl creates an informational network between Native American artists & art organizations as well as between mainstream institutions & emerging organizations. Maintains a National Registry of Native American Artists which currently includes more than 1500 artists
Collections: Native American Artists files
Exhibitions: Hiapsi Wami Seewam: Flowers of Life
Publications: Quarterly newsletter
Activities: Workshops & training sessions; circulates audiovisual materials such as slides sets & videotapes by Native American artists; originate exhibitions of Native American art to a variety of institutions including tribal museums, community & university galleries & fine art museums

O **AUDUBON ARTISTS, INC,** * 32 Union Sq E, Rm 1214, New York, NY 10003. Tel 212-260-5706; *Pres* Marion Roller; *Sr VPres* William Spinka; *Treas* Open; *VPres Aqua Media* Nessa Grainger; *VPres Graphics* Takayo Noda; *VPres Oils* Gary Erbe; *VPres Sculpture* Andrew Pitynski
Open during exhib. Estab 1940 as a national organization for the presentation of annual exhibitions in all media, oil, acrylics, watercolors, graphics, sculpture; open to nonmembers. Exhibitions held at the National Arts Club. Mem: 650; mem by invitation; dues $40, assoc mem $30; annual meeting in Apr
Income: $15,000 (financed by mem)
Exhibitions: Annual exhibitions lasting four weeks
Publications: Illustrated catalog of exhibitions, annual
Activities: Demonstrations in all media; medals & $10,000 in cash awards

C **AUTOZONE**, Autozone Corporation Collection, 123 S Front St, PO Box 2198, Memphis, TN 38103. Tel 901-495-6763; FAX 901-495-8300; *Cur* Lynda Ireland
Estab 1978 to support local artists & artists of the United States. 20th century collection of American art in a variety of media highlighting the work of artists in the South

O **COALITION OF WOMEN'S ART ORGANIZATIONS**, 123 E Beutel Rd, Port Washington, WI 53074-1103. Tel 414-284-4458; FAX 414-284-8875; *Pres* Dorothy Provis; *VPres-Nominations* Christine Buth-Furness; *VPres-Programs* Kyra Sullivan
Estab 1977 as a national advocacy organization dedicated to the achievement of equality for all in the arts. Mem: 22 national organizations, 30 individuals; dues $25 organizations, $10 individuals; annual meeting in Feb at College Art Association Conference
Income: Financed by mem & contributions
Publications: Coalition of Women's Art Organization News, monthly
Activities: Lect open to public

O **COLLEGE ART ASSOCIATION**, 275 Seventh Ave, New York, NY 10001. Tel 212-691-1051; FAX 212-627-2381; Elec Mail caa@tmn.com. *Pres* Judith Brudsky; *VPres* Leslie King-Hammond; *Exec Dir* Susan L Ball; *Deputy Dir* Jeffrey Larris; *Publications Dir* Virginia Wageman; *Fel Coordr* Angela Montague
Estab 1911 as a national organization to further scholarship & excellence in the teaching & practice of art & art history. Mem: 12,000, open to all individuals & institutions interested in the purposes of the Assoc; dues life $1000, institution $125, individual $40-$75 (scaled to salary), student $25; annual meeting in Feb
Income: Financed by mem
Publications: The Art Bulletin, quarterly; Art Journal, quarterly; CAA Newsletter, bimonthly
Activities: Awards: Distinguished Teaching of Art History Award; Distinguished Teaching of Art Award; Charles Rufus Morey Book Award; Frank Jewett Mather Award for Distinction in Art & Architectural Criticism; Arthur Kingsley Porter Prize for Best Article by Younger Scholar in The Art Bulletin; Alfred H Barr, Jr Award for Museum Scholarship; Distinguished Artist Award for Lifetime Achievement; Award for a Distinguished Body of Work, Exhibition, Presentation or Performance

O **COLOR ASSOCIATION OF THE US**, 409 W 44th St, New York, NY 10036. Tel 212-582-6884; FAX 212-757-4557; *Pres* Bill Bonnellgal; *Exec Dir* Marielle Bancou; *Dir Membership* Hugh Sang; *Assoc Dir* Margaret Walch
Open Mon - Fri 9 AM - 4 PM. Estab 1915 for the purpose of forecasting fashion colors & standards in the United States. Mem: 1500; dues $600
Income: Financed by mem
Collections: Colored Swatch Archives date back to 1915
Publications: CAUS Newsletter, 8 times per year; The Color Compendium; The Standard Color Reference of America
Activities: Lect open to public, 12 vis lectr per year

O **CONGRESSIONAL ARTS CAUCUS**, Rayburn HOB, House Annex 2, H2-347, Washington, DC 20515. Tel 202-226-3615; FAX 202-225-7822; *Acting Chmn* Louise Slaughter
Estab 1980 to keep members informed of the progress of arts legislation in Congress & provide them with analyses of issues affecting the arts community as a whole & within their own districts. Mem: The Caucus, which is bipartisan, is open to any member of the House of Representatives or Senate who is interested in supporting the arts

O **THE DRAWING SOCIETY**, 15 Penn Plaza, PO Box 66, New York, NY 10001. Tel 212-563-4822; FAX 212-563-4829; *Pres* Micheal Flack
Estab 1959 to encourage interest in, & understanding of, drawing of all periods & cultures. Mem: Dues $100 & up for patrons, institutional $75, associate $45
Exhibitions: Theodore Roszak: The Drawings
Publications: Drawing, bi-monthly; Books & catalogues
Activities: Originate traveling exhibitions to museums in United States

O **FEDERATION OF MODERN PAINTERS & SCULPTORS**, 234 W 21st St, New York, NY 10011. Tel 212-568-2981, 255-4858; *Pres* Haim Mendelson; *Pres* Ahmet Gursoy; *VPres* Theo Hios; *Treas* John Servetas
Estab 1940 as a national organization to promote the cultural interests of free progressive artists working in the United States. Mem: 60; selected by mem comt; dues $25; meeting every 2 months
Income: Financed by mem
Exhibitions: Exhibition at Art Students League; A Decade for Renewal, at Lever House, New York.
Publications: Exhibit catalog
Activities: Lect open to public, 1-2 vis lectr per year; symposium; originate traveling exhibitions

O **GENERAL SERVICES ADMINISTRATION**, Art-in-Architecture Program, 33162 & F Sts NW, Rm 1300, Washington, DC 20405. Tel 202-501-1812; FAX 202-501-3393; *Chief Art-in-Architecture Prog* Susan Harrison
The Art-in-Architecture program commissions artists to design & execute sculpture, murals, tapestries & other art works to be incorporated as part of the design of Federal Buildings Nationwide. The scope of work is determined by the size & character of the building with allowances up to .5 percent of the estimated construction cost. Artists are commissioned by direct selection by the government upon recommendation by a panel of distinguished art professionals & community advisors
Income: $1,000,000
Collections: National Collection of Public Art

O **GUILD OF BOOK WORKERS**, 521 Fifth Ave, New York, NY 10175. Tel 212-873-4315, 914-657-3348; *Pres* Frank Mowery; *VPres* Bernadette Callery
Estab 1906 as a national organization to establish & maintain a feeling of kinship & mutual interest among workers in the several hand book crafts. Mem: 620; mem open to all interested persons; dues national $40, chapter (New York City Area Guild, New England Guild, Midwest Guild, Lone Star, Delaware Valley, Potomac) $10 additional; annual meeting in Oct
Income: Financed by mem
Exhibitions: 80th Anniversary Exhibition consisting of fine bindings, artists' books, restorations, calligraphy & decorated papers
Publications: Guild of Book Workers Journal, 2 times per year; membership list, annually; newsletter, 6 times per yr; supply list, biennially; Opportunities for

Study in Hand Bookbinding & Calligraphy, directory & supplement
Activities: Lect open to members only; tours; workshops; annual seminar on Standards of Excellence in Hand Bookbinding open to public; book traveling exhibitions; originate traveling exhibitions
L **Library,** Univ of Iowa, Conservation Dept, Boston, IA 52242. Tel 319-335-5908; FAX 319-335-5900; *Librn* Pamela Spitzmueller
Open to Guild members for lending & reference
Library Holdings: Vols 700
Special Subjects: Related to handbook binding, binding videotapes, bookbinding, exhibition catalogs, manuals on book & paper making

O **INDUSTRIAL DESIGNERS SOCIETY OF AMERICA,** 1142 Walker Rd, Ste E, Great Falls, VA 22066. Tel 703-759-0100; FAX 703-759-7679; Elec Mail idsa@erols.com;
Internet Home Page Address http://www.idsa.org. *Pres* Craig Vogel; *Exec Dir* Robert T Schwartz
Open daily 9 AM - 5 PM. No admis fee. Estab & inc 1965 as a nonprofit national organization representing the profession of industrial design. Mem: 2400; dues full, affiliate & international $238, assoc $140
Publications: Innovation, quarterly; IDSA Newsletter, monthly; Membership Directory; other surveys & studies
Activities: IDSA Student Chapters; IDSA Student Merit Awards; lect; competitions; scholarships offered

O **INTERMUSEUM CONSERVATION ASSOCIATION,** Allen Art Bldg, Oberlin, OH 44074. Tel 216-775-7331; *Pres* Bill Lipscomb; *VPres* Ted Alfied; *Treas & Dir* Bill Pusta
Estab 1952 as a non-profit conservation laboratory to aid in the maintenance of the collections of its member museums. Maintains a technical conservation library. Mem: 28; must be non-profit cultural institution; dues $100-$1000; meetings biannually
Activities: Lect open to public; 3-6 vis lectr per year; seminars twice a year; scholarships for advanced training of conservators

O **INTERNATIONAL CENTER FOR ADVANCED STUDIES IN ART,** NY Univ Dept of Art & Art Professions, 34 Stuyvesant St, New York, NY 10003. Tel 212-998-5700; FAX 212-995-4320; *Co-Dir* Angiola Churchill; *Co-Dir* Jorge Glusberg; *Chmn* Leonard Lehrer
Estab 1979 to provide international studies through which the complex & multi-faceted field of visual arts can be viewed, examined, researched & developed on the highest scholarly & professional level The most significant aspect of the Center is the firsthand contact with critics, theorists, aestheticians & other specialists & the opportunity to work with artists & other thinkers
Activities: Lect open to public; symposia

O **INTERNATIONAL FOUNDATION FOR ART RESEARCH, INC,** 500 Fifth Ave, Ste 1234, New York, NY 10110. Tel 212-391-6234; FAX 212-391-8794; *Exec Dir* Constance Lowenthal
Open Mon - Fri 9:30 AM - 5:30 PM. Estab 1968 to provide a service for impartial consideration by experts of questions concerning attribution & authenticity of major works of art; expanded in 1975 to include an Art Theft Archive for collection & cataloguing of information on art theft. In 1990, helped form the Art Loss Register, an international database of stolen & missing art
Income: Financed by donations, mem & fees
Publications: IFAR reports, 10 per year
Activities: Lect & symposia are conducted throughout the year on subjects relating to connoisseurship, authenticity & art theft & fraud
—**Art Loss Register,** 500 Fifth Ave, Ste 1234, New York, NY 10110. Tel 212-391-8791; FAX 212-391-8794; Elec Mail alrnewyork@aol.com. *Dir* Anna J Kisluk
The Art Loss Register at the International Foundation for Art Research is devoted to collecting & cataloguing records of art thefts & providing information on stolen objects to individuals, institutions, government agencies & others in order to prevent the circulation of stolen art & aid in its recovery. The Register contains over 70,000 items from a wide range of domestic & international sources. Stolen art reports are published in IFAR's monthly IFAR reports
Income: Financed by fees & subscriptions
—**Authentication Service,** 500 Fifth Ave, Ste 1234, New York, NY 10110. Tel 212-391-6234; FAX 212-391-8794; *Dir* Dr Constance Lowenthal
Through this service, the resources of leading institutional experts, both scholarly & scientific, are made available to the pub in order to answer questions relating to authenticity & proper attribution of works of art

O **INTERNATIONAL SOCIETY OF COPIER ARTISTS (ISCA),** 759 President St, No 2H, Brooklyn, NY 11215. Tel 718-638-3264; Elec Mail isca4art2b@aol.com. *Dir* Louise Neaderland
Open by appt. Estab 1981 to promote use of copier as a creative tool. Mem: 150; dues international $110, subscriber $90, $30 & $40; mem open to artists using the copier for printmaking & bookmaking
Income: $10,000 (financed by mem & subscriptions to Quarterly)
Collections: Slide Archive of Xerographic Prints & Books
Exhibitions: ISCA GRAPHICS; Using the Copier as a Creative Tool
Publications: ISCA Quarterly
Activities: Classes for adults & children; lect open to public; individual prints, books & original objects of art lent to university, library & community galleries; originate traveling exhibitions

O **INTER-SOCIETY COLOR COUNCIL,** Data Color Intl, 5 Princess Rd, Lawrenceville, NJ 08648. Tel 609-924-2189, Ext 7427; *Secy* Dr Danny C Rich
Estab 1931 as a national organization to stimulate & coordinate the study of color in science, art & industry; federation of 29 national societies & individuals interested in colors. Mem: 900; members must show an interest in color & in the aims & purposes of the Council; dues individual $25; annual meeting usually Apr
Income: Financed by mem
Publications: Inter-Society Color Council Newsletter, bimonthly
Activities: Lect open to public; lect at meetings; gives Macbeth Award and Godlove Award

O **KAPPA PI INTERNATIONAL HONORARY ART FRATERNITY,** 9321 Paul Adrian Dr, Crestwood, MO 63126. Tel 314-843-1273; *Pres* Arthur B Kennon; *VPres* Dr Ralph M Hudson
Estab 1911 as an international honorary art fraternity for men & women in colleges, universities & art schools
Income: Financed by mem
Publications: Sketch Board Newsletter, annually in the fall; Sketch Book, annual spring magazine
Activities: Sponsors competition in photography; annual scholarships available to active members

O **LANNAN FOUNDATION,** 5401 McConnell Ave, Los Angeles, CA 90066-7027. Tel 310-306-1004; FAX 310-578-6445; *Dir, Art Prog* Kathleen Merrill; *Prog Asst, Art Prog* Jenee A Misraje
Estab 1970; awards granted to qualifying art institutions within the US

O **ARTHUR MANLEY SOCIETY,** 12712 DuPont Circle, Tampa, FL 33626. Tel 813-855-4636; *Pres* Beverley Manley
Open Sept - May, Mon - Fri 10 AM - 8 PM, Sat 10 AM - 4 PM. Inc 1984; provides facilities for art activities at the American Fine Arts Society building. Gallery used only for art students. Average Annual Attendance: 9000 - 10,000. Mem: Annual meeting May
Activities: Sponsors lect by prominent people in the art world

O **MID AMERICA ARTS ALLIANCE & EXHIBITS USA** (Formerly ExhibitsUSA), 912 Baltimore Ave, Ste 700, Kansas City, MO 64105. Tel 816-421-1388; FAX 816-421-3918; *Chmn* Wallace Richardson; *Dir* Mary Kennedy McCabe
A national division of Mid America Arts Alliance created to organize & tour exhibits throughout the Unites Sates & beyond
Income: $1,000,000 (financed by federal & state grants, private contributions & exhibition fees)
Exhibitions: American Indian Realism (photographs); Artists of the American West (handcolored prints); Buildings & Landscapes (prints, watercolors, photographs); Built, Thrown, & Touched: Contemporary Clay Works (ceramics); By a Clearer Light: Commemorating the 75th Anniversary of the National Park Service (photographs); Crossing Borders: Contemporary Australian Textile Art (mixed media); Enlightening the Classics: 18th-Century Etchings of Ancient Roman Architecture (etchings); First Quilt/Last Quilt: Ten Contemporary Quiltmakers (textiles); From Plastic Form to Printer's Plate: 16 Contemporary Sculptor/Printmakers (mixed media & installations); From the Hip: A Celebration of Youth Activism & Service (photographs); Gathering Medicine: Works by Coast to Coast, National Women Artists of Color (mixed media); Generations of Kentucky: An Exhibition of Folk Art with Photographs by Guy Mendes (mixed media); The Good Earth: Folk Art & Artifacts from the Chinese Countryside (paintings & artifacts); Hand, Mind, & Spirit: An Art Experience of the Senses (mixed media); Hmong Artistry: Preserving a Culture on Cloth (textiles); In Praise of Pattern: The Art of Alfredo Arreguin (paintings); In the Realm of the Senses: The Works of Mel Chin (mixed media & installations); Luis Jimenez (sculpture, maquettes, working drawings); Elizabeth Layton: Drawing on Life (drawings); Alfred Leslie: The Complete Prints (prints); Living Traditions: Mexican Popular Arts (mixed media & installations); Masks from Guerrero (masks & costumes); Mennonite Furniture: A Migrant Tradition (1766-1910) (furniture & decorative arts); Mojo: Photographs by Keith Carter (photographs); Moving the Fire: The Removal of Indian Nations to Oklahoma (mixed media); The National Council on Education for the Ceramic Arts: 1995 Clay National (ceramics); Nature Watercolors USA: Works by Mario Reis (paintings & photographs); Navajo Weaving from the Harmsen Collection (textiles); Objects of Personal Significance (mixed media); On the Land: Three Centuries of American Farmlife (photographs); Picasso Posters: A Study in Design (linocuts, offset reproductions); Rags to Riches: Recycled Rugs (rugs); Betye Saar: Personal Icons (mixed media & installations); Sacred Ground/Sacred Sky: An Eco-Experience by Daniel Dancer (photographs & eco-sculpture); Saddlemaking in Wyoming: History, Utility, & Art (historic & contemporary saddles); Shared Stories: Exploring Cultural Diversity (illustrations); Street Engagements: Social Landscape Photography of the 1960's (photographs); Tales from the Nuclear Age (photographs); Telling Tales: Children's Book Illustrations from the 1950s (illustrations); Through the Looking Glass: Drawings by Elizabeth Layton (drawings); A True Likeness: The Black South of Richard Samuel Roberts, 1920-1936 (photographs); Vision Quest: Men, Women, & Sacred Sites of the Sioux Nation (photographs); The Works of Louis Monza (paintings, drawings, prints); Benedicte Wrensted: An Idaho Photographer in Focus (photographs); Please Touch! (mixed media); Howardena Pindell: A Retrospective (mixed media); Ribs, Rods and Splits: Appalachian Oak Basketry (basketry); Sacred Ground/Sacred Sky (mixed media); Textile Diaries: Quilts as Cultural Markers (quilts); Through the looking Glass; Tutavoh: Learning the Hopi Way (photography); Waterways West (photography); Welty (photography); Woven Vessels (mixed media)
Publications: Exhibition catalogs
Activities: Book traveling exhibitions; originate traveling exhibitions

O **MIDWEST ART HISTORY SOCIETY,** Coll of Wooster, Wooster, OH 44691. Tel 330-263-2150; Elec Mail lhuts@acs.wooster.edu. *Pres* Linda C Huts
Estab 1973 to further art history in the Midwest as a discipline & profession. Average Annual Attendance: 150 at meetings. Mem: 550; mem is open to institutions, students & academic & mus art historians in the Midwest; dues institution $10, professional $5; annual meeting in Mar
Income: $1200 (financed by mem)
Publications: Midwest Art History Society Newsletter, Oct & Apr
Activities: Lect provided

O **NAMES PROJECT FOUNDATION,** 310 Townsend St, San Francisco, CA 94107. Tel 415-882-5500; FAX 415-882-6200; Elec Mail info@aidsquilt.org; Internet Home Page Address www.aidquilt.org. *Exec Dir* Anthony Turney
Estab 1987
Collections: AIDS Memorial Quilt, over 40,000 individual memorial panels commemorating people lost to AIDS
Publications: On Display, newsletter

O **NATIONAL ACADEMY OF DESIGN,** 1083 Fifth Ave, New York, NY 10128. Tel 212-369-4880; FAX 212-360-6795; *Cur Drawings, Prints & Paintings* Dita Amory; *Cur* David Daringer
Open Wed - Sun Noon - 5 PM, Fri evening until 8 PM, cl Mon, New Year's, Thanksgiving & Christmas. Admis $2.50. Estab 1825, honorary arts organization for American artists & architects. Mem: 425
Collections: Permanent collection consists of 5000 watercolors, drawings & graphics 2000 paintings, 250 sculptures, mostly the gifts of the artist & architectural members of the Academy from 1825 to present; American art from mid-nineteenth century to the present
Exhibitions: Annual juried exhibition of contemporary art; exhibitions of permanent collection & loan exhibitions
Publications: Annual exhibition catalogue; catalogues of exhibitions of permanent collection; catalogues of special loan exhibitions
Activities: Lect open to public; tours by appointment; individual paintings & original objects of art lent to other museums; museum shop sells books, posters, catalogues & postcards
L **Archives,** 1083 Fifth Ave & 89th St, 10128. Tel 212-369-4880; FAX 212-360-6795; *Cur* David Daringer; *Archival Asst* Lois H Woodyatt
Open by appointment only. Admis general $3.50, senior citizens & students $2. For reference
Library Holdings: Biographical files on all members; records on The National Academy of Design; Other — Clipping files, exhibition catalogs, manuscripts, memorabilia, original art works, pamphlets, photographs, prints, sculpture
Collections: Diploma works of artists elected to membership
Activities: Classes for adults & children; docent training; lect open to public; concerts; gallery talks; tours; competitions with prizes; scholarships & fels offered; exten dept serves art students; individual paintings & original objects of art lent to other museums; lending collection contains original art works, original prints, paintings & sculpture; book traveling exhibitions; originate traveling exhibitions

O **NATIONAL ALLIANCE FOR MEDIA ARTS & CULTURE,** 346 Ninth St, San Francisco, CA 94103. Tel 415-431-1391; FAX 415-431-1392; Elec Mail namac@sigc.apc.org. *National Coordr* Helen DeMichiel
Estab for the purpose of furthering diversity & participation in all forms of the media arts, including film, video, audio & multimedia production
Income: $200,000 (financed by grants)
Publications: Main newsletter, bimonthly; NAMAC Member Directory, biennial

O **NATIONAL ANTIQUE & ART DEALERS ASSOCIATION OF AMERICA, INC,** 12 E 56th St, New York, NY 10022. Tel 212-826-9707; FAX 212-319-0471; *Pres* Anthony Victoria; *VPres* Fiti Halle; *Secy* Andrew Chait; *Treas* Andrew Chait
Estab 1954 to promote the best interests of the antique & art trade; to collect & circulate reports, statistics & other information pertaining to art; to sponsor & organize antique & exhibitions; to promote just, honorable & ethical trade practices
Exhibitions: International Fine Art & Antique Dealers Show
Publications: NAADA Directory, biannual
Activities: Lect

O **NATIONAL ARCHITECTURAL ACCREDITING BOARD, INC,** 1735 New York Ave NW, Washington, DC 20006. Tel 202-783-2007; FAX 202-783-2822; Elec Mail archbd@aol.com. *Exec Dir* John Maudlin-Jeronimo
Estab 1940 to produce & maintain a current list of accredited programs in architecture in the United States & its jurisdictions, with the general objective that a well-integrated program of architectural educ be developed which will be national in scope
Publications: Criteria and Procedures, pamphlet; List of Accredited Programs in Architecture, annually

O **NATIONAL ART EDUCATION ASSOCIATION,** 1916 Association Dr, Reston, VA 20191. Tel 703-860-8000; *Pres* Sarah Tambucci; *Pres-Elect* Michael Day; *Exec Dir* Dr Thomas A Hatfield
Estab 1947 through the affiliation of four regional groups, Eastern, Western, Pacific & Southeastern Arts Associations. The NAEA is a national organization devoted to the advancement of the professional interests & competence of teachers of art at all educational levels. Promotes the study of the problems of teaching art; encourages research & experimentation; facilitates the professional & personal cooperation of its members; holds public discussions & programs; publishes desirable articles, reports & surveys; integrates efforts of others with similar purposes. Mem: 29,000 art teachers, administrators, supervisors & students; fee institutional comprehensive $150, active $50
Income: Programs financed through mem, sales of publications & occasional grants for specific purposes
Publications: Art Education, 6 issues per year; NAEA Advisory, 4 issues per year; NAEA News, 6 issues per year; Studies in Art Education, 4 times per year; special publications

O **NATIONAL ARTISTS EQUITY ASSOCIATION INC,** Central Sta, PO Box 28068, Washington, DC 20038-8068. Tel 202-628-9633; FAX 202-628-0034; Elec Mail naea@capaccess.org. WATS 800-628-9633. *Pres* George C Koch; *VPres* Carol Sky; *Membership Dir* Craig Kittner
Estab 1947 as a national nonprofit, aesthetically nonpartisan organization working for social, economic & legislative change for all visual artists. Mem: 4500 who are or ask to be recognized as professional contributors to the development of visual art & culture; dues chapter $60, at-large $40
Income: $100,000 (financed by mem & grants)
Publications: The Artist Advocate, quarterly; Pen, Pencil & Paint, quarterly
Activities: Works for legislation & public policy favorable to visual artists; chapters occasionally organize & circulate traveling exhibitions or conduct conferences, seminars, or other educational programs

O **NATIONAL ASSEMBLY OF STATE ARTS AGENCIES,** 1010 Vermont Ave NW, Ste 920, Washington, DC 20005. Tel 202-347-6352; FAX 202-737-0526; *Chmn* Barbara Robinson; *Pres* Marvin Cohen; *Exec Dir* Jonathan Katz
Estab 1975 to enhance the growth & development of the arts through an informed & skilled mem; to provide forums for the review & development of national arts policy. Mem: 56; members are the fifty-six state & jurisdictional arts agencies, affiliate memberships are open to public; annual meeting in the fall
Income: Financed by mem & federal grants
Publications: Annual survey of state appropriations to arts councils; NASAA Notes, monthly

O **NATIONAL ASSOCIATION OF ARTISTS' ORGANIZATIONS (NAAO),** 918 F St NW, Ste 611, Washington, DC 20004. Tel 202-347-6350; Elec Mail naoo@artswire.org. *Exec Dir* Roberto Bedoya; *Prog & Mem Serv Coordr* Victoria Reis
Estab for the advancement of artist-run & artist-directed contemporary art organizations

O **NATIONAL ASSOCIATION OF SCHOOLS OF ART & DESIGN,** 11250 Roger Bacon Dr, Ste 21, Reston, VA 20190. Tel 703-437-0700; FAX 703-437-6312; *Executive Dir* Samuel Hope
Formerly the National Conference of Schools of Design, holding its first conference in 1944. Changed name in 1948, at which time its constitution & by-laws were adopted. Changed its name again in 1960 from National Association of Schools of Design to National Association of Schools of Art. Name changed again in 1981 to National Association of Schools of Art & Design. NASAD is the national accrediting agency for higher educational institutions in the visual arts & design & is so recognized by the US Department of Educ & the Council on Postsecondary Accreditation. The organization was established to develop a closer relationship among schools & departments of art & design for the purpose of educating designers & artists in the visual arts & giving evidence of permanence & stability, possessing an approved organization, administration, faculty & facilities & maintaining standards agreed upon by the Association. Mem: 190 institutions; to qualify for mem, institutions must meet accreditation standards (peer evaluation process), open to any individual; annual meeting in Oct
Income: $300,000 (financed by mem)
Publications: Directory of Member Institutions, annually; Handbook of Accreditation Standards, biennial
Activities: Awards given

O **NATIONAL ASSOCIATION OF WOMEN ARTISTS, INC,** 41 Union Sq W, Rm 906, New York, NY 10003. Tel 212-675-1616; Elec Mail nawomena@msn.com. *Pres* Janet Indick
Estab 1889 as a national organization to provide opportunities for member women artists, to exhibit their work. Mem: 800; member work is juried prior to selection; dues $45; meetings in Nov & May
Income: Financed by mem
Exhibitions: Annual members' exhibition in spring with awards; annual traveling exhibitions of oils, acrylics, works on paper, printmaking; annual New York City shows of oils, acrylics, works on paper, printmaking & sculpture
Publications: Annual Exhibition Catalog
Activities: Lect open to public, 1 vis lectr per year; awards given to members during annual exhibition; originate traveling exhibitions

O **NATIONAL CARTOONISTS SOCIETY,** Columbus Circle Sta, PO Box 20267, New York, NY 10023-1484. Tel 212-627-1550; *Info Contact* Joe Duffy; *Pres* Bruce Beattie
Estab 1946 to advance the ideals & standards of the profession of cartooning; to assist needy, or incapacitated cartoonists; to stimulate interest in the art of cartooning by cooperating with estab schools; to encourage talented students; to assist governmental & charitable institutes. Mem: 480; annual Reuben Awards Dinner in Apr
Collections: Milt Gross Fund; National Cartoonists Society Collection
Publications: The Cartoonist, bimonthly
Activities: Educ dept to supply material & information to students; individual cartoonists to lect, chalktalks can be arranged; cartoon auctions; proceeds from traveling exhibitions & auctions support Milt Gross Fund assisting needy cartoonists, widows & children; gives Reuben Award to Outstanding Cartoonist of the Year, Silver Plaque Awards to best cartoonists in individual categories of cartooning; original cartoons lent to schools, libraries & galleries; originate traveling exhibitions

O **NATIONAL COUNCIL ON EDUCATION FOR THE CERAMIC ARTS (NCECA),** 668 W Tenth, PO Box 158, Bandon, OR 97411. Tel 541-347-7505; *Exec Secy* Regina Brown
Estab 1967 as a non-profit organization to promote & improve ceramic art, design, craft & educ through the exchange of information among artists, teachers & individuals in the ceramic art community
Income: Financed by annual conferences & mem
Exhibitions: Annual Conference Exhibitions
Publications: Journal, annual; Information Annual Conference, spring; Newsletter, 4 times a year

O **NATIONAL ENDOWMENT FOR THE ARTS,** 1100 Pennsylvania Ave NW, Washington, DC 20506. Tel 202-682-5400; *Chmn* Jane Alexander; *Sr Deputy Chmn* Ana Steele; *Deputy Chmn Prog* Susan Clampitt; *Deputy Chmn Partnership* Scott Sanders
Open 9 AM - 5:30 PM. No admis fee. Estab 1965 to encourage & support American arts & artists. Information is to foster the excellence, diversity & vitality of the arts in the United States & to help broaden their ability & appreciation
Income: $170,225,000
Publications: Annual Report; Guide to the National Endowment for the Arts
Activities: Educ dept; scholarships & fels offered

L Library, 1100 Pennsylvania Ave NW, 20506. Tel 202-682-5485; FAX 202-682-5651; *Librn* Jeanne McConnell
Open Mon - Thurs 8:30 AM - 5 PM. Estab 1971 to provide an effective information service to staff which will support division activities & contribute to the accomplishment of agency goals
Income: Financed by federal appropriation
Library Holdings: Vols 8000; Per subs 150; Other — Clipping files
Special Subjects: Arts in contemporary America, arts administration, cultural policy; government & the arts

O NATIONAL FOUNDATION FOR ADVANCEMENT IN THE ARTS, 800 Brickell Ave, Miami, FL 33131. Tel 305-377-1140; FAX 305-377-1149; *Pres* William Banchs
Estab 1981 to identify & reward young artists at critical stages in their development
Publications: Quarterly newsletter

O NATIONAL INSTITUTE FOR ARCHITECTURAL EDUCATION, 30 W 22nd St, New York, NY 10010. Tel 212-924-7000; FAX 212-366-5836; *Chmn* Robert Fox; *VChmn* Stephen Potters; *Exec Dir* Joan Bassin; *Treas* Susan Swan
Open Mon - Fri 9 AM - 5 PM. Inc 1894 as Society of Beaux-Arts Architects, which was dissolved Dec 1941; Beaux-Arts Institute of Design estab 1916, name changed 1956 to present name. Average Annual Attendance: 2500. Mem: 400; dues $50; annual meeting end of Oct
Exhibitions: Prize-winning drawings of competitions held during year
Publications: Yearbook, annually in October
Activities: Lect open to public, 4-5 vis lectr per year; competitions with awards; Trustee for the Lloyd Warren Fellowship (Paris Prize in Architecture) for study & travel abroad; William Van Alen Architect Memorial Award (international competition) annual scholarship for further study or research project of some architectural nature; & other trust funds for prize awards for study & travel abroad & educational activities in the United States; individual paintings & original objects of art lent; lending collection contains 200 original prints; book traveling exhibitions 3-4 per year; originate traveling exhibitions

O NATIONAL INSTITUTE FOR THE CONSERVATION OF CULTURAL PROPERTY, 3299 K St NW, Ste 602, Washington, DC 20007. Tel 202-625-1495; FAX 202-625-1485; *Pres* Lawrence L Reger
Estab 1974 as a national forum for conservation & preservation activities in the United States

O NATIONAL LEAGUE OF AMERICAN PEN WOMEN, 1300 17th St NW, Washington, DC 20036. Tel 202-785-1997; FAX 202-785-1997; *National Pres* Elaine Waidelich
Estab 1897 to support women office arts. Maintains member reference library. Mem: 5000; 200 local branches; dues $40
Income: Financed by mem dues & legacies
Collections: Purchase award
Exhibitions: NLAPW Biennial Arts Show at national Biennial Convention
Publications: The Pen Women, bi-monthly magazine (6 times per year)
Activities: Lect open to public; concerts; competitions with awards; scholarships offered

O NATIONAL OIL & ACRYLIC PAINTERS SOCIETY, PO Box 676, Osage Beach, MO 65065. Tel 573-346-3897, 348-9986 (Pres), 348-1189 (Secy-Treas); FAX 573-346-0040; *Pres* Donald Ruthenberg PhD
Open 10 AM - 5 PM. No admis fee. Estab to promote the work of exceptional living artists working in oil & acrylic paint & to expand the pub awareness, knowledge & appreciation of fine art, particularly in these two mediums. Mem: Dues $40
Exhibitions: Annual exhibit
Publications: Annual catalog; semiannual newsletter
Activities: Originates traveling exhibitions

O NATIONAL SCULPTURE SOCIETY, 1177 Avenue of the Americas, New York, NY 10036. Tel 212-764-5645; FAX 212-764-5651; *Pres* Richard McDermott Miller; *VPres* Elliot Offner; *Exec Dir* Gwen M Pier
Open Mon - Fri 10 AM - 5 PM. No admis fee. Estab 1893 as a national organization to spread the knowledge of good sculpture. Average Annual Attendance: 40,000. Mem: 5000; work juried for sculptor mem; vote of Board of Directors for allied professional & patron mem; dues $40-$150; annual meeting second Tues in Jan
Income: Financed by endowment, mem & donations
Exhibitions: 7-8 exhibitions annually on a rotating basis; open to all United States residents
Publications: Membership book, triennial; Sculpture Review Magazine, quarterly
Activities: Educ programs; lect open to public, 2 vis lectr per year; gallery talks; tours; competitions with prizes; scholarships & fels offered; sculptures & educational videos lent to tenants in Americas Tower; originate traveling exhibitions 1 per year; sales shop sells books, magazines, original art
L Library, 1177 Avenue of the Americas, New York, NY 10036. Tel 212-764-5654; FAX 712-764-5651; *Bus Mgr* Amy Frushour Kelly; *Exec Dir* Gwen Pier
Open to the pub for reference; 2500 volumes & periodicals, photographic & original archival materials. For reference only
Library Holdings: Per subs 50; Micro — Fiche; AV — Motion pictures, slides, v-tapes; Other — Clipping files, exhibition catalogs, manuscripts, memorabilia, original art works, pamphlets, photographs, reproductions, sculpture
Special Subjects: Sculpture, American Sculpture

O NATIONAL SOCIETY OF MURAL PAINTERS, INC, c/o American Fine Arts Society, 215 W 57th St, New York, NY 10019. Tel 212-247-4510, 777-8570; *Pres* Jack Stewart
Estab and incorporated 1895 to encourage and advance the standards of mural painting in America; to formulate a code for decorative competitions and by-laws to regulate professional practice. Mem: 200; dues $25, non-res $20
Publications: Biographies and articles pertinent to the mural painting profession; Press Sheets of photographs and articles of the executed work of the members of

society
Activities: Exhibitions held in collaboration with allied professions; available for booking - a traveling show of color sketches for murals on the subject of momentous events in American History

O NATIONAL SOCIETY OF PAINTERS IN CASEIN & ACRYLIC, INC, 969 Catasauqua Rd, Whitehall, PA 18052. Tel 610-264-7472; *Pres* Douglas Wiltrout; *VPres* Robert Dunn
Open in March during exhibition. Estab 1952 as a national organization for a showcase for artists in casein & acrylic. Galleries rented from National Arts Club. Average Annual Attendance: 800 during exhibition. Mem: 120; mem by invitation, work must pass three juries; dues $20; annual meeting in Apr
Income: $3000 (financed by mem)
Exhibitions: Annual Exhibition
Publications: Exhibition Catalog, annually
Activities: Demonstrations; medals & $2500 in prizes given at annual exhibition; originate traveling exhibitions

O NATIONAL WATERCOLOR SOCIETY, 7937 E Fourth Pl, Downey, CA 90241. Tel 310-923-4933; *Pres* Will Ellyn McFarland; *First VPres* Libby Tolley; *Treas* Carol Vink; *Dir Communications* Loa Spnung
Estab 1921 to sponsor art exhibits for the cultural & educational benefit of the pub. Mem: 1560; dues $25-$30 beginning each yr in Mar (must be juried into mem); annual meeting in Jan
Collections: Award-winning paintings from 1954 to present
Exhibitions: Spring Membership Exhibition; National Annual Exhibition.
Publications: Society's newsletter; color annual catalog
Activities: Sponsor yearly grant to children's art program of LA Southwest Museum; originate traveling exhibitions

O NEW ENGLAND WATERCOLOR SOCIETY, 162 Newbury St, Boston, MA 02116. Tel 617-536-7660; *Pres* Thomas Rebok
Estab 1886 to advance the fine art of aqua media. Mem: 200, assoc mem 80; annual meeting in Mar
Income: Financed by mem
Exhibitions: Annual winter membership exhibit; Biennial-North America National Show-Juried Exhibit; 2-3 exhibits per year
Activities: Demonstrations, lect & gallery works open to the public during exhibitions

O PASTEL OF THE WEST COAST, Sacramento Fine Arts Center, 5330-B Gibbons Dr, Carmichael, CA 95608. Tel 916-971-3713; *Pres* Don Paganco; *VPres* Thelma Davis; *Memberships* Dianna Rossi
Estab 1985 to promote soft pastel medium & exhibitions, workshops. Mem: 350; dues $20; quarterly meetings in Jan, Apr, July & Oct 3rd Wed
Income: $20,000 (financed by mem & donations)
Library Holdings: AV — V-tapes
Publications: PSWC newsletter, quarterly; exhibit catalogs
Activities: Classes for adults; lect open to public, 3-4 vis lectr per year; competitions with awards; scholarships offered

O PASTEL SOCIETY OF AMERICA, National Arts Club Gallery, 15 Gramercy Park S, New York, NY 10003. Tel 212-533-6931; *Pres* Flora B Giffuni, MFA
Estab 1972 to promote & encourage pastel painting/artists. Mem: 600; initiation fee $100, dues full $40, assoc $35; jury fee $10; mem open to professional artists; monthly meetings
Library Holdings: AV — A-tapes, slides, v-tapes; Other — Clipping files, exhibition catalogs, original art works
Collections: Raymond Kintsler, Robert Phillip, Constance F Pratt & other master pastellists
Publications: Pastelagram, bi-annual
Activities: Classes for adults; lect open to public, 10 vis lectr per year; gallery talks; competitions with awards; scholarships offered; exten dept serves lending collection of paintings; book traveling exhibitions 3-4 per year; originate traveling exhibitions to galleries & museums

O PASTEL SOCIETY OF OREGON, PO Box 105, Roseburg, OR 97470. Tel 541-440-9171; *Pres* Laura Block
Estab 1987 to promote pastel as an art medium & to educate the pub on pastel. Mem: 80; dues $20 per yr; mem open to artists working in pastels; monthly working meetings
Income: $2000 (financed by mem & shows)
Publications: Pastel Newsletter, bi-monthly
Activities: Classes for adults; hands on exhibitions for schools

O THE PRINT CENTER, 1614 Latimer St, Philadelphia, PA 19103. Tel 215-735-6090; FAX 215-735-5511; *Pres* F Michael Medway; *VPres* Thomas Scuvvia; *Dir* Kathleen Edwards; *Asst Dir* Joan Wetmore; *Treas* Donald McThail
Open Tues - Sat 11 AM - 5:30 PM. No admis fee. Estab 1915 as a non-profit, educational organization dedicated to the promotion of fine prints & the support & encouragement of printmakers, photographers & collectors. Average Annual Attendance: 2000. Mem: 800; dues contributing $50, artist $30, student $20; annual meeting in Mar
Income: $200,000 (financed by mem, private & government grants)
Collections: The Print Center Permanent Collection (prints & photograph collection held at the Philadelphia Museum of Art); The Print Club Archives (documents, books & catalogues held at the Historical Society of Pennsylvania)
Exhibitions: Changing monthly exhibitions of prints & photographs; Annual International Competition (since 1924)

O PRINT COUNCIL OF AMERICA, c/o The Yale Univ Art Gallery, Box 208271, New Haven, CT 06520-8271. Tel 203-432-0628; FAX 203-432-8150; *Pres* Richard Field; *VPres* Suzanne Boorsch
Estab 1956 as a nonprofit organization fostering the study & appreciation of fine prints, new & old. Mem: 100 museum & university professionals interested in prints; annual meeting in Apr or May
Income: Financed by dues & publication royalties
Publications: Occasional publications on old & modern prints; The Print Council Index to Oeuvre-Catalogues of Prints by European & American Artists

O **SALMAGUNDI CLUB,** 47 Fifth Ave, New York, NY 10003. Tel 212-255-7740; *Chmn Board* John McCarthy; *Pres* Richard Pionk; *Chmn Scholarship Members* Gaye Elise Beda; *Chmn Jr Members* Louis DeDonato
Open daily 1 - 5 PM, cl holidays. No admis fee. Estab 1871, incorporated 1880, to enhance the advancement of art appreciation, building purchased 1917. Clubhouse restaurant & bar 2 galleries, Billiard room, library & board room. Average Annual Attendance: 10,000. Mem: 600; dues resident layman & resident artist $500, scholarship graduated to scale, Honorary & Emeritus
Income: Financed by dues, donations, bequests
Collections: Club collection of past & present members
Exhibitions: Seven per year by artist members with cash awards; two per year by non-members (artists, photographers, sculptors) with cash awards; Annual Junior/Scholarship exhibition in February
Publications: Centennial Roster published in 1972; Salmagundi Membership Roster, every three years; Salmagundian, three per yr
Activities: Classes for adults; demonstrations; lect, 8 vis lectr per year; gallery talks; scholarships & fels offered; sales shop sells earrings, necklace, patch, ties & tie tack
L **Library,** 47 Fifth Ave, New York, NY 10003. Tel 212-255-7740; *Librn* Keneth Fitch
For reference only
Library Holdings: Vols 10,000; Per subs 10; Steinway Player piano with 100 rolls; Other — Exhibition catalogs, original art works, photographs, sculpture
Special Subjects: Architecture, Art History, Drawings, Folk Art, Graphic Arts, Historical Material, History of Art & Archaeology, Illustration, Landscapes, Painting - American, Photography, Posters, Sculpture, Watercolors, Woodcuts

O **SCULPTORS GUILD, INC,** Soho Bldg No 603, 110 Greene St, New York, NY 10012. Tel 212-431-5669; FAX 212-431-5669; *Pres* Stephen Keltner; *VPres Publications* Phyllis Mark; *VPres Annual Exhib* Barbara Lekberg; *VPres Admissions* Renata Manasse Schwebel; *Treas* Pamela Endacott
Open Tues & Thurs 10 AM - 5 PM & by appointment. No admis fee. Estab 1937 to promote sculpture & show members' work in an annual show & throughout the country. Mem: 120; qualifications for mem, quality of work & professionalism; dues $125; annual meeting in May
Income: Financed by mem dues, donations, & commissions on sales
Exhibitions: Various exhibitions of small works are held in the Sculptors Guild office every two months; Annual Exhibition at Lever House. (1997) Fordham University Exhibition
Publications: Brochure 1985; exhibit catalogs, every other year for annual exhibitions; 50th Anniversary Catalog 1937-1938; The Guild Reporter, Vol. 1, No. 1, 1986, annually
Activities: Speakers bureau; lect open to public; competitions; original objects of art lent; lending collection contains sculptures; book traveling exhibitions

O **SOCIETY FOR FOLK ARTS PRESERVATION, INC,** * 308 E 79th St, New York, NY 10021. Tel 212-436-4053; *Exec Dir* Evelyn Stern
Estab 1977 to document on film and video, living folk art and craft traditions, worldwide. Mem: 350; dues $40
Income: Financed by donations
Collections: Folk toys & objects; Indian Textiles
Exhibitions: Warli Womens Wall Paintings from Maharashtra, India; A Sense of Beauty; Multi Image Slide Presentations - Crafts and People of Asia
Publications: Newsletter, twice a year
Activities: Educ dept; lect open to public, 3 vis lectr per year; tours; originate traveling exhibitions
L **Library,** * 308 E 79th St, New York, NY 10021. Tel 914-436-4053; Estab 1979. Reference only
Library Holdings: Vols 500; AV — A-tapes, slides 14,000, v-tapes; Other — Clipping files, exhibition catalogs, memorabilia, original art works, pamphlets, photographs
Special Subjects: Living folk arts and crafts
Collections: Indian textiles; folk art

O **SOCIETY OF AMERICAN GRAPHIC ARTISTS,** 32 Union Sq, Rm 1214, New York, NY 10003. Tel 212-260-5706; *Pres* Martin Levine; *VPres* Susan Carter-Carter; *VPres* Florence Putterman; *Treas* Linda Adato
Estab 1916 as a society of printmakers, now a society of graphic artists. Mem: 250 voted in by merit; dues $20; annual meeting May
Income: Financed by mem & associate mem
Exhibitions: Semi-annual Open Competition National Print Exhibition; Semi-annual Closed Members Exhibit; National Traveling Exhibitions every two years
Publications: Exhibition Catalog, annually; Presentation Prints for Associate Membership
Activities: Lect open to public, 1 vis lectr per year; sponsors competitive & members' exhibits with awards; original objects of art lent, lending collection contains original prints; originate traveling exhibitions

O **SOCIETY OF AMERICAN HISTORICAL ARTISTS,** 146 Dartmouth Dr, Osysterbay, NY 11801. Tel 516-681-8820; *Pres* John Duillo; *VPres* James Muir; *Treas* Ron Tunison
Estab 1980 for furthering American Historical Art, especially authenticity. Mem: 13; dues $150; meetings 3-4 per yr
Activities: Awards for excellence

O **SOCIETY OF ARCHITECTURAL HISTORIANS,** 1365 N Astor St, Chicago, IL 60610-2144. Tel 312-573-1365; FAX 312-573-1141; Elec Mail l-torrance.nwu.edu. *Pres* Patricia Waddy; *First VPres* Richard Longstreth; *Exec Dir* Pauline Saliga
Open daily 9 AM - 5 PM. Estab to provide an international forum for those interested in architecture & its related arts, to encourage scholarly research in the field & to promote the preservation of significant architectural monuments throughout the world. Mem: 3500; show an interest in architecture, past, present & future; dues $80; annual meeting Apr
Income: Financed by mem
Publications: Journal, quarterly; Newsletter, bimonthly; Preservation Forum, biannual

Activities: Sponsors competitions; Alice Davis Hitchcock Book Award, Founders' Award, Antoinette Forrester Downing Award & Architectural Exhibition Catalogue Award given annually; scholarships offered; sales shop sells architectural guides & booklets & also back issues of the Journal

O **SOCIETY OF ILLUSTRATORS,** 128 E 63rd St, New York, NY 10021. Tel 212-838-2560; FAX 212-838-2561; *Pres* Vincent DiFate; *Dir* Terrence Brown
Open Mon, Wed, Thurs, Fri 10 AM - 5 PM, Tues 10 AM - 8 PM. No admis fee. Estab 1901 as a national organization of professional illustrators and art directors. Gallery has group, theme, one-man & juried shows, approximately every four weeks. Mem: 850
Publications: Illustrators Annual
Activities: Lect open to public; holds annual national juried exhibition of best illustrations of the year; awards scholarships to college level art students; originate traveling exhibitions; sales shop sells books

O **SOCIETY OF NORTH AMERICAN GOLDSMITHS,** 5009 Londonderry Dr, Tampa, FL 33647. Tel 813-977-5326; FAX 813-977-8462; Elec Mail rmitchel@cftnet.com. *Pres* Billie Jean Theide; *Treas* Becky Thatcher; *Bus Mgr* Robert Mitchell
Maintains rental library. Mem: 2800; dues $55; annual meeting in Apr
Income: $600,000 (financed by mem)
Exhibitions: Distinguished Members of SNAG; Jewelry USA
Publications: Metalsmith magazine, 5 per year; bi-monthly newsletter
Activities: Lect open to members only; competitions; scholarships; lending collection contains motion pictures, videotapes & 10,000 slides; originate traveling exhibitions

O **SOCIETY OF PHOTOGRAPHERS & ARTISTS REPRESENTATIVES,** 60 E 42nd St, No 166, New York, NY 10165. Tel 212-779-7464; FAX 203-886-3321; Estab 1965 as an association of professional representatives of illustrators, photographers & related talent. Mem: must be representative in industry for at least 1 year & provide references
Publications: Membership directory, biannual

O **SPECIAL LIBRARIES ASSOCIATION,** Museum, Arts & Humanities Division, c/o Dir of Communications, 1700 18th NW, Washington, DC 20009. Tel 202-234-4700; *Pres* Sylvia E A Piggott; *Exec Dir* David R Bender; *Bulletin Educ* Sharise Esh; *Dir Public Relations* Jennifer Stoe
Estab 1929 to provide an information forum & exchange for librarians in the specialized fields of museums, arts & humanities. Mem: 1400; dues $105; annual meeting in early June
Publications: Museums, Arts & Humanities Division Bulletin, semi-annual

O **THE STAINED GLASS ASSOCIATION OF AMERICA,** PO Box 22642, Kansas City, MO 64113. FAX 816-361-9173, 333-6690; Elec Mail sgaofa@aol.com. WATS 800-888-7422. *Exec Secy* Kathy Murdock
Estab 1903 as an international organization to promote the development & advancement of the stained glass craft. Mem: 550; dues accredited $350, active $150, affiliate $75, student $50 (various criteria apply to each mem)
Income: Financed by mem dues
Publications: Stained Glass magazine, quarterly
Activities: Educ dept with two & three week courses

O **UKIYO-E SOCIETY OF AMERICA, INC,** * PO Box 665, New York, NY 10150. *Pres* Rosemary Torre; *VPres* Gustin Tan; *Treas* Paul Steier
Estab 1972 as soc of collectors of Japanese woodblock prints. Average Annual Attendance: 350. Mem: 300; dues benefactor $500, supporting $100, contributing $50, individual $40; ten monthly meetings
Income: $10,000 (financed by mem, dues & donations)
Publications: Impressions, scholarly journal; President's Newsletter, 10 per year
Activities: Lect open to public, 8-10 vis lectr per year; awards; original Japanese woodblock prints owned by members lent to institutions sponsoring exhibitions on the subject

O **UNITED STATES DEPARTMENT OF THE INTERIOR,** Indian Arts & Crafts Board, 1849 C St NW, Rm 4004-MIB, Washington, DC 20240. Tel 202-208-3773; *Dir* Geoffrey E Stamm
Open Mon - Fri 8 AM - 5 PM. No admis fee. Estab 1935 to promote contemporary arts by Indians & Alaska Natives of the United States. Board administers the Southern Plains Indian Museum, Anadarko, OK; Museum of the Plains Indian, Browning, MT; Sioux Indian Museum, Rapid City, SD. Average Annual Attendance: 150,000
Income: Financed by federal appropriation
Collections: Contemporary American Indian & Alaska Native Arts
Exhibitions: Twelve special exhibitions among the three museums
Publications: Source Directory of American Indian & Alaska Native owned & operated arts & crafts businesses
Activities: Information & advice on matters pertaining to contemporary Indian, Eskimo & Aleut arts & crafts

O **VISUAL ARTISTS & GALLERIES ASSOCIATION (VAGA),** 521 Fifth Ave, Ste 800, New York, NY 10175. Tel 212-808-0616; FAX 212-808-0064; *Exec Dir* Robert Panzer
Open daily 9 AM - 5 PM, by appointment. Estab 1976 to help artists control the reproduction of their works, from sculptures to photographs in textbooks; to act as a clearinghouse for licensing reproduction rights & set up a directory of artists & other owners of reproduction rights for international use. Mem: European 10,000, American 500; dues gallery & associate $300, estates $75, artist $50
Income: Financed by mem & royalties
Special Subjects: Copyright Law, Moral Rights, Fair Use, Droite Morale
Publications: Newsletter

O **WASHINGTON SCULPTORS GROUP,** 2735 McKinley St NW, Washington, DC 20015. Tel 202-362-7707; *Pres* Mariah Josephy; *VPres* Tom Rooney; *VPres* Sam Noto; *Treas* Serena Litofsky
Estab 1983 to promote sculpture. Use pub & corporate space for exhibitions;

members' juried exhibitions available for exchange shows. Average Annual Attendance: 1000. Mem: 300; dues $30

Income: $6500 (financed by mem & occasional grants)

Exhibitions: 2-3 juried exhibitions per year. (1997) Sculpture 97; Landscapes-An Exhibition of Sculpture

Activities: Lect open to public, 10 vis lectr per year; originate traveling exhibitions

O **WOMEN'S CAUCUS FOR ART,** * Moore College of Art, 1920 Race St, Philadelphia, PA 19103. Tel 215-854-0922; FAX 215-854-0915; *Pres* Helen Kiebvesadel; *Exec Dir* Essie Karp
Estab 1972 as a non-profit women's professional & service organization for visual arts. Average Annual Attendance: 500. Mem: 4000; annual meeting in Feb
Income: $55,000 (financed by mem)
Publications: Membership Directory, Honors Catalogue (all annual); National Update (quarterly)
Activities: Honor awards for senior women in the arts

ALABAMA

ANNISTON

M ANNISTON MUSEUM OF NATURAL HISTORY, 800 Museum Dr, PO Box 1587, 36202-1587. Tel 205-237-6766; FAX 205-237-6776; *Asst Dir* Cheryl Bradd; *Develop Officer* Lindie K Brown; *Cur Exhibits* Paul Siboroski; *Marketing Mgr* Paige Moreland
Open Tues - Fri 9 AM - 5 PM, Sat 10 AM - 5 PM, Sun 1 - 5 PM, cl Mon. Admis adults $3, children $2. Estab 1930, nationally accredited mus with the purpose of enhancing pub knowledge, understanding & appreciation of living things & their environments. Permanent exhibit halls interpret the theme Adaptation the Environment; changing exhibit gallery features exhibitions focusing on interrelationships between nature & art. Average Annual Attendance: 100,000. Mem: 1600; dues family $25, individual $20; annual meeting in Sept
Income: Financed by mem, earned income, donations & city appropriations
Collections: Archaeology; Ethnology; Natural Science; Wildlife Art
Activities: Classes for adults & children; docent programs; lect open to public, 8 vis lect per year; book traveling exhibitions 5 per year; retail store sells books, original art & reproductions

BIRMINGHAM

M BIRMINGHAM MUSEUM OF ART, 2000 Eighth Ave N, 35203. Tel 205-254-2565; *Dir* Gail Trechsel; *Cur Edu* Dr Kate Bennett; *Cur Oriental Art* Dr Don Wood
Open Tues - Fri 10 AM - Noon & 1 - 4 PM. No admis fee. Estab 1951 as a general art mus with collections from earliest manifestation of man's creativity to contemporary work. Its goal is to illustrate the highest level of man's artistic work in an art historical context. The 36 galleries are climate controlled; lighting system is modern & controlled to latest safety standards. Average Annual Attendance: 100,000. Mem: 6000; dues $35 - $500
Income: $3,500,000 (financed by mem, city appropriation & annual donations)
Purchases: $650,000
Collections: English ceramics & silver; American painting & sculpture; American decorative arts 19th-20th centuries; Ethnographic Collection; African, American Indian, Pre-Columbian works; Oriental Collection; Indian, Korean, Chinese & Southeast Asian works; Oriental Rug Collection; European paintings; Renaissance to 20th century art; Wedgewood Collection; photography; prints and drawings, 18th-19th centuries
Publications: Annual bulletin; bi-monthly calendar; Zorn Catalogue
Activities: Classes for adults & children; docent training; lect open to public, 12-15 vis lectr per year; concerts; gallery talks; tours; competitions; individual paintings lent to other museums; organize & circulate traveling exhibitions; museum shop sells reproductions, prints and gifts
L Clarence B Hanson, Jr Library, 2000 Eighth Ave N, 35203-2278. Tel 205-254-2982; FAX 205-254-2714; *Librn* Grace Reid
Income: Financed by city & private funding
Library Holdings: Vols 10,500; Per subs 63; Other — Exhibition catalogs
Special Subjects: American Indian Art, American Western Art, Art History, Asian Art, Ceramics, Decorative Arts, Painting - American, Painting - European, Porcelain, Pre-Columbian Art, Primitive Art, Traditional Arts (Pre-Columbian, African & American Indian)

L BIRMINGHAM PUBLIC LIBRARY, Arts, Music & Recreation Department, 2100 Park Pl, 35203. Tel 205-226-3670; FAX 205-226-3737; Elec Mail kralya@bham.lib.al.us. *Head Librn* Kelyn Ralya; *Librn* Susan Richardson
Open Mon - Tues 9 AM - 8 PM, Thurs - Sat 9 AM - 6 PM, Sun 2 - 6 PM. Estab 1909 to serve the Jefferson County area
Library Holdings: Vols 40,000; Per subs 155; Micro — Fiche; AV — A-tapes, cassettes, rec; Other — Framed reproductions 200
Special Subjects: Architecture, Art History, Asian Art, Decorative Arts, Folk Art, Graphic Design, History of Art & Archaeology, Islamic Art, Mixed Media, Pewter, Porcelain, Portraits, Pottery, Pre-Columbian Art, Sculpture, Applied Arts

M BIRMINGHAM SOUTHERN COLLEGE, Doris Wainwright Kennedy Art Center, * 900 Arkadelphia Rd, PO Box A21, 35254-0001. Tel 205-226-4928; FAX 205-226-4627; *Dir* Robert Shelton
Open Mon - Fri 8:30 AM - 5 PM
Exhibitions: Faculty show (all medias); juried student show; BFA show

M SLOSS FURNACES NATIONAL HISTORIC LANDMARK, PO Box 11781, 35202. Tel 205-324-1911; *Dir* Jim Burnham; *Asst Dir* Paige Wainwright; *Asst Cur* Lenny Bates
Open Tues - Sat 10 AM - 4 PM, Sun Noon - 4 PM. No admis fee. Estab as an industrial mus, former blast furnace plant; temporary exhibitions, especially in metal arts

M UNIVERSITY OF ALABAMA AT BIRMINGHAM, Visual Arts Gallery, 900 13th St S, 35294-1260. Tel 205-934-4941; FAX 205-975-6639; Telex 88-8826. *Pres* Claude Bennett; *Exec VPres* Kenneth Roozen; *Cur* Antoinette Nordan
Open Mon - Fri 1 - 6 PM, Sun 2 - 6 PM except between exhibitions, holidays & vacation. No admis fee. Estab 1973 to exhibit works of students, faculty & nationally & internationally known artists & to form & exhibit a permanent collection of art since 1750. Two galleries, each 1200 sq ft & adjacent storage all on first floor of Humanities building with adjacent sculpture courtyard. All are temperature, humidity controlled & secured by alarms. Average Annual Attendance: 4100
Income: Financed by university & private donations
Collections: †Contemporary art; †Student & faculty works since 1950; †Works on paper since 1750
Exhibitions: Contemporary Cast Iron Art; Hans Grohs: Prints & Watercolors; Tales from the Nuclear Age: Photographs by James Lerager; Timed Exposure: Early 20th Century Photographs & African-Americans in Anniston, AL; Felix Vallotton: Prints & Preparatory Drawings
Publications: Exhibit catalogs
Activities: Lect open to pub, 2 vis lectr per year; gallery talks; tours; competitions; awards; individual and original objects of art lent to qualified mus & galleries; book traveling exhibitions; mus shop sells gallery publications & posters

M WATERCOLOR SOCIETY OF ALABAMA, PO Box 43011, 35243-0011. Tel 205-822-3721; *Pres* Nanette L Jones; *Treas* Mary Ann Kohn; *Pres-Elect* Jennifer Faust
Estab 1940 to promote watercolor painting. Mem: 708; dues $25; annual meeting in Sept
Income: $24,000 (financed by mem & award donations)
Exhibitions: (1997) Annual Alabama Members Exhibition; 56th Annual National Exhibition
Publications: Newsletters & prospectus
Activities: Classes for adults; lect open to public, 2 vis lectr per year; competitions with prizes; scholarships offered

DECATUR

M JOHN C CALHOUN STATE COMMUNITY COLLEGE, Art Gallery, Hwy 31 N, PO Box 2216, 35609-2216. Tel 205-306-2500, 306-2699; *Pres* Dr Richard Carpenter; *Dir* Helen C Austin, PhD; *Cur* Dr Art Bond
Open Mon - Fri 8 AM - 3 PM, special weekend openings. No admis fee. Estab 1965 to provide temporary exhibits of fine art during the school year for the benefit of the surrounding three county area & for the students & faculty of the college. Located in a fine arts building completed June 1979, the gallery has 105 linear ft of carpeted wall space with adjustable incandescent track lighting & fluorescent general lights in a controlled & well-secured environment. Average Annual Attendance: 20,000
Collections: Permanent collection consists of graphics collection as well as selected student & faculty works
Exhibitions: Student Art Exhibit; Student Photographs
Publications: Announcements; exhibition catalogs
Activities: Classes for adults; lect open to public, 3 vis lectr per year; gallery talks; tours; competitions with awards; scholarships and fels offered; individual paintings & original objects of art lent to museums, galleries & college art departments; lending collection contains 40 original art works & 85 original prints; book traveling exhibitions, biannually

DOTHAN

M WIREGRASS MUSEUM OF ART, 126 Museum Ave, PO Box 1624, 36302-1624. Tel 334-794-3871; FAX 334-671-0380; *Dir* Sam W Kates; *Educ Coordr* Alberta Keener; *Cur* Carolyn Shafer
Open Tues - Sat 10 AM - 5 PM, Sun 1 - 5 PM, cl Mon. No Admis fee. Estab 1988 to provide exhibits & educational programs. Maintains library. Average Annual Attendance: 15,000. Mem: 600; dues $20 - $1000
Income: $250,000 (financed by mem, city appropriation, special events & fees)
Collections: 19th & 20th century works on paper, decorative arts, paintings & sculpture
Exhibitions: (1997) Art for Art's Sake Auction; Local Color: Dothan Wiregrass Art League; 19th & 20th Century Works from a Private Collection; Frank Stella: A Collection of Prints, 1967-1995; Stella's Contemporaries: Works on Paper from the 1960s & 70s; Permanent Collection & Staff Favorites. (1998) African-American Ceramicists; The Art of Africa; Beverly B Erdreich; A Flash of Brilliance: American Cut Grass; Glass from a Private Collection; Marc Chagall: Works on Paper; The Navy Art of Thomas Hart Benton; The Posh Purse: A Decorative Accessory, circa 1780-1940; A Silver Setting: Victorian Silver, 1860-

1890; The Style of Pauline Burdeshaw; Surrealist Works on Paper; Tropical Rhythms: The Collage of Beth Appleton
Activities: Classes for children; docent programs; lect open to public, 6 vis lectr per year; competitions with prizes; originate traveling exhibitions; museum shop sells books, original art, reproductions, prints, art related items, stationary & children's items

FAIRHOPE

A **EASTERN SHORE ART ASSOCIATION, INC,** Eastern Shore Art Center, 401 Oak St, 36532. Tel 334-928-2228; FAX 334-928-5188; *Pres* Jim Gambil; *Mgr* B G Hinds
Open Mon - Sat 10 AM 4 PM, cl Sun, New Years Day, Thanksgiving & Christmas. No admis fee. Estab Assoc 1952, Center 1963 features local, regional & nationally known artist; sponsor cultural, educational & social activities. Four galleries change monthly, a fifth gallery is for members only. Maintains library. Average Annual Attendance: 100,000. Mem: 8000; dues $1500, $500, $200, $100, $34, $20; annual meeting in May
Income: $200,000 (financed by gifts, dues, tuition fees & purchases)
Collections: Herman Bischoff, drawings, oils & watercolors; Maria Martinez, pottery; Emily Woodward Collection; contemporary American paintings from Gulf coast area; primarily southern artist
Publications: Bi-monthly newsletter; Yearbook
Activities: Classes for adults & children; concerts; gallery talks; tours; competitions with awards; outreach educational program arranges gallery tours, slide programs & portable exhibits; sales shop sells original art, reproductions, prints, photographs, pottery
L **Library,** 401 Oak St, PO Box 443, 36533-0443. Tel 334-928-2228; FAX 334-928-5188; *Librn* Peggy Richardson; *Registrar & Public Relations Coordr* Debbie Hanson
Open Mon - Sat 10 AM - 4 PM, cl Sun, New Years Day, Thanksgiving & Christmas. For lending & reference for members
Library Holdings: Vols 700; Other — Clipping files, exhibition catalogs, memorabilia, original art works, pamphlets

FAYETTE

M **FAYETTE ART MUSEUM,** 530 N Temple Ave, 35555. Tel 205-932-8727; FAX 205-932-8788; *Board Chmn & Cur* Jack Black
Open Mon, Tues, Thurs & Fri 9 AM - Noon & 1 - 4 PM, also by appointment. No admis fee. Estab 1969 to offer on continuous basis exhibits of visual arts free to the pub. All facilities are at Fayette Civic Center: six multi-purpose galleries, five folk art galleries plus lobby & corridors; 1200 running ft of exhibition space
Income: Financed by city appropriation & Annual Art Festival
Purchases: Very limited purchases of works by local & regional artists
Collections: 3300 paintings, 2600 by Lois Wilson, a former resident; Margarette Guinther & by local folk artists Jimmy Lee Sudduth, Benjamin Perkins, Fred Webster & Sybil Gibson
Exhibitions: Jimmy Lee Sudduth (folk art); Rev Benjamin Perkins (folk art); Fred Webster & Sybil Gibson
Activities: Lect open to public; gallery talks; tours; individual paintings & original objects of art lent to museums & galleries; originate traveling exhibitions to qualified museums

GADSDEN

M **GADSDEN MUSEUM OF FINE ARTS, INC,** 2829 W Meighan Blvd, 35904-1717. Tel 205-546-7365; *Dir* Sherrie Hamil; *Pres* Jerry E Baker; *VPres* Janie Terrell
Open Mon - Fri 10 AM - 4 PM, Thurs 10 AM - 8 PM, Sun 1 - 5 PM. No admis fee. Estab 1965 to promote, foster, & preserve the collection of paintings, sculpture, artifacts & antiques. 4500 sq ft. Average Annual Attendance: 10,000. Mem: 2500; dues individual $25
Income: Financed by mem, local government & grants
Collections: Fowler Collection (paintings, sculpture & porcelain); Snelgrove Historical Collection
Exhibitions: Quilt exhibit; antique radios; annual juried art show
Activities: Classes for adults & children; workshops; lect open to public, 500 vis lectr per year; competitions with awards

HUNTSVILLE

A **HUNTSVILLE ART LEAGUE,** 2801 Memorial Pkwy, Ste 8B, 35801. Tel 205-534-3860; *Pres* Jimmy Temple; *First VPres* Harriet Smith; *Educ Chmn* Marty Vinc; *Exec Dir* Susan Sefton; *Treas* Sally McDonell; *Office Mgr* Karen Dewhitt
Open Mon - Sat 10 AM - 7 PM, Sun 1 - 6 PM. No admis fee. Estab 1957. The League is a nonprofit organization dedicated to promoting & stimulating the appreciation of the visual arts. 81 artists exhibiting, all mediums, special exhibitions. Average Annual Attendance: 4600. Mem: 200; dues $25; meetings held first Mon each month
Income: Financed by mem, commissions, grants
Exhibitions: Annual Fall & Spring Shows; annual juried show; continuous exhibitions throughout Huntsville; featured artist each month; Southern Exposure
Publications: Newsletter on activities & exhibition opportunities in the Southeast, monthly; mem books
Activities: Classes for adults & children; lect open to public, 12 vis lectr per year; competitions; tours; individual paintings & original objects of art leased to banks, restaurants, theaters; lending collection contains original art works, original prints, paintings, photographs, sculpture; sales shop sells original art, reproductions, prints, small hand made art objects as special seasonal gifts

M **HUNTSVILLE MUSEUM OF ART,** 700 Monroe St, 35801. Tel 205-535-4350; FAX 205-532-1743; *Pres* Richard Loring; *Chief Cur* Peter Baldaia; *Educ Dir* Deborah Taylor; *Registrar* David Reyes; *Admin* Laura Marshall; *Develop Dir* Wendy Tucker
Open Tues - Fri 10 AM - 5 PM, Sat 9 AM - 5 PM, Sun 1 - 5 PM, cl Mon. No admis fee. Estab 1970. Mus is part of the Von Braun Civic Center ; 23,000 sq ft total including 9000 sq ft exhibition galleries. Atmospherically controlled galleries & storage; 10-12 special exhibitions per year. Average Annual Attendance: 57,000. Mem: 1200; dues Champion $5000, Sustaining $2500, Participating $1000, Benefactor $500, Sponsor $200, Patron $100, Contributing $25
Income: $1,000,000 (financed by mem, city appropriation, grants & support groups)
Purchases: $25,000
Collections: †American art, 1700-present, including paintings & works on paper; local & regional art; African art; Oriental art
Exhibitions: Annual Youth Art Month & Holiday Celebrations Exhibitions
Publications: Brochures; catalogs, occasionally; Museum Calendar, quarterly
Activities: Classes for adults & children; docent training; Partnership in Art Education program; lect open to public, 3-4 vis lectrs per year; concerts; gallery talks; tours; competitions with awards; scholarships offered; collection loan program; book traveling exhibitions 8-10 per year; originate traveling exhibitions
L **Reference Library,** 700 Monroe St SW, 35801. Tel 205-535-4350; FAX 205-532-1743; *Chief Cur* Peter J Baldaia; *Educ Dir* Deborah Taylor
Open Tues - Sat 10 AM - 5 PM, Sun 1 - 5 PM. No Admis fee. Estab 1970 to bring art & people together. 8000 sq ft of gallery space in 5 galleries. Average Annual Attendance: 40,000. Mem: 1800; dues $30
Library Holdings: Vols 3000; Per subs 20; AV — Slides; Other — Clipping files, exhibition catalogs 2000, pamphlets
Special Subjects: Antiquities-Greek, Architecture, Bronzes, Ceramics, Crafts, Decorative Arts, Etchings & Engravings, Glass, Graphic Arts, Metalwork, Miniatures, Oriental Art, Photography, Pottery, Sculpture, Contemporary American Art, Museum Management
Collections: 19th & 20th century American art with an emphasis on the region of the South Asian art; African art; postwar graphics
Exhibitions: Biennial Red Clay Survey Exhibition, southern contemporary art; Chip Cooper: On Common Ground (cibachromes); Chip Cooper: Mighty Fortress (cibachromes); Kathryn Windham Photographs (silver prints)
Activities: Classes for adults & children; docent training; lect; films; symposia; lect open to public, 10-12 vis lectr per year; gallery talks; tours; competitions with awards; scholarships offered; originate traveling exhibitions

M **UNIVERSITY OF ALABAMA AT HUNTSVILLE,** Gallery of Art, 35899. Tel 205-890-6114; *Gallery Adminr* Karen Haynes
Open Mon - Fri 1 - 4:30 PM. No admis fee. Estab 1975. An intimate & small renovated chapel with a reserved section for exhibits located in the University Center. Average Annual Attendance: 1800
Income: Financed by administration
Exhibitions: Contemporary artwork (US & international); annual juried exhibition
Activities: Lect open to public, 7-10 vis lectr per year; gallery talks; competitions with awards; individual paintings & original objects of art lent; book traveling exhibitions 3 per year; originate traveling exhibitions

MOBILE

M **MOBILE MUSEUM OF ART,** Museum Dr, PO Box 8426, 36689. Tel 334-343-2667; FAX 334-343-2680; *Cable* FAMOS. *Dir* Joseph B Schenk
Open Tues - Sun 10 AM - 5 PM. Admis for special exhibitions only. Estab 1964 to foster the appreciation of art & provide art educ programs for the community. Primarily American 19th & 20th Century. Average Annual Attendance: 100,000. Mem: 1100; dues business mem $1500, benefactor $500, associate $250, patron $100, supporting $50, family $25, individual $15
Income: Financed by mem, city appropriation & state grants
Purchases: $35,000
Collections: American Crafts; African Art; 19th & 20th century American & European paintings, sculpture, prints, & decorative arts; Oriental art; Miller Oriental porcelain, Indian miniatures, Chinese ceramics, Medieval art, European paintings & sculpture; 16th to 20th century and classical art; Southern furniture; Wellington Collection of Wood Engravings; †1930s - 1940s paintings & graphics
Exhibitions: Mobile Artist Asn Juried Exhibition; Watercolor Society Juried Exhibition; Best of Mobile (invitational); Southeastern Juried Exhibition
Publications: Art Patrons League Calendar, quarterly
Activities: Classes for adults & children; docent training; lect open to public, 15-25 lectr per year; gallery talks, tours, competitions with awards; individual paintings & objects of art lent; lending collection includes art works, original prints, paintings, photographs, sculpture; museum shop sells books, reproductions, jewelry, toys, posters, baskets, pottery, puzzles, glass art
L **Library,** Langan Park, PO Box 8426, 36689. Tel 334-343-2667; FAX 334-343-2680; *Educ Cur* Ann Pond
For reference only
Library Holdings: Vols 1800; Per subs 20; AV — Slides; Other — Clipping files, exhibition catalogs, framed reproductions, pamphlets, photographs, prints, reproductions
Collections: American & European paintings & decorative arts; contemporary crafts; Southern decorative arts; wood engraving

M **MUSEUM OF MOBILE,** 355 Government St, 36602. Tel 334-434-7569; FAX 334-434-7686; *Dir* Barbara E Taylor; *Cur Coll* John Gavin; *Cur Exhibits* Robert McClendon; *African-American Cur* Sheila Flanagan; *Researcher* Charles Torrey
Open Tues - Sat 10 AM - 5 PM, Sun 1 - 5 PM, cl Mon & city holidays. Estab 1964 to interpret Mobile's history. Consists of three mus incl: The Carlen House built in 1842 is a beautiful example of that style of architecture unique to this area, the Creole Cottage; the Phoenix Fire Mus occupies the home station house of the Phoenix Steam Fire Company No 6, which was organized in 1838; the Bernstein-Bush House built in 1872. Mus is located in elegantly restored Bernstein-Bush townhouse, the mus houses exhibits bearing upon the history of

Mobile & the Gulf Coast area since its founding as a French colony in 1702. This building is listed on the National Register of Historic Places. Displays illustrate life in Mobile under French, British & Spanish colonial rule, the rapid growth of the city in the pre-Civil War period, the rise & fall of the fortunes of Mobile of the best defended Confederate city & the ever international seaport & center of culture, business & scholarly institutions. Average Annual Attendance: 60,000

Income: Financed by city appropriation

Collections: CSS Hunley; Queens of Mobile Mardi Gras; Admiral Raphael Semmes collection includes probably the finest Confederate presentation sword in existence, along with a presentation cased revolver & accessories, books, paintings, documents, personal papers & ship models; Mardi Gras Gallery; 80,000 items reflecting the entire span of the history of Mobile

Publications: Exhibition & collection catalogs

Activities: Classes for children; docent training; lect open to pub; tours; original objects of art lent to other mus; mus shop sells books, reproductions & slides

L **Reference Library,** 355 Government St, 36602. Tel 334-434-7569; FAX 334-434-7686; *Dir* Barbara E Taylor
For reference only
Library Holdings: Vols 3000; Per subs 12; AV — Slides; Other — Clipping files, memorabilia, original art works, photographs, prints, sculpture

M **Carlen House,** 54 Carlen St, 36606. Tel 334-434-7569; *Dir* Barbara E Taylor
Open Tues - Sat 10 AM - 5 PM, Sun 1 - 5 PM, cl Mon. Estab 1970 to preserve an authentic representation of Southern architecture. The Carlen House is an important representation of Mobile's unique contribution to American regional architecture. It is a fine example of the Creole Cottage as it evolved from the French Colonial form & was adapted for early American use. The house was erected in 1842; furnishings are from the collections of the Museum of the City of Mobile & are typical of a house of that period. Average Annual Attendance: 6200

Exhibitions: Sleeping Under the Stars: Exhibition of star quilts 1820-1990, guest curator Mary Elizabeth Johnson

Activities: Lect open to pub; group tours are conducted by guides in period costumes who emphasize aspects of everyday life in Mobile in the mid-nineteenth century. The making of material is demonstrated by the guide who cards wool, spins fibers & weaves cloth; individual paintings & original objects of art lent to other mus; sales shop sells books, slides & souvenirs

L **UNIVERSITY OF SOUTH ALABAMA,** Ethnic American Slide Library, Dept Arts & Art History, 172 VAB, 36688. Tel 334-460-6335; FAX 334-414-8294; *Acting Chmn* John H Cleverdon
Open daily 8 AM - 5 PM. Estab for the acquisition of slides of works produced by Afro-American, Mexican-American & Native American artists & the distribution of duplicate slides of these works to educational institutions & individuals engaged in research

Library Holdings: AV — Slides

Collections: 19th & 20th centuries ethnic American art works in ceramics, drawing, painting, photography, printmaking, sculpture

Publications: Slide Catalog

MONTEVALLO

M **UNIVERSITY OF MONTEVALLO,** The Gallery, Sta 6400, 35115. Tel 205-665-6400; *Acting Gallery Dir* Scott Stephens
Open Mon - Fri 10 AM - 4 PM. No admis fee. Estab Sept 1977 to supply students & pub with high quality contemporary art. The gallery is 27 x 54 ft with track lighting; floors & walls carpeted; no windows. Average Annual Attendance: 3000

Income: Financed by state appropriation & regular dept budget

Publications: High quality catalogs & posters

Activities: Management classes; lect open to pub, 6 vis lectr per year; gallery talks; originate traveling exhibitions

MONTGOMERY

M **ALABAMA DEPARTMENT OF ARCHIVES & HISTORY,** Museum Galleries, 624 Washington Ave, 36130. Tel 334-242-4363; FAX 334-240-3433; *Dir* Edwin C Bridges; *Asst Dir Spec Coll* Alden Monroe; *Asst Dir Public Services* Debbie Pendleton
Open Mon - Fri 8 AM - 5 PM, Sat 9 AM - 5 PM. No admis fee. Estab 1901. Reference only. Average Annual Attendance: 78,000

Income: Financed by state appropriation

Collections: Early Alabama Indians; Children's Gallery & Grandma's Attic (for children of all ages); Military Room; the 19th Century Room; William Rufus King Room; Archives Sampler Room

Exhibitions: History of Alabama

Activities: Classes for adults; docent training; lect open to public, 15 vis lectr per year; tours; exten dept serves Records Retention facility for state government records; individual paintings & original objects of art lent to museums with in state, state capitol, governor's offices & Governor's Mansion; lending collection contains paintings; sales shop sells books, Civil War & Civil Rights related materials, reproduced arrowheads, jewelry & posters

L **Library,** 624 Washington Ave, 36130. Tel 334-242-4152; FAX 334-240-3433; *Readi Reference Librn* Frazine Taylor; *Archival Librn* Dr Norwood Kerr
Open Mon - Fri 8 AM - 5 PM, Sat 9 AM - 5 PM, reference room cl Mon. Estab 1901. American Indian gallery, Military & Flag galleries, 19th century galleries & Hands On gallery with Grandma's Attic & Discovery Boxes. Average Annual Attendance: 50,000

Library Holdings: Vols 32,000; Micro — Fiche, reels; AV — A-tapes, cassettes, fs, lantern slides, motion pictures, rec, v-tapes; Other — Clipping files, manuscripts, pamphlets, photographs

Special Subjects: Historical Material, Manuscripts, Maps

Collections: Alabama Subjects 1700-1989; Political & Social Events; State Government Records

AMERICAN SOCIETY OF PORTRAIT ARTISTS (ASOPA)
For further information, see National and Regional Organizations

C **BLOUNT INC,** Blount Corporate Collection, 4520 Executive Park Dr, PO Box 949, 36116. Tel 334-244-4000; FAX 334-271-8188; *Exec Asst to Chmn* Shirley Milligan
Open 8 AM - 5 PM by appointment only. Estab 1973, original collection began in response to commemorate America's bicentennial. Collection displayed at Corporate Headquarters Building

Collections: †American art—200 years; †international sculpture; †regional artists; †works by American artists from Revolutionary period to present

Exhibitions: Greenville Co Museum of Art; Selections from the Blount Collection; Highlights of the Blount Collection

Publications: Blount Collection Vol I, II & III, catalog; Blount Collection, quarterly newsletter

Activities: Lect; concerts; gallery talks; tours; poster employee art competition with award; individual paintings & original objects of art lent to museums; instrumental in the formation of Art, Inc, a traveling exhibition of corporate art

M **MONTGOMERY MUSEUM OF FINE ARTS,** One Museum Dr, 36117. Tel 334-244-5700; FAX 334-244-5774; *Pres* John Walter Stowers; *Dir* Mark M Johnson; *Deputy Dir Operations* Grace M Hanchrow; *Asst Dir* Shirley Woods; *Registrar* Pamela Bransford; *Cur, Paintings & Sculpture* Margaret Ausfeld; *Cur Educ* Tara Sartorius
Open Tues - Sat 10 AM - 5 PM, Thurs evening until 9 PM, Sun Noon - 5 PM. No admis fee. Estab 1930 to generally promote the cultural artistic & higher educ life of the city of Montgomery by all methods that may be properly pursued by a mus or art gallery. Mus open in new 45,000 sq ft facility located on 35 acres of landscaped park, adjacent to the Alabama Shakespeare festival. Galleries occupy lower & upper levels of two story neopalladian structure. A new educ wing. Artworks occupies 3000 sq ft & includes a hands-on, interactive gallery & studio. A recent gift of 41 American Paintings from the Blount Inc. Collection of American Art is permanently installed in spacious Blount Wing of the new mus; 240 seat auditorium. Average Annual Attendance: 50,000. Mem: 2700; dues Director's Circle $100-$5000, patron $100-$500, general $15-$50; annual meeting in Oct

Income: Financed by mem, city & county appropriations & grants

Collections: †American & European Works on Paper; †Contemporary graphics & other works on paper by artists living in the South; decorative arts; master prints of the 15th & 19th Centuries; †paintings by American artists from early 19th Century through the present; 41 paintings from the Blount Collection of American Art

Publications: Annual Report; Calendar of Events, monthly; exhibitions catalogs for selected shows

Activities: Classes for children; docent training; lect open to public, 20 vis lectr per year; films; concerts; gallery talks; tours; scholarships & fels offered; individual paintings & original objects of art lent to galleries which meet AAM standards for security & preservation; lending collection contains 300 original prints, 250 paintings, photographs, sculpture & 3500 slides; book traveling exhibitions 12 per year; originate traveling exhibitions, national & international; museum shop sells books, original art, reproductions, prints & gift items

L **Library,** One Museum Dr, PO Box 230819, 36123. Tel 334-244-5700; FAX 334-244-5774; *Librn* Alice T Carter
Open Tues - Fri 10 AM - 5 PM. Estab 1975 to assist the staff & community with reliable art research material. For reference

Income: Financed by City of Montgomery & Mus Assoc

Library Holdings: Vols 3000; Per subs 16; AV — Slides, v-tapes; Other — Clipping files, exhibition catalogs, pamphlets, photographs, prints

Special Subjects: American Art

SELMA

M **STURDIVANT HALL,** 713 Mabry St, PO Box 1205, 36702. Tel 334-872-5626; *Pres* Lawrence Hughen; *Cur* Mrs George Tate Jr; *Cur* Pat Tate; *Cur* Marie Barker
Open Tues - Sat 9 AM - 4 PM, Sun 2 - 4 PM. Admis adults $4, student $2, children under 6 free. Estab 1957 as a mus with emphasis on the historical South. Period furniture of the 1850s in a magnificent architectural edifice built 1852-53. Average Annual Attendance: 10,000. Mem: 480; dues $15 - $1000; annual meeting in Apr

Income: Financed by mem, city & state appropriations

Collections: Objects of art; †period furniture; textiles

Publications: Brochure

Activities: Lect open to public; tours

THEODORE

M **BELLINGRATH GARDENS & HOME,** 12401 Bellingrath Gardens Rd, 36582. Tel 334-973-2217; FAX 334-973-0540; *Exec Dir* J Robert Pearson; *Museum Dir* Thomas C McGehee
Open daily 8 AM - dusk. Admis home & garden $14.70, children 6-11 $11.56, garden only $6.83. Estab 1932 to perpetuate an appreciation of nature & display man-made objects d'art. The gallery houses the world's largest public display of Boehm porcelain & the Bellingrath Home contains priceless antiques. Average Annual Attendance: 200,000

Income: Financed by Foundation & admissions

Collections: Early-mid 19th Century American antique furnishings from South, silver & crystal; separate Boehm Gallery from Bellingrath Home: porcelains by Meissen, Dresden, Copeland, Capo di Monte, Sevres

Activities: Classes for children; tours; lending collection contains kodachromes, motion pictures, slides; sales shop sells books, magazines, prints, reproductions & slides

TUSCALOOSA

A ARTS COUNCIL OF TUSCALOOSA COUNTY, INC, 600 Greensboro, 35401. Tel 205-758-8083; FAX 205-345-2787; *Exec Dir* Gail Skidmore
Open Mon - Fri 8 AM - 5 PM. No admis fee. Estab 1970 for the develop, promotion & coordination of educational, cultural & artistic activities of the city & county of Tuscaloosa. Mem: 410 individual, 30 organization; dues organization $25, individual $15; annual meeting Oct, meetings quarterly
Income: Financed by endowment, mem, city, state & county appropriation
Publications: Arts calendar, monthly newsletter
Activities: Dramatic programs; concert series, Bama Fanfare (professional performances for students K - 12); sponsor of educ program called SPECTRA (Special Teaching Resources in the Arts)

M UNIVERSITY OF ALABAMA, Sarah Moody Gallery of Art, 103 Garland Hall, PO Box 870270, 35487-0270. Tel 205-348-5967; FAX 205-348-9642; Elec Mail wdooley@uaivm.ua.edu. *Dir* William Dooley
Open Mon - Fri 8:30 AM - 4:30 PM, Sun 2 - 5 PM. No admis fee. Estab 1946
Collections: Small collection of paintings, prints, photography, drawings, primarily contemporary
Exhibitions: Approx 15 exhibitions per year
Publications: Exhibit catalogs
Activities: Originate traveling exhibitions

TUSCUMBIA

A TENNESSEE VALLEY ART ASSOCIATION & CENTER, 511 N Water St, PO Box 474, 35674. Tel 205-383-0533; *Exec Dir* Mary Settle-Cooney; *Admin Asst* Norma Burns; *Dir Visual Arts* Shirley Maize; *Exhibit Coordr* Lucie Ayers
Open Mon - Fri 9 AM - 5 PM, Sun 2 - 4 PM. No admis fee. Chartered 1963 to promote the arts in the Tennessee Valley. Building completed 1973. Main Gallery 60 x 40 ft; West Gallery for small exhibits, meetings and arts and crafts classes. Located one block from the birthplace of Helen Keller in Tuscumbia. During the Helen Keller Festival, TVAC sponsors the Arts and Crafts Fair. Average Annual Attendance: 10,000. Mem: Dues benefactor $100, family $50, sustaining $15, regular $15, student $10
Income: $200,000 (financed by appropriations, donations, grants & mem)
Collections: †Reynolds Collection (paintings); †TVAA Crafts Collection
Exhibitions: Exhibition South (paintings, sculpture, prints), annual fall juried art show for mid-south states; Spring Photo Show, annual juried; exhibits feature work by national artists, members & students; handcraft exhibits
Activities: Classes for adults & children; dramatic programs; class instruction in a variety of arts and crafts; workshops & performances in drama; lect open to public; concerts; competitions with awards; individual paintings lent; book traveling exhibits

TUSKEGEE INSTITUTE

M TUSKEGEE INSTITUTE NATIONAL HISTORIC SITE, George Washington Carver & The Oaks, PO Drawer 10, 36087. Tel 334-727-6390; FAX 334-727-4597; *Park Supt* Willie C Madison; *Museum Technician* Tyrone Brandyberg
Open 9 AM - 5 PM, cl Thanksgiving, Christmas & New Year's. Original mus estab 1941 & National Park in 1976 to interpret life & work of George Washington Carver & the history of Tuskegee Institute. Maintains small reference library
Income: Financed by federal funds
Collections: Artifacts interpreting life & work of George Washington Carver & history of Tuskegee Institute; life & contributions of Booker T Washington
Activities: Lect open to public; gallery talks; guided tours; sponsor competitions with awards; individual & original objects of art lent to other parks & museums; lending limited to photos, films, slides & reproductions; book traveling exhibitions; originate traveling exhibitions; sales shop sells books, reproductions, prints & slides

ALASKA

ANCHORAGE

A ALASKA WATERCOLOR SOCIETY, PO BOX 90714, 99502. Tel 907-274-5965; *Pres* Kim Donofrio; *Librn* Jean Shadrach; *Librn* Suzanne Boch
No admis fee. Estab 1977. Maintains library
Income: Financed by mem
Exhibitions: Annual juried watercolor exhibit at the Anchorage Museum of History & Art
Activities: Workshops; scholarships offered; originate traveling exhibitions

M ANCHORAGE MUSEUM OF HISTORY & ART, 121 W Seventh Ave, 99501. Tel 907-343-4326; FAX 907-343-6149; *Dir* Patricia B Wolf; *Cur Educ* Sharon Abbott; *Cur Exhibits* Dave Nicholls; *Cur Coll* Walter Van Horn; *Archivist* M Diane Brenner; *Cur Public Art* Jocelyn Young
Open winter Tues - Sat 10 AM - 6 PM, Sun 1 - 5 PM, summer daily 9 AM - 6 PM. Admis adults $4, sr citizens $3.50, under 18 free. Estab 1968 to collect & display Alaskan art & artifacts of all periods; to present changing exhibitions of the art of the world. Average Annual Attendance: 300,000. Mem: 3000
Income: $1,900,000
Purchases: $50,000
Collections: †Alaskan art; †Alaskan Eskimo & Indian art; Alaskan history; American art; Primitive Art (non-American)
Publications: Painting in the North: Alaskan art in the Anchorage Museum of History & Art; exhibition catalogs; monthly newsletters; occasional papers
Activities: Classes for adults & children; docent training; lect open to pub; gallery talks; tours; competitions; awards; individual paintings & original works of art lent to AMA accredited mus; lending coll contains original art works, original prints, paintings, photographs, sculpture & slides; book traveling exhibitions 100 per year; originate traveling exhibitions; mus shop sells books, magazines, original art, prints, slides & Alaskan Native art

L Archives, 121 W Seventh Ave, 99501. Tel 907-343-6189; FAX 907-343-6149; Elec Mail anmdb@orion.alaska.edu. *Museum Archivist* M Diane Brenner
Open winter Tues - Fri 10 AM - Noon, summer Mon - Fri 9 AM - Noon, afternoons by appointment. No admis fee. Estab 1968 to maintain archives of Alaska materials, particularly the Cook Inlet area. Reference only
Purchases: $4000
Library Holdings: Vols 6000; Per subs 10; Original documents; Micro — Fiche, reels; AV — Kodachromes, slides, v-tapes; Other — Clipping files, exhibition catalogs, memorabilia, pamphlets, photographs
Special Subjects: American Indian Art, American Western Art, Anthropology, Eskimo Art, Historical Material, American art, Alaska history & culture, Alaska native peoples, museum techniques
Collections: Hinchey Alagco Photograph Collection of approximately 4000 pictures of the Copper River area; Alaska Railroad Collection, 19,000 historical photos; Reeve Collection, historical maps; Ward Wells Anchorage Photo Collection 1950-80, 125,000 items; FAA 1973-1975, 10,000 photos; Lu Liston Photo Collection 1920-1950, 6,000 photos; Steve McCutcheon Photo Collection, 70,000; J N Wyman (Upper Koyukon) 1989, 500 glass plates

BETHEL

M YUGTARVIK REGIONAL MUSEUM & BETHEL VISITORS CENTER, Third Ave, PO Box 388, 99559. Tel 907-543-2911; FAX 907-543-2255; *Museum & Visitors Center Coordr* Open; *Museum Shop Mgr & Arts & Crafts Dir* Sophie Charles
Open Tues - Sat 10 AM - 5:30 PM. No admis fee. Estab 1967 to help preserve the native culture & lifestyle of the Central Yupik Eskimos of the Yukon-Kuskokwin delta. Average Annual Attendance: 10,500. Mem: 50; dues $25
Income: $165,000 (financed by city appropriation & occasional grants)
Purchases: $5000
Collections: †Traditional handmade objects of the Yupik Eskimo, both artifacts & contemporary art objects (included are full-size kayak, ivory carvings & wooden masks, wooden bowls, stone & ivory implements, grass baskets, Yupik toys, fishskin, sealgut, birdskin & fur clothing); black & white photographs
Activities: Classes for adults & children; lect open to the public; book traveling exhibitions, 3-4 times per year; museum shop sells baskets, ivory jewelry, beaded work, skin & fur garments, wooden & ivory masks, books & posters relating to Yupik Eskimos

FAIRBANKS

A FAIRBANKS ARTS ASSOCIATION, Alaskan Land Civic Ctr, PO Box 72786, 99707. Tel 907-456-1225; FAX 907-456-4112; *Pres* Diane Borgeson; *VPres* Phil Younker Sr; *VPres* Arnold Tornell; *Exec Dir* June Rojers; *Treas* Dick Wadlow
Open Mon - Sat Noon - 8 PM, gallery Sat & Sun Noon - 5 PM. No admis fee. Estab 1965 to provide assistance & to help coordinate & promote the programs of arts organizations; to encourage & develop educational progams designed to strengthen & improve the climate for the arts; to inform the community of performing & creative arts awareness & develop in the Fairbanks area. 4000 sq ft contemporary art gallery. Average Annual Attendance: 22,000. Mem: 500; dues $25 & up; annual meeting in Sept
Income: Financed by city & state appropriations, nation grants, contributions
Activities: Classes for adults & children; performing arts programs; docent training; professional workshops; lect open to public, 10 vis lectr per year; gallery talks; tours; competitions with awards; scholarships & fels offered; book traveling exhibitions semi-annually; originate traveling exhibitions; museum shop sells books, magazines, original art, reproductions & prints

A INSTITUTE OF ALASKA NATIVE ARTS, INC, 455 Third Ave, PO Box 70769, 99707. Tel 907-456-7491; FAX 907-451-7268; Elec Mail iana@tmn.com. *Exec Dir* Susheila Khera; *Prog Dir* Janet Steinbright; *Office Admin* Tammy Young
Open daily 9 AM - 5 PM. Estab 1976 to stimulate & encourage the study & presentation of Alaska performing, literary & visual arts, & pub participation therein. Registry of Aleut, Inuit (Eskimo) & Indian artists; small reference library. Mem: 184
Income: Financed by Alaska State Council on the Arts, Alaska Department of Educ, Alaska Department of Community & Regional Affairs, National Endowment for the Arts, earned & contributed sources
Collections: Athabascan Art Collection; Interwoven Expressions Works by Contemporary Alaska Native Basketmakers
Exhibitions: Alaskameut '86, exhibition of contemporary Alaska Mask; Bending Traditions
Publications: Calendar; Earth Dyes, catalog; exhibit catalogs; From Skins, Trees, Quills & Beads: The Work of Nine Athabascans, book; Journal of Alaska Native Arts, quarterly; posters
Activities: Workshops & residencies; conferences; seminars; scholarships offered; sales shop sells books

UNIVERSITY OF ALASKA

M Museum, 907 Yukon Dr, 99775-1200. Tel 907-474-7505; FAX 907-474-5469; *Dir* Dr Aldona Jonaitis; *Asst to Dir* Hazel E Daro; *Coordr Exhib & Exhib Designer* Wanda W Chin; *Coordr Public Servs & Educ* Terry P Dickey; *Co-Dir Alaska Native Heritage Film Center* Sarah M Elder; *Cur Ethnology* Molly Lee; *Coordr Fine Arts* Barry J McWayne; *Co-Dir Alaska Native Heritage Film Center* Leonard J Kamerling
Open Mon - Fri May 9 AM - 5 PM, June - Aug 9 AM - 7 PM, Sept 9 AM - 5 PM, Oct - Apr 9 AM - 5 PM, Sat & Sun Noon - 5 PM. Estab 1929 to collect, preserve & interpret the natural & cultural history of Alaska. Gallery contains 10,000 sq ft of exhibition space. Average Annual Attendance: 120,000. Mem: 220; annual meeting in Nov

Income: Financed by state appropriation, pub & private donations, grants & contracts
Collections: †Contemporary Alaska photography; †ethnographic collection; †paintings & lithographs of Alaska subjects
Exhibitions: Temporary exhibits rotate every two to three months
Activities: Classes for adults & children; docent training; monthly children's program; lect open to public, 3 vis lectr per year; docent tours for grades 1-12; museum shop sells notecards, slides, exhibition catalogues, pamphlets, charts, posters

L **Elmer E Rasmuson Library,** PO Box 756800, 99775-1000. Tel 907-474-7224; FAX 907-474-6841; *Interim Dir* Joseph Kan; *Head Bibliographic Access Management* Debbie Kalvee; *Head Alaska & Polar Regions Colls* David Hales; *Acting Head Instructional Media Serv* Diane Ruess; *Coll Develop Officer* Dennis Stephens
Open Mon - Thurs 7:30 AM - 11 PM, Fri 7:30 AM - 10 PM, Sat 10 AM - 6 PM, Sun 10 AM - 10 PM, when school is not in session 8 AM - 5 PM. Estab 1922 to support research & curriculum of the university. Circ 147,000
Income: Financed by state appropriation
Library Holdings: Vols 2,260,000; Audio tapes; Film; Government documents; AV — Slides, v-tapes; Other — Manuscripts, photographs
Collections: Lithographs of Fred Machetanz; paintings by Alaskan artists; C Rusty Heurlin; photographs of Early Alaskan bush pilots; print reference photograph collection on Alaska & the Polar Regions

HAINES

M **CHILKAT VALLEY HISTORICAL SOCIETY,** Sheldon Museum & Cultural Center, 11 Main St, PO Box 269, 99827. Tel 907-766-2366; FAX 907-766-2368; Elec Mail sheldmus@seaknet.alaska.edu. *Dir & Cur Sheldon Museum* Cynthia L Jones; *Pres Chilkat Valley Historical Society* Jim Heaton; *Pres Museum Board Trustees* Jan Hill
Open summer daily 1 - 5 PM, winter Sun, Mon & Wed 1 - 4 PM, Tues, Thurs & Fri 3 - 5 PM. Admis adults $3, children free. Estab 1924, under operation of Chilkat Valley Historical Society since 1975, for the purpose of collecting, preserving & interpreting through exhibits, educational programs, artifacts & memorabilia the history & culture of the Chilkat Valley & Tlingit Indian People. Maintains small reference library. Average Annual Attendance: 19,500. Mem: 124; dues $10; meetings second Thurs of Jan, Mar, May, July, Sept, Nov
Income: Financed by mem, user fees, Haines Borough appropriations, federal & state grants
Collections: Chilkat blankets; Tlingit Indian artifacts; ivory, silver, wood carvings; native baskets, pioneer artifacts, photos, maps, oral histories, archival
Exhibitions: (1997) Reaching Home: Pacific Salmon, Pacific People
Publications: Haines - The First Century; A Personal Look at the Sheldon Museum & Cultural Center; Journey to the Tlingits
Activities: Classes for adults & children; docent training; gallery tours; book traveling exhibitions; museum store sells books, prints, slides, jewelry, wood crafts; Children's Corner

JUNEAU

L **ALASKA STATE LIBRARY,** Alaska Historical Collections, PO Box 110571, 99811-0571. Tel 907-465-2925; FAX 907-465-2990; *Head Librn* Kay Shelton; *Photographs Librn* India Spartz
Open Mon - Fri 9 AM - 5 PM. Estab 1900
Library Holdings: Vols 34,000; Per subs 75; Other — Photographs 110,000
Special Subjects: American Indian Art, Anthropology, Eskimo Art, Ethnology, Historical Material, Manuscripts, Maps, Photography, Alaska
Collections: Winter & Pond; Wickersham Historical Site Collection; Skinner Collection; Grainger Post Card Collection
Publications: Books about Alaska, annual; Inventories for Individual Collections

M **ALASKA STATE MUSEUM,** 395 Whittier St, 99801-1718. Tel 907-465-2901; FAX 907-465-2976; Elec Mail bkato@educ.state.ak.us. *Chief Cur* Bruce Kato; *Cur Coll* Steve Henrickson; *Cur Museum Serv* Ken DeRoux; *Cur Exhib* Mark Daughhetee; *Registrar* Donna Baron; *Temporary Exhibits* Paul Gardinier; *Admin Asst* Pat Montgomery; *Graphic Designer* Elizabeth Knecht; *Visitor Serv* Lisa Golisek; *Visitor Serv* Mary Irvine; *Visitor Serv* Marilyn Doyle
Open Mon - Sat 10 AM - 4 PM (Sept 16 - May 15), daily 9 AM - 6 PM (May 16 - Sept 15). Admis $3, students free. Estab 1900 to collect, preserve, exhibit & interpret objects of special significance or value in order to promote pub appreciation of Alaska's cultural heritage, history, art & natural environment. Gallery occupies two floors housing permanent & temporary exhibits on 9000 sq ft. Average Annual Attendance: 80,000 with more than 200,000 including outreach program
Income: Financed by state appropriation & grants
Collections: †Alaskan ethnographic material including Eskimo, Aleut, Athabaskan, Tlingit, Haida & Tsimshian artifacts; †Gold Rush & early Alaskan industrial & historical material; †historical & contemporary Alaskan art
Exhibitions: Governor's Gallery: (1997) And the Bead Goes On; Bradford Washburn: Glory of the Greatland; Earth, Fire & Fibre. (1998) Earth 2U; 6th International Shoebox Sculpture; North Galleries: (1997) Submerged-Carolyn Reed: Alaska Artist Solo Exhibition; Jim Schoppert Retrospective. (1998) Alaska Positive 1998; Chihuly Baskets; Lounge Gallery: (1997) Dale De Armond: The Nondalton Legends
Activities: Classes for adults & children; docent training; circulate learning kits to Alaska public schools; lect open to public, 4-6 vis lectr per year; gallery talks & demonstrations; individual paintings & original objects of art lent to other museums, libraries, historical societies; lending collection contains original prints, photographs; originate traveling exhibits of photographs & prints organized & circulated; sales shop sells books, reproductions, prints, Alaskan Native arts & crafts

KETCHIKAN

M **TONGASS HISTORICAL MUSEUM,** 629 Dock St, 99901. Tel 907-225-5600; FAX 907-225-5602
Open summer Mon - Sat 8:30 AM - 5 PM, Sun 1 - 5 PM, winter Wed - Sun 1 - 5 PM. Admis adults $1. Estab 1967 to collect, preserve & exhibit area articles & collect area photographs. Maintains reference library. Average Annual Attendance: 34,000
Income: $250,000 (financed by municipal funds)
Purchases: $9950
Collections: North West Indian Collection; †ethnographic & development history, local artists contemporary artwork; †local area history artifacts; †works from local & Alaskan artists, photographs, manuscripts & newspaper archives
Publications: Art class listings; Calendar; Newsletter
Activities: Classes for adults; docent training; lect open to public, 5 vis lect per year; book traveling exhibitions

M **TOTEM HERITAGE CENTER,** 629 Dock St, 99901. Tel 907-225-5600
Open summer daily 8 AM - 5 PM, winter Wed - Fri 1 - 5 PM. Admis $3, children under 5 free. Estab 1976 to preserve & teach traditional Northwest Coast Indian Arts. Average Annual Attendance: 140,000
Income: $200,000
Collections: Indian arts; original totem poles; monumental sculpture
Activities: Classes for adults & children; docent training; workshops; lect open to public, 20 lectr per year; gallery talks; tours; arts & crafts festival; scholarships & work-study awards offered; museum shop sells books, magazines, original art, reproductions, prints, slides & native art

L **Library,** 629 Dock St, 99901. Tel 907-225-5600;
For reference only
Library Holdings: Vols 250; Per subs 5; Micro — Fiche; AV — A-tapes, cassettes, Kodachromes, slides, v-tapes; Other — Clipping files, exhibition catalogs, manuscripts, original art works
Special Subjects: Northwest Coast Indian Art, Totem Poles

NOME

M **CARRIE MCLAIN MUSEUM,** 200 E Front St, PO Box 53, 99762. Tel 907-443-2566; FAX 907-443-6663; *City Mgr* Paul Day; *Dir* Janet Williams
Open Tues - Fri 10 AM - 5 PM, Sat & Sun Noon - 6 PM. No admis fee. Estab to show the prehistory & history of Northwest Alaska
Income: Financed by City of Nome & supplemental grant projects & donations
Collections: Coons Collection; McLain Collection; Mielke Collection; permanent collection includes examples of art from 1890-1990, including basketry, carved ivory, ink, oil, skin drawings, stone carving, woodworking; extensive photography collection on database; gold rush & dog sledding memorabilia
Exhibitions: Permanent exhibitions
Activities: Demonstrations; workshops; school tours

SITKA

M **ALASKA DEPARTMENT OF EDUCATION, DIVISION OF LIBRARIES, ARCHIVES & MUSEUMS,** Sheldon Jackson Museum, 104 College Dr, 99835. Tel 907-747-8981; FAX 907-747-3004; *Cur Coll* Peter Corey; *Interpretation Specialist* Rosemary Carlton; *Visitor Servs* P Lisa Bykonen
Open summer May 15 - Sept 15, 8 AM - 5 PM daily, winter Sept 16 - May 14 Tues - Sat 10 AM - 4 PM, cl Mon & Sun. Admis $3 over 18. Estab 1888, the first permanent mus in Alaska, for the purpose of collecting & preserving the cultural heritage of Alaskan Natives in the form of artifacts. The mus, a division of Alaska State Museums, occupies a concrete, octagonal structure from 1895 with permanent displays concerning Tlingit, Tsimshian, Haida, Aleut, Athabaskan & Eskimo cultures. Average Annual Attendance: 50,000
Income: $30,000 (financed by admis fee, sales, donation, State of Alaska)
Collections: Ethnographic material from Tlingit, Haida, Tsimshian, Aleut, Athabaskan & Eskimo people; Alaskan ethnology produced through 1930
Publications: Brochures; catalogs of Ethnological Collection
Activities: Classes for adults & children; gallery interpreters & demonstrations; lect open to public, 4-6 vis lectr per year; gallery talks; exten dept serves entire state through Division of Museums; original works of art lent to qualified museums; book traveling exhibitions; museum shop sells books, original art, reproductions, prints, Alaskan Native arts & crafts

L **Stratton Library,** 801 Lincoln St, 99835. Tel 907-747-5259; FAX 907-747-5237; *Dir Library Servs* Evelyn K Bonner
Estab 1944 with Collection Library for curriculum support & meeting the needs of patrons interested in the arts
Library Holdings: Micro — Reels; AV — A-tapes, cassettes, fs, Kodachromes, lantern slides, motion pictures, rec, slides, v-tapes; Other — Clipping files, exhibition catalogs, framed reproductions, memorabilia, original art works, pamphlets, photographs, reproductions, sculpture
Special Subjects: Alaskan & Native American Art Books, Alaska & the Northwest Pacific Coast, Harmon original pictures
Collections: Alaska Reference Collection (containing works on Native Arts & Crafts); E W Merrill Glass Plate Photo Collection (representative of Sitka at the turn of the century)
Activities: Annual programs held in April, include dramatic presentations; lect; demonstrations

M **SITKA HISTORICAL SOCIETY,** Isabel Miller Museum, 330 Harbor Dr, 99835. Tel 907-747-6455; *Adminr* Dr Orriene First Denslow; *Pres* Thelma Carter; *VPres* Stephen Brenner; *Colls Mgr* John Hallum
Open summer daily 9 AM - 5 PM, winter Mon - Fri 10 AM - Noon & 1 - 4 PM. No admis fee. Estab 1959 to preserve the history of Sitka, its people & industries. Average Annual Attendance: 80,000. Mem: 100; dues $10-$100; annual meeting in Oct
Income: Financed by grants, mem, donations & shop sales
Collections: Copy of warrant that purchased Alaska; 2000 documents & mss;

furniture from the Russian-American era; library paintings of Alaska scenes; 6000 photographs; Russian artifacts
Exhibitions: Alaska Purchase; Diorama of Sitka in 1867 (Year of the Transfer); Fishing Industry Exhibit; Forest Products Exhibit; Historic Diving Suit; Tourism Industry Exhibit
Activities: Lect open to pub, 4 vis lectr per year; sales shop sells books, original art, reproductions, reproductions of Tlingit totem poles, prints, video tapes & postcards

SKAGWAY

M TRAIL OF '98 MUSEUM, Second & Broadway, PO Box 521, 99840. Tel 907-983-2420; FAX 907-983-2151
Open 8 AM - 6 PM, May - Sept; Oct - Apr on request. Admis adults $2, students $1. Estab 1961 to preserve & display items relating to our gold rush & Skagway. Average Annual Attendance: 25,000
Income: Financed by admis
Collections: Gold Rush Era artifacts
Publications: Brochures
Activities: Sales shop sells reproductions of old newspapers & postcards

ARIZONA

BISBEE

L BISBEE ARTS & HUMANITIES COUNCIL, Lemuel Shattuck Memorial Library, 5 Copper Queen Plaza, PO Box 14, 85603. Tel 520-432-7071; *Cur Archival Coll* Carrie Gustavson
Open Mon - Fri 10 AM - 4 PM, Sat & Sun by appointment. Estab 1971 to provide research facilities on copper mining & social history of Bisbee, Arizona, Cochise County & Northern Sonora, Mexico. For reference only
Income: $300 (financed by mem)
Purchases: $600
Library Holdings: Vols 1600; Per subs 3; Micro — Reels; AV — Cassettes; Other — Clipping files, manuscripts, photographs 23,000
Special Subjects: Historical Material, Manuscripts, Maps, Photography
Activities: Classes for adults & children; docent training; lect open to public, 5 vis lectr per year; originate traveling exhibitions

COTTONWOOD

A ART QUESTERS, 201 E Mingus Ave No 221, 86326-3637. Tel 520-639-1661; *Owner* Richard Lambard
Estab 1987
Collections: Artist Employment/Referrals; Artist Registry; Exhibition/ Performance Referrals; Information Services; Marketing/Presentation; Mixed/ Multi-Disciplinary, Fundraising; Organization Services; Programs/Encourage New Art Forms

DOUGLAS

L COCHISE COLLEGE, Charles Di Peso Library, Art Dept, 4190 W Hwy 80, 85607-9724. Tel 520-364-7943; FAX 520-364-0320; *Libr Dir* Catherin Lincer
Open Mon - Fri 8 AM - 9 PM. Estab 1965
Income: Financed by state & local funds
Library Holdings: Other — Exhibition catalogs, framed reproductions, memorabilia, original art works, photographs, prints, reproductions, sculpture
Special Subjects: Oriental Art
Collections: Oriental originals (ceramics & paintings); 19th century American & European Impressionists

M DOUGLAS ART ASSOCIATION, Little Gallery, * 625 Tenth St, 85607. Tel 520-364-3182; *Pres* Terry Mason; *Dir* Brenda Romero
Open Tues - Sat 1:30 - 4 PM. No admis fee. Estab 1960 as a non-profit tax exempt organization dedicated to promoting the visual arts & general cultural awareness in the Douglas, Arizona & Agua Prieta, Sonora area. Little Gallery is operated in a city owned building with city cooperation. Average Annual Attendance: 2000. Mem: 100; dues $10 & $7.50
Income: Financed by mem & fundraising events
Collections: †Two Flags Festival International Festival of the Arts for the cities of Douglas & Agua Prieta, Mexico
Publications: Monthly newsletter
Activities: Classes for adults & children; workshops in painting & various art activities; lect open to pub; gallery talks; competitions with cash awards; sales shop sells books & donated items

DRAGOON

A AMERIND FOUNDATION, INC, Amerind Museum, Fulton-Hayden Memorial Art Gallery, Dragoon Rd, PO Box 400, 85609. Tel 520-586-4679; FAX 520-586-4679; Elec Mail amerindinc@aol.com. *Pres* William Duncan Fulton; *VPres* Peter L Formo; *Treas* Michael W Hard; *Foundation Dir* Anne I Woosley
Open Sept - May daily 10 AM - 4 PM, June - Aug Wed - Sun 10 AM - 4 PM. Admis adults $3, sr citizens & children (12-18) $2, under 12 free. Estab 1937 as a private, nonprofit archeological research facility & mus focusing on the native people of the Americas. Works on western themes, paintings & sculptures by 19th & 20th century Anglo & Native American artists. Average Annual Attendance: 20,000

Income: Financed by endowment income, grants, gifts
Collections: Archaeological & ethnological materials from the Americas; antique furniture; archives on film; ivory & scrimshaw; oil paintings; research & technical reports; santos; sculpture
Exhibitions: Dance in Ceremony; Southwest Art; Prehistoric Peoples of the American Southwest
Publications: Amerind Foundation Publication Series; Amerind New World Studies Series
Activities: Docent training; seminars; tours for school groups; fels offered; museum shop sells books, original art, Native American Arts & Crafts

L Fulton-Hayden Memorial Library, Dragoon Rd, PO Box 400, 85609. Tel 520-586-3666; FAX 520-586-4679; *Pres* Duncan Fulton; *VPres* Peter L Formo; *Treas* Michael W Hard; *Foundation Dir* Anne I Woosley
Estab 1961. Open to scholars by appointment
Income: Financed by endowment income, grants, gifts
Library Holdings: Vols 20,000; Per subs 60; Micro — Cards, fiche, prints, reels; AV — Fs, Kodachromes, lantern slides; Other — Clipping files, exhibition catalogs, manuscripts, original art works, pamphlets, prints, sculpture
Special Subjects: Archaeology, Ethnology
Collections: Parral Archives on microfilm; collections of research & technical reports

FLAGSTAFF

M MUSEUM OF NORTHERN ARIZONA, 3101 N Fort Valley Rd, 86001. Tel 520-774-5211; FAX 520-779-1527; *Pres Board Trustees* Wes Ward; *Dir* Michael J Fox; *Deputy Dir* Dr Edwin L Wade; *Research Archaeologist & Spec Asst to Deputy Dir* Dr David R Wilcox; *Assoc Cur Geology* Dr Michael Morales; *Comptroller* Judy Leary
Open Mon - Sun 9 AM - 5 PM, cl Thanksgiving, Christmas & New Year's Day. Admis adults $5, senior citizens $4, children $2. Estab 1928 to study, preserve & interpret the art & cultural & natural history of the Colorado Plateau. Maintains reference library. Average Annual Attendance: 100,000. Mem: 5500; dues $35-$500; annual meeting in Sept
Income: $2,500,000 (financed by endowment, mem & earned income)
Collections: †Works of Southwestern Native American artists; †non-Indian art depicting Colorado Plateau subjects; †archaeological & ethnographic artifacts & natural history specimens of the Colorado Plateau
Publications: Bulletin, irregular; Canon Journal, semiannual; Museum Notes, quarterly
Activities: Classes for adults & children; adult back-country expeditions; trips; docent training; lect open to public, 5-10 vis lectr per year; gallery talks; tours; competitions with prizes; scholarships offered; individual paintings & original objects of art lent to various institutions; lending coll contains 2200 original art works; book traveling exhibitions one per year; originate traveling exhibitions to other museums; museum shop sells books, magazines, reproductions, prints, Native American art, games, posters, T-shirts, videos, cassettes & jewelry

M NORTHERN ARIZONA UNIVERSITY, Art Museum & Galleries, PO Box 6021, 86011-6021. Tel 520-523-3471; FAX 520-523-1424; *Dir* Dr Joel S Eide; *Admin Asst* Linda Stromberg
Open Mon - Fri 8 AM - 5 PM, Tues & Wed 6:30 - 8:30 PM, Sat & Sun 1 - 4 PM, special holiday hours. No admis fee. Estab 1968 for the continuing education & service to the students & the Flagstaff community in all aspects of fine arts & to national & international fine arts communities
Collections: †Contemporary ceramics; Master prints of the 20th century & American painting of the Southwest
Activities: Lect open to public, national & international workshops & conferences; concerts; tours; competitions with awards; scholarships; originate traveling exhibitions; museum shop sells books, original art works, prints & posters

GANADO

M NATIONAL PARK SERVICE, Hubbell Trading Post National Historic Site, PO Box 150, 86505. Tel 520-755-3475; *Supt* Charles D Wyatt; *Cur* Shirley Hardine
Open May - Sept 8 AM - 6 PM, Oct - Apr 8 AM - 5 PM. No admis fee. Estab 1967 to set aside Hubbell Trading Post as a historic site as the best example in Southwest of a Trader, an Indian Trading Post & people he served. Average Annual Attendance: 200,000
Income: Financed by federal appropriation
Collections: Contemporary Western artists; ethnohistoric arts & crafts; furnishings; photographs
Exhibitions: Photo contests
Activities: Educ dept; lect open to public; tours; presentations; competitions; individual paintings & art objects are lent to certified museums; sales shop sells books, Indian arts & crafts, magazines, original art, prints & slides

KINGMAN

M MOHAVE MUSEUM OF HISTORY & ARTS, 400 W Beale, 86401. Tel 520-753-3195; *Dir* Robert Yost
Open Mon - Fri 9 AM - 5 PM, Sat & Sun 1 - 5 PM. Admis adults $2, children free. Estab 1960 to preserve & present to the pub the art & history of Northwest Arizona. Average Annual Attendance: 30,000. Mem: 550; dues $20-$125; annual meeting in Apr
Income: Financed by endowment, mem, city & state appropriation, sales & donations
Collections: American Indian Art; art & history of Northwest Arizona
Activities: Classes for children; docent programs; lect open to public; museum shop sells books, prints, original art, craft items, reproductions

MESA

M GALERIA MESA, Mesa Arts Center, 155 N Center, PO Box 1466, 85211-1466.
Tel 602-644-2056; *Supv* Robert Schultz; *Cur* Richard Wager
Open Tues - Fri Noon - 8 PM, Sat Noon - 5 PM. No admis fee. Estab 1981 to
provide an exhibition space for emerging & mid-career artists. Average Annual
Attendance: 7500. Mem: 160; dues vary; annual meeting in Spring
Income: Financed by city appropriation
Collections: †Permanent collection
Activities: Classes & workshops for adults & children; lect open to public, 4 vis
lectr per year; gallery talks; tours; competitions with awards; book traveling
exhibitions annually; originate traveling exhibitions; sales shop sells original art

A XICANINDIO, INC, PO Box 1242, 85211-1242. Tel 602-833-5875; *Pres* Gema
Duarte; *VPres* Jorge Eagar; *Secy* Bryon Barabe; *Exec Dir* Dina Lopez-Woodward
Open daily 9 AM - 5 PM. Estab 1977 as a non-profit organization of Native
American & Hispanic artists to promote cross cultural understanding, preserve
tradition, and develop grass roots educational programs. Average Annual
Attendance: 28,000. Mem: 20; annual meeting in Sept
Income: $64,000 (financed by endowment, city & state appropriation)
Publications: Papel Picado (paper cut-out techniques)
Activities: Lect open to public, 1 vis lectr per year

NOGALES

A PIMERIA ALTA HISTORICAL SOCIETY, 136 N Grand Ave, PO Box 2281,
85621. Tel 520-287-4621; FAX 520-287-5201; *Acting Dir* Patricia Berrones-
Molina
Open Tues - Fri 10 AM - 5 PM, Sat 10 AM - 4 PM, Sun 1 - 4 PM. Estab 1948
to preserve the unique heritage of northern Sonora Mexico & southern Arizona
from 1000 AD to present; art is incorporated into interpretive exhibits. Also
maintains a photo gallery. Average Annual Attendance: 15,000. Mem: 850; dues
adults $7.50; meeting in Jan
Income: $55,000 (financed by mem, fundraising events, educ programs & grants)
Collections: Art & artifacts of Hohokam & Piman Indians, Spanish
conquistadores & Mexican ranchers & Anglo pioneer settlement
Publications: Centennial Book of Nogales; newsletter, 10 per year; annual
calendar on historic subjects
Activities: Classes for adults & children; lect open to public, 3 vis lectr per year;
tours; competitions; originate traveling exhibitions; sales shop sells books, maps &
pins
L Library, 136 N Grand Ave, PO Box 2281, 85628-2281. Tel 520-287-4621; FAX
520-287-5201; *Acting Dir* Patricia Berrones-Molina
Collects books & archival material on Pimeria Alta, Northern Sonora & Southern
Arizona
Income: $1000
Purchases: $500
Library Holdings: Vols 1000; Per subs 3; AV — Cassettes; Other — Clipping
files, manuscripts, memorabilia, pamphlets, photographs
Collections: The Jack Kemmer Memorial Collection, books on the cattle industry
of Texas, New Mexico, Arizona and California

PHOENIX

A ARIZONA ARTIST GUILD, 8912 N Fourth St, 85020. Tel 602-944-9713; *Pres*
Diane Kent; *First VPres* Joyce Froncek; *Second VPres Exhib* Tom Hurbet; *Treas*
Don Kirscher
Estab 1928 to foster guild spirit, to assist in raising standards of art in the
community & to assume civic responsibility in matters relating to art. Average
Annual Attendance: 550. Mem: 295 juried, 90 assoc; dues $25; mem by jury;
monthly meetings
Income: Financed by endowment & mem
Exhibitions: Horizons (annually in spring, members only); fall exhibition for
members only; juried exhibition
Publications: AAG news, monthly
Activities: Classes for adults; lect sometimes open to public, 12 or more vis lectr
per year; gallery talks; competitions with awards; workshops by vis professionals
offered; paint-outs; sketch groups; demonstrations; scholarship offered
L Library, 8912 N Fourth St, 85020. Tel 602-944-9713, 948-8565; *Pres* Cynthia
Ganem
Open to members for reference only
Library Holdings: Vols 200

A ARIZONA COMMISSION ON THE ARTS, 417 W Roosevelt St, 85003. Tel
602-255-5882; FAX 602-256-0282; Elec Mail artscomm@indirect.com. *Chmn*
Gerald Murphy; *Exec Dir* Shelley Cohn; *Artists in Educ Dir* Sandie Campolo;
Deputy Dir Gary Delago; *Visual Arts Dir* Dora Hernandez; *Performing Art Dir*
Claire West; *Public Information & Locals Dir* Mollie Lakin-Hayes; *Expansion
Arts Dir* Rudy Guglielmo; *Presenting, Touring & Literature Dir* Jill Bernstein;
Anti-Drug APPLE Corps Dir Rose Devine
Open 8 AM - 5 PM. No admis fee. Estab 1966 to promote & encourage the arts
in the State of Arizona. Maintains reference library. Mem: Meetings, quarterly
Income: $1,152,800 (financed by state & federal appropriation)
Publications: Artists' Guide to Programs; monthly bulletin guide to programs
Activities: Workshops; conferences; artists-in-education grants program;
scholarships & fels offered; originate traveling exhibitions 20-30 per year
L Reference Library, 417 W Roosevelt St, 85003. Tel 602-255-5882; FAX 602-256-
0282; *Public Information & Locals Dir* Mollie Lakin-Hayes
Topics related to the business of the arts. For reference only
Library Holdings: Vols 750; Per subs 25; AV — Slides; Other — Pamphlets

A ARIZONA WATERCOLOR ASSOCIATION, PO Box 37071, 85069. Tel 602-
584-2710, 943-6265; *Pres* James Farrah; *Treas* Don Miller; *First VPres* Penny
Peterson; *Second VPres* Sally Dallas; *Third VPres* Glorianne Michaels; *Mem-at-Large* Hazel Stone; *Western Representative* Sue Hunter

Estab 1960 to further activity & interest in the watermedia, promote growth of
individuals & group & maintain high quality of professional exhibits. Average
Annual Attendance: 600. Mem: 500; qualifications for juried mem must be
accepted in three different approved juried shows; all members who pay dues are
considered members; dues $30
Income: Financed by dues & donations
Exhibitions: Two exhibitions yearly: Membership Show
Publications: AWA Newsletter, monthly; Directory, annual
Activities: Workshops; lect for members only; paint outs; competitions with
awards

ATLATL
For Further Information see National and Regional Organizations

C BANK ONE ARIZONA, Fine Arts Department, PO Box 71, A-960, 85001. Tel
602-221-4693; *Cur Art* Catherine Trapp
Open to pub. Estab 1933 to support emerging artists throughout the state;
encourage & promote talented high school students with Scholastic Art Awards;
provide the pub with beautiful, integrated art in branch banks. Several thousand
pieces of art collection displayed in over 200 branches, business offices & support
facilities throughout the state of Arizona
Collections: Primarily Western, Southwestern art featuring many of the now
classic Western artists; earliest lithograph dates back to the 1820s & coll
continues through the present
Activities: Lect; gallery talks; tours by appointment; competitions, since 1942
state sponsor for Scholastic Art Awards throughout Arizona; purchase awards
throughout the state, sponsor Employees' Art Show annually, with juried &
popular choice awards, underwrite local art exhibitions on the Concourse of the
Home Office Building; individual objects of art lent contingent upon bank policy

M HEARD MUSEUM, 22 E Monte Vista Rd, 85004-1480. Tel 602-252-8840;
FAX 602-252-9757; *Dir* Martin Sullivan; *Cur Colls* Diana Pardue; *Dir Research*
Ann Marshall; *Marketing Coordr* Kim Figgins-Fuchs; *Cur of Fine Arts* Margaret
Archuleta; *Registrar* Debra Slaney; *Pub Information Coordr* Juliet Martin; *Asst
Cur* Gloria Lomahaftewa; *Exhibit Coordr* Lisa MacCollum; *Educ Servs Mgr*
Gina Laczko; *Librn* Mario Nick Klimiades; *Community Affairs Dir* Judith V
Shannon; *Bus Mgr* Karl Almquist
Open Mon, Tues, Thurs & Sat 9:30 AM - 5 PM, Wed 9:30 AM - 8 PM, Sun
Noon - 5 PM. Admis general $6, senior citizens 65 & up $5, children 4-12 $3,
children under 4 free, Wed evenings 5-8 PM free. Estab 1929 to collect, preserve
& exhibit Native American art & artifacts, offering an expansive view of the
Southwest as it was thousands of years ago & is today & to increase general
awareness about Native American cultures, traditions & art. Art Galleries:
Gallery of Indian Art, Native Peoples Gallery, North Gallery, COMPAS
Gallery, World Cultures Gallery, South Gallery & Sandra Day O'Connor
Gallery. Average Annual Attendance: 250,000. Mem: 5000; dues varies
Collections: Barry M Goldwater Photograph Collection; Fred Harvey Fine Arts
Collection; C G Wallace Collection; Archaeology; †Native American fine arts;
†sculpture, †primitive arts from the cultures of Africa, Asia & Oceania;
†American Indian
Exhibitions: Annual Heard Museum Guild Indian Fair & Market; Native Peoples
of the Southwest; Old Ways, New Ways; Annual World Championship Hoop
Dance Contest. (1996-97) Mayan Life: Source & Symbol. (1997) Inventing the
Southwest: The Fred Harvey Company & Native American Art; Recent
Acquisitions from the Heard Museum Collection; Heard Museum Guild Native
American Student Art & Craft Show; Contemporary Southwestern Jewelry.
(1997-98) Following the Sun & Moon; Hopi Katsina Dolls; The 7th Native
American Fine Arts Invitational
Publications: Earth Song Calendar; The Heard Museum Newsletter, quarterly;
exhibition catalogs
Activities: Classes for adults & children; docent training; outreach programs; lect
open to public, 8-10 vis lectr per year; concerts; gallery talks; tours; competitions
with awards; scholarships & fels offered; exten dept serves Southwest; individual
paintings & original objects of art lent to other art institutions & museums for
exhibits; book traveling exhibitions; originate traveling exhibitions to other art
institutions & museums; museum shop sells books, magazines, original art work,
reproductions & prints
L Library & Archives, 22 E Monte Vista Rd, 85004-1480. Tel 602-252-8840; FAX
602-252-9757; *Library Archives Mgr* Mario Nick Klimiades; *Assoc Archivist* Jim
Reynolds; *Documenting Coll Archivist & Automation Coordr* Richard Pearce-
Moses
Open Mon - Fri 10 AM - Noon & 1 - 4:45 PM. Estab 1929 as a research library
for mus staff, mem & the pub (in-house only). For reference only
Income: $11,000 (financed by mem & mus budget)
Library Holdings: Vols 26,500; Per subs 250; Micro — Fiche, prints, reels; AV —
A-tapes, cassettes, fs, Kodachromes, lantern slides, motion pictures, rec, slides, v-
tapes; Other — Clipping files, exhibition catalogs, manuscripts, memorabilia,
pamphlets, photographs 28,000, prints, reproductions
Special Subjects: American Indian Art, Anthropology, Archaeology, Crafts,
Eskimo Art, Ethnology, Folk Art, Mexican Art, Painting - American, Pre-
Columbian Art, Primitive Art, Southwestern Art, Native American Writings
Collections: Fred Harvey Company Research Collection; †Native American
Artists Resource Collection

A MOVIMIENTO ARTISTICO DEL RIO SALADO, INC (MARS)
ARTSPACE, 126 S Central Ave, PO Box 20431, 85004. Tel 602-253-3541; FAX
602-253-3550; *Chmn* James Bucanek; *Pres* Ralph Cordova; *Art Dir* Jerry
Gilmore
Open Tues - Fri 11 AM - 2 PM, Sat & Sun Noon - 3 PM. No admis fee. Estab
1976 to promote Arizona, Mexican-American, Chicano artists through visual,
literary & performance art. Nonprofit artist cooperative art space. Average
Annual Attendance: 15,000. Mem: Open to Mexican American &/or Arizona
artist, must volunteer at gallery; dues $75; meeting 3rd Wed each month
Income: $33,000 (financed by mem, National Endowment for the Arts, county &
state appropriation)
Exhibitions: (1997) La Phoeniquera; Rock & Roll in Art
Publications: MARS Newsletter, monthly
Activities: Classes for children; lect open to public; sales shop sells prints, T-
shirts & small art works

M PHOENIX ART MUSEUM, 1625 N Central Ave, 85004. Tel 602-257-1880;
FAX 602-253-8662; *Pres* John Bouma; *Dir* James K Ballinger
Open Tues - Sun 10 AM - 5 PM, Thurs & Fri 10 AM - 9 PM, cl Mon. Admis to
exhibition adults $5, senior citizens $4, students $2, members & school tours
free. Estab 1925, mus constructed 1959. Average Annual Attendance: 250,000.
Mem: 7000; dues $50 & up; annual meeting in June
Income: $4,000,000 (financed by pub & private funds
Collections: Asian art; decorative arts; fashion design; 14th-20th century
European & American art; Latin American art; Spanish Colonial art; Thorne
Miniature Rooms; Western American art; Renaissance; Thorne Miniature
Rooms; Western American art; Medieval art
Publications: Annual report; exhibition catalogs; quarterly newsletter
Activities: Classes for adults & children; docent training; lect open to public, 12
vis lectr per year; concerts; gallery talks; tours; competitions; originate traveling
exhibitions; museum shop sells books, magazines, reproductions, prints, jewelry,
slides & gifts from around the world
L Art Research Library, 1625 N Central Ave, 85004-1685. Tel 602-257-1880;
FAX 602-253-8662; *Librn* Genni Houlihan
Open Tues - Fri 10 AM - 4:30 PM. Estab 1959 to serve reference needs of the
mus staff, docents, mem, students & pub. For reference only
Income: Financed by Museum operating funds
Purchases: $22,000
Library Holdings: Vols 40,000; Per subs 97; Auction Records; Ephemera; AV —
Slides; Other — Clipping files, exhibition catalogs, memorabilia, pamphlets,
reproductions
Special Subjects: Art History, Asian Art, Ceramics, Conceptual Art, Decorative
Arts, Drawings, Etchings & Engravings, Fashion Arts, Folk Art, Graphic Arts,
Islamic Art, Ivory, Jade, Latin American Art, Manuscripts, Costume Design,
18th, 19th & 20th Century Western American Painting, 18th, 19th & 20th
Century Chinese Painting, Ceramics, Glass
Collections: Ambrose Lansing Egyptian Collection; Arizona Artist Index; auction
catalogs; museum archives; Rembrandt print catalogs; Whistler Prints

M TEMPLE BETH ISRAEL, Sylvia Plotkin Judaica, 3310 N Tenth Ave, 85013.
Tel 602-264-4428; FAX 602-264-0039; *Assoc Dir* Pamela Levin; *Registrar*
Thelma Bilsky
Open daily 10 AM - 3 PM. Admis donations accepted. Estab 1970 to promote
education of Judaism. Tunisian Synagogue Gallery. Maintains library. Average
Annual Attendance: 10,000. Mem: 500; dues $20 - $250; annual meeting Mar
Income: $20,000 (financed by endowment, mem & gifts)
Collections: Contemporary art reflecting the Jewish experience; Holiday Judaica;
†Jewish Life Cycles; Synagogue Period Room; †Tunisian
Exhibitions: (1997) Jews of Ethiopia
Publications: HA-OR, three times a year
Activities: Classes for adults & children; docent programs; lect open to public, 3
vis lectr per year; concerts; tours; films; individual paintings & original objects of
art are lent to other museums; book traveling exhibitions 3 per year; originate
traveling exhibitions 1 per year

C WELLS FARGO (Formerly First Interstate Bank of Arizona), 100 W
Washington, 85003. Tel 602-229-4688; *Cur* Connie Wahlin
Open Mon - Fri 10 AM - 3 PM. Collection displayed in Old West Gallery, three
room gallery on second floor of Tucson Main
Collections: Western scenes
Activities: Tours; awards to various art associations around the state; objects of
art lent to Tucson Museum & Phoenix Art Museum

PRESCOTT

M GEORGE PHIPPEN MEMORIAL FOUNDATION, Phippen Museum of
Western Art, 4701 Hwy 89 N, 86301. Tel 520-778-1385; FAX 520-778-4524;
Dir Sue Willoughby; *Asst Dir* Bob Hallenbeck
Open daily 10 AM - 4 PM, Sun 1 - 4 PM, cl Tues. Admis adults $3, seniors $2,
students $1. Estab 1974 to exhibit art of the Americans West, collect & educ.
Gallery has 4000 sq ft. Maintains reference library. Average Annual Attendance:
15,000. Mem: 800; dues $35; annual meeting in Aug
Income: $100,000 (financed by mem & admis)
Collections: Permanent collection contains fine art depicting art of the American
West
Exhibitions: Phippen Memorial Day Art Show Annual Art Show, juried with
144 artists
Activities: Classes for adults & children; lect open to public, 6 vis lectr per year;
gallery talks; tours; competitions & awards; individual paintings & original objects
of art lent to various museums in the country; lending collection contains original
art works, paintings & sculpture; book traveling exhibitions; originate traveling
exhibitions; museum shop sells books, magazines, original art, reproductions,
prints, original art & southwestern gifts

A PRESCOTT FINE ARTS ASSOCIATION, Gallery, 208 N Marina St, 86301.
Tel 520-445-3286; *Pres* Jerry Schuster; *VPres* Ralph Hess
Open Wed - & Sat 11 AM - 4 PM, Sun Noon - 4 PM. No admis fee, donations
accepted. Estab 1968 as a nonprofit gallery & theatre to promote arts within the
county & local community. Art Gallery is one large room below theater section
in what was previously a Catholic Church. Average Annual Attendance: 16,000.
Mem: 400; dues family $50, individual $25
Income: $30,000 (financed by mem & grants from Arizona Arts & Humanities
Council)
Activities: Classes for children; concerts; scholarship competitions with awards;
scholarships & fels offered; book traveling exhibitions; sales shop sells original
art, prints, pottery, jewelry, glass & woven items

SCOTTSDALE

A COSANTI FOUNDATION, 6433 Doubletree Ranch Rd, 85253. Tel 602-948-
6145; *Pres* Paolo Soleri; *Asst to the Pres* Scott M Davis; *Dir of Design* Tomiaki
Tamura; *Admin* Mary Hoadley
Open Mon - Sun 9 AM - 5 PM. Suggested donation $1. Estab 1956 as a
nonprofit educational organization by Paolo Soleri pursuing the research &
develop of an alternative urban environment. A permanent exhibit of original
sketches, sculptures & graphics by Paolo Soleri. Average Annual Attendance: 50,
000
Income: Financed by tuition, private donations & sales of art objects
Collections: Permanent coll of architectural designs & drawings by Paolo Soleri
Activities: Classes for adults & college students; academic conferences,
experimental workshops; lect open to public; concerts; gallery talks; tours;
scholarships offered; traveling exhibits organized & circulated; sales shop sells
books, original art, prints, reproductions, slides

A Arcosanti, HC74 Box 4136, Mayer, 86333. Tel 520-632-7135; FAX 520-632-
6229; Elec Mail America Online: Arcosanti, arcosanti@aol.com. *Pres* Paolo
Soleri; *Admin* Mary Hoadley; *Pub Relations & Exec Asst to Pres* Lori Carroll;
Planning & Exhib Coordr Tomiaki Tamura
Open Mon - Sun 9 AM - 5 PM, tours on the hour 10 AM - 4 PM. Suggested
donation for tour $5. Estab 1970 for architecture & urban design research &
practical Handson experience, cultural events. A prototype arcology for 7000
people, combining compact urban structure with large scale, solar greenhouses on
10 acres of a 4000 acre preserve. Average Annual Attendance: 40,000
Income: Financed by art & crafts sales, tuition, volunteer labor & donations
Publications: Arcosanti Newsletter, 2 per year
Activities: Classes for adults & children; lect open to public, vis lectr vary;
concerts; tours; scholarships & fels offered; originate traveling exhibitions
circulated to museums, corporate space, exhibit halls attached to conventions;
sales shop sells books, original art, reproduction, prints, slides, t-shirts, postcards
& videos

A FRANCHISE FINANCE CORPORATION OF AMERICA, The Fleischer
Museum, 17207 N Perimeter Dr, 85255-5402. Tel 602-585-3108; FAX 602-585-
2225; WATS 800-528-1179. *Exec Dir* Donna H Fleischer; *Asst to Dir* Annabelle
Markstein
Open 10 AM - 4 PM. No admis fee. Estab 1989 to provide a permanent home
for the coll & develop a scholarly forum for educ on the art period. Average
Annual Attendance: 25,000
Income: Financed by private funds
Collections: American Impressionism, California School from 1880 to 1940s;
Russian & Soviet Impressionism 1930-1970s
Exhibitions: (1997) East Meets West American Impressionism, Fleischer
Museum coll of California Impressionism & Paintings from the Hartford Stem
Boiler
Publications: Masterworks of California Impressionism, book; exhibition catalogs
Activities: Lect provided; tours by reservation only; museum shop sells books &
prints
L Fleischer Museum Library, 85255-5402 FAX 602-585-2225;
For reference only
Income: $18,000 (financed by private collection)
Library Holdings: Vols 800; Per subs 12; AV — Kodachromes, slides, v-tapes; Other —
Clipping files, exhibition catalogs, framed reproductions, memorabilia, original art
works, pamphlets, photographs, prints, reproductions, sculpture

A SCOTTSDALE ARTISTS' LEAGUE, PO Box 1071, 85252. Tel 602-946-0139;
Pres Melissa Showalter
Estab 1961 to encourage the practice of art & to support & encourage the study
& application of art as an avocation, to promote ethical principals & practice, to
advance the interest & appreciation of art in all its forms & to increase the
usefulness of art to the public at large. Gallery in Scottsdale Memorial Hospital.
Average Annual Attendance: 100 per month. Mem: 225; dues $20; monthly
meetings first Tues Sept - June
Exhibitions: Yearly juried exhibition for members only; yearly juried exhibition
for all Arizona artists (open shows)
Publications: Art Beat, monthly
Activities: Classes for adults; lect open to public, 6 vis lectr per year; gallery
talks; tours; scholarships offered to art students

L SCOTTSDALE ARTISTS' SCHOOL LIBRARY, 3720 N Marshall Way, PO
Box 8527, 85252-8527. Tel 602-990-1422; FAX 602-990-0652; WATS 800-333-
5707.
Library Holdings: Vols 2500; Per subs 20; AV — V-tapes; Other — Clipping
files, exhibition catalogs, framed reproductions, original art works, pamphlets,
prints, reproductions, sculpture
Special Subjects: Afro-American Art, American Indian Art, American Western
Art, Art History, Commercial Art, Decorative Arts, Drawings, Etchings &
Engravings, Graphic Design, Illustration, Oriental Art, Photography, Portraits,
Prints, Watercolors

M SCOTTSDALE CENTER FOR THE ARTS, 7380 E Second St, 85251. Tel 602-
994-2787, 874-4610; FAX 602-874-4699; *Dir* Frank Jacobson; *VPres Visual Arts*
Robert Knight; *Asst Dir Visual Arts* Debra Hopkins
Open Tues - Fri 10 AM - 8 PM, Sat Noon - 8 PM, Sun Noon - 5 PM. No admis
fee. Estab 1975 to provide a varied program of performance events & art
exhibits. Center is a large contemporary space including two climate controlled
galleries allowing viewing of large & small works in various media. Average
Annual Attendance: 130,000. Mem: 2500; dues $20 & up
Income: $1,250,000 (financed by mem, city appropriation & corporate
sponsorship)
Collections: Paintings, prints, sculptures
Publications: Exhibition catalogs
Activities: Docent training; lect open to public, 10 vis lectr per year;
competitions with awards; exten dept serves local schools; book traveling
exhibitions; originates traveling exhibitions; sales shop sells books, original art,
reproductions, prints & craft items

SECOND MESA

M **HOPI CULTURAL CENTER MUSEUM,** Rte 264, Box 7, 86043. Tel 520-734-6650; *Dir* Anna Silas
Open Mon - Fri 8 AM - 5 PM
Collections: Hopi arts & crafts; pre-historic & historic pottery; weavings; wood carvings; silver

TEMPE

ARIZONA STATE UNIVERSITY

M **ASU Art Museum,** Nelson Fine Arts Ctr, 85287-1202. Tel 602-965-2787; FAX 602-965-5254; *Elec Mail* artmuse@asuvm.inre.asu.edu. *Dir* Marilyn A Zeitlin; *Cur* Heather Lineberry; *Registrar* Mary Jane Williams; *Installationist* Stephen Johnson
Open Tues 10 AM - 9 PM, Wed - Sat 10 AM - 5 PM, Sun 1 - 5 PM. No admis fee. Estab 1950 to provide esthetic & educational service for students & the citizens of the state. Permanent installations, changing galleries & various changing area; 48 shows annually. Average Annual Attendance: 55,000
Income: $250,000 (financed by state appropriations, donations & earnings)
Collections: †American crafts, especially ceramics & glass; †American painting & sculpture, 18th Century to present; †Contemporary; †print collection, 15th Century to present; †Latin American Art; Folk Art; 20th century ceramics
Exhibitions: (1997) Elinas & Jamex de la Torre; Art on the Edge of Fashion
Publications: Too Late for Goya: Works by Francesc Torres; Art Under Duress: El Salvador 1980-Present; Bill Biola: Buried Secrets; Art of the Edge of Fashion
Activities: Educ dept; docent training; student docent program; special events; lect open to public, 12 vis lectr per year; gallery talks; tours; competitions; originate traveling exhibitions; museum shop sells books, original art & crafts, jewelry, cards
L **Hayden Library,** PO Box 871006, 85287-1006. Tel 602-965-6164, 965-3605; *Dean University Libraries* Sherri Schmidt; *Assoc Dean Coll Develop* Dora Biblarz; *Art Specialist* Winberta Yao; *Architecture Librn* Berna Neal
Open Mon - Thurs 7 AM - 11:30 PM, Fri 7 AM - 7 PM, Sat 9 AM - 5 PM, Sun Noon - 11:30 PM
Income: Financed by state
Library Holdings: Vols 2,826,679; Per subs 31,694; Micro — Cards, fiche, reels; AV — Cassettes
Special Subjects: American Indian Art, American Western Art, Anthropology, Archaeology, Architecture, Art Education, Art History, Coins & Medals, History of Art & Archaeology, Interior Design
M **Memorial Union Gallery,** PO Box 870901, 85287-0901. Tel 602-965-6649; FAX 602-727-6212; *Prog Coordr* Rosalyn Munk
Open Mon - Fri 9 AM - 5 PM. Estab to exhibit work that has strong individual qualities from the United States, also some Arizona work that has not been shown on campus. Gallery is contained in two rooms with 1400 sq ft space; fireplace; one wall is glass; 20 ft ceiling; 26 4 x 8 partitions; track lighting; one entrance and exit; located in area with maximum traffic. Average Annual Attendance: 30,000
Income: Financed by administrative appropriation
Purchases: $3000
Collections: Painting, print & sculpture, primarily Altma, Gorman, Mahaffey, Schoulder & Slater
Activities: Internships; lect open to public, 4 vis lectr per year; gallery talks; competitions; originate traveling exhibitions
L **Architecture & Environmental Design Library,** Arizona State University, 85287-1705. Tel 602-965-6400; FAX 602-965-1594; *Elec Mail* bneal@asu.edu; madden@asu.edu. *Dept Head* Berna E Neal; *Archivist* Dennis Madden
Open Mon - Thurs 9 AM - 10 PM, Fri 9 AM - 5 PM, Sat Noon - 4 PM, Sun 2 - 10 PM. Estab 1959 to serve the College of Architecture & Environmental Design & the university community with reference & research material in the subjects of architecture, planning, landscape architecture, industrial design & interior design. Circ 35,000
Income: Financed by state appropriation
Library Holdings: Vols 30,000; Per subs 130; Architectural models; Micro — Fiche, prints, reels; AV — A-tapes, cassettes, slides, v-tapes; Other — Manuscripts, memorabilia, photographs, prints
Special Subjects: Architecture, Furniture, Industrial Design, Interior Design, Landscape Architecture
Collections: †Paolo Soleri & †Frank Lloyd Wright Special Research Collections; Victor Olgyzy, Paul Schweikher, Litchfield Park, Will Bruder, Albert Chase MacArthur, other drawings & documents
L **Architectural Image Library,** College of Architecture, 85287. Tel 602-965-5469; FAX 602-965-1594; *Coordr* Diane Upchurch
Circ 75,000
Library Holdings: Vols 30,000; AV — Slides 110,000; Other — Prints
Special Subjects: Architecture, Art History, Asian Art, Etchings & Engravings, Furniture, Graphic Design, Interior Design, Islamic Art, Landscape Architecture, Painting - American, Painting - Dutch, Painting - European, Painting - Flemish, Painting - French, Painting - German, Painting - Italian, Period Rooms, Photography, Pottery, Primitive Art, Printmaking, Sculpture, Tapestries, Textiles, Woodcuts

A **TEMPE ARTS CENTER,** 54 W First St, PO Box 549, 85280-0549. Tel 602-968-0888; *Exec Dir* Vicki Stouffer; *Exhib Coordr* Patty Haberman; *Prog Coordr* Margaret Brunning
Open Tues - Sun Noon - 5 PM. No admis fee. Estab 1982. Contemporary craft & sculpture - Main Gallery & outdoor sculpture garden featuring contemporary large scale sculpture on a rotating basis; Satellite Gallery in Tempe Public Library. Average Annual Attendance: 250,000. Mem: 200; dues $30, $50, $100, $250; annual meeting in Sept
Income: Financed by mem, city & state appropriation
Activities: Children's classes; lect open to public, 6 vis lectr per year; scholarships & fels; book traveling exhibitions 1 per year; originate traveling exhibitions 1 per year; retail store sells original art & craft only

TUBAC

A **SANTA CRUZ VALLEY ART ASSOCIATION,** Tubac Center of the Arts, PO Box 1911, 85646. Tel 520-398-2371; FAX 520-398-9511; *Pres* Virginia Cochrane; *Dir* Nancy James
Open Tues - Sat 10 AM - 4:30 PM, Sun & holidays 1 - 4:30 PM, cl Mon. No admis fee. Estab 1963 to promote interest in regional art. Three galleries, one a Spanish Colonial Building, 139 running ft of exhibit space. Average Annual Attendance: 40,000. Mem: 800; dues $25-$500; annual meeting in Apr
Collections: Works by present & former Tubac artists
Exhibitions: Invitationals; members' & non-members' shows; Arizona Glass Artists
Activities: Classes for adults & children; docent training; lect for members only, 2-4 vis lectr per year; competitions with awards; sales shop sells books, original art, pottery, jewelry, ethnic crafts (Indian, Mexican)
L **Library,** PO Box 1911, 85646. Tel 520-398-2371; FAX 520-398-9511; *Dir* Nancy James
Library Holdings: Vols 850; Micro — Cards; AV — Slides; Other — Exhibition catalogs
Special Subjects: Art History

TUCSON

M **DINNERWARE ARTIST'S COOPERATIVE,** 135 E Congress St, 85701. Tel 520-792-4503; FAX 520-792-4503; *Exec Dir* Nora Kuhl
Open Tues - Sat Noon - 5 PM. No admis fee. Estab 1979 to present & promote contemporary art. 2000 sq ft. Average Annual Attendance: 20,000
Activities: Lect open to public, 5 vis lectr per year; concerts; gallery talks; competitions with prizes; book traveling exhibitions 3 per year

A **NATIONAL NATIVE AMERICAN CO-OPERATIVE,** North American Indian Information & Trade Center, PO Box 27626, 85726. Tel 520-622-4900; FAX 520-292-0779; *Dir & Consultant* Fred Synder; *International Representative* Carole J Garcia
Open Mon - Sat 10 AM - 7 PM. No admis fee. Estab 1969 to provide incentive to 2700 American Indian artists representing over 410 tribes for the preservation of their contemporary & traditional crafts, culture & education through involvement in Indian cultural programs, including dances, traditional food, fashion shows & performances. Also sponsors various Indian events. Average Annual Attendance: 50,000-100,000. Mem: 2700; meetings in Nov & Jan
Income: Financed through sales
Collections: †Native American arts & crafts, including jewelry, basketry, wood & stone carving, weaving, pottery, beadwork, quill-work, rug-making, tanning & leatherwork, dance & cookery
Exhibitions: Dance/Craft Competition
Publications: Native American Directory: Alaska, Canada, United States; Native American Reference Book (1982); Pow-Wow on the Red Road
Activities: Classes for adults; lect open to public, 5-10 vis lectr per year; concerts; competitions with prizes; scholarships offered; artmobile; book traveling exhibitions 40-50 per year; originate traveling exhibitions; museum shop sells books, magazines, original art & authentic American Indian crafts, books & tapes

M **TUCSON MUSEUM OF ART & HISTORIC BLOCK,** 140 N Main Ave, 85701. Tel 520-624-2333; FAX 520-624-7202; *Dir* Robert A Yassin; *Pres* Burton Lazar; *Dir Public Relations & Marketing* Laurie Swanson; *Bus Mgr* Carol Bleck; *Controller* Ruth Sons; *School Mgr* Judith D'Agostino; *Registrar* Susan Dolan; *Librn* Sheila Mortonson; *Dir Develop* Sandy Napombejra; *Cur Exhib* Joanne Stuhr; *Shop Mgr* John McNulty; *Admin Asst* Tisa Rodriquez Sherman
Open Mon - Sat 10 AM - 4 PM, Sun Noon - 4 PM, cl Mon in June, July & Aug. Admis adults $2, senior citizens & students $1, under 12 & Tues free. Estab 1924 to operate a private nonprofit civic art gallery to promote art educ, to hold art exhibitions & to further art appreciation for the pub. Galleries display permanent collections & changing exhibitions. Average Annual Attendance: 141,068. Mem: 2500; dues Director's Circle $1000, President's Circle $500, patron $250, sustaining $100, sponsor $60, senior couple $35, individual/senior/student $30; annual meeting in June
Income: $1,793,353 (financed by grants, endowment, mem, city & state appropriations, contributions & generated income)
Collections: Contemporary & decorative arts; †contemporary Southwest, folk, Mexican, †Pre-Columbian, †Spanish Colonial, Western American & 20th century art
Exhibitions: Arizona Biennial '97; Harvey Brown, Duane Bryers, Don Crowley, Tom Hill, Bob Kuhn, Ken Riley, Howard Terpning: The Tucson 7; El Nacimiento; Lasting Impressions; Drawings by Thomas Hart Benton; Joan P Schaefer Photography; Seven Years in Tiret: The Photos of Heinric Harrer; Symbols of Life: Ceremonial Art of the Amazon People; Jim Waid: Natural Elements; Women Artists & the West
Publications: Quarterly Preview; exhibition catalogs
Activities: Classes for adults & children; docent training; lect open to public; concerts; gallery talks; tours; awards; scholarships & fels offered; exten dept serving Tucson school districts; book traveling exhibitions 4-6 per year; originate traveling exhibitions; museum & sales shop sells books, magazines, original art, reproductions, prints & area crafts
L **Library,** 140 N Main Ave, 85701. Tel 520-388-4723; *Librn* Sr Sheila Mortonson
Open Mon, Wed & Thurs 10 AM - 2 PM. Estab 1974 for bibliographic & research needs of Mus staff, faculty, students & docents. Open to public for research & study
Income: Financed by gifts & fund allocations
Library Holdings: Vols 4000; Per subs 25; Indexes; Museum archives; Micro — Fiche, reels; AV — Kodachromes, slides 25,000, v-tapes; Other — Clipping files, exhibition catalogs 500, manuscripts, pamphlets 3000, photographs, prints, reproductions, sculpture
Special Subjects: Aesthetics, American Indian Art, American Western Art, Art Education, Art History, Ceramics, Conceptual Art, Decorative Arts, Drawings, Etchings & Engravings, Folk Art, Furniture, Glass, Gold, History of Art & Archaeology, Pre-Columbian Art, Art of Africa, Oceania, Western art, Contemporary Art, Spanish Colonial, Arizona Artists
Collections: Biographic material documenting Arizona artists

UNIVERSITY OF ARIZONA

M **Museum of Art,** Park & Speedway Sts, 85721. Tel 520-621-7567; *Dir & Chief Cur* Dr Peter Bermingham; *Asst Dir* Adeline Karpiscak; *Cur Educ* Joshua Goldberg; *Assoc Cur Educ* Lisa Hastreiter; *Cur Coll* Dr Peter Briggs; *Admin Asst* Chris Jackson; *Registrar* Richard Schaffer; *Asst Registrar* Kevin Gillian
Open Sept 1 - May 15 Mon - Fri 9 AM - 5 PM, Sun Noon - 4 PM, cl Sat; May 15 - Sept 1 Mon - Fri 10 AM - 3:30 PM, Sun Noon - 4 PM, cl Sat. Estab 1955 to share with the Tucson community, visitors & the university students the treasures of three remarkable permanent collections: the C Leonard Pfeiffer Collection, the Samuel H Kress Collection & the Edward J Gallagher Jr Collection. One of the museums' most important functions is to reach out to schools around Tucson through the educ dept. Special exhibitions are maintained on the first floor of the mus; the permanent collections are housed on the second floor. Average Annual Attendance: 45,000
Income: Financed by state appropriation
Collections: Edward J Gallagher Collection of over a hundred paintings of national & international artists; Samuel H Kress Collection of 26 Renaissance works & 26 paintings of the 15th century Spanish Retablo by Fernando Gallego; C Leonard Pfeiffer Collection of American Artists of the 30s, 40s & 50s; Jacques Lipchitz Collection of 70 plaster models
Publications: Fully illustrated catalogs on all special exhibitions
Activities: Docent training; lect open to public, 10 vis lectr per year; tours; gallery talks; out reach tours; book traveling exhibitions 2-3 per year; originate traveling exhibitions; sales shop sells books, cards & poster reproductions

L **Museum of Art Library,** Speedway & Olive, 85721. Tel 520-621-7567; *Librn* Barbara Kittle
Estab to assist staff & students working at mus with reference information. Not open to pub; telephone requests for information answered
Library Holdings: Vols 5000; Per subs 16; AV — Cassettes, slides; Other — Clipping files, exhibition catalogs, pamphlets
Special Subjects: Art History, Museum Studies

M **Center for Creative Photography,** University of Arizona, 85721. Tel 520-621-7968; FAX 520-621-9444; *Dir* Terence Pitts; *Cur* Trudy Wilner Stack; *Registrar* Anne Sullivan; *Archivist* Amy Rule; *Librn* Tim Troy
Open Mon - Fri 9 AM - 5 PM, Sun Noon - 5 PM. Estab 1975 to house & organize the archives of numerous major photographers & to act as a research center in 20th century photography. Gallery exhibitions changing approximately every six weeks. Average Annual Attendance: 30,000
Income: Financed by state, federal, private & corporate sources
Collections: Archives of Ansel Adams, Wynn Bullock, Harry Callahan, Aaron Siskind, W Eugene Smith, Frederick Sommer, Paul Strand, Edward Weston, Richard Aredon & others
Publications: The Archive, approx 3 times per year; bibliography series; exhibitions catalogs; guide series
Activities: Lect open to pubic; gallery talks; tours; original objects of art lent to qualified museums; originate traveling exhibitions

L **Library,** Center for Creative Photography, 85721. Tel 520-621-7968; FAX 520-621-9444; *Librn* Tim Troy
Open Mon - Fri 10 AM - 5 PM, Sun Noon - 5 PM. Open to the pub for print viewing & research
Library Holdings: Vols 15,000; Per subs 95; Micro — Fiche, reels; AV — A-tapes, cassettes, slides, v-tapes; Other — Clipping files, exhibition catalogs, manuscripts, memorabilia, original art works, pamphlets, photographs
Special Subjects: Photography as an art form in the 20th century
Collections: Limited edition books; hand-made books; books illustrated with original photographs; artists' books

L **College of Architecture Library,** 85721. Tel 520-621-2498; FAX 520-621-8700; *Librn* Ann Lally; *Archives* Jeffrey Brooks
Open Mon - Thurs 9 AM - 9 PM, Fri 9 AM - 5 PM, Sat Noon - 5 PM, Sun Noon - 9 PM. Estab 1965
Income: $34,700 (financed by state appropriation)
Library Holdings: Vols 14,000; Per subs 125; AV — Slides, v-tapes; Other — Clipping files
Special Subjects: Architecture, Drafting, Landscape Architecture, Arid Lands Architecture, Design Communications

M **WOMANKRAFT,** 388 S Stone Ave, 85701. Tel 520-629-9976; *Contact* Linn Lane
Open Tues, Wed & Sat 1 - 5 PM. No admis fee. Estab 1974 to claim & validate women artists. Craft area, topic gallery, gallery of the month & child-run gallery of art made by children. Average Annual Attendance: 5000. Mem: 100; dues $30 & up
Collections: Members art collection
Activities: Classes for adults & children; dramatic programs; workshops & workshop series-poetry readings & performance; lect open to public

WICKENBURG

M **MARICOPA COUNTY HISTORICAL SOCIETY,** Desert Caballeros Western Museum, 21 N Frontier St, 85390. Tel 520-684-2272; FAX 520-684-5794; Elec Mail dcwm@aol.com. *Dir* Cheryl Taylor; *Cur* Sheila Kollasch; *Public Relations* Kathy Wortman; *Treas* Stephen Morris
Open Mon - Sat 10 AM - 4 PM, Sun 1 - 4 PM. Admis general $4, sr citizens $3, children 6-16 $1, under 6 free. Estab 1960 to show the development of Wickenburg from prehistoric to present day. The museum houses western art gallery, mineral room, Indian room, period rooms & gold mining equipment. Average Annual Attendance: 30,000. Mem: 600; dues $25-$30; annual meeting in Jan
Income: $200,000 (financed by mem, private donations, endowments)
Collections: 19th Century Decorative arts, textiles, Navajo rugs; Cowboy Art, bronze & paintings; Native American Art, minerals & gems; Western American Art
Exhibitions: Sole of the West: The Art & History of Cowboy Boots
Publications: A History of Wickenburg to 1875 by Helen B Hawkins; The Right Side Up Town on the Upside Down River; Museum Highlights, newsletter bimonthly
Activities: Lect open to public, 4 vis lectr per year; gallery talks; tours; individual paintings & original objects of art lent to museum; book traveling exhibitions two per year; museum shop sells books & prints

L **Eleanor Blossom Memorial Library,** 21 N Frontier St, PO Box 1446, 85358. Tel 520-684-2272; FAX 520-684-5794; Elec Mail dcwm@aol.com. *Dir* Cheryl Taylor
Open to members for reference only
Library Holdings: Vols 2000; Per subs 25
Special Subjects: American Western Art, History of Art & Archaeology, Manuscripts, History of Wickenburg, AZ, General Arizona history

WINDOW ROCK

L **NAVAJO NATION LIBRARY SYSTEM,** PO Box 9040, 86515. Tel 520-871-6376; *Librn* Irving Nelson
Library Holdings: Vols 21,000
Special Subjects: History, culture & arts of Navajo Indians

M **NAVAJO NATION MUSEUM,** Hwy 264, PO Box 9000, 86515. Tel 520-871-6673
Open Mon - Fri 9 AM - 5 PM, cl national & tribal holidays. No admis fee. Estab 1961 to collect & preserve items depicting Navajo history & culture & natural history of region. Exhibit area approx 2500 ft. Average Annual Attendance: 16,000
Income: Financed by tribal budget & donations
Collections: †Works in all media by Navajo Indian artists, & non-Navajo artists who depict Navajo subject matter
Publications: Artist's directory & biographical file
Activities: Individual paintings & original works of art available for loan to other museums; lending collection contains 4000 nature artifacts, 300 original works of art & 30,000 photographs; sales shop sells books

YUMA

M **ARIZONA HISTORICAL SOCIETY-YUMA,** Century House Museum & Garden, 240 Madison Ave, 85364. Tel 520-782-1841; FAX 520-783-0680; *Div Dir* Megan Reid; *Cur* Carol Brooks; *Admin Secy* Karen Roberts
Open Tues 10 AM - 4 PM. No admis fee. Estab 1963 to collect, preserve & interpret the history of the lower Colorado River Regions. Average Annual Attendance: 1400. Mem: 300; dues $40; annual meetings in Apr & Oct
Income: Financed by mem, state appropriation & donations
Collections: †Archives; †Clothing; †Furniture & Household Items; †Photos & Maps; †Trade & Business Items
Exhibitions: Lower Colorado River Region from 1540-1940; History Exhibits; Period Rooms
Publications: Newsletter
Activities: Lect; tours; living history; slide shows; walking tours; lending collection contains books, artifacts, album-scrapbooks, linear feet archives & 12,400 photographs; museum shop sells books, reproductions, prints & gifts

M **YUMA FINE ARTS ASSOCIATION,** Art Center, 301 Main St, 85364. Tel 520-783-2314; *Dir* Shawn Davis; *Educ Coordr* Cynthia Rouillard
Open Tues - Sun 10 AM - 5 PM. Admis adult $1, children $.50, free Tues. Estab 1962 to foster the arts in the Yuma area & to provide a showing space for contemporary art & art of the Southwest. Gallery is housed in restored Southern Pacific Railway depot built in 1926. Average Annual Attendance: 30,000. Mem: 350; dues $25 - $5000
Income: Financed by endowment, mem & city appropriation, grants & fundraising events
Collections: Contemporary Art; Art of the Southwest
Publications: Art Notes Southwest, quarterly
Activities: Classes for adults & children; lect open to public, 10 vis lectr per year; concerts; gallery talks; tours; competitions; $3000 awards annually; individual paintings & original objects of art lent to other museums for specific exhibitions; book traveling exhibitions 6-10 times per year; originate traveling exhibitions; museum shop sells original art & art of the Southwest

ARKANSAS

CLARKSVILLE

UNIVERSITY OF THE OZARKS

L **Robson Memorial Library,** 415 N College Ave, 72830. Tel 501-754-3839; FAX 501-979-1355; *Library Dir* Stuart Stelzer
Estab 1891
Library Holdings: Vols 1750; Per subs 12; Micro — Fiche, reels; AV — Cassettes, rec, slides 7000, v-tapes 17

M **Stephens Gallery,** Walton Fine Arts Bldg, 72830. Tel 501-754-7119; FAX 501-754-3839, Ext 351; *Gallery Dir* Nancy Farrell
Open Mon - Fri 10 AM - 3 PM & by special arrangement. Estab 1986
Collections: Gould Ivory Collection; Pfeffer Moser Glass Collection
Exhibitions: Monthly exhibitions
Activities: Educ dept; lect open to public; concerts; gallery talks; tours

EL DORADO

A **SOUTH ARKANSAS ARTS CENTER,** 110 E Fifth St, 71730. Tel 501-862-5474; *Pres* Steve Jones; *Exec Dir* Linda Boyston
Open Mon - Fri 9 AM - 5 PM. No admis fee. Estab 1965 for the promotion, enrichment & improvement of the visual & performing arts by means of exhibits, lectures & instruction & through scholarships to be offered whenever possible. Gallery maintained. New 2000 sq ft gallery. Mem: 500; dues individual $25, seniors minimum $15; board of directors meeting second Tues every month

Income: Financed by mem, city & state appropriation
Collections: Japanese block prints (including Hokusai, Utamarro, Hiroshig); regional watercolorists; Indian Jewelry (Hopi, Zuni, Navaho)
Exhibitions: Various art shows in this & surrounding states; gallery shows, ten guest artists annually. One show monthly, featuring regional or national artists
Publications: Newsletter, quarterly
Activities: Classes for adults & children; theater & dance workshops; guitar lessons; visual arts classes; lect open to public; gallery talks; competitions; scholarships offered
L **Library,** 110 E Fifth St, 71730. FAX 501-862-5474; *Exec Dir* Linda Boydston
Income: $250,000 (financed by mem, grants, sales & sponsorships)
Library Holdings: Vols 2000
Special Subjects: Painting - American, Painting - Japanese, Porcelain, Pottery, Southwestern Art
Exhibitions: Changing exhibits regularly
Publications: Quarterly newsletter

FAYETTEVILLE

UNIVERSITY OF ARKANSAS

L **Fine Arts Library,** FNAR-104, 72701. Tel 501-575-4708; *Librn* Norma Johnson
Open Mon - Thurs 8 AM - 11 PM, Fri 8 AM - 6 PM, Sat 10 AM - 6 PM, Sun 1 - 11 PM. Estab 1951 to support the curriculum in music, art & architecture. Circ 36,000
Library Holdings: Vols 33,000; Per subs 146; Micro — Fiche, reels; AV — Slides; Other — Exhibition catalogs
Special Subjects: Architecture, Art Education, Art History, Landscape Architecture

FORT SMITH

M **FORT SMITH ART CENTER,** 423 N Sixth St, 72901. Tel 501-784-2787, 782-1156; FAX 501-784-9071; *Pres Board* Dr Amy Jordon; *Dir* Julie A Lind
Open daily 9:30 AM - 4:30 PM, Sun 2 - 4 PM, cl Mon, July 4, Labor Day, Thanksgiving & Christmas Eve-New Years. No admis fee. Estab 1957 to provide art museum, art association and art education. Art Library maintained. Average Annual Attendance: 24,000. Mem: 930; dues $40
Income: $100,000 (financed by grants, mem, contributions & sales)
Collections: †American painting, graphics and drawings; †Boehm porcelain; local & regional art
Exhibitions: Five exhibitions monthly
Publications: Bulletin, monthly
Activities: Classes for children; competitions with awards; artmobile; gallery & gift shop sells books, original art & art related gift items

HELENA

M **PHILLIPS COUNTY MUSEUM,** 623 Pecan St, 72342. Tel 501-338-7790; *Pres* Mary A Burke
Open Mon - Sat 9 AM - 5 PM, cl national holidays. No admis fee. Estab 1929 as an educational & cultural museum to impart an appreciation of local history & to display objects of art from all over the world. Average Annual Attendance: 5000. Mem: 250; dues $3-$5; annual meeting first Fri in May
Income: Financed by endowment, mem & city appropriation
Collections: China; glassware; paintings; Indian artifacts; Civil War memorabilia; Thomas Alva Edison Historical Display
Exhibitions: Blues Exhibition Chuck Berry

HOT SPRINGS

M **HOT SPRINGS ART CENTER,** Fine Arts Center, 514 Central Ave, 71901. Tel 501-624-0489; *Dir* Bob Lake
Open Mon - Sat 10 AM - 4 PM, Sun 1:30 - 5 PM. No admis fee. Estab 1946 as a multi-disciplinary Arts Center. The Center constitutes an amalgam of arts organizations from throughout the region, representing all forms of fine & applied art as well as performing, instructional & crafts groups. Two galleries; twenty exhibits per year of local area artists. Average Annual Attendance: 5000. Mem: 550; dues benefactor $1000, sustaining $500, sponsor $250, subscriber $100, patron $50, family $25, individual $15; annual meeting in Oct
Income: Financed by individual & corporate mem, grants from the Arkansas Arts Council & National Endowment for the Arts
Exhibitions: Annual Open Competition; regional, state & local artist exhibition
Publications: Class schedule brochures; monthly exhibit announcements; newsletters, 4 times per year
Activities: Classes for adults & children in art, dance, theatre & music; dramatic programs; concerts; competitions with awards; scholarships offered; individual paintings & original objects of art lent to other institutions; lending collection contains books & photographs

HOT SPRINGS NATIONAL PARK

M **THE ART FOUNDATION,** * 520 Central Ave, 71901. Tel 501-623-9847, 623-0474; *Chmn* Lorraine Benini
No admis fee. Estab 1984
Collections: †Contemporary paintings & sculpture

JONESBORO

M **ARKANSAS STATE UNIVERSITY-ART DEPARTMENT, JONESBORO,**
Fine Arts Center Gallery, * Caraway Rd (Mailing add: PO Box 1920, State University, 72467). Tel 501-972-3050; FAX 501-972-3932; Elec Mail cspeele@aztec.astate.edu. *Dir* Steven Mayes; *Chair Art Dept* Curtis Steele
Open weekdays 10 AM - 4 PM. No admis fee. Estab 1967 for educ objectives; recognition of contemporary artists & encouragement to students. Located in the Fine Arts Center, the well-lighted gallery measures 40 x 45 ft plus corridor display areas. Average Annual Attendance: 10,500
Income: $3956 (financed by state appropriation)
Collections: Contemporary paintings; contemporary sculpture; †historical & contemporary prints; †photographs
Publications: Exhibition catalogs
Activities: Lect open to public, 4-6 vis lectr per year; gallery talks; competitions; originate traveling exhibitions
L **Library,** * 2040 Caraway Rd (Mailing add: PO Box 2040, State University, 72467). Tel 501-972-3077; FAX 501-972-5706; *Reference Librn* Terrie Sypoelt
Library Holdings: Vols 9100; Per subs 79; Micro — Fiche, reels; AV — Cassettes, fs, Kodachromes, motion pictures, slides
Collections: Microfilm collection for 19th century photography

LITTLE ROCK

M **ARKANSAS ARTS CENTER,** Mac Arthur Park, PO Box 1137, 72203-2137. Tel 501-372-4000; FAX 501-375-8053; *Dir & Chief Cur* Townsend D Wolfe III; *Cur* Ruth Pasquine; *Cur Decorative Arts* Alan DuBois; *Registrar* Thom Hall; *Bus Mgr* Paul Hayes
Open Mon - Sat 10 AM - 5 PM, Sun & holidays Noon - 5 PM. No admis fee to galleries & Decorative Arts Mus, admis charged for theatre activities. Estab 1937 to further the development, the understanding & the appreciation of the visual & performing arts. Six galleries, two for permanent collections, four for temporary exhibits, & eight at the Decorative Arts Mus. Average Annual Attendance: 350,000. Mem: 4000; dues from benefactor $20,000 to basic $40; annual meeting in Aug
Income: Financed by endowment, mem, city & state appropriation & earned income & private corporate, state, local & federal grants
Purchases: Peter Paul Rubens, Hygieia Goddess of Health Feeding the Serpent; Giacomo Manzu, Bust of Woman; Alison Saar, Invisible Man; Joseph Stella, Head of a Woman in Profile; William T Wiley, Gift of Ms Givings; John Himmelfarb, Broad Daylight Meeting; Morris Graves, Chalices; Mark Tobey, Untitled, ca 1940; Hans Hofmann, Study for Fruit Bowl; Benny Andrews, Portrait of a Model & Cools
Collections: †Drawings from the Renaissance to present, with major collection of American & European drawings since 1900; 19th & 20th century paintings & prints; 20th century sculpture & photographs; Oriental & American decorative arts; †contemporary crafts & †toys designed by artists
Exhibitions: (1997) Twentieth Century Russian Drawings from a Private Collection; Imperial Russian Porcelain 1744-1917 from the Raymond F Piper Collection; Forum on Decorative Arts; Still Life: The Object in American Art, 1915-1995 Selections From the Metropolitan Museum of Art; 27th Annual Mid-Southern Watercolorists Exhibition; The Barrett Hamilton Young Arkansas Artists Competition & Exhibition; The Art of Toshiko Takaezu; Irwin Kremen: Collage & Sculpture; 24th Annual Prints, Drawings & Photographs Exhibition; Boehm Birds & Botanical Illustrations at Kate Nessler; Josiah Wedgwoud: Experimental Potter; 40th Annual Delta Exhibition of Painting & Sculpture; Permanent Collection; William Wegman: Photographs, Paintings, Drawings & Video; Winners of the 1996 Arkansas Women Artists State Exhibition; Ruth Bernhard at Ninety: Known & Unknown; Re-Aligning Vision: South American Drawings 1960-1990; National Objects Invitational. (1997-98) Hot Dry Men, Cold Wet Women: The Theory of Humors & Depictions of Men & Women in Western European Art of the 1600s; Collector's Show & Sale; 25th Annual Toys Designed by Artists Exhibition; Annual Collectors Show & Sale
Publications: Members Bulletin, monthly; annual membership catalog; annual report; catalogue selections from the permanent collection; exhibit catalogues & brochures
Activities: Classes for adults & children; dramatic programs; children's theatre; docent training; lect open to public, 6-10 vis lectr per year; gallery talks; tours; competitions with awards; exten dept serving the state of Arkansas; artmobile; individual paintings & original objects of art lent to schools, civic groups & churches; lending collection contains motion pictures, original prints, paintiings, 4300 phonorecords & 16,000 slides; book traveling exhibitions; originates traveling exhibitions; museum shop sells books, original art, reproductions, jewelry, crafts, cards & calendars
L **Elizabeth Prewitt Taylor Memorial Library,** MacArthur Park, PO Box 2137, 72203. Tel 501-372-4000; *Librn* Betty Lane
Open Mon - Fri 10 AM - 5 PM. Estab 1963 to provide resources in the arts for students, educators & interested pub. For reference only
Income: $25,120
Purchases: $6800
Library Holdings: Vols 5500; Per subs 100; AV — A-tapes, cassettes, Kodachromes, motion pictures, rec, slides; Other — Clipping files, exhibition catalogs, pamphlets, photographs
Special Subjects: Afro-American Art, American Indian Art, American Western Art, Asian Art, Decorative Arts, Eskimo Art, Folk Art, Historical Material, History of Art & Archaeology, Latin American Art
Collections: †George Fisher Cartoons; John Reid Jazz Collection

M **ARKANSAS TERRITORIAL RESTORATION,** 200 E Third St, 72201. Tel 501-324-9351; FAX 501-324-9345; *Dir* William B Worthen Jr; *Cur* Swannee Bennett; *Educ Coordr* Starr Mitchell; *Public Relations* Nancy W Long
Open daily 9 AM - 5 PM, Sun 1 - 5 PM. Admis to mus houses adults $2, senior citizens (65 & over) $1, children under 16 $.50. Reception Center free. Restoration completed 1941. The Restoration is a group of homes including a recently restored log house, that represent the early & mid-19th century of Arkansas

history. Average Annual Attendance: 50,000
Income: Financed by state & private funding
Collections: †Arkansas made guns & furniture; Audubon prints; furnishing of the period; porcelain hands, prints & maps from the 19th century; silver collection; watercolors
Publications: Arkansas Made: The Decorative Mechanical & Fine Arts Produced in Arkansas 1819-1870; Territorial Times, 3 times a year
Activities: Classes for children; docent training; Log House activities include educational program for students & adults in candle dipping, cooking & needlework; Reception Center has slide show, exhibits & art gallery; tours; individual paintings & original objects of art lent to other museums & cultural institutions; lending collection contains books, motion pictures, original prints, paintings, photographs, loan box (artifacts) & 2000 slides; originate traveling exhibitions to area museums & schools; craft store sells books, reproductions & early Arkansas crafts

L **Library,** 200 E Third St, 72201. FAX 501-324-9345; *Dir* W B Worthen Jr; *Cur* Swannee Bennett; *Educ Coordr* Starr Mitchell; *Public Relations* Nancy Long
Open Mon - Sat 9 AM - 5 PM, Sun 1 - 5 PM. Admis adults $2, senior citizens $1, children $.50. Estab 1941 to preserve & promote Arkansas history. Arkansas Artist Gallery contains Arkansas artists with new display monthly, Cromwell Hall contains historical exhibits 3 times a year. Average Annual Attendance: 50,000
Income: Financed by the state & private funds
Library Holdings: Vols 500; Per subs 8; Micro — Reels; AV — A-tapes, cassettes, slides; Other — Clipping files, framed reproductions, manuscripts, original art works, pamphlets, photographs, prints, reproductions
Special Subjects: Antiques, Art, Furniture, Gardening, Historical Material, Houses, Living History
Collections: Arkansas-made decorative, mechanical & fine art
Exhibitions: Contemporary art; historical exhibits
Publications: Arkansas Made: The Decorative, Mechanical and Fine Art Produced in Arkansas 1819-1870
Activities: Classes for adults & children; dramatic programs; docent training; lect open to public, 3 vis lectr per year; tours; individual paintings & original objects of art lent to other museums; museum shop sells books, original art, reproductions, prints

C **FIRST COMMERCIAL BANK IN LITTLE ROCK,** 400 W Capitol, PO Box 1471, 72201. Tel 501-371-7000; FAX 501-371-7413; *In Charge Art Coll & Prog* Kevin Sabin
Open Mon - Fri 9 AM - 4 PM. Estab 1960 to support art community. Collection displayed in two bank buildings & 20 branch offices; annual amount of contributions & grants $5000-$15,000
Purchases: $5000
Collections: Arkansas art, chiefly paintings; some sculpture and weavings, pottery
Exhibitions: One major exhibit per year

M **QUAPAW QUARTER ASSOCIATION, INC,** Villa Marre, 1321 Scott St, 72202. Tel 501-371-0075; FAX 501-374-8142; *Exec Dir* Cheryl G Nichols
Open Mon - Fri 9 AM - 1 PM, Sun 1 - 5 PM, & by appointment. Admis adults $3, senior citizens & students $2. Estab 1966. The Villa Marre is a historic house mus which, by virtue of its extraordinary collection of late 19th century decorative arts, is a center for the study of Victorian styles. Average Annual Attendance: 5000. Mem: 1000; dues $25 & up; annual meeting in Nov
Income: $95,000 (financed by mem, corporate support, grants & fundraising events)
Collections: Artwork by Benjamin Brantley; curioes appropriate to an 1881 Second Empire Victorian home, late 19th & early 20th century furniture, textiles
Publications: Quapaw Quarter Chronicle, bimonthly
Activities: Classes for adults & children; docent training; lect open to public, vis lectr; tours; book traveling exhibitions; originate traveling exhibitions; sales shop sells books & magazines

L **Preservation Resource Center,** 1315 Scott St, 72202. Tel 501-371-0075; *Exec Dir* Cheryl G Nichols
Open Mon - Fri 9 AM - 5 PM. Estab 1976 for the assembly of materials relevant to historic buildings & neighborhoods in the greater Little Rock area
Purchases: $500
Library Holdings: Vols 250; Per subs 12; Maps; AV — Kodachromes, lantern slides; Other — Clipping files, manuscripts, pamphlets, photographs
Collections: Architectural drawings

L **UNIVERSITY OF ARKANSAS,** Art Slide Library, Fine Arts Bldg, Rm 202, 2801 S University, 72204-1099. Tel 501-569-8976; *Chmn* Floyd Martin; *Slide Cur* Laura Grace
Open Mon - Fri 9 AM - 5 PM, Sun 1 - 4 PM. No admis fee. Estab 1978 for educational purposes. Gallery I, 2500 sq ft, is a two story space; Gallery II, 500 sq ft, is a glassed on three sides; Gallery III is a hallway for student works
Income: Financed by state funds & private donations
Library Holdings: Vols 360; Per subs 15; AV — Fs, Kodachromes, slides 50,000; Other — Clipping files, exhibition catalogs, pamphlets
Special Subjects: Western & Non-Western Art & Architecture
Collections: Photographs & other works on paper
Activities: Docent training; lect open to public, 3 vis lectr per year; gallery talks; student competitions with awards; scholarships offered; originate traveling exhibitions

MAGNOLIA

M **SOUTHERN ARKANSAS UNIVERSITY,** Art Dept Gallery & Magale Art Gallery, 100 E University, SAU Box 1309, 71753-5000. Tel 501-235-4242; *Pres* Steven G Gamble; *VPres* Dan Ball; *Chmn Art Dept* Jerry Johnson; *Asst Prof* Steven Ochs; *Instructor* Ralph Larmann
Open Mon - Thurs 8 AM - 10 PM, Fri 8 AM - 5 PM, Sat 10 AM - 4 PM, Sun 2 - 10:30 PM (McGale Gallery). Mon, Wed & Fri 8 AM - 5 PM (Brinson Gallery). No admis fee. Estab 1970. Magale Library Art Gallery, foyer type with 120 running ft exhibition space, floor to ceiling fabric covered. Caraway Gallery preview type gallery, about 80 ft. Average Annual Attendance: 2000

Income: Financed partially by state funds
Collections: †American printmakers
Exhibitions: Faculty exhibit; six student shows
Activities: Classes for adults & children; lect open to public; gallery talks; tours; scholarships & fels offered; individual paintings & original objects of art lent to schools, non-profit organizations

MONTICELLO

M **DREW COUNTY HISTORICAL SOCIETY,** Museum, * 404 S Main, PO Box 797, 71655-0797. Tel 501-367-7446, 362-5156; *Dir* Henri Mason
No admis fee. Estab 1969. Average Annual Attendance: 3000. Mem: dues $100, commercial $15, individual $5; monthly meetings
Income: Financed by endowment, mem, city & county appropriation
Collections: Antique Toys & Dolls; Civil War Artifacts; Indian Artifacts; Handwork & Clothing from early 1800s; Woodworking Tools
Exhibitions: Antique Quilts, Trunks, Paintings by Local Artists; Leather Parlor Furniture from late 1800s
Publications: Drew County Historical Journal, annually

MOUNTAIN VIEW

L **OZARK FOLK CENTER,** Ozark Cultural Resource Center, Hwy 382, PO Box 500, 72560. Tel 501-269-3851; FAX 501-269-2909; *Gen Mgr* Bill Young; *Asst Gen Mgr* Phillip Hogue; *Music Dir* Elliott Hancock; *Crafts Dir* Kay Thomas; *Folklorist & Archivist* W K McNeil
Archives: Open Tues - Sat 10 AM 6 PM. Admis $7.50. Estab 1973 to demonstrate various aspects of traditional culture of the Ozark Mountain region. For reference only. Average Annual Attendance: 160,000
Income: $1,800,000 (financed by state appropriation & auxiliary committee)
Library Holdings: Vols 8500; Per subs 50; AV — A-tapes, cassettes, fs, motion pictures, rec, slides, v-tapes; Other — Clipping files, exhibition catalogs, memorabilia, original art works, pamphlets, photographs, prints
Special Subjects: Architecture, Art Education, Art History, Crafts, Decorative Arts, Drawings, Embroidery, Folk Art, Furniture, Glass, Laces, Landscape Architecture, Landscapes, Photography, Portraits
Collections: †Traditional Ozark crafts; †music folios & sheet music
Activities: Classes for adults & children; lect open to public; concerts; tours; awards; workshops; sales shop sells books, magazines, slides

PINE BLUFF

A **ARTS & SCIENCE CENTER FOR SOUTHEAST ARKANSAS,** 701 Main, 71601. Tel 501-536-3375; FAX 501-536-3380; *Dir* Helen M Brooks; *Dir Science & Educ* Erin Branham; *Dir Performing Arts* Hubert Rolling; *Business Mgr* Nell Brown; *Dir Public Relations* Gina Teel
Open Mon - Fri 8 AM - 5 PM, Sat 10 AM - 4 PM & Sun 1 - 4 PM. No admis fee. Opened in 1968 in Civic Center Complex; mission is to provide for the practice, teaching, performance & understanding of the Arts & Sciences, opened new facility 1994. 22,000 sq ft facility containing four art galleries, a science gallery & a 232 seat theatre, instructional studio. Average Annual Attendance: 55,000. Mem: 1400; dues family $35
Income: $450,000
Collections: †John M Howard Memorial Collection of works by black American artists; Collection of botanical paintings by Elsie Mistie Sterling; Photographs by J C Coovert of the Southern Cotton Culture, early 1900s; †Works on paper by local, national & international artists; art deco/noveau bronze sculptures
Exhibitions: Art Gallery Exhibitions; Biennial Regional Competition
Activities: Classes for adults & children; dramatic programs; docent training; lect open to public, 12 vis lectr per year; concerts; gallery talks; tours; book traveling exhibitions; originate traveling exhibitions

M **JEFFERSON COUNTY HISTORICAL MUSEUM,** 201 E Fourth, 71601. Tel 501-541-5402; *Interim Dir* Sue Trulock
Open daily 9 AM - 5 PM. No admis fee. Estab 1980 to collect, preserve & interpret artifacts showing the history of Jefferson County. One room in County Courthouse. Average Annual Attendance: 11,200; dues $5-$15
Income: $16,000 (financed by county Quorum Court appropriation)
Collections: Clothing dating from 1870; personal artifacts; photographs; tools & equipment; Quapau Indian artifacts
Exhibitions: Bottle Collection; Made in Pine Bluff AR; exhibit of dolls dressed in gowns worn by governors' wives; Quapace Indian Artifacts; Settlers Exhibit; Civil War Exhibit
Publications: The Jeffersonian, quarterly newsletter
Activities: Lect; competitions

SPRINGDALE

M **ARTS CENTER OF THE OZARKS GALLERY,** 214 S Main, PO Box 725, 72765. Tel 501-751-5441; *Dir* Kathi Blundell; *Visual Arts Dir* Garrett Hunt; *Dir of Theatre* Harry Blundell
Open Mon - Fri 8 AM - 4 PM, gallery open Mon - Fri 9 AM - 4 PM. No admis fee. Estab 1948, merged with the Springdale Arts Center of the Ozarks in 1973 to preserve the traditional handcrafts, to promote all qualified contemporary arts & crafts, to help find markets for artists & craftsmen
Income: Financed by mem & state appropriations
Exhibitions: Exhibitions change monthly
Publications: Arts Center Events, monthly; newsletter, bimonthly
Activities: Adult & children's workshops; instruction in the arts, music, dance & drama run concurrently with other activities; evening classes in painting; eight theater productions per year; concerts & arts & crafts

M CITY OF SPRINGDALE, Shiloh Museum, 118 W Johnson Ave, 72764. Tel 501-750-8165; FAX 501-750-8171; Elec Mail shiloh@cavern.urark.edu. *Dir* Bob Besom; *Educ Coordr* Marc Reif; *Exhib Designer* Michelle Westfall-Edwards; *Project Planner* Susan Young
Open Mon - Sat 10 AM - 5 PM. No admis fee. Estab 1968 to exhibit history & culture of Northwest Arkansas. Displays in main exhibit hall of 4500 sq ft, halls, meeting room & a restored 19th century home. Average Annual Attendance: 15,000. Mem: 1000; dues $10
Income: $200,000 (financed by endowment, mem, city appropriation, private & pub grants)
Collections: †Folk Arts; †Ozarks Photographers; †Charles Summey Oils; †Essie Ward Primitive Paintings
Exhibitions: Essie Ward; Charles Summey
Publications: Newsletter, quarterly
Activities: Programs & workshops for adults & children; lect open to public, 10 vis lectr per year; lending collection contains 500 items; book traveling exhibitions 2 per year; originate traveling exhibitions 1 per year; retail store sells books, magazines & original art

STUTTGART

A GRAND PRAIRIE ARTS COUNCIL, INC, Arts Center of the Grand Prairie, 108 W 12th St, PO Box 65, 72160. Tel 501-673-1781; *Pres* Linda Fischer
Open Mon - Fri 10 AM - 12:30 PM & 1:30 - 4:30 PM, cl Mon. No admis fee. Estab 1956 & incorporated 1964 to encourage cultural development in the Grand Prairie area, to sponsor the Grand Prairie Festival of Arts held annually in Sept at Stuttgart. Estab as an arts center for jr & sr citizens. Average Annual Attendance: 2500. Mem: 250; dues $10 - $100; monthly meetings
Income: Financed by mem & donations
Collections: Very small permanent collection started by donations
Exhibitions: Monthly exhibitions of Arkansas artists
Publications: Festival invitations; newsletter, monthly; programs
Activities: Classes for adults & children; dramatic programs; lect open to public, 4-6 vis lectr per year; gallery talks; competitions with awards; originate traveling exhibitions

CALIFORNIA

ALHAMBRA

AMERICAN SOCIETY OF BOOKPLATE COLLECTORS & DESIGNERS
For further information, see National and Regional Organizations

BAKERSFIELD

M BAKERSFIELD ART FOUNDATION, Bakersfield Museum of Art, 1930 R St, 93301. Tel 805-323-7219; FAX 805-323-7266; *Exec Dir* Sherry Dillard; *Admin Asst* Candis Gibson
Open Tues - Sat 10 AM - 4 PM, Sun Noon - 4 PM, cl Mon. Admis adult $3, seniors $2, students & children under 12 free. Estab to provide the facilities & services of a municipal art museum which will nurture & develop the visual arts in Kern County. Gallery is a one story building located in Camellia Garden of Central Park; maintains reference library. Average Annual Attendance: 50,000. Mem: 500; dues $15-$35; Board meeting second Mon each month
Income: Financed by corporate, state & local public, & private non-profit sources
Collections: California oils & watercolors, emphasis on impressionistic art
Publications: Catalogues with each exhibit (6 yrly); Perspective, monthly
Activities: Classes for adults & children; docent training; lect open to public; gallery talks; tours; juried competitions with prizes; scholarships offered; book traveling exhibitions; originate traveling exhibitions; museum shop sells books, magazines, gifts, crafts & art-related items

M KERN COUNTY MUSEUM, 3801 Chester Ave, 93301. Tel 805-861-2132; FAX 805-322-6415; *Dir* Carola R Enriquez; *Cur* Jeff Nickell
Open Mon - Fri 8 AM - 5 PM, Sat, Sun & holidays 10 AM - 5 PM. Admis adults $5, senior citizens $4, children 3-12 $3, under 3 free. Estab 1945 to collect & interpret local history & culture, mainly through a 14 acre outdoor mus. Also has Lori Brock Children's Discovery Center. One main building, 1929 Chamber of Commerce Building, houses changing exhibitions on assorted topics; modern track lighting, temporary walls. Average Annual Attendance: 82,000. Mem: 550; dues family $50, Basic $30
Income: $750,000 (financed by county appropriation, earned income & non-profit foundation)
Purchases: Archival, occasionally decorative arts
Collections: †60-structure outdoor museum covering 14 acres; †Photographic Image Collection; †Material Culture; †Paleontology; †Natural History
Publications: Brochure on the Museum; The Forgotten Photographs of Carleton E Watkins
Activities: Classes for adults & children; docent training; lect open to public; concerts; tours; Candlelight Christmas & Heritage Days celebrations; competitions with awards; book traveling exhibitions 2 per year; gift shop sells books, reproductions, slides & handicrafts; junior museum located at Children's Discovery Center
L Library, 3801 Chester Ave, 93301. Tel 805-861-2132; FAX 805-322-6415; *Cur* Jeff Nickell
Open Mon - Fri 8 AM - 5 PM by appointment only. Estab 1950 to support the work of the mus. Open for reference only by appointment
Library Holdings: Vols 2200; AV — Fs, v-tapes; Other — Clipping files, manuscripts, memorabilia, pamphlets, photographs
Special Subjects: Costume Design & Construction, Ethnology, Furniture, Historical Material, Crafts, Decorative Arts, History of Art & Archaeology,

Maps, Period Rooms, Restoration & Conservation, Textiles, Native American Arts
Collections: More than 200,000 photos relating to Kern County
Publications: Courier, quarterly newsletter
Activities: Classes for children; docent training; gift shop sells books, prints & slides

BELMONT

A SAN MATEO COUNTY ARTS COUNCIL, 1219 Ralston Ave, 94002. Tel 415-593-1816; *Pres* Sheila Bilich
Open Mon - Fri 9 AM - 5 PM, Sun 1 - 4 PM. No admis fee. Estab 1972 to promote the cultural life of San Mateo County through programs in schools, advocacy with business & government, to provide services for artists & arts organizations. Galleries maintained on premises & at the Hall of Justice in Redwood City, Calif. Each holds about 100 works of art. Average Annual Attendance: 100,000. Mem: 1000; dues $25; annual meeting July
Income: $200,000 (financed by mem, state & county appropriation, corporate & foundation support & programs)
Exhibitions: Bi-monthly exhibits in three galleries by local & invited artists both regional & international
Publications: Arts Talk; cultural calendar
Activities: Classes for adults & children; volunteer & docent training; lect open to public, 3-5 vis lectr per year; concerts; gallery talks; tours; competitions with awards; book traveling exhibitions; originate traveling exhibitions; gift shop sells crafts, fine arts, posters

BERKELEY

A BERKELEY ART CENTER, 1275 Walnut St, 94709. Tel 510-644-6893; *Exec Dir* Robbin Henderson
Open Thurs - Sun Noon - 5 PM, cl Mon - Wed & holidays. No admis fee. Estab 1965 to display art works of Bay Area artists. Average Annual Attendance: 12,000. Mem: 250; dues $20 - $2500; annual meeting Jan 1
Income: Financed by city appropriation and other grants
Collections: Paintings; sculptures; environments; prints
Exhibitions: Rotating loan exhibitions & shows by Bay Area artists
Activities: Lect open to public, 8 vis lectr per year; concerts; gallery talks; competition with prizes; original objects of art lent to non-profit & educational institutions; originate traveling exhibitions; sales shop sells prints

A BERKELEY CIVIC ARTS PROGRAM, 2118 Milvia St, Ste 200, 94704. Tel 510-705-8183; FAX 510-883-6554; TDD 510-644-6915. *Arts Specialist* Sonia Manjon
Estab 1980. Provides grants to art organizations, cultural service contracts, community outreach, business & technical assistance to artists & organizations, information referrals to the arts community; conducts on-going efforts to promote the importance of the arts & actively participates in regional & national local art agency development
Income: $264,500
Exhibitions: Exhibits 14 different showings annually by artists & art organizations in the Addison Street storefront windows
Publications: Arts Education Resource Directory; arts events list; quarterly newsletter

L BERKELEY PUBLIC LIBRARY, Art & Music Dept, 2090 Kittredge St, 94704. Tel 510-649-3928; *Head Reference* Patricia Mullan; *Librn* Lynn Murdock Wold; *Librn* Marti Morec; *Librn* Andrea Segall
Open Mon - Thurs 10 AM - 9 PM, Fri & Sat 10 AM - 6 PM, Sun 1 - 5 PM
Income: $60,000
Library Holdings: Vols 22,560; Per subs 146; Compact discs 4500; AV — Cassettes 4200, rec 15,000, slides 22,000
Activities: Lectr on art four times a year

A KALA INSTITUTE, 1060 Heinz Ave, 94710. Tel 510-549-2977; FAX 510-540-6914; *Exec Dir* Archana Horsting; *Artistic Dir* Yuzo Nakano
Open Tues - Fri Noon - 5 PM, Sat Noon - 4 PM. No admis fee. Estab 1974 to provide equipment, space, exhibition opportunities to artists. Maintains Ray Abel Memorial Library of Fine Arts Books. Average Annual Attendance: 5000. Mem: 50; mem open to artists with proficiency in printmaking; studio rental $200-$300 per month
Income: $210,000 (financed by mem, city & state appropriation, art sales, classes & private foundations)
Collections: Kala Institute Archive; †Works on Paper
Exhibitions: On going: Works on Paper
Activities: Classes for adults & children; lect open to public, 1 vis lectr per year; scholarships & fels offered; book traveling exhibitions 1 per year; originate traveling exhibitions 1 per year; retail store sells prints & original art

M JUDAH L MAGNES MUSEUM, 2911 Russell St, 94705. Tel 510-549-6950; FAX 510-849-3673; *Dir* Seymour Fromer; *Cur Emertius* Ruth Eis; *Registrar* Marni Welch; *Public Relations* Paula Friedman; *Archivist* Susan Morris; *Cur* Sheila Braufman; *Cur* Florence Helzel; *Librn* Tora Gazit; *Membership* Michelle Ackerman; *Photo Archivist* Laura O'Hara; *Develop & Traveling Exhib* Brad Berman; *Cur Judaica* Michal Friedlander
Open Sun - Thurs 10 AM - 4 PM, cl Jewish & legal holidays. No admis fee. Estab 1962 to preserve, collect & exhibit Jewish artifacts & art from around the world; the mus also contains the Blumenthal Rare Books & Manuscripts Library & the Western Jewish History Center Archives on the Jewish community in the Western United States since 1849. Museum's first floor has changing exhibition galleries (including the Jacques & Esther Reutlinger Gallery estab 1981. The second floor contains the permanent exhibition area. Average Annual Attendance: 18,000
Income: Financed by mem, donations, & foundation grants
Purchases: Ethnic Costumes & Folk Art Pieces; Ceremonial & Fine Art; Rare Judaic books; Western US Jewish history rarities

Collections: †Hannukah lamps; †Synagogue art & objects; †spice boxes; †graphics; †manuscripts; †prints; †rare books; †textiles; †genre paintings; †art & ceremonial objects from Sephardic & Indian Jewish communities
Exhibitions: A Vanished World: Roman Vishniac; The Jewish Illustrated Book; Nupcias Sefardies (Sephardic Wedding); Winners of the Interfaith Forum on Religion, Art & Architecture Awards; Jewish Themes/Northern California Artists; Witnesses to History: The Jewish Poster, 1770-1985; Contemporary Jewish Themes Triennial; 30th Anniversary Exhibition; Faith & Survival: Jews of Ethiopia; Shtetl Life; Breaking the Mold: Harold Paris; First-Third Jewish Video Competitions-Winning Entries; Works by Louis Lozowick; Jerusalem; People's Art Movement of the '30s & '40s
Publications: Bibliographies; books of Western Jewish historical themes; exhibition catalogs; memoirs; poetry; triannual newsletter; trade books on recent European Jewish history
Activities: Lect open to public; gallery talks; tours; Rosenberg inteenational poetry award; annual numismatics series; individual paintings & original objects of art lent internationally & nationally to museums, synagogues, exhibition halls & Jewish organizations; originate traveling exhibitions organized & circulated; museum shop sells books original art, jewelry, note cards, posters, & gifts for home religious ceremonies

L **Blumenthal Rare Book & Manuscript Library,** 2911 Russell St, 94705. Tel 510-549-6939; *Librn* Tova Gazit
Estab 1966 as a center for the study & preservation of Judaica. For reference only. Changing & permanent exhibitions of painting, sculpture, photography, ceremonial objects
Income: Financed by mem & private gifts
Library Holdings: Vols 12,000; Per subs 15; Original documents; AV — Fs, motion pictures, slides; Other — Clipping files, exhibition catalogs, manuscripts, memorabilia, pamphlets, reproductions
Special Subjects: Art History, Bookplates & Bindings, Calligraphy, Cartoons, Illustration, Judaica, Manuscripts, Maps, Jewish art & music, special emphasis on Yiddish theater music, History of Jewish communities throughout the world, particularly Sephardic, rare books & manuscripts
Collections: Community collections from Cochin, Czechoslovakia, Egypt, India & Morocco; Holocaust Material (Institute for Righteous Acts); Karaite Community (Egypt); Passover Haggadahs (Zismer); 16th to 19th century rare printed editions, books & manuscripts; Ukrainian programs (Belkin documents)
Exhibitions: Jewish Illustrated Book
Publications: Exhibition catalogues; Jewish Illustrated Book; The Jewish Printed Book in India: Imprints of the Blumenthal Library
Activities: Docent training; lect open to public, 15 vis lectr per year; concerts; gallery talks; tours; awards; book traveling exhibitions; originate traveling exhibitions nationwide

UNIVERSITY OF CALIFORNIA

M **Berkeley Art Museum & Pacific Film Archive,** 2626 Bancroft Way, 94720-2250. Tel 510-642-0808; FAX 510-642-4889; *Dir* Jacquelynn Baas; *Assoc Dir* Stephen Gong; *Cur Film* Edith Kramer; *Installation & Design* Nina Zurier; *Cur* Lawrence Rinder; *Cur Educ* Sherry Goodman; *Coll & Exhib Admin* Lisa Calden; *Cur* James Steward; *Asst Cur Video* Steve Seid; *Film Coll Mgr* Mona Nagai; *Develop Dir* Janine Sheldon; *Cur Film* Kathy Geritz
Open Wed - Sun 11 AM - 5 PM, Thurs 11 AM - 9 PM. Admis $4-$6. Estab 1963, new mus building opened in 1970. Mus designed by Mario Ciampi, Richard Jorasch & Ronald E Wagner of San Francisco; eleven exhibition galleries, a sculpture garden & a 234 seat theater. Average Annual Attendance: Gallery 100,000, Pacific Film Archive 100,000. Mem: 2800; dues vary
Income: $4,200,000 (financed by university sources, federal & foundation grants, earned income & private donations)
Collections: Gift of 45 Hans Hoffman paintings housed in the Hans Hoffman Gallery; pre-20th century paintings & sculpture; Chinese & Japanese paintings; 20th century European & American paintings & sculpture; over 7000 films & video tapes; 16th-20th century works on paper; conceptual art study center
Exhibitions: Twenty exhibitions annually; Matrix Project (a changing exhibition of contemporary art), 600 film programs
Publications: The Calendar, bi-monthly; catalogs; handbills; exhibition brochures; Matrix artists sheets
Activities: Educ dept; lect open to public, 50 vis lectr per year; concerts; gallery talks; on-site performances; film programs for classes & research screening; film study center & library; book traveling exhibitions 3-4 per year; originate traveling exhibitions to other art museums; museum shop sells books, magazines, posters, jewelry, rental facilities available, cafe

M **Phoebe Apperson Hearst Museum of Anthropology,** 103 Kroeber Hall No 3712, 94720-3712. Tel 510-642-3681, 642-3682; FAX 510-642-6271; *Dir* Rosemary Joyce
Exhibition Hall Open Wed - Sun 10 AM - 4:30 PM, Thurs 10 AM - 9 PM, cl major national holidays; access to research collections by appointment Sat & Sun. Admis adults $2, seniors $1, children $.50, no admis fee Thurs. Estab 1901 as a research mus for the training & educating of undergraduate & graduate students, a resource for scholarly research & to collect, preserve, educate & conduct research. Average Annual Attendance: 800,000
Income: Financed principally by state appropriations
Special Subjects: Afro-American Art, American Indian Art, American Western Art, Anthropology, Antiquities-Assyrian, Flasks & Bottles, Folk Art, Furniture, Glass, Gold, Photography, Porcelain, Portraits, Pottery, Pre-Columbian Art
Collections: Over four million objects of anthropological interest, both archaeological & ethnological. Ethnological collections from Africa, Oceania, North America (California, Plains, Arctic & Sub-Arctic); Archaeological Collections from Egypt, Peru, California, Africa & Oceania
Publications: Occasional papers of the Phoebe A Hearst Museum of Anthropology, newsletter
Activities: Classes for children; docent training; family days; lect open to public, 12 vis lectr per year; gallery talks; tours; originate traveling exhibitions varies; museum shop sells books, magazines, reproductions & slides

L **Pacific Film Archive,** 2625 Durant Ave, 94720. Tel 510-642-1412, 642-1437; FAX 510-642-4889; *Cur Film* Edith Kramer; *Library Head* Nancy Goldman; *Film Coll Mgr* Mona Nagai; *Assoc Film Cur* Kathy Geritz
Open Mon - Fri 1 - 5 PM; nightly film screenings 6 - 11 PM. Estab 1971, the Archive is a cinematheque showing a constantly changing repertory of films; a research screening facility; a media information service & an archive for the storage & preservation of films
Income: Financed by earned box office income, grants, students fees & benefits
Library Holdings: Vols 5500; Per subs 75; Posters 7000; Stills 25,000; AV — Motion pictures 6000; Other — Clipping files 60,000, photographs
Special Subjects: Film
Collections: Japanese film collection; Soviet Silents; experimental & animated films
Publications: Bi-monthly calendar
Activities: Nightly film exhibition; special daytime screening of films; lect, 50-57 vis filmmakers per year

L **Architecture Slide Library,** 232 Wurster Hall, 94720-1800. Tel 510-642-3439; FAX 510-643-5607; Elec Mail slides@ced.berkeley.edu; Internet Home Page Address http://www.mip.berkely.edu/query_forms/browse_spiro_form.html. *Librn* Maryly Snow; *Library Asst* Claire Dannenbaum; *Photographer* Steven Brooks
Open Mon - Fri 10 AM - Noon & 1 - 4 PM. Estab 1951 for instructional support for the Department of Architecture. Library permits circulation on a 24 hour basis for educational presentations. No duplication of slides permitted
Income: Financed by state educational funds
Library Holdings: AV — Slides; Other — Photographs
Special Subjects: Art History, History of Architecture, Slides & Photographs, Topography, Urbanism, Design
Collections: Denise Scott Brown & William C Wheaton Collections: City Planning; Herwin Schaefer Collection: visual design

L **Environmental Design Library,** 210 Wurster Hall, 94720-6000. Tel 510-642-4818; FAX 415-643-7891; Elec Mail ebyrne@library.berkeley.edu. *Head* Elizabeth Byrne; *Architectural Librn* Kathryn Wayne
Open Sept - May Mon - Thurs 9 AM - 9 PM, Fri 9 AM - 5 PM, Sat 1 - 5 PM, Sun 3 - 7 PM. Estab 1903. Circ 135,000
Library Holdings: Vols 173,000; Per subs 1250; Micro — Fiche, reels; AV — V-tapes
Special Subjects: Architecture, Landscape Architecture, City Planning
Collections: Architecture, city & regional planning, landscape architecture; Beatrix Jones Farrand

BEVERLY HILLS

L **BEVERLY HILLS PUBLIC LIBRARY,** Fine Arts Library, 444 N Rexford, 90201. Tel 310-288-2231; FAX 310-278-3387; *Supv Fine Arts Servs* Dr Stefan Klima; *Fine Art Librn* Jeri Byrne; *Fine Arts Librn* Suzy Chen; *Fine Arts Librn* Carl Baker
Open Mon - Thurs 10 AM - 9 PM, Fri & Sat 10 AM - 6 PM, Sun Noon - 5 PM. Estab 1973 to make art materials available to the general public. The library concentrates on 19th & 20th century American & West European art
Income: Financed by city appropriation and Friends of Library
Library Holdings: Vols 20,000; Per subs 200; Micro — Fiche, reels; AV — Cassettes, Kodachromes, motion pictures, slides, v-tapes; Other — Clipping files, exhibition catalogs, pamphlets, photographs
Special Subjects: Architecture, Art History, Decorative Arts, Drafting, Etchings & Engravings, Fashion Arts, History of Art & Archaeology, Painting - American, Painting - European, Painting - French, Painting - German, Painting - Italian, Period Rooms, Photography, Printmaking, Art, Costume, Dance
Collections: †Dorothi Bock Pierre Dance Collection; Artists Books

BREA

M **BREA CIVIC & CULTURAL CENTER GALLERY,** One Civic Center Circle, 92821. Tel 714-990-7713; FAX 714-990-2258; *Cultural Arts Mgr* Emily Keller
Open Wed - Sat Noon - 5 PM, cl holidays. No admis. Estab 1980
Exhibitions: Western Sagas; American Quilt Exhibit; The Real Thing (juried realistic multimedia show); Photography Exhibit; Artists of Northern Mexico; National Watercolor Juried Show
Activities: Docent training; lect; tours; gallery talks; concerts; workshops

BURBANK

A **BURBANK PUBLIC LIBRARY,** Warner Research Collection, 110 N Glenoaks Blvd, 91502. Tel 818-238-5615; FAX 818-238-5553; *Librn in Charge* Jerri Thomson; *Clerk* Susan Hurlbert
Open Mon - Fri 10 AM - 5 PM by appointment only. Estab 1936 to provide visual & historical documentation for use in the pre-production phase of motion picture & television production. Also used for prototype research by artist & architects
Library Holdings: Vols 39,000; Per subs 80; License Plate Files; Other — Clipping files, exhibition catalogs, pamphlets, photographs, reproductions
Special Subjects: Period Rooms, Stage Design, Theater Arts
Activities: Lect open to the public

CARMEL

M **CARMEL MISSION & GIFT SHOP,** 3080 Rio Rd, 93923. Tel 408-624-3600; FAX 408-624-0658; *Cur* Richard J Menn; *Shop Mgr* Katherine Ambrosio
Open Mon - Sat 9:30 AM - 4:30 PM, Sun 10:30 AM - 4:30 PM, cl Thanksgiving & Christmas. No admis fee; donations accepted. Estab 1770
Collections: California's first library, founded by Fray Junipero Serra, 1770; library of California's first college, founded by William Hartnell, 1834; Munras Memorial Collection of objects, papers, furnishings of early California; large collection of ecclesiastical art of Spanish colonial period; large collection of ecclesiastical silver & gold church vessels, 1670-1820; paintings, sculpture, art objects of California Mission period
Activities: Sales shop sells religious articles, souvenir books & postcards

L **Archive of Old Spanish Missions, Diocese of Monterey,** 3080 Rio Rd, 93923. Tel 408-624-1271; *Cur* Richard J Menn
Estab 1931 for research for Mission Restoration & documents. Open to scholars by special appointment
Library Holdings: Vols 200; AV — Cassettes; Other — Clipping files, manuscripts, pamphlets, photographs
Special Subjects: Early California reference & photo library

CARMICHAEL

PASTEL SOCIETY OF THE WEST COAST
For further information, see National and Regional Organizations

CHERRY VALLEY

M **RIVERSIDE COUNTY MUSEUM,** Edward-Dean Museum, 9401 Oak Glen Rd, 92223-3799. Tel 909-845-2626; *Dir* Cathy Gilbert
Open Tues - Fri 1 - 4:30 PM, Sat & Sun 10 AM - 4:30 PM. Admis adults $3, children under 12 free. Built in 1957 & given to the county of Riverside in 1964. The South Wing of the gallery displays antiques & decorative arts as permanent collections; the North Wing has changing exhibits including contemporary artists. Average Annual Attendance: 20,000. Mem: 250; monthly meetings
Income: Financed by county funding
Collections: 17th & 18th Century European & Oriental decorative arts; Fine Arts including series of original watercolors by David Roberts
Publications: Museum catalog
Activities: Classes for children; docent training; lect open to public; tours; outdoor art shows; cultural festivals; concerts; gallery talks; original objects of art lent to local universities & colleges; museum shop sells books, original art, reproductions & prints
L **Library,** 9401 Oak Glen Rd, 92223-3799. Tel 909-845-2626; *Vol Docent Librn* Margaret Mueller
Open by appointment for reference only
Library Holdings: Vols 2000; Per subs 3; Micro — Cards; Other — Manuscripts, original art works, prints
Special Subjects: Art History, Asian Art, Ceramics, Costume Design & Construction, Decorative Arts, Furniture, Glass, History of Art & Archaeology, Jade, Painting - British, Painting - European, Porcelain, Watercolors, David Roberts (original lithograph set of Holy Land)

CHICO

M **CALIFORNIA STATE UNIVERSITY, CHICO,** University Art Gallery, Art Dept, 95929-0820. Tel 916-898-5331; *Chmn* Vernon Patrick
Open Mon - Fri 10 AM - 4 PM, Sun 1 - 5 PM. No admis fee. Estab to afford broad cultural influences to the massive North California region
Income: Financed by state appropriations & private funds
Collections: University Art Collection includes Masters of Graduate Artwork Study collection of fine art print
Activities: Lect open to public, 6-12 vis lectr per year; competitions with awards; individual & original objects of art lent to offices on campus
L **Meriam Library,** First & Hazel, 95929. Tel 916-898-6878; *Art Librn* Carolyn Dusenbury
Open to students & the pub
Library Holdings: Vols 16,600; Per subs 72; Micro — Cards, fiche, prints, reels; AV — A-tapes, cassettes, fs, motion pictures, rec, slides, v-tapes; Other — Framed reproductions, original art works, pamphlets, photographs, prints, reproductions, sculpture
Collections: Janet Turner Print Collection
M **Third Floor Gallery,** Bell Memorial Union, 95929-0750. Tel 916-898-5079; FAX 916-898-4717; *Coordr* Marlys Williams
Estab 1945. 100 linear ft of enclosed area & two gallery halls
Income: Financed by associated students & university
M **Janet Turner Print Gallery & Collection,** Laxson Auditorium, 95929-0820. Tel 916-898-4476; *Cur* Catherine Sullivan Sturgeon; *Registrar* Sue Richardson; *Coll Mgr* Denise Devine; *Curatorial Asst* Jesse Brown
Open Mon - Fri 11 AM - 4 PM. Estab 1981. Located in Laxson Auditorium; displays seven thematic exhibitions per academic year from the Print Gallery's Collection of over 2000 original prints. Average Annual Attendance: 6000. Mem: 40; dues $2-$100
Income: $33,000 (financed by endowment, mem & state appropriation)
Purchases: Contemporary prints, mixed media, 18th century Dutch
Collections: †General collection of prints historical to contemporary, international in scope, includes all technologies
Activities: Educ dept; lect to CSU Chico classes; competitions with prizes; scholarships offered; original objects of art lent in traveling exhibitions; lending collection contains 2000 original prints; originate traveling exhibitions to other CSU system colleges; sales shop sells cards & catalogs

M **1078 GALLERY,** 738 W Fifth St, 95928. Tel 916-343-1973; *Co-Dir* Lynette Krehe; *Co-Dir* John Ferrell
Open Tues - Sat 12:30 - 5:30 PM. No admis fee. Estab as a Nonprofit artist run arts organization showing contemporary art exhibitions & installations by artists of cultural & geographic diversity

CHULA VISTA

M **SOUTHWESTERN COLLEGE,** Art Gallery, 900 Otay Lakes Rd, 91910. Tel 619-421-6700; *Gallery Dir* Larry Urrutia
Open Mon - Fri 10 AM - 2 PM; Wed - Thurs 6 - 9 PM. No admis fee. Estab 1961 to show contemporary artists' work who are of merit to the community & the school, & as an educational service. Gallery is approx 3000 sq ft. Average Annual Attendance: 10,000
Income: Financed by city and state appropriations

Collections: Permanent collection of mostly contemporary work
Activities: Classes for adults; lect open to public, 3 vis lectr per year; gallery talks; competitions; individual paintings & original objects of art lent; lending collection contains color reproductions, photographs & original art works; junior museum

CITY OF INDUSTRY

M **WORKMAN & TEMPLE FAMILY HOMESTEAD MUSEUM,** 15415 E Don Julian Rd, 91745-1029. Tel 818-968-8492; FAX 818-968-2048; *Dir* Karen Graham Wade; *Asst Dir* Max A van Balgooy; *Public Prog Mgr* Mary Roberts
Open Tues - Fri 1 - 4 PM, Sat - Sun 10 AM - 4 PM, group tours by appointment, cl 4th wkend of every month & holidays. No admis fee. Estab 1981 to collect & interpret Southern California history from 1830 to 1930. Contemporary exhibition gallery; mid-19th century Workman Family House; late 19th century watertower; 1922-27 Spanish Colonial Revival Temple Family Residence. Maintains reference library. Average Annual Attendance: 15,000
Income: Financed by city appropriation
Collections: 1830-1930 costumes, decorative arts, furnishings, textiles †photographic archives; interior decorative elements (metal work, tile, wood carvings, stained glass)
Publications: The Homestead, quarterly; News 'N Notes, monthly; A Journey Through Time Teachers' Manual; A guide to El Campo Santo & the Walter Temple Memorial Mausoleum; San Gabriel Valley Historian, annual; Workman & Temple Family of Southern California
Activities: Classes for adults & children; dramatic programs; docent training; architectural crafts fair; films; workshops; lect open to public; concerts; museum shop sells books, prints & museum-related postcards & booklets

CLAREMONT

M **GALLERIES OF THE CLAREMONT COLLEGES,** 91711-6344. Tel 909-621-8283; *Dir* Marjorie L Harth; *Curatorial Asst* Elizabeth Villa; *Cur Exhib* Mary McNaughton; *Galleries Mgr* Gary Keith; *Registrar* Steve Comba; *Admin Asst* Barbara Senn; *Galleries Asst* Douglas Humble
Open Wed - Sun 1 - 5 PM, cl national & college holidays. No admis fee. Estab 1974 to present balanced exhibitions useful not only to students of art history & studio arts, but also to the general pub. Galleries consist of Montgomery Gallery of Pomona College & Lang Gallery of Scripps College. Average Annual Attendance: 15,000
Income: Financed jointly by Pomona & Scripps Colleges, support group, & endowment grants
Collections: Samuel H Kress Collection of Renaissance paintings; 19th century American painting; contemporary ceramics; Old Master & contemporary graphics; photographs; Oriental art; African art; Native American art
Publications: Art Publications List, annual
Activities: Lect open to public, 2-3 vis lectr per year; gallery talks; tours; individual paintings & original objects of art lent to qualified museums & galleries; book traveling exhibitions biennially; originates traveling exhibitions

M **SCRIPPS COLLEGE,** Clark Humanities Museum, 91711. Tel 909-607-3606; *Dir* Eric Haskell; *Admin Asst* Nancy Burson
Open Mon - Fri 9 AM - Noon & 1 - 5 PM, cl holidays & summer. No admis fee. Estab 1970 to present multi-disciplinary exhibits in conjunction with Scripps College's humanities curriculum & to maintain a study collection. Mus has large room with storage & study area; reception desk
Collections: Nagel Collection of Chinese, Tibetan Sculpture & Textiles; Wagner Collection of African Sculpture
Exhibitions: Hatian art; Japanese prints; masks & musical instruments
Publications: Exhibition catalogues
Activities: Lect open to public

CUPERTINO

M **DE ANZA COLLEGE,** Euphrat Museum of Art, 21250 Stevens Creek Blvd, 95014. Tel 408-864-8836; *Dir* Jan Rindfleisch; *Asst* Diana Argabrite
Open Tues - Thurs 11 AM - 4 PM, Wed 7 - 9 PM, Sat 11 AM - 2 PM. No admis fee. Estab 1971. 1700 sq ft contemporary gallery located on De Anza College Campus. Average Annual Attendance: 15,000
Income: $125,000 (financed by mem, grants, endowment, college)
Publications: Art Collectors in & Around Silicon Valley; Art of the Refugee Experience; Art, Religion & Spirituality; Content Contemporary Issues; The Power of Cloth (Political Quilts 1845-1986); Staying Visible: The Importance of Archives
Activities: Classes for children; docent programs; lect open to public; competition with awards; sales shop sells books

CYPRESS

M **CYPRESS COLLEGE,** Fine Arts Gallery, 9200 Valley View St, 90630. Tel 714-826-5593; FAX 714-527-8238; *Dir* Betty Disney; *Secy* Maureen King
Open Mon - Thurs 10 AM - 2 PM, Tues & Wed 6 - 8 PM, cl Fri, except by appointment. No admis fee. Estab 1969 to bring visually enriching experiences to the school & community. Average Annual Attendance: 5000
Income: Financed by school budget, donations & sales
Collections: †Donor gifts; †purchase awards; †student works
Publications: Exhibition catalogs
Activities: Lect open to public, 2 vis lectr per year; competitions; scholarships

DAVIS

M PENCE GALLERY, 212 D St, 95616. Tel 916-758-3370; *Pres* Rosalie Paine; *Dir* Nancy M Servis; *Gallery Educator* Lois Morris; *Board Pres* Regina Hamel
Open Tues - Sat Noon - 4 PM & by appointment, except holidays & between shows. No admis fee. Estab 1976 to foster & stimulate awareness of the arts & cultural heritage of California through changing exhibitions of art & objects of artistic, aesthetic & historical significance. Gallery has 90 running ft of wall space & 650 sq ft of floor space. An outdoor performing space with a small stage lies behind the Gallery. Average Annual Attendance: 2500. Mem: 300; dues sustaining member $150, benefactor $125, sponsor $75, business $50, patron $50, family $35, individual $25, student $15
Income: $21,000 (financed by mem, city appropriation & fund raisings)
Exhibitions: Rotating exhibitions exploring contemporary California art & history
Publications: Newsletters, 10 per year
Activities: Classes for adults & children; docent training; artist lect series; lect open to public, 8 vis lectr per year; concerts; gallery talks; tours; scholarships offered; museum shop sells books & original art

UNIVERSITY OF CALIFORNIA

M Memorial Union Art Gallery, Memorial Union, 2nd Flr, 95616. Tel 916-752-2885; *Dir* Roger Hankins
Open Mon - Fri 9 AM - 5 PM, also by appointment. No admis fee. Estab 1965 to provide exhibitions of contemporary & historical concerns for the students, staff & community. Gallery consists of North Gallery & South Gallery
Collections: Northern California contemporary art
Exhibitions: Sacramento Valley Landscapes
Publications: Exhibition catalogs
Activities: Classes for adults; lect; concerts; poetry readings; films; competitions; internships offered
M Richard L Nelson Gallery & Fine Arts Collection, Dept of Art, 95616. Tel 916-752-8500; FAX 916-752-0795; *Dir* L Price Amerson Jr; *Coll Mgr & Registrar* Carol Rosset
Open Mon - Fri Noon - 5 PM, Sun 2 - 5 PM. No admis fee. Estab 1976 to provide exhibitions of contemporary art as well as historical importance as a service to teaching program of the department of art, the university & pub. Contains main gallery & small gallery. Average Annual Attendance: 15,000. Mem: 175; dues $25 & up; annual meeting in May
Income: Financed by university appropriation, grants & Nelson ARTfriends
Collections: Fine Arts Collection of the Department of Art; general collection representing various periods of historical & contemporary art, with emphasis on Northern California art; also special collection includes: The Nagel Collection of Oriental Ceramics & Sculpture
Exhibitions: New World (Dis) Order, Robert Arneson: Palace at 9 AM & works on paper from the Alice Street series
Publications: Exhibition catalogues
Activities: Lect open to public, 3-5 vis lectr per year; gallery talks; originate traveling exhibitions; sales shop sells books & reproductions
L Art Dept Library, University of California, Davis, 95616. Tel 916-752-0152; *Book Librn* Bonnie Holt; *Slide Librn* Leah Theis
Slide Library Open Mon - Fri 8 AM - Noon & 1 - 5 PM, Book Library Open Mon - Thurs 9 AM - 4 PM, Fri 9 AM - Noon. Estab 1966 to make readily accessible reference & research material to Art Department faculty, students & the general pub
Income: Financed by state appropriation & college funds
Purchases: $3500
Library Holdings: Vols 20,000; Per subs 15; DIAL (Decimal Index of Art of the Low Countries) photographs; Micro — Fiche, prints; AV — A-tapes, fs, Kodachromes, lantern slides, motion pictures, slides, v-tapes; Other — Clipping files, exhibition catalogs, photographs, reproductions
Special Subjects: Aesthetics, Afro-American Art, American Indian Art, American Western Art, Architecture, Art History, Asian Art, Conceptual Art, Film, Folk Art, Mexican Art, Oriental Art, Painting - American, Painting - British

DESERT HOT SPRINGS

M CABOT'S OLD INDIAN PUEBLO MUSEUM, Pueblo Art Gallery, * 67-616 E Desert View Ave, PO Box 1267, 92240. Tel 619-329-7610; FAX 619-329-1956; *Pres* Cole H Eyraud
Open Wed - Mon 9:30 AM - 4:30 PM, cl Tues. Admis adults $2.50, sr citizens $2, juniors $1. Estab 1968 as a source of reference. 1100 sq ft art gallery representing contemporary artists through a variety of media. Artifacts of past cultures & Americana along with native American work. Average Annual Attendance: 10,000. Mem: 50; dues lifetime $1000, patron $500, donor $300, organization $100, supporting $75, family $35, individual $20, student $10
Income: Financed by donations
Purchases: Cahuilla baskets, Navajo blankets & rugs acquired
Special Subjects: Advertising Design, American Indian Art, Architecture, Carpets & Rugs, Coins & Medals, Flasks & Bottles, Furniture, Handicrafts, Historical Material, Maps, Photography, Southwestern Art
Collections: †The Theosophical Society Collection
Exhibitions: Full Moon Shaman Ceremonies
Activities: Concerts; museum shop sells books, magazines, original art, reproductions, prints, fine mineral specimens & fossils

DOMINGUEZ HILLS

M UNIVERSITY ART GALLERY OF CALIFORNIA STATE UNIVERSITY AT DOMINGUEZ HILLS, 1000 E Victoria, 90747. Tel 310-243-3334; Elec Mail kzimmerer@ahvx20.csudh.edu. *Gallery Dir* Kathy Zimmerer
Open Mon - Thurs 9:30 AM - 4:30 PM. Estab 1973 to exhibit faculty, student, contemporary California art & multi-cultural exhibits. New 2000 sq ft gallery in 1978. Average Annual Attendance: 10,000
Income: Financed by yearly grants from CSUDH Student Assoc,; support from Friends of the Gallery, City of Carson

Exhibitions: (1997) Tony Gleaton: American Cowboy Revisited, En Recuerdo de Henry
Publications: Exhibition catalogues published three times per yr; yearly newsletter
Activities: Lect open to public, 10 vis lectr per year; gallery talks; tours; book traveling exhibitions 1-2 per year

DOWNEY

M DOWNEY MUSEUM OF ART, 10419 Rives Ave, 90241. Tel 310-861-0419; *Dir* Scott Ward
Open Wed - Sun Noon - 5 PM. No admis fee. Estab 1957 as an aesthetic & educational facility. Located in Furman Park, it is the only art mus with a permanent collection in Southeast Los Angeles, which includes in its area 27 neighboring communities of significant ethnic range & a total population close to one million. The Mus is continuing a prog for new emerging multi-ethnic artists. The facility has five gallery areas plus classroom space. Gallery I covers 15 x 39 ft, Gallery II covers approx 12 x 24 ft, Gallery III covers 15 x 20 ft, Gallery IV covers 23 x 39 ft, and Gallery V covers 24 x 24 ft. Average Annual Attendance: 12,500. Mem: 475; dues $15 - $1000; annual meeting Apr
Income: $45,000 (financed by mem, grants, donations & fundraising)
Collections: Many pieces produced by Southern California artists over the past 20 years, including Billy Al Bengston, Corita Kent, Don Emery, Sabato Fiorello, Stephen Longstreet, Anna Mahler, Shirley Pettibone, Betye Saar, Boris Duetsch & Frederick Wight
Publications: Exhibition catalogs
Activities: Lect open to public, 4 vis lectr per year; gallery talks; tours; traveling exhibitions organized & circulated; museum shop selling reproductions & prints

EL CAJON

M GROSSMONT COMMUNITY COLLEGE, Hyde Gallery, 8800 Grossmont College Dr, 92020-1799. Tel 619-465-1700, Ext 299; FAX 619-461-3396; *Chmn Art Dept* Harry Lum; *Cur* James Wilsterman
Open Mon - Fri 10 AM - 2 PM & by appointment. No admis fee. Estab 1970 as a co-curricular institution which cooperates with & supports the Art Department of Grossmont College & which provides a major cultural resource for the general pub in the eastern part of the greater San Diego area. Two galleries, one 30 x 40 ft; one 30 x 20 ft. Average Annual Attendance: 20,000
Income: Financed through College
Collections: Prints; photographs; clay objects; large Tom Holland painting
Publications: Exhibition catalogs; posters
Activities: Lect open to public, 6 vis lectr per year; concerts; original objects of art lent to institutions; lending collection photographs; originate traveling exhibitions

ESCONDIDO

M CALIFORNIA CENTER FOR THE ARTS MUSEUM, 340 N Escondido Blvd, 92025. Tel 619-738-4170; FAX 619-743-6472; *Dir* Reesey Shaw
Open Tues - Sat 10 AM - 5 PM, Sun Noon - 5 PM, cl Mon. Admis adults $4. Estab 1994 committed to presenting & promoting the art of California. Maintains reference library. Mem: Minimum $50 annual mem dues
Collections: Collection of decorative arts, paintings, photography & sculpture in California from 1900 to present
Exhibitions: Exhibits draw on a distinct theme or idea in the visual arts of the 10th century
Publications: Exhibition specific catalogues
Activities: Classes for adults & children; docent training; lect open to public, 2-4 vis lectr per year; book traveling exhibitions; sales shop sells books, gifts, magazines

EUREKA

A HUMBOLDT ARTS COUNCIL, Corner of Seventh & F Sts, 95501. Tel 707-442-0278; *Exec Dir* Open; *Prog Dir* Halimah Collingwood
Estab 1966 to encourage, promote & correlate all forms of activity in the visual & performing arts & to make such activity a vital influence in the life of the community. Mem: 250; annual meeting in Oct
Income: $10,000 (financed by mem)
Collections: Art Bank, other purchase & donated works of art; photograph collection; Premier Collection of North Coast Art (traveling display); traveling import museum exhibits
Exhibitions: Annual Youth Art Exhibit
Activities: Concerts; competitions; scholarships offered; individual paintings & original objects of art lent; originate traveling exhibitions

FREMONT

M CITY OF FREMONT, Olive Hyde Art Gallery, 123 Washington Blvd, PO Box 5006, 94537. Tel 510-791-4357, 494-4228 (Dir); FAX 510-494-4753; *Dir* Cynthia Abraham
Open Wed - Sun 12:30 - 5:00 PM, Thurs 6 - 8:30 PM. No admis fee. Estab 1964 for community exposure to artistic awareness. Historical former home of Miss Olive Hyde, a well-known San Francisan art patron. This is the only fine arts gallery open to the public between Hayward & San Jose, located across from the Historical Mission San Jose in Fremont. Exhibits are displayed in 5 galleries with 1000 sq ft of space. Average Annual Attendance: 10,000. Mem: 200; dues $10-$50; annual meeting in June
Income: $20,000 (financed by city appropriation)
Exhibitions: 10 exhibits per year in fine arts, crafts, photography, textiles, sculpture; local, regional, national & international artists
Publications: Full color exhibit postcards
Activities: Classes for adults & children; docent programs; lect open to both the public & members only, 10 vis lectr per year; competitions with cash prizes & awards; book traveling exhibitions 1 per year

FRESNO

M FRESNO ARTS CENTER & MUSEUM, 2233 N First St, 93703. Tel 209-485-4810; FAX 209-441-4227; *Dir & Chief Cur* Robert Barrett
Open Tues - Sun 10 AM - 5 PM. Admis adults $2, students & senior citizens $1, children 16 & under, school tours & mus mem free, Sat free to pub. Estab 1949 as a visual arts gallery to provide Fresno & its environs with a community oriented visual arts center. The Center exhibits works of internationally known artists & arranges shows of local artists. Three galleries plus entry for exhibits. Average Annual Attendance: 98,000. Mem: 2500; dues $35; annual meeting in May
Income: Financed by mem & fundraising efforts
Collections: Works of prominent California artists; contemporary American artists; Mexican folk art; Mexican graphic arts; permanent collection, National & International artists; extensive Pre-Columbian folk art
Exhibitions: Contemporary exhibitions changing every six to eight weeks
Activities: Classes for adults & children; docent training; lect open to public, 12 vis lectr per year; gallery talks; concerts; tours; competitions; scholarships offered; individual paintings & objects of art lent to city & county offices & other institutions; lending collection contains framed reproductions, original art works, original prints & slides; book traveling exhibitions; traveling exhibitions organized & circulated; museum shop sells books, magazines, original art, reproductions, prints, cards & local crafts

M FRESNO METROPOLITAN MUSEUM, 1515 Van Ness Ave, 93721. Tel 209-441-1444; *Pres & Board Trustees* Richard Johanson; *Exec Dir* Edwin J C Sobey, PhD; *Dir Exhib* Kaywin Feldman; *Business Adminr* Sally Irestone; *Develop Dir* Elizabeth Olson Looney
Open daily 11 AM - 5 PM. Admis adults $4, senior citizens, students & children 4-12 $3, members & children under 4 free. Estab 1984 to increase the availability of fine & educational arts to the Fresno area. Mus is housed in a refurbished 1922 newspaper plant, two stories, with other floors marked for development; equipped with elevtors & facilities for the handicapped. Average Annual Attendance: 180,000. Mem: 5000; dues $20-$1000
Income: $1,300,000 (financed by mem, donations, service fees & grants)
Collections: Frank & Mary Alice Diener Collection of ancient snuff bottles; Oscar & Maria Salzer Collection of still life & trompe L'oeil paintings; Oscar & Maria Collection of 16th & 17th century Dutch & Flemish paintings; Charles Small Puzzle Collection
Publications: MetReport, monthly
Activities: Children's classes & summer day camps; dramatic programs; docent training; lect open to public; tours; individual paintings & original objects of art lent; book traveling exhibitions; originate traveling exhibitions; museum shop sells books & prints

FULLERTON

M CALIFORNIA STATE UNIVERSITY, FULLERTON, Art Gallery, Visual Arts Center, 800 N State College Blvd, 92634-9480. Tel 714-773-3471; FAX 714-773-3005; *Dir* Mike McGee; *Asst to Dir* Marilyn Moore; *Equipment Technician* Martin Lorigan
Open during exhibits, Mon - Fri Noon - 4 PM, Sun 2 - 5 PM, cl Sat. No admis fee. Estab 1963 to bring to the campus carefully developed art exhibits that instruct, inspire & challenge the student to the visual arts; to present to the student body, faculty & community exhibits of historical & aesthetic significance; to act as an educational tool, creating interaction between various departmental disciplines & promoting pub relations between campus & community. Four to five exhibits each year stemming from the Museum Studies & Exhibition Design Program. Undergraduate & graduate students have the opportunity to focus within a professionally oriented program directed toward the mus profession. Activity incorporates classes, art gallery & local mus. The Department of Art & the Art Gallery are the holders of the permanent collection. Average Annual Attendance: 15,000-20,000
Income: Financed by state appropriation, grants & donations
Collections: Contemporary Lithographs (Gemini); works by artists in the New York Collection for Stockholm executed by Styria Studio; lithographs by Lita Albuquerque, Coy Howard, Ed Rusha & Alexis Smith; Pre-Columbian artifacts; environmental & site-specific sculpture by Lloyd Hamrol, Ray Hein, Bernard Rosenthal, Michael Todd, Jay Willis
Exhibitions: Connie Zehr: Threshold; Six Views: Contemporary Landscape Architecture; Ten Years Later: Richard Shaw, Ed Blackburn, Tony Costanzo, Robert Rasmussen (Redd Ekks), John Roloff; The Infamous Image (photography); Animals; Contemporary Humanism: Reconfirmation of the Figure; Betye Saar: Resurrection; Nature: Two Views; Models: Hand-Held Ideas
Publications: Exhibition catalogs
Activities: Lect open to public, 8-10 vis lectr per year; workshops; production of slide/sound interpretation programs in conjunction with specific exhibitions; gallery talks; tours; scholarships offered; exten dept 4-6 major exhibitions per year; originate traveling exhibitions

A MUCKENTHALER CULTURAL CENTER, 1201 W Malvern, 92633. Tel 714-738-6595; FAX 714-738-6306; *Center Adminr* Betty Tesman; *Exhib Adminr* Mel Andrews; *Educ Adminr* Suzanne Lockhart
Open Tues - Sat 10 AM - 4 PM, Sun Noon - 5 PM. Suggested donation $1. Estab 1966 for the promotion & development of a public cultural center for the preservation, display & edification in the arts. Gallery is a National Historic Building, contains 2500 sq ft & is on 8 1/2 acres of land; outdoor theatre facilities. Average Annual Attendance: 60,000. Mem: 500; dues $10 & up; annual meeting in Apr
Income: $230,000 (financed by endowment, mem & city appropriation)
Publications: Exhibition catalogs
Activities: Classes for adults & children; dramatic programs; docent training; lect open to public, 12 vis lectr per year; concerts; gallery talks; tours; book traveling exhibitions; museum shop sells original art, reproductions, prints & gifts

GILROY

M GAVILAN COLLEGE, Art Gallery, 5055 Santa Teresa Blvd, 95020. Tel 408-847-1400, 848-4833; *Gallery Advisor & Humanities Div Dir* Kent Child; *Community Services Dir* Ken Cooper; *Gallery Dir* Sylvia Rios
Open Mon - Fri 8 AM - 5 PM. No admis fee. Estab 1967 to serve as a focal point in art exhibitions for community college district & as a teaching resource for the art department. Gallery is in large lobby of college library with 25 ft ceiling, redwood panelled walls & carpeted floor
Income: Financed through college
Collections: Approx 25 paintings purchased as award purchase prizes in college art competitions
Exhibitions: Monthly exhibits of student, local artist & traveling shows
Activities: Lending collection contains books, cassettes, color reproductions, film strips, Kodachromes, paintings, sculpture

GLENDALE

L BRAND LIBRARY & ART GALLERIES, 1601 W Mountain St, 91201-1209. Tel 818-548-2051; FAX 818-548-5079; *Library Mgr* Joseph Fuchs; *Asst Mgr & Gallery Dir* Jill Conner; *Librn* Blair Whittington
Open Tues & Thurs 1 - 9 PM, Wed 1 - 6 PM, Fri & Sat 1 - 5 PM. No admis fee. Estab 1956 to exhibit Southern California artists. Large gallery, foyer gallery, glass & concrete sculpture court. Average Annual Attendance: 120,000. Mem: 375; dues $10 - $500
Income: Financed by city & state appropriations
Library Holdings: Vols 55,000; Color slides 25,000; Compact discs 12,000; Micro — Fiche; AV — Rec 30,000, slides; Other — Exhibition catalogs, framed reproductions, original art works, prints, reproductions
Special Subjects: Painting - American, Prints
Collections: Indexes & other guides to art music literature
Exhibitions: 8 exhibits per year
Activities: Classes for adults & children; concerts; tours; competitions

M FOREST LAWN MUSEUM, 1712 S Glendale Ave, 91205. Tel 213-254-3131; *Dir* Frederick Llewellyn; *Mgr* Margaret Burton
Open daily 10 AM - 5 PM. No admis fee. Estab 1951 as a community museum offering education and culture through association with the architecture and the art of world masters. There are four galleries in the museum and several smaller galleries in buildings throughout the four parks. Recreation of room under the Medici Chapel in Florence, Italy, where Michelangelo's drawings were recently discovered. Average Annual Attendance: 200,000
Collections: American Western Bronzes; Ancient Biblical and Historical Coins; Crucifixion by Jan Styka (195 x 45 ft painting); Resurrection (Robert Clark), painting; reproductions of Michelangelo's greatest sculptures; stained glass window of the Last Supper by Leonardo da Vinci; originals and reproductions of famous sculptures, paintings, and documents
Exhibitions: History of Forest Lawn
Activities: Scholarships offered; lending collection contains reproductions of the crown jewels of England; originate traveling exhibitions; memento shop sells books and art works

L Library, 1712 Glendale Ave, 91205. Tel 213-254-3131; *Chmn* Frederick Llewellyn; *Cur* Margaret Burton
Open 10 AM - 5 PM. Estab 1952. For use of employees
Library Holdings: Vols 3000
Special Subjects: Bronzes, Mosaics, Painting - Polish, Sculpture, Stained Glass

C GLENDALE FEDERAL BANK, 401 N Brand Blvd, 91203. Tel 818-500-2000; FAX 818-409-5062; *Architectural Admin* Dennis Kailey
Open 9 AM - 4 PM. Collection displayed in branches

GLEN ELLEN

M JACK LONDON STATE HISTORIC PARK, House of Happy Walls, 2400 London Ranch Rd, 95442. Tel 707-938-5216
Open daily 10 AM - 5 PM; cl Thanksgiving, Christmas, New Year's Day. Admis $20 - $40 per bus, $5 per car, sr citizens $4. Estab 1959 for the interpretation of the life of Jack London; the fieldstone home was constructed in 1919 by London's widow. The collection is housed on two floors in the House of Happy Walls, and is operated by Calif Dept of Parks & Recreation. Average Annual Attendance: 80,000
Income: Financed by state appropriation
Collections: Artifacts from South Sea Islands; original illustrations
Activities: Tours; sales shop sells some of London's books

GREENBRAE

A MARIN COUNTY WATERCOLOR SOCIETY, 364 Via Casitas, 94904-2344. Tel 415-461-5871; *Treas-Membership* Marjorie L Pirie; *Newsletter Ed* Bee Bofinger; *Site Selector* Marion Lafkas; *Mailing Coordr* Lisa Guthrie; *Publicity* Jennifer Pelham; *Special Events Coordr* Maggi Manca
Estab 1970 to provide a way for members to share painting experiences in outdoor landscape. Mem: Open to painters, ranging from beginner to professional, in Marin County & San Francisco Bay area; dues $10-$20
Exhibitions: Marin County Civic Center Show
Publications: Monthly bulletin

HAYWARD

M CALIFORNIA STATE UNIVERSITY, HAYWARD, University Art Gallery, 94542. Tel 510-885-3111; FAX 510-885-2281; *Pres* Dr Norma Rees; *Prof* James Perrizo; *Prof* Lew Carson
Open Mon - Wed 11 AM - 4 PM, Thurs 11 AM - 7 PM, Sun 1 - 4 PM, time/days vary - check announcements. No admis fee. Estab 1970 to provide a changing exhibition program for the university & general public. Gallery contains 2200 sq ft. Average Annual Attendance: 11,000
Income: $13,500
Publications: Usually one catalog a yr; flyers for each show
Activities: Lect open to public, 6 vis lectr per year; exten dept; artmobile; book traveling exhibitions
M C E Smith Museum of Anthropology, 94542. Tel 510-885-3104; FAX 510-885-3353; *Elec Mail* gmiller@csuhayward.edu. *Dir* George Miller, PhD
Open Mon - Fri 11 AM - 5 PM. No admis fee. Estab 1974 as a teaching museum. Three converted classrooms; one main entrance from center room; alarm system; smoke detectors. Average Annual Attendance: 2500. Mem: 200
Income: $22,000 (financed by state appropriation)
Collections: Krone Collection: Philippine artifacts; Lee Collection: Hopi Kachinas, baskets, Navajo Mat
Activities: Lect open to public, 12 vis lectr per year

M HAYWARD AREA FORUM OF THE ARTS, Sun Gallery, 1015 E St, 94541. Tel 510-581-4050; FAX 510-581-3384; *Dir* Dr Maria Ochoa
Open Wed - Sat 11 AM - 5 PM, cl major holidays. No admis fee. Estab 1975. Mem: dues sustaining $65, family $40, single $30, student & senior citizen $20
Income: Financed by city, county & mem funds, corporate & foundation grants
Collections: †Contemporary art by Northern California artists
Exhibitions: San Francisco Alumni Association exhibition (photography); recent works in Monotype; contemporary Mexican painters (from Santiago Garza collection); Jack & Marilyn da Silva (metalware); art programs for the physically limited; Roger Hankins (painting, assemblage); Dicksen Schneider; Southern Alameda County Art Educators; Corita Kent; Artistas del Grupo Hermes (paintings, drawings); Recent Work in Metal; Artists With Creative Growth; The Picture: As Object, As Image (painting, assemblage, photography); Shrine & Koan (painting, sculpture); Corita & Southern Alameda County Art Educators (multi-media); HAFA members exhibition (multi-media); Art in the News (photojournalists, editorial cartoonists); Forms In Space (2-D, 3-D); Felted Fibers
Activities: Educ dept; docent training; lect open to public; 3 vis lectr per year; concerts; gallery talks; tours; art festivals with awards; scholarships offered; individual paintings & original objects of art lent to city offices; sales shop sells original art, prints & crafts

HOLLYWOOD

A LOS ANGELES CENTER FOR PHOTOGRAPHIC STUDIES, * 6518 Hollywood Blvd, 90028. Tel 213-466-6232; FAX 213-466-3203; *Pres* Adrienne Goldstone; *Dir* Joe Smoke; *Assoc Dir* Susan Sayre
Open Mon - Fri 10 AM - 5 PM. Estab 1974 to promote photography within the visual arts. Mem: 600; dues patron $250 - $1000, friend $100, regular $30, student & sr citizen $15
Income: $110,000 (financed by mem, city & state appropriation, federal funds, corporations & foundations)
Exhibitions: Members exhibition; group exhibitions
Publications: Frame/Work, 3 times per yr, Photo Calendar, bi-monthly
Activities: Workshops for adults; symposia; lect open to public, 8-12 vis lectr per year; competitions with awards; originates traveling exhibitions; sales shop sells magazines & original art

M LOS ANGELES CONTEMPORARY EXHIBITIONS, 6522 Hollywood Blvd, 90028. Tel 213-957-1777; FAX 213-957-9025; *Exec Dir* Brian Karl; *Presentations Coordr* Elissa Levy; *Mem Coordr* Bridget DuLong
Open (gallery) Wed - Sun Noon - 5 PM, Thurs Noon - 8 PM; (office) Mon - Fri 10 AM - 6 PM. Admis $2 suggested donation. Estab 1978, artist run interdisciplinary space. Average Annual Attendance: 25,000. Mem: 1000; dues $40-$2500
Publications: Exhibit catalogs
Activities: Lect open to public; educational programs; originates traveling exhibitions

HUNTINGTON BEACH

M HUNTINGTON BEACH ART CENTER, 538 Main St, 92648. Tel 714-374-1650; FAX 714-374-1654; *Dir* Naida Osline; *Dir Operations* Randy Pesqueira; *Dir Programming* Tyler Stallings; *Studio Dir* Carole Frances
Open Tues - Sun Noon - 6 PM. Admis $3. Estab 1995 to provide community art center. Three large galleries, store gallery, studio & one educational gallery. Average Annual Attendance: 3000. Mem: 300
Activities: Classes for adults & children; performance art venue; lect open to public; sales shop sells books & magazines

IRVINE

M CITY OF IRVINE, Irvine Fine Arts Center, 14321 Yale Ave, 92604-1901. Tel 714-724-6880; FAX 714-552-2137; *Dir* Tony Pang; *Educ Coordr* Tim Jahns
Open Mon - Thurs 9 AM - 9 PM, Fri 9 AM - 5 PM, Sat 9 AM - 3 PM, Sun 1 - 5 PM. Estab 1980 to make the arts integral in the lives of people. Gallery contains 5000 sq ft. Average Annual Attendance: 65,000. Mem: 250; dues $25 - $100
Income: $600,000 (financed by city appropriation, grants & donations)
Exhibitions: All Media, annual competition for Orange County artists.
Publications: Art Beat, quarterly
Activities: Classes for adults & children; docent programs; open studios; lect open to public, 4 vis lectr per year; competitions; originate annual traveling exhibition; retail store sells books & original art

M UNIVERSITY OF CALIFORNIA, IRVINE, Fine Art Gallery, * Dept Studio Art, 92717-2775. Tel 714-824-6610; FAX 714-824-2450; *Dir* Catharine Lord
Open Oct - June, Tues - Sun Noon - 5 PM. No admis fee. Estab 1965 to house changing exhibitions devoted to contemporary art
Income: Financed by city & state appropriations & by interested private collectors
Exhibitions: Nick Vaughn (1983-1987); Wayne Thiebaud: Works on Paper (1947-1987); Peter Shelton: Environmental Sculpture; Michael Hardesty, NY Artist - Site Installation; Sigmund Freud Antiquities: Fragments from a Varied Past
Publications: Exhibition catalogs; mailers
Activities: Monthly lect on each exhibit; performances; tours; field trips

KENTFIELD

M COLLEGE OF MARIN, Art Gallery, College Ave, 94904. Tel 415-485-9494; *Dir* Duane Aten
Open Mon - Fri 8 AM - 10 PM; open also during all performances for drama, music & concert. No admis fee. Estab 1970 for the purpose of educ in the college district & community. Gallery is housed in the entrance to Fine Arts Complex, measures 3600 sq ft of unlimited hanging space; has portable hanging units & locked cases. Average Annual Attendance: 100 - 300 daily
Income: Financed by state appropriation & community taxes
Collections: Art student work; miscellaneous collection
Exhibitions: Faculty & Art Student; Fine Arts & Decorative Arts
Publications: Catalogs, 1-2 per year
Activities: Gallery Design-Management course; gallery talks; tours

LAGUNA BEACH

L ART INSTITUTE OF SOUTHERN CALIFORNIA, Ruth Salyer Library, 2222 Laguna Canyon Rd, 92651. Tel 714-497-3309; FAX 714-497-4399; *Pres* John W Lottes; *Chmn Visual Communications* Vito Leonard Scarola; *Chmn Fine Arts* Jonathan Burke; *Chmn Liberal Arts* Helene Garrison
Open 8 AM - 5 PM. No admis fee. Estab 1962. For lending. Circ 5000
Purchases: $9000
Library Holdings: Vols 14,471; Per subs 69; AV — Slides 23,787, v-tapes 97; Other — Clipping files, exhibition catalogs 400
Special Subjects: Advertising Design, Anthropology, Architecture, Art Education, Bronzes, Ceramics, Commercial Art, Etchings & Engravings, Film, Graphic Arts, History of Art & Archaeology, Mixed Media, Painting - American, Photography, Portraits
Publications: Catalog, annual; newsletters, semi-annual

M LAGUNA ART MUSEUM OF THE ORANGE COUNTY MUSEUM OF ART, Pacific Coast Hwy at 307 Cliff Dr, 92651. Tel 714-494-6531; *Acting Dir & Cur Exhib* Susan Anderson; *Cur Colls* Bolton Colburn; *Pub Relations* Karen Drum; *Finance Officer* Nancy Hightower; *Bookstore Mgr* Monte Butler
Open Tues - Sun 11 AM - 5 PM, cl Mon. Admis adults $4, children free. Estab 1918 as an art assoc. Two large galleries, six small galleries, mus store & offices. Average Annual Attendance: 75,000. Mem: 1800; dues $35-$1000; annual meeting in Sept
Income: Financed by endowment & mem
Collections: American Art with focus on contemporary & early 20th century California painting
Activities: Classes for adults & children; docent training; lect open to public, 10 vis lectr per year; gallery talks; tours; competitions with awards; book traveling exhibitions; originate traveling exhibitions; sales shop sells books, magazines, original art, reproductions & prints

LA JOLLA

L LIBRARY ASSOCIATION OF LA JOLLA, Athenaeum Music & Arts Library, 1008 Wall St, 92037. Tel 619-454-5872; FAX 619-454-5835; *Exec Dir & Librn* Erika Torri; *Prog Dir* Daniel Atkinson; *Mem Asst* Renetta Happe; *Reference Librn* Beth Deahl; *Public Relations* Susan Dilts
Open Tues, Thurs, Fri & Sat 10 AM - 5:30 PM, Wed 10 AM - 8:30 PM. No admis fee. Estab 1899 to provide the La Jolla & San Diego communities with library resources in music & arts & an on going schedule of cultural programs, classes, concerts & exhibitions. No estab gallery; changing exhibitions every six weeks. Circ 34,000. Average Annual Attendance: 45,000. Mem: 1900; dues $40-$5000; annual meeting third Tues in July
Income: $420,000 (financed by trust fund, rents, dues, gifts, admis & tuitions)
Purchases: $27,000
Library Holdings: Vols 10,000; Per subs 85; AV — A-tapes, cassettes 4000, rec 8000, v-tapes 1000; Other — Clipping files 1800, exhibition catalogs, pamphlets, photographs
Special Subjects: Advertising Design, Aesthetics, Afro-American Art, Architecture, Art History, Asian Art, Bookplates & Bindings, Bronzes
Exhibitions: Changing shows every six weeks
Publications: Bimonthly newsletter
Activities: Classes for adults & children; lect open to public, 10 vis lectr per year; concerts; library tours; panel discussions; vis artists workshops; outreach programs for children; bi-monthly book sales; competitions with prizes

M MUSEUM OF CONTEMPORARY ART, SAN DIEGO, * 700 Prospect St, 92037. Tel 619-454-3541; FAX 619-454-6985; *Develop Dir* Anne Farrell; *Pres Bd Trustees* Carolyn P Farris; *Cur* Louis Grachos; *Dir* Hugh M Davies; *Assoc Dir* Charles Castle; *Educ Cur* Seonaid McArthur
Estab 1941 to collect, preserve & present post-1950 art. Maintains two locations, a 500 seat auditorium, 16,000 sq ft total exhibition space. See also listing for San Diego facility. Average Annual Attendance: 195,000. Mem: 2500; dues $40
Income: $2,200,000 (financed by endowment, mem, city & state appropriation, grants from the National Endowment for the Arts, Institute of Museum Services & private foundations)

Collections: †Contemporary Art, International, 1950 to the present
Exhibitions: Vernon Fisher; Emilio Ambasz; Ann Hamilton; Alfredo Jaar.
Publications: Exhibition catalogs; newsletter, quarterly
Activities: Classes for adults & children; docent training; lect open to the public, 10-15 lectr per year; films; gallery talks; tours; concerts; individual paintings & original objects of art lent to museums & qualified art organizations; lending collection contains original art works, original prints, paintings, photographs, sculpture; book traveling exhibitions 3-4 per year; originate traveling exhibitions; museum bookstore sells books, magazines, posters, design objects

L Geisel Library, 700 Prospect St, 92037. Tel 619-454-3541; FAX 619-454-6985; *Librn* Virginia Abblitt
Open Tues - Fri 10 AM - 4PM. Estab 1941. For reference use by staff, docents & mus members
Income: Financed by mem, gifts & grants
Library Holdings: Vols 4500; Per subs 56; Micro — Cards; AV — A-tapes, cassettes, slides 9000, v-tapes; Other — Clipping files 2000, exhibition catalogs 6000, pamphlets
Special Subjects: Art History, Conceptual Art, Drawings, Latin American Art, Painting - American, Painting - British, Painting - Japanese, Photography, Sculpture, Video, Contemporary Art, international in scope

M UNIVERSITY OF CALIFORNIA-SAN DIEGO, University Art Gallery, 9500 Gilman Dr, Mail Code 0327, 92093-0327. Tel 619-534-2864; *Dir* Kathleen Stoughton
Open Tues - Sun Noon - 5 PM, cl Mon, July, Aug & Christmas break. No admis fee. Estab 1967 to provide changing exhibitions of interest to the visual arts majors, university personnel & the community at large, including an emphasis on contemporary art. Located on the west end of Mandeville Center, flexible open space approximately 40 x 70 ft. Average Annual Attendance: 15,000. Mem: 200; dues $35 & up; bi-monthly meetings
Income: Financed by state appropriations, member contributions & student registration fees
Collections: Small Impressionist Collection owned by UC Foundation, presently on loan to San Diego Fine Arts Gallery, Balboa Park
Publications: UC San Diego Catalog: At Home with Architecture; exhibit catalogs
Activities: Lect open to public, 3-4 vis lectr per year; gallery talks; tours; originate traveling exhibitions

L UNIVERSITY OF CALIFORNIA, SAN DIEGO, Art & Architecture Library, Geisel Library, 0175F, 92093-0175. Tel 619-534-4811; FAX 619-534-0189; *Head* Leslie Abrams; *Visual Arts Librn* Susan Jurist
Open Mon - Fri 8 AM - 5 PM. No admis fee. Estab 1992. Circ 60,000
Income: Financed by state appropriation
Purchases: $100,000
Library Holdings: Vols 60,000; Per subs 180; AV — A-tapes 10, slides 250,000, v-tapes 10; Other — Clipping files, exhibition catalogs
Special Subjects: Afro-American Art, American Indian Art, Architecture, Art History, Conceptual Art, Ethnology, History of Art & Archaeology, Landscape Architecture, Manuscripts, Mixed Media, Photography, Religious Art, Video, Performance Art
Publications: Art & Architecture Library, general guide; Contemporary Artists, Education & Careers; Guide to Architectural Information; Notes from the Underground; irregular newsletter; Resources for Having Slides Made; Searching BHA, RILA, RAA

M UNIVERSITY OF CALIFORNIA, SAN DIEGO, Stuart Collection, 9500 Gilman Dr, 92093-0010. Tel 619-534-2117; FAX 619-534-9713; Elec Mail mbeebe@ucsd.edu, jfuller@sucsd.edu. *Dir* Mary Livingstone Beebe; *Prog Representative* Julia F Kindy; *Project Mgr* Mathieu Gregoire
Estab 1981 to commission contemporary sculptures for UCSD campus. Maintains library
Collections: Outdoor sculptures
Activities: Lect open to public

LONG BEACH

M CALIFORNIA STATE UNIVERSITY, LONG BEACH, University Art Museum, 1250 Bellflower Blvd, 90840-1901. Tel 310-985-5761; FAX 310-985-7602; Elec Mail uam@csulb.edu. *Dir & Chief Cur* Constance W Glenn; *Assoc Dir* Ilee Kaplan; *Educ Consultant* Liz Harvey; *Registrar* Marina Freeman; *Cur* Gwen Hill; *Dir Pub Relations & Publ* Kirsten Schmidt
Open Tues - Thurs Noon - 8 PM, Fri - Sun Noon - 5 PM, cl Mon. Admis $1 donation suggested. Estab 1949 to be an academic & community visual arts resource. North Campus Library. Average Annual Attendance: 50,000
Income: Financed by university appropriation & private funding
Purchases: Site specific sculpture, works of art on paper
Collections: 1965 Sculpture Symposium; contemporary prints, drawings & photographs; site-specific sculpture
Exhibitions: Jim Dine Figure Drawings: 1975-1979; Kathe Kollwitz at the Zeitlin Bookshop 1937: CSULB 1979; Roy Lichtenstein: Ceramic Sculpture; Nathan Oliveira Print Retrospective; Lucas Samaras: Photo Transformations; George Segal: Pastels 1957 - 1965; Frederick Sommer at Seventy-five; The Photograph as Artifice; Renate Ponsold-Robert Motherwell: Apropos Robinson Jeffers; Francesco Clemente Recent Works; Paul Wonner: Recent Works; Jacques Hurtubise: Oeuvres Recentes-Recent Works; Bryan Hunt: A Decade of Drawings; Anders Zorn Rediscovered; Robert Longo: Sequences-Men in the Cities; A Collective Vision: Clarence White & His Students; Hirosada: Osaka Printmaker; Eric Fischl: Scenes Before the Eye; Lorna Simpson; Imagenes Liricas: New Spanish Visions; James Rosenquist: Time Dust, The Complete Graphics 1962 - 1992
Publications: Exhibition catalogs & brochures, 3-4 per year
Activities: Classes for children; docent training; lect open to public, 4-6 vis lectr per year; concerts; gallery talks; tours; competitions with awards; book traveling exhibitions 3-6 per year; originate traveling exhibitions to other museums; museum shop sells books, original art & reproductions

L University Library, 1250 Bellflower Blvd, 90840-1901. Tel 562-985-4047; FAX 562-985-1703; *Acting Dir* Roman V Kochan; *Art Bibliographer* Henry J DuBois
Open Mon - Thurs 7:45 AM - 12 AM, Fri 7:45 AM - 5 PM, Sat 10 AM - 4 PM, Sun 12:30 PM - 12 AM. Estab 1949 for delivery of information & related services to the campus & surrounding communities. For lending & reference. Circ 340,248
Income: Financed by state appropriation
Purchases: $17,722
Library Holdings: Vols 1,022,263; Art per subs 116; Art vols 37,000; Micro — Cards, fiche, reels; AV — Cassettes, fs, motion pictures, rec, slides, v-tapes; Other — Exhibition catalogs, pamphlets, prints, reproductions
Special Subjects: Art Education, Art History, Asian Art, Photography, Prints, Video
Collections: Modern Photography Collection (Edward Weston, Ansel Adams), original photographic prints; Kathe Kollwitz Collection, original prints

A CALIFORNIA STATE UNIVERSITY, LONG BEACH FOUNDATION, 6300 State Univ Dr E, Ste 332, 90815. Tel 310-985-5537; FAX 310-985-7951; Elec Mail svanderh@csulb.edu. *Exec Dir* Sandra Vanderhaden
Estab 1955 existing solely to advance the mission of the University. Serves to complement & strengthen the University's teaching, research, scholarly, creative & public service goals
Activities: Lect open to public, 8 vis lectr per year; grants offered

M LONG BEACH JEWISH COMMUNITY CENTER, Center Gallery, 3801 E Willow St, 90815. Tel 310-426-7601; FAX 310-424-3915; *Pres* Dr David Tillman; *Exec Dir* Joe Parmet; *Asst Dir* Lynne Rosenstein
Open Sun - Fri 9 AM - 5 PM, Mon - Thurs evenings 7:30 - 10 PM. Estab to provide a community service for local artists & the broader community as well as offering exhibits of particular interest to the Jewish Community. The gallery is located in the large lobby at the entrance to the building; panels & shelves are for exhibit displays
Income: Financed by mem, United Jewish Welfare Fund, United Way & fundraising events
Exhibitions: Monthly exhibits throughout the year; Annual Holiday Craft & Gift Show; Annual Youth Art Show; Paintings; Photography; Portraits; Sculpture
Publications: Center News, monthly; Jewish Federation News, bimonthly
Activities: Classes for adults & children; dramatic programs; lect open to the public; concerts; competitions with awards; sales shop sells books, Israeli & Jewish Holiday art objects & gift items

M LONG BEACH MUSEUM OF ART, 2300 E Ocean Blvd, 90803. Tel 310-439-2119; FAX 310-439-3587; *Dir* Harold Nelson; *Develop Officer* Susan Reeder; *Cur* Harold Nelson; *Media Arts Cur* Carole Ann Klonarides; *Educator* Sue Ann Robinson; *Mgr Media Arts Center* Joe Leonardi; *Business Mgr* Jim Wilson
Open Wed - Sun Noon - 5 PM; cl New Year's, July 4, Thanksgiving & Christmas. Admis $2. Opened in 1951 as a Municipal Art Center under the city library department; in 1957 the Long Beach City Council changed the center to the Long Beach Museum of Art; managed by Foundation since 1985. Eight galleries & a screening room with changing exhibitions & selections from Permanent Collection. Average Annual Attendance: 50,000. Mem: 1600; dues $35
Income: Financed by annual contribution by City of Long Beach & through grants from National Endowment for the Arts, California Arts Council & private foundations & through individual & corporate contributions
Collections: †Paintings, †sculpture, †prints, †drawings, crafts & photography; 1000 items with emphasis on West Coast & California modern & contemporary art; sculpture garden; Milton Wichner Collection includes Kandinsky, Jawlensky, Feininger, Moholy-Nagy; Major collection of video art
Exhibitions: Pioneers in Paradise; Hollis Frampton: The Blue Four; Art Moderne Architecture; A Passage Repeated; Drawing & Sculpture; Life: The Second Decade; Laddie John Dill; Japan-America; Video Poetics; Art of Music Vidio; Masami Teraoka; Gary Hill Retrospective; Alexej Jawlensky Retrospective; Afro-American Quilts; Relocations & Revisions: The Japanese-American Internment Reconsidered
Publications: Announcements; exhibit catalogs; quarterly bulletin
Activities: Workshops for adults & children; docent training; screening & lect series open to public, 12 - 20 vis lectr per year; concerts; gallery talks; tours; video art Open Channels competition; awards; book traveling exhibitions, 4 per year; originate traveling exhibitions that circulate to museums

L Library, 2300 E Ocean Blvd, 90803. Tel 310-439-2119; FAX 310-439-3587
Open Wed - Sun Noon - 5 PM. Admis $2. Estab 1957 to promote understanding & appreciation of the visual & media arts; to collect & facilitate the production of significant works of art; to manage & support an institution where these works of art may be housed & displayed for the education & enjoyment of the public. Open for staff reference with restricted lending of books, publications & slides. Average Annual Attendance: 47,000
Library Holdings: Vols 2000; Per subs 4; AV — V-tapes; Other — Clipping files, exhibition catalogs
Special Subjects: Art History
Exhibitions: Annual Dia de los Muertos & Children's Cultural Festival
Activities: Four-part lect series, 2 - 4 vis lectr per year; poetry readings; concerts; gallery talks; tours; individual paintings & original objects of art lent to other art institutions, corporations & organizations with art programs; museum lobby sells catalogues, cards & posters

L LONG BEACH PUBLIC LIBRARY, 101 Pacific Ave, 90822. Tel 310-570-7500; FAX 310-590-6956; *Dir Libr Servs* Cordelia Howard; *Assoc Dir Adult Servs* Eleanore Schmidt; *Fine Arts Librn* Ruth Stewart
Open Mon 10 Am - 8 PM, Tues - Sat 10 AM - 5:30 PM, Sun Noon - 5 PM. Estab 1897
Income: Financed by municipality
Library Holdings: Vols 16,000; Per subs 45; AV — A-tapes, cassettes, rec, v-tapes; Other — Clipping files, pamphlets
Collections: Miller Special Collections Room housing fine arts books with an emphasis on Asian Art & Marilyn Horne Archives

A PUBLIC CORPORATION FOR THE ARTS, Visual & Performing Arts Registry, 100 W Broadway, Ste 360, 90802. Tel 310-570-1366; FAX 310-570-1367; *Exec Dir* Sandra Gibson; *Public Arts Mgr* Jorge Pardo; *Member Serv Liaison* Susan Malmstrom; *Corporate Press Officer* Deborah Robinson
Open Mon - Fri 9 AM - 5 PM, cl Sat & Sun. Admis free. Estab 1977, non-profit, official arts advisory council for city of Long Beach
Income: $750,000 (financed by endowment, mem, city appropriation, private corporations & foundations)
Collections: Contemporary & archival slides; Library of Long Beach & area resident artists' work; all media 300 artists performing & visual
Publications: Newsletter, bi-monthly; quarterly events calendar; monthly media sheets
Activities: Enrichment & alternative arts programs; technical assistance; lect open to public, 3 vis lectr per year; individual & community art grants

LOS ALTOS

M GALLERY 9, 143 Main St, 94022. Tel 415-941-7969; *Treas* Elaine B Rothwell; *Exhibits Chmn* Carol Hake; *Staff* Jean Pell Morton; *Publicity* Louise Freund
Open Tues - Sat Noon - 5 PM. No admis fee. Estab 1970 to exhibit local fine art. Average Annual Attendance: 1200. Mem: 23; dues $480; meetings first Mon each month
Exhibitions: Exhibit changes each month. Member artists featured once every two years
Activities: Sales shop sells original art

LOS ANGELES

L ART IN ARCHITECTURE, Joseph Young Library, 7917 1/2 W Norton Ave, 90046. Tel 213-656-2286, 654-0990; *Dir* Dr Joseph L Young
Estab 1955 to provide background to history of art in architecture. Only availabe to students, associates and apprentices for reference only
Purchases: $2000
Library Holdings: Vols 2000; Per subs 10; AV — Kodachromes, motion pictures, slides, v-tapes; Other — Clipping files, exhibition catalogs, memorabilia, original art works, pamphlets, photographs, prints, reproductions, sculpture
Special Subjects: Architecture, Art History, Calligraphy, Drawings, Judaica, Mexican Art, Mixed Media, Mosaics, Painting - American, Painting - Dutch, Painting - European, Painting - French, Painting - Italian, Photography, Religious Art, Sculpture, Stained Glass, Mural Painting
Activities: Two vis lectr per year; tours; scholarships & fels offered; lending collection contains 2000 books, 200 color reproductions, 2000 Kodachromes, motion pictures, 100 original art works, 500 original prints, paintings, 500 photographs, sculpture & 2000 slides; book traveling exhibitions 1 per year; originate traveling exhibitions

M CALIFORNIA AFRICAN-AMERICAN MUSEUM, 600 State Dr Exposition Park, 90037. Tel 213-744-7432; FAX 213-744-2050; *Dir* Jamesina Henderson; *Deputy Dir & Assoc Ed Publs* Nancy McKinney; *Cur History* Rick Moss
Open daily 10 AM - 5 PM, cl Mon. No admis fee. Estab to examine, collect, preserve & display art, history & culture of Blacks in The Americas with concentration on Blacks in California
Publications: Calendar of Events, every 2 months; exhibition catalogs

M CALIFORNIA MUSEUM OF SCIENCE AND INDUSTRY, 700 State Dr, 90037. Tel 213-744-7400; *Dir* Jeffrey Rudolph; *Deputy Dir* Bob Campbell; *Deputy Dir* Ann Muscat; *Deputy Dir* Vahe Simonian
Open daily 10 AM - 5 PM. Dynamically tells the story of science, industry and commerce to the public by tempting each visitor to take part in a sensory learning experience and education adventure. The museum has 9 halls housing 20 permanent exhibits & more than 60 temporary exhibits among which are Sister Cities Youth Art Exhibit & Sister Cities in Focus which appear throughout the year; auditorium seating 500
Income: Financed by state appropriation and California Museum Foundation
Exhibitions: Temporary-Annual Union Artist (painting & sculpture by all unions in AFL-CIO; Bonsai, Care & Growing; children's Gametime playground exhibit; Key Art Awards (annual showing of posters, logos, word-styles promoting movies or TV shows); props from motion picture Alien
Publications: Notices of temporary exhibits, maps, pamphlets
Activities: Formal science-art educ programs for school groups & public; competitions; scholarships offered

M CALIFORNIA STATE UNIVERSITY, LOS ANGELES, Fine Arts Gallery, 5151 State University Dr, 90032. Tel 213-343-4023; *Dir* Daniel Douke
Open Mon - Thurs Noon - 5 PM. No admis fee. Estab 1954 as a forum for advanced works of art & their makers, so that educ through exposure to works of art can take place. Gallery has 3500 sq ft, clean white walls, 11 ft high ceilings with an entry & catalog desk. Average Annual Attendance: 30,000
Income: Financed by endowment & state appropriation
Exhibitions: American Landscape Painting; Mark Lere; Peter Liashkoy; New Talent Exhibitions; California Painting; The Essential Modernist Framework
Publications: Exhibition catalogs, three per year
Activities: Educ dept; lect open to public, 10-20 vis lectr per year; gallery talks; exten dept

M CITY OF LOS ANGELES, Cultural Affairs Dept, 433 S Spring St, 10th Flr, 90013. Tel 213-485-2433; *General Mgr* Adolfo V Nodal; *Performing Arts Dir* Ernest Dillihay; *Pres Cultural Affairs Commission* Arthur Pfefferman; *Pres Cultural Heritage Commission* Mary Z George; *Community Arts Dir* Dr Earl Shevburn
Estab 1925 to bring to the community the cultural & aesthetic aspects of Los Angeles; to encourage citizen appreciation & participation in cultural activities & developing art skills. Operates facilities, programs & classes throughout the city. Sponsors festivals, special events. Average Annual Attendance: 250,000
Income: $3,000,000 (financed by city appropriation)
Collections: Works by local area artists; Portraits of Mayors of Los Angeles; gifts to the city from other countries
Exhibitions: Various at different venues
Activities: Classes for adults & children; dramatic programs; docent training; lect open to public; concerts; gallery talks; tours; competitions; historic preservation; street murals; grants program; folk arts program; sales shop sells books, original art, reproductions & prints

M CRAFT & FOLK ART MUSEUM, 5800 Wilshire Blvd, 90036. Tel 213-937-5544; FAX 213-937-5576; *Acting Dir* Nancy Fister; *Librn* Joan Benedeth; *Exhibition Designer* Carol Fulton; *Controller* Lorraine Trippett; *Project Dir* Marcia Page
Open Tues - Sun 11 AM - 5 PM. Admis general $4, students & seniors $2.50, children under 12 free. Estab 1973 as The Egg & The Eye Gallery
Collections: Contemporary American Crafts; Contemporary Design; International Folk Art including Japanese, East Indian & Mexican works; masks of the worlds
Exhibitions: Annual International Festival of Masks; Intimate Appeal: The Figurative Art of Beatrice Wood; Ed Rossbach: 40 Years of Exploration & Innovation in Fiber Art
Publications: Quarterly calendar
Activities: Classes for adults & children; docent training; lect open to public, 5 vis lectr per year; gallery talks; tours; community outreach programs; book traveling exhibitions 1-2 per year; originate traveling exhibitions; museum shop sells books, magazines, original art, reproductions, prints, jewelry, folk art, ceramics, glass

L Edith R Wyle Research Library, 5800 Wilshire Blvd, 90036. Tel 213-857-4682, 937-5544; FAX 213-937-5576; *Museum Librn* Joan M Benedetti
Open by appointment only. Estab 1975 to support & supplement the documentation & information activities of the Museum in regard to contemporary crafts, international folk art, design. Visual material collected equally with print. For reference only
Income: Financed by the museum & grants
Library Holdings: Vols 7000; Per subs 100; Posters; AV — A-tapes, cassettes, fs, Kodachromes, motion pictures, rec, slides, v-tapes; Other — Clipping files, exhibition catalogs, memorabilia, pamphlets, photographs
Special Subjects: Aesthetics, Anthropology, Architecture, Ceramics, Costume Design & Construction, Decorative Arts, Ethnology, Folk Art, Glass, Historical Material, Industrial Design, Metalwork, Mixed Media, Fiber Art, Japanese Folk Art, Masks & Masking, Mexican Folk Art, Vernacular & Domestic Architecture, Wood Art
Collections: Preserving Ethnic Traditions Project Archive (slides, cassette, a-tapes & reports of LA folk artists); †Slide Registry of Contemporary Crafts people

A CULTURAL AFFAIRS DEPARTMENT CITY OF LOS ANGELES, Junior Arts Center, 4814 Hollywood Blvd, 90027. Tel 213-485-4474; *Dir* Harriet S Miller; *Teacher Outreach Coordr* Laura Stickney; *Handicapped Servs Coordr* Dr Mary J Martz; *Sunday Coordr* Gayle Gale; *International Child Art Coordr* Patty Sue Jones
Open Tues - Sun 12:30 - 5 PM. No admis fee. Estab 1967 to stimulate & assist in the development of art skills & creativity. The gallery offers exhibitions of interest to children & young people & those who work with the young. Average Annual Attendance: 60,000. Mem: 200; dues $25 ; annual meeting June 1
Income: Financed by city appropriation & Friends of the Junior Arts Center
Collections: International Child Art Collection; Two-dimensional works on paper; 8mm film by former students
Exhibitions: 12 exhibitions a year
Publications: Schedules of art classes, quarterly; exhibition notices
Activities: Art classes for young people in painting, dramatic programs drawing, etching, general printmaking, photography, filmmaking, photo silkscreen, ceramics, film animation; workshops for teachers; lect, 2-4 vis lectr per year; films; musical instrument making, design, video festivals for students & the general public; gallery talks; tours; scholarships offered

L Library, 4814 Hollywood Blvd, 90027. Tel 213-485-4474, 485-8396; FAX 213-485-7456; *Dir* Harriet S Miller
Staff use only
Library Holdings: Vols 700; AV — Slides 15,000

A FELLOWS OF CONTEMPORARY ART, 777 S Figueroa St, 44th Flr, 90017-2513. Tel 213-243-4154; FAX 213-243-4092, 243-4199; Elec Mail focal@aol.com. *Admin Dir* Carole Kim
Supports contemporary art in California by initiating & sponsoring exhibitions & videos at selected institutions. Mem: 140
Exhibitions: At least one major exhibition per year
Activities: One day educ programs; guest speakers; domestic & international tours

A FOUNDATION FOR ART RESOURCES, PO Box 29422, 90029. Tel 310-289-4181; *Chair* Karen Bonsigli; *Treas* Karen Schwenkmeyer
No admis fee. Estab 1977 to represent artists & art criticism theory not normally represented in main stream galleries. Full Moon Gallery, outdoor window installations. Average Annual Attendance: 10,000
Income: $15,000 (financed by endowment)
Activities: Lect open to public, 6 vis lectr per year

C GOLDEN STATE MUTUAL LIFE INSURANCE COMPANY, Afro-American Art Collection, 1999 W Adams Blvd, 90018. Tel 213-731-1131; *Cur & Cunsultant* Harold Toliver
Open to public by appointment through Personnel Department. Estab 1965 to provide a show place for Afro-American Art; to assist in the development of ethnic pride among the youth of our community. Collection displayed throughout building
Income: Financed by the Company
Collections: Drawings, lithographs, paintings and sculpture
Publications: Afro-American Art Collection Brochure; Historical Murals Brochure
Activities: Tours by appointment

M **HEBREW UNION COLLEGE**, Skirball Cultural Center, 2701 N Sepulveda Blvd, 90049. Tel 310-440-4600; FAX 310-440-4695; *Dir* Nancy Berman; *Adminr* Peggy Kayser; *Educ Dir* Adele Burke; *Cur* Grace Cohen Grossman; *Cur* Barbara Gilbert; *Media Resources Coordr* Susanne Kester; *Asst Cur* Monica Billeit; *Asst Cur* Debbie Freund
Open Tues, Wed & Fri 10 AM - 4 PM, Thurs 10 AM - 9 PM, Sat Noon - 5 PM, Sun 10 AM - 5 PM. Admis general $6, students & seniors $4, children under 12 free. Estab 1972 to interpret American Jewish experience & nurture American Jewish identity & encourage cultural pluralism. 4000 years of Jewish historical experience. Average Annual Attendance: 100,000. Mem: 4368; dues $45-$1200
Income: Financed by mem admis, private & pub grants, progams & fees
Collections: American Jewish Ethnographic Collection (paintings, prints, drawings, coins, sculpture); 2000 archaeological objects from the Near East, primarily Israeli; Biblical Archaeology; 6000 ceremonial objects, primarily Western Europen, but some exotic Oriental & indian pieces as well; Chinese Torah & India Torah cases; †2500 ethnographic objects of American Jewish Life; Judaica Collection; 4000 prints & drawings from Western Europe, spanning 4-5 centuries
Exhibitions: Vision & Values: Jewish Life from Antiquity to America. (1997) George Segal: The Bible Sculptures
Publications: Exhibition brochures & catalogs
Activities: Classes for adults & children; dramatic programs; docent training; film series; lect open to public, 5 vis lectr per year; concerts; gallery talks; tours; book traveling exhibitions 5-8 per year; originate traveling exhibitions; museum shop sells books, original art, reproductions, prints, jewelry & children's items

M **JAPANESE AMERICAN CULTURAL & COMMUNITY CENTER**, George J Doizaki Gallery, 244 S San Pedro St, Ste 505, 90012-3895. Tel 213-628-2725; FAX 213-617-8576; *Gallery Dir* Robert Hori

LANNAN FOUNDATION
For further information, see National and Regional Organizations

A **LA ART ASSOCIATION**, 825 N LaCienega Blvd, 90069. Tel 310-652-8272; FAX 310-652-9251; *Pres* Joan Carl; *Dir* Richard Campbell; *VPres* Ruth Eyrich; *Treas* Bob Jesburg
Open Tues - Sat Noon - 5 PM. No admis fee. Estab 1925 to discover & present young professional artists & to exhibit the work of established California artists. Average Annual Attendance: 5000. Mem: 350; dues $60 per yr; biannual meetings in Apr & Oct
Income: Financed by investments; partly by mem dues
Exhibitions: All Creatures Great & Small: The Animal in Art; Burden Collection of Famous Photographers; Jubilee Show of Artists of the Forties & Fifties; Los Angeles, Yesterday & Today; Graphics, Painting & Sculpture by Southern California Artists, monthly
Publications: Announcements of exhibitions & lectures, monthly; newsletter, monthly
Activities: Exhibition receptions & gallery lect, open to the public

M **LOS ANGELES COUNTY MUSEUM OF ART**, 5905 Wilshire Blvd, 90036. Tel 213-857-6111; FAX 213-931-7347; *Dir* Graham W J Beal; *Pres & Chief Exec Officer* Andrea L Rich; *Asst Dir Operations* Arthur Owens; *Head Conservation* Pieter Meyers; *Cur Costumes & Textiles* Dale Carolyn-Gluckman; *Asst Dir Facilities* Romalis Taylor; *Sr Cur Prints & Drawings* Victor Carlson; *Cur 20th Century Art* Stephanie Barron; *Cur Contemporary Art* Howard Fox; *Cur Far Eastern Art* George Kuwayama; *Cur European Paintings & Sculpture* Philip Conisbee; *Cur Photo* Robert A Sobieszek; *Dir Film Progs* Ronald Haver; *Dir Music Progs* Dorrance Stalvey; *Public Information Progs* Pamela Jenkinson; *Registrar* Renee Montgomery; *Librn* Eleanor Hartman; *Cur American Art* Michael Quick; *Sr Cur 20th Century Art* Maurice Tuchman; *Cur Indian & Southeast Asian Art* Pratapaditya Pal; *Cur Decorative Arts* Leslie Greone Bowman; *Asst Dir Exhib* Elizabeth Algermissen
Open Tues - Thurs 10 AM - 5 PM, Fri 10 AM - 9 PM, Sat & Sun 11 AM - 6 PM, cl Mon, Thanksgiving, Christmas & New Year's Day. Admis adults $5, students & senior citizens with ID $3.50, young people 6-12 $1, free day second Tues of each month, mus members & children under 5 free. Estab 1910 as Division of History, Science & Art; estab separately in 1961, for the purpose of acquiring, researching, publishing, exhibiting & providing for the educational use of works of art from all parts of the world in all media, dating from prehistoric times to the present. Maintains reference library. Average Annual Attendance: 1,000,000. Mem: 80,000; dues $45-$5000
Income: $30,000,000 (financed by endowment, mem & county appropriation)
Collections: †American art; †ancient & Islamic art; †contemporary art; †decorative arts; †European painting & sculpture; †Far Eastern art; †Indian & South Asian art; †textiles & costumes; †modern art; †prints & †drawings; †photography
Exhibitions: (1997) Exiles & Emigren's: The Flight of European Artists from Hitler; Galanos
Publications: Members Calendar, monthly, exhibition catalogs, 6-8 yearly; exhibition education brochures, 6 yearly, permanent collection catalogs, 3 yearly
Activities: Classes for adults & children; dramatic programs; docent training; lect open to public, 50 vis lectr per year; concerts; gallery talks; tours; films; individual paintings & original objects of art lent to other AAM-accredited museums for special exhibitions; lending collection contains original art work, original prints, paintings & 130,000 slides; originate traveling exhibitions organized & circulated; museum shop sells books, magazines, reproductions, prints, gifts, posters, postcards, calendars & jewelry
L **Allan C Balch Art Research Library**, 5905 Wilshire Blvd, 90036. Tel 213-857-6118; FAX 213-936-5755; Elec Mail library@lacma.org. *Librn* Deborah Barlow
Open Tues - Fri 10 AM - 5 PM. No admis fee. Estab 1965 to support research needs of mus staff & outside scholars, pub by appointment. For reference only
Library Holdings: Vols 105,000; Per subs 450; Artists' Files; Auction catalogs 27,000; AV — Slides, v-tapes; Other — Clipping files, exhibition catalogs, manuscripts
Special Subjects: Aesthetics, Afro-American Art, Antiquities-Assyrian, Archaeology, Asian Art, Crafts, Drawings, Etchings & Engravings, Furniture, Graphic Arts, Interior Design, Mosaics, Photography, Prints, Sculpture

L **Robert Gore Rifkind Center for German Expressionist Studies**, 5905 Wilshire Blvd, 90036. Tel 213-857-6165; FAX 213-936-5755; Elec Mail strauger@art.lacma.org. *Assoc Cur* Timothy Benson; *Librn* Susan Trauger; *Asst Registrar* Christine Vigiletti
Open by appointment. Reference library
Library Holdings: Vols 6000; Other — Exhibition catalogs, original art works, prints
Special Subjects: Art History, Decorative Arts, Drawings, Etchings & Engravings, Graphic Arts, Painting - German, Photography, Portraits, Posters, Printmaking, Prints, Sculpture, Watercolors, Woodcuts, German expressionism, Lithographs
Collections: German expressionist prints, †drawings, †books & periodicals
Publications: Publications relating to German Expressionist studies
Activities: Scholarships offered; individual graphics & illustrated books; periodicals lent to qualified institutions; book traveling exhibitions

M **LOS ANGELES MUNICIPAL ART GALLERY**, 4804 Hollywood Blvd, 90027. Tel 213-485-4581; FAX 213-485-8396; TDD: 213-660-4254. *Prog Dir* Noel Korten
Open Tues - Sun 12:30 - 5 PM. Admis $1.50. Estab to show Los Angeles artists

L **LOS ANGELES PUBLIC LIBRARY**, Arts & Recreation Dept, 630 W Fifth St, 90071-2002. Tel 213-228-7225; FAX 213-228-7229; *Dept Mgr* Romaine Ahlstrom
Open Mon, Wed, Fri & Sat 10 AM - 5:30 PM, Tues & Thurs Noon - 8 PM, cl Sun. No admis fee. Estab 1872
Income: Financed by municipality
Library Holdings: Vols 200,000; Per subs 800; Prints including original etchings, woodcuts, lithographs & drawings; Other — Clipping files, exhibition catalogs, framed reproductions, original art works, photographs, prints
Collections: Twin Prints; Japanese prints, including a complete set of Hiroshige's Tokaido Series
Exhibitions: Museum's Artists Scrapbooks, NY Public Artist's File

M **LOYOLA MARYMOUNT UNIVERSITY**, Laband Art Gallery, 7900 Loyola Blvd, 90045-8346. Tel 310-338-2880; FAX 310-338-6024; Elec Mail gfuglie@lmumail.lmu.edu. *Dir* Gordon Fuglie
Open Wed - Fri 11 AM - 4:30 PM, Sat Noon - 4 PM, cl Sun & Tues. No admis fee. Estab 1971 to hold exhibitions. The new gallery which opened in 1984, is 40 ft by 50 ft with 20 ft ceilings, track lighting & closeable skylights. Average Annual Attendance: 10,000
Exhibitions: Biennial national exhibitions of the Los Angeles Printmaking Society; (1997) The Eloquent Line: Contemporary Japanese Calligraphy. (1998) Divine Carriers: Contemporary Art from India
Publications: Catalogs, 2-3 per year
Activities: Lect open to public, 4-5 vis lectr per year; concerts; gallery talks; films; competitions with awards; originate traveling exhibitions

M **MOUNT SAINT MARY'S COLLEGE**, Jose Drudis-Biada Art Gallery, Art Dept, 12001 Chalon Rd, 90049. Tel 310-476-2237, 471-9584 (gallery); FAX 310-476-9296; *Gallery Dir* Olga Seem
Open Mon - Fri Noon - 5 PM. No admis fee. Estab to present works of art of various disciplines for the enrichment of students & community
Income: Financed by College
Collections: Collection of works by Jose Drudis-Blada
Exhibitions: Geno Mako Collection; Sedivy & Zokosky: Recent Paintings; Works on Paper; Drucker: Constructions; Geer Installation
Publications: Exhibitions catalogs, 1 per year
Activities: Lect open to public, 2-3 vis lectr per year; scholarships

M **THE MUSEUM OF CONTEMPORARY ART**, 250 S Grand Ave at California Plaza, 90012. Tel 213-621-2766; FAX 213-620-8674; *Chmn* David Laventhol; *Dir* Richard Koshalek; *Dir Admin* Kathleen Bartels; *Dir Develop* Erica Clark
Open Tues, Wed, Fri - Sun 11 AM - 5 PM, Thurs 11 AM - 8 PM, cl Mon. Admis general $6, sr citizens & students $4, children under 12 & MOCA members free. Estab 1979, emphasizing the arts since mid century, encompassing traditional & non-traditional media. Permanent building designed by Arata Isozaki opened in 1986. Average Annual Attendance: 300,000. Mem: 13,000; dues $45
Income: Financed by donations & admis fees, grants (private, corporate, NEA)
Collections: El Paso Collection; The Barry Lowen Collection; The Panza Collection; The Schreiber Collection; General Permanent Collection
Activities: Classes for children; docent training; lect open to public; gallery talks; tours; individual paintings lent to other institutions; originate traveling exhibitions; museum shop sells books, magazines, original art, posters, gifts

M **MUSEUM OF NEON ART**, 501 W Olympic Blvd, 90015. Tel 213-489-9918; FAX 213-489-9932; *Dir* Mary Carter
Open Wed - Sat 11 AM - 5 PM, Sun Noon - 5 PM, 2nd Thurs of month 11 AM - 8 PM. Admis adults $5, seniors & students $3.50. Estab 1981 to exhibit, document & preserve works of neon, electric & kinetic art. Consists of large main gallery for group or theme exhibitions & a small gallery for solo shows. Average Annual Attendance: 15,000. Mem: 300; dues $35 & up; annual meetings in Dec
Income: Financed by mem, donations, admis fees, gifts & grants
Collections: †Antique electrical signs; contemporary neon art
Exhibitions: Ladies of the Night; Victoria Rivers: Neon/Fabric Construction; Electro-Kinetic Box Art.
Publications: Transformer, quarterly
Activities: Classes for adults; lect open to public; concerts; gallery talks; tours; book traveling exhibition; originates travelings exhibitions; museum shop sells books, magazines, original art, reproductions, prints, slides, electronic jewelry & posters

M **NATURAL HISTORY MUSEUM OF LOS ANGELES COUNTY**, 900 Exposition Blvd, 90007. Tel 213-744-3414; FAX 213-744-2999; *Dir* Dr James Powell; *Chief Exhib* James Olson
Open Tues - Sun 10 AM - 5 PM, cl Mon, Thanksgiving, Christmas & New

Year's Day. Admis adults $6, senior citizens & students 12-17 $3.50, children 4-12 $2, members, children under 5 & first Tues of each month free. Estab 1913 to collect, exhibit & research collection in history, art & science; now focuses on American history, science & earth science. Average Annual Attendance: 1,400,000. Mem: 11,000; dues $25-$100; annual meeting in Sept
Income: Financed by county appropriation & private donations
Collections: †American historical works & decorative arts; †California & western paintings & prints; pre-Columbian artifacts
Exhibitions: Permanent exhibits: American History Halls; Chaparral: A Story of Life from Fire; Dinosaur Fossils; Egyptian Mummy; Gem & Mineral Hall; Habitat Halls; Lando Hall of California & Southwest History; Marine Biology Hall; Megamouth; Pre-Columbian Hall; Ralph M Parsons Children's Discovery Center; Ralph M Parsons Insect Zoo; The Ralph W Schreiber Hall of Birds
Publications: Science Bulletin; Contributions in Science; Terra, bi-monthly magazine
Activities: Classes for adults & children; docent training; lect open to public; gallery talks; tours; artmobile; individual & original objects of art lent to recognized museums, educational galleries & similar institutions; lending collection contains 30,000 color reproductions, 8653 native artifacts, 35,670 slides, 5500 small mammals, historical & scientific models; originate traveling exhibitions; museum & sales shops sell books, magazines, original art, reproductions, prints, slides & ethnic art objects
L **Research Library,** 900 Exposition Blvd, 90007. Tel 213-744-3388; *Chief Librn* Donald W McNamee; *Asst Librn* Mark E Herbert
Open to staff & pub by appointment for reference only
Library Holdings: Vols 102,000; Per subs 350; Micro — Reels 472; AV — Slides; Other — Clipping files, exhibition catalogs, memorabilia, pamphlets, photographs, prints
Special Subjects: Anthropology, Archaeology, Bookplates & Bindings, Coins & Medals, Decorative Arts, Dioramas, Dolls, Ethnology, Film, Folk Art, Maps, Pre-Columbian Art, Southwestern Art, Textiles

M **OCCIDENTAL COLLEGE,** Weingart & Coons Galleries, 1600 Campus Rd, 90041. Tel 213-259-2749 (art dept), 259-2714 (galleries); Elec Mail minta@edu. Open Mon - Fri 9 AM - 4:30 PM. No admis fee. Estab 1938 to acquaint students & visitors with contemporary concerns in the visual arts. Average Annual Attendance: 50,000
Activities: Lect open to public; gallery talks

M **OTIS COLLEGE OF ART & DESIGN,** 9045 Lincoln Blvd, 90045. Tel 213-251-0555, 251-0525 (Pres office); FAX 213-480-0059; *Dir* Anne Ayres; *Gallery Coordr* Jinger Heffner
Open Tues - Sat 10 AM - 5 PM. No admis fee. Estab 1954 as a forum for contemporary art. Gallery is white drywall; two rooms measuring 35 x 40 ft each with 16 ft ceilings. Average Annual Attendance: 20,000
Income: Financed by endowment
Collections: Contemporary art
Activities: Lect open to public, 2-3 vis lectr per year; gallery talks; book traveling exhibitions; originate traveling exhibitions to other university museums & galleries
L **Library,** 2401 Wilshire Blvd, 90057. Tel 213-251-0560; FAX 213-480-0059; *Dir* Sue Maberry
Open daily 9 AM - 5 PM for student & faculty use; open to pub by appointment only; cl weekends. Estab 1918 as a visual arts library
Library Holdings: Vols 30,000; Per subs 150; AV — A-tapes, cassettes, motion pictures, rec 150, slides 100,000, v-tapes 100; Other — Clipping files, exhibition catalogs, original art works, pamphlets, prints, reproductions 2500
Special Subjects: Advertising Design, Art History, Conceptual Art, Costume Design & Construction, Decorative Arts, Graphic Arts, Mixed Media, Photography, Contemporary Art

A **PLAZA DE LA RAZA CULTURAL CENTER,** 3540 N Mission Rd, 90031-3195. Tel 213-223-2475; FAX 213-223-1804; Elec Mail admin@plazaraza.org. *Exec Dir* Rose Cano; *School Coordr* Maria Jimenez-Torres
Open 9 AM - 6 PM, Boathouse Gallery open by appointment. No admis fee. Estab 1969 to preserve, promote & present Chicano/Mexican/Latino art & culture & promote new works. Boathouse Gallery houses Plaza's permanent collection of Latino art & also hosts temporary exhibits of the work of Chicano artists. Average Annual Attendance: 10,000. Mem: 100; dues $35 - $500
Income: $800,000 (financed by endowment, mem, city & state appropriation, grants from private & pub foundations)
Collections: Permanent collection of works by nationally known Latino visual artists
Activities: Adult classes in folk arts, dance & music; children classes in music, dance, visual arts, theatre & folk arts; dramatic programs; competitions; retail store sells prints, original art, reproductions & crafts

A **SAVING & PRESERVING ARTS & CULTURAL ENVIRONMENTS,** 1804 N Van Ness, 90028. Tel 213-463-1629; *Dir* Seymour Rosen
Open by appointment only. Estab 1978 for documentation & preservation of folk art environments. Mem: Dues $15-$250
Collections: Archival material about America's contemporary folk art environments
Publications: Occasional newsletter
Activities: Lect open to public, 6 vis lectr per year; gallery talks; tours; lending collection contains 20,000 photographs; originates traveling exhibitions; sales shop sells books, magazines, prints
L **Spaces Library & Archive,** 1804 N Van Ness, 90028. Tel 213-463-1629; *Dir* Seymour Rosen
Open by appointment only. Estab 1978 to provide reference for scholars, artists, preservations concerned with folk art environments. For lending & reference
Income: Financed by mem, individual appropriation, government & private grants
Library Holdings: Vols 300; AV — A-tapes, slides; Other — Clipping files, exhibition catalogs, manuscripts, memorabilia, photographs, sculpture
Special Subjects: Architecture, Art History, Collages, Constructions, Folk Art, Intermedia, Landscape Architecture, Folk art environments
Collections: Watts Tower Collection - photographs, documentation, archive,

letters, clippings, history
Exhibitions: Divine Disorder: Folk Art Environments in California
Publications: Spaces: Notes on America's Folk Art Environments, three times per year
Activities: Lect open to public, 5 vis lectr per year; originate traveling exhibitions

A **SELF HELP GRAPHICS,** 3802 Cesar E Chavez Ave, 90063. Tel 213-264-1259; FAX 213-881-6447; *Cur* Cristina Ochoa
Open Tues - Sat 10 AM - 4 PM. Estab 1972 to provide art opportunities for Chicano & all artists

M **SOUTHWEST MUSEUM,** 234 Museum Dr, PO Box 41558, 90041-0558. Tel 213-221-2164; FAX 213-224-8223; Elec Mail swmuseum@annex.com. *Exec Dir* Dr Duane King; *Chief Cur* Kathleen Whitaker; *Asst Dir* Jeannette O'Malley; *Cur Coll* Cheri Doyle; *Controller* Cheryl Petersen
Open Tues - Sun 10 AM - 5 PM, cl Mon. Admis adults $5, children $2, students & senior citizens $3, under 7 yrs free. Estab 1907. Four permanent halls focus on Native American culture. Average Annual Attendance: 60,000. Mem: 5300; dues $40 & up
Income: $1,360,000 (financed by endowment & mem)
Special Subjects: American Indian Art, American Western Art, Anthropology, Archaeology, Eskimo Art, Ethnology, Mexican Art, Photography, Pre-Columbian Art, Primitive Art, Southwestern Art
Collections: Anthropology & the science of man in the New World; prehistoric, historical, Spanish Colonial & Mexican provincial arts
Exhibitions: Permanent exhibits of Plains, Northwest Coast, California & Southwest Indian art & culture, plus three changing special exhibitions
Activities: Classes for children & adults; docent training; lect open to public, 10 vis lectr per year; tours; exten dept serves Los Angeles School District, individual paintings & original objects of art lent to other museums; book traveling exhibitions; museum shop sells books, magazines, original art & prints
L **Braun Research Library,** 234 Museum Dr, PO Box 41558, 90041-0558. Tel 213-221-2164; FAX 213-224-8223; Elec Mail swmuseum@annex.com. *Librn & Dir* Kim Walters
Open Wed - Sat 1 - 4:45 PM, cl Sun, Mon & Tues by appointment preferred. Estab 1907. For reference only
Library Holdings: Vols 50,000; Per subs 300; Micro — Cards, fiche, reels; AV — A-tapes, cassettes, fs, Kodachromes, lantern slides, motion pictures, rec, slides, v-tapes; Other — Clipping files, exhibition catalogs, framed reproductions, manuscripts, memorabilia, original art works, pamphlets, photographs, prints, reproductions
Special Subjects: Man in the New World, Indians of the Western Hemisphere, Anthropology of the Americas, Western Americana
Collections: George Wharton James's Collection; Joseph Amasa Munk's Collection; Charles F Lummis's Collection; Frederick Webb Hodge Collection

C **SUNAMERICA, INC,** The SunAmerica-Kaufman & Broad Home Corporation Collection, One SunAmerica Ctr, 90067-6022. Tel 310-772-6000; *Acting Cur* Joanne Heyler
Corporate collection estab in 1981 to bring contemporary art into the corporate workplace & support the local art community
Income: Financed by corporate budget
Collections: †Selection of works primarily by Southern California artists; emphasis on artists who had not had a major retrospective prior to 1975

C **TIMES MIRROR COMPANY,** Times Mirror Square, 90053. Tel 213-237-3819; *Supv Corporate Admin Serv* Elke G Corley
Annual amount of contributions and grants $100,000; supports museums by providing funds for acquisitions, constructions and operating (mostly in Southern California)
Collections: Primarily contemporary art, including works by Picasso, Steinberg, Tamayo, Helen Frankenthaler, Richard Diebenkorn, Frank Stella, Roy Lichtenstein & Peter Ellenshaw

UNIVERSITY OF CALIFORNIA, LOS ANGELES
M **Fowler Museum of Cultural History,** 405 Hilgard Ave, 90024-1549. Tel 310-825-4361; FAX 310-206-7007; *Dir* Dr Christopher B Donnan; *Asst Dir & Cur Africa, Oceania & Indonesia* Doran H Ross; *Admin Asst* Betsy Escandor; *Consulting Cur Costumes & Textiles* Patricia Anawalt; *Registrar* Sarah J Kennington; *Conservator* Jo Hill; *Photographer* Denis J Nervig; *Colls Mgr* Owen Moore; *Educ Dir* Betsy Quick; *Exhib Designer* David Mayo; *Publications Dir* Daniel R Brauer
Open Wed, Fri - Sun Noon - 5 PM, Thurs Noon - 8 PM. Estab in 1963 to collect, preserve & make available for research & exhibition objects & artifacts from cultures considered to be outside the Western tradition. Changing exhibitions on view Wed - Sun Noon - 5 PM
Income: Financed by endowment, state appropriation & private donations
Collections: Archaeological & ethnographic collections; 150,000 objects primarily from non-Western cultures - Africa, Asia, the Americas, Oceania, The Near East & parts of Europe
Publications: Exhibition catalogues; filmstrips; monographs; pamphlets; papers; posters; slide sets
Activities: Satellite Museum Program; Early Man Program; Chumash Indian Program; Publications Program; lect open to public, 1-3 vis lectr per year; tours; book traveling exhibitions; originate traveling exhibitions; museum shop sells books, jewelry, magazines, textiles
M **Grunwald Center for the Graphic Arts,** 10899 Wilshire Blvd, 90024. Tel 310-443-7076; FAX 310-443-7099; *Dir* David S Rodes; *Office Mgr* Caludine Dixon; *Dir Educ & Community Develop* Cindi Dale; *Assoc Dir & Cur* Cynthia Burlingham; *Registrar* Anne Bennett
Open Tues 11 AM - 8 PM, Wed - Fri 11 AM - 5 PM, Sat & Sun 1 - 5 PM, cl Mon & during Aug. No admis fee. Estab 1956. Gallery serves the university & pub; program is integrated with the University curricula. Average Annual Attendance: 175,000
Collections: Grunwald Center for the Graphic Arts: 35,000 prints, drawings, photographs & illustrated books from the 13th through 20th Centuries, including old master prints & drawings, Frank Lloyd Wight Collection of Japanese Prints,

Tamarind Lithography Archive; Fred Grunwald Collection of Daumier, The Rudolf L Baumfeld Collection of Landscape Drawings & Prints
Exhibitions: Three exhibitions annually
Publications: Exhibition catalogues; Jasper Johns, French Caricature, The Rudolf L Baumfeld Collection of Landscape Drawings & Prints
Activities: Gallery talks; tours daily; book traveling exhibitions; originate traveling exhibitions; museum shop sells books, magazines, original art, reproductions & various gift items

M **UCLA at the Armand Hammer Museum of Art & Cultural Center,** 10899 Wilshire Blvd, 90024. Tel 310-443-7000; FAX 310-443-7099; *Dir* Henry T Hopkins; *Assoc Dir* Paula Berry; *Admin Mgr* Patricia Capps; *Dir Educ & Community Develop* Cindi Dale; *Cur Exhibit* Elizabeth Shepherd; *Registrar* Susan Melton Lockhart
Open Tues, Wed, Fri & Sat 11 AM - 7 PM, Thurs 11 AM - 9 PM, Sun 11 AM - 5 PM, cl Mon, Thanksgiving, Christmas & July 4. Admis adults $4.50, senior citizens (65 & over), non-UCLA students, UCLA faculty & staff $3, UCLA students $1, mus members, children 17 & under free. Estab 1990. Gallery serves the university & pub; program is integrated with the University curricula. Average Annual Attendance: 150,000. Mem: 3000; dues fellow $1000, patron $500, sustaining $250, participating $100, active $45, UCLA faculty & staff & senior citizen $25, students $20
Collections: 300 paintings, including the Willitts J Hole Collection of the Italian, Spanish, Dutch, Flemish & English schools from the 15th-19th century; Franklin D Murphy Sculpture Garden: 70 sculptures from the 19th-20th centuries, including Arp, Calder, Lachaise, Lipchitz, Moore, Noguchi, Rodin & Smith; The Armand Hammer Collection includes approximately 100 paintings, primarily 19th century French artists; the Armand Hammer Daumier & Contemporaries Collection includes over 7000 works by 19th century French artist Honore Daumier & his contemporaries
Exhibitions: Ten exhibitions annually; operates in close conjunction with the UCLA Grunwald Center for the Graphic Arts
Publications: Exhibition catalogues; The Macchiaioli, California Assemblage; Silk Route & the Diamond Path; Chicano Art
Activities: Gallery talks; tours daily; book traveling exhibitions; originate traveling exhibitions; museum shop sells books & prints

L **Visual Resource Collection,** Department of Art History, 200 Dodd Hall, 90095-1417. Tel 310-825-3725; FAX 310-206-1903; Elec Mail ziegler@humnet.ucla.edu. *Dir* David Ziegler; *Asst Cur* Susan Rosenfeld
Library Holdings: AV — Fs, slides 300,000
Special Subjects: Afro-American Art, American Indian Art, American Western Art, Antiquities-Assyrian, Archaeology, Architecture, Asian Art, Costume Design & Construction, Decorative Arts, Etchings & Engravings, Ethnology, Film, Folk Art, Furniture, Graphic Arts

L **Arts Library,** Box 951392, 90095-1392. Tel 310-825-3817, 206-5426; *Head, Arts Library* Alfred Willis; *Arts Special Coll Librn* Brigitte Kueppers
Founded 1952
Library Holdings: Vols 180,000; Per subs 7000; Ephemera files; Micro — Fiche, reels; Other — Exhibition catalogs, manuscripts, photographs
Special Subjects: Architecture, Art History, Film, Theatre Arts, Television, Press Kits, Renaissance, Scripts
Collections: †One of four copies of Princeton's Index of Christian Art; †Elmer Belt Library of Vinciana; Judith A Hoffberg Collection of Bookworks & Artists' Publications

L **Elmer Belt Library of Vinciana,** Box 951392, 90095-1392. Tel 310-825-3817, 206-5425
Open by appointment Mon - Fri 9 AM - 5 PM. Estab 1961
Income: Financed by state appropriation
Library Holdings: Vols 10,000; Original documents; Micro — Reels; AV — Cassettes, fs, motion pictures; Other — Clipping files, exhibition catalogs, framed reproductions, manuscripts, memorabilia, original art works, pamphlets, photographs, prints, reproductions, sculpture
Special Subjects: Architecture, Art History, Graphic Arts, Painting - French, Painting - Italian, Sculpture, Leonardo da Vinci
Collections: Special collection of †rare books, †incunabula & related materials in Renaissance studies, with a focus on †Leonardo da Vinci, his manuscripts, miliu, art & thought

UNIVERSITY OF SOUTHERN CALIFORNIA

M **Fisher Gallery,** 823 Exposition Blvd, 90089-0292. Tel 213-740-4561; FAX 213-740-7676; *Dir* Dr Selma Holo; *Assoc to Dir* Kay Allen; *Exhib Designer* Trevor Norris; *Exhib Coordr* Jennifer Jaskowiak
Open Tues - Fri Noon - 5 PM, except for special exhibitiions. No admis fee. Estab 1939 as the art mus of the University. Fisher Gallery consists of three rooms, for changing exhibitions. Average Annual Attendance: 10,000
Income: Financed by endowment
Collections: Elizabeth Holmes Fisher Collection; Armand Hammer Collection; galleries house the permanent collections of paintings of 17th century Dutch, Flemish & Italian, 18th century British, 19th century French & American landscape & portraiture schools
Exhibitions: Keepers of the Flame: The Unofficial Artists of Leningrad
Publications: Exhibition catalogs, three annually
Activities: Lect open to public; concerts; gallery talks; tours; awards; individual paintings & original objects of art lent; lending collection contains original prints, paintings, sculpture; originate traveling exhibitions

L **Helen Topping Architecture & Fine Arts Library,** Watt Hall 4, 90089-0182. Tel 213-740-1956; FAX 213-749-1221; Elec Mail aciccone@usc.edu; Internet Home Page Address http://www-lib.usc.edu/info/afa. *Head Librn* Amy Navratil Ciccone; *Slide Cur* Howard Smith; *Reference & Instruction Librn* Aniko Halverson
Open Mon - Thurs 10 AM - 10 PM, Fri 10 AM - 5 PM, Sun 1 - 8 PM, cl Sat, summer hours Mon - Thurs 10 AM - 4 PM. Estab 1925 to provide undergraduate & graduate level students & the teaching & research faculty materials in the areas of architecture & fine arts needed to achieve their objectives. Branch library in the central library system is supported by the University, lending library. Circ 65,000
Income: Financed by University funds
Purchases: $95,000

Library Holdings: Vols 72,000; Per subs 285; Architectural drawings 1000; Artist's books 400; Micro — Reels; AV — Slides 260,000, v-tapes 90; Other — Clipping files, exhibition catalogs, pamphlets
Special Subjects: Antiquities-Roman, Architecture, Art History, Decorative Arts, Landscape Architecture, Latin American Art, Photography, California Art & Architecture, Museum Studies
Publications: Exhibit catalogs

L **Cinema-Television Library & Archives of Performing Arts,** University Library, 90089-0182. Tel 213-206-8013; FAX 213-749-1221; *Dir* Robert Rosen
Open academic semester 8:30 AM - 10 PM. No admis fee. Estab 1960
Library Holdings: Vols 18,000; Per subs 225; Micro — Cards, reels; AV — A-tapes, cassettes, rec, v-tapes; Other — Clipping files, manuscripts, memorabilia, pamphlets
Special Subjects: Film, Video
Collections: Film & television: scripts, stills, posters, production records, correspondence

A **FREDERICK R WEISMAN ART FOUNDATION,** 275 N Tarolwood Dr, 90077. Tel 310-277-5321; FAX 310-277-5075; *Registrar* Mary Eleen Powell
Estab 1982 as a non-profit foundation focusing on exhibition, workshop & award programs
Income: Financed by endowment
Collections: Contmporary Art: Installation Work; Mixed Media; Painting; Sculpture; Works on Paper
Publications: Workshop publication, semi-annual
Activities: Art purchase & curatorial achievement awards distributed annually to museum collections & professionals involved in contemporary art

C **WELLS FARGO & CO,** History Museum, 333 S Grand Ave, 90071. Tel 213-253-7166; *Cur* Lacinda Luther; *Asst Cur* Vicki L Marino
Open Mon - Fri 9 AM - 5 PM. Museum estab to demonstrate impact of Wells Fargo on California & American West. 6500 sq ft; approx 1000 objects on display. Average Annual Attendance: 30,000
Income: Financed by private funds
Collections: Authentic 19th century Concord Stagecoach; display of firearms; Dorsey Gold Collection of gold quartz ore; $50 gold piece; original Spanish language documents giving Los Angeles its city status in 1835; Perils of Road; Pony Express exhibit; two-pound gold nugget; Wells Fargo office
Exhibitions: Staging; mining; express; banking; South California
Publications: Various publications concerning Wells Fargo in US history
Activities: Dramatic programs; tours & off-site presentations; lect open to public; museum shop sells books, reproductions of memorabilia & prints

MENDOCINO

A **MENDOCINO ART CENTER,** Gallery, 45200 Little Lake St, PO Box 765, 95460. Tel 707-937-5818; FAX 707-937-1764; Internet Home Page Address http://www.mcn.org@mendoart. *Exec Dir* Elaine Beldin-Reed
Open Mon - Thurs 10 AM - 4 PM, Fri - Sun 10 AM - 5 PM, winter hours daily 10 AM - 5 PM. No admis fee. Estab 1959 as a rental-sales gallery for exhibition & sales of member work; also to sponsor traveling & mus exhibits. Two major gallery rooms, one gallery room available for rental of one-man shows. Average Annual Attendance: 25,000. Mem: 1000; dues $35
Collections: Graphics, paintings & sculpture
Publications: Arts & Entertainment, monthly
Activities: Classes for adults & children; docent training; lect open to public, 4-10 vis lectr per year; concerts; competitions; scholarships offered; individual paintings & original objects of art lent to business & public places; sales shop sells books, original art, reproductions, prints & crafts

L **Library,** 45200 Little Lake St, PO Box 765, 95460. Tel 707-937-5818; *Exec Dir* Elaine Beldin-Reed
Open Tues - Sat 11 AM - 2 PM. Estab 1975 to provide members with access to art books & magazines. Lending library for members of Art Center only. Circ 1350 books & 18 magazines
Income: Financed by donations & mem
Library Holdings: Vols 2500; Per subs 4; Picture File; Other — Prints, reproductions

MISSION HILLS

A **SAN FERNANDO VALLEY HISTORICAL SOCIETY,** 10940 Sepulveda Blvd, 91345. Tel 818-365-7810; *Cur* Lori Underwood
Open by appointment. No admis fee. Estab 1943. The Soc manages the Andres Pico Adobe (1834) for the Los Angeles City Department of Recreation & Parks, where they house their collection. Mem: dues life $100, active, sustaining & organization $15
Income: Financed by mem & donations
Collections: Historical material; Indian artifacts; paintings; costumes; decorative arts; manuscripts
Exhibitions: Permanent & temporary exhibitions
Activities: Lect; films; guided tours

L **Andres Pico Adobe Library,** 10940 Sepulveda Blvd, PO Box 7039, 91346. Tel 818-365-7810; *Pres* Ralph Herman; *Cur* Lori Underwood; *VPres* Neal Longen; *Newsletter Ed* Glenn Thornhill
Open by appointment. Estab 1970
Income: Financed by mem & gifts
Library Holdings: Vols 1000; AV — Cassettes; Other — Clipping files, manuscripts, memorabilia, original art works, pamphlets, photographs, prints
Collections: Citrus; Communities; Historical landmarks; Olive; Pioneers; San Fernando Mission; San Fernando Valley
Exhibitions: Ethnic contributions to valley history (for local school dist); 200 years valley agriculture (for SFV Fair), Valley history (local malls)
Publications: The Valley, monthly newsletter

MONTEREY

M CASA AMESTI, 516 Polk St, 93940. Tel 408-372-8173; *Pres* Luis Senton
Open Sat & Sun 2 - 4 PM, cl 2 wks July. Admis $1, children & members no
charge. Bequeathed to the National Trust in 1953 by Mrs Frances Adler Elkins.
It is an 1833 adobe structure reflecting phases of the history & culture of the part
of California owned by Mexico, after the period of Spanish missions & before
development of American influences from the Eastern seaboard. It is a prototype
of what is now known as Monterey style architecture. The Italian-style gardens
within the high adobe walls were designed by Mrs. Elkins, an interior designer, &
her brother, Chicago architect David Adler. The furnishings, largely European,
collected by Mrs. Elkins are displayed in a typical 1930s interior. The property is
a National Trust historic house. The Old Capital Club, a private organization,
leases, occupies & maintains the property for social & educational purposes
Collections: Elkins Collection of largely European furnishings
Activities: Monterey History & Art Association volunteers provide interpretive
services for visitors on weekends

A MONTEREY HISTORY & ART ASSOCIATION, 5 Custom House Plaza,
93940. Tel 408-372-2608; FAX 408-655-3054; *Pres* Jack Holt
No admis fee. Estab 1931. The Assoc owns the 1845 Casa Serrano Adobe, the
1865 Doud House, the 1845 Fremont Adobe, the Mayo Hayes o'Donnell Library
& the newly constructed Stanton Center - Monterey's Maritime Mus & History
Center. The Assoc celebrates the birthday of Monterey (June 3, 1770) with the
Merienda each year on the Sat nearest that date. The Assoc commemorates the
landing at Monterey by Commodore John Drake Sloat in 1846. Mem: 1800; dues
individual life mem $500, sustaining couple $75, sustaining single $50, couple
$25, single $15, junior $1
Income: Financed by mem, donations & fundraising activities
Collections: †Costumes, manuscripts & paintings, sculpture, †antique furniture,
†books, †photographs
Exhibitions: Permanent & temporary exhibitions; Fourth Grade History & Art
Contest
Publications: Noticias Del Puerto De Monterey, quarterly bulletin
Activities: Guided tours; competitions
M Maritime Museum of Monterey, 5 Custom House Plaza, 93942. Tel 408-375-
2553; *Dir* Donna Penwell
Open Sun - Sat 1 - 5 PM. Admis adults $5, children 3-17 $3, children 6-11 $2,
under 6 free. Estab 1971, moved 1992 into new facility along waterfront.
Maritime related artifacts & artwork; features operating light from Point Sur
Lighthouse. Average Annual Attendance: 12,000. Mem: 1800; dues $30 - $50;
annual meeting in Sept
Collections: Marine Artifacts, ship models, paintings, photographs, Fresnel First
Order Lens from Point Sur, California (on loan from US Coast Guard)
Exhibitions: Permanent & temporary exhibitions
Activities: Lect open to public, 12 vis lectr per year; gallery talks; tours;
competitions with awards; museum shop sells books, prints, original art,
reproductions & gift items
L Library, 5 Custom House Plaza, 93940-2430. Tel 408-372-2608; FAX 408-655-
3054; *Librn* Faye Messinger
Open Wed, Fri, Sat & Sun 1:30 - 3:30 PM. No admis fee. Estab 1971. Open for
research on the premises
Library Holdings: Vols 2500; Per subs 2; Local History archive; Other —
Manuscripts, memorabilia, original art works, photographs, prints
Special Subjects: Maritime history
Publications: Brochure of Museum with map

A MONTEREY MUSEUM OF ART ASSOCIATION, 559 Pacific St, 93940. Tel
408-372-7591, 372-5477; FAX 408-372-5680; *Dir* Richard W Gadd; *Pres* Jess
Brown; *VPres* Mary Green; *VPres* Peter Toyce; *VPres* Steve Hauk; *Treas* Bill
Keland; *Develop Dir* Donna Kneeland; *Dir Educ* Sandra Still
Open Wed - Sat 11 AM - 5 PM, Sun 1 - 4 PM, cl Mon, Tues, New Year's,
Christmas & Thanksgiving. No admis fee, donations requested. Estab 1959 to
perpetuate knowledge of & interest in the arts; to encourage a spirit of fellowship
among artists & to bring together the artist & the community at large. It
recognizes the need for the collection, preservation & exhibition of art works,
especially the best of those done in the area. The Frank Work Gallery (30 x 60
ft) houses temporary exhibitions; Maurine Church Coburn Gallery, temporary
exhibitions of painting, graphics & photography; five additional galleries which
are used to show permanent collection as well as temporary exhibitions. Average
Annual Attendance: 45,000. Mem: 2700; dues $35-$1000; annual meeting in July
Income: Financed by endowment, mem & fundraising functions
Collections: Armin Hansen Collection; William Ritschel Collection; American
art; Asian & Pacific; international fold ethnic & tribal arts; photography &
graphics; regional art, past & present
Exhibitions: Juried exhibitions; theme shows
Publications: Quarterly newsletter
Activities: Classes for adults & children; docent training; lect open to public;
concerts; dramatic programs; gallery talks; tours; in service training for teachers;
outreach program; scholarships; artmobile; Museum on Wheels teaches folk craft
classes in schools; book traveling exhibitions 1 per year; originate traveling
exhibitions; museum shop sells books, magazines, original art, reproductions,
prints, museum replicas & folk art objects

L MONTEREY PUBLIC LIBRARY, Art & Architecture Dept, 625 Pacific St,
93940. Tel 408-646-3932; *Dir* Paula Simpson
Open Mon - Thurs 9 AM - 9 PM; Fri 9 AM - 6 PM; Sat 9 AM - 5 PM; Sun 1 -
5 PM. Estab 1849
Income: Financed by mem & city appropriation
Purchases: $750,000
Library Holdings: Vols 100,000; Per subs 300; Micro — Reels; AV — Cassettes,
rec; Other — Clipping files, manuscripts, original art works, photographs,
reproductions
Special Subjects: Local history

M SAN CARLOS CATHEDRAL, 550 Church St, 93940. Tel 408-373-2628; *Rector*
Joseph Occhiuto
Open daily 8 AM - 6 PM. No admis fee. Built in 1770, now a branch of the
Monterey Diocese. The art museum is housed in the 1794 Royal Presidio Chapel
Collections: Spanish religious paintings and sculpture of the 18th and 19th
century
Activities: Guided tours

MONTEREY PARK

M EAST LOS ANGELES COLLEGE, Vincent Price Gallery, 1301 Avenide Nida
Csar Chevez Ave, 91754. Tel 213-265-8841; *Dir* Thomas Silliman
Estab 1958 as an institutional art gallery serving the East Los Angeles area
Collections: Includes art from Africa, Peruvian & Mexican artifacts dating from
300 B C, North American Indian Art; important works from the Renaissance to
the present day; Leonard Baskin; Daumier; Delacroix; Durer; Garvarni;
Hiroshige I; Rico Lebrun; Maillol; Picasso; Piranesi; Redon; Utrillo; Howard
Warshaw; Anuskiewicz; Bufano; Rouault; Tamayo
Exhibitions: Selections from the private collection of The Vincent Price Art
Collection

MORAGA

M SAINT MARY'S COLLEGE OF CALIFORNIA, Hearst Art Gallery, PO Box
5110, 94575-5110. Tel 510-631-4379; *Elec Mail* ahaslow@stmarys-ca.edu. *Dir*
Ann Harlow; *Cur* Marvin Schenck
Open Wed - Sun 11 AM - 4:30 PM, cl Mon & Tues & between exhibitions.
Suggested admis donation $1. Estab 1977 to exhibit a variety of the visual arts
for the benefit of college students, staff & members of surrounding communities.
Maintains two rooms with connecting rampway (1640 sq ft) for temporary
exhibitions, William Keith Room for permanent collection. Average Annual
Attendance: 11,000. Mem: 350; dues donor $50 & up, family $30, individual $20
Income: $275,000 (financed by college, donations, grants & earned income)
Collections: †Paintings by William Keith (1838-1911) & other California
landscapes; icons; medieval sculpture; †thematic print collection
Publications: Exhibition catalogues, 1 - 2 per yr
Activities: Lect open to public, 4-8 vis lectr per year; gallery talks; tours;
individual paintings & original objects of art lent to museums; book traveling
exhibitions 1 per year; originate traveling exhibitions to museums

NEVADA CITY

A ARTIST'S ALLIANCE OF CALIFORNIA, PO Box 2424, 95959. Tel 916-272-
7357; FAX 916-272-7357; *Pres* Bonnie Hall; *Ed-Asst* Katie Harrison; *Asst*
Dianne Lutz
Open by appointment. No admis fee. Estab 1993. Provides discounts on supplies
for artists; organizes exhibitions & sales. Mem: 250; dues single $45
Income: Financed by mem & sales
Publications: Review, newsletter 3-4 per year
Activities: Competitions

NEWHALL

M LOS ANGELES COUNTY MUSEUM OF NATURAL HISTORY, William S
Hart Museum, William S Hart Park, 24151 San Fernando Rd, 91321. Tel 805-
254-4584; FAX 805-254-6499; *Col Mgr* John Cahoon
Open winter Wed - Fri 10 AM - 1 PM, Sat - Sun 11 AM - 4 PM; summer mid-
June to mid-Sept Wed - Sun 11 AM - 4 PM. No admis fee. Estab through the
bequest of William S Hart (1946) & opened 1958 for use as a public park &
museum. The retirement home of William S Hart is maintained as it was during
his lifetime, his extensive collection of Western art is on display throughout the
house. Average Annual Attendance: 250,000. Mem: 250; dues $35; meetings
second Wed of every month
Income: Financed by county appropriation & private donations
Collections: Charles Cristadoro Sculpture Collection; Joe DeYong Collection of
paintings; Clarence Ellsworth Collection of watercolor & oil paintings; James M
Flagg Collection of oil & watercolor paintings, drawings; Gene Hoback
Collection of woodcarvings; Robert L Lambdin Collection of oil paintings;
Frederic Remington Collection of watercolor & oil paintings; Charles M Russell
Collection of oil & watercolor paintings, gouache, pen & ink; Charles
Schreyvogel Collection of oil paintings decorative arts; Navajo rugs
Activities: Classes for Adults; docent training; school outreach program; Classes
for adults; docent training; school outreach program; museum shop sells books,
videotapes, souvenirs

NEWPORT BEACH

M ORANGE COUNTY MUSEUM OF ART, Newport Harbor Art Museum, 850
San Clemente Dr, 92660. Tel 714-759-1122; FAX 714-759-5623; *Dir* Naomi
Vine; *Chief Cur* Bruce Guenther; *Dir Educ* Maxine Gaiber; *Dir Design &
Facility* Brian Gray; *Registrar* Tom Callus; *Dir Develop* Joan Van Hooten
Open Tues - Sun 10 AM - 5 PM, cl Mon. Admis adults $4, student, senior
citizen, military, groups of 10 $2, children 6-17 $1, children under 6 & Tues free.
Estab 1962 as a mus of the Art of our Time serving Orange County & Southern
California. Building completed in 1977 contains four galleries of various sizes;
5000; 1600; 500 sq ft plus lobby & sculpture garden area. Average Annual
Attendance: 100,000. Mem: 5500; dues business council $500, patron $150,
general mem $35, student $25
Income: $1,500,000 (financed by special events, mem, government grants, private
sector, sales from restaurant & bookstore)
Purchases: $100,000
Collections: Collections of contemporary American art; California artists
Publications: Bimonthly calendar; exhibition catalogs; posters

Activities: Docent training; in-service training sessions for teachers, docent tours for school & adult groups; lect series, special guest lectr & meet-the-artist programs; gallery talks; creative art workshops; concerts & performances; film & video programs; individual paintings & original objects of art lent to qualified art museums; lending collection contains original prints; paintings & sculptures; traveling exhibitions organized & circulated; museum shop sells books, magazines, original art

L **Library,** 850 San Clemente Dr, 92660. Tel 714-759-1122; *Librn* Ruth Roe
Open for reference by appointment
Income: Financed by Museum
Library Holdings: Vols 5000; Per subs 11; AV — A-tapes, cassettes, slides, v-tapes; Other — Clipping files, exhibition catalogs
Special Subjects: Contemporary art

NORTH HOLLYWOOD

L **WARNER BROS RESEARCH LIBRARY,** 5200 Lankershim Blvd, No 100, 91601. Tel 818-506-8693; FAX 818-506-8079; *Dir* Anne G Schlosser; *Research Librn* Barbara Poland
Open Mon - Fri 9 AM - 6 PM. Estab 1929 for picture & story research
Income: Financed by endowment
Library Holdings: Vols 35,000; Per subs 85; Other — Clipping files, pamphlets, photographs
Special Subjects: Costume Design & Construction, Fashion Arts, Film, Interior Design, Military, Travel & Description, Western History
Collections: †Art & Architecture History; †Costumes; †Interior Design; †Military & Police; †Travel & Description

NORTHRIDGE

M **CALIFORNIA STATE UNIVERSITY, NORTHRIDGE,** Art Galleries, 18111 Nordhoff St, 91330. Tel 818-677-2156, 677-2226; FAX 818-677-4545; *Dir* Louise Lewis; *Exhib Coordr* Ann Burroughs
Open Mon Noon - 4 PM, Tues - Fri 10 AM - 4 PM. No admis fee. Estab 1971 to serve the needs of the four art departments & to provide a source of cultural enrichment for the university & the community at large. Exhibitions in Main & South Galleries have average duration of four weeks. North Gallery for weekly MA candidate solo exhibitions. Average Annual Attendance: 35,000. Mem: Arts Council for CSUN 300; dues $25; annual meeting May
Income: $30,000 (financed by city & state appropriation, community support organizations)
Exhibitions: Nomads of the Niger; Images of the Barrio; Michael C McMillen: The Pavilion of Rain; Helen Hardin: Art as Spirit; Icons of the Divine: Lisa Lyon; Body Parts: Ilene Segalove; Women Redefining Power: International Graphics; International Chair Design; Jean Cocteau: Personalities; Artquest 87; Variations III: Emerging Artists in Southern California; Chicana Art; The Monumental Print; Dreamtime: Art of the Australian Aborigine; California Art Pottery 1895-1920; Beverly Naidus: Activating the Audience; The Art of Fly Tying
Publications: Exhibition catalogs, 2 per yr
Activities: Docent training; 2-3 art performances per year; lect open to public, 5-7 vis lectr per year; gallery talks; tours; competitions; sales shop sells books, magazines, original art, prints, reproductions, slides, folk art objects & gifts

OAKLAND

M **CALIFORNIA COLLEGE OF ARTS & CRAFTS,** Steven Oliver Art Center, 5212 Broadway, 94618. Tel 510-594-3650; FAX 510-428-1346; *Dir* Dyana Curreri
Open Mon - Fri 10 AM - 4 PM, Sat Noon - 4 PM. No admis fee. Estab 1989 to exhibit work of contemporary artists, craftspersons, architects & designers. 3600 sq ft exhibition area with 20 ft ceilings. Average Annual Attendance: 20,000. Mem: 2500
Income: $125,000 (financed by grants & tuition)
Collections: Alumni Collection, Contemporary Art
Publications: CCAC News, quarterly
Activities: Classes for adults & children; docent training; lect open to public, 10-15 vis lectr per year; book traveling exhibitions 2 per year

L **CALIFORNIA COLLEGE OF ARTS & CRAFTS LIBRARY,** 5212 Broadway & College Aves, 94618. Tel 510-653-8118, Ext 175; FAX 510-655-3541; *Dir Libraries* Mary Manning; *Librn* Nina Saab; *Librn* Michael Lordi
Open Mon - Thurs 8 AM - 9 PM, Fri 8 AM - 5 PM, Sat 11 AM - 6 PM. Estab 1907 to support the studio & academic requirements for BFA, BArchit & MFA; Branch Library in architecture & design
Income: $334,198 (financed by tuition)
Purchases: $61,850
Library Holdings: Vols 42,208; Per subs 230; AV — A-tapes 320, rec, slides 12,000
Special Subjects: Aesthetics, Architecture, Art History, Ceramics, Drawings, Film, Furniture, Glass, Graphic Design, Illustration, Industrial Design, Interior Design, Jewelry, Metalwork, Photography
Collections: Jo Sinel Collection of pioneering work in industrial design

M **CREATIVE GROWTH ART CENTER,** 355 24th St, 94612. Tel 510-836-2340; FAX 510-836-2349; Elec Mail creativg@dnai.com. *Exec Dir* Irene Ward Brydon; *Studio Mgr* Ron Kilgore; *Gallery Mgr* Bonnie Haight; *Business Mgr* Timothy Sauer
Open Mon - Fri 10 AM - 4 PM. No admis fee. Estab 1974 to professionally exhibit the art of Creative Growth & art work by outsider & well-known artists. Average Annual Attendance: 4000
Income: $800,000
Collections: Permanent collection includes art works in all media on traditional & contemporary subjects
Exhibitions: Individual & group shows; 9 exhibitions held per year in house

gallery; 10 exhibitions in variety of locations
Publications: Creative Growth Art Center newsletter, 3-4 issues per year
Activities: Docent programs; lect open to public, 6-8 vis lectr per year; competitions with awards; scholarships & fels offered; retail store sells prints, original art, reproductions

M **EAST BAY ASIAN LOCAL DEVELOPMENT CORP,** Asian Resource Gallery, 310 Eighth St, Ste 309, 94607. Tel 510-287-5353; FAX 510-763-4143; *Admin Coordr* Ann G Yee
Open Mon - Fri 8 AM - 6 PM. No admis fee. Estab 1983 to promote Asian art & Asian artists
Income: $3000
Collections: Collection of photographs, paintings, mixed media; history exhibits on Asian groups from China, Japan & Korea

L **LANEY COLLEGE LIBRARY,** Art Section, 900 Fallon St, 94607. Tel 510-464-3500; *Art Librn* Shirley Coaston
Open Mon - Thurs 8 AM - 9 PM, Fri 8 AM - 2 PM, Sat 8:30 AM - 1:30 PM, cl Sun. Estab 1954. Circ 78,000
Library Holdings: Vols 81,000; Per subs 300; Compact discs; Laser discs; AV — A-tapes, cassettes, fs, Kodachromes, lantern slides, motion pictures, rec, slides, v-tapes; Other — Prints, reproductions
Exhibitions: Ceramics, community persons, fabrics, paintings, photography by students & faculty, sculpture
Publications: Monthly newsletter

M **MILLS COLLEGE,** Art Gallery, 5000 MacArthur Blvd, 94613. Tel 510-430-2164; FAX 510-430-3168; *Dir* Dr Katherine B Crum; *Asst Dir* Keith Lachowicz
Open Tues - Sat 11 AM - 4 PM, Sun Noon - 4 PM. No admis fee. Estab 1925 to show contemporary & traditional painting, sculpture & ceramics, exhibitions from permanent & loan collections. Gallery is Spanish colonial architecture & has 5500 sq ft main exhibition space, with skylight full length of gallery. Average Annual Attendance: 24,000
Income: Financed by college funds; grants & gifts
Purchases: Nagle, DeFeo, Bellows, Kales
Collections: †Asian & Guatemalan Collection (textiles); †European & American Collection (prints, drawings & ceramics); †Regional California Collection (paintings, drawings & prints); †photographs
Publications: Annual bulletin; exhibition catalogs
Activities: Lect open to public, 3 vis lectr per year; gallery talks; individual paintings & original objects of art lent; book traveling exhibition; originate traveling exhibition

M **OAKLAND MUSEUM OF CALIFORNIA,** Art Dept, 1000 Oak St, 94607. Tel 510-238-3005 (art); FAX 510-238-2258, 238-2200 (general information); *Sr Cur Art* Harvey L Jones; *Sr Cur* Karen Tsujimoto; *Registrar* Arthur Monroe; *Chief Cur Art* Philip Linhares
Open Wed - Sat 10 AM - 5 PM, Sun Noon - 7 PM, cl Mon, Tues, New Year's, Thanksgiving & Christmas. Admis general $5, seniors & students $3, 5 yrs & under free & 4-7 PM Sun. The Oakland Mus of California comprises three departments: Natural Sciences (formerly the Snow Mus of Natural History, founded 1922); History (formerly the Oakland Pub Mus, founded 1910); & the Art Department (formerly the Oakland Art Mus, founded 1916). Internationally recognized as a brilliant contribution to urban mus design. The Oakland Mus occupies a 4 sq block, three-storied site on the south shore of Lake Merritt. Designed by Kevin Roche, John Dinkeloo & Associates, the mus is a three-tiered complex of exhibition galleries, with surrounding gardens, pools, courts & lawns, constructed so that the roof of each level becomes a garden & a terrace for the one above. The Art Department has a large hall with 20 small exhibition bays for the permanent collection & 3 galleries for one-person or group shows as well as the Oakes Gallery. Average Annual Attendance: 500,000
Income: Financed by city funds, private donations & Oakland Mus of California Foundation
Collections: Paintings, sculpture, prints, illustrations, photographs, by California artists & artists dealing with California subjects, in a range that includes sketches & paintings by early artist-explores; gold Rush genre pictures; massive Victorian landscapes; examples of the California Decorative Style, Impressionist, Post-Impressionist, Abstract Expressionist, & other contemporary works
Exhibitions: (1997) This Is Our Land! Teens Speak Out on Nature & Community in the City; In Front of the Lens: Portraits of California Photographers; Expressions in Woods: Masterworks from the Warnick Collection; Hello Again: A New Wave of Recycled Art & Design; Memory & Imagination: The Legacy of Maidu Indian Artist Frank Day; California Species: Biological Art & Illustrations; California Wildflower Show; The Art of John Cederquist: Reality of Illusion; William T Wiley (working title). (1997-98) A Poetic Vision: The Photography of Anne Brigman. (1998) California Gold Rush; Art of the Gold Rush; Silver & Gold: Cased Images of the California Gold Rush; Farewell, Promised Land; Maidu Paintings by Dal Castro: From the Aeschliman-McGreal Collection of the Oakland Museum of California. (1998-99) California Caves (working title); Chinese American Women; Transformation: The Art of Joan Brown (working title)
Publications: The Museum of California, quarterly; Oakland Museum of California, bimonthly calendar of exhibitions & events
Activities: Docent training; lect open to public; gallery talks; tours; individual paintings & original objects of art lent to other museums & galleries for specific exhibitions; originate traveling exhibitions; museum shop sells books, magazines, reproductions, prints, slides & jewelry

L **Library,** 1000 Oak St, 94607-4892. Tel 510-238-3005; FAX 510-238-2258; Library maintained on archives of California art & artists. For in-house use only, cl to the pub at this time
Income: Financed by city & state appropriation
Library Holdings: Per subs 19; Bk vols & catalogues 7000; Other — Clipping files, photographs
Special Subjects: American Western Art, Crafts, Decorative Arts, Photography, Printmaking

L **OAKLAND PUBLIC LIBRARY,** Art, Music & Recreation Section, Main Library, 125 14th St, 94612. Tel 510-238-3134, 238-3178 (art dept); *Dir Library Servs* Martin Gomez; *Sr Librn in Charge* Jean Blinn
Open Mon - Thurs 10 AM - 8:30 PM, Fri Noon - 5:30 PM, Sat 10 AM - 5:30 PM, Sun 1 - 5 PM, cl holidays. Library cooperates with the Oakland Mus & local groups
Purchases: $30,000
Library Holdings: Vols 1,000,000; Per subs 2745; Posters; AV — A-tapes, cassettes, rec; Other — Framed reproductions, reproductions
Collections: Picture Collections
Publications: Museum catalogs

M **PRO ARTS,** 461 Ninth St, 94607. Tel 510-763-4361; FAX 510-763-9425; *Board Pres* Randolph Belle
Open Wed & Thurs Noon - 6 PM, Fri & Sat 11 AM - 5 PM. Estab 1974 as a contemporary art exhibition space for static & non-static works, non-profit. Store-front gallery located in restored Old Oakland, 2500 sq ft, 14 ft ceilings. Average Annual Attendance: 20,000. Mem: 600; dues $20 & up

A **SURFACE DESIGN ASSOCIATION, INC,** PO Box 20799, 94620. Tel 707-829-3110; FAX 707-829-3285; *Pres* Jason Pollen; *VPres* Jani Mohr; *Treas* Kay Campbell; *Ed Surface Design Journal* Patricia Malarcher
No admis fee. Estab 1976. Mem: 2200; dues regular $45, students $25, outside USA $6
Income: Financed by mem
Publications: SDA Newsletter, quarterly; Surface Design Journal, quarterly
Activities: Classes for adults; national conference; lect open to members only; competitions with cash prizes; scholarships & fels offered; originate traveling exhibitions

OJAI

A **OJAI VALLEY ART CENTER,** 113 S Montgomery, PO Box 331, 93023. Tel 805-646-0117; *Pres* Rupert Goodspeed; *Mgr* Teri Mettala
Open Tues - Sun Noon - 4 PM. No admis fee. Estab 1936 to foster all art disciplines in community. Gallery is 40 x 50 ft, high ceilings, with a large hanging area. Average Annual Attendance: 60,000. Mem: 400; dues family $25, adult $10; annual meeting in Jan
Income: Financed by mem, class & special event fees
Exhibitions: Twelve monthly exhibitions; Annual Watercolor Competition
Publications: Newsletter, monthly; Ojai Review, quarterly
Activities: Classes for adults & children; dramatic programs; lect open to public; concerts; gallery talks; competitions with awards; scholarships offered; museum shop sells books, magazines & original art

OROVILLE

M **BUTTE COLLEGE,** Coyote Gallery, 3536 Butte Campus Dr, 95965. Tel 916-895-2208; FAX 916-895-2346; *Dir* Idie Adams
Estab 1981, a contemporary college art gallery. Average Annual Attendance: 2000
Exhibitions: Annual Juried Student Art Exhibit; contemporary art of a local, regional & national orientation
Activities: Classes for adults; lect open to public, 3-4 vis lectr per year

OXNARD

M **CARNEGIE ART MUSEUM,** * 424 S C St, 93030. Tel 805-385-8157; *Dir* Andrew Voth; *Cur* Mary S Bellah
Open Thurs, Fri & Sat 10 AM - 5 PM, Sun 1 - 5 PM. Admis $2 donation suggested. Estab 1980 to serve as a city museum and to house permanent collection. 5000 sq ft of gallery space. Average Annual Attendance: 15,000
Income: $190,000 (financed by endowment, city appropriation, city & non-profit support)
Purchases: $8500
Collections: †California Painters: 1920 to present; Art in Public Places Program
Publications: Master of the Miniature: The Art of Robert Olszewski; Municipal Art Collection Catalogue; Quechuan Rug Catalogue; Theodor Lukits Catalogue
Activities: Classes for adults & children; docent programs; lect open to public, 6 vis lectrs per year; book traveling exhibitions, 4 per year; originate traveling exhibitions that circulate to other US & foreign museums

PACIFIC GROVE

A **PACIFIC GROVE ART CENTER,** 568 Lighthouse Ave, PO Box 633, 93950. Tel 408-375-2208; *Office Mgr* Connie Pearlstein; *Preparator* Michael Kainer; *Pres Board* Joanna Chapman
Open Tues - Sat Noon - 5 PM, Sun 1 - 4 PM. No admis fee. Estab 1969 to promote the arts & encourage the artists of the Monterey Peninsula & California. Four galleries consist of 6000 sq ft of exhibition space, showing traditional & contemporary fine art & photography; galleries are available for classes & lectures. Average Annual Attendance: 25,000. Mem: 550; dues business & club $100, family $25, single $20, annual meeting in Nov
Income: Financed by grants, donations & income from lease of studio space
Collections: †Photography; †painting
Exhibitions: Multiple exhibits every 6 weeks throughout the year
Publications: Monthly newsletter
Activities: Educ dept; classes for adults & children; dramatic programs; concerts; lect open to public, 6-12 vis lectr per year; concerts; gallery talks; tours; competitions; sales shop sells books, original art, prints, photos, jewelry, t-shirts & frames

PALM SPRINGS

M **PALM SPRINGS DESERT MUSEUM,** 101 Museum Dr, PO Box 2288, 92263. Tel 619-325-7186; FAX 619-327-5069; *Dir* Dr Janice Lyle; *Dir Educ* Sidney Williams; *Cur Natural Science* James W Cornett; *Dir Coll & Exhib* Katherine Plake Hough; *Dir Performing Arts* Dick Horner; *Dir Performing Arts* Lynne Stuart
Open Tues - Thurs 10 AM - 5 PM, Fri 10 AM - 8 PM, Sat & Sun 10 AM - 5 PM, cl Mon. Admis adults $6, students & children 6-17 $2, members & children under 6 free; free admis the first Fri of every month. Estab 1938 to offer culture & educational opportunities to all interested persons. Includes Annenberg Theater. Average Annual Attendance: 200,000. Mem: 5000; dues sustaining benefactor $75000, sustaining patron $3500, President's Circle $1000, patron $500, contributing $250, business & supporting $100, family/dual $60, individual $40
Income: Financed by private funds
Collections: Steve Chase Collection; William Holden Collection; Interpretation of natural sciences of the desert; 19th-20th century American painting, prints & sculpture specializing in California artists; Southwestern Native American art
Exhibitions: Artist's Council National Juried Exhibition; Fine Arts Creativity Program; Science Fair; Approximately 30 exhibitions per year
Publications: Calendar of Events, bi-monthly; special exhibiton catalogs each season
Activities: Classes for adults & children; docent training; student visits to museum; out-reach docent art classes; on-site child/adult classes; lect open to public, 30 vis lectr per year; concerts; gallery talks; tours; competiitons with awards; exten dept servs Adult university Ar/Natural Science Classes; book traveling exhibitions 4 per year; originate traveling exhibitions; museum shop sells books, magazines, original art, reproductions, jewelry, educational childrens toys & cards

L **Library,** 101 Museum Dr, PO Box 2288, 92263. Tel 619-325-7186; FAX 619-327-5069; *Dir* Janice Lyle, PhD; *Cur* Katherine Hough; *Educ* Sidney Williams; *Natural Sciences* James W Cornett
Open for reference only; art & natural science books available for use on premises by members
Library Holdings: Vols 6000; Per subs 82; Other — Photographs
Special Subjects: American Indian Art, American Western Art, Anthropology, Archaeology, Art Education, Art History, Bronzes, Folk Art, Graphic Arts, History of Art & Archaeology, Islamic Art, Mexican Art, Mixed Media, Oriental Art, Photography, Porcelain, Portraits, Pottery, Pre-Columbian Art, Printmaking, Religious Art
Publications: Exhibition Catalogs

PALO ALTO

A **PALO ALTO CULTURAL CENTER,** 1313 Newell Rd, 94303. Tel 415-329-2366; FAX 415-326-6165; *Dir* Linda Craighead; *Vol Coordr* Shiela Pastore; *Cur* Signe Mayfield; *Workshop Supv* Gary Clarien; *Office Mgr* Jean Dickson; *Children's Prog* Larnie Fox
Open Tues - Sat 10 AM - 5 PM, Tues - Thurs evenings 7 - 10 PM, Sun 1 - 5 PM, cl Mon. No admis fee. Estab 1971 to stimulate aesthetic expertise & awareness in the Palo Alto & surrounding communities. Average Annual Attendance: 86,000. Mem: 625; dues $1000, $500, $250, $100, $50, $25, $15
Income: $700,000 (financed by municipal funds, private donations & earned income)
Collections: Contemporary & historical art
Publications: Palo Alto Cultural Center Newsletter/Calendar, quarterly; exhibit catalogues
Activities: Classes for adults & children; dramatic programs; docent training; lect open to public, 6-8 vis lectr per year; concerts; gallery talks; tours; competitions; museum shop sells books, original art, reproductions, prints & objects for sale related to exhibitions

M **PALO ALTO JUNIOR MUSEUM & ZOO,** 1451 Middlefield Rd, 94301. Tel 415-329-2111; *Dir* John Walton; *Instructor Arts & Crafts* Debbie Hillyer
Open Tues - Sat 10 AM - 5 PM, Sun 1 - 4 PM, cl New Years, Easter, July 4, Thanksgiving & Christmas; Baylands Interpretive Center: Wed - Fri 2 - 5 PM, Sat & Sun 10 AM - 5 PM, cl Thanksgiving & Christmas. No admis fee. Estab 1932, completely renovated in 1969. Average Annual Attendance: 100,000
Income: Financed by city appropriation
Collections: Art & artifacts
Publications: Notes, monthly; Prehistoric Palo Alto (brochure)
Activities: Classes; guided tours; exten dept; sciencemobile

PASADENA

L **ART CENTER COLLEGE OF DESIGN,** James Lemont Fogg Memorial Library, 1700 Lida St, 91103-1999. Tel 818-396-2233; FAX 818-568-0428; *VPres & Dir* Elizabeth Galloway; *Catalog Librn* Alison Holt; *Slide Cur* Theresa Pendlebury; *Acquisitions Librn* George Porcari; *Circulation Supv* Arlene Sanchez-Walsh; *Circulations Supv* Steven Hanson; *Reference Librn* Michelle Betty; *Photo Research Cur* Tess Norbut
Open Mon - Thurs 8:30 AM - 10 PM, Fri 8:30 AM - 5 PM, Sat 8:30 AM - 4 PM, cl Sun. Estab to provide reference & visual resources for the designers who study & teach at Art Center College of Design. For lending & reference. Circ 90,000
Income: Financed by institution & private grants
Purchases: $85,000 (books); $45,000 (periodicals); $30,000 (videos & slides)
Library Holdings: Vols 46,072; Per subs 450; AV — Cassettes, motion pictures 100, slides 90,000, v-tapes 2200; Other — Clipping files 28,000, exhibition catalogs 1850, reproductions
Special Subjects: Advertising Design, Commercial Art, Graphic Design, Illustration, Industrial Design, Photography, Environmental Design, Fine Arts, History of Design, Moving Pictures, Packaging Design

M PACIFIC - ASIA MUSEUM, 46 N Los Robles Ave, 91101. Tel 818-449-2742; *Exec Dir* David Kamansky; *Dir Develop* Jan Saiget; *Dir Admin* Edward Prohaska; *Communications Coordr* Paul Little; *Educ Coordr* Betty Wan; *Registrar* Debra J Bailey; *Asst Cur* Dorothy Roraback; *Vol Coordr* Liz Corey
Open Wed - Sun 10 AM - 5 PM, cl holidays. Admis adults & non-members $3, senior citizens & students $1.50, under 12 free. Estab 1971 to promote understanding of the cultures of the Pacific & Far East through exhibitions, lectures, dance, music & concerts. Through these activities, the mus helps to increase mutual respect & appreciation of both the diversities & similarities of Asian/Pacific & Western cultures. The building was designed by Marston, Van Pelt & Mayberry, architects for Grace Nicholson. The building is listed in the national register of historic places as the Grace Nicholson Building. There is 11,000 sq ft of exhibition space. Average Annual Attendance: 50,000. Mem: 1600; dues benefactor $1000. donor $600, sponsor $350, patron $150, contributor $75, active $37
Collections: Bronzes; Buddhist sculptures; Chinese & Japanese paintings & ceramics; Chinese textiles; †Oriental art objects; Southeast Asian ceramics
Publications: Exhibit catalogs
Activities: Classes for adults & children; docent training; lect open to public; gallery talks; tours; original objects of art lent to other museums & limited number of libraries; originate traveling exhibitions to schools, libraries & other museums; museum shop sells books, magazines, original art, reproductions & prints

M PASADENA CITY COLLEGE, Art Gallery, Art Dept, 1570 E Colorado Blvd, 91106. Tel 818-585-7238; *Dir* Allen Harrison
Open Mon - Fri 11 AM - 3 PM, Mon & Tues evenings 7 - 9 PM. No admis fee. Estab to show work that relates to class given at Pasadena City College. Gallery is housed in separate building; 1000 sq ft. Average Annual Attendance: 20,000. Mem: 2800 (financed by school budget)
Collections: Small permanent collection of contemporary art
Exhibitions: Clothing Design; painting; sculpture; Faculty Show; Advertising Design; Student Show; Print Show
Publications: Mailers for each show
Activities: Educ dept; lect open to public, 5-10 vis lectr per year; gallery talks; competitions; book traveling exhibitions occasionally

M PASADENA HISTORICAL MUSEUM, 470 W Walnut St, 91103. Tel 818-577-1660; FAX 818-577-1662; *Exec Dir* James Auerbach; *Archivist* Tania Rizzo; *Educator* Ardis Willwerth
Open Thurs - Sun 1 - 4 PM. Admis adults $4, students & senior citizens $3, children under 12 free. Estab 1924 for the preservation & collection of historical data relating to Pasadena. Historical house with American Impressionist Art. Average Annual Attendance: 10,000. Mem: 750; dues $35, annual meeting fourth Sun in Jan
Income: $159,000 (financed through mem, endowment & contributions)
Library Holdings: Vols 10,000; Other — Clipping files, manuscripts, memorabilia, original art works, photographs
Collections: Collection of documents & artifacts relating to Pasadena; Collection of paintings by California artists European & American furniture (antiques & reproductions); 750 photographs; rare books & manuscripts; Turn of the Century Life Style on Millionaire's Row
Publications: Quarterly newsletter
Activities: Classes for adults; docent & junior docent training; lect open to public, 4-8 vis lectr per year; gallery talks; tours; sales shop sells books, magazines, prints & gift items

L PASADENA PUBLIC LIBRARY, Fine Arts Dept, 285 E Walnut St, 91101. Tel 818-405-4052; *Dir* Luis Herrera; *Head Reference* Robin Weed-Brown
Open Mon - Thurs 9 AM - 9 PM, Fri & Sat 9 AM - 6 PM, Sun 1 - 5 PM. No admis fee. Art dept estab 1927
Income: Financed by endowments & gifts, for materials only
Library Holdings: Vols 22,000; Per subs 60; Compact Discs 3600; Micro — Fiche, reels; AV — Cassettes 4200, rec 2000, v-tapes 2279; Other — Photographs, reproductions

M NORTON SIMON MUSEUM, 411 W Colorado Blvd, 91105. Tel 818-449-6840; FAX 818-796-4978; *Exec VPres* Walter Timoshuk; *Cur* Gloria Williams; *Dir Art* Sara Campbell; *Registrar* Andrea Clark; *Rights & Reproductions* Marcy Guzman
Open Thurs - Sun Noon - 6 PM. Admis Thurs - Sat: adults $4, students & senior citizens $2; members & children under 12 accompanied by adult free. Estab 1974; this museum brings to the western part of the United States one of the worlds great collections of paintings, tapestries, prints & sculptures for the cultural benefit of the community at large; the museum is oriented toward the serious & meticulous presentation of masterpiece art. Average Annual Attendance: 150,000. Mem: Dues $35-$1000
Income: Financed by endowment, mem, city appropriation, tours, admis, contributions, bookshop & grounds maintenance
Collections: Art spanning 14 centuries: including paintings, sculptures, tapestries & graphics from the early Renaissance through the 20th century; Indian & Southeast Asian sculpture
Exhibitions: Degas bronze sculptures; Goya prints; Picasso; Vangogh: Painter, Printmaker, Collector; etchings of Rembrandt; Southeast Asian and Indian Sculpture
Publications: Masterpieces from the Norton Simon Museum
Activities: Private guided tours; museum shop sells books, magazines reproductions, slides & postcards

PENN VALLEY

A ARTNETWORK, 18757 Wildflower Dr, PO Box 1268, 95946. Tel 916-432-7630; FAX 916-432-7633; *Dir* Constance Smith
Open daily 9 AM - 5 PM. Estab 1986 to publish marketing information for fine artists & art world professionals
Publications: Art Marketing 101; Art Marketing Sourcebook, biannual; Art Source Quarterly newsletter; Artworld Hotline; Encyclopedia of Living Artists, biannual; semimonthly newsletter
Activities: Marketing seminars; lect open to public; competitions

QUINCY

M PLUMAS COUNTY MUSEUM, 500 Jackson, PO Box 10776, 95971. Tel 916-283-6320; FAX 916-283-6415; *Dir* Scott Lawson; *Asst Cur* Evelyn Whisman
Open winter Mon - Fri 8 AM - 5 PM, summer Mon - Fri 8 AM - 5 PM, Sat 10 AM - 4 PM. No admis fee. Estab 1964 to preserve the past for the enjoyment & edification of the present & future generations. 1878 historical home next door has been restored & opened to the pub with period rooms. Average Annual Attendance: 18,000. Mem: 300; dues life $100, general per yr $5; meetings held bi-annually
Income: Financed by members & county budget
Purchases: $300
Collections: Antique period furnishings, Indian (Maidu) artifacts, dolls, clothing, mining & logging artifacts, domestic, jewelry, guns, period furniture, Historic Home Museum adjacent; railroad collection, memorabilia; Coburn Variel Home
Exhibitions: Steam Forever: James E Boynton Collection
Publications: Plumas County Museum Newsletter, two times a year
Activities: Lect open to public

L Museum Archives, 500 Jackson, PO Box 10776, 95971. Tel 916-283-6320; FAX 916-283-6415; *Dir* Scott Lawson; *Asst Cur* Evelyn Whisman
Open Mon - Fri 8 AM - 5 PM, May-Sept 10 AM - 4 PM. Admis adults $1, 17 & under $.50, children & members free. Estab 1964 to preserve Plumas County's rich heritage & history. Library for reference use only. Average Annual Attendance: 25,000. Mem: 300; dues $10 & up; annual meeting in June
Income: $80,000 (financed by county, memorial donations, mem, book store sales & personal donations)
Library Holdings: Vols 2000; Per subs 1000; Negatives; Micro — Prints, reels; AV — A-tapes, cassettes, Kodachromes, motion pictures, slides; Other — Clipping files, exhibition catalogs, memorabilia, original art works, pamphlets, photographs, prints, reproductions
Special Subjects: Logging, Mining, Railroad
Collections: Indian jewelry; Maidu Indian Basket Collection; agriculture; bottles; china; crystal; dolls; furniture; logging; mining; musical instruments; railroad items; toys; Coburn Variel home
Activities: Docent training; demonstrations; lect open to public; gallery talks; tours; sales shop sells books, original art, reproductions, photographs

RANCHO PALOS VERDES

A PALOS VERDES ART CENTER, 5504 W Crestridge Rd, 90275. Tel 310-541-2479; FAX 310-541-9520; *Prog Dir* Mary Drosny; *Educ Dir* Janene Ferguson; *Pub Relations Dir* June Romine; *Exhib Dir* Anne Morris
Open Mon - Fri 9 AM - 4 PM, Sat & Sun 1 - 4 PM, cl Christmas & New Year's. No admis fee. Estab 1931 to provide cultural enrichment thru art educ, exhibitions & outreach. Changing exhibits in 4 galleries. Average Annual Attendance: 15,000. Mem: dues $50-$1000; annual meeting in June
Income: Financed by mem & private donations
Exhibitions: Twenty-four temporary exhibits per year
Publications: Exhibit catalogs; The Quarterly
Activities: Classes for children; docent training; lect open to public, 25 vis lectr per year; gallery talks; library tours; competitions with awards; sales shop sells prints & wearable art

RED BLUFF

M KELLY-GRIGGS HOUSE MUSEUM, 311 Washington St (Mailing add: 1248 Jefferson St, CA 96080). Tel 916-527-1129; *Pres* Helen McKenzie Owens
Open Thurs - Sun 1 - 4 PM, cl holidays. Admis donations accepted. Estab 1965, a Victorian history museum in a home built in 1880s. Mem: dues associate $10, sustaining $50, charter $100 plus $10 annually, memoriam $100, life $200, patron $500, benefactor $1000
Collections: Collection of paintings spanning a century of art; Indian artifacts; antique furniture; Victorian costumes
Exhibitions: Permanent and temporary exhibitions
Publications: Brochure; Kellygram (guides' newsletter and schedule)
Activities: Guided tours

REDDING

M REDDING MUSEUM OF ART & HISTORY, 56 Quartz Hill Rd, PO Box 990427, 96099-0427. Tel 916-243-8801; FAX 916-243-8929; *Pres* Jan Cameron; *Treas* Bryan Russell; *Dir* Alice Hoveman; *Exhib Cur* Jim Gilmore; *Public Prog Cur* Beverly Becker; *Arts Outreach Coordr* Rosemarie Orwig
Open Tues - Sun 10 AM - 5 PM, cl Mon. Estab 1963 to encourage understanding & appreciation of human accomplishments throughout history & pre-history. Two galleries present changing contemporary art & history exhibits. Average Annual Attendance: 20,000. Mem: 800; dues $20-$100; annual meeting third Wed in Sept
Income: Financed by mem, city appropriation, fundraising activities
Purchases: Contemporary fine arts, Native American baskets & artifacts
Collections: †Native American baskets; †Shasta County historical artifacts & documents †Contemporary Regional art; †photography
Exhibitions: (1997) Barbed Wire to Hard Wired: Ranching in the 21st Century; History gallery exhibition
Publications: Historical calendar; occasional papers; winter ethnography
Activities: Classes for adults & children; docent training; lect open to public, 10 vis lectr per year; gallery talks; tours; competitions with awards; Children's Lawn Festival; Art Fair; Native American Heritage Day; Christmas Craft Show; scholarships offered; affiliated natural science museum; Community Art Rental Program; original works of art lent to other museums; originate book traveling exhibitions 10-12 per year; museum shop sells books, magazines & original art, consignment from local craftspeople & artists, reproductions, gifts

L Shasta Historical Society Research Library, 56 Quartz Hill Rd, PO Box 990427, 96099-0427. Tel 916-243-3720; *Librn* Hazel McKim
Open Tues - Wed 10 AM - 5 PM. Open for reference only by appointment
Special Subjects: Shasta County history

REDLANDS

L LINCOLN MEMORIAL SHRINE, 125 W Vine St, 92373. Tel 909-798-7636, 798-7632; FAX 909-798-6566; *Cur* Donald McCue; *Assoc Archivist* Christie Hammond
Open Tues - Sat 1 - 5 PM, other hours by appointment; cl Sun, Mon & holidays. No admis fee. Estab 1932, operated as a section of the Smiley Public Library. Reference use only
Library Holdings: Vols 4500
Collections: Sculptures, paintings, murals
Publications: Lincoln Memorial Association Newsletter, quarterly
Activities: Docent training; lect; guided tours by appointment; sales shop sells pamphlets & postcards

A REDLANDS ART ASSOCIATION, 215 E State St, 92373-5273. Tel 909-792-8435; *Pres* Frederick C Edwards
Open Mon - Fri 10 AM - 5 PM, Sat 10 AM - 2 PM. No admis fee. Estab 1964 to promote interest in the visual arts & to provide a gallery for artists. Average Annual Attendance: 3000. Mem: 290; dues $20; annual meeting in May
Income: Financed by dues, gifts, grants
Exhibitions: Multimedia mini juried show
Publications: Bulletin, monthly
Activities: Classes for children & adults; lect open to public, 4 vis lectr per year; tours; competitions with prizes; gallery talks; scholarships offered; lending collection contains nature artifacts & original prints; gallery shop sells original art, reproductions, glass & ceramics

M SAN BERNARDINO COUNTY MUSEUM, Fine Arts Institute, 2024 Orange Tree Lane, 92374. Tel 909-798-8570; *Pres* Anne-Marie Perks; *VPres* Sandra Kramer; *Dir* Dr Allan Griesemer; *Cur Natural History* Robert McKernan; *Registrar* Noella Benvenuti; *Artist* Vicky Hipsley; *Cur of Educ* Maggie Foss
Open Tues - Sat 9 AM - 5 PM, Sun 1 - 5 PM. Admis adults $3, senior citizens, students & children 2-12 $2, mus mem free. Estab 1952 for education. Maintains upper & lower dome galleries & foyer. Average Annual Attendance: 300,000. Mem: 2100; dues Fine Arts Institute $40, Mus Assoc $15 & up; annual Fine Arts Institute meeting Feb; annual Mus Assoc meeting in May
Income: $280,000 (financed by mem)
Purchases: $2000
Collections: Collection consists primarily of representational art pertaining to Wildlife or the history of Southern California, & annual purchase awards from Fine Arts Institute's Annual International Exhibit & Southern California Open Exhibit
Exhibitions: Three juried art members exhibits; one annual international open exhibit; one regional Southern California open exhibit; one featured artists group exhibit
Publications: Newsletter, bi-monthly
Activities: Classes for children; docent training; lect open to public, 150 vis lectr per year; art competitions with cash & purchase awards totaling $45,000 annually; book traveling exhibition; originate traveling exhibitions; museum shop sells books, magazines, original art reproductions, prints & slides, jewelry, items pertaining to natural history

M UNIVERSITY OF REDLANDS, Peppers Gallery, 1200 E Colton Ave, 92373. Tel 909-793-2121; *Gallery Dir* Barbara Thomason
Open Tues - Fri Noon - 4 PM, Sat & Sun 2 - 5 PM, cl summer. No admis fee. Estab 1963 to widen students interest in art. Gallery is one large room with celestial windows & movable panels for display. Average Annual Attendance: 1500
Income: Financed by endowment
Collections: Ethnic Art; graphics; a few famous artists works
Exhibitions: Exhibitions during fall, winter, spring
Publications: Exhibition catalogs & posters
Activities: Lect open to public, 4-5 vis lectr per year; gallery talks; tours; talent awards

RICHMOND

A NATIONAL INSTITUTE OF ART & DISABILITIES (NIAD), 551 23rd St, 94804. Tel 510-620-0290; FAX 510-620-0326, 415-441-1537; Elec Mail niadektz@thecity.sfsu.edu. *Admin Dir* Pat Claytor; *Develop Dir* Heather Thomson
NIAD & Florence Ludins - Katz Gallery open Mon - Fri 9 AM - 3 PM, Creative Spirit Gallery open Tues - Sun 11 AM - 6 PM. No admis fee. Estab 1984 to provide a program to meet the needs of disabled adults for creative self-expression in the arts. Currently there are 27 similar centers throughout the US & Canada. Maintains professional exhibition galleries which display the work of NIAD artists, often alongside the work of established artists from outside the NIAD setting in order to bring the art of NIAD artists to the attention of the general public. Mem: 250; dues $15-$100
Collections: Resource room in arts & disabilities, †books, †pamphlets, †posters, †videotapes
Exhibitions: NIAD artist work
Publications: Art & Disabilities, Freedom to Create, the Creative Spirit; Freedom to Create (videotape series)
Activities: Classes for adults & children; interdisciplinary visual art studio program; professional training in art & disabilities field; research, training & technical assistance; lect open to public; concerts; gallery talks; tours; originate traveling exhibitions of NIAD artist work to regional galleries, museums, colleges, community centers & businesses; sales shop sells books, original art, reproductions & prints

A RICHMOND ART CENTER, Civic Center Plaza, 2540 Barrett Ave, 94804. Tel 510-620-6772; FAX 510-620-6771; *Exec Dir* Jeff Nathanson
Open Tues - Fri 10 AM - 4:30 PM, Sat Noon - 4:30 PM, cl Sun, Mon & holidays. No admis fee. Estab preliminary steps 1936-44; formed in 1944 to establish artists studios & community center for arts; to offer to the community

an opportunity to experience & to improve knowledge & skill in the arts & crafts at the most comprehensive & highest level possible. A large gallery, small gallery & entrance gallery total 5000 sq ft & a rental gallery covers 1628 sq ft; an outdoor sculpture court totals 8840 sq ft. Average Annual Attendance: 8000.
Mem: 800; dues $30 & up
Income: $300,000 (financed by mem, tuition, donation, grants, events, in-kind services from city & Art Center Assoc)
Collections: †Primarily contemporary art & crafts of Bay area
Exhibitions: Rotating: group theme, solo, invitational & juried annuals
Publications: Catalog for annual shows; newsletter, quarterly; show announcements for exhibitions
Activities: Classes for adults & children; lect open to public, 5 vis lectr per year; gallery talks; tours; scholarships offered; outreach program serving community; rental gallery, paintings & original objects of art lent to offices, businesses & homes, members of Art Center

RIVERSIDE

M RIVERSIDE ART MUSEUM, 3425 Mission Inn Ave, 92501. Tel 909-684-7111; FAX 909-684-7332; *Pres* D Gregg Brown; *Dir* Bobbie Powell
Open Mon 10 AM - 3 PM, Tues - Fri 10 AM - 5 PM, Sat 10 AM - 4 PM, cl Sun. No admis fee. Estab 1935 to display art, collect & preserve art created in the West. Three spaces - Main Gallery 72 ft x 35 ft; Upstairs Gallery 18 ft x 30 ft; Art Alliance Gallery 72 ft x 35 ft. Average Annual Attendance: 20,000. Mem: 1000; dues life mem $1000 & up, patron $200, supporting $100, family $50, individual $35, senior citizens $10; annual meeting fourth Thurs in Feb
Income: Financed by mem, grants & donations
Collections: Mixture of media dating from the late 1800s to the present; 300 pieces; art by Southern California artists (past & present) living in the west (Andrew Molles Collection); Works on paper
Publications: Artifacts, monthly
Activities: Classes for adults & children; docent training; lect open to public, 5 vis lectr per year; gallery talks; demonstrations; special events; competitions with prizes; tours; scholarships & fels offered; individual paintings & original objects of art lent; sales shop sells magazines, original art & reproductions

L Library, 3425 Mission Inn Ave, 92501. Tel 909-684-7111; *Dir* Bobbie Powell
Open for reference upon request
Library Holdings: Vols 600; Per subs 15; Other — Exhibition catalogs, framed reproductions, pamphlets, photographs, reproductions

M RIVERSIDE MUNICIPAL MUSEUM, 3580 Mission N St, 92501. Tel 909-782-5273; *Historic Resources International Dir* Richard Esparza; *Admin Cur* Alan Curl; *Cur Anthropology* Christopher L Moser; *Cur History* H Vincent Moses; *Restoration Specialist* Gary Ecker; *Exhib Designer* Dasia Bytnerowicz
Open Tues - Fri 9 AM - 5 PM, Sat & Sun 1 - 5 PM. No admis fee. Estab 1924 to collect, preserve & display local & California prehistory, natural history & local history. Permanent galleries on local geodesy, paleontology, Indians, history & animals. Mem: 600; dues $10
Collections: History photo archive; Indian art; Native American Basketry historic house, 1891 Heritage House; photo & document archives
Activities: Classes for children; docent training; lect open to members only, 6-10 vis lectr per year; tours; artmobile; original objects of art lent to other public museums & art galleries; museum shop sells books, original art, reproductions & prints

UNIVERSITY OF CALIFORNIA

M University Art Gallery, Watkins House, 92521. Tel 909-787-3755, 787-3786; Elec Mail kvwarren@ucracl.ucr.edu. *Dir* Katherine V Warren; *Admin Asst* Virginia Field
Open Wed - Fri 11 AM - 4 PM, Sat & Sun Noon - 4 PM. No admis fee. Estab 1963, gallery presents major temporary exhibitions. Gallery contains 2000 sq ft. Average Annual Attendance: 5000. Mem: dues patron $1000 & up, supporting $500, contributor $100, family $45, individual $30, student $15
Income: $100,000 (financed by mem & state appropriation)
Purchases: $30,000 (print collection)
Collections: Works on paper-portfolios of prints, sculpture
Exhibitions: Master Prints from the Age of Durer; Art Department Faculty Exhibitions; Photo-Mechanical Printmaking Competition; Claire Falkenstein: The Continuing Vision; Form Over Function; Companeras De Mexico: Women Photograph Women; Relationship: New Work by Sandra Rowe; Site Specific Sculpture Competition
Publications: Exhibition catalogs
Activities: Lect open to public, 1-2 vis lectr per year; gallery talks; tours; competitions; book traveling exhibitions 1-2 per year; originate traveling exhibitions to appropriate institutions, other campus galleries; sales shop sells catalogs & posters

M California Museum of Photography, 92521. Tel 909-787-4787; FAX 909-787-4797; *Assoc Dir New Media & Colls* Edward W Earle; *Dir* Jonathan W Green; *Cur Educ* Lori Fiacco; *Assoc Dir Develop & Admin* Cathleen Walling; *Exhib Cur* Kevin Boyle
Open Wed - Sat 11 AM - 5 PM, Sun Noon - 5 PM. Admis adult $2, senior citizens & youth $1, children under 12 & AAM members free. Estab 1973 to preserve, protect & exhibit photography. Mus has five exhibition galleries which display changing exhibitions related to historical & contemporary photography & emerging technologies. Average Annual Attendance: 20,000. Mem: 1200; dues $35
Income: $800,000 (financed by university funds, grants, private donations & mem)
Collections: Bingham camera & apparatus; Keystone-Mast stereo negatives & prints; photographs of the 19th & 20th centuries
Activities: Classes for adults & children; lect open to public, 2 vis lectr per year; gallery talks; tours; competitions with awards; film series; Riverside Film Festival; symposia; original objects of art lent to other art institutions; lending collection contains 400,000 photographs; book traveling exhibitions 3 per year; originate traveling exhibitions; museum shop sells books, magazines, reproductions, exhibition catalgogues & prints

L **Tomas Rivera Library,** PO Box 5900, 92517. Tel 909-787-3703; FAX 909-787-3285; *University Librn* James C Thompson; *Art Selector* Richard Vierich
Open Mon - Thurs 8 AM - Noon, Fri 8 AM - 6 PM, Sat 10 AM - 6 PM, Sun 1 PM - 12 AM. Open to faculty, students & staff
Library Holdings: Vols 38,000; Per subs 172; Micro — Cards, fiche, reels; AV — A-tapes, cassettes, fs, motion pictures, rec, slides, v-tapes; Other — Exhibition catalogs, manuscripts, original art works
Special Subjects: Photography

ROHNERT PARK

M **SONOMA STATE UNIVERSITY,** Art Gallery, 1801 E Cotati Ave, 94928. Tel 707-664-2295; FAX 707-664-2505; Elec Mail art.gallery@sonoma.edu; Internet Home Page Address http://www.sonoma.edu/artgallery/. *Dir* Michael Schwager
Open Tues - Fri 11 AM - 4 PM, Sat & Sun Noon - 4 PM. No admis fee. Estab 1978 to provide exhibitions of quality to the university & Northern California community. 2800 sq ft of exhibition space designed to house monumental sculpture & painting
Income: Financed through University & private funds
Collections: Asnis Collection of Prints; Garfield Collection of Oriental Art
Publications: Bulletins and announcements of exhibitions; exhibition catalog
Activities: Docent training; educ-outreach program; vis lectr; gallery talks; tours; annual benefit auction; book traveling exhibitions 1-2 per year; originate traveling exhibitions to national art museums; sales shop sells books, T-shirts & posters

ROSS

A **MARIN SOCIETY OF ARTISTS INC,** Sir Francis Drake Blvd, PO Box 203, 94957. Tel 415-454-9561; *Pres* Sidnii Woods; *Office Mgr* Jo Smith
Open Mon - Thurs 11 AM - 4 PM; Sat & Sun 1 - 4 PM, cl Fri. No admis fee. Estab 1926 to foster cooperation among artists & to continually develop pub interest in art. Gallery is located in a garden setting. It is approximately 3500 sq ft of well lighted exhibit space. Average Annual Attendance: 75,000. Mem: 400; Qualifications for mem: Previous exhibition in a juried show & must reside in Bay Area if active; dues $40; meetings in May & Sept
Income: Financed by mem, sale & rental of art
Publications: Monthly newsletter
Activities: Lect open to public, 2-3 vis lectr per year; competitions with cash awards; sales shop sells original art, original prints, handcrafted jewelry ceramics & fiberworks

SACRAMENTO

A **CALIFORNIA CONFEDERATION OF THE ARTS,** 704 O St, 2nd Flr, 95814. Tel 916-447-7811; FAX 916-447-7891, 415-826-6850; *Exec Dir* Susan Hoffman; *Assoc Dir* Ken Larsen
Open 10 AM - 5 PM. Estab 1975 as a non-profit partnership to improve cultural opportunities. Mem: 1000; dues individual $50, organizations by budget; annual meeting May, Congress of the Arts
Income: $100,000 (financed by mem, corporate & foundation grants
Publications: Publications correspond to government & local arts activity
Activities: Referral services; lect open to public, over 10 vis lectr per year

CALIFORNIA STATE UNIVERSITY AT SACRAMENTO

L **Library - Humanities Reference Dept,** 2000 Jed Smith Dr, 95819. Tel 916-278-6218; FAX 916-278-7089; *Dean* Charles Martell; *Dept Head* Clifford P Wood; *Humanities Reference Librn* Kay Muther; *Humanities Reference & Slide Librn* Susan Beelick
Open Mon - Thurs 7:45 AM - 11 PM, Fri 7:45 AM - 5 PM, Sat 10 AM - 6 PM, Sun 1 - 9 PM (during school year), summer sessions vary during week. Estab 1947
Income: Financed through the University
Library Holdings: Per subs 250; Micro — Cards, fiche, reels; AV — A-tapes, cassettes, fs, slides, v-tapes; Other — Clipping files, exhibition catalogs, pamphlets, reproductions
Special Subjects: Book Arts, Decorative Arts
Publications: Women Artists: A Selected Bibliography; bibliographic handouts
M **University Union Exhibit Lounge,** University Union, CSUS, 6000 J St, 95819-6017. Tel 916-278-6595; FAX 916-278-6278; *Assoc Dir* Richard Schiffers
Open Mon - Fri 10:30 AM - 3:30 PM, Wed & Thurs 5 - 8 PM, during school year, summer hours vary. No admis fee. Estab 1975 to expose students to a variety of visual arts & techniques. The Exhibit Lounge is located on the second floor of the University Union. It has 67 running ft of display space. Gallery run by students. Average Annual Attendance: 8250
Income: Student fees & commissions
Purchases: Works purchased for permanent collection annually from artists with a relationship, past or present, with the University
Collections: Various prints, photographs, paintings by students; sculpture by Yoshio Taylor: Tsuki, painting by Jack Ogden: American Grove, Bronze original by John Battenberg J G Sheds His Wolf's Clothing
Exhibitions: Annual student competition, other various exhibits encompassing a variety of media & subjects
Activities: Lect open to public, 9 vis lectr per year; gallery talks; competitions; Book traveling exhibitions once a year

M **CROCKER ART MUSEUM,** 216 O St, 95814. Tel 916-264-5423; FAX 916-264-7372; Elec Mail crocker@sacto.org. *Dir* Stephen C McGough; *Cur* Janice T Driesbach; *Registrar* Paulette Hennum; *Cur Educ* K D Kurutz
Open Tues - Sun 10 AM - 5 PM, Thurs 10 AM - 9 PM, cl Mon. Admis adults $4.50, children 7-17 $2, 6 & under free. Estab 1873; municipal art mus since 1885; original gallery building designed by Seth Babson completed in 1873; R A Herold Wing opened in 1969; Crocker Mansion Wing opened in 1989. Average Annual Attendance: 110,000. Mem: 5500; annual meeting in June
Income: $750,000 (financed by Crocker Art Mus Assoc & city appropriation)

Collections: †19th century California painting; American decorative arts; †contemporary California painting, sculpture & crafts; †prints & photographs; European decorative arts; †European painting 1500 - 1900; †Old Master drawings; †Oriental art
Exhibitions: (1997) The Middle Path: Buddhist Sculpture from South & Southeast Asia; Uelsmann: Yosemite; Regional Contemporary Show; California Impressionists. (1998) The Art of the Gold Rush
Publications: Calendar, 6 times per year
Activities: Seminars for adults; children's programs; docent training; lect open to the public, 10 vis lectr per year; concerts; tours; annual juried competitions; individual paintings & original objects of art lent to other museums; book traveling exhibitions; originate traveling exhibitions; museum shop sells books, original art, cards & miscellaneous gifts
L **Research Library,** 216 O St, 95814. Tel 916-264-5423; FAX 916-264-7372
Open Tues - Sun 10 AM - 5 PM, Thurs 10 AM - 9 PM, cl Mon. Open to staff, docent, interns and others upon application
Library Holdings: Vols 2000; Per subs 30; Dissertations; Micro — Fiche; Other — Exhibition catalogs
Activities: Classes for adults & children; dramatic programs; docent training; lect open to public, some open to members only, vis lectr; concerts; artmobile; individual paintings lent

M **LA RAZA-GALERIA POSADA,** 704 O St, 95814. Tel 916-446-5133; FAX 916-447-7891; *Exec Dir* Luis Chabolla; *Admin Asst* Christina Tarango
Open Tues - Fri 11 AM - 6 PM, Sat Noon - 5 PM. Estab 1971 as a Chicano art & culture center. 2000 sq ft gallery. Average Annual Attendance: 10,000. Mem: 150; dues $15-$100
Activities: Lect open to public; gallery talks; tours

SAINT HELENA

M **SILVERADO MUSEUM,** 1490 Library Lane, PO Box 409, 94574-0409. Tel 707-963-3757; FAX 707-963-0917; *Dir* Edmond Reynolds
Open Tues - Sun Noon - 4 PM, cl Mon & holidays. No admis fee. Estab 1968; the mus is devoted to the life & works of Robert Louis Stevenson, who spent a brief but important time in the area; the object is to acquaint people with his life & works & familiarize them with his stay. The mus has five wall cases & three large standing cases, as well as numerous bookcases. Average Annual Attendance: 5500
Income: Financed by the Vailima Foundation, set up by Mr & Mrs Norman H Strouse
Collections: All material relating to Stevenson & his immediate circle
Exhibitions: A different exhibition devoted to some phase of Stevenson's work is mounted every three months
Activities: Dramatic programs; lect open to public; tours; sales desk sells books
L **Reference Library,** 1490 Library Lane, PO Box 409, 94574. Tel 707-963-3757; FAX 707-963-8131; *Interim Cur* Ed Reynolds
Open Tues - Sun Noon - 4 PM. 1970. For reference only
Income: Financed by Vailima Foundation
Library Holdings: Vols 3000; AV — Kodachromes 300, motion pictures
Special Subjects: Painting - American, Painting - British, Photography
Collections: †First editions, †variant editions, †fine press editions of Robert Louis Stevenson, †letters, †manuscripts, †photographs, †sculptures, †paintings and memorabilia
Exhibitions: Exhibits of two months duration 6 times a year; Christmas Exhibit
Publications: The Silverado Squatters; Prayers Written at Vailima

SALINAS

M **HARTNELL COLLEGE GALLERY,** 156 Homestead Ave, 93901. Tel 408-755-6700, 755-6791; *Dir* Gary T Smith
Open Mon 10 AM - 1 PM & 7 - 9 PM, Tues - Thurs 10 AM - 1 PM, cl Fri - Sun. No admis fee. Estab 1959 to bring to students & the community the highest quality in contemporary & historical works of all media. Main gallery is 40 x 60 ft, south gallery is 15 x 30 ft, brick flooring. Average Annual Attendance: 7500
Collections: Approx 45 works on paper from the San Francisco Bay Area WPA; FSA photographs; Mrs Virginia Bacher Haichol Artifact Collection; Mrs Leslie Fenton Netsuke Collection
Exhibitions: Edward Weston; Claes Oldenburg; Edward Curtis; Oriental Porcelain from the Albert & Pat Scheopf Collection; Charles Russell & Frederick Remington; Russian Lacquer Boxes; Selections from the Hartnell Farm Security Admin Photography Collection; Christo: Wrapped Coast
Activities: Classes for adults; gallery management training; individual paintings & original objects of art lent to qualified institutions, professional galleries or museums; lending collection contains original art works; book traveling exhibitions; traveling exhibitions organized & circulated

SAN BERNARDINO

M **CALIFORNIA STATE UNIVERSITY, SAN BERNARDINO,** University Art Galleries, 5500 University Pky, 92407-2397. Tel 909-880-5823, 880-7373 (Fullerton Mus); FAX 909-880-7068; *Chmn Art Dept & Gallery Dir* Richard Johnston
Open Mon - Fri 9 AM - Noon & 1 - 4 PM. No admis fee. Estab 1972 for the purpose of providing high quality exhibitions on varied subjects suitable for both campus & community. Gallery 2 opened 1978 as an exhibit area for senior shows & student work. Average Annual Attendance: 5500
Income: Financed by mem, city & state appropriations
Collections: Small collection of prints
Publications: Catalogs; Personas de los Tumbas - West Mexican tomb sculpture, 2-3 per year
Activities: Classes for adults; lect open to public, 1-3 vis lectr per year; gallery talks; competitions

A SAN BERNARDINO ART ASSOCIATION, INC, 780 North E St, PO Box 3574, 92404. Tel 909-885-2816; *Pres* Doris M Jacka; *VPres* Maureen Reinen; *Second VPres* Yolanda Voce; *Treas* Evelyn Franeasis
Open Mon - Fri 11 AM - 3 PM. No admis fee. Estab 1934 as a non-profit organization to generate interest in art for all ages. Open to the public; maintains gallery of paintings & ceramics by local artists. Mem: 120; dues $20; meetings on first of each month
Exhibitions: Inland Exhibits
Publications: Newsletter
Activities: Classes for adults; artist presentations; lect open to public, 8 vis lectr per year; gallery talks; competitions with awards; scholarships; individual paintings & original objects of art lent; sales shop sells original art, ceramics & photographs

SAN DIEGO

A BALBOA ART CONSERVATION CENTER, Balboa Park, 1649 El Prado, PO Box 3755, 92163-1755. Tel 619-236-9702; FAX 619-236-0141; *Pres* Dr James Lasry; *General Mgr & Chief Paper Conservator* Janet Ruggles; *Chief Paintings Conservator* Elizabeth Court; *Paper Conservator* Laura Downey; *Paintings Conservator* Sarah Murray; *Frames Technician* Janos Novak
Open Mon - Fri 9 AM - 4:30 PM. No admis fee. Estab 1975 for research & educ in art conservation; services in exams, treatment & consulation in art conservation. Mem: 14; non-profit institutions are members, their members may contract for services; annual meeting in May
Income: $300,000 (financed by services performed)
Collections: †Illustrative photographs, †memorabilia, tools, equipment of profession; paintings for experimental & didactic purposes
Publications: BACC Newsletter, quarterly
Activities: Lect open to public & some for members only; gallery talks; tours
L Richard D Buck Memorial Library, Balboa Park, PO Box 3755, 92163-1755. Tel 619-236-9702; FAX 619-236-0141; *General Mgr* Janet Ruggles
Library not open to pub
Income: Financed by Mellon Grant
Library Holdings: Vols 700; Per subs 35; Micro — Reels; AV — Cassettes, slides; Other — Clipping files, exhibition catalogs, memorabilia, pamphlets, photographs
Special Subjects: Art Conservation, Scientific Analysis of Materials

M CENTRO CULTURAL DE LA RAZA, 2125 Park Blvd, 92101. Tel 619-235-6135; FAX 619-595-0034; *Board Pres* Daniel Hernandez; *Board VPres* Connie Hernandez; *Board Exec Dir* Larry Baza; *Cur* Luis Stand
Open Wed - Sun Noon - 5 PM. No admis fee, donations requested. Estab 1970 to create, promote & preserve Mexican, Indian & Chicano art & culture. 2500 sq ft of gallery space with five sections & 8 X 15 ft walls. Average Annual Attendance: 65,000. Mem: 500; dues $10-$1000
Income: $150,000 (financed by mem, city & state appropriation, sales & services, private grants, National Endowment for the Arts)
Purchases: $1500
Collections: †Historical artifacts of Mexican & Indian culture; †contemporary artwork by Chicano artists
Exhibitions: Native American Contemporary Photography; solo exhibitions of local & regional artists; group shows; invitational group exhibitions
Publications: Exhibit catalogues, 3 per year; literary publications, 2 per year
Activities: Classes for adults & children; lect open to public, 5-7 vis lectr per year; exten dept; lending collection includes 15 pieces of original art & prints; book traveling exhibitions 1-2 per year; originate traveling exhibits that circulate to other galleries & cultural centers; sales shop sells books, magazines, original art, reproductions, prints

A INSTALLATION GALLERY, PO Box 2552, 92112. Tel 619-544-1482; FAX 619-544-1486; Elec Mail dreo@insite97.org. *Exec Dir* Michael Krichman; *Assoc Dir* Danielle Reo
No admis fee. Estab 1980 as a vital alternative space for San Diego, a forum for provocative ideas outside the boundaries of the mus & traditional gallery; an umbrella for community & educational outreach, for interaction with other community organizations & for art in pub context. Installation is important as a dynamic intertwining of art & life & in focusing new perspectives on pub issues; dedicated to promoting challenging & diverse art making without restrictions as to individuals, medium or content
Exhibitions: In Site 97, emphasizing artists from San Diego & Tijuana areas
Activities: Classes for adults & children; docent training; lect open to public, 3 vis lectr per year; tours

M MINGEI INTERNATIONAL, INC, Mingei International Museum Satellite of World Folk Art, 4405 La Jolla Village Dr, I-7 (Mailing add: 1439 El Prado, 92101). Tel 619-239-0003 (OFC); FAX 619-239-0605; *Pres* Roger C Cornell, MD; *VPres* Elizabeth Bergan; *VPres* Albert N Williams; *Treas* Armand LaBey; *Asst Dir* Rob Sidner; *Registrar* John Digesare; *Coll Gallery Mgr* Susan Fast; *Dir Public Relations* Martha Ehringer; *Exec Secy & Operations Mgr* Carol Clich
Open Tues - Sat 11 AM - 5 PM, Fri evenings to 9 PM, Sun 2 - 5 PM. Admis fee donation $2. Estab 1978 to further the understanding of arts of the people from all parts of the world. 6000 sq ft mus, architecturally designed space, white interior, hardwood floors, track lighting. Average Annual Attendance: 40,000. Mem: 1500; dues $20-$1000; annual meeting in May
Income: Financed by mem, grants & contributions
Collections: †International Folk Art (in all media including textiles, ceramics, metals, woods, stone, paper, bamboo & straw); African, American, Ethiopian, East Indian, Indonisian, Japanese, Pakistani, Himalayan & Mexican Folk Art
Exhibitions: The Beaded Universe - International Strands of Culture; Yunta - The Art of a Nomad's Hearth & Home in Central Asia
Publications: Exhibition related publications
Activities: Docent training; illustrated lectures; films; gallery talks; tours; originate traveling exhibitions; collectors gallery sells original folk art
L Reference Library, 1439 El Prado, 92101. Tel 619-239-0003; FAX 619-239-0605; *Librn* Nancy Andrews
Library Holdings: AV — A-tapes, cassettes, fs, Kodachromes, lantern slides, motion pictures, slides, v-tapes; Other — Clipping files, exhibition catalogs, framed reproductions, manuscripts, memorabilia, photographs

M MUSEUM OF CONTEMPORARY ART, SAN DIEGO-DOWNTOWN, 1001 Kettner Blvd, 92101. Tel 619-234-1001; FAX 619-234-1070; *Pres Board Trustees* Carolyn P Farris; *Develop Dir* Anne Farrell; *Cur* Louis Grachos; *Dir* Hugh M Davies; *Assoc Dir* Charles Castle; *Educ Cur* Seonaid McArthur
Open Tues - Sun 10:30 AM - 5:30 PM, Fri 10:30 AM - 8 PM. Admis $3. Estab 1941 to collect, preserve & present post-1950 art. Average Annual Attendance: 195,000. Mem: 2500; dues $40
Income: $2,200,000 (financed by endowment, mem, city & state appropriation, grants from the National Endowment for the Arts, Institute of Mus Services & private foundations)
Collections: Contemporary art, all media; post-1950 art, all media
Publications: VIEW, quarterly newsletter; exhibition catalogues
Activities: Classes for adults & children; docent programs; lect open to public; internships offered; book traveling exhibitions 1 per year; originate traveling exhibitions 2 per year; museum shop sells books, magazines, posters, original art & design objects

M MUSEUM OF PHOTOGRAPHIC ARTS, 1649 El Prado, 92101. Tel 619-238-7559; FAX 619-238-8777; *Dir* Arthur Ollman; *Admin Dir* Cathy Boemer; *Dir Develop* Charles Reilly; *Exhibit Designer* Vera Westergaard; *Registrar* Hetty Tye
Open daily 10 AM - 5 PM. Admis $3.50. Estab 1983 to collect & exhibit photographic works of art. Average Annual Attendance: 75,000. Mem: 1600; dues $25-$10,000
Income: $850,000 (financed by city, state, & federal appropriation, endowments, mem, grants & corporations)
Purchases: $20,000
Collections: Photographic collection includes examples from earliest to most recent photographs
Publications: Points of Entry
Activities: Classes for adults; docent training; educator workshop; summer workshops with guest artists; lect open to public, 10-12 vis lectr per year; gallery talks; tours; Lou Stovman prize for photography; Century Award for Lifetime Achievement; book traveling exhibitions 5-6 per year; originate traveling exhibitions; museum shop sells books, magazines, prints & photography related gifts

M SAN DIEGO MARITIME MUSEUM, 1306 N Harbor Dr, 92101. Tel 619-234-9153; FAX 619-234-8345; *Develop Dir* Joe Ditler; *Pres* Chas Allen; *Cur* David Brierley; *Librn* Craig Arnold
Open daily 9 AM - 8 PM. Admis family $10, adults $6, service personnel, children 13-17 & senior citizens $4, children under 12 $2, discount to adult groups. Estab 1948 for preservation & educ of San Diego related maritime history. A maritime mus in a fleet of three ships: Star of India (1863 bark); Berkeley (1898 ferryboat) & Medea (1904 steam Yacht). Average Annual Attendance: 180,000. Mem: 1600; dues life $2000, benefactor/corporate $1000, patron $500, associate $250, friend $100, active $50, family $35, individual $25; annual meeting in Nov
Collections: Antiques; maritime art; maritime artifacts; clothing; navigation instruments
Exhibitions: Temporary exhibitions
Publications: Mains'l Haul, quarterly historical journal; Books: Euterpe, MEDEA The Classic Stream Yacht, Star of India, They Came by Sea, Transpac 1900-1979
Activities: Educ dept; docent training; lect for members & guests, 5 vis lectr per year; tours; special programs; competitions for children with awards; museum store sells books, magazines, reproductions, prints, slides & related maritime items, including video tapes

M SAN DIEGO MUSEUM OF ART, Balboa Park, PO Box 2107, 92112-2107. Tel 619-232-7931; FAX 619-232-9367; Telex 88-3594. *Dir* Steven L Brezzo; *Dep Dir* Jane G Rice; *Head Design & Installation* Mitchell Gaul; *Cur Modern Art* Mary Stofflet; *Cur Educ* Barney J Malesky; *Public Affairs* Marilen Sedlock; *Marketing Dir* Dennis Cushman; *Chief Financial Officer* John Paterniti; *Registrar* Louis Goldich; *Grant Officer* Caroline Harwood
Open Tues - Sun 10 AM - 4:30 PM; cl Mon. Admis general pub $5, children 6-12 $1. Estab 1925. Gallery built in 1926 by a generous patron in a Spanish Plateresque design; the West wing was added in 1966 & the East wing in 1974. Average Annual Attendance: 417,000. Mem: 10,000, dues; benefactor $10,000; President's Circle donor & business donor $5000, business partner $1500, President's Circle $1250, sponsoring friend $600, business associate $500, friend of mus $125, active $45, senior citizens $25, students $24
Income: $3,712,391 (financed by investment income, contributions, admis, city & county appropriations & sales)
Purchases: $300,000
Collections: Renaissance & Baroque paintings; with strong holdings in Spanish; 19th & 20th century American & European sculpture & paintings; Asian arts - sculpture, paintings, ceramics, decorative arts; American furniture & glass, English silver; Spanish Baroque, Flemish, Dutch & English schools;
Exhibitions: Pacific Parallels: Artists & the Landscape in New Zealand; Sanchez Cotan; Silver, Wood, Clay, Gold: San Diego Crafts & NCECA Clay National 1993; Art Alive; The William S Paley Collection; Artists Guild Open Juried Exhibition; Helen Frankenthaler; Bruno Schulz; Giorgione: Songs of My People; Florentine Drawings; Gerald Brockhurst; Balboa's Ark; Young Art '94; Deborah Butterfield; Russian Music Covers; Passionate Visions of the American South
Publications: Biennial Reports port; catalogs of collections; exhibition catalogs; membership calendar, monthly; gallery guide
Activities: Classes for adults & children; docent training; lect open to public; gallery talks; tours; competitions; originate traveling exhibitions; sales shops sells books, reproductions, prints, cards, jewelry & ceramics
L Art Reference Library, Balboa Park, PO Box 2107, 92112-2107. Tel 619-696-1959; FAX 619-232-9367; Elec Mail nemerson@class.org. *Library Mgr* Nancy Emerson
Call for hours. Estab 1926 for curatorial research. Noncirculating. Available to public on limited basis. For Reference Only
Library Holdings: Vols 25,000; Per subs 90; AV — A-tapes, cassettes, slides 15,000, v-tapes; Other — Clipping files, exhibition catalogs, manuscripts, memorabilia, original art works, pamphlets, photographs
Special Subjects: Art History, Asian Art, Islamic Art, Latin American Art,

Oriental Art, Painting - American, Painting - European, Painting - Italian, Painting - Japanese, Painting - Spanish, Prints, Religious Art, Sculpture, Watercolors, Italian Renaissance, Spanish Baroque, American & Latin American Contemporary
Collections: Bibliography of artists in exhibition catalogues

L **SAN DIEGO PUBLIC LIBRARY,** Art & Music Section, 820 E St, 92101. Tel 619-236-5810; *Sr Librn* Kathleen Griffin; *Picture Specialist* Jacqueline Adams; *Librn* Christina Clifford
Open Mon - Thurs 10 AM - 9 PM, Fri & Sat 9:30 AM - 5:30 PM, Sun 1 - 5 PM. No admis fee. Estab 1966 to make art available to students & the community. Two gallery spaces: smaller gallery is basically for student & classroom work; larger gallery is for invited guests. Average Annual Attendance: 8000
Income: Financed by city and state appropriation
Purchases: $32,000
Library Holdings: Vols 85,000; Per subs 200; Postcards; AV — Rec 23,000; Other — Clipping files, exhibition catalogs
Collections: Former libraries of William Templeton Johnson, architect & Donal Hord, sculptor; emphasis is on Spanish, Mediterranean, Italian & French Renaissance architecture & Oriental art, sculpture & ceramics; books on the theatre including biographies of famous actors and actresses as well as histories of the American, London and European stages, gift of Elwyn B Gould, local theatre devotee
Activities: Student show with prizes; individual paintings & original objects of art lent to faculty members on campus; book traveling exhibitions 1 or 2 per year; sales shop sells books

M **SAN DIEGO STATE UNIVERSITY,** University Gallery, 5402 College Ave, 92182-0214. Tel 619-594-6511; FAX 619-594-1217; *Dir* Fredrick Orth; *Gallery Dir* Tina Yapelli
Open Mon - Thurs & Sat Noon - 4 PM, cl Fri & Sun. No admis fee. Estab 1977 to provide exhibitions of importance for the students, faculty & pub of the San Diego environment; for study & appreciation of art & enrichment of the University. Average Annual Attendance: 35,000. Mem: 270; dues $35
Income: Supported by student fees, SDSU Art Council & grants
Collections: Crafts collection; contemporary print collection; graduate student sculpture & painting
Exhibitions: Contemporary national & international artists
Publications: Exhibit catalogs
Activities: Lect open to public, 4 vis lectr per year; gallery talks; book traveling exhibitions 2 per year; originate traveling exhibitions; sales shop sells books & exhibition catalogs

L **Art Department Slide Library,** San Diego State University, 5500 Campani Dr, 92182-1606. Tel 619-594-6511; FAX 619-594-1217; *Slide Cur* Lilla Sweatt
Open Mon - Thurs 7:30 AM - 11 PM, Fri 7:30 AM - 5 PM, Sat 10 AM - 5 PM, Sun Noon - 10 PM. Estab 1957 to aid & facilitate the faculty in teaching art & art history as well as aiding students in class reports
Library Holdings: Micro — Cards, fiche, prints, reels; AV — Cassettes, Kodachromes, slides 122,000; Other — Clipping files, exhibition catalogs, framed reproductions, manuscripts, memorabilia, pamphlets, reproductions
Exhibitions: Special Art collections, student & women's art shows

M **SUSHI-PERFORMANCE & VISUAL ART GALLERY,** 320 11th Ave, 92101-7413. Tel 619-235-8466; *Dir* Lynn Schuette; *Managing Dir* Vicki Wolf; *Visual Arts Coordr* Open
Estab 1980 to present contemporary visual & performance art. Visual art gallery is 6 ft x 40 ft; performance gallery is 35 x 55 ft. Average Annual Attendance: 5000. Mem: 300; dues $15-$500
Income: $80,000 (financed by endowment, mem, city & state appropriation)
Activities: Educ dept; dramatic programs

M **TIMKEN MUSEUM OF ART,** 1500 El Prado, 92101. Tel 619-239-5548; FAX 619-233-6629; *Dir* John Peterson; *Pres* Robert Ames; *VPres* John Thiele
Open Tues - Sat 10 AM - 4:30 PM, Sun 1:30 - 4:30 PM, cl Mon & month of Sept. No admis fee. Estab to display & preserve European Old Masters, 18th & 19th centuries American paintings & Russian icons. Six galleries. Average Annual Attendance: 90,000
Income: Financed by endowment
Collections: Dutch & Flemish, French, Spanish & American Italian paintings; Russian icons; all paintings owned by Putnam Collection are on permanent display; Pissarro, Bords de l'Oise a Pontoise; Il Guercino - Return of the Prodigal Son; Copley, Mrs Thomas Gage
Publications: Gallery Guides; exhibit catalogs; Gabriel Metsu's The Letter monograph; Eastman Johnson's The Cranberry Harvest; Island of Nantucket; Corot: View of Volterra
Activities: Lect; tours available by request

M **UNIVERSITY OF SAN DIEGO,** Founders' Gallery, 5998 Alcala Park, 92110. Tel 619-260-4600; *Dir* Derrick Cartwright
Open Mon - Fri Noon - 5 PM. Estab 1971 to enrich the goals of the Fine Arts department & university by providing excellent in-house exhibitions of all eras, forms & media & to share them with the community. Gallery is an architecturally outstanding facility with foyer, display area and patio, parking in central campus. Average Annual Attendance: 1500
Income: Financed by Fine Arts department & private endowment
Collections: 17th, 18th & 19th century French tapestries & furniture; South Asian textiles & costumes of 19th & 20th centuries; Tibetan & Indian looms, Ghandi spinning wheels; 19th Century French bronze sculpture; 20th Century Paintings
Exhibitions: Seven shows each year
Publications: The Impressionist as Printmaker; Child Hassam 1859-1935; Arbol de la Vida, The Ceramic Art of Metepec
Activities: Educ dept; seminars in art history; lect open to public, 4 vis lectr per year; concerts; tours; awards; originate traveling exhibitions

SAN FRANCISCO

L **ACADEMY OF ART,** College Library, 180 New Montgomery St, 6th Flr, 94105. Tel 415-274-2270; FAX 415-957-9411; *Dir* Carol M Block; *AV Coordr* Lillian Hetherington
Open Mon - Wed 8:30 AM - 8 PM, Thurs 8:30 AM - 6 PM, Fri & Sat 8:30 AM - 5 PM. Estab 1929
Library Holdings: Vols 16,000; Per subs 140; Indexed image files; AV — Slides 70,000; Other — Clipping files, exhibition catalogs
Special Subjects: Advertising Design, Fashion Arts, Graphic Design, Illustration, Industrial Design, Interior Design, Photography, Sculpture, Fine Arts, Motion Pictures, Product Design

A **AFRICAN AMERICAN HISTORICAL & CULTURAL SOCIETY,** Fort Mason Ctr, Bldg C, Rm 165, 94123. Tel 415-441-0640; FAX 415-441-2847; *Dir & Pres* Netra Roston-Warren; *Gift Shop Mgr* Vonnel Black
Open Wed - Sun 5 PM. Estab 1955 as an archival & presentation institution of African American thought & culture
Income: $100,000 (financed by mem & donations)
Collections: African artifacts, sculpture; Allensworth; Azania/Southern Africa; Black Businesses; Blacks in the West; Curriculum Studies; Fraternal Organizations & Benevolent Societies; Haitian Art; Protest Movements 1960s-1970s; Sargeant Johnson
Exhibitions: Unity Then & Now, Prison Art-Under Lock & Key
Publications: Ascension, biennial; Praisesinger, newsletter
Activities: Classes for adults & children; lect open to public, 12 vis lectr per year; gallery talks; tours; originate traveling exhibitions; sales shop sells books, magazines, original art, reproductions, prints, t-shirts, African art

L **Library,** 762 Fulton St, 94123. Tel 415-292-6172; FAX 415-441-2847; Elec Mail aahs@sfpl.lib.ca.us. *Librn* Amy Holloway
For reference only
Library Holdings: Vols 5000; Oral history
Collections: African-American newspapers; 1000 periodicals

A **AMERICAN INDIAN CONTEMPORARY ARTS,** 23 Grant Ave, 6th Flr, 94108. Tel 415-989-7003; FAX 415-989-7025; *Exec Dir* Janeen Antoime
Open Tues - Sat 10 AM - 5:30 PM. No admis fee. Estab 1983 to bring to the public eye perspectives on a new generation of American Indian artists. Managed by an American Indian staff & board, it is an advocacy & development organization for today's Indian artists trying to bridge the gap between traditional & contempory art & native & non-native people
Activities: On site lect; lect at schools & universities

A **ARCHIVES OF MOCA (MUSEUM OF CONCEPTUAL ART),** 657 Howard St, 94105. Tel 415-495-3193; FAX 415-495-3793; *Dir* Tom Marioni
Open by appointment. No admis fee. Estab 1970 for research, study & organization of exhibitions & events. Average Annual Attendance: 2000
Income: Financed by endowment
Exhibitions: Vito Acconci; Robert Barry; Bar Room Video; Chris Burden; Lowell Darling; Howard Fried; Paul Kos; Masashi Matsumoto; Restoration of Back Wall; Miniatures from San Francisco & Kyoto; Social Art, Cafe Society
Publications: Vision, 1975-1982
Activities: Classes for adults; lect, 2 vis lectr per year; concerts; artmobile; original objects of art lent to museums & art centers; original traveling exhibitions

L **Library,** 657 Howard St, 94105. Tel 415-495-3193; *Dir* Tom Marioni
For reference only
Library Holdings: Vols 1000; Original documents; Micro — Reels; AV — A-tapes, cassettes, fs, Kodachromes, motion pictures, rec, slides, v-tapes; Other — Exhibition catalogs, original art works, pamphlets, photographs, prints, sculpture
Exhibitions: Inspired by Leonardo

A **ART COM-LA MAMELLE, INC,** 70 12th St, PO Box 193123 Rincon, 94119-3123. Tel 415-431-7524, 431-7672; *Exec Dir* Carl E Loeffler; *Asst Dir* Jennifer Bender; *Distribution* Jen Tait
Open Mon - Fri 10:30 AM - 6:30 PM. Estab 1975 to support network for contemporary art
Income: Financed by endowment, mem & state appropriation
Collections: Artists' books, marginal works, video & television art, tape collection
Exhibitions: On Going - Artists Software; Artists Computer Graphics
Publications: Performance Anthology: Source book for a decade of California performance art; Correspondence Art: Source Book for the Network of International Postal Art Activity; ACEN (Art Com Electronic Network); Art Com Magazine; BBS
Activities: Distributes artists' video & television art world wide; maintains ACEN, an online artists' network for information sharing & distribution of art information; traveling exhibitions organized and circulated

L **Contemporary Art Archives,** 70 12th St, PO Box 193123 Rincon, 94119. *Dir* Carl E Loeffler
For reference only
Special Subjects: Video, Artists' books, Alternative publishing, Performance

M **ASIAN ART MUSEUM OF SAN FRANCISCO,** Avery Brundage Collection, Golden Gate Park, 94118-4598. Tel 415-668-8921; FAX 415-668-8928; Cable SANCEMOR. *Deputy Dir* Emily Sano; *Cur Indian Art* Terese Tse Bartholomew; *Cur Japanese Art* Yoko Woodson; *Cur Educ* Brian Hogarth; *Cur Chinese Art* Michael Knight; *Conservator* Tracy Power; *Cur Korean Art* Kumja Kim; *Librn* John Stucky
Open Wed - Sun 10 AM - 5 PM, first Wed of each month 10 AM - 8:45 PM, cl Mon, Tues & Christmas. Admis adults (18-64) $5, senior citizens $3, youth (12-17) $2, children under 12, recognized educational group & first Wed of each month free. Founded in 1969 by the City & County of San Francisco to collect, care for, exhibit & interpret the fine arts of Asia. 40,000 sq ft of exhibition space. Average Annual Attendance: 425,000. Mem: 40,000; dues $50
Income: Financed by city & county appropriation & the Asian Art Mus Foundation
Collections: Nearly 12,000 objects from China, Japan, Korea, India, Southeast

Asia, The Himalayas & Middle East; †architectural elements, †ceramics, †decorative arts, †paintings, †sculpture; †textiles, †works on paper
Publications: Exhibition catalogs; handbooks & catalogs on museum collections
Activities: Classes for children; docent training; lect open to public, 6 vis lectr per year; concerts; gallery talks; tours; original objects of art lent to other museums for exhibitions; originate traveling exhibitions to other museums; museum shop sells books, magazines, original art, reproductions & slides

L **Library,** Golden Gate Park, 94118-4598. Tel 415-668-8921; FAX 415-668-8928; *Librn* John Carl Stucky
Open Wed - Fri 10 AM - 4:45 PM. Estab 1967. For reference only
Income: Financed by mem, city appropriation & private gifts
Library Holdings: Vols 23,000; Per subs 160; Micro — Fiche, reels; AV — A-tapes, Kodachromes, lantern slides, motion pictures, slides; Other — Clipping files, exhibition catalogs, manuscripts, memorabilia, pamphlets, photographs
Special Subjects: Antiquities-Oriental, Antiquities-Persian, Archaeology, Architecture, Art History, Asian Art, Bronzes, Calligraphy, Carpets & Rugs, Ceramics, Decorative Arts, Dolls, Drawings, Embroidery, Enamels, Folk Art, Furniture, Glass, Gold, Goldsmithing, Handicrafts, Historical Material, History of Art & Archaeology, Islamic Art, Ivory, Jade, Jewelry, Landscape Architecture, Leather, Metalwork, Miniatures, Oriental Art, Painting - Japanese, Porcelain, Pottery, Printmaking, Prints, Religious Art, Restoration & Conservation, Sculpture, Silver, Silversmithing, Tapestries, Textiles, Watercolors, Woodcarvings, Woodcuts
Collections: Chinese painting collection; Khmer Art Collection

ASSOCIATION OF INDEPENDENT COLLEGES OF ART & DESIGN
For further information, see National and Regional Organizations

C **BANK OF AMERICA GALLERIES,** 555 California St, Art Program 3021, PO Box 37000, 94137. Tel 415-622-1265; *Cur* Bonnie Earls-Solari
Open Plaza Gallery Mon - Fri 8 AM - 5:30 PM, Concourse Gallery Mon - Fri 8 AM - Midnight, A P Giannini Gallery Mon - Fri 8 AM - 7 PM. Estab 1970 to operate as a pub service by Bank America Corporation for the downtown, financial district audience & art community. Average Annual Attendance: 520,000
Collections: Collection contains contemporary art in all media
Activities: Individual paintings & original objects of art lent to bonafide exhibitions & exhibiting bodies which can protect & properly install the art

M **CAPP STREET PROJECT,** 525 Second St, 94107. Tel 415-495-7101; FAX 415-495-7059; *Pres* Ann Hatch; *Prog Dir* Mary Ceruti; *Exec Dir* Linda Blumberg
Open Tues - Sat Noon - 6 PM. Estab 1983 as a non-profit arts organization providing three month residencies in San Francisco for installation art. Average Annual Attendance: 20,000
Publications: Capp Street Project Catalog, biennally
Activities: Lectr open to public, 8-10 vis lectr per year; tours; originate traveling exhibitions

M **CARTOON ART MUSEUM,** 814 Mission St, 94103. Tel 415-227-8666; FAX 415-243-8666; *Dir* Paola Muggia Stuff; *Asst Dir* Lara Pepp
Open Wed - Fri 11 AM - 5 PM, Sat 10 AM - 5 PM, Sun 1 - 5 PM. Admis adult $4, student & senior citizens $3, children $2. Estab 1984 to exhibit original cartoon art. 3000 sq ft exhibition space. Average Annual Attendance: 20,000. Mem: 500; dues individual $35
Income: $28,000
Collections: 11,000 pieces of original cartoon art
Exhibitions: 40 Years of Peanuts; Visions of a Floating World: The Cartoon Art of Japan
Publications: Cartoon Times
Activities: Classes for adults & children; lect open to public, 4 vis lectr per year; gallery talks; tours; cartoon contests for children kindergarten through 12th grade with money & gift certificates; individual paintings & original objects of art lent to other museums, galleries & corporations; lending collection contains color reproductions, original art works, original prints & paintings; retail store sells books, prints, magazines

A **CENTER FOR CRITICAL ARCHITECTURE,** AAES (Art & Architecture Exhibition Space), 450 Irwin St, 94107. Tel 415-703-9568; *Dir* Sarah Herdy
Estab 1988 to establish awareness of design excellence & provide vehicle for exchange of critical ideas in architecture. Average Annual Attendance: 3500. Mem: 100; 1600 mailing list; dues firms $100, individual $25
Income: Financed by endowment & mem
Publications: Cafe Talks, annual
Activities: Lect open to public, 6 vis lectr per year; competitions, conferences; book traveling exhibitions

M **CENTER FOR THE ARTS AT YERBA BUENA GARDENS,** 701 Mission St, 94103-3138. Tel 415-978-2700; FAX 415-978-9635; Elec Mail yerbabuena@aol.com. *Artistic Dir Visual Arts* Renny Pritikin; *Asst Artistic Dir Visual Arts* Rene de Guzman
Open Tues - Sun 11 AM - 6 PM. Admis $4. Estab 1993
Exhibitions: The Art of Star Wars; Rooms for the Dead

M **CHINESE CULTURE FOUNDATION,** Chinese Culture Center Gallery, 750 Kearny St, 3rd Flr, 94108. Tel 415-986-1822; FAX 415-986-2825; Internet Home Page Address http://www.c-c-c.org. *Pres* Albert Cheng; *Exec Dir* John H Seto
Open Tues - Sun 10 AM - 4 PM, cl holidays. No admis fee. Estab 1965 to promote the understanding & appreciation of Chinese & Chinese-American culture in the United States. Traditional & contemporary paintings, sculpture by Chinese & Chinese American artists, photographs & artifacts illustrating Chinese-American history & major international & cultural exchanges from China make the center a local & national focus of Chinese artistic activities. Mem: 800
Income: Financed by mem, city appropriation & grants
Exhibitions: Stories from China's Past; Beyond the Open Door; Landscapes of the Mind: Paintings of C C Wang; The Art of Wu Gaunzhong.
Publications: Chinese Culture Center Newsletter, quarterly; Exhibition catalogs
Activities: Classes for adults & children; dramatic programs; docent training; lect open to public; concerts; gallery talks; tours; film programs; museum shop sells books, original art, reproduction, prints, jewelry, pottery, jade, material & papercuts

C **EMBARCADERO CENTER LTD,** 4 Embarcadero Ctr, Ste 2600, 94111. Tel 415-772-0500; *Pub Relations Dir* Maureen Barry
Open to public at all hours. Estab 1971, modern art has been a key element in the planning & development of the Embarcadero Center complex; evidence of a desire to provide beauty on a smaller scale amid the harmony of its massive structures; to enhance the total environment & provide a variety of dramatic views for pedestrians as they circulate through the complex. Collection displayed throughout the Center complex; Center supports San Francisco DeYoung Museum, Fine Arts Museum Downtown Center, American Conservatory Theatre, San Francisco Symphony, San Francisco Center for the Performing Arts, and others
Collections: Willi Gutmann, Two Columns with Wedge; Francoise Grossen; Michael Gibbers, Steel Sculptures; Nicholas Schoffer, Chronos XIV; Lia Cook, Space Continuum Two; Olga de Amaral, Citurs Wall; Anne Van Kleeck, Blocks, Stacks; Louise Nevelson, Sky Tree; Barbara Shawcroft, Yellow Leggs; Robert Russin, Chthonodynamis; Jean Dubuffet, La Chiffonniere; Sheila Hicks, Cristobal's Trapeze & Itaka's Cascade; John Portman Jr, The Tulip; Elbert Weinberg, Mistral; Charles O Perry, Eclipse; Adolph Gottlieb, Burst; Francoise Grossen; Olga de Amaral, Hojarasca en mil Rojos; Jagoda Buic, Souvenir en Blue; Josef Grau Garriga, Lapell D'un Poble; Candace Crockett, Revival; Armand Vaillancourt, 101 precast aggregate concrete boxes that allow visitors to walk over, under & through its waterfalls

A **EXPLORATORIUM,** 3601 Lyon St, 94123. Tel 415-563-7337; FAX 415-561-0307; *Dir* Goery Delacote; *Artist Coordr* Peter Richards; *Museum Liaison* Sally Duensing
Open winter Tues - Sun 10 AM - 5 PM, Wed 10 AM - 9:30 PM, summer Wed - Sun 11 AM - 5 PM, Wed 5 - 9 PM. Admis adult $8.50, senior citizens $6.50, 6-18 $4.50. Estab 1969 to provide exhibits & art works centering around the theme of perception, which are designed to be manipulated & appreciated at a variety of levels by both children & adults. Average Annual Attendance: 500, 000. Mem: 1500; dues $35
Income: Financed by National city & state appropriation, private foundations & corporation contributions
Publications: The Exploratorium Magazine, monthly; exhibition catalogs
Activities: Classes for artists in residence program, performing artists in residence program & teachers; lect open to the public; concerts; tours; originate traveling exhibitions; museum shop sells books, magazines, reproductions, prints, slides & science related material

A **EYES & EARS FOUNDATION,** * 642 Natoma, 94103. Tel 415-621-2300; *Exec Dir* Mark Rennie; *Pres* Freddie Hahne
Estab 1976 to sponsor pub visual performance art projects, mostly outdoor large-scale billboard art shows & the theatre projects. Average Annual Attendance: 100,000 per day. Mem: 100; dues $15
Income: $57,000 (financed by endowment, mem, fundraising, individual & corporate contributions)
Exhibitions: Artists Television Access; Lynn Hershman & Lisa English's Endangered Species; Sando Counts, Sideshow; weekly exhibitions.

M **FINE ARTS MUSEUMS OF SAN FRANCISCO,** c/o de Young Museum, Golden Gate Park, 94118. Tel 415-750-3636, 750-3641 (March); FAX 415-750-7686; *Deputy Dir* Paula March
Estab 1971 as a mem organization for Fine Arts Museum of San Francisco & the Asian Art Mus of San Francisco & the Asian Art Mus of San Francisco. Mem: 45,000; dues $50
Income: $2,770,000 (financed by mem & bookshop revenues)
Publications: Triptych, bimonthly magazine
Activities: Museum shop sells books, reproductions, prints & slides

M **M H de Young Memorial Museum & California Palace of the Legion of Honor,** Golden Gate Park, 94118. Tel 415-750-3600; *Dir* Harry S Parker III; *Deputy Dir Admin* Stephen E Dykes; *Assoc Dir & Chief Cur* Steven Nash; *Cur African, Oceania & the Americas* Kathleen Berrin; *Mgr Exhib* Bill White; *Cur Interpretation* Renee Dreyfus; *Cur Textiles* Melissa Leventon; *Registrar* Ted Greenberg; *Conservator Paper* Robert Futernick; *Assoc Cur American Painting* Patti Junker; *Publs Mgr* Ann Karlstrom; *Cur Rugs* Cathryn Cootner; *Gen Mgr Museum Stores* Couric Payne; *Ed Dir Media Relations* Pamela Forbes; *Audio & Visual Dir* Linda Jablon
Open Wed - Sun 10 AM - 5 PM. Admis adults $5, seniors & youth 12-17 $3, under 12 free. Estab 1895 to provide museums of historic art from ancient Egypt to the 20th century. Two separate buildings are maintained, one in the Golden Gate Park (de Young Mus) with 65 galleries & the other in Lincoln Park (California Palace of the Legion of Honor) with 22 galleries. Average Annual Attendance: 800,000. Mem: 50,000; dues patron $1000, sponsor $500, donor $250, supporting $100, sustaining $60, individual $25, senior dual $20, s
Collections: African art; American art; Ancient art; Art from Central & South America & Mesoamerica; textiles; graphic arts of all schools & eras; primitive arts of Africa, Oceania & the Americas; Rodin sculpture collection
Exhibitions: (1997) The Shape of Belief. African Art; American paintings (various artists)
Publications: Triptych, bimonthly magazine; exhibition & collection catalogues
Activities: Classes for adults & children; docent training; lect open to public; tours; museum shop sells books, magazines, reproductions, prints, slides & jewelry

L **Library,** Golden Gate Park, 94118. Tel 415-750-7603; *Librn* Allison Pennell
Estab 1955 to serve mus staff in research on collections, conservation, acquisition, interpretations. Graphic arts are housed in the Achenbach Foundation Library in the California Palace of the Legion of Honor
Income: Financed by mem & city appropriation
Library Holdings: Vols 45,000; Per subs 125; Micro — Fiche 613, reels; AV — Slides 30,000; Other — Exhibition catalogs
Special Subjects: American Indian Art, African, American, French & Oceanic Art
Collections: Achenbach Foundation for Graphic Arts (prints & drawings)

A **THE FRIENDS OF PHOTOGRAPHY,** Ansel Adams Center for Photography, 250 Fourth St, 94103. Tel 415-495-7000; FAX 415-495-8517; *Exec Dir* Andy Grundberg; *Pres* Carla Emil; *Pres* Tony Hooker; *Treas* Roy Eisenhardt; *Treas* Geoffrey Yang
Open Tues - Sun 11 AM - 5 PM & first Thurs of every month 11 AM - 8 PM. Admis adults $4, students $3, senior citizens & youth 12-17 $2, members & children free. Estab 1967 to promote creative photography through exhibitions, workshops, publications & critical inquiry. Maintains an art gallery with continuous exhibitions. Average Annual Attendance: 36,400. Mem: 5500; dues $35
Income: $1,000,000 (financed by endowment, mem, city & state appropriations, federal grants & patrons)
Collections: Photographs by Ansel Adams
Publications: Untitled, book series published by the Friends of Photography, 2 times per year; newsletter, 6 issues per year; monographic publications
Activities: Classes for adults; educational outreach to children; lect open to the public, 6 vis lectr per year; competitions with awards; scholarships offered; book traveling exhibitions; originate traveling exhibitions; sales shop sells books

M **GALERIA DE LA RAZA,** Studio 24, 2851 & 2857 24th St, 94110. Tel 415-826-8009; FAX 415-826-5128; *Exec Dir* Liz Lerma; *Dir* Maria Pinedo; *Asst Dir* Mia Gonzalez; *Asst Cur & Gallery Coordr* Ruben Guzman; *Technical Asst* Richard Sanchez; *Gallery Docent* Jose R Lernia
Open Tues - Sat Noon - 6 PM. Donations accepted. Estab 1969 as a community gallery & mus to exhibit works by Chicano-Latino artists, contemporary as well as cultural folk art. Two rooms in the Mission District of San Francisco, the heart of the Latino Community. Average Annual Attendance: 35,000. Mem: 135; dues $35
Income: Financed by NEA, California Arts Council, private foundations & earned income from sales in studio
Exhibitions: Changing monthly
Publications: Exhibition catalogs, small publications, yearly calendar, children's coloring book & postcards; bi-monthly newsletter
Activities: Docent training; lect open to public, 8-15 vis lectr per year; gallery talks; tours; originate traveling exhibitions 1 per year; museum shop sells folk art
L **Chicano-Latino Arts Resource Library,** 2857 24th St, 94110. Tel 415-826-8009; FAX 415-826-5128
Open Mon - Fri Noon - 6 PM. Estab 1978 as a reference & archives of Chicano & Latino arts
Income: $1000
Purchases: $500
Library Holdings: Vols 300; Per subs 5; AV — Slides; Other — Clipping files, exhibition catalogs, memorabilia, original art works, pamphlets, photographs, prints, reproductions
Special Subjects: El Dia de Los Muertos artifacts and resources
Collections: Chicano & Latino murals; Chicano Latino Youth; car clubs Mexican Folk Art; Mexican & Latin American Contemporary Art

A **INTERSECTION FOR THE ARTS,** 446 Valencia, 94103. Tel 415-626-2787; FAX 415-626-1636; *Dir* Francis Phillips
Open Tues - Sat Noon - 4:30 PM. Estab 1965 to represent visual & performing arts. Average Annual Attendance: 10,000

A **JAPANTOWN ART & MEDIA WORKSHOP,** 1840 Sutter St, Ste 102, 94115. Tel 415-922-8700; *Exec Dir* Dennis Taniguchi
Open daily 10 AM - 5 PM. No admis fee. Estab 1977 as an Asian-American art center. Mem: 120; dues $20
Income: $100,000 (financed by endowment, mem, foundations, city & state appropriations)
Collections: Silkscreen posters & other art works
Exhibitions: Layer Exhibition; Asia-American Film & Video Exhibit
Publications: Enemy Alien; Yoisho
Activities: Classes for adults & children; concerts; competitions with awards; lending collection contains posters

M **THE LAB,** 2948 16th St, 94103. Tel 415-864-8855; FAX 415-864-8855; *Admin Dir* Elisabeth Beaird; *Artistic Dir* Laura Brun; *Asst Develop Dir* Zoey Kroll
Open Wed - Sat Noon - 5 PM. No admis fee. Estab 1983 to support the development & presentation of experimental & interdisciplinary art of emerging or mid-career artists
Income: $130,000 (financed by mem, city & state appropriations, federal funding & private foundations)
Exhibitions: Installations; Interdisciplinary & Experimental Art
Activities: Classes for adults & youth; digital sound editing classes; lect open to public; concerts; dance; performance art events; exhibitions

L **MECHANICS' INSTITUTE LIBRARY,** 57 Post St, 94104. Tel 415-421-1750; FAX 415-421-1770; *Dir* K T Pabst; *Reference Librn* Craig Jackson
Open for members only Mon - Thurs 9 AM - 9 PM, Fri 9 AM - 6 PM, Sat & Sun 1 - 5 PM. Estab 1854 to serve the needs of 7000 members with a general collection emphasizing the humanities. Circ 285,000
Income: Financed by city appropriation, building rents, endowment
Library Holdings: Vols 180,000; Per subs 685; Newspapers; Micro — Fiche; AV — Cassettes, v-tapes; Other — Clipping files
Special Subjects: American Western Art, Architecture, Art History, Crafts, Decorative Arts, Embroidery, Etchings & Engravings, Fashion Arts, Furniture, Handicrafts, Painting - American, Painting - Australian, Painting - British, Painting - French, Painting - German, Japanese Painting, Photography, Watercolors

M **MEXICAN MUSEUM,** Fort Mason Ctr, Bldg D, Laguna & Marina Blvd, 94123. Tel 415-441-0445; *Exec Dir* Marie Acosta-Colon; *Deputy Dir* Lilia Villanueva; *Cur* Tere Romo; *Develop Dir* Nancy Young; *Financial Dir* Carol Wells; *Acting Dir Develop* Amy Schoenborn
Open Wed - Sun Noon - 5 PM. Admis adults $3, students & senior citizens $2. Estab 1975 to foster the exhibition, conservation & dissemination of Mexican & Mexican-American & Chicano culture for all people. Average Annual

Attendance: 60,000. Mem: 720, dues $25
Income: Financed by state grants, corporate & individual support, earned income through gift shop, mem, educational tours & work shops
Collections: Chicano, Colonial, Folk, Mexican, Mexican-American & Pre-Hispanic Fine Arts
Publications: Exhibit catalogs
Activities: Summer internship program; docent program; lect open to public; gallery talks; tours; exten dept serves San Francisco Bay area; lending collection contains slides & educational kits; book traveling exhibitions; museum shop sells books, original art, reproductions & prints

M **MUSEO ITALO AMERICANO,** Fort Mason Ctr, Bldg C, 94123. Tel 415-673-2200; FAX 415-673-2292; *Pres* Annette De Nunzio; *VPres* Peter Gumina; *VPres* Paola Bagnatori; *Treas* Claudio Tarchi; *Cur* Robert Whyte; *Adminr* Michela DiPilla
Open Wed - Sun Noon - 5 PM. Admis $2, senior citizens & full-time students $1. Estab 1978 to research, preserve & display works of Italian & Italian-American artists & to foster educational programs for the appreciation of Italian & Italian-American art, history & culture. 3700 sq ft of exhibit space; The Fontana Gallery & The Lanzone Gallery. Average Annual Attendance: 25,000. Mem: 1034; dues $35-$1000
Income: Financed by mem, city appropriation, foundations & corporate contributions
Collections: 20th Century paintings, sculptures, prints & photographs
Exhibitions: The Work of David Bottini (sculpture); J DeFeo (The Florentine Works); Napoli Naples (photography); Frank Spadarella (photography); Palcoscenico e Spazio Scenico (stage design); Emerging Artists Show
Publications: Calendar of Events, monthly
Activities: Classes for adults & children; school outreach art program; lect open to public; concerts; awards; individual paintings & original objects of art lent to museums; museum shop sells books, magazines, Italian pottery, blown glass & gift items
L **Library,** Fort Mason Ctr, Bldg C, 94123-1380. Tel 415-673-2200; FAX 415-673-2292; *Cur* Robert A Whyte
Estab 1978 to serve as a resource center of Italian & Italian-American culture & art
Library Holdings: Vols 300

NAMES PROJECT FOUNDATION
For further information, see National and Regional Organizations

NATIONAL ALLIANCE FOR MEDIA ARTS & CULTURE
For further information, see National and Regional Organizations

M **NEW LANGTON ARTS,** 1246 Folsom St, 94103. Tel 415-626-5416; FAX 415-255-1453; *Elec Mail* nla:arts@sirius.com. *Exec Dir* Susan Miller; *Prog Assoc* Lareli Stewart; *Operations Mgr* Misha Myers; *Develop Assoc* Amy Hicks
Estab 1975 to support artists in experimental art, non-profit organization
Exhibitions: David Wilson: Museum of Jurassic Technology.

M **RANDALL MUSEUM JUNIOR MUSEUM,** 199 Museum Way, 94114. Tel 415-554-9600; FAX 415-668-3330; *Dir* Amy Dawson; *Cur Natural Sciences* John Dillon; *Cur Natural Sciences* Carol Preston; *Cur Arts* Chris Boetcher; *Art Instr* Dennis Treanor; *Art Instr* Julie Dodd Tetzlaff
Open Tues - Sat 10 AM - 5 PM, cl holidays. No admis fee. Estab 1937 as part of the San Francisco Recreation & Park Dept. Average Annual Attendance: 50,000. Mem: 300; dues $15-$250; annual meeting in June
Collections: Animals; Children's Art; Indian Artifacts; Insects, Minerals
Activities: Classes for adults & children; dramatic programs; docent training; lect open to public; concerts; tours; competitions with awards; scholarships offered

L **SAN FRANCISCO ACADEMY OF COMIC ART,** Library, * 2850 Ulloa St, 94116. Tel 415-681-1737; *Dir* Bill Blackbeard
Open daily by appointment 10 AM - 10 PM. Estab 1967 to locate, preserve and house all elements of American popular narrative culture in danger of destruction through oversight or misunderstanding. Gallery maintained
Income: Financed by grants, donations, fees from personnel writing and lect, research charges
Library Holdings: Vols 28,000; Per subs 42; AV — Cassettes, motion pictures, rec, slides, v-tapes; Other — Clipping files, exhibition catalogs, framed reproductions, manuscripts, memorabilia, original art works, pamphlets, photographs, prints, reproductions
Collections: †Adventure fiction; †the American comic strip; †the American newspaper; †the American popular fiction magazine; †children's books since 1850; †detective fiction; †motion pictures; †the popular illustrated periodical; radical and underground publications; †science fiction; †Victorian illustrated book; western fiction
Exhibitions: Permanent collection: Original art in the comic strip and popular fiction; comic strip exhibit; national science fiction
Activities: Lect, 10 visiting lectr per year; gallery talks; tours; originate traveling exhibitions

M **SAN FRANCISCO ART COMMISSION,** Gallery & Slide Registry, 401 Van Ness Ave, 155 Grove St, 94102. Tel 415-554-6080; FAX 415-252-2595; *Elec Mail* sfacgallery@sfpl.lib.ca.us;
Internet Home Page Address http://thecity.sfsu.edu/sfac. *Dir* Rupert Jenkins; *Asst Dir* Cheryl Coon
Open Wed - Sat Noon - 5:30 PM. No admis fee. Estab 1970. Average Annual Attendance: 20,000. Mem: dues $10
Income: Financed by mem & city appropriations
Exhibitions: (1997) Jehanne-Marie Gavirini, Ann Chamberlain; Mary Ellen Pleasant (African-American photo archive); San Francisco Arts Education Project (group show); Time & Space: Awareness into Art: Cynthia Lenssen, Annette Tosti, Robert Ortbal, Betsie Miller-Kusz (1997-98) Street Artists 25th Anniversary Show; Board (group show); Fahrenheit 451 (book show); Jim Goldberg
Activities: Classes for children; lect open to public; lending collection contains slides

M SAN FRANCISCO ART INSTITUTE, Galleries, 800 Chestnut St, 94133. Tel 415-749-4564; *Gallery Dir* Jean-Edith Weiffenbach
Open Tues - Sat 10 AM - 5 PM, Thurs evening until 8 PM, Sun Noon - 5 PM. No admis fee. Estab 1871, incorporated 1889 to foster the appreciation & creation of the fine arts & maintain a school & mus for that purpose. Walter McBean Gallery; two-level, used for exhibitions of contemporary artists of international repute; Diego Rivera Gallery, one room with Rivera miral, used for exhibitions of work by SFAI students; SFAI Photo Gallery, for photo students.
Average Annual Attendance: 60,000
Exhibitions: Walter McBean (six exhibitions per year)
Publications: Exhibition catalogs
Activities: Lect open to public, 20 vis lectr per year; gallery talks; tours; scholarships & fels offered; exten dept; sales shop sells art supplies

L Anne Bremer Memorial Library, 800 Chestnut St, 94133. Tel 415-749-4559; *Media Dir* Charles Stephanian; *Librn* Jeff Gunderson; *Catalog Librn* Carolyn Franklin; *Library Asst* Claudia Marlowe
Open Mon - Thurs 8:30 AM - 8:30 PM, Fri 8:30 AM - 6 PM, Sat 11 AM - 5:30 PM, Sun Noon - 4 PM & during school sessions. Estab 1871 to develop a collection & services which will anticipate, reflect & support the objectives & direction of the San Francisco Art Institute & the contemporary arts community. Circ 12,795
Library Holdings: Vols 26,000; Per subs 200; AV — Cassettes 600, fs, Kodachromes, motion pictures, slides 70,000; Other — Clipping files, exhibition catalogs, manuscripts, memorabilia, pamphlets, photographs
Collections: Archives documenting the history of the Art Institute; artists' books
Exhibitions: Artists' Book Contest; 1960's Rock Posters
Activities: Poetry-Book Readings; current events roundtable

A SAN FRANCISCO ARTSPACE & ARTSPACE ANNEX, 123 S Park, 94103. Tel 415-546-9100; FAX 415-546-0236; *Dir* Anne MacDonald; *Prog Dir* Maureen Keefe
Open Tues - Sat by appointment only. Estab 1985 for contemporary exhibitions & installations; video editing & sound systems. Two galleries, 3000 sq ft
Income: Financed by endowment, mem, city & state appropriation
Exhibitions: Jessica Diamond
Publications: Art Space Book, semiannual
Activities: Lect open to public, 5 vis lectr per year; 2 book signings; grants offered; retail store sells books, magazines

A SAN FRANCISCO CAMERAWORK INC, 115 Natoma St, 94105. Tel 415-764-1001; FAX 415-764-1063; *Dir* Marnie Gillett; *Assoc Dir* Beth Goldberg; *Prog & Educ Coordr* Michael Rauner; *Gallery Bookstore Mgr* Corey Cohen
Open Tues - Sat Noon - 5 PM. Estab 1973 to encourage & display contemporary photography & related visual arts through exhibitions, lectures, publications & communication services. Two large galleries in a loft space as well as bookstore display area. Average Annual Attendance: 35,000. Mem: 1400; dues $40 & up
Income: Financed by government agencies & private contributions, mem
Exhibitions: James D Phelan Art Award in Photography
Publications: San Francisco Camerawork Quarterly
Activities: Lect open to public, 10 vis lectr per year; workshops; gallery talks; competitions; book traveling exhibitions 1-3 per year; museum shop sells books & magazines, postcards, limited edition artists' books

A SAN FRANCISCO CITY & COUNTY ART COMMISSION, 25 Van Ness Ave, Ste 240, 94102. Tel 415-252-2590; FAX 415-252-2595; *Pres* Anne Healy; *Dir Cultural Affairs* Joanne Winship; *Asst Dir* Richard Newirth; *Dir Neighborhood Art Prog* Sonia Gray; *Dir Street Artist Prog* Howard Lazar; *Dir Pub Art Prog* Jill Manton; *Art Commission Gallery* Jason Tannen; *Mgr Civic Art Coll* Debra Lehane; *Dir Cultural Equity Grants* Lawrence Thoo
Open daily 8 AM - 5 PM. No admis fee. Estab 1932. Average Annual Attendance: 100,000. Mem: Consists of nine professional & three lay-members appointed by the Mayor with advice of art societies & five ex-officio members; monthly meetings
Activities: Classes for adults & children; dramatic programs; docent training; neighborhood arts program; lect open to public; concerts; competitions; individual paintings & original objects of art lent to city agencies; lending collection contains 28,000 original artworks

M SAN FRANCISCO CRAFT & FOLK ART MUSEUM, Fort Mason Ctr, Landmark Bldg A, 94123-1382. Tel 415-775-0990; FAX 415-775-1861; *Dir* J Weldon Smith, PhD; *Cur* Carole Austin; *Adminr* Mary Ann McNicholas
Open Tues - Sun 11 AM - 5 PM, Sat 10 AM - 5 PM, first Wed of month 11 AM - 7 PM. Admis $1, seniors & teens 12-17 $.50, children free. Estab 1983 to provide a permanent showplace for contemporary craft, folk art & traditional ethnic art. Maintains reference library. Average Annual Attendance: 90,000. Mem: 856; dues $35-$250
Income: $250,000 (financed by endowment, mem fees, city & state appropriations & private foundations)
Publications: A Report, scholarly quarterly; 1989-90 The Arts & Crafts Studio of Dirk Van Erp; The Quiet Eye; Pottery of Shoji Hamada & Bernard Leach
Activities: Classes for adults; slide programs; docent training; lect open to public, 5 vis lectr per year; gallery talks; special events; originate traveling exhibitions; museum shop sells books, handmade jewelry & art objects

M SAN FRANCISCO MARITIME NATIONAL HISTORICAL PARK, National Maritime Museum, Bldg E, Lower Fort Mason, Rm 265, 94123. Tel 415-556-1659; FAX 415-556-1624; Elec Mail williamthomas@npsgov. *Supt* William G Thomas; *Librn* David Hull
Open winter daily 10 AM - 5 PM, summer daily 10 AM - 6 PM. Admis adults $3, senior citizens & children free. Estab 1951; mus built in 1939; a terazzo & stainless steel structure with a nautical theme
Income: Financed by federal funding, private support from National Maritime Mus Assoc, Golden Gate National Park Assoc & donations
Purchases: A S Palmer Film Collection
Collections: Historic photographs; paddlewheel ferry; paddlewheel tug; paintings; scow schooner; small craft; †ship models; square-rigged sailing ship: steam schooner; steam tug; 3-mast schooner

Exhibitions: Tugboats; San Francisco Bay Ferryboats
Publications: Sealetter; booklets, irregular
Activities: Slide lect; environmental living program; sales shop sells books, magazines, reproductions & miscellaneous materials

L J Porter Shaw Library, Lower Fort Mason, Bldg E, 94123. Tel 415-556-9870; FAX 415-556-3540; Elec Mail golibgo@well.sf.ca.usa. *Principal Librn* David Hull; *Reference* Irene Stachura; *Technical Services* Herbert Beckwith; *Library Technician* Bill Koolman; *Library Technician* Debbie Grace; *Library Technician* Mark Goldstein
Open to the public for research on premises
Income: $275,000 (financed by federal & friends group)
Purchases: $7500 (collection development)
Library Holdings: Vols 18,000; Per subs 150; Archives; Oral History; Vessel Plans; Micro — Fiche, reels; AV — A-tapes, cassettes, motion pictures; Other — Clipping files, manuscripts, memorabilia, pamphlets, photographs 250,000
Special Subjects: Historical Material, Marine Painting

M SAN FRANCISCO MUSEUM OF MODERN ART, 151 Third St, 94103-3159. Tel 415-377-4000; FAX 415-357-4158; *Dir* John R Lane; *Dir Curatorial Affairs* Lori Fogarty; *Chief Cur* Gary Garrels; *Controller* Ikuko Satoda
Open Mon, Tues & Thurs - Sun 11 AM - 6 PM, & Thurs 11 AM - 9 PM, cl Wed. Admis adults $7, senior citizens & students $3.50, members & children under 13 free. Estab 1935 to collect & exhibit art of the 20th century. Mus occupies its own 225,000 sq ft building. Average Annual Attendance: 750,000. Mem: 36,000; dues $20-$150
Income: Financed by endowment, mem, city hotel tax, earnings & grants
Collections: Clyfford Still; †painting, †photography, †sculpture †architecture & design, †media & video works
Publications: Monthly Calendar
Activities: Classes for adults & children; docent training; lect open to public; 40 vis lectr per year; gallery talks; tours; competitions; originate traveling exhibitions organized & circulated; museum shop sells books, magazines, original art, reproductions, prints & slides

L Library, 151 Third St, 94103-3159. Tel 415-357-4120; FAX 415-357-4038; *Librn* Eugenie Candau
Open to the pub for reference, Tues & Thurs 11 AM - 4 PM, by appointment
Library Holdings: Vols 30,000; Per subs 400; Artists files; Museum archives; Other — Exhibition catalogs
Special Subjects: Modern & contemporary art including photography, architecture & design
Collections: Margery Mann Collection of books in the history of photography

M Rental Gallery, Fort Mason Bldg A, 94123. Tel 415-441-4777; FAX 415-441-0614; *Dir* Marian Wintersteen Parmenter; *Corporate Consultant* Sue Sproule; *Gallery Coordr* Andrea Voinot
Open Tues - Sat 11:30 AM - 5:30 PM. No admis fee. Estab 1978 for the support & exposure of Northern California artists. Over 1000 artists represented
Exhibitions: Eleven exhibitions per year, all media; one person & group exhibitions

L SAN FRANCISCO PUBLIC LIBRARY, Art & Music Center, Civic Ctr, 94102. Tel 415-557-4525; FAX 415-557-4524; *Dir* Kenneth E Dowlin; *Art & Music* Marilyn Thieme
Open Mon - Thurs 9 AM - 8 PM, Fri 11 AM - 5 PM, Sat 9 AM - 5 PM, Sun Noon - 5 PM. Estab 1878
Income: Financed by city & state appropriations
Library Holdings: Vols 45,000; Per subs 250; Micro — Cards, fiche, reels; AV — A-tapes, motion pictures, rec, v-tapes; Other — Clipping files, exhibition catalogs

L SAN FRANCISCO STATE UNIVERSITY, J Paul Leonard Library, 1630 Holloway, 94132. Tel 415-338-2188; FAX 415-338-6199; Elec Mail dtong@sfsu.edu. *Dir* Open ; *Art Librn* Darlene Tong
Open Mon - Wed 8:30 AM - 10 PM, Thurs 8:30 AM - 9 PM, Fri 8:30 AM - 4 PM, Sat & Sun Noon - 5 PM. Estab 1890
Library Holdings: Vols 800,000; Per subs 4500; Bound Periodial Vol 110,000; Micro — Cards, fiche, prints, reels; AV — A-tapes, cassettes, fs, motion pictures, rec, v-tapes; Other — Exhibition catalogs, framed reproductions, manuscripts, memorabilia, original art works
Special Subjects: Antiquities-Etruscan, Antiquities-Roman, Art History, Graphic Design, Industrial Design, Intermedia, Jewelry
Collections: John Magnani Collection of Arts & Crafts; Frank deBellis Collection on Italian Culture; Juliet Bredon Collection of Chinese Textiles; H Wilder Bentley Brush Painting Collection; Simeon Pelenc Collection of Paintings & Drawings
Activities: Book traveling exhibitions; originate traveling exhibitions; sales shop sells books & reproductions

M SOUTHERN EXPOSURE GALLERY, 401 Alabama St, 94110. Tel 415-863-2141; FAX 415-863-1841; *Dir* Mike Blackstein
Estab to give exposure of contemporary California art by emerging and established artists

M TATTOO ART MUSEUM, 841 Columbus Ave, 94133. Tel 415-775-4991; FAX 707-462-4406; *Dir* Lyle Tuttle; *Consultant* Judith Tuttle
Open daily Noon - 6 PM. Admis donations. Estab 1974. Average Annual Attendance: 5000
Collections: Lyle Tuttle Collection, tattoo art, Memorabilia & Equipment, especially tattoo machines & primitive tools; George Burchett Collection
Publications: Magazine of the Tattoo Art Museum; Tattoo Historian, biannual
Activities: Lect open to public, 12 vis lectr per year; awards; Tattoo Hall of Fame; individual paintings & objects of art lent; bookstore sells books, original art work, reproductions & prints

C WELLS FARGO BANK, Wells Fargo History Museum, 420 Montgomery St, 94163. Tel 415-396-2619; FAX 415-391-8644; *Cur* Charles LaFontaine
Open Mon - Fri 9 AM - 5 PM, cl Bank holidays. Estab 1960 to provide information on Wells Fargo, California & San Francisco. For reference only. Average Annual Attendance: 65,000

Collections: Wiltsee Collection of Postal Franks; Califonia History; 19th & 20th Century Banking; San Francisco History
Exhibitions: Great Ships of California
Activities: Concerts; tours; museum shop sells books

SAN JOSE

M **ROSICRUCIAN EGYPTIAN MUSEUM & ART GALLERY,** 1342 Naglee Ave, 95191-0001. Tel 408-947-3636; FAX 408-947-3638; *Dir* Julie Scott
Open daily 9 AM - 5 PM. Admis adults $6.75, senior citizens $5, children 7-15 $3.50, under 7 free. Estab 1929, in present location 1966, to publicly show a collection of the works of ancient Egyptians, reflecting their lives & culture. Collections include Bronzes of Egyptian Gods & Goddesses; Funerary Models; full size walk-in tomb replica; human & animal mummies; Tel-El-Armana room with amulets, cosmetics & writing implements; jewelry, pottery & King Zoser's tomb complex; Mesopotanian collection - cuneiform tablets & seals from Babylon, Sumer & Assyna; a contemporary art gallery. Average Annual Attendance: 100,000
Income: Financed by Rosicrucian Order, AMORC
Purchases: Regular acquisitions of Egyptian antiquities
Collections: Collections include Bronzes of Egyptian Gods & Goddesses; Funerary Models; full size walk-in tomb replica; human & animal mummies; Tel-El-Armana room; amulets, cosmetics, writing implements, jewelry, pottery, scale model of King Zoser's tomb complex; Mesopotanian collection - cuneiform tablets & seals from Babylon
Exhibitions: Monthly contemporary exhibitions in Art Gallery; mainly one-man
Publications: The Hieroglphic Coloring Book Magazine; quarterly magazine
Activities: Tours; lect; gift shop sells books, magazines, reproductions, prints, slides, jewelry & posters

M **SAN JOSE INSTITUTE OF CONTEMPORARY ART,** 451 S First St, 95113. Tel 408-998-4310, 283-8155; *Dir* Preston Metcalf
Open Tues, Wed, Fri & Sat 11 AM - 5 PM, Thurs 11 AM - 8 PM & by appointment. No admis fee. Estab 1980, SJICA is a non-profit visual arts organization highlighting emerging & estab artists from the Greater Bay Area. One large store front space plus mezzanine. Average Annual Attendance: 20,000. Mem: 700; dues $25 & up
Income: Financed by mem & cultural grants
Exhibitions: Monthly exhibitions
Activities: Lect open to public; gallery talks; tours by appointment

M **SAN JOSE MUSEUM OF ART,** 110 S Market St, 95113-2383. Tel 408-294-2787, 271-6881; FAX 408-294-2977;
Internet Home Page Address http://www.sjliving.com/sjma. *Dir* Josi I Callan; *Deputy Dir* Deborah Norberg; *Dir Develop* Angela McConnell; *Dir Public Relations* Diane Maxwell; *Dir Marketing* Yvonne Nevens; *Dir Mem* Linda Larkin; *Cur* Peter Gordon; *Book & Gift Shop Mgr* Madelon Palma
Open Tues, Wed, Fri, Sat & Sun 10 AM - 5 PM, Thurs 10 AM - 8 PM. Admis adults $6, senior citizens, students with ID & children under 6 free. Estab 1969 to foster awareness, appreciation & understanding of 20th century art. An 1892 Richardson-Romanesque building with a striking contemporary new wing, totaling more than 18,000 sq ft of exhibition space. Average Annual Attendance: 200,000. Mem: 4500; dues $45-$250; annual meeting in June
Income: Financed by City of San Jose, private sector contributions, state & federal government
Collections: Permanent Collection features work by †nationally recognized artists, †artists of the California region, †American prints, †sculptures, & †paintings by American masters
Exhibitions: (1997) The Eureka Fellowship Awards: 1996-1998; Two in Montana: Deborah Butterfield & John Buck, Sculpture & Woodblock Prints; Basil Blackshaw-Painter; William Wegman: Photographs, Paintings, Drawings & Videos; Manuel Neri: Early Works, 1953-1978; New Art in China, Post-1989. (1997-98) American Art in the Age of Technology: Selections from the Permanent Collection of The Whitney Museum of American Art
Publications: Exhibition catalogs; Framework Newsletter, quarterly
Activities: Classes for adults & children; docent training; family programs; school outreach; lect open to public, 13 vis lectr per year; concerts; gallery talks; tours; competitions with awards; individual paintings lent to non-profit institutions for educational & scholarly purposes; book traveling exhibitions; originate traveling exhibitions to other museums in the US; museum shop sells books, magazines, reproductions, prints, jewelry, gifts, toys & cards
L **Library,** 110 S Market St, 95113. Tel 408-271-6840; FAX 408-294-2977; *Librn* Jean Wheeler
Open to the mus staff & volunteers for reference only
Income: Financed by donations
Library Holdings: Vols 2300; AV — Slides 1200, v-tapes; Other — Clipping files, exhibition catalogs 3750, pamphlets, photographs
Special Subjects: Children's Art Books
Publications: SJMA Frameworks, 6 times a year

SAN JOSE STATE UNIVERSITY
M **Art Gallery,** Art Dept, 95192-0089. Tel 408-924-4328; FAX 408-924-4326; *Dir* Andy Ostheimer
Open Tues - Fri 11 AM - 4 PM during term. No admis fee. Estab 1960 as part of the university Art Dept. Gallery is 34 x 28 ft with 12 ft ceiling. Average Annual Attendance: 9000
Income: Financed by city & state appropriations & private endowment
Exhibitions: Robert Brady, Design, Contemporary Issues
Publications: Exhibition catalogs; brochures
Activities: Lect open to public, 6 vis lectr per year; concerts; gallery talks; tours; scholarships offered
L **Robert D Clark Library,** One Washington Square, 95192-0028. Tel 408-924-2738; FAX 408-924-2701; Elec Mail ecrowe@email.sjsu.edu;
Internet Home Page Address bantrim0email.sjsu.edu. *Art Reference Librn* Edith Crowe; *Slide Cur* Elizabeth Antrim
Purchases: $44,205
Library Holdings: Vols 36,500; Per subs 88; Micro — Cards, fiche, prints, reels; AV — A-tapes, cassettes, fs, lantern slides, motion pictures, rec, slides, v-tapes; Other — Exhibition catalogs, framed reproductions, original art works, photographs, prints, reproductions

SAN LUIS OBISPO

L **CALIFORNIA POLYTECHNIC STATE UNIVERSITY,** College of Architecture & Environmental Design-Art Collection, Media Resource Ctr, 93407. Tel 805-756-2165; FAX 805-756-5986; *Asst* Vickie Aubourg
Open Mon - Fri 9 AM - 5 PM, cl Sat & Sun. No admis fee. Estab 1969; 180,000 slides for lending & reference. Circ 20,000 (slides)
Income: $11,500 (financed by state appropriation)
Library Holdings: Vols 1000; Per subs 30
Special Subjects: Architecture, Constructions, Intermedia, Landscapes, City Planning
Collections: Architecture & Landscape Architecture slide collection

L **CUESTA COLLEGE,** Cuesta College Art Gallery, PO Box 8106, 93403-8106. Tel 805-546-3202; FAX 805-546-3904; *Dir* Marta Peluso
Open Mon - Thurs 7:30 AM - 9 PM, Fri 7:30 AM - 4 PM, Sun Noon - 6 PM, vacation hrs vary. Estab 1966 to support the educational program of the college. Contemporary fine art gallery featuring rotating exhibitions of national, regional & local artists. Average Annual Attendance: 10,000
Library Holdings: Vols 3130; Per subs 18; Micro — Fiche, reels; AV — A-tapes, cassettes, fs, motion pictures, rec, slides, v-tapes; Other — Pamphlets
Collections: 20 works of art primarily of California artists; 2 Japanese artists
Activities: Educ dept; lect open to public, 6 vis lectr per year; gallery talks; tours; originate traveling exhibitions

A **SAN LUIS OBISPO ART CENTER,** 1010 Broad St (Mailing add: PO Box 813, 93406-0813). Tel 805-543-8562; FAX 805-543-4518; *Exec Dir* Carol Dunn; *Cur* Arne Nybak
Gallery open Tues - Sun 11 AM - 5 PM. Estab 1952 to promote the visual arts through educ, expression & interaction. Average Annual Attendance: 40,000. Mem: 700; dues $15-$100
Income: $100,000 (financed by mem, earnings & donations)
Collections: Small collection of regional artists
Exhibitions: Gray Wing Gallery: (1997) Brushstrokes '97; 30 By 30: A Celebration; Geo-Political Landscapes; Craftmakers '97; Prints; Realm of Courage; Denial
Publications: Calendar of Events Newsletter, monthly
Activities: Classes for adults & children; docent programs; lect open to public, 50 vis lectr per year; scholarships offered; sales shop sells original art, reproductions, cards & jewelry

SAN LUIS REY

M **MISSION SAN LUIS REY DE FRANCIA,** Mission San Luis Rey Museum, 4050 Mission Ave, 92068. Tel 619-757-3651; FAX 619-757-4613; *Local Minister* Father Warren Rouse; *Cur* Mary Whelan; *Admnr* Ed Gabarra
Open Mon - Sat 10 AM - 4 PM, Sun Noon - 4 PM. Admis adults $3, children $1. Estab 1798 to protect, conserve & display artifacts which reflect the history of the Mission. Average Annual Attendance: 75,000
Income: Financed by property of Franciscan Friars Inc of California
Collections: Artifacts, furniture, paintings, statuary, religious vestments & vessels & other historical objects from early mission days in California
Activities: Individual paintings & original objects of art lent to qualified museums; sales shop sells books, slides & religious items

SAN MARCOS

M **PALOMAR COMMUNITY COLLEGE,** Boehm Gallery, 1140 W Mission Rd, 92069. Tel 619-744-1150; *Gallery Dir* Harry Bliss
Open Mon - Thurs 8 AM - 8 PM, Fri 8 AM - 4 PM, Sat 10 AM - 2 PM. No admis fee. Estab 1964 to provide the community with fine art regardless of style, period or approach. The gallery is 35 x 35 ft, no windows, 18 in brick exterior, acoustic ceiling & asphalt tile floor. Average Annual Attendance: 50,000
Income: $8000 (exhibition budget). Financed by city & state appropriations
Collections: †Contemporary art by nationally acclaimed artists; 16th - 20th century art; California artists
Exhibitions: Annual Student Art Show; Three Photographers: Edward, Cole and Kim Weston; Roland Reiss, The Morality Plays: An Installation Work; Eleanor Antin, A Look-Back 1969-1975; Robert Freeman; Native American; Etchings and Richard White; Table; Kazuo Kadonaga; Sculpture; D J Hall; Recent Paintings and Drawings Richard Allen Morris: Painting Retrospective; Christine Oatman: Fantasy Landscapes; Sam Richardson: Ten Year Retrospective of Sculpture and Drawing; Italo Sconga: Recent Sculpture; Masami Teraoka: Recent Paintings and Prints; Wayne Thiebaud: Recent Paintings and Drawings; William Wiley: Recent Sculpture and Drawings
Activities: Lect open to public, 12 vis lectr per year; competitions; individual paintings & original objects of art lent to reputable museums & galleries; lending collection contains original paintings, prints & sculpture

SAN MARINO

M **CALIFORNIA HISTORICAL SOCIETY,** El Molino Viejo, 1120 Old Mill Rd, 91108-1840. Tel 818-449-5450; *Pres* David Hudnut
Open Tues - Sun 1 - 4 PM, cl holidays. Historic adobe grist mill with changing exhibit room. Mem: dues centennial $1000, benefactor $500, associate $250, patron $150, contributing $75, sustaining $40, active $25, student $15
Income: Financed by mem dues & contributions
Collections: Fine arts include California lithography & other graphics; oils; watercolors; drawings; furniture & artifacts to 1915; research materials both original & published on California & Western artists
Exhibitions: National traveling photographic exhibitions; The American Farm; changing thematic exhibits relating to California history in the galleries of the Whittier House from the society's collection. Permanent exhibition in San Francisco from the Society's collections
Publications: California History, quarterly magazine

Activities: Classes for adults; docent training; programs; lect; tours & films throughout the state; lect open to the public; concerts; gallery talks; tours; awards given for participation in the field of California history; traveling exhibitions organized & circulated

L **Schubert Hall Library,** 678 Mission St, San Francisco, 94109-2235. Tel 415-567-1848; *Dir* Michael McCone
Estab 1922 to collect books, manuscripts, photographs, ephemera, maps and posters pertaining to California and Western history. For in-house reference & research only
Library Holdings: Vols 45,500; Per subs 150; Original documents; 3-dimensional artifacts; Micro — Fiche, reels; AV — A-tapes, cassettes, Kodachromes, lantern slides, motion pictures, slides; Other — Clipping files, framed reproductions, manuscripts, memorabilia, original art works, pamphlets, photographs 500,000, prints, reproductions
Special Subjects: Early California imprints; county and municipal histories; early voyages of exploration, Genealogy; Gold Rush; Printing; Publishing
Collections: C Templeton Crocker Collections; Florence Keen Collection of Western Literature; San Francisco Chronicle Collection; Kemble Collection of Western Printing & Publishing
Exhibitions: The American Farm; Executive Order 9006

M **THE HUNTINGTON LIBRARY, ART COLLECTIONS & BOTANICAL GARDENS,** 1151 Oxford Rd, 91108. Tel 818-405-2100; FAX 818-405-0225; *Pres* Robert Allen Skotheim; *VPres Develop* Marylynn Warren; *VPres Financial Affairs* Alison Sowden; *Dir Art Division* Edward J Nygren; *Dir Library* David Zeidberg; *Dir Botanical Gardens* James Folsom; *Dir Research* Robert Ritchie; *Dir Communications* Catherine M Babcock; *Cur American Art* Amy Meyers; *Cur British & Continental Art* Shelley Bennett
Open Tues - Fri Noon - 4:30 PM, Sat & Sun 10:30 AM - 4:30 PM, cl Mon & major holidays. Suggested donation adults $7.50, senior citizens 65 & older $6, students 12 & older $4. Estab 1919 by the late Henry E Huntington as a free research library, art gallery, mus & botanical garden; exhibitions open to the pub in 1928 for educational & cultural purposes. Virginia Steel Scott Gallery for American art opened in 1984. Average Annual Attendance: 500,000. Mem: 7500; supporters of the institution who give $45-$1000 annually are known as the Friends of the Huntington Library, Fellows give $2000 or more per yr
Income: Financed by endowment & gifts
Collections: Ellesmere manuscript of Chaucer's Canterbury Tales; Gutenberg Bible on vellum; Birds of America by Audobon; British, European & American art collections; Rich Collection of rare books & manuscripts
Publications: The Calendar, bimonthly; Huntington Library Quarterly; various monographs & exhibition catalogs
Activities: Classes for children; dramatic programs; docent training; lect open to public, 25 vis lectr per year; concerts; gallery talks; tours; scholarships & fels offered; museum shop sells books, calendars, gift items, note cards, postcards, prints, puzzles, reproductions, slides

L **Art Reference Library,** 1151 Oxford Rd, 91108. Tel 818-405-2228; FAX 818-405-0634; *Head Art Reference Library* Linda Kay Zoeckler
Open Mon - Fri 8:30 AM - Noon & 1 - 5 PM. No admis fee. Estab 1940 for research. Open to qualified scholars for reference. Average Annual Attendance: 1500
Income: Financed by endowments & gifts
Library Holdings: Vols 682,094; Per subs 1200; Photographic archive 100,000; Micro — Cards, fiche, prints, reels; Other — Exhibition catalogs, manuscripts, memorabilia, pamphlets, prints
Special Subjects: American Western Art, Art History, Bronzes, Carpets & Rugs, Ceramics, Decorative Arts, Drawings, Etchings & Engravings, Furniture, History of Art & Archaeology, Illustration, Interior Design, Landscape Architecture, Landscapes, Manuscripts
Collections: British drawings & watercolors; probably the largest collection of books, photographs & other materials for the study of British art that exists outside London

L **UNIVERSITY OF SOUTHERN CALIFORNIA,** Greene & Greene Library of the Arts & Crafts Movement, The Scott Gallery of the Huntington Library, 1151 Oxford Rd, 91108. Tel 818-405-2232; *Dir* Randel Makinson; *Library Chmn* Louise Millis
Open Tues & Thurs 1 - 4 PM by appointment. Estab 1968 as a concentrated collection of archival material on the work of architects Charles & Henry Greene, their contemporaries & the Arts & Crafts movement. For research only
Library Holdings: Vols 800; Per subs 12; Blueprints; Client files; Drawings; AV — Rec, slides 800; Other — Clipping files, exhibition catalogs, manuscripts 10, memorabilia, pamphlets, photographs
Special Subjects: Architecture, Decorative Arts, Historical Material
Collections: †Art, architecture, and decorative arts of architects Charles Sumner Greene and Henry Mather Greene
Activities: Docent training; lect open to members only

SAN MIGUEL

M **MISSION SAN MIGUEL MUSEUM,** 775 Mission St, PO Box 69, 93451. Tel 805-467-3256; FAX 805-467-2448; *Dir* Father John Vaughn; *Pastor* Salvador Parisi
Open daily 9:30 AM - 4:30 PM, cl New Year's, Easter, Thanksgiving & Christmas. Admis by donation. Estab 1797 as The Old Mission church, the original still in use as the parish church. The Mission contains paintings dating back to the 18th century, also original, untouched frescoes. Average Annual Attendance: 50,000
Income: Financed by Franciscan Friars
Activities: Concerts; tours; sales shop sells books, reproductions, prints, slides, gifts & religious articles

SAN PEDRO

M **ANGELS GATE CULTURAL CENTER,** The Gate Gallery, 3601 S Gaffey St, PO Box 1471, 90733. Tel 310-519-0936; FAX 310-519-8698; *Exec Dir* Pamela Siers; *Asst to Dir* Lydia Dickerson; *Facilities Mgr* Ted Rosenthal; *Admin Asst* Lynne Mori
Open Wed - Sun 11 AM - 4 PM. No admis fee. Estab 1981 dedicated to innovation & cultural diversity. 3000 sq ft interdisciplinary space, contains four galleries. Mem: 400; dues $10-$1500; annual meeting in Sept
Income: $150,000 (financed by mem, studio rentals, workshop tuition, donations & grants)
Publications: The Gate, quarterly; Oversight at the Gate
Activities: Classes for adults; internships; outreach workshops; lect open to public; director's tours; dialogue with artists; competitions with prizes; scholarships & fels offered

SAN RAFAEL

M **CITY OF SAN RAFAEL,** Falkirk Cultural Center, 1407 Mission Ave, 94901. Tel 415-485-3328; FAX 415-485-3404; *Dir* Carol Adney; *Cur* Cameron Cartiere
Gallery Open Tues - Fri 10 AM - 5 PM, Thurs 10 AM - 9 PM, Sat 10 AM - 1 PM. Estab 1974 to provide classes, lectures, concerts. Contemporary art gallery. Average Annual Attendance: 45,000. Mem: Dues Business/Corporate $1000, patron $500, donor $250, sponsor $100, family $50, regular $30, sr citizen & student $15
Income: Financed by City of San Rafael appropriation, rentals, classes & grants
Publications: Exhibition catalogues
Activities: Classes for adults & children; docent training; lect open to public, 6 vis lectr per year; concerts; tours; juried annual competitions with cash awards; bookstore sells books, prints, & poetry readings

M **PUBLIC ART WORKS,** PO Box 150435, 94915-0435. Tel 415-457-9744; FAX 415-457-9749; *Exec Dir* Bill Morrison
Estab 1979 to sponsor art in pub places

SANTA ANA

M **BOWER'S MUSEUM,** 2002 N Main St, 92706. Tel 714-567-3600; FAX 714-567-3603; *Registrar* Teresa M Ridgeway; *Exec Dir* Dr Peter Keller; *Chief Cur* Armand J Labbe; *Cur Native American Art* Paul Opodocer; *Chief Cur of Educ* Janet Baker; *Cur of Exhibit* Paul Johnson; *Dir Develop & Marketing* Pat House
Open Tues - Sat 10 AM - 4 PM, Sun 1 - 5 PM, cl Mon. Admis adults $4.50, students & sr citizens $3, children $1.50. Estab 1934 to provide an active cultural arts museum for the community. Housed in an authentic California mission-style structure amid expansive fountain-studded grounds, originally devoted to the display of antique furniture, Indian relics & historical items of early California families, is currently undergoing a major expansion of its physical plant. The new 51,000 sq ft addition includes major galleries, new collection storage rooms, administrative offices, library, restaurant peoples of the Americas & the Pacific rim. Average Annual Attendance: 225,000. Mem: 1800; dues from student $15 - life $1000
Income: Financed by city appropriation
Collections: Pre-Columbian, North American Indian, Asian, Pacific & African; California history; late 19th century Oriental costumes; 19th & early 20th century North & South American costumes; Northwest American Indian; 19th & 20th century American Indian baskets; 19th century American textiles, decorative arts & patterned glass; Oceania; Orange County history
Publications: Brochures; Calendar, monthly; exhibition catalogs
Activities: Classes for adults & children; docent guild; lect open to public; films; gallery talks; tours; study clubs; paintings & original art objects lent to other museums; originate traveling exhibitions organized & circulated; sales shop sells books, magazines, original art, reproductions, prints, jewelry, imported clothing, gift items

M **ORANGE COUNTY CENTER FOR CONTEMPORARY ART,** PO Box 1892, 92701-1892. Tel 714-549-4989; *Dir* Jefferey Frisch; *Advisor to Board* Gene Isaacson; *Treas* Russell Sasaki
Open Wed - Sun 11 AM - 4 PM. No admis fee. Estab 1980 as a non-profit exhibit space, alternative to commercial galleries & to provide support & exposure to contemporary work in visual arts; gallery houses artists slide registry. Average Annual Attendance: 3000. Mem: 200; general mem requires only annual dues, affiliate is a juried process; dues affiliate $48, general $25
Income: Financed by mem & donations
Exhibitions: The gallery shows run 4 wks & 3 artists are shown concurrently
Publications: Art Week, monthly; Art Scene, monthly
Activities: Lect open to public; concerts; gallery talks; sponsors juried exhibit annually; awards donated by local businesses

SANTA BARBARA

L **BROOKS INSTITUTE PHOTOGRAPHY LIBRARY,** 1321 Alameda Padre Serra (Mailing add: 801 Alston Rd, 93108). Tel 805-966-3888; *Librn* Isabelle Higgins
Open Mon - Fri 8 AM - 5 PM. Lend to students only, reference to non-students
Income: Financed by school tuition
Library Holdings: Vols 6953; Per subs 92; CD-ROMs; AV — Fs, v-tapes
Special Subjects: Photography

A **SANTA BARBARA CONTEMPORARY ARTS FORUM,** 653 Paseo Nuevo, 93101. Tel 805-966-5373; FAX 805-962-1421; Internet Home Page Address http://artscenecal.com. TDD 805-965-9727. *Pres Board of Dir* Paul Roberts; *Dir* Nancy Doll; *VPres* Susan Jorgensen; *VPres* Keith Puccinelli; *Treas* Christian White
Open Wed - Sat 10 AM - 5 PM, Sun Noon - 5 PM. Estab 1976; committed to the presentation of contemporary art. Klausner Gallery 2345 sq ft & Norton

Gallery 378 sq ft. Mem: 800; dues start at $25

Income: $265,000 (financed by federal, state, county & city grants, corporate & private contributions, fund raising events)

Publications: Addictions; Carl Cheng: exhibit catalogues; Carroll Dunham: paintings; Focus/Santa Barbara; Jene Highstein: Gallery/Landscape; Teraoka Erotica

Activities: Classes for adults & children; docent training; lect open to public, 15 vis lectr per year; gallery talks; tours; book traveling exhibitions; originate traveling exhibitions to other non-profit galleries; sales shop sells artist designed plates, books, exhibition catalogs, Yoko Ono Artist book

M **SANTA BARBARA MUSEUM OF ART,** 1130 State St, 93101-2746. Tel 805-963-4364; FAX 805-966-6840; *Acting Dir* Robert Frankel; *Deputy Dir & Asst Dir Admin* Barbara Luton; *Asst Dir Curatorial Servs* Robert Henning Jr; *Cur Educ* Deborah Borrowdule-Cox; *Registrar* Cherie Summers; *Cur 20th Century Art* Diana duPont; *Cur Asian Art* Susan Shin-Tsu Tai; *Cur Photo* Karen Sinsheimer; *Public Relations* Virginia Cochran

Open Tues - Sun 11 AM - 5 PM. Admis adults $4, senior $3, students & children 6-17 $1.50. Estab 1941 as an art mus with exhibitions & educ programs. 14 galleries totaling 16,500 sq ft of exhibition space. Maintains reference library. Average Annual Attendance: 125,000. Mem: 3600; dues director's circle $1250 & up, patron $600, master member $300, gallery guild $150, assoc $60, general $40, student $20

Income: $2,600,000 (financed by earnings, including endowment, mem, grants, government & foundations & contributions)

Collections: Preston Morton Collection of American Art; Asian Art; Classical Art; International Modern Art; 19th Century French Art; prints & drawings; photography; 20th Century Art

Exhibitions: Prized Possessions: Selections from the Permanent Collection; Venice: The City of All Seasons; Santa Barbara's Own: The Architecture of Lutah Maria Riggs; Cambios: The Spirit of Transformation in Spanish Colonial Art; Mexican Colonial Paintings: From the Old World to the New; Photographs of China by Loris Conner; In Dialogue: The Art of Elsa Rady & Robert Mapplethorpe; Brushstrokes: Styles & Techniques of Chinese Painting; Auguste Rodin: Selections from the Fine Arts Museums of San Francisco; In Rodin's Studio: Photographs; Seeing Straight: The F/64 Revolution in Photography; Egypt Through the Lens; Werner Bischof; The Splendid Centuries: 18th & 19th Century French Paintings From the Fine Arts Museums of San Francisco; 19th Century French Prints from the Permanent Collection; The Santa Barbara Connection: Contemporary Photography

Publications: Bulletin, bi-monthly newsletter; exhibit & collection catalogs; Update, semi-annual periodical

Activities: Classes for adults & children; docent training; outreach classes & programs; lect open to public, 4-6 vis lectr per year; concerts; gallery talks; tours; scholarships offered to children's art classes only; artmobile; individual paintings original objects of art lent to other museums only for exhibition; book traveling exhibitions 3-5 per year; originate traveling exhibitions; museum shop sells books, original art, reproductions

L **Library,** 1130 State St, 93101. Tel 805-963-4364; FAX 805-966-6840; *Dir* Robert H Frankel

Open to pub on an appointment basis. For reference only

Library Holdings: Vols 40,000; Per subs 20; AV — Kodachromes, slides; Other — Clipping files, exhibition catalogs, manuscripts, pamphlets

L **SANTA BARBARA PUBLIC LIBRARY,** Faulkner Memorial Art Wing, 40 E Anapamu St, PO Box 1019, 93102. Tel 805-962-7653; FAX 805-962-8972; *Dir* Carol Keator; *Reference Librn* Margot Collin

Open Mon - Thurs 10 AM - 9 PM, Fri & Sat 10 AM - 5:30 PM, Sun 1 - 5 PM. Estab 1930 & administered by the library trustees as a municipal art reading room & gallery

Library Holdings: Vols 200,000; Per subs 500; Micro — Fiche, prints, reels; AV — Cassettes, rec; Other — Clipping files, framed reproductions, pamphlets, reproductions

Exhibitions: Local contemporary paintings & sculpture

Activities: Lect, programs & meetings; lending collection contains reproduction paintings

UNIVERSITY OF CALIFORNIA, SANTA BARBARA

M **University Art Museum,** Arts Bldg, 1626-B, 93106. Tel 805-893-2951; FAX 805-893-3013; *Dir* Marla Berns; *Cur* Elizabeth Brown; *Designer Exhib* Paul Prince; *Cur Educ* Corinne Gillet Horowitz; *Registrar* Sandra Rushing; *Pub Relations Coordr* Sharon Major; *Preparator* Rollin Fortier; *Cur Architectural Drawings* Dr David Gebhard; *Adjunct Cur Ethnic Art* Dr Herbert M Cole; *Adjunct Cur Photo* Dr Ulrich Keller; *Adjunct Cur Drawings* Dr Alfred Moir

Open Tues - Sat 10 AM - 4 PM, Sun & holidays 1 - 5 PM, cl Mon, New Year's, Thanksgiving, Christmas, Easter & between exhibits. No admis fee. Estab 1959 & direct at both the needs of the university & the community; with a wide range of contemporary & historical exhibitions. Located in the UCSB campus Arts Building complex; three galleries for changing exhibits; two which exhibit part of the permanent collection. Average Annual Attendance: 30,000

Income: Financed by university funds

Collections: Collection of Architectural Drawings by Southern California Architects, including Irving Gill, R M Schindler, George Washington Smith & Kem Weber; Morgenroth Collection of Renaissance Medals & Plaquettes; Sedgwick Collection of 16th-18th Century Italian, Flemish & Dutch Artists; Ala Story Print Collection; Grace H Dreyfus Collection of Ancient Peruvian & Middle Eastern Art; Fernand Lungren Bequest

Publications: Exhibition catalogs, 3 - 6 per year

Activities: Classes for adults & children; lect upon request; regular schedule of docent tours; gallery talks; originate traveling exhibitions; sales shop sells exhibition catalogs, books, prints, slides, reproductions, t-shirts, gifts

L **Library,** 93106. Tel 805-893-3613; Elec Mail korenic@library.ucsb.edu. *Head Arts Library* Lynette Korenic

Open Mon - Thurs 9 AM - 10 PM, Fri & Sat 9 AM - 6 PM, Sun 2 - 10 PM. Estab 1966 to support academic programs. Circ 60,000

Income: Financed by state appropriation

Library Holdings: Vols 86,000; Per subs 520; Auction Catalogs 42,000; Micro —

Fiche 75,000, reels 1400; AV — V-tapes 180; Other — Exhibition catalogs 80,000, pamphlets 11, photographs 5000

Special Subjects: Aesthetics, American Western Art, Antiquities-Byzantine, Antiquities-Greek, Architecture, Art History, Drawings, Etchings & Engravings, Furniture, History of Art & Archaeology, Painting - American, Painting - Dutch, Photography, Pre-Columbian Art, Prints, Art Theory & Criticism, Greek, Roman & Etruscan Art, Islamic Art & Architecture, Medieval Art & Architecture, Primitive & Exotic Art, Renaissance & Baroque Art

Publications: Catalogs of the Art Exhibition, Catalogs of the Arts Library, University of California, Santa Barbara; Cambridge, England, Chadwyck-Healey, 1978

Activities: Tours

SANTA CLARA

A **ARTS COUNCIL OF SANTA CLARA COUNTY,** 4 N Second St, Ste 210, 95513. Tel 408-998-2787; FAX 408-971-9458; Elec Mail artsfund@aol.com. *Dir* Bruce Davis

Estab 1982 as the regional art support/planning agency for Santa Clara County, The Arts Council is the principal funding agency within the county for small, mid-size & multi-cultural arts groups & individual independent artists

Income: $1,000,000 (financed by county, California Arts Council, San Jose & other county municipalities, local, private & community foundations, Silicon Valley corporations, individual gifts & interest from two endowments)

Activities: Annual Music & Arts Campaign

M **SANTA CLARA UNIVERSITY,** de Saisset Museum, 500 El Camino Real, 95053. Tel 408-554-4528; FAX 408-554-7840; *Academic Pres* Rev Paul Locatelli, SJ; *Assoc VPres Academic Affairs* Jo Ann Vasquez; *Dir* Rebecca M Schapp; *Preparator* Fred Shepard; *Coll Mgr & Public Relations Officer* Anna Koster; *Admin Asst* Vicky Lee; *Cur Exhibits & Coll* Jo Anne Severns Northrup

Open Tues - Sun 11 AM - 4 PM, cl Mon & all holidays. No admis fee. Estab 1955 as a major cultural resource in Northern California. In recent years the museum has dramatically broadened its scope, exhibiting some of the world's leading avant-garde artists while not losing sight of the traditional. The gallery has 20,000 sq ft of floor space in a concrete structure adjacent to the Mission Santa Clara, two stories of galleries with a mezzanine for small exhibitions, plus offices & workrooms. Average Annual Attendance: 25,000. Mem: dues friend $500, benefactor $250, sponsor $100, family $50, individual $35, student & senior citizen $20

Income: Financed by endowment, mem, University operating budget & grants

Purchases: All media

Collections: Kolb Collection of 17th & 18th century graphics; Arnold Mountfort Collection; D'Berger Collection of French furniture & ivories; African Collection; New Deal art repository; photography, paintings, antiques, sculpture, prints, china, silver & ivory collections; 17th & 18th century tapestries; Henrietta Shore Collection (paintings & prints); Focus Gallery Collection: Helen Johnston Bequest (photographs)

Exhibitions: Quarterly exhibitions of contemporary & modern art

Publications: Newsletter, quarterly; exhibition catalogs

Activities: Lect open to public; gallery talks; tours; paintings lent to campus offices; originate traveling exhibitions

M **TRITON MUSEUM OF ART,** 1505 Warburton Ave, 95050. Tel 408-247-3754; FAX 408-247-3796; *Dir & Pres* Richard Gourley; *Asst Dir & Chief Cur* George Rivera

Open Wed - Fri 10 AM - 5 PM, Sat & Sun Noon - 5 PM, Tues 10 AM - 9 PM, cl Mon. No admis fee. Estab 1965 to offer a rich & varied cultural experience to members of the community through the display of 19th & 20th century American art, particularly artists of California & through related special events & programs. The mus consists of a new state of the art facility designed by San Francisco architect Barcelon Jang. The building opened in Oct, 1987 & sits on a 7 acre park site with four Oriental/Spanish style pavilions & sculpture garden. Average Annual Attendance: 120,000. Mem: 1000; dues $15-$1000

Income: $550,000 (financed by endowment, mem & city appropriation)

Collections: Paintings by Frank Duveneck; The Austen D Warburton Native American Art & Artifacts Collection; American paintings, prints & sculpture; oil paintings by Theodore Wores; international folk art

Publications: Exhibition catalogs; newsletter, bimonthly

Activities: Classes for children; docent training; lect open to public, 4 vis lectr per year; concerts; gallery talks; tours; competition with prizes; individual paintings & original objects of art lent to museums, non-profit galleries & educational institutions; lending collection contains original art works; original prints; paintings & sculpture; book traveling exhibitions 2 per year; originates traveling exhibitions; museum shop sells books, postcards, handmade jewelry & gift items

L **Library,** 1505 Warburton Ave, 95050. Tel 408-247-3754; FAX 408-247-3796; *Acting Dir* George Rivera

Open by appointment only. Estab 1967 to enhance the resource of the art mus. Open to members for reference

Library Holdings: Vols 800; Per subs 10; AV — Slides; Other — Clipping files, exhibition catalogs

Special Subjects: Folk Art, Twentieth Century American Art

Collections: †Special collection of artists books

Exhibitions: Working with Glass: A Survey of Bay Area Artists; Art of New Guinea; The Art of Instruments: 1450-1800; Scientific Inventions & Curiosities by Clayton Bailey; Miniatures

Publications: Exhibition catalogs; bimonthly newsletter

SANTA CLARITA

L **CALIFORNIA INSTITUTE OF THE ARTS LIBRARY,** 24700 McBean Pky, 91355. Tel 805-253-7885; FAX 805-254-4561; Elec Mail fred@muse.calarts.edu. *Dean* Frederick Gardner; *Music Librn & Cataloger* Joan Anderson; *Info Resources & Dance & Theater Librn* Susan Lowenberg; *Film & Reference Librn* Margie Hanft; *Art & Slide Librn* Evelyn Horigan
Open Mon - Thurs 9 AM - Midnight, Fri 9 AM - 9 PM, Sat Noon - 5 PM, Sun 1 PM - Midnight. Estab 1961, first classes 1970, designed to be a community of practicing artists working in schools of art, design, film, music, theatre & dance
Income: Financed by endowment
Library Holdings: Vols 63,204; Per subs 565; Performance music 19,738; Micro — Cards 3900, fiche 991, reels 5041; AV — A-tapes 1773, cassettes, fs 731, motion pictures 1150, rec 13,147, slides 109,165, v-tapes 3296; Other — Exhibition catalogs 12,494, pamphlets
Special Subjects: Film, Theatre Arts, Video, Art & Design, Critical Studies, Dance, Music
Exhibitions: Student work, approximately 20 per year
Publications: California Institute of the Art Library Handbook
Activities: Scholarships & fels offered

SANTA CRUZ

A **CHILDREN'S ART FOUNDATION,** Museum of International Children's Art, 765 Cedar St, Ste 201, PO Box 83, 95063. Tel 408-426-5557; FAX 408-426-1161; Elec Mail editor@stonesoup.com. *Pres* William Rubel; *VPres* Gerry Mandel; *Admin Asst* Laurie Gabriel
Open Mon - Fri 9 AM - 5:30 PM & by appointment. No admis fee. Estab 1973 to improve the quality of American art education. Gallery has 800 sq ft with rotating displays of art by children from around the world. Average Annual Attendance: 3500. Mem: 20,000; dues $26; quarterly meetings
Income: $5000
Purchases: $5000
Collections: American children's art; drawings, paintings & prints from 40 countries
Exhibitions: Exhibit of 55 works from international children's art collection at Portland Art Museum; Exhibit of 50 paintings by Nelly Toll, made when she was a 10-year-old in hiding from the Nazis in Poland in 1943-44, at the University of California, Santa Cruz
Publications: Stone Soup, magazine 5 times per yr
Activities: Classes for children; individual paintings & original objects of art lent; originates traveling exhibitions; sales shop sells magazines & reproductions

M **MUSEUM OF ART & HISTORY** (Formerly Art Museum of Santa Cruz County), 705 Front St, 95060. Tel 408-429-1964; FAX 408-429-1954; Elec Mail mah@cruzio.com. *Exec Dir* Charles Hilger
Admis adults $2 (in county) $3 (out of county). Estab 1981 to encourage & develop the study of fine arts & to foster & support educational & artistic interests in the county. 2200 sq ft galleries. Average Annual Attendance: 40,000. Mem: 1200; dues $15-$5000
Income: $100,000
Publications: Catalogues; quarterly newsletter
Activities: Docent training; lect open to public, 12 vis lectr per year; gallery talks; tours; originate traveling exhibitions; Art Box, a mobile museum which travels to county elementary schools

A **SANTA CRUZ ART LEAGUE, INC,** Center for the Arts, 526 Broadway, 95060. Tel 408-426-5787; *Pres* Bill Bagnall; *Office Mgr* Kim Scheibraur
Open Tues - Sun 11 AM - 4 PM, cl Mon. No admis fee, $1 donation. Estab 1919, Incorporated 1949, to further interest in visual & arts performing in community. 2000 sq ft of gallery space, off-site exhibits, 65 seat performance hall. Average Annual Attendance: 10,000. Mem: 700; dues $35
Income: Financed by donations
Collections: Local historical & contemporary works
Exhibitions: Annual Statewide Juried Show; Open Studios Preview
Publications: Bimonthly bulletin
Activities: Classes for adults & children; classes in painting, drawing & sculpture; dramatic programs; docent training; demonstration by professional artist at monthly meetings; 12 vis lectr per year; gallery talks; competitions with awards; scholarships offered to senior high schools in Santa Cruz County; sales shop sells original art, reproductions & prints

UNIVERSITY OF CALIFORNIA AT SANTA CRUZ
M **Eloisa Pickard Smith Gallery,** Cowell College, 95064. Tel 408-459-2953; *Dir* Linda Pope
Open Tues - Sun 11 AM - 5 PM
Exhibitions - Futzie Nutzle; Tobin Keller; Barbara Guenther
Publications: Exhibition catalog, annually

M **Mary Porter Sesnon Art Gallery,** Porter College, 95064. Tel 408-459-2314; FAX 408-459-3535; Elec Mail sesnon@cats.ucsc.edu. *Dir* Pamela Bailey; *Asst Dir* Bridget Barnes
Open Tues - Sun Noon - 5 PM. No admis fee. Estab 1974 for curricular support through exhibitions & programs. Average Annual Attendance: 6000
Income: $51,000 (financed by endowment, state appropriation, donor support & catalog sales)
Exhibitions: Pilar Aguero: Absence of Gravity; Hung Liu: Identity Fragments
Publications: Exhibition catalogs, periodically
Activities: Classes for adults & children; lect open to public, 3-5 vis lectr per year; book traveling exhibitions; originate traveling exhibitions

SANTA MONICA

A **18TH STREET ARTS COMPLEX,** 1639 18th Street, 90404. Tel 310-453-3711; FAX 310-453-4347; Elec Mail arts18thst@aol.com; Internet Home Page Address http://www.ecafe.com. *Exec Dir* Clayton Campbell; *Gen Mgr* Jan Williamson
Provides art services to the pub & services to artists & art organizations engaged with contemporary issues of community & diversity
Collections: High Performance Magazine Archives
Publications: Traffic Report, annual

L **GETTY CENTER FOR THE HISTORY OF ART & THE HUMANITIES TRUST MUSEUM,** 17985 Pacific Coast Hwy (Mailing add: 401 Wilshire Blvd, Ste 700, 90401-1455). Tel 310-458-9811; FAX 310-458-6661; Telex 82-0268; TWX 910-343-6873. *Assoc Dir* Debra Gribbon; *Cur of European Sculpture & Works of Art* Peter Fusco; *Cur Paintings & Drawings* David Jaffe; *Cur Antiquities* Marion True; *Cur Photographs* Weston Naef; *Cur Decorative Arts* Gillian Wilson; *Cur Manuscripts* Thom Kren; *Head Public Information* Sue Runyard
Open by appointment only. No admis fee, parking reservations required, call 310-458-2003. Estab 1983 for the purpose of advancing research in art history & related disciplines. The mus building is a re-creation of an ancient Roman villa & consists of 47 galleries. Average Annual Attendance: 400,000
Income: Financed by Foundation
Library Holdings: Vols 650,000; Per subs 1500; Micro — Fiche, reels; Other — Exhibition catalogs, pamphlets
Special Subjects: Architectural treatises, antiquities reference works, early 20th century archival & library materials
Collections: Art historical archives; photo archives
Publications: Calendar, monthly; Museum Journal, annually
Activities: Docent training; slide show for children; classroom materials; research scholar program by invitation only, 20 vis scholars per year; original objects of art lent to other museums for special exhibitions; museum shop sells books, reproductions, slides & museum publications

L **The J Paul Getty Museum,** 17985 Pacific Coast Hwy (Mailing add: PO Box 2112, Santa Monica, 90265-5799). Tel 310-459-7611; FAX 310-454-6633; *Dir* John Walsh Jr; *Cur European Sculpture & Works of Art* Peter Fusco; *Cur Paintings & Drawings* David Jaffe; *Cur Antiquities* Marion True; *Cur Photographs* Weston Naef; *Cur Decorative Arts* Gillian Wilson; *Cur Manuscripts* Thomas Kren; *Head Public Information* Sue Runyard
Open Tues - Sun 10 AM - 5 PM, cl New Year's Day, Independence Day, Thanksgiving & Christmas. No admis fee, parking reservations required, call 310-458-2003. Founded 1953. Research in fields pertaining to collections & conservation. The mus building is a re-creation of ancient Roman villa with interior & exterior gardens. Average Annual Attendance: 400,000
Income: Financed by endowment
Library Holdings: Vols 450,000; Per subs 1500; Micro — Fiche, reels; Other — Exhibition catalogs, pamphlets
Special Subjects: Architectural treatises, antiquities reference works, early 20th century archival & library materials
Collections: †Greek & Roman antiquities; †French decorative arts; †Western European paintings, drawings, sculpture; illuminated manuscripts; deocrative arts; 19th & 20th century photographs
Publications: Calendar, quarterly; Museum Journal, annually
Activities: Classes for adults & children; lect; concerts; gallery talks; scholarships & fels offered; museum shop sells books

M **SANTA MONICA COLLEGE ART GALLERY,** 1900 Pico Blvd, 90405. Tel 310-452-9230, Ext 9550; FAX 310-396-4970; *Gallery Chmn* Mauricio Baraetucci
Open Tues - Fri 10 AM - 3 PM, Mon 5:30 - 8:30 PM, Sat 10 AM - 4 PM, cl academic holidays. No admis fee. Estab 1973 to provide a study gallery for direct contact with contemporary & historic works of art. Average Annual Attendance: 25,000
Income: Financed by mem, city & state appropriations
Collections: Southern California prints & drawings
Exhibitions: Eight per year
Activities: Lect open to public; gallery talks; tours; original art objects lent

SANTA ROSA

SANTA ROSA JUNIOR COLLEGE
M **Art Gallery,** 1501 Mendocino Ave, 95401. Tel 707-527-4298, 527-4011, Ext 4575; FAX 707-527-4298; *Dir* Donna Larsen
Open Mon - Fri & Sun Noon - 4 PM. No admis fee. Estab 1973. 1700 sq ft exhibit space with movable walls. Average Annual Attendance: 10,000
Exhibitions: Four exhibits during the school year generally of contemporary artists of national & local prominence & of emerging new artists
Activities: Lect open to public, 1-2 vis lectr per year; gallery talks

SARATOGA

A **MONTALVO CENTER FOR THE ARTS,** 15400 Montalvo Rd, PO Box 158, 95071. Tel 408-741-3421; FAX 408-741-5592; *Exec Dir* Elizbeth Challener
Open Tues - Sun 1 - 4 PM, cl Mon & holidays; call ahead for hrs. Estab 1930; administered by Montalvo Association, Villa Montalvo is part of a cultural center for the development of art, literature, music & architecture by artists & promising students. There are facilities for five artists-in-residence. The home of the late US Senator & Mayor of San Francisco, James Duval Phelan, was bequeathed as a cultural center & is conducted as a non-profit enterprise by the Board of Trustees of the Montalvo Association. Average Annual Attendance: 7000. Mem: 1250; dues $25 & up; annual meeting in Nov
Income: $350,000 (financed by donation, grants & investments)
Exhibitions: 20 solo exhibitions per year of emerging artists in all media; occasional special or group exhibitions
Publications: Calendar, monthly
Activities: Lect open to public, 8 vis lect per year; concerts; gallery talks; tours; competitions with awards; plays; winter workshops; scholarships offered; museum shop sells books, original art, reproductions, prints & gift items

SAUSALITO

A HEADLANDS CENTER FOR THE ARTS, 944 Fort Barry, 94965. Tel 415-331-2787; FAX 415-331-3857; *Exec Dir* Kathryn Reasoner; *Prog Dir* Donna Gravef; *Facilities Mgr* Christopher Doyle
Open daily Noon - 5 PM. No admis fee. Estab 1982 to support artists in their research of the Marin Headlands, a National Park. Average Annual Attendance: 18,000. Mem: 300
Income: $380,000 (financed by endowment, city appropriation, donations from foundations & corporations)
Publications: Bi-monthly calendar, annual journal

STANFORD

M STANFORD UNIVERSITY, Museum of Art, 94305-5060. Tel 415-723-4177; FAX 415-725-0464;
Internet Home Page Address http://www.leland.stanford.edu/dept/suma/. *Dir* Thomas K Seligman; *Assoc Dir & Chief Cur* Bernard Barryte; *Cur of Prints & Drawings* Betsy G Fryberger; *Cur of Oriental Art* Patrick Maveety; *Cur of Photography* Joe Leivick; *Head Registration-Conservation* Susan Roberts-Manganelli; *Cur Educ* Patience Young; *Cur of Modern & Contemporary* Dr Hilarie Faberman; *Cur of African & Oceanic Art* Ruth Franklin; *Assoc Dir External Affairs* Mona Duggan
Open Tues - Fri 10 AM - 5 PM, Sat & Sun 1 - 5 PM. No admis fee. Estab 1894 as a teaching mus & laboratory for University's Department of Art. Average Annual Attendance: 85,000. Mem: 1600; dues $10 - $200; annual meeting in May
Income: Financed by endowment, mem & university funds
Collections: B G Cantor Gallery of Rodin Sculpture; Cesnola Collection of Cypriote antiquities, prints & drawings since the Renaissance; Stanford Family Collection; †African art; †American art of 19th & 20th centuries; †ancient art; †contemporary art; †European art 16th-20th century; †Native American Art; †photography including major holdings by Robert Frank & Eadwaerd Muybridge; †Pre-Columbian art; †Western Art of the 20th century
Exhibitions: Recent Acquisitions, 1984 - 1990; paintings, sculpture, drawings, prints, photographs & decorative arts; Summer Fields - Montotypes by Kritina Brancy; Mark Tobey: Works on Paper; Barbara Morgan - paintings & photographs.
Publications: The Stanford Museum, biennial journal; exhibition catalogs; handbook of the collection
Activities: Classes for adults & children; docent training; lect open to the public, 15 vis lectr per year; gallery talks; tours; book traveling exhibitions; originate traveling exhibitions
L Art & Architecture Library, 102 Cummings Art Bldg, 94305-2018. Tel 415-723-3408; FAX 415-725-0140; Elec Mail cn.art@forsythe.stanford.edu. *Head Librn* Alex Ross; *Asst Librn* Peter Blank
Open Mon - Thurs 9 AM - 10 PM, Fri & Sat 9 AM - 5 PM, Sun 1 - 10 PM. Limited service to non-Stanford patrons
Library Holdings: Vols 150,000; Per subs 529; Micro — Fiche; Other — Exhibition catalogs
Special Subjects: Aesthetics, Afro-American Art, American Indian Art, American Western Art, Antiquities-Assyrian, Antiquities-Byzantine, Antiquities-Egyptian, Antiquities-Etruscan, Antiquities-Greek, Antiquities-Oriental, Antiquities-Persian, Antiquities-Roman, Archaeology, Architecture, Art History

STOCKTON

M SAN JOAQUIN PIONEER & HISTORICAL SOCIETY, The Haggin Museum, 1201 N Pershing Ave, 95203-1699. Tel 209-462-4116, 462-1566; FAX 209-462-1404; *Dir & Cur of History* Tod Ruhstaller; *Controller* Setsuko Ryuto; *Exhib Design* Mike Ferrell; *Cur Educ* Marillyn Guiby; *Registrar* Karen Jahnke; *Librn & Archivist* Susan Benedetti
Open Tues - Sun 1:30 - 5 PM. No admis fee. Estab 1928 to protect, preserve & interpret for present & future generations historical & fine arts collections that pertain to the museum's disciplines. The mus covers 34,000 sq ft of exhibit space housing art & history collections. Average Annual Attendance: 69,000. Mem: 1500; dues $25 & up; annual meeting third Tues in Jan
Income: $500,000 (financed by endowment, mem, city & county appropriation & foundation grant)
Collections: 19th Century French, American & European paintings; Oriental & European decorative arts; graphics; Japanese woodblock prints; American Illustrators
Exhibitions: Six - eight temporary exhibits per year; Stockton National Print & Drawing juried exhibition; Stockton Art League Exhibition; Robert T McKee Student Art Exhibition
Publications: Museum Calendar, quarterly
Activities: Summer art classes for children; docent training; lect open to public; concerts; gallery talks; tours; competitions with awards; individual paintings & original objects of art lent; book traveling exhibitions 2-3 per year; sales shop sells books, postcards, posters, notecards
L Petzinger Memorial Library, Victory Park, 1201 N Pershing Ave, 95203-1699. Tel 209-462-4116, 462-1566; FAX 209-462-1404; *Dir* Tod Ruhstaller
Open Tues - Sat by appointment only. Estab 1941 to supply material to those interested in the research of California & San Joaquin County history as well as the history of Stockton. For reference only
Income: $15,000 (financed by endowment for Historical Libraries)
Purchases: $400
Library Holdings: Vols 7000; Original documents; AV — Cassettes, Kodachromes, lantern slides, motion pictures, slides; Other — Clipping files, exhibition catalogs, manuscripts, memorabilia, pamphlets, photographs, prints
Special Subjects: California, Central San Joaquin Valley & Stockton History
Collections: Earl Rowland Art Reference Library

M UNIVERSITY OF THE PACIFIC, 3601 Pacific Ave, 95211. Tel 209-946-2011
Open Mon - Fri 9 AM - 8 AM, Sat & Sun 3 - 9 PM. No admis fee. Estab 1975 to expose the University community to various art forms. Gallery is 1200 sq ft with 80 ft wall space, well equiped ceiling spots and flat panels. Average Annual Attendance: 10,000
Income: Financed by student fees & sales
Exhibitions: Rotating schedule of contemporary California artists
Activities: Lect open to public, 3-4 vis lectr per year; gallery talks; juried contests; awards; tours

SYLMAR

M COUNTY OF LOS ANGELES, Century Gallery, 13000 Sayre St, 91342. Tel 818-362-3220; FAX 818-364-7755; *Dir* John Cantley
Open Mon - Fri 9 AM - 5 PM, Sat Noon - 4 PM. No admis fee. Estab 1977 for contemporary art exhibits & to bring educational value to the community. Average Annual Attendance: 7500
Income: Financed by city, county & state appropriation
Exhibitions: Seven curated theme exhibits of contemporary art
Activities: Gallery talks; competitions

THOUSAND OAKS

M CONEJO VALLEY ART MUSEUM, PO Box 1616, 91358. Tel 805-373-0054; *Pres* Maria Dessornes; *VPres* Gayle Simpson; *Exhibit Dir* Ginger Worthley; *Develop Dir* Ray Dion
Open Wed - Sun Noon - 5 PM. No admis fee, donation suggested. Estab 1975 to exhibit works of nationally & internationally known artists. Average Annual Attendance: 10,000. Mem: 350; dues family $25, single $15
Income: Financed by mem, donations & grants
Collections: Large Serigraph by Ron Davis
Exhibitions: Artwalk; Juried Fine Art & Designer Crafts Outdoor Exhibition
Activities: Lectr open to public, 6 vis lectr per year; concerts; gallery talks; competitions with awards; scholarships offered; museum shop sells books, magazines, prints, jewelry & folk art

TORRANCE

M EL CAMINO COLLEGE ART GALLERY, 16007 Crenshaw Blvd, 90506. Tel 310-532-3670, Ext 4568; *Dir* Susanna Meiers
Open Mon - Fri 9 AM - 3 PM, Mon & Thurs 5:30 - 8:30 PM. No admis fee. Estab 1970 to exhibit professional, historical & student art. Gallery has 2300 sq ft of exhibit space located on the ground floor of the Art Building on campus. Average Annual Attendance: 5000
Collections: Small print collection; small sculpture collection
Exhibitions: Juried student exhibit; organizational & guild competitions
Publications: Exhibit catalogs
Activities: Classes for adults; docent training; lect open to public, 25 vis lectr per year; concerts; gallery talks; tours; competitions with awards; scholarships offered through the Library; exten dept serves the South Bay Community; collections or parts of collections are exchanged; lending collection contains books & sculpture; sales shop sells original art & posters

TURLOCK

CALIFORNIA STATE UNIVERSITY STANISLAUS
M University Art Gallery, 801 W Monte Vista, 95382. Tel 209-667-3186
Open Mon - Wed Noon - 4 PM, Thurs Noon - 7 PM. No admis fee. Estab 1967, for the purpose of community & cultural instruction. Gallery is small, covering 250 ft running. Average Annual Attendance: 10,000
Income: Financed by state appropriation
Collections: †Permanent collection of graphics & small contemporary works; Chinese pottery & artifacts; contemporary paintings, graphics; ancient Egyptian & Greek artifacts; Japanese artifacts; Italian Renaissance Jewelry; Pre-Conquest artifacts; William Wendt paintings (California landscapes)
Exhibitions: Six exhibitions annually
Publications: Exhibition catalogs
Activities: Classes for adults; lect open to public, 11 vis lectr per year; concerts; gallery talks; tours; exten dept serving summer school; individual paintings & original objects of art lent to qualified museums & galleries & campus community; lending collection contains film strips, 35mm lantern slides, motion pictures, original art works, original prints; book traveling exhibitions 1-2 per year; originate traveling exhibitions to University Art Galleries
L Vasche Library, 801 W Monte Vista Ave, 95382. Tel 209-667-3232; FAX 209-667-3164; *Dean Library Serv* John Amrhein
Open Mon - Thurs 9 AM - 11 PM, Fri 9 AM - 5 PM, Sat 9 AM - 5 PM, Sun 1 - 5 PM. Estab 1960, a regional state university
Purchases: $8800
Library Holdings: Vols 11,000; Per subs 37; Micro — Fiche, prints, reels; AV — A-tapes, cassettes, v-tapes
Special Subjects: 19th & 20th Century Art

UKIAH

M CITY OF UKIAH, Grace Hudson Museum & The Sun House, 431 S Main St, 95482. Tel 707-467-2836; *Dir* Rob Wilson; *Cur* Sherrie Smith-Ferri; *Cur* Karen Holmes
Open Wed - Sat 10 AM - 4:30 PM, Sun Noon - 4:30 PM. Admis adults $2, senior citizens & children $1. Estab 1975. Average Annual Attendance: 11,500. Mem: 450; dues $5-$500; annual meeting in June
Income: $220,000 (financed by endowment, mem, city appropriation & grants)
Collections: Hudson & Carpenter Family Collection; Grace Hudson Art Collection; Collection of Pomo Indian arts & material cult; Photographic &

manuscript archives

Exhibitions: Grace Hudson (art); History & Anthropology of Native Americans; regional artists

Activities: Classes for adults & children in docent programs; lect open to public, 2-3 vis lectr per year; book traveling exhibitions 1 per year; originates traveling exhibitions 1 per year; museum shop sells books, magazines, slides, original art, reproductions & jewelry

VAN NUYS

M **LOS ANGELES VALLEY COLLEGE,** Art Gallery, 5800 Fulton Ave, 91401. Tel 818-781-1200, Ext 400; *Dir* Samuel Jossredo
Open Mon - Thurs Noon - 3 PM & 7 - 9 PM. No admis fee, donation requested. Estab 1960 to show changing exhibitions of ethnic, historical, & contemporary art. Single gallery
Income: $25,000 (financed by state appropriation & fundraising)
Exhibitions: Student Exhibition
Activities: Lect open to public, 2 vis lectr per year

VENICE

A **BEYOND BAROQUE FOUNDATION,** Beyond Baroque Literary/Arts Center, 681 Venice Blvd, 90291. Tel 310-822-3006; *Dir* Tosh Berman; *Prog Dir* Erica Bornstein
Open Tues - Fri 10 AM - 5 PM, Sat Noon - 4 PM. Admis $8 non-members, $4 members & students. Estab 1968 to promote & support literary arts projects, writers & artists in Southern Calif & nationally. Mem: 1200; dues $30 annually for 2 people
Income: $200,000 (financed by grants from National Endowment for the Arts, California Art Council, City of Los Angeles, other government & private grants as well as donations from the public)
Publications: Annual magazine
Activities: All types of writing workshops; art lect open to public; weekly reading & performance series; art gallery; film program

A **SOCIAL & PUBLIC ART RESOURCE CENTER,** (SPARC), 685 Venice Blvd, 90291. Tel 310-822-9560; *Artistic Dir* Judith F Baca; *Assoc Dir* Debra Padilla
Open Mon - Fri 9:30 AM - 5:30 PM, Sat 10 AM - 4 PM. Admis donations requested. Estab 1976 as a non-profit multi-cultural art center that produces, exhibits, distributes & preserves public artworks. Average Annual Attendance: 10,000. Mem: 200; dues $25 & up; mem open to public
Exhibitions: Neighborhood Pride Program-Mural Competition
Publications: California Chicano Muralists; Signs from the Heart
Activities: Classes for adults & children; lect open to public, 6-10 vis lectr per year; gallery talks; mural tours; competitions; scholarships & fels offered; individual paintings & original objects of art lent to museums; lending collection contains books, framed reproductions, original art works, original paintings, paintings, photographs & slides; originate traveling exhibitions; sales shop sells books, reproductions, prints, slides & postcards

VENTURA

M **VENTURA COLLEGE,** Art Galleries, 4667 Telegraph Rd, 93003. Tel 805-648-8974; FAX 805-654-6466; *Gallery Dir* Debra McKillop
Call ahead for hours. No admis fee. Estab 1970s to showcase faculty & student artworks, as well as prestigious artists from throughout the country. Gallery 2 & New Media Gallery
Exhibitions: (1997) Art History Projects Show; Interactions: Man & Nature; Ventura College Art Department Annual Student Awards Exhibition
Activities: Originate traveling exhibitions

M **VENTURA COUNTY HISTORICAL SOCIETY,** Museum of History & Art, 100 E Main St, 93001. Tel 805-653-0323; *Pres* William Orcutt; *VPres* W B Mariott Jr; *VPres* Gregory H Smith; *Exec Dir* Edward Robings; *Cur* Tim Schiffer; *Res Librn* Charles Johnson
Open Tues - Sun 10 AM - 5 PM, cl Mon. No admis fee. Estab 1913 to collect, study, & interpret the history of Ventura County. Hoffman Gallery houses changing exhibits every 6-8 weeks. Average Annual Attendance: 30,000. Mem: 1800; dues $25 - $500; annual meeting in May
Income: $300,000 (financed by endowment, mem, county appropriation)
Collections: Farm implements & machines; fine arts; historical artifacts; historical figures; prehistorical artifacts
Exhibitions: George Stuart Historical Figures; Annual Assembly of the Arts; changing history & art exhibitions; permanent collection
Publications: Heritage & History, monthly; Ventura County Historical Quarterly
Activities: Docent training & networking; school outreach; lect open to public, 6 vis lectr per year; competitions with awards; museum shop sells books, original art, jewelry, and clothing

WALNUT CREEK

A **CALIFORNIA WATERCOLOR ASSOCIATION,** PO Box 4631, 94596. Tel 510-934-2535; Internet Home Page Address http://ideswww.artscope.com. *Pres* Karen Mason; *VPres* Judi Greenberg; *Treas* Margaret Fago
Estab 1968. Maintains video library & art gallery at Blackhawk Plaza in Danville. Average Annual Attendance: Over 500. Mem: dues $25
Income: Financed by mem
Library Holdings: AV — Slides, v-tapes; Other — Exhibition catalogs
Exhibitions: Annual Open Watercolor Exhibitions
Publications: Annual catalog; monthly newsletter
Activities: Workshops; scholarships offered

M **DEAN LESHER REGIONAL CENTER FOR THE ARTS** (Formerly Walnut Creek Regional Center for the Arts), Bedford Gallery, 1601 Civic Dr, 94596. Tel 510-295-1400; FAX 510-943-7222; *Cur* Carrie Lederer
Open Tues - Sun Noon - 5 PM, Fri 7:30 - 9 PM, cl Mon & national holidays. No admis fee. Estab 1963 to offer varied & education changing exhibitions to the community & surrounding area. Gallery contains 396 running ft, 2300 sq ft, including mezzanine gallery. Average Annual Attendance: 24,000. Mem: 1200; dues Diablo Regional Arts Assoc mem $35
Income: Funded by city, pub & private grants
Purchases: $2000
Exhibitions: 5-6 exhibits on view at the gallery each year
Publications: City Scene Newsletter; three catalogs per year; The Diablo Magazine, quarterly
Activities: Classes for adults & children; dramatic programs; docent training; lect open to public, 6-10 vis lectr per year; concerts; gallery talks; tours; competitions; sales shop sells books, original art, slides & catalogs

WESTPORT

A **MENDOCINO COUNTY ARTS COUNCIL,** PO Box 98, 95488. Tel 707-459-7897; Elec Mail al4art@aol.com. *Dir* Alex Leeder
No admis fee. Estab 1972 to collect, interpret & exhibit multicultural artists of Mendocino County. Rural arts delivery service. Preparing to open premiere exhibition gallery to showcase Northern California contemporary fine artist. Average Annual Attendance: 20,878. Mem: 367; dues $25; meetings 4 times per year
Income: $49,000 (financed by county funds)
Collections: Encourages general collections relating to Mendocino County History including Pomo Indian & contemporary objects
Exhibitions: Pride & Spirit of Americans for the Arts; Recycled Arts; rotating exhibitions of contemporary fine arts
Activities: Educ dept; docent training; technical services to artists including grantwriting workshops; lect open to public, 4 vis lectr per year; concerts; gallery talks; tours; competitions with awards; exten dept serves inland & coastal communities; individual paintings & original objects of art lent by request, allocate resources in advance & insure artwork; book traveling exhibitions 1 or more per year; originate traveling exhibitions; sales shop sells original art, prints, cards, posters & ceramics

WHITTIER

M **RIO HONDO COLLEGE ART GALLERY,** 3600 Workman Mill Rd, 90601-1699. Tel 310-908-3428; FAX 310-908-3446; *Gallery Dir* Chris Akuna-Hanson; *Div Dean* Lance Carlton
Open Mon - Fri 11 AM - 4 PM & 6:30 - 9 PM. No admis fee. Estab 1967 to bring to the college students a wide variety of art experiences that will enhance & develop their sensitivity & appreciation of art. Small gallery about 1000 sq ft located within the art facility. Average Annual Attendance: 8000
Income: Financed through college
Collections: Contemporary paintings and graphics by Southern California artists
Exhibitions: Landscapes by Paul Donaldson, Carl Aldana, James Urstrom; Sculptures by Joyce Kohl; Self Portraits by Selected California Artists; student shows and area high school honor show
Activities: Classes for adults; lect open to public

YOSEMITE NATIONAL PARK

M **YOSEMITE MUSEUM,** National Park Service, PO Box 577, 95389. Tel 209-372-0281, 372-0297; *Chief Cur* David M Forgang; *Cur Ethnography* Craig D Bates; *Registrar* Martha J Lee; *Coll Mgr* Barbara Beroza
Open daily summer 9 AM - 5 PM, winter Fri - Tues 9 AM - 5 PM. No admis fee. Estab 1926 to interpret the natural sciences & human history of the Yosemite area. Mem: 1700; dues $10 & up
Income: Financed by federal appropriation
Collections: Indian cultural artifacts; †original paintings & photos of Yosemite; photographs (special collection on early Yosemite); pioneer artifacts; Yosemite related emphemera
Activities: Classes for adults & children; lect open to public; paintings & original art objects lent on special exhibits only; lending collection contains prints, photographs; sales shop sells books, magazines, reproductions, prints, slides; junior museum
L **Research Library,** PO Box 577, 95389. Tel 209-372-0280;
For reference only
Library Holdings: Vols 10,000; Per subs 100; Micro — Fiche, reels; AV — Lantern slides, slides; Other — Clipping files, exhibition catalogs, manuscripts, memorabilia, pamphlets, photographs, reproductions
Special Subjects: Yosemite history

COLORADO

ASPEN

M **THE ASPEN ART MUSEUM,** 590 N Mill St, 81611. Tel 970-925-8050; FAX 970-925-8054; Elec Mail aam@rof.net. *Dir* Suzanne Farver
Open Tues - Sat 10 AM - 6 PM, free reception & gallery tours Thurs 6 - 8 PM, cl Mon. Admis $3, seniors & students $2, members & children under 12 free. Estab 1979 to provide the community with a variety of cultural & educational experiences through exhibits, lectures & classes. Maintains small reference library. Average Annual Attendance: 15,000. Mem: 800; dues $35-$5000; annual meeting in Aug

Exhibitions: (1997) Private Worlds: 200 Years of American Still Life Painting; Animals in Antiquity; Young Artists of the Roaring Fork Valley; Nancy Rubins Installation; Howl at the Moon Benefit; Tony Oursler; Roaring Fork Open/ Annual exhibit of Artists of the Roaring Fork Valley; Spanish Colonial Exhibition

Activities: Classes for adults & children; docent training; lect open to public, 10 vis lectr per year; gallery talks; tours; museum shop sells books, cards, catalogues, hats, mugs, posters, t-shirts

BOULDER

A BOULDER HISTORICAL SOCIETY INC, Museum of History, 1206 Euclid Ave, 80302. Tel 303-449-3464; FAX 303-938-8322; *Dir* Tom Meier; *Assoc Dir* Wendy Gordon; *Cur Costumes* Phyllis Plehaty
Open Tues - Sat Noon - 4 PM. Admis adults $1. Estab 1944 to promote history of Boulder Valley. Average Annual Attendance: 5000. Mem: 400; dues $15 - $100; annual meeting in Nov
Income: $90,000 (financed by endowment & mem)
Purchases: Quilts, photographs, costumes, agricultural tools, glass
Collections: Costumes; Local Historical Material; Manuscripts & Photographs
Exhibitions: Period Kitchen & Sitting Room; 19th Century Businesses; Bicycles; Millenary Shop; Agriculture; Mining; Education
Publications: Quarterly newsletter
Activities: Adult classes; lect open to public, 400 vis lectr per year; lending collection contains 5000 paintings; book traveling exhibitions 1 per year; originate traveling exhibitions 2 per year; retail store sells books, local history artifacts & costumes

A BOULDER MUSEUM OF CONTEMPORARY ART, 1750 13th St, 80302. Tel 303-443-2122; FAX 303-447-1633; *Pres* Ross Cooney; *Dir* Cydney Payton; *Office Mgr* Dona Uyeno
Open Tues - Sat 11 AM - 5 PM, Sun 1 - 5 PM. Admis exhibitions free, lectures $1-$5. Estab 1972 to promote contemporary visual arts & appreciation of quality in the community. Two galleries totaling 5000 sq ft; lecture space; exhibitions focus on contemporary, experimental, Colorado & regional art. Average Annual Attendance: 20,000. Mem: 700; dues from $12-$1000; annual meeting in Oct
Income: $180,000 (financed by endowment, mem, city appropriation & grants)
Collections: Tom Hicks, Another Boulder, large outdoor sculpture; Doug Wilson, untitled, large outdoor sculpture
Publications: The 13th Street Journal, 8 times annum
Activities: Classes for adults & children; docent training; lect open to public, 3-5 vis lectr per year; concerts; gallery talks; tours; competitions with awards; sales shop sells magazines

L BOULDER PUBLIC LIBRARY & GALLERY, Dept of Fine Arts Gallery, 1000 Canyon Blvd, PO Drawer H, 80306. Tel 303-441-3100; FAX 303-442-1808; *Library Dir* Marcelee Gralapp; *Asst Library Dir* Randy Smith; *Exhib Coordr* Karen Ripley; *City of Boulder Arts Commission* Donna Gartenmann
Open Mon - Fri 9 AM - 9 PM, Sat 9 AM - 6 PM, Sun Noon - 6 PM. Estab to enhance the personal development of Boulder citizens by meeting their informational needs. Bridge Gallery, three shows change monthly. Average Annual Attendance: 300,000
Income: Financed by city appropriations, grants & gifts
Library Holdings: Micro — Cards, fiche, prints; AV — A-tapes, cassettes, fs, slides, v-tapes; Other — Clipping files, exhibition catalogs, framed reproductions, manuscripts, original art works, pamphlets, photographs, prints, reproductions, sculpture
Special Subjects: Colorado Artists Register
Activities: Classes for adults & children; lect open to public; concerts; tours; competitions; awards

M LEANIN' TREE MUSEUM OF WESTERN ART, PO Box 9500, 80301. Tel 303-530-1442; FAX 303-530-7283;
Internet Home Page Address http://www.leanintree.com. *Assoc Museum Dir* Sara Sheldon
Open Mon - Fri 8 AM - 4:30 PM, Sat 10 AM - 4 PM, cl Sun & holidays. No admis fee. Estab 1974. Two floors of paintings & bronzes. Average Annual Attendance: 40,000
Purchases: Bears Nest, Polychrome Bronze by Dave McGary (1956-), Hidden River, Oil by Bill Hughes (1932-1993)
Collections: Contemporary western cowboy & Indian art; western bronze sculptures; paintings by major contemporary western artists, 1950 to present day
Activities: Self guided tours; sales shop sells reproductions prints, greeting cards, coffee mugs, t-shirts with western art & magnets

M UNIVERSITY OF COLORADO, Art Galleries, Sibell-Wolle Fine Arts Bldg, Campus Box 318, 80309-0318. Tel 303-492-8300; FAX 303-492-4886; *Dir* Susan Krane
Open Mon - Fri 8 AM - 5 PM; Tues till 8 PM, Sat Noon - 4 PM. No admis fee. Estab 1939 to maintain & exhibit art collections & to show temporary exhibits. The galleries have 450 linear ft of wall space & a total of 5000 sq ft
Income: Financed through University, gifts & grants
Collections: †19th & 20th century paintings & †prints; †photographs, †prints, drawings, watercolors, sculptures & ceramics
Publications: Brochures; exhibition catalogs
Activities: Lect open to public, 15 vis artists per year; paintings & original art objects lent to museums; lending collection contains original art works & prints, paintings, photographs, sculpture, original drawings
L Art & Architecture Library, PO Box 184, 80309. Tel 303-492-7955; FAX 303-492-4886; *Head Art & Architecture Library* Liesel Nolan; *Library Technician* Mary Larson; *Library Asst* Anna Frajzyngier
Open Mon - Fri 8 AM - midnight, Sat 10 AM - 5 PM, Sun Noon - midnight; summer hrs Mon - Thurs 7:30 AM - 10 PM, Fri 7:30 AM - 5 PM, Sat 10 AM - 5 PM, Sun Noon - 10 PM. Estab 1966 to support the university curriculum in the areas of fine arts, art history, environmental design, architecture, planning, landscape & interior design. For lending only

Income: Financed by state appropriation
Library Holdings: Vols 89,000; Per subs 500; MFA thesis statements; Museum & gallery publications; Micro — Fiche 5950, reels; Other — Exhibition catalogs
Special Subjects: Afro-American Art, American Indian Art, American Western Art, Eskimo Art, Folk Art, History of Art & Archaeology, Latin American Art, Mexican Art, Oriental Art, Painting - American, Religious Art, Southwestern Art, Artists books

BRECKENRIDGE

M COLORADO MOUNTAIN COLLEGE, Fine Arts Gallery, 103 S Harris St, 80424. Tel 970-453-6757; FAX 970-453-2209; *Dir* Tim Hoopingarner; *Head Fine Arts* Tom Hart

BRIGHTON

M ADAMS COUNTY HISTORICAL SOCIETY, Museum & Cultural Center, 9601 Henderson Rd, 80601. Tel 303-659-7103; *Adminr* Patricia Erger
Open Tues - Sat 10 AM - 4:30 PM, cl Mon & Sun. Admis donations requested. Historical Soc estab 1974, mus estab 1987. Maintains reference library. Average Annual Attendance: 5750. Mem: 155; dues family $15, individual $10; meetings Jan, Mar, May, Sept, Nov, Dec & when needed
Income: $50,000 (financed by mem, bazaars, gift shop & donations)
Purchases: Five small bronze pieces
Collections: Blacksmith Shop/Earth Science; Barber Shop Equipment; 1940's Doll House; Uniforms; Spanish & American/WW I & WW II; 1930 Conoco Gas Station
Exhibitions: Photographs; Carvings; Quilts; Indian
Publications: Hi Story News, quarterly newsletter
Activities: Educ dept; docent training; school tours; Heritage days; lect opn to public, 6 vis lectr per year; gallery talks; tours; lending collection consists of lantern slides; originate traveling exhibitions; museum shop sells books, rocks, fossils & related items & hand crafted jewelry
L Library, 9601 Henderson Rd, 80601. Tel 303-659-7103;
For reference. Different artists & groups exhibited throughout the year
Income: $50,000 (financed by mem, dues, craft shows, gifts & grants)
Library Holdings: Vols 200; AV — Lantern slides, rec; Other — Clipping files, pamphlets
Special Subjects: Art Education, Art History, Historical Material, Southwestern Art, Watercolors

CANON CITY

A FREMONT CENTER FOR THE ARTS, 505 Macon Ave, PO Box 1006, 81215-1006. Tel 719-275-2790; FAX 719-275-4244; *Exec Dir* Monica R Hinson
Open Tues - Sat 10 AM - 4 PM. No admis fee. Estab 1947. Average Annual Attendance: 10,000. Mem: 400
Income: Financed by mem, individual donations, local small businesses, grants, fundraising
Activities: In-house classes for beginning & advanced artisans; drama & design workshop; watercolor workshop

CENTRAL CITY

A GILPIN COUNTY ARTS ASSOCIATION, Eureka St, PO Box 98, 80427. Tel 303-582-5574, 642-7800; *Pres* Robert G Koropp; *Gallery Mgr* Diane Sill
Open Tues - Sat 11 AM - 5:30 PM, June 22 - Aug 10 Sun Noon - 5:30 PM, cl Mon. No admis fee. Estab 1947 to offer a juried exhibition of Colorado artists & to support the local school arts program. Six wings on two floors; outdoor sculpture garden; memorial fountain in Newbury Wing sculpted by Angelo di Benedetto; gallery is open June - Sept 15; oldest juried art exhibition in Colorado; non-profit organization. Average Annual Attendance: 25,000. Mem: 200; dues $1000; annual meeting, third Sun in Aug
Income: Financed by mem, sales & entry fee
Purchases: Over $60,000 annually
Publications: Annual exhibit catalog
Activities: Juried competitions with awards; sponsor elementary & secondary school art program

COLORADO SPRINGS

AMERICAN NUMISMATIC ASSOCIATION
For further information, see National and Regional Organizations

L ARJUNA LIBRARY, 1025 Garner St, D, Space 18, 80905. *Dir* Joseph A Uphoff Jr
Estab 1963. For reference only
Library Holdings: Vols 2100; AV — Slides 1100; Other — Manuscripts, original art works, sculpture
Special Subjects: Aesthetics, Archaeology, Ceramics, Coins & Medals, Conceptual Art, Decorative Arts, Historical Material, Manuscripts, Painting - European, Surrealism
Collections: Manuscripts & Proceedings, Differential Logic, Mathematical Surrealistic Theory; Mathematical Proceedings in Criticism for Drama, Poetics, Dance, Martial Arts & Yoga; Metamathematics, Calculus, Abstract Algebra
Publications: Journal of Regional Criticism, irregular

M COLORADO SPRINGS FINE ARTS CENTER, 30 W Dale St, 80903. Tel 719-634-5581; FAX 719-634-0570; *Dir* David Turner; *Dir Exhib* Cathy Wright; *Dir Public Relations* West Royal; *Dir Sales Shop* Chris Jones; *Dir Museum Servs* R E Zendejas; *Dir Performing Arts* Robert Geers; *Librn* Rod Dew; *Bemis Art School Dir* John Lawson
Open Tues - Fri 9 AM - 5 PM, Sat 10 AM - 5 PM, Sun 1 - 5 PM, cl Mon.

Admis adults, senior citizens, students between 13 & 21 $1.50; children 6-12 $1, 5 & under free. Estab 1936 as a forum, advocate & programmer of visual & performing arts activities & art school for the community. Eleven galleries range in size from quite small to large. Exhibits range from international to national to regional. Average Annual Attendance: 122,000. Mem: 3150; dues $20-$1000; annual meeting in Oct
Income: $1,600,000 (financed by endowment, mem, business & industry contributions, revenue producing enterprises, city, state & federal appropriations)
Library Holdings: Vols 27,000; Per subs 50; Other — Clipping files, exhibition catalogs, memorabilia, pamphlets
Collections: †Taylor Museum Collection of Southwestern Spanish Colonial & Native American Art; †American paintings, sculptures, graphics & drawings with emphasis on art west of the Mississippi; ethnographic collections; fine arts collections; 19th & 20th century art
Exhibitions: Sacred Land: Indian & Hispanic Cultures of the Southwest
Publications: Artsfocus, bi-monthly calendar; educational programs and tours; exhibition catalogs; gallery sheets; scholarly publications; catalogue of the collections
Activities: Art classes for pre-school arts program; gifted & talented classes (grades 3-6) in visual arts & drama; docent lect/presentations to children & adults; creative dramatics; docent training; lect open to public; concerts; films; gallery talks; competitions; art lent to AAM accredited museums; sales shop sells books, art & gifts
L **Library,** 30 W Dale St, 80903. Tel 719-634-5581; FAX 719-634-0570; *Librn* Roderick Dew
Open Tues - Fri 9 AM - Noon & 1 - 5 PM, Sat 10 AM - Noon & 1 - 5 PM, cl Mon & Sun. Estab 1936 as a fine arts reference library in support of the museum's collection & activities. Open for pub reference, lending is restricted to members of the center & local university students & faculty
Income: Financed by endowment & mem
Library Holdings: Vols 30,000; Per subs 50; Other — Clipping files, exhibition catalogs, memorabilia, pamphlets
Special Subjects: Aesthetics, American Indian Art, American Western Art, Anthropology, Art Education, Art History, Ceramics, Collages, Crafts, Decorative Arts, Embroidery, Eskimo Art, Etchings & Engravings, Ethnology, Folk Art, Art & anthropology of the Southwest; Guatemalan textiles; Mexican Folk Art; Santos of the Southwestern US
Collections: Taylor Museum Collection on the art & anthropology of the Southwest
Activities: Tours

M **UNITED STATES FIGURE SKATING ASSOCIATION,** World Figure Skating Museum & Hall of Fame, 20 First St, 80906. Tel 719-635-5200; FAX 719-635-9548; *Cur* Beth Davis
Open winter Mon - Fri 10 AM - 4 PM & first Sat of month, summer Mon - Sat 10 AM - 4 PM. No admis fee. Estab 1979 to preserve the art & history of figure skating. Maintains 10,000 sq ft exhibition area. Average Annual Attendance: 20,000
Income: Financed by Association's general fund & mem
Collections: Skating in Art, the Gillis Grafstrom Collection; costumes of the champions; On Edge (exhibit of technical aspects of skating); Pierre Brunet Collection, Gladys McFerron Collection, Kloss Photo Collection, Dorothy Stevens Collection
Exhibitions: Scott Hamilton: Portraiture of a Champion; Sonja Henie Remembered
Publications: Skating Magazine
Activities: Gallery talks; tours; competitions with awards; video tape showings; originate traveling exhibitions to skating organizations, clubs & members; gift shop sells books, reproductions, jewelry, decals, cards, decorations
L **Library,** 20 First St, 80906. Tel 719-635-5200; FAX 719-635-9548; *Cur* Beth Davis
Open winter Mon - Fri 10 AM - 4 PM & 1st Sat of month, summer Mon - Sat 10 AM - 4 PM
Library Holdings: Micro — Reels; AV — A-tapes, cassettes, fs, lantern slides, motion pictures, rec, slides, v-tapes; Other — Clipping files, exhibition catalogs, framed reproductions, memorabilia, original art works, pamphlets, photographs, prints
Special Subjects: Skating, the best reference collection in the world
Collections: First books published in English, French & German on skating

M **UNIVERSITY OF COLORADO AT COLORADO SPRINGS,** Gallery of Contemporary Art, Austin Bluffs Pkwy, PO Box 7150, 80933-7150. Tel 719-593-3567; FAX 719-593-3183; Elec Mail griggs@uccs.edu. *Dir & Cur* Gerry Riggs; *Admin Asst* Grace Gerstner
Open Mon - Fri 10 AM - 4 PM, Sat 1 - 4 PM. Admis fee adults $1, sr citizen & students $.50, children under 12 free. Estab 1981 to organize & host exhibitions primarily of contemporary art by artists of international, national, & regional significance. 411 linear ft & 6000 sq ft of exhibition space; adjoining classroom, auditorium & workshop/storage room. Average Annual Attendance: 25,000
Income: $140,000 (financed by state appropriation, private donations & grants)
Exhibitions: 6 to 7 group exhibitions annually based on themes or surveys of particular mediums
Publications: Gallery of Contemporary Art News, spring, summer & fall; Sin Frontiers, Crossing Borders; Crossovers: Contemporary Fibers; Colorado Collects: Art of the 20th Century
Activities: Classes for adults & children; docent training; museum training program; lect open to public, 7 vis lectr per year; concerts; book traveling exhibitions, 4 per year; museum shop sells catalogs, postcards & posters

CRIPPLE CREEK

M **CRIPPLE CREEK DISTRICT MUSEUM,** * 500 E Bennett Ave, PO Box 1210, 80813. Tel 719-689-2634; *Dir* Erik Swanson
Open Fall & Summer daily 10 AM - 5:30 PM, Spring & Winter weekends only. Admis adults $2.25, children 7 - 12 $.50, children under 7 free. Estab 1953 as a showplace for local artists. Average Annual Attendance: 35,000
Income: Financed by donations
Collections: Archival Collection; small collection of locally produced paintings
Exhibitions: Victorian Gambling; Gold Ore
Activities: Museum shop sells books

DENVER

M **AURARIA HIGHER EDUCATION CENTER,** Emmanuel Gallery, Campus Box Y, PO Box 173361, 80217-3361. Tel 303-556-8337; FAX 303-556-8349; *Dir* Carol Keller
Open Mon - Fri 11 AM - 5 PM. Estab 1976. Gallery is in the oldest standing church structure in Denver which has been renovated for exhibit space. This historically designated building is used by the Community College of Denver, Metropolitan State College, the University of Colorado at Denver & the Denver community. Average Annual Attendance: 30,000
Income: Financed by above colleges & Auraria Higher Education Center
Activities: Book traveling exhibitions

M **BLACK AMERICAN WEST MUSEUM & HERITAGE CENTER,** 3091 California St, 80205
Estab 1971. Average Annual Attendance: 10,000. Mem: 200; dues vary; annual meeting in Feb
Income: $100,000 (financed by mem, donations, gift shop sales, rentals & grants)
Activities: Docent training; lect open to public; tours; originates traveling exhibitions; museum shop sells books, magazines, prints & reproductions

M **COLORADO HISTORICAL SOCIETY,** Colorado History Museum, 1300 Broadway, 80203. Tel 303-866-3682; FAX 303-866-5739; Elec Mail chssysop@usa.net. *VPres* Andrew E Masich; *State Archaeologist* Susan Collins; *Cur Decorative & Fine Arts* Georgianna Contiguglia; *Cur Photog* Eric Paddock; *Dir Publications* David Wetzel; *Dir Educ* Martha Dyckes; *Cur Material Culture* Anne Wainstein Bond; *Cur Books & Manuscripts* Stan Oliner; *Coll Mgr* Jeanne Brako; *Dir Coll Servs* Katherine Kane; *Dir Design & Production* Allyson Smith; *Dir General Serv* Joseph Dean
Open Mon - Sat 10 AM - 4:30 PM, Sun Noon - 4:30 PM, cl Christmas. Admis adults $3, children 6-16 yrs & senior citizens $1.50, children under 6 free. Estab 1879 to collect, preserve & interpret the history of Colorado. 15,000 sq ft for temporary exhibits; 25,000 sq ft for permanent exhibits. Average Annual Attendance: 200,000. Mem: 7500; dues $30; annual meeting in Dec
Income: $1,600,000 (financed by endowment, mem, state & federal appropriations)
Collections: †William H Jackson Photo Collection; painting, sculpture, fine & decorative arts relating to Colorado & West America
Exhibitions: 20th Century Colorado; Artist of America
Publications: Colorado Heritage, quarterly; Colorado History News, monthly; Essays & Monographs
Activities: Classes for children; docent training; lect open to public; 12 vis lectr per year; gallery talks; tours; competitions with awards; individual paintings & original objects of art lent to qualified museums; lending collection contains film strips & motion pictures; museum shop sells books, magazines, original art, reproductions, prints & slides
L **Stephen H Hart Library,** 1300 Broadway, 80203. Tel 303-866-2305; FAX 303-866-5739; *Librn* Rebecca Lintz
Open to public for reference
Library Holdings: Vols 45,000; Per subs 600; maps; Micro — Reels; AV — A-tapes, motion pictures, v-tapes; Other — Clipping files, manuscripts 9,000,000, memorabilia, original art works, pamphlets, photographs 500,000, prints
Special Subjects: American Western Art, Archaeology, Architecture, Maps, Painting - American, Photography, Southwestern Art
Collections: William Henry Jackson Glass Plate Negatives of Views West of the Mississippi

M **COLORADO PHOTOGRAPHIC ARTS CENTER,** Alcott Sta, PO Box 12616, 80212-0616. Tel 303-278-3693; FAX 303-278-3693; *Pres* R Skip Kohloff
Estab 1963 to foster the art of photography. Mem: 100; dues family $25, individual $15, meetings in Jan, Apr, Sept & Nov
Income: $15,000 (financed by mem & grants)
Purchases: $1000 (Carole Gallaoher print from American Ground Zero project)
Collections: Permanent collection, 500-600 photographs
Exhibitions: Members exhibit; National Juried Exhibit
Activities: Lect open to public & members; exhibits; workshops; competitions

M **DENVER ART MUSEUM,** 100 W 14th Ave Pky, 80204. Tel 303-640-2793; FAX 303-640-5627; *Dir* Lewis Sharp; *Public Relations Dir* Deanna Person
Open Tues - Sat 10 AM - 5 PM, Sun Noon - 5 PM. Admis adults $3, senior citizens & students $1.50, children under 6 & members free. Estab 1893, new building opened 1971, to provide a number of permanent & rotating art collections for pub viewing, as well as a variety of art educ programs & services. The Mus, a seven story building contains 210,000 sq ft of space, 117,000 of which is exhibit space. Average Annual Attendance: 400,000. Mem: 19,000; dues family $40, individual $30; annual meeting in Apr
Income: Financed by mem, city & state appropriations & private funding
Collections: †American art; †contemporary art; design & architecture; †European art; †Native American art; †Native arts; †New World art; †Oriental art; Western art
Publications: Calendar, monthly; catalogues for exhibitions
Activities: Classes for adults & children; dramatic programs; docent training; lect open to public, 10 vis lectr per year; concerts; gallery talks; tours; book traveling exhibitions 2-3 per year; originate traveling exhibitions to national & international museums & galleries; museum shop sells books, magazines, original art, reproductions, prints, jewelry, rugs & children's art projects
L **Library,** 100 W 14th Ave Pky, 80204. Tel 303-640-1613; FAX 303-640-5627; *Dir* Nancy Simon; *Reference Librn* Margaret Goodrich
Open Mon - Thurs 10 AM - 5 PM, by appointment for research. Estab 1935 to facilitate research in anthropology & native arts. Reference only
Purchases: $1000
Library Holdings: Vols 25,000; Per subs 50; Basketry; Pottery; Other — Clipping files, exhibition catalogs, manuscripts, memorabilia, original art works, pamphlets, photographs, sculpture
Special Subjects: Afro-American Art, American Indian Art, American Western Art, Anthropology, Archaeology, Asian Art, Folk Art, History of Art & Archaeology, Islamic Art, Latin American Art, Mexican Art, Oriental Art, Painting - American, Pre-Columbian Art, Southwestern Art, Africa, American Indians, Native American linguistics, Oceania
Collections: †Native American; †African & Oceanic linguistics

L DENVER PUBLIC LIBRARY, General Reference, 10 W 14th Ave Pky, 80203. Tel 303-640-6280; FAX 303-640-6207; *Librn* Rick J Ashton; *Head Dept* James Kroll

Open Mon - Wed 10 AM - 9 PM, Thurs - Sat 10 AM - 5:30 PM, Sun 1 - 5 PM. No admis fee. Estab 1889

Income: Financed by city & county taxes

Library Holdings: Vols 80,000; Per subs 100; Original documents; Micro — Fiche, reels; AV — A-tapes, cassettes, fs, rec 1500; Other — Clipping files, exhibition catalogs, manuscripts, memorabilia, original art works, pamphlets 177,726, photographs 14,752, prints 1384, reproductions, sculpture

Special Subjects: American Western Art

Collections: †Western art

Exhibitions: Frequent exhibitions from the book & picture collections

Activities: Lect open to public; tours

M METROPOLITAN STATE COLLEGE OF DENVER, Center for the Visual Arts, 1701 Wazee St, 80202. Tel 303-294-5207; FAX 303-294-5209; *Dir* Sally L Perisho

Estab 1990 for temporary exhibitions of contemporary art. 5000 sq ft in historic building. Average Annual Attendance: 22,000. Mem: 250; annual meeting in July

Income: $300,000 (financed by mem, state appropriation, grants & revenues)

Publications: Quarterly newsletter

Activities: Classes for adults & children; lect open to public, 8 vis lectr per year; book traveling exhibitions 2 per year; originate traveling exhibitions 5 per year

M MUSEO DE LAS AMERICAS, 861 Santa Fe Dr, 80211. Tel 303-571-4401; FAX 303-607-9761; *Exec Dir* Jose Aguayo; *Cur & Dir Public Relations* Tariana Navas; *Dir Educ* Patricia Sigaca

Open Tue - Sat 10 AM - 5 PM. Admis $1-$3. Estab 1991 to collect, preserve & interpret Latin American art, history & culture. Average Annual Attendance: 12,000. Mem: 500; dues $10-$500

Income: $190,000 (financed by mem, foundation, corporation & pub funding)

Collections: †Folk Art Collection; †Historical Objects Collection; †paintings; †photography; †sculpture

Exhibitions: Eppie Archuleta: Master Weaver of the San Luis Valley; Cuba Siempre Vive; Alberto Gironela: Madonna Series; Luis Jimenez: Man On Fire

Publications: Notitas Newsletter, bimonthly

Activities: Classes for children; docent training; lect open to public, 5 vis lectr per year; book traveling exhibitions 5 per year; museum shop sells books, prints, original art & historical objects

M MUSEUM OF WESTERN ART, 1727 Tremont Pl, 80202. Tel 303-296-1880; FAX 303-296-7621; *Pres* William C Foxley; *Dir Public Relations & Educ* Judith Toliver

Open Tues - Sat 10 AM - 4:30 PM. Admis adults $3, seniors & students $2, members & children under 7 free, group discounts, guided tours available. Estab 1983 to collect, preserve & interpret the art of the American West. Listed on the National Register of Historical Places, the museum is located in the Historical Navarre Building, one elegant Victorian gambling hall & bordello. The museum is handicapped accessible & features 8000 sq ft of temperature & humidity controlled exhibit space, plus museum store specializing in Western mints, jewelry, rare & out of print books. Maintains reference library. Average Annual Attendance: 30,000. Mem: 250; dues commercial $100, family $35, single $25

Income: Financed by admis, sales, rental income, sponsorships

Collections: Collection of master works spanning the period from pre-Civil War to World War II, including works by many of the West's major artists such as Bierstadt, Moran, Remington, Russell, Blumenschein & Dixon

Publications: Frontier Spirit, catalogue

Activities: Classes for adults & children; docent training; lect open to public, 30 vis lectr per year; concerts; gallery talks; tours; competitions; individual paintings lent to various museums or traveling exhibition; museum shop sells books, magazines, rare & out of print books, reproductions, prints, Native American jewelry, Zuni fetishes, notecards & postcards

M PIRATE-A CONTEMPORARY ART OASIS, * 1370 Verbena, 80220. Tel 303-458-6058; *Dir* Phil Bender

Open Sat & Sun Noon - 5 PM. No admis fee. Estab 1980. Average Annual Attendance: 2000. Mem: 15

Income: Financed by mem

Publications: Blackspot, quarterly newsletter

Activities: Sales shop sells original art, hats, t-shirts, buttons & bumper stickers

C SLA ARCH-COUTURE INC, Art Collection, 2088 S Pennsylvania St, 80210. Tel 303-733-5157; *Pres* Leslie Alcott Temple; *Exec Asst* Sara Church; *Asst* Cecil Burns

Open by appointment only. Estab 1990 for educ & enjoyment. Sculpture, paintings, artifacts, African art, New Guinea, bone, skull & skeleton collections, BC & AD coins, art library, Native American, extensive photo & slide collection of Tarahumara Indians of Old Mexico. Maintains reference library. Average Annual Attendance: 500. Mem: contribution $20

Purchases: Rhinoceros Skin Shield, African & Bird Wing Collection

Collections: †SLA Corporate Collection: African & New Guinea; Animal; Artifacts; Figurative; Landscape; Portraits; drawing, etching, litho, oil & watercolor; clay, sculpture/bronze, stone & wood

Exhibitions: Deceased Artists 1890 - 1930; Evolving Young Artists

Activities: Classes for adults & children; lect open to public, 4-6 vis lectr per year; concerts; gallery talks; tours by appointment; art appraisals; art brokering & locating; art collection consulting; environmental enrichment design; individual paintings & original objects of art lent to government offices & institutions; book traveling exhibitions 3 per year; originate traveling exhibitions; sales shop sells original art, reproductions & prints

M SPARK GALLERY, * 1535 Platte St, 80202. Tel 303-455-4435

Open Fri & Sat 7 - 10 AM, Sun 1 - 5 PM. No admis fee. Estab 1979 as an artist's cooperative. Average Annual Attendance: 6000. Mem: 25; mem open to professional artist with reasonable body of work; dues $360; meeting first Sun each month

Income: $10,000 (financed by mem & grants)

Activities: Classes for adults & children; classes for AIDS patients; lect open to public, 3 vis lectr per year

M THE TURNER MUSEUM, 773 Downing St, 80218-3428. Tel 303-832-0924; FAX 303-832-0924; *Founder & Treas* Douglas Graham; *Dir & VPres* Linda Graham; *Dir & Secy* K L Vaggalis

Open Mon - Fri 2 - 5 PM, Sun Noon - 3 PM. Admis $7.50 including tour. Estab 1973 to carry out the last will of J M W Turner & to publicly display his works & also his principal admirer's (Thomas Moran) works. The Atlantic Richfield Gallery; The Mediterranean Gallery; The Kurt Pantzer Gallery. Average Annual Attendance: 5000. Mem: 800; dues corporate $100, family $25; annual meeting first Sun in Dec

Income: $10,000 (financed by endowment, mem & fund raising)

Purchases: J M W Turner; Thomas Moran

Collections: Thomas Moran Collection; J M W Turner Collection

Publications: Turner & Moran, yearly; Turner's Angels; Turner's Children; Turner's Powerful Allegories; Turner's Rainbows

Activities: Classes for adults & children; seminars, courses in art appreciation; lect open to public, 6 vis lectr per year; concerts; gallery talks; tours; individual paintings & original objects of art lent to other museums & similar organizations; lending collection contains books, color reproductions, original art works, original prints, slides & posters; originate traveling exhibitions; museum shop sells books, magazines, original art, reproductions, prints & posters

EVERGREEN

M JEFFERSON COUNTY OPEN SPACE, Hiwan Homestead Museum, 4208 S Timbervale Dr, 80439. Tel 303-674-6262; FAX 303-670-7746; *Adminr* John Steinle; *Educ Coordr* Sue Ashbaugh; *Cur* Brian Lang

Open Tues - Sun Noon - 5 PM, cl Mon. No admis fee. Estab 1975 to collect, preserve & exhibit Jefferson County history. History House furnished to 1900; 17 room log mansion with original furnishings & displays on local history. Average Annual Attendance: 18,000. Mem: 175; dues couple $15, individual $10; monthly meetings

Income: $20,000 (financed by mem & memorial donations)

Collections: †Decorative & fine arts; farm machinery; manuscripts; †Native American Arts & Crafts; Photographs; Textiles

Exhibitions: (1997) Indian Hills County, Pueblo & Pottery

Publications: The Record, quarterly

Activities: Classes for children; docent training; historic lect series open to public, 4 vis lectr per year

FORT COLLINS

M COLORADO STATE UNIVERSITY, Curfman Gallery, Lory Student Ctr, 80523. Tel 970-491-5412; FAX 970-491-3746; *Dir* Miriam B Harris

Open Mon - Fri 8:30 AM - 4:30 PM & 7 - 9:30 PM, Sat 1 - 4 PM. No admis fee. Estab 1965 to exhibit multi-cultural works from all over the world plus student works. 20 x 26 ft with fabric covered movable interior walls; some wood paneling on outer walls; handicapped accessible. Average Annual Attendance: 50,000

Income: $10,000 (financed by student government money, state appropriated funds through college administration)

Activities: Lect open to public

C FIRST NATIONAL BANK, 205 W Oak, 80521-2712. Tel 970-482-4861; FAX 970-495-9507; *Dir Marketing* Duane Rowe

Open 9 AM - 5:30 PM. Estab 1977 to invest in art for enjoyment of bank customers. Collection displayed in lobby & mezzanine of main bank; supports Council on Arts & Humanities, Colorado State University, Symphony, Theater

Collections: Prints by Boulanger, Calder, Sam Francis, Jasper Johns, Pali, Rauschenberg, Vasarely, Dave Yurst & local artists

Activities: Originate traveling exhibitions; sponsors Colorado State University Traveling Print Collection

M ONE WEST ART CENTER, 201 S College Ave, 80524. Tel 303-482-2787; *Exec Dir* Angela Brayham

Open Tues - Sat 10 AM - 5 PM. No admis fee. Estab 1990 a non-profit art mus dedicated to educ & exhibition of visual art. 2 galleries, 5000 sq ft housed in former 1911 post office on historic register. Average Annual Attendance: 10,000. Mem: 300

Income: $150,000 (financed by mem, fundraisers & tenant rent)

Exhibitions: Colorado-Wyoming Biennial Competition

Activities: Docent training; lect open to public, 5 vis lectr per year; gallery talks; tours; competitions; book traveling exhibition 1 per year; museum shop sells original art

FORT MORGAN

M FORT MORGAN HERITAGE FOUNDATION, 414 Main St, PO Box 184, 80701. Tel 970-867-6331; FAX 970-867-2988; *Pres Heritage Foundation* Sue Spencer; *VPres* Gerald Danford; *Dir* Marne Jurgemeyer; *Admin Asst* Michelle David

Open Mon - Fri 10 AM - 5 PM, Tues - Thurs evenings 6 - 8 PM, Sat 1:30 - 4:30 PM. No admis fee. Estab 1975 to interpret the history & culture of the area. Mus exhibits on a temporary basis fine art exhibits, both local artists & traveling exhibits. Average Annual Attendance: 10,000. Mem: 275; dues $10-$500; annual meeting fourth Thurs in Jan

Income: $110,000 (financed by endowment, mem, city appropriation & local, state & federal grants)

Collections: Hogsette Collection; primarily cultural & historical material; Native Arts

Activities: Classes for adults & children; docent programs

GOLDEN

A **COLORADO WATERCOLOR SOCIETY,** 1021 Homesteak Dr. 80401. Tel 303-273-5793; *Pres* Evelyn Lombardi-Lail
Estab 1954
Exhibitions: Colorado State Watermedia Exhibit
Publications: Monthly newsletter

A **FOOTHILLS ART CENTER, INC,** 809 15th St, 80401. Tel 303-279-3922; FAX 303-279-9470; *Exec Dir* Carol V Dickinson
Open Mon - Sat 9 AM - 4 PM, Sun 1 - 4 PM, cl holidays. No admis fee. Estab 1968 to provide a cultural center which embraces all the arts, to educate & stimulate the community in the appreciation & understanding of the arts, to provide equal opportunities for all people to participate in the further study & enjoyment of the arts & to provide artists & artisans with the opportunity to present their work. Housed in the former First Presbyterian Church of Golden, the original structure was built in 1872, the manse (a part of the whole layout) was built in 1892; there are five galleries, offices, a kitchen and classrooms. Average Annual Attendance: 15,000. Mem: 950; dues $20; annual meeting in Dec
Income: $165,000 (financed by mem, city appropriation, donations, commissions & rental of rooms)
Exhibitions: North American Sculpture Exhibitions; Rocky Mountain National Watermedia Exhibition; numberous open juried competitions
Publications: Bimonthly newsletter; one chapbook per year-winner of poetry; Catalogs of major national shows
Activities: Classes for adults & children; lect open to public, 2-3 vis lectr per year; concerts; tours; competitions with awards; individual paintings & original objects of art lent to businesses
L **Art Library,** 809 15th St, 80401. Tel 303-279-3922;
Open to members only
Library Holdings: Vols 800; Per subs 3

GRAND JUNCTION

L **MUSEUM OF WESTERN COLORADO,** 248 S Fourth St, PO Box 20000-5020, 81502-5020. Tel 970-242-0971; FAX 970-242-3960; *Coll & Information Mgr* Judy Prosser; *Dir* Richard S Sims
Open Mon - Fri 10 AM - 4:45 PM, cl Sun, Christmas wk & major holidays. Admis $2. Estab 1965 to collect preserve, interpret social & natural history of Western Colorado. For reference only. Mem: dues benefactor $1000, patron $500, sponsor $150, contributor & business $50, family $25, retired adult $15
Income: Financed by Mesa County, admis, gift shop revenues, grants, mem, donations, programs & special events
Library Holdings: Vols 2500; Per subs 15; Micro — Prints, reels; AV — Cassettes, lantern slides, motion pictures, slides; Other — Manuscripts, memorabilia, original art works, pamphlets, photographs
Special Subjects: Natural History; Social History of Western Colorado
Collections: Frank Dean Collection; †Al Look Collection; †Warren Kiefer Railroad Collection; Wilson Rockwell Collection; artwork, books, manuscripts & photographs on the history & natural history of Western Colorado; †Mesa County Oral History Collection
Exhibitions: Denny Sanders Exhibit; Country School Legacy; Otavolo Indian Exhibit; Keith Phillips/Sheri Dunn Art Show; Lydia & Bob Maurer Art Show; World War I Exhibition & Lecture Series; Pearl Harbor Exhibition & Lecture Series; Classic Film Festival; Al Look Lecture Series
Publications: A Bibliography of the Dinosauria; Cross Orchards Coloring Book; Dinosaur Valley Coloring Book; Familiar Insects of Mesa County, Colorado; Footprints in the Trail; Mesa County, Colorado: A 100 Year History; Mesa County Cooking with History; More Footprints in the Trail; Museum Times, monthly newsletter; Paleontology & Geology of the Dinosaur Triangle
Activities: Classes for children; docent training; lect open to public, 10 vis lectr per year; concerts; tours; Cross Ranch Apple Jubilee; Cross Ranch Artisan's Festival; slides/tape & video tape presentations

A **WESTERN COLORADO CENTER FOR THE ARTS, INC,** 1803 N Seventh, 81501. Tel 970-243-7337; *Dir* Richard Helm
Open Tues - Sat 10 AM - 5 PM. No admis fee. Art Center - Mus incorporated in 1952 to provide an appropriate setting for appreciation of & active participation in the arts. Two exhibition galleries of 2000 sq ft each; small stage; four studio classrooms. Average Annual Attendance: 24,000. Mem: 800; dues family $15, individual $7.50; annual meeting in Feb
Income: Financed by endowment, mem, tuition, gifts & grants
Collections: Ceramics; needlework; paintings; Navajo weavings
Exhibitions: Changing exhibits only in gallery
Publications: Newsletter for members, monthly
Activities: Classes for adults & children; dramatic programs; Childrens Theatre Company & Class Program; Community Theatre; docent training; lect open to public, 4-5 vis lectr per year; concerts; gallery talks; tours; competitions; book traveling exhibitions 8-10 per year; originate traveling exhibitions; sales shop sells books, magazines, original art, reproductions, Southwest Indian & contemporary craft items & notecards
L **Library,** 1803 N Seventh, 81501. Tel 970-243-7337;
Open to members & pub for reference
Library Holdings: Vols 1000; Other — Exhibition catalogs

GREELEY

M **MADISON & MAIN GALLERY,** 801 Eighth Plaza St, 80631. Tel 970-351-6201; *Treas* Susan B Anderson
Open Tues - Sat 10:30 AM - 5:30 PM. No admis fee. Estab 1987 as an artists' cooperative
Income: $30,000 (financed by city appropriation)
Exhibitions: Six shows per year plus work of members & consignees

M **UNIVERSITY OF NORTHERN COLORADO,** John Mariani Art Gallery, Department of Visual Arts, Eighth Ave & 18th St, 80639. Tel 970-351-2184; FAX 970-351-2299; *Dir* Patricia Reubain
Open Mon - Fri 9 AM - 4 PM. No admis fee. Estab 1973, to provide art exhibitions for the benefit of the University & the surrounding community
Income: Financed by endowment & city & state appropriations
Publications: Schedule of Exhibitions, quarterly
Activities: Classes for adults; lect open to public; gallery talks; tours; competitions with awards

GUNNISON

M **WESTERN STATE COLLEGE OF COLORADO,** Quigley Hall Art Gallery, 81231. Tel 970-943-2045; *Chmn* Charles Tutor; *Art Area Coordr* Lee Johnson; *Gallery Dir* Harry Heil
Open Mon - Fri 1 - 5 PM. No admis fee. Estab 1967 for the purpose of exhibiting student, staff & traveling art. Nearly 300 running ft composition walls, security lock-up iron grill gate is contained in the gallery. Average Annual Attendance: 7500
Income: Financed by state appropriation
Collections: Original paintings and prints
Activities: Competitions; originates traveling exhibitions

LA JUNTA

M **KOSHARE INDIAN MUSEUM, INC,** 115 W 18th, PO BOX 580, 81050. Tel 719-384-4411; *Exec Dir* Joe Clay; *Office Mgr* Linda Root; *Gift Shop Mgr* Jo Ann Jones; *Develop Dir* Linda Powers
Open summer 9 AM - 5 PM, winter 12:30 - 4:30 PM. No admis fee. Estab 1949 for the exhibition of Indian artifacts & paintings. 15,000 sq ft display space. For reference to members only or by special arrangement. Average Annual Attendance: 100,000. Mem: 250; annual meeting second Tues in Dec
Income: Financed by donations & shows
Collections: †Indian arts & crafts, of & by Indians; Taos Ten; †prominent southwestern artists
Exhibitions: Exhibits change monthly
Activities: Classes for children; tours; paintings & original art works lent to qualified museums; book traveling exhibitions; museum shop sells books, original art, reproductions, souvenirs, Indian jewelry & pottery
L **Library,** 115 W 18th, 81050. Tel 719-384-4411; *Exec Dir* Joe Clay
Open for reference only to members
Library Holdings: Vols 1700; Other — Clipping files
Special Subjects: American Indian Art, American Western Art, Anthropology, Archaeology, Eskimo Art, History of Art & Archaeology, Pottery, Primitive Art, Southwestern Art

LEADVILLE

A **LAKE COUNTY CIVIC CENTER ASSOCIATION, INC,** Heritage Museum & Gallery, * 100-102 E Ninth St, PO Box 962, 80461. Tel 719-486-1878, 486-1421; *Pres Board of Dir* Carl Schaeffer; *VPres* Ray Stamps
Open Memorial Day - Sept 30 daily 10 AM - 4:30 PM, May 2 - Oct daily 10 AM - 6 PM, July 15 - Aug 31 daily 10 AM - 8 PM. Admis adults $1.50, sr citizens $1, children 6 - 16 $.75, under 6 free, members free. Estab 1971 to promote the preservation, restoration & study of the rich history of the Lake County area & to provide display area for local & non-local art work & also to provide an educational assistance both to public schools & interested individuals. The Museum & Gallery own no art work, but display a variety of art on a changing basis. Average Annual Attendance: 10,000. Mem: 250; dues donor $100, contributing $50, patron $25, associate $12.50; annual meeting Feb
Income: $15,000 (financed by mem & admis fee)
Purchases: $1000
Collections: Diorama of Leadville history; mining & Victorian era artifacts; Victorian furniture
Exhibitions: Changing displays of paintings, photography and craft work
Publications: Mountain Diggings, annual; The Tallyboard, newsletter, quarterly
Activities: Lect open to public; competitions; sales shop sells books, slides, papers, postcards, rock samples

M **TABOR OPERA HOUSE MUSEUM,** 306-310 Harrison Ave (Mailing add: 815 Harrison Ave, 80461). Tel 719-486-1147; *Cur* Evelyn E Furman
Open June - Oct Sun - Fri 9 AM - 5:30 PM, Nov - May by appointment only. Admis adults $4, children under 12 $2. Estab 1955 as a historic theatre museum
Collections: Costumes; paintings
Exhibitions: Original scenery live shows
Activities: Lect; tours; films; concerts; arts festivals; sales shop sells books, cards, pictures & souvenirs

LITTLETON

M **ARAPAHOE COMMUNITY COLLEGE,** Colorado Gallery of the Arts, 2500 W College Dr, PO Box 9002, 80160. Tel 970-797-5650; FAX 970-797-5935; *Dir* Wayne Henry
Open Mon - Thurs 9 AM - 2 PM & 6 - 9 PM, Fri 9 AM - 2 PM, Sat 1 - 4 PM. Admis adults $1, senior citizens & students $.50, Arapahoe students, staff, gallery members & children under 12 free. Gallery contributes significantly to the cultural growth of the Denver-metro area. Average Annual Attendance: 13,000. Mem: 550; dues patron $100, associate $35-$99, family $20, individual $15, student & senior citizens $10
Income: $80,000 (Financed by mem, state & federal grants, corporate & private donations)
Collections: Small Costume Collection (for educational purposes & outreach program)
Publications: Artline, quarterly newsletter; Clay: Beyond Function, catalog
Activities: Classes for children; docent training; workshops; lect open to public, 10 vis lectr per year; tours; concerts; book traveling exhibitions

LOVELAND

M LOVELAND MUSEUM GALLERY, Fifth & Lincoln, 80537. Tel 970-962-2410; FAX 970-962-2910; *Dir* Susan Ison; *Cur Exhibits* Lynn Verschoor; *Cur Interpretation* Tom Katsimpalis; *Cur Coll* Jennifer Slichter; *Museum Preparator* David Phelps; *Events Coordr* Jan Schendel
Open Tues, Wed & Fri 10 AM - 5 PM, Thurs 9 AM - 9 PM, Sat 10 AM - 4 PM, Sun Noon - 4 PM. No admis fee. Estab 1956 to preserve & interpret history of Loveland area. Average Annual Attendance: 40,000. Mem: 120; dues individual $15
Income: Financed by city appropriation
Collections: Archaeology; art; dioramas; historical material; period rooms
Exhibitions: Victorian period rooms; pioneer cabin; Bureau of Reclamation relief map of Big Thompson Project; art gallery
Publications: Exhibition catalogues; history books; newsletter
Activities: Classes for adults & children; lect open to public; tours; inter-museum loan programs; museum shop sells books, magazines, original art, reproductions & prints

PUEBLO

M ROSEMOUNT MUSEUM, INC, 419 W 14th St, PO Box 5259, 81002. Tel 719-545-5290; FAX 719-545-5291; *Exec Dir* William T Henning; *Bus Mgr* Monica L Moore; *Cur & Registrar* Martha Valle; *Pres* Alan Kuykendall
Open June - Aug, Tues - Sat 10 AM - 4 PM, Sun 2 - 4 PM, Sept - May Tues - Sat 1 - 4 PM, Sun 2 - 4 PM. Admis adults $5, senior citizens $4, children 6-16 $2, under 6 free. Estab 1968 as a historic house museum devoted to portraying lifestyle of a wealthy Victorian family. 37 room Victorian mansion contains 80 percent of original furnishings including many decorative objects & art from late 19th century. Average Annual Attendance: 26,000. Mem: 650; dues $15-$500; annual meeting in Apr
Income: $503,000 (financed by endowment, mem, rental, gift shop, auxiliary organization, fundraisers, admis, donations & grants)
Purchases: $503,000
Collections: Permanent collections are displayed in a 37 room Victorian mansion & are one of the finest intact collections of the American Aesthetic Movement; Collections include furnishings, decorative objects, paintings, sculpture, drawings, photographs, all pertaining to the life of the Thatcher Family
Publications: Rosemount News, quarterly
Activities: Classes for adults & children; docent training; lect open to public, 4-6 vis lectr per year; concerts; tours; museum shop sells books, magazines, prints & deorative art objects

A SANGRE DE CRISTO ARTS & CONFERENCE CENTER, 210 N Santa Fe, 81003. Tel 719-543-0130; FAX 719-543-0134; *Dir* Maggie Divelbiss; *Asst Dir* David Zupancic; *Visual Art Cur* Jennifer Cook; *Rentals Coordr* Lorrie Marquez; *Marketing Coordr* Tressa Panepinto; *Dir Educ* Donna Stinchcomb
Open Mon - Sat 11 AM - 4 PM. No admis fee. Estab 1972 to promote the educational & cultural activities related to the fine arts in Southern Colorado including four gallery spaces & a hands on children's museum, a conference area with over 7000 sq ft of rentable space for conventions, receptions, meetings, including a 500 seat theater. The Helen T White Gallery provides four gallery spaces with changing exhibitions by local, regional & international artists, including the Francis King Collection of Western Art on permanent display. PAWS Children's Mus displays over 2 dozen hands-on exhibits. Average Annual Attendance: 80,000. Mem: 1900; dues $15-$1500
Income: $993,000 (financed by mem, city & County appropriation, grants, grants, private underwriting, donations & in-kind services)
Collections: Francis King Collection of Western Art, on permanent display
Publications: Town & Center Mosaic, nine times a yr; Catalogue of Francis King Collection, annual report exhibition catalogues; brochures for workshop & dance classes, quarterly; performing arts series, children's series, children's museum
Activities: Year-round workshop program, wide selection of disciplines for children & adults; special facilities for ceramics, painting & photography; school of dance; artists-in-residence; lect & seminars coinciding with exhibits; Theatre Arts - Town & Gown Performing Arts Series; Children's Playhouse Series; outdoor summer concerts, Repertory Theatre Company presenting 2 performances a year, resident modern dance company; scholarships offered; individual paintings & objects of art lent to museums, galleries & art centers; lending collection contains 320 original art works, 50 original prints, 150 paintings, photographs, nature artifacts & sculptures; book traveling exhibitions 1-3 per year; sales shop sells hand-crafted & imported gifts & southwestern artifacts, posters, jewelry

M UNIVERSITY OF SOUTHERN COLORADO, College of Liberal & Fine Arts, 2200 Bonforte, 81001-4901. Tel 719-549-2100; *Art Dept Chmn* Carl Jensen; *Gallery Dir* Dennis Dolton
Open daily 10 AM - 4 PM. No admis fee. Estab 1972 to provide educational exhibitions for students attending the University. Gallery has a 40 x 50 ft area with 16 ft ceiling; vinyl covered wooden walls; carpeted & adjustable track lighting. Average Annual Attendance: 6000
Income: Financed through University & student government
Collections: Basketry of the Plains Indian, clothing of the Plains Indian; Orman Collection of Indian Art of the Southwest including Indian blankets of the Rio Grande & Navajo people; pottery of the Pueblo Indians (both recent & ancient)
Exhibitions: Art Director's Club of Denver Exhibition; Art Resources of South Colorado; Colorado Invites
Publications: Catalogs
Activities: Lect open to public; individual paintings & original objects of art lent; book traveling exhibitions 2-6 per year; originate traveling exhibitions organized & circulated

TRINIDAD

M ARTHUR ROY MITCHELL MEMORIAL INC, Museum of Western Art, 150 E Main St, 81082-0095. Tel 719-846-4224; *Pres* Bernard Parsons; *VPres* Clara Dunning; *Dir* Peggy Weurding; *Treas* Eugene Aiello
Open daily 10 AM - 4 PM, cl Sun Apr - Sept. No admis fee. Estab 1981 to preserve & display art of the American West. 5000 sq ft. Average Annual Attendance: 18,000. Mem: 950
Income: $45,000 (financed by endowment, mem, donations, gifts, grants & gift shop)
Collections: A R Mitchell Collection; Almeron Newman Collection of photography; The Aultman Collection of photography; Harvey Dienn Collection
Exhibitions: Santa Fe Trail Regional
Activities: Classes in docent programs; lect open to public, 1 vis lectr per year; concerts; gallery talks; tours; competitions with prizes; individual paintings & original objects of art lent to University of Colorado at Boulder, Colorado Community College & other museums; lending collection contains original art works & paintings; book traveling exhibitions; originate traveling exhibitions 4 per year; museum shop sells books, original art, Indian jewerly & Indian rugs

CONNECTICUT

AVON

A FARMINGTON VALLEY ARTS CENTER, Avon Park N, 25-27 Arts Center Lane, 06001. Tel 860-678-1867; FAX 860-678-1867; *Exec Dir* Betty Friedman; *Admin Coordr* Jean Swanson; *Shop Mgr* Sally Bloomberg; *Educ Dir* Wendy Rappaport
Open Mon - Fri 10 AM - 4 PM. No admis fee. Estab 1972 to provide a facility with appropriate environment & programs, to serve as a focal point for public awareness of & participation in the visual arts by furthering quality arts education & exposure to dedicated artists & their works. Maintains 20 studios. Average Annual Attendance: 30,000. Mem: 1200; dues family $25, individual $20, Board of Directors annual meeting in Apr
Income: $500,000 (financed by shop, mem, grants, tuitions, donations from corporations & individuals, special event earning)
Exhibitions: American artists/craftspeople featured in Fisher Gallery & Shop
Activities: Classes for adults & children; lect open to public; tours; visits to artist's studios; annual holiday sale of fine crafts

BRIDGEPORT

M THE BARNUM MUSEUM, 820 Main St, 06604. Tel 203-331-1104; FAX 203-339-4341; *Acting Dir* Barbara Kram; *Cur* Robert Pelton
Open Tues - Sat 10 AM - 4:30 PM, Sun Noon - 4:30 PM. Admis adults $5, senior citizens $4 & children $3. Estab 1893 to exhibit the life & times of P T Barnum. Average Annual Attendance: 50,000. Mem: 500; dues family $45, individual $25
Income: Financed by City of Bridgeport, corporate individual, mem & endowments
Exhibitions: Bridgeport Industrial History Circus (Barnum)
Publications: The Barnum Hearld newsletter, 2 times per year
Activities: Tours; films; workshops; lect open to public; book traveling exhibitions 1 per year; originate traveling exhibitions; sales shop sells books, souvenirs

M DISCOVERY MUSEUM, 4450 Park Ave, 06604. Tel 203-372-3521; *Develop* Mary Ann C Freeman; *Pres* Elaena DeMurias; *Dir Admin* Jennifer Getty; *Cur Art* Benjamin Ortiz
Open Tues - Sat 10 AM - 5 PM, Sun Noon - 5 PM, cl major holidays. Admis adults $6, children, senior citizens & students $4, members free. Estab 1958 to provide exhibitions & educational programs in the arts & sciences for a regional audience. Average Annual Attendance: 90,000. Mem: 1500; dues $20-$1000; annual meeting in June
Collections: Paintings, prints & works on paper
Exhibitions: Temporary & permanent exhibitions; hands-on physical science exhibits; New Hands-on Art Gallery; Challenger Space Station; Fine Art Gallery; Planetarium
Publications: American Artists Abroad, catalog; Milton Avery, catalog
Activities: Classes for adults & children; docent training; lect open to public, 6 vis lectr per year; gallery talks; competitions with awards; planetarium shows; individual paintings & original objects of art lent to other museums & galleries; book traveling exhibitions 1 per year; museum shop sells books, reproductions, cards, calendars, gifts, jewelry, dishware & toys for children & adults

M HOUSATONIC COMMUNITY-TECHNICAL COLLEGE, Housatonic Museum of Art, 900 Lafayette Blvd, 06604-4704. Tel 203-579-6550; FAX 203-579-6993; *Dir* Jeanne DuBois
Average Annual Attendance: 12,000
Income: Financed by state & donations
Collections: Extensive 19th & 20th Century drawings, paintings & sculpture: Avery, Baskin, Calder, Cassat, Chagall, Daumier, DeChirico, Derain, Dubuffet, Gottlieb, Lichtenstein, Lindner, Marisol, Matisse, Miro-Moore, Pavia, Picasso, Rauchenberg, Rivers, Shahn, Vasarely, Warhol, Wesselmann & others; extensive ethnographic collections, including Africa, South Seas & others; smaller holdings from various historical periods
Exhibitions: Several exhibitions per year
Publications: Exhibition catalogs
Activities: Classes for adults; college art courses; lect open to public, 2-4 vis lectr per year; concerts; gallery talks; tours; scholarships offered; individual paintings & original objects of art lent to institutions; limited lending collection contains 2000 paintings. 25,000 slides; book traveling exhibitions; originate traveling exhibitions

L **Library,** 900 Lafayette Blvd, 06604. Tel 203-332-5070; FAX 203-332-5252; *Dir* Bruce Harvey
Extensive art section open to students & community
Library Holdings: Vols 30,000; Micro — Fiche

M **UNIVERSITY OF BRIDGEPORT GALLERY,** Bernhard Ctr, 06601. Tel 203-576-4239; FAX 203-576-4051; *Art Dept Chmn* Thomas Juliusburger; *Operations Mgr* Kaz McCue
Open Mon - Fri 11 AM - 5 PM, Sat & Sun 1 - 5 PM. No admis fee. Estab 1972
Collections: Contemporary art; prints
Activities: Lect open to public; gallery talks; concerts; individual paintings & original objects of art lent; originates traveling exhibitions

BROOKFIELD

M **BROOKFIELD CRAFT CENTER, INC,** Gallery, Rte 25, PO Box 122, 06804. Tel 203-775-4526; FAX 203-740-7815; Elec Mail brkfldcrft@aol.com. *Exec Dir* John I Russell
Open daily 10 AM - 5 PM. No admis fee. Estab 1954 to provide a wide spectrum of craft education & exhibition to the local & national audiences. Average Annual Attendance: 10,000. Mem: 1200; dues $35-$50
Exhibitions: Contemporary craft exhibitions changing every 8 weeks
Publications: Catalogs
Activities: Classes for adults & children; lect open to public, 300 vis lectr per year; concerts; scholarships offered; book traveling exhibitions to other craft organizations; sales shop sells original art & handmade craft items
L **Video Library,** Rte 25, PO Box 122, 06804. Tel 203-775-4526; FAX 203-740-7815; *Registrar* Dee Wagner
Open Mon - Sat 10 AM - 4 PM, Sun 2 - 5 PM. Estab 1954 to aid students & members of the Center with resource craft information. Reference only
Purchases: $250
Library Holdings: Per subs 25; Other — Exhibition catalogs

BROOKLYN

M **NEW ENGLAND CENTER FOR CONTEMPORARY ART,** Rte 169, PO Box 302, 06234. Tel 860-774-8899; FAX 860-774-4840; *Dir* Henry Riseman; *Cur* Eva Pape
Open Apr - Dec Mon - Sat 10 AM - 5 PM, Sun Noon - 5 PM, cl Christmas. No admis fee. Estab 1975. Mem: dues corporate $100, supporting $50, family $15, individual $10, senior citizen $6
Collections: Contemporary paintings & sculpture; print collection by Russian artists; woodblock print collection from the People's Republic of China
Activities: Classes for adults & children; lect; tours; films; gallery talks; originate traveling exhibitions; sales shop sells paintings, prints & books

COS COB

M **HISTORICAL SOCIETY OF THE TOWN OF GREENWICH, INC,** Bush-Holley House Museum, 39 Strickland Rd, 06807. Tel 203-869-6899; FAX 203-869-6727; *Chmn* Claire F Vanderbilt; *Exec Dir* Debra Walker Mecky; *Pres* William C Crooks
Open Tues - Fri Noon - 4 PM, Sun 1 - 4 PM. Admis adults $4, senior citizens & students $3. 18th century wealthy Bush family home. Maintains reference library. Average Annual Attendance: 2000. Mem: 1500; dues $30 & up; annual meeting 3rd Tues in Sept
Income: Financed by contributions, mem, special events, fees
Collections: Outbuilding houses collection of John Rogers groups; 18th & 19th century decorative arts; paintings of American impressionists; antiques
Publications: Pamphlets
Activities: Classes for children; docent training; children's summer program; lect open to public; tours; individual paintings & original objects of art lent

DANBURY

M **DANBURY SCOTT-FANTON MUSEUM & HISTORICAL SOCIETY, INC,** 43 Main St, 06810. Tel 203-743-5200; *Dir* Maryann Root
Mus open Wed - Sun 2 - 5 PM, cl Mon, Tues & holidays; office open Tues - Fri 10 AM - 5 PM. No admis fee. Estab June 24, 1941 as historic house. Merged with Mus & Arts Center by Legislative Act 1947. Operates the 1785 John & Mary Rider House as a mus of early Americana & the 1790 Dodd Hat Shop with exhibits relating to hatting. Huntington Hall houses frequently changing exhibits. Ives Homestead, located at Rogers Park in Danbury is to be restored & opened to the pub as a memorial to American composer Charles Edward Ives. At present there is a Charles Ives Parlor in the Rider House, recreating the period with Ives furnishings & memorabilia. Average Annual Attendance: 5000. Mem: 500; dues student $2 up to life $1000; annual meeting in Nov
Income: Financed by endowment & mem
Publications: Newsletter, monthly; reprints
Activities: Classes for adults & children; dramatic programs; lect open to public; concerts; open house; special exhibits; gallery talks; tours; slide shows
L **Library,** 43 Main St, 06810. Tel 203-743-5200; *Dir* Maryann Root
Historic information & photographs for reference only
Library Holdings: City Directories; Other — Clipping files, manuscripts, memorabilia, photographs
Collections: Charles Ives Photograph Collection

A **WOOSTER COMMUNITY ART CENTER,** 73 Miry Brook Rd, 06810. Tel 203-744-4825; *Exec Dir* Nancy M Rogers; *Asst Dir* Judy Kagan
Open Mon - Fri 9:30 AM - 10 PM, Sat 10 AM - 2 PM. Estab 1965 as a Community Art Center. Reception center gallery 500 sq ft. Average Annual Attendance: 1500. Mem: 400; dues $35
Exhibitions: Nancy Tholen; P Warfield; A Werner; Faculty Exhibits Art exhibits change monthly in Lobby Gallery, Area artists exhibit artwork in varied media,

indoor & outdoor photography, painting & sculpture
Publications: Arts News (newsletter), 3 times a yr
Activities: Classes for adults & children; lect open to public, 5 vis lectr per year; scholarships & fels offered; originate traveling exhibitions; sales shop sells art supplies
L **Library,** 73 Miry Brook Rd, 06810. Tel 203-744-4825; *Exec Dir* Nancy M Rogers
For reference only
Library Holdings: AV — Slides 2200

ESSEX

A **ESSEX ART ASSOCIATION, INC,** * N Main St, PO Box 193, 06426. Tel 860-767-8996; *Pres* Boyce Price; *Treas* Jesse Mayer
Open daily 1 - 5 PM June - Labor Day. No admis fee. Estab 1946 as a non-profit organization for the encouragement of the arts & to provide & maintain suitable headquarters for the showing of art. Maintains a small, well-equipped one-floor gallery. Average Annual Attendance: 2500. Mem: 360; dues artists $25, assoc $20; annual meeting in Fall
Income: Financed by mem & donations
Exhibitions: Three annual exhibits each year plus one or two special exhibits

FAIRFIELD

A **FAIRFIELD HISTORICAL SOCIETY,** 636 Old Post Rd, 06430. Tel 203-259-1598; FAX 203-255-2716; *Cur* Ellen Endslow
Open Mon - Fri 9 AM - 5 PM, Sun 1 - 5 PM. Suggested donation adults $1, children $.50. Estab 1902 to collect, preserve & interpret artifacts & information relating to the history of Fairfield. Average Annual Attendance: 3000. Mem: 750; dues $20 - $500; meeting date varies
Income: $100,000 (financed by endowment, mem, admis, donation & town contributions)
Collections: Ceramics, furniture, greeting cards, jewelry, paintings, photographs, prints, silver; local history; textiles & costumes
Publications: Newsletter, quarterly
Activities: Classes for adults & children; dramatic programs; docent training; docent lect open to public for a fee; gallery talks; tours
L **Library,** 636 Old Post Rd, 06430. Tel 203-259-1598; FAX 203-255-2716; *Dir* Steve Young
Open Mon - Fri 9:30 AM - 4:30 PM Sat & Sun 1 - 5 PM. Estab 1902. Open to the pub for reference only. Mem: 1000; dues $25; annual meeting in Oct
Library Holdings: Vols 10,000; Diaries; Documents; Maps; Micro — Fiche; AV — A-tapes, cassettes, lantern slides, motion pictures, slides; Other — Clipping files, manuscripts, original art works, pamphlets, photographs, prints
Special Subjects: Landscape Architecture, Genealogy & local history
Activities: Classes for adults & children; docent training; lect; gallery talks; tours; individual paintings & original objects of art lent; museum shop sells books, original art, prints

M **FAIRFIELD UNIVERSITY,** Thomas J Walsh Art Gallery, Quick Ctr for the Arts, N Benson Rd, 06430. Tel 203-254-4242; FAX 203-254-4113; *Dir Walsh Art Gallery* Dr Philip Eliasoph; *Asst Cur* Dale Skaggs
Open Tues - Sat 11 AM - 5 PM, Sun Noon - 4 PM. No admis fee. Estab 1990. Multi-purpose space with state of the art security & environmental controls requirement; 2200 sq ft
Income: Financed by endowment & university funds
Exhibitions: Thematic & social context art exhibitions; Renaissance Baroque, 19th & 20th centuries.
Publications: Educational materials; exhibition catalogues
Activities: Adult classes; lect open to public; book traveling exhibitions 3 per year; originate traveling exhibitions two per year

FARMINGTON

A **THE ART GUILD,** Church St, 06032. Tel 860-677-6205; *Pres* William Godfrey; *Exec Dir* Donna Gorman; *Guild Dir* Nancy Donagen
Open Tues - Fri 11 AM - 4 PM, when exhibits are ongoing. No admis fee. Estab 1976 to provide instruction in art & crafts & provide facilities for local artists. 18 ft x 18 ft with moveable walls. Displaying painting, sculpture, crafts, photography. Mem: 300; dues $25
Income: $40,000 (financed by mem, state, local & corporate grants, sales & fees)
Exhibitions: Faculty show; Xmas Crafts Show; individual & group shows; Members Show; Distinguished Artists Exhibition
Activities: Classes for adults & children; lect open to public, 1 vis lectr per year; competitions with awards

A **CONNECTICUT WATERCOLOR SOCIETY,** PO Box 1313, 06034-1313. *Pres* John Atwateraws; *Treas* Joan Roof
Estab 1938. Mem: Over 200; dues $15
Exhibitions: Two annual exhibits

M **FARMINGTON VILLAGE GREEN & LIBRARY ASSOCIATION,** Stanley-Whitman House, 37 High St, 06032. Tel 860-677-9222; *Chmn* Mary Grace Reed; *Dir* Jean Martin
Open May - Oct Wed - Sun Noon - 4 PM; Nov - Apr, Sun Noon - 4 PM & by appointment. Admis adults $5, senior citizens $4, children $2, mem & AAM free. Estab 1935 to collect, preserve, educate about 18th century Farmington. A separate building, has space for art exhibits. Maintains reference library. Average Annual Attendance: 2000. Mem: 200; dues $18-$500
Income: Financed by endowment interest, special events, mem & admis
Collections: American decorative arts; †ceramics; costumes & †textiles; 18th century; decorative arts; dooryard & herb garden; †furniture; †glass; household utensils; musical instruments; photographs; †weaving equipment
Exhibitions: Permanent & changing exhibitions
Publications: A Guide to Historic Farmington, Connecticut; A Short History of

Farmington, Connecticut
Activities: Classes for adults & children; dramatic programs; docent training; family & schoool programs; lect open to public, 3 vis lectr per year; gallery talks; tours; competitions with awards; scholarships offered; individual paintings & original objects lent to other museums; lending collection contains cassettes, over 80 original art works, paintings, over 1000 photographs & 300 slides; museum shop sells books, magazines, original art, reproductions, prints, needle kits & related to collection books, toys, games & cards

M **HILL-STEAD MUSEUM,** 35 Mountain Rd, 06032. Tel 860-677-4787; FAX 860-677-0174; *Pres* Prudence Robertson; *Trustee* Charles Parkhurst; *Trustee* John C Pope; *Trustee* Saren Langmann; *Trustee* R Kelley Brown
Hours change seasonally, call for current schedule. Admis adults $6, senior citizens & students over 12 $5, under 12 $3. Estab 1946. Colonial Rivival style house designed by Theodate Pope in collaboration with McKim, Mead & White & built around 1900 for industrialist Alfred Atmore Pope. Set on 150 acres including a sunken garden designed by Beatrix Farrand, the house contains Mr Pope's early collection of French Impressionist paintings and decorative arts. Average Annual Attendance: 15,000
Income: Financed by endowment, contributions, individual, corporate & foundations, admis & sales
Collections: Paintings by Cassatt, Degas, Manet, Monet & Whistler; prints by Durer, Piranesi, Whistler & other 19th century artists; American, English & other European furniture Oriental & European porcelain ; Japanese prints
Publications: Catalog of Hill-Stead Paintings; Theodate Pope Riddle, Her Life & Work; Hill-Stead Museum House Guide
Activities: Guide training; concerts; museum talks; tours; shop sells books, postcards, posters & gifts

GOSHEN

M **GOSHEN HISTORICAL SOCIETY,** Old Middle Rd, 06756-2001. Tel 860-491-2665, 491-8612; *Pres* N Terry Hall; *Cur* Hazel Wadhams
Open year round Tues 10 AM - Noon, July & Aug Sat 2 - 4 PM, by appointment on same day. Estab 1955 to interpret the past & present of our area. Average Annual Attendance: 400. Mem: 300; meetings in May & Oct
Income: Financed by endowment
Collections: Collection of Indian art, farm tools, household items used through town's history & photographs
Exhibitions: Exhibits focused on 250 years of town's history
Activities: Classes for children; 2 vis lectr per year

GREENWICH

M **THE BRUCE MUSEUM,** One Museum Dr, 06830. Tel 203-869-0376; FAX 203-869-0963; *Dir* John B Clark; *Cur Art* Nancy Hall-Duncan
Open Tues - Sat 10 AM - 5 PM, Sun 2 - 5 PM, cl Mon & major holidays. Admis adults $3.50, seniors & children 5-12 $2.50. Estab 1909 by Robert M Bruce. Recently expanded & completely renovated. Museum features changing exhibits in fine & decorative arts & environmental history. Changing exhibits in fine & decorative arts in four galleries; small reference library for staff use only. Average Annual Attendance: 80,000. Mem: 2500; dues $35-$5000; annual meeting in May
Income: $1,100,000 ($500,000 financed by town of Greenwich & $600,000 by Bruce Museum, Inc)
Collections: 19th & 20th century American paintings & costumes; North American Indian ethnology; Orientalia; American natural sciences
Publications: Exhibition Catalogs, 6 per yr; calender of events, 12 per yr
Activities: Classes for adults & children; docent training; lect open to public, 8-10 vis lectr per year; concerts; gallery talks; tours; individual paintings & original objects of art lent to other museums; originate traveling exhibitions; museum shop sells books, reproductions, prints & slides

A **GREENWICH ART SOCIETY INC,** 299 Greenwich Ave, 06830. Tel 203-629-1533; FAX 203-622-3980; *Co-Pres* Janet Jones; *Co-Pres* Adrienne Camilli; *Treas* Herbert Egli
Estab 1912 as a nonprofit organization to further art educ & to awaken & stimulate broader interest in arts in the town of Greenwich. Art Center studio is used for classes & E C Pottery Gallery meetings & exhibitions. Mem: 300; dues family $35, regular $25, student 19-24 yrs $10
Income: Financed by mem, fees & contributions
Exhibitions: Members' Juried Exhibition in Hulbutt Gallery (annual); Spring or Winter Juried members Exhibition, Greenwich Arts Center (annual); Art & Nature Show, Garden Education Center of Greenwich (annual); (1997) Presidents' Choice Show; 80th Annual Members' Juried Exhibition; GAS Scholarship Awards Show; GAS Faculty Show
Publications: The History of the Greenwich Art Society, booklet; bulletin of program for the year & class schedule
Activities: Day & evening classes for adults, special classes for children; critiques & demonstrations; lect open to public; scholarships

L **GREENWICH LIBRARY,** 101 W Putnam Ave, 06830-5387. Tel 203-622-7900; FAX 203-622-7939;
Internet Home Page Address www.greenwich.lib.cp.us. *Dir* Elizabeth Mainiero
Open Mon - Fri 9 AM - 9 PM, Sat 9 AM - 5 PM, Sun 1 - 5 PM Oct - May. Estab 1878 to provide free & convenient access to the broadest possible range of information & ideas. Hurlbutt Gallery features exhibits of paintings, prints, sculpture, photos, antiques & objects d'art, sponsored by Friends of the Greenwich Library. Circ 1,063,950
Income: $3,378,992 (financed by city appropriation)
Purchases: Art & Music $19,925, video $39,913, records & audio cassettes $46,285
Library Holdings: Vols 313,824; Per subs 600; Art related books 16,990; Compact discs 10,000; AV — Cassettes 6550, v-tapes 10,000; Other — Framed reproductions 326
Collections: †Book arts collection (fine press books)

Exhibitions: Six different exhibits per year
Publications: Monthly book lists
Activities: Lect open to public, 3-5 vis lectr per year; individual paintings lent to Greenwich residents; lending collection contains approx 438 items

HAMDEN

L **PAIER COLLEGE OF ART, INC,** Library, 20 Gorham Ave. 06514. Tel 203-777-7319, 287-3023 (library); *Pres* Jonathan E Paier; *VPres* Daniel Paier; *Library Dir* Gail J Nochin
Open daily 8 AM - 8 PM. Admis free. Estab 1946, library estab 1978
Library Holdings: Vols 14,000; Per subs 85; AV — A-tapes, slides 20,000, v-tapes 25; Other — Clipping files, exhibition catalogs 500, pamphlets, prints, reproductions
Special Subjects: Advertising Design, Architecture, Art History, Calligraphy, Commercial Art, Conceptual Art, Decorative Arts, Drawings, Folk Art, Graphic Arts, Graphic Design, History of Art & Archaeology, Illustration, Interior Design, Lettering

HARTFORD

A **CONNECTICUT HISTORICAL SOCIETY,** One Elizabeth St, 06105. Tel 860-236-5621; FAX 860-236-2664; *Exec Dir* David Kahn; *Asst Dir* Paul B Parvis; *Cur* Elizabeth P Fox; *Dir Educ* Christine Ermenc; *Cur Prints & Photographs* Kate Steinway; *Registrar* Richard C Malley; *Ed* Everett C Wilkie Jr; *Public Information Officer* Diana McCain
Open Tues - Sun 12 - 5 PM; cl Sat (June 1 - Sept 1). Admis fee $2, children 3 -12 $1, members free. Estab 1825 to collect & preserve materials of Connecticut interest & to encourage interest in Connecticut history. Exhibition space totals 6500 sq ft, half of which is devoted to permanent exhibitions, the other half to changing exhibits. Average Annual Attendance: 20,300. Mem: 2300; dues $20; annual meeting in Oct
Income: Financed by endowment & mem
Collections: Historical Collections (decorative arts)
Exhibitions: Connecticut History Day
Publications: Connecticut Historical Society Bulletin, quarterly; Annual Report; Notes and News, five times a year
Activities: Classes for adults & children, dramatic programs, docent training; lect open to public, 12 vis lectr per year; gallery talks; tours; competitions with awards; exten dept serves Connecticut State; individual paintings & original objects of art lent; lending collection contains books, lent to qualified institutions; book traveling exhibitions annually; originate traveling exhibitions; museum shop sells books, reproductions, prints

L **Library,** One Elizabeth St, 06105. Tel 860-236-5621; FAX 860-236-2664; Elec Mail cthist@ix.netcom.com. *Head Librn* Everett C Wilkie Jr
Open Tues - Sat 9 AM - 5 PM, cl Sun, Sat & holidays (June 1 - Sept 1). Reference only
Library Holdings: Vols 100,000; Per subs 62; AV — Lantern slides, rec, v-tapes; Other — Clipping files, exhibition catalogs, framed reproductions, original art works, pamphlets, photographs, prints, reproductions
Special Subjects: Connecticut structures & artists
Collections: Frederick K & Margaret R Barbour Furniture Collection; George Dudley Seymour Collection of Furniture; Morgan B Brainard Tavern Signs
Publications: Bulletin, quarterly; Notes & News, three times per year
Activities: Docent training; lect open to public, 10 vis lectr per year; gallery talks; tours

L **CONNECTICUT STATE LIBRARY,** Museum of Connecticut History, 231 Capitol Ave, 06106. Tel 860-566-3056; FAX 860-566-2133; *Museum Adminr* Dean Nelson; *Cur* David J Corrigan; *Cur* Deborah Barone
Open Mon - Fri 9 AM - 4:45 PM, Sat 9 AM - 1 PM, cl holidays. Estab 1910 to collect, preserve & display artifacts & memorabilia reflecting the history & heritage of Connecticut. For reference only
Library Holdings: Vols 500,000; Original documents; Micro — Fiche, reels; AV — Cassettes, motion pictures, v-tapes; Other — Clipping files, manuscripts, memorabilia, original art works, pamphlets, photographs, prints
Special Subjects: Coins & Medals, Connecticut, firearms
Collections: Collection of Firearms; Portraits of Connecticut's Governors
Exhibitions: Changing exhibits

L **HARTFORD PUBLIC LIBRARY,** Art Dept, 500 Main St, 06103. Tel 860-543-8628; *Dept Head* Kathleen L Brophy
Open hours vary. Estab 1774 as a free pub library
Income: Financed by endowment, mem & city appropriation
Library Holdings: Compact discs; Pictures 300,000; Micro — Reels; AV — Cassettes, motion pictures, rec, v-tapes; Other — Clipping files, framed reproductions

C **HEUBLEIN, INC,** 450 Columbus Blvd, PO Box 778, 06142-0778. Tel 860-702-4000; FAX 860-702-4169; *Corporate VPres* Peter M Seremet; *Admin Serv* K Gaillard
Open to pub by appointment. Estab 1973 for the benefit of employees & to complement the building interior design
Purchases: $15,000
Collections: Contemporary American art, large oils & sculptures, acrylics, watercolors, drawings, prints, photographs & tapestries
Activities: Selected pieces are loaned to qualifying organizations who must provide for all necessary packing requirements, insurance & transportation

M **OLD STATE HOUSE,** 800 Main St, 06103. Tel 860-522-6766; FAX 860-522-2812; *Chmn* David Whelehan; *Pres* David Coffin; *Exec Dir* Wilson H Faude
Open Tues - Sat 10 AM - 5 PM, Sun Noon - 5 PM. No admis fee. Estab 1975 to preserve oldest state house in the nation & present variety of exhibitions on historic & contemporary subjects. Former exec wing is used for exhibitions of contemporary artists & craftsmen, paintings, decorative arts on a rotating basis. Average Annual Attendance: 200,000. Mem: 1500; dues life $1000, family $15,

individual $10; annual meeting in the fall
Income: Financed by endowment, mem & appeals
Collections: †Connecticut portraits; documents; Restored Senate Chamber
Activities: Educ dept; lect open to the public, 25 vis lectr per year; concerts; gallery talks; tours; individual paintings & original objects of art lent to museums for special exhibitions; museum shop sells books, magazines, original art, reproductions, prints, slides, Connecticut arts & crafts

M **REAL ART WAYS (RAW),** 56 Arbor St, 06106. Tel 860-232-1006; FAX 860-233-6691; *Dir* Will K Wilkins; *Gallery Cur* J Anderson
Open Tues - Fri 10 AM - 5 PM, Sat Noon - 5 PM. No admis fee. Estab 1975 to present artists of many disciplines working at the forefront of creative activity in their respective fields

A **HARRIET BEECHER STOWE CENTER,** 77 Forest St, 06105. Tel 860-522-9258; FAX 860-522-9259; *Dir* Jo Blatti; *Cur* Debra Fillos
Open Tues - Sat 9:30 AM - 4 PM, Sun Noon - 4 PM, Mon 9:30 AM - 4 PM, June 1 - Columbus Day & Dec. Estab 1941 to maintain & open to the pub the restored Harriet Beecher Stowe House. The Foundation operates the Stowe-Day Library, oversees a publishing program of reprints of H B Stowe's works & new books & provides workshops & lect. Average Annual Attendance: 22,000. Mem: 300; dues sustaining $150, supporting $50, family $30, individual $20; fall & spring meetings
Special Subjects: Canadian Art, Contemporary Art, Inuit Art
Collections: 19th Century Decorative Arts, Domestic Furnishing, Fine Arts; Wallpaper & Floor Treatment Sample Collections
Publications: The Harriet Beecher Stowe House & Library Newsletter, 6 times per year; catalog available upon request
Activities: Classes for adults; teacher workshops; lect open to public, 1-2 vis lectr per year; paintings & original decorative, domestic or fine art objects lent to institutions; sales shop sells books, prints, slides, Victorian gift items

L **Stowe-Day Library,** 77 Forest St, 06105. Tel 860-522-9258; FAX 860-522-9259; *Dir* Jo Blatti; *Librn* Diana Royce
Open Mon - Fri 9 AM - 4:30 PM, cl national holidays. Estab 1941 to concentrate on the architecture, decorative arts, history & literature of the United States in the 19th century emphasizing a Hartford neighborhood known as Nook Farm. Reference only
Library Holdings: Vols 15,000; Per subs 18; Original documents 160,000; Micro — Fiche, reels 100; AV — Lantern slides 60, slides 3500; Other — Clipping files, exhibition catalogs, manuscripts, memorabilia, pamphlets 5000, photographs 5000
Special Subjects: Architecture, Decorative Arts, Furniture, Historical Material, Landscape Architecture, Photography, Restoration & Conservation, Textiles, Hartford 19th Century Literature Community, Nook Farm & Residents; Mark Twain; Harriet Beecher Stowe; Chas Dudley Warner, William Gillette
Collections: †Architecture & Decorative Arts of 19th Century: books, plans, drawings, trade catalogs; †Hartford 19th Century Literary Community, Nook Farm & Residents; Mark Twain; Harriet Beecher Stowe; Chas Dudley Warner; William Gillette
Activities: Library tours; interlibrary loans

M **TRINITY COLLEGE,** Austin Arts Center, 300 Summit St, 06106-3100. Tel 860-297-2498; FAX 860-297-5380; *Dir* Jeffry Walker; *Cur* Felice Caivano
Open Sept - May Mon - Fri 12:30 - 5:30 PM, Sat & Sun 1 - 5 PM. No admis fee. Estab 1965. A building housing the teaching & performing aspects of music, theater dance & studio arts at a liberal arts college. Widener Gallery provides exhibition space mainly for student & faculty works, plus outside exhibitions. Average Annual Attendance: 12,000
Income: Financed by college appropriation
Collections: Edwin M Blake Memorial & Archive; College Collection; Samuel H Kress Study Collection; George Chaplin Collection
Activities: Classes for adults; dramatic programs; lect open to public, 6-8 vis lectr per year; concerts; lending collection contains 500 original art works & 100,000 slides

M **MARK TWAIN MEMORIAL,** 351 Farmington Ave, 06105. Tel 860-247-0998 (admin office), 525-9317, 525-9318 (visitor center); FAX 860-278-8148; *Exec Dir* John Boyer; *Cur* Marianne Curling
Open Mon - Sat 9:30 AM - 5 PM, Sun Noon - 5 PM, Memorial Day through Columbus Day & month of Dec, cl Tues rest of year. Admis adults $7.50, senior citizens $7, children 6-12 $3.50. Estab 1929 to foster an appreciation of the legacy of Mark Twain as one of our nation's culturally defining figures; to demonstrate the continuing relevance of his work, life & times. Maintains Historic House Mus with period interiors, mus room of memorabilia. National Historic Landmark status, US Dept of Interior. Average Annual Attendance: 55,000. Mem: 900; dues $25-$5000; annual meeting in Nov
Collections: Lockwood deForest Collection; Mark Twain memorabilia (photographs, manuscripts); period & original furnishings; Tiffany Collection; Candace Wheeler Collection
Exhibitions: National Symposia
Publications: Exhibition catalogues
Activities: Classes for adults & children; docent training; symposia; internship programs; lect open to public, 5 vis lectr per year; concerts; gallery talks; tours; college internships offered; individual paintings & original objects of art lent to approved museums & organizations; lending collection contains books, color reproductions, film strips, lantern slides, prints, paintings, photographs, sculpture & slides; museum shop sells books, reproductions, prints & slides; junior museum

L **Mark Twain House Research Library,** 351 Farmington Ave, 06105. Tel 860-247-0998 (admin office); FAX 860-278-8148; *Exec Dir* John Boyer; *Cur* Marianne Curling
For reference only
Library Holdings: Vols 6000; Per subs 15; Micro — Fiche, reels; AV — A-tapes, fs, lantern slides, motion pictures, rec, slides, v-tapes; Other — Clipping files, manuscripts, memorabilia, original art works, pamphlets, photographs, reproductions, sculpture

M **WADSWORTH ATHENEUM,** 600 Main St, 06103-2990. Tel 860-278-2670; FAX 860-527-0803; *Dir* Peter C Sutton; *Cur Educ* Cynthia Cormier; *Head Conservator* Stephen Kornhauser; *Cur Contemporary Art* Andrea Miller-Keller; *Cur Costume & Textiles* Carol Krute; *Cur Decorative Arts* William Hosley; *Registrar* Martha Small
Open Tues - Sun 11 AM - 5 PM, cl Mon. Estab 1842 by Daniel Wadsworth as Atheneum Gallery of Fine Arts. There are more than 60 galleries in five interconnected buildings, plus lecture room, classrooms & 299-seat theater. 1968 renovation of facilities includes James Lippincott Goodwin Building, along with sculpture court, restaurant, additional classrooms & offices. Average Annual Attendance: 160,000. Mem: 6000; dues $35 & up; annual meeting in Nov
Income: Financed by private funds
Collections: Archival materials (Wadsworth Atheneum); titles from the Watkinson Library of Reference, 19th century; Hetty Gray Baker Bookplate Collection
Publications: Newsletter, monthly to members; collections and exhibitions catalogs
Activities: Lect & gallery talks by staff; docent talks; seasonal concerts; gallery tours; outside lect; members' exhibition previews & various special events; Atheneum shop sells books, reproductions, photographs, cards & gifts

L **Auerbach Art Library,** 600 Main St, 06103. Tel 860-278-2670, Ext 3115; FAX 203-527-0803; Elec Mail j__teahan@hartnet.org. *Librn* John W Teahan; *Asst Librn* Anne Lyons
Open Tues, Thurs, Sat 11 AM - 5 PM, cl Sun, Mon, Wed, Fri. Estab 1934 as a reference service to the mus staff, members & pub; to provide materials supporting work with mus collection. For reference only
Library Holdings: Vols 32,000; Per subs 150; Micro — Fiche, reels; AV — Lantern slides, rec; Other — Clipping files, exhibition catalogs, pamphlets
Special Subjects: Decorative Arts, Art sales and collections, museology
Collections: Sol Lewitt (contemporary art); Elizabeth Miles (English silver); Watkinson Collection (pre-1917 art reference)

KENT

M **CONNECTICUT HISTORICAL COMMISSION,** Sloane-Stanley Museum, Route 7 (Mailing add: Connecticut Historical Commission, 59 S Prospect St, Hartford, 06106). Tel 860-566-3005; *Dir* John W Shannahan; *Museum Dir* David O White
Open May - Oct Wed - Sun 10 AM - 4:30 PM. Admis adults $3, senior citizens & children $1.50. Estab 1969 to collect, preserve, exhibit historic American tools, implements & paintings of American scenes. Average Annual Attendance: 4000
Income: Financed by state appropriation
Collections: Eric Sloane Collection (paintings) American tools & implements
Activities: Museum shop sells books & prints

A **KENT ART ASSOCIATION, INC,** Gallery, * 21 S Main St, PO Box 202, 06757. Tel 860-927-3989; *Pres* Constance Horton; *VPres* Gloria Malcolm-Arnold; *Second VPres* Charles Dransfield; *Treas* Lee Bardenheuer
Open during exhibitions only Tues - Sun , cl Mon. Estab 1923, incorporated 1935. Maintains gallery for changing exhibitions. Average Annual Attendance: 2000. Mem: 400; dues life $200, patron $40, sustaining $25, assoc $15; annual meeting in Oct
Income: Financed by mem, donations
Exhibitions: Spring Show; Member's Show; President's Show; Fall Show
Publications: Exhibition catalogues, 4 per year
Activities: Lect; demonstrations

LITCHFIELD

A **LITCHFIELD HISTORICAL SOCIETY,** On-the-Green, PO Box 385, 06759. Tel 860-567-4501; FAX 860-567-3565; *Dir* Catherine Keene Fields; *Cur* Jennifer Jacobs; *Educ Coordr* Kelli Green
Open mid Apr - Nov Tues - Sat 11 AM - 5 PM, Sun 1 - 5 PM. Admis $3, children under 16 free. Estab 1896, incorporated 1897 for the preservation & interpretation of local historical collections. A gallery of portraits by Ralph Earl is maintained. Average Annual Attendance: 12,000. Mem: 450; dues benefactor $250, donor $100, contributing $50, family $25, individual $15; annual meeting second Fri in Sept
Income: $220,000 (financed by endowment, mem & fundraising)
Collections: American & Connecticut fine & decorative arts, pewter, costumes, textiles, †paintings, silver, pottery & graphics; †furniture; †textiles; †household goods
Exhibitions: Changing exhibitions on area art & history
Activities: Classes for adults & children; docent training; curriculum units; workshops; lect open to public, 4 vis lectr per year; gallery talks; tours; individual & original objects of art lent to accredited museums with board approval; sales shop sells books, reproductions & prints

L **Ingraham Memorial Research Library,** On-the-Green, PO Box 385, 06759. Tel 860-567-4501; FAX 860-567-3565; *Dir* Catherine Keene Fields; *Librn* Nancy Beveridge
Open Tues - Sat 10 AM - Noon & 1 - 4 PM. Estab 1896 as a center of local history & genealogy study
Income: $10,000 (financed by endowment & mem)
Library Holdings: Vols 10,000; Per subs 10; Original documents 50,000; Micro — Reels; Other — Clipping files, exhibition catalogs, manuscripts, memorabilia, pamphlets, photographs, prints
Special Subjects: Litchfield & Connecticut history 1700-1975
Collections: †40,000 manuscripts in local history

MERIDEN

A ARTS & CRAFTS ASSOCIATION OF MERIDEN INC, Gallery 53, 53
Colony St, PO Box 348, 06450. Tel 203-235-5347; *Pres* Stuart Grandy
Open Tues - Fri Noon - 4 PM, weekends on special exhibits. No admis fee.
Estab 1907 to encourage appreciation of the arts in the community. One floor
gallery to hold exhibits & art work studios above with meeting room. Average
Annual Attendance: 1000. Mem: 400; dues $12 & up; annual meeting in June
Income: Financed by mem & fund raising
Collections: †Permanent collection of paintings & sculptures includes works by
Eric Sloan, Emile Gruppe, Stow Wengenroth as well as works by Meriden artists
Exhibitions: Annual Members Show; Photography Show; Student Show; One
man & group shows; theme shows & alternating exhibits of works from
permanent collection
Activities: Classes for adults & children; dramatic programs; lect open to public,
8 vis lectr per year; workshops; gallery talks; tours; competitions with awards;
scholarships offered; individual paintings & original objects of art lent to banks &
public buildings; originate traveling exhibitions; sales shop sells original art &
crafts
L Library, PO Box 348, 06450. Tel 203-235-5347; *Librn* Edna Pison
Library Holdings: Vols 650
Collections: Indiana Thomas Book Collection

MIDDLETOWN

M WESLEYAN UNIVERSITY, Davison Art Center, 301 High St, 06459-0487.
Tel 860-685-2500; FAX 860-685-2501; *Cur* Ellen G D'Oench; *Registrar* Robert
C Lancefield
Open Tues - Fri Noon - 4 PM, Sat & Sun 2 - 5 PM, cl Mon & academic
vacations. No admis fee. Part of the collection was presented to Wesleyan
University by George W & Harriet B Davison. Since 1952 the collection with its
reference library has been housed in the historic Alsop House, now the Davison
Art Center
Collections: The print collection, extending from the 15th century to present day
includes Master E S, Nielli, Mantegna, Pollaiuolo, Durer, Cranach, Rembrandt,
Canaletto, Piranesi, Goya, Millet, Meryon, Jim Dine, & others; Japanese &
contemporary American prints; 1840s to present, photographs
Exhibitions: Regularly changing exhibitions of prints, drawings, photographs &
other works on paper
Publications: Exhibition catalogues
Activities: Lect open to public, 5-10 vis lectr per year; gallery talks; tours;
original objects of art lent; lending collection contains 25,000 original prints,
drawings & photographs; traveling exhibitions organized & circulated
—Art Library, 06459-0487. Tel 860-685-3327; *Art Librn* Susanne Javorski
Open Mon - Thurs 9 AM - 11 PM, Fri 9 AM - 5 PM, Sat Noon - 5 PM, Sun 1 -
11 PM. Estab 1950 as research/reference library primarily supporting university
courses in art history
Library Holdings: Vols 24,000; Per subs 125
Collections: †Print Reference Collection (books pertaining to the history of the
graphic arts)
A Friends of the Davison Art Center, 301 High St, 06459-0487. Tel 860-685-2500;
FAX 203-685-2501; *Pres* Peter M Frenzel
Estab 1961 for the support & augmentation of the activities & acquisition fund of
the Davison Art Center by its members
Income: Financed by mem dues & contributions
Purchases: Photographs, Prints
Activities: Gallery talks
M Ezra & Cecile Zilkha Gallery, Ctr for the Arts, 06459-0442. Tel 860-685-2694;
Cur Exhib Nina Felshin
Open Tues - Fri Noon - 4 PM, Sat & Sun 2 - 5 PM, cl Mon & academic
vacations. No admis fee. Estab 1974. Exhibitions of contemporary art. Average
Annual Attendance: 10,000
Exhibitions: Changing exhibitions of contemporary art
Publications: Exhibition catalogs & brochures
Activities: Educ Dept; lect, 4 vis lectr per year; gallery talks; tours; sales shop
sells catalogs

MYSTIC

A MYSTIC ART ASSOCIATION, INC, 9 Water St, 06355. Tel 860-536-7601;
FAX 860-536-0610; Elec Mail maa@mystic-art.org. *Exec Dir* Joanne K
Newman; *Pres* Mary Anne Stets; *Treas* Peter F Stuart; *VPres* Willa T Schuster
Open daily 11 AM - 5 PM. Admis adults $2, children & members free. Estab
1914 to maintain an art mus to promote cultural educ, local philanthropic &
charitable interests. The assoc owns a colonial building on the bank of Mystic
River with spacious grounds; there is one small gallery & one large gallery with
L-shaped corridor. Average Annual Attendance: 10,000. Mem: 900; artist mem
must have high standards of proficiency & be jurored in four shows; dues active
$25, assoc $20; meeting held in Apr
Income: Financed by mem, grants & leases
Collections: Mystic Art Colony Paintings; original artwork by notable artists
Exhibitions: Juried Members' Show (all media); Annual Regional (all media)
Activities: Classes for adults & children; dramatic programs; lect open to public,
2 vis lectr per year; concerts; gallery talks; scholarships offered

NEW BRITAIN

M CENTRAL CONNECTICUT STATE UNIVERSITY, Art Dept Museum, 1615
Stanley St, 06050. Tel 860-832-2620; FAX 860-832-2634; *Gallery Dir* Ron Todd
Estab to collect, display & interpret works of art & ethnic materials relating to
the art educ program. Center will be constructed within two years & collection
will be on display in center, whole collection will not be on permanent display
Exhibitions: Changing exhibitions every month

M NEW BRITAIN MUSEUM OF AMERICAN ART, 56 Lexington St, 06052.
Tel 860-229-0257; FAX 860-229-3445; *Dir* Laurene Buckley; *Business Mgr* Mel
Ellis; *Coll Mgr* Renee T Williams; *Develop Coordr* Claudia 1 Thesing
Open Tues 1 - 5 PM, Sat 10 AM - 5 PM, Sun Noon - 5 PM. Admis adults $3,
senior citizens & students $2, children under 12, Sat 10 AM - Noon & members
free. Estab 1903 to exhibit, collect & preserve American art. 19 galleries.
Average Annual Attendance: 24,000. Mem: 1400; dues patron $100, contributing
$50, family $25, individual $15
Income: Financed by endowment
Collections: Sanford D D Low Illustration Collection (paintings, graphics &
sculpture); Collections from Fredrick Church, Thomas Cole, Child Hassam,
Thomas Hart; Traces the History of American Art from 1740 to Present
Publications: Newsletter, quarterly
Activities: Educ dept; docent training; lect open to public, 6 vis lectr per year;
concerts; gallery talks; tours; competitions with prizes; original objects of art lent
to other museums; originate traveling exhibitions; museum shop selling books,
reproductions, prints, slides & postcards & gifts

NEW CANAAN

M NEW CANAAN HISTORICAL SOCIETY, 13 Oenoke Ridge, 06840. Tel 203-
966-1776; *Exec Dir* Janet Lindstrom; *Librn* Marilyn O'Rourke
Open Wed, Thurs, Sun 2 - 4 PM, Town House open Tues - Sat 9:30 AM - 12:30
PM & 2 - 4:30 PM. Admis $2. Estab 1889 to bring together & arrange historical
events & genealogies, collect relics, form a museum & library. Society consists of
seven museums & library. Rogers' studio contains sculpture groups by John
Rogers. Exhibit room houses changing displays of costumes, photos & paintings.
Average Annual Attendance: 5000. Mem: 900; dues family $35, individual $25;
meetings second Mon in Mar, June, Sept, Dec
Income: Financed by mem & contributions
Collections: Costume collection, including fans, purses & shoes; document
collections; pewter; period furniture; photo collection; Rogers' sculpture groups;
quilts
Exhibitions: Costume & History; permanent exhibition of Rogers' sculptures
Publications: New Canaan Historical Society Annual; Philip Johnson in New
Canaan; John Rogers (1829-1904) & the Rogers Groups by John Rogers (1945-
present)
Activities: Seminars; children's classes; docent training; lect open to public, 4 vis
lectr per year; Bayles Award (Presidential Classroom), biannual & Award to New
Canaan High School Junior for outstanding achievement in history, annual;
museum shop sells New Canaan Historical Society Annual, Christmas cards,
maps, postcards & stationery

L NEW CANAAN LIBRARY, 151 Main St, 06840. Tel 203-801-2665; FAX 203-
801-2654; *Dir* David Bryant; *Chair Art Committee (Exhibits)* Jane Perkins
Open Mon - Thurs 10 AM - 8 PM, Fri & Sat 10 AM - 5 PM, Sun 1 - 5 PM
except summer. Estab 1877
Income: $1,293,000 (financed by mem, city & state appropriation)
Purchases: $190,600
Library Holdings: Vols 146,000; Per subs 407; Audio & Video tapes 7338; Micro —
Reels; AV — A-tapes
Special Subjects: Crafts, Landscape Architecture, Oriental Art, Painting -
American, Painting - European, Painting - Japanese, Photography, Sculpture,
Video
Collections: Alfandari Collection-European from fall of Rome Impressionism;
Chinese-Japanese art; general collection of art books & videos

M SILVERMINE GUILD ARTS CENTER, Silvermine Galleries, 1037 Silvermine
Rd, 06840. Tel 203-966-5617; FAX 203-966-2763; *Exec Dir* Robert Meyer;
School Dir Ann Connell
Open Tues - Sat 11 AM - 5 PM, Sun 12:30 - 5 PM, cl Mon. No admis fee. Estab
1922 as an independent art center to foster, promote & encourage activities in
the arts & art educ & to provide a place for member artists & invited artists to
show & sell their work & to offer the community a wide variety of artistic,
cultural & educational activities. Four exhibition galleries & Farrell Gallery
which contains paintings & sculpture for purchase. Average Annual Attendance:
20,000. Mem: 800; dues sustaining $125, individual $25
Income: Financed by mem, sale of art, contributions & tuitions
Collections: †Permanent print collection containing purchase prizes from
International Print Exhibition
Exhibitions: Biennial International Print Exhibition; Art of Northwest USA -
Exhibition of Painting & Sculpture (juried); 14 one-person exhibitions (juried); 2
group shows (juried); 2 invitational exhibitions (juried)
Publications: Exhibition catalogs; member newsletter, quarterly
Activities: Classes for adults & children; docent training; workshops; lect open to
public, 10 vis lectr per year; concerts; gallery talks; tours; competitions with
awards; scholarships offered; individual paintings & original objects of art lent to
corporations & banks; lending collection contains books & original prints;
originate traveling exhibitions; museum shop sells books, original art,
reproductions & prints
L Library, 1037 Silvermine Rd, 06840. Tel 203-966-5617; *Asst Dir* Ann Connell
Library Holdings: Vols 2000; Per subs 6; AV — Slides

NEW HAVEN

M KNIGHTS OF COLUMBUS SUPREME COUNCIL, Headquarters Museum,
One Columbus Plaza, 06510-3326. Tel 203-772-2130; FAX 203-777-0114; *Cur &
Registrar* Mary Lou Cummings
Open Mon - Fri 8:30 AM - 4 PM. No admis fee. Estab 1982 as a corporate
history museum revealing the history & activities of the Knights of Columbus.
Average Annual Attendance: 3000
Collections: Fine & decorative arts
Exhibitions: Christopher Columbus; Founder Father Michael J McGivney; gifts
& items from Knights of Columbus state & local councils; Knights of Columbus
War Activities; Tributes (interactions with the Catholic Church & the Vatican)
Publications: Postcards; museum tour brochures
Activities: Lect open to the public; corporate archives research history of Knights
of Columbus; individual paintings & original objects of art lent under special
arrangements & careful consideration

A **NEW HAVEN COLONY HISTORICAL SOCIETY,** 114 Whitney Ave, 06510. Tel 203-562-4183; FAX 203-562-2002; *Pres* Carlton Loucks; *Dir* Robert Egleston; *Cur* Amy Trout
Open Tues - Fri 10 AM - 5 PM, Sat, Sun 2 - 5 PM, cl Mon & major holidays. Admis adults $2, senior citizens $1.50, children 6-16 $1, members & Tues free. Estab 1862 for the preservation, exhibition & research of local history. Average Annual Attendance: 11,300. Mem: 1100; annual meeting in Nov
Income: $250,000 (financed by private contributions)
Collections: Morris House (c 1685 - 1780); decorative arts; ceramics; 18th & 19th Century Collection of portraits of the New Haven area personages; maritime collection of shops paintings; paintings by local artists Corne, Durrie, Jocelyn, Moulthrop
Exhibitions: Permanent exhibition includes paintings by local artists such as Jocelyn, Moulthrop & George H Durrie; landscape portraits; maritime historicl paintings; New Haven Illustrated: From Colony, Town to City; Maritime New Haven; Table Wares 1640 - 1840; Ingersoll Collection of Furniture & Decorative Arts; Two changing exhibitions per year minimumm
Publications: Newsletter; Quarterly Journal
Activities: Classes for adults & children; hands-on programs; docent training; lect open to public, 4 vis lectr per year; slideshows; concerts; gallery talks & tours; individual paintings & objects of art lent to other approved museums; museum shop sells reproductions, prints, antiques & collectibles

L **Whitney Library,** 114 Whitney Ave, 06510-1025. Tel 203-562-4183; FAX 230-562-2002; *Librn* James Campbell
Open Tues - Fri 1 - 5 PM. Admis $2 for nonmembers for library use. Estab 1862 to collect, preserve, make available & publish historical & genealogical material relating to the early settlement & subsequent history of New Haven, its vicinity & incidentally, other parts of the USA. Four departments: mus, library-archives, photograph & educational, with the mus staff taking care of the galleries, the library is primarily for reference
Income: Financed by endowment, mem & grants
Library Holdings: Vols 30,000; Per subs 55; Glass plate negatives 30,000; Original documents; Micro — Fiche, reels; AV — A-tapes, cassettes, fs, motion pictures, rec, v-tapes; Other — Clipping files, exhibition catalogs, manuscripts, memorabilia, pamphlets, photographs, prints
Special Subjects: Architecture, Art History, Decorative Arts, Historical Material, Landscape Architecture, Marine Painting, Painting - American, Period Rooms, Portraits, Pottery, Genealogy
Collections: Afro-American Collection; Architectural Drawings; John W Barber Collection; Dana: New Haven Old & New; Durrie Papers; Ingersoll Papers; National & Local Historical Figures, A-Z; Ezra Stiles Papers; Noah Webster Collection
Publications: Journal, irregular; News and Notes, irregular; monographs; exhibition catalogs
Activities: Arrangement with local colleges for internship programs & work-study programs; lect open to public & members; tours; individual paintings & objects of art lent to other institutions; museum shop sells books, reproductions, prints & antiques

A **NEW HAVEN PAINT & CLAY CLUB, INC,** The John Slade Ely House, 51 Trumbull St, 06510. Tel 203-624-8055; *Pres* Dolores Gall
Open Tues - Fri 1 - 4 PM; Sat & Sun 2 - 5 PM; cl Mon. No admis fee. Estab 1900 to provide opportunities for artists in New England to exhibit their work, inc in 1928. Two floors of an historic house. Average Annual Attendance: 350. Mem: 270; open to artists working in any media whose work has been accepted two times in the Annual Juried Show; dues life $100, active $15, assoc $10; annual meeting in May
Income: $4000 (financed by dues)
Purchases: $3000
Collections: 250 2-D pictures & 10 sculptures
Exhibitions: Annual March-April Exhibition (New England & New York artists); Annual Fall Exhibition (active members only); Permanent Collection
Publications: Exhibition catalogs; newsletter
Activities: Lect at annual meeting; awards $500 members show, $2500 juried exhibition; scholarships; individual paintings & original objects of art lent to local organizations

PRINT COUNCIL OF AMERICA
For further information, see National and Regional Organizations

M **SOUTHERN CONNECTICUT STATE UNIVERSITY,** Art Gallery, * 501 Crescent St, PO Box 3144, 06515. Tel 203-392-6652; *Dir* Tony Bonadies
Estab 1976 to build a collection of works of art for educational purposes, gallery developing now. Mem: 750; dues $5 & up
Income: $10,000 (financed by mem, state appropriation & fundraising)
Collections: African & Pre-Columbian art
Activities: Travelogues; lect open to public, 6 vis lectr per year; gallery talks; national & international tours; original objects of art lent to administrative offices

YALE UNIVERSITY
M **Art Gallery,** 1111 Chapel St, Yale Sta, PO Box 2006, 06520. Tel 203-432-0600; *Dir* Susan M Vogel; *Cur Prints, Drawings & Photographs* Richard S Field; *Assoc Cur Ancient Art* Susan Matheson; *Cur American Painting* Helen Cooper; *Cur American Decorative Arts* Patricia Kane; *Registrar* Susan Frankenbach; *Mem* Debbie Cook; *Supt* Richard Moore; *Cur Educ* Janet S Dickson; *European & Contemporary* Sasha Newran; *Sales* Howard Yasin; *Public Relations* Marie Weltzien; *Asian* Colin Mackenzie
Open Tues - Sat 10 AM - 5 PM, Sun 2 - 5 PM, cl Mon. No admis fee. Estab 1832 to exhibit works of art from ancient times to present. Building designed by Louis Kahn & completed in 1953. Average Annual Attendance: 120,000. Mem: 1500; dues $25 & up
Income: Financed by endowment, mem & annual fundraising
Collections: †American & European painting & sculpture; †Chinese painting & ceramics; Dura-Europos Archaeological Collection; †Garvan Collection of American Decorative Arts History paintings & miniatures by John Trumbull; †Japanese painting & ceramics; Jarves Collection of Italian Renaissance Painting; Societe Anonyme Collection of Twentieth century art; Stoddard Collection of Greek Vases; 20th Century Art; †25,000 prints, drawings & photographs
Publications: Exhibition catalogues; Yale University Art Gallery Bulletin, 2 times a year
Activities: Sunday programs; gallery tours three times per week; Art a la Carte (lunchtime mini-lect); museum shop sells books, children's games, jewelry, prints, reproductions, scarves, slides

M **Yale Center for British Art,** 1080 Chapel St, PO Box 208280, 06520-8280. Tel 203-432-2800, 432-2850; FAX 203-432-9695; *Dir* Duncan Robinson; *Asst Dir* Constance Clement; *Cur Paintings* Susan Casteras; *Cur Prints Drawings & Rare Books* Patrick Noon; *Registrar* Timothy Goodhue; *Librn* Dr Anne-Marie Logan
Open Tues - Sat 10 AM - 5 PM, Sun Noon - 5 PM, cl Mon. No admis fee. Estab 1977 to foster appreciation & knowledge of British art; to encourage interdisciplinary use of the collections. Reference library & photograph archive for reference;. Average Annual Attendance: 100,000. Mem: 1800
Income: Financed by endowment, annual gifts, mem & mus shop
Collections: Paintings; drawings; prints; rare books & sculpture
Publications: Calendar of Events-Preview of Exhibitions, bi-annually; exhibition catalogues, five per year
Activities: Docent & information volunteer training; lect; concerts; gallery talks; tours; films open to public; sympsosia; scholarships & fels offered; individual paintings & objects of art lent to other museums; originate traveling exhibitions; museum shop sells books, reproductions, postcards & exhibitions catalogs
—**Art Reference Library,** 1080 Chapel St, PO Box 208280, 06520-8280. Tel 203-432-2818; FAX 203-432-9695; *Librn* Dr Anne-Marie Logan
Open Tues - Fri 10 AM - 4:30 PM. No admis fee. Estab 1977 to support collection of British Art. Reference library
Library Holdings: Vols 20,000; Per subs 38; Micro — Cards, fiche 75,000, reels 860; AV — V-tapes; Other — Exhibition catalogs, pamphlets, photographs 150,000
Special Subjects: Art History, Drawings, Etchings & Engravings, Maps, Marine Painting, Painting - British, Portraits, Restoration & Conservation, British Art since 16th century
Collections: British Art from age of Holbein to present
Activities: Classes for adults & children; docent training; lect open to public; concerts; gallery talks; tours; scholarships offered; originate traveling exhibitions; museum shop sells books, reproductions, slides

L **Art & Architecture Library,** 180 York St, PO Box 208242, 06520-8242. Tel 203-432-2640; FAX 203-432-0549; Elec Mail max.marmor@yale.edu; christine.devallet@yale.edu. *Librn* Max Marmor; *Asst Librn* Christine deVallet; *Slide & Photograph* Helen Chillman
Estab 1868. Serves Schools of Art & Architecture, History of Art Department & the Yale University Art Gallery
Library Holdings: Vols 100,000; Photographs & color prints 182,000; Micro — Fiche; AV — Slides 312,000; Other — Exhibition catalogs
Collections: †Faber Birren Collection of Books on Color
Publications: Faber Birren Collection of Books on Color: A Bibliography

L **Beinecke Rare Book & Manuscript Library,** 121 Wall St, PO Box 208240, 06520-8240. Tel 203-432-2977; FAX 203-432-4047; *Dir* Ralph W Franklin
Open Mon - Fri 8:30 AM - 5 PM. Estab 1963. Non-circulating
Library Holdings: Vols 600,000; Other — Clipping files, manuscripts, memorabilia, original art works, pamphlets, photographs, prints, sculpture
Special Subjects: Afro-American Art, American Indian Art, American Western Art, Art History, Bookplates & Bindings, Calligraphy, Drawings, Etchings & Engravings, Graphic Arts, Graphic Design, Historical Material, History of Art & Archaeology, Illustration, Islamic Art, Judaica
Collections: Osborn Collection of English literary & historical manuscripts from the Anglo-Saxon period to 20th century; Collection of America Literature of 19th & early 20th century writings; German Literature Collection of rare books & first editions of 17th-19th century; Western Americana Collection of books, manuscripts, maps, art, prints & photographs of Trans-Mississippi West through World War I; General collection of Early Books & Manuscripts includes Greek & Roman papyri, medieval & Renaissance manuscripts; modern books & manuscripts in English literature & history from 17th-20th century
Exhibitions: (1997) Annotated Books; Contested Terrain (Mexican War); Thorton Wilder Centenary; David Plowden, photographs
Publications: Exhibition catalogs
Activities: Scholarships & fels offered; sales shop sells books

NEW LONDON

M **LYMAN ALLYN ART MUSEUM,** 625 Williams St, 06320. Tel 860-443-2545; FAX 860-442-1280; *Dir* Charles A Shepard III; *Conservator* Lance Mayer; *Conservator* Gay Myers; *Public Relations Officer* Susan Hendricks; *Dir Develop* Nancy Hileman
Open Tues & Thurs - Sat 10 AM - 5 PM, Wed 10 AM - 9 PM, Sun 1 - 5 PM, cl Mon. Admis adults $3, students & seniors $2, children under 12 free. Estab 1932 for the educ & enrichment of the community & others. The current building consists of nine permanent galleries & four galleries for changing exhibitions. Average Annual Attendance: 100,000. Mem: 1500; dues range from individual $35 to life $10,000
Income: $220,000 (financed by endowment, mem & gifts)
Purchases: $10,000
Collections: Egyptian, Greek & Roman antiquities; Medieval & Renaissance art; Oriental material primitive art; American & European paintings; furniture; silver; decorative arts; Baratz Collection of dolls, doll houses & toys
Exhibitions: Museology: Photographs of Richard Ross; Ladies Fashion Emporium & Victorian Toy Shop; Afro-American; 4 corporate collections; The Devotion Family of 18th Century Connecticut: In Life & in Art; Lines, Letters, Image: An International Calligraphy Exhibition; Connecticut Women Artists; The Artist Sees New London
Publications: Handbook of the Museum's Outstanding Holdings; New London County Furniture from 1640-1840; New London Silver
Activities: Classes for adults & children; docent training; school tours & programs; lect open to public; gallery talks; tours; individual paintings & original objects of are lent; museum shop sells small antiques, books & reproductions

L **Library,** 625 Williams St, 06320. Tel 860-443-2545; FAX 860-442-1280; *Librn* Lissa Van Dyke
Open Tues - Sat 11 AM - 5 PM. Estab 1932 to provide an art reference library as an adjunct to the material in the Lyman Allyn Art Museum. Reference only
Library Holdings: Vols 10,000; Per subs 32; Micro — Fiche; AV — Slides; Other — Clipping files, exhibition catalogs, pamphlets, photographs, reproductions
Special Subjects: Decorative Arts, Artists & Related Areas; Art Objects
Collections: Decorative arts, furniture, drawings
Activities: Docent training; lect open to public, 2 vis lectr per year; gallery talks; tours

A **NEW LONDON COUNTY HISTORICAL SOCIETY,** * 11 Blinman St, 06320. Tel 860-443-1209; *Adminr* Alice D Sheriff
Open Wed - Fri 1 - 4 PM, Sat 10 AM - 4 PM by appointment. Admis $3. Estab 1871 for preservation of New London County history. 300; dues $20; annual meeting in Sept. Average Annual Attendance: 2000
Income: $6000 (financed by endowment, mem, admis)
Purchases: Manuscripts
Collections: Six Portraits by Ralph Earle; furniture & decorative arts owned by Shaw & Perkins families; furniture made in New London County; miscellaneous portraits, miniatures
Exhibitions: Temporary Exhibitions
Publications: NLCHS Bulletin, biannually
Activities: Lect open to public, 6 vis lectr per year; retail store sells books

M **US COAST GUARD MUSEUM,** US Coast Guard Academy, 15 Mohegan Ave, 06320-4195. Tel 860-444-8511, 444-8444; FAX 860-444-8289; *Cur* Cindee Herrick
Open Mon - Fri 9 AM - 4:30 PM, Sat 10 AM - 5 PM, Sun Noon - 5 PM. No Admis fee. Estab 1967 to preserve historical heritage of US Coast Guard, US Life Saving Service and US Lighthouse Service. Average Annual Attendance: 20,000
Income: Financed by federal appropriations and private donations
Purchases: $12,000
Collections: Ship & aircraft models; paintings; photographs & manuscripts representing the Coast Guard; military artifacts from WWI, WWII & Vietnam;
Activities: Museum studies internships, graduate level; individual paintings & original objects of art lent to federal museums & qualified organizations for educational purposes only; lending collection contains 200 framed reproductions, 300 paintings, sculpture; book traveling exhibitions, biennial; originate traveling exhibitions to other Coast Guard facilities; Sales shop sells Coast Guard souvenirs

NEW MILFORD

M **MUSEUM OF CONTEMPORARY IMPRESSIONISM,** 29 Church St, PO Box 67, 06776-0067. Tel 860-354-2550; *Dir* Richard Salter
Estab to preserve & display Contemporary Impressionist Art. One main gallery & 2 additional; 4th gallery that alternates as a classroom when needed
Collections: Fannie Lager Collection; Bernard Lennon Collection

NORFOLK

M **NORFOLK HISTORICAL SOCIETY INC,** Museum, 13 Village Green, PO Box 288, 06058-0288. Tel 860-542-5761, 542-5231; *Pres & Dir* Richard Byrne; *Archivist* Ann Havemeyer; *Cur Photography* Michaela A Murphy; *Cur Rare Books* Laura Byers; *Exhib Designer* Kathleen Bordelon
No admis fee. Estab 1960
Collections: †Marie Kendall Photography Collection (1884 - 1935), era during which she worked in Norfolk; Collection of works by Alfred S G Taylor, noted architect - his blueprints, drawings, photographs plus documents for 40 of his buildings in Norfork listed as a Thematic Group in the National Register of Historic Places; Small collection of Connecticut clocks; Fine 1879 dollhouse with elegant original furnishings; photographs & memorabilia of the Norfolk Downs, one of the very first New England golf courses (1897)
Exhibitions: Norfolk General Stores, Post Offices & Early Norfolk Merchants
Publications: Exhibition catalogs; books, pamphlets & maps, irregularly

NORWALK

M **LOCKWOOD-MATHEWS MANSION MUSEUM,** 295 West Ave, 06850. Tel 203-838-9799; *Dir* Zachary Studenroth; *Asst Dir* Kathleen Maher
Open Tues - Fri 11 AM - 3 PM, Sun 1 - 4 PM. Admis, suggested donation $5, students & senior citizens $3. Estab 1968 to completely restore this 19th century 50-room mansion as a historic house mus. Now a registered National Historic Landmark. Average Annual Attendance: 25,000. Mem: 1200; annual meeting May
Income: $37,000 (financed by mem, city & state appropriation, federal grant)
Collections: †Furniture original to the mansion; 19th century decorative arts, painting & textiles
Exhibitions: Permanent collection
Publications: Newsletter, quarterly
Activities: Classes for adults & children; docent training; lect open to public, 6 vis lectr per year; gallery talks; tours; book traveling exhibitions 1-2 per year; museum shop sells books & magazines

NORWICH

M **SLATER-NORTON CORPORATION** (Formerly Norwich Free Academy), Slater Memorial Museum & Converse Art Gallery, 108 Crescent St, 06360. Tel 860-887-2506; *Dir* Joseph P Gualtieri; *Asst to Dir* Frances E Kornacki; *Cur Educ* Mary-Anne Hall
Open Sept - June Tues - Fri 9 AM - 4 PM, Sat & Sun 1 - 4 PM, July - Aug Tues - Sun 1 - 4 PM, cl Mon & holidays. Admis $2, Friends of Museum & children

under 12 free. Estab 1888. The collection is housed in two buildings. Average Annual Attendance: 37,000. Mem: 600; lifetime individual $300, patron $100, contributing $50, family $30, individual $20, senior citizen $10; annual meeting usually in Apr
Income: Financed by endowment
Collections: Vanderpoel Collection of Asian Art; African Art; American Art & Furniture from the 17th - 20th Centuries; Native American Artifacts; Egyptian Art Objects & Textiles; Greek, †Roman & Renaissance Plaster Cast Collection (major collection)
Exhibitions: Special exhibitions changed every 4 - 6 wks; Work of the Norwich Art School children & students displayed
Publications: Catalogue of the Plaster Cast Collection; Discovering Ellis Ruley; Charlotte Fuller Eastman, Artist & Teacher; Greek Myths for Young People; Gualtieri, a Retrospect; NORWICH, a Photographic Essay; Renaissance Art for Young People
Activities: Lect open to public; competitions; individual paintings and original objects of art lent to museums and historical societies; sales shop sells Connecticut crafts, prints, books, cards & art work

OLD LYME

L **LYME ACADEMY OF FINE ARTS,** 84 Lyme St, 06371. Tel 860-434-5232; *Pres* Henry E Putsch; *Acad Dean* Sharon Hunter
Lending to students & faculty only
Library Holdings: Vols 3500; Per subs 23; AV — Slides, v-tapes; Other — Clipping files, exhibition catalogs, original art works, pamphlets, sculpture
Publications: Brochure; catalog

A **LYME ART ASSOCIATION, INC,** * 90 Lyme St, PO Box 222, 06371. Tel 860-434-7802; *Pres* Norman Legassie; *VPres* Rachel Armstrong; *Treas* Kay Chester
Open Tues - Sat Noon - 5 PM, Sun & holidays 1 - 5 PM. No admis fee, donations accepted. Estab 1914 to promote art & advance educ. Four large sky-lighted galleries are maintained. Present building built in 1922 by early Lyme artists. Average Annual Attendance: 2000. Mem: 38; dues invitational juried members $35, associate mem, $10; meetings in May & Sept
Income: Financed by mem & associate members dues, donations & sales commissions
Collections: Collection is under custodianship of Florence Griswold Museum
Exhibitions: Six annual exhibitions: 3 open, 3 member only
Activities: Lect for members only, 2 vis lectr per year; concerts; tours; competitions with awards; sales shop sells original art

M **LYME HISTORICAL SOCIETY,** Florence Griswold Museum, 96 Lyme St, 06371. Tel 860-434-5542; *Pres* Anthony C Thurston; *Dir* Jeffrey W Andersen; *Cur & Librn* Jack Becker
Open June - Oct, Tues - Sat 10 AM - 5 PM, Sun 1 - 5 PM; Nov - May, Wed - Sun 1 - 5 PM. Admis $3. Estab 1936 for the purpose of collecting, preserving & exhibiting the art & history of the Lyme region. Average Annual Attendance: 16,000. Mem: 1530; dues family $40, individual $25; annual meeting in June
Income: $519,000 (financed by endowment, mem, grants & town appropriation)
Collections: Clara Champlain Griswold Toy Collection; Evelyn McCurdy Salisbury Ceramic Collection; Old Lyme Art Colony Paintings; decorative arts & furnishings; local historical collections
Exhibitions: The Ancient Town of Lyme; The Art Colony at Old Lyme; 19th Century Period Rooms; Walker Evans Photographs; Clark Voorhees 1971 - 1933; Old Lyme: The American Barbizon; Dressed for Any Occasion: Patterns of Fashion in the 19th Century; Thomas W Nason, 1889-1971, The Notable Women of Lyme; The Whites of Waterford: An American Landscape Tradition; Childe Hassam in Connecticut; En Plein Air: The Art Colonies of East Hampton & Old Lyme; The Harmony of Nature: Frank Vincent DuMond
Publications: The Connecticut Impressionists at Old Lyme; The Lieutenant River; The Lymes Heritage Cookbook; Hamburg Cove: Past & Present; The Lyme Ledger, quarterly; Report of the Lyme Historical Society, annually; Miss Florence & The Artists of Old Lyme; A New Look at History
Activities: Classes for adults & children; docent training; lect open to public; tours; museum shop sells books

L **Archives,** 96 Lyme St, 06371. Tel 860-434-5542; FAX 860-434-6259; *Cur* Jack Becker
Open Mon - Fri 10 AM - 5 PM. Estab 1953 as a research facility for mus programs & for the pub. Open to the public for reference by appointment
Purchases: $1500
Library Holdings: Vols 1200; Per subs 15; AV — Cassettes, Kodachromes, motion pictures, slides; Other — Clipping files, exhibition catalogs, manuscripts, memorabilia, pamphlets, photographs, prints, reproductions
Special Subjects: The Art Colony at Old Lyme, American landscape paintings, local history

RIDGEFIELD

M **ALDRICH MUSEUM OF CONTEMPORARY ART,** 258 Main St, 06877. Tel 203-438-4519; FAX 203-438-0198; *Chmn* Joel Mallin; *Dir* Jill Snyder; *Asst Dir* Richard Klein
Open Tues - Sun 1 - 5 PM; group visits by appointment. Admis adults $3, students & seniors $2. Estab 1964 for the presentation of contemporary painting & sculpture & allied arts; to stimulate public awareness of contemporary art through exhibitions & educ programs. Nine galleries on three floors, auditorium, gift shop. Renovated colonial building with modern addition, sculpture garden. Average Annual Attendance: 16,000. Mem: 650; dues $35 & up
Income: $130,000 (financed by mem, federal & state grants, corporate & private foundations)
Exhibitions: (1997) Making it Real; Bruce Nauman - Works on Paper & Related Sculpture 1985-96
Publications: Exhibition catalogs; quarterly newsletter
Activities: Classes for adults & children; docent training; lect open to public, 10 vis lectr per year; concerts; gallery talks; tours; film; competitions with prizes; book traveling exhibitions; originate traveling exhibitions; museum shop sells books, jewelry, gift items & decorative objects

STAMFORD

L FERGUSON LIBRARY, One Public Library Plaza, 06904. Tel 203-964-1000; Elec Mail admin@ferg.lib.ct.us. *Pres* Ernest A DiMattia Jr; *Dir Admin Servs* Nicholas Bochicchio Jr; *Dir Human Resources* Kevin McCarthy; *Dir Pub Relations* Melanie McMillan; *Dir Pub Servs* Katherine Golomb; *Information Serv Supv* Lee Jaworski; *Business Office Supv* Marie Giuliano; *Adult Servs Supv* Phyllis Massar; *Dir Computer Serv* Gary Giannelli
Open Mon - Thurs 10 AM - 9 PM, Fri 10 AM - 6 PM, Sat 10 AM - 5 PM, mid Sept - mid May Sun 1 - 5 PM. Estab 1880 as a public library dedicated to serving the information needs of the community
Income: Financed by city appropriation
Purchases: $8000 (art & music books), $50,000 (video cassettes), $22,000 (tapes & compact discs)
Library Holdings: Vols 15,500; Circulating sculpture; Frame art; AV — Cassettes, motion pictures, rec, slides, v-tapes; Other — Framed reproductions
Collections: Photography of Old Stamford
Exhibitions: Painting, sculpture, photography & posters under sponsorship of Friends of Ferguson Library
Publications: Focus on Ferguson quarterly newsletter, Art Currents for the Whitney Museum, Musical Notes for the Stamford Symphony and the Connecticut Grand Opera

M STAMFORD MUSEUM & NATURE CENTER, 39 Scofieldtown Rd, 06903. Tel 203-322-1646; *Pres* Norman Lotstein; *Dir* Gerald E Rasmussen; *Asst Dir* Philip Novak; *Dir of Art* Dorothy Mayhall
Open Mon - Sat 9 AM - 5 PM, Sun & holidays 1 - 5 PM, cl Thanksgiving, Christmas & New Year's Day. Admis adults $2.50, Stamford residents $1.25, Children accompanied by adult $.75, mem free. Estab 1936, Art Department 1955. Museum has an art wing for changing exhibitions of 19th & 20th century art. Average Annual Attendance: 250,000. Mem: 3000; dues $35 & up; annual meeting in June
Income: Financed by mem, private & corporate donations & city appropriation
Collections: †American crafts; American Indian drawings, photography, prints; 19th & 20th century painting, sculpture
Exhibitions: Annual Connecticut Artists; Four Winners Exhibition; Ellen Lanyon: Strange Games; Private Expressions: Personal Experiences; Color: Pure & Simple; American Art at the Turn of the Century; American Printmaking; The Natural Image; New American Paperworks; Connecticut Craftsmen; Bernstein; Button; Johnson; Margolies; Krushenick; Fiberforms; Contemporary Iroquois Art
Publications: American Art: American Women; Animals; brochures; exhibit catalogs; Folk Art: Then & Now; monthly newsletter
Activities: Educ dept, classes for adults & children in art, dance, nature & science; docent training; lectures open to public, 12 vis lectr per year; concerts; gallery talks; tours; competitions with awards; individual paintings & original objects of art lent to other museums; originate traveling exhibitions; museum shop sells books, magazines, slides, & 19th century collectibles & gifts

M WHITNEY MUSEUM OF AMERICAN ART AT CHAMPION, One Champion Plaza, 06921. Tel 203-358-7652; FAX 203-358-2975; *Dir* Eugenie Tsai; *Public Relations & Spec Events Coordr* Jessica Varner; *Educ Coordr* Janice Romley; *Mgr* Cynthia Roznoy
Open Tues - Sat 11 AM - 5 PM. No addmis fee. Estab 1981
Income: Financed by Champion International Corporation
Activities: Educ dept; docent training; lect open to public; concerts; gallery talks; sales shop sells books, notecards & postcards

C XEROX CORPORATION, Art Collection, 800 Long Ridge Rd, 06904. Tel 203-968-3000; *VPres Xerox Foundation* Joseph M Cahalan; *Prog Mgr* Evelyn Shockley
Collection on display at Xerox Headquarters
Collections: The art collection represents a broad spectrum of American fine art as well as art forms from other countries. The works range from abstraction to realism & consist of sculpture by David Lee Brown located in the lobby, fiberwork by Gerhardt Knodel located in the dining facility, collages, etchings, lithographs, graphics, mezzotints, mono-prints, montages, pastels, photography, pochoir, silkscreens, watercolors & xerography

STORRS

UNIVERSITY OF CONNECTICUT
M William Benton Museum of Art, 245 Glenbrook Rd, 06269-2140. Tel 860-486-4520; FAX 860-486-0234; *Acting Dir* Thomas P Bruhn; *Registrar* George Mazeika; *Museum Shop Mgr* Jennifer Jeffreys
Open during exhibitions Tues - Fri 10 AM - 4:30 PM, Sat & Sun 1 - 4:30 PM, cl Mon. No admis fee. Estab 1966, a mus of art, operating as an autonomous department within the University, serving the students, faculty & general pub; contributing to the field at large through research, exhibitions & publications & by maintaining a permanent collection of over 3500 objects. The main gallery measures 36 x 116 ft, galley II 33 x 36 ft. Average Annual Attendance: 25,000. Mem: 600; dues double $25
Income: $700,000 (financed by mem, state appropriation, grants & gifts & donations)
Collections: †American painting & graphics 19-20th Century; †German & French graphics late 19th & 20th Century; †selected 17th & 18th Century European paintings, sculptures & graphics; Western European & American c 1600 to present; paintings, graphics
Publications: Exhibition catalogs,annually
Activities: Lect open to public, 5-8 vis lectr per year; gallery talks; tours; individual paintings & original objects of art lent to accredited institutions for exhibition purposes; lending collection contains original prints, paintings & sculpture; book traveling exhibitions; originate traveling exhibitions; sales shop sells books, original art, prints, reproductions & museum related art objects & jewelry

M Jorgensen Gallery, 2132 Hillside Rd, Box U-104, 06269-3104. Tel 860-486-4228; Elec Mail rock@jorg.anj.uconn.edu. *Dir* Rodney Rock; *Operations Dir* Gary Yakstis
Open Mon - Fri 9 AM - 4 PM, cl Sat & Sun. No admis fee. Estab 1967 to present work by leading contemporary North American artists. Serves the pub as well as the university community. The gallery is 2872 square ft. Average Annual Attendance: 25,000
Activities: Gallery talks

L Art & Design Library, Box U-5AD, 06269-1005. Tel 860-486-2787; FAX 860-486-3593; Elec Mail tom.jacoby@uconnm.uconn.edu. *Head* Thomas J Jacoby; *Asst Head* Heidi N Abbey
Open Mon - Thurs 9 AM - 10 PM, Fri 9 AM - 5 PM, Sat 9 AM - 10 PM, Sun Noon - 10 PM. Estab 1979 to support the Department of Art, Art History, Landscape Architecture & William Benton Mus of Art. Circ 16,000
Income: Financed by state appropriation & private funds
Library Holdings: Vols 68,000; Per subs 180; Micro — Cards, fiche; Other — Exhibition catalogs, pamphlets
Special Subjects: Afro-American Art, Antiquities-Assyrian, Antiquities-Byzantine, Antiquities-Egyptian, Antiquities-Etruscan, Antiquities-Greek, Antiquities-Oriental, Antiquities-Roman, Architecture, Art History, Asian Art, Commercial Art, Costume Design & Construction, Decorative Arts, Drawings, American Art, Artistic Photography, Western European Art

STRATFORD

M STRATFORD HISTORICAL SOCIETY, Katherine Mitchel Museum, 967 Academy Hill, PO Box 382, 06497. Tel 203-378-0630; *Cur* Hiram Tindall
Open Wed, Sat & Sun 11 AM - 4 PM, mid May - Oct. Admis adults $2, senior citizens & children $1. Estab 1925 to preserve Stratfords past. Museum contains local history; Judson House, 1750 house with period furnishings. Average Annual Attendance: 1500. Mem: 350; dues $7; meetings in Sept, Nov, Jan, Mar & May, last Fri of month
Income: Financed by endowment, fundraising & mem
Collections: Local Indians; 18th century house with period furnishings; collection of baskets, ceramics, cooking items, paintings, quilts, military items & weapons
Exhibitions: Calvin Curtis; Stratford Artist
Publications: Newsletter
Activities: Classes for children; docent training; lect open to public, 5 vis lectr per year; tours; individual paintings & original objects of art lent to accredited museums & galleries; lending collection contains books, original art, paintings, photographs & slides; sales shop sells books, reproductions, cards, prints & souvenirs

L Geneological Library, 967 Academy Hill, PO Box 382, 06497. Tel 203-378-0630
Office open Tues & Thurs. For reference & geneological research
Income: $50,000 (financed by mem & city appropriation)
Library Holdings: Vols 1000; AV — A-tapes, fs, Kodachromes, slides, v-tapes; Other — Clipping files, exhibition catalogs, manuscripts, memorabilia, original art works, pamphlets, photographs, prints, reproductions
Special Subjects: American Indian Art, Art History, Ceramics, Drawings, Flasks & Bottles, Folk Art, Furniture, Glass, Manuscripts, Marine Painting, Miniatures, Oriental Art, Painting - American, Period Rooms, Pewter

WASHINGTON DEPOT

A WASHINGTON ART ASSOCIATION, 4 Bryan Plaza, PO Box 173, 06794-0173. Tel 860-868-2878; *Pres* Gwen Kley; *VPres* Barbara Kraut; *VPres* James Hogue; *Admin* Delancey Watts
Open Mon - Sat 10 AM - 5 PM, Sun 2 - 5 PM, cl Wed. Estab 1952 to make available to the community a variety of art experiences through exhibitions & activities. Three connected galleries downstairs for individual & group shows; small members sales gallery upstairs. Average Annual Attendance: 10,000. Mem: 850; dues family $30, individual $20; annual meeting third Sun in Aug
Income: $32,000 (financed by endowment, mem & fund-raising events)
Publications: Events Bulletin, quarterly
Activities: Classes for adults & children; lect open to public, 8 vis lectr per year; gallery talks; sales shop sells original art & crafts by members

L Library, 4 Bryan Plaza, PO Box 173, 06794-0173. Tel 860-868-2878; *Admin* Delancey Watts
Open to members, teachers & pub for reference only
Library Holdings: Vols 800; Per subs 2; Other — Clipping files, exhibition catalogs
Special Subjects: Aesthetics, Crafts, Decorative Arts, Graphic Arts, Illustration, Landscapes, Painting - American, Photography, Porcelain, Portraits, Printmaking

WATERBURY

L SILAS BRONSON LIBRARY, Art, Theatre & Music Services, 267 Grand St, 06702. Tel 203-574-8222; FAX 203-574-8055; *Dir* Leo Flanagan; *Fine Arts* Eugenia Benson
Open Mon & Wed 9 AM - 9 PM, Tues, Thurs & Sat 9 AM - 5:30 PM, Fri 9 AM - 5:30 PM. Estab 1869 to provide a free public library for the community. A spotlighted gallery wall & locked glass exhibition case used for art exhibits
Income: Financed by endowment & city appropriation
Library Holdings: Vols 188,000; Per subs 550; AV — Cassettes, v-tapes
Exhibitions: Local artists in various media
Publications: Books & Happenings, monthly newsletter
Activities: Lect open to the public; concerts; individual framed art prints lent

M MATTATUCK HISTORICAL SOCIETY, Mattatuck Museum, 144 W Main St, 06702. Tel 203-753-0381; FAX 203-756-6283; *Chmn* Orton P Camp Jr; *Pres* Sharon Drubner; *VPres* Judy Staubo; *Cur* Ann Smith; *Dir Administration* Laurie Ryer; *Cur Educ Servs* Dorothy Cantor
Open Tues - Sat 10 AM - 5 PM, Sun Noon - 5 PM, cl Mon, cl Sun in July & Aug. No admis fee. Estab 1877 to collect & preserve the arts, history of the state of Connecticut, especially of Waterbury & adjacent towns. An art gallery is

maintained. Average Annual Attendance: 100,000. Mem: 1300; dues $40-$5000; annual meeting in Nov
Income: Financed by endowment, mem & grants
Collections: †Connecticut artists collection; †decorative arts collection; †local history & industrial artifacts; †period rooms
Publications: Annual Report
Activities: Classes for adults & children; dramatic programs; docent training; lect; gallery talks; group tours by appointment; competitions; individual paintings & original objects of art lent to other museums; lending collection contains paintings, photographs & slides; museum shop sells books, original art, reproductions, prints, decorative arts
L **Library,** 144 W Main St, 06702. Tel 203-753-0381; FAX 203-756-6283; Open for reference by appointment only
Income: Financed by grants & research fees
Library Holdings: Vols 3000; Per subs 10; CT artist files; AV — A-tapes, cassettes, fs, lantern slides, slides, v-tapes; Other — Clipping files, exhibition catalogs, manuscripts, memorabilia, original art works, pamphlets, photographs, prints, sculpture
Special Subjects: Architecture, Art History, Ceramics, Coins & Medals, Crafts, Decorative Arts, Drawings, Etchings & Engravings, Furniture, Historical Material, Industrial Design, Painting - American, Period Rooms, Restoration & Conservation, Sculpture, Local industrial history

WEST HARTFORD

M **NOAH WEBSTER HOUSE, INC,** Noah Webster House, 227 S Main St, 06107-3430. Tel 860-521-5362; *Dir* Sally Whipple; *Educ Coordr* Deborah O'Loughlin; *Office Mgr* Anne Kierstead
Open daily 1 - 4 PM, extended hours July & Aug. Admis adult $5, senior citizens & AAA members $4, children 6-12 $1. Estab 1965 to preserve & promote 18th-century daily life, Noah Webster & West Hartford history. Average Annual Attendance: 15,000. Mem: 500; annual meeting in Jan
Exhibitions: Permanent Noah Webster exhibit & temporary exhibits on West Hartford history
Publications: The Spectator, quarterly member newsletter
Activities: Classes for adults & children; docent training; family programs; school & scout programs; lect open to public; tours; competitions with prizes; lending collection contains film strips; sales shop sells books, reproductions, prints & educational items

M **UNIVERSITY OF HARTFORD,** Joseloff Gallery, Harry Jack Gray Ctr, 200 Bloomfield Ave, 06117. Tel 860-768-4090; FAX 860-768-5159; *Dir* Zina Davis
Open Tues - Fri 11 AM - 4 PM, Sat & Sun Noon - 4 PM. No admis fee. Comprehensive exhibition program focusing on established & emerging artists
Activities: Classes for adults

L **Anne Bunce Cheney Library,** Mortensen Library, University of Hartford, 200 Bloomfield Ave, 06117. Tel 860-768-4397; FAX 860-768-5165; *Library Coordr* Anna Bigazzi
Open Mon - Thurs 8 AM - Noon, Fri 8 AM - 6 PM, Sat Noon - 6 PM, Sun Noon - 9 PM. Estab 1964
Income: Financed through university library
Library Holdings: Vols 15,500; Per subs 80; Other — Exhibition catalogs, pamphlets, reproductions
Special Subjects: Advertising Design, Aesthetics, American Indian Art, Archaeology, Art History, Ceramics, Drawings, Etchings & Engravings, Furniture, Graphic Arts, History of Art & Archaeology, Judaica, Oriental Art, Photography, Sculpture

L **UNIVERSITY OF HARTFORD,** Mortensen Library, 200 Bloomfield Ave, 06117. Tel 860-768-4397; FAX 860-768-5165; Elec Mail bigazzi@uhavax.hartford.edu. *Art Coordr* Anna Bigazzi
Open Mon - Thurs 8 - 12 AM, Fri 8 AM - 6 PM, Sat 10 AM - 6 PM, Sun Noon - 12 AM. Estab 1964
Purchases: $3000
Library Holdings: Per subs 80; AV — V-tapes; Other — Exhibition catalogs, pamphlets, reproductions
Special Subjects: Afro-American Art, American Indian Art, Art History, Conceptual Art, Decorative Arts, Drawings, Graphic Arts, History of Art & Archaeology, Mexican Art, Oriental Art, Portraits, Pre-Columbian Art, Primitive Art, Sculpture, Watercolors

WESTPORT

L **WESTPORT PUBLIC LIBRARY,** Arnold Bernhard Plaza, 06880. Tel 203-227-8411; Elec Mail wpl@nai.net. *Dir* Sally H Poundstone; *Head AV Services* Jerri Lynch
Open Sept - May Mon, Tues & Thurs 9 AM - 9 PM, Wed & Fri 9 AM - 6 PM, Sat 9 AM - 5 PM, Sun 1 - 5 PM. Estab 1907. Circ 496,659
Income: $2,484,445 (financed by endowment, city & state appropriations, fines, rentals & gifts)
Purchases: $327,614
Library Holdings: Vols 176,576; Per subs 399; Micro — Fiche; AV — Cassettes, fs, rec, v-tapes; Other — Clipping files, memorabilia, pamphlets, photographs
Collections: Picture collection (for pictorial research by artists, illustrators, & designers)
Publications: News from Your Library, bi-monthly
Activities: Lect open to public

WETHERSFIELD

M **WETHERSFIELD HISTORICAL SOCIETY INC,** Museum, 200 Main St, 06109. Tel 860-529-7656; *Dir* Brenda Milkofsky
Open Tues - Sat 10 AM - 4 PM, Sun 1 - 4 PM. Estab 1932 to preserve local history. Two changing exhibit rooms. Average Annual Attendance: 18,000. Mem: 800; dues family $35, individual $23; annual meeting in mid-May
Income: $190,000 (financed by endowment, mem, programs & fundraising)
Collections: Local history/culture
Exhibitions: Changing monthly exhibits
Publications: Newsletter, quarterly
Activities: Children's programs; docent programs; lect open to public, 4 vis lectr per year; book traveling exhibitions 8 per year; retail store sells books & prints
L **Old Academy Library,** 150 Main St, 06109. Tel 860-529-7656; *Dir* Brenda Milkofsky
Open Tues - Fri 10 AM - 4 PM, Sat 1 - 4 PM & by appointment. Estab 1932
Income: $150,000 (financed by endowment, mem, programs, donations & rentals)
Library Holdings: Vols 2000
Collections: Wethersfield history & genealogy
Exhibitions: Woodworkers Guild; Embroiderer's Guild; Wethersfield History
Publications: Newsletter, quarterly
Activities: Classes for adults & children; docent programs; lect open to public, 4 vis lectr per year; book traveling exhibitions 4 per year; retail store sells books, prints & more

WILTON

M **NATIONAL PARK SERVICE,** Weir Farm National Historic Site, 735 Nod Hill Rd, 06897. Tel 203-834-1896; FAX 203-834-2421; *Exec Dir, Weir Farm Heritage Trust* Constance Evans; *Supt* Sarah Olson
Open 8:30 AM - 5 PM. No admis fee. Estab 1990. Visitor center has changing exhibits in two small rooms. Average Annual Attendance: 12,000. Mem: 200; annual meeting in May
Collections: J Alden Weir Archive & Manuscript Collection; †American Impressionist paintings; †Decorative Arts Collection
Activities: Classes for children; docent training, visiting artist program for professional artists; lect open to public, 5 vis lectr per year; museum shop sells books & prints

DELAWARE

DOVER

M **HISTORICAL & CULTURAL AFFAIRS,** Delaware State Museums, 102 S State St, PO Box 1401, 19903. Tel 302-739-5316; FAX 302-739-6712; *Div Dir* Daniel Griffith; *Cur Coll* Ann Horsey; *Cur Exhib* Dominique Coulet du Gard; *Cur Educ* Madeline Thomas; *Adminr* James A Stewart; *Cur Registration* Claudia F Melson; *Cur Historic Bldgs* Steven Curtis
John Dickinson Plantation: Tues - Sat 10 AM - 3:30 PM, Apr - Dec 1:30 - 4:30 PM; Johnson Victrola Museum, Meeting House Galleries I & II: Tues - Sat 10 AM - 3:30 PM; Old State House, Zwaanendael, New Castle Courthouse: Tues - Sat 8:30 AM - 4:30 PM, Sun 1:30 - 4:30 PM. No admis fee. Historic house museums were opened in the 1950s, Zwaanendael Museum 1931, to reflect the pre-historic & historic development of Delaware by exhibiting artifacts & interpreting the same through various facilities-those of early times. Average Annual Attendance: 100,000
Income: $1,500,000 (state appropriations)
Collections: Meeting House Galleries I & II: Prehistoric & Historic Archaeology; Main Street Delaware; John Dickinson Plantation: Decorative arts, furniture & Dickinson family artifacts; New Castle Court House: Portraits of famous Delawareans, archaeological artifacts, furniture & maps; Old State House: legislative judicial & governmental furniture & decorative arts; Zwaanendael Museum: HMS Debraak Artifacts, Mary Gregory Glass, Dolls etc; Commemorative gifts to the State of Delaware from Holland, china, glass, & silver; Johnson Victrola Museum: Talking machines, Victrolas, early recordings & Johnson memorabilia associated with the Victor Talking Machine Company (RCA)
Publications: Delaware State Museum Bulletins; Delaware History Notebook; miscellaneous booklets & brochures
Activities: Classes for children; docent training; special educational programs for school groups & adults which reflect the architecture, government, educ & aspects of social history relevant to Delaware; individual paintings are lent to governmental facilities; inservice programs relating to Delaware history are offered to Delaware teachers; traveling trunk program circulated to elementary schools; museum shop sells books, magazines, prints & Delaware souvenirs

NEWARK

UNIVERSITY OF DELAWARE
M **University Gallery,** 114 Old College, 19716-2509. Tel 302-831-8242; FAX 302-831-8251; Elec Mail belena.chapp@mvs.udel.edu. *Dir* Belena S Chapp; *Asst Cur* Jan Broske
Open Tues - Fri 11 AM - 5 PM, Sat & Sun 1 - 5 PM, cl university holidays. No admis fee. Estab 1978 to promote excellence in arts & humanities at the University of Delaware through exhibitions, acquisitions, preservation, interpretation of art collection & through providing support system to Mus studies curriculum. Average Annual Attendance: 15,000
Collections: 19th & 20th century American works on paper; Pre-Columbian textiles & ceramics; African Artifacts; early 20th century photographs
Exhibitions: (1998) P H Polk: American Photographer

Publications: Exhibit catalog
Activities: Lect open to public, 5 vis lectr per year; gallery talks; competitions with awards; individual & original objects of art lent to other museums & universities; book traveling exhibitions 1 per year; originate traveling exhibitions which circulate nationally to museums & universities

L **Morris Library,** S College Ave, 19717-5267. Tel 302-831-2965, 831-2231; FAX 302-831-1046; *Dir Libraries* Susan Brynteson; *Subject Librn (Art & Art History)* Susan A Davi; *Head Reference Dept* Shirley Branden
Income: Financed through the University
Purchases: $121,886
Library Holdings: Vols 2,259,718; Per subs 11,781; Micro — Cards, fiche, prints, reels; AV — A-tapes, cassettes, fs, motion pictures, rec, slides, v-tapes; Other — Exhibition catalogs, manuscripts, pamphlets, photographs, prints
Collections: American art & architecture; early 20th century European art; material on ornamental horticulture

ODESSA

L **CORBIT-CALLOWAY MEMORIAL LIBRARY,** 115 High St, PO Box 128, 19730-0128. Tel 302-378-8838; FAX 302-378-7803; *Dir* Steven J Welch
Open Mon - Sat. Estab 1847
Library Holdings: Vols 21,000; Per subs 58; AV — A-tapes, slides, v-tapes
Collections: †Delawareana

REHOBOTH BEACH

A **REHOBOTH ART LEAGUE, INC,** 12 Dodds Lane, Henlopen Acres, 19971. Tel 302-227-8408; FAX 302-227-4121; *Pres Board* Marcia Marvel; *Dir* Charles Palmer; *Exec Secy* Carolyn Wright
Open mid May - mid Oct, Mon - Sat 10 AM - 4 PM, Sun 1 - 4 PM. No admis fee. Estab 1938 to provide art education & creative arts in Rehoboth Beach community & Sussex County, Delaware. Two galleries, the Corkran & the Tubbs built for exhibitions; plus Homestead, circa 1743, gallery & studio. Average Annual Attendance: 30,000. Mem: 1200; dues $30 & up
Income: Financed by mem, donation & fund raising & sales of paintings
Collections: Small permanent collection from gifts, includes many Ethel P B Leach, Orville Peats & Howard Pyle
Exhibitions: Annual Members Fine Arts Crafts Exhibition; Annual Members Fine Arts Exhibition; Outdoor Fine Art
Publications: Brochure of yearly events
Activities: Classes for adults & children; lect open to public, 3 vis lectr per year; concerts; gallery talks; competitions with awards; sales shop sells original art & prints

WILMINGTON

M **DELAWARE ART MUSEUM,** 2301 Kentmere Pky, 19806-2096. Tel 302-571-9590; FAX 302-571-0220; *Dir* Stephen T Bruni; *Assoc Dir & Chief Cur* Nancy Miller Batty; *Dir Educ* Lial Jones; *Registrar* Mary Holahan
Admis adults $4, senior citizens & students $2.50, children 8 & under free. Incorporated 1912 as the Wilmington Soc of Fine Arts; present building expanded 1987; a privately funded, non-profit cultural & educational institution dedicated to the increase of knowledge & pleasure through the display & interpretation of works of art & through classes designed to encourage an understanding of & a participation in the fine arts. Nine galleries are used for exhibitions; six usually hold permanent or semi-permanent exhibitions which change at six week intervals. Average Annual Attendance: 100,000. Mem: 3200; dues family $50, individual $30; annual meeting in Mar
Income: $1,800,000 (financed by endowment, mem & grants)
Purchases: $20,000
Collections: †Bancroft Collection of English Pre-Raphaelite Paintings; †Copeland Collection of Work by Local Artists; Phelps Collection of Andrew Wyeth Works; †American paintings & sculpture, including many Howard Pyle works & complete etchings & lithographs of John Sloan; †American illustrations
Publications: DAM Magazine, quarterly
Activities: Classes for adults & children; docent training; workshops; lect open to public & occasionally to members only, 3-4 vis lectr per year; concerts; gallery talks; competitions; exten dept serving schools & community groups offering two-week programs in visual educ; originate traveling exhibitions; museum & sales shops sell books, candles, jewelry, note cards, paper, original art, prints, reproductions, slides & crafts

L **Helen Farr Sloan Library,** 2301 Kentmere Pky, 19806. Tel 302-571-9590; FAX 302-571-0220; *Head Librn* Harriet B Memeger
Open, Wed, Thurs & Fri 1 - 4 PM, by appointment during other hours. Estab 1923. Open to public for reference only
Library Holdings: Vols 50,000; Per subs 70; AV — V-tapes 30; Other — Clipping files, exhibition catalogs, manuscripts, memorabilia, original art works, pamphlets, photographs, prints
Special Subjects: Art History, Illustration, Painting - American, American Art 19th - 20th Century, American Illustration, Pre-Raphaelite Art
Collections: John Sloan Archives and Library; †Howard Pyle Archives and Library; †Samuel Bancroft Pre Raphaelite Library; †Everett Shinn Archives; Frank Schoonover Archives

HISTORICAL SOCIETY OF DELAWARE

M **Delaware History Museum,** 504 Market St, 19801. Tel 302-655-7161; FAX 302-655-7844; *Exec Dir* Dr Barbara E Benson; *Dir Museum Div* Timo May Mullin; *Registrar* Thomas Beckman
Open Tues - Fri Noon - 4 PM, Sat 10 AM - 4 PM. No admis fee. Estab 1864 to preserve, collect & display material related to Delaware History. Delaware History Mus & Old Town Hall Mus are the main mus galleries for the Historical Soc of Delaware. Mem: 1200; dues $35; annual meeting in Apr
Collections: Regional decorative arts; children's toys; costumes
Publications: Delaware Collections by Deborah D Waters; Delaware History, twice a year
Activities: Lect open to public, 3-7 vis lectr per year; concerts; gallery talks; tours; originate traveling exhibitions in conjunction with other history museums; museum shop sells books, reproductions, prints

M **George Read II House,** 42 The Strand, New Castle, 19720. Tel 302-322-8411; *Cur Museums* Timothy J Mullin; *Site Dir* Timothy J Mullin
Open Tues - Sat 10 AM - 4 PM, Sun Noon - 4 PM, cl New Year's, Thanksgiving & Christmas. Admis adults $3, children $1.50. Average Annual Attendance: 20,000. Mem: 1000; dues $10 & up
Collections: Federal Period decorative arts & architecture
Activities: Walking tours; sales shop sells books & crafts

L **Library,** 505 Market St, 19801. Tel 302-655-7161; FAX 302-655-7844; Elec Mail hsd@dca.net.com. *Exec Dir* Dr Barbara E Benson
Open Mon 1 - 9 PM, Tues - Fri 9 AM - 5 PM
Income: $1,100,000 (financed by endowment, annual support & grants)
Purchases: $15,000
Library Holdings: Vols 75,000; Per subs 73; Micro — Fiche, reels; AV — Cassettes, fs, Kodachromes, lantern slides, motion pictures, rec, slides; Other — Clipping files, exhibition catalogs, manuscripts, memorabilia, pamphlets, photographs, prints
Special Subjects: American & Delaware history
Publications: Delaware History, twice a year; Newsletter, twice a year

M **NEMOURS MANSION & GARDENS,** Rockland Rd, PO Box 109, 19899. Tel 302-651-6912; *Tour Supv* B J Whiting
Open May - Nov tours Tues - Sat 9 & 11 AM, 1 & 3 PM, Sun 11 AM, 1 & 3 PM. Admis fee. Estab 1977. 300 acre estate of Alfred du Pont; 102 room modified Louis XVI chateau built 1909 - 10; formal French-style gardens and natural woods
Collections: Collection of European furniture, tapestries, & paintings dating back to the 15th century

C **WILMINGTON TRUST COMPANY,** * Rodney Square N, 19890. Tel 302-651-8381; *VPres* Lewis B Hyman; *Art Consultant* Jean Athan
Open to public by appointment only. Estab 1942 to support regional artists. Collection displayed statewide in branch offices
Collections: Primarily Delaware scenes by Delaware artists

WINTERTHUR

M **WINTERTHUR MUSEUM,** Rte 52, 19735. Tel 302-888-4600, 888-4907; FAX 302-888-4880; WATS 800-448-3883. *Chmn* Samuel Schwartz; *Dir* Dwight P Lanmon; *Deputy Dir Coll* Brock Jobe; *Deputy Dir Finance & Adminr* Richard F Crozier; *Head of Gardens* Thomas Buchter; *Registrar* Open ; *Dir Public Relations* Janice Roosevelt; *Deputy Dir External Affairs* Open
Open Mon - Sat 9 AM - 5 PM, Sun Noon - 5 PM, cl New Year's, Thanksgiving & Christmas. Admis adults $8, senior citizens & youth 12-16 $6, children 5-11 $4. Corporation estab in 1930, mus opened in 1951. Mus collection housed in two buildings, the Period Rooms (guided tours) & the Galleries (self guided) featuring decorative arts made or used in America from 1640-1860; vast naturalistic garden. Average Annual Attendance: 165,000. Mem: 20,000
Income: Financed by endowment, mem, grants for special projects, admis, commercial activities
Collections: Over 89,000 American decorative arts made or used from 1640-1860; ceramics, furniture, glassware, interior architecture, metals, needlework, paintings, prints & textiles
Exhibitions: Point to Point Steeplechase Race
Publications: Publications & articles by staff, including Winterthur Portfolio, quarterly; Annual Report
Activities: School programs for K-12; classes for adults & children; Winterthur Program in Early American Culture; Winterthur Program in the Conservation of Artistic & Historic objects & PhD programs in the History of American Civilization, all graduate programs co-sponsored with the University of Delaware; lect open to public & to members; Yuletide tours; competitions; fels offered; individual paintings & original objects of art lent to museum & historical societies; museum shop sells books, gifts, postcards, plants & slides; Winterthur reproduction gallery sells over 200 reproductions of museum objects

L **Library,** Rte 52, 19735. Tel 302-888-4681; FAX 302-888-4870; *Dir* Gary Kulik; *Assoc Conservator Librn Coll* Lois Price; *Librn in Charge Visual Resources Coll* Bert Denker; *Librn in Charge Joseph Downs Coll of Manuscripts & Printed Ephemera* Richard McKinstry; *Librn in Charge Printed Books & Periodical Coll* Neville Thompson
Open Mon - Fri 8:30 AM - 5 PM. Estab in 1951 to support advanced study in American artistic, cultural, social & intellectual history up to the early twentieth century. For reference only
Library Holdings: Vols 72,000; Per subs 300; Auction Catalogs; Architectural Drawings; Micro — Cards, fiche 9200, reels 3450; AV — Lantern slides, slides 170,000, v-tapes; Other — Exhibition catalogs, manuscripts 73,000, memorabilia, pamphlets, photographs 150,000, prints
Special Subjects: Architecture, Decorative Arts, Painting - American, Museology
Collections: †Waldron Phoenix Belknap, Jr Research Library of American Painting; †Edward Deming Andrews Memorial Shaker Collection; †Decorative Arts Photographic Collection; Henry A duPont & Henry F duPont Papers; †Thelma S Mendsen Card Collection; †Maxine Waldron Collection of Children's Books & Paper Toys
Publications: Catalogs of collections of printed books: General (9 volumes); Trade Catalogs; Andrews Shaker Collection; America Cornucopia (thematic guide to library collections)

M **Historic Houses of Odessa,** Main St, PO Box 507, Odessa, 19730. Tel 302-378-4069; FAX 302-378-4050; *Site Adminr* Steven M Pulinka; *Exhib & Prog Coordr* Deborah Buckson
Open Tues - Sat 10 AM - 4 PM, Sun 1 - 4 PM, cl Mon & holidays. Admis adults (combined) $6, (house) $3, students & sr citizens (combined) $5, (house) $2.25. Estab 1958 for interpretation of regional lifestyle, architecture & material culture. Historic Houses of Odessa is a cluster of 18th & 19th century domestic structures composing a historic village within the community of Odessa. Gallery is humidity-controlled & contains seven gallery spaces. Average Annual Attendance: 20,000
Income: Financed by endowment
Collections: Corbit-Sharp House containing Chippendale, Federal & Queen Anne furniture; Wilson-Warner House; 19th century Brick Hotel Gallery; Federal Decorative Arts †Brick Hotel contains largest collection of early Victorian Belter Furniture in Nation
Activities: Tours

DISTRICT OF COLUMBIA

WASHINGTON

M AMERICAN ARCHITECTURAL FOUNDATION, The Octagon, 1799 New York Ave NW, 20006-5292. Tel 202-638-3105 (information), 638-3221 (museum); FAX 202-879-7764; *Dir* Eryl J Platzer
Open Tues - Fri 10 AM - 4 PM, Sat & Sun Noon - 4 PM. Admis by donation; groups over 10 charges $3 per person except student & senior citizens groups $1 per person. Opened as house mus in 1970; formerly a federal townhouse designed by the first architect of the United States Capitol, Dr William Thornton for Col John Taylor III to serve as a winter home; used by President & Mrs Madison as temporary White House during war of 1812. Furnished with late 18th & early 19th centuries decorative arts; changing exhibition program in second floor galleries. Average Annual Attendance: 25,000
Collections: Permanent collection of furniture, paintings, ceramics, kitchen utensils
Exhibitions: (1997) AIGA Awards; Kremlin Models (tentative); AIA Honor Awards; Veiled Doorways: Paintings by Anil Revri; Portraits of Great Places: Photographs by Victoria Cooper; Passonneau's Magnificent Maps of Washington, DC
Publications: Competition 1792-Designing a Nation's Capitol, 1976 book; exhibition catalogs; Octagon being an Account of a Famous Residence: Its Great Years, Decline & Restortaion , 1976 book; William Thornton: A Renaissance Man in the Federal City, book; The Architect & the British Country House, book; Architectural Records Management, 1985 booklet; the Architecture of Richard Morris Hunt, 1986 book; Building the Octagon, 1989 book; Ambitious Appetites: Dining, Behavior & Patterns of Consumption in Federal Washington, 1990 book; In the Most Fashionable Style: Making a Home in the Federal City, 1991 book; Creating the Federal City, 1774-1800: Potomac Fever, 1988 book; The Frame in American, 1700-1900: A survey of Fabrication, Techniques & Styles, 1983 catalog; Robert Mills, Architect, 1989 book; Sir Christopher Wren: The Design of St Paul's Catherdral, 1987 book; & exhibit catalogs
Activities: Educ dept; docent training; lect open to public, 6 vis lectr per year; tours; museum shop sells books & reproductions
M The Octagon Museum, The Octagon, 1799 New York Ave, NW, 20006-5292. Tel 202-638-3105; FAX 202-879-7764; *Dir* Eryl J Platzer
Open to the pub for reference but primarily used by staff
Exhibitions: (1997) Mounmental Miniatures: Souvenir Buildings from the Collection of Ace Architects. (1998) Facets & Reflections: Painting the Octagon's History

AMERICAN ASSOCIATION OF MUSEUMS
For further information, see National and Regional Organizations

AMERICAN ASSOCIATION OF UNIVERSITY WOMEN
For further information, see National and Regional Organizations

AMERICAN INSTITUTE FOR CONSERVATION OF HISTORIC & ARTISTIC WORKS (AIC)
For further information, see National and Regional Organizations

AMERICAN INSTITUTE OF ARCHITECTS
For further information, see National and Regional Organizations

AMERICANS FOR THE ARTS
For further information, see National and Regional Organizations

M AMERICAN UNIVERSITY, Watkins Collection, 4400 Massachusetts Ave NW, 20016. Tel 202-885-1670, 885-1064; FAX 202-885-1132; *Dir* Ron Haynie; *Asst Dir* Tom Raneses
Open Mon - Fri 10 AM - Noon & 1 - 4 PM. No admis fee. Estab 1945 to exhibit art of interest to pub & university art community; schedule includes shows by comtemporary artists & student exhibits. Maintains 15' x 15' gallery with 130 linear ft of exhibit space. Average Annual Attendance: 2000 plus art students
Collections: Watkins Collection of 19th & 20th century American & European paintings, drawings & prints
Activities: Lect open to the public, 3 - 5 vis lectr per year; individual paintings & original objects of art lent to museums & university galleries; traveling exhibitions organized & circulated on occassion

L AMERICAN UNIVERSITY, Jack I Dorothy G Bender Library, 4400 Massachusetts Ave NW, 20016-8046. Tel 202-885-1000; Internet Home Page Address http://www.american.edu. *University Librn* Patricia A Wand; *Asst University Librn* Linda Chase; *Asst University Librn* Diana Vogelsong; *Head Reference* Mary Mintz; *Head Coll Develop* Martin Shapiro
Estab 1893. Circ 292,817
Library Holdings: Vols 653,505; Per subs 3084; Compact Discs; Videodiscs; Micro — Fiche, reels; AV — A-tapes, cassettes, fs, motion pictures, rec, v-tapes; Other — Manuscripts
Special Subjects: Advertising Design, Anthropology, Archaeology, Architecture, Art History, Film, Graphic Design, History of Art & Archaeology, Painting - American, Photography, Printmaking, Sculpture, Video
Collections: General Academic Collection supporting Art Fields

M ANACOSTIA MUSEUM, 1901 Fort Pl SE, 20020. Tel 202-287-3369; FAX 202-287-3183; *Dir* Steven Newsome; *Deputy Dir* Sharon Reinckens; *Acting Dir Educ & Outreach* Robert Hall; *Historian* Portia P James
Open daily 10 AM - 5 PM, cl Christmas. No admis fee. Estab 1967, as a non-profit federally chartered corporation to record & research African, Black American & Anacostia history & urban problems; the first federally funded, community-based museum
Income: Financed by federally funded bureau of Smithsonian Institute
Collections: Afro-American & African art; Afro-American history; exhibits & artifacts of the Black Diaspora in the Western Hemisphere

Publications: Educational booklets; exhibit programs; museum brochures accompany each major exhibit
Activities: Programs for children & adults; lect; tours; gallery talks; art festivals; competitions; extension department serves groups unable to visit the museum; traveling exhibitions organized and circulated
L Branch Library, 1901 Fort Pl SE, 20020. Tel 202-287-3380; FAX 202-287-3183; *Branch Librn* Thomas Bickley
Open to public for research on the premises; call for appointment
Library Holdings: Vols 2000; Per subs 16

M ARCHIVES OF AMERICAN ART, AA-PG Bldg Smithsonian Institute, Room 331, Balcony, 20560. Tel 202-357-4251; FAX 202-786-2608; *Dir* Richard J Wattenmaker
Open Mon - Fri 9 AM - 5 PM. No admis fee. The Archives of American Art, founded in 1954, has assembled the world's largest collection of material documenting the history of the visual arts in this country. Eight million items of original source material are available on microfilm to scholars, students, writers & researchers. Affiliated with the Smithsonian Institution since 1970, the Archives preserves its original documents in Washington with microfilm copies in its regional branches. Mem: 2000; dues benefactor $2500, fellow $1000, patron $500, sponsor $250, associate $125, sustaining $65, student $25
Income: Financed by federal appropriation, private contributions, gifts & foundation grants
Collections: †Manuscript collection pertinent to the study of art in America
Publications: Finding aids & guides, video: From Reliable Sources - The Archives of American Art
—New York Regional Center, 1285 Avenue of the Americas, Lobby Level, New York, NY 10019. Tel 212-399-5015; FAX 212-399-6890; *Dir* Stephen Polcari; *Supv & Archivist* Valerie Komor
Open daily 9 AM - 5 PM. Estab 1956 to collect papers of artists, critics, dealers & collectors. 3000 sq ft. Average Annual Attendance: 5000. Mem: 1200; dues $65; annual meeting varies
Collections: Letters, diaries, artwork, writings, photographs & oral histories of the American art world
Exhibitions: American Art of the 19th & 20th centuries; four yearly from our collections: Dorothy Miller, Frank Stella, Louise Bourgeois, Jacob Kainen, Katherine Kuh
Activities: Lect open to members only, 1500 vis lectr per year; gallery talks
—Midwest Regional Center, 5200 Woodward Ave, Detroit, MI 48202. Tel 313-226-7544; FAX 313-226-7620; Elec Mail aaaemill@sivm.si.edu. *Librn* Cynthia Williams
Open Mon - Fri 9 AM - 5 PM. No admis fee. Estab 1954 to locate, preserve & make accessible primary sources for study of American Art; maintains lending library
Income: Financed trust funds
Activities: Lect open to public, 3-4 vis lectr per year
—New England Regional Center, 87 Mount Vernon St, Boston, MA 02108. Tel 617-565-8444; FAX 617-565-8466; Elec Mail aaabos02@sivm.si.edu. *Dir & Journal Ed* Robert F Brown
This office is now limited to collecting, editorial & telephone/written inquiries; un-restricted AAA microfilm is now available for research use in the Fine Arts Dept of the Boston Public Library, main branch
Publications: Archives of American Art Journal, quarterly
—Archives of American Art, 1151 Oxford Rd, San Marino, CA 91108. Tel 818-583-7847; FAX 818-583-7207; *Regional Dir* Paul J Karlstrom
Open by appointment only Mon - Fri 9 AM - Noon & 1 - 5 PM. Estab 1954 as a manuscript repository of American artists. Reference only
Library Holdings: Micro — Reels; AV — Fs
Special Subjects: Art History, American Art History
Collections: Manuscripts, correspondence, journals, diaries of American painters, sculptors, craftsmen, designers & architects
Publications: The Archives of American Art Journal, quarterly

M ART MUSEUM OF THE AMERICAS, 201 18th St, NW (Mailing add: 1889 F St, NW, 20006). Tel 202-458-6016; FAX 202-458-6021; *Dir* Ana Maria Escallon; *Cur Reference Center* Maria Leyva
Open Tues - Sat 10 AM - 5 PM, cl holidays. No admis fee. Estab 1976 by organization of American States to bring about an awareness & appreciation of contemporary Latin American art. The mus maintains an art gallery with the focus on contemporary Latin American art. Average Annual Attendance: 100,000
Collections: Contemporary Latin American & Caribbean art including paintings, prints, drawings & sculpture
Activities: Lect open to public, 10 vis lectr per year; gallery talks; tours; paintings & original art objects lent to museums & educational institutions; originate traveling exhibitions; sales shop sells films on Latin American art & artists
L Archive of Contemporary Latin American Art, 20006. Tel 202-458-6016; *Cur* Maria Leyva
Open to scholars for research only
Library Holdings: Vols 100; Micro — Fiche, reels; AV — A-tapes, slides, v-tapes; Other — Clipping files, exhibition catalogs, pamphlets, photographs, reproductions
Special Subjects: Aesthetics, Art History, Film, Latin American Art, Mexican Art, Painting - Spanish

A ART PAC, 408 Third St SE, 20003. Tel 202-546-1804; FAX 202-543-2405; *Treas* Robert J Bedard
Estab 1981 to lobby for art's legislation & assist federal candidates supporting the arts. Mem: dues $40
Income: Financed by mem
Publications: Newsletter/ART PAC News, quarterly
Activities: Legislator of Year Award

A ART RESOURCES INTERNATIONAL, 5813 Nevada Ave NW, 20015. Tel 202-363-6806; FAX 202-244-6844; *Exec Dir* Donald H Russell; *Dir Spec Projects* Helen M Brunner
Estab 1987 to provide curatirical & technical consulting in contemporary visual art
Publications: Money to Work: Grants for Visual Artists

M ARTS CLUB OF WASHINGTON, James Monroe House, 2017 I St NW, 20006. Tel 202-331-7282; FAX 202-857-3678; *Pres* Evelyn Woolston; *Mgr* Linda Cassell
Open Tues & Thurs 10 AM - 5 PM, Wed & Fri 2 - 5 PM, cl Mon. No admis fee. Founded 1916. The James Monroe House (1803-1805) was built by Timothy Caldwell of Philadelphia. It is registered with the National Register of Historic Places, the Historical Survey 1937 & 1968 & the National Trust for Historic Preservation. James Monroe, fifth President of the United States, resided in the house while he was Secretary of War & State. During the first six months of his Presidency (1817-1825) the house served as the Exec Mansion, since the White House had been burned in the War of 1812 & had not yet been restored. Garden, rooms & stairhalls serve as galleries. Average Annual Attendance: 10,000. Mem: 350; annual meeting in Apr
Income: Financed by mem, catering functions & fundraising
Purchases: Obtained through gifts & bequests
Collections: Washington, DC art
Publications: Monthly news bulletin to members
Activities: Lect open to public & for members, 40 vis lectr per year; concerts; gallery talks; tours; awards; scholarships offered

ASSOCIATION OF COLLEGIATE SCHOOLS OF ARCHITECTURE
For further information, see National and Regional Organizations

M B'NAI B'RITH INTERNATIONAL, B'nai B'rith Klutznick National Jewish Museum, 1640 Rhode Island Ave NW, 20036. Tel 202-857-6583; *Dir* Ori Z Soltes; *Asst Dir* Lisa Rosenblatt; *Shop Mgr* Beverly Goldman
Open Sun - Fri 10 AM - 5 PM, cl Sat & legal & Jewish holidays. No admis fee; suggested donation adults $2, children, students & sr citizens $1. Estab 1957 to exhibit & preserve Jewish art & culture. Three changing exhibition galleries; five permanent collection galleries, including Life & Holiday cycles; sculpture garden; Jewish American Sports Hall of Fame. Average Annual Attendance: 40,000. Mem: 1000; dues $25-$5000
Income: General operations financed by parent organization; private & corporate donations; programs & exhibitions financed by mem members
Collections: Permanent collection of Jewish ceremonial & folk art; ancient coins; archives of B'nal B'rith; contemporary paintings; lithographs; photographs; sculptures
Exhibitions: Jews in Sports
Publications: Exhibitions brochures & catalogues; members newsletter, semi-annual; permanent collection catalogue
Activities: Multicultural educational outreach program; children's program; docent training; lect open to public; concerts; individual paintings lent to museums; originate traveling exhibitions; museum shop sells books, original art, reproductions, posters, Judaica & giftware

M CANADIAN EMBASSY, Art Gallery, 501 Pennsylvania Ave NW, 20001. Tel 202-682-1740; FAX 202-682-7791; *Cultural Counsellor* Louise Blais
Open Mon - Fri 10 AM - 5 PM. No admis fee
Publications: Cultural Calendar, every 4 months

L CATHOLIC UNIVERSITY OF AMERICA, Humanities Div, Mullen Library, 620 Michigan Ave NE, 20064. Tel 202-319-5075; *Head Humanities Div* B Gutekunst
Open fall & spring terms Mon - Thurs 8 AM - 10 PM, Fri & Sat 9 AM - 5 PM, Sun Noon - 10 PM. Estab 1958 to offer academic resources & services that are integral to the work of the institution
Library Holdings: Vols 12,000
Special Subjects: Early Christian & Medieval Art

CONGRESSIONAL ARTS CAUCUS
For further information, see National and Regional Organizations

M CORCORAN GALLERY OF ART, 17th St & New York Ave NW, 20006. Tel 202-639-1700; FAX 202-639-1768; *Pres & Dir* David C Levy; *Deputy Dir & Chief Cur* Jack Cowart; *Cur* Terrie Sultan; *Registrar* Cynthia Rom
Open Tues - Sun 10 AM - 5 PM. No admis fee. Founded 1869 primarily for the encouragement of American art. The nucleus of the collection of American Paintings was formed by its founder, William Wilson Corcoran, early in the second half of the 19th century. In 1925 a large wing designed by Charles A Platt was added to house the European collection bequested by Senator William Andrews Clark of Montana. The Walker Collection, formed by Edward C and Mary Walker, added important French Impressionists to the collection upon its donation in 1937. Average Annual Attendance: 400,000. Mem: 4500; dues contributing $500 & up, sponsor $250, Friends of the Corcoran $125, family $50, single $35, student & senior citizens $15
Collections: The American collection of paintings, watercolors, drawings, sculpture & photography from the 18th through 20th centuries; European collection includes paintings & drawings by Dutch, Flemish, English & French artists; 18th century French salon, furniture, laces, rugs, majolica; Gothic & Beauvais tapestries; Greek antiquities; 13th century stained glass window & bronzes by Antoine Louise Barye; tryptich by Andrea Vanni; Walker Collection of French Impressionists
Exhibitions: Changing exhibitions of Contemporary Art; Fine Art Photography; works by regional artists; works drawn from the permanent collection
Publications: Calendar of Events (for members); Corcoran Shop Catalogue
Activities: Classes for adults & children; docent training; lect open to public; concerts; gallery talks; tours; originates traveling exhibitions; sales shop sells books, magazines, reproductions, prints & slides
L Corcoran Museum & School of Art Library, 500 17th St NW, 20006-4899. Tel 202-639-1826; FAX 202-639-1768; *Head Librn* Deborah Barlow; *Technical Servs Technician* Pat Reid
Research & lending resource for mus & school, staff, faculty & student. Provides interlibrary loan to other institutions & open for pub use by appointment only
Purchases: $49,000
Library Holdings: Vols 18,000; Per subs 140; Micro — Fiche; AV — Slides; Other — Exhibition catalogs
Special Subjects: Ceramics, Drawings, Graphic Design, Painting - American, Photography, Pottery, Printmaking, Sculpture
Collections: Artists books

A CULTURAL ALLIANCE OF GREATER WASHINGTON, 410 Eighth St NW, No 600, 20004. Tel 202-638-2406; FAX 202-638-3388; *Exec Dir* Jennifer Cover Payne
Open 9 AM - 5 PM. Estab 1978 to increase appreciation & support for the arts in Washington DC region. Mem: 647; mem open to artists, arts administrator or patron; dues individual $60, organization-scaled to annual income; annual meeting in the fall
Income: $82,663 (financed by mem & donations)
Exhibitions: Tony Taylor Award
Publications: Arts Washington, newsletter 10 times per year; Cultural Alliance Directory, biennial
Activities: Lect open to public for fee, free to members

M DAR MUSEUM, National Society Daughters of the American Revolution, 1776 D St NW, 20006. Tel 202-879-3241; FAX 202-879-3252; *Dir & Chief Cur* Diane Dunkley
Open Mon - Fri 8:30 AM - 4 PM, Sun 1 - 5 PM. No admis fee. Estab 1890 for collection & exhibition of decorative arts used in America from 1700-1840; for the study of objects & the preservation of Revolutionary artifacts & documentation of American life. There are 33 period rooms which reflect the decorative arts of particular states, also a mus which houses large collections grouped by ceramics, textiles, silver, glass, furniture & paintings. Average Annual Attendance: 12,000. Mem: 215,000; dues $15 - $17; annual meeting in Apr
Income: $200,000 (financed by mem)
Collections: †Ceramics, †furniture, †glass, †paintings, †prints, †silver, †textiles
Exhibitions: Special exhibitions arranged & changed periodically, usually every 6 months
Activities: Classes for adults & children; docent training; lect open to public; tours; paintings & original art works lent to museums & cultural institutions for special exhibitions; museum shop sells books, stationery, dolls & handcrafted gift items
L Library, 1776 D St NW, 20006-5392. Tel 202-879-3241; FAX 202-879-3227; *Librn* Eric Grundset
Open to pub by advance notice; for reference only
Purchases: $1000
Library Holdings: Vols 2500; Per subs 4
Special Subjects: American Decorative Arts

M EVANS-TIBBS COLLECTION, 1910 Vermont Ave NW, 20001. Tel 202-234-8164; *Dir* Thurlow Evans-Tibbs Jr
Open by appointment only. Estab 1980. For reference only
Collections: Evans-Tibbs Archives; African-American Artists, †books, †catalogs, †news articles, brochures, slides, resumes
Exhibitions: African-American Printmakers 1925-1955; H O Tanner & Two of His Students-Harper & Scott
Activities: Lect open to public; individual paintings & original objects of art lent; book traveling exhibitions
L Archives, 1910 Vermont Ave NW, 20001. Tel 202-234-8164; *Dir* Thurlow Evans-Tibbs Jr
Estab 1980. For reference only
Library Holdings: Items 19,585; AV — Slides, v-tapes; Other — Clipping files, exhibition catalogs, manuscripts, memorabilia, original art works, pamphlets, photographs, prints, reproductions

M FEDERAL RESERVE BOARD, Art Gallery, 20th & C Sts, 20551. Tel 202-452-3686; FAX 202-452-3102; *Dir* Mary Anne Goley
Open daily 11:30 AM - 2 PM. Estab 1975 to promote art in the work place. Two story atrium space with travertine, marble walls. Works are hung on four landings & one very long hall. Average Annual Attendance: 800. Mem: 1500
Income: Financed by the Federal Reserve Board
Collections: American & European paintings; 19th century - present sculpture; Works on paper
Exhibitions: Swiss Folk Art
Publications: Exhibition catalogs
Activities: Docent programs; book traveling exhibitions 4 per year; originate traveling exhibitions 4 per year

L FOLGER SHAKESPEARE LIBRARY, 201 E Capitol St SE, 20003. Tel 202-544-4600; FAX 202-544-4623; *Dir* Werner Gundersheimer; *Librn* Richard J Kuhta
Open (exhibition gallery) Mon - Sat 10 AM - 4 PM. Estab 1932 as a private, independent research library & international center for the study of all aspects of the European Renaissance & civilization in the 16th & 17th centuries. Maintains an exhibition gallery & a permanent display of Shakespearean items, with changing topical exhibits of books, manuscripts, paintings & sculpture
Income: Financed by endowment
Library Holdings: Vols 250,000; Per subs 180; Rare books 120,000; Micro — Reels 10,000; AV — A-tapes, fs, motion pictures, rec, slides; Other — Exhibition catalogs, manuscripts 55,000, memorabilia, original art works 3700, pamphlets, photographs 3000, prints 20,000, reproductions, sculpture
Collections: Shakespeare, playbills & promptbooks; Continental & English Renaissance, 1450-1700
Exhibitions: (1997) Impressions of Wenceslaus Hellar; Shakespeare's Unruly Women
Publications: The Folger Edition of the Complete Plays of William Shakespeare; Shakespeare Quarterly, newsletter, 3 times per year
Activities: Seminars for advanced graduate students; lect open to public; concerts; gallery talks; fels offered

M FONDO DEL SOL, Visual Art & Media Center, 2112 R St NW, 20008. Tel 202-483-2777; *Exec Dir* W Marc Zuver; *Asst Dir Spec Projects* Irma Talabi Francis
Estab 1973 to promote Latin American culture, non-profit organization
Collections: Permanent collection, Religious artifacts of artistry, ceramics, sculpture, paintings Pre-Columbian
Exhibitions: Pre-Columbian art by Santos

M FREER GALLERY OF ART GALLERY, Arthur M Sackler Gallery, 1050 Independence Ave SW, 20560. Tel 202-357-4880; *Dir* Milo C Beach
Open daily 10 AM - 5:30 PM, cl Christmas Day. No admis fee. Estab 1987 for exhibition, research & educ on the arts of Asia. Average Annual Attendance: 500,000
Income: Financed by endowment & federal appropriation
Collections: Chinese, Japanese, Islamic, Ancient Near Eastern & South & Southeast Asian Art
Exhibitions: Sackler Gallery: The Arts of China; Luxury Arts of the Silk Route Empires; Metalwork & Ceramics from Ancient Iran; Puja: Expressions of Hindu Devotion; Sculpture of South & Southeast Asia. (1997) The Bridge: Illusion in Clay; King of the World: A Mughall Manuscript from the Royal Library, Windsor Castle. (1997-98) Art & Patronage under Shah Jahan; Freed Gallery: (1997) Beyond Paper: Chinese Calligraphy on Objects, Choice Spirits; Crosscurrents in Chines & Islamic Ceramics; Telling Tales in Japanese Art; Art for Art's Sake; Armenian Gospels; At the Margins; Islamic Art; The Natural World in Indian Paintings; Seto & Mino Ceramics; The Evolution of Chinese Celadon; Japanese Art in the Meiji Period (1868-1912); The Seven Thrones of Jami. (1997-98) An Invitation to Tea; Chinese Gardens in the Painter's Imagination
Publications: Asian Art, quarterly; Arthur M Sackler Gallery Calendar, bi-monthly
Activities: Programs for adults & children; dramatic programs; docent training; lect open to public, 5-6 vis lectr per year; concerts; gallery talks; tours; films; individual paintings & original objects of art lent to other art institutions; originate traveling exhibitions; museum shop sells books, magazines, reproductions, prints, slides, jewelry, cards & gifts
L Library, 1050 Independence Ave SW, 20560. Tel 202-357-4880; FAX 202-786-2936; *Head Librn* Lily C J Kecskes; *Librn* Kathryn D Phillips; *Librn* Reiko Yoshimura; *Archivist* Colleen Hennessey
Open to public for reference
Library Holdings: Vols 56,000; Per subs 400; Sales catalogs; Micro — Fiche, reels; AV — A-tapes, cassettes, lantern slides, slides; Other — Clipping files, exhibition catalogs, reproductions
Special Subjects: Antiquities-Assyrian, Antiquities-Oriental, Archaeology, Carpets & Rugs, Crafts, Drawings, Embroidery, Etchings & Engravings, Folk Art, Gold, History of Art & Archaeology, Islamic Art, Ivory, Jewelry, Manuscripts

GENERAL SERVICES ADMINISTRATION
For further information, see National and Regional Organizations

M GEORGETOWN UNIVERSITY, Art & History Museum, Hoya Sta, 20057. Tel 202-687-4406; FAX 202-687-4452; *Cur* Clifford T Chieffo; *Assoc Cur* Patricia H Chieffo
Open during University hours according to yearly schedule, cl holidays. No admis fee. University estab 1789. The museum is on the Georgetown University campus in Healy Hall (1879)
Income: Financed by University budget
Collections: American portraits; Works by Van Dyck & Gilbert Stuart; graphics, historical objects, paintings, religious art
Exhibitions: 3-4 exhibitions per year
Publications: Collection catalog, exhibit catalogs
Activities: Educational programs for undergraduate students; gallery talks, guided tours; art festivals, temporary exhibitions
L Lauinger Library-Special Collections Division, 3700 O St NW, 20057-1006. Tel 202-687-7475; FAX 202-687-7501; Elec Mail barringg@gunet.georgetown.edu; Internet Home Page Address http://gulib.lausun.georgetown.edu/dept/speccoll/. *Special Collections Librn* George M Barringer
Open Mon - Fri 9 AM - 5:30 PM. Estab 1796 to support Georgetown's academic programs
Library Holdings: Other — Original art works, photographs, prints
Special Subjects: Bookplates & Bindings, Cartoons, Drawings, Illustration, Woodcuts
Collections: †Editorial Cartoon Collection - Originals (American) c 1910 to present; Elder Collection - Artist Self - Portraits, prints, drawings, watercolors, paintings , c 1925-1975; †Jesuit Collection - American fine prints, c 1900-1950 Eric F Menke Collection - prints, drawings, watercolors, paintings; Murphy Collection - American Fine Prints, c 1900-1950; †Eric Smith Collection - original editorial cartoon; Lynd Ward Collection - prints, drawings, watercolors, paintings, c 1925-1980; †Printmakers' Collections: John DePol, Werner Drewes, Isac Friedlander, Norman Kent, Clare Leighton, William E C Morgan, Barry Moser, Philip Riesman, Prentiss Taylor
Publications: Annual print exhibition handlists; Graphic Arts in the Special Collections Division, Georgetown University Library; Special Collections at Georgetown (1996)

M GEORGE WASHINGTON UNIVERSITY, The Dimock Gallery, Lower Lisner Auditorium, 730 21st St NW, 20052. Tel 202-994-1525; FAX 202-994-1632; *Dir* Lenore D Miller; *Asst Cur* Penny Dwyer
Open Tues - Fri 10 AM - 5 PM. No admis fee. Estab 1967 to enhance graduate & undergraduate programs in fine art & research in art history; documentation of permanent collections; feature historical & contemporary exhibitions related to university art dept programs. Average Annual Attendance: 10,000
Collections: U S Grant Collection; Joseph Pennell Collection of Prints; W Lloyd Wright Collection of Washingtoniana; graphic arts from the 18th, 19th & 20th centuries, with special emphasis on American art; historical material; paintings; prints; sculpture; works pertaining to George Washington
Exhibitions: 6-8 temporary exhibitions staged per year, including faculty, alumni, student, permanent collection shows & Washington DC area invitational exhibitions
Publications: Exhibition catalogs
Activities: Lect open to public; gallery talks; tours; individual paintings & original objects of art lent

M HARVARD UNIVERSITY, Dumbarton Oaks Research Library & Collections, 1703 32nd St NW, 20007. Tel 202-339-6400; *Dir* Angeliki Laiou
Open daily (Gardens) Apr - Oct 2 - 6 PM, Nov - Mar 2 - 5 PM, (Collections) Tues - Sun 2 - 5 PM, cl holidays. Conveyed in 1940 to Harvard University by Mr & Mrs Robert Woods Bliss as a research center in the Byzantine & Medieval humanities & subsequently enlarged to include pre-Columbian studies & studies in landscape architecture. Average Annual Attendance: 100,000
Collections: Byzantine devoted to early Christian & Byzantine mosaics, textiles, bronzes, sculpture, ivories, metalwork, jewelry, glyptics & other decorative arts of the period; pre-Columbian devoted to sculpture, textiles, pottery, gold ornaments & other objects from Mexico, Central & South America, dating from 800 BC to early 16th century; European & American paintings, sculpture & decorative arts
Publications: Handbooks & catalogs of the Byzantine & pre-Columbian collection; scholarly publications in Byzantine, pre-Columbian & landscape architecture studies
Activities: Lect; conferences
L Byzantine Library, 1703 32nd St NW, 20007. Tel 202-339-6980; *Librn* Irene Vaslef; *Serials Librn* Ronald Schwertfeger; *Asst Reader's Servs* Mark Zapatka
Important resources for Byzantine research
Library Holdings: Vols 123,500; Per subs 870; Micro — Fiche, reels; Other — Exhibition catalogs
Special Subjects: Landscape Architecture, Pre-Columbian Art, Byzantine Studies
Collections: Dumbarton Oaks Census of Early Christian and Byzantine Objects in American Collection; Photographic copy of the Princeton Index of Christian Art; collection of photographs
L Studies in Landscape Architecture & Garden Library, 1703 32nd St NW, 20007. Tel 202-339-6450, 339-6460 (garden library); *Librn* Linda Lott-Gerlach; *Librn* Anne Thacher; *Acting Dir Studies* Terence Young
For reference
Library Holdings: Vols 14,756; Per subs 46; Drawings of Garden; Seed catalogs; Micro — Fiche, reels; AV — Slides; Other — Exhibition catalogs, manuscripts, memorabilia, original art works, pamphlets, photographs, prints
Special Subjects: Architecture, Landscape Architecture, History of Landscape Architecture, History of Horticulture, History of Botanical Illustration
Collections: †Rare books (3535)
Exhibitions: The French Garden; The Poetic Dimension in Contemporary Garden Design: Ian Hamilton Findlay & Bernard Lassus; The Regional American Gardener's Library; New World Symphony: The Introduction of Exotic Plants into European Culture; From Art to Comic: A Glimpse into Five Centuries of Discussion about Garden Design
Publications: Dumbarton Oaks Reprints & Facsimiles in Landscape Architecture; History of Landscape Architecture (Colloquium Series); other titles in garden history
Activities: Departmental lect; roundtables; symposium

M HIRSHHORN MUSEUM & SCULPTURE GARDEN, Seventh & Independence Ave SW, 20560. Tel 202-357-3091; FAX 202-786-2682; Elec Mail hmspa001@sivm.si.edu. *Dir* James Demetrion; *Adminr* Beverly Pierce; *Dir Public Programs & Chief Cur* Neal Benezra; *Sr Educator* Teresia Bush; *Registrar* Brian Kavanagli; *Chief Exhib* Edward Schelsser; *Chief Conservator* Lawrence Hoffman; *Chief Photography* Lee Stalsworth; *Head Public Affairs* Sidney Lawrence
Open Mon - Sun 10 AM - 5:30 PM, cl Christmas Day. No Admis fee. Estab 1966 under the aegis of the Smithsonian Institution; building designed by Gordon Bunshaft of the architectural firm Skidmore, Owings & Merrill. Opened in 1974. Average Annual Attendance: 800,000
Income: Financed by federal funds
Collections: †American art beginning with a strong group of Thomas Eakins & going on to De Kooning, Gorky, Hartley, Hopper, Johns, Elizabeth Murray, Rothko, Frank Stella, Warhol; †European paintings & mixed media work of the last 5 decades represented by Bacon, Balthus, Kiefer & Korenellis, Leger, Miro, Polke & Richter; †extensive sculpture collection includes works by Bourgeois, Brancusi, Calder, Cragg, Giacometti, Hessi, Merz, Moore, Oldenburg & David Smith; †12,000 paintings, sculptures, mixed media works, drawings & prints, the nucleus donated to the nation by Joseph H Hi emphasizing contemporary art & the development of modern art from the latter half of the 19th century to present
Exhibitions: Permanent collection & special loan exhibitions
Publications: Exhibit catalogs; collection catalogs; seasonal events calendar, three times per yr
Activities: Classes for children; docent training; workshops for teachers; outreach; lect open to public, 4 vis lectr per year; gallery talks; tours; individual paintings & original objects of art lent to accredited museums that meet security & conservation standards, loans, subject to approval by curators; lending contains original art works, original prints & sculpture; book traveling exhibitions 1-2 per year; originate traveling exhibitions 1-2 per year; museum shop sells books, reproductions, slides, jewelry by artists, CD's sculptural toys
L Library, Seventh & Independence Ave SW, 20560. Tel 202-357-3222; *Librn* Anna Brooke
Estab 1974. For reference only by appointment
Income: Financed by federal funds
Library Holdings: Vols 44,400; Auction catalogs; Micro — Fiche, reels; AV — A-tapes, cassettes, slides, v-tapes; Other — Clipping files, exhibition catalogs, memorabilia, photographs
Special Subjects: American Painting, Contemporary Art, International Modern Sculpture
Collections: Armory Show Memorabilia; Eakins Memorabilia; 5 Samuel Murray Scrapbooks

M HISTORICAL SOCIETY OF WASHINGTON DC, Heurich House Museum, 1307 New Hampshire Ave NW, 20036. Tel 202-785-2068; FAX 202-887-5785; *Chair* Gary Henrich; *Exec Dir* Barbara Franco; *Cur* Candace Shireman
Open Wed - Sat Noon - 4 PM. Admis adults $3, children, students & senior citizens $1.50. Estab 1894 to preserve & interpret local history of Washington, DC. Historic house mus, 1894 Richardsonian Romanesque, with ornate interiors & furnishings original to house; painted ceilings, wallstenciling & carved mantels, woodwork, furniture, two changing exhibition spaces. Maintains reference library. Average Annual Attendance: 8000. Mem: 1800; dues $40-$2000

Income: $385,000 (financed by endowment, mem, grants & earned income)
Exhibitions: Small exhibitions, largely using photographs, mss, maps, memorabilia from Washington history library colls
Publications: Washington History, semi-annual magazine
Activities: Classes for adults & children; lect open to public; tours; awards; originate traveling exhibitions; museum shop sells books, reproductions & crafts
L **Research Collections,** 1307 N Hampshire Ave, 20036. Tel 202-785-2068; *Exec Dir* Barbara Franco
Open Wed, Fri, Sat 10 AM - 4 PM. Estab 1894 for collection of materials related to Washington, DC history. For reference only
Library Holdings: Vols 14,000; Micro — Cards, fiche, reels; AV — Lantern slides, slides; Other — Clipping files, exhibition catalogs, manuscripts, memorabilia, original art works, pamphlets, photographs, prints
Special Subjects: Architecture of Washington, DC
Activities: Individual paintings & original objects of art lent; sales shop sells books, magazines & prints

M **HOWARD UNIVERSITY,** Gallery of Art, College of Fine Arts, 2455 Sixth St NW, 20059. Tel 202-806-7047; FAX 202-806-9258; *Chmn* Dr Tritobia Benjamin; *Asst Dir* Scott Baker; *Registrar* Eileen Johnston
Open Mon - Fri 9 AM - 5 PM, cl Sat & Sun. No admis fee. Estab 1928 to stimulate the study & appreciation of the fine arts in the University & community. Three air-conditioned art galleries are in Childers Hall, James V Herring Heritage Gallery, James A Porter Gallery & the Student Gallery along with Gumbel Print Room. Average Annual Attendance: 24,000
Collections: †Agnes Delano Collection of contemporary American watercolors & prints; Irving R Gumbel Collection of prints; Kress Study Collection of Renaissance paintings & sculpture; Alain Locke Collection of African art; †University collection of painting, sculpture & graphic arts by Afro-Americans
Exhibitions: Changing tri-monthly exhibits
Publications: Catalogue of the African & Afro-American collections; exhibition catalogues; informational brochures; Native American Arts (serial)
Activities: Bimonthly gallery lect & community programs
L **Architecture & Planning Library,** 2366 Sixth St NW, 20059. Tel 202-806-7424; *Librn* Dr Arthuree Wright
Library Holdings: Vols 27,000; Per subs 400; Documents 600; Micro — Reels 1,300; AV — Fs, lantern slides, slides 29,000; Other — Photographs
Special Subjects: Architectural History, Construction & Design, City Planning, Environmental Design
Collections: Dominick Collection of pre-1900 books & periodicals on architecture; K Keith Collection of books & photographs on indigenous African architecture

M **INTERNATIONAL SCULPTURE CENTER,** 1050 17th St NW, Ste 250, 20036. Tel 202-785-1144; FAX 202-785-0810; Elec Mail sculpt@dgsys.com. *Exec Dir* Jeanne C Dond; *Deputy Dir* Carla M Hanzal
Open Mon - Fri 9 AM - 5 PM. Estab 1960, dedicated to expand the base of understanding & support of contemporary sculpture through its programs & services. The ISC serves the needs & interests of sculptors, educators, arts supporters & the general public. Mem: 11,000; dues $65
Income: Financed by mem dues, private donations & grants
Publications: Sculpture, 10 times year
Activities: Lect open to public; tours; competitions with prizes; scholarships offered; originate traveling exhibitions

A **THE JOHN F KENNEDY CENTER FOR THE PERFORMING ARTS,** New Hampshire Ave & F St, 20566. Tel 202-416-8000; FAX 202-416-8421; *Chmn* James A Johnson
Open Mon - Sun 10 AM - 12 midnight. No admis fee for building, ticket prices vary. The Center opened in Sept 1971. Facilities include the 2200-seat Opera House, 2750-seat Concert Hall, 1130-seat Eisenhower Theater, 500-seat Terrace Theater, 224-seat film theater & 350-seat Theater Lab operated by the American Film Institute. Estab in 1958 by Act of Congress as the National Cultural Center. A bureau of the Smithsonian Institution, but administered by a separate independent Board of Trustees; the Center is the sole official memorial in Washington to President Kennedy. Although the Center does not have an official collection, gifts in the form of art objects from foreign countries are on display throughout the Center. Average Annual Attendance: 1,500,000 ticketed, 2,500,000-3,000,000 visitors. Mem: Friends of the Kennedy Center 40,000; dues from $30-$2000
Income: $30,000,000 (financed by ticket revenue & private contributions)
Exhibitions: Changing exhibits on the performing arts are displayed in the Center's Performing Arts Library, a cooperative effort between Kennedy Center & the Library of Congress. Exhibits frequently include portraits, prints, engravings, sketches, etc, of relevence to the performing arts
Publications: John F Kennedy Center for the Performing Arts; Kennedy Center News, bi-monthly
Activities: Classes for adults & children; dramatic programs; performing arts series for young audiences; lect open to public, 50 vis lectr per year; concerts; tours; originate traveling exhibitions to Library of Congress; sales shop sells books, original art, reproductions, slides, souvenirs, needle point & posters
L **Education Resources Center,** Roof Terrace Level, 20566. Tel 202-416-8780; *Head Educ Dept* Derek Gordon
Open Tues - Fri 11 AM - 8:30 PM, Sat 10 AM - 6 PM, cl Mon & Sun. Estab 1979 to provide a national information & reference facility for all areas of the performing arts, including film & broadcasting. For reference only. Access to all Library of Congress collections
Library Holdings: Vols 7000; Per subs 400; Micro — Fiche, reels; AV — A-tapes, cassettes, rec, slides, v-tapes; Other — Clipping files, exhibition catalogs, framed reproductions, manuscripts, memorabilia, pamphlets, reproductions
Special Subjects: Kennedy Center History, performing arts information

A **LAWYERS COMMITTEE FOR THE ARTS,** Volunteer Lawyers for the Arts, 918 16th St, NW, Ste 400, 20006. Tel 202-429-0229; *Exec Dir* Joshua Kaufman
Open Mon - Fri 9 AM - 5 PM. Estab 1977 to provide pro bono legal referral services. A small library provides access to art law books & forms
Activities: Lect open public or groups on request

L **LIBRARY OF CONGRESS,** Prints & Photographs Division, Madison Bldg, Rm 339, 101 Independence Ave SE, 20540-4730. Tel 202-707-6394 (reference), 707-5836 (offices); FAX 202-707-6647; *Librn* James H Billington; *Chief* Stephen E Ostrow; *Asst Chief* Elizabeth Parker; *Head Reference Section* Mary M Ison; *Head Curatorial Section* Bernard Reilly; *Head Processing Section* Helena Zinkham; *Cur Architecture* C Ford Peatross; *Cur Architecture* Christine Carlone; *Photographs* Beverly W Brannah; *Photographs* Verna Curtis; *Popular & Applied Graphic Arts* Harry Katz; *Posters* Elena G Millie
Exhibit Halls open Mon, Wed & Thurs 8:30 AM - 9:30 PM, Tues, Fri & Sat 8:30 AM - 5 PM, cl Sun, Reading Room of the Division open Mon - Fri 8:30 AM - 5 PM, cl legal holidays. Estab 1897. For reference only
Income: Financed by congressional appropriation, gifts & endowments
Purchases: Fine prints, master photographs, posters, architectural drawings & historical prints & drawings
Library Holdings: Architectural items 2,000,000; Fine prints 100,000; Master photographs 3800; Photographic images 10,500,000; Popular & applied graphic art items 110,000; Posters 80,000
Special Subjects: Americana
Collections: Archive of Hispanic Culture; Japanese Prints; †Pennell Collection of Whistleriana; †Civil War drawings, prints, photographs & negatives †early American lithographs; †pictorial archives of early American architecture; †Historic American Buildings Survey; Historic American Engineering Record; Cabinet of American Illustration; †original fine prints of all schools & periods; Yanker Collection of Propaganda posters; †originally designed posters for all periods, dating 1840s - present; Seagram County Court House Collection: †Swann Collection of Caricatures & Cartoons; †American Political Cartoons; †outstanding among the collection of photographs & photographic negatives are the Brady-Handy Collection, Farm Security Administration Collection, Alexander Graham Bell Collection, Arnold Genthe, J C H Grabill, F B Johnston, Tony Frissell, Detroit Photographic Co, W H Jackson Collection, George Grantham Bain Collection, H E French Washington Photographs, Matson Near Eastern Collection; NY World-Telegram & Sun, US News & World Report; †Presidential, †geographical, †biographical & †master photograph groupings, captured German photographs of the WW II period & panorama photographs
Exhibitions: Permanent collection
Publications: A Century of Photographs, 1846-1946; American Prints in the Library of Congress; American Revolution in Drawings & Prints; Graphic Sampler; Historic America: Buildings, Structures & Sites; Historic American Buildings Survey; Middle East in Pictures; Viewpoints; Special Collections in the Library of Congress; Fine Prints in the Library of Congress; The Poster Collection in the Library of Congress; Popular & Applied Graphic Art in the Library of Congress

M **MARINE CORPS MUSEUM,** Art Collection, Marine Corps Historical Ctr, Bldg 58 Washington Navy Yard, 20374. Tel 202-433-3840; FAX 202-433-7265; *Dir* E H Simmons; *Deputy Dir* Colonel W J Davis; *Cur Art* J T Dyer
Open Mon - Sat 10 AM - 4 PM, Sun & holidays Noon - 5 PM. No admis fee. Estab 1970, special exhibit gallery for major art & artifacts shows. Large 20 ft x 100 ft gallery available for temporary exhibits; maintains 30,000 volume library directly relating to military & Naval history; art is in hanging storage throughout Marine Corps Historical Center, HQMC & Pentagon; maintains reference library. Average Annual Attendance: 25,000
Income: Financed by US government
Collections: Marine Corps art (original art work by, of & about Marines with the major emphasis of the collection on the Vietnam War & peace time operations); military music; personal papers; combat art, historical illustrations, prints cartoons, recruiting posters, sculptures
Publications: Exhibit publications
Activities: Vis lectr varies per year; awards given through Marine Corps Historical Foundation; research grants; individual paintings & original art objects lent, request are handled individually, internal (USMC & government) & external (museums, etc); lending collection contains books, color reproductions, original art work, original prints, paintings, photographs & sculptures; book traveling exhibition; museum shop sells books, magazines, art reproductions, art prints, jewelry, shirts, videos, office & household items

M **MERIDIAN INTERNATIONAL CENTER,** Cafritz Galleries, 1624-30 Crescent Pl NW, 20009. Tel 202-939-5568; FAX 202-319-1306; Elec Mail meridian@dgs.dgsys.com. *Pres, Ambassador* Walter L Cutler; *VPres for Develop* Patricia Johnson; *VPres for Mgt* Bruce Clark; *VPres for Arts* Nancy Matthews
Open Wed - Sun 2 - 5 PM. Estab 1960 to promote international understanding through exchange of ideas & the arts. 3000 sq ft, 5 rooms in renovated historic mansion. Average Annual Attendance: 20,000. Mem: donations
Income: Financed by endowment & contributions
Exhibitions: (1997) Imagining the World through Native Art; Europe Vivante; A Winding River: The Journey to Contemporary Art in Vietnam
Publications: Exhibit catalogues; newsletter, 3 per year
Activities: Lect open to public, 2-3 vis lect per year

M **NATIONAL ACADEMY OF SCIENCES,** Arts in the Academy, 2101 Constitution Ave, NW, 20418. Tel 202-334-2436; FAX 202-334-1687; *Dir* Fredrica W Wechsler
Open Mon - Fri 9 AM - 5 PM. No admis fee
Exhibitions: (1997) Betsy Bauer (painting); Christopher Pelley (painting)
Activities: Concerts; individual paintings & original objects of art lent to other galleries

M **NATIONAL AIR AND SPACE MUSEUM,** Sixth & Independence Ave SW, 20560. Tel 202-357-2700, 357-1745; *Dir* Donald D Engen; *Public Relations* Mike Fetters
Open daily 10 AM - 5:30 PM, cl Dec 25. No admis fee. Estab 1946 to memorialize the national development of aviation & space flight. One gallery comprised of 5000 sq ft devoted to the theme, Flight & the Arts. Average Annual Attendance: 8,000,000
Income: Financed through the Smithsonian Institute
Collections: Paintings, prints & drawings include: Alexander Calder, Lamar Dodd, Richard Estes, Audrey Flack, Francisco Goya, Lowell Nesbitt, Robert

Rauschenberg, James Wyeth; major sculptures by Richard Lippold, Alejandro Otero, Charles Perry; Stuart Speiser Collection of Photo Realist Art
Exhibitions: Exhibitions change annually. (1997) Star Wars (film trilogy)
Publications: Various publications relating to aviation & space science
Activities: Educ dept; handicapped services; regional resource program; lect open to public, 15-20 vis lectr per year; concerts; gallery talks; tours; scholarships offered; individual paintings & original objects of art lent to non-profit educational institutions; book traveling exhibitions; originate traveling exhibitions; museum shop sells books, magazines, reproductions, prints, slides, posters, stamp covers, kites, models & jewelry

L **Library MRC 314,** Sixth & Independence Ave SW, 20560. Tel 202-357-3133; *Reference Librn* Paul McCutcheon
Open Mon - Fri 10 AM - 4 PM. Estab 1972 to support research in aerospace field; Library is part of the Smithsonian Institution Libraries system. For reference. Average Annual Attendance: 4000
Income: Financed by federal funds
Library Holdings: Vols 40,000; Per subs 300; Micro — Fiche 200,000, reels 2000
Special Subjects: Ballooning (prints), Earth & Aerospace, Astronomy and Planetary Science
Collections: Aerospace Event Files; Aviation & Space Art; Illustrated Sheet Music; Archives of Personalities
Publications: NASM Library Guide; NASM Library Periodical Index
Activities: Educ dept; classes for children; docent training; lect open to public; tours; awards; scholarships

NATIONAL ARCHITECTURAL ACCREDITING BOARD, INC
For further information, see National and Regional Organizations

NATIONAL ARTISTS EQUITY ASSOCIATION INC
For further information, see National and Regional Organizations

NATIONAL ASSEMBLY OF STATE ARTS AGENCIES
For further information, see National and Regional Organizations

NATIONAL ASSOCIATION OF ARTISTS' ORGANIZATIONS (NAAO)
For further information, see National and Regional Organizations

NATIONAL ENDOWMENT FOR THE ARTS
For further information, see National and Regional Organizations

M **NATIONAL GALLERY OF ART,** Constitution Ave at Fourth St NW, 20565. Tel 202-737-4215; FAX 202-842-2356; TDD 202-842-6176. *Chmn Board Trustees* Ruth Carter Stevenson; *Pres* Robert H Smith; *Dir* Earl A Powell III; *Deputy Dir* Alan Shestack; *Dean, Center for Advanced Study in Visual Arts* Henry A Millon; *Chief Librn* Neal Turtell; *Special Events Officer* Genevra Higginson; *Cur Photo Archives* Ruth Philbrick; *Cur American Art* Nicholai Cikovsky; *Cur Northern Baroque Painting* Arthur Wheelock; *Cur Renaissance Painting* David Brown; *Cur Southern Baroque Painting* Diane DeGrazia; *Sr Cur Print, Drawing & Sculpture* Andrew Robison; *Cur Sculpture* C Douglas Lewis; *Cur Educ* Linda Downs; *Chief of Design & Installation* Gaillard Ravenel; *Chief Photographic Services* Richard Amt; *Head Educ Resources Progs* Ruth Perlin; *Horticulture* Donald Hand; *Ed* Frances Smyth; *Chief Conservation* Ross Merrill; *Gallery Archivist* Maygene Daniels; *Secy & Gen Counsel* Philip C Jessup; *Treas* Ann Leven; *Registrar* Sally Freitag; *Coordr of Photography* Ira Bartfield; *Asst to Dir of Music* George Manos; *Public Information Officer* Ruth Kaplan; *Corporate Relations Officer* Elizabeth Perry; *Develop Officer* Laura Smith-Fisher; *Visitor Services* Sandra Creighton; *Public Sales Mgr* Keith Webb
Open Mon - Sat 10 AM - 5 PM; Sun 11 AM - 6 PM; cl Christmas & New Years Day. No admis fee. Administered by a board of trustees which consists of Chairman, US Chief Justice, US Secretary of State, Treasury, Smithsonian Institution, Robert Smith Alexander M Laughin & Ruth Carter Stevenson. Estab 1941; East Building opened 1978. West Building was a gift from Andrew W Mellon; the East Building was a gift of Paul Mellon, Ailsa Mellon Bruce & Andrew Mellon Foundation. Average Annual Attendance: 6,500,000
Income: Financed by private endowment & federal appropriation
Collections: The Andrew W Mellon Collection of 126 paintings & 26 pieces of sculpture includes Raphael's Alba Madonna, Niccolini-Cowper's Madonna & St George & the Dragon; van Eyck Annunciation; Botticelli's Adoration of the Magi; nine Rembrants. Twenty-one of these paintings came from the Hermitage. Also in the original gift were the Vaughan Portrait of George Washington by Gilbert Stuart & The Washington Family by Edward Savage. The Samuel H Kress Collection, given to the nation over a period of years, includes the great tondo The Adoration of the Magi by Fra Angelico & Fra Filippo Lippi, the Laocoon by El Greco & fine examples by Giorgione, Titian, Grunewald, Durer, Memling, Bosch, Francois Clouet, Poussin, Watteau, Chardin, Boucher, Fragonard, David & Ingres. Also included are a number of masterpieces of Italian & French sculpture; In the Widener Collection are paintings by Rembrandt, van Dyck & Vermeer, as well as major works of Italian, Spanish, English & French painting & Italian & French sculpture & decorative arts. The Chester Dale Collection includes masterpieces by Braque, Cezanne, Degas, Gauguin, Manet, Matisse, Modigliani, Monet, Picasso, Pissarro, Renoir, Toulouse-Lautrec, van Gogh & such American painters as George Bellows, Childe Hassam & Gilbert Stuart. Several major works of art by Cezanne, Gauguin, Picasso & the American painter Walt Kuhn were given to the Gallery in 1972 by the W Averell Harriman Foundation in memory of Marie N Harriman. Paintings to round out the collection have been bought with funds provided by the late Ailsa Mellon Bruce. Most important among them are: portrait of Ginevra de' Benci (the only generally acknowledged painting by Leonardo da Vinci outside Europe), Georges de la Tour's Repentant Magdalen, Picasso's Nude Woman-1910, Ruben's Daniel in the Lions' Den, Claude Lorrain's Judgment of Paris, St George & the Dragon attributed to Rogier van der Weyden & a number of American paintings, including Thomas Cole's second set of the Voyage of life. The National Gallery's rapidly expanding graphic arts holdings, in great part given by Lessing J Rosenwald, numbers about 50,000 items & dates from the 12th century to the present. The Index of American Design contains over 17,000 watercolor renderings & 500 photographs of American crafts & folk arts. The National Gallery's Collection continues to be built by private donation, rather than through government funds, which serve solely to operate & maintain the Gallery
Exhibitions: Temporary exhibitions from collections both in the United States & abroad
Publications: A W Mellon Lectures in the Fine Arts; Studies in the History of Art; exhibition catalogs; annual report; monthly calendar of events
Activities: Sunday lect by distinquished quest speakers & members of the staff are given throughout the year; the A W Mellon Lect in the Fine Arts are delivered as a series each spring by an outstanding scholar; concerts are held in the West Garden Court, West Building each Sunday evening between October & June at 7 PM without charge; general tours & lect are given in the Gallery by members of the Educ Dept throughout the week; special tours are arranged for groups; films on art are presented on a varying schedule; color slide programs, films & video cassettes on gallery exhibitions & collections, free of charge, free catalog; sponsors Metropolitan Opera auditions; programs to 4900 communities; exten dept provides art loans to galleries around the world; lending cllection contains books, cassettes, color reproductions, film strips, framed reproductions, Kodachromes, sculpture & slides; museum shop sells books, magazines, reproductions, prints, slides & video-cassettes

L **Library,** Constitution Ave at Fourth St NW, 20565. Tel 202-737-4215; FAX 202-408-8530; *Exec Librn* Neal Turtell; *Reader Services Librn* Lamia Doumato; *Catalogue Librn* Roger Lawson; *Acquisitions* Anna Rachwald
Open Mon Noon - 4:30 PM, Tues - Fri 10 AM - 4:30 PM. Estab 1941 to support the national curatorial, educational & research activities & serve as a research center for graduate & undergraduate students, vis scholars & researchers in the visual arts. Supports the research programs of the Center for Advanced Study in the Visual Arts. For reference only
Income: Financed by federal appropriations & trust funds
Library Holdings: Vols 225,000; Per subs 950; Vertical Files 125,000; Micro — Fiche, reels; AV — A-tapes; Other — Exhibition catalogs, manuscripts, pamphlets, photographs
Special Subjects: Western European & American art & architecture, illuminated manuscripts; surrealism, Leonardo da Vinci, auction catalogues
Collections: Art exhibition, art auction & private art collection catalogs; artist monographs; Leonardo da Vinci, catalogues raisonne
Publications: NGA Library Guide, 1994 & 1996
Activities: Library tours on request

L **Photographic Archives,** Constitution Ave at Fourth St NW, 20565. Tel 202-842-6027; FAX 202-789-2681; *Cur* Ruth Philbrick
Open daily 10 AM - 4:30 PM. Reference only
Library Holdings: Micro — Cards, fiche 5,807,800, prints, reels; Other — Photographs 1,375,000
Special Subjects: Black-white photographs & microforms of American & Western European art

L **Slide Library,** Constitution Ave at Fourth St NW, 20565. Tel 202-842-6099; FAX 202-408-8530; *Chief Slide Librn* Gregory P J Most
Library Holdings: CD-ROM 30; AV — Slides 165,000
Special Subjects: Graphic Arts, Western European & American painting & sculpture

L **Index of American Design,** Constitution Ave at Sixth NW, 20565. Tel 202-842-6605; FAX 202-842-6859; *Asst Cur* Carlotta Owens; *Asst Cur* Charles Ritchie
Open daily 10 AM - Noon & 2 - 4 PM. No admis fee. Acquired by National Gallery in 1943 to serve as a visual archive of American decorative arts, late 17th through 19th centuries. Study room with National Gallery print galleries available for exhibitions; offices; storeroom
Library Holdings: Watercolors 17,000; Micro — Fiche; Other — Photographs
Special Subjects: Architecture, Ceramics, Costume Design & Construction, Decorative Arts, Folk Art, Furniture, Glass, Jewelry, Religious Art, Silver, Textiles, Woodcarvings
Activities: Original objects of art lent to institutions complying with National Gallery lending rules; lending collection contains 11 slide programs available through National Gallery dept of exten programs

NATIONAL INSTITUTE FOR THE CONSERVATION OF CULTURAL PROPERTY
For further information, see National and Regional Organizations

NATIONAL LEAGUE OF AMERICAN PEN WOMEN
For further information, see National and Regional Organizations

M **NATIONAL MUSEUM OF AFRICAN ART,** 950 Independence Ave SW, 20560. Tel 202-357-4600; FAX 202-357-4879; *Acting Dir* Patricia L Fiske; *Chief Cur* Philip Ravenhill; *Pub Affairs Dir* Janice Kaplan
Open Mon - Sun 10 AM - 5:30 PM, cl Christmas Day. No admis fee. Estab 1964 to foster public understanding & appreciation of the diverse cultures & artistic achievements in Africa; museum joined the Smithsonian Institution in 1979. Moved in 1987 to the Smithsonian's new museum complex, the Quadrangle on the National Mall. Average Annual Attendance: 500,000
Income: $4,013,000 (financed by federal funding, mem & contributions)
Collections: African art works in wood, metal, ceramic, ivory & fiber (7000 objects); Eliot Elisofon Photographic Archives of 200,000 slides & 78,000 black & white photographs & 140,000 ft of motion picture film & videotape
Exhibitions: Permanent Exhibitions: Images of Power & Identity; The Art of the Personal Object; Purpose & Perfection: Pottery as a Woman's Art in Central Africa; The Ancient West African City of Benin, AD 1300-1897. (1997) Adire: Resist-Dyed Cloths of the Yoruba; Treasures of the Tervuren Museum: The Royal Museum of Central Africa, Tervuren, Belgium. (1997-98) The Nsukka Group: Tradition, Innovation & Experimentation in Nigerian Modern Art
Publications: Exhibition Catalogs; multimedia slide kit; pamphlets; booklets, videotapes
Activities: Classes for adults & children; docent training; lect open to public; concerts; gallery talks; films; tours; residency fellowship program; museum sales shop sells books, magazines, reproductions, prints, slides, quality crafts, original art, cassettes & CD's, jewelry & other imports from Africa

L **Branch Library,** 950 Independence Ave SW, 20560. Tel 202-357-4875; FAX 202-357-4879;
Internet Home Page Address www.siris.si.edu. *Librn* Janet L Stanley
Open Mon - Fri 9 AM - 5 PM. Estab 1971 to provide major resource center for African art and culture; Library is part of the Smithsonian Institution Libraries system. For reference only
Income: Financed through Smithsonian budget
Library Holdings: Vols 25,000; Per subs 200; Other — Clipping files, exhibition catalogs, pamphlets
Special Subjects: Afro-American Art, African Art: African artistic retentions in the New World
Publications: Libr Acquisitions List, monthly

M **NATIONAL MUSEUM OF AMERICAN ART,** Eighth & G Sts NW, 20560. Tel 202-357-1959; FAX 202-357-2528;
Internet Home Page Address http://www.nmaa.si.edu. *Dir* Elizabeth Broun; *Deputy Dir* Charles Robertson; *Chief Cur* Jacquelyn Serwer; *Renwick Gallery Cur-in-Charge* Ken Trapp; *Research & Scholars Center Chief* Rachel Allen; *Educ Prog Chief* Nora Panzer; *Registrar* Melissa Kroning; *Design & Production Chief* John Zelenik; *Admin Officer* Maureen Damaska; *External Affairs Chief* Robert Johnston; *Develop Officer* Katie Ziglar; *Info Technology Chief* Thornton Staples
Open daily 10 AM - 5:30 PM, cl Christmas. Estab 1829 & later absorbed by the Smithsonian Institution, it was designated the National Gallery of Art in 1906. The museum's name was changed to the National Collection of Fine Art in 1937 & in 1980, to the National Museum of American Art. With the largest collection of American art in the world, it is the leading center for study of the nation's heritage. Barney Studio House, administered by the museum, is a unique showplace built by artist Alice Pike Barney as her home, studio and salon; it is open for guided tours by reservation only and for special programs. Average Annual Attendance: 500,000
Income: $7,000,000 annually (financed by federal appropriation, gifts, grants & trust income)
Collections: All regions, cultures & traditions in the United States are represented in the museum's holdings, research resources, exhibitions & public programs. Colonial portraiture, 19th century landscapes, American impressionism, 20th century realism & abstraction, New Deal projects, sculpture, photography, graphic arts, works by African Americans, contemporary art & the creativity of self-taught artists are featured in the galleries. Major collections include those of Harriet Lane Johnston (1906), William T Evans (1907), John Gellatly (1929), the SC Johnson & Son Collection (1967), Container Corporation of America Collection (1984), Sara Roby Foundation Collection (1984), Herbert Waide Hemphill Jr Collection (1986) & the Patricia & Phillip Frost Collection. Research resources include 300,000 listings on the Inventory of American Painting & Sculpture
Exhibitions: A representative selection of works from the collection are on permanent display in the galleries, providing a comprehensive view of the varied aspects of American art. Most temporary exhibitions, some 12 per year, are originated by the staff, many as part of the program to investigate less well-known aspects of American art. They include both studies of individual artists & thematic studies. (1997) Singular Impressions: The Monotype in America; Miriam Shapiro: A Woman's Way; Pre-World War II Watercolors from the Collection; The Bard Brothers: Painting America Under Steam & Sail. (1997-98) The Paintings of Charles E Burchfield; Ansel Adams, A Legacy. (1998) Posters American Style
Publications: American Art, journal; calendar of events; quarterly member newsletter; major exhibitions are accompanied by authoritative publications; smaller exhibitions are accompanied by checklists & often brochures
Activities: The Office of Education Programs carries on an active program with the schools & the general public, offering imaginative participatory tours for children, as well as lect & symposia for adults. A research program in American art is maintained for vis scholars & training is carried on through internships in general museum practice & conservation; fels offered; circulates exhibitions throughout the United States on a regular basis

L **Library of the National Museum of American Art & the National Portrait Gallery,** Eighth & G Sts NW, 20560. Tel 202-357-1886; FAX 202-786-2565; *Chief Librn* Cecilia Chin; *Asst Librn* Patricia Lynagh
Open Mon - Fri 10 AM - 5 PM. Estab 1964 to serve the reference & research needs of the staff & affiliated researchers of the National Museum of American Art, The National Portrait Gallery, the Archives of American Art & other Smithsonian bureaus. Open to graduate students & other qualified adult researchers
Income: $160,000 (financed by federal appropriation)
Purchases: $65,000
Library Holdings: Vols 100,000; Per subs 900; Original documents; Micro — Fiche, reels; AV — V-tapes; Other — Clipping files, exhibition catalogs, manuscripts, pamphlets
Special Subjects: American Art, especially printing, drawing, sculpture & graphic arts; American History & Biography
Collections: Ferdinand Perret Art Reference Library: collection of scrapbooks of clippings & pamphlets; special section on California art & artists consisting of approximately 325 ring binders on art & artists of Southern California; vertical file of 400 file drawers of material on art & artists, with increasing emphasis on American art & artists

M **Renwick Gallery,** 17th St & Pennsylvania Ave NW, 20560. Tel 202-357-2531; FAX 202-786-2810; *Cur-in-Charge* Kenneth Trapp
Open daily 10 AM - 5:30 PM, cl Christmas. Designed in 1859 by architect James Renwick, Jr as the original Corcoran Gallery of Art, the building was renamed for the architect in 1965 when it was transferred by the Federal government to the Smithsonian Institution for restoration. Restored to its French Second Empire elegance after 67 years as the United States Court of Claims, the building has two public rooms with period furnishings, the Grand Salon & the Octagon Room, as well as eight areas for its permanent collection & temporary exhibitions of American crafts, design & decorative arts
Collections: American crafts, design & decorative arts
Exhibitions: (1997) The Renwick at Twenty-Five. (1997-98) Michael Lucero: Sculpture. (1998) The Arts & Crafts in Boston. (1998-99) Daniel Brush: Objects of Virtue; The Stonewares of Charles Fergus Binns

Publications: Major exhibitions are accompanied by publications, smaller exhibitions by checklists & brochures
Activities: Docent training; film programs; lect & workshops emphasizing the creative work of American craft artists; tours; concerts

M **NATIONAL MUSEUM OF AMERICAN HISTORY,** 14th St & Constitution Ave NW, 20560. Tel 202-357-2700; *Dir* Spencer Crew
Open daily 10 AM - 5:30 PM, cl Christmas Day. No admis fee. Estab 1964. The Mus, a bureau of the Smithsonian Institution, is devoted to the collection, care, study & exhibition of objects that reflect the experience of the American people. Average Annual Attendance: 6 million
Collections: Agriculture, armed forces, automobiles, †ceramics, †glass, locomotives, musical instruments, †numismatics, †philately, political history, †textiles
Exhibitions: American Encounters; American Pressed Pattern Glass; First Ladies: Political Role & Public Image; Yeoman F; The Tool Chest; From Parlor to Politics: Women & Reform in America; We the People: Winning the Vote; A More Perfect Union: Japanese Americans & the United States Constitution; Field to Factory: Afro-American Migration 1915 - 1940; What are Archives: Who Uses Archives; After the Revolution: Everyday Life in America; Information Age: People, Information & Technology; The Ceremonial Court; A Material World; Engines of Change: The American Industrial Revolution 1790 - 1860; Infantry Machine Guns in the United States Service 1861 - present.
Publications: Exhibition brochures & catalogs; related research publications
Activities: Classes for adults & children; docent training; internship & fellowship programs; lect open to public, 2 vis lectr per year; competitions; museum shop sells books, magazines, reproductions, prints & slides

A **Society for Commercial Archeology,** PO Box 2423, 20560. Tel 202-882-5424; Estab 1976 to promote pub awareness, exchange information & encourage selective conservation of the commercial landscape. Mem: 800; dues institutional $40, individual $25; annual meetings
Income: Financed by mem & dues
Publications: Journal, two times a year; newsletter, quarterly

L **Branch Library,** 14th St & Constitution Ave NW, 20560. Tel 202-357-2036, 357-2414; *Librn* Rhoda Ratner
Open Mon - Fri 9 AM - 5 PM. Library is part of the Smithsonian Institution Libraries system. Open to staff & vis scholars
Income: Financed through SIL budgets
Library Holdings: Vols 165,000; Per subs 450; Micro — Fiche, reels
Special Subjects: Carpets & Rugs, Decorative Arts, Furniture, Graphic Design, Historical Material, Metalwork, Photography, Pottery, Silver, Textiles, Historical Trade Literature

M **NATIONAL MUSEUM OF WOMEN IN THE ARTS,** 1250 New York Ave NW, 20005. Tel 202-783-5000; FAX 202-393-3235;
Internet Home Page Address http://www.nmwa.org. *Admin Dir* Rebecca Phillips-Abbott
Open Mon - Sat 10 AM - 5 PM, Sun Noon - 5 PM, cl Thanksgiving, Christmas & New Year's Day, group tours by appointment. Admis suggested donation adults $3, seniors, students & children $2. Estab 1981 to promote knowledge & appreciation of women artists through exhibits, publications, educ programs & library services. Maintains library. Average Annual Attendance: 120,000. Mem: 60,000
Income: Private non-profit
Collections: Over 15,000 works by women from the Renaissance to the present. Includes paintings, sculpture & pottery
Exhibitions: A History of Women Photographers (1997-98) American Indian Pottery: The Legacy of Generations; Establishing the Legacy: From the Renaissance to Modernism
Publications: Exhibit catalogs
Activities: Classes for adults & children; dramatic programs; docent training; films; lect open to public, 4 vis lectr per year; concerts; tours; individual paintings & original objects of art lent; book traveling exhibitions 1 per year; originate traveling exhibitions; museum shop sells books, prints & reproductions

L **Library & Research Center,** 1250 New York Ave NW, 20005. Tel 202-783-5000; FAX 202-393-3235; *Head Librn* Krystyna Wasserman; *Research Asst* Michelle Weber; *Library Asst* Leah Davis
Open Mon - Fri 10 AM - 5 PM, by appointment only. Admis suggested donation adults $3, srs & students $2. Estab 1982, to highlight the artistic achievement of women past, present & future. Gallery has over 1500 works by more than 500 artists from Renaissance to the present, in a variety of media. Average Annual Attendance: 95,000. Mem: 60,000; dues $20 & up
Library Holdings: Vols 8000; Per subs 60; AV — A-tapes 32, cassettes, slides, v-tapes; Other — Clipping files, exhibition catalogs, manuscripts, memorabilia, original art works, pamphlets, photographs, prints, reproductions, sculpture
Special Subjects: Asian Art, Bookplates & Bindings, Bronzes, Calligraphy, Ceramics, Crafts, Decorative Arts, Drawings, Embroidery, Etchings & Engravings, Jewelry, Laces, Baroque Art, Costumes, Hispanic Art
Collections: Irene Rice Pereira Library; Collection of Artists' Books; Collection of Bookplates; Archives of the International Festival of Women Artists in Copenhagen, Denmark, 1980
Activities: Lect; concerts; gallery talks; tours; original objects of art & individual paintings lent to museums; book traveling exhibitions 2-3 per year; originate traveling exhibition to museums; museum shop sells books, magazines, reproductions, prints, slides

M **NATIONAL PORTRAIT GALLERY,** F St at Eighth NW, 20560. Tel 202-357-2700; *Dir* Alan Fern; *Deputy Dir* Carolyn Carr; *Assoc Dir Admin* Barbara A Hart; *Cur Paintings & Sculpture* Ellen G Miles; *Chief Design & Production* Nello Marconi; *Cur Exhib* Beverly Cox; *Cur Photographs* Mary Panzer; *Cur Prints & Drawings* Wendy W Reaves; *Registrar* Suzanne Jenkins; *Keeper Catalog of American Portraits* Linda Thrift; *Ed Charles Willson Peale Papers* Lillian B Miller; *Conservator* Cindylou Ockershausen; *Chief Photographer* Rolland White; *Public Affairs Officer* Brennan Rash; *Publications Officer* Frances Stevenson
Open daily 10 AM - 5:30 PM, cl Dec 25. No admis fee. The National Portrait Gallery was estab by Act of Congress in 1962 as a mus of the Smithsonian Institution for the exhibition & study of portraiture depicting men & women who

have made significant contributions to the history, development & culture of the people of the United States. One of the oldest government structures in Washington, the former US Patent Office Building constructed between 1836 & 1867, on the very site which Pierre L'Enfant, in his original plan for the city, had designated for a pantheon to honor the nation's immortals. The first floor is devoted to changing exhibitions & images of performing artists & sports figures from the permanent collection. Second floor features the permanent collection of portraits of eminent Americans & the Hall of Presidents, containing portraits & associative items of our Chief Executives. Also houses a collection of photographs by Mathew Brady, silhouettes by Auguste Edouart & portrait sculptures by Jo Davidson. The two-story Victorian Renaissance Revival Great Hall on the third floor is used for special events & pub programs. The third floor mezzanine houses a permanent collection civil gallery with portraits, engravings & photographs. Average Annual Attendance: 414,000
Income: $3,000 (financed by federal appropriation & private contributions)
Collections: The collections, which are constantly being expanded, include portraits of significant Americans, preferably executed from life, in all traditional media: oils, watercolors, charcoal, pen & ink, daguerreotypes, photographs; portraits of American Presidents from George Washington to Bill Clinton 1600 original works of art from the Time Magazine Cover collection; more than 5000 glass plate negatives by Mathew Brady & studio in the Meserve Collection
Exhibitions: (1997) Image of the President: Photographs by George Tames; Red Hot & Blue: A Salute to American Musicals
Publications: Large-scale, richly illustrated publications accompany major shows & provide comprehensive analysis of exhibition themes; descriptive brochures about the gallery; documentary, audio & visual materials designed to be used as teaching guides; illustrated checklist; American portraiture; biographies
Activities: Outreach programs for elementary & secondary schools, senior citizens groups, hospitals & nursing homes; docent training; scheduled walk-in tours for special groups, adults, families & schools; programs for handicapped & other special audiences; films; lect; Cultures In Motion, (special musical & dramatic events); museum shop sells books, magazines, reproductions, recordings, CDs, cassettes, jewelry & gifts, prints, & slides

L **Library,** Ninth & G Sts NW, 20560. Tel 202-357-1886; FAX 202-633-9189; Elec Mail maars017.si.edu. *Chief Librn* Cecilia H Chin; *Asst Librn* Pat Lynagh; *Cataloger* Kimball Clark
Shared with the National Mus of American Art; see library entry under National Mus of American Art
Library Holdings: Vols 100,000; Per subs 900; Micro — Fiche, reels; Other — Clipping files, exhibition catalogs, manuscripts, reproductions

M **NATIONAL TRUST FOR HISTORIC PRESERVATION,** 1785 Massachusetts Ave NW, 20036. Tel 202-588-6000; FAX 202-588-6082; *Pres* Richard Moe
Open to the pub, hrs & fees vary with the property, cl Christmas, New Year's, call for information. Founded 1949, the National Trust for Historic Preservation is the only national, non-profit, private organization chartered by Congress to encourage pub participation in the preservation of sites, buildings & objects significant in American history & culture. Its services, counsel & educ on preservation & historic property interpretation & administration, are carried out at national & regional headquarters in consultation with advisors in each state & U S Territory. Mem: 265,000; dues sustaining $100, active $20, student $15
Income: Financed by mem dues, contributions & matching grants from the US Department of the Interior, National Park Service, under provision of the National Historic Preservation Act of 1966
Collections: Fine & decorative arts furnishing nine historic house museums: Chesterwood, Stockbridge, MA; Cliveden, Philadelphia, PA; Decatur House & Woodrow Wilson House, Washington, DC; Drayton Hall, Charleston, SC; Lyndhurst, Tarrytown, NY; Oatlands, Leesburg, VA; The Shadows-on-the-Teche, New Iberia, LA; Woodlawn/Pope-Leighey Plantation House, Mt Vernon, VA. (For additional information, see separate listings)
Publications: Preservation Magazine, bi-monthly

M **Decatur House,** 748 Jackson Pl NW, 20006. Tel 202-842-0920; FAX 202-842-0030; *Exec Dir* Paul Reber; *Asst Dir* Chris Slusher
Open Tues - Fri 10 AM - 2:30 PM, Sat & Sun Noon - 3:30 PM, cl Mon. Admis adults $4, students & senior citizens $2.50, National Trust Members free. Estab 1958, bequeathed to National Trust for Historic Preservation by Mrs Truxton Beale to foster appreciation & interest in the history & culture of the city of Washington, DC. The House is a Federal period townhouse designed by Benjamin Henry Latrobe & completed in 1819. Average Annual Attendance: 19, 000. Mem: National Trust members
Income: Financed by endowment & mem
Collections: Furniture & memorabilia of the Federal period; Victorian house furnishings
Exhibitions: Special exhibits
Activities: Lect open to public, 2-3 vis lectr per year; concerts; individual paintings & original objects of art lent; sales shop sells books, magazines, reproductions, prints & Christmas decorations

M **NAVAL HISTORICAL CENTER,** The Navy Museum, * Washington Navy Yard, 901 M St SE, 20374-0571. Tel 202-433-4882; FAX 202-433-8200; *Dir* Dr Oscar P Fitzgerald; *Assoc Dir* Claudia L Pennington; *Cur* Dr Edward Furgol; *Pub Prog* Susan Silverstein Scott
Open Sept - May Mon - Fri 9 AM - 4 PM, June - Aug daily 9 AM - 5 PM. Parking & admis free. Estab 1961 to present history & preserve heritage of US Navy. 48,000 sq ft exhibit area. Average Annual Attendance: 300,000
Income: Financed by federal appropriations
Collections: History of US Navy from 1775 to Space Age; Naval Art; Paintings; Prints; Watercolors; Naval Artifacts; Fighting Top of Constitution; WW II Corsair (744 plane)
Exhibitions: Changing art exhibitions; Polar Exploration; Perry & Japan; Submarine Museum Annex; WW II; Civil War
Activities: Docent training; tours; internships; individual paintings & original objects of art lent to public institutions; museum shop sells books, reproductions, prints, postcards, jewelry, t-shirts, models & nautical accessories

M **THE PHILLIPS COLLECTION,** 1600 21st St NW, 20009. Tel 202-387-2151, Ext 238/239, 387-3036 (membership); FAX 202-387-2436; Elec Mail phillipsco@aol.com. *Dir* Charles S Moffett; *Exec Asst to Dir* Johanna Halford-MacLeoud; *Chief Cur* Eliza Rathbone; *Cur* Elizabeth Hutton Turner; *Asst Cur* Katherine Rothkopf; *Asst Cur* Stephen Phillips; *Dir Music* Mark Carrington; *Registrar* Joseph Holbach; *Librn* Karen Schneider; *Dir Public Relations* Kristin Krathwohl; *Dir External Affairs* Marilyn Montgomery; *Dir Corporate & Foundation Relations* Joy Halinan; *Dir Finanical Affairs* Michael Bernstein; *Human Resources* Oscar Iraheta; *Visual Resources Coordr* Pamela Steele; *Educ Dir* Donna McKee; *Facilities & Security Mgr* Tom Gilleylen; *Dir Retail Operations* Thora Colet; *Dir Membership* Deana Ciatto
Open Tues - Sat 10 AM - 5 PM, Thurs 5 - 8:30 PM & Sun Noon - 7 PM, cl Christmas, Thanksgiving, July 4 & New Year's. Weekday admis is suggested contribution, weekend admis adults $6.50, senior citizens & studentd $3.25. Open to the pub 1921 to show & interpret the best of contemporary painting in the context of outstanding works of the past; to underscore this intent throught the presentation of concerts & lectures. The original building, a Georgian Revival residence designed in 1897 by Hornblower & Marshall, was added to in 1907 & renovated in 1983-84. A modern annex connected by a double bridge to the old gallery was opened to the public in 1960 & renovated in 1987-89. Average Annual Attendance: 150,000. Mem: 4000; dues corporate mem $10,000, $5000 & $500, individual $45-$5000 & up
Income: $4,000,000 (financed by endowment, mem, contributions, grants, sales, rental fees & exhibition fees)
Collections: 19th & 20th century American & European painting with special emphasis on units of particular artists such as Bonnard, Braque, Cezanne, Daumier, de Stael, Dufy, Rouault & Americans such as Avery, Dove, Gatch, Knaths, Marin, O'Keeffe, Prendergast, Rothko & Tack. The best known painting is Renoir's Luncheon of the Boating Party
Publications: The Phillips Collection: A Summary Catalogue; News & Events, bi-monthly; childrens guides; exhibition catalogs & brochures; membership brochures & communications
Activities: Classes for adults & children; lect open to public & to mem only, 10-15 vis lectr per year; weekly concerts; gallery talks; tours; individual paintings & original objects of art lent to national & international museums; book traveling exhibitions three per year; originate traveling exhibitions to national & international museums; museum sales shop sells books, magazines, reproductions, prints, slides, jewelry & original crafts

L **Library,** 1600 21st St NW, 20009. Tel 202-387-2151, Ext 212; FAX 202-387-2436; Elec Mail phillipsco@aol.com. *Chief Cur* Eliza Rathbone; *Librn* Karen Schneider
Available to serious students, researchers & mus professionals, by appointment. Reference only
Library Holdings: Vols 6500; Per subs 20; Vertical files; Micro — Reels 60; AV — Fs; Other — Clipping files, exhibition catalogs, pamphlets
Special Subjects: Aesthetics, Afro-American Art, Art Education, Art History, Asian Art, Collages, Decorative Arts, Drawings, Etchings & Engravings, Folk Art, Furniture, Graphic Arts, History of Art & Archaeology, Latin American Art, Mexican Art, Painting-American, Painting-Australian, Painting-British, Painting-Canadian, Painting-Dutch, Painting-European, Painting-Flemish, Painting-French, Painting-Italian, Painting- Japanese

M **MARJORIE MERRIWEATHER POST FOUNDATION OF DC,** Hillwood Museum, 4155 Linnean Ave NW, 20008. Tel 202-686-8500, 686-5807; FAX 202-966-7846; *Pres* Ellen MacNeile Charles; *Cur* Anne Odom; *Dir* Fred J Fisher
Open Tues - Sat 9:30 - 10:45 AM, 12:30 - 1:45 & 3 PM for tours. Admis adults $10, students $5, children under 12 not admitted. Estab 1977 to enable the general public to see extensive collection of Russian & French decorative art. Mansion in the Georgian style, home of the late Marjorie Merriweather Post, situated on 25 acres of landscaped grounds. Average Annual Attendance: 25,000. Mem: 300; dues $35-$50
Income: Financed by endowment & admis
Collections: French decorative arts, furnishings & memorabilia; Russian decorative arts
Publications: Notes on Hillwood
Activities: Lect open to public; concerts; gallery talks; tours; museum shop sells books, gifts, reproductions, prints & slides

PUBLIC LIBRARY OF THE DISTRICT OF COLUMBIA

L **Art Division,** Martin Luther King Memorial Library, 901 G St NW, 20001. Tel 202-727-1291; FAX 202-727-1129; *Dir Library* Dr Hardy R Franklin; *Chief Art Division* George McKinley-Martin
Open winter & summer Mon, Wed & Thurs 10 AM - 7 PM, Tues 10 AM - 9 PM, Fri & Sun 10 AM - 5:30 PM. No admis fee
Income: Financed by city government appropriation
Library Holdings: Vols 41,648; Per subs 95; Micro — Reels; Other — Clipping files, exhibition catalogs, pamphlets
Special Subjects: Aesthetics, Afro-American Art, American Indian Art, American Western Art, Antiquities-Assyrian, Antiquities-Byzantine, Antiquities-Egyptian, Antiquities-Etruscan, Antiquities-Greek, Antiquities-Oriental, Architecture, Art History, Asian Art, Bronzes, Calligraphy, Antiques, Collectibles
Collections: †Reference & circulating books & periodicals on architecture, painting, sculpture, photography, graphic & applied arts; †extensive pamphlet file including all art subjects, with special emphasis on individual American artists & on more than 1151 artists active in the area; †circulating picture collection numbering over 81,519 mounted reproductions
Exhibitions: Special exhibitions held occasionally

L **Audiovisual Division,** Martin Luther King Memorial Library, 901 G St NW, Room 226, 20001. Tel 202-727-1265; *Chief* Eric White
Open Mon - Thurs 9 AM - 9 PM, Fri 9 AM - 5:30 PM
Purchases: 16 mm, VHS
Library Holdings: Per subs 15; Books-on-tape; AV — Cassettes, motion pictures, rec, v-tapes

M SMITHSONIAN INSTITUTION, 1000 Jefferson Dr, 20560. Tel 202-357-2700; TTY 357-1729; Dial-a-Museum 357-2020 (English), 633-9126 (Spanish). *Secy* Ira Michael Heyman; *Under Secy* Constance Berry Newman; *Asst Secy Arts & Humanities* Tom Freudenheim; *Asst Secy for the Sciences* Dr Robert Hoffmann; *Asst Secy Educ & Pub Serv* James Early; *Asst Secy External Affairs* Thomas Lovejoy; *Asst Secy Institutional Initiatives* Alice Green Burnette; *Asst Secy Finance & Admin* Nancy Suttenfield; *Dir Traveling Exhib Serv* Anna Cohn
Open daily 10 AM - 5:30 PM, cl Dec 25. Estab 1846, when James Smithson bequeathed his fortune to the United States, under the name of the Smithsonian Institution, an establishment in Washington for the increase & diffusion of knowledge. To carry out the terms of Smithson's will, the Institution performs fundamental research; preserves for study & reference approx 140 million items of scientific, cultural & historical interest; maintains exhibits representative of the arts, American history, aeronautics & space exploration; technology; natural history & engages in programs of education & national & international cooperative research & training. The Smithsonian Institution is the world's largest museum complex composed of 14 museums & the National Zoo in Washington, DC & the Cooper-Hewitt, National Design Museum & the National Museum of the American Indian in New York City; see separate listings for complete information on the bureaus listed below. Average Annual Attendance: 26,000,000
Income: Financed by federal appropriations & private monies
Activities: Classes for adults & children; dramatic programs; docent training; lect open to the public; concerts; gallery talks; tours; awards; scholarships & fels; museum shops sell books, magazines, original art, reproductions, prints, slides & gifts; museum shop sells books, magazines, original art, reproductions, prints, slides, & gifts
 —**Anacostia Museum,** 1901 Fort Pl SE, 20020
 —**Archives of American Art,** AA-PG Bldg Smithsonian Inst, 20560
 —**Cooper-Hewitt Museum**
See separate entry in New York, NY
 —**Hirshhorn Museum & Sculpture Garden,** Seventh & Independence Aves, SW, 20560
 —**John F Kennedy Center for the Performing Arts,** 20566
Administered under a separate Board of Trustees
 —**National Air & Space Museum,** Seventh & Independence Ave, SW, 20560
 —**National Museum of American Art,** Eighth & G Sts, NW, 20560
Includes the Renwick Gallery
 —**National Gallery of Art,** Constitution Ave at Fourth St NW, 20565
 —**National Museum of American History,** 14th St & Constitution Ave, 20560
 —**National Portrait Gallery,** F St at Eighth, NW, 20560
 —**Arthur M Sackler Gallery,** 1050 Independence Ave SW, 20560
 —**Freer Gallery of Art,** Jefferson Dr at 12th St SW, 20560
 —**National Museum of African Art,** 20560
 —**National Museum of the American Indian**
See separate listing in New York, NY

M SOCIETY OF THE CINCINNATI, Museum & Library at Anderson House, 2118 Massachusetts Ave NW, 20008-2810. Tel 202-785-2040; *Museum Dir* Katheleen Betts; *Library Dir* Sandra L Powers
Open Tues - Sat 1 - 4 PM; Library open weekdays by appointment. No admis fee. Museum estab 1938. Serves as the National Headquarters Museum & Library of the Society of the Cincinnati. Average Annual Attendance: 10,000
Special Subjects: Etchings & Engravings, Manuscripts, Maps, Painting - American, Painting - British, Painting - European, Painting - French, Painting - Japanese, Period Rooms, Porcelain, Portraits, Sculpture, Silver, Tapestries, Textiles, American Revolution; Art of War, 18th Century
Exhibitions: Temporary exhibitions change every six months
Publications: Annual Report of the Museum & Library Directors
Activities: Docent training; concert series

SPECIAL LIBRARIES ASSOCIATION
For further information, see National and Regional Organizations

M STUDIO GALLERY, 2108 R St NW, 20008. Tel 202-232-8734; FAX 202-232-9222; Elec Mail studiog@erols.com. *Dir* June Linowitz; *Assoc Dir* Shira Keyes; *Co-Chmn* Micheline Frank; *Co-Chmn* Bob Monahan
Open Wed - Sat 11 AM - 5 PM, Sun 1 - 5 PM. No admis fee. Estab 1964 as a showcase for local artists. Average Annual Attendance: 20,000. Mem: 30; dues $920; monthly meetings
Income: Nonprofit
Activities: Lect open to public; gallery talks; individual paintings & original works of art lent

M SUPREME COURT OF THE UNITED STATES, US Supreme Court Bldg, One First St NE, 20543. Tel 202-479-3298; FAX 202-479-2926; *Cur* Gail Galloway; *Coll & Exhibits Coordr* Catherine Fitts; *Visitor Prog Coordr* Jane Yarborough; *Photograph Coll Coordr* Franz Jantzen
Open Mon - Fri 9 AM - 4:30 PM, cl federal holidays. No admis fee. Curator's office estab 1973. Two exhibit spaces on ground floor; portrait collection displayed on ground floor & in restricted areas of the building. Average Annual Attendance: 798,233
Collections: Portraits of all former Justices throughout history; marble busts of the Chief Justices and certain Associate Justices; historic images such as photos, etchings & drawings of the Justices & the architecture of the building; memorabilia, archival & manuscript materials on the Supreme Court history; 18th & 19th centuries American & English furniture & decorative arts
Exhibitions: Permanent & temporary exhibits
Publications: Exhibit brochures
Activities: Lect in the courtroom every hour on the half hour; continuously running film describing the functions of the Supreme Court; tours; individual paintings & original objects of art lent to museums & historical organizations; sales shop operated by Supreme Court Historical Society sells gift items

M TEXTILE MUSEUM, 2320 S St NW, 20008-4088. Tel 202-667-0441; FAX 202-483-0994; *Pres & Board Trustees* David Fraser; *Dir* Ursula E McCracken; *Cur Eastern Hemisphere* Carol Bier; *Cur Western Hemisphere* Ann P Rowe
Open Mon - Sat 10 AM - 5 PM, Sun 1 - 5 PM. No admis fee, suggested contribution $5. Estab 1925 to further the understanding of mankind's creative achievements in textile arts. Mus is devoted exclusively to the handmade textile arts. Average Annual Attendance: 35,000. Mem: 3600; dues Mid-Atlantic & foreign $50, national $45, students $25
Income: Financed by endowment, mem & grants
Collections: Collection of oriental carpets including, Caucasian, Chinese, Egyptian (Mamluk), Persian, Spanish & Turkish; Collections of African, Chinese, Coptic, India, Indonesian, Islamic, pre-Columbian Peruvian & 20th century ethnographic textiles
Exhibitions: (1997) Looping & Knitting, A History; Avant Garde by the Yard
Publications: The Textile Museum Bulleting, quarterly membership newsletter; The Textile Museum Journal, semiannual
Activities: Workshops for adults & children; seminars & demonstrations; lect open to public, 50 vis lectr per year; concerts; gallery talks; tours; individual textiles & original objects of art lent; originate traveling exhibitions; museum shop sells books, magazines, original art, ethnographic textiles, jewelry & one of a kind items

L Arthur D Jenkins Library, 2320 S St NW, 20008. Tel 202-667-0441; FAX 202-483-0994; *Librn* Mary Mallia Samms
Open Wed - Fri 10 AM - 2 PM. Estab 1925 as a reference library dealing with ancient & ethnographic textiles & rugs of the world
Income: Financed by endowment, mem & gifts
Library Holdings: Vols 15,000; Per subs 164; AV — Cassettes, slides, v-tapes; Other — Clipping files, exhibition catalogs, manuscripts, pamphlets, photographs
Special Subjects: Afro-American Art, American Indian Art, Anthropology, Antiquities-Assyrian, Antiquities-Byzantine, Archaeology, Architecture, Art Education, Art History, Asian Art, Carpets & Rugs, Costume Design & Construction, Crafts, Decorative Arts, Embroidery, Textile Techniques
Collections: Art, Costume, Cultural History; Rugs & Textiles of the traditional Cultures of the Americas, Asia, Africa, the Middle East & the Pacific Rim

L TRINITY COLLEGE LIBRARY, 125 Michigan Ave NE, 20017. Tel 202-884-9351; FAX 202-884-9362; *Dir* Karen Leider; *Pub Serv* Christel Vonderscheer; *Periodicals* Doris Gruber
Open during school semesters, Mon - Thurs 9 AM - 11 PM, Fri 9 AM - 8 PM, Sat 10 AM - 5 PM, Sun Noon - 11 PM. Estab 1897 as an undergraduate college library, serving the college community
Income: $253,548 (financed by college budget)
Library Holdings: Vols 175,000; Per subs 600; Micro — Reels; AV — Cassettes, slides
Special Subjects: Art collection in both books & slides is general in content, including works on painting, sculpture & architecture principally

M UNITED STATES CAPITOL, Architect of the Capitol, 20515. Tel 202-228-1222; *Acting Architect of the Capitol* William L Ensign; *Chief Cur* Dr Barbara A Wolanin
Open daily 9 AM - 4:30 PM. No admis fee. Cornerstone layed 1793. Capitol is working building with mus value. Restored historic chambers; paintings & sculptures scattered through rooms & halls of Congress; reference library. Average Annual Attendance: 1,500,000
Income: Financed by United States Congressional appropriation & appropriate donations
Collections: Works by Andrei, Brumidi, Crawford, Cox, Franzoni, French, Greenough, Leutze, Peale, Powers, Rogers, Trumbull, Vanderlyn, Weir; 800 paintings & sculptures, manuscripts, 60,000 photographs & 100,000 architectural drawings
Exhibitions: Art & Architecture of the United States Capitol, changes periodically. Congressional Student Annual Exhibition; Hall of the House of Representatives; changing exhibitions sponsored by Members of Congress
Publications: Art in the Capitol, periodically; catalog of collections; occasional pamplets & books; press releases
Activities: US Capitol Guide Service tours; fellowships offered

A UNITED STATES COMMISSION OF FINE ARTS, Pension Bldg, Ste 312, 441 F St NW, 20001. Tel 202-504-2200; FAX 202-504-2195, 347-1906; *Chmn* J Carter Brown; *Secy* Charles H Atherton
Open daily 8:30 AM - 5 PM. Estab by Act of Congress in 1910 to advise the President, members of congress & various governmental agencies on matters pertaining to the appearance of Washington, DC. The Commission of Fine Arts is composed of seven members who are appointed by the President for four-year terms. Report issued periodically, principally concerned with architectural review. Plans for all new projects in the District of Columbia under the direction of the Federal & District of Columbia Governments which affect the appearance of the city & all questions involving matters of design with which the Federal Government may be concerned must be submitted to the Commission for comment & advice before contracts are made. Also gives advice on suitability of designs of private buildings in certain parts of the city adjacent to the various departments & agencies of the District & Federal Governments, the Mall, Rock Creek Park & Georgetown
Income: Financed by annual appropriations enacted by Congress
Publications: 15 publications on area architecture, 1964-1978; Commission of Fine Arts, 1910-1985

M US DEPARTMENT OF STATE, Diplomatic Reception Rooms, 2201 C St NW, 20520. Tel 202-647-1990; FAX 202-736-4231; Tour reservations 202-647-3241. *Dir* Gail F Serfaty; *Museum Technician* Todd Sudbrink; *Fine Arts Support Specialist* Patricia Heflin; *Chmn Fine Arts Committee* John F W Rogers
Open for three public tours by reservations only Mon - Fri 9:30 AM, 10:30 AM & 2:45 PM. No admis fee. Estab 1961 to entertain foreign dignitaries. These rooms allow foreign & American visitors to view furniture & art of the American & Federal periods. Furnished in 18th & early 19th Century American furniture, silver, Chinese export porcelain, antique Oriental rugs, American portraits & paintings, Tour Mon - Fri. Average Annual Attendance: 100,000
Income: Financed by private donations, foundation & corporate grants & loans of furnishings & paintings
Purchases: American Fine & decorative arts
Collections: †American furniture 1740-1825; †American portraits & paintings; †American silver; †Chinese export porcelain
Publications: Treasures of the US Dept of State; PBS documentary film: America's Heritage

UNITED STATES DEPARTMENT OF THE INTERIOR, Indian Arts & Crafts Board
For further information, see National and Regional Organizations

M **UNITED STATES DEPARTMENT OF THE INTERIOR MUSEUM,** 1849 C St NW, MS-1221, Dept of the Interior, 20240. Tel 202-208-4743; FAX 202-208-6950; Elec Mail dberke@ios.gov. *Museum Cur* Debra Berke; *Museum Specialist* Anne James; *Museum Specialist* Kim Robinson
Open Mon - Fri 8 AM - 5 PM. No admis fee. Estab 1938 to explain through works of art & other media the history, aims & activities of the Department. Museum occupies one wing on the first floor of the Interior Department Building. Average Annual Attendance: 26,000
Income: Federally funded
Collections: Leland Curtis (paintings); Colburn Collection of Indian basketry; collection of Indian, Eskimo, South Sea Islands & Virgin Islands arts & crafts, documents, maps, charts, etc; Gibson Collection of Indian materials; Indian arts & crats; murals; dioramas of Interior history scenes; oil paintings of early American survey teams by William Henry Jackson; oil paintings of western conservation scenes by Wilfrid Swancourt Bronson; sculpture groups; watercolor & black & white illustrations; wildlife paintings by Walter Weber
Exhibitions: Changing exhibits gallery at museum entrance has new exhibits every three months; Permanent exhibits include: Overview of Interior history & activities; architectural history of the headquarters building; interpretation of a turn of the century totem pole
Activities: Educ dept; lect open to public, 10-12 vis lectr per year; gallery talks; tours

M **UNITED STATES NAVY,** Art Gallery, Bldg 67, Washington Navy Yard, Ninth & M St SE, 20374-5060. Tel 202-433-3815; FAX 202-433-9553; *Acting Cur* Lisa Rayse
Open Mon - Fri 8 AM - 4 PM. Estab 1941. Average Annual Attendance: 3000
Income: Financed by Naval Historical Center
Collections: Graphic arts, paintings, sketches
Exhibitions: US Naval History
Publications: United States Navy Combat Art
Activities: Lending collection contains original objects of art

A **UNITED STATES SENATE COMMISSION ON ART,** United States Capitol Bldg, Rm S-411, 20510-7102. Tel 202-224-2955; Elec Mail curator@sec.senate.gov;
Internet Home Page Address senate.gov/curator/index.html. *Chmn* Trent Lott; *VChmn* Thomas A Daschle; *Cur* Diane Skvarla; *Coll Mgr* John B Odell; *Registrar* Melinda K Smith; *Museum Specialist* Richard L Doerner; *Adminr* Scott M Strong
Rooms in Capitol under jurisdiction of Commission are open daily 9 AM - 4:30 PM. No admis fee. Commission estab 1968 to acquire, supervise, hold, place & protect all works of art, historical objects & exhibits within the Senate wing of the United States Capitol & Senate Office Buildings. Average Annual Attendance: 3,000,000
Income: Financed by United States Senate appropriation
Collections: Paintings, sculpture, historic furnishings & memorabilia located within the Senate wing of the Capitol & Senate Office Buildings; Preservation Projects: Old Senate & Old Supreme Court Chamber restored to their appearances 1850
Exhibitions: Senate Art & Stamps; The Supreme Court of the United States, the Capitol Years 1801-1935; Isaac Bassett, The Venerable Doorkeeper, 1831-1895; The Political Cartoons from Puck
Publications: The Senate Chamber 1810-1859; The Supreme Court Chamber 1810-1860; A Necessary Fence: The Senate's First Century; An Assembly of Chosen Men: Popular Views of the Senate's Chambers 1847-1886; U S Senate graphic Arts Collection: An Illustrated Checklist
L **Reference Library,** United States Capitol Bldg, Rm S-411, 20510-7102. Tel 202-224-2976; Elec Mail curator@sec.senate.gov;
Internet Home Page Address senate.gov/curator/index.html. *Cur* Diane Sklarva
A reference collection on fine & decorative arts; supplemented by the United States Senate Library
Income: $1000 (financed by United States Senate appropriation to the Commission)
Library Holdings: Vols 250,000; Per subs 30; Micro — Cards; AV — Slides; Other — Clipping files, exhibition catalogs, manuscripts, memorabilia, pamphlets, photographs
Special Subjects: Architecture, Decorative Arts, United States Senate

M **WASHINGTON CENTER FOR PHOTOGRAPHY,** 406 Seventh St NW, 20004. Tel 202-737-0406; FAX 202-737-0419; *Exec Dir* Cynthia Rowland
Open Wed - Sat Noon - 6 PM, cl Sun, Mon & Tues. No admis fee. Estab 1986 as an educational resource center. Office space, 1200 sq ft of exhibition wall space. Average Annual Attendance: 5000. Mem: 300; dues $25-$1000 ; annual meeting in Aug
Income: Financed by mem & grants
Publications: Contact, periodic; Update, quarterly
Activities: Classes for adults; workshops; lect open to public, 1-2 vis lectr per year; gallery talks; competitions; exhibitions; portfolio review; book traveling exhibitions semi-annually

WASHINGTON SCULPTORS GROUP
For further information, see National and Regional Organizations

M **WESLEY THEOLOGICAL SEMINARY CENTER FOR THE ARTS & RELIGION,** Dadian Gallery, 4500 Massachusetts Ave, NW, 20016. Tel 202-885-8674; FAX 202-885-8683; *Artistic Dir* Catherine Kapinan; *Admin Dir* Elly Sparks Brown; *Cur* Deborah Soklove
Open Mon - Fri 11 AM - 7 PM. No admis fee. Estab 1989 to provide visual demonstration of intrinsic relationship between art & religion. Average Annual Attendance: 5000
Income: $40,000 (financed by gifts & grants, subsidized partly by parent institution)

Exhibitions: (1997) The Prodigal Son; Portraits on the Street (photographs); Kidstuff, Homestuff & Other Stuff: Porcelaines by Ginger Geyer
Activities: Classes for adults; dramatic programs; poetry readings; dance & music concerts; lect open to public, 5 vis lectr per year; lending collection contains paintings & art objects; book traveling exhibitions; originate traveling exhibitions

M **WHITE HOUSE,** 1600 Pennsylvania Ave NW, 20500. Tel 202-456-2550; FAX 202-456-6820; *Cur* Rex W Scouten; *Assoc Cur* Betty C Monkman
Open Tues - Sat 10 AM - Noon, cl Sun, Mon & most holidays. No admis fee
Income: Financed by federal government appropriation
Collections: †18th & 19th century period furniture; 18th, 19th & 20th century †paintings & †prints; †glassware; †manuscripts; †porcelain; †sculpture
Exhibitions: Temporary & permanent exhibits on White House & its collections
Publications: Art in the White House: A Nation's Pride; The First Ladies; The Living White House; The President's House: A History; The Presidents of the United States; Thite House Glassware: Two Centuries of Presidential Entertaining; The White House: A Historic Guide; White House History, magazine

M **WOODROW WILSON HOUSE,** 2340 S St, NW, 20008. Tel 202-387-4062; FAX 202-483-1466; Elec Mail wilsondc@worldweb.net. *Dir* Michael T Sheehan; *Asst Dir* Frank J Aucella
Open Tues - Sun 10 AM - 4 PM, cl Mon. Admis adults $5, students & senior citizens $4, National Trust members free. Estab 1963, owned by the National Trust for Historic Preservation, it works to foster interest & appreciation of the 28th President, Woodrow Wilson. Wilson House is a 1915 Georgian-Revival townhouse designed by Waddy B Wood, with formal garden. From 1921 it served as the home of President & Mrs Wilson. Average Annual Attendance: 16,000. Mem: 350; dues $35 & up
Income: Financed by endowment, mem, admis, sales & fundraising
Collections: Early 20th century art, furnishings, clothing; presidential memorabilia; decorative arts
Publications: Woodrow Wilson News, quarterly
Activities: Provide lect; individual paintings & objects of art lent to qualified museums; museum shop sells books & reproductions

FLORIDA

BELLEAIR

A **FLORIDA GULF COAST ART CENTER, INC,** 222 Ponce de Leon Blvd, 34616. Tel 813-584-8634; FAX 813-586-0782; *Exec Dir* Ken Rollins; *Cur Educ* Elaine Georgilas; *Registrar* Rebecca Kiphuth; *Controller* Edgardo Leon; *Admin Asst* Sue Cimerman
Open Mon - Fri 10 AM - 4 PM, Sat & Sun Noon - 4 PM, cl holidays. No admis fee, donations accepted. Estab 1936 as a regional center for the visual arts. Gallery has 2200 sq ft of space, teaching studio classrooms 8000 sq ft. Average Annual Attendance: 35,000. Mem: 800; dues $35-$1000
Income: Financed by tuition, mem dues, donations, grants & endowment
Purchases: Contemporary Florida Art
Collections: American Fine Crafts; Contemporary Florida Art
Exhibitions: Average 15 exhibitions per year including regional artists, traveling exhibits & those organized by Art Center
Publications: Bulletin, bi-monthly newsletter; catalogue; exhibition brochures
Activities: Book traveling exhibitions 2 per year
L **Art Reference Library,** 222 Ponce de Leon Blvd, Belleair, 34616. Tel 813-584-8634; FAX 813-586-0782; *Cur Educ* Elaine Georgilas
Open Tues - Sat 10 AM - 4 PM, Sun 2 - 5 PM, cl Aug. Estab 1949 to provide reference material & current periodicals to Art Center members & students. Average Annual Attendance: 8000. Mem: 1300; dues $20 and up; annual meeting in March or April
Library Holdings: Vols 1200; Per subs 3; AV — Fs, slides; Other — Exhibition catalogs

BOCA RATON

A **BOCA RATON MUSEUM OF ART,** 801 W Palmetto Park Rd, 33486. Tel 561-392-2500; FAX 561-391-6410; *Pres* Norman Codo; *Exec VPres* William Wolgin
Open Tues, Thurs & Fri 10 AM - 4 PM, Wed 10 AM - 9 PM, Sat & Sun Noon - 4 PM, cl Mon & holidays. Admis adults $3, seniors $2, students $1, members & children under 12 free. Estab 1951 to foster & develop the cultural arts. Large Main Gallery, mus shop contained in one building. Second building houses art school & storage. 4500 sq ft expansion houses a permanent collection. Average Annual Attendance: 40,000. Mem: 2036; dues single $45, family $65; annual meeting in Apr
Income: Financed by mem, fundraising, art school & grants
Collections: John J Mayers Collection, works by Braque, Demuth, Glackens, Matisse & Picasso; Photography from 19th century to present; African & Pre-Columbian art & contemporary sculpture
Exhibitions: Changes every 4-6 weeks; state-wide competition & show; annual outdoor art festival
Publications: Exhibition catalogues; quarterly newsletter
Activities: Classes for adults & children; docent training; lect for members & guests; tours; juried exhibition; national outdoor art festival with awards given for Best in Show & Merit; museum shop sells books, original art, reproductions, prints
L **Library,** 801 W Palmetto Park Rd, 33486. Tel 561-392-2500; *Dir Communications* Mary Jane Wood
Open Tues, Thurs & Fri 10 AM - 4 PM, Wed 10 AM - 9 PM, Sat & Sun Noon - 4 PM, cl Mon. Estab 1970
Library Holdings: Vols 4000

M FLORIDA ATLANTIC UNIVERSITY, Ritter Art Gallery, 777 Glades Rd, PO Box 3091, 33431-0991. Tel 561-367-2660; *Dir* Robert Watson
Open Tues - Fri 10 AM - 4 PM. No admis fee. Estab 1970 to provide exhibit space for faculty & students & to provide an opportunity to bring to the area exhibits which would expand the cultural experience of the viewers. Gallery is located at the center of the University campus. Average Annual Attendance: 15,000
Income: Financed by city, state & county appropriations & student activities fees
Collections: Slide collection; student work
Exhibitions: Annual juried student show; faculty & former students; work from area junior colleges; traveling exhibitions; Dre Devens: Dutch Constructivist; Arnulf Rainer: the Self -Portraits; Jan Schoonhoven: A Retrospective
Publications: We Call This Art, newsletter; exhibit catalogues
Activities: Classes for adults; dramatic programs; lect open to public & some for members only; concerts; gallery talks; tours; competitions with awards; originate traveling exhibitions; traveling exhibitions organized & circulated

M INTERNATIONAL MUSEUM OF CARTOON ART, 200 Plaza Real, PO Box 1643, 33429. Tel 407-391-2200; *Chmn* Mort Walker; *Pres* Joseph D'Angelo; *Dir Develop* Fritz Jellinghaus
Estab 1974 to make available to the general public the largest cartoon collection
Income: Financed by contributions & earned income
Collections: Animated Film Collection, videotape; Cartoon Hall of Fame; Comics collection from 1896 to the present; early and contemporary original cartoon art
Exhibitions: Original artwork from all of the various genres of illustration Peanuts Retrospective; Uncle Sam; Defenders of the Earth; Disney '86/'87
Publications: Tad Dorgan, Story of America in Cartoons; Dick Tracy: The Art of Chester Gould
Activities: Classes for adults; docent training; lect open to public, 3 vis lectr per year; competitions; originate traveling exhibitions to community colleges, museums, historical societies & universities; museum shop sells books, magazines, original art, reproductions, prints & collectibles
L Library, PO Box 1643, 10573. Tel 407-391-2200; *Coll Mgr* Debra Hyman
Income: $160,000 (financed by contributions)
Library Holdings: Vols 1500; AV — Motion pictures, slides, v-tapes; Other — Clipping files, memorabilia, photographs, prints, reproductions
Collections: Archives collection
Activities: Celebrity Guest Cartoonist program

BRADENTON

A ART LEAGUE OF MANATEE COUNTY, Art Ctr, 209 Ninth St W, 34205. Tel 941-746-2862; *Office Mgr* Maureen Zaremba; *Office Asst* Ann Hall
Open Sept - July Mon - Fri 9 AM - 4:30 PM, cl Aug & holidays. No admis fee. Estab 1937 to offer opportunities in further educ in the visual arts by providing space for exhibitions, classes, demonstrations, critiques & the exchange of ideas & information by vis artists. Average Annual Attendance: 25,000. Mem: 600; dues $5 & up; annual meeting in April
Exhibitions: Work by members & local artists one person shows & circulating exhibitions changing at three week intervals from Oct to May
Activities: Art school instruction in painting, drawing, clay techniques & variety of handcrafts; creative development for children; special art programs; gallery talks
L Library, Art League of Manatee County, 209 Ninth St W, 33505. Tel 813-746-2862; *Mgr* Maureen Zaremba; *Office Asst* Ann Medlin Hall
Open Mon - Fri 9 AM - 4:30 PM
Income: Financed by donations
Library Holdings: Vols 850; Other — Clipping files

CLEARWATER

M NAPOLEONIC SOCIETY OF AMERICA, Museum & Library, 1115 Ponce de Leon Blvd, 34616. Tel 813-586-1779; *Pres* Robert M Snibbe
Open 9 AM - 5 PM. No admis fee. Estab 1983. Mem: 1800; dues $36
Income: $309,199 (financed by mem)
Publications: Members bulletin, quarterly

CORAL GABLES

M UNIVERSITY OF MIAMI, Lowe Art Museum, 1301 Stanford Dr, 33124. Tel 305-284-3536; *Dir* Brian Dursum; *Cur Exhib* Denise Gersan; *Registrar* Susan Lucke
Open Tues - Sat 10 AM - 5 PM, Sun Noon - 5 PM, cl Mon. Admis general $4, senior citizens $3, students $2, members, University of Miami students & children under 6 free, group rates available. Estab 1952 to bring outstanding exhibitions & collections to the community & to the University; gallery maintained. Average Annual Attendance: 95,000
Collections: †African Art; Washington Allston Trust Collection; †Virgil Barker Collection of 19th & 20th Century American Art; Alfred I Barton Collection of Southwestern American Indian Art; Esso Collection of Latin American Art; Samuel H Kress Collection of Renaissance & Baroque Art; Samuel K Lothrop Collection of Guatemalan Textiles; Asian Art; †Pre-Columbian; American & European Paintings; Cintas Foundation Collection of Spanish Old Master Paintings
Exhibitions: Varied, changing exhibitions throughout the year.
Publications: Exhibition catalogs; newsletter, bimonthly
Activities: Classes for children; docent training; lect open to public, 6 vis lectr per year; concerts; gallery talks; tours; individual paintings & original objects of art lent to other museums; originate traveling exhibitions; museum shop sells books, magazines, ceramics, jewelry, children's art toys; decorative gifts
L Lowe Art Museum Reference Library, 1301 Stanford Dr, 33124-6310. Tel 305-284-3535, 284-2211; *Assoc Dir* Denise Gersan
For reference only
Library Holdings: Vols 5000; Per subs 1500; Micro — Cards; AV — Kodachromes, slides; Other — Clipping files, exhibition catalogs, photographs

Special Subjects: Art History
Publications: Newsletter, quarterly
Activities: Classes for children; docent training; lect open to public, 6 vis lectr per year; concerts; gallery talks; tours

DAYTONA BEACH

M DAYTONA BEACH COMMUNITY COLLEGE, Southeast Museum of Photography, 1200 International Speedway Blvd, PO Box 2811, 32120-2811. Tel 904-254-4475, 255-8131, Ext 3680; FAX 904-254-4487; *Dir* Alison Nordstrom
Open Tues 10 AM - 3 PM & 5 - 7 PM, Wed - Fri 10 AM - 3 PM, Sun 1 - 4 PM, cl Mon. Estab 1960
Collections: Photographic Collection of Karsch, Chartier - Breson, Friedlander, Perlmutter

M HALIFAX HISTORICAL SOCIETY, INC, Halifax Historical Museum, 252 S Beach St, 32114. Tel 904-255-6976; *Pres* Robert B Wood; *Pres Emeritus* William L Wood; *First VPres* Dr William Doremus; *Second VPres* Judge Shawn Briese; *Third VPres* William McKemie; *Acting Dir* Elizabeth B Baker
Open Tues - Sat 10 AM - 4 PM. Admis adult $2, children 12 & under $.50, members & children free on Sat. Estab 1949 to preserve & interpret history of the Halifax area. Ames Gallery contains modern art. Average Annual Attendance: 18,000. Mem: 423; dues $18 & up; annual meeting first Thurs in Jan
Income: Financed by dues, donations, grants, gift shop, fund raising
Collections: Digget Collection of wooden models of boats, cars & trains; †18th century Spanish & English artifacts; Indian arrowheads, canoe, pottery; racing memorabilia; Victorian clothing & furniture
Publications: Monthly newsletter, Six Columns & Fort New Smyrna; various pamphlets
Activities: Educ dept; lect open to public, 7 vis lectr per year; recognition plaques; tours; book traveling exhibitions 4 per year; museum shop sells books, magazines, reproductions, plates

M THE MUSEUM OF ARTS & SCIENCES INC, 1040 Museum Blvd, 32114. Tel 904-255-0285; FAX 904-255-5040; *Dir* Gary Russell Libby; *Cur* David Swoyer; *Registrar* Jennifer Perry
Open Tues - Fri 9 AM - 4 PM, Sat & Sun Noon - 5 PM, cl Mon & national holidays. Admis $4, museum members free. Estab 1971. Large hexagonal main exhibition galleries, hall gallery & lobby gallery are maintained; Mus includes Planetarium, A Frischer Sculpture Garden, Gallery of American Art, Root Hall & Gallery, Gallery of African Art, Gallery of Florida History & Prehistory of Florida Gallery. Average Annual Attendance: 160,000. Mem: 6000; dues $35; annual meeting in Dec
Income: $1,500,000 (financed by endowment, mem, city & county appropriations, donations, earned income)
Purchases: American Contemporary Art 1720-1900, American Decorative Arts, Cuban Art, European Art
Collections: Aboriginal Art including Florida Indian; African Art; American Art 1620-1900; American Fine Art; American Illustration: Norman Rockwell; Cuban Collection; Decorative arts including silver & furniture; Florida Contemporary Collection; Pre-Columbian Art
Publications: Arts & Sciences Magazine, 3 times per year; catalogs, monthly
Activities: Classes for adults and children; docent training; lect open to public, 15 vis lectr per year; gallery talks; concerts; tours; competitions with awards; scholarships offered; exten dept serves Volusia County; individual paintings & original objects of art lent to other museums, municipalities & public spaces; lending collection contains 1000 nature artifacts, 1000 original art works, 1000 original prints, paintings, photographs & sculptures; book traveling exhibitions 4 per year; origianle traveling exhibitions; museum shop sells books, magazines, original art, reproductions, prints
L Library, 1040 Museum Blvd, 32114. Tel 904-255-0285; *Librn* Marge Sigerson
Open to members & school children; reference library
Income: Financed by Mus
Purchases: Periodicals & reference materials
Library Holdings: Vols 10,000; Per subs 2000; AV — Slides, v-tapes; Other — Clipping files, exhibition catalogs, manuscripts, original art works, photographs, prints
Special Subjects: Aesthetics, Afro-American Art, American Indian Art, American Western Art, Anthropology, Archaeology, Architecture, Art Education, Art History, Asian Art, Bronzes, Calligraphy, Ceramics, Decorative Arts, Drawings, Cuban Art
Collections: Cuban: Jose Marti Library

DELAND

M DELAND MUSEUM OF ART, 600 N Woodland Blvd, 32720-3447. Tel 904-734-4371; *Exec Dir* Michael Sarden
Open Tues - Sat 10 AM - 4 PM, Sun 1 - 4 PM. Admis adults $2, children $1. Estab 1951 to provide art educ. Lower gallery: 12 ft carpeted walls, 3100 sq ft; upper gallery: 12 ft carpeted walls, 2100 sq ft. Average Annual Attendance: 15,000. Mem: 800; dues family $50, individual $30, senior citizens $25
Income: $152,000 (financed by mem, city & state appropriation & Volusia County)
Purchases: $1000
Collections: Contemporary Florida Artists 1900 - Present; North American Indian Baskets
Activities: Classes for adults & children; docent programs; lect open to public, 8 vis lectr per year; competitions with awards; book traveling exhibitions 1 per year; originate traveling exhibitions 5 per year; retail store sells books, original art & reproductions

M STETSON UNIVERSITY, Duncan Gallery of Art, Campus Box 8252, 32720. Tel 904-822-7266; Elec Mail khansen@suvax1.stetson.edu. *Dir* Gary Bolding
Open Mon - Fri 10 AM - 4 PM, Sat & Sun 1 - 4 PM. No admis fee. Estab 1964 as an educational gallery to augment studio teaching program. There is a large main gallery, 44 x 55 ft, with a lobby area 22 x 44 ft. Average Annual

Attendance: 10,000
Income: University art budget
Purchases: $1000
Collections: 20th Century American Prints, Ceramics, Drawings, Oils, Watercolors
Exhibitions: Various regional & national artists exhibitions; themed group exhibitions
Publications: Catalogs; monthly exhibition announcements
Activities: Lect open to public, 8 vis lectr per year, gallery talks; student competitions with prizes

DELRAY BEACH

M PALM BEACH COUNTY PARKS & RECREATION DEPARTMENT, Morikami Museum & Japanese Gardens, 4000 Morikami Park Rd, 33446. Tel 561-495-0233; FAX 561-499-2557; *Dir* Larry Rosensweig; *Cur* Thomas Gregersen; *Educ Dir* Reiko Nishioka; *Museum Store Mgr* Helene Buntman; *Admin Assoc* Debbie Towers; *Garden Cur* Bob Nelson; *Cur Exhib* Shoko Brown; *Dir Develop* Nancy N Goerler
Open Tues - Sun 10 AM - 5 PM, cl Mon & holidays. Admis adults $4.25, senior citizens $3.75, children 6-18 $2. Estab 1977 to preserve & interpret Japanese culture & Japanese-American culture. Five small galleries in Japanese style building & main museum building. Average Annual Attendance: 150,000. Mem: 850; dues $35; annual meeting June
Income: $650,000 (financed by mem & county appropriation)
Purchases: $9000
Collections: †Japanese folk arts (ceramics, dolls, tools, baskets, home furnishings); †Japanese art (paintings, prints, textiles); †Japanese-American historical & art objects
Exhibitions: (1997) Emblems of Celebration: An Exhibition in Recognition of the Morikami's 20th Anniversary; The Morikami Portraits; Photographs by Akira Suwa; Twenty Years of the Morikami
Publications: Newsletter, quarterly; Calendar bi-monthly; Exhibition catalogs 1-2 per yr
Activities: Classes for adults & children; docent training; lect open to public; concerts; tours; book traveling exhibitions biannually; originate traveling exhibitions; museum shop sells books, magazines, reproductions, prints & slides
L Donald B Gordon Memorial Library, Morikami Museum, 4000 Morikami Park Rd, 33446. Tel 561-495-0233; FAX 561-499-2557; *Coll Cur* Shoko Brown
Open by appointment. Estab 1977 to provide printed & recorded materials on Japan. For reference only
Income: Financed by donations
Purchases: $1000
Library Holdings: Vols 3000; Per subs 40; AV — Cassettes, fs, Kodachromes, rec, slides, v-tapes; Other — Clipping files, exhibition catalogs, memorabilia, pamphlets
Special Subjects: Anthropology, Antiquities-Oriental, Architecture, Asian Art, Calligraphy, Ceramics, Commercial Art, Costume Design & Construction, Crafts, Decorative Arts, Dolls, Ethnology, Film, Folk Art, Graphic Arts
Collections: Memorabilia of George S Morikami

FORT LAUDERDALE

L ART INSTITUTE OF FORT LAUDERDALE, Technical Library, 1650 SE 17th St, 33316. Tel 954-463-3000, Ext 541; FAX 954-463-1339; Elec Mail http://www.seflin.org.aifl. *Library-LRC Dir* Diane Rider; *Librn* Rick Fought; *Assoc Dir* Art McKinney
Open daily 7:45 AM - 5:15 PM. Estab 1973 as a techinical library for the applied & fine arts
Purchases: $8000
Library Holdings: Vols 1200; Per subs 157; AV — A-tapes, cassettes 50, fs, Kodachromes, motion pictures, v-tapes 600; Other — Clipping files 2000
Activities: Educ dept; lect open to public; competitions; scholarships & fels offered; sales shop sells books, prints & supplies

A BROWARD COUNTY BOARD OF COMMISSIONERS CULTURAL AFFAIRS DIVISON, 100 S Andrews Ave, 33301. Tel 954-357-7457; FAX 954-357-5769;
Internet Home Page Address http://www.co.broward.fl.us/arts.htm. *Dir* Mary A Becht; *Asst Dir* Michael G Brew; *Admin Asst* Will E Groves; *Public Serv Intern* Jennifer Clark; *Public Art & Design Asst* Doris Brown Penn; *Grants Adminr* Sara Nickels; *Grants Financial Analyst* Carole Lechoco; *Grants Asst* Hanan Okosh; *Marketing Adminr* Jody Horne-Leshinsky; *Marketing Asst* Ros Weiner; *FAU Marketing Intern* Marianne Schmandt
Estab 1976 to enhance the cultural environment of Broward County through development of the arts; develops & distributes government & private resources for the visual arts, performing arts, literary arts, museums & festivals; acts as the liaison between cultural organizations, all levels of government & the private sector in incouraging & promoting cultural development
Publications: Annual Calendar; Arts Education Directory; Cultural Directory; Cultural Quarterly; Cultural Treasures of Broward County Brochure; Voices & Venues Newsletter, bi-monthly
Activities: Scholarships & grants offered

M MUSEUM OF ART, FORT LAUDERDALE, One E Las Olas Blvd, 33301-1807. Tel 954-525-5500; FAX 954-524-6011; *Exec Dir* Dr Kenworth W Moffett; *Cur Coll* Jorge Santis; *Cur Exhib* Laurence Pamer
Open Tues, Thurs & Fri 10 AM - 9 PM, Sat 10 AM - 5 PM, Sun Noon - 5 PM, cl Mon & national holidays. Admis non-members $6, senior citizens 65 & over $5, student with identification card $3, members & children under 12 free. Estab 1958 to bring art to the community & provide cultural facilities & programs. Library, exhibit space & auditorium are maintained. Average Annual Attendance: 150,000. Mem: 3500; dues corporate $5000, $2500 & $1000, benefactor $1000, patron $500, contributing $250, sustaining $125, family-dual $60, individual $40
Collections: Golda & Meyer B Marks Cobra Art Collection; William Glackens Collection; American & European paintings, sculpture & graphics from late 19th

century-present; pre-Columbian & historic American Indian ceramics, basketry & stone artifacts; Modern Cuban Collection; West African tribal sculpture
Publications: Annual Report; Bulletin, quarterly; Calendar of Events, quarterly; Exhibition Catalogs
Activities: Classes for adults & children; docent training; slide lect program in schools by request; lect; gallery talks; tours; films; competitions; individual paintings & original objects of art lent to other museums
L Library, One E Las Olas Blvd, 33301-1807. Tel 954-525-5500; FAX 954-524-6011; *Librn* Elaine Newland
Founded 1958. Staff, members & schools only; for educational purposes only
Library Holdings: Vols 7500; Per subs 15; AV — Slides

M MUSEUM OF DISCOVERY & SCIENCE, 401 SW Second St, 33312-1707. Tel 954-467-6637; FAX 954-467-0046; *Exec Dir* Kim L Maher; *Trustee Pres* Terry W Stiles
Open Mon - Fri 10 AM - 5 PM, Sat 10 AM - 8:30 PM, Sun Noon - 5 PM, cl Christmas Day, open all on other holidays; Blockbuster IMAX Theater open Mon - Sun with daily showings. Admis adults $6, senior citizens $5, children 3-12 $5, special group rates available. Estab 1977 to increase science literacy. Average Annual Attendance: 534,000. Mem: 5500; dues $55; annual meeting in Sept
Income: $5,000,000
Exhibitions: Choose Health; Florida EcoScapes; Gizmo City; Great Gravity Clock; KidScience; No Place Like Home; Science Fair; Sound; Space Base
Publications: Modulations, quarterly
Activities: Classes for adults & children; camps; sleepovers; outreach programs; films daily; docent training; lect open to public, some to members only, 8-10 vis lectr per year; gallery talks; tours; book traveling exhibitions 5 per year; originate traveling exhibitions to other museums; museum shop sells books, original art, reproductions, prints & science related activities

FORT MYERS

M EDISON COMMUNITY COLLEGE, Gallery of Fine Art, 8099 College Pky, PO Box 60210, 33906. Tel 941-489-9314; FAX 941-489-9482; *Cur & Dir* Marta Mieras
Open Tues - Fri 10 AM - 4 PM, Sat 11 AM - 3 PM, Sun 1 - 5 PM. No admis fee. Estab 1979 to provide exhibitions of national & regional importance & related educational programs. Main gallery 2000 sq ft, high security; adjunct performing arts hall gallery. Average Annual Attendance: 15,000. Mem: 200; dues $30
Income: Financed by endowment & state appropriation
Activities: Tours for adults & children; docent training; lect open to public, 2 - 4 vis lectr per year; gallery talks; scholarships & fels offered; book traveling exhibitions 2 - 4 per year; originate traveling exhibitions to other museums in Florida; sales shop sells posters & catalogs

GAINESVILLE

M CITY OF GAINESVILLE, Thomas Center Galleries - Cultural Affairs, 302 NE Sixth Ave, PO Box 490, 32602-0490. Tel 904-334-2197; FAX 904-334-2314; *Mgr* Coni Gesualdi; *Gallery Coordr* Amy Vigilante Dickerson, PhD
Open Mon - Fri 8 AM - 5 PM, Sat & Sun 1 - 4 PM. Estab 1979 to increase local arts awareness. Two small galleries in a historic building. Average Annual Attendance: 9000
Income: $8000 (financed by city appropriation, grants & donations)
Exhibitions: Contemporary American Artists, predominantly Floridian 9 shows per year in main gallery; 11 shows per year in mezzanine gallery
Publications: Exhibition brochures
Activities: Lect open to public, 4 vis lectr per year; gallery talks; tours; competitions with prizes; workshops & receptions for artists

UNIVERSITY OF FLORIDA
M University Gallery, PO Box 115803, 32611. Tel 352-392-0201; *Acting Dir* Karen W Valdes; *Registrar* Janice Everidge
Open Tues 10 AM - 8 PM, Wed - Fri 10 AM - 5 PM, Sat & Sun 1 - 5 PM, cl Mon & holidays. No admis fee. Estab 1965 as an arts exhibition gallery, open 11 months of the year, showing monthly exhibitions with contemporary & historical content. Gallery located in independent building with small lecture hall, limited access & completely secure with temperature & humidity control, adjustable track lighting; display area is in excess of 3000 sq ft. Average Annual Attendance: 8000. Mem: 50; dues professional $100 & up, family $35, individual $20; annual meeting in May
Income: $97,000 (financed by state appropriation & community mem)
Purchases: $2000
Collections: †European & American prints, paintings & photographs; †pre-Columbian & Latin American art (also folk art)
Exhibitions: Changing monthly exhibitions; Annual University of Florida Art Faculty (January)
Publications: Exhibition catalogs; periodic bulletins
Activities: Lect open to public; exten dept serves area schools; lending collection contains cassettes, original art works, photographs & slides; originate traveling exhibitions organized & circulated
L Architecture & Fine Arts Library, 201 FAA, PO Box 11017, 32611. Tel 352-392-0222; Elec Mail edteag@nervm.nerdc.ufl.edu. *Architecture Fine Arts Bibliographer & Head Librn* Edward H Teague
Open Mon - Thurs 8 AM - 10 PM, Fri 8 AM - 5 PM, Sat 1 - 5 PM, Sun 2 - 10 PM. Estab 1853 as a state art & architecture information center
Library Holdings: Vols 85,000; Per subs 600; Micro — Fiche, reels; AV — V-tapes; Other — Exhibition catalogs, manuscripts, pamphlets, photographs, reproductions
Special Subjects: Advertising Design, Afro-American Art, American Indian Art, American Western Art, Architecture, Asian Art, Decorative Arts, Folk Art, Gold, Graphic Arts, History of Art & Archaeology, Intermedia, Interior Design, Landscape Architecture, Latin American Art
Collections: Rare book collection

M Samuel P Harn Museum of Art, Hull Rd & SW 34th St, PO Box 112700, 32611-2700. Tel 352-392-9826; FAX 904-392-3892; *Dir* Budd Harris Bishop; *Cur Coll* Larry David Perkins; *Cur Exhib* Dede Young; *Cur Educ* Kerry Oliver-Smith
Open Tues - Fri 11 AM - 5 PM, Sat 10 AM - 5 PM, Sun 1 - 5 PM. No admis fee. Estab 1981 to collect, preserve, display & interpret art. Five spacious galleries surround a large exhibition hall & a Rotunda with a gallery off that. Also a museum store off the Galleria (entrance). Maintains a reference library available to Alliance members & staff only. Average Annual Attendance: 75,000. Mem: 667; dues $35-$1000
Income: $1,500,000 (financed by endowment, mem & state appropriation)
Purchases: $700,000
Collections: African Art; American Art; Asian Ceramics; Papua New Guinea; Pre-Columbian
Publications: Harn Monthly Bulletin
Activities: Docent programs; lect open to public, 22 vis lectr per year; book traveling exhibitions 10-12 per year; originate traveling exhibitions 4-5 per year; museum shop sells books & prints

HOLLYWOOD

M ART & CULTURE CENTER OF HOLLYWOOD, 1650 Harrison St, 33020. Tel 954-921-3274, 921-3275; *Chmn* Johnnie Sue Glantz; *Chief Exec Officer & Pres* Rick Arrowwood; *Dir Musical Prog* Matthew Janpol; *Educ Cur* Carolyn Kossan
Open Tues - Sat 10 AM - 4 PM, Thurs 7 - 9 PM, Sun 1 - 4 PM. Admis Wed - Sat $2, Sun $3, Tues free. Estab 1975 for the study, educ & enjoyment of visual & performing arts. Great Gallery, major exhibit space, is 6300 sq ft with 400 running ft; concerts are also held there. Two Hall galleries. Average Annual Attendance: 30,000. Mem: 1250; dues $25-$500
Income: $200,000 (financed by mem, city appropriation, private & pub contributions, grants)
Collections: 19th & 20th century American & contemporary Florida artists; African & 18th - 19th century European silver
Exhibitions: Exhibitions change year round
Publications: Calendar of Events, bi-monthly; exhibit catalogs
Activities: Educ dept; lect open to public, 8 vis lectr per year; competitions with awards; individual paintings & original objects of art lent to museums; lending collection contains 50 motion pictures & 100 original art works; originate travelling exhibitions

L Art Reference Library, 1650 Harrison St, 33020. Tel 954-921-3275
Open by appointment or request. Estab 1983 as an art research facility for staff, docents & members. For reference only. Average Annual Attendance: 43,000
Income: $1000
Purchases: $1000
Library Holdings: Vols 1200; Per subs 3; Micro — Cards; AV — Motion pictures; Other — Exhibition catalogs, pamphlets
Collections: African Collection of English Silver; International, national & regional artists
Activities: Classes for adults & children; docent training; lect open to public, 6 vis lectr per year; concerts; gallery talks; tours; original paintings & original objects of art lent to other museums & children's museums; originate traveling exhibitions to national, state & regional institutions

A FLORIDA PASTEL ASSOCIATION, 2442 Rodman St, 33020. Tel 954-923-7591; *Exec Dir* Michelle M Camp; *Pres* Linda M Gershen
Estab 1980
Income: $2000 (financed by mem)
Exhibitions: Annual Art League Exhibition
Publications: Quarterly newsletter

M HOLLYWOOD ART MUSEUM, * 4000 Hollywood Blvd, Ste 120, 33021. *Dir* Herbert Tulk; *Treas* Lilyan Beckerman
Open Sept - June Mon - Fri 1 - 4 PM. No admis fee. Estab 1962 to encourage artists, instruct students & establish mus arts, science & technology. On site have limited art showcases in prominent locations. Mem: dues $5-$20
Income: Financed by fund raising events - i.e. Golf Classics etc
Collections: Bakuba Collection
Exhibitions: Permanent & temporary exhibits
Publications: H.A.M., annual magazine
Activities: Classes for children; docent training; teach in school; lect open to public; gallery talks; tours; competitions with awards; scholarships offered to children; artmobile; originate traveling expeditions to schools in Broward County

HOLMES BEACH

M ISLAND GALLERY WEST, 5348 Gulf Dr, 34217. Tel 941-778-6645
Open Mon - Sat 10 AM - 5 PM. No admis fee. Estab 1991 to exhibit & sell local artists' work. Art work by local & regional artists working in a wide variety of media. Mem: 30; juried in by current artist members
Activities: Museum shop sells original art

JACKSONVILLE

M CUMMER MUSEUM OF ART & GARDENS, DeEtte Holden Cummer Museum Foundation, 829 Riverside Ave, 32204. Tel 904-356-6857; FAX 904-353-4101; *Dir* Dr Kahren Arbitman; *Asst to Dir* Michael Richell
Open Tues & Thurs 10 AM - 9 PM, Wed, Fri & Sat 10 - 5 PM, Sun Noon 5 PM. Admis adults $5, seniors, military & students $3, members & children under 5 free. Estab 1960 to build the foremost survey collection of art in the Southeast. Eleven galleries of paintings & decorative arts surround garden court sited on two acres of formal gardens. Average Annual Attendance: 100,000. Mem: 3000; dues $40-$150
Income: $1,000,000
Purchases: $600,000
Collections: †Europeaan & American painting, sculpture, graphic arts, tapestries

& decorative arts; Netsuke, Inro & porcelains; Oriental Collection of jade, ivory; Early Meissen porcelain
Publications: Collection handbooks; exhibition catalogs; yearbooks
Activities: Classes for adults & children; docent training; lect open to public; concerts; gallery talks; tours; awards; individual paintings lent to other museums & galleries; book traveling exhibitions 6 per year; museum shop sells books, prints & small objects of art associated with museum collections

L Library, 829 Riverside Ave, 32204. Tel 904-356-6857; FAX 904-353-4101;
Open for reference
Income: $8500
Purchases: $3500
Library Holdings: Vols 3600; Per subs 17; AV — Slides 10,000; Other — Exhibition catalogs 1200
Special Subjects: German porcelain, Meissen

M FLORIDA COMMUNITY COLLEGE AT JACKSONVILLE, South Gallery, 11901 Beach Blvd, 32246-7625. Tel 904-646-2023; FAX 904-646-2396; *Dir* Mary Joan Hinson; *Docent* Mary N Worthy
Open Mon 10 AM - 9 PM, Tues - Thurs 10 AM - 5 PM, Fri 10 AM - 1 PM, cl weekends. No admis fee. Estab 1985
Collections: FCCJ Permanent Collection

M JACKSONVILLE MUSEUM OF CONTEMPORARY ART, 4160 Boulevard Ctr Dr, 32207. Tel 904-398-8336; *Dir* Henry Flood Robert Jr; *Art Librn* Barbara Salvage
Open Tues, Wed & Fri 10 AM - 4 PM, Thurs 10 AM - 10 PM, Sat & Sun 1 - 5 PM, cl Mon, holidays. No admis fee. Estab 1947 as an art center for the greater Jacksonville area. Average Annual Attendance: 100,000. Mem: 3200; dues $25; annual meeting spring
Income: Financed by mem
Collections: Pre-Columbian art; 20th century paintings, prints & sculpture
Exhibitions: Photons; Phonons - Kinetic Art; The Nature of Sculpture; Wyeth Family Exhibition
Publications: Calendar, monthly; exhibition catalogues
Activities: Classes for adults & children; docent training; art enrichment program; dramatic programs; lect open to public, 10 vis lectr per year; concerts; gallery talks; tours; competitions; scholarships offered; book traveling exhibitions; originate traveling exhibitions; museum shop sells books, magazines, original art, reproductions, prints, jewelry & children's toys

L Library, 4160 Boulevard Center Dr, 32207. Tel 904-398-8336; FAX 904-348-3167; *Registrar* Barbara Salvage
Open to teachers in Duval County schools
Library Holdings: Vols 200

L JACKSONVILLE PUBLIC LIBRARY, Fine Arts & Recreation Dept, 122 N Ocean St, 32202. Tel 904-630-2665; FAX 904-630-2431; *Acting Dir* Sylvia Cornell; *Dept Head* Tricia Coutant
Open Mon - Thurs 10 AM - 8 PM, Fri & Sat 10 AM - 6 PM, most Sun 1 - 5 PM. No admis fee. Estab 1905 to serve the pub by giving them free access to books, films, recordings, pamphlets, periodicals, maps, plus informational services & free programming
Income: Financed by city appropriation
Library Holdings: Vols 48,000; Per subs 200; Compact discs 6000; AV — Motion pictures 2000, rec 10,000, slides 3500, v-tapes 6000
Publications: Annual Report
Activities: Weekly film programs

M JACKSONVILLE UNIVERSITY, Alexander Brest Museum & Gallery, 2800 University Blvd, 32211. Tel 904-744-3950, Ext 7371; FAX 904-745-7375; *Dir* M Lauderdale
Open Mon - Fri 9 AM - 4:30 PM, Sat Noon - 5 PM. No admis fee. Estab 1972 to exhibit decorative arts collection. Three galleries exhibiting decorative arts. One gallery contains contemporary art on rotating schedule. Average Annual Attendance: 18,000
Income: Financed by endowment & private funds
Collections: Porcelain; Ivory; †Pre-Columbian; †Steuben; Tiffany
Publications: Museum catalog
Activities: Classes for adults; docent training; lect open to public; competitions

M MUSEUM SCIENCE & HISTORY, 1025 Museum Circle, 32207. Tel 904-396-7062, Ext 214; FAX 904-396-5799; *Exec Dir* Margo Dundon
Open Mon - Fri 10 AM - 5 PM, Sat 10 AM - 6 PM, Sun 1 - 6 PM. Admis $5, seniors & military $4, children (3-12) $3. Estab 1941. Lobby & three floors contain exhibit areas, classrooms & studios. Average Annual Attendance: 225,000. Mem: 2000; dues vary
Income: Financed by mem, city appropriation & grants
Collections: Historical; Live Animal Collection; Physical Science Demonstrations
Exhibitions: Alexander Brest Planetarium (16th largest in US); health; science; wildlife
Publications: Teacher's Guide, annually; brochures, bimonthly; annual report
Activities: Classes for adults & children; dramatic programs; docent training; lect open to public; tours; Art in the Park; traveling exhibitions organized and circulated; museum shop and sales shop selling books, prints, museum-oriented items and toys for children

KEY WEST

M KEY WEST ART & HISTORICAL SOCIETY, East Martello Museum & Gallery, 3501 S Roosevelt Blvd, 33040. Tel 305-296-3913; FAX 305-296-6206; *Exec Dir* Kevin O'Brien; *Pres* Bob Feldman; *VPres* Joseph Bryan, Jr; *VPres* Kitty Clements; *Cur* Stacey Rousseau; *Corresp Secy* Scotti Merrill; *Treas* Marua Green
Open Mon - Sun 9:30 AM - 5 PM. Admis $3 adults, children 7-15 $1, active military free. Estab 1962 to preserve history of the Florida Keys. Two air-conditioned contiguous galleries with arched ceilings. Average Annual Attendance: 25,000. Mem: 1200; dues $25, individual $15, student $2; annual meeting in Apr

Income: Financed by mem, donations, admis & gift shop sales
Collections: Carvings & paintings of Mario Sanchez; folk art of Stanley Papio
Exhibitions: Monthly exhibits by Key West artists during winter; Art & History Fair
Publications: Martello; two newsletters
Activities: Lect open to public, 6 vis lectr per year; competitions with prizes; individual paintings & original objects of art lent to qualifying museums; book traveling exhibitions; originate traveling exhibitions; museum shop sells books, magazines, original art, reproductions, prints

M **OLD ISLAND RESTORATION FOUNDATION INC,** Wrecker's Museum - Oldest House, 322 Duval St (Mailing add: 1501 Olivia St, 33040). Tel 305-294-9502; *Dir* Nancy O Jameson
Open 10 AM - 4 PM. Admis $4. Estab 1976 to present the maritime history of Key West's wrecking industry in the 19th century. Furnished period house with paintings throughout. Average Annual Attendance: 14,000. Mem: 200; dues $15-$20; annual meeting in Apr
Income: $36,000 (financed through admis fees & fundraising)
Purchases: $1500 (three 19th century ship models)
Collections: Oil on canvas by Edward Moran; All Sailing Ships & Scenes; Watercolors by Marshall Joyce; Watercolors by unknown artists

LAKELAND

M **ARTS ON THE PARK,** * 115 N Kentucky Ave, 33801. Tel 941-680-2787; *Pres* Lo Alexander; *VPres* Penelope Pinson; *Exec Dir* Dudley Uphoff; *Treas* Steve Hamic
Open Tues - Fri 10 AM - 5 PM. No admis fee. Estab 1979 to encourage Florida artists through shows, competitions, classes. 1600 sq ft ground floor, plus second floor library, office, studio in restored contributing structure in Lakeland's Munn Park Historic District. Average Annual Attendance: 30,000. Mem: 1200; dues sponsor $100-$999, individual $35, senior citizens $25
Income: $80,000 (financed by mem, city, business & industry)
Publications: Art Paper, quarterly newsletter; Onionhead, quarterly literary magazine
Activities: Classes for adults & children; docent training; lect open to public, 2 vis lectr per year; concerts; gallery talks; tours; competitions with awards; scholarships & fels offered; exten dept serves county; originate traveling exhibitions

M **FLORIDA SOUTHERN COLLEGE,** Melvin Art Gallery, 111 Lake Hollingsworth Dr, 33802. Tel 941-680-4224, 680-4225, 680-4111; *Dir* Downing Barnitz
Open Mon - Fri 1:30 - 4:30 PM. No admis fee. Estab 1971 as a teaching gallery. Large 3000 sq ft main gallery; small one room adjacent gallery. Average Annual Attendance: 3000 - 5000
Collections: Brass Rubbings Collection in Roux Library; Laymon Glass Collection in Annie Pfeiffer Chapel; permanent collection in various offices & buildings
Activities: Lect open to public, 3 vis lectr per year; gallery talks; concerts; awards

M **POLK MUSEUM OF ART,** 800 E Palmetto, 33801. Tel 941-688-7743; FAX 941-688-2611; *Exec Dir* Daniel Stetson; *Dir Develop* Judy Barger; *Pres* George Truitt; *Cur Coll* Eden Wilson; *Cur Educ* Jane Parkerson; *Controller* Ken Bailey
Open Tues - Fri 9 AM - 5 PM, Sat 10 AM - 4 PM, Sun Noon - 4 PM. No admis fee. Estab 1966 to collect, exhibit, interpret & preserve the visual arts. 12,000 sq ft of exhibition space, including outdoor sculpture garden. Average Annual Attendance: 125,000. Mem: 1600; dues gold patron $2500, patron $1000, benefactor $500, advocate $250, sponsor $100, general $35, 10% discount on all senior citizen mem; annual meeting in June
Income: Financed by mem, cities of Lakeland, Bartow, Auburndale & Winter Haven, Polk County School Board, grants, endowment & special projects
Collections: Ellis Verink Collection of photographs; 15th-19th Century European Collection of ceramics; Pre-Columbian Collection; assorted decorative arts; †Asian arts; contemporary paintings, photographs, prints & sculpture featuring Florida artists
Exhibitions: Changing exhibitions; 6 student gallery exhibitions including 12th Congressional District Competition & juried competition for high school students 12th Congressional District Competition, juried competition for high school students
Activities: Official school site; classes for adults & children; dramatic programs; docent training; workshops; circulating exhibits; lect open to public; concerts; gallery talks; docent-guided tours; competitions with awards; art films; outreach programs; annual outdoor art festival; scholarships & fels offered; book traveling exhibitions 4 per year; originate traveling exhibitions to other museums in Florida; museum shop sells books, magazines, prints & gift items
L **Penfield Library,** 800 E Palmetto, 33801. Tel 813-688-7743; *Chmn & Librn* Martha Bier
Open Fri only. Estab 1970 as a reference library for Polk County residents
Library Holdings: Vols 1750; Per subs 28; Other — Clipping files, exhibition catalogs, photographs, prints
Special Subjects: American Indian Art, American Western Art, Architecture, Art Education, Art History, Folk Art, History of Art & Archaeology, Latin American Art, Mexican Art, Oriental Art, Pre-Columbian Art, Southwestern Art

LAKE WORTH

M **PALM BEACH COMMUNITY COLLEGE FOUNDATION,** Museum of Art, 601 Lake Ave, 33460. Tel 407-582-00006; *Dir* Kip Eagen
Open Noon - 5 PM. Admis $2 donation. Estab 1989 for exhibition of contemporary art. Mus is a renovated 1939 Art Deco Movie Theatre with five separate galleries on two floors. Average Annual Attendance: 4000. Mem: 500; average dues $100
Income: Financed by endowment, mem
Collections: Contemporary Ceramics; Contemporary Glass; Kinetic Sculpture
Exhibitions: Changing exhibits & permanent collection

Publications: Catalogs; posters
Activities: Classes for children; docent training; lect open to public, some to members only, 3 vis lectrs per year; lending collection contains art objects; book traveling exhibitions 1-2 per year

MAITLAND

M **MAITLAND ART CENTER,** 231 W Packwood Ave, 32751-5596. Tel 407-539-2181; FAX 407-539-1198; *Exec Dir* James G Shepp; *Educ Coordr* Ann E Spalding; *Prog Coordr* Robin Ambrose; *Membership & Staff Coordr* Carol B Shurtleff; *Cur Traveling Exhib & Registrar* Leslie Tate Boles
Open Mon - Fri 10 AM - 4:30 PM, Sat & Sun Noon - 4:30 PM, cl major holidays. No admis fee. Estab 1938 to promote exploration & educ in the visual arts & contemporary crafts; listed in National Register of Historic Places. Four galleries totaling 202 running ft. Average Annual Attendance: 45,000. Mem: 625; dues $20-$1000; annual meeting in Sept
Income: Financed by mem, city & state appropriations, donations, special events, endowment
Collections: Architectural work including 6-acre compound & memorial chapel designed by Smith; graphics; paintings & sculptures of Andre Smith; etchings & drawings
Publications: Exhibit catalogs; quarterly class schedules; quarterly newsletter
Activities: Classes for adults & children; docent training; lect open to public, 4 vis lectr per year; gallery talks; tours; individual paintings & original objects of art lent to museums & art centers; book traveling exhibitions 1-2 per year; originate traveling exhibitions to museums, art centers, libraries & universities; museum shop sells original art, reproductions, cards, jewelry & children's items
L **Library,** 231 W Packwood Ave, 32751-5596. Tel 407-539-2181; FAX 407-539-1198; *Dir* James G Shepp; *Cur Traveling Exhib & Registrar* Leslie Tate Boles; *Membership & Staff Coordr* Carol B Shurtleff; *Community Relations Coordr* Catherine T Simmons
Open Mon - Fri 10 AM - 4:30 PM, Sat & Sun Noon - 4:30 PM, cl major holidays. No admis fee. Estab 1970 to promote knowledge & educ in American Art. Open for reference. Average Annual Attendance: 55,000
Income: Financed by City of Maitland, mem, tuition, special events, grants, contributions, gallery donations
Library Holdings: Vols 3000; Per subs 10; Other — Exhibition catalogs
Special Subjects: Painting - American, Photography, Porcelain, Portraits, Posters, Pottery, Printmaking, Prints, Sculpture, Watercolors, Woodcarvings, Woodcuts
Collections: †Works by Andre Smith (1880 - 1959); exhibiting artists

MELBOURNE

M **BREVARD MUSEUM OF ART & SCIENCE,** 1463 Highland Ave, 32935. Tel 407-242-0737; FAX 407-242-0798; *Exec Dir* Randall Hayes
Open Tues - Fri 10 AM - 5 PM, Sat 10 AM - 4 PM, Sun Noon - 4 PM, cl Mon. Estab 1978 to exhibit art for the educ, information, & enjoyment of the pub. Exhibition facility with three changing & two permanent collection galleries with approx 6000 sq ft of exhibition space. Average Annual Attendance: 40,000. Mem: 1700; dues patron $100 & up, family $35, individual $20; annual meeting third Tues in May
Income: $400,000 (financed by mem, city & county appropriation, corporate gifts & grants)
Purchases: $1500
Collections: †Contemporary regional & national artists; drawings, paintings, prints of Ernst Oppler; small objects collection of Ethnic Art
Exhibitions: Ernst Oppler & the Russian Ballet; Annual Members Juried Exhibition
Publications: Bi-monthly newsletter; calendar for members; handouts & catalogues for changing exhibitions
Activities: Classes for adults & children; docent training; artist-in-residence program; lect open to public; concerts; gallery talks; tours; competitions with awards; book traveling exhibitions 6-8 per year; museum shop sells original art, reproductions, prints, small objects & cards

MIAMI

THE AMERICAN FOUNDATION FOR THE ARTS
For further information, see National and Regional Organizations

M **BAKEHOUSE ART COMPLEX, INC,** 561 NW 32nd St, 33127. Tel 305-576-2828; *Dir* Pola Reydburd; *Admnr* Donna Wilt Sperow
Open Tues - Fri 10 AM - 4 PM. No admis fee. Estab 1985. Cultural complex with artist studios, galleries & classrooms; main gallery: 3200 sq ft, 16 ft ceilings, track lighting; Swenson Gallery: 800 sq ft, carpeted floor. Average Annual Attendance: 8000. Mem: 200; dues donor $500, supporter $100, family $50, friend $35
Income: $135,000 (financed through mem, studio rents, grants & contributions)
Exhibitions: (1997) Bakehouse Three: Medlock, Nicklas, Regis; Bakehouse Seventh Annual Membership Show
Activities: Classes for adults & children; lect open to public, 6 - 8 vis lectr per year; competitions; scholarships & fels; retail store sells original art

M **FLORIDA INTERNATIONAL UNIVERSITY,** The Art Museum at FIU, University Park, PC 110, 33199. Tel 305-348-2890; FAX 305-348-2762; *Dir* Dahlia Morgan; *Asst Dir* Regina C Bailey; *Cur Educ* Chris Ingalls; *Registrar* Edward G Russo
Open Mon 10 AM - 9 PM, Tues - Fri 10 AM - 5 PM, Sat Noon - 4 PM. No admis fee. Estab 1977. 2500 sq ft of flexible exhibition space in the main administration building & outdoor art park. Average Annual Attendance: 50,000. Mem: 150; dues $250 & up
Income: Financed by state appropriation & supported by Friends of the Art Mus, private foundations & municipal councils
Collections: Cintas Foundation Collection; The Metropolitan Collection;

Margulies Sculpture Collection
Exhibitions: Art Park, 57 total sculptures
Publications: Exhibition catalogues
Activities: Dade County Public Schools Museum Education Program; lect open to public, 4 vis lectr per year; gallery talks; tours; book traveling exhibitions; originate traveling exhibitions

M **THE FLORIDA MUSEUM OF HISPANIC & LATIN AMERICAN ART,**
One NE 40th St, 33137. Tel 305-576-5171; FAX 305-530-9262; *Dir* Raul Oyuela; *Asst Dir* Lina Velazquez; *Treas* Adam D Fischer
Open Tues - Sat 11 AM - 5 PM. Admis $2, senior citizens $1. Estab 1991. 3500 sq ft. Average Annual Attendance: 10,000. Mem: 100
Income: $75,000 (financed by mem & sponsors)
Collections: Contemporary Spanish & Latin American art
Exhibitions: 11 exhibits per year
Publications: Quarterly newsletter
Activities: Lect open to public; museum shop sells prints, reproductions & T-shirts

M **METRO-DADE,** Miami Art Museum of Dade County, 101 W Flagler St, 33130. Tel 305-375-3000, 375-1700; FAX 305-375-1725; *Interim Dir* Vivian Rodriguez; *Asst Dir* Jorge Gonzalez; *Registrar* Arlene Dellis
Open Tues - Sat 10 AM - 5 PM, Thurs 10 AM - 9 PM, Sun Noon - 5 PM, cl Mon. Admis adults $5, children $2, groups $2.50 (20 or more). Estab 1984 to originate & receive major traveling art exhibitions. 16,000 sq ft of gallery space on two levels; 3300 sq ft sculpture court; 1800 sq ft auditorium. Average Annual Attendance: 15,000. Mem: 6800; dues $40
Publications: CFA News, bi-monthly; exhibit brochures
Activities: Docent programs; films; concerts; dance performances; lect open to public, 12 vis lectr per year; book traveling exhibitions 10 per year; originate traveling exhibitions; museum shop sells books, reproductions, prints, jewelry, art-greeting cards, posters

M **MIAMI-DADE COMMUNITY COLLEGE,** Kendal Campus, Art Gallery, 11011 SW 104th St, 33176-3393. Tel 305-237-2322; FAX 305-237-2901; *Dir* Robert J Sindelir; *Asst Dir* Lilia M Fontana
Open Mon, Thurs & Fri 8 AM - 4 PM, Tues - Wed 12 - 7:30 PM. No admis fee. Estab 1970 as a teaching laboratory & pub service
Income: Financed by state appropriation
Purchases: $250,000
Collections: Contemporary American paintings, photographs, prints, sculpture includes: Beal, Boice, Bolotowsky, Christo, Ferrer, Fine, Gibson, Henry, Hepworth, Hockney, Judd, Komar, Lichtenstein, Marisol, Melamid, Michals, Motherwell, Nesbitt, Oldenburg, Parker & Pearlstein
Exhibitions: Tom Doyle; Max Cole; Ed McGowin; Lynn Gelfman; Vito Acconci; Marilyn Pappas; Tom Balbo; Phillip Tsiaras; Jene Highstein; Jim Jacobs; Robert Peterson; Saul Kamenter; Harriet Bell
Publications: 6 catalogs per year
Activities: Lect open to public, 4-6 vis lectr per year; gallery talks; individual paintings & original objects of art lent; lending collection contains original art works, original prints, paintings, photographs, sculpture; traveling exhibitions organized & circulated

M **MIAMI-DADE COMMUNITY COLLEGE,** Frances Wolfson Art Gallery, 300 NE Second Ave, 5th Flr, 33132. Tel 305-237-3278; FAX 305-237-3603; *Gallery Dir* Amy Cappellazzo; *Dir Cultural Affairs* Olga Garay
No admis fee. Gallery estab 1976 to exhibit contemporary art for students & community. Atrium lobby space; 2000 sq ft & 157 linear ft; two smaller secured galleries. Average Annual Attendance: 3000
Income: $230,000, as part of Wolfson Campus Galleries (financed by endowment, annual grants & state appropriation)
Exhibitions: Second Time Around; First Exhibit; Transforms: Mixed-Media Student Exhibit; Glen Gentele: The Genetic Trail, sculptures
Activities: Educational packets; workshops; symposia; lect open to public, 12 vis lectr per year

M **InterAmerican Art Gallery,** 627 SW 27th Ave, No 3104 (Mailing add: c/o Centre Gallery, 300 NE Second Ave, 33132). Tel 305-237-3278; FAX 305-237-3603; *Gallery Dir* Amy Cappellazzo; *Dir Cultural Affairs* Olga Garay
No admis fee. Gallery estab 1986 to exhibit contemporary art for students & community. Large main gallery, small side gallery, secured space; 1214 sq ft & 136 linear ft. Average Annual Attendance: 2000
Income: $230,000, as part of Wolfson Campus Galleries (financed by endowment, annual grants & state appropriation)
Exhibitions: Linda Matalon: Gathering & Protecting, Carol Sun
Activities: Educational packets; workshops; symposia

M **Wolfson Galleries,** 300 NE Second Ave, No 1365, 33132. Tel 305-237-3278; FAX 305-237-3603; *Gallery Dir* Amy Cappellazzo; *Dir Cultural Affairs* Olga Garay
Open Mon - Fri 9 AM - 5 PM. No admis fee. Gallery estab 1990 to exhibit contemporary art, host residencies; educational art. Secured spaces with alarm systems, no windows; 2700 sq ft, 1100 sq ft, 600 sq ft (3 spaces). Average Annual Attendance: 20,000
Income: $299,000, as part of Wolfson Campus Galleries (financed by endowment, annual grants & state appropriation)
Collections: Centre Gallery - Youth Matters; Edurance: The Information (The History of the Body in performance Arts; Inter-American Gallery - Linda Matalon: Gathering & protecting, Carol Sun
Publications: Exhibition catalogs
Activities: Educational packets; workshops; symposia; lect open to public, 12 vis lectr per year; book traveling exhibitions 3 per year; originate traveling exhibitions 1 per year

L **MIAMI-DADE PUBLIC LIBRARY,** 101 W Flagler St, 33130. Tel 305-375-2665; *Dir* Mary R Somerville; *Asst Dir* Harriet Schwanke; *Asst Dir* Raymond Santiago; *Asst Dir* William Urbizu; *Asst Dir* Manny Lomba; *Technical Serv Adminr* Susan Mead-Donaldson; *Supv Branches* Carol Gawron; *Supv Branches* Sharon Bart; *Art Servs Librn* Barbara Young; *Youth Serv Adminr* Sylvia

Mavrogenes
Open Mon - Wed & Fri - Sat 9 AM - 6 PM, Thurs 9 AM - 9 PM, Sun (Oct - May) 1 - 5 PM. No admis fee. Estab 1947 to provide the informational, educational and recreational needs of the community. Gallery maintained, Artmobile maintained
Income: Financed by special millage
Library Holdings: Per subs 140; Micro — Fiche, reels; AV — Cassettes 2000, motion pictures 5500, rec 4000, v-tapes 6000; Other — Clipping files, exhibition catalogs, framed reproductions 800, original art works 1200, pamphlets, photographs, prints
Special Subjects: Afro-American Art, Latin American Art
Collections: African American original graphics; Latin American original graphics; Oriental collection of original graphics
Publications: Exhibition catalogs
Activities: Lectures open to public; concerts; gallery talks; tours; exten dept; artmobile; reproductions lent; book traveling exhibitions, 1-2 per year; originate traveling exhibitions, permanent collection of works on paper

A **MIAMI WATERCOLOR SOCIETY, INC,** PO Box 561953, 33156-1953. Tel 305-361-6016; *Pres* Virginia Munz; *VPres* Mary Bennett; *VPres* Sandra Miot; *Treas* Daisy Armas-Garcia
Exhibitions: Two annual juried exhibitions; several unjuried exhibitions
Activities: Workshops

NATIONAL FOUNDATION FOR ADVANCEMENT IN THE ARTS
For further information, see National and Regional Organizations

M **NEW WORLD SCHOOL OF THE ARTS,** Gallery, 25 NE Second St (Mailing add: 300 NE Second Ave, 33132-2297). Tel 305-237-3620; FAX 305-237-3794; Elec Mail nwsapost.mel@mdcc.edu. *Dean Visual Arts* Dr Mel Alexenberg; *Asst Dean* Louise Romeo; *Gallery Dir* Randell Von Bloomberg
Open 9 AM - 5 PM. No admis fee. Estab 1990 to exhibit contemporary art & design. Major gallery in downtown Miami showing contemporary art & design from USA & abroad & faculty & student art work. Average Annual Attendance: 54,000
Income: Financed by county & state appropriation
Exhibitions: (1997) Rising Stars
Publications: Exhibition catalogs
Activities: High School & BFA programs; lect open to public, 25 vis lectr per year; concerts; gallery talks; tours; juried student exhibitions; scholarships offered; book traveling exhibitions 2 per year; originate traveling exhibitions 1 per year

A **SOUTH FLORIDA CULTURAL CONSORTIUM,** Metropolitan Dade County Cultural Affairs Council, 111 NW First St, Ste 625, 33128-1964. Tel 305-375-4634; FAX 305-375-3068; *Exec Dir* Michael Spring; *Deputy Dir* Deborah Margol
Estab 1976 to provide planning, coordination, promotion & advocacy, as well as funding support & technical assistance to & marketing for Dade County's & South Florida's cultural organizations & activities; create a nurturing environment for the development of cultural excellence & diversity; address the needs of cultural community that includes the visual & performing arts, history, historic preservation & folklife, the sciences, festivals & special events, & the literary & media arts

M **VIZCAYA MUSEUM & GARDENS,** 3251 S Miami Ave, 33129. Tel 305-250-9133; FAX 305-285-2004; *Dir* Richard Farwell; *Cur* Michele A McDonald; *Chief Conservator* Emilio Cianfoni
Open daily 9:30 AM - 5 PM, cl Christmas. Admis house & gardens $10, children 6-12 $5. Estab 1952 to increase the general public's appreciation of the European decorative arts, architecture & landscape design through lectures with tours conducted by trained volunteer guides. Vizcaya is a house mus with a major collection of European decorative arts & elaborate formal gardens. The Villa, formerly the home of James Deering, was completed in 1916 & contains approximately 70 rooms. Average Annual Attendance: 200,000. Mem: 1500; dues $35 & up; annual meeting third Wed in Apr
Income: $1,450,000 (financed by admis fees)
Collections: Italian & French Furniture of the 16th-18th & early 19th centuries; Notable Specialized Collections of Carpets. Tapestries, Furniture, Roman Antiques & Bronze Mortars
Publications: Vizcayan Newsletter, quarterly
Activities: Tours for children; docent training; lect open to public; concerts; tours; individual paintings & original objects of art lent to accredited museums; museum shop sells books, magazines, original art, reproductions, prints & slides

L **Library,** 3251 S Miami Ave, 33129. Tel 305-250-9133, Ext 2252; FAX 305-285-2004; *Vol Librn* Don Gayer
Open to mus volunteers & students of the decorative arts for reference only
Income: Financed by donations
Library Holdings: Vols 4000; Per subs 8; Archival material; AV — Cassettes, Kodachromes, slides; Other — Exhibition catalogs, memorabilia, photographs
Special Subjects: Decorative Arts, Furniture, Interior Design
Collections: Slide collection for reference & teaching

MIAMI BEACH

M **BASS MUSEUM OF ART,** 2121 Park Ave, 33139. Tel 305-673-7530; FAX 305-673-7062; *Dir* Diane W Camber
Open Tues - Sat 10 AM - 5 PM, Sun 1 - 5 PM. Admis adults $5, students $4, donations on Tues. Estab 1964 for the collection & exhibition of works of art. Collection features European art, architectural drawings & contemporary art. The museum is a two-story 1930 art deco structure. Average Annual Attendance: 100,000
Income: $1,150,000 (financed by city, mem & grants from state, county & federal government)
Collections: Permanent collection of European textiles, Old Master paintings, Baroque sculpture, Oriental art, ecclesiastical artifacts, 19th & 20th century

graphics, paintings & architectural drawings & arts
Publications: Quarterly magazine; exhibition catalogues; permanent collection catalogue
Activities: Lect open to public; concerts; films; individual & original objects of art lent to other museums; originate traveling exhibitions; sales shop selling cards, jewelry & objects of fine design

L **MIAMI DADE PUBLIC LIBRARY,** Miami Beach Branch, 2100 Collins Ave, 33139. Tel 305-535-4219; *Library Serv Supv* Gia Thompson
Open Mon & Wed 10 AM - 8 PM, Tues, Thurs & Sat 9:30 AM - 5:30 PM. Estab 1927 to serve the citizens of Miami Beach. Circ 350,000
Income: $850,000 (financed by city appropriation)
Purchases: $125,000
Library Holdings: Vols 80,000; Per subs 298; Micro — Reels; AV — A-tapes, motion pictures, rec, v-tapes; Other — Clipping files, pamphlets

A **WOLFSONIAN FOUNDATION,** 1001 Washington Ave, 33139. Tel 305-535-2602; FAX 305-531-2133; *Dir* Peggy A Loar; *Assoc Dir* James J Kamm; *Head Librn* James Findlay; *Head Register* Christine Giles
Estab 1986
Income: Financed by private foundation
Collections: †Architecture & Design Arts; †Decorative & Propaganda Arts (pertaining to period 1885-1945); †Fine Arts; †Rare & Reference Library

NAPLES

M **NAPLES ART GALLERY,** 275 Broad Ave S, 33940. Tel 941-262-4551; *Pres* William B Spink; *VPres & Treas* Warren C Nelson
Open Mon - Sat 9:30 AM - 5 PM. No admis fee. Estab 1965 to present works of prominent American artists for display in home or office. Contains foyer with fountain & four additional gallery rooms & sculpture garden; 4600 sq ft of gallery space. Average Annual Attendance: 15,000
Income: $1,000,000 (financed by sales)
Exhibitions: One or two-person shows
Publications: Exhibit brochures

NORTH MIAMI

M **MUSEUM OF CONTEMPORARY ART** (Formerly COCA - Center of Contemporary Art), 770 NE 125th St, 33161. Tel 305-893-6211; *Dir* Lou Anne Colodny
Open Mon - Fri 10 AM - 4 PM, Sat 11 AM - 4 PM, Sun 1 - 4 PM. No admis fee. Estab 1981 to feature national, international & Florida artists. Average Annual Attendance: 10,000. Mem: 500; dues $20-$150
Income: Financed by mem, city appropriation, private donations, corporations foundations
Publications: Catalogs; newsletter, semi-annually
Activities: Docent programs; film videos; lect open to public; originate traveling exhibitions & performances

NORTH MIAMI BEACH

M **SAINT BERNARD FOUNDATION & MONASTERY,** 16711 W Dixie Hwy, 33160. Tel 305-945-1462; *Exec Dir* Barbara Bambrick
Open Mon - Sat 10 AM - 5 PM, Sun Noon - 5 PM. Admis adults $4, sr citizens $2.50, children 7-12 $1, under 6 free. A reconstruction of a monastery built in Segovia, Spain, in 1141, with original stones brought to the United States by William Randolph Hearst
Income: Financed by members & donations of visitors
Collections: Historic and Religious Material; paintings; sculpture
Activities: Tours; arts festivals; sales shop sells books, slides & religious objects

OCALA

M **CENTRAL FLORIDA COMMUNITY COLLEGE ART COLLECTION,** 3001 SW College Rd, PO Box 1388, 32678. Tel 352-237-2111; FAX 904-237-0510; *Pres* William Campion
Open Mon - Fri 8 AM - 4:30 PM. No admis fee. Estab 1962 as a service to the community. Gallery is the lobby to the auditorium. Average Annual Attendance: 5000
Income: Financed by state appropriations
Collections: Contemporary Artists of Varies Media; CFCC Foundation Permanent Collection
Exhibitions: Student Art Exhibitions
Activities: Classes for adults; scholarships offered

M **FLORIDA STATE UNIVERSITY FOUNDATION - CENTRAL FLORIDA COMMUNITY COLLEGE FOUNDATION,** The Appleton Museum of Art, 4333 NE Silver Springs Blvd, 34470-5000. Tel 352-236-7100; FAX 352-236-7136; *Dir* Sandra Talarico; *Registrar* Brenda McNeal; *Facilities Dir* Russell Days; *Cur Museum Educ* Angela Fortunas-Whatley; *Cur Exhib & Programs* Tom Larose
Open Tues - Sat 10 AM - 4:30 PM, Sun 1 - 5 PM. Admis adults $3, students with ID $2, children under 18 free. Estab 1987 to provide cultural & educational programs. Average Annual Attendance: 60,000. Mem: 2500; dues $10-$500
Income: $1,000,000 (financed by endowment, mem & state appropriation)
Collections: †Appleton Museum of Art Collection; Antiquities, Asian, Pre-Columbian & African; Decorative Arts; European Painting & Sculpture
Exhibitions: (1997) American Academy of Equine Art Invitational Show; British Watercolors & Drawings; Children's International Peace Murals; Ailene Fields - The Timeless Truth; Kathryn Myers; Bill Schaaf-Horses
Publications: Gallery guides; museum catalog; quarterly newsletter
Activities: Educ dept; classes for adults & children; docent training; lect open to public, 10 vis lectr per year; concerts; gallery talks; tours; individual paintings &

original objects of art lent to other institutions; lending collection contains books, photographs & slides; book traveling exhibitions 8-10 per year; originate traveling exhibitions to state institutions; museum shop sells books, original art, reproductions, posters & jewelry

ONECO

A **INTERNATIONAL SOCIETY OF MARINE PAINTERS,** PO Box 13, 34264. Tel 941-758-0802; FAX 941-755-1042; *Pres* Jerry McClish; *VPres* Wanda Coady
Estab 1984
Income: Financed by dues & contributions
Exhibitions: United States Merchant Marine Museum, Kings Point, NY
Publications: Seascaped, every 3 months

ORLANDO

M **ORLANDO MUSEUM OF ART,** 2416 N Mills Ave, 32803-1483. Tel 407-896-4231; FAX 407-896-9920; *Dir* Marena Grant Morrisey
Open Tues - Sat 9 AM - 5 PM, Sun Noon - 5 PM, cl Mon. Admis adults $4, children 4-11 $2, members & children under 4 free. Estab 1924 to encourage the awareness of & participation in the visual arts. Accredited by the American Assoc of Museums. 81,884 sq ft mus; seven galleries including exhibitions of 19th & 20th Century American Art, Pre-Columbian & African Art. Average Annual Attendance: 341,066. Mem: 3216; dues $40 & up; annual meeting in Sept
Income: Financed by mem, United Arts of Central Florida, Inc & State of Florida
Collections: †19th & 20th Century American painting, sculpture, prints & photography; †Pre-Columbian from Central & South America; African Art
Publications: Members Magazine, 2 times per year; mem newsletter, 6 times per year; exhibition catalogues
Activities: Classes for adults & children; dramatic programs; docent training; lect open to public, 6 vis lectr per year; concerts, gallery talks, tours; competitions with awards; scholarships offered; individual prints & original objects of art lent to museums; book traveling exhibitions 3-4 per year; originate traveling exhibitions; museum shop sells books, magazines, reproductions, art exhibit & art related merchandise

L **Orlando Sentinel Library,** 2416 N Mills Ave, 32803-1483. Tel 407-896-4231; FAX 407-896-9920; *Exec Dir* Marena Grant Morrisey
Library Holdings: Vols 3200; Per subs 10; Other — Clipping files, exhibition catalogs, pamphlets
Special Subjects: Aesthetics, Afro-American Art, American Western Art, Art Education, Art History, Ceramics, Decorative Arts, Furniture, Glass, History of Art & Archaeology, Landscape Architecture, Mexican Art, Painting - American, Pre-Columbian Art, Prints
Exhibitions: (1997) Imperial Tombs of China

A **PINE CASTLE FOLK ART CENTER,** 6015 Randolph St (Mailing add: 731 E Fairlane Ave, 32809). Tel 407-855-7461; FAX 407-855-7461; *Dir* Joan H Pyle
Open by appointment only. No Admis fee, tours $3. Estab 1965 as a non-profit community cultural center which provides programs in visual arts, folk crafts, local history, music & drama, & sponsors special projects for handicapped & senior citizens. One room 15 x 15 ft in main building; 85 yr old cracker farm house; 208 yr old log cabin. Average Annual Attendance: 25,000
Income: Financed by private citizens
Collections: Oral histories of area Old-timers, along with photographs, memorabilia & antiques
Exhibitions: Festival
Publications: Pioneer Days Annual Historical Magazine
Activities: Classes for adults & children; dramatic programs; concerts in the park

M **VALENCIA COMMUNITY COLLEGE,** Art Gallery-East Campus, 701 N Econlockhatchee Trail, PO Box 3028, 32802. Tel 407-299-5000, Ext 2298; *Chmn* Qurentia Throm; *Pres* Paul Gianini
Open Mon - Fri 12:30 - 4:30 PM. No admis fee. Estab 1982
Income: Financed by state appropriation, grants & private donations
Purchases: $1500
Collections: †Permanent collection: Mixed Media; Small Works: Mixed Media
Exhibitions: Art of Healing: National Invitational; Small Works Competition
Activities: Individual paintings & original objects of art lent; lending collection contains 250 items; originate traveling exhibitions 2 per year

ORMOND BEACH

M **ORMOND MEMORIAL ART MUSEUM AND GARDENS,** 78 E Granada Blvd, 32176. Tel 904-676-3347; *Dir* Anne Burt
Open Tues - Fri 11 AM - 4 PM, Sat & Sun Noon - 4 PM, cl Mon & month of Aug. No admis fee. Estab 1946 to house the symbolic oil paintings of Malcolm Fraser. Four connecting rooms; rear gallery opens with French doors onto wooden patio deck with a gazebo; lattice work windows. Average Annual Attendance: 8000. Mem: 350; dues $15 - $500; monthly meetings & annual meeting in Jan
Income: $32,000 (financed by endowment, mem & city appropriation)
Collections: Malcolm Fraser Symbolic Paintings - permanent collection; Catherine Combs lusterware
Exhibitions: Paintings, photography, crafts, sculpture & multi-media exhibits
Activities: Classes for adults & children; lect open to the public; workshops & children's events; private tours available; gallery tours

PALM BEACH

M HENRY MORRISON FLAGLER MUSEUM, Whitehall Mansion, Cocoanut Row, PO Box 969, 33480. Tel 407-655-2833; FAX 407-655-2826; *Dir* John Blades
Open Tues - Sat 10 AM - 5 PM, Sun Noon - 5 PM, cl Mon. Admis adults $5, children 6-12 $2, under 6 free. Estab 1960 for preservation & interpretation of the Whitehall mansion, the 1901 residence built for Standard Oil partner & pioneer developer of Florida's east coast, Henry Morrison Flagler. Fifty-five room historic house with restored rooms & special collections, special events & exhibitions. Average Annual Attendance: 130,000. Mem: 1700; dues $35-$1000; annual meeting Fri preceding first Sat in Feb
Income: Financed by endowment, mem & admis
Collections: †Original family furnishings, †china, †costumes; †furniture; †glassware; †paintings & †silver
Exhibitions: Various temporary exhibits
Publications: The Henry Morrison Flagler Museum booklet; Members' Newsletter, bimonthly
Activities: Guide training; lect open to public; gallery talks; concerts; tours; competitions; museum sells books & postcards contains gift shop

M EDNA HIBEL ART FOUNDATION, Hibel Museum of Art, 150 Royal Poinciana Plaza, PO Box 10607, 33480. Tel 561-833-6870; FAX 561-848-9640; Elec Mail hibel@worldnef.aff.net. *Dir* Mary Johnson; *Asst Dir* Janet E Tanis; *Pres* Theodore Plotkin; *Exec Trustee* Andy Plotkin, PhD
Open Tues - Sat 10 AM - 5 PM, Sun 1 - 5 PM, cl Mon. No admis fee. Estab 1977 to extend the appreciation of the art of Edna Hibel specifically & visual art in general. 14 galleries & spaces devoted to paintings, lithographs, sculpture & porcelain art by artist Edna Hibel, also features antique furniture, snuff bottles, paper weights & art book collections. Average Annual Attendance: 25,000. Mem: 10,000; dues $20; meeting Feb & Mar
Income: $80,000 (financed by mus store sales & private donations)
Purchases: $80,000
Collections: Craig Collection of Edna Hibel's Work; English & Italian 18th century furniture; ancient Chinese snuffbottles; 18th & 19th century paperweights; Japanese dolls; 19th & 20th century library art books; Paintings; Porcelain Art, Lithographs, Serigraphs, Sculpture
Exhibitions: Graphics, paintings, porcelains & sculptures
Publications: Edna Hibel Society Newsletter, 3 per year; exhibition catalogs; exhibition posters
Activities: Classes for children; docent training; lect open to public, 4 vis lectr per year; concerts; gallery talks; tours; book traveling exhibitions; originate traveling exhibitions; museum shop sells books & reproductions
L Gallery, 311 Royal Poinciana Plaza, 33480. Tel 561-655-2410; FAX 561-833-9370; *Dir* Mary Johnson; *Exec Trustee* Andy Plotkin, PhD; *Asst Dir & Dir Educ* Janet E Tanis
Open Tues - Sat 10 AM - 5 PM, Sun 1 - 5 PM. No admis fee. For reference only. Average Annual Attendance: 25,000
Purchases: $300
Library Holdings: Vols 400; AV — A-tapes, cassettes, fs, motion pictures, slides, v-tapes; Other — Clipping files, exhibition catalogs, framed reproductions, memorabilia, original art works, pamphlets, photographs, prints, reproductions, sculpture
Special Subjects: Antique art books on European & Oriental art; Stone lithography
Exhibitions: Annual Festival of Animals. Hibel's Russian Palette, Award Wining Documentary
Activities: Classes for adults & children; docent training; lect open to public, 2 vis lectr per year; lect to school classes & cultural activities for elementary school children; museum shop sells books, reproductions, collectable art plates, gift boxes, jewelry, posters

A THE SOCIETY OF THE FOUR ARTS, 4 Arts Plaza, 33480. Tel 407-655-7226; FAX 407-655-7233; *Pres* F Eugene Dixon Jr; *VPres* Robert M Grace; *VPres* Wiley R Reynolds; *VPres* Robert A Magowan; *VPres* Hollis M Baker; *Dir* Robert W Safrin; *Deputy Dir* Nancy Mato; *Treas* Henry P McIntosh IV
Open Dec - mid-Apr Mon - Sat 10 AM - 5 PM, Sun 2 - 5 PM. Admis to exhibition galleries free; $3 donation suggested. Estab 1936 to encourage an appreciation of the arts by presentation of exhibitions, lectures, concerts, films & programs for young people & the maintenance of a fine library & gardens. Five galleries for exhibitions, separate general library, gardens & auditorium. Average Annual Attendance: 40,000 (galleries & library). Mem: 1500; dues life $10,000, sustaining $550; annual meeting third Fri in Mar
Income: Financed by endowment, mem, city appropriation toward maintenance of library & contributions
Exhibitions: 56th Annual National Exhibition of Contemporary American Paintings; French Oil Sketches & The Academic Tradition: Nostalgic Journeys; American Illustration from the Delaware Art Museum; Augustus Vincent Tack; Landscape of the Spirit Organized by the Philips Collection, Washington DC
Publications: Calendar; schedule of events, annual
Activities: Programs for young people; lect open to public when space permits, otherwise limited to members, 13 vis lectr per year; concerts; films; competitions open to artists resident in United States; juror selects about 70 paintings for inclusion in annual exhibition
L Library, 4 Arts Plaza, 33480. Tel 561-655-2766; FAX 561-659-8510; *Librn* Joanne Rendon; *Art Reference Librn* Victoria Galban
Open Mon - Fri 10 AM - 5 PM, cl Sat May - Nov. Estab 1936. Circ 40,000
Income: Financed by endowment, mem & city appropriation
Library Holdings: Vols 40,000; Per subs 75
Special Subjects: Aesthetics, Architecture, Art Education, Art History, Ceramics, Decorative Arts, Drawings, Etchings & Engravings, Folk Art, Glass, Graphic Arts, Handicrafts, Landscapes, Mixed Media, Oriental Art
Collections: John C Jessup Collection; Henry P McIntosh Collection; James I Merrill Collection; Addison Mizner Collection, over 300 reference books & scrapbooks
Publications: Booklist, semi annual
Activities: Library tours

PANAMA CITY

M VISUAL ARTS CENTER OF NORTHWEST FLORIDA, 19 E Fourth St, 32401. Tel 904-769-4451; FAX 904-785-9248; *Exec Dir* K Kelly Keltner; *Admin Dir* Denise Walker; *Cur Educ* Kimberly Hudson
Open Tues - Sat 9 AM - 4 PM, Thurs 9 AM - 8 PM, cl Sun & Mon. No admis fee. The Center occupies the old city hall, jail & fire station on the corner of Fourth St & Harrison Ave in downtown Panama City. Main gallery hosts contemporary artists, juried competitions & mus coordinated collections. The lower galleries feature emerging artists & community sponsored competitions & collections. Impressions Gallery for children. Average Annual Attendance: 35,000. Mem: 475; family $40, individual $25, student $10
Income: $95,000 (financed by mem, grants & corporate sponsors)
Collections: †Permanent collection contains works of artists from Northwest Florida
Exhibitions: Rotating exhibits of all types of art
Publications: Images, newsletter, every 6 weeks
Activities: Classes for adults & children; docent programs; lect open to public, 125 vis lectr per year; concerts; gallery talks; tours; competitions with prizes; scholarships offered; individual paintings & original objects of art lent to businesses; book traveling exhibitions 2 per year; junior museum
L Visual Arts Center Library, 19 E Fourth St, 32401. Tel 904-769-4451; *Exec Dir* K Kelly Keltner; *Cur Educ* Linda Slayton
For reference & limited lending
Library Holdings: Vols 200; AV — V-tapes

PEMBROKE PINES

M BROWARD COMMUNITY COLLEGE - SOUTH CAMPUS, Art Gallery, 7200 Hollywood Blvd, 33024. Tel 954-963-8895, 963-8969; FAX 954-963-8802; *Gallery Dir* Dr Kyra Belan
Open Mon - Fri 10 AM - 2 PM. No admis fee. Estab 1991 to offer contemporary art exhibitions & cultural enrichment activities to college students & to the surrounding community. Gallery is 31 ft x 31 ft with a glass wall & high ceilings
Income: Financed by grants
Exhibitions: Studio Art Club Annual Juried Exhibition
Activities: Lect open to public, 6 vis lectr per year; competitions

PENSACOLA

A HISTORIC PENSACOLA PRESERVATION BOARD, Historic Pensacola Village, 120 Church St, 32501. Tel 904-444-8905; FAX 904-444-8641; *Dir* John P Daniels; *Museum Adminr* Tom Muir
Open Mon - Sat 10 AM - 4 PM, cl New Year's, Thanksgiving, Christmas. Admis adult $6, seniors $5, children 4-16 $2.50. Estab 1967 for collection, preservation & interpretation of artifacts dealing with the history & culture of Pensacola & West Florida. Multi-building complex includes two museums & three historic houses; main gallery includes history of development of West Florida as well as area for temporary exhibits. Average Annual Attendance: 45,000
Income: $500,000 (financed by city, county & state appropriations, sales & rentals)
Collections: Archives; costumes; decorative arts; Early 19th & 20th centuries local artists; Marine lumbering & farming tools & equipment
Activities: Docent training; sales shop sells books, reproductions & local crafts
L Library, 120 Church St, 32501. Tel 904-444-8905; FAX 904-444-8641; *Museum Adminr* Tom Muir
Open to the public for reference
Library Holdings: Vols 800; Per subs 15; AV — Slides; Other — Photographs
Special Subjects: Architecture, Decorative Arts, Historical Material, Regional history

M PENSACOLA JUNIOR COLLEGE, Visual Arts Gallery, 1000 College Blvd, 32504. Tel 904-484-1000; FAX 904-484-1826; *Dir* Allan Peterson; *Asst Dir* Carol Horigan
Open Mon - Thurs 8 AM - 9 PM, Fri 8 AM - 3:30 PM, cl weekends. No admis fee. Average Annual Attendance: 20,000
Income: Financed by state appropriation
Collections: †Contemporary ceramics, †glass, †drawings, †paintings, †prints, †photographs, †sculpture
Exhibitions: The Glassmaker: Historic and Contemporary; Pensacola National Crafts Exhibition; Pensacola National Printmaking Exhibition; Pensacola National Watermedia Exhibition; New Orleans Sculpture Invitational; Realism: A Close Look; Kim Irwin & Lisa Williamson-Fabric Collage; Texas Sculpture Invitational; Pensacola National Portrait Exhibition; Robert Fichter photography; Pensacola National Calligraphy Exhibition; Pensacola National Landscape Exhibition
Publications: Catalog, brochure or poster for each exhibition
Activities: Lect open to public, 3-6 vis lectr per year; workshops; gallery talks; competitions with awards given; scholarships offered; individual paintings & original objects of art lent to other museums & lending collection contains original art works; traveling exhibitions organized & circulated

M PENSACOLA MUSEUM OF ART, 407 S Jefferson St, 32501. Tel 904-432-6247; FAX 904-469-1532; *Admin Asst* Sandra Gentry
Open Tues - Fri 10 AM - 5 PM, Sat 10 AM - 4 PM, Sun 1 - 4 PM, cl Mon. Admis adults $2, students & military $1, members free. Estab 1954 to further & disseminate art history & some studio instruction with regard to the general pub & to increase knowledge & appreciation thereof. Mus is a historical building, old city jail built in 1908 & has 13,000 sq ft of exhibition area. Average Annual Attendance: 85,000. Mem: 850; dues $20-$500; annual meeting in Oct
Income: Financed by mem
Collections: Art, African pieces, contemporary art, glass
Exhibitions: Changing loan exhibitions

Publications: Monthly newsletter
Activities: Classes for adults & children; docent training; lect open to public, lectr varies; concerts; gallery talks; tours; individual paintings & original objects of art lent to other museums or galleries; book traveling exhibitions 9 per year; originate traveling exhibitions to regional museums; museum shop sells books, magazines, jewelry, cards, stationery, children's items & puzzles

L **Harry Thornton Library,** 407 S Jefferson St, 32501. Tel 904-432-6247; FAX 904-469-1532
Open Tues - Fri 10 AM - 5 PM, Sat 10 AM - 4 PM, Sun 1 - 4 PM. Estab 1968 to provide reference material for public & members. Reference library
Income: Financed by mem, city appropriation & grants by state & federal government
Purchases: $250
Library Holdings: Vols 1500; Per subs 10; AV — A-tapes, slides; Other — Exhibition catalogs
Special Subjects: Afro-American Art, Glass, Painting - American, Photography, Sculpture
Collections: Complete set of E Benezit's Dictionaire des Peintres, Sculpteurs, Dessinateurs et Graveurs; Encyclopedia of World Art and other art references books
Publications: Exhibitions catalogs; newsletter, 10 per year
Activities: Lect open to public, lectr varies; concerts; gallery talks; purchase & category awards

M **UNIVERSITY OF WEST FLORIDA,** Art Gallery, 11000 University Pky, 32514. Tel 904-474-2696; *Dir* Duncan E Stewart; *Asst Dir* E George Norris
Open Tues - Thurs 10 AM - 5 PM; Fri - Sat 10 AM - 1 PM; cl Sun. No admis fee. Estab 1970 to hold exhibitions which will relate to our role as a senior level university. Galleries include a foyer gallery 10 x 40 ft & a main gallery of 1500 sq ft. It is fully air-conditioned & has carpeted walls with full facilities for construction & display. Average Annual Attendance: 8500
Income: Financed by state appropriation
Collections: Photographs & prints by a number of traditional & contemporary artists
Activities: Lect open to public, 3 vis lectr per year; gallery talks; tours; competitions with awards; films; scholarships offered; individual paintings & original objects of art lent to university offices; book traveling exhibitions
L **Library,** 11000 University Pky, 32514-5750. Tel 904-474-2213; FAX 904-474-3338; Elec Mail ddebolt@neptune.icd.uws.edu/. *Dir Spec Coll* Dean DeBolt
Estab 1967
Income: Financed by state appropriations & Friends of the Library
Library Holdings: Vols 8345; Per subs 176; AV — Fs; Other — Memorabilia
Special Subjects: George Washington Sully, Watercolor sketches, Mardi Gras Float Designs
Collections: Includes collections of papers about Gulf Coast artists & art organizations

M **T T WENTWORTH JR MUSEUM,** Florida State Museum, 120 Church St, 32501. Tel 904-444-8586, 444-8905; FAX 904-444-8641; *Cur* Tom Muir; *Deputy Dir & Secy* T W Wentworth
Open Sat - Sun 2 - 6 PM. No admis fee. Estab 1957 to conserve historical items & make them available to the public; art sections to encourage art & exhibit local art work. Three floors of exhibits; collections change from floor to floor. Mem: Annual meeting Aug
Income: Financed by mem & founder's contributions
Collections: Works of local & some nationally famous artists; Indian artifacts; coins; porcelain
Exhibitions: Special yearly art exhibit of some distinguished local artist

SAFETY HARBOR

M **SAFETY HARBOR MUSEUM OF REGIONAL HISTORY,** 329 S Bayshore Blvd S, 34695. Tel 813-726-1668; *Pres* Marilyn Bartz; *VPres* Guy Waters; *Treas* Carol Wood; *Historical Preservation Dir* Hector Borghetty
Open daily 10 AM - 4 PM. Admis adult $1, children $.50. Estab 1977 to promote, encourage, maintain & operate a mus for the preservation of knowledge & appreciation of Florida's history; to display & interpret historical materials & allied fields. Indian art in the form of murals, pottery & artifacts. Average Annual Attendance: 8000. Mem: 60; dues $15 - $500; quarterly meetings
Income: $2000 (financed by mem & donations)
Collections: †Fossils; †dioramas, Heritage Gallery furniture; †Indian artifacts; †natural history exhibits; possessions of Count Philippe: Antiques; Spanish artifacts
Activities: Docent training; lect open to public, 7 vis lectr per year; gallery talks; tours; originate traveling exhibitions

SAINT AUGUSTINE

A **HISTORIC SAINT AUGUSTINE PRESERVATION BOARD,** PO Box 1987, 32085. Tel 904-825-5033; FAX 904-825-5096; *Cur* Tracy Spikes; *Exec Dir* Earle W Newton; *Info Officer* Cookie O'Brien
Open daily 9 AM - 5:15 PM, cl Christmas. Admis to six buildings adults $2.50, students $1.25, children under 6 free. Estab 1959 to depict daily life in the 1740s (Spanish) through its living history mus
Collections: Spanish artifacts; fine & decorative arts; restored & reconstructed colonial buildings from the 18th & 19th centuries
Exhibitions: Permanent & temporary exhibitions
Publications: Brochures & booklets

M **LIGHTNER MUSEUM,** 75 King St, Museum-City Hall Complex, PO Box 334, 32085. Tel 904-824-2874; *Exec Dir* Robert W Harper III; *Cur* James McBeth; *Registrar* Irene L Lawrie; *Chief Visitors Services* Helen Ballard
Open 9 AM - 5 PM, cl Christmas. Admis adults $4, students $1, children under 12 free when accompanied by adult. Estab 1948. Average Annual Attendance: 160,000
Income: Financed by admis

Collections: 19th century material culture & decorative arts
Activities: Classes for adults & children; dramatic programs; docent training; lect open to public, 4 vis lectr per year; concerts; gallery talks; tours; individual paintings & original objects of art lent to museums; book traveling exhibitions; originate traveling exhibitions to other museums; museum shop sells books, magazines, reproductions, prints, slides, dolls, jewelry, procelain, games & cards

L **Library,** PO Box 334, 32085-0334. Tel 904-824-2874; *Exec Dir* Robert W Harper III
Library for reference only
Income: Financed by the mus
Library Holdings: Vols 4600; Per subs 10; Other — Clipping files, exhibition catalogs, memorabilia, original art works, pamphlets, photographs, prints, reproductions, sculpture
Special Subjects: 19th Century Decorative Arts

A **SAINT AUGUSTINE ART ASSOCIATION GALLERY,** 22 Marine St, 32084. Tel 904-824-2310; *Pres* Len Weeks; *VPres* Alice Murphree; *Treas* Richard Waler; *Dir* Kay Burtin
Open Tues - Sat Noon - 4 PM, Sun 2 - 5 PM, cl Mon & holidays. No admis fee. Estab 1924, incorporated 1934 as a non-profit organization to further art appreciation in the community by exhibits & instructions, also to provide a gallery where local artists may show their work & pub & tourists may see them free. Gallery is 50 ft x 90 ft with carpeted walls for exhibition. Average Annual Attendance: 5000. Mem: 450; dues $25 & up; annual meeting in Mar
Income: Financed by mem & develop grant
Collections: Donations of art works by St Augustine artists or members representing St Augustine
Activities: Classes for adults & children; docent training; workshops; lect open to public, 8-10 vis lectr per year; gallery talks; tours; competitions with prizes; concerts on a rental basis

SAINT AUGUSTINE HISTORICAL SOCIETY

M **Oldest House & Museums,** 14 Saint Frances St, 32084. Tel 904-824-2872; Elec Mail oldhouse@aug.com. *Dir* Page Edwards; *Vol Coordr* Eddie Joyce Geyer
Open Mon - Fri 9 AM - 5 PM; cl Christmas Day. Admis adults $3.50, students $1.75. Estab 1883 to preserve the Spanish heritage of the United States through exhibits in historic mus with collection of furnishings appropriate to the periods in Saint Augustine history (1565 to date). The Oldest House was acquired in 1918; it is owned & operated by the Saint Augustine Historical Soc; it has been designated a National Historic Landmark by the Department of the Interior & is listed in the national registrar of historic sites & places. Average Annual Attendance: 90,000. Mem: 600; dues $20; annual meeting in Jan
Income: Financed by admis
Collections: Archaeological material recovered from this area, both aboriginal & colonial; period furnishings: Spanish America (1565-1763 & 1783-1821); British (1763-1783); American (1821-present)
Exhibitions: Saint Johns Railway
Publications: El Escribano, annual; East Florida Gazette, quarterly
Activities: Classes for adults & children; docent training; lect open to public, 9 vis lectr per year; original objects of art lent; museum shop sells books, reproductions, prints & slides

L **Library,** 12 Aviles St, 32084. Tel 904-825-2333; FAX 904-824-2569; Elec Mail sahs@aug.com. *Library Dir* Taryn Rodrigues-Boette; *Reference* Charles Tingley; *Cataloger* Dorothy Lyon
Open Tues - Fri 9 AM - 4:30 PM, cl holidays. Research library
Income: Financed by endowment & admis from Oldest House
Library Holdings: Vols 10,000; Per subs 40; Original documents; Micro — Reels; AV — A-tapes, cassettes, Kodachromes, motion pictures, rec, slides; Other — Clipping files, manuscripts, memorabilia, original art works, pamphlets, photographs, prints, reproductions, sculpture
Special Subjects: Anthropology, Archaeology, Architecture, Ceramics, Coins & Medals, Costume Design & Construction, Furniture, Glass, Historical Material, History of Art & Archaeology, Manuscripts, Maps, Painting - American - Spanish, Period Rooms, Pottery, Religious Art, Restoration & Conservation, Florida history (to 1821) with emphasis on early periods of Saint Augustine history to the present
Collections: Paintings of early artist & of early Saint Augustine; 200 linear feet of maps, photographs, documents & photostats of Spanish Archival Materials as touching directly on Saint Augustine's History during the early Spanish, British & American periods (1565 to present)
Publications: East Florida Gazette, quarterly; El Escribano, annually
Activities: Lect open to public, 9 vis lectr per year

SAINT PETERSBURG

M **MUSEUM OF FINE ARTS, SAINT PETERSBURG, FLORIDA, INC,** 255 Beach Dr NE, 33701. Tel 813-896-2667; FAX 813-894-4638; Elec Mail musfinarts@earthlink.net. *Dir* Michael Milkovich; *Cur Coll & Exhib* Jennifer Hardin; *Admin Asst* Barbara Somerville; *Mem Coordr* Donna Fletcher; *Coordr Exhib* Gale C Laubach; *Registrar* Margarita Laughlin; *Accounting Officer* Ruth Wells; *Museum Shop* Donna Dontale; *Cur Educ* Rebecca Russell; *Photog & Installations* Thomas Gessler
Open Tues - Sat 10 AM - 5 PM; Sun 1 - 5 PM; cl Mon. Admis $5. Estab 1962 to increase & diffuse knowledge & appreciation of art; to collect & preserve objects of artistic interest; to provide facilities for research & to offer popular instruction & opportunities for esthetic enjoyment of art. Twenty galleries of works from the collection including period rooms. Average Annual Attendance: 100,000. Mem: 3200; dues $25 & higher; annual meeting in May
Income: $1,100,000 (financed by endowment, mem, fundraising, city & state grants)
Collections: Art: African, American, Ancient, Asian, European, Native American & Pre-Columbian; †decorative arts; 19th & 20th Century photographs; †paintings; †photographs; †prints; †sculpture
Publications: Mosaic, quarterly newspaper; brochures & exhibition catalogues; catalogue of the collection
Activities: Classes for adults & children; docent training; lect open to public; 30 vis lectr per year; films; tours; performing arts; dance; concerts; theatre;

storytellers; individual paintings & original objects of art lent to other museums; lending collection contains color reproductions, films on art; originate traveling exhibitions; museum shop sells books, museum reproductions, prints, museum replicas, jewelry, pottery & crafts by local & national artisans, stationery, children's art educational games & puzzles, t-shirts with museum logo

L **Art Reference Library,** 255 Beach Dr N, 33701. Tel 813-896-2667; FAX 813-894-4638; *Library Vol* Muriel S Kirk
Open Tues - Fri 10 AM - 5 PM, cl Mon. Estab 1962 as reference library
Income: Financed by grants & contributions
Library Holdings: Vols 10,210; Per subs 30; AV — A-tapes, slides 20,000, v-tapes; Other — Exhibition catalogs, reproductions
Special Subjects: Architecture, Art History, Bronzes, Carpets & Rugs, Ceramics, Folk Art, Glass, Gold, Graphic Design, History of Art & Archaeology, Islamic Art, Painting - European, Painting - Flemish, Painting - French, Painting - German, Stained Glass, Tapestries, East Indian Art
Collections: †Photography
Publications: Mosaic, quarterly-mem bulletin; Pharos, biennial; catalogue of the collection
Activities: Classes for adults & children; lect open to the public, 6 vis lectr per year; concerts; gallery talks; exten dept serves public schools

M **SALVADOR DALI MUSEUM,** 1000 Third St S, 33701. Tel 813-823-3767, 822-6270; FAX 813-894-6068; Elec Mail daliweb@mindspring.com. *Chmn* A Reynolds Morse; *Exec Dir* T Marshall Rousseau; *Pres* Thomas A James; *Vol Coordr* Gwenda Barnitz; *Bookstore Mgr* Kathy White
Open Tues - Sat 10 AM - 5 PM, Sun Noon - 5 PM, cl Mon. Admis $3. Estab 1971 to share the private Dali Collection of Mr & Mrs A Reynolds Morse with the pub; formerly in Cleveland, Ohio, the museum re-opened Mar 7, 1982 in Saint Petersburg, Fla. Average Annual Attendance: 75,000
Income: Financed by private collector, State University Systems & donations
Collections: †93 oils and 5 large masterworks by Dali make up a retrospective of his work from 1914 to the present; numerous drawings and watercolors
Exhibitions: (1997) Dali by the books; Salvador Dali Prints & Processes; Works of Kenny Scharf; Visionary State Surrealist Prints from Gilbert Kaplan Collection Dali Alchemy; Dali Les-Chants-De Maldoror; Alice in Wonderland
Publications: Dali Adventure; Dali - A Panorama of His Art; Dali Draftmanship; Guide to Works by Dali in Public Museums; Introductionto Dali; Dali-Picasso; Poetic Homage to Gala-Dali; Dali Primer; Dali's World of Symbols: Workbook for Children; Dali Newsletter; exhibition catalogues
Activities: Adult classes; docent training; lect open to public, 2 vis lectr per year; film series; gallery talks; tours; museum shop sells books, reproductions, prints, slides, postcards

L **Library,** 1000 Third St S, 33701. Tel 813-823-3767; FAX 813-894-6068; *Librn* Joan R Kropf
Restricted use at present; contains 5000 references to Dali in books, periodicals & newspapers
Income: Financed privately by Salvador Dali Foundation
Purchases: $20,000
Library Holdings: Vols 32; Per subs 20; Illustrated editions; AV — A-tapes, cassettes, Kodachromes 3000, motion pictures 10, slides, v-tapes 50; Other — Clipping files, exhibition catalogs, framed reproductions 1028, manuscripts, memorabilia, original art works 165, pamphlets, photographs, prints 750
Collections: Films & Tapes on or by Dali

SARASOTA

L **RINGLING SCHOOL OF ART & DESIGN,** Verman Kimbrough Memorial Library, 2700 N Tamiami Trail, 34234. Tel 813-359-7587; FAX 813-359-7632; *Library Dir* Deborah Johnson; *AV Librn* Allen Novak; *Technical Servs Librn* Frances Adams-O'Brien
Open Mon - Thurs 8 AM - 10 PM, Fri 8 AM - 4:30 PM, Sat 2 - 6 PM, Sun 2 - 10 PM. Estab 1932 to serve the curriculum needs of an undergraduate, visual arts college. Art gallery is maintained. Circ 30,000
Income: $100,000 (financed by library assoc, parent institution & capital expense)
Purchases: $100,000
Library Holdings: Vols 20,000; Per subs 350; AV — Cassettes 600, fs 24, slides 60,000, v-tapes; Other — Exhibition catalogs
Special Subjects: Advertising Design, Aesthetics, American Indian Art, Architecture, Art Education, Art History, Asian Art, Commercial Art, Conceptual Art, Decorative Arts, Drawings, Film, Graphic Arts, Graphic Design, History of Art & Archaeology, Computer Design, Fine Arts

A **SARASOTA VISUAL ART CENTER,** 707 N Tamiami Trail, 34236. Tel 941-365-2032; FAX 941-366-0585; *Pres* Charles Meyrick; *Co-Gallery Dir* Elaine Summers; *Co-Gallery Dir* Davidson Gigliotti
Open Mon - Fri 10 AM - 4 PM, Sat & Sun 1 - 4 PM. No admis fee. Estab 1926, incorporated 1940, to promote the educational & cultural advantages of Sarasota in the field of contemporary art. Three galleries: east & sales galleries supports small exhibits & one-man shows; west gallery for member shows. Average Annual Attendance: 15,000. Mem: 500; dues $40
Income: Financed by mem & donations
Publications: Bulletin, monthly; yearbook
Activities: Classes for adults & children; docent training; workshops; lect open to public, 25 vis lectr per year; gallery talks; tours; demonstrations; scholarships offered; book traveling exhibitions 5 per year; originate traveling exhibitions; museum shop sells books, original art, reproductions & prints

M **STATE ART MUSEUM OF FLORIDA,** John & Mable Ringling Museum of Art, 5401 Bay Shore Rd, PO Box 1838, 34243. Tel 941-359-5700; *Dir* David Ebitz; *Registrar* Edward Amatore; *Conservator* Michelle Scalera; *Dir Public Affairs* Barbara Linick; *Dept Dir Finance & Admin* Gary Lamm; *Dir Adult Educ* Elisa Hansen; *Dir Student Educ* Susan Hazelroth; *Librn* Linda McKee
Open daily 10 AM - 5:30 PM. Admis adults $8.50, children 12 & under free. Estab 1928. Bequeathed to the State of Florida by John Ringling & operated by the state; built in Italian villa style around sculpture garden on 60 plus landscaped acres; original 19th century theater from Asolo, near Venice, in adjacent building; Ringling Residence & Circus Galleries on grounds. Average Annual Attendance: 250,000 paid combination, 700,000 free attendance & special events. Mem: 3000; dues benefactor $10,000, patron $5000, fellow $1000, friend $250, centennial $100, family $50, individual $30
Collections: Archaeology of Cyprus; Baroque pictures, especially those of Peter Paul Rubens; European painting, sculpture, drawings & prints from the 16th, 17th & 18th centuries; medals & 18th century decorative arts; developing collection of 19th & 20th century painting, sculpture, drawings & prints
Exhibitions: Selections from the Permanent Collection: Old Masters.
Publications: Calendar, bi-monthly; Collection Catalogues; Exhibition Catalogues; Newsletter, quarterly
Activities: Educ dept; docent training; state services; lect open to public & some for members only; concerts; gallery talks; exten dept serves the state; individual paintings & original objects of art lent to affiliates & other qualified museums nationally & internationally on board approval; lending collection contains 1000 individual paintings, 1000 objects of art; originate traveling exhibitions to affiliates; sales shop sells books, reproductions, prints & slides

L **Ringling Museum Library,** 5401 Bay Shore Rd, 34243. Tel 941-359-5743; FAX 941-351-7959; *Librn* Linda R McKee; *Archivist* Deborah Walk
Open Mon, Wed & Fri 1 - 5 PM. Reference only
Library Holdings: Vols 35,000; Per subs 100; Art auction catalogues; Rare books; Other — Exhibition catalogs
Special Subjects: Art History, Painting - Dutch, Painting - Flemish, Painting - Italian, Emblem Books, Iconography, Renaissance & Baroque Art, 20th Century Art
Collections: John Ringling Library of Circus Books

STUART

M **HISTORICAL SOCIETY OF MARTIN COUNTY,** Elliott Museum, 825 NE Ocean Blvd, 34996-1696. Tel 561-225-1961; *Dir* Elizabeth Press
Open daily 11 AM - 4 PM including holidays. Admis adults $4, children between 6 & 13 $.50. Estab 1961. Average Annual Attendance: 30,000. Mem: 1000; dues $25-$1000
Collections: Contemporary American artists (realistic): Walter Brightwell, Nina D Buxton, Cecilia Cardman, E I Couse, James Ernst, Jo Gabeler, Diana Kan, Hui Chi Mau, Rose W Traines
Activities: Concerts; local school tours, morning; bookstore sells jewelry & children items

TALLAHASSEE

A **FLORIDA DEPARTMENT OF STATE, DIVISION OF CULTURAL AFFAIRS,** Florida Arts Council, The Capitol, 32399-0250. Tel 904-487-2980; FAX 904-922-5259; Telex 488-5779. *Dir* Peyton C Fearington; *Asst Dir* JuDee Pettijohn; *Arts Adminr* Lee Modica
Open 8 AM - 5 PM. Estab 1969 to advise the Secretary of State in fostering the arts in Florida
Activities: Scholarships & fels offered to individual artists

A **FLORIDA FOLKLIFE PROGRAMS,** Grey Bldg, Rm 402, 500 S Bruno St, 32399-0250. FAX 904-397-2915; WATS 800-847-7278. *Dir* Susan Walker; *Folklife Adminr* Teresa Hollingsworth; *Folk Arts Coordr* Tina Bucubusa
Open Mon - Fri 8 AM - 5 PM. No admis fee. Estab 1979. The Bureau is under Secretary of Jim Smith & carries on a year-round calendar of folk activities in an effort to encourage statewide pub interests & participation in the folk arts & folklore
Activities: Classes for adults & children; lect open to public; concerts; Florida Folk Heritage Award; apprenticeships offered; originate traveling exhibitions

L **Library,** Grey Bldg, Rm 402, 500 S Bruno St, 32399-0250. FAX 904-397-2915; WATS 800-847-7278. *Archivist* David Reddy
Open to pub for reference Mon - Fri 8 AM - 5 PM
Library Holdings: Vols 500; Per subs 12; Micro — Cards; AV — A-tapes, cassettes, fs, Kodachromes, rec, slides, v-tapes; Other — Clipping files, exhibition catalogs, manuscripts, original art works, pamphlets, photographs
Special Subjects: Ethnology, Folk Art, Florida folklife

M **FLORIDA STATE UNIVERSITY,** Museum of Fine Arts, 250 Fine Arts Bldg, Copeland & Tennessee Sts, 32306-2055. Tel 904-644-6836; FAX 904-644-7229; Elec Mail apcraig@mailer.fsu.edu. *Dir* Allys Palladino-Craig; *Fiscal Officer & Designer. Museum Press* Julienne T Mason; *Preparator* Richard Fett; *Registrar & Cur Exhib* Viki D Wylder
Open Mon - Fri 10 AM - 4 PM, Sat & Sun 1 - 4 PM & 7 - 8 PM preceding Mainstage performances; cl school holidays. No admis fee. Estab 1950. Three upper galleries; two lower galleries, one for permanent collection; sculpture courtyard. Average Annual Attendance: 55,000. Mem: 300, friends of the Gallery; 150, Artists' League
Income: Financed by state appropriations, grants & private sector
Collections: Asian prints; Carter Collection of pre-Columbian Art; contemporary American graphics, photography & paintings; European painting
Exhibitions: Permanent Collections; changing schedule of major art historical works & contemporary American & European art; Combined Talents: The Florida National, juried competition
Publications: Exhibition catalogues
Activities: Lect open to public, 4-6 vis lectr per year; tours & lect for children; concerts; gallery talks; tours; competitions with awards; exten dept; individual paintings & original objects of art lent by appropriate request; book traveling exhibitions 1-2 per year; originate traveling exhibitions

M **LEMOYNE ART FOUNDATION, INC,** 125 N Gadsden St, 32301. Tel 904-222-8800; *Pres* Thomas A Deans; *Dir* Richard L Puckett
Open Tues - Sat 10 AM - 5 PM; Sun 2 - 5 PM; cl Mon. No admis fee. Estab 1964 as a non-profit organization to serve as gallery for contemporary, quality art; class center; sponsor the visual arts in Tallahassee; an educational institution in the broadest sense. Located in Meginnes-Munroe House, built c 1840; four main galleries and gallery shop. Average Annual Attendance: 7000. Mem: 800;

dues $25 - $1000
Income: Financed by mem, sales, classes & fund raisers
Collections: Contemporary Florida Artists; William Watson Collection of Ceramics; Karl Zerbe Serigraphs
Publications: Newsletter, bi-monthly
Activities: Classes for adults and children; lect open to public, 4 vis lectr per year; gallery talks; tours; competitions; individual paintings and original objects of art lent to businesses and members; lending collection contains original art works, original prints; paintings and sculpture; sales shop sells original fine art, craft items and prints

M **TALLAHASSEE MUSEUM OF HISTORY & NATURAL SCIENCE,** 3945 Museum Dr, 32310. Tel 904-575-8684; FAX 904-574-8243; *Dir* Russell S Daws; *Dir Admin* Dan Hughen; *Educ Dir* Jennifer Golden; *Cur Coll & Exhib* Linda Deaton; *Animal Cur* Mike Jones
Open Mon - Sat 9 AM - 5 PM; Sun 12:30 - 5 PM. Admis adults $6, children 4-15 $3, members free. Estab 1957 to educate children & adults about natural history, native wildlife, North Florida history, art & culture. Facilities include 1880's farm, historic buildings, exhibit & class buildings, 40 acres of nature trails & animal habitats. Average Annual Attendance: 120,000. Mem: 5000; dues $40; annual meeting third Thurs in Oct
Income: $1,000,000 (financed by mem, fundraisers, admis & government appropriation)
Collections: Pre-Columbia Florida Indian Pottery; Historic Buildings; Furnishings
Exhibitions: Changing exhibit on art, clothing, crafts, history & science; permanent or semi-permanent (3 years) exhibits on local history & natural history
Publications: Guidebook Series; Newsletter, monthly; School Handbook
Activities: Classes for adults & children; docent training; lect open to public, 8-12 vis lectr per year; concerts; gallery talks; tours; scholarships offered; museum shop sells books, reproductions & prints
L **Library,** 3945 Museum Dr, 32310. Tel 904-575-8684; FAX 904-574-8243; *Chief Exec Officer & Exec Dir* Russell S Daws
Open to members
Income: $1,500,000 (financed by earned income, donations, grants & special events)
Library Holdings: Vols 500; Per subs 7
Collections: Ivan Gundrum Pre-Columbian Florida Indian Artifacts (reproductions) representing the Weeden Island culture 500 - 1500 AD
Publications: Monthly Tallahassee Museum Newsletter

TAMPA

C **CASPERS, INC,** Art Collection, 4908 W Nassau St, 33607. Tel 813-287-2231; *Pres* Joseph Casper; *VPres* Chuck Peterson; *Marketing Mgr* Molly Lawrence
Open Mon - Fri 8 AM - 5 PM. Estab 1981 to enhance the employees' environment
Collections: Collection features works by artists with some relationship to Florida

A **CITY OF TAMPA,** Art in Public Places, 1420 N Tampa St, 33602. Tel 813-227-7736; FAX 813-227-7744; *Prog Coordr* Barbara A Hill; *Dir Recreation Dept* Joe Abrahams
Estab 1985 to visually enhance & enrich the public environment for both residents & visitors of Tampa. Mem: Public Art Committee meets monthly
Collections: Permanent collection of outdoor works including environmental park, murals & sculpture; interior works including drawings, mixed media, 50 paintings, prints
Publications: Public Art Brochure; Save Outdoor Sculpture, Tampa Bay
Activities: Lect open to public; tours; competitions with prizes

ARTHUR MANLEY SOCIETY
For further information, see National and Regional Organizations

M **MUSEUM OF AFRICAN AMERICAN ART,** 1308 N Marion St, 33602. Tel 813-272-2466; FAX 813-272-2325; *Founder* Dr Samella Lewis
Estab as a national resource dedicated to the presentation of the rich cultural heritage of people of African descent; educates the broadest possible audience; serves as a vehicle through which it promotes & fosters scholarship in art history with a particular interest in the contemporary & historical contributions of African American artists
Collections: Arts of the African & African-descendant people; Soapstone Sculpture of Shona; People of Southeast Africa; Makonde Sculpture of East Africa; Traditional Sculpture of West Africa; Sculpture, Paintings, Ceramics of the Caribbean & the South American Peoples; Contemporary North American Artists

SOCIETY OF NORTH AMERICAN GOLDSMITHS
For further information, see National and Regional Organizations

M **TAMPA MUSEUM OF ART,** 600 N Ashley, 33602. Tel 813-274-8130; FAX 813-274-8732; *Dir* Emily S Kass; *Chief Cur* Michael J Bennett; *Preparator* Bob Hellier; *Registrar* Kay T Morris
Open Mon - Sat 10 AM - 5 PM, Wed 10 AM - 9 PM, Sun 1 - 5 PM. Admis adults $5, senior citizens & students $4, children 6-18 $3, under 6 free. Estab 1970 to educate the pub through the display of art. 7 galleries with antiquities, sculpture, photography & paintings. Average Annual Attendance: 75,000. Mem: 1800; dues $50
Income: $1,250,000 (financed by local government, grants, mem & contributions)
Collections: Greek & Roman antiquities; 20th century painting, sculpture & photographyy; 19th century photography & sculpture
Exhibitions: Eye For Antiquity Photography, 1850s-1995 with Classical Antiquities as Reference; Liberated Image Photography Since 1970 (primarily American)
Publications: Catalogs; Newsletter, bi-monthly; school calender
Activities: Classes for adults & children; docent training; films; workshops; lect open to public; concerts; gallery talks; tours; individual paintings & original

objects of art lent to fellow museums, lending collection contains cassettes, color reproductions, Kodachromes, phonorecords, photographs, slides & videos; book traveling exhibitions 10 per year; originate traveling exhibitions to other museums; museum shop sells books, original art, reproductions, prints, jewelry, toys, t-shirts, cards & stationary
L **Library,** 600 N Ashley Dr, 33602. Tel 813-274-8130; FAX 813-274-8732; *Registrar* Kay T Morris; *Dir* Emily S Kass; *Sr Cur* Michael J Bennett
For reference only. Average Annual Attendance: 70,550. Mem: 1800; dues $35 & up
Library Holdings: Vols 1200; Per subs 32; CD Rom programs; Micro — Fiche; AV — A-tapes, cassettes, slides, v-tapes; Other — Exhibition catalogs 700, pamphlets
Special Subjects: Antiquities-Etruscan, Antiquities-Greek, Antiquities-Roman, Art Education, Art History, Coins & Medals, Painting - American, Painting - European, Photography, Pre-Columbian Art, Prints, Sculpture, Florida Artists

M **UNIVERSITY OF SOUTH FLORIDA,** Contemporary Art Museum, College of Fine Arts, 4202 E Fowler Ave, 33620-7360. Tel 813-974-2849; *Dir & Chief Cur* Margaret A Miller; *Assoc Dir* Alexa A Favata; *Coordr Pub Art* Vincent Ahern
Open Mon - Fri 10 AM - 5 PM, Sat 1 - 4 PM. No admis fee. Estab 1961 to provide exhibitions of contemporary art. Mus located on W Holly Dr on Tampa Campus. Average Annual Attendance: 55,000. Mem: dues corporate $1000-$100,000, private $5-$1000
Income: Financed by state appropriation, grants, mem fees & corporate art program
Collections: African art, Pre-Columbian artifacts; art bank collection of loan traveling exhibitions (approx 60 small package exhibitions); contemporary photography; †contemporary works on paper; †painting; sculpture
Exhibitions: (1997) Rapture; 21st Annual Juried USF Student Art Exhibition; Dennis Oppenheim: Landscape; Crossings: Contemporary African Art; Shouts from the Wall
Publications: Exhibition catalogs
Activities: Docent training; lect open to public, 4 vis lectr per year; gallery talks; tours; through Art Bank program original prints are lent to institutions, universities & arts organizations; book traveling exhibitions 2 per year; originate traveling exhibitions organized & circulated to universities, galleries & colleges; museum shop sells books, magazines, artists' created jewelry, architecture related products
L **Library,** 4202 E Fowler Ave, 33620. Tel 813-974-2729; FAX 813-974-9875; *Dir* Sam Fustukian; *Art Reference Librn* Irene Frank
Open to students & pub
Library Holdings: Vols 865,276; Per subs 5041; Micro — Cards, fiche, reels; AV — A-tapes, cassettes, fs, motion pictures, v-tapes; Other — Clipping files, framed reproductions, manuscripts, pamphlets, photographs, prints, reproductions
Special Subjects: Historical Material, Contemporary
Collections: Rare art books

UNIVERSITY OF TAMPA
M **Henry B Plant Museum,** 401 W Kennedy Blvd, 33606. Tel 813-254-1891, Ext 3400; *Dir* Cynthia Gandee; *Cur & Registrar* Susan Carter; *Museum Relations* Darby Miller; *Cur Educ* Harriett Lenfestey; *Museum Store Mgr* Sue Blankinship
Open Tues - Sat 10 AM - 4 PM, Sun Noon - 4 PM, cl holidays. Admis suggested donation $3. Estab 1933 in the former Tampa Bay Hotel built in 1891, to explain the importance of the Tampa Bay Hotel & Henry Plant to the area. This building which contains Victorian furnishings & artifacts, original to the Tampa Bay Hotel, is now on the register as a National Historical Landmark built by the railroad industrialist H B Plant. Average Annual Attendance: 25,000. Mem: 500
Income: Financed by city appropriation, University of Tampa, mem & donations
Collections: †Late Victorian furniture & objects d'art of same period; Venetian mirrors; Wedgwood, Oriental porcelains
Exhibitions: Exhibits relating to 19th century life; Plant system railroads & steamships, Annual Christmas Stroll
Publications: Henry B Plant Museum, Today & Moments In Time, a pictorial history of the Tampa Bay Hotel; Tampa Bay Hotel: Florida's First Magic Kingdom (video); member newsletter, quarterly
Activities: Docent training; lect open to public & lect for members only, 4 vis lectr per year; tours; museum store sells books, original art reproductions, Victorian style gifts, Chinese & Japanese artifacts, antique estate jewelry, estate silver, linens
M **Lee Scarfone Gallery,** 401 W Kennedy Blvd, 33606. Tel 813-253-3333, 253-6217; *Pres* Ron Vaughn; *Dir* Dorothy Cowden
Open Fri 10 AM - 4 PM, Sat 1 - 4 PM, cl June - July. No admis fee. Estab 1977 to exhibit works of art as an extension of the classroom & to utilize the space for pub functions which would benefit from the artistic environment created by showing current trends of all art forms of artistic merit. Average Annual Attendance: 12,000. Mem: 75; donation dues $25-$400
Income: Financed by donations & fundraisers
Collections: Contemporary artists
Exhibitions: Studio F; Monotype Exhibition; George Sugarman, Susan Gott, Lynn Davison Student & Faculty Exhibitions
Publications: Exhibiton brochures, 10 times a yr
Activities: Classes for adults; lect open to public; gallery talks; awards; scholarships offered; lend artwork to other art or educational institutions; lending collection contains 100 pieces of original art; originate traveling exhibitions

TEQUESTA

M **LIGHTHOUSE GALLERY & SCHOOL OF ART,** 373 Tequesta Dr, Gallery Sq N, 33469. Tel 561-746-3101; FAX 561-746-3241; *Acting Dir* Margaret Inserra
Open Mon - Sat 9:30 AM - 4:30 PM. No admis fee. Estab 1964 to create pub interest in all forms or the fine arts. Average Annual Attendance: 50,000. Mem: 800; dues $50; annual meeting in Apr
Exhibitions: Temporary & traveling exhibitions; Celebration of the Arts juried exhibit
Publications: Calendar of Events, monthly
Activities: Classes for adults & children; workshops; Fine Arts Festival; Jazz Concert; Formal Beaux Art Ball; Holiday Tea; lect open to public, 10 vis lectr

per year; concerts; tours; competitions with awards; scholarships offered; individual paintings & original objects of art lent to local doctors offices, local restaurants & banks; lending collection contains books, original art works, original prints, paintings & sculptures; sales shop sells original art, gift shop items

L **Library,** 373 Tequesta Dr, Gallery Sq N, 33458. Tel 561-746-3101; FAX 561-746-3241; *Acting Dir* Margaret Inserra
Small library of art books & art magazines
Library Holdings: Vols 600; Per subs 10; Other — Clipping files, exhibition catalogs, pamphlets, prints, reproductions

VALPARAISO

M **HERITAGE MUSEUM ASSOCIATION, INC,** 115 Westview Ave, PO Box 488, 32580. Tel 904-678-2615; *Dir* Mrs Christian S LaRoche; *Educ Cur* Kay McNeese
Open Tues - Sat 11 AM - 4 PM. No admis fee. Estab 1971 to collect, preserve, & display items related to the history & development of the area. Average Annual Attendance: 6000. Mem: 130; dues $20
Income: $30,000 (financed by mem, city & county appropriation, fundraising & donations)
Collections: Paleo & archaic stone artifacts; pioneer household utensils, agricultural implements, artisans' tools, tools used in the turpentine & lumber industries; photos & files of research materials
Activities: Adult & children's classes; docent programs; lectures open to the public; gallery talks; tours; museum shop sells books

VERO BEACH

A **FLORIDA ART MUSEUM DIRECTORS ASSOCIATION,** 1990 Sand Dollar Lane, 32963. Tel 561-388-2428; FAX 561-388-9313; *Pres & Dir Museum Arts* Gary R Libby; *Exec Dir Norton Museum* Dr Christina Orr-Cahall; *Coordr* Ruth Myers
Estab 1977 to promote the development of a scholarly & creative role for Florida visual arts museums & their directors in the cultural life of the State of Florida & to apply its members' knowledge & experience to the field of art to the promotion of the pub good; to encourage communication among visual arts museums & their directors. Mem: 62,839

WEST PALM BEACH

A **HISTORICAL SOCIETY OF PALM BEACH COUNTY,** 400 N Dixie Hwy, 33401-4210. Tel 561-832-4164; FAX 561-832-7965; *Adminr* Ellen L Donovan; *Bookkeeper* Sue Wagner
Open Tues - Fri 10 AM - 3 PM. No admis fee. Estab 1937 to preserve & disseminate history of Palm Beach County. Average Annual Attendance: 1000. Mem: 700; dues $35-$1000; annual meeting in Apr
Income: $90,000 (financed by mem, donations & grants)
Collections: Addison Mizner architectural drawings; History of Palm Beach County; other local architect drawings
Publications: Newsletter, monthly Oct - May
Activities: Lect open to public, 6 vis lectr per year; tours; competitions-Judge James R Knott Award for excellence in historical research-public history; original objects of art lent to qualified non-profit organizations; lending collection contains film strips, framed reproductions, original art works, original prints, photographs, slides & artifacts from permanent collection; sales shop sells books & reproductions

M **NORTON GALLERY & SCHOOL OF ART, INC,** Norton Museum of Art, 1451 S Olive Ave, 33401. Tel 561-832-5194, 832-5196; FAX 561-659-4689; Internet Home Page Address http://www.norton.org. *Dir* Christina Orr-Cahall; *Pres* R B Snyder; *Dir Develop* Sara Smith; *Cur* David Setford; *Dir Membership* Graham Russell; *Public Relations Dir* Sarah Flynn; *Supt* Franklyn Slocumb; *Registrar* Pamela Parry; *Cur Educ* Brian MacFarland
Open Tues - Sat 10 AM - 5 PM; Sun 1 - 5 PM. Admis voluntary donation. The Norton Gallery of Art was founded in 1940, dedicated in 1941 for the educ & enjoyment of the pub; additions were made in 1946, 49, 52 & 66. Acquisitions & gifts are continually being made to the mus. Building & major collections were given by Ralph Hubbard Norton & Elizabeth Calhoun Norton. The Gallery, designed by the Palm Beach architects, Wyeth, King & Johnson, opened to the pub in 1941, with an original collection of one hundred paintings. Mr Norton continued to acquire works of art for the mus until his death in 1953, when the remainder of his private collection was given to the mus. Sculptures are exhibited throughout the Gallery & in the patio garden. Average Annual Attendance: 120,000. Mem: 4000; dues family $60 & $40; annual meeting Nov
Income: Financed by endowment, mem, city appropriation, Palm Beach County Tourist Development Council, donations & fundraising events
Collections: French Collection contains late 19th & early 20th century paintings including Impressionist & Post-Impressionist masterpieces; American holdings include works of art from 1900 to the present; Chinese collections contain archaic bronzes, archaic jades, Buddhist sculpture, jade carvings & ceramics
Publications: Monthly calendar; exhibition catalogs
Activities: Public school tours; dramatic programs; docent training; lect open to public, 8 vis lectr per year; films; concerts; gallery talks; tours; competitions with awards; individual paintings & original objects of art lent to museums around the world; originate traveling exhibitions; museum shop sells books, magazines, reproductions, prints & slides

L **Library,** 1451 S Olive Ave, 33401. Tel 561-832-5196; FAX 407-659-4689; Internet Home Page Address http://www.norton.org. *Dir* Dr Christina Orr-Cahall; *Cur* David F Setford Sr
Open Tues - Sat 10 AM - 5 PM, Sun 1 - 5 PM. Admis $5. Estab 1941
Library Holdings: Vols 3800; Per subs 30; Micro — Fiche, reels; AV — A-tapes, fs, Kodachromes, slides; Other — Clipping files, exhibition catalogs, memorabilia, pamphlets, photographs
Collections: †Individual Artist Reviews, †Catalogues, etc

Publications: Visions magazine, 3 times per year; Images newsletter, 6 times per year
Activities: Classes for adults & children; dramatic programs; docent training; lect open to public, 10 vis lectr per year; concerts; gallery talks; tours; original & individual paintings lent; museum shop sells books, reproductions, prints, slides, table art

A **PALM BEACH COUNTY CULTURAL COUNCIL,** 1555 Palm Beach Lakes Blvd, Ste 900, 33401. Tel 407-471-2901; FAX 407-687-9484; *VPres* Norree Boyd; *Dir* Will Ray; *Dir Information Serv* Glen Miller
Estab 1978 by Alex W Dreyfoos Jr as the Palm Beach County Council of the Arts to develop, coordinate, & promote the arts & cultural activities throughout Palm Beach County; recognized by the Board of County Commissioners as the county's advisory agency for cultural development & administers a portion of local tourist development funds under contract with county government. Mem: Dues $50
Income: Financed by donations

WHITE SPRINGS

M **FLORIDA DEPARTMENT OF ENVIRONMENTAL PROTECTION,** Stephen Foster State Folk Culture Center, PO Drawer G, 32096. Tel 904-397-2733; *Park Mgr* Darrell R Krause
Open 8 AM - Sunset daily. Admis Florida resident vehicle operator $1, each passenger $.50, children under 6 free; out-of-state vehicle operator $2, each passenger $1. Estab 1950 as a memorial to Stephen Collins Foster; operated by the State Department of Natural Resources. Mus contains eight dioramas of Foster's best known songs. The North wing holds a collection of minstrel materials; the South wing 19th century furniture & musical instruments; the 200 foot tall Foster Tower, a collection of pianos. Average Annual Attendance: 90,000
Collections: Dioramas; furniture; minstrel materials; musical instruments; pianos

WINTER PARK

A **ARCHITECTS DESIGN GROUP INC,** 333 N Knowles Ave, PO Box 1210, 32790. Tel 407-647-1706; FAX 407-645-5525; *Pres* I S K Reeves V
Open by appointment 9 AM - 3 PM. Estab 1971 to exhibit Native American antique art. Corporate headquarters for architecture firm
Collections: †Antique American Indian Art; Florida Contemporary Art; Native American Art
Activities: Originate traveling exhibitions to museums in the Southeast

M **CHARLES MORSE MUSEUM OF AMERICAN ART,** 445 Park Ave N, 32789. Tel 407-644-8355; FAX 407-647-1284; *Pres* Dr Keith McCain; *Dir* Laurence Ruggiero; *Pres Assoc* Ann Saurman
Open Tues - Sat 9:30 AM - 4 PM, Sun 1 - 4 PM, cl Mon, Christmas Day, New Year's Day, Fourth of July, Thanksgiving, Labor Day & Memorial Day. Admis adults $2.50, students & children $1, members free. Estab to display work of Louis Comfort Tiffany & his contemporaries from an extensive collection on a rotating basis. A small, intimate jewel box of a gallery consists of nine rooms & display areas. New mus will have 14 galleries. Mem: 732; dues sustaining $1000, student $5
Income: $1,000,000 (financed through admis, mem & gifts)
Collections: Louis Comfort Tiffany Collection of blownglass, lamps, metalware, paintings, personal correspondence & effects, personal windows & photographs; Tiffany & other American art pottery numbering some 500 items; 4000 objects focusing on American art from 1800-1950 including art glass, drawings, paintings & prints
Publications: INSIDER, monthly newletter to members
Activities: Classes for adults; docent training; lect; concerts; gallery talks; tours; competitions with awards; exten dept serves schools, nursing homes & public parks; original objects of art lent to nursing homes, bank lobbies & art center; museum shop sells books, prints, slides, postcards, posters & notepaper

M **ROLLINS COLLEGE,** George D & Harriet W Cornell Fine Arts Museum, 32789. Tel 407-646-2526; FAX 407-646-2524; *Dir* Dr Arthur R Blumenthal; *Registrar* Mary Ann Bowie; *Exhibit Designer* Richard D Colvin; *Admin Asst* Vicki Brodnax; *Mem Coordr* Micki Evans; *Educ Coordr* Becky Savill
Open Tues - Fri 10 AM - 5 PM, Sat & Sun 1 - 5 PM, cl Mon. No admis fee. Formerly the Morse Gallery of Art, estab 1942. New Fine Arts Center completed in 1976, dedicated & opened on Jan 29, 1978. Rollins College is a liberal arts college & the Cornell Fine Arts Mus is part of the college. Cornell Fine Arts Mus was accredited by the American Assoc of Museums in 1981. The mus houses the college's permanentcollection of more than 6000 works & provides a focus for the arts in Central Florida. Mus consists of the McKean, the Yust & Knapp Galleries. Average Annual Attendance: 24,000. Mem: Dues President's Club $1000, Director's Club $500, benefactor $300, sponsor $150, family $70, friend/partner (combined individual) $55, partner (individual) $35, friend (individual) $30
Income: $520,000 (funded by endowment & grants)
Purchases: Over 500 contemporary American & European artworks
Collections: American paintings & portraits; European paintings from the 15th to 20th centuries; print; bronzes; decorative arts; Smith Watch Key Collection of 1200 keys
Exhibitions: (1997-98) The Art of Nancy Jay; Milton Avery's, Ebb & Flow; Blankelock: Visionary in Context; Modern American Realism: The Sara Roby Foundation Collection; Sandy Skoglund: A Photographic Installation; Treasures of the Chinese Nobility: Chauncey P Love Collection. (1998) Senior Art Show
Publications: Exhibit catalogs, 3 per year; newsletter, 5 per year
Activities: Lect, 5 vis lectr per year; concerts; gallery talks; tours; originate traveling exhibitions

GEORGIA

ALBANY

M ALBANY MUSEUM OF ART, 311 Meadowlark Dr, 31707. Tel 912-439-8400, 435-0977; FAX 912-434-4289; *Exec Dir* Tim Close; *Cur* Cory Micots
Open Tues - Sat 10 Am - 5 PM, Sun 1 - 4 PM, cl Mon, also by special appointment. No admis fee. Estab 1964; new museum facility opened 1983. Average Annual Attendance: 35,000. Mem: 1200; dues patron family $250, young patron family $150, patron individual $125, family $35
Income: $500,000 (financed by state, federal & foundation grants, mem & special events)
Purchases: Recent purchases include photographs by Henri Cartier Besson
Collections: African Collection; Ancient Art-Greek, Roman & Egyptian; Art of the Southern Region; Community Collection; 20th Century American Art
Exhibitions: Children's Art Fair
Publications: Bimonthly newsletter; exhibition catalogs
Activities: Classes for adults & children; workshops; docent training; lect open to public, 6 vis lectr per year; gallery; films; talks; tours; Children's Art Fair; individual paintings & original objects of art lent to other museums; originate traveling exhibitions to other museums

AMERICUS

M GEORGIA SOUTHWESTERN STATE UNIVERSITY, Art Gallery, 800 Wheatly St, 31709-4693. Tel 912-931-2204; FAX 912-931-2927; *Chmn Fine Arts* Duke Jackson; *Art Coordr* Jack R Lewis
Open Mon - Fri 8 AM - 5 PM. No admis fee. Estab 1971
Collections: Contemporary prints; Indian art of the southwest

ATHENS

M US NAVY SUPPLY CORPS SCHOOL, US Navy Supply Corps Museum, 1425 Prince Ave, 30606-2205. Tel 706-354-7349; FAX 706-354-7239; *Cur* Dan Roth
Open Mon - Fri 9 AM - 5 PM, cl federal holidays. No admis fee. Estab 1974. Exhibits depict the history & activities of US Navy Supply Corps & commemorate noteworthy individuals associated with the Corps. Mus housed in National Register Carnegie Library building (c1910). Average Annual Attendance: 2000
Income: Financed by federal appropriation
Collections: Nautical paintings, ship models, gallery gear, navigational equipment, uniforms, personal memorabilia; Archives: official records, manuals, photographs, yearbooks, scrap books, newsletter, directories

UNIVERSITY OF GEORGIA

M Georgia Museum of Art, 90 Carlton St, 30602-1719. Tel 706-542-4662; FAX 706-542-1051; Elec Mail wcooper@uga.cc.uga.edu. *Acting Museum Adminr* William Eiland; *Acting Preparator* Jim Stipe Maas; *Cur Educ* Victoria Lepka; *Registrar* Lynne Perdue; *Dir Publications* Bonnie Ramsey; *Coordr Public Relations* Wendy Cooper; *Cur Paintings* Donald Keyes; *Cur Prints & Drawings* Patricia Phagan
Open Mon - Thurs & Sat 10 AM - 5 PM, Fri 10 AM - 9 PM, Sun 1 - 5 PM. No admis fee. Estab 1945; open to the pub 1948 as a fine arts mus. 10 exhibition galleries. Maintains reference library. Average Annual Attendance: 40,000. Mem: 565; dues $15 - $1000; annual meeting Feb
Income: Financed through university, mem & grants
Purchases: American & European prints & paintings
Collections: †American & European Paintings (19th & 20th century); †Drawings; † European & American Graphics, †Japanese Graphics, 15 century to the present
Exhibitions: (1997) A Palette in a Pen's World; A Delicate Bouquet: French Floral Studies
Publications: Newsletter, four times annually; gallery notes, biannually; exhibtion catalogs; annual report bulletin
Activities: Classes for adults & children; docent training; senior citizen programs; volunteer docents program; lect open to public, 3-5 vis lectr per year; concerts; tours; gallery talks; competitions with awards; individual paintings & original objects of art lent to other museums & galleries; originate traveling exhibitions; museum shop sells books, prints & reproduction jewelry

L University of Georgia Libraries, * Fine Arts Collection, Jackson St, 30602. Tel 706-542-7463; *Art Librn* Marilyn Halkovic
Open Mon - Thurs 7:30 AM - midnight, Fri 7:30 AM - 9 PM, Sat 9 AM - 6 PM, Sun 1 PM - midnight; between quarters Mon - Fri 8 AM - 6 PM, Sat 9 AM - 6 PM, cl Sun. Reference library only
Income: Financed by state appropriation
Library Holdings: Vols 58,500; Per subs 265; Micro — Cards, fiche, prints, reels; AV — A-tapes, cassettes, motion pictures, rec, slides, v-tapes; Other — Clipping files, exhibition catalogs, manuscripts, pamphlets, photographs
Special Subjects: History of Art & Architecture, History of Photography
Collections: †Rare books & manuscripts collection; †Illustration archives on microfiche; stereographs from William C Darrah Collection; †private press collection; †handmade paper collections

L Dept of Art Lamar Dodd School of Art, Visual Arts Bldg, Jackson St, 30602. Tel 706-542-1618; FAX 706-542-0226; *Librn* Janet Williamson; *Dir* Evan R Firestone
Open 8 AM - 5 PM and by special arrangement. Estab 1955 to house slides & AV equipment for use by faculty & students for classroom lecturing. Reference & instructional library
Library Holdings: AV — Cassettes, slides 165,000, v-tapes
Special Subjects: American Western Art, Antiquities-Assyrian, Archaeology, Asian Art, Ceramics, Coins & Medals, Decorative Arts, Etchings & Engravings, Furniture, Islamic Art, Latin American Art, Mexican Art, Oriental Art, Painting - American, Photography, 19th Century Albumen Prints

ATLANTA

L ALTANTA-FULTON PUBLIC LIBRARY, Art-Humanities Dept, One Margaret Mitchell Sq NW, 30303. Tel 404-730-1700; FAX 404-730-1757; *Dir* Ronald A Dubberly; *Mgr* Mavis Jackson
Open Mon - Thurs 9 AM - 9 PM; Fri & Sat 9 AM - 6 PM, Sun 2 - 6 PM. Estab 1950 to provide materials in the fine arts. Some exhibit space maintained
Income: Financed by city & state appropriation
Library Holdings: Vols 300,000; Compact discs 5000; AV — Cassettes 10,000, rec 4000; Other — Prints
Activities: Classes for adults; lect open to public

A ARTS FESTIVAL OF ATLANTA, 999 Peachtree St NE, 30309. Tel 404-885-1125; FAX 404-876-1791; *Exec Dir* Pat Gann; *Artistic Dir* Leslie Gordon; *Marketing Develop Dir* Michael Foden; *Dir Opera* Bob Keil
Estab 1944 to foster the creation, presentation & understanding of contemporary arts; enriches the cultural life of metropolitan Atlantans by bringing together artists & audiences from all over the world in an annual festival. Average Annual Attendance: 1,000,000
Income: $900,000 (financed by donations)

ASSOCIATION OF MEDICAL ILLUSTRATORS
For further information, see National and Regional Organization

L ATLANTA COLLEGE OF ART, Georgia Artists Registry, 1280 Peachtree St NE, 30309. Tel 404-733-5025; FAX 404-733-5201; *Dir* Anne Cox
Open Tues - Thurs 11 AM - 4 PM, by appointment. Estab 1978. For reference only
Library Holdings: AV — Slides; Other — Clipping files, exhibition catalogs, photographs
Special Subjects: Bronzes, Calligraphy, Ceramics, Conceptual Art, Crafts, Decorative Arts, Drawings, Graphic Design, Landscapes, Metalwork, Painting - American, Photography, Portraits, Pottery, Sculpture
Collections: 8000 slides of artists' works in Georgia
Publications: Artists Proof, semiannual newsletter

L ATLANTA COLLEGE OF ART LIBRARY, 1280 Peachtree St NE, 30309. Tel 404-733-5020; FAX 404-733-5012; *Dir* Barbara Hutsell; *Visual Coll Cur* Kevin Fitzgerald; *Asst Librn* Jozina Fish
Open Mon - Thurs 8:45 AM - 9 PM, Fri 8:45 AM - 3:30 PM, Sat Noon - 5 PM. Estab 1950 to provide art information & research facility to the Atlanta College of Art community & the southeast art community. Circ 12,000
Purchases: $22,800
Library Holdings: Vols 29,000; Per subs 320; Artists' books; AV — Slides, v-tapes; Other — Clipping files, exhibition catalogs
Special Subjects: Graphic Design, Interior Design
Collections: †Artists' Books; †rare books
Activities: Films; vis artists program

M ATLANTA HISTORICAL SOCIETY INC, Atlanta History Center, 130 W Paces Ferry Rd, 30305. Tel 404-814-4000; FAX 404-814-4186; Internet Home Page Address http://www.atlhist.org. *Exec Dir* Rick Beard; *Dir Research & Educ* Patricia Suhrcke; *Dir Exhib & Coll* Darlene Roth; *Dir Communications* Kim Resnik; *Dir Develop* David Buchanan; *Dir Finance & Admin* Glenn Fite
Open Mon - Sat 10 AM - 5:30 PM, Sun Noon - 5:30 AM, Library/Archives open Mon - Sat 10 AM - 5 PM. Admis $7, discount for sr citizens, youth, children & groups; $1 additional to tour each historic house; library/archives free. Estab 1926, dedicated to presenting the stories of Atlanta's past, present & future through exhibits, programs, collections & research. Atlanta History Museum with state-of-the-art exhibits, shop, cafe, classrooms, 100 seat theater; two National Historic Register houses: Swan House, a 1928 classically styled mansion with original furnishings & the 1840's Tullie Smith Farm with outbuildings & livestock; 1890s Victorian playhouse; 33 acres of gardens & woodland trails labeled for self-guided tours; McElreath Hall, housing an extensive library/archives; member's room & a 400 seat auditrium. Average Annual Attendance: 175,000. Mem: 7500; dues $30-$1000; annual meeting in mid-Oct
Income: $4,200,000 (financed through endowment, mem, county appropriation, donations, admis & shop sales
Purchases: $22,500
Collections: Burrison Folklife Collection; Thomas S Dickey Civil War Ordnance Collection; DuBose Civil War Collection; Philip Trammell Shutze Collection of Decorative Arts; costumes & textiles; general Atlanta history
Exhibitions: Metropolitan Frontiers: Atlanta, 1835-2000; Shaping Traditions: Folk Arts in a Changing South; Turning Point: The American Civil War; (1997) The American South: Past, Present, Future. (1998) Gone With the Wind: A Worldwide Fascination
Publications: Atlanta History: A Journal of Georgia & the South, quarterly; Atlanta History Center News, quarterly; Atlanta History Programs Calendar, quarterly
Activities: Classes for adults & children; family programs; docent programs; lect open to public, 15 vis lectr per year; symposia; workshops; special events; guided tours; book traveling exhibitions; originate traveling exhibitions; retail store sells books, prints, magazines, slides, original art, reproductions, folk crafts, educational toys & Atlanta history memorabilia

M ATLANTA MUSEUM, * 537-39 Peachtree St NE, 30308. Tel 404-872-8233; *Dir* J H Elliott Jr; *Cur* Mary Gene Elliot
Open Mon - Fri 10 AM - 5 PM, cl Sat, Sun & holidays. Admis adults $2, children $1, special group rates. Estab 1938
Collections: Bronzes; Confederate Money; Decorative Arts; Early Chinese Art; Furniture; Indian Artifacts; Paintings; Porcelains; Sculpture; Glass
Activities: Lect; tours; sales shop sells antiques, china, furniture, gifts, glass, paintings, porcelain, rugs and silver

M CENTER FOR PUPPETRY ARTS, 1404 Spring St NW, 30309. Tel 404-873-3089; FAX 404-873-9907; Elec Mail puppet@mindspring.com. *Exec Dir* Vincent Anthony; *Admin Dir* Lisa Rhodes; *Producer* Bobby Box; *Museum Dir* Don Aaron; *Co-Educ Dir* Lesley Potts; *Co-Educ Dir* Robin Jacobs
Open 9 AM - 5 PM. Admis adult $3, children $2. Estab 1978 to educate pub of the art of puppetry. Puppetry - International Exhibits. Mem: dues $25 - $1000 & up
Income: $1,300,000 (financed by endowment, mem, city & state appropriations)
Collections: Global collection of puppets
Exhibitions: Permanent Collection: Puppet Power Wonders (200 puppets); (1997) Centre for Puppetry Arts, Retrospective. (1997-98) Tribute to Jim Rowland
Publications: Articles, brochures, catalogs & reports
Activities: Classes for adults & children; dramatic programs; lect open to public, 3 vis lectr per year; scholarships offered; artmobile; lending collection contains art objects; book traveling exhibitions 3 per year; originate traveling exhibitions 2 per year; museum shop sells books & prints
L Library, 1404 Spring St NW, 30309. Tel 404-873-3089; FAX 404-873-9907; *Museum Dir* Dona Aaron; *Exec Dir* Vincent Anthony
For reference only. Library estab 1978
Library Holdings: Vols 1500; AV — A-tapes, cassettes, rec, slides, v-tapes; Other — Clipping files, exhibition catalogs, framed reproductions, memorabilia, original art works, pamphlets, photographs, reproductions
Special Subjects: Puppetry

A CITY OF ATLANTA, Bureau of Cultural Affairs, 675 Ponce deLeon Ave (City Hall East), 5th Flr, 30308. Tel 404-817-6815; FAX 404-817-6827; *Dir* Barbara Bowser; *Dir Asst* Eloise Joyner; *Project Coordr, Contracts for Art Servs* Sophia Lyman; *Project Coordr, Public Relations & Fund Develop* Pauline Caesar; *Project Coordr, Public Art Prog* Lamar Renford; *Project Supv, Public Art Prog* David Vogt; *Project Coordr, Public Art Prog* Lisa Walker; *Admin Asst* Susan Bowen
Estab 1974 to improve the social fabric & quality of life for Atlanta's citizen & visitors by supporting the arts & cultural activities & by nurturing the arts community
Activities: Contracts for art services; music programs; public art programs; special projects
M City Gallery East, 675 Ponce de Leon Ave NE, 30308. Tel 404-817-6981; FAX 404-817-6827; *Dir* Eddie Granderson
Open Mon - Sat 8:30 AM - 5:30 PM. Estab to present contemporary fine art produced by regional, national & international professional artists; focused primarily on Atlanta-based artists; goal: display work that is stimulating & innovative & that presents a new persepective or cross-collaboration with other art disciplines. 7000 sq ft exhibition space
Activities: Sponsors lect, forums, demonstrations & performances in collaboration with service agencies
M Atlanta Cyclorama, 800 Cherokee Dr SE, 30315. Tel 404-658-7625; FAX 404-658-7045; *Dir* Pauline Smith
Open June 1 - Labor Day 9:30 AM - 5:30 PM, Labor Day - May 9:30 AM - 4:30 PM. Admis adults $5, children 6-12 $3, children under 6 free. Estab 1886. Located in Grant Park & listed in the National Historic Register; 184-seat revolving platform
Collections: Civil War artifacts; lifelike figures in Civil War costume & period props; panoramic painting depicting the Battle of Atlanta
Activities: Sales shop sells books, videos & Civil War era souvenirs
A Chastain Arts Center, 135 W Wieuca Rd NW, 30342. Tel 404-252-2927; FAX 404-851-1270; *Dir* Jim Berry
Estab 1975. Located in Chastain Park; oldest City-operated arts facility in Atlanta
Activities: Classes for adults; workshops
M City Gallery at Chastain, 135 W Wieuca Rd NW, 30342. Tel 404-257-1804; FAX 404-851-1270; *Dir* Debra Wilbur
Open Tues - Sat 1 - 5 PM. Estab to expose the Atlanta community to exhibitions that address the social & personal political issues of our time. Venue for display of contemporary art by local, regional & national artists & designers
Exhibitions: Exhibitions addressing design, architecture & popular culture in educational manner
Activities: Lect; gallery tours; symposiums in conjunction with exhibitions
M Gilbert House, 2238 Perkerson Rd SW, 30315. Tel 404-766-9049; FAX 404-765-2806; *Dir* Erin Bailey
Estab 1984. Built in 1865 by Jeremiah Gilbert immediately after the Civil War; registered historic landmark located on 12 acres
Activities: Art classes for adults & children; exhibitions of art work
A Southeast Arts Center, 215 Lakewood Way SE, 30315. Tel 404-658-6036; FAX 404-624-0746; *Dir* Alberta Ward
Center known for its state-of-the-art photography studio which provides professional instruction for young people & adults; near Lakewood Amphitheater; other classes include: Ceramics, Handbuilt Pottery & Raku Firing, Jewelrymaking, Sewing & Art for Youth
L Arts Clearinghouse, 887 W Marietta St NW, 30318. Tel 404-853-3261; FAX 404-853-3262; *Dir* Laura Lieberman
Estab as a comprehensive arts information & resources referral center. Offers open files on all Hotline presenters: listings of available studio space in Atlanta, health insurance policies for self-employed artists, sets of grant guidlines from National Endowment for the Arts & local arts funding agencies, as well as information on pub art commissions nationwide
Library Holdings: Vols 150; Per subs 30
Activities: Art in education program; professional development workshops; arts hotline; materials for the arts program

M EMORY UNIVERSITY, Michael C Carlos Museum, * 571 S Kilgo, 30322. Tel 404-727-4282; FAX 404-727-4292; *Dir* Dr Maxwell L Anderson; *Asst Dir* Catherine Howett Smith; *Exhib Design Supv* W Clayton Bass; *Coordr Educ Progs* Elizabeth S Hornor
Open Tues - Sat 10 AM - 5 PM, Fri 10 AM - 9 PM, Sun Noon - 5 PM. Admis suggested donation $3. Mus redesigned in 1985 by Michael Graves, Post-Modernist architect; 15,400 sq ft; permanent exhibition galleries & special

exhibition galleries. Average Annual Attendance: 43,055. Mem: 400; dues $25 & up
Income: $1,072,000
Collections: †Art collection from Renaissance to present, African, classical Greek & Egyptian; †Old World art & archaeology, including works from Egypt, Mesopotamia, ancient Palestine; Pre-Columbian, American Indian & Far Eastern holdings
Publications: Exhibition catalogues
Activities: Classes for adults & children; classes for teachers; lect open to public; concerts; gallery talks; tours; scholarships & fels offered; exten dept; original objects of art lent to other institutions; book traveling exhibitions 2-4 per year; originate traveling exhibitions; museum shop sells books, magazines, reproductions, prints, gifts, jewelry, CD ROMs, videos & catalogues

A GEORGIA COUNCIL FOR THE ARTS, 530 Means St NW, Ste 115, 30318. Tel 404-651-7920; *Exec Dir* Caroline Ballard Leake
Open Mon - Fri 8 AM - 5 PM. Estab 1968 as a state agency providing funding to non-profit, tax-exempt organizations & individual Georgia artists for arts programming. Mem: 24 members appointed by governor; meetings four times per yr
Income: $3,900,000 (financed by state appropriation plus federal funding)
Publications: Guide to Programs, annual (one for organizations & one for artists)

L GEORGIA INSTITUTE OF TECHNOLOGY, College of Architecture Library, Georgia Institute of Technology, 30332-0155. Tel 404-894-4877; FAX 404-894-4651; Elec Mail kathy.brackney@library.gatech.edu. *Librn* Kathryn S Brackney
Income: Financed by state appropriation
Library Holdings: Vols 33,800; Per subs 160; Architectural drawings; Micro — Fiche, reels; AV — Slides, v-tapes; Other — Pamphlets
Collections: Neel Reid & Associates Drawings Collection

L GEORGIA STATE UNIVERSITY, School of Art & Design, Visual Resource Center, University Plaza, 30303. Tel 404-651-2257; *Cur* Ann England
Open Mon - Fri 8:30 AM - 5 PM. No admis fee. Estab 1970 to make visual & literary resource materials available for study, teaching & research. Two galleries for student & facility exhibits, national & international travelling shows. Average Annual Attendance: 20,000
Library Holdings: Vols 300; Per subs 18; AV — Slides 255,000, v-tapes 45; Other — Exhibition catalogs, original art works, pamphlets, reproductions
Special Subjects: Aesthetics, Afro-American Art, Native American Art
Collections: Rare book collection, original prints emphasis impressionism, 19th - early 20th century artists; extensive Pre-Columbian slide collection, History of textile, Metalsmithing & jewelry making, History of photography
Activities: Lect open to public, 5-10 vis lectr per year; films; artist's slide presentations; discussions
M Art Gallery, University Plaza, 30303. Tel 404-651-2257; FAX 404-651-1779; *Dir* Teri Williams
Open Mon - Sat 8 AM - 8 PM, Sun 10 AM - 8 PM during exhibitions. No admis fee
Publications: Catalogues
Activities: Gallery talks

A GEORGIA VOLUNTEER LAWYERS FOR THE ARTS, INC, * 675 Ponce De Leon Ave NE, 30308. Tel 404-873-3911; FAX 404-730-5798; *Exec Dir* Gail Centini; *Dep Dir* Patricia Prusak PhD
Open Mon - Fri 10 AM - 5 PM. Estab 1975 as legal reference for the arts
Income: Financed by city & state funds & private foundations
Collections: Copyrights; fundraising; art law related to literature
Publications: An Artists Handbook on Copyright; Handbook on the Georgia Print Law
Activities: Educ dept; lect open to public, 5 vis lectr per year

M HIGH MUSEUM OF ART, 1280 Peachtree St NE, 30309. Tel 404-733-4200; FAX 404-898-9578; *Dir* Ned Rifkin; *Chmn Board of Dir* John Wieland; *Deputy Dir & Chief Cur* Michael E Shapiro; *Cur American Art* Judy L Larson; *Cur Decorative Art* Donald Peirce; *Cur European Art* David Brenneman; *Cur Folk Art* Joanne Cubbs; *Cur Modern & Contemporary Art* Carrie Przybilla; *Cur Photography* Ellen Dugan; *Cur Media Art* Linda Dubler; *Registrar* Frances Francis; *Mgr Exhib & Design* Marjorie Harvey
Open Tues - Thurs & Sat 10 AM - 5 PM, Fri 10 AM - 9 PM, Sun Noon - 5 PM, cl Mon. Admis adults $6, senior citizens & students $4, children ages 6-17 $2, children under 6 & members free, Thurs 1 - 5 PM free. Estab 1926 to make the best in the visual arts available to the Atlanta public in exhibitions & supporting programs. Four floors (46,000 sq ft) exhibition space; top floor for traveling exhibitions; semi-flexible space (moveable walls); ramp & elevator for accessibility. Average Annual Attendance: 500,000. Mem: 23,000; dues $25 & up
Income: $7,500,000 (financed by endowment, mem, Members Guild of the High Museum of Art, city & state appropriations, museum shop sales, grants & foundations, ticket sales & operating income)
Collections: American painting & sculpture; European painting & sculpture, 20th Century painting, photography & sculpture; African Art; Works on Paper; 18th & 19th Century decorative art featuring Herter Brothers, William Whitehead & John Henry Belter; contemporary crafts; 20th Century furniture; regional historical decorative arts & English ceramics; 19th Century American landscape paintings; contemporary art since 1970 †Western art early Renaissance - present; decorative arts; graphics; sculpture; African & sub-Saharan; †19th - 20th century photography
Publications: HighLife, bi-monthly mem magazine; exhibition catalogues
Activities: Workshops for adults, children & families; docent training; lect open to public; family days; tours; performing arts programs; sr citizen programs; gallery talks; speakers bureau; traveling exhibitions organized and circulated; two museum shops sell books, reproductions, slides, prints, stationery, children's books & toys, crafts, jewelry & gift items; junior museum
L Library, 1280 Peachtree St NE, 30309. Tel 404-733-4528; FAX 404-733-4503; Elec Mail colkim@woodruff-arts.org. *Librn* Kim Collins
Library Holdings: Vols 8500; Per subs 50; AV — Slides; Other — Clipping files, exhibition catalogs

Special Subjects: Aesthetics, Afro-American Art, American Western Art, Antiquities-Oriental, Architecture, Art Education, Art History, Ceramics, Conceptual Art, Constructions, Crafts, Decorative Arts, Drawings, Etchings & Engravings, Film, Folk Art, Furniture, Glass, Graphic Arts, Graphic Design

M **NEXUS CONTEMPORARY ART CENTER,** 535 Means St, 30318. Tel 404-688-1970; FAX 404-577-5856; Elec Mail nexusart@mindspring.com. Nexus Gallery 404-688-2500, 688-1605, Nexus Press 577-3579. *Exec Dir* Louise E Shaw; *Dir Nexus Gallery* Teresa Bramlette; *Dir Nexus Press* Jo Anne Paschall; *Dir Develop* Kathy Mashke; *Bus Mgr* Mike Priegel; *Public Relations Coordr* Chinyere Gonzales; *Develop Asst* Nikki Tucker; *Gallery Assoc* Dejay Byrd
Open Tues - Sat 11 AM - 5 PM. Admis non-mem $3, students $1, members free. Estab 1973 as a non-profit & multidisciplinary facility committed to promoting experimentation, education & excellence in visual, performing & book arts. Average Annual Attendance: 50,000. Mem: 1300; dues $25-$50; annual meeting in June
Income: $650,000
Exhibitions: (1997) Atlanta Biennial-Presentation of works by Atlanta's newest & most promising artists
Publications: Artist books; exhibit catalogs; Nexus News, quarterly newsletter
Activities: Classes for adults & children; lect open to public, 4 vis lectr per year; gallery talks; video tours; theatre; media programs; docent & internship programs; book traveling exhibitions 3 per year; originate traveling exhibitions; sales shop sells Nexus artist books, Nexus catalogs

C **RITZ-CARLTON HOTEL COMPANY,** Art Collection, 3414 Peachtree Rd NE, Ste 300, 30326. Tel 404-237-5500; FAX 404-237-9169; *Chmn* William B Johnson; *Design Coordr* Marilyn Bowling
Open 24 hrs. Estab 1983 to reflect & communicate the history & tradition of Ritz-Carlton Hotels
Purchases: $7,500,000
Collections: †18th & 19th century European & American paintings, prints, sculpture †18th & 19th century English & Continental antiques & decorations
Publications: The Ritz-Carlton Art Collections, catalogs
Activities: Lect open to public on request; sales shop sells books & reproductions

M **SYMMES SYSTEMS,** Photographic Investments Gallery, 3977 Briarcliff Rd NE, 30345-2647. Tel 404-320-1012; *Pres* Edwin C Symmes Jr
Open by appointment. No admis fee. Estab 1979 to display & produce traveling exhibits of classical photography
Collections: 19th century photographic images in all media; 20th century black & white & color photos by masters
Exhibitions: 19th Century Albumen Prints of Westminster Cathedral; Netsuke: An Insight into Japan; Color Photography by E C Symmes; 19th & 20th Century Images of China.
Activities: Lect open to public; original objects of art lent; lending collection contains 1500 19th century Albumen prints; originate traveling exhibitions; museum shop sells original art

AUGUSTA

M **AUGUSTA RICHMOND COUNTY MUSEUM,** 560 Reynolds St, 30901-1430. Tel 706-722-8454; *Dir* Richard Wescott
Open Tues - Sat 10 AM - 5 PM, Sun 2 - 5 PM, cl holidays. No admis fee. Estab 1937; owns 1850 historic Brahe House at 426 Telfair St. Mem: dues $5-$250
Collections: Archaeology; Decorative Arts; Graphics; Historical Material; Paintings; Sculpture
Activities: Training program for professional museum personnel; workshops; films; lect; guided tours; volunteer council; book traveling exhibitions

M **GERTRUDE HERBERT INSTITUTE OF ART,** 506 Telfair St, 30901. Tel 706-722-5495; FAX 706-722-3670; *Dir* Sharon White Gruber
Open Tues - Fri 10 AM - 5 PM, Sat 10 AM - 2 PM, groups by special appointment, cl Sun & Mon, Thanksgiving, Christmas & New Year's. Admis $2. Estab 1937 for the advancement & encouragement of art & educ in art. Main gallery located on first floor of historic home. Average Annual Attendance: 5000. Mem: 300
Exhibitions: Circulating exhibitions; monthly exhibitions; one-person and group exhibitions; the Southeastern Annual Juried Exhibition
Activities: Classes for adults & children; docent training; lect open to public, 4 vis lectr per year; concerts; gallery talks; tours; competitions with awards; scholarships offered; book traveling exhibitions

C **MORRIS COMMUNICATIONS CORPORATION,** Corporate Collection, 725 Broad St, PO Box 936, 30913. Tel 706-724-0851; FAX 706-722-7125; *Chmn & Chief Exec Officer* W S Morris III
Collections: Alaskan Art; Western Bronzes; Wildlife (birds)

M **MORRIS MUSEUM OF ART,** One Tenth St, 30901-1134. Tel 706-724-7501; FAX 706-724-7612; Elec Mail mormuse@csra.net. *Dir* Louise Keith Claussen; *Deputy Dir* J Richard Gruber; *Chmn Board* W S Morris III; *Store Mgr* Melinda Murphy; *Cur* Estill Curtis Pennington
Open Tues - Sat 10 AM - 5:30 PM, Sun 12:30 - 5:30 PM. Admis adults $2, senior citizens 65 & over $1, students $1. Estab 1992 to emphasize painting in the South. Maintains reference library. Average Annual Attendance: 30,000. Mem: dues $15-$5000
Income: Financed by endowment, mem, foundation funds & fundraising activities
Purchases: Southern Art permanent collection
Collections: Bird Paintings; Birds of North America; Robin Hill; †Southern American Art
Exhibitions: A Southern Collection: Masterworks from a Permanent Collection of Painting in the South
Publications: Exhibition catalogs
Activities: Docent training; lect open to public, 6 vis lectr per year; gallery talks; tours; book traveling exhibitions; originate traveling exhibitions 1 per year; museum shop sells books

BRUNSWICK

A **GOLDEN ISLES ARTS & HUMANITIES ASSOCIATION,** 1530 Newcastle St, 31520. Tel 912-262-6934; FAX 912-262-1029; *Exec Dir* Bryan Thompson
Open Mon - Fri 10 AM - 4 PM. Estab 1989 as a county coordinating arts council & presenter. The Ritz Theatre Lobby. Average Annual Attendance: 10,000. Mem: 375; dues family $30, single $15; annual meeting in June
Income: $105,000 (financed by mem, programs, services & grants)
Activities: Children's classes; dramatic programs; lect open to public, 4-5 vis lectr per year; photographic & visual arts competitions; ribbons & cash awards; scholarships offered; book traveling exhibitions 1 per year

COLUMBUS

M **COLUMBUS MUSEUM,** 1251 Wynnton Rd, 31906. Tel 706-649-0713; FAX 706-649-1070; *Dir* Charles T Butler; *Chief Cur* Karol Anne Peard Lawson; *Dir Educ* Gay Carney; *Cur Archaeology* Frank T Schnell; *Dir Develop* Betsy Covington; *Museum Resource Specialist* Elinor Winn; *Asst to the Dir* Patricia Butts; *Art Handler* Chris Land; *Preparator* Chris Lofton; *Mem Coordr* Juli Means; *Registrar* Danielle Funderburk; *Exhibit Designer* Steve Ellis; *Bus Mgr* Kimberly Beck
Open Tues - Sat 10 AM - 5 PM, Sun 1 - 5 PM, cl Mon, Thanksgiving & Christmas. No admis fee. Estab 1954 to build a permanent collection; encourage work by Georgia & Southern artists; establish loan shows & traveling exhibitions in all fields of American art & history. 11,000 sq ft history gallery, 2000 sq ft interactive gallery, 25,000 sq ft art gallery. Maintains reference library. Average Annual Attendance: 75,000. Mem: 2400; dues $35-$1000; annual meeting in Sept
Collections: †American art from all periods & all media; †Artifacts relating to the culture of the Chattahoochee Valley & Southeastern United States permanent collection includes Landscapes, Paintings & Portraits by Early & Contemporary American Painters, with strong Collection of American Impressionism paintings
Publications: Annual report; gallery guides; newsletter, quarterly
Activities: Classes for adults & children; docent training; workshops; lect open to public, 5-6 vis lectr per year; concerts; gallery talks; tours; scholarships offered; individual paintings & original objects of art lent to qualified institutions which are recognized & meet facilities accreditation standards; book traveling exhibitions 6-10 per year; originate traveling exhibitions to other museums; museum shop sells books, original art, reproductions, jewelry & children's toys & gift items; junior museum

M **COLUMBUS STATE UNIVERSITY,** The Gallery, Dept of Art, 4225 University Ave, 31907-5645. Tel 706-568-2047; FAX 706-569-3123; *Dept Head* Jeff Burden
Open Mon - Fri 9 AM - 5 PM. No admis fee. Average Annual Attendance: 6000
Income: $11,000 (financed by student activities)
Purchases: Permanent collection
Exhibitions: Annual art students show; faculty show; regional guest artist & nationally prominent artists (1997) Annual Student Art Exhibition
Activities: Classes for adults & college students; lect open to public, 1-5 vis lectr per year; tours; competitions with awards; scholarships offered

DALTON

A **CREATIVE ARTS GUILD,** 520 W Waugh St, PO Box 1485, 30722-1485. Tel 706-278-0168; FAX 706-278-6996; *Pres* Nancy Harrison; *Dir* Ann Treadwell
Open Mon - Fri 9 AM - 5 PM. No admis fee. Estab 1963 to recognize, stimulate & popularize creative excellence in the arts for the benefit of the entire community. Average Annual Attendance: 121,000. Mem: 1000; dues family $35, annual meeting in June
Income: $500,000 (financed by mem, commissions, grants, tuitions & fund raising events)
Collections: Permanent collection of regional art
Exhibitions: Changing monthly shows of crafts; graphics; photography; original art; sculpture; fiber
Publications: Bulletins to members, monthly
Activities: Classes for adults & children; dramatic programs; visual & performing arts programs for schools; concerts; gallery talks; competitions with awards; arts & crafts festivals; individual paintings & original objects of art lent to area schools & organizations

DECATUR

M **AGNES SCOTT COLLEGE,** Dalton Gallery, 141 E College Ave, 30030. Tel 404-638-6000; FAX 404-638-6177; *Chmn Art Dept* Terry McGehee
Open Mon - Fri 9 AM - 9 PM; Sat 9 AM - 5 PM; Sun 2 - 5 PM. No admis fee. Estab 1965 to enhance art program. Gallery consists of four rooms, 300 running ft of wall space, light beige walls & rug; Dana Fine Arts Bldg designed by John Portman
Income: Financed by endowment
Collections: Clifford M Clarke; Harry L Dalton; Steffen Thomas; Ferdinand Warren
Activities: Lect open to public

DULUTH

A **HANDWEAVERS GUILD OF AMERICA,** 3327 Duluth Hwy, Ste 201, 30136. Tel 770-495-7702; FAX 203-242-3982; Elec Mail compuserve: 73744,202. *Exec Dir & Ed* Sandra Bowles
Estab 1969 to promote fiberarts. Mem: 10,000; dues $30; annual meeting in summer
Income: Financed by mem dues, contributions, advertising & conferences
Publications: Shuttle, Spindle & Dyepot, quarterly publication for members
Activities: Fiber programs for adults, classes for children; awards to selected fiber art shows; scholarships & fels offered; originate traveling exhibitions to fiber guilds

FORT BENNING

M **NATIONAL INFANTRY MUSEUM,** Bldg 396, Baltzell Ave, 31905-5593. Tel 706-545-2958; FAX 706-545-5158; *Dir & Cur* Frank Hanner
Open Tues - Fri 10 AM - 4:30 PM; Sat - Sun 12:30 - 4:30 PM. No admis fee. Estab 1959 to honor the infantryman & his two centuries of proud history. Gallery contains 30,000 sq ft; Hall of Flags, Gallery of Military Art, Benning Room, West Gallery: 1750-1865, Center Galleries 1870-1970, Medal of Honor Hall & Airborne Diorama. Average Annual Attendance: 110,000. Mem: 9000; dues $2
Income: $200,000 (financed by federal funds)
Collections: †Military related art; Presidential Documents & Memorabilia; Regimental Quartermasters Sales Store
Activities: Lect open to public; concerts; gallery talks; tours; individual paintings & original objects of art lent; museum shop sells books, reproductions & prints
L **Library,** Bldg 396, Baltzell Ave, 31905-5273. Tel 706-545-2958; *Dir* Frank Hanner
Open Mon - Fri 8 AM - 4:30 PM, Sat & Sun 12:30 - 4:30 PM. Estab 1959 to preserve the collection of military artifacts
Income: Financed by Department of Army
Library Holdings: Vols 8000; AV — Fs, motion pictures, slides; Other — Clipping files, manuscripts, memorabilia, original art works, pamphlets, photographs, prints, sculpture
Special Subjects: The Infantryman
Exhibitions: WWII Through the Artists eye

FORT VALLEY

L **FORT VALLEY STATE COLLEGE,** H A Hunt Memorial Library, 1005 State College Dr, 31030-3298. Tel 912-825-6342; FAX 912-825-6916; *Elec Mail* fvsclib@uscn.cc.uga.edu. *Library Dir* Carole Taylor
Open 8 AM - 5 PM. No admis fee. Estab 1939
Income: Financed by state assistance
Special Subjects: Afro-American Art, Art Education, Art History, Historical Material
Collections: Afro - American Art; Graphic Arts
Exhibitions: History of College
Activities: Classes for adults; lending collection contains books

JEKYLL ISLAND

M **JEKYLL ISLAND MUSEUM,** 375 Riverview Dr, 31527. Tel 912-635-4036 (Tours), 635-2119 (Office); FAX 912-635-4420; *Exec Dir Jekyll Island* James A Bradley; *Dir Museum & Historic Preservation* F Warren Murphey; *Cur of Educ* Leslie Hicks
Open Memorial Day - Labor Day Mon - Sun 9:30 AM - 5 PM, Labor Day - Memorial Day Mon - Sun 9:30 AM - 4 PM. Admis adults $10, students 6-18 years $6. Estab 1954. Average Annual Attendance: 51,000
Income: Financed by fees & admis
Collections: 1890 Furniture; Tiffany Stained Glass Windows; portraits
Activities: Programs for adults & children; lect open to public; tours; museum shop sells books, reproductions, slides & turn-of-the century related items

LAGRANGE

M **CHATTAHOOCHEE VALLEY ART MUSEUM,** 112 Hines St, 30240. Tel 706-882-3267; *Exec Dir* Keith Rasmussen; *Cur Educ* Gregory Morton; *Asst Cur* Anise Morrison; *Finance Officer* Diane Frazier; *Admin Officer* Owen Holleran
Open Tues - Fri 9 AM - 5 PM, Sat 11 AM - 5 PM, cl Sun & Mon. Estab 1963 to provide visual art experience & educ to people of West Georgia. 100 year old former Troup County Jail refurbished for use as galleries having about 350 running ft of wall space & 7000 sq ft of floor space on two floors. Average Annual Attendance: 22,000. Mem: 380; dues $10 - $5000; annual meeting in Jan
Income: $150,000 (financed by foundation grant, civic organizations & fundraisers)
Purchases: $10,000, Purchase Awards, LaGrange National Competition
Collections: Contemporary American art of all types & media
Publications: Quarterly newsletter
Activities: Classes for adults & children; lect open to public, 2-4 vis lectr per year; gallery talks; tours; competitions with awards; individual paintings & original objects of art lent to business patrons; book traveling exhibitions 1-4 per year; originate traveling exhibitions; museum shop sells prints, original art & reproductions

M **LA GRANGE COLLEGE,** Lamar Dodd Art Center Museum, 30240. Tel 706-882-2911; FAX 706-884-6567; *Dir* John D Lawrence
Estab 1988
Collections: 20th Century Photography; American Indian Collection; Retrospective Collection
Exhibitions: Two shows every six weeks

MACON

M **MUSEUM OF ARTS & SCIENCES, INC,** 4182 Forsyth Rd, 31210. Tel 912-477-3232; FAX 912-477-3251; *Exec Dir* Nancy B Anderson; *Dir of Educ* Mary Ann Ellis; *Dir of Fine Arts* Suzanne Harper
Open Mon - Thurs 9 AM - 5 PM, Fri 9 AM - 9 PM, Sat 9 AM - 5 PM, Sun 1 - 5 PM. Admis adults $5, seniors $4, students $3, children $2, members free; No admis fee Mon 9 AM - 5 PM & Fri 5 - 9 PM. Estab 1956 as a general art & science museum with a planetarium. South Gallery 50 ft x 60 ft; North Gallery 25 ft x 35 ft; Hall Gallery 8 ft x 32 ft; Newberry Hall 1759 sq ft. Average Annual Attendance: 70,000. Mem: 1700; dues $15-$1000
Collections: American art with emphasis on the Southeast drawings, paintings, prints & sculpture; gems & minerals; doll collection; quilt collection;

ethnographic
Publications: Museum Muse, bi-monthly newsletter; catalogues
Activities: Classes for adults & children; docent training; lect open to public, 2-6 vis lectr per year; concerts; gallery talks; guided tours; movies; special events; summer children's camps; individual paintings & original objects of art lent to other museums; book traveling exhibitions, 5 - 10 per year; originate traveling exhibitions to circulate to schools or appropriate institutions in Georgia & Southeast; museum shop sells books, magazines, original art, reproductions, prints, small educational toys, t-shirts, gem & minerals, gift items, rocks, shells, science kits

M **TUBMAN AFRICAN AMERICAN MUSEUM,** 340 Walnut St, 31201. Tel 912-743-8544; FAX 912-743-9063; *Exec Dir* Carey Pickard; *Asst Dir* Anita Ponder; *Operations Coordr* Angela Brooks; *Prog Coordr* Wilfred Stroud
Open 9 AM - 5 PM. Admis $2. Estab 1981, emphasis on regional contemporary art & historical objects. Nine galleries, one mural entitled from Africa to America. Average Annual Attendance: 35,000. Mem: 500; dues $10-$1000; annual meeting in Dec
Income: $250,000 (financed by endowment, mem, city & state appropriation, store)
Purchases: $10,000
Collections: African & African-American art & artifacts; 70 foot long mural is signature possession
Activities: Classes for children; dramatic programs; docent training; lect open to public; scholarships & fels offered; museum shop sells books, magazines, original art, prints, reproductions & African crafts
L **Keil Resource Center,** 340 Walnut St, 31201. Tel 912-743-8544; FAX 912-743-9063;
Estab 1987. For reference only
Library Holdings: Vols 2500; AV — V-tapes
Special Subjects: Afro-American Art, Art Education, Art History, Film, Folk Art, Mixed Media, Painting - American, Photography, Pottery, Printmaking, Prints, Sculpture, Textiles, Theatre Arts

MADISON

M **MORGAN COUNTY FOUNDATION, INC,** Madison-Morgan Cultural Center, 434 S Main St, 30650. Tel 706-342-4743; *Chmn Board* Ruth Bracewell; *Exec Dir* Cassandra Baker; *Admin Dir* Peggy Kempton; *Dir Visual Arts* Ann Laura Parks
Open Tues - Sat 10 AM - 4:30 PM, Sun 2 - 5 PM. Admis fee adults $3, students $2, members free. Estab 1976 to enhance the educational & cultural life of Georgia & the Southeast. Four galleries for changing exhibits, housed in former classrooms (approx 25 ft x 35 ft of historic 1895 school facility; heart pine floors, no daylight, tungsten track lighting only, with heat, air conditioning & electronic security. Average Annual Attendance: 30,000. Mem: 1500; dues $10-$1000; annual meeting second Mon in July
Income: $460,000 (financed by endowment, mem, state grants, admis fees for services & sponsorship contributions)
Exhibitions: Usually two simultaneous exhibits, each 8-12 wks, of work by regional artists &/or collections of museums & private collections from the region or across the nation; Annual Juried Regional Art Exhibit
Publications: Exhibit brochures & catalogs, 4-5 per yr; Madison Georgia - An Architectural Guide
Activities: Performing arts programs; docent training; gallery tours; demonstrations; lect open to public, 5-10 vis lectr per year; competitions with awards; book traveling exhibitions 5-10 per year; originate traveling exhibitions; museum shop sells books, posters, note cards, postcards

MARIETTA

M **MARIETTA-COBB MUSEUM OF ART,** 30 Atlanta St NE, 30060. Tel 770-528-1444; FAX 770-528-1440; *Dir* Donna Colebeck
Estab 1990 to provide the communities of Cobb County, the city of Marietta & visitors to the area exposure to the visual arts through a diversity of visual art experiences, educational services & outreach activities based upon visiting exhibitions & the acquisition, conservation & exhibition of a permanent collection focused on American Art
Income: Financed by mem & donations
Activities: Classes for children; lect open to public

MOUNT BERRY

M **BERRY COLLEGE,** Moon Gallery, Art Dept Berry College, 30149. Tel 706-236-2219; FAX 706-236-2248; *Pres* Dr Gloria Shatto; *VPres* Dr Doyle Mathis
Open weekdays 9 AM - 4 PM. No admis fee. Estab 1972. Medium size gallery, carpeted floors & walls, tracking spots. Average Annual Attendance: 3500
Exhibitions: Guest lecturer & juror for student Honors show
Activities: Classes for adults & children; lect open to public, 6-8 vis lectr per year; gallery talks; competitions with awards; scholarships offered; individual paintings & original objects of art lent; lending collection contains books, cassettes, color reproductions, 20 original prints, paintings, records, photographs & 5000 slides; book traveling exhibitions; originate traveling exhibitions
L **Memorial Library,** 30149. Tel 706-236-2221; FAX 706-236-9596; *Elec Mail* lfoldes@berry.edu. *Dir* Lance Foldes; *Prof of Art* Dr T J Mew III
Open Mon - Thurs 8 AM - Midnight, Fri 8 AM - 8 PM, Sat 1 - 6 PM, Sun 1 PM - Midnight during academic year, Mon - Thurs 8 AM - 10 PM, Fri 8 AM - 5 PM during summer. Estab 1926 for educational purposes
Library Holdings: Vols 350; Per subs 25; AV — A-tapes, cassettes, fs, motion pictures, rec, slides, v-tapes; Other — Clipping files, exhibition catalogs, manuscripts, memorabilia, original art works, pamphlets, photographs, prints
Special Subjects: Ceramics, Contemporary women artists

RABUN GAP

M HAMBIDGE CENTER GALLERY, Betty's Creek Rd, PO Box 339, 30568. Tel 706-746-5718; FAX 706-746-9933; *Exec Dir* Judith Barber; *Gallery Coordr* Peggy McBride
Open 6 days per wk 10 AM - 4 PM. No admis fee. Estab 1934
Collections: Hambidge Collection (books, papers & textiles)
Exhibitions: Folk Art changing exhibitions; Jugtown Pottery (annual); Metal Morphosis (metal art); Southern Folk Expressions (annual)
Activities: Workshops; speakers' forums open to public; guided nature walks; fels offered

SAINT SIMONS ISLAND

A GLYNN ART ASSOCIATION, 319 Mallory St, PO Box 20673, 31522. Tel 912-638-8770; *Dir* Kay W Wayne; *Pres* Mary Garrison
Open 9 AM - 5 PM. No admis fee. Estab 1953. 1100 sq ft, largest portion devoted to local art, smaller portion for one man exhibits, traveling shows & competitions. Average Annual Attendance: 8000. Mem: 600; dues $20-$500; annual meeting in June
Income: $100,000 (financed by mem, state appropriation & commission on sales of art)
Exhibitions: Miniature competition from all over & more than 100 local artists
Publications: Glynn Art News, monthly newsletter
Activities: Classes for adults & children; docent training; lect open to public, 4 vis lectr per year; competitions with prizes; scholarships & fels offered; sales shop sells books, prints & original art

SAVANNAH

M KIAH MUSEUM, 505 W 36th St, 31401. Tel 912-236-8544; *Dir & Founder* Virginia J Kiah
Open Tues - Thurs 11 AM - 5 PM. No admis fee. Estab 1959 to expose this type of culture to the masses; to teach the relationship of art to everyday life
Collections: Civil War Period Collection; Harmon Foundation Collection of African Wood Carvings; Howard J Morrison Jr Osteological Collection; Marie Dressler Collection; Fine Arts Exhibit of all art work of students and adult artists from 18 countries; Folk Art; 18th & 20th Century Furniture; Hobby Collection; Indian Artifacts
Exhibitions: Ten paintings from the House of Representatives
Activities: Docent training; gallery talks; tours; paintings & original objects of art lent to schools

M SHIPS OF THE SEA MARITIME MUSEUM, 41 MLK St, 31401. Tel 912-232-1511; FAX 912-234-7363; *Exec Dir* Jeff Fulton
Open Mon - Sun 10 AM - 5 PM. Admis adults $2, senior citizens $1, children between 7 & 12 $.75. Estab 1966 to bring a greater awareness to the general pub of the great part in history that ships have played. Four floors of ship models & items which pertain to the sea with an outstanding exhibit of ships-in-bottles & scrimshaw. Average Annual Attendance: 50,000
Income: Financed privately
Collections: Figureheads; Porcelains; Scrimshaw; Ships Models, etc
Activities: Classes for children; museum shop sells books, magazines & slides
L Library, 41 MLK St, 31401. Tel 912-232-1511; *Exec Dir* David T Guernsey Jr; *Librn* Open
Reference only
Library Holdings: Vols 500; Per subs 10; Micro — Cards; Other — Clipping files, framed reproductions, memorabilia, original art works, pamphlets, photographs, prints
Special Subjects: Maritime
Activities: Children summer classes in nautical lore

M TELFAIR MUSEUM OF ART, 121 Barnard St, PO Box 10081, 31401. Tel 912-232-1177; FAX 912-232-6954; *Admin* Sandra S Hadaway; *Designer* Miutin Pavovic; *Cur Educ* Harry H DeLorme
Open Tues - Sat 10 AM - 5 PM; cl Mon & some holidays. Admis adults $5, senior & AAA $3, students $2, children 6-12 $1. Estab 1875 to collect & to preserve, exhibit & interpret. 4 galleries 2400 sq ft, Rotunda gallery 3400 sq ft, Sculpture gallery 2700 sq ft. Maintains reference library. Average Annual Attendance: 45,000. Mem: 1400; dues $25-$10,000; annual meeting in Apr
Income: Financed by endowment, mem, city & state appropriation, banks & corporate foundations & federal government
Collections: American decorative arts; American & European artists; Late 18th century to present; 19th & 20th century American & European paintings; works on paper
Exhibitions: Special & traveling exhibitions
Publications: The Octagon Room; We Ain't What We Used to Be; Christopher P H Murphy (1869-1939): A Retrospective
Activities: Docent training; programs & tours for children; lect open to public, 4-10 vis lectr; individual paintings & original objects of art lent to other musems internationally; lending collection contains 4000 original art works, 100-4000 sculptures, 2400 furniture, furnishings & drawings; book traveling exhibitions 5 per year; originate traveling exhibitions; museum shop sells books, posters, postcards
L Telfair Academy of Arts & Sciences Library, 121 Barnard St, PO Box 10081, 31412. Tel 912-232-1177; FAX 912-232-6954; *Dir* Diane Lesko, PhD
For reference only, for scholars & the public
Library Holdings: Vols 3500; Per subs 130; Other — Exhibition catalogs
Special Subjects: American Art

VALDOSTA

M VALDOSTA STATE UNIVERSITY, Art Gallery, N Patterson St, 31698-0110. Tel 912-333-5835; FAX 912-245-3799; *Gallery Dir* Stephen Andersen; *Head Art Dept* Dr Lanny Milbrandt
Open Mon - Thurs 10 AM - 4 PM, Fri 10 AM - 3 PM. No admis fee. Estab 1970 for educational purposes serving students, faculty, community & region. Gallery is an open rectangular room with approximately 122 running ft of exhibition space. Average Annual Attendance: 20,000
Income: Financed by state appropriations
Collections: African art; Lamar Dodd
Exhibitions: 8-9 exhibitions per year; national juried Valdosta works on paper exhibition
Activities: Classes for adults; dramatic programs; docent training; lect open to public, 3-5 vis lectr per year; concerts; gallery talks; tours; competitions; scholarships offered; originate traveling exhibitions

WAYCROSS

M OKEFENOKEE HERITAGE CENTER, INC, 1460 N August Ave, PO Box 406A, 31503-4954. Tel 912-285-4260, 285-0733; FAX 912-283-2858; *Dir* Ann Tweedy
Open Mon - Sat 10 AM - 5 PM, Sun 1 - 5 PM, cl holidays. Admis adults $2, youth 5-18 $1, under 4 & members free. Estab 1975 to house displays on arts & history. Two gallery areas. Average Annual Attendance: 10,000. Mem: 250
Income: $85,000 (financed by endowment, mem, grants, contributions, admis, special activities, gift shop)
Collections: 1912 Baldwin Steam Locomotive train & caboose; 1940's Homestead; 1870's house exhibit; 1890's printshop; prints, crafts, paintings & photographs
Exhibitions: Annual art show
Publications: Quarterly exhibit catalogues; newsletter
Activities: Classes for adults & children; demonstrations; workshops; lect open to public; concerts; gallery talks; tours; competitions; purchase awards; book traveling exhibitions 6-12 per year; museum shop sells books, original art, reproductions, prints gifts & souvenirs

HAWAII

HAWAII NATIONAL PARK

M VOLCANO ART CENTER, PO Box 104, 96718-0104. Tel 808-967-7511 (gallery), 967-8222 (office); FAX 808-967-8512; *Exec Dir* Marilyn L Nicholson; *Gallery Mgr* Natalie Pfeifer
Open daily 9 AM - 5 PM. No admis fee. Estab 1974 to promote Hawaii's fine arts & crafts. Average Annual Attendance: 250,000. Mem: 800; dues $25-$50; annual meeting first week in Nov
Income: $1,375,000
Collections: Hawaiian fine arts & crafts; art-to-wear, books, ceramics, glass, jewelry, native woods, painting, photographs, prints, sculpture
Publications: Volcano Gazette, bi-monthly
Activities: Classes for adults & children; performing arts programs; Elderhostel; literary readings; marathon run; lect open to public; concerts; gallery talks; tours; book traveling exhibitions 1-2 per year; retail store sells books, prints, original art, reproductions, crafts, clothes & jewelry

HILO

M STATE OF HAWAII, DEPT OF LAND & NATURAL RESOURCES, Wailoa Visitor Center, Piopio St, PO Box 936, 96721. Tel 808-933-4360; *Dir* Kathleen Lassiter; *Asst Dir* Betty L King
Open Mon, Tues, Thurs & Fri 8 AM - 4:30 PM, Wed Noon - 8:30 PM, Sat 9 AM - 3 PM, cl Sun & State holidays. Estab 1968 as a place of interest in Hilo for local residents as well as visitors to the island. Average Annual Attendance: 32,000
Activities: Classes for adults & children; workshops on cultural events; lect open to public; competitions with awards; exten dept serves airport departures; individual paintings & original objects of art lent to the State of Hawaii

HONOLULU

A ASSOCIATION OF HAWAII ARTISTS, PO Box 10202, 96816. Tel 808-923-1711; FAX 808-923-1711; *Pres* Elisabeth Knoke
Estab 1926 to promote congeniality & stimulate growth by presenting programs; to contribute to the cultural life of the State of Hawaii. Average Annual Attendance: 1000. Mem: 250; dues $15-$30; monthly meeting every second Tues
Income: Financed by mem
Exhibitions: (1997) 24th Annual Aloha Show
Publications: Paint Rag, monthly
Activities: Lect open to public, 2-3 vis lectr per year; demonstrations; competitions with cash awards, plaques & rossettes

M BERNICE PAUAHI BISHOP MUSEUM, 1525 Bernice St, PO Box 19000-A, 96817-0916. Tel 808-847-3511; FAX 808-841-8968; *Dir* W Donald Duckworth
Open Mon - Sun 9 AM - 5 PM, cl Christmas. Estab 1889 to preserve & study the culture & natural history of Hawaii
Exhibitions: Awesome Treasures of Hawaii & the Pacific: A Hands-On Adventure; Treasures; Ocean Planet

L   Library, 1525 Bernice St, 96817-0916. Tel 808-848-4147; FAX 808-841-8968; *Head Librn* Duane Wenzel
Open Mon - Fri 10 AM - 3 PM, Sat 9 AM - Noon. Estab 1889
Library Holdings: Vols 40,000
Special Subjects: Anthropology, Archaeology, Ethnology, Folk Art, Historical Material, History of Art & Archaeology, Hawaii & the Pacific Cultural & Natural History

L   Archives, 1525 Bernice St, 96817-0916. Tel 808-848-4182; FAX 808-841-8968; *Archivist* Betty Lou Kam
Open Mon - Fri 10 AM - 3 PM, Sat 9 AM - Noon. Estab 1991
Library Holdings: Other — Manuscripts 3500, photographs 1,000,000
Collections: Cylinders, discs & reel to reel tapes; Maps; Moving Images; Oils on Canvas; Works of Art on Paper

M   THE CONTEMPORARY MUSEUM, 2411 Makiki Heights Dr, 96822. Tel 808-526-1322; FAX 808-536-5973; *Dir* Georgianna M Lagoria; *Assoc Dir* James Jensen
Open Tues - Sat 10 AM - 4 PM, Sun Noon - 4 PM, cl Mon. Admis adults $5, children under 13 & members free. Estab 1961 as Contemporary Arts Center to provide a showcase for contemporary artists of Hawaii. Reorganized & open in 1988 in present facility situated in 3 1/2 acres of gardens; five galleries comprise 5000 sq ft of exhibitions space. Also includes exhibition annex. Honolulu Advertiser Gallery & First Hawaiian Center in downtown Honolulu. Average Annual Attendance: 45,000. Mem: 2500; dues $35 & up
Income: $1,500,000 (financed by endowment, mem, grants, contributions & earned income)
Collections: Permanent collection of over 1200 works from 1940 to present in all media by local, national & international artists; stage set by David Hockney on permanent view
Exhibitions: Approximately 25 temporary exhibitions annually of artists of local, national & international reputation;
Publications: Masami Teraoka: Waves & Plagues (90 page catalogue)
Activities: Educ dept; docent training; lect open to public; gallery talks; tours; museum shop sells books, original art, reproductions, prints & jewelry

M   HONOLULU ACADEMY OF ARTS, 900 S Beretania St, 96814. Tel 808-532-8700; FAX 808-532-8787; Cable HONART. *Dir* George R Ellis; *Assoc Dir* David de la Torre; *Cur Western Art* Jeniffer Saville; *Cur Textile Coll* Reiko Brandon; *Cur Asian Art* Julia White; *Cur Educ* Karen Thompson; *Cur Art Center* Carol Khewhok; *Keeper, Lending Center* Gwen Harcada; *Registrar* Sanna Deutsch
Open Tues - Sat 10 AM - 4:30 PM, Sun 1 - 5 PM, cl Mon & major holidays. Admis $5. Estab 1927 as the only art museum of a broad general nature in the Pacific; to provide Hawaii's people of many races with works of art representing their composite cultural heritage from both East and West. Main building is a Registered National Historic Place. Average Annual Attendance: 250,000. Mem: 7000; dues $15 & up
Income: $8,261,641
Collections: European and American Decorative Arts, Painting, Prints, Sculpture; Ancient Mediterranean and Medieval Christian Art; Kress Collection of Italian Renaissance Painting; Chinese Bronze, Ceramics, Furniture, Lacquerware, Painting, Sculpture; Islamic Ceramics; Japanese Ceramics, Folk Arts, Painting, Prints, Screens, Sculpture; Korean Ceramics; Traditional Arts of Africa, Oceania and the Americas; Western and Oriental Textiles
Exhibitions: Approx 50 temporary exhibitions annually
Publications: Art Books and Pamphlets; Catalog of the Collection; Catalogs of Special Exhibitions; Honolulu Academy of Arts Journal
Activities: Classes for children; lectr; films & videos illustrating contemporary & historic range of the medium; guided tours; gallery talks; arts festivals; workshops; music programs; research in Asian & Western Art; lending collection contains paintings, prints, textiles, reproductions, photographs. slides and ethnographic objects (about 21,000); sales shop sells books and gifts

L   Robert Allerton Library, 900 S Beretania St, 96814. Tel 808-532-8755; FAX 808-532-8787; *Librn* Kimberly B Bridges
Open Tues - Sat 10 AM - Noon & 1 - 4 PM, cl Sun & Mon. Estab 1927.
Reference library for staff & members
Library Holdings: Vols 40,000; Per subs 250; Micro — Fiche, reels; AV — Slides; Other — Clipping files, exhibition catalogs, pamphlets, photographs
Special Subjects: Art History, Oriental Art, National Palace Museum Photographic Archives

M   JUDICIARY HISTORY CENTER, 417 S King St, 96813. Tel 808-539-4999; FAX 808-539-4996; *Dir* Lani Lapilio; *Educ Specialist* Matt Mattice; *Cur* Susan Shaner
Open Tues - Thurs 10 AM - 3 PM. No admis fee. Estab to interpret the history of Hawaii's courts & legal system. Average Annual Attendance: 40,000. Mem: 150; dues $15-$1000
Income: Financed by appropriation
Collections: Art (paintings, prints); Artifacts; Documents (judicial & legal); furniture
Exhibitions: The Monarchy Courts; Martial Law in Hawaii 1941 - 1944; Restored Court Room 1913
Activities: Educ dept; dramatic programs; docent programs; tours

C   PERSIS CORPORATION, Art Collection, 605 Kapiolani Blvd, 3rd Flr, 96813. Tel 808-525-8015, 525-8061; FAX 808-521-7691; *Cur* Sharon Twigg-Smith
Open 7:30 AM - 5:30 PM. Art Collection estab 1961 for contemporary art. Gallery located on first floor near entrance; changing exhibits every six weeks: local artists, nationally known artist, group shows & annual showcase of recent corporate acquisitions
Purchases: Jennifer Bartlett painting, Richard Estes print, Paul Wonner painting
Activities: Docent training; lect open to public; many purchases & prizes awarded to local exhibits, special projects funded

M   QUEEN'S MEDICAL CENTER AUXILIARY, Queen Emma Gallery, 1301 Punchbowl St, PO Box 861, 96813. Tel 808-547-4397; FAX 808-547-4646; *Dir* Masa Morioka Taira; *Treas* Gretchen Aona
Open daily 8 AM - 4 PM. No admis fee. Estab 1977 as a showcase for local & regional artists. 13 ft x 24 ft alternative space in largest, oldest hospital in Hawaii. Average Annual Attendance: 15,000
Income: Financed by sales & donations
Collections: Nicholas Bleeker sculptures; Hawaiian Moon Calendar (pastels); Queen Emma's Medallion (wall mural); Lei Sanne Doo monoprint; Dietrick Varez linocut prints; batik hangings; glass spheres
Exhibitions: Human Form Traveling Exhibit; monthly exhibits
Activities: Lect open to public; originate traveling exhibitions

M   TENNENT ART FOUNDATION GALLERY, 203 Prospect St, 96813. Tel 808-531-1987; *Dir* Elaine Tennent
Open Tues - Sat 10 AM - Noon; Sun 2 - 4 PM or by appointment. No admis fee. Estab 1954; dedicated to aesthetic portrayal of Hawaiian people and to house works of Madge Tennent. Gallery is set in a terraced garden with a variety of plants & trees. Mem: 300; dues family $25, individual $15; annual meeting in Feb
Income: Financed by trust
Collections: Madge Tennent's Personal Art Books Collection
Publications: Prospectus, quarterly newsletter
Activities: Special exhibitions and social events sponsored by Friends of Tennent Art Gallery; lect; tours; concerts; museum shop sells note cards & reproductions

L   Library, 203 Prospect St, 96813
Open for reference
Library Holdings: Vols 350

M   UNIVERSITY OF HAWAII AT MANOA, Art Gallery, 2535 The Mall, 96822. Tel 808-956-6888; FAX 808-956-9043; Elec Mail gallery@hawaii.edu. *Dir* Tom Klobe; *Assoc Dir* Sharon Tasaka; *Design Asst* Wayne Kawamoto
Open Mon - Fri 10 AM - 4 PM; Sun Noon - 4 PM; cl Sat. No admis fee. Estab 1976 to present a program of regional, national & international exhibitions. Gallery is seen as a major teaching tool for all areas of specialization. It is located in the center of the art building & is designed as a versatile space with a flexible installation system that allows all types of art to be displayed. Average Annual Attendance: 50,000
Income: Financed by state government
Collections: Japanese & Polish posters
Publications: Exhibition catalogs
Activities: Lect open to public; gallery talks; competitions; scholarships & fels offered; book traveling exhibitions; 1 biannually; originate traveling exhibitions; sales shop sells exhibit catalogs

KANEOHE

M   HAWAII PACIFIC UNIVERSITY (Formerly The Gallery a Hawaii Loa College), Gallery, 45-045 Kamehameha Hwy, 96744. Tel 808-233-3167; FAX 808-223-3190; *Gallery Dir* Sanit Khewhok
Open Mon - Sat 8 AM - 5 PM. No admis fee. Estab 1983 as a cultural & academic resource for students & community. Average Annual Attendance: 5000
Income: Financed by college funds & private donations
Exhibitions: 6 exhibitions per year featuring contemporary artists' working in Hawaii
Activities: Lect open to public; gallery talks; competitions

LAHAINA

A   LAHAINA ARTS SOCIETY, Art Organization, 649 Wharf St, 96761. Tel 808-661-0111; *Pres* Sherry Barnhard; *VPres* Eileen Jones; *Bookkeeper* John Capone; *Gallery Dir* Mona Harris
Open daily 9 AM - 5 PM. No admis fee. Estab 1968 as a nonprofit organization interested in perpetuating culture, art & beauty by providing stimulating art instruction, lectures & art exhibits. Gallery located in old Lahaina Courthouse; Main Gallery is on ground floor; Old Jail Gallery is in the basement. Average Annual Attendance: 36,000. Mem: 350; dues $30; annual meeting Oct
Income: $12,000 (financed by mem & annual fundraising event, Beaux Arts Ball)
Exhibitions: Exhibits change each month; group, special or theme exhibits in Main Gallery; one or two-person member shows are in Old Jail Gallery
Publications: Newsletter, monthly; exhibition catalogs
Activities: Classes for children; lect for members only; gallery talks; competitions with scholarships; workshops; scholarships offered; gallery sales shop sells original art, prints, cards, ceramics, handcrafted jewelry & sculptures

LAIE

A   POLYNESIAN CULTURAL CENTER, 55-370 Kamehameha Hwy, 96762. Tel 808-293-3005; FAX 808-293-3022; *Chmn Board* Dallin H Oaks; *Pres & Gen Mgr* Lester Moore; *Dir* Bryan Bowles
Open Mon - Sat 11 AM - 9 PM, cl Sun, Thanksgiving, New Year's & Christmas. Admis adults $14, children $7. Estab 1963 by the Church of Jesus Christ of Latter Day Saints as an authentic Polynesian village. Center is a 42 acre living mus with two amphitheaters, it represents villages of Hawaii, Samoa, Tonga, Fiji, Tahiti, New Zealand & the Marquesas. Average Annual Attendance: 1,000,000
Income: Financed by admis
Collections: Decorative arts, ethnic material, graphics, paintings & sculpture
Publications: Polynesia in a Day, magazine
Activities: Classes for adults & children; workshop training in Polynesian arts & crafts; lect open to public; scholarships offered; sales shop sells Polynesian handicrafts, books, reproductions, prints, slides, tapa cloth, Hawaiian quilting & pandanus-leaf items

LIHUE

M KAUAI MUSEUM, PO Box 248, 96766. Tel 808-245-6931; FAX 808-245-6864; *Pres* Clifford Nakea; *Dir* Carol Lovell; *Cur* Margaret Lovett; *Mgr Museum Shop* Laverne Silva
Open Mon - Fri 9 AM - 4 PM, Sat 10 AM - 4 PM, cl Sun. Admis adults $5, seniors $4, students $3, children 6-12 $1. Estab 1960 to provide the history through the permanent exhibit, the Story of Kauai & through art exhibits; ethnic cultural exhibits in the Wilcox Building to give the community an opportunity to learn more of ethnic backgrounds. Average Annual Attendance: 30,000. Mem: 1700; dues $15-$350; annual meeting in Dec
Collections: Hawaiian artifacts; Oriental works
Exhibitions: Downstairs: Hawaiian History; Quilts; Upstairs
Publications: Hawaiian Quilting on Kauai; Early Kauai Hospitality; Amelia; Moki Goes Fishing; Kauai: The Separate Kingdom
Activities: Classes for adults & children; docent training; lect open to public, 8 vis lectr per year; concerts; tours; book traveling exhibitions 3 per year; museum shop sells books, magazines, original art, reproductions, prints

L KAUAI PUBLIC LIBRARY, 4344 Hardy St, 96766. Tel 808-241-3222; FAX 808-241-3225; *Librn* Carol White
Open Mon - Wed 8 AM - 8 PM, Thurs - Fri 8 AM - 4:30 PM, Sat 8 AM - Noon. Estab 1922 to serve the pub of Kauai through a network of a regional library, three community libraries, community-school library, reading room in community center & a bookmobile service. These libraries provide exhibition space for a variety of art works & individual art shows as well as participate in joint art exhibits with the local schools, community college & mus. Gallery provides display & exhibit area for one-man & group art shows. Circ 431,678
Income: $794,942 (financed by state appropriation)
Library Holdings: Vols 126,285; Per subs 280; AV — A-tapes, cassettes, fs, rec, slides, v-tapes; Other — Clipping files, pamphlets
Collections: Curator for art in State Buildings Collection for the Island of Kauai funded through the statewide program by the State Foundation on Culture and the Arts. This collection is a revolving collection available for all state buildings and public schools
Exhibitions: Series of small one-man exhibits; average 13 per year
Activities: Dramatic programs; film programs; lectr open to public, 4 - 8 vis lectr per year; library tours; craft exhibits; contests

WAILUKU

M MAUI HISTORICAL SOCIETY, Bailey House, 2375A Main St, 96793. Tel 808-244-3326, 242-5080 (Research); FAX 808-244-3920; *Pres* Linda Decker; *Adminr* Cathy F Riley; *Cultural Research Specialist* Kealii Reichel
Open daily 10 AM - 4 PM, cl Sun. Donation requested adults $2, students $.50. Estab 1957 to preserve the history of Hawaii, particularly Maui County; housed in former residence of Edward Bailey (1814-1903). Average Annual Attendance: 21,000. Mem: 800; dues $10-$100; annual meeting in Jan
Income: $100,000 (financed by mem, gift shop purchases & admis fees)
Collections: Landscape Paintings (1860-1900); Paintings of Hawaiian Scenes by Edward Bailey; Prehistoric Hawaiian Artifacts
Exhibitions: Exhibits depicting missionary life, throughout the year
Publications: LaHaina Historical Guide; La Perouse on Maui; Hale Hoikeike - A House and Its People; Index to the Maui News 1900-1932
Activities: Classes for children; docent training; lect open to public, 4-6 vis lectr per year; tours; originate traveling exhibitions to schools & other museums; museum shop sells books, reproductions, prints, slides & arts & crafts

IDAHO

BOISE

M BOISE ART MUSEUM, 670 S Julia Davis Dr, 83702. Tel 208-345-8330; FAX 208-345-2247; Elec Mail boiseart@micron.net. *Dir* Dennis O'Leary; *Assoc Dir* Nancy McDaniel; *Cur Exhib* Sandy Harthorn
Open Tues - Fri 10 AM - 5 PM, Sat & Sun Noon - 5 PM, cl Mon & holidays. Admis general $3, sr citizens & college students $2, grades 1 - 12 $1, children under 6 free, first Thurs of month free. Estab 1931, inc 1961, gallery opened 1936. Average Annual Attendance: 147,000. Mem: 2000; dues family $40, individual $30; annual meetings in May
Income: Financed by mem, Beaux Arts Societe, grants, private & corporate donations, art festival
Collections: Glenn C Janss; African Sculpture (masks); American Ceramics; American, †European & Oriental Collections of Painting, The Minor Arts, Sculpture; American Realism; Arranged Image Photography; collection of works by Northwest Artists; Contemporary Prints
Exhibitions: Triennial exhibition for Idaho artists; 16 exhibitions annually of all media, regional to international; Contemporary & Historical rotating shows
Publications: Annual report; quarterly bulletin; occasional catalogs & posters of exhibitions
Activities: Classes in art; docent tours; concerts; films; outdoor arts festival; Beaux Arts Societe (fund raising auxiliary); exten dept serves 50 mile radius; originate traveling exhibitions statewide & Northwest region; museum shop sells books, original art, reproductions, cards & jewelry

A IDAHO COMMISSION ON THE ARTS, 304 W State, PO Box 83720, 83720-0008. Tel 208-334-2119; FAX 208-334-2488; Elec Mail bgarrett@ica.state.id.us. *Exec Dir* Margot H Knight; *Mgr Visual Arts & Crafts* Barbara Garrett; *Dir Literature* Diane Peaney; *Dir Arts Educ* Ruth Piispanen
Estab 1966 to promote artistic development within the state & to make cultural resources available to all Idahoans
Publications: Newsletter 6 times a year

M IDAHO HISTORICAL MUSEUM, 610 N Julia Davis Dr, 83702. Tel 208-334-2120; FAX 208-334-4059; *Museum Adminr* Kenneth J Swanson; *Registrar* Jody Ochoa; *Cur* Joe Toluse
Open Mon - Sat 9 AM - 5 PM, Sun & holidays 1 - 5 PM. No admis fee
Collections: History artifacts
Exhibitions: Story of Idaho

CALDWELL

M ALBERTSON COLLEGE OF IDAHO, Rosenthal Art Gallery, * 2112 Cleveland Blvd, 83605. Tel 208-459-5426; FAX 208-454-2077; *Dir* Lynn Webster; *Asst Dir* Stephen Fisher
Open Tues, Thurs & Sun 1 - 4 PM, cl academic holidays. No admis fee. Estab 1980
Collections: Luther Douglas, Sand Paintings; Paintings; Prints Collection
Exhibitions: Temporary & traveling exhibitions on an inter-museum loan basis
Publications: Exhibit Brochures
Activities: Lect; gallery talks; guided tours; films

MOSCOW

M APPALOOSA MUSEUM, INC, Moscow-Pullman Hwy, PO Box 8403, 83843. Tel 208-882-5578; FAX 208-882-8150; Elec Mail aphc@appaloosa.com. *Pres* King Rockhill; *Cur* Sue Emory
Open Mon - Fri 8 AM - 5 PM, June - Sept Sat 9 AM - 3 PM. No admis fee donations appreciated. Estab 1974 to collect, preserve, study & exhibit those objects that illustrate the story of the Appaloosa Horse. Average Annual Attendance: 5000. Mem: 22,000; annual meeting on May 1
Income: $6000 (financed by grants from Appaloosa Horse Club & fundraising)
Purchases: $1600
Collections: Bronzes by Shirley Botoham, Less Williver, Don Christian & William Menshew; reproductions of Chinese, European & Persian Art relating to Appaloosas; reproductions of Charles Russellart; original Western by George Phippen, Reynolds; Native American Items, saddle & other tack art work; Trace History of Appaloosa Horses from prehistoric times to present
Exhibitions: Horse demonstrations; programs with groups
Activities: Lect open to the public; tours; museum shop sells books, jewelry, cards & games, toys, clothing & Appaloosa Horse reproductions

POCATELLO

M IDAHO STATE UNIVERSITY, John B Davis Gallery of Fine Art, PO Box 8004, 83209. Tel 208-236-2361; FAX 208-236-4741; *Dir* Gail Dial
Open Mon - Fri 10 AM - 4 PM. No admis fee. Estab 1956 to exhibit art. Gallery contains 130 running ft of space with 8 ft ceilings. Average Annual Attendance: 2600
Income: $2600 (financed by city appropriation)
Purchases: $350
Collections: †Permanent collection
Exhibitions: Big Sky Biennial Exhibit; Regional Group Graduate Exhibit; exhibitions & national exhibitions; MFA Thesis Exhibits, bi-weekly one-man shows; student exhibits
Activities: Lect open to public, 5-10 vis lectr per year; gallery talks; tours; competitions with awards; scholarships offered; exten dept servs surrounding communities; individual paintings lent to school offices & community; originate traveling exhibitions

TWIN FALLS

M COLLEGE OF SOUTHERN IDAHO, Herrett Center for Arts & Science, 315 Falls Ave, PO Box 1238, 83303. Tel 208-733-9554, Ext 2355; FAX 208-734-2362; *Dir* James Woods; *Colls Mgr* Phyllis Oppenheim; *Art Gallery Mgr* Mike Green; *Exhibits Mgr* Bill West; *Display Technician* Nick Peterson; *Office Mgr* Wilma Titmus
Open Tues 9:30 AM - 8 PM, Wed - Fri 9:30 AM - 4:30 PM, Sat 1 - 4:30 PM, cl holidays. No admis fee. Estab 1965. Art Gallery, Natural History Gallery, four anthropology galleries (700-2400 sq ft). Average Annual Attendance: 10,000
Collections: Pre-Columbian, Prehistoric & Ethnographic Indian Artifacts
Activities: Classes for adults & children; lect open to public, 6-12 vis lectr per year; gallery talks; tours; original objects of art lent to other public institutions; originate traveling exhibitions to schools, libraries & museums

WEISER

M SNAKE RIVER HERITAGE CENTER (Formerly Intermountain Cultural Center & Museum), 2295 Paddock Ave, PO Box 307, 83672. Tel 208-549-0205; *Mgr* Carol Odoms
Open summer Thurs - Mon Noon - 4:30 PM, winter Fri - Mon Noon - 4:30 PM. Admis by donation. Estab 1962 to preserve the history of Washington County, Idaho. Housed in a 1923 three story, solid concrete building of the Intermountain Institute. Average Annual Attendance: 2200. Mem: 200; dues $15
Income: $20,000 (financed by mem, county appropriation, gifts & fundraising)
Collections: Washington County memorabilia & artifacts of Snake River Country
Publications: Museum newsletter; quarterly bulletin
Activities: Tours; sales shop sells books, magazines & gift items

ILLINOIS

AURORA

M AURORA UNIVERSITY, Schingoethe Center for Native American Cultures, * Dunham Hall, 1400 Marseillaise, 347 S Gladstone, 60506-4892. Tel 630-844-5402; FAX 630-844-5463; *Cur* Marcia Lautanen-Raleigh; *Asst Cur* Denyse M Cunningham; *Educ Mgr* Rachel Kay Schimelfenig; *Cur Asst* Elizabeth Crane
Open Mon, Tues, Thurs & Fri 10 AM - 4:30 PM, Sun 1 - 4 PM. No admis fee. Estab 1990 to advance cultural literacy about Native peoples. Two permanent exhibit galleries with rotating displays from the mus collection; one temporary exhibit gallery with mus collection displays & borrowed materials. Total of 3500 sq ft. Average Annual Attendance: 10,000. Mem: 50; dues donor $50-$500, individual $30; annual meeting second weekend in Dec
Income: $78,000 (financed by mem & endowment)
Collections: †Ethnographic material from North, Central & South America; †Native American Fine Art; Prehistoric/Pre-Columbian material
Exhibitions: Storyteller Pottery; Biennial Native American Fine Arts Show.
Publications: Spreading Wings; quarterly newsletter to membership
Activities: Workshops for adults; summer classes for children; outreach materials for educators; docent programs; lect open to public, 3 - 4 vis lectr per year; competitions with awards

BISHOP HILL

M ILLINOIS HISTORIC PRESERVATION AGENCY, Bishop Hill State Historic Site, PO Box 104, 61419. Tel 309-927-3345; *Site Mgr* Martha J Downey; *Asst Site Mgr* Cheryl Dowell
Open daily Mar - Oct 9 AM - 5 PM, Nov - Feb 9 AM - 4 PM. Admis suggested donation adult $2, ages 17 & younger $1. Estab 1946 to preserve & interpret the history of Bishop Hill Colony 1846-1861. Restored Colony church, 1848 & restored Colony hotel, 1860. Average Annual Attendance: 80,000
Income: Financed by state appropriation
Collections: Bishop Hill Colony artifacts-agricultural items, furniture, household items, textiles & tools; Olof Krans Collection of folk art paintings
Activities: Lect open to public

BLOOMINGTON

M ILLINOIS WESLEYAN UNIVERSITY, Merwin & Wakeley Galleries, School of Art, 61702-2899. Tel 309-556-3150; FAX 309-556-3411; Elec Mail mdutka@titan.iw.edu. *Dir* Marie Dutka
Open Mon - Fri Noon - 3 PM, Tues 7 - 9 PM, Sat & Sun 1 - 4 PM. Estab 1945
Income: Financed by endowment & mem
Collections: 250 drawings, paintings & prints including works by Baskin, Max Beckmann, Helen Frankenthaler, Philip Guston, John Ihle, Oliviera, Larry Rivers & Whistler
Exhibitions: Gary Justis; Dann Nardi
Publications: Exhibition Posters; Gallery Schedule, monthly;
Activities: Dramatic programs; lect open to public, 5 vis lectr per year; concerts; tours; competitions with awards; original objects of art lent, on campus only; book traveling exhibitions; originate traveling exhibitions organized & circulated
L Slide Library, 201 E University St, 61702-2899. Tel 309-556-3077; *Fine Arts Librn* Robert C Delvin
Library Holdings: AV — Slides 35,000

A MCLEAN COUNTY ART ASSOCIATION, Arts Center, 601 N East St, 61701. Tel 309-829-0011; *Item Dir* Laura Merwin
Open Tues 10 AM - 7 PM, Wed - Fri 10 AM - 5 PM, Sat Noon - 4 PM, Dec only Sun Noon - 4 PM. No admis fee. Estab 1922 to enhance the arts in McLean County. Provides display galleries, sales & rental gallery featuring local professional artists. Brandt Gallery is 2500 sq ft hosting local shows & traveling exhibits. Mem: 600; annual meeting first Fri in May
Income: Financed by mem, art & book sales
Exhibitions: Annual Amateur Competition & Exhibition; Annual Holiday Show & Sale; 10-2 other exhibits, local & traveling
Publications: Quarterly newsletter
Activities: Classes for adults & children; lect open to public; gallery talks; tours; competitions with awards; gift shop sells fine crafts & original art, conservation framing shop

M MCLEAN COUNTY HISTORICAL SOCIETY, 200 N Main, 61701. Tel 309-827-0428; FAX 309-827-0100; *Exec Dir* Greg Koos; *Librn & Archivist* Michele McNabb; *Cur* Susan Hartzold; *Museum Educ* Patty Wagner
Open Mon - Sat 10 AM - 5 PM, Sun 10 AM - 9 PM. Admis adults $2, children $1, members free. Estab 1892 to promote history of McLean County. Average Annual Attendance: 25,000. Mem: 1500
Income: $325,000 (financed by endowment, government & mem)
Collections: Civil War; Illinois History; local history; Material Culture
Exhibitions: Encounter on the Prairie
Activities: Classes for adults & children; lect open to public; retail store sells books, prints & locally trademarked items

CARBONDALE

M SOUTHERN ILLINOIS UNIVERSITY, University Museum, 62901-6632. Tel 618-453-5388; FAX 618-453-3000; *Dir* Dr John J Whitlock; *Museology Dr* Robert Lorinskas; *Prog Educational-Community Servs Coordr* Robert De Hoet; *Cur Colls* Lorilee Huffman; *Exhibits Designer* Alan Harasimowicz; *Adjunct Cur Archaeology* Dr Robert L Rands; *Adjunct Cur Anthropology* Dr Joel Maring; *Adjunct Cur Botany* Dr Donald Ugent; *Adjunct Cur Zoology* Dr Brooks Burr; *Adjunct Cur Geology* Harvey Henson
Open Tues - Sat 9 AM - 3 PM, Sun 1:30 - 4:30 PM. No admis fee. Estab 1874

to reflect the history & cultures of southern Illinois & promote the understanding of the area; to provide area schools & the University with support through educational outreach programs; to promote the fine arts in an unrestricted manner through exhibitions & provide support to the School of Art MFA program through exhibition of MFA graduate students. One art gallery of 1700 sq ft, shared gallery spaces totalling 1500 sq ft, sculpture garden & two semi-permanent exhibit halls with 3500 sq ft featuring exhibitis on southern Illinois. Average Annual Attendance: 50,000
Income: Financed by state appropriated budget, federal, state & private grants, donations & University Mus associates
Purchases: Michael Dunbar; Richard Hunt; Ke Francis
Collections: Decorative Arts; European & American paintings, drawing & prints from 13th-20th century with emphasis on 19th & 20th century; photography, sculpture, blacksmithing & art & crafts; Oceanic Collection; Southern Illinois history; 20th century sculpture, metals, ceramics; Asiatic holdings; archaeology; costumes; textiles; geology; zoology
Exhibitions: A variety of changing exhibitions in all media; ethnographic arts; fine & decorative arts; history & the sciences
Publications: Annual report; annual museum newsletter; exhibition catalogs
Activities: Classes for children; docent training; lect open to public, 15 vis lectr per year; gallery talks; tours; competitions with awards; outdoor sculpture exhibitions; exten dept serves southern thirty counties; individual paintings & original objects of art lent to campus offices only; lending collection contains film strips & slides; book traveling exhibitions 2 per year; originate traveling exhibitions circulated to museums, art centers, libraries & schools; museum gift shop sells original art, reproductions, jewelry, pottery & crafts
L Morris Library, 62901-6632. Tel 618-536-3391; FAX 618-453-8109; *Humanities Librn* Loretta Koch
Primarily lending
Library Holdings: Vols 32,500; Per subs 150; Micro — Cards, fiche, reels; AV — Cassettes 475, rec; Other — Exhibition catalogs, framed reproductions

CHAMPAIGN

M PARKLAND COLLEGE, Art Gallery, 2400 W Bradley Ave, 61821-1899. Tel 217-351-2485; *Gallery Dir* Denise Seif
Open Mon - Fri 10 AM - 3 PM. No admis fee. Estab 1981 to exhibit contemporary fine art. Average Annual Attendance: 10,000
Income: Non-profit, supported by Parkland College & in part by Illinois Arts Council, a state agency
Exhibitions: State of the Art - Biennial National Watercolor Invitational; Midwest Ceramics Invitational - Biennial, 2-person shows
Publications: Bi-annual exhibitional catalogs & brochures
Activities: Concerts; tours; originate traveling exhibitions

UNIVERSITY OF ILLINOIS

M Krannert Art Museum, 500 E Peabody Dr, 61820. Tel 217-333-1860; *Dir* Maarten van de Guchte; *Assoc Dir* Brigette D Scott; *Dir Educ* Linda Duke; *Cur* Eunice Maguire; *Registrar* Kathleen Jones
Open Tues - Sat 10 AM - 5 PM, Wed evenings until 8 PM, Sun 2 - 5 PM. No admis fee. Estab 1961 to house & administer the art collections of University of Illinois, to support teaching & research programs & to serve as an area art mus. Gallery is 48,000 sq ft, with 30,000 devoted to exhibition space. Average Annual Attendance: 111,000. Mem: 800; dues $35 & up
Income: Financed by mem, state appropriation & grants
Collections: †American paintings, †sculpture, †prints & drawings; †Ancient Near Eastern Classical & Medieval Art; European Paintings; European & American Decorative Arts; Pre-Columbian Art; †Asian Art; African Art
Publications: Catalogs, 3 or 4 annually
Activities: Classes for adults & children; docent training; lect open to public; concerts; gallery talks; tours; individual paintings & original objects of art lent to museums & university galleries; book traveling exhibitions; originate traveling exhibitions; museum shop sells books, cafe, jewelry & prints
M World Heritage Museum, 484 Lincoln Hall, 702 S Wright St, Urbana, IL 61801. Tel 217-333-2360, 333-1000; *Dir* Dr Barbara E Bohen; *Cur Numismatics* Dr James Dengate; *Finance & Mem* Amber Eslick; *Project Coordr* Diana Johnson
Open Mon - Fri 9 AM - 5 PM, Sun 2 - 5 PM when classes in session. No admis fee. Estab 1911. Galleries devoted to different historic & ethnographic cultures. Average Annual Attendance: 30,000. Mem: 800
Income: $120,000
Purchases: John Needles Chester Vase - Apulian Krater ca 320 BC
Collections: Original works & reproductions of Greek, Roman, Egyptian, Mesopotamian, African, Oriental & European art, including sculpture, pottery, glass, implements, coins, seals, clay tablets, inscriptions & manuscripts
Exhibitions: Of Kings, Crusaders & Craftsmen; Beyond the Himalayas
Publications: Heritage, bi-annual newsletter; exhibition brochures
Activities: Lect open to public, 1-2 vis lectr per year; concerts; gallery talks; tours; bus trips; workshops; competitions with awards; original objects of art lent for special shows in established museums; book traveling exhibitions; museum shop sells books & reproductions
M Museum of Natural History, 1301 W Green, Urbana, 61801. Tel 217-333-2517; FAX 217-244-9419; *Dir* Douglas Brewer; *Cur* Steven Sroka; *Cur & Outreach* Ann Hutflies; *Graduate Cur* Rossana de la Noval; *Graduate Cur* Rui Wang; *Graduate Cur* John Werner; *Discovery Room Mgr* Michelle Jensen
Open Mon - Sat 9 AM - 4 PM, cl Sun. No admis fee. Estab 1868 for research & educ in anthropology, botany, geology & zoology. Hall of the Past: Native North Americans, especially Midwest. Average Annual Attendance: 40,000. Mem: 100
Income: Financed by State University support
Collections: Anthropology, Herpetology, Malacology, Mammalology & Paleontology collections, 400,000 specimens
Activities: Classes for children; docent training; lect open to public, 2-3 vis lectr per year; tours; original objects of art lent to other museums
L Ricker Library of Architecture & Art, 208 Architecture Bldg, 608 E Lorado Taft Dr, 61820. Tel 217-333-0224; FAX 217-244-5169; *Librn* Dr Jane Block
Open Mon - Thurs 8:30 AM - 10 PM, Fri 8:30 AM - 5 PM, Sat 10 AM - 5 PM, Sun 1 - 10 PM. Estab 1878 to serve the study & research needs of the students & faculty of the university & the community. Ricker Library lends material through

UIUC Interlibrary Loan. Circ 50,000
Income: $85,000 (financed by state appropriation, blanket order, gifts & UIUC Library Friends)
Purchases: $65,000
Library Holdings: Vols 45,000; Per subs 350; Micro — Fiche, reels; Other — Clipping files, exhibition catalogs, pamphlets, photographs, reproductions, sculpture
Special Subjects: Architecture, Art Education, Art History, Asian Art, Ceramics, Collages, Conceptual Art, Crafts, Decorative Arts, Drawings, Graphic Design, Handicrafts, History of Art & Archaeology, Illustration, Interior Design, History of Art & Architecture; Philosophy of Art, Practice & History of Painting, Vernacular Architecture
Collections: Architectural Folio; Prairie School Architects; Ricker Papers; Frank Lloyd Wright
Publications: Acquisitions list, 4 per year; annual periodicals list

CHARLESTON

M **EASTERN ILLINOIS UNIVERSITY,** Tarble Arts Center, 600 Lincoln Ave, 61920-3099. Tel 217-581-5832, 581-2787; *Dir* Michael Watts; *Cur Educ* Kit Morice; *Registrar* David Pooley
Open Tues - Fri 10 AM - 5 PM, Sat 10 AM - 4 PM, Sun 1 - 4 PM, cl Mon & major holidays. No admis fee. Estab 1982 to encourage the understanding of & participation in the arts. Main Gallery consists of fifteen 20 ft x 20 ft modular units with natural & incandescent lighting; Brainard Gallery, 20 ft x 50 ft; Reading Room, 20 ft x 20 ft; Sales/Rental Gallery, 20 ft x 20 ft. Average Annual Attendance: 18,000. Mem: 300; dues $10 - $1000
Income: Financed by state appropriation, mem contributions, sales & rental commissions, grant & foundation funds
Collections: †Contemporary Printmaking by Midwest artists; †American Scene Prints; Paul Turner Sargent paintings; †Contemporary American Art; †Indigenous Contemporary Illinois Folk Arts
Exhibitions: Solo Exhibitions: Lasting Impressions: Drawings by Thomas Hart; Recent Paintings by William Conger Group Shows: Echo Press: A Decade of Printmaking; Old Master Prints from Collegiate Collections; Spirited Visions: Portraits of Chicago Artists; A Celebration of Contemporary Illinois Folk Arts; African American Prints from the Ruth Waddy Collection; Wall Ceramics: Cary Esser, Karen Gunderman & Jim Stephenson; Portraits & Prospects: British & Irish Drawings & Watercolors; Annual Exhibitions: Art Faculty Exhibition, All-Student Show (juried, undergraduate), Graduate Art Exhibition (group thesis), Watercolor: Illinois (biennial juried competition), International Children's Exhibition; Folk Arts from the Collection
Publications: Exhibition catalogs
Activities: Classes & workshops for children & adults; docent training; lect open to public; concerts; gallery talks; tours; competitions with awards; films & videos;; individual paintings & original objects of art lent to qualified professional galleries, arts centers & museums; book traveling exhibitions 2-4 per year; originate traveling exhibitions; sales shop sells books, original art & craft pieces; Sales/Rental Gallery rents & sells original works

CHICAGO

AMERICAN CENTER FOR DESIGN
For further information, see National and Regional Organizations

A **AMERICAN JEWISH ART CLUB,** 6301 N Sheridan Rd, Apt 8E, 60660-1711. Tel 312-676-3187; *Pres* Mrs Irmgard Hess Rosenberger; *VPres* Nina Turner; *Treas* Ruth Zwick; *Publicity Dir* Irene Poll; *Publicity Dir* Sylvia Schnitmann
No admis fee. Estab 1928 to expose work of members & educate pub. Average Annual Attendance: 600. Mem: 80; mem based on professional standing & jurying by general mem; dues $35; 6-8 meetings per yr
Income: Financed by mem dues & contributions
Exhibitions: Exhibitions at various galleries
Publications: Exhibition catalogs; newsletter, 11 per year
Activities: Educ dept; lect open to public, 5 vis lectr per year; give awards, 5 per year; individual paintings & original objects of art lent; lending collection contains original art works, original prints, paintings, photographs & sculpture; sales shop sells original art

AMERICAN SOCIETY OF ARTISTS, INC
For further information, see National and Regional Organizations

M **ARC GALLERY,** 1040 W Huron St, 60622. Tel 312-733-2787; *Pres* Julia Morrisroe
Open Wed - Sat 11 AM - 5 PM. No admis fee. Estab 1973 for the exhibition of alternative artworks & education to the public about contemporary art
Exhibitions: ARC Regional Women's view on the Nude, National Photo Show & Solo Shows, 66 exhibitions annually, six per month in six separate galleries How I Didn't Spend My Summer Vacation
Activities: Educ dept; lect open to public; gallery talks; juried exhibitions; originate traveling exhibitions; sales shop sells original art

M **ARTEMISIA GALLERY,** 700 N Carpenter, 60622. Tel 312-226-7323; FAX 312-226-7756; *Co-Pres* Carrie Seid; *Co-Pres* Susan Sensemann; *Coordr* Nora Donnelly
Open Tues - Sat 11 AM - 5 PM. No admis fee. Estab 1973 to promote public awareness of & leadership opportunities for women artists. Five areas to show five different artists or group shows. Average Annual Attendance: 12,000. Mem: 12, associate mem 15; dues $600-$900; mem is judged by quality of art work
Income: Financed by grants, donations, member dues, gallery rental & benefits
Exhibitions: Annual exhibit of established contemporary women artists; emerging artists & educational exhibits; international exchanges; regular exhibitions by members
Publications: Anniversary catalog of members & alumnae work every 5 years; quarterly newsletter
Activities: Lect open to public, 5-7 vis lectr per year; gallery talks; competitions with prizes; performance art; international exchanges; mentor program: scholarships offered; originate traveling exhibitions 1-2 per year; shop sells original art, magazines & exhibition catalogs

A **THE ART INSTITUTE OF CHICAGO,** Michigan Ave at Adams St, 60603. Tel 312-443-3600; FAX 312-443-0849; *Chmn Board Trustees* John D Nichols; *Pres & Dir* James N Wood; *School Pres* Anthony Jones; *Exec VPres Admin Affairs* Robert E Mars; *Exec VPres Develop & Public Affairs* Edward W Horner Jr; *Deputy Dir* Teri J Edelstein; *Cur American Arts* Judith Barter; *Cur European Painting* Douglas Druick; *Cur European Painting Before 1750* Martha Wolff; *Exec Dir Conservation* Frank Zuccari; *Exec Dir Museum Educ* Ronne Hartfield; *Exec Dir Imaging & Technical Serv* Alan B Newman; *Cur Photography* David Travis; *Cur Africa, Oceania & the Americas* Richard F Townsend; *Cur Prints & Drawings* Douglas Druick; *Cur Prints & Drawings* Suzanne McCullagh; *Cur Architecture* John Zukowsky; *Dir Foundations & Corporate Relations* Gregory Cameron; *Cur Textiles* Christa C Mayer Thurman; *Cur European Decorative Arts, Sculpture & Classical Art* Ian Wardropper; *Cur 20th Century Painting & Sculpture* Jeremy Strick; *Exec Dir of Museum Registration* Mary Solt; *Exec Dir Pub Affairs* Eileen E Harakal; *Exec Dir Publications* Susan F Rossen; *Dir Government Relations* Karin Victoria; *Exec Dir Graphics & Communications* Lyn Delli Quadri
Open Mon, Wed, Thurs & Fri 10:30 AM - 4:30 PM, Tues 10:30 - 8 PM, Sat 10 AM - 5 PM, Sun & holidays Noon - 5 PM, cl Christmas & Thanksgiving. Admis adults $7 suggested, senior citizens & children $3.50 suggested, Tues no admis fee. Estab & incorporated 1879 to found, build, maintain & operate museums of fine arts, schools & libraries of art, to form, preserve & exhibit collections of objects of art of all kinds & to carry on appropriate activities conducive to the artistic development of the community. Maintains reference library. Average Annual Attendance: 1,300,000. Mem: 163,000; dues life $1500, family $60, individual $50, national associates & students $35
Income: $97,000,000 (financed by endowments, gifts & grants)
Collections: Paintings, sculpture, Asian art, prints & drawings, photographs, decorative arts, architectural fragments, tribal arts & textiles; The painting collection reviews Western art, with an especially fine sequence of French Impressionists & Post Impressionists; the print collection illustrates the history of printmaking from the 15th-20th centuries with important examples of all periods. It is particularly rich in French works of the 19th century including Meryon, Redon, Millet, Gauguin & Toulouse-Lautrec; textiles are displayed in the Agnes Allerton Textile Galleries which includes a study room & new conservation facilities; collections also include African, Oceanic & ancient American objects; The Architecture Collection includes 19th & 20th century drawings & architectural fragments in the Institute's permanent collection including the more than 40,000 architectural drawings from the Burnham Library of Architecture; The Columbus Drive Facilities include the reconstructed Trading Room from the Chicago Stock Exchange; Arthur Rubloff Paperweight collection is on view; the America Windows, monumental stained glass windows designed by Marc Chagall are on view in the gallery overlooking McKinlock Court; decorative arts & sculpture range from medieval to the twentieth century; the Asian collection contains a world renowned collection of Ukiyo-e prints
Exhibitions: Max Ernst: Dada & the Dawn of Surrealism; Thinking is Form: The Drawings of Joseph Beuys; I Tell My Heart: The Art of Horace Pippin; John James Audubon: The Watercolors for The Birds of America; Goya: Truth & Fantasy, The Small Paintings. Chicago's Dream, A World's Treasure: The Art Institute of Chicago, 1893-1993 Max Ernst: Dada & the Dawn of Surrealism; Chicago's Dream, A World's Treasure: The Art Institute of Chicago 1893 - 1993; Thonet Furniture from the Collection of Mr & Mrs Manfred Steinfeld & German & Austrian Textiles from the Permanent Collection 1900 - 1930s
Publications: News & Events every two months; Museum Studies; catalogs; Annual Report
Activities: Classes & workshops for adults & children; teacher training; docent training; lect open to public; concerts; gallery walks & talks; guided lect tours; individual paintings & original objects of art lent to museums around the world; originate traveling exhibitions to selected museums; museum shop sells books, magazines, original art, reproductions, prints, slides, decorative accessories, crafts, jewelry, greeting cards & postcards; junior museum at Kraft Education Center

L **Ryerson & Burnham Libraries,** 111 S Michigan Ave, 60603-6110. Tel 312-443-3666; FAX 312-443-0849; Elec Mail ryerson@artic.edu;
Internet Home Page Address www.artic.edu. *Dir of Libraries* Jack Perry Brown; *Head Reader Servs* Maureen Lasko; *Head Technical Servs* Anne Champagne; *Head Slide Librn* Leigh Gates; *Serials Librn* Ann Jones; *Architecture Librn* Mary Woolever; *Archivist* Bart Ryckbosch
Open Wed - Fri 10:30 AM - 4:30 PM, Tues 10:30 AM - 7:45 PM, Sat 10 AM - 4:45 PM, cl Sat from June - Labor Day & legal holidays. Open to mus members, staff of mus, students & faculty of the School of Art Institute & vis scholars & curators, for reference only
Income: $1,410,000
Purchases: $410,000
Library Holdings: Vols 225,000; Per subs 1500; Micro — Fiche, reels; AV — A-tapes, cassettes, Kodachromes, lantern slides, slides 410,000, v-tapes; Other — Clipping files, exhibition catalogs, manuscripts, memorabilia, pamphlets, photographs
Special Subjects: Architecture, Art History, Asian Art, Bronzes, Carpets & Rugs, Ceramics, Conceptual Art, Crafts, Decorative Arts, Drawings, Embroidery, Enamels, Etchings & Engravings, Folk Art, Furniture, Glass, Gold, Goldsmithing, Graphic Arts, History of Art & Archaeology, Ivory, Jade, Jewelry, Laces, Latin American Art, Marine Painting, Metalwork, Mexican Art, Oriental Art, Painting - American
Collections: Burnham Archive: Chicago Architects, letters, reports; including special Louis Sullivan, Frank Lloyd Wright & D H Burnham Collections; Percier & Fontaine Collection; Chicago Art & Artists Scrapbook: newspaper clippings from Chicago papers from 1880 to 1993 Mary Reynolds Collection: Surrealism; Bruce Goff Archive; Collins Archive of Catalan Art & Architecture
Publications: Architectural Records In Chicago, research guide; Burnham Index to Architectural Literature (1990)

A **Woman's Board,** 111 S Michigan Ave, 60603-6110. Tel 312-443-3629; *Pres* Mrs William R Jentis
Estab 1952 to supplement the Board of Trustees in advancing the growth of the Institute & extending its activities & usefulness as a cultural & educational institution. Mem: 98; annual meeting May
Income: Financed by contributions

A **Auxiliary Board,** 111 S Michigan Ave, 60603. Tel 312-443-3674; *Pres* Elizabeth Souder Louis
Estab 1973 to promote interest in programs and activities of the Art Institute amoung younger men and women. Mem: 60; dues $500; annual meeting in June

A **Antiquarian Society,** 111 S Michigan Ave, 60603. Tel 312-443-3641; *Pres* Judith York
Open daily 9 AM - 5 PM. Estab 1877. Support American Arts & European Decorative Arts. Mem: 600; by invitation; annual meeting in Nov
Income: Financed by donations, benefits, annual dues
Exhibitions: Preview of Charles Renmie Mackintosh
Publications: Antiquarian Society Catalogue, every 10 years
Activities: Lect & seminars for members; tours; trips

A **Print & Drawing Dept,** 111 S Michigan Ave, 60603. Tel 312-443-3660; FAX 312-443-0849; *Pres* Edward Blair Sr; *Prince Trust Cur Prints & Drawings & Searle Cur European Drawings* Dr Douglas W Druick
Estab & incorporated 1922 to study prints & drawings & their purchase for the institute. Mem: 190; dues $35-50
Income: Financed by mem contributions
Activities: Lect; gallery talks

A **Society for Contemporary Arts,** 111 S Michigan Ave, 60603. Tel 312-443-3630; FAX 312-443-1041; *Pres* Daryl Gerber
Estab & incorporated 1940 to assist the Institute in acquisition of contemporary works. Mem: 160; dues $300-$500; annual meeting in Apr
Income: Financed by mem contributions
Activities: Lect; seminars & biennial exhibition at the Institute

A **Department of Asian Art,** 111 S Michigan Ave, 60603. Tel 312-443-3834; *Pritzker Cur Asian Art* Stephen Little; *Assoc Cur Chinese Art* Elinor Pearlstein; *Asst Cur Japanese Art* Bernd Jesse
Estab 1925 to promote interest in the Institute's collection of Asian art. Mem: 50; dues $50
Purchases: Tang Dynasty Lu-shan Ware, Ninth Century Chinese Ceramics
Collections: Chinese furniture; bronze; jade; ceramics; Buddhist arts & paintings Collections; Clarence Buckingham Japanese Woodblock Print Collection; Japanese Buddhist art; ceramic & painting Collection; Korean Ceramics Collection
Exhibitions: Alsdorf Indian Sculpture Collection; Ice & Green Clouds: Traditions of Chinese Celadon; Roger Weston: Inro Collection
Publications: Exhibition catalogues
Activities: Lect open to public; symposia on exhibitions

A **Textile Society,** 111 S Michigan Ave, 60603. Tel 312-443-3696; *Pres* Mrs John K Notz
Open daily 10:30 AM - 4 PM by appointment only. Estab 1978 to promote appreciation of textiles through lectures, raising of funds, special publications & exhibitions for the Department of Textiles

M **Kraft Education Center,** 111 S Michigan Ave, 60603. Tel 312-443-3680; *Assoc Dir of Museum Educ* Jean Sousa
Open Mon, Wed - Fri 10:30 AM - 4:30 PM, Tues 10:30 AM - 8 PM, Sat 10 AM - 5 PM, Sun & holidays Noon - 5 PM. Admis free with Art Institute of Chicago discretionary admis, no admis fee Tuesday. Estab 1964. The new center includes a main exhibition gallery, family room, classrooms, a Teacher Resource Center, a seminar room, an auditorium, conference room & staff offices. Average Annual Attendance: 150,000
Income: Financed by grants, gifts & endowment; renovation financed by Kraft General Foods & the Woman's Board; exhibitions supported by grants from John D & Catherine T MacArthur Foundation & NEA
Exhibitions: Telling Images: Stories in Art
Publications: Family Self Guides & teacher packets to permanent collections & special exhibitions; gallery games; yearly publications; Volunteer Directory; Information for Students & Teachers; quarterly brochures on family programs, teachers' services, school & general programs
Activities: Docent training; teacher & family workshops; lect open to the public; gallery walks & games; tours; performances; artist demonstrations

L **Teacher Resource Center,** 111 S Michigan Ave, 60603. Tel 312-443-7290; *Head Resource Center* Jeanne Poole
Open Tues 2 - 7 PM, Sat 10 AM - 3 PM. Open for reference only. Average Annual Attendance: 20,000
Income: Financed by endowment
Library Holdings: Vols 1500
Activities: Junior museum activities such as gallery games & architectural walks

A **THE ARTS CLUB OF CHICAGO,** 201 E Ontario St, 60611. Tel 312-787-3997; FAX 312-787-8664; *Dir* Kathy S Cottong; *Pres* Stanley M Freehling; *First VPres* John D Cartland
Open 10 AM - 5 PM. No admis fee. Estab 1916 to maintain club rooms for members & provide pub galleries for changing exhibitions. Gallery has 230 running ft of wall space. Average Annual Attendance: 15,000. Mem: 1000; annual meeting in Nov
Income: Financed by mem dues
Purchases: Occasional purchases gifts & bequests
Publications: Exhibition Catalogs
Activities: Lect open to public, 3-4 vis lectr per year; concerts; gallery talks; tours; book traveling exhibitions 1 per year; traveling exhibitions organized and circulated

L **Reference Library,** 109 E Ontario St, 60611. *Dir* Kathy Cottong
Library Holdings: Vols 3000; Per subs 6; Other — Exhibition catalogs
Special Subjects: 20th Century paintings, sculpture, drawings, prints & photography

M **BALZEKAS MUSEUM OF LITHUANIAN CULTURE,** 6500 S Pulaski Rd, 60629. Tel 773-582-6500; FAX 773-582-5133; *Pres* Stanley Balzekas Jr; *VPres* Joseph Katauskas; *Exec Dir* Loreta Visomirskyte
Open daily 10 AM - 4 PM. Admis adults $4, senior citizens & students $3, children $1. Estab 1966 as a repository for collecting and preserving Lithuanian cultural treasures. Average Annual Attendance: 34,800. Mem: 2700; dues $25-$35
Income: $10,000 (financed by mem & donations)
Collections: †Amber; archeology; archives; †coins; fine art; folk art; †graphics; †maps; †numismatics; philately; photography; rare books; rare maps; †textiles; †wooden folk art †Textiles; †Wooden folkart; †Maps; †Paintings; †Graphics
Exhibitions: Various exhibits of paintings, graphics & sculpture

Publications: Lithuanian Museum Review, bimonthly
Activities: Classes for adults & children; demonstrations; folk art workshops; lect open to public, 10 vis lectr per year; tours; original objects of art lent to other museums & galleries; lending collection contains books, nature artifacts, original art works, paintings, photographs & slides; originate traveling exhibitions; museum shop sells books, magazines, original art, reproductions, prints, folk art, amber jewelry, souvenirs & t-shirts

L **Research Library,** 6500 S Pulaski Rd, 60629. Tel 312-582-6500; FAX 312-582-5133; *Pres* Stanley Balzekas; *Librn* Jessie Daraska; *Cur* Danas Lapkus
Open daily 10 AM - 4 PM. Estab 1966 to preserve Lithuanian-American literature & culture. Open to pub for reference only
Library Holdings: Vols 40,000; Micro — Cards, prints; AV — A-tapes, cassettes, rec, slides, v-tapes; Other — Clipping files, exhibition catalogs, framed reproductions, manuscripts, memorabilia, original art works, pamphlets, photographs, prints, reproductions, sculpture
Special Subjects: Anthropology, Archaeology, Architecture, Art History, Decorative Arts, Ethnology, Folk Art, Furniture, Graphic Arts, Historical Material, History of Art & Archaeology, Maps, Photography, Prints
Collections: Original art work: painting, sculpture & rare maps; †reproductions of Lithuanian artists; †Information on Lithuanian artists & their works
Exhibitions: Rare Book & Map Exhibits

C **BANK OF AMERICA-ILLINOIS,** Art Collection, 200 W Jackson, 26th Flr, 60697. Tel 312-974-6751; FAX 312-974-6898; *Art Consultant* Lowanzer Reed
Collections: †Vintage photographs; †contemporary master prints; †folk art; †American Indian art & artifacts; †Pre-Columbian art & artifacts; †African art; †ancient art; †art of the American West

M **BOULEVARD ARTS CENTER,** 1525 W 60th St, 60636. Tel 773-476-4900; FAX 773-476-5951; *Exec Dir* Pat Devine-Reed; *Artistic Dir* Marti Price
Estab 1986. Gallery shows, music with AAMC, dance, visual arts, wood carving, stone carving. Mem: Dues $30
Income: Financed by endowment, mem, city appropriation & state appropriation
Exhibitions: (1997) Anniversary Tribute (Honore to be Announced) Art Auction; Emerging Artist Exhibit; Boulevard Arts Student Exhibit; Boulevard Arts/AACM Student Recital-Awards Day; Gallery 60 Arts Employment Training For Youth; Young Artist Festival; 13th Annual Tribute to the Creativity of Youth
Activities: Classes for adults & children; dramatic programs; lect open to public & members; sales shop sells original art

M **ROY BOYD GALLERY,** 739 N Wells St, 60610-3520. Tel 312-642-1606; FAX 312-642-2143; *Co-Dir* Ann Boyd; *Co-Dir* Roy Boyd
Open Tues - Sat 10 AM - 5:30 PM. No admis fee. Estab 1972 to exhibit art
Collections: Contemporary American paintings; Russian & Baltic photography; sculpture & works on paper

M **CHICAGO ARCHITECTURE FOUNDATION,** 224 S Michigan Ave, 60604. Tel 312-922-3432; FAX 312-922-0481; Elec Mail architecture.org. *Pres* Lynn J Osmond
Open Mon - Sat 9 AM - 7 PM, Sun 9 AM - 6 PM. Comprehensive program of tours, lectures, exhibitions & special events to enhance pub awareness & appreciation of Chicago architecture. Average Annual Attendance: 160,000. Mem: 6000; dues $35
Income: Financed by mem, shop & tour center, foundation, government & private grants
Publications: In Sites Newsletter, quarterly
Activities: Classes for adults; docent training; lect open to pub, 35 vis lectr per year; concerts; tours; competitions; sales shop sells books, magazines, architecturally inspired gift items, stationery & posters

A **CHICAGO ARTISTS' COALITION,** 11 E Hubbard St, 7th Flr, 60611. Tel 312-670-2060; FAX 312-670-2521; *Exec Dir* Arlene Rakoncay; *Ed* Jeff Abell
Open Mon - Fri 10 AM - 5 PM. Estab 1975 to provide services, benefits, information & support to visual artists. Resource center includes reference books, pamphlets & catalogs. Mem: 2800; mem open to professional fine & graphic artists; dues $35, monthly board meetings; annual meeting in Sept
Income: $130,000 (financed by mem, city & state appropriation, donations, earned income projects, corporations & foundations)
Publications: Artists' Gallery Guide; Artists' Bookkeeping Book; Artists Yellow Pages; Chicago Artists News, 11 times per yr
Activities: Lect open to public, 25 vis lectr per year

M **CHICAGO ATHENAEUM,** Museum of Architecture & Design, 6 N Michigan Ave, 60626. Tel 312-251-0175; FAX 312-251-0176; *Dir & Pres* Christian K Narkiewicz-Laine; *Deputy Cur* Leonard M Kliwinski; *Dir Exhib* Ioannis Karalias
Open Tues - Sat 11 AM - 6 PM, Sun Noon - 5 PM, cl Mon. Admis $3. Estab 1988; dedicated to all areas in the art of design - architecture, industrial & product design, graphics & urban planning. Two floors of temporary exhibit galleries; Landmark Chicago Gallery (permanent) & Made in Chicago Gallery. Average Annual Attendance: 500,000. Mem: 2500; dues $50-$250
Income: Financed by mem & grants
Collections: Architectural Drawings & Models, International Collection; Design-Chicago (1910-1960) Collection; Design-International Product & Graphic Collection; Japanese Graphic Design Collection
Exhibitions: The Children of Chernobyl; Denmark Through Design; Landmark Chicago
Activities: Seminars; lect open to public, 15 vis lectr per year; competitions; book traveling exhibitions 8 per year; originate traveling exhibitions 6 per year; museum shop sells books, original art, architectural models, drawings & industrial design

M **CHICAGO CHILDREN'S MUSEUM,** 700 E Grand Ave, 60611. Tel 312-527-1000; FAX 312-527-9082; *Pres* Dianne L Sautter; *Assoc Exec Dir* Judy Chiss
Open Tues - Fri 12:30 - 4:30 PM, Sat & Sun 10 AM - 4:30 PM, cl Mon. Admis adults $3, children $2, Thurs 5 - 8 PM free. Estab 1982 to inspire discovery & self-expression in children through interactive exhibits & programs. Average

Annual Attendance: 3500 families. Mem: dues $35
Income: $1,200,000 (financed by mem, foundation, corporate, government, individual support, earned income)
Exhibitions: City Hospital; Touchy Business; The Art & Science of Bubbles; Lies About Animals; Magic & Masquerades; Grandparents Exhibit: The Stinking Truth about Garbage, News Brief
Activities: Classes for adults & children; docent programs; retail store sells books, prints, educational toys & games

M **CHICAGO DEPARTMENT OF CULTURAL AFFAIRS,** Chicago Cultural Center, 78 E Washington St, 60602. Tel 312-744-6630; FAX 312-744-2089; TTY/TTD 312-744-2947. *Commissioner* Lois Weisberg; *First Deputy Commissioner* John Small; *Dir Visual Arts* Gregory G Knight; *Assoc Cur* Edward Maldonado; *Assoc Cur* Lanny Silverman
Open Mon - Thurs 10 AM - 7 PM, Fri 10 AM - 6 PM, Sat 10 AM - 5 PM, Sun Noon - 5 PM, cl holidays. No admis fee. Estab 1991 as an architectural showplace for lively & visual arts. Exhibit Hall; Sidney R Yates Gallery; Michigan Avenue Galleries; Chicago Rooms; Renaissance Court; Randolph Gallery; 'Round & About the Loop; Pedway Art Showcases; Landmark Chicago Gallery. The Chicago Cultural Center is a landmark building, dating from 1897 that includes rare imported marbles, fine hardwood, stained glass, polished brass, as well as mosaics of Favrile glass, colored stone & mother of pearl. The building's most notable features are its spectacular stained glass domes; a 38-ft Tiffany dome; & a second stained glass dome, executed in an intricate Renaissance pattern. Average Annual Attendance: 800,000
Income: $100,000 (financed by city & state appropriation, corporate sponsors & foundation)
Exhibitions: Represent a wide range of media: paintings, sculpture, photography, graphics, crafts, architecture & design. A variety of contemporary, historical & cultural offerings include national traveling exhibitions as well as one-person shows by local artists. Overall the exhibition schedule reflects a commitment to showcasing cultural diversity in the arts
Activities: Classes for children; demonstrations; workshops; lect open to public; gallery talks; panel discussions; concerts; screenings; receptions; performances; book traveling exhibitions 9 per year; originate traveling exhibitions 1 per year; sales shop sells exhibition catalogs, T-shirts, notecards, postcards & miscellaneous

A **CHICAGO HISTORICAL SOCIETY,** Clark St at North Ave, 60614. Tel 312-642-4600; FAX 312-266-2077; *Chmn* Philip Hummer; *VChmn* Richard Jaffee; *VChmn* Charlie Brumback; *Treas* Sharon Gist Gilliam; *Pres* Douglas Greenberg; *Cur Decorative Arts* Olivia Mahoney; *Cur Costumes* Susan Samek; *Ed* Rosemary Adams; *Cur Architecture* Maggie Kelly; *Cur Manuscripts Coll* A J Motley; *Librn* Janice McNeill; *Deputy Dir Research* Russell Lewis; *VPres Finance* Robert Nauert; *VPres Develop & External Affairs* Jay Frey
Open Mon - Sat 9:30 AM - 4:30 PM, Sun & holidays Noon - 5 PM. Admis adults $3, senior citizens & students $2, children (6-17) $1, no admis fee Mon. Estab 1856 to maintain a museum and library of American history with special emphasis on the Chicago region. Average Annual Attendance: 175,000. Mem: 8500; dues $50; annual meeting in Oct
Income: $7,200,000 (financed by endowment, mem, city & state appropriations & public donations)
Collections: Architectural Archive; costumes; decorative arts; industrial photographs; manuscripts; paintings; sculpture
Exhibitions: Chicago History Galleries; We the People; America in the Age of Lincoln
Publications: Books, Calendar of Events & newsletter, quarterly; catalogs; Chicago History, quarterly
Activities: Classes for adults and children; lect open to public, 15-20 vis lectr per year; gallery talks; tours; sales shop selling books, magazines, prints, reproductions, slides

L **CHICAGO PUBLIC LIBRARY,** Harold Washington Library Center, Art Info Ctr, Visual & Performing Arts Div, 400 S State St, 60605. Tel 312-747-4800; FAX 312-747-4832; Elec Mail sloane@mcs.com. *Commissioner* Mary A Dempsey; *Head Visual & Performing Arts Div* Rosalinda I Hack; *Head Spec Projects* Gerald Zimmerman; *Head Art Information Center* Yvonne S Brown; *Picture Coll Librn* Margarete K Gross; *Coll Develop* Karen Kuntz; *Serials* Laura Morgan; *Dance Librn* Robert Sloane
Open Mon 9 AM - 7 PM, Tues & Thurs 11 AM - 7 PM, Wed, Fri & Sat 9 AM - 5 PM, Sun 1 - 5 PM. Estab 1872 as a free public library & reading room. The original building was built in 1897. New location of central library. The Harold Washington Library Center was opened to the public in 1991. Audio-visual materials are restricted for use by Chicago area residents
Income: $321,343 (financed by city & state appropriations)
Library Holdings: Vols 116,335; Per subs 529; Videodiscs; Micro — Fiche 6192, reels 4230; AV — Cassettes, rec, slides, v-tapes 464; Other — Clipping files, exhibition catalogs, memorabilia, original art works, pamphlets, photographs, reproductions, sculpture
Special Subjects: Afro-American Art, American Indian Art, American Western Art, Decorative Arts, Folk Art, Historical Material, Islamic Art, Judaica, Oriental Art, Painting - American, Chicago Architecture; Dance
Collections: †Chicago Artists Archives; Maurice S Weigle Photography Collection of videodiscs; †exhibition catalogues beginning in 1973, primarily English language catalogues; folk dance collection of 50 loose leaf volumes; †dance videocassettes documenting history, styles & local choreography; †picture collection of over one million items of secondary source material covering all subject areas
Publications: Chicago Artists' Archives Brochure; Collecting Black Americana: A Bibliography Brochure; Guide To the Central Library Brochure; Pathfinders, Dance Brochure; Pathfinders, Polish Arts & Crafts Brochure; Visual & Performing Arts Division Brochure
Activities: Dramatic programs; lect open to public; concerts; interlibrary loan

COLUMBIA COLLEGE

L **Library,** 600 S Michigan Ave, 60605. Tel 312-663-1600; FAX 312-663-1707; *Dir* Mary Schellhorn; *Head Technical Serv* Patricia Smith; *Fine Arts Librn* Wendy Hall
Open Mon - Thurs 8 AM - 9:30 PM, Fri 8 AM - 6 PM, Sat 9 AM - 5 PM. Estab 1893 to provide library & media services & materials in support of the curriculum & to serve the college community as a whole. For lending & reference
Library Holdings: Vols 107,000; Per subs 300; Micro — Fiche, reels; AV — Cassettes, slides, v-tapes; Other — Clipping files, exhibition catalogs, pamphlets
Special Subjects: Advertising Design, Art Education, Commercial Art, Film, Graphic Arts, Theatre Arts, Video
Collections: †George Lurie Fine Arts Collection; Film & Television Script Collection
Publications: Film/Videotape List; Index to Filmscripts; Periodicals List

M **The Museum of Contemporary Photography,** 600 S Michigan Ave, 60605-1996. Tel 312-663-5554; FAX 312-360-1656; *Dir* Denise Miller Clark; *Asst Dir* Martha Alexander-Grohman; *Curatorial Asst Preparator* Nancy Fewkes; *Mus Coordr & Chmn Dept Art & Photog* John Mulvany
Open Sept - May Mon - Fri 10 AM - 5 PM, Sat Noon - 5 PM, June & July Mon - Fri 10 AM - 4 PM, Sat Noon - 4 PM, cl Aug. Estab 1976 to exhibit, collect & promote contemporary photography. 4000 sq ft on two levels; newly designed 1500 sq ft main exhibition gallery permits a spacious installation of 200 photographs; upper level gallery can accommodate an additional 200-300 prints. Mem: 450; dues $10-$1000
Collections: Contemporary American photography, including in-depth holdings of works by Harold Allen, Harry Callahan, Barbara Crane, Louise Dahl-Wolfe, Dorothea Lange, Danny Lyon, Barbara Morgan, David Plowden, Anne Noggle & Jerry Uelsmann
Publications: Exhibit catalogs
Activities: Lect open to public, 6 vis lectr per year; lending collection contains photographs; book traveling exhibitions 1-2 per year; originate traveling exhibitions; museum shop sells books, catalogs & posters

A **CONTEMPORARY ART WORKSHOP,** 542 W Grant Pl, 60614. Tel 773-472-4004; *Pres* John Kearney; *Dir* Lynn Kearney
Open daily 12:30 - 5 PM, Sat 2 - 5 PM. No admis fee. Estab 1949 as an art center & a Workshop-Alternative Space for artists; it is the oldest artist-run art workshop in the country. Studios for 20 artists & two galleries for exhibition of developing & emerging artists from Chicago & other parts of the country are maintained. Average Annual Attendance: 7000
Income: Financed by contributions, foundations, Illinois Arts Council, Chicago Council on Fine Arts, National Endowment for the Arts, & earnings by the workshop fees
Exhibitions: Catherine Arnold; Denise Falk; Tom Gengler; Doug Jeck; Jared Joslin; John Kearney; Anna Kunz; Didier Nolet; Mark Ottens; Ron Porter; Peggy Robinson; Peter Roos; Joe Seigenthaler; John Slavik; Tim Stegmaier; Frank Trankina; Suen Wong
Activities: Classes for adults; lect open to public, 5 vis lectr per year; gallery talks; tours; gallery sells artwork

M **DUSABLE MUSEUM OF AFRICAN AMERICAN HISTORY,** 740 E 56th Pl, 60637. Tel 312-947-0600; FAX 312-947-0677; *Founder* Margaret T Burrough; *Chief Cur* Ramon Price; *Registrar* Theresa Christopher
Open Mon - Fri 9 AM - 5 PM, Sat & Sun Noon - 5 PM. Admis adults $2, children & students $1, groups by appointment. Estab 1961 as history & art museum on African American history. Mem: Dues corp $1000, family $35, general $25, student & senior citizen $15
Collections: Historical archives; paintings; photographs; prints; sculpture
Publications: Books of poems, children's stories, African & African-American history; Heritage Calendar, annual
Activities: Lect; guided tours; book traveling exhibitions; sales shop sells curios, sculpture, prints, books & artifacts

C **EXCHANGE NATIONAL BANK OF CHICAGO,** 135 S LaSalle St, 60603. Tel 312-781-8076; FAX 312-750-6142; *Cur* Herbert Kahn
Open Mon - Fri 8 AM - 4 PM. Estab 1968 as a community service by making a meaningful cultural contribution to the community. Collection displayed in pub areas of the bank
Collections: Approximately 2000 photographs by important photographers since the founding of photography up to the present
Activities: Tours

M **FIELD MUSEUM,** Roosevelt Rd at Lake Shore Dr, 60605. Tel 312-922-9410; FAX 312-922-0741; *Pres Emeritus* Willard L Boyd; *Pres* John W McCarter Jr
Open daily 9 AM - 5 PM, cl Thanksgiving, Christmas, New Year's. Admis family (maximum) $10, adults $3, senior citizens & students $2, no charge on Wed. Estab 1893 to preserve & disseminate knowledge of natural history. 22 anthropological exhibition halls, including a Hall of Primitive Art are maintained. Average Annual Attendance: 1,400,000. Mem: 23,172; dues $30 & $35
Income: $20,000,000 (financed by endowment, mem, city & state appropriations & federal & earned funds)
Collections: Anthropological, botanical, geological & zoological collections totaling over 19,000,000 artifacts & specimens, including 100,000 art objects from North & South America, Oceania, Africa, asia & prehistoric Europe
Exhibitions: Permanent exhibitions: Ancient Egypt Exhibition; Prehistoric Peoples Exhibition; Dinosaur Hall; The American Indian; Pacific Exhibition
Publications: In the Field, monthly; Fieldiana (serial)
Activities: Classes for adults & children; lect open to public, 25 vis lectr per year; concerts; gallery talks; tours; exten dept serving Chicago area; original objects of art lent to qualified museum or other scholarly institutions; traveling exhibitions organized & circulated; museum shop selling books, magazines, prints, slides

L **Library,** Roosevelt Rd at Lake Shore Dr, 60605. Tel 312-922-9410, Ext 280; FAX 312-427-7269; *Librn & Spec Coll Librn* Benjamin Williams
Open Mon - Fri 8:30 AM - 4:30 PM
Library Holdings: Vols 250,000; Per subs 4000
Special Subjects: American Indian Art, Anthropology, Antiquities-Egyptian, Archaeology, Asian Art, Illustrated Zoological Volumes, Pacific Art
Collections: Rare Book Room housing 6500 vols

C **THE FIRST NATIONAL BANK OF CHICAGO,** Art Collection, One First National Plaza, Ste 0523, 60670. Tel 312-732-5935; *Dir Art Prog* John Hallmark Neff; *Cur* Lisa K Erf; *Registrar* John W Dodge; *Cur Asst* Robert Bridges
Open to public by appointment only. Estab 1968 to assemble works of art to serve as a permanent extension of daily life. Collection displayed throughout bank building and overseas offices
Collections: Art from Africa, America, Asis, Australia, the Caribbean Basin, Europe, Latin America, Near East & the South Seas ranging from Sixth Century BC to the present
Activities: Individual objects of art lent only to major exhibitions in museums; originate traveling exhibitions

L **HARRINGTON INSTITUTE OF INTERIOR DESIGN,** Design Library, 410 S Michigan Ave, 60605. Tel 312-939-4975; FAX 312-939-8005; *Library Dir* Craig Davis; *Asst Librn Cataloging* Elaine Lowenthal; *Library Technical Asst* Nevin Peters
Open Mon, Wed & Fri 8 AM - 4 PM, Tues & Thurs 8 AM - 9:45 PM, summer daily 9 AM - 5 PM. Estab 1960
Purchases: 30,000 (books, periodicals & AV materials)
Library Holdings: Vols 17,000; Per subs 90; AV — Slides 23,000, v-tapes 120; Other — Clipping files, exhibition catalogs, pamphlets 200
Special Subjects: Afro-American Art, Architecture, Display, Furniture, Graphic Design, Industrial Design, Interior Design, Landscape Architecture, Painting - American, Period Rooms, Photography, Pottery, Primitive Art, Restoration & Conservation, Stained Glass, Watercolors, Pure Design, 20th Century Design
Collections: †Furniture Manufacture Catalogs (current dates only)
Publications: Current Awareness; recent acquisitions; subject bibliographies

M **HYDE PARK ART CENTER,** 5307 S Hyde Park Blvd, 60615. Tel 312-324-5520; *Exec Dir* Eva M Olson; *Educ Dir* Jacqueline Terrassa; *Public Relations Coordr* Arthur Fournier
Open Mon - Sat 11 AM - 5 PM. No admis fee. Estab 1939 to stimulate an interest in art. Average Annual Attendance: 14,000. Mem: 800; dues family $35
Income: $239,000 (financed by endowment, mem, city & state appropriation, foundations, corporations & private contributions)
Exhibitions: (1997) How to Describe a Suspect, self portraits; upcoming guest curated events/exhibitions
Publications: Quarterly newsletter, exhibition catalogues
Activities: Classes for adults & children; lect open to public; gallery talks; scholarships offered; sales shop sells original art

M **ILLINOIS STATE MUSEUM,** Illinois Art Gallery, 100 W Randolph, Ste 2-100, 60601. Tel 312-814-5322; FAX 312-814-3471; *Admin Asst & Registration* Jane Stevens; *Preparations* Luke Dohner; *Educ & Public Relations* Judith Lloyd
Open Mon - Fri 9 AM - 5:30 PM. No admis fee. Estab 1985 for the purpose of promoting an awareness of the variety of art found & produced in Illinois. Three large galleries & three smaller galleries provide a flexible space for a diverse exhibition program. Exhibits are produced by the Illinois State Mus & the State of Illinois Art Gallery. Average Annual Attendance: 47,000
Publications: Exhibit catalogs
Activities: Internships offered; book traveling exhibitions 6 per year; originate traveling exhibitions; museum shop sells books & original art

M **Illinois Artisans Shop,** 100 W Randolph St, 60601. Tel 312-814-5321; FAX 312-814-2439; *Dir ILL Artisans Prog* Ellen Gantner; *Mgr ILL Artisans Shop* Maryanne Miceli
Open Mon - Fri 9 AM - 5 PM. No admis fee. Estab 1985. A not-for-profit program to showcase the craft work of Illinois artisans accepted in a consignment shop & to educate the pub about the scope of craft art. Mem: 1400 artists in program; qualification for mem; juried art work
Income: Financed by state appropriation & retail sales of art work
Publications: Craft Events in Illinois, biannual; Illinois Artisan Newsletter, periodic
Activities: Educ dept; public demonstrations; monthly workshops; lect open to public; sales shop sells original art

M **Illinois Artisans & Visitors Centers,** 14967 Gun Creek Trail, Whittington, 62897-1000. Tel 618-629-2220; FAX 618-629-2704; *Dir ILL Artisans Prog* Ellen Gantner; *Dir SIACM* Leo Packard; *Mgr IL Artisans Shop* Mary Lou Galloway
Open daily 9 AM - 5 PM. No admis fee. Estab 1990. A not-for-profit program to showcase the craft work of Illinois artisans accepted in a consigment shop & to educate the pub about the scope of craft art. Mem: 1100 artists in program; qualification for mem: juried art work
Income: Financed by state appropriation & retail sales of art work
Activities: Demonstrations; lect open to public

M **Museum Shop,** Spring & Edwards St, Springfield, 62704. Tel 217-782-0979; *Dir* Bruce McMillian; *IL Artisans Prog* Ellen Gantner; *IL Artisans Shop* Linda Kloppe
Open Mon - Sat 8:30 AM - 5 PM, Sun Noon - 5 PM. No admis fee. Estab 1990. A not-for-profit program to showcase the craft work of Illinois artisans accepted in a consignment shop & to educate the pub about the scope of craft art. Mem: 1100 artists in program
Income: Financed by state appropriation & retail sales of art work
Activities: Demonstrations; lect open to public

M **LOYOLA UNIVERSITY OF CHICAGO,** Martin D'Arcy Gallery of Art, 6525 N Sheridan Rd, 60626. Tel 312-508-2679; FAX 312-508-2993; *Acting Dir* Rita E McCarthy; *Gallery Asst* Jennifer Oatess
Open Mon - Fri Noon - 4 PM (during school yr), cl summers. No admis fee. Estab 1969 to display the permanent university collection of Medieval, Renaissance & Baroque decorative arts & paintings. One gallery set up as a large living room with comfortable seating, classical music, view of Lake Michigan & art objects in view. Average Annual Attendance: 5500. Mem: 300; dues $50
Income: Financed by donations, endowment, mem & university support
Collections: Decorative arts, furniture, liturgical objects, paintings, sculptures & textiles
Publications: Exhibition catalogs
Activities: Educ dept; lect open to public, 9 vis lectr per week; concerts; gallery talks; tours on request; paintings & original objects of art lent to qualified museums; lending collection contains original art works, paintings & sculpture

M **MEXICAN FINE ARTS CENTER MUSEUM,** 1852 W 19th St, 60608. Tel 312-738-1503; FAX 312-738-9740; *Pres* Helen Valdez; *Exec Dir* Carlos Tortolero; *Visual Arts Coord* Rene Arceo
Open Tues - Sun 10 AM - 5 PM. No admis fee. Estab 1982. Average Annual Attendance: 70,000. Mem: 1100; dues $20
Income: $535,000 (financed by mem, city, state & federal appropriation, corporation & foundations)
Collections: Mexican prints, photography & folk art collection; Latino art collection
Exhibitions: Jose Guadalupe Posada
Activities: Classes for children in docent programs; lect open to the public, 4 vis lectr per year; museum shop sells books, original art, folk art & prints

M **MUSEUM OF CONTEMPORARY ART,** 220 E Chicago Ave, 60611. Tel 312-280-2660; FAX 312-397-4095; *Chief Cur* Richard Francis; *Dir* Kevin Consey; *Dir Marketing* Lori Kleinerman; *Educ Dir* Wendy Woon; *Adminr* Helen Dunbeck; *Cur Spec Projects* Lynne Warren; *Dir Develop* Carolyn Stolper; *Registrar* Lela Hersh; *Store Mgr* Lynn Davis; *Controller* Janet Alberti; *Dir Public Relations* Maureen King
Open Tues - Sat 10 AM - 5 PM, Sun Noon - 5 PM, cl Mon, Thanksgiving, Christmas & New Year's Day. Suggested admis adults $6.50, students, senior citizens & children under 16 $4, members & children under 10 free, 1st Tues of month free. Estab 1967 as a forum for contemporary arts in Chicago. Average Annual Attendance: 350,000. Mem: 15,000
Income: $11,300,000 (financed by endowment, mem, pub & private sources)
Collections: Permanent collection of 20th century & contemporary, constantly growing through gifts & purchases
Publications: Bimonthly calendar, exhibition catalogs, membership magazine
Activities: Docent training; teacher workshops; lect; performance; tours; films; book traveling exhibitions; originate traveling exhibitions; museum store sells books, designer jewelry & other gifts, magazines, original art & reproductions

L **Library,** 220 E Chicago Ave, 60611. Tel 312-397-3894; FAX 312-397-4099; Elec Mail akaiser@mcachicago.org. *Librn* Amanda M Kaiser
Library collection, non-circulating; for reference
Library Holdings: Vols 15,000; Per subs 110; Artist Files 125 drawers; Artists' Books 4300; AV — Cassettes 400, slides 45,000, v-tapes 300
Special Subjects: Art History, Conceptual Art

M **MUSEUM OF HOLOGRAPHY - CHICAGO,** 1134 W Washington Blvd, 60607. Tel 312-226-1007; FAX 312-829-9636; *Dir* Loren Billings; *VPres* Patrick McCallig; *Dir Display & Design* Constance Kasprzak; *Dir Educ* Dr Ted Niemiec; *Dir Research* John Hoffmann; *Dir System Develop* Terry Kay; *Dir Electronics & Kinetics* John General
Open Wed - Sun 12:30 - 5 PM, group tours Mon, Tues by appointment. Admis $2.50. Estab 1976 to perform all functions of a mus. 15,000 sq ft of exhibition space, oak panel walls, special display wings, sales gallery; school facilities comprise 4600 sq ft of fully equipped laboratories & darkrooms with additional lecture facilities. Average Annual Attendance: 25,000
Income: $780,000 (financed by sales, research grants, teaching, consulting, mus store, school, tours & rentals)
Collections: Holograms from throughout the world
Exhibitions: Holography.
Publications: Holography; class text books
Activities: Classes for adults; lect open to public, 6 vis lectr per year; book traveling exhibitions; museum shop sells books, originals & holograms

L **David Wender Library,** 1134 W Washington Blvd, 60607. Tel 312-226-1007; FAX 312-829-9636; *Exec Dir* Loren Billings
Open Wed - Sun 12:30 - 5 PM
Library Holdings: Vols 350; Per subs 10; AV — Kodachromes, motion pictures, slides, v-tapes; Other — Exhibition catalogs, framed reproductions

M **MUSEUM OF SCIENCE & INDUSTRY,** 5700 S Lake Shore Dr, 60637. Tel 773-684-1414; FAX 773-684-7141; *Pres & Chief Exec Officer* Dr James S Kahn; *VPres Admin* George Smith; *VPres Prog* Marvin Pinkert; *Dir Educ* Sheridan Turner; *Dir Exhibits* Joe Shacter
Open summer Mon - Sun 9:30 AM - 5:30 PM, winter Mon - Fri 9:30 AM - 4 PM, Sat, Sun & holidays 9:30 AM - 5:30 PM. No admis fee. Estab 1926 to further pub understanding of science, technology, industry, medicine & related fields. Visitor-participation exhibits depicting scientific principles, technological applications & social implications in fields of artscience. Average Annual Attendance: 2,000,000. Mem: 59,470; dues life $1500, family $75, individual $50
Income: $16,200,000 (financed by endowment, mem, city & state appropriation, contributions & grants from companies, foundations & individuals)
Exhibitions: AIDS: The War Within; The Coal Mine; Imaging: The Tools of Science; Colleen Moore Fair Castle; Take Flight; U-505 Submarine
Publications: AHA! quarterly
Activities: Classes for adults & children; dramatic programs; field trips; summer camps; teacher workshops; lect open to public, 4 vis lectr per year; competitions; outreach activities; lending collection contains communications, transportation & textile equipment; book traveling exhibitions; originate traveling exhibitions; museum shop sells books, magazines, prints, slides, postcards & souvenirs

M **NAB GALLERY,** 1117 W Lake, 60607. Tel 312-738-1620; *Assoc Dir* Robert Horn; *Assoc Dir* Craig Anderson
Open Sat & Sun Noon - 5 PM. No admis fee. Estab 1974 as an artist-run space to show original artworks. Average Annual Attendance: 3000. Mem: 5; open to artists with portfolio; dues $500; monthly meetings
Income: $15,000 (finaced by mem)
Exhibitions: Local Artists Juried Exhibit: Cleveland, Dallas, Kryczka, Williams
Activities: Classes for adults; lect open to public; concerts; competitions

M **NAME GALLERY,** 1255 S Wabash, 60605. Tel 312-554-0671; *Exec Dir* Laxzlo Sulyok
Open Tues - Sat Noon - 6 PM. Estab 1973, as a non-profit alternative art gallery. Gallery has 4500 sq ft of space. Average Annual Attendance: 10,000. Mem: 260; dues sliding
Income: Financed by city, state & federal grants, private donations & corporate/

foundation grants

Collections: Series of portfolios, includes the work of: Othello Anderson, Lynda Benglis, Ron Gorchov, Freya Hansell, Barry Holden, Michiko Itatani, Jerry Saltz, Jack Tworkov, Guy Whitney & William T Wiley
Exhibitions: Developing projects in painting, sculpture, video, mixed media installation & innovating public project addressing the changing nature of exhibitions
Publications: Exhibition catalogues
Activities: Seminars; lect open to public, 3 vis lectr per year; gallery talks; book traveling exhibitions; originate traveling exhibitions

L Documents, 1255 S Wabash, 60605. Tel 312-554-0671; *Exec Dir* Laszlo Sulyok
Open Tues - Sat Noon - 6 PM. Estab 1973
Library Holdings: AV — A-tapes, cassettes, fs, slides, v-tapes; Other — Clipping files, exhibition catalogs, original art works

L NEWBERRY LIBRARY, 60 W Walton St, 60610-3394. Tel 312-943-9090; *Pres & Librn* Charles T Cullen; *VPres Research & Educ* Fredrick E Hoxie; *Librn* Mary Wyly; *VPres Finance & Admin* Jim Burke; *VPres Develop* Toni M Markness
Open Tues - Thurs 10 AM - 6 PM, Fri & Sat 9 AM - 5 PM. Estab 1887 for research in the history & humanities of Western Civilization. For reference only. Two small galleries are maintained for exhibitions. Mem: 1950; dues $35; annual meeting in Oct
Income: $4,500,000 (financed by endowment, mem, gifts, federal, corporate & foundation funds)
Purchases: $400,000
Library Holdings: Vols 1,400,000; Per subs 900; Micro — Cards, fiche, reels; AV — A-tapes, motion pictures, rec, v-tapes; Other — Clipping files, exhibition catalogs, manuscripts 5,000,000, memorabilia, original art works, pamphlets, photographs
Special Subjects: American Indian Art, American Western Art, Art History, Ethnology, Graphic Arts, History of Art & Archaeology, Manuscripts, Maps, Southwestern Art
Collections: †Edward Ayer Collection, manuscripts & maps related to European expansion to the Americas & the Pacific; †Everett D Graff Collection of Western Americana books & manuscripts; †John M Wing Foundation Collection on history of printing & aesthetics of book design; †Rudy L Ruggles Collection on American constitutional & legal history
Publications: A Newberry Newsletter, quarterly; Center for Renaissance Studies Newsletter, 3 times per yr; Mapline, quarterly newsletter; Meeting Ground, bi-annual newsletter; Origins, quarterly newsletter
Activities: Classes for adults; dramatic programs; docent training; lect open to public, some open to members only, 35 vis lectr per year; concerts; gallery talks; tours; scholarships & fels offered; individual paintings & original objects of art lent to museums & libraries on restricted basis; book traveling exhibitions 1-2 per year; sales shop sells books, reproductions, slides

M NORTHEASTERN ILLINOIS UNIVERSITY, Gallery, Art Dept, 5500 N Saint Louis Ave, 60625. Tel 312-583-4050, Ext 3324; *Dir* Mary Stoppert
Open Mon - Fri 1 - 5 PM. No admis fee. Estab Feb 1973 for the purpose of providing a link between the University & the local community on a cultural & aesthetic level, to bring the best local & midwest artists to this community. Gallery is located in the commuter center on the University campus. Average Annual Attendance: 5000
Income: Financed by Department of Art funds and personnel
Publications: Flyers on each show
Activities: Competitions

M NORTHERN ILLINOIS UNIVERSITY, Art Gallery in Chicago, 215 W Superior St, 3rd Flr, 60610. Tel 312-642-6010; *Acting Dir* Sarah Peak
Open Tues - Sat 11 AM - 5 PM. No admis fee. Estab 1985. 1700 sq ft, 200 linear ft, movable walls, 10.5 ft ceilings. Average Annual Attendance: 3000
Income: Financed by state appropriation
Publications: Occasional catalogues
Activities: Lect open to public, 5 vis lectr per year; panel discussions & seminars; gallery talks; book traveling exhibitions; originate traveling exhibitions

M NORTH PARK COLLEGE, Carlson Tower Gallery, 3225 W Foster, 60625. Tel 312-244-6200; FAX 312-583-0858; *Gallery Dir* Tim Lowly
Open Mon - Fri 9 AM - 4 PM, occasional weekend evenings. No admis fee. Educational development of aesthetic appreciation
Collections: Original contemporary Christian, Illinois & Scandinavian art
Activities: Classes for adults; lect open to public, 1-2 vis lect per year; concerts; exten dept serves Chicago; book traveling exhitions, 1-2 per year

M PALETTE & CHISEL ACADEMY OF FINE ARTS, 1012 N Dearborn St, 60610. Tel 312-642-4400; FAX 312-642-4317; *Pres* Cable Spence; *Exec Dir* Patricia Randel
Gallery open Fri 2 - 6 PM, Sat 12 - 4 PM, workshops are open to the pub on a regular basis. No admis fee. Estab & incorporated 1985 to provide a meeting/work place for the visual arts. Building contains galleries, classrooms, studios & library. Mem: 203; dues $200; patron & nonresident mem available
Collections: Permanent Collection: works by James Montgomery Flag; J Jeffery Grant; A W Mauach; Richard Schmid & others
Exhibitions: Five Members Award Shows; guest artists & organizations frequently exhibited
Publications: The COW BELL, quarterly
Activities: Educ events; classes for artists; lect open to public; tours; competitions with awards; scholarships & fels offered

M PEACE MUSEUM, 314 W Institute Pl, 60610. Tel 312-440-1860; FAX 312-440-1267; *Dir* Diane Grams
Open Tues - Sat 11 AM - 5 PM, cl Sun & Mon. Admis adults $3.50, senior citizens, students & children $2, members free. Estab 1981 to provide peace educ through the arts; presents issue-oriented exhibits. 2500 sq ft space featuring small display of permanent collection & 4-6 changing exhibits. Average Annual Attendance: 20,000. Mem: 2500; dues $25 - $500

Income: Financed by foundation grants, donations & mem
Collections: 10,000 artifacts from civil rights, domestic violence prevention, peace, social justice, violence prevention efforts
Publications: The Peace Release: A Handbill of the Peace Museum
Activities: Classes for adults & children; docent training; lect open to public, 10-15 vis lectr per year; competitions; individual paintings & original objects of art lent to other galleries, art directors of publications & universities; lending collection contains 2000 books, 300 cassettes, 500 framed reproductions, 100 original art works, 100 original prints, 150 photographs, 2000 slides & peace posters; book traveling exhibitions; originate traveling exhibitions to library exhibit spaces, galleries, schools & community centers; museum shop sells books, magazines & prints

C PLAYBOY ENTERPRISES, INC, 680 N Lake Shore Dr, 60611. Tel 312-751-8000; FAX 312-751-2818; *VPres & Art Dir* Tom Staebler; *Bus Mgr & Art Cur* Barbara Hoffman
Open to pub by appointment only in groups. Estab 1953 to gather & maintain works commissioned for reproduction by Playboy Magazine
Collections: Selected works from 4000 illustrations & fine art pieces, works include paintings & sculpture representing 20th Century artists such as Robert Ginzel, Roger Hane, Larry Rivers, James Rosenquist, Seymour Rosofsky, Roy Schnackenberg, George Segal, Andy Warhol, Robert Weaver, Tom Wesselman, Karl Wirsum & others
Publications: Catalogs pertaining to Beyond Illustration - The Art of Playboy; The Art of Playboy - from the First 25 Years
Activities: Lect; tours; annual illustration awards; individual paintings & original objects of art lent to museums & schools; originate traveling exhibitions to galleries, universities, museums & cultural centers

L Library, 680 N Lake Shore Dr, 60611. Tel 312-751-8000, Ext 2420; FAX 312-751-2818; *Librn* Mark Durand
Library Holdings: Vols 10,000; Per subs 75; Other — Clipping files, exhibition catalogs, original art works, photographs

M POLISH MUSEUM OF AMERICA, 984 N Milwaukee Ave, 60622. Tel 773-384-3352; FAX 773-384-3799; *Pres* Joanna Kosinski; *Dir* Jan M Lorys
Open daily 11 AM - 4 PM. No admis fee, suggested donation adults $2, children $1. Estab 1937, to promote & preserve Polish & Polish-American culture. A specialized mus & gallery containing works of Polish artists & Polish-American culture artists is maintained. Average Annual Attendance: 6000. Mem: dues $25
Income: Financed by donations & fundraising
Collections: Originals dating to beginning of 20th century, a few older pieces; Pulaski at Savannah (Batowski); works of Polish artists, Polish-American artists & works on Polish subject; Nikifor, Jan Styka, Wojciech Kossak; paintings from the collection of the Polish Pavilion from 1939 World's Fair in NY; large collection of Paderewski memorabilia, including the last piano he played on
Exhibitions: Modern Polish Art; folk art; militaria
Publications: Exhibit Catalogs; Art Collection Catalog
Activities: Lect open to public, 5 vis lectr per year; tours; museum shop sells books, reproductions, prints, Polish Folk items, amber & crystal

L Research Library, 984 N Milwaukee Ave, 60622. Tel 773-384-3352; FAX 773-384-3799; *Librn* Malgorzata Kot; *Cur* Jan M Lorys
For reference only; interlibrary circulation
Library Holdings: Vols 63,000; Per subs 125; Micro — Fiche, reels; AV — A-tapes, cassettes, fs, motion pictures, rec, slides 2000, v-tapes; Other — Clipping files, exhibition catalogs, framed reproductions, manuscripts, memorabilia, original art works, pamphlets, photographs 3000, prints, reproductions 1000, sculpture
Special Subjects: Maps, Coins & Medals, Posters, Poland & works by Polish-American authors, philatelic, kosciuszko
Collections: Haiman; Paderewski; Polish Art
Activities: Lect

M PRAIRE AVENUE HOUSE MUSEUMS, Glesser House, 1800 S Prairie Ave, 60616. Tel 312-326-1480; *Cur* Janice Griffin; *Exec Dir* David Crosson
Open Wed & Fri Noon -3 PM, Sat & Sun Noon - 4 PM. Admis adults $5, students & senior citizens $3. Estab 1967 to save & restore Glessner House, the last remaining building in Chicago designed by renown late 19th century architect Henry Hobson Richardson. Glessner House was completed in 1887 on Prairie Avenue. Chicago's most elegant residential neighborhood. The mus is furnished with original period furnishings in the English Arts & Crafts & Aesthetic Movement styles. Average Annual Attendance: 10,000. Mem: 4400; dues $35
Activities: Original objects of art lent to galleries which are mounting exhibitions on architecture; lending collection contains architectural ornaments; sales shop sells books, magazines, reproductions, prints, posters, stationery & small gift items

M Henry B Clarke House Museum, 1800 S Prairie Ave, 60616. Tel 312-326-1480; FAX 312-326-1397; *Exec Dir* David Crosson; *Prog Dir* Micki Leventhal; *Cur* Jsnice Griffin
Open Wed - Sun Noon - 4 PM. Admis $8. Estab 1994. The oldest building in Chicago; includes period rooms. Average Annual Attendance: 12,000. Mem: 600; dues $35

M RANDOLPH STREET GALLERY, 756 N Milwaukee Ave, 60622. Tel 312-666-7737; FAX 312-666-8986; *Exec Dir* Gusteavo Paredes; *Asst Dir* Guy Nickson; *Communications Coordr* Marie Shurkus
Open Tues - Sat Noon - 6 PM. Estab 1979 dedicated to the development & understanding of new & innovative art. 1600 sq ft, 14 ft ceiling height, white walls, sprung wood floors; exhibition space in one room, performance space in adjoining room of same dimensions with lighting grid, basic theatrical lighting & sound system, video playback equipment. Average Annual Attendance: 10,000
Income: $190,000 (financed by endowment, mem, city & state appropriation & private foundation grants)
Exhibitions: Audio Install: Janet Cardiff; Four Walls, Two Windows & A Door
Publications: Performance Art Journal, bi-monthly
Activities: Educ dept; panel discussions with artists; gallery talks

A **THE RENAISSANCE SOCIETY,** Bergman Gallery, 5811 S Ellis, 60637. Tel 773-702-8670; FAX 773-702-9669; Elec Mail pscott@midway.uchicago.edu. *Dir* Susanne Ghez
Open Tues - Fri 10 AM - 5 PM, Sat & Sun Noon - 4 PM, cl summer. No admis fee. Founded 1915 to advance the understanding & appreciation of the arts in all forms. Mem: 500; dues $40; annual meeting in June
Exhibitions: Six changing exhibitions per yr
Publications: Exhibit catalogs
Activities: Lect open to public; gallery talks; film programs; performances

L **SAINT XAVIER UNIVERSITY,** Byrne Memorial Library, Art Dept, 3700 W 103rd St, 60655. Tel 773-779-3300, Ext 365; FAX 773-779-5231; *Dir* JoAnn Ellingson
Open daily 8 AM - 10 PM. Estab 1847
Library Holdings: Vols 160,600; Per subs 890; Micro — Cards; AV — Kodachromes, motion pictures, rec, slides 10,000, v-tapes; Other — Original art works
Collections: Permanent art collection

L **SCHOOL OF ART INSTITUTE OF CHICAGO,** Video Data Bank, 112 S Michigan Ave, 60603. Tel 312-345-3550; FAX 312-541-8073; Elec Mail mfaber@artic.edu. *Dir* Kate Horsfield; *Assoc Dir* Mindy Faber
Open Mon - Fri 9 AM - 6 PM. No admis fee. School estab 1892, library estab 1976 to distribute, preserve & promote videos by & about contemporary artists. Average Annual Attendance: 500,000
Income: $550,000 (finance by grants & earned income)
Library Holdings: AV — V-tapes 3000
Special Subjects: Art History, Film, Mixed Media, Painting - American, Painting - British, Painting - German, Photography, Sculpture, Video, On Art & Artists - over 200 interviews with contemporary artists on video, performance
Collections: †Video Tapes: Eary Video History, Independent Video/Alternative Media, Latin/South America, Media Literacy, On Art & Artists
Publications: Annual catalog of holdings

L **SCHOOL OF THE ART INSTITUTE OF CHICAGO,** John M Flaxman Library, 37 S Wabash, 60603. Tel 312-899-5097; FAX 312-899-1465; Elec Mail ceike@artic.edu. *Dir* Claire Eike; *Head Readers Services* Roland Hansen; *Head Technical Services* Fred Hillbruner; *Bibliographer* Henrietta Zielinski
Open Mon - Thurs 8:30 AM - 9 PM, Fri 8:30 AM - 6 PM, Sat 10 AM - 4 PM, Sun Noon - 6 PM. Estab 1967 to provide a strong working collection for School's programs in the visual & related arts. Circ 47,045
Income: $574,800 (financed by the operational budgets of the School of Art Institute of Chicago)
Purchases: $118,900
Library Holdings: Vols 46,081; Per subs 632; Artists' books 2826; Compact discs 323; Microforms 164; Vertical files 53 linear ft; Micro — Fiche; AV — Cassettes 1377, fs, motion pictures 663, rec 880, v-tapes 332; Other — Clipping files, exhibition catalogs, prints
Special Subjects: Afro-American Art, American Indian Art, American Western Art, Anthropology, Architecture, Decorative Arts, Eskimo Art, Folk Art, History of Art & Archaeology, Latin American Art, Mexican Art, Oriental Art, Painting - American, Photography, Porcelain, Artists' Books, Contemporary Art, Time Arts
Collections: Joan Flasch Artists' Books Collection; Whitney Halstead Art History; †Mary McCarty Art History Collection; †Film Study Collection
Publications: Ferret Collection Guides; International Artists Book Show Catalog; Library handbook for patrons, annually

M **SCHOOL OF THE ART INSTITUTE OF CHICAGO,** Gallery 2, 847 W Jackson Blvd, 60607. Tel 312-563-5162; FAX 312-563-0510; *Dir* Douglas Grew; *Asst Dir Exhibitions & Events* Claire Broadfoot; *Asst Dir Exhibitions & Events* Valerie Cassel
Open Tues - Sat 11 AM - 6 PM. No admis fee. Estab 1984. Showcase work by students, faculty & alumni. Present artists lectures, performances, screenings & other time arts events. Maintains reference library. Average Annual Attendance: 8000
Income: Financed by school
Exhibitions: Student Group Show
Activities: Lect open to public, 25 vis lect per year

A **SCULPTURE CHICAGO, INC,** 20 N Michigan Ave, Ste 400, 60602. Tel 312-456-7140; FAX 312-456-0056; *Asst Dir* Karen A Paluzzi
Estab 1983 to serve as a catalyst for the creation of innovative pub art projects. Sculpture Chicago, a unique visual arts organization, is devoted to enabling artists to create & showcase their works & to educ the pub about the creative process through innovative education programs. With an emphasis on collaboration & community involvement, Sculpture Chicago seeks to enhance Chicago's reputation as a world-class center for the arts
Income: Financed by foundations, corporations, government agencies & individuals
Publications: Catalogs documenting biennial programs
Activities: Pritzer Park educational programs

SOCIETY OF ARCHITECTURAL HISTORIANS
For further information, see National and Regional Organizations

M **SPERTUS INSTITUTE OF JEWISH STUDIES,** Spertus Museum, 618 S Michigan Ave, 60605. Tel 312-322-1747; *Dir* Howard Sulkin; *Dir Design* Mark Akgulian; *Assoc Dir* Betsy Gomberg; *Asst Cur Educ* Paula Chaiken; *Registrar & Cur of Exhib* Olga Weiss; *Educ Coordr* Devorah Heitner; *Asst Artifact Center Cur* Doug Irvine; *Educational Cur* Susan Youdovin; *Artifact Center Cur* Susan Bass Marcus
Open Sun - Thurs, 10 AM - 5 PM, Fri 10 AM - 3 PM. Artifact Center open Sun - Thurs 1 - 4:30 PM. Admis adults $4, children, students & senior citizens $2, Fri free. Estab 1967 for interpreting & preserving the 3500-year-old heritage embodied in Jewish history. Mus houses a distinguished collection of Juddaica from many parts of the world, containing exquisitely designed ceremonial objects of gold, silver, bronze & ivory. Average Annual Attendance: 25,000
Income: Financed by contributions & subsidy from Spertus Institute
Collections: A pertinent collection of sculpture, paintings & graphic art; ethnographic materials spanning centuries of Jewish experience; a permanent Holocaust memorial; Judaica, paintings, ceremonial silver, textiles, archaeology
Exhibitions: Ongoing schedule of changing exhibitions
Publications: Special publications with exhibits; Calendar of Events
Activities: Educ dept; docent training; lect; gallery talks; tours; biennial competition for contemporary Jewish ceremonial art; lending collection contains 1500 slides & archaeological replicas; traveling exhibitions organized & circulated; museum store selling books, original art reproductions, slides and jewelry from Israel; The Artifact Center is a hands on exhibit on art & archaeology in ancient Israel

L **Asher Library,** 618 S Michigan Ave, 60605. Tel 312-922-8248; FAX 312-922-0455; Elec Mail ahserlib@spertus.edu. *Assoc Dir* Kathleen Bloch; *Reference Librn* Dan Sharon; *Dir* Michael Terry; *Cataloger* Angela Ricetti; *Public Serv* Andrew Wertheimer; *Serials & Archivist* Joy Kingsolver; *Conservator* Melissa Oresky
Reference library open to public. Includes Badona Spertus Art Library
Library Holdings: Vols 100,000; Per subs 556; Micro — Fiche, reels; AV — A-tapes, cassettes, rec, slides, v-tapes; Other — Exhibition catalogs, manuscripts, pamphlets, photographs
Special Subjects: Judaica

M **SWEDISH AMERICAN MUSEUM ASSOCIATION OF CHICAGO,** 5211 N Clark St, 60640. Tel 773-728-8111; FAX 773-728-8870; *Pres* Joan Papadopoulos; *Exec Dir* Kerstin B Lane; *First VPres* Paul Rimington; *Treas* Russell Holmguist
Open Tues - Fri 10 AM - 4 PM, Sat & Sun 10 AM - 3 PM. No admis fee, donations appreciated. Estab 1976 to display Swedish arts, crafts, artists, scientists, and artifacts connected with United States, especially Chicago. Material displayed in the four story museum in Andersonville, once a predominantly Swedist area in Chicago. Average Annual Attendance: 30,000. Mem: 12,000; dues $5-$500; meetings in Apr, June & Oct
Income: $400,000 (financed by mem & donations)
Collections: Artifacts used or made by Swedes, photographs, oils of or by Swedes in United States
Publications: SAMAC News, quarterly
Activities: Classes for adults & children; lect open to public, 3-4 vis lectr per year; concerts; tours; awards; individual paintings lent; book traveling exhibitions 2-3 per year; museum shop sells books, reproductions, prints & gifts; junior museum

M **TERRA MUSEUM OF AMERICAN ART,** 664 N Michigan Ave, 60611. Tel 312-664-3939; FAX 312-664-2052; *Founder* Daniel J Terra; *Dir & Chief Financial Officer* Stuart Popowcer; *Museum Store Mgr* Mary Messersmith; *Admin Servs Mgr* Stephanie Grais; *Cur Educ* Virginia Spindler; *Mgr School & Teacher Progs* Scott Sikkema; *Librn* Amy Henderson; *Dir Develop & Membership* Stephanie Leese; *Coordr, Membership & Vols* Mary Kay Williams; *Cur* D Scott Atkinson; *Librn* Catherine Wilson; *Mem Coordr* Mark Robinson
Open Tues Noon - 8 PM, Wed - Sat 10 AM - 5 PM, Sun Noon - 5 PM, cl Mon. Admis adults $4, senior citizens $2, students with ID, educators, members & children under 14 free. Estab 1980 to educate the public through the exhibition of the Terra Collection and visiting exhibitions of American paintings. Average Annual Attendance: 100,000. Mem: 1000; dues $25-$2000
Income: Financed by endowment & mem
Collections: †Terra Collection of 18th, 19th & 20th Century American oil, watercolor & pastel paintings & prints
Exhibitions: (1997) An American Century of Photography: The Hallmark Photographic Collection
Publications: Exhibition catalogues
Activities: Docent training; gallery talks; guided tours; individual and original objects of art lent to other museums; sales shop sells books, prints, slides and posters

L **Library,** 664 N Michigan Ave, 60611. Tel 312-664-3939; FAX 312-664-2052; *Librn* Amy Henderson
Open Mon, Wed & Fri 9 AM - 5 PM. For reference only
Income: Privately financed
Library Holdings: Vols 5000; Per subs 13; Auction Catalogs; Other — Exhibition catalogs, pamphlets
Special Subjects: American Western Art, Art History, Painting - American, Printmaking, Watercolors

M **TEXTILE ARTS CENTRE,** 916 W Diversey, 60614. Tel 773-929-5655; FAX 773-929-9837; *Chair Board* Nina Bliese; *Exec Dir* Karen Carlson
Open Noon - 5 PM. No admis fee. Estab 1986 to support & promote textile arts. Maintains reference library. Average Annual Attendance: 17,000. Mem: 500; dues $35 & up; annual meeting in Feb
Income: $900,000 (financed by mem, city appropriation, state appropriation, donations & fundraising)
Exhibitions: Virginia Davis: A Survey
Publications: Quarterly newsletter
Activities: Classes for adults & children; lect open to public, 6 vis lectr per year; originate traveling exhibitions; museum shop sells original art, fiber items & wearable art

L **Library,** 916 W Diversey, 60614
For reference only
Library Holdings: Vols 350; AV — Slides
Special Subjects: Embroidery, Fashion Arts, Textiles, Fiber
Exhibitions: 4-6 exhibitions per year

M **UKRAINIAN NATIONAL MUSEUM & LIBRARY,** 721 N Oakley Blvd, 60612. Tel 312-421-8020; *Dir & Pres* Dr George Hrycelak; *Cur* Oksana Teodorowych
Open Sun 11 AM - 4 PM. Estab 1954, to collect & preserve Ukrainian cultural heritage
Income: Financed through mem & donations
Library Holdings: Vols 18,000; Per subs 100; Micro — Cards; AV —

Kodachromes, slides; Other — Clipping files, framed reproductions, manuscripts, memorabilia, original art works, pamphlets, photographs, sculpture
Special Subjects: Large collection of Ukrainian Folk Arts: easter egg painting, embroidery, woodcarving
Collections: Ukrainian Folk Art
Activities: Classes for adults & children; tours; book traveling exhibitions; traveling exhibitions organized & circulated

UNIVERSITY OF CHICAGO
M **Lorado Taft Midway Studios,** 6016 Ingleside Ave, 60637. Tel 312-753-4821; *Dir* Thomas Mapp
Open Mon - Fri 9 AM - 5 PM, cl Sun. Studios of Lorado Taft and Associates, a Registered National Historic Landmark; now University of Chicago, Committee on Art & Design
Exhibitions: Graduate MFA Exhibitions
Activities: Special performances
M **David & Alfred Smart Museum of Art,** 5550 S Greenwood Ave, 60637. Tel 312-702-0200; FAX 312-702-3121; *Dir* Kimerly Rorschach; *Cur* Richard Born; *Registrar* Martha Sharma; *Preparator* Rudy Bernal; *Marketing Mgr* Stefanie White; *Operations Mgr* Priscilla Stratton; *Educ Dir* Kathleen Gibbons; *Asst Cur* Courtenay Smith
Open Tues, Wed, Fri 10 AM - 4 PM, Sat - Sun Noon - 6 PM. No admis fee. Estab 1974 to assist the teaching & research programs of the University of Chicago by maintaining a permanent collection & presenting exhibitions & symposia of scholarly & general interest. Gallery designed by E L Barnes; exhibit space covers 9500 sq ft & also contains print & drawing study room, Elden Sculpture Garden. Average Annual Attendance: 35,000. Mem: 400; dues individual $35
Income: Financed by mem, university, special funds, corporations, foundations & government grants
Collections: †American, †Ancient, †Baroque, †decorative arts, †drawings, †Medieval, †Modern European, †Oriental & Renaissance paintings , †photographs, †prints, †sculpture
Activities: Docent training; lect open to public, 5-10 vis lectr per year; symposia; gallery talks; tours; concerts; individual paintings & original objects of art lent to professional art museums; book traveling exhibitions 1-3 per year; originate traveling exhibitions; sales shop sells books, post cards, posters, papers & photographs
M **Oriental Institute Museum,** 1155 E 58th St, 60637. Tel 773-702-9521; FAX 773-702-9853; Elec Mail oi-museum@uchicago.edu. *Museum Dir* Karen L Wilson; *Registrar* Raymond Tindel; *Archivist* John Larson; *Assoc Cur* Emily Teeter
Open Tues, Thurs & Fri 11 AM - 5:30 PM, Wed 11 AM - 6 PM, Sat 10 AM - 4 PM, Sun Noon - 4 PM, cl Mon. No admis fee. Estab 1894 as a mus of antiquities excavated from Egypt, Mesopotamia, Assyria, Syria, Palestine, Persia, Anatolia & Nubia, dating from 7000 years ago until the 18th Century AD. Average Annual Attendance: 62,000. Mem: 2650; dues $30 & up
Income: Financed by parent institution, admis donations, federal, state grants & proceeds from sales
Collections: Ancient Near Eastern antiquities from pre-historic times to the beginning of the present era plus some Islamic artifacts; Egypt: colossal statue of King Tut, mummies; Iraq; Assyrian winged human-headed bull (40 tons); Mesopotamia temple & house interior, reconstructions, sculpture, jewelry; Iran: Persepolis bull; column & capital; Palestine: Megiddo ivories & horned alter
Publications: Annual report; News & Notes, bimonthly; museum guidebook; brochures
Activities: Classes for adults & children; dramatic programs; docent training; family programs; lect open to public, 8-10 vis lectr per year; gallery talks; tours; competitions with awards; original objects of art lent to museums & institutions; lending collection contains kodachromes, original art works & mini museum boxes; book traveling exhibitions; museum shop sells books, magazines, reproductions, prints, slides, original art, crafts & near Eastern jewelry
—**Oriental Institute Research Archives,** 1155 E 58th St, 60637-1569. Tel 773-702-9537; FAX 773-702-9853; Elec Mail oi_library@uchicago.edu. *Librn* Charles E Jones
Open to staff, students & members for reference
Library Holdings: Vols 30,000; Per subs 500; Micro — Cards, fiche, reels; AV — A-tapes, cassettes, Kodachromes, lantern slides, motion pictures, slides; Other — Clipping files, exhibition catalogs, manuscripts, memorabilia, pamphlets, photographs
Special Subjects: Anthropology, Antiquities-Assyrian, Antiquities-Byzantine, Antiquities-Egyptian, Antiquities-Greek, Antiquities-Persian, Archaeology, Asian Art, Historical Material, History of Art & Archaeology, Islamic Art, Textiles, The Ancient Near East
L **Art Slide Collection,** 5540 S Greenwood, 60637. Tel 773-702-0261; FAX 773-702-5901; *Cur* John L Butler-Ludwig
Open Mon - Fri 8:30 AM - 4 PM; cl Sat & Sun. Estab 1938. For reference only
Library Holdings: AV — Slides 310,000
L **Max Epstein Archive,** 420 C Joseph Regenstein Library, 60637. Tel 773-702-7080; *Cur* Rob Rush
Open Mon - Fri 9 AM - 5 PM, cl Sat & Sun. Estab 1938. For reference only
Income: Financed by gifts & donations
Library Holdings: Vols 55,500; Mounted photographs of art 500,000; catalogued & mounted photographs added annually 8000; auction sales catalogs, Union Catalog of Art Books in Chicago
Collections: Photographs of architecture, sculpture, painting, drawing & decorative arts illustrating Far Eastern, South Asian & Western art history; illustrated Bartsch Catalogue; DIAL Index; Marburger Index; Papal Medals Collection; Courtauld Institute Illustrated Archive; Courtauld Photo Survey
M **UNIVERSITY OF ILLINOIS AT CHICAGO,** Gallery 400, 400 S Peoria, 60607. Tel 312-996-6114; FAX 312-996-5378; *Dir* Karen Indeck
Open Mon - Fri 9 AM - 5 PM, Sat Noon - 4 PM. No admis fee. Estab 1983 to highlight current trends in art & architecture including all medium. Loft space approx 130 ft x 30 ft serving primarily as exhibition hall, as well as for lectures, films & video screenings. Average Annual Attendance: 10,000
Income: $150,000 (financed by state & federal grants, college of A&A, private

donations & foundations)
Publications: Exhibit Catalogs, 2 per year
Activities: Lect open to public, 20 vis lectr per year; concerts; gallery talks; tours; book traveling exhibitions 1 per year; originate traveling exhibitions
M **UPTOWN CENTER HULL HOUSE ASSOCIATION,** 4520 N Beacon, 60640. Tel 312-561-3500; *Cur* Margaret Luft
Open Mon - Fri 10 AM - 5 PM. No admis fee. Estab 1983 as a contemporary arts & folk art gallery. Average Annual Attendance: 40,000
Income: Financed by endowment, city & state appropriation
Exhibitions: Cultural Heritage Exhibit
Activities: Classes for adults & children; dramatic programs

DANVILLE

M **VERMILION COUNTY MUSEUM SOCIETY,** 116 N Gilbert St, 61832. Tel 217-442-2922; *Cur* Susan Richter
Open Tues - Sat 10 AM - 5 PM, Sun 1 - 5 PM, cl Mon, Thanksgiving & Christmas. Admis 15 yrs & older $1, 6-14 $.50, under 6 yrs free, school & scout groups free. Estab 1964; in 1855 doctor's residence & carriage house. Average Annual Attendance: 5500. Mem: 1001; dues life $180, patron $50, contributing $25, organization & family $15, individual $12, student & senior citizens $10
Collections: Costumes; decorative arts; graphics; historical material; paintings; sculpture
Publications: Heritage, quarterly magazine
Activities: Lect open to public, 2 vis lectr per year; tours; children competitions; museum shop sells books, magazines & prints
L **Library,** 116 N Gilbert St, 61832. Tel 217-442-2922; *Prog Dir* Susan E Richter
Open to the public for reference
Income: Financed by endowment fund
Library Holdings: Vols 400; AV — Slides, v-tapes; Other — Clipping files, photographs
Collections: Medical equipment, furniture, photographs, arrowheads
Publications: The Heritage of Vermilion County, quarterly; bimonthly newsletter

DECATUR

M **MILLIKIN UNIVERSITY,** Perkinson Gallery, Kirkland Fine Arts Ctr, 1184 W Main St, 62522. Tel 217-424-6227; FAX 217-424-3993; *Dir* James Schietinger
Open Mon - Fri Noon - 5 PM. No admis fee. Estab 1970. Gallery has 3200 sq ft & 224 running ft of wall space
Income: Financed by university appropriation
Collections: Drawings; painting; prints; sculpture; watercolors
Publications: Monthly show announcements
Activities: Lect; guided tours; gallery talks

DE KALB

M **NORTHERN ILLINOIS UNIVERSITY,** NIU Art Museum, Altgeld Hall, 2nd Flr, 60115. Tel 815-753-1936; *Dir* Peggy M Doherty
Open Mon - Fri 10 AM - 5 PM, Thurs 10 AM - 7 PM, Sat Noon - 4 PM. No admis charge. Estab 1970. Main Gallery is 6000 sq ft. Average Annual Attendance: 50,000
Income: Financed by state appropriation & grants from public agencies & private foundations
Collections: †Contemporary & †Modern paintings, †prints, †sculptures, & †photographs, †Burmese Art; Native American Art
Activities: Lect open to public; gallery talks; tours; original objects of art lent to accredited museums; book traveling exhibitions
L **Library,** 60115. Tel 815-753-1634; *Arts Librn* Charles Larry
Estab 1977 to provide reference service & develop the collection
Library Holdings: Vols 40,000; Per subs 164; Art book titles 963; Rare bks 250; Micro — Cards, fiche, reels; AV — Motion pictures, slides, v-tapes; Other — Exhibition catalogs

EDWARDSVILLE

L **SOUTHERN ILLINOIS UNIVERSITY,** Lovejoy Library, Fine Arts Dept, PO Box 1063, 62026. Tel 618-692-2695; FAX 618-692-2381; Elec Mail dbardon@sive.edu, tdickma@sive.edu. *Friends of Lovejoy Librn* Donna Bardon; *Fine Arts Librn* Therese Zoski Dickman
Open Mon - Thurs 8 AM - 11:30 PM, Fri 8 AM - 9 PM, Sat 9 AM - 5 PM, Sun 1 - 9 PM. Estab 1957, as a source for general University undergraduate & graduate instruction, & faculty research
Library Holdings: Vols 500,000; Per subs 6000; Illustrated sheet music covers; Micro — Fiche, reels; AV — Motion pictures, rec, slides, v-tapes
Special Subjects: Advertising Design, Aesthetics, Afro-American Art, American Indian Art, American Western Art, Anthropology, Archaeology, Architecture, Art Education, Art History, Asian Art, Bookplates & Bindings, Bronzes, Calligraphy, Carpets & Rugs, African Art, Fibers
Exhibitions: Louis Sullivan Collection of Terra Cotta
Activities: Photography contest; tours; scholarships

ELMHURST

M **ELMHURST ART MUSEUM,** 130 W Madison, PO Box 23, 60126. Tel 630-834-0202; FAX 630-834-0234; *Exec Dir* Mary Moy-Gregg; *Cur* Teresa J Parker; *Office Mgr* Tara Esposito
Open Tues - Thurs 10 AM - 5 PM, Thurs 6:30 - 9:30 PM, Sat 11 AM - 3 PM. No admis fee. Estab 1981 to exhibit contemporary art, Chicago vicinity to national. 14,000 sq ft; 3 exhibition galleries, 1 artists' guild gallery & entrance gallery. Mem: 400; dues individual $15-$20
Income: Financed by endowment, mem, city & state appropriation

Collections: Contemporary Art-American & Chicago vicinity
Exhibitions: Annual competitions; children's exhibits; one person & group shows; permanent collections; traveling exhibits. (1997) Hal Rogoff
Activities: Classes for adults & children; docent training; lect open to public, 4-6 vis lectr per year; individual paintings lent; book traveling exhibitions 2-3 per year; museum shop sells books & prints

M **LIZZADRO MUSEUM OF LAPIDARY ART,** 220 Cottage Hill Ave, 60126. Tel 630-833-1616; *Dir* John S Lizzadro; *Prog Dir* Dorothy Anderson
Open Tues - Sat 10 AM - 5 PM, Sun 1 - 5 PM, cl Mon. Admis adults $2.50, senior citizens $1.50, students $1, under 13 free, no charge on Fri. Estab 1962 to promote interest in the lapidary arts & the study & collecting of minerals & fossils. Main exhibit area contains hardstone carvings, gemstone materials, minerals; lower level contains education exhibits. Average Annual Attendance: 30,000. Mem: 350; dues $30 per yr
Income: Financed by endowment
Collections: Hardstone Carving Collection
Exhibitions: Educational exhibits
Publications: Biannual
Activities: Lect open to the public, 12 vis lectr per year; educational films; tours; demonstrations; sales shop sells books, jewelry, magazines, hardstone & gemstone souvenirs

ELSAH

M **PRINCIPIA COLLEGE,** School of Nations Museum, 62028. Tel 618-374-2131, Ext 312; FAX 618-374-5122; *Cur* Bonnie Gibbs
Open Tues & Fri by appointment only
Collections: American Indian collection including baskets, bead work, blankets, leather, pottery, quill work and silver; Asian art collection includes arts and crafts, ceramics, textiles from China, Japan and Southeast Asia; European collections include glass, metals, snuff boxes, textiles and wood; costumes and dolls from around the world
Exhibitions: Changing exhibits on campus locations; permanent exhibits in School of Nations lower floor
Activities: Special programs offered throughout the year; objects available for individual study

EVANSTON

A **EVANSTON ART CENTER,** 2603 Sheridan Rd, 60201. Tel 847-475-5300; FAX 847-475-5330; *Dir School* Michelle Rowe-Scheel
Open Tues - Sat 10 AM - 4 PM, Thurs evening 7 - 10 PM, Sun 2 - 5 PM. No admis fee. Estab 1929 as a community visual arts center with exhibits, instructions & programs. Focuses primarily on the contemporary visual arts with emphasis on emerging & under-recognized Midwest artists. Average Annual Attendance: 35,000. Mem: 1500; dues $30, annual meeting in Apr
Income: Financed by state & city arts councils & mem
Exhibitions: Primarily artists of the Midwest, all media
Publications: Concentrics, quarterly; exhibition catalogs
Activities: Classes for adults & children; lect, 6 vis lectr per year

M **EVANSTON HISTORICAL SOCIETY,** Charles Gates Dawes House, 225 Greenwood St, 60201. Tel 847-475-3410; FAX 847-475-3599; *Dir* Joan M Costello
Open Tues - Sat 1 - 5 PM. Admis $5, sr citizens & children $3. Estab 1898 to collect, preserve, exhibit & interpret Evanston's history. Average Annual Attendance: 4000. Mem: 1050; dues $25-$500; annual meeting in June
Income: Financed by mem & private donations
Collections: Historical collections reflecting the history of Evanston & its people, especially since the mid 1800s, including costumes & archival material
Exhibitions: Charles Gates Dawes House permanent exhibit; other rotating exhibits year round; Evanston Takles the Woman Question, the Story of Evanston women who influenced the National Women's Movement; The Sick Can't Wait, the story of Evanston Community Hospital; Your Presence Is Requested, the Story of African-American Social Organization
Publications: TimeLines, mem newsletter, quarterly; annual report
Activities: Docent training; school outreach & in-house educational programs; lect open to public; tours; individual paintings & original objects of art lent to other cultural institutions; lending collection contains 60 paintings & 30 sculptures; originate traveling exhibitions; museum shop sells books & museum & Victorian related gifts

M **C G JUNG INSTITUTE OF CHICAGO,** 1567 Maple Ave, 60201. Tel 847-475-4848; FAX 847-475-4970; *Exec Dir* Peter Mudd; *Asst Dir & Ed* Mary Nolan; *Exhibit Coordr* Barbara Zaretsky; *Librn & AV Production Mgr* Mark Swanson
Open Mon - Fri 10 AM - 5 PM, Sat 10 AM - 4 PM. No admis fee. Estab 1965. For reference only
Library Holdings: Vols 4000; AV — A-tapes, motion pictures, slides, v-tapes; Other — Clipping files, exhibition catalogs, manuscripts, pamphlets, reproductions
Special Subjects: American Indian Art, Anthropology, Archaeology, Asian Art, Ethnology, Film, Folk Art, History of Art & Archaeology, Islamic Art, Judaica, Oriental Art, Pre-Columbian Art, Religious Art, Archetypal Symbolism, Mythology, Psychology, Religion
Collections: Archive for Research in Archetypal Symbolism (ARAS), photographs & slides
Publications: Transformation, quarterly

NORTHWESTERN UNIVERSITY
M **Mary & Leigh Block Gallery,** 1967 S Campus Dr, 60208. Tel 847-491-4000; FAX 847-491-2261; *Dir* David Mickenberg; *Cur* Amy Winter; *Public Relations & Develop* Mary Stewart; *Educ & Tours* Julie Collins
Open Tues & Wed Noon - 5 PM, Thurs - Sun Noon - 8 PM. No admis fee. Estab 1980, to serve the university, Chicago & North Shore communities. Average Annual Attendance: 30,000. Mem: 500; dues $25-$1000
Publications: Exhibition catalogs
Activities: Lect open to public; concerts; gallery talks; tours; book traveling exhibitions; originate traveling exhibitions circulated through other university galleries & museums; sales shop sells catalogs & posters

L **Art Library,** 1935 Sheridan Rd, 60208-2300. Tel 847-491-7484, 491-3635; *Head Spec Art Library* R Russell Maylone; *Bibliographer* Rochelle S Elstein
Open Mon - Thurs 8:30 AM - 10 PM, Fri & Sat 8:30 AM - 5 PM, Sun 1 - 10 PM. Estab 1970 as a separate collection. Serves curriculum & research needs of the Art & Art History Departments
Income: Financed through the university & endowment funds
Library Holdings: Vols 64,000; Other — Exhibition catalogs
Special Subjects: Architecture, Art History, Etchings & Engravings, Graphic Arts, History of Art & Archaeology, Painting - American, Painting - Dutch, Painting - European, Painting - Flemish, Painting - French, Painting - German, Painting - Italian, Photography, Prints, Sculpture, 20th Century Art Movements

FREEPORT

M **FREEPORT ARTS CENTER,** 121 N Harlem, 61032. Tel 815-235-9755; FAX 815-235-9755; *Dir* Becky Connors; *Office Mgr* Doris Green
Open Tues Noon - 7 PM, Wed - Sun Noon - 5 PM, cl Mon. Admis adults $1, senior citizens & students $.50. Estab 1975 to house W T Rawleigh Art Collection & to promote the arts in the region. Five permanent galleries & three galleries featuring temporary exhibitions. Average Annual Attendance: 13,000. Mem: 500; dues $30; annual meeting in May
Income: $130,000 (financed by endowment, mem, grants & corporate support)
Collections: Native American pottery, basketry & beadwork; art from Madgascar; European 19th century oil paintings & sculpture; antiquities from Egypt, Greece, Rome & MesoAmerica; Oriental art; 20th century American prints & paintings; Oceanic Cultures
Activities: Classes for adults & children; docent training; lect open to public; gallery talks; tours; competitions; scholarships offered; exten dept serves Ogle, Carroll, Jo Daviess Counties; individual paintings & original objects of art lent to bona fide galleries with full insurance; lending collection contains paintings & sculptures; book traveling exhibitions; originate traveling exhibtiions organized & circulated

L **Library,** 121 N Harlem Ave, 61032. Tel 815-235-9755; *Dir* Becky Connors
Open to members & pub for research & reference
Library Holdings: Vols 500; Per subs 10
Special Subjects: Afro-American Art, American Indian Art, Antiquities-Egyptian, Antiquities-Greek, Antiquities-Oriental, Flasks & Bottles, Historical Material, Laces, Painting - American, Painting - British, Southwestern Art, Textiles
Publications: Annual report; quarterly newsletter

GALESBURG

A **GALESBURG CIVIC ART CENTER,** 114 E Main, 61401. Tel 309-342-7415; *Dir* Carrie J Inness; *Pres* Judy Swanson; *Office Mgr* Roberta Wood
Open Tues - Fri 10:30 AM - 4:30 PM, Sat 10:30 AM - 3 PM, cl Sun & Mon. No admis fee. Estab 1923 as a non-profit organization for the furtherance of art. The main gallery has about 100 running feet of wall space for the hanging of exhibits. The sales-rental gallery runs on a commission basis & is open to professional artists as a palace to sell their work under a consignment agreement. Average Annual Attendance: 20,000. Mem: 400; dues begin at $15; annual meeting second Wed in June
Income: Financed by mem & grants
Collections: Regional artists in a variety of media (change monthly)
Exhibitions: GALEX - national juried competition all media
Publications: The Artifacts, newsletter
Activities: Classes for adults & children; gallery talks; tours; competitions with awards; lending collection contains original art works, paintings, photographs & sculpture; museum shop sells original art, prints

GREENVILLE

M **GREENVILLE COLLEGE,** Richard W Bock Sculpture Collection, 62246. Tel 618-664-1840, Ext 4560; *Dir & Cur* Guy M Chase
Open Mon - Wed 3:30 - 5:30 PM, Sat 10:30 AM - 12:30 PM & by appointment, cl summer & holidays. No admis fee. Estab 1975 to display an extensive collection of the life work of the American sculptor in a restored home of the mid-19th century period. Five large rooms and two hallways have approximately 320 running ft of exhibition space. Average Annual Attendance: 5000
Income: Financed by endowment, college appropriation, gifts and donations
Collections: Furniture and furnishings of the 1850-1875 era; Japanese prints; late 19th and early 20th century drawing, painting and sculpture; late 19th and early 20th century posters; Frank Lloyd Wright artifacts, designs and drawings
Publications: General museum brochures
Activities: Lect open to the public, 1-2 vis lectr per year; gallery talks; individual paintings and original objects of art lent to museums only; lending collection contains original art works, paintings, photographs, sculpture and drawings; traveling exhibitions organized and circulated; museum shop sells books, magazines

L **The Richard W Bock Sculpture Collection & Art Library,** 62246. Tel 618-664-1840, Ext 4353; *Librn* Guy M Chase
For reference only
Library Holdings: Vols 1000; AV — Rec; Other — Exhibition catalogs
Special Subjects: Richard W Bock, The Prairie School of Architecture, Frank Lloyd Wright

JACKSONVILLE

M **ART ASSOCIATION OF JACKSONVILLE,** David Strawn Art Gallery, 331 W College, PO Box 1213, 62651. Tel 217-243-9390; *Pres* Donna Cody; *Dir* Kelly M Gross
Open Sept - May, Tues - Sat 4 - 6 PM, Sun 1 - 3 PM. No admis fee. Estab 1873, endowed 1915, to serve the community by offering monthly shows of visual arts and weekly classes in a variety of media. The two main rooms house the monthly

exhibitions and a third large room houses a collection of Pre-Columbian pottery. The Gallery is in a large building, previously a private home. Average Annual Attendance: 1800. Mem: 550; dues $10 & up; annual meeting July
Income: Financed by endowment & mem
Collections: Pre-Columbian Pottery; pottery discovered in the Mississippi Valley
Activities: Classes for adults and children; lect workshops open to public

JOLIET

M **JOLIET JUNIOR COLLEGE,** Laura A Sprague Art Gallery, J Bldg, 1215 Houbolt Ave, 60436. Tel 815-729-9020, Ext 2423, 2223; *Gallery Dir* Joe B Milosevich
Open Mon - Fri 9 AM - 8 PM. No admis fee. Estab 1978, to present exhibitions related to academic programs, the college & the community. Gallery, approx 20 x 25 ft, has burlap covered panels mounted on the walls, & also has track lighting; located on second floor of Spicer-Brown Hall
Income: Financed by college appropriations
Collections: Permanent collection of student work, annual
Exhibitions: (1997) Lois R Gruberger & Salvatore Ventura; Joliet Junior College Art Students' Juried Exhibition
Activities: Lect open to public, 2-3 vis lect per year; gallery talks; tours; sponsor student competitions with awards

LAKE FOREST

L **LAKE FOREST LIBRARY,** Fine Arts Dept, 360 E Deerpath, 60045. Tel 847-234-0636; FAX 847-234-1453; *Admin Librn* Kaye Grabbe; *Adult Servs Coordr* Cynthia Infantino; *Graphic Artist* Patricia Kreischer
Open Mon - Thurs 9 AM - 9 PM, Fri 9 AM - 6 PM, Sat 9 AM - 5 PM, Sun 1 - 5 PM (Sept - May). Estab 1898 to make accessible to the residents of the city, books & other resources & services for educ, information & recreation. Gallery carries sculpture reproductions Circ 341,497
Income: $1,799,718 (financed by city & state appropriations)
Purchases: $205,000 (materials); $1,796,190 (total expenditure)
Library Holdings: Pamphlets; Sculpture reproductions
Special Subjects: Local architects
Collections: Folk art; painting
Publications: The Open Book, four times per year

LOMBARD

L **HELEN M PLUM MEMORIAL LIBRARY,** 110 W Maple St, 60148. Tel 630-627-0316; FAX 630-627-0336; *Dir* Robert A Harris; *Readers' Services* Donna Slyfield
Open Mon - Fri 9 AM - 9 PM, Sat 9 AM - 5 PM, cl Sun. Estab as a pub library. Art gallery maintained for monthly displays by Addison Art League. Circ 451, 978
Income: $1,427,162 (financed by local government)
Purchases: $722,485
Library Holdings: Vols 189,498; Per subs 416; Micro — Fiche, prints, reels; AV — A-tapes, cassettes, fs, motion pictures, rec, slides, v-tapes; Other — Framed reproductions, pamphlets, prints, reproductions, sculpture
Special Subjects: Art History, Crafts, Decorative Arts, Folk Art, Handicrafts, Painting - American
Publications: Brochure, annual
Activities: Lect open to public; original objects of art lent to public

MACOMB

M **WESTERN ILLINOIS UNIVERSITY,** Art Gallery-Museum, 61455. Tel 309-298-1587; FAX 309-298-2400; *Pres* Donald Spencer; *Cur Exhib* John R Graham
Open Mon, Wed - Fri 9 AM - 4 PM & Tues 6 - 8 PM. No admis fee. Estab 1945 to present art as an aesthetic and teaching aid. Building has three galleries with 500 running ft. Average Annual Attendance: 20,000
Income: Financed through state appropriation
Collections: WPA & 20th Century: Prints, Drawing, Paintings & Ceramics; Old Masters Prints
Activities: Classes for adults; lect open to public, 8 vis lectr per year; gallery talks; tours; competitions with awards; individual paintings lent; lending collection contains 100 paintings; traveling exhibitions organized & circulated

MOLINE

C **DEERE & COMPANY,** John Deere Rd, 61265. Tel 309-765-8000; FAX 309-765-4735; *Coll Conservator* Laurence Jonson AACR
Guided tours Mon - Fri 10:30 AM - 1:30 PM. Estab 1964 to complement the offices designed by Eero Saarinen & Kevin Roche; to provide opportunities for employees & visitors to view & enjoy a wide variety of art pieces from many parts of the world. Collection displayed at Deere & Company Administrative Center
Collections: Artifacts, paintings, prints, sculpture & tapestries from over 25 countries
Activities: Concerts; tours

MOUNT VERNON

M **MITCHELL MUSEUM,** Richview Rd, PO Box 923, 62864. Tel 618-242-1236; FAX 618-242-9530; *Elec Mail* mitchell@midwest.net. *Cur* Bonnie Speed
Open Tues - Sat 10 AM - 5 PM, Sun 1 - 5 PM, cl Mon & national holidays. No admis fee. Estab 1973 to present exhibitions of paintings, sculpture, graphic arts, architecture & design representing contemporary art trends; to provide continued learning & expanded educ. Marble faced structure houses two galleries for

exhibition, 3000 sq ft & 1300 sq ft; flexible designs. Average Annual Attendance: 60,000. Mem: 800; dues $40; annual meeting in Nov
Income: Financed by endowment & mem
Collections: Paintings by late 19th & early 20th century American artists; some drawings & small sculptures; silver, small stone, wood & ivory carvings; jade; small bronzes; 85 acre Cedarhurst Sculpture Park
Exhibitions: Changing exhibits; Southern Illinois Artists Open Competition
Publications: Form Beyond Function: Recent Sculpture by North American Metalsmiths; quarterly newsletter; Recent Graphics from American Print Shops; Sculpture at Cedarhurst, catalogue
Activities: Classes for adults & children; dramatic programs; docent training; workshops; demonstrations; field trips; lect open to public, 8-10 vis lectr per year; concerts; gallery talks; tours; competitions with awards; scholarships offered; book traveling exhibitions 1 per year; originate traveling exhibitions to qualified museums & college galleries with adequate staff & facilities; sales shop sells books, reproductions, slides, postcards & small items for children
L **Cedar Hurst Library,** Richview Rd, PO Box 923, 62864. *Librn* Beth Brennan
Open to public for reference only
Library Holdings: Vols 1250; Per subs 20; AV — A-tapes, Kodachromes, rec, slides, v-tapes; Other — Exhibition catalogs, pamphlets
Special Subjects: Painting - American

NAPERVILLE

L **NORTH CENTRAL COLLEGE,** Oesterle Library, 320 E School Ave, 60540. Tel 630-637-5700; FAX 630-637-5716; *Dir* Carolyn A Sheehy; *Technician* Belinda Cheek; *Pub Servs Librn* Kelly Collins; *Pub Servs Librn* Jacklyn Egolof; *System Librn* Sharon Takacs
Open Mon - Thurs 8 AM - 11 PM, Fri 8 AM - 6:30 PM, Sat 9 AM - 5:30 PM, Sun Noon - 11 PM. Estab 1861 to provide academic support. For lending & reference. Art Gallery houses 4-5 exhibitions per yr
Library Holdings: Vols 120,000; Per subs 751; Micro — Fiche, reels; AV — A-tapes, cassettes, fs, motion pictures, rec, v-tapes; Other — Clipping files, manuscripts, memorabilia, original art works, pamphlets, photographs
Collections: Sang Collection of Fine Bindings
Exhibitions: Barry Skurkis; Hopi Art
Activities: Book traveling exhibitions 4 per year

NILES

M **THE BRADFORD MUSEUM OF COLLECTOR'S PLATES,** 9333 Milwaukee Ave, 60714. Tel 847-966-2770; FAX 847-966-2121
Open Mon - Fri 10 AM - 5 PM, Sat & Sun 9 AM - 4 PM. Admis adult $2, senior citizens $1, children under 12 accompanied by adult free. Estab 1978 to house and display limited-edition collector's plates for purposes of study, education and enjoyment
Income: Financed by The Bradford Exchange
Collections: Limited-Edition Collector's Plates, approximately 800

NORMAL

ILLINOIS STATE UNIVERSITY

L **Museum Library,** 61790-5620. Tel 309-438-8800; *Cur* Debra Risberg
Museum library open to scholars, students & staff
Library Holdings: Vols 150; Per subs 8
Special Subjects: Decorative Arts, American Indian Art, Pre-Columbian Art, African Art & History

M **University Galleries,** 110 Ctr For Visual Arts, Beaufort St Campus Box 5620, 61790-5620. Tel 309-438-5487; FAX 309-438-8318; *Dir* Barry Blinderman; *Cur* Debra Risberg
No admis fee. Estab 1973 to provide changing exhibits of contemporary art for the students & community at large. The main gallery I contains rotating exhibitions; gallery II & III display student & faculty work, graduate exhibitions, studio area shows & works from the permanent collection. Average Annual Attendance: 29,000
Income: $100,000 (financed by university)
Collections: †Contemporary art emphasis †prints & drawings & 1500 object collection of African Art, primarily West African
Publications: Exhibition catalogs
Activities: Lect open to public, 7 vis lectr per year; gallery talks; tours; individual paintings & original objects of art lent for other exhibitions; lending collection contains original art works, original prints, paintings, photographs & sculpture; book traveling exhibitions 1 per year; originate traveling exhibitions

OAKBROOK

C **MCDONALD'S CORPORATION,** Art Collection, One McDonald's Plaza, 60521. Tel 630-623-3585; FAX 630-623-5361; *Cur* Susan Pertl
Open to group tours by appointment. Estab 1971
Collections: Collection of contemporary paintings & sculpture & of works by established & emerging artists; glass sculptures
Activities: Lect; The Spirit of McDonald's Competition; individual paintings & original objects of art lent; lending collection consists of more than 1000 pieces

PARIS

M **BICENTENNIAL ART CENTER & MUSEUM,** * 132 S Central Ave, 61944. Tel 217-466-8130; *Exec Coordr* Thelma M Sturgeon
Open Tues - Fri Noon - 4 PM, Sat & Sun 1 - 3 PM. No admis fee. Estab 1975 to encourage & bring art to area. Four galleries, 1037 sq ft. Average Annual Attendance: 3000. Mem: 300; annual meeting in Oct
Income: $30,000 (financed by mem, contributions & fundraising)
Collections: Paintings & sculpture primarily 20th century period, including

extensive collection of Alice Baber work
Exhibitions: Changing exhibits each month
Publications: Monthly newsletter
Activities: Classes for adults & children; lect open to public, 6 vis lectr per year; originate traveling exhibitions 2 per year

PEORIA

M **BRADLEY UNIVERSITY,** Heuser Art Center, 1400 Bradley Ave, 61625. Tel 309-677-2967; FAX 309-677-3505; *Dir Div of Art* James Ludwig; *Dir Art & Cur Gallery* John Heintzman
Open Mon - Fri 9:30 - Noon & 1 - 4 PM. Exhibition space 639 sq ft. Average Annual Attendance: 2000
Income: Financed by University
Activities: Classes for adults; lect open to the public; gallery talks; tours; competitions with awards; master print program; individual paintings lent on campus

M **LAKEVIEW MUSEUM OF ARTS & SCIENCES,** 1125 W Lake Ave, 61614-5985. Tel 309-686-7000; FAX 309-686-0280; *Dir* John B Clark; *Cur* Kristan McKinsey; *Cur Exhib* Cory Tibbitts; *Cur Educ* Barbara Melcher-Brethorst; *Science Planetarium Dir* Sheldon Schafer
Open Tues - Sat 10 AM - 5 PM, Sun 1 - 5 PM, Wed 10 AM - 8 PM, cl Mon. Admis adults $2.50, students & sr citizens $1.50, kids 3 & under free. Estab 1965, new building opened 1965, to provide enjoyment & educ by reflecting the historical, cultural & industrial life of the Central Illinois area. Two changing exhibition galleries, Illinois Folk Art Gallery & Children's Discovery Center. Average Annual Attendance: 250,000. Mem: 3600; dues family $40, individual $25, student $10; annual meeting in June
Income: $500,000
Collections: Archaeological; †decorative arts; Regional American Fine & Folk Art; paintings & graphics; fine arts; anthropology, natural sciences
Exhibitions: Changing exhibitions dealing with the arts & sciences
Publications: Bi-monthly bulletin, Lake Views, bi-monthly; exhibition catalogues
Activities: Classes for adults & children; docent training; lect open to public, 8-10 vis lectr per year; concerts; gallery talks; tours; competitions with awards; individual & original objects of art lent to sister institutions; museum shop sells books, magazines, original art, reproductions, prints & craft items; junior museum

A **PEORIA ART GUILD,** 1831 N Knoxville, 61603. Tel 309-685-7522; *Dir* Tyson Joye
Open Tues - Sat 10 AM - 5 PM, cl Mon. No admis fee. Estab 1878 to encourage development of the arts. Average Annual Attendance: 10,000. Mem: 500; dues $25
Income: Financed by mem, Illinois Arts Council, sales & rental, private donations & Peoria Area Arts & Sciences Council
Collections: †Framed & unframed 2-D design, ceramics, sculpture, jewelry, weaving & wood designs; winning works from the Bradley National Print & Drawing Exhibition
Exhibitions: One-person shows; group theme shows, 11 shows annually
Activities: Classes for adults & children; workshops; lect open to public, 5-6 vis lect per year; gallery talks; tours; awards; individual paintings rented to business & members of the community; lending collection contains original art work, prints, paintings, photographs & sculptures; sales shop sells books, magazines, original art & prints

M **PEORIA HISTORICAL SOCIETY,** 942 NE Glen Oak, 61603. Tel 309-674-1921; *Pres* David Puterbaugh
Judge John C Flanagan House open for tours Mon - Fri 10 AM - 3 PM; Pettengill-Morron House open Tues - Sat 10 AM - 3 PM. Admis adults $3, children 15 & under $1. Estab 1934 to acquire, preserve & display artifacts & records relating to the history of Peoria & the Central Illinois Valley; to encourage & support historical research & investigation & to promote & sustain pub interest in history of Peoria & the Central Illinois Valley. Two historic house museums: Flanagan House is post-colonial, Pettingill-Morron house is Victorian. Average Annual Attendance: 5000. Mem: 700; dues $25; annual meeting in May
Income: Financed by mem, endowments; private gifts & grants
Collections: Household items & artifacts from 1840; Library housed in special collections center of Bradley University; Peoria Pottery
Exhibitions: Rennick Award (art works relating to historic sites).
Publications: Monthly Newsletter to members
Activities: Classes for children; lect open to public, 6 vis lectr per year; monthly meetings Sept - May relating to history of the area; competitions with prizes; Boutique at Pettengill-Morron House; museum shop sells books, cards, reproductions

QUINCY

A **QUINCY ART CENTER,** 1515 Jersey St, 62301. Tel 217-223-5900; *Exec Dir* Julie D Nelson
Open Tues - Sun 1 - 4 PM, cl Mon & holidays. Donations accepted. Estab 1923, incorporated 1951 to foster pub awareness & understanding of the visual arts. Average Annual Attendance: 6000. Mem: 650; dues sustaining $150, annual patron $50, family $30, individual $20, student $5; annual meeting in June
Income: Financed by grants, donations, mem fees & Beaux Art Ball
Collections: Crafts, graphics, †paintings & sculpture by contemporary American & European artists
Exhibitions: Annual Quad-State Juried Exhibition, Annual High School Student Exhibition
Publications: Calendar, brochures &/or catalogs for temporary exhibitions
Activities: Classes for adults & children; docent training; lect open to public, 6 vis lect per year; films; gallery talks; tours; competitions with awards; scholarships offered; inter-museum loan; traveling exhibitions organized & circulated; museum shop sells original art

A **QUINCY SOCIETY OF FINE ARTS,** 300 Civic Ctr Plaza, Ste 244, 62301-4162. Tel 217-222-3432; FAX 217-228-2787; Elec Mail info@artsqcy.org. *Dir* Rob Dwyer
Open Mon - Fri 8 AM - 5 PM. Estab 1947 as a community arts council to coordinate & stimulate the visual & performing arts in Quincy & Adams County. Mem: 30 art organizations
Income: Financed by endowment, mem & contribution, Illinois Arts Council, National Endowment for the Arts
Publications: Cultural Calendars, monthly; pamphlets & catalogs
Activities: Workshops for adults & students in visual & performing arts

M **QUINCY UNIVERSITY,** The Gray Gallery, 1800 College Ave, 62301-2699. Tel 217-228-5371; *Gallery Dir* Robert Lee Mejer
Open Mon - Thur 8 AM - 10 PM, Fri 8 AM - 8 PM, Sat 11 AM - 5 PM, Sun 1 - 10 PM. No admis fee. Estab 1968 for cultural enrichment & exposure to contemporary art forms in the community. Exhibitions are held in the Brenner library foyer & The Gray Gallery. Average Annual Attendance: 6000
Income: Financed through the coll & student activities assoc
Collections: †19th century Oriental & European prints; †permanent collection of student & faculty works; †20th century American prints & drawings
Publications: Brochures, 1-2 times annually; gallery calendars, annually
Activities: Lect open to public, 1 vis lectr per year; gallery talks; tours; student show with awards; individual paintings & original objects of art lent; book traveling exhibitions 1-2 per year

L **Brenner Library,** 1800 College Ave, 62301. Tel 217-222-8020; FAX 217-228-5354; *Dir* Victor Kingery
Reference only for pub; lending for faculty & students
Income: $1600 (financed by college revenues)
Purchases: $1600 annually for books
Library Holdings: Vols 7269; Per subs 20; AV — Cassettes, fs, lantern slides, motion pictures, rec, slides, v-tapes; Other — Exhibition catalogs, prints

ROCKFORD

A **ROCKFORD ART MUSEUM,** 711 N Main St, 61103. Tel 815-968-2787; FAX 815-968-0164; *Dir* Carolyn Deluca; *Cur Exhib* Scott Snyder; *Financial Officer* Curtis Kleckler; *Cur Coll* Matt Herbig
Open Tues - Sat 11 AM - 5 PM, Sun 1 - 5 PM, cl Mon & holidays. Admis suggested donation adults $2, students & children $1. Estab 1913 to promote & cultivate an active interest in all fields of fine & applied art, past & present in the surrounding area. 20,000 sq ft exhibition space. Average Annual Attendance: 100,000. Mem: 1000
Income: Financed by mem, state appropriation & private donations
Collections: Permanent collection 19th & 20th century American oil paintings, graphics, sculpture, photography, ceramics, glassware, textiles, watercolors & mixed media
Exhibitions: Annual Rockford & Vicinity Show; Annual Young Artist's Exhibition; numerous one-person and group shows
Publications: Exhibition brochures & catalogs; newsletter, semi-monthly
Activities: Classes for adults & children; docent training; artist-in-residence; museum school program; lect open to public, 5 vis lectr per year; gallery talks; tours; competitions with cash awards; book traveling exhibitions; museum shop sells books, original art, reproductions, prints, jewelry, ceramics & crafts

L **Library,** 711 N Main St, 61103. Tel 815-968-2787; FAX 815-968-0164; Elec Mail cram1@1x.net.com.com. *Exec Dir* Carolyn DeLuca; *Educ Dir* Laura Johnson; *Cur* Scott Snyder
Open to the pub & members by appointment. For reference only
Library Holdings: Vols 500; Per subs 15
Special Subjects: The visual arts

M **ROCKFORD COLLEGE ART GALLERY,** Clark Arts Ctr, 5050 E State St, 61108. Tel 815-226-4034; FAX 815-226-4119; *Dir* Maureen Gustafson
Open daily 2 - 5 PM (academic calendar). Estab 1970. Average Annual Attendance: 5000
Activities: Gallery & group tours; lect open to public, 6 vis lectr per year; originate traveling exhibitions 1 per year

ROCK ISLAND

M **AUGUSTANA COLLEGE,** Art Gallery, NW Corner Seventh Ave & 38th St, 61201. Tel 309-794-7469; FAX 309-794-7678; Elec Mail armaurer@augustana.edu. *Gallery Dir* Sherry C Maurer
Open Tues - Sat Noon - 4 PM. No admis fee. Estab 1973 for the display of visual arts exhibits commensurate with a liberal arts college curriculum. Main gallery serves as an entrance to large auditorium; lower gallery is smaller than main gallery; two galleries total 217 ft wall space. Average Annual Attendance: 50,000
Income: $53,785
Purchases: $3000
Collections: Contemporary, Eastern & Western prints; Swedish American Art; modern Oriental
Exhibitions: (1997) Twenty-first Annual Rock Island Fine Arts Exhibition
Publications: Exhibit catalogs
Activities: Classes for children; lect open to public; 3-4 vis lectr per year; concerts; gallery talks; tours; competitions with prizes; individual paintings & original objects of art lent upon requests considered on individual basis; book traveling exhibitions, 2-3 per year

SKOKIE

L SKOKIE PUBLIC LIBRARY, 5215 Oakton, 60077. Tel 847-673-7774; FAX 847-673-7797; *Dir* Carolyn Anthony; *Assoc Dir Public Servs* Barbara Kozlowski; *Asst Dir for Technical Servs* Camille Cleland
Open Mon - Fri 9 AM - 9 PM, Sat 9 AM - 5 PM, Sun 1 - 5 PM. Estab 1941 as a general pub library serving the residents of Skokie; reciprocal borrowing privileges offered to members of pub libraries in North Suburban Library System. Art gallery is maintained
Income: $2,800,000 (financed by independent tax levy)
Purchases: 450,000
Library Holdings: Vols 360,954; Per subs 789; Compact discs; Micro — Fiche, reels; AV — A-tapes, cassettes, slides, v-tapes; Other — Clipping files, framed reproductions, original art works, pamphlets, reproductions, sculpture
Special Subjects: Architecture, Art History, Crafts, Dolls, Embroidery, Handicrafts, Painting - American, Painting - European, Sculpture, Watercolors
Activities: Lect open to public; framed art prints & posters lent; book traveling exhibitions

SPRINGFIELD

M ILLINOIS STATE MUSEUM, Illinois Art Gallery & Lockport Gallery, Spring & Edwards St, 62706. Tel 217-782-7440; FAX 217-782-1254; *Dir* R Bruce J McMillan; *Dir Art* Kent J Smith; *Cur Decorative Arts* Janice Wass; *Cur Asst Decorative Art* Irene Boyer; *Registrar Art* Carole Peterson; *Admin* Amy Jackson; *Exhibits Designer Art* Philip Kennedy; *Cur Art* Robert Sill
Open Mon - Sat 8:30 AM - 5 PM, Sun Noon - 5 PM. No admis fee. Estab 1877 as mus of natural history, art added in 1928. Collection, exhibition & publication of art produced by or of interest to Illinois & its citizens. Six major changing exhibitions annually. Changing exhibition space: Springfield Art Gallery 3000 sq ft; Arts of Science Gallery (six changing exhibitions), 1364 sq ft; permanent collection galleries present fine, decorative & ethnographic arts, 6400 sq ft permanent exhibit of Illinois Decorative Arts, At Home in The Heartland 3000 sq ft. Average Annual Attendance: 300,000. Mem: 650; dues $25-$500
Income: $266,000. Art Section only (Springfield program financed by state appropriations, Chicago & Lockport programs privately funded)
Purchases: $5000
Collections: Decorative art including †ceramics, †metal work, †textiles, †glass, †furniture; fine art including †paintings, †sculpture, †prints, †drawings, †photography, †contemporary crafts, †folk art
Exhibitions: 18 exhibitions annually featuring contemporary & historical paintings, sculpture, photography, graphics, decorative arts & history, with emphasis on Illinois material
Publications: Living Museum (also in Braille), quarterly; exhibit & collection catalogs; Biennial report
Activities: Programs for adults & children; dramatic programs; lect & symposia open to public; concerts; gallery talks; tours; competitions with awards; film series; individual paintings lent to other museums, historical sites & galleries; book traveling exhibitions 3 per year; originate traveling exhibitions organized & circulated 3 per year; museum shop sells books & original art; Illinois Artisans Shop sells consigned work by Illnois Artisans, facilities in Chicago, Springfield & near Rend Lake
L Library, Spring & Edwards St, 62706. Tel 217-782-6623; *Librn* Ronald Sauberli
Open Mon - Sat 8:30 AM - 5 PM, Sun Noon - 5 PM. Estab to provide informational materials & services to meet the requirements of the mus staff in fields pertinent to the purpose & work of the mus. Circ 100 per month
Income: Financed by state appropriation
Purchases: $2600
Library Holdings: Vols 1500; Per subs 27; AV — Slides, v-tapes; Other — Clipping files, exhibition catalogs, manuscripts, memorabilia, pamphlets
Special Subjects: Anthropology, Art & Natural Sciences
Collections: Anthropology and Ornithology

A SPRINGFIELD ART ASSOCIATION OF EDWARDS PLACE, 700 N Fourth, 62702. Tel 217-523-2631, 523-3507; FAX 217-523-3866; Elec Mail spiartassc@aol.com. *Exec Dir* Michel Krevenas
Open Daily 9 AM - 4 PM, Sat 1 - 3 PM. No admis fee. Estab 1913 to foster appreciation of art, to instruct people in art & to expose people to quality art. Mem: 1000; dues $40-$500; monthly meeting
Income: $200,000 (financed by mem & grants, interest, tuition & benefits)
Collections: †Contemporary American Indian; African sculpture; early American paintings; furniture; Mexican; Oriental & Japanese artifacts & textiles; †paintings; †pottery; †prints; †textiles
Exhibitions: Seven to ten exhibitions are scheduled annually with two or three juried exhibitions; work is borrowed from museum & artist nationwide
Publications: Membership brochures, quarterly; newsletters
Activities: Classes for adults & children; docent training; art outreach program in school in community; lect open to public; gallery talks; tours; scholarships offered; book traveling exhibitions
L Michael Victor II Art Library, 700 N Fourth, 62702. Tel 217-523-3507; FAX 217-523-3866; *Librn* Joan Ekiss
Open 9 AM - 4 PM daily, Mon - Thurs evenings 6:30 - 9:30 PM, Sat 9 AM - Noon, cl Sun. Estab 1965 to provide total community with access to art & art related books
Income: $900
Purchases: $700
Library Holdings: Vols 5000; Per subs 20; Micro — Cards; AV — Slides; Other — Clipping files, exhibition catalogs, pamphlets, reproductions
Special Subjects: Aesthetics, Afro-American Art, American Indian Art, American Western Art, Architecture, Art Education, Art History, Asian Art, Calligraphy, Carpets & Rugs, Cartoons, Ceramics, Collages, Commercial Art, Conceptual Art
Activities: Lect series; film program

VERNON HILLS

M CUNEO FOUNDATION, Museum & Gardens, 1350 N Milwaukee, 60061. Tel 847-362-3042; *Dir* Barbara Hirschfeld
Open Tues - Sun 10 AM - 5 PM. Estab 1991
Income: $300,000 (financed by endowment, mem & admis)
Collections: Architecture; decorative arts; furniture; paintings

WATSEKA

M IROQUOIS COUNTY HISTORICAL SOCIETY MUSEUM, Old Courthouse Museum, * 103 W Cherry, 60970. Tel 815-432-2215; *Pres* Hubert Lytle; *VPres* Mary Hartke
Open Mon - Fri 10:30 AM - 4:30 PM, Sat & Sun 1 - 4:30 PM. Estab 1967 to further the interest in history, art & genealogy. Two rooms for county artists. Average Annual Attendance: 10,000. Mem: 800; dues $5 - $100
Income: Financed by donations by visitors, artists & art committee sells crafts
Collections: Paintings, prints, posters & pictures
Publications: Genealogical Stalker, quarterly; newsletter, monthly; historic reprints
Activities: Lectures open to public; concerts; tours; competitions with awards; museum shop sells books, original art, maps & Indian items

WHEATON

A DUPAGE ART LEAGUE SCHOOL & GALLERY, 218 W Front St, 60187. Tel 630-653-7090; *Pres* Tony Junes; *Treas* Carol Kincaid; *VPres Educ* Jill Sengel; *VPres Exhibits* Kay Walhgren; *VPres Organization* Mary Gerthman; *VPres Buildings & Grounds* Kathy Young
Open daily 9 AM - 5 PM, Sat 9 AM - 2 PM. No admis fee. Estab 1957 primarily as an educational organization founded to encourage artists & promote high artistic standards through instruction, informative programs & exhibits. Three galleries are maintained where members exhibit & sell their work. Mem: 450; dues $30; annual meeting in May
Income: Financed through mem, gifts & donations
Exhibitions: Monthly exhibits; nine juried shows per yr; holiday gift gallery; Fine Art Gallery with monthly exhibits of local artists (Gallery I), one-man or one-woman shows (Gallery II), Fine Crafts (Gallery III)
Publications: Monthly newsletter
Activities: Classes for adults & children; programs; demonstrations; lect open to public, 8 vis lectr per year; gallery talks; competitions; awards; scholarships offered; individual paintings & original objects of art lent to local libraries & businesses; sales shop sells original art & fine crafts (jewerly, ceramics, woodworks fiber & glass)

WINNETKA

A NORTH SHORE ART LEAGUE, Winnetka Community House, 620 Lincoln Ave, 60093. Tel 847-446-2870; *Pres* Rita Price; *First VPres* Nancy Koltun; *Second VPres* Sissy Allwenss
Open Mon - Fri 9 AM - 5 PM, Sat 9 AM - Noon. Estab 1924, inc 1954, to promote interest in creative art through education, exhibition opportunities, scholarship & art programs. Average Annual Attendance: 100,000. Mem: 500; dues $35; annual meeting in May
Income: Financed by mem dues, shows & tuition from classes
Exhibitions: Old Orchard Art Festival - Members Show; Old Orchid Craft Festival - New Horizons in Art; Midwest Print Show
Publications: Art League News, quarterly
Activities: Classes for adults & children; sponser juried competitions with awards; scholarships offered for children

C STROUD WRIGHT ASSOCIATES, 180 Scott Ave, 60093. Tel 847-835-4676, 835-8424; FAX 847-835-4616; *Partner* Jane Stroud
Estab 1994
Collections: AT&T Midwest Corp Center; United Stationers Inc; W W Grainger Inc; Illinois Tool Works Inc; McDermott, Will & Emery Law Offices; Chapman & Culter Law Offices; Katten, Muchin & Zavis Law Offices

INDIANA

ANDERSON

A ANDERSON FINE ARTS CENTER, 226 W Historical Eighth St, 46016. Tel 317-649-1248; FAX 317-649-0199; *Exec Dir* Deborah McBratney-Stapleton; *Pres Board Trustees* Thomas F Lyons; *Educ Coordr* Carol Heger; *Gallery Asst* Tim Swain
Open Sept - July Tues - Sat 10 AM - 5 PM, Sun 2 - 5 PM, cl Mon & national holidays. No admis fee. Estab 1967 to serve the community by promoting & encouraging interest in the fine arts through exhibitions, programs & education activities & the development of a permanent collection. Three galleries contain 1705 sq ft; also a small sales & rental gallery & a studio/theatre. Average Annual Attendance: 30,000. Mem: 700; dues sponsor $1000 or more, sustaining $500-$999, benefactor $250-$499, patron $100-$249, contributor $50-$99, friend $25-$49; annual meeting in May
Income: Financed by mem, endowments, grants, individual & corporate contributions
Special Subjects: Contemporary American Art
Collections: Midwestern & 20th century American prints, paintings & drawings
Exhibitions: Annual Winter Show Exhibits; annual Christmas Tree Exhibit; annual Indiana Artists - Local Exhibit; annual photo exhibits; one-man shows

Publications: Calendar of Events, quarterly; catalogue of the permanent collection; exhibition catalogs
Activities: Classes for adults & children; dramatic programs; docent training; educational outreach; lect open to public, 4-6 vis lectr per year; concerts; gallery talks; tours; competitions with awards; Art Lady Project in the Public Schools; individual paintings & original objects of art lent to businesses, educational facilities & other museums; lending collection contains 300 original art works, 150 original prints, 300 paintings, 10 sculpture & 1000 slides; book traveling exhibitions; museum shop sells books, original art, reproductions, prints, slides, pottery, handcrafted items, glass, fine cards & note papers
L **Library,** 226 W Historical Eighth St, 46016. Tel 317-649-1248
Open Tues - Sat 10 AM - 5 PM, Sun 2 - 5 PM. Estab 1967 for reference needs & enjoyment by members of Arts Center & the community
Purchases: $500
Library Holdings: Vols 400; Per subs 14; AV — Cassettes, Kodachromes, motion pictures, slides; Other — Clipping files, exhibition catalogs, pamphlets
Collections: Contemporary American art

BLOOMINGTON

INDIANA UNIVERSITY

M **Art Museum,** E Seventh St, 47405. Tel 812-855-5445; FAX 812-855-1024; Elec Mail iuartmus@indiana.edu. Cable ARTMUSEUM INDVERS. *Dir* Adelheid Gealt; *Assoc Dir Develop* Eileen Savage; *Assoc Dir Editorial Servs* Linda Baden; *Assoc Dir Curatorial Services & Cur African & Oceanic Pre-Columbian Art* Diane Pelrine; *Cur Ancient Art* Adriana Calinescu; *Registrar* Fran Huber; *Cur Educ* Ed Maxedon; *Asst Registrar* Anita Bracalente; *Cur 19th & 20th Century Art* Kathleen Foster
Open Wed - Sat 10 AM - 5 PM, first of the month Fri 10 AM - 8 PM, Sun Noon - 5 PM, cl Mon & Tues. No admis fee. Estab 1941 to serve as a teaching & cultural resource for the University community & the public at large. Average Annual Attendance: 100,000
Collections: †African, †ancient to modern, Far Eastern, Oceanic, the Americas, †prints, drawings & photographs
Publications: Guide to the collection, exhibition catalogs, occasional papers, newsletter
Activities: Classes for adults & children; docent training; lect open to public; gallery talks; tours; concerts series; competition with awards; Book traveling exhibitions; originate traveling exhibitions; museum shop sells books, magazines, reproductions, prints, slides
M **William Hammond Mathers Museum,** 601 E Eighth St, 47405. Tel 812-855-6873; FAX 812-855-0205; Elec Mail iuartmus@indiana.edu. *Dir* Geoffrey W Conrad; *Designer* Elaine Gaul; *Coll Mgr* William Scott; *Exhibits Mgr* David Bruker; *Conservator* Judith Sylvester; *Asst Dir* Judith Kirk; *Cur Coll* Thomas Kavanagh; *Business Mgr* Sandra Warren; *Designer* Matthew Sieber
Open Tues - Fri 9 AM - 4:30 PM, Sat & Sun 1 - 4:30 PM. No admis fee. Estab 1964 as Indiana University Mus, institute renamed in 1983. Mus of World Cultures housing over 30,000 artifacts
Collections: Anthropology, folklore & history with collections of American primitives, Latin American primitives & folk art
Exhibitions: Museum features changing exhibitions
Publications: Papers & monograph series
Activities: Docent program; museum training classes; lect; tours; film series; school loan collection

L **INDIANA UNIVERSITY,** Fine Arts Library, Art Museum Bldg, 47405. Tel 812-855-3314; FAX 812-855-3443; Elec Mail irvine@indiana.edu. *Head Librn* Betty Jo Irvine; *Slide Librn* Eileen Fry
For lending
Income: Financed by state & student fees
Library Holdings: Vols 90,000; Per subs 390; Micro — Fiche 24,000; AV — Slides 325,000; Other — Clipping files 50,000, exhibition catalogs, reproductions 58,000
Special Subjects: Aesthetics, Afro-American Art, Antiquities-Byzantine, Antiquities-Etruscan, Antiquities-Greek, Antiquities-Oriental, Antiquities-Roman, Architecture, Art History, Asian Art, Bronzes, Calligraphy, Ceramics, Collages, Commercial Art

ELKHART

M **MIDWEST MUSEUM OF AMERICAN ART,** 429 S Main St, PO Box 1812, 46515. Tel 219-293-6660; *Dir* B Jane Burns; *Admin Asst* Martha Culp; *Cur Exhib & Educ* Brian D Byrn
Open Tues - Fri 11 AM - 5 PM, Sat - Sun 1 - 4 PM. Admis adults $2, student & sr citizens $1. Estab 1978 to provide high quality exhibitions, educational programs & permanent collection of 19th & 20th century American art for the public. Seven galleries on two floors (approx 9000 sq ft of exhibit space). Average Annual Attendance: 25,000. Mem: 659; dues $10-$250
Income: $100,000 (financed through mem, grants, foundations, contributions)
Collections: Paintings: Arthur Bowen Davies; Joan Mitchell; Robert Natkin; Maurice Pendergast; †Grant Wood; Red Grooms; Carl Olaf Seltzer; Norman Rockwell; LeRoy Neiman; Roger Brown; Art Green; George Luks; Glen Cooper Henshaw; Pennerton West; Robert Reid; Sculpture: Louise Nevelson; Mark DiSuvero; Felix Eboigbe; Frederick MacMonnies;
Exhibitions: Changing Walls; Tactile Environment; Midwest Photo '80; Northern Indiana & Southern Michigan Competition
Publications: Midwest Museum Bulletin, bimonthly
Activities: Classes for adults and children; dramatic programs; docent training; lect open to public, 8-10 vis lectr per year; concerts; gallery talks; tours; competitions with awards; individual paintings & original objects of art lent to other museums only; originate traveling exhibitions to other museums & university galleries; museum shop sells books, magazines, reproductions, prints & original crafts

EVANSVILLE

A **ARTS COUNCIL OF SOUTHWESTERN INDIANA,** 201 NW Fourth St, Ste 305, 47708. Tel 812-422-2111; FAX 812-422-2357; *Dir* Lori Kissinger; *Asst* Linda O'Connor
Estab 1970 to increase the awareness & accessibility of the arts in Southwestern Indiana through community programs, arts in educ & festivals; serves as an umbrella organization for over 50 cultural organizations, providing technical assistance, marketing & linkage with local, state & national arts organizations. Mem: 400; $20 & up
Income: Financed by endowment, mem, city appropriation & state appropriation
Exhibitions: Business/Arts Month
Publications: Artist directory; artist registry; Arts Talk Newsletter, quarterly; cultural calendar; cultural directory; media directory
Activities: Classes for general community; arts-in-education program; artist residencies in elementary schools; art workshops; lect open to public; concerts; festivals; outreach program provided to six rural counties

M **EVANSVILLE MUSEUM OF ARTS & SCIENCE,** 411 SE Riverside Dr, 47713. Tel 812-425-2406, 421-7506 (TTY); FAX 812-421-7507; *Pres Board Dir* Patrick Shoulders; *Dir* John W Streetman; *Dir Emeritus* Siegfried Weng; *Cur Educ* Sam Longmire; *Cur of Coll* Mary Schnepper; *Registrar* Susan P Colaricci; *Asst Cur* Thomas R Lonnberg; *Science Planetarium Dir* Mitch Luman
Open Tues - Sat 10 AM - 5 PM, Sun Noon - 5 PM, cl Mon. No admis fee. Estab 1926 to maintain & perpetuate a living mus to influence & inspire the taste & cultural growth of the community, to provide facilities for the collection, preservation & exhibition of objects, data & programs related to the arts, history, science & technology. First Level: 19th century village of homes, shops, offices & town hall, America at War Gallery, two science & technology galleries, classrooms; Second Level: furnished Gothic Room with linefold paneling; Sculpture Gallery: galleries for Dutch & Flemish art, 18th century English art, 19th & 20th century American & European art, Anthropology Gallery; two galleries for monthly exhibits; Third Level: Planetarium. Average Annual Attendance: 100,000. Mem: Dues benefactor $1000, sponsor $500, donor $250, patron $100, contributing $50, family $25, individual $15; annual meeting third Tues in May
Income: $174,000 (financed by mem, city & state appropriations)
Collections: †American Art; Dutch & Flemish, 16th & 17th centuries; 18th Century English Art; 19th & 20th Century European Art; Local History; State & Regional Historical Artifacts & Decorative Arts
Publications: Bulletin, monthly; catalogs of exhibitions
Activities: Classes for adults & children; docent training; lect open to public, 6 vis lectr per year; concerts; gallery talks; tours; competitions with prizes; museum shop sells books, original art
L **Henry R Walker Jr Memorial Art Library,** 411 SE Riverside Dr, 47713. Tel 812-425-2406; FAX 812-421-7509; *Cur* Mary Schnepper
Open Tues - Sat 10 AM - 5 PM, Sun Noon - 5 PM. For reference only
Library Holdings: Vols 4000; Per subs 25; AV — Slides; Other — Clipping files, exhibition catalogs, manuscripts, memorabilia, original art works, pamphlets, photographs, prints, reproductions, sculpture

UNIVERSITY OF EVANSVILLE

M **Krannert Gallery,** 1800 Lincoln Ave, 47722. Tel 812-479-2043; FAX 812-479-2101; Elec Mail lm23@evansvill.edu. *Chmn Art Dept* Les Miley
Open Mon - Sat 9 AM - 5 PM. No admis fee. Estab 1969-70 to bring to the University & pub communities exhibitions which reflect the contemporary arts, ranging from crafts through painting & sculpture. Pub access exhibition space 80 x 40 & located in Fine Arts Building
Income: Financed by Department of Art funds
Exhibitions: Drawing Exhibition; Indiana Ceramics; New Aquisitions; Student Scholarship Exhibition; Undergraduate BFA Exhibition; Faculty Exhibition; Painting Invitational; Sculpture Invitational; Evansville Artists Guild Show; Photography Exhibition
Activities: Lect open to public, 2 vis lectr per year; gallery talks; competitions with awards; individual paintings & original objects of art lent to university community
L **University Library,** 1800 Lincoln Ave, 47722. Tel 812-479-2247; FAX 812-471-6996; Elec Mail mg28@evansville.edu. *Acquistions Librn* Marvin Guilfoyle
Open 8 AM - 11 PM
Library Holdings: Micro — Fiche, prints

L **WILLARD LIBRARY,** Dept of Fine Arts, 21 First Ave, 47710. Tel 812-425-4309; FAX 812-421-9742, 425-4303; *Head Librn* Brian Rhodes; *Spec Coll* Lyn Martin; *Children's Librn* Anne Wells
Open Tues 9 AM - 8 PM, Wed - Fri 9 AM - 5:30 PM, Sat 9 AM - 5 PM, Sun 1 - 5 PM. Estab 1885
Income: $3360 (financed by endowment & city appropriation)
Library Holdings: Vols 1000; Per subs 16; AV — Rec; Other — Original art works, photographs

FORT WAYNE

L **ALLEN COUNTY PUBLIC LIBRARY,** Art, Music & Audiovisual Services, 900 Webster St, 46801. Tel 219-424-7241, Ext 2275; FAX 219-422-9688; Elec Mail spearson@everest.acpl.lib.in.us. *Dir* Jeffrey R Krull; *Assoc Dir* Steven Fortreide; *Art, Music & Audiovisual Mgr* Stacey Pearson
Open Mon - Thurs 9 AM - 9 PM, Fri 9 AM - 6 PM, Sat 9 AM - 6 PM, Sun 1 - 6 PM. Estab 1968 to provide a reference collection of the highest quality & completeness for the community & its colleges, a place where local artists & musicians could exhibit their works & perform, to provide a circulating collection of art prints, slides & musical scores sufficient to meet the demand. The gallery is reserved for painting, sculpture, graphics, photography, ceramics & other art crafts
Income: $170,000 (financed by local property taxes)
Library Holdings: Vols 75,000; Per subs 170; Compact discs 9500; AV — A-tapes, cassettes 11,000, fs, motion pictures, rec 25,000, slides 23,000, v-tapes

9300; Other — Clipping files, exhibition catalogs, memorabilia, original art works, pamphlets
Activities: Lect open to public, 3 vis lectr per year; concerts; lending collection contains books, slides, videos, CDs, cassettes & books-on-tape; sales shop sells books, posters, videos, CDs & cassettes

A **ARTS UNITED OF GREATER FORT WAYNE,** The Canal House, 114 E Superior St, 46802. Tel 219-424-0646; FAX 219-424-2783; *Pres* Geoff Gephart; *Chmn* Alex Jokay; *Comptroller* Christine Jones; *Mgr Facility* Janet McCaulay; *Coordr Community Servs* Carla Nunez; *Dir Develop* Mark Gilmore
Estab 1955 to raise funds for cultural organizations in Fort Wayne & to foster a positive atmosphere for arts growth
Income: Financed by pub allocations & private donations
Collections: Bicentennial Collection
Publications: Discovery, quarterly newspaper; fine arts calendar
Activities: Own & manage the Performing Arts Center, umbrella organization for 36 arts organizations

M **FORT WAYNE MUSEUM OF ART, INC,** 311 E Main St, 46802. Tel 219-422-6467; FAX 219-422-1374; *Interim Dir* Gregory Manifold
Open Tues - Sat 10 AM - 5 PM, Sun Noon - 5 PM. No admis fee. Estab 1921 to heighten visual perception of fine arts & perception of other disciplines. Average Annual Attendance: 65,000. Mem: 1550; dues $30 for an individual & up; annual meeting in July
Income: Financed by endowment, mem, Arts United & grants
Collections: Dorsky & Tannenbaum Collection (contemporary graphics); Fairbanks Collection (paintings & prints); Hamilton Collection (paintings & sculpture); Thieme Collection (paintings); Weatherhead Collection (contemporary paintings & prints); contemporary pieces by living America artists; paintings, sculptures & works on paper from 1850 to present by artists from the US & Europe; works by significant regional artists
Publications: Books; calendar, bi-monthly; catalogs; fact sheets; posters
Activities: Classes for adults & children; docent training; lect open to public; 15 vis lectr per year; gallery talks; tours; book traveling exhibitions 5-6 per year; originate traveling exhibitions; museum & sales shop sells books, magazines, original art, reproductions & prints

C **LINCOLN NATIONAL LIFE INSURANCE CO,** Lincoln Museum, 200 E Berry St, 46801-7838. Tel 219-455-3864; FAX 219-455-6922; *Asst* Joan Flinspach
Open Mon - Thurs 9 AM - 5 PM, Fri 8 AM - 12:30 PM, May - Sept Mon - Fri 8 AM - 4:30 PM, Sat 10 AM - 4:30 PM. Estab 1928 for collection of Lincolniana; as research library & mus. Average Annual Attendance: 14,000
Collections: †Lincolniana; †Civil War; †19th Century Art (1809-1865)
Publications: Lincoln Lore, monthly; R Gerald McMurry Lecture, annually
Activities: Lect open to public; 1 vis lectr per year; individual paintings & original objects of art lent to qualified institutions; originate traveling exhibitions

M **SAINT FRANCIS COLLEGE,** John Weatherhead Gallery, 2701 Spring St, 46808. Tel 219-434-3100; FAX 219-434-7444; Elec Mail rcartwri@sfc.edu.
Open Mon - Fri 10 AM - 5 PM. No admis fee. Estab 1965 to provide art programs to students & community. Gallery, approx 25 x 15 ft each, is maintained in two rooms, located on the third floor, Bonaventure Hall. Average Annual Attendance: 2000
Activities: Lect open to public, 1-2 vis lectr per year; tours; competitions with awards; traveling exhibitions organized & circulated

HAMMOND

M **PURDUE UNIVERSITY CALUMET,** Bicentennial Library Gallery, 46323-2094. Tel 219-989-2249; *Secy Art Committee* Barbara R Stoddard
Open Mon - Thurs 8 AM - 9:30 PM, Fri 8 AM - 5 PM, Sat 10 AM - 4 PM, Sun 1 - 5 PM. No admis fee. Estab 1976 to present varied art media to the university community & general public. Average Annual Attendance: 25,000
Income: $3000
Collections: 19th century Chinese Scroll collection; 1930 art deco bronze sculptured doors from City Hall
Exhibitions: Area Professional Artists & Students Shows; group shows; traveling shows (Smithsonian Institution, French Cultural Services, Austrian Institute)
Activities: Book traveling exhibitions

HUNTINGTON

M **HUNTINGTON COLLEGE,** Robert E Wilson Art Gallery, Merillat Centre for the Arts, 2303 College Ave, 46750-1299. Tel 219-356-6000, Ext 2061; FAX 219-356-9448; Elec Mail dericsso@huntcol.edu. *Dir* Dwight Ericsson
Open Mon - Fri 8 AM - 5 PM. No admis fee. Estab 1990 to provide community with art shows & support college art program. Gallery is 25 x 44 ft. Average Annual Attendance: 3000
Income: $5000 (financed by gifts)
Collections: Wilson Collection (paintings)
Activities: Art in the schools; docent programs; book traveling exhibitions four per year

INDIANAPOLIS

M **CHILDREN'S MUSEUM,** Rauh Memorial Library, 3000 N Meridian, PO Box 3000, 46208. Tel 317-924-5431; FAX 317-921-4019; *Pres* Peter Sterling; *VPres* Paul Richard; *VPres* Margaret Maxwell; *VPres* John Grogan; *Staff Librn* Greg Jackson
Open 10 AM - 5 PM. Admis $3 - $4. Estab 1926 to enrich the lives of children. History, physical science, natural science, world cultures, pastimes, center of exploration, trains, dolls, playscape, planetarium, theater. Average Annual Attendance: 1,100,000. Mem: 6800; dues family $50; annual meeting Apr
Income: $10,000,000 (funded by endowment, mem, fundraising)

Collections: Caplan Collection
Publications: Quarterly newsletter
Activities: Children's classes; dramatic programs; docent programs; lect open to public, 6 vis lectr per year; competitions in theatre, visual arts, vocal music, literature, dance & instrumental music; lending collection contains 730 educational kits; book traveling exhibitions 3 per year; retail store sells books

M **EITELJORG MUSEUM OF AMERICAN INDIANS & WESTERN ART,** 500 W Washington, 46204. Tel 317-636-9378; FAX 317-264-172; Internet Home Page Address http://www.eiteljorg.org. *Chmn* Harrison Eiteljorg; *Pres & Chief Exec Officer* John Vanausdall
Open Tues - Sat 10 AM - 5 PM, Sun Noon - 5 PM. Dedicated to the preservation & interpretation of the history of the American frontier experience, particularly as it relates to the culture & art of North American Indians & to the exploration, settling & development of the continent. Average Annual Attendance: 102,000. Mem: 2000
Collections: Collections of Taos Artists; 19th & 20th Century Art Work
Exhibitions: (1997) In Search of Frederic Remington; In the Presence of the Past: The Miami Indians of Indiana; Birds & Beasts of Ancient Latin America; Luis Jimenez, Working Class Heroes: Images from the Popular Culture. (1997-98) Cuando Hablan Los Santos: Contemporary Santero Traditions from Northern New Mexico
Activities: Classes for adults & children; dramatic programs; docent training; lect open to public; gallery talks; tours; museum shop sells books, magazines, original art, prints, jewelry

M **HISTORIC LANDMARKS FOUNDATION OF INDIANA,** Morris-Butler House, 1204 N Park Ave, 46202. Tel 317-636-5409; FAX 317-636-2630; *Admnr* Tiffany C Sallee
Open Tues - Sat 10 AM - 4 PM, Sun 1 - 4 PM (tours on the half hour), cl Mon. Admis adult $3, students & children $1. Home built 1865 & restored by Historic Landmarks Foundation of Indiana. Estab in 1969 to document age of picturesque eexlecticism in architecture & interior decoration. Interpretation, exhibition & preservation of Victorian lifestyle, customs & objects (1850-1890). 16 rooms completely furnished. Facilities for receptions & meetings. All paintings by Indiana artists previously owned by Mid-Victorian homeowners (1850-1890). Average Annual Attendance: 10,000. Mem: Annual dues $15-$100
Income: Financed by private funds & admis fees
Collections: †Rococo, †Renaissance & Gothic Revival furniture; †paintings by early Indiana artists; †Victorian ceramics, silver & glass; †Victorian textiles
Publications: Victorian Wedding Primer; Victorian Christmas Sampler
Activities: Classes for children & adults; dramatic programs; docent training; lect open to public, 10 vis lectr per year; tours; individual paintings & original objects of art lent to professional museums; lending collection contains original art work & paintings

L **Information Center Library,** 340 W Michigan St, 46202. Tel 317-639-4534; FAX 317-639-6734; *Pres* J Reid Williamson Jr; *VPres* James D Conley; *Dir Community Servs* Marsh Davis
For Reference only
Library Holdings: Vols 3000; Per subs 100; AV — A-tapes, Kodachromes, motion pictures, slides, v-tapes; Other — Clipping files

A **HOOSIER SALON PATRONS ASSOCIATION,** Hoosier Salon Art Gallery, 6434 N College Ave, 46220. Tel 317-253-5340; *Pres* Pam Hicks; *First VPres* Harry Riser; *Treas* Mack McKinzie; *Exec Dir* Pat Templin
Main gallery open Mon - Fri 9:30 AM - 4 PM. No admis fee. Estab 1925 to promote work of Indiana artists. Average Annual Attendance: 60,000. Mem: 850 (artists), 700 (patrons); dues patrons $40 & up, artists $20; annual meeting in June
Income: Financed by mem & art sales
Collections: Paintings, prints, sculpture
Exhibitions: Hoosier Salon Annual Exhibition
Publications: Annual Salon Exhibition Catalog; History of the Hoosier Salon; Hoosier Salon Newsletter, three times a year
Activities: Educ dept; gallery talks & tours at annual exhibit; juried competition with awards; original prints & paintings lent to qualified organizations; originate traveling exhibitions; sales shop sells books

A **INDIANAPOLIS ART CENTER,** Churchman-Fehsenfeld Gallery, 820 E 67th St, 46220. Tel 317-255-2464; FAX 317-255-0486; Elec Mail inartctr@inetdirect.net. *Exec Dir* Joyce Sommers; *Assoc Dir* David Thomas; *Exhib Cur* Julia Muney Moore
Open Mon - Fri 9 AM - 3 PM, Sat 9 AM - 3 PM, Sun Noon - 3 PM. No admis fee, suggested donation $2. Estab 1934 to engage, enlighten & enhance community through art educ, participation & observation. Maintains collection for on-site reference only. Average Annual Attendance: 185,000. Mem: 2000
Income: Financed by endowment, mem, city & state appropriation
Publications: Periodic exhibition catalogues
Activities: Over 90 art classes offered for all ages & skill levels in all medias. Outdoor river front stage has music theatre & dance; summer fine arts camps; workshops; lect open to public, 20 vis lect per year; concerts; gallery talks; tours; competitions with awards; scholarship & fels offered; exten dept; sales shop sells books, original art & prints

L **INDIANAPOLIS MARION COUNTY PUBLIC LIBRARY,** Arts Division, 40 E Saint Clair St, PO Box 211, 46206-0211. Tel 317-269-1764; FAX 317-269-1768; *Div Head* Dan Gann; *Ref Librn* Sue Chatman
Open Mon - Fri 9 AM - 9 PM, Sat 9 AM - 5 PM, Sun 1 - 5 PM. Estab 1873
Income: Financed by state appropriation and county property tax
Library Holdings: Vols 25,000; Per subs 200; Micro — Reels; AV — Cassettes, fs 1250, motion pictures, rec 25,000; Other — Clipping files, exhibition catalogs, framed reproductions, pamphlets, photographs, prints
Collections: Julia Connor Thompson Collection on Finer Arts in Homemaking
Activities: Lect open to public; concerts; tours

M **INDIANAPOLIS MUSEUM OF ART,** 1200 W 38th St, 46208-4196. Tel 317-923-1331; FAX 317-926-8931; *Dir* Bret Waller; *Deputy Dir* Tim Boruff; *Chief Cur* Ellen Lee; *Cur Asian Art* Dr James Robinson; *Assoc Cur Textiles & Costumes* Niloofar Imami-Paydar; *Cur Contemporary Art* Holliday T Day; *Cur Decorative Arts* Barry Shifman; *Cur Prints & Drawings* Martin F Krause; *Cur African, S Pacific, Pre-Columbian* Theodore Celenko Jr; *Interim Dir Educ* Brian Hogarth; *Dir Curatorial Support Servs* Martin J Radecki; *Dir Marketing & Communications* Alice M Irvan; *Dir Institutional Advancement* Mack P McKinzie; *Controller* Matthew Conacchione II; *Cur Asian Art* Jane Weldon Myers; *Dir Horticulture* Charles T Gleaves; *Cur Painting & Sculpture* Ronda J Kasl; *Research Cur* A Ian Fraser
Open Tues, Wed, Fri & Sat 10 AM - 5 PM, Thurs 10 AM - 8:30 PM, Sun Noon - 5 PM, cl Mon & major holidays. No admis fee to permanent collection; Charge for special exhibitions. Estab 1883 to maintain a mus, the grounds, pavilions & other facilities for the display of art, a library for the collection of books, manuscrpits, periodicals, photographs & other similar data or facilities relating to art of all kinds; to promote interest in art of all kinds by lectures, exhibitions, publications, prog & general sponsorship of art & artists in the City of Indianapolis & State of Indiana; to cooperate with national state & city government & civic, educational & artistic groups foundations. Maintains 4 pavilions, the Krannert, Hulman, Clowes & Lilly Pavilions, as part of a 152 acre complex. Average Annual Attendance: 500,000. Mem: 10,000
Income: Financed by corporations, foundations, private individuals & endowment
Collections: J M W Turner Collection of prints, watercolors & drawings; W J Holliday Collection of neo-impressionist art; Clowes Fund Collection of Old Master paintings; Eli Lilly Collection of Chinese art & the Eiteljorg Collection of African art; European & American painting & sculpture, †contemporary art, †textiles & costumes, †decorative arts
Publications: Brochures; handbook of permanent collections; Bi-monthly magazine (Previews) for members; catalogues for IMA-organized exhibitions
Activities: Classes for adults & children; dramatic programs; docent training; lect open to public, 15-30 vis lectr per year; concerts; gallery talks; tours; book traveling exhibitions 12-20 per year; originate traveling exhibitions; museum shop & sales shop sell books, magazines, original art, reproductions, prints, slides & jewelry; Alliance Art Rental Gallery rents paintings to members & sells to members & public

M **Clowes Fund Collection,** Clowes Pavilion, 1200 W 38th St, 46208. Tel 317-923-1331; FAX 317-931-1978; Elec Mail ima@indy.net. *Cur* A Ian Fraser
Open Tues, Wed, Fri & Sat 10 AM - 5 PM, Thurs 10 AM - 8:30 PM, Sun Noon - 5 PM, cl Mon. No admis fee. Mem: 10,000
Income: Financed by endowment
Collections: Italian Renaissance: Duccio, Fra Angelico, Bellini, Luini, Tintoretto & others; Spanish-El Greco, Goya & others; Northern Renaissance-17th & 18th century Dutch, Hals, Rembrandt & others; French-Clouet, Corneille de Lyon; English-Reynolds, Constable & others; Flemish-Breughel, Bosch & others
Activities: Classes for adults & children; dramatic programs; docent training; lect open to public, 30 vis lectr per year; concerts; gallery talks; tours; book traveling exhibitions 12-20 per year; originate traveling exhibitions to other art museums; museum shop sells books

L **Stout Reference Library,** 1200 W 38th St, 46208. Tel 317-923-1331, Ext 276; FAX 317-926-8931; *Reference Librn* Ursual Kolmstetter; *Librn Asst* Anne Marie Quets
Open Tues - Fri 10 AM - 5 PM, Sat & Sun 1 - 4 PM. Estab 1908 to serve needs of Mus staff & Indianapolis community. For reference only
Income: Financed by endowment, mem, city appropriation & federal grants
Library Holdings: Vols 35,000; Per subs 150; Micro — Reels; AV — Slides, v-tapes; Other — Clipping files, exhibition catalogs, pamphlets
Special Subjects: Architecture, Decorative Arts, Ethnology, Oriental Art, Painting - American, Sculpture, Textiles, Indiana Artists
Collections: Indiana Artists
Publications: Exhibition catalogs as needed; Indianapolis Museum of Art Bulletin, irregularly; newsletter, bimonthly; 100 Masterpieces

L **Slide Collection,** 1200 W 38th St, 46208. Tel 317-923-1331, Ext 226; FAX 317-926-8931; *Slide Coordr* Jane Ferger
Open Tues - Sat 1 - 5 PM. Estab 1972 to provide visuals on the history of art & to document & record the mus prog & activities. Circ 50,000
Income: Financed by endowment and museum budget
Purchases: $5000
Library Holdings: AV — Slides 150,000, v-tapes 400
Special Subjects: Art History
Collections: Exhibits & installation documentation of programs

M **Columbus Gallery,** 390 The Commons, 47201. Tel 812-376-2597; FAX 812-375-2724; *Dir* Susie Saunders
Open Tues - Sat 10 AM - 5 PM, Fri 10 AM - 8 PM, Sun Noon - 4 PM. No admis fee. Estab 1974. Gallery contains 2400 sq ft of exhibit space on Second floor of The Commons. Average Annual Attendance: 8500. Mem: 250; dues family $50, individual $35; annual meeting in Feb
Income: Financed by auction & donations, including annual fund campaign
Exhibitions: Five exhibitions a year of IMA permanent collection & of local interest
Activities: Classes for adults & children; school programs; lect open to public, 6-8 vis lectr per year; gallery talks; tours; museum shop sells books, original art, reproductions

M **INDIANA STATE MUSEUM,** 202 N Alabama St, 46204. Tel 317-232-1637; FAX 317-232-7090; *Exec Dir* Richard A Gantz; *Dir Develop* Margaret Kauffmann-Hay; *Dir Budget & Finance* Willard Bruggen; *Cur in Charge* Ronald Richards; *Cur Fine Arts* Jim Moy; *Cur Costumes & Flat Textiles* Kathleen McLary; *Cur History* Dale Ogden; *Cur Popular Culture* William Wepler; *Registrar* Jeffrey Tenuth; *Coll Mgr* Linda Badger; *Dir Design & Graphics* Tony Garcia; *Dir Public Relations* Cindy Busch; *Dept Educ* Cynthia Ewick
Open daily 9 AM - 4:45 PM, Sun Noon - 4:45 PM. No admis fee. Estab 1869 for collections; current mus building opened 1967 to collect, preserve & interpret the natural & cultural history of the state. Numerous galleries. Average Annual Attendance: 260,000. Mem: 1300; dues $5 & up; annual meeting in Apr
Income: Financed by state appropriation
Exhibitions: Three Indiana art shows annually; Pottinger Amish Quilt Collection; Indiana Sports Hall of Fame
Publications: On-the-Move, quarterly; brochures for individual historic sites
Activities: Docent training; in-school programs; lect open to public, 4 vis lectr per year; sales shop selling books, reproductions & prints

INDIANA UNIVERSITY - PURDUE UNIVERSITY AT INDIANAPOLIS

M **Indianapolis Center for Contemporary Art-Herron Gallery,** 1701 N Pennsylvania St, 46202. Tel 317-920-2420; FAX 317-920-2401; *Dir & Cur Art Gallery* William Adkins; *Gallery Asst* Open
Open Mon - Thurs 10 AM - 7 PM, Fri 10 AM - 5 PM, Sat 10 AM - 2 PM. No admis fee. School estab 1860. Gallery estab 1978 & is located in the Mus Building & exhibits contemporary art on an international scale. 3000 sq ft, 14 ft ceilings, marble floors, climate control. Average Annual Attendance: 40,000. Mem: 250; dues $25-$500
Income: Financed by state appropriation, grants & private support
Exhibitions: Biannual Faculty Show; Senior Show & Student Show
Activities: Docent training; tours; lect open to public; 15 vis lectr per year; gallery talks; tours; competitions; awards; exten dept serving Indianapolis & surrounding communities; facilitators of civic art projects; book traveling exhibitions 2 per year; originate traveling exhibitions; museum shop sells t-shirts, posters, catalogs
—**Herron School of Art Library,** 1701 N Pennsylvania St, 46202-2402. Tel 317-920-2433; FAX 317-920-2430; *Head Librn* Ophelia Roop; *Assoc Librn* Jennifer Hehman
Open Mon - Thurs 8 AM - 7 PM, Fri 8 AM - 5 PM, Sat 8:30 AM - 12:30 PM. Estab 1970 as a visual resource center for the support of the curriculum of the Herron School of Art. Circ 110,000
Income: $35,000 (financed by state appropriation)
Purchases: $17,000
Library Holdings: Vols 27,500; Per subs 100; Laser disc; AV — A-tapes 615, lantern slides, slides 143,000, v-tapes; Other — Clipping files, exhibition catalogs, pamphlets, photographs, prints, reproductions
Special Subjects: Advertising Design, Afro-American Art, American Indian Art, American Western Art, Antiquities-Greek, Architecture, Art Education, Art History, Ceramics, Collages, Commercial Art, Conceptual Art, Crafts, Display, Drawings, Visual communication, painting, Woodworking

C **LAUGHNER BROTHERS, INC,** 4004 S East St (US Hwy 31 S), 46227. Tel 317-783-2907; FAX 317-783-3126; *Pres* Richard Tierney
Open Mon - Sun 11 AM-8:30 PM. Estab 1960 to promote Indiana artists. Collection displayed in dining establishments, Mr Laughner uses original paintings from several artists as his main decor in all 10 locations in Indiana
Purchases: $2000
Collections: Original paintings from several artists

M **MARIAN COLLEGE,** Allison Mansion, 3200 Cold Spring Rd, 46222. Tel 317-929-0299, 929-0123; FAX 317-929-0263, 929-0288; *Dir Conferences & Events* Vicky Welch
Conference Center open by appointment. Donations accepted. Estab 1970, in the National Register of Historical Places. The interior of the mansion is a work of art with its magnificent treatment of walls of hand carved marble & wood: oak, white mahogany & walnut. The grand stairway in the main hall leads to the balcony overlooking the hall, all hand-carved walnut. A private collection of 17th century paintings complement its beauty
Income: Financed by donations
Collections: 17th century paintings
Activities: Concerts; tours; corporate meeting site

M **NATIONAL ART MUSEUM OF SPORT,** Univ Pl, 850 W Michigan St, 46202-5198. Tel 317-274-3627; FAX 317-274-3878; Elec Mail uplace@wpo.iupui.edu. *Admin* Ann M Rein
Open Mon - Fri 9 AM - 5 PM, Sat 10 AM - 4 PM. No admis free, donations accepted. Estab 1959 as a fine art mus covering sports. Mem: 167
Collections: Works by George Bellows, Fletcher Martin, Winslow Homer, Alfred Boucher, Willard Mullin, John Groth
Publications: News from the Museum, quarterly newsletter; catalogs
Activities: Docent training; teach workshops; lect open to public; gallery talks; tours; individual paintings & original objects of art lent to archivally sound institutions with adequate security & qualified staff; book traveling exhibitions 5-6 per year; originate traveling exhibitions; museum shop sells books, reproductions, prints, clothing, games, cards & stationery, jewelry

M **UNIVERSITY OF INDIANAPOLIS,** Christel DeHaan Fine Arts Gallery, 1400 E Hanna Ave, 46227. Tel 317-788-3253; *Dir* Open; *Chmn* Dee Schaad
Open Mon - Fri 9 AM - 4 PM. No admis fee. Estab 1964 to serve the campus & community. Average Annual Attendance: 40,000
Income: Financed by institution support
Purchases: $15,000
Collections: †Art Department Collection; †Krannert Memorial Collection
Exhibitions: Student, faculty & local artists exhibits
Publications: Announcements; annual catalog & bulletin
Activities: Classes for adults; lect open to public; concerts; gallery talks; competitions with prizes; scholarships offered

LAFAYETTE

M **GREATER LAFAYETTE MUSEUM OF ART,** 101 S Ninth St, 47901. Tel 317-742-1128; FAX 317-742-1120; *Pres* Doug Gutridge; *Cur* Ellen E Fischer; *Registrar* Michal Hathaway; *Asst to Dir* Jennifer Leighton
Open Tues - Sun 11 AM - 4 PM, cl Mon & major holidays. No admis fee. Estab 1909 to encourage & stimulate art & to present exhibitions of works of local, regional & national artists & groups as well as representative works of American & foreign artists. Average Annual Attendance: 17,000. Mem: 1000; dues $15-$1000; annual meeting in Oct
Income: Financed by art assoc foundation, endowment, mem, school of art & special events

Collections: Permanent collection of over 600 works of art obtained through purchase or donation since 1909; Laura Anne Fry American Art Pottery & Art Glass; Alice Baber Collection of Contemporary American Art; American art collection specializing in Hoosier artist's work
Publications: Annual report; exhibition catalog; Visions, quarterly newsletter
Activities: Classes for adults & children; lect open to public, 2-5 vis lectr per year; gallery talks; tours; competitions with awards; Akeley Memorial lect series; scholarships & fels offered; individual paintings & original objects of art lent to Museum members on a monthly basis & to corporations; sales shop sells books, cards, childrens material, crafts, jewelry, original art, prints, reproductions
L **Library,** 101 S Ninth St, 47901. Tel 317-742-1128; FAX 317-742-1120; *Pres* Doug Gutride
Open to members
Library Holdings: Vols 1000; Per subs 15; AV — A-tapes, cassettes, motion pictures, slides, v-tapes; Other — Clipping files, exhibition catalogs, framed reproductions, original art works, pamphlets, photographs, prints, reproductions, sculpture
Special Subjects: American Indian Art, American Western Art, Art Education, Art History, Crafts, Decorative Arts, Etchings & Engravings, Folk Art, Graphic Arts, Latin American Art, Oriental Art, Painting - American, Painting - European, Painting - Japanese, Photography

M **TIPPECANOE COUNTY HISTORICAL MUSEUM,** 909 South St, 47901. Tel 317-742-8411; FAX 317-742-1851; *Exec Dir* Phillip C Kwiatkowski; *Cur Educ* Paula Woods; *Asst Cur Educ* Cindy Bedell; *Exhib Dir* William Dichtl
Open daily 1 - 5 PM, cl Mon. No admis fee. Estab 1925 to collect, preserve, research & interpret the history of Tippecanoe County & the immediate surrounding area. Housed in a Victorian house (1851-52), there are exhibits of various phases of county history in nine rooms. Average Annual Attendance: 20, 000. Mem: 1000; dues $10 - $500; annual meeting in Jan
Income: Financed by endowment, mem, county & state appropriation, sales & programs
Collections: Broad range, incorporating any object relative to county history
Exhibitions: Changing exhibits; fixed exhibits include Pioneer Development, Woodland Indians, The Building Years 1840-1900, miniature rooms, paintings & porcelains
Publications: Tippecanoe Tales, occasional series on various phases of Tippecanoe County history; Weatenotes, 11 times a year; Books on various historical topics, every 2 yrs
Activities: Classes for adults & children; docent training; lect open to public; tours; individual paintings & original objects of art lent to other museums; sales shop selling books, reproductions, original crafts on consignment
L **Alameda McCollough Library,** 1001 South St, 47901. Tel 317-742-8411; *Librn* Nancy Weirich; *Archivist* Mary Anthrop
Open to serious researchers for reference only
Library Holdings: Vols 7000; Per subs 21; Maps; Micro — Reels 575; AV — A-tapes; Other — Clipping files, manuscripts, pamphlets, photographs

MADISON

M **JEFFERSON COUNTY HISTORICAL SOCIETY MUSEUM,** 615 W First St, 47250. Tel 812-265-2335; *Pres* John Wurtz
Open Fri, Sat & Sun 1 - 4 PM. Estab 1900 to preserve & display art & artifacts worthy of note & pertinent to local area history & culture. Mus is on the grounds of the Madison Jefferson County Pub Library & was the carriage house for the owners of the original mansion which later became the library. Average Annual Attendance: 1500. Mem: 45; dues patron $10, family $5, single $2; monthly meetings fourth Thurs
Collections: William McKendree Snyder Collection, paintings, portraits; Jefferson County artifacts-textiles, primitives; 1895 Madison Railroad Station
Activities: Lect open to public, 6 vis lectr per year; paintings & art objects are lent to organization sponsored events

MUNCIE

BALL STATE UNIVERSITY
M **Museum of Art,** Corner of Warwick & Riverside, 47306. Tel 317-285-5242; FAX 317-285-5275; *Dir* Alain Joyaux; *Office Mgr & Asst to Dir* Lisa Carmichael; *Asst Dir & Cur Educ* Nancy Huth; *Exhib Design & Preparator* Terrence McIntee
Open Tues - Fri 9 AM - 4:30 PM, Sat & Sun 1:30 - 4:30 PM, cl legal holidays. No admis fee. Estab 1936 as an university & community art mus. Four galleries, sculpture court & mezzanine. Average Annual Attendance: 29,000
Income: Financed by university, community & federal government
Collections: Ball-Kraft Collection of Roman & Syrian glass; Italian Renaissance art & furniture; 18th, 19th & 20th century European & American paintings, prints & drawings
Exhibitions: Annual Art Student Exhibit; Art That Works: Decorative Arts of the 80's Crafted in America; Biennial Art Faculty Exhibit; Contemporaries Servies; Gods, Saints, Hero & Villians; WPA exhibitions
Publications: Biennial report; exhibition catalogs
Activities: Art for lunch talks; children's activity sheets; docent training; lect open to public, 2-5 vis lectr per year; gallery talks; tours; book traveling exhibitions 6-7 per year; originate traveling exhibitions; museum shop sells posters, postcards & catalogues
L **Architecture Library,** College of Architecture & Planning, McKinley at Neely, 47306-0160. Tel 317-285-5857, 285-5858; Elec Mail oowhmeyer@bsuvc.bsu.edu. *Librn* Wayne Meyer
Open Mon - Thurs 8 AM - 10 PM, Fri 8 AM - 5 PM, Sat 9 AM - 5 PM, Sun 1 - 10 PM; hours vary during academic vacations, interims & summer sessions. Estab 1965 to provide materials necessary to support the academic programs of the College of Architecture & Planning. Average Annual Attendance: 66,000
Income: Financed through University
Library Holdings: Vols 28,000; Per subs 100; Manufacturers' catalogs; Maps & student theses; Micro — Fiche 7050, reels 340; AV — Cassettes, slides 100,000; Other — Clipping files, pamphlets
Special Subjects: Architecture, Decorative Arts, Drafting, Drawings, Furniture, Graphic Design, Industrial Design, Interior Design, Landscape Architecture, Restoration & Conservation, Landscape architecture

NASHVILLE

A **BROWN COUNTY ART GALLERY ASSOCIATION INC,** Brown County Art Gallery & Museum, One Artist Dr, PO Box 443, 47448. Tel 812-988-4609; *Pres* Dr Emanuel Klein; *First VPres* Richard Hess; *Second VPres* Kaye McLeod; *Exec Secy & Mgr* John Henry
Open 10 AM - 5 PM, Fri, Sat & Sun in Jan & Feb only. No admis fee. Estab 1926 to unite artists and laymen in fellowship; to create a greater incentive for development of art and its presentation to the public; to estab an art gallery for exhibition of work of members of the Association. Average Annual Attendance: 35,000. Mem: 40 artists; 500 supporting members; dues life $500, individual $10, annual meeting in Oct
Income: Financed by mem, foundation and trust
Collections: 81 paintings & pastels by the late Glen Cooper Henshaw; over 200 paintings by early Brown County Artists
Exhibitions: Three exhibits each year by the artist members
Publications: Annual catalog
Activities: Competitions with awards

M **T C STEELE STATE HISTORIC SITE,** 4220 S TC Steele Rd, PO Box 256, 47448. Tel 812-988-2785; FAX 812-988-8457; *Cur* Andrea Smith
Open Tues - Sat 9 AM - 5 PM, Sun 1 - 5 PM, cl Mon, holidays & mid Dec - mid Mar. No admis fee, donations requested. Estab 1945 to protect, collect & interpret the art & lifestyle of T C & Selma Steele. 1200 sq ft, with 80 T C Steele paintings on display at any one time. Average Annual Attendance: 17,000
Income: Financed by state appropriation
Collections: 347 paintings, historic furnishing, decorative arts photos, books. No purchases, all part of willed estate
Activities: Lect open to public; concerts; gallery talks; tours; four annual special events; individual paintings & original objects of art lent to other museums & universities; lending collection contains original art works & paintings; framed reproductions; originate traveling exhibitions to other museums & historic sites; museum shop sells books & prints

NEW ALBANY

M **FLOYD COUNTY MUSEUM,** 201 E Spring St, 47150. Tel 812-944-7336; FAX 812-944-9238; *Pres* Kerry Stemler; *Art Dir* Julie Schweitzer; *Coordr* Sally Newkirk
Open Tues - Sat 10 AM - 4 PM. No admis fee. Estab 1971, to exhibit regional professional artists work on a monthly basis & to promote the arts & history of our community. Two galleries are maintained, approx dimensions: 18 x 25 ft & 15 x 25 ft. Average Annual Attendance: 7000. Mem: 400; dues $10-$500; annual meeting in Dec
Income: Financed by county appropriation, mem & fundraising
Collections: Permanent collection of †historical items
Exhibitions: Floyd County in World War I; 1920s to Depression Years; A History Sampler; Annual July Juried Art Exhibit; Hand Carved, Animated Folk Art Diorama on permanent display
Publications: Bulletins
Activities: Classes for adults & children; lect open to public; concerts; tours; competitions with awards; book traveling exhibitions annually

NEW HARMONY

M **NEW HARMONY GALLERY OF CONTEMPORARY ART,** 506 Main St, 47631. Tel 812-682-3156; FAX 812-682-4313; *Acting Dir* Scott Knauer; *Exhibits Preparator* Michelle Peterlin
Open Tues - Sat 9 AM - 5 PM (Sun by appointment only), cl Mon. No admis fee. Estab 1975 for exhibition of contemporary midwest art & artists. Average Annual Attendance: 25,000
Income: Financed by contributions & grants
Exhibitions: Monthly changing exhibitions
Activities: Lect open to the public, 4 vis lectr per year; gallery talks; tours; awards; book traveling exhibitions; originate traveling exhibitions; sales shop sells magazines & original art

NOTRE DAME

M **SAINT MARY'S COLLEGE,** Moreau Galleries, 46556. Tel 219-284-4655; FAX 219-284-4716; *Gallery Dir* K Johnson Bowles
Open Tues - Fri 10 AM - Noon & 1 - 4 PM, Sun 1 - 3 PM, Sat 10 AM - Noon. Estab 1956 for educ, community-related exhibits & contemporary art. Gallery presently occupies two spaces; all exhibits rotate. Average Annual Attendance: 6000
Collections: Cotter Collection; Dunbarton Collection of prints; Norman LaLiberte; various media
Publications: Catalogs, occasionally
Activities: Lect open to public; tours; concerts; gallery talks; competitions with awards; individual paintings & original objects of art lent; originate traveling exhibitions

UNIVERSITY OF NOTRE DAME
M **Snite Museum of Art,** 46556. Tel 219-631-5466; *Dir* Dean A Porter; *Cur* Stephen B Spiro; *Cur* Douglas Bradley; *Cur* Stephen Muriarty; *Cur* James Flanagan; *Educ Coordr* Gina Zachman; *Coordr Community Prog* Diana Matthias; *Registrar* Robert Smogor; *Head Preparator* Greg Denby; *Exec Secy* Anne Mills; *Auditorium Mgr & Book Store Mgr* Iris Mensing; *Exhib Designer* John Phegley; *Secy* Sue Fitzpatrick
Open Tues - Sat 10 AM - 4 PM, Thurs 4 - 8 PM, Sun 1 - 4 PM (when classes are in session). No admis fee. Estab 1842; Wightman Memorial Art Gallery estab 1917; O'Shaughnessy Art Gallery estab 1952; Snite Museum estab 1980 to educate through the visual arts; during a four year period it is the objective to expose students to all areas of art including geographic, period & media, open 1980. Galleries consist of 35,000 sq ft. Average Annual Attendance: 95,000.

Mem: 650; dues from $15 - $5000; annual meeting in May
Income: $600,000 (financed by endowment, university appropriation & gifts)
Purchases: $600,000
Collections: †African art; American Indian & pre-Columbian art; Baroque paintings, northern & Italian; 18th & 19th century American, English, 17th, 18th & 19th Century French paintings & Master drawings; Kress Study Collection 19th century French oils; Reilly Collection of Old Master Drawings through 19th century; Sanderson Collection of Rembrandt Collections
Exhibitions: Annual Faculty Exhibition; Annual Student Exhibition
Publications: Exhibition catalogs, 3-5 times per yr; Calendar of Events, semi-annually
Activities: Docent training; lect open to public, 4-6 vis lectr per year; concerts; gallery talks; tours; individual paintings & original objects of art lent to qualified institutions; book traveling exhibitions 2-3 per year; originate traveling exhibitions; museum shop sells books, posters, post cards, sweat shirts, tote bags & T-shirts
L **Snite Museum Library,** 46556. Tel 219-631-5466; FAX 219-239-8501
Open Tues - Sat 10 AM - 4 PM, Sun 1 - 4 PM. No admis fee. Estab 1980. Open to students and faculty for reference only
Library Holdings: Vols 10,000; Per subs 20; Other — Exhibition catalogs
L **Architecture Library,** 46556. Tel 219-631-6654; *Librn* Sheila Curl; *Library Assoc* Debra Webb
Open Mon - Thurs 8 AM - 10 PM, Fri 8 AM - 5 PM, Sat 9 AM - 5 PM, Sun 1 - 10 PM, vacations Mon - Fri 8 AM - 5 PM. Estab 1890 as a branch of the university library. Circ 10,000
Income: $70,000 (financed by university)
Purchases: $25,000
Library Holdings: Vols 15,500; Per subs 107; Micro — Fiche, reels; AV — Fs; Other — Clipping files, pamphlets, reproductions
Special Subjects: Architecture, History of Art & Archaeology, Landscape Architecture, Restoration & Conservation, art, engineering, planning environment
Collections: Rare folio books on architecture
Exhibitions: Models of Student Work; Student Thesis Projects; visiting exhibits
Publications: Architecture Library New Books List, monthly
Activities: Lect open to public, 8 vis lectr per year; tours; awards; scholarships; exten dept serves Rome

PORTLAND

M **JAY COUNTY ARTS COUNCIL,** Hugh N Ronald Memorial Gallery, 138 E Main, PO Box 804, 47371-0804. Tel 219-726-4809; FAX 219-726-4791; *Exec Dir* Eric Rogers; *Dir Visual Arts* William Adkins; *Staff Performing Artist* Kathleen Byrd; *Dir Admin* Carol Stephenson; *Dir Develop & Center Operations* Dan Snyder
No admis fee. Estab 1967. Local, regional, national & international contemporary art in a wide range of media
Exhibitions: Contemporary regional art
Activities: Classes for adults & children; dramatic programs; scholarships offered; originate traveling exhibitions 4-8 per year

RICHMOND

A **ART ASSOCIATION OF RICHMOND,** Richmond Art Museum, 350 Hub Etchison Pky, 47374. Tel 317-966-0256, 973-3369; *Dir* Ruth B Mills-Varnell
Open Sept - Dec & Feb - May Mon - Fri 9 AM - 4 PM, Sun 1 - 4 PM, cl Sat & school holidays. No admis fee. Estab 1898 to promote creative ability, art appreciation & art in pub schools. Maintains an art gallery with four exhibit rooms: two rooms for permanent collection & two rooms for current exhibits. Average Annual Attendance: 10,000. Mem: 600; dues students $5-$1000
Income: Financed by mem
Collections: Regional & state art; American, European, Oriental art
Exhibitions: Amateur Area Artists Exhibition; Annual Area Professional Artists Exhibition; Annual Photographic Exhibition; Crafts Exhibition; Hands-On Exhibition for grade school children High School Art Exhibition
Publications: Art in Richmon - 1898-1978; quarterly newsletter
Activities: Lect open to public, 6 vis lectr per year; gallery talks; tours; competitions with merit & purchase awards; scholarships offered; individual paintings & original objects of art lent to corporations that annually support the museum or to other galleries for exhibition; lending collection contains books, original art works, original prints & photographs; originate traveling exhibitions
L **Library,** 350 Hub Etchison Pky, 47374. Tel 317-966-0256; *Dir* Ruth B Mills-Varnell
Open to members
Library Holdings: Vols 200; Per subs 3
Special Subjects: Art History, Ceramics, Decorative Arts, Graphic Arts, Landscapes, Painting - American, Painting - British, Painting - Dutch, Painting - European, Painting - Flemish, Photography, Pottery, Printmaking, Reproductions, Sculpture, Art museums, art techniques

M **EARLHAM COLLEGE,** Leeds Gallery, National Rd W, 47374-4095. Tel 317-983-1410; FAX 317-983-1304; *Pres College* Gene Mills; *Art Dept Convener* Richard Rodgers; *Dir Permanent Coll* Beth Lykins
Open daily 8 AM - Noon. No admis fee. Estab 1847 as a liberal arts college; Leeds Gallery estab 1970
Collections: Regional artist: George Baker, Bundy (John Ellwood), Marcus Mote; prints by internationally known artists of 19th & 20th centuries; regional artists; rotating collections from all areas
Activities: Dramatic programs; lect open to public, 5-6 vis lectr per year; concerts; individual paintings & original objects of art lent; traveling exhibitions organized & circulated; sales shop sells books

ROCHESTER

M **FULTON COUNTY HISTORICAL SOCIETY INC,** Fulton County Museum, 37 E 375 N, 46975-8384. Tel 219-223-4436; *Pres* Shirley Willard; *Treas* Wilma Thomas; *Admin Asst* Melinda Clinger
Open 9 AM - 5 PM. No admis fee. Estab 1963 to preserve Fulton County & Northern Indiana history. 64 X 144 ft; new exhibit quarterly. Average Annual Attendance: 20,000. Mem: 700; dues $15; annual meeting third Mon in Nov
Income: $72,000 (financed by mem, sales & festivals, grants & donations)
Collections: Antiques; Elmo Lincoln, first Tarzan; old farm equipment; old household furniture; Woodland Indians
Exhibitions: Traditional & Indian Crafts; Round Barn Festival; Trail of Courage; Redbud Trail. (1997) Hoosier Her Heritage Art Exhibit & Sale
Publications: Fulton County Images, annual
Activities: Classes for adults & children; dramatic programs; docent programs; Indian dances; living history festivals, 10,000 vis lectr per year; lect open to public; competitions with prizes; retail store sells books, prints, magazines, original art & reproductions

SOUTH BEND

A **SOUTH BEND REGIONAL MUSEUM OF ART,** 120 S Saint Joseph St, 46601. Tel 219-235-9102; FAX 219-235-5782; *Exec Dir* Susan R Visser; *Cur* Leisa Rundquist
Warner & Art League Permanent & Community Gallery open Tues - Fri 11 AM - 5 PM, Sat & Sun Noon - 5 PM. No admis fee, $3 donation recommended. Estab in 1947 for museum exhibitions, lectures, film series, workshops, and studio classes. The Art Center is located in a three-story building designed by Philip Johnson. There are four galleries: the Warner Gallery features traveling shows or larger exhibits organized by the Art Center & the Art League Gallery features one or two-person shows by local or regional artists; also a community & permanent gallery. Average Annual Attendance: 40,000. Mem: 1000; dues sustaining $100, family $45, active $30, student & senior citizens $25
Income: Financed by mem, corporate support, city & state appropriations
Collections: European and American paintings, drawings, prints and objects; †20th century American art with emphasis on regional and local works
Publications: Checklists; exhibition catalogues; quarterly newsletter
Activities: Studio classes for adults & children; docent training & tours; outreach educational program conducted by Art League; workshops; lect open to public, 3 vis lectr per year; gallery talks; artist studio tours; competitions with prizes; film series; paintings and original works of art lent to accredited museums; lending collection contains prints, paintings, phono records and sculpture; museum shop sells gift items and original works of art
L **Library,** 120 S Saint Joseph St, 46601. Tel 219-235-9102; *Exec Dir* Susan R Visser
Estab 1947 to provide art resource material to members of the Art Center
Library Holdings: Vols 963; Per subs 49; AV — Motion pictures, rec; Other — Exhibition catalogs

TERRE HAUTE

M **INDIANA STATE UNIVERSITY,** Turman Art Gallery, Fine Arts Bldg, 47809. Tel 812-237-3697; *Chmn Art Dept* Wayne Enstice; *Dir* Craig Zollars
Open Tues - Fri Noon - 4:30 PM, Sun 1 - 5 PM, cl last two wks in Aug. No admis fee
Collections: Paintings & sculpture
Exhibitions: Changing exhibitions of national & regional contemporary art during school terms; periodic student & faculty exhibitions
Activities: Lect

M **SHELDON SWOPE ART MUSEUM,** 25 S Seventh St, 47807-3692. Tel 812-238-1676; FAX 812-238-1677; *Dir* David Butler; *Cur Educ* Graeme Reid; *Bus Mgr* Katie Wood; *Registrar* Elizabeth Petrulis
Open year round Tues - Fri 10 AM - 5 PM, Sat - Sun Noon - 5 PM. No admis fee. Estab 1942 to present free of charge American art of the 19th & 20th centuries. Average Annual Attendance: 15,000. Mem: 750; dues individual $30; annual meeting third Wed in Sept
Income: $130,000 (financed by mem & trust fund)
Collections: American art of 19th & 20th centuries
Publications: Membership newsletter; catalogs to special exhibitions
Activities: Docent training; lect open to public, 10 vis lectr per year; concerts; gallery talks; tours; competitions with awards; individual paintings & original objects of art lent to other museums; originate traveling exhibitions; museum shop sells books, original art, reproductions, note cards, gift items & prints
L **Research Library,** 25 S Seventh St, 47807-3692. Tel 812-238-1676; FAX 812-238-1677; *Dir* David Butler
Open Tues - Fri 10 AM - 5 PM, Sat & Sun Noon - 5 PM. Open to pub
Library Holdings: Vols 1500
Collections: American 19th & 20th centuries

UPLAND

M **TAYLOR UNIVERSITY,** Chronicle-Tribune Art Gallery, Art Dept, 500 W Reade Ave, 46989. Tel 317-998-2751, Ext 5322; FAX 317-998-4910; Elec Mail inkautman@tayloru.edu. *Chmn* Lon Kaufmann
Open Mon - Sat 8 AM - 5 PM, cl Sun. No admis fee. Estab 1972 as an educational gallery
Income: Financed by educational funding
Exhibitions: Four Visiting Artists Exhibits
Activities: Scholarships offered; originate traveling exhibitions

VALPARAISO

M VALPARAISO UNIVERSITY, Brauer Museum of Art, 46383. Tel 219-464-5365; FAX 219-464-5381; *Dir* Dr Robert L Gambone; *Asst Cur* Juliet Istrabadi; *Registrar* Gloria Ruff; *Exhibits Preparator* Carl Galow
Open Tues - Fri 10 AM - 5 PM, Wed 6:30 - 8:30 PM, Sat & Sun Noon - 5 PM, cl Mon. No admis fee. Estab 1953 to present significant art to the University community & people of northwest Indiana
Income: $14,000 (financed by endowment)
Purchases: $35,000
Collections: †Sloan Collection: 19th & 20th Century American Paintings, Prints & Drawings
Exhibitions: Rotating Exhibits
Activities: Lect open to the public; gallery talks; individual paintings and original objects of art lent to museums and art centers

WEST LAFAYETTE

M PURDUE UNIVERSITY GALLERIES, Creative Arts Bldg 1, 47907-1352. Tel 317-494-3061, 494-9335; FAX 317-496-1198; *Gallery Dir* Mona Berg; *Asst Dir* Michael Atwell
Open Mon - Fri 10 AM - 5 PM & 7 - 9 PM, Sun 1 - 5 PM. No admis fee. Estab 1972 to provide aesthetic & educational programs for art students, the university & greater Lafayette community. Galleries are located in four different buildings to provide approximately 5000 sq ft of space for temporary exhibitions. Average Annual Attendance: 60,000
Income: Financed through the university
Purchases: $1500
Collections: American Indian baskets; †photographs; Contemporary paintings, †prints, sculpture; †ceramics; Pre-Columbian textiles
Exhibitions: 40 per yr including work by faculty, students, regionally & nationally prominent artists
Publications: Exhibit catalogs
Activities: Lect open to public; concerts; gallery talks; competitions with awards; individual paintings & original objects of art lent to university administrative offices; book traveling exhibitions, 1-2 per year; traveling exhibitions organized & circulated

IOWA

AMES

M IOWA STATE UNIVERSITY, Brunnier Art Museum, Scheman Bldg, 50011. Tel 515-294-3342; FAX 515-294-7070; Elec Mail museums@muse.adp.iastate.edu. *Dir* Lynette Pohlman; *Collections Mgr* Mary Atherly; *Educ Coordr* Renee Senter; *Publicity* Stacy Brothers; *Shop Mgr* Pamela Butler
Open Tues, Wed & Fri 11 AM - 4 PM, Thurs 11 AM - 4 PM & 5 - 9 PM, Sat & Sun 1 - 4 PM, cl Mon. No admis fee. Estab 1975, to provide a high level of quality, varied & comprehensive exhibits of national & international scope & to develop & expand a permanent decorative arts collection of the western world. Gallery is maintained & comprised of 10,000 sq ft of exhibit space, with flexible space arrangement. Average Annual Attendance: 50,000
Income: $400,000 (financed through state appropriations & grants)
Collections: Permanent collection of ceramics, dolls, furniture, glass, ivory, wood, sculpture, fine arts
Activities: Classes for children; docent training; lect open to public, 10 - 15 vis lectr per year; book traveling exhibitions, 3-4 per year; traveling exhibitions organized & circulated; museum shop sells books, magazines, catalogs, jewelry, dolls, glass & original works

A OCTAGON CENTER FOR THE ARTS, 427 Douglas, 50010-6213. Tel 515-232-5331; FAX 515-232-5088; *Pres* George C Christensen; *VPres* Ellen Landon; *Exec Dir* Patrice K Beam; *Treas* Robert Parker; *Dir Educ* Kathy Timmer; *Registrar/Cur* Michelle Deal; *Public Relations Dir* Carla J Murphy; *Shop Mgr* Alissa Hansen
Open Mon - Sat 10 AM - 5 PM, Sun 2 - 5 PM. Admis suggested donation or contribution, family (up to five people) $3, individual $2. Estab 1966 to provide year-round classes for all ages; exhibitions of the work of outstanding artists from throughout the world & also special programs in the visual & performing arts. Average Annual Attendance: 33,000. Mem: 485, open to anyone interested in supporting or participating in the arts; dues $15-$500 & up; annual meeting in May
Income: $300,000 (financed by mem, city and state appropriations, class fees and fund raising)
Collections: Feinberg Collection of Masks from Around the World
Exhibitions: (1997) The Octagon's Clay, Fiber, Paper, Glass, Metal & Wood Exhibition; Ames High School Seniors Art Show; Iowa Watercolor Society Exhibition; The Two Bill Zimmermans: Portraits, Landscapes & Wildlife Art; ART in the PARK-art festival of over 125 Midwest artists; Ohio Star Quilts: New Quilts From An Old Favorite; Fifth Annual Community of Artists Exhibition
Publications: Exhibition catalogs; newsletter, bimonthly
Activities: Classes in the arts for adults & children; special classes for senior citizens & physically & emotionally challenged; outreach programs; lect open to public, 5-8 vis lectr per year; gallery talks; tours; competitions with awards; scholarships offered; book traveling exhibitions; museum shop sells books, original art, prints & original fine crafts

ANAMOSA

A PAINT 'N PALETTE CLUB, Grant Wood Memorial Park & Gallery, RR 3, 52205. Tel 319-462-2680; *Pres* Joyce Dusanek; *VPres* Wilbur Evarts
Open June 1 - Oct 15; Sun 1 - 4 PM; other times by appointment. No admis fee (donations accepted). Estab 1955 to maintain Antioch School, the school attended by Grant Wood, a famous Iowa artist; to provide a studio & gallery for local artists & for pub enjoyment. A log cabin art gallery on the grounds of the Grant Wood Memorial Park contains the work of some local & vis artists. Average Annual Attendance: 3000. Mem: 37, members must have art experience; dues $10
Income: $800 (financed by endowment & donations)
Collections: Prints of Grant Wood, Iowa's most famous artist; original amateur art
Exhibitions: Special exhibits throughout the season
Activities: Occasional classes for adults & children; lect open to public, 6-7 vis lectr per year; tours; competitions; films; sales shop sells magazines, original art, prints, reproductions, memorial plates, coins & postcards

BURLINGTON

A ART GUILD OF BURLINGTON, Arts for Living Center, Seventh & Washington St, PO Box 5, 52601. Tel 319-754-8069; FAX 319-754-4731; *Dir* Lois Rigdon; *Pres* Pam Brocker; *VPres* Jim Hilkin
Open Tues - Fri Noon - 5 PM, weekends 1 - 4 PM, cl Mon & all major holidays, with the exception of Thanksgiving. No admis fee. Estab 1966, the Art Guild purchased the Center (a church building built 1868) in 1974, which has now been placed on the National Register of Historic Places. Average Annual Attendance: 8000. Mem: 425; dues benefactor $1000, down to student $5
Income: Financed by mem & donations
Exhibitions: Exhibitions of regional professional artists
Publications: Monthly newsletter
Activities: Classes for adults & children; films; special workshops; lect open to public, 6 vis lectr per year; concerts; gallery talks; tours; scholarships & fels offered; book traveling exhibitions 2-3 per year; traveling exhibitions organized & circulated; sales shop sells books, original art, reproductions, prints

CEDAR FALLS

M CITY OF CEDAR FALLS, IOWA, James & Meryl Hearst Center for the Arts, 304 W Seerley Blvd, 50613. Tel 319-273-8641; FAX 319-273-8659; *Dir* Mary Huber
Open Tues - Fri 10 AM - 5 PM, Tues & Thurs evenings 5 - 9 PM, Sat & Sun 1 - 4 PM. No admis fee. Estab 1988
Income: $290,000 (financed by city appropriation, individual contributions, program fees & grants)
Exhibitions: Annual competition exhibition; 28 exhibitions per year
Activities: Classes for adults & children; dramatic programs; docent training; lect open to public, 3 - 5 vis lectr per year

M UNIVERSITY OF NORTHERN IOWA, Gallery of Art, 50614-0362. Tel 319-273-2077; FAX 319-273-2731; *Dir* Blair Benz
Open Mon - Thurs 9 AM - 9 PM, Fri 9 AM - 5 PM, Sat & Sun Noon - 5 PM. No admis fee. Estab 1978 to bring to the University & the community at large the finest quality of art from all over the world. The 4700 sq ft gallery is divided into five separate exhibition rooms; high security mus space with climate control & a highly flexible light system; the Gallery adjoins a pub reception space & a 144 seat auditorium; the facility also has two permanent collections' storage areas, a work shop, a general storage room & a fully accessible loading dock. Average Annual Attendance: 11,000
Income: Financed by state appropriation
Purchases: 20th century art work
Collections: †20th century American & European Art
Publications: Exhibition catalogs
Activities: Docent training; lect open to public, 5 vis lectr per year; concerts; gallery talks; tours; competitions; individual paintings & original objects of art lent; book traveling exhibitions 2-8 per year; originate traveling exhibitions; sales shop sells catalogs, postcards, posters

L Art & Music Section Rod Library, 50613-3675. Tel 319-273-6252; FAX 319-273-2913; *Dir* Herbert D Safford; *Asst Dir* Robert Rose; *Librn* Dr Alberto Hernandez
Open Mon - Thurs 7:30 AM - midnight, Fri 7:30 AM - 9 PM, Sat 10 AM - 6 PM, Sun 9 AM - midnight. Main Library estab 1964, additions 1975 & 1995; to serve art & music patrons. For lending & reference. Circ 18,872
Income: Financed by state
Purchases: $38,099
Library Holdings: Vols 50,245; Per subs 141; Compact discs 766; Micro — Fiche, prints; AV — A-tapes, cassettes 830, rec 10,028, slides 6012; Other — Clipping files, exhibition catalogs, original art works, pamphlets, prints, reproductions 692

CEDAR RAPIDS

M CEDAR RAPIDS MUSEUM OF ART, 410 Third Ave SE, 52401. Tel 319-366-7503; FAX 319-366-4111; *Dir* Dr Donald Doe; *Cur* Leslie Wright
Open Tues - Sat 10 AM - 4 PM, Thurs 10 AM - 7 PM, Sun Noon - 3 PM. Estab art assoc 1905, art center 1966. First & second floors maintain changing exhibits & the third floor maintains the Permanent Collection. Mem: 1000; dues family $35, individual $25, students & senior citizens $15
Income: Financed by endowment, mem, city & state appropriations
Collections: Largest concentrated collection of Grant Wood, Marvin Cone and Mauricio Lasansky art in existencne; print collection
Exhibitions: (1997) A Time of Malfeasance; Lynn Geesaman, Belgium & France; Richard D Pinney: Retrospective; Painting Abstract: Gregory Amenoff, John L Moore, Katherine Porter; Drawing Power; Anita Lappi; Jazz Images by David

Spitzer; Paintings by Charlie Emmert; Great Plains; Of Nature & Knowledge: Art by 7 Fairfield Artists; New Work by Robert L Kocher; Sara Bell; Photographs by Bob Campagna. (1997-98) St Louis City Show. Rotating exhibitions
Publications: Newsletter, bi-monthly
Activities: Classes for adults & children; docent training; lect open to public, 2-3 vis lectr per year; gallery talks; tours; book traveling exhibitions 15-25 per year; originate traveling exhibitions; museum shop sells books, original art, reproductions, prints & craft items including pottery, weaving, jewelry

L Herbert S Stamats Library, 410 Third Ave SE, 52401. Tel 319-366-7503; FAX 319-366-4111; *Dir* Dr Donald Doe
Open Tues - Sat 10 AM - 4 PM, Thurs 10 AM - 7 PM, Sun Noon - 3 PM. For reference
Library Holdings: Vols 3000; AV — Cassettes, fs
Special Subjects: Archival materials on American Regionalism, Grant Wood, James Swann, Chicago Society of Etchers, Prairie Printmakers, Mauricio Lasansky, Bertha Jaques, Malvina Hoffman, Marvin Cone

M COE COLLEGE, Gordon Fennell Gallery & Marvin Cone Gallery, 1220 First Ave NE, 52402. Tel 319-399-8559; *Chmn Art Dept* John Beckelman; *Gallery Dir* Shirley A Donaldson
Open daily 3 - 5 PM. No admis fee. Estab 1942 to exhibit traveling exhibitions & local exhibits. Two galleries, both 60 x 18 ft with 125 running ft of exhibit space & 200 works on permanent exhibition. Average Annual Attendance: 5000
Income: $6555 (financed through college)
Collections: Coe Collection of art works; Marvin Cone Alumni Collection; Marvin Cone Collection; Conger Metcalf Collection of paintings; Hinkhouse Collection of contemporary art; Grant Wood Collection
Exhibitions: Circulating exhibits; one-person & group shows of regional nature
Publications: Exhibition brochures, 8-10 per year
Activities: Lect open to public, 5-6 vis lectr per year; gallery talks; tours; competitions; individual paintings & original objects of art lent to colleges & local galleries; lending collection contains original art work, original prints, paintings, sculpture & slides; traveling exhibitions organized & circulated

M Stewart Memorial Library & Gallery, 1220 First Ave NE, 52402-5092. Tel 319-399-8023; FAX 319-399-8019; *Dir Library Services & Academic Computing* Richard Doyle
Open Mon - Thurs 8 - Noon, Fri 8 AM - 10 PM, Sun 1 PM - 12 AM; June - Aug Mon - Fri 8 AM - 4 PM
Collections: 200 permanent collection works

M MOUNT MERCY COLLEGE, McAuley Gallery, 1330 Elmhurst Dr NE, 52402. Tel 319-363-8213; FAX 319-363-5270; *Dir* David Van Allen
Open Mon - Thurs 7 AM - 9 PM. No admis fee. Estab 1970 to show work by a variety of fine artists. The shows are used by the art department as teaching aids. They provide cultural exposure to the entire community. One room 22 x 30 ft; two walls are glass overlooking a small courtyard. Average Annual Attendance: 1000
Income: Financed through the college
Purchases: $300
Collections: †Small collection of prints & paintings
Exhibitions: Annual High School Art Exhibit; Senior Thesis Exhibit
Publications: Reviews in Fiber Arts; American Craft & Ceramics Monthly
Activities: Classes for adults; dramatic programs; lect open to public; gallery talks; competitions with awards; scholarships

L Library, Art Dept, 1330 Elmhurst Dr NE, 52402-4797. Tel 319-363-8213, Ext 244; FAX 319-363-9060; *Librn* Marilyn Murphy
Library Holdings: Vols 1000; Per subs 30; Micro — Cards, fiche, prints, reels; AV — A-tapes, cassettes, fs, Kodachromes, lantern slides, motion pictures, rec, slides, v-tapes; Other — Exhibition catalogs, framed reproductions, original art works, pamphlets, photographs, prints, reproductions, sculpture

CLINTON

M CLINTON ART ASSOCIATION GALLERY, 708 25th Ave N, PO Box 132, 52733. Tel 319-243-3300, 242-8055; *Dir* Hortense Blake
Open Sat & Sun 1 - 5 PM, cl Christmas & New Year. No admis fee. Estab 1968 to bring visual art to the community. Small gallery is housed in an abandoned building of an army hospital complex and is loaned to the association by the Clinton Park and Recreation Board. A separate Pottery School has been maintained since 1975. Average Annual Attendance: 15,000. Mem: 400; dues single membership $10; annual meeting first Tues in May
Income: Financed by mem & through grants from the Iowa Arts Council
Collections: Painting (watercolor, oil, acrylic, pastel); beaded loin cloth; photographs; lithograph; engraving; sculptures; etching; prints; pottery; fabric; pencil; wood; slate; Ektaflex Color Printmaking System; glass; ink; lucite; rugs; woodcarving
Exhibitions: Change from month to month
Publications: Newsletter every two months
Activities: Classes for adults & children in watercolor, oil, rosemaling, macrame, photography & pottery making; docent training; lect open to public; gallery talks; tours; individual paintings lent by members to businesses; lending collection contains books, lantern slides and slides; sales shop sells original art & prints

DAVENPORT

M DAVENPORT MUSEUM OF ART, 1737 W 12th St, 52804. Tel 319-326-7804; FAX 319-326-7876; *Dir* Wm Steven Bradley; *Dir Develop* Carol Ehlers; *Cur Coll & Exhib* Brady Roberts; *Cur Educ* Ann Marie Hayes; *Librn* Sheryl Haut; *Supt* E J Johnson; *Curatorial Registrar* Patrick Sweeney; *Asst Cur Coll* Jane Milsoch; *Asst Cur Educ* Linda Lewis
Open Tues - Sat 10 AM - 4:30 PM, Sun 1 - 4:30 PM, cl Mon & holidays. Admis charged for some main gallery exhibitions. Estab 1925 as a mus of art & custodian pub collection & an educ center for the visual arts. Consists of three levels including a spacious main gallery, exhibition area & two additional floors with galleries; six multipurpose art studios, printmaking & ceramic gallery, studio workshop & an outdoor studio-plaza on the lower level. Average Annual

Attendance: 100,000. Mem: 1009; dues household $50, individual $30, senior citizens $20, student $15; annual meeting in June
Income: $900,000 (financed by private & city appropriation)
Collections: 19th & 20th Century American; Regionalism including Grant Wood, Thomas Hart Benton, John Steuart Curry; European; Mexican- Colonial; Haitian; Oriental
Exhibitions: Beverly Pepper: The Moline Makers; Byron Burford; Mississippi Corridor; Grandma Moses; Selections: The Union League of Chicago Collection; Thomas Eakins (photographs); Joseph Sheppard; Mauricio Lasansky; Sol LeWitt; Stephen Antonakos - Neons; Frederic Carder: Portrait of a Glassmaker; Paul Brach Retrospective; David Hockney (photographs); Rudie (holograms); McMichael Canadian Collection; Kassebaum Medieval & Renaissance Ceramics; Collected Masterworks; The International Collections of the Davenport Museum of Art; Mexico Nueve; A Differnt War: Vietnam In Art; Judaica: Paintings by Nathan Hilu & Ceramics by Robert Lipnick; Faith Ringgold: 25 Year Survey
Publications: Quarterly newsletter; biennial report; Focus 1: Michael Boyd - Paintings from the 1980s; Focus 2: Photo Image League - Individual Vision/ Collective Support; Focus 3: A Sense of Wonder - The Art of Haiti; Focus 4: Artists Who Teach: Building our Future; Haitian Art: The Legend & Legacy of the Naive Tradition; Three Decades of Midwestern Photography, 1960 - 1990
Activities: Classes for adults & children; docent training; lect open to public; concerts; gallery talks; tours; competitions with prizes; scholarships & fels offered; book traveling exhibitions organized & circulated; originate traveling exhibitions; museum shop sells books & original art; Arterarium environmental installation

L Art Reference Library, 1737 W 12th St, 52804. Tel 319-326-7804; FAX 319-326-7876; *Librn* Sheryl Haut
Open for reference
Library Holdings: Vols 6000; Per subs 20; AV — V-tapes
Special Subjects: General visual arts

M PUTNAM MUSEUM OF HISTORY & NATURAL SCIENCE, 1717 W 12th St, 52804. Tel 319-324-1933; FAX 319-324-6638; *Dir* Christopher J Reich; *Asst Dir Mus Servs* Janice Hall; *Asst Dir Educ* Karen Larson; *Exhibits Mgr* Michael Murphy
Open Tues - Fri 9 AM - 5 PM, Sat 10 AM - 5 PM, Sun Noon - 5 PM, cl Mon & national holdiays. Admis adults $4, senior citizens $3, ages 5-17 $1.50, members & children 4 & under free. Estab 1867 as Davenport Academy of Natural Sciences. To provide educational & enriching experiences through interpretive exhibits & mus programming. Average Annual Attendance: 78,000. Mem: 2091; dues contributing $75, family $35, individual $25, senior citizen $22
Income: $2,200,000 (financed by contributions, grants, endowments, mem & earned income)
Collections: Natural history; American Indian, pre-Columbian; anthropology; arts of Asia, Near & Middle East, Africa, Oceanic; botany; ethnology; paleontology; decorative arts; local history
Exhibitions: Permanent & changing exhibition programs
Activities: Formally organized educ programs for children & adults; films; lect; gallery talks; guided tours; theatre presentations; individual paintings & original objects of art lent to museums & educational organizations for special exhibitions only; book traveling exhibitions 4 per year; originate traveling exhibitions aimed at other musems only; musem shop sells books, original art, prints, miscellaneous collections-related merchandise for children & adults

L Library, 1717 W 12th St, 52804. Tel 319-324-1933; FAX 319-324-6638;
Available for use by special request; for reference only
Library Holdings: Vols 25,000; AV — Lantern slides, motion pictures, rec; Other — Original art works, photographs, prints

DECORAH

M LUTHER COLLEGE, Fine Arts Collection, 700 College Dr, 52101-1042. Tel 319-387-1195; FAX 319-387-1657; Elec Mail kempjane@luther.edu. *Supv* Jane Kemp; *Gallery Coordr* David Kamm
Open Sept - June 8 AM - 5 PM. Estab 1900. Five galleries on campus. Average Annual Attendance: 10,000
Income: $4000
Collections: Gerhard Marcks Collection (drawings, prints & sculpture); Marguerite Wildenhain Collection (drawings & pottery); contemporary & historic prints; Inuit sculpture; pre-Columbian poetry; Scandinavian immigrant painting
Publications: Occasional catalogs & brochures
Activities: Lect open to public; lending collection contains individual paintings & original objects of art; book traveling exhibitions 12 per year

M VESTERHEIM NORWEGIAN-AMERICAN MUSEUM, 502 W Water St, 52101. Tel 319-382-9682; FAX 319-382-8828; *Dir* Darrell D Henning; *Registrar* Carol Hasvold; *Textiles Cur & Conservator* Laurann Figg; *Asst Cur & Site Mgr* Steven Johnson
Open May - Oct 9 AM - 5 PM daily, Nov - Apr 10 AM - 4 PM, cl Thanksgiving, Christmas, Easter & New Year's. Admis adults $4, children (7-18) $2, (summer); adults $3, children $1.50 (winter) special rates for sr citizens & groups. Estab 1877 for the collection, preservation & exhibition of artifacts relating to the life of people in the United States of Norwegian birth & descent, in their home environment in Norway & in their settlements in America. Numerous historic buildings, including two from Norway, make up the complex of Vesterheim. Average Annual Attendance: 30,000. Mem: 8000; dues basic mem $15; annual meeting in Oct
Income: $400,000 (financed by endowment, mem, donations, admis, sales)
Collections: Through 21,000 objects including Norwegian & Norwegian-American house furnishings, costumes, tools & implements, church furniture, toys & the like, the Museum tells the story of the Norwegian immigrant
Exhibitions: Annual competitive exhibitions in Norwegian rosemaling, weaving & woodcarving; American rug hooking
Publications: Newsletter, quarterly; Norrona Sketchbook; Norwegian Tracks, quarterly; Time Honored Norwegian Recipes; Rosemaling Letter, quarterly; Vesterheim: Samplings from the Collection; Rosemaler's Recipes Cookbook; Woodworker's Newsletter, quarterly
Activities: Classes for adults; docent training; lect open to public, 4 vis lectr per

year; gallery talks; tours; book traveling exhibitions; originate traveling exhibitions for museums, special events; museum shop sells art & craft supplies, books, original art, prints, related gift items, woodenware, artist supplies for rosemaling & woodworking

L **Reference Library,** 502 W Water St, 52101. Tel 319-382-9681; FAX 319-382-8828; *Dir* Darrell D Henning; *Textiles Cur & Conserv* Lauran Gilbertson; *Asst Cur & Site Mgr* Steven Johnson
Reference library open to the public
Library Holdings: Vols 10,000; Per subs 75; AV — Fs; Other — Clipping files, memorabilia, photographs
Special Subjects: Anthropology, Architecture, Calligraphy, Carpets & Rugs, Ceramics, Coins & Medals, Costume Design & Construction, Crafts, Decorative Arts, Dioramas, Dolls, Drawings, Embroidery, Etchings & Engravings, Ethnology, Norwegian history, culture, crafts, genealogy

DES MOINES

M **EDMUNDSON ART FOUNDATION, INC,** Des Moines Art Center, 4700 Grand Ave, 50312-2099. Tel 515-277-4405; FAX 515-279-3834; *Dir* I Michael Danoff; *Pres Board Trustees* Robert Helmick
Open Tues, Wed, Fri & Sat 11 AM - 4 PM, Thurs 11 AM - 9 PM, Sun Noon - 4 PM, cl Mon. Admis $4, students & senior citizens $2, Thurs free, members, children 12 & under & scheduled docent tours free. Estab 1948 for the purpose of displaying, conserving & interpreting art. Large sculpture galleries in I M Pei-designed addition; the main gallery covers 36 x 117 ft area. New Meier wing, opened 1985, increased space for exhibitions 50 percent. Average Annual Attendance: 140,000. Mem: 3000, dues $25 & up
Income: $935,000 (financed by endowment, mem, state appropriation)
Collections: African art; graphics; American & European sculpture & painting of the past 200 years
Publications: Bulletin, bimonthly; annual report; catalogs of exhibitions
Activities: Classes for adults & children; docent training; lect open to members only, 6 vis lectr per year; concerts; gallery talks; tours; competitions; traveling exhibitions organized & circulated; traveling exhibitions organized and circulated; museum shop sells books, original art, prints & postcards

L **Des Moines Art Center Library,** 4700 Grand Ave, 50312-2099. Tel 515-277-4405; FAX 515-279-3834; *Librn* Mary Morman-Graham
Open Tues - Fri 11 AM - 5 PM. Estab 1948 for research of permanent collection, acquisitions, exhibition preparation, class preparation & lectures. Open to the public for reference by appointment
Purchases: $12,000
Library Holdings: Vols 14,000; Per subs 70
Special Subjects: Iowa Artists, Twentieth Century Art

M **IOWA STATE EDUCATION ASSOCIATION,** Salisbury House, 4025 Tonawanda Dr, 50312. Tel 515-279-9711; FAX 515-279-2659; *Exec Dir* Fred Comer; *Assoc Exec Dir* C William Pritchard
Open daily 8 AM - 4:30 PM. Admis adults $2, 12 years & under $1. Estab 1954 as a cultural center. Gallery is maintained as a replica of King's House in Salisbury, England & contains Tudor age furniture, classic paintings, & sculpture from East & West, tapestries, Oriental rugs. Average Annual Attendance: 17,000
Income: Financed through mem & endowment
Collections: Collection of paintings by Raeburn, Romney, Sir T Lawrence, Van Dyck; permanent collection of tapestries by Brussels Brabant, Flemish, French Verdure; permanent collection of sculpture by Archapinko, Bordelle, Martini; permanent collection of Chinese, India & Oriental (Persian) rugs
Exhibitions: Permanent collection
Activities: Lect; tours; individual paintings & original objects of art lent; lending collection contains motion pictures, original art works, paintings; museum shop sells reproductions, brochures, postcards, stationery

L **PUBLIC LIBRARY OF DES MOINES,** Central Library Information Services, 100 Locust St, 50309-1791. Tel 515-283-4152, Ext 3; FAX 515-237-1654; Elec Mail dsmlib@netins.net. *Head Librn* Pam Deitrick; *Art Librn* Carla Tibboel
Open Mon - Wed 10 AM - 9 PM, Thurs & Fri 10 AM - 6 PM, Sat 10 AM - 5 PM, cl Sun. Estab 1866, dept estab 1970 to serve art & music patrons. Circ 80, 150
Income: Financed by city appropriation
Purchases: $5000
Library Holdings: Vols 5000; Per subs 12; AV — V-tapes

DUBUQUE

M **DUBUQUE ART ASSOCIATION,** Dubuque Museum of Art, 36 E Eighth St, 52001. Tel 319-557-1851; *Pres* Dr Darryl Moezena; *Dir* Lantz Caldwell
Open Tues - Fri 10 AM - 5 PM, Sat & Sun 1 - 5 PM, cl Mon. No admis fee. Estab 1911, inc 1956 to preserve, collect, exhibit, interpret & teach the fine arts to those in the Dubuque area & surrounding communities. Occupies Old County Jail (now National Historic Landmark), built in 1857, converted in 1976. Average Annual Attendance: 20,000. Mem: 400; dues $15-$4000; annual meeting in May
Income: Financed by dues & donations
Collections: †Permanent collection consists of regional & historic art, drawings, paintings, prints, sculptures & watercolor
Exhibitions: Crafts show; ceramics, drawing, paintings, sculptures
Publications: Art News, quarterly
Activities: Classes for adults & children; lect open to public, 12-14 vis lectr per year; concerts; gallery talks; tours; competitions with awards; museum shop sells prints

FAIRFIELD

L **FAIRFIELD ART ASSOCIATION,** 114 S Court, 52556. *Librn* Suzan Kessel
Open Mon - Thurs 9:30 AM - 8:30 PM, Fri 9:30 AM - 6 PM, Sat 9:30 AM - 4:30 PM, winter Sun 1:30 - 4:30 PM, cl national holidays. No admis fee
Income: Financed by endowment & mem
Library Holdings: Per subs 180
Collections: †Graphics; †paintings
Activities: Classes for adults & children; lect open to the public; competitions

A **MAHARISHI UNIVERSITY OF MANAGEMENT** (Formerly Institute for Creative Arts), Department of Fine Arts, c/o MIU-Faculty Mail, 1000 N Fourth St, PO Box 1019, 52557. Tel 515-472-6966; *Dir* C Gregory Thatcher; *Cur* Terrence Kennedy
Open daily 10 AM - Noon June - Aug for children's art classes. No admis fee. Estab 1985 to foster development of the arts in the region. One gallery 20 ft X 40 ft for exhibition of contemporary & historic art; 20 artist studios; event room for lectures & performances; classrooms for teaching visual arts courses. Average Annual Attendance: 2000
Income: Financed by endowment
Collections: Contemporary art in all media
Exhibitions: Annual Juried Show; David Hanson: Coal Strip, Montana (photography); Sales & Rental Exhibition; Selected Masterworks
Publications: Exhibit catalogues
Activities: Classes for adults & children; dramatic programs; lect open to public, 15 vis lectr per year; competitions with awards

FORT DODGE

M **BLANDEN MEMORIAL ART MUSEUM,** 920 Third Ave S, 50501. Tel 515-573-2316; FAX 515-573-2317; *Dir* Margaret Skove; *Educ* Meg Adams
Open Tues, Wed & Fri 10 AM - 5 PM, Thurs 10 AM - 8:30 PM, Sat & Sun 1 - 5 PM. No admis fee. Estab 1930 as a permanent municipal, non-profit institution, educational & aesthetic in purpose; the mus interprets, exhibits & cares for a permanent collection & traveling exhibitions. Houses works of art in permanent collection. Average Annual Attendance: 14,000. Mem: 400; dues $15-$500
Income: $290,000 (financed by city & state appropriation, mem, Blanden Art Gallery Charitable Foundation & private support)
Collections: †Arts of China & Japan; †15th - 20th Century Works on Paper; Pre-Columbian & African Art; †Regional Art; †Twentieth century American & European masters, paintings & sculpture
Exhibitions: (1997) Focus on Spain; Personal Sightings II; I Have A Dream; Range of Possibilities; Woman!; Mingei: Japanese Folk Art from the Montgomery Collection
Publications: Annual report; exhibition catalogues; handbook of the permanent collection; membership information; quarterly bulletin
Activities: Classes for adults & children; art appreciation program in the community schools; lect open to public, 5-10 vis lectr per year; gallery talks; tours; competitions; scholarships offered; exten outreach art appreciation program; loans to art museums meeting necessary professional requirements including climate conditions, security & other physical needs specifications of the art collection; book traveling exhibiitions; originate traveling exhibitions

L **Museum Library,** * 920 Third Ave S, 50501. Tel 515-573-2316; FAX 515-573-2317; *Dir* Margaret Skove
Open Tues, Wed & Fri 10 AM - 5 PM, Thurs 10 AM - 8:30 PM, Sat & Sun 1 - 5 PM. Estab 1972 as reference library for museum
Income: $90,000 (financed by mem, city appropriation & charitable foundation)
Library Holdings: Vols 4100; Per subs 12; Micro — Cards; AV — Fs, slides, v-tapes; Other — Clipping files, exhibition catalogs, framed reproductions 148, pamphlets, reproductions, sculpture 9

GRINNELL

M **GRINNELL COLLEGE,** Print & Drawing Study Room/Gallery, 50112. Tel 515-269-3371; FAX 515-269-4283; Elec Mail Jenkins@AC.Grin.Edu. *Dir* Kay Wilson
Open Sun - Fri 1 - 5 PM. No admis fee. Estab 1983 for exhibition & study of art on paper. Average Annual Attendance: 4000
Income: $75,000 (financed by endowment)
Purchases: $30,000
Collections: Works of Art on Paper
Exhibitions: (1997) Lawrence Collection of Eat European Prints; John Pittman Paintings; Eric Pervukhin Art on Paper; A Graphic Odyssey: Romare Bearden
Publications: Exhibition catalogs
Activities: Lect open to public, 8 vis lectr per year; book traveling exhibitions 8 times per year; originate traveling exhibitions 4 times per year; museum shop sells original art

INDIANOLA

M **SIMPSON COLLEGE,** Farnham Gallery, 701 NC, 50125. Tel 515-961-1561; FAX 515-961-1498; Elec Mail heinicke@simpson.edu. *Head Art Dept* Janet Heinicke
Open Mon - Fri 8 AM - 4:30 PM. No admis fee. Estab 1982 to educate & inform the public. Two small gallery rooms each 14 ft, 4 in x 29 ft. Average Annual Attendance: 1200
Special Subjects: Advertising Design, Aesthetics, Architecture, Art History, Ceramics, Commercial Art, Decorative Arts, Drawings, Graphic Arts, Interior Design, Islamic Art, Landscapes, Lettering, Painting - American, Painting - European
Collections: Small permanent collection being started
Exhibitions: (1997) Beyond Heaven & Earth (prints); Color-A Many Splendor Thing; Senior Shows Faculty show - recent work by Mary Schaeffer (sculpture); Janet Heinicke (painting & drawing); Senior shows - Kris Coltrain, Waverly; Cori

Brown, Farragut; Craig Brown, Eldora; Edith Kuitert, Pella; Thad White, Indianola; Sue Curtis, Indianola; Dollie Stout, Randolph; Indianola Area Artists Show; critique with guest artist
Activities: Classes for adults; lect open to public, 4 vis lectr per year; gallery talks; scholarships offered; individual paintings lent; originate traveling exhibitions

IOWA CITY

A ARTS IOWA CITY, Art Center & Gallery, 129 E Washington St, 52240. Tel 319-337-7447; *Pres* Carol Spaziani; *Pres-Elect* Tom Wegman; *Treas* Holly Hotchkiss
Open Tues - Sat 11 AM - 4 PM. No admis fee. Estab 1975. Large gallery space for group or theme shows; solo rooms for single artist shows; installation space. Average Annual Attendance: 5000. Mem: 250-300; dues family $35, individual $25; meeting first Mon of month
Income: $70,000 (financed by mem, sales & grants)
Exhibitions: Ten exhibitions per year are mounted. In April a national exhibition of works using paper &/or fiber as a medium is organized & installed. Monthly exhibitions include works of local artists & from local collections; each group show is accompanied by a solo show & an installation in separate gallery spaces
Publications: Paper Fiber Show Catalog, annually; membership pamphlet; bi-monthly newsletter
Activities: Classes for adults & children; dramatic programs; concerts; gallery talks; competitions; workshops; fiscal agent for individual artists; participant in arts festival

UNIVERSITY OF IOWA

M Museum of Art, 150 N Riverside Dr, 52242. Tel 319-335-1727; FAX 319-335-3677; *Dir* Stephen S Prokopoff; *Cur Educ* Emily J G Vermillion; *Cur* Victoria Rovine; *Cur* Pamela White Trimpe; *Technical Dir* David Dennis; *Registrar* Jeff Martin
Open Tues - Sat 10 AM - 5 PM, Sun Noon - 5 PM, cl Thanksgiving, Christmas & New Year's Day. No admis fee. Estab 1969 to collect, exhibit & preserve for the future, works of art from different cultures; to make these objects as accessible as possible to people of all ages in the state of Iowa; to assist the pub, through educational programs & publications, in interpreting these works of art & expanding their appreciation of art in general. 48,000 sq ft in 16 galleries, including a central sculpture court. Average Annual Attendance: 50,000. Mem: 1000; dues directors circle $1000, benefactor $500, patron $250, sponsor $125, household $50, individual $35, senior citizen $25, student $10
Income: Financed by mem, state appropriation & private donations
Collections: †African & Pre-Columbian art; Chinese & Tibetan bronzes; Oriental jade; 19th & 20th century European & †American paintings & sculpture; †prints, †drawings, †photography, silver
Exhibitions: The Elliott Collection of 20th Century European paintings, silver & prints; a major collection of African sculpture; Approximately 24 changing exhibitions each year, both permanent collection, original & traveling exhibitions; From the Ocean of Painting; Michael Mazur's Inferno; Alan Sonfist Retrospective; Phillip Guston: Working Through the Forties
Publications: Calendar (brochure), twice/year; exhibition catalogs; newsletter
Activities: Docent training; lect open to public, 35 vis lectr per year; concerts; gallery talks; tours; works of art lent to other museums; originate traveling exhibitions; sales shop sells posters, postcards & catalogs
L Art Library, W 145 Art Bldg, 52242. Tel 319-335-3089; *Librn* Rijn Templeton
Open Mon - Fri 8 AM - 5 PM, Mon - Thurs evenings 7 - 10 PM, Sat & Sun 1 - 4 PM. Estab 1937 to support the University programs, community & state needs. Circ 40,000
Income: Financed by state appropriation
Purchases: $76,000
Library Holdings: Vols 70,000; Per subs 230; Micro — Fiche, reels; Other — Clipping files, exhibition catalogs, memorabilia, pamphlets

KEOKUK

A KEOKUK ART CENTER, Keosippi Mall, PO Box 862, 52632. Tel 319-524-8354; *Pres* Rae Zweertz; *Dir* Tom Seabold; *VPres* Jim Wells; *Treas* Rita Noe
Open Tues - Sat 9 AM - Noon. No admis fee. Estab 1954 to promote art in tri-state area. Gallery maintained in Keokuk Public Library, 210 N Fifth St. Average Annual Attendance: 2000. Mem: dues sustaining $50, patron $25, family $12, individual $6, student $2; annual meeting first Mon in May
Collections: Paintings, sculpture
Publications: Newsletter, quarterly
Activities: Classes for adults & children; docent training; lect open to public; gallery talks; tours; competitions with cash awards; scholarships; book traveling exhibitions; originate traveling exhibitions

LEMARS

M TEIKYO WESTMAR UNIVERSITY, Westmar Art Gallery, 51031. Tel 712-546-7081; *Gallery Dir* Randy Becker
Open daily 8 AM - 5:30 PM, Sat 2 - 5 PM; inactive during summer. No admis fee. Estab 1973 to provide a forum for cultivating the sensitivity of our student body & the community to a variety of visual arts through a regular schedule of art exhibits. Gallery covers 2000 sq ft floor space, 170 linear ft of display space, with track lighting. Average Annual Attendance: 7500
Income: Financed by endowment, college appropriation & private gifts
Collections: Haitian Art Collection
Publications: Westmar College Fine Arts Schedule of Events
Activities: Educ dept; lect open to public; concerts; gallery talks
L Mock Library Art Dept, 51031. Tel 712-546-7081; *Dir* Randy Becker
Open to students
Library Holdings: Vols 1675; Per subs 9; AV — Slides

MARSHALLTOWN

A CENTRAL IOWA ART ASSOCIATION, INC, Fisher Community Ctr, 709 S Center, 50158. Tel 515-753-9013; *Dir* Marty Bowman
Open Mon - Fri 8 AM - 11 PM, Sat 8 AM - 5 PM, Sun 2 - 5 PM. Estab 1942, incorporated 1959. The large auditorium has changing monthly exhibitions of varied art; glass cases in corridor & studio display contemporary ceramics of high quality. Average Annual Attendance: 3000. Mem: 330; dues $15; annual meeting June 30
Income: Financed by mem, contributions & United Way
Collections: Fisher Collection—Utrillo, Cassatt, Sisley, Vuillard, Monet, Degas, Signac, Le Gourge, Vlaminck and Monticelli; sculpture—Christian Petersen, Rominelli, Bourdelle; ceramic study collection—Gilhooly, Arneson, Nagle, Kottler, Babu, Geraedts, Boxem, Leach, Voulkos; traditional Japanese wares
Exhibitions: Monthly art & crafts in Fisher Community Center Auditorium
Publications: Newsletter, monthly; brochures
Activities: Classes for adults & children in ceramics, sculpture, jewelry, painting; lect open to public, 3 vis lectr per year; gallery talks; tours; awards; individual paintings & original objects of art lent; book traveling exhibitions; originate traveling exhibitions; sales shop sells original art, reproductions, prints, pottery, wood, fiber & metal
L Art Reference Library, Fisher Community Ctr, 50158. Tel 515-753-9013; *Dir* Marty Bowman
For reference only
Library Holdings: Vols 300; AV — Cassettes, slides; Other — Original art works, photographs, sculpture

MASON CITY

M CHARLES H MACNIDER MUSEUM, 303 Second St SE, 50401-3988. Tel 515-421-3666; FAX 515-423-2615; *Dir* Richard E Leet; *Coordr Educ* Mary Mello-nee; *Registrar & Cur Asst* Dana Michels
Open Tues & Thurs 10 AM - 9 PM, Wed, Fri & Sat 10 AM - 5 PM, Sun 1 - 5 PM, cl Mon & holidays. No admis fee. Estab 1964, opened 1966 to provide experience in the arts through development of a permanent collection, through scheduling of temporary exhibitions, through the offering of classes & art instruction, through special programs in film, music & other areas of the performing arts. The mus was estab in an English-Tudor style of brick & tile, enhanced by modern, design coordinated additions. It is located in a scenic setting, two & a half blocks from the main thoroughfare of Mason City. Gallery lighting & neutral backgrounds provide a good environment for exhibitions. Average Annual Attendance: Over 30,000. Mem: 800; dues from contributions $20-$1000 or more
Income: $360,000 (financed by mem, city appropriation & grants)
Collections: Permanent collection being developed with an emphasis on American art, with some representation of Iowa art; contains paintings, prints, pottery; artists represented include Baziotes, Benton, Burchfield, Burford, Bricher, Cropsey, Davies, De Staebler, Dove, Flannagan, Francis, Gottlieb, Graves, Guston, Healy, Hurd, Lasansky, Levine, Marin, Maurer, Metcalf, Sloan & Oliveira; Bil Baird: World of Puppets
Exhibitions: Annual Area Competitive Show; Annual Iowa Crafts Competition
Publications: Annual report; newsletter, bi-monthly; occasional exhibit fliers or catalog
Activities: Classes for adults & children; docent training; lect open to public; concerts; gallery talks; tours; competitions; individual paintings & original objects of art lent to other museums & art centers; museum shop sells original art
L Library, 303 Second St SE, 50401. Tel 515-421-3666; FAX 515-423-2615; Reference library within the structure of the mus for reference only
Library Holdings: Vols 1500; Per subs 30; AV — Motion pictures, slides, v-tapes; Other — Clipping files, exhibition catalogs
Special Subjects: American Indian Art, American Western Art, Architecture, Art Education, Art History, Drawings, Folk Art, Graphic Design, Landscapes, Painting - American, Photography, Portraits, Pottery, Printmaking, Prints, American art

L MASON CITY PUBLIC LIBRARY, 225 Second St SE, 50401. Tel 515-421-3668; *Dir* Andrew Alexander; *Reference* Bev Elder; *Children's Room* Jeaneal Weeks; *Young Adult* Fern Robinson; *Art Librn* Elizabeth Camarigg
Open Mon - Thurs 9 AM - 9 PM; Fri & Sat 9 - 5 PM; Sun 1 - 5 PM. No admis fee. Estab 1869 to service pub in providing reading material & information. Permanent collection of regional artists on display in auditorium; monthly exhibits of local & regional artists located in main lobby of library. Circ 197,635
Income: $327,909 (financed by city, county appropriation & Federal Revenue Sharings)
Purchases: $85,000
Library Holdings: Vols 103,000; Per subs 325; Original documents; Micro — Fiche, reels; AV — Cassettes, fs 350, motion pictures, rec; Other — Clipping files, framed reproductions, memorabilia, original art works, pamphlets, prints
Collections: Permanent collection of regional artists; signed letters of authors
Exhibitions: Rotating exhibitions
Activities: Exten dept serves general public; gallery holdings consist of art works & reproductions paintings which are lent to public

MOUNT VERNON

M CORNELL COLLEGE, Armstrong Gallery, 600 First St W, 52314. Tel 319-895-4137; *Dir Gallery* Christina McOmber; *Chmn Dept Art* Anthony Plant
Open Mon - Fri 9 AM - 4 PM, Sun 2 - 4 PM. Estab to display artists work
Income: Financed by Cornell College
Collections: Thomas Nast drawings & prints; Sonnenschein Collection of European Drawings of the 15th - 17th Century
Exhibitions: Three exhibits per year plus 10-20 student thesis shows
Activities: Lect open to public, 1 vis lectr per year

MUSCATINE

M MUSCATINE ART CENTER, 1314 Mulberry Ave, 52761. Tel 319-263-8282;
FAX 319-263-4702; *Pres* Mike Knott; *Dir* Barbara C Longtin
Open Tues - Fri 10 AM - 5 PM, Sat & Sun 1 - 5 PM, Thurs evenings 7 - 9 PM,
cl Mon & legal holidays. No admis fee. Estab 1965 to collect, preserve &
interpret work of art & objects of historical & aesthetic importance. Average
Annual Attendance: 11,000. Mem: 500; dues sponsor $500-$999, supporting
$200-$499, contributing $100-$199, sustaining $50-$99, family $30, individual
$20, senior citizens $12.50 or senior citizen couple $20; annual meeting in June
Income: Financed by city appropriation & Muscatine Art Center Support
Foundation
Collections: Muscatine History; Button Collection; Paperweight Collection;
†American painting prints, especially Mississippi River views; †American art
pottery; †children's books; decorative arts; †glassware; graphics; oriental carpets;
toys
Publications: Newsletter, quarterly
Activities: Classes for adults & children; docent training; lect open to public, 6
vis lectr per year; concerts; gallery talks; tours; individual paintings & original
objects of art lent to qualified museums for exhibition purposes; book traveling
exhibitions 5-7 per year; originate traveling exhibitions 1-2 per year
L Library, 1314 Mulberry Ave, 52761. Tel 319-263-8282;
For reference only
Library Holdings: Vols 2500; Per subs 10; Other — Memorabilia, pamphlets

ORANGE CITY

M NORTHWESTERN COLLEGE, Te Paske Gallery, Student Ctr, 51041. Tel 712-
737-7000, 737-7003; *Exhib Coordr* John Kaericher
Open Mon - Sat 8 AM - 10 PM. No admis fee. Estab 1968 to promote the visual
arts in northwest Iowa and to function as a learning resource for the college and
community. Average Annual Attendance: 2000
Income: Financed by school budget
Collections: Approx 75 original works of art: etchings, woodcuts, serigraphs,
lithographs, mezzotints, paintings, sculpture and ceramics by modern and old
masters of Western World and Japan
Exhibitions: Contemporary American Artists Series; student shows
Activities: Classes for adults; lect open to public, 2-3 vis lectr per year; gallery
talks; competitions

OTTUMWA

L AIRPOWER MUSEUM LIBRARY, 22001 Bluegrass Rd, 52501. Tel 515-938-
2773;
Estab 1971
Library Holdings: AV — Fs, v-tapes; Other — Photographs
Special Subjects: Drawings, Film, Maps, Photography, Video
Collections: Aviation Collection, blueprints, books, brochures, clothing, drawings,
films, lithographs, maps, models, paintings, periodicals, photographs, videos
Publications: Airpower Museum bulletin, annual

SIOUX CITY

A SIOUX CITY ART CENTER, 225 Nebraska St, 51101. Tel 712-279-6272; FAX
712-255-2921; *Board Trustees* John Lawrence; *Board Dirs Pres* John Day;
Interim Dir Janet Brown
Open Tues - Sat 10 AM - 5 PM, Sun 1 - 5 PM, cl Mon & holidays. No admis
fee. Estab 1938 to provide art experiences to the general pub. Four exhibition
galleries consisting of nationally known artists from the midwest regional area;
includes a graphics gallery & changing exhibitions. Average Annual Attendance:
40,000. Mem: 450; dues $15-$5000; monthly meetings
Income: Financed by mem, city & state appropriation
Collections: Permanent collection of over 700 works; consists of †paintings &
†prints of nationally known regional artists, contemporary photography &
sculpture & crafts
Exhibitions: Youth Art Month Exhibition; Annual Juried Exhibition
Publications: Annual Report; Artifact, bi-monthly magazine; class brochures,
quarterly; exhibition catalogs; exhibition announcements
Activities: Classes for adults & children; docent training; workshops; outreach
programs to schools; lect open to public; gallery talks; tours; concerts;
competitions; scholarships offered; original objects of art & individual paintings
lent to qualified institutions with approved facilities & security; book traveling
exhibitions 3-4 per year; traveling exhibitions organized & circulated to regional
art museums; museum shop sells books, magazines, original art, prints, jewelry &
property items
L Library, 513 Nebraska St, Sioux City, 51101. Tel 712-279-6272; FAX 712-279-
6267; *Dir* Jim Zimmer
Reference library - non-circulating
Library Holdings: Vols 1500; Per subs 20; AV — Cassettes, slides; Other —
Exhibition catalogs

STORM LAKE

M WITTER GALLERY, 609 Cayuga St, 50588. Tel 712-732-3400; *Pres* Jolene
Dentelinger; *Dir* Andriette Wickstrom; *Educ Coordr* Judy Ferguson
Open Mon - Fri 1:30 - 4 PM, Sat 10 AM - Noon. No admis fee. Estab 1972 to
encourage the appreciation of fine arts & to support fine arts educ, exhibits,
lectures & workshops. Gallery occupies a wing of the Storm Lake Pub Library
building. It has about 1800 sq ft of floor space & 120 linear ft of hanging wall
space. Average Annual Attendance: 10,000. Mem: 300; dues sponsor $250,
supporting $100, sustaining $50, active $25
Income: $20,000 (financed by endowment, mem, city appropriation, fundraising
projects)
Collections: Paintings & collected artifacts of Miss Ella Witter; prints by

Dorothy D Skewis
Exhibitions: Iowa Women in Art: Pioneers of the Past- touring exhibition of
work by Ella Witter and Dorothy Skewis
Publications: Witter Gallery News & Events, monthly
Activities: Classes for adults & children; art appreciation programs in area
schools; lect open to public, 10 vis lectr per year; gallery talks; concerts; tours;
biennial juried competition with cash awards; originate traveling exhibitions;
museum shop sells notecards & tote bags

WATERLOO

A WATERLOO ART ASSOCIATION, 2745 E Big Rock Rd, 50703. Tel 319-232-
1984; *Pres* Russell Caruthers
Open Tues - Sat 10 AM - 4 PM. No admis fee. Estab 1944 to encourage area
artists & provide for the exhibition of their work. Gallery is maintained in a
rented building providing gallery rooms, workshop, art supply sales room &
storage. Average Annual Attendance: 2000. Mem: 150; dues $10-$20; annual
meeting last Tues in Jan
Income: Financed by mem
Collections: Small collection of work by former members
Exhibitions: Amateur Iowa Artists Regional Show; Black Hawk County Art
Show; Monthly exhibits by area professionals
Publications: Bulletin published six times a yr
Activities: Classes for adults; workshops; lect open to public, 8-10 vis lectr per
year; gallery talks; tours; competitions with awards; sales shop sells original art,
prints, pottery & sculpture & gift shop items

M WATERLOO MUSEUM OF ART, 225 Commercial St, 50701. Tel 319-291-
4491; FAX 319-291-4270; *Dir* Cammie V Scully
Open Mon - Fri 10 AM - 5 PM, Sat & Sun 1 - 5 PM. No admis fee. Estab 1957
to provide an art forum for the Waterloo area. Average Annual Attendance: 60,
000, plus junior art gallery attendance of 16,000. Mem: 500; dues individual $15
& up; annual meeting second Thurs of July
Income: Financed by city funds, mem, grants & donations
Collections: American Decorative Arts; Contemporary American paintings,
prints & †sculpture; †Haitian/Caribbean paintings & sculpture
Exhibitions: Schedule changing exhibitions of regional painting, sculpture, prints
& fine crafts
Activities: Classes for preschool through senior adults; dramatic programs; docent
training; lect open to public; concerts; gallery talks; tours; competitions;
scholarships & fels offered; individual paintings & original objects of art lent to
other museums; originate traveling exhibitions; museum shop sells books &
original art; junior museum

WEST BRANCH

L HERBERT HOOVER PRESIDENTIAL LIBRARY & MUSEUM, Parkside
Dr, 52358. Tel 319-643-5301; FAX 319-643-5825; *Library Dir* Timoth Walch;
Reference Archivist Pat Wildenberg
Open daily 9 AM - 5 PM, cl Thanksgiving, Christmas, New Year's Day. Admis
$1, children 15 & under free. Estab 1962 as a research center to service the
papers of Herbert Hoover & other related manuscript collections; a museum to
exhibit the life & times of Herbert Hoover from his 90 years of public service &
accomplishments
Income: Financed by federal appropriation
Library Holdings: Vols 20,934; Per subs 30; Original documents; Still
photographs; Micro — Reels; AV — A-tapes, motion pictures, rec, slides; Other —
Clipping files, manuscripts, memorabilia, pamphlets
Collections: 64 Chinese porcelains; oil paintings; 190 Original Editorial Cartoons;
340 posters; 26 World War I Food Administration; 464 World War I Painted and
Embroidered Flour Sacks
Exhibitions: Permanent exhibits on Herbert & Lou Henry Hoover; subjects
related to Hoover & the times; temporary exhibits cover subjects related to the
memorabilia collection, the decades & activities of Hoover's life & state &
national interest
Activities: Lect open to public, 2-3 vis lectr per year; sales shop sells books,
prints, slides and medals

KANSAS

ABILENE

L DWIGHT D EISENHOWER PRESIDENTIAL LIBRARY, 200 SE Fourth St,
67410. Tel 913-263-4751; FAX 913-263-4218; *Dir* Daniel Holt; *Museum Cur*
Dennis Medina
Open daily 9 AM - 4:45 PM, cl Thanksgiving, Christmas & New Year's. Admis
$2, sr citizens $1.50, under 16 free. Estab 1961 as library, in 1954 as museum.
Average Annual Attendance: 126,000
Income: Financed by Federal Government appropriation
Library Holdings: Vols 22,850; Micro — Prints, reels; AV — A-tapes, cassettes,
fs, motion pictures, rec, slides, v-tapes; Other — Clipping files, manuscripts,
memorabilia, original art works, photographs, prints, sculpture
Collections: Research Library and Museum contains papers of Dwight D
Eisenhower and his associates, together with items of historical interest
connected with the Eisenhower Family. Mementos and gifts of General Dwight
D Eisenhower both before, during, and after his term as President of the United
States
Activities: Educ dept; docent training; lect open to the public, 5 vis lectr per
year; libr tours; individual paintings & original objects of art lent; lending
collection contains original art work & prints, paintings & sculpture; originate
traveling exhibitions; museum shop sells books, prints, reproductions & slides

ALMA

M WABAUNSEE COUNTY HISTORICAL MUSEUM, 227 Missouri, PO Box
387, 66401. Tel 913-765-2200; *Cur* Lila Beasterfeld
Open Tues - Sat 10 AM - 4 PM, Sun 1 - 4 PM. No admis fee. Estab 1968 for
the purpose of preserving art in Wabaunsee County. Paintings are hung
throughout the museum in available space. Maintains reference library. Average
Annual Attendance: 2000. Mem: 230; lifetime $100, yr $10; annual meeting last
Sat in May
Income: $30,000 (financed by mem & endowment)
Collections: General Louis Walt display, blacksmith shop, clothing, farm tools &
equipment; Indian arrowhead display; mainstreet USA-historical town; 1923 Reo
firetruck; old time telephone shop; postal display
Publications: Historical Society Newsletter, quarterly
Activities: Sales shop sells books, postcards, stationery, t-shirts, sweat shirt &
caps

ASHLAND

M CLARK COUNTY HISTORICAL SOCIETY, Pioneer - Krier Museum, 430 W
Fourth St, PO Box 862, 67831-0862. Tel 316-635-2227; *Cur* Floretta Rogers
Open daily 1 - 5 PM. Admis donations requested. Estab 1967 to collect &
preserve Southwest Kansas history. Displays set up as mortuary, bank, general
store, barber shop, doctor's office, saddle shop, blacksmith shop; rooms in homes,
such as bedroom, parlor, kitchen, music room, craft room; aerobatic plane; farm
machinery; buggies. Average Annual Attendance: 1400. Mem: 300; lifetime $10;
annual meeting in Nov
Income: $20,277 (financed by mem, county taxes & donations)
Collections: Archeological Collection; Barbed Wire Collection; Early Settlers
Collection; Elephant Collection; Gun Collection
Publications: Notes on Eary Clark County, Kansas, book; Kings & Queens of the
Range, book
Activities: Demonstrations & group tours; sales shop sells books

ATCHISON

M MUCHNIC FOUNDATION & ATCHISON ART ASSOCIATION, Muchnic
Gallery, 704 N Fourth St, PO Box 308, 66002. Tel 913-367-4278; *Cur* Nancy
Kaiser-Kaplan
Open Mar - Nov Sat & Sun 1 - 5 PM. Admis $2. Estab 1970 to bring fine arts to
the people of Atchison. 19th century home furnished with original family
belongings downstairs; upstairs there are five rooms devoted to the art gallery.
Average Annual Attendance: 3000. Mem: 120; board meeting second Tues of
each month
Income: Financed by Muchnic Foundation, Atchison Art Asn art shows
Purchases: $7000
Collections: †Paintings by regional artists: Don Andorfer; Thomas Hart Benton;
John Stuart Curry; Raymond Eastwood; John Falter; Jim Hamil; Wilbur Niewald;
Jack O'Hara; Roger Shimomura; Robert Sudlow; Grant Wood; Jamie Wyeth;
Walter Yost
Activities: Classes for adults; docent training; lect open to public; tours;
scholarships & fels offered; individual paintings lent to local museums; book
traveling exhibitions 3 per year; originate traveling exhibitions; sales shop sells
books, original art & prints

BALDWIN CITY

M BAKER UNIVERSITY, Old Castle Museum, 515 Fifth St, PO Box 65, 66006.
Tel 913-594-6809; FAX 913-594-2522; *Dir* Brenda Day
Open Tues - Sat 10 AM - 4:30 PM, cl Mon. Admis by donation. Estab 1953 to
display items related to life in early Kansas. Average Annual Attendance: 1500
Income: Financed by endowment, University & donations
Collections: Country store; Indian artifacts & pottery; 19th century print shop;
quilts; silver & pewter dishes & table service; tools; old quilts; old cameras; Santa
Fe Trail Artifacts
Exhibitions: John Brown material; Indian Pottery; Indian artifacts; old guns
Activities: Lect open to public

CHANUTE

M MARTIN & OSA JOHNSON SAFARI MUSEUM, INC, 111 N Lincoln Ave,
66720. Tel 316-431-2730; *Dir* Conrad G Froehlich; *Cur* Barbara E Henshall
Open Mon - Sat 10 AM - 5 PM, Sun 1 - 5 PM. Admis adults $2.50, students $1,
children under 12 free with adult. Estab 1961 to be the repository of the Johnson
Archives. Average Annual Attendance: 7500. Mem: 350; dues $15; annual
meeting in Oct
Income: $100,000 (financed by mem, city appropriation, donations & gifts shop)
Publications: Empty Masks; Exploring with Martin & Osa Johnson (book); Wait-
A-Bit News, quarterly newsletter
Activities: Educ dept; tours; museum boxes for school use; individual paintings &
original objects of art lent to qualified institutions; museum shop sells books,
imported carvings, brass, fabric & ethnic toys
M Imperato Collection of West African Artifacts, 66720. Tel 316-431-2730; *Dir*
Conrad G Froehlich
Estab 1974
Collections: West African sculpture including masks, ancestor figures & ritual
objects, household items, musical instruments
Exhibitions: African culture exhibit of East & West African items; narrow strip
loom; ceremonial masks
Publications: Collection catalogs
M Johnson Collection of Photographs, Movies & Memorabilia, 66720. Tel 316-
431-2730; *Dir* Conrad G Froehlich
Collections: Photographs & movie footage of the South Seas, Borneo & East
Africa between 1917-1936; Manuscript material, archival collection, & artifacts
collected by the Johnsons
Exhibitions: Life of the Johnsons

M Selsor Gallery of Art, 66720. Tel 316-431-2730; *Dir* Conrad G Froehlich
Estab 1981
Collections: Original paintings; scratch boards & sketches; bronze, ivory & amber
sculpture; lithographs
L Scott Explorers Library, 66720. Tel 316-431-2730; *Dir* Conrad G Froehlich
Estab 1980 for research and reference
Library Holdings: Vols 14,000
Special Subjects: Natural History, Exploration

EL DORADO

M COUTTS MEMORIAL MUSEUM OF ART, INC, 110 N Main St, 67042. Tel
316-321-1212; FAX 316-321-1212; *Chmn Board* Rhoda Hodges
Open Mon - Fri 1 - 5 PM & by special arrangements. No admis fee. Estab 1970
as a Fine Arts museum. Average Annual Attendance: 4000
Income: Financed by endowment & gifts
Collections: Frederick Remington sculpture collection completed in 1992
(recasts)
Exhibitions: Frederick Remington Traveling Exhibit; Kansas Camera '96
Midwest Artists; Kansas Quilt Traditions
Activities: Classes for adults & children; lect open to public, 1-2 vis lectr per
year; concerts gallery talks; tours; competitions with awards; scholarships offered

EMPORIA

M EMPORIA STATE UNIVERSITY, Norman R Eppink Art Gallery, 1200
Commercial, 66801. Tel 316-343-1200, 341-5246; Elec Mail
perrydon@esumail.emporia.edu. *Dir* Donald Perry
Open Mon - Fri 9 AM - 3 PM, cl university holidays. No admis fee. Estab 1939
to bring a variety of exhibitions to the campus. Main Gallery is 25 x 50 ft & has
a 50 ft wall for hanging items; adjacent gallery is 16 x 50 ft; display gallery
contains eighteen 40 inch x 28 inch panels. Average Annual Attendance: 10,000
Income: Financed by state, grant & endowment funds
Purchases: Annual purchase of contemporary drawings from the Annual
National Invitational Drawing Exhibition, and works on paper from the Annual
Summer Art Festival
Collections: Artifacts; †contemporary drawings and paintings; †sculpture
Exhibitions: John Baeder: Dineis, spring prints; Plainstates, changing
Publications: Exhibition catalogs
Activities: Lect open to public, 6 vis lectr per year; concerts; gallery talks; tours;
scholarships offered; individual paintings & original objects of art lent to
university offices; book traveling exhibitions 4-6 per year; originate traveling
exhibitions to schools

HAYS

M FORT HAYS STATE UNIVERSITY, Moss-Thorns Gallery of Arts, 600 Park
St, 67601. Tel 913-628-4247; FAX 913-628-4087; *Chmn* Gary Coulter
Open Mon - Fri 8:30 AM - 4 PM, weekends on special occasions. No admis fee.
Estab 1953 to provide constant changing exhibitions for the benefit of students,
faculty & other interested people in an educ situation. Rarick Hall has 2200 sq ft
with moveable panels that can be used to divide the gallery into four smaller
galleries. Mem: 88
Income: Financed by state appropriation
Purchases: $2000
Collections: Vyvyan Blackford Collection; †contemporary prints; †national
exhibition of small paintings, prints & drawings; regionalist collection (1930s);
Oriental scroll collection
Publications: Exhibitions brochures; Art Calendar, annually
Activities: Lect open to public, 4 vis lectr per year; gallery talks; tours;
competitions with prizes; concerts; exten dept servs western Kansas; individual
paintings & original objects of art lent to individuals, organizations & institutions;
lending collection contains original art works & prints, paintings, sculpture &
slides; traveling exhibitions organized & circulated
L Forsyth Library, 600 Park St, 67601. Tel 913-628-4431; FAX 913-628-4096; *Dir*
Lawrence M Caylor; *Reference Librn* Chris Gibson
Reference Library
Library Holdings: Vols 6000; Per subs 1181; AV — Fs; Other — Exhibition
catalogs

HUTCHINSON

A HUTCHINSON ART ASSOCIATION, Hutchinson Art Center, 405 N
Washington, 67501. Tel 316-663-1081, 662-8652; *Dir & VPres* Del Knauer; *Pres*
Ruth Dillon; *Exhibits* Manuel Senti
Open Tues - Fri 9 AM - 5 PM, Sat & Sun 2 - 4 PM. Estab 1949 to bring
exhibitions to the city of Hutchinson & maintain a permanent collection in the
pub schools. Two galleries. Average Annual Attendance: 3000. Mem: 300; dues
$10-$1000; monthly meetings
Income: Financed by mem, profits on spring fair, corporations, gallery sales
Collections: †Permanent collection of watercolors, prints, ceramics, glass, wood,
oils & metals
Exhibitions: Two all-member shows per yr; one traveling show per month
Activities: Lect open to public, 3 vis lectr per year; gallery talks; tours; annual art
fair with prizes; monthly public receptions to meet artists currently exhibiting;
scholarships offered; book traveling exhibitions; sales shop sells original art,
prints, cards, ceramics, handblown glass, jewelry, sculpture, carved wood &
stoneware

INDEPENDENCE

M INDEPENDENCE MUSEUM (Formerly Ladies Library & Art Association), Eighth & Mrytle, PO Box 294, 67301. Tel 316-331-3515; *Coordr* Ossie E Tranbarger
Open Thurs - Sat 10 AM - 2 PM, cl holidays. Admis by donation. Estab 1882 to secure an art collection for the community. The mus has a large 19 ft gallery which contains original paintings; Indian art & artifacts; Mexican Room, late 1800 & early 1900 costume room, country store, War & Peace Room, Oriental room, period bedroom, early 1900 kitchen, childrens room, William Inge Memorabilia Room, historical oil room, & blacksmith shop. Average Annual Attendance: 5000. Mem: 125; dues $20-$50; meeting monthly Oct-May
Income: Financed by mem, bequests, gifts, art exhibits, various projects & donations
Collections: †William Inge Memorabilia Collection; American Indian Collection; †Oriental Collection
Exhibitions: Annual Art Exhibit: Quilt Fair; various artists & craftsmen exhibits
Activities: Classes for adults & children; lect open to public, 9 vis lectr per year; tours; competitions with awards

LAWRENCE

M UNIVERSITY OF KANSAS, Spencer Museum of Art, 66045. Tel 913-864-4710; FAX 913-864-3112; *Dir* Andrea Norris; *Asst Dir* Douglas Tilghman; *Cur Prints & Drawings* Stephen Goddard; *Cur Photog* John Pultz; *Registrar* Janet Dreiling; *Exhib Designer* Mark Roeyer; *Managing Ed & Public Relations* Sally Hayden; *Programs* Lori Eklund; *Docents* Betsy Weaver; *Bookshop* Bernadette Traiger; *Cur European & American Art* Susan Earle; *Cur Educ* Pat Villenueve; *Graphic Designer* Valerie Spicher
Open Tues - Sat 10 AM - 5 PM, Thurs 8:30 AM - 9 PM, Sun Noon - 5 PM, cl Mon. No admis fee. Dedicated in Spooner Hall 1928, Spencer dedicated 1978. The Mus has traditionally served as a laboratory for the visual arts, supporting curricular study in the arts. Primary emphasis is placed on acquisitions & publications & with a regular schedule of changing exhibitions. Mus has a two level Central Court, seven galleries devoted to the permanent collections & three galleries for temporary exhibitions; altogether affording 29,000 sq ft. Mem: Dues $35
Income: Financed by mem, state appropriation & state & federal grants, contributions
Collections: †American paintings; ancient art; †Asian art; †graphics; †Medieval art; †17th & 18th century art, especially German; †19th century European & American art; †20th century European & American art
Publications: Calendar, monthly; Murphy Lectures, annually; The Register of the Spencer Museum of Art, annually; exhibition catalogs, 1-2 per year
Activities: Docent training; lect open to public, 24 vis lectr per year; gallery talks; tours; traveling exhibitions organized & circulated; museum shop sells books, magazines, posters, postcards & gifts
L Murphy Library of Art & Architecture, University of Kansas, 66045. Tel 913-864-3020; FAX 913-864-4608; Elec Mail Bitnet: scraig@ukans.edu. *Librn* Susan V Craig
Open Mon - Thurs 8 AM - 10 PM, Fri 8 AM - 8 PM, Sat Noon - 5 PM, Sun 1 - 10 PM. Estab 1970 to support academic programs & for research. Open to faculty, students & pub
Library Holdings: Vols 110,000; Per subs 700; Auction catalogs; Micro — Fiche, reels; Other — Exhibition catalogs, pamphlets
Special Subjects: Architecture, Art Education, Art History, Asian Art, Decorative Arts, Graphic Design, Painting - American, Painting - Dutch, Painting - Flemish, Painting - Japanese, Photography, Prints, Textiles
L Architectural Resource Center, School of Architecture & Urban Design, 66045. Tel 913-864-3244; FAX 913-864-5393; *Dir* Ursula Stammler
Open Mon - Fri 9 AM - Noon & 5 PM, Sun - Thurs evenings 7:30 - 9:30 PM. Slide Library, estab 1968, is primarily a teaching tool for faculty, but also accessible to students; Donald E & Mary Bole Hatch Architectural Reading Room, estab 1981, is adjacent to studios in School of Architecture & supports the immediate reference needs of students. For reference only
Income: Financed by endowment & state appropriation
Library Holdings: Vols 2600; Per subs 30; AV — Slides 73,000
Special Subjects: Architecture

LINDSBORG

BETHANY COLLEGE
L Library, 235 E Swensson, 67456. Tel 913-227-3311, Ext 8342; *Dir* John Stratton; *Librn* Denise Carson; *Inter-Library Loan Librn* Gretchen Esping-Swanson
Open Mon - Thurs 7:30 AM - 10:30 PM, Fri 7:30 AM - 5 PM, Sat 11 AM - 4 PM, Sun 2:30 - 10:30 PM. Estab 1881. For reference only
Library Holdings: Vols 121,000; Other — Exhibition catalogs
Special Subjects: Art Education, Art History, Ceramics, Painting - American, Painting - British, Painting - European, Painting - Scandinavian, Printmaking
M Mingenback Art Center, 421 N Second St, 67456. Tel 913-227-3311, Ext 8146; *Chmn Dept* Caroline Kahler; *Asst Prof* Mary Kay; *Assoc Prof* Dr Bruce Kahler; *Asst Prof* Frank Shaw; *Asst Prof* Jennifer Torres
Open daily 8 AM - 5 PM, cl summer & holidays. Estab 1970 as an educational gallery for student & professional exhibitions. Materials are not for pub display, for educational reference only. Average Annual Attendance: 1500
Collections: Oil paintings, watercolors, prints, etchings, lithographs, wood engravings, ceramics & sculpture
Exhibitions: Lucia Student Exhibition; Messiah Exhibition
Activities: Classes for adults; lect open to public; gallery talks; competitions with prizes; scholarships offered

M BIRGER SANDZEN MEMORIAL GALLERY, 401 N First St, PO Box 348, 67456. Tel 913-227-2220; *Dir* Larry L Griffis
Open Wed - Sun 1 - 5 PM, cl Mon, Tues & major holidays. Admis adults $2, grade & high school students $.50. Estab 1957 to permanently exhibit the paintings & prints by the late Birger Sandzen, teacher at Bethany College for 52 years. Ten exhibition areas. Average Annual Attendance: 9000. Mem: 350; dues $5-$1000; annual meeting May for Board of Directors
Income: Financed by admis fees, sales & mem
Collections: H V Poor, Lester Raymer, Birger Sandzen, John Bashor, Elmer Tomasch, Doel Reed & Carl Milles
Exhibitions: Spring & Fall: Guest artist & special exhibits; Winter & Summer: Work from permanent collections
Publications: Birger Sandzen: An Illustrated Biography; The Graphic Work of Birger Sandzen
Activities: Classes for children; docent training; lect open to public, 2-4 vis lectr per year; concerts; gallery talks; tours; sales shop sells books, reproductions, stationary

LOGAN

M DANE G HANSEN MEMORIAL MUSEUM, PO Box 187, 67646. Tel 913-689-4846; FAX 913-689-4833; *Dir* JoAnn Sammons
Open Mon - Fri 9 AM - Noon & 1 - 4 PM, Sat 9 AM - Noon & 1 - 5 PM, Sun & holidays 1 - 5 PM, cl Thanksgiving, Christmas & New Year's. No admis fee. Estab 1973. Traveling exhibitions. Average Annual Attendance: 9000. Mem: dues sustaining $50, patron $15, benefactor $5
Collections: Coins; guns; paintings; prints; sculptures
Activities: Classes for adults & children; lect open to public, 3 vis lectr per years; concerts; tours

MANHATTAN

L KANSAS STATE UNIVERSITY, Paul Weigel Library of Architecture Planning & Design, 323 Seaton Hall, College of Architecture Planning & Design, 66506. Tel 913-532-5968; *Librn* Patricia Weisenburger; *Library Asst* Judy Wyatt; *Ref Librn* Ann Scott
Open Mon - Thurs 8 AM - 10 PM, Fri 8 AM - 5 PM, Sat 11 AM - 5 PM, Sun 2 - 10 PM. Estab 1917. Circ 29,861
Income: $40,000 (financed by state appropriations & gifts)
Library Holdings: Vols 38,806; Per subs 225; Micro — Fiche, reels; Other — Clipping files
Special Subjects: Architecture, Drafting, Graphic Design, Historical Material, Landscape Architecture, Restoration & Conservation, Architectural history, Community & regional planning, Historic preservation, Interior architecture, Landscape architecture
Publications: Subject catalog

M RILEY COUNTY HISTORICAL SOCIETY, Riley County Historical Museum, 2309 Claflin Rd, 66502. Tel 913-565-6490; *Dir* D Cheryl Collins; *Archivist* Jeanne C Mithen
Open Tues - Fri 8:30 AM - 5 PM; Sat & Sun 2 - 5 PM. No admis fee. Estab 1916 to exhibit history & current & historical arts & crafts. Maintains reference library. Average Annual Attendance: 25,000. Mem: 900; dues $10; dinner meetings in Jan, Apr, July & Oct
Income: Financed by Riley County budget
Exhibitions: Household Work Week
Publications: Tracing Traditions, a coloring book for children
Activities: Classes for children, dramatic programs, docent programs; lect open to public; book traveling exhibitions 2 per year; originate traveling exhibitions to schools & club meetings; sales shop sells books, Kansas crafts, wheatweaving, wood cuts, pottery & wood carvings
L Seaton Library, 2309 Claflin Rd, 66502. Tel 913-565-6490; *Archivist* Jeanne C Mithen
Reference, non-circulating collection
Library Holdings: Vols 4000; AV — A-tapes, lantern slides, motion pictures, slides, v-tapes; Other — Clipping files, manuscripts, memorabilia, pamphlets, photographs
Special Subjects: Architecture, Historical Material, Manuscripts, Maps, Manhattan/Riley County Architecture - homes & buildings
Collections: Photo Collection

MCPHERSON

M MCPHERSON COLLEGE GALLERY, Friendship Hall, 1600 E Euclid, 67460. Tel 316-241-0731; FAX 316-241-8443; *Dir* Wayne Conyers
Open Mon - Fri 8 AM - 10 PM. No admis fee. Estab 1960 to present works of art to the college students & to the community. A long gallery which is the entrance to an auditorium, has four showcases & 11 panels 4 x 16 ft. Average Annual Attendance: 2500
Income: Financed through college
Collections: Oils, original prints, watercolors
Activities: Classes for adults; scholarships offered; book traveling exhibitions

M MCPHERSON MUSEUM, 1130 E Euclid, 67460. Tel 316-245-2574; *Museum Dir* Shirley Ade; *Display Arrangement* Nadine Logback; *Office* Patty Johnson
Open Tues - Sun 1 - 5 PM, cl Mon & holidays. Admis adult $1. Estab 1890. Average Annual Attendance: 7000
Income: Financed by city appropriation
Collections: Fossils of mammoths, mastodons, saber tooth tigers & many other fossils; oriental & African collection; Pioneer artifacts & Indian artifacts
Exhibitions: Fall Festival; Victorian Christmas; Quilt Show
Publications: McPherson Museum Memoranda

NORTH NEWTON

L BETHEL COLLEGE, Mennonite Library & Archives, PO Drawer A, 67117-9989. Tel 316-284-5304; FAX 316-284-5286; Elec Mail mla@bethelks.edu. *Archivist* John D Thiesen
Open Mon - Thurs 10 AM - 5 PM. No admis fee. Estab 1936 to preserve resources related to Mennonite history for the use of researchers
Income: $70,000 (financed by college & church conference support)
Library Holdings: Micro — Fiche, reels; AV — A-tapes, cassettes, fs, Kodachromes, lantern slides, motion pictures, rec, slides, v-tapes; Other — Clipping files, exhibition catalogs, framed reproductions, manuscripts, memorabilia, original art works, pamphlets, photographs, prints, reproductions
Special Subjects: Ethnology, Historical Material, Manuscripts, Painting - American, Painting - Dutch, Painting - German, Photography, Religious Art
Collections: 500 paintings and etchings by Mennonite artists
Exhibitions: Photographs of Hopi and Cheyenne Indians; The Dutch Setting: Mennonite Personalities & Their Environment; Children of Yesterday; Weddings of Yesterday
Publications: Mennonite Life, quarterly journal

NORTON

C FIRST STATE BANK, 105 W Main, 67654. Tel 913-877-3341; FAX 913-877-5808; *Pres* L O Concannon; *VPres* Ann R Hazlett
Open Mon - Fri 9 AM - 3 PM. Estab 1965 as a gallery of those who ran for President of the United States & lost
Collections: Also Ran Gallery; Elephants display

SALINA

A ASSOCIATION OF COMMUNITY ARTS AGENCIES OF KANSAS, PO Box 1363, 67402-1363. Tel 913-825-2700; FAX 913-823-1992; Elec Mail acaakshar@aol.com, acaaeeilen@aol.com. *Exec Dir* Ellen Morgan
Estab 1970 to work with community arts agencies & organizations to develop an environment in which the arts can flourish; facilitator & advocate for the growth of the arts in Kansas communities

M SALINA ART CENTER, 242 S Santa Fe, PO Box 743, 67402-0743. Tel 913-827-1431; *Dir* Saralyn Reece Hardy
Open daily Noon - 5 PM, cl Mon. No admis fee. Estab 1979 as an international & national private non-profit, non-collecting contemporary art & educ center. Average Annual Attendance: 30,000. Mem: 500; dues $30
Income: $350,000 (financed by mem & private donations)
Exhibitions: Contemporary Art; changing exhibitions; Annual Juried Show
Publications: Brochures; newsletters
Activities: Classes for adults & children; docent programs; lect open to public, 6-8 vis lectr per year; competitions; traveling exten dept serves rural Kansas; book traveling exhibitions 4 per year; originate traveling exhibitions 5 per year

TOPEKA

M KANSAS STATE HISTORICAL SOCIETY, Kansas Museum of History, 6425 SW Sixth Ave, 66615-1099. Tel 913-272-8681; FAX 913-272-8682; *Exec Dir* Ramon Powers; *Museum Dir* Robert Keckeisen; *Cur Fine Art* Anne Marvin; *Cur of Decorative Art* Blair Tarr
Open Mon - Sat 9 AM - 4:30 PM, Sun 12:30 - 4:30 PM. No admis fee. Estab 1875 to collect, preserve & interpret the historical documents & objects of Kansas history. Average Annual Attendance: 140,000. Mem: 3400; dues life $1000, special $50 - $1000, family $35, individual $25, student $15; meetings in spring & fall
Income: $784,000 (financed by endowment & state)
Collections: Regional collection for period from middle 19th century to present, especially portraiture, native art, political cartoons & folk art
Exhibitions: Rotating Exhibits
Publications: Kansas History: Journal of the Central Plains, quarterly; exhibit catalogs
Activities: Classes for adults & children; dramatic programs; docent training; craft demonstration program; lect open to public, 4 vis lectr per year; provided by staff to public organizations on request; tours; slide tape programs; exten dept serves entire state of Kansas; traveling trunks on Kansas topics; book traveling exhibitions 1-2 per year; sales shop sells books, prints, cards, slides, postcards, folk art, crafts, souvenirs and jewelry; junior museum

M TOPEKA & SHAWNEE COUNTY PUBLIC LIBRARY, Gallery of Fine Arts, 1515 SW Tenth St, 66604-1374. Tel 913-231-0527; FAX 913-233-2055; *Dir* David L Leamon; *Dept Dir* Tom J Muth; *Gallery Dir* Larry D Peters
Open Mon - Fri 9 AM - 9 PM, Sat 9 AM - 6 PM, Sun 2 - 6 PM (Labor Day - Memorial Day). No admis fee. Estab 1870 to serve the city & the Northeast Kansas Library System residents with public information, both educational & recreational; to be one of the areas cultural centers through services from the Gallery of Fine Arts within the library. Gallery is 40 ft x 30 ft, with track lighting, carpet covered walls & security system; gallery furniture. Average Annual Attendance: 2400
Purchases: $72,713
Collections: Art Mouveau Glass, 19th Century Chinese Decorative Arts; Hirschberg Collection of West African Arts; Johnson Collection of Art; Wilder Collection of Art Glass & Pottery; †Contemporary American Ceramics; †Glass paperweight collection; New Mexican Woodcarving; Rare Book Room; †Regional painting, drawing & prints
Publications: Creative Expression in Rural West Africa; Rookwood Pottery: One Hundred Year Anniversary
Activities: Lect open to public, 1-2 vis lectr per year; concerts; gallery talks; tours; competitions with awards; individual paintings & original objects of art lent to other qualified museums; book traveling exhibitions annually; sales shop sells books, magazines, records, tapes & CDs

M WASHBURN UNIVERSITY, Mulvane Art Museum, 17th & Jewell, 66621. Tel 913-231-1010, Ext 1324; FAX 913-234-2703; *Dir* Robert T Soppelsa; *Asst to Dir* Judith L Lennox; *Educ Coordr* Kathleen R Hughes; *Office Asst* Elizabeth V Wunder
Open Tues & Wed 10 AM - 7 PM, Thurs & Fri 10 AM - 4 PM, Sat & Sun 1 - 4 PM, cl holidays. No admis fee. Estab 1922. Building gift of Joab Mulvane: provides three galleries with 319 running ft of hanging space with carpeted walls & temperature & humidity controlled. Average Annual Attendance: 30,000. Mem: 600; dues $25 & up
Income: $250,000
Purchases: $10,000
Collections: 18th-19th Century Japanese Fine & Decorative Art; 19th & 20th Century American Art; 16th-20th Century European Prints
Exhibitions: Contemporary Mountain-Plains regional painting, prints, sculpture, ceramics; changing exhibitions include a Kansas Artist Exhibit & Annual Mountain-Plains Art Fair
Publications: Exhibition brochures
Activities: Classes for adults & children; outreach programs: Art in School, Art After School; docent training; lect open to public, 4-6 vis lectr per year; gallery talks; tours; scholarships; individuals painting & original objects of art lent to accredited art museums; book traveling exhibitions; museum shop sells original art, reproductions, wide range of art-related & educational gift items

WICHITA

FRIENDS UNIVERSITY

M Whittier Fine Arts Gallery, 2100 University, 67213. Tel 316-261-5877; FAX 316-262-5027; *Cur* Annie Lowrey
Open daily 7:45 AM - 10 PM. No admis fee. Estab 1963 to bring art-craft exhibits to campus as an educational learning experience & to supply the local community with first class exhibits. 1224 sq ft of exhibit space. Average Annual Attendance: 20,000
Publications: Exhibition catalogs
Activities: Lect open to public, 4 vis lectr per year; gallery talks; tours; exten dept

L Edmund Stanley Library, 2100 University Ave, 67213. Tel 316-261-5880; FAX 316-263-1092; *Dir* David Pappas; *Asst to Dir* Max Burson
Estab 1979. 500 sq ft of exhibition space, ideal for crafts & locked cases
Library Holdings: Vols 85,000; Per subs 640

M GALLERY XII, 412 E Douglas Ave, Ste A, 67202. Tel 316-267-5915; *Pres* Judy Dove
Open Mon - Sat 10 AM - 4 PM. No admis fee. Estab 1977 as art cooperative. Average Annual Attendance: 10,000. Mem: dues $400
Income: $40,000 (financed by mem)
Activities: Sales shop sells original art

A KANSAS WATERCOLOR SOCIETY, Wichita Art Museum, PO Box 1796, Hutchinson, 67504-1796. Tel 316-662-1517; *Pres* Shirley G Johnson
Estab 1968 to promote watercolor in Kansas. Mem: 185; dues $20, annual meeting in June
Income: Financed by mem, entry fees & patrons
Exhibitions: KWS 7-State Exhibition
Publications: Newsletter, quarterly
Activities: Demonstrations & workshops; lect open to public; gallery talks; tours; competions with awards; traveling exhibitions organized & circulated

M MID-AMERICA ALL-INDIAN CENTER, Indian Center Museum, 650 N Seneca, 67203. Tel 316-262-5221; FAX 316-262-4216; Elec Mail icm@southwind.net. *Exec Dir* John Ortiz; *Museum Dir* Jerry P Martin
Open Mon - Sat 10 AM - 5 PM, Sun 1 - 5 PM, cl Mon Oct 1 - May 1. Admis adults $2, children 6-12 $1, under 6 free. Estab 1976 to preserve the Indian heritage, culture & traditions. Average Annual Attendance: 60,000. Mem: 400; dues benefactor $500 & up, patron $250 - $499, friend $100 - $249, contributor $50 - $99, family $35 - $49, individual $25 - $34
Income: Financed by admis, donations, mem & gift shop sales
Collections: Native American arts and artifacts; Mildred Many Memorial Collection; Lincoln Ellsworth Collection; Plains beadwork; Northwest Coast & Eskimo crafts; Southwest pottery, paintings, sculpture, carvings & basketry
Exhibitions: Four changing exhibits per year, prehistory or speciality exhibits; three dimensional traditional art; two & three dimensional contemporary art
Publications: Gallery Notes, quarterly newsletter
Activities: Classes for adults & children; docent training; lect open to the public; gallery talks; tours; museum shop sells books, magazines, original art, reproductions & prints

L Library, 650 N Seneca, 67203. Tel 316-262-5221; Elec Mail icm@southwind.net. *Dir* Jerry P Martin; *Registrar* Sue Cowdery
Reference only
Library Holdings: Vols 400; AV — Fs, motion pictures, slides; Other — Pamphlets
Collections: Indian art & history

A NATIONAL SOCIETY OF TOLE & DECORATIVE PAINTERS, INC, 393 N McLean Blvd, PO Box 808, 67203. Tel 316-269-9300; FAX 316-269-3535; Elec Mail nstdp@aol.com. *Team Adminr* Julie Vosberg; *Team Adminr* Doris Hawkey; *Team Adminr* Marshall Williams
Open Mon - Fri 8:30 AM - 4:30 PM. No admis fee. Estab 1972 to provide information about decorative painting activities, stimulate interest in the art form. Mem: 28,000; dues $30; 5 day convention in May
Income: $132,370 (financed by mem & gifts)
Collections: Decorative Arts Collection - antique & contemporary decorative art; various media
Publications: The Decorative Painter, magazine 6 times a year
Activities: Lending collection; originate traveling exhibitions

M **WICHITA ART MUSEUM,** 619 Stackman Dr, 67203. Tel 316-268-4921; FAX 316-268-4980; *Dir* Inez Wolins; *Chief Cur* Novelene Ross; *Registrar* Barbara Odevseff
Open Tues - Sat 10 AM - 5 PM, Sun Noon - 5 PM, cl Mon & holidays. No admis fee. Estab 1935 to house & exhibit art works belonging to permanent collection; to present exhibits of loaned art works, to ensure care & maintain the safety of works through security, environmental controls & appropriate curatorial functions & to interpret collections & exhibitions through formal & educational presentations. Facility designed by Edward Larrabee Barnes opened Oct 1977. Average Annual Attendance: 85,000. Mem: dues $25 up
Income: $1,200,000
Collections: Roland P Murdock, American Art; M C Naftzger Collection of Charles M Russell (paintings, drawings & sculpture); Kurdian Collection of Pre-Columbian Mexican Art; Virginia & George Ablah Collection of British Watercolors; L S & Ida L Naftzger Collection of Prints & Drawings; Gwen Houston Naftzger Collection of Boehm & Doughty Porcelain Birds; Florence Naftzger Evans Collection of Porcelain & Faience
Publications: Catalog of Roland P Murdock Collection; bi-monthly newsletter; exhibition brochures & catalogues
Activities: Classes for adults & children; docent training; lect open to public; gallery talks; tours; museum shop sells books, magazines, original art, reproductions, slides, jewelry & art related objects
L **Library,** 619 Stackman Dr, 67203. Tel 316-268-4921; FAX 316-268-4980; *Librn* Lois F Crane
Open Tues - Fri 10 AM - 5 PM. Estab 1963 as research library for mus staff. Reference only
Library Holdings: Vols 7000; Per subs 15; Auction catalogs; Museum handbooks; Micro — Fiche; AV — V-tapes; Other — Clipping files, exhibition catalogs, manuscripts, pamphlets
Special Subjects: American Indian Art, American Western Art, Art History, Decorative Arts, Drawings, Etchings & Engravings, Folk Art, Landscapes, Painting - American, Pre-Columbian Art, Prints, Sculpture, Watercolors, History of American Art
Collections: Elizabeth S Navas Collection; Gene Morse Collection

A **WICHITA CENTER FOR THE ARTS,** 9112 E Central, 67206. Tel 316-634-2787; FAX 316-634-0593; *Chmn Board* Hal Ross; *Exec Dir* Sally Luallen; *Treas* Kathy Galichia
Open Tues - Fri 10 AM - 5 PM, Sat & Sun 1 - 5 PM, cl national holidays & week of July 4th. No admis fee. Estab 1920, incorporated 1932, as an educational & cultural institution. Gallery contains 1000 running ft of exhibit space; up to five exhibits each six-week period. Average Annual Attendance: 55,000. Mem: 1250; dues $35 & up
Income: Financed by private contributions
Collections: Prints and drawings, paintings, sculpture, †American decorative arts & contemporary crafts
Exhibitions: Exhibitions change each six weeks; one man shows; special programs; Biennial National Craft Exhibit
Publications: Quarterly newsletter
Activities: Visual & performing arts classes for adults & children; theatre productions; docent training; lect open to public, up to 6 vis lectr per year; gallery talks; classic film series; competitions with awards; scholarships; individual paintings & original objects of art lent to other art museums; book traveling exhibitions; originate traveling exhibitions; sales shop sells books & original art

L **WICHITA PUBLIC LIBRARY,** 223 S Main, 67202. Tel 316-262-0611; *Head Librn* Richard J Rademacher; *Asst Librn* Gary D Hime; *Adult Serv Div Coordr* Myrna Hudson; *Pub Support Serv* Diana Williams; *Youth Serv Div Coordr* Judy Nichols
Open Mon - Thurs 10 AM - 9 PM, Fri & Sat 10 AM - 5:30, Sun 1 - 5 PM. Estab 1876 & grown to be informational center & large free public library to improve the communiy with educational, cultural & recreational benefits through books, recordings, films, art works & other materials. Circ 1,100,000
Income: $4,000,000 (from local taxes)
Library Holdings: Micro — Reels; AV — Motion pictures, rec; Other — Framed reproductions
Special Subjects: Advertising Design, Afro-American Art, American Indian Art, American Western Art, Architecture, Coins & Medals, Crafts, Decorative Arts, Film, Folk Art, Furniture, Glass, Graphic Arts
Collections: Kansas Book Collection; John F Kennedy Collection; Harry Mueller Philately Book Collection; Driscoll Piracy Collection
Exhibitions: Preview of Academy Award Short Subjects
Activities: Lect; tours

M **WICHITA STATE UNIVERSITY,** Edwin A Ulrich Museum of Art, 1845 Fairmount, 67260-0046. Tel 316-978-3664; FAX 316-978-3898; Elec Mail knaub@twsuvm.uc.twsu.edu. *Dir* Donald E Knaub; *Cur Exhib* Dana Self; *Asst Cur Coll Management* Gabriela Magnuson; *Asst Cur Exhibition Serv* Kevin Mullins
Open daily Noon - 5 PM, cl major holidays. No admis fee. Estab 1974 to provide exhibitions of contemporary & 20th century art for the benefit of the university & community. The museum was established to provide members of the university community with an educational & research facility for art, to exhibit traveling shows by nationally & internationally recognized artists & to organize touring exhibitions from the permanent collection. Galleries consist of 4160 sq ft collection gallery & 1860 sq ft in temporary exhibition galleries
Income: Financed by endowment & state funds
Purchases: Claes Oldenburg, invented Q (T P White); Ed Hendricks, untitled, 1992-III; Jaune Quick-To-See Smith, Survival, Suite of four lithographs; 10 x 10; portfolio of 10 prints by 10 women
Collections: The Bloomfield Collection; †The Martin Bush Outdoor Sculpture Collection of 60 pieces featuring a 28x52 ft mosaic mural designed by Joan Miro; The Charles Grafly Memorial Collection; The Harris Klein African Collection; The H E Platt Jr Collection of Asian Ceramics; The Elizabeth Sprague Collection; The Harold Weston Memorial Collection; The Permanent Collection, with emphasis on contemporary & 20th century American & European artwork;

Ulrich Collection of Frederick J Waugh (painting); collection of prints by Honore Daumier, Arthur B Davies, Albrecht Altdorfer, Harry Sternberg, Anthony van Dyck; collections of sculpture by Ernest Trova & Charles Grafly; prints & drawings by William Gropper; paintings by Josef Presser
Publications: The Sculptor's Clay, Charles Grafly (1862-1929); Subversive Domesticity
Activities: Originate traveling exhibitions

WINFIELD

L **SOUTHWESTERN COLLEGE,** Memorial Library - Art Dept, 100 College, 67156. Tel 316-221-8225; FAX 316-221-8382; *Dir* Gregory J Zuck
Open school year Mon - Thurs 8 AM - 10 PM, Fri 8 AM - 4 PM, Sat Noon - 4 PM, Sun 3 - 10 PM, summer Mon - Fri 8 AM - 4 PM. Estab 1885 as a four-year liberal arts college. Circ 30,000
Income: Financed by college budget
Library Holdings: Vols 62,000; Per subs 300; Micro — Fiche, reels
Collections: Arthur Covey Collection of paintings, mural sketches, etchings, lithographs, drawings and watercolors; Cunningham Asian Arts Collection of books, catalogues & exhibition catalogs
Activities: Tours

KENTUCKY

ASHLAND

C **ASHLAND OIL, INC,** PO Box 391, 41114. Tel 606-329-3333; FAX 606-329-3559; *Corporate Art Admin* Tim Heaberlin
Collection may be viewed through special arrangements. Estab 1972, primary function is decorative art, but also to establish a creative atmosphere; to enhance community cultural life. Collection displayed in public areas of corporate office buildings
Collections: Mainly contemporary printmaking, emphasis on Americans; paintings, sculpture, wall hangings
Activities: Tours; competitions, sponsorship consists of purchase awards for local art group & museum competitions; provides purchase & merit awards for certain museum & university competitions; individual objects of art lent; originate traveling exhibitions to museums, colleges, universities & art centers in general marketing areas

BEREA

M **BEREA COLLEGE,** Doris Ulmann Galleries, Art Dept, CPO 2342, 40404. Tel 606-986-9341, Ext 5530; Elec Mail robert_f.boyce@berea.edu. *Dir* Robert Boyce
Open Mon - Fri 8 AM - 5 PM, Sun 1 - 5 PM. No admis fee. Estab 1936 for educational purposes. Three gallery areas; exhibitions change monthly; loan & rental shows, regional artists, work from Berea College collection. Average Annual Attendance: 6500
Income: Financed by college budget
Collections: Kress Study Collection of Renaissance art; Doris Ulmann photographs; prints, textiles, paintings, sculpture, ceramics; Asian Art
Activities: Educ Dept; lect open to public, 2-6 vis lectr per year; gallery talks; tours; scholarships offered; individual paintings & original objects of art lent to other colleges, museums & galleries; lending collection contains 500 framed reproductions
L **Art Dept Library,** CPO 2342, 40404. Tel 606-986-9341, Ext 5276; *Dept Chair* Walter Hyleck
Open Mon - Fri 8 AM - 5 PM. Estab 1936. Reference library only
Income: Financed by college budget
Purchases: $1200 annually
Library Holdings: Vols 3500; Per subs 30; AV — Cassettes, fs, Kodachromes, lantern slides, rec, slides, v-tapes; Other — Clipping files, exhibition catalogs, framed reproductions, manuscripts, memorabilia, original art works, pamphlets, photographs, prints, reproductions, sculpture

M **BEREA COLLEGE,** Appalachian Museum, 103 Jackson St, 40404. Tel 606-986-9341, Ext 6078; FAX 606-986-4506; Elec Mail christopher_a.miller@berea.edu. *Dir* Christopher A Miller; *Cur* Juliette Sowell
Open Mon - Sat 9 AM - 6 PM, Sun 1 - 6 PM, cl Jan. Admis $.50 -1.50. Estab 1969 to collect, preserve & interpret history of Berea College & Appalachian Region. Mem: 50; dues $15-$300
Income: Financed by earned revenue & support from College
Collections: †Appalachian Crafts; †Berea College & Related Crafts; Kentucky Crafts & Folk Art
Activities: Museum shop sells books, magazines & music

A **KENTUCKY GUILD OF ARTISTS & CRAFTSMEN INC,** * 128 Main St, 40403. Tel 606-986-3192; FAX 606-985-9114; *Dir* Anna Reiss
Open Mon - Fri 10 AM - 4 PM. No admis fee. Estab 1961 for the pursuit of excellence in the arts & crafts & to encourage the pub appreciation thereof. Average Annual Attendance: 20,000. Mem: 500; must be a Kentucky resident & be juried for exhibiting status; dues individual $25; annual meeting in Nov
Income: $100,000 (financed by grants, contributions, admis & mem fees)
Exhibitions: Two annual fairs include a members exhibit
Publications: The Guild Record, 4 times per yr
Activities: Classes for adults & children; docent training; workshops; lect open to public; demonstrations; competitions with awards; 2 annual retail fairs; traveling exhibitions organized & circulated

BOWLING GREEN

WESTERN KENTUCKY UNIVERSITY
M **Kentucky Museum**, 42101. Tel 502-745-2592; FAX 502-745-4878; *Dept Head* Riley Handy; *Cur Exhib* Donna Parker; *Cur Coll & Registrar* Sandra Staebell; *Cur Educ* Dianne Watkins
Open Tues - Sat 9:30 AM - 4 PM, Sun 1 - 4 PM. Admis family $5, adult $2, children $1, members free. As well as offering exhibits & programs of wide interest, the mus also serves as a research & educational resource for scholars, specialists & academic units of the University. The museum's subject area is the history & art of Kentucky, with supportive areas in American art & decorative arts & European art. Average Annual Attendance: 36,000
Income: Financed by state appropriation & university
Activities: Workshops for adults & children; docent training; lect open to public, 2 vis lectr per year; gallery talks; tours; individual paintings & original objects of art lent to public institutions & museums; originate traveling exhibitions; museum shop sells books, magazines, reproductions, contemporary arts & crafts, toys, textiles
L **Kentucky Library**, 42101. Tel 502-745-5083; FAX 502-745-4878; *Dept Head* Riley Handy
Open to the public for reference
Library Holdings: Vols 70,000; Per subs 1800; Broadsides; Maps; Postcards; Micro — Reels; AV — A-tapes, cassettes, Kodachromes, lantern slides, rec, slides; Other — Clipping files, framed reproductions, manuscripts, memorabilia, original art works, pamphlets, photographs
Collections: Ellis Collection of steamboat pictures; Gerard Collection of Bowling Green Photographs; McGregor Collection of rare books; Neal Collection of Utopian materials
M **University Gallery**, Ivan Wilson Ctr for Fine Arts, Rm 443, 42101. Tel 502-745-3944; *Dir* Leo Fernandez
Open Mon - Fri 8:30 AM - 4:30 PM. No admis fee. Estab 1973 for art exhibitions relating to university instruction & regional cultural needs. Average Annual Attendance: 12,000
Income: Financed by state appropriation

CRESTVIEW

M **THOMAS MORE COLLEGE**, TM Gallery, 333 Thomas More Pky, 41017. Tel 606-344-3420, 344-3419; FAX 606-344-3345; *Dir* Barb Rauf; *Asst Dir* Joan Enzweiler
Open Mon - Sat 8:30 AM - 10 PM. No admis fee. Estab for cultural & educational enrichment for the institution & area. Average Annual Attendance: 2000
Exhibitions: Full academic season of exhibitions
Activities: Lect open to public, 1-2 vis lectr per year; scholarships & fels offered; book traveling exhibitions

DANVILLE

M **EPHRAIM MCDOWELL-CAMBUS-KENNETH FOUNDATION**, McDowell House & Apothecary Shop, 125 S Second St, 40422. Tel 606-236-2804; *Cur* George Grider; *Dir* Carol Johnson Senn; *Asst Dir* Alberta Moynahan
Open Mon - Sat 10 AM - Noon & 1 - 4 PM, Sun 2 - 4 PM, cl Mon Nov 1 - Mar 1. Admis adults $3, senior citizens $2, students $1, children under 12 $.50, group rates available. Estab 1935 to preserve the home of the Father of Abdominal Surgery in Danville, 1795 - 1830. Average Annual Attendance: 5000. Mem: 600; dues $20-$1000
Income: $36,000 (financed by endowment, mem, private contribution from groups & individuals)
Collections: All furnishings pre-1830; apothecary collection: late 18th & early 19th Century, 320 pieces; portraits & folk art, 1795-1830
Publications: Annual newsletter
Activities: Docent training; lect open to public, 50 vis lectr per year; tours; sales shop sells books, prints, slides, pewter mugs

FORT KNOX

M **CAVALRY - ARMOR FOUNDATION**, Patton Museum of Cavalry & Armor, 4554 Fayette Ave, PO Box 208, 40121-0208. Tel 502-624-3812; FAX 502-624-2364; *Dir* John M Purdy; *Cur* Charles R Lemons
Open year round weekdays 9 AM - 4:30 PM, holidays & weekends May 1 - Sept 30 10 AM - 6 PM, Oct 1 - Apr 30 10 AM - 4:30 PM, cl Dec 24 & 25 & Dec 31 - Jan 1. No admis fee. Estab 1975 to preserve historical materials relating to Cavalry & Armor & to make these properties available for public exhibit & research. The Museum is administered by the US Army Armor Center, Fort Knox & is one of the largest in the US Army Museum System. Galleries feature a variety of armored equipment & vehicles, weapons, art & other memorabilia which chronologically present the development of the Armor branch from the beginning of mechanization to the present
Activities: Retail store sells books & prints

FRANKFORT

M **KENTUCKY HISTORICAL SOCIETY**, Old State Capitol & Annex, PO Box 1792, 40602. Tel 502-564-3016; FAX 502-564-4701; *Dir* Dr James Klotter
Open Mon - Sat 9 AM - 4 PM, Sun 1 - 5 PM. No admis fee. Estab 1836 as a general history & art mus emphasizing the history, culture & decorative arts of the Commonwealth of Kentucky & its people. The Old Capitol Galleries located in the Old State House consist of two rooms totaling 2740 sq ft which are used by the Mus to display its fine arts exhibitions, painting, silver, furniture & sculpture, one temporary exhibits gallery in Old Capitol Annex. Average Annual Attendance: 50,000. Mem: 6000; dues for life $300 individual $25
Income: $560,000 (financed by state appropriation)
Collections: Kentucky & American furniture coverlets, furniture, paintings, quilts,

silver, textiles
Publications: The Register, The Bulletin, quarterly
Activities: Lect open to public, 4 vis lectr per year; tours; individual paintings & original objects of art lent to qualified museums; lending collection consists of original art works, original prints; paintings; sculpture & historical artifacts; book traveling exhibitions; traveling exhibitions organized and circulated; museum shop sells books & reproductions
L **Library**, PO Box 1792, 40602. Tel 502-564-3016; FAX 502-564-4701; *Head Librn* Anne McDonnell
Library Holdings: Vols 85,000

M **KENTUCKY NEW STATE CAPITOL**, Division of Historic Properties, Capitol Ave, 700 Louiville Rd, 40601. Tel 502-564-3000; Capitol Tour Desk 502-564-3449. *Cur* Lou Karibo
Open Mon - Fri 8 AM - 4:30 PM, At 9 AM - 4 PM, Sun 1 - 4 PM. No admis fee
Income: Funded by city appropriation
Collections: First Lady, Miniature Dolls; Oil Paintings of Chief Justices; Statues of Famous Kentuckians including Abraham Lincoln & Jefferson Davis
Publications: Brochures; exhibition catalogs

M **KENTUCKY STATE UNIVERSITY**, Jackson Hall Gallery, Art Dept, 40601. Tel 502-227-5995, 227-5994; *Area Head* John Batter
Open Mon - Fri 8 AM - 4:30 PM. No admis fee. Gallery. Average Annual Attendance: 2000
Income: Financed through small grants & university appropriations
Collections: A small collection of students & faculty work
Exhibitions: Rotating exhibits
Activities: Lect open to public, 4 vis lectr per year; competitions; scholarships offered; book traveling exhibitions 2-3 per year

M **LIBERTY HALL HISTORIC SITE**, Liberty Hall Museum, 218 Wilkinson St, 40601. Tel 502-227-2560; *Dir* Carter Lively; *Cur* Mary Elizabeth Smith
Open Tues - Sat 10 AM - 5 PM, Sun 2 - 5 PM, cl Mon & holidays. Admis adults $2, children & students $.50. Estab 1937 as an historic museum. A Georgian house built in 1796, named Historic Landmark in 1972
Collections: 18th century furniture; china; silver; portraits
Activities: Guided tours
L **Library**, 218 Wilkinson St, 40601. Tel 502-227-2560; *Dir* Carter Lively
Open Tues 11 AM - 3PM. Non-circulating library
Library Holdings: Vols 2000
Collections: Books belonging to John Brown, Kentucky's first US senator & builder of Liberty Hall
M **Orlando Brown House**, 220 Wilkinson St, 40601. Tel 502-875-4952; *Dir* Carter Lively
Open Tues - Sat 10 AM - 4 PM, Sun 2 - 4 PM, cl Mon and holidays. Admis adults $1.50, children $.50. Estab 1956. Built in 1835 by architect Gilbert Shryock
Collections: Paul Sawyier paintings; original furnishings
Activities: Guided tours

GEORGETOWN

M **GEORGETOWN COLLEGE GALLERY**, Mullberry St, PO Box 201, 40324. Tel 502-863-8106; FAX 502-868-8888; Elec Mail jmccormi@gtc.georgetown.ky.us. *Chmn* James McCormick
Open Mon, Wed & Fri Noon - 4:30 PM. No admis fee. Estab 1959 as educational gallery with various mediums & styles. Gallery has 100 running ft wall space, portable screens. Average Annual Attendance: 1200
Collections: †Contemporary graphics; †contemporary painting & sculpture; crafts; artifacts
Activities: Classes for children; lect open to public; 1-2 vis lectr per year;; scholarships & fels offered; exten dept; individual paintings & original objects of art lent to museums

HARRODSBURG

M **OLD FORT HARROD STATE PARK MANSION MUSEUM**, S College St, PO Box 156, 40330. Tel 606-734-3314; *Supt* Susan T Barrington
Open daily 9 AM - 5:30 PM. Admis $2. Estab 1925. Average Annual Attendance: 60,000
Collections: Antique China; Confederate Room; Daniel Boone & George Rogers Clark Room; furniture; gun collection; Indian artifacts; Lincoln Room; musical instruments; silver
Exhibitions: Permanent collection

M **SHAKER VILLAGE OF PLEASANT HILL**, 3501 Lexington Rd, 40330. Tel 606-734-5411; FAX 606-734-5411; *Pres & Chief Exec Officer* James C Thomas; *Dir Museum* Larrie Curry; *Public Relations Dir* Marcheta Sparrow; *Educ Specialist* Susan Hughes
Open Apr - Oct daily 9:30 AM - 6 PM, hours vary in winter. Admis adults $9, children 12-high school $4.50, children between 6 & 11 $2.50. Estab 1961 to restore, preserve & interpret the architecture, artifacts & culture of Shakers. 2800 acres, 33 historic buildings (1805-1855); Primary exhibition building: 40 room centre family dwelling (1824-1834); stone, three story dwelling full of artifacts & furniture of Shakers. Average Annual Attendance: 140,000. Mem: 2300; dues family $50, individual $30; annual meeting in Feb
Income: Financed by mem, endowment, inn & lodging, sales, village-generated income
Collections: Shaker culture including †furniture, †textiles, †manuscripts, †cultural artifacts, architecture, period rooms & shops
Activities: Classes for adults & children; dramatic programs; docent training; lect open to public, 15-25 vis lectr per year; concerts; tours; lending collection contains videos; museum shop sells reproductions, prints & slides

HIGHLAND HEIGHTS

M **NORTHERN KENTUCKY UNIVERSITY GALLERY**, Nunn Dr, 41099-1002.
Tel 606-572-5421; FAX 606-572-6051; *Dir* David Knight
Open Mon - Fri 9 AM - 6 PM. No admis fee. Estab 1968, new location 1990, to
provide an arts center for the University & community area. Two galleries are
maintained, the smaller 15 X 30. Average Annual Attendance: 20,000
Income: Financed by university & state funds
Collections: Permanent collection of Red Grooms Monumental Sculpture in
Metal; Donald Judd Monumental Sculpture; earth works, other outdoor
sculpture, prints, painting, photographs, folk art
Exhibitions: Student exhibitions; state, regional & national visiting artists
Publications: Bulletins, 4-5 per year
Activities: Lect open to public, 3-5 vis lectr per year; gallery talks; individual
paintings & original objects of art lent to university members to be used in their
offices only; lending collection contains 379 prints, paintings, photographs &
ceramics

LEXINGTON

M **HEADLEY-WHITNEY MUSEUM**, 4435 Old Frankfort Pike, 40510. Tel 606-
255-6653; FAX 606-255-8375; *Pres* James Frazier; *Dir* Diane C Wachs; *Cur* Lisa
K Blackadar
Open Tues - Fri 10 AM - 5 PM, Sat & Sun Noon - 5 PM. Admis adults $4,
senior citizens $3, AAA $3, students $2, members & children 5 & under free.
Estab 1968 in central Kentucky for the collection, preservation & interpretation
of fine examples of visual arts with an emphasis on the decorative arts.
Five principal galleries are maintained. Average Annual Attendance: 9800. Mem: 500;
dues $100, $45, $35, $25 & $10; annual meeting in July
Income: Financed by admis, mem, benefits, grants, contributions & trust
Collections: Antique boxes, gemstones, jeweled bibelots, Oriental porcelains &
textiles: American Jewelry
Exhibitions: Monthly exhibitions
Publications: Headley Treasure of Bibelots & Boxes (catalog of Bibelot
Collection); newsletters, quarterly, for mem
Activities: Classes for adults & children; docent training; symposia; lect open to
public, 6 vis lectr per year; concerts; gallery talks; tours; competitions with prizes;
individual paintings & original objects of art lent; lending collection contains
slides, selected works from permanent collections by special arrangement;
museum shop sells books, original art, reproductions, slides, jewelry & porcelains

L **Library**, 4435 Old Frankfort Pike, 40510. Tel 606-255-6653; FAX 606-255-8375;
Chmn Board James Frazier; *Dir* Diane C Wachs; *Cur* Lisa Blackadar
Open Tues - Fri 10 AM - 5 PM, Sat & Sun Noon - 5 PM. Estab 1968. For
reference, research, visitors' & scholars'
Income: Financed by state government, foundations, admis, mem, benefits,
grants, contributions & trust
Library Holdings: Vols 1500; AV — Kodachromes, slides, v-tapes; Other —
Clipping files, exhibition catalogs, memorabilia, original art works, pamphlets,
photographs, reproductions
Special Subjects: Antiquities-Egyptian, Antiquities-Greek, Antiquities-Oriental,
Antiquities-Persian, Antiquities-Roman, Art History, Asian Art, Bronzes,
Ceramics, Decorative Arts, Embroidery, Enamels, Fashion Arts, Furniture,
Glass, Gemstones, Minerals
Publications: The Jewel, quarterly for mem

A **LEXINGTON ART LEAGUE, INC**, Loudoun House, 209 Castlewood Dr,
40505. Tel 606-254-7024; *Exec Dir* Jerry McGee
Open Tues - Fri Noon - 4 PM, Sat & Sun 1 - 4 PM. No admis fee. Estab 1957,
to encourage an active interest in the visual arts among its members &
community as a whole. Three visual art galleries. Average Annual Attendance:
5000. Mem: 420; dues $25; annual meeting in Apr
Income: Financed by mem, art fairs, donations, grants
Exhibitions: Changing monthly exhibitions; member, group, one person
exhibitions
Publications: Annual Membership Book; newsletter, quarterly
Activities: Classes for adults & children; lect, 4 vis lectr per year; gallery talks;
tours; competitions; originate traveling exhibitions

M **LIVING ARTS & SCIENCE CENTER, INC**, * 362 N Martin Luther King
Blvd, 40508. Tel 606-252-5222; *Dir* Marty Henton; *Cur* Jim Brancaccio
Open Mon - Fri 9 AM - 4 PM, Sat 10 AM - 1 PM. No admis fee. Estab 1968 to
provide enrichment opportunities in the arts & sciences. Gallery features 8-10
exhibits per year with regional art. Average Annual Attendance: 25,000. Mem:
400; dues $15-500; annual meetings
Income: Financed by grants & fundraising events
Exhibitions: Ten temporary art exhibits per year.
Publications: Exhibition catalogs
Activities: Classes for adults & children; lect open to public; tours; design &
children's art competition with cash awards; class scholarships offered; book
traveling exhibitions once per year

M **TRANSYLVANIA UNIVERSITY**, Morlan Gallery, Mitchell Fine Arts Ctr, 300
N Broadway, 40508. Tel 606-233-8210; *Dir* Nancy Wolsk
Open Mon - Fri Noon - 5 PM. No admis fee. Gallery is housed in The Mitchell
Fine Arts Building. Average Annual Attendance: 3000
Income: Financed by endowment
Collections: 19th century natural history works; 19th century portraits
Exhibitions: Temporary exhibitions, primarily contemporary works, various
media
Activities: Lect open to public, 2 vis lectr per year; concerts; gallery talks; tours;
competitions; originate traveling exhibitions

UNIVERSITY OF KENTUCKY

M **Art Museum**, Ctr for the Arts, 40506-0241. Tel 606-257-5716; FAX 606-323-
1994; *Dir* Harriet Fowler; *Registrar* Barbara Lovejoy; *Preparator* Frank Jones;
Cur Rachel Sadinsky; *Ed Coordr* Kerry Zack
Estab 1975 to collect, preserve, exhibit & interpret world art for the benefit of
the university community & the region. New building completed & opened Nov
1979; 20,000 sq ft of galleries & work space. Average Annual Attendance: 30,
000. Mem: 485; dues $25 & up
Income: $278,010 (financed by state appropriation & gifts)
Collections: African; American Indian; Decorative Arts; American paintings,
sculpture & graphics, 15th-20th Century; Oriental; Pre-Columbian
Publications: Museum Newsletter; exhibitions catalogs; posters
Activities: Classes for children; docent training; lect open to public, 5 vis lectr
per year; concerts; gallery talks; book traveling exhibitions 5 per year; originate
traveling exhibitions; museum shop sells books

L **Edward Warder Rannells Art Library**, M King Library N, 40506. Tel 606-257-
3938; FAX 606-257-4908; Elec Mail megshaw@ukcc.uky.edu. *Librn* Meg Shaw
Open to students, faculty & general public
Library Holdings: Vols 47,454; Per subs 198; Micro — Fiche 812, reels 223; AV —
V-tapes 18; Other — Clipping files, pamphlets
Special Subjects: Art Education, Art History, Photography, Theatre Arts

L **Photographic Archives**, M King Library Annex, 40506-0039. Tel 606-257-8611,
257-9611; FAX 606-257-1563; Elec Mail lwood@pop.uky.edu. *Dir Spec Coll &
Archives* William J Marshall; *Photographic Archivist* Lisa R Wood
Library Holdings: Vols 100,000; Per subs 60; Manuscript materials; AV — A-
tapes, motion pictures; Other — Exhibition catalogs
Collections: Over 300,000 photographs documenting the history of photography
as well as Kentucky, Appalachia & surrounding areas

L **UNIVERSITY OF KENTUCKY**, Hunter M Adams Architecture Library, 200
Pence Hall, 40506-0041. Tel 606-257-1533; FAX 606-257-4305; *Librn* Faith
Harders; *Library Technician* Jo Staggs
Open Mon - Thurs 8 AM - 10 PM, Fri 8 AM - 6 PM, Sat 2 - 5 PM, Sun 3 - 10
PM, summer Mon - Fri 8 AM - 4:30 PM
Library Holdings: Vols 30,000; Per subs 114; Architectural drawing; Micro —
Cards 1828, fiche 1903, reels 606; AV — A-tapes, cassettes, slides; Other —
Clipping files, exhibition catalogs, sculpture
Special Subjects: Architecture, Furniture, Interior Design, Landscape
Architecture, Construction, Historic preservation, LeCorbusier, Urbanism
Publications: News of the Hunter M Adams Architecture Library, quarterly

LOUISVILLE

A **ARTSWATCH**, 2337 Frankfort Ave, 40206-2467. Tel 502-893-9661; FAX 502-
893-9661; Elec Mail artswatch2@aol.com. *Exec Dir* Andy Perry
Open Tues - Sat 1 - 5 PM, cl Christmas & New Year's. Estab 1985. Average
Annual Attendance: 2000. Mem: 175; dues $15-$100
Income: $100,000 (financed by mem, city & state appropriation)
Exhibitions: Annual member show

C **BANK ONE GALLERY** (Formerly Liberty National Bank), 416 W Jefferson,
40202. Tel 502-566-2081; FAX 502-566-1800; *Dir* Jacque Parsley; *Gallery
Coordr* Karen Denham
Open Mon - Thurs 9 AM - 4 PM, Fri 9 AM - 5 PM. Estab 1976. Non-profit
gallery, local & regional exhibits
Income: Financed by Bank One Kentucky
Exhibitions: (1997) Town & Countryscapes by Cheryl Correll (oil on canvas);
Landscape-Based Abstractions by Dudley Zopp (mixed media); Beth Reitmeyer-
Geometric Abstractions on Canvas; Mary Reid Drawings; Computer-Generated
Art - 22 Major Invitational Exhibition. (1997-98) Artists Portraits by Geoff Carr.
(1998) Louisville Craftsmen's Guild Juried Exhibition
Publications: Catalogues, 1 - 2 per yr
Activities: Craft instruction; lect open to public; gallery talks; school tours;
invitational exhibits with purchase awards; individual paintings & original objects
of art lent; lending collection also contains Kentucky watercolors

A **THE FILSON CLUB**, 1310 S Third St, 40208. Tel 502-635-5083; FAX 502-
635-5086; *Dir* Dr Mark V Wetherington
Open Mon - Fri 9 AM - 5 PM, cl national holidays. Admis $3 non-member fee.
Estab 1884 to collect, preserve & publish historical material, especially pertaining
to Kentucky. Average Annual Attendance: 15,000. Mem: 4100; dues $35
Income: Financed by mem dues & private funds
Collections: †Books & †manuscripts; large collection of portraits of Kentuckian;
artifacts, textiles, silver, photographs, maps, prints
Publications: Filson Club History Quarterly; Series 1 & Series 2 Publications (39
volumes)
Activities: Lect open to public, 6 vis lectr per year; gallery talks; tours; individual
paintings lent to art museum & Historical Society exhibitions; sales shop sells
books, reproductions & prints

L **Reference & Research Library**, 1310 S Third St, 40208. Tel 502-635-5083; *Librn*
Judith Partington
Open Mon - Fri 9 AM - 5 PM, Sat 9 AM - Noon. Estab 1884 to collect,
preserve & publish Kentucky historical material & associated material
Income: Financed by endowments, mem & gifts
Library Holdings: Vols 55,000; Micro — Reels; Other — Clipping files,
manuscripts, memorabilia, original art works, pamphlets, photographs, prints,
sculpture
Collections: Extensive Civil War Collection
Exhibitions: Portraits of Kentuckians
Publications: Filson Club History Quarterly; Series & Series 2 publication (40
vols)
Activities: Lect open to public 6 - 10 per year; tours; individual paintings &
original objects of art lent to other organizations for special exhibits; museum
shop sells books, reproductions & prints

M KENTUCKY ART & CRAFT GALLERY, 609 W Main St, 40202. Tel 502-589-0102; FAX 502-589-0154; *Exec Dir* Rita Steinberg; *Cur* Brian Clinkingbeard; *Dir Marketing* Vallery Kramer
Open Mon - Sat 10 AM - 4 PM. Estab 1981 to advance & perpetuate Kentucky's art & craft heritage. Works by over 400 Kentucky Crafts people displayed & sold in restored 19th century building. Average Annual Attendance: 60,000. Mem: 600; dues $500, $250, $100 & $25
Income: Financed by mem dues, state appropriation, corporations, foundations & fund-raising events
Exhibitions: Rotating Exhibits
Publications: Made in Kentucky, newsletter three times yearly
Activities: Adult classes; dramatic programs; workshops for artists & crafts people; lect open to public, 2 vis lectr per year; scholarships & fels offered; book traveling exhibitions, 6 per year; originate traveling exhibitions annually; sales shop sells original art & crafts

M KENTUCKY DERBY MUSEUM, 704 Central Ave, PO Box 3513, 40201. Tel 502-637-1111; FAX 502-636-5855; *Interim Exec Dir* Judy Bortner; *Dir Marketing & Develop* Lynn Ashton; *Cur Exhib* Joe McGee; *Cur Coll* Candace Perry; *Dir Cur Services* Jay R Ferguson
Open Mon - Fri 9 AM - 5 PM, cl Sat & Sun, Christmas & Thanksgiving. Admis adult $5, senior citizen $4, children 5-12 $2, children under 5 free. Estab 1985 to expand appreciation for Kentucky Derby & Thoroughbred racing. Maintains reference library. Average Annual Attendance: 170,000. Mem: 1100; dues $20-$2000
Income: $1,000,000 (financed by Earned revenues)
Collections: Archives from industry; †Kentucky Derby memorabilia; 19th & 20th century Equine Art; Thoroughbred Racing Industry Collection (artifacts)
Exhibitions: Permanent exhibits about Derby & Thoroughbred Racing Industry; African-Americans in Thoroughbred Racing
Publications: Inside Track newsletter, quarterly
Activities: Classes for children; competitions with prizes; individual paintings lent to qualified museums; originate traveling exhibits; originate traveling exhibitions statewide; museum shop sells books, original art, prints

A LOUISVILLE VISUAL ART ASSOCIATION, 3005 River Rd, 40207. Tel 502-896-2146; FAX 502-896-2148; *Pres* Frank Weisberg; *Exec Dir* John P Begley; *Gen Mgr* Lisa Work
Open Mon - Fri 9 AM - 5 PM, Sat 9 AM - 3 PM, Sun Noon - 4 PM. No admis fee. Estab 1909 to provide programs for local & regional artists, adults & children; slide registry. Located at designated national historic landmark building, the water tower at Louisville's original water pumping station 1; Gallery area: Price Gallery 125-150 running ft, Brown Hall 125-150 running ft, 3500 sq ft total. Average Annual Attendance: 200,000. Mem: 5000; dues $20-$500; monthly meeting of Board of Dir
Income: $750,000 (financed by endowment, mem, state appropriation, Louisville Fund for the Arts, grants, rental of space & annual fundraising events)
Exhibitions: Group Invitational; regional artist emphasis; regional competitions
Publications: Visual Art Review, quarterly; exhibit catalogs
Activities: Classes & workshops for adults & children; docent; lect open to public, 50 vis lectr per year; concerts; gallery talks; tours; competitions with awards; scholarships offered; exten dept serves Jefferson, Bullitt, Oldham & Shelby Counties in Kentucky & Clark, Floyd & Harrison Counties in Indiana; individual paintings & original objects of art lent to prospective buyers; book traveling exhibitions 1-2 per year; originate traveling exhibitions; sales shop sells magazines, original art, prints, jewelry, pottery, glass & hand crafted items

M SOUTHERN BAPTIST THEOLOGICAL SEMINARY, Joseph A Callaway Archaeological Museum, 2825 Lexington Rd, 40280. Tel 502-897-4141; FAX 502-897-4880; *Cur* Dr Joel F Drinkard Jr
Open Mon - Fri 8 AM - 5 PM, other hours by special arrangement. No admis fee. Estab 1961
Collections: Biblical archeology; coptic religious materials; glass; materials excavated from Jerico, AI & Jerusalem; mummy; numismatics; ostraca; pottery; sculpture; textiles
Activities: Guided tours; films

M J B SPEED ART MUSEUM, 2035 S Third St, PO Box 2600, 40201-2600. Tel 502-636-2893; FAX 502-636-2899; *Chmn Board of Governors* Sarah McNeal Few; *Pres Board Governor* John S Speed; *Dir* Peter Morrin; *Registrar* Charles Pittenger; *Communications Officer* Mark Stewart; *Business Mgr* David Knopf; *Cur* Ruth Cloudman
Open Tues - Sat 10 AM - 4 PM, Sun 1 - 5 PM. Donation. Estab 1925 for the collection & exhibition of works of art of all periods & cultures, supported by a full special exhibition program & educational activities. Galleries are arranged to present painting, sculpture & decorative arts of all periods & cultures; special facilities for prints & drawings. Average Annual Attendance: 120,000. Mem: 4500; dues family $40
Income: Financed by endowment
Collections: Comprehensive permanent collection
Exhibitions: In Pursuit of Perfection: The Art of J A D Ingres; Breaking the Rules: Audrey Flack, A Retrospective 1950 - 1990
Publications: Newsletter, quarterly; Bulletin, occasional
Activities: Classes for children; docent training; lect open to public, 10-12 vis lectr per year; concerts; gallery talks; tours; competitions; individual paintings & original objects of art lent to members; lending collection contains 200 paintings; museum shop sells books, original art, reproductions

L Art Reference Library, 2035 S Third St, PO Box 2600, 40201-2600. Tel 502-636-2893; FAX 502-636-2899; *Librn* Mary Jane Benedict
Open Tues - Fri 10 AM - 4 PM by appointment only
Income: Financed by general budget
Purchases: $10,000
Library Holdings: Vols 15,615; Per subs 63; Vertical files 48; AV — Slides; Other — Clipping files, exhibition catalogs, manuscripts, pamphlets, photographs, reproductions
Special Subjects: Aesthetics, Afro-American Art, American Indian Art, American Western Art, Antiquities-Greek, Antiquities-Roman, Architecture, Art Education, Art History, Asian Art, Bronzes, Carpets & Rugs, Ceramics, Conceptual Art, Crafts
Collections: J B Speed's Lincoln Books; Frederick Weygold's Indian Collection
Publications: Acquisitions list, bibliographies, in-house periodical index, index to J B Speed Art Museum bulletins, index to dealers catalogs

UNIVERSITY OF LOUISVILLE
M Allen R Hite Art Institute Gallery, Belknap Campus, 40292. Tel 502-852-6794; FAX 502-852-6791;
Internet Home Page Address http://www.louisville.edu/a-s/finearts. *Chmn* James Grubola; *Publicity Officer* Matt Landus
Open Mon - Fri 8:30 AM - 4:30 PM, cl Sat & Sun by appointment only. No admis fee. Estab 1935 for educ & enrichment. There are three galleries: Morris Belknap Gallery, Dario Covi Gallery & SAL Gallery
Income: Financed by endowment & state appropriation
Collections: †Teaching collection; paintings; drawings; prints
Publications: Exhibition catalogs
Activities: Lect open to public, 9-12 vis lectr per year; gallery talks; tours; Winthrop Allen Memorial Prize for creative art; scholarships offered; original objects of art lent to other departments on campus & to other institutions; lending collection includes 1000 prints, 36 drawings, 36 paintings; book traveling exhibitions

L Margaret M Bridwell Art Library, Belknap Campus, 40292. Tel 502-852-6741; Elec Mail grgilb01@ulkyvm.louisville.edu. *Head Art Library* Gail R Gilbert; *Asst Librn* Kathleen A Moore
Open Mon - Thurs 8 AM - 9 PM, Fri 8 AM - 5 PM, Sat 10 AM - 2 PM, Sun 1 - 6 PM. Estab 1956 to support the programs of the art department. For reference only
Income: Financed by endowment & state appropriation
Purchases: $92,520
Library Holdings: Vols 65,000; Per subs 300; Micro — Fiche, reels; AV — Rec; Other — Clipping files, exhibition catalogs, manuscripts, memorabilia, pamphlets
Special Subjects: Advertising Design, Afro-American Art, Antiquities-Byzantine, Antiquities-Etruscan, Antiquities-Greek, Antiquities-Roman, Archaeology, Architecture, Art Education, Art History, Bronzes, Carpets & Rugs, Ceramics, Coins & Medals, Collages, American Art
Collections: †Original Christmas cards; †posters

L Photographic Archives, 40292. Tel 502-852-6752; FAX 502-852-8753; Elec Mail bitney:jcand01&@ulkyvm. *Cur* James C Anderson; *Assoc Cur* Cynthia Stevenson
Open Mon - Fri 10 AM - 4 PM. No admis fee. Estab 1967 to collect, preserve, organize photographs & related materials; primary emphasis on documentary photography
Income: Financed through the University
Library Holdings: Vols 750; Micro — Reels; Other — Clipping files, exhibition catalogs, photographs 800,000
Collections: Antique Media & Equipment; Lou Block Collection; Will Bowers Collection; Bradley Studio--Georgetown; Theodore M Brown--Robery J Doherty Collection; Caldwell Tank Co Collection; Caulfield & Shook, Inc; Lin Caulfield Collection; Cooper Collection; Flexner Slide Collection; Erotic Photography; Fine Print Collection; Arthur Y Ford Albums; Forensic Photographic Collection; Vida Hunt Francis Collection; K & IT Railroad Collections; Mary D Hill Collections; Goiswold Collections; Joseph Krementz Collection; Kentucky Mountain Schools Collection; The Macauley Theater Collection; Manvell Collection of Film Stills; Boyd Martin Collection; Kate Matthews Collection; J C Rieger Collections; Roy Emerson Stryker Collections
Publications: Exhibition catalogues; collections brochures
Activities: Lect open to public, vis lectr per year varies; gallery talks; educational groups; individual paintings lent to museums & galleries; book traveling exhibitions; originates traveling exhibitions; sales shop sells reproductions, prints, slides & postcards

L Slide Collection, 40292. Tel 502-852-5917; Elec Mail ascoat01@ulkyvm.bitnet. *Cur Slides* Ann S Coates; *Asst to Cur* Karen Knowles
Open Mon - Fri 8:30 AM - 4:30 PM. Estab 1930s to provide comprehensive collection of slides for use in the University instructional program; 400,000 catalogued slides primarily illustrating history of Western art. Circ 50,000
Library Holdings: AV — Kodachromes, slides 400,000; Other — Clipping files
Special Subjects: Architecture, Painting - American, Photography, Porcelain, Pottery, Decorative Arts
Collections: American Studies; Calligraphy; Manuscript of Medieval Life

MAYSVILLE

M MASON COUNTY MUSEUM, 215 Sutton St, 41056. Tel 606-564-5865; FAX 606-564-4237; *Dir* Jean W Calvert; *Pres* Bill Hendrickson; *Librn* Myra Hardy; *Cur* Sue G Case; *Asst Cur* Mary V Clarke; *Bus Mgr* Gayle H McKay; *Museum Asst* Roger Gillespie; *Adminr* Louis N Browning
Open Mon - Sat 10 AM - 4 PM. Admis adults $2, children $.50. Estab 1878 to maintain historical records & artifacts for area. Average Annual Attendance: 3000. Mem: 200; dues $15-$35
Income: $30,000 (financed by endowment and members)
Collections: Paintings & maps related to area; †genealogical library
Activities: Gallery talks; tours; individual paintings & original objects of art lent; book traveling exhibitions; museum shop sells books, prints, postcards & souvenirs

MOREHEAD

MOREHEAD STATE UNIVERSITY
M Claypool-Young Art Gallery, Art Dept, 40351. Tel 606-783-2193; *Dir* Robert Franzini
Open Mon - Fri 8 AM - 4 PM, by appointment. Estab 1922 to provide undergraduate & graduate programs in studio & art educ. An exhibition gallery is maintained for traveling exhibitions, faculty & student work. The Claypool-Young Art Gallery is tri-level with 2344 sq ft of exhibition space. Average Annual Attendance: 8000
Income: Financed by appropriation

Collections: Establishing a permanent collection which to date consists principally of prints by major contemporary figures; several works added each year through purchase or bequest. Additions to lending collection include: The Maria Rilke Suite of lithographs by Ben Shahn consisting of 23 pieces; the Laus Pictorum Suite by Leonard Baskin, consisting of 14 pieces; & three lithographs by Thomas Hart Benton: Jesse James, Frankie & Johnny, & Huck Finn; Permanent display of several hundred Eastern Kentucky Folk Art pieces
Exhibitions: A large number of solo exhibitions along with invitational shows & group exhibits
Activities: Educ dept; lect open to public, 5 vis lectr per year; concert; gallery talks; tours; competitions; individual paintings lent to schools; lending collection contains items, prints & photographs; originate traveling exhibitions organized & circulated; museum shop sells folk art

MURRAY

M MURRAY STATE UNIVERSITY, Eagle Gallery, Price Doyle Fine Arts Ctr, PO Box 9, 42071-0009. Tel 502-762-3052; FAX 502-762-6335; *Gallery Dir* Albert Sperath; *Chmn* Dick Dougherty
Open Mon, Wed & Fri 8 AM - 6 PM, Tues & Thurs 8 AM - 7:30 PM, Sat 10 AM - 4 PM, Sun 1 - 4 PM, cl University holidays. No admis fee. Estab 1971. Gallery houses the permanent art collection of the University: the Main Gallery is located on the fourth floor & its dimensions are 100 x 40 ft; the Upper Level is divided into three small galleries that may be used as one or three. Average Annual Attendance: 10,000
Income: Financed by state appropriation and grants
Collections: Asian Collection (given by Asian Cultural Exchange Foundation); Collection of Clara M Eagle Gallery; Harry L Jackson Print Collection; WPA prints, drawings
Exhibitions: Biennial Magic Silver Show (even years); Annual Student Exhibition; Biennial Faculty Exhibitions (odd years)
Publications: Brochures and posters for individual shows
Activities: Vis artists; workshops; demonstrations; lect open to public, 8 vis lectr per year; gallery talks; tours; competitions with merit & purchase awards; exten dept serving Jackson Purchase Area of Kentucky; individual paintings & original objects of art lent; lending collection consists of original prints, paintings, photographs & sculpture; books traveling exhibitions; traveling exhibitions organized and circulated

OWENSBORO

M BRESCIA COLLEGE, Anna Eaton Stout Memorial Art Gallery, 717 Frederica, 42301. Tel 502-685-3131; *Chmn Dept Art* Sr Mary Diane Taylor; *Gallery Dir* Lance Hunter
Open Mon - Fri 8 AM - 4:30 PM, Sat 8 AM - Noon. No admis fee. Estab 1950. Gallery space is 20 x 30 ft, walls are covered with neutral carpeting. Average Annual Attendance: 4000
Activities: Lect open to public, 2-3 vis lectr per year; competitions with awards; scholarships offered; book traveling exhibitions; originate traveling exhibitions

M OWENSBORO MUSEUM OF FINE ART, 901 Frederica St, 42301. Tel 502-685-3181; *Dir* Mary Bryan Hood; *Asst Dir* Jane Wilson; *Dir Operations* Larry Myles; *Bus Mgr* Terri Melton; *Registrar* Ron Hardesty; *Educ Dir* Louise Halsey
Open Tues - Fri 10 AM - 4 PM, Sat & Sun 1 - 4 PM, cl Mon & national holidays. No admis fee, donations accepted. Estab 1977. Average Annual Attendance: 65,000. Mem: 1000; dues $5-$10,000
Income: Financed by endowment, mem, city & county appropriations, grants
Collections: 14th-18th century European drawings, graphics, decorative arts; 19th-20th century American, French & English paintings, sculpture & stained glass
Publications: Exhibition catalogues; newsletters
Activities: Classes for adults & children; docent training; dramatic programs; seminars & critiques led by major American artists; lect open to public, 4-6 vis lectr per year; concerts; gallery talks; tours; competitions with awards; pre-tour visits to the classroom; film series; individual & original objects of art lent to museums; book traveling exhibitions 2-3 per year; originate traveling exhibitions to museums; museum shop sells original art
L Art Library, 901 Frederica St, 42301. Tel 502-685-3181; *Dir* Mary Bryan Hood
Books for reference
Library Holdings: Vols 2000; Other — Clipping files, exhibition catalogs, manuscripts, pamphlets, photographs, reproductions

PADUCAH

M MUSEUM OF THE AMERICAN QUILTER'S SOCIETY, 215 Jefferson St, PO Box 1540, 42002-1540. Tel 502-442-8856; FAX 502-442-5448; *Exec Dir* Victoria Faoro; *Cur & Registrar* Susan Morgan
Open Apr - Oct, Tues - Sat 10 AM - 5 PM, Sun 1 - 5 PM. Admis adult $5, student $3, children 12 & under free. Estab 1991. Three climate controlled galleries - Gallery A (7000 sq ft) displays selection from MAQS/Schroeder Collection. Gallery B (2900 sq ft) displays temporary exhibit of antique quilts. Gallery C (3500 sq ft) displays temporary exhibits of contemporary quilts. Average Annual Attendance: 45,000
Income: $802,069 (financed by private & corporate donations, small amount of state funding & earned income)
Exhibitions: Quilts in the MAQS/Scroeder Collection
Publications: MAQS Friends, quarterly newsletter; exhibit catalogs published jointly with the American Quilter's Society
Activities: Classes for adults & children; docent training; lect open to public; school tours; annual schoolblock contest; scholarships offered; originate traveling exhibitions; museum shop sells books & magazines

A YEISER ART CENTER INC, 200 Broadway. 42001-0732. Tel 502-442-2453; *Exec Dir* Dan Carver
Open Tues - Sat 10 AM - 4 PM, Sun 1 - 4 PM, cl Mon & major holidays. Admis $1. Estab 1957 as a non profit cultural and educational institution to provide the community and the membership with visual art exhibitions, classes and related activities of the highest quality. Average Annual Attendance: 16,000. Mem: 600; monthly programs & mem meetings
Income: $80,000 (financed by mem fees, donations, commissions & grants)
Collections: Primarily regional/contemporary with some 19th century works on paper & Japanese prints; teaching collection; Collection includes R Haley Lever; Matisse; Goya; Emil Carlsen; Philip Moulthrop; Ron Isaacs
Exhibitions: Fantastic Fibers, Annual National Fibers Exhibit; Six State Annual Competition; changing exhibitions of historical & contemporary art of regional, national & international nature
Publications: Exhibit catalog; Monthly newsletter
Activities: Classes for adults & children; dramatic programs; docent training; lect open to public; gallery talks; tours; competitions with awards; scholarships offered; individual and original objects of art lent to qualified institutions; lending collection contains original art works, prints and paintings; originate traveling exhibitions; sales shop sells original art & regional crafts

WHITESBURG

C APPALSHOP INC, Appalshop Films Media Center, 306 Madison St, 41858. Tel 606-633-0108; FAX 606-633-1009; Elec Mail appalshop@aol.com. 800-545-7467 (orders only). *Admin Dir* Ray Moore
Open 9 AM - 6 PM. Estab 1969 as the Community Film Workshop of Appalachia, part of a national program to train poor & minority young people in the skills of film & television production, now a incorporated non-profit media arts center. In 1982 a renovated 13,000 sq ft warehouse, became the Appalshop Center with offices, video & radio editing suites, a 150 seat theater, an art gallery & educational facilities. Recently a community radio station was added
Publications: Newsletter, annual
Activities: Films, plays, music & educational programs to schools, college, museums, libraries, churches, festivals, conferences & community in the region, throughout the US & in Europe, Asia & Africa

WILMORE

M ASBURY COLLEGE, Student Center Gallery, One Macklem Dr, 40390. Tel 606-858-3511; FAX 606-858-3921; *Head Art Dept* Dr Rudy Medlock; *Prof* Cliff Davis; *Prof* Kevin Sparks
Open 11 AM - 1 PM & 6 - 9 PM. No admis fee. Estab 1976 for the purpose of exhibiting the works of national, local, and student artists. Tract lighting in a 20 x 20 ft space. Average Annual Attendance: 2000
Publications: Newsletter
Activities: Classes for adults; lect open to public, 4 vis lectr per year; gallery talks; tours; scholarships offered

LOUISIANA

ALEXANDRIA

M ALEXANDRIA MUSEUM OF ART, 933 Main St, PO Box 1028, 71309-1028. Tel 318-443-3458; *Dir* Mark Tullos; *Cur* Bryan F Lafaye; *Cur Educ* Dorinda J Gifford
Open Tues - Fri 9 AM - 5 PM, Sat 10 AM - 4 PM. Admis fee. Estab 1977 to explore American art of 20th century with emphasis on contemporary art of the south. National Register Building in Downtown Historic District; 2900 sq ft gallery remodeled in 1984; 933 window works - installation gallery visible through 8 x 8 street front window; accredited by AAM. Average Annual Attendance: 35,000. Mem: 600; dues individual $15-$500; business $250-$5000
Income: 250,000 (financed by mem, grants & donations)
Purchases: $30,000
Collections: †Contemporary Louisiana Art; N Louisiana Folk Crafts; †Contemporary Southern Art; Prints & Drawings; †Artist's Books
Publications: Catalogs: Doing it Right & Passing it on; North Louisiana Folk Crafts; Lynda Benglis & Keith Sonnier; Robert Gordy & Robert Warrens; Lin Emery & Emery Clark; quarterly newsletter; September Competition catalog, annual; Richard Johnson/John Scott (Mar, 1991)
Activities: Classes for adults & children; docent training; workshops; lect open to public, 6 vis lectr per year; gallery talks; tours; annual Sept competition, international, all media with awards; exten dept serves 7 parishes in Central Louisiana; individual paintings & original objects of art lent; lending collection contains color reproductions, 1500 kodachromes, original art works & video cassettes; book traveling exhibitions; traveling exhibitions organized & circulated; museum shop sells books, original art; junior museum located at 927 Main St

M LOUISIANA STATE UNIVERSITY AT ALEXANDRIA, University Gallery, Student Ctr, Highway 71 S, 71302. Tel 318-473-6449; *Gallery Dir* Roy V de Ville
Open Mon - Fri 10 AM - 3 PM. No admis fee. Estab 1960 as university art department gallery. Gallery located in student union for both students & public. Meets all state & university guidelines for climate control. Average Annual Attendance: 600
Income: Financed by university
Exhibitions: Mixed Media of Michael David Elvestrom, OSG
Publications: University Gallery Catalogue, quarterly
Activities: Classes for children; docent training; lect open to public, 3-4 vis lectr per year; competitions; individual paintings & original objects of art lent

BATON ROUGE

M EAST BATON ROUGE PARKS & RECREATION COMMISSION, Baton Rouge Gallery Inc, 1442 City Park Ave, 70808-1037. Tel 504-383-1470; FAX 540-336-0943; *Dir* Kathleen Pheney; *Asst Dir* Nancy Stapleton; *Publicity Dir* Lori Jefferson
Open Tues - Sun Noon - 6 PM. Estab 1966 to educate & promote contemporary art. Non-profit, cooperative, contemporary gallery made up of general members from community & artist members. Average Annual Attendance: 10,000. Mem: 40 artist, 200 community; dues $35; annual meeting in Nov
Income: $50,000 (financed by mem & East Baton Rouge Parks & Recreation Commission)
Collections: Southern regional artists based around Baton Rouge & New Orleans
Activities: Docent training; lect open to public; concerts; gallery talks; tours; competitions with awards; individual paintings & original objects of art lent to State of Louisiana

M LOUISIANA ARTS & SCIENCE CENTER, 100 S River Rd, PO Box 3373, 70821. Tel 504-344-5272; FAX 504-344-9477; *Exec Dir* Carol S Gikas; *Asst Dir* Sam Losavio; *Museum Cur* Mala Jalenak; *Art Educ Cur* Karen Farbo; *Science Educ Cur* Susan Tittlebaum; *Art Prog Cur* Wendy Post; *Challenger Center Sr Flight Dir* Gayle Glusman; *Challenger Center Asst Flight Dir* Wanda Williams; *Public Relations Coordr* Carole Wilson; *Registrar* Margo Laville; *Cur Old Governor's Mansion* Catherine McKenzie
Open Tues - Fri 10 AM - 3 PM, Sat 10 AM - 4 PM, Sun 1 - 4 PM, cl Mon. Admis adults $3, university students, senior citizens & children 2-12 $2, members, children under 2 & 1st Sat of the month free. Estab 1960. General mus - art, history & science. Center administers the Riverside Mus in the renovated Old Illinois Central Railroad Station with an auditorium & sculpture garden. Mus contains changing & permanent exhibits of art, Louisiana history & science, a science gallery & a Challenger Learning Center. Center administers Old Governor's Mansion, a restored historic house. Average Annual Attendance: 95,000. Mem: Dues $20-$1000
Income: Financed by mem, city appropriation & donations
Collections: 18th & 20th century European & American paintings; contemporary photographs; Clementine Hunter paintings; Ivan Mestrovic; sculpture; Egyptian artifacts; Eskimo graphics & soapstone carvings; North American Indian crafts; Tibetan religious art; memorabilia of former Louisiana governors
Exhibitions: Discovery Depot, a participatory gallery that introduces children to art; Egyptian Mummies & Artifacts; Miniature Train
Publications: LASC Calendar
Activities: Classes for adults & children; docent training; lect open to public, 5-10 vis lectr per year; gallery talks; competitions with awards; individual paintings & original objects of art lent to other museums; book traveling exhibitions 10 per year; museum shop sells books & magazines
L Museum, 100 S River Rd, PO Box 3373, 70821. Tel 504-344-5272; FAX 504-344-9477; *Exec Dir* Carol S Gikas
Small reference library open to staff only

LOUISIANA STATE UNIVERSITY

M Museum of Arts, 114 Memorial Tower, 70803. Tel 504-388-4003; *Pres* Nadine Russell; *Dir & Cur* H Parrott Bacot; *Admin Asst* Sheridan Wilkes
Open Mon - Fri 8 AM - 4:30 PM, Sat 9 AM - Noon & 1 - 4 PM, Sun 1 - 4 PM. No admis fee. Estab 1959 to serve as a constant reminder of the major cultural heritage the United States received from the British People. Two temporary galleries house loan exhibitions & local art work. Average Annual Attendance: 55,000. Mem: 400; dues $10 - $500
Income: Financed by endowment, mem & state funds
Collections: Hogarth & Caroline Durieux graphic works; early Baton Rouge subjects; early New Orleans-made silver; English & American drawings, decorative arts, paintings, watercolors; Newcomb Crafts: 19th century lighting devices
Publications: Catalogues; newsletter
Activities: Lect, 2 vis lectr per year; gallery talks; tours; competitions; originate traveling exhibitions
L Library, 114 Memorial Tower, 70803. Tel 504-388-4003; *Dir* H Perrott Bacot
Open Mon - Fri 8 AM - 4 PM, Sat 10 AM - Noon & 1 - 4 PM, Sun 1 - 4 PM, cl university holidays. No admis fee, guided tours $2 per person. Reference library. Average Annual Attendance: 7500. Mem: 480; dues $20, $25-$100; annual meeting in spring
Library Holdings: Vols 700; Other — Clipping files, exhibition catalogs, original art works, photographs, prints, sculpture
Special Subjects: Anglo-American Decorative Arts
Collections: English - American decorative arts, drawings, paintings
Exhibitions: English period rooms 17th & 19th century; American period rooms 18th & 19th centuries; Collection of Newcomb Crafts; New Orleans made Silver; Hogarth Prints; Works by Caroline Durieux; 18th century lighting devices
Publications: Exhibit catalogs
Activities: Lect for members only, 1-2 per year; tours; individual paintings & objects of art lent to other museums
M Union Art Gallery, PO Box 25123, 70894-5123. Tel 504-388-5162; *Art Dir* Judith R Stahl
Open Mon - Fri 9 AM - 9 PM, Sat & Sun 11 AM - 5 PM. Estab 1964, designed for exhibitions for university & community interests. Gallery is centrally located on the main floor of the LSU Union with 1725 sq ft. Average Annual Attendance: 55,000. Mem: 4000; dues $35
Income: Financed by student activity fee, fundraising & grants
Exhibitions: Annual Student Art Exhibition
Publications: Brochures for local exhibitions, quarterly
Activities: Classes for adults & children; lect open to public, 2 vis lectr per year; concerts; gallery talks; competitions with awards
M School of Art Gallery, 123 Art Bldg, 70803-3208. Tel 504-388-5411; *Dir* Michael Crespo
Open Mon - Fri 10 AM - 4 PM, Sun 1 - 5 PM. No admis fee. Estab 1934 for special exhibitions planned by faculty committee. Circulates exhibitions of student's arts consisting of 30-40 works by students. Average Annual Attendance: 10,000

Collections: Department collection of contemporary graphic works, prints & drawings
Activities: Lect open to public, 5 vis lectr per year; gallery talks; scholarships & fels offered
L Design Resource Center, 104 Design Bldg, 70803-7010. Tel 504-388-2665; FAX 504-388-6992; Elec Mail notstm@lsuvm.sncc.lsu.edu. *Librn* Sandra Mooney
Estab 1959. Lending library
Library Holdings: Vols 12,800; Per subs 100; Vertical files 12 drawers
Special Subjects: Advertising Design, Architecture, Commercial Art, Decorative Arts, Drafting, Drawings, Furniture, Graphic Arts, Graphic Design, History of Art & Archaeology, Industrial Design, Interior Design, Landscape Architecture, Photography, Restoration & Conservation, Sculpture

L SOUTHERN UNIVERSITY, Art & Architecture Library, Southern University Post Office Branch, 70813. Tel 504-771-3290; *Librn* Dorothy Davis; *Librn* Lucille Bowie
Open Mon - Fri 8 AM - 10:45 PM. Estab 1971 to encourage support of fine arts & architecture. Circ 12,000
Income: Financed by state appropriation
Library Holdings: Vols 7500; Per subs 87; Micro — Fiche, reels; AV — Cassettes, motion pictures, slides; Other — Pamphlets

COVINGTON

A ST TAMMANY ART ASSOCIATION, 129 N New Hampshire St, PO Box 704, 70434. Tel 504-892-8650; FAX 504-898-0976; *Pres* Madeline Gill; *Coordr* Marie-Louise Adams
Open Tues - Fri 10 AM - 4 PM. No admis fee. Estab 1958 to act as a center for art in the community. Average Annual Attendance: 5000. Mem: 850; dues family $30, individual $20; annual meeting in May
Income: $45,000 (financed by endowment & mem)
Exhibitions: Crafts Conference; monthly exhibits; Photographic Club
Publications: Newsletter, 3 times per yr
Activities: Classes for adults & children, Artists in the Schools Program; docent training; lect open to public, 10 vis lectr per year; gallery talks; tours; competition with cash awards

CROWLEY

A CROWLEY ART ASSOCIATION, The Gallery, 220 N Parkerson, PO Box 2003, 70527-2003. Tel 318-783-3747; *Coordr* Jean Oubre
Open daily 10 AM - 4 PM. No admis fee. Estab 1980 to promote art in all forms. Average Annual Attendance: 500. Mem: 250; dues $10; monthly meetings
Income: Financed by mem
Exhibitions: Juried Art Show
Publications: Monthly newsletter
Activities: Classes for adults & children; lect open to public, 3 vis lectr per year; competitions; retail store sells original art

JENNINGS

M ZIGLER MUSEUM, 411 Clara St, 70546. Tel 318-824-0114; *Pres Board Trustees* Richard Boisture; *Cur* Dolores Spears
Open Tues - Sat 9 AM - 5 PM, Sun 1 - 5 PM, cl Mon. No admis fee. Estab 1963 to place the art of western civilization & the area in a historical context. West Wing has permanent collection of American & European paintings & sculptures. East Wing contains a gallery of wildlife art. Central galleries are reserved for a new art exhibit each month. Average Annual Attendance: 20,000
Purchases: 23 paintings by William Tolliver; One painting by Vlaminck; One painting by Whitney Hubbard; One painting by van Dyck; One painting by Herring
Collections: Bierstadt; Chierici; Constable; Crane; Gay; Heldner; George Inness Jr; Pearce; Pissarro; Reynolds; Sloan; Frank Smith; Vergne; Whistler; Gustave Wolff; Robert Wood; Sculpture: J Chester Armstrong; Wildlife Art; Louisiana Art
Exhibitions: Rotating exhibits
Publications: Brochure
Activities: Classes for adults; docent training; lect open to public; tours; individual paintings & original objects of art lent; originates traveling exhibitions that travel to other museums; sales shop sells books, magazines, reproductions; prints

LAFAYETTE

M LAFAYETTE MUSEUM ASSOCIATION, Lafayette Museum-Alexandre Mouton House, 1122 Lafayette St, 70501. Tel 318-234-2208; *Pres* Yvonne D Bienvenu
Open Tues - Sat 9 AM - 5 PM. Admis $3, student $2. Estab 1954 as a historical house. Average Annual Attendance: 3000
Income: $35,000 (financed by endowment, city appropriation)
Purchases: Refurbishing two rooms in mus
Collections: Historical †Costumes & Dress, †Documents, †Furnishings, †Objects
Activities: Children's tours

M LAFAYETTE NATURAL HISTORY MUSEUM, PLANETARIUM & NATURE STATION, 637 Girard Park Dr, 70503. Tel 318-291-5544; FAX 318-291-5464; *Dir* Joe S Hays; *Cur Exhibits* Cliff Deal; *Cur Natural Science* Bill Fontenot; *Cur Planetarium* David Hostetter; *Registrar* Kathy Ball; *Secy* Karen Miller; *Marketing Coordr* Rita Case; *Museum & Planetarium Tech* Dexter LeDoux
Open Mon, Wed, Fri 9 AM - 5 PM, Tues, Thurs 9 AM - 9 PM, Sat, Sun 1 - 5 PM. No admis fee. Estab 1969 to provide a focus on the physical world in order to benefit the citizens of the community. 30 by 130 ft space with architectural glass window walls, interior walls constructed as needed. Average Annual

Attendance: 100,000. Mem: 700; annual meeting in Dec
Income: $500,000 (financed by mem & city & parish appropriation)
Purchases: $4000
Collections: Acadian artifacts; Audubon prints; Historical Louisiana maps; Louisiana Indian artifacts; Louisiana landscape art; Louisiana moths & butterflies; Louisiana related Harper's Weekly prints; Louisiana shells
Exhibitions: Rain or Shine: Louisiana Weather; Travailler C'est Trop Dur: The Tools of Cajun Music; Audubon's World: A Window Into Nature; Louisiana Snakes Alive; Louisiana Crawfish: Perspectives on a New World Traveler Outlook Universe; Waterways of Louisiana; Wildflowers of Louisiana; Rain or Shine: Louisiana Weather
Activities: Classes for adults & children; docent training; tours; lending collection contains 20 nature artifacts, original art works, 400 photos, 1000 slides, 200 Louisiana Indian & Acadian artifacts; book traveling exhibitions; originate traveling exhibitions in Louisiana; museum shop sells books, reproductions, prints, t-shirts & educational gifts

LAKE CHARLES

M **IMPERIAL CALCASIEU MUSEUM,** 204 W Sallier St, 70601. Tel 318-439-3797; FAX 318-439-6040; *Dir* Mary June Malus
Open Tues - Fri 10 AM - 5 PM, Sat & Sun 1 - 5 PM. Admis adults $1, students $.50. Estab Mar 1963 by the Junior League of Lake Charles & housed in City Hall. After several moves in location, the mus is now housed in a building of Louisiana Colonial architecture which incorporates in its structure old bricks, beams, balustrades & columns taken from demolished old homes. In Dec 1966 administration was assumed by the Fine Arts Center & Mus of Old Imperial Calcasieu Mus, Inc, with a name change in 1971. Site of the building was chosen for its historic value, having been owned by the Charles Sallier family, the first white settler on the lake & the town named for him. The mus depicts the early history of the area. Average Annual Attendance: 12,500. Mem: 350; dues $50-$1500
Income: Financed by mem
Collections: Artifacts of the Victorian Period, especially Late Victorian
Exhibitions: American Indian Artifacts in Calcasieu Collections; Antique Quilts & Coverlets; Calcasieu People & Places in 19th Century Photographs; Christmas Around The World; special exhibitions every six weeks, with smaller exhibits by other organizations at times
Activities: Docent training; lect open to members only, 2-3 vis lectr per year; gallery talks; book traveling exhibitions 1 per year; originate traveling exhibitions; sales shop sells books, original art
M **Gibson-Barham Gallery,** 204 W Sallier St, 70601. Tel 318-439-3797; FAX 318-439-6040; *Coordr* Mary June Malus
Open Tues - Fri 10 AM - 5 PM, Sat & Sun 1 - 5 PM, cl Mon. Admis adults $1, students $.50. Estab to collect & display history & artifacts at five parishes in the original Imperial Land Grant. 1000 running ft. Average Annual Attendance: 5000. Mem: 500; dues $25-$1500
Activities: Lect open to public, 2 vis lectr per year; gallery talks; tours; individual paintings & original objects of art lent to established museums or collectors; book traveling exhibitions; originate traveling exhibitions; sales shop sells books & original art
L **Gibson Library,** 204 W Sallier St, 70601. Tel 318-439-3797; FAX 318-439-6040; *Coordr* Mary June Malus
Open Mon - Fri 10 AM - 5 PM, Sat & Sun 1 - 5 PM. Estab 1971, to display early school books & bibles. Reference Library
Income: Financed by mem, memorials & gifts
Library Holdings: Vols 100; Per subs 100; AV — A-tapes, cassettes, slides, v-tapes; Other — Memorabilia, original art works, pamphlets, photographs, sculpture
Collections: Audubon animal paintings; Audubon bird paintings; Calcasieu photographs; Boyd Cruise
Exhibitions: History of Imperial Calcasieu Parish, with settings & objects

MINDEN

L **WEBSTER PARISH LIBRARY,** 521 East & West Sts, 71055. Tel 318-371-3080; *Librn* Eddie Hammonter; *Asst Librn* Beverly Hammett
Open Mon, Wed, Thurs 8:15 AM - 8 PM, Tues, Fri, Sat 8:15 AM - 5 PM. Estab 1929 to serve as headquarters & main branch for county. Circ 145,508
Income: $221,353 (financed by parish tax)
Library Holdings: Vols 60,000; Per subs 800; Micro — Reels; AV — Cassettes, fs, rec, slides, v-tapes; Other — Clipping files, framed reproductions, original art works, pamphlets, photographs
Activities: Exten dept serves the elderly; individual paintings lent to registered borrowers, lending collection contains 54 art prints & 50 b & w photographs depicting parish history

MONROE

M **NORTHEAST LOUISIANA UNIVERSITY,** Bry Gallery, 700 University Ave, Stubbs 141, 71209-0310. Tel 318-342-1053; FAX 318-342-1369; *Head* Ron J Alexander, MFA
Open 8 AM - 4:30 PM. No admis fee. Estab 1931. Gallery is 24 sq ft x 26 sq ft with 14 ft ceilings. Average Annual Attendance: 8000
Collections: Kit Gilbert; Pave Brou of New Orleans
Activities: Classes for adults & children; docent training; 6 vis lectr per year; gallery talks; exten dept

M **TWIN CITY ART FOUNDATION,** Masur Museum of Art, 1400 S Grand St, 71202. Tel 318-329-2237; FAX 318-329-2847; *Dir* Marion M Callis
Open Tues - Thurs 9 AM - 5 PM, Fri - Sun 2 - 5 PM. No admis fee. Estab 1963 to encourage art in all media & to enrich the cultural climate of this area. Gallery has 500 running ft hanging space. Average Annual Attendance: 5000. Mem: 380; dues $250, $100, $35
Income: $225,000 (financed by mem & appropriations)

Purchases: $3000
Collections: †Contemporary art all media, approximately 100 works
Publications: Brochures of shows, monthly
Activities: Classes for adults & children; lect open to public, 4 vis lectr per year; tours; competitions; book traveling exhibitions

NEW IBERIA

M **SHADOWS-ON-THE-TECHE,** 317 E Main St, 70560. Tel 318-369-6446; FAX 318-365-5213; *Dir* Shereen H Minvielle; *Operations Mgr* Shala Carlson
Open daily 9 AM - 4:30 PM, cl Christmas, New Year's Day & Thanksgiving Day. Admis adults $4, children 6-11 $2, group rates available. The Shadows is a property of the National Trust for Historic Preservation. Preserved as a historic house mus; operated as a community preservation center, it is a National Historic Landmark. On the Bayou Teche, it faces the main street of modern New Iberia, but is surrounded by three acres of landscaped gardens shaded by live oaks. Built in 1831, the Shadows represents a Louisiana adaption of classical revival architecture. The life & culture of a 19th century southern Louisiana sugar plantation are reflected in the possessions of four generations of the Weeks family on display in the house. It fell into ruin after the Civil War, but was restored during the 1920s by Weeks Hall, great-grandson of the builder Mr Hall bequeathed the Shadows to the National Trust in 1958. Property serves as a focal point for advancement of historic preservation, it develops new relationships among cultural community preservation groups and National Trust members in its area. Responds to community preservation needs by acting as a link between community and appropriate regional or headquarters offices of National Trust. Average Annual Attendance: 30,000. Mem: 300
Income: Financed by mem in Friends of the Shadows, admis fees & special events
Collections: Paintings by Louisiana's itinerant artist Adrien Persac & period room settings (1857-72) paintings by Weeks Hall; furnishings typical of those owned by a planter's family between 1830 and 1865
Activities: Docent training; interpretive programs which are related to the Shadows historic preservation program; Members Day during National Historic Preservation Week; concerts; tours; museum shop sells books, original art and prints

NEW ORLEANS

A **ARTS COUNCIL OF NEW ORLEANS,** 225 Baronne St, Ste 1712, 70112. Tel 504-523-1465; FAX 504-529-2430; *Exec Dir* Shirley Trusty Corey
Estab 1975 to support & expand the opportunities for diverse artistic expression & to bring the community together in celebration of rich multicultural heritage; provides a variety of Cultural Planning, Advocacy, Public Art, Economic Development, Arts Education, Grants & Service Initiatives focused on its vision of New Orleans as a flourishing cultural center. Average Annual Attendance: 1000. Mem: Dues organization $154, individuals free with qualifications
Activities: Lect open to public & members; workshops

A **CONTEMPORARY ARTS CENTER,** 900 Camp St, 70130. Tel 504-523-1216; FAX 504-528-3828; *Exec Dir* Ted Potter
Open Mon - Fri 10 AM - 5 PM, Sat & Sun 11 AM - 5 PM. Admis $3, members free. Estab 1976 to support experimentation & innovative products of work in visual arts & performing arts. Interdisciplinary arts center. Average Annual Attendance: 55,000. Mem: 3200; dues $25 & up; annual meeting in May
Exhibitions: (1997) Glass - Dale Chihuly; William Christenberry Art, L A Major Works; Works by William Wegman
Activities: Classes for adults & children; concerts; gallery talks; tours; competitions with awards

M **LONGUE VUE HOUSE & GARDENS,** 7 Bamboo Rd, 70124. Tel 504-488-5488; FAX 504-486-7015; *Dir* Gainor Davis; *Asst Dir* Mary E D'Aquin Fergusson; *Cur* Lydia H Schmalz; *Museum Shop Mgr* Kathryn B Youngberg; *Vol Dir* Angelle Thompson
Open Tues - Fri 10 AM - 4:30 PM, Sat 10 AM - 4:30 PM, Sun 1 - 5 PM, cl Mon except for group tours. Admis adults $5, students & children $3. Estab 1980 to preserve & interpret Longue Vue House & Gardens & collect decorative & fine arts. Period 1930-40 house. Average Annual Attendance: 45,000. Mem: 1000; dues family $25, individual $12, student & senior citizens $7; biannual meetings in spring & fall
Income: $450,000 (financed by endowment)
Collections: 18th - 19th century English & American furniture; textile collection of 18th - 20th century English, French, & American fabrics, needlework, Karabagh & Aubusson rugs, 19th - 20th century French wallpapers; 18th - 20th century British ceramics; Chinese exports; contemporary & modern art, including Vasarely, Gabo, Picasso, Michel, Agam, Hepworth, & Laurens
Publications: The Decorative Arts at Longue Vue; The Queen's Table
Activities: Docent programs; lect open to public, 8-10 vis lectr per year; museum shop sells books, reproductions, prints, slides, decorative arts

M **LOUISIANA DEPARTMENT OF CULTURE, RECREATION & TOURISM,** Louisiana State Museum, 751 Chartres St, PO Box 2448, 70176. Tel 504-568-6968; FAX 504-568-4995;
Internet Home Page Address www.crt.state.la.us/crt/museum/lsmnet3.htm.
Chmn Dr E Ralph Lupin; *Dir Spec Projects* Vaughn L Glasgow; *Dir Coll* Milita Rios-Samaniego; *Dir Progs* Tamra Carboni; *Registrar* Patricia Eischen; *Museum Dir* James F Sefcik; *Marketing & Public Relations Dir* Claire H Brown; *Dir Interpretive Servs* Karen Leathem
Open Tues - Sun 9 AM - 5 PM. Admis adult $4, student $3, educational groups free by appointment. Estab 1906, to collect, preserve & present original materials illustrating Louisiana's heritage. Gallery is maintained & has eight historic buildings containing paintings, prints, maps, photographs, decorative arts, furniture, costumes & jazz. Average Annual Attendance: 320,000. Mem: 3000; dues $20-$35; annual meeting in May
Income: $2,000,000 (financed by state appropriation)
Purchases: $40,000

Collections: Carnival costumes (2000 items); Colonial documents (500,000 folios); †decorative art (8000 items); †flat textiles (1000 items); historic costumes (6000 items); jazz & Louisiana music (40,000 objects); Louisiana silver (300); maps & cartography (3000); Newcomb pottery & allied arts (750); †paintings (1500 canvases); †photography (70,000 images); †post Colonial manuscripts (500, 000); †prints (3000 works); †rare Louisiana books (40,000); Sculpture (125 works)
Publications: Louisiana's Black Heritage; Louisiana Portrait Gallery, Vol I; A Social History of the American Alligator; exhibit catalogs
Activities: Classes for adults & children; docent training; dramatic programs; lect open to public, 6-10 vis lectr per year; tours; individual paintings & original objects of art lent to museums; book traveling exhibitions 2-3 per year; originate traveling exhibitions; museum shop sells books, original art, reproductions, prints, maps & crafts
L Louisiana Historical Center Library, 400 Esplanade (Mailing add: PO Box 2448, 70176). Tel 504-568-8214; FAX 504-568-6969; *Dir* James F Sefcik; *Cur Maps & Documents* Kathryn Page
Archives open Tues - Fri 10 AM - 4 PM, or by appointment. Estab 1930, to collect materials related to Louisiana heritage
Library Holdings: Vols 40,000; Per subs 5; Non-circulating Louisiana historical material; Other — Clipping files
Special Subjects: Colonial judicial documents

A LOUISIANA HISTORICAL ASSOCIATION, Confederate Museum, 929 Camp St, 70130. Tel 504-523-4522; *Chmn Memorial Hall Committee* Bill Meneray; *Cur* Pat Ricci
Open Mon - Sat 10 AM - 4 PM. Admis adults $2, students & senior citizens $1, children $.50. Estab 1891 to collect & display articles, memorabilia & records surrounding the Civil War. Gallery is maintained in a one story brick building; one main hall paneled in cypress, one side hall containing paintings of Civil War figures & display cases containing artifacts. Average Annual Attendance: 15,000. Mem: 2000; dues $15; annual meeting Mar
Income: Financed by mem & admis
Publications: Louisiana Historical Association Newsletter; Louisiana History, quarterly
Activities: Lect open to public; competitions; sales shop sells books, reproductions & novelties

M NEW ORLEANS ACADEMY OF FINE ARTS, Academy Gallery, 5256 Magazine St, 70115. Tel 504-899-8111; *Pres* Dorothy J Coleman; *Academy Dir* Auseklis Ozolis; *Gallery Dir & Admin* Patsy Collins Baker
Open Mon - Fri 9 AM - 4 PM, Sat 10 AM - 4 PM. No admis fee. Estab 1978 to provide instruction in the classical approaches to art teaching adjunct to school. Average Annual Attendance: 300
Activities: Classes for adults; lect open to members only, 3 vis lectr per year; academic awards in painting, drawing, sculpture

M NEW ORLEANS MUSEUM OF ART, One Collins Diboll Circle, PO Box 19123, 70124. Tel 504-488-2631; FAX 504-484-6662; *Pres Board* Francoise Richardson; *Dir* E John Bullard; *Asst Dir Art* William A Fagaly; *Asst Dir Admin* Jacqueline Sullivan; *Asst Dir Develop* Sharon Litwin; *Asst Dir Educ* Lee Morais; *Chief Cur Exhib* Daniel Piersol; *Cur Decorative Arts* John W Keefe; *Cur Photog* Nancy Barrett; *Ed Arts Quarterly* Wanda O'Shello; *Asst Cur Educ* Ann Moore; *Public Relations Officer* Virginia Weaver; *Registrar* Paul Tarver; *Asst Registrar & Cur Traveling Exhib* Patricia Pecoravo; *Asst to Dir* Alice Rae Yelen; *Librn* Carl Penny; *Chief Preparator* Thomas E Herrington
Open Tues - Sun 10 AM - 5 PM, cl Mon & legal holidays. Admis adults (18-64) $6, children (3-17) $3. Estab 1910; building given to city by Issac Delgado, maintained by municipal funds & private donations to provide a stimulus to a broader cultural life for the entire community. Stern Auditorium, Ella West Freeman wing for changing exhibitions; Wisner Educ wing for learning experiences; Delgado Building for permanent display. Mus opens April 1993 after complete renovations & expansion; gallery space doubled & new Courtyard Cafe restaurant & expanded shop. Average Annual Attendance: 150, 000. Mem: 10,000; dues $35-$1000; annual meeting in Nov
Income: Financed by mem, city appropriation, federal, state & foundation grant, corporate contributions & individual donations
Collections: Old Master paintings of various schools; Kress Collection of Italian Renaissance & Baroque Painting; Chapman H Hyams Collection of Barbizon & Salon Paintings; Pre-Columbian & Spanish colonial painting & sculpture; works by Edgar Degas; 20th century English & Continental art, including Surrealism & School of Paris; Japanese Edo period painting; African Art; photography; graphics; Melvin P Billups Glass Collection; 19th & 20th century United States & Louisiana painting & sculpture; Latter- Schlesinger Collection of English & Continental Portrait Miniatures; Victor Kiam Collection of African, Oceanic, American Indian, & 20th century European & American Painting & Sculpture; The Matilda Geddings Gray Foundation Collection of Works by Peter Carl Faberge; Rosemonde E & Emile Kuntz Federal & Louisiana Period Rooms; 16th - 20th century French art; Bert Piso Collection of 17th century Dutch painting; Imperial Treasures by Peter Carl Faberge from the Matilda Geddings Gray Foundation Collection; 18th, 19th & 20th Century French Paintings; Morgan-Whitney Collection of Chinese Jades; Rosemonde E & Emile Kuntz Rooms of Late 18th - Early 19th Century American Furniture
Exhibitions: (1997) Contemporary Botanical Artists: The Shirley Sherwood Collection; Hockney to Hodgkin: British Master Prints 1960-1980; A Connoisseur's Eye: Old Master Paintings from the Collection of Mr & Mrs Henry H Weldon; Artists of Mardi Gras: The Golden Age of Carnival, 1870-1930; eossem Porcelain Figures from the H Lloyd Hawkins Collection
Publications: Arts Quarterly; catalogs of New Orleans Museum of Art organized exhibitions; History of New Orleans Museum of Art
Activities: Classes for children; docent training; teacher workshops; lectr open to public, 20 vis lectr per year; concerts; gallery talks; tours including multi-language; VanGo Museum on Wheels; competitions; individual paintings & original objects of art lent to museums; book traveling exhibitions 5 per year; originate traveling exhibitions; museum shop sells books, original art, reproductions, prints, cards, toys & jewelry

L Felix J Dreyfous Library, PO Box 19123, 70179. FAX 504-488-2631; *Librn* Carl O Penny
Open Mon - Fri 9 AM - 5 PM. Estab 1971 to provide information for reference to the curators, mus members & art researchers. Open to staff & members; general pub by appointment
Income: Financed by mem, donations & gifts
Library Holdings: Vols 20,000; Per subs 50; Micro — Fiche, reels; AV — A-tapes, cassettes, slides, v-tapes; Other — Clipping files, exhibition catalogs, memorabilia, pamphlets
Special Subjects: Photography, African art, Pre-Columbian art
Collections: WPA Project - New Orleans Artists

M NEW ORLEANS SCHOOL OF GLASSWORKS, GALLERY & PRINTMAKING STUDIO, 727 Magazine St, 70130. Tel 504-529-7277; FAX 504-539-5417; *Pres* Jean duP Blair
Open Mon - Sat 11 AM - 5 PM. Estab 1991 to educate visitors about glassworking & printmaking. Average Annual Attendance: 20,000. Mem: 35; dues $20
Income: Financed by mem, sale of art works, tax deductible donations, grants & classes
Exhibitions: Thomas & Mathew Beuchner; Curtiss Brock; Andrew Brott; Dale Chihuly; Josh Cohen; Brent Cole; Erwin Eisch; Harvey Littleton; Carol B Rice; Adam Ridge; Richard Royal; Karoline Schleh; Pino Signoretto; Paul Stankard; Frank Van Denham; Udo Zembok
Activities: Classes for adults & children; tours; demonstrations; gallery sells original art, glasswork & prints made in school's glass sculpture & printmaking studio

TULANE UNIVERSITY
M University Art Collection, Tulane University Library, 7001 Freret St, 70118. Tel 504-865-5699; *Cur* Gary Van Zante
Open Mon - Fri 8:30 AM - 5 PM, cl school holidays & Mardi Gras. No admis fee. Estab 1980
Collections: Architectural Drawings; 17th century to present; Architectural books 17th century to current; maps; Photograph Collection
Activities: Gallery talks; tours; original objects of art lent to other institutions; book traveling exhibitions; originate traveling exhibitions
M Dept Art Newcomb Col Art Galleries, Newcomb Art Dept, 70118. Tel 504-865-5327; FAX 504-862-8710; *Asst Dir* Sally Main; *Admin* Linda Turpie
Open Mon - Fri 10 AM - 5:00 PM, Sat (during exhibitions) Noon - 5 PM. No admis fee. Estab 1918. Committed to best contemporary & historical exhibits in which visitors can experience, learn from & be inspired by art works of high quality. Average Annual Attendance: 7000
Collections: Newcomb Decorative & Minor Arts; †Newcomb Pottery
Activities: Lect open to public, 6-7 vis lectr per year; gallery talks; tours; awards; scholarships offered; individual paintings & original objects of art lent to AAM certified/accredited institutions; book traveling exhibitions 3-4 per year; originate traveling exhibitions
L Architecture Library, Howard-Tilton Memorial Library, Richardson Memorial Hall, Rm 202, 70118. Tel 504-865-5391; FAX 504-865-6773; Elec Mail heckerf@mailhost.tcs.tulane.edu. *Head* Frances E Hecker
Open fall & spring Mon - Thurs 8 AM - 9:50 PM, Fri 8 AM - 4:50 PM, Sat 10 AM - 4:50 PM, Sun 2 - 9:50 PM; summer Mon - Fri 8:30 AM - Noon & 1 - 4:50 PM, cl Sat & Sun. For reference only
Library Holdings: Vols 14,000; Per subs 235; Other — Clipping files, exhibition catalogs
Special Subjects: Architecture
M Gallier House Museum, 1118-1132 Royal St, 70116. Tel 504-523-6722; *Dir* Lee Warner; *Cur* Mary Strickland; *Bus Mgr* Barbara Lopez; *Educ Coordr* Catherine Schupp
Open Mon - Sat 10 AM - 4:30 PM, Sun Noon - 4:30 PM. Admis family $9, adult $4, children $2.25. Estab 1971 to preserve & exhibit the house of James Gallier Jr & 19th century decorative arts. Average Annual Attendance: 20,000. Mem: 150; dues $10-$250
Library Holdings: Vols 1000; Per subs 10; AV — Slides, v-tapes; Other — Clipping files, manuscripts, original art works, pamphlets, photographs, prints, sculpture
Special Subjects: Architecture, Art History, Decorative Arts, Furniture, Period Rooms, Porcelain, Silver, Textiles
Collections: 19th century architecture, art, decorative arts, New Orleans lifestyles
Exhibitions: Architectural Details; Architectural displays & house exhibitions
Publications: Quarterly newsletter
Activities: Classes for adults & children; docent training; lect open to pubic; 2 vis lectr per year; retail store sells books, prints, slides, Victorian gifts

M UNIVERSITY OF NEW ORLEANS, Fine Arts Gallery, 2000 Lake Shore Dr, 70148. Tel 504-280-6493; Elec Mail vatfa@wno.ed. *Gallery Dir* Richard Johnson
Open Mon - Fri 8 AM - 4:30 PM. No admis fee. Estab 1974 to expose the students & community to historic & contemporary visual arts. Gallery consists of 1800 sq ft, 165 lineal ft of wall space, 20 ft ceilings, natural & artificial lighting. Average Annual Attendance: 15,000
Income: Financed by state appropriation
Activities: Credit & non-credit classes for adults in conjunction with University of New Orleans; lect open to public, 10 vis lectr per year
L Earl K Long Library, Lakefront, 70148. Tel 504-280-6354; FAX 504-286-7277; *Chair Reference Servs* Robert T Heriard
Open Mon - Thurs 8 AM - 12 AM; Fri 8 AM - 4:30 PM, Sat 9 AM - 5 PM, Sun 1 PM - 9 PM. Estab 1958 for scholarly & professional research. For lending & reference. Circ 110,140
Income: $2,401,104 (financed by state appropriation)
Purchases: $797,407
Library Holdings: Vols 394,729; Per subs 4500; Art per subs 250; Art vols 12, 974; Micro — Cards, fiche, reels

M KEMPER & LEILA WILLIAMS FOUNDATION, 533 Royal St, 70130. Tel 504-523-4662; *Pres of Board* Mary Louise Christovich; *Dir Emerita* Dode Platou; *Dir* Jon Kukla; *Dir Museum Prog* John Lawrence; *Cur Manuscripts* Alfred Lemmon; *Systems Dir* Charles Patch; *Coll Mgr* Priscilla Lawrence; *Registrar* Maureen Donnelly; *Public Relations Dir* Elsa Schneider; *Dir Public & Academic Affairs* Patricia Brady; *Head Librn* Florence Jumonville
Open Tues - Sat 10 AM - 4:45 PM. No admis fee to Gallery, admis to Williams Residence & Louisiana History Galleries, tour by guide $2. Estab in 1792 by Jean Francois Merieult; renovated by Koch & Wilson to accommodate the Louisiana History galleries which house a collection of paintings, prints, documents, books & artifacts relating to the history of Louisiana from the time of its settlement, gathered over a number of years by the late L Kemper Williams & his wife. The foundation was estab with private funds to keep original collection intact & to allow for expansion. Research Center for State & Local History / Mus. Average Annual Attendance: 35,000
Income: Financed by endowment
Collections: Charles L Franck, photographs (1900-1955); Dan Leyrer, photographs (1930-1970); Clarence Laughlin, photographs (1935-1965); James Gallier Jr & Sr, architectural drawings (1830-1870); Morries Henry Hobbs, prints (1940); B Lafon, drawings of fortifications (1841); B Simon, lithographs of 19th-century businesses; Alfred R & William Waud, drawings of Civil War & post-war; †maps, †paintings, †photographs, †prints, †three-dimensional objects
Exhibitions: The Long Weekend: The Arts & the Vieux Carre, 1918-1941, Part I: The 1920s from Armistice to the Crash, Part II: The 1930s from the Crash to Pearl Harbor; Place Settings from the Permanent Collections; Sheet Music from the 1920s; Tennessee Williams' New Orleans; Monumental New Orleans: Letting the Past Inform the Future; Gone But Not Forgotten; Tokens of Immortality; Letter Perfect: Three Centuries of Louisiana Correspondence; Alvyk Boyd Cruise (1909-1986): Selected Works & Recent Gifts; Seasons' Greetings from the Collection; Through a Lens Softy: The Photographs of Eugene Delcroix; From Bank to Shore: 19th Century Development Neighborhoods; The Grand American Avenue: 1850-1920; Eugene Delcroix's Contemporaries; Creole Dining: An Exhibition of Menus, Product Labels & Silver Serving Pieces; Recent Acquisitions: Paintings
Publications: Guide to Research at the Historic New Orleans Collection; exhibition brochures & catalogs; historic publications; monograph series; quarterly newsletter
Activities: Docent training; lect open to public; tours; competitions with awards; gallery talks; individual paintings & original objects of art lent to museums, institutions, foundations, libraries & research centers; sales shop sells books, original art, reproductions and prints; research collections

L Historic New Orleans Collection, 533 Royal St, 70130. Tel 504-523-4662; *Head Librn* Florence M Jumonville; *Reference Librn* Pamela D Arceneaux; *Reference Librn* Jessica Travis
Open Tues - Sat 10 AM - 4:30 PM. Open to researchers
Income: Financed by private endowment
Library Holdings: Vols 18,000; Per subs 30; Maps 500; AV — Motion pictures 100; Other — Pamphlets 10,000
Special Subjects: Historical Material, Louisiana History
Collections: Manuscripts Division: unique textual sources on New Orleans & Louisiana History & Culture (family papers & other collections, †newspapers); Curatorial Division: †visual materials, biographical information on regional artists
Publications: Guide to The Vieux Carre Survey, a guide to a collection of material on New Orleans architecture; Bibliography of New Orleans Imprints, 1764-1864

PORT ALLEN

M WEST BATON ROUGE HISTORICAL ASSOCIATION, Museum, 845 N Jefferson Ave, 70767. Tel 504-336-2422; FAX 504-336-2448; *Dir* Caroline Kennedy
Open Tues - Sat 10 AM - 4:30 PM, Sun 2 - 5 PM. No admis fee. Estab 1968, Museum opened 1970, to foster interest in history, particularly that of West Baton Rouge Parish; to encourage research, collection & preservation of material illustrating past & present activities of the parish; to operate one or more museums; to receive gifts & donations; to accept historical & historical materials on loan. A large room housing a scale model of a sugar mill (one inch to one ft, dated 1904) & parish memorabilia; restored French creole cottage (circa 1830); a room 31 X 40 ft for art exhibits; restored plantation quarters cabin (1850). Average Annual Attendance: 10,000. Mem: 300; dues $10; annual meeting in Jan
Income: $250,000 (financed by mem, gifts & millage levied on parish)
Collections: †Art collection of parish artists; c1830 French Creole Cottage; †Contemporary Louisiana (drawings, paintings, prints & sculpture); †Needlework; †Newcomb Pottery; Old Duck Decoys
Exhibitions: Gallery with six shows yearly
Publications: Ecoutez, twice a year
Activities: Classes for children; docent training; lect open to public, 1 vis lectr per year; tours; book traveling exhibitions semi-annually

SAINT MARTINVILLE

M LONGFELLOW-EVANGELINE STATE COMMEMORATIVE AREA, Hwy 31, 1200 N Main, 70582. Tel 318-394-4284, 394-3754; *Mgr* Reinaldo Barnes; *Site & Museum Cur* Suzanna Lavioette
Open daily 9 AM - 5 PM, cl Thanksgiving, Christmas & New Year. Admis adults $2, children free. Estab 1931 to display & describe 18th & 19th century French lifeways & folk items. Artworks are displayed in an 18th & 19th century plantation home, in the interpretive center of the site & in the 18th century cabin. Average Annual Attendance: 50,000
Income: Financed by state appropriations
Collections: Early 19th century portraits; 18th, 19th & 20th centuries textile arts; religious art of the 19th century; wood carvings; local craft & folk art
Activities: Docent training; lect open to public; tours

SHREVEPORT

M CENTENARY COLLEGE OF LOUISIANA, Meadows Museum of Art, 2911 Centenary Blvd, PO Box 41188, 71134-1188. Tel 318-869-5169; FAX 318-869-5730; Elec Mail jgodfrey@beta.centenary.edu. *Dir* Judy Godfrey
Open Tues - Fri Noon - 4 PM, Sat & Sun 1 - 4 PM. No admis fee. Estab 1975 to house the Indo-China Collection of Drawings & Paintings by Jean Despujols. Eight galleries; main gallery on first floor 25 x 80 ft; other galleries 25 x 30 ft; linen walls, track lights and no windows. Average Annual Attendance: 18,000
Income: $80,000 (financed by endowment)
Collections: 360 works in Indo-China Collection, dealing with Angkor Region, The Cordillera, Gulf of Siam, Laos, The Nam-Te, The Thai, Upper Tonkin, Vietnam
Exhibitions: Degas Pastel Society; Dutch & Flemish; Italian Renaissance Paintings; Souchon, painting; Twentieth Century Art
Publications: Partial Catalog of Permanent Collection with 21 color plates
Activities: Docent training; lect open to public, 4 vis lectr per year; gallery talks; tours; individual paintings & original objects of art lent to qualified museums; lending collection includes one motion picture

M LOUISIANA STATE EXHIBIT MUSEUM, PO Box 38356, 71133. Tel 318-632-2020; FAX 318-632-2056; *Dir* Dr George Ward Shannon Jr; *Dir Educ* Mary R Zimmerman
Open Tues - Sat 9 AM - 4:30 PM, cl Christmas. No admis fee. Estab 1939 to display permanent & temporary exhibitions demonstrating the state's history, resources & natural beauty. Art Gallery is maintained. Average Annual Attendance: 200,000
Income: Financed by state appropriation
Collections: Archaeology; dioramas; historical artifacts; Indian artifacts; murals
Publications: History of Art; brochures
Activities: Public Archaeology program; films; concerts

M R W NORTON ART GALLERY, 4747 Creswell Ave, 71106-1899. Tel 318-865-4201; FAX 318-869-0435; Elec Mail norton@softdisk.com. *Pres Board* Mrs Richard W Norton Jr; *VPres Board* A W Coon; *Secy Board* Jerry M Bloomer
Open Tues - Fri 10 AM - 5 PM, Sat & Sun 1 - 5 PM, cl Mon & holidays. No admis fee. Estab 1946, opened 1966. To present aspects of the development of American & European art & culture through exhibition & interpretation of fine works of art & literature, both from the Gallery's own collections & from those of other institutions & individuals. Average Annual Attendance: 30,000
Income: Financed by endowment
Collections: American miniatures & colonial silver; contemporary American & European painting & †sculpture; painting & sculpture relating to Early American history; †Paintings by 19th century American artists of the Hudson River School; Portraits of famous confederate leaders; 16th Century Flemish tapestries; Wedgwood pottery; paintings & sculpture by western American artists Frederic Remington & Charles M Russell
Publications: Announcements of special exhibitions; catalogs (47 through 1992); catalogs of the Frederic Remington & Charles M Russell Collections & of the Wedgwood Collection
Activities: Educ dept; lect open to public; gallery talks; tours; museum shop sells magazines, exhibition catalogs, catalogs of permanent collection

L Library, 4747 Creswell Ave, 71106-1899. Tel 318-865-4201; FAX 318-869-0435; *Librn* Jerry M Bloomer
Open Tues - Sat 1 - 5 PM. Estab 1946 to acquire and make available for public use on the premises, important books, exhibition catalogs, etc relating to the visual arts, literature, American history and genealogy, as well as other standard reference and bibliographic works for reference only
Income: Financed by endowment
Library Holdings: Vols 7000; Per subs 100; Original documents; Auction catalogs; Micro — Reels; AV — Slides; Other — Clipping files, exhibition catalogs, manuscripts, memorabilia, pamphlets, photographs
Special Subjects: American Western Art, Architecture, Art History, Bronzes, Carpets & Rugs, Ceramics, Coins & Medals, Crafts, Decorative Arts, Dolls, Drawings, Etchings & Engravings, Folk Art, Painting - European, Painting - Flemish, Furniture, Painting - French, Glass, Painting - German, Goldsmithing, Graphic Arts, History of Art & Archaeology, Illustration, Pewter, Photography, Porcelain, Portraits, Pottery, Printmaking, Prints, Landscapes, Manuscripts, Sculpture, Silver, Marine Painting, Silversmithing, Metalwork, Southwestern Art, Miniatures, Stained Glass, Tapestries, Watercolors, Painting - American, Painting - British, Bibliography, fine arts, history, literature, ornithological works by J J Audubon (elephant folio edition of Birds of America) and John Gould (complete set), rare books and atlases
Collections: James M Owens Memorial Collection of Early Americana (725 volumes on Colonial history, particularly on Virginia)

L SOUTHERN UNIVERSITY LIBRARY, 3050 Martin Luther King Jr Dr, 71107. Tel 318-674-3400; *Dir* Orella R Brazile
Estab 1967 to supplement the curriculum & provide bibliographic as well as reference service to both the academic community & the pub
Library Holdings: Vols 47,302; Per subs 375; Micro — Fiche 24,308, reels; AV — Cassettes 1121, fs 414, motion pictures 59, rec 293, slides 22,874, v-tapes 240; Other — Clipping files, framed reproductions, original art works, pamphlets 750, prints, reproductions 12, sculpture
Collections: Black Collection, pictures, clippings & motion pictures; Louisiana Collection
Exhibitions: Show Local Artists Exhibitions
Activities: Book traveling exhibition annually; originate traveling exhibitions to YWCA

MAINE

AUGUSTA

M UNIVERSITY OF MAINE AT AUGUSTA, Jewett Hall Gallery, University Heights, 04330. Tel 207-621-3207; *Dir* Karen Guig
Open Mon - Thurs 10 AM - 7 PM, Fri 10 AM - 5 PM. No admis fee. Estab 1970 to provide changing exhibitions of the visual arts for the university students and faculty and for the larger Augusta-Kennebec Valley community; the principal exhibition area is a two level combination lounge and gallery. Average Annual Attendance: 9000
Income: Financed by university budget
Collections: Drawings, paintings, outdoor sculpture
Exhibitions: Six major art exhibits
Activities: Lect open to public, 2-3 vis lectr per year; gallery talks; tours

BATH

M MAINE MARITIME MUSEUM, 243 Washington St, 04530. Tel 207-443-1316; FAX 207-443-1665; *Exec Dir* Thomas R Wilcox Jr; *Library Dir* Nathan Lipfert; *Cur* Robert Webb
Open daily 9:30 AM - 5 PM, cl Thanksgiving, Christmas, New Year's Day. Admis adults $7.50, children under 17 $4.75, under 6 free, group rates available. Estab 1964 for the preservation of Maine's maritime heritage. Average Annual Attendance: 55,000. Mem: 1800; dues $25 & up; annual meeting in Aug
Income: Financed by mem, gifts, grants & admis
Collections: †Marine art; †navigational instruments; †ship models; †shipbuilding tools; †shipping papers; †traditional watercraft
Exhibitions: Historical Percy & Small Shipyard; Lobstering & the Maine Coast; Maritime History of Maine; small watercraft; other rotating exhibits
Publications: Rhumb Line, quarterly
Activities: Classes for adults & children; docent training; lect open to public, 20 vis lectr per year; group tours; concerts; gallery talks; individual paintings & original objects of art lent to non-profit institutions with proper security & climate control; museum shop sells books, reproductions, prints & related novelties
L Archives Library, 243 Washington St, 04530. Tel 207-443-1316; *Library Dir* Nathan Lipfert
Open Mon - Fri & by appointment. Small reference library
Income: Financed by mem, admis, gifts & grants
Library Holdings: Vols 6500; Per subs 50; Manuscripts; AV — A-tapes, Kodachromes, motion pictures, slides, v-tapes; Other — Clipping files, memorabilia, original art works, pamphlets, photographs
Special Subjects: Historical Material, Manuscripts, Maps, Marine Painting, Painting - American, Painting - Australian, Scrimshaw, Maine maritime history & art, especially shipbuilding
Collections: Sewall Ship Papers, shipbuilding firms business papers
Exhibitions: Maritime History of Maine, Lobstering & the Maine Coast

BLUE HILL

M PARSON FISHER HOUSE, Jonathan Fisher Memorial, Inc, 04614. Tel 207-374-2459
Open July - Sept Mon - Sat 2 - 5 PM. Admis $2. Estab 1965 to preserve the home & memorabilia of Jonathan Fisher. The house was designed & built by him in 1814. Average Annual Attendance: 300. Mem: 260; dues endowment $1000, contributing $100, sustaining $25, annual $10; annual meeting in Aug
Income: Financed by admis fees, dues, gifts & endowment funds
Purchases: Original Fisher paintings or books
Collections: Furniture, Manuscripts, †Paintings & †Articles made by Fisher
Activities: Lect open to public, 1-2 vis lectr per year; individual paintings & original objects of art lent to state museum or comparable organizations for exhibit; sales shop sells reproductions

BOOTHBAY HARBOR

A BOOTHBAY REGION ART FOUNDATION, 7 Townsend Ave (Mailing add: PO Box 124, 04538). Tel 207-633-2703; *Pres* Roger Roche; *VPres* Diane Esterly
Open Apr 15 - Oct Mon - Sat 11 AM - 5 PM, Sun Noon - 5 PM. Estab 1956, originated to help develop an art curriculum in the local schools, presently functions to bring art of the region's artists to enrich the culture of the community. Located in historic Brick House, built in 1807, two exhibition rooms on the first floor & the second, one of which features prints, drawings & small watercolors. Average Annual Attendance: 3000. Mem: 465; dues $25 & up; annual meeting first Tues in Oct
Income: Financed by mem, contributions & commissions
Exhibitions: Seven juried & invitational shows of graphics, paintings & sculpture by artists of the Boothbay Region & Monhegan Island
Activities: Adult & children workshop, Jan, Feb & Mar (fee); scholarships offered

BRUNSWICK

M BOWDOIN COLLEGE, Peary-MacMillan Arctic Museum, 04011. Tel 207-725-3416, 725-3062; FAX 207-725-3499; *Dir* Susan A Kaplan; *Cur* Genevieve LeMoine; *Exhib Coordr* David Maschino
Open Tues - Sat 10 AM - 5 PM, Sun 2 - 5 PM, cl Mon & holidays. No admis fee. Estab 1967. Museum consists of 3 galleries containing ivory, fur & soapstone Inuit artifacts, Arctic exploration equipment, natural history specimens, prints & paintings. Average Annual Attendance: 18,000
Collections: †Inuit artifacts & drawings; †exploration equipment; †Arctic photos & films; †Arctic related manuscripts & books
Exhibitions: One permanent exhibition on Arctic exploration & Inuit culture;

temporary exhibits annually
Activities: Docent training; lect open to public, 3-7 vis lectr per year; tours; individual paintings & original objects of art or ethnographic objects lent to other museums; museum shop sells books, cards & original art
M Museum of Art, Walker Art Bldg, 04011. Tel 207-725-3275; FAX 207-725-3762; *Dir* Katharine J Watson; *Asst Dir* Suzanne K Bergeron; *Cur* Alison Ferris
Open Tues - Sat 10 AM - 5 PM, Sun 2 - 5 PM, cl Mon & holidays. No admis fee. Estab 1891-1894. Ten galleries containing paintings, medals, sculpture, decorative arts, works on paper & antiquities. Average Annual Attendance: 28,000
Collections: Assyrian reliefs; European & American paintings, decorative arts, drawings, prints, sculpture & photographs; Far Eastern ceramics; Greek & Roman antiquities; Kress Study Collection; Molinari Collection of Medals & Plaquettes; Winslow Homer memorabilia
Exhibitions: 14 - 20 temporary exhibitions per year; three major exhibitions per year
Activities: Docent training; lect open to public, 6-10 vis lectr per year; gallery talks; tours; individual paintings & original objects of art lent to accredited museums; book traveling exhibitions 3 per year; originate traveling exhibitions to other accredited museums; museum shop sells books, reproductions, slides, jewelry

DAMARISCOTTA

M ROUND TOP CENTER FOR THE ARTS INC, Arts Gallery, PO Box 1316, 04543. Tel 207-563-1507; *Pres* Nancy Freeman
Open Mon - Sat 9 AM - 5 PM. Estab 1988 for presentation & participation in quality arts with emphasis on educ. Average Annual Attendance: 16,000. Mem: 1300; dues $20-$1000; annual meeting in Mar
Income: $150,000 (financed by mem)
Collections: All facets & eras of visual arts history; classical music collection; theatre script collection
Publications: Catalogues, gallery booklets & newsletters
Activities: Classes for adults & children; dramatic programs; lect open to public, 5-10 vis lectr per year; museum shop sells prints, crafts & paintings
L Round Top Library, PO Box 1316, 04543. Tel 207-563-1507; *Pres* Nancy Freeman
Estab 1989 for arts research & reference. For reference only
Income: $150,000 (financed by endowment)
Library Holdings: Vols 2500; AV — Rec; Other — Exhibition catalogs, original art works, pamphlets, sculpture
Special Subjects: Afro-American Art, American Indian Art, American Western Art, Architecture, Art History, Historical Material, Mexican Art, Mixed Media, Oriental Art, Primitive Art

DEER ISLE

M HAYSTACK MOUNTAIN SCHOOL OF CRAFTS, Gallery, PO Box 518, 04627-0518. Tel 207-348-2306; FAX 207-348-2307; *Chmn Board* Arline Fisch; *Pres* Marlin Miller; *Dir* Stuart J Kestenbaum; *Treas* Ingrid Menken
Open 10 AM- 4 PM daily. No admis fee. Estab 1950 to provide exhibition space for artists & instructors. Gallery maintained for continuous summer exhibition of important American and other national craftsmen, one room 24' X 40' ft. Average Annual Attendance: 1000
Income: Financed by tuition income plus annual donations
Collections: †American Ceramics; †Jewelry
Publications: Annual brochure
Activities: 13 week summer session in ceramics, graphics, glass, jewelry, weaving, blacksmithing, papermaking & fabrics; lect open to public, 40 vis lectr per year; gallery talks; concerts; scholarships offered; individual artwork & original objects of art lent to schools & banks; sales shop sells books
L Library, PO Box 518, 04627-0518. Tel 207-348-2306; *Dir* Stuart J Kestenbaum
For reference only
Library Holdings: Vols 1000; Per subs 10; AV — Kodachromes; Other — Exhibition catalogs

ELLSWORTH

M COLONEL BLACK MANSION, PO Box 1478, 04605. Tel 207-667-8671; *Pres* Stephen C Shea; *House Committee Chmn* Terri Smith
Open Jun 1 - Oct 15 Mon - Sat 10 AM - 5 PM; cl Sun, July 4th & second Wed in Aug. Admis adults $5, students under 12 $2. Estab 1929. Historical mansion operated by the Hancock County Trustees of Pub Reservations. Average Annual Attendance: 3000. Mem: 225; annual meeting second Wed in Aug
Income: Financed by private trust fund, donations & admis
Collections: Authentic period china, decorative objects, glass, furniture in original setting; carriages & sleighs
Publications: Colonel John Black of Ellsworth (1781 - 1856); David Cobb an American Patriot; Legacy of the Penobscot Million
Activities: Docent training; guided tours; museum shop sells books, magazines, post cards & dried arrangements

HALLOWELL

A KENNEBEC VALLEY ART ASSOCIATION, Harlow Gallery, * 160 Water St, PO Box 213, 04347. Tel 207-622-3813; *Gallery Dir* Adele Nichols; *Treas* Madge Ames
Open Tues - Sat 1 - 4 PM, cl Mon & Sun. No admis fee. Estab 1963 to foster an interest in and appreciation of fine art. Single gallery on ground level having central entrance and two old storefront windows which provide window display space, peg board covering walls, with two large display screens providing extra display area. Average Annual Attendance: 700. Mem: Approx 100; dues $15; annual meeting first Mon in Jan
Income: Financed by mem and donations
Publications: Newsletter, monthly
Activities: Classes for adults; lect open to the public, 10 - 12 vis lectrs per year; gallery talks; scholarshps & fels offered; museum shop sells original art

KENNEBUNK

M **BRICK STORE MUSEUM & LIBRARY,** 117 Main St, PO Box 177, 04043.
Tel 207-985-4802; *Dir* Susan C S Edwards; *Manuscrips Cur* Joyce Butler;
Registrar Kathryn Hussey
Open Apr - Dec Tues - Sat 10 AM - 4:30 PM, Jan - Mar Tues - Fri 10 AM -
4:30 PM. Admis adults $3, children 6-16 $1. Estab 1936 to preserve & present
history & arrt of southern Maine. Non-circulating reference library only; museum
owns the former home of artist Edith Cleaves Barry. Includes her studio (in situ),
her paintings, book plates designed by her, sculpture, art library, etc. Average
Annual Attendance: 12,500. Mem: 900; dues vary
Library Holdings: Vols 4000; Architectural drawings & plans; Micro — Reels; AV —
Fs; Other — Clipping files, exhibition catalogs, framed reproductions,
manuscripts, memorabilia, original art works, pamphlets, photographs, prints,
reproductions, sculpture
Special Subjects: Maritime History
Collections: Art Library of Edith Cleaves Barry; Maritime - Kenneth Roberts,
Booth Tarkington & Maine authors in general; Papers of Architect William E
Barry; †40,000 items: photographs, documents, fine art & decorative arts
Exhibitions: Edith Cleaves Barry Art Award to Graduating High School Senior
China, furniture, portraits & ships portraits in William Lord Gallery, plus
changing exhibitions in other galleries
Publications: Chapters in Local History, semi-annual
Activities: Docent training; occasional workshops; lect open to public, 15 vis
lectr per year; concerts; gallery talks; tours; individual paintings & original
objects; originate traveling exhibitions to schools & senior citizen groups

KINGFIELD

M **STANLEY MUSEUM, INC,** School St, PO Box 280, 04947. Tel 207-265-2729;
FAX 207-265-4700; *Dir* Susan S Davis, MA; *Secy* Ann Gordon
Admis $2. Estab 1982. Average Annual Attendance: 2000. Mem: 525; dues $10 -
$1000; annual meetings in July
Income: $50,000 (financed by endowment, mem, donations & grants)
Purchases: $35,000 (steam car)
Collections: Collection of †steam cars, †photography & †violins
Publications: Newsletter; quarterly
Activities: Classes for adults & children in dramatic & docent programs; lect
open to public, 2 vis lectr per year; museum shop sells books, magazines & prints

LEWISTON

M **BATES COLLEGE,** Museum of Art, Olin Arts Ctr, 04240-6028. Tel 207-786-
6158; FAX 207-786-6123; *Dir* Genetta McLean; *Asst Cur* Bill Low; *Educ
Coordr* Anthony Shostak
Open Tues - Sat 10 AM - 5 PM, Sun 1 - 5 PM; cl Mon & major holidays. No
admis fee. Estab in the Olin Arts Center, Oct 1986 to serve Bates College & the
regional community
Collections: Marsden Hartley Memorial Collection; 19th & 20th Century
American & European Collection (painting, prints & scultpure)
Exhibitions: (1997) Paul Heroux (ceramics); Anthony Panzera (drawings). (1998)
Jonathan Borofsky (prints); Phil & Jan Sultz
Activities: Lect open to public; gallery talks; individual paintings & original
objects of art lent to museums, college & university galleries

NEW GLOCESTER

M **UNITED SOCIETY OF SHAKERS,** Shaker Museum, 707 Shaker Rd, 04260.
Tel 207-926-4597; *Dir* Leonard L Brooks; *Archivist* Alexandra Regan; *Cur*
Michael Graham
Open Mon - Sat 10 AM - 4:30 PM. Admis for tours: adults $3, children (6-12)
$1.50, under 6 free with adult. Estab 1931, incorporated 1971, to preserve for
educational & cultural purposes Shaker artifacts, publications, manuscripts &
works of art; to provide facilities for educational & cultural activities in
connection with the preservation of the Shaker tradition; to provide a place of
study & research for students of history & religion
Collections: †Drawings & paintings by Shaker artists; †Shaker textiles;
†community industries; †furniture; †manuscripts; †metal & wooden ware
Exhibitions: Shaker Oval Box Making; Winter Life
Publications: The Shaker Quarterly
Activities: Classes for adults; workshops in summer for herb dyeing, oval box
making, cultivating, weaving, spinning, photography, baskets; lect open to public;
concerts; tours; individual paintings & original objects of art lent to institutions
mounting exhibits; museum shop sells books, reproductions, prints, slides, herbs
produced in the community, yarn from flock, woven items
L **The Shaker Library,** RR 1 Box 640, 04274. Tel 207-926-4597; *Dir* Leonard
Brooks; *Archivist* Alexandra Regan; *Cur* Michael Graham
Open Mon - Fri 8:30 AM - 4:30 PM. For reference only
Library Holdings: Vols 10,000; Per subs 70; Ephemera; Micro — Prints 317,
reels 353; AV — A-tapes, cassettes, fs, motion pictures, rec, slides, v-tapes; Other —
Clipping files, exhibition catalogs, manuscripts, photographs, prints
Special Subjects: Architecture, Crafts, Folk Art, Furniture, Historical Material,
History of Art & Archaeology, Manuscripts, Maps, Mixed Media, Photography,
Posters, Textiles, Video, Woodcuts, American Communal Societies, Early
American Technology, Herbology
Collections: The Koreshan Unity; The Religious Society of Friends
Publications: The Shaker Quarterly

OGUNQUIT

M **OGUNQUIT MUSEUM OF AMERICAN ART,** 183 Shore Rd, PO Box 815,
03907. Tel 207-646-4909; FAX 207-646-4909; *Dir* John Dirks; *Assoc Dir & Cur*
Michael Culver
Open July - Sept Mon - Sat 10:30 AM - 5 PM, Sun 2 - 5 PM, cl Labor Day.
Admis adults $3, senior citizens & students $2, children under 12 free. Estab
1953 to exhibit, collect & preserve 20th century American art. Museum consists
of five interior galleries with 6000 sq ft; central gallery provides an expansive
view of the Atlantic Ocean & the rockbound coast; outdoor sculpture garden.
Average Annual Attendance: 10,000. Mem: 550; dues benefactor $5000, patron
$1000, donor $500, business $250, associate $100, couple $50, individual $25
Income: Financed by endowment, mem, donations
Purchases: Recent additions to Collection: works by Will Barnet, Gertrude Fiske,
Edward Hopper, John Hultberg, Jack Levine
Collections: Paintings, drawings & sculpture by 20th Century contemporary
Americans, including Marsh, Burchfield, Hartley, Lachaise, Tobey, Kuhn, Strater,
Graves, Levine & Marin
Exhibitions: (1997) Realism in 20th Century American Painting
Publications: Exhibition catalog, annually; Museum Bulletin
Activities: Classes for adults; docent training; lect open to public, 4 vis lectr per
year; gallery talks; tours; individual paintings & original objects of art lent to
other museums; lending collection contains 1100 original art works; originate
traveling exhibitions; museum shop sells books, original art, reproductions, prints,
posters, postcards, museum catalogs & art books
L **Reference Library,** PO Box 815, 03907. Tel 207-646-4909; *Dir* John Dirks
For reference only
Library Holdings: Vols 400; Other — Clipping files, exhibition catalogs,
manuscripts, memorabilia, pamphlets, photographs, reproductions

ORONO

M **UNIVERSITY OF MAINE,** Museum of Art, 109 Carnegie Hall, 04469-5712.
Tel 207-581-3255; FAX 207-581-3083; Elec Mail art@maine.maine.edu. *Admin
Asst* Jen Boucher; *Exhibits Preparator* Stephen Ringle
Open Mon - Sat 9 AM - 4:30 PM & by appointment. Estab 1946 to add to the
cultural life of the university student; to be a service to Maine artists; to promote
good & important art, both historic & modern. Average Annual Attendance: 23,
450
Income: Financed by state appropriation to university, donations & grants
Collections: The University Collection has grown to a stature which makes it a
nucleus in the state for historic & contemporary art. It includes more than 5400
original works of art & 13 paticularly strong in American mid-20th century
works on paper
Publications: Biennial catalogs & exhibition notes
Activities: Lect open to public, 4-6 vis lectr per year; gallery talks; awards;
scholarships & fels offered; museums by mail program; individual paintings &
original objects of art lent to qualified museums & campus departments; lending
collection contains books, cassettes, color reproductions, filmstrips, kodachromes,
lantern slides, motion pictures, original art works, original prints, paintings,
phono records, photographs, sculptures & slides; book traveling exhibitions;
originate traveling exhibitions to public schools & libraries

PEMAQUID POINT

A **PEMAQUID GROUP OF ARTISTS,** Pemaquid Art Gallery, Lighthouse Park
(Mailing add: PO Box 105, South Bristol, 04568-0105). Tel 207-644-8105, 677-
2752; *Pres* Julia Babb; *Gallery Hostess* Sheila Jackovich; *Treas* Maude Olson
Open Mon - Sat 10:30 AM - 5 PM, Sun 1 - 5 PM. Admis by donation. Estab
1929 to exhibit & sell paintings, sculpture, carvings by members & give
scholarships. Maintains an art gallery, open July through Columbus Day.
Average Annual Attendance: 8000. Mem: 31; must be residents of the Bristol
Peninsula; dues $25; annual meeting in Sept
Income: Financed by dues, patrons, commissions on paintings & sculpture
Exhibitions: Summer members exhibition
Activities: Scholarships offered; gallery sells original art

PORTLAND

M **DANFORTH GALLERY, THE MAINE ARTISTS' SPACE,** 34 Danforth St,
04101. Tel 207-775-6245; FAX 207-775-6550; *Dir* Helen Rivres
Open Wed - Sun. No admis fee. Estab 1986

L **MAINE COLLEGE OF ART,** Library, 619 Congress St, 04101. Tel 207-775-
5153; Elec Mail kdoty@saturn.caps.maine.edu. *Librn* Kristin Doty
Open Mon - Thurs 8 AM - 9:30 PM, Fri 8 AM - 5 PM, Sat & Sun 11 AM - 4
PM. Estab 1973, to support the curriculum & serve the needs of students &
faculty. Circ 12,000
Income: $20,000
Purchases: $15,000
Library Holdings: Vols 18,000; Per subs 110; AV — A-tapes 56, cassettes,
lantern slides, slides 45,000, v-tapes 70; Other — Clipping files, exhibition
catalogs, pamphlets
Special Subjects: Advertising Design, Art History, Crafts, Decorative Arts,
Etchings & Engravings, Furniture, Graphic Arts, Graphic Design, Printmaking,
Prints, Sculpture, Textiles, Woodcuts, Antiquities, Costumes, Crafts, Decorative
Arts, Dolls, Drafting, Drawings, Enamels, Etchings & Engravings, Ethnology
M **The Institute of Contemporary Art,** 522 Congress St, 04101. Tel 207-775-5152;
FAX 207-772-5069; *Dir* Jennifer Gross
Open Tues, Wed, Fri - Sun 11 AM - 4 PM, Thurs 11 AM - 9 PM. No admis fee.
Gallery estab 1983 to present temporary exhibitions of contemporary art &
design. 1800 sq ft gallery located on third floor of Romanesque revival building.
Average Annual Attendance: 10,000
Income: $38,700
Publications: Exhibition catalogues, 2 yearly
Activities: Tours of exhibitions; lect open to public; originate traveling exhibitions

A **MAINE HISTORICAL SOCIETY,** 485 Congress St, 04101. Tel 207-774-1822; FAX 207-775-4301;
Internet Home Page Address http://www.mainehistory.com. *Exec Dir* Richard D'Abate; *Asst Dir* Nan Cumming
Maine History Gallery open June - Oct Tues - Sun 10 AM - 4 PM, Nov - May Wed - Sat Noon - 4 PM, cl state & federal holidays. Admis charged. Estab 1822 to collect, preserve & teach the history of Maine; the Soc owns & operates a historical research library & the Wadsworth - Longfellow House of 1785. Average Annual Attendance: 30,000. Mem: 2700; dues $30; annual meeting in May or June
Collections: Architecture; books archival; material culture; photographs; special collection-prints
Exhibitions: James Phinney Baxter Award, history article
Publications: Maine Historical Society, quarterly; tri-annual monograph
Activities: Classes for adults; docent training; lect open to public, 4 vis lectr per year; gallery talks; tours; individual paintings & original objects of art lent; museum shop sells books, reproductions & prints

M **Wadsworth-Longfellow House,** 485 Congress St, 04101. Tel 207-879-0427; *Asst Dir* Nan Cumming
Open June - Oct Tues - Sat 10 AM - 4 PM. Admis adults $4, children $1. Average Annual Attendance: 9500
Income: Financed by donations, admis, dues & endowment income
Collections: Maine furniture; glass; historic artifacts; paintings; photographs; pottery; prints; textiles; Maine artists; Maine portraits, seascapes
Publications: Quarterly, special publications
Activities: Educ dept; docent training; individual paintings & original objects of art lent to museums; museum shop sells books, reproductions, prints & slides

L **Library,** 485 Congress St, 04101. Tel 207-774-1822; FAX 207-775-4301; *Dir Library Servs* Nicholas Noyes; *Reference Asst* William D Barry; *Reference Asst* Stephanie Phillbrick; *Cataloger* Margot McLaren
Open Tues - Fri 10 AM - 4 PM, Second & Fourth Sat of each month 10 AM - 4 PM. Admis $10. Estab 1822. For reference only. Average Annual Attendance: 5500. Mem: 2500
Library Holdings: Vols 65,000; Other — Manuscripts
Special Subjects: American Indian Art, Architecture, Cartoons, Costume Design & Construction, Decorative Arts, Folk Art, Goldsmithing, Graphic Arts, Historical Material, Interior Design, Marine Painting, Miniatures, Painting - American, Photography, Printmaking
Activities: Classes for adults & children; docent training; lect open to public; gallery talks; tours; lending collection contains original objects of art; museum shop sells books, prints & reproductions

M **Maine History Gallery,** 485 Congress St, 04101. Tel 207-879-0427
Open June - Oct Tues - Sun 10 AM - 4 PM, Nov - May Wed - Sat 1 - 4 PM. Admis adults $2, children under 12 $1. Estab 1993 to teach, preserve & present the history of Maine. Changing exhibitions; one or two exhibitions at a time. Average Annual Attendance: 10,000. Mem: 2000; dues $35; annual meeting in the Spring
Collections: Archaeological artifacts; †costumes; †decorative arts; †folk art; †history artifacts; †paintings
Publications: Classes for adults & children; docent training
Activities: Lect open to public, 5 vis lectr per year; individual paintings & original objects of art lent to other museums & historical societies; lending collection contains original art works, paintings & sculptures; museum shop sells books, magazines, reproductions & prints

M **PORTLAND MUSEUM OF ART,** 7 Congress Square, 04101. Tel 207-775-6148; *Dir* Daniel O'Leary; *Cur Coll* Jessica Nicoll; *Registrar* Michelle Butterfield; *Educ Dir* Dana Baldwin; *Pub Relations Dir* Kristen Levesque; *Develop Dir* Marilyn Lalumiere; *Financial Officer* Elena Murdoch
Open Tues - Sat 10 AM - 5 PM, Thurs until 9 PM, Sun Noon - 5 PM. Admis adults $3.50 sr citizens & students $2.50, children 6 -16 yrs $1, children under 6 free, Thurs 5 - 9 free. Estab 1882 as a non-profit educational institution based on the visual arts & critical excellence. The Museum includes the McLellan-Sweat House, built in 1800, a Registered National Historic Landmark; the LDM Sweat Memorial Galleries, built in 1911; & the Charles Shipman Payson Building, built in 1983, designed by Henry N Cobb. This building is named for Mr Charles Shipman Payson, whose gift of 17 Winslow Homer paintings spurred expansion. Average Annual Attendance: 100,000. Mem: 3400; dues $20 - $5000
Income: $1,291,855 (financed by endowment, mem, private & corporate donations, grants from national, state & municipal organizations)
Purchases: $62,000
Collections: †19th & 20th century American & European paintings; neo-classic American sculpture; †contemporary prints; †State of Maine Collection of artists associated with Maine including Winslow Homer, Andrew Wyeth & Marsden Hartley; †American decorative arts of the Federal period; †American glass
Publications: Bulletin, monthly; exhibition catalogs; general information brochure
Activities: Classes for adults & children; docent training; lect open to public; tours; gallery talks; concerts; films; competitions; members' openings of exhibitions; individual paintings & original objects of art lent to museums; museum shop sells books, reproductions, prints, posters, cards, jewelry, gifts & items by Maine craftsmen

L **PORTLAND PUBLIC LIBRARY,** Art - Audiovisual Dept, 5 Monument Square, 04101. Tel 207-871-1725; FAX 207-871-1714; *Dir* Sheldon Kaye; *Art & AV Librn* Steven Goldberg; *AV Mgr* Tom Wilsbach
Open Mon, Wed & Fri 9 AM - 6 PM, Tues & Thurs Noon - 9 PM, Sat 9 AM - 5 PM. Estab 1867 as the public library for city of Portland. Circ 51,700
Income: Financed by endowment, city & state appropriation
Purchases: $32,000
Library Holdings: Vols 17,400; Per subs 96; Micro — Fiche, reels; AV — Cassettes, motion pictures, rec, v-tapes; Other — Clipping files, exhibition catalogs, original art works, pamphlets, sculpture
Collections: †Costume Book Collection; †Maine Sheet Music; Press Books; †Anthoensen Press, Mosher Press
Exhibitions: Monthly exhibits concentrating on Portland & Maine artists
Activities: Lect open to the public; gallery talks

M **VICTORIA MANSION, INC,** Victoria Mansion - Morse Libby House, 109 Danforth St, 04101-4504. Tel 207-772-4841; *Pres* Edward G Asherman; *Dir* Donna M Ridewood
Open Tues - Sat 10 AM - 4 PM, Sun 1 - 4 PM June - Aug, Tues - Sat 10 AM - 1 PM, Sun 1 - 4 PM Sept, other months by appointment. Admis adults $2, children under 12 $.50. Estab 1943 to display Italian Villa, Victorian Period, built by Henry Austin of New Haven, Connecticut in 1858-1860. Average Annual Attendance: 9000. Mem: 550; dues $15; annual meeting in Apr
Income: Financed by mem, tours & special activities, grants & donations
Collections: Mid 19th Century Decorative Arts (luxury) & Architecture; Original Interior-Exterior & Original Furnishings, Gifts of the Victorian Period
Exhibitions: Christmas Opening Exhibition
Activities: Classes for children; dramatic programs; docent training; lect open to public; 2 vis lectr per year; concerts; tours; museum shop sells books & slides

ROCKLAND

M **WILLIAM A FARNSWORTH LIBRARY & ART MUSEUM,** 19 Elm St, PO Box 466, 04841. Tel 207-596-6457; *Dir* Christopher B Crosman; *Cur* Susan Larson; *Develop Dir* Sara Sasoldt; *Develop Dir* Mary Alice Bird; *Registrar* Edith Murphy; *Educ Coordr* Debra Vendetti
Open Tues - Sat 10 AM - 5 PM, Sun 1 - 5 PM, Mon (June - Sept) 10 AM - 5 PM. Admis $5. Estab 1948 to house, preserve & exhibit American art. Seven galleries house permanent & changing exhibitions. Average Annual Attendance: 40,000. Mem: 2200; dues $35 & up
Income: Financed by endowment & public support
Collections: American Art; two historic houses
Publications: Exhibition catalogs & brochures 6-8 per year; quarterly newsletter for members
Activities: Classes for adults & children; lect open to public; concerts; gallery talks; tours; films; outreach programs; individual paintings & original objects of art lent to other museums & galleries; originate traveling exhibitions; museum shop sell books, reproductions, notecards, educational toys & contemporary design objects

L **Library,** 19 Elm St, 04841. Tel 207-596-6457; FAX 207-596-0509; *Dir* Christopher B Crosman; *Cur* Susan Larson; *Vol Librn* Barbara Watson
Estab 1948. Art reference only. Archives on American artists, including papers of Louise Nevelson, Andrew Wyeth, N C Wyeth, George Bellows, Robert Indiana & Waldo Peirce
Library Holdings: Vols 4000; Per subs 15; American artists' file; Other — Clipping files, exhibition catalogs
Special Subjects: Art History, Etchings & Engravings, Folk Art, Marine Painting, Painting - American, Printmaking, Prints, Watercolors, Local History, Victorian
Collections: American art with an emphasis on Maine Art; paintings, works on paper, prints, sculpture, photography, decorative arts, artifacts & manuscripts

ROCKPORT

A **MAINE COAST ARTISTS,** Art Gallery, Russell Ave, PO Box 147, 04856. Tel 207-236-2875; *Dir* John Chandler; *Cur* Bruce Brown
Open Tues - Wed & Fri - Sun 10 AM - 5 PM, Thurs 10 AM - 9 PM (May 23 - Sept 27). Admis $2. Estab 1952 to show the works of contemporary Maine artists. Gallery building was an old livery stable & fire station overlooking Rockport Harbor. Average Annual Attendance: 15,000. Mem: 800; dues $15-$50; annual meeting in Nov
Income: Financed by mem, contributions, grants, handling fees, annual art auction
Exhibitions: Seasonal: varied exhibitions of contemporary Maine art; Annual Juried Craft Fair
Publications: Quarterly newsletter; exhibition catalogues; brochures
Activities: Classes for adults & children; docent training; lect open to public, 5 vis lectr per year; concerts; gallery talks; tours; originate traveling exhibitions to museums, galleries & universities who meet facility requirements; sales shop sells books, magazines, original art, prints, fine crafts & t-shirts

A **MAINE PHOTOGRAPHIC WORKSHOPS,** 2 Central St, 04856. Tel 207-236-8581; FAX 207-236-2558; *Founder & Dir* David H Lyman
Open Mon - Sun 9 AM - 5 PM & 7 - 9 PM June - Aug. Admis lectures $2.50. Estab 1973 as photographic center. Contains four separate spaces for the display of vintage & contemporary photographers. Average Annual Attendance: 10,000. Mem: 1400; dues $20; annual meetings Nov
Income: $2,000,000 (financed by mem, tuitions, sales & accommodations)
Collections: Eastern Illustrating Archive containing 100,000 vintage glass plates; The Kosti Ruohomaa Collection, prints of Life photographers; Master Work Collection; Paul Caponigro Archive, prints
Exhibitions: Forty photographic exhibitions
Publications: The Work Print, bi-monthly newsletter; Catalogues - Programs, semi-annual
Activities: Classes for adults & children; dramatic programs; lect open to public, 50 vis lectr per year; competitions with awards; scholarships offered; lending collection contains photographs; book traveling exhibitions; originate traveling exhibitions; sales shop sells books, magazines, original art, reproductions, prints, photographic equipment & supplies

L **Carter-Haas Library,** Union Hall, 2 Central St, 04856. Tel 207-236-8314; Elec Mail lib@meworkshops.com. *Librn* Anne Holmes
Open Mon - Wed 1 - 10 PM, Thurs 10 AM - 3 PM. Estab 1975 to support student studies
Purchases: $5000
Library Holdings: Vols 6500; Per subs 45; Micro — Cards, prints; AV — A-tapes, cassettes, fs, Kodachromes, lantern slides, motion pictures, rec, slides, v-tapes; Other — Clipping files, exhibition catalogs, framed reproductions, memorabilia, original art works, pamphlets, photographs, reproductions
Special Subjects: Film, Photography, Photographic technical & esthetic subjects, photographic history
Activities: Scholarships offered

SACO

M YORK INSTITUTE MUSEUM, 371 Main St, 04072. Tel 207-282-3031, 283-3861; FAX 207-283-0754; *Cur* Tina Toomey; *Cur* Thomas Hardiman
Open Tues, Wed & Fri Noon - 4 PM, Thurs Noon - 8 PM, Sun 1 - 4 PM. Admis adult $2, senior citizens, students & groups $1. Estab 1867 as a museum of regional history & culture. Permanent collections feature Maine furniture, decorative arts & paintings, 1750-1880. Special exhibitions on regional art, social history & student art. Average Annual Attendance: 5000. Mem: 300; dues perpetual $1000, life $500, contributing $50, family $25, senior citizen family $20, single $15
Income: Financed by endowment, private & corporate contributions, federal, state & municipal support
Collections: Federal period Maine books, ceramics, decorative arts, glass, manuscripts, maps, natural history paintings, pewter, sculpture, silver
Exhibitions: (1997) Contemporary Women Artists; The Fire of '47
Activities: Classes for adults & children; art workshops; dramatic programs; docent training; lect open to public, 3-4 vis lectr per hear; concerts; gallery talks; historica walking tours; house tour; individual paintings & original objects of art lent to other museums; museum shop sells books, Maine-made crafts, original art, prints & reproductions

SEARSPORT

M PENOBSCOT MARINE MUSEUM, Church St, PO Box 498, 04974-0498. Tel 207-548-2529; FAX 207-548-2520; *Dir* Renny A Stackpole; *Museum Teacher* Abigail E Zelz; *Dir Develop* Judith Demott; *Store Mgr* Ann Moffitt; *Librn* John Arrison; *Cur* Samuel W Shogren
Open Memorial Day weekend - Oct 15, Mon - Sat 9:30 AM - 5 PM, Sun 1 - 5 PM. Admis adults $5, senior citizens $3.50, youth 7-15 $1.50, 6 & under free. Estab 1936 as a memorial to the maritime record of present & former residents of the State of Maine in shipbuilding, shipping & all maritime affairs. The Mus consists of eight historic buildings, including the Old Town Hall (1845), Nickels-Colcord Duncan House (1880); Fowler True Ross House (1825); Cap Merithew House; Dutch House; two new buildings: Stephen Phillips' Memorial Library (1983) & Douglas & Margaret Carver Memorial Art Gallery/Auditorium (1986) & a Educ Center. Average Annual Attendance: 15,000. Mem: 1000; dues $25 & up; annual meeting in June
Income: Financed by endowment, mem, grant, gifts & admis
Collections: Marine Artifacts; China Trade Exports; 450 paintings & prints; Ship Models; water craft; decorative arts; ceramics; glass; textiles & extensive archives
Exhibitions: Permanent exhibit: The Challenge of the Downeasters; Marine Painting of Thomas & James Buttersworth; Working the Bay; Bound for Whampoa-The China Trade
Publications: Searsport Sea Captains, 1989; Lace & Leaves: The Art of Dolly Smith, 1994 (exhibit catalogue); annual report; newsletter, 3 times per year
Activities: Classes for adults & children; docent training; lect open to public, 12 vis lectr per year; concerts; scholarships offered; individual paintings & original objects of art lent to other institutions in accordance with museum policies; originate traveling exhibitions; sales shop sells Marine books, magazines, original art & reproductions & prints
L Stephen Phillips Memorial Library, Church St, PO Box 498, 04974-0498. Tel 207-548-2529; *Librn* John Arrison
Open for reference to researchers
Library Holdings: Vols 6000; Per subs 30; Nautical charts; Micro — Fiche, reels; AV — A-tapes, cassettes, fs, lantern slides, slides, v-tapes; Other — Clipping files, exhibition catalogs, manuscripts, memorabilia, original art works, pamphlets, photographs, prints
Special Subjects: Architecture, Art History, Asian Art, Ceramics, Decorative Arts, Drafting, Etchings & Engravings, Flasks & Bottles, Folk Art, Furniture

SOUTHWEST HARBOR

M WENDELL GILLEY MUSEUM, Main St & Herrick Rd, PO Box 254, 04679. Tel 207-244-7555; *Pres* Steven C Rockefeller; *Exec Dir* Nina Z Gormley; *VPres* Robert L Hinckley
Open June, Sept & Oct Tues - Sun 10 AM - 4 PM, July - Aug Tues - Sun 10 AM - 5 PM, May, Nov & Dec Fri - Sun 10 AM - 4 PM. Admis adults $3. Estab 1981 to house collection of bird carvings & other wildlife related art. Gallery occupies 3000 sq ft on one floor of a solar heated building; handicapped access. Average Annual Attendance: 17,000. Mem: 2000; dues $15-$500; annual meeting in Nov
Income: $166,000 (financed by mem, admis, sales & fundraising events)
Collections: Decorative wood carvings of birds & working decoys by Wendell Gilley; Birds of America, 1972 ed J J Audubon; Birds of Mt Desert Island by Carroll S Tyson (prints); Photos by Eliot Porter
Exhibitions: Bird Carvings by Wendell Gilley (rotating); Audubon prints (rotating)
Publications: The Eider, bi-annual newsletter
Activities: Classes for adults & children; films; lect open to public, 12 vis lectr per year; gallery talks; scholarships offered; original objects of art lent to other museums; book traveling exhibitions 1-2 per year; museum shop sells books, original art, carving tools, gift items, jewelry, posters & toys

WATERVILLE

M COLBY COLLEGE, Museum of Art, 04901-4799. Tel 207-872-3228; FAX 207-872-3141; *Dir* Hugh J Gourley III; *Asst Dir* Lynn Marsden-Atlass; *Preparator* Greg Williams
Open Mon - Sat 10 AM - 4:30 PM, Sun 2 - 4:30 PM, cl major holidays. No admis fee. Estab 1959 to serve as an adjunct to the Colby College Art Program & to be a mus center for Central Maine. Mem: Friends of Art at Colby, 700; dues $25 & up
Income: Financed by college funds, mem & donations
Collections: Bernat Oriental ceramics & bronzes; American Heritage collection;

The Helen Warren & Willard Howe Cummings Collection of American Art; American Art of the 18th, 19th & 20th centuries; Jette Collection of American painting in the Impressionist Period; John Marin Collection of 25 works by Marin; Adelaide Pearson Collection; Pre-Columbian Mexico; Etruscan art; The Alex Katz Wing (417 works)
Publications: Exhibition catalogs; periodic newsletter
Activities: Docent training; lect open to public; gallery talks; tours; individual paintings lent to other museums; originate traveling exhibitions; museum shop sells books, note cards, postcards & posters
L Bixler Art & Music Library, 04901. Tel 207-872-3232; FAX 207-872-3141; *Librn* Anthony P Hess
For reference & academic lending to college community
Library Holdings: Vols 15,000; Per subs 68; Music; Micro — Reels; AV — A-tapes, cassettes, Kodachromes, lantern slides, rec, slides 50,000, v-tapes; Other — Clipping files, exhibition catalogs, prints
Special Subjects: Afro-American Art, American Indian Art, American Western Art, Asian Art, Folk Art, History of Art & Archaeology, Islamic Art, Judaica, Latin American Art, Mexican Art, Oriental Art

M THOMAS COLLEGE ART GALLERY, 180 W River Rd, 04901. Tel 207-873-0771; FAX 207-877-0114; *Dir* Amy Warner
Open Mon - Fri 8 AM - 5 PM. No admis fee. Estab 1968 for presentation of instructional shows for student & community audiences. Average Annual Attendance: 1500
Exhibitions: Monthly exhibitions by local artists
L Library, 180 W River Rd, 04901. Tel 207-873-0771; FAX 207-877-0114; *Librn* Steven Larochelle
For reference only
Library Holdings: Vols 21,500; Per subs 400; AV — Slides

M WATERVILLE HISTORICAL SOCIETY, Redington Museum, 64 Silver St, 04901. Tel 207-872-9439; *Pres Historical Society* Willard B Arnold III; *Resident Cur* Harry Finnemore; *Resident Cur* Donnice Finnemore; *Librn* Caroline Waldman; *Librn* Diane Johnson
Open Memorial Day - Labor Day Tues - Sat 10 AM - 2 PM. Admis adults $3, children 12 & under $2. Estab 1903. Average Annual Attendance: 1500. Mem: 450; dues sponsor $100, family $30, single $15; annual meeting second Thurs in June
Income: Financed by mem & city appropriation & limited endowment
Collections: Early Silver & China; 18th & 19th century furniture; 19th century apothecary; portraits of early local residents; Victorian clothing
Activities: Lect open to public, 3 vis lectr per year; tours

WISCASSET

A LINCOLN COUNTY HISTORICAL ASSOCIATION, INC, Pownalborough Court House, PO Box 61, 04578. Tel 207-882-6817; *Dir* Anne R Dolan
Open July - Aug Wed - Sat 10 AM - 4 PM, Sun Noon - 4 PM. Admis adults $3, children 13 & under $1. Incorporated 1954, to preserve buildings of historic interest. Presents 200 years of Maine's crafts & skills including the work of craftsmen who spend part of the year in Maine. Gallery presents the works of contemporary professional artists, working in Maine, by means of two juried summer exhibitions. Two museums & one art gallery maintained. Average Annual Attendance: 3000. Mem: 650; dues $20 & up; annual meeting in July
Income: Financed by dues, fundraisers, admis
Collections: Furniture; hand tools; household articles; prison equipment; textiles
Exhibitions: Changing exhibits on 200 years of Maine crafts & skills; Lincoln County Museum, permanent exhibit on history of punishment
Publications: Newsletter; occasional monographs
Activities: School programs; lect; tours; slide shows
L Library, 04578. Tel 207-882-6817; *Dir* Anne R Dolan
Open by appointment for reference & research
Library Holdings: Vols 200
M Old Lincoln County Jail & Museum, Federal St, PO Box 61, 04578. Tel 207-882-6817; *Dir* Anne R Dolan
Open July - Aug Sun 11 AM - 4 PM. Admis adults $2, children 13 & under $1. Estab 1954 for historical preservation. Average Annual Attendance: 2000. Mem: 600; dues $20 & up, annual meeting in July
Income: Financed by mem, donations, restricted funds & bequests
Collections: Early American tools; jail artifacts; quilts; samplers; textiles
Activities: Lect open to public, over 5 vis lectr per year; tours; museum shop sells books
M Maine Art Gallery, Old Academy, Warren St, PO Box 315, 04578. Tel 207-882-7511; *Chmn & Dir* Anne R Dolan; *Treas* Linda Stetson
Open summer daily 10 AM - 4 PM, Sun 1 - 4 PM, winter Fri & Sat 10 AM - 4 PM, Sun 1 - 4 PM. No admis fee, donations appreciated. Estab 1958 as a cooperative, non-profit gallery created by the Artist Members of Lincoln County Cultural & Historical Assoc to exhibit the work of artists living or working in Maine. Gallery occupies a red brick federal two-story building built in 1807 as a free Academy. The building is now on National Historical Register. Average Annual Attendance: 6000. Mem: 185; dues $0; annual meeting in Sept
Income: Financed by patrons
Exhibitions: Summer Exhibition: A juried show in parts of 8 weeks featuring approx 100 painters & sculptors living or working in Maine. Winter series of one-person invited exhibitions
Activities: Lect open to public; gallery talks; school art classes visits

YORK

A OLD YORK HISTORICAL SOCIETY, PO Box 312, 03909. Tel 207-363-4974; FAX 207-363-4021; *Acting Dir & Cur* Thomas B Johnson; *Mem & Vol Coordr* Cheryl St Germain; *Dir Educ* Jennifer Lapp; *Registrar* Cynthia Young-Gome
Open mid-June - Sept Tues - Sat 10 AM - 5 PM, Sun 1 - 5 PM. Admis adults $8, children 6-16 $4, children under 6 free. Estab 1900 to operate buildings of historical interest & to inspire an awareness & appreciation of York's past in order to protect the town's environment for the present & the future. Administers

Old Gaol, oldest jail in US; 18th Century Jefferds Tavern; Elizabeth Perkins House; John Hancock Warehouse; Emerson-Wilcox House; Schoolhouse. Maintains reference library. Average Annual Attendance: 22,000. Mem: 600; dues $35 & up; annual meeting in Aug
Collections: American & European furniture; decorative arts from southern Maine; ceramic & glass collection; tools & maritime artifacts
Activities: Classes for adults & children; docent training; lect open to public, 3 per year; concerts; tours; fellowship; originate traveling exhibitions that circulate to other museums; sales shop sells books, reproductions, prints, Maine crafts & books & other gift items

M **Old Gaol Museum,** Lindsey Rd, 03909. Tel 207-363-4974; FAX 207-363-4021; *Acting Dir & Cur* Thomas B Johnson; *Cur* John Labranche; *Educator* Jennifer Lapp
Open June - Sept Mon - Fri 10:30 AM - 4:30 PM, Sun 1:30 - 4:30 PM. Admis $3. Estab 1900 as a local history mus to maintain, care for & develop historical collections of a regional nature & to promote historic research & historically educational programs. Mus consists of the oldest jail in the United States & an 18th century tavern arranged as period rooms. Two gallery rooms house traveling shows & temporary exhibitions of an historical nature; thirty-two period rooms in 3 other buildings. Average Annual Attendance: 10,000. Mem: 600; dues family $15, single $10; annual meeting Aug
Income: $70,000 (financed by endowment)
Collections: Regional collection of American furniture & decorative arts; rare books; manuscripts
Exhibitions: Changing exhibitions
Publications: Old Gaol Museum (history), E H Pendleton; York Maine Then & Now; Enchanted Ground, George Garrett; Old York Newsletter, quarterly
Activities: Classes for adults & children; dramatic programs; docent training; lect open to public, 6 vis lectr per year; scholarships offered; museum shop sells books, magazines, original art, reproductions, prints

L **Administration Building & Library,** 207 York St, 30909. Tel 207-363-4974; *Librn* Virginia Speller
Open Tues - Fri 9 AM - 5 PM. Reference only
Library Holdings: Vols 8000; Per subs 16; Original documents; Micro — Fiche, prints, reels; AV — A-tapes, cassettes, Kodachromes, lantern slides, motion pictures, rec, slides, v-tapes; Other — Clipping files, exhibition catalogs, manuscripts, memorabilia, original art works, pamphlets, photographs, prints
Special Subjects: Decorative Arts, History of York County, Maine
Activities: Educ dept; lect open to public, 6 vis lectr per year; gallery talks; tours; scholarships offered; individual paintings & original objects of art lent; museum shop sells books, reproductions & prints

MARYLAND

ANNAPOLIS

M **HAMMOND-HARWOOD HOUSE ASSOCIATION, INC,** 19 Maryland Ave, 21401. Tel 410-263-4683; FAX 410-267-6891; *ExecDir* Vickie Watson-Sopher
Open Mon - Sat 10 AM - 4 PM, Sun 1 - 4 PM. Admis adults $4, students between 6 & 18 $3. Estab 1938 to preserve the Hammond-Harwood House (1774), a National Historic Landmark; to educate the pub in the arts & architecture of Maryland in the 18th century. Average Annual Attendance: 15,000. Mem: 400; dues varied; meeting May & Nov
Income: Financed by endowment, mem, attendance & sales
Collections: Paintings by C W Peale; Chinese export porcelain; English & American furnishings, especially from Maryland; prints; English & American silver; colonial architectural interiors designed by William Buckland
Publications: Maryland's Way (Hammond-Harwood House cookbook); Hammond-Harwood House Guidebook
Activities: Interpretive programs; docent training; lect open to public; individual paintings & original objects of art lent to bonafide museums within reasonable transporting distance; museum shop sells books & prints

M **MARYLAND HALL FOR THE CREATIVE ARTS,** Cardinal Gallery, 801 Chase St, 21401. Tel 410-263-5544; FAX 410-263-5114; Elec Mail mdhall@annap.infi.net;
Internet Home Page Address www.mdhallarts.org. *Exec Dir* Linnell R Bowen
Open Mon - Sat 9 AM - 5 PM. No admis fee. Estab 1979 to exhibit work of contemporary regional artists. Two room post modern space with 100 ft of wall space & 1100 sq ft of floor area. Contemporary grid-track lighting. Limited, portable, double sided walls for larger exhibits. Average Annual Attendance: 6000. Mem: 2000; dues $25 & up
Income: Financed by local, state & special grant funds
Publications: Exhibition catalog
Activities: Classes for adults & children; dramatic programs; concerts; gallery talks; competitions

M **SAINT JOHN'S COLLEGE,** Elizabeth Myers Mitchell Art Gallery, 60 College Ave, 21404-2800. Tel 410-263-2371, Ext 256, (Direct line) 626-2556; FAX 410-263-4828; *Dir* Hydee Schaller; *Exhibit Preparator* Sigrid Trumpy; *Outreach Coordr* Lucinda Edinberg
Open Sept - May Tues - Sun Noon - 5 PM, Fri 7 - 8 PM. No admis fee. Estab 1989 for museum quality exhibits for the area. One gallery of 1300 sq ft, rectangle with corner windows, one gallery of 525 sq ft, rectangular, no windows. Average Annual Attendance: 10,000. Mem: 77; dues $5-$1000
Exhibitions: (1997) Nancy Graves: Excavations in Print, 1972-1992; Peleliu: WWII Drawings & Paintings by Donald McBride. (1998) From Earth & Soul: The Evans Collection of Asian Ceramics: Small Paintings by Arthur Dove, 1942-

43; St John's College Community Art Exhibition
Publications: Catalogs; exhibition programs; gallery guides
Activities: Educ dept offers studio courses in painting, lifedrawing & sculpture for adults & children; lectr open to public, 7 vis lectr per year; gallery talks; tours; book traveling exhibitions 3-4 per year; originate traveling exhibitions

M **UNITED STATES NAVAL ACADEMY MUSEUM,** 118 Maryland Ave, 21402-5034. Tel 410-293-2108; *Dir* William B Cogar; *Sr Cur* James W Cheevers; *Cur Ship Models* Robert F Sumrall; *Cur Robinson Coll* Sigrid Trumpy; *Sr Exhibit Specialist* Ronald Corder
Open Mon - Sat 9 AM - 5 PM, Sun 11 AM - 5 PM. No admis fee. Estab 1845 as Naval School Lyceum for the purpose of collecting, preserving & exhibiting objects related to American naval history. Mus contains two large galleries totaling 9000 sq ft, with other exhibits in other areas of the campus. Average Annual Attendance: Approx 600,000
Income: Financed by federal government appropriations & private donations
Purchases: $36,170
Collections: †Ceramicwares; Drawings; †Medals; †Naval Uniforms; †Paintings, †Prints, †Sculpture of Naval Portraits & Event; †Ship Models; †Silver; †Weapons
Exhibitions: Selections from the Permanent Art Collection; John Sloan, A Printmaker; Dutch Seapower in the 17th Century; The Bradshaw Collections of Marine Paintings; Target Angle Zero; Selections from the Permanent Art Collection; Edward Seager (1809-86)
Publications: Collection catalogs & special exhibition brochures, periodically
Activities: Lect; tours upon request; individual paintings & original objects of art lent to other museums & related institutions for special, temporary exhibitions; originate traveling exhibitions

L **Library,** 118 Maryland Ave, 21402-5034. Tel 410-293-2108; FAX 410-293-5220; *Dir* William B Cogar
Open to students, scholars & public with notice, reference only
Library Holdings: Vols 200; Per subs 15; Other — Exhibition catalogs
Special Subjects: Naval History, Marine Art

BALTIMORE

M **BALTIMORE CITY COMMUNITY COLLEGE,** Art Gallery, Fine & Applied Arts Dept, 2901 Liberty Heights Ave, 21215. Tel 410-462-8000; *Coordr Arts* Carlton Leverette
Open Mon - Fri 10 AM - 4 PM. No admis fee. Estab 1965 to bring to the Baltimore & college communities exhibitions of note by regional artists & to serve as a showplace for the artistic productions of the college art students & faculty. Consists of one large gallery area, approx 120 running ft, well-lighted through the use of both natural light (sky domes) & cove lighting which provides an even wash to the walls
Income: Financed through the college
Collections: Graphics from the 16th century to the present; paintings by notable American artists & regional ones
Exhibitions: Groups shows & three-man shows representing a broad cross section of work by regional artists; art faculty show; three-man show featuring graphic designs & paintings; exhibition of portraits by 15 artists; annual student show
Publications: Gallery announcements
Activities: Lect open to public; gallery talks

M **BALTIMORE CITY LIFE MUSEUMS,** 335 Front St, 21202-2605. Tel 410-396-3524; FAX 410-396-1806; *Acting Dir* Sally Zinno
Hours vary by site. No admis fee. Estab 1931 to collect, interpret & exhibit objects related to Baltimore history. Five sites: Carroll Mansion, Peale Museum, H L Mencken House, 1840 House, Baltimore Center for Urban Archaeology. Average Annual Attendance: 50,000. Mem: 300; dues $20; annual meeting in Sept
Income: Financed by city government & other sources
Collections: †Archaeological artifacts; †Baltimore historic photographs; †Baltimore paintings; †H L Mencken's personal effects; †Peale family paintings; †prints of Baltimore
Publications: City Past-Time, quarterly newsletter
Activities: Dramatic programs; docent training; lect open to public, 5-10 vis lectr per year; gallery talks, tours; individual paintings & original objects of art lent to other museums; museum shop sells books & postcards

L **Library,** 225 Holliday St, 21202. Tel 410-396-1149; *Supv* Mary Markey
Open to staff & pub for reference, by appointment only
Library Holdings: Vols 1400; Per subs 20; Maps; Printed Ephemera; Micro — Reels; AV — Lantern slides, motion pictures, rec, slides, v-tapes; Other — Clipping files, exhibition catalogs, framed reproductions, manuscripts, memorabilia, original art works, pamphlets, photographs, prints, reproductions
Special Subjects: Architecture, Baltimore History, Maritime

M **BALTIMORE MUSEUM OF ART,** Art Museum Dr, 21218. Tel 410-396-7101; FAX 410-396-7153; *Dir* Arnold L Lehman; *Dir Educ* Bridiged Globensky; *Deputy Dir Admin* Kathleen Basham; *Pub Relations & Marketing* Becca Seitz; *Deputy Dir & Cur Modern Paintings & Sculpture* Brenda Richardson; *Deputy Dir External Affairs* Paul Papich; *Dir Mem & Develop* Roger Marquis; *Cur Decorative Arts* James Abbott; *Consultant Cur Decorative Arts* William Voss Elder III; *Cur Prints, Drawings & Photographs* Jay Fisher; *Assoc Cur Prints Drawings & Photographs* Jan Howard; *Asst Cur Decorative Arts* M B Munford; *Cur Painting & Sculpture Before 1900* Sona Johnston; *Consultant Cur Textiles* Dena Katzenberg; *Assoc Cur Textiles* Anita Jones; *Cur Art of Africa, Americas, Oceania* Frederick Lamp; *Assoc Cur Art Of Africa, Americas, Oceania* Katharine Ferstrom
Open Wed, Thurs & Fri 10 AM - 4 PM, Sat & Sun 11 AM - 6 PM, cl Mon, Tues & holidays. Admis $5.50 for non-members over 19. Estab 1914 to house & preserve art works, to present art exhibitions, art-related activities & offer educational programs & events. The original building was designed by John Russell Pope in 1929; addition in 1982 with cafe, auditorium & traveling exhibition galleries; sculpture gardens opened in 1980 & 1988; new wing for Modern Art opened 1994. Average Annual Attendance: 300,000. Mem: 17,000; dues $15-$50
Income: $8,000,000 (financed by city & state appropriation; corporate, individual

& foundation gifts; mem, earned revenue & endowment income; county support)
Collections: Blanche Adler Collection of Graphic Art; Antioch Mosaics; Ellen H Bayard Collection of 18th & 19th Century American Paintings, European Ceramics, Chinese Export Porcelain, American & English Silver; General Lawrason Riggs Collection of Old Master Prints & Chinese Ceramics; Thomas E Benesch Memorial Collection of Drawings by 20th Century American & European artists; Harry A Bernstein Memorial Collection of Contemporary American Paintings; Cone Collection of 19th & 20th Century French Paintings, Sculpture; Drawings & Prints, Near Eastern & European Textiles Laces, Jewelry, Furniture & other Decorative Arts; Elise Agnus Daingerfield Collection of 18th Century English, French & American Paintings with emphasis on Portraiture; Hanson Rawlings Duval Jr Memorial Collection of 19th Century Baltimore Architectural Elements, American Furniture, Paintings, European & Chinese Ceramics; Helen & Abram Eisenberg Collection of Paintings, primarily 19th Century French; Jacob Epstein Collection of Old Master Paintings; Edward Joseph Gallagher III Memorial Collection of American Paintings between 1921 & 1955; T Harrison Garrett Collection of Graphic Art 15th - 19th Century; Nelson & Juanita Greif Gutman Memorial Collection of 20th Century Paintings, Sculpture & Drawings; Charles & Elsa Hutzler Memorial Collection of Contemporary Sculpture; Mary Frick Jacobs Collection of 15th - 18th Century European Paintings, Tapestries, Furniture & Objects d'Art; Julius Levy Memorial Fund Collection of Oriental Art; George A Lucas Collection of 19th Century Drawings, Prints, Paintings & Bronzes; Saidie A May Collection of 20th Century Paintings, Sculpture & Graphics, Ancient, Medieval & Renaissance Sculpture & Textiles; McLanahan Memorial Collection of 1720 Bedchamber & its Furnishings; Samuel & Tobie Miller Memorial Collection of Contemporary Painting & Sculpture; J G D'Arcy Paul Collection of 18th Century American Furniture; Peabody Institute Collection of 19th & 20th Century American Paintings; White Collection of Ceramics, Furniture, Needlework, Glass & Decorative Art Books; White Collection of Early Maryland Silver; William Woodward Collection of 18th & 19th Century Paintings of English Sporting Life; Wurtzburger Collection of Art of Africa, the Americas & Oceania; Janet & Alan Wurtzburger Collection of 20th Century Sculpture; Robert H and Ryda Levi Collection of Contemporary Sculpture
Exhibitions: Painting, sculpture, textiles, furniture & other decorative arts, prints, drawings and photography
Publications: Exhibition catalogs; monthly calendar; members newsletter; posters & postcards
Activities: Classes for children; docent training; lect open to public; concerts; gallery talks; tours; competitions; dance performances; film series; museum shop sells books, original art, reproductions, prints, slides & art-related gifts

L **E Kirkbride Miller Art Library,** Art Museum Dr, 21218. Tel 410-396-6317; FAX 410-396-6562; *Librn* Wendy Thompson; *Asst* Alene D Oestreicher
Open by appointment: Wed - Fri 10 AM - 4 PM, 1st Thurs each month 5 - 9 PM, 2nd Sat each month 1 - 5 PM
Library Holdings: Vols 44,511; Per subs 291; Auction catalogs; Other — Clipping files, exhibition catalogs, pamphlets
Special Subjects: Decorative Arts, Drawings, Painting - American, Prints, Arts of Africa, Contemporary Art, 19th & 20th Century French Art, The Americas & Oceania

M **THE CONTEMPORARY,** Museum for Contemporary Arts, 601 N Howard St, 21201. Tel 410-333-8600; FAX 410-333-8602; Elec Mail thecontemporary@softaid.net. *Dir* Gary Sangster; *Cur & Educator* Lisa Corrin; *Mus Admin* Dana Johns
Estab 1989 to explore connections between the art of our time & our world. Average Annual Attendance: 25,000. Mem: 400; dues $35; annual meeting in June
Income: Financed by endowment, mem, grants, private donations & IMS
Exhibitions: Mining the Museum: an installation by Fred Wilson; Catfish Dreamin'; A Sculpture on a Truck by Alison Saar; Going Baroque (Collaboration with Walters Art Gallery); Hung Liu Paintings
Publications: Mining the Museum; Outcry; Artists Answer AIDs
Activities: Classes for adults & children; volunteer programs; lect open to public, 5 vis lectr per year; book traveling exhibitions 1 per year; originate traveling exhibitions 1 per year

M **GOUCHER COLLEGE,** Rosenberg Gallery, Department of Art, 1021 Dulaney Valley Rd, 21204. Tel 410-337-6333, 337-6073; FAX 410-337-6405; Elec Mail hglazer@goucher.edu. *Exhib Dir & Coll Coordr* Helen Glazer
Open Mon - Fri 9 AM - 5 PM during the academic calendar & on evenings & weekends of pub events. No admis fee. Estab 1964 to display temporary & continuously changing exhibitons of contemporary & historically important visual arts. Gallery spaced located in the lobby of the Kraushaar Auditorium; 144 running ft of wall space. Average Annual Attendance: 90,000
Income: Financed privately
Collections: Ceramics; coins; drawings; paintings; prints; sculpture; photography
Exhibitions: (1997) After the Fire: Clipper Mill & Hollins Exchange Artists; In to The Woods: Eliot Cohen & Dan Kuhne; Woodcuts from The 1930s by Eloise Hampton Wilson
Publications: Exhibit brochures, 4 per year
Activities: Lect open to public; gallery talks; individual paintings & original objects of art lent to museums & university galleries; book traveling exhibitions 1 per year

JOHNS HOPKINS UNIVERSITY

M **Archaeological Collection,** 3400 N Charles St, 21218. Tel 410-516-7561, 659-2540; *Cur* Dr Lori-Ann Touchette; *Cur Near Eastern & Egyptian Art* Dr Betsy Bryan
Estab 1876. Small exhibit space in Gilman Hall
Collections: Egyptian through Roman material 3500 BC to 500 AD

M **Evergreen House,** 4545 N Charles St, 21210. Tel 410-516-0341; FAX 410-516-0864; *Dir* Lili Ott
Open Mon - Fri 10 AM - 4 PM, Sat & Sun 1 - 4 PM. Admis fee $6. Estab 1952 for promotion of cultural & educational functions & research. Formerly the residence of Ambassador John W Garrett which he bequeathed to the University. Average Annual Attendance: 10,000. Mem: Dues $25
Collections: Bakst Theater Decorations; European Ceramics; Japanese Inro, Netsuke & Lacquer: Chinese Ceramics; Oriental Rugs; Rare Book Collection; Tiffany Glass; Twentieth Century European Paintings
Exhibitions: Changing exhibitions
Activities: Classes for adults; docent training; lect open to public; concerts; individual paintings & original objects of art lent to other museums, national & international; museum shop sells books, reproductions & prints

L **George Peabody Library,** 17 E Mount Vernon Pl, 21202. Tel 410-659-8179; FAX 410-659-8137; *Librn* Carolyn Smila; *Librn Asst* Jeanette Harden
Open Mon - Fri 9 AM - 3 PM
Library Holdings: Vols 250,000
Special Subjects: Architecture, Decorative Arts

M **Homewood House Museum,** 3400 N Charles St, 21218. Tel 410-516-5589; FAX 410-516-7859; *Dir* Lili Ott
Open 11 AM - 5 PM. Admis $5. Estab 1987; a historic house mus. Restored Federal Period country seat of Charles Carroll, Jr, with period furnishings. Average Annual Attendance: 10,000. Mem: Annual dues $25
Collections: English & American decorative arts of the late 18th & early 19th Century
Activities: Classes for adults; historically relevant activities for children & young people; concerts; tours; internships offered; museum shop sells books, original art, object reproductions, prints, slides, exclusive Homewood items & jewelry

M **MARYLAND ART PLACE,** 218 W Saratoga St, 21201. Tel 410-962-8565; FAX 410-244-8017; Elec Mail map@charm.net. *Exec Dir* Jack Rasmussen; *Develop Dir* Coleen West; *Prog Dir* Tex Andrews
Open Tues - Sat 11 AM - 5 PM. No admis fee. Estab 1981, to provide opportunities for artists to exhibit work, nurture & promote new ideas & forms. Three floors of exhibition space, including the 14 Karat Caberet used for performance art, music, films & dance. Maintains reference library. Average Annual Attendance: 30,000. Mem: 900; dues $25-$1000
Income: $330,000 (financed by mem, federal, state & corporate appropriation)
Exhibitions: Varies
Publications: Annual catalogs; exhibition brochures, 4-6 per year; quarterly newsletter
Activities: Critics' residencies including writing workshop & annual public forum; lect open to public, 4 vis lectr per year; concerts; gallery talks; tours; book traveling exhibitions 1 per year; originate traveling exhibitions 1-2 per year

M **MARYLAND HISTORICAL SOCIETY,** Museum of Maryland History, 201 W Monument St, 21201. Tel 410-685-3750, Ext 70; FAX 410-385-2105; *Dir* Dennis Fiori; *Cur & Coll* Nancy Davis
Open Tues - Fri 10 AM - 4:30 PM, Sat 9 AM - 4:30 PM. Admis adults $3.50, seniors & student $2.50, children $1.50. Estab 1844 to collect, display & interpret the history of the State of Maryland. Average Annual Attendance: 70, 000. Mem: 6500; dues family $45; annual meeting in June
Income: Financed by endowment, mem, city & state appropriations
Collections: †Architectural drawings; †crystal & glassware; †ethnic artifacts, all of Maryland origin or provenance; †metalwork; †paintings, both portrait & landscape; †porcelain & †pottery; †silver; †textiles & †costumes; †furniture
Exhibitions: Continually changing exhibitions refelecting the history & culture of the state
Publications: Maryland Historical Society Magazine, quarterly; News & Notes, bimonthly
Activities: Classes for adults; docent training; lect open to public; conerts; gallery talks; tours; competiitons with awards; exten dept; individual paintings & original objects of art lent to other organizations; originate traveling exhibitions; museum shop sells books, magazines, original art, reproductions, prints, slides, crafts, decorative arts items, jewelry

L **Library,** 201 W Monument St, 21201. Tel 410-685-3750; FAX 410-385-2105; *Dir* Dennis Fiori; *Cur & Coll* Nancy Davis
Open Tues - Fri 10 AM - 5 PM, Sat 9 AM - 5 PM. Estab 1844. Library for reference only. Average Annual Attendance: 80,000. Mem: 6000
Library Holdings: Vols 60,000; Per subs 125; Micro — Fiche, reels; AV — A-tapes, cassettes, fs, Kodachromes, lantern slides, motion pictures, rec, slides, v-tapes; Other — Clipping files, exhibition catalogs, manuscripts, memorabilia, pamphlets, photographs, prints, reproductions

M **MARYLAND INSTITUTE,** College of Art Exhibitions, 1300 Mount Royal Ave, 21217. Tel 410-225-2280; FAX 410-225-2229; *Pres* Fred Lazarus IV; *Gallery Mgr* Thomas Sakoulas; *Asst Dir* Maryann Savige
Open Mon - Wed & Sat 10 AM - 5 PM, Thurs & Fri 10 AM - 9 PM, Sun Noon - 5 PM. No admis fee. Estab 1826, including the Decker & Meyerhoff Galleries, the Graduate Thesis Gallery & 2 student galleries. Average Annual Attendance: 10,000
Income: Financed by endowment & student tuition
Exhibitions: Changing exhibitions of contemporary work in Meyerhoff & Decker Galleries; (1997) Alumni Exhibition; Artists: Doug Hall, Dennis Oppenheim, Not Vital, Robert Morris, Nancy Davidson, Ellen Driscoll; Juried Undergraduate Exhibition; Graduate School Exhibition; Mt Royal Graduate School of Painting Exhibit; Reinhart Graduate School of Sculpture Exhibit; Spaces & Forms, Part 2
Publications: Several small catalogs; two major publications per year
Activities: Lect open to public; concerts; gallery talks; tours; original objects of art lent

L **Decker Library,** 1400 Cathedral St, 21201. Tel 410-225-2311; FAX 410-225-2316; *Library Dir* Marjorie Chenoweth
Open Mon - Thurs 8:30 AM - 9 PM, Fri 8:30 AM - 4:30 PM, Sat & Sun 1 - 5 PM during the academic year; call for summer & holiday hours. Open to the pub for reference only.
Library Holdings: Vols 50,000; Per subs 310

M **MEREDITH GALLERY,** 805 N Charles St, 21201. Tel 410-837-3575; FAX 410-837-3577; *Dir* Judith Lippman; *Assoc Dir* Terry Heffner
No admis fee. Estab 1977 to exhibit a variety of contemporary art by living American artists, including art furniture, ceramics, glass, handmade paper, paintings & prints. The building is divided into two floors with regular monthly exhibits & ongoing representation of gallery artists.

Average Annual Attendance: 4000
Exhibitions: Ed Baynard; Gene Davis; Dorothy Gillespie; Paul Jenkins; Margie Hughto; Alex Katz; David Lund; Robert Motherwell; Bennett Bean; John Dunnigan; Elizabeth Osborne; Michael Graves; Judy Kensley McKie; Alphonse Mattia; Rosanne Somerson; Stanley Tigerman; Robert Stern
Activities: Classes for adults & children; educational lect on current exhibitions; lect open to public; gallery talks; tours

MORGAN STATE UNIVERSITY
M **James E Lewis Museum of Art,** Cold Spring Lane & Hillen Rd, 21251. Tel 410-319-3030, 319-3306; FAX 410-319-3835; *Dir & Cur* Gabriel S Tenabe
Open Mon - Fri 9 AM - 5 PM, Sat, Sun, holidays by appointment only, cl Easter, Thanksgiving, Christmas. No admis fee. Estab 1950. Average Annual Attendance: 5000
Income: $5500
Collections: 19th & 20th centuries American & European sculpture; graphics; paintings; decorative arts; archaeology; African & New Guinea Sculptures
Publications: Monthly catalogs
Activities: Lect open to public, vis lectr; lending collection contains kodachromes; originate traveling exhibitions organized & circulated
L **Library,** Cold Spring Lane & Hillen Rd, 21251. Tel 410-319-3488; *Dir* Karen Robertson
Library Holdings: Vols 8800; Other — Photographs

M **NATIONAL SOCIETY OF COLONIAL DAMES OF AMERICA IN THE STATE OF MARYLAND,** Mount Clare Mansion, Carroll Park, 1500 Washington Blvd, 21230. Tel 410-837-3262; *Admin* Joan Feldman
Open Tues - Fri 10 AM - 4:30 PM, Sat & Sun Noon - 4:30 PM. Admis adults $3, students & senior citizens $2, children under 12 $.50. Estab 1917 to preserve the home of Charles Carroll, Barrister & teach about the colonial period of Maryland history. Maintained by the National Soc of Colonial Dames. Rooms of the house are furnished with 18th & early 19th century decorative arts, much of which belonged to the Carroll family who built the house in 1756. Average Annual Attendance: 8000
Income: Financed by admis, gift shop sales & contributions from pub & private sectors
Collections: American paintings; 18th & early 19th century English & American furniture; English silver; Irish crystal; Oriental export porcelain; archaeological artifacts found on property; other English & American decorative arts
Publications: Brochure on Mount Clare; Mount Clare: Being an Account of the Seat Built by Charles Carroll, Barrister Upon His Lands at Patapsco; booklet on the house
Activities: Historical slide shows for schools & organizations; tours; original objects of art lent to historical societies; museum shop sells books, reproductions, slides, gift items & historical replicas
L **Library,** Carroll Park, 1500 Washington Blvd, 21230. Tel 410-837-3262; Open to members & the pub for reference only
Library Holdings: Vols 1000; AV — Slides; Other — Framed reproductions, original art works, pamphlets, photographs
Special Subjects: Decorative Arts, 18th Century Culture
Collections: 18th century furniture; decorative arts; part of the library of Charles Carroll, Barrister-at-law, builder of the house, 1756

L **ENOCH PRATT FREE LIBRARY OF BALTIMORE CITY,** Fine Arts Dept, 400 Cathedral St, 21201. Tel 410-396-5430; *Dir* Carla Hayden; *Chief Pub Relations Div* Averil Kadis; *Dept Head* Ellen Luchinsky
Open Mon, Tues & Wed 10 AM - 8 PM, Sat 10 AM - 5 PM, Sun 1 - 5 PM Oct - Apr, cl Fri. Estab 1882 to provide materials, primarily circulating on the visual arts and music. Exhibition space in display windows, interior display cases, corridors and special departments
Income: Financed by city and state appropriation
Purchases: $32,000
Library Holdings: Framed prints; Unframed pictures; AV — Fs, rec, slides; Other — Framed reproductions, reproductions
Publications: Booklets, periodically
Activities: Lect & film showings

A **SCHOOL 33 ART CENTER,** 1427 Light St, 21230. Tel 410-396-4641; FAX 410-625-2634; *Dir* Claudia Amory
Open Tues - Sat 11 AM - 4 PM. Estab 1979 to promote the development & growth of contemporary visual art. Provide services & special events for artists & the public

A **STAR-SPANGLED BANNER FLAG HOUSE ASSOCIATION,** Flag House & 1812 Museum, 844 E Pratt St, 21202. Tel 410-837-1793; *Pres* Charles Steiff; *VPres* Hall Worthington; *Treas* Harry F Reid
Open Mon - Sat 10 AM - 4 PM, cl Sun. Admis adults $1.50, students 13 - 18 $1, children 6 - 12 $.50, under 6 free. Estab 1928 for the care & maintenance of 1793 home of Mary Pickersgill, maker of 15 star, 15 stripe flag used at Fort McHenry during Battle of Baltimore, War of 1812, which inspired Francis Scott Key to pen his famous poem, now our national anthem; also to conduct an educational program for pub & private schools. Mus houses artifacts, portraits & library. 1793 house furnished & decorated in Federal period to look as it did when Mary Pickersgill was in residence. Average Annual Attendance: 15,000. Mem: 500; dues $15; annual meeting in May
Income: Financed by mem, admis, special events fund-raisers & sales from mus shop
Collections: Flag collection; original antiques of Federal period
Publications: The Star (newsletter), quarterly
Activities: Educ dept; lect open to public; concerts; gallery talks; tours; museum sales shop sells books, reproductions, prints, slides, Baltimore souvenirs, flags from all nations, maps, country crafts & small antiques
M **Museum,** 844 E Pratt St, 21202. Tel 410-837-1793, 837-1812; *Dir* Sally S Johnston
Open Tues - Sat 9:30 AM - 4:30 PM. Admis $.50-$4. Estab 1927. Mem: 375; dues $30; annual meeting in Apr
Collections: House furnished in authentic federal period furniture & artifacts
Publications: The Star, quarterly
Activities: Lect open to public, 5 vis lectr per year; museum shop sells books & flags of all descriptions

M **UNITED METHODIST HISTORICAL SOCIETY,** Lovely Lane Museum, 2200 Saint Paul St, 21218. Tel 410-889-4458; *Pres* Millard B Knowles; *Dir* Arthur D Thomas Jr
Open Mon & Fri 10 AM - 4 PM, Sun after church; groups by appointment. No admis fee. Estab 1855; a religious collection specializing in Methodism. The main mus room contains permanent exhibits; three other galleries are devoted largely to rotating exhibits. Average Annual Attendance: 5000. Mem: 623; dues $10-$200; annual meeting in May
Income: $43,000 (financed by mem & religious denomination)
Collections: Archaeological items from Evans House; Artifacts with Methodist significance; medallions; †Methodist Library & Archives; oil portraits & engraving of United Methodist leader, quilts; †Papers of Leading Methodists
Publications: Third Century Methodism, quarterly; annual report
Activities: Docent training; lect open to public, 1-2 vis lectr per year; tours; competitions with awards; individual paintings & original objects of art lent to institutions able to provide proper security upon application & approval by Board of Directors; originate traveling exhibitions to United Methodist Churches & Conferences; museum shop sells books, prints, reproductions
L **Library,** Lovely Lane Museum, 2200 Saint Paul St, 21218. Tel 410-889-4458; *Librn* Edwin Schell; *Asst Librn* Betty Ammons
Open Mon & Fri 10 AM - 4 PM & by appointment. Estab 1855 specializing in United Methodist history & heritage. Open to general pub for reference. Average Annual Attendance: 4000. Mem: 700
Income: $43,000
Purchases: $700
Library Holdings: Vols 5000; Per subs 20; Archives; Micro — Reels; AV — A-tapes, cassettes, fs, Kodachromes, lantern slides, motion pictures, rec, slides; Other — Clipping files, manuscripts, memorabilia, original art works, pamphlets, photographs, prints, reproductions, sculpture
Special Subjects: Archaeology, Architecture, Bookplates & Bindings, Etchings & Engravings, Film, Prints, Religious Art, Historical Material, Manuscripts, Maps, Painting - American, Portraits, Posters, Textiles, United Methodist History, Local Church History, Baltimore Conference Archives
Publications: Third Century Methodism, 3 per year

M **WALTERS ART GALLERY,** 600 N Charles St, 21201. Tel 410-547-9000; FAX 410-783-7969; *Pres Board Trustees* Adena Testa; *Dir* Dr Gary Vikan; *Assoc Dir* William R Johnston; *Asst Dir Admin* John Caugant; *Asst Dir Curatorial Affairs & Cur Medieval Art* Shrebe Simpson; *Cur Ancient Art* Ellen Reeder; *Research Cur Manuscripts & Rare Books* Lilian M C Randall; *Dir Develop* Joy Heyrmon; *Dir Educ* Diane Brandt Stillman; *Ed Publications* Maria Lalima; *Dir Conservation & Technical Research* Terry Drayman Weisser; *Registrar* Joan Elizabeth Reid; *Sales Mgr* William O'Brien
Open Tues - Sun 11 AM - 5 PM, cl Mon, New Year's Day, Fourth of July, Thanksgiving, Christmas Eve, Christmas. Admis adults $4, senior citizens $3, members, students & children free, free admis on Sat 11 AM - Noon. Estab 1931 by the will of Henry Walters & opened in 1934 as an art mus. Hackerman House Mus of Asian Art opened in 1990. A Renaissance revival mus of 1905 with a contemporary wing of five floors opened in 1974, covering 126,000 sq ft of exhibition space with auditorium, library & conservation laboratory. Average Annual Attendance: 222,000. Mem: 5000; dues $15-$5000
Income: $2,850,000 (financed by endowment, mem, city & state appropriation & grants)
Collections: The Collection covers the entire history of art from Egyptian times to the beginning of the 20th century. It includes important groups of Roman sculpture, Etruscan, Byzantine & medieval art; Oriental art; Sevres porcelains; Near Eastern Art & Euorpean paintings
Exhibitions: Sharing Traditions: Five Black Artists in Nineteenth-Century America, from the Collection of the National Museum of American Art; Harlem Portraits: Photographs by Carl Van Vechten; Silver Treasure from Early Byzantium; Renaissance to Rococo: Italian Paintings from the Walters Collection; Master Drawings from Titian to Picasso: The Curtis O Baer Collection; Dutch Masterworks from The Bredius Museum: A Connoisseur's Collection; Northern European Masterworks from the Walters Collection; Frederick Carder: Portrait of a Glassmaker; Objects of Adornment: Five Thousand Years of Jewelry from The Walters Art Gallery; Stories from China's Past, Han Dynasty Pictorial Tomb Tiles from Sichuan, People's Republic of China; Time Sanctified; Holy Image, Holy Space; From Alexander to Cleopatra
Publications: Bulletin, bi-monthly; journal, annually; exhibition catalogues
Activities: Classes for adults & children; dramatic programs; docent training; seminars; lect open to public; concerts; gallery talks; tours; films; exten dept serves Baltimore City & nearby counties; book traveling exhibitions 3-4 per year; originate traveling exhibitions; museum shop sells books, reproductions, slides, Christmas cards, notepaper
L **Library,** 600 N Charles St, 21201. Tel 410-547-9000, Ext 274; FAX 410-752-4797; *Head Librn* Elise Calvi; *Asst Librn* Elizabeth Fishman
Open Tues - Fri 11 AM - 5 PM. Estab 1934 serves staff of the mus & open to the pub by appointment. Non-circulating
Income: $154,000
Purchases: $73,000
Library Holdings: Vols 104,000; Per subs 450; Auction catalogs
Special Subjects: American Western Art, Antiquities-Assyrian, Archaeology, Architecture, Ceramics, Decorative Arts, Drawings, History of Art & Archaeology, Painting - American, Religious Art, Restoration & Conservation, Sculpture, Silver, Silversmithing, Stained Glass, History of art from prehistoric times to the end of the 19th century, with emphasis on manuscript illumination & decorative arts

CHESTERTOWN

A **HISTORICAL SOCIETY OF KENT COUNTY,** 101 Church Alley, PO Box 665, 21620. Tel 410-778-3499; *Exec Dir* Nancy Nunn
Open May - Oct weekdays by appointment, Sat & Sun 1 - 4 PM. Admis adults $1, children & students $.50. Estab 1936 to foster an appreciation of our colonial heritage, to encourage restoration, to enlighten and to entertain. Headquarters are in an early 18th century town house, beautifully restored and furnished. Mem: 660; dues family $25, single $15; annual meeting in Apr

Income: Financed by mem and a Candlelight Tour
Collections: Furniture, pictures; Indian artifacts; fans
Exhibitions: Permanent house museum
Activities: Classes for adults & children; lect for members & community; tours; open house with traditional costuming; competitions with awards; book scholarships offered

COLLEGE PARK

M UNIVERSITY OF MARYLAND, COLLEGE PARK, Art Gallery, Art-Sociology Bldg, 20742. Tel 301-405-2763; FAX 301-314-7774; Elec Mail cg17@umail.umd.edu. *Dir* Terry Gips; *Asst to Dir & Registrar* Robert Blitz; *Designer* Karen Werth; *Exhib Asst* Kimberly Gladfelter
Open Mon - Fri Noon - 4 PM, Wed evening until 9 PM, Sat & Sun 1 - 5 PM, cl summer & holidays. No admis fee. Estab 1966 to present historic & contemporary exhibitions. Gallery has 4000 sq ft of space, normally divided into one large & one smaller gallery. Average Annual Attendance: 10,000
Income: Financed by university & department funds, grants, catalog sales
Collections: 20th century paintings, prints & drawings, including WPA mural studies, paintings by Warhol, Prendergast & Gottlieb; prints by Hundertwasser, Appel, Kitaj, Rivers & Chryssa; 20th century Japanese prints by Hiratsuka, Kosaka, Matsubara, Iwami, Ay-O & others; West African sculpture
Exhibitions: (1997) Department of Art: New Works by the Faculty, MFA & Undergraduate Students; Masters of Fine Arts Thesis Exhibitions; Crosscurrents 97: Regional Artists. (1998) Masters of Fine Arts Thesis Exhibition
Publications: Exhibition catalogs, 1 - 2 per year
Activities: Lect, symposiums & films open to public; 3-5 vis lectr per year; gallery talks; tours; individual paintings & original objects of art lent; lending collection contains original art work & print, paintings, photographs & sculpture; originate traveling exhibitions; exhibition catalogs sold in gallery
L Art Library, Art-Sociology Bldg, 20742. Tel 301-405-9061; FAX 301-314-9725; *Head Art Library* Lynne Woodruff; *Acting Asst Librn* Louise Green; *Library Asst* Amrita Kavr; *Library Technical Asst II* Pat deLaubenfels
Open Mon - Thurs 8:30 AM - 10 PM, Fri 8:30 AM - 5 PM, Sat 10 AM - 5 PM, Sun 1 - 10 PM. Estab 1979 in new building to serve the needs of the art & art history departments & campus in various art subjects
Income: Financed by university library system
Library Holdings: Vols 90,000; Per subs 234; Micro — Fiche, reels; Other — Exhibition catalogs, reproductions 33,000
Special Subjects: Advertising Design, Afro-American Art, American Indian Art, American Western Art, Art Education, Carpets & Rugs, Ceramics, Folk Art, Furniture, Graphic Arts, Painting - American, Photography, Portraits, Posters, Pottery
Collections: Art & Architecture in France; Index photographic de l'art de France; Index Iconologicus; Decimal Index to art of Low Countries; †Marburg index; Index of American Design; Deloynes Collections; Southeast Asia Collection
Publications: Bibliography; Checklist of Useful Tools for the Study of Art; Western Art; Asian Art
Activities: Tours
L Architecture Library, 20742. Tel 301-405-6317 (architecture), 405-6320 (Libr Colls); *Head* Anita Carrico
Open Mon - Thurs 8:30 AM - 10 PM, Fri 8:30 AM - 5 PM, Sat 1 - 5 PM, Sun 5 - 10 PM. Estab 1967 for lending & reference. Circ 25,000
Library Holdings: Vols 36,000; Per subs 180; Bd per 6200; Micro — Fiche 200, reels 600; AV — Fs; Other — Clipping files
Special Subjects: Architecture, Interior Design, Landscape Architecture, Urban Planning & Design
Collections: †World Expositions: books & pamphlets on buildings, art work & machinery
Publications: Architecture Library (brochure), annual; Access to Architectural Literature: Periodical Indexes, annual
L National Trust for Historic Preservation Library Collection, McKeldin Library, 20742. Tel 301-405-6319; FAX 301-405-9191; *Librn* Sally Sims Stokes
Open Mon - Fri 9 AM - 5 PM. For reference only
Income: Financed by the University of Maryland
Library Holdings: Vols 11,000; Per subs 300; Micro — Fiche; AV — A-tapes, cassettes, motion pictures, v-tapes; Other — Clipping files, pamphlets
Special Subjects: Architecture, Historical Material, Period Rooms, Restoration & Conservation, all aspects of preservation of historic buildings

COLUMBIA

M AFRICAN ART MUSEUM OF MARYLAND (Formerly Maryland Museum of African Art), 5430 Vantage Point Rd, Historic Oakland at Town Ctr, PO Box 1105, 21044. Tel 410-730-7105; FAX 410-715-3047; *Dir* Doris Hillian Ligon
Open Tues - Fri 10 AM - 4 PM, Sun Noon - 4 PM. Admis adults $2, sr citizens & under 12 $1, members free. Estab 1980 working towards better understanding of African art & culture. Average Annual Attendance: 40,000. Mem: dues contributing $100, family $40, individual $25, students & senior citizens $20
Collections: African art consisting of household items, jewelry, masks, musical instruments, sculpture & textiles
Publications: Museum Memos, quarterly
Activities: Workshops for children & families; docent training; lect open to public, 5-10 vis lectr per year; concerts; gallery talks; tours; awards given; original objects of art lent to distinctive level members; museum shop sells books, original art, reproductions, jewelry, textiles & crafts

CUMBERLAND

M ALLEGANY COUNTY HISTORICAL SOCIETY, History House, 218 Washington St, 21502. Tel 301-777-8678; *Dir* Sharon Nealis; *Pres* Roseanne Shuttleworth; *VPres* J Scott Geare
Open Tues - Sat 11 AM - 4 PM, May - Oct, Sun 1:30 - 4 PM. Admis $3. Estab 1937. 18 room Victorian house, each room furnished with furniture, antiques, pictures. Average Annual Attendance: 4000. Mem: 600; dues individual $25,

couple $20; meetings in Jan, May, Sept & Nov
Income: $16,000 (financed by mem)
Publications: Quarterly newsletter
Activities: Originates traveling exhibitions to area schools; sales shop sells books & prints

EASTON

M ACADEMY OF THE ARTS, 106 South St, 21601. Tel 410-822-0455; FAX 410-822-5997; *Dir & Cur* Christopher Brownawell
Open Mon, Tues, Fri & Sat 10 AM - 4 PM, Wed 10 AM - 9 PM, Sun 1 - 4 PM, cl bank holidays. No admis fee. Estab 1958 to promote the knowledge, appreciation & practice of all the arts; a private non-profit art center. Two large rooms in a historic building (old schoolhouse) in Easton's historic district. The Academy is housed in two 18th century structures - the original schoolhouse in Easton & an adjacent residence that has been renovated & linked with new construction. Begun in 1989, the renovation project expands the Academy's 6500 sq ft to 26,000 sq ft & includes five galleries, five studios, a 1000 volume resource center & an Artist's slide registry. Average Annual Attendance: 46,000. Mem: 1500; dues benefactor $5000, patron $1000, sustaining $500, contributing $250, friend $100, dual family $50, individual $35
Income: Financed by mem, contributions, government, corporate & foundation grants, admis, tuitions, endowment & investments
Collections: Permanent art collection includes 19th & 20th century prints & paintings, including artists Felix Burot, James McNeill Whistler, Anders Lorn-the majority & other historically important 19th & 20th century artists
Exhibitions: The Academy mounts 24 exhibits per year featuring local, regional & nationally known artists
Publications: Academy of the Arts Newsletter, bimonthly
Activities: Classes in drawing, painting, sculpture, fine crafts plus weekend workshops & open studio sessions; dance & music classes for all ages; childrens' summer arts program in all disciplined & arts media; dramatic programs; annual members shows with prizes awarded; exten dept serving Mid-Shore Talbot, Caroline, Queen Annes, Dorchester & Kent

ELKTON

A COUNCIL OF DELAWARE ARTISTS, 1034 Old Field Point Rd, 21921. Tel 410-392-7803; *Pres* Sally Cooper March
Estab 1955 to educate the mem & the pub about significant aspects of the creative arts including discussions, lectures & exhibitions pertaining to the visual arts & to provide continuous exposure of member's work through exhibitions; to establish an atmosphere of fellowship & cooperation among professional artist members. Mem: 100; dues $20; meetings once per month
Income: Financed by mem dues
Publications: Newsletter, 9 per year
Activities: Lect open to public; 9 vis lectr per year; individual paintings lent to schools, public offices, retirement homes, banks & museums; originate traveling exhibitions

ELLICOTT CITY

A HOWARD COUNTY ARTS COUNCIL, 8510 High Ridge Rd, 21043. Tel 410-313-2787; FAX 410-313-2790; *Exec Dir* Mary Toth; *Deputy* Viviana Holma; *Office Mgr* Barbara Worthington
Estab 1981 to serve pub fostering arts, artists & art organizations. Average Annual Attendance: 30,000. Mem: Dues $25-$250; annual meeting in Sept
Income: $400,000

FORT MEADE

M FORT GEORGE G MEADE MUSEUM, 4674 Griffin Ave, Attn: Bev, 20755-5094. Tel 301-677-7054; FAX 301-677-2953; Elec Mail johnsono@meade-emh2.army.mil. FTS 923-6966. *Cur* Robert S Johnson; *Exhibits Specialist* Barbara Dlugokinski
Open Wed - Sat 11 AM - 4 PM, Sun 1 - 4 PM, cl Mon, Tues & holidays. No admis fee. Estab 1963 to collect, preserve, study & display military artifacts relating to the United States Army, Fort Meade & the surrounding region. Average Annual Attendance: 40,000
Income: Financed by federal and military funds
Collections: Military art; World War I, World War II & Civil War Periods
Exhibitions: Development of Armor, 1920-1940; History of First US Army; History of Fort George G Meade
Activities: Lect open to the public, 4 vis lectr per year; gallery talks; tours; living history programs

FROSTBURG

M FROSTBURG STATE UNIVERSITY, The Stephanie Ann Roper Gallery, 21532. Tel 301-687-4000; *Head* Dustin P Davis; *Coordr* Jackie Brown
Open Sat - Tues 1 - 4 PM, Wed 7 - 9 PM. No admis fee. Estab 1972 for educational purposes. Average Annual Attendance: 3000
Income: Financed by state appropriation
Collections: Folk art; prints
Activities: Educ dept; lect open to public, 5 vis lectr per year; gallery talks; competitions with awards; book traveling exhibitions 4 per year; junior museum
L Lewis J Ort Library, 21532. Tel 301-687-4395; FAX 301-687-7069; *Dir* Dr David M Gillespie; *Exhib Librn* Mary Jo Price
Library Holdings: Vols 500,000; Per subs 1300; Micro — Fiche; AV — A-tapes, cassettes, fs, Kodachromes, motion pictures, slides, v-tapes; Other — Exhibition catalogs, prints, reproductions

HAGERSTOWN

M WASHINGTON COUNTY MUSEUM OF FINE ARTS, City Park, PO Box 423, 21741. Tel 301-739-5727; FAX 301-745-3741; *Dir* Jean Woods; *Admin Asst* Christine Shives
Open Tues - Sat 10 AM - 5 PM, Sun 1 - 6 PM, cl Mon. No admis fee. Estab 1930 to exhibit, interpret & conserve art. The mus consists of the William H Singer Memorial Gallery, Sculpture Court, Concert Gallery, South Gallery & North Gallery. Average Annual Attendance: 40,000. Mem: 800; dues $25
Income: Financed by government, mem & donations
Collections: American pressed glass; antique laces; †contemporary painting, drawing, prints & sculpture; †European & †American sculpture, †prints & drawings; Oriental jades & art; †ethnographic art; decorative art; textiles; folk art; 19th & 20th century American art
Exhibitions: Exhibits Drawn from the Permanent Collection - 19th & 20th Century American Art; (1997) Art by American Women; Chinese Export Porcelain Deitrich Collection; Lee Reiss-Retrospective; The Sellers Collection
Publications: The Fiftieth Year; American Pressed Glass; Old Master Drawings; annual reports; bulletin, monthly; catalogs of major exhibitions; catalog of the permanent collection; bi-monthly bulletin
Activities: Classes for adults & children; dramatic programs; docent training; lect open to public, 10 vis lectr per year; concerts; gallery talks; tours; competitions with awards; original objects of art lent to accredited museums; originate traveling exhibitions; sales shop sells books & original art
L Library, City Park, PO Box 423, 21741. Tel 301-739-5727; FAX 301-745-3741; *Dir* Jean Woods
Open Tues - Sat 10 AM - 5 PM, Sun 1 - 6 PM. Open to the pub for reference only
Library Holdings: Vols 5000; Per subs 7; Micro — Cards; AV — Cassettes, fs, motion pictures, slides, v-tapes; Other — Clipping files, exhibition catalogs, pamphlets

LAUREL

M MARYLAND-NATIONAL CAPITAL PARK & PLANNING COMMISSION, Montpelier Cultural Arts Center, 12826 Laurel-Bowie Rd, 20708. Tel 301-953-1993, 410-792-0664; FAX 301-206-9682; *Dir* Richard Zandler; *Asst Dir* Nancy Sausser; *Office Mgr* Janet Henderson
Open daily 10 AM - 5 PM. No admis fee. Estab 1979 to serve artists regionally & to offer high quality fine arts experiences to pub. Main Gallery houses major invitational exhibitions by artists of regional & national reputation; Library Gallery houses local artists' exhibitions; Resident Artists' Gallery provided to artists who rent studio space; Small library of donated volumes. Average Annual Attendance: 35,000
Income: $300,000 (financed by county appropriation, grants, classes & studio rentals)
Publications: Exhibit catalogs; promotional invitations, monthly
Activities: Classes for adults & children; lect open to pub, 5 vis lectr per year; competitions with award; book traveling exhibitions, annually; originate traveling exhibitions

RIVERDALE

A PYRAMID ATLANTIC, 6001 66th Ave, Ste 103, 20737. Tel 301-459-7154; *Artistic Dir* Helen C Frederick; *Resident Printer* Susan Goldman; *Resident Printer* Elen Hill; *Resident Letter Press* Terry Chouinard
Open Mon - Sat 10 AM - 4 PM. Estab 1981 to support artists, foster the art of hand papermaking, printmaking & book arts
Income: Financed by grants from federal, state & local funding agencies, foundations & corporate support, mem
Collections: Archives of Prints, paper works & books
Exhibitions: Art Book Fair (held at the Corcoran Gallery of Art, Washington DC); Art of Work/Work of Art; Crossing Over/Changing Places, by Jane Former (international tour)
Publications: Biannual newsletter

ROCKVILLE

M JEWISH COMMUNITY CENTER OF GREATER WASHINGTON, Jane L & Robert H Weiner Judaic Museum, 6125 Montrose Rd, 20852. Tel 301-881-0100; *Pres* Samuel Lehrman; *Exec Dir* Michael Witkes; *Gallery Dir* Karen Falk
Open Mon - Thurs Noon - 4 PM & 7:30 - 9:30 PM, Sun 2 - 5 PM. No admis fee. Estab 1925 to preserve, exhibit & promulgate Jewish culture. Center houses mus & Goldman Fine Arts Gallery. Average Annual Attendance: 25,000
Income: Financed by endowment, corporate, private & pub gifts, grants & sales
Exhibitions: Monthly exhibits, Sept-June; Fine art, fine craft, documentary photography; seven to eight temporary exhibitions yearly including Israeli Artists & American & emerging artist
Publications: Exhibition catalogues; brochures
Activities: Classes for adults & children; docent training; lect open to public; concerts; gallery talks; tours; book traveling exhibitions; originate traveling exhibitions; museum shop sells books, original art, reproductions & prints

SAINT MARY CITY

M ST MARY'S COLLEGE OF MARYLAND, The Dwight Frederick Boyden Gallery, SMC, 20686. Tel 301-862-0246; FAX 301-862-0958; *Dir* David Emerick; *Gallery Asst* Casey Page; *Registrar* Jan Kiphart
Open Mon - Thurs 10:30 AM - 5 PM, Fri 10:30 AM - 4:30 PM. No admis fee. 1600 sq ft exhibition space for temporary exhibits of art; five bldgs with art hung in public areas
Income: Financed by St Mary's College
Purchases: Collection is from donation
Collections: Study; developmental; Long Term Loan; SMC; Permanent
Activities: Gallery talks; individual paintings & original objects of art lent to local, non-profit organizations; lending collection contains original art works & prints, paintings & sculptures

SAINT MICHAELS

M CHESAPEAKE BAY MARITIME MUSEUM, Navy Point, PO Box 636, 21663. Tel 410-745-2916; FAX 410-745-6088; *Dir* John R Valliant; *Cur* Pete Lesher
Open Jan - Mar weekends & holidays only 10 AM - 4 PM, Apr - Oct daily 10 AM - 5 PM, Nov - Dec daily 10 AM - 4 PM. Admis adults $7.50, children $3. Estab 1965 as a waterside mus dedicated to preserving the maritime history of the Chesapeake Bay. Consists of twenty buildings on approx 18 acres of waterfront property including Hooper's Strait Lighthouse, 1879. Average Annual Attendance: 85,000. Mem: 4500; dues $25 - $60
Income: Financed by mem, admis & endowment
Collections: Paintings; ship models; vessels including skipjack, bugeye, log canoes, & many small crafts; waterfowling exhibits; working boat shop
Publications: Weather Gauge (newsletter), semi-annually
Activities: Classes for adults & children; docent training; lect open to public, 15 vis lectr per year; concerts; gallery talks; tours; competitions with prizes; individual paintings & original objects of art lent to other museums; museum shop sells books, magazines, original art, reproductions, prints & slides
L Howard I Chapelle Memorial Library, Navy Point, PO Box 636, 21663. Tel 410-745-2916; FAX 410-745-6088; *Cur* Pete Lesher
Open Tues - Thurs 10 AM - 4 PM, other times by appointment. Estab 1965 for preservation of Chesapeake Bay maritime history & culture. Non-circulating research facility. Average Annual Attendance: 85,000
Income: Financed by endowment
Library Holdings: Vols 3500; Per subs 5; Micro — Cards; Other — Clipping files, pamphlets
Special Subjects: Local art, maritime history

SALISBURY

SALISBURY STATE UNIVERSITY
M University Gallery, 1101 Camden Ave, 21801. Tel 410-543-6271; *Gallery Dir* Kenneth Basile; *Gallery Asst* Rachel Shedaker
Open Sept - Dec & Feb - May Mon & Wed 10 AM - 8 PM, Tues & Thurs 10 AM - 5 PM, Sat & Sun 1 - 5 PM, cl Fri. No admis fee. Estab 1967 to provide a wide range of art exhibitions to the University & community, with emphasis on educational value of exhibitions. Gallery open to pub & is located on the second floor of Blackwell Library. Average Annual Attendance: 4000
Income: Financed mainly by Salisbury State University with additional support from the Maryland State Arts Council, The Salisbury/Wicomico Arts Council & other agencies
Exhibitions: Annual faculty & student shows; wide range of traveling exhibitions from various national & regional arts organizations & galleries; variety of regional & local exhibitions; speakers & special events; annual spring art & flower show; sculpture gardens
Publications: Announcements
Activities: Workshops for children, students & general public; film series; lect open to public, 1-2 vis lectr per year
L Blackwell Library, 1101 Camden Ave, 21801. Tel 410-543-6130; *Library Dir* James R Thrash
Open Mon - Thurs 8 AM - midnight, Fri 8 AM - 10 PM, Sat 10 AM - 8 PM, Sun Noon - midnight. Estab 1925, to support the curriculum of Salisbury State University. Library has total space of 66,000 sq ft. Circ 2500
Library Holdings: Vols 235,336; Per subs 1673; Micro — Cards 2278, fiche 617,436, reels 12,936; AV — A-tapes 451, cassettes 435, fs, motion pictures, rec, slides, v-tapes 39; Other — Clipping files, pamphlets

M WARD FOUNDATION, Ward Museum of Wildfowl Art, 909 S Schumaker, 21801. Tel 410-742-4988; FAX 410-742-3107; *Acting Exec Dir* Ned White; *Mem* Charity Shankle; *Archives* Barbara Gehrm; *Gift Shop Mgr* Crystal Viens; *Events Coordr* Jane Rollins; *Cur Educ* Tod Hall; *Public Information Coordr* Mary Tyler; *Business Mgr* Teresa Boyd
Open Mon - Sat 10 AM - 5 PM, Sun 1 - 5 PM. Admis adults $7, seniors $5, students $3. Estab 1968 as a non-profit organization dedicated to preservation & conservation of wildfowl carving. Main gallery & balcony contain 2000 carvings, prints & paintings of wildfowl-related items, including World Championship carvings. Average Annual Attendance: 8000. Mem: 7000; dues family $60, individual $35
Income: $1,000,000 (financed by mem, city & state appropriations, grants, donations, gift shop sales)
Exhibitions: Annual Fall Exhibition of paintings & sculptures; Antique decoy auction; The Ward Exhibition of Wildfowl Art; World Carving Championship; Society of Animal Artists
Publications: Wildfowl Art Journal, quarterly; Ward Foundation News, quarterly
Activities: Classes for adults & children, docent training; lect open to public; tours; competition with awards; carving workshops held in Apr, June & Feb; individual paintings & original objects of art lent; lending collection contains color reproductions, framed reproductions, original art works, original prints, paintings, photographs, sculpture; museum shop sells books, magazines, original art, reproductions, prints, slides, decoys and video shows

SILVER SPRING

L MARYLAND COLLEGE OF ART & DESIGN LIBRARY, 10500 Georgia Ave, 20902. Tel 301-649-4454; *Head Librn* David DuPuy
Open Mon - Fri 8 AM - 5 PM. Estab 1977 to facilitate & encourage learning by the students & to provide aid for the faculty. College maintains Gudelsky Gallery. Circ 7200
Purchases: $7000
Library Holdings: Vols 11,000; Per subs 25; AV — Cassettes 25, motion pictures, slides 27,000; Other — Clipping files
Special Subjects: Art History, Calligraphy, Commercial Art, Graphic Design, Illustration, Painting - American, Painting - British, Painting - Canadian, Painting - Dutch, Painting - European, Painting - Flemish, Painting - French, Painting - German, Painting - Italian, Painting - Japanese, Painting - New Zealander, Painting - Polish, Painting - Russian, Painting - Scandinavian, Painting - Spanish, Posters, Woodcuts, French, German, Italian, Photography, Spanish

SOLOMONS

M CALVERT MARINE MUSEUM, PO Box 97, 20688. Tel 410-326-2042; FAX 410-326-6691; *Dir* C Douglass Alves Jr; *Registrar* Robert J Hurry; *Exhib Designer* Tom Ewart; *Master Woodcarver* James LeRoy Langley; *Cur Educ* Karen E Stone; *Cur Maritime History* Richard J Dodds; *Cur Estuarine Biology* Kenneth Kaumeyer; *Cur Paleontology* Michael D Gottfried
Open Mon - Sun 10 AM - 5 PM. Admis $4 & $3. Estab 1970, to provide the public with a marine oriented museum on maritime history, estuarine natural history, marine paleontology and natural & cultural history of the Patuxent River region. 5,500 sq ft gallery is maintained on maritime history of the region, three to four shows per yr. Average Annual Attendance: 50,000. Mem: 2200; dues family $35, individual $20
Income: $1,700,000 (financed by county appropriation & Calvert Marine Society)
Purchases: $1000
Collections: J S Bohannon Folk Art Steamboat Collection; local Chesapeake Bay Ship Portraits; Tufnell Watercolor Collection; Louis Feuchter Collection A Aubrey Bodine Collection; C Leslie Oursler Collection; August H O Rolle Collection
Publications: Bugeye Times, quarterly newsletter; Cradle of Invasion: A History of the US Amphibious Training Base, Solomons, Maryland, 1942-45; The Drum Point Lighthouse, brochure; Early Chesapeake Single-Log Canoes: A Brief History & introduction to Building Techniques; The Last Generation: A History of a Chesapeake Shipbuilding Family; The Othello Affair; The Pursuit of French Pirates on the Patuxent River, Maryland, August 1807; War on the Patuxent, 1814: A Catalog of Artifacts; Watercraft Collection, brochure; Working the Water: The Commercial Fisheries of Maryland's Patuxent River; Solomons Island & Vicinity An Illustrated History & Walking Tour; miscellaneous special publications on history
Activities: Classes for adults and children; docent training; lect open to the public, 8 lectrs per year; concerts; gallery talks; tours; individual paintings & original objects of art lent to other appropriately qualified non-profit organizations; lending collection contains 3000 black & white photographs, lantern slides, art works, original prints, 2800 slides; originate traveling exhibitions, circulated to other professional museums; sales shop sells books, magazines, original art, prints, reproductions, slides, hand crafts
L Library, PO Box 97, 20688. Tel 410-326-2042; FAX 410-326-6691; *Librn* Paul Berry
Open Mon - Fri 9 AM - 4:30 PM, cl weekends. Estab 1970. Library open for research and reference
Income: $1000 (finance by Calvert County government, mem, gift shop, donations & grants)
Purchases: $800
Library Holdings: Vols 6000; Per subs 25; Micro — Fiche; AV — A-tapes, fs, Kodachromes, motion pictures, rec, slides, v-tapes; Other — Clipping files, exhibition catalogs, manuscripts, memorabilia, original art works, pamphlets, photographs, prints, reproductions
Special Subjects: Southern Maryland, Patuxent River, Chesapeake Bay

TOWSON

TOWSON STATE UNIVERSITY
M The Holtzman Art Gallery, Osler Dr, 21204. Tel 410-321-2808; *Dir & Prof* Christopher Bartlett
Open Tues - Sat Noon - 4 PM. Estab 1973 to provide a wide variety of art exhibitions, primarily contemporary work, with national importance. The main gallery is situated in the new fine arts building directly into the foyer. It is 30 x 60 ft with 15 ft ceiling & 15 x 30 ft storage area. Average Annual Attendance: 10,000
Income: $18,000 (financed by state appropriation, cultural services fees & private gifts)
Collections: African art; †Asian arts, through Roberts Art Collection; †contemporary painting & sculpture
Exhibitions: Annual Summer Exhibition; Bi-annual Faculty Exhibition; Crisis Of Memory; Sports Graphics; Whirligigs & Weathervances
Publications: Calendar, each semester; exhibition posters & catalogs
Activities: Lect open to public, 5-10 vis lectr per year; gallery talks; tours; book traveling exhibitions 2-3 per year; sales shop sells exhibition catalogs & posters
M Asian Arts Center, Fine Arts Bldg, Osler Dr & Cross Campus Dr, 21252-7097. Tel 410-830-2807; *Cur* Suewhei T Shieh
Open during academic year Mon - Fri 10 AM - 4 PM, Sat hours posted for each exhibition, summer Mon - Fri 11 AM - 3 PM. No admis fee. Estab 1972 to provide an area to display the Asian art collections of the University & for the benefit of both the university community & the pub. The gallery is located on the second floor of the Fine Arts Building; also includes a small reference library. Average Annual Attendance: 3500. Mem: Dues Dragon Circle $1000 & up, Phoenix Circle $500-$999, Tiger Soc $250-$499, Crane Club $100-$249, general mem $30-$99, student $5
Income: Financed by state funding
Collections: Asian Ceramics; ivory; metalwork; furniture; paintings; prints; textiles; sculptures
Exhibitions: Permanent collection; special loan exhibitions
Activities: Lect open to public, 2 vis lectr per year; gallery talks; tours; workshops; concerts; performances; individual & original objects of art lent to educational & cultural institutions

WESTMINSTER

M WESTERN MARYLAND COLLEGE, Esther Prangley Rice Gallery, Dept of Art, 21157. Tel 410-848-7000, Ext 596; *Dir* Michael Losch
Open Mon - Fri Noon - 4 PM. No admis fee. Estab to expose students to original works by professional artists
Income: Financed by college funds
Exhibitions: Six visiting artists shows; student shows; faculty & alumni show

MASSACHUSETTS

AMESBURY

M THE BARTLETT MUSEUM, 270 Main St, PO Box 692, 01913. Tel 508-462-6467, 388-0233; *Pres* John McCone; *Cur* Hazele Kray
Open Memorial Day - Labor Day Fri - Sun 1 - 4 PM. Estab 1968. Two-room Victorian-style Ferry School built in 1870. Name later changed to The Bartlett School in honor of Josiah Bartlett, signer of America's Declaration of Independence, near whose home the school was sited. Mem: dues patron $100 & up, contributing $25, family $15, individual $5, student $1
Collections: Natural science artifacts
Activities: Workshops

AMHERST

M AMHERST COLLEGE, Mead Art Museum, 01002. Tel 413-542-2335; FAX 413-542-2117; *Dir* Martha Sandweiss; *Cur American Art* Susan Danly
Open Mon - Fri 10 AM - 4:30 PM, Sat & Sun 1 - 5 PM (summer) Tues - Sun 1 - 4 PM, cl Mon. No admis fee. Estab 1949. Average Annual Attendance: 13,500. Mem: 500; annual meetings in the spring
Collections: †American art; Ancient art; †English art; Western European & †Oriental Collections
Publications: American Art at Amherst: A Summary Catalogue of the Collection at the Mead Art Gallery; American Watercolors & Drawings from Amherst College; Mead Museum Monographs; catalogues for major exhibitions
Activities: Educ dept; lect open to public, 3 vis lectr per year; gallery talks; tours; individual paintings & original objects of art lent for exhibition only to other museums
L Frost Library, 01002. Tel 413-542-2677; FAX 413-542-2662; *Reference & Fine Arts Librn* Michael Kasper
Circulating to Amherst College students & five college faculty
Library Holdings: Vols 40,000; Per subs 82; Micro — Fiche; AV — Slides; Other — Exhibition catalogs

ARTS EXTENSION SERVICE
For further information, see National & Regional Organizations

L JONES LIBRARY, INC, 43 Amity St, 01002. Tel 413-256-4090; FAX 413-256-4096; *Dir* Bonnie Isman; *Asst Dir* Sondra M Radosh; *Reference Librn* Pauline M Peterson; *Adult Service Librn* Beth Girshman; *Cur* Dan Lombardo
Open Mon, Wed, Fri & Sat 9 AM - 5:30 PM, Tues & Thurs 9 AM - 9:30 PM; Special Collections has limited hours. Estab 1919 as a public library. Gallery. Circ 500,000. Average Annual Attendance: 500,000
Income: Financed by endowment & city appropriation
Library Holdings: Micro — Reels; AV — A-tapes, cassettes, rec, slides; Other — Clipping files, framed reproductions, manuscripts, memorabilia, original art works, pamphlets, photographs, sculpture
Collections: Ray Stannard Baker; †Emily Dickinson; †Robert Frost; Julius Lester; Harlan Fiske Stone; †Sidney Waugh Writings; †local history & geneology
Activities: Lect open to public; concerts; tours

UNIVERSITY OF MASSACHUSETTS, AMHERST
M University Gallery, Fine Arts Ctr, Room 35 D, 01003. Tel 413-545-3670; FAX 413-545-2018; *Dir* Betsy Siersma; *Cur* Regina Coppola; *Registrar* Jennifer Lind; *Gallery Mgr* Craig Allaben; *Preparator* Justin Griswold
Open Tues - Fri 11 AM - 4:30 PM, Sat & Sun 2 - 5 PM during school yr. No admis fee. Estab 1975. Main Gallery 57-1/2 x 47 ft, East Gallery 67-1/2 x 20-1/2 ft, West Gallery 56-1/2 x 23-1/2 ft, North Gallery 46-1/2 x 17-1/2 ft. Average Annual Attendance: 15,000. Mem: 150; dues $25 & up
Collections: †20th century American works on paper including drawings, prints & photographs
Publications: Exhibition catalogs
Activities: Lect open to public, 2-3 vis lectr per year; gallery talks; tours; individual art works from the permanent collection loaned to other institutions; originate traveling exhibitions
L Dorothy W Perkins Slide Library, Bartlett Hall, 01003. Tel 413-545-3314; FAX 413-545-3880; *Cur Visual Coll* Louise Bloomberg; *Slide Librn* Nathalie Sulzner
Open Mon - Fri 12:15 PM - 3:30 PM. Circ 60,000 (slides)
Library Holdings: Interactive video disks; Magnetic disks 50; Study Plates 7000; AV — Slides 270,000

ANDOVER

A ANDOVER HISTORICAL SOCIETY, 97 Main St, 01810. Tel 508-475-2236; *Dir* Barbara Thibault
Exhibitions: An Andover Photographer: Charles Henry Newman (1872-1944); Main Street, Andover; Store to Door-Andover Merchants (1860-1920); Time of Transition: Andover (1820-1850)
Activities: Originate traveling exhibitions

M PHILLIPS ACADEMY, Addison Gallery of American Art, Chapel Ave, 01810. Tel 508-749-4015; *Dir & Cur Photo* Jock Reynolds; *Asst Dir & Cur Paintings, Sculpture, Prints & Drawings* Susan Faxon; *Registrar* Denise Johnson; *Asst Cur* Allison Kemmerer; *Curatorial Asst Preparator* Leslie Maloney; *Mem Pub Relations* Duncan Will
Open Tues - Sat 10 AM - 5 PM, Sun 1 - 5 PM. No admis fee. Estab 1931 in memory of Mrs Keturah Addison Cobb, to enrich permanently the lives of the students by helping to cultivate & foster in them a love for the beautiful. The gift also included a number of important paintings, prints & sculpture as a nucleus for the beginning of a permanent collection of American art. Maintains small reference library for mus use only. Average Annual Attendance: 35,000
Income: Financed by endowment
Collections: 18th, 19th & 20th centuries drawings, paintings, prints, sculpture; photographs; film; videotapes
Activities: Lect open to public, 8-10 vis lectr per year; concerts

ASHLAND

M ASHLAND HISTORICAL SOCIETY, Two Myrtle St, PO Box 145, 01721. Tel 508-881-8183; *Pres* Clifford Wilson
Open by appointment. Estab 1909
Publications: Monthly newsletter for members

ATTLEBORO

M ATTLEBORO MUSEUM, CENTER FOR THE ARTS, 86 Park St, 02703. Tel 508-222-2644; *Pres Board Trustees* Sarah Mott; *Treas* Scott Smith; *Dir* James Russell
Open Tues - Fri 12:30 - 5:30 PM, Sat 9 AM - 5 PM, Sun 12:30 - 5 PM, cl Mon. No admis fee. Estab 1927 to exhibit the works of contemporary New England artists, as well as the art works of the museum's own collection. These are pub openings plus several competitive exhibits with awards & an outdoor art festival. Three galleries with changing monthly exhibits of paintings, drawings, sculpture, ceramics, jewelry, glass, metals & prints. Mem: 230; dues life mem $1000, benefactor $500, patron $250, sponsor $200, supporting & corporate $1000, assoc $40, family $35, artist mem $25 student & senior citizen $15
Income: Financed by mem, gifts, local & state grants
Collections: Paintings & prints
Exhibitions: Holiday Show; Annual Area Artist Exhibit; Individual & Group Exhibits of Various Media & Subject; Competitive Painting Show; Summer Members Show; Competitive Photography Show; Selections from the Permanent Collection
Publications: Newsletter
Activities: Classes for adults & children; lect open to public; concerts; gallery talks; competitions, painting & photography; original objects of art lent

BEVERLY

M BEVERLY HISTORICAL SOCIETY, Cabot, Hale & Balch House Museums, 117 Cabot St, 01915. Tel 508-922-1186; *Pres* Daniel M Lohnes; *Dir & Cur* David K Goss; *Treas* Frederick Shale; *Asst Dir* Mary Ellen Smiley
Cabot Museum open yearly Wed - Fri 10 AM - 4 PM & alternate Sat; Balch House open May 20 - Oct 15; Hale House open June - Sept. Admis adults $2 (all three museums for $5), children under 16 $.50 (all three museums for $1). The Balch House built in 1636 by John Balch contains period furniture. The Hale House was built in 1694 by the first minister, John Hale. Cabot House built in 1781-82 by prominent merchant & private owner, John Cabot. Average Annual Attendance: 2000. Mem: 450; dues families $15, single $10; annual meeting in Oct
Collections: 120 paintings containing portraits, folk & Revolutionary War scenes; 1000 pieces furniture, toys, doll houses, military & maritime items & pewter, books, manuscripts & photographs
Exhibitions: Beverly Mariners & the China Trade; Two Hundred Years at the House of Cabot; Collection of 19th century Accessories
Publications: Quarterly newsletter
Activities: Docent training; lect open to public & some for members only; gallery talks by arrangement; tours; individual paintings & original objects of art lent to other museums & libraries; sales shop sells books & postcards
L Library, 117 Cabot St, 01915. Tel 508-922-1186; *Dir* David K Goss
Library Holdings: Vols 4000; Per subs 2; AV — A-tapes, motion pictures, slides; Other — Clipping files, manuscripts, memorabilia, pamphlets, photographs, prints, sculpture
Special Subjects: Beverly History; New England Maritime & Transportation History

BOSTON

ARCHAEOLOGICAL INSTITUTE OF AMERICA
For further information, see National and Regional Organizations

M THE ART INSTITUTE OF BOSTON, Main Gallery, 700 Beacon St, 02215. Tel 617-262-1223; FAX 617-437-1226; *Pres* Stan Trecker; *Dir Gallery & Exhib* Bonnell Robinson
Open Mon - Fri 9 AM - 4:30 PM, Sat Noon - 4 PM. No admis fee. Estab 1969 to present major contemporary & historical exhibitions of the work of established & emerging artists & to show work by students & faculty of the Institute. 3000 sq ft of gallery. Average Annual Attendance: 4000
Exhibitions: Aardman Animations; Neo-Artists; Edward Sorel
Activities: Classes for adults & children; professional programs in fine & applied arts & photography; lect open to public, 5 vis lectr per year; lect series coordinated with exhibitions; gallery talks; competitions, local & regional; exten dept serves Greater Boston area; individual paintings & original objects of art lent to other galleries; curate & mount exhibitions for major public spaces
L Library, 700 Beacon St, 02215. Tel 617-262-1223; *Librn* Valda Bolis
Open Mon - Thurs 7:30 AM - 9 PM, Fri 7:30 AM - 5 PM, Sat 11 AM - 4 PM, Sun Noon - 5 PM. Estab 1969 to support school curriculum
Purchases: $14,500
Library Holdings: Vols 8500; Per subs 65; Vertical File 350; AV — Kodachromes, slides 30,000, v-tapes 200; Other — Clipping files 10,000, exhibition catalogs
Special Subjects: Architecture, Art Education, Art History, Ceramics, Commercial Art, Crafts, Decorative Arts, Drawings, Etchings & Engravings, Folk Art, Graphic Arts, Graphic Design, History of Art & Archaeology, Illustration, Industrial Design

C BANK BOSTON, Gallery, 100 Federal St, 02110. Tel 617-434-2200, 434-6314; *Dir & Cur* Lillian Lambrechts
Collections: Contemporary paintings; non-contemporary paintings & textiles, sculpture
Publications: Exhibition catalogues, 6-10 times per yr

A BOSTON ARCHITECTURAL CENTER, 320 Newbury St, 02115. Tel 617-536-3170; FAX 617-536-5829; *Interim Pres* William Dill; *Office Coordr* Diane Sparrow; *Dean* Arcangelo Cascieri
Open Mon - Thurs 9 AM - 10:30 PM, Fri & Sat 9 AM - 5 PM, Sun Noon - 5 PM. No admis fee. Estab 1889 for educ of architects & designers. Small exhibition space on first floor. Average Annual Attendance: 2000. Mem: 300; dues $40; annual meeting in June
Activities: Classes for adults; lect open to public, 16 vis lectr per year; competitions; exten dept servs professional architects; traveling exhibitions organized & circulated
L Memorial Library, 320 Newbury St, 02115. Tel 617-536-9018; FAX 617-536-5829; *Chief Librn* Susan Lewis; *Asst Librn* Sarah Dickinson
Open by appointment only
Income: $2000
Library Holdings: Vols 2000
Special Subjects: 19th Century European & American Architecture
Collections: 18th, 19th & early 20th centuries architectural books from the collections of practicing architects

A BOSTON ART COMMISSION OF THE CITY OF BOSTON, Boston City Hall, Rm 712, 02201. Tel 617-635-3245; FAX 617-635-3031; *Chmn* Robert Cormier; *Dir* M Mildred Farrell; *Commissioner* Bruce R Rossley; *Commissioner* Henry Lee; *Commissioner* Bruce Beal
Estab 1890 to accept & maintain the art collection owned by the City of Boston. Mem: 5; one representative from each organization: Boston Soc of Architects, Commissioner of Cultural Affairs, Boston Pub Library, Copley Soc, & Boston Mus of Fine
Income: Financed by city appropriation
Purchases: Commissions through private trust fund
Collections: City of Boston art collection, including fountains, paintings, sculpture, statuary
Publications: Catalog and guide to the art work owned by the City of Boston, in preparation; Passport to Public Art
Activities: Competitions

L BOSTON ATHENAEUM, 10 1/2 Beacon St, 02108. Tel 617-227-0270; *Dir & Librn* Richard Wendorf; *Assoc Dir* Ruth Morley; *Assoc Dir* John Lannon; *Cur of Coll* Michael Wentworth; *Research Librn* Steve Nonack; *Print Dept Cur* Sally Pierce
Open Mon - Fri 9 AM - 5:30 PM, Sat 9 AM - 4 PM; cl Sun also Sat June 1 - Oct 1. Estab 1807 to exhibit fine arts & crafts of New England & national artists. Large exhibition gallery in conjunction with library. Average Annual Attendance: 20,000
Income: $1,400,000 (financed by endowment & mem)
Purchases: $75,000
Library Holdings: Vols 100,000; Per subs 100; Original documents; Micro — Reels; Other — Clipping files, exhibition catalogs, manuscripts, memorabilia, original art works, pamphlets, photographs, prints, reproductions, sculpture
Collections: †19th century Boston prints & photographs; †American & European painting & sculpture; †World War I posters
Exhibitions: Change monthly
Publications: Exhibition catalogs
Activities: Lect open to public, 15 vis lectr per year; concerts; tours; individual paintings & original art lent to qualified museums & institutions; book traveling exhibitions; originate traveling exhibitions

M THE BOSTONIAN SOCIETY, Old State House Museum, 206 Washington St, 02109. Tel 617-720-3290; *Exec Dir* Joan C Hull
Open daily 9:30 AM - 5 PM. Admis adults $3, seniors & students $2, children ages 6-18 $1. Estab 1881 to collect & preserve the history of Boston. Average Annual Attendance: 90,000. Mem: 1250; dues benefactor $500, supporter $100, family $50, individuals $30, students $20, senior citizens $20
Income: Financed by endowment, mem, admis, grants, state & federal appropriations
Collections: Paintings & artifacts relating to Boston history; Maritime art; Revolutionary War artifacts; prints
Exhibitions: Ongoing exhibitions
Publications: Proceedings of The Bostonian Society; The Bostonian Society Newsletter
Activities: Classes for children; lect open to public; concerts; gallery talks; walking tours; individual paintings & original objects of art lent to other museums; museum shop sells books, decorative arts, reproductions, prints & toys
L Library, 15 State St, 3rd Flr (Mailing add: Old State House, 206 Washington St, 02109). Tel 617-720-3285; FAX 617-720-3289; *Librn* Doug Southard
Open Mon - Fri 9:30 AM - 4:30 PM. Estab 1881 to collect & preserve material related to the history of Boston. For reference only
Purchases: $1500
Library Holdings: Vols 6000; Per subs 10; Documents; Ephemera; Postcards; Scrapbooks; Micro — Fiche; AV — Lantern slides, slides 1000; Other — Clipping files, manuscripts, memorabilia, original art works, pamphlets, photographs 8500, prints 2000, reproductions
Special Subjects: History of Boston
Publications: Bostonian Society Newsletter, quarterly

A BOSTON PRINTMAKERS, c/o Emmanuel College, 400 The Fenway, 02115. Tel 617-735-9898; *Pres* Marjorie Javan
Estab 1947 to aid printmakers in exhibiting their work; to bring quality work to the public. Average Annual Attendance: 15,000. Mem: 200; dues $25; annual meeting June
Income: Financed by mem, entry fees, and commission on sales
Purchases: $4700
Exhibitions: Prints, artist books, etchings, lithograph, mixed media, monotypes, serigraph & woodcut
Publications: Exhibition catalogs
Activities: Lect open to the public; gallery talks; competitions with awards and prizes; individual paintings and original objects of art lent to local museums, galleries, libraries and schools; book 5 traveling exhibitions per year; traveling exhibitions organized and circulated

BOSTON PUBLIC LIBRARY

L **Central Library,** PO Box 286, 02117. Tel 617-536-5400; *Dir* Arthur Curley
Building contains mural decorations by Edwin A Abbey, John Elliott, Pierre Puvis de Chavannes, & John Singer Sargent; bronze doors by Daniel Chester French; sculptures by Frederick MacMonnies, Bela Pratt, Louis Saint Gaudens; paintings by Copley & Duplessis; & bust of John Deferrari by Joseph A Coletti
Income: Financed by city & state appropriation
Library Holdings: Vols 6,000,000; Per subs 16,704
Publications: Exhibition catalogues
Activities: Lect open to public; concerts; tours

L **Fine Arts Dept,** Copley Sq, 02117. Tel 617-536-5400, Ext 275; *Cur of Fine Arts* Janice Chadbourne
Open Mon - Thurs 9 AM - 9 PM, Fri & Sat 9 AM - 5 PM, Oct - May Sun 1 - 5 PM. For reference only
Library Holdings: Vols 162,000; Per subs 425; Auction catalogs; Micro — Fiche 71,749, reels 5852; Other — Clipping files, exhibition catalogs, manuscripts, memorabilia, pamphlets, photographs, reproductions
Collections: Connick Stained Glass Archives; W G Preston Architectural Drawings; Peabody & Stearns Architectural Drawings; Clarence Blackall scrapbooks & sketchbooks; Archives of American Art (unrestricted) Microfilm; Society of Arts & Crafts Archives; Vertical files on local artists, architects & architecture organizations
Publications: Fine Arts Department (a description)

M **Albert H Wiggin Gallery & Print Department,** Copley Sq, 02117. Tel 617-536-5400, Ext 280; FAX 617-262-0461; *Librn* Jane E Duggan; *Keeper of Prints* Sinclair H Hitchings; *Asst Keeper of Prints* Karen Smith Shafts; *Photographs* Aaron Schmidt
Open Gallery Mon - Thurs 9 AM - 9 PM, Fri & Sat 9 AM - 5 PM, cl Sun; Print Study Room Mon - Fri 9 AM- 5 PM, cl Sat & Sun
Library Holdings: Vols 2100; Architectural drawings 100,023; Drawings, prints & paintings 76,000; Negatives 40,810; Postcards 500,000; AV — Lantern slides 6,623; Other — Clipping files, exhibition catalogs, photographs 650,379
Collections: Collection of 18th, 19th & 20th centuries French, English & American prints & drawings, including the Albert H Wiggin Collection; 20th century American prints by Boston artists; 19th century photographs of the American West & India & Middle East; Boston Pictorial Archive; paintings; postcards; Boston Herald Traveler Photo Morgue; ephemera
Exhibitions: Eight or nine per year drawn from the print department's permanent collections
Activities: Lect open to public, 1-2 vis lectr per year; Internships offered

L **Rare Book & Manuscripts Dept,** Copley Square, 02117. Tel 617-536-5400, Ext 425; *In Charge & Cur Rare Books* Roberta Zonghi; *Cur Manuscripts* Giusseppe Bissaccia; *Librn* Eugene Zepp
Open 9 AM - 5 PM Weekdays. Estab 1934. Average Annual Attendance: 1400
Income: Financed by trust funds
Purchases: Books, manuscripts, maps, prints & photographs relevant to our current subject strengths
Library Holdings: Vols 276,000; Per subs 4; Micro — Prints, reels; AV — Lantern slides; Other — Manuscripts, memorabilia, photographs
Special Subjects: Antiquities-Greek, Antiquities-Roman, Bookplates & Bindings, Calligraphy, Coins & Medals, Costume Design & Construction, Etchings & Engravings, Ethnology, Fashion Arts, Landscape Architecture, Audubon, Book & Graphic Design, Civil War Photographs & Prints, History of Book Illustration, W A Dwiggins
Collections: †FEER World's Fair Collection †Americana; †book arts; †Boston theater; †history of printing; †juvenilia; †landscape & gardening; †theater costume design
Exhibitions: Exhibits change every 3-4 months & feature book, manuscripts, maps & prints that make up department collections; (1997) Boston Theatre; Religion in 19th Century America
Activities: Seminars; lect open to public, 3 vis lectr per year; concerts; tours; sales shop sells postcards & pamphlets

M **BOSTON UNIVERSITY,** Art Gallery, 855 Commonwealth Ave, 02215. Tel 617-353-3329; Elec Mail gallery@acs.bu.edu;
Internet Home Page Address http://web.bu.edu/art. *Dir* Kim Sichel; *Asst Dir* John R Stomberg
Open Tues - Fri 10 AM - 5 PM, Sat & Sun 1 - 5 PM. No admis fee. Estab 1960. One exhibition space, 250 running ft, 2500 sq ft
Collections: Contemporary & New England Art
Publications: Annual exhibition catalogs
Activities: Lect open to public; gallery talks; book traveling exhibitions 2 per year; originate traveling exhibitions

M **BROMFIELD ART GALLERY,** 560 Harrison Ave, 02118-2436. Tel 617-451-3605; *Pres* Florence Montgomery
Open Tues - Sat Noon - 5 PM. No admis fee. Estab 1974 to exhibit art. Three galleries, about 2500 sq ft. Average Annual Attendance: 3000. Mem: 20; dues $750; monthly meetings
Income: Financed by mem
Activities: Lect open to public; 5 vis lectr per year; gallery talks

M **CRANE COLLECTION GALLERY,** 218 Newbury St, 02116. Tel 617-262-4080; FAX 617-262-7854, 235-1166; *Pres* Bonnie L Crane; *Asst to Pres* Gael Crasco
Open Mon - Sat 10 AM - 5 PM. Estab 1983 to exhibit 19th & early 20th century American paintings. Five rooms in 19th century building with period furnishings. Average Annual Attendance: 2500
Collections: 19th century & early 20th century American paintings, including Hudson River School, Boston School & regional artists
Exhibitions: Boston School: Then & Now; Summer Scenes II; Bruce Crane; Tonalism; Inspiration of Cape Ann; City Scenes; Little Picture Show; American Barbizon; Interiors

C **FEDERAL RESERVE BANK OF BOSTON,** PO Box 2076, 02106-2076. Tel 617-973-3454, 973-3368; FAX 617-973-3621;
Internet Home Page Address http://www.bos.frb.org. *Cultural Affairs Coordr* Anne M Belson; *Cultural Affairs Asst* Holly Giannino
Open Mon - Fri 9 AM - 5 PM by appointment only. Estab 1978 for educational & cultural enrichment. Collection displayed throughout building. A permanent gallery, 28 x 183 ft with an adjoining 420 seat auditorium, located on the ground floor, open Mon - Fri 10 AM - 4 PM, is reserved for temporary exhibitions
Collections: †Focus of the collection is on United States art since the mid-1950s
Publications: Art at the Federal Reserve Bank of Boston; Lithographs: The Federal Reserve Bank of Boston Collection
Activities: Lect; gallery talks; tours by advance appointment only; book temporary exhibitions by New England groups

M **ISABELLA STEWART GARDNER MUSEUM,** 280 Fenway (Mailing add: 2 Palace Rd), 02115). Tel 617-566-1401; FAX 617-566-7653; *Dir* Anne Hawley; *Cur* Hilliard T Goldfarb; *Bus* Christopher Mekal
Open Tues - Sun 11 AM - 5 PM, cl Mon & national holidays. Admis adults $9, students $5, children between 12-17 & Wed $3, children under 3 free. Estab 1903, the mus houses Isabella Stewart Gardner's various collections. Mus building is styled after a 16th century Venetian villa; all galleries open onto a central, glass-roofed courtyard, filled with flowers that are changed with the seasons of the year. Average Annual Attendance: 170,000. Mem: 3000; dues $25 & up
Income: Financed by endowment, fundraising, mem donations & door charge
Collections: Gothic & Italian Renaissance, Roman & classical sculpture; Dutch & Flemish 17th century; Japanese screens; Oriental & Islamic ceramics, glass, sculpture; 19th century American and French paintings; major paintings of John Singer Sargent & James McNeill Whistler
Publications: Guide to the Collection; Oriental & Islamic Art in the Isabella Stewart Gardner Museum; European & American paintings in the Isabella Steward Gardner Museum; Drawings-Isabella Stewart Gardner Museum; Mrs Jack; A Checklist of the Correspondence of Isabella Stewart Gardner at the Gardner Museum; Sculpture in the Isabella Stewart Gardner Museum; Textiles - Isabella Stewart Gardner Museum; children's books - Isabella Stewart Gardner Museum; Fenway Court; History and Companion Guide; Special Exhibition Catalogs
Activities: Programs for children; lect open to public, 10 vis lectr per year; concerts; gallery talks; tours; symposia; sales shop selling books, reproductions, prints, slides, postcards & annual reports, jewelry, gifts

L **Rare Book Collection & Archives,** 2 Palace Rd, 02115. Tel 617-278-5133; FAX 617-278-5177; *Librn & Archivist* Susan Sinclair
Open by appointment Mon, Wed, Fri & Sat. Estab 1903. Open to scholars who need to work with mus archives; building designed in style of 15th century Venetian palace. Mem: 2000; dues $40 & up
Library Holdings: Vols 800; Per subs 19; Other — Clipping files, exhibition catalogs, manuscripts, memorabilia, photographs
Special Subjects: Art History
Collections: Objects spanning 30 centuries; 1000 rare books spanning 6 centuries including papers of museum founder; rich in Italian Renaissance painting
Activities: Educ program; lect open to public, 6-8 vis lectr per year; symposia; concerts; gallery talks; tours; sales shop sells books, gifts, reproductions, prints, slides & postcards

M **GIBSON SOCIETY, INC,** Gibson House Museum, 137 Beacon St, 02116-1504. Tel 617-267-6338; *Dir* Edward Gordon
Open May - Oct, Wed - Sun, Nov - Apr, Sat & Sun 2 - 5 PM, cl holidays. Admis $4. Estab 1957 as a Victorian House museum; memorial to Gibson family. Victorian time capsule, early Back Bay Town House, eight rooms with Victorian & Edwardian era furnishings. Average Annual Attendance: 1500
Income: Financed by trust fund & admis
Collections: Decorative arts; paintings; sculpture; Victorian period furniture; objects associated with Gibson & related families
Activities: Lect open to public, 5 vis lectr per year; guided tours; original objects of art lent to museums & galleries; sales shop sells postcards

A **GUILD OF BOSTON ARTISTS,** 162 Newbury St, 02116. Tel 617-536-7660; *Gallery Mgr* Barbara A Dahill; *Treas* William Ternes; *Gallery Mgr* Barbara A Smith
Open Tues - Sat 10 AM - 5 PM; cl Sun, Mon & July & Aug. No admis fee. Estab & incorporated 1914, cooperative organization. Guild owns building; one gallery with continuous exhibitions in which each member is entitled to show one work; second gallery devoted to one-man shows, each member by turn at regular intervals. Mem: Active 65-80, associates under 100; annual meeting Apr
Income: Financed by mem dues
Exhibitions: Three yearly general exhibitions; two educational exhibits

M **INSTITUTE OF CONTEMPORARY ART,** 955 Boylston St, 02115-3194. Tel 617-266-5152; FAX 617-266-4021; *Dir* Milena Kalinovska; *Asst to Dir* Christine McCarthy; *Marketing Coordr* Nicola Rinne; *Cur* Christoph Grunenberg; *Exhib Mgr* Tim Obetz; *Asst Cur Registrar* Lia Gangitano; *Mgr Pub Information* Joann Barrett; *Develop Assoc* Susan Weiss; *Dir Finance & Operations* Kara Keller; *Asst Finance* Komar Manbooh
Open Wed Noon - 5 PM, Thurs Noon - 9 PM, Fri, Sat & Sun Noon - 5 PM. Admis $5.25, students with ID $3.25, senior citizens & children $2.25, members free. Estab 1936 to organize, document, & exhibit works of contemporary masters of new & innovative talents, showing a range of artistic media, including paintings, sculpture, photography, film & video performance. Average Annual Attendance: 55,000. Mem: 2500; dues $30 & up; annual meeting in Sept
Income: Financed by mem, gifts & grants, earned income
Publications: Exhibition catalogs
Activities: Educ dept; dramatic programs; docent training; lect open to public, 20 vis lectr per year; film series; video; concerts; gallery talks; tours; competitions; book traveling exhibitions annually; originate traveling exhibitions; circulating to other national & international contemporary art museums; museum shop sells books, magazines, t-shirts, catalogues, cards, posters

MASSACHUSETTS COLLEGE OF ART
L **Morton R Godine Library,** 621 Huntington Ave, 02115. Tel 617-232-1555; *Dir* George Morgan; *Librn* Margot Isabelle; *Librn* Mary Curtin-Stevenson; *Slide Cur* Staci Stull; *Archivist* Paul Dobbs; *Librn* John Keating; *Librn* Mary Van Winkle; *Assoc Circulation Mgr* Peter Madden
For lending
Library Holdings: Vols 95,000; Per subs 491; Micro — Cards, fiche 8000; AV — A-tapes, cassettes, fs, motion pictures, rec, slides, v-tapes 1200; Other — Exhibition catalogs, memorabilia, original art works, pamphlets, photographs, prints, sculpture
Special Subjects: Art Education, Art History

A **MASSACHUSETTS HISTORICAL SOCIETY,** 1154 Boylston St, 02215. Tel 617-536-1608; FAX 617-859-0074; Elec Mail mg.masshist@nelinet.org. *Dir* Louis L Tucker
Open Mon - Fri 9 AM - 4:45 PM, cl Sat, Sun & holidays. No admis fee. Estab 1791
Income: Financed by endowment
Collections: Archives; historical material; paintings; sculpture
Exhibitions: Temporary exhibitions
Publications: Annual brochure; irregular leaflets; various books
Activities: Lect; special exhibits for members & their guests
L **Library,** 1154 Boylston St, 02215. Tel 617-536-1608 & 1608; FAX 617-859-0074; *Librn* Peter Drummey; *Photo* Chris Steele; *Reference Librn* Jennifer Tolpa
Open Mon - Fri 9 AM - 4:45 PM. Average Annual Attendance: 3000
Library Holdings: Vols 250,000; Other — Manuscripts 3500, prints
Special Subjects: Coins & Medals, Manuscripts, Maps, Miniatures, Painting - American, Photography, Portraits, Prints
Publications: Portaits in the Massachusetts Historical Society, Boston 1988 (one edition)
Activities: Lect

A **MOBIUS INC,** 354 Congress St, 02210. Tel 617-542-7416; FAX 617-451-2910; Elec Mail mobius1@world.std.com;
Internet Home Page Address http://www.artswire.org/mobius/mobius.html.
Co-Dir Marilyn Arsem; *Co-Dir* Jed Speare
Estab 1977 to support artists producing experimental work in all media. Average Annual Attendance: 6000
Exhibitions: Weekly exhibition for Boston & Regional Artists in experimental work in all media; installations & performances throughout the year
Publications: Newsletter, biannually

M **MUSEUM OF AFRO-AMERICAN HISTORY,** Abiel Smith School, 46 Joy St, 02114. Tel 617-742-1854; *Exec Dir* Sylvia Watts McKinney
A non-profit educ institution founded to study the social history of New England's Afro American communities & to promote an awareness of that history by means of educational programs, publications, exhibits & special events. The African Meeting House is the chief artifact of the Mus of Afro American History
Activities: Lect open to public, 4 vis lectr per year; concerts; gallery talks; tours; individual sculptures & original objects of art lent; book traveling exhibitions; museum shop sells books

M **MUSEUM OF FINE ARTS,** 465 Huntington Ave, 02115. Tel 617-267-9300; FAX 617-247-6880;
Internet Home Page Address http://www.mfa.org. *Dir* Malcolm Rogers; *Deputy Dir Operations* John Stanley; *Deputy Dir Marketing & Develop* Patricia Jacoby; *Dir Exhibit* Katie Getchell; *Comptroller* Thomas Fitzgerald; *Registrar* Patricia Loiko; *Cur American Decorative Arts* Jonathan Fairbanks; *Cur European Decorative Arts & Sculpture* Anne Poulet; *Cur Asiatic Art* Wu Tung; *Cur European Paintings* George Shackelford; *Cur Prints & Drawings* Clifford Ackley; *Deputy Dir Curatorial Affairs* Brent Benjamin; *Cur Classical Art* John Herrmann; *Cur American Painting* Theodore E Stebbins Jr; *Cur Egyptian & Ancient Near Eastern* Rita Freed; *Dir Research* Arthur Beale; *Dir Educ* William Burback; *Cur Contemporary Art* Trevor Fairbrother
Open Mon & Tues 10 AM - 4:45 PM, Wed - Fri 10 AM - 9:45 PM, Sat & Sun 10 AM - 5:45 PM, Thurs & Fri after 5 PM only West Wing is open. Admis adults $10, senior citizens & college students $8, children 17 & under & members free. Estab & incorporated in 1870; present building opened 1909. Average Annual Attendance: 800,000. Mem: 55,000; dues assoc $125, family $75, individual $55
Collections: Ancient Nubian & Near Eastern art; Chinese, Japanese & Indian art; Egyptian, Greek & Roman art; European & American decorative & minor arts, including period rooms, porcelains, silver, Western & Asian tapestries, costumes & musical instruments; master paintings of Europe & America; print collection from 15th century to present; sculpture
Exhibitions: Specially organized exhibitions are continually on view; exhibitions of the permanent collections; (1997) Herb Ritts: Work; Tales from the Land of Dragons; 1000 Years of Chinese Painting; Alfred Stieglitz & Early Modern Photography; The Art of John Biggers: View from the Upper Room; IKAT: Splendid Silks of Central Asia; Karsh Portraits: The Searching Eye; Face & Figure: Contemporary Art; Roy Lichtenstein: Landscapes in the Chinese Style; This is the Modern World: Furnishings of the 20th Century, The Big City: Prints, Drawings, Photographs; Durer in his Time; Dressing Up: Children's Fashions 1720-1920; Chinoiserie
Publications: Journal, yearly; calendar of events, bi-monthly; exhibition catalogs; collection catalogs
Activities: Classes for adults & children; lect open to public; concerts; gallery talks; tours; films; museum shop sells books, magazines, original art, reproductions, prints & slides
L **William Morris Hunt Memorial Library,** 465 Huntington Ave, 02115. Tel 617-267-9300; FAX 617-267-0280; *Chief Librn* Nancy S Allen
Admis adults $10, senior citizens & students $8, children 17 & under free. Estab 1870 to house, preserve, interpret & publish its collections. For reference only. Average Annual Attendance: 1,000,000. Mem: 59,000
Income: $290,000 (financed by endowment & mem)
Purchases: $105,000

Library Holdings: Vols 138,902; Per subs 650; Other — Clipping files, exhibition catalogs, pamphlets 117,000
Special Subjects: Carpets & Rugs, Ceramics, Decorative Arts, Drawings, Etchings & Engravings, Furniture, Painting - American, Prints, Sculpture, Textiles, Mosaics, Painting - European, Restoration & Conservation, Antiquities
Activities: Classes for adults & children; docent training; dramatic programs; lect open to public; concerts; gallery talks; tours; book traveling exhibitions
L **Dept of Photographic Services,** Slide & Photographic Library, 465 Huntington Ave, 02115. Tel 617-267-9300; FAX 617-247-2312; *Dir* Janice Sorkow
Library Holdings: AV — Slides 120,000
Special Subjects: Architecture, Decorative Arts, Painting - American, Photography, Prints, Sculpture

M **MUSEUM OF THE NATIONAL CENTER OF AFRO-AMERICAN ARTISTS,** 300 Walnut Ave, 02119. Tel 617-442-8014; FAX 617-445-5525; *Dir & Cur* Edmund B Gaither; *Asst to Dir* Gloretta Baynes; *Artistic Dir* Elma Lewis
Open June - Aug daily 1 - 6 PM, Sept - May daily 1 - 5 PM. Admis adult $1.25, children $.50. Estab 1969 to promote visual art heritage of Black people in the Americas and Africa. Suite of three special exhibition galleries; suite of three African Art Galleries; suite of three permanent collection galleries; one local artist gallery. Average Annual Attendance: 10,000. Mem: 250; dues $25
Income: $250,000 (financed by private gifts, contracts, etc)
Collections: Art from Western Africa; Early 20th century Afro-American Prints & Drawings; visual fine arts of the black world
Exhibitions: African Artists in America; Stone Churches of Ethiopia; Praying Shoes, Praying Shoes-A Video Installation, James Mintford; African Outlook; Recent Fashion Design, C S Okkeke; Afro-American Artists in Paris 1919-1937
Publications: Newsletter, quarterly
Activities: Dramatic programs; lect open to the public; concerts; gallery talks; tours; competitions with awards (Edward Mitchell Barrister Award); book traveling exhibitions; traveling exhibitions organized and circulated; sales shop sells books, magazines, prints and small sculpture

M **NATIONAL ARCHIVES & RECORDS ADMINISTRATION,** John F Kennedy Library & Museum, Columbia Point, 02125. Tel 617-929-4500; *Dir* Bradley Gerratt; *Cur* Frank Rigg
Open daily 9 AM - 5 PM. Admis adults $6, senior citizens & students $4, children 5-15 $2. Estab 1964 to preserve collections of Kennedy papers & other material pertaining to his career; to educate public about J F Kennedy's career & political system; to make materials available to researchers. Library is a nine-story building overlooking Boston Harbor, has two theaters & an exhibition floor. Average Annual Attendance: 250,000
Income: Financed by federal government & national archives trust fund
Library Holdings: Micro — Cards, fiche, prints; AV — A-tapes, cassettes, fs, lantern slides, motion pictures, slides, v-tapes; Other — Memorabilia, original art works, pamphlets, photographs, prints, reproductions
Collections: 32,000,000 documents & personal papers of John F Kennedy, Robert Kennedy & many others associated with life & career of John F Kennedy; 6,000,000 ft of film relating to political career, 150,000 photographs, 1200 oral histories, 11,000 paintings & museum objects (personal); manuscripts of Ernest Hemingway, 10,000 photographs of him with family & friends; 800 glass plates collection of Josiah Johnson Hawes
Activities: Tours; fels & research grants; museum shop sells books, reproductions, prints and slides

L **NEW ENGLAND SCHOOL OF ART & DESIGN AT SUFFOLK UNIVERSITY,** Library, 81 Arlington St, 02116. Tel 617-536-0383; *Librn* Brian Tynemouth, MLS
For lending
Purchases: $5000
Library Holdings: Vols 5500; Per subs 55; AV — Slides, v-tapes; Other — Clipping files, pamphlets
Special Subjects: Advertising Design, Architecture, Art History, Calligraphy, Cartoons, Commercial Art, Decorative Arts, Drafting, Drawings, Furniture, Graphic Design, Illustration, Interior Design, Landscape Architecture
Activities: Scholarships & fels offered

NEW ENGLAND WATERCOLOR SOCIETY
For further information, see National and Regional Organizations

M **NICHOLS HOUSE MUSEUM, INC,** 55 Mount Vernon St, 02108. Tel 617-227-6993; FAX 617-227-4045; *Cur* William H Pear
Open Noon - 4:15 PM. Admis $5. Estab 1961. Historic house museum. Average Annual Attendance: 2000. Mem: 315; dues $25; annual meeting in May
Income: $50,000 (financed by endowment, admis sales, donations, mem & rentals)
Collections: Decorative Arts Collection
Activities: Lect for members only, 5 vis lectr per year; tours; museum shop sells books

L **PAYETTE ASSOCIATES ARCHITECTS PLANNERS,** Library, 285 Summer St, 02210. Tel 617-342-8201, Ext 234; FAX 617-342-8202; *Librn* Ardys Kozbial
Library Holdings: Vols 1500; Per subs 120; AV — Slides; Other — Clipping files
Special Subjects: Architecture
Collections: Interiors Sample Library; †Manufacturer's Catalogs; †Medical & Laboratory Planning

M **PHOTOGRAPHIC RESOURCE CENTER,** 602 Commonwealth Ave, 02215-2400. Tel 617-353-0700; FAX 617-353-1662; *Dir* John P Jacob; *Cur* Robert E Seydel; *Mem & Develop* Lauriann Serra
Open Tues - Sun Noon - 5 PM, Thurs Noon - 8 PM. Admis general $3, sr & students $2, free Thurs 5 PM - 8 PM. Estab 1977 for the photographic arts. Mem: 2600; dues $30
Library Holdings: Vols 4000; Other — Exhibition catalogs
Publications: Views: The New England Journal of Photography, triannual; monthly newsletter
Activities: Photography workshops with guest artists; lect open to public, 5 vis lectr per year; gallery talks; tours; competitions; book traveling exhibitions 2 - 3 per year; originate traveling exhibitions

A SOCIETY FOR THE PRESERVATION OF NEW ENGLAND ANTIQUITIES, Harrison Gray Otis House, 141 Cambridge St, 02114. Tel 617-227-3956; FAX 617-227-9204; *Dir* Jane Nylander
Open Tues - Fri 12 - 5 PM, Sat 10 AM - 5 PM. Admis adults $4, children under 12 $2. Estab & incorporated 1910, the Otis House serves as both headquarters & mus for the Soc. Soc owns over 30 historic houses throughout New England, 23 of which are open to the pub. Average Annual Attendance: 3000. Mem: 3200; dues $25 & up; annual meeting in June
Collections: American & European decorative arts & antiques with New England history; photographs; houses
Publications: Old Time New England, occasional bulletin; SPNEA News, quarterly; house guide, annual
Activities: Classes for adults; lect open to public, 5-10 vis lectr per year; originate traveling exhibitions; museum shop sells books/merchandise

L Archives, Harrison Gray Otis House, 141 Cambridge St, 02114. Tel 617-227-3956; FAX 617-227-9204; *Cur Archives* Lorna Condon
Admis nonmembers $5, students $3, members free. Estab 1910 to document New England architecture from the 17th century to the present. For reference. Mem: 3000; dues $25; annual meeting in June
Library Holdings: Other — Clipping files, manuscripts, memorabilia, original art works, pamphlets, photographs, prints
Collections: Study collections of New England Architecture in the form of decorative arts, interior decoration, landscape; 350,000 photographs, builders guides & pattern books
Exhibitions: Scouting a Perch: The Photographer Views the City, Boston photographs by David Bohl
Activities: Lect open to public; concerts; tours; museum shop sells books & reproductions

A THE SOCIETY OF ARTS & CRAFTS, 175 Newbury St, 02116. Tel 617-266-1810; *Exec Dir* Beth Gerstein; *Gallery Mgr* Randi Lathrop
Open Mon, Tues, Thurs & Fri 10 AM - 6 PM, Wed 10 AM - 7 PM, Sat 10 AM - 5 PM, Sun Noon - 5 PM. No admis fee. Estab 1897 to promote high standards of excellence in the arts & crafts & to educate the pub in the appreciation of fine craftsmanship. Two galleries on the second level house special exhibitions. Average Annual Attendance: 8000. Mem: 800; dues party or joint $50, single $30; annual meeting in May or June
Income: $110,000 (financed by mem, gallery sales, grants)
Collections: Contemporary one-of-a-kind furniture
Exhibitions: Special exhibitions on a single craft medium presented year round; Furniture Interiors I, II & III
Publications: Newsletter, semiannual
Activities: Lect open to public, vis lectr; gallery talks; awards; sales shop sells fine handmade crafts in ceramics, wood, glass, metal, fiber & leather

C STATE STREET CORPORATION, Concourse Gallery, 225 Franklin St, 02110. Tel 617-654-3938; *Art Cur* Ann Cyr
Collections: American maritime fold art, 19th century; lithographs; ship models & figureheads; maritime artifacts

M USS CONSTITUTION MUSEUM, Bldg 22, Charlestown Navy Yard, PO Box 1812, 02129. Tel 617-426-1812; FAX 617-242-0496; *Exec Dir* Burt Logan; *Cur* Anne Gimes Rand; *Dir Educ* Marilyn W Cruickshank
Open 9 AM - 5 PM, varies by season. Admis $4 & under. Estab 1972 to collect, preserve & display items relating to the sailing frigate USS Constitution. Average Annual Attendance: 70,000. Mem: 2800; dues $25-$1000; annual meeting in the fall
Income: $1,850,000 (financed by endowment, mem, admis, gift shop, federal, state & private grants)
Collections: †Documents relating to the sailing frigate USS Constitution; †Personal possessions of crew members; †Shipbuilding & navigational tools; †Souvenirs depicting Old Ironsides; †USS Constitution images (paintings, prints & photos)
Exhibitions: Around the World Aboard Old Ironsides; Old Ironsides in War & Peace; Annual Juried Ship Model Show
Publications: Chronicle, quarterly newsletter
Activities: Classes for adults & children; family programs; docent programs; summer teen internship program; teachers' workshops; lect open to public, 4-6 vis lectr per year; tours; originate traveling exhibitions; sales store sells books, prints, magazines, slides, reproductions, clothing, souvenirs & sponsors book signings

A VOLUNTEER LAWYERS FOR THE ARTS OF MASSACHUSETTS INC, PO Box 8784, 02114. Tel 617-523-1764; FAX 617-523-1764;
Estab 1989 to provide arts related legal assistance to artists & arts organizations
Activities: Lect open to public

L WENTWORTH INSTITUTE OF TECHNOLOGY LIBRARY, 550 Huntington Ave, 02115-5901. Tel 617-989-4040; FAX 617-989-4091; Elec Mail walkerr@admin.wit.edu. *Dir* Rosemary Walker; *Technical Servs* Elizabeth Holmes; *Archival Librn* Priscilla Biondi; *Archivist* Mary Ellen Flaherty; *Reference* Pia Romano
Library Holdings: Vols 75,000; Per subs 600; AV — A-tapes, v-tapes; Other — Clipping files, memorabilia, photographs
Special Subjects: Architecture, Industrial Design, Interior Design, Facilities Management

BROCKTON

L BROCKTON PUBLIC LIBRARY SYSTEM, Joseph A Driscoll Art Gallery, 304 Main St, 02401-5390. Tel 508-580-7890; *Acting Dir* Diana Pacheco
Open Mon - Thurs 9 AM - 9 PM, Fri & Sat 9 AM - 5 PM, cl Sun. No admis fee. Special room for monthly art exhibitions. Average Annual Attendance: 20,000
Library Holdings: Vols 258,768
Collections: W C Bryant Collection of 19th & 20th century American paintings, chiefly by New England artists; gifts of 20th century paintings which includes

four paintings by Hendricks Hallett & an oil painting by Mme Elisabeth Weber-Fulop; loan collection of 20th century painters from the Woman's Club of Brockton; mounted photographs of Renaissance art & watercolors by F Mortimer Lamb
Exhibitions: Monthly exhibitions by local & nationally known artists

M FULLER MUSEUM OF ART, 455 Oak St, 02401-1399. Tel 508-588-6000; FAX 508-587-6191; *Dir* Caroline Graboys; *Cur* Jennifer Atkinson; *Dir Develop* Ken Medd; *Dir Educ* Linda Marcus
Open Tues - Sun Noon - 5 PM. Admis by donation. Estab 1969 to provide a variety of art exhibitions & educ programs of regional & national interest. The center houses six galleries. Average Annual Attendance: 35,000. Mem: 850; dues $30
Income: $784,000 (financed by endowment, mem, gifts & government grants)
Collections: Contemporary American art; Early American & Sandwich glass; 19th & 20th century American paintings; contemporary regional crafts
Publications: Quarterly newsletter & calendar of events
Activities: Classes for adults & children; dramatic programs; docent training; special programs for children; lect open to public, 4 vis lectr per year; gallery talks; tours; concerts; individual paintings & original objects of art lent to accredited museums of the American Association of Museums; lending collection contains paintings & art; book traveling exhibitions 1-2 per year; originate traveling exhibitions; museum shop sells book, original art, reproductions, prints, contemporary crafts, t-shirts & mugs

L Library, 455 Oak St, 02401. Tel 508-588-6000;
Open to members, staff & students
Library Holdings: Vols 500; Other — Exhibition catalogs, pamphlets

CAMBRIDGE

A CAMBRIDGE ART ASSOCIATION, 25 R Lowell St, 02138. Tel 617-876-0246; FAX 617-876-1880; *Dir* Kathryn Zuckerman
Open Tues - Sat 11 AM - 5 PM, cl July & Aug. No admis fee. Estab 1944 to exhibit, rent & sell members' work & to encourage an interest in fine arts & crafts in the community. Mem: 400; dues artist $65, friends $40, students $15
Exhibitions: Invited shows in Rental Gallery & Craft Gallery; foreign exhibition each year; members' juried exhibitions in Main Gallery every month
Publications: Bulletin, monthly
Activities: Classes for adults; dramatic programs; open workshops; lect & demonstrations; competitions with prizes; sales shop sells books, original art, prints, cards, jewelry & crafts

L CITY OF CAMBRIDGE HISTORICAL COMMISSION, City Hall Annex, 57 Inman St, 02139. Tel 617-349-4683; FAX 617-349-4669; *Exec Dir* Charles M Sullivan; *Preservation-Planner* Sally Zimmerman; *Survey Dir* Susan Maycock; *Asst Dir* Kathleen Rawlins
Open Mon - Fri 9 AM - 5 PM. No admis fee. Estab 1963
Income: $190,000 (financed by city appropriation)
Library Holdings: Vols 1000; Other — Photographs
Special Subjects: Architecture
Collections: Survey of architectural history in Cambridge
Exhibitions: The City at Work, 1846-1896; Photographic History of Cambridge
Publications: Cambridgeport (1971); Northwest Cambridge (1977); Photographic History of Cambridge (1984); East Cambridge (1988)

HARVARD UNIVERSITY

M Harvard University Art Museums, 32 Quincy St, 02138. Tel 617-495-9400; FAX 617-495-9936; Elec Mail artmuseum@fas.harvard.edu. *Dir* James Cuno; *Deputy Dir* Frances A Beane; *Registrar* Jane Montgomery; *Mem, Dir Fellows & Spec Prog* Mary Rose Bolton; *Visitor Servs* Margaret Howland; *Dir Straus Center Conservation* Henry Lie; *Pub Realtions* Kate McShea
Open Mon - Sat 10 AM - 5 PM, Sun 1 - 5 PM, cl national holidays. Admis (applies to all three museums) adults $5, senior citizens $4, students $3, children under 18 free, Sat AM free. 225,000 vol fine arts library (Fogg Art Mus) & Rubel Asiatic Research Collection (Sackler) available for use by request only; extensive visual collection; reading room; classrooms. Average Annual Attendance: 83,696. Mem: 2700; dues patron $1000, donor $500, contributor $100, couple $50, individual $35, student $25, admis only $20
Income: Financed by endowment, mem & federal grants
Publications: Director's report, quarterly newsletter; exhibit catalogs; gallery guides
Activities: Lect; gallery talks; tours; seminars; concerts; museum shop sells books, magazines, reproductions & prints
—**Busch-Reisinger Museum,** 32 Quincy St, 02138. Tel 617-495-9400; FAX 617-495-9936; Elec Mail artmuseums@fas.harvard.edu. *Cur* Peter Nisbet; *Asst Cur* Emilie Norris; *Cur Asst* Tawney Becky
Open Mon - Sat 10 AM - 5 PM, Sun 1 - 5 PM, cl national holidays. Admis adult $5, seniors $4, students $3, under 18 & Sat AM free. Estab 1901 & opened in 1920, it has one of most important & extensive collections of Central & European art outside of Europe, ranging from the Romanesque to the present day. This coll serves the teaching prog of the Dept of Fine Arts, outside scholars & the gen pub. Werner Otto Hall contains 7 galleries, 6 for German Art (1880-1980), 1 for rotating exhibits. Average Annual Attendance: 83,696. Mem: 2700; dues individual $35
Collections: 18th Century Painting Collection; Late Medival, Renaissance & Baroque Sculpture Collection; 16th Century Porcelain Collection; 20th Century German Works Collection; largest collection of Bauhaus material outside Germany; drawings; paintings; prints; sculpture
Publications: Newsletter
Activities: Classes for children; lect open to public; concerts; gallery talks; tours; symposia; individual paintings & original objects of art lent to other museums, considered on request; book traveling exhibitions 1-2 per year; originate traveling exhibitions; museum shop sells books, reproductions, prints & small gift items
—**William Hayes Fogg Art Museum,** 32 Quincy St, 02138. Tel 617-495-9400; FAX 617-495-9936; Elec Mail artmuseums@fas.harvard.edu. *Dir* James Cuno; *Deputy Dir* Frances A Beane; *Cur Drawings* William W Robinson; *Cur Prints* Marjorie B Cohn; *Cur Painting* Ivan Gaskell

Open Mon - Sat 10 AM - 5 PM, Sun 1 - 5 PM, cl national holidays. Admis adults $5, sr citizens $4, students $3, Sat morning free. University estab 1891; mus estab 1927; serves both as a pub mus & as a laboratory for Harvard's Dept of Fine Arts, which trains art history mus professionals. The Straus Center for Conservation operates a training program for conservators & technical specialists. Average Annual Attendance: 83,696. Mem: 2700; dues $35 & up
Income: Financed by endowment, mem & federal grants
Collections: Maurice Wertheim Collection of Impressionist & Post-Impressionist Art; European & American paintings, sculpture, decorative arts, photographs, prints & drawings; English & American silver; Wedgwood
Exhibitions: (Permanent) Circa 1874: The Emergence of Impressionism; France & The Portait, 1799-1870; Subliminations: Art & Sensuality in the Nineteenth Century. (1997) Fragments of Antiquity: Drawing Upon Greek Vases; From Lowlife to Rustic Idyll: The Peasant Genre in Seventeenth-Century Dutch Drawings & Prints
Publications: Annual report; newsletter, 4 - 5 per year
Activities: Docent training; lect open to public; concerts; gallery talks; tours; individual paintings & original objects of art lent to other museums, considered on individual basis; book traveling exhibitions 1-2 per year; originate traveling exhibitions; museum shop sells books, reproductions, prints & small gift items
—**Arthur M Sackler Museum,** 485 Broadway, 02138. Tel 617-495-9400; FAX 617-495-9936; Elec Mail artmuseums@fas.harvard.edu. *Dir* James Cuno; *Deputy Dir* Frances A Beane; *Cur Chinese Art* Robert Mowry; *Cur Ancient Art* David Gordon Mitten
Estab 1985 to serve both as a pub mus & a laboratory for Harvard's Dept of Fine Arts, which trains art historians & mus professionals
Collections: Ancient coins; Asian bronzes, ceramics, jades, painting, prints & sculpture; Egyptian antiquities; Greek red & black figure vases; Greek & Roman bronze & marble sculpture; Greek, Roman & Near Eastern jewelry & metalwork; Islamic & Indian ceramics, illuminated manuscripts; metalwork, paintings & textiles
Exhibitions: (Permanent) Serveran Silver Coinage. (1997) Sewn Together by Peace of Mind: Islamic Album Pages from Harvard's Collection; Worlds Within Worlds: The Richard Rosenblum Collection of Chinese Scholars' Rocks
Activities: Museum shop sells books, prints & reproductions

L **Fine Arts Library,** 02138. Tel 617-495-3373; FAX 617-496-4889; Elec Mail falhub@harvarda.harvard.edu. *Librn* Jeffrey L Horrell; *Chief Cataloguer* Susan Myerson
Open to Harvard Community Mon - Thurs 9 AM - 10 PM, Fri 9 AM - 6 PM, Sat 10 AM - 5 PM, Sun 1 - 6 PM. Estab 1895 to support the teaching dept of fine arts & the research needs of the curatorial depts of Fogg Art Mus & an international community of scholars in art history. Circ 116,000
Income: $1,956,510 (financed by endowment)
Purchases: $520,688
Library Holdings: Vols 262,744; Per subs 1152; Ephemera; Micro — Fiche 67,855, reels; AV — Slides 654,897; Other — Exhibition catalogs, pamphlets 57,435, photographs 424,549
Special Subjects: All areas of art history with emphasis on Italian primitives, architectural history, art & architecture of western & eastern Europe, conservation & restoration of works of art, Dutch 17th century, history of photography, master drawings, Romanesque sculpture, Far Eastern art, Islamic art & architecture
Collections: DIAL Index; Marburger Index; The Index of Jewish Art; The Knoedler Libray Library on Microfiche; Manuscript Archives of American artists and art scholars; Oriental and Islamic Art; Rubel Asiatic Research Collection: Library collection on the arts of the Far East; 40,000 catalogued auction sales catalogs
Publications: Catalog of Auction Sales Catalogs; Fine Arts Library Catalog (1971); Dictionary Catalog; The Catalogs of the Rubel Asiatic Research Collection (microfiche editions, 1984); Guide to the Card Catalogs of Harvard University, 1895 - 1981 (1984); Iconographic Index to Old Testament (1987); Iconographic Index to New Testament (1992); Vol I: Narrative Paintings of the Italian School (1992)

L **Frances Loeb Library,** Graduate School of Design, Gund Hall, 02138. Tel 617-495-2574; FAX 617-496-5929; *Librn* Hinda F Sklar
Estab 1900 to serve faculty & students of graduate school of design. Circ 55,000
Income: $1,100,000 (financed by endowment & tuition)
Purchases: $208,381
Library Holdings: Vols 260,020; Per subs 1200; Drawings; Micro — Fiche; AV — A-tapes 350, cassettes 326, fs 65, Kodachromes, lantern slides, motion pictures, rec, slides 169,515, v-tapes; Other — Clipping files, exhibition catalogs, manuscripts, pamphlets, photographs
Special Subjects: Architecture, City & Regional Planning; Landscape Architecture; Urban Design
Collections: Cluny Collection; Le Corbusier Collection; Edward Larrabee Barnes Collection; Charles Elliot Collection; Daniel Kiley Collection; John C Olmsted Collection; H H Richardson Collection; Charles Mulford Robinson Collection; Hugh Stubbins Collection; Joseph Lluis Sert Collection
Publications: Frances Loeb Library Users' Guide, annual
Activities: Tours

M **Semitic Museum,** 6 Divinity Ave, 02138. Tel 617-495-4631; FAX 617-496-8904; Elec Mail green5@fas.harvard.edu;
Internet Home Page Address
http://www.fas.harvard.edu/~semitic/museum_semitic.html. *Dir* Lawrence Stager; *Asst Dir* Joseph A Greene; *Asst Cur* James A Armstrong; *Cur Cuneiform Coll* Piotr Steinkeller
Open Mon - Fri 10 AM - 4 PM, Sun 1 - 4 PM. No admis fee, donations requested. Estab 1889 to promote sound knowledge of Semitic languages & history; an archaeological research mus. Average Annual Attendance: 3000-5000. Mem: 250; dues $30 & up
Income: Financed by endowment, mem, private research grants, gifts
Collections: Excavated archaeological & excavation archives materials from Egypt, Mesopotamia, Syma-Palestine, Cypres, Arabia, North Africa; ethnographic collection (Ottoman period)
Exhibitions: The Pyramids & the Sphinx: 100 Years of American Archaeology at Giza
Publications: Harvard Semitic Series; exhibit catalogs; Harvard Semitic Monographs; Semitic Museum Newsletter, quarterly
Activities: Classes for adults & children; docent training; teacher workshop; lect-film series; lect open to public, 5-8 vis lectr per year; gallery talks; tours; scholarships offered; exten dept serves Harvard University; original objects of art lent to universities & museums; museum shop sells books, reproductions & prints

M **LONGFELLOW NATIONAL HISTORIC SITE,** 105 Brattle St, 02138. Tel 617-876-4491; *Cur* Jim Shea; *Asst Cur* Michelle Clark
Open daily 10 AM - 4:30 PM. Admis $2 (under 16, over 62 free). Estab 1972 to acquaint the pub with the life, work & time of the American poet Henry W Longfellow. Average Annual Attendance: 18,000
Income: Financed by US Department of the Interior
Collections: Paintings, sculpture, prints, letters, furniture & furnishings once belonging to Henry W Longfellow & his daughter Alice; 19th century photographic collection including views of China & Japan; American, European & Asian Collections
Activities: Lect open to public; concerts; tours; individual paintings & original objects of art lent to qualified institutions; sales shop sells books

MASSACHUSETTS INSTITUTE OF TECHNOLOGY

M **List Visual Arts Center,** Wiesner Bldg E 15 - 109, 20 Ames St, 02139. Tel 617-253-4680; FAX 617-258-7265; *Dir* Katy Kline; *Cur* Helaine Posner; *Registrar* Jill Aszling; *Admin Officer* Toby Levi; *Gallery Mgr* Jon Roll
Open Tues - Thurs Noon - 6 PM, Fri Noon - 8 PM, Sat & Sun Noon - 6 PM. No admis fee. Estab 1963 to organize exhibitions of contemporary art in all media. Average Annual Attendance: 15,000
Income: Financed by MIT, pub & private endowments, art councils, corporations & individuals
Collections: Major public sculpture, paintings, drawings, prints, photographs & site-specific commissions all publicly sited through the campus. All collections are being enlarged through donations & purchases
Exhibitions: Nine exhibitions per year of contemporary art in all mediums
Publications: Exhibition catalogs
Activities: Educ Dept; tours; films; lect open to public, 10 vis lectr per year; gallery talks; tours; lending collection of original art; Student Loan Print Collection of over 300 pieces; book traveling exhibitions 2 per year; originate traveling exhibitions to major museums 2 per year; museum shop sells exhibition catalogues

M **MIT Museum,** Bldg N52, 2nd Flr, 265 Massachusetts Ave, 02139. Tel 617-253-4444; FAX 617-253-8994; *Acting Dir* Mary Leen; *Keeper History Coll* Michael Yeates; *Mgr Exhibits* Donald Stidsen; *Asst Dir Marketing* Kathleen Thurston-Lighty; *Coll & Information Mgr* Kara Schneiderman; *Cur Architecture* Kimberly Shilland; *Cur Hart Nautical Coll* Kurt Hasselbalch
Open Tues - Fri 10 AM - 5 PM, Sat & Sun Noon - 5 PM. Admis for people outside MIT community $3. Estab 1971 as a mus facility documenting the development of the Institute & of 19th & 20th centuries science & technology & the interrelationships of art, science & technology. Main exhibition facility & two campus galleries. Average Annual Attendance: 20,000
Income: Financed by University & outside funding
Collections: Architectural drawings; biographical information; furniture; holograms; maritime; objects d'art; paintings; photographs; portraits; scientific instruments & apparatus
Publications: Exhibition catalogs; gallery exhibition notes
Activities: Classes for adults & children; lect open to public; gallery talks; tours; book traveling exhibitions 2-4 per year; originate traveling exhibitions; museum shop sells books, prints, MIT - & exhibit-related items
—**Hart Nautical Galleries & Collections,** 55 Massachusetts Ave, 02139. Tel 617-253-5942; FAX 617-258-9107; *Cur* Kurt Hasselbalch
Gallery open daily 9 AM - 8 PM; reference Mon - Fri 9 AM - 5 PM by appointment only. Estab 1922 to preserve history of naval architecture, shipbuilding, yachts. Galleries include permanent exhibit of ship models & changing exhibits
Income: Financed by University
Collections: Forbes Collection of whaling prints; rigged models & half models of merchant & warships, engine models, marine paintings, drawings & photographs
Activities: Lect open to public, 5 vis lectr per year; individual paintings & original objects of art lent to qualified museums; lending collection contains prints, slides & models; museum shop sells books

L **Rotch Library of Architecture & Planning,** 77 Massachusetts Ave, Rm 7-238, 02139-4307. Tel 617-258-5594, 258-5599; FAX 617-253-9331; Elec Mail depopolo@mit.edu. *Librn* Margaret DePopolo; *Assoc Librn & Col Mgr* Merrill W Smith; *Librn Aga Khan Program for Islamic Architecture* Omar Khalidi; *Architecture Librn* Michael Leininger; *Art Librn* Patricia Flanagan; *Real Estate Librn* Ragnhild Bairnsfather; *Visual Coll Librn* Katherine K Poole
Open Mon - Thurs 8:30 AM - 10 PM, Fri 8:30 AM - 7 PM, Sat 10 AM - 6 PM, Sun 2 - 10 PM, special hours when school is not in session. Estab 1868 to serve the students & faculty of the School of Architecture & Planning & other members of the MIT community
Library Holdings: Vols 192,690; Per subs 1960; Micro — Fiche, reels; AV — A-tapes, cassettes, Kodachromes, lantern slides, motion pictures, slides, v-tapes; Other — Exhibition catalogs, pamphlets, photographs
Special Subjects: Architecture, Art History, Decorative Arts, Film, Photography, Architectural Design History & Theory, Contemporary Islamic Architecture, Urban & Environmental Design

CHATHAM

M **CHATHAM HISTORICAL SOCIETY,** Old Atwood House Museum, 347 Old Harbor Rd, PO Box 381, 02633. Tel 508-945-2493, 945-1205; *Pres* Daniel Buckley; *Cur* Joseph Nickerson
Open June - Sept Tues - Fri 1 - 4 PM. Admis $3, student with ID $1. Estab 1926 to preserve local Chatham history. Murals Barn houses Alice Stallknecht murals of Chatham people. The New Gallery houses Frederick Wight paintings of local sea captains. Average Annual Attendance: 1500. Mem: 1000; dues family $15; meetings in Feb & Aug
Income: Financed by mem
Purchases: Local historical artifacts & paintings

Collections: †Harold Brett, paintings; Harold Dunbar, paintings; Frederick Wright, paintings; Sandwich Glass; 17th & 18th century furnishings; antique tools; china; items brought back by Chatham sea captains; maritime paintings; ship models
Exhibitions: Exhibits change every year
Publications: Exhibition catalogs
Activities: Docent training; talks & slideshows (winter only); scholarships & fels offered; museum shop sells books & prints

CHESTNUT HILL

M **BOSTON COLLEGE,** Museum of Art, Devlin Hall 108, 02167. Tel 617-552-8587; FAX 617-552-8577; *Dir* Nancy Netzer; *Cur* Alston Conley; *Adminr* Helen Swartz
Open Mon - Fri 11 AM - 4 PM, Sat & Sun Noon - 5 PM. Estab 1986 to enhance the teaching mission of the University & extend it to a wider audience. Two floors; flexible galleries. Average Annual Attendance: 45,000. Mem: 200; dues $35
Income: Financed through University funds
Activities: Classes for adults & children; docent training; lect open to public, 10 vis lectr per year; gallery talks; tours; individual paintings & original objects of art lent to other exhibitions; book traveling exhibitions 3 per year; originate traveling exhibitions to other museums 3 per year

COHASSET

M **COHASSET HISTORICAL SOCIETY,** Caleb Lothrop House, 14 Summer St, 02025. Tel 617-383-1434; *Pres* David Pottenger; *Sr Cur* David Wadsworth
Headquarters open by appointment only; Maritime Museum & Wilson House open daily 1:30 - 4:30 PM, cl Mon June - Sept. Admis by donations. Estab 1974 as the headquarters house of the Cohasset Historical Society. Paintings of local significance are displayed in various rooms; Cohasset Historical Society's library & archives located here. Mem: 400; dues sustaining $50, family $30, single $20; annual meetings in Nov & Mar
Collections: Old furniture, local art work
Publications: Historical Highlights, newsletter 4 times per yr
Activities: Educ dept
M **Cohasset Maritime Museum,** Elm St (Mailing add: 14 Summer St, 02025). Tel 617-383-1434
Open Tues - Sun 1:30 - 4:30 PM, cl Mon June-Sept. Estab 1957 to display the seafaring history of Cohasset. Average Annual Attendance: 800. Mem: 370
Collections: Local maritime history, fishing gear of 19th century, lifesaving, shipwreck memorabilia, pictures & charts
Activities: Tours
M **Captain John Wilson Historical House,** Elm St (Mailing add: 14 Summer St, 02025). Tel 617-383-1434; *Pres* David Pottenget; *Cur* David H Wadsworth
Open July - Aug 1:30 - 4:30 PM, cl Mon. No admis fee. Estab 1936. Paintings of local subjects & topics, some by local artists, are displayed upon walls of the several rooms; maintains reference library. Average Annual Attendance: 700. Mem: 375; annual meeting in Nov
Income: Financed by mem, donations & grants
Collections: Old household furnishings, toys, kitchenware & artwork from the old homes of Cohasset
Activities: 2 vis lectr per year; tours; sales shop sells books

CONCORD

A **CONCORD ART ASSOCIATION,** 37 Lexington Rd, 01742. Tel 508-369-2578; *Pres* Mary A Bramhall; *VPres* George Nick; *Cur* Patsy B McVity; *Secy* Kris Guarll
Open Tues - Sat 10 AM - 4:30 PM, Sun 2 - 4:30 PM, cl Mon. No admis fee. Estab 1916 for the encouragement of art & artists. Housed in a 1740 house with four galleries, rent out to weddings & meetings. Average Annual Attendance: 10,000. Mem: 900; dues life member $500, business & patron $100, family $50, individual $40, artist $30, student $5
Income: Financed by mem
Collections: Bronze sculptures; colonial glass
Exhibitions: Changing exhibition per year
Publications: Exhibition notices
Activities: Classes for adults; lect open to public, 4-6 vis lectr per year; tours; competitions with prizes; original objects of art lent; sales shop sells original art, reproductions, prints

M **CONCORD MUSEUM,** 200 Lexington Rd, PO Box 146, 01742. Tel 508-369-9609; FAX 508-369-9660; *Pres* Jean Hogan; *Exec Dir* Desiree Caldwell; *Cur* David Wood; *Business Mgr* Cathy Tilney; *Coordr of Educ* Jayne Gordon; *Public Relations Officer* Carol Haines
Open Apr - Dec Mon - Sat 9 AM - 5 PM, Sun 12 - 5 PM, Jan - Mar Mon - Sat 11 AM - 4 PM, Sun 1 - 4 PM. Admis adults $6, senior citizens $5, children $3, family $12, members free. Estab 1886 to collect & preserve objects of antiquarian interest to Concord & towns originally a part of Concord; to interpret life in Colonial America, range of American decorative arts, role of Concord in the American Revolution & contributions of Concord authors-Thoreau, Emerson, Alcotts & Hawthorne-to American literature. Fifteen period rooms & galleries. Average Annual Attendance: 40,000. Mem: 950; dues $30 & up; annual meeting in Mar
Income: $500,000 (financed by mem, admis, grants, endowment & giving)
Publications: Newsletter, quarterly; Concord: Climate for Freedom by Ruth Wheeler; Forms to Sett On: A Social History of Concord Seating Furniture; Musketaquid to Concord: The Native & European Experience; Native American Source Book: A Teacher's Guide to New England Natives; The Concord Museum: Decorative Arts from a New England Collection
Activities: Classes for adults & children; docent training; lect open to public; 8 vis lectr per year; concerts; gallery talks; tours; museum shop sells books, reproductions, prints, slides, gift items and crafts made by local craftspeople which compliment the museum collection

L **Library,** 200 Lexington Rd, 01742. Tel 508-369-9763; FAX 508-369-9660; *Cur* David Wood
Open to members only for research
Purchases: American Decorative Arts
Library Holdings: Vols 800; Per subs 14
Special Subjects: Decorative Arts, Concord Collection, Costumes, Early American Decorative Arts

A **LOUISA MAY ALCOTT MEMORIAL ASSOCIATION,** Orchard House, 399 Lexington Rd, PO Box 343, 01742. Tel 508-369-4118; *Dir* Stephanie Upton; *Asst Dir* Cara Shapiro; *Cur* Heather Wager
Open Apr - Oct Mon - Sat 10 AM - 4:30 PM, Sun 1 - 4:30 PM, Nov - Mar Mon - Fri 11 AM - 3 PM, Sat 10 AM - 4:30 PM, Sun 1 - 4:30 PM, cl Easter, Thanksgiving, Christmas & Jan 1 - 15. Admis adults $5.50, senior citizens/students $4.50, children $3.50. Estab 1911, preservation of house & family effects for educational purposes. Historic House Museum. Maintains reference library. Average Annual Attendance: 30,000. Mem: 500; dues family $40, individual $25
Income: Financed by mem, admis, gift shop sales, donations & grants
Collections: Books & photographs of Alcott's; Household furnishings; House where Little Women was written; May Alcott's paintings & sketches
Publications: Exhibit catalogs
Activities: Classes for adults & children; dramatic programs; docent training; lect open to public, 5 vis lectr per year; tours; competitions with prizes; original objects of art lent to other museums; lending collection contains books, original art works, original prints, paintings, photographs & sculpture; sales shop sells books, magazines, prints & exclusive reproductions

CUMMINGTON

M **TOWN OF CUMMINGTON HISTORICAL COMMISSION,** Kingman Tavern Historical Museum, 42 Main St, 01026. Tel 413-634-5335; *Chmn* Merrie Bergmann; *Archivist* Daphne Morris; *VChmn* Stephen Howes
Open 2 - 5 PM, Sat July & Aug by appointment. Admis donation suggested. Estab 1968 to have & display artifacts of Cummington & locality. 17 rm house with artifacts of Cummington & area including 17 miniature rms, two flr barn, tools, equipment, carriage shed, cider mill. Average Annual Attendance: 300. Mem: 7, appointed by selectmen
Income: $5000 (financed by endowment & donations)
Publications: Only One Cummington, history of Cummington
Activities: Demonstrators; sales shop sells books & souvenirs

DEERFIELD

M **HISTORIC DEERFIELD, INC,** The Street, PO Box 321, 01342. Tel 413-774-5581; FAX 413-773-7415; *Pres* Henry N Flynt Jr; *VPres* Jeptha H Wade; *Exec Dir & Secy* Donald R Friary; *VPres* Mary Maples Dunn; *Dir Acad Progs* Kenneth Hafertepe; *Business Mgr* Carol Wenzel; *Deputy Dir & Cur* Philip Zea
Open Mon - Sun 9:30 AM - 4:30 PM. Admis adult $12, children $6. Estab 1952 to collect, study & interpret artifacts related to the history of Deerfield, the culture of the Connecticut Valley & the arts in early American life. Maintains 14 historic house museums. Average Annual Attendance: 45,000. Mem: dues $35; annual meeting 2nd or 3rd Sun in Oct
Income: $1,923,527 (financed by endowment, mem, rental, royalty & museum store income)
Purchases: $163,694
Collections: †American & English silver; †American & European textiles & costume; †American needlework; †American pewter; †Chinese export porcelain; †early American household objects; †early American paintings & prints; †early New England furniture; †English ceramics
Publications: Historical Deerfield Quarterly; Annual Report
Activities: Educ dept; lect open to public, 17 vis lectr per year; gallery talks; tours; scholarships & fels; museum shop sells books, reproductions, slides & local crafts
L **Henry N Flynt Library,** 6 Memorial St, PO Box 53, 01342. Tel 413-774-5581, Ext 125; FAX 413-773-7415; *Librn* David C Bosse; *Assoc Librn* Sharman Prouty; *Library Aide* Shirley Majewski
Open Mon - Fri 8:30 AM - 5 PM. Estab 1970 to support research on local history & genealogy & the museum collections; also for staff training. For reference & research
Income: Grants & Historic Deerfield budget
Purchases: 1000 vols per year
Library Holdings: Vols 17,400; Per subs 57; Micro — Cards, fiche, reels 550; AV — A-tapes, cassettes, fs, v-tapes 25; Other — Clipping files, exhibition catalogs, manuscripts, pamphlets
Special Subjects: Architecture, Ceramics, Decorative Arts, Folk Art, Furniture, Glass, Historical Material, Landscape Architecture, Landscapes, Painting - American, Porcelain, Pottery, Silver, Silversmithing, Textiles
Collections: †Decorative Arts; †Works dealing with the Connecticut River Valley
Publications: Research at Deerfield, An Introduction to the Memorial Libraries, irregular
Activities: Museum sales shop sells books, reproductions, prints & slides

A **POCUMTUCK VALLEY MEMORIAL ASSOCIATION,** Memorial Hall, Memorial St, PO Box 428, 01342. Tel 413-774-7476; *Pres* Amelia Miller; *Secy* Donald Frizzle; *Dir* Timothy C Neumann; *Cur* Suzanne Flint
Open May 1 - Oct 31 Mon - Sun 10 AM - 4:30 PM. Admis adults $2, students $1.50, children (6-12) $.75, tour $1. Estab 1870 to collect the art & other cultural artifacts of Connecticut River Valley & western Massachusetts. Maintains 15 galleries. Average Annual Attendance: 17,000. Mem: 800; dues $10; annual meeting last Tues in Feb
Income: $400,000 (financed by endowment, mem, sales & fundraising)
Collections: Folk art; furniture; Indian artifacts; paintings; pewter; textiles; tools; toys; dolls
Publications: PVMA Newsletter, quarterly
Activities: Classes for children; lect open to the public; concerts; tours; artmobile; individual paintings & original objects of art lent to other museums; lending collection contains original art works, original prints, paintings & artifacts; museum shop sells books, original art, reproductions & slides

DUXBURY

M ART COMPLEX MUSEUM, 189 Alden St, PO Box 2814, 02331. Tel 617-934-6634; FAX 617-934-5117; *Mus Dir* Charles A Weyerhaeuser; *Cur Colls* Nancy Whipple Grinnell; *Communications Coordr* Bonnie Jernigan; *Educ Coordr* Diane Muliero; *Preparator* Laura Brown; *Cur Exhib* Lisa Greenberg; *Office Mgr* Patricia O'Donnell
Open Wed - Sun 1 - 4 PM. No admis fee. Estab 1971 as a center for the arts. Average Annual Attendance: 10,000
Income: Financed by endowment
Collections: American paintings, prints & sculpture; European paintings & prints; Asian art; Native American art; Shaker furniture
Publications: Complexities (newsletters); exhibit catalogues
Activities: Educ dept; workshops for children & adults; docent training; lect open to public; concerts; gallery talks; tours of vis groups; individual art works lent to other institutions

L Library, 189 Alden St, PO Box 2814, 02331. Tel 617-934-6634;
Open to the pub for reference
Income: Financed by endowment
Library Holdings: Vols 5000; Per subs 20; AV — Slides, v-tapes; Other — Clipping files, exhibition catalogs, pamphlets
Special Subjects: Asian Art, Prints, American Art, Shakers
Activities: Docent reading group

ESSEX

M ESSEX HISTORICAL SOCIETY, Essex Shipbuilding Museum, 28 Main St, PO Box 277, 01929. Tel 508-768-7541; *Cur* James Witham; *Pres* John D Cushing; *Historian* Dana A Story; *Treas* Charlotte Bengston
Open Mon, Thurs - Sat 11 AM - 4 PM, Sun 1 - 4 PM. Admis $3, senior citizens $2.50, children 6-12 $2, members & Essex residents free. Estab 1976 to preserve & interpret Essex history with special emphasis on its shipbuilding industry. Average Annual Attendance: 4500. Mem: 525; dues $15, annual meeting second Tues in May
Income: $55,000 (financed by endowment, mem, business, individual contributions & grants)
Purchases: $11,500 (climate control & Macintosh printer); $350,000 (story shipyard site)
Collections: Collection of shipbuilding tools, documents, paintings, plans & photographs, models-both scale & builders; fishing schooner hull; shipyard site 300 years old
Exhibitions: Five rigged ship models & 15 builder's models on loan from the Smithsonian Institution's Watercraft Collection; Frame-Up (on going); Caulker's Art (on going).
Publications: A list of vessels, boats & other craft built in the town of Essex 1860-1980, a complete inventory of the Ancient Burying Ground of Essex 1680-1868; Essex Electrics, 1981; Dubbing, Hooping & Lofting, 1981
Activities: Classes for adults & children; docent training; lect open to public, 5-7 vis lectr per year; gallery talks; tours; exten dept lends paintings, art objects, tools & models; museum shop sells books, prints, original art, reproductions, & audio-video cassettes, t-shirts, models, plans, magazines & notecards

FALL RIVER

M FALL RIVER HISTORICAL SOCIETY, 451 Rock St, 02720. Tel 508-679-1071; *Cur* Michael Martins; *Pres* Elizabeth Denning; *VPres* Andrew Mann Lizak
Open Tues - Fri 9 AM - 4:30 PM, Sat & Sun 2 - 4 PM. Admis adult $3, children under 12 $1.50. Estab 1921 to preserve the social & economic history of Fall River. Average Annual Attendance: 6000. Mem: 659; dues $20
Income: Financed by endowment, mem
Collections: †Fall River School Still Life Paintings & Portraits; Antonio Jacobsen marine paintings; †Period costumes, furs, fans; †Victorian furnishings & decorative arts; Victorian Decorative Stenceling: A Lost Art Revived
Exhibitions: Victorian Decorative Stenceling: A Lost Art Revived; More Than Just Mourning: Fashionable Black in the Collection of the Fall River Historical Society
Activities: Small private tours for local schools; lect open to public, 4 vis lectr per year; individual paintings lent; shop sells books, prints, postcards, paperweights

FITCHBURG

M FITCHBURG ART MUSEUM, 185 Elm St, 01420. Tel 508-345-4207; *Pres* Georgia Barnhill; *VPres* Andre Gelinas; *Dir* Peter Timms; *Prog Coordr* Mary Ann Menger; *Treas* Parker Rice; *Dir of Docents* Ursula Pitman; *Bus Mgr* Sheryl Demers
Open Tues - Sat 11 AM - 4 PM, Sun 1 - 4 PM. Admis fee $3. Estab 1925. Three building complex incl two museums, with eight large galleries & two entrance halls & one administration building. Average Annual Attendance: 20,000. Mem: 1300; dues $25 - 1000; annual meeting Dec
Income: Financed by endowment & mem
Collections: †Drawings, †paintings & †prints; †A Walk Through The Ancient World (household & sacred articles from ancient cultures)
Publications: Exhibitions catalogs; event notices
Activities: Classes for adults & children; docent training; lect open to public, 12 vis lectr per year; gallery talks; tours; competitions with awards; scholarships; individual paintings & original objects of art lent to colleges & museums

M FITCHBURG HISTORICAL SOCIETY, 50 Grove St, PO Box 953, 01420-0953. Tel 508-345-1157; *Exec Dir* Ruth Penka
Open Mon 10 AM - 4 PM, 6 - 9 PM, Tues - Thurs 10 AM - 4 PM, Sept - June Sun 2 - 4 PM. Admis members free, non-members $2. Estab 1892 to preserve & transmit local history. Three floors of Fitchburg items. Mem: 450; dues individual $15, family $25, $50 & $100; annual meeting third Mon in May
Income: Financed by endowment & mem
Collections: Books, printed items, artifacts of all kinds made in or living in Fitchburg
Exhibitions: Fitchburg artifacts (some permanently displayed, others changing)
Publications: Newsletter, 5 per year
Activities: Lect open to public, 6 vis lectr per year; gallery talks; tours; competitions

FRAMINGHAM

M DANFORTH MUSEUM OF ART, 123 Union Ave, 01702. Tel 508-620-0050; *Dir* Linda Stegleder; *Assoc Dir Develop & Membership* Rika Clement; *Educ Coordr* Ann I Person; *Financial Dir* Antionette Matisoo; *Mus School Dir* Beverly Snow; *Assoc Dir Develop* Lisa Poller
Open Wed - Sun Noon - 5 PM, cl first three wks of Aug each yr. Admis adults $3, students & senior citizens $2, children free. Estab 1975 to provide fine arts & art-related activities to people of all ages in the South Middlesex area. There are seven galleries, including a children's gallery with hands-on activities. Average Annual Attendance: 30,000. Mem: 1000; dues vary from $15-$45, annual meeting in Oct
Income: Financed by mem, Framingham Sate College & Town of Framingham, federal & state grants; foundations & corporate support
Collections: †Old master & contemporary prints, drawings & photography; †19th & 20th centuries American paintings; African & Oceanic art
Exhibitions: Varied program of changing exhibitions, traveling shows, selections from the permanent collection, in a variety of periods, styles & media
Publications: Newsletter; exhibition brochures & catalogues, museum school brochure
Activities: Classes for adults & children; docent training; programs for area schools; lect open to public; concerts; gallery talks; tours; trips; book traveling exhibitions 2-3 per year; originate traveling exhibitions to other museums & galleries nationally; museum shop sells publications, original art, prints, art glass, crafts, jewelry & ceramics; junior gallery

L Library, 123 Union Ave, 01701. Tel 508-620-0050; *Dir* Linda Stegleder
Open Wed - Sun Noon - 5 PM. Estab 1975 as an educational resource of art books & catalogues. For reference only; research as requested
Library Holdings: Vols 4500; Other — Clipping files, exhibition catalogs, pamphlets
Special Subjects: Rare & Valuable Books; Whistler Books & Catalogues
Collections: Bibliographies for the museum exhibitions; museum school book collection

GARDNER

M MOUNT WACHUSETT COMMUNITY COLLEGE, Art Galleries, 444 Green St, 01440. Tel 508-632-6600, Ext 168; *Chmn Dept Art* Jean C Tandy; *Dir Fine Arts Gallery* Gene Cauthen
Open Mon - Thurs 8 AM - 9 PM, Fri 8 AM - 5 PM. No admis fee. Estab 1971 to supply resources for a two-year art curriculum; develop an art collection. Well-lighted gallery with skylights & track lighting, white panelled walls; two open, spacious levels with Welsh tile floors. Average Annual Attendance: 8000-10,000
Income: Financed by city & state appropriations
Purchases: Pottery by Makato Yabe, print by Bob Boy, 17 student paintings, ten student prints, five student ceramic works, eight student sculpture, two bronze works
Collections: †Approximately 100 works; framed color art posters & reproductions; prints; ceramic pieces; student collection
Exhibitions: Annual student competition of painting, sculpture, drawing, ceramics, printmaking; local, national & international artists & former students' works
Publications: Annual brochure
Activities: Lect open to public, 8-10 vis lectr per year; gallery talks; tours; competitions with awards; exten dept serves Mount Wachussett

L Library, 444 Green St, 01440. Tel 508-632-6600, Ext 126; FAX 508-632-1210; *Dir* Linda R Oldach; *Asst Librn* Christina Coolidge
Open Mon - Thurs 8 AM - 9:30 PM, Fri 8 AM - 5 PM, Sun 2 - 6 PM (when school is in session). Estab 1964. Circ 12,998
Income: Financed by state appropriation
Library Holdings: Vols 70,000; Per subs 325; Micro — Fiche, reels; AV — Cassettes, fs, rec, slides; Other — Memorabilia, pamphlets
Exhibitions: Periodic exhibitions

GLENDALE

M NATIONAL TRUST FOR HISTORIC PRESERVATION, Chesterwood Museum, 4 Williamsville Rd (Mailing add: PO Box 827, Stockbridge, 01262-0827). Tel 413-298-3579; FAX 413-298-3973; *Dir* Paul W Ivory
Open daily 10 AM - 5 PM, May 1 through Oct 31. Admis adults $7, children 13-18 $3.50, 6-12 $1.50, National Trust & Friends of Chesterwood members free; group rates available by advanced arrangement. Estab 1955 to preserve & present the summer home & studio of Daniel Chester French. Chesterwood, a National Trust Historic Site, was the former estate of Daniel Chester French (1850-1931), sculptor of the Lincoln Memorial, Minute Man & Leading figure the American Renaissance. The 150 acre property includes: French's Studio (1898) & Residence (1900-1901), both designed by Henry Bacon, architect of the Lincoln Memorial; Barn Gallery, a c1825 barn adapted for use as exhibition space, a museum gift shop in a c1925 garage & country estate garden with woodland walk laid out by French. Average Annual Attendance: 33,000. Mem: 155,000; individual dues $25
Collections: Decorative arts, memorabilia, plaster models, marble & bronze casts of French's work & paintings
Exhibitions: Annual Outdoor Contemporary Sculpture Exhibition; Annual Antique Car Show; Christmas at Chesterwood; special exhibits dealing with aspects of historic preservation in the Berkshire region & French's life, career, social & artistic milieu & summer estate
Publications: The Pedestal, quarterly newsletter
Activities: College intern programs; volunteer & guide training; lect open to public; gallery talks; tours; museum shop sells books, cards, reproductions & gift items

L Chesterwood Museum Archives, 4 Williamsville Rd (Mailing add: Glendale Rd, PO Box 827, Stockbridge, 01262-0827). Tel 413-298-3579; *Archivist* Wanda Magdeleine Styka
Open by appointment only. Estab 1969. Library consists of books on sculpture, historic preservation, decorative arts, history of art, architecture, garden & landscape design, including books collected personally by sculptor Daniel Chester French, Mary Adams French (wife) & Margaret French Cresson (daughter) as well as archival material; serves art, social, landscape & architectural historians & historic preservationists
Library Holdings: Vols 5000; Per subs 5; Micro — Reels; AV — A-tapes, cassettes, lantern slides, motion pictures, slides, v-tapes; Other — Clipping files, exhibition catalogs, manuscripts, memorabilia, original art works, pamphlets, photographs, prints, sculpture
Special Subjects: Architecture, Art History, Coins & Medals, Bronzes, Decorative Arts, Furniture, Historical Material, History of Art & Archaeology, Landscape Architecture, Painting - American, Period Rooms, Photography, Portraits, Restoration & Conservation, Sculpture, Chesterwood, late 19th & early 20th centuries classical sculpture, Lincoln Memorial, American Renaissance, Country Place Era
Collections: Oral histories: Daniel Chester French & his summer estate Chesterwood; blueprints & plans of sculpture commissions & of Chesterwood; period photographs of French & his family, summer estate & sculptures; papers, correspondence, photograph albums & scrapbooks of D C French & Margaret French Cresson, sculptor, writer & preservationist; literary manuscripts of Mary Adams French
Publications: The Chesterwood Pedestal, newsletter 4 times a year; educational brochures; annual exhibit catalogues
Activities: Intern archivist program

GLOUCESTER

M CAPE ANN HISTORICAL MUSEUM, 27 Pleasant St, 01930. Tel 508-283-0455; *Dir* Judith McCulloch
Open Tues - Sat 10 AM - 5 PM, cl Feb. Admis adults $3.50, senior citizens $3, students $2 & members free. Estab 1873 to foster appreciation of the quality & diversity of life on Cape Ann past & present. Fine arts, decorative arts & American furniture; Fisheries/maritime galleries; granite industry gallery; 1804 furnished house; maintains reference library. Average Annual Attendance: 10, 000. Mem: 1700; dues $15-$1000
Collections: Fitz Hugh Lane Collection, paintings
Activities: Lect open to public, 3-4 vis lectr per year; individual paintings & original objects of art lent to museums, galleries & local businesses; museum shop sells books, magazines, reproductions, prints, slides, jewelry, postcards & note papers
L Library, 27 Pleasant St, 01930. *Dir* Judith McCulloch
Estab 1876. Reference only
Library Holdings: Vols 2000; AV — Motion pictures, rec; Other — Clipping files, exhibition catalogs, manuscripts, memorabilia, original art works, pamphlets, photographs, prints, reproductions, sculpture
Special Subjects: Art History, Decorative Arts, Historical Material, Manuscripts, Maps, Marine Painting, Painting - American, Period Rooms, Photography, Porcelain, Portraits, Sculpture, Silver, Watercolors

M HAMMOND CASTLE MUSEUM, 80 Hesperus Ave, 01930. Tel 508-283-2080, 283-2081, 283-7673; *Exec Dir & Cur* John W Pettibone
Open daily June - Aug 10 AM - 5 PM, weekends Sept - May 10 AM - 5 PM. Admis adults $6, sr & students $5, children between 4 & 12 $4. Estab 1931 by a famous inventor, John Hays Hammond Jr. Incorporated in 1938 for the public exhibition of authentic works of art, architecture and specimens of antiquarian value and to encourage and promote better education in the fine arts, with particular reference to purity of design and style. Built in style of a medieval castle with Great Hall, courtyard and period rooms, Dr Hammond combined elements of Roman, Medieval and Renaissance periods in his attempt to recreate an atmosphere of European beauty. Average Annual Attendance: 60,000
Income: Financed by tours, concerts, special events & rentals
Collections: Rare collection of European artifacts; Roman, Medieval and Renaissance Periods
Publications: Exhibition catalogs; Hammond Biography
Activities: Classes for children; docent training; educational & teacher workshops; lect open to public; concerts; self guided & group tours; exten dept servs neighboring schools; sales shop sells books, reproductions, crafts, jewelry, art cards & postcards

A NORTH SHORE ARTS ASSOCIATION, INC, Art Gallery, Rear 197 E Main St, 01930. Tel 508-283-1857; *Pres* Tom O'Keefe; *VPres* Harold Kloongian; *Treas* Carleen Muniz; *Gallery Mgr* Ruth A Brown
Open daily 10 AM - 5 PM, Sun 1 - 5 PM, June - Aug & Sept - mid Oct. No admis fee. Estab 1923 by the Cape Ann Artists to promote American art by exhibitions. Gallery owned by association; maintains reference library. Average Annual Attendance: 4000. Mem: 350; dues artist $40, patron $20, associate $15; annual meeting in Aug
Income: Financed by dues, contributions & rentals
Collections: Member paintings
Publications: Calendar of Events
Activities: Classes for adults & children; docent training; lect open to public, 3 vis lectr per year; concerts; gallery talks; tours; awards given; museum shop sells magazines, original art & artists cards

GREAT BARRINGTON

M SIMON'S ROCK COLLEGE OF BARD, 84 Alford Rd, 01230. Tel 413-528-0771; FAX 413-528-7365; Elec Mail wjackson@simons-rock.edu. *Chmn Art Dept* Bill Jackson
Open Mon - Thurs 8 AM - Midnight, Fri 8 AM - 9 PM, Sat Noon - 9 PM, Sun Noon - Midnight. No admis fee. Estab 1964 as a liberal arts college
Exhibitions: A continuing exhibition program of professional & student works in

drawing, painting, graphics, sculpture & crafts; Graphic Design Workshop of Simon's Rock (poster); Barbara Baranowska (photographs); Jim Cave (prints); Peter Homestead (sculpture); Tom Shepard (sculpture & drawings); Evan Stoller (sculpture); Niki Berg (photograph); Dennis Connors (sculpture); Cynthia Picchi (painting); Lyalya (painting & sculpture); Nick Farina (photography); Richard Webb (painting); William Jackson (sculpture); Jane Palmer (ceramics); Arthur Hillman (prints); The African-Afro-American Connection (photos); Brigitte Keller (painting); Harriet Eisner (painting); Linda Kaye-Moses (jewelry); Taff Fitterer (painting)
Activities: Gallery talks; tours
L Library, 84 Alford Rd, 01230. Tel 413-528-7274; Elec Mail goodkind@simons_rock.edu. *Librn* Joan Goodkind
Library Holdings: Vols 60,000; Per subs 300; Micro — Fiche, reels; AV — Cassettes, rec
Exhibitions: In the Atrium Gallery, exhibits change monthly

HADLEY

M PORTER-PHELPS-HUNTINGTON FOUNDATION, INC, Historic House Museum, 130 River Dr, 01035. Tel 413-584-4699; *Exec Dir* Susan J Lisk; *Pres* Peter G Wells; *VPres* Elizabeth Carlisle
Open May 15 - Oct 15 Sat - Wed 1 - 4:30 PM. Admis fee $4, children under 12 $1. Estab 1955. Historic house built in 1752; twelve rooms house the accumulated belongings of ten generations of one family; carriage house; corn barn; historic gardens; sunken garden. Average Annual Attendance: 5500. Mem: 500; dues $25-$500; annual meeting in Nov
Income: $65,000 (financed by endowment, grants, programs & mem)
Collections: Porter-Phelps-Huntington family collection of 17th, 18th & 19th century furniture, paintings, papers, decorative arts; clothing collection; archives at Amherst
Publications: Annual report; Forty Acres, newsletter, quarterly
Activities: Dramatic programs; lect open to public, 1 vis lectr per year; concerts; tours; individual paintings & objects of art lent to other museums; museum shop sells books, cards & pamphlets

HARVARD

M FRUITLANDS MUSEUM, INC, 102 Prospect Hill Rd, 01451. Tel 508-456-3924; FAX 508-456-9393; *Dir* Robert D Farwell; *Asst to Dir* Joanne Myers; *Cur* Michael Volinar
Open mid-May - mid-Oct Tues - Sun 10 AM - 5 PM, cl Mon. Admis adults $6, students $4, ages 7-16 $3. Estab 1914, incorporated 1930 by Clara Endicott Sears. Fruitlands was the scene of Bronson Alcott's Utopian experiment in community living. The Fruitlands Farmhouse contains furniture, household articles, pictures, handicrafts, books & valuable manuscript collection of Alcott, Lane & Transcendental group. The Shaker House, built in 1794 by the members of the former Harvard Shaker Village, was originally used as an office. Moved to its present location, it now forms the setting for the products of Shaker Handicrafts & Community Industries. American Indian museum contains ethnological exhibits. Picture gallery contains portraits by itinerant artists of the first half of the 19th century & landscapes by Hudson River School. Average Annual Attendance: 18,000. Mem: 650; schedule of mem fees; annual meeting in June
Income: Financed by earned income, Sears Trust, mem fees, gifts & grants
Purchases: Books, paintings & ethnographic materials
Publications: Under the Mulberry Tree, quarterly
Activities: Docent training; lect open to public, 2-4 vis lectr per year; concerts; individual & original objects of art lent to other museums in the area; lending collection includes original art works, prints, paintings; book traveling exhibitions; museum shop sells books, magazines, reproductions & prints
L Library, 102 Prospect Hill Rd, 01451. Tel 508-456-3924; *Dir* Robert D Farwell
Open year round by appointment. Estab 1914 for staff resource & scholarly research
Library Holdings: Vols 10,000; Per subs 10; Micro — Reels; AV — Fs, motion pictures, rec, slides, v-tapes; Other — Manuscripts, memorabilia, original art works, photographs
Special Subjects: Art History, Transcendental Movement, Shakers, American Indian North of Mexico

HAVERHILL

L HAVERHILL PUBLIC LIBRARY, Art Dept, 99 Main St, 01830. Tel 508-373-1586
Open Mon, Thurs & Sat 10 AM - 1 PM & 2 - 5 PM, Mon & Tues 6 - 9 PM, cl Fri & Sun. Estab 1873
Income: Financed by private endowment
Library Holdings: Vols 8600; Per subs 16; AV — A-tapes, cassettes, fs, Kodachromes, lantern slides, motion pictures, v-tapes; Other — Clipping files, manuscripts, original art works, photographs, prints, sculpture
Special Subjects: Manuscripts, Photography, Prints
Collections: Illuminated manuscripts; mid-19th century photographs, work by Beato and Robertson, Bourne, Frith, Gardner, Naya, O'Sullivan, and others; small group of paintings including Joseph A Ames, †Henry Bacon, †Sidney M Chase, †William S Haseltine, Thomas Hill, Harrison Plummer, Winfield Scott Thomas, Robert Wade
Exhibitions: Matthew Brady, photographer, from the National Portrait Gallery
Publications: Architectural Heritage of Haverhill
Activities: Slide presentations; lect open to public; concerts; periodic films

HOLYOKE

M **WISTARIAHURST MUSEUM,** 238 Cabot St, 01040. Tel 413-534-2216; FAX 413-534-2344; *Chmn Holyoke Historical Commission* Jill Hodnicki; *Dir* Sandra Christoforidis
Open Wed - Sun 1 - 5 PM, cl national & state holidays. Admis adult $2, sr citizen $1.50, members & children under 12 free. Historic house museum estab to show history of Holyoke 1850-1930. Sponsored by the City of Holyoke under the jurisdiction of the Holyoke Historical Commission. Average Annual Attendance: 8000. Mem: annual meeting May
Income: $73,963 (financed by city appropriation)
Collections: Late 19th & early 20th centuries furniture, paintings, prints, decorative arts & architectural details; period rooms; natural history & native Armenian ethno-graphic material
Activities: Workshops, courses & special programs for adults & children; contemporary art exhibits and historic exhibits; gallery talks; lectures; concerts; special events and holiday programs; group and school tours

LEXINGTON

M **MUSEUM OF OUR NATIONAL HERITAGE,** * 33 Marrett Rd, PO Box 519, 02173. Tel 617-861-6559; *Dir* Thomas Lovett; *Dir Educ* Robert MacKay; *Cur of Exhibits* Cara Sutherland; *Gen Servs* June Cobb; *Cur Colls* John Hamilton; *Designer* Serena Furman
Open Mon - Sun 10 AM - 5 PM. No admis fee. Estab 1972 as an American history museum, including art and decorative art. Five modern galleries for changing exhibits, flexible lighting & climate control. Two galleries of 3000 sq ft, two 1500 sq ft, atrium area used for print & photo exhibits. Average Annual Attendance: 60,000. Mem: 200; dues friend for life $250, family $20, individual $15
Income: $1,500,000 (financed by endowment & appeal to Masons)
Collections: General American & American Paints; American decorative art; objects decorated with Masonic, patriotic & fraternal symbolism
Publications: Exhibition catalogs
Activities: Docent training; lect open to public; concerts; gallery talks; tours for school groups; paintings and art objects lent; originate traveling exhibitions; museum shop sells books and a variety of gift items related to exhibit program

LINCOLN

M **DECORDOVA MUSEUM & SCULPTURE PARK,** 51 Sandy Pond Rd, 01773-2600. Tel 617-259-8355; FAX 617-259-8249; *Dir* Paul Master-Karnik; *Assoc Dir Develop* Denise Trapani; *Cur* Rachel Lafo; *Pub Relations Dir* Michael Sockol; *Assoc Dir Educ* Eleanor Lazarus
Open Tues - Sun Noon - 5 PM. Admis adults $4, 6-21 & senior citizens $3, students & members free. Estab 1948 to exhibit, to interpret, collect & preserve modern & contemporary American art. 8000 sq ft is broken into five galleries. Average Annual Attendance: 95,000. Mem: 2500; dues $35-$1000
Income: $2,500,000 (financed by endowment, individual/corporate mem, foundation & government grants)
Purchases: $60,000
Collections: American art; 20th century American painting, graphics, sculpture & photography; emphasis on artists associated with New England
Publications: Exhibition catalogs; newsletter
Activities: Classes for adults & children; docent training; lect open to public; concerts; gallery talks; guided tours; arts festivals; outreach programs; individual paintings & original objects of art lent to corporate program members; book traveling exhibitions 2-3 per year; originate traveling exhibitions; museum shop sells books, magazines, original art, art supplies & contemporary crafts
L **DeCordova Museum Library,** 51 Sandy Pond Rd, 01773-2600. Tel 617-259-8355; FAX 617-259-3650;
Internet Home Page Address http//www.decordova.org. *Librn* Barbara Stecker
Open Tues - Sun Noon - 5 PM for visitors of the mus only. For reference only. Average Annual Attendance: 80,000
Library Holdings: Vols 3000; Per subs 10; Museum catalogs; Other — Exhibition catalogs
Special Subjects: Fine Arts & Studio Arts, 20th Century Contemporary Art

LOWELL

M **AMERICAN TEXTILE HISTORY MUSEUM** (Formerly Museum of American Textile History), 491 Dutton St, 01854. Tel 508-441-0400; FAX 508-441-1412; *Pres* Edward B Stevens; *Dir* Paul Rivard; *Cur* Diane Fagan-Affleck; *Textile Conservator* Deirdre Windsor Bailey
Estab 1960 to preserve artifacts, documents & pictorial descriptions of the American textile industry & related development abroad
Income: Financed by endowment
Collections: Hand looms, industrial machinery, spinning wheels, textile collection; books, manuscripts, prints & photographs
Exhibitions: Textiles in America
Publications: Exhibition catalogs; Linen Making in America
Activities: Classes for adults; docent training; tours; competitions; lending collection contains slides; sales desk sells textiles, books, prints & postcards
L **Library,** 491 Dutton St, 01854. Tel 508-441-0400; FAX 508-441-1412; *Librn* Clare Sheridan
Open by appointment. For reference only
Income: Financed by endowment
Library Holdings: Vols 25,000; Per subs 56; Ephemera; Original documents; Trade literature; Micro — Reels; AV — Motion pictures; Other — Exhibition catalogs, manuscripts, memorabilia, original art works, pamphlets, photographs, prints, reproductions, sculpture
Special Subjects: History of Textile Industry, Textile Design & Manufacturing, Textile Mill Architecture
Publications: Checklist of prints and manuscripts

M **THE BRUSH ART GALLERY & STUDIOS,** 256 Market St, 01852. Tel 508-459-7819; *Exec Dir* E Linda Poras
Estab 1982. Non-profit; in national historic park. Gallery with changing exhibitions plus 13 artist studios. Average Annual Attendance: 200,000. Mem: dues $25-$40
Income: Financed by mem, grants, fundraising & sales
Activities: Classes for adults & children; lect open to public; scholarships offered; sales shop sells original art

A **WHISTLER HOUSE MUSEUM OF ART** (Formerly Lowell Art Association), 243 Worthen St, 01852. Tel 508-452-7641; *Exec Dir* Flavia Cigliano
Open Wed - Fri 11 AM - 4 PM & Sun 1 - 4 PM, cl Mon. Admis $3. Estab 1878 to preserve the birthplace of James McNeil Whistler; to promote the arts in all its phases & to maintain a center for the cultural benefit of all the citizens of the community. Average Annual Attendance: 5000. Mem: 500; dues adults $25, senior citizens & students $15
Income: Financed by endowment, mem, admis, grants & earned income
Collections: Mid 19th through early 20th century American Art: Hibbard, Benson, Noyes, Spear, Paxton, Phelps; Whistler etchings & lithographs
Exhibitions: Galleries of works from permanent collection & periodic exhibits by contemporary artists
Publications: Brochures; S P Howes: Portrait Painter, catalog
Activities: Classes for adults & children; docent training; lect open to public, 3 vis lectr per year; concerts; gallery talks; tours; programs of historical interest; book traveling exhibitions 1-2 per year; originate traveling exhibitions to small museums & schools; museum shop sells books, original art, reproductions, prints & postcards

MALDEN

L **MALDEN PUBLIC LIBRARY,** Art Dept & Gallery, 36 Salem St, 02148. Tel 617-324-0218; FAX 617-324-4467; *Librn* Dina G Malgeri
Open Mon - Thurs 9 AM - 9 PM, Fri & Sat 9 AM - 6 PM, cl Sun & holidays, cl Sat during summer months. Estab 1879, incorporated 1885 as a public library and art gallery. Maintains an art department with three galleries. Circ 239,493
Income: $421,530 (financed by endowment, city and state appropriations)
Purchases: $91,000
Library Holdings: Other — Exhibition catalogs, framed reproductions, manuscripts, memorabilia, original art works, pamphlets, photographs, prints, reproductions, sculpture
Publications: Thirty Paintings in the Malden Collection (art catalog); annual report; art reproduction note cards
Activities: Lect open to public, 6-12 vis lectr per year; concerts; gallery talks; tours

MARBLEHEAD

A **MARBLEHEAD ARTS ASSOCIATION, INC,** King Hooper Mansion, 8 Hooper St, 01945. Tel 617-631-2608; *Pres* Pat Richwagen; *Exec Dir* Nancy Fergusen
Open Mon - Sat 10 AM - 4 PM, Sun 1 - 5 PM. Admis free donations only for tours, no admis to art galleries. Estab 1922. Owns & occupies the historic King Hooper Mansion, located in historic Marblehead. Contains fine paneling, ballroom, gallery & garden by Shurclif. Maintains an art gallery. Mem: 500 assoc members; mem upon application (open); dues family $25, individual $20; annual meeting in June
Income: Financed by mem & mansion rentals
Publications: Newsletter, monthly
Activities: Classes for adults & children; lect open to public; concerts; gallery talks; tours competitions with cash & ribbon awards

A **MARBLEHEAD HISTORICAL SOCIETY,** 161 Washington St, PO Box 1048, 01945. Tel 617-631-1069; *Admin Dir* Donald Gardner
Open mid-May - Oct Mon - Sat 10 AM - 4 PM, Sun 1 - 4 PM. Admis $4. Estab 1898, incorporated 1902 for the preservation of Lee Mansion & historical material & records of Marblehead. Georgian mansion built in 1768 with elegant rococo interior carving & original hand-painted wallpaper. Average Annual Attendance: 3000. Mem: 600; dues based on sliding scale
Income: Financed by endowment, mem & admis
Collections: Ceramics, documents, folk art, furniture, glass, military items, nautical items, portraits, ship paintings
Activities: Lect open to public, 4 vis lectr per year; sales shop sells books, prints & postcards
L **Library,** 161 Washington, PO Box 1048, 01945. Tel 617-631-1069; *Historian* Janice Rideout; *Research* Karen MacInnis
Open Mon - Fri 10 AM - 4 PM. Admis non-members $3, members free. Estab 1898 to collect & maintain artifacts of Marblehead history. No galleries. Art & decorative art displayed in historic 1768 mansion. Average Annual Attendance: 4000. Mem: 850; dues $15-$100
Special Subjects: Historical Material, Manuscripts, Local history
Collections: Art, artifacts, furniture & documents pertaining to Marblehead
Publications: Members semiannual newsletter
Activities: Classes for adults & children; docent training; lect open to public, 3 vis lectr per year; tours; sales shop sells books, original art, reproductions, prints & postcards

MARION

A **MARION ART CENTER,** 80 Pleasant, PO Box 602, 02738. Tel 508-748-1266; *Pres* Trudy Kingery; *Dir* Wendy Bidstrup
Open Tues - Fri 1 - 5 PM, Sat 10 AM - 2 PM. Estab 1957 to provide theater, concerts & visual arts exhibitions for the community & to provide studio art, theater arts, music & dance classes for adults & children. Two galleries, 125 ft of wall space, 500 sq ft floor space; indirect lighting; entrance off Main St. Average Annual Attendance: 2000. Mem: 650; dues patron $500, sponsor $100, family

$50, basic $25; annual meeting in Jan
Income: Financed by mem dues, donations & profit from ticket & gallery sales
Collections: Cecil Clark Davis (1877-1955), portrait paintings
Exhibitions: Monthly one person & group shows
Publications: Annual mem folder; monthly invitations to opening; monthly newsletter
Activities: Classes for adults & children; dramatic programs; lect open to public, 6 vis lectr per year; concerts; gallery talks; competitions; scholarships; student art competition held annually; awards for student art & best portfolio; sales shop sells fine crafts, small paintings, prints, cards, original art and reproductions

MEDFORD

M TUFTS UNIVERSITY, Art Gallery, Aidekman Arts Ctr, 02155. Tel 617-627-3518; *Interim Dir* Susan Masuoka
Open fall & spring semesters, Wed - Sat Noon - 8 PM, Sun Noon - 5 PM. No admis fee. Estab 1955 to display works of art by university students & faculty & special exhibitions of traditional & experimental works in all visual art media. Average Annual Attendance: 5000
Income: Financed through the Fine Arts Dept, private, corporate & foundation sources, state & federal agencies
Purchases: Roger Kizik, Animal; Danny Lyon, photographs; Paul Stopforth, oils & drawings
Collections: Primarily 19th & 20th centuries American paintings, prints & drawings; contemporary paintings, photographs & works on paper
Exhibitions: Fourteen shows annually, including thesis exhibits of candidates for the MFA degree offered by Tufts in affiliation with the School of the Boston Museum of Fine Arts; Added Dimensions; Danny Lyon: Pictures from Films/Films from Pictures; Collaborations/Rugg Road; Private Lives: Personal Narrative Painting; Chuck Close: Handmade Paper Editions; Olga Antonova, Susan Schwall & Pauna Blacklow: Three Women, Three Visions; Mitchell Gordon Exterior/Interior: Alice Neel; The Life & Art of Esphyr Slobodkina
Publications: Exhibition brochures
Activities: Lect open to pub, 1-2 vis lectr per year; gallery talks; tours; competitions; individual & original objects of art lent to locations on campus & occasionally outside sources; book traveling exhibitions

MILTON

M CAPTAIN ROBERT BENNET FORBES HOUSE, 215 Adams St, 02186. Tel 617-696-1815; *Dir* Dana D Ricciardi, PhD; *Outreach Coordr* Kerry Keser; *Exec Secy* Nadine Leary
Open Wed & Sun 1 - 4 PM, Tues & Thurs by appointment. Admis $3, sr citizens & students $1.50, children under 12 free. Estab 1964 as a Historic House museum; for preservation, research, education: 19th century through Forbes family focus. Average Annual Attendance: 1000. Mem: 400; dues life member $500, sponsor $250, donor $100, friend $50, family $30, individual $20
Income: $70,000 (financed by endowment, mem & fundraising)
Library Holdings: Vols 2500; Per subs 6; Micro — Prints; Other — Exhibition catalogs, manuscripts, memorabilia, original art works, pamphlets, photographs, prints
Collections: Abraham Lincoln Civil War Collections & Archives; Forbes Family Collection of China trade & American furnishings
Exhibitions: Annual Abraham Lincoln essay contest for grades 5 - 12
Publications: Forbes House Jottings, four times per year
Activities: Classes for adults & children; docent training; lect open to public, 3 vis lectr per year; competitions & awards; lending collection contains decorative arts, Lincoln memorabilia, original art works, original prints & sculpture; museum shop sells books, cards, gifts & prints

NANTUCKET

A ARTISTS ASSOCIATION OF NANTUCKET, PO Box 1104, 02554. Tel 508-228-0722; *Pres* Donna Tillotson; *Dir* Melissa Macleod
Open Mon - Sat 10 AM - 5 PM & 7 - 10 PM, Sun 1 - 5 PM & 7 - 10 PM. No admis fee. Estab 1945 to provide a place for Nantucket artists of all levels & styles to show their work & encourage new artists. Maintains one gallery: The Little Gallery, two floors in historic building. Average Annual Attendance: 50,000 - 70,000. Mem: 500; dues patron $50 - $500, artist $50; annual meeting Aug
Income: $75,000 - $100,000 (financed by mem, fundraising & commissions, large patron gifts)
Collections: 160 pieces, most by Nantucket artists
Exhibitions: Annual Craft Show; juried shows; changing one-person & group member shows during summer; occasional off-season shows
Publications: Monthly newsletter; annual brochure
Activities: Classes for adults & children; workshops; lect open to public, 5-6 vis lectr per year; gallery talks; competitions with awards; scholarships; individual paintings & original objects of art lent to local hospital & public offices; sales shop sells original art, prints & lithographs

M NANTUCKET HISTORICAL ASSOCIATION, Historic Nantucket, PO Box 1016, 02554. Tel 508-228-1894; FAX 508-228-5618; *Exec Dir* Jean M Weber
Open June - Oct 10 AM - 5 PM. Admis a vistor pass to all buildings, adults $10, children 5-14 $5, individual building admis $2-$5. Estab 1894 to preserve Nantucket & maintain history. Historic Nantucket is a collection of 13 buildings throughout the town, open to the pub & owned by the Natucket Historical Assoc. Together they portray the way people lived & worked as Nantucket grew from a small farming community to the center of America's whaling industry. Mem: 3000; dues families $50, individuals $30; annual meeting in July
Income: $450,000 (financed by endowment, mem & admis)
Collections: Portraits, Oil Paintings, Watercolors, Needlework Pictures & all other manner of artifacts related to Nantucket & Maritime History; all objects exhibited in our historic houses & museums which cover the period 1686-1930
Publications: Art on Nantucket; Historic Nantucket, quarterly, magazine for members

Activities: Classes for children; lect open to public; 12 vis lectr per year; tours; individual paintings lent to other museums; museum shop sells books, reproductions, prints, slides, period furniture, silver, bone & ivory scrimshaw, candles & children's toys

NEW BEDFORD

L NEW BEDFORD FREE PUBLIC LIBRARY, Art Dept, 613 Pleasant St, 02740. Tel 508-991-6275; *Dir* Terry Coish; *Dept Head Reference* Martine Hargraves; *Dept Head Genealogy & Whaling Coll* Paul Cyr; *Dept Head Technical Service* Vicki A Lukas
Open Mon 9 AM - 9 PM, Tues 9 AM - Sat 9 AM - 5 PM, Wed 9 AM - 9 PM, cl Sun & holidays. Estab 1852. Circ 399,947
Income: $1,038,291 (financed: $108,515 by endowment; $829,726 by city, $100,050 by state appropriation)
Library Holdings: Micro — Reels; AV — Cassettes, fs, motion pictures, rec, slides, v-tapes; Other — Framed reproductions, photographs
Special Subjects: American Western Art, Etchings & Engravings, Landscapes, Marine Painting, Painting - American, Watercolors, Woodcarvings, Whaling, New Bedford Artists
Collections: Paintings by Clifford Ashley, Albert Bierstadt, F D Millet, William Wall
Activities: Scholarships offered; individual & original objects of art lent to city offices

M OLD DARTMOUTH HISTORICAL SOCIETY, New Bedford Whaling Museum, 18 Johnny Cake Hill, 02740. Tel 508-997-0046; FAX 508-997-0018; *Dir* Anne Brengle; *Cur* Judith N Lund
Open Mon - Sat 9 AM - 5 PM, Sun 1 - 5 PM. Admis $4.50, youth & senior citizens $4. Estab 1903 to collect, preserve & interpret objects including printed material, pictures & artifacts related to the history of the New Bedford area & American whaling. Average Annual Attendance: 50,000. Mem: 2100; dues $15-$850; annual meeting in May
Income: $713,000 (financed by endowment, mem, private gifts, grants, special events & admis)
Collections: Paintings, watercolors, drawings, prints, photographs, whaling equipment, ship models, including 89 foot 1/2 scale model of whaler Lagoda
Exhibitions: Highlights From the Glass Museum's Collection; Two Brothers Gowlart; changing exhibits every 6 months
Publications: Bulletin from Johnny Cake Hill, quarterly; exhibition catalogs; calendar, quarterly
Activities: Classes for adults & children; docent training; lect open to public, 12 vis lectr per year; gallery talks; tours; individual paintings & original objects of art lent to other museums; lending collection contains microfilm, nature artifacts, original art works, original prints, paintings, photographs & sculptures; traveling exhibitions organized & circulated; museum shop sells books, magazines, reproductions, prints, slides & gift items

L Whaling Museum Library, 18 Johnny Cake Hill, 02740. Tel 508-997-0046; FAX 508-994-4350; *Librn* Judith Downey
For reference only
Income: Financed by private gifts & grants
Library Holdings: Vols 15,000; Per subs 12; Micro — Reels; AV — Fs; Other — Clipping files, exhibition catalogs, manuscripts, memorabilia, pamphlets
Special Subjects: Whaling, New Bedford History

NEWBURYPORT

M HISTORICAL SOCIETY OF OLD NEWBURY, Cushing House Museum, 98 High St, 01950. Tel 508-462-2681; *Dir* William Barton; *Cur* John H Wright
Open Tues - Sat 10 AM - 4 PM, cl Sun & Mon. Admis adults $3. Estab 1877 to preserve heritage of Old Newbury, Newbury, Newburyport & West Newbury. Average Annual Attendance: 3000. Mem: 600; dues benefactor $100, sustaining $50, family $35, individual $20
Income: $50,000 (financed by dues, tours, endowments, fund-raisers)
Collections: China; dolls; furniture; glass; miniatures; needlework; paintings; paperweights; sampler collection; silver; military & other historical material
Publications: Old-Town & The Waterside, 200 years of Tradition & Change in Newbury, Newburyport & West Newbury - 1635-1835
Activities: Docent training; lect open to public, 8 vis lectr per year; gallery talks; tours for children; Garden Tour; annual auction; scholarships & fels offered; exten dept serves Merrimack Valley; individual paintings & original objects of art lent to nonprofit cultural institutions; museum shop sells books

M NEWBURYPORT MARITIME SOCIETY, Custom House Maritime Museum, 25 Water St, 01950. Tel 508-462-8681; *Dir & Cur* William Barton; *Admin Asst* Celeste Johnson
Open Mon - Sat 10 AM - 4 PM, Sun 1 - 5 PM. Admis adults $1.50, children to 15 $.75, under 5 free. Estab 1975 to exhibit the maritime heritage of the Merrimack Valley. Housed in an 1835 custom house designed by Robert Mills. The structure is on the National Register of Historic Places. Average Annual Attendance: 8000. Mem: 600; dues $2-$1000, annual meeting in Dec
Income: $75,000 (financed by mem, admis, fundraisers, pub, private & government grants)
Collections: Collection of portraits, ship models & decorative art objects 1680-1820; original collection of ethnographic items owned by Newburyport Marine Society Members, half hull models of Merrimack River Valley Ships; portraits of sea captains; navigational instrument & models
Publications: Newsletter, bimonthly
Activities: Classes for adults & children; lect open to public, 10 vis lectr per year; gallery talks; tours; individual paintings & original objects of art lent to other museums & historical agencies; book traveling exhibitions; museum shop sells nautical items

NEWTON

A BOSTON VISUAL ARTISTS UNION, PO Box 399, 02160. Tel 617-695-1266;
Dir Carol Spack; *Spec Projects* Martin Ulman
Estab 1970 to bring the artist out of the studio & into the market. A small
reference library, slide registry & print bins of members' works are maintained at
a members home. Mem: 50; dues $40
Income: Financed by dues & occasional Massachusetts Cultural Council Support
Publications: BVAU News, every other month
Activities: Scholarships & fels offered

NORTHAMPTON

L FORBES LIBRARY, 20 West St, 01060. Tel 413-584-8550, 586-0489; *Dir*
Blaise Bisaillon; *Arts & Music Librn* Faith Kaufmann
Open Mon - Tues 9 AM - 6 PM, Wed 9 AM - 9 PM, Fri & Sat 9 AM - 5 PM, cl
Thurs & holidays. Estab 1894 to serve the residential and academic community
as a general public library and a research facility. Gallery and exhibit cases for
regional artists, photographers and craftspeople. Circ 292,950
Purchases: $53,500
Library Holdings: Vols 150,000; Per subs 47; Compact discs 3000; Original
Documents; Micro — Reels; AV — Cassettes 2000; Other — Clipping files,
exhibition catalogs, original art works, photographs, prints
Special Subjects: Costume Design & Construction, Posters, Art, music
Collections: Bien Edition of Audubon Bird Prints; Library of Charles E Forbes;
Walter E Corbin Collection of Photographic Prints & Slides; The Coolidge
Collection; Connecticut Valley History; Genealogical Records; Official White
House Portraits of President Calvin Coolidge & Grace Anna Coolidge; World
War I & II Poster Collection; Local History Photograph Collection & Print
Collection
Exhibitions: Monthly exhibits of works by regional artists, photographers and
craftspeople
Activities: Concerts; exten dept serves elderly & house bound

M HISTORIC NORTHAMPTON MUSEUM, 46 Bridge St, 01060. Tel 413-584-
6011; *Trustee* Stanley Elkins; *Cur Colls* Lynne Bassett
Open Mon - Fri 9 AM - 5 PM. Estab 1905 to collect, preserve & exhibit objects
of human history in Northhampton & Connecticut Valley. The mus maintains
three historic houses from about 1728, 1798 & 1813; a barn from about 1825
with newly added educ center; a non-circulating reference library. Average
Annual Attendance: 9500. Mem: 500; dues business $100 - $500, individual $20
- $100, annual meeting in Nov
Income: $95,000 (financed by endowment, mem, gifts)
Collections: Collections focus on material culture of Northampton & the upper
Connecticut River Valley, costumes, textiles, ca. 1900 Howes Brothers
photographs; archaeological artifacts from on-site excavation, decorative arts; oil
paintings of local personalities & scenes; Collection of costumes, textiles,
furniture & decorative art
Publications: Newsletter, quarterly; booklets on local subjects; brochures & flyers
Activities: Classes for adults & children; docent programs; workshops;
internships; lect open to public; gallery talks; scholarships offered; museum shop
sells books, merchandise related to museum's collections, reproductions of
collection items, maps, period toys & games

M SMITH COLLEGE, Museum of Art, Elm Street at Bedford Terrace, 01063. Tel
413-585-2760; FAX 413-585-2782; Elec Mail artmuseum@ais.smith.edu. TTY
413-585-2786. *Dir & Chief Cur* Suzannah J Fabing; *Cur Educ* Nancy Rich;
Assoc Cur Prints Ann H Sievers; *Assoc Cur Paintings* Linda Muehlig; *Prog
Coordr & Archivist* Michael Goodison
Open Sept - June, Tues, Fri & Sat 9:30 AM - 4 PM; Wed & Sun Noon - 4 PM,
Thurs Noon - 8 PM; July & Aug, Tues - Sun Noon - 4 PM, cl Mon, New Year's
Day, July 4, Thanksgiving, Christmas Eve & Christmas Day, hours vary around
holidays, please call. No admis fee. Collection founded 1879; Hillyer Art Gallery
built 1882; Smith College Museum of Art established 1920; Tryon Art Gallery
built 1926; present Smith College Museum of Art in Tryon Hall opened 1973.
Average Annual Attendance: 36,000. Mem: 1200; dues student $10 & up
Collections: Examples from most periods and cultures with special emphasis on
European and American paintings, sculpture, drawings, prints, photographs and
decorative arts of the 17th-20th centuries
Exhibitions: Temporary exhibitions and installations 12-24 annually
Publications: Catalogues
Activities: Lect; gallery talks; tours; concerts; individual works of art lent to
other institutions; sales desk selling publications, post and note cards, posters
L Hillyer Art Library, Elm Street at Bedford Terrace, 01063. Tel 413-585-2940;
FAX 413-585-2904; Elec Mail bpolowy@library.smith.edu. *Librn* Barbara
Polowy
Open Mon - Thurs 8 AM - 11 PM, Fri 8 AM - 9 PM, Sat 10 AM - 9 PM, Sun
Noon - Midnight. Estab 1900 to support courses offered by art department of
Smith College. For reference use only
Income: Financed by endowment
Library Holdings: Vols 74,200; Per subs 260; Micro — Fiche 32,041, reels; AV —
Cassettes; Other — Clipping files, exhibition catalogs
Special Subjects: Antiquities-Etruscan, Antiquities-Greek, Antiquities-Oriental,
Antiquities-Roman, Architecture, Art History, Drawings, Etchings & Engravings,
History of Art & Archaeology, Painting - American, Painting - British, Painting -
European, Painting - Italian, Painting - Spanish, Sculpture

M WORDS & PICTURES MUSEUM, 140 Main St, 01060. Tel 413-586-8545;
FAX 413-586-9855; Elec Mail comics@wordsandpictures.org. *Exec Dir*
Maryann Meeks; *Cur* Fiona Russell; *Retail Dir* Tonya Talbot
Estab 1990. Average Annual Attendance: 45,000. Mem: 300
Income: $530,000 (financed by mem, gifts, admis & gift shop sales)
Collections: †Classic pin-ups; †comic books; †contemporary comic artwork;
†contemporary fantasy illustration; †ephemera
Exhibitions: Change every eight weeks
Publications: Words about Pictures, quarterly
Activities: Individual paintings & original objects of art lent; book traveling
exhibitions, 1 per year; museum shop sells books, magazines, original art,
reproductions & prints

NORTH GRAFTON

M WILLARD HOUSE & CLOCK MUSEUM, INC, 11 Willard St, 01536-2011.
Tel 508-839-3500; FAX 508-839-3599; *Pres* Dr Roger W Robinson; *VPres*
Sumner Tilton; *Dir* Imogene Robinson; *Cur* John R Stephens
Open Tues - Sat 10 AM - 4 PM, Sun 1 - 5 PM, cl Mon & holidays. Admis adults
$3, children $1. Estab 1971 for educ in the fields of history, horology, decorative
arts & antiques. Maintains nine rooms open in house mus. Average Annual
Attendance: 3000. Mem: 100; dues $25; annual meeting in house museum
Income: Financed by endowment, mem, admis, gifts & sales
Collections: Native American Artifacts Collection; Willard Clockmaking Family
Collection, furnishings, memorabilia & portraits; 17th & 18th Early Country
Antique Furniture Collection; 18th Century Embroidery Collection; 18th & 19th
Century Firearms Collection; 19th Century Children's Toy Collection; 19th
Century Costume Collection; 19th Century Oriental Rug Collection
Exhibitions: Annual Clock Collectors Workshop; Annual Christmas Open House
(1997) 30 Hour Grafton Clocks
Publications: Mem newsletter, quarterly
Activities: Museum shop sells books, clocks, antiques & gifts

NORTON

WHEATON COLLEGE
M Watson Gallery, E Main St, 02766. Tel 508-286-3578; FAX 508-285-8270; Elec
Mail a__murray@wheatonma.edu. *Dir* Ann H Murray
Open daily 12:30 - 4:30 PM. No admis fee. Estab 1960, gallery program since
1930 to provide a wide range of contemporary one person & group shows as well
as exhibitions from the permanent collection of paintings, graphics & objects.
Gallery is of fireproof steel-frame, glass & brick construction; there are no
windows. Average Annual Attendance: 5000
Income: Financed by college budget & occasional grants
Purchases: Marble portrait bust of Roman boy; Etruscan antefix head; Head of
Galienus, Roman c 260 AD; Cycladic Figurine, 2500-1100 BC Greek Black
Figure Amphora, 6th c BC
Collections: 19th & 20th centuries prints, drawings, paintings & sculpture;
decorative arts; Wedgewood, 18th & 19th centuries glass; ancient bronzes,
sculptures & ceramics
Exhibitions: Changing exhibitions
Publications: Exhibition catalogs; Prints of the 19th Century: A Selection from
the Wheaton College Collection; Collage; Eleanor Norcross; Amy Cross; Edith
Loring Getchell; Hugh Townley; Patterns: Period Costumes; Francesco Spicuzza;
Waterworks; Dime Store Deco; Spirituality in Contemporary Art by Women
Activities: Lect open to public, 5-8 vis lectr per year; concerts; gallery talks;
tours; individual paintings & original objects of art lent to colleges, other
museums & galleries; originate traveling exhibitions organized & circulated

PAXTON

M ANNA MARIA COLLEGE, Saint Luke's Gallery, Moll Art Ctr, Sunset Lane,
01612. Tel 508-849-3441; *Chmn Art Dept* Alice Lambert
Open 10 AM - 3 PM. No admis fee. Estab 1968 as an outlet for the art student
and professional artist, and to raise the artistic awareness of the general
community. Main Gallery is 35 x 15 ft with about 300 sq ft of wall space.
Average Annual Attendance: 600
Collections: Small assortment of furniture, paintings, sculpture
Exhibitions: Annual senior art exhibit; local artists; faculty & students shows
Publications: Exhibit programs
Activities: Educ Dept; lect open to public; individual paintings & original objects
of art lent to campus offices

PITTSFIELD

L BERKSHIRE ATHENAEUM LIBRARY, Reference Dept, One Wendell Ave,
01201. Tel 413-499-9488; *Dir* Ron Latham; *Music & Arts Librn* Mary Ann
Knight; *Supv Reference* Madeline Kelly
Open Mon - Thurs 10 AM - 9 PM, Fri & Sat 10 AM - 5 PM. Estab 1872, music
and arts dept 1937
Income: Financed by city & state appropriations
Library Holdings: Vols 15,800; Compact discs 500; AV — Cassettes 1200, rec
6000; Other — Prints 2000
Collections: Mary Rice Morgan Ballet Collection: a reference room of programs,
artifacts, prints, original art, rare & current books on dance & costume design
Exhibitions: Changing monthly exhibits of fine arts, crafts, antiques &
collectables

M BERKSHIRE MUSEUM, 39 South St, 01201. Tel 413-443-7171; *Dir of
Develop* Tracy Wilson; *Dir Art Educ* Marion Grant; *Aquarium Dir* Thomas G
Smith; *Librn* Rollin Hotchkiss; *Registrar* Tim Decker
Open to pub Tues - Sat 10 AM - 5 PM, Sun 1 - 5 PM, Mon 10 AM - 5 PM, July
& Aug. Admis adults $3, senior citizens & students $2, children 12-18 $1,
members & children under 12 free. Estab 1903 as a mus of art, natural science &
history. Average Annual Attendance: 85,000. Mem: 2400; dues sustaining $60 &
up, family $40, single $20; annual meeting in Jan
Income: Financed by endowment, mem, fundraising & gifts
Collections: Paintings of the Hudson River School (Inness, Moran, Blakelock,
Martin, Wyant, Moran, Church, Bierstadt & others); American Abstract: Art of
the '30s; early American portraits; Egyptian, Babylonia & Near East arts; grave
reliefs from Palmyra; Paul M Hahn Collection of 18th century English &
American silver; Old Masters (Pons, de Hooch, Van Dyck & others);
contemporary painting & sculpture; two Norman Rockwell paintings
Publications: Schedule of events, quarterly
Activities: Classes for adults & children; lect open to the public, 40 vis lectr per
year; concerts gallery talks; individual paintings & original objects of art lent to
corporate & individual members; book traveling exhibitions 1-2 per year;
originate traveling exhibitions primarily to New England institutions; museum
shop sells gifts

M CITY OF PITTSFIELD, Berkshire Artisans, 28 Renne Ave, 01201-4720. Tel 413-499-9348; *Commissioner of Cultural Affairs & Artistic Dir* Daniel M O'Connell, MFA
Open Mon - Fri 11 AM - 5 PM. No admis fee. Estab 1976. Three story 100 yr old brownstone, municipal gallery. Average Annual Attendance: 5100. Mem: 1200; dues $5000; annual meeting in Sept
Income: $100,000 (financed by endowment, mem, city, state & federal appropriations)
Exhibitions: Doe, Warner Freidman, Dave Novak, Jay Tobin, Daniel Galvez, John Dilg, Sally Fine, Linda Bernstein, David Merritt
Publications: The Berkshire Review
Activities: Classes for adults & children; dramatic programs; docent training; lect open to public, 12 vis lectr per year; competitions; scholarships & fels offered; artmobile; lending collection contains paintings, art objects; traveling exhibition 12 per year; originate traveling exhibitions 12 per year; museum shop sells books, prints, magazines, slides, original art, public murals

M HANCOCK SHAKER VILLAGE, INC, US Rte 20, PO Box 898, 01202. Tel 413-443-0188; FAX 413-447-9397; Elec Mail info@shancockshakervillage.org; Internet Home Page Address http://www.hancockshakevillage.org. *Dir* Lawrence J Yerdon; *Cur Coll* June Sprigg; *Interpretation & Educ* Todd Burdick; *Mus Shop Mgr* Rebecca Petore
Open June 1 - Nov 1 9:30 AM - 5 PM daily. Admis adults $6, senior citizens & students $5.50, children between 6-12 $2. Estab 1960 for the preservation & restoration of Hancock Shaker Village & the interpretation of Shaker art, architecture & culture. Period rooms throughout the village. Exhibition Gallery contains Shaker inspirational drawings & graphic materials. Average Annual Attendance: 50,000. Mem: 1300; dues individual $20
Income: Financed by mem, donations
Collections: Shaker architecture, furniture & industrial material; Shaker inspirational drawings
Publications: Newsletter, quarterly; specialized publications
Activities: Classes for adults & children; docent training; workshops; seminars; lect open to public; gallery talks; tours; individual paintings & original objects of art lent to qualified museums with proper security & environmental conditions; museum shop sells books, magazines, reproductions, prints & slides
L Library, US Rte 20, PO Box 898, 01202. Tel 413-443-0188;
Reference library open to students & scholars by appointment
Library Holdings: Vols 3800; Graphics; Maps; Micro — Fiche, reels; AV — Rec; Other — Clipping files, exhibition catalogs, framed reproductions, manuscripts, photographs, prints
Special Subjects: Argricultural & Mechanical Books, Shaker Crafts & Culture
Collections: Buildings; †furniture; †farm & crafts artifacts; inspirational drawings; over 10,000 Shaker objects

PLYMOUTH

M PILGRIM SOCIETY, Pilgrim Hall Museum, 75 Court St, 02360. Tel 508-746-1620; FAX 508-747-4228; *Pres* Christopher Hussey; *Dir & Librn* Peggy M Baker; *Cur Exhib* Karen Goldstein
Open daily 9:30 AM - 4:30 PM. Admis adults $4, senior citizens $3.50, children $1.50. Estab 1820 to depict the history of the Pilgrim Colonists in Plymouth Colony. Average Annual Attendance: 27,000. Mem: 809; dues $20; annual meetings in Dec
Income: Financed by endowment, mem & admis
Special Subjects: Historical Material, Manuscripts, Maps, Painting - American
Collections: Arms & armor, decorative arts, furniture & paintings relating to the Plymouth Colony settlement (1620-1692) & the later history of Plymouth
Exhibitions: Permanent collections; exhibitions change year round
Publications: The Pilgrim Journal, bi-annually
Activities: Lect open to public, 8 vis lectr per year; museum shop sells books, magazines, reproductions, prints, slides, ceramics, souvenir wares
L Library, 75 Court St, 02360. Tel 508-746-1620; FAX 508-747-4228; *Dir & Librn* Peggy M Baker
Open Apr - Nov daily 9:30 AM - 4:30 PM, Dec - Mar Noon - 4:30 PM. Admis adults $5, children $2.50. Estab 1820 to collect material relative to the history of Plymouth. For reference only
Library Holdings: Vols 10,000; Per subs 5; Micro — Reels; AV — A-tapes, cassettes, Kodachromes, lantern slides, motion pictures, rec, slides; Other — Clipping files, exhibition catalogs, manuscripts, memorabilia, original art works, pamphlets, photographs, prints, reproductions, sculpture

A PLYMOUTH ANTIQUARIAN SOCIETY, * PO Box 1137, 02362. Tel 508-746-0012; *Dir & Cur* Barbara J Milligan Ryan; *Asst to Dir* Nancy Gedraicis; *Pres* Annette Talbot
Open May, June & Sept Wed - Sun Noon - 5 PM, July & Aug daily Noon - 5 PM. Admis adults $2.50, children $.50. Estab 1919 to maintain & preserve the three museums: Harlow Old Fort House (1677), Spooner House (1747) & Antiquarian House (1809). Average Annual Attendance: 5000. Mem: 500; dues family $25, individual $15; annual meeting in Nov
Income: Financed by mem & donations
Collections: Antique dolls, artwork, china, furniture, costumes, toys & textiles
Activities: Classes for adults & children; lect open to public; sales shop at Harlow House sells selected items

PROVINCETOWN

A PROVINCETOWN ART ASSOCIATION & MUSEUM, 460 Commercial St, 02657. Tel 508-487-1750; FAX 508-487-4372; Elec Mail paam@capecod.net. *Dir* Robyn S Watson
Open daily Noon - 5 PM & 8 - 10 PM. Admis adult $3, senior citizens & children $1. Estab in 1914 to promote & cultivate the practice & appreciation of all branches of the fine arts, to hold temporary exhibitions, forums & concerts for its members & the pub. Four galleries are maintained. Average Annual Attendance: 30,000. Mem: 800; mem open; dues $40
Income: $250,000 (financed by mem, private contributions, state agencies, IMS,

NEA & others)
Collections: Permanent collection consists of artists work who have lived or worked on the Lower Cape
Exhibitions: Permanent collection, members' exhibitions
Publications: Exhibitions catalogues & newsletters
Activities: Classes for adults & children; lect open to public, 6 vis lectr per year; concerts; gallery talks; individual paintings & original objects of art lent to other museums; book traveling exhibitons; originate traveling exhibition; museum shop sells books, magazines, original art, prints, reproductions, slides
L Library, 460 Commercial St, 02657. *Dir* Robyn S Watson
Open to members & researchers by appointment
Library Holdings: Vols 500; Other — Clipping files, exhibition catalogs, pamphlets, photographs
Special Subjects: Provincetown artists
Collections: Memorabilia of WHW Bicknell; Provincetown Artists

QUINCY

M ADAMS NATIONAL HISTORIC SITE, 135 Adams St, PO Box 531, 02269. Tel 617-773-1177; FAX 617-471-9683; *Cur* Judith McAlister-Curtis; *Supt* Marianne Peak
Open daily April 19 - Nov 10 9 AM - 5 PM. Admis adults $2, children under 16 admitted free if accompanied by an adult. Estab 1946. The site consists of a house, part of which dates to 1731; a library containing approx 14,000 books, a carriage house, a woodshed & grounds which were once owned & enjoyed by four generations of the Adams family. Average Annual Attendance: 31,000
Income: Financed by Federal Government
Collections: Original furnishings belonging to the four generations of Adamses who lived in the house between 1788 and 1937
Activities: Lect (one week each spring); tours

ROCKPORT

A ROCKPORT ART ASSOCIATION, Old Tavern, 12 Main St, 01966. Tel 508-546-6604; FAX 508-546-9767; *Exec Dir* Carol Linsky; *Pres* Stapleton Kearns
Open summer daily 10 AM - 5 PM, Sun Noon - 5 PM, winter daily 10 AM - 4 PM, Sat 10 AM - 5 PM, Sun Noon - 5 PM. No admis fee. Estab 1921 as a non-profit educational organization established for the advancement of art. Four galleries are maintained in the Old Tavern Building; two large summer galleries are adjacent to the main structure. Average Annual Attendance: 75,000. Mem: 1300; mem open to Cape Ann resident artists (minimum of one month), must pass mem jury; contributing mem open to public; photography mem subject of resident/jury restrictions
Income: Financed by endowment, mem, gifts, art programs & sales
Collections: Permanent collection of works by Cape Ann artists of the past, especially those by former members
Exhibitions: Special organized exhibitions are continually on view; fifty exhibitions scheduled per year
Publications: Quarry Cookbook; Rockport Artists Book 1990; Reprints (recent); Rockport Artists Book 1940; Rockport Sketch Book
Activities: Classes & workshops for adults & children; lect open to the public; painting lectr/demonstrations; Tavern Door shop sells books, cards & notes by artist members

A SANDY BAY HISTORICAL SOCIETY & MUSEUMS, Sewall Scripture House-Old Castle, 40 King St & Castle Lane, PO Box 63, 01966. Tel 508-546-9533; *Cur* Cynthia A Peckam
Open summer 2 - 5 PM. No admis fee. Estab 1925. Average Annual Attendance: 300. Mem: 500; dues $7; annual meeting first Fri in Sept
Income: $8000 (financed by endowment & mem)
Collections: Extensive Granite Tools & Quarry Materials; 55 local paintings in oil, prints, watercolor; old quilts, samplers, textiles
Exhibitions: A Town That Was; Some Rockporters Who Were (for the Sesqui-centennial of the town)
Publications: Mem bulletins, 3-4 annually; brochures

SALEM

M PEABODY ESSEX MUSEUM, East India Sq, 01970. Tel 508-745-1876; FAX 508-744-6776; Elec Mail pem@pem.org. *Exec Dir* Dan L Monroe; *Dir Admin & Finance* Susan Davy; *Dir Curatorial Operations* Peter Fetchko; *Dir Develop* Jim Forbes; *Dir Marketing* Dorothy Chen-Courtin; *Dir Educ* Rick Guttenberg
Open summer daily 10 AM - Thurs & Sat 10 AM - 5 PM, Fri 10 AM - 8 PM, Sun Noon - 5 PM, cl Thanksgiving, Christmas, New Year's Day & Mon Nov 1 - Memorial. Admis family $18, adults $7.50, seniors & students $6.50, children 6-16 $4, mus members & children under 6 free. Estab 1799. 18,000 sq ft of exhibition plus historic properties; the nation's oldest continuously operating mus, with nearly half a million objects collected over the past two centuries, 28 historic properties & 30 galleries of permanent & changing exhibitions. The Museum's Philips Library contains a million photographs & negatives, 400,000 volumes & original court documents form the Salem witch trials of 1692. Maintains reference library. Average Annual Attendance: 150,000. Mem: 4200; dues $30-$65; annual meeting in Nov
Income: $6,000,000 (financed by endowment, mem, gifts & admis)
Collections: American Decorative Arts; Asian Export Art: porcelain, silver, furniture, Asian, Oceanic & African-Large, Japanese, Korean & Pacific Island Collection; Early American Architecture; Maritime history: paintings, models, scrimshaw, instruments; Native American Art & Archaeology: Early collection of northeast & northwest; Native American artifacts; Natural History Local flora & fauna
Exhibitions: (1997) Gifts of the Spirit: Works by 19th Century & Contemporary Native American Artists; Views of the Pearl River Delta: Macao, Canton, Hong Kong; Prize Goods: Recent Acquisitions of Maritime Art & Artifacts; American Furniture Essex County Landscape Artist; Fashions and Draperies for Windows and Beds; Library Exhibit - Conservation: Some Problems and Solutions; Life

and Times in Shoe City: The Shoe Workers of Lynn; Nathaniel Hawthorne Exhibition;
Publications: Peabody Essex Museum Collections, quarterly; The American Neptune, quarterly; The Review of Archaeology, semiannually; member's magazine, quarterly; occasional books
Activities: Classes for adults & children; docent training; lect open to public, 12 vis lectr per year; concerts; gallery talks; tours; shops sell jewelry, folk art, books, magazines, reproductions, posters, prints & art objects reflecting our global collections

L **Phillips Library**, E India Sq, 01970. Tel 508-745-1876; FAX 508-744-0036; *Librn* William T La Moy; *Librn* James Duncan Phillips; *Librn* Stephen Phillips
Open Mon - Wed & Fri 10 AM - 5 PM, Thurs 1 - 8 PM, cl Mon from Labor Day to Memorial Day. For reference only
Library Holdings: Vols 400,000; Per subs 150; Micro — Fiche; AV — Kodachromes, lantern slides, motion pictures, slides; Other — Clipping files, exhibition catalogs, manuscripts, memorabilia, original art works, pamphlets
Special Subjects: American Indian Art, Anthropology, Archaeology, Architecture, Asian Art, Bookplates & Bindings, Ceramics, Crafts, Decorative Arts, Etchings & Engravings, Ethnology, Folk Art, Furniture, Glass, Ivory
Collections: The library supports the entire range of the collections of this international & multi-disciplinary museum of arts & cultures
Publications: Peabody Essex Museum Collections

M **Gardner-Pingree House**, 132 Essex St, 01970. Tel 508-745-9500; FAX 508-744-6776; Elec Mail pem@pem.org. *Cur* Robert Saarnio
Open May 30 - Oct 31 Tues - Sat 10 AM - 5 PM, Sun Noon - 5 PM. Admis adults $7.50, senior citizens & students $6.50, children 4-14 $4, under 4 free. Built in 1804-1805 & illustrates the Federal Style of Salem master-builder & carver, Samuel McIntire; furnished in that period

M **Crowninshield-Bentley House**, 132 Essex St, 01970. Tel 508-745-9500; FAX 508-744-6776; Elec Mail pem@pem.org. *Cur* Robert Saarnio
Open May 30 - Oct 31 Tues - Sat 10 AM - 5 PM, Sun Noon - 5 PM. Admis adults $7.50, senior citizens & students $6.50, children 4-14 $4, under 4 free. Built in 1727, added to & remodeled after 1800. It illustrates the styles of interior architecture & furnishings of much of the 18th century in Salem

M **John Ward House**, 132 Essex St, 01970. Tel 508-744-3390; FAX 508-744-0036; *Cur* Dean Lahikainen
Open June 1 - Oct 31 Tues - Sat 10 AM - 4 PM, Sun 1 - 4:30 PM. Admis adults $1.50, senior citizens $1, children $.75. Built 1684, restored 1910-1912 under direction of George Francis Dow, architectural historian. Furnished in the manner of the time. The rear lean-to contains a later apothecary's shop, a weaving room with operable loom & a small cent shop

M **Andrew-Safford House**, 13 Washington Sq, 01970. Tel 508-744-3390; FAX 508-744-0036; *Cur* Dean Lahikainen
Open Thurs 2 - 4:30 PM. Admis $1.50. Built in 1818-1819 & purchased by the Institute in 1947 for the purpose of presenting a vivid image of early 19th century urban life. It is the residence of the Institute's director

M **Peirce-Nichols House**, 80 Federal St, 01970. Tel 508-744-3390; FAX 508-744-0036
Open Tues - Sat 2 - 4:30 PM, open to pub by appointment only. Admis adults $1.50, senior citizens $1, children $.75. Built in 1782 by Samuel McIntire. Maintains some original furnishings & a counting house

M **Cotting-Smith-Assembly House**, 138 Federal St, 01970. Tel 508-744-3390; FAX 508-744-0036
Open for functions & by special appointment. Admis adults $1.50, senior citizens $1, children $.75. Built in 1782 as a hall for social assemblies; remodeled in 1796 by Samuel McIntire as a home residence. Not open to pub

M **Lyle-Tapley Shoe Shop & Vaughn Doll House**, 132 Essex St, 01970. Tel 508-744-3390; FAX 508-744-0036
Open June 1 - Oct 31 Tues - Sat 9 AM - 4:30 PM, Sun 1 - 5 PM. Accommodates special collections

M **Derby-Beebe Summer House**, 132 Essex St, 01970. Tel 508-744-3390; FAX 508-744-0036;
The Summer House (c. 1800) is the focal point of the Institute Gardens

SANDWICH

M **THORNTON W BURGESS SOCIETY, INC**, Museum, 4 Water St, PO Box 972, 02563. Tel 508-888-4668; *Exec Dir* Jeanne Johnson; *Pres* David Pape; *VPres* David O'Conner
Open Mon - Sat 10 AM - 4 PM, Sun 1 - 4 PM. Admis by donation. Estab 1976 to inspire reverence for wildlife & concern for the natural environment. 1756 house. Average Annual Attendance: 80,000. Mem: 2900; dues family $20, individual $12; annual meeting in Feb
Income: Financed by mem, gift shop & mailorder sales
Collections: Collection of Thornton Burgess' writings; the original Harrison Cady illustrations from the writings of the children's author & naturalist
Publications: Newsletter, 3 times per yr; program schedule, 4 times per yr
Activities: Classes for adults & children; docent programs; lect open to public

M **HERITAGE PLANTATION OF SANDWICH**, 67 Grove & Pine Sts, PO Box 566, 02563. Tel 508-888-3300; FAX 508-888-9535; *Dir* Gene A Schott; *Asst Dir* Nancy Tyrer; *Cur Military History* James Cervantes; *Cur Botanical Science* Jean Gillis; *Registrar* Allota Whitney; *Cur Art Mus* Jennifer Younginger; *Cur Antique Auto Mus* Robert Rogers
Open daily 10 AM - 5 PM, May - Oct. Admis adults $5, children $2. Estab 1969 as a mus of Americana. Heritage Plantation is a Massachusettes charitable corporation. Maintains three galleries which house collections. Average Annual Attendance: 100,000. Mem: 3000; dues $25-$1000
Income: Financed by endowment, mem & admis
Collections: †American Indian artifacts; folk art; primitive paintings; †Scrimshaw Antique Automobiles; †Folk Art; †Fine Arts; Tools; Weapons; Military Miniatures; Native American Art
Exhibitions: Western Art; Landscape Paintings; Pennsylvania German Art; Young American Chinese Experimental Art Antique & Classic Automobiles; Hand painted Military Miniatures & Antique Firearms; Restored 1912 Charles I D Looff Carousel; Currier & Ives prints.
Publications: Exhibit catalogues; quarterly newsletter

Activities: Classes for adults & children; docent training; lect for members only, 7-10 vis lectr per year; concerts; gallery talks; tours; exten dept serving Cape Cod area; artmobile; individual paintings & original objects of art lent; lending coll includes fs, original prints, paintings & nature artifacts; museum shop sells books, original art, reproductions, prints, slides

M **THE SANDWICH HISTORICAL SOCIETY, INC**, Sandwich Glass Museum, 129 Main St, PO Box 103, 02563. Tel 508-888-0251; FAX 508-888-4941; *Dir* Bruce Courson; *Cur Glass* Kirk J Nelson, MA; *Cur Hist* Lynne M Horton, BA
Open Apr - Oct daily 9:30 AM - 4:30 PM, Nov, Dec, Feb & Mar, Wed - Sun 9:30 AM - 4 PM, cl Mon & Tues, Thanksgiving, Christmas & Jan. Admis adults $3.50, children 6-16 $1. Estab 1907 to collect, preserve local history. Thirteen galleries contain the products of the glass companies that operated in Sandwich from 1825-1907. Also displayed are artifacts and memorabilia relating to the history of Sandwich. Average Annual Attendance: 63,000. Mem: 605; dues family $25, individual $15; meeting dates: third Tues in Feb, Apr, June, Aug & Oct
Income: $382,000 (financed by endowment, mem, admis & retails sales)
Collections: Glass-Sandwich, American, European; Artifacts relating to the history of Sandwich
Publications: Acorn, annual; The Cullet, 3 times per year
Activities: Classes for adults & children; docent training; lect open to public, 10 vis lectr per year; individual paintings & original objects of art lent; museum shop sells books, reproductions & glass

L **Library**, 129 Main St, PO Box 103, 02563. Tel 508-888-0251; FAX 508-888-4941; *Dir* Bruce Courson
For reference only
Purchases: $900
Library Holdings: Vols 3000; Per subs 21; Micro — Reels; AV — A-tapes, lantern slides, motion pictures, slides, v-tapes; Other — Clipping files, exhibition catalogs, manuscripts, memorabilia, photographs, prints
Special Subjects: Ceramics, Decorative Arts, Embroidery, Furniture, Glass, Historical Material, Jewelry, Manuscripts, Maps, Reproductions

SHARON

M **KENDALL WHALING MUSEUM**, 27 Everett St, PO Box 297, 02067. Tel 617-784-5642; Internet Home Page Address http://www.kwm.org. *Dir* Stuart M Frank; *Cur* Michael P Dyer; *Registrar* Louise Dembrowsky
Open Tues - Sat 10 AM - 5 PM, Sun 1 - 5 PM, cl Mon & holidays, New Year's, Memorial Day, Independence Day, Thanksgiving & Christmas. Admis family $5, adults $2, student $1.50, children under 14 $1. Estab 1956 to collect, preserve & interpret art works & artifacts relating to the history & fine arts of whaling & the natural history of the whale. Twelve galleries hold the maritime collections. Average Annual Attendance: 20,000. Mem: 750; dues $20
Income: Financed by foundations, grants, admis, gifts & publ
Collections: †Dutch & Flemish marine painting of 17th -18th century; †American, British, European & Japanese prints & paintings, 16th-20th century; †Scrimshaw; †ship models; †tools; †small craft; †decorative arts & carvings; †Eskimo (Inuit) art; †maritime art
Exhibitions: Recent acquisitions (annual): Ancient Treasures Dutch Golden Age; Dutch Old Master paintings: Japanese Whaling Art, 1680-1980; Northwest Coast Indian Art; Afro-American Contributions to the Whaling Industry
Publications: Kendall Whaling Museum Newsletter, quarterly; original publications; exhibition catalogs; monograph series
Activities: Classes for adults & children; musical programs; lect open to public, 30 vis lectr per year; concerts; gallery talks; tours; awards; scholarships offered; exten dept serves New England & anywhere else by arrangement; individual paintings & original objects of art lent to qualified museums; museum shop sells books, magazines, original art, reproductions, prints, slides, records, jewelry, crockery, stationery, gifts, curriculum kits & educational material

L **Library**, 27 Everett St, PO Box 297, 02067. Tel 617-784-5642; *Dir* Stuart M Frank; *Librn* Michael P Dyer
For reference only
Library Holdings: Vols 9000; Per subs 15; Micro — Cards, fiche, prints, reels; AV — A-tapes, cassettes, fs, Kodachromes, lantern slides, motion pictures, rec, slides, v-tapes; Other — Clipping files, exhibition catalogs, framed reproductions, manuscripts, memorabilia, original art works, pamphlets, photographs, prints, reproductions, sculpture
Special Subjects: Whaling history & literature; maritime art 17th - 20th century; natural history: 15th century to present; marine mammal preservation, seal hunting, cetology, fine arts
Collections: Whaling (all histories/eras & peoples, worldwide); voyager of exploration; natural history before 1800; literature; maritime history; art history
Publications: Monographic series, 3 per year; quarterly newsletter

SOUTH HADLEY

M **MOUNT HOLYOKE COLLEGE**, Art Museum, 01075-1499. Tel 413-538-2245; FAX 413-538-2144; *Dir* Marianne Doezema; *Cur* Wendy Watson; *Bus Mgr* Amy Wehle; *Registrar & Preparator* Sean Tarpey
Open Tues - Fri 11 AM - 5 PM, Sat - Sun 1 - 5 PM. No admis fee. Estab 1876, mus now occupies a building dedicated in 1970. In addition to its permanent collections, mus also organizes special exhibitions of international scope. Art mus with five galleries houses the permanent collection & special exhibitions. Mem: Dues $25-$1000
Income: Financed by endowment, mem & college funds
Collections: †Asian art, †European & American paintings, †sculpture, †prints & drawings; †Egyptian, †Greek, †Roman, †Pre-Columbia
Publications: Newsletter, bi-annually; exhibition catalogues; calendar, bi-annual
Activities: Educ dept; docent training; lect open to public, 5-6 vis lectr per year; concerts; gallery talks; tours; individual paintings lent to qualified museums; book traveling exhibitions 1-2 per year; originate traveling exhibitions to qualified museums; museum shop sells exhibition catalogues, cards

L **Art Library**, 50 College St, 01075-6404. Tel 413-538-2225; FAX 413-538-2370; Elec Mail sperry@mtholyoke.edu. *Dir* Susan L Perry
Open to college community only
Library Holdings: Vols 15,550; Per subs 64; AV — Slides

SOUTH SUDBURY

M LONGFELLOW'S WAYSIDE INN MUSEUM, Wayside Inn Rd off Rte 20, 01776. Tel 508-443-1776; *Innkeeper* Robert H Purrington; *Chmn Trustees* Richard Davidson
Open daily 9 AM - 6 PM cl Christmas Day. Admis $.50; no charge for dining room and overnight guests. Estab 1702 as the oldest operating Inn in America. The ancient hostelry continues to provide hospitality to wayfarers from all over the world. 18th century period rooms including Old Barroom, Longfellow Parlor, Longfellow Bed Chamber, Old Kitchen, Drivers and Drovers Chamber. Historic buildings on the estate include Redstone School of Mary's Little Lamb fame, grist mill, and Martha Mary Chapel. Average Annual Attendance: 170,000
Collections: Early American furniture and decorative arts; Howe family memorabilia; paintings; photographs of the Inn; prints
Activities: Classes for adults; docent training; colonial crafts demonstrations and workshops; lect open to public, 5 vis lectr per year; gallery talks; tours; sales shop selling books, original art, reproductions, prints and slides

SPRINGFIELD

M MUSEUM OF FINE ARTS, 49 Chestnut St, 01103. Tel 413-263-6800; FAX 413-263-6814; *Dir* Gail Colglazier; *Dir Public Progs* Kay Simpson; *Coll Mgr* Wendy Stayman; *Cur Coll* Heather Haskell; *Spec Events Coordr* Laurie Darby
Open Wed - Sun Noon - 4 PM, cl Mon, Tues & holidays. Admis adults $4, children $1. Estab 1933 as a unit of the Springfield Library & Mus Assoc through the bequests of Mr & Mrs James Philip Gray, to collect, preserve & display original artwork. Building contains 18 galleries, theater, offices. Average Annual Attendance: 76,000. Mem: 4500; dues $50
Collections: †American paintings, sculpture & graphics, primitive to contemporary; †European paintings & sculpture, early Renaissance to contemporary; †Japanese woodblock prints
Exhibitions: Special exhibitions, historic to contemporary are continually on view in addition to permanent collection; changing exhibitions
Publications: Handbook to the American & European Collection, Museum of Fine Arts, Springfield; exhibition catalogs
Activities: Classes for adults & children; dramatic programs; docent training; lect open to public, 65 vis lectr per year; concerts; gallery talks; tours; scholarships offered; individual paintings & original objects of art lent to museums & galleries; lending collection contains original art works, original prints, paintings, sculpture, color transparencies & black & white photographs; book traveling exhibitions 1-3 per year; originate traveling exhibitions; museum shop sells books, children's items, gift items, jewelry, posters, reproductions, prints & slides
L Reference Library, 49 Chestnut St, 01103. Tel 413-263-6800; FAX 413-734-3688; *Asst to Registrar* Stephen Fisher
Library Holdings: Vols 2800; AV — Slides; Other — Photographs

M GEORGE WALTER VINCENT SMITH ART MUSEUM, 222 State St, 01103. Tel 413-263-6890; *Chmn Trustee Committee* Janee Armstrong-Friedmann; *Dir* Hollister Sturges; *Registrar* Karen Papineau; *Dir Educ* Kay Simpson; *Asst Cur Educ* Mary Franks; *Asst Cur Educ* Maren Brown; *Conservator* Emil G Schnorr
Open Thurs - Sat Noon - 4 PM. Admis adults $4, children $1. Estab 1889 to preserve, protect, present, interpret, study & publish the collections of fine & decorative arts; administered by the Springfield Library & Museums Assoc. Maintains eleven galleries housing permanent collection & one gallery reserved for changing exhibitions. Average Annual Attendance: 35,000. Mem: 2000; dues $15 & up; annual meeting in June
Income: Financed by endowment, mem, city & state appropriations
Collections: 19th century American & European Paintings; Japanese Bronzes-Arms & Armor; Near Eastern Carpets; Oriental Arts (calligraphy, ceramics, lacquer, painting, sculpture, textiles); Oriental Cloisonne; plaster casts of ancient & Renaissance sculptural masterworks
Exhibitions: Annual Juried Exhibition; Art League Exhibition
Publications: Annual report; quadrangle calendar; special exhibition catalogs
Activities: Classes for adults & children; dramatic programs; demonstrations; gallery walks; public programs; activity rooms; docent training; lect open to public, 50 vis lectr per year; concerts; gallery talks; tours; competitions with awards; scholarships & fels offered; lending collection contains books, slides & videos; book traveling exhibitions 5-10 per year; originate traveling exhibitions to other museums; museum shop sells books, magazines, original art, reproductions, prints & slides

A SPRINGFIELD ART LEAGUE, George Walter Vincent Smith Art Museum, 222 State St, 01103. Tel 413-263-6890; *Pres* Diana Papas
Estab 1918 to stimulate art expression & appreciation in Springfield. Mem: dues $15; annual meeting in May
Income: Financed solely by mem
Exhibitions: Non-juried show in Oct open to all members
Activities: Lectr open to public; demonstrations; tours; workshops

M SPRINGFIELD COLLEGE, Hasting Gallery, Visual & Performing Arts Dept, 263 Alden St, 01109. Tel 413-748-3000; *Chmn* Bill Blizard; *Coordr* Ronald Maggio
Open Mon - Thurs 8 AM - 12 AM, Fri 8 AM - 8 PM, Sat 9 AM - 8 PM, Sun Noon - 12 AM. Estab 1975 to bring a wide range of quality exhibits in all areas of the visual arts to the Springfield College campus & surrounding community
Income: Financed by Cultural Affairs Committee
Library Holdings: Vols 112,000; Per subs 10; Micro — Prints; AV — Cassettes, fs, motion pictures, v-tapes; Other — Original art works, prints
Activities: Dramatic programs; lect open to public; original prints, color reproductions, photographs lent to faculty & administration on campus

SPRINGFIELD LIBRARY & MUSEUMS ASSOCIATION
M Connecticut Valley Historical Museum, 194 State St, 01103. Tel 413-263-6895; *Dir* Gail N Colglazier; *Cur Educ* Alice Smith; *Head Library & Archive Coll* Margaret Humberston
Open Thurs - Sun Noon - 4 PM. Admis adults $4, children $1, under 6 free.

Includes admis to all four mus at Quadrangle. Estab 1876 to interpret history of Connecticut River Valley. Average Annual Attendance: 15,000. Mem: 3900; dues $30; annual meeting in Sept
Collections: Decorative arts of Connecticut Valley, including furniture, paintings & prints, pewter, firearms, glass, silver; early games
Exhibitions: Many exhibits pertaining to history & decorative arts of Connecticut River Valley
Publications: Musical Memories: Springfield Symphony Orchestra 50th Anniversary Commemorative Book; Say Goodbye to the Valley
Activities: Classes for adults & children; lect open to public; gallery talks; tours; book traveling exhibitions 1-2 per year; museum shop sells books, note cards, genealogy shirts & tote bags

M Springfield Science Museum, Quadrangle, Corner of State & Chestnut Sts (Mailing add: 220 State St, 01103). Tel 413-263-6800; FAX 413-263-6898; *Dir* Galil Nessel Colglazier; *Cur Anthropology* John Pretola PhD; *Public Prog* Kay Simpson; *Cur Natural Science* David Stier
Open Wed - Sun Noon - 4 PM. Admis adults $4, child $1. Estab 1859 to collect, preserve & exhibit material related to natural & physical science. Average Annual Attendance: 100,000. Mem: 4500; dues $35 & up; annual meeting in Sept
Income: Financed by mem, city appropriation, admis & program fees, local, state & federal grants
Collections: Aquarium; Dinosaur Hall; early aviation artifacts; Exploration Center; habitat groupings of mounted animals; Native American & African artifacts; Planetarium
Activities: Classes for adults & children; docent programs; outreach programs; lect open to public; book traveling exhibitions 2-3 per year; museum shop sells books & gift items

A SPRINGFIELD LIBRARY & MUSEUMS ASSOCIATION, Art & Music Dept, 220 State St. Tel 413-263-6800; FAX 413-263-6825; *Head Adult Information Serv* Arthur Messier; *Dir* Emily Bader; *Assoc Dir* Lee Fogerty
Open Mon - Thurs 10 AM - 8 PM, Fri Noon - 5 PM, Sat 9 AM - 5 PM, Sun Noon - 4 PM, cl holidays & weekends in summer. No admis fee. Estab 1857, Department opened 1905. In addition to the City Library system, the Springfield Library & Mus Assoc owns & administers, as separate units, the George Walter Vincent Smith Mus, the Mus of Fine Arts, the Science Mus & the Connecticut Valley Historical Mus
Library Holdings: Vols 700,000; Per subs 1000; Compact discs 15,000; AV — Cassettes 1000, rec 5000; Other — Clipping files, exhibition catalogs, pamphlets, reproductions
Exhibitions: Occasional exhibitions from the library's collections & of work by local artists

STOCKBRIDGE

M NORMAN ROCKWELL MUSEUM AT STOCKBRIDGE, 9 Glendale Rd, PO Box 308, 01262. Tel 413-298-4100; FAX 413-298-4142; *Pres* David L Klausmeyer; *Dir* Laurie Norton Moffatt; *VPres* Bobbie Crosby; *Asst Dir Prog & Educ* Maud V Ayson; *Assoc Dir External Relations* Philip S Deely; *Cur* Maureen Hart Hennessey
Open May - Oct daily 10 AM - 5 PM, Nov - Apr Mon - Fri 11 AM - 4 PM, Sat & Sun 10 AM - 5 PM, cl Thanksgiving, Christmas, New Year's Day. Admis adult $9, youth 6-18 $2, children 5 & under free, Stockbridge residents & mus members free. Estab 1967 to collect, manage, preserve, study, interpret & present to the public material pertaining to the life & career of Norman Rockwell. Consists of a main building (1993), situated on 36 acres in a country setting with galleries for permanent & changing exhibitions, classrooms, the Norman Rockwell Reference Center, meeting room & store. The Norman Rockwell Studio is adjacent. Average Annual Attendance: 200,000. Mem: 2000; dues $35-$5000; annual meeting in Sept
Income: Financed by admis, mem, donations, sales & grants
Collections: Largest permanent collection of original Rockwell art (more than 500 original paintings & drawings); artifacts & furnishings of Norman Rockwell's studio; archives including business letters, memorabilia, negatives & photographs
Exhibitions: Mirror on America: My Adventures as an Illustrator; My Best Studio Yet; changing exhibits 3 times yearly
Publications: Norman Rockwell: A Definitive Catalogue; The Portfolio, quarterly newsletter; Programs & Events, quarterly calendar
Activities: Docent training; lect open to public; tours; educator's seminars, art workshops for adults & children; school programs; family days; special performances & events; free admission days; scholarships & internships offered; individual paintings & original objects of art lent to qualifying not for profit educational institutions; originate traveling exhibitions; museum shop sells books, prints & gift items
L Library, PO Box 308, 01262. Tel 413-298-4100; FAX 413-298-4145; *Cur* Maureen Hart Hennessey; *Asst Cur* Linda Szekely
Open Tues, Thurs & Sat 1 - 5 PM & by appointment
Library Holdings: Vols 300; Per subs 10; AV — A-tapes, cassettes, lantern slides, motion pictures, rec, slides, v-tapes; Other — Clipping files, manuscripts, memorabilia, photographs, prints, reproductions
Special Subjects: Norman Rockwell

M THE TRUSTEES OF RESERVATIONS, The Mission House, PO Box 792, 01262. Tel 413-298-3239; *Adminr* Mark Baer
Open Memorial Day through Columbus Day Tues - Sun 11 AM - 5 PM. Admis adults $5, children 6-12 $2.50. Built 1739, the home of John Sergeant, first missionary to the Stockbridge Indians, it is now an Early American Mus containing an outstanding collection of Colonial funishings. Mus opened in 1930. Average Annual Attendance: 3000
Publications: Yearly brochure

TAUNTON

M OLD COLONY HISTORICAL SOCIETY, Museum, 66 Church Green, 02780. Tel 508-822-1622; *Pres* Marcus A Rhodes Jr; *Dir* Katheryn P Viens; *Cur* Jane Emack-Cambra
Open Tues - Sat 10 AM - 4 PM, mus tours 10:30 AM, 1:30 PM & 2:30 PM. Admis adults $2, sr citizens & children 12-18 $1. Estab 1853 to preserve & perpetuate the history of the Old Colony in Massachusetts. Four exhibition halls. Average Annual Attendance: 7000. Mem: 700; dues $10-$250; annual meeting third Thurs in Apr
Income: $120,000 (financed by endowment, mem, service fees, grants)
Collections: Fire fighting equipment; furniture, household utensils, Indian artifacts, military items; portraits, silver, stoves
Publications: Booklets; pamphlets
Activities: Classes for adults & children; docent training; workshops; lect open to public, 8-10 vis lectr per year; fels offered; museum shop sells books & souvenirs
L Library, 66 Church Green, 02780. Tel 508-822-1622; *Dir* Katheryn P Viens; *Library Asst* Greta Smith; *Cur* Jane Emack-Cambra
Open Tues - Sat 10 AM - 4 PM. Admis genealogy $5, other research $2. Estab 1853. For reference only; research services available for a fee
Library Holdings: Per subs 10; Micro — Reels; AV — A-tapes, slides; Other — Exhibition catalogs, manuscripts, memorabilia, pamphlets, photographs, prints
Special Subjects: Architecture, Art History, Ceramics, Coins & Medals, Decorative Arts, Dolls, Flasks & Bottles, Folk Art, Furniture, Glass, Manuscripts, Maps, Metalwork, Painting - American, Pewter, Genealogy

TYRINGHAM

M SANTARELLA (Formerly Tyringham Art Galleries), Tyringham's Gingerbread House, 75 Main Rd, PO Box 414, 01264. Tel 413-243-3260; *Dir* Hope C Talbert
Open 10 AM - 4:30 PM. No admis fee. Estab 1953 to exhibit & sell paintings, prints & sculptures by recognized artists, including world masters. The building was designed as a sculpture studio by the late Sir Henry Kitson. Average Annual Attendance: 15,000
Income: Financed privately
Collections: Santarella Sculpture Gardens
Exhibitions: One-person shows by established artists
Activities: Gallery talks; tours; museum shop sells books & prints

WALTHAM

A AMERICAN JEWISH HISTORICAL SOCIETY, 2 Thornton Rd, 02154. Tel 617-891-8110; FAX 617-899-9208; *Pres* Justin L Wyner; *Dir* Dr Michael Feldberg
Open summer Mon - Fri 8:30 AM - 5 PM, winter Mon - Thurs 8:30 AM - 5 PM, Fri 8:30 AM - 2 PM. No admis fee. Estab 1892 to collect, preserve, catalog & disseminate information relating to the American Jewish experience. Two galleries with exhibitions mounted, 15 x 50 ft. Average Annual Attendance: 3000. Mem: 3300; dues $50; annual meeting in May
Income: $500,000 (financed by endowment, mem, Jewish Federation allocations, grants & donations)
Collections: Manuscripts; Portraits; Yiddish Motion Pictures; Yiddish Theater Posters
Exhibitions: Gustatory Delights in the New World; German Jews in America; Emma Lazarus, Joseph Pulitzer & The Statue of Liberty; Yiddish Theatre in America; American Jewish Colonial Portraits; Sebhardim in America
Publications: American Jewish History, quarterly; Heritage; Local Jewish Historical Society News; books; newsletters
Activities: Lect open to public, 10 vis lectr per year; gallery talks; tours; competitions with awards; individual paintings & original objects of art lent to museums & historical societies; lending collection contains motion pictures, paintings, books, original art works, original prints & photographs; originate traveling exhibitions
L Lee M Friedman Memorial Library, 2 Thornton Rd, 02154. Tel 617-891-8110; FAX 617-899-9208; *Librn* Michele Feller-Kuppman
Open Mon - Fri 8:30 AM - 5 PM; winter Fri 8:30 AM - 2 PM, Sun 2 - 5 PM. Estab 1892 to collect, preserve & catalog material relating to American-Jewish history. Open to qualified researchers for reference
Income: $514,000 (financed by endowment, mem, contributions, grants, allocations from Jewish welfare funds)
Purchases: $10,000
Library Holdings: Vols 90,000; Per subs 100; Archives; AV — Cassettes, motion pictures, rec, slides; Other — Exhibition catalogs, manuscripts, memorabilia, original art works, pamphlets, photographs, prints, reproductions, sculpture
Special Subjects: Colonial American Jewry, philanthropic institutions, synagogues
Collections: Stephen S Wise Manuscripts Collection; Archives of Major Jewish Organizations
Exhibitions: Colonial American Jewry; 19th Century Jewish Families; On Common Ground: The Boston Jewish Experience, 1649-1980; Statue of Liberty; German American Jewry; Moses Michael Hays & Post- Revolutionary Boston
Publications: American Jewish History, quarterly; Heritage, bi-annually
Activities: Lect open to public, 2-3 vis lectr per year; gallery talks; tours; sponsor competitions with awards; originate traveling exhibitions to libraries, museum societies, synagogues

M BRANDEIS UNIVERSITY, Rose Art Museum, PO Box 9110, 02254. Tel 617-736-3434; FAX 617-736-3439; *Dir* Carl I Belz; *Cur* Susan Stoops; *Registrar* John Rexine; *Preparator* Roger Kizik; *Coordr Educ Patrons & Friends* Corinne Zimmermann
Open Tues - Sun 1 - 5 PM, Thurs 1 - 9 PM. No admis fee. Estab 1961 for the organization of regionally & nationally recognized exhibits of contemporary painting & sculpture. All galleries are used for changing exhibitions; there are no permanent exhibitions; two levels & wing gallery. Average Annual Attendance: 20,000
Collections: The permanent collections consist of: African art; American Indian

art; contemporary art (post World War II); Japanese prints; modern art (1800 to World War II), including the Riverside Museum Collections & the Teresa Jackson Weill Collection; Pre-Columbian art; pre-modern art (before 1800); Mr & Mrs Edward Rose Collection of early ceramics; Helen S Slosberg Collection of Oceanic art; Tibetian art
Exhibitions: Stephen Antonakos; William Beckman & Gregory Gillespie; Eva Hesse; Katherine Porter; Friedel Dzubas; Dorothea Rockburne; Lester Johnson; Jake Berthot; Jene Highstein; More Than Minimal: Feminism & Abstraction in the '70s
Publications: Exhibition catalogs
Activities: Classes for children; docent training; lect open to public; gallery talks; tours; individual paintings & original objects of art lent to students & individuals within the university; lending collection contains original art works, original prints, paintings; book traveling exhibitions 1 per year
L Leonard L Farber Library, Norman & Rosita Creative Arts Ctr, 415 South St, PO Box 9110, 02254-9110. Tel 617-736-4681; FAX 617-736-4675
Open Mon - Fri 8:30 AM - 1 AM, Sat 9 AM - 10 PM, Sun Noon - 1 AM. Estab 1948 to provide materials & services for the teaching, research & pub interest in the arts of the Brandeis community. For lending & reference
Library Holdings: Vols 40,000; Per subs 130; Micro — Cards, fiche, prints, reels; AV — Cassettes, rec; Other — Exhibition catalogs, photographs
Special Subjects: Art History
Collections: †Dr Bern Dibner Collection of Leonardo Da Vinci - Books; Benjamin A & Julia M Trustman Collection of Honore Daumier Prints (4000); extensive collection of books on Daumier
Exhibitions: Rotating exhibition of Daumier Prints

WELLESLEY

WELLESLEY COLLEGE

M Davis Museum & Cultural Center, 106 Central St, 02181. Tel 617-235-0320, Ext 2034; FAX 617-283-2064; *Dir* Susan Taylor; *Cur* Lucy Flint-Gohlke; *Asst Dir Museum Develop* Nancy Gunn; *Cur* Judith Hoos Fox; *Assoc Dir* Kathleen Harleman; *Dir Information* Peter Walsh
Open Mon - Sat 10 AM - 5 PM; Sun 2 - 5 PM; cl New Year's Day, Thanksgiving, Dec 24, 25 & 31, mid-June, July & Aug. No admis fee. Estab 1889, dedicated to acquiring a collection of high quality art objects for the primary purpose of teaching art history from original works. Main gallery houses major exhibitions; Corridor Gallery, works on paper; Sculpture Court, permanent installation, sculpture, reliefs, works on wood panel. Average Annual Attendance: 18,000. Mem: 650; dues donor $100, contributor $50, regular $25
Income: Financed by mem, through college & gifts
Collections: Paintings; sculpture; graphic & decorative arts; Asian, African, ancient, medieval, Renaissance, Baroque, 19th & 20th century European & American art; photography
Publications: Exhibition catalogs; Wellesley College Friends of Art Newsletter, annually
Activities: Docent training; lect open to public & members only; gallery talks; tours; original objects of art lent to students; lending collection contains original prints; book traveling exhibitons; originate traveling exhibitions; sales shop sells catalogs, postcards & notecards
L Art Library, 106 Central St, 02181. Tel 617-283-3258; FAX 617-283-3647; Elec Mail rmcelroy@lucy.wellelsy.edu. *Librn* Richard McElroy
Circ 18,000
Income: Financed by College appropriation
Purchases: $48,000
Library Holdings: Vols 48,500; Per subs 158; Micro — Fiche 1700; AV — Kodachromes, lantern slides; Other — Exhibition catalogs, pamphlets, photographs
Special Subjects: Antiquities-Greek, Antiquities-Roman, Archaeology, Architecture, Art History, Asian Art, History of Art & Archaeology, Oriental Art, Painting - American, Painting - European, Painting - Italian, American art & architecture, Western European art & architecture, Far Eastern art, Ancient art & architecture

WELLFLEET

M WELLFLEET HISTORICAL SOCIETY MUSEUM, Main St, PO Box 58, 02667. Tel 508-349-9157; *Cur* Joan Hopkins Coughlin; *Co-Cur* Durand Echeverria
Open late June - early Sept, Tues - Sat 2 - 5 PM, Tues & Fri 10 AM - Noon. Admis $1. Estab 1953. Average Annual Attendance: 200. Mem: 350; dues $3.50; 5 general meetings per yr
Income: $4000 (financed by mem)
Purchases: $1000
Collections: Books; china & glass; documents; Indian artifacts; paintings & photographs; personal memorabilia of Wellfleet; pewter; shellfish & finfish exhibit; shop models; shipwreck & marine items
Publications: Beacon, annual
Activities: Lect open to public, 5 vis lectr per year; walking tours during summer

WENHAM

A WENHAM MUSEUM, 132 Main St, 01984. Tel 508-468-2377; *Dir* Eleanor E Thompson; *Pres* Elizabeth Stone; *Office Admin* Felicia Connolly; *Doll Cur* Diane Hamblin; *Cur* Bar Browdo
Open Mon - Fri 11 AM - 4 PM, Sat 1 - 4 PM, Sun 2 - 5 PM, groups by appointment. Admis adults $1.50, children (6-14) $.50. Estab 1921 as Historical Soc, incorporated 1953, to acquire, preserve, interpret & exhibit collections of literary & historical interest; to provide an educational & cultural service & facilities. Maintains three permanent galleries & one gallery for changing exhibits. Average Annual Attendance: 10,000. Mem: 650; dues family $10, individual $5; annual meeting Apr
Income: Financed by endowment, mem, earned income
Collections: Dolls; doll houses; figurines; costumes & accessories 1800-1960;

embroideries; fans; needlework; quilts; toys

Exhibitions: Ice Cutting Tool Exhibit; 19th Century Shoe Shops; Still Lifes; Quilts Old & New; Samplers; Tin & Woodenware; Weavers; Wedding Dresses

Publications: Annual report; newsletter

Activities: Classes for children; lect open to the public; gallery talks; tours; museum shop sells books, miniatures, original needlework, dolls & small toys

L **Timothy Pickering Library,** 132 Main St, 01984. Tel 508-468-2377; *Librn* Marilyn Corning

Open to members & the pub for reference

Library Holdings: Vols 2200; Other — Manuscripts, memorabilia, pamphlets, photographs

WESTFIELD

M **WESTFIELD ATHENAEUM,** Jasper Rand Art Museum, 6 Elm St, 01085. Tel 413-568-7833; *Pres* James Rogers; *Dir* Patricia T Cramer; *Treas* Mark Morin

Open Mon - Thurs 8:30 AM - 8 PM, Fri & Sat 8:30 AM - 5 PM, cl Sat in summer. No admis fee. Estab 1927 to provide exhibitions of art works by area artists & other prominent artists. Gallery measures 25 x 30 x 17 feet, with a domed ceiling & free-standing glass cases & wall cases. Average Annual Attendance: 13,500. Mem: Annual meeting fourth Mon in Oct

Income: Financed by endowment, city appropriation

Exhibitions: Changing exhibits on a monthly basis

WESTON

M **REGIS COLLEGE,** Fine Arts Center, 235 Wellesley St, 02193. Tel 617-893-1820, Ext 2706; *Dir* Rosemary Noon

Open Mon - Fri 9 AM - 4:30 PM. No admis fee. Estab 1964 for educ, vis exhibits & students use. Gallery is one room, 20 x 30 ft. Average Annual Attendance: 1500

Income: Financed by donations

WILLIAMSTOWN

M **STERLING & FRANCINE CLARK ART INSTITUTE,** 225 South St, PO Box 8, 01267. Tel 413-458-9545; FAX 413-458-2336; Elec Mail clark.williams.edu. *Dir* Michael Conforti; *Assoc Dir* John H Brooks; *Cur of Paintings* Steven Kern; *Cur Decorative Arts* Beth Carver Wees; *Registrar* Martha Asher; *Asst Comptroller* Valerie Schueckler; *Asst Comptroller* Karin Watkins; *Supt* Alan Chamberland; *Asst Dir Publications & Spec Projects* Mary Jo Carpenter

Open Tues - Sun 10 AM - 5 PM, cl Mon, New Year's Day, Thanksgiving & Christmas. No admis fee. Estab 1955 as a mus of fine arts with galleries, art research library & pub events in auditorium. Average Annual Attendance: 120,000

Collections: Antique silver; Dutch, Flemish, French, Italian Old Master paintings from the 14th-18th centuries; French 19th century paintings, especially the Impressionists; 19th century sculpture; Old Master prints & drawings; porcelains; selected 19th century American artists (Homer & Sargent)

Exhibitions: The Permanent Collection & Traveling Exhibitions

Publications: Calendar of Events, quarterly

Activities: Docent training; lect open to public, 10 vis lectr per year; concerts; gallery talks; tours for school children; individual paintings & original objects of art lent to other museums whose facilities meet criteria, for exhibitions of academic importance; book traveling exhibitions 1-4 per year; museum shop sells books, reproductions, prints, slides, jewelry, glass, games, puzzles

L **Clark Art Institute Library,** 225 South St, PO Box 8, 01267. Tel 413-458-9545; FAX 413-458-2336; *Librn* Sarah S Gibson; *Photograph & Slide Librn* J Dustin Wees

Open Mon - Fri 9 AM - 5 PM, cl holidays. Estab 1962. For reference only

Purchases: $150,000

Library Holdings: Vols 150,000; Per subs 640; Auction sale catalogues 30,000; Micro — Fiche, reels; AV — Slides; Other — Exhibition catalogs, photographs, reproductions

Special Subjects: Art History, Drawings, Etchings & Engravings, Graphic Arts, History of Art & Archaeology, Painting - American, Painting - British, Painting - Dutch, Painting - European, Painting - Italian, Painting - Polish, Painting - Russian, Painting - Scandinavian, Restoration & Conservation, Silver, European and American Art

Collections: †Mary Ann Beinecke Decorative Art Collection; Duveen Library & Archive; Juynboll Collection

M **WILLIAMS COLLEGE,** Museum of Art, Main St, 01267-2566. Tel 413-597-2429; FAX 413-458-9017; *Dir* Linda Shearer; *Asst Dir* Marion Goethals; *Public Relations-Develop Dir* Open ; *Prendergast Cur* Nancy Mowll Mathews; *Assoc Cur Exhib* Deborah Menaker Rothschild; *Dir Educ* Barbara Robertson; *Pub Relations Asst* Open ; *Assoc Cur Coll* Vivian Patterson; *Registrar* Diane Hart-Agee; *Asst to Dir* Judith M Raab; *Preparator* Scott Hayward

Open Tues - Sat 10 AM - 5 PM, Sun 1 - 5 PM. No admis fee. Estab 1926 for the presentation of the permanent collection & temporary loan exhibitions for the benefit of the Williams College community & the general pub. Original 1846 Greek Revival building designed by Thomas Tefft; 1983 & 1986 additions & renovations designed by Charles Moore & Robert Harper of Centerbrook Architects & Planners. Building also houses Art Department of Williams College. Average Annual Attendance: 50,000

Collections: Ancient & medieval art; Asian & African art; modern & contemporary art; 18th-20th century American art; 20th century American photography

Publications: Brochures; exhibition catalogs, 3-4 per year

Activities: Lect open to public; gallery talks; tours; individual paintings & original objects of art are lent to other museums; museum shop sells books, jewelry, magazines, posters & postcards

L **Sawyer Library,** Main St, 01267-2566. Tel 413-597-2504; FAX 413-597-4106; *Librn* Phyllis L Cutler

Income: $22,367

Library Holdings: Vols 697,023; Per subs 3024; AV — Slides 22,800

L **Chapin Library,** Stetson Hall, PO Box 426, 01267-0426. Tel 413-597-2462; FAX 413-597-2929; Elec Mail wayne.g.hammond@williams.edu. *Head Librn* Robert L Volz; *Asst Librn* Wayne G Hammond

Open Mon - Fri 10 AM - Noon & 1 - 5 PM. Library estab 1923. For reference only

Income: Financed by Williams College, endowments & gifts

Library Holdings: Vols 50,000; Per subs 20; AV — A-tapes, cassettes, Kodachromes, motion pictures, rec, slides, v-tapes; Other — Clipping files, exhibition catalogs, manuscripts, memorabilia, original art works, pamphlets, photographs, prints, sculpture

Special Subjects: Advertising Design, Architecture, Art History, Calligraphy, Cartoons, Commercial Art, Decorative Arts, Drawings, Etchings & Engravings, Film, Graphic Arts, Graphic Design, Historical Material, Illustration, Lettering

A **WILLIAMSTOWN ART CONSERVATION CENTER,** 225 South St, 01267. Tel 413-458-5741; FAX 413-458-2314; Elec Mail wacc@clark.williams.edu. *Dir* Gary Burger

Estab 1977

Income: $1,000,000 (financed by state appropriation & earned income)

Activities: Internships; lect open to public, 2-4 vis lectr per year

WINCHESTER

M **ARTHUR GRIFFIN CENTER FOR PHOTOGRAPHIC ART,** 67 Shore Rd, 01890. Tel 617-729-1158; FAX 617-721-2765; *Exec Dir* Glenn Doyle

Open Tues - Sun Noon - 4 PM. Admis $3. Estab 1992 to promote historic & contemporary photography through photographic exhibitions. Average Annual Attendance: 5000. Mem: 1000

Exhibitions: Annual Juried Photography Show

Publications: The Griffin News, newsletter

Activities: Classes for adults & children; sales shop sells books, original art & prints

WORCESTER

AMERICAN ANTIQUARIAN SOCIETY
For further information, see National and Regional Organizations

M **CLARK UNIVERSITY,** The University Gallery at Goddard Library, 950 Main St, 01610. Tel 508-793-7113; FAX 508-793-8844; *Dir* Sarah Walker

Open Tues - Sun Noon - 5 PM, cl University holidays & vacations. No admis fee. Estab 1976 to provide the Clark community & greater Worcester community the opportunity to view quality exhibitions of art, primarily, but not exclusively, contemporary. Gallery 24 ft x 32 ft, 9 ft ceiling height, with moveable panels. Average Annual Attendance: 5000

Income: Financed through the University

Exhibitions: Six to eight exhibitions per year of, primarily emerging artists & well-known artists

Publications: Announcements of exhibitions

Activities: Lect open to public; gallery talks; Senior Art Purchase Award

L **COLLEGE OF THE HOLY CROSS,** Dinand Library, One College St, 01610-2349. Tel 508-793-3372; FAX 508-793-2372; Elec Mail jhogan@holycross.edu. *Dir & Col Librn* Dr James Hogan; *Assoc Dir* Karen Reilly

Estab 1843 to support the academic study & research needs of a liberal visual arts department

Library Holdings: Vols 527,128; Per subs 2052; AV — Slides 50,000; Other — Exhibition catalogs, original art works, sculpture

Special Subjects: Antiquities-Byzantine, Antiquities-Greek, Architecture, Art Education, Art History, Commercial Art, Decorative Arts, Fashion Arts, Film, Graphic Arts, Industrial Design, Painting - American, Theatre Arts

Publications: Art reference bibliographies, semi-annual

M **HIGGINS ARMORY MUSEUM,** 100 Barber Ave, 01606-2444. Tel 508-853-6015; FAX 508-852-7697; *Pres* J C Donnelly Jr; *Dir* Kent durRussell

Open Tues - Sat 10 AM - 4 PM, Sun Noon - 4 PM, cl Mon & legal holidays. Admis adults $4.75, senior citizens $4, children 6-16 $3.75. Estab 1929 to collect & maintain arms, armor & related artifacts. Museum has a Gothic Hall with high vaulted ceilings. Average Annual Attendance: 40,000-50,000. Mem: 500; dues $15-$1000; annual meeting in Apr

Income: Financed by admis, mem, grants, gift shop & endowment

Collections: Arms & armor from antiquity through the 1800s art from related periods; paintings; tapestries; stained glass; woodcarvings

Publications: Quarterly calendar

Activities: Classes for adults & children; dramatic programs; docent training; lect open to public, 2 vis lectr per year; concerts; gallery talks; original objects of art lent to other museums; lending collection contains paintings, sculptures & several thousand objects of armor; museum shop sells books, magazines, reproductions & souvenirs

L **Library,** 100 Barber Ave, 01606-2444. Tel 508-853-6015; FAX 508-852-7697; *Cur & Librn* Walter J Karcheski Jr

Library closed at present due to renovations; no opening date set

Library Holdings: Vols 3000; Other — Clipping files, exhibition catalogs, manuscripts, memorabilia, photographs

Special Subjects: Archaeology, Art History, Bronzes, History of Art & Archaeology, Islamic Art, Metalwork, Mixed Media, Painting - European, Portraits, Stained Glass, Woodcuts, Arms & armor, medieval & Renaissance history & warfare to c1870

Publications: Higgins Catalogue of Armor (out-of-print); Higgins Catalogue of Books; Knightly News quarterly

M **WORCESTER ART MUSEUM,** 55 Salisbury St, 01609-3196. Tel 508-799-4406; FAX 508-798-5646; *Dir* James A Welu; *Deputy Dir* Anthony G King; *Dir Develop & Mem* Susan Courtemanche; *Assoc Dir Develop* Clare O'Connell; *Asst Dir Develop* Sarah Cecil; *Dir Pub Affairs* Gina Lionette; *Dir Pub Information* Barbara Feldstein; *Dir Pub* Ann McCrea; *Dir Educ* Honee A Hess; *Dir*

Curatorial Affairs Susan E Strickler; *Cur Asian Art* Elizabeth de Sabato Swinton; *Cur Contemporary Art* Donna Harkavy; *Cur Photography* Stephen B Jareckie; *Cur Prints & Drawings* David L Acton; *Registrar* Joan-Elisabeth Reid; *Chief Preparator & Exhib Designer* John R Reynolds; *Chief Conservator* Jennifer Spohn; *Dir Bldg Servs* James Sanders; *Coordr Spec Events* Brenda Welch
Open Wed & Fri 11 AM - 4 PM, Thurs 11 AM - 8 PM, Sat 10 AM - 5 PM, Sun 1 - 5 PM, cl Mon & major holidays. Admis adult $4, sr citizens & full-time students with current ID $2.50 members & children under 18 free, Sat 10 AM - noon free to all. Estab Museum 1896, School 1898. The Museum and School were founded for the promotion of art and art education in Worcester; for the preservation and exhibition of works and objects of art and for instruction in the industrial, liberal and fine arts. There are 42 galleries housed in a neoclassical building. The Higgins Education Wing, built in 1970, houses studios and classrooms and contains exhibition space for shows sponsored by the Education Department. Average Annual Attendance: 130,000. Mem: 4500; dues $15 - $1000 & over; annual meeting in Nov
Income: $4,000,000 (financed by endowment, mem, private corporate contributions & government grants)
Collections: John Chandler Bancroft Collection of Japanese Prints; †American Paintings of 17th - 20th Centuries; †British Paintings of 18th and 19th Centuries; †Dutch 17th and 19th Century Paintings; †Egyptian, Classical, Oriental and Medieval Sculpture; †French Paintings of 16th - 19th Centuries; †Flemish 16th - 17th Century Paintings; †Italian Paintings of the 13th - 18th Centuries; Mosaics from Antioch; †Pre-Columbian Collection; 12th Century French Chapter House
Publications: American Portrait Miniatures: The Worcester Art Museum Collection; In Battle's Light: Woodblock Prints of Japan's Early Modern Wars; Calendar of Events, quarterly; The Second Wave: American Abstractions of the 1930s & 1940s; A Spectrum of Innovation: American Color Prints, 1890 - 1960
Activities: Classes for adults & children; docent training; lect open to public, 10-15 vis lectr per year; symposia; concerts; gallery talks; tours; film series; videos; scholarships offered; museum shop sells books, reproductions, prints, jewelry & exhibition-related merchandise

L **Library,** 55 Salisbury St, 01609-3196. Tel 508-799-4406, Ext 3070; FAX 508-798-5646; *Librn* Kathy L Berg; *Slide Librn* Debby Aframe; *Asst* Donna Winant; *Cataloger* Pauline McCormick
Open Tues & Thurs 11 AM - 4 PM, & by appointment during academic year. Estab 1909 to provide resource material for the Museum Departments. Participate in Worcester Area Cooperating Libraries. Maintains non-circulating collection only
Income: $85,200 (financed by endowment, grants and gifts)
Purchases: $25,000
Library Holdings: Vols 34,000; Per subs 106; Auction & sale catalogues; Micro — Fiche; AV — Kodachromes, lantern slides, slides; Other — Exhibition catalogs, pamphlets
Special Subjects: European & American paintings, prints & drawings; Japanese prints; auction & sale catalogues; museum exhibition catalogues
Exhibitions: Periodic book displays related to museum exhibitions and special library collections
Activities: Tours

M **WORCESTER CENTER FOR CRAFTS,** 25 Sagamore Rd, 01605. Tel 508-753-8183; FAX 508-797-5626; *Exec Dir* Maryon Attwood
Open Mon - Thurs 9 AM - 8 PM, Sat 9 AM - 5 PM. No admis fee. Estab 1856 for educational exhibits of historic & contemporary crafts. Professionally lighted & installed 40 x 60 gallery with six major shows per yr in main gallery. Atrium Gallery hosts four to six smaller exhibitions per year. Average Annual Attendance: 10,000. Mem: 800; dues $35 & up
Income: Financed by mem, grants, contributions & endowment
Collections: Collection contains 200 books, 2000 Kodachromes, 300 photographs
Exhibitions: (1997) Sandra Brownlee (metal); Myra Mimlitsch Gray (fiber); New Traditions: Val Cushing (clay); Bob Troutman (wood); School for Professional Crafts Exhibitions; Arts Worcester Biennial
Publications: On-Center, newsletter; school for professional crafts brochures; 3 course catalogs, yearly
Activities: Classes for adults & children; weekend professional workshops; 2 year full-time program in professional crafts; lect open to public, 12 vis lectr per year; gallery talks; tours; scholarships offered; book traveling exhibitions 2 per year; traveling exhibitions organized and circulated; supply shop & gift shop sells books, original craft objects

MICHIGAN

ADRIAN

M **SIENA HEIGHTS COLLEGE,** Klemm Gallery, Studio Angelico, 1247 E Siena Heights Dr, 49221. Tel 517-264-7860; FAX 517-264-7704; *Dir* Christine Reising
Open Mon - Fri 9 AM - 4 PM, Tues evening 6 - 9 PM, cl major holidays & summers. No admis fee. Estab 1970's to offer cultural programs to Lenawee County & others. Average Annual Attendance: 6000
Collections: Drawings; graphics; paintings; sculptures; textiles
Exhibitions: Invitational Artists Shows; major national culturally-based exhibitions; professional artists & student shows
Activities: Classes for adults; lect open to public, 6 vis lectr per year; gallery talks; tours; competitions with awards; performances; scholarships & fels offered
L **Art Library,** 1247 E Siena Heights Dr, 49221. Tel 517-264-7151; FAX 517-264-7711; *Dir Instructional Servs* Mark Dombrowski; *Public Servs Librn* Melissa M Sissen
Library Holdings: Vols 10,000; Per subs 35; Micro — Cards, fiche, reels; AV — A-tapes, cassettes, fs, rec, slides, v-tapes; Other — Clipping files, pamphlets, photographs

ALBION

M **ALBION COLLEGE,** Bobbitt Visual Arts Center, 611 E Porter, 49224. Tel 517-629-0246; *Chmn* Doug Goering
Open Mon - Thurs 9 AM - 4:45 PM & 6:30 - 10 PM, Fri 9 AM - 4:45 PM, Sat 10 AM - 1 PM, Sun 2 - 5 PM. No admis fee. Estab 1835 to offer art education at college level & general art exhibition program for campus community & public. Maintains one large gallery & three smaller galleries
Income: Privately funded
Purchases: $2000 - $4000
Collections: African Art; ceramics; glass; †prints
Exhibitions: From the Print Collection; Pieces from the Permanent Collection; various one-man & group shows;
Activities: Lect open to public, 2 - 4 vis lectr per year; gallery talks; original objects of art lent to faculty and students

ALPENA

M **JESSE BESSER MUSEUM,** 491 Johnson St, 49707-1496. Tel 517-356-2202; FAX 517-356-3133; Elec Mail jbmuseum@northland.lib.mi.us. *Pres* Joanne Gallagher; *Dir* Dennis R Bodem; *First VPres* John Milroy; *Treas* Lillian Banas
Open Mon - Fri 10 AM - 5 PM, Thurs 10 AM - 9 PM, Sat & Sun Noon - 5 PM. Admis family group rate $5, adults $2, seniors, students & children $1. Estab assoc 1962, building open to pub 1966, an accredited mus of history, science & art serving northern Michigan. Mus has a research library, a planetarium, a Foucault Pendulum, Indian artifact collection, Avenue of shops, lumbering exhibits & preserved furnished historical buildings on grounds. Also on grounds, sculptured fountain by artist Glen Michaels. Three galleries are utilized for shows, traveling exhibits, & changing exhibitions of the Museum's collection of modern art & art prints, decorative arts & furniture. There are 260 running ft of wall space on lower level, 1250 sq ft & 16 45 sq ft on upper level galleries. Average Annual Attendance: 29,000
Income: Financed by Besser Foundation, federal & state grants, private gifts & donations, Museums Founders Soc, Operation Support Grant from Michigan Council for the Arts, & other sources
Collections: †Art prints; †Clewell pottery; †contemporary native american art; †maps of the Great Lakes; †modern art; †photography
Exhibitions: Changing exhibitions of all major collecting areas & touring exhibits; Northeast Michigan Juried Art
Activities: Classes for adults & children; art workshops; seminars; docent training; lect open to public, 5 vis lectr per year; gallery talks; tours; competitions with awards; book traveling exhibitions 8 per year; originate traveling exhibitions; museum shop sells books, magazines, original art, handicrafts
L **Philip M Park Library,** 491 Johnson St, 49707. Tel 517-356-2202; *Dir* Dennis R Bodem; *Librn* Sandy Mitchell
Open to pub for reference only
Library Holdings: Vols 4100; Per subs 46; Micro — Fiche, reels; AV — Cassettes, v-tapes; Other — Clipping files, exhibition catalogs, manuscripts, pamphlets
Special Subjects: American Indian Art, Architecture, Art History, Ceramics, Decorative Arts, Dolls, Flasks & Bottles, Folk Art, Glass, Painting - American, Pottery, Printmaking, Prints, Restoration & Conservation, Antiques, Astronomy, Indian History, Local History, Museum Management

ANN ARBOR

A **ANN ARBOR ART ASSOCIATION,** Art Center, 117 W Liberty, 48104. Tel 313-994-8004; FAX 313-994-3610; Elec Mail azartcen@aol.com. *Pres* Damien Farrel; *Exhibit Gallery Dir* Heather Graham; *Exec Dir* Marsha Chamberlin; *Dir of Operations* Susan Monaghan; *Gallery Dir* Liz Lemire; *Educ Dir* Kim Roberts; *Develop Dir* Deborah Jahn
Open Tues - Sat 10 AM - 6 PM, Sun Noon - 5 PM, cl Mon. Estab 1909 to provide for the well-being of the visual arts through programs that encourage participation in & support for the visual arts, as well as foster artistic development. Maintains 750 sq ft of exhibit gallery space with monthly shows; & 1300 sq ft sales - rental gallery next to exhibit areas; classes in studio art & art appreciation; special events. Average Annual Attendance: 52,000. Mem: 1000; dues $35; annual meeting in Feb
Income: Financed by mem, Michigan Council for the Arts grant, rental of studios & retail sales
Exhibitions: Michigan Artists for the Home, 2 week show in art furnished new home with all works for sale
Publications: Class catalog, quarterly; gallery announcements, monthly; lecture listings, quarterly; newsletter, quarterly
Activities: Classes for adults & children; artist workshops on professional development; lect open to public, 4-6 vis lectr per year; gallery talks; tours; competitions with prizes; scholarships offered; exten dept lends individual paintings & original objects of art to organizations & community facilities; sales shop sells original art & fine contemporary crafts

A **ARTRAIN, INC,** N E W Ctr, 1100 N Main St, Ste 102, 48104. Tel 313-747-8300; *Chmn* Ronald Weiser; *Exec Dir* Debra Polich
No admis fee. Estab 1971 to tour major art exhibits throughout the nation & provide catalyst for community arts development. Traveling art museum in a train; consists of converted railroad cars with large walls & cases. Average Annual Attendance: 122,000
Income: Financed by endowment, state appropriation, individual foundation & corporation campaigns
Publications: Exhibition catalogs; newsletter
Activities: Classes for children; docent training; lect open to public; competitions; book traveling exhibitions; museum shop sells exhibit related items

A **MICHIGAN GUILD OF ARTISTS & ARTISANS,** Michigan Guild Gallery, 118 N Fourth Ave, 48104. Tel 313-662-3382; *Exec Dir* Kaye Sirotti; *Gallery Coordr* Marilyn Govin; *Art Fair Dir* Shary Brown
Open Mon - Fri 9 AM - 5 PM. No admis fee. Estab as an art service organization offering exhibition opportunities, referrals, educational programs; specializing in contemporary work of all media by member artists. Average Annual Attendance: 1000. Mem: 1700; dues $45-$55; annual meeting in Jan
Income: Financed by mem fees & art fair fees
Publications: Mem newsletter, bi-monthly
Activities: Educ dept provides workshops

UNIVERSITY OF MICHIGAN
M **Museum of Art,** 525 S State St, 48109-1354. Tel 313-764-0395; FAX 313-764-3731; *Dir* William Hennessey; *Cur of Asian Art* Marshall Wu; *Admin* Kathryn Huss; *Registrar* Carole A McNamara; *Cur Western Art* Annette Dixon
Open (Sept - May) Tues - Sat 10 AM - 5 PM, Thurs 10 AM - 9 PM, Sun Noon - 5 PM; (June - Aug) Tues - Sat 11 AM - 5 PM, Thurs 11 AM - 9 PM, Sun Noon - 5 PM. No admis fee. Estab 1946, as a university art mus & mus for the Ann Arbor community. Average Annual Attendance: 100,000. Mem: 800; dues individual $35
Income: Financed by state appropriation
Collections: Arts of the Western World from the Sixth Century AD to the Present; Asian, Near Eastern, African & Oceanic, including ceramics, contemporary art, decorative art, graphic arts, manuscripts, painting, sculpture
Exhibitions: (1997) Common Ground: African Art & Affinities; Ellen Driscoll: Ahab's Wife; Images d'Epinal; Komar, Melamid & Renee; Michigan Collectors; Ukiyo-e Prints; Venice, Traditions Transformed: Works from the Sarah Campbell Blaffer Foundation & the University of Michigan
Publications: Bulletin of the Museum of Art & Archaeology, irregular; bimonthly Calendar of Events; Catalogues & Gallery Brochures, irregular
Activities: Educ dept; dramatic programs; children programs; university-accredited museum practice program; lect open to public, 10 vis lectr per year; gallery talks; tours; concerts; scholarships offered; individual paintings & original objects of art lent to other museums; originate traveling exhibitions to national & international museums; museum shop selling publications, posters, postcards & gifts
M **Kelsey Museum of Archaeology,** 434 State St, 48109-1390. Tel 313-763-3559; FAX 313-763-8976; *Dir* Elaine K Gazda; *Vis Cur* Janet Richards; *Vis Cur* Terry Wilfong; *Assoc Cur* Thelma Thomas; *Assoc Cur Photo & Slides* Robin Meador-Woodruff; *Assoc Dir & Assoc Cur Educ* Lauren E Talalay; *Conservator* Geoffrey Brown; *Exhibit Preparator* Dana Buck
Open Sept - Apr Mon - Fri 9 AM - 4 PM, Sat & Sun 1 - 4 PM; May - Aug Tues - Fri 11 AM - 4 PM, Sat & Sun 1 - 4 PM, cl Mon. No admis fee. Estab 1928. Four small galleries are maintained. Average Annual Attendance: 37,000
Collections: †Objects of the Graeco-Roman period from excavations conducted by the University of Michigan in Egypt & Iraq; Greece, Etruria, Rome & provinces: sculpture, inscriptions, pottery, bronzes, terracottas; Egyptian antiquities dynastic through Roman; Roman & Islamic glass, bone & ivory objects, textiles, coins; 19th century photographs
Publications: Biannual newsletter; Bulletin of the Museums of Art & Archaeology, irregular; Kelsey Museum Studies Series, irregular
Activities: Educ dept; docent training; traveling educational kits; lect open to public, 5 vis lectr per year; tours; original objects of art lent to other museums upon request; book traveling exhibitions; originate traveling exhibitions to museums with similar collections; sales shop sells books & exhibition catalogs
M **Slusser Gallery,** School of Art, 2000 Bonisteel Blvd, 48109. Tel 313-936-2082; FAX 313-936-0469; *Dean* Allen Samuels
Open Tues - Sat 11 AM - 5 PM. No admis fee. Estab 1974, primarily used as an educational facility with high volume of student & faculty participation. Gallery is located on the main floor of the Art & Architecture Building. Comprised of 3600 sq ft of exhibition space in a well lit area. Average Annual Attendance: 11, 000
Income: Financed by School of Art general fund & gifts of the Friends of the Jean Paul Slusser Gallery
Collections: Artifacts of the School's history; works by faculty & alumni of the University of Michigan School of Art
Exhibitions: Faculty Exhibition; Upper Class Student Exhibition
Publications: Occasional catalogues
Activities: Lect open to public, 10-15 vis lectr per year; gallery talks
L **Asian Art Archives,** 48109-1357. Tel 313-763-2874; FAX 313-647-4121; Elec Mail wholden@umich.edu. *Sr Assoc Cur* Wendy Holden
Open Mon - Fri 9 AM - 5 PM. Estab 1962 for study & research. Contains 180, 000 black & white photographs of Asian art objects or monuments. Library also houses the Asian Art Photographic Distribution, a non-profit business selling visual resource materials dealing with Chinese & Japanese art. Houses Southeast Asia Art Foundation Collection of 100,000 slides & photographs of Southeast Asian art
Income: $5000 (financed by endowment, federal funds)
Purchases: $4000 - $5000
Library Holdings: Vols 50; Black/white negatives 26,000; Micro — Fiche 10,000, reels; AV — Slides; Other — Clipping files, exhibition catalogs, photographs 80,000, reproductions 3000
Special Subjects: Architecture, Art History, Asian Art, Bronzes, Calligraphy, Ceramics, Coins & Medals, Decorative Arts, Glass, Gold, Graphic Arts, Islamic Art, Ivory, Jade, Landscapes, Chinese Painting
Collections: National Palace Museum, Taiwan, photographic archive; †Chinese art, painting, decorative arts; †Southeast Asian Art Archive, sculpture, architecture; Islamic Art Archive; †Asian Art Archive, Chinese & Japanese arts, painting
Publications: Newsletter, East Asian Art & Archaeology (three issues per year)
L **Fine Arts Library,** 260 Tappan Hall, 48109. Tel 313-764-5405; FAX 313-647-4121; *Head Fine Arts Library* Deirdre Spencer; *Library Technical Asst* Michael Donovan
Open Mon - Thurs 8 AM - 11 PM, Fri 8 AM - 5 PM, Sat 10 AM - 6 PM, Sun 1 - 10 PM, summer hrs vary. Estab 1949, to support the academic programs of the History of the Art Department, including research of faculty & graduate students. Circ 17,200
Income: Financed by state appropriation
Library Holdings: Vols 71,227; Per subs 232; Marburger index of photographic documentation of art in Germany; Micro — Fiche, reels; Other — Exhibition catalogs, pamphlets
Special Subjects: Afro-American Art, Antiquities-Byzantine, Antiquities-Etruscan, Antiquities-Greek, Antiquities-Roman, Art History, History of Art & Archaeology, Islamic Art, Oriental Art, Painting - American, Painting - British, Painting - Dutch, Painting - European, Painting - Flemish
L **Slide & Photograph Collection,** History of Art Department, 20A Tappan Hall, 48109. Tel 313-763-6114; FAX 313-747-4121; *Cur* Joy Blouin; *Sr Assoc Cur* Rebecca Hoort; *Photographer* Patrick Young; *Sr Assoc Cur & Asian Art Archives* Wendy Holden; *Assoc Cur* Tina Bissell; *Asst Cur* David Hogge
Open Mon - Fri 8 AM - 5 PM. Estab 1911, as a library for teaching & research collection of slides & photos of art objects; limited commercial distribution; non-profit slide distribution projects; (Asian Art Photographic Distribution; Univ of Mich Slide Distribution). Circ 3,600 weekly
Income: Financed by state appropriation
Library Holdings: AV — Lantern slides, slides 290,000; Other — Photographs 200,000, reproductions
Special Subjects: History of Art & Archaeology
Collections: Berenson's I Tatti Archive; Courtauld Institute Illustration Archive; †Islamic Archives; Palace Museum Archive (Chinese painting); Romanesque Archive (sculpture & some architecture concentrating on Burgundy, Southwestern France, †Spain & southern Italy); †Southeast Asian & Indian Archives
Activities: Materials lent only to University of Michigan faculty & students
L **Art Media Union Library,** 2281 Bonisteel Blvd, 48109-2069. Tel 313-936-3191; FAX 313-764-4487; *Asst Librn* D H Shields; *Head Librn* Paul Grochowski
Estab to support the teaching & research activities of the School of Art & the College of Architecture & Urban Planning
Library Holdings: Vols 72,000; Per subs 560; Micro — Cards, fiche 1000, prints, reels 150; AV — A-tapes, cassettes, fs, Kodachromes, lantern slides 1000, slides 60,000, v-tapes; Other — Clipping files, exhibition catalogs, manuscripts 1000, original art works, pamphlets, photographs, sculpture 10
Special Subjects: Architecture of all places & periods, Contemporary art & design, History of Photography, Studio art collections in graphic design
Collections: Jens Jensen Archive of Landscape Architecture & Drawings
Activities: Computer workstations with various software

BATTLE CREEK

M **ART CENTER OF BATTLE CREEK,** 265 E Emmett St, 49017. Tel 616-962-9511; FAX 616-969-3838; *Dir* Ann Worth Concannon; *Educ Dir* Susan Eckhardt; *Cur* Caral Snapp
Open Tues - Sat 10 AM - 5 PM, Sun Noon - 5 PM, cl Aug & legal holidays. No admis fee. Estab 1948 to offer classes for children & adults & to present monthly exhibitions of professional work. Four galleries of varying sizes with central vaulted ceiling gallery, track lighting & security. Average Annual Attendance: 30, 000. Mem: 750; dues $15; annual meeting in Sept
Income: Financed by mem, endowment fund, grants, UAC, special projects, tuition, sales of artwork
Collections: Michigan Art Collection featuring 20th century Michigan artists
Exhibitions: Group & Solo Shows: Paintings; Photography; Prints; Sculpture; Crafts; American Art 40s & 50s; Artist's competitions
Publications: Newsletter, bi-monthly
Activities: Classes for adults & children; docent training; workshops & programs; lect open to public, 5 vis lectr per year; gallery talks; tours; competitions with prizes; scholarships offered; individual paintings & original objects of art lent to qualified institutions; book traveling exhibitions 1-2 per year; originate traveling exhibitions to museums & art centers; museum shop sells original art by Michigan artists; KidSpace hands-on gallery
L **Michigan Art & Artist Archives,** 265 E Emmett St, 49017. Tel 616-962-9511; FAX 616-969-3838; *Dir* Ann Concannon; *Operations Dir* Angela Hartung
Library Holdings: Vols 450; Per subs 5; AV — Slides; Other — Clipping files, exhibition catalogs, original art works, photographs, sculpture
Special Subjects: Afro-American Art, American Indian Art, Antiquities-Egyptian, Art History, Middle American Art

BAY CITY

M **BAY COUNTY HISTORICAL SOCIETY,** Historical Museum of Bay County, 321 Washington Ave, 48708. Tel 517-893-5733; *Dir* Gay McInerney
Open Mon - Fri 10 AM - 5 PM, Sun 1 - 5 PM. No admis fee. Estab 1919 to preserve, collect, & interpret the historical materials of Bay County. Average Annual Attendance: 12,000. Mem: 500; dues corporate $500, patron $100, small business $50, sustaining $25; annual meeting in Apr
Income: Financed by mem, state grant, county funds
Collections: Hand crafts, photographs, portraits, quilts; mid-1800s - post WW II historical material; native American materials & paintings
Publications: Anishinabe - People of Saginaw; Ghost Towns & Place Names; Vanished Industries; Women of Bay County
Activities: Classes for adults & children; home tours; historical encampment; living history programs; traveling displays & educational kits; lect open to public, 2-3 vis lectr per year; gallery talks; tours; museum shop sells books, reproductions, hand crafts, historical gifts

BIRMINGHAM

A **BIRMINGHAM-BLOOMFIELD ART ASSOCIATION,** 1516 S Cranbrook Rd, 48009. Tel 810-644-0866; FAX 810-644-7904; *Pres* Chris Parfitt; *VPres* Tina Parfitt; *VPres* Harry Cendrowski; *Exec Dir* Janet E Torno; *Asst Dir* Cynthia Mills; *Business Mgr* Diane Brayton
Open Mon - Thurs 9 AM - 10 PM, Fri 9 AM - 5 PM, Sat 9 AM - 5 PM, cl Sun. No admis fee. Estab 1956 to provide a community-wide, integrated studio-gallery art center. Average Annual Attendance: 10,000. Mem: 2400; dues $30 & up;

annual meeting in May

Income: $1,200,000 (financed by mem, tuitions, special events funding & donations)

Exhibitions: Annual Michigan Fine Arts Competition; juried exhibits & competitions; local high school exhibits

Publications: Quarterly class brochure; quarterly newsletter

Activities: Classes for adults & children; Picture Lady Program; lect open to public, 2-3 vis lectr per year; local & international art tours; competitions with prizes; poetry readings; Holiday Sale show; children's art camp; Annual Shain Park Art Fair; scholarships offered; sales shop sells original art

BLOOMFIELD HILLS

M CRANBROOK ART MUSEUM, 1221 N Woodward, Box 801, 48303-0801. Tel 810-645-3312; FAX 810-646-0046; *Dir* Greg Wittkopp; *Cur Educ* David D J Rau; *Asst Cur* Irene Hofmann
Open Wed, Fri & Sat 10 AM - 5 PM, Thurs 10 AM - 9 PM, Sun Noon - 5 PM, cl Mon, Tues & major holidays. Admis adults $3, students & senior citizens $2, group rates available. Estab 1942 as part of Cranbrook Academy of Art. Average Annual Attendance: 30,000. Mem: 800; dues family $45, general $35

Collections: Artists associated with Cranbrook Academy of Art: ceramics by Maija Grotell; architectural drawings & decorative arts by Eliel Saarinen; porcelains by Adelaide Robineau; sculpture by Carl Milles; contemporary paintings; 19th century prints; study collection of textiles; prints & ceramics

Exhibitions: 15 exhibitions annually of contemporary art, architecture & design

Activities: Classes for adults & children; docent training; lect open to public, 30 vis lectr per year; gallery talks; tours; exten dept serves Detroit area 4th grades; individual paintings & original objects of art lent to other institutions; book traveling exhibitions; originate traveling exhibitions & circulate to other museums national & international; museum shop sells books, magazines, slides, gift items & cards

L Library, 1221 Woodward Ave, PO Box 801, 48303-0801. Tel 810-645-3355; FAX 313-646-0046; *Head Librn* Judy Dyki
Open Mon - Fri 9 AM - 5 PM & 7 PM - 10 PM, Sat & Sun 1 - 5 PM. Estab 1928 to support research needs of Art Academy & Mus. Library is for Academy students, faculty & staff; open to pub for reference only

Income: Financed by academy

Library Holdings: Vols 25,000; Per subs 150; Masters theses; AV — A-tapes, cassettes 600, slides 32,500, v-tapes; Other — Clipping files, exhibition catalogs

Special Subjects: Architecture, Art History, Ceramics, Graphic Arts, Metalwork, Photography, Printmaking, Sculpture, Design, Fiber Arts, Photography, Printmaking

DEARBORN

C FORD MOTOR COMPANY, Henry Ford Museum & Greenfield Village, 20900 Oakwood Blvd, PO Box 1970, 48121-1970. Tel 313-271-1620, Ext 599, 538; *Publicist* Molly Zink; *Marketing* Marlene Manseau
Collection not available for pub viewing

DETROIT

A CASA DE UNIDAD UNITY HOUSE, 1920 Scotten, 48209. Tel 313-843-9598; FAX 313-843-7307; *Co-Dir* Marta Lagos
Estab 1981 as a cultural arts & media center exhibiting works of Latino artists

Income: Financed by city & state appropriation, individual & corporate donations

Activities: Annual Unity in the Community Festival; Sales shop sells books & poetry

L CENTER FOR CREATIVE STUDIES, College of Art & Design Library, 201 E Kirby, 48202-4034. Tel 313-872-3118, Ext 263; *Librn* Jean Peyrat; *Slide Librn* Donna Rundels
Open Mon - Thurs 8:30 AM - 9 PM, Fri 8:30 AM - 4:30 PM, Sat 1 - 4 PM. Estab 1966 to serve students & faculty of an undergraduate art school. Primarily a how-to, illustrative collection. Gallery has three rooms located at 15 E Kirby

Income: Financed by private school

Library Holdings: Vols 23,000; Per subs 72; AV — Slides 70,000; Other — Exhibition catalogs

Special Subjects: Advertising Design, Crafts, Graphic Design, Industrial Design, Photography

M CENTRAL UNITED METHODIST CHURCH, Swords Info Plowshares Peace Center & Gallery, 33 E Adams, 48226. Tel 313-963-7575; FAX 313-965-4328; *Exec Dir* James W Bristah; *Outreach Coordr* Lois St Aubin White
Open Tues, Thurs & Sat 11 AM - 3 PM. No admis fee. Estab 1985 to use the arts for peace in the world. Main gallery 1475 sq ft, height 13 ft 7 inches; multipurpose gallery 1043 sq ft, height 7 ft 8 inches; second floor balcony gallery 357 sq ft, height 7 ft 3 inches. Maintains reference library. Average Annual Attendance: 10,000. Mem: annual meeting in Mar

Income: $55,000 (financed by endowment, individuals, city & state appropriation, grants, sales, local churches)

Collections: Peace Art Collection (permanent)

Exhibitions: Peace Quilting; juried 2-3 dimensional art from Michigan & Ontario

Publications: Harbinger Newsletter, 3-4 times per year; periodic exhibit catalogues

Activities: Classes for adults & children; individual paintings & original objects of art lent; book traveling exhibitions 5-6 per year; museum shop sells books, original art, reproductions, cards, t-shirts & posters

M DETROIT ARTISTS MARKET, 300 River Pl, Ste 1650, 48207. Tel 313-393-1770; FAX 313-393-1772; *Board Chmn* A David Mikesell; *VChmn* Mike Schwartz; *VChmn* Jeffrey Abt; *VChmn* Thomas Cox; *VChmn* Joan Ferguson; *VChmn* Evie Wheat; *VChmn* David Penny; *VChmn* Matthew Holland; *Exec Dir* Maria Luisa Belmonte; *Exhib Coordr* Mary Jane Smith
Open Mon - Sat 11 AM - 5 PM. No admis fee. Estab 1932 to educate pub &

bring work by local artists within 90 mile radius to the attention of the pub. Average Annual Attendance: 10,000. Mem: 1300; dues $15-$1000

Income: $250,000 (financed by endowment, mem, state appropriation, mini-grants, MCA, contributions, percent of art work sales)

Exhibitions: Small Group Exhibition; All Media Juried Exhibition; The Garden Sale.

Publications: Catalogs, 1-2 per yr; quarterly newsletter; Journal of exhibitions available for each exhibition including an essay & biographical information of participating artists

Activities: Educ program; lect open to public; tours; competitions with awards; scholarships offered; sales shop sells magazines, original art

M DETROIT FOCUS, 33 E Grand River, PO Box 32823, 48232-0823. Tel 313-965-3245; *Gallery Mgr* Robert Crise Jr
Open Thurs - Sat 11 AM - 5 PM, summer to 6 PM. No admis fee. Estab 1978 as an exhibition space for Michigan visual artists. Average Annual Attendance: 10,000. Mem: 400; dues from $25; meetings annually

Income: $21,000 (financed by mem, city & state appropriation, fundraising)

Exhibitions: Juried exhibitions, visual & performance art

Publications: Detroit Focus Quarterly; exhibition catalogues

Activities: Lect open to public, 5 vis lectr per year; competitions with awards; originate traveling exhibitions

M DETROIT INSTITUTE OF ARTS, 5200 Woodward Ave, 48202. Tel 313-833-7900; FAX 313-833-2357; *Dir* Samuel Sachs II; *Deputy Dir* Maurice Parrish; *Cur American Art* Nancy Rivard-Shaw; *Cur Ancient Art* William H Peck; *Cur African, Oceanic & New World Cultures Art* Michael Kan; *Cur European Painting* George Keyes; *Cur Educ* Nancy Jones; *Graphic Arts* Ellen Sharp; *Acting Cur Twentieth Century* MaryAnn Wilkinson; *Cur of Asian Art* Laurie Barnes; *Photographer* Dirk Bakker; *Head Conservator* Barbara Heller; *Cur European Sculpture & Decorative Arts* Alan Darr; *Registrar* Pam Watson
Open Wed - Fri 11 AM - 4 PM, Sat - Sun 11 AM - 5 PM, cl Mon, Tues & holidays. Estab & incorporated 1885 as Detroit Mus of Art; chartered as municipal department 1919 & name changed; original organization continued as Founders Soc Detroit Institute of Arts; present building opened 1927; Ford Wing addition completed 1966; Cavanagh Wing addition opened 1971. Midwest area office of Archives of American Art

Collections: Elizabeth Parke Firestone Collection of 18th Century French Silver; William Randolph Hearst Collection of Arms & Armor & Flemish Tapestries; Grace Whitney Hoff Collection of Fine Bindings, German Expressionist Art, African, Oceanic & New World Cultures; Graphic Art, Photography; Modern Art; 20th century Art; American Art: Painting, Sculpture, Furniture, and Decorative Arts; European Painting, sculpture and Decorative Art; Asian Art; Ancient Art

Exhibitions: Changing Spaces: Projects from the Fabric Worshop; Discovering Ellis Ruley; Detroit Public Schools Exhibition; Harry Callahan; Images in Ivory: Precious Objects of the Gothic Age; Edward Steichen; An American Modern/The Conde Nast Years 1923-1938; Splendors of Egypt; 20th Century printmakers from DIA & area collections; The Wealth of the Thracians

Publications: Exhibition catalogues; bulletin; annual report; collection catalogues

Activities: Classes for adults & children; dramatic programs; docent training; lect open to public; gallery talks; tours; concerts, Detroit filmtheatre; scholarships & fels offered; book traveling exhibitions; originate traveling exhibitions; museum shop sells books, calendars, games, jewelry, prints, slides & t-shirts

L Research Library, 5200 Woodward Ave, 48202. Tel 313-833-7926; FAX 313-833-9169; Elec Mail jmoldwi@cms.cc.wayne.edu.Internet; jmoldwi@waynestl.Bitnet. *Library Consultant* Jennifer L S Moldwin; *Library Asst* Ryan S Wieber; *Intern* Mary D Galvin
Open by written request only. Estab 1905 to provide material for research, interpretation & documentation of mus collection. For reference only

Income: Financed by city & The Founders Society

Library Holdings: Vols 500,000; Per subs 205; AV — Lantern slides; Other — Exhibition catalogs, pamphlets, photographs

Special Subjects: Afro-American Art, American Indian Art, Antiquities-Assyrian, Antiquities-Byzantine, Antiquities-Egyptian, Antiquities-Etruscan, Antiquities-Greek, Antiquities-Oriental, Antiquities-Persian, Antiquities-Roman, Archaeology, Architecture, Art History, Asian Art, Bookplates & Bindings, applied arts

Collections: Albert Kahn Architecture Library; Paul McPharlin Collection of Puppetry; Grace Whitney-Hoff Collection of Fine Bindings

A Founders Society, 5200 Woodward Ave, 48202. Tel 313-833-7900; FAX 313-833-9169; Cable DETINARTS. *Pres* Joseph Hudson; *Exec VPres* Joseph P Bianco; *VPres* Margaret K Gillis; *VPres* Henry B Frank; *Treas* Gilbert B Silverman
Estab & incorporated 1885; pub mem philanthropic soc contributing to the growth of the Detroit Institute of Arts; underwrites Educ Dept activities, publications, special exhibitions & purchases of works of art. Mem: 26,000; dues corporate patron $10,000, corporate sponsor $5000, corporate contributor $1000, corporate $250, patron $150, family $40, individual $25

Activities: Museum shop rents original work by Michigan artists & reproductions

L DETROIT PUBLIC LIBRARY, Art & Literature Dept, 5201 Woodward Ave, 48202-4093. Tel 313-833-1470; FAX 313-833-1474; Elec Mail jcompor@cms.cc.wayne.edu. *Interim Library Dir* Maurice Wheeler; *Mgr Art & Literature Dept* Jean Comport
Open Tues, Thurs, Fri & Sat 9:30 AM - 5:30 PM, Wed 1 - 9 PM. Estab 1865. Serves residents of Michigan with circulating and reference materials

Income: Financed by city and state appropriation

Purchases: $40,000

Library Holdings: Vols 71,000; Per subs 200; Micro — Fiche, reels; Other — Clipping files, exhibition catalogs, pamphlets, photographs

Special Subjects: Afro-American Art, American Indian Art, American Western Art, Architecture, Art History, Calligraphy, Ceramics, Decorative Arts, Etchings & Engravings, Furniture, Industrial Design, Landscape Architecture, Painting - American, Photography, Sculpture

Activities: Tours

M DETROIT REPERTORY THEATRE GALLERY, 13103 Woodrow Wilson, 48238. Tel 313-868-1347; FAX 313-868-1702; *Gallery Dir* Gilda Snowden
Estab 1957 to show Detroit Art
Income: Financed by endowment & state appropriation
Exhibitions: One person shows for emerging Detroit Area Artists; Amy Kelly, Robert Hyde, Jay Jurma, Kris Essen, Kathy Arkley, Renee Dooley, Albert Nassar, Sabrina Nelson
Publications: Exhibition catalogs
Activities: Adult classes; dramatic programs

M NATIONAL CONFERENCE OF ARTISTS, Michigan Chapter Gallery, 216 Fisher Bldg, 3011 W Grand Blvd, 48202. Tel 313-875-0923; *Gallery Dir & Mgr* Celia Woodson; *Cur Exhib* Bamidele Demerson; *Asst Proj Dir* Esther Vivian Brewer
Open Mon - Fri 11 AM - 5 PM, Sat 11 AM - 4 PM. Estab 1985 to promote cultural support for artists & community through visual arts. Average Annual Attendance: 4500. Mem: 300; monthly meetings
Income: $50,000 (financed by mem, city & state appropriation, corporate, National Endowment for the Arts & private donations)
Publications: NCA Newsletter, quarterly
Activities: Classes for adults & children; docent programs; lect open to public, 15 vis lectr per year; originate traveling exhibitions 3 per year; sales shop sells art videos, books, original art & prints

M PEWABIC SOCIETY INC, Pewabic Pottery, 10125 E Jefferson, 48214. Tel 313-822-0954; *Exec Dir* Ronald Streitz Jr
Open Mon - Sat 10 AM - 6 PM. Estab 1903 to continue its tradition of leadership in the areas of ceramic & education. Average Annual Attendance: 50,000. Mem: 1200
Collections: The work of the founder (Mary Chase Stratton)
Activities: Classes for adults & children; residencies & internships; lect open to public; tours; competitions; original objects of art lent; originate traveling exhibitions; sales shop sells original art

M WAYNE STATE UNIVERSITY, Community Arts Gallery, 150 Community Arts Bldg, Rm 150, 48202. Tel 313-577-2985, 577-2203; *Acting Dir* Mary Jane Smith
Open Mon - Fri 9 AM - 5 PM. No admis fee. Estab 1956 as a facility for university & community oriented exhibitions & programs. Has a slide library
Collections: Small collection of American & European graphics, painting, sculpture
Activities: Lect open to public; concerts; scholarships offered

M YOUR HERITAGE HOUSE, 110 E Ferry St, 48202. Tel 313-871-1667; *Dir* Josephine Harreld Love
Open weekdays 11:30 AM - 5:30 PM, weekends by appointment. Estab 1969. Average Annual Attendance: 15,000. Mem: 500; regular dues $50; annual meetings in Sept
Income: Financed by mem, city & state appropriation, individuals, groups & business donations, foundation support
Collections: †Art for Youth; Black Heritage; graphics; Puppetry; Paintings; objects & works of interest to children; dolls; many works of art by renowned artists
Publications: Catalogues; imprints
Activities: Classes for adults & children; lect open to public, 3-6 vis lectr per year; concerts; gallery talks; tours; scholarships offered; sales shop sells books, cards & catalogues of exhibits
L Library, 110 E Ferry St, 48202. Tel 313-871-1667; *Dir* Josephine Harreld Love
Open Mon - Fri 11 AM - 4 PM. Estab 1940's to provide fine arts material for children. For reference only
Library Holdings: Rare books & music scores; Micro — Cards; Other — Clipping files, exhibition catalogs, manuscripts, memorabilia, pamphlets, photographs, prints
Special Subjects: Fine Arts for Youth
Collections: Black Heritage; Puppetry of the World

EAST LANSING

M MICHIGAN STATE UNIVERSITY, Kresge Art Museum, 48824. Tel 517-355-7631; FAX 517-355-6577;
Internet Home Page Address http://www.msu.edu/unit/kamuseum. *Dir* Dr Susan Bandes; *Dir Emeritus* Joseph Ishikawa; *Educ Coordr* Dr Carol Fisher; *Registrar* Lynne Campbell; *Cur* Dr Phylis Floyd
Open Mon - Wed & Fri 9:30 AM - 4:30 PM, Thurs Noon - 8 PM, Sat & Sun 1 - 4 PM; summer hours: Mon - Fri 11 AM - 4 PM, Sat & Sun 1 - 4 PM, cl Aug - mid-Sept. No admis fee. Estab 1959. Average Annual Attendance: 35,000. Mem: 500; dues $15 - $1000
Income: Financed by Michigan State University & Friends of Kresge Art Museum
Purchases: Paolo di Giovanni Fei triptych, 1985; John Marin watercolor, 1986; Gaston Lachaise, 1987; Jasper Johns
Collections: †Work from neolithic period to present; †European paintings & sculpture; †American paintings & sculpture; †prints from 1500 to present; †complete prints of Peter Takal; Small †Asian, African, †pre-Columbian collections
Exhibitions: Shows making up a yearly calendar of about 12 exhibitions supplementing the permanent collection; special exhibits; staff and student shows
Publications: Kresge Art Museum Bulletin; Exhibition calendar & publications
Activities: Docent training; workshops; lect open to public; symposia; gallery talks; tours; off-campus breakfast lectures; scholarships offered; individual paintings and original objects of art lent to qualified institutions or galleries; originate traveling exhibitions; sales shop sells books, prints, cards & miscellaneous items
L Fine Arts Library, 48824-1048. Tel 517-353-4593; FAX 517-432-1445; Elec Mail thomps54@pilot.msu.edu;
Internet Home Page Address
http://www.lib.msu.edu/coll/main/finearts/index.htm. *Head Art Library* Patricia

T Thompson; *Library Asst* Annette Haines
Open Mon - Thurs 8 AM - 11 PM, Fri 8 AM - 6 PM, Sat 10 AM - 6 PM, Sun Noon - 11 PM. Estab 1973 to support the research and teaching needs in the visual arts of Michigan State University. Primarily reference & non-circulating
Income: Financed by state appropriation
Library Holdings: Vols 65,000; Per subs 175; Picture files; Micro — Fiche, reels; Other — Clipping files, exhibition catalogs
Special Subjects: Architecture, Art History, Decorative Arts, Furniture, Graphic Arts, History of Art & Archaeology, Interior Design, Painting - American, Painting - British, Painting - Dutch, Painting - European, Painting - Flemish, Painting - German, Painting - Italian, African Art; Illuminated Manuscript Facsimiles

ESCANABA

M WILLIAM BONIFAS FINE ART CENTER GALLERY, Alice Powers Art Gallery, 700 First Ave S, 49829. Tel 906-786-3833; *Gallery Dir* Pasgua Warstler; *Adminr* Vicki Soderberg
Open Mon - Fri 10 AM - 5 PM, Sun Noon - 4 PM. No admis fee. Estab 1974 to advance the arts in the area. 40 x 80, small gallery inside Center. Mem: Dues club $50, patron $30 & up, family $25, individual $15, student & senior citizens $10
Collections: Local artists work
Exhibitions: Northern Exposure; Smithsonian Matthew Brady Photographs; Michigan Watercolor Society; Regional & Touring Exhibits
Publications: Passage North, monthly newsletter
Activities: Classes for adults & children; dramatic programs; lect open to public, 3 vis lectr per year; tours; individual paintings & original objects of art lent to arts organizations & businesses in return for promotional assistance

FLINT

M BUCKHAM FINE ARTS PROJECT, Gallery, 134-1/2 W Second St, 48502. Tel 810-239-6334; *Pres* S E Morello; *VPres* C J Smith
Open Mon - Fri Noon - 5 PM. No admis fee. Estab 1984 to present contemporary arts. 40 x 60 ft gallery with 14 ft arched ceiling, no permanent interior walls. Average Annual Attendance: 5000. Mem: 250; dues $15-$200; annual meeting in first week of Mar
Income: $35,000 (financed by mem, state appropriation, grants, gifts, commissions from sales)
Exhibitions: New exhibitions on rotating monthly basis, twelve each year
Activities: Exhibitions; performances; readings; lect open to public; competitions with prizes; book traveling exhibitions 1 per year; museum shop sells original art

M FLINT INSTITUTE OF ARTS, 1120 E Kearsley St, 48503. Tel 810-234-1695; FAX 810-234-1692; *Dir* John B Henry; *Asst to Dir* Deborah S Gossel; *Cur* Christopher R Young; *Cur of Educ* Jean Forell; *Pub Relations & Mem Coordr* Suzanne G Walters; *Bus Mgr* Michael Melenbrink; *Museum Shop Mgr* Peggy Shedd; *Registrar* Kristie Everett
Open Tues - Sat 10 AM - 5 PM, Sun 1 - 5 PM, Fri (May - Oct) 7 - 9 PM. No admis fee. Estab 1928 as a community art mus serving the citizens of the area. Average Annual Attendance: 70,000. Mem: 2200; dues $15 & up; annual meeting third Tues in June
Collections: African Sculpture; French Paperweights; Modern Art; 19th Century Germanic Glass; Oriental Gallery; 17th - 20th Century European & American Art; Renaissance & Baroque Gallery
Publications: Exhibition catalogs; monthly calendar for members
Activities: Classes for adults & children; docent training; lect open to public, 12 vis lectr per year; concerts; gallery talks; tours; Flint Art Fair; individual paintings & original objects of art lent to other museums; museum shop sells books, gift items, stationery, cards & jewelry; original art, reproductions
L Library, 48503. Tel 810-234-1695; FAX 810-234-1692; *Registrar* Kristie Everett
Library open to the pub for reference by appointment
Library Holdings: Vols 4500; Per subs 19; Other — Exhibition catalogs
Special Subjects: American Indian Art, Architecture, Asian Art, Ceramics, Crafts, Decorative Arts, Drawings, Etchings & Engravings, Folk Art, Furniture, Oriental Art, Painting - American, Painting - European, Photography, Pottery

GRAND RAPIDS

M CALVIN COLLEGE, Center Art Gallery, 3201 Burton St SE, 49546. Tel 616-957-6326; FAX 616-957-8551; *Dir Exhib* Virginia Bullock
Open Sept - May Mon - Thurs 9 AM - 9 PM, Fri 9 AM - 5 PM, Sat Noon - 4 PM, summer 9 AM - 4:30 PM, cl Sun. No admis fee. Estab 1974 to provide the art students, & the college community & the pub at large with challenging visual monthly exhibitions. Gallery is well lighted, air-conditioned 40 x 70 ft with 10 ft ceiling along the sides & 8 ft ceiling in the center. Average Annual Attendance: 12,000
Income: Financed through private budget
Collections: Dutch 17th & 19th centuries paintings & prints; Japanese prints; †contemporary paintings, prints, drawings, sculpture, weaving & ceramics
Exhibitions: Invitational exhibits by various artists, exhibits of public & private collections & faculty & student exhibits
Publications: Various exhibition brochures
Activities: Classes for adults; lect open to public; concerts; gallery talks; competitions; scholarships offered

M GRAND RAPIDS ART MUSEUM, 155 Division N, 49503. Tel 616-459-4677; FAX 616-459-8491; *Acting Dir* Ann Van Tassel; *Acting Dir* Linda Thompson
Open Tues & Sun Noon - 4 PM, Wed, Fri & Sat 10 AM - 4 PM, Thurs 10 AM - 9 PM, cl Mon & legal holidays. Admis adults $3, students, senior citizens & children $.50. Museum allocated a 1910 Beaux Arts former post office & courthouse, renovated & opened in Sept 1981. Average Annual Attendance: 100,000. Mem: 2750; dues corporate benefactor $2500, corporate patron $1000, corporate donor $600, corporate $300, benefactor $2500, grand patron $500 -

$1000, collections patron $300, donor $150, patron $74, family $45, individual $35, full-time student $15; annual meeting in Sept
Income: $919,000 (financed by endowment, mem, state appropriation & federal grants)
Purchases: $30,000
Collections: Staffordshire Pottery; American 19th & 20th centuries paintings; decorative arts; drawings; French 19th century paintings; German expressionist paintings; master prints of all eras; Renaissance paintings; sculpture
Publications: Catalogs of major exhibitions; bi-monthly newsletter
Activities: Classes for children; docent training; lect open to public, 15 vis lectr per year; concerts; gallery talks; tours; exten dept serves elementary schools; individual paintings & original objects of art lent to museums; lending collection contains books, original art works, original prints, paintings, photographs, sculpture & slides; book traveling exhibitions; museum & sales shops sell books, original art, reproductions, gift items & prints; Gram for Kids

L **McBride Art Reference Library,** 155 Division N, 49503. Tel 616-459-4677; FAX 616-459-8491; *Library Chmn* Luci King
Open Tues & Sun Noon - 4 PM, Wed, Fri & Sat 10 AM - 4 PM, Thurs 10 AM - 9 PM. Estab 1969. Reference library
Income: Financed by mem, gifts, museum general budget allowance
Purchases: $2000
Library Holdings: Vols 6000; Per subs 12; AV — A-tapes, cassettes, slides, v-tapes; Other — Clipping files, exhibition catalogs 10,000, pamphlets, reproductions
Special Subjects: Advertising Design, Aesthetics, Afro-American Art, American Western Art, Anthropology, Art Education, Art History, Asian Art, Bronzes, Calligraphy, Ceramics, Coins & Medals, Collages, Commercial Art, Constructions
Activities: Docent Training

L **GRAND RAPIDS PUBLIC LIBRARY,** Music & Art Dept, 60 Library Plaza NE, 49503. Tel 616-456-3600, 456-3622; *Dir Library* Robert Raz
Open Mon, Tues & Wed 9 AM - 9 PM, Thurs, Fri & Sat 9 AM - 5:30 PM. No admis fee. Estab 1871 to provide information & library materials for people in Grand Rapids & Lakeland Library Cooperative area. Circ 1,031,274
Income: $4,064,791 (financed by city & state appropriations)
Purchases: $200,000
Library Holdings: Vols 250,000; Per subs 800; Micro — Fiche, reels; AV — Cassettes, motion pictures, rec; Other — Clipping files, exhibition catalogs, original art works, pamphlets
Special Subjects: Furniture
Collections: The Furniture Design Collection
Activities: Tours

L **KENDALL COLLEGE OF ART & DESIGN,** Frank & Lyn Van Steenberg Library, 111 Division Ave N, 49503-3194. Tel 616-451-2787; FAX 616-451-9867; *Pres* Oliver Evans; *Chmn Art History & Liberal Arts* Ruth O Keefe; *Chmn Foundation & Fine Arts* Jay Constantine; *Chmn Design Studies* Bruce Mulder
Open Mon - Thurs 7 AM - 10 PM, Fri 7 AM - 5 PM. Estab 1928 to serve Kendal students & faculty; also available to artists & designers as a reference library
Income: Financed by tuition
Library Holdings: Vols 16,000; Per subs 98; Micro — Fiche, prints, reels; AV — A-tapes, cassettes, rec, slides, v-tapes; Other — Clipping files, reproductions
Special Subjects: Art History, Asian Art, Ceramics, Commercial Art, Drafting, Folk Art, Graphic Arts, History of Art & Archaeology, Interior Design, Landscapes, Painting - American, Photography, Pre-Columbian Art, Prints, Sculpture
Collections: Furniture Collection

M **PUBLIC MUSEUM OF GRAND RAPIDS,** 272 Pearl NW, 49504. Tel 616-456-3977; FAX 616-456-3873; *Dir* Timothy J Chester; *Asst Dir* Kay A Zuris; *Cur Coll* Christian Carron; *Cur Exhib* Thomas Bantle; *Colls Mgr* Marilyn Merdzinski
Open daily 9 AM - 5 PM. Admis adults $5, senior citizens $4, children $2. Estab 1854 for the interpretation of environment & culture of West Michigan & Grand Rapids. Maintains reference library. Average Annual Attendance: 400,000. Mem: 4000; dues $30-500; annual meeting in May
Income: $4,000,000 (financed by endowment, mem, city & state appropriations, grants, contributions & foundations)
Collections: Costumes & household textiles; Decorative arts; Ethonogical; Furniture of the 19th & 20th centuries; Industrial & agricultural artifacts
Exhibitions: Permanent exhibitions: Furniture City; Habitats (1997) Gold, Jade & Forests: Costa Rica Anishinabek: People of This Place
Publications: Museum, quarterly; Discoveries, monthly
Activities: Classes for adults & children; dramatic programs; docent training; lect open to public; concerts; gallery talks; tours; individual paintings lent to non-profit educational institutions; museum shop sells books, original art, reproductions, prints, jewelry, decorative arts, stationery, toys & games

M **URBAN INSTITUTE FOR CONTEMPORARY ARTS,** 88 Monroc Ave NW, 49503. Tel 616-454-7000; FAX 616-454-7013; Elec Mail uica@iserv.net. *Exec Dir* Margorie Kuipers
Open Tues, Thurs, Fri Noon - 5 PM, Wed Noon - 8 PM, Sat 1 - 5 PM. No admis fee. Estab 1976, dedicated to the development of a vital cultural community. Visual arts gallery. Average Annual Attendance: 15,000
Income: Financed by grants, donations, mem, ticket sales, studio rental & fundraising events
Publications: Monthly newsletter
Activities: Film program & literature readings; lect open to public, 3 vis lectr per year; dance events; book traveling exhibitions; sales shop sells t-shirts

GROSSE POINTE SHORES

M **EDSEL & ELEANOR FORD HOUSE,** 1100 Lake Shore Rd, 48236. Tel 313-884-4222; FAX 313-884-5977; Elec Mail kgormley@bizserve.com. *Pres* Open ; *Head Cur & Registrar* Maureen Devine; *Dir Tours* Donna Oliver; *Dir Marketing* Kate Gormley
Open Wed - Sun 1 - 5 PM, Apr - Dec Wed - Sun Noon - 5 PM. Admis adult $5, senior citizen $4, children $3. Estab 1978 to help educate public on local history, fine & decorative arts. Average Annual Attendance: 38,000
Income: Financed by endowment
Collections: Collection paintings, prints, archival photographs, French & English antique furniture, silver, glass, ceramics, historic textiles
Exhibitions: (1997) In the Spirit of Resistance: African American Modernists & the Mexican Muralist School
Publications: Exhibit catalogs
Activities: Classes for adults & children, seasonal children's programs; docent training.; lect open to public, 4 - 6 vis lectr per year; tours; individual paintings & original objects of art lent to other museums; book traveling exhibitions 2 - 3 per year; museum shop sells books, reproductions, souvenirs & postcards

HARTLAND

A **HARTLAND ART COUNCIL,** PO Box 530126, 48353. Tel 810-229-0869; *Pres* Nadine Cloutier
Estab 1973 to promote arts in Hartland community. Gallery space in local library & adjacent school building. Mem: 35; dues $10 - $100; annual meeting in May
Income: $3000-$4000 (financed by mem & summer art camp)
Collections: Paintings, photographs, sculptures, fibers, works of Michigan artists exhibited in local public buildings
Exhibitions: Local artists exhibit annually
Publications: Recollections, exhibit catalog
Activities: Classes for adults & children; lect open to public; competitions with awards; scholarships; exten dept serving Michigan art councils and schools, lending collection contains kodachromes & photographs; originate traveling exhibitions

HOLLAND

M **HOPE COLLEGE,** De Pree Art Center & Gallery, 275 Columbia Ave, 49423. Tel 616-395-7500; FAX 616-395-7499; Elec Mail @hope.cit.hope.edu. *Dir* John Montgomery Wilson
Open Mon - Thurs 10 AM - 10 PM, Fri & Sat 10 AM - 7 PM, Sun 1 - 10 PM. No admis fee. Estab as a place for the college & community to enjoy art. Average Annual Attendance: 5000
Exhibitions: Days of Saints & Souls: A Celebration of the Day of the Dead; Government Art of the 30s & 40s; Movers & Shakers: Sculpture That Affects Change in Time; New Deal; Power over the Clay; Pre-modern Art of Vienna; Prints of Japan
Publications: Exhibition catalogs
Activities: Lect open to public; tours; gallery talks; individual paintings & original objects of art lent to faculty; lending collection contains original art works, original prints, paintings & sculpture

INTERLOCHEN

L **INTERLOCHEN CENTER FOR THE ARTS,** PO Box 199, 49643. Tel 616-276-7200, Ext 7420; FAX 616-276-6321; *Head Librn* Evelyn R Weliver
Open daily 8 AM - 5 PM & 6:30 - 9:30 PM. Estab 1963. Special music library with over 50,000 titles. Circ 9000
Library Holdings: Vols 20,000; Per subs 140; Micro — Reels; AV — Cassettes, fs, rec
Publications: Interlochen Review, annual
Activities: Dramatic programs; lect open to public; concerts; tours; competitions; awards; scholarships & fels offered; originate traveling exhibitions

JACKSON

M **ELLA SHARP MUSEUM,** 3225 Fourth St, 49203. Tel 517-787-2320; *Dir* David Mitchell; *Dir Pub Relations* Kathy Spring; *Office Mgr* Cynthia Parker; *Outreach Coordr* Lynnea Lottis
Open Tues - Fri 10 AM - 4 PM, Sat & Sun 11 AM - 4 PM, cl Mon & major holidays. Admis family $5, adults $2.50, senior citizens $2, children $1. Estab 1965 to serve the people of Jackson & to provide a place for cultural educ in the community & a temporary gallery where a variety of exhibits are held. Included are a large & small gallery; small library is maintained. Average Annual Attendance: 200,000. Mem: 2000; dues $1600, $1000, $500, $250, $125, $75, $50, $30, $20; annual meeting in June
Income: Financed by endowment & mem along with grants
Collections: China; coverlets & quilts; furniture from Victorian period; †oil paintings; porcelain; †prints
Publications: Annual Report; bulletins and catalogs; newsletter, monthly; research material as requested
Activities: Classes for adults & children; dramatic programs; lect open to public, 7 vis lectr per year; concerts; gallery talks; tours; competitions; art objects lent to schools; lending collection contains photographs

KALAMAZOO

M KALAMAZOO INSTITUTE OF ARTS, 314 S Park St, 49007. Tel 616-349-7775; FAX 616-349-9313; *Exec Dir* James A Bridenstine
Open Tues - Sat 10 AM - 5 PM, Sun 1 - 5 PM, cl Aug, Sun during June, July & holidays. No admis fee. Incorporated 1924 to further interest in the arts, especially in the visual arts; new building opened in 1961. There is one large gallery, four small exhibition galleries, with exhibitions changed monthly. One or more galleries always devoted to pieces from the permanent collection. Average Annual Attendance: 150,000. Mem: 1800; dues $25 & up; annual meeting Sept
Income: $800,000 (financed by endowment & mem)
Collections: †Art on Paper - drawings, graphics, photographs & watercolors; †sculpture; †20th century American art
Exhibitions: Bronson Park Art Fair; Kalamazoo Area Show;
Publications: Exhibition catalogs, issued irregularly; newsletters, monthly
Activities: Classes for adults & children; docent training; lect open to public; concerts; tours; scholarships; individual paintings & original objects of art lent to other institutions; lending collection contains books & slides; originate traveling exhibitions; museum shop sells craft items, jewelry & cards

L Library, 314 S Park St, 49007. Tel 616-349-7775; FAX 616-349-9313; *Head Librn* Rebecca D Steel
Open Tues - Sat 10 AM - 5 PM. Estab 1961, reference for Kalamazoo Institute of Arts curatorial staff & school faculty. For public reference only, open to members for circulation
Library Holdings: Vols 8500; Per subs 60; AV — Fs, slides, v-tapes; Other — Clipping files 1000, exhibition catalogs, pamphlets
Special Subjects: Art History, Ceramics, Etchings & Engravings, Folk Art, Jewelry, Lettering, Painting - American, Painting - British, Painting - European, Photography, Pottery, Printmaking, Watercolors, Woodcuts, American Art, especially art of the 20th century printmaking, history, technique & Weaving
Activities: Lect; tours

M WESTERN MICHIGAN UNIVERSITY-ART DEPT, Dept of Art Galleries, Department of Art, 49008. Tel 616-387-2455; FAX 616-387-2477; Elec Mail jacquelyn.ruttinger@wmich.edu. *Exhib Dir* Jacquelyn Ruttinger
Open Mon - Fri 10 AM - 5 PM. Estab 1965 to provide visual enrichment to the university & Kalamazoo community. The Department of Art Galleries are located in various buildings on campus. Gallery II is a space located on the ground floor of Sangren Hall; Space Gallery is on the ground floor of Knauss Hall & the Student Art Gallery is in East Hall. Sculpture Tour is a rotating outdoor exhibit of traveling sculpture for which a catalog is available. Average Annual Attendance: 50,000
Income: Financed by state appropriation
Collections: Contemporary print collection; 19th & 20th century American & European Art
Exhibitions: Rotating exhibition on contemporary arts
Publications: Sculpture Tour 92-93, 93-94, 94-95
Activities: Classes for adults; lect open to public, 4 vis lectr per year; gallery talks; tours; awards; scholarships offered; collection contains 1900 original art works, 350 original prints; book traveling exhibitions 4 per year

LAKESIDE

M LAKESIDE STUDIO, 15251 S Lakeshore Rd, 49116. Tel 616-469-1377; FAX 616-469-1101; *Exec Dir* John Wilson
Open daily 9 AM - 5 PM. Estab 1968, international. Represents international artists, American, Soviet, Chinese, Dutch work done by Artists-in-Residence
Activities: Award placement in Artist-in-Residence Program through selection process; museum shop sells original art

LANSING

M LANSING ART GALLERY, 425 S Grand Ave, 48933. Tel 517-374-6400; *Dir* Martha Brownscombe; *Pres* Marge Malarney
Open Tues - Fri 10 AM - 4 PM, Sat & Sun 1 - 4 PM. No admis fee. Estab 1965 as a private non-profit gallery to promote the visual arts in their many forms to citizens of the greater Lansing area. Maintains large exhibit area, gallery shop & rental gallery. Average Annual Attendance: 18,000. Mem: 500; dues $20-$2500; annual meeting in June
Income: $180,000 (financed by mem, sales, grants, contributions & fees)
Exhibitions: Monthly invitational shows & competitions
Publications: Gallery News, monthly
Activities: Docent training; lect open to public, 10 vis lectr per year; gallery talks; tours; competitions with awards; individual paintings & original objects of art available for lease or purchase, including original art works, original prints, paintings, photographs & sculpture; book traveling exhibitions, 1-2 per year; sales shop sells books, sculpture

LELAND

M LEELANAU HISTORICAL MUSEUM, 203 E Cedar St, PO Box 246, 49654. Tel 616-256-7475; *Cur & Adminr* Laura Quackenbush
Open June 15 - Labor Day Tues - Sat 10 AM - 4 PM, Labor Day - June 14, Fri, Sat & Sun 1 - 4 PM. Admis adult $1, student $.50. Estab 1959 for the preservation & exhibition of local history. One gallery for temporary exhibits of traditional & folk arts, 40 ft x 20 ft. Average Annual Attendance: 5,000. Mem: 450; dues $15; annual meeting last Mon in Aug
Income: $52,000 (financed by endowment, mem, fundraising & activities)
Collections: Small collection of local paintings, both folk and fine art; small collection of Leelanau County Indian baskets, birch bark crafts
Publications: Lee Muse newsletter, 2 per yr
Activities: Educ dept; Sales shop sells books, reproductions, local crafts & original needlework kits

MARQUETTE

M NORTHERN MICHIGAN UNIVERSITY ART MUSEUM, 49855. Tel 906-227-1481; *Gallery Dir* Wayne Francis
Open Mon - Fri 9 AM - 5 PM, Sun 1 - 4 PM. No admis fee. Estab 1975 to bring exhibits of the visual arts to the University, community & the upper peninsula of Michigan. Gallery covers approx 2000 sq ft of space, with security system & smoke detectors. Average Annual Attendance: 10,000
Income: $6500 (financed by University funds)
Collections: Contemporary printing & sculpture; student collection; Japanese & American illustration; Japanese prints & artifacts; †permanent collection
Exhibitions: Average of one to two major exhibits each month
Publications: Exhibit Announcement, monthly
Activities: Educ dept; lect open to public, 5 vis lectr per year; gallery talks; competitions; individual paintings & original objects of art lent; traveling exhibitions organized & circulated

MIDLAND

A ARTS MIDLAND GALLERIES & SCHOOL, 1801 W St Andrews, 48640. Tel 517-631-3250; FAX 517-631-7890; *Dir* B B Winslow; *Prog Coordr* Judy Mullison; *Office Mgr* Gail Wilson
Open Mon - Sun 10 AM - 5 PM. Admis adults $3, students $1, members free. Estab 1956 to generate interest in & foster understanding & enjoyment of the visual arts. Exhibition space consists of three galleries, one 40 x 80 ft & two smaller 20 x 40 ft space; spot tracking lighting. Average Annual Attendance: 20,000. Mem: 650; dues family $40, senior citizen $25; annual meeting in fall; monthly board meetings
Income: $200,000 (financed by endowment, mem, grants, fees for services, fundraising events)
Exhibitions: Great Lakes Regional Art Exhibition; Annual All Media Juried Competition & Exhibition (open to all Michigan artists age 18 & over)
Publications: Calendar of events; quarterly newsletter for members; yearly report
Activities: Classes for adults & children; docent training; workshops; Picture Parent; lect open to public, 4 vis lectr per year; gallery talks; self-guiding tours; tours; juried art fairs; competitions with awards; scholarships offered; book traveling exhibitions 5-10 per year; originate traveling exhibitions; museum shop sells books, magazines, original art, jewelry, children's art toys, reproductions, original crafts

L GRACE A DOW MEMORIAL LIBRARY, Fine Arts Dept, 1710 W Saint Andrews, 48640. Tel 517-835-7151; FAX 517-835-9791; *Dir* James Alsip; *Fine Arts Reference Librn* Margaret Allen
Open Mon - Fri 10 AM - 9 PM, Sat 10 AM - 5 PM; during school year, Sun 1 - 5 PM. Estab 1955 as a pub library. Maintains art gallery
Income: Financed by city appropriation & gifts
Purchases: $27,000
Library Holdings: Vols 12,000; Per subs 80; Compact discs; AV — A-tapes, cassettes, motion pictures, rec, v-tapes; Other — Clipping files, framed reproductions, original art works, pamphlets, prints, reproductions
Collections: Alden B Dow Fine Arts Collection
Exhibitions: Exhibits form local artists, art groups & schools
Activities: Films

M MIDLAND COUNTY HISTORICAL SOCIETY, 1801 W Saint Andrews Rd, 48640. Tel 517-835-7401; *Dir* Gary Skory, BS; *Asst Dir* Shelley Wegner, BS
Open 9 AM - 5 PM. Estab 1952. Average Annual Attendance: 100. Mem: 350; dues $100, $50, $35, $25 & $20
Income: $105,000 (financed by endowment & mem)
Collections: Collection of local history photographs; Collection of local books
Exhibitions: Oriental Dolls: Blair-Murrah
Publications: Salt of the Earth, Yates; Midland Log
Activities: Classes for children; docent programs; lect open to public, 3 vis lectr per year; museum shop sells books, original art & reproductions

MONROE

A MONROE COUNTY COMMUNITY COLLEGE, Fine Arts Council, 1555 S Raisinville Rd, 48161. Tel 313-242-7300, Ext 345; *Chmn* Dr William McCloskey
Estab 1967 to promote the arts. Average Annual Attendance: 120. Mem: 50; dues $5
Income: $3000 (financed by endowment, mem & county appropriation)
Activities: Classes for children; gallery talks; competitions with awards; scholarships

MOUNT CLEMENS

A THE ART CENTER, 125 Macomb Pl, 48043. Tel 810-469-8666; FAX 810-469-4529; *Exec Dir* Jo-Anne Wilkie
Open Tues - Fri 11 AM - 5 PM, Sat 9 AM - 2 PM, cl Mon. No admis fee. Estab 1969 to foster art appreciation and participation for people of Macomb County. The only public facility of its kind in the northeast Detroit metro area; The Center has two rooms, 17 x 27 ft, connected by lobby area in the former Carnegie Library Bldg, a Historical State Registered building. Average Annual Attendance: 10,000. Mem: 500; dues individual $25; annual meeting in June
Income: Financed by mem, city & state appropriation, commissions from sales, class fees & special fundraising events
Exhibitions: Several all state open competitive exhibitions, including painting, sculpture & crafts; county wide student show; regional scholastic art awards shows
Publications: Newsletter, quarterly
Activities: Classes for adults and children; docent training; tours; competitions; gallery & gift shops sell original art

MOUNT PLEASANT

M CENTRAL MICHIGAN UNIVERSITY, Art Gallery, Whitman 132, 48859. Tel 517-774-3974, 774-3800; *Dir* Mary Dole
Open Mon - Sat 10 AM - 5 PM, cl school holidays. No admis fee. Estab 1987 to serve Mount Pleasant & university community; offer contemporary & traditional forms of art. Corner of Franklin & Preston Streets. 125 ft of wall space & 900 sq ft of unobstructed floor space. Average Annual Attendance: 5000
Income: Financed by art dept
Exhibitions: All Michigan Student Competitions; Art Faculty Show; MFA Show; three other shows on various themes or mediums
Activities: Lect open to public, 4 vis lectr per year; gallery talks; tours; competitions with awards

MUSKEGON

M MUSKEGON MUSEUM OF ART, 296 W Webster Ave, 49440. Tel 616-722-2600; FAX 616-722-3041; *Dir* Henry Matthews; *Public Relations Coordr* Melissa Freye; *Educ Coordr* Gail Phinney; *Registrar* Babs Vaughn; *Gift Shop Mgr* Amy Inglat
Open Tues - Fri 10 AM - 5 PM, Sat, Sun Noon - 5 PM. Estab 1912, Hackley Gallery designed by S S Beman, Chicago architect. Average Annual Attendance: 40,000. Mem: 1100; dues benefactor $1000, patron $250, sponsor $100, family $45, individual $35
Income: $500,000 (financed by endowment, underwriting, mem & fundraising)
Collections: American paintings; glass by Louis Comfort Tiffany, Harvey Littleton, Lipofsky, & others; The Home Signal by Winslow Homer; Impressionist paintings; modern & Old Masters prints; Study in Rose & Brown by James Whistler; Tornado Over Kansas by John Steuart Curry; New York Restaurant by Edward Hopper
Publications: Catalogs of American & European paintings from the Permanent Collection
Activities: Classes for adults & children; docent training; workshops; lect open to public; gallery talks; tours; competitions with awards; individual & original objects of art lent to qualified museums; book traveling exhibitions; originate traveling exhibitions; museum shop sells books & reproductions
L Library, 296 W Webster Ave, 49440. Tel 616-722-2600; FAX 616-722-3041; *Librn* Lucille Meier
Estab 1977. Open to pub

OLIVET

M OLIVET COLLEGE, Armstrong Museum of Art & Archaeology, 320 S Main St, 49076. Tel 616-749-7000; FAX 616-749-7178; *Pres* Michael Bassis; *Dir* Donald Rowe
Open Mon - Fri 9 AM - 5 PM, while college is in session. Estab 1960 to collect artifacts & display for educational purposes. Average Annual Attendance: 1200
Collections: American Indian, Mesopotamian, Philippine & Thailand Artifacts; Modern American Prints; Primitive Art; Sculpture
Exhibitions: Invitational shows; one-man shows; student shows; traveling shows
Activities: Book traveling exhibitions
L Library, 320 S Main St, 49076. Tel 616-749-7608; FAX 616-749-7178; *Library Dir* Hoda Mahmoudi
Library Holdings: Vols 75,000; Micro — Prints

ORCHARD LAKE

M ST MARY'S GALERIA, 3535 Indian Trail, 48324. Tel 810-682-1885; *Dir* Marian Owczarski
Open Mon - Fri 1 - 5 PM, first Sun of the month 1 - 4 PM & anytime upon request. No admis fee. Estab to house major Polish & Polish-American art. Average Annual Attendance: 8000
Collections: Contemporary Polish Painting by Andrzej Luczynski; John Paul II: The First Year (Pictorial exhibit); Sculpture by Marian Owczarski; History of Polish Printing: Rare Books & Documents; Polish Folk Art; Polish Tapestry; Paintings of A Wierusz Kowalski; Watercolors by J Falat; Watercolors by Wojciech Gierson; Louvre by Night, a sketch by Aleksander Gierymski; oil paintings by Jacek Malczewski; lithographs by Irene Snarski & Barbara Rosiak
Activities: Lect open to public; concerts; tours

PETOSKEY

M CROOKED TREE ARTS COUNCIL, Virginia M McCune Community Arts Center, 461 E Mitchell St, 49770. Tel 616-347-4337; FAX 616-347-3429; *Dir* Michelle Conklin; *Pres* Joe Hickey; *VPres* Joe Burgin
Open Mon - Sat 10 AM - 5 PM. No admis fee. Estab 1981 as a non-profit arts council & arts center. 40 ft x 25 ft exhibition gallery featuring monthly shows, modern lighting & security systems; 85 x 45 ft gallery featuring work of Michigan artists on consignment. Average Annual Attendance: 30,000. Mem: 1600; dues family $40, individual $20; annual meeting in Sept
Income: $300,000 (financed by endowment, city & state appropriation, ticket sales, tuition income, fundraisers)
Exhibitions: Monthly exhibits shown
Publications: Art news, bimonthly
Activities: Classes for adults & children; dramatic programs; docent programs; music & dance classes; 3 competitions per year (crafts, fine arts, photography); cash prizes; book traveling exhibitions 7 per year; sales shop sells original art, reproductions, prints, art postcards

PONTIAC

A CREATIVE ARTS CENTER, 47 Williams St, 48341. Tel 810-333-7849; FAX 810-333-7841; *Exec Dir* Carol Paster; *Exhib Coordr* Debbie Agdanowski
Open Tues, Thurs & Sat 10 AM - 4 PM, cl holidays. No admis fee. Estab 1964 to present the best in exhibitions, educational activities, & community art outreach. Main gallery is a two storey central space with carpeted walls; Clerestory Gallery is the second floor balcony overlooking the main gallery. Average Annual Attendance: 80,000. Mem: 160; dues organizational $50, general $35, artists & citizens $20, annual meeting in Mar
Income: Financed by endowment, mem, city & state appropriation, trust funds, United Way, Michigan Council for the Arts
Exhibitions: Temporary exhibits of historic, contemporary & culturally diverse works
Publications: Biannual newsletter
Activities: Classes for adults & children; dramatic programs, music, dance, visual arts programs; lect open to the public, 30 vis lectr per year; gallery talks; concerts; tours; competitions with awards; book traveling exhibitions semi-annually; originate traveling exhibitions; sales shop sells books & original art work

PORT HURON

M MUSEUM OF ARTS & HISTORY, 1115 Sixth St, 48060. Tel 810-982-0891; FAX 810-982-0053; *Dir* Stephen R Williams
Open Wed - Sun 1 - 4:30 PM. Admis adults $1.50, sr citizens $1, students $.50. Estab 1968 to preserve area historical & marine artifacts; exhibit living regional artists; exhibit significant shows of national & international interest. Maintains reference library. Two galleries are maintained for loaned exhibitions & the permanent collection; also a decorative arts gallery & a sales gallery. Average Annual Attendance: 120,000. Mem: 1400; dues family $25, individual $15
Income: $200,000 (financed by endowment, mem, city appropriation, state & federal grants & earned income through program fees)
Collections: Thomas Edison Collection; Civil War Collection; marine artifacts; 19th century American decorative arts (paintings & prints)
Publications: Exhibit catalogs; monthly newsletter
Activities: Classes for adults & children; docent training; lect open to public, 6 vis lectr per year; concerts; gallery talks; tours; competitions with awards; film series; festivals; music & theatre programs; book traveling exhibitions, 8 per year; museum shop sells books, magazines, original art

M SAINT CLAIR COUNTY COMMUNITY COLLEGE, Jack R Hennesey Art Galleries, 323 Erie St, PO Box 5015, 48061-5015. Tel 810-984-3881; *Coordr of Galleries* John Henry
Open Mon - Fri 8 AM - 4:30 PM. No admis fee. Estab 1975 to serve the community as an exhibition site & to serve the faculty & students of the college as a teaching tool. Maintains three galleries connected by common hall with approximately 2,000 sq ft. Average Annual Attendance: 3000
Collections: Paintings, print, and sculpture (wood and metal)
Activities: Educ dept; lect open to public; concerts; competitions with awards; scholarships offered

ROCHESTER

M OAKLAND UNIVERSITY, Meadow Brook Art Gallery, 48309-4401. Tel 810-370-3005; *Dir & Cur* Kiichi Usui
Open Mon - Fri 1 - 5 PM, Sat & Sun 2 - 6:30 PM, evening 7 - 9:30 PM in conjunction with Meadow Brook Theater Performances. No admis fee. Estab 1966 to provide a series of changing exhibitions & to develop an art collection to serve the university community & the greater community of Southern Michigan. 2000 sq ft across hallway from theatre auditorium. Average Annual Attendance: 50,000. Mem: 300; dues $20 - $500
Income: Financed by university budget, mem, fees & contributions
Collections: Art of Africa, Oceania and Pre-Columbian America; contemporary art and Sculpture Park; Oriental art
Publications: Exhibition catalogs
Activities: Lect open to public, 2 vis lectr per year; gallery talks; slide presentations in conjunction with exhibitions; paintings & original art objects lent within university; originate traveling exhibitions

SAGINAW

M SAGINAW ART MUSEUM, 1126 N Michigan Ave, 48602. Tel 517-754-2491; FAX 517-754-9387; *Dir* Ann M Knoll
Open Tues - Sat 10 AM - 5 PM, Sun 1 - 5 PM. No admis fee. Estab 1947 as an art exhibition center & education department. Housed in 1899, former residence of Clark L Ring family, designed by Charles Adams Platt. Average Annual Attendance: 19,300. Mem: 547; dues $10 - $1000; annual meetings on second Thurs of Sept
Income: $164,500 (financed by endowment, mem & grants)
Collections: 14th century through present European & American paintings; contemporary graphics; Visionarea (children's hands-on)
Publications: Annual report
Activities: Classes for adults & children; docent training; lect open to public; gallery talks; tours; competitions with awards; exten dept serves grade schools; individual paintings & objects of art lent to other museums; book traveling exhibitions 10 per year; originate traveling exhibitions which circulate to other museums
L Couse Memorial Library, 1126 N Michigan Ave, 48602. Tel 517-754-2491; FAX 517-754-9387; *Dir* Ann Knoll
Open to public for reference only by appointment
Library Holdings: Vols 3000; Per subs 15; AV — Kodachromes, slides; Other — Clipping files, exhibition catalogs, original art works, pamphlets, photographs, prints, sculpture

TRAVERSE CITY

M **NORTHWESTERN MICHIGAN COLLEGE,** Dennos Museum Center, 1701 E
Front St, 49686. Tel 616-922-1055; FAX 616-922-1597; *Museum Dir* Eugene A
Jenneman; *Cur* Jacqueline Shinners
Open Mon - Sat 10 AM - 5 PM, Sun 1 - 5 PM. Estab 1991. 40,000 sq ft
complex features three changing exhibit galleries & a sculpture court; a hands on
Discovery Gallery; & a Gallery of Inuit Art, the museum's major permanent
collection. The 367 seat Milliken Auditorium offers theater & musical
performances throught-out the year
Income: $650,000 (financed by earned income/endowment)
Library Holdings: Other — Prints
Collections: †Canadian Inuit sculpture & prints
Activities: Docent training; lect open to public, 12-15 vis lectr per year; concerts;
individual paintings & original objects of art lent to museums; lending collection
contains original art works & original prints; originate traveling exhibitions to
museums; museum shop sells books, magazines, original art & prints

YPSILANTI

M **EASTERN MICHIGAN UNIVERSITY,** Ford Gallery, 48197. Tel 313-487-
1268; FAX 313-481-1095;
Internet Home Page Address http//:www.art.acad.emich.edu/. *Dept Head* Roy
Johnson; *Gallery Dir* Martha Gelarden
Open Mon - Fri 9 AM - 5 PM. No admis fee. Estab 1925, in present building
since 1982, for educational purposes. Art Dept gallery is maintained displaying
staff & student exhibitions from a wide variety of sources; also on large, well-
lighted gallery with lobby & a satellite student-operated gallery are maintained
Income: Financed by state appropriation
Purchases: $500
Exhibitions: Seven changing exhibitions annually. Annual Faculty Exhibition;
Annual Juried Student Exhibition; Bi-annual Michigan Drawing Exhibition; Paul
Suttman: Encounters in Bronze
Publications: Exhibition catalogs
Activities: Classes for adults; lect open to public; gallery talks; competitions
L **Art Dept Slide Collection,** Ford Hall, Rm 214, 48197. Tel 313-487-1213; Elec
Mail fa__pawloski@online.emich.edu. *Librn* Carole Pawloski
Open 8 AM - 5 PM. Estab 1978 as reference source for faculty & graduate
students
Library Holdings: Vols 350; AV — Slides 92,000
Special Subjects: Afro-American Art, American Indian Art, American Western
Art, Furniture, History of Art & Archaeology, Mexican Art, Oriental Art,
Painting - American, Pre-Columbian Art, Restoration & Conservation, Western
European Art

MINNESOTA

BLOOMINGTON

M **BLOOMINGTON ART CENTER,** 10206 Penn Ave S, 55431. Tel 612-948-
8746; FAX 612-948-8744; *Dir* Susan Anderson
Open Mon - Fri 9 AM - 5 PM, Sat 10 AM - 1 PM. No admis fee. Estab 1976 to
serve emerging local artists. Average Annual Attendance: 12,000. Mem: 700;
dues individual $25, family 35; annual meeting in Jan
Income: $228,000 (financed by mem & city appropriation)
Exhibitions: Ongoing
Activities: Classes for adults & children in dramatic programs; lect open to
public, 3 vis lectr per year; competitions with prizes

BRAINERD

M **CROW WING COUNTY HISTORICAL SOCIETY,** 320 W Laurel St, PO Box
722, 56401. Tel 218-829-3268; *Exec Dir* Mary Lou Moudry
Open June - Aug, Mon - Fri 9 AM - 5 PM & Sat 9 AM - 1 PM, Sept - May,
Mon - Fri 1 - 5 PM & Sat 9 AM - 1 PM. Admis adult $3, seniors $2. Estab 1927
to preserve & interpret county history. Average Annual Attendance: 6000. Mem:
750; dues $10-$500; annual meeting 2nd Tues in Apr
Income: $90,000 (financed by mem, county, state grants, private donations)
Exhibitions: 19th Century Uses of Rails; Sarah Thorp Heald & Freeman Thorp
Paintings: Home & Community: Rotating Artifacts Reflecting County Life;
Native American Tools & Beadwork; When Lumber Was King
Publications: The Crow Wing County Historian, quarterly newsletter
Activities: Docent training; lect open to public; tours; competitions with awards;
museum shop sells books, reproductions, prints

BROOKLYN PARK

M **NORTH HENNEPIN COMMUNITY COLLEGE,** Art Gallery, 7411 85th Ave
N, 55445. Tel 612-424-0811, 424-0702; *Dir* Susan McDonald
Open Mon - Fri 8 AM - 7:30 PM. No admis fee. Estab 1966 to make art
available to students & community. Two gallery spaces: smaller gallery is for one
person exhibitions & installation; larger gallery is for group exhibitions. Average
Annual Attendance: 8000
Income: Financed by state appropriation & foundation grants
Collections: Student works & local artists in Minnesota
Exhibitions: Mid-West Artist on regular basis
Activities: Lect open to the public; concerts; gallery talks; tours; student show
with prizes; individual paintings & original objects of art lent to faculty members
on campus; book traveling exhibitions 1-2 per year; sales shop sells books

DULUTH

M **SAINT LOUIS COUNTY HISTORICAL SOCIETY,** 506 W Michigan St,
55802. Tel 218-733-7580; *Dir* JoAnne Coombe
Open Mon - Sat 10 AM - 5 PM, Sun Noon - 5 PM. Admis family $15, adults
$5, senior citizens & juniors $3, 3 & under free. Estab in 1922. Housed in the
Saint Louis County Heritage & Arts Center along with A M Chisholm Mus,
Duluth Ballet, Duluth-Superior Symphony, Duluth Playhouse, Duluth Art
Institute, Matinee Musicale & Lake Superior Mus of Transportation. Soc exhibit
areas consist of three galleries interspersed in viewing areas. Average Annual
Attendance: 100,000. Mem: 900; dues $9 & up
Income: $236,000 (financed by pub support, dues, earned profit, & volunteer
service)
Collections: E Johnson Collection; drawings; paintings; Ojibwe & Sioux
beadwork, quillwork, basketry; Logging Exhibit; Herman Melheim hand-carved
furniture
Exhibitions: Changing exhibits on topics related to the history of northeastern
Minnesota & Lake Superior region
Publications: Books & pamphlets on topics related to the history of northeastern
Minn; quarterly newsletter
Activities: Workshops; lect; tours to places of historical interest within the region

M **UNIVERSITY OF MINNESOTA, DULUTH,** Tweed Museum of Art, 10
University Dr, 55812. Tel 218-726-8222; FAX 218-726-8503; *Dir* Martin
DeWitt; *Technician* Larry Gruenwald; *Asst Cur* Peter Spooner
Open Tues - Fri 9 AM - 4:30 PM, Sat & Sun 1 - 5 PM. No admis fee. Estab
1950 to serve both the university & community as a center for exhibition of
works of art & related activities. Nine galleries within the mus. Average Annual
Attendance: 80,000. Mem: 680; dues $10-$250
Income: Financed by mem, state appropriation & foundation
Purchases: $10,000-$50,000
Collections: Jonathan Sax Collections of 20th Century American Prints; George
P Tweed Memorial Art Collections of 500 paintings with emphasis on Barbizon
School and 19th Century American; †20th century American paintings &
sculptures; Old Master European paintings
Exhibitions: Contemporary Photographers Seriies; Sara Singer: New Work;
Minnesota Ceramics Today: Other Traditions; Joan Simmons: Paintings & Works
on Paper; Annual Art Student Juried Exhibition; American Art from the
Frederick R Weismann Collection; Craig Blacklock: Lake Superior Images
Publications: Catalogues, irregular
Activities: Docent training; lect open to public, 6-8 vis lectr per year; concerts;
gallery talks; tours; individual paintings & original objects of art lent to qualifying
museums & institutions; lending collection contains original art works, original
prints & paintings; traveling exhibitions organized & circulated; museum shop
sells books, reproductions, craft objects & cards

ELK RIVER

A **ELK RIVER AREA ARTS COUNCIL,** 400 Jackson Ave, Ste 205, 55330-1363.
Tel 612-441-4725; *Exec Dir* David Beauvais; *Strings Dir* Rhonda Johnson
Estab 1989 to promote the arts. Elk River Chamber of Commerce Building &
Sherburne County Government Center. Mem: 145; dues $15-$1000; annual
meeting in Nov
Income: $38,000 (financed by mem, city appropriation & grants)
Collections: A Day in the Life of Elk River Photography Collection
Exhibitions: Arts in Harmony (juried exhibition)
Publications: The Eddy, bimonthly newsletter
Activities: Competitions with prizes; book traveling exhibitions 6 per year;
originate traveling exhibitions 1 per year

ELYSIAN

M **LESUEUR COUNTY HISTORICAL MUSEUM,** Chapter One, PO Box 240,
56028-0240. Tel 507-267-4620, 362-8350; *VPres* Michael LaFrance; *Dir &
Museologist* David Woolin
Open May - Sept Sat & Sun 1 - 5 PM; June - Aug Wed - Sun 1 - 5 PM. No
admis fee. Estab 1966 to show the works of Adolf Dehn, Roger Preuss, David
Maass; Lloyd Herfindohl & Albert Christ-Janer to preserve early heritage &
artifacts of the pioneers of LeSueur County. Mus is depository of Dehn, Preuss,
Maass & Lloyd Herfindahl; examples of originals, prints & publications of the
artists are on display. Average Annual Attendance: 1000. Mem: 700; dues life
$25, annual $1; annual meeting quarterly
Income: $17,000 (financed by mem, county appropriation, county government &
grants)
Purchases: $51,000
Collections: †Adolf Dehn; David Maass; Roger Preuss; Lloyd Herfindahl; Albert
Christ-Janer
Exhibitions: Exhibitions of works by Adolf Dehn, David Maass, Roger Preuss,
Lloyd Herfindohl, Albert Christ-Janer
Publications: Newsletters, quarterly
Activities: Slide carousel to show the sites & early history of the County & works
of the Artists; lect open to public; gallery talks; tours; lending collection contains
books, cassettes, color reproductions, latern slides, original prints, paintings,
motion pictures & 1000 photographs; museum shop sells books, original art &
prints
L **Collections Library,** PO Box 240, 56028-0240. Tel 507-267-4620, 362-8683; *Dir*
David Woolin
Open by appointment only. Estab 1970 to collect locally & state-wide for
purposes of genealogy; history of the artists
Library Holdings: Vols 300; Per subs 3; Micro — Reels 120; AV — A-tapes,
cassettes, lantern slides, slides; Other — Clipping files, framed reproductions,
original art works, reproductions
Special Subjects: Prints of four Artists
Collections: Original Adolf Dehn Watercolors & Lithographs; Duck Stamp Prints
of Roger Preuss & David Maass; Lloyd Herfindahl: All Media
Exhibitions: Lloyd Herfindahl
Publications: Newsletters, 4 per yr

FOUNTAIN

A FILLMORE COUNTY HISTORICAL SOCIETY, Rt 1, Box 81D, 55935. Tel
507-268-4449; *Exec Dir* Jerry D Henke; *Asst Dir* Alma Syvertson
Open 9 AM - 4 PM. No admis fee, donations accepted. Estab 1934 to preserve
& illustrate the written & photographic history. Average Annual Attendance:
8000. Mem: 350; dues $5-$150; annual meeting second Sat in Oct
Income: $50,000 (financed by mem, county appropriations, donations)
Purchases: An Original Bernard Pietenpol Airplane
Collections: Bue Photography; Antique Agricultural Equipment; Hand Made
Wooden Tools; Vintage Clothing & Tractors
Publications: Rural Roots, quarterly
Activities: Gift shop sells books

GLENWOOD

M POPE COUNTY HISTORICAL SOCIETY, Pope County Museum, S Hwy 104
(Mailing add: 809 S Lakeshore Dr, 56334). Tel 320-634-3293; *Pres* Merlin
Peterson; *VPres* Jayne Nyhammer; *Office Supv* Margaret Kettells
Open Mon - Fri 10 AM - 5 PM, Sat & Sun 1 - 5 PM. Admis adults $3, children
under 12 $.50. Estab 1932 to display & preserve artifacts & geneology files.
Average Annual Attendance: 4500. Mem: 325; dues $5; annual meeting second
Sat in Feb
Income: $36,000 (financed by county appropriation, admis & gifts)
Publications: Semi-annual newsletter
Activities: Educ dept; guided tours for students

INTERNATIONAL FALLS

M KOOCHICHING COUNTY HISTORICAL SOCIETY MUSEUM, 214 Sixth
Ave, PO Box 1147, 56649. Tel 218-283-4316; *Exec Dir* Sarah Williams; *Chair*
Buck Johnson
Open Mon - Sat 11 AM - 5 PM, Sun 1 - 5 PM. Admis adults $3, senior citizens
$2, students $1. Estab 1967 to collect, preserve & interpret the history of
Koochiching County & of the state of Minnesota
Income: Financed by county, mem & admis funds
Collections: 50 paintings relating to the history of the county, including many by
local artists & six of which were commissioned for the museum
Exhibitions: Permanent collection
Publications: Gesundheit, monthly newsletter; descriptive brochure about
paintings
Activities: Classes for adults & children; dramatic programs; lect open to public,
4 vis lectr per year; tours; originate traveling exhibitions; sales shop sells books,
Indian craft items, note & post cards

LESUEUR

M LESUEUR MUSEUM, 208 N Main St, 56058. Tel 612-357-4488; *Pres* Helen
Meyer; *Cur* Mary Gartner; *Treas* Ann Burns
Open Memorial Day - Labor Day 1 - 4:30 PM. No admis fee. Estab 1976.
Average Annual Attendance: 1500. Mem: dues $3; annual meeting in Oct
Income: Financed by County allotment & donations
Exhibitions: Green Giant & Canning; Agriculture; Veterinary Medicine; War in
the Valley
Publications: Biannual newsletter
Activities: Docent training; lect open to public, 1 vis lectr per year; tours; sales
shop sells books & cards

MANKATO

M MANKATO AREA ARTS COUNCIL, Carnegie Art Center, 120 S Broad St,
56001. Tel 507-625-2730; *Pres* Wendy Cramer; *Shop Coordr* Jan Odden;
Grantsperson-Historian Rosemary Froem; *Treas* Joan Turtle; *Building Consultant*
Jon Carlstrom; *Gallery Coordr* Hope Cook
Open Mon, Wed & Fri 1 - 4 PM or by appointment. No admis fee. Estab 1980
to provide exhibition space for regional artists. Two galleries (Rotunda Gallery &
Fireplace Gallery) housed in historic Carnegie Library. Average Annual
Attendance: Over 500. Mem: 300; dues $20 & up; annual meeting in Oct
Exhibitions: (1997) See Art, Hear Art, Speak Art-Katherine Nordby, Rebecca
Nosbush & Nadine Schreyer
Activities: Classes for children; sales shop sells books, original art, prints &
reproductions

M MANKATO STATE UNIVERSITY, Conkling Gallery Art Dept, MSU Box 42,
PO Box 8400, 56002-8400. Tel 507-389-6412; *Dir* Brian Frank
Open Mon - Wed 9 AM - 9 PM, Thurs & Fri 9 AM - 5 PM, Sun 1 - 4 PM. No
admis fee. Estab 1979 to provide cultural enrichment in the visual arts to the
campus & community through a program of exhibitions from local, regional &
national sources & student exhibitions. Gallery has 150 running ft of carpeted
display area, track lighting & climate controlled
Income: Financed by university
Collections: American bookplates; contemporary prints, drawings, paintings,
photographs, sculpture & crafts; student works in all media

MINNEAPOLIS

M AMERICAN SWEDISH INSTITUTE, 2600 Park Ave, 55407. Tel 612-871-
4907; FAX 612-871-8682; *Dir* Bruce Karstadt
Open Tues, Thurs, Fri & Sat Noon - 4 PM, Wed Noon - 8 PM, Sun 1 - 5 PM, cl
Mon & national holidays. Admis adults $3, students under 18 & senior citizens
$2, children under 6 free. Estab & incorporated 1929 to preserve, collect, procure
& exhibit objects related to the Swedish-American in the Midwest from 1845.
Building donated by Swan J Turnblad & contains, in a home setting, a fine
collection of Swedish artifacts, plus many items of general cultural interest
pertaining to Scandinavia. The Grand Hall, paneled in African mahogany, is
considered to be the finest example in US. Throughout the mansion there are
eleven procelain tile fireplaces; nine Swedish & two German design. Average
Annual Attendance: 50,000. Mem: 7000; dues, life $2000, patron $175,
supporting $125, sustaining $85, family (husband, wife & all children under age
18, living at home) $45, regular (single) $33, non-resident single, or husband &
wife outside of fifty mile radius of Twin Cities $25, students attending school,
below the age of 18 $30
Collections: Paintings, sculpture, tapestries, ceramics, china, glass, pioneer items
& textiles, immigration related objects
Publications: ASI Posten (newsletter), monthly; ASI catalog
Activities: Classes for adults & children; dramatic programs; docent training; lect
open to public; concerts; gallery talks; tours; scholarships offered; individual
paintings lent to other museums; book traveling exhibitions 1-2 per year;
bookstore sells books, magazines & original art

A ARTS MIDWEST, 528 Hennepin Ave, Ste 310, 55403-1899. Tel 612-341-0755;
FAX 612-341-0902; Elec Mail general@arts.midwest.org;
Internet Home Page Address http://www.artsmidwest.org. TDD 612-341-0901.
Exec Dir David J Fraher
Estab 1985, provides funding programs, conferences & publications to individuals
& organizations in Illinois, Indiana, Iowa, Michigan, Minnesota, North Dakota,
Ohio, South Dakota & Wisconsin. Works in collaboration with corporations,
foundations, state government arts agencies, the National Endowment for the
Arts & art enthusiasts to connect the arts to audiences, enabling individuals &
families to share in & enjoy the arts & cultures of the region & the world
Publications: Inform, bimonthly newsletter; Insights on Jazz, booklets; Midwest
Jazz, quarterly newsmagazine

C FEDERAL RESERVE BANK OF MINNEAPOLIS, 250 Marquette Ave,
55401-2171. Tel 612-340-6928; Elec Mail cpower@res.mpls.frb.fed.us. *Cur*
Christine T Power
Open to public by appointment with Art Dir or Asst. Estab 1973 to enhance the
working environment of bank; to support the creative efforts of ninth district
artists. Collection displayed throughout the bank in offices, lounges, public areas
and work areas
Collections: Regional collection consists of works by artists living & working in
the Ninth Federal Reserve District
Activities: Tours; individual objects of art loaned for special exhibitions upon
request

C FIRST BANK SYSTEM, Art Collection, 601 Second Ave S, 55402-4302. Tel
612-973-0393; *Cur* James Becker
Estab 1980
Collections: European & American Contemporary Art
Activities: Tours available by appointment only during business hours; individual
paintings & original objects of art lent to art organizations, institutions, museums
& galleries worldwide

C HONEYWELL INC, Art Collection, 2701 Fourth Ave S Honeywell Plaza,
55408. Tel 612-951-3394; *Cur* Caren Olsen; *Asst Cur* Patricia Ryan
Open Mon - Fri 9 AM - 4 PM. Collection displayed in main lobby, second &
fifth floors
Collections: Variety of paintings, abstracts & statues

M INTERMEDIA ARTS MINNESOTA, 425 Ontario St SE, 55414. Elec Mail
iam@maroon.tc.umn.edu. *Exec Dir* Tom Borrup; *Managing Dir* Kathleen
Maloney; *Presenting Progs Mgr* Nicky Tamrong
Open 9 AM - 5 PM. No admis fee. Estab 1973. 2000 sq ft space used for
installations, screenings & performances. Average Annual Attendance: 5000.
Mem: 250; dues $35
Income: Financed by endowment
Exhibitions: Dia de los Muertos; Jerome Installation Art Commissions; Midwest
Masala
Activities: Classes for adults; lect open to public, 3 vis lectr per year; gallery
talks; scholarships & fels offered

M LUTHERAN BROTHERHOOD GALLERY, Gallery of Religious Art, 625
Fourth Ave S, 55415. Tel 612-340-7000; *Consultant & Cur* Richard L Hillstrom
Open Mon - Fri 10 AM - 4 PM. No Admis fee. Estab 1982 as a cultural &
educational gallery. Art is exhibited in a modest sized gallery & in the corporate
library
Collections: Bing & Grondahl Plate Collection; Martin Luther Commemorative
Medals 16th-20th centuries; collection restricted to religious prints & drawings
(15th-20th centuries)
Exhibitions: 8-10 Exhibitions per year
Activities: Originate traveling exhibitions

M MHIRIPIRI GALLERY, 1020 Nicollet Mall, 55403. Tel 612-332-7406;
Co-Owner Rex Mhiripiri; *Co-Owner* Julie Mhiripiri
Open 10 AM - 8 PM. Estab 1986

L MINNEAPOLIS COLLEGE OF ART & DESIGN, Library, 2501 Stevens Ave
S, 55404. Tel 612-874-3791; *Acting Dir* Suzanne Degler; *Slide Librn* Allan Kohl
Open Mon - Thurs 8:30 AM - 10 PM, Fri 8:30 AM - 5 PM, Sat & Sun Noon -
4:30 PM, summer 11:30 AM - 4:30 PM, slide library has different hours. Estab
to provide library & materials in support of the curriculum of the College;
includes a library & slide library. Circ 32,000, circulation limited to students,
staff & alumni
Income: Financed by student tuition, grants & gifts
Library Holdings: Vols 56,000; Per subs 201; AV — Cassettes, rec, slides, v-
tapes; Other — Clipping files, exhibition catalogs, pamphlets
Special Subjects: Drawings, Film, Graphic Design, Illustration, Photography,
Printmaking, Sculpture, Video, Contemporary painting, Product design
Publications: Quarterly accessions list; guide to MCAD Library (irregular);
annual serials list; bibliographic guides to collection

M **MINNEAPOLIS INSTITUTE OF ARTS,** 2400 Third Ave S, 55404. Tel 612-870-3000, 870-3046; FAX 612-870-3004; *Dir* Evan Maurer; *Assoc Dir* Patricia Grazzini; *Chmn Educ* Kathryn C Johnson; *Cur Prints & Drawings* Richard Campbell; *Cur Photo* Carroll T Hartwell; *Cur Oriental Arts* Robert Jacobsen; *Registrar* Catherine Ricciardelli; *Chief Cur & Cur Decorative Arts* Christopher Monkhouse; *Cur Paintings* Charles Stuckey; *Cur Textiles* Lotus Stack; *Cur Ethnographic Arts* Louise Lincoln
Open Tues - Sat 10 AM - 5 PM, Thurs 10 AM - 9 PM, Sun Noon - 5 PM, cl Mon. Admis to museum's permanent collection free; exhibitions adults $2, student $1, free to members, senior citizens, those under 12 & AFDC Cardholders. Estab 1883 to foster the knowledge, understanding & practice of the arts. The first gallery was opened in 1889 & the original building was constructed in 1911-15. The south wing was added in 1926 & the entire structure features the classical elements of the day. The mus was expanded to twice the original size in 1972-74 & has incorporated modern themes designed by Kenzo, Tange & URTEC of Tokyo. Average Annual Attendance: 570,000. Mem: 21,000; dues household $40, individual $30; annual meeting in Oct
Income: Financed by endowment, mem, county & state appropriations & admis
Collections: Collection representing all schools & periods of art: American & European paintings, decorative arts, period rooms, photography, prints & drawings, sculpture; Ancient, African, Oceanic, Oriental & native North & South American arts & textiles
Exhibitions: Images of a Queen's Power: Royal Tapestries of France; The Westward Migration of Chinese Blue & White Porcelain; American Masters: Selections from the Collection of Richard Lewis Hillstrom; Two Lives: Georgia O'Keefe & Alfred Stieglitz - A Conversation in Paintings & Photographs; Alfred Stieglitz's Camera Notes; Minnesota 1990. Visions of Antiquity: Neoclassic Figure Drawings
Publications: Bulletin, biannually; exhibitions catalogs; member's magazine, monthly
Activities: Classes for adults & children; docent training; workshops; lect open to public, 15 vis lectr per year; concerts; gallery talks; tours; paintings & original art objects lent to other professional arts organizations; originate traveling exhibitions; museum shop sells books, magazines, original art, reproductions, prints, slides & jewelry

L **Library,** 2400 Third Ave S, 55404. Tel 612-870-3117; FAX 612-870-3004; *Librn* Harold Peterson; *Assoc Librn* Michael Boe; *Asst Librn* Alice Wernimont Bodnar; *Slide Librn* Heidi Raatz
Open winter Tues, Wed, Fri & Sat Noon - 5 PM, Thurs Noon - 8 PM, summer Tues - Fri Noon - 5 PM. Estab 1915 to provide a reference collection based around the museum's collection of works of art. Has exhibitions of books & prints. For reference only
Library Holdings: Vols 50,000; Per subs 125; Other — Exhibition catalogs, pamphlets
Special Subjects: History of books & printing, decorative arts, prints & photography
Collections: Leslie Collection: History of Books & Printing; Minnick Collection: Botanical, Floral & Fashion Books
Exhibitions: Jean Cocteau
Publications: Five Hundred years of Sporting Books, Manuscripts, Prints & Drawings, by Harold Peterson & Michael Boe; History & Guide to the Library; I Tatti by Jane Satowski; Long Chain of Words by John Parker

A **Friends of the Institute,** 2400 Third Ave S, 55404. Tel 612-870-3046; FAX 612-870-3004; *Pres* Carol Burton
Estab 1922 to broaden the influence of the Institute in the community & to provide volunteer support within the mus. Mem: 1900; annual meeting in May
Activities: Coordinates docent program, museum shop, sales & rental gallery, speaker's bureau, information desk, special lect, exhibitions & fundraising projects

C **NORWEST CORPORATION, MINNEAPOLIS,** Arts Program, Sixth & Marquette Ave, 55479-1025. Tel 612-667-5136; FAX 612-667-2112; *Cur Coll* David Ryan
Open Mon - Fri 8 AM - 5 PM. Estab 1987 to acquire a core collection focusing on modernism comprised of 19th & early 20th century decorative & applied arts & paperworks. Twenty vitrines are installed on the first & second floors of Norwest Center
Purchases: 400 acquisitions to date
Collections: Decorative & applied arts & paperworks dating from 1880 to 1940
Exhibitions: (1996-97) Modernist Metalwork: 1900-1940. (1997-98) Scandinavian Moderne: 1900-1960 The American Moderne: 1920-1940. Art Nouveau in Europe
Publications: Exhibition brochures
Activities: Lect open to employees only; tours; original objects of art lent to other museums

C **THE PILLSBURY COMPANY,** Art Collection, Pillsbury Ctr, 200 S Sixth St, 55402. Tel 612-330-4718; *Pres & Chief Exec Officer* Paul Walsh; *Mgr Bldg Servs* Jean Hardginski
Estab to create exciting & attractive environment & support the arts. Collection displayed on internal walls of corporate headquarters building
Collections: Contemporary & Western American art, primarily oil paintings, prints & watercolors

UNIVERSITY OF MINNESOTA

M **Weisman Art Museum,** 333 E River Rd, 55455. Tel 612-625-9494; FAX 612-625-9630; Elec Mail kingx001@maroon.pc.umn.edu. *Dir* Lyndel King; *Develop Dir* Kathleen Fluegel; *Cur* Patricia McDonnell; *Educ Dir* Colleen Sheehy; *Registrar* Karen Duncan; *Public Affairs* Robert Bitzan; *Technical Dir* William Lampe; *Museum Shop Mgr* Kay McGuire; *Accounts Supvr* Rose Blixt
Open Tues, Wed & Fri 10 AM - 5 PM, Thurs 10 AM - 8 PM, Sat & Sun 11 AM - 5 PM, cl Mon. Estab 1934; the program of the University Art Mus is one geared to meet broad objectives of an all-University mus, as well as the specific teaching & research needs of various University of Minnesota departments. Average Annual Attendance: 120,000
Income: Financed by state appropriation, grants & gifts
Collections: Paintings, drawings & prints by American artists working in the first half of the 20th century, & contains notable works by Avery, Dove, Feininger, Hartley, MacDonald-Wright, Marin, Maurer & O'Keefe; Nordfeldt collection on extended loan from Mrs B J O Nordfeldt; print collection includes works by artists of all schools & periods; sculpture collection of major works by contemporary artists including: Baizerman, Bertoia, Richie, David Smith & others; Third Ave El at 14th St, 1931: Edward Laning; Study of New York 1939 Worlds Fair Mural, 1938; Ilya Bolotowsky; decorative arts; 18th century Italian & Austrian paintings, decorative arts; ancient vases
Exhibitions: The University Art Museum stresses a program of major loan exhibitions, held concurrently with smaller exhibitions organized for specific teaching purposes or from the permanent collection
Activities: Programs; lending program to University, staff & students of Minnesota faculty of framed two-dimensional material; originate traveling exhibitions

M **Coffman Union Third Floor Gallery,** 300 Washington Ave SE, 55455. Tel 612-625-9918, 625-9617; FAX 612-626-3547; *Coordr* Diana J Eicher
Open Mon - Thurs 7 AM - 9 PM, Fri & Sat 7 - 1 AM, cl Sun. No admis fee. Estab 1976 to make art accessible to university community & general pub. Average Annual Attendance: 30,000
Income: Financed by student fees
Exhibitions: 7-10 Exhibitions, annually
Activities: Educ dept; lect; gallery talks

L **Art Book Collection,** 4 Wilson Library, 55455. Tel 612-624-7343; Elec Mail herbert.g.scherer-1@tc.umn.edu. *Librn* Herbert G Scherer
Open Mon - Fri 7 AM - 1 PM, Sat & Sun 9 - 1 AM. Estab 1950 to serve undergraduate & graduate teaching programs in Art History & Humanities to PhD level & in Studio Art to MA level; to provide art related books to other departments & to the entire academic community as best we can
Library Holdings: Vols 85,000; Per subs 339; Micro — Fiche 7000; AV — Cassettes 52; Other — Exhibition catalogs 5000, pamphlets
Special Subjects: Art History, Scandinavian art history
Activities: Lect; tours

L **Architecture & Landscape Library,** 89 Church St SE, 55455. Tel 612-624-6383; *Library Head* Joon Mornes
Open Mon - Fri 8 AM - 4:30 PM. Circ 20,641
Income: Financed by University
Library Holdings: Vols 38,000; Per subs 198; Micro — Reels 244; Other — Manuscripts
Special Subjects: Architecture, Decorative Arts, Graphic Arts, Interior Design, Landscape Architecture, Energy Conservation, Environmental Psychology

L **Children's Literature Research Collections,** 109 Walter Library, 117 Pleasant St SE, University of Minnesota Libraries, 55455. Tel 612-624-4576; FAX 612-625-5525; Elec Mail k-holy@tc.umn.edu, k-holy@vml.spcs, umh.edu. *Cur* Karen Nelson Hoyle
Open Mon - Fri 9 AM - 4 PM. Estab 1949 to collect books, manuscripts & illustrations for use by researchers & for exhibits. For reference & research only
Income: Financed by endowment, University of Minnesota libraries
Library Holdings: Vols 140,000; Per subs 37; Toys; Micro — Fiche; AV — A-tapes, cassettes, fs, rec, slides, v-tapes; Other — Clipping files, exhibition catalogs, manuscripts, original art works, pamphlets, photographs
Special Subjects: Illustration, Manuscripts, Painting - American, Posters
Collections: Figurine Collection
Publications: Kerlan Newsletter, 4 times per yr
Activities: Classes for adults; lect open to public, 6 vis lectr per year; competitions with awards; scholarships offered; individual paintings lent to art galleries; travelling exhibits; lending collection contains books, original art work, manuscript material; book traveling exhibitions 6 per year; originate traveling exhibitions in Sweden, Spain & US; sales shop sells notecards, posters, books, keepsakes & catalogs, publications

M **James Ford Bell Museum of Natural History,** 10 Church St SE, 55455-0104. Tel 612-624-7083; FAX 612-626-7704; *Cur Exhib* Donald T Luce; *Touring Exhib Coordr* Ian Dudley; *Cur Natural History Art* Bryan G Webster
Open Tues - Fri 9 AM - 5 PM, Sat 10 AM - 5 PM, Sun Noon - 5 PM. Admis adults $3, seniors & students $2, children under 3 & members free, free admis Thurs. Estab 1872 to explore the diversity of life in the natural world. Average Annual Attendance: 60,000. Mem: 600; dues $20-$35
Collections: †Owen T Gromme Collection; †Francis Lee Jaques Collection; three separate Audubon collections; †works by other artist-naturalists
Exhibitions: Exotic Aquatics; Francis Lee Jaques-Images of the North Country; The Peregrine Falcon-Return of an Endangered; The Photography of Jim Brandenburg 18 touring exhibits
Publications: Imprint & Calendar, quarterly
Activities: Classes for adults & children; docent training; lect open to public, 2 vis lectr per year; gallery talks; tours; competitions; lends to other non-profit art museums; lending collection contains original art works, original prints, paintings & sculpture; originate traveling exhibitions to libraries, art museums, nature centers, environmental learning centers & schools; museum shop sells books, magazines, original art, prints & reproductions

M **WALKER ART CENTER,** Vineland Pl, 55403. Tel 612-375-7600; FAX 612-375-7618; *Pres* Ralph W Burnet; *Chmn Board* H Brewster Atwater; *Dir* Kathy Halbreich; *Admin Dir* David Galligan; *Chief Cur* Richard Flood; *Publication & Design Mgr* Michelle Piranio; *Registrar* Gwen Bitz; *Dir Develop* Katie DeShaw; *Design Dir* Matt Eller; *Dir Film & Video* Bruce Jenkins; *Pub Information* Margaret Patridge
Open Tues, Wed, Fri & Sat 10 AM - 5 PM, Thurs 10 AM - 8 PM, Sun 11 AM - 5 PM, cl Mon. Admis $3. Estab 1879 by T B Walker, reorganized 1939 as Walker Art Center, Inc; building erected 1927; new museum building opened 1971. The Center consists of nine galleries, three sculpture terraces, the Center Bookshop 11 acre Sculpture Garden, Conservatory & the Gallery 8 Restaurant. Average Annual Attendance: 906,605. Mem: 8000; dues household $45, individual $35, special $25; annual meeting in Sept
Income: Financed by corporate & individual contributions, endowment, mem, state & federal appropriation, grants, book shop, museum admis & prog ticket sales
Collections: Joseph Beuys Collection; Jasper Johns Collection; Sigmar Polke Collection; Complete Archive of Tyler Graphics: Contemporary Print Collection; Edmond R Ruben Film Study Collection

Exhibitions: Selections from Permanent Collection; (1997) Mark Luyten; No Place (like home); Frank Stella & Kenneth Tyler: A Unique Collaboration; Joseph Beuys Multiples. (1997-98) The Architecture of Reassurance: Designing Disney's Theme Parks. (1998) Siah Armajani Retrospective
Publications: Brochures; calendar of events; exhibition catalogs
Activities: Classes for adults & children; docent training; internships; lect open to public, 25 vis lectr per year; concerts; gallery talks; school & adults tours; films; individual paintings & original objects of art lent to museums; book traveling exhibitions; traveling exhibitions organized & circulated; museum shop selling books, magazines, posters, jewelry & gift items
L Staff Reference Library, Vineland Pl, 55403. Tel 612-375-7680; FAX 612-375-7590; Elec Mail rachel@walker.mus.mn.us. *Librn* Rosemary Furtak
Open to museum personnel & scholars by appointment. For reference only
Library Holdings: Vols 12,000; Per subs 140; Artists' books; AV — A-tapes 1700, cassettes, fs, motion pictures, slides, v-tapes; Other — Clipping files, exhibition catalogs
Special Subjects: Architecture, Film, Graphic Arts, Graphic Design, Photography, Sculpture
Collections: Catalogs dating back to 1940

MOORHEAD

M HERITAGE HJEMKOMST INTERPRETIVE CENTER, 202 First Ave N, PO Box 157, 56561. Tel 218-233-5604; *Exec Dir* Bev Woodward; *Cur* Pete Conlin
Open Mon - Sat 9 AM - 5 PM, Thurs 9 AM - 9 PM, Sun Noon - 5 PM. Admis adults $3.50, senior citizens $3, youths 5-17 $1.50. Estab 1986 to interpret River Valley heritage. 7000 sq ft exhibition area for traveling exhibits. Average Annual Attendance: 40,000. Mem: Dues $25; annual meeting in Mar
Income: $280,000 (financed by mem & attendance)
Exhibitions: Focus on humanities, but are supplemented by art and/or science exhibits
Publications: Heritage Press, bimonthly
Activities: Docent programs; lect open to public; book traveling exhibitions 3 per year; sales shop sells books, prints, slides & Scandinavian items

NORTHFIELD

A NORTHFIELD ARTS GUILD, 304 Division St, 55057. Tel 507-645-8877; *Exec Dir* Danette Caldwell; *Prog-Shop Mgr* Mary Ericksen; *Theater Mgr* Patsy Dew; *Theater Technical Mgr* Chuck Sandstrom; *Bookkeeper* Kathy Peterson
Open Mon - Wed & Fri 9 AM - 5 PM, Thurs 9 AM - 8 PM, Sat 10 AM - 5 PM. Estab 1958 as a non-profit organization which offers classes in visual arts, theater, music & other areas. Has gallery, theater, chorus, orchestra & shop
Publications: NAG Notes, quarterly

OWATONNA

A OWATONNA ARTS CENTER, Community Arts Center, 435 Dunnell Dr, PO Box 134, 55060. Tel 507-451-0533; *Dir & Cur* Silvan A Durben; *Pres* Kim Clark; *VPres* Qwen Buscho; *Dir Educ* Judy Srsen; *Treas* John Hylle
Open Tues - Sat 1 - 5 PM, Sun 2 - 5 PM. No admis fee except for specials. Estab 1974 to preserve local professional artists' work & promote the arts in the community. The West Gallery (32 x 26 x 12 ft) & the North Gallery (29 x 20 x 12 ft) provide an interesting walk through space & a versatile space in which to display two & three dimensional work; the two galleries can be combined by use of moveable panels & the Sculpture Garden which was completed in 1979 of multi-level construction. Average Annual Attendance: 7000. Mem: 400; dues basic $25 & up, sustaining $200 & up; annual meeting third Sun in Oct
Income: $80,000 (financed by mem & fund raising activities plus sustaining fund from industries & business)
Collections: Marianne Young World Costume Collection of garments & jewelry from 27 countries; painting, prints, sculpture by local professional artists; 3 Bronzes by John Rood, Paul Grandland & Charles Gagnon
Exhibitions: Annual Christmas Theme Display; Annual Outdoor Arts Festival; Annual Steele County Show
Publications: Monthly newsletter to members & other Arts Organizations
Activities: Classes for adults & children; festivals; concerts monthly; tours; original objects of art & Costume Collection lent to other arts organizations
L Library, 435 Dunnell Dr, PO Box 134, 55060. Tel 507-451-0533; FAX 612-224-8854;
Open to members only; for reference
Library Holdings: Vols 255

PARK RAPIDS

M NORTH COUNTRY MUSEUM OF ARTS, Third & Court Streets, PO Box 328, 56470. Tel 218-732-5237; *Cur* Johanna M Verbrugghen; *Treas* Blanche Szuszitzky
Open May - Oct Tues - Sun 11 AM - 5 PM. Admis $1. Estab 1977 to provide a cultural and educational center to house a permanent study collection of old school European paintings & to house traveling exhibitions for the benefit of persons of all ages through contact & work with art in its many forms. Maintains Great Gallery, Members Gallery, four Revolving Galleries & studio. Average Annual Attendance: 6000. Mem: 120; dues family $20, individual $15; annual meeting in Oct
Income: $25,000 (financed by mem, individual & corporate grants & gifts)
Collections: †160 Nigerian arts, crafts & artifacts; †45 Old School European paintings; †18 Contemporary Prints; 10 Contemporary paintings & artwork; 19 Drawings of Native American Children
Exhibitions: Annual Juried High School Fine Arts Exhibition
Activities: Classes for adults & children; docent training; lect open to the public, 2-3 lectr per year; concerts; gallery talks; tours; competitions; book traveling exhibitions 5-6 per year; originate traveling exhibits; museum shop selling original art

ROCHESTER

A ROCHESTER ART CENTER, 320 E Center St, 55904. Tel 507-282-8629; *Dir* B J Shigaki
Open Tues - Sat 10 AM - 5 PM, Sun Noon - 5 PM, cl Mon. No admis fee. Estab 1946 as a center for contemporary visual arts & crafts, Rochester Art Center sponsors an on-going program of exhibitions, educational classes, lectures, workshops & community services in the arts. Two separate galleries offer a combined exhibition space of 8000 sq ft. Average Annual Attendance: 25,000. Mem: 1000; dues $20-$50; annual meeting in Nov
Income: Financed by endowment, contributions, city & state appropriations, fund raising & tuition
Collections: Local & regional artists' work, including prints, sculpture & watercolors
Exhibitions: Varied exhibits in Contemporary Fine Arts & Crafts
Publications: Quarterly newsletter
Activities: Classes for adults & children; lect open to public; gallery talks; tours; scholarships & fels offered; original objects of art lent to corporations & other arts organizations; originate traveling exhibitions

SAINT CLOUD

A SAINT CLOUD COMMUNITY ARTS COUNCIL, PO Box 323, 56302-0323. Tel 320-259-4015; *Exec Dir* Charlene Hopela
Estab 1973 to serve as an advocate & a resource for artists, art groups, educators & the community
Publications: Saint Cloud Community Arts Calendar, quarterly
Activities: Scholarships offered

SAINT CLOUD STATE UNIVERSITY

M Atwood Center Gallery Lounge, Atwood Ctr, 720 Fourth Ave S, 56301-4498. Tel 320-255-2205; FAX 320-654-5190; Elec Mail http://tigger.stcloud.msus.edu. *Prog Dir* Jessica Ostman; *Asst Dir* Toshiko Schwerdtfeger
Open Mon - Fri 7 AM - 11 PM, Sat 8 AM - 11 PM, Sun Noon - 11 PM. No admis fee. Estab 1967 as a university student union facility. Gallery area is part of program, designed for maximum exposure, where students may relax or study while enjoying exhibits; space is flexible; also area for music listening and small theatre; additional exhibits displayed in prominent area
Income: Financed by student enrollment fee assessment
Collections: Collections of artists work from the central Minnesota area
Exhibitions: Monthly exhibits in various media
Activities: Artists' residencies, lect & workshops that coincide with exhibits
M Kiehle Gallery, 720 S Fourth Ave, 56301. Tel 320-255-3605; FAX 320-654-5337; *Dir* Virginia Bradley
Open Mon - Fri 8 AM - 4 PM. No admis fee. Estab 1974 to expose college community to ideas & attitudes in the field of visual arts. The gallery has 1600 sq ft of enclosed multi use gallery floor space & 2500 sq ft outside sculpture court. Average Annual Attendance: 15,000
Income: Financed by student fund appropriation
Activities: Lect open to public, 5 vis lectr per year; gallery talks; competitions; individual paintings & original objects of art lent to other departments on campus; lending collection contains original prints, paintings, photographs & sculpture; traveling exhibitions organized & circulated

SAINT JOSEPH

M COLLEGE OF SAINT BENEDICT, Art Gallery, Benedict Arts Ctr, 56374-2099. Tel 612-363-5777; *Chmn Art Dept* Gordon Goettemann; *Exhib Coordr* Kathleen Stevenson
Open daily 9 AM - 4:30 PM. No admis fee. Estab 1963
Income: Financed by college
Collections: Contemporary collection of crafts, drawings, paintings, prints and sculpture; East Asian Collection of ceramics, crafts, drawings, fibers and prints; Miscellaneous African, New Guinea, Indian and European
Exhibitions: Ongoing exhibitions
Activities: Lect open to the public, 8 vis lectr per year; gallery talks; tours; scholarships offered; individual paintings & originial objects of art lent to faculty & staff members of the college

SAINT PAUL

M ARCHIVES OF THE ARCHDIOCESE OF ST PAUL & MINNEAPOLIS, 226 Summit Ave, 55102. Tel 612-291-4429; FAX 612-290-1629; *Archivist* Steven T Granger
Open Mon - Fri 9 AM - 5 PM. No admis fee. Estab 1987 to collect & preserve materials of archival value relating to the Catholic church of the Archdiocese of Saint Paul & Minneapolis. Average Annual Attendance: 300
Income: Financed by Diocesan funds
Collections: Artifacts; documents; letters; painting; papers & photographs
Activities: Lect, 2 vis lectr per year

M COLLEGE OF VISUAL ARTS, Gallery, 173 Western Ave, 55102. Tel 612-224-3416; FAX 612-224-8854; *Pres* Chris R Kabella
Open Mon - Fri 8:30 AM - 3 PM, Sat 10 AM - 3 PM. No admis fee. Estab 1948; galleries were established in adjunct to art education. Average Annual Attendance: 1200
Income: Financed by endowment
Exhibitions: Ten shows per year of the work of local artists, visiting artists, faculty, students, traveling shows & work from our own collection. The emphasis on contemporary art
Activities: Lect open to public, varied vis lectr per year; gallery talks; competitions with prizes

L **Library,** 344 Summit Ave, 55102. Tel 612-224-3416; *Librn* Mary Beth Frasczak
Open Mon - Thurs 8 AM - 11:30 PM, Fri 8 AM - 4:30 PM. Estab 1924 to have
reference material for our own students. Not open to pub. Maintains an art
gallery
Library Holdings: Vols 3500; Per subs 30; AV — Slides 9600, v-tapes 100; Other —
Original art works, pamphlets, photographs, reproductions
Special Subjects: Afro-American Art, American Indian Art, American Western
Art, Architecture, Art History, Asian Art, Bookplates & Bindings, Conceptual
Art, Drawings, Etchings & Engravings, Graphic Design, Illustration, Mixed
Media, Oriental Art, Sculpture
Activities: Classes for adults & children; lect open to public; gallery talks; tours;
scholarships offered

M **HAMLINE UNIVERSITY LEARNING CENTER GALLERY,** 1536 Hewitt
Ave, MSB-1801, 55104. Tel 612-641-2387, 641-2296; *Cur Permanent Colls &
Exhib Dir* Debra Seigal
Open Mon - Fri 8:30 AM - 10 PM. No admis fee. Estab 1943 to display
outstanding works of art in all media for instruction of & appreciation by the pub
& students. Average Annual Attendance: 12,000
Income: Financed by the University
Collections: Contemporary paintings, prints, drawings & sculpture
Publications: Exhibition catalog
Activities: Classes for adults; lect open to public, 6 vis lectr per year; gallery
talks; individual paintings & original objects of art lent to faculty & staff;
originate traveling exhibitions to galleries, historical societies & colleges
L **Library,** 1536 Hewitt Ave, 55104. Tel 612-641-2373, 641-2375; *Chmn* Leonardo
Lasansky; *Dir & Cur* Jack King
Rental Library of original modern works & reproductions; extensive color slide
library of paintings, architecture, sculpture, minor arts & graphics

M **MACALESTER COLLEGE,** Galleries, 1600 Grand Ave, 55105. Tel 612-696-
6416; FAX 612-696-6253; *Cur* Trevor Richardson
Open Mon - Fri 10 AM - 9 PM, Sat & Sun 1 - 5 PM, cl June - Aug, national
holidays & school vacations. No admis fee. Estab 1964 as a college facility to
bring contemporary art exhibitions to the students, faculty & community.
Average Annual Attendance: 18,000
Collections: African Art; Oriental Art; contemporary & historical prints,
paintings, sculpture & crafts
Exhibitions: Temporary, traveling & student exhibitions with special emphasis on
international & multi-cultural
Activities: Lect open to the public; concerts; gallery talks; tours; competitions
with awards; individual paintings & original objects of art lent; lending
collections contains original prints, paintings & sculpture; book traveling
exhibitions; traveling exhibitions organized and circulated; sales shop sells art
books & supplies
L **DeWitt Wallace Library,** 1600 Grand Ave, 55105. Tel 612-696-6345; *Library
Dir* Joel Clemmer
Circ 66,531
Library Holdings: Vols 273,668; Per subs 1311; Micro — Cards, fiche, reels;
AV — Cassettes; Other — Framed reproductions, pamphlets
Special Subjects: Art History
Activities: Individual paintings & original objects of art lent to faculty & staff of
the college

A **MINNESOTA HISTORICAL SOCIETY,** 345 Kellogg Blvd W, 55102-1906.
Tel 612-296-2747, 296-6126; FAX 612-296-1004; *Pres* Karen Humphrey; *Dir*
Nina M Archabal; *Deputy Dir* Ian R Stewart; *Asst to Dir for Libraries &
Museum Coll* Lila J Goff; *Media Relations Mgr* Barbara Averilo
Open Tues, Wed, Fri & Sat 10 AM - 5 PM, Thurs 10 AM - 9 PM, Sun Noon - 5
PM, cl Mon except state holidays. Estab 1849 to collect, preserve & make
available to the pub the history of Minnesota. 40,000 sq ft of exhibition space.
Average Annual Attendance: 200,000. Mem: 14,000; dues household $45,
individual $35, senior citizens $30; annual meeting in Nov
Income: Financed by endowment, mem & state appropriation
Collections: Archives; †art works; †books; †maps; †manuscripts; †museum
artifacts relating to the history of Minnesota; newspapers; †photographs
Exhibitions: Minnesota A to Z; Exhibits on families, stories of wild ricing,
communities
Publications: Minnesota History, quarterly; Member News, 6 issues per year;
books & exhibit catalogs
Activities: Classes for adults & children; lect open to the public; tours; gallery
talks; book traveling exhibitions; originate traveling exhibitions; sales shop sells
books, magazines, prints, reproductions, original art & slides
L **Library,** 345 Kellogg Blvd W, 55102. Tel 612-296-2143; *Cur Art* Thomas
O'Sullivan; *Head Reference Serv* Denise Carlson
Open Mon - Sat 10 AM - 5 PM, Thurs 10 AM - 9 PM, Sun Noon - 5 PM. No
admis fee. For reference
Library Holdings: Vols 500,000; Micro — Fiche, reels; AV — A-tapes, cassettes,
fs, Kodachromes, motion pictures, rec, slides, v-tapes; Other — Clipping files,
exhibition catalogs, manuscripts, memorabilia, pamphlets, prints, sculpture
Special Subjects: Minnesota Art
Collections: 19th & 20th centuries art relating to Minnesota
Activities: Classes for adults & children; dramatic programs; docent training; lect
open to public; concerts; gallery talk; tours; competitions with awards;
scholarships offered; exten dept serves Minnesota local & county Historical
Societies; individual paintings & original objects of art lent only to museums &
similar constructional institutions; lending collection contains 6000 original works
of art, 4500 original paintings & 1500 paintings; museum shop sells books,
magazines, reproductions, prints & slides

M **MINNESOTA MUSEUM OF AMERICAN ART,** Landmark Ctr, 75 W Fifth
St, 55102-1486. Tel 612-292-4355; FAX 612-292-4340; *Dir* Ruth Stevens
Appelhof, PhD; *Assoc Cur* Lin Nelson-Mayson; *Media Relations Supv* William
Hegeman; *Personnel Supv* Jodi Royce
Open Tues - Sat 11 AM - 4 PM, Thurs 11 AM - 7:30 PM, Sun 1 - 5 PM. cl
Mon, major holidays & between exhibits. Admis by donation. Estab 1927 as the
Saint Paul Gallery & School of Art. All mus programs are in its Landmark

Center Galleries. MMAA hosts traveling exhibitions of regional & national
importance. Average Annual Attendance: 120,000. Mem: 1200; dues household
$35, individual $25; annual meeting in Sept
Income: $1,042,000 (financed by endowment, individual contributions, mem,
allocation from United Arts Fund & foundation & government grants)
Collections: American Art; contemporary art of the Upper Midwest; E S Curtis
collection; Paul Manship collection & several non-western cultures: Korean,
Japanese, Chinese, Oceanic, African, Native American
Exhibitions: (1997) Toward Diversity: A Decade of Collecting by the Minnesota
Museum of American Art; Shared Stories: Exploring Cultural Diversity; Old
Turtle: Watercolors by Cheng-Khee Chee; Abuelita's Heart: Illustrations by Amy
Cordova. (1997-98) Regional Invitational. (1998) Half-Past Autumn: The Art of
Gordon Parks; Bearing Witness: Art by Contemporary African American
Women; Strong Hearts: Native American Visions & Voices Seeing Straight: The
F64 Revolution in Photography
Publications: Annual report; exhibition catalogs; periodic gallery guides;
quarterly newsletter
Activities: Classes for adults & children; docent training; lect open to public, 12
vis lectr per year; gallery talks; tours; circulating exhibitions, program (9
exhibitions titles); originate traveling exhibitions nationally to museums,
regionally to other sites; museum shop sells books

C **NORTH CENTRAL LIFE INSURANCE COMPANY,** Art Collection, 445
Minnesota St, PO Box 64139, 55164. Tel 612-227-8000, Ext 290; *Exec VPres*
Frank McCarthy
Not open to public
Collections: Works by Charles Beck, Alexis Fournier, John Gordon, Michael
Heindorf, Catherine Ingebretsen, Valerie Jaudon, Bruce McClain, William
Murray, Malcolm Myers, Roger Laux Nelson, John Page, Bela Petheo, Marjorie
Pohlman, Birney Quick, Joan Seifert, Cynthia Starkweather Nelson, Terry
Striech, Richard Sussman

L **SAINT PAUL PUBLIC LIBRARY,** Art, Music & Video Dept, 90 W Fourth St,
55102. Tel 612-292-6186; FAX 612-292-6283; Elec Mail suee@stpaul.lib.mn.us.
Dir Library Carol Williams; *Supv Art, Music & Video* Sue A Ellingwood
Open Mon 11:30 AM - 8 PM, Tues, Wed & Fri 9 AM - 5:30 PM, Thurs 9 AM -
8 PM, Sat 11 AM - 4 PM. Estab 1882. Circ 92,642
Income: Financed by city appropriation
Purchases: $42,700
Library Holdings: Vols 16,000; Per subs 95; Compact discs 4000; AV — Rec,
slides 2000, v-tapes 4500; Other — Clipping files, exhibition catalogs
Collections: Field collection of popular sheet music

C **3M,** Art Collection, 3M Ctr, Bldg 225-1S-01, 55144-1000. Tel 612-737-3335;
FAX 612-737-4555; *Cur. Art Coll* Charles Helsell
Estab 1902, dept estab 1974. Concourse Gallery provides changing exhibitions
drawn from the collection
Collections: Collection of paintings, drawings, sculpture, watercolors, original
prints, photographs & textiles
Publications: Exhibition brochures
Activities: Tours by appointment only & must be scheduled two weeks in
advance; individual paintings & original objects of art lent to scholarly
exhibitions

M **UNIVERSITY OF MINNESOTA,** Paul Whitney Larson Gallery, 2017 Buford,
55108. Tel 612-625-7200, 625-0214; FAX 612-624-8749; Elec Mail
hanc0005@gold.tc.umn.edu. *Gallery Cur* Jason Hancock; *Prog Dir* Marlene
Vernon
Open Mon - Fri 10 AM - 4 PM, Wed 10 AM - 7 PM, Sun 1 - 5 PM, cl Sat. No
admis fee. Estab 1979 to bring art of great variety into the daily lives of students
& university community. Intimate gallery featuring traditional & contemporary
visual arts
Income: Financed by student fees
Publications: Annual report & activity summary
Activities: Mini-courses; lect open to public, arts & crafts sales; films & videos
M **Goldstein Gallery,** Dept of Design, Housing & Apparel, 244 McNeal Hall, 1985
Buford Ave, 55108. Tel 612-624-7434; FAX 612-624-2750; *Dir* Dr Suzanne
Baizerman; *Costume Cur* Dr Marilyn DeLong; *Textile Cur* Karen LaBat
Open Mon - Fri 10 AM - 4 PM, Thurs until 8 PM, Sat & Sun 1:30 - 4:30 PM.
No Admis fee. Estab 1976 as an exhibit facility serving as an educational tool in
teaching & research. Maintains reference library. Mem: 315; mem $20 & up;
annual meeting in June
Income: Financed by private gifts, mem & grants
Collections: †Historic costumes; †20th century designer garments; †historic &
contemporary decorative arts; †furniture; †glass; †metal ceramics; †textiles
Publications: Exhibition catalogs
Activities: Educ dept; lect open to public, 4 vis lectr per year; concerts; gallery
talks; tours; awards; original objects of art lent to other institutions; book
traveling exhibitions 1 per year; museum shop sells books

A **WOMEN'S ART REGISTRY OF MINNESOTA GALLERY,** 2402 University
Ave W, 55114. Tel 612-649-0059; *Admin Dir* Vicki MacNabb
Estab 1975. Office only. Mem: 2800; dues $30
Income: Financed by mem, grants for projects & operating expenses
Collections: Members work on display in one area
Exhibitions: Local & national exhibitions; Annual Juried Members Exhibit
Publications: Quarterly newsletter
Activities: Educ dept; lect open to the public; competitions with awards;
scholarships & fels offered; individual paintings lent & original objects of art lent
to non-profit groups for fee; originate traveling exhibitions

WORTHINGTON

A NOBLES COUNTY ART CENTER GALLERY, 407 12th St, PO Box 313, 56187. Tel 507-372-8245; *Co-Dir* Jean Bunge; *Co-Dir* Martin Bunge
Open Mon - Fri 2 - 4:30 PM, cl Sat & holidays. No admis fee. Estab 1960 to nourish the arts & to bring arts & cultures of other communities & nations, civilizations to Nobles County & the surrounding area so residents become more universal in their thinking. Located on the ground floor. Maintains lending & reference library. Average Annual Attendance: 3000. Mem: 140; dues $7.50-$100; annual meeting in Jan
Income: Financed by mem dues, donations, memorial gifts, county appropriation bequest
Special Subjects: Lect open to public; concerts; tours; competitions with prizes
Collections: Midwestern art
Exhibitions: Art in the Courtyard; monthly exhibitions; two juried fine art shows per year; annual student exhibition the work of area artists
Publications: Advance, monthly; monthly newsletter; monthly press release
Activities: Workshops; gallery talks; tours; competitions with awards; originate traveling exhibitions

MISSISSIPPI

BILOXI

A BILOXI ART ASSOCIATION INC & GALLERY, 137 Lameuse St, PO Box 667, 39530. Tel 601-432-5682; *Pres* Clovis Kelly; *VPres* Sue Henry; *Treas* Lilly Holliman
Open Thurs - Sat 11:30 AM - 4:30 PM. No admis fee. Estab 1965 to promote art, educate general pub & to encourage local people to view & buy art at a very nominal fee. Gallery maintained on volunteer basis by 23 members of Biloxi Art Assn & Gallery. Average Annual Attendance: 5000. Mem: 48; mem open to artists at all levels; dues $15, students $10; meetings third Tues of each month
Income: $750 (financed by mem)
Collections: Works by local artists
Publications: Biloxi Art Assn & Gallery Newsletter, monthly
Activities: Workshops; lect open to public; competitions with awards; individual paintings & original objects of art lent; lending collection contains original art works, original prints, paintings & sculpture; revolving art exhibit in 10 locations on Mississippi Gulf Coast; sales shop sells & exhibits original art & prints

CLARKSDALE

M CARNEGIE PUBLIC LIBRARY, Delta Blues Museum, 114 Delta Ave, PO Box 280, 38614. Tel 601-627-6820; FAX 601-627-7263;
Internet Home Page Address www.deltabluesmuseum.org. *Dir* Ronald H Gorsengner; *Cur* John Ruskey
Open Mon - Fri 9 AM - 5:30 PM, Sat 10 AM - 5 PM. No admis fee. Estab 1979 to preserve & promote understanding of MS Delta blues music & heritage. Average Annual Attendance: 16,000
Income: $125,000 (financed by gift shop, federal & state grants, mem & corporate donors)
Collections: Books & tapes; †Interpretative exhibits; †memorabilia; †photography & art (sculpture, paintings); †recordings; †stage & music; †videos
Exhibitions: All Shook Up; Bancas to Blues: West African Stringed Instrument traditions & the origin of pre-civil War American Music; MS Roots of American Music; Vintage American Guitar Collection
Publications: Delta Blues Museum Brochure
Activities: Monthly Blues performances; lect open to public, 10 vis lectr per year; sales shop sells books, compact discs, prints, magazines, original art, reproductions, souvenirs, gifts, audiotapes

CLEVELAND

M DELTA STATE UNIVERSITY, Fielding L Wright Art Center, PO Box D-2, 38733. Tel 601-846-4720; *Chmn Dept* Collier B Parker; *Exhib Chmn* Patricia Brown; *Chmn Art Educ* Carolyn Stone, PhD
Open Mon - Fri 8 AM - 5 PM, Sun 3 - 5 PM on opening shows, cl school holidays. No admis fee. Estab 1968 as an educational gallery for the benefit of the students, but serves the entire area for changing art shows; it is the only facility of this nature in the Mississippi Delta Region. Three gallery areas. Average Annual Attendance: 3000
Income: Financed by state appropriation
Collections: Delta State University permanent collection; Ruth Atkinson Holmes Collection; Marie Hull Collection; Smith-Patterson Memorial Collection; Whittington Memorial Collection; Joe & Lucy Howorth Collection; John Miller Photography Collection; James Townes Medal Collection; Photography Study Collection
Publications: Announcements of exhibitions, monthly during fall, winter & spring; exhibit catalogs
Activities: Classes for adults & children; lect open to public, 10 vis lectr per year; gallery talks; tours; competitions; exten dept serving the Mississippi Delta Region; individual paintings & original objects of art lent to offices of campus; lending collection contains color reproductions, film strips, motion pictures, original art works, 30,000 slides; traveling exhibitions organized & circulated
L Library, 38733. Tel 601-846-4440; FAX 601-846-4443; *Dir Library Servs* Terry S Latour
Library Holdings: Vols 25,000; Per subs 52; Micro — Cards, fiche, prints, reels; AV — A-tapes, cassettes, fs, Kodachromes, motion pictures, rec, slides, v-tapes; Other — Clipping files, exhibition catalogs, framed reproductions, original art works, photographs, prints
Special Subjects: Art Education, Art History, Drawings, Etchings & Engravings, Film, Graphic Design, Historical Material, History of Art & Archaeology, Illustration, Interior Design, Painting - European, Photography, Portraits, Pottery, Printmaking

COLUMBUS

M COLUMBUS & LOWNDES COUNTY HISTORICAL SOCIETY, Blewett-Lee Museum, 316 Seventh St N, 39701. Tel 601-327-8888; *Cur* Carolyn Neault
Open Fri 10 AM - 4 PM or by appointment. Admis $5, students free. Estab 1960 for a memorabilia 1832-1907 pertaining to Lowndes County preserved & exhibited. Average Annual Attendance: 2000. Mem: 210; dues $5; annual meeting third Thurs in Sept
Income: $600 (financed by mem, bequests, donations, memorials, sale of souvenirs)
Collections: 100 years of artifacts, books, china, crystal, clothes, flags, furniture, jewelry, pictures, portraits, swords, wedding gowns
Activities: Docent training; tours for school children; awards; museum shop sells books & souvenirs

M MISSISSIPPI UNIVERSITY FOR WOMEN, Fine Arts Gallery, Fine Arts Bldg, 39701. Tel 601-329-7341; *Dir Gallery, Cur Museum & Permanent Coll* Larry Feeney
Open Mon - Fri 8 AM - 5 PM. No admis fee. Estab 1948. Average Annual Attendance: 1200
Income: Financed by state appropriation & private funds
Collections: †American Art; †paintings, sculpture, photographs, drawings, ceramics, prints; †Permanent collection of Mississippi artists
Exhibitions: Frequent special and circulating exhibitions; Selections from permanent collection, periodically
Activities: Visiting artists program; workshops; lect open to public, 4 vis lectrs per year; gallery talks; tours; scholarships; individual paintings & original objects of art lent to offices & public student areas on the campus; lending collection contains 400 original prints, 300 paintings, 100 records; book traveling exhibitions; originate traveling exhibitions

GREENWOOD

M COTTONLANDIA MUSEUM, 1608 Hwy 82 W, 38930-2725. Tel 601-453-0925; FAX 601-453-6680; *Exec Dir* Robin Seage
Open Mon - Fri 9 AM - 5 PM, Sat - Sun 2 - 5 PM. Admis adults $2.50, children $.50. Estab 1969 as a mus for tourism & learning facility for schools. Two well lighted rooms plus available space in mus for temporary & competition, permanent hangings in some corridors. Average Annual Attendance: 15,000. Mem: 500; dues vary; annual meeting early Dec
Income: Financed by mem, county appropriation, donations
Collections: †Permanent collection of works of past Cottonlandia Collection; competition winners; other accessions by Mississippi Artists
Publications: Cottonlandia newsletter, bimonthly
Activities: Classes for adults; lect open to the public, 2 vis lectr per year; talks; tours; competitions with awards; individual paintings lent; lending collection contains nature artifacts; museum shop sells books, original art, reproductions, prints & natural stone jewelry

HATTIESBURG

M TURNER HOUSE MUSEUM, 500 Bay, 39401. Tel 601-582-1771; *Dir & Cur* David Sheley
Open by appointment. No admis fee. Estab 1970
Collections: 18th century furniture; silver; crystal chandelier; Persian rugs; old masters; tapestries
Activities: Tours

L UNIVERSITY OF SOUTHERN MISSISSIPPI, McCain Library & Archives, Hardy St & US Rte 49, PO Box 5148, 39406-5148. Tel 601-266-7011; *Dir* Kay L Wall MLS; *Cur* Dolores A Jones MLS; *Archivist* Dr Bobs M Tusa; *Librn* David Richards, MLS
Open Mon, Wed & Thurs 8 AM - 6 PM, Tues 8 AM - 8 PM, Fri 8 AM - 5 PM, Sat 10 AM - 2 PM. No admis fee. University estab 1912, library estab 1976. For reference only
Collections: De Grummond Children's Literature Research Collection (historical children's literature & illustrations); Mississippiana Collection (all documentary media); Editorial Cartoon Collection
Publications: Juvenile Miscellany, 2 times per year

JACKSON

M CRAFTSMEN'S GUILD OF MISSISSIPPI, INC, Agriculture & Forestry Museum, 1150 Lakeland Dr, 39216. Tel 601-981-0019, 981-2499; FAX 601-981-0488; *Exec Dir* Kit Barksdale
Estab 1973 to preserve, promote, educate, market & encourage excellence in regional crafts. Two galleries: Mississippi Crafts Center, Natchez Trace Pkwy PO Box 69, Ridgeland 39158, sales demonstrations, festival of regional crafts; Chimneyville Craft Gallery. Average Annual Attendance: 100,000. Mem: 361; dues $50; annual meeting in Jan
Income: $360,000 (financed by mem, state arts commission grant, corporate & private contributions & earned income)
Activities: Classes for adults; suit case museum for schools & civic groups; lect open to public, 2 vis lectr per year; individual paintings & original objects of art lent to Mississippi schools & civic groups, could arrange in Southeastern region; lending collection contains original art works, video tapes, script & lesson plan; originate traveling exhibitions; sales shop sells original art

M MISSISSIPPI DEPARTMENT OF ARCHIVES & HISTORY, Old Capitol Museum, 100 S State St, PO Box 571, 39201. Tel 601-359-6920; FAX 601-359-6981; *Dir* Donna Dye; *Cur Exhib* Cavett Taff; *Cur Colls* Mary Lohrenz; *Progs Coordr* Lucy Allen
Open Mon - Fri 8 AM - 5 PM, Sat 9:30 AM - 4:30 PM, Sun 12:30 - 4:30 PM. No admis fee. Estab 1961 for educ in Mississippi history & culture through interpretation of the collection. Oil portraits hung throughout the 3-story Greek

Revival former capitol; four rooms set aside for temporary exhibits. Average Annual Attendance: 55,000

Income: $692,520 (financed by state appropriations)

Collections: 177 oil portraits; artifacts of Mississippi history & culture from earliest times to the present

Activities: Talks for children & adult groups; docent training; concerts; gallery talks; tours; dramatic programs; statewide social studies teachers workshop; lect open to public, 4-5 vis lectr per year; book traveling exhibitions 3-4 per year; originate traveling exhibitions; circulate to institutions throughout the state; museum shop sells books, magazines, original art, prints, reproductions, slides & Mississippi Craftsmen's Guild items; films; school films loan service

L **Library,** 100 S State St, PO Box 571, 39205-0571. Tel 601-359-6850, 359-6877, 359-6964; *Pres Board Trustees* William F Winter; *Dir* Elbert R Hilliard; *Dir State Historical Museum* Donna Dye; *Dir Archives & Library* H T Holmes; *Dir Historic Preservation* Kenneth M P'Pool; *Dir Public Information* Christine Wilson; *Dir Spec Projects* Dr Patricia Galloway; *Dir Historic Properties* James F Barnett Jr; *Dir Records Management* William J Hanna

Open Mon - Fri 8 AM - 5PM, Sat 9:30 AM - 4:30 PM, Sun 12:30 - 4:30 PM. Estab 1902 for the care & custody of official archives; to collect material relating to the history of the state from the earliest times & to impart a knowledge of the history & resources of the state. Maintains the State Historical Mus. Maintains a portrait gallery of distinguished Mississippians & holds monthly exhibitions, concerts & lectures. Average Annual Attendance: 65,000

Income: Financed by state appropriation

Library Holdings: Vols 40,000; Per subs 250; Original documents; Micro — Fiche, reels; AV — A-tapes, cassettes, fs, motion pictures, rec, slides, v-tapes; Other — Clipping files, exhibition catalogs, manuscripts, pamphlets, photographs, prints

Special Subjects: Archaeology, Civil War, genealogy, Mississippiana

Collections: Maps, museum artifacts, newspapers, photographs; all pertaining to Mississippi

Exhibitions: Beyond the Porches; Biloxi's Ethnic Heritage; Delta Blues Today; Eudora; Gold of El Dorado; The Natchez Passion for Greek Revival Architecture; Eudora Welty (photographs); Steamboating in Style; Walthall County; Welty I; Welty II

Publications: Journal of Mississippi History, quarterly; Mississippi History Newsletter, monthly

Activities: Folk crafts programs; lect; concerts; gallery talks; tours; exten dept serves other museums & libraries; individual paintings & original objects of art lent; book traveling exhibitions 3-4 per year; originate traveling exhibitions circulated; sales shop sells books, original art, reproductions, prints, slides & folk crafts

M **MISSISSIPPI MUSEUM OF ART,** 201 E Pascagoula St, 39201. Tel 601-960-1515; FAX 601-960-1505; *Exec Dir* R Andrew Maass; *Office Mgr* Julie Norris; *Asst Cur & Registrar* Renee Barilleaux; *Dir Admin* Michele Harris

Open Mon - Sat 10 AM - 5 PM, Sun Noon - 5 PM. Admis fee. Chartered in 1911. Mus opened 1978; East Exhibition Galleries 6500 sq ft; West Exhibition Galleries 2600 sq ft; Graphics Study Center 800 sq ft, houses exhibitions area, study & storage rooms; Impressions Gallery 400 sq ft; Open Gallery 2000 sq ft, includes special power, lighting & water requirements for technological media; Upper & Lower Atrium Galleries 4500 sq ft & outdoor Sculpture Garden; Nonprofit Corporation. Average Annual Attendance: 110,000. Mem: 3400; dues Rembrandt Soc $1000, benefactor $500, donor $250, patron $100, family $25, artist $20, individual $15

Income: $130,000 (financed by endowment, mem, contributions, pub sector grants & appropriations, earned income)

Purchases: A Bierstadt, Edward Potthast, Eugene Auffrey, Birney Imes III (45 color photographs) Thomas Salley Croprey, A B Davies

Collections: 19th & 20th Century American; Smaller non-western art collection, oceanic, Eskimo, Native American, Asian, African; Southern Photographers; Western art history sample collection

Exhibitions: Overstreet: Two Generations of Architecture in the South; Annual Spring Symposium & Antique Show; Scholastic Art Awards; William Dunlap - Reconstructed Recollections; Mississippi Craft Exhibit; Official Images: New Deal Photographs; Songs of My People; Mississippi National Watercolors Grand Exhibition. Discoveries - African Art from the Smiley Collection; Master Silver by Paul Storr & his Contemporaries; Privileged Eye - Photographs by Carl Vechten

Publications: Bi-monthly newsletter; selected exhibition catalogs

Activities: Classes for adults & children; docent training; lect open to public, some for members only, 6 vis lectr per year, 10 vis artists per year; tours; competitions; music series; scholarships offered; Art Cart; travel lect program; original objects of art lent to accredited museums; branches in Biloxi & Tupelo; book traveling exhibitions 4-6 per year; originate traveling exhibitions; museum shop sells books, magazines, reproductions, prints, slides, paper goods, designer items, Mississippi crafts

L **Media Center Library,** 201 E Pascagoula St, 39201. Tel 601-960-1515; *Cur Educ* Joanna Sternberg

For reference only, open to the general pub

Library Holdings: Vols 10,000; Per subs 12; AV — Slides, v-tapes; Other — Clipping files, exhibition catalogs, pamphlets

Collections: Walter Anderson Collection on Slides; Marie Hull Collection of Art Reference Books; Metropolitan Miniature Album; Museums permanent collection

LAUREL

M **LAUREN ROGERS MUSEUM OF ART,** Fifth Ave & Seventh St, PO Box 1108, 39441. Tel 601-649-6374; FAX 601-649-6379; Elec Mail lrma@teclink.net. *Dir* George Bassi; *Registrar* Tommie Rodgers; *Marketing Dir* Kim Thomson; *Asst Dir* Marna Ward; *Head Librn* Donna Smith

Open Tues - Sat 10 AM - 5 PM, Sun 1 - 4 PM, cl Mon. No admis fee. Estab 1923 as a reference library & mus of art for pub use & employment. Six smaller galleries open off large American Gallery; these include European Gallery, Catherine Marshall Gardiner Basket collection, Gibbons Silver Gallery plus 2 temporary exhibit galleries. Average Annual Attendance: 20,000. Mem: Dues $15-$1000

Income: Financed by endowment (Eastman Memorial Foundation), mem,

donations, fundraising, events government appropriations, grants

Collections: European Artists of the 19th Century; 18th Century English Georgian Silver; 18th & 19th Century Japanaese Ukiyo-e Woodblock Prints; 19th & 20th Century American Paintings Native American

Exhibitions: Annual schedule of exhibitions by regional & nationally recognized artists; collections exhibits

Publications: Gibbons Silver Catalog; Jean Leon Gerome Ferris, 1863-1930: American Painter Historian; Handbook of The Collections; Mississippi Portraiture

Activities: Workshop for adults & children; musical concerts; docent training; lect open to public; concerts; gallery talks; tours; individual art objects lent to AAM Accredited museums or galleries; museum shop sells books, prints, slides, Choctaw baskets, silver, jewelry, Polish boxes & t-shirts

L **Library,** PO Box 1108, 39441. Tel 601-649-6374; *Head Librn* Donna Smith

For reference only

Income: Financed by endowment (Eastman Memorial Foundation), mem, donations

Library Holdings: Vols 10,000; Per subs 60; Micro — Fiche, reels 200; AV — A-tapes, cassettes, slides 500, v-tapes; Other — Clipping files, exhibition catalogs, manuscripts, memorabilia, pamphlets, photographs, reproductions

Special Subjects: Painting - American, Painting - European, Prints, Silver, Art, Mississipiana, Laurel history

Collections: Museum archives

MERIDIAN

M **MERIDIAN MUSEUM OF ART,** Seventh St at Twenty-Fifth Ave, PO Box 5773, 39302. Tel 601-693-1501; FAX 601-485-7471; *Dir* Terence Heder

Open Tues - Sun 1 - 5 PM, cl Mon. No admis fee. Estab 1970 to provide exhibition space for local, state & nationally known artists. Mus has four galleries. Housed in a national landmark building, the mus offers over twenty exhibitions annually in four galleries. Average Annual Attendance: 10,500. Mem: 350; dues $25-$1000; annual mem meeting mid-Jan

Income: Financed by mem & appropriation

Collections: 20th century Southern fine arts & photography; 18th century European portraits; contemporary & traditional crafts & decorative arts

Exhibitions: (1997) Mississippi Collegiate Art Competition; Valery Kosorukov Paintings; Claudia Cartee (stoneware & raku); 6th Annual People's Choice Art Competition; Robin Smith Nance (watercolors & mixed media); Annabelle Meacham (paintings & prints); Art Auction Preview Exhibition; 5th Annual MMA Art Auction; Bob Deen (photographs); Mississippi Art Colony; Museum Members Show

Activities: Classes for adults & children; youth art classes held each summer; symposia lect open to public; gallery talks; tours; competitions with awards; original objects of art lent to museums, traveling shows & offices in the city; book traveling exhibitions 2 per year; originate traveling exhibitions for circulation to museums & galleries; museum shop sells original art, reproductions & crafts

OCEAN SPRINGS

M **WALTER ANDERSON MUSEUM OF ART,** 510 Washington Ave, 39564. Tel 601-872-3164; FAX 601-875-4494; *Exec Dir* Clayton Bass; *Coordr Educ* Debbie Kanz; *Art Specialist & Cur* Joey Rice

Open Mon - Sat 10 AM - 5 PM, Sun 1 - 5 PM. Estab 1991 to exhibit the works of Walter Anderson & other artists. Average Annual Attendance: 30,000. Mem: 800; dues $20-$1000

Income: $366,000 (financed by mem, attendance, grants, shop proceeds & donations)

Purchases: $40,000

Collections: Work of Walter Inglis Anderson; ceramics; textiles; wood carving; works of art on paper

Exhibitions: Spirit Line: Graphite Images of Gendron Jensen & Walter Inglis Anderson

Publications: Motif, quarterly newsletter

Activities: Classes for adults & children; docent programs; lect open to members & to public, 5-20 vis lectr per year; 3 state educational outreach programs; museum shop sells books, prints, reproductions, games & educational materials

OXFORD

M **UNIVERSITY OF MISSISSIPPI,** University Museums, University Ave & Fifth St (Mailing add: University of Mississippi, University, 38677). Tel 601-232-7073; Elec Mail bkrause@vm.ca.olemiss.edu. *Dir* Bonnie J Krause; *Coll Mgr* William Griffith; *Prog Coordr* Susan Hannah

Open Tues - Sat 10 AM - 4:30 PM, cl Mon. No admis fee. Estab 1977 to collect, conserve & exhibit objects related to history of the University of Mississippi & to the cultural & scientific heritage of the people of the state & region. Main gallery contains 3000 sq ft with 12 ft ceilings for permanent collections & 800 sq ft with 18 ft ceilings for temporary exhibits; meeting room has 1100 sq ft for temporary wall hung exhibits; each of the four galleries of the Mary Buie Mus contains 400 sq ft for permanent collection. Average Annual Attendance: 12,000. Mem: 325

Income: $190,000 (financed by state appropriation)

Collections: Theora Hamblett Collection (paintings, glass, drawings); Lewisohn Collection of Caribbean Art; Fulton-Meyer Collection of African Art; Millington-Barnard Collection of 18th & 19th Century Scientific Instruments; David Robinson Collection of Greek & Roman antiquities; antique dolls; Victorian memorabilia; American decorative arts; Southern folk art

Exhibitions: (1997) A New Picture: American Modernism New Deal Art: Images of Mississippi

Publications: Department essays; exhibit catalogs

Activities: Classes for children; docent training; gallery talks; tours; school outreach program

L University Museums Library, 38677. Tel 601-232-7073; Elec Mail bkrause@vm.cc.olemiss.edu. *Dir* Bonnie J Krause
Open to members, students, researchers for reference
Library Holdings: Vols 600
Special Subjects: Antiquities-Greek, Antiquities-Roman, Art History, Graphic Arts, American Art, American Folk Art; Victorian Decorative Arts
M University Gallery, Bryandt Hall, 38677. Tel 601-232-7193; FAX 601-232-5013; Elec Mail art@sunset.backbone.oldmiss.edu. *Dir* Margaret Gorove
Open daily 8:30 AM - 4:30 PM. No admis fee. Estab 1954 as a teaching gallery. Average Annual Attendance: 1000
Income: Financed by state appropriation & tuition
Collections: Faculty & student work; some work bought from traveling exhibitions
Exhibitions: Faculty, students, alumni & visiting artist
Publications: Gallery Schedule, annual
Activities: Lect open to public, 1-2 vis lectr per year; gallery talks; individual paintings & original objects of art lent to departments within the University Complex; lending collection contains original art works, original prints, paintings & sculpture

PASCAGOULA

A MISSISSIPPI ART COLONY, 2207 Beach Blvd, 39567. Tel 601-482-2827; *Dir* Mrs Jamie Tate; *Pres* George Ann McCulla; *VPres* Amelia Crumbley; *Treas* Jean R Loeb; *Secy* Lyn Brown
Estab 1945 to hold workshops at least twice yearly, for painting & drawing instruction and occasionally other areas; to organize juried show, with prizes awarded, that travels state of Mississippi between workshops. Average Annual Attendance: 40 at each of the two four-day workshops. Mem: 55; dues $15; annual fall workshop last week of Sept
Income: Financed by mem
Exhibitions: Two travel exhibitions each year
Publications: Bulletin, newsletter
Activities: Competitions sponsored; awards; scholarships; traveling exhibitions organized & circulated to libraries & museums in Mississippi

RAYMOND

M HINDS COMMUNITY COLLEGE DISTRICT, Marie Hull Gallery, 39154. Tel 601-857-3275; *Dir* Gayle McCarty; *Chmn* Russell Schneider
Open Mon - Thurs 8 AM - 3 PM, Fri 8 AM - Noon. No admis fee. Estab 1971 as a community service & cultural agent for the visual arts. Main gallery measures 60 x 60 ft; an adjacent gallery 8 x 45 ft; reception area 15 x 25 ft. Average Annual Attendance: 2500
Income: $2900 (financed by Art Department budget)
Collections: †Permanent collection of state artist, with 200 pieces in prints, sculptures & paintings
Exhibitions: Sponsors 7 exhibits during college session
Activities: Lect open to public, 3 vis lectr per year; gallery talks; tours; scholarships & fels offered

RIDGELAND

M CRAFTSMEN'S GUILD OF MISSISSIPPI CRAFTS CENTER MISSISSIPPI, INC, Natchez Trace Pky, PO Box 69, 39158. Tel 601-856-7546; *Dir* Martha Garrott
Open Mon - Sun 9 AM - 5 PM. No admis fee. Estab 1975. Average Annual Attendance: 30,000. Mem: 250; dues $50; annual meeting in Dec
Income: Financed by sales & grants
Collections: †Choctaw Indian crafts created by members; crafts created by members
Activities: Classes for adults & children; craft demonstration, lect & festivals; lect open to public; gallery talks; artmobile; original objects of art lent by negotiation in response to requests; lending collection contains original art works, photographs & slides; originate traveling exhibitions; sales shop sells original art, primarily original craft objects (Native American to contemporary)

TOUGALOO

TOUGALOO COLLEGE
M Art Collection, 39174. Tel 601-977-7743; FAX 601-977-7714; *Pres* Joe A Lee; *Dir* Ron Schnell; *VPres Academic Affairs* Dr Lewis L Jones; *Photographer* John Wright
Open by appointment. No admis fee. Estab 1963 to service the community & the metropolitan Jackson area. Located in Student Union Building & Library. Average Annual Attendance: 2500
Income: Financed by endowment & department budget
Collections: †Afro-American; African; International Print Collection with emphasis on European art; New York School (abstract, expressionism, minimal art, surrealism)
Exhibitions: African Collection; Afro-American Collection; Faculty & Student Show; Local artists;
Publications: Mississippi Museum of Art, African Tribal Art; Calder-Hayter-Miro; G M Designs of the 1960s; Hans Hofmann, Light Prints; brochure; catalog; newspaper of special events
Activities: Classes for adults; dramatic programs; lect open to public, 2-3 vis lectr per year; concerts; gallery talks; tours by appointment; scholarships offered; exten dept; individual paintings & original objects of art lent to libraries, universities & museums; lending collection contains 8000 lantern slides, 700 original art works, 350 original prints, 140 paintings, 150 sculpture, industrial designs & typography; book traveling exhibitions; originate traveling exhibitions; museum shop sells original art

L Coleman Library, 39174. Tel 601-977-7704; FAX 601-977-7714; *Dir Library Services* Charlene Cole
Open Mon - Thurs 8 AM - midnight, Fri 8 AM - 5 PM, Sat 1 - 4 PM, Sun 3 - 9 PM. No admis fee. Estab 1963. Open to students & faculty
Income: Financed by rental fees
Library Holdings: Vols 135,000; Per subs 432; Micro — Cards, fiche, reels; AV — A-tapes, cassettes, fs, Kodachromes, motion pictures, rec, slides; Other — Clipping files, exhibition catalogs, framed reproductions, manuscripts, memorabilia, original art works, pamphlets, photographs, prints, reproductions, sculpture
Special Subjects: Advertising Design, Aesthetics, Afro-American Art, American Indian Art, American Western Art, Anthropology, Antiquities-Egyptian, Antiquities-Greek, Antiquities-Oriental, Antiquities-Persian, Antiquities-Roman, Archaeology, Folk Art, Glass, Graphic Arts
Collections: Tracy Sugerman (wash drawings, civil rights studies 1964); African masks & sculpture
Exhibitions: Four major exhibits per year
Publications: Tougaloo College Art Collections
Activities: Lect open to public, 2 vis lectr per year; symposium; gallery talks; tour

TUPELO

C BANK OF MISSISSIPPI, Art Collection, One Mississippi Plaza, PO Box 789, 38802. Tel 601-680-2000; *Pres* Aubrey B Patterson Jr
Open Mon - Thurs 9 AM - 4:30 PM, Fri 9 AM - 5:30 PM. Estab to encourage local artists & provide cultural enrichment for customers & friends
Purchases: $500
Collections: Oils, prints, watercolors
Activities: Grants available

L LEE COUNTY LIBRARY, 219 N Madison, 38801. Tel 601-841-9029; *Dir* Louann Hurst; *Technical Services Librn* Barbara Anglin
Open Mon - Thurs 9:30 AM - 8:30 PM, Fri & Sat 9 AM - 5 PM, cl Sun. Estab 1941 to provide books & other sources of information to serve the intellectual, recreational & cultural needs of its users. Maintains art gallery; The Mezzanine Gallery & Helen Foster Auditorium are used as exhibit space for works by University Art students, local professional artists & traveling exhibitions
Income: $469,000 (financed by city, state & county appropriations)
Library Holdings: AV — Cassettes, rec; Other — Framed reproductions
Collections: The Tupelo Gum Tree Festival purchase prizes, these include †paintings and pottery
Publications: Bi-monthly newsletter
Activities: Book traveling exhibitions

MISSOURI

ARROW ROCK

M ARROW ROCK STATE HISTORIC SITE, 65320. Tel 816-837-3330; *Admin* Mike Dickey
Tours available daily June - Aug, Apr, May, Sept & Oct Sat & Sun only & by appointment. Admis $4, children $1, GRP rates available. Estab 1923 to preserve, exhibit & interpret the cultural resources of Missouri, especially those associated with George Caleb Bingham & his era in central Missouri. The 1837 home of G C Bingham serves as a mus house & the 1834 Tavern has exhibition space for the Bingham Collection. Average Annual Attendance: 80,000
Income: Financed by state appropriation
Collections: Bingham Collection; Central Missouri Collection (textiles, furnishing & glass of the 19th century)
Exhibitions: Annual Art Fair; Annual Summer Workshop Exhibit; Annual Craft Festival
Publications: Friends of Arrow Rock Letter, quarterly
Activities: Classes for children; tours

CAPE GIRARDEAU

L SOUTHEAST MISSOURI STATE UNIVERSITY, Kent Library, One University Plaza, 63701. Tel 573-651-2235; *Dir* James Zink
Open Mon - Thur 7:45 AM - 11:30 PM, Fri 7:45 AM - 6 PM, Sat 9 AM - 5 PM, Sun 1:30 - 11:30 PM. Exhibition areas on second & third levels; Artium Gallery on fourth level. The Jake K Wells Mural, 800 sq ft covers the west wall of the library foyer, depicting the nature & the development of the southeast region of the state
Collections: Charles Harrison Collection (rare books including some of the finest examples of the book arts); books & manuscripts from the 13th to the 20th centuries
Exhibitions: Exhibits by local artists
Activities: Tours

COLUMBIA

L DANIEL BOONE REGIONAL LIBRARY, 100 W Broadway, 65203. Tel 573-443-3161; *Dir* Melissa Carr
Open Mon - Thurs 9 AM - 9 PM, Fri 9 AM - 6 PM, Sat 9 AM - 5 PM, Sun 1 - 5 PM. Estab 1959
Library Holdings: AV — Cassettes
Exhibitions: Exhibits by local artists through the year

A STATE HISTORICAL SOCIETY OF MISSOURI, 1020 Lowry, 65201. Tel 573-882-7083; FAX 573-884-4950; Elec Mail shfofmo@ext.missouri.edu. *Exec Dir* Dr James W Goodrich; *Cur* Sidney Larson
Open Mon - Fri 8:30 AM - 4:30 PM, Sat 9 AM - 4:30 PM. No admis fee. Estab 1898 to collect, preserve, make accessible & publish materials pertaining to the history of Missouri & the Middle West. Major art gallery 54 ft x 36 ft; corridor galleries. Average Annual Attendance: 30,000. Mem: 6800; dues $10; annual meeting in fall
Income: Financed by state appropriation
Collections: Works by Thomas Hart Benton, George C Bingham, Karl Bodmer, Fred Geary, Carl Gentry, William Knox, Roscoe Misselhorn, Frank B Nuderscher, Charles Schwartz, Fred Shane, Frederick Sylvester; contemporary artists collection containing work of over fifty outstanding Missouri related artists; original cartoon collection of works by Tom Engelhardt, Daniel Fitzpatrick, Don Hesse, Bill Mauldin, S J Ray and others
Publications: Missouri Historical Review, quarterly; R Douglas Hurt & Mary K Dains, eds; Thomas Hart Benton: Artist, Writer & Intellectual (1989)
Activities: Individual paintings lent, loans based on submitted requests
L Library, 1020 Lowry St, 65201-7298. Tel 573-882-7083; FAX 573-884-4950; Elec Mail shsofmo@ext.missouri.edu. *Dir & Librn* James W Goodrich
Open to public for reference use only
Income: Financed by state appropriation
Library Holdings: Vols 450,000; Per subs 984; Micro — Fiche, reels; AV — A-tapes, cassettes, lantern slides, rec, slides, v-tapes; Other — Clipping files, exhibition catalogs, manuscripts, original art works, pamphlets, photographs, prints
Special Subjects: Historical Material, Manuscripts, Maps, Photography, Cartoons, Missouri & the Midwest
Collections: George Caleb Bingham Paintings Collection; The Thomas Hart Benton Collection; Karl Bodmer Ninety colored engravings Eugene Field Collection; Mahan Memorial Mark Twain Collection; Bishop William Fletcher McMurray Collection; Francis A Sampson Collection of rare books

M STEPHENS COLLEGE, Lewis James & Nellie Stratton Davis Art Gallery, 1200 Biway, 65215. Tel 573-876-7627; FAX 573-876-7248; *Cur* Irene Alexander; *Dir* Rosalind Kimball-Moulton
Open Mon - Fri 10 AM - 4 PM, cl school holidays & summer. No admis fee. Estab 1964 to provide exhibitions of art for the general interest of the local community & for the education of the student body in general. Average Annual Attendance: 500
Income: $2000 (financed by endowment)
Collections: †Modern graphics; †modern paintings; primitive sculpture
Exhibitions: Elizabeth Layton's Drawing on Life; Ron Meyers: Ceramics; Margaret Peterson Paintings
Activities: Lect open to public, 6 vis lectr per year; gallery talks; exhibitions; competitions with awards

UNIVERSITY OF MISSOURI

M Museum of Art & Archaeology, One Pickard Hall, 65211. Tel 573-882-3591; FAX 573-884-4039; Elec Mail muswww@showme.missouri.edu. *Dir* Marlene Perchinske; *Cur European & American Art* Christine Crafts Neal; *Cur Ancient Art* Jane C Biers; *Registrar* Jeffrey Wilcox; *Asst Conservator* Aimee Leonhard; *Cur Educ* Luann Andrews; *Preparator* Greig Thompson; *Grad Res Asst* Debra Page; *Fiscal Officer* Debbie Fridrich; *Receptionist & Tour Coordr* Beth Cobb
Open Tues - Fri 9 AM - 5 PM, Thurs 6 - 9 PM, Sat & Sun Noon - 5 PM, cl Mon & holidays. No admis fee. Estab 1957 to exhibit a study collection for students in Art History & Archaeology; a comprehensive collection for the enjoyment of the general area of Missouri. Housed in renovated 1890's building. Ten galleries for permanent collection & special exhibitions. Average Annual Attendance: 35,000. Mem: 600
Income: $1,088,667 (financed by mem, grants & state appropriation)
Collections: †Ancient Art—Egypt, Western Asia, Greek & Roman; European & American painting & sculpture; †Early Christian—Byzantine & Coptic; †Modern paintings & sculpture; †Prints & drawings; African, Pre-Columbian; Oriental—Chinese & Japanese; South Asian—Indian, Thai, Tibetan, Nepalese
Exhibitions: Expressions of Africa, ongoing; Reinstallation of the Weinberg Gallery of Ancient Art, ongoing. Africa Through the Eyes of Women Artists; Waterways West: Photographs from Missouri River Portfolios
Publications: Muse, annually; exhibition catalogues; The News, 3 per year; calendars, 3 per year
Activities: Classes for adults & children; docent training; workshops on conservation; lect open to public, 5-10 vis lectr per year; tours; gallery talks; original objects of art lent to institutions; book traveling exhibitions 2-3 per year; originate traveling exhibitions; museum shop sells books, prints, reproductions
L Art, Archaeology & Music Collection, Ellis Library, Ninth & Lowry St, 65201. Tel 573-882-4581; FAX 314-882-8044; *Librn* Michael Muchow
Estab 1841 to house material for the faculty & students of the University
Income: Financed by state appropriation
Library Holdings: Vols 81,000; Per subs 300; Micro — Fiche, reels; AV — Rec; Other — Exhibition catalogs
Special Subjects: European prehistory, Near Eastern & Mediterranean art & archeology, Renaissance art history

CRESTWOOD

KAPPA PI INTERNATIONAL HONORARY ART FRATERNITY
For further information, see National and Regional Organizations

FENTON

L MARITZ, INC, Library, 1400 S Highway Dr, 63099. Tel 314-827-1501; FAX 314-827-5505; *Mgr* Jan Meier; *Librn* Jeffrey L Sherk
Estab 1968. For reference & lending. Circ 12,000
Library Holdings: Vols 6000; Per subs 250
Special Subjects: Graphic Arts, Illustration

FULTON

M WESTMINSTER COLLEGE, Winston Churchill Memorial & Library in the United States, 501 Westminster Ave, 65251. Tel 573-642-3361, 642-6648; *Dir* Judith Novak Pugh; *Asst to the Dir* Randy P Hendrix; *Archivist* Warren Hollrah
Open Mon - Sat 10 AM - 4:30 PM, Sun 12:30 - 4:30 PM. Admis adults $2.50, senior citizens $2, children 12 & under free; group rates. Estab 1969 to commemorate life & times of Winston Churchill & attest to ideals of Anglo-American relations. Special exhibits gallery changes quarterly; ecclesiastical gallery contains historic robes & communion vessels; connecting gallery houses historic map collection. Average Annual Attendance: 22,000. Mem: 900
Income: Financed by endowment, mem, admis, friends fundraising, gift shop sales
Collections: Churchill & family memorabilia, including documents, manuscripts & photographs; Churchill oil paintings; rare maps
Exhibitions: Churchill paintings; Iron Curtain speech memorabilia
Publications: MEMO, quarterly newsletter
Activities: Churchill classes for WC students; docent training; lect open to public; concerts; tours; scholarships & fels offered; individual paintings & original objects of art lent to other museums & libraries; book traveling exhibitions 2-4 per year; originate traveling exhibitions; museum shop sells books, original art, reproductions, prints, slides, Churchill busts & memorabilia, English china, posters, collectible English toy soldiers

M WILLIAM WOODS COLLEGE, Art Gallery, 65251. Tel 314-642-2251, Ext 367; *Dir* Terry Martin
Open Mon - Fri 9 AM - 4:30 PM. No admis fee. Estab 1967 to be used as a teaching aid for the Art Center. Maintains 3200 sq ft sky-lighted gallery with a mezzanine
Income: Financed by endowment
Activities: Lect open to public, 2 vis lectr per year; gallery talks; scholarships

HOLLISTER

L WORLD ARCHAEOLOGICAL SOCIETY, Information Center & Library, 120 Lakewood Dr, 65672. Tel 417-334-2377; *Dir* Ron Miller
Not open to public. Estab 1971 to study related areas of archaeology, authropology & art history & to reach worldwide mail & telephone queries. Lending & reference by special arrangement
Income: Financed by endowment & newsletter sales
Library Holdings: Vols 6000; Per subs 32; AV — Slides; Other — Clipping files, original art works, photographs, prints
Special Subjects: Anthropology, Antiquities-Egyptian, Antiquities-Greek, Antiquities-Oriental, Antiquities-Roman, Archaeology, Architecture, Art History, Asian Art, Ethnology, History of Art & Archaeology, Illustration, Pre-Columbian Art, Primitive Art, Sculpture, Religious Art
Collections: Steve Miller Library of Archaeology
Publications: WAS Newsletter, occasional; special publications, occasional
Activities: Educ dept; special tapes on request; consulting; competitions with awards; exten dept answers questions globally

INDEPENDENCE

M CHURCH OF JESUS CHRIST OF LATTER DAY SAINTS, Mormon Visitors' Center, 937 W Walnut, 64050. Tel 816-836-3466; *Dir* Robert Parker
Open daily 9 AM - 9 PM. No admis fee. Estab 1971 as a center of Latter Day Saints beliefs & history for residents of Missouri, Ohio & Illinois. Average Annual Attendance: 50,000
Collections: Large 30 ft mural of Christ; painting; computer reproductions; two & a half ton statue
Exhibitions: Paintings; audio-visual shows; historical maps exhibits
Publications: Brochures
Activities: Lect open to public; tours; sales shop sells books & reproductions

M JACKSON COUNTY HISTORICAL SOCIETY, The 1859 Jail, Marshal's Home & Museum, 217 N Main St, 64050. Tel 816-252-1892; FAX 816-461-1897; *Dir* Gay Clemenson; *Operating Committee Chmn* Jake Simonitsch
Open Mon - Sat 10 AM - 5 PM, Sun 1 - 4 PM, Mar, Nov & Dec Mon 10 AM - 4 PM, cl Jan & Feb. Admis adults $2.50, senior citizens $1.75, children under 12 $.50, group rates available. Estab 1958 for interpretation of Jackson County history. 1859 Federal town house of county marshal, attached limestone jail which served as federal headquarters during the Civil War. Restored historical interior c 1860s. Restored cell of Frank James c 1882. Average Annual Attendance: 12,000. Mem: 1000; dues $15-$500
Income: Financed by mem, tours, fundraising events
Collections: Jackson County history, 1800-present; home furnishings of mid-19th century in restored areas
Exhibitions: Permanent exhibits on Jackson County history; changing exhibits
Publications: Jackson County Historical Society Journal, bi-annual
Activities: Classes for children; docent training; lect open to public; tours; museum shop sells books
L Research Library & Archives, Independence Sq Courthouse, Rm 103, 64050. Tel 816-252-7454; FAX 816-461-1510; *Dir Archives* Kelly Chambers
Open Mon & Wed 9:30 AM - 2:30 PM, Tues & Fri Noon - 5 PM, Sat Noon - 3 PM. Estab 1966
Income: Financed by mem, fees, donations, sales
Library Holdings: Vols 2000; Per subs 15; Micro — Reels; AV — A-tapes, fs, Kodachromes, lantern slides, motion pictures, slides, v-tapes; Other — Clipping files, photographs
Special Subjects: Collection limited to the history of Jackson County & surrounding region
Collections: Photograph collection for reference; extensive manuscript collection

M John Wornall House Museum, 146 W 61 Terrace, 64113. Tel 816-444-1858; FAX 816-444-1858; *Dir* Betsy Johnson; *Asst to Dir* Janet Russell
Open Tues - Sat 10 AM - 4 PM, Sun 1 - 4 PM. Admis adults $3, senior citizens $2.50, children under 12 $1, group rates available. Estab 1972 restored to interpret the daily lives of frontier farm families in the 1830s-1860s in early Kansas City. House was used as field hospital during the Civil War. Built in 1858; opened to pub in 1972. Average Annual Attendance: 7000. Mem: 400; dues $25-$500
Income: Financed by mem, tours & fund raisings
Collections: Home furnishings of prosperous farm families
Exhibitions: Special exhibitions on subjects dealing with interpretation of home & Civil War period
Activities: Classes for adults & children; docent training; tours; museum shop sells books, holiday & gift items

L NATIONAL ARCHIVES & RECORDS ADMINISTRATION, Harry S Truman Library, 24 Hwy & Delaware, 64050. Tel 816-833-1400; *Dir* Larry J Hackman; *Asst Dir* George H Curtis
Open Mon - Sat 9 AM - 5 PM, Thurs 9 AM - 9 PM, Sun Noon - 5 PM. Admis adults $4, seniors $4.50, children 6-18 $3, under 6 free. Estab 1957 to preserve & make available for study & exhibition the papers, objects & other materials relating to President Harry S Truman & to the history of the Truman administration. Gravesite of President & Mrs Truman in the courtyard. Administered by the National Archives & Records Administration of the Federal Government. Average Annual Attendance: 150,000
Income: Financed by federal appropriation, federal trust fund & private donations
Library Holdings: Vols 40,000; Per subs 23; Documents; Micro — Reels; AV — A-tapes, motion pictures, rec, slides; Other — Clipping files, framed reproductions, manuscripts, memorabilia, original art works, pamphlets, photographs, prints, sculpture
Collections: Papers of Harry S Truman, his associates, and of officials in the Truman administration; Portraits of President Truman; paintings, prints, sculptures & artifacts presented to President Truman during the Presidential & Post-Presidential periods; original political cartoons; mural by Thomas Hart Benton
Exhibitions: Permanent & temporary exhibits relating to the life & times of Harry S Truman; the history of the Truman administration; the history & nature of office of the Presidency
Publications: Historical materials in the Truman Library
Activities: Educ dept; lect; conferences & commemorative events; tours to tour groups; film series; research grants; sales shop sells books, reproductions, slides & postcards

JEFFERSON CITY

M DEPARTMENT OF NATURAL RESOURCES OF MISSOURI, Missouri State Museum, State Capitol, Room B-2, 65101. Tel 573-751-2854; FAX 573-526-2927; *Dir* John Cunning; *Cur Exhib* Bill Fannin; *Cur Coll* L T Shelton
Open daily 8 AM - 5 PM, cl holidays. No admis fee. Estab 1920. Average Annual Attendance: 250,000
Income: Financed by state appropriation, affiliated with Missouri Department of Natural Resources
Collections: Art murals by T H Benton, Berninghaus, Frank Brangwyn, N C Wyeth; historical material and natural specimens representing Missouri's natural and cultural resources; Indian artifacts; History hall & reference center
Exhibitions: Permanent and temporary exhibits
Publications: Pamphlets
Activities: Guided tours of Capitol; audio-visual presentations; book traveling exhibitions, 4-5 per year
M Elizabeth Rozier Gallery, State Capitol, Rm B-2, 65101. Tel 573-751-4210; FAX 573-526-2927; *Dir* John Cunning
Open 10 AM - 4 PM. No admis fee. Estab 1981 to provide art, crafts & educational exhibits. Located in mid-nineteenth century building with a large & small gallery. Average Annual Attendance: 6000
Activities: Lect open to public; 15 vis lectr per year; concerts; gallery talks; tours; competitions with awards; book traveling exhibitions

JOPLIN

L WINFRED L & ELIZABETH C POST FOUNDATION, Post Memorial Art Reference Library, 300 Main St, 64801. Tel 417-782-7678; FAX 417-624-5217; Elec Mail simpso2@vm.mssc.edu. *Dir* Leslie T Simpson
Open Mon & Thurs 9:30 AM - 7:30 PM, Tues, Wed, Fri & Sat 9:30 AM - 5:30 PM. No admis fee. Estab 1981 to provide information on the fine & decorative arts to members of the community. Located in a wing of the Joplin Public Library. Average Annual Attendance: 6500
Income: Financed by private endowment
Library Holdings: Vols 3500; Per subs 25; Other — Clipping files, exhibition catalogs, original art works, pamphlets, photographs, reproductions, sculpture
Special Subjects: Architecture, Art History, Decorative Arts, Furniture, Historical Material, Photography
Collections: 16th-17th Century Antiques & Artworks; †Joplin, Missouri historic architecture collection; †fine arts books collections; †mounted reproductions
Exhibitions: Monthly exhibits of works by area artists
Activities: Educ dept; film & slide programs

A GEORGE SPIVA CENTER FOR THE ARTS, 222 W Third St, 64801. Tel 417-623-0183; *Dir* Darlene Brown
Open Tues - Sat 10 AM - 5 PM, Sun 1 - 5 PM, Thurs evening until 8 PM, cl Mon & national holidays. Estab June 1959, incorporated 1969, as a non-profit, cultural center with the purpose of increasing knowledge & appreciation of the visual arts in Joplin & surrounding area; to offer educational classes, workshops & to exhibit works of educational & artistic value. Average Annual Attendance: 15,000. Mem: 600; dues $15-$1000; annual meeting in Dec
Exhibitions: Thespiva; 46th Annual Membership Show; Tribal Art; National Spiva Annual
Publications: Calendar; newsletter
Activities: Classes for adults & children; docent training; lect open to public, 3 vis lectr per year; tours; competitions with awards

KANSAS CITY

M AVILA COLLEGE, Thornhill Art Gallery, 11901 Wornall Rd, 64145. Tel 816-942-8400; FAX 816-942-3362; *Acadmic Dean* Sr Marie Joan Harris; *Chmn Humanities* Daniel Larson; *Pres* Larry Kramer; *Dir* George Chrisman
Open Mon - Fri 10 AM - 5 PM. No admis fee. Estab 1978 to present the visual arts in a contemporary sense to the student community as well as the Greater Kansas City community. Gallery space 60 x 35 ft is maintained with carpeted floor and walls, an Artist-in-Residence studio, and track lighting. Average Annual Attendance: 2000
Income: Financed through school budget
Activities: Classes for adults; dramatic programs; lect open to public; gallery talks

C COMMERCE BANCSHARES, INC, Art Collection, 1000 Walnut St, PO Box 13686, 64199. Tel 816-234-2968; FAX 816-234-2356; *Chief Exec Officer & Pres* David W Kemper; *Dir Art Coll* Laura Kemper Fields; *Cur Art Coll* Robin Trafton
Open Mon - Sat 8 AM - 5 PM. Estab 1964. 125 ft barrel vaulted gallery with 13 ft ceiling to exhibit mus quality paintings
Exhibitions: Contemporary American Realist Art, paintings & drawings
Activities: Individual paintings lent on restricted basis

EXHIBITSUSA
For further information, see National and Regional Organizations

HALLMARK CARDS, INC
C Fine Art Programs, 2501 McGee, 64141. Tel 816-274-4726; FAX 816-545-6591; *Dir Fine Art Prog* Keith F Davis
Estab 1949
Collections: Hallmark Photographic Collection; Hallmark Art Collection; drawings; paintings; photographs; prints
Publications: Exhibition catalogs; New Acquisitions brochures, annually
Activities: Lect; purchase awards for art shows; individual objects of art lent to reputable institutions for temporary exhibitions; originate traveling exhibitions
L Creative Library, 2501 McGee, No 146, Kemo, 64108. Tel 816-274-5525; FAX 816-274-7245; *Mgr Library Serv* Carol Carr; *Reference Librn* Mary Knebel
Open to Hallmark personnel only. Estab to provide pictorial research
Income: Financed by corp funds
Library Holdings: Vols 22,000; Per subs 150
Special Subjects: Illustration, Design, Fine Arts, Children's Books
Collections: Old & rare collection

M KANSAS CITY ART INSTITUTE, Kemper Museum of Contemporary Art & Design, 4420 Warwick Blvd, 64111-1821. Tel 816-753-5784; FAX 816-753-5906; *Chmn of Board* R Crosby Kemper; *Cur* Dana Self
Open Mon - Fri 10 AM - 4 PM, Sat 10 AM - 5 PM, Sun 11 AM - 5 PM. No admis fee. Estab 1994 as a regional resource for modern & contemporary art in all medias. 24,000 sq ft, 2 galleries plus atrium & open areas & courtyard. Average Annual Attendance: 105,000. Mem: 600; dues $35-$1000
Collections: Bebe & Crosby Kemper Collection
Exhibitions: Changing contemporary art exhibitions
Activities: Educ Dept; dramatic programs; docent training; lect open to public; concerts; gallery talks; tours; individual paintings & original objects of art lent to other museums; book traveling exhibitions; originate traveling exhibitions; museum shop sells books & original art
L Library, 4415 Warwick Blvd, 64111-1821. Tel 816-561-4852; *Library Dir* Allen Morrill
Open Mon - Thurs 8:30 AM - 9 PM, Fri 8:30 AM - 5 PM, Sat Noon - 5 PM, Sun 1 - 5 PM. Estab 1924 to serve students & faculty of Art Institute
Income: $75,622 (financed by Art Institute budget)
Library Holdings: Vols 30,000; Per subs 120; Picture file; Other — Exhibition catalogs
Special Subjects: Photography, Fine arts

M KANSAS CITY ARTISTS COALITION, 201 Wyandotte, 64105. Tel 816-421-5222; FAX 816-421-0656; *Exec Dir* Janet F Simpson; *Asst Dir* Bridget Stewart
Open Wed - Sat 11 AM - 4 PM. No admis fee. Estab 1972 to promote contemporary art & artists from Kansas City & the Midwest; non-profit organization. Mem: 500; dues $40
Exhibitions: Exhibitions of high-quality, innovative work by emerging & mid-career artists; exhibition series features a diverse combination of local, regional & national artists
Publications: Forum, 5 times a year; newsletter, 6 times a year
Activities: Lect open to public, 1-2 vis lectr a year; competitions with awards

A KANSAS CITY MUNICIPAL ART COMMISSION, 414 E 12th St, City Hall, 17th Flr, 64106. Tel 816-274-1515; FAX 816-274-1515; *Public Art Adminr* Heidi Iverson Bilardo
Estab 1926. Administers the One-Percent-for-Art Program in Kansas City, setting aside one percent of all construction costs for new building & renovation projects for artwork
Exhibitions: Shown at various public locations, such as libraries, college campuses & museums on a rotating basis
Activities: Originate traveling exhibitions

L KANSAS CITY PUBLIC LIBRARY, 311 E 12th St, 64106. Tel 816-221-2685; *Central Reference Coordr* Lillie Brack
Open Mon - Thurs 9 AM - 9 PM, Fri & Sat 9 AM - 5 PM, Sun 1 - 5 PM. Established 1873
Library Holdings: Vols 1,459,336; Per subs 1575; Micro — Fiche, reels; AV — Motion pictures, rec, slides; Other — Clipping files, exhibition catalogs, framed reproductions, memorabilia, pamphlets, prints, reproductions

M LIBERTY MEMORIAL MUSEUM & ARCHIVES, 100 W 26th St, 64108. Tel 816-221-1918; *Dir* Doran L Cart; *Archivist* Lynn Ward
Open Site 1: Tues - Sun 10 AM - 6 PM, Site 2: Mon - Fri 10 AM - 6 PM. No admis fee. Estab 1919 to exhibit World War I memorabilia. Two rectangular

spaces 45 x 90 ft; permanent & temporary exhibits
Income: Financed by city appropriation & private donations
Collections: †WWI: books, documents, militaria, original sketches & paintings, photos, posters, sheet music
Exhibitions: Trench Warfare; Aviation; Artillery; Medical Care; Uniforms; Women at War
Publications: Signals, quarterly newsletter
Activities: Children's programs

M **NELSON-ATKINS MUSEUM OF ART,** 4525 Oak St, 64111-1873. Tel 816-561-4000; FAX 816-561-7154; *Dir & Chief Cur Oriental Art* Marc F Wilson; *Acting Dir Develop* Judith M Cooke; *Registrar* Ann E Erbacher; *Samuel Sosland Cur American Art* Margaret Conrads; *Cur Decorative Arts* Christina H Nelson; *Head Librn* Susan Malkoff-Moon; *Dir Capital Campaign* Michael Churchuan; *Cur Prints, Drawings & Photography* George L McKenna; *Cur European Painting & Sculpture* Dr Roger B Ward; *Sanders Sosland Cur 20th Century Art* Deborah Emont Scott; *Assoc Cur Southeast Asian & Indian Art* Dr Doris Srinivasan; *Cur, Arts of Africa, Oceania & the Americas* Dr David A Binkley; *Cur Ancient Art* Dr Robert Cohon; *Consult Cur Medieval Art* Dr Marilyn Stokstad; *Res Cur Far Eastern Art* Chu-tsing Li; *Chief Conservator* Forrest Bailey; *Assoc Conservator of Paper* Open; *Conservator Paintings* Scott Heffley; *Dir Educ* Ann Brubaker; *Asst Cur 20th Century Art* Jan Schall; *Conservator of Objects* Kathleen Garland; *Cur Early Chinese Art* Xiaoneug Yang; *Asst Cur American Art* Julie Aronson
Open Tues - Thurs 10 AM - 4 PM, Fri 10 AM - 9 PM, Sat 10 AM - 5 PM, Sun 1 - 5 PM. Admis adults $4, adult students with ID $2, children 6-18 $1, children under 5 free. Estab 1933 to enrich, enliven & present the arts of the ancient & modern world to the Midwest & the remainder of the US; develop activities relating to art educ, the interpretation of the collections & their general enjoyment. Maintains reference library. Average Annual Attendance: 350,000. Mem: 13,000; dues $40-$2750
Income: Financed by endowment, mem & gifts
Collections: †Burnap Collection of English pottery, Oriental ceramics, paintings, sculpture, bronze, Egyptian tomb sculpture, American painting, period rooms & furniture; Coloisters; †contemporary works of art; †Impressionist painting; the finest Oriental furniture collection outside of the Orient; sculpture garden; †Oriental Art
Publications: Calendar, 10 times per year
Activities: Classes for adults & children; docent training; lect open to public, 50 vis lectr per year; concerts; gallery talks; tours; individual paintings and original objects of art lent to qualified organizations & exhibitions; museum shop sells books, magazines, original art, reproductions & slides

L **Spencer Art Reference Library,** 4525 Oak St, 64111-1873. Tel 816-751-1216; FAX 816-561-7154; *Head Librn* Susan Malkoff Moon; *Sr Oriental Cataloger* Jane Cheng; *Sr Cataloger* Jane Zander; *Slide Librn* Jan B McKenna; *Reference Librn* Josephine Gordon; *Assoc Librn Technical Servs* Martha P Childers
Open Tues - Fri 10 AM - 4 PM, Sat 10 AM - 2 PM. For reference only
Library Holdings: Vols 75,000; Per subs 500; International auction catalogues; Per titles 1200; Micro — Fiche, reels; AV — A-tapes, cassettes, fs, motion pictures, slides 60,000, v-tapes; Other — Clipping files, exhibition catalogs, manuscripts, pamphlets, photographs
Special Subjects: American Indian Art, Asian Art, Decorative Arts, Etchings & Engravings, Graphic Arts, Historical Material, Oriental Art, Painting - American, Period Rooms, Photography, Pre-Columbian Art, Prints, Sculpture, Southwestern Art
Collections: Bender Library on prints & drawings; Oriental study collection with emphasis on Chinese art
Publications: Calendar, 10 times per year

A **Friends of Art,** 4525 Oak St, 64111-1873. Tel 816-561-4000, Ext 246; FAX 816-561-7154; *Dir* Marc Wilson; *Asst Dir of Develop & Mem* Judith M Cooke
Open Tues - Sat 10 AM - 5 PM, Sun 1 - 5 PM. Admis adults $2, children free. Estab 1934 as a non-profit organization supporting the Nelson Gallery & now serves as mem department. Mem: 7000; dues $35-$250
Income: Financed by mem and contributions
Publications: Mem communication
Activities: Classes for adults & children; docent training; lect open to public; gallery talks; tours; sales shop sells books, magazines, reproductions and slides; junior museum

M **Creative Arts Center,** 4525 Oak St, 64111-1873. Tel 816-751-1236; FAX 816-561-7154; *Dir* Lisa Silagyi
Open Tues - Thurs 10 AM - 4 PM, Fri 10 AM - 9 PM, Sun 1 - 5 PM
Activities: Art classes for children ages 3-18 & adults; workshops for schools; family workshops & events; tours

M **PRINT CONSORTIUM,** 6121 NW 77th St, 64151. Tel 816-587-1986; *Exec Dir* Dr William S Eickhorst
Estab 1983 to promote printmaking as a fine art. Mem: 300; mem open to professional printmaking artists; dues $25
Income: Financed by mem & exhibition rental
Collections: Prints by established professional artists from the US & 9 foreign countries
Publications: Artist's Proof, quarterly newsletter
Activities: Book traveling exhibitions 5-6 per year; originate traveling exhibitions 2 per year

THE STAINED GLASS ASSOCIATION OF AMERICA
For further information, see National and Regional Organizations

C **UMB FINANCIAL CORPORATION,** PO Box 419226, 64141-6226. Tel 816-860-7000; *Chmn* R Crosby Kemper
Estab 1973 to provide good art for viewing by customers. Collection is displayed in lobbies & customer access areas in various UMB Banks
Collections: Americana Collection, including American portraits (George Caleb Bingham, Benjamin Blythe, Gilbert Stuart, Charles Wilson Peale), regional collection (William Commerford, Peter Hurd, J H Sharp, Gordon Snidow), modern art (Fran Bull, Olive Rush, Wayne Thiebaud, Ellsworth Kelly)
Activities: Objects of art lent to galleries for special exhibits

M **UNIVERSITY OF MISSOURI-KANSAS CITY,** Gallery of Art, 5100 Rockhill Rd, 64110. Tel 816-235-1502; FAX 816-235-5507; *Dir* Craig Subler
Open Tues - Fri Noon - 5 PM, Sat & Sun 1 - 5 PM, Summer Tues - Fri Noon - 5 PM. No admis fee. Estab 1977 to bring a broad range of art to both students and the community. Average Annual Attendance: 5000. Mem: 100; dues $50
Income: Financed by endowment, city & state appropriation, contribution
Publications: Exhibition catalogues
Activities: Adult classes; lect open to public; book traveling exhibitions; originate traveling exhibitions that circulate to museums & galleries in US & abroad

M **LEEDY VOULKO'S ART CENTER GALLERY,** 2012 Baltimore Ave, 64108. Tel 816-474-1919; FAX 816-474-1919; *Dir* Sherry Leedy; *Asst Dir* Emily Eddins
Open Thurs - Sat 11 AM - 5 PM or by appointment. Estab 1985 to showcase contemporary arts & crafts. 10,000 sq ft of exhibition space. Average Annual Attendance: 50,000
Exhibitions: Showcase contemporary art in all media-changing exhibits every six weeks
Activities: Lect open to public; originate traveling exhibitions 1 per year; sales shop sells books, original art & prints

MARYVILLE

M **NORTHWEST MISSOURI STATE UNIVERSITY,** DeLuce Art Gallery, Dept of Art, 64468. Tel 816-562-1326; FAX 816-562-1900, 816-562-1346; *Chmn Dept Art Mgr* Lee Hageman; *Olive DeLuce Art Gallery Coll Cur* Philip Laber; *Percival DeLuce Art Gallery Coll Cur* Robert Sunkel
Open Mon - Fri 1 - 4 PM. No admis fee. Estab 1965 to provide exhibitions of contemporary works in all media as part of the learning experiences in the visual arts. Gallery is maintained with 150 running ft exhibition space with high security, humidity-controlled air conditioning & flexible lighting. Average Annual Attendance: 6000
Income: Financed by state appropriation
Collections: Percival DeLuce Memorial Collection consisting of American paintings, drawings, prints and decorative arts; some European furniture and prints
Activities: Classes for adults; lect open to public, 6 vis lectr per year; gallery talks; tours; scholarships offered; individual & original objects of art lent within the institution; lending collection contains original art works, original prints, paintings & drawings; book traveling exhibitions 3 per year

MEXICO

M **AUDRAIN COUNTY HISTORICAL SOCIETY,** Graceland Museum & American Saddlehorse Museum, 501 S Muldrow Ave, PO Box 3, 65265. Tel 573-581-3910; *Exec Dir* Roberta Cooney
Open Tues - Sat 2 - 5 PM, Sun 1 - 4 PM, cl Mon, Jan & holidays. Admis $2, children 12 & under $.50. 1959. Average Annual Attendance: 2500. Mem: 766; dues $5 & up
Income: $25,000 (financed by endowment & mem)
Collections: Currier & Ives; Photographs; Lusterware; Dolls; Tom Bass Artifacts

L **MEXICO-AUDRAIN COUNTY LIBRARY,** 305 W Jackson, 65265. Tel 573-581-4939; *Dir* Kurt H Lamb; *Children's Librn* Margaret Jones; *Acquisitions Librn* Violet Lierheimer; *Reference Librn* Christal Brunner
Open winter hours, Mon - Thurs 9 AM - 9 PM, Fri & Sat 9 AM - 5:30 PM. No admis fee. Estab 1912 to provide library services to the residents of Audrain County, Missouri. Exhibit room with different exhibits each month; childrens department has a continuously changing exhibit
Income: Financed by donations
Library Holdings: Vols 112,529; Per subs 127; Art print reproductions; Newspapers; AV — Fs, Kodachromes, motion pictures, rec
Collections: Audrain County history; paintings by Audrain County artists
Exhibitions: Local Federated Womens Club sponsored a different exhibit each month during the fall, winter & spring, these included local artists, both adult & young people, & recognized artists of the area; The Missouri Council of the Arts also provide traveling exhibits that we display
Activities: Classes for children; story hour - one hour four days a week; individual paintings & original objects of art lent

OSAGE BEACH

NATIONAL OIL & ACRYLIC PAINTERS SOCIETY
For further informations, see National and Regional Organizations

SAINT CHARLES

M **LINDENWOOD COLLEGE,** Harry D Hendren Gallery, Department of Art, 63301. Tel 314-949-4862; *Chmn* Elaine Tillinger
Open Mon - Fri 9 AM - 5 PM, Sat & Sun Noon - 4 PM. No admis fee. Estab 1969 as a college exhibition gallery. Gallery is approximately 3600 sq ft with skylight & one wall of side light. Average Annual Attendance: 4000
Income: Financed by endowment
Collections: Contemporary American & European prints in various media including Works by Paul Jenkins, William Hayter, Will Barnet, Mauricio Lazansky
Exhibitions: Women's Caucus For Art, St Louis Artist Guild Visiting Artist Program's
Activities: Lect open to public, 5-6 vis lectr per year; gallery talks; tours; original objects of art lent; lending collection contains photographs; traveling exhibitions organized & circulated through the Missouri State Council on the Arts

SAINTE GENEVIEVE

M ST GENEVIEVE MUSEUM, Merchant & DuBourgh St, 63670. Tel 573-883-3461; *Pres* Jim Baker; *Treas* Delores Koetting
Open winter Noon - 4 PM, summer 9 - 11 AM, Noon - 4 PM. Admis adults $1.50, students $.50. Estab 1935. Average Annual Attendance: 8000. Mem: Dues family $10, individual $5
Income: Financed by mem, admis, sales

SAINT JOSEPH

M THE ALBRECHT-KEMPER MUSEUM OF ART, 2818 Frederick Blvd, 64506. Tel 816-233-7003; FAX 816-233-3413; Elec Mail akma@albrecht-kemper.org. *Dir* Mark J Spencer; *Registrar* Ann Tootle; *Public Events Dir* Robyn Enright
Open Tues - Sat 10 AM - 4 PM, (open until 8 PM on Thurs), Sun 1 - 4 PM, cl Mon. Admis adult $3. Estab 1914 to increase public knowledge & appreciation of the arts. Mem: 550; dues $35 & up, students $15; annual meeting in Apr
Income: Financed by mem & fundraising events
Collections: Collections of American Art consisting of paintings by George Bellows, Thomas Hart Benton, Albert Bierstadt, Alfred Bricher, William Merritt Chase, Francis Edmonds, George Hall, Robert Henri, Edward Hopper, George Inness, Eatsman Johnson, Fitz Hugh Lane, Ernest Lawson, William Paxton, Rembrandt Peale, John Sloan, Gilbert Stuart, Andrew Wyeth; drawings by Leonard Baskin, Isabel Bishop, Paul Cadmus, Kenneth Callahan, William Gropper, Gabor Peterdi, Robert Vickrey & John Wilde; prints by John Taylor Arms, George Catlin, Thomas Nason; sculpture by Deborah Butterfield, L E Gus Shafer & Ernest Trova
Publications: Annual report including catalog of year's acquisitions, exhibition catalogs & brochures; Artmail, monthly newsletter
Activities: Classes for adults & children; docent training; lect open to public, 8 vis lectr per year; performances & programs in fine arts theater; concerts; gallery talks, tours, competitions; individual paintings & original objects of art lent to other museums; originate traveling exhibitions to other museums; museum shop sells books, magazines & miscellaneous items

A ALLIED ARTS COUNCIL OF ST JOSEPH, 118 S Eighth St, 64501. Tel 816-233-0231; FAX 816-233-6704; Elec Mail wbloff@stjoearts.org. *Exec Dir* Wally Bloff; *Campaign-Marketing Mgr* Christy Barber
Estab 1963 to bring the Arts & people together. Mem: 1800
Income: Financed by state appropriation

M MISSOURI WESTERN STATE COLLEGE, Fine Arts Gallery, 4525 Downs Dr, 64507. Tel 816-271-4282; *Pres* Dr Janet Murphy; *VPres* Dr James Roever; *Chmn Dept of Art* William Eickhorst, EdD
Open Mon - Fri 8 AM - 4 PM. No admis fee. Estab 1971 to bring an awareness of contemporary directions in art to students & to the community. Foyer gallery is in front of building, next to theater; 120 ft long, 30 ft wide, with 25 ft high ceiling; rug paneling on walls; modern decor, gallery 206 is on second floor; 25 sq ft, 10 ft ceiling; rug paneling on walls, carpeted. Average Annual Attendance: 10,000
Income: Financed by state appropriation
Exhibitions: Invitational of juried art exhibitions
Activities: Classes for adults; lect open to public, 3-4 vis lectr per year; gallery talks; tours; book traveling exhibitions

M SAINT JOSEPH MUSEUM, 11th & Charles, PO Box 128, 64502. Tel 816-232-8471; FAX 816-232-8482; *Dir* Richard A Nolf; *Registrar & Cur Coll* Carol Wills; *Cur Ethnology* Marilyn S Taylor; *Cur Hist & Librn* Sarah M Elder
Open Mon - Sat 9 AM - 5 PM, Sun & holidays 1 - 5 PM. Admis adults $2, children between 7 & 15 $1, under 7 free. Estab 1927 to increase & diffuse knowledge & appreciation of history, art & the sciences & to aid the educational work that is being done by the schools of Saint Joseph & other educational organizations. Mini-gallery, usually for small, low security traveling exhibits. Average Annual Attendance: 100,000. Mem: 209; dues $25 & up; annual meeting in Jan
Income: $100,000 (financed by mem & city appropriation)
Collections: †Harry L George Collection of Native American Art
Publications: The Happenings (newsletter), bimonthly
Activities: Classes for children; craft program; lect open to public; museum shop sells books, reproductions, prints, slides & gift items

L Library, 1100 Charles, PO Box 128, 64502-0128. Tel 816-232-8471; FAX 816-232-8482; *Dir* Richard A Nolf
Open Mon - Sat 9 AM - 5 PM, Sun 1 - 5 PM. Estab 1926 to hold mus collections. Mini gallery for traveling exhibits
Purchases: $1200
Library Holdings: Vols 5000; Per subs 40; Other — Clipping files, framed reproductions, manuscripts, memorabilia, original art works, photographs, prints, sculpture
Special Subjects: Area History; Native American; Natural History
Publications: The Happenings, bi-monthly newsletter
Activities: Classes for children; docent training; tours; originate traveling exhibitions to schools

SAINT LOUIS

M AMERICAN KENNEL CLUB (Formerly The Dog Museum), Museum of the Dog, 1721 S Mason Rd, 63131. Tel 314-821-3647; FAX 314-821-7381; *Cur & Mgr* Barbara Jedda
Open Tues - Sat 9 AM - 5 PM, Sun Noon - 5 PM. Admis $3. Estab 1984. Average Annual Attendance: 12,000. Mem: 650; dues $25 minimum; annual meeting in Oct
Purchases: Kathy Jacobson - Dog Walking in Central Park
Collections: Fine Art: art, artifacts & literature dedicated to the dog
Exhibitions: Artists' Registry Exhibition
Publications: SIRIUS, quarterly newsletter
Activities: Classes for adults; docent programs; lect open to public; book traveling exhibitions 2 per year; museum shop sells books & prints

L Reference Library, 1721 S Mason Rd, 63131. Tel 314-821-3647, 821-7381; For reference only
Income: $400,000 (financed by endowment, mem & gift shop sales)
Library Holdings: Vols 2000; Per subs 10; AV — Cassettes, motion pictures, slides, v-tapes; Other — Exhibition catalogs, framed reproductions, memorabilia, original art works, photographs, prints, sculpture

A ARTS & EDUCATION COUNCIL OF GREATER SAINT LOUIS, 3526 Washington Ave, 63103. Tel 314-535-3600; *Chmn* Charles Schukai; *Pres* Patricia Rich; *Communications Coordr* Jennifer Gross
Estab 1963 to coordinate, promote & assist in the development of cultural & educational activities in the Greater St. Louis area; to offer planning, coordinating, promotional & fundraising service to eligible organizations & groups, thereby creating a valuable community-wide assoc. Mem: 145
Income: Financed by funds from private sector
Exhibitions: Saint Louis Arts Awards
Publications: Annual report; calendar of cultural events, quarterly; quarterly newsletter

M ATRIUM GALLERY, 7638 Forsyth Blvd, 63105. Tel 314-726-1066; FAX 314-726-5444; *Dir* Carolyn Miles
Open Mon - Sat 10 AM - 5:30 PM; also by appointment. Estab 1986. Commercial gallery featuring contemporary artists who are active regionally & nationally featuring one-person shows
Activities: Buffet luncheon/lect art series; 15 vis lectr per year

C THE BOATMEN'S NATIONAL BANK OF ST LOUIS, Art Collection, One Boatmen's Plaza, 800 Market St, 63101. Tel 314-466-6000; *Pres & Chmn* Andrew B Craig; *Sr VPres Advertising & Public Relations* Alfred S Dominick Jr
Open Mon - Fri 8 AM - 4 PM. Bank estab 1938; corporate art collection estab for purposes of investment & the pleasure of art. Art emphasizes Western theme & bank's affiliation with opening of the West
Collections: The Political Series by George Caleb Bingham; †Transportation Series by Oscar E Berninghause; Exhibition into the Rockies Mountains - watercolors by Alfred Jacob Miller; Tarahumara Series by George Carlson

M CHATILLON-DEMENIL HOUSE FOUNDATION, DeMenil Mansion, 3352 DeMenil Pl, 63118. Tel 314-771-5828; *Dir* Graff Marcia
Open Tues - Sat 10 AM - 4 PM. Admis $4. Estab 1965 to educate & inform the community on 19th century life & culture. Average Annual Attendance: 8000. Mem: 500; dues $35-$1000; annual meeting in May
Income: Financed by mem, grants & donations
Collections: Decorative art from c1770 through 19th century; period rooms with furnishings; paintings
Activities: Educ programs; retail store sells books

M CONCORDIA HISTORICAL INSTITUTE, 801 DeMun Ave, 63105. Tel 314-721-5934; *Dir* Dr August R Suelflow
Open Mon - Fri 8 AM - 4:30 PM, cl international holidays. No admis fee. Estab 1847, to collect & preserve resources on the history of Lutheranism in America. Affiliated with The Lutheran Church, Missouri Synod. Average Annual Attendance: 12,000. Mem: 1600; dues Life $500, over 65 $300, organization $75, patron $50, sustaining $30, active & subscription $20
Collections: Church archives & vast historical materials; crafts; handcrafts; Reformation & Lutheran coins & medals; Works by Lutheran artists & paintings & artifacts for Lutheran worship; Native artwork from Foreign Mission Fields, especially China, India, Africa & New Guinea
Exhibitions: Temporary exhibitions
Publications: Concordia Historical Institute Quarterly; Historical Footnotes, a quarterly newsletter; Regional Archivist, a newsletter and 'how to' serial for archives; bulletins
Activities: Lect open to public; competitions with awards; Distinquished Service Award & awards of commendation for contributions to Lutheran History & archives; sales shop sells books, slides & craft items

M CRAFT ALLIANCE GALLERY & EDUCATION CENTER FOR THE VISUAL ARTS, 6640 Delmar Blvd, 63130. Tel 314-725-1151, 725-1177; FAX 314-725-1180; *Exec Dir* Sharon McPherron; *Chief Cur* Barbara Jordon; *Dir Educational Center* Leslie Wood
Open Tues - Fri Noon - 5 PM, Sat 10 AM - 5 PM. No admis fee. Estab 1964 for exhibition & sales of craft objects. Average Annual Attendance: 12,000. Mem: 650
Income: Financed by mem, Missouri Arts Council, St Louis Arts & Educ Council, National Endowment for the Arts, Regional Arts Commission
Exhibitions: Monthly exhibits by national artists.
Publications: Animals of Power, (1991); Exhibition catalogs; Old & New Faces, Vols 1 & 2 (1987 & 88); Works Off The Lathe
Activities: Classes for adults & children; lect open to public, 3 vis lectr per year; book traveling exhibitions 1 per year; originate traveling exhibitions; sales shop sells books, magazines & original art

A FORUM FOR CONTEMPORARY ART, 3540 Washington Ave, 63103. Tel 314-535-4660; FAX 314-535-1226; Elec Mail forum@inlink.com. *Pres* Donna Moog Nussbaum; *Exec Dir* Elizabeth Wright Millard; *Cur* Mel Watkin
Open Tues - Sat 10 AM - 5 PM. No admis fee, donations accepted. Estab 1980 to promote & advocate contemporary arts. Multi-disciplinary visual arts center. Average Annual Attendance: 150,000. Mem: 500; dues $35 & up
Income: $450,000 (financed by mem, corporations & foundation funds)
Exhibitions: Altered States: American Art in the 90s; History 101: The Re-Search for Family
Publications: Exhibit catalog; quarterly newsletter
Activities: Educational outreach; workshops; lect open to public; 12 - 15 vis lectr per year; concerts; gallery talks; tours; book traveling exhibitions; originates traveling exhibitions

M **LAUMEIER SCULPTURE PARK & MUSEUM,** 12580 Rott Rd, 63127. Tel 314-821-1209; FAX 314-821-1248; *Dir* Dr Beej Nierengarten-Smith; *Public Relations Dir* Debbie Lakin; *Cur* Susan Brown; *Cur* Porter Arneill
Park open daily 8 AM - half hour past sunset; Museum open Tues - Sat 10 AM - 5 PM, Sun Noon - 5 PM. Estab 1976 to exhibit contemporary sculpture by internationally acclaimed artists. Average Annual Attendance: 350,000. Mem: 1000; dues benefactor $2500, patron $1000, sustaining $500, contributing $250, associate $60, family $40, senior $10
Income: Financed by mem, corporate gifts & grants
Collections: Outdoor contemporary sculpture collection by Vito Acconci, Jackie Ferrara, Ian Hamilton Finlay, Richard Fleischner, Charles Ginnever, Dan Graham, Hera, Jene Highstein, Richard Hunt, Donald Judd, William King, Alexander Liberman, Robert Lobe, Mary Miss, Robert Morris, David Nash, Manuel Neri, Dennis Oppenheim, Beverly Pepper, George Rickey, Tony Rosenthal Richard Serra, Judith Shea, Michael Steiner, Mark Di Suvero, Ernest Trova, Ursula von Rydingsvard, David Von Schlegell, Meg Webster
Activities: Classes for adults & children; docent training; lect open to public, 3 vis lectr per year; concerts; gallery talks; tours; original objects of art lent to established institutions; lending collection contains 40 sculptures; book traveling exhibitions; originate traveling exhibitions; museum shop sells books, original art, slides

C **MARK TWAIN BANCSHARES,** 8820 Ladue Rd, 63124. Tel 314-727-1000; *Cur* Rick Barcheck
Collections: Sculpture; American paintings; graphics; photography

M **MARYVILLE UNIVERSITY SAINT LOUIS,** Morton J May Foundation Gallery, 13550 Conway Rd, 63141. Tel 314-576-9300; *Gallery Dir* Nancy N Rice
Open Mon - Thurs 9 AM - 10 PM, Fri & Sat 8 AM - 5 PM, Sun 2 - 10 PM. No admis fee. Estab to show work of artists, many of whom have no gallery affiliation. Average Annual Attendance: 3000
Income: $2901
Activities: Lect open to public, 4 vis lectr per year; gallery talks; individual paintings & original objects of art lent to organizations, art guilds & schools

M **MISSOURI HISTORICAL SOCIETY,** Jefferson Memorial Bldg, PO Box 11940, 63112-0040. Tel 314-746-4599; FAX 314-454-3162; *Pres* Dr Robert Archibald; *Exec VPres* Karen M Goering; *VPres* Marsha Bray; *Dir Educ* Kris Runberg Smith; *Cur Photographs* Duane Sneddeker
Open Tues - Sun 9:30 AM - 5 PM. No admis fee. Estab 1866 to collect & preserve objects & information relating to the history of St Louis, Missouri & the Louisiana Purchase Territory. Estab 1866 to preserve the history of St Louis & the American West. Circ 6000; dues from $45 & up; annual meeting in Sept. Average Annual Attendance: 200,000. Mem: 5500; dues from $35; annual meeting Sept
Income: Financed by private endowment, mem, special events, city & county taxes
Collections: †19th & 20th century art of St Louis and the American West; †paintings; †photographs; †prints
Exhibitions: Linbergh Memorabilia; St Louis Memory & History: 1904 Worlds Fair; St. Louis Gilded Age
Publications: Focus, quarterly; Gateway Heritage, quarterly journal
Activities: Classes for adults & children; dramatic programs; docent training; outreach program festivals; lect open to public, 30 vis lectr per year; concerts; gallery talks; tours; individual paintings & original objects of art lent to qualified museums & galleries that meet AAM standards; book traveling exhibitions; originate traveling exhibitions; sales shop sells books, prints, slides, souvenirs, china

L **Library & Research Center,** 225 S Skinker Blvd, PO Box 11940, 63112-0040. Tel 314-746-4599; *Pres* Robert R Archibald
Open Mon - Sat 10 AM - 5 PM. Estab 1866 to provide history of St. Louis, Missouri & Westward expansion
Library Holdings: Vols 75,000; Per subs 503; Micro — Reels; AV — Cassettes; Other — Clipping files, manuscripts, pamphlets, photographs 500,00, prints 2000, sculpture 150
Special Subjects: Midwestern and Western Artists: Bodmer, Catlin and Russell
Publications: Gateway Heritage, quarterly
Activities: Museum shop sells books, magazines, reproductions & prints

A **MISSOURI STATE COUNCIL ON THE ARTS,** 111 N Seventh St, Ste 105, 63101. Tel 314-340-6845; Internet Home Page Address http://www.ecodev.state.mo.us/moartscouncil/. *Exec Dir* Flora Maria Garcia; *Develop Mgr* Don Dyer
Estab 1965 to promote & develop cultural resources on the arts & as sets in Missouri
Income: Financed by state appropriation
Activities: Some internships offered

A **SAINT LOUIS ARTISTS' GUILD,** Two Oak Knoll, 63105. Tel 314-727-9599; FAX 314-727-9190; *Pres* Richard T Silverman; *Exec Dir* Jody Barksdale
Open Tues - Sun Noon - 4 PM, cl Mon. No admis fee. Estab for the purpose of promoting excellence in the arts. Maintains reference library. Average Annual Attendance: 30,000. Mem: 800, dues $45
Income: Financed by mem
Exhibitions: 15-20 exhibits per yr
Publications: Monthly newsletter
Activities: Classes for adults & children; lect open to public, 5 vis lectr per year; gallery talks; tours; competitions with awards; sales shop sells original art

M **THE SAINT LOUIS ART MUSEUM,** One Fine Arts Dr, 63110-1380. Tel 314-721-0067; FAX 314-721-6172;
Internet Home Page Address http://www.slam.org. *Dir* James D Burke
Open Tues 1:30 - 8:30 PM, Wed - Sun 10 AM - 5 PM, cl Mon. No admis fee except for special exhibitions. Estab 1907, erected as Palace of Art for 1904 World's Fair; designed by Cass Gilbert in Beaux Arts architecture style. The main sculpture hall is fashioned after Roman Baths of Caracalla. Average Annual

Attendance: 650,000. Mem: 16,000; dues $2500, $1000, $500, $100, $50, $45, $25
Income: Property tax provides 65% of operating income & balance from grants & private donations
Collections: A comprehensive museum of global interest with collections ranging from prehistoric times to the present. A new department of prints, drawings & photographs display works from the Museum's 6000 holdings; art collection of works from Oceania, Africa, Pre-Columbian & American Indian objects; paintings emphasize Northern European works from the Renaissance to Rembrandt as well as colonial to contemporary American, French Impressionist & Post Impressionist & German Expressionist works; 20th century European sculpture, American & European decorative art; Chinese bronzes & porcelains
Publications: The St Louis Art Museum Bulletin, semi-annual; annual report; bi-monthly magazine/calendar
Activities: Classes for adults & children; docent training; lect open to public, 26 vis lectr per year; concerts; gallery talks; tours; comptitions with prizes; exten dept serves state of Missouri; individual paintings & origianl objects of art lent ot other museums; book traveling exhibitions; traveling exhibitions organized & circulated; museum shop sells books, magazines, prints & reproductions

L **Richardson Memorial Library,** One Fine Arts Dr Forest Park, 63110-1380. Tel 314-721-0072; FAX 314-721-6172; Elec Mail library@slam.org. *Librn* Stephanie C Sigala; *Assoc Librn* Marianne L Cavanaugh; *Archivist* Norma Sindelar; *Archives Technician* Ann Shuck; *Admin Asst* Clare Vasquez; *Slide Cur* Cheryl Vogler; *Technical Servs Asst* Davina Harrison
Open Tues - Fri 10 AM - 5 PM. Estab 1915 to provide reference & bibliographical service to the mus staff & the adult pub; to bibliographically support the collections owned by the mus
Income: Financed by endowment & city appropriation
Library Holdings: Vols 70,000; Per subs 300; Art auction catalogs since 1824; Micro — Fiche, reels; AV — Slides 41,000; Other — Clipping files, exhibition catalogs, pamphlets
Collections: Museum Archives, includes records of Louisiana Purchase Expo (1904) & papers of Morton D May

L **SAINT LOUIS PUBLIC LIBRARY,** Fine Arts Dept, 1301 Olive St, 63103. Tel 314-241-2288; FAX 314-241-3840; *Mgr Fine Arts Dept* Suzy Enns Frechette
Open Mon 10 AM - 9 PM, Tues - Fri 10 AM - 6 PM, Sat 9 AM - 5 PM. Estab Art Dept in 1912
Library Holdings: Vols 115,000; Micro — Fiche, reels; AV — Cassettes, motion pictures, rec, slides 17,500; Other — Clipping files 135, exhibition catalogs, pamphlets, reproductions
Special Subjects: Afro-American Art, Architecture, Art History, Decorative Arts, Graphic Arts, Illustration, Interior Design, Photography, Collectibles
Collections: Steedman Architectural Library; Local Architects & Buildings Files; Local Artists Files

M **UNIVERSITY OF MISSOURI, SAINT LOUIS,** Gallery 210, Art Dept, 8001 Natural Bridge Rd, 63121. Tel 314-516-5000; *Chmn* Ruth Bohan; *Dir* Terry Suhre
Open Tues Noon - 8 PM, Wed - Fri 10 AM - 5 PM, Sat 10 AM - 2 PM, cl Sun & Mon. Estab 1972 to exhibit contemporary art of national importance & to provide visual enrichment to campus & community. Average Annual Attendance: 5000
Income: Financed by state appropriation & grants
Publications: Exhibition catalogs: Color Photography; Light Abstractions
Activities: Educ dept on art history; lect open to public; originate traveling exhibitions

WASHINGTON UNIVERSITY
M **Gallery of Art,** Steinberg Hall, Campus Box 1214, 63130. Tel 314-935-5490; *Dir* Joseph D Ketner; *Cur* Connie Homburg; *Registrar* Marie Nordimann; *Facilities Tech* Jan Hessel; *Admin* Jane Neidhardt
Open Mon - Fri 10 AM - 5 PM, Sat & Sun 1 - 5 PM, cl Mon from mid-May - Labor Day. No admis fee. Estab 1881, present building opened 1960, for the students of Washington University & the community at large. A modern building containing two floors of gallery space for exhibit of the permanent collection & special exhibitions. Also houses a library of art, archaeology, architecture & design
Income: Financed by university & private support
Collections: Emphasis on †modern artists, including Miro, Ernst, Picasso, Leger, Moore; many †Old Masters, 19th & 20th century European & American paintings, sculpture, drawings & prints
Publications: Exhibition catalogs
Activities: Lect open to public, 24 vis lectr per year by artists, art historians & architects; symposia; music concerts; films; scholarships; book traveling exhibitions; originate traveling exhibitions; sales shop sells exhibition catalogs & postcards

L **Art & Architecture Library,** One Brookings Dr, PO Box 1060, 63130. Tel 314-935-5268; FAX 314-935-4045; Elec Mail dana-beth@library.wustle.edu. *Art & Architecture Librn* Dana Beth; *Circulation & Reserve Supv* Betty Daniel
Open Mon - Thurs 8:30 AM - 11 PM, Fri 8:30 AM - 5 PM, Sat 11 AM - 5 PM, Sun 1 - 9 PM, cl nights & weekends during vacations & intersessions. Supports the academic programs of the School of Art, the School of Architecture & the Department of Art History & Archaeology
Income: Financed through the university
Library Holdings: Vols 80,000; Per subs 340; Micro — Cards, fiche 1354, prints, reels 245; Other — Exhibition catalogs, pamphlets, reproductions

M **WEBSTER UNIVERSITY,** Cecille R Hunt Gallery, 470 E Lockwood Ave, 63119. Tel 314-968-7171; Elec Mail langtk@websteruniv.edu. *Adminr* Tom Lang
Open Mon - Fri 10 AM - 4 PM, Sat 10 AM - 2 PM, cl Christmas. No admis fee. Estab 1950. Average Annual Attendance: 3500
Publications: Monthly news releases; exhibition catalogs; books
Activities: Lect open to public, 6 vis lectr per year; competitions with awards; Hunt Awards for student shows; individual paintings & original objects of art lent

L Library, 475 E Lockwood Ave, 63119. Tel 314-968-6951; FAX 314-968-7113; For reference & lending
Library Holdings: Vols 204,421; Per subs 966; Micro — Cards, fiche, prints, reels; AV — A-tapes, cassettes, fs, motion pictures, rec, slides, v-tapes; Other — Exhibition catalogs, manuscripts, pamphlets, photographs, prints, reproductions
Special Subjects: 20th century paintings, prints, sculpture and photography

SPRINGFIELD

A SOUTHWEST MISSOURI MUSEUM ASSOCIATES INC, 1111 E Brookside Dr, 65807. Tel 417-837-5700; *Pres* Samuel O King
Estab 1928 to inform & interest citizens in appreciation of art & to maintain an art mus as an essential pub institution. Mem: 1300; dues sustaining life $1000, life $500, supporting $50, family $40, at large $30, art group: resident $20, extension groups $10
Income: $14,000 (financed by mem)
Publications: Bi-monthly newsletter, in cooperation with the Museum
Activities: Gift shop sells books, original art, prints, reproductions, stationary & gift items; maintain a sales gallery

M SPRINGFIELD ART MUSEUM, 1111 E Brookside Dr, 65807. Tel 417-837-5700; FAX 417-837-5709; *Dir* Jerry A Berger; *Cur Coll* Debbie Sehlier; *Cur Educ* Faity Yorty; *Registrar* Winifred Clement; *Admin Asst* Tyra Knox
Open Mon - Sat 9 AM - 5 PM, Wed 6:30 - 9 PM, Sun 1 - 5 PM, cl Mon. No admis fee. Estab 1928 to encourage appreciation & foster educ of the visual arts. Mus has four temporary exhibition galleries for traveling & special exhibitions totaling approx 7500 sq ft; new wing opened in 1994 with 13,400 sq ft including four galleries for the permanent collection; 40-seat auditorium & sales gallery. Average Annual Attendance: 50,000. Mem: 1300; dues $15-$1000; annual meeting second Wed in May
Income: $500,000 (financed by mem, city & state appropriations)
Purchases: $40,000
Collections: †American & European decorative arts; †American drawing & photography; †American painting & sculpture of all periods; †American prints of all periods with emphasis on the 20th Century; †European prints, drawings & paintings from the 17th-20th Centuries
Activities: Classes for adults & children; lect open to public; concerts; gallery talks; tours; competitions with awards; originate traveling exhibition; museum shop sells books, original art, reproductions, pottery, jewelry, cards, stationary & t-shirts

L Library, 1111 E Brookside Dr, 65807-1899. Tel 417-837-5700; FAX 417-837-5704
Open Tues - Sat 9 AM - 5 PM, Thurs 9 AM - 8 PM, Sun 1 - 5 PM. Estab 1928 to assist those persons interested in securing information regarding art & artists, craftsmen from ancient times to the present. Lending & reference library. Circ 1800. Average Annual Attendance: 1000
Income: Financed by city
Purchases: $6000 (library acquisitions), $60,000 (artwork acquisitions)
Library Holdings: Vols 5000; Per subs 53; Art access kits; Exhibition cards; Multimedia kits; Slide kits; AV — Cassettes, slides, v-tapes; Other — Clipping files, exhibition catalogs, manuscripts, pamphlets
Special Subjects: Afro-American Art, American Indian Art, American Western Art, Archaeology, Architecture, Art Education, Art History, Bronzes, Calligraphy, Carpets & Rugs, Cartoons, Ceramics, Decorative Arts, Folk Art, Painting - American
Collections: †American & European paintings, prints & sculpture-primarily 19th & 20th century
Exhibitions: WUSA - Watercolor USA, open to US residents & MOAK (Missouri, Oklahoma, Arkansas, Kansas)
Publications: Exhibition catalogs; bimonthly newsletter; watercolor USA Catalog, annually
Activities: Classes for adults & children; docent training; lect open to public, 1-2 vis lectr per year; gallery talks; tours; competitions with prizes; lending collection contains 5000 books, 430 slide sets

ST LOUIS

M TROVA FOUNDATION, Philip Samuels Fine Art, 8112 Maryland Ave, 63105. Tel 314-727-2444; FAX 314-727-6084; *Pres* Philip Samuels; *Dir* Clifford Samuels
Open Mon - Fri by appointment only. Estab 1988. Contemporary painting, collage, drawing & sculpture

STOUTSVILLE

M MARK TWAIN BIRTHPLACE STATE HISTORIC SITE BIRTHPLACE MUSEUM, PO Box 54, 65283. Tel 314-565-3449
Open Mon - Sat 10 AM - 4 PM, Sun Noon - 5 PM. Admis adults $2, children between 6 & 12 $1.25. Estab 1960 to preserve the birth cabin of Samuel L Clemens, interpret his life and inform visitors of local history. Foyer and two large exhibit areas. Average Annual Attendance: 24,000
Income: Financed by state appropriation
Collections: Samuel Clemens memorabilia; manuscripts; period furnishings and paintings
Exhibitions: Permanent exhibits depicting the life of Samuel Clemens
Activities: Lects; tours; craft demonstrations

WARRENSBURG

M CENTRAL MISSOURI STATE UNIVERSITY, Art Center Gallery, 217 Clark St, 64093. Tel 816-543-4498; FAX 816-543-8006; *Gallery Dir* Morgan Dean Gallatin
Open Sept - Aug Mon, Wed - Fri 8 AM - 5 PM, Tues 8 AM - & 7 PM, Sat 10 AM - 2 PM, Sun 1 - 5 PM, June & July Mon - Fri 8 AM - 4 PM. No admis fee. Estab 1984 for the purpose of education through exhibition. Small outer gallery

& large main gallery located in the university Art Center. Average Annual Attendance: 3500
Income: Financed by state appropriation & university funding
Collections: †University permanent collection
Exhibitions: (1995) Greater Midwest International Annual Visual Art Competition
Activities: Classes for adults; 4 vis lectr per year; gallery talks; competitions with awards

MONTANA

ANACONDA

A COPPER VILLAGE MUSEUM & ARTS CENTER, 401 E Commercial, 59711. Tel 406-563-2422; *Dir* Linda Talbott; *Pres & Board Dir* Liz Willett
Open Tues - Fri 10 AM - 5 PM, Sat & Sun 11 AM - 4 PM, cl Mon & holidays. No admis fee. Estab 1971 as Community Arts Center, gallery & regional historical mus. Average Annual Attendance: 15,000. Mem: 150; dues $5-$100
Income: Financed by endowment, mem, city appropriation, fundraising events & individual donations
Collections: Permanent collection holds paintings & prints
Exhibitions: Monthly exhibits of local, national & international art work
Publications: Quarterly newsletters, brochures
Activities: Classes for adults & children; dramatic programs; docent training; lect open to public, 4 vis lectr per year; concerts; gallery talks; tours; awards; book traveling exhibitions 4-8 per year; originate traveling exhibitions which circulate to Montana Galleries; sales shop sells books, original art, prints, pottery, glass & jewelry

L Library, 401 E Commercial, 59711. Tel 406-563-2422; *Dir* Linda Talbott
Library open to the pub for reference
Library Holdings: Vols 45; Per subs 11; AV — Motion pictures, slides; Other — Clipping files, memorabilia, pamphlets, reproductions, sculpture
Special Subjects: Western History and Art
Publications: Newletters, quarterly; brochures
Activities: Book traveling exhibitions

BILLINGS

M PETER YEGEN JR YELLOWSTONE COUNTY MUSEUM, Logan Field, PO Box 959, 59103. Tel 406-256-6811; *Dir* Art Gaudet
Open Mon - Fri 10:30 AM - 5 PM, call for weekend hours. No admis fee. Estab 1953. Average Annual Attendance: 15,000. Mem: dues lifetime $1000, corporate $100, family $25, individual $20, senior $15; annual Open House in Sept/Oct
Income: $22,000 (financed by county, mem, memorials, donations & grants)
Collections: Dinosaur bones; Montana Pioneers; Native American; Northern Pacific Steam Switch Engine; rocks; Yellowstone Valley
Exhibitions: Dinosaur bones; Leory Greene (local artist) paintings of Crow Indians, 1930-1968; Indian artifacts; military items; Western memorabilia
Publications: Cabin Chat, quarterly newsletter
Activities: Lect for members only; tours; originate traveling exhibitions; museum shop sells books, magazines, postcards, prints & gift items

A YELLOWSTONE ART CENTER, 401 N 27th St, 59101. Tel 406-256-6804; FAX 406-256-6817; *Pres Board* Cal Northam; *Dir* Donna M Forbes; *Asst Dir & Sr Cur* Gordon McConnell; *Cur* Robert Durden
Open Tues - Sat 11 AM - 5 PM, Sun Noon - 5 PM, Thurs 11 AM - 8 PM. No admis fee. Estab 1964 to offer a broad program of art exhibitions, both historical & contemporary, of the highest quality, to provide related educ programs. Two large galleries and four smaller ones in a large brick structure. Average Annual Attendance: 25,000. Mem: 850; dues $20 & up; annual meeting third Wed in June
Income: $700,000 (financed by mem, contributions, county appropriations, grants, mus shop & fundraising events)
Purchases: Current work by Montana artists
Collections: †Contemporary Print Collection; Poindexter Collection of Abstract Expressionists; †Contemporary Montana Artists
Exhibitions: Portfolios of Edward Weston & Ansel Adams; Theodore Waddell, John Buck, Clarice Dreyer: In Context; Northern Rockies: New Visions; 27th Annual Auction (paintings, sculpture, works on paper)
Publications: Bi-monthly exhibition announcements; newsletter, bi-monthly; exhibition catalogues, 4-6 per yr
Activities: Classes for children; docent training; lect open to public, 4-6 vis lectr per year; concerts; gallery talks; tours; individual paintings & original art objects lent to museums & art centers; originate traveling exhibitions; museum shop sells books, original art, reproductions, jewelry & small gift items

BOZEMAN

MONTANA STATE UNIVERSITY
M Museum of the Rockies, 600 W Kagy, 59717. Tel 406-994-2251; FAX 406-994-2682; *Asst Dir* Judy Weaver; *Cur Art & Photo* Steve Jackson
Open 9 AM - 9 PM Memorial Day - Labor Day; winter, Tues - Sat 9 AM - 5 PM, Sun 1 - 5 PM, cl Mon. Admis adults $5, children 5-18 & MSU students $3, children under 5 free; planetarium admis $2.50. Estab in 1958 to interpret the physical & cultural heritages of the Northern Rockies region. Average Annual Attendance: 160,000. Mem: 4200; dues directors circle $500, sustaining $250, contribution $100, family $50, non-resident family $40, individual $25, MSU student $15
Income: Financed by MSU, fundraising, grants & revenue
Collections: Art Works by R E DeCamp; Edgar Paxton; C M Russell; O C Seltzer; William Standing; geology; paleontology; astronomy; archaeological

artifacts; history & western art; regional native Americans
Exhibitions: Rotation Gallery features changing exhibitions
Publications: Quarterly newsletter; papers
Activities: Classes for adults & children; docent training; programs in science, history & art; lect open to public, 20 vis lectr per year; planetarium shows; field trips; field schools; gallery talks; tours; traveling portable planetarium, book traveling exhibitions; originate traveling exhibitions; museum shop sells books, magazines, original art, reproductions, prints, slides, crafts, toys, hats, t-shirts, stationery

M **Helen E Copeland Gallery,** School of Art, Haynes Hall Rm 213, 59717. Tel 406-994-4501; FAX 406-994-6696; *Gallery Dir* John Anacker
Open Mon - Fri 8 AM - 5 PM. No admis fee. Estab 1974 to present exhibitions of national interest. A new building with a small gallery space adjacent to offices & studio classrooms. Average Annual Attendance: 10,000
Income: Financed by university appropriation
Collections: Japanese Patterns; Native American Ceramics; WPA Prints
Exhibitions: 7-8 exhibitions annually including graduate & undergraduate exhibitions
Activities: Lect open to public, 5 vis lectr per year; gallery talks; competitions

L **Creative Arts Library,** 207 Cheever Hall, Creative Arts Complex, 59717. Tel 406-994-4091; FAX 406-994-2851; Elec Mail alikk@montana.edu. *Librn* Kathy Kaya
Open Mon - Thurs 8 AM - 10 PM, Fri 8 AM - 5 PM, Sat & Sun 1 - 10 PM. Estab 1974 to support the Schools of Architecture & Art
Income: Financed by state appropriation
Library Holdings: Vols 14,677; Per subs 100; Matted reproductions; AV — Slides 80,000

BROWNING

M **MUSEUM OF THE PLAINS INDIAN & CRAFTS CENTER,** US Hwy 89 & 2, 59417. Tel 406-338-2230; *Cur* Loretta F Pepion
Open June - Sept, daily 9 AM - 5 PM, Oct - May Mon - Fri 10 AM - 4:30 PM, cl New Year's Day, Thanksgiving Day and Christmas. No admis fee. Estab 1941 to promote the development of contemporary Native American arts & crafts, administered and operated by the Indian Arts and Crafts Board, US Dept of the Interior. Average Annual Attendance: 80,000
Income: Financed by federal appropriation
Collections: Contemporary Native American arts & crafts; historic works by Plains Indian craftsmen & artists
Exhibitions: Historic arts created by the tribal peoples of the Northern Plains; Traditional costumes of Northern Plains men, women & children; Art forms related to the social & ceremonial aspects of the regional tribal cultures; Winds of Change: Five Screen Multi-Media Presentation of the Evolution of Indian Cultures on the Northern Plains; One-Person exhibitons of Native American artists & craftsmen; Architectural decorations, including carved wood panels by sculptor John Clarke & a series of murals by Victor Pepion
Publications: Continuing series of brochures for one-person shows, exhibition catalogues
Activities: Gallery talks; tours; demonstrations of Native American arts & crafts; traveling exhibitions organized and circulated; sales shop sells books, original art

BUTTE

M **BUTTE SILVER BOW ARTS CHATEAU,** 321 W Broadway, 59701. Tel 406-723-7600; *Dir* Sharon Knauth
Open Sept - May Tues - Sun 1 - 4 PM, June - Aug Tues - Sat 10 AM - 5 PM, Sun 1 - 4 PM, cl major holidays. Admis donation. Estab 1977 to further all forms of art. 1898 French Chateau converted to galleries. Mem: 350; dues Business: benefactor $1000, patron $750, sustaining $500, contributing $100, active $10; Individual: benefactor $1000, patron $500, sustaining $100, contributing $50, family $25, active $10; annual meeting Jan
Collections: Contemporary regional art
Publications: Newsletter
Activities: Classes for adults, dramatic programs; lect open to public, 10 vis lectr per year; gallery talks; tours; book traveling exhibitions 4 per year; sales shop sells original art, reproductions & prints

CHESTER

M **LIBERTY VILLAGE ARTS CENTER & GALLERY,** 402 S Main St, PO Box 269, 59522. Tel 406-759-5652; *Dir* Trudy Skari
Open Tues, Thurs & Sun Noon - 4 PM, Wed & Fri Noon - 2 PM winter hours, cl New Years, Easter, Thanksgiving & Christmas. No admis fee. Estab 1976 to provide community with traveling exhibitions & educ center. Average Annual Attendance: 1500-2000. Mem: 50; dues patron $100 & up, Friend of the Arts $50 - $99, family $25, individual $20; annual meeting Oct
Collections: Works by local artists, paintings & quilts
Activities: Classes for adults & children; workshops; film series; lect open to public, 5 vis lectr per year; gallery talks; competitions with awards; book traveling exhibitions; originate traveling exhibitions; museum shop sells books, original art & prints

DILLON

M **WESTERN MONTANA COLLEGE,** Art Gallery/Museum, 710 S Atlantic, 59725-3958. Tel 406-683-7126; WATS 800-WMC-MONT. *Dir* Randy Horst
Open Mon - Fri 10 AM - 3 PM, Tues & Thurs 7 - 9 PM. No admis fee. Estab 1970 to display art works of various kinds, used as an educational facility. Located in the south end of Old Main Hall Seidensticker Wildlife Collection. Average Annual Attendance: 7000
Income: Financed through college funds
Collections: †Emerick Art Book Collection; Seidensticker Wildlife
Activities: Educ dept; scholarships offered; originate traveling exhibitions

L **Lucy Carson Memorial Library,** 710 S Atlantic, 59725-3598. Tel 406-683-7541; FAX 406-683-7493; *Head Librn* Mike Shultz
Library open to the pub
Library Holdings: Vols 4500; Per subs 12; AV — V-tapes 140

GREAT FALLS

M **CASCADE COUNTY HISTORICAL SOCIETY,** Cascade County Historical Museum & Archives, 1400 First Ave N, 59401. Tel 406-452-3462; *Dir & Cur* Cindy Kittredge; *Cur Colls* Barbara Brewer; *Archives* Julianne Ruby; *Bookkeeper* Kim Hulten; *Gift Shop Mgr* Claudette Bourcier
Open summer, Mon - Fri 10 AM - 5 PM, Sat & Sun Noon - 5 PM, winter, Tues - Fri 10 AM - 5 PM, Sat & Sun Noon - 5 PM, cl holidays. No admis fee. Estab 1976 to preserve & interpret the history of the Cascade County area & the diverse area heritage. The historical mus is housed in a school building built in 1895, which is functioning as an art center & historical mus. Auxiliary site open in the summer at State Fairgrounds. Average Annual Attendance: 57,000. Mem: 400; dues corporate $250; patron $200; sustainer $50; sponsor $100; family $20; individual $15; senior citizen $10; annual meeting third Thurs in Feb
Income: $220,000 (financed by mem dues, donations, memorials, sales shop & grants)
Collections: Art, documents, manuscripts, photographs, objects reflecting the history of the local area; clothing, furniture & memorabilia from Great Falls & Cascade County
Exhibitions: Exhibits from the permanent collections, changed quarterly
Activities: Classes for adults & childrens; lect open to public, 10 vis lectr per year; tours; individual paintings & original objects of art lent to other museums; Book traveling expedition 1 per year; originate traveling expedition to schools & smaller areas town businesses; museum shop sells books, original arts, reproductions & prints

M **PARIS GIBSON SQUARE,** Museum of Art, 1400 First Ave N, 59401. Tel 406-727-8255; *Dir* Bonnie Laing-Malcolmson; *Cur* Jessica Hunter
Open Tues - Fri 10 AM - 5 PM, Sat & Sun Noon - 5 PM, cl Mon. No admis fee. Estab 1976 to exhibit contemporary & historical art. Maintains 3 galleries which consist of 1100 ft of running wall space. Average Annual Attendance: 57,000. Mem: 550-650; mem open to public; dues $20; annual meetings in June
Income: $300,000 (financed by mem, grants, contributions & county mill)
Collections: †Contemporary regional artists; Montana folk-art naive sculptures (polychromed wood), Lee Steen
Exhibitions: (1997) Talking Quilts; Signs of Spring, Art Equinox: A Regional Survey of Contemporary Art; Stephen Schultz The Archie Bray Foundation: A Ceramic Tradition; Great Falls All-City Student Show; Seeing the Light; Shades of Difference: Five Contemporary Western Photographers
Publications: Artist postcards, bi-monthly exhibition announcements, Exhibition Quarterly
Activities: Classes for adults & children; docent training; lect open to public, 6-12 vis lectr per year; gallery talks; tours; scholarships & fels offered; individual paintings & original objects of art lent to other museums; lending collection contains original art works, original prints, paintings & photographs; book traveling exhibitions 1-2 per year; originate traveling exhibitions to regional art institutions; museum shop sells Montana original art, reproductions, prints, ceramics, museum cards & gift items

M **C M RUSSELL MUSEUM,** 400 13th St N, 59401. Tel 406-727-8787; FAX 406-727-2402; *Dir* Lorne E Render; *Cur* Elizabeth Dear; *Registrar* Nancy Wheeler
Open during winter Tues - Sat 10 AM - 5 PM, Sun 1 - 5 PM, cl Mon; summer (May 1 - Oct 30) Mon - Sat 9 AM - 6 PM, Sun 1 - 5 PM. Admis adults $4, students $2, senior citizens $3, children under 5 free. Estab 1953 to preserve art of Charles M Russell, western painter. Mus includes Russell's home & original studio; has seven galleries of Western art/photographs & Indian artifacts. Maintains reference library. Average Annual Attendance: 65,000. Mem: 1750; dues $25 - $3000 & up; annual meeting in May
Income: Financed by operating budget
Collections: Works by Charles M Russell & other Western works including Seltzer, Couse, Wieghorst, SHARP, Heikka, Reiss, Farny; Historical & contemporary; Contemporary & western art; Native American art
Exhibitions: Traveling exhibitions of western art; permanent exhibitions
Publications: Magazine, semi-annually; newsletter, quarterly
Activities: Classes for adults & children; docent training; Tipi Camp; lect for members only, 0-6 vis lectr per year; gallery talks; tours; individual paintings & original objects of art lent to qualified museums; book traveling exhibitions 1 per year; museum store sells books, magazines, reproductions, prints, jewelry, pottery

L **Frederic G Renner Memorial Library,** 400 13th St N, 59401. Tel 406-727-8787; FAX 406-727-2402; *Registrar* Nancy Wheeler
Open same hrs as museum. Estab 1965 to provide research material on Western art & artists, primarily C M Russell & The History of Montana & The West. For reference only
Income: $2500 (financed by private contributions)
Library Holdings: Vols 2700; Per subs 4; Micro — Prints; AV — A-tapes, Kodachromes, motion pictures, slides, v-tapes; Other — Clipping files, exhibition catalogs, manuscripts, memorabilia, pamphlets, photographs, prints, reproductions
Special Subjects: American Western Art, Art History, Painting - American, Southwestern Art
Collections: Joseph Henry Sharp Collection of Indian Photographs; Yost Archival Collection; Flood Archival Collection
Publications: C M Russell Museum Newsletter, quarterly; Russell's West, semi-annual magazine

HAMILTON

M RAVALLI COUNTY MUSEUM, 205 Bedford, Old Court House, 59840. Tel 406-363-3338; *Dir* Helen Ann Bibler; *Treas* Candace George
Open summer Mon, Thurs, Fri & Sat 10 AM - 4 PM, Sun 1 - 4 PM, winter Mon & Thurs 1 - 4 PM, cl Tues & Wed. Admis donations appreciated. Estab 1979 to preserve the history of the Bitterroot Valley. Museum contains Flathead Indian exhibit, Rocky Mt Spotted Fever display, pioneer rooms, schoolroom, tack & trophy room, veterans room, rotating exhibits in old court room; extensive archives. Average Annual Attendance: 10,000. Mem: 300; dues family $10, regular $5, senior $2; meetings third Mon each month
Income: Financed by county appropriation & gifts from Bitterroot Valley Historical Society
Purchases: $5000
Collections: Home furnishings reflecting early life of the Bitterroot Valley; Indian Railroad
Exhibitions: Special Exhibits of International Interest; Porcelain Artists Exhibit; Special Local Collection Exhibit; Veterans Exhibit; December Christmas Exhibit
Publications: An Old Bitter Rooters Thoughts in Poetry, Joe Hughes; Bitterroot Trails, Bitterroot Historical Society; McIntosh Apple Cookbook; Historic Survey of Hamilton Buildings 1890-1940; The Vicbor Story, Jeffrey H Langton; The Yellow Pine; May Vallance; Newsletter
Activities: Educ dept; docent training, Sunday lect, cultural programs; lect open to public, 48 vis lectr per year; concerts; competitions with awards; museum shop sells books, original art, reproductions, prints, porcelain, jewelry & gifts

HELENA

A MONTANA HISTORICAL SOCIETY, 225 N Roberts, 59620. Tel 406-444-2694, 444-4710; FAX 406-444-2696; *Dir* Brian Cockhill; *Cur* Sue Near; *Business Mgr* Sharon McCabe
Open Mon - Fri 8 AM - 5 PM, Sat 9 AM - 5 PM, Sun (Memorial Day - Labor Day) 9 AM - 5 PM. No admis fee. Estab 1865 to collect, preserve & present articles relevant to history & heritage of Montana & the Northwest. Mackay Gallery of C M Russell Art; temporary exhibits gallery. Average Annual Attendance: 93,000. Mem: 4000; dues $40
Income: $27,000 (financed by State of Montana General Fund, private gifts & grants, federal grants, earned revenue)
Collections: †Haynes Collection of Art & Artifacts; MacKay Collection of C M Russell Art; Poindexter Collection of Contemporary Art; Montana artists; late 19th & 20th century Western art; ethnographic & decorative arts
Exhibitions: Bronzes of the American West; Mackay Gallery of C M Russell Art
Publications: Montana, Magazine of Western History, quarterly; Montana Post (newsletter), quarterly
Activities: Educational programs for adults & children; docent training; lect open to public, 10 vis lectr per year; concerts; gallery talks; tours; scholarships & fels; individual paintings & original objects of art lent to museums, galleries, historical societies, bonafide organizations & corporations; lending collection includes 300 color transparencies, 200 original art works, 500,000 photographs, 40 sculptures, 1000 slides; book traveling exhibitions; traveling exhibitions organized & circulated; sales shop selling books, magazines, prints, reproductions, slides

L Library, 225 N Roberts, 59620. Tel 406-444-2681; *Dir* Brian Cockhill; *Head Librn & Archivist* Bob Clark; *Photograph Cur* Delores Morrow; *Cur Coll* Kirby Lambert
For reference and research only
Income: Financed by State of Montana
Library Holdings: Vols 4000; Per subs 100; Other — Clipping files, exhibition catalogs, manuscripts, pamphlets, photographs
Special Subjects: American Indian Art, American Western Art, Anthropology, Archaeology, Ethnology, Historical Material, Painting - American, Montana history
Collections: Historical artifacts; Late 19th & 20th century art; photo collection; manuscripts
Publications: Montana: The Magazine of Western History, quarterly

KALISPELL

A HOCKADAY CENTER FOR THE ARTS, Second Ave E & Third St, PO Box 83, 59901. Tel 406-755-5268; FAX 406-755-2023; *Interim Dir* Joan Baucus
Open Tues - Fri 10 AM - 4 PM, Sat 10 AM - 3 PM. Estab 1968 to foster & encourage a growing interest in & understanding of all the arts; to provide the opportunity to take a place in the main current of the arts today, as well as to observe & learn from the arts of the past. Center is housed in the former Carnegie Library near downtown Kalispell; has four spacious exhibition galleries & a sales gallery. Mem: 1000; dues Friends of the Arts $100; assoc mem $50, general mem $25
Income: $100,000 (financed by mem, contributions, grants, exhibition sponsors, corporate donations & city funds)
Collections: Main collection includes eight portrait studies by Hugh Hockaday, artist of regional significance & the center's late namesake, as well as the works of Theodore Waddell, David Shaner, Russell Chatham & others
Exhibitions: Eight to twelve traveling & regional exhibitions per yr
Publications: Exhibition catalogs; newsletter
Activities: Classes for adults & children; drama programs; docent training; suitcase art program; lect open to public; 10 vis lectr per year; gallery talks; tours; summer & winter art festival; book traveling exhibitions 3-7 per year; museum shop sells books, original art, reproductions, prints & crafts from local artists

LEWISTOWN

A LEWISTOWN ART CENTER, 801 W Broadway, 59457. Tel 406-538-8278; *Dir* Ellen Gerharz
Open Tues - Sat 11:30 AM - 5:30 PM, cl Mon. Estab 1971 for advancement & educ in the arts. The gallery exhibitions change monthly showing a variety of local, state & national artwork. A sales gallery features Montana artists & local artists. Average Annual Attendance: 5000. Mem: 500; dues $10 & up; annual meeting in July
Income: $65,000 (financed entirely by mem, donations, sponsorships by local businesses, art grants, sales from gift shop, auction & market room)
Collections: Collection of art work from artists from Central Montana, bronze & all other mediums
Exhibitions: In-state shows; Juried Art Auction; juried show; regional shows
Publications: Newsletter, bimonthly
Activities: Arts classes & workshops for adults & children; docent training; lect open to public, 1-2 vis lectr per year; gallery talks; tours; competitions with awards; scholarships offered; originate traveling exhibitions to rural communities in Central Montana; sales shop sells books, original art, reproductions, prints, sculpture, pottery, wall hangings, jewelry, fiber arts & wood crafts

MILES CITY

A CUSTER COUNTY ART CENTER, Water Plant Rd, PO Box 1284, 59301. Tel 406-232-0635, 232-0637; *Exec Dir* Mark Browning; *Admin Asst* Brenda Kneeland
Open Tues - Sun 1 - 5 PM, cl holidays. No admis fee. Estab 1977 to provide an arts program of exhibits and educational activities to residents of Southeastern Montana. Maintains The Water Works Gallery, located in the former holding tanks of the old Miles City Water Works. Average Annual Attendance: 10,000. Mem: 500; dues benefactor $500, patron $300, sponsor $100, sustaining $75, contributing $50, family $30, individual $20, student & sr citizens $10
Income: $100,000 (financed by mem, fundraising events & grants)
Collections: Edward S Curtis Photographic Collection; Andrew Hofmeister Painting Collection; William Henry Jackson Photochrome Collection; Contemporary Montana Artists
Exhibitions: Custer County Art Center annual juried art exhibit; annual Art Auction Exhibit; plus eight additional temporary exhibits per year; Western Art Roundup & Quick Draw during Bucking Horse Sale Weekend
Publications: Biannual exhibit catalogs; quarterly newsletter
Activities: Classes for adults & children; lect open to public, 4 vis lectr per year; gallery talks; tours; competitions; films; book traveling exhibitions; museum store sells pottery, jewelry, books, prints, original art & gifts from regional crafts people

MISSOULA

M ART MUSEUM OF MISSOULA (Formerly Missoula Museum of the Arts), 335 N Pattee, 59802. Tel 406-728-0447; FAX 406-543-8691; *Dir* Laura J Millin; *Cur* Deborah Mitchell; *Adminr* Billie Bloom; *Educ Cur* Stephen Glueckert; *Museum Shop Mgr* Kate Likvan
Open Mon - Sat Noon - 5 PM. No admis fee. Estab 1975 to collect, preserve & exhibit international art; to educate through exhibits, art school, special programs & forums. Housed in renovated Carnegie Library (1903) featuring soft-panel covered walls; moveable track lighting; approx 3500 sq ft of exhibits space on two floors; fire and security alarm systems; meeting rooms. Average Annual Attendance: 25,000. Mem: 800
Income: $265,000 (financed by mem, grants, fund raising events & annual permissive mill levy by Missoula County)
Purchases: Contemporary Art of Western United States
Collections: Contemporary Art of Western United States with an emphasis on Montana
Exhibitions: Paintings, Prose, Poems & Prints: Missouri River Interpretations; 23rd Annual Art Auction Exhibition; Jacob Lawrence: Thirty Years of Prints (1963-1993); Beth Lo: Sabbatical Exhibition. Narrative Painting; Talking Quilts: Possibilities in Response. Jim Todd: Portraits of Printmakers; David Regan: WESTAF Fellowship Winner; Art Museum of Missoula Permanent Collection; Lucy Capehart: Interiors
Publications: Exhibit catalogs; membership newsletter; mailers & posters advertising shows
Activities: Classes for adults & children; lect open to public, 10-15 vis lectr per year; concerts; gallery talks; tours; book traveling exhibitions 3-5 per year; originate traveling exhibitions to museums in region; museum shop sells books, prints, artist made jewelry & other objects of design emphasis

M HISTORICAL MUSEUM AT FORT MISSOULA, Bldg 322, Fort Missoula, 59801. Tel 406-728-3476; FAX 406-728-5063; Elec Mail ftmslamuseum@marsweb.com. *Dir* Robert Brown; *Sr Cur* L Jane Richards; *Educ Cur* Darla Wilson
Open Memorial Day to Labor Day Mon - Sat 10 AM - 5 PM, Sun Noon - 5 PM. Admis adult $2, seniors & children $1, children under 6 free. Estab July 4, 1976 to collect and exhibit artifacts related to the history of western Montana. Changing gallery, 900 sq ft used for temporary exhibits; Meeting room gallery, 200 sq ft; Permanent gallery, 1200 sq ft. Average Annual Attendance: 40,000. Mem: 225; dues $20; quarterly meetings
Income: $200,000 (financed by mem, county appropriation & fundraising events)
Collections: Forest industry artifacts from Western Montana; Fort Missoula & the military presence in Western Montana; Missoula history
Exhibitions: Missoula: A Community Evolves; Fort Missoula, 1877-1947.
Activities: Classes for adults & children; docent training; lect open to public; 9 vis lectr per year; gallery talks; tours; awards given; book traveling exhibitions; sales shop sells books, magazines, original art

UNIVERSITY OF MONTANA
M **Gallery of Visual Arts,** School of Fine Arts, 59812. Tel 406-243-2813; *Dir* Dennis D Kern; *Admin Officer* Bryan D Spellman
Open Tues - Sat 11 AM - 3 PM. No admis fee. Estab 1981 to present faculty, student & outside exhibitions of contemporary emphasis for community interest. Gallery has 220 linear ft, 2800 sq ft; adjustable lighting. Average Annual Attendance
Exhibitions: Jeff Key & Bruce Guttin (sculpture); Bachelor of Fine Art Exhibit; MFAThesis Exhibits
Activities: Internships for gallery management; lect open to public, 1-3 vis lectr per year; gallery talks; tours; competitions; campus art awards; Thomas Wickes Award
M **Paxson Gallery,** School of Fine Arts, Performing Arts/Radio-TV Bldg, 59812. Tel 406-243-2019; *Dean* James D Kriley; *Dir* Dennis D Kern; *Admin Officer* Bryan D Spellman
Open Mon - Fri 9 AM - Noon & 1 - 4 PM. No admis fee. Estab 1985 to exhibit permanent art collection & selected traveling exhibitions. Gallery has 190 linear ft, 670 sq ft; adjustable space & lighting. Average Annual Attendance: 50,000-60,000
Collections: Autio Ceramics Collection; Dana Collection; Duncan Collection; McGill Collection; contemporary †ceramic sculpture & †paintings; historical furniture; Western genre paintings
Exhibitions: Centennial Exhibit; Ron Klien (sculpture); MFA Thesis Exhibit
Activities: Internships for collection & gallery management; lect open to public; original objects of art lent to Montana Art Gallery Directors' Association members; loans of historical objects to Montana museums; lending collection contains original prints, paintings & photographs; book traveling exhibitions 1-5 per year; originate traveling exhibitions to any museum or gallery meeting staff & security requirements

PRYOR

M **CHIEF PLENTY COUPS MUSEUM,** PO Box 100, 59066. Tel 406-252-1289; *Dir* Rich Pittsley
Open May 1 - Sept 30 daily 10 AM - 5 PM. Admis $3 per vehicle (park entrance fee includes museum). Estab 1972. Average Annual Attendance: 5000
Income: Financed by state appropriation; affiliated with Montana Fish, Wildlife & Parks
Collections: Ethnographic materials of the Crow Indians; paintings; drawings; prehistoric artifacts
Exhibitions: Crow clothing and adornment
Activities: Tours; sales shop sells books, prints, stationary notes, Crow crafts & beadwork

SIDNEY

M **MONDAK HERITAGE CENTER,** 120 Third Ave SE, PO Box 50, 59270. Tel 406-482-3500; *Exec Dir* Bert Sawyer; *Exec Dir* Marie Sawyer; *Admin Asst* Becky Dige
Open Tues - Sun 1 - 5 PM. No admis fee. Estab 1972 to preserve history of area & further interest in fine arts. Average Annual Attendance: 13,000. Mem: 300; dues $5 & up; annual meeting in Mar
Income: Financed by county appropriations, mem dues, grants & donations
Collections: J K Ralston originals; Mortensen woodcut prints
Publications: MonDak Historical & Arts Society Newsletter, 6 times yearly
Activities: Classes for adults & children; dramatic programs; docent training; lect open to public, 2 vis lectr per year; gallery talks; tours; competitions with awards; individual paintings & original objects of art lent to other museums & galleries; lending collection contains books; sales shop sells books, magazines, original art, reproductions, prints, pottery & calendars
L **Willo Ralston Library for Historical Research,** 120 Third Ave SE, PO Box 50, 59270. Tel 406-482-3500; *Exec Dir* Bert Sawyer; *Exec Dir* Marie Sawyer
Open to the pub for historical reference
Income: Financed by County Mill levy
Library Holdings: Vols 1500; Micro — Reels; Other — Clipping files, exhibition catalogs, manuscripts, memorabilia, pamphlets, photographs
Activities: Tours

NEBRASKA

AURORA

M **PLAINSMAN MUSEUM,** 210 16th, 68818. Tel 402-694-6531; *Dir* Gwen Allen; *Asst Dir* John Green
Open Apr 1 - Oct 31 Mon - Sat 9 AM - 5 PM, Sun 1 - 5 PM, Nov 1 - Mar 31 Mon - Sun 1 - 5 PM. Admis adult $4, senior citizen $3. Estab 1976 to tell the story of Plainsman using mosaics, murals, & period homes, boardwalk with many shops, other settings to add to use of artifacts. Free standing panels in area of Historical Mus (5 large folding panels). Maintains reference library. Average Annual Attendance: 15,000. Mem: 350; dues family $25, singles $10; annual meeting 2nd Thurs in Jan
Income: $60,000 (financed by mem, county allowance & individual donations)
Collections: Sidney E King Collection of murals; †Pioneer Scene Mosaic floor murals; two large murals by Ernest Ochsner; one large pen & ink mural (20 ft x 8 ft) by Larry Guyton; blacksmith artifacts; homestead; horse drawn implements; Indian collections; fossils, plains wild-life cases; machinery; military memorabilia, fire arms; music machines; player pianos & jukebox; railroad artifacts; vintage automobiles
Publications: Events Past & Upcoming, Historical Stories of County, Plainsman newsletter, 3 times yearly; Volunteer News
Activities: Lect open to public; concerts; gallery talks; tours; originate traveling exhibitions; museum shop sells books, original art, reproductions, prints, Hamilton County Bicentennial plates, postcards & note cards

CHADRON

M **CHADRON STATE COLLEGE,** Arts Gallery, 1000 Main St, 69337. Tel 308-432-6000; *Coordr* Richard Bird
Open Mon - Fri 8 AM - 5 PM. No admis fee. Estab 1967 to offer opportunities for students, faculty & local artists to present their works; to bring in shows to upgrade the cultural opportunities of students & the general pub. Main gallery has space for traveling & larger shows; little gallery suffices for small shows. Average Annual Attendance: 5000
Income: Financed by college budget & state appropriation
Exhibitions: Arts & Crafts Fair; Bosworth, Rickenbach Exhibits; Da Vinci Model Show by IBM; Edges: Hard & Soft; Faculty Art Show; Former Students Works; Hands in Clay; Greg Lafler: Ceramics & Crafts; Photographs of the Farm Security Administration; Roten Galleries: Graphics Show; National Cone Box Traveling Show; Iowa Arts & Crafts; Mathew Brady, photographs State of the Print; Student Art Show; Of Dustbowl Descent
Activities: Lect open to public; gallery talks; competitions with awards

CHAPPELL

L **CHAPPELL MEMORIAL LIBRARY AND ART GALLERY,** 289 Babcock, PO Box 248, 69129. Tel 308-874-2626; *Head Librn* Dixie Riley; *Asst Librn* Doris McFee
Open Tues - Thurs 1 - 5 PM, Tues & Thurs evening 7 - 9 PM, Sat 2 - 5 PM. No admis fee. Estab 1935 by gift of Mrs Charles H Chappell
Income: Financed by city of Chappell
Library Holdings: Vols 10,398; Per subs 31
Collections: Aaron Pyle Collection; permanent personal collection of art works from many countries, a gift from Mrs Charles H Chappell
Activities: Gallery talks; library tours

GERING

M **OREGON TRAIL MUSEUM ASSOCIATION,** Scotts Bluff National Monument, Hwy 92 W, PO Box 27, 69341. Tel 308-436-4340; FAX 308-436-7611; *Supt* Larry Reed; *Chief Ranger* Open; *Business Mgr* Jolene Kaufman; *Historian* Dean Knudsen
Open June - Sept 8 AM - 8 PM, Oct - May 8 AM - 5 PM, cl Christmas & New Year's Day. Admis $4 per vehicle. Estab 1919 to preserve & display Oregon Trail landmark, artifacts, art & natural resources. 3 exhibit rooms. Average Annual Attendance: 125,000. Mem: 75; dues $10, renewal $5
Income: Financed by sales of Oregon Trail Museum Association
Collections: Watercolors, drawings, & photographs by William H Jackson; surface finds from the Oregon Trail vicinity; paleontological specimens from within Monument boundaries
Exhibitions: 6 exhibits depicting geological, prehistoric, archaeological, ethnological history of the area; 15 exhibits depicting history of western migration from 1840-1870s; photos, drawings & paintings by W H Jackson; 2 dioramas depicting interaction between white men & buffalo
Publications: The Overland Migration; brochures & handbooks
Activities: Slide presentation of history of Oregon Trail & Scotts Bluff; Living History presentation of life on the trail; lect open to public; museum shop sells books, prints, slides, postcards

HASTINGS

M **HASTINGS MUSEUM,** 1330 N Burlington Ave, 68901. Tel 402-461-2399; FAX 402-461-2379; *Dir* Jerry Dierfeldt; *Pres Board of Trustees* O J McDougal Jr; *Cur Exhib* Burton R Nelson; *Museum Coordr* Marty Harrold; *Cur Astronomy* Dan Glonski; *Educ Coordr* Joan Janzen
Open Mon - Sat 9 AM - 5 PM, Sun 10 AM - 5 PM. Admis adults $2, children (7-15) $1, tots free. Estab 1926 for a program of service & exhibits to augment & stimulate the total educative program of schools & the general pub. Animal displays in natural habitat settings; IMAX Theater. Average Annual Attendance: 35,000. Mem: 1750; dues family $35, individual $4
Income: Financed by city appropriation
Collections: Glassware; Irma Kruse Collection; Richards Coin Collection; George W Cole Smith & Wesson Gun Collection; American Indian Artifacts
Exhibitions: People on the Plains; Natural Habitats
Publications: Yester News, monthly except July, August & Sept
Activities: Sales shop selling books & selected gift items

HOLDREGE

M **PHELPS COUNTY HISTORICAL SOCIETY,** Phelps County Museum, PO Box 164, 68949-0164. Tel 308-995-5015; *Pres* Harry Dahlstrom; *VPres* Eileen Schrock; *Treas* Robert Slater
Open Mon - Sat 10 AM - 5 PM, Sun 1 - 5 PM, cl Jan 1, July 4, Thanksgiving, Armistice Day & Christmas. No admis fee. Estab 1966 for preservation of County history & artifacts. Average Annual Attendance: 9500. Mem: 450; dues life $100, annual $5; annual meeting in May
Income: Financed by mem, county mill levy, state contributions & estate gifts
Collections: Agriculture equipment, china, furniture, historical items, photos
Publications: Centennial History of Holdrege, 1883; History of Phelps County, 1873-1980; Holdrege Centennial Coloring Book; Prisoners On The Plains; Stereoscope, quarterly
Activities: Lect open to public, 4 vis lectr per year; tours; book traveling exhibitions; sales shop sells books, labels, souvenir plates, original art
L **Library,** PO Box 164, 68949-0164. Tel 308-995-5015; *Pres* Harry D Dahlstrom; *Librn* Sandra Slater
Open Mon - Sat 10 AM - 5 PM, Sun 1 - 5 PM. Admis donations only. Estab 1966 for historic preservation & educ. Collections available for in mus research only. Average Annual Attendance: 10,000. Mem: 350; dues $5; annual meeting in May

Income: $40,000 (financed by taxes, investment earnings & contributions
Library Holdings: Vols 1000; AV — A-tapes, cassettes, Kodachromes, lantern slides, motion pictures, v-tapes; Other — Clipping files, manuscripts, pamphlets, photographs, prints
Activities: Classes for adults & children; lect open to public, 4 vis lectr per year; tours; sales shop sells books, reproductions, prints, toys, ceramics

LEXINGTON

M DAWSON COUNTY HISTORICAL SOCIETY, Museum, PO Box 369, 68850-0369. Tel 308-324-5340; *Dir* Bob Wallace; *Asst Dir* Genice Gordening; *Cur* Open
Open Mon - Sat 9 AM - 5 PM, Sun 1 - 4:30 PM. Admis $1. Estab 1958 to preserve Dawson County's heritage. Art gallery features exhibits by local artists; exhibits change monthly. Average Annual Attendance: 6000. Mem: 450; dues life $100, family $7.50, individual $5
Income: Financed by endowment, mem, grants, county appropriation
Collections: Agricultural Equipment; Furniture; Glassware; Household Implements; Textiles; Tools
Exhibitions: 1919 McCoto Aeroplane
Publications: Dawson County Banner newsletter, quarterly
Activities: Docent programs; lect open to public, 3 vis lectr per year; book traveling exhibitions 4 per yr; retail store sells books, original art, fossils

LINCOLN

A LINCOLN ARTS COUNCIL, 920 O St, 68508. Tel 402-434-2787; *Pres* Steve Clymer; *Exec Dir* Margaret Berry
Open 9 AM - 5 PM. Estab 1966 to promote & encourage the community at large & all its arts organizations to grow, develop, use all the resources available, avoid overlapping of energy, money, talent; clearing house for arts activities scheduling. Mem: 400; 60 groups; dues prorated; meetings monthly Sept-May
Income: Financed by endowment, mem, city & state appropriation, community arts fund
Publications: Arts calendar; newsletter
Activities: Originate traveling exhibitions

M NEBRASKA STATE CAPITOL, 1445 K St, 68509-4924. Tel 402-471-3191; FAX 402-471-0421; *Mgr Capitol Restoration & Promotion* Robert C Ripley; *Preservation* Thomas L Kaspar
Open Mon - Fri 8 AM - 5 PM, Sat 10 AM - 5 PM, Sun & holidays 1 - 5 PM. Stone carvings of BAS reliefs; mosaic tile vaulting & floor panels; painted & mosaic murals; vernacular architectural ornamentation. Average Annual Attendance: 100,000
Income: Financed by state appropriation & private donations
Purchases: Eight murals commissioned to complete Capitol Thematic Program
Collections: Lee Lawrie, building sculptor; Hildreth Meiere, mosaicist; muralists - Augustus V Tack, Kenneth Evett, James Penny, Elizabeth Dolan, Jean Reynal, Reinhold Marxhausen, F John Miller, Charles Clement
Publications: A Harmony of the Arts - The Nebraska State Capitol
Activities: Univ of Nebraska lect & service organization lect; retail store sells books & prints

M NEBRASKA WESLEYAN UNIVERSITY, Elder Gallery, 50th & Huntington, 68504. Tel 402-466-2371, 465-2230; FAX 402-465-2179; *Dir* Dr Donald Paolatta
Open Tues - Fri 10 AM - 4 PM, Sat & Sun 1 - 4 PM. No admis fee. Estab 1966 as a cultural addition to college & community. Average Annual Attendance: 10,000
Collections: Campus collection; †permanent collection of prints, paintings & sculpture
Exhibitions: Annual Fred Wells National Juried Exhibition; Nebraska Art Educators; faculty show; students shows; other changing monthly shows
Activities: Classes for adults

M NOYES ART GALLERY, 119 S Ninth St, 68508. Tel 402-475-1061; *Dir* Julia Noyes
Open Mon - Sat 10 AM - 5 PM, cl Sun. No admis fee. Estab 1994 as a commercial, cooperative profit organization to exhibit, promote & sell works by regional artists. Located in 100 yr old building near downtown Lincoln; main floor includes over 1200 sq ft exhibit area, office, storage & kitchen; second floor contains rented artist studios & classrooms
Income: Financed by mem, commissions on sales
Exhibitions: Monthly exhibits of gallery artists' work
Publications: Exhibit announcements, monthly
Activities: Classes for adults & children; competitions with awards

UNIVERSITY OF NEBRASKA, LINCOLN
M Sheldon Memorial Art Gallery & Sculpture Garden, 12th & R Sts, 68588-0300. Tel 402-472-2461; FAX 402-472-4258; *Dir* George W Neubert; *Cur Educ* Karen Janovy; *Cur* Daniel Siedell; *Adminr* P J Jacobs
Open Tues - Sat 10 AM - 5 PM, Thurs, Fri & Sat 7 - 9 PM, Sun 2 - 9 PM. No admis fee. Estab 1888 to exhibit the permanent collections owned by the University & to present temporary exhibitions on an annual basis. These activities are accompanied by appropriate interpretive programs. The Sheldon Gallery, a gift of Mary Frances & Bromley Sheldon, was opened in 1963 & is the work of Philip Johnson. Facilities in addition to 15,000 sq ft of exhibition galleries, include an auditorium, a print study, members room a 25 acre outdoor sculpture garden. Average Annual Attendance: 125,000
Income: Financed by endowment, state appropriation & Nebraska Art Assoc
Purchases: $200,000
Collections: †Frank M Hall Collection of contemporary paintings, sculpture, prints, drawings, photographs & ceramics; Nebraska Art Association Collection of American paintings & drawings; University Collections; Permanent collection includes more than 12,000 objects in various media
Exhibitions: (1997) Torn Notebook: The Project, Claes Oldenburg & Coosje van

Bruggen; European Master Sculptors; Wearable Art: Contemporary Artists' Jewelry; Proud Possessions: Selected Acquisitions; Irwin Kremen: Collage & Sculpture, Mark Rothko: The Spirit of Myth; Sheldon Solo: Frederick Brown & Manuel Neri
Publications: Exhibition catalogs & brochures; sculpture collection catalogue
Activities: Classes for adults, docent training; lect open to public, 4-5 vis lectr per year; gallery talks; tours; campus loan program; exten dept serves State of Nebraska; individual paintings & original objects of art lent to campus offices & other museums; originate traveling exhibitions; gift shop sells reproductions of works of original art within the permanent collection, prints, jewelry, ceramics & unique gifts

L Architecture Library, 308 Architecture Hall, 68588-0108. Tel 402-472-1208; FAX 402-472-0665; *Assoc Prof* Kay Logan-Peters
Open Mon - Thurs 8 AM - 10 PM, Fri 8 AM - 5 PM, Sat 1 - 5 PM, Sun 2 - 10 PM, summer Mon - Fri 8 AM - 5 PM. Circ 21,000
Purchases: $25,000
Library Holdings: Vols 48,000; Per subs 203; Micro — Fiche, reels; AV — A-tapes, cassettes, fs, rec, slides 30,000; Other — Clipping files, exhibition catalogs, photographs
Special Subjects: Architecture, Architecture; Community and Regional Planning
Collections: American Architectural Books (microfilm); Architecture: Urban Documents (microfiche); Fowler Collection of Early Architectural Books (microfilm); National Register of Historic Places (microfiche); Historic American Building Survey Measure & Drawings

M The Gallery of the Department of Art & Art History, 102 Richards Hall, Tenth & T Sts, 207 NC Woods Hall, 68588-0114. Tel 402-472-5541, 472-2631 (Main Art Office); FAX 402-472-9746; *Chmn & Dir* Joseph M Ruffo
Open Mon - Thurs 9 AM - 5 PM. No admis fee. Estab 1985 to exhibit contemporary art by national artists; student & faculty exhibitions. 2300 sq ft with 238 running feet of exhibition space in two spacious rooms; track lights. Average Annual Attendance: 8000
Collections: Collection of UNL Student Work from BFA & MFA degree program
Exhibitions: Undergraduate, graduate & faculty exhibitions
Publications: Exhibition catalogues

MCCOOK

M HIGH PLAINS MUSEUM, 423 Norris Ave, 69001. Tel 308-345-3661; *Chmn Board* Russell Dowling
Open Tues - Sat 1 - 5 PM, Sun 1:30 - 5 PM, cl Mon & holidays. No admis fee, donations accepted. Estab 1963 to preserve the items pertaining to local history & to interpret them for the pub. Mus is located in new building. New additions include complete pioneer kitchen; railroad section (inside & out); complete Old Time Pharmacy; 1942 Airbase; George W Norris Room; Governors From Nebraska; AM tours by appointment. Average Annual Attendance: 8000. Mem: 210; mem qualification is art display by local art club; dues $5-$200; annual meeting in Mar
Income: Financed by mem
Collections: Paintings made on the barracks walls of prisoner of war camp near McCook; paintings donated by local artists
Exhibitions: Quilt Show
Activities: Lect open to public, 8 vis lectr per year; tours; competitions; original objects of art lent; lending collection contains books, framed reproductions & motion pictures; museum shop sells books, magazines & original art; repair shop

MINDEN

M HAROLD WARP PIONEER VILLAGE FOUNDATION, PO Box 68, 68959-0068. Tel 308-832-1181; FAX 308-832-2750; WATS 800-445-4447. *Pres* Harold Warp; *Gen Mgr* Marvin Mangers
Open daily 8 AM - sundown. Admis adults $6, children 6-15 $3, children under 6 free; special group rates. Estab 1953 to preserve man's progress from 1830 to present day. Foundation includes a 90 unit motel, 350 seat restaurant & 135 site campground; Elm Creek Fort; The People's Store; Bloomington Land Office; fire house; Lowell Depot; country school; sod house; China house; church; merry-go-round; horse barn; homes & shops building; antique farm machinery building; antique tractor & 350 auto's & trucks; livery stable; agricultural building; blacksmith shop; Pony Express barn; Pony Express station; home appliance building; hobby house. Average Annual Attendance: 100,000
Collections: Airplanes; automobiles; bath tubs; bicycles; boats; clocks; fire wagons; guns; harvesters; horse drawn rigs; kitchens; lighting; locomotives; musical instruments; numismatics; paintings; plows; rare china; sculpture; street cars; telephones; threshers; toys; tractors; trucks
Publications: 500 Fasinating Facts; History of Man's Progress (1830-present); Pioneer Cookbook; Sister Clara's Letters (Over Our Hill-Past Our Place)
Activities: Classes for adults; elder hostel; lect for members only; tours; museum shop sells books, reproductions, prints & slides

NEBRASKA CITY

M GAME AND PARKS COMMISSION, Arbor Lodge State Historical Park, PO Box 15, 68410. Tel 402-873-7222; *Supt* Randall Fox; *Asst Supt* Mark Kemper
Open Apr - May Mon - Sun 11 AM - 5 PM, May - Sept Mon - Sun 9 AM - 5 PM, Sept, Oct & Nov Mon - Sun 1 - 4 PM, Dec call for hours, cl Jan & Feb. Admis adults $3, children 6-15 $1, children under 5 free. Estab 1923. Art collection of members of the J S Morton family & outdoor scenes spread through a 52 room mansion. Average Annual Attendance: 90,000
Income: Financed by state appropriation
Activities: Lect open to public; tours; awards; Arbor Day Tree plantings on last weekend in April; sales shop sells books, Arbor Day tree pins & postcards

OMAHA

M ARTISTS' COOPERATIVE GALLERY, 405 S 11th St, 68102. Tel 402-342-9617; *Pres* Pam King; *VPres* Maria Meares; *Board Dir* Dottie Seymour; *Board Dir* Alessandra Petersen; *Board Dir* Zenaide Luhr; *Board Dir* Carol Ellington; *Board Dir* Margie Schimenti
Open Wed & Thurs 11 AM - 5 PM, Fri & Sat 11 AM - 10 PM, Sun Noon - 5 PM. No admis fee. Estab 1975 to be gathering place for those interested in visual art; to display quality local, contemporary art; to offer programs, panels & discussions on related issues to the pub. Gallery contains 4000 sq ft consisting of large open area with 1 small, self-contained gallery. Average Annual Attendance: 21,000. Mem: 29; dues $300; monthly meetings
Income: $10,000
Exhibitions: Each month a different show features 2 - 4 members of the gallery with a major show. December features an all member show; exchange exhibits & special exhibits are featured by arrangement
Activities: Lect open to public, 2 vis lectr per year; concerts; gallery talks; tours; originate traveling exhibitions to other cooperative galleries

M BEMIS CENTER FOR CONTEMPORARY ARTS, New Gallery, 724 S 12th St, 68102-3202. Tel 402-341-7130; FAX 402-341-9791; *Dir* Ree Schonlau; *Dir Asst* Mimi Schneider; *Admin Asst* Cheri Lund
Open daily 11 AM - 5 PM. No admis fee. 5000 sq ft, 14 ft ceilings, cement floors, off-white walls. Maintains research library. Average Annual Attendance: 20,000
Collections: Bemis collection of international contemporary art
Publications: Swivel, newsletter
Activities: Lect open to public, 25-30 vis lectr per year; concerts; awards; educational programs; art leasing program

M CREIGHTON UNIVERSITY, Fine Arts Gallery, 2500 California Plaza, 68178. Tel 402-280-2509, Ext 2831; FAX 402-280-2320; *Dir* G Ted Bohr; *Chmn Fine & Performing Arts Dept* Roger Aikin
Open Mon - Sun Noon - 4 PM. Mus estab 1973. Gallery handles 8 exhibits per academic year; space provided for student thesis exhibits; 150 running ft. Average Annual Attendance: 2000
Income: $6600 (financed by school's general funding)
Collections: Ceramics; drawings; graphics; paintings; photography; pottery & sculpture; printmaking
Exhibitions: Bonnie Manriquez & Nancy Samotis (painting); John Thein (painted glass); Senior Thesis Exhibits; Creighton University Faculty Exhibit; Chris Weaver (sculpture); Student Juried Exhibit
Activities: Lect open to public

M JOSLYN ART MUSEUM, 2200 Dodge St, 68102. Tel 402-342-3300; FAX 402-342-2376; Elec Mail info@joslyn.org. *Dir* John Schloder; *Deputy Dir* Audrey Kauders; *Chief Cur, Cur Material Culture* Marsha V Gallagher; *Dir Marketing & Public Relations* Linda Rejcevich; *Assoc Cur 20th Century Art* Janet Farber; *Coll & Exhib Mgr* Theodore James; *Museum Shop Mgr* Martha Lattie; *Assoc Cur European Art* Claudia Einecke; *Art Librn* Kathryn Corcoran
Open Tues - Sat 10 AM - 5 PM, Thurs 10 AM - 8 PM, Sun Noon - 5 PM, cl Mon & holidays. Admis adults $4, children under 12 & senior citizens $2, Sat AM free, members free. Estab in 1931 as a cultural center for the community. Joslyn houses works from antiquity to the present, with a special emphasis on 19th & 20th century European & American art. In addition to the art galleries, there is the 1200 seat Witherspoon Concert Hall, the 200 seat Lecture Hall, Members Room & the Storz Fountain Court. Mus was a gift of Mrs Sarah H Joslyn in memory of her husband, George A Joslyn. Mus is a marble building covering a two-block area; contains large galleries with small exhibit areas surrounding the large central Storz Fountain Court & 1200-seat Witherspoon Concert HHll on the main floor. The concert hall is used for programs by major community music & cultural organizations. The ground floor includes exhibit areas, library, classroom, lecture hall, museum shop & office. Average Annual Attendance: 130,000. Mem: 7000; dues $17.50-$40
Collections: †Ancient through modern art, including European & American paintings, sculpture, graphics; †Art of the Western Frontier; †Native American art
Exhibitions: Temporary exhibitions include traveling shows of national significance; Joslyn-organized shows; one-person & group shows in all media; Midlands Invitational
Publications: Members calendar, bi-monthly; exhibition catalogs; art books
Activities: Creative & art appreciation classes for adults & children (pre-school through high school); special workshops; film programs; special tour program of permanent collections & special exhibitions maintained for public school children; lect & exhibition gallery talks; tours of the collections & special exhibitions; museum shop sells books, magazines, reproductions, slides, cards, collectibles, posters & gifts
L Art Reference Library, 2200 Dodge St, 68102. Tel 402-342-3300; FAX 402-342-2376; Elec Mail kcorcora@joslyn.org. *Reference Librn* Janice Bolte
Open Tues - Sat 10 AM - 5 PM. Estab 1931 for research only
Library Holdings: Vols 27,000; Per subs 100; Vertical files 150; Micro — Fiche, reels; AV — Slides 24,500; Other — Clipping files, exhibition catalogs, pamphlets
Special Subjects: Afro-American Art, American Indian Art, Anthropology, Decorative Arts, Etchings & Engravings, Folk Art, Landscapes, Latin American Art, Painting - American, Painting - European, Painting - Flemish, Painting - French, Painting - German, Painting - Italian, Painting - Spanish, American West History, 19th & 20th Century European & American Art

M OMAHA CHILDRENS MUSEUM, INC, 500 S 20th St, 68102. Tel 402-342-6164; FAX 402-342-6165; *Dir* Elizabeth Brownrigg; *Finance Mgr* Jim O'Conner; *Marketing, Publications Coordr* Renee Buroker; *Cur Science Educ* Martin Fisher; *Cur Arts, Humanities Educ* Tom Arndorter; *Visitor Services Mgr* Andy Fenoglio; *Fund Develop Mgr* Karen Doerr
Open Tues - Sat 10 AM - 5 PM, Sun 1 - 5 PM, cl Mon. Admis $4. Estab 1977 to provide high-quality participation & educational experiences in the arts, humanities & science. Average Annual Attendance: 100,000. Mem: 2500 families; dues $40

Income: Financed by mem, admis, grants, donations from individuals, foundations & corporations
Exhibitions: Hands-on exhibits which promote learning in the arts, science & humanities; traveling exhibits; workshops by local professional educators & artists
Publications: Bimonthly calendar; museum newsletter, quarterly
Activities: Classes for children; summer camp; exten dept serves local metro area; book traveling exhibitions 1 per year; museum shop sells books, educational games & toys

M UNION PACIFIC RAILROAD, Historical Museum, 1416 Dodge St, 68179. Tel 402-271-3530; FAX 402-271-5572; *Museum Dir* Donald Snoddy
Open Mon - Fri 9 AM - 3 PM, Sat 9 AM - Noon, cl major holidays

M UNIVERSITY OF NEBRASKA AT OMAHA, Art Gallery, Fine Arts Bldg, Rm 137, 68182-0012. Tel 402-554-2796; *Dir* Nancy Kelly
Open Mon - Fri 10 AM - 4:30 PM, Sat 1 - 4 PM. No admis fee. Estab 1967 to heighten cultural & aesthetic awareness of the metropolitan & midlands area. Average Annual Attendance: 14,000
Income: Financed by state appropriation
Purchases: $5000
Collections: University Visiting Printmaker's Collection
Exhibitions: Wayne Kimball, lithographs; Dennis Guastella, paintings; Juergen Strunck, relief prints; Drawings: Terry Allen, Power Boothe, Harold Boyd, Ann Karlsen, Fran Noel & Jim Roche
Publications: Exhibition catalogs
Activities: Lect open to public, 2 vis lectr per year; gallery talks; tours; competitions; scholarships

SEWARD

M CONCORDIA COLLEGE, Marx Hausen Art Gallery, 800 N Columbia Ave, 68434. Tel 402-643-3651, Ext 7435; *Dir* Lynn Soloway
Open weekdays 8 AM - 5 PM, Sun 2 - 5 PM. No admis fee. Estab 1959 to provide the college & community with a wide variety of original art; both monthly exhibitions & permanent collection serve primarily an educational need; spacious gallery has additional showcases
Collections: Ceramics; †Contemporary Original Prints
Exhibitions: Wood: A Common Material; Nebraska Places & Spaces; 1 & 2 artists exhibitions; shows drawn from Permanent Collection & Annual Student Exhibitions; The Art of Cartoons; Animal Show; The Computer & its Influence on Art & Design: Part II; Contemporary Artists Christian Themes; The Human Image (from the permanent collection)
Activities: Gallery talks; original objects of art lent; lending collection of framed reproductions, original prints & paintings; book traveling exhibitions, 6 per year

WAYNE

M WAYNE STATE COLLEGE, Nordstrand Visual Arts Gallery, Fine Arts Div, 1111 Main St, 68787. Tel 402-375-7000; FAX 402-375-7204; *Division Chmn of Fine Arts* Dr Jay O'Leary
Open Mon - Fri 9 AM - 5 PM. No admis fee. Estab Jan 1977 to provide art students with a space to display work; to enhance student's educ by viewing incoming regional professional work; to enrich cultural atmosphere of college & community. Small gallery, carpeted floors & walls, ceiling spotlights on tracts. Average Annual Attendance: 800
Income: Financed by city & state appropriation, as well as Wayne State Foundation
Collections: †Wayne State Foundation Print Collection
Activities: Lect open to public, 1-2 vis lectr per year; competitions

WILBER

M WILBER CZECH MUSEUM, 321 S Harris, PO Box 253, 68465. Tel 402-821-2485 (AM), 821-2183 (PM); *Pres* Irma Ourecky
Open daily 1 - 4 PM & by appointment, cl holidays. No admis fee. Estab 1962 to preserve Czech culture & artifacts. Average Annual Attendance: 4000. Mem: annual meeting in Dec
Income: Financed by donations & shop sales
Collections: Model rooms of homes & businesses of pioneer days
Activities: Tours for adult & school groups; sales shop sells books, quilted items, Czech crystal & crafts

NEVADA

ELKO

M NORTHEASTERN NEVADA HISTORICAL SOCIETY MUSEUM, 1515 Idaho St, 89801. Tel 702-738-3418; *Dir* Lisa Seymour
Open Mon - Sat 9 AM - 5 PM, Sun 1 - 5 PM. No admis fee; admis charge for theatre program. Estab 1968; general mus concentrating on Northeastern Nevada; also area cultural center. Gallery is 4000 sq ft, 12 exhibits per year local, state, regional & national artists. Average Annual Attendance: 100,000. Mem: 1300; dues $10-$1000; annual meeting date varies
Income: $18,000 (financed by grants, contributions, dues, sales shop & memorials)
Collections: History; Pre-Hsitory; Natural History; Art
Exhibitions: Annual statewide touring photography exhibitions; sound slide show - Nevada subjects
Publications: Historical, quarterly; Northeastern Nevada Historical Society Quarterly

Activities: Classes for children; docent training; lect open to public, 15 vis lectr per year; concerts; gallery talks; tours; photography competitions with awards; Nevada photography exhibit tours to 13 Nevada communities; exten dept serving Nevada; lending collection of 35 film strips, 4000 slides (complete programs); 5000 photographs; 1700 books & 12 cassettes; originate traveling exhibitions; museum shop sales books, magazines, prints, & local craft items

L **Library,** 1515 Idaho St, 89801. Tel 702-738-3418; *Dir* Lisa Seymour
Open Mon - Sat 9 AM - 5 PM, Sun 1 - 5 PM. Rotating art exhibits, two local artists display at all times
Income: $5000 (financed by contributions, dues, sales shop, memorials)
Library Holdings: Vols 5000; Per subs 10; AV — A-tapes, cassettes, fs, slides, v-tapes; Other — Clipping files, exhibition catalogs, framed reproductions, manuscripts, memorabilia, original art works, pamphlets, photographs 25,000, prints, reproductions
Special Subjects: American Indian Art, American Western Art, Film, Flasks & Bottles, Folk Art, Historical Material, History of Art & Archaeology, Period Rooms, Southwestern Art, Theatre Arts, Video, Concentration on Northeastern Nevada History
Collections: Newspaper and negative files
Publications: Quarterly historical publication

LAS VEGAS

M **LAS VEGAS ART MUSEUM,** 9600 W Sierra Ave, 89117. Tel 702-259-4458; FAX 702-259-8464; *Dir* Sharon King; *Dir* Joseph Palermo; *Cur* James Mann
Open Tues - Sat 10 AM - 5 PM, Wed evening 5 - 9 PM, Sun 1 - 5 PM. Admis adults $5, senior citizens $3, children & students $1, members free. Estab 1950 to offer fine arts to the community of Las Vegas; to offer artists a place to show, work & study; to offer good educ in fine arts to adults & children of the community. Three galleries that change monthly. Average Annual Attendance: 9000. Mem: 500; dues benefactor $50,000, patron $500, family $50, individual $40, student & seniors $25; meetings third Thurs each month
Income: Financed by mem, donation & commissions on sales gift shop
Collections: Contemporary artists
Exhibitions: State & County Art Show; local & international exhibits; National Finals Art Show
Publications: The Art Beat Newsletter, monthly; Monthly bulletin
Activities: Classes for adults presented by leading artists & craftsmen; museum sponsors classes for youths; self-help workshops; docent training; competitions; museum shop sells exhibit catalogs, fine-art prints, posters, slides, postcards & gifts; junior museum

L **LAS VEGAS-CLARK COUNTY LIBRARY DISTRICT,** 4101 E Flamingo Rd, 89119. Tel 702-733-7810; 382-3493; *Dir* Darrell Batson; *Asst Dir* Gene Nelson; *Extension Serv* Ann Langevin; *Branch Adminr* Beryl Andrus; *Branch Adminr* Sally Feldman; *Branch Adminr* Darrell Batson; *Branch Adminr* Jane Lorance; *Bus Serv* Irene Voit; *Library Develop* Stan Colton
Open Mon - Thurs 9 AM - 9 PM, Fri & Sat 9 AM - 5 PM, Sun 1 - 5 PM. Estab 1965 to provide informaton in all its varieties of form to people of all ages; nine branch libraries, including three art galleries. Galleries provide regularly rotating art exhibitions of regional & national repute as well as ten solo shows a year, & a regional mixed media competition every spring. Circ 1,770,951
Income: $5,500,000 (financed by state & county appropriation)
Purchases: $700,000
Library Holdings: Per subs 586; Micro — Fiche, reels; AV — A-tapes, cassettes, fs, motion pictures, rec; Other — Clipping files, framed reproductions, original art works, pamphlets, photographs, prints, reproductions, sculpture
Collections: Model ship collection; †Nevada materials
Exhibitions: Art-a-Fair; Nevada Watercolor Society; All Aboard: Railroads, Memorabilia; Neon: Smithsonian Exhibition; Expressions in Fiber; Graham & Breedlove; Sand & Water; Dottie Burton; Woodworks: Christian Brisepierre & Jack Daseler; KNPR Craftworks; It's a Small, Small World: Dollhouses, Kimberly House
Publications: Exhibition brochures, monthly; library program, bimonthly
Activities: Lect open to public; concerts; tours; competitions with awards; exten dept & regional servs dept serving the area; individual paintings & original objects of art lent; book traveling exhibitions; originate traveling exhibitions; used book store sells books, magazines, original art & handcrafts

M **Flamingo Gallery,** 4101 E Flamingo Rd, 89119. Tel 702-733-7810; FAX 702-732-7271; *District Gallery Mgr* Denise Shapiro
Open Mon - Thurs 9 AM - 9 PM, Fri 9 AM - 5 PM, Sat 9 AM - 5 PM, Sun 1 - 5 PM. Estab 1970. Gallery is located in Clark County Library, main gallery has 80 running ft of exhibit space, upstairs gallery is used for photographic displays. Average Annual Attendance: 36,000-40,000. Mem: 500; dues $15, annual meeting in summer
Income: Financed by tax support, federal & state grants
Exhibitions: Art-A-Fair (judged and juried); Spirit Impressions; The Potter & the Weaver; Nevada Watercolor Society Annual exhibit
Publications: Bi-monthly library calendar of events
Activities: Classes for adults & children; dramatic programs; string quartet; feature films; lect open to public, 10 vis lectr per year; concerts; Art-A-Fair competition; monetary awards

M **UNIVERSITY OF NEVADA, LAS VEGAS,** Donna Beam Fine Art Gallery, 4505 Maryland Pky, 89154-5002. Tel 702-895-3893; FAX 702-895-4346; *Dir* Jerry Schefcik
Open yr-round Mon - Fri 9 AM - 5 PM; cl holidays. No admis fee. Estab 1968. Gallery measures 1400 sq ft, 175 linear ft with track lighting. Average Annual Attendance: 10,000
Income: Financed by mem & appropriation
Collections: †Ceramics; †Paintings; †Prints; †Sculpture
Exhibitions: Karen Carson (drawings & paintings); Scott Grieger (mixed media); Jim Shaw (drawings)
Activities: Classes for adults & children; dramatic programs; lect open to public, 4 vis lectr per year; gallery talks; tours; student-juried competitions; awards given for student work; individual painting & original objects of art lent; lending collection includes 150 original art works; book traveling exhibitions 1 per year; originate traveling exhibitions to other universities & galleries

RENO

M **NEVADA MUSEUM OF ART,** 160 W Liberty St, 89501. Tel 702-329-3333; FAX 702-329-1541; *Pres* Nancy Fennell; *Prog Cur* Laurie Macfee; *Development Officer* Jenny Rudy; *Public Relations Officer* Amy Oppio; *Exec Dir* Steven S High; *Cur* Howard DaLee Spencer; *Cur Educ* Wendy Thomas Felling; *ARTLINKS Coordr* Leslie Dandois
Open Tues - Sat 10 AM - 4 PM, Sun 12 - 4 PM. Admis adult $3, senior citizens $1.50, children $.50, free admis Fri. Estab 1931 to collect, conserve & exhibit 19th & 20th century American art with an emphasis on artwork which articulates our interaction with the land & environment. The collections are divided into five focus areas including a contemporary collection & altered landscape collection. The facility is a 15,000 sq ft state of the art building which holds three exhibitions simultaneously. Average Annual Attendance: 45,000. Mem: 1200; dues corporation $250, family $35; annual meeting in Apr
Income: Financed by endowment, mem, federal & private foundation grants, individual grants & earned income
Collections: †E L Wiegand Art Collection (emphasis on the American work ethic); †Altered Landscape Collection (photography); †Contemporary collection; Historical Collection; Sierra Nevada Collection
Exhibitions: Robert Beckmann: The Body of a House; California Impressionist Paintings; Ingrid Evans: Paper Sculpture; Roger Shimomura: Paintings
Publications: Annual Bulletin; brochures; catalogues; calendar newsletter, quarterly; postcards for events, twice a month
Activities: Classes for adults & children; dramatic programs; hands on exhibits; lect open to the public, 20 vis lectr per year; gallery talks; tours; concerts; outreach services to schools, senior citizens & other community groups in Greater Reno-Carson-Tahoe area; exchange program with other museums; originate traveling exhibitions; museum shop sells books, original art & reproductions

L **Art Library,** 160 W Liberty St, 89501. Tel 702-329-3333; FAX 702-329-1541; *Exec Dir* Steven High; *Cur Educ & Assoc Dir* Wendy Felling
Open Tues - Sat 10 AM - 4 PM, Sun Noon - 4 PM & by appointment. Admis adults $3, students & seniors $1.50, children 6-12 yrs $.50, members & under 6 yrs free; free admis on Fri. Estab 1931
Library Holdings: Vols 1400; Per subs 6; Other — Clipping files, exhibition catalogs, manuscripts, memorabilia, pamphlets, photographs, reproductions
Special Subjects: Advertising Design, Aesthetics, Afro-American Art, American Indian Art, American Western Art, Anthropology, Antiquities-Byzantine, Antiquities-Egyptian, Antiquities-Etruscan, Antiquities-Greek, Antiquities-Oriental, Antiquities-Roman, Archaeology, Architecture, Art Education, Papermaking

A **SIERRA ARTS FOUNDATION,** 200 Flint St, 89501. Tel 702-329-1324; FAX 702-329-1328; *Pres* Brad Van Woert; *VPres* Robin Holabind; *Exec Dir* Patricia Smith; *Prog Dir* Jill Cordi; *Services Dir* Christine Ohr
Open Mon - Fri 8:30 AM - 5 PM. No admis fee. Estab 1971 as a non-profit, private community arts agency, advocates for & supports the arts. Mem: 800; dues $20-$10,000 & up; annual meeting in May
Income: Financed by endowment, corporate & individual mem, grants & fund raising activities
Exhibitions: 6-week exhibitions of contemporary artworks throughout the year
Publications: Art Resource Guide; Artist Registry, current list of culture organizations, facilities list & media list; Encore, monthly community arts magazine; Master Calendar; Services Booklet
Activities: Classes for children in elementary school; classes for at-risk youths in local detention facility shelter for run-away kids & alternative high school; concerts; competitions; grants offered; exten dept; Endowment Income Grants Program for local individual artists; museum shop sells original art on consignment

M **UNIVERSITY OF NEVADA,** Sheppard Fine Art Gallery, Church Fine Arts Bldg, Art Dept, Mail Stop 224, 89557. Tel 702-784-6682; FAX 702-784-6655; *Dir & Cur* Suzanne Kanatsiz; *Art Dept Chmn* Edward Martinez; *Asst* Sandra Ward
Open Mon - Fri 9 AM - 5 PM, cl Sat, Sun & holidays. No admis fee. Estab 1960. University Art Gallery has 1800 sq ft finished exhibition space. Average Annual Attendance: 15,000-24,000
Income: $10,000
Exhibitions: Annual Student Exhibition
Activities: Lect open to public, 360 vis lectr per year; gallery talks; tours; competitions with awards

NEW HAMPSHIRE

BOSCAWEN

A **NEW HAMPSHIRE ART ASSOCIATION, INC,** PO Box 3096, 03303. Tel 603-796-6414, 431-4230; *Admin* Angus Locke
Estab 1940, incorporated 1962, as a non-profit organization, to promote the public's understanding & appreciation of the arts; to provide artists with a forum for their work & ideas. If offers a year-round exhibition & sales gallery at its headquarters in Boscawen & Portsmith; an August exhibition at Sunapee State Park. Mem: 400; dues $60; annual meeting in June
Income: Financed by grants, dues, patrons, rental art & sales
Exhibitions: Annuals at Currier Gallery of Art; Summer Annual combined with New Hampshire League of Arts & Crafts at Mount Sunapee State Park; Summer Annual Juried Exhibition at Prescott Park; Year-Round exhibits at N E Center; Durham NH; various one-person & group shows
Activities: Educ program for schools; patron program; lect demonstrations by member artists; awards; originate traveling exhibitions

CENTER SANDWICH

M **SANDWICH HISTORICAL SOCIETY,** 4 Maple St, 03227. Tel 603-284-6269; *Dir & Cur* Robin Dustin
Open June - Sept Tues - Sat 11 AM - 5 PM. Admis donations accepted. Estab 1917
Collections: Paintings by Albert Gallatin Hoit (oil & water); Paintings by E Wood Perry (oil)
Publications: Annual Excursion Bulletin 1920, annually; Newsletter, 4 per year

CONCORD

A **LEAGUE OF NEW HAMPSHIRE CRAFTSMEN,** League Gallery, 205 N Main St, 03301. Tel 603-224-1471; FAX 603-225-8452; *Dir* Carl Richardson
Open Mon - Fri 9 AM - 5 PM. Estab 1932 to encourage the economic development & educ of the crafts; gallery displaying exhibits of members' works. Average Annual Attendance: 5000. Mem: 3000; dues $20-individual; annual meeting in Oct
Exhibitions: Annual Craftsmen's Fair; Living with Crafts; Annual Juried Exhibit
Publications: Newsletter, quarterly
Activities: Classes for adults;; exhibits; competitions with awards; lending collection of books
L **Library,** 205 N Main St, 03301. Tel 603-224-1471; FAX 603-225-8452; *Dir* Carl Richardson
Open to members
Income: Financed by league operating funds
Library Holdings: Vols 1100; Per subs 30; AV — Cassettes
Special Subjects: Crafts, Marketing Crafts

A **NEW HAMPSHIRE HISTORICAL SOCIETY,** 30 Park St, 03301. Tel 603-225-3381; FAX 603-224-0463; *Pres* Hiliary P Clevand; *Dir* John Frisbee; *Cur* Donna Bell-Garvin; *Librn* William Copeley
Open Mon - Fri 9 AM - 4:30 PM, Sat & Sun Noon - 4:30 PM. Admis $2 donation suggested. Estab 1823 to collect, preserve & make available books, manuscripts & artifacts pertaining to the history of New Hampshire; art gallery maintained. Exhibition gallery maintained. Average Annual Attendance: 20,000. Mem: 3000; dues family $50, active $30; annual meeting first Sat in Apr
Income: $700,000 (financed by endowment, mem, grants & sales)
Purchases: $20,000
Collections: †Artifacts made or used in New Hampshire including collections of †glass, †furniture, †metals, †paintings, †silver and †textiles; †Fine and Decorative Arts; †Historical Memorabilia
Exhibitions: Highways & Hotels: On the Road in New Hampshire. At What Cost: Land use in NH
Publications: Historical New Hampshire, quarterly; annual report; exhibition catalogues; bi-monthly newsletter
Activities: Classes for adults & children; docent training; lect open to public, 4 vis per year; programs & tours for children; gallery talks; bus tours; museum shop sells books, reproductions, prints
L **Library,** 30 Park St, 03301. Tel 603-225-3381; FAX 603-224-0463; *Librn* William Copeley
Admis $5 per day. Reference library only
Library Holdings: Vols 50,000; Per subs 150; Newspapers; Micro — Reels; AV — A-tapes, cassettes, motion pictures, rec, slides, v-tapes; Other — Exhibition catalogs, manuscripts, memorabilia, original art works, pamphlets, photographs, prints
Special Subjects: Bookplates & Bindings, Manuscripts, Maps, Photography, New Hampshire History
Collections: †History & genealogy of New Hampshire & New England

M **SAINT PAUL'S SCHOOL,** Art Center in Hargate, 325 Pleasant St, 03301. Tel 603-225-3341, Ext 258; FAX 603-225-8491; *Dir Art Center* Karen Burgess Smith; *Gallery Asst* Carol Shelton
Open Tues - Sat 10 AM - 4:30 PM, during school year. Estab 1967 to house the Art Department of St Paul's School, to provide a cultural center for the school community as well as central New Hampshire. Secure gallery, 50 X 40 ft. Average Annual Attendance: 10,000
Income: Financed by endowment
Collections: Collection represents varied periods & nationlities, chiefly gifts to the school, drawings, graphics, painting & sculpture
Exhibitions: Winnie Owens-Hart, Ceramic Works: Helena Chapellin-Wilson, Gum bichromate Images; Works on Paper; Yoshiaki Shimizu; Joyce Tenneson
Activities: Lect & classes for students & school community only; Gallery receptions & lect open to the public; tours; original objects of art lent to qualifying institutions
L **Ohrstrom Library,** 325 Pleasant St, 03301. Tel 603-229-4860; FAX 603-229-4888; *Librn* Robert H Rettew
Estab 1967 for art reference only. Circ 600
Income: $1000
Purchases: Approx $1000
Library Holdings: Vols 50,000; Per subs 150; AV — Slides; Other — Exhibition catalogs, reproductions

CORNISH

M **SAINT-GAUDENS NATIONAL HISTORIC SITE,** New Hampshire Route 12A (Mailing add: RR 3, PO Box 73, 03745). Tel 603-675-2175; FAX 603-675-2701;
Internet Home Page Address wwwnps.gov/saga. *Supt & Cur* John H Dryfhout
Open daily 8:30 AM - 4:30 PM (end of May - Oct 31). Admis 16 & over $.50. Estab 1926, transferred to Federal Government (National Park Service) in 1965 to commemorate the home, studios & works of Augustus Saint-Gaudens (1848-1907), one of America's foremost sculptors. The site has historically (1907) furnished rooms, studios & gardens displaying approximately half of the work of Augustus Saint-Gaudens. Average Annual Attendance: 40,000

Income: Financed by federal appropriation (National Park Service)
Purchases: Works by Augustus Saint Gaudens; original furnishings of the Cornish Property
Collections: Historic furnishings & sculpture; plaster, bronze & marble works by Augustus; Saint Gaudens
Exhibitions: (1997) The Shaw Memorial: 54 Massachusetts Regiment of African American Volunteers
Publications: Brochures
Activities: Individual paintings & original objects of art lent to museums & societies; sales shop sells books, slides & souvenir items
L **Library,** New Hampshire Rte 12A (Mailing add: RR 3, PO Box 73, 03745). Tel 603-675-2175; FAX 603-675-2701; *Cur* John H Dryfhout
Open for reference
Library Holdings: Vols 100
Special Subjects: 19th and early 20th Century American art

DURHAM

M **UNIVERSITY OF NEW HAMPSHIRE,** The Art Gallery, Paul Creative Arts Ctr, 30 College Rd, 03824-3538. Tel 603-862-3712, 3713 (outreach); FAX 603-862-2191; *Dir* Vicki C Wright; *Asst Dir* Anne Goslin; *Educ Coordr* Helen K Reid
Open Mon - Wed 10 AM - 4 PM, Thurs 10 AM - 8 PM, Sat & Sun 1 - 5 PM, cl Fri, University holidays & June - Aug. No admis fee. Estab 1960 renovated 1973, teaching collection for university faculty & students outreach & pub service functions for the non-university community. Upper mezzanine & lower level galleries with a total of 3800 ft of exhibition space; 900 ft storage room to house permanent collection & temporary loans; additional storage & office space. Average Annual Attendance: 12,000. Mem: 200
Collections: 19th century American landscapes, 19th century Japanese prints & 20th century works on paper
Exhibitions: Temporary exhibitions; the Art Gallery features exhibitions from Sept through May each year
Publications: Exhibition catalogs
Activities: Educational program for area schools; workshops; docent training; lect open to public, 8-10 vis lectr per year; concerts; gallery talks; tours; fels offered; original works of art lent to other qualified museums for exhibitions; lending collection contains slides & video tapes; book traveling exhibitions 1-3 per year; originate traveling exhibitions; sales shop sells books, magazines & note cards
L **Dept of the Arts Slide Library,** Paul Creative Arts Ctr, 03824. Tel 603-862-1366; FAX 603-862-2191; *Slide Librn* Barbara Steinberg
Estab as a teaching collection for the university. Slides do not circulate off-campus
Library Holdings: AV — Slides 132,000
Special Subjects: Western art

EXETER

M **PHILLIPS EXETER ACADEMY,** Frederic R Mayer Art Center & Lamont Gallery, Front St & Tan Lane, 03833. Tel 603-772-4311, Ext 324; *Interim Dir* Barbara R Jenny; *Principal* Kendra O'Donnell; *Asst* Tadaye Nishimura
Open Mon - Sat 9 AM - 5 PM, Wed 9 AM - 1 PM & Sun by appointment. No admis fee. Estab 1953 to provide an Art Center & studios for art instruction dedicated to the memory of Thomas William Lamont II, lost in action in 1945. Four bays with moveable walls to alter number & size of bays, sky lit with sol-r-veil screen
Activities: Classes for Academy students; dramatic programs; lect open to public, 4 vis lectr per year; gallery talks; scholarships offered; lending collection contains color reproductions, framed reproductions, original art works, original prints paintings & sculpture; book traveling exhibitions 1 - 2 per year

HANOVER

M **DARTMOUTH COLLEGE,** Hood Museum of Art, 03755. Tel 603-646-2808; FAX 603-646-1400; *Dir* Timothy Rub; *Assoc Dir* Suzanne Gandell; *Sr Cur Ethnographic Art* Tamara Northern; *Cur European Art* Richard Rand; *Cur Exhib* Evelyn Marcus; *Cur American Art* Barbara MacAdam; *Registrar* Kellen Haak; *Financial Mgr* Nancy McLain; *Assoc Registrar* Kathleen O'Malley; *Asst Registrar* Cynthia Gilliland; *Cur Educ* Lesley Wellman; *Cur Academic Progs* Katherine Hart; *Museum Educator* Anne Marie Manning; *Exhib Coordr* Juliette Bianco; *Public Relations Coordr* Christine Crabb; *School & Community Outreach Coordr* Vivian Ladd; *School & Community Outreach Asst* Samantha Hightower; *Tour Coordr* Joan Monroe; *Chief Preparator* Nicolas Nobili; *Asst Cur* Kelly Pask; *Bus Mgr* Theresa Delemare; *Admin Asst to Dir* Mary McKenna
Open Tues - Sat 10 AM - 5 PM, Sun Noon - 5 PM, Wed evening until 9 PM. No admis fee. Estab 1772 to serve the Dartmouth community & Upper Valley region. New building, designed by Charles Moore & Chad Floyd of Centerbrook, completed in 1985, houses ten galleries. Average Annual Attendance: 70,000. Mem: 2100; dues $30 - $1000; annual meeting in July
Income: Financed through Dartmouth College, endowment income, contributions & grants
Collections: The Hood Museum has about 24,000 fine art objects & about 28,000 historical anthropological objects; especially strong in areas such as 19th & 20th century American art, 17th century paintings & European & American prints; also has a survey of Native American, African, Asian & Pre-Columbian artifacts
Exhibitions: Approximately fifteen temporary exhibitions per year on a wide range of subjects. Exhibitions include those organized by the museum, traveling exhibitions & exhibitions drawn from permanent collections
Publications: Museum catalogues, annually
Activities: Classes for adults & children; docent training; lect open to public, 8-10 vis lectr per year; gallery talks; tours; awards; individual paintings & original objects of art lent to other museums & campus depts; book traveling exhibitions 1-2 per year; museum shop sells books, cards, posters & jewelry

L Sherman Art Library, 6033 Carpenter Hall, 03755-3570. Tel 603-646-2305; FAX 603-646-1218; *Librn* Barbara E Reed
Open Mon - Thurs 8 AM - 12 PM, Fri 8 AM - 6 PM, Sat 9 AM - 6 PM, Sun 1 - 12 PM, during school terms (reduced hours in summer & during intersessions). Estab 1928
Library Holdings: Vols 90,000; Per subs 500; Videodiscs; Micro — Cards 328, fiche 100,000, prints 1529, reels 111; Other — Exhibition catalogs, pamphlets
Special Subjects: Architecture, Photography

HOPKINTON

M NEW HAMPSHIRE ANTIQUARIAN SOCIETY, 300 Main St, 03229. Tel 603-746-3825; *Exec Dir* Caroline Yoder
Open Thurs & Fri 10 AM - 5 PM, Sat 10 AM - 2 PM. No admis fee. Estab 1875 to preserve local & state historical & genealogical records & collections, & to provide the community with cultural & historical programs of local significance. Gallery houses primative portraits of local citizens by itinerant artists. Average Annual Attendance: 2000. Mem: 425; dues $15-$200
Income: $7000
Collections: Early American furniture, clothing, china, portraits; local historical material
Exhibitions: 18th-20th century local handicrafts
Activities: Children's classes; docent training; lect open to public

KEENE

M HISTORICAL SOCIETY OF CHESHIRE COUNTY, Archive Center of the Society, 246 Main St, PO Box 803, 03431. Tel 603-352-1895; *Dir* Alan Rumrill, MLS
Open Mon - Fri 9 AM - 4 PM. Estab 1927 as a reference library. Average Annual Attendance: 7000. Mem: 700; dues $15-$100; annual meeting fourth Mon in Apr
Income: $3000 (financed by endowment & mem)
Purchases: $1000
Publications: Newsletter, 5 times annually
Activities: Lect open to public, 8 vis lectr per year; tours; book traveling exhibitions 1-2 per year; museum shop sells books & reproductions

M KEENE STATE COLLEGE, Thorne-Sagendorph Art Gallery, Wyman Way, 03435-3501. Tel 603-352-1909, Ext 382, 358-2720; *Dir* Maureen Ahearn
Open Sept - May Mon - Fri Noon - 4 PM, Wed evenings 6 - 8 PM, June - Aug Mon - Thurs 9 AM - 3 PM. No admis fee. Estab 1965 to provide a year-round calendar of continuing exhibitions; to sponsor related programs of artistic & educational interest & to maintain small permanent collection displayed on campus. Two adjacent galleries occupy space in a wing of Mason Library on campus. Average Annual Attendance: 9000. Mem: 400; dues $10
Income: Financed by endowment, state appropriation & annual college budget
Collections: Paintings & Prints of Historical Interest included: Pierre Alechinsky; Milton Avery; Chuck Close; Robert Mapplethorpe; Paul Pollero; Gregorio Prestopino; George Rickey; Sidney Twardowicz Artists of National Prominence; Paintings by Regional Artists
Exhibitions: New Art/New Hampshire IV
Publications: Small catalogs or brochures to accompany exhibitions
Activities: Lect open to public; concerts; gallery talks; competitions; individual paintings lent to departments on campus, other museums & galleries; lending collection consists of original prints, paintings & sculpture; book traveling exhibitions; originate traveling exhibitions; sales shop sells catalogues

MANCHESTER

M THE CURRIER GALLERY OF ART, 201 Myrtle Way, 03104. Tel 603-669-6144; FAX 603-669-7194; *Dir* Susan Stryklin; *Pres* Kimon S Zachos; *VPres* John Swope; *Treas* James R Griswold; *Clerk* Mrs Norman F Milne; *Marketing & Public Relations* Kathleen Williams; *Mgr Museum Progs* Virginia H Eshoo; *Dir Educ* Britt Sten Zunita; *Cur* P Andrew Spahr; *Dir Develop* Tina Andrad; *Deputy Dir* Susan Leidy
Open Mon, Wed, Thurs, Sat & Sun 11 AM - 5 PM, Fri 11 AM - 9 PM, cl Tues. Admis adults $4, senior citizens & students 18 & older $3, children under 18 & members free. Estab & incorporated 1915 by will of Mrs Hannah M & Governor Moody Currier, which included endowment, building opened in 1929. Building contains six galleries, library & auditorium, two pavilions. Currier Art Center is housed in adjacent building acquired in 1938 & offers after school & Sat classes for children. Average Annual Attendance: 50,000. Mem: 2500; dues $15 & up
Income: Financed by endowment
Collections: American Furniture, glass & textiles 18th - 20th century; †American Paintings & Sculpture 18th century to present; European Paintings, prints & sculpture, 13th - 20th century; †European Masters 13th - 20th century; †Fine American Decorative Art 17th - 19th century including furniture, glass textiles & silver; Frank Lloyd Wright designed Zimmerman House, opened seasonally for tours
Exhibitions: (1997) The Prints of Peter Milton; The Currier Art Center Student Exhibition; American Art from the Currier Gallery of Art; Direct from Nature: Oil Sketches by Thomas Hill
Publications: Bulletin, semi-annually; calendar, quarterly; exhibition catalogs, occasionally; Annual Report
Activities: Classes for children; docent training; lect open to public, 10 vis lectr per year; concerts; gallery talks; tours; competitions; scholarships & fels offered; exten dept serves New Hampshire schools; individual paintings & original objects of art lent to art institutions worldwide; lending collection contains original art works, original prints, paintings, photographs & sculpture; book traveling exhibitions 1 per year; originate traveling exhibitions to art museums; museum shop sells baskets, books, jewelry, prints, reproductions, slides, toys
L Library, 201 Myrtle Way, 03104. Tel 603-669-6144; *Librn* Katharine L Ritter
Library Holdings: Vols 11,000; Per subs 26; Vertical files; Other — Clipping files, exhibition catalogs
Special Subjects: Antiquities-Greek, Antiquities-Roman, Architecture, Art Education, Art History, Asian Art, Carpets & Rugs, Ceramics, Crafts, Decorative Arts, Drawings, Enamels, Etchings & Engravings, Flasks & Bottles, Folk Art

L MANCHESTER CITY LIBRARY, 405 Pine St, 03104. Tel 603-624-6550; FAX 603-624-6559; *Fine Arts Librn* Beverly M White
Open Mon, Tues & Thurs 9:30 AM - 9 PM, Wed 12:30 - 5:30 PM, Fri 9:30 AM - 5:30 PM, Sat 9 AM - 5 PM
Income: Financed by city appropriations
Purchases: $6000
Library Holdings: Vols 22,694; Compact discs 1800; AV — Cassettes 6010, rec 5477, v-tapes 2200; Other — Framed reproductions 99
Exhibitions: Patron's art works, crafts, collectibles

A MANCHESTER HISTORIC ASSOCIATION, 129 Amherst St, 03101. Tel 603-622-7531; FAX 603-622-0822; *Pres* Charles Whittemore; *Dir* John Mayer
Open Tues - Fri 9 AM - 4 PM, Sat 10 AM - 4 PM, cl Sun & Mon, national & state holidays. Estab 1896 to collect, preserve & make known Manchester's historical heritage. Average Annual Attendance: 10,000. Mem: 500; dues $25
Income: $100,000
Collections: Amoskeag Manufacturing Company records; artifacts, books, documents, maps & photographs on Manchester History
Exhibitions: Permanent & changing exhibitions reflecting all aspects of Manchester history
Publications: Annual report; newsletter, calendar of events, exhibit texts
Activities: Educ dept; lect open to public, 10 vis lectr per year; tours; competitions with prizes; individual & original objects of art lent to educational, business organizations & other museums; book traveling exhibitions; museum shop sells books, original art, reproductions
L Library, 129 Amherst St, 03101. Tel 603-622-7531; FAX 603-622-0822; *Head Librn* Kevin Shupe; *Librn* Elizabeth Lessard; *Asst Librn* Arlene Crossett
Library Holdings: Vols 5000; Per subs 14; Maps 500; AV — Cassettes; Other — Clipping files, manuscripts, memorabilia, pamphlets, photographs 20,000, prints, reproductions
Special Subjects: Amoskeag Manufacturing Company, Dignam Music Collection
Collections: Amoskeag Manufacturing Company Archives; cloth samples; early textile mill records; 19th century music; publications of local history
Exhibitions: Quarterly exhibits reflecting history of city of Manchester.
Publications: Annual report; Manchester Historic Association Calendar of events

M MANCHESTER INSTITUTE OF ARTS & SCIENCES GALLERY, 148 Concord St, 03104. Tel 603-623-0313; *Pres* Jay Svedlow, PHD; *Program & Educ Coordr* Kim Keegan; *Admin Asst* Nancy Banaian; *Public Relations & Membership Coordr* Linda Seabury
Open Mon - Sat 9:30 AM - 5 PM. No admis fee. Estab 1898, as a private non-profit educational institution in order to promote, encourage & stimulate educ in the arts & sciences. Gallery has limited space which is devoted to a variety of exhibitions including historical as well as contemporary themes. Mem: 670; dues family $35, individual $25; annual meeting in June
Income: Financed by endowment, mem, tuition & grants
Publications: Exhibition catalogs; schedule of courses, exhibitions & programs, 2 or 3 times per year
Activities: Classes for adults & children; lect open to public, 7 vis lectr per year; concerts; competitions with prizes; scholarships & fels offered; sales shop sells handcrafted items & books

M SAINT ANSELM COLLEGE, Chapel Art Center, Saint Anselm College, 100 Saint Anselm Dr, 03102. Tel 603-641-7470; FAX 603-641-7116; *Dir* Dr Donald Rosenthal; *Asst Dir* Adrian LaVallee
Tues - Sat 10 AM - 4 PM, Thurs until 9 PM. No admis fee. Estab 1967. Large gallery, formerly college chapel with painted, barrel-vaulted ceiling, stained glass windows. Average Annual Attendance: 5000
Income: Financed through College
Collections: New Hampshire artists & craftsmen; Prints
Exhibitions: Family Pictures: Restructuring the Family Album; Latin American Colonial Religious Art from the Mabee-Gerrer Museum; recent landscape painting; contemporary religious art
Publications: Exhibition catalogues, occasional
Activities: Lect open to public; 4 vis lectr per year; gallery talks; concerts; individual paintings lent to faculty & staff of Saint Anselm College; lending collection contains paintings; book traveling exhibitions 1-2 per year; originate traveling exhibitions

PETERBOROUGH

M SHARON ARTS CENTER, RR2 Box 361, 03458. Tel 603-924-7256; FAX 603-924-6074; *Dir* Marshall Lawton; *Cur* Randall Hoel; *Registrar* Lajla Kraichnan; *Shop Mgr* Carol Underwood
Open Mon - Sat 10 AM - 5 PM, Sun Noon - 5 PM. No admis fee. Estab 1947 to promote the educ, sales & enjoyment of the arts. Center consists of a gallery, store, & classroom facility. Average Annual Attendance: 19,000. Mem: 750; dues family $45, individual $30; annual meeting in Sept
Income: Financed by endowment, mem & state appropriation
Collections: Nora S Unwin Collection of Wood Engravings, Drawings, Watercolors
Exhibitions: Annual juried exhibition of paintings, drawings & sculpture; eight exhibits per year featuring fine artists & craftsmen throughout New England; (1997) William & Lee Kaula (1870-1950), New England landscape painters; The Banquet: Works from the New Hampshire Pottery Guide; 20th Annual Juried Exhibition
Publications: Exhibit catalogs
Activities: Classes for adults & children; lect open to public; gallery talks; tours; competitions with awards; scholarships offered; individual paintings & original artworks lent to art museums & art centers; lending collection contains original prints & paintings; originate traveling exhibitions; sales shop sells crafts

PLYMOUTH

L PLYMOUTH STATE COLLEGE, Herbert H Lamson Library, 03264. Tel 603-535-2258; FAX 603-535-2446; *Dir Library Services* Todd Trevorrow; *Coordr Public Servs* Gary McCool; *Slide & Ill Librn* William Kietzman
Open Mon - Thurs 7 AM - 11:30 PM, Fri 7 AM - 9 PM, Sat 10 AM - 9 PM, Sun Noon - 11:30 PM. Estab 1871 to serve the academic and personal needs of the college's students and faculty. Maintains exhibition space, an 18 ft exhibition wall. Circ 106,000
Income: $705,000 (one-fourth financed by state appropriation)
Purchases: $250,000
Library Holdings: Audio discs 6300; Micro — Fiche 275,000, reels 7600; AV — Cassettes 1770, fs 3200, rec 6000, slides 32,700; Other — Pamphlets
Exhibitions: Lucien Aigner; Patricia Benson; James Fortune; Margaret Houseworth; Winthrop Pratt; Leslie Snow; Viola Sutton; John McDonnell; Warren Mason
Publications: Brochures; handbook
Activities: Lect open to public; library tours; bibliographic instruction

PORTSMOUTH

A LA NAPOULE ART FOUNDATION, 799 South St, 03801. Tel 603-436-3040; FAX 603-633-6302; *Pres* Christopher S Clews
Estab 1958 as a French-American organization to sponsor a wide range of educational & cultural programs. Foundation's programs & artists' residencies take place year-round at the Chateau de la napoule, situated immediately west of Cannes on the shores of the Mediterranean
Income: Financed by private & pub funds by governmental agencies; private foundations & individuals

A THE NATIONAL SOCIETY OF THE COLONIAL DAMES OF AMERICA IN THE STATE OF NEW HAMPSHIRE, Moffatt-Ladd House, 154 Market St (Mailing add: 74 Ocean Blvd, 03862). Tel 603-436-8221; *Pres* Dorothy Orr Cole
Open Mon 10 AM - 4 PM, Sun 2 - 5 PM. Admis adults $4, children & garden $1; free to school groups. Soc estab 1892, mus estab 1913. Moffatt-Ladd House was completed in 1763. Average Annual Attendance: 2000. Mem: 215; annual meeting in June
Income: $54,000 (financed by endowment, mem, rents & donations)
Collections: Original china & porcelain, furniture, documents, letters & papers, portraits, wallpaper & documented wallpaper
Publications: George Mason & Gunston Hall (video); George Mason & The Bill of Rights (video); The Great Seal (audiotape)
Activities: School tours; lect open to members only, 4 vis lectr per year; guided tours open to the public; competitions with awards; scholarships offered; individual paintings lent to Currier Gallery of Art; sales table sells books, prints & historic related items

M PORTSMOUTH ATHENAEUM, 9 Market Square, PO Box 848, 03801. Tel 603-431-2538; *Pres* Jack McGee; *Treas* John N Welch; *Librn* Lynn Aber; *Keeper* Jane M Porter; *Cataloger* Robin Silva
Historic Reading Room open yearly Thurs 1 - 4 PM or by appointment. No admis fee. Estab 1817 to house mus of historical objects of local, statewide & national interest & is listed on National Register of Historical Sites. Maintains local history research library. Average Annual Attendance: 8500. Mem: 320; dues $125; annual meeting 2nd Wed in Jan
Income: Financed by endowment & mem
Collections: American paintings; Colonial & later portraits; ship models & half-models; New England history; maritime history
Exhibitions: (1997) The Black Elders of 20th Century Portsmouth; A Victorian Photographer's View of Portsmouth & Vicinity; The Isles of Shoals
Activities: Lect; gallery talks; tours
L Library, 6-8 Market Square, PO Box 848, 03801. Tel 603-431-2538; *Librn & Archivist* Lynn Aber; *Keeper* Jane Porter; *Cataloger* Robin Silva; *Cur* Rita Conant
Open Tues & Thurs 1 - 4 PM, Sat 10 AM - 4 PM, or by appointment. Estab 1817. For reference only
Purchases: New book purchases relating to interests of the institution
Library Holdings: Vols 40,000; Per subs 45; AV — Cassettes, lantern slides; Other —Clipping files, manuscripts, memorabilia, original art works, pamphlets, photographs, prints
Special Subjects: Architecture, Art History, Decorative Arts, Embroidery, Folk Art, Furniture, Historical Material, Manuscripts, Maps, Marine Painting, Painting - American, Portraits, Textiles, 18th Century American Shipping; United States Marine History
Collections: 18th Century American Shipping Collection; Portsmouth & Piscataqua Regional History; United States Marine History Collection; Local imprints, manuscripts, maps, newspapers, periodicals, photographs; †fine art & artifacts related to maritime & regional history
Activities: Lect open to public, 9 vis lectr per year; gallery talks; individual paintings & original objects of art lent

M PORTSMOUTH HISTORICAL SOCIETY, John Paul Jones House, Middle & State St, PO Box 728, 03802-0728. Tel 603-436-8420; *Pres* Thomas R Watson; *Dir* Virginia E Morin
Open Mon - Sat 10 AM - 4 PM, Sun Noon - 4 PM. Admis adults $4, children $2, children under 6 free. Estab 1920 to identify & retain local history. The House was built in 1758 by Gregory Purcell, a merchant sea-captain. Purchased & restored in 1920 by the Portsmouth Historical Society. Average Annual Attendance: 7000. Mem: 250; dues $15; annual meeting Apr
Income: Financed by mem, investment & admis fees
Collections: Guns, books, china, costumes, documents, furniture, glass, portraits and silver pertaining to the early history of Portsmouth
Activities: Lect, 3-4 vis lectr per year; daily tours; original objects of art lent to other museums; lending collection contains looking glass & furniture; museum shop sells books, prints, slides, cards & jewelry

M WARNER HOUSE ASSOCIATION, MacPheadris-Warner House, 150 Daniel St, PO Box 895, 03802-0895. Tel 603-436-5909; *Chmn* Evelyn Barrett; *Cur* Joyce Volk
Open June - Oct, Tues - Sat 10 AM - 4:30 PM, Sun 1 - 4:30 PM, cl Mon. Admis $4. Estab 1931
Income: $30,000 (financed by endowment, mem & admis)
Collections: Joseph Blackburn Collection (portraits); Portsmouth Furniture; Stair murals (1720); complete set of English Copperplate bed hangings made in America (1780-85)
Exhibitions: Joseph Blackburn: Portraits (1761)
Activities: Lect open to public, 5 vis lectr per year; tours; original objects of art lent to museums & other historic houses; sales shop sells books reproductions, prints & slides

NEW JERSEY

ATLANTIC CITY

L PRINCETON ANTIQUES BOOKSERVICE, Art Marketing Reference Library, 2915-17 Atlantic Ave, 08401. Tel 609-344-1943; FAX 609-344-1944; *Pres* Robert E Ruffolo Jr; *Cur* Martha Ireland; *Adminr* Robert Eugene
Open by appointment 10 AM - 4 PM. Estab 1974 for pricing documentation of books and antiques. Open by appointment only; maintains art gallery. Average Annual Attendance: 1000
Income: $25,000 - $30,000
Purchases: $20,000
Library Holdings: Vols 12,500; Per subs 20; Exhibition catalogs; Original art works & prints; AV — Slides
Special Subjects: The function in US of art and the book market, Price information history from 1900
Collections: 19th century art; Post-card Photo Library Information Bank, 1900 - 1950, consisting 250,000 post-cards
Activities: Sales shop sells books & original art

BAYONNE

L BAYONNE FREE PUBLIC LIBRARY, Art Dept, 697 Avenue C, 07002. Tel 201-858-6981; *Library Dir* Sneh Bains
Open Mon & Thurs 1 - 5 PM & 6 - 9 PM, Tues 9 AM - Noon, 1 - 5 PM, 6 - 9 PM, Wed, Fri & Sat 9 AM - Noon & 1 - 5 PM. Estab 1894. Art Gallery has 194 running feet exhibition space
Income: Financed by city appropriation & state aid
Library Holdings: Vols 222,000; Per subs 517; AV — Fs, rec 8101, slides 736; Other — Clipping files
Activities: Adult & children film programs weekly; concerts

BERKELEY HEIGHTS

L BERKELEY HEIGHTS FREE PUBLIC LIBRARY, 290 Plainfield Ave, 07922-1438. Tel 908-464-9333; FAX 908-464-7098; *Dir* Stephanie Bakos; *Asst Dir* Laura Fuhro; *Reference Head* Linda Fox
Estab 1953
Income: $603,356 (financed by mem & city appropriation)
Purchases: $3000
Library Holdings: Vols 3500; Per subs 32; Micro — Fiche, reels; AV — A-tapes, cassettes, fs, slides, v-tapes; Other — Clipping files, pamphlets
Special Subjects: Advertising Design, Aesthetics, Afro-American Art, American Indian Art, American Western Art, Anthropology, Art Education, Art History, Costume Design & Construction, Decorative Arts, Drawings, Graphic Arts, Graphic Design, Handicrafts, Lettering
Collections: †Art & art history prints

BLOOMFIELD

M HISTORICAL SOCIETY OF BLOOMFIELD, 90 Broad St, 07003. Tel 201-429-9292; FAX 201-429-0170; *Pres* Richard West; *2nd VPres* Richard Pohli; *Treas* Dorothy Greenfield; *Cur* Lucy Sant Ambrogio
Open Wed 2 - 4:30 PM by appointment. No admis fee. Estab circa 1968 to collect, preserve & exhibit items which may help to establish or illustrate the history of the area. Mus located in the gallery of the Bloomfield Pub Library. Average Annual Attendance: 1436. Mem: 115; dues life $50, commercial organization $25, non-profit organization $10, couple $8, individual $5, student under 18 $3; meeting 2nd Wed of alternate months Sept-May
Income: Financed by mem, Ways & Means Committee & bequests
Collections: Miscellaneous items of books, †clothing & accessories, †deeds & other documents, †dioramas, †early maps & newspapers, furniture, †household articles, letters, †memorabilia, †paintings, postcards, posters, tools, toys
Exhibitions: Revolving Charles Warren Eaton (items donated by people of Bloomfield and/or heirs)
Activities: Lect open to public, 5 vis lectr per year; tours; sales shop sells books, prints, postcards, mugs, notepaper, medallions, & fruit cake (seasonal)

BLOOMSBURY

C M GRUMBACHER INC, Rte 173W, 08804. Tel 609-655-8282; *Dir Human Resources* Dennis Richardson; *Public Relations* Dawn Lerch
Exhibitions: Emerging Artists Exhibition
Publications: Palette Talk magazine, quarterly
Activities: Lect; factory tours; cash awards; medallions; certificates to various art societies

BURLINGTON

A BURLINGTON COUNTY HISTORICAL SOCIETY, 457 High St, 08016. Tel 609-386-4773; FAX 609-386-4828; *Pres* Canon James J Greene; *VPres* Louis Colaguori; *Dir* M M Pernot
Open Mon - Thurs 1 - 4 PM, Sun 2 - 4 PM. Admis $5. Estab 1915 to preserve & interpret Burlington County history. Average Annual Attendance: 5000. Mem: 1000; dues $15 & up; annual meeting fourth Thurs in May
Income: Financed by endowment & donations
Collections: Clocks; Decorative Arts; Delaware River Decoys; Quilts; Samplers
Exhibitions: Ingenuity & Craftmanship
Publications: Quarterly newsletter
Activities: Tours for children; docent training; lect open to public, several vis lectr per year; tours; museum shop sells books, magazines & reproductions

CALDWELL

M CALDWELL COLLEGE, Art Gallery, 9 Ryerson Ave, 07006. Tel 201-228-4424; *Dir* Judith Croce
Open Mon - Fri 8:30 AM - 5 PM, weekends by appointment. No admis fee. Estab 1970 to provide students & area community with exposure to professional contemporary talent, to afford opportunities for qualified artists to have one-person shows
Income: Financed by college budget
Exhibitions: George Mueller (painting); Mary Ansgar of Norway Painting; Bob Lahm (painting); Alan Brown (painting); Alumni Show
Activities: Educ dept in connection with the college art dept; lect open to public, 3 vis lectr per year; lending collection contains 12,000 kodachromes, motion pictures

CAMDEN

C HENRY FRANCIS DUPONT WINTER THUR (Formerly Campbell Museum), 19735. Tel 302-888-4600; *Dir* Catherine Magee
Open Mon - Fri 9 AM - 4:30 PM. .. Estab 1966, a non-profit educational institution chartered by State of New Jersey, to collect soup tureens of silver, porcelain & pewter from the royal European houses of 18th & 19th centuries. Collection displayed at Campbell Museum. Museum has red velvet walls and Plexiglas cases. Average Annual Attendance: 35,000
Income: Financed by Campbell Soup Company
Purchases: Soup tureens & eating vessels from European houses of 18th & 19th centuries
Collections: 18th Century soup tureens by leading porcelain makers & silversmiths
Exhibitions: Juried tureen exhibitions
Publications: Catalogue
Activities: Lect; gallery talks; tours; film; competitions with awards; original objects of art lent; book traveling exhibitions; originate traveling exhibitions to museums only

M RUTGERS UNIVERSITY, Stedman Art Gallery, Fine Arts Ctr, 08102. Tel 609-225-6245, 225-6350; FAX 609-225-6330; TTY 609-225-6648. *Dir & Cur* Virginia Oberlin Steel; *Asst Dir & Assoc Cur* Nancy Maguire; *Cur Educ* Noreen Scott Garrity
Open Mon - Sat 10 AM - 4 PM. No admis fee. Estab 1975 to serve educational needs of the campus & to serve community of southern New Jersey. Average Annual Attendance: 14,000
Income: Financed by endowment, state appropriation & gifts from private sources
Collections: Modern & contemporary art; †works on paper
Exhibitions: Changing exhibitions of visual arts & interdisciplinary exhibitions
Publications: Catalog for a major exhibition, yearly
Activities: Vis lectr; symposia, concerts & gallery talks open to public; competition with purchase prizes

CHESTER

A NEW JERSEY WATER-COLOR SOCIETY, PO Box 53, 07930. Tel 908-879-7079; *Pres* Patrick G Bannigan; *First VPres* Debbie Tintle; *Second VPres* Margaret Crawford; *Treas* Pat Shamy
Estab 1938 to bring to the pub the best in New Jersey watercolorists - teachers. Mem: 129; dues $25; open to exhibitors in the Annual Open Exhibition whose work conforms to standards of the Soc & are legal residents of the State of New Jersey
Exhibitions: Annual Members Show in spring; Annual Open Statewide Juried Exhibition in fall - alternating between Nabisco Brands USA Gallery, East Hanover, NJ & the Monmouth Museum, Lincroft, NJ
Publications: Illustrated Catalogue; Newsletter, 2 per yr
Activities: Classes for adults & children; workshops; lect open to public, 2-4 vis lectr per year; competitions with awards; annual dinner; reception for Open & Members Shows

CLINTON

A HUNTERDON ART CENTER, 7 Lower Center St, 08809. Tel 908-735-8415; FAX 908-735-8416; *Exec Dir* Marjorie Frankel Nathanson; *Pres* Anthony Martino; *VPres* Kimberlee Hoey; *VPres* Wm Anderson; *Dir Exhibitions* Kristin Accola; *Dir Educ* David Leese
Open Wed - Sun 11 AM - 5 PM. Donation requested. Estab 1952 as a non-profit organization to provide arts enrichment through fine & performing arts. The first, second & third floors provide gallery space. The old stone mill has been remodeled retaining the original atmosphere with open broad wooden beams, white walls & plank flooring. Average Annual Attendance: 22,000. Mem: 700; dues patron $500, sponsor $250, contributor $100, family $50, individual $35,

senior $20; annual meeting in Apr
Income: $Financed by mem, city, state & county appropriations, donations, tuitions
Purchases: $100
Collections: †Print collection
Exhibitions: National Print Exhibition
Activities: Classes for adults & children; lect open to public, 3 vis lectr per year; gallery talks; competitions with cash awards; annual juried members show; works from print collection lent to nearby corporations; lending collection contains 200 original prints; originate traveling exhibitions to Newark Museum and corp membership; sales shop sells books, original art, reproductions & crafts

M HUNTERDON HISTORICAL MUSEUM, 56 Main St, PO Box 5005, 08809-0005. Tel 908-735-4101; FAX 908-735-0914; *Dir* Andrew Drysdale; *Cur Educ* Joan Jensen
Open early Apr - late Oct, Tues - Sun 10 AM - 4 PM. Admis adults $3, seniors $2, children under 12 $1, pre-schoolers free. Estab 1960 for the preservation & display of artifacts from the 18th & 19th century & early 20th century for educational & cultural purposes. Four-floor grist mill, blacksmith shop, general store, schoolhouse, log cabin, herb garden & quarry buildings. Average Annual Attendance: 26,000. Mem: 630; dues $15-$2500; annual meeting in May
Income: $150,000 (financed by mem & donations)
Collections: Artifacts pertaining to 18th, 19th & early 20th centuries
Exhibitions: Variety of Special Events
Activities: Classes for children; docent training; lect; concerts; tours; sales shop sells books & gift items

DENVILLE

A BLACKWELL STREET CENTER FOR THE ARTS, PO Box 808, 07834. Tel 201-337-2143; FAX 201-337-2143; *Dir* Annette Adrian Hanna
Estab 1983. Average Annual Attendance: 2100. Mem: 10 artists, 12 pub; qualifications for mem: artists members juried by Credentials Commission; dues $100; monthly meeting third Thurs of month
Income: $5000 (financed by mem, grants & donations)
Exhibitions: Six or more exhibitions scheduled per year

EAST HANOVER

C NABISCO, INC, 100 DeForest Ave, 07936. Tel 201-503-4425, 503-2000; *Archivist* David Stivers; *Art* Mary Ellen Walsh; *Art* Mary Shandor
Art collection viewed only while on tour
Collections: A History of the Golden Age of Illustration; Illustrations for Cream of Wheat Cereal Advertising in Magazines, on Posters & Signs, from 1900-1955, includes oil on canvas, oil on board, watercolors, sketches & photo montages
Exhibitions: Cream of Wheat Art Collection Traveling Exhibit

ELIZABETH

L FREE PUBLIC LIBRARY OF ELIZABETH, Fine Arts Dept, 11 S Broad St, 07202. Tel 908-354-6060; *Dir* Joseph Keenan
Open Mon - Fri 9 AM - 9 PM, Sat 9 AM - 5 PM, cl Sun. No admis fee. Estab 1913, the art department functions within the Linx library system; it offers free service to patrons of Elizabeth & Union County. Special exhibit area displays paintings & miscellaneous objects d'art
Income: Financed by city and state appropriation
Library Holdings: Vols 15,000; Photographs & Illustrations 200,000; Other — Reproductions 800
Collections: Japanese prints by various artists
Exhibitions: Works by artists & photographers; other special exhibitions from time to time
Activities: Dramatic programs; lect open to the public, 15 vis lectr per year; concerts; material available to patrons of Union County; lending collection contains film strips, projection equipment & motion pictures; printed catalogues of film strips & films available to the public - 4500 VHS videotapes (circulating)

ENGLEWOOD

L ENGLEWOOD LIBRARY, Fine Arts Dept, 31 Engle St, 07631. Tel 201-568-2215; FAX 201-568-8199; *Dir Library* Don Jacobsen
Open Mon - Thurs 9 AM - 9 PM, Fri & Sat 9 AM - 5 PM, Sun 1 - 5 PM (Oct-May). Estab 1901 to estab a free pub library for citizens
Income: $510,000 (financed by endowment, city & state appropriation)
Library Holdings: Micro — Reels; AV — Cassettes, fs, motion pictures, rec, slides; Other — Clipping files, framed reproductions, original art works, pamphlets
Exhibitions: Members of Salurre to Women In The Arts; Quilts; Rare Books & Manuscripts; World of Renaissance
Activities: Lect open to public; concerts

HOPEWELL

M HOPEWELL MUSEUM, * 28 E Broad St, 08525. Tel 609-466-0103; *Pres* David Mackey; *Cur* Beverly Weidl
Open Mon, Wed & Sat 2 - 5 PM, cl national holidays. No admis fee, donations suggested. Estab 1922 as a mus of local history from early 1700-1900, to show what the community was like for almost 300 years. Average Annual Attendance: 2000
Income: Financed by endowment, mem & donations
Collections: Antique china, glass, silver & pewter; colonial furniture; colonial parlor; early needlework; Indian handicrafts; photograph collection; Victorian parlor
Publications: Hopewell Valley Heritage; Pioneers of Old Hopewell; maps

JERSEY CITY

M JERSEY CITY MUSEUM, 472 Jersey Ave, 07302. Tel 201-547-4514; *Chmn* Carlos Hernandez; *Dir* Nina S Jacobs; *Cur* Alejandro Anreus
Open Tues - Sat 10:30 AM - 5 PM, Wed evening until 8 PM, cl Sun & legal holidays. No admis fee. Estab 1901 for the purpose of preserving & interpreting its permanent collection of art & historical objects. Maintains three gallery spaces for contemporary & historical exhibitions. Average Annual Attendance: 25,000. Mem: 500; dues $25-$100, students & senior citizens $10
Income: Financed by state, county, city, federal appropriations as well as foundation, corporate & private support
Collections: Paintings, drawings & watercolors by 19th century artist August Will; 19th & 20th century paintings & prints; Jersey City & New Jersey related artifacts, documents, decorative & historical objects
Exhibitions: Changing exhibitions
Publications: Exhibition catalogs, posters, reproductions of art work on cards
Activities: Classes for adults & children; workshops; lect open to public; gallery talks; tours; slide & panel talks; historical tours; video & performance arts

M JERSEY CITY STATE COLLEGE, Courtney Art Gallery, Dept of Art Gross Nickel Hall, 1st Flr, 2039 Kennedy Blvd, 07305. Tel 201-200-3214; *Dir* Dr Harold Lemmerman
Open Mon - Fri 10 AM - 5 PM. No admis fee. Estab 1969 to bring examples of professional work to the campus in each of the areas in which students are involved: Painting, sculpture, film, photography, textiles, weaving, ceramics, graphic design. Gallery is operated by students & with the Jersey City Mus for a student internship training program. Average Annual Attendance: 5000
Income: Financed by city, state appropriation & Art Department
Collections: Small collection of prints & paintings
Activities: Lect open to public, 5 vis lectr per year; gallery talks; exten dept serving community organizations; individual paintings & original objects of art lent; lending collection contains color reproductions, film strips, Kodachromes, motion pictures, photographs; originate traveling exhibitions organized & circulated

M Art Space, Hepburn Hall, 3rd Flr, 2039 Kennedy Blvd, 07305. Tel 201-200-3214; *Dir* Dr Harold Lemmerman
Gallery maintained for student & professional exhibitions

M SAINT PETER'S COLLEGE, Art Gallery, 2641 Kennedy Blvd, 07306. Tel 201-333-4400; *Dir* Oscar Magnan
Open Mon, Tues, Fri & Sat 11 AM - 4 PM, Wed & Thurs 11 AM - 9 PM. No admis fee. Estab 1971 to present the different art trends. Gallery is maintained with good space, lighting and alarm systems
Income: Financed by the college
Activities: Classes for adults; docent training; lectures open to public, 20 vis lectrs per year; concerts; gallery talks; tours; exten dept serving students

LAKEWOOD

M GEORGIAN COURT COLLEGE GALLERY, M Christina Geis Gallery, 900 Lakewood Ave, 08701-2697. Tel 908-364-2200, Ext 348, 364-2181; FAX 908-905-8571; *Dir* Sr Mary Christina Geis
Open Mon - Fri 9 AM - Noon & 1 - 4 PM. No admis fee. Estab 1964 to offer art students the opportunity to view the works of professional artists & also to exhibit student work. Gallery is one large room with 100 running ft of wall area for flat work; the center area for sculpture. Average Annual Attendance: 1000
Income: Financed through the college
Exhibitions: Monthly exhibitions

LAWRENCEVILLE

INTER-SOCIETY COLOR COUNCIL
For further information, see National and Regional Organizations

M RIDER UNIVERSITY, Art Gallery, 2083 Lawrenceville Rd, PO Box 6400, 08648-3099. Tel 609-896-5192, 896-5168; FAX 609-895-5440; *Assoc Prof of Art & Dir* Harry I Naar
Open Mon - Thurs Noon - 2 PM & 6 - 8 PM, Fri - Sun 2 - 5 PM (subject to change). No admis fee. Estab 1970 to afford members of the community & college the opportunity to expand their knowledge & exposure to art. Gallery has 1513 sq ft of space divided into two rooms of different height. Average Annual Attendance: 5000
Income: $8000 (college funded)
Collections: †African Art, statues & masks; contemporary art; paintings; drawings; sculpture
Publications: Exhibit catalogues
Activities: Classes for adults; docent training; internships; lect open to public, 4 vis lectr per year; concerts; gallery talks; tours; individual paintings lent to museums, group shows, one person shows, major exhibitions; book traveling exhibitions

LAYTON

L PETERS VALLEY CRAFT CENTER, 19 Kuhn Rd, 07851. Tel 201-948-5200; FAX 201-948-0011; *Exec Dir* Kenneth Jones; *Asst Dir* Sandra Ward
Open 10 AM - 5 PM. Estab 1970 as a non profit craft educ center to promote & encourage traditional & contemporary crafts through exhibitions, demonstrations, workshops & educational programs. For reference only. Mem: 350; dues $25; annual meeting in Oct
Income: Financed in part by a grant from NJ State Council on the Arts/Department of State, the Geraldine R Dodge Foundation & members, friends, corporations & local companies
Library Holdings: Vols 500; AV — Slides; Other — Exhibition catalogs, original art works, pamphlets, photographs
Special Subjects: Ceramics, Crafts, Decorative Arts, Handicrafts, Metalwork,

Photography, Silversmithing, Textiles, Woodcarvings
Collections: Teaching collection of craft works/art & photographs
Publications: Summer Workshop Catalog, annual; Valley Views Newsletter, three times a year
Activities: Educ dept; classes for adults & children; lect open to public, 80 vis lectr per year; tours; workshops; juried craft fair; scholarships & fels offered; sales shop sells original art

LINCROFT

M MONMOUTH MUSEUM & CULTURAL CENTER, PO Box 359, 07738. Tel 908-747-2266; FAX 908-747-8592; *Prog Adminr* Catherine Jahos; *Pres* Dorothy V Morehouse; *First VPres* Jane McCosker; *Second VPres* Barbara Goldfarb
Open Tues - Sat 10 AM - 4:30 PM, Sun 1 - 5 PM. Admis adults $3, children & senior citizens $2.50, free to Museum members & Brookdale Community College students. Estab 1963 to advance interest in art, science & nature. Mus houses two large galleries & the Becker Children's Wing. Exhibitions are changed eight times a year; also an educational area & a conference area. Average Annual Attendance: 50,000. Mem: 1600; dues family $30, individual $20; annual meeting in Jan
Income: $450,000 (financed by mem, donations, county funds & benefits)
Exhibitions: Annual Monmouth County Arts Council Juried Exhibition; Paintings of Michael Lenson; 52nd Annual NJ Watercolor Society Exhibition; The Nutcracker & Friends Backstage; The Energy Puzzle; All Aboard at the Monmouth Museum
Publications: Calendar of events; catalogues of exhibitions; newsletter
Activities: Classes for adults & children; docent training; lect open to public; originate traveling trunks for use in schools; museum shop sells books & gift items

LONG BRANCH

M LONG BRANCH HISTORICAL MUSEUM, 1260 Ocean Ave, 07740. Tel 908-229-0600; *Pres* Edgar N Dinkelspiel
Open by appointment only. No admis fee. Estab 1953 as post Civil War historical museum. Average Annual Attendance: 10,000. Mem: Dues $1
Collections: Period furniture

MADISON

M ARCHIVES & HISTORY CENTER OF THE UNITED METHODIST CHURCH (Formerly United Methodist Church Commission on Archives & History), PO Box 127, 07940. Tel 201-408-3189; FAX 201-408-3909; Elec Mail cyrigoye@drew.edu. *Archivist* L Dale Patterson; *Librn* Kenneth E Rowe
Open Mon - Fri 9 AM - 5 PM. No admis fee. Estab 1885 as a religious history mus. The Archives & History Center is located on Drew University Campus & it contains a mus, a library & a spacious 180,000 cubic ft archival vault. Maintains reference library
Income: Financed by general church funds
Collections: Letters; Photographs
Exhibitions: Chinese Missionaries
Publications: Historian's Digest, bimonthly; Methodist History, quarterly
Activities: Lect open to public, 1 vis lectr per year; tours; sales shop sells books, plates, cards, slides & prints

L Library, PO Box 127, 07940. Tel 201-408-3590; FAX 201-408-3909; *Head Librn* Kenneth Rowe
For reference only
Library Holdings: Vols 70,000; Per subs 600; Micro — Fiche, reels; AV — A-tapes, cassettes, fs, lantern slides, motion pictures, rec, slides, v-tapes; Other — Manuscripts, memorabilia, original art works, pamphlets, photographs, prints
Collections: Methodist materials; pamphlets & manuscripts of John Wesley & his associates; materials pertaining to women & ethnic minorities

M DREW UNIVERSITY, Elizabeth P Korn Gallery, 07940. Tel 201-408-3553; *Dean* Paolo Cucchi; *Chmn Art Dept* Livio Saganic
Open Tues - Fri 12:30 - 4 PM & by appointment. No admis fee. Estab 1968 to provide exhibitions each school year to augment program of courses & to serve the community
Income: Financed by University instructional budget
Collections: Ancient Near-East archaeological collection; colonial America; †contemporary abstraction; native American artifacts; 19th century academic; Oriental art
Activities: Lect open to public. 3-4 vis lectr per year; gallery talks

L Art Dept Library, Rt 24, 07940. Tel 201-408-3588; FAX 201-408-3770; *Dir* Jean Schoenthaler; *Reference Librn* Jody Caldwell
Library maintained for art history courses
Purchases: $7400 annually (for purchases to support art history courses at the college level)
Library Holdings: Vols 350,000; Per subs 1900; Micro — Fiche; AV — A-tapes, fs, rec, slides, v-tapes; Other — Exhibition catalogs, manuscripts, original art works, pamphlets, photographs

L FAIRLEIGH DICKINSON UNIVERSITY, Florham Madison Campus Library - Art Dept, 285 Madison Ave, 07940. Tel 201-593-8500; FAX 201-593-8525; *Libr Dir* James Fraser
Open Mon - Fri 8:30 AM - 10:30 PM. Estab 1958. Circ 40,000
Library Holdings: Vols 200,000; Per subs 960; Archives of NY Cultural Art Center 30,000; AV — Rec 5000, slides 50,000; Other — Exhibition catalogs 6000, original art works 6000, photographs 50,000
Collections: †Czech Graphic Design, 1919-1939; †Cartoon & Graphic Satire; †Outdoor Advertising; †book arts
Publications: Exhibition catalogues

MAHWAH

M **THE ART GALLERIES OF RAMAPO COLLEGE,** 505 Ramapo Valley Rd, 07430. Tel 201-529-7587; *Dir* Shalom Gorewitz
Open Mon - Fri 11 AM - 2 PM, Wed 5 - 7 PM, cl Sat & Sun. No admis fee. Estab 1979 as outreach for community, faculty, staff & students to support undergraduate curriculum. Three galleries: thematic changing exhibitions gallery; permanent collection gallery; alternate space gallery. Average Annual Attendance: 5000. Mem: 300 (friends); dues $15
Income: Financed by state appropriation & grants
Collections: †Rodman Collection of Popular Art, Art by Haitians; †Study Collection of Prints; fine art printmaking from 15th century to present
Publications: Exhibit catalogs
Activities: Classes for adults & children; dramatic programs; docent training; lect open to public, 10 vis lectr per year; competitions; scholarships & fels offered; individual paintings lent to institutions, colleges & museums; book traveling exhibitions; originate traveling exhibitions

MAPLEWOOD

A **FEDERATED ART ASSOCIATIONS OF NEW JERSEY, INC,** 17 Maplewood Ave, 07040. Tel 201-763-3335; FAX 201-262-0928; *Pres* Helen Poulos; *VPres for North Jersey* Eugenia Gore
Estab 1969 to provide communications & exchange of ideas among visual art groups. Mem: 9000 (50 member groups); dues per club $25, individuals $15; composed of four districts which meet separately, annually
Publications: Directory of Visual Art Organizations in New Jersey, periodically; FAA NJ Views, quarterly; Judge & Jury Selector; Living Library of New Jersey Visual Artists; Videos of Artists in Their Own Studios
Activities: Lect open to public, 8 vis lectr per year

MERCERVILLE

L **JOHNSON ATELIER TECHNICAL INSTITUTE OF SCULPTURE,** Johnson Atelier Library, 60 Ward Ave Extension, 08619. Tel 609-890-7777; FAX 609-890-1816; *Librn* Eden R Bentley
Not open to public. Estab 1977 to provide an information center for apprentices, instructors & staff on sculpture, art appreciation & art history. Library provides space for lectures, movies, slides & critique sessions
Income: Financed by appropriation from the Johnson Atelier Technical Institute of Sculpture
Library Holdings: Vols 3355; Per subs 23; AV — Slides; Other — Clipping files, exhibition catalogs
Special Subjects: Bronzes, Sculpture, Art Appreciation
Collections: Exhibition catalogues on sculptors & group shows; slides of about 50 sculptor's work

MILLVILLE

M **WHEATON CULTURAL ALLIANCE INC,** Wheaton Village, 1501 Glasstown Rd, 08332. Tel 609-825-6800; FAX 609-825-2410; *Pres* Barry Taylor
Estab 1970, a cultural center dedicated to American folklore, craft & heritage

MONTCLAIR

M **MONTCLAIR ART MUSEUM,** 3 S Mountain Ave, 07042-1747. Tel 201-746-5555; FAX 201-746-9118; *Pres* James Mills; *Dir* Ellen Harris; *Dir Communications* Anne-Marie Nolin; *Curatorial Registrar* Randy Black; *Comptroller* Diane Parisien; *Dir Develop* Elyse Reissman; *Cur Educ* Twig Johnson; *Cur Coll* Gail Stavitsky
Open Tues, Wed, Fri & Sat 11 AM -5PM, Thurs & Sun 1 - 5 PM. Admis suggested contribution $4. Estab 1914. Five galleries of changing exhibitions; one gallery of permanent exhibitions; student gallery. Average Annual Attendance: 70,000. Mem: 2700; individual $30
Income: Financed by endowment & mem
Collections: American costumes; The Rand Collection of American Indian Art; Whitney Silver Collection; †American paintings, 18th - 20th century; bookplate collection; †prints & drawings
Exhibitions: The American Landscape: From Cole to Blakelock Dottie Atty: The Anxious Object; Three Hispanic-American Masters; Robert Kushner: Seasons; Brave Against the Enemy: Plains Indian Art from the Montclair Art Museum; Arctic Imagery: Contemporary Inuit Drawing from a Private New Jersey Collection; Hans Weingaertner: A Retrospective; The Crayon; June Brides; Currier & Ives: Selections from the George Raimes Beach Collection; Henri & The Ash Can School
Publications: Bulletin, bi-monthly; exhibition catalogues
Activities: Classes for adults & children; docent training; workshops coordinated programs with school groups; dramatic programs; lect open to public; concerts; gallery talks every Sunday; tours; museum shop sells books, notecards, reproductions, slides, Native American jewelry & crafts, jewelry & games/toys for children
L **LeBrun Library,** 3 S Mountain Ave, 07042-1747. Tel 201-746-5555; FAX 201-746-9118; *Librn* Edith A Rights
Open Wed 10 AM - 5 PM, Thurs & Fri 9 AM - 5 PM. Estab 1916 to support research & exhibitions of the mus. For reference only
Library Holdings: Vols 13,000; Per subs 50; Bookplates; Micro — Fiche; AV — A-tapes, slides 20,000; Other — Clipping files, exhibition catalogs
Special Subjects: American Art, American Indian
Collections: Over 7000 bookplates

MOORESTOWN

M **PERKINS CENTER FOR THE ARTS,** 395 Kings Hwy, 08057. Tel 609-235-6488; FAX 609-235-6624; *Dir* Alan Willoughby; *Asst Dir* Denise Creedon
Open Thurs - Sun. No admis fee. Estab 1977 as a multi-disciplinary art center. A tudor mansion built in 1910 on 5-1/2 acre lot. The building is listed on the National Register of Historic Places. Average Annual Attendance: 10,000. Mem: 1200; dues family $40, adult $25, individual $15
Income: $430,000 (financed by mem, state appropriation, corporate, foundation & earned income)
Exhibitions: Annual Photography Exhibition; Annual Works on Paper Exhibition; Director's Choice; Members Faculty; Young at Art
Publications: Perkinsight, quarterly newsletter/class catalog
Activities: Classes for adults & children; docent programs; lect open to public, 5 vis lectr per year; awards given; scholarships & fels offered

MORRISTOWN

L **COLLEGE OF SAINT ELIZABETH,** Mahoney Library, 2 Convent Rd, 07960-6989. Tel 201-605-7000; *Dir Library* Bro Paul B Chervenie
Open Mon - Thurs 8:30 AM - 10 PM, Fri 8:30 AM - 6 PM. Estab 1899 for academic purposes
Income: Financed by private funds
Library Holdings: Vols 7200; Per subs 40; Micro — Fiche, reels; AV — Cassettes, fs, rec; Other — Exhibition catalogs, original art works, photographs, prints, reproductions, sculpture
Special Subjects: The Madonna
Exhibitions: Sculpture, paintings, prints by the Art Dept faculty
Activities: Original objects of art lent

M **MORRIS MUSEUM,** 6 Normandy Heights Rd, 07960. Tel 201-538-0454; FAX 201-538-0154; *Exec Dir* Steven Klindt; *Dir Exhib & Coll* Suzanne Gyorgy; *Cur Educ* Martha Wilcox O'Connor; *Artistic Dir The Bickford Theatre* Walker Joyce
Open Mon - Sat 10 AM - 5 PM, Thurs until 8 PM, Sun 1 - 5 PM, cl major holidays. Admis adults $4, students, senior citizens & children $2; groups of 20 or more $2 per person. Estab 1913 to educate diverse pub on topics in art, humanities & the sciences. Average Annual Attendance: 300,000. Mem: 2500; dues $35-$60; annual meeting in Sept
Collections: Antique dolls & toys; ethnographic materials of New Guinea, Africa & the Americas; fine & decorative arts; geology; mineralogy; paleontology; textiles; zoology
Exhibitions: History Gallery features early American kitchen & general store; North American Indian & Woodland Indian Galleries; Rock & Mineral Gallery; Live Animal Gallery; Dinosaur Gallery; Children's Room; Mammal Gallery; Model Train Gallery; juried art exhibitions
Activities: Classes for adults & children; dramatic programs; docent training; lect open to public, 6-10 vis lectr per year; concerts; gallery talks for schools; tours; competitions with prizes; exten dept serves schools, senior centers & hospitals; artmobile; individual paintings & original objects of art lent to other local organizations & museums; book traveling exhibitions; originate traveling exhibitions; museum shop sells books, reproductions, prints, exhibitions-related gifts & toys
L **Library,** 6 Normandy Heights Rd, 07960. Tel 201-538-0454; FAX 201-538-0154; *Librn* Elizabeth Addison
Library Holdings: Vols 2500; Per subs 10; AV — Slides
Special Subjects: Anthropology, Archaeology, Art Education, Ceramics, Costume Design & Construction, Decorative Arts, Dolls, Painting - American, Painting - British, Painting - Dutch, Painting - European, Painting - Flemish, Painting - French, Painting - German, Painting - Italian, Painting - Japanese, Painting - Scandinavian, Painting - Spanish, Pottery, Pre-Columbian Art, Textiles

M **SCHUYLER-HAMILTON HOUSE,** 5 Olyphant Pl, 07960. Tel 201-267-4039; *Regent* Dorothy Graef
Open Tues & Sun 2 - 5 PM, other times by appointment. Admis adults $2, children under 12 free. Estab 1923 for preservation of historical landmark. House is furnished with 18th Century antiques; five large portraits of General & Mrs Philip Schuyler, their daughter, Betsey Schuyler Hamilton, Alexander Hamilton & Dr Jabez Campfield; old lithographs, silhouette of George Washington, needle & petit point. Average Annual Attendance: 1500. Mem: 90; dues $30; annual meeting 1st Thurs in May, Chapter meets Oct - May
Income: Financed by mem, Friends of Schuyler-Hamilton, foundations & matching gifts
Collections: China - Canton, blue willow; Staffordshire; doll china; pewter; brass candlesticks; rugs; tunebooks
Activities: Docent training; lect for members; tours; competitions with awards; sales shop sells stationery, cards & reproductions

NEWARK

A **ALJIRA CENTER FOR CONTEMPORARY ART,** 2 Washington Pl, 4th Flr, PO Box 7506, 07102. Tel 201-643-6877; *Exec Dir* Victor Davson; *Art Dir* Carl Hazelwood
Open Wed - Sun Noon - 6 PM. Estab 1983 as a multi-cultural visual art organization
Exhibitions: Living Space - Interior Exterior; Decorative Impulse

M **NEWARK MUSEUM ASSOCIATION,** The Newark Museum, 49 Washington St, PO Box 540, 07101. Tel 201-596-6550; FAX 201-642-0459; *Pres & Chmn Board of Trustees* Kevin Shanley; *Dir* Mary Sue Sweeney Price; *Deputy Dir Prog & Coll* Ward Mintz; *Deputy Dir Finance* Meme Omogbai; *Cur Classical Coll* Dr Susan H Auth; *Cur Coin Coll* Dr William L Bischoff; *Cur Decorative Arts* Ulysses G Dietz; *Cur Asian Coll* Valrae Reynolds; *Cur Africa, Americas & Pacific* Anne M Spencer; *Cur Painting & Sculpture* Joseph Jacobs; *Dir Educ* Lucy Brofman; *Lending Dept Supv* Helene Konkus; *Arts Workshop Supv* Stephen McKenzie; *Dir Mem & Museum Servs* Kristine Hood; *Merchandise Mgr*

Lorelei Rowars; *Dir Exhib* David Palmer; *Prog Coordr* Jane Stein; *Dir Develop* Peggy Dougherty; *Spec Events* Ellen G Trama
Open Wed - Sun Noon - 5 PM, cl Christmas, New Year's Day, July 4 & Thanksgiving. No admis fee. Estab 1909 to exhibit articles of art, science & technology & for the study of the arts & sciences. The building was a gift of Louis Bamberger, opened 1926; held in trust by the Mus Assoc for the City of Newark, which gave the site. The adjoining buildings were acquired by the Mus in 1937 & 1982. Major renovation designed by Michael Graves reopened in 1989, with 60,000 sq ft of gallery space, as well as new educ facilities & a 300 seat auditorium & won the 1992 American Institute of Architects Honor Award for Design Excellence. The Ballantine House, the 1885 beer brewer's mansion designated a National Historic Landmark in 1985, showcases the museum's decorative arts collection, 8 period rooms & 6 thematic galleries. Average Annual Attendance: 350,000. Mem: 4750; dues $35 & up; annual meeting in Jan
Income: $6,400,000 (financed by city & state appropriations, county funds)
Collections: †African, †American Indian, †Chinese, †Indian, †Islamic, †Japanese, †South Pacific, †Tibetan; †American painting & sculpture of all periods with primitives well represented; †decorative arts; †Mediterranean Antiquities, including Eugene Schaefer Collection of ancient glass; †numismatics; †Pre-Columbian material
Exhibitions: American Folk Art; American paintings and sculptures; Tibet: A Lost World; Japanese Art; Chinese Ceramics; Ritual & Ceremony in African Life; Victorian Furniture; The Ballantine House; Art of Coptic Egypt; Southwest Indian Pottery; Japan The Enduring Heritage; 2000 Years of Chinese Ceramics; Murals Without Walls; Arshile Gorky's Aviation Murals Rediscovered; American Art Pottery; American Bronze Sculpture; American Silver; Navajo Textiles; American Impressionists; Edmondson/Butler Folk Art; Twentieth Century Afro-American Artists; Money & Medals of Newark; Against the Odds; Dragon Threads; In the Wake of Columbus: American Treasure, Demographic Upheavel, Global Economy
Publications: Newsletter, bimonthly; catalogs & bulletins on major exhibitions
Activities: Extensive educational programs including classes for adults & children; docent training; lect open to public; films; concerts; gallery talks; tours; competitions; exten dept servs community neighborhoods; individual paintings & original objects of art lent to other museums; lending collection contains cultural, scientific & historic objects & models; museum shop sells catalogues, reproductions, prints, original craft items from around the world

L **Newark Museum Library,** 49 Washington St, PO Box 540, 07101. Tel 201-596-6622; FAX 201-642-0459; *Librn* William A Peniston
Open Wed - Fri 9 AM - 5 PM by appointment. Estab 1926 to serve the Mus staff & to provide information on the collections
Library Holdings: Vols 28,000; Per subs 200; AV — Kodachromes, lantern slides, slides; Other — Clipping files, exhibition catalogs, pamphlets, photographs
Special Subjects: Afro-American Art, American Indian Art, Antiquities-Egyptian, Antiquities-Oriental, Asian Art, Decorative Arts, Ethnology, Folk Art, Historical Material, Oriental Art, Painting - American, Period Rooms, Pre-Columbian Art, Primitive Art, Sculpture, Native American Art, Natural Sciences, Numismatics

M **Junior Museum,** 53 Washington St, PO Box 540, 07101. Tel 201-596-6605; FAX 201-642-0459; *Jr Museum Supv* Jane Caffrey Reid; *Asst Supv* Kevin Heller; *Art Asst* Enola R Romano
Open Oct - Dec & Feb - May Tues - Fri 9 AM - 5 PM, Sat 9 AM - 1 PM. No admis fee. Estab 1926 to provide art & science programs designed to stimulate the individual child in self discovery & exploration of the world & to teach effective use of the Mus as a whole, which may lead to valuable lifetime interests. Average Annual Attendance: 17,000. Mem: 3500 active; **dues** $10 lifetime mem; annual meeting in May
Income: Financed through the Newark Mus
Exhibitions: Changing exhibitions of children's artwork; annual spring & summer exhibitions in Junior Gallery
Activities: Weekday pre-school & after school; Saturday morning & summer workshops for ages 3-16; parents' workshops; community outreach & school enrichment programs; special events workshops & holiday festivals & hospital outreach; Junior Gallery offering a self-guided gallery game & art activity sessions, weekend Sept-June & weekdays in summer

L **NEWARK PUBLIC LIBRARY,** Art & Music Div, 5 Washington St, PO Box 630, 07101-0630. Tel 201-733-7840; FAX 201-733-5648; *Supv Art & Music Div* Frances Beiman
Open Sept - June Tues - Thurs 9 AM - 8:30 PM, Mon, Fri & Sat 9 AM - 5:30 PM, July - Aug Mon, Tues, Thurs & Fri 9 AM - 5:30 PM, Wed 9 AM - 8:30 PM, Sat 10 AM - 1 PM. Estab 1888, provides materials on all aspects of the visual arts to the New Jersey Library Network of New Jersey. Maintains an art gallery: a total of 200 running ft. Circ 70,000
Income: Financed by city & state appropriations
Library Holdings: Vols 75,000; Per subs 150; Original documents; Micro — Fiche, reels; AV — Slides 18,000; Other — Clipping files, exhibition catalogs, manuscripts, original art works, photographs, prints
Special Subjects: Bookplates & Bindings, Artist's Books, Fine Prints, Illustrated Books, Japanese Books & Prints, Shopping Bags, Shopping Bags
Collections: †Autographs; †Bookplates; †Fine Print Collection (22,000); †Picture Collection (750,000 illustrations); †Posters (4000)
Exhibitions: Posters from the Olympic Games: 1964-1984; Prints by Clarence Carter: A 60 year retrospective; Movable Books: A Paradise of Pop Ups, A Feast of Fold Outs, & a Mix of Mechanicals Melded with a Marvelous Melange on the Same Theme; A Celebration of Great Books from the Limited Editions Club, 1988; Prints by Joseph Pennell: 1857-1926; Charles Breed: Early Photographs, 1900-1923, 1989; Contemporary American Printmaking 1989; Poster & Prints from Puerto Rico, 1950-1990
Publications: Calendar of events, bimonthly
Activities: Gallery talks; tours

M **NEW JERSEY HISTORICAL SOCIETY,** 52 Park Pl, 07102. Tel 201-483-3939; FAX 201-483-1988; *Chmn Board* James M Porter; *Cur Coll* Elizabeth DeRosa; *Coll Mgr* Catherine Quintana; *Head Librn* Elaine Harger; *Archivist* Gregg Williams
Open Wed - Sat 10 AM - 4 PM. Admis adults $2.50, students & senior citizens $2, groups $1.50 per person. Estab 1845 to collect, preserve, exhibit & make available for study the materials pertaining to the history of New Jersey & its people. The mus has five period rooms & lobby display cases on the main floor; three galleries on second floor totaling 3900 sq ft devoted to permanent or changing exhibitions. Average Annual Attendance: 45,000. Mem: 3163; dues adults $25 & up; annual meeting third Wed in Apr
Income: Financed by endowment, mem, gifts, grants & benefits
Collections: Ceramics; glassware; furniture; important technical drawings from 1790-1815; Indian relics; New Jersey portraits, landscapes, prints & photographs; sculpture; silhouettes & miniatures; silver; toys; World War I posters; New Jersey History Artifacts
Exhibitions: (1997) From Sinatra to the Shirelles & Springstein, NJ Works, Teenage NJ 1945-1975
Publications: Exhibition catalogs; New Jersey History, quarterly; New Jersey Messenger, monthly newsletter; Instructional Bulletin; Crossroads, Jersey Journeys
Activities: Classes for children; docent training; school history clubs; lectr open to the public; tours; competitions; individual paintings & original objects of art lent to established institutions; traveling exhibitions organized & circulated; sales shop sells books, reproductions, prints & items for children

L **Library,** 230 Broadway, 07104. Tel 201-483-3939; FAX 201-483-1988; *Exec Dir* Hope Alswang; *Asst Dir Museum* Janet Rassweiler; *Cur Educ* Claudia Ochele; *Cur Coll* Libby DeRosa; *Head Librn* Elaine Harger; *Asst Dir Research* Kennett Myers
Open Tues - Sat 10 AM - 4 PM
Library Holdings: Vols 75,000; Per subs 300; Manuscript material 2000 linear feet; Micro — Fiche, reels; AV — Cassettes, motion pictures, rec, v-tapes; Other — Clipping files, exhibition catalogs, manuscripts, memorabilia, pamphlets
Special Subjects: Afro-American Art, American Indian Art, Anthropology, Archaeology, Decorative Arts, Drawings, Etchings & Engravings, Folk Art, Historical Material, History of Art & Archaeology, Illustration, Interior Design, Landscape Architecture, Landscapes, Marine Painting

L **NEW JERSEY INSTITUTE OF TECHNOLOGY,** Architecture Library, 323 Martin Luther King Blvd, 07102-1982. Tel 201-642-4390 (reference); FAX 201-643-5601; Elec Mail robertson@tesla.njit.edu. *Architecture Coordr* Anthony Grimaldi; *Architecture Librn* Jim Robertson
Open Mon - Thurs 8 AM - 8:30 PM, Fri 8 AM - 6 PM, Sat & Sun 1 - 5 PM. Estab 1975 to serve the needs of the school of architecture. For lending & reference
Purchases: $20,000
Library Holdings: AV — A-tapes, cassettes, fs, slides; Other — Clipping files, pamphlets
Special Subjects: Architecture, Art History, Constructions, History of Art & Archaeology, Interior Design, Landscape Architecture, Maps, Period Rooms, Photography, Restoration & Conservation

C **PRUDENTIAL ART PROGRAM,** 100 Mulberry St, Gateway Center 2-17th Flr, 07102. Tel 201-367-7151; *Dir Art Program* Helene Zucker Seeman; *Mgr* Naomi Baigell
Estab 1969 to enhance the surroundings & living up to social responsibility in supporting art as a genuinely important part of life
Collections: Approximately 12,000 holdings of paintings, sculptures & unique works on paper; 2558 signed graphics; 1182 posters; 241 billboards; 200 photographs

NEW BRUNSWICK

C **JOHNSON & JOHNSON,** Art Program, One Johnson & Johnson Plaza, 08933. Tel 908-524-0400; *Art Cur* Michael J Bzdak
Collections: Works on paper from the 1960s, 70s & 80s; photographs; works by New Jersey artists
Exhibitions: Paul Robeson: Artist & Activist; Images of an Icon: Photographs of the Statue of Liberty Stated as Fact; Photographic Documents of New Jersey

RUTGERS, THE STATE UNIVERSITY OF NEW JERSEY

M **Jane Voorhees Zimmerli Art Museum,** George & Hamilton Sts, 08903. Tel 908-932-7237; FAX 908-932-8201; Elec Mail surname@zimmerli.rutgers.edu. *Dir* Phillip Dennis Cate; *Assoc Dir* Ruth Berson; *Sr Cur* Jeffrey Wechsler; *Cur Educ* Katherine Tako-Girard; *Cur Prints & Drawings* Trudy Hansen; *Registrar* Barbara Trelstad; *Cur of Russian & Soviet Art* Alla Rosenfeld
Open Tues - Fri 10 AM - 4:30 PM, Sat & Sun Noon - 5 PM, cl Mon, Dec 25 - Jan 1, Sat in July, Aug. No admis fee. Estab 1966 to house Fine Arts Collection & present exhibitions through the school yr. Average Annual Attendance: 30,000. Mem: 900; dues $35, $10 student
Income: Financed by state appropriation & pub & private sources
Purchases: $150,000
Collections: Japonisme: Western Art Influenced by Japanese Art; 19th & 20th Century French & American Prints; Russian Art; Rutgers Archives for Printmaking Studios; Rutgers Collection of Original Illustrations for Children's Literature; The Herbert D & Ruth Schimmel Rare Book Library; Soviet Nonconformist Art
Exhibitions: (1997) Asian Traditions/Modern Expressions: Asian American Artists & Abstraction; The Three Billy Goats Gruff: Illustrations of Robert Bender; Emily Mason: Works on Paper; Sequences, As You Can See: Conceptual Works from the Dodge Collection; Vadim Rokhlin. (1997-98) The Great American Pop Store: Multiples of Sixties. (1998) Paul Robeson Centennial Exhbition
Publications: Exhibition catalogs; Friends Newsletter; International Center for Japonisme Newsletter
Activities: Classes for adults & children; docent tours; lect open to public; concerts; gallery talks; individual paintings & original objects of art lent to museums; originate traveling exhibitions organized & circulated; museum shop sells books

L Art Library, Voorhees Hall, 08903. Tel 908-932-7739; FAX 908-932-6743; *Art Librn* Halina Rusak; *Asst Librn* Beryl K Smith
Open Mon - Thurs 9 AM - 10 PM, Fri & Sat 9 AM - 5 PM, Sun 1 - 10 PM. Estab 1966 for academic research. For reference only
Library Holdings: Vols 65,000; Per subs 240; Micro — Fiche; Other — Clipping files, exhibition catalogs, pamphlets
Special Subjects: Architectural History; Western Art
Collections: Mary Barlett Cowdrey Collection of America Art; Howard Hibbard Collection; George Raibou Collection of Russian Art; Louis E Stern Collection of Contemporary Art; Western Art-Architectural History
Activities: Bibliographic instruction; lect; tours
M Mary H Dana Women Artists Series, Mabel Smith Douglass Library, Chapel Dr, 08903. Tel 908-932-9346; *Dir* Francoise S Puniello; *Cur* Ferris Olin
Open Mon - Thurs 8 AM - 1 PM, Fri 8 AM - 9 PM, Sat 10 AM - 6 PM, Sun Noon - 1 PM. No admis fee. Estab 1971 to exhibit the work of living women artists. Located in lobby of Mabel Smith Douglass Library on women's campus of Rutgers University
Income: Financed from gifts from endowment, student groups & departmental funds
Exhibitions: Four exhibits each academic year, all are one or two-women exhibits
Publications: Annual exhibition catalogue
Activities: Lect open to public; vis lectr; artists selected by jury
L Mabel Smith Douglass Library, Tel 908-932-9346; FAX 908-932-6777; Elec Mail olin@rci.rutgers.edu; puniello@rci.rutgers.edu. *Dir* Francoise Puniello
Open Mon - Thurs 8 AM - 1 PM, Sat 10 AM - 6 PM, Sun Noon - 1 PM. Estab 1918
Special Subjects: Graphic Arts, Graphic Design, Photography, Theatre Arts, Women Artists

NEW PROVIDENCE

M CAMBRIA HISTORICAL SOCIETY, 121 Chanlon Rd, 07974. Tel 908-665-2846; *Dir* Tamika Borden; *Cur* Donald Bruce
Open Mon - Thurs & Sat 10 AM - 4 PM. Admis adult $3. Estab 1950 as a historic house museum. Average Annual Attendance: 10,000. Mem: 1600; dues $70; annual meeting in Oct
Income: $160,000 (financed by mem)
Collections: China; dolls; furniture; glass; paintings

NORTH BRANCH

A PRINTMAKING COUNCIL OF NEW JERSEY, 440 River Rd, 08876. Tel 908-725-2110; FAX 908-725-2484; *Exec Dir* Nancy Boney; *Admin Dir* Sarah M Muccifori; *Gallery Dir* Wink Einthoven
Open Wed - Fri 11 AM - 4 PM, Sat 1 - 4 PM, cl Sun. No admis fee. Estab 1973 to promote & educate the fine art of printmaking, photography & papermaking. Average Annual Attendance: 50,000. Mem: 350; dues $35 & up; annual meeting in Jan
Income: Financed by mem & individual, foundation & corporate gifts including NJ State Council on the Arts & Somerset County Parks Commission
Exhibitions: 9 exhibitions per year, national juried exhibits
Activities: Classes for adults & children; lect open to public; competitions with awards; lending collection contains art objects, lent to corporate members & libraries; book traveling exhibitions 9 per year; originate traveling exhibitions 9 per year; sales shop sells original art

NORTH BRUNSWICK

A MIDDLESEX COUNTY CULTURAL & HERITAGE COMMISSION, 841 Georges Rd, 08902. Tel 908-745-4489; *Exec Dir* Anna M Aschkenes; *Treas* Edmund Spiro; *Exhibit Chmn* Wend Enger Gibson
Estab 1979 to provide exhibition opportunities & information services for members & educational & cultural opportunities for the general pub. Slide file of members' art work is maintained. Mem: 177; dues family or friend $25, mem $15, students & senior citizens $10; monthly board meetings
Income: Financed by mem, state grants, fundraising
Exhibitions: New Brunswick Tommorrow; Annual Statewide Show
Publications: ALCNJ Newsletter, monthly
Activities: Demonstrations open to public; competitions with awards

OCEAN CITY

A OCEAN CITY ART CENTER, 1735 Simpson Ave, 08226. Tel 609-399-7628; *Exec Dir* Eunice Bell; *Board Pres* Jack Devine
Open Mon - Thurs 9 AM - 9 PM, Fri 9 AM - 4 PM, Sat 9 AM - Noon, cl Sun. Estab 1967 to promote the arts. Teaching studios & a gallery for monthly changing exhibitions throughout the year. Average Annual Attendance: 10,000. Mem: 1200; dues individual $15, family $30; annual meeting in Feb
Income: 70,000 (financed by mem, city appropriation, New Jersey State Council on the Arts Grant 1981)
Exhibitions: Annual: Membership Show, Juried Show, Boardwalk Art Show Winners Exhibition, Christmas Crafts Fair, Juried Photography Show
Publications: Newsletters, quarterly
Activities: Classes for adults & children; lect open to the public, 12 vis lectr per year; concerts; competitions with awards; museum shop sells books, original art & crafts
L Art Library, 1735 Simpson Ave, PO Box 97, 08226. Tel 609-399-7628; *Exec Dir* Eunice Bell
Open Mon - Thurs 9 AM - 9 PM, Fri 9 AM - 4 PM, Sat 9 AM - Noon, cl Sun
Income: $70,000
Library Holdings: Vols 400; AV — Slides; Other — Exhibition catalogs
Special Subjects: Art History, Photography

OCEANVILLE

M NOYES MUSEUM, Lily Lake Rd, 08231. Tel 609-652-8848; FAX 609-652-6166; *Dir* Bonnie L Pover; *Cur Coll & Exhib* Stacy Smith
Open Wed - Sun 11 AM - 4 PM. Admis adults $3, senior citizens $1.50, full-time students & children $.50, Fri free. Estab 1983 to foster awareness & appreciation of contemporary American art & crafts & folk art from the mid-Atlantic region. Four wing galleries & central gallery space devoted to rotating exhibitions of contemporary American art, folk art & crafts. Average Annual Attendance: 12,000-15,000. Mem: 750; dues corporate sponsor $500 - $1500, benefactor $250, sponsor $125, patron $75, family $35, individual $20, students $10
Income: $335,000 (financed by endowment, mem & state appropriation)
Purchases: Purple Martin Palace by Leslie Christofferson; Crazy Quilt for T C W by Ephraim Watson; Final Resting Places Compared by Judith K Brodsky
Collections: Contemporary American Fine Art & Crafts; 19th & 20th century folk art from the mid-Atlantic region
Exhibitions: (1997) Recent Works by David Ambrose; Treasures of Art History from the New Jersey State Museum; Easy Access: Highlights from the Noyes Museum's Collection of Contemporary Art; Concert: Ben Arnold; For the Love of Art: Carvings & Paintings by South Jersey Folk Artist Albert Hoffman; Photographs by Dwight Hiscano; Immortal Beauty: Artists Capture Miss America in Art
Activities: Free tours, educational handouts for classes K - 12; Meet the Artist Days; family festivals; educ outreach programs; lect & special programs open to public; gallery talks; tours; individual paintings & original objects of work lent to other professional museums or exhibition spaces; book traveling exhibitions 2 - 6 per year; originate traveling exhibitions to other professional museums or exhibition spaces; gift shop sells posters, tote bags, notecards, handmade crafts, jewelry, baskets, glassware, ornaments
L Library, Lily Lake Rd, 08231. Tel 609-652-8848; FAX 609-652-6166; *Dir* Bonnie L Pover
Estab 1983
Special Subjects: Art Education, Art History, Folk Art, American Art, American Bird Decoys
Collections: †Contemporary American Art rotating exhibitions; crafts, folk art; Meet the Artist Days
Exhibitions: Crafts & folkart
Publications: Exhibition catalogs
Activities: Tours available for school & community groups; concerts; gallery talks; lect open to public; 4 vis lectr per year

PARAMUS

M BERGEN MUSEUM OF ART & SCIENCE, 327 E Ridgewood Ave, 07652. Tel 201-265-1248, 265-1255; *Dir* David Messer
Open Tues - Sat 9:30 AM - 4:30 PM, Sun 1 - 5 PM, cl Mon. Admis suggested donation adults $2.50, senior citizens & students $1. Estab May 1956 to maintain a mus which will provide a creative & recreative mus to stimulate youth & adult interest in art & science. Average Annual Attendance: 15,000. Mem: 800
Income: Financed by mem, contributions, county appropriations, grants & corporation
Collections: Mainly works of New Jersey artists; painting, sculpture, prints
Publications: Newsletter, quarterly
Activities: Classes for adults & children; dramatic programs; docent training; lect open to public, some to members only; concerts; gallery talks; tours; competitions; individual paintings & original objects of art lent to local organizations; museum shop sells books, prints & slides

PATERSON

M PASSAIC COUNTY HISTORICAL SOCIETY, Lambert Castle, Valley Rd, 07503-2932. Tel 201-881-2761; FAX 201-357-1070; *Acting Dir* Andrew Shick
Open Wed - Sun 1 - 4 PM. Admis adults $1.50, seniors $1, children under 15 free. Estab 1926. Located in Lambert Castle built in 1892. Average Annual Attendance: 25,000. Mem: Dues sustaining $50, family $35, regular $20, seniors $15, student $5
Collections: Koempel Spoon Collection; textiles; local historical material; paintings; photographs; decorative arts; folk art
Exhibitions: A Needle for Her Brush: Passaic County Textile Arts 1800-1950; Gaetano Federici; Heroes; Latch Key to the White House: The Lives of Garret & Jennie Hobart; Myths & Icons: The Print Collections of PCHS; Passaic County Folk Art, Life & Times in Silk City; Passaic Falls; Paterson Means Business; quilts & coverlets; The World of Catholina Lambert & His Castle; World War I posters
Publications: Castle Lite, bi-monthly newsletter; pamphlets; exhibition catalogues
Activities: Lect open to public. 4-5 vis lectr per year; gallery talks; tours; individual paintings & original objects of art lent to qualified museums by written request; book traveling exhibitions; museum shop sells books, reproductions, prints, publications, postcards, souvenirs, gifts
L Library, Lambert Castle, Valley Rd, 07503-2932. Tel 201-881-2761; FAX 201-357-1070; *Acting Dir* Andrew Shick
Open Mon - Fri 9 AM - 4 PM by appointment only
Library Holdings: Vols 10,000
Special Subjects: Local History. Silk Industry, Local Genealogy

PLAINFIELD

L PLAINFIELD PUBLIC LIBRARY, Eighth St at Park Ave, 07060-2514. Tel 908-757-1111; FAX 908-754-0063; *Dir* Joseph H Da Rold
Open Mon - Thurs 9 AM - 9 PM; Fri - Sat 9 AM - 5 PM, Sun 1 - 5 PM. Estab 1881. Maintains an art gallery with original artworks on permanent display, group shows as scheduled. Circ 135,000
Income: Financed by endowment, city & state appropriation & federal funds
Library Holdings: Vols 210,000; Per subs 475; Micro — Fiche; AV — Cassettes,

fs, motion pictures 500, rec, v-tapes 1600; Other — Exhibition catalogs
Special Subjects: Historical Material
Collections: Winslow Homer Collection; Jonas Lie Collection; Lincoln Fine Arts Collection

PRINCETON

C BRISTOL-MYERS SQUIBB PHARMACEUTICAL GROUP, Gallery at Bristol-Myers Squibb, PO Box 4000, 08543-4000. Tel 609-252-6275; FAX 609-252-6713; *Cur. Cultural & Community Relations* Pamela V Sherin; *Asst. Cultural & Community Relations* Lisa Russell
Open Mon - Fri 9 AM - 5 PM, Thurs 9 AM - 7 PM, Sat, Sun & holidays 1 - 5 PM. Estab 1972 to enrich, educate & entertain employees & outside visitors. 5560 sq ft, glass-walled fine arts gallery overlooking a 12-acre lake, mounts five professional, two employee & one in-house exhibition each year. Average Annual Attendance: 8000
Collections: Begun in 1991, consists of 2600 works in all mediums displayed in lobbies, executive floors, dining centers & offices of Bristol-Myers Squibb Pharmaceutical Group in Princeton & Plainsboro, NJ. Concentration on NJ artists & artists of diverse cultural heritages, predominantly works on paper
Activities: Gallery talks; competitions; individual paintings & original objects of art lent; book traveling exhibitions 1 or less per year; originate traveling exhibitions

PRINCETON UNIVERSITY

M The Art Museum, 08544-1018. Tel 609-258-3788; FAX 609-258-5949; *Dir* Allen Rosenbaum; *Assoc Dir* Charles Steiner; *Assoc Cur* Michael Padgett; *Assoc Cur* Betsy Rosasco; *Assoc Cur* Barbara Ross; *Registrar* Maureen McCormick; *Managing Ed* Jill Guthrie
No admis fee. Estab 1890 to make original works of art available to students in the Department of Art & Archaeology & also for the enjoyment of the University, community & general pub. About 65,600 sq ft of gallery space for permanent, semi- permanent & changing installations. Average Annual Attendance: 70,000. Mem: 1250; dues $25 & up
Income: Financed by endowment, university & by government, corporate & private sources
Collections: †Ancient Mediterranean; †British & American; †Chinese ritual bronze vessels; †Far Eastern, especially Chinese & Japanese paintings; †medieval & later European; †Pre-Columbian; Northwest Coast Indian; African
Publications: Catalogs, occasionally; Record of the Art Museum, semi-annually; newsletter, three times per yr
Activities: Docent training; lect; gallery talks; tours

L Index of Christian Art, 107 McCormick Hall, 08544-1018. Tel 609-258-3773; *Dir* Brendan Cassidy
Open Mon - Fri 9 AM - 5 PM, cl holidays. Estab 1917 as a division of the Department of Art & Archaeology. It is a research & reference collection of cards & photographs designed to facilitate the study of Christian iconography in works of art before 1400. Duplicate copies exist in Washington, DC in the Dumbarton Oaks Research Center & in Los Angeles in the Library of the University of California. European copies are in Rome in the Vatican Library & in Utrecht in the University

L Marquand Library of Art & Archaeology, McCormick Hall, 08544. Tel 609-258-3783; FAX 609-258-0103; Elec Mail jjpowell@phoenix.princeton.edu. *Librn* Janice J Powell; *Asst Librn* Denise Gavio Weinheimer
Not open to pub. Estab 1908 to serve study & research needs of the students & faculty of Princeton University in the History of Art, Architecture, Photography, Classical & Archaeology. For reference only
Income: Financed by endowments
Library Holdings: Vols 200,000; Per subs 900; Film titles 837; Micro — Fiche 12,728
Special Subjects: Archaeology, Architecture, Art History, Decorative Arts, Drawings, Eskimo Art, Etchings & Engravings, Historical Material, Landscape Architecture, Mosaics, Photography, Pottery, Sculpture

RINGWOOD

M RINGWOOD MANOR HOUSE MUSEUM, Sloatsburg Rd, PO Box 1304, 07456. Tel 201-962-7031; FAX 201-962-7658; *Cur* Elbertus Prol
Open Wed - Fri 10 AM - 4 PM, Sat & Sun 10 AM - 5 PM, cl Thanksgiving, Christmas & New Years. No admis fee. Estab 1935
Income: Financed by state appropriation & funds raised by private organization sponsored special events
Collections: Decorative arts; furniture; graphics; historical material; paintings; New Jersey iron making history
Activities: Guided tours; special events; sales shop sells books, magazines, reproductions & prints

RIVER EDGE

M BERGEN COUNTY HISTORICAL SOCIETY, Steuben House Museum, 1209 Main St, PO Box 55, 07661. Tel 201-343-9492, 487-1739 (museum); *Cur* Kevin Wright
Open Wed - Sat 10 AM - 5 PM, Sun 2 - 5 PM. No admis fee. Estab 1902 to collect & preserve historical items of Bergen County. Average Annual Attendance: 10,000. Mem: 535; dues $12; annual meeting in June
Income: Financed by mem, grants & corporate support
Collections: Collection of artifacts of the Bergen Dutch 1680-1914
Publications: In Bergen's Attic, quarterly newsletter
Activities: Classes for children; docent programs; lect open to public, 8 vis lectr per year; gift shop

SOUTH ORANGE

M SETON HALL UNIVERSITY, 400 S Orange Ave, 07079. Tel 201-761-9460, 761-9000 (main); FAX 201-752-2368; *Dir* Petrateu Doesschate Chu
Open Mon - Fri 10 AM - 5 PM, Sat & Sun 2 - 4 PM. No admis fee. Estab 1963. Troast Memorial Gallery, estab 1974, houses permanent collection of contemporary American art; Wang Fang-Yu Collection of Oriental art was estab in 1977. Average Annual Attendance: 35,000
Collections: †Archaeology Collections
Activities: Lect open to public; gallery talks

L Library, 400 S Orange Ave, 07079. Tel 201-761-9005; FAX 201-761-9432; *Acting Dean* Sr Anita Talar; *Assoc Dean* Paul Chao; *Art Librn* Beth Bloom
Open Mon - Thurs 8 AM - 12 PM, Fri 8 AM - 5 PM, Sat 9 AM - 5 PM, Sun 1 - 11 PM
Library Holdings: Vols 500,000; AV — Slides 12,000

SPRINGFIELD

L SPRINGFIELD FREE PUBLIC LIBRARY, Donald B Palmer Museum, 66 Mountain Ave, 07081-1786. Tel 201-376-4930; FAX 201-376-1334; *Head Circulation Dept* Rose Searles; *Head Technical Servs* Joan L Meyer; *Ref Dept* Henriann Robins
Open Mon, Wed, Thurs 10 AM - 9 PM, Tues, Fri, & Sat 10 AM - 5 PM. No admis fee. Estab 1975 as a museum addition to a public library established to preserve local history. The library, including a meeting room, serves as a cultural center
Collections: †Permanent collection of circulating framed art reproductions
Activities: Lect; films; puppet shows; individual reproductions lent to library patrons; lending collection contains books, framed reproductions, records, photographs, slides & periodicals

SUMMIT

A NEW JERSEY CENTER FOR VISUAL ARTS, 68 Elm St, 07901. Tel 908-273-9121; FAX 908-273-1457; *Pres* Betse Gump; *Exec Dir* Joan Good; *Dir Educ* Jennifer Koenig; *Assoc Develop & Public Relations* Amy Martin
Open weekdays 9 AM - 10 PM (includes hrs for exhibitions & for classes), weekends 9 AM - 4 PM. No admis fee. Estab 1933 to educate thru gallery exhibition & classes for diverse audience. Two gallery spaces, containing 5000 ft of exhibition space, specializing in visual art. Three exhibition spaces, 2 plus new art Park/sculpture garden. Maintains reference library. Average Annual Attendance: 50,000. Mem: 1500; Friends mem 354; dues Friends $45, general $35; annual meeting 4th wk of Apr
Exhibitions: Changing exhibitions of contemporary visual art; Members' Show; Juried Show; Outdoor Show
Publications: Class & exhibition catalogs; monthly newsletter
Activities: Classes for adults & children; docent training; Broadrange; lect open to public & members; concerts; gallery talks; tours; competitions with awards; scholarships offered; exten dept servs OUTREACH Programs; sales shop sells original art, jewelry, cards

TRENTON

A ARTWORKS, The Visual Art School of Princeton & Trenton, 19 Everett Alley, 08611. Tel 609-394-9436; *Co-Chmn Board Trustees* Nancy Myers; *Co-Chmn Board Trustees* Pamela Mount
Open Tues - Fri 11 AM - 4 PM, call for Sat hours. Estab 1964 to establish & maintain educational & cultural programs devoted to visual arts. Skylit gallery, 2000 sq ft, in downtown Trenton. Average Annual Attendance: 7500. Mem: 1000; dues $35-$50; annual meeting in May
Income: Financed by friends, class fees, workshops & demonstration fees, trip fees, entry fees, grants, corporate & private contributions
Exhibitions: Exhibitions are held at the Trenton Gallery & at various locations throughout the community
Publications: The Artworks Reader, quarterly
Activities: Classes for adults & children; lect open to public, 3-10 vis lectr per year; tours; competitions with awards; scholarships offered

L Library, 19 Everett Alley, 08611. Tel 609-394-9436; FAX 609-394-9551; *Co-Chmn Board Trustees* Nancy Myers; *Co-Chmn Board Trustees* Pamela Mounty
Reference library
Library Holdings: Vols 200; AV — Slides

M COLLEGE OF NEW JERSEY (Formerly Trenton State College), Art Gallery, Holman Hall CN 4700, Hillwood Lakes, 08650-4700. Tel 609-771-2198, 771-2652; *Pres* Dr Harold Eickoff; *Chmn & Prof* Ruane Miller; *Gallery Coordr* Judith P Masterson
Open Mon - Fri Noon - 3 PM, Thurs 7 - 9 PM, Sun 1 - 3 PM. No admis fee. Estab to present students & community with the opportunity to study a wide range of artistic expressions & to exhibit their work. Average Annual Attendance: 2000
Income: Financed by art department budget & grants including NJ State Council on the Arts, Mercer County Cultural & Heritage Commission
Purchases: Works from National Print Exhibition, National Drawing Exhibition & Mercer County Photography Exhibition
Collections: Purchases from National Print & Drawing Show
Exhibitions: Craft Show; Faculty Show; Mercer County Competitive Art; Mercer County Competitive Photography; National Drawing Exhibition; National Print Exhibition; Selections from the State Museum; Sculpture Shows; Student Show; Contemporary Issues; African Arts
Publications: Catalog for African Arts; Catalog for Contemporary Issues; Catalog for National Drawing Exhibition; Catalog for National Print Exhibition
Activities: Classes for adults & children; lect open to public, 5 vis lectr per year; gallery talks; tours; competitions with awards; individual paintings & original objects of art lent to other offices & departments on campus; lending collection contains original art works; original prints; paintings; traveling exhibitions organized & circulated to other state colleges & art schools

L FREE PUBLIC LIBRARY, Art & Music Dept, 120 Academy St, 08608-1302.
Tel 609-392-7188, Ext 24; FAX 609-396-7655; *Dir* Robert E Coumbe; *Head Art
& Music Dept* Shirley Michael
Open Mon, Wed & Thurs 9 AM - 9 PM, Tues, Fri & Sat 9 AM - 5 PM, cl Sun
& holidays. Estab 1900
Income: Financed by city appropriation
Library Holdings: Vols 8000; Per subs 35; Mounted pictures 5500; Micro —
Reels; AV — Motion pictures 300, rec; Other — Clipping files, exhibition
catalogs, memorabilia, pamphlets, photographs, prints, reproductions
Special Subjects: Advertising Design, Aesthetics, Afro-American Art, American
Indian Art, American Western Art, Antiquities-Greek, Antiquities-Roman,
Archaeology, Architecture, Art Education, Art History, Asian Art, Bookplates &
Bindings, Bronzes, Calligraphy
Exhibitions: Paintings; photographs; crafts; antiques collections

M MERCER COUNTY COMMUNITY COLLEGE, The Gallery, 1200 Old
Trenton Rd, 08690. Tel 609-586-4800, Ext 589, 588; *Gallery Dir* Henry Hose
Open Mon - Sat 11 AM - 3 PM, Thurs 5 - 8 PM. No admis fee. Estab 1971 as
an educational resource for students. Gallery of 2000 sq ft primarily for
exhibiting work by New Jersey artists. Average Annual Attendance: 3600
Income: Financed by pub funding & sales commissions
Purchases: Annual purchases from exhibits
Collections: Cybis Collection; Painting by Wolf Kahn; Sculptures by Salvadore
Dali & Isaac Whitkin; Paintings by Reginald Neal; Darby Bannard; B J
Nordfeldt; NJ artist collection; Art Work by Frank Ivera
Exhibitions: (1997) A Retrospective of Paintings by Eleanor Barnett
Activities: Classes for adults & children; dramatic programs; lect open to public,
12 vis lectr per year; concerts; gallery talks by appointment; tours; competitions
with purchase awards; scholarships offered; individual paintings & original objects
of art lent to other galleries & museums; lending collection contains original
prints
L Library, 1200 Old Trenton Rd, 08690. Tel 609-586-4800; *Library Dir* Pam Price
Estab 1891 to provide library services for the college; portion of the main floor is
devoted to permanent display cabinets. In addition display panels are used for
faculty exhibits, community exhibits & traveling exhibits
Library Holdings: Vols 64,518; Per subs 718; CD-ROMS 200; AV — A-tapes
1460, fs, rec 3107, slides 17, v-tapes 2878; Other — Pamphlets 644
Publications: Library handbook, annually; Videocassette catalog, annually

M NEW JERSEY STATE MUSEUM, 205 W State St, CN-530, 08625. Tel 609-
292-6308; FAX 609-599-4098; *Dir* Leah P Sloshberg; *Cur Fine Arts* Zoltan Buki;
Cur Cultural History Susan Finkel; *Cur Exhibits* John Mohr; *Cur Education*
Karen Cummins; *Cur Archaeology-Ethnology* Lorraine Williams; *Cur Science*
David Parris
Open Tues - Sat 9 AM - 4:45 PM, Sun Noon - 5 PM, cl Mon & most state
holidays. No admis fee. Estab 1895 by legislation to collect, exhibit & interpret
fine arts, cultural history, archaeology-ethnology & science with a New Jersey
focus; changing exhibit gallery, Hall of Natural Science, fine & decorative arts
galleries; ethnology gallery. Average Annual Attendance: 350,000. Mem: 1000;
dues $25 & up; annual meeting in June
Income: $2,000,000 (financed by state appropriation)
Collections: American fine & decorative arts of the 18th, 19th & 20th century;
†American painting from 1910-1950 with special emphasis on the Steiglitz Circle
Regionalist, Abstract Artists; New Jersey fine & decorative arts
Exhibitions: Changing exhibitions focus on New Jersey artists & cultural history;
Long-term exhibition galleries on the fine & decorative arts, ethnology & the
natural sciences
Publications: Annual report; catalogs & irregular serials; quarterly calendar;
reports
Activities: Classes for adults & children; dramatic programs; docent training; lect
open to public; concerts; gallery talks; tours; individual paintings & original
objects of art lent to other insitutions; lending collections contains 3000 motion
picture titles, 2613 reels, nature artifacts, original art works, original prints,
paintings, photographs, sculpture, slides; book traveling exhibitions; museum shop
sells books, international folk crafts or items related to collection
M Historical Morven, 55 Stockton St, Princeton, 08540. Tel 609-683-4495; FAX
609-497-6339; *Site Adminr* Mary Alice Quigley; *Sr Interpreter* Barbara Soganic
Open Wed 11 AM - 2 PM, other weekdays by advance request. No admis fee,
donations accepted. Built c.1758 by Richard Stockton, a signer of the
Declaration of Independence & later the residence of New Jersey Governors;
tours & exhibitions highlight Stockton Family & architectural preservation.
Average Annual Attendance: 5000
Income: Program of the New Jersey State Museum; financed by gifts, grants &
benefits
Collections: Artifacts Archaeology
Exhibitions: Period Rooms of Federal & Jacksonian Eras
Activities: Classes for adults; docent training; lect open to public, 6 vis lectr per
year; tours

M OLD BARRACKS MUSEUM, Barrack St, 08608. Tel 609-396-1776; FAX 609-
777-4000; *Dir* Richard Patterson; *Cur* Danielle Riebel; *Cur Educ & Military
Historian* Lawrence Schmidt; *Chief Historical Interpreter* Jeffrey Macechak
Open Tues - Sat 11 AM - 5 PM, Sun 1 - 5 PM, Mon by appointment. Admis
adults $2, children 12 & under $.50, educational groups free. Built 1758, estab
1902 as museum of history & decorative arts. Located in English barracks that
housed Hessian Soldiers Dec 1776. Average Annual Attendance: 28,000. Mem:
460; dues $10 - $200; annual meeting May
Income: Financed by mem, state appropriation & donations
Collections: †American decorative arts 1750-1820; Archaeological materials;
†early American tools & household equipment; †military artifacts; 19th century
New Jersey Portraits; patriotic paintings & prints
Exhibitions: The Trenton Barrack 1758-1918; Washington & The Battle of
Trenton; 18th century Period Rooms & Soldiers Quarters; changing exhibitions;
Of War, Law & the Third Amendment; Hail the Conquering Hero Comes:
Washington's Triumphal Entry into Trenton; The Restoration of the Old
Barracks
Publications: The Barracks Bugle, quarterly newsletter; The Old Barracks at

Trenton, book
Activities: Classes for children; dramatic programs; docent training; lect open to
public, 3 vis lectr per year; tours; exten dept serves elementary schools;
individual paintings & original objects of art lent to museums; lending collection
contains slides & reproduction military objects/costumes; book traveling
exhibitions; museum shop sells books, reproductions, prints, slides, historical toys,
ceramics

M TRENTON CITY MUSEUM, Cadwalader Park, 319 E State St, 08608. Tel
609-989-3632; FAX 609-989-3624; *Dir* Theresa McNichol
Open Tues - Sat 11 AM - 3 PM, Sun 2 - 4 PM. No admis fee. Estab 1978 to
provide a cultural window into the ongoing life of the city & its people. Mus is a
historical site, an Italiante Revival Mansion; only remaining example of John
Notman architecture in Trenton & is located in historic Cadwalder Park,
designed by Frederick Law Olmstead. Average Annual Attendance: 5000. Mem:
Dues $15-$100
Income: Financed by endowment & city appropriation
Collections: †Trenton-made Ceramics; objects made in or pertaining to Trenton;
full set of Trenton directories
Exhibitions: (1997) Potteries: The Story of Trenton's Ceramic Industry
Activities: Classes for adults & children accompany changing exhibits; lect open
to public, 10 vis lectr per year; sales shop sells books, prints, original art, jewelry
& toys for children

UNION

M KEAN COLLEGE OF NEW JERSEY, College Gallery, Morris Ave, 07083. Tel
908-527-2307,527-2347; *Pres* Ronald Applebaun; *Gallery Dir* Alec Nicolescu
Open Mon - Thurs 10 AM - 2 PM, 5 - 7 PM, by appointment at other times. No
admis fee. Estab 1971 as a forum to present all art forms to students & the
community through original exhibitions, catalogues, fine art, by guest curators,
art history & mus training students. One gallery 22 x 34 ft plus an alcove 8 x 18
ft on first floor of arts & humanities building. Average Annual Attendance: 3000
Income: Financed by state appropriation & private grants
Collections: American painting, prints sculpture by Audobon, L Baskin, Robert
Cooke, Max Ernst, Lamar Dodd, W Homer, P Jenkins, J Stella, Tony Smith,
Walter Darby Bannard, Werner Drewes, B J O Norfeldt, James Rosenquist,
Robert Rauschenberg, Odilon Redon; photographs, rare books, and 1935-50
design and furniture; Ben Yamimoto Art Work
Exhibitions: (1997) Nancy Dreyfuss: A Dedication; George Seigle; 60th
Anniversary: American Abstract Artist
Publications: Catalogues for exhibitions
Activities: Dramatic programs; lect open to public; individual paintings lent to
colleges, institutions, corporations & departments on the campus
L Nancy Thompson Library, Morris Ave, 07083. Tel 908-527-2017; *Librn* Barbara
Simpson
Open Mon - Thurs 8 AM - 11:30 PM, Fri 8 AM - 10 PM, Sat 8 AM - 5 PM,
Sun 1 - 8 PM. Estab 1855 to support instruction
Purchases: $6000
Library Holdings: Vols 243,000; Per subs 1350; AV — A-tapes 150, fs, slides; Other —
Exhibition catalogs, pamphlets

UPPER MONTCLAIR

M MONTCLAIR STATE UNIVERSITY, Art Galleries, 07043. Tel 201-655-5113;
FAX 201-655-5279; *Dir* Lorenzo Pace; *Pres* Irvin Reid; *VPres* Richard Lynde;
Dean Geoffrey Newman; *Dir Art Dept* John Luttropp
Open Mon, Wed & Fri 10 AM - 4 PM, Tues & Thurs 10 AM - 6 PM. No admis
fee. Estab 1973. Three galleries with 1200 sq ft, 600 sq ft & 600 sq ft. Average
Annual Attendance: 5000
Collections: Cosla Collection of Renaissance Art, Lida Hilton Print Collection,
Wingert Collection of African & Oceanic Art
Exhibitions: Contemporary East Indian Artists; Japanese Expressions in Paper
Activities: Classes for adults; lect open to public; concerts; gallery talks;
scholarships offered
L Calcia Fine Arts Slide Library, Calcia Fine Arts Bldg Rm 214, 07043. Tel 201-
655-4151; *Slide Librn Cur* Lynda Hong
Open Mon - Fri 9 AM - 4:30 PM. Circ 40,000
Library Holdings: Vols 13,600; Per subs 35; AV 300; AV — Cassettes, fs, slides,
v-tapes; Other — Exhibition catalogs
Special Subjects: Afro-American Art, American Indian Art, American Western
Art, Antiquities-Assyrian, Antiquities-Byzantine, Antiquities-Egyptian,
Antiquities-Etruscan, Antiquities-Greek, Antiquities-Oriental, Antiquities-
Persian, Antiquities-Roman, Architecture, Asian Art, Ceramics, Decorative Arts,
Prehistoric to contemporary art

WAYNE

M WILLIAM PATERSON COLLEGE OF NEW JERSEY, Ben Shahn Galleries,
300 Pompton Rd, 07470. Tel 201-595-2654; FAX 201-595-3273; *Dir* Nancy
Einreinhofer
Open Mon - Fri 10 AM - 5 PM. No admis fee. Estab 1969 to educate & instruct
students & visitors through exhibits & programs. 5000 sq ft space divided into
three gallery rooms specializing in the exhibition of contemporary art. Average
Annual Attendance: 10,000
Collections: Permanent collection of WPC 19th century landscapes; paintings &
sculptures from 1950's to present
Exhibitions: Three gallery rooms of rotating exhibits of contemporary art that
change twice during each semester
Publications: Exhibition catalogs
Activities: Art at Lunch program; docent programs; lect open to public, 15 vis
lectr per year

WOODBRIDGE

M **WOODBRIDGE TOWNSHIP CULTURAL ARTS COMMISSION,** Barron
Arts Center, 582 Rahway Ave, 07095. Tel 908-634-0413; *Chmn* Dr Dolores
Gioffre; *Dir* Stephen J Kager; *Prog Coordr* Nancy Casteras
No admis fee. Estab 1977 to provide exhibits of nationally recognized artists,
craftsmen & photographers, & of outstanding NJ talent. Gallery is housed in an
1877 Richardsonian Romanesque Revival building on the National Register of
Historic Places. Average Annual Attendance: 8000
Income: $71,000 (financed by endowment & city appropriation)
Activities: Lect open to public, 1-2 vis lectr per year; awards; concerts; poetry
readings

NEW MEXICO

ABIQUIU

M **GHOST RANCH LIVING MUSEUM,** Carson National Forest, Canjilon
District, General Delivery, 87510. Tel 505-685-4312; *Dir* Ray Martinez;
Environmental Educ Diego Martinez
Open April - Sept 8 AM - 5:30 PM, Oct - Mar 8 AM - 4:30 PM, cl Mon. No
admis fee. Estab 1959 as an outdoor interpretive project for the conservation of
natural resources. Average Annual Attendance: 105,000
Income: $140,000 (financed by government appropriations & corporate
contributions)
Collections: Paintings & prints related to natural resources conservation; art
objects
Publications: Ghost Ranch Museum & More, bulletin; Museum at Ghost Ranch,
bulletin; We Called it Ghost Ranch, book
Activities: Classes for children; lect open to public; tours; museum shop sells
books & prints; gift shop
L **Conference Center Library,** HC 77, Box 11, 87510. Tel 505-685-4333; FAX 505-
685-4519; *Librn* Edgar W Davy
Estab 1955. Reference library
Library Holdings: Vols 15,000; Per subs 42; AV — Cassettes, fs, motion pictures,
slides, v-tapes; Other — Clipping files, original art works
Special Subjects: American Indian Art, American Western Art, Anthropology,
Archaeology, Art History, Calligraphy, Ceramics, Crafts, Decorative Arts,
Ethnology, Folk Art, Handicrafts, Historical Material, Painting - American,
Photography, Conservation

ALBUQUERQUE

M **ALBUQUERQUE MUSEUM OF ART & HISTORY,** 2000 Mountain Rd NW,
PO Box 1293, 87103. Tel 505-243-7255; FAX 505-764-6546; *Dir* James C
Moore; *Admin Mgr* Thomas C O'Laughlin; *Cur Art* Ellen J Landis; *Cur History*
John Grassham; *Cur Exhib* Robert Woltman; *Cur Coll* Tom Lark; *Cur Educ*
Chris Steiner
Open Tues - Sun 9 AM - 5 PM. No admis fee. Estab 1967 as a city mus with the
purpose of diffusing knowledge & appreciation of history & art, establishing &
maintaining a museum & related reference library, collecting & preserving objects
of historic & artistic interest, protecting historic sites, works of art & works of
nature from needless destruction, providing facilities for research & publication &
offering popular instruction & opportunities for aesthetic enjoyment. Average
Annual Attendance: 123,000. Mem: 1075; dues patron $250, friend $100, family
$40, senior citizen family $30
Income: Financed by city appropriation & Albuquerque Museum Foundation
Collections: Decorative arts; costumes; †fine arts and crafts; objects and artifacts
relevant to our cultural history from 20,000 BC to present; photography
Publications: Las Noticias, monthly
Activities: Classes for adults & children; docent training; lect; gallery talks; tour;
competition with awards; original objects of art lent to other museums; book
traveling exhibitions 3 per year; originate traveling exhibitions; sales shop selling
books, original magazines, reproductions, prints, Indian jewelry, local crafts &
pottery

M **ALBUQUERQUE UNITED ARTISTS,** PO Box 1808, 87103. Tel 505-243-
0531; *Pres* Allan Rosenfield; *Office Mgr* Carol Adamec
Estab 1978 to represent/show work of member artists, statewide shows. Various
locations, shows held at galleries around Albuquerque as donated spaces.
Average Annual Attendance: 1200. Mem: open to contemporary artists; dues $30
Exhibitions: Visions of Excellence; exhibits at various locations
Publications: Monthly newsletter

A **INDIAN ARTS & CRAFTS ASSOCIATION,** 122 La Veta Dr NE, Ste B,
87108. Tel 505-265-9149; Elec Mail iaca@ix.netcom.com. *Exec Dir* Susan
McGuire
Estab 1974 to promote, preserve, protect & enhance the understanding of
authentic handmade American Indian arts & crafts. Mem: 710; quarterly
meetings in Jan, Apr, July & Oct
Income: Financed by mem dues, markets
Exhibitions: Annual Indian IACA Artists of the Year
Publications: Annual directory; brochures on various Indian arts & crafts;
newsletter, 6 times per year
Activities: Marketing seminars for Indian artists & crafts persons; lect are open
to public, 4-5 vis lectr; competitions

M **INDIAN PUEBLO CULTURAL CENTER,** 2401 12th St NW, 87104. Tel 505-
843-7270; *Dir* Rafael Gutierrez; *VPres* Joyce Merrill; *Museum Coordr* Pat Reck;
Retail Marketing Mgr Keith Lucero
Open 9 AM to 5:30 PM. Admis adults $3, senior citizen $2, student $1. Estab
1976 to advance understanding & insure perpetuation of Pueblo culture. Pueblo

Gallery houses monthly Native American artist exhibits. Average Annual
Attendance: 300,000. Mem: 800-1000; dues family $25, individual $15, students
& senior citizens $7.50; annual meeting 3rd Tuesday in Feb
Income: Financed by admis, restaurant revenue & office space rental
Collections: †Jewelry, †paintings, †photos, †pottery, †rugs, †sculptures, †textiles
Exhibitions: Monthly exhibits of Native American art; Pueblo Children's Art
Contest
Publications: Pueblo Horizons, 4 times per yr
Activities: Classes for adults & children; docent training; lect open to public, 6-12
vis lectr per year; competitions with awards; museum shop sells books, original
art, reproductions, prints, slides, Native American arts & crafts (pots, rugs,
kachinas)

C **LOVELACE MEDICAL FOUNDATION,** Art Collection, 5400 Gibson Blvd,
SE, 87108. Tel 505-262-7000; FAX 505-262-7729; *Chief Exec Officer* John
Lucas
Estab 1940. Foundation utilizes patient waiting lobbies throughout medical clinic
& hospital complex to display collection
Collections: Indian (American Southwest) Textiles; Santa Fe School paintings;
Taos School paintings
Activities: Tours; individual paintings lent to requesting museums

A **NEW MEXICO ART LEAGUE,** Gallery, 3407 Juan Tabo NE, 87111. Tel 505-
293-5034; *Pres* Lucille M Miera; *VPres* Thomson B Baure; *Treas* Sue Sterling
Open Tues - Sat 10 AM - 4 PM, Sun 1 - 4 PM, cl Mon. No admis fee. Estab
1929 to promote artwork of New Mexico; art gallery. Members' works exhibited in
space 1400 sq ft. Average Annual Attendance: 2500. Mem: 325; dues $35;
monthly mem meetings
Income: Financed by mem & sales
Collections: National Small Paintings Exhibit
Exhibitions: 24th Annual Small Painting Exhibit (national competition)
Publications: Catalog of National Small Painting Show; newsletter, monthly
Activities: Classes for adults & children; docent training; lect open to the public;
6 vis lectr per year; gallery talks; tours; competitions with awards; individual
paintings lent to schools & museums; lending collection contains original art
works & prints, paintings, sculptures & slides; sales shop sells original art

A **SOCIETY OF LAYERISTS IN MULTI MEDIA (SLMM),** 1408 Georgia NE,
87110. Tel 505-268-1100; *Founder* Mary Carroll Nelson
Estab 1981
Income: $2500 (financed by mem)
Collections: Mixed Media

UNIVERSITY OF NEW MEXICO

M **University Art Museum,** Fine Arts Ctr, 87131. Tel 505-277-4001; FAX 505-277-
7315; *Dir* Peter Walch; *Registrar* Kitty Longstreth-Brown; *Cur Exhibits* Lee
Savary; *Assoc Dir* Linda Bahm; *Cur Educ* Jeanette Entwistle; *Cur Prints/Photos*
Kathleen Howe
Open Tues - Fri 9 AM - 4 PM, & Tues evening 5 - 8 PM, Sun 1 - 4 PM. No
admis fee. Estab 1963. Maintains four galleries; a print & photograph room
which is open to the pub at certain hours. Average Annual Attendance: 49,000.
Mem: 200; dues $10-$500; annual meeting in May
Income: Financed by university appropriations, grants & donations
Collections: Field Collection of Spanish Colonial Silver; Tamarind Archive of
lithographs; 19th & 20th century American painting & sculpture, drawings; prints
by American & European masters; 19th & 20th century lithographs &
photography
Exhibitions: (1997) French Oil Sketches & the Academic Tradition; Eyedazzlers:
20th Century Painting & 19th Century Navajo Weaving; Into the Nineties: Prints
from the Tamarind Institute
Publications: Bulletin; exhibition catalogs
Activities: Lect open to public; inter-museum loans; traveling exhibitions
organized & circulated; museum shop sells books, catalogs, magazines, cards
M **Jonson Gallery,** 1909 Las Lomas Rd NE, 87131-1416. Tel 505-277-4967; FAX
505-277-3188; *Cur* Joseph Traugott; *Assoc Cur* Tiska Blankenshop
Open Tues - Fri 9 AM - 4 PM; Tues 5 - 9 PM; cl Sat & Sun & holidays. No
admis fee. Estab 1950 for the assemblage & preservation of a comprehensive
collection of the works of Raymond Jonson; a depository for works of art by
other artists & their preservation, with emphasis on the Transcendental Painting
Group (1938-42); the exhibition of contemporary works of art. The structure
includes a main gallery, four storage rooms, work room & office, a reception
room & living quarters for the curator. Average Annual Attendance: 10,000
Income: Financed through University & Jonson Trust
Collections: Jonson reserved retrospective collection; †other artists works &
works by Jonson students
Exhibitions: Media/Contra/Media, Paula Hocks Retrospect; Living with the
Enemy; Annual Summer Raymond Johnson Exhibition
Publications: Exhibition announcements; The Art of Raymond Jonson; The
Transcendental Painting Group, New Mexico 1938-1941
Activities: Lect open to public, 5 vis lectr per year; gallery talks; tours;
scholarships offered; individual paintings & original works of art lent to museums
& campus president's office; lending collection contains color reproductions,
original prints, slides, sculpture, 1000 books, 2000 original art & 2000 paintings;
originate traveling exhibitions; books sold by order
L **Jonson Library,** 1909 Las Lomas Rd NE, 87131-1416. Tel 505-277-4967, 277-
1844; FAX 505-277-3188; *Assoc Cur* Tiska Blankenship
For reference only, exceptions made for special projects
Library Holdings: Vols 500; AV — Slides; Other — Clipping files, exhibition
catalogs, manuscripts, memorabilia, pamphlets, photographs, reproductions
Special Subjects: Transcendentalism
Collections: The Jonson Archives containing books & magazines relating to
Raymond Jonson, his letters, his diaries, catalogs, clippings, hotographs & slides
of works
L **Fine Arts Library,** Fine Arts Ctr, 87131-1501. Tel 505-277-2357; FAX 505-277-
6019; *Dir* James Wright; *Assoc Dir* Nancy Pistorius
Open Mon - Thurs 8 AM - 10 PM, Fri 8 AM - 6 PM, Sat 10 AM - 6 PM, Sun
Noon - 8 PM. Estab 1963 to provide library assistance, literature, microforms &

sound recording materials to support the programs of the university in the areas of art, architecture, music & photography

Library Holdings: Vols 109,000; Per subs 237; Micro — Cards, fiche, reels; AV — A-tapes, cassettes, fs, rec, v-tapes; Other — Exhibition catalogs, pamphlets
Special Subjects: American Indian Art, American Western Art, Architecture, Art Education, Art History, Ceramics, Conceptual Art, Decorative Arts, Drafting, Drawings, Furniture, Goldsmithing, Graphic Arts, Islamic Art, Jewelry, History of Photography, Modern American & European, Native American, Spanish Colonial, Southwest Music, Opera

M VERY SPECIAL ARTS NEW MEXICO, Very Special Arts Gallery, 2015 Yale Blvd SE, PO Box 7784, 87194. Tel 505-245-8545; FAX 505-843-8262; *Exec Dir* Beth Rudolph; *Dir Enabled Arts Center* Deborah Mashibini; *Exhib Coordr* Richard Garriott-Stejskal
Estab 1994. Small gallery focusing on the art of individuals with disabilities, outsider, visionary & intuitive art. Exhibits the work of emerging & established artists
Exhibitions: 15th Anniversary Exhibit; Holiday Exhibition; Those That Can: Teach II
Publications: Arts Access, quarterly
Activities: Lect open to public, 2-3 vis lectr per year

ARTESIA

M ARTESIA HISTORICAL MUSEUM & ART CENTER, 505 W Richardson Ave, 88210. Tel 505-748-2390; FAX 505-746-3886; *Dir* Nancy Dunn; *Curatorial Asst* Lee Macaw; *Registrar* Merle Rich
Open Tues - Sat 8 AM - 5 PM. No admis fee. Estab 1970 to preserve & make available local history; maintains reference & research library. Gallery showcases local & regional artists, exhibits drawn from permanent art collection, traveling exhibits
Income: Financed by city appropriation
Collections: Art; early Area Histroy; Farm; Kitchen; Ranch; Native American Artifacts; Oil & Mineral; WWI & WWII
Exhibitions: Russell Floore Memorial Southwest Art Show (competition)
Activities: School & civic club programs; lect open to public, 1-3 vis lectr per year; competitions with awards; individual paintings lent to other museums & organizations; book traveling exhibitions 1-3 per year

CHURCH ROCK

M RED ROCK STATE PARK, Red Rock Museum, PO Box 328, 87311. Tel 505-863-1337; *Museum Clerk* Maxine A Touchine
Open Mon - Fri 8 AM - 4:30 PM, Memorial Day - Labor Day daily 8 AM - 7 PM. Admis adults $1, children $.50. Estab 1951 to acquaint visitors with the arts & crafts of the Navajo, Zuni & Hopi Indians & other tribes of the Four Corners area. A small mus manned by Red Rock State Park; displaying Indian arts & crafts & exhibitions on natural history. Average Annual Attendance: 20,000.
Income: Financed by city of Gallup, private contributions & admis fees
Collections: Kachina Carving Doll Collection; Anasazi relics; arts & crafts of Navajo, Zuni, Hopi & other Pueblos; specimens of geological, herbarium, archaeological & cultural materials of the Four Corners area
Exhibitions: Permanent exhibits: Navajo Hogan; Pueblo Culture; Elizabeth Andron Houser Collection of Native American Arts; Gallup Intertribal Indian Ceremonial Posters, Jewelry, Basketry, Navajo Rugs; temporary exhibits vary
Publications: Exhibitions catalog; quarterly newsletter
Activities: Lect open to public; gallery talks; tours; concerts; rodeos; individual paintings & original objects of art lent to other museums; book traveling exhibitions 1-4 per year; originate traveling exhibitions circulate to museums & arts & educational organizations; sales shop sells books, reproductions, magazines, prints, sandpaintings, pottery, jewelry & other Native American crafts, cassettes & compact discs of Native American music
L Library, PO Box 328, 87311. Tel 505-863-1337; *Museum Cur* Joan Barnette; *Museum Clerk* Rae Lynn Francisco
Open Mon - Fri 8 AM - 4:30 PM, Memorial Day - Labor Day daily 8 AM - 9 PM. Admis suggested donation adults $1, children $.50
Income: Municipally sponsored
Library Holdings: Vols 350; Micro — Cards; Other — Clipping files, exhibition catalogs, manuscripts, pamphlets, photographs, prints
Special Subjects: Anthropology, Geology, Indians, Science, Sociology, Southwest

CIMARRON

M PHILMONT SCOUT RANCH, Philmont Museum, Philmont Scout Ranch, 87714. Tel 505-376-2281; FAX 505-376-2281; *Dir* Stephen Zimmer
Open Mon - Fri 8 AM - 5 PM. No admis fee. Estab 1967 to exhibit art & history of Southwest United States. Average Annual Attendance: 30,000
Income: Financed by endowment & sales desk revenue
Collections: Art by Ernest Thompson Seton; American Indian Art; History of Boy Scouts of America; History of New Mexico
Exhibitions: Ernest Thompson Seton's Collection of Plains Indian Art
Activities: Docent programs; lect open to public; lending collection contains over 6000 items; retail store sells books, magazines, prints, slides
L Seaton Memorial Library, Philmont Scout Ranch, 87714. Tel 505-376-2281; *Dir* Stephen Zimmer
Estab as a lending & reference facility
Income: Financed by endowment
Library Holdings: Vols 6500; Per subs 17; Other — Clipping files, exhibition catalogs, framed reproductions, manuscripts, memorabilia, original art works, pamphlets, photographs, prints

DEMING

M DEMING-LUNA MIMBRES MUSEUM (Formerly Luna County Historical Society, Inc), 301 S Silver St, 88030. Tel 505-546-2382; *Coordr* Katy Hofacket; *Dir* Ruth Brown; *Archives* Dolly Shannon
Open Mon - Sat 9 AM - 4 PM, Sun 1:30 - 4 PM, cl Thanksgiving & Christmas Day, open by appointment during evenings for special interest groups. Admis free with donations. Estab 1955, moved into Old Armory 1978, to preserve Luna County history, historical items & records for reference. Art gallery is in a passageway 50 ft x 10 ft, no windows; open to local artists for displays. Average Annual Attendance: 20,000. Mem: 200; dues $3; annual meeting in Jan
Income: Financed by donations & endowment earnings
Collections: Chuck wagon, vintage clothing, dolls, frontier life objects & other items on the local history; Mimbres Indian artifacts; mine equipment; minerals; paintings & saddles; camera display; phone equipment; quilt room; old lace display; National Guard display; Bataan-Corregidor display & momument; facsimile of front of Harvey House; bell collection; bottle collection, china, ceramics & silver displays; antiques; Military Room; Art Gallery
Publications: History of Luna County & Supplement One
Activities: Dramatic programs; docent training; tours; service awards; museum shop sells Indian jewelry, postcards & pottery

LAS CRUCES

M NEW MEXICO STATE UNIVERSITY, University Art Gallery, PO Box 30001, MSC 3572, 88001. Tel 505-646-2545; FAX 505-646-8036; Elec Mail artglry@nmsu.edu. *Gallery Dir* Charles Lovell; *Museum Educator* Rosemary McLoughlin; *Registrar* Cathy Brockman; *Preparator* Matt Lynch
Open Tues - Fri 10 AM - 5 PM, Thurs 10 AM - 7 PM, Sun 1 - 4 PM. No admis fee. Gallery estab in 1974 as an educational resource for the University & southern New Mexico. 4000 sq ft exhibition space. Average Annual Attendance: 18,000. Mem: 100; dues $10 & up; annual meeting in June
Purchases: Eric Avery, Sue Coe, Luis Jimenez & Frances Whitehead
Collections: †19th Century Retablos from Mexico; †20th century prints, photographs, works on paper, graphics & paintings
Exhibitions: (1997) James Drake; Gregory Amgnoff
Publications: Visiones, biannual arts newsletter; semiannual exhibit catalogs
Activities: Docent training; school tours & outreach; family day; lect open to public, 12 vis lectr per year; gallery talks; tours; competitions with awards; individual paintings & original objects of art lent to museums with appropriate security & climate control conditions; lending collection contains original art works, original prints, paintings & photographs; book traveling exhibitions up to 5 per year; originate traveling exhibitions

LAS VEGAS

M NEW MEXICO HIGHLANDS UNIVERSITY, Arrott Art Gallery, Donnelly Library, National Ave, 87701. Tel 505-425-7511, 454-3338; *Art Dir* Bob Read
Open Mon - Fri 8 AM - 5 PM. No admis fee. Estab 1956 to acquaint University & townspeople with art of the past & present. Gallery dimensions approx 20 x 40 ft. Average Annual Attendance: 4000-5000
Income: Financed by state appropriation
Collections: †Permanent collection
Exhibitions: Twelve individual & group shows; one statewide show
Publications: University general catalog, annually
Activities: Classes for adults & children; lect open to public, 1 vis lectr per year; concerts; gallery talks; tours; competitions; book traveling exhibitions, 1-2 per year; originate traveling exhibitions

LOS ALAMOS

M FULLER LODGE ART CENTER & GALLERY, 2132 Central, PO Box 790, 87544. Tel 505-662-9331; FAX 505-662-6455; *Dir* Gloria Gilmore-House
Open Mon - Sat 10 AM - 4 PM, Sun 1 - 4 PM. No admis fee. Estab 1977 to provide an art center to the regional area; to foster the interests of the artists & art interested pub in the Community. Center is approx 210 running ft; located in (1995) storefront, west of Bradbuary Science Mus; gallery area has been renovated. Average Annual Attendance: 12,000. Mem: 460; dues memorial $1500, life $1000, corporate $300, patron $100, sponsor $50, contributing $30, member $20
Income: Financed by mem, county appropriation, grants, gallery shop sales, annual art sale
Collections: †Northern New Mexico Art (all media)
Exhibitions: Los Alamos Studio Tour Club Exhibition; New Mexico Sculptors' Guild; UNM Faculty & Student Exhibition; Que Pasa: Art in New Mexico-all media, juried show for New Mexico artists; Society of Layerists in Multi-Media; Biennial Crafts 6-State Juried Exhibition; Art through the Loom Exhibition featuring Art through the Loom Weavers Guild; Summer Fair; Through the Looking Glass National Photography Juried Exhibition; Art Meets Science Exhibition; Early Christmas Fair; Art Benefit Sale; New Mexico Las Tejedoras Weavers Guild.
Publications: Bulletin, quarterly
Activities: Classes for children; docent training; seminars for artists; competitions with awards; gallery talks; individual paintings & original objects of art lent; book traveling exhibitions; originate traveling exhibitions; museum shop sells original art by member artists, jewelry, cards & posters

MESILLA

M GADSDEN MUSEUM, W Barker Rd, PO Box 147, 88046. Tel 505-526-6293;
Owner Mary Veitch Alexander
Open Mon - Sun 9 - 11 AM & 1 - 5 PM, cl Easter, Thanksgiving, Christmas.
Admis ages 12 & up $2.14, ages 6-11 $1.07. Estab 1931 to preserve the history
of Mesilla Valley. Average Annual Attendance: 3000
Income: $2000 (financed by donations)
Collections: Civil War collection; clothing; gun collection; Indian artifacts,
including pottery; paintings; Santo collection
Activities: Tours; museum shop sells books

PORTALES

M EASTERN NEW MEXICO UNIVERSITY, Dept of Art, Dept of Art 105, Sta
19, 88130. Tel 505-562-2510; *Dir* Greg Erf
Open 7 AM - 9 PM. No admis fee. Estab 1935 for exhibiting student artwork;
gallery is room coverted for student works
Income: Financed by University funds
Collections: Student works in Art Department Collection
Exhibitions: Seen & Unseen
Activities: Individual paintings & original objects of art lent to the university
L Golden Library, Sta 32, 88130. Tel 505-562-2624; *Dir Art Dept* Greg Erf
Public exhibitions & artist presentations
Income: $3000 (financed by University & grants)
Purchases: Some student art is purchased
Library Holdings: Vols 10,000; Per subs 35; Micro — Cards, fiche, prints, reels;
AV — A-tapes, cassettes, fs, Kodachromes, motion pictures, rec, slides, v-tapes;
Other — Exhibition catalogs, framed reproductions, original art works, pamphlets,
photographs, prints, sculpture

ROSWELL

M ROSWELL MUSEUM & ART CENTER, 100 W 11th St, 88201. Tel 505-624-
6744; FAX 505-624-6765; *Pres Board Trustees* Robert Cress; *VPres* John
Hultman; *Treas* Henry Lucero; *Dir* William D Ebie; *Asst Dir* Laurie J Rufe; *Cur
Coll* Wesley A Rusnell; *Cur Painting/Registrar* Theresa Ebie
Open Mon - Sat 9 AM - 5 PM, Sun & holidays 1 - 5 PM, cl Thanksgiving,
Christmas Eve, Christmas & New Year's Day. No admis fee. Estab 1937 to
promote & cultivate the fine arts. The basis of the fine arts collection being
paintings & sculptures with emphasis on the artistic heritage of the Southwest. 16
galleries are maintained for art works; plus Robert H Goddard rocket display; 24,
000 sq ft of exhibition space. Average Annual Attendance: 60,000. Mem: 1340;
dues $15 & up
Income: $650,000 (financed by mem, city & county appropriation)
Collections: †Regional & Native American fine arts & crafts & Western historical
artifacts; †international graphics collection; †20th century Southwestern paintings
& sculpture, drawings; †Hispanic Art
Exhibitions: Permanent collection plus 10-14 temporary exhibitions annually
Publications: Bulletin, quarterly; Exhibition Catalogs
Activities: Classes for adults & children; docent training; school outreach
program; lect open to public, 8-10 vis lectr per year; concerts; gallery talks; tours;
scholarships for children's classes offered; individual paintings & original art
objects lent to qualified museums; book traveling exhibitions 3-4 per year;
museum shop sells books, magazines, original art, reproductions & prints
L Library, 100 W 11th St, 88201. Tel 505-624-6744; FAX 505-624-6765;
Reference only
Library Holdings: Vols 7500; Per subs 35; Micro — Cards; AV — A-tapes 187,
cassettes, motion pictures, slides 6000, v-tapes 137; Other — Exhibition catalogs,
prints
Special Subjects: American Indian Art, Historical Material, Painting - American,
Photography, Southwestern Art

SANTA FE

A THE CENTER FOR CONTEMPORARY ARTS OF SANTA FE, 1050 Old
Pecos Trail, 87501. Tel 505-982-1338; FAX 505-982-9854
Gallery open 1 PM - 8 PM, open evenings for performances or cinema
screenings. no admis fee for gallery, media arts admis $3.50-$5, other $6-$15.
Estab 1979, as a multidisciplinary contemporary arts organization. Hosts
performance art: dance, poetry, musical, mixed media. Exhibition space for
changing shows; theatre; dance space; new performance space & Teen Project
space. Average Annual Attendance: 65,000 (all events)
Exhibitions: Visual arts exhibitions
Activities: Teen Project-performing, visual, mixed media, music, radio & video
workshops & projects for teens; lect open to public, 12 vis lectr per year;
concerts

M GUADALUPE HISTORIC FOUNDATION, Santuario de Guadalupe, 100 S
Guadalupe St, 87501. Tel 505-988-2027; *Pres* Joe J Martinez; *VPres* Donald J
Ortiz; *Treas* Waldo Anton; *Dir* Emilio I Ortiz
Open Mon - Sat 9 AM - 4 PM, cl weekends Nov - Apr. Admis - donation. Estab
1790, became an international mus 1975 to preserve & extend the community's
awareness through educ & in culture areas. Gallery space is used for exhibits of
local artists, with emphasis on Hispanic art. Average Annual Attendance: 37,000.
Mem: 435; dues $15 & up; annual meeting in Apr
Income: $41,000 (financed by mem, grants, corporate & private donations)
Collections: Archdiocese Santa Fe Collection, 16th century books, 18th -19th
century religious artifacts; Mexican Baroque paintings; Our Lady of Guadalupe
mural by Jose de Alzibar; Renaissance Venetian painting
Publications: Flyers; noticias; quarterly newsletter
Activities: Dramatic programs; docent training; performing arts; visual arts;
poetry readings; lect open to public, 1-2 vis lectr per year; concerts; tours

M INSTITUTE OF AMERICAN INDIAN ARTS MUSEUM, 108 Cathedral Pl,
87501. Tel 505-988-6281; FAX 505-988-6273; WATS 800-476-1281. *Dir* Paul
Gonzales; *Assoc Dir* Jane Piasecki
Open Mon - Sat 10 AM - 5 PM, Sun Noon - 5 PM, cl Mon in Jan & Feb. Admis
adults $4, seniors $2, children under 16 & members free. Estab 1962 to train
Native American students to own, operate & manage their own museums; to
collect, preserve & exhibit materials relating to the Native American; act as a
resource area for Indian Museums nationwide. 2100 sq ft of exhibition galleries,
15,000 sq ft outdoor Art Park Performance Gallery. Average Annual
Attendance: 100,000
Income: $1,100,000 (financed by Congressional appropriation)
Purchases: $50,000
Collections: National collection of contemporary Indian arts America; Vital &
comprehensive collection in fields of paintings, graphics, textiles, ceramics,
sculpture, jewelry, photographs, printed textiles, costumes, ethnological materials
such as drums & paraphernalia for general living
Exhibitions: Semi Annual Student Exhibitions; Triennial Faculty Exhibitions;
Special Exhibitions 6-8 per year, Installation Pieces Quarterly, Semi- Annual
Exhibitions of the Permanent Collection
Publications: Exhibition catalogs
Activities: Classes for adults & children; lect open to public, 25-30 vis lectr per
year; concerts; gallery talks; tours; competitions with awards; scholarships;
individual paintings & original objects of art lent to museums, state capital &
colleges; book traveling exhibitions 6-8 per year; originate traveling exhibitions;
museum shop sells jewelry, pottery, fashions, books, magazines, original art &
prints all of a contemporary nature
L Alaska Native Culture & Arts Development, PO Box 20007, 87504. Tel 505-
988-6423; FAX 505-986-5509; *Asst Librn* Grace Nuvayestewa
Open Mon - Fri 8 AM - 5 PM & 6 - 9 PM, Sat 11 AM - 3 PM, Sun 1 - 5 PM.
Estab 1962 to support college curriculum. For reference only. Circ 30,000
Income: $31,000 (financed by private fundraising & government)
Purchases: $2500
Library Holdings: Vols 400; Per subs 25; Artists Files, Oral Histories on video-
tape; AV — Slides, v-tapes 957
Special Subjects: American Indian Art, Eskimo Art, Native American subjects

M MUSEUM OF NEW MEXICO, 113 Lincoln Ave, PO Box 2087, 87504-2087.
Tel 505-827-6451; FAX 505-827-6427; *Dir* Thomas Livesay; *Deputy Dir* Marsha
Jackson
Open daily 10 AM - 5 PM, cl Mon, Christmas, New Year's Day, Easter &
Thanksgiving. Admis multiple visits & 2-Day pass $8, adults single visit $5,
children under 17 free. Estab 1909. Mus is a state institution & operates in four
major fields of interest: Fine Arts, International Folk Art, History &
Anthropology. Four separate buildings, each with galleries: Southwestern art,
Indian art & crafts. Average Annual Attendance: 850,000. Mem: 800; dues $35-
$1000; board of regents meeting in July
Income: Financed by state appropriation, federal grants & private funds
Collections: Over 500,000 objects, artifacts & works of art in the fields of art,
archaeology, folk art & history
Publications: Annual report; books; El Palacio, quarterly; exhibition catalogs;
guides; magazines; monographs; pamphlets
Activities: Educ kits with hands-on materials are sent to schools throughout the
state; docent program serving 15,000 school children; films; lect open to public,
12 vis lectr per year; gallery talks; tours; extension dept serves United States &
Mexico; original objects of art lent to other cultural institutions; lending
collection 7000 original art works; book traveling exhibitions 2-3 per year;
originate traveling exhibitions; museum shop sells books, magazines,
reproductions, prints, slides, posters & Indian arts & crafts
L Fray Angelico Chavez History Library, 120 Washington, PO Box 2087, 87504-
2087. Tel 505-827-6470; FAX 505-827-6521; *Librn* Orlando Romero
Mus houses four separate research libraries on folk art, fine arts, history &
anthropology
Library Holdings: Vols 15,000; Journals 40
Special Subjects: Spanish Colonial History, Southwestern Art & Archaeology
M Museum of Fine Arts, 107 W Palace, PO Box 2087, 87503. Tel 505-827-4470;
FAX 505-827-4473; *Dir* Stuart Ashman; *Cur 20th Century Painting* Joseph
Traugott; *Cur Painting* Sandra D'Emilio; *Cur Photo* Steve Yates; *Asst Cur
Contemporary Art* Aline B; *Registrar* Joan Tafoya; *Librn* Mary Jebsen;
Preparator Charles Sloan
Open Tues - Sun 10 AM - 5 PM, cl Mon. Admis adults $5, 4-day & annual
passes available for $8, children free. Estab 1917 to serve as an exhibitions hall,
chiefly for New Mexican & Southwestern art. Building is of classic Southwestern
design (adobe); attached auditorium used for performing arts presentations.
Average Annual Attendance: 290,000
Income: Financed by state appropriation
Collections: Drawings, paintings, photographs, prints & sculpture with emphasis
on New Mexican & regional art, including Native American artists
Publications: Exhibition catalogs; gallery brochures
Activities: Classes for adults & children; dramatic programs; docent training; lect
open to public, 10 vis lectr per year; concerts; gallery talks; tours; competitions;
individual paintings & original objects of art lent to art museums; lending
collection contains original prints, paintings, photographs & sculpture; originate
traveling exhibitions; museum shop sells books, original art, reproductions &
prints
L Museum of Fine Arts Library, 107 W Palace, PO Box 2087, 87504-2087. Tel
505-827-4453; FAX 505-827-4473; *Librn* Mary Jebsen
Open Tues - Fri 10 AM - 4:30 PM & by appointment, cl Mon. Estab 1917 to
provide fine arts research materials to mus staff, artists, writers & community
Purchases: $4000
Library Holdings: Vols 6000; Per subs 45; AV — Slides; Other — Clipping files,
exhibition catalogs, manuscripts, pamphlets
Special Subjects: American Art & Artists with Emphasis on Southwestern Art &
Artists
Collections: Biography files of artists

M Museum of International Folk Art, 706 Camino Lejo, PO Box 2087, 87504-2087. Tel 505-827-6350; FAX 505-827-6349;
Internet Home Page Address http://www.state.nm.us/moifa. *Dir* Charlene Cerny; *Asst Dir* Joyce Ice PhD; *Cur Latin American Folk Art* Barbara Mauldin; *Cur European & American Coll* Judith Chiba Smith; *Cur Spanish Colonial Coll* Robin Farwell Gavin; *Cur Textiles & Costumes* Nora Fisher; *Asst Cur Textiles* Tamara Tjardes; *Cur Southwestern Hispanic* Mariah Sacoman; *Prog Coordr* Hope Connors; *Librn* Judith Sellars; *Cur Middle Eastern-Asian Coll* Frank Korom PhD; *Dir Educ* Laura Temple-Sullivan; *School Arts Coordr* Ariela Gomez; *Unit Registrar* Debbie Garcia; *Collections* Paul Smutko
Open daily 10 AM - 5 PM, cl Mon. Admis adults multiple visits $8, single visit $5, children under 17 free. Estab 1953 to collect, exhibit & preserve worldwide folk art. Average Annual Attendance: 100,000
Income: Financed by endowment, grants & state appropriation
Collections: †Arts of Traditional Peoples, with emphasis on Spanish Colonial & Hispanic-related cultures; †costumes & textiles
Exhibitions: (Permanent) Familia y Fe/Family & Faith; Multi-Visions: A Common Bond. (1997) At Home Away from Home: Tibetan Culture in Exile. (1997-98) A Kind & Gentle Life: The Narrative Folk Paintings of Maria Hesch
Publications: American Folk Masters, 1992; The Spirit of Folk Art, 1989; Mud, Mirror & Thread: Folk Traditions of Rural India, 1993; Traditional Arts of Spanish New Mexico, 1994; Rio Grande Textiles, 1994; Recycled, Re-Seen: Folk Art from the Global Scrap Heap, 1996
Activities: Classes for children; lect open to public; gallery talks; original objects of art lent to responsible museums nationwide; originate traveling exhibitions; museum shop sells books & original art

L Library, 706 Camino Lejo, PO Box 2087, 87504-2087. Tel 505-827-6359, Ext 623; FAX 505-827-6349; *Librn* Judith Sellars; *Archivist* Eleanore Voutselas
Open Tues - Fri 10 AM - Noon & 1 - 5 PM. Estab 1953 to support museum's research needs. Reference library
Income: Financed by private & state support
Purchases: $5500
Library Holdings: Vols 12,500; Per subs 180; AV — A-tapes, cassettes, rec, slides; Other — Clipping files, exhibition catalogs, manuscripts, pamphlets, photographs
Special Subjects: Afro-American Art, Anthropology, Asian Art, Calligraphy, Carpets & Rugs, Crafts, Decorative Arts, Dolls, Embroidery, Ethnology, Folk Art, Handicrafts, Islamic Art, Jewelry, Latin American Art, Folk Costume Design & Construction, Folk Art of Various Countries, Religious Folk Art of New Mexico
Collections: †Folk literature & music of the Spanish Colonist in New Mexico circa 1800-1971

M Palace of Governors, PO Box 2087, 87504-2087. Tel 505-827-6473; FAX 505-827-6521; *Assoc Dir* Thomas Chavez
Built in 1610
Exhibitions: Society Defined; Another Mexico

M Laboratory of Anthropology, 708 Camino Lajo, 87501. Tel 505-827-6344; FAX 505-827-6497; *Librn* Laura Holt
Open Mon - Fri 10 AM - 5 PM. Estab 1936 as a research laboratory in archaeology & ethnology
Collections: Materials from various Indian cultures of the Southwest: jewelry, pottery & textiles
Exhibitions: (1997) Here, Now & Always

M MUSEUM OF NEW MEXICO, Office of Cultural Affairs of New Mexico, The Governor's Gallery, State Capitol, PO Box 2087, 87503. Tel 505-827-3089; FAX 505-827-3026; *Cur* Terry Bumpass
Open Mon - Fri 8 AM - 5 PM. No admis fee. Estab 1977 to promote New Mexico artists. Gallery located in Governor's reception area in the State Capitol. Average Annual Attendance: 50,000
Income: Financed by state appropriation & the Mus of New Mexico
Exhibitions: Exhibits of New Mexico Art (all media); New Mexican Governor's Awards Show
Activities: Educ dept; docent training; lect open to public, 200 vis lectr per year; gallery talks; tours; A Governor's Award for Excellence in the Arts; individual paintings & original objects of art lent to other museums; book traveling exhibitions 1 per year; originate traveling exhibitions to other public galleries; museum shop sells books, original art & prints

A NEW MEXICO ARTISTS' ASSOCIATION, 4350 Airport Rd, Ste 5-239, 87505. Tel 505-982-5639; FAX 505-473-4718;
Estab 1987
Activities: Workshops offered for ceramics, drawing, jewelry, painting, photography, printmaking, sculpture, silversmithing & weaving

M PUEBLO OF SAN ILDEFONSO, Maria Martinez Museum, Rte 5, Box 315-A, 87501. Tel 505-455-2031 (business office), 455-3549 (visitors' center); *Tourism Mgr* Harold Torres
Open Mon - Fri 8 AM - 4 PM. Mus admis is included with $3 entrance fee to the Pueblo. Estab to display pottery: history, artists & methods of pottery making
Collections: Arts & Crafts; Clothing; Painting; Pottery

M SCHOOL OF AMERICAN RESEARCH, Indian Arts Research Center, PO Box 2188, 87504. Tel 505-982-3584; FAX 505-989-9809; Elec Mail iarc@sarsf.org. *Pres* Douglas W Schwartz; *Dir* Michael J Hering; *VPres* Duane Anderson
Open to members & special scholars by appointment. Estab 1907. Dedicated to advance studies in anthropology, support advanced seminars for post-doctoral scholars, archaeological research, anthropological publication & a pub educ program. Southwest Indian Arts Building houses collections for research. Mem: 1100; dues family $50, individual $40
Income: Financed by endowment, mem, special grants & individuals
Collections: Basketry, Kachinas, paintings, silver jewelry, Southwest Indian pottery, textiles
Publications: Publications of Advanced Seminar Series
Activities: Lect for members only, 5 vis lectr per year

L Library, PO Box 2188, 87504. Tel 505-982-3583; *Librn* Jane Gillentine
Open to scholars of the School of American Research; staff & members by appointment
Library Holdings: Vols 6000; Per subs 50
Special Subjects: Anthropology

M WHEELWRIGHT MUSEUM OF THE AMERICAN INDIAN, PO Box 5153, 87502. Tel 505-982-4636; FAX 505-989-7386; *Dir* Jonathan Batkin; *Asst Dir* Mary Branham; *Cur* Janet Fragua Hevey
Open Mon - Sat 10 AM - 5 PM, Sun 1 - 5 PM. Admis by donation. Estab 1932 to record & present creative expressions of Native American people. Main gallery is shaped like inside of Navajo hooghan or house. Skylight Gallery is smaller exhibit space. Average Annual Attendance: 54,000. Mem: 1300; dues $25-$35
Income: Financed by endowment & mem
Collections: American Indian art & ethnographic material of Southwestern US, Navajo, Apache & Pueblo people
Exhibitions: Native American Youth Invitational; (1997) Dan Namingha Sculpture. (1997-98) Charlene Teeters
Publications: Bulletins & books on Navajo culture; exhibition catalogs
Activities: Classes for adults & children; dramatic programs; docent training; tours; lect; children's reading hours; slide-lect; lect open to public, 10 vis lectr per year; gallery talks; tours; competitions with awards; scholarships offered; individual paintings & original objects of art lent to museums; lending collection contains books, color reproductions, framed reproductions, Kodachromes, nature artifacts, original art works, original prints, paintings & phonorecords; museum shop sells books, magazines, original art, reproductions, prints, pottery, jewerly, textiles, beadwork (all original)

L Mary Cabot Wheelwright Research Library, 704 Camino Lejo, PO Box 5153, 87502. Tel 505-982-4636; FAX 505-989-7386; *Dir* Jonathan Batkin; *Cur* Janet Fragua Hevey
Open to researchers for reference
Library Holdings: Vols 4000; Per subs 3000; Per Issues 3000
Special Subjects: American Indian Art, Anthropology, Archaeology, Architecture, Art History, Carpets & Rugs, Ceramics, Costume Design & Construction, Crafts, Eskimo Art, Ethnology, Folk Art, Historical Material, Jewelry, Painting - American

TAOS

M BENT MUSEUM & GALLERY, 117 Bent St, PO Box 153, 87571. Tel 505-758-2376; *Owner* Otto T Noeding; *Owner* Faye S Noeding
Open daily 10 AM - 4 PM. Admis adults $1, children 8 - 15 $.50, under 8 free. Estab 1959. Home of the first territorial governor of New Mexico - Site of his death in 1847
Collections: American Indian Art; old Americana; old Taos art
Activities: Sales shop sells books, prints, Indian jewelry, pottery & dolls

M KIT CARSON HISTORIC MUSEUMS, PO Drawer CCC, 87571. Tel 505-758-0505; FAX 505-758-0330; *Bus Mgr* Mike Williams; *Co-Dir* Skip Miller; *Co-Dir* Karen S Young
Estab 1949 to maintain & operate the home of Kit Carson & to perpetuate his name & deeds. The Kit Carson Home is now classified as a Registered National Historic Landmark. In 1962 the home of Ernest L Blumenschein was given to the Foundation by Miss Helen C Blumenschein; it is now classified as a Registered National Landmark. In 1967 Mrs Rebecca S James gave the Foundation the Ferdinand Maxwell House & Property. In 1972, acquired the Hacienda de Don Antonio Serverino Martinez, pominent Taos merchant & offical during the Spanish Colonial Period; designated a Registered National Historic Landmark. Acquired in 1972, site of the Simeon Turley Trading Post, Grist Mill & Distillery, built in 1830 & destroyed in Taos Rebellion of 1847; entered in National Register of Historic Places Acquired in 1977 La Morada de Don Fernando de Taos, Chapel and meeting place of Los Penitentes, an early religious organization; entered in National Register of Historic Places. Average Annual Attendance: 90,000. Mem: 200; dues patron $1000, sponsor $500, benefactor $250, sustaining $100, contributing $50, family $30, individual $15, annual meeting in Apr
Income: $400,000 (financed by admis, museum shops, rentals, donations & grants)
Purchases: $70,000
Collections: †Historical and Archaeological Collection; Western Americana
Publications: Director's annual report; Taos Lightnin Newsletter, quarterly; publications on the historic sites; technical reports
Activities: Tours; lect

L Archives, PO Drawer CCC, 87571. Tel 505-758-5440; FAX 505-758-0330; Elec Mail nitkit@laplaza.org, wow—joan@laplaza.org. *Co-Dir* Skip Miller; *Co-Dir* Karen S Young; *Librn* Nita Murphy; *Registrar-Archivist* Joan Phillips
Open by appointment only. For reference only
Purchases: $500-$1000
Library Holdings: Vols 500; Maps; AV — Cassettes, Kodachromes, lantern slides, slides; Other — Clipping files, exhibition catalogs, manuscripts, pamphlets, photographs, reproductions
Special Subjects: American Western Art, Anthropology, Archaeology, Historical Material, Maps, Southwestern Art, Kit Carson
Collections: †Photograph archives; †vertical files

M Ernest Blumenschein Home & Studio, PO Drawer CCC, 87571. Tel 505-758-0505; FAX 505-758-0330; *Co-Dir* Skip Miller; *Co-Dir* Karen S Young
Open daily 9 AM - 5 PM, cl Christmas, Thanksgiving & New Year's Day. Admis family rate $8, adults $4, senior citizens $3, youths $2.50, children under 6 years free with parents, group tour rates available & combination tickets available to Martinez Hacienda & Kit Carson Mus. Home of world renowned artist & co-founder of famous Taos Soc of Artists. Restored original mud plaster adobe dating to 1789 with traditional furnishings of New Mexico & European furnishings. Average Annual Attendance: 17,000. Mem: 195; dues $15-$500; annual meeting in Apr
Collections: Tacos Society of Artists Collection; fine art paintings
Exhibitions: Temporary exhibits of arts and crafts of the Taos area and of New

Mexico

Activities: Docent training; lect open to public, 2 vis lectr per year; tours; annuals founder art show; book traveling exhibitons; museum shop sells books, reproductions & prints

M **Home & Museum,** PO Drawer CCC, 87571. Tel 505-758-4741; FAX 505-758-0330; *Co-Dir* Skip Miller; *Co-Dir* Karen S Young

Open daily 9 AM - 5 PM. Admis family rate $8, adults $4, senior citizens $3, youths $2.50, children under 6 years free with parents, group tours available. Home of the famous Western Scout & Fur Trapper. Built in 1825, bought by Kit in 1843 as a wedding gift for his beautiful bride, Josefa Jaramillo, member of prominent Taos family. They lived in the home for 25 years, their lifetime together as both died in 1868. Average Annual Attendance: 44,000. Mem: 200

Income: Financed by donations & admis

Collections: Period furniture and furnishings

Exhibitions: Life of Kit Carson & Personal Items including clothing, guns, saddles, tools; Mountain Man Exhibits; Spanish articles; archaeological artifacts

Activities: Museum shop sells books, reproductions, prints, furs, original crafts, mountain-man fur trade items

M **Hacienda Martinez,** PO Drawer CCC, 87571. Tel 505-758-1000; FAX 505-758-0330; *Co-Dir* Skip Miller; *Co-Dir* Karen S Young

Open Mon - Sun 9 AM - 5 PM. Admis family rate $8, adults $4, senior citizens $3, youth $2.50, children under 6 free with parents, group tours rates & combination tickets available to Kit Carson Mus & Blumenschein Home. Estab 1972, built & occupied by Don Antonio, Martinez 1800-1827. Last remaining hacienda open to pub in New Mexico. Martinez, an important trader with Mexico, also served as Alcalde of Northern New Mexico. Spanish Colonial fortress hacienda having 21 rooms & two large patios. Living mus program. Average Annual Attendance: 30,000

Income: Financed by admis & donations

Collections: †Furniture, †tools & †articles of Spanish Colonial period & personal family articles

Exhibitions: Various art & craft exhibits, irregular schedule

Activities: Docent training; lect open to public, 6 vis lectr per year; tours; The Annual Taos Trade Fair; museum shop sells books, original art, reproductions & prints

M **MILLICENT ROGERS MUSEUM OF NORTHERN NEW MEXICO,** PO Box A, 87571. Tel 505-758-2462; FAX 505-758-5751; *Exec Dir* David R McFadden; *Prog Mgr* Vincente Martinez; *Coll Mgr* Guadalupe Tafoya; *Financial Mgr* Susan Strong

Open Mon - Sun 10 AM - 5 PM, cl holidays. Admis family groups $12, adults $6, students, seniors & groups of 10 or more $5, children under 16 $1. Estab 1956 for the acquisition, preservation, research, display & interpretation of art & material cultures of the southwest focusing on New Mexico. The museum's permanent home is a traditional adobe building, once the private residence of Claude J K Anderson. Average Annual Attendance: 20,000. Mem: 600; quarterly Board of Directors meeting in spring & fall

Income: Financed by endowment, mem, donations, admis, grants & revenue from mus store

Collections: American Indian Art of Western United States, emphasis on Southwestern groups; paintings by contemporary Native American artists; religious arts and non-religious artifacts of Hispanic cultures; nucleus of collection formed by Millicent Rogers

Exhibitions: Tutavoh; Learning the Hopi Way; Hozhoogo Nitsehakees; Thoughts of Beauty; Abiquin Country; Photographs by Mark Kane. Hispanic Women of New Mexico

Publications: Las Palabras, quarterly newsletter for members of the museum

Activities: Classes for adults & children; lect open to public, 2-3 vis lectr per year; gallery talks; tours; field trips; seminars; original works of art lent to similar institutions; museum shop sells books, magazines, original art, prints, art & craft work by contemporary Southwest artisans & artists

L **Library,** 1504 Museum Rd, PO Box A, 87571. Tel 505-758-2462; FAX 505-758-5751; Elec Mail mrm@laplaza.org. *Exec Dir* David R McFadden

Open daily 9 AM - 5 PM, Nov - Mar cl Mon. Estab 1956, emphasis on Native American, Chicano/Hispanic northern New Mexican Anglo artists. Average Annual Attendance: 45,000. Mem: 500

Income: Financed by admis, mem & mus store

Library Holdings: Vols 6000; Per subs 25; Other — Clipping files, exhibition catalogs, manuscripts, pamphlets

Special Subjects: American Indian Art, Archaeology, Art Education, Art History, Decorative Arts, Eskimo Art, Folk Art, Historical Material, Latin American Art, Mexican Art, Primitive Art, Southwestern Art, Art & Architecture, Material Culture & Art, Museology, Southwestern Hispanic History

Collections: Limited edition, special edition & out of print books on Southwestern Americana; Maria Martinez pottery; over 600 Native American & Hispanic textiles; Native American costumes

Activities: Classes for adults & children; docent training; lect open to public, 10 vis lectr per year; gallery talks; tours; book traveling exhibitions; originate traveling exhibitions

A **TAOS ART ASSOCIATION INC,** Stables Art Center, 133 Paseo de Pueblo Norte, 87571. Tel 505-758-2052, 758-2036; *Pres* Stan Crawford; *Exec Dir* Julie Layer; *Museum Shop Mgr* Vikki Madd

Open Mon - Sat 10 AM - 5 PM, Sun Noon - 5 PM. No admis fee. Estab Oct 1981 as a nonprofit community art center to promote the arts in Taos for the benefit of the entire community. Average Annual Attendance: 30,000. Mem: 1000; annual meeting Apr

Income: Financed by mem, contributions, grants & sales of art works

Exhibitions: Annual Awards Show for Taos County; 14 exhibitions per year, including Artists of Taos; Taos Impressionism; Spirit in Art; SW Furniture; Taos Non Representational Technology

Publications: Monthly calendar of events to membership & with map to hotels

Activities: Classes for adults & children; children's program in painting & theater; dramatic programs; lect open to public; concerts; competitions; originate traveling exhibitions; sales shop sells books, magazines, original art, reproductions, prints, slides & posters

L **TAOS PUBLIC LIBRARY,** 402 Camino De La Placita, 87571. Tel 505-758-3063; FAX 505-758-7864; *Librn* Tracy McCallum

Open Tues - Thurs 10 AM - 8 PM, Fri & Sat 10 AM - 5 PM. Estab 1936. Circ 59,000

Library Holdings: Vols 45,000; Per subs 70; AV — Slides; Other — Clipping files, exhibition catalogs, original art works, pamphlets, photographs, prints, reproductions

Special Subjects: American Indian Art, American Western Art, Archaeology, Art History, Southwestern Art, Southwestern History

Activities: Lect; concerts; films; plays

M **UNIVERSITY OF NEW MEXICO,** The Harwood Foundation, PO Box 4080, 87571. Tel 505-758-9826; FAX 505-758-1475; *Dir* Robert M Ellis; *Cur* David Witt

Open Mon - Fri Noon - 5 PM, Sat 10 AM - 4 PM. No admis fee. Estab 1923, Buildings & contents given to the University by Elizabeth Case Harwood, 1936, to be maintained as an art, educational & cultural center; maintained by the University with all activities open to the pub. Building was added to the National Register of Historic Places in 1976; two main galleries plus smaller display areas

Income: Financed by University of New Mexico, private contributions & grants, government grants, endowment income

Collections: †Permanent collection of works by Taos artists

Exhibitions: Four changing exhibits each year; New Mexico Impressions; Three Generations of Hispanic Photographers; (1997-98) Traveling Exhibition Spirit Acerdent; The Art & Life of Patrocino Barela

Publications: Exhibit catalogs; quarterly newsletter

Activities: Tours; individual paintings & original objects of art lent to museums; lending collection contains original prints, paintings, photographs & sculpture

NEW YORK

ALBANY

M **ALBANY INSTITUTE OF HISTORY & ART,** 125 Washington Ave, 12210. Tel 518-463-4478; FAX 518-462-1522; *Chmn* Alan Goldberg; *Dir* Christine M Miles; *Chief Librn* Sandra Markham; *Chief Cur* Tammis Groft; *Cur History* Wes Balla

Open Wed - Sun Noon - 5 PM, cl most NY state holidays. Admis adults $3, seniors & students $2, children under 12 free, mem free, Wed free. Estab 1791, inc 1793 as the Society for the Promotion of Agriculture, Arts & Manufactures; 1829 as Albany Institute; 1900 as Albany Institute & Historical & Art Soc. Present name adopted 1926. Maintains luncheon gallery, mus shop & sales-rental gallery. Average Annual Attendance: 100,000. Mem: 2000; dues $35 & up; annual meeting in May

Income: Financed by endowment, mem, sales, foundation, city, county, state & federal grants & special gifts

Collections: Art, decorative arts & historical artifacts related to the art, history & culture of Upper Hudson Valley Region from the 17th century to present; 18th & 19th century paintings; Hudson River School; Ceramics; New York (especially Albany) costumes, furniture, glass, pewter, silver & other regional decorative arts; textiles

Exhibitions: Hudson River School paintings from the Institute's collection; Dutch Rooms, 1737 Limmer Gallery; All Aboard: Railroad Images; Cast with Style: 19th Century Cast-iron Stoves; Visions & Vistas; City Neighbor: An Albany Community Album; Made in Albany: 18th & 19th Century Decorative Arts

Publications: Catalogues; several books about the history of New York State; Remembrance of Patria: Dutch Arts & Culture in Colonial America; Thomas Cole: Drawn to nature members' newsletter & calendar

Activities: Classes for adults & children; docent training; lect open to public, 10 vis lectr per year; gallery talks; tours; individual paintings & original objects of art lent to other museums; book traveling exhibitions 4 per year; sales-rental gallery sells books, original art & prints

L **McKinney Library,** 125 Washington Ave, 12210. Tel 518-463-4478; FAX 518-462-1522; Elec Mail 75701.2362@compuserve.com. *Chief Librn* Sandra Markham

Open Wed - Fri Noon 4 PM. Estab 1793 to collect historical material concerning Albany & the Upper Hudson region, as well as books on fine & decorative art related to the Institute's holdings. For reference only

Library Holdings: Vols 14,000; Per subs 60; Architectural Plans; Deeds; Ephemeral; Maps; Posters; Micro — Reels; Other — Clipping files, exhibition catalogs 50, manuscripts, memorabilia, pamphlets, photographs

Special Subjects: Architecture, Art History, Carpets & Rugs, Ceramics, Crafts, Decorative Arts, Folk Art, Furniture, Glass, Historical Material, Silver, Textiles, Albany social and political history, American painting and sculpture, Dutch in the Upper Hudson Valley, 17th to 19th century manuscripts

M **COLLEGE OF SAINT ROSE,** Picotte Hall Art Gallery, 324 State St, 12210. Tel 518-485-3902; FAX 518-485-3920; *Dir* Jeanne Flanagan

Open Mon - Fri 10 AM - 4:30 PM, Mon - Thurs 6 - 8 PM, Sun Noon - 4 PM, cl Sat. No admis fee. Estab 1969 to act as a forum for contemporary art in the downtown Albany area. Average Annual Attendance: 1200

Income: Financed by college funds

Collections: Paintings, prints, sculpture

Activities: Classes for adults; lect open to public, 6-8 vis lectr per year; gallery talks; tours; scholarships offered

M **HISTORIC CHERRY HILL,** 523-1/2 S Pearl St, 12202. Tel 518-434-4791; *Dir* Liselle La France; *Cur* Christine Heidorf; *Educ Dir* Rebecca Watrous

Open Tues - Sat 10 AM - 3 PM, Sun 1 - 3 PM. Admis adults $3.50, senior citizens $3, students $2, children $1. Estab 1964 to preserve & research the house & contents of Cherry Hill, built for Philip Van Rensselaer in 1787 & lived in by him & four generations of his descendents until 1963. Georgian mansion having 14 rooms of original furniture, ceramics, paintings and other decorative

arts spanning all five generations & garden. Average Annual Attendance: 5000.
Mem: 250; dues $15 & up
Income: Financed by endowment fund, admis, mem, program grants, sales shop revenue
Collections: Catherine Van Rensselaer Bonney Collection of Oriental decorative arts; New York State furniture; silver; ceramics; textiles and paintings dating from the early 18th thru 20th centuries
Publications: New Gleanings, quarterly newsletter
Activities: Educ dept; docent training; classroom materials; lect open to public; tours; paintings and art objects are lent to other museums and exhibitions; museum shop sells books, postcards & reproductions

A **NEW YORK OFFICE OF PARKS, RECREATION & HISTORIC PRESERVATION,** Natural Heritage Trust, Empire State Plaza, Agency Building One, 12238. Tel 518-474-0456; *Deputy Commissioner Admin & Fiscal Prog Affairs* Nancy Palumbo; *Chief of Grants, State of NY* Kevin Burns
Estab to administer individual gifts & funds; funding appropriated by state legislatures for various purposes
Exhibitions: Letchworth Art & Crafts Show

L **NEW YORK STATE LIBRARY,** Manuscripts & Special Collections, Cultural Educ Ctr, 11th Flr, Empire State Plaza, 12230. Tel 518-474-6282; FAX 518-474-5786; Elec Mail baul@unix2.nysed.gov. *Dir* GladysAnn Wells; *Sr Librn* Billie Aul; *Assoc Librn* James Corsaro
Open Mon - Fri 9 AM - 5 PM
Income: Financed by State
Special Subjects: Art History, Historical Material, Manuscripts, New York State History
Collections: Over 50,000 items: black & white original photographs, glass negatives, daguerreotypes, engravings, lithographs, bookplates, postcards, original sketches & drawings, cartoons, sterograms & extra illustrated books depicting view of New York State & Portraits of its citizens past & present
Exhibitions: Exhibit program involves printed & manuscript materials

M **NEW YORK STATE MUSEUM,** Cultural Education Ctr, Empire State Plaza, 12230. Tel 518-474-5877; *Dir & Asst Commissioner* Louis D Levine
Open Mon - Sun 10 AM - 5 PM. Donation suggested. Estab 1836 to research, collect, exhibit & educate about the natural & human history of New York State for the people of New York; to function as a cultural center in the Capital District of the Empire State. Museum has 1 1/2 acres of exhibit space; three permanent exhibit halls devoted to people & nature (history & science) themes of Adirondack Wilderness, Metropolitan New York, Upstate New York; three temporary exhibit galleries of art, historical & technological artifacts. Average Annual Attendance: 900,000
Income: $5,700,000 (financed by state appropriation, government & foundation grants & private donations)
Collections: Ethnological artifacts of Iroquois-Algonkian (New York area) Indians; circus posters, costumes, decorative arts, paintings, photographs, postcards, prints, toys, weapons
Activities: Classes for adults & children; lect open to public; concerts; individual paintings & original objects of art lent to museums; lending collection contains nature artifacts, original art works, original prints, paintings, photographs & slides; book traveling exhibitions, 6 per year; originate traveling exhibitions; museum shop sells books, magazines, original art, reproductions, prints, slides, toys, baskets, pottery by local artists, jewelry, stationery & posters

A **PRINT CLUB OF ALBANY,** 140 N Pearl St (Mailing add: Ft Orange Sta, PO Box 6578, 12206-6578). Tel 518-432-9514; Elec Mail pcaprint@crisny.org; Internet Home Page Address http://crisny.org/not-for-profit/pcaprint/index.htm. *Pres* Charles Semowich; *Librn & Archivist* William Clarkin; *VPres* Diana Westercook; *Print Selection Committee Chmn* Thomas Andress; *Facilities Chmn* James Otis; *Treas* Donald Bolon
Varies. No admis fee. Estab 1933 for those interested in all aspects of prints & printmaking. Maintains reference library. Average Annual Attendance: 2000.
Mem: 200; dues $60; mem open to artists who have national recognition, non-artists need interest in prints; annual meeting in May
Income: Financed by mem, city & state appropriation, sales, commissions & auction
Purchases: Prints & printmakers' archives
Special Subjects: Art History, Drawings, Etchings & Engravings, Prints, Woodcuts
Collections: †Drawings; †Plates; Prints from all periods & countries concentrating on 20th century America
Exhibitions: Internet Exhibitions; Joint Exhibitons with Albany Symphony Orchestra; Members Exhibitions; Triannal National Print Exhibition 17th National Open Competitive Print Exhibition
Publications: Exibition catalogues; newsletter, 5 per year
Activities: Educ dept; workshops; lect open to public, 3 vis lectr per year; talks; competition with prizes; objects of art lent to state capital & county offices; lending collection contains 5000 original prints; originate traveling exhibitions; sales shop sells original art

M **SCHUYLER MANSION STATE HISTORIC SITE,** 32 Catherine St, 12202. Tel 518-434-0834; FAX 518-434-3821; *Site Mgr* Susan Haswell; *Historic Site Asst* Mary Ellen Grimaldi
Open Wed - Sat 10 AM - 5 PM, Sun 1 - 5 PM, cl Mon & Tues, mid-Apr - Oct, call for winter hrs. Admis adult $3, New York seniors $2, children 5-12 $1. Estab 1917 for the preservation and interpretation of the 18th century home of Philip Schuyler, one of the finest examples of Georgian architecture in the country. The house boasts a substantial collection of Schuyler family pieces & fine examples of Chinese export porcelain, delftware & English glassware. Average Annual Attendance: 12,000
Income: Financed by state appropriation
Collections: American furnishings of the Colonial & Federal Periods, predominantly of New York & New England origins
Publications: Schuyler Mansion; A Historic Structure Report; Schuyler Genealogy: A Compendium of Sources Pertaining to the Schuyler Families in America Prior to 1800; vol 2 prior to 1900
Activities: Educ dept; lect; tours; special events

M **UNIVERSITY AT ALBANY, STATE UNIVERSITY OF NEW YORK,** University Art Museum, 1400 Washington Ave, 12222. Tel 518-442-4035; FAX 518-442-5075; *Dir* Marijo Dougherty; *Exhib Designer* Zheng Hu; *Admin Asst* Joanne Lue
Open Tues - Fri 10 AM - 5 PM, Sat & Sun Noon - 4 PM. No admis fee. Estab 1968. The University Art Mus at the University at Albany, State University of New York, is a window to both the University & soc, a place where contemporary art & artifacts reflecting the diversity of peoples, cultures & life experiences are exhibited. As such, the mus is a resource for all of Albany's academic programs supporting the core curriculum with world class exhibitions & scholarships. Students, faculty & staff who visit the mus draw inspiration from the exhibitions it hosts, which contribute to their understanding & appreciation of differing cultures & ideas. Average Annual Attendance: 25,000
Income: Financed by state appropriation
Collections: Paintings, prints, drawings & sculpture of 20th century contemporary art; photographs
Exhibitions: (1997) Once Upon a Drawing: The Picture Book Illustrations of Marcia Brown; Master of Arts & Master of Fine Arts Thesis Exhibitions; Artists of the Mohawk Hudson Region Juried Exhibition; Memory & Mourning: Shared Cultural Experience; Master of Arts & Master of Fine Arts Thesis Exhibition. (1998) Witness & Legacy: Contemporary Art About the Holocaust; University at Albany Juried Undergraduate Art Show; Master of Fine Arts Thesis Exhibition & Master of Arts Thesis Exhibition; Beauty & Truth; Thom O'Connor & Friends: An Artist/Teacher's Legacy; The University at Albany Foundation Carol & Marvin Brown Photography Collection; Master of Fine Arts Thesis Exhibition & Master of Arts Thesis Exhibition
Publications: Exhibition catalogs
Activities: Lect open to public; gallery talks; tours; competitions with awards; individual art works lent to offices on the university campus only; book traveling exhibitions; originate traveling exhibition

L **Art Dept Slide Library,** Fine Arts Bldg, Rm 121, 12222. Tel 518-442-4018; *Art Historian* Roberta Bernstein; *Art Historian* Sarah Cohen; *Slide Librn* Kendra Wells
Open daily 9 AM - 4 PM. Estab 1967 to provide instruction & reference for the university & community
Library Holdings: AV — Fs, Kodachromes, lantern slides, slides 80,000; Other — Exhibition catalogs, pamphlets, photographs
Collections: Slides, mainly of Western art & architecture

ALFRED

L **NEW YORK STATE COLLEGE OF CERAMICS AT ALFRED UNIVERSITY,** Scholes Library of Ceramics, 2 Pine St, 14802-1297. Tel 607-871-2494; FAX 607-871-2349; Elec Mail Bitnet: freemanc@ceramics, Internet: freemanc@bigvax.alfred.edu. *Dir* Carla C Freeman; *Public Serv Librn* Kim Donius; *Technical Serv Librn & Engineering Bibliographer* Paul T Culley; *Art Reference Librn & Archivist* Elizabeth Gulacsy; *Information Systems Librn* Mark A Smith; *Visual Resource Cur* Suzanne O Roberts; *Access Serv Librn* Bruce E Connolly
Open academic year Mon - Thurs 8 AM - 11 PM, Fri 8 AM - 8 PM, Sat 10 AM - 6 PM, Sun 10 AM - 10 PM, other periods Mon - Fri 8 AM - 4:30 PM. Estab 1947 to service art educ to the Master's level in fine art & the PhD level in engineering & science related to ceramics. The College has a 2500 sq ft Art Gallery which is managed by the Art & Design Division
Income: $671,884 (financed by endowment & state appropriation)
Purchases: $55,000
Library Holdings: Vols 60,830; Per subs 678; Art books 24,197; Audio cassettes 171; College archives; NCECA archives; Video discs 28; Micro — Fiche, reels; AV — A-tapes 51, cassettes 393, fs, lantern slides 200, motion pictures, slides 145,316, v-tapes 15; Other — Clipping files, exhibition catalogs, original art works, pamphlets
Special Subjects: Art History, Asian Art, Bronzes, Ceramics, Commercial Art, Crafts, Decorative Arts, Folk Art, Glass, Graphic Design, History of Art & Archaeology, Painting - American, Painting - European, Photography, Printmaking, Fine Art, Media Art, Wood Design
Publications: Scholes Library Bulletin, biannual
Activities: Tours

ALMOND

M **ALMOND HISTORICAL SOCIETY, INC,** Hagadorn House, The 1800-37 Museum, 7 Main St, PO Box 209, 14804. Tel 607-276-6465, 276-6781; *Pres* Harriett Ide; *VPres* Virginia Allen; *Treas* Frederick Bayless
Open Fri 2 - 4 PM & by appointment. Admis by donations. Estab 1965 to preserve local history, genealogy & artifacts. The Little Gallery 4 ft x 12 ft, burlap covered walls, 4 display cases, 8-track lighting system. Average Annual Attendance: 2000. Mem: 385; mem open to those interested in local history; life member $100, business or professional $10, family $6, dues $2.50; annual meeting in Nov
Income: $25,908 (financed by endowment, mem, city appropriations)
Collections: 1513 genealogies of local families; town & village records; slide collection of local houses; 1500 costumes & hats; 50 quilts; toys; school books; maps; cemetary lists; photographs, scrapbooks
Exhibitions: Local architecture: drawings & photographs; history of the local post office
Publications: The Cooking Fireplace in the Hagadorn House; Forgotten Cemeteries of Almond; My Father's Old Fashioned Drug Store; Recollections of Horace Stillman; School Days
Activities: Classes for children; lect open to public, 4 vis lectr per year

AMENIA

A AGES OF MAN FELLOWSHIP, Sheffield Rd, Box 5, 12501. Tel 914-373-9380; *Pres* Dr Nathan Cabot Hale; *VPres* Niels Berg
Open 10 AM - 5 PM. Estab 1968 for the building & design of a sculpture chapel based on the thematic concepts of the Cycle of Life. Mem: 20; dues $100; meetings May & Nov
Income: Financed by mem & contributions
Collections: Sculpture & architectural models of the chapel
Publications: Project report, yearly
Activities: Art history; apprenticeship & journeyman instruction in Cycle of Life design; lect open to public, 20 vis lectr per year; gallery talks; original objects of art lent to museums, art associations, educational institutions; originate traveling exhibitions

AMHERST

M AMHERST MUSEUM, 3755 Tonawanda Creek Rd, 14228-1599. Tel 716-689-1440; FAX 716-689-1409; *Exec Dir* Lynn S Beman; *Sr Cur* Sharon L Gray; *Educ Cur* Jean W Neff; *Textile Cur* Mary Iannone; *Librn* Mary Lou Kinyon
Open Nov - Mar Tues - Fri 9:30 AM - 4:30 PM, Apr - Oct Tues - Fri 9:30 AM - 4:30 PM, Sat & Sun 12:30 - 4:30 PM, cl Mon & Municipal Holidays. Admis adult $2, children between 5 & 12 $1, members & children under 4 free, 50% discount for Town of Amherst residents. Estab 1972 to preserve town of Amherst history. Maintains reference library. Average Annual Attendance: 34,000. Mem: 825; dues family $30, individual $15; annual meeting in Jan
Income: $550,000 (financed by mem, town appropriation, earned income)
Collections: American Material Culture; 19th Century Historic Buildings; WNY Aviation; textiles & costumes
Exhibitions: Amherst: Our Town; Children's Discovery Room; Gallery of the Senses; Niagara Frontier Wireless Radio Gallery; Something Old, Something Blue: Wedding Gowns 1850-1950
Publications: Ephemera, quarterly newsletter; researching Amherst House Histories, booklet
Activities: Classes for adults & children; docent training; special events; lect open to public, 2-5 vis lectr per year; museum shop sells books & prints
L Neiderlander Research Library, 3755 Tonawanda Creek Rd, 14228-1599
For reference only
Library Holdings: Vols 3000; Micro — Fiche, reels; Other — Clipping files, manuscripts, memorabilia, pamphlets, photographs, prints

M DAEMEN COLLEGE, Fanette Goldman & Carolyn Greenfield Gallery, Duns Scotus Hall, 4380 Main St, 14226. Tel 716-839-3600, Ext 241; *Dir* James Allen
Open Mon - Fri 9 AM - 4 PM. No admis fee. Estab to add dimension to the art program and afford liberal arts students opportunity to view art made by established artists as well as art students. Gallery area is part of main building (Duns Scotus Hall), recently renovated exterior & entrance. Average Annual Attendance: 1500
Income: Financed by College Art Department
Activities: Lect open to public, 4 - 5 vis lectr per year
L Marian Library, 4380 Main St, 14226-3592. Tel 716-839-8243; FAX 716-839-8475; *Head Librn* Glenn V Woike; *Ref Librn* Mary Joan Gleason; *Ref Librn* Randolph Chojecki; *Technical Servs Librn* Frank Carey
Library Holdings: Vols 140,000; Per subs 940; Micro — Cards; AV — Slides; Other — Pamphlets
Special Subjects: Art Education, Art History, Calligraphy, Graphic Arts, Graphic Design, Painting - American, Textiles

AMSTERDAM

M MOHAWK VALLEY HERITAGE ASSOCIATION, INC, Walter Elwood Museum, 300 Guy Park Ave, 12010-2228. Tel 518-843-5151; *Pres* Bryan Buchanan; *Dir* Mary M Gage; *Supt Greater Amsterdam School Dist* H Arthur P Cotugno
Open Sept - June Mon - Fri 8:30 AM - 4 PM & weekend by appointment; July 1 - Labor Day Mon - Thurs 8:30 AM - 3:30 PM, Fri 8:30 AM - 1 PM. Estab 1940 to preserve local heritage & natural history. Gallery displays changing exhibits, local & professional collections & museum's works of art. Mem: 675; dues $5 - $500; annual meeting 3rd Tues in June
Income: $25,000 (financed by mem & fundraisers)
Collections: Oil paintings by turn of the century local artists; photographs of early Amsterdam & vicinity; steel engravings by turn of the century artists
Exhibitions: Paintings by the Monday Art Group (local area artists)
Activities: Adult classes; museum shop sells books, maps

ANNANDALE-ON-HUDSON

M BARD COLLEGE, William Cooper Procter Art Center, 12504. Tel 914-758-6822; *Dir* Tom Wolf
Open daily 10 AM - 8 PM. No Admis fee. Estab 1964 as an educational center. Art center has a gallery, slide library and uses the college library for its teaching
Exhibitions: Four guest-curated exhibitions of contemporary art & two student exhibitions per year
Publications: Catalogs
Activities: Gallery talks

M BARD COLLEGE, Center for Curatorial Studies Museum, 12504-5000. Tel 914-758-7598; FAX 914-758-2442; Elec Mail ccs@bard.edu. *Dir* Vasif Kortun; *Assoc Dir* Marcia Acita
Open Wed - Sun 1 - 5 PM. No admis fee. Estab 1992 for the presentation of contemporary art. 9500 sq ft of exhibition space, changing exhibitions. Average Annual Attendance: 8000
Collections: Marieluise Hessel Collection of Late 20th Century Art; contemporary art from 1960s to the present in all media, including installations & video

Exhibitions: (1997) Tunga: A Survey
Activities: Educ programs; teacher training programs; lect open to public, 20 vis lectr per year; individual paintings & original objects of art lent to museums in Europe & the United States, 10 outgoing loans per year; book traveling exhibitions 1 per year; originate traveling exhibitions
L Library, 12504-5000. Tel 914-758-7590; FAX 914-758-7590; *Librn* Susan Leonard
Estab 1990. For reference only; non-circulating research collection supporting the graduate program in Curatorial Studies
Library Holdings: Vols 9000; Per subs 49; AV — Slides, v-tapes; Other — Clipping files, exhibition catalogs, memorabilia, pamphlets
Special Subjects: Aesthetics, Art History, Conceptual Art, Historical Material, Painting - American, Painting - European, Painting - German, Photography, Restoration & Conservation, Video, Late Twentieth Century Art

ASTORIA

M AMERICAN MUSEUM OF THE MOVING IMAGE, 35 Ave at 36 St, 11106. Tel 718-784-4520; FAX 719-784-4681; *Dir* Rochelle Slovin, MA; *Sr Historian* Richard Kaszarski PhD; *Chief Cur Film & Video* David Schwartz; *Cur Digital Media* Carl Goodman
Open Tues - Fri Noon - 5 PM, Sat & Sun 11 AM - 6 PM. Admis adults $7, children $4. Estab 1988, devoted to art, history, technique & technology of moving image media. Temporary gallery on first floor, 1800 sq ft; 2nd & 3rd floors 5500 sq ft of permanent exhibition space. Average Annual Attendance: 80,000. Mem: 1500; dues $50-$1000
Collections: The museum has a collection of over 70,000 artifacts relating to the material art form of movies & television, magazines, dolls, costumes, clothing
Exhibitions: Behind the Screen; Computer Space; Television Set Design: Late Show with David Letterman
Publications: Behind the Screen; Who Does What in Motion Pictures & Television
Activities: Classes for children; ESL programs; docent training; adult tours; lect open to public, 50 vis lectr per year; gallery talks; tours; originate traveling exhibitions; museum shop sells books, magazines, & reproductions

AUBURN

M CAYUGA MUSEUM OF HISTORY & ART, 203 Genesee St, 13021. Tel 315-253-8051; FAX 315-253-9829; *Interim Dir* Stephanie Przybylek; *Cur S* Przybylek; *Educator* Heather Gunsalus
Open Mon - Sat Noon - 5 PM, Sun 1 - 5 PM, cl New Year's, Labor Day, Thanksgiving, Christmas. No admis fee. Estab 1936 for research & Cayuga County history. Average Annual Attendance: 45,000. Mem: 200; dues $30-$250; annual meeting in May
Income: Financed by endowment, mem, county & city appropriation
Collections: Fine & Decorative Arts; Native American Collection; Soundfilm
Exhibitions: Ongoing series of changing exhibits
Activities: Classes for adults & children; docent training; lect open to public; tours; lending collection contains motion pictures & slides; museum shop sells reproductions & small gifts
L Library, 203 Genesee St, 13021. Tel 315-253-8051; *Librn* Stephanie Przybylek
Open to researchers for reference
Library Holdings: Vols 16,000; Per subs 10
Special Subjects: Indians, local history
Collections: Clarke Collection

M SCHWEINFURTH ART CENTER, 205 Genesee St, 13021. Tel 315-255-1553; Elec Mail smac@relex.com. *Dir* David Kwasigroh; *Educ Coordr* Jude Valentine; *Admin Asst* Mary Ellen Kliss
Open Tues - Fri Noon - 5 PM, Sat 10 AM - 5 PM, Sun 1 - 5 PM. Estab 1981 to exhibit & sponsor multi arts activities for a rural audience. 700 sq ft contemporary gallery & 5 galleries 250 sq ft. Average Annual Attendance: 15,000. Mem: 400; dues $15-$1000
Income: $143,000 (financed by endowment, mem, city & state appropriation, federal & private)
Exhibitions: Annual adult exhibitions; local artist solo exhibitions; Made in New York, annual juried exhibition; Quilts
Publications: Monthly calendar
Activities: Classes for adults & children; lect open to public, 2 vis lectr per year; concerts; gallery talks; tours; competitions with prizes; scholarships offered; originate traveling exhibitions; sales shop sells books, original art, prints & hand made artists crafts

AURIESVILLE

M KATERI GALLERIES, The National Shrine of the North American Martyrs, 12016. Tel 518-853-3033; *Dir* John J Paret; *Asst Dir* John M Doolan
Open 9 AM - 4 PM. No admis fee. Estab 1885 as a religious & historic shrine. Average Annual Attendance: 100,000
Publications: The Pilgrim, quarterly

BALDWIN

M BALDWIN HISTORICAL SOCIETY MUSEUM, 1980 Grand Ave, 11510. Tel 516-223-6900, 223-8080 (Chamber of Commerce); *Pres* Vincent B Schuman; *Cur* Glenn F Sitterly
Open to the pub Mon, Wed, Fri 9 - 11:30 AM, Sun 1 - 4 PM by appointment. No admis fee. Estab 1971, mus estab 1976 to preserve Baldwin history memorablia including historical photographs. Average Annual Attendance: 500. Mem: 225; dues family $10, individual $5; monthly meetings except Jan, Feb, July & Aug
Income: $5000 (financed by mem, fundraising)
Collections: Collection of local history photographs, postal cards, advertising

objects, decorative art objects, manuscripts
Exhibitions: Selection of Baldwin's memorabilia
Publications: Newsletter
Activities: Classes for adults & children in local history programs; lect open to public, 4 vis lectr per year; gallery talks; annual American History award given to a senior in History; museum shop sells books, reproductions, prints & post cards

BALLSTON SPA

A **SARATOGA COUNTY HISTORICAL SOCIETY,** Brookside Museum, Six Charlton St, 12020. Tel 518-885-4000; *Exec Dir* Jennifer Ley; *Colls Mgr* William Garrison; *Education Dir* Claudia McLaughlin
Open Tues, Thurs & Fri Noon - 8 PM, Wed 10 AM - 4 PM, Sat & Sun Noon - 4 PM, cl Mon. Admis family $5, adults $2, senior citizens, $1.50, children $1. Estab 1965 to inform pub on the history of Saratoga County. 4 small galleries. Average Annual Attendance: 10,000. Mem: 500; dues individual $15
Income: $100,000 (financed by endowment, mem, city appropriation & grants)
Collections: History of Saratoga County, books, manuscripts, objects, photographs
Exhibitions: Dairying in Saratoga County
Publications: Gristmill, 4 per year
Activities: Classes for adult & children; lect open to public, 4 vis lectr per year; sales shop sells books & gifts

BAYSIDE

M **QUEENSBOROUGH COMMUNITY COLLEGE,** Art Gallery, 222-05 56th Ave, 11364-1497. Tel 718-631-6396, 281-5095; FAX 718-423-9620; *Dir* Faustino Quintanilla; *Gallery Conservator* Oscar Sossa
Open 9 AM - 5 PM. No admis fee. Estab 1981 to provide the college & Queens Community with up to date documentation outline on the visual arts. Average Annual Attendance: 12,000. Mem: 500; dues $25
Income: $214,793 (financed by endowment & mem)
Purchases: Ruth Rothschild & Hampton Blake
Collections: Contemporary art; works on paper; Richard Art Schwager; Roger Indiana; Paul Jenkins; R Dichtenstein; Larry Rives; Frank Stella; Judy Ritka; Alfonso Ossorio; Jules Allen; Jimmy Ernst; Josef Albers; Sirena
Exhibitions: Siri Berg-Suzane Winkler; The Priva B Gross International Works On/Of Paper; Permanent Collection: Larry Rives
Publications: Signal; Politics & Gender; Romanticism & Classicism; Power of Popular Imagery; Art & Politics
Activities: Lect open to public, 4-8 vis lectr per year; competitions with awards; scholarships offered; individual paintings & original objects of art lent for exhibit purposes to organizations that follow loan criteria; lending collection contains original art works, photographs, sculptures & videos (art-New York & others); originate traveling exhibitions annually; junior museum

L **QUEENSBOROUGH COMMUNITY COLLEGE LIBRARY,** 56th Ave & Springfield Blvd, 11364. Tel 718-631-6226; FAX 718-428-0802; *Chief Librn* Kyu Hugh Kim; *Music & Art Librn* Devin Feldman
Open Mon - Thurs 9 AM - 9 PM, Fri 9 AM - 5 PM, Sat 10 AM - 5 PM. Estab 1961 to serve the students and faculty of the college
Income: $1,000,000
Purchases: $80,000
Collections: Book & periodical collection includes material on painting, sculpture & architecture; print collection; reproductions of famous paintings; reproductions of artifacts & sculpture; vertical file collection
Publications: Library Letter, biannual

BINGHAMTON

M **ROBERSON MUSEUM & SCIENCE CENTER,** 30 Front St, 13905. Tel 607-772-0660; FAX 607-771-8905; *Dir* David Chesbrough; *Dir Exhib & Prog* Tim Weidner; *Dir Science* Carol Stowell; *Chief Designer* Peter Klosky; *Registar* Eve Daniels; *Cur History & Art* Timothy Weidner; *Cur Folklife* Catherine Schwoeffermann
Open Tues - Thurs & Sat 10 AM - 5 PM, Fri 10 AM - 9 PM, Sun Noon - 5 PM, cl Mon. Admis adults $4, senior citizens & students $3. Estab 1954 as a regional museum of art, history, folklore & science educ center. The Roberson Mus & Science Center, built in 1905-06 contains eight galleries; the Martin Building, built in 1968, designed by Richard Neutra, contains five galleries; the A Ward Ford Wing, completed in 1983 contains the Irma M Ahearn Gallery. Average Annual Attendance: 100,000. Mem: 1500; dues $35-$45
Income: $1,500,000 (financed by endowment, mem, city, county & state appropriations, federal funds & foundations)
Collections: Loomis Wildlife Collection: Northeastern Birds & Mammals; Regional fine & decorative arts, crafts, furniture; archeological & ethnological collections; natural history specimens; historical archives & photographic collections; Hands-on science displays & interactive art
Exhibitions: Threaded Memories: A Family Quilt Collection; Barbara Insalaco; Exceptional Artworks; Climbing Jacob's Ladder; Bell Watch Collection; Childhood From Field to Factory
Publications: Exhibition catalogs; quarterly newsletter
Activities: Classes for adults & children; school programs; public programs & workshops; lect open to the public; 5 vis lectr per year; concerts; gallery talks; tours; scholarships offered; programs sent to schools in eleven counties; individual paintings & original objects of art lent; lending collection contains slide tape programs with hands-on-activities for groups; book traveling exhibitions 2-3 per year; originate traveling exhibitions to other museums; museum & sales shops sell books, original art, reproductions, prints, slides & a wide range of contemporary crafts

BLUE MOUNTAIN LAKE

M **ADIRONDACK HISTORICAL ASSOCIATION,** Adirondack Museum, 12812. Tel 518-352-7311; FAX 518-352-7653; *Pres* Robert R Worth; *Dir* Jacqueline Day; *Cur* Caroline Welsh; *Cur* Hallie Bond; *Educ Dir* Susan Carroll; *Registar* Tracy Meehan; *Librn* Jerold Pepper; *Bus Mgr* Tom Proulx; *Dir Public Affairs* Ann Carroll; *Dir Develop* Hillarie Logan-Dechene
Open Memorial Day - mid Oct daily 9:30 AM - 5:30 PM. Estab 1957 to interpret the history & culture of the Adirondack Park. Museum contains two large galleries for paintings. Average Annual Attendance: 85,000. Mem: 3000; annual meeting in Aug
Collections: Drawings, †Paintings, †Prints, †Photographs
Exhibitions: Special exhibitions each has (included the work of Frederic Remington, A F Tait, Winslow Homer, J K Kensett, Thomas Cole, Asher Durand, Rockwell Kent)
Publications: Newsletters, books
Activities: Classes for adults & children; lect open to public, 8-10 vis lectr per year; concerts; tours; individual paintings & original objects of art lent to museums & galleries; sales shop sells books, magazines, reproductions, prints, slides & postcards

L **Library,** 12812. Tel 518-352-7311; FAX 518-352-7603; *Librn* Jerold L Pepper
Open Mon - Fri 9:30 AM - 5 PM by appointment. Estab to provide research materials for mus staff (exhibit documentation) & researchers interested in the Adirondack & to preserve written materials relating to the Adirondack. For research only
Library Holdings: Vols 8000; Per subs 13; Maps; Micro — Fiche, reels; AV — A-tapes 25, cassettes, Kodachromes, lantern slides, slides; Other — Clipping files, exhibition catalogs, manuscripts
Special Subjects: All Adirondackiana

A **ADIRONDACK LAKES CENTER FOR THE ARTS,** 12812. Tel 518-352-7715; *Dir* Robert C Lilly; *Prog Coordr* Daisy Kelley
Open Mon - Fri 9 AM - 5 PM, summer Sat & Sun 10 AM - 5 PM. Admis films $3-$5, concerts $10-$12. Estab 1967; this Community Art Center offers both community & artist - craftsmen the opportunity for creative exchange. 7000 sq ft facility with 4 studios & black-box theatre. Average Annual Attendance: 30,000. Mem: 600; annual meeting in July
Income: $180,000 (financed by private contributions, county, state & federal assistance, foundations, local businesses, government, mem & fundraising events)
Exhibitions: Exhibits change every month
Publications: Newsletter - Program, quarterly
Activities: Classes for adults & children; lect open to public, 8 vis lectr per year; concerts; competitions; gallery talks; tours; scholarships offered; exten dept serves Adirondack Park; sales shop sells original art, prints, crafts made locally & records by musicians appearing at the art center

BOLTON LANDING

A **MARCELLA SEMBRICH MEMORIAL ASSOCIATION INC,** Opera Museum, Lake Shore Dr, PO Box 417, 12814-0417. Tel 518-644-9839; *Admin Dir* Anita Richards; *Assoc Pres* Ernest Hillman Jr; *Cur* Richard Wargo
Open June 15 - Sept 15 10 AM - 12:30 PM & 2 - 5:30 PM. No admis fee, donations requested. Estab 1937 to exhibit memorabilia of Marcella Sembrich & the Golden Age of Opera. Exhibits in Sembrich's former teaching studio on the shore of Lake George. Average Annual Attendance: 1600. Mem: 120; dues $35 & $50; annual meeting in Jan
Income: $30,000 (financed by mem & gifts)
Collections: Memorabilia of the life & career of Marcella Sembrich, opera star of international acclaim (1858 - 1935); paintings, sculpture, furnishings, photographs, costumes, art works, gifts & trophies from colleagues & admirers
Publications: Newsletter, annual; Recollection of Marcella Sembrich, Biography
Activities: Lect open to public, 4 vis lectr per year; retail store sells books, postcards & cassettes

BROCKPORT

M **STATE UNIVERSITY OF NEW YORK, COLLEGE AT BROCKPORT,** Tower Fine Arts Gallery, Dept of Art, 14420. Tel 716-395-2209; FAX 716-395-2588; *Dir* Roger Rowley
Open Tues - Sat Noon - 5 PM, Tues & Wed evenings 7 - 9 PM. Estab to present quality exhibitions for purpose of educ. 160 running ft, 1900 sq ft. Average Annual Attendance: 9000
Income: Financed by state appropriation & student government
Collections: E E Cummings paintings & drawings
Exhibitions: The Faculty Selects: Alumni Invitational III
Activities: Lect open to public, 6 vis lectr per year; book traveling exhibitions 1-2 per year; originate traveling exhibitions

BRONX

M **BARTOW-PELL MANSION MUSEUM & GARDENS,** 895 Shore Rd, Pelham Bay Park, 10464. Tel 718-885-1461; FAX 718-885-1461; *Pres* Joan Taubner
Open Wed, Sat & Sun 12 - 4 PM, cl 3 wks in summer. Admis adults $2.50, seniors & students $1.25, children under 12 free. Estab 1914
Collections: Greek revival restoration; period furnishings; paintings; sunken gardens

M **BRONX COUNCIL ON THE ARTS,** Longwood Arts Gallery, 965 Longwood Ave (Mailing add: 1738 Hone Ave, 10461-1486). Tel 718-931-9500; FAX 718-409-6445; Elec Mail bronxart@panix.comx. *Council Dir* William Aguado; *Longwood Dir* Betti-Sue Hertz
Open Thurs - Fri Noon - 5 PM, Sat Noon - 4 PM, also by appointment. No admis fee. Estab 1985 for exhibits of interest to artists & the Bronx communities. The Gallery, housed in a former Bronx Pub School building at 925 Longwood Ave, presents solo & group exhibitions centering on contemporary themes of

interest to artists & the Bronx communities
Income: Financed by city, state & federal grants, foundation & corporate support
Exhibitions: Vietnamese Artists; Post-Colonialism; Feminism & the Body; Puerto Rican Taino Imagery in Contemporary Art; Real Life Comics; Like Butter; Maze-phantasm; Mini-Murals; Sovereign State; Here & Now, Now & Then
Publications: Catalogues, 2 per year
Activities: Lect open to public, 3 vis lectr per year; fel; originate traveling exhibitions 2 per year

M **BRONX MUSEUM OF THE ARTS,** 1040 Grand Concourse, 166th St, 10456. Tel 718-681-6000; FAX 718-681-6181; *Chmn Board* George N Benoit; *Exec Dir* Jane Delgado
Open Wed 3 - 9 PM, Thurs & Fri 10 AM - 5 PM, Sat & Sun 1 - 6 PM, cl Mon & Tues. Admis adults $3, students $2, senior citizens $1, children under 12 & members free. Estab 1971 with a primary purpose of making arts & educational programming more accessible & relevant to the Borough's 1.2 million ethnically diverse residents; to stimulate community participation through the visual arts within a central mus space & a network of four Satellite Galleries in pub spaces in the Bronx; exhibiting diverse collections & schools of art with special concern accorded Bronx artists; to provide educational programs in the arts while serving as a catalyst for its continued creative development. Mem: 987; corporate sponsor $1000, patron $500, associate $250, sustaining $100, family $50, individual $35, student & senior citizen $25
Income: Financed by mem, city, state & federal appropriations, foundations & corporations
Collections: Collection of 20th century works on paper by artists from the geographical areas of Latin America, Africa & Southeast Asia as well as works by American descendents of these areas; File on Bronx artists
Publications: Exhibition catalogs; educational workbooks; walking tours of the Bronx
Activities: Classes for adults, children & seniors; lect open to public; concerts; gallery talks; tours; films; annual arts & crafts festival; originate traveling exhibitions; museum shop sells books, posters, catalogs, original art, prints, jewelry, childrens & museum gift items

M **BRONX RIVER ART CENTER,** Gallery, 1087 E Tremont Ave, 10460. Tel 718-589-5819, 589-6379; *Exec Dir* Walter C Jackson; *Gallery Coordr* Amir Bey
Open Tues - Thurs 3 - 6 PM. No admis fee. Estab 1980 as a professional, multi-cultural art center. 2000 sq ft, handicapped accessible, ground floor gallery. Two main gallery rooms, natural light. Average Annual Attendance: 5000
Exhibitions: Exhibitions of contemporary artists focusing on innovative multi-cultural, multi-media work
Activities: Classes for adults & children; lect open to public, 16 vis lectr per year; originate traveling exhibitions 1 per year

M **CIAO,** Gallery & Art Center, 278 City Island Ave, 10464. Tel 718-885-9316; *Pres* Georgine Sheridan; *VPres* Rena Hansen; *Treas* Rick DeWitt
Open Thurs Noon - 7 PM, Fri & Sat Noon - 9 PM, Sun Noon - 7 PM. No admis fee. Estab 1995 to promote arts in the community. Mem: 55; dues $50; monthly meetings
Exhibitions: Two juried exhibits annually; bimonthly changing exhibitions
Activities: Classes for adults; lect open to public; concerts; competitions with prizes; individual paintings & original objects of art lent to local library & museum; lending collection contains original art works, original prints, paintings & photographs; sales shop sells original art, reproductions & prints

M **EN FOCO, INC,** 32 E Kingsbridge Rd, 10468. Tel 718-584-7718; FAX 718-584-7718; *Exec Dir* Charles Biasiny-Rivera; *Managing Dir* Miriam Romais
Open Mon - Wed 9:30 AM - 4:30 PM. No admis fee. Estab 1974 to support photographers of color via exhibits & publications. Mem: dues basic $25, insitutional $45
Collections: Photographs & posters by leading photographers of color
Exhibitions: Annual Seminar in Puerto Rico & Touring Gallery Programs; Saving the Light
Publications: Critical Mass Newsletter, quarterly; Nueva Luz, annual bilingual photography journal
Activities: Lect open to public; 2-3 vis lectr per year; gallery talks; competitions; originate traveling exhibitions; sales shop sells magazines

M **FOCAL POINT GALLERY,** 321 City Island Ave, 10464-1348. Tel 718-885-1403; *Dir* Ron Terner
No admis fee. Estab 1974 to give exposure to photographic artists. Average Annual Attendance: 5200
Exhibitions: Photography by Ron Terner & Watercolors by Nirn Terner; The Winners of Focal Point National Juried Exhibition (photography)
Publications: Viewfinder, annual exhibit catalog
Activities: Museum shop sells books, original art, prints & reproductions

A **HOSTOS CENTER FOR THE ARTS & CULTURE,** 500 Grand Concord, 10451. Tel 718-518-4444; FAX 718-518-6688; Internet Home Page Address www.hostos.cuny.edu. *Dir* Wallace I Edgecombe; *Theater Mgr* Gregory S Shanck; *Production Mgr* Jack Jacobs; *Dean* Wilda Orta; *Cur* Betty Wilde
Estab 1993 to present artists of national & international renown; presents emerging & estab local artists; offers workshops in drama, folk arts & dance to community residents; serves as a forge for new art, & thus has estab an individual artists' program consisting of commissions & residencies. Center consists of a museum-grade art gallery, 367-seat theater & 907-seat concert hall. Average Annual Attendance: 33,000
Income: Financed by mem, city appropriation, state appropriation, government sources, corporations
Activities: Dramatic programs; originate traveling exhibitions

M **LEHMAN COLLEGE ART GALLERY,** 250 Bedford Park Blvd W, 10468. Tel 718-960-8731; FAX 212-960-8212; *Dir* Susan Hoeltzel; *Assoc Dir* Mary Ann Siano
Open Tues - Sat 10 AM - 4 PM. No admis fee. Estab 1985 to exhibit work of

20th century artists. Two galleries housed in Fine Arts building on Lehman College campus, City University NY, designed by Marcel Breuer. Average Annual Attendance: 19,000. Mem: 200; dues $30-$1000
Income: Financed by endowment, mem, city & state appropriation & private foundations
Publications: Exhibition catalogs; gallery notes
Activities: Classes for children; docent training; lect open to public, 6 vis lectr per year; book traveling exhibitions; originate traveling exhibitions

M **VAN CORTLANDT HOUSE MUSEUM,** W 246th & Broadway, 10471. Tel 718-543-3344; FAX 718-543-3315; *Dir* Laura Correa
Tues - Fri 10 AM - 3 PM, Sun 11 AM - 4 PM, cl Mon. Admis adult $2, children under 14 free, Fri & Sat free to all. Estab 1898. Average Annual Attendance: 30,000
Collections: Furniture & objects of the 18th century
Activities: Classes for children; slide programs for visitors

M **WAVE HILL,** 675 W 252 St, 10471. Tel 718-549-3200, 549-2055; FAX 718-884-8952; *Pres* Kate Pearson French; *Public Relations Dir* Marilyn Oser
Open Tues - Sun 9 AM - 4:30 PM. No admis weekdays, weekends adults $4, senior citizens & students $2, children under 6 free. Estab 1960 as a pub garden & cultural center. Wave Hill House Gallery; Glyndor Gallery; Outdoor Sculpture Garden. Average Annual Attendance: 80,000. Mem: 2000; dues $30
Income: Financed by mem, city & state appropriation, private funding
Collections: †Toscanini Collection: Recordings, Tapes, Photos, Memorabilia
Publications: Calendar, 4 per yr; exhibit catalogues, annually
Activities: Classes for adults & children; dramatic programs; natural history/environmental workshops; lect open to public, 3 vis lectr per year; concerts; originate traveling exhibitions; sales shop sells books, magazines, reproductions

BRONXVILLE

L **BRONXVILLE PUBLIC LIBRARY,** 201 Pondfield Rd, 10708. Tel 914-337-7680; *Dir Library* Roxane Campagna
Open winter Mon, Wed & Fri 9:30 AM - 5:30 PM, Tues 9:30 AM - 9 PM, Thurs 1 - 9 PM, Sat 9:30 AM - 5 PM, Sun 1 - 5 PM, summer Mon, Wed, Thurs & Fri 9:30 AM - 5:30 PM, Sat 9:30 AM - 1 PM. No admis fee
Income: Financed by city & state appropriations
Special Subjects: Painting - American, Prints
Collections: American painters: Bruce Crane, Childe Hassam, Winslow Homer, William Henry Howe, Frederick Waugh; Japanese Art Prints; 25 Original Currier and Ives Prints
Exhibitions: Current artists, changed monthly; original paintings and prints

L **SARAH LAWRENCE COLLEGE LIBRARY,** Esther Raushenbush Library, Glen Washington Rd, 10708. Tel 914-395-2474; FAX 914-395-2473; *Librn* Charlin Chang Fagan; *Exhibits Librn* Carol Shaner; *Slide Librn* Renee Kent
Open 9 AM - 5 PM. Estab to provide library facilities for students & members of the community with an emphasis on art history. Slide collection closed to the pub; non-circulating reference materials available to the pub
Library Holdings: Vols 225,000; Per subs 1073; AV — Slides 88,000
Exhibitions: Changing exhibits
Activities: Lect in connection with exhibits; tours on request

BROOKLYN

A **BROOKLYN ARTS COUNCIL,** 195 Cadman Plaza W, 11201. Tel 718-625-0080; *Dir* Lorraine Boyd
Gallery Open Tues - Sat 1 - 6 PM, theater Fri & Sat 8 - 11 PM. No admis fee to gallery, theater $5-$8. Estab 1979 to promote experimentation, excellence & exchange in the visual & performing arts. Two professionally equipped galleries exhibit recent work by contemporary artists working in all media; painting, sculpture, video, installation, mixed media & performance are presented through solo, group & thematic guest-curated shows. Average Annual Attendance: 150,0000
Income: $200,000 (financed by endowment, city & state appropriation, theater admis, gallery sales, corporate & foundation support)
Exhibitions: Solo exhibitions by Brooklyn-based, non-affiliated artists; Artist & Guest-curated group & thematic exhibitions
Publications: BACA Downtown Calendar, bimonthly
Activities: Workshops for adults & children; lect open to public, seminars; gallery talks; competitions with awards

A **BROOKLYN HISTORICAL SOCIETY,** 128 Pierrepont St, 11201. Tel 718-624-0890; Elec Mail webmaster@brooklynhistorical.org; Internet Home Page Address http://www.brooklyn.org. *Pres* Jessie Kelly; *Acting Dir* Irene Tichenor
Open Tues - Sat 10 AM - 5 PM. Estab in 1863 to collect, preserve & interpret documentary & other materials relating to the history of Brooklyn & the adjoining geographical areas. Gallery used for exhibits on Brooklyn history. Average Annual Attendance: 15,000. Mem: 1750; dues $15 - $1000; annual meeting May
Income: $650,000 (financed by grants, endowment & mem)
Collections: Paintings, drawings, watercolors, prints, sculpture, decorative arts, archeological artifacts relating to Brooklyn's history & key citizens
Exhibitions: (1998) Brooklyn Works!: History of the Bourough Through the Eyes of the Working People
Publications: Bimonthly newsletter
Activities: Educ dept; docent training; lect open to the public, 15 vis lectr per year; gallery talks; individual paintings & original objects of art lent to other institutions; lending collection contains 3000 original prints, 275 paintings, sculptures

L **Library,** 128 Pierrepont St, 11201. Tel 718-624-0890; *Acting Head Librn* Clara Lamers
Open Tues - Sat 10 AM - 4:45 PM. Admis $2. Estab 1863 for the purpose of collecting, preserving & interpreting the history of Brooklyn. Open to general

pub. Mem: dues $25
Library Holdings: Vols 170,000; Other — Clipping files, manuscripts, original art works, pamphlets, photographs 90,000
Special Subjects: Brooklyn History; Genealogy
Activities: Classes for adults & children; lect open to public

M **BROOKLYN MUSEUM,** 200 Eastern Pky, 11238-6052. Tel 718-638-5000; FAX 718-638-3731; Elec Mail bklynmus@echonyc.com. Telex 12-5378; Cable BRKLYN-MUSUNYK. *Chmn Board of Trustees* Robert S Rubin; *Acting Dir & Chief Cur* Linda S Ferber; *Acting Pres* Roy R Eddey; *Vice Dir Develop* Darcy Gilpin; *Public Information Officer* Sally Williams; *Cur Egyptian & Classical Art* Richard Fazzini; *Vice Dir Publications* Elaine Koss; *Government & Community Relations Officer* Deborah Schwartz; *Vice Dir Educ Div* Deorah Schwartz; *Cur European Paintings & Sculpture* Sarah Faunce; *Cur American Paintings & Sculpture* Linda Ferber; *Cur Contemporary Art* Charlotta Kotik; *Cur Asian Art* Amy Poster; *Cur Decorative Arts* Kevin Stayton; *Cur Arts of Africa & Pacific* William Siegmann; *Vice Dir Coll & Chief Conservator* Ken Moser; *Chmn Arts of Africa, Pacific & Americas* Diana Fane; *Registrar* Liz Reynolds; *Librn* Deirdre Lawrence; *VDir Marketing* Sallie Stutz
Open daily 10 AM - 5 PM, cl Mon & Tues. Voluntary admis fee. Estab 1823 as the Apprentices Library Assoc. Five floors of galleries maintained, seventh largest mus of art in the United States. Average Annual Attendance: 300,000. Mem: 9000; dues donor $600, patron $300, contributor $125, family $65, individual $45, senior citizens & students $30
Income: $14,374,000 (financed by endowment, mem, city & state appropriation, gifts)
Collections: Art from the Americas & South Pacific; American period rooms; European & American paintings, sculpture, prints, drawings, costumes, textiles & decorative arts; major collections of Egyptian & Classical; Asian, Middle Eastern & African art; Americas & the Pacific; sculpture garden of ornaments from demolished New York buildings
Exhibitions: (Permanent) The Arts of China; The Arts of the Pacific; European Paintings Reinstallation. (1997) Recent Acquisitions: The James Brooks Gift; Symbolist Prints; Mistress of House, Mistress of Heaven: Women in Ancient Egypt; American Paintings: Ashcan & Modernist; 18th & 19th Century American Paintings; Old Bags: Handbags from the Permanent Collection. (1997-98) Monet & the Mediterranean; Invention & Innovation in the 19th Century: The Furniture of George Hunzinger; Artists in Action: BAM Visual Arts Initiative, MINE by Rona Pondick. (1998-99) The Qajar Epoch: 200 Years of Painting from the Royal Persian Courts; Vital Forms in America, 1941-1962
Publications: Newsletter, bimonthly; catalogues of major exhibitions; handbooks
Activities: Classes for adults & children; concerts; film; lect open to public; gallery talks; tours; individual paintings & original objects of art lent to other museums; originate traveling exhibitions; museum shops sell books, original objects, reproductions, prints, slides for adults & children
L **Libraries/Archives,** 200 Eastern Pky, 11238-6052. Tel 718-638-5000, Ext 307; FAX 718-638-3731; Elec Mail rlini-mailbm.gml. rlini-mailbm.bml. *Principal Librn Libraries & Archives* Deirdre E Lawrence
Open by appointment, call in advance. Estab 1823 to serve the staff of the mus & pub for reference
Income: Financed by city, state & private appropriation
Purchases: $50,000
Library Holdings: Vols 200,000; Per subs 400; Micro — Fiche; AV — A-tapes, v-tapes; Other — Clipping files, exhibition catalogs, pamphlets
Special Subjects: Anthropology, Antiquities-Assyrian, Antiquities-Egyptian, Antiquities-Greek, Antiquities-Roman, Archaeology, Art History, Asian Art, Decorative Arts, Drawings, Painting - American, Sculpture, African, Oceanic & Art of the Americas, Costumes & textiles, 19th & 20th century prints, drawings & photographs
Collections: Fashion plates; original fashion sketches 1900-1950; 19th century documentary photographs
Publications: Newsletter, bi-monthly
Activities: Classes for children; docent training; programs relating to current exhibitions; lect open to public, 30 vis lectr per year; gallery talks; tours; originate traveling exhibitions to other museums
L **Wilbour Library of Egyptology,** 200 Eastern Pky, 11238-6052. Tel 718-638-5000, Ext 215; FAX 718-638-3731; *Librn* Diane Guzman
Open by appointment. Estab 1934 for the purpose of the study of Ancient Egypt. For reference by appointment only
Income: Financed by endowment & city, state & private appropriation
Purchases: $16,000
Library Holdings: Vols 37,000; Per subs 150; Original documents; Micro — Fiche; Other — Exhibition catalogs, pamphlets
Special Subjects: Egypt, Greece, Rome & Ancient Near East
Collections: Seyffarth papers
Publications: Wilbour Monographs; general introductory bibliographies on Egyptian art available to visitors

L **BROOKLYN PUBLIC LIBRARY,** Art & Music Division, Grand Army Plaza, 11238. Tel 718-780-7784; *Division Chief* Sue Sharma
Open Mon 10 AM - 6 PM, Tues - Thurs 9 AM - 8 PM; Fri & Sat 10 AM - 6 PM, Sun 1 - 5 PM. No admis fee. Estab 1892
Income: Financed by city & state appropriation
Library Holdings: Vols 260,000; Per subs 420; Mounted pictures; Micro — Cards, prints, reels; AV — A-tapes, cassettes, fs, motion pictures, rec, slides, v-tapes; Other — Exhibition catalogs, pamphlets
Collections: Checkers Collection; Chess Collection; Costume Collection
Publications: Brooklyn Public Library Bulletin, bimonthly
Activities: Classes for children; programs; films

M **FUND FOR THE BOROUGH OF BROOKLYN,** Rotunda Gallery, 33 Clinton St, 11201. Tel 718-875-4047; FAX 718-488-0609; *Dir* Janet Riker; *Dir Educ* Meridith McNeal; *Gallery Asst* Robert Caldwell
Open Tues - Fri Noon - 5 PM, Sat 11 AM - 4 PM. No admis fee. Estab 1981 to exhibit the works of professional Brooklyn affiliated artists. Average Annual Attendance: 14,000
Income: $250,000 (financed by federal, state & municipal sources, private

foundations, corporations & individuals)
Exhibitions: Abstraction; Informed Choices (all media); Kidsart; Luminous Bodies (contemporary lightwork); untitled group exhibition (stitching & sewing)
Activities: Classes for adults & children; lect open to public, 6-10 vis lectr per year; gallery talks; computerized slide registry

INTERNATIONAL SOCIETY OF COPIER ARTISTS (ISCA)
For further information, see National and Regional Organizations

M **KINGSBOROUGH COMMUNITY COLLEGE, CITY UNIVERSITY OF NEW YORK,** Art Gallery, 2001 Oriental Blvd, 11235. Tel 718-368-5000; FAX 718-368-5573; *Dir* Lilly Wei; *Gallery Asst* Peter Malone
Open Mon - Fri 9 AM - 4 PM. No admis fee. Estab 1975 to show a variety of contemporary artistic styles. 44 ft x 44 ft gallery with moveable walls & 30 ft x 25 ft outdoor sculpture courtyard. Average Annual Attendance: 10,000
Income: Financed by Kingsborough Community College Assn
Exhibitions: Annual Student Exhibition
Activities: Lectures open to public, 4 - 8 vis lectr per yr; competitions with awards

M **KURDISH MUSEUM,** 144 Underhill Ave, 11238. Tel 718-783-7930; FAX 718-398-4365; *Dir* Vera Beaudin Saeedpour
Estab 1988. Maintains library
Collections: Costumes, jewelry, photos, slides
Exhibitions: Jews of Kurdistan
Publications: International Journal of Kurdish Studies, semiannual
Activities: Originate traveling exhibitions

L **NEW YORK CITY TECHNICAL COLLEGE,** Namm Hall Library and Learning Resource Center, * 300 Jay St, 11201. Tel 718-260-5469; FAX 718-260-5467; *Chief Librn* Darrow Wood; *Admin Services Librn* Prof Paul T Sherman; *Chief Cataloguer* Morris Hownion; *Reference Coordr* Joan Grissano
Open Mon - Fri 9 AM - 9 PM, Sat & Sun 10 AM - 2 PM. Estab 1947
Library Holdings: Other — Reproductions
Special Subjects: Advertising Design, Graphic Arts
Publications: Library Alert & Library Notes, occasional publications
Activities: Tours; Library Instruction; BRS Data Base Searching

L **PRATT INSTITUTE LIBRARY,** Art & Architecture Dept, 200 Willoughby Ave, 11205. Tel 718-636-3545, 636-3685; *Dean* F William Chickering; *Chmn* Dr Sydney Starr; *Art & Architecture Librn* Paul Glassman; *Art & Architecture Librn* Greta Earnest
Open Mon - Thurs 9 AM - 9 PM, Fri 9 AM - 7 PM, Sun Noon - 7 PM for students, faculty & staff, others by appointment from METRO or ALB card. Estab 1887 for students, faculty, staff & alumni of Pratt Institute. The school has several galleries, the library has exhibitions in display cases
Income: $50,000
Library Holdings: Vols 85,000; Per subs 150; Micro — Fiche, reels; AV — Slides; Other — Clipping files, exhibition catalogs, prints, reproductions
Special Subjects: Architecture, Photography, Contemporary Art, Design
M **Rubelle & Norman Schafler Gallery,** 200 Willoughby Ave, Brooklyn, 11205. Tel 718-636-3517; FAX 718-636-3785; *Dir Exhib* Eleanor Moretta; *Registrar* Nicholas Battis; *Exhibit Designer* Katherine Davis
Open Mon - Fri 9 AM - 5 PM, summer 9 AM - 4 PM. No admis fee. Estab 1960. Average Annual Attendance: 14,000
Collections: Permanent collection of fiber art, paintings, pottery, prints, photographsm sculpture
Activities: Lect open to public, 2 vis lectr per year; traveling exhibitions 1 per year; originate traveling exhibitions

A **PROMOTE ART WORKS INC (PAWI),** Laziza Videodance Lumia Project, 123 Smith St (Mailing add: PO Box 154, New York, 10012-0003). Tel 718-797-3116; FAX 718-797-3116; Elec Mail laziza4@gramercy.ios.com; Internet Home Page Address http://www.onlinegallery.com/laziza. *Artistic Dir* Kathleen Laziza; *Technical Dir* William Laziza; *Assoc Producer* Samantha Twyford; *Chmn* Alan Glousky; *Technician* Leonardo Monteolive
Open by appointment. Admis 0-$25. Estab 1980. Average Annual Attendance: 1200
Income: $15,000 (financed by contributions)
Exhibitions: Micro Museum
Activities: Classes for adults & children; internships; archival program for public television; lect open to public, 5 vis lectr per year; book traveling exhibitions 1 per year
Videodance Archives, 123 Smith St (Mailing add: PO Box 154, New York, 10012-0003)
Library Holdings: AV — A-tapes, cassettes, Kodachromes, lantern slides, rec, slides; Other — Manuscripts, memorabilia, original art works, photographs, prints, reproductions, sculpture

A **URBAN GLASS** (Formerly New York Contemporary Glass Center), 647 Fulton St, 11217. Tel 718-625-3685; *Dir* John Perreault
Open every day Noon - 5 PM. No admis fee. Estab 1978 to provide facility for artists who work in glass
Publications: Glass Magazine, quarterly
Activities: Classes for adults; lect open to public, 7 vis lectr per year; gallery talks; tours; competitions

BROOKVILLE

M **C W POST CAMPUS OF LONG ISLAND UNIVERSITY,** Hillwood Art Museum, North Blvd, 11548. Tel 516-299-4073; FAX 516-299-4180; *Assoc Dir* Barry Stern; *Coordr* Nicole Cox
Open Tues - Thurs 9:30 AM - 4:30 PM, Fri & Sat Noon - 8 PM, Sun Noon - 4 PM, cl Mon. No admis fee. Estab 1973. Museum has great appeal to the surrounding North Shore community as well as the student body. It is located in a multimillion dollar student complex and occupies a space of approx 46 x 92 ft.

Average Annual Attendance: 25,000
Income: Financed by university budget, grants & donations
Collections: Contemporary graphics, including works by Rauschenberg, Max Ernst, Pearlstein, Mark di Suvero and Salvador Dali
Exhibitions: Monumental Drawings, including R Serra, R Nonas, M Westerlund-Roosen, J Highstein; Painting from the Mind's Eye, including B Jensen, T Nozkowski, N Brett, P Brown, D Nelson, L Fishman; The Raw Edge: Ceramics of the 80's, including M Lucero, T Rosenberg, P Gourfain, A Gardner, V Frey; Floored, including L Benglis, C Andre, T Girouard, K Park, H Hammond; The Expressionist Vision, including A Rattner, J Solmon, M Hartley, K Schrag, Ben-Zion, U Romano, K Zerbe; Futurism and Photography; The Artist in the Theatre, including R Grooms, R Lichtenstein, J Shea, E Murray, V James, R Kushner, A Katz Reflections: New Conceptions of Nature, including P Norvell, J Bartlett, L Nesbitt, A Sonfist, M Stuart, T Winters, J Robbins; Michelle Stuart, Donald Lipski & Seymour Lipton, sculpture
Publications: Exhibition catalogs
Activities: Educ dept; lect open to public, 30 vis lectr per year; gallery talks; tours; individual paintings & original objects of art lent; lending collection contains books, cassettes, 3000 prints; originate traveling exhibitions; museum shop sells books & original art

BUFFALO

M **ART STUDIOS OF WESTERN NEW YORK,** 2495 Main St, Ste 500, 14214. Tel 716-833-4450; *Founder & Dir* Joanna Angie; *Gallery Co-Cur* Bryan Hopkins; *Gallery Co-Cur* Maggie Parks
Open 11 AM - 5 PM. No admis fee. Estab 1990 to provide space that enriches the artist & community. 75 x 25, shared with urban arts; opening 5 galleries, shared art center. Average Annual Attendance: 5000
Income: $100,000 (financed by mem, city appropriation, state appropriation, Arts Council of Buffalo, county, city, Yaeger Foundation, Wendt Foundation, County of Erie, corporations, private donations)
Exhibitions: Annual member exhibit; monthly exhibits
Activities: Classes for adults & children; lect open to public; summer, city wide mural program; museum shop sells prints, original art, pottery & sculptures

L **BUFFALO & ERIE COUNTY PUBLIC LIBRARY,** Lafayette Square, 14203. Tel 716-858-8900; FAX 716-858-6211; *Dir* Daniel L Walters; *Deputy Dir Public Services* Diane J Chrisman; *Deputy Dir Finance* Kenneth H Stone
Open Mon - Wed, Fri & Sat 8:30 AM - 6 PM, Thurs 8:30 AM - 8 PM. Estab 1954 through a merger of the Buffalo Pub, Grosvenor & Erie County Pub Libraries
Income: $25,000,000 (financed by county appropriation & state aid)
Library Holdings: Vols 3,000,000; Per subs 3200; AV — V-tapes; Other — Exhibition catalogs, manuscripts 4178, original art works, photographs, prints
Special Subjects: Drawings, Etchings & Engravings, Prints, Woodcuts
Collections: Fritz Eichenberg Collection (drawings); J J Lankes Collection (original woodcuts); William J Schwanekamp Collection (etchings); Niagara Falls Collection (prints); Rare book room with emphasis on fine printing
Publications: Bimonthly library bulletin
Activities: Dramatic programs; consumer programs; gallery talks; tours; concerts; book talks; architectural programs

M **THE BUFFALO FINE ARTS ACADEMY,** Albright-Knox Art Gallery, 1285 Elmwood Ave, 14222. Tel 716-882-8700; FAX 716-882-1958; *Pres* Charles E Balbach; *VPres* Mrs John T Elfvin; *VPres* Northrup R Knox; *VPres* William J Magavern II; *Treas* Richard W Cutting; *Dir* Douglas G Schultz; *Cur* Marc Mayer; *Cur* Cheryl A Brutuan; *Cur Educ* Jennifer Bayles; *Registrar* Laura Catalano
Open Tues - Sat 11 AM - 5 PM, Sun Noon - 5 PM, cl Thanksgiving, Christmas & New Year's Day. Admis adults $4, students & senior citizens $3, children 12 & under free. Estab 1862 as The Buffalo Fine Arts Academy. Gallery dedicated in 1905, with a new wing added in 1962. Center of modern art, the collection offers a panorama of art through the centuries, dating from 300 BC. Average Annual Attendance: 200,000. Mem: 7800; dues individual $45; annual meeting in Oct
Income: $3,300,000 (financed by contributions, mem, endowment, county appropriations, individual & corporate grants, earned income & special projects)
Collections: †Painting & drawings; †prints & sculpture ranging from 3000 BC to the present with special emphasis on †American & European contemporary art; †sculpture & constructions
Exhibitions: Being & Time: The Emergence of Video Projection; The Buffalo & San Francisco Collections; Clyfford; The Paintings of Sylvia Pilmack Mangold
Publications: Annual report; calendar (monthly); exhibition catalogs
Activities: Classes for adults & children; docent training; family workshops & programs; programs for the handicapped; lect open to public, 12 vis lectr per year; concerts; gallery talks; tours; individual paintings & original objects of art lent to major museums world wide; lending collections contain paintings, photographs & sculptures; book traveling exhibitions; originate traveling exhibitions; museum shop sells books, reproductions, slides, jewelry, gift items & toys

L **G Robert Strauss Jr Memorial Library,** 1285 Elmwood Ave, 14222. Tel 716-882-8700, Ext 225; FAX 716-882-8773; *Librn* Kari E Horowicz; *Asst Librn* Janice Lurie
Open Tues - Sat 1 - 5 PM & by appointment. Estab 1933 to support the staff research & to document the Gallery collection, also to serve the fine art & art history people doing research in the western New York area. Exhibits are prepared in a small vestibule, rare items in the library collection & print collection are displayed
Library Holdings: Vols 31,000; Per subs 100; Original documents; Micro — Fiche; AV — A-tapes, cassettes, v-tapes; Other — Clipping files, exhibition catalogs, manuscripts, memorabilia, original art works, pamphlets, photographs, prints, reproductions
Special Subjects: History of Art & Archaeology, Painting - American, Photography, Pre-Columbian Art, Printmaking, Prints, Sculpture, American Art; Contemporary Art; Artists' Books; Illustrated Books
Collections: †Artists books; †Graphic Ephemera; †Illustrated books
Exhibitions: Books and Prints of Maillol; Photography in Books; Rare Art Periodicals; Woodcuts from the Library Collection; Artists' Books; Illustrated Books; Derriere Le Mirroir; From the Gallery Archives; General Ide; Books with a Diffrence Circle Press Publications

L **BUFFALO MUSEUM OF SCIENCE,** Research Library, 1020 Humboldt Pky, 14211. Tel 716-896-5200, Ext 280; FAX 716-897-6723; *Research Librn* Lisa A Seivert
Open Tues - Fri 10 AM - 5 PM (by appointment only). Estab 1861 to further the study of natural history among the people of Buffalo. Museum has exhibition space for permanent & temporary exhibitions
Income: Financed by endowment, mem, county & state appropriation, grants, gifts
Purchases: $12,000
Library Holdings: Vols 30,000; Per subs 600; Micro — Fiche, reels; AV — A-tapes, fs, v-tapes; Other — Clipping files, exhibition catalogs, manuscripts, pamphlets, photographs
Special Subjects: Afro-American Art, American Indian Art, Anthropology, Archaeology, Dioramas, Ethnology, Jade, Laces, Oriental Art, Southwestern Art
Collections: African, Asian, American, European, Oceanic & Oriental Art; E W Hamlin Oriental Library of Art & Archaeology
Publications: Bulletin of the Buffalo Society of Natural Sciences, irregular; Collections, quarterly
Activities: Classes for adults & children; docent training; travel talks; lect open to public, 5 vis lectr per year; tours; sponsor Camera Club Photo Contests; book traveling exhibitions 2-3 per year; museum shop sells books & reproductions

M **BURCHFIELD-PENNEY ART CENTER,** Buffalo State College, 1300 Elmwood Ave, 14222. Tel 716-878-6011; FAX 716-878-6003; Elec Mail burchsld@snybuffaa.cs.snybuf.edu. *Charles Cary Rumsey Cur* Nancy Weekly; *Registrar* Mary Helen Miskuly; *Admin Asst* Jenn Doran; *Business Operations Mgr* Micheline Lepine; *Exhib Cur* Gerald Mead
Open Tues - Sat 10 AM - 5 PM, Sun 1 - 5 PM. No admis fee. Estab 1966 to develop a regional arts center for the exhibition, study & encouragement of artistic expression in the Western New York area. This includes a permanent collection of works by Charles Burchfield & other historic & contemporary artists who have lived or worked in the area. Museum has eight exhibition galleries. Average Annual Attendance: 40,000. Mem: 1600; dues associate $50, family $35, regular $25, student, artist & senior citizens $15
Income: Financed by grants, endowment, mem, SUNY & other sources
Collections: †Charles Burchfield collection; †works by contemporary & historical artists of the western New York area
Publications: Exhibition catalogues
Activities: Docent training; lect open to public; concerts; symposia; tours; poetry readings; competitions; exten dept serves area schools & community organizations; original objects of art lent to teachers; lending collection contains books, cassettes, color reproduction, film strips, framed reproductions, slides, magazine articles, periodicals; originates traveling exhibitions; sales shop sells books, catalogues, craft art, reproductions & wallpapers designed by Charles Burchfield

L **Archives,** Buffalo State College, 1300 Elmwood Ave, 14222. Tel 716-878-4143; FAX 716-878-6003; *Registrar* Mary Helen Miskuly
Open Mon - Fri 10 AM - 5 PM. Estab 1967. For pub reference only. Significant donations by Charles Vand Penney
Library Holdings: Vols 2500; Monographs; Periodicals; AV — A-tapes, cassettes, motion pictures, slides, v-tapes; Other — Clipping files, exhibition catalogs, manuscripts, memorabilia, photographs
Special Subjects: Architecture, Art Education, Art History, Historical Material, Manuscripts, Painting - American, Photography, Printmaking, Watercolors, Western New York State Regional Arts
Collections: Archives relating to Charles E Burchfield, George William Eggers, Charles Cary Rumsey, Frank K M Rehn Gallery, J J Lankes, Martha Visser't Hooft, Buffalo Society of Artists, Patteran Society; Artpark; Artist Gallery
Exhibitions: Archival materials relating to the life & career of Charles Burchfield

M **CENTER FOR EXPLORATORY & PERCEPTUAL ART,** CEPA Gallery, 700 Main St, 4th Flr, 14202. Tel 716-856-2717; FAX 716-856-2720; *Pres* Biff Henrich; *Assoc Dir* Gail Nicholson; *Exec Dir* Robert Hirsch
Open Tues - Fri 10 AM - 5 PM, Sat Noon - 4 PM. No admis fee. Estab 1974 as a non-profit art center for the advancement of contemporary ideas & issues expressed through photographically related work. Five gallery rooms, 225 running ft of wall space, tracklight, hardwood floors. Average Annual Attendance: 50,000. Mem: 200; dues $20 - $1000
Income: $100,000 (financed by mem, city & state appropriation, NY State Council on the arts, National Endowment for the Arts)
Exhibitions: A View from Within; Keepers of the Western Door/Works by Native American Artists; Ritual Social Identity
Publications: CEPA Quarterly; Artist Project Publications, 2 artist books per year
Activities: Adult classes; lect open to public, vis lectr; competitions with awards; book traveling exhibitions 1 per year; shop sells books, original art

L **CEPA Library,** 700 Main St, 4th Flr, 14202. Tel 716-856-2717;
Reference library only
Library Holdings: AV — Lantern slides, rec, slides, v-tapes; Other — Clipping files, exhibition catalogs, pamphlets
Special Subjects: Photography

M **HALLWALLS CONTEMPORARY ARTS CENTER,** 2495 Main St, Ste 425, 14214. Tel 716-835-7362; FAX 716-835-7364; Elec Mail hallwall@pce.net. *Dir* Edmund Cardoni; *Visual Arts Dir* Sara Kellner
Open Tues - Fri 11 AM - 6 PM, Sat by appointment. No admis fee. Estab 1974 to provide exhibition space for artists whose careers are just beginning to emerge into the mainstream of art activity; besides exhibitions, programming includes film, literature, music, performance art & video. The gallery is comprised of 1 large & 2 smaller viewing galleries. Average Annual Attendance: 25,000. Mem: 800; dues $20-$300; annual meeting in Nov
Income: Financed by the National Endowment for the Arts, city, county & state

appropriations, New York State Council on the Arts, contributions from private corporations & foundations
Collections: 400 tape video library
Publications: Consider the Alternatives: 20 Years of Contemporary Art at Hallwalls
Activities: Lectures open to the public; gallery talks; fellowships offered; book traveling exhibitions 1 per year; originate traveling exhibitions

CANAJOHARIE

M **CANAJOHARIE LIBRARY & ART GALLERY,** 2 Erie Blvd, 13317. Tel 518-673-2314; FAX 518-673-5243; *Pres of Board* Oliver Simonsen; *Dir* Eric Trahan; *Cur & Historical Cur* James Crawford
Open Mon - Wed 10 AM - 4:45 PM, Thurs 1:30 - 8:30 PM, Fri 1:30 - 4:45 PM, Sat 10 AM - 1:30 PM, cl Sun. No admis fee. Estab 1914 as a memorial to Senator James Arkell. Two galleries total area 1500 sq ft exhibit works from permanent collection including major collection of paintings by Winslow Homer. Average Annual Attendance: 50,000. Mem: Annual meeting in Jan
Income: Financed by endowment & village grants
Collections: Archival Materials & Artifacts on Regional History; †Paintings by American artists, colonial period-present
Exhibitions: Permanent collection
Publications: Catalog of Permanent Art Collection varies
Activities: Lect provided, 5 vis lectr per year; concerts; gallery talks; tours; individual paintings & original objects of art lent to other museums & galleries; lending collection contains 28,617 books, 831 cassettes, color reproductions, paintings, 682 phono records, 376 slides, 523 video cassettes; museum shop sells books, original art, prints & reproductions
L **Library,** 2 Erie Blvd, 13317. Tel 518-673-2314; FAX 518-673-5243; *Dir Library* Eric Trahan; *Pres of Board* Oliver Simonsen; *Cur* James Crawford
Open Mon, Tues, Wed & Fri 10 AM - 4:45 PM, Thurs 10 AM - 8:30 PM, Sat 10 AM - 1:30 PM. No Admis fee. Estab 1914 to represent American Art
Library Holdings: Vols 28,617; Per subs 146; Micro — Reels; AV — A-tapes, cassettes, rec, slides, v-tapes; Other — Clipping files, exhibition catalogs, framed reproductions, pamphlets, photographs
Activities: Lect open to public, 5 vis lectr per year; concerts; gallery talks; tours; lending collection contains 29,022 books, cassettes, framed reproductions & 788 phono records; museum shop sells books, magazines, original art, reproductions, prints, slides, notecards & postcards

CANTON

M **ST LAWRENCE UNIVERSITY,** Richard F Brush Art Gallery, Romoda Dr, 13617. Tel 315-379-5174; *Dir* Catherine Tedford; *Coll Mgr* Carole Mathey
Open Mon - Thurs Noon - 8 PM, Fri & Sat Noon - 5 PM, cl for the summer. No admis fee. Estab 1968 as an adjunct of the Department of Fine Arts. The Gallery's programs are intended to complement the University's curriculum as well as benefit the general pub of Northern New York state & Southern Canada
Income: Financed by university funds
Collections: Oriental & African Art; 16th-20th Century European & American paintings, sculpture & prints; †20th Century American & European prints, drawings & photographs
Publications: Annual report; exhibition brochures
Activities: Lect open to public, 6 vis lectr per year; art objects lent to museums

CAZENOVIA

M **CAZENOVIA COLLEGE,** Chapman Art Center Gallery, 13035. Tel 315-655-8283, Ext 162; FAX 315-655-2190; *Dir* John Aistars
Open Mon - Thurs 1 - 4 PM & 7 - 9 PM, Fri 1 - 4 PM, Sat & Sun 2 - 6 PM. No admis fee. Estab 1977 as a college gallery for students & community. Gallery is 1084 sq ft with track lighting. Average Annual Attendance: 1000
Income: Financed by College
Collections: A small permanent collection of work donated to college
Exhibitions: Annual shows of faculty, students & invitational work; Cazenovia Watercolor Society

CHAUTAUQUA

M **CHAUTAUQUA CENTER FOR THE VISUAL ARTS,** PO Box 999, 14722. Tel 716-357-2771; *Pres* Bob Ivers; *VPres* Jan Friend Davis; *Dir* Alberto Rey
Open Mon - Sun 10 AM - 5 PM July - Aug. No admis fee. Estab 1952 to promote quality art, culture & appreciation of the arts. Main gallery with 3 smaller galleries. Average Annual Attendance: 10,000. Mem: 250; dues $20; monthly meetings
Income: Financed by mem, grants, donations & fundraising activities
Exhibitions: 15 exhibitions per year including prints, paintings, glass, metals & sculpture; Annual Chautauqua National Exhibition of American Art (entering 40th year)
Publications: Chautauqua National, annual catalog; Calendar of Events, annual; Chautauqua National Prospectus, annual; annual report; promotional materials; exhibition brochures; membership brochures
Activities: Classes for adults & children; art appreciation; docent training; lect open to public, 17 vis lectr per year; concerts; gallery talks; docent tours; competitions with awards; annual juried National Exhibition of American Art; individual paintings & original objects of art lent to Chautauqua institution, area libraries, exhibition sites, area galleries & theatres; book traveling exhibitions annually; originate traveling exhibitions; sales shop sells books, original art, reproductions, prints, original jewelry, small gifts & handicraft from around the world

CLINTON

M **HAMILTON COLLEGE,** Fred L Emerson Gallery, 13323. Tel 315-859-4396; FAX 315-859-4969; *Dir* Lise Holst
Open Sept - May Mon - Fri Noon - 5 PM, Sat & Sun 1 - 5 PM, cl weekends June - Aug. No admis fee. Estab 1982. Housed in 1914 building. Average Annual Attendance: 20,000
Income: Financed by Hamilton College appropriations
Purchases: Martin Lewis, Rainy Day on Murray Hill, etching; George Bellows Between Rounds 1916, lithograph; Jefferson David Chalfant Working Sketch for the Chess Players, pencil; Roman, c 2nd Century AD; Two Sarcophagi Fragments, marble
Collections: Greek vases, Roman glass; Native American artifacts; †16th-20th century prints, †19th-20th century paintings
Exhibitions: Josh Simpson: New Work, New Worlds
Publications: Exhibition catalogues
Activities: Lect open to public, 2-3 vis lectr per year; concerts; gallery talks; tours; individual paintings & original objects of art lent; originate traveling exhibitions

A **KIRKLAND ART CENTER,** E Park Row, PO Box 213, 13323. Tel 315-853-8871; *Dir* Matthew Mielnick
Open Tues - Fri 9:30 AM - 5 PM, Sun 2 - 5 PM, cl Mon; Tues - Fri 9:30 - 3 PM, Sun 2 - 5 PM July & Aug. No admis fee. Estab 1960 to promote the arts in the town of Kirkland & surrounding area. The center has a large main gallery, dance studio & studio space for classes. Average Annual Attendance: 15,000 - 17,000. Mem: 1350; dues adults $15; annual meeting June
Income: Financed by endowment, mem, state, county & town appropriation, fund raising events, thrift, gallery shop, United Way & United Arts Funds
Exhibitions: Works by contemporary artists
Publications: Newsletter, monthly
Activities: Classes for adults & children; performances for children; bluegrass & folk music series; film series; lect open to public; competitions

COBLESKILL

A **SCHOHARIE COUNTY ARTS COUNCIL,** 54 E Main (Mailing add: PO Box 730, 12043). Tel 518-234-7380; *Dir* Emily Rauch; *Folklorist* Ellen McHale
Open Mon - Fri 9 AM - 5 PM, Sat 10 AM - 2 PM, cl Sun. Estab 1977. Average Annual Attendance: 5000. Mem: 265; mem open to individual artists & business donations of $25 or more; dues individual/artist $25, seniors $10; annual meeting 3rd Tues in May
Income: $150,000 (financed by mem, government, corporate & foundation support)
Exhibitions: Annual National Small Works Exhibition
Activities: Classes for children; dramatic programs; benefit concerts; acoustic jams; book traveling exhibitions 1 per year; originate traveling exhibitions 1 per year; sales shop sells books, original art & reproductions

COLD SPRING

M **PUTNAM COUNTY HISTORICAL SOCIETY,** Foundry School Museum, 63 Chestnut St, 10516. Tel 914-265-4010; *Cur* Charlotte B Eaton; *Admin Asst* Jean Rosenwald
Open Tues - Wed 10 AM - 4 PM, Thurs 1 - 4 PM, Sun 2 - 5 PM, cl Mon, Fri & Sat. No admis fee. Estab 1906 to present local history artifacts. Average Annual Attendance: 1000. Mem: 500; dues family $25, individual $15, seniors & students $10, juniors 10-13 $1; annual meeting in Feb
Income: $40,000 (financed by endowment, mem & fundraising events)
Collections: Country Store; Furnishings & Hudson River Paintings; 19th Century Country Kitchen; West Point Foundry
Exhibitions: (1997) Fahnstalk Mines; Jean Saunders History Contest Entries; Contest Winners; Prints From Our Attic
Activities: School programs; lect open to public, 2 vis lectr per year; competitions with awards; individual paintings & original objects of art lent

COOPERSTOWN

A **COOPERSTOWN ART ASSOCIATION,** 22 Main St, 13326. Tel 607-547-9777; FAX 607-547-9777; *Dir* Janet Garber
Open Mon, Wed - Sat 11 AM - 4 PM, Sun 1 - 4 PM, cl Tues, extended summer hours. Estab 1928 to provide a cultural program for the central part of New York State. An art gallery is maintained. Average Annual Attendance: 14,000. Mem: 300; dues $5 & up
Income: Financed by mem
Collections: †Crafts; †paintings; †sculpture
Exhibitions: Annual Regional & National Juried Exhibitions
Publications: Annual newsletter
Activities: Classes for adults; lect open to public, 1-3 vis lectr per year; concerts; awards; scholarships offered; individual paintings & original objects of art lent; lending collection contains paintings, sculpture, crafts

M **GALLERY 53,** 118 Main St, 13326. Tel 607-547-5655; FAX 607-547-2570; *Dir* Brian Millen; *Fiscal Mgr* Marci Schwartzman
Open Mon - Sat 10 AM - 5 PM, cl Tues & Sun. No admis fee. Estab 1981 to expand appreciation for contemporary art. Main Gallery & Downstairs Garden Gallery in restored historic storefront, 90 linear ft of wall space (total); outdoor sculpture gardens. Average Annual Attendance: 15,000. Mem: 600; dues $20-$1000, depending on level
Income: $250,000 (financed by mem, state appropriation, gift gallery sales, fundraising & corporate grants)
Exhibitions: Artists' Toys; Baseball-Related Contemporary Fine Art; Constructions/Assemblages; Contemporary Folk Art
Publications: An Agricultural Legacy: Farm Outbuildings of Central NY
Activities: Classes for adults & children; dramatic programs; lect open to public, 10 vis lectr per year; internships offered; individual paintings lent; book traveling exhibitions; originate traveling exhibitions; sales shop sells books, original art, prints, reproductions, pottery, jewelry & fiber-art

A LEATHERSTOCKING BRUSH & PALETTE CLUB INC, PO Box 446, 13326. Tel 607-547-8044; *Publicity* Dorothy V Smith
Estab 1965 to encourage original arts and crafts work and foster general art appreciation and education. Mem: 55; dues $10; meetings quarterly
Income: Financed by mem & outdoor show revenues
Exhibitions: Annual Labor Day Weekend Outdoor Arts & Crafts Show; Annual Fine Arts Exhibition; Leatherstocking Gallery Arts & Crafts Shop
Publications: Information Bulletin, quarterly
Activities: Classes for adults; All activities offered to public; member tours to art museums & exhibits; originate traveling exhibitions

M NATIONAL BASEBALL HALL OF FAME & MUSEUM, INC, Art Collection, 25 Main St, PO Box 590, 13326. Tel 607-547-7200; FAX 607-547-5980; *Pres* Donald C Marr Jr; *VPres* William J Guilfoile; *Registrar* Peter P Clark; *Librn* James L Gates Jr; *Cur Exhibits* William T Spencer; *VPres* Frank Simio
Open May - Oct daily 9 AM - 9 PM, Nov - Apr daily 9 AM - 5 PM. Admis adults $9.50, children ages 7-15 $4.50. Estab 1936 to collect, preserve & display memorabilia pertaining to the national game of baseball. Maintains reference library. Average Annual Attendance: 300,000
Income: $1,500,000 (financed by admis & gift shop sales, Hall of Fame Game & contributions)
Collections: Baseball & sport-related art & memorabilia
Publications: National Baseball Hall of Fame & Museum Yearbook, annually; quarterly newsletter
Activities: Classes for children; originate traveling exhibitions to museums, banks, baseball clubs, shopping malls; bookstore sells books, reproductions, prints, t-shirts, caps, glassware, postcards, mugs & jackets

NEW YORK STATE HISTORICAL ASSOCIATION
M Fenimore House Museum, Rte 80, Lake Rd, PO Box 800, 13326. Tel 607-547-1400; FAX 607-547-5384; *Pres* Kent Barwick; *VPres* Milo V Stewart; *Dir Coll* A Bruce McLeish
Open May - Labor Day daily 9 AM - 5 PM, Labor Day - Oct 31 daily 10 AM - 4 PM, Nov & Dec Tues - Sun 10 AM - 4 PM, cl Jan - Apr. Admis adults $6, children 7-12 $2.50, members free. Estab 1899 as a historical soc whose purpose is to promote the study of New York State through a state wide educational program, the operation of two museums & graduate programs offering master's degree in conjunction with the State University of New York at Oneonta. Fenimore House is an art & history museum with an extensive collection of folk, academic, decorative art & American Indian Art. Opening a new American Indian Art wing in 1995 to house the Eugene & Clare Thaw Collection of American Indian Art. Average Annual Attendance: 45,000. Mem: 6200; dues $35 & up; annual meeting in July
Collections: †American folk art; †American Indian Art; Browere life masks of famous Americans; James Fenimore Cooper (memorabilia); genre paintings of New York State; landscapes; portraits
Exhibitions: Worlds of Art-Worlds Apart
Publications: Annual Report; New York History, quarterly journal; Heritage, quarterly membership magazine, occasional manuscripts; exhibit catalogues
Activities: Classes for adults & children; docent training; seminars on American culture; junior program; conferences; lect open to public; gallery talks; tours; individual paintings & original objects of art lent to selected museums; museum shop sells books & magazines

M Farmers' Museum, Inc, Rte 80, Lake Rd, PO Box 800, 13326. Tel 607-547-1400, 547-1450; FAX 607-547-1404; Elec Mail nyshal@aol.com. *Pres* Kent Barwick; *VPres & Dir Museums* Dr Gilbert T Vincent; *Dir Coll* A Bruce Macleish
Open June - Labor Day daily 9 AM - 5 PM, Labor Day - Oct 31 daily 10 AM - 4 PM, Nov, Dec & Apr Tues - Sun 10 AM - 4 PM, cl Jan - Mar. Admis adults $9, children between 7-12 $4, under 7 & members free. Estab 1943 as an outdoor mus of rural life in upstate New York. Main exhibit building with exhibits & craft demonstrations; recreated 1845 village with 10 buildings brought in from nearby areas. Average Annual Attendance: 100,000
Income: Financed by endowment, self-sustaining
Collections: 19th century tools & implements; horse-drawn vehicles & farm equipment; 19th century rural homes & business interior furnishings
Exhibitions: The Sheltered Nest: Mechanizing the Victorian Household; Textile Area; Tradesman's Tool Chest (22 New York Crafts)
Activities: Classes for adults & children; docent training; lect open to public, 2-3 vis lectr per year; concerts; tours; special events; book traveling exhibitions; museum shop sells reproductions & gifts

L Library, Lake Rd, PO Box 800, 13326. Tel 607-547-1470; FAX 607-547-1405; *Dir* Amy Barnum; *Assoc Dir* Wayne Wright
Open to public for reference only
Library Holdings: Vols 80,000; Per subs 160; Micro — Reels; AV — Cassettes, rec; Other — Manuscripts
Special Subjects: American Indian Art, Decorative Arts, Folk Art, Historical Material, Painting - American, New York State History

CORNING

A ARTS OF THE SOUTHERN FINGER LAKES, One Baron-Steuben Pl, Ste 8, 14830. Tel 607-962-5871; FAX 607-936-2235; Elec Mail thearts@servtech.com. *Exec Dir* Kevin Geoghan; *Folklorist* Peter Voorheis; *Marketing Support* Stephen Miller; *Arts Educ Dir* Ann Hazlitt; *Grants Coordr* Susan Peck; *Marketing Dir* Ann Campbell; *Admin Support* Sandra Nolan
Open Mon - Fri 9 AM - 5 PM. No admis fee. Estab to increase resident participation in the arts. Mem: 42; annual meeting in June
Exhibitions: Festival of Art. The Crafts of the Southern Finger Lakes; The Westend Gallery (Local Artists)
Publications: Artscope, 6 times per year; See, Hear, Do, 6 times per year
Activities: Educ dept; infuses art into education in area schools; lect open to public; partnership awards given

M CORNING MUSEUM OF GLASS, One Museum Way, 14830-2253. Tel 607-937-5371; FAX 607-937-3352; Elec Mail cmg@servtech.com. *Dir* David Whitehouse; *Research Scientist* Robert H Brill; *Cur 20th Century Glass* Susanne Frantz; *Cur American Glass* Jane Spillman; *Registrar* Priscilla B Price; *Managing*

Editor Richard W Price; *Cur European Glass* Dr Jutta-Annette Bruhn
Open all year daily 9 AM - 5 PM. Admis family $13, adult $5, senior citizens $4, children 6-17 $3, children under 6 free. Estab 1951 to collect & exhibit the finest glass from 1500 BC to the present. New building opened May 1980. Average Annual Attendance: 450,000. Mem: 800; dues $125 & up
Income: $3,000,000 (financed by gifts, interest & sales)
Collections: †Over 25,000 objects representing all periods of glass history from 1500 BC to the present
Exhibitions: (1997) Italian Glass 1930-1970; Master Pieces of Design from Murano to Milan. (1998) The Glass Skin
Publications: Annual catalog for special exhibitions; Journal of Glass Studies, annual; New Glass Review, annual
Activities: Classes for children; docent training; annual seminar on glass; lect open to public, 20 vis lectr per year; film series; gallery talks; tours; competitions; awards; scholarships & fels offered; original art objects lent to the other museums; lending collection contains 50,000 books, 350 lantern slides; originate traveling exhibitions; sales shop sells books, postcards, prints & slides

L Rakow Library, One Museum Way, 14830-3352. Tel 607-937-5371; FAX 607-937-3352; *Librn* Patricia J Rogers; *Assoc Librn* Virginia L Wright
Open Mon - Fri 9 AM - 5 PM. Estab 1951 for the purpose of providing comprehensive coverage of the art, history, archaeology & early manufacture of glass. The library is primarily for research reference only
Library Holdings: Vols 42,000; Per subs 850; Original documents; Rare books 670; Micro — Fiche 13,200, reels 800; AV — A-tapes, cassettes, motion pictures, slides 20,000, v-tapes 780; Other — Clipping files, exhibition catalogs, original art works, pamphlets, photographs, prints 550
Special Subjects: Antiquities-Assyrian, Antiquities-Byzantine, Antiquities-Egyptian, Antiquities-Etruscan, Antiquities-Greek, Antiquities-Oriental, Antiquities-Persian, Antiquities-Roman, Archaeology, Crafts, Decorative Arts, Flasks & Bottles, Glass, Glass history, manufacturing, painting and staining, glassware, ornamental glass
Collections: Archival & historical materials relating to glass & its manufactures; 5000 manufacturers' trade catalogs on microfiche
Activities: Scholarships & fels offered

M THE ROCKWELL MUSEUM, 111 Cedar St, 14830. Tel 607-937-5386; FAX 607-974-4536; *Dir* Richard B Bessey; *Registrar* Maria E McWilliams; *Cur* Robyn G Peterson; *Asst Dir Admin* Mercedes C Skidmore; *Public Relations & Marketing Mgr* Lilita Bergs; *Supv Public Programs* P Jensen Monroe; *Museum Shop Mgr* Juanita Malavet
Open Mon - Sat 9 AM - 5 PM, Sun Noon - 5 PM. Admis family $10, adults $4, senior citizens $3.60, students 6-17 $2. Estab 1976 to house & exhibit the collection of the Robert F Rockwell family & to collect & exhibit American Western art, Carder glass, antique toys. The 3rd floor Western art gallery has bronzes, paintings, antique firearms & artifacts & Reifschlager Gallery displays Carder Steuben glass. Average Annual Attendance: 35,000. Mem: 700; dues $25 - $1000; meetings in June & Dec
Income: $400,000 (financed by a grant from the Corning Glass Works)
Purchases: $50,000
Collections: †Carter Steuben glass (1903-1933); bronzes; †19th & 20th century American Western paintings & illustrations; Plains Indian beadwork & artifacts; prints; †Pueblo Indian pottery; Navajo rugs
Exhibitions: Finding New Worlds: American Frontier Photography; Red Grooms' Ruckus Rodeo; Brilliance in Glass: The Lost Wax Castings of Frederick Carder
Publications: Exhibition catalog; Newsletter, 3 times per yr
Activities: Classes for adults & children; docent training; lect open to public; annual symposia on Carder Steuben glass; gallery talks; tours; paintings, original objects of art lent to established museums; lending collection contains reproductions, original art works, original prints, Victorian toys, Carder Steuben Glass; originate traveling exhibitions; shop sells books, magazines, reproductions, prints, Indian jewelry, postcards, crafts from the Southwest, T-shirts, Pueblo pottery, Hopi Kachinas, toys, glass

L Library, 111 Cedar St, 14830. Tel 607-937-5386; FAX 607-974-4536; *Dir* Richard B Bessey
For reference only
Income: Financed by mem, bequests, grants, corporate donations from Corning Glass Works
Library Holdings: Vols 3000; Per subs 40; Micro — Cards; AV — Cassettes, fs, slides, v-tapes; Other — Clipping files, exhibition catalogs, manuscripts, original art works, pamphlets, photographs

CORNWALL ON HUDSON

M MUSEUM OF THE HUDSON HIGHLANDS, The Boulevard, PO Box 181, 12520. Tel 914-534-7781; *Pres* Edward Hoyt; *Dir* Charles Keene; *Admin Dir* Susan Brander
Open Mon - Thurs 11 AM - 5 PM, Sat Noon - 5 PM, Sun 1:30 - 5 PM, cl Fri. Admis $1 suggested donation. Estab 1962; primarily a children's natural history & art mus. A large octagonal gallery & a small gallery. Average Annual Attendance: 33,000. Mem: 450; artists qualify by approval of slides; dues $15-$25
Income: $140,000 (financed by mem, city appropriation & grants)
Collections: Richard McDaniels: Hudson River Drawings
Activities: Classes for adults & children; lect open to public, 2 vis lectr per year; competitions with awards; lending collection contains nature & history kits; book traveling exhibitions, annually; museum shop sells books, magazines, original art, reproductions, prints, toys, pottery, jewelry, batik scarfs

CORTLAND

M CORTLAND COUNTY HISTORICAL SOCIETY, Suggett House Museum, 25 Homer Ave, 13045. Tel 607-756-6071; *Pres* James Sarvay; *Treas* Robert Ferris; *Dir* Mary Ann Kane
Open Tues - Sat 1 - 4 PM, mornings by appointment. Admis adults (16 & up) $2. Estab 1925 to collect, store & interpret the history of Cortland County through programs, exhibits & records in our 1882 Suggett House. Some art displayed in period settings, 1825-1900. Average Annual Attendance: 2000. Mem: 750; dues $15; meetings second Sat of Jan, Apr, June & Oct
Income: $60,000 (financed by endowment, mem, county appropriations, grants, sales & fundraisers)
Collections: †Antique furniture, †children's toys, †china, †folk art, †glass, †military memorabilia, †paintings, †textiles & clothing
Publications: Roots & Branches, 2 times per yr; books on local history; bulletin, 3 times per yr; newsletter, 3 times per yr
Activities: Classes for adults & children; docent training; lect open to public; individual paintings & original objects of art lent to other museums & college galleries; museum shop sells books
L Kellogg Memorial Research Library, 25 Homer Ave, 13045. Tel 607-756-6071; *Exec Dir* Mary Ann Kane; *Coll Mgr* Anita Wright
Open Tues - Sat 1 - 5 PM, mornings by appointment. Estab 1976 to collect, preserve & interpret information about the history of Cortland County. For reference only
Purchases: $500
Library Holdings: Vols 5000; Micro — Fiche, reels; AV — Cassettes, lantern slides, rec, slides, v-tapes; Other — Clipping files, exhibition catalogs, manuscripts, memorabilia, original art works, pamphlets, photographs, prints, reproductions, sculpture

L CORTLAND FREE LIBRARY, 32 Church St, 13045. Tel 607-753-1042; FAX 607-758-7329; *Dir* Warren S Eddy
Open Mon - Thurs 10 AM - 8:30 PM, Fri 10 AM - 5:30 PM, Sat 10 AM - 4 PM, cl Sun. No admis fee. Estab 1938
Purchases: $1800
Library Holdings: Vols 1600
Exhibitions: Occasiional monthly exhibitions held

M 1890 HOUSE-MUSEUM & CENTER FOR THE ARTS, 37 Tompkins St, 13045-2555. Tel 607-756-7551; *Dir* John H Nozynski; *Admin Asst* Grace Nicholas
Open daily 9 AM - 5 PM, tours 9 AM - 5 PM. Estab 1978
Collections: †Decorative arts; †Oriental Furnishings; †Paintings; †1890 - 1900 Documentary Photographs; †Victorian Furniture; †Victorian Silver
Exhibitions: Late Victorian Cast Iron Lawn Ornaments; Victorian Lighting; Documentary Photographs of Restoration
Publications: Whispers Near the Inglenook, quarterly
L Kellogg Library & Reading Room, 37 Tompkins St, 13045-2555. Tel 607-756-7551; *Admin Asst* Grace Nicholas
For lending & reference
Library Holdings: Vols 1800; Per subs 12

L STATE UNIVERSITY OF NEW YORK COLLEGE AT CORTLAND, Art Slide Library, 13045. Tel 607-753-4318; FAX 607-753-5999; Elec Mail schafferj@snycurva.cortland.edu. *Cur* Jo Schaffer
Open Mon - Fri 8:30 AM - 5 PM & by appointment. Estab 1967 to provide visual resources to faculty, students & community
Income: Financed by state appropriation
Library Holdings: Vols 1000; Per subs 10; Micro — Fiche; AV — Fs, Kodachromes, lantern slides 5000, slides 125,000, v-tapes 100; Other — Exhibition catalogs, photographs 10,000
Special Subjects: Pop Art

COXSACKIE

M GREENE COUNTY HISTORICAL SOCIETY, Bronck Museum, Rte 9W, 12051. Tel 518-731-6490, 731-6822; *Pres* Charles Schaefer; *Librn* Raymond Beecher; *Cur* Shelby Kriele
Open June - Sept 10 AM - 4 PM. Admis $3. Estab 1929
Exhibitions: Catskills of Green County, photographs
Publications: Greene County Historical Journal, quarterly

DOUGLASTON

A NATIONAL ART LEAGUE INC, 44-21 Douglaston Pky, 11360. Tel 718-229-9495; *Pres* Nat Bukar; *VPres* Al Camurati
Estab 1932, inc 1950, as Art League of Long Island, Inc. Mem: 230
Income: Financed by mem dues & contributions
Exhibitions: Six annual major shows, one national; gallery exhibitions
Publications: Brochures; bulletins; catalogs; newsletter, monthly
Activities: Art classes for adults & children; demonstrations; lect open to public, 10 vis lectr per year; gallery talks; competitions with awards

EAST HAMPTON

L EAST HAMPTON LIBRARY, Pennypacker Long Island Collection, 159 Main St, 11937. Tel 516-324-0222; FAX 516-329-5947; *Dir* Beth Gray; *Librn* Dorothy King; *Library Asst* Diana Dayton
Open Mon - Sat 1 - 4:30 PM, cl Sun. Estab 1897
Library Holdings: Maps; Other — Clipping files, exhibition catalogs, manuscripts, original art works, pamphlets, prints
Collections: Pennypacker Long Island Collection contains material relating to the history & people of Long Island; Thomas Moran Biographical Art Collection contains original pen & ink & pencil sketches by Thomas Moran, lithographs, etchings & engravings by Moran & other members of the family, biographical material, exhibit catalogues, books & pamphlets

M GUILD HALL OF EAST HAMPTON, INC, Guild Hall Museum, 158 Main St, 11937. Tel 516-324-0806; FAX 516-324-2722; *Exec Dir* Henry Korn; *Chmn* Melville Strauss; *VChmn* Michael Lynne; *Treas* M Bernard Aidinoff; *Cur* Donna Stein; *Assoc Cur & Registrar* Heather Dimon
Open Winter - Spring Wed - Sat 11 AM - 5 PM, Sun Noon - 5 PM, Summer open daily 11 AM - 5 PM, Fall same as Spring. No admis fee for members, non-members $3. Estab 1931 as a cultural center for the visual & performing arts with a State Board of Regents Educational Charter. Emphasis in art collection & exhibitons is chiefly on the many artists who live or have lived in the area. Mus has four galleries, art library & a sculpture garden. Average Annual Attendance: 80,000. Mem: 4000; dues $30-$2500; annual meeting in May
Income: $1,400,000 (financed by mem, federal, state, county & town appropriations, corporate, foundation, individual contributions, benefits, fund drives & mus shop)
Collections: Focuses on American artists associated with the region of Eastern Long Island, including James Brooks, Jimmy Ernst, Adolf Gottlieb, Childe Hassam, William de Kooning, Roy Lichtenstein, Thomas Moran, Jackson Pollock, Larry Rivers, as well as contemporary artists such as Eric Fischl, Donald Sultan & Lynda Benglis, paintings, works on paper, prints, photographs, sculpture
Publications: Newsletter, exhibition catalogues, annual report, monthly calendar
Activities: Classes for adults; docent training; cooperative projects with area schools; lect open to public, 12 vis lectr per year; concerts, gallery talks; tours, competitions; original art objects lent to museums, libraries, schools, public building; lending collection contains cassettes, original art works & prints, paintings, photographs, sculpture, slides; book traveling exhibitions; originate traveling exhibitions; museum shop sells mainly posters created for Guild Hall by artists of region; also gift items and local crafts

EAST ISLIP

M ISLIP ART MUSEUM, 50 Irish Lane, 11730. Tel 516-224-5402; *Exec Dir* Mary Lou Cohalan; *Dir Coll & Exhib* Catherine Valenza; *Cur* Karen Shaw
Open Wed - Sat 10 AM - 4 PM, Sun 2 - 4:30 PM. No admis fee, suggested donation $2. Estab 1973 for group showings of contemporary art from local & city based artists. 3000 sq ft of exhibition space divided among 4 rooms & a hallway on the Brookwood Hall estate. The main building housing the mus also houses the town offices & the Islip Arts Council. Average Annual Attendance: 9500. Mem: 250; dues $25-$5000
Income: $150,000 (financed by mem, city & state appropriation, & National Endowment for the Arts)
Exhibitions: Satellite Gallery & a Project Space
Publications: Exhibition brochures; Newsletter
Activities: Classes for adults & children; internships; lect open to public, 3-5 vis lectr per year; museum shop sells books, handmade gifts, jewelry, original art, postcards, posters, reproductions

EAST OTTO

A ASHFORD HOLLOW FOUNDATION FOR VISUAL & PERFORMING ARTS, Griffis Sculpture Park, 6902 Mill Valley Rd, 14729. Tel 716-257-9344; *Exec Dir* Simon Griffis; *Dir* Mark B Griffis; *Chief Exec Officer* Larry Griffis
Open May - Oct 9 AM - dusk. No admis fee, donations welcomed. Estab 1966 to promote the visual & performing arts by sponsoring exhibitions & performances. Funds for the 400 acre sculpture park donated by Ruth Griffis in memory of her husband, L W Griffis Sr. The original park accomodates the work of Larry Griffis Jr. The expanded areas now include works of numerous other sculptors. Materials include welded steel, wood, aluminum & bronze, most of which has been cast at the Essex St Foundry. Sculpture park festival stage is an open-air platform for regional artist's performance of dance, music, poetry & drama
Income: Financed by donations, mem & pub funds
Exhibitions: Twelve distinctly different groups of work by Larry Griffis Jr are displayed
Publications: Brochure; postcards
Activities: Concerts; tours; sales shop sells prints, original art, reproductions, metal sculptures; junior museum, Big Orbit, 30 Essex St, Buffalo, NY

ELMIRA

M ARNOT ART MUSEUM, 235 Lake St, 14901. Tel 607-734-3697; FAX 607-734-5687; *Dir* John D O'Hern
Open Tues - Sat 10 AM - 5 PM, Sun 2 - 5 PM, cl Mon & national holidays. Admis $2, Sat & Sun no admis fee. Estab 1911 to serve the people of the community with a regular schedule of changing exhibits of the permanent collection, traveling shows & regional artists, as well as providing other free cultural activities not ordinarily available in the area. Permanent installations: 17th to 19th-century European art in period room of original donor, Matthias H Arnot; 19th-20th century American paintings. Average Annual Attendance: 50,000. Mem: 850; dues $25 & up
Collections: †American & European sculpture; Flemish, Dutch, †French, English, German, Italian, Spanish & †American paintings & works on paper Matthias H Arnot Collection, permanent installation in restored picture gallery
Exhibitions: Annual Regional Art Exhibition with prizes; Annual Arts & Crafts Exhibition with prizes
Publications: Books; catalogs
Activities: Classes for adults & children, two wk summer adult painting school, docent training, & outreach programs for community groups through educ center; lect & gallery talks open to public; tours; competitions; individual paintings lent; book traveling exhibitions 5-8 per year; originate traveling exhibitions to US museums; museum shop sells books, catalogues, original art & craft work, reproductions, slides, prints

M ELMIRA COLLEGE, George Waters Gallery, One Park Pl, 14901. Tel 607-735-1800; FAX 607-735-1723; *Dir* Leslie Kramer
Open Tues - Sat 1 - 4 PM, cl Mon & Sun. No admis fee. The Gallery is located in the Elmira Campus Center. Average Annual Attendance: 1000
Income: Financed by school budget
Exhibitions: Annual Student Exhibition

FLUSHING

A BOWNE HOUSE HISTORICAL SOCIETY, 37-01 Bowne St, 11354. Tel 718-359-0528; *Pres* Douglas Bauer; *VPres* Dominick Alaggia; *Dir* Yvonne Engglezos; *Treas* Vincent Tsang
Open Tues, Sat & Sun 2:30 - 4:30 PM. Admis adults $2, senior citizens, students & children $1. Estab 1945 for historic preservation, educ, collection of 17th, 18th & 19th century furnishing & decorative & fine art. Examples of colonial life. Average Annual Attendance: 5000. Mem: 620; dues $250, $100, $50, $25, $10; annual meeting third Tues in May
Income: Financed by mem, private & pub contributions
Collections: Furnishings from the 17th, 18th & early 19th centuries Furniture, pewter, fabrics, china, portraits, prints & documents
Exhibitions: Photo Documentation of ongoing Restoration
Publications: Booklets regarding John Bowne & the House; quarterly newsletter
Activities: Classes for adults & children; docent training; lect open to public; museum shop sells books, reproductions, prints, slides, products of herb garden, plates & tiles

M QUEENS COLLEGE, CITY UNIVERSITY OF NEW YORK,
Godwin-Ternbach Museum, 405 Kalpper Hall, 11367. Tel 718-997-4747; *Dir & Cur* Jerold Green
No admis fee. Estab 1957 for a study collection for Queens College students & in 1981 independently chartered. Collection located in one large exhibition gallery on Queens College Campus. Average Annual Attendance: 10,000. Mem: 60, dues $25
Income: Financed by state appropriation, Friends of the Mus, federal state & local grants
Collections: Ancient & antique glass; Egyptian, Greek, Luristan antiquities, Old Master & WPA prints; Renaissance & later bronzes; 16th - 20th century paintings
Exhibitions: 20th Century Prints; Joseph Ternback: Collector, Connoisseur; Italian Art; 15th - 18th Century Art of the East; Recent Acquisitions 1981 - 1985; Herb Aach Memorial Exhibition; Summerscape; Ancient & Islamic Art: Selections from the Godwin-Ternbach Museum; Gerald Hahn A Memorial Exhibition; Helen Benz Schiavo: A Memorial Exhibition; Alliance of Queens Artists
Publications: Brochures, exhibition catalogs; newsletter
Activities: Classes for adults; high school creative arts program; lect open to public, 3-4 vis lectr per year; gallery talks; individual paintings & original objects of art lent to qualified art organization & museums
M Queens College Art Center, 65-30 Kissena Blvd, 11367. Tel 718-997-3770; FAX 718-997-3753; Elec Mail sbsqc@cunyvm.cuny.edu; adlqc@cunyvm.cuny.edu; Internet Home Page Address http://www.qu.edu/library/acpage.html. *Dir* Dr Suzanna Simor; *Cur* Alexandra de Luise
Open Mon - Thurs 9 AM - 7 PM, Fri 9 AM - 5 PM. No admis fee. Estab 1937. Average Annual Attendance: 20,000
Exhibitions: (1997) Jolyn Hofstead: 30 Years at Queens College
Publications: exhibition catalogues
Activities: Gallery talks; lect open to public, 2-3 vis lectr per year
L Art Library, 65-30 Kissena Blvd, 11367. Tel 718-997-3770; FAX 718-997-3753; Elec Mail sbsqc@cunyvm.cuny.edu; adlqc@cunyvm.cuny.edu; Internet Home Page Address http://www.qc.edu/library/acpage.html. *Head* Dr Suzanna Simor; *Art Librn* Alexandra de Luise
Open 52 hrs wk when classes are in session. Estab 1937 to support instruction. Circ 35,000
Library Holdings: Vols 65,000; Per subs 200; Exhibition catalogs & pamphlets 40,000; Micro — Fiche 2000, reels; AV — Slides 15,000; Other — Clipping files, photographs, reproductions 51,000
Activities: Lending collection contains 30,000 books, 30,000 color reproductions & 12,000 slides

A QUEENS HISTORICAL SOCIETY, Kingsland Homestead, 143-35 37th Ave, 11354-5729. Tel 718-939-0647; FAX 718-539-9885; *Exec Dir* Byron C Saunders; *Exec Asst* Joyce A Cook; *Coll Mgr* Laura Zelasnic; *Research Analyst* James Driscoll
Open 9:30 AM - 5 PM. Admis adults $2, seniors & students $1. Estab 1968 as a historical society to collect Queens history. Two parlor rooms; first floor for changing exhibits, second floor permanent. Maintains reference library. Average Annual Attendance: 5000. Mem: 600; dues business $100-$750, family $40, individual $15, students & seniors $10; annual meeting second Sun in June
Income: $150,000 (financed by mem, city & state appropriation)
Exhibitions: (1997) Horticulture Industry of Queens
Publications: Quarterly newsletter
Activities: Docent training; lect open to public; museum shop sells books

M THE QUEENS MUSEUM OF ART, New York City Bldg, Flushing Meadows-Corona Park, 11368-3398. Tel 718-592-9700; FAX 718-592-5778; *Exec Dir* Carma Funtleroy; *Asst Dir* Marilyn Simon; *Dir Exhib* Jane Farver; *Dir Educ* Sharon Vatsky; *Public Information Officer* Robert Mahones; *Dir Admin* Mary Brown; *Pres* Constance B Cooke
Open Wed - Fri 10 AM - 5 PM, Sat & Sun Noon - 5 PM, cl Mon. Admis adult $3, seniors & children $1.50, children under 5 & members free. Estab 1972 to provide a vital cultural center for the more than 2.5 million residents of Queens County; it provides changing, high-quality, fine art exhibitions & a wide-range of educational & public programs. Museum has approx 25,000 sq ft gallery space, The Panorama of New York City (9,335 sq ft architectural scale model of New York City), theatre, workshops, offices. Average Annual Attendance: 50,000. Mem: 700; dues family $55, individual $35, seniors & students $20
Income: $2,000,000 (financed by mem, city & state appropriation, corporate &

foundation grants, earned income)
Collections: The Panorama of New York City (world's largest architectural scale model); Small collection of paintings, photographs & prints; Collection of materials from 1939 - 1940 & 1964 - 1965 New York World's Fairs
Exhibitions: Tiffany Art from the Egon & Hildegard Museum of Tiffany Art (permanent display). (1997) Queen's Artists: Highlights of the 20th Century; Out of India
Publications: Catalogs; quarterly newsletter; Panorama brochure
Activities: Guided tours for adults & children; docent training; projects involving elementary school children; films; drop-in arts & crafts workshops on Sun during school year & certain weekdays in summer; lect open to public, 10 vis lectr per year; concerts; gallery talks; tours; competitions; satellite gallery at Bulova Corporate Center in Jackson Heights, NY; book traveling exhibitions 4 per year; museum shop sells books, reproductions, prints, exhibition catalogs, children's items & 1939-40 & 1964-65 World's Fair memorabilia

FREDONIA

M STATE UNIVERSITY OF NEW YORK COLLEGE AT FREDONIA, M C Rockefeller Arts Center Gallery, 14063. Tel 716-673-3537; FAX 716-673-3397; *Gallery Dir* Marvin Bjurlin
Open Wed - Sun 2 - 8 PM. No admis fee. Estab 1963 and relocated in 1969 to new quarters designed by I M Pei and Partners. The gallery serves as a focal point of the campus, uniting the college with the community. Average Annual Attendance: 5000
Income: Financed by state appropriation and student groups
Collections: Primarily 20 century American art and architectural archival material, with an emphasis on prints and sculpture
Exhibitions: Graduating Seniors I; Graduating Seniors II; Graduating Seniors III; curated & traveling shows
Publications: Exhibition catalogs
Activities: Individual paintings and original objects of art lent to offices and public lobbies on campus; traveling exhibitions organized and circulated

GARDEN CITY

L ADELPHI UNIVERSITY, Fine & Performing Arts Library, 11530. Tel 516-877-3560; FAX 516-877-3592; *Performing Arts Librn* Gary Cantrell
Open Mon - Thurs 8:30 AM - 11 PM, Fri & Sat 10 AM - 6 PM, Sun 1 - 11 PM. The Fine & Performing Arts Library builds print & nonprint collections & provides reference service in fine & applied arts, music, dance, theater, photography, university archives & special collections
Income: Financed by state appropriations & through the University
Library Holdings: Vols 35,000; Per subs 125; Original documents; Micro — Fiche, reels; AV — Cassettes, fs, motion pictures, rec 9000, slides 1500, v-tapes 50; Other — Exhibition catalogs, manuscripts, memorabilia, original art works, pamphlets, photographs, prints, reproductions
Collections: Americana; William Blake; Cuala Press; Expatriate Writers; Cobbett; Morley; Hauptmann; University Archives; Spanish Civil War Robert McMillian Papers; Christopher Morley
Exhibitions: 85 Golden Florins
Activities: Lect
M Swirbul Library Gallery, 11530. Tel 516-877-3000; FAX 516-877-3592
Open Mon - Thurs 8 AM - 11 PM, Sat 10 AM - 6 PM, Sun 1 - 11 PM. No admis fee. Estab 1963 to enrich cultural life, provide a showcase for faculty research & art works & interdisciplinary exhibitions. Average Annual Attendance: 30,000. Mem: 150
Collections: †William Blake
Exhibitions: Walt Whitman Exhibition
Publications: Exhibit catalogs
Activities: Lect open to public, 4 vis lectr per year; gallery talks; individual & original objects of art lent to university offices only

M NASSAU COMMUNITY COLLEGE, Firehouse Art Gallery, 11530. Tel 516-572-7165; FAX 516-572-7302; *Dir* Janet Marzo
Open Sept - May Mon & Thurs 11:30 AM - 4:30 PM, Tues & Wed 11:30 AM - 7 PM, Sat & Sun 1 - 5 PM. Estab 1964 to exhibit fine art & varied media. Two exhibition spaces, carpeted fabric walls, & track lighting
Income: Financed by state, college & county appropriation
Collections: Painting; sculpture; prints; photography
Exhibitions: Invitational exhibits, national or regional competition; faculty & student exhibits per year
Activities: Lect open to public; competitions with awards

GARRISON

L ALICE CURTIS DESMOND & HAMILTON FISH LIBRARY, Hudson River Reference Collection, Routes 9D & 403, PO Box 265, 10524. Tel 914-424-3020; FAX 914-424-4061; *Library Dir* Carol Donick
Open by appointment only. No admis fee. Estab 1983
Library Holdings: Vols 18,000; Per subs 100
Special Subjects: Art Education, Art History, Dioramas, Display, Landscape Architecture, Landscapes, Painting - American, Photography, Restoration & Conservation
Collections: Slide Archive: Hudson River views in 19th century painting
Exhibitions: Shows annually: Contemporary artists as well as Hudson River School Works

GENESEO

M **LIVINGSTON COUNTY HISTORICAL SOCIETY,** Cobblestone Museum, 30 Center St, 14454. Tel 716-243-9147; *Pres* Alberta S Dunn
Open May - Oct Sun & Thurs 2 - 5 PM. No admis fee. Estab 1877 to procure, protect & preserve Livingston County history. Average Annual Attendance: 1500. Mem: 230; dues $10; meetings first Sun in Nov & May
Income: $2500 (financed by mem & donations)
Collections: China & Silver; Indian Artifacts; primitive tools; Shaker items; toy collection; war items
Activities: Lect open to public, 6 vis lectr per year

M **STATE UNIVERSITY OF NEW YORK AT GENESEO,** Bertha V B Lederer Gallery, 14454. Tel 716-245-5814; FAX 716-245-5005; *Dir & Chmn Exhib Committee* Jan Jackson
Open 2 - 5 PM for exhibitions. No admis fee. Estab 1967; the gallery serves the college and community. Average Annual Attendance: 6000
Income: Financed by state appropriation
Collections: Ceramics, furniture, graphics, paintings, sculpture
Exhibitions: African Roots in the Western Hemisphere; Function & Metaphore-New Art Faculty; Annual Student Art Exhibition
Publications: Exhibition catalogs
Activities: Lect open to public; lending collection contains 400-600 books

GLENS FALLS

M **HYDE COLLECTION TRUST,** 161 Warren St, 12801. Tel 518-792-1761; FAX 518-792-9197; *Dir* Kathleen Monaghan
Open Tues - Sun 10 AM - 5 PM, cl Mon. No admis fee, call for guided tour information & cost. Estab 1952 to promote & cultivate the study & improvement of the fine arts. Average Annual Attendance: 34,000. Mem: 900; dues $15-$5000
Income: Financed by endowment, mem, contributions, municipal support & grants
Collections: Drawings by da Vinci, Degas, Tiepolo, Matisse, Lorraine and others; Paintings by El Greco, Rembrandt, Rubens, Botticelli, Tintoretto, Renoir, Picasso, Homer and others; furniture, sculpture, tapestries
Exhibitions: Six temporary exhibitions throughout the year; Regional Juried High School Art
Publications: Exhibit catalogs
Activities: Classes for adults & children; docent training; lect open to public, 5 vis lectr per year; concerts; gallery talks upon request; tours; scholarships offered; original objects of art lent to accredited museums; book traveling exhibitions; originate traveling exhibitions; museum shop sells books, magazines, original art & reproductions

L **Library,** 161 Warren St, 12801. Tel 518-792-1761; FAX 518-792-9197; *Dir* Kathleen Monaghan
For reference only
Income: Financed by the Hyde Collection Trust
Purchases: Books & periodicals
Library Holdings: Vols 1000; Per subs 8; Original documents 3000; AV — Fs; Other — Clipping files, exhibition catalogs, memorabilia, photographs
Collections: Hyde Family Archives

GOSHEN

M **HARNESS RACING & HALL OF FAME** (Formerly Trotting Horse Museum), 240 Main St, 10924. Tel 914-294-6330; FAX 914-294-3463; *Dir* Gail Cunard
Open Mon - Sat 10 AM - 5 PM, Sun & holidays Noon - 5 PM. Admis adults $1.50, children $.50. Estab 1951 to preserve the artifacts of harness racing. There are two galleries; one usually has the museum's permanent collection; the smaller one is used for visiting art shows. Average Annual Attendance: 10,000. Mem: 800; dues $100, $50, $35; annual meeting in July
Income: Financed by endowment & mem
Collections: Large collection of lithographs by Currier and Ives pertaining to harness racing, plus other leading printers of the 19th century; bronzes, dioramas, statuary, wood carvings
Exhibitions: Visiting art shows
Publications: Quarterly newsletter
Activities: Classes for children; lect open to public; concerts; gallery talks; tours; museum shop sells books, reproductions, prints, jewelry, harness racing memorabilia & other horse-related items

HAMILTON

M **COLGATE UNIVERSITY,** Picker Art Gallery, Charles A Dana Arts Ctr, 13346. Tel 315-824-7634; FAX 315-824-7932; *Dir* Dewey F Mosby, PhD; *Registrar* Jennifer Olson-Rudenko; *Educ Coordr* Lisa Jarvinen
Open daily 10 AM - 5 PM. No admis fee. Estab 1966, as an educative adjunct to study in the fine arts & liberal arts curriculum. Building designed by architect Paul Rudolph. Average Annual Attendance: 15,000. Mem: 147; dues lifetime $5000, patron $1000, sustaining $500, supporting $100, sponsoring $50, contributing $25, student $10
Income: Financed by the University & Friends of the Visual Arts at Colgate
Collections: Herman Collection of Modern Chinese Woodcuts; †Gary M Hoffer '74 Memorial Photography Collection; Luis de Hoyos Collection of pre-Columbian Art; paintings; photographs; posters; prints; †sculpture
Publications: Annual report; bulletins; exhibition catalogs
Activities: Lect open to public & some for members only; individual paintings & original objects of art lent; book traveling exhibitions; originate traveling exhibitions

A **GALLERY ASSOCIATION OF NEW YORK STATE,** PO Box 345, 13346-0345. Tel 315-824-2510; FAX 315-824-1683; *Exec Dir* Hugh Bradford; *Transit Coordr* Donna Lamb; *Exhibits Coordr* Donna Ostrzewski; *Designer* Ted Anderson

Estab 1972 to facilitate cooperation among exhibiting institution in state/region. Mem: 200; mem open to exhibiting organization; dues $100-$500; annual meeting in Sept
Income: $800,000 (financed by mem, grants, services provided & traveling exhibits)
Exhibitions: Inspiration & Context: The Drawing of Albert Paley & More: Out of the Ordinary: Community Tastes & Values in Contemporary Folk Art; Private Art/Public Art: Photographs from Johnson & Johnson & Citibank; Twenty-Five Years of African American Art-Studio Museums in Harlem
Publications: Bulletin, 3 times per year
Activities: Originate traveling exhibitions 6 per year

HASTINGS ON HUDSON

A **HUDSON VALLEY ART ASSOCIATION,** Newington-Cropsey Fourndation Gallery, Cropsey Lane, 10706. Tel 914-478-1213; *Pres* Mary LaGreca; *Treas* Perry Alley
Estab 1928, incorporated 1933 to perpetuate the artistic traditions of American artists such as made famous the Hudson River School of painting through exhibitions of painting & sculpture with pub support. Mem: 300; mem by invitation; dues $30, special exhibits extra; annual meeting in May
Exhibitions: Annual juried exhibition each May, open to all artists of the US who work in realistic tradition, to compete for money awards & gold medals of honor; other exhibits from time to time
Activities: Lect; free demonstrations; exhibitions

HEMPSTEAD

M **FINE ARTS MUSEUM OF LONG ISLAND,** 295 Fulton Ave, 11550. Tel 516-481-5700; FAX 516-481-8007; *Dir* Anthony Pollera; *Registrar* Paul Andersen
Open 10 AM - 4:30 PM. Admis $2. Estab 1979. A contemporary hall for rotating exhibits; a computer imaging center with hand-on equipment; a pre-columbian & primitive art hall; a window environment for solo shows; 20,000 sq ft exhibition space. Average Annual Attendance: 25,000. Mem: 1400; dues $35
Income: $379,000 (financed by endowment, mem, state appropriation)
Exhibitions: Selections from FAMIL's Permanent Collection: Pre-Columbia Artifacts, Photography, Paintings, Sculpture, Computer art; Annual Juried Art Exhibitions; Beyond Outsider Thread: Multi Artist Exhibition
Activities: Classes for adults & children; docent programs; lect open to public, 5 vis lectr per year; competitions with awards; originate traveling exhibitions 2 per year; retail store sells books, prints, original art

M **HOFSTRA UNIVERSITY,** Hofstra Museum, 112 Hofstra University, 11550. Tel 516-463-5672, 463-5673; *Dir* David C Christman; *Cur Coll* Elearnor Rait; *Exhibit Designer & Preparation* Karen Albert; *Registrar* Mary Wakeford
Open Wed - Fri 10 AM - 5 PM, Tues 10 AM - 9 PM, Sat & Sun 1 - 5 PM. No admis fee. Estab 1963; a university mus that serves the needs of its student body & the surrounding Nassau County community. Mus includes 5 exhibition facilities. Average Annual Attendance: 15,000. Mem: 250; dues $35-$5000
Income: Financed by university, mem & grants
Collections: †American paintings & prints; African, Pre-Columbian, New Guinea, Japanese & Indian art; 17th & 18th century European painting; contemporary prints, painting & photographs
Exhibitions: Mother & Child: the Art of Henry Moore; Shapes of the Mind: African Art from L I Collections; People at Work: 17th Century Dutch Art; Seymour Lipton; 1979 - 1989: American, Italian, Mexican Art for the Collection of Francesco Pellizzi; The Coming of Age of America: The First Decades of the Sculptors Guild; The Transparent Thread: Asian Philosophy in Recent American Cart. Street Scenes: 1930's - '50's; Leonard Bramer's Drawing of the 17th Century Dutch Life T.V. Sculpture; R.B. Kitaj (Art and Literature); Indian Miniatures; Maelstrom; Preserving Our Heritage: A Celebration of the Restoration of Hofstra's Collection of Currier & Ives Prints; The Mountain Retreat: Modern Chinese Landscape Paintings
Publications: Exhibition catalogs
Activities: Lect open to public, 10-15 vis lectr per year; gallery talks; tours for school groups & community organizations; originate traveling exhibitions

HEWLETT

L **HEWLETT-WOODMERE PUBLIC LIBRARY,** 1125 Broadway, 11557. Tel 516-374-1967; FAX 516-569-1229; *Art Librn* Nancy Delin
Open Mon - Thurs 9 AM - 9 PM, Fri 9 AM - 6 PM, Sat 9 AM - 5 PM, Sun 1 - 5 PM (except summer). Estab 1947 as a Co-Center for art & music. Gallery maintained
Income: Financed by state appropriation & school district
Library Holdings: Vols 160,000; Per subs 520; Micro — Reels; AV — Fs, Kodachromes, motion pictures, rec, slides; Other — Exhibition catalogs, pamphlets, photographs, reproductions
Special Subjects: Architecture, Crafts, Film, Photography, antiques
Exhibitions: Hold local exhibits
Publications: Index to Art Reproductions in Books (Scarecrow Press)
Activities: Classes for adults & children; lect open to the public; concerts; gallery talks; tours

HOWES CAVE

M **IROQUOIS INDIAN MUSEUM,** Caverns Rd, PO Box 7, 12092. Tel 518-296-8949; FAX 518-296-8955; *Dir* Thomas Elliot; *Dir Children's Museum* Colette Lemmon; *Cur* Stephanie Shultes; *Museum Educator* Mike Tarbell; *Nature Park Mgr* Mike Butler
Open 10 AM - 5 PM. Admis adults $5, senior citizens & students 13-17 $4, children 7-12 $2.50. Estab 1980 to teach about Iroquois culture today & in the past. Exhibits follow a time line from the earliest times to present day. Archaeology exhibits trace the development of native culture from the time of

Paleo-Indians (8000 BC) through the 1700s, when the Iroquois & colonists lived side-by-side in the Schoharie Valley. Mem: 900; dues donor $45, family $25, individual $20, seniors $10
Income: $300,000 (financed by mem, admis, sales shop, fundraising & grants)
Collections: †Historic beadwork & cornhusk work; †extensive collection of contemporary art (painting & sculpture) & crafts (baskets, woodwork items & beadwork); †Paleo Indian to 18th century artifacts mainly from known sites in Schoharie County, NY
Exhibitions: Indian Stereotypes as External Avatars. Art on the Longhouse Wall
Publications: Exhibition catalogs; Museum Notes, quarterly
Activities: Classes for adults & children; school programs; lect open to public; internships offered; exten dept includes lending collection; museum shop sells books, prints, magazines, slides & original art; Iroquois Indian Children's Museum

HUDSON

M **OLANA STATE HISTORIC SITE,** RD 2, Off Route 9-G, 12534. Tel 518-828-0135; *Cur* Karen Zukowski; *Historic Site Mgr* James Ryan; *Site Asst* Heidi Hill
Open May 1 - Labor Day, Wed - Sat 10 AM - 4 PM, Sun Noon - 4 PM, by tour only, Wed after Labor Day - Oct 31 Wed - Sun Noon - 4 PM. Opened as a museum 1967 to promote interest in & disseminate information of the life, works & times of Frederic Edwin Church, landscape painter of the Hudson River School. The building is a Persian-style residence overlooking the Hudson River. Average Annual Attendance: House 24,000; Grounds 200,000. Mem: 615; dues $25 - $5000; annual meeting May or June
Income: Financed by state appropriation
Collections: Extensive 19th Century Furniture Collection; Oil Sketches & Drawings by Church; †Paintings by Church †and other artists; Textile Collection; Decorative Arts
Publications: The Crayon, quarterly (journal produced by Friends of Olana)
Activities: Lect; slide programs; concerts; original objects of art lent to other institutions who qualify
L **David Huntington Archive,** Rd 2, Off Route 9-G, 12534. Tel 518-828-0135; *Historic Site Mgr* James Ryan
Open to the pub with approval of Site Manager; for reference only
Library Holdings: Other — Exhibition catalogs 10, memorabilia 200, original art works, photographs, prints
Collections: Family papers, photographs, books, correspondence diaries, receipts
Publications: Crayon, quarterly

HUNTINGTON

M **HECKSCHER MUSEUM OF ART,** 2 Prime Ave, 11743-7702. Tel 516-351-3250; FAX 516-423-2145; *Chmn Board Trustees* Donald E Gundermann; *Dir* Dr John E Coraor; *Cur* Anne Cohen DePietro; *Coordr Educ* Beth Levinthal; *Registrar* William Titus; *Development Officer* Lori Gordon
Open Tues - Fri 10 AM - 5 PM, Sat & Sun 1 - 5 PM, cl Mon & holidays. No admis fee, suggested donation $2. Estab 1920, incorporated 1957, for the maintenance, preservation & operation of the mus building together with the preservation, exhibition & display of all objects & works of art therein. Four galleries, each 20 x 40 ft with 15 ft ceilings, track incandescent & diffused ultraviolet-free fluorescent lighting. Two galleries are used for changing exhibition & two for permanent collections. Average Annual Attendance: 40,000. Mem: 680; dues $35 & up; annual meeting in June
Income: $740,000 (financed by endowment, mem, town appropriations & grants)
Collections: Major works by the Moran family, George Grosz, Lucas Cranach the Elder, R A Blakelock, Arthur Dove, Helen Torr, Thomas Eakins, James M & William Hart, Asher B Durand; paintings, sculpture, drawings & prints by 16th-20th century artists, primarily American with some European
Exhibitions: The Art of Thomas Anshutz; Baudelaire's Voyages: The Poet & His Painters; The Collector's Eye: American Art from Long Island Collections; Garden of Earthly Delights; Huntington Township Art League Island Artists Exhibition; INSIGHTS Ron Schwerin: Paintings & Studies; regional artists are featured in contemporary exhibitions
Publications: Bi-monthly newsletter; Catalog of the collection; exhibition catalogs
Activities: Classes for adults & children; docent training; lect open to public, 15 vis lectr per year; concerts; gallery talks; tours; awards given; individual paintings lent to scholarly museum exhibitions; book traveling exhibitions 2-3 per year; originate traveling exhibitions to other museums; museum shop sells books, stationery, playing cards, jewelry, children's games & toys
L **Library,** 2 Prime Ave, 11743-7702. Tel 516-351-3250; FAX 516-423-2145; *Vol Librn* Mary Mazeau
Open by appointment only. Estab to provide range of research materials & unique resources. Open to researchers & pub by appointment. For reference only
Library Holdings: Vols 2828; Micro — Cards; AV — A-tapes, slides; Other — Clipping files, exhibition catalogs, memorabilia, pamphlets, reproductions
Special Subjects: Painting - American, Painting - British, Painting - Dutch, Painting - European, Painting - Flemish, Painting - French, Painting - German, Photography, Prints, Museum & dealer exhibit catalogs, 19th Century - present American & European art

HYDE PARK

M **NATIONAL ARCHIVES & RECORDS ADMINISTRATION,** Franklin D Roosevelt Museum, 511 Albany Post Rd, 12538. Tel 914-229-8114; FAX 914-229-0872; Elec Mail library@roosevelt.nara.gov. *Dir* Verne W Newton
Open daily 9 AM - 5 PM, cl Thanksgiving, Christmas & New Year's Day. Admis adults $5 for combination ticket to the Roosevelt Home & Museum, children, senior citizens & school groups fee. Estab 1939; contains displays on President & Mrs Roosevelt's lives, careers & special interests, including personal items, gifts & items collected by President Roosevelt. Average Annual Attendance: 175,000
Income: $1,002,000 (financed by congressional appropriation, trust fund)
Purchases: $154,000
Collections: Papers of President & Mrs Roosevelt & of various members of his

administration; prints, paintings & documents on the Hudson Valley; paintings, prints, ship models, documents & relics of the history of the United States Navy as well as other marine items; early juvenile books
Publications: The Museum of The Franklin D Roosevelt Library; Historical Materials in the Franklin D Roosevelt Library; The Era of Franklin D Roosevelt
Activities: Classes for adults & children; docent training; lect open to public; gallery talks; tours to school groups competitions with prizes; scholarships & fels offered; individual paintings & original objects of art lent to museums; lending collection contains 23,000 artifacts; sales shop sells books, prints, reproductions & slides
L **Franklin D Roosevelt Library,** 511 Albany Post Rd, 12538. Tel 914-229-8114; FAX 914-229-0872; Elec Mail library@roosevelt.nara.gov. *Dir* Verne W Newton
Open May - Oct 9 AM - 6 PM, Nov - Apr 9 AM - 5 PM, cl Thanksgiving, Christmas & New Year's Day. Estab 1939 to preserve, interpret & make available for research archives & memorabilia relating to Franklin & Eleanor Roosevelt, their families & associates. Open to scholars on appointment only
Income: Financed by Federal government & trust fund
Library Holdings: Broadsides; Newspapers; Maps; Micro — Fiche, reels; AV — A-tapes, cassettes, fs, motion pictures, rec, slides, v-tapes; Other — Clipping files 500, exhibition catalogs, manuscripts, memorabilia 300, original art works, pamphlets, photographs 200, prints, sculpture
Special Subjects: Portraits, Posters, Pre-Columbian Art, Prints, Scrimshaw, Sculpture, Silver, Textiles, Franklin-Eleanor Roosevelt; American History & Politics, 1913-45; NY Colonial History; Hudson Valley History; US Naval History
Collections: Naval history; Hudson River Valley history; early juvenile books; illustrated ornithology; Eleanor and Franklin Roosevelt; US History: 20th Century
Exhibitions: Permanent exhibitions on lives & times of Franklin & Eleanor Roosevelt
Publications: The Era of Franklin D Roosevelt: A Selected Bibliography of Periodicals, Essays & Dissertation Literature, 1945-1971; Franklin D Roosevelt and Foreign Affairs

M **ROOSEVELT-VANDERBILT NATIONAL HISTORIC SITES,** 519 Albany Post Rd, 12538. Tel 914-229-9115; FAX 914-229-0739; *Supt* Paul Cole
Open daily 9 AM - 5 PM Apr - Oct, cl Tues & Wed Nov - Mar, cl Thanksgiving, Christmas & New Year's Day, Eleanor Roosevelt NHS open daily Nov, Dec, Mar & Apr, by appt only Thurs - Sun, Jan - Mar, Groups of 10 or more require reservations. Admis $1.50, under 16, over 62 & school groups free admis. Vanderbilt Mansion NHS estab 1940; home of Franklin D Roosevelt NHS 1944; Eleanor Roosevelt NHS, 1977. Average Annual Attendance: 330,000
Income: Financed by Federal Government
Collections: Vanderbilt & Home of FDR collections consist of original furnishings; Eleanor Roosevelt site collections are combination of originals, reproductions & like items
Exhibitions: Annual Christmas Exhibition; Antique Car Show
Publications: Vanderbilt Mansion, book; Art in the Home of Franklin D Roosevelt, brochure
Activities: Tours; sales shop sells books, postcards & slides

ISLAND PARK

A **LONG BEACH ART LEAGUE,** PO Box 123, 11558. Tel 516-431-5082; *Pres* Naomi Diracles
Estab in 1952 by a group of interested residents determined to form an organization to promote art activity & appreciation with emphasis on quality
Exhibitions: North by South
Publications: Exhibitions brochures
Activities: Workshops; demonstrations; lect; discussions

ITHACA

M **CORNELL UNIVERSITY,** Herbert F Johnson Museum of Art, 14853-4001. Tel 607-255-6464; FAX 607-255-9940; *Co-Dir* Richard J Schwartz; *Co-Dir* Franklin W Robinson; *Asst Dir Coll & Progs & Cur Prints, Drawings & Photographs* Nancy E Green; *Assoc Cur Painting & Sculpture* Sean Ulmer; *Cur Asian Art* Martie Young; *Registrar* Carol DeNatale; *Chief Adminr* Cheryl L H Muka; *Ames Cur Educ* Cathy Klimaszewski; *Asst Dir Public Affairs* Ellen McCollister; *Asst Dir Finance & Admin* Jerry Regan; *Publicity/Publications Coordr* Sarah Benson
Open Tues - Sun 10 AM - 5 PM, cl Mon. No admis fee. Estab 1973, replacing the Andrew Dickson White Mus of Art, originally founded in 1953 as Cornell University's Art Mus to serve students, the Tompkins County community & the Finger Lakes region. The collection & galleries are housed in an I M Pei designed building on Cornell University campus overlooking downtown Ithaca & Cayuga Lake. Average Annual Attendance: 70,000. Mem: 1000; dues $20 - $2500
Income: Financed by endowment, mem, grants & university funds
Collections: †Asian art; †arts of ethnographic societies; †European & American paintings, †drawings, †sculpture, †graphic arts, †photographs, †video
Publications: Collections handbook; exhibition catalogs; seasonal newsletter; annual report
Activities: Workshops for adults & children; lect open to public, 5-10 vis lectr per year; gallery talks; tours; individual paintings & original objects of art lent to other institutions for special exhibition; originate traveling exhibitions; museum shop sells exhibition catalogs, postcards & notecards
L **Museum Library,** 14853. Tel 607-255-6464; FAX 607-255-9940; *Dir* Franklin W Robinson
Open Tues - Sun 10 AM - 5 PM, print room open to pub by appointment only. Estab 1956. Open to scholars & students by special appointments. Average Annual Attendance: 16,000
Library Holdings: Vols 3000; Per subs 15; Monographs; Other — Exhibition catalogs

L Fine Arts Library, Sibley Dome, 14853. Tel 607-255-3710; FAX 607-255-6718; Elec Mail fineartsref@cornell.edu. *Librn* Judith Holliday; *Asst Librn* Barbara Prior
Open Sat 10 AM - 5 PM, Sun 1 - 11 PM, Mon - Thurs 9 AM - 11 PM, Fri 9 AM - 6 PM, hrs change for University vacation & summer session. Estab 1871 to serve Cornell students. Circ 110,000
Income: Financed through University funds
Purchases: $190,000
Library Holdings: Vols 160,000; Per subs 1800; Micro — Fiche 5928, reels 424; Other — Exhibition catalogs

M DEWITT HISTORICAL SOCIETY OF TOMPKINS COUNTY, 401 E State St, 14850. Tel 607-273-8284; FAX 607-273-6107; Elec Mail dhs@lakenet.org. *Dir* Michael Koplinka-Loehr; *Cur* Laurie Rush
Open Tues - Sat 11 AM - 5 PM. No admis fee. Estab 1935 to collect, preserve & interpret the history of Tompkins County, New York. Average Annual Attendance: 5000. Mem: 750; dues $25-$500; annual meeting in last quarter
Income: $280,000 (financed by endowment, mem, county appropriation, state & federal grants, earned income & foundations)
Collections: Decorative arts; local historical objects; painting & sketches by local artists; portraits; photographers - Louise Boyle, Joseph Burritt, Curt Foerster, Charles Howes, Charles Jones, Henry Head, Robert Head, Verne Morton, Sheldon Smith, John Spires, Trevor Teele, Marion Wesp
Publications: DeWitt Historical Society Newsletter, quarterly; DeWitt Historical Society Calender & Newsnotes
Activities: Classes for adults & children; lect open to public, 12 vis lectr per year; museum shop sells books, reproductions of photographs; gift items

M HINCKLEY FOUNDATION MUSEUM, 410 E Seneca St, 14850. Tel 607-273-7053; *Dir* Macleah Carlisle
Open Sat 10 AM - 4 PM & by appointment. Admis donations accepted. Estab 1970 to collect & preserve 18th, 19th & early 20th century domestic, decorative & folk arts artifacts. One main gallery with three small galleries. Average Annual Attendance: 500. Mem: 150; dues family $15, individual $10; annual meeting in Mar
Income: $19,000 (financed by endowment, mem, grants & rent)
Purchases: 19th century washing machine, c1870 log cabin quilt; three bonnets
Collections: Clothing; lighting devices; pewter; quilts; toys; trivets
Exhibitions: Toys
Activities: Classes for children; lect open to public, 1-2 vis lectr per year; lending collection contains approx 20 art objects; book traveling exhibition 1 per year; retail store sells books

JACKSON HEIGHTS

A OLLANTAY CENTER FOR THE ARTS, PO Box 720636, 11372-0636. Tel 718-565-6499; FAX 718-446-7806; Elec Mail ollantaypm@aol.com. *Exec Dir* Pedro Monge-Rasuls
Estab 1977 as an Hispanic Art Heritage Center
Income: Financed by city & state appropriations, pub donations & NEA
Publications: Biennial journal; Ollantay Press books-Latino writers
Activities: Conferences, seminars, workshops 2-3 per year

JAMAICA

M JAMAICA ARTS CENTER, 161-04 Jamaica Ave, 11432. Tel 718-658-7400; FAX 718-658-7922; *Board Pres* David McCean; *Exec Dir* Veronique LeMelle; *Dir Public Prog* Howard Asch; *Performing Arts Dir* Claudia Bostick; *Visual Arts Dir* Robert Craddock; *Dir Public Relations* Michele Hollow
Open Tues, Thurs, Fri & Sat 9 AM - 5 PM, Mon & Wed 9 AM - 9 PM. Estab 1974 to provide educational opportunity in the visual & performing arts, exhibitions & performances. Five story landmark building; workshop studios for painting, drawing, maskmaking, ceramics, silkscreen & photography; two dance studios; three art galleries; 75 seat black box theater; two multi-purpose spaces. Average Annual Attendance: 65,000. Mem: 500; dues busin
Income: $939,000 (financed by New York City Deptment of Cultural Affairs, New York State Council on the Arts, foundations, corporations & workshop tuitions)
Exhibitions: Up to 12 changing exhibitions annually in three museum quality galleries
Publications: Exhibition catalogs & posters
Activities: Classes for adults, teens & children; dramatic programs; concerts; gallery talks; tours; competitions; scholarships offered; exten dept serves New York City; photographs & blow ups of original photographs lent; book traveling exhibitions annually

L QUEENS BOROUGH PUBLIC LIBRARY, Fine Arts & Recreation Division, 89-11 Merrick Blvd, 11432. Tel 718-990-0755; FAX 718-658-8312; Elec Mail username@queens.lib.ny.us. *Dir* Gary Strong; *Division Mgr* Claire Kach; *Asst Mgr* Sharon Kugler
Open Mon - Fri 10 AM - 9 PM, Sat 10 AM - 5:30 PM, Sun, Sept - May, Noon - 5 PM. Estab 1933 to serve the general public in Queens, New York
Income: Financed by city & state appropriations
Library Holdings: Vols 129,800; Per subs 398; Compact discs 10,000; Micro — Fiche, reels 4100; AV — A-tapes, cassettes 10,500, rec 5000; Other — Clipping files, exhibition catalogs, original art works, pamphlets, photographs, prints, reproductions 500,000
Collections: The WPA Print Collection
Activities: Concerts

M SAINT JOHN'S UNIVERSITY, Chung-Cheng Art Gallery, Sun Yat Sen Hall, Grand Central & Utopia Parkways, 11439. Tel 718-990-1526; FAX 718-990-1881; *Cur* Abraham P Ho
Open Mon - Fri 10 AM - 8 PM, Sat & Sun 10 AM - 4 PM. No admis fee. Estab 1977 to make available Oriental art objects to the pub & to expose the metropolitan area to the Oriental culture through various exhibits & activities.

Gallery displays contemporary as well as ancient objects, mainly Oriental with a few western subjects. Average Annual Attendance: 50,000
Income: Financed by the University, endowments & private contributions
Collections: Harry C Goebel Collection containing 595 pieces of rare & beautiful art objects dating from the 7th-19th century - jades; ivory carvings; netsuke; porcelains; lacquerware & paintings from Japan & China; permanent collection contains 700 pieces of Chinese porcelain, paintings, textiles, calligraphy & paper cuttings dating from 7th-20th century
Exhibitions: Two Great Textiles of Modern Chinese Paintings; The Chinese Ancient Coin Exhibit
Publications: Exhibition catalogues
Activities: Lect open to public, 3 vis lectr per year; concerts; gallery talks; tours; competitions with awards; individual paintings & original objects of art lent; lending collection contains 200 original art works; original prints; 200 paintings; traveling exhibitions organized & circulated

L Asian Collection, Grand Central & Utopia Parkways, 11439. Tel 718-990-6161, Ext 6722; *Librn* Kenji Niki
Open to the pub for reference only
Library Holdings: Vols 50,500; Per subs 90; Micro — Cards, fiche, prints, reels; Other — Exhibition catalogs, manuscripts
Collections: Collected Works of Chinese & Japanese Calligraphy; Japan Foundation Collection includes 200 volumes on various Japanese art subjects; Series of Chinese Arts

JAMESTOWN

M JAMESTOWN COMMUNITY COLLEGE, The Forum Gallery, 525 Falconer St, 14701. Tel 716-665-9107; FAX 716-665-9110; *Dir* Michelle Henry; *Asst to Dir* Michelle Henry
Open Tues - Sat 11 AM - 5 PM, Thurs evenings until 7 PM. No admis fee. Estab 1969 to show significant regional, national & international contemporary art. Facility includes 2000 sq ft exhibition area
Income: $93,000 (financed through Faculty Student Association & private foundation funds)
Exhibitions: PhotoNominal
Publications: Exhibition catalogs, semiannual
Activities: Lect open to public, 200 vis lectr per year

L JAMES PRENDERGAST LIBRARY ASSOCIATION, 509 Cherry St, 14701. Tel 716-484-7135; FAX 716-483-6880; *Dir* Murray L Bob; *Gallery Coordr* Anne Plyler
Open Mon - Fri 9 AM - 9 PM, Sat 9 AM - 5:30 PM, Sun 1 - 4 PM, shorter hours in summer. Estab 1891 as part of library. Maintains art gallery
Income: Financed by state & local funds
Library Holdings: Vols 265,454; Per subs 410; Micro — Prints; AV — Motion pictures, rec, slides; Other — Reproductions, sculpture
Special Subjects: Prints
Collections: Prendergast paintings, 19th & 20th century paintings; Roger Tory Peterson, limited edition print collection; Alexander Calder mats
Exhibitions: Traveling Exhibitions; local one-person and group shows
Publications: Mirror Up To Nature, collection catalog
Activities: Lectures open to the public; concerts; competitions; lending collection contains books, cassettes, film strips, framed reproductions, Kodachromes, phonorecords & slides; books traveling exhibitions

KATONAH

M CARAMOOR CENTER FOR MUSIC & THE ARTS, INC, Caramoor House Museum, Girdle Ridge Rd, PO Box 816, 10536. Tel 914-232-5035; FAX 914-232-5521; *Chmn Board of Trustees* Michael E Gellert; *Exec Dir* Howard Herring; *Gen Mgr* Paul Rosenblum
Open winter Mon - Fri by appointment; summer Wed & Fri by appointment, Thurs & Sat 11 AM - 4 PM, Sun 1 - 4 PM. Admis adults $4, children $2. Estab 1970 to preserve the house & its collections, the legacy of Walter T Rosen & to provide interpretive & educ programs. Period rooms from European palaces are showcase for art collection from Europe & the Orient, spanning 6 centuries
Income: $42,000
Collections: Period rooms - European & fine & decorative arts from Europe & the Orient (1400-1950)
Publications: Guidebook to collection
Activities: Classes for children; docent training; concerts; lect open to public, 6-8 vis lectr per year; museum shop sells books, prints, slides

M KATONAH MUSEUM OF ART, Rte 22 at Jay St, 10536. Tel 914-232-9555; FAX 914-232-3128; *Exec Dir* George G King; *Pres* Athena Kimball; *VPres* Leslie Jacobson; *Treas* Donald Herdrich
Open Tues - Fri 2 - 5 PM, Sat 10 AM - 5 PM, Sun 1 - 5 PM, cl Mon. No admis fee. Estab 1953 to present exhibitions created with loaned works of art, programs for schools, films, lectures, demonstrations & workshops. The Katonah Museum consists of 3000 sq ft of exhibition space with a sculpture garden. Average Annual Attendance: 50,000. Mem: 1200; dues $35 & up
Income: $700,000 (financed by mem, contributions & grants)
Exhibitions: Fairfield Porter; Navajo Weavings; Navajo Ways; Bloomsbury Artists at Charleston; An American Luminist; Charles Henry Gifford; Edouard Vuillard, Master of Intimism; Odilon Redon; George Rickey
Publications: Exhibition catalogs; Forgotten Instruments, 1980; Many Trails: Indians of the Lower Hudson Valley, 1983; Shelter: Models of Native Ingenuity, 82
Activities: Docent training; teacher workshops; programs for schools; lect & films open to public, 2-10 vis lectr per year; gallery talks; tours; originate traveling exhibitions; member school lending collection contains AV programs & slides; originate traveling exhibitions; museum shop sells books, reproductions & jewelry gifts

M NEW YORK STATE OFFICE OF PARKS RECREATION & HISTORIC PRESERVATION, John Jay Homestead State Historic Site, New York State Rte 22, PO Box 832, 10536. Tel 914-232-5651; FAX 914-232-8085; *Historic Site Mgr III* Linda E McLean; *Interpretive Programs Asst* Julia M Warger
Open Wed - Sat 10 AM - 4 PM, Sun Noon - 4 PM, May - Sept; after Labor Day call for fall and winter hours. No admis fee. Estab 1968 to inform public on John Jay and his contributions to national, state & local history. Ten restored period rooms reflecting occupancy of the Jay family at its height; art distributed throughout. Average Annual Attendance: 25,000. Mem: 400; dues $15 & up; annual meeting in Apr
Income: Financed by state appropriation
Collections: American art and American decorative arts; John Jay memorabilia and archives; Westchester mansion with estate & out-buildings
Exhibitions: Federal Period Decorations; Period Home, Federal decor including art, decorative arts furnishings & memorabilia
Publications: John Jay and the Constitution, a Teacher's Guide; John Jay 1745-1829; The Jays of Bedford; The Jay Genealogy
Activities: Classes for adults & children; docent training; lect open to public; concerts; gallery talks; group tours by advance reservation; school outreach; craft demonstrations; special exhibits

KENOZA LAKE

M MAX HUTCHINSON'S SCULPTURE FIELDS, Fulton Hill Rd, PO Box 94, 12750. Tel 914-482-3669; FAX 914-482-3669; *Pres* Max Hutchinson
Open by appointment. No admis fee. Estab 1986 to exhibit large scale & outdoor sculpture. permanent & changing exhibits of sculpture mostly oriented to outdoor locations
Exhibitions: Twenty-five sculptures by Ju Ming; Eight sculptures by Charles Ginnever; individual works by Mel Chin, Linda Howard, Peter Barton, Ronald Bladen, Donna Byers, Jackie Ferrara, Ann Gillen, Ruth Hardinger, Marcia Kaplan, Marion Kaselle, Bridget Kennedy, Bernard Kirschenbaum, Henner Kuckuck, Wendy Lehman, John Pohanka, Christy Rupp, Frank Sansome, Heidi Schlatter, Robert Stackhouse, William Tucker, Brian Wall, Mac Whitney, Robert Wick, Roger Williams
Activities: Original art sold

KINDERHOOK

M COLUMBIA COUNTY HISTORICAL SOCIETY, Columbia County Museum, 5 Albany Ave, PO Box 311, 12106. Tel 518-758-9265; FAX 518-758-2499; *Pres* H Neal Conolly; *Exec Dir* Sharon S Palmer; *Cur* Helen McLallen
Open Mon - Fri 10 AM - 4 PM. No admis fee. Estab 1916 as House of History & Van Alen House to interpret local & regional, colonial & federal period history, including art of 18th & 19th century & decorative arts. In large hall, wall space 40 ft x 38 ft used for 3 exhibitions of paintings per yr. Average Annual Attendance: 12,000. Mem: 700; dues $15-$500; annual meeting third Sat in Oct
Income: $125,000 (financed by mem, endowment, activities, projects, events, private donations, admis, government & corporate grants)
Collections: Historical objects pertaining to history of county; †New York regional decorative arts; furniture & costumes; paintings of 18th & 19th centuries
Exhibitions: Local history & cultural exhibit; Black history Columbia County 1750-1900
Publications: Brochures; exhibit catalogs; quarterly newsletter
Activities: Classes for children; docent training; lect open to public, 4 vis lectr per year; concerts; originate traveling exhibitions; museum shop sells books, gifts, prints
L Library, 5 Albany Ave, PO Box 311, 12106. Tel 518-758-9265; FAX 518-758-2499; *Dir* Sharon S Palmer; *Cur* Helen M McLallen
Open Mon - Fri 10 AM - 4 PM, June - Aug Sat 11 AM - 5 PM, Sun 1 - 5 PM. Estab 1926 to maintain research files on the county & regional art history. For reference only
Library Holdings: Vols 3300; AV — Cassettes, Kodachromes, slides; Other — Clipping files, exhibition catalogs, manuscripts, memorabilia, original art works, pamphlets, photographs, prints
Special Subjects: Architecture, Decorative Arts, Folk Art, County History
Collections: †County & Regional history; †Hudson Valley architecture; Dutch culture; †Local & Regional paintings & decorative arts; Federalists

KINGSTON

M PALISADES INTERSTATE PARK COMMISSION, Senate House State Historic Site, 296 Fair St (Mailing add: 312 Fair St, 12401). Tel 914-338-2786; *Historic Site Mgr* Rich Goring
Open Apr - Oct Wed - Sat 10 AM - 5 PM, Sun 1 - 5 PM, Jan - Mar Sat 10 AM - 5 PM, Sun 1 - 5 PM. No admis fee. Estab 1887 as an educational community resource which tells the story of the growth of state government as well as the stories of the lives & works of local 19th century artists. Average Annual Attendance: 20,000
Collections: 18th & 19th century decorative arts; 18th & 19th century paintings & other works of art, particularly those by James Bard, Jervis McEntee, Ammi Phillips, Joseph Tubb & John Vanderlyn
Publications: Exhibition catalogs
Activities: Classes for adults & children; docent training; lect open to public, 2 vis lectr per year; individual paintings & original objects of art lent to well-established institutions; lending collection contains color reproductions, original art works, original prints, paintings & sculptures; book traveling exhibitions
L Reference Library, 312 Fair St, 12401. Tel 914-338-2786; *Historic Site Mgr* Rich Goring
Open Wed - Sat 10 AM - 5 PM, Sun 1 - 5 PM, cl Jan - Mar. Estab 1887. Open by appointment to scholars, students & researchers for reference only
Library Holdings: Vols 10,000; Per subs 10; Other — Exhibition catalogs, manuscripts, memorabilia, pamphlets
Special Subjects: Ulster County history; government; genealogies; local artists
Collections: Collection of letters relating to the artist John Vanderlyn
Publications: Exhibit catalogs

LAKE GEORGE

M LAKE GEORGE ARTS PROJECT, Courthouse Gallery, Canada St, 12845. Tel 518-668-2616; *Dir* John Strong; *Asst Dir* Rachel Seligman
Open Tues - Fri Noon - 5 PM. Estab 1977, gallery estab 1985 to provide income & exposure for regional artists. 30 ft by 30 ft. Average Annual Attendance: 400. Mem: 400; dues $15-$100; annual meeting in Dec
Income: $90,000 (financed by mem & by city & state appropriation)

LEROY

A LEROY HISTORICAL SOCIETY, 23 E Main St, 14482. Tel 716-768-7433; *Dir* Lynne Belluscio
Open Tues - Fri 10 AM - 4 PM, Sun 2 - 4 PM. Admis adult $2, children $1. Estab 1940. Mem: 400; dues $18-$30; annual meeting in May
Income: $42,000 (financed by endowment, mem, city & state appropriations)
Collections: Decorative Arts; †Jell-O; †LeRoy related; 19th Century Art; Textiles; Tools; Western NY Redware
Publications: Quarterly newsletter
Activities: Classes for adults & children; docent training; lect open to public; tours; individual paintings & original objects of art lent to other museums; museum shop sells books & reproductions

LONG BEACH

L LONG BEACH PUBLIC LIBRARY, 111 W Park Ave, 11561. Tel 516-432-7201; FAX 516-889-4641; *Dir* George Trepp
Open Oct - May Mon, Wed, Thurs 9 AM - 9 PM, Tues & Fri 9 AM - 6 PM, Sat 9 AM - 5 PM, Sun 1 - 5 PM. Estab 1928 to serve the community with information & services, including recreational, cultural & informational materials. The Long Beach Art Association in cooperation with the library presents monthly exhibits of all types of media
Library Holdings: Vols 96,000; Per subs 300; Micro — Fiche, reels; AV — Cassettes, fs, rec, v-tapes; Other — Memorabilia, pamphlets, photographs
Collections: Local history; 300 photographs of Long Beach
Exhibitions: Local talent; membership shows; juried exhibitions
Publications: Monthly newsletter
Activities: Dramatic programs; lect open to public, 18-20 vis lectr per year; concerts; gallery talks; films; tours

LONG ISLAND CITY

C CITIBANK, NA, One Court Sq, 8th Flr, 11120. Tel 718-248-1864; FAX 718-248-1834; *Cur* Suzy Lemakis
Estab to enhance the environment. Collection displayed in offices of the corporate headquarters
Collections: Art reflects the working environment of the various departments, including international, American and New York themes
Activities: Individual objects of art lent for museum exhibitions

M INSTITUTE FOR CONTEMPORARY ART, Project Studio One (P S 1), 46-01 21st St, 11101. Tel 718-784-2084; FAX 718-482-9454; *Exec Dir* Alanna Heiss; *Managing Dir* Martin Fritz; *Building Dir* Hank Stahler; *Publications Dir* Carole Kismaric
Open Wed - Sun Noon - 6 PM. Admis donation $2. Estab 1972 as artist studios & exhibition contemporary & experimental art. Located in a vast renovated 19th century Romanesque schoolhouse, the gallery contains 46,000 sq ft of exhibition space. Maintains reference library. Average Annual Attendance: 60,000. Mem: Dues leadership council $5000, patrons council $1000
Income: Financed by city & state appropriations, corporate & private donations, National Endowment for the Arts
Collections: Architecture; fashion; film; painting; photography; sculpture; video
Exhibitions: International Studio Exhibition; Alternating 1-100 & Vice Versa by Alighiero e Boetti; Gilles Peress Farewell to Bosnia; Stalin's Choice Soviet Socialistic Realism; The Winter of Love
Activities: Classes for adults & children; dance; film; video; photography; fashion; architectural presentations; lect open to public; concerts; gallery talks; tours; competitions for studio program with awards of studio residency; scholarships offered; original works of art lent to not-for-profit institutions with appropriate facilities; book traveling exhibitions; originate traveling exhibitions; sales shop sells books, catalogues, posters, postcards

M ISAMU NOGUCHI FOUNDATION, Isamu Noguchi Garden Museum, 32-37 Vernon Blvd, 11106. Tel 718-721-1932; *Dir* Bruce Altshuler; *Admin Dir* Lawre Stone; *Dir Coll* Bonnie Rychlak
Open Apr 1 - Oct 31 Wed, Thurs & Fri 10 AM - 5 PM, Sat & Sun 11 AM - 6 PM. Admis suggested contribution $4, senior citizens & students $2. Estab 1985 to preserve, protect & exhibit important sculptural, environmental & design work of Isamu Noguchi. Twelve galleries & a garden exhibiting over 250 sculptures, models, drawings & photos. 24,000 sq ft factory converted by the artist. Average Annual Attendance: 18,000
Income: $400,000 (financed by Noguchi Foundation, New York City Department of Cultural Affairs & private donations)
Collections: Sculptures in stone, wood, metal, paper, clay; models and drawings; photos of Noguchi's gardens and plazas; stage sets
Exhibitions: Permanent exhibition
Activities: Classes for adults & children; tours; workshops; lect open to public; concerts; museum shop sells books & Noguchis Akari light sculptures

M SOCRATES SCULPTURE PARK, 31-34 Vernon Blvd, 11106. Tel 718-956-1819; FAX 718-626-1533; *Dir* Kathleen Gilrain; *Asst Dir* Mimi Mingalone; *Asst Ad* Carlos Celdran
Open 10 AM - Sunset. No admis fee. Estab 1986. Outdoor park. Average Annual Attendance: 30,000
Collections: Large-scale public art
Exhibitions: 10th Anniversary Exhibit Part II
Publications: Biannual exhibition catalog

MOUNTAINVILLE

M STORM KING ART CENTER, Old Pleasant Hill Rd, 10953. Tel 914-534-3115; FAX 914-534-4457; *Dir* David R Collens
Open daily 11 AM - 5:30 PM, Apr 1 - Nov 16. Admis adults $7, seniors $5, students $3, children 5 & under free. Estab 1960. Average Annual Attendance: 50,000. Mem: Dues $35 individual, $50 family, $100 contributor, $250 donor, $500 sponsor, $1000 patron
Collections: 500 acre sculpture park with over 100 large scale 20th century American & European sculptures, including works by Abakanowicz, Aycock, Armajani, Bourgeois, Calder, Caro, di Suvero, Grosvenor, Hepworth, LeWitt, Liberman, Moore, Nevelson, Noguchi, Paik, Rickey, Serra, David Smith, Snelson, Streeter, Witkin
Exhibitions: Four-week exhibitions of gallery artists & special out-reach exhibitions
Activities: Educ dept; lect open to public, lectr series, courses in sculpture history & modern art; concerts; gallery talks, guided tours of sculpture park, outdoor concerts; museum shop sells books, slides, postcards, posters, t-shirts, totes & maps

MOUNT VERNON

L MOUNT VERNON PUBLIC LIBRARY, Fine Art Dept, 28 S First Ave, 10550. Tel 914-668-1840; *Dir* Mary Brown
Open Mon - Thurs 9 AM - 9 PM, Fri 9 AM - 6 PM, Sat 9 AM - 5 PM, Sun 1 - 5 PM, cl Sat & Sun during July and Aug. No admis fee. Estab 1854. Library contains Doric Hall with murals by Edward Gay, NA; Exhibition Room with frescoes by Louise Brann Soverns; & Norman Wells Print Alcove, estab 1941
Income: $2,200,000 (financed by city & other funds)
Library Holdings: Vols 450,000; Per subs 750; Art books 17,000; AV — A-tapes 1293, cassettes 1293, rec 12,500; Other — Photographs 11,700
Special Subjects: Architecture, Ceramics, Costume Design & Construction, Decorative Arts, Painting - American, Photography, Prints
Exhibitions: Costume dolls; fans; metalwork; one-man shows of painting, sculpture & photographs porcelains; silver; woodcarving; jewelry; other exhibits changing monthly cover a wide range of subjects from miniatures to origami
Activities: Lect open to public, 6 vis lectr per year; concerts; gallery talks; tours; individual paintings & original objects of art lent to library members

MUMFORD

M GENESEE COUNTRY MUSEUM, John L Wehle Gallery of Sporting Art, 1410 Flint Hill Rd, PO Box 310, 14511. Tel 716-538-6822; FAX 716-538-2887; *Chief Exec Officer & Pres* Douglass W McDonald; *Cur* Diane E Jones
Open Tues - Fri 10 AM - 4 PM, Sat, Sun, holidays, May, June, Sept & Oct 10 AM - 5 PM, Tues - Sun July & Aug 10 AM - 5 PM. Admis adult $10, children between 4 & 16 $8.50, members free. Estab 1976. Gallery has over 600 paintings & sculptures dealing with wildlife, sporting art & western art. Average Annual Attendance: 120,000. Mem: 2000; dues Hosmer Inn Society $500, Crier $325, Selectman $150, Family $75, Friend & one $75, Friends $50
Income: Financed by self-generated income
Collections: Decorative arts, restored 19th Century buildings, paintings & sculpture
Publications: Booklets; Four Centuries of Sporting Art; Genesee Country Museum; monthly newsletter
Activities: Classes for adults & children; docent training; lect open to public; concerts; gallery talks; tours; museum shop sells books, magazines, original art, reproductions, prints & slides

NEW CITY

M HISTORICAL SOCIETY OF ROCKLAND COUNTY, 20 Zukor Rd, 10956. Tel 914-634-9629; *Exec Dir* Sarah E Henrich; *Cur* Melanie Solomon; *Cur Educ* Jean Wortman; *Publications* Marianne Leese
Open Tues - Fri 9:30 AM - 5 PM, Sat & Sun 1 - 5 PM. Admis by donation. Estab 1965 to preserve & interpret history of Rockland County. Average Annual Attendance: 15,000. Mem: 2000; dues $25
Income: $250,000 (financed by endowment, mem & state appropriation)
Collections: Archaeological Collection; Educational Materials Collection/ Reproductions; General Collections; Historical Structures; Special Archival Collections
Activities: Classes for adults & children; docent programs; lect open to public, 4-6 vis lectr per year; concerts; gallery talks; tours; competitions; History Awards Program for high school seniors; individual paintings & original objects of art lent to other museums; originate traveling exhibitions in Rockland County; museum shop sells books & educational gifts

NEW PALTZ

M HUGUENOT HISTORICAL SOCIETY OF NEW PALTZ GALLERIES, PO Box 339, 12561. Tel 914-255-1660; *Dir* Timothy F Harley
Open late May - Sept, Wed - Sun 9 AM - 4 PM, cl Mon & Tues. Admis house alone $2.75, full tour (outbuildings) $7. Estab 1894 to preserve memory & material culture of Huguenot settlers. Includes three galleries: Huguenot Street National Historic Landmark District; Locust Lawn & Terwiller House, Quaker Meeting House. Primarily ancestral portraits - Vanderlyn, Waldo & Dewett. Maintains reference library. Average Annual Attendance: 5000. Mem: 5000; dues $15; annual meeting in June
Income: Financed by mem, endowment
Collections: American primitive paintings; early 19th century furnishings, paintings, decorative arts & documents
Exhibitions: Revolving in-house displays
Publications: genealogies & histories
Activities: Lect open to public, 2 vis lectr per year; concerts; tours; scholarships offered; individual paintings are lent to institutions & galleries; museum shop sells books, magazines, original art, reproductions, prints & slides

M STATE UNIVERSITY OF NEW YORK AT NEW PALTZ, College Art Gallery, 75 S Manheim Blvd, 12561. Tel 914-257-3844; FAX 914-257-3854; *Dir* Neil C Trager; *Registrar* Christine DeLape
Open Mon - Thurs 10 AM - 4 PM, Sat & Sun 1 - 4 PM, cl school holidays. No admis fee. With an exhibition schedule of 10 exhibitions per year, the College Art Gallery provides support for the various art curricula & serves as a major cultural resource for the College & surrounding community. There are two adjoining galleries, South Gallery 59 x 56 ft, North Gallery 42 x 23 ft. Average Annual Attendance: 16,000
Collections: Artifacts, Folk Art, Oriental Prints; Painting, principally 20th century America; †Photographs; Posters; Pre-Columbian Art; Prints, Primative African & New Guinea; Sculpture
Exhibitions: Hot Spots: America's Volcanic Landscape; Photographs by Diane Cook & Len Jenshel; Puerto Rican Silkscreen Posters
Activities: Lect open to public; concerts; gallery talks; competitions; individual paintings & original objects of art lent to museums & galleries; lending collection contains artifacts, original prints, paintings, photographs, sculpture, folk art, textiles, drawings, posters

L Sojourner Truth Library, 12561. Tel 914-257-3719; FAX 914-257-3712; Elec Mail leec@npvm.newpaltz.edu. *Dir* Chui-Chun Lee; *Team Leader Information Resources & Delivery* Wilma Schmidt; *Team Leader Coll & Facilities* Nancy Nielson; *Team Leader Record Develop & Management* Michael Zackheim; *Coll Develop* Gerlinde Barley
For lending & reference. Circ 258,000
Income: Financed by state appropriation
Purchases: $436,000
Library Holdings: Vols 420,000; Per subs 1300; Micro — Cards, fiche, prints, reels; AV — Rec; Other — Exhibition catalogs, pamphlets
Special Subjects: Anthropology, Art Education, Art History, Drawings, Oriental Art, Painting - American, Painting - European, Painting - Japanese, Photography, Silversmithing, Theatre Arts, Watercolors
Publications: Newsletter, biannual

NEW ROCHELLE

M COLLEGE OF NEW ROCHELLE, Castle Gallery, Castle Pl, 10805. Tel 914-654-5423; FAX 914-654-5290; *Exec Dir* Susan Shoulet; *Assoc Dir* Anne Roberston; *Asst Dir* Karen Convertino
Open Tues - Fri 10 AM - 5 PM, weekends Noon - 4 PM. No admis fee. Estab 1979 as a professional art gallery to serve the college, city of New Rochelle & lower Westchester & provide exhibition & interpretation of fine arts, material culture. Located in Leland Castle, a gothic revival building, listed in National Register of Historic Places; gallery is modern facility, with flexible space
Publications: Newsletter
Activities: Docent training; lect open to public, 6 vis lectr per year; originate traveling exhibitions

L NEW ROCHELLE PUBLIC LIBRARY, Art Section, One Library Plaza, 10801. Tel 914-632-7878; FAX 914-632-0262; *Dir* Patricia Anderson; *Head of Reference* Marjorie Sha
Open Oct - May Mon 10 AM - 6 PM, Tues 10 AM - 9 PM, Wed Noon - 6 PM, Thurs Noon - 9 PM, Fri & Sat 10 AM - 5 PM, Sun 1 - 5 PM. Estab 1894
Library Holdings: Vols 8000; Micro — Fiche, reels; AV — Cassettes, rec, slides, v-tapes; Other — Clipping files, exhibition catalogs, original art works, pamphlets, photographs
Exhibitions: All shows, displays & exhibits are reviewed & scheduled by professional advisory panel
Activities: Lect; demonstrations; lending collection contains framed prints & art slides

A New Rochelle Art Association, One Library Plaza, 10801. Tel 914-632-7878; *Pres* Theresa A Cavanaugh
Estab 1912 to encourage art in the area. Mem: 200; dues $20; monthly meeting
Income: Financed by mem
Exhibitions: Four exhibitions per year
Activities: Classes for adults; lect open to public, 4 vis lectr per year; competitions with awards

NEW YORK

A ACTUAL ART FOUNDATION, 7 Worth St, 10013. Tel 212-226-3109; *Pres* Valerie Shakespeare; *Treas* Perry Fugate-Wilcox
Estab 1983 to promote Actual Art
Income: $75,000 (financed by endowment & pub fund raising)

A AESTHETIC REALISM FOUNDATION, 141 Greene St, 10012-3201. Tel 212-777-4490; FAX 212-777-4426; *Class Chmn Aesthetic Realism* Ellen Reiss; *Exec Dir* Margot Carpenter
Open Mon - Fri 10 AM - 7:30 PM, Sat 10 AM - 5 PM. Estab 1973 as a not-for-profit educational foundation to teach Aesthetic Realism, the philosophy founded in 1941 by the great American poet & critic Eli Siegel (1902-1978), based on his historic principle - The world, art & self explain each other: each is the aesthetic oneness of opposites
Special Subjects: Art Criticism
Publications: The Right of Aesthetic Realism to Be Known, weekly periodical
Activities: Weekly public seminars & dramatic presentations; classes in the visual arts, drama, poetry, music, educ, marriage; class for children; individual consultations in person & by telephone worldwide

M Terrain Gallery, 141 Greene St, 10012. Tel 212-777-4490; FAX 212-777-4426; *Coordr* Marcia Rackow
Open Sat 1 - 3:15 PM & other times by appointment. Estab 1955 with a basis in this principle stated by Eli Siegel: All beauty is a making one of opposites, and the making one of opposites is what we are going after in ourselves
Collections: Permanent collection of paintings, prints, drawings & photographs with commentary
Activities: Gallery talks free to public every Sat at 2:30 PM & by appointment for organizations & schools

L **Eli Siegel Collection,** 141 Greene St, 10012-3201. Tel 212-777-4490; FAX 212-777-4426; *Librn* Richita Anderson; *Librn* Leila Rosen; *Librn* Meryl Simon
Open to faculty, students & qualified researchers by appointment. Estab 1982.
The Collection houses the books & manuscripts of Eli Siegel
Library Holdings: Vols 30,000; AV — A-tapes; Other — Manuscripts
Special Subjects: Aesthetics, Anthropology, Art History, Film, Photography, Sculpture, Theatre Arts, Art Criticism, History, Literature, Painting - All Periods, Sciences

L **Aesthetic Realism Foundation Library,** 141 Greene St, 10012-3201. Tel 212-777-4490; FAX 212-777-4426; *Librn* Richita Anderson
Open to faculty, students & qualified researchers by appointment. Estab 1973
Special Subjects: Aesthetics, Anthropology, Architecture, Art Education, Art History, Photography, Theatre Arts, Literature, Music, Painting - All Periods
Collections: Published poems & essays by Eli Siegel; published & unpublished lectures by Eli Siegel

M **A I R GALLERY,** 40 Wooster St, 2nd Flr, 10013. Tel 212-966-0799; *Dir* Alissa Schoenfeld
Open Tues - Sat 11 AM - 6 PM. No admis fee. Estab 1972 as cooperative women's gallery representing 35 American women artists; also provides programs & services to women artists community. Average Annual Attendance: 10,000.
Mem: Dues $110; monthly meetings
Income: Financed by mem, city and state appropriation
Collections: Contemporary Women Artists
Exhibitions: One-woman exhibitions; invitational which can be international, regional and performance or theme shows
Publications: Invitational exhibition catalogues, bi-annually
Activities: Lect open to public; concerts; gallery talks; competitions with awards; individual paintings & original objects of art lent; lending collection contains original art works, original prints, paintings, photographs, sculpture, slides & videos

THE ALLIED ARTISTS OF AMERICA, INC
For further information, see National and Regional Organizations

M **ALTERNATIVE MUSEUM,** 594 Broadway, 10012-3234. Tel 212-966-4444; FAX 212-226-2158; *Dir* Romy Phillips; *Asst Dir* Jan Rooney; *Asst Cur* Kenseth Armstead; *Chief Adminr* David Freilach; *Cur Asst* Elisa White; *Dir Advertising* Geno Rodriguez
Open Tues - Sat 11 AM - 6 PM, cl Aug & Christmas. Admis suggested contribution $3. Estab 1975. 3500 sq ft. Average Annual Attendance: 70,000.
Mem: 2000; dues $35-$1000
Income: $300,000
Exhibitions: Expansion Arts: Artists of our Times; Luminous Image Convergence; The New Clans Group Exhibition (paintings)

AMERICAN ABSTRACT ARTISTS
For further information, see National and Regional Organizations

AMERICAN ACADEMY OF ARTS & LETTERS
For further information, see National and Regional Organizations

AMERICAN ARTISTS PROFESSIONAL LEAGUE, INC
For further information, see National and Regional Organizations

M **AMERICAN CRAFT COUNCIL,** American Craft Museum, 40 W 53rd St, 10019. Tel 212-956-3535; FAX 212-459-0926; *Dir* Holly Hotchner; *Registrar* Marcia Veitchman
Open Wed - Sun 10 AM - 5 PM, Tues 10 AM - 8 PM. Estab 1956 by the American Craft Council (see National Organizations). Gallery displays contemporary art in craft media. Average Annual Attendance: 47,000. Mem: 35,000; dues benefactors $1000, patrons $500, friends $250, sponsors $100, family/dual $50, subscribing $39.50
Income: Financed by mem, government grants, private & corporate donations
Collections: Works of American craftsmen since 1900 in ceramics, paper, fiber, wood, metal, glass, plastics, enamels
Exhibitions: Montly rotating exhibitions
Publications: American Craft, bi-monthly magazine; exhibition catalogs; bibliographies, directories and manuals on crafts
Activities: Docent training; lect open to public, 30 vis lectr per year; gallery talks; tours; competitions with awards; meet the Artist program; book traveling exhibitions annually; sales shop sells books, magazines, slides

AMERICAN CRAFT COUNCIL
For further information see National and Regional Organizations

THE AMERICAN FEDERATION OF ARTS
For further information, see National and Regional Organizations

AMERICAN FINE ARTS SOCIETY
For further information, see National and Regional Organizations

AMERICAN INSTITUTE OF GRAPHIC ARTS
For further information, see National and Regional Organizations

A **AMERICAN JEWISH CONGRESS,** 15 E 84th St, 10028. Tel 212-879-4500; FAX 212-249-3672; *Pres* David Kahn
Open to pub. Estab 1965 to advance Jewish art & aid Jewish artists. Average Annual Attendance: 500. Mem: 200; dues $15-$100
Income: Financed by mem & grants
Collections: Bibliographic & resource files
Publications: First Jewish Art Annual; Art in Judaism; art pamphlets
Activities: Classes for adults; lect open to public; sales shop sells books, original art, prints & slides

L **Shad Polier Memorial Library,** 15 E 84th St, 10028. Tel 212-879-4500; FAX 212-249-3672; *Librn* Sarah Witt
Open Mon - Fri by appointment. Estab 1978
Library Holdings: Micro — Cards; Other — Clipping files, exhibition catalogs, manuscripts, memorabilia, pamphlets, reproductions
Special Subjects: Archaeology, Decorative Arts, Ethnology, Graphic Arts, History of Art & Archaeology, Judaica, Maps, Mixed Media, Painting - American, Painting - European, Painting - Israeli, Prints

M **AMERICAN MUSEUM OF NATURAL HISTORY,** Central Park West at 79th St, 10024-5192. Tel 212-769-5000; FAX 212-769-5018; *Pres* Ellen V Futter; *VPres Communications* Jeanne Collins
Open Mon - Thurs & Sun 10 AM - 5:45 PM, Fri & Sat 10 AM - 8:45 PM, cl Thanksgiving & Christmas. Admis by contribution (suggested, adults $8, children $4.50). Estab 1869 as a mus for the study & exhibition of all aspects of natural history. Exhibition spaces include Roosevelt Memorial Hall, Gallery 3, Naturemax Gallery, Akeley Gallery, Gallery 1. Average Annual Attendance: 3,000,000. Mem: 500,000
Income: Financed by special presentations, contributions
Exhibitions: Permanent exhibitions include: Hall of Asian Peoples; Hall of Ocean Life & Biology of Fishes; Arthur Ross Hall of Meteorites; Guggenheim Hall of Minerals; Margaret Mead Hall of Pacific Peoples. Shark! Fact & Fantasy
Publications: Natural History, magazine; Curator; Bulletin of the American Museum of Natural History; Anthropological Papers of the American Museum of Natural History; American Museum of Natural History Novitates; annual report
Activities: Classes for adults & children; dance & music programs; lect open to public; tours; scholarships

L **Library,** Central Park West at 79th St, 10024. Tel 212-769-5400; FAX 212-769-5009; *Dir Library Servs* Nina J Root
Library Holdings: Vols 450,000; AV — A-tapes, fs, Kodachromes, lantern slides, motion pictures, rec, slides, v-tapes; Other — Clipping files, manuscripts, memorabilia, original art works, pamphlets, photographs, prints, sculpture
Special Subjects: Afro-American Art, American Indian Art, Anthropology, Archaeology, Architecture, Bronzes, Carpets & Rugs, Ceramics, Eskimo Art, Etchings & Engravings, Ethnology, Gold, Goldsmithing, Historical Material, Mexican Art

AMERICAN NUMISMATIC SOCIETY
For further information, see National and Regional Organizations

A **AMERICAN-SCANDINAVIAN FOUNDATION,** 725 Park Ave, 10021. Tel 212-879-9779; FAX 212-249-3444; *Pres* Edward Gallagher; *Dir* Lynn Carter; *Prog Dir* Patricia Splendore
Foundation estab 1910 since 1980 exhibitions of contemporary art from Denmark, Finland, Iceland, Norway & Sweden have been presented. Mem: 3500; dues $40
Exhibitions: Contemporary Scandinavian painting, sculpture, design and crafts; artwork is selected for exhibition by a committee of professional art advisors
Publications: Calendar of Nordic Events, 2 times a year; The Scandinavian Review, 3 times a year; SCAN, newsletter 4 times a year
Activities: Lect open to public; awards

AMERICANS FOR THE ARTS
For further information, see National and Regional Organizations

AMERICAN SOCIETY OF CONTEMPORARY ARTISTS (ASCA)
For further information, see National and Regional Organizations

AMERICAN WATERCOLOR SOCIETY
For further information, see National and Regional Organizations

M **AMERICAS SOCIETY ART GALLERY,** 680 Park Ave, 10021. Tel 212-249-8950; FAX 212-249-5668; Telex 42-9169. *Head Visual Arts Dept* Elizabeth Ferrer
Open Tues - Sun Noon - 6 PM, cl Mon (during exhibitions). Admis suggested $2 contribution. Estab 1967 to broaden understanding & appreciation in the United States of the art & cultural heritage of other countries in the Western Hemisphere. One large gallery with 3-4 exhibitions a year of Latin American, Caribbean & Canadian art. Maintains reference library. Average Annual Attendance: 25,000. Mem: 900; dues $75
Income: $120,500
Collections: Collection of Mexican art & furniture as well as contemporary Latin American
Exhibitions: Canadian Impressionism, 1885-1925
Publications: Exhibition catalogs
Activities: Classes for adults & children in conjunction with exhibitions; lect open to public, 50-100 vis lectr per year; gallery talks; concerts; tours; book traveling exhibitions 1 per year; originate traveling exhibitions; exhibition catalogues available for purchase at front desk

A **ARCHITECTURAL LEAGUE OF NEW YORK,** 457 Madison Ave, 10022. Tel 212-753-1722; FAX 212-371-6048; *Pres* Walter F Chatham; *Exec Dir* Rosalie Genevro
Admis seminars $7, members free. Estab 1881 to promote art & architecture; serves as a forum for new & experimental ideas in the arts. Mem: 1000; dues over 35 years $85, under 35 years $50, students $25; annual meeting in June
Exhibitions: Annual Juried Exhibition of Young Architects Competition
Publications: Exhibition catalogs; posters
Activities: Lect; slide lect; competitions; awards

A **ART COMMISSION OF THE CITY OF NEW YORK,** City Hall, 3rd Flr, 10007. Tel 212-788-3071; FAX 212-788-3086; *Pres* Nicholas Quennell; *Exec Dir* Deborah Bershad
Open by appointment only. No admis fee. Estab 1898 to review designs for city buildings landscape architecture & works of art proposed for city owned property. Portraits are installed in Governors Room and other areas in City Hall. Mem: 11

Income: Financed by city appropriation
Collections: 100 portraits of historic figures, state, city and national
Publications: The Art Commission & Municipal Art Society Guide to Outdoor Sculpture by Margot Gayle & Michele Cohen; Imaginary Cities, European Views from the Collection of the Art Commission; National Directory of Design Review Agencies (1991); New York Re-Viewed, Exhibition Catalogue of 19th & 20th Century Photographs from the Collection of the Art Commission

A **Associates of the Art Commission, Inc,** City Hall, 3rd Flr, 10007. Tel 212-788-3071; FAX 212-788-3086;
Estab 1913 to advise and counsel Art Commission as requested. Mem: 35; dues $35; annual meeting in Jan
Income: Financed by mem

ART DEALERS ASSOCIATION OF AMERICA, INC
For further information, see National and Regional Organizations

ART DIRECTORS CLUB, INC
For further information, see National and Regional Organizations

A **ART INFORMATION CENTER, INC,** 148 B Duane St, 10013. Tel 212-227-0282; *Pres & Dir* Dan Concholar; *VPres* Gail Swithenbanik; *Treas* Edward Enck; *Board Dir Member* Jacob Lawrence
Open 10 AM - 5 PM. Organized 1959, inc 1963, as a tax-deductible clearing house of contemporary fine arts. Files of galleries, their rosters of artists & catalogs of current & recent shows (c 550 in New York, 300 in other US cities, 50 in foreign cities); files of slides of work by unaffiliated artists (c 750 artists & 8-12 slides each) for use by dealers looking for new talent. The Center helps to channel the many artists in New York, & those coming to New York, seeking New York outlets for their work. Advise artist seeking galleries in New York City. Work with Art Initiatives as a alternative exhibition space showing emerging unaffiliated artists
Income: $20,000 (financed by donations & small grants)

A **ART IN GENERAL,** 79 Walker St, 10013-3523. Tel 212-219-0473; FAX 212-219-0511; *Exec Dir* Holly Block; *Gallery Coordr* Joanna Spitzner; *Writer* Kerri Sakamoto
Open Thurs - Sat Noon - 6 PM. No admis fee. Estab 1981 as a nonprofit organization. Non-profit arts organization which relies on private & public support to meet its expenses. Average Annual Attendance: 10,000. Mem: 90; dues vary
Income: Financed by endowment, state & private funds
Exhibitions: Salon Show
Publications: Manual of exhibitions & programs, annual
Activities: Educ dept; interactive discussions & art workshops; lect open to public; gallery talks; tours; originate traveling exhibitions; sales shop sells books

A **ARTIST-CRAFTSMEN OF NEW YORK,** 165 E 83rd St, 10028. Tel 212-777-0062, 831-4259; *Pres* Monona Rossol; *VPres* Trudy Jeremias
Estab 1958 as successor to New York Soc of Craftsmen & New York Soc of Ceramic Arts. Exhibitions & demonstrations are arranged for the purpose of broadening pub interest in & knowledge of crafts; developing standards of taste in design & workmanship. Affiliated with American Craftsmen's Council. Mem: 300; qualification for member: by submission of work by artist-craftsman member to mem jury with emphasis laid upon professional standards of craftsmanship & the quality of work; non-craftsman may become associate or contributing member on election by the Board of Governors; annual meeting in Mar, with six mem meetings per yr
Exhibitions: Annual exhibition in New York City; periodic exhibitions at National Design Center & other New York City locations
Publications: Newsletter

ARTISTS' FELLOWSHIP, INC
For further information, see National and Regional Organizations

A **ARTISTS SPACE,** 38 Greene St, 3rd Flr, 10013. Tel 212-226-3970; FAX 212-966-1434; Elec Mail http://www.avsi.com. *Dir* Claudia Gould; *Pres* Virginia Cowles; *VPres* Carolyn Alexander; *Treas* Richard Shebairo; *Develop Assoc* Elizabeth Metcalf
Open Tues - Sat 11 AM - 6 PM. Estab 1973 as a non-profit contemporary art exhibition space & artists services organization that provides artists with professional & financial support while presenting the most exciting new art developments to the pub
Activities: Administers two grant programs

M **Artists Space Gallery,** 38 Greene St, 3rd Flr, 10013. Tel 212-226-3970; FAX 212-966-1434; *Dir* Claudia Gould; *Developmental Assoc* Lisa Metcalf
Open Tues - Sat 11 AM - 6 PM. No admis fee for exhibitions, films & events $4. Estab 1973 to assist emerging & unaffiliated artists. Five exhibition rooms & hall gallery. Average Annual Attendance: 20,000
Income: Financed by National Endowment for the Arts, New York State Council, corporate & foundation funds & private contributions
Activities: Gallery talks by appointment; financial aid to artists for public presentation; book traveling exhibitions; originate traveling exhibitions; junior museum

L **Unaffiliated Artists File,** 38 Greene St, 3rd Flr, 10013. Tel 212-226-3970; *Cur* Pip Day
Open Tues - Sat 11 AM - 4 PM. Slide file of over 2500 New York state artists. Available to dealers, critics, curators & artists for reference only

A **ARTISTS TALK ON ART,** * 280 Broadway, Ste 412, 10007. Tel 212-385-2862; FAX 212-334-2143; *Exec Dir & Pres* Vernita Nemec; *Board of Dir* Doug Sheer
Open Fri 7 AM - 10 PM, call for appointment. Estab 1979 to promote dialog in the arts. Average Annual Attendance: 4000. Mem: dues season pass $25-$150
Income: $20,000 (financed by mem, state appropriation, admis, contributions & corporate funding)
Exhibitions: Recycling with Imagination: Art from Detritus, curated by Vernita N Cognita; 30 US artists, F Palzia, R Castoro, K Miller, J Jelenfy, C Manley, C Rosen, E A Racette, M Dingus, S Benitez, J Volunius

Publications: Artists Talk on Art Calendar, semi-annually
Activities: Classes for adults; docent training & internships; lect open to public, 40-200 vis lectr per year; book traveling exhibitions 1-3 per year; originate traveling exhibitions 1-3 per year

A **ART STUDENTS LEAGUE OF NEW YORK,** 215 W 57th St, 10019. Tel 212-247-4510; FAX 212-541-7024; *Admin Mgr* Ira Goldberg
Gallery open 10 AM - 8 PM. No admis to members. Estab 1875 to maintain art school & mem activities. Maintains an art gallery open to pub for league exhibits. Average Annual Attendance: 8000-9000. Mem: 6000; dues $10; annual meeting in Dec
Income: Financed by tuitions & investments
Exhibitions: Exhibitions by members, students & instructors
Publications: Art Students League News, monthly
Activities: Lect open to public, 12 vis lectr per year; individual paintings & original objects of art lent to museums

L **Library,** 215 W 57th St, 10019. Tel 212-247-4510; *Admin Mgr* Ira Goldberg
Reference library for students & members
Library Holdings: Vols 60,000; AV — A-tapes, cassettes, fs, slides, v-tapes; Other — Clipping files, exhibition catalogs, manuscripts, original art works, pamphlets, photographs, prints, reproductions, sculpture

A **ASIAN-AMERICAN ARTS CENTRE,** 26 Bowery, 3rd Flr, 10013. Tel 212-233-2154; FAX 212-766-1287; *Dir* Robert Lee
Open Mon - Fri 10 AM - 6 PM. No admis fee. Estab 1974 to promote Asian-American artists & preserve Asian heritage. Gallery has multi-purpose exhibition space. Average Annual Attendance: 12,000. Mem: 500; dues $25
Income: Public & private grants, sponsorships, donations
Collections: Permanent collection of works commemorating Tiananmen Square; China June 4; collection of works by contemporary Asian-American artists; folk arts collection (predominantly Chinese)
Publications: Arts Spiral, bi-annual
Activities: Educ dept; lect open to public, 15 vis lectr per year; gallery talks; tour; competitions with awards; originate traveling exhibitions; sales shop sells books, magazines & original art

M **THE ASIA SOCIETY GALLERIES,** 725 Park Ave, 10021. Tel 212-288-6400; Telex 22-4953 ASIA URCable ASIAHOUSE NEW YORK. *Dir Galleries* Vishakha Desai; *Pres* Nicholas Platt; *Chmn Society Board Trustees* Marice R Greenberg; *Cur Galleries* Carion Smith
Open Tues - Sat 11 AM - 6 PM, Sun Noon - 5 PM. Admis fee $3, seniors & students $1. Estab 1956 as a non-profit organization to further greater understanding & mutual appreciation between the US & peoples of Asia. The Asia House Gallery was inaugurated in 1960 to acquaint Americans with the historic art of Asia. In 1981 the Asia Society came into possession of its permanent collection, the Mr & Mrs John D Rockefeller 3d Collection of Asian Art, which is shown in conjunction with three to four temporary exhibitions each year. Average Annual Attendance: 60,000. Mem: 6000; dues $50 & up; annual meeting in May
Income: $750,000 (financed by endowment, mem, & grants from foundation, individual, federal & state government)
Collections: †Mr & Mrs John D Rockefeller 3D Collection of Asian Art; loans obtained from the US & foreign collections for special exhibitions
Publications: Archives of Asian Art, annually
Activities: Lect by guest specialists in connection with each exhibition & recorded lect by the gallery educ staff available to visitors, 40 vis lectr per year; concerts; gallery talks; tours; loan exhibitions originated; book traveling exhibitions 2 per year; sales shop sells books, magazines, prints, slides

A **ASSOCIATION OF ARTIST-RUN GALLERIES,** 591 Broadway, Ste 2A, 10012. Tel 212-924-6520; FAX 212-924-7945; *Exec Dir* Geoff Homan
No admis fee. Estab 1974 as a non-profit mem assoc composed of artist-run galleries & spaces. Sponsors an information resource center for member galleries, artists & general pub. Thirty five artist-run galleries
Exhibitions: Museum of the City of New York; US Customhouse-World Trade Center
Publications: AAR Guide; Fly Tracks, reviews; How to Begin & Maintain an Artist Run Space; newsletter; Time & Space Concepts in Art
Activities: Educ program in conjunction with various schools off-campus programs; lect open to public; concerts; gallery talks; tours

ASSOCIATION OF ART MUSEUM DIRECTORS
For further information, see National and Regional Organizations

A **ASSOCIATION OF HISPANIC ARTS,** 173 E 116 St, 10029. Tel 212-860-5445; FAX 212-427-2787; *Exec Dir* Sandra M Perez
Estab 1975, the Assoc of Hispanic Arts, Inc is a not-for-profit art service organization dedicated to the advancement of Latino arts. We highlight & promote the achievements of Latino artists & provide technical assistance to Latino arts organizations. AHA is an innovative forum for cultural exchange, with programs designed to foster the appreciation, development & stability of the Latino cultural community
Income: Financed by grants & contracts from pub & private sector
Publications: Hispanic Arts News, 9 times per yr; monthly listing of arts activities (in English & Spanish)

M **ATLANTIC GALLERY,** 475 Broome St, 10013. Tel 212-219-3183; *Dir* Nancy Balliet
Open Tues - Sat Noon - 6 PM. No admis fee. Estab 1971 as an artist-run gallery presenting the work of members & guests artists in solo exhibitions & group shows. 1 large gallery, 2 large gallery spaces. Average Annual Attendance: 10,000. Mem: 25; dues $100; annual meeting in May
Income: Financed by mem & artists of the gallery
Publications: Periodic flyers
Activities: Lect open to public; life-drawing sessions; concerts; gallery talks; tours; poetry readings; individual paintings & original objects of art lent; sales shop sells original art

AUDUBON ARTISTS, INC
For further information, see National and Regional Organizations

M AUSTRIAN CULTURAL INSTITUTE GALLERY, 950 Third Ave, 20th Flr
(Mailing add: 11 E 52nd St, 10022). Tel 212-759-5165; FAX 212-319-9636;
Telex 17-7142; Cable AUSTRO-CULT. *Dir* Dr Wolfgang Waldner
Open Mon - Fri 9 AM - 5 PM. Estab 1962 for presentaiton of Austrian Art &
culture in America. 10 exhibitions per year, focus on contemporary Austrian art
mainly
Publications: Austria Kultur, bi-monthly; monthly calendar

A LEO BAECK INSTITUTE, 129 E 73rd St, 10021. Tel 212-744-6400; FAX 212-
988-1305; *Exec Dir* Carol Kahn Strauss; *Pres* Ismar Schorsch; *Art Cur* Renata
Stein; *Librn* Dr Julia Bock; *Chief Archivist* Dr Frank Mecklenburg
Open Mon - Thurs 9:30 AM - 4:30 PM, Fri 9:30 AM - 2:30 PM. No admis fee.
Estab 1955 for history of German-Speaking Jewry. Center includes library &
archives; about 180 running ft, various display cases for books & documents.
Average Annual Attendance: 2000. Mem: 2000; dues $50
Collections: Drawings, paintings, prints, sculpture, ritual objects, textiles from
15th - 20th centuries; 19th - 20th Century German-Jewish Artists, including Max
Liebermann, Lesser Ury, Ludwig Meidner, Hugo Steiner-Prag
Exhibitions: Portraits of German Jews
Publications: Year Book; LBI News, semi-annually
Activities: Lect open to public, 10 vis lectr per year; concerts; gallery talks; tours;
scholarships & fels offered; individual paintings & original objects of art lent to
cultural art institutions; lending collection contains paintings, sculptures, 50,000
books, 5000 original art works, 2500 original prints, 40,000 photographs
L Library, 129 E 73rd St, 10021. Tel 212-744-6400; *Dir* Carol Kahn Strauss;
Archivist Frank Mecklenburg, PhD; *Cur* Renata Stein
Open winter Mon - Fri 9:30 AM - 4:30 PM, Fri 9:30 AM - 2:30 PM, July - Aug
9:30 AM - 3:30 PM. Estab 1955 to collect & preserve materials by & about
history of German-speaking Jews. For reference only
Income: Financed by endowment & mem
Library Holdings: Vols 50,000; Per subs 150; Micro — Fiche; Other — Original
art works 6300, photographs 30,000, prints 5000, sculpture 30
Special Subjects: Drawings, Folk Art, Historical Material, History of Art &
Archaeology, Judaica, Painting - German, Portraits, Prints, Stage Design,
Watercolors
Collections: †Archival collections relating to German-Jewish life

M BARUCH COLLEGE OF THE CITY UNIVERSITY OF NEW YORK, Sidney
Mishkin Gallery, 135 E 22nd St (Mailing add: D-0100, PO Box 821, NY 10010).
Tel 212-387-1006; *Dir* Sandra Kraskin, PhD
Open Mon - Fri Noon - 5 PM, Thurs Noon - 7 PM. No admis fee. Estab 1983.
2400 sq ft. Average Annual Attendance: 10,000
Income: Financed by the Baruch College Fund & federal, state & private grants
Collections: American & European drawings, paintings, photographs, prints &
sculptures
Publications: Exhibition catalogues
Activities: Lect open to public, 3-7 vis lectr per year; gallery talks; tours; book
traveling exhibitions 1-2 per year

M BLUE MOUNTAIN GALLERY, 121 Wooster St, 10012. Tel 212-226-9402; *Dir*
Morgan Taylor; *Co-Dir* Helene Manzo; *Treas* Meg Leveson
Open Tues - Sun Noon - 6 PM. No admis fee. Estab 1968, an artist supported
coop gallery exhibiting works of gallery members. 15 ft x 33 ft, white walls, grey
floor, & black ceiling. Mem: 28; members must be artists willing to exhibit & sell
own work & must be chosen by existing members; dues $840; 8 meetings a yr
Activities: Lect open to public; gallery talks; competitions

A BUSINESS COMMITTEE FOR THE ARTS, INC, 1775 Broadway, Ste 510,
10019-1942. Tel 212-664-0600; FAX 212-956-5980; *Pres* Judith A Jedlicka
Estab 1967 by David Rockefeller to encourage businesses to support the arts &
provide them with the resources necessary to do so
Publications: The Art of Leadership; BCA Case Studies; BCA News; A BCA
Report: 1993 Survey of Arts Organizations' Business Support; The BCA Report:
1995 National Survey of Business Support to the Arts; A BCA Report: 1996
Survey of Member Companies; A BCA Report: Foreign-Based Business Giving
to American Arts Organizations; Business & the Arts: Building Partnerships for
the Future; Business in the Arts Award Winners: 1993 to 1996; A Businesses
Guide to Investing in the Arts: Invest A Little - Get A Lot; Involving the Arts in
Advertising, Marketing & Public Relations: A Business Strategy; Why Business
Invests in the Arts: Facts, Figures, Philosophy (Fifth Edition-1996)

A CARIBBEAN CULTURAL CENTER, Cultural Arts Organization & Resource
Center, 408 W 58th St, 10019. Tel 212-307-7420; FAX 212-315-1086; *Dir*
Melody Capote; *Deputy Dir* Laura Moreno; *Dir Spec Projects* Mora Byrd
Open Mon - Fri 11 AM - 6 PM. Admis $2. Estab 1976. Resource center for
reference only. Average Annual Attendance: 100,000. Mem: dues $25
Income: Financed by federal, state & city appropriations, mem, foundation &
corporate support
Library Holdings: AV — A-tapes, cassettes, slides, v-tapes; Other — Exhibition
catalogs, framed reproductions, manuscripts, original art works, photographs
Publications: Caribe Magazine, irregular; occasional papers
Activities: Adult & children classes; concerts; conferences; curriculum
development; cultural arts programs; lect open to public, 5-10 vis lectr per year;
original objects of art lent to non-profit organizations, universities & colleges;
originate traveling exhibitions; retail store sells books, reproductions, artifacts
from the Caribbean, Latin America & Africa

M CATHEDRAL OF SAINT JOHN THE DIVINE, 1047 Amsterdam Ave,
10025. Tel 212-316-7493 (office), 316-7540 (visitors center)
Open daily 7 AM - 6 PM. Admis individuals no fee, donations accepted; groups
$1 per person. Estab 1974. The mus building was erected in the 1820's & forms
part of the complex of the Cathedral of Saint John the Divine. Average Annual
Attendance: 500,000
Income: Financed by federal government appropriations & Cathedral assistance

Collections: Old Master Paintings; decorative arts; sculptures; silver; tapestries;
vestments
Exhibitions: Monthly Photography Exhibitions; annual exhibitions planned to
spotlight specific areas of the Cathedral's permanent art collection
Activities: Lect open to public, 10 vis lectr per year; concerts; gallery talks; tours
L Library, 1047 Amsterdam Ave, 10025. Tel 212-316-7495; *Vol Librn* Madeleine
L'Engle
Open 9:30 AM - 4:30 PM. No admis fee. For reference only
Income: $3000

M CENTER FOR BOOK ARTS, 626 Broadway, 10012. Tel 212-460-9768; *Dir*
Brian Hannon
Open Mon - Fri 10 AM - 6 PM, Sat 10 AM - 4 PM. Estab 1974, dedicated to
contemporary bookmaking. Mem: 800; mem qualifications, must submit 5 slides
of their work along with current resume; dues $35
Collections: †Archive of Book Arts Collection
Exhibitions: Annual Chapbook Poetry Competition; 3-4 changing exhibitions
annually
Publications: Koob stra, quarterly; exhibition catalogues
Activities: Classes for adults & children; lect open to public, 8-10 vis lectr per
year; gallery talks; tours; competitions with prizes; sales shop sells books &
exhibition catalogs

L CENTER FOR SAFETY IN THE ARTS, 155 Avenue of the Americas, 10013.
Tel 212-366-6900; FAX 212-366-1778; *Exec Dir* Michael McCann
Open Mon - Fri 9:30 AM - 5:30 PM, or by appointment. Estab to make more
available research in art hazards. For reference only
Library Holdings: Vols 500
Special Subjects: Health & Safety, Performing Arts, Visual Arts
Activities: Adult classes; lectures

M THE CHAIM GROSS STUDIO MUSEUM, 526 LaGuardia Pl, 10012. Tel
212-529-4906; FAX 212-529-4906; *Pres* Irwin Hersey; *Dir* Mrs Chaim Gross;
Coll Cur April Paul
Open Tues - Sat Noon - 6 PM, cl Sun, Mon & Major holidays. No admis fee.
Estab 1989 to demonstrate the continuity of Gross's personal vision in sculpture
over 70 years of work. Three floors including the intact studio where he worked
for over 30 years. Average Annual Attendance: 5000. Mem: 250; dues $25-$125
& up; annual meetings in June & Dec
Income: $30,000 (financed by endowment, mem & gifts)
Purchases: Ebony carved figural group of two rabbits; carved marble head of a
woman; carved wood torso (all 1930's)
Collections: Permanent collection consists of 70 years of Chaim Gross's (1904-
91) sculpture in wood, stone & bronze, drawings, prints & watercolors
Activities: Docent guided tours for groups; lect open to public, 4 vis lectr per
year

C CHASE MANHATTAN (Formerly Chemical Bank), 600 Fifth Ave, 6th Flr,
10020. Tel 212-270-6000; *VPres & Cur* Claudia Mengel
Collections: 19th century American paintings & prints; 20th century &
contemporary paintings; sculpture; graphics; antique furniture; decorative arts;
textiles

C THE CHASE MANHATTAN BANK, NA, Art Collection, One Chase
Manhatten Plaza, 56th Flr, 10081. Tel 212-552-6728, 552-2222; FAX 212-552-
0695; *Exec Dir & VPres* Manuel Gonzalez; *Registrar* Katherine Gass; *Asst Cur*
Stacy Gershon
Estab 1959 to support young & emerging artists & enhance bank offices world-
wide. Collection displayed in branches, offices in New York City, state & world-
wide
Collections: Largely contemporary American, 12,000 works in all media
Exhibitions: Selection from the Chase Manhattan Bank Art Collection
Publications: Acquisitions report, annual; Art at Work: The Chase Manhattan
Bank
Activities: Lect for employees; individual objects of art lent to museum & gallery
exhibitions; originate traveling exhibitions

M CHILDREN'S MUSEUM OF MANHATTAN, 212 W 83rd St, 10024. Tel 212-
721-1223; *Assoc Dir* Robert Blandford; *Educ Dir* Valerie Winkler; *Public
Program Dir* Beth Weintraub
Open Tues - Fri 2 - 5 PM, Sat, Sun & holidays 10 AM - 5 PM. Admis $4. Estab
1973 as a children's museum & art center featuring participatory art, science, &
nature exhibits. Average Annual Attendance: 150,000. Mem: 1700; dues $40 -
$5000
Income: $2,300,000 (financed by city, state, federal, corporate & foundation
support, admis, mem, donations, program fees & tuition, sales shop)
Exhibitions: Ooh-La-La! Award Winning author Maira Kalman's delightful
characters from her series of books come to life in a new exhibition; Tar Beach
Exhibition: Flying Upon Dreams & Imagination; Special Preview of Sounds fun:
Exhibition on Sound
Publications: Monthly calendars; program brochures
Activities: Educ dept with parent/child workshops, toddler programs, summer
day camp, outreach, performing artists, intern/training, teacher training
program; museum sales shop sells books, games, toys

M CHINA INSTITUTE IN AMERICA, China Institute Gallery, 125 E 65th St,
10021. Tel 212-744-8181; FAX 212-628-4159; *Dir* Page Shaver
Open Mon, Wed - Sat 10 AM - 5 PM, Tues 10 AM - 8 PM, Sun 1 - 5 PM.
Contribution. Estab 1966 to promote a knowledge of Chinese culture. Two-room
gallery. Average Annual Attendance: 12,000. Mem: 1500; dues resident $50,
non-resident $35, academic $30, student, $20
Income: $30,000 (financed by mem, government grants & sponsors)
Exhibitions: Art at the Dragon Court: Chinese Embroidered Mandarin Squares from
the Schuyler V R Cammann Collection. Animals of the Chinese Zodiac:
Celebrating Chinese New Year; Politics & Decorative Schemes on Seventeenth
Century Chinese Porcelains; On Flying Hooves: The Horse in Chinese Art.
Brown & Black Wares; Through a Patron's Eye: Zhou Lianggong's Lives of

Painters & 17th Century China. The Resonance of the Qin; The Painter as Poet
Publications: Exhibition catalogs
Activities: Classes for adults & children; lect open to public; concerts; gallery talks; tours; originate traveling exhibitions; sales shop sells books

A   **CHINESE-AMERICAN ARTS COUNCIL,** 456 Broadway, 10013. Tel 212-431-9740; FAX 212-431-9789; *Exec Dir* Alan Chow; *Prog Dir* Beth Shu
Estab 1975 to provide exhibition space to Chinese-American artists. Average Annual Attendance: 600-800. Mem: 300; dues $10-$100
Income: Financed by endowment, city & state appropriation & private funds
Activities: Classes for children

L   **CITY COLLEGE OF THE CITY UNIVERSITY OF NEW YORK,** Morris Raphael Cohen Library, Convent Ave & 138th St, 10031. Tel 212-650-7292; FAX 212-650-7604; *Chief Librn* Pamela Gillespie; *Chief Reference Division* Loren Mendelsohn
Open Mon - Thurs 9 AM - 8 PM, Fri 9 AM - 5 PM, Sat Noon - 6 PM. Estab 1847 to support the educ at the City College
Library Holdings: Vols 22,000; Per subs 40; Micro — Fiche; Other — Clipping files, exhibition catalogs, memorabilia, pamphlets
Collections: History of Costume
L   **Architecture Library,** 408 Shepard Hall, Convent Ave & 138th St, 10031. Tel 212-650-8768; *Librn* Judy Connorton
Reference use for public; circulation for patrons with CUNY ID's
Library Holdings: Vols 20,000; Per subs 60; Micro — Fiche, reels; AV — A-tapes; Other — Clipping files
Special Subjects: Architecture, Landscape Architecture, Construction Technology, Urban Planning

COLLEGE ART ASSOCIATION
For further information, see National and Regional Organization

COLOR ASSOCIATION OF THE US
For further information, see National and Regional Organizations

L   **COLUMBIA UNIVERSITY,** Avery Architectural & Fine Arts Library, 1172 Amsterdam Ave, MC-0301, 10027. Tel 212-854-2425; FAX 212-854-8904; *Dir* Angela Giral; *Assoc Dir* Kitty Chibnik; *Rare Books Cur* William O'Malley; *Cur Drawings & Archives* Janet Parks; *Ed* Ted Goodman
Open Mon - Thurs 9 AM - 11 PM, Fri 9 AM - 9 PM, Sat Noon - 6 PM, Sun 2 - 10 PM. Estab 1890. Primarily for reference
Library Holdings: Vols 300,000; Per subs 1000; Original documents; Micro — Fiche, reels; Other — Manuscripts, memorabilia, photographs, prints
Special Subjects: Architecture, Art History, City Planning
Collections: Over 400,000 original architectural drawings, mainly American
Publications: Catalog of Avery Memorial Architectural Library; Avery Index to Architectural Periodicals, annually, also available as a data base
L   **Dept of Art History & Archeology,** Visual Resources Collection, 820-825 Schermerhorn Hall, 10027. Tel 212-854-3044; FAX 212-854-7329; *Cur Visual Resources Coll* Linda Strauss
Library Holdings: Gallery announcements 15,000; Other — Photographs 250,000
Collections: Berenson I-Tatti Archive; Dial Icongraphic Index; Haseloff Archive; Bartsch Collection; Gaigleres Collection; Arthur Kingsley Porter Collection; Ware Collection; Courtauld Collection; Marburger Index; Windsor Castle; Chatsworth Collection; Millard Meiss Collection
M   **Miriam & Ira D Wallach Art Gallery,** Schermerhorn Hall, 8th Flr, 10025. Tel 212-854-7288; FAX 212-854-7329; *Dir* Sarah Elliston Weiner
Open Wed - Sat 1 - 5 PM. No admis fee. Estab 1987 to complement the educational goals of Columbia University & to embody the research interests of faculty & graduate students in art history. 5 rooms, 2300 sq ft, 310 running ft. Average Annual Attendance: 4000
Income: $60,000 (financed by endowment & university)
Exhibitions: Temporary exhibitions only; 4 exhibitions annually during academic year
Publications: Exhibition catalogs
Activities: Lect open to public; gallery talks

M   **CONGREGATION EMANU-EL,** One E 65th St, 10021-6596. Tel 212-744-1400; FAX 212-570-0826; *Dir* Reva G Kirschberg; *Cur* Cissy Grossman, MA
Open daily 10 AM - 5 PM. No admis fee. Estab 1928 as a Judaica mus & to show history of congregation. Building is a landmark & is open for touring
Income: Financed by subvention from congregation
Collections: Congregational Memorabilia; Graphics; Judaica; Paintings
Exhibitions: Seasonal exhibits; Congregational History; Photographic exhibit of stained glass; A Temple Treasury, The Judaica Collection of Congregation Emanu-El of the City of New York

M   **COOPER-HEWITT,** National Design Museum, 2 E 91st St, 10128. Tel 212-860-6868, 860-6865; FAX 212-860-6909;
Internet Home Page Address http://www.si.edu/ndm/. *Dir* Dianne Pilgrim; *Cur Applied Arts* Deborah Shinn; *Cur Drawings & Prints* Marilyn Symmes; *Cur Textiles* Milton Sonday; *Cur Contemporary Design* Ellen Lupton; *Cur Wallcoverings* JoAnne Warner; *Asst Dir Public Prog* Susan Yelavich; *Librn* Stephen Van Dyk
Open Tues 10 AM - 9 PM, Wed - Sat 10 AM - 5 PM, Sun Noon - 5 PM, cl Mon & federal holidays. Admis Adults $3, seniors & students $1.50, free admis to members & after 5 PM on Tues. Founded 1897 as the Cooper Union Mus, to serve the needs of scholars, artisans, students, designers & everyone who deals with the built environment. Mus is based on large & varied collections of historic & contemporary design & a library strong in those fields; changing exhibitions are based on the museum's vast collections or loan shows illustrative of how design affects everyone's daily life; its emphasis on educ is expanded by special courses & seminars related to design in all forms & of all periods; the galleries occupy the first & second floors; (1998) exhibitions relate to the collections & other aspects of design. Maintains library. Average Annual Attendance: 150,000. Mem: 4500; dues $35-$2500

Income: Financed by private contributions, mem & partly Smithsonian Institution
Collections: Drawings including works by Frederic Church, Winslow Homer, Thomas Moran & other 19th century American artists; ceramics, furniture & woodwork, glass, original drawings & designs for architecture & the decorative arts; 15th-20th century prints; textiles, lace, wallpaper; 300,000 works representing a span of 300 years; wallcoverings
Exhibitions: (1997) Disegno: Italian Renaissance Designs for the Decorative Arts; Henry Dreyfuss: Directing Design, The Jewelry of the Vigeland; Under the Sun: An Outdoor Exhibition of Light. (1997-98) Design for Life: A Centennial Celebration; Arquitectonica: The Times Square Project. (1998) Todd Oldman; The Jewels of Lalique; Helen Drutt
Publications: The Smithsonian Illustrated Library of Antiques; books on decorative arts; collection handbooks; exhibition catalogues; magazine
Activities: Classes for adults & children; dramatic programs; performances; docent training; Master's Degree program in Decorative Arts through Parsons; lect open to public, 50-100 vis lectr per year; concerts; gallery talks; tours; fels offered; paintings & original objects of art lent to other museums; lending collection contains original art works, original prints & 40,000 books; book traveling exhibitions; originate traveling exhibitions; museum shop sells books, magazines & objects related to historical & contemporary design
L   **Cooper-Hewitt Museum Branch Library,** 2 E 91st St, 10128. Tel 212-860-6887; FAX 212-860-6339; *Librn* Stephen Van Dyk
Open Mon - Fri 9 AM - 5:30 PM. Interlibrary lending only
Income: Financed through SIL budgets
Library Holdings: Vols 50,000; Per subs 300; Original documents; Pictures & photographs 1,500,900; Micro — Cards, fiche, prints, reels; AV — Kodachromes, lantern slides, slides, v-tapes; Other — Clipping files, exhibition catalogs, manuscripts, memorabilia, original art works, pamphlets, photographs, prints, reproductions
Special Subjects: Advertising Design, Decorative Arts, Graphic Design, Industrial Design, Interior Design, Color, Materials of Design
Collections: Donald Deskey Archive; Henry Dreyfuss Archive; Nancy McCelland Archive; Ladislav Sutnar Archive

L   **COOPER UNION FOR THE ADVANCEMENT OF SCIENCE & ART,** Library, 30 Cooper Square, 10003. Tel 212-353-4186; Elec Mail vajda@cooper.edu. *Head Librn* Elizabeth Vajda; *Art & Architecture* Ulla Volk; *Slide & Picture* Tom Micchelli; *Engineering & Science* Carol Salomon; *Electronic Serv* Julie Castelluzzo
Estab 1859 to support the curriculum of the three professional schools: Art, Architecture, Engineering
Library Holdings: Vols 86,500; Per subs 370; Micro — Fiche 3500, reels 3800; AV — Lantern slides, slides 50,000; Other — Clipping files 90,000
Special Subjects: Architecture, Calligraphy, Collages, Commercial Art, Drawings, Etchings & Engravings, Film, Graphic Arts, Graphic Design, Islamic Art, Landscape Architecture, Manuscripts, Maps, Painting - American, Painting - British, Painting - Dutch, Painting - Flemish, Painting - French, Painting - German, Painting - Italian, Painting - Japanese, Painting - Russian, Painting - Spanish, Photography, Posters, Pre-Columbian Art, Prints, Sculpture, Photography
Activities: Non-degree classes for adults; lect open to public, 20-30 vis lectr per year

A   **CREATIVE TIME,** 131 W 24th St, 10011. Tel 212-206-6674; FAX 212-255-8467; *Exec Dir* Anne Pasternak; *Dir Development* Susan Kennedy
Open Mon - Fri 10 AM - 5 PM, exhibition hrs vary depending on site. Admis performances $8, exhibitions usually free. Estab 1973 to present visual, architecture & performing art programs in public spaces throughout New York City. Spaces include a variety of temporarily unused public locations. Average Annual Attendance: 50,000. Mem: 200; members give tax-deductible contributions
Income: $500,000 (financed by National Endowment for the Arts, NY State Council of the Arts, NYC Dept of Cultural Affairs, private corporations & foundations)
Exhibitions: Art in the Anchorage
Publications: Creative Time; biannual program/project catalogs
Activities: Multi-media, dance & performance art events

M   **CULTURAL COUNCIL FOUNDATION,** Fourteen Sculptors Gallery, Broadway, 10012. *Chmn Board Dir* John Cino
No admis fee. Estab 1973 to exhibit emerging & estab sculptors. Invitational, curated & traveling exhibitions held annually of artists throughout the US. Average Annual Attendance: 35,000. Mem: 22; mem qualifications: reviewed & interviewed by current gallery artists; dues $1200; annual meeting in June
Income: Financed by mem
Publications: Catalogs

M   **DAHESH MUSEUM,** 601 Fifth Ave, 10017. Tel 212-759-0606; FAX 212-759-1235; *Dir* J David Farmer; *Deputy Dir* Tara P Davey; *Cur* Stephen Edidin; *Asst Cur* Cristina Portell; *Adminr* Maria Celi; *Registrar* Martin Beck
Open Tues - Sat 11 AM - 6 PM. No admis fee. Estab 1987. Maintains reference library. Average Annual Attendance: 20,000
Collections: †European 19th & 20th Century Academic Art (paintings, sculpture & works on paper)
Exhibitions: (1997) Religion & the Rustic Image
Publications: Dahesh Muse, newsletter 3 per year
Activities: Lect open to public, 20 vis lectr per year; museum shop sells books, prints, reproductions, jewelry, figurines, stationery, educational toys & gifts

A   **DIA CENTER FOR THE ARTS,** 548 W 22nd St, 10011. Tel 212-989-5566; FAX 212-989-4055; Elec Mail diacentr@pannix;.
Internet Home Page Address http://www.diacenter.org. *Exec Dir* Michael Govan; *Cur* Lynne Cooke
Open Thurs - Sun Noon - 6 PM. Admis fee $4. Estab 1974 for planning, realization & presentation of important works of contemporary art. Committment to artist's participation in display of works in long term, carefully maintained

installations. Galleries: Dan Flavin Art Institute, Bridgehampton, NY; The Lightning Field, Quemado, NM
Income: Financed by grants
Collections: Works by 13 contemporary American & European artists, retrospective in nature; works by Joseph Beuys, Walter De Maria, Dan Flavin, Fred Sandback, Cy Twombly, Andy Warhol
Exhibitions: Dan Graham. (1997) Hanne Darboven; Juan Munoz
Publications: The Foundation has published collections of poetry & translations of poetry
Activities: Educ dept; lect open to public, 3 vis lectr per year; Exhibit catalogues; Series of discussions on contemporary cultural issues; museum shop sells books & original art

M **DIEU DONNE PAPERMILL, INC,** 433 Broome St, 10013. Tel 212-226-0573; *Exec Dir* Mina Takahashi; *Prog Dir* Helen Hiebert
Exhibitions: Essential Material (Book show of books made with Dieu Donne handmade papers)
Activities: Residencies offered; originate traveling exhibitions

A **DRAWING CENTER,** 35 Wooster St, 10013. Tel 212-219-2166; FAX 212-966-2976; *Dir* Ann Philbin; *Dir Operations* Peter Gilmore; *Dir Develop* Caroline Harris; *Registrar* Meryl Cohen
Open Tues, Thurs & Fri 10 AM - 6 PM; Wed 10 AM - 8 PM; Sat 11 AM - 6 PM, cl Sun & Mon. Estab 1977 to express the quality & diversity of drawing through exhibition & educ. 200 linear ft historic building; special facility considerations for works-on-paper. Maintains reference library. Average Annual Attendance: 125,000. Mem: 300; dues dual/household $75, individual $40
Exhibitions: Group shows of emerging artists: Selections; The Northern Landscape: Flemish, Dutch, & British Drawings From The Courtauld Collections
Publications: Exhibition catalogs
Activities: Classes for adults & children; teacher training workshops; lect open to public, 50 vis lectr per year; gallery talks; tours; work study program offered; book traveling exhibitions 1-2 per year; originate traveling exhibitions; museum shop sells books

THE DRAWING SOCIETY
For further information, see National and Regional Organizations

A **ELECTRONIC ARTS INTERMIX, INC,** 536 Broadway, 9th Flr, 10012. Tel 212-966-4605; FAX 212-941-6118; *Dir* Lori Zippay
Open daily 9:30 AM - 5:30 PM. Estab as a non-profit corporation to assist artists seeking to explore the potentials of the electronic media, particularly television, as a means of personal expression
Income: Financed by videotape & editing fees & in part by federal & state funds & contributions
Collections: Several hundred video cassettes
Publications: Electronic Arts Intermix Videocassette Catalog, annual

M **EL MUSEO DEL BARRIO,** 1230 Fifth Ave, 10029. Tel 212-831-7272; FAX 212-831-7927; *Exec Dir* Susana Torruella Leval
Open Wed - Sun 11 AM 5 - PM, cl Mon & Tues. Admis adults $2, senior citizens & students with ID $1, children under 12 free when accompanied by adult. Estab 1969 to conserve & display works by Puerto Rican artists & other Hispanic artists. Located on Museum Mile. Gallery space divided into 4 wings: Northwest Wing houses Santos de Palo, East Gallery will house Pre-Columbian installation, F-Stop Gallery devoted to photography & Childrens Wing opened fall of 1982. Average Annual Attendance: 19,450. Mem: 250; patron, organization & business $1000, associate $500, sustaining $250, support $100, contributing $50, family $35, individual $25, special $15
Collections: 16mm Films on History, Culture and Art; †300 Paintings and †5000 Works on Paper, by Puerto Rican and other Latin American Artists; Pre-Columbian Caribbean Artifacts; Santos (Folk Religious Carvings)
Exhibitions: Art of the Other Mexico
Activities: Classes for adults & children; dramatic programs; children's workshops; lect open to public, 25 vis lectr per year; concerts; gallery talks; tours; awards; scholarships; individual & original objects of art lent to other museums & galleries; originate traveling exhibitions; Junior Museum

M **AMOS ENO GALLERY,** 594 Broadway, Ste 404, 10012. Tel 212-226-5342; *Dir* Jane Harris
Open Tues - Sat 11 AM - 6 PM. No admis fee. Estab 1974
Collections: Contemporary Art

C **EQUITABLE LIFE ASSURANCE SOCIETY,** The Equitable Gallery, 787 Seventh Ave, 10019. Tel 212-554-4818; *Cur* Pari Stave; *Asst Cur & Registrar* Nancy Deihl
Equitable Gallery open Mon - Fri 11 AM - 6 PM, Sat Noon - 5 PM. Estab 1992 to exhibit traveling exhibitions organized by nonprofit institutions. Average Annual Attendance: 110,000
Collections: 19th & 20th century paintings, sculpture & works on paper, American emphasis; Commissioned Art Works by; Roy Lichetenstein, Scott Burton, Sol Lewitt, Sandro Chia
Activities: Support technical assistance programs; lect open to public; gallery talks; library tours; individual paintings & original objects of art lent to museums for short-term exhibitions

M **EXIT ART-THE FIRST WORLD, INC,** 548 Broadway, 2nd Flr, 10012. Tel 212-966-7745; FAX 212-925-2928; *Dir* Jeannette Ingberman; *Asst Dir* Stuart Anthony; *Co-Founder-Official Poet* Papo Colo
Open Tues - Thurs 10 AM - 6 PM, Fri 10 AM - 8 PM, Sat 11 AM - 8 PM. Voluntary contribution. Estab 1982, dedicated to multi-cultural, multi-media enlightenment through presentations & publications, film festivals, exhibitions, music performances & theater. Mem: 250; dues $30 & up
Exhibitions: Wide range of varied exhibitions
Activities: Lect open to public; concerts; originate traveling exhibitions to museums, cultural spaces & university galleries; museum shop sells magazines, original art & artist made products

M **FASHION INSTITUTE OF TECHNOLOGY,** Museum at FIT, Seventh Ave at 27th St, 10001-5992. Tel 212-760-7970; FAX 212-760-7978; *Dir* Dorothy Twining Globus
Open Tues - Fri Noon - 8 PM, Sat 10 AM - 5 PM, cl Sun, Mon & holidays. No admis fee. Estab 1967 to bring to the student body & the community at large a variety of exhibitions in fashion & the applied arts. Gallery contains 11,500 sq ft of space divided into four galleries. The galleries on the main floor are used for smaller exhibits from the collections & for student projects while the three galleries located in the lower level are used for major exhibitions. Average Annual Attendance: 70,000
Income: Financed by endowment & grants
Purchases: Costumes & textile collections, The Mus at FIT
Collections: Largest working costume & textile collection in the world focusing on the 20th century
Exhibitions: (1997) Dreams on Paper; Gio Pomodoro Ornamenti, 1954-1996
Publications: Exhibit catalogs
Activities: Classes for adults; docent training; lect open to public, gallery talks; tours; clothing & textiles lent to major museums & art institutions; originate traveling exhibitions organized & circulated

L **Gladys Marcus Library,** Seventh Ave at 27th St, 10001-5992. Tel 212-760-7590; FAX 212-760-7268; *Dir* Rochelle Sager; *Reference Head* Beryl Rentof; *Reference & Spec Coll* Joshua Walker; *Reference & Systems* Lorraine Weberg; *Reference & ILL* Stephen Rosenberger; *Acquisition Head* Judy Wood; *Catalog Head* Janette Rozene
Open Mon - Thurs 9:30 AM - 9:30 PM, Fri 9:30 AM - 6:30 PM, Sat & Sun Noon - 5 PM. Estab 1944 to meet the academic needs of the students & faculty & to serve as a resource for the fashion industry. For reference only
Library Holdings: Vols 118,984; Per subs 507; Artist Books; Micro — Cards, fiche 1947, prints, reels; AV — A-tapes 98, cassettes 98, fs 357, motion pictures 295, slides 101,096, v-tapes; Other — Clipping files, exhibition catalogs, memorabilia, original art works 184, pamphlets, photographs, prints, reproductions
Special Subjects: Artists Books
Collections: Oral History Project on the Fashion Industry; several sketchbook collections

FEDERATION OF MODERN PAINTERS & SCULPTORS
For further information, see National and Regional Organizations

M **55 MERCER,** 55 Mercer St, 10013. Tel 212-226-8513; *Co-Pres* Ethelyn Honig; *Co-Pres* Bill Hochhausen
Open Tues - Sat 10 AM - 6 PM. No admis fee. Estab 1970 to give unaffiliated artists a space to show their work. Average Annual Attendance: 8000. Mem: 16; dues $1200; meeting every 2 months
Income: Financed by mem dues
Exhibitions: One Person & Group shows including Anne Barnard, Eric Deiratsch, Hank DeRicco, Charles Farless, Bill Giersbach, Gloria Greenberg, Betti-Sue Hertz, Eliot Label, Mike Metz, Nancy Olivier, Joyce Robins, Robert Segall, Carol Steen, Robert Sussman, Joy Walker, Diane Whitcomb, Tyler Smith, Carl Plansky, Leslie Wayne, Fran Schalom, Ethlin Honig, Joan Gardner, Bill Hochhausen, Pierre Louaver
Activities: Apprenticeship program; competitions; individual paintings & original objects of art lent to college shows

M **FIRST STREET GALLERY,** 560 Broadway, 10012. Tel 212-226-9127; *Acting Dir* Rallou Hamshaw; *Asst Mgr* Allen Petrulis
Estab 1969 to promote figurative art & artists throughout the US. Artist-run cooperative exhibiting contemporary Realist work. Mem: 25; dues $100; open to Realist artists only; monthly meetings
Exhibitions: Aros: Group Exhibition; David Rich, Wendy Gittler, Mary Napolitano, Stephen Gaffney
Activities: Originate traveling exhibitions

C **FORBES MAGAZINE, INC,** 62 Fifth Ave, 10011. Tel 212-206-5549; FAX 212-620-2426; *Dir* Margaret Kelly
Open Tues, Wed, Fri & Sat 10 AM - 4 PM, Thurs group tours. Estab 1985
Collections: Antique Toys; Faberge Imperial Eggs Collection; French Military Paintings; Presidential Papers; Toy Soldiers
Activities: Gallery talks; individual paintings & original objects of art lent to museums & galleries

A **FOTOGRAFICA,** 484 W 43rd St, Ste 22T, 10036. Tel 212-244-5182; *Exec Dir* Perla de Leon; *Asst Dir* Evelyn Collazo, AA
Estab 1982 to promote Latin American photography. Average Annual Attendance: 500. Mem: dues individual $25, group $50, associate $250, patron $500, corporate $1500
Collections: El Dia de Los Muertos

L **FRANKLIN FURNACE ARCHIVE, INC,** 112 Franklin St, 10013. Tel 212-925-4671; *Executive Dir* Martha Wilson; *Prog Coordr* Nathan Blake; *Admin Coordr* Anita Chao
Open Tues - Sat Noon - 6 PM. No admis fee. Estab 1976 as a non-profit corporation dedicated to the cataloging, exhibition & preservation of book-like work by artists, performance art & temporary installations. Mem: Dues $35
Library Holdings: Other — Original art works
Special Subjects: Performance art documentation
Publications: FLUE, irregular periodical
Activities: Classes for children; lect open to public; gallery talks; tours; original objects of art lent to qualified institutions; originate traveling exhibitions

M **FRAUNCES TAVERN MUSEUM,** 54 Pearl St, 10004-2429. Tel 212-425-1778; FAX 212-509-3467; *Dir* Lauren Kaminsky; *Development Dir* Kelly Whalen; *Public Relations Officer* Nicole Colanoelo; *Assoc Cur* Maureen Sarro
Open Mon - Fri 10 AM - 4:45 PM, Sat & Sun Noon - 4 PM. Admis adults $2. 50, students, children & senior citizens $1. Estab 1907 for focus on early American history, culture, historic preservation & New York City history. Museum is housed in the site of eighteenth-century Fraunces Tavern and four

adjacent nineteenth-century buildings. The museum houses two fully furnished period rooms: the Long Room, site of George Washington's farewell to his officers at the end of the Revolutionary War, and the Clinton Room. a nineteenth-century dining room. Mem: 500; dues $20-$1000

Collections: 17th, 18th, 19th & 20th century prints, paintings, artifacts & decorative arts relating to early American history, culture & historic preservation; New York City history; George Washington & other historic figures in American history

Exhibitions: Capital City; The Changing Image of George Washington; Colonial Revival; Come All You Gallant Heroes; Education in the Young Republic; English Naive Art The Healing Arts in Early America; Much Depends on Dinner: Culinary Customs in Early New York; NY After the Revolution; Picturing History; Tavern Revels; To Establish Justice; To Please Every Taste; The 200th Anniversary of the US District Court in New York; Wall Street: Changing Fortunes; Watercolors of Harry Ogden

Publications: Exhibit catalogs

Activities: Educ dept; docent training; lectures open to public; tours; demonstrations; films; off-site programs; individual paintings lent to qualified museums & historical organizations, lending collection contains 750 original works of art, 150 original prints, & 1300 decorative art & artifacts; book traveling exhibitions; museum shop sells books, reproductions, prints & slides

L **FRENCH INSTITUTE-ALLIANCE FRANCAISE,** Library, 22 E 60th St, 10022-1077. Tel 212-355-6100; FAX 212-935-4119; *Librn* Katherine Branning; *Library Technical Asst* Ronda Murdock
Open Mon 4 - 8 PM, Tues Noon - 8 PM, Wed & Thurs 1 - 8 PM, Sat 10 AM - 1:30 PM. Admis first visit free, $5 daily use fee for non-members. Estab 1911 to encourage the study of the French language & culture. Library lends to members, reference only for non-members; maintains art gallery
Income: Financed by endowment & mem, tax deductible contributions & foundation grants
Library Holdings: Vols 45,000; Per subs 110; AV — Cassettes 900, rec 1350; Other — Exhibition catalogs
Special Subjects: Film, French Art
Collections: †Architecture, †costume, †decorative arts, †paintings
Exhibitions: Rogi Andre: Portraits; Sam Levin: French Stars, portraits; Andre Ostier, portraits
Publications: Acquisitions list, quarterly
Activities: Classes given; lect open to public, 25 vis lectr per year; concerts; weekly film showings; closed circuit TV screenings

L **FRICK ART REFERENCE LIBRARY,** 10 E 71st St, 10021. Tel 212-288-8700; *Andrew W Mellon Librn* Patricia Barnett; *Assoc Librn* Marie C Keith; *Cataloguer* Patricia D Siska; *Reference Librn* Irene Avens; *Reference Letters* Lydia Dufour
Open Mon - Fri 10 AM - 4:45 PM (Sept - July), Sat 9:30 AM - 1 PM (Sept - May), cl Sun, holidays & month of Aug. Estab 1920 as a reference library to serve adults & graduate students interested in the history of European & American painting, drawing, sculpture, illuminated manuscripts. For reference only
Library Holdings: Vols 108,284; Micro — Fiche 61; Other — Exhibition catalogs 82,148, photographs 421,495
Publications: Frick Art Reference Library Original Index to Art Periodicals; Frick Art Reference Library Sales Catalogue Index (microform); The Story of the Frick Art Reference Library; The Early Years, by Katharine McCook Knox

M **FRICK COLLECTION,** One E 70th St, 10021. Tel 212-288-0700; FAX 212-628-4417; *Pres* Henry Clay Frick II; *Dir* Charles Ryskamp; *Cur* Edgar Munhall; *Assoc Cur* Susan Grace Galassi; *Deputy Dir Admin* Robert B Goldsmith; *Mgr Sales & Info* Kate Gerlough; *Mgr Bldgs & Secy* Robert J Brady; *Registrar* William G Stout
Open Tues - Sat 10 AM - 6 PM, Sun 1 - 6 PM; cl Jan 1, July 4, Thanksgiving, Dec 24 & 25. Admis adults $5, students & senior citizens $3, children under 10 not admitted. Estab 1920; opened to public 1935 as a gallery of art. The Frick Collection is housed in the former residence of Henry Clay Frick (1849-1919), built in 1913-14 & alterations & additions were made 1931-1935 & further extension & garden were completed in 1977. The rooms are in the style of English & French interiors of the 18th century. Maintains art reference library. Average Annual Attendance: 250,000. Mem: 600 Fellows; dues $600 minimum contribution
Income: $10,430,000 (financed by endowment, mem & admis)
Collections: 15th-18th century sculpture, of which Renaissance bronzes are most numerous; 14th-19th century paintings, with fine examples of Western European masters & suites of Boucher & Fragonard decorations; Renaissance & French 18th century furniture; 17th-18th century Chinese & French procelains; 16th century Limoges enamels; 16th-19th century drawings & prints
Exhibitions: (1997) Italian Drawings from the Ratjen Foundation
Publications: Artin the Frick Collection (paintings, sculpture & decorative arts); exhibition catalogs; The Frick Collection, illustrated catalog; guide to the galleries; handbook of paintings; Ingres & the Comtesse d'Haussonville; paintings from the Frick Collection
Activities: Lect open to public; concerts; museum shop selling books, prints, slides, postcards, greeting cards

C **FRIED, FRANK, HARRIS, SHRIVER & JACOBSON,** Art Collection, One New York Plaza, 10004. Tel 212-820-8000; Telex 747-1526. *Chmn* Arthur Fleischer Jr; *Cur* Brooke Alexander; *Cur* Paula Cooper
Open by appointment. Estab 1979 intended as a survey
Purchases: Over 750 pieces in all offices (NY, DC & LA)
Collections: †Fried, Frank, Harris, Shriver & Jacobson Art Collection; Contemporary Art
Exhibitions: Permanent exhibition
Activities: Tours

M **GALLERY OF PREHISTORIC PAINTINGS,** 30 E 81st St, 10028. Tel 212-861-5152; *Dir* Douglas Mazonowicz
Open by appointment. No admis fee. Estab 1975 to make available to the pub the art works of prehistoric peoples, particularly the cave paintings of France, Spain & the Sahara Desert. Large display area. Average Annual Attendance: 10,000
Income: Financed by private funds
Collections: Early American Indian Rock Art; Rock Art of Eastern Spain; Rock Art of the Sahara; serigraph reproduction editions of Cave Art of France and Spain
Publications: Newsletter, quarterly
Activities: Classes for adults & children; Cave Art-in-Schools Program; lect open to the public; gallery talks; tours; lending collection contains books, cassettes, framed reproductions, 1000 Kodachromes, motion pictures, original prints, 1000 photographs, 2000 slides; originate traveling exhibitions organized & circulated; sales shop selling books, magazines

L **Library,** 30 E 81st St, 10028. Tel 212-861-5152; *Dir* Douglas Mazonowicz
Open Mon - Fri 9 AM - 5 PM, Sat 9 AM - Noon. Estab 1975 to make information available to the general public concerning the art works of prehistoric peoples. For reference only
Library Holdings: Vols 250; Per subs 9; AV — Cassettes, Kodachromes, motion pictures, slides; Other — Clipping files, exhibition catalogs, framed reproductions, manuscripts, pamphlets, photographs, prints, reproductions, sculpture

C **THE GILMAN PAPER COMPANY,** 111 W 50th St, 10020. Tel 212-246-3300; FAX 212-582-7610; *Cur* Pierre Apraxine
Collections: Al Reinhardt; Robert Mangold; Ellsworth Kely; Dan Flavin; Robert Morris; conceptual art; Robert Smithsons Script for the Spiral Jetty; Claes Oldenburg drawing Potatoe; architectural drawings; photography
Activities: Tours

A **GRAPHIC ARTISTS GUILD,** 11 W 20th St, 10011. Tel 212-463-7730; FAX 212-463-8779; *Exec Dir* Paul Basista
Open 10 AM - 6 PM. Estab 1967 to improve the economic & social condition of graphic artists; to provide legal & credit services to members; to increase pub appreciation of graphic art (including illustration, cartooning & design) as an art form. Mem: 1300
Income: Financed by mem & publication sales
Publications: Cartooning books; GAG Directory of Illustration, annual; GAG Handbook, Pricing & Ethical Guidelines, biennial; monthly newsletter
Activities: Walter Hortens Memorial Awards for Distinguished Service & Outstanding Client

L **GREENWICH HOUSE,** Pottery Library, 16 Jones St, 10014. Tel 212-242-4106; FAX 212-645-5486; *Dir* Elizabeth Zawada; *Asst Dir* Lynne Lerner
Estab 1909. For reference only
Library Holdings: Vols 700; Per subs 10; AV — Slides; Other — Exhibition catalogs
Special Subjects: Ceramics

L **GROLIER CLUB LIBRARY,** 47 E 60th St, 10022. Tel 212-838-6690; FAX 212-838-2445; *Librn* Martin Antonetti
Open Mon - Sat 10 AM - 5 PM, cl Sun, Sat in the Summer & pub in Aug. No admis fee. Estab 1884, devoted to the arts of the book. Mem: 700; annual meetings fourth Thurs of Jan
Purchases: $15,000
Library Holdings: Vols 100,000; Per subs 35; Other — Prints
Special Subjects: Bibliography
Collections: †Bookseller & auction catalogs from 17th century
Exhibitions: Contemporary American Bookbindings; Italian & French 16th Century Bookbindings; Modern German Fine Printing; With Weapons & Wits (WW II)
Publications: Exhibition catalog (1989); Rudolph Ruzicka: Speaking Reminiscently (1986)
Activities: Lect for members only

A **JOHN SIMON GUGGENHEIM MEMORIAL FOUNDATION,** 90 Park Ave, 10016. Tel 212-687-4470; FAX 212-697-3248; *Pres* Joel Conarroe; *VPres & Secy* G Thomas Tanselle; *Dir Planning & Latin America Prog* Peter Kardon; *Assoc Secy* Sue Schwager; *Treas* Coleen Higgins-Jacob; *Development Officer* Nancy McCabe
Estab & incorporated 1925; offers fellowships to further the development of scholars & artists by assisting them to engage in research in any field of knowledge & creation in any of the arts, under the freest possible conditions & irrespective of race, color or creed. For additional information see section devoted to Scholarships and Fellowships

M **GUGGENHEIM MUSEUM SOHO,** 575 Broadway, 10012. Tel 212-423-3500; FAX 212-423-3650; *Dir* Thomas Krens; *Deputy Dir & Sr Cur* Diane Waldman; *Deputy Dir Financed & Admin* Robert Gebbie; *Cur Coll & Exhib* Lisa Dennison; *Conservator* Paul Schwartzbaum; *Photographer* David Heald; *Asst to Dir* Ann Kraft; *Dir Public Affairs* Scott Gutterman; *Assoc Cur* Nancy Spector
Open Wed - Fri & Sun 11 AM - 6 PM, Sat 11 AM - 8 PM, cl Mon, Tues & Christmas, open Christmas Eve & New Years Eve 11 AM - 5 PM. Admis $6, seniors (65+) & student with valid ID $4, children under 12 free, members free. Estab 1992. Housed in a nineteenth century landmark building in SOHO's historic cast-iron district, which was designed by renowned architect Arata Isozaki
Exhibitions: Special exhibitions that complement those at Solomon R Guggenheim Museum with emphasis on multi-media & interactive art; ongoing virtual reality & CD-ROM installations related to art & architecture
Activities: Dramatic programs; docent training; symposia; family activities; teacher training; lect open to public, 6 vis lectr per year; concerts; gallery talks; tours; competitions with prizes

M **SOLOMON R GUGGENHEIM MUSEUM,** 1071 Fifth Ave, 10128. Tel 212-423-3500; FAX 212-423-3650; *Dir* Thomas Krens; *Deputy Dir Finance & Adminr* Robert Gebbie; *Cur Col & Exhib* Lisa Dennison; *Conservator* Paul Schwartzbaum; *Photographer* David Heald; *Asst to Dir* Ann Kraft; *Dir Cmmunications* Scott Gutterman; *Assoc Cur* Nancy Spector
Open Sun - Wed 10 AM - 6 PM, Fri & Sat 10 AM - 8 PM, cl Thurs & holidays. Admis general $7, students with valid ID cards & visitors over 65 $4, group rates for students when accompanied by a teacher, children under 12 free, Fri evening free. Estab 1937 as a nonprofit organization which is maintained by the Solomon R Guggenheim Foundation; founded for the promotion & encouragement of art & educ in art; to foster an appreciation of art by acquainting mus visitors with significant paintings & sculpture of our time. The gallery was designed by architect Frank Lloyd Wright. Average Annual Attendance: 700,000. Mem: 7000; dues $30-$5000
Income: Financed by endowment, mem & state & federal appropriations
Collections: Reflects the creative accomplishments in modern art from the time of the Impressionists to the constantly changing experimental art of today. The collection of nearly four thousand works, augmented by the Justin K Thannhauser Collection of 75 Impressionists & Post-Impressionist masterpieces, including the largest group of paintings by Vasily Kandinsky; one of the largest & most comprehensive collection of paintings by Paul Klee; largest number of sculptures by Constantin Brancusi in any New York museum; paintings by Chagall, Delaunay, Lager, Marc, Picasso, Bacon, Bonnard, Braque, Cezanne, Malevitch, Modigliani, Moore, Reusseau & Seurat, with concentration of works by Dubuffet, Miro & Mondrian among the Europeans; Americans such as Davis, deKooning, Diebenkorn, Gottlieb, Guston, Johns, Lichenstein, Agnes Martin, Motherwell, Nevelson, Noguchi, Pollack, younger artists include Andre, Flavin, Judd, Christenson, Hamilton, Hesse, Mangold, Nauman, Stella & Serra; paintings, drawings & sculpture collections are being enlarged
Exhibitions: (1997) A Century of Sculpture: The Nasber Collection
Publications: Exhibition catalogs, Guggenheim Museum Magazine (2 times per year)
Activities: Lect open to the public; concerts; gallery talks; acoustiguide tours; individual paintings & original objects of art lent to other museums & galleries; lending collection contains original art works, original prints, painting, sculpture; originates traveling exhibitions; museum shop sells books, jewelry & t-shirts
L **Library,** 1071 Fifth Ave, 10128. Tel 212-423-3500; *Librn* Eileen Majaras
Open by telephone appointment only, Mon - Fri 11 AM - 5 PM. Estab 1952 to document the Museum's collection of 20th century art. For reference only
Library Holdings: Vols 26,000; Per subs 40; Artist Files; Early Avant-Grade Periodicals; Other — Exhibition catalogs, pamphlets, reproductions
Special Subjects: Early 20th Century European Art
Collections: Rebay Library

GUILD OF BOOK WORKERS
For further information, see National and Regional Organizations

A **HARVESTWORKS, INC,** 596 Broadway, Ste 602, 10012. Tel 212-431-1130; FAX 212-431-8473; Elec Mail jfxm@echonyc.com. *Dir* Carol Parkinson; *Studio Mgr* Alex Noyes; *General Mgr* John McGeehan
Open Mon - Fri 10 AM - 6 PM. Estab 1977 to provide support & facilities for audio art & experimental music. Average Annual Attendance: 2000. Mem: 250; dues $35
Income: $150,000 (financed by endowment, mem, city & state appropriations, recording studio)
Purchases: Pro-tools by Digi Design, Digital Audio Editing
Publications: TELLUS, the Audio Series, biannual
Activities: Adult classes; artist in residence program; lect open to public, 12 vis lectr per year; competitions; retail store sells audio art & music cassettes & CDs

M **HEBREW UNION COLLEGE-JEWISH INSTITUTE OF RELIGION,** One W Fourth St, 10012-1186. Tel 212-674-5300, Ext 209; FAX 212-533-0129; *Exhib Dir* Jean Bloch Rosensaft; *Chair, Exhib Advisory Committee* Laura Kruger
Open Mon - Thurs 9 AM - 6 PM & selected Sun. No admis fee. Estab 1875 to present 4000 years of Jewish art with stress on contemporary art expressing Jewish identity & themes. 5000 sq ft of space, rare book room gallery for book arts. Average Annual Attendance: 10,000
Income: Financed by annual budget & fundraising
Collections: Biblical archaeology; contemporary art expressing Jewish identity & themes; Jewish ritual art
Exhibitions: Sherry Karver, Generation to Generation; Ben Katchor, Drawings from Julius Knipl; Ran Oron, Planes; Arlene Slauin, Genesis in the Beginning
Publications: Exhibition catalogs, brochures & posters
Activities: Classes for adults & children; dramatic programs; docent training; lect open to public, 15 vis lectr per year; book traveling exhibitions 3 per year; originate traveling exhibitions 6 per year

M **HENRY STREET SETTLEMENT ART CENTER,** Abrons Art Center, 466 Grand St, 10002. Tel 212-598-0400; FAX 212-505-8329; *Dir* Susan Fleminger
Open Tues - Sat Noon - 6 PM. No admis fee. Estab 1975 as a multi discipline community arts center for the performing & visual arts programs. Photo gallery for solo shows. Average Annual Attendance: 150,000
Exhibitions: Contemporary art by emerging artists, women artists & artists of color, changing thematic exhibitions
Activities: Classes for adults & children in all arts disciplines; dramatic programs; docent training; gallery educ program for groups; lect open to public; concerts; gallery talks; tours

M **HISPANIC SOCIETY OF AMERICA,** Museum, Broadway, Between 155th and 156th Sts, 10032. Tel 212-926-2234; *Pres* Theodore S Beardsley; *Dir* Mitchell A Codding; *Cur Paintings & Metalwork* Marcus Burke; *Cur Archaeology & Sculpture* Constancio del Alamo; *Cur Iconography* Patrick Lenaghan
Open Tues - Sat 10 AM - 4 PM, Sun 1 - 4 PM. No admis fee. Estab 1904 by Archer Milton Huntington as a free public museum and library devoted to the culture of Hispanic peoples. Average Annual Attendance: 15,000. Mem: 100 plus 300 corresponding members; membership by election
Income: Financed by endowment
Purchases: Hispanic objects in various media
Collections: †Archaeology; †costumes; customs; †decorative arts of the Iberian peoples; †paintings; †photographic reference files; †sculpture; †prints
Exhibitions: Permanent gallery exhibits are representative of the arts and cultures of Iberian Peninsula from prehistory to the present. Sorolla, an 80th Anniversary Exhibition
Publications: Works by members of the staff and society on Spanish art, history, literature, bibliography, with special emphasis on the collections of the society
Activities: Sales shop sells books, prints & slides
L **Library,** 613 W 155th St, 10032. Tel 212-926-2234; *Cur* Gerald J MacDonald; *Cur Manuscripts & Rare Books* John O'Neill
Open Tues - Fri 1 - 4:15 PM, Sat 10 AM - 4:15 PM, cl Aug, Christmas holidays & other holidays. Estab 1904 as a free reference library to present the culture of Hispanic peoples. Reference only
Income: Financed by endowment
Library Holdings: Vols 250,000; Other — Clipping files, exhibition catalogs, manuscripts 200,000, memorabilia, original art works, pamphlets, photographs, prints, reproductions, sculpture
Special Subjects: Antiquities-Roman, Art History, Costume Design & Construction, Historical Material, History of Art & Archaeology, Laces, Manuscripts, Maps, Metalwork, Painting - Spanish, Porcelain, Prints, Religious Art, Silversmithing, Textiles, General culture of Spain & Portugal, Liberian Art, Literature
Activities: Sales shop sells reproductions, prints & slides

M **HUDSON GUILD,** Joe & Emily Lowe Art Gallery, 441 W 26th St, 10001. Tel 212-760-9800; *Gallery Dir* James Furlong
Open Mon & Fri 4 - 7 PM. No admis fee. Estab 1948 for exhibition of contemporary art. A modern facility within the Hudson Guild Building. The Art Gallery is also open for all performances of the Hudson Guild Theatre
Income: Financed by the Joe & Emily Lowe Foundation

M **ILLUSTRATION HOUSE INC,** Gallery Auction House, 96 Spring St, 7th Flr, 10012. Tel 212-966-9444; FAX 212-966-9425; Elec Mail illushse@interport.net; Internet Home Page Address http://www.intetport.net/-illushe. *Pres* Walt Reed; *VPres* Roger Reed; *Asst Dir* Fred Taraba; *Gallery Mgr* Jim Pratzon; *Painting Restorer* Jill Pratzon
Open 10:30 AM - 5:30 PM. Estab 1974 devoted to exhibition & selling original paintings & drawings of America's great illustrators (1880-1990)
Collections: Illustration Art Reference
Exhibitions: Art Pertaining to Illustration (1880-1980); An Eye for Character: The Illustrations of E F Ward; 100 Years of Comic Art; Pulps & Paperbacks: Sensational Art from the Twenties to the Fifties; semi-annual action of original illustration art of full range of media & genre
Publications: The Illustration Collector, subscription
Activities: Sales shop books & original art

A **INDEPENDENT CURATORS INC,** 799 Broadway, Ste 205, 10003. Tel 212-254-8200; FAX 212-477-4781; Elec Mail ici@inch.com. *Exec Dir* Sandra Lang; *Assoc Dir* Judith Olch Richards; *Registrar* Jack Coyle
Estab 1975 as a non-profit traveling exhibition service specializing in contemporary art
Income: $750,000
Exhibitions: After Matisse; After Perestroika: Kitchenmaids or Stateswomen; After Photography; The American Experience: Contemporary Immigrant Artists; The Analytical Theatre: New Art from Britain; At the Threshold of the Visible: Minuscule & Small-Scale Art, 1964-1996; Contemporary Illustrated Books: Word & Image, 1967-1988; Content & Discontent in Today's Photography; Critiques of Pure Abstraction; Dark Decor; Departures: Photography 1923-1990; A Different War: Vietnam in Art; Do It; Drawn in the Nineties; Embedded Metaphor; Empty Dress: Clothing as Surrogate; Eternal Metaphors: New Art from Italy; Eye for I: Video Self-Portraits; First Generation: Women & Video; Good Stories Well Told; From Media to Metaphor: Art About AIDS; Image & Memory: Latin American Photography 1880-1992; Large Scale Drawings; Liquiform: Visualizing Liquidity; Imagenes Liricas; Life & Image; Making it Real; Matters of Fact: New Art from Glasgow; Monumental Propaganda; Multiple Exposure; New Spanish Visions; No Laughing Matter; Of Two Minds: Asian-American Video: 1977-1993; Meret Oppenheim: Beyond the Teacup; Presence of Absence (wallworks); Print Portfolio: Selections from the Sol Lewitt Collection; David Smith: Medals for Dishonor; Team Spirit; Through the Path of Echoes: Contemporary Art in Mexico; Tradition & Conflict: Images of a Turbulent Decade; Transformers; Unfaithful Realities: Six Artists from Brazil; Video Transformations
Publications: Exhibition catalogs
Activities: Originate traveling exhibitions

M **INTAR LATIN AMERICAN GALLERY,** 420 W 42nd St, 10036. Tel 212-695-6135; FAX 212-268-0102; *Dir* Eduardo Casares
Open Mon - Fri Noon - 6 PM. No admis fee. Estab 1978. Assists & exhibits artists of diverse racial backgrounds. Devoted to artists who inhabit a dimension of their own in which the tension between singularity & universality has been acknowledged successfully. Only Hispanic gallery in area. Average Annual Attendance: 7000
Income: Financed by endowment
Publications: Exhibition catalogues
Activities: Lect open to public; gallery talks; originates traveling exhibitions

M **THE INTERCHURCH CENTER,** Galleries at the Interchurch Center, 475 Riverside Dr, 10115. Tel 212-870-2933; FAX 212-870-2440; *Cur* Dorothy Cochran
Open daily 9 AM - 5 PM. No admis fee. Estab 1969. Two exhibit spaces Treasure Room Gallery 2000 sq ft, Corridor Gallery 20 self-lite cases which line North & South Corridor each approximately 36 x 50
Exhibitions: Rotating exhibits, 10 per year
Publications: 475, monthly

L   The Interchurch Center, 475 Riverside Dr, 10115. Tel 212-870-2933; FAX 212-870-2440; Elec Mail icelib1@metgate.metro.org. *Dir & Cur Galleries* Dorothy Cochran; *Pres Exec Dir of Interchurch Center* Mary McNamara
Open Mon - Fri 9 AM - 5 PM. Estab 1959 to enhance the employee environment & be a New York City neighborhood art resources. 2000 sq ft (Treasure Room Gallery) & twenty (46 x 36) built in, self-light wall display cases. Average Annual Attendance: 4000
Income: $6,000,000
Purchases: $6000
Library Holdings: Vols 14,000; Per subs 95
Exhibitions: Changing exhibitions on a 10 month schedule
Publications: 475 Newsletter, monthly
Activities: Noon time music & arts programming; lect open to public, 5 vis lectr per year; concerts; gallery talks; tours

INTERNATIONAL CENTER FOR ADVANCED STUDIES IN ART
For further information, see National and Regional Organizations

A   INTERNATIONAL CENTER OF MEDIEVAL ART, INC, The Cloisters, Fort Tryon Park, 10040. Tel 212-928-1146; FAX 212-928-1146; Elec Mail 73430.2037@compuserve.com. *Pres* Charles T Little; *VPres* Dorothy F Glass; *Treas* Paula Gerson
Estab 1956 as The International Center of Romanesque Art, Inc. The International Center of Medieval Art was founded to promote greater knowledge of the arts of the Middle Ages, & to contribute to & make available the results of new research. Sponsor sessions at the annual conferences of the Medieval Institute of Western Michigan University, Kalamazoo the College Art Association Annual Conference & the International Medieval Congress at Leeds, England; keeps its members informed as to events of interest to medievalists; sponsors the Limestone Sculpture Provenance Project. Mem: 1400; dues benefactor $1000, supporting $500, contributing $100, institutions $50, active foreign countries $40, active US $35, student $15; annual meeting in Feb, in conjunction with College Art Association of America
Publications: Gesta (illustrated journal), two issues per year; ICMA Newsletter, 3 issues per year; Romanesque Sculpture in American Collections, New England Museums; Gothic Sculpture in American Collections
Activities: Lect open to public; exhibitions & symposia

M   INTERNATIONAL CENTER OF PHOTOGRAPHY, 1130 Fifth Ave, 10128. Tel 212-860-1777; FAX 212-360-6490; *Dir* Willis Hartshorn; *Dir Educ* Philip Block; *Deputy Dir for Development* Ann Doherty; *Deputy Dir for Adminr* Steve Rooney; *Public Information Dir* Phyllis Levine; *Cur of Coll* Miles Barth; *Traveling Exhibits Coordr* Marion Kocot
Open Tues 11 AM - 8 PM, Wed - Sun 11 AM - 6 PM, cl Mon. Admis adults $4, students & senior citizens $2.50, volunteer contributions Tues 6 - 8 PM. Estab 1974 to encourage & assist photographers of all ages & nationalities who are vitally concerned with their world & times, to find & help new talents, to uncover & preserve forgotten archives & to present such work to the pub. Maintains five exhibition galleries showing a changing exhibition program of photographic expression & experimentation by over 350 photographers. Average Annual Attendance: 100,000. Mem: 7000; dues $50 & up
Income: Financed by public & private grants
Collections: The core of the collection is 20th century documentary photography, with a companion collection of examples of master photographs of the 20th century including Siskind, Abbott, Capa, Callahan, Feininger, Hine & Cartier-Bresson. Major holdings include works from the documentary tradition as well as fashion & other aesthetic genres
Exhibitions: Along the Frontier-Ann Hamilton, Bruce Nauman, Francesc Torres, Bill Viola; Chim, The Photographs of David Seymour; Feeling the Spirit-Searching the World for the People of Africa by Chester Higgins Jr; Annie Leibovitz Photographs 1970-1994; David Levinthal 1975-1996; Talking Pictures-People Speak about the Photographs that Speak to Them; Weegee's World-Life, Death & the Human Drama; Written in Memory-Portraits of the Holocaust, Photographs by Jeffrey Wolin
Publications: Annual report; monographs; exhibition catalogs, programs guide
Activities: Classes for adults & children; docent training; lect open to public; gallery talks; tours; awards; book traveling exhibitions; originate traveling exhibitions; museum shop sells books, magazines, original art
L   Library, 1130 Fifth Ave, 10128. Tel 212-860-1787; FAX 212-360-6490; *Public Information Dir* Phyllis Levine
Reference only
Library Holdings: Vols 9000; Per subs 100; AV — A-tapes, cassettes, fs, Kodachromes, slides, v-tapes; Other — Clipping files, exhibition catalogs, pamphlets
Special Subjects: Photography
Collections: Archives contains films, video tapes & audio recordings of programs related to photographs in the collections as well as programs about the subject & history of photography
M   Midtown, 1133 Avenue of the Americas, 10036. Tel 212-768-4682; FAX 212-368-4688; *Dir* Willis Hartshorn
Open Tues 11 AM - 8 PM, Wed - Sun 11 AM - 6 PM, cl Mon. Admis $4, students & senior citizens $2.50. Estab 1989. Maintains eight exhibition galleries
Activities: Classes for adults & children; docent training; lect open to public; gallery talks; tours; originate traveling exhibitions; museum shop sells books, magazines, prints & slides

INTERNATIONAL FOUNDATION FOR ART RESEARCH, INC
For further information, see National and Regional Organizations

JAPAN SOCIETY, INC
M   Japan Society Gallery, 333 E 47th St, 10017. Tel 212-832-1155, 755-6752; FAX 212-715-1262; *Pres Japan Society* William H Gleysteen Jr; *Dir* Dr Gunhild Avitabile; *Asst Dir* Elizabeth Rogers
Open Tues - Sun 11 AM - 5 PM, cl Mon. No admis fee; suggested contribution. Estab 1907, bi-cultural membership organizations to deepen understanding and friendship between Japan and the United States. Reference library. Average Annual Attendance: 100,000. Mem: 3000 individual; dues $1500, $750,

$500, $250, $125, $75, $55, $30; annual meeting in Oct
Income: Financed by mem & donations
Collections: Japan Society permanent collection: ceramics, paintings, prints, sculpture & woodblocks
Exhibitions: Modern Japanese Ceramics in American Collections. Japan: A Cartographic Vision, European Printed Maps from the Early 16th to 19th Century
Publications: Japan Society Newsletter, monthly; exhibition catalogs accompaning each exhibition
Activities: Educ dept; docent training; lect open to public; gallery talks; originate traveling exhibitions; sell books & catalogues
L   Library, 333 E 47th St, 10017. Tel 212-832-1155; FAX 212-715-1279; *Dir* Reiko Sassa; *Asst Librn* Merle Okada
Open Tues - Thurs 10 AM - 5 PM. Estab 1971
Income: Financed by mem
Library Holdings: Vols 14,000; Per subs 35; Other — Clipping files, pamphlets
Publications: What Shall I Read on Japan

M   THE JEWISH MUSEUM, 1109 Fifth Ave, 10128. Tel 212-423-3200; FAX 212-423-3232; *Dir* Joan H Rosenbaum; *Adminr* Samantha Gilbert; *Chief Cur* Susan T Goodman; *Deputy Dir Adminr* Jane Dunne; *Dir Public Relations* Anne J Scher; *Dir Educ* Judith Siegel; *Deputy Dir Curatorial Affairs* Eric Zafron; *Dir Museum Shop* Debbie Schwab; *Deputy Dir External Affairs* Lynn Thommen; *Cur Fine Arts* Norman Kleeblatt; *Cur of Judaica* Dr Vivian B Mann
Open Sun, Mon, Wed & Thur 11 AM - 5:45 PM, Tues 11 AM - 8 PM. Admis adults $7, students with ID cards & senior citizens $5, members & children under 12 free. Estab 1904 to preserve & present the Jewish cultural tradition. Three exhibition floors devoted to the display of ceremonial objects & fine art in the permanent collection, special exhibitions from the permanent collections & photographs & contemporary art on loan. Average Annual Attendance: 189,000. Mem: 13,000; dues $60 & up
Income: Financed by mem, grants, individual contributions & organizations
Collections: †Contemporary art; graphics; †Jewish ceremonial objects; †paintings; †textiles; comprehensive collection of Jewish ceremonial art; Harry G Friedman Collection of Ceremonial Objects; Samuel Friedenberg Collection of Plaques & Medals; Rose & Benjamen Mintz Collection of Eastern European Art; Harry J Stein-Samuel Freidenberg Collection of Coins from the Holy Land
Exhibitions: Gardens & Ghettos: The Art of Jewish Life in Italy; Too Jewish: Challenging Traditional Identities
Publications: Annual report; exhibition catalogs; newsletter, quarterly; poster & graphics; program brochures
Activities: Classes & programs for children; dramatic programs; docent training; lect open to public, 6 vis lectr per year; concerts; gallery talks; tours; originate traveling exhibitions organized & circulated museum trips to Europe, once or twice per year; museum shop sells books, magazines, original art, reproductions, prints, slides, needlecrafts, posters, catalogs & postcards
L   Library, 1109 Fifth Ave, 10128. Tel 212-423-3200; FAX 212-423-3232; *Cur of Judaica* Dr Vivian B Mann
Reference library open to staff only
Income: Financed by Jewish Museum budget & private sources
Purchases: $3000
Library Holdings: Vols 1250; AV — A-tapes, cassettes, slides, v-tapes; Other — Clipping files, exhibition catalogs, pamphlets, photographs
Special Subjects: Judaica
Collections: Esther M Rosen Slide Library (contains slides of objects in the museum's collection)

A   KENKELEBA HOUSE, INC, Kenkeleba Gallery, 214 E Second St, 10009. Tel 212-674-3939; *Dir* Corrine Jennings; *Art Dir* Joe Overstreet
Open Wed - Sat 11 AM - 6 PM. No admis fee. Committed to the goals of presenting, preserving & encouraging the development of art excluded from the cultural mainstream. Supports experimental & interdisciplinary approaches. Features exhibitions of contemporary & modern painting, sculpture, experimental media, performance, poetry readings & literary forums
Collections: 20th Century African American Artists
Exhibitions: Eleanor Magid & Tom Kendall; Frank Stewart & Adal (photography)

M   KENNEDY GALLERIES, Art Gallery, 730 Fifth Ave, 10019. Tel 212-541-9600; FAX 212-333-7451; *Chmn* Lawrence Fleischman
Open to public with restrictions
Publications: American Art Journal

M   THE KITCHEN CENTER, 512 W 19th St, 10011. Tel 212-255-5793; FAX 212-645-4258; *Exec Dir* Bernadette Speach; *Prog Dir* Scott Macaulay; *Publicity Dir* Eric Latzki
Estab 1971 as a center for video art & a showcase for experimental & avant-garde music
Exhibitions: Exhibitions held in the gallery, often incorporating video, audio & experimental performing arts, including dance & performance art

L M KNOEDLER & CO, INC, Library, 19 E 70th St, 10021. Tel 212-794-0567; FAX 212-772-6932; *Librn* Melissa DeMedeiros
Open Mon - Fri 10 AM - 5 PM to researchers by appointment only. Research by appointment on a fee basis, for scholars, museum curators & students use
Income: Financed by usage fees
Library Holdings: Vols 55,000; Per subs 27; Auction catalogs; Micro — Fiche; Other — Clipping files, exhibition catalogs, pamphlets, photographs
Special Subjects: Painting - American, Painting - European, Modern & Contemporary Art

M   LAMAMA LA GALLERIA, 6 E First St, 10003. Tel 212-505-2476; *Dir & Cur* Lawry Smith
Open Tues - Sun 1 - 6 PM. Admis by donation. Estab 1983 for exhibition of emerging artists. 2500 sq ft, bi-level. Average Annual Attendance: 10,000. Mem: 3000; dues $20; biennial meetings in Oct & May
Activities: Classes for adults & children; lectures open to public, 6 vis lectr per year; concerts; gallery talks

M **LINCOLN CENTER FOR THE PERFORMING ARTS,** Cork Gallery, 70 Lincoln Ctr Plaza, 9th Flr, 10023. Tel 212-875-5151; FAX 212-875-5122; *Pres* Nathan Leventhal; *Gallery Dir* Jenneth Webster
Open Mon - Sun 10 AM - 10 PM. No admis fee. Estab in 1971 to provide a show case for young & unknown artists. One 60 ft x 10 ft wall covered in white linen, two smaller walls, 11 ft & 8 ft 6 inches, respectively, plus two 15 ft bay windows. Average Annual Attendance: 15,000
Exhibitions: 26 annual exhibitions (all self-produced by art group that exhibiting)

M **LOWER EAST SIDE PRINTSHOP, INC,** 59-61 E Fourth St, 6th Flr, 10003. Tel 212-673-5390; FAX 212-673-5390; *Exec Dir* Dusica Kirjakovic
Open Mon, Wed & Fri Noon - 6 PM. No admis fee. Estab 1968
Collections: Lower East Side Printshop Archive, prints created by artists involved in LESP programs since 1972

MANHATTAN PSYCHIATRIC CENTER
M **Sculpture Garden,** Ward's Island, 10035. Tel 212-369-0500, Ext 3022; *Project Coordr* Helen Thomas-Williams
Open Mon - Sun 10 AM - sundown. No admis fee. Estab 1977 to enhance hospital environment & offer exhibition area to new as well as estab sculptors. Hospital grounds are used to site outdoor sculpture, mostly on temporary basis. Artists may contact Manhattan Psychiatric Center directly to arrange for possible display of work
Exhibitions: Clovis, Glen Zwygardt; The Emerging Sun, Vivienne Thaul Wechter; The Gazebo, Helene Brandt; Map of Time, Time of Map, Toshio Sasaki; Rock Garden Sanctuary, Gigi & Paul Franklin; Roman Garden Sites Continued; Steel Toys, Elizabeth Egbert
M **East River Gallery,** Meyers Bldg, 13th Flr, Ward's Island, 10035. Tel 212-369-0500, Ext 3250; *Sr Recreation Therapist* Jill Brock
Open Mon, Wed & Fri 1 - 3 PM & by appointment. No admis fee. Estab 1994 to publicly display & sell resident artist's works. Professionally organized, publicly accessible artspace, uniquely located in a psychiatric hospital & representing the residents' creative work. The gallery is set up for the pub to view & purchase artwork, conduct research & select works for outside exhibition
Exhibitions: Recent Work: Painting, Drawing, Sculpture; Art Works! Soho (paintings, drawings & sculpture)
Activities: Classes for resident artists only; lect for members only; individual paintings & original objects of art lent to gallery & restaurant owners for public shows & researchers of approved studies; sales shop sells original art

M **THE MARBELLA GALLERY INC,** 28 E 72nd St, 10021. Tel 212-288-7809; *Dir* Mildred Thaler Cohen
Estab 1971 to buy & sell American art of the 19th century & early 20th century
Activities: Lect open to public; book traveling exhibitions 2 per year

M **MARYMOUNT MANHATTAN COLLEGE GALLERY,** 221 E 71 St, 10021. Tel 212-517-0400; FAX 212-517-0413; *Dir* Karen Harris
Open 12:30 - 8 PM. No admis fee. Estab 1982 as a showcase for unaffiliated artists. Gallery is 30 x 40 ft. Average Annual Attendance: 2500
Exhibitions: Dorothy Gillespie; Liz Whitney Quisgar
Activities: Lect by artist

M **THE METROPOLITAN MUSEUM OF ART,** Main Bldg, 1000 Fifth Ave, 10028. Tel 212-535-7710 (General Information), 879-5500 (Museum Offices); FAX 212-570-3879; *Chmn Board Trustees* Arthur Ochs Sulzberger; *Pres* William H Luers; *Dir* Philippe de Montebello; *Assoc Dir* Doralynn Pines; *Assoc Dir Educ* Kent Lydecker; *Dir Communiations* Harold Holzer; *Assoc Dir Exhibits* Mahrukh Tarapor; *VPres Operations* Richard Morsches; *VPres Finance & Treas* Diana T Murray; *VPres Development & Membership* Emily Rafferty; *VPres Merchandising Activities* John Curran; *Admin Human Resources* Carol S Cantrell; *Chmn American Art Dept* John K Howat; *Cur American Decorative Art* Morrison H Hecksher; *Chmn Ancient Near Eastern Art* Prudence O Harper; *Cur Arms & Armor* Stuart Pyhrr; *Chief Librn* William B Walker; *Assoc Cur Drawings* Helen Mules; *Cur Egyptian Art* Dorothea Arnold; *Lila Acheson Wallace Research Cur Egyptology* Christine Lilyquist; *Chmn European Paintings* Everett Fahy; *Cur-in-Charge Prints & Illustrated Books* Colta Ives; *Chmn European Sculture & Decorative Arts* Olga Raggio; *Sr Cur Asian Art* James C Y Watt; *Cur Asian Art* Martin Lerner; *Cur-in-Charge Greek & Roman Art* Carlos A Picon; *Cur Greek & Roman Art* Joan R Mertens; *Cur Robert Lehman Collection* Laurence Kanter; *Cur Musical Instruments* Laurence Libin; *Cur American Paintings & Sculpture* H Barbara Weinberg; *Cur Arts of Africa, Oceania & the Americas* Julie Jones; *Cur Costume Institute* Richard Martin; *Special Consultant for Asian Affairs* Wen Fong; *Cur Islamic Art* Daniel Walker; *Chmn Medieval Art & the Cloisters* William D Wixom; *Chmn Twentieth Century Art* William S Lieberman; *Conservator Objects* James H Frantz; *Conservator Paintings* Hubert von Sonnenberg; *Conservator-in-Charge Paper* Helen K Otis; *Conservator Textiles* Nobuko Kajitani; *Cur Photographs* Maria Hambourg; *Program Mgr Concerts & Lectures* Hilde Limondjian
Open Tues - Thurs & Sun 9:30 AM - 5:15 PM, Fri & Sat 9:30 AM - 8:45 PM, cl Mon. Admis suggested for adults $6, students & senior citizens $3. Estab 1870 to encourage & develop the study of the fine arts & the application of arts to life; of advancing the general knowledge of kindred subjects & to that end of furnishing popular instruction & recreation. Average Annual Attendance: 4,700,000. Mem: 97,245; dues patron $4000, sponsor $2000, donor $900, contributing $600, sustaining $300, dual $125, individual $70, student $30, national associate $35
Income: $78,146,461 (financed by endowment, mem, city & state appropriations & other)
Collections: †Acquisitions-Departments: Africcna, Oceanic; American decorative arts, paintings & sculpture; †Ancient Near Eastern art; †arms & armor; †Asian art; †Costume Institute; †drawings; †Egyptian art; †European paintings, sculpture & decorative arts; †Greek & Roman art; †Islamic art; Lehman Collection, †medieval art & The Cloisters; †musical instruments; †prints; †photographs; †Twentieth Century Art Exhibitions
Exhibitions: (1997) Following the Stars: Images of the Zodiac in Islamic Art, The Florene M Schoenborn Collection; The Glory of Byzantium; Indian Court Painting: 16th-19th Century; The Four Seasons; Cartier: 1900-1939; The Human Figure in Transition, 1900-1945: American Sculpture from the Museum's Collection; The Iris & B Gerald Cantor Roof Garden; Prints in the Age of Albrecht Durer & Lucas Van Layden; The New Chinese Galleries; Ivan Albright: Magic Realist; Georgia O'Keeffe: A Portrait by Alfred Stieglitz; Picasso: The Engraver, 1900-1942. (1997-98) Jackson Pollock: Sketchbooks & Drawings; Filippino Lippi & His Circle; Flowers Underfoot: Indian Carpets of the Mughal Era; King of the World, A Mughal Manuscript from the Royal Library, Windsor Castle; Richard Pousette-Dart in the Metropolitan Museum of Art: Works from the Artist's Estate
Publications: Bulletin, quarterly; Calendar, bi-monthly; The Journal, annually; exhibition catalogs, scholarly books
Activities: Classes for adults & children; docent training; films; programs for the disabled touch collection; lect open to public; concerts; gallery talks; tours; outreach; exten dept serves community programs for greater New York City area; color reproductions, individual paintings & original objects of art lent to other institutions; book traveling exhibitions; originate traveling exhibitions to US museums; museum shop sells books, magazines, original art, reproductions, prints, slides, children's activities, records, post cards & posters
L **Thomas J Watson Library,** 1000 Fifth Ave, 10028-0198. Tel 212-650-2221; FAX 212-570-3847; Elec Mail Internet: metart4@metgate.metro.org. *Chief Librn* Doralynn S Pines; *Acquisitions Librn & Bibliographer* Kenneth Soehner; *Systems Librn* Patricia J Barnett; *Serials Librn* Evalyn Stone; *Reader Servs Librn* Linda Seckelson; *Conservation Librn* Mindell Dubansky
Open Tues - Fri 10 AM - 4:40 PM, cl holidays & Aug. Estab 1880 for the use of the curatorial, educational & other staff; privileges are extended to qualified researchers & graduate students with appropriate identification. Reference library
Income: Financed by endowment
Library Holdings: Vols 350,000; Per subs 2250; Auction catalogs; Original documents; Micro — Fiche, reels; AV — Fs; Other — Clipping files, exhibition catalogs, manuscripts, memorabilia, pamphlets
Special Subjects: Aesthetics, Afro-American Art, American Western Art, Antiquities-Assyrian, Antiquities-Byzantine, Antiquities-Egyptian, Antiquities-Etruscan, Antiquities-Greek, Antiquities-Oriental, Antiquities-Persian, Painting, Prints and Drawings of all Countries and Periods
Collections: Art Auction Catalogs
L **Dept of Drawings & Prints,** 1000 Fifth Ave, 10028-0198. Tel 212-570-3920; FAX 212-570-3879; *Cur in Charge* Dr George R Goldner
Open Tues - Fri 10 AM - 12:30 PM & 2 - 5 PM by appointment. Estab 1917 to collect & preserve prints, illustrated books & drawings for ornament & architecture. Has 3 exhibition galleries
Library Holdings: Other — Original art works, prints
Special Subjects: Architecture, Art History, Decorative Arts, Drawings, Etchings & Engravings, Illustration, Landscape Architecture, Portraits, Printmaking, Prints, Woodcuts, Bookplates, Lithographs, Illustrated Books
L **Photograph & Slide Library,** 1000 Fifth Ave, 10028. Tel 212-879-5500, Ext 3261; FAX 212-861-2458; *Chief Librn* Priscilla Farah; *Assoc Museum Librn* Mary Doherty; *Assoc Museum Librn* Beatrice Epstein; *Assoc Museum Librn* Susan M Bresnan; *Asst Museum Librn* Ann Vollmann Bible; *Asst Museum Librn* Lenora Paglia
Open Tues - Fri 10 AM - 4:30 PM, cl holidays & Aug. Estab 1907 to provide a circulation (rental) library of slides covering the history of art; to provide color transparencies & photographs of the collections of the Metropolitan Mus of Art for publication purposes. Circ 100,000
Library Holdings: Color transparencies; AV — Lantern slides, slides 400,000; Other — Photographs
Special Subjects: Art History, Collections of the Metropolitan Museum of Art, particularly complete coverage of Western decorative arts
Collections: William Keighley Slide Collection covering Asia Minor, Austria, France, Germany, Italy and Spain; architecture and other arts of various periods
L **Robert Goldwater Library,** 1000 Fifth Ave, 10028-0198. Tel 212-570-3707; FAX 212-570-3879; Elec Mail indigene@interport.net. *Head Librn* Ross Day; *Librn* Barbara Mathe
Open Tues - Fri 10 AM - 4:30 PM, cl Aug. Estab 1957 as the library of the Mus of Primitive Art; holding of the Metropolitan Mus as of 1976; open Feb 1982. Primarily for reference
Income: Financed by endowment
Library Holdings: Vols 35,000; Per subs 175; Micro — Fiche, reels
Special Subjects: Anthropology, Archaeology, Ethnology, African, American Indian, Eskimo, Oceanic, Pre-Columbian and Primitive art
Publications: Primitive Art Bibliographies (1963 - 1971); Catalog of the Robert Goldwater Library (1982, 4 vols)
L **Robert Lehman Collection Library,** 1000 Fifth Ave at 82nd St, 10028. Tel 212-879-5500, Ext 3662; FAX 212-650-2542; *Librn* Tanya Pakhlazhgan
Estab 1975 to provide mus staff & researchers with a resource from which to obtain information about the Lehman Collection. Open by appointment only
Income: Financed by endowment
Library Holdings: Vols 10,000; Per subs 10; Original documents; Other — Clipping files, exhibition catalogs, manuscripts, memorabilia, pamphlets, photographs, reproductions
Special Subjects: Western European arts from the 13th-20th centuries with special emphasis on the art of Siena & Renaissance decorative arts
Collections: Archives containing books, correspondence, manuscripts and reproductions; photograph collection
L **The Costume Institute Library,** 1000 Fifth Ave, 10028-0198. Tel 212-650-2723; FAX 212-570-3970; Elec Mail ded8@ix.netcom.com, ilcrl@interport.net. *Cur* Richard Martin; *Library Coordr* Deirdre Donohue
Open Mon - Fri by appointment. Estab 1946 to study costume history, fashion & theatre design & any subject related to the subject of dress. For reference only
Income: Financed by bequest
Library Holdings: Vols 15,000; Per subs 40; Fashion plates; Original fashion sketches; Micro — Cards; AV — V-tapes; Other — Clipping files, exhibition catalogs, framed reproductions, manuscripts, memorabilia, original art works, photographs, prints
Special Subjects: Costume Design & Construction, Crafts, Decorative Arts, Display, Embroidery, Fashion Arts, Gold, Goldsmithing, Illustration, Jewelry, Laces, Metalwork, Textiles, Theatre Arts, Contemporary Fashion
Collections: Bergdorf-Goodman Fashion Sketches; Fashion Textile Archives; Mainbocher Fashion Sketches

L **Uris Library & Resource Center,** 1000 Fifth Ave. 10028. Tel 212-570-3788
Open Tues - Thurs, Sun 10 AM - 4:30 PM, Fri & Sat 10 AM - 8:30 PM. The
Uris Library & Resource Center is part of the educ department
Library Holdings: Vols 5000; Per subs 30
Special Subjects: Art Education, Art History, Painting - American, Painting -
European, Portraits, Sculpture, Antiquities, Portraits, Primitive art, Sculpture,
Tapestries

M **The Cloisters,** Fort Tryon Park, 10040. Tel 212-923-3700; FAX 212-795-3640;
Cable CLOMUSE. *Chmn & Cur* William D Wixom; *Cur* Timothy Husband; *Asst
Mgr* Jose Ortiz
Open Tues - Sat 10 AM - 4:45 PM, Sun & holidays Oct - Apr 1 - 4:45 PM, May
- Sept Noon - 4:45 PM. Estab 1938 to display in an appropriate setting works of
art & architecture of the Middle Ages. Medieval French cloisters incorporated
into the building, as well as the chapter house, a chapel & Romanesque apse; also
Medieval herb garden. Average Annual Attendance: 240,000
Collections: Frescoes, ivories, precious metalwork, paintings, polychromed
statues, stained glass, tapestries, and other French and Spanish architectural
elements
Exhibitions: The Wild Man: Medieval Myth and Symbolism; The Royal Abbey
of Saint-Denis in the Time of Abbot Suger (1122-1151)
Publications: A Walk Through The Cloisers; exhibition catalogs
Activities: Classes for adults and children; dramatic programs; lect open to
public; concerts; original objects of art lent to other museums; museum shop sells
books, reproductions and slides

L **The Cloisters Library,** Fort Tryon Park, 10040. Tel 212-923-3700, Ext 154;
FAX 212-795-3640; *Assoc Museum Librn* Lauren Jackson-Beck
Open Tues - Fri 9:30 AM - 4:30 PM. Estab 1938 to be used as a small highly
specialized reference library for the curatorial staff at The Cloisters; scholars &
accredited graduate students are welcome & qualified researchers by appointment
only. Reference library for the staff at The Cloisters; scholars & accredited
graduate students are welcome by appointment only
Income: Financed by endowment
Library Holdings: Vols 12,000; Per subs 58; Original documents; Micro — Fiche
9000, reels; AV — Slides 20,000; Other — Photographs 22,000
Special Subjects: Architecture, Art History, Enamels, Sculpture, Stained Glass,
Tapestries, Illuminated Manuscripts
Collections: George Grey Barnard Papers; Harry Bober Papers; Joseph & Ernest
Brummer Papers; Summer McKnight Crosby Papers; Demotte Photograph
Archive; Archives of the Cloisters

L **MIDMARCH ASSOCIATES,** Women Artists News Archive, 300 Riverside Dr,
Apt 8A, 10025. Tel 212-666-6990; *Ed* Sylvia Moore; *Exec Dir* Cynthia
Navaretta; *Ed* Judy Seigel
Open by appointment. Estab 1975 to maintain archival material on women artists
world wide
Income: Financed by public funding & contributions
Library Holdings: Other — Clipping files, exhibition catalogs, manuscripts,
memorabilia, original art works, pamphlets, photographs, sculpture
Special Subjects: Architecture, Art History, Ceramics, Conceptual Art,
Constructions, Crafts, Decorative Arts, Drawings, Film, Latin American Art,
Mixed Media, Pre-Columbian Art, Sculpture, Theatre Arts, Watercolors
Publications: Essays on Women Photographers 1840 - 1930; guide to Women's
Art Organizations & Directory for the Arts, bi-annually; Regional Series on
Women Artists (New England, Texas, California, Pacific Northwest), annually;
Voices of Women; Women Artists of the World; Women Artists News,
bimonthly; Talk That Changed Art, 1975 - 1990; Beyond Walls & Wars: Art,
Politics & Multiculturalism
Activities: Educ dept; lect provided

L **PIERPONT MORGAN LIBRARY,** 29 E 36th St, 10016. Tel 212-685-0008;
FAX 212-685-4740; *Pres* S Parker Gilbert; *Dir* Dr Charles E Pierce Jr; *Cur
Printed Books & Bindings* H George Fletcher; *Cur Medieval & Renaissance
Manuscripts* Dr John H Plummer; *Cur Medieval & Renaissance Manuscripts*
William M Voelkle; *Emeritus Cur Drawings & Prints* Felice Stampfle; *Cur
Drawings & Prints* Cara D Denison; *Cur Autograph Manuscripts* Robert Parks;
Cur Music Manuscripts J Rigbie Turner; *Cur Gilbert & Sullivan Coll* Frederic W
Wilson; *Assoc Cur Printed Books* Anna Lou Ashby; *Head Reader Serv* Inge
Dupont; *Registrar* David W Wright; *Public Affairs* Elizabeth Wilson; *Honorary
Cur Seals & Tablets* Dr Edith Porada
Open Tues - Sat 10:30 AM - 6 PM, Sun Noon - 6 PM, cl Mon during July &
Aug; reading room open to scholars Mon - Fri 9:30 AM - 4:45 PM. No admis
fee; suggested donation $5. Estab 1924 for research & exhibition purposes. The
Gallery has changing exhibition with Old Master drawings, Medieval &
Renaissance illuminated manuscripts, rare printed books & literary, historical, &
music manuscripts. Average Annual Attendance: 200,000. Mem: 1100; dues $35,
$50
Income: $4,000,000 (financed by endowment & mem)
Purchases: $1,000,000
Library Holdings: Vols 50,000; Per subs 170; Original documents; AV — Slides;
Other — Manuscripts, original art works
Collections: Ancient written records including seals, cuneiform tablets and
papyri; art objects; †autograph manuscripts; †book bindings; †early children's
books; †Medieval & Renaissance illuminated manuscripts; †later printed books;
†letters and documents; mezzotints; modern calligraphy; †music manuscripts;
†original drawing from 14th-19th centuries; †printed books before 1500;
Rembrandt prints
Exhibitions: Small Mischief; Master Drawings from the Albertina; Drawings
from the E V Thaw collection; the Apocalypse: 950 - 1800; Italian drawings from
the collection of Duke Roberto Ferretti; Merchants to Emperors: British Artists
in India; Mahler & Liszt
Publications: Report to the Fellows, triennial; books; catalogs; facsimiles
Activities: Lect open to the public, 8 vis lectr per year; tours; sales shop sells
books, reproductions, prints, slides, cards, calendars, address books and posters

M **MORRIS-JUMEL MANSION, INC,** 65 Jumel Terrace, 10032. Tel 212-923-
8008; *Pres* Thomas Morris; *Dir* Peter Apgar
Open Wed - Sun 10 AM - 4 PM. Estab 1904
as a Historic House Museum. Morris-Jumel Mansion consists of twelve period
rooms which are restored to represent the colonial, revolutionary & nineteenth-
century history of the mansion, highlighting its owners & inhabitants (the Morris
family, George Washington, Eliza Jumel & Aaron Burr). Average Annual
Attendance: 30,000. Mem: 200; contributors 500; dues $35-$2500
Income: Financed by mem, contributions & private sources
Collections: Architecture; †decorative art; †furniture of the 18th & 19th centuries
Publications: Morris-Jumel News, quarterly; exhibitions catalogs
Activities: Educ dept; docent training; lect open to public; concerts; tours;
originate traveling exhibitions; sales shop sells books, postcards, souvenirs

A **MUNICIPAL ART SOCIETY OF NEW YORK,** 457 Madison Ave, 10022. Tel
212-935-3960; FAX 212-753-1816; *Chmn* Brendan Sexton
Estab 1892, incorporated 1898. The Soc is the one organization in New York
where the layman, professional & business firm can work together to encourage
high standards for pub art, architecture, planning, landscaping & preservation in
the five boroughs. Mem: 4500; dues $25 & up; annual meeting in June
Collections: Photographs
Exhibitions: Reviewing the City's Edge; Rare Photographs by Stanford White
Publications: The Livable City, quarterly

L **Information Exchange,** 457 Madison Ave, 10022. Tel 212-935-3960; FAX 212-
753-1816; *Acting Dir* Ann Anielewski
Open Mon - Fri 10 AM - 1 PM. Estab 1979. For reference only
Library Holdings: Vols 1000; Per subs 100; Other — Clipping files
Special Subjects: Architecture, Historic Preservation, Landscape Architecture,
Public Art, Urban Planning in New York City
Publications: Information sheets, irregular

M **MUSEUM OF AFRICAN ART** (Formerly International Museum of African
Art), 593 Broadway, 10012. Tel 212-966-1313; FAX 212-966-1432; *Exec Dir*
Grace Stanislaus; *Co-Chmn* Adrian Munchin; *Assoc Cur* Carol Thompson;
Deputy Dir Open; *Comptroller* Patricia Cochran; *Cur Exhib* Erica Blumenfeld;
Educ Coordr Open
Open Tues 10 AM - 8 PM, Wed - Fri 10 AM - 5 PM, Sat 11 AM - 5 PM, Sun
Noon - 5 PM. Voluntary contribution adults $2.50, students, senior citizens &
children $1.50. Estab 1983 to exhibit the best in traditional African art. 5
galleries housed in 2 adjacent recently-restored turn-of- century townhouses.
Average Annual Attendance: 12,500. Mem: 800; dues vary
Income: $1,100,000 (financed by mem, foundation grant entrance fees, exhibition
fee & tours)
Purchases: $425,000
Exhibitions: Exhibitionism: Museums & African Art; Artists & Ancestors in
African Art; Animals in African Art: From the Familiar to the Marvelous
Publications: African Masterpieces from the Musee de L'Homme; Sets, Series &
Ensembles in African Art; Exhibition Catalogues
Activities: Docent training; lect Sundays open to public, 5-10 vis lectr per year;
tours; gallery talks; book traveling exhibitions 1-2 per year; originate traveling
exhibitions to circulate to other museums; museum shop sells catalogues, books

M **MUSEUM OF AMERICAN FOLK ART,** 2 Lincoln Square, 10023. Tel 212-
977-7298, Gallery 595-9533; *Dir* Gerard C Wertkin; *Public Relations Dir* Susan
Slamm
Open Tues - Sun 11:30 AM - 7:30 PM, cl Mon. No admis fee, suggested
donation $2. Estab 1961 for the collection & exhibition of American folk art in
all media, including painting, sculpture, textiles & painted & decorated furniture.
Single floor, cruciform shape gallery approx 3000 sq ft. Average Annual
Attendance: 100,000. Mem: 5000; dues $35 & up
Income: Financed by mem, state appropriation, personal donations
Collections: American folk paintings & watercolors; folk sculpture including shop
& carousel figures, shiphead figures, decoys, weathervanes, whirligigs, wood
carvings & chalkware; painted & decorated furniture; tradesmen's signs; textiles
including quilts, coverlets, stenciled fabrics, hooked rugs & samplers; works from
18th, 19th & 20th centuries
Publications: The Clarion, quarterly magazine
Activities: Educ dept; classes for adults; docent training; lect open to public;
gallery talks; tours; outreach programs; book traveling exhibitions; originate
traveling exhibitions to qualifying art & educational institutions; museum shop
sells books, reproductions & prints

L **Library,** 61 W 62nd St, 10023. Tel 212-977-7298, 977-7170; *Librn* Jill Keefe
Not open to pub except by appointment. Reference library
Library Holdings: Vols 10,000; Per subs 32; AV — Fs, motion pictures, slides, v-
tapes; Other — Clipping files, exhibition catalogs, manuscripts, memorabilia,
pamphlets, photographs, prints, reproductions

M **MUSEUM OF CHINESE IN THE AMERICAS,** 70 Mulberry St, 2nd Flr,
10013. Tel 212-619-4785; Elec Mail 212-619-4720. *Exec Dir* Winston J Dong Jr;
Deputy Dir Fabiana Chiu; *Prog Dir* Adrienne Cooper; *Co-Founder* Dr John K W
Tchen; *Co-Founder* Charlie Lai
Open Tues - Sun 10:30 AM - 5 PM, archives by appointment only. Admis adults
$3, seniors & students $1, members & children under 12 free. Estab 1980
dedicated to preserving 180 years of Chinese American history. Located in an
historic, century-old school building. Mem: Dues $35-$1000
Income: Financed by mem, pub & private funds
Collections: Archives: Chinese American history & culture, including oral
histories, photographs, documents, personal & organizational records, sound
recordings, textiles, artifacts & a library of over 2000 volumes covering Asian
American topics
Exhibitions: (1997) A Good Place to Land One's Feet: Brooklyn's Sunset Park
Chinese Community
Activities: Workshops; lect; walking tours; family events; museum shop sells
exhibition posters, gift items & over 80 titles of poetry, drama, fiction & non-
fiction on the culture & history of Chinese Americans & other Asian Americans

M **MUSEUM OF MODERN ART,** 11 W 53rd St, 10019-5498. Tel 212-708-9400, (Exhibit & Film Info) 708-9480; FAX 212-708-9889; Internet Home Page Address www.moma.org. Telex 6-2370; Cable MODERNART. *Pres & Chmn Board* Agnes Gund; *Chmn Emeritus* David Rockefeller; *VChmn Emeritus* Mrs Henry Ives Cobb; *VChmn* Mrs Frank Y Larkin; *VChmn* Donald B Marron; *VChmn* Richard E Solomon; *VChmn* Ronald S Lauder; *Treas* John Parkinson III; *Dir Museum* Glenn D Lowry; *Deputy Dir, Planning & Prog Support* James Snyder; *Chief Cur, Dept Film & Video* Mary Lee Bandy; *Coordr Exhib* Richard Palmer; *Acting Dir International Prog* Elizabeth Streibert; *Dir Public Information* Jessica Schuartz; *Dir Publications* Osa Brown; *Dir Development* Daniel Vecchitto; *Dir Visitor Servs* Jo Pike; *Chief Cur, Dept Painting & Sculpture* Kirk Varnedoe; *Chief Cur, Drawings* Margot Rowell; *Chief Cur, Dept Architecture & Design* Terence Riley; *Chief Cur, Dept Photography* Peter Galassi; *Chief Cur, Prints & Illustrated Books* Riva Castleman

Open daily 11 AM - 6 PM, Thurs & Fri Noon - 8:30 PM, cl Wed, Thanksgiving & Christmas. Admis adults $8, students & senior citizens $5, children under 16 accompanied by adult free, Thurs & Fri 5:30-8:30 pay what you wish. Estab 1929, the Mus offers an unrivaled survey of modern art from 1880 to the present. Designed in 1939 by Phillip Goodwin & Edward Durell Stone, the building is one of the first examples of the International Style in the US. Subsequent expansions took place in the 1950s & 1960s under the architect Philip Johnson, who also designed the Abby Aldrich Rockefeller Sculpture Garden. A major renovation, completed in 1984, doubled the Museum's gallery space & enhanced visitor facilities. Average Annual Attendance: 1,500,000. Mem: 52,000; dues student $25, others $45 & up

Income: Financed by admis, mem, sales of publications & other services & contributions

Collections: †Painting & sculptures over 2963; †drawings 5090; †prints 15,822; †illustrated books 20,423; †photographs 15,000; †architectural drawings 20,000; †architectural models 60; †design objects 3000; †posters & graphics 4000; films 10,000; †film stills over 3,000,000

Exhibitions: Robert Ryman; A Preview: The New Austrian Cultural Institute by Raimund; Joan Miro; Designed for Speed: 3 Automobiles by Ferrari; Masters of the Bauhaus: Wasily Kandinsky, Paul Klee & Lyonel Feininger; Frank Lloyd Wright: Architect; American Surrealist Photography; Masterpieces from the David & Peggy Rockefeller Collection: from Manet to Picasso; A Century of Artists Books; American Politicians; Mapping; Thresholds/O.M.A. at MoMA: Rem Koolhaas & the Place of Public Architecture. Jacob Lawrence: The Migration Series; Max Beckmann Prints from the Museum of Modern Art; Kandinsky: Compositions; Bruce Nauman: Inside/Out; Master Works for the Louise Reinhardt Smith Collection; Mutant Materials in Contemporary Design; Video Spaces; Stieglitz at Lake George; Transparencies. Piet Mondian: 1872-1944; Annette Messager; Roy de Carva; Antonin Artaud; Picasso & Portraiture: Representations & Transformation; Thinging Print: The Role of Prints, Books & Other Editions in Contemporary Art; Philip Johnson; Jasper Johns Retrospective

Publications: Annual report; books on exhibitions & artists; Members Quarterly; Members Calendar; monographs; catalogs; exhibitions catalogs

Activities: Classes for adults & children; lect open to public; concerts; gallery talks; tours; film showings, international in scope, illustrating the historic and esthetic development of the motion picture; scholarships & fels offered; art advisory service; originates traveling exhibitions; circulating film programs and video programs; sales shop sells publications, postcards, note & seasonal cards, posters, slides, calendars, design objects & furniture

L **Library,** 11 W 53rd St, 10019-5498. Tel 212-708-9433, 708-9430; FAX 212-333-1122; Elec Mail eimm@moma.org. *Chief Librn Adminr* Janis Ekdahl; *Chief Librn Technical Servs & Planning* Daniel Starr; *Assoc Librn Reference* Eumie Imm-Stroukoff

Open Mon - Fri 11 AM - 5 PM. Estab 1929 as a research library. For mus staff, art researchers & the pub

Library Holdings: Vols 140,000; Per subs 300; Artists files 70,000; Micro — Reels; AV — Cassettes, v-tapes; Other — Clipping files, exhibition catalogs, manuscripts, pamphlets

Special Subjects: Architecture, Art History, Collages, Conceptual Art, Drawings, Film, Graphic Design, Industrial Design, Intermedia, Latin American Art, Mixed Media, Photography, Posters, Prints, Sculpture, Design, Painting, Intermedia

Collections: †Archives of artists' groups; †artists' books; †avant-garde art; †Dada & Surrealism; †archive of museum publications; †Latin American art; personal papers of artists, writers, dealers; political art documentation/archives

Exhibitions: Fluxus: Selections from the Gilbert & Lila Silverman Collection, 1988-89 (catalog)

Publications: Annual Bibliography of Modern Art; catalog of the Library of the Museum of Modern Art

M **MUSEUM OF THE CITY OF NEW YORK,** 1220 Fifth Ave, 10029. Tel 212-534-1672; FAX 212-423-0758; *Dir* Robert R Macdonald; *Deputy Dir Admin & Finance* Ed Henry; *Assoc Dir Coll* Dr Jan Ramirez; *Deputy Dir Membership & Develop* Monica Willon

Open Wed - Sat 10 AM - 5 PM, Sun & holidays 1 - 5 PM, cl Mon. Admis suggested contribution. Estab 1923 to preserve the cultural accomplishments of New York City & to meet the needs & interests of the community of today. Permanent & temporary exhibition galleries on subjects related to mission. Average Annual Attendance: 350,000. Mem: 2500; dues $35 & up

Income: $3,000,000 (financed by private & non-profit institutions, individual contributions, city, state & federal funds)

Collections: †Costume collection; †decorative arts collection; marine collections; †paintings, sculpture, prints & †photographs collection; theatre & †music collection; †toy collection

Exhibitions: New York City History Fair; Jews in Colonial New York - The Levy Franks Family Portraits; Growing Old in Spanish Harlem; Broadway - 125 Years of Musical Theatre; Songs of My People - An African-American Self-Portrait

Publications: Annual report; exhibit catalogs; quarterly newsletter; quarterly programs brochure for members

Activities: Classes for adults & children; docent training; lect open to public; gallery talks; concerts; city walking tours; competitions with awards; original objects of art lent to affiliated institutions; lending collection contains sculptures, 40,000 books, 5000 original art works, 15,000 original prints, 2000 paintings & 300,000 photographs; book traveling exhibitions 1-2 per year; originate traveling exhibitions to other museums; museum shop sells books, reproductions, prints & slides

L **Library,** 1220 Fifth Ave, 10029. Tel 212-534-1672; FAX 212-534-5974; *Rights & Reproductions* Marguerite Lavin; *Assoc Dir Coll* Dr Jan S Ramirez

Library Holdings: Vols 8000; Per subs 10; Other — Clipping files, manuscripts, memorabilia, original art works, photographs, prints, reproductions

Special Subjects: History of New York City; History of New York Theatre

NATIONAL ACADEMY OF DESIGN
For further information, see National and Regional Organizations

NATIONAL ANTIQUE & ART DEALERS ASSOCIATION OF AMERICA, INC
For further information, see National and Regional Organizations

NATIONAL ASSOCIATION OF WOMEN ARTISTS, INC
For further information, see National and Regional Organizations

NATIONAL CARTOONISTS SOCIETY
For further information, see National and Regional Organizations

NATIONAL INSTITUTE FOR ARCHITECTURAL EDUCATION
For further information, see National and Regional Organizations

M **NATIONAL MUSEUM OF THE AMERICAN INDIAN,** George Gustav Heye Center, One Bowling Green, 10004. Tel 212-825-6700; FAX 212-825-8180; *Dir* W Richard West Jr; *Deputy Dir* Douglas E Evelyn; *Dir Public Affairs* Liz Hill; *Asst Dir Public Progs* Charlotte Heth; *Asst Dir Administration* Donna A Scott; *Deputy Asst Dir Public Progs* John Haworth; *Deputy Asst Dir Exhib* James Volkert; *Deputy Asst Dir Cultural Resources* George Horse Capture; *Dir NMAI National Campaign* John Colonghi; *Asst Dir NMAI National Campaign* Maggie Bertin; *Exhib Prog Mgr* Karen Fort; *Head Exhib NY* Peter S Brill; *Public Prog Coordr* Carolyn Rapkievian; *Head Publications* Terence Winch; *Resource Center Mgr* Marty Kreipe de Montano; *Head Film & Video Center* Elizabeth Weatherford; *Community Serv Coordr* Keevin Lewis; *Training Coordr* Alyce Sadongei; *Head Photo Archives* Pamela Dewey; *Acting Head Curatorial* Mary Jane Lenz; *Head Coll* Scott Merritt; *Head Conservation* Marian Kaminitz; *Repatriation Prog Mgr* Betty White; *Technology Prog Coordr* Robert Billingsley; *Facilities Planning Mgr* Duane Blue Spruce; *Budget Analyst* Kelly Bennett; *Human Resources Specialist* Carol Belovitch; *Admin Officer NY* Marty Lathan; *Facilities Mgr NY* Myroslaw Riznyk; *Museum Shop Mgr* Lilli Liell

Open daily 10 AM - 5 PM, Thurs until 8 PM, cl Christmas. No admis fee. Estab 1989 to recognize & affirm the historical & contemporary cultures & cultural achievements of the Native peoples of the Western Hemisphere. 20,000 sq ft exhibition galleries. Average Annual Attendance: 250,000. Mem: dues $20, $35, $100 charter mem

Income: Financed by trust, endowments & revenues, gifts, grants, contributions, mem & funds appropriated by Congress

Collections: Pre-Columbian art & historical materials; world's largest collection of art & the culture of the Indians of North, Central & South America

Exhibitions: (1997) Creations Journey: Native Americans Identity & Beliefs All Roads Are Good: Native Voices on Life & Culture;

Publications: Books, occasionally; brochures; catalogs; recordings; Smithsonian Runner Newsletter

Activities: Guided tours for children; lect open to public; concerts; gallery talks; tours; scholarships offered; individual paintings & original objects of art lent to museums, including tribal museums & cultural centers, non-profit institutions & other appropriate sites; originate traveling exhibitions; museum shop sells Indian crafts, jewelry, masks, pottery, beadwork, basketry, weavings, carvings, paintings, prints, books, slides, postcards & notepaper

M **THE NATIONAL PARK SERVICE, UNITED STATES DEPARTMENT OF THE INTERIOR,** The Statue of Liberty National Monument, Liberty Island, 10004. Tel 212-363-7620, 363-5804; FAX 212-363-8347, 363-6304; *Chief Cur* Diana Pardue; *Cur Coll* Geradine Santoro; *Cur Exhibits* Carl Rutberg; *Libr Technician* Barry Moreno

Open 9:30 AM - 5 PM. No admis fee, donations accepted. Estab 1972. Exhibit areas in base of Statue of Liberty & in Ellis Island Immigration Museum

Collections: Ellis Island Collection; Statute of Liberty Collection; Furniture Art Work, oral histories, prints, manuscripts, films & videos, books, periodicals, historic structures

Exhibitions: AMI exhibition on the immigration history of the USA; Statue of Liberty exhibit

Activities: Classes for children; dramatic programs; docent training; lect open to public; gallery talks; tours; individual paintings & original objects of art lent to other museums; book traveling exhibitions; sales shop sells books, magazines, original art, prints & slides

NATIONAL SCULPTURE SOCIETY
For further information, see National and Regional Organizations

NATIONAL SOCIETY OF MURAL PAINTERS, INC
For further information, see National and Regional Organizations

M **THE NEW MUSEUM OF CONTEMPORARY ART,** 583 Broadway, 10012. Tel 212-219-1222; FAX 212-431-5328; Elec Mail newmuseum@thorn.net. *Dir* Marcia Tucker

Open Wed - Fri & Sun Noon - 6 PM, Sat Noon - 8 PM, cl Mon & Tues. Estab 1977 to present to the pub new, provocative art that does not yet have wide pub exposure or critical acceptance. Average Annual Attendance: 80,000. Mem: 800; dues $35 & up

Income: Financed by endowment, mem, state appropriation, corporations, foundations & federal grants

Collections: Semi-permanent collections of paintings, prints, photos, sculptures

Publications: Exhibition catalogs; newsletter

Activities: Docent training; lect open to public, 3-4 vis lectr per year; gallery talks; tours; exten dept serves high schools in metropolitan area; book traveling exhibitions 1-2 per year; originate traveling exhibitions

L **The Soho Center Library,** 627 Broadway, 10012. Tel 212-219-1222; FAX 212-431-5328; *Dir* Marcia Tucker
Open Wed - Sun Noon - 6 PM, Sat Noon - 8 PM, 2 free hrs from 6 - 8 PM. Admis $4, students, seniors & artists $3.50. Estab 1985. Reference library, cl to pub
Income: Financed by mem & city appropriation
Library Holdings: Vols 200; Per subs 150
Special Subjects: Architecture, Art History, Conceptual Art, Film, Painting - American, Painting - Australian, Painting - British, Painting - Canadian, Painting - Dutch, Painting - European, Painting - French, Painting - German, Painting - Italian, Painting - Japanese, Painting - New Zealander

A **NEW YORK ARTISTS EQUITY ASSOCIATION, INC,** 498 Broome St, 10013. Tel 212-941-0130; *Exec Dir* Regina Stewart; *Pres* Arnold Gold; *Treas* Violet Baxter; *VPres* Bernard Olshan; *VPres* Donald Pierce; *VPres* Geoffrey Homan; *VPres* Brenda Tribush
Open 11 AM - 6 PM. Estab 1947 as a politically non-partisan group to advance the cultural, legislative, economic and professional interest of painters, sculptors, printmakers, and others in the field of visual arts. Various committees concerned with aims. Administrators of the Artists Welfare Fund, Inc. Mem: Over 3000; dues $30, meetings monthly
Income: Financed by dues
Publications: The Artists Proof newsletter, quarterly
Activities: Lect open to public; 6 - 8 vis lectr per year; symposiums & seminars Oct - May Art Thursday; trips to cultural institutions; advocacy; information services; artists benefits

A **NEW YORK HISTORICAL SOCIETY,** 2 W 77th St, 10024-5194. Tel 212-873-3400; FAX 212-874-8706; *Exec Dir* Betsy Gotbaum; *Asst to Dir* Gloria Yuen; *Sr Cur* Jack Rutland
Open Tues - Sun 10 AM - 5 PM, cl Mon & national holidays. Admis adults $3, senior citizens $2, children under 12 $1. Estab 1804 to collect & preserve material relating to the history of New York City & State. Maintains art gallery. Average Annual Attendance: 50,000. Mem: 2870; dues benefactor $25,000, patron $10,000, associate $5000, pintard friend $1000, pintard fellow $250, New-Yorker $100, participating $50, individual $35, senior citizen, non-resident & student $25
Income: $8,000,000 (financed by endowment, grants, contributions, federal, state & local government, mem, admis)
Collections: The Birds of America: Audubon's 433 original watercolors; architectural drawings, decorative arts, drawings, paintings, photographs, prints & sculpture. American paintings from the Colonial period to 20th century, including genre scenes, portraits & landscapes by major artists of this period
Activities: Classes for adults & children; lect open to public; concerts; gallery talks; tours; individual paintings & original objects of art lent to museums; lending collection contains 2700 paintings, 5000 drawings, 675 sculptures, 800 miniatures; book traveling exhibitions 3 per year; museum shop sells books, magazines, prints, reproductions, cards

L **Library,** 2 W 77th St, 10024. Tel 212-873-3400; FAX 212-875-1591; *Library Dir* Margaret Heilbrun
Open Wed - Fri Noon - 5 PM
Library Holdings: Vols 650,000; Per subs 150; AV maps 15,000, Micro film 50,000, Vertical files 10,000 (including menus); Micro — Cards 10,000, fiche, reels; AV — Fs 7500; Other — Clipping files, exhibition catalogs, manuscripts, memorabilia, original art works, pamphlets, photographs, prints, sculpture
Special Subjects: American History; New York City & State; Naval History, New York Genealogy
Collections: American Almanacs; American Genealogy; American Indian (accounts of & captivities); Early American Imprints; Early Travels in America; Early American Trials; Circus in America (Leonidas Westervelt); Civil War Regimental Histories & Muster Rolls; Jenny Lind (Leonidas Westervelt) Maps; Military History (Military Order of the Loyal Legion of the United States, Commandery of the State of New York) Military History & Science (Seventh Regiment Military Library); Naval & Marine History (Naval History Society); 18th & 19th Century New York City & New York State Newspapers; Slavery & the Civil War; Spanish American War (Harper); Among the Manuscript Collections; Horatio Gates, Alexander McDougall, Rufus King, American Fur Company, Livingston Family, American Art Union, American Academy of Fine Arts

L **THE NEW YORK PUBLIC LIBRARY,** Astor, Lenox & Tilden Foundations, Fifth Ave & 42nd St, 10018. Tel 212-930-0830; *Pres* Paul LeClerc
Estab 1895. Entire library contains over 30,000,000 items

L **Print Room,** Fifth Ave & 42nd St, Rm 308, 10018. Tel 212-930-0817; FAX 212-930-0530; *Cur Prints* Roberta Waddell; *Cur Photographs* Julia Van Haaften
Open by application to Special Collection Office, Tues - Sat 1 - 6 PM, cl Sun, Mon & holidays. Estab 1899
Library Holdings: Vols 25,000; Stereographs 72,000; Other — Photographs 15,000, prints 175,000
Special Subjects: Graphic artists and catalogs of their works, original fine prints of the past six centuries with special emphasis on 19th century French and American, contemporary American and European, prints, techniques and illustrated books, photographers & history of photography, original 19th century topographical photographs & photo-illustrated books, American & European
Collections: Samuel Putnam Avery Collection (primarily 19th century prints); Radin Collection of Western European bookplates; British & American caricatures; Beverly Chew bequest of Milton & Pope portraits; Eno Collection of New York City Views McAlpin Collection of George Washington Portraits; Smith Collection of Japanese Prints; Phelps Stokes Collection of American Views; Lewis Wickes Hine Collection; Robert Dennis Collection of Stereoscopic Views; Pageant of America Collection; Romana Javitz Collection

L **Spencer Collection,** Fifth Ave & 42nd St, Rm 308, 10018. Tel 212-930-0817; FAX 212-930-0530; *Asst Dir for Art, Prints & Photographs & Cur Spencer Coll* Robert Rainwater
Open by application to Special Collection Office, Tues - Sat 1 - 6 PM, cl Sun & holidays
Library Holdings: Vols 9000
Special Subjects: Rare illustrated books & illuminated manuscripts in all languages of all countries & of all periods, constituting the development of book illustration & fine bindings

L **Art, Prints & Photographs Division,** Fifth Ave & 42nd St, Rm 313, 10018. Tel 212-930-0834; *Cur Art & Arch Coll* Paula A Baxter
Open Tues 11 AM - 7:30 PM, Wed 11 AM - 6 PM, Thurs, Fri & Sat 10 AM - 6 PM, cl Sun & Mon. Estab 1911 for reference
Library Holdings: Vols 275,000; Other — Clipping files, exhibition catalogs, pamphlets
Special Subjects: Architecture, Art History, Ceramics, Costume Design & Construction, Decorative Arts, Drawings, Furniture, Glass, Goldsmithing, Interior Design, Ivory, Jade, Jewelry, Latin American Art, Metalwork, Mexican Art, Oriental Art, Painting - American, Pewter, Porcelain
Collections: †Private & public collection catalogs; individual artists & architects
Exhibitions: Life in a Boundless Land: The Gancho Scenes of Juan Manuels Blanes. Canadian Impressionism: 1885-1925. Casta Painting. School of the North: Torres-Garcia, Adolph Gottlieb, Louise Nevelson

L **Schomburg Center for Research in Black Culture,** 515 Malcolm X Blvd, 10037. Tel 212-491-2200; *Chief* Howard Dodson
Open for research & exhibitions Mon - Wed Noon - 8 PM, Thurs - Sat 10 AM - 6 PM. A reference library devoted to Black people throughout the world; small gallery in lobby for rotating exhibition program
Library Holdings: Vols 130,000; Broadsides; Maps; Playbills; Programs; Micro — Reels; AV — Fs, rec; Other — Clipping files, photographs, prints
Special Subjects: Black people throughout the world with major emphasis on Afro-American, Africa and Caribbean, nucleus of collected rarities of Arthur A Schomburg, a Puerto Rican of African descent
Collections: One of the largest collections in the country of books on Black Culture & Art; a research collection containing African Art, American Art by Black artists, Afro-Caribbean art & artifacts
Activities: Lect open to public; gallery talks; tours; fel offered; originate traveling exhibitions; sales shop sells books, reproductions, exhibition catalogs & cards

L **Mid-Manhattan Library, Art Collection,** 455 Fifth Ave, 10016. Tel 212-340-0871;
Open Mon & Wed 9 AM - 9 PM, Tues & Thurs 11 AM - 7 PM, Fri & Sat 10 AM - 6 PM
Library Holdings: Vols 40,000; Per subs 200; Vertical files of clippings on artists & New York City art institutions; Micro — Fiche, reels; AV — V-tapes; Other — Clipping files

—**Mid-Manhattan Library, Picture Collection,** 455 Fifth Ave, 10016. Tel 212-340-0878, 340-0849; *Supervising Librn* Constance Novak
Estab 1915
Collections: Approximately 5,000,000 classified pictures; Encyclopedic in scope; Approximately half of collection available for loan with a valid NYPL card; remainder available for studying & copying, not for classroom or exhibition use

M **Shelby Cullom Davis Museum,** 40 Lincoln Ctr Plaza, 10023. Tel 212-870-1608; *Exec Dir* Robert Marx; *Cur Exhib* Barbara Stratyner; *Head & Chief Designer* Donald Vlack; *Dance Cur* Madeleine Nichols; *Theatre Cur* Robert Taylor; *Recordings Cur* Donald McCormick; *Chief Librn Circulations Coll Mgr* Susan Sommer
No admis fee. Estab 1965 to present exhibitions of high quality pertaining directly with the performing arts. Main Gallery is 140 x 40 x 20 ft & has large glass space designed by Saarinsen. Astor Gallery measures 25 x 57 x 12 ft; Amsterdam Gallery is 30 x 48 x 10 ft
Income: Financed by endowment & city appropriation
Collections: Prints; letters; documents; photographs; posters, films; video tapes; memorabilia; dance music; recordings
Exhibitions: (1997) Alternative Rock Music; Henry Cowell, Composer; Caribbean Music
Activities: Docent training; symposia; lect open to public, 20 vis lectr per year; concerts; gallery talks; tours; awards; lending collection contains books, cassettes, motion picture videos & phono records; book traveling exhibitions 1 per year; originate traveling exhibitions 3 per year; museum shop sells books, magazines, original art, reproductions & prints

L **NEW YORK SCHOOL OF INTERIOR DESIGN LIBRARY,** 170 E 70th St, 10021. Tel 212-472-1500; FAX 212-472-3800; *Librn* Jean Hines
Open Mon - Thurs 9 AM - 7 PM, Fri 9 AM - 2 PM. Estab 1924 to supplement the courses given by the school & to aid students & faculty in their research & projects
Income: $4484 (financed by New York State grant)
Purchases: $6345
Library Holdings: Vols 5200; Per subs 68; AV — Slides; Other — Exhibition catalogs
Special Subjects: Interior Design, Architecture

A **NEW YORK SOCIETY OF ARCHITECTS,** 10 Columbus Circle, Ste 1030, 10019. Tel 212-581-6398; FAX 212-675-5922; *Pres* Hal Dorfman; *Second VPres* Shirley Klein; *Treas* Sal Bracco; *Exec Dir* Diane Elmendorf
Open 9:30 AM - 4:30 PM. Incorporated 1906. Mem: 750; dues $125
Income: $100,000 (financed by dues & sales)
Publications: Bulletin, bi-monthly; New York City Building Code Manual; New York City Fire Prevention Code
Activities: Educational programs; educational seminars; lect open to public, 6-10 per year; Matthew W DelGaudio Award for Excellence in Design to architectural students, Honorary Membership Certificate to other than architect, Distinguished Service Award to members, Sidney L Strauss Memorial Award to architect or layman, Fred L Uebmann Book Award; scholarships

M **NEW YORK STUDIO SCHOOL OF DRAWING, PAINTING & SCULPTURE,** Gallery, 8 W Eighth St, 10011. Tel 212-673-6466; *Chmn* David Mckee; *Dean* Graham Nickson
Open daily 10 AM - 6 PM. No admis fee. Estab 1964, a non-profit organization. Gallery is located on ground floor of the Studio School, site of the original Whitney Mus of Art; 2 large rooms on courtyard. Average Annual Attendance: 1000
Income: Financed by private funding
Exhibitions: Founding Faculty Show, including works by Meyer Schapiro, Esteban Vicente, Mercedes Matter, Nicholas Carone, Peter Agostini; occasional drawing exhibitions. Works from the Drawing Marathon; works are rotated monthly, including student works as well
Activities: Classes for adults; drawing instruction; lect open to public, 52 vis lectr per year; scholarship & fels offered; exten dept

L **Library,** 8 W Eighth St, 10011. Tel 212-473-5932, 673-6466; FAX 212-777-0996; *Dean* Graham Nickson
Estab 1964 for pedagogical purposes. Not open to pub
Library Holdings: Vols 4700; AV — A-tapes, cassettes, slides, v-tapes; Other — Clipping files, exhibition catalogs, reproductions
Activities: Lectures open to public, weekly

NEW YORK UNIVERSITY
M **Grey Art Gallery & Study Center,** 100 Washington Sq E, 10003. Tel 212-998-6780; FAX 212-995-4024; *Dir* Lynn Gumpert; *Asst to Dir & Librn* Open ; *Registrar* Michele Wong; *Gallery Mgr & Assoc Dir* Frank Poveymrov
Open Tues, Thurs & Fri 11 AM - 6:30 PM, Wed 11 AM - 8:30 PM, Sat 11 AM - 5 PM; summer Mon - Fri 11 AM - 6 PM. No admis fee; suggested contribution. Estab 1975 as university art mus to serve pub as well as university community. The New York University Art Collection of approx 3500 works is now under the Grey Art Gallery. Gallery space of approx 4000 sq ft used for changing exhibitions. Average Annual Attendance: 50,000. Mem: 250
Collections: American & European 20th Century Paintings, Watercolors & Prints; Ben & Abby Grey Foundation Collection of Contemporary Asian & Middle Eastern Art; New York University Art Collection
Exhibitions: Modern Redux: Critical Alternatives for Architecture in the Next Decade; A E Gallatin & His Circle/Abstract Appropriations
Publications: Exhibition catalogs
Activities: Lect open to public, 2-3 vis lectr per year; individual paintings & original objects of art lent to other cultural institutions & sister organizations for exhibitions; originate traveling exhibitions; sales shop sells exhibition catalogs
M **Washington Square East Galleries,** 80 Washington Square E, 10003. Tel 212-998-5747; FAX 212-998-5752; *Faculty Dir* Dr Marilynn Karp; *Dir* Ruth D Newman
Open Tues 11 AM - 7 PM, Wed & Thurs 11 AM - 6 PM, Fri & Sat 11 AM - 5 PM. No admis fee. Estab 1975 for exhibitions of works by graduate student artists. Eight gallery rooms containing solo shows. Average Annual Attendance: 10,000
Exhibitions: 70 one man shows annually; Annual Small Works Competition
Publications: Press releases
Activities: Annual International Art Competition, Small Works
L **Stephen Chan Library of Fine Arts,** One E 78th St, 10021. Tel 212-772-5825; FAX 212-772-5807; *Elec Mail* chcknzff@is2.nyu.edu; stacy@is.nyu.edu; hillsnov@is.nyu.edu; *Dir* Sharon Chickanzeff; *Supvr* Robert Stacey; *Reference Librn* Clare Hills-Nova
Estab to provide scholarly materials for graduate studies in art history, archaeology & conservation of works of art. Reference library
Library Holdings: Vols 140,000; Per subs 460; Micro — Fiche, reels
Special Subjects: Antiquities-Assyrian, Antiquities-Byzantine, Antiquities-Egyptian, Antiquities-Etruscan, Antiquities-Greek, Antiquities-Oriental, Antiquities-Persian, Antiquities-Roman, Archaeology, Art History, Asian Art, Painting - European
L **Institute of Fine Arts Visual Resources Collection,** One E 78th St, 10021. Tel 212-772-5800; FAX 212-772-5807; *Elec Mail* Internet: roddaj@is2.nyu.edu. *Cur* Jenni Rodda; *Asst Cur* Dorothy Simon; *Photographer* Nita Roberts; *Reference* David Basson; *Photo Archives* Peter Emerick
Open Mon - Fri 9 AM - 5 PM by appointment. Library open to qualified researchers
Library Holdings: B&W photographs, mounted & unmounted 750,000; 35mm slides 350,000; AV — Lantern slides 500,000
Collections: Biblioteca Berensen; Frank Caro Archives (b&w, Oriental); Census; Gertrude Achenbach Coor Archives; D.I.A.L.; Walter Friedlaender Archives; Corpus Gernsheim (85,000 pieces; drawings); Henry Russell Hitchcock Archives (b&w, architecture); Richard Offner Archives (b&w, Italian painting); James Stubblebine Archives (b&w, Italian painting); Emile Wolf Archives (b&w, Spanish art) scope of collection: art, art history, archaeology, architectural history; photographs are used for teaching & research purposes only

M **NIPPON CLUB GALLERY,** 145 W 57th St, 10019. Tel 212-581-2223; FAX 212-581-3332; *Dir* Thom Donovan
Open Mon - Sat 11 AM - 7 PM, cl Sun & holidays. No admis fee. Estab 1981 for the purpose of international cultural exchange of arts & crafts from Japan & US. Located in the main lobby of a 6 storey club house; gallery space is 900 sq ft with high ceiling & multiple lighting system. Mem: 2700; dues $400
Income: Financed by mem
Collections: Japanese arts & crafts
Publications: The Nippon Club Dayori, monthly; The Nippon Club Directory, annual; The Nippon Club News, annual
Activities: Classes for adults; lect for members only, 5 vis lectr per year

A **THE ONE CLUB FOR ART & COPY,** 32 E 21st St, 10010. Tel 212-979-1900; *Exec Dir* Mary Warlick; *Asst to Dir* Kristin Overson
Open Mon - Fri 10 AM - 6 PM. Estab 1975 to support the craft of advertising, informal interchange among creative people, develop advertising excellence through advertising students who are tomorrow's professionals. Exhibits feature different advertising agencies. Mem: 700; dues individual $75, student $45; annual meeting in Jan
Income: $200,000 (financed by mem & awards show)
Publications: The One Show Annual, Advertising's Best Print, Radio & TV, annually
Activities: Educ dept; lect open to public & some for members only; gallery talks; competitions with awards; scholarships offered; individual ads lent to various ad clubs & sometimes to various schools; sales shop sells books & TV reels

A **ORGANIZATION OF INDEPENDENT ARTISTS,** 19 Hudson St, No 402, 10013. Tel 212-219-9213; FAX 212-219-9216; *Pres* Susan Fetterolf; *Prog Dir* Miriam Romais; *Membership Coordr* Elizabeth Rogers
Open Tues 1 - 7 PM, Wed - Fri 1 - 5 PM. Estab 1976 to facilitate artist-curated group exhibitions in public spaces throughout NY. Exhibit in public spaces. Maintains reference library. Average Annual Attendance: 20,000. Mem: 1100; patrons $500, sponsors $100, friends & artists $35
Income: $80,000 (financed by mem, state appropriation, federal funds, corporate

& foundation funds)
Exhibitions: Raw Materials; Landscape: Seen & Remembered; Paint & Circumstance; 5 Women Sculptors; Fire Without Gold
Publications: Quarterly newsletter
Activities: Classes for adults; lect open to public; tours; competitions with prizes; workshops; scholarships offered; individual paintings lent; slide registry; originate traveling exhibitions

C **PAINE WEBBER INC,** 1285 Avenue of the Americas, 10019. Tel 212-713-2869; FAX 212-713-1087; *Chief Exec Officer* Donald B Marron; *Cur* Matthew Armstrong
Collection displayed throughout offices
Collections: Contemporary American & European drawings, sculptures, paintings & prints
Activities: Tours; individual paintings & objects of art lent

L **PARSONS SCHOOL OF DESIGN,** Adam & Sophie Gimbel Design Library, 2 W 13th St, 10011. Tel 212-229-8914; FAX 212-229-2806; *Elec Mail* kirkingc@newschool.edu. *Libr Dir* Clayton C Kirking; *Reference Librn* Jennifer Tobias
Open Mon - Thurs 10 AM - 9 PM, Fri & Sat 10 AM - 6 PM, Sun Noon - 8 PM, summer hours vary. Estab as a school in 1896, The Gimbel Library moved to its present location in 1974; collections & services support the curriculum of the school as well as general design research. Lending to Parsons students & library consortium members; limited reference to general public
Library Holdings: Vols 47,000; Per subs 180; Pictures 55,000; AV — Slides 79,000; Other — Exhibition catalogs, memorabilia, original art works, prints
Special Subjects: Architecture, Art History, Crafts, Fashion Arts, Furniture, Graphic Design, Historical Material, Illustration, Industrial Design, Interior Design, Jewelry, Metalwork, Oriental Art, Photography, Textiles, Design Concepts, Typography
Collections: Claire McCardell Fashion Sketchbooks

PASTEL SOCIETY OF AMERICA
For further information, see National and Regional Organizations

A **PEN & BRUSH, INC,** 16 E Tenth St, 10003-5958. Tel 212-475-3669; FAX 212-475-6018; *Pres* Vinni Marie D'Ambrosio; *VPres* May Rolstad Triek; *Treas* Annette Needle
Open Tues - Sun 2 - 6 PM, cl July & Aug. No Admis fee. Estab 1893, incorporated 1912 for encouragement in the arts. The Clubhouse was purchased in 1923, and contains rooms, dining room and 3 exhibition galleries. Mem: 225; dues $130 professional women writers, artists, sculptors, craftsmen, musicians; annual meeting in Apr
Collections: Collages; crafts; graphics; mixed media; oil; paintings; pastels; sculpture; watercolor
Exhibitions: Ten annual exhibitions of members' work; one man shows; solo winner shows
Publications: Pen & Brush bulletin, semiannual
Activities: Lect open to public, 17-19 vis lectr per year; concerts; gallery talks; competitions with awards; scholarships offered; sales shop sells original art, paintings, sculpture & craft items
L **Library,** 16 E Tenth St, 10003. Tel 212-475-3669; FAX 212-475-6018; *Pres* Vinni Marie D'Ambrosio
For members only
Library Holdings: Vols 1000; Per subs 5
Publications: Bulletin, monthly

C **PHILIP MORRIS COMPANIES INC,** 120 Park Ave, 10017. Tel 212-880-3470; FAX 212-878-2167; *VPres Corporate Contributions & Cultural Programs* Stephanie French; *Mgr Cultural Affairs* Jennifer Goodale
Estab 1960's to enhance the creative & aesthetic environments of offices. Collection displayed in offices & corridors. Since 1958, Philip Morris' support of the arts focuses on contemporary & multi cultural visual & performing arts. One of the most comprehensive cultural programs in the world
Collections: Paintings, photography, sculptures, works on paper; 500 works by established & emerging artists with a focus on contemporary art
Activities: Individual objects of art lent to museums exhibitions only. Organizations that present breakthrough ideas & explore new ground in artistic expression

M **PHOENIX GALLERY,** 568 Broadway, Ste 607, 10012. Tel 212-226-8711; FAX 212-343-7307;
Internet Home Page Address http://www.gallery-guide.com/gallery/phoenix. *Dir* Linda Handler
Open Tues - Sat 11 AM - 5:30 PM. No admis fee. Estab 1958. 190 linear ft of exhibition walls. Average Annual Attendance: 10,000. Mem: 30; dues non-active $2500, active $1940; meetings one per month
Income: $64,000 (financed by mem)
Collections: Contemporary Art - 30 members from all over the United States, Venezuela & Germany
Activities: Dramatic programs; poetry & dance programs; lect open to public, 5 vis lectr per year; competitions

L **PLAYERS,** Hampden-Booth Theatre Library, 16 Gramercy Park, 10003. Tel 212-228-7610; *Cur & Librn* Raymond Wemmlinger
Open Mon - Fri 10 AM - 5 PM & by appointment. Estab 1957 to provide scholarly & professional research on American & English theater with emphasis on 19th century
Purchases: $10,000
Library Holdings: Vols 10,000; Micro — Reels; AV — A-tapes, cassettes, rec; Other — Clipping files, exhibition catalogs, framed reproductions, manuscripts, memorabilia, original art works, pamphlets, photographs, prints, reproductions, sculpture
Special Subjects: Coins & Medals, Costume Design & Construction, Etchings & Engravings, Painting - American, Painting - British, Photography, Portraits, Prints, Sculpture, Stage Design, Reproductions, Theatre Arts
Collections: Documents, letters, photos, paintings, memorabilia, promptbooks of †Walter Hampden, †Edwin Booth, Union Square Theater; English playbill (18th & 19th century)

M PORT AUTHORITY OF NEW YORK & NEW JERSEY, Art Collection, One World Trade Ctr, Ste 82W, 10048. Tel 212-435-7000; FAX 212-435-3382; *Adminr* Christine M Lassiter; *Cur* Christine Moss Lassiter; *Registrar* Kimberly Beard
Open 24 hrs. Estab 1969 as a pub arts program. John F Kennedy International Airport, International Arrivals Building; World Trade Center; Port Authority Bus Terminal. Average Annual Attendance: 10,000,000
Purchases: $250,000
Exhibitions: Memories of Surrealism, Salvador Dali; Wind Circus of Susumu Shingu (World Trade Center); Barrier Murals by Franco the Great Gaskin; The Wonder Woman Wall by Graupe Pillard (Port Authority Bus Terminal); American - for the People of Bathgate by Tim Rollins & KOS (Bathgate Industrial Park); Smug by Tony Smith (Saint John's Rotary, Holland Tunnel)
Publications: Art for the Public, collection catalog
Activities: Competitions sponsored, awards given; lending collection of original objects of art & paintings; book traveling exhibitions 6 per year; originate traveling exhibitions

M PRINCE STREET GALLERY, 121 Wooster St, 10012. Tel 212-226-9402; *Dir* Flavia Bacarella
Open Tues - Sun Noon - 6 PM. Estab 1970 to provide a showing place for members, mainly figurative art; cooperative artist run gallery. Gallery has about 30 members who have shown in New York as well as throughout the country & internationally. Average Annual Attendance: 8000. Mem: 30; mem enrollment fees $450, mem $75 per month for 12 months; 6 meetings per yr
Income: Financed by mem
Exhibitions: Gallery Artists: Flavia Bacarella, Janice Becker, Monica Bernier, Suzanne Biggins, Tina Brown, Paul Carrellas, Carol Diamond, Pamela Ervin, Karen Frances Fitch, Mary Flinn, Lynn Kotula, Anni Kruger, Barbara Kulicke, Leslie Hertzog, Elizabeth Higgins, Marion Lerner-Levine, Gerald Marcus, Maria Pia Marella, Fred McCarthy, Mary Parkman, Nancy Prusinowski, Mary Salstrom, Bill Scott, Norma Shatan, Paula Stark, Michel Tombelaine, Evelyn Twitchell, Gina Werfel
Publications: Annual catalog

C PRINTED MATTER, INC, 77 Wooster St, 10012. Tel 212-925-0325; *Dir* David Dean
Open Tues - Fri 10 AM - 6 PM, Sat 11 AM - 7 PM, cl major holidays. Estab 1976. Average Annual Attendance: 100,000
Income: $400,000
Exhibitions: Conceptual artists books from the 70's & early 80's
Publications: Annual catalog
Activities: Classes for adults & children; lect open to public, 6 vis lectr per year; originate traveling exhibitions 6-8 per year; sales shop sells books, magazines & original art

A PRINTMAKING WORKSHOP, 55 W 17th St, 10011. Tel 212-989-6125, 242-9884; FAX 212-206-8398; *Exec Dir* Robert Blackburn; *Admin Dir* Judy Collischan; *Studio Mgr* Darin Forehand; *Bookkeeper* Lawanda Graves; *Cur & Registrar* Debbie Cullen
Open Mon - Fri 8 AM - midnight, Sat & Sun 10 AM - 7 PM. Estab 1949 as a workshop space for artists to print etchings & lighographs, relief printing, photographics, including night classes & edition printing; outreach program. Mem: 800; dues vary
Income: Financed by earned income, mem, city, federal & state appropriation, donations from individuals, mem some foundation & corporate support
Collections: Impressions-Expressions, Black American Graphics; Artists Who Make Prints, Independent Artists; Prints & Monotypes by Bob Blackburn
Exhibitions: Elizabeth Harington: The Tao of Physics (etchings); Prints from the 1930s & 1940s
Activities: Classes for adults & children; lect, tours & demonstrations by appointment; scholarships & fels offered; traveling exhibitions organized & circulated

M PS 122 GALLERY, 150 First Ave, 10009. Tel 212-228-4249;
Estab 1978 to show work by emerging artists. 600 sq ft ground floor space. Average Annual Attendance: 20,000
Income: Financed by NYSCA & private funds
Activities: Competitions

A PUBLIC ART FUND, INC, One E 53rd St, 10022. Tel 212-980-4575; FAX 212-980-3610; *Pres* Susan K Freedman; *Dir* Tom Eccles; *Project Mgr* Gregor Clark
Open Mon - Fri 10 AM - 6 PM. Estab 1977 to incorporate contemporary art at sites throughout New York City; one of the first organizations solely dedicated for its pioneering support of temporary pub art installation
Income: $220,000 (financed by National Endowment for the Arts, New York State Council of the Art, endowments, private & corporate contributions)
Exhibitions: Magdelena Abakanowicz; Fernando Botero: Botero in NY; Alexander Brodsky: Canal Street Project; Urban Paradise: Garden in the City
Publications: Catalogues; manuals on public art; newsletter; postcards
Activities: Competitions to commission new works of art; site assistance; temporary exhibition program
L Library, One E 53rd St, 10022. Tel 212-980-4575; FAX 212-980-3610; *Comm Dir* Lynn Richardson
Open by appointment only. Estab as a reference library on pub art
Library Holdings: Documentation of public art projects; AV — Slides 4000
Collections: Murals; outdoor sculpture; sponsors temporary installations throughout New York City

C R J R NABISCO, INC, 1301 Avenue of the Americas, 34th Flr, 10019. Tel 212-258-5600; *Facilities Dept* Harvey Brundage
Collection shown in Corporate Headquarters Plaza & Reynolds Buildings
Collections: Works of living 20th century artists, including paintings, prints, photography, sculpture, crafts & mixed media; glass cases display Art Deco smoking memorabilia; 30 ft mural tracing the history of tobacco by Dennis Abbe

M NICHOLAS ROERICH MUSEUM, 319 W 107th St, 10025. Tel 212-864-7752; FAX 212-864-7704; Elec Mail roerich@igc.apc.org. *Pres* Edgar Lansbury; *Exec Dir* Daniel Entin
Open daily 2 - 5 PM; cl Mon & holidays. No admis fee. Estab 1958 to show a permanent collection of paintings by Nicholas Roerich, internationally known artist, to promote his ideals as a great thinker, writer, humanitarian, scientist, and explorer, and to promote his Pact and Banner of Peace. Average Annual Attendance: 8000. Mem: Dues patron $100, contributing $50, associate $25
Income: Financed by mem & donations
Collections: Permanent collection of paintings by Nicholas Roerich
Publications: Altai-Himalaya, A Travel Diary; Flowers of Morya, The Theme of Spiritual Pilgrimage in the Poetry of Nicholas Roerich; The Invincible; Nicholas Roerich, An Annotated Bibliography; Nicholas Roerich, A Short Biography; Nicholas Roerich 1874-1974 Centenary Monograph; Roerich Pact & Banner of Peace; Shambhala
Activities: Lect open to public; concerts; tours; museum shop selling books, reproductions and postcards

C RUDER FINN INC, 301 E 57th St, 10022. Tel 212-593-6400; FAX 212-715-1507; *Pres* Philippa Polskin
Estab to link corporations which support the arts with museum exhibitions and performing arts events, to develop major corporate sponsored exhibitions and special projects created for public spaces. Assistance given for marketing and publicity assignments for cultural institutions and the selection, installation and documentation of corporate art collections
Activities: Originate traveling exhibitions to museums nationwide

SALMAGUNDI CLUB
For further information, see National and Regional Organizations

M SCALAMANDRE MUSEUM OF TEXTILES, 942 Third Ave, 10022. Tel 718-361-8500; FAX 212-688-7531; *Mgr* Susan Branch
Open Mon - Fri 9 AM - 5 PM. Estab 1947 to encourage interest in textile design for decoration
Collections: Contemporary textiles showing modern motifs in textured weaves of today; reproductions of old textiles; 2000 old documentary pieces of textile
Exhibitions: Permanent display of textiles used in Historic Restorations
Activities: Lect given on history of textile design, including the classification of textiles, both period & modern; traveling exhibits in the various periods of decorative art for circulation throughout the United States to museums only

M SCHOOL OF VISUAL ARTS, Visual Arts Museum, 209 E 23rd St, 10010-3994. Tel 212-592-2144; FAX 212-592-2095; *Dir* Francis Di Tommaso; *Asst Dir* Meg Asaro; *Gallery Mgr* Lane Twitchell
Open Mon - Wed & Fri 9 AM - 6:30 PM, Thurs 9 AM - 8 PM, Sat 10 AM - 5 PM. No admis fee. Estab 1961. Average Annual Attendance: 8000
Exhibitions: 4th Annual Digital Salon; The Master's Series: Mary Ellen Mark; Sculptors Drawings, World's Most Memorable Posters
Publications: Exhibition catalogs & posters

L SCHOOL OF VISUAL ARTS LIBRARY, 380 Second Ave (Mailing add: 209 E 23rd St, 10010). Tel 212-592-2660; FAX 212-592-2655; *Chief Librn* Robert Lobe; *Catalog Librn* Rosyln D Mylorie; *Reference* Nina Nazionale; *Slide Cur* Lorraine Kuczek
Open Mon - Thurs 9 AM - 9 PM, Fri 9 AM - 7 PM, Sat 10:30 AM - 5:30 PM. Estab 1962 to serve needs of School of Visual Arts students and faculty. Exclusively for student & faculty use, lending to students. Circ 50,000
Income: Financed by tuition
Purchases: $80,000
Library Holdings: Vols 65,000; Per subs 260; AV — A-tapes, cassettes, rec, slides, v-tapes; Other — Clipping files, exhibition catalogs, pamphlets, photographs, reproductions, sculpture
Special Subjects: Advertising Design, Art History, Commercial Art, Film, Graphic Design, Illustration, Photography, media arts, painting
Publications: Library Handbook; accessions lists

SCULPTORS GUILD, INC
For further information, see National and Regional Organizations

M SCULPTURE CENTER SCHOOL & STUDIOS, 167 E 69th St, 10021. Tel 212-737-9870; *Pres* Armand Bartos; *VPres* Edwin Nochberg; *VPres* Jan Abrams; *Treas* Arthur Abelman; *Gallery Dir* Marion Giffiths; *School Dir* Michael Cochran; *Asst Dir* Jay Gibson; *Asst Dir* Elizabeth Eder
Open Tues - Sat 11 AM - 5 PM. No admis fee. Estab 1928 as Clay Club of New York to further the interest of student & professional sculptors. Incorporated in 1944 as the Sculpture Center, a nonprofit organization for the promotion of the art of sculpture & to provide work facilities. Moved into the new building in 1950, when the present name was adopted. Slide file maintained for unaffiliated sculptors for use by consultants, curators, collectors & architects. A gallery is maintained & has represented in it professional sculptors. School & studio space can be provided for beginning, intermediate & advanced students. Average Annual Attendance: 35,000
Exhibitions: Solo & group exhibitions of emerging & mid-career sculptors; selection from the Sculptor Center Slide File; Video Installations; ongoing series of installations on AIDS as well as monthly readings by poets & writers
Publications: Announcements (for the gallery and school); brochures; exhibition catalogs
Activities: Classes for adults & children; lect open to public; concerts; gallery talks; tours; scholarships offered; original objects of art lent to private galleries & corporate lobbies; sales shop sells tools & supplies for sculptors
L Gallery, 167 E 69th St, 10021. Tel 212-879-3500; FAX 212-879-7155; *School Dir* Michael Cochran
Library Holdings: Vols 200; Per subs 3; Other — Exhibition catalogs, memorabilia, original art works, pamphlets, photographs, sculpture

C **JOSEPH E SEAGRAM & SONS, INC,** Gallery, 375 Park Ave, 10152. Tel 212-572-7379; FAX 212-572-7510; *Cur* Carla Caccamise Ash; *Asst Cur* Barry M Winiker
Open to public. Estab 1958 for the enjoyment of Seagram employees. Collection displayed in offices & reception areas; permanent gallery on 4th floor, used for temporary art exhibitions, both loan & in-house
Collections: 19th & 20th century American photographs of urban life; antique glass, European & American; 20th century drawings, graphics, paintings, posters & tapestries
Exhibitions: Temporary installations of notable sculpture on Plaza; several loan exhibitions
Activities: Lect; tours of public areas Tues 3 PM; individual objects of art lent for selected musuem exhibitions; originate traveling exhibitions

A **SEGUE FOUNDATION,** Reading Room-Archive, 303 E Eighth St, 10009. Tel 212-674-0199; FAX 212-254-4145; WATS 800-869-7553. *Pres* James Sherry; *Exec Dir* Daniel Machlin
Open by appointment. Estab 1977. For reference only
Library Holdings: Vols & per subs 2000; AV — A-tapes, cassettes, v-tapes; Other — Manuscripts, memorabilia, reproductions
Collections: Language poetry books; periodicals; rare archival materials manuscripts; reading series footage
Publications: Poetry, literary criticism, film & performance texts

M **ABIGAIL ADAMS SMITH MUSEUM,** 421 E 61st St, 10021. Tel 212-838-6878; *Dir* Barbara Hayward; *Cur* Jennifer Anderson Lawrence; *Prog & Public Information* Anthony Bellov; *Educ Coordr* Laurie Brown
Open Mon - Fri Noon - 4 PM, Sun 1 - 5 PM, groups Mon - Fri 10 AM - Noon. Admis adults $3, seniors (65 & up) & students (with ID $2, under 13 free. Estab 1939, historic house museum representing early 19th century New York City. Nine period rooms in original 1826 interiors; 1799 Landmark building. Average Annual Attendance: 10,000. Mem: 600; dues $35-$500; annual meeting in Spring
Collections: †Decorative arts-furniture, †ceramics, †metals, †porcelain, †silver, †textiles; †documents & †manuscripts
Exhibitions: Period rooms in original 1820s interiors; American Decorative Arts
Publications: Biannual newsletter
Activities: Classes for adults & children; dramatic programs; docent programs; musical performances; craft demonstrations; lect open to public, 25 vis lectr per year; scholarships & fels offered; museum shop sells books, reproductions, slides, toys & craft items

SOCIETY FOR FOLK ARTS PRESERVATION, INC
For further information, see National and Regional Organizations

SOCIETY OF AMERICAN GRAPHIC ARTISTS
For further information, see National and Regional Organizations

SOCIETY OF ILLUSTRATORS
For further information, see National and Regional Organizations

M **SOCIETY OF ILLUSTRATORS,** Museum of American Illustration, 128 E 63rd St, 10021. Tel 212-838-2560; FAX 212-838-2561; *Dir* Terrence Brown; *Asst Dir* Phillis Harvey
Open Mon, Wed, Thurs & Fri 10 AM - 5 PM, Tues 10 AM - 8 PM, cl Aug & legal holidays. No admis fee. 1901. Average Annual Attendance: 30,000
Collections: Original illustrations from 1838 to present, all media
Exhibitions: Seventeen exhibitions a year; Annual Illustrators Show
Activities: Lect open to public, 18 vis lectr; sponsor competitions for professional illustrators; awards; individual paintings & original objects of art lent to museums & universities; lending collection contains 1200 art works; original traveling exhibitions; museum shop sells books, prints, t-shirts & gift items

SOCIETY OF PHOTOGRAPHERS & ARTISTS REPRESENTATIVES
For further information, see National and Regional Organizations

A **SOCIETY OF SCRIBES, LTD,** 207 W 25th St, PO Box 933, 10150. Tel 212-741-2717; *Pres* Margaret Neiman Harber; *VPres* Caroline Paget Leake; *Treas* Judith B Kastin
Estab 1974. Mem: 1000; dues overseas $32, Canada & Mexico $30, USA $25; annual meeting in Feb, annual Fair in Dec
Publications: NEWS.S
Activities: Adult classes in calligraphy & lettering arts & calligraphy in the graphic arts; lect & demonstrations open to public; 2-4 vis lectr per year; gallery talks; competitions

M **SOHO 20 GALLERY,** 545 Broadway, 3rd Flr, 10012. Tel 212-226-4167; *Dir* Thomas Slaughter
Open Tues - Sat Noon - 6 PM. Estab 1973 as a women's co-operative gallery. 1400 sq ft for exhibition. Main gallery 1000 sq ft invitational space. Average Annual Attendance: 50 per day. Mem: 27; dues $1320; meetings first Tues each month
Income: Financed by funding programs, sponsored exhibitions
Exhibitions: Soho 20 Strikes Gold
Activities: Lect open to public, 52 vis lectr per year; gallery talks; tours; individual paintings & original objects of art lent to corporations, universities & other galleries; originate traveling exhibitions to other museums

M **SOUTH STREET SEAPORT MUSEUM,** 207 Front St, 10038. Tel 212-669-9400; FAX 212-732-5168; *Pres* Peter Neill; *Dir Educ* Catrin Perih; *Historian & Librn* Norman Brouwer
Open daily 11 AM - 5 PM. Admis adults $3.50, children $1.50, members no charge. Estab 1967 to preserve the maritime history & traditions of the Port of New York. Several gallery spaces: The Seaport Gallery for art exhibits; the printing press gallery at Bowne & Co Staioners; the mus children's center. Average Annual Attendance: 300,000. Mem: 9000; dues family $25, individual $15; annual meeting May
Income: Financed by mem & corporate grants

Collections: Restored historic buildings; fleet of historic ships; permanent collection of marine art & artifacts; collections of ship models; archive of ship plans, photos & negatives
Exhibitions: Travelling In Style, ongoing; My Hammer Hand; Mens Lives; New York Trades Transformed; Peking At Sea; Recent Archeology in Lower Manhattan; Titanic!; Waterfront Photography
Publications: Seaport Magazine, quarterly
Activities: Educ dept; docent training; lect open to public; gallery talks; tours; individual paintings and original objects of art lent to institutions; museum shop sells books & prints; junior museum

L **Library,** 207 Front St, 10038. Tel 212-748-8648; FAX 212-748-8610; *Historian & Librn* Norman Brouwer
For reference
Library Holdings: Vols 20,000; Per subs 30; Negatives; Micro — Reels; AV — A-tapes, Kodachromes, motion pictures, slides; Other — Clipping files, exhibition catalogs, manuscripts, memorabilia, original art works, pamphlets, photographs, prints, reproductions
Special Subjects: Archaeology, Folk Art, Historical Material, Industrial Design, Maps, Marine Painting, Painting - American, Painting - British, Scrimshaw, Woodcarvings

A **SPANISH INSTITUTE, INC,** Center for American-Spanish Affairs, 684 Park Ave, 10021. Tel 212-628-0420, 628-0423 (class prog); FAX 212-734-4177; *Asst Dir* Maria Ruana
Estab 1954 to promote understanding of Spanish culture, past & present, & current Spanish pub affairs & economic issues in the United States; enhance an understanding of the influence of Spanish culture in Americas. Housed in a McKim, Mead & White landmark building donated by Margaret Rockefeller Strong de Larrin, Marquesa de Cuevas
Income: Financed by individual & corporate mem fees, donations, foundation grants & endowment
Exhibitions: Exhibits of rich & varied traditions of the visual arts of Spain
Activities: Spanish language classes; lect open to public; symposia

C **STERLING PORTFOLIO INC,** 444 E 58th St, 10022. Tel 212-755-2733; FAX 212-753-6634; *Cur* Lois Wagner
Open by appointment only. Estab 1978
Collections: American Impressionism & Realism Collection (1880-1930); Contemporary Realism Collection; figurative, landscape & still-life paintings

M **STOREFRONT FOR ART & ARCHITECTURE,** 97 Kenmare St, 10012. Tel 212-431-5795; *Dir* Shirin Neshat; *Founder* Kyong Park; *Spec Dir Ecotec* Amerigo Murras
Open Tues - Sat 11 AM - 6 PM. No admis fee. Estab to show interdisciplinary & experimental works of art & architecture, often never previously shown in New York. Organizes large events or competitions of an experimental nature
Exhibitions: Ecotec Forum, held in Corsica, France; Future Systems; Gunther Domeney (Austrian architect); Mark West (Canadian artist)
Publications: Exhibition catalogs; monthly bulletin; quarterly reports

M **THE STUDIO MUSEUM IN HARLEM,** 144 W 125th St, 10027. Tel 212-864-4500; FAX 212-666-5753; *Dir* Kinshasha Holman Conwill; *Deputy Dir Progs* Patricia Cruz; *Cur* Dr Valerie J Mercer; *Museum Shop Mgr* Sheila Singleton
Open Wed - Fri 10 AM - 5 PM, Sat & Sun 1 - 6 PM. Admis adults $1.50, children, students & senior citizens $.50, members free. Estab 1967 to exhibit the works of contemporary Black American artists, mount historical & informative exhibitions & provide culturally educational programs & activities for the general pub. 10,000 sq ft of exhibition & educ space. Average Annual Attendance: 40,000. Mem: 11,000; dues $15 - $1000
Income: Financed by mem, city & state appropriation, corporate & foundation funding, federal funding, rental income, gift shop sales & individual contributions
Collections: James Van Der Zee Collection of Photography; over 1000 works of art by African-American artists including sculpture, painting & works on paper; Caribbean art
Exhibitions: Emma Amos: Paintings & Prints; Sam Gilliam: Recent Monoprints
Publications: Catalogues of major black artists; exhibition catalogues
Activities: Classes for adults & children; docent training; workshops; panel discussions; demonstrations; cooperative school program; internship program; lect open to public, 10 vis lectr per year; concerts; gallery talks; tours; scholarships offered; book traveling exhibitions; originate traveling exhibitions; museum shop sells books, magazines, original art, reproductions, prints, jewelry, baskets, crafts, pottery & catalogues

M **SWISS INSTITUTE,** 495 Broadway, 3rd Flr, 10012. Tel 212-925-2035; FAX 212-925-2040; Elec Mail swissins@dti.net. *Dir* Carin Kuoni
Open Tues - Sat 11 AM - 6 PM, cl Sun & Mon. No admis fee. Estab 1986 to promote artistic dialogue between Switzerland & the United States. 2000 sq ft. Average Annual Attendance: 10,000. Mem: 300; dues $25-$1000; annual meeting in Fall
Income: Financed by mem, corporate contributions, sponsors & foundations
Publications: Exhibition catalogs, 3 per year
Activities: Educ dept; lect open to public, 4 vis lectr per year; concerts; gallery talks; tours; originate traveling exhibitions

L **TAIPEI ECONOMIC & CULTURAL OFFICE,** Chinese Information & Culture Center Library, 1230 Avenue of the Americas, 10020-1513. Tel 212-373-1800; FAX 212-373-1867; *Dir* Yun-feng Pai
Open Mon - Thurs 9 AM - 6 PM, Fri 9 AM - 7 PM. Estab 1991
Library Holdings: Vols 37,000; Per subs 1167; Micro — Reels; AV — Motion pictures, v-tapes; Other — Clipping files, pamphlets, prints, reproductions
Special Subjects: Oriental Art
Publications: CICC Currents, monthly

M THREAD WAXING SPACE, 476 Broadway, 10013. Tel 212-966-9520; FAX 212-274-0792; *Exec Dir* Ellen Salpeter; *Asst Dir* Samantha Tsao; *Dir Visual Arts Prog* Timothy Nye
Open 10 AM - 6 PM. Estab 1991. Average Annual Attendance: 25,000. Mem: 200; dues $35
Exhibitions: Pieter Schoolwerth Astrid's Secret Banana (main gallery), Charles Spurrier (Project Room); Violence & Women: Artists Speak on the Visual Language of Survival; Logo Non Logo (group exhibition); Sand, Sea, Sky; Managing Mortality; Poetry Reading by Dr Marc Straus (from his book One Word)
Publications: Catalogs, 3-4 per year
Activities: Classes for children; lect open to public; book traveling exhibitions 1 per year; originate traveling exhibitions 1 per year

A LOUIS COMFORT TIFFANY FOUNDATION, c/o American Federation of Arts, 42 E 65th St, PO Box 480, 10013. Tel 212-431-3685; *Pres* Angela K Westwater; *VPres* Paul Smith; *Secy* Gerard Jones
Estab 1918 to encourage talented artists - painters, sculptors & crafts artists - by awarding a limited number of grants biennially. Mem: Annual meeting May
Income: Financed by endowment
Activities: Bi-annual grants selected from nominations of professionals around the US; This is a closed competition; no direct applications accepted

UKIYO-E SOCIETY OF AMERICA, INC
For further information, see National and Regional Organizations

A UKRAINIAN INSTITUTE OF AMERICA, INC, 2 E 79th St, 10021. Tel 212-288-8660, 772-8489; *Admin Dir* Wolodymyr Lysniak; *Cur* Daria Hoydysh
Open Tues - Sat 11 AM - 6 PM, Sun by appointment. Admis by contribution. Estab 1948 to develop, sponsor & promote educational activities which will acquaint the general public with history, culture & art of Ukrainian people. Average Annual Attendance: 8500. Mem: 280; dues life $100, associate $25; annual meeting Nov 6
Income: $60,000 (financed by endowment, mem & contributions)
Purchases: $2500
Collections: Church & religious relics; folk art, ceramic & woodwork; patents of Ukrainian-American engineers; Gritchenko Foundation Collection; sculptures by Archipenko, Kruk, Mol & others; Ukrainian paintings
Exhibitions: Arka Petryshyn, International Art Exhibit
Publications: UIA Newsletter, monthly; Fifteenth Anniversary of UIA; Thirtieth Anniversary of UIA
Activities: Classes for adults; dramatic programs; seminars; symposiums; workshop seminars; literary evenings; lect open to public, concerts; gallery talks; tours

M THE UKRAINIAN MUSEUM, 203 Second Ave, 10003. Tel 212-228-0110; FAX 212-228-1947; *Dir* Maria Shust; *Admin Dir* Daria Bajko; *Educational Dir* Lubow Wolynetz; *Public Relations* Lydia Hajduczok; *Archivist* Chrystyna Pevny
Open Wed - Sun 1 - 5 PM. Admis adults $1, senior citizens, students & children $.50. Estab 1976 to collect, preserve, maintain & exhibit its permanent collection of Ukrainian folk art, fine art & its photographic & document collection of Ukrainian immigration; special exhibitions organized on various aspects of the Ukrainian culture. Average Annual Attendance: 25,000. Mem: 1700; dues family $60, adults $35, senior citizens & students $10
Income: $295,000 (financed by mem, donations & grants)
Collections: †Major crafts in Ukrainian folk art: woven & embroidered textiles (including costumes & kilms), woodwork, ceramics, metalwork, Ukrainian Easter Eggs; †fine arts; †photographic/documentary archival collection†/ on Ukrainian cultural heritage, among them photographs of individuals in their native dress, architectural landmarks as well as photographic records of historic events
Exhibitions: Two Folk Art Exhibitions; Masterpieces in Wood: Houses of Worship in Ukraine; Pysanky-Ukrainian Easter Eggs; To Preserve a Heritage: The Story of the Ukrainian Immigration in the USA; Ukrainian Kilims
Publications: Annual report; bulletins; bilingual exhibition catalogs or brochures
Activities: Classes for adults & children; lect open to public, 2-3 vis lectr per year; gallery talks; tours; individual paintings & original objects of art lent; lending collection contains 3000 Ukrainian Folk Art, including costumes & textiles, 1000 original prints, 500 paintings, 200 works on paper; originate traveling exhibitions; museum shop sells books, magazines, original art & reproductions

L Library, 203 Second Ave, 10003. Tel 212-228-0110; FAX 212-228-1947; *Dir* Maria Shust
Library for internal use only. For reference by appointment
Library Holdings: Vols 4000; AV — Slides 600, v-tapes; Other — Exhibition catalogs, pamphlets, photographs
Special Subjects: Archaeology, Architecture, Art History, Crafts, Drawings, Etchings & Engravings, Folk Art, Jewelry, Landscapes, Leather, Portraits, Pottery, Religious Art, Sculpture, Woodcarvings, Ukrainian Fine & Folk Art & Ukrainian Culture
Collections: †Historical photographic documentary archives; †Folk Art; †Ukrainian Fire
Publications: Extensive catalogues with major exhibitions; Annual reports

L UNION OF AMERICAN HEBREW CONGREGATIONS, Synagogue Art & Architectural Library, 838 Fifth Ave, 10021. Tel 212-249-0100; FAX 212-734-2857; *Dir* Dale Glasser
Open Mon - Fri 9:30 AM - 5 PM; cl Sat & Sun & Jewish holidays. Estab 1957. Books for use on premises only
Income: Financed by budgetary allocation plus rental fees for slides
Library Holdings: Vols 350; AV — Slides 3400
Special Subjects: Synagogue architecture, ceremonial objects & Judaic art
Publications: An American Synagogue for Today & Tomorrow (book); Contemporary Synagogue Art (book)
Activities: Slide rental service

L UNIVERSITY CLUB LIBRARY, One W 54th St, 10019. Tel 212-572-3418; FAX 212-572-3452; *Dir* Andrew Berner; *Asst Dir* Jane Reed; *Librn* Susan Grant; *Conservator* Laurie Bolger; *Art Asst* Andrew Townsend
Open to members & qualified scholars (inquire by letter or telephone first) Mon - Fri 9 AM - 6 PM. Estab 1865 for the promotion of the arts & culture in post-university graduates. Art is displayed in all areas of the building. Average Annual Attendance: 7000. Mem: 4250
Income: Financed by endowments & mem
Library Holdings: Vols 90,000
Collections: Art; architecture, fine printing, book illustration, works by George Cruikshank
Publications: The Illuminator, occasional

M VIRIDIAN ARTISTS INC, 24 W 57th St, 10019. Tel 212-245-2882; FAX 212-245-2882; *Dir* Joan Krawczyk; *Asst to Dir* Fran Kornfeld
Open Tues - Sat 10:30 AM - 6 PM. Estab 1968 to exhibit work by emerging artists. Exhibits & sells prints by The Paris Review. Average Annual Attendance: 10,000
Exhibitions: Juried exhibitions every spring, curator from a contemporary museum
Publications: Gallery Artists; Gallery Catalogue
Activities: Exten dept lends paintings, sculpture & photographs; book traveling exhibitions 1 per year; originate traveling exhibitions 2 per year

VISUAL ARTISTS & GALLERIES (VAGA)
For further information, see National and Regional Organizations

M WARD-NASSE GALLERY, 178 Prince St, 10012. Tel 212-925-6951; FAX 212-334-2095;
Internet Home Page Address http://www.wardnasse.org. *Chmn of the Board* Harry Nasse; *Dir* Robert Curcio
Open Tues - Sat 11 AM - 6 PM, Sun 1 - 4 PM. Estab 1969 to provide an artist-run gallery; also serves as resource center for artists & pub; to provide internships for students. First floor, 2000 sq ft space. Average Annual Attendance: 7000. Mem: 300; dues $30
Income: Financed by mem
Exhibitions: Seventeen exhibitions per year ranging from 3 person shows, up to large salon shows with 100 artists
Publications: Brochure; gallery catalog, every two years
Activities: Work study programs; lect open to public; concerts; poetry readings; multi-arts events; sales shop sells original art

M WHITE COLUMNS, 154 Christopher St, 10014. Tel 212-924-4212; *Exec Dir* Paul Ha; *Gallery Mgr* Elaine TinNyo
Open Wed - Sun Noon - 6 PM. Estab 1970 to showcase the works of emerging artists. Average Annual Attendance: 12,000. Mem: 500; dues $35-$250
Activities: Lect open to public, 8 vis lectr per year

M WHITNEY MUSEUM OF AMERICAN ART, 945 Madison Ave, 10021. Tel 212-570-3600; *Alice Pratt Brown Dir* David Ross; *Deputy Dir* Willard Holmes; *Chief Financial Officer* Michael Wolfe; *Dir Human Resources* Martha Koletar; *Dir Develop & External Affairs* Susan Courtmanche; *Dir Communications* Mary Haus; *Dir. Coll Management* Nancy McGary; *Assoc Dir Pub Prog* Constance Wolf; *Operations Mgr* Donald Maclean; *Cur* Barbara Haskell; *Cur* Lisa Phillips; *Cur* Elisabeth Sussman; *Cur. Permanent Coll* Adam Weinberg; *Head Publ* Mary DelMonico; *Librn & Assoc Cur Spec Coll* May Castleberry; *Independent Study Prog Dir* Ron Clark; *Branch Dir, Philip Morris & Assoc Cur* Thelma Golden; *Branch Dir, Champion* Eugene Tsai; *Assoc Cur Permanent Coll* Beth Venn; *Asst Cur, Film & Video* Matthew Yokobosky; *Head, Mus Sales* Kaarin Lemstrom-Sheedy
Open Wed, Fri - Sun 11 AM - 6 PM, Thurs 1 - 8 PM, cl Mon, Tues & national holidays. Admis $8, seniors 62 & over & students with ID $6, children under 12 free. Estab 1930, inc 1931 by Gertrude Vanderbilt Whitney for the advancement of contemporary American art; Museum opened 1931 on Eighth Street & moved to 54th Street in 1954; new building opened in 1966. Average Annual Attendance: 500,000. Mem: 5000; dues $65 & up
Income: Financed by endowment, admis, grants, mem
Purchases: Numerous annual acquisitions
Collections: †Drawings, †paintings, †prints, †sculpture of mainly 20th century American artists
Exhibitions: Figurative Works from the Permanent Collection; Trans-Voices; Alfonso Ossorio Drawings, 1940-48: The Anatomy of a Surrealist Sensibility; Jean-Michel Basquiat; Robert Gardner: The Impulse to Preserve; Agnes Martin; Jonas Mekas; The Geometric Tradition in 20th Century American Art; Thersea Hak Kyung Cha; 1993 Biennial Exhibition; In the Spirit of Fluxus; Hand-Painted Pop: American Art in Transition, 1955-62
Publications: Annual report; brochures, cards, posters; calendars; exhibition catalogues; gallery brochures
Activities: Classes for adults; docent training; symposia & panel discussions; teachers' workshops; lect open to public; gallery talks; tours; Artreach provides introductory art education to elementary & high school students; individual paintings & original objects of art lent; originate traveling exhibitions for museums here & abroad; sales shop sells books, magazines, reproductions, slides, cards & posters

L Library, 945 Madison Ave, 10021. Tel 212-570-3648; *Librn* May Castleberry
Open Tues - Fri 10 AM - Noon & 2 - 5 PM by appointment for advanced research. No admis fee. Estab 1931 for encouragement & advancement of American art & art scholarship
Purchases: $30,000
Library Holdings: Vols 35,000; Per subs 100; Micro — Fiche, reels; AV — A-tapes, cassettes, rec, slides; Other — Clipping files, exhibition catalogs, manuscripts, memorabilia, pamphlets, photographs, reproductions
Special Subjects: Focuses on 20th century American drawing, graphics, painting and sculpture

M **Whitney Museum at Philip Morris,** 120 Park Ave at 42nd St, 10017. Tel 212-878-2550, 878-2453; *Branch Dir* Thelma Golden
Sculpture court open Mon - Sat 7:30 AM - 9:30 PM, Sun & holidays 11 AM - 7 PM, gallery open Mon - Fri 11 AM - 6 PM, Thurs 11 AM - 7:30 PM. No admis fee. Estab 1982 to extend American art to wider audience. Sculpture court with major works & adjacent gallery for changing exhibitions. Average Annual Attendance: 45,000
Income: Financed by Philip Morris Companies Inc
Exhibitions: Mathew McCaslin; Beverly Semmes-She Moves
Publications: Free brochures for each exhibition
Activities: Gallery talks Mon, Wed & Fri at 1 PM; films; performances

A **CATHARINE LORILLARD WOLFE ART CLUB, INC,** 802 Broadway, 10003. Tel 212-254-2000; *Pres* Jean T Kroeber
Estab 1896, incorporated in as a non-profit club to further fine, representational American Art. A club of professional women painters, graphic artists & sculptors. Mem: 325; dues $40 associate mem $20; monthly meetings
Income: Financed by mem
Exhibitions: Members Exhibition (spring); Open Annual Exhibition (fall)
Activities: Metropolitan Museum Benefit, annually; lect; demonstration programs

A **WOMEN IN THE ARTS FOUNDATION, INC,** 1175 York Ave, No 2G, 10021. Tel 212-751-1915; *Exec Coordr* Roberta Crown; *Recording Coordr* Sari Menna; *Newsletter Ed* Erin Butler; *Financial Coordr* Alice Philipps
Estab 1971 for the purpose of overcoming discrimination against women artists both in government & the private sector. Sponsors discussions, workshops, panels and exhibits the work of women artists, both established & unknown. Average Annual Attendance: 800. Mem: 200; dues $40
Income: $12,000 (financed by endowment & mem)
Exhibitions: Brooklyn Botanic Gardens '94
Publications: Women in the Arts, bulletin-newsletter, quarterly
Activities: Public educ as to the problems & discrimination faced by women artists; lect open to public; individual paintings & original objects of art lent to museum & university art galleries for special exhibitions; original art works for exhibitions are obtained from member artists

M **WOMEN'S INTERART CENTER, INC,** Interart Gallery, 549 W 52 St, 10019. Tel 212-246-1050; *Dir Programming* Ronnie Geist; *VPres* Bill Perlman; *Artistic Dir* Margot Lewitin
Open Mon - Fri 1 - 6 PM. No admis fee. Estab 1970 to present to the pub the work of significant, emerging women artists. Average Annual Attendance: 9000. Mem: Dues $35
Income: Financed by state appropriation, National Endowment for the Arts, private foundations, corporations & individuals
Exhibitions: Community as Planner
Publications: Women's Interart Center Newsletter, quarterly
Activities: Classes for adults; lect open to public, 2 vis lectr per year; originate traveling exhibitions

M **YESHIVA UNIVERSITY MUSEUM,** 2520 Amsterdam Ave at W 185th St, 10033. Tel 212-960-5390, 960-5268; FAX 212-960-5406; *Dir* Sylvia A Herskowitz; *Cur Educ* Rochelle Bradt; *Asst Cur Educ* Elizabeth Diament; *Office Mgr* Eleanor Chiger; *Cur & Registrar* Bonni-Dara Michaels; *Deputy Dir* Randi Glickberg; *Contemporary Exhib Coordr* Reba Wulkan
Open Tues - Thurs 10:30 AM - 5 PM, Sun Noon - 6 PM. Admis adults $3, students & senior citizens $2. Estab 1973 to collect, preserve & interpret Jewish art & objects of material culture in the light of Jewish history. 8000 sq ft of upper & lower galleries; maintains reference library. Average Annual Attendance: 40,000. Mem: 500; dues $18-$1000
Collections: Architectual models, ceremonial objects, documents, ethnographic material, fine & decorative art, manuscripts, photographs, sculpture, textiles
Exhibitions: Jewish Women's Clothing from the 18th through the 20th Centuries; Remnants: Jewish Life in the Former Soviet Union Photographs by David Blumenfeld; A Love Affair With Wood: Sculpture & Judaica by Robert Richter. Die Velt Fun A Moler: A Painter's World by Anthony Dubovsky; A Jeweler's Edition Of Judaica by Hanna Bechar-Paneth; Give Luck A Chair: Wood Sculpture by Aaron Ben Arieh; Prayers, Proverbs & Psalms: Paintings by Philip Pearlman; Quilted Visions: Modern Quilts with Jewish Themes; Mountains Round About: Jerusalem In Israeli Printmaking from the Seventies & The Eighties; The Story of the S S Quanza Refugees: A Prelude to The Holocaust; Around The World In Eighty Years: Photographs by Leni Sonnenfeld
Publications: Catalogs
Activities: Classes for children; dramatic programs; docent training; craft workshops; lect open to public; concerts; gallery talks; tours; individual paintings & original objects of art lent for purposes of exhibitions to institutions which provide specified levels of care; book traveling exhibitions 1 per year; originate traveling exhibitions; museum shop sells books, original art, reproductions, Judaica & children's toys

NIAGARA

M **NIAGARA UNIVERSITY,** Castellani Art Museum, 14109. Tel 716-286-8200; FAX 716-286-8289; *Dir* Dr Sandra H Olsen; *Registrar* Kathleen Fraas; *Gallery Mgr* Kurt VonVoetcsch; *Museum Shop* Anne LaBarbera; *Museum Shop* Carla Castellani
Open Wed - Sat 11 AM - 5 PM, Sun 1 - 5 PM. No admis fee. Estab 1978. The gallery is a 10,000 sq ft museum that displays the permanent collection of over 3000 works of art encompassing 19th century to present with a concentration on contemporary art. Mem: 300
Income: $120,000
Collections: Modern paintings, sculpture & works on paper (19th -20th centuries); Pre-Columbian Pottery
Exhibitions: Glass art: Arnold Mesches; John Moore; Michael Kessler; Arcadia Revisted: Niagara River & Falls from Lake Erie to Lake Ontario, Photographs by John Pfahl

Publications: Exhibition catalogs, 4 per yr
Activities: Classes for adults & children; Public Art Project on Underground Railroad; docent training; learning disabled prog; senior citizen outreach prog; lect open to the public, 1-6 vis lectr per year; concerts; gallery talks; tours; competitions; awards; scholarships & fels offered; individual paintings & original objects of art lent to qualified museums; originate traveling exhibitions

NORTHPORT

L **NORTHPORT-EAST NORTHPORT PUBLIC LIBRARY,** Art Dept, 151 Laurel Ave, 11768. Tel 516-261-6930; FAX 516-261-6718; *Dir* Stephanie Heineman; *Asst Dir* Eileen Minogue
Open Sept - June Mon - Fri 9 AM - 9 PM, Sat 9 AM - 5 PM, Sun 1 - 5 PM. Estab 1914. Circ 968,285
Income: $3,630,054
Purchases: $406,820
Library Holdings: Vols 214,613; Per subs 700; Compact discs; Micro — Fiche; AV — A-tapes, cassettes, fs, rec, v-tapes; Other — Clipping files, exhibition catalogs, manuscripts, pamphlets, prints, reproductions, sculpture
Publications: Library, monthly
Activities: Lect open to public, 5 vis lectr per year; concerts; competitions

NORTH SALEM

M **HAMMOND MUSEUM & JAPANESE STROLL GARDEN,** Cross-Cultural Center, Deveau Rd, 10560. Tel 914-669-5033; FAX 914-669-8221; *Exec Dir* Abigail Free
Open Apr - Dec, Wed - Sat Noon - 4 PM. Admis to Museum adult $4, seniors $3, members & children under 12 free; to the Gardens adult $4, children $2. Estab 1957. A museum of the Humanities, it presents changing exhibitions of international scope & varied historic periods & topics, supplemented by programs of related special events. The Oriental Stroll Gardens comprising 15 individual gardens on 3 1/2 acres, include a lake, a reflecting pool, a dry landscape, a waterfall & a Zen Garden. Maintains library. Average Annual Attendance: 25,000. Mem: 700; dues $35-$100, open to all who are in sympathy with its aims & purposes
Income: Financed by mem, matching funds, private foundations & corporations
Collections: Carl Van Vechten Photographs
Exhibitions: (1997) Costumes of China; Apres Monet
Activities: Classes for adults & children; lect open to public, 5 vis lectr per year; concerts; gallery talks; tours; competitions with prizes; documentary films; exten dept serves schools; individual paintings & original objects of art lent to other museums; lending collection contains photographs & slides

NYACK

A **OIL PASTEL ASSOCIATION,** PO Box 587, 10960. Tel 914-353-2483; FAX 914-358-3821; *Pres* John T Elliott; *Executive Dir* Sheila Elliott
Estab 1983 exhibition forum for new & traditional types of pastel paintings. Average Annual Attendance: 2000. Mem: 350; dues $25 per year
Income: $4000 (financed by donations & mem)
Exhibitions: Oil pastels; soft pastels; water soluble pastels
Publications: Art & Artists, USA
Activities: Classes for adults; workshops; scholarships offered

OGDENSBURG

M **FREDERIC REMINGTON ART MUSEUM,** 303 Washington St, 13669. Tel 315-393-2425; FAX 315-393-4464; *Exec Dir* Lowell McAllister; *Cur* Laura Foster; *Museum Educ Specialist* Laura Bennett; *Museum Shop Mgr* Lynn Clark-Stone
Open May 1 - Oct 31 Mon - Sat 10 AM - 5 PM, Sun 1 - 5 PM, Nov 1 - Apr 30 Wed - Sat 10 AM - 5 PM, Sun 1 - 5 PM, cl legal holidays. Admis adults $3, senior citizens & youth $2, under 5 & members free; organized tour groups $2 per person. Estab 1923 to house & exhibit works of art of Frederic Remington (1861-1909), a native of northern New York. The mus is in the converted Parish Mansion, built 1809-1810 & the recently constructed Addie Priest Newell Wing. Remington's last studio has been reconstructed with most of the original furnishings. Average Annual Attendance: 15,000
Income: Financed by endowment & city appropriation
Collections: Remington paintings, bronzes, watercolors, drawings, photographs, letters & personal art collection; studies in plaster by Edwin Willard Deming; sculpture by Sally James Farnham; Haskell Collection of 19th century American and European paintings; Parish Collection of Belter furniture; Sharp Collection of period glass, china, silver and cameos
Exhibitions: The Children's Exhibit; The Frederic Remington Exhibit
Activities: Classes for adults & children; docent training; lect open to public; gallery talks; tours; museum shop sells books, reproductions, prints, Remington related merchandise & Native American items

L **Library,** 303 Washington St, 13669. Tel 315-393-2425; FAX 315-393-4464; *Exec Dir* Lowell McAllister; *Cur* Laura Foster
Remington's own personal library for viewing purposes only
Library Holdings: Vols 200; Per subs 5

OLD CHATHAM

M **SHAKER MUSEUM & LIBRARY,** 88 Shaker Museum Rd, 12136. Tel 518-794-9100; FAX 518-794-8621; *Dir* Mary Ellen W Hern; *Finance Mgr* Susan Linton
Open May - Oct daily 10 AM - 5 PM, cl Tues. Admis adults $6, reduced rates for senior citizens, children & groups. Estab 1950 to promote interest in & understanding of the Shaker cultural heritage. The exhibits are housed in a complex of eight buildings. Average Annual Attendance: 16,000. Mem: 325; dues

$35 - $1000
Income: $430,000 (financed by earned revenue, endowment, contributions, private & public grants)
Purchases: $3000
Collections: 35,000 artifacts & archival material representing 200 years of Shaker history & culture including, baskets, furniture, metal work, personal artifacts, stoves, textiles, tools & equipment, transportation
Exhibitions: Orientation to Shaker History; Shakers in the 20th Century; Shaker Cabinetmakers and Their Tools; study storage related to individual collections
Publications: Members update; The Shaker Adventure; Shaker Seed Industry; pamphlets; booklets; gallery guide; catalogs; postcards, reprints, and broadsides
Activities: Classes for adults & children; docent training; seminars; lect open to public; concerts; adult tours; symposia; festivals; family events; originate traveling exhibitions; museum shop sells Shaker reproduction furniture, craft items & publications
L **Emma B King Library,** 88 Shaker Museum Rd, 12136. Tel 518-794-9100, Ext 111; FAX 518-794-8621; *Dir* Mary Ellen Hern; *Librn* Virginia McEwen
Open by appointment Mon - Fri, cl holidays. Admis research use fee. For reference only
Library Holdings: Vols 2000; Micro — Reels 189; AV — A-tapes, cassettes, fs, Kodachromes, motion pictures, rec, slides, v-tapes; Other — Clipping files, manuscripts, memorabilia, original art works 100, pamphlets, photographs 3500, prints
Special Subjects: Shakers Art, Crafts, Design & Theology
Collections: Manuscripts and records; Photographic and map archive

OLD WESTBURY

M **NEW YORK INSTITUTE OF TECHNOLOGY,** Gallery, 11568. Tel 516-686-7542; *Chmn* Lynn Oddo
Open Mon - Fri 9 AM - 5 PM. Estab 1964. Gallery maintained for the many exhibits held during the year. Average Annual Attendance: 5000
Exhibitions: Annual faculty & student shows; some traveling exhibitions
Publications: Graphic Guild Newsletter, quarterly
Activities: Classes in custom silk-screen printmaking; gallery talks; awards; scholarships offered; exten Dept serves all areas
L **Art & Architectural Library,** Education Hall, 11568. Tel 516-686-7579; *Librn* Leslie Goldstein
Open Mon - Thurs 9 AM - 9 PM, Fri 9 AM - 5 PM, Sat Noon - 4 PM. No admis fee. Estab 1976
Library Holdings: Vols 1808; Per subs 258; Micro — Reels 1384; AV — Cassettes, motion pictures 23, slides 30,000, v-tapes 80; Other — Clipping files, exhibition catalogs, pamphlets
Special Subjects: Afro-American Art, American Western Art, Antiquities-Egyptian, Art History, Asian Art, Calligraphy, Cartoons, Decorative Arts, Folk Art, Mexican Art, Southwestern Art
Exhibitions: Architecture dept student projects
Activities: Tours

M **STATE UNIVERSITY OF NEW YORK COLLEGE AT OLD WESTBURY,** Amelie A Wallace Gallery, Rte 107 (Broadway), PO Box 210, 11568-0210. Tel 516-876-3148; *Dir* Christine Griffin
Open Mon - Thurs & Sat 1 - 5 PM. No admis fee. Estab 1976 to serve as a teaching aid & for community enlightenment. 334 sq ft on three levels. Average Annual Attendance: 3000
Income: $1300 (financed by endowment & HYS)
Publications: Exhibit catalogues
Activities: Lect open to public, 4 vis lectr per year; originate traveling exhibitions

ONEIDA

M **MADISON COUNTY HISTORICAL SOCIETY,** Cottage Lawn, 435 Main St, PO Box 415, 13421. Tel 315-363-4136; *Pres* Dorothy Willsey; *VPres* Diane Mordus; *Exec Dir* Thomas Kernan
Open summer Tues - Sat 9 AM - 4 PM; winter Mon - Fri 9 AM - 4 PM & by appointment. Admis adults $2, seniors $1, discounts for school groups. Estab 1898 to collect, preserve & interpret artifacts indigenous to the history of Madison County. 1849 A J Davis gothic dwelling with period rooms, library & craft archive. Average Annual Attendance: 4000. Mem: 600; dues $12-$15; annual meeting second Tues in Nov
Income: $87,000 (financed by endowment, mem, county, city & state appropriation, Annual Craft Fair)
Collections: Locally produced & or used furnishings, paintings, silver, textiles & ceramics
Exhibitions: Permanent exhibit in the barn: The Hops Exhibit
Publications: Quarterly Newsletter; Madison County Heritage, published annually; Country Roads Revisited
Activities: Educational outreach programs for nursing homes & schools; lect open to public, 6 vis lectr per year; slides; tapes & movies documenting traditional craftsmen at work; individual paintings & original objects of art lent to qualified museums & galleries for special exhibits; sales shop sells books, magazines, prints & slides
L **Library,** 435 Main St, PO Box 415, 13421. Tel 315-363-4136; *Librn* Mary King
Open summer Tues - Sat 9 AM - 4 PM, winter Mon - Fri 9 AM - 4 PM. Estab 1975 as a reference library of primary & secondary sources on Madison County History
Library Holdings: Vols 2500; Per subs 5; Other — Clipping files, exhibition catalogs, manuscripts, memorabilia, pamphlets, photographs, prints
Special Subjects: Madison County and New York State History, Civil War, Oneida Indians
Collections: Gerrit Smith family papers

ONEONTA

M **HARTWICK COLLEGE,** Foreman Gallery, Anderson Ctr for the Arts, 13820. Tel 607-431-4483; FAX 607-431-4468; Elec Mail winelandj@hartwick.edu. *Cur* John Wineland; *Coll Mgr* Charles Clausen
Open daily Noon - 9 PM, or by appointment, cl last half of Dec. No admis fee. Estab 1928, contemporary exhibitions for benefit of faculty, students & community
Exhibitions: Changing exhibitions; rotating art displays
Publications: Exhibition catalogues
M **Museum at Hartwick,** Hartwick College, 13820. Tel 607-431-4480; FAX 607-431-4457; *Dir* Jane des Grange; *Asst to Dir* Patricia Gladstone; *Coll Mgr* Alan Francisco
Open Mon - Sat 10 AM - 4 PM, Sun 1 - 4 PM. No admis fee. Estab 1928
Collections: Collection of North American, Mexican & South American Indian art & artifacts & mask collection
Exhibitions: Changing exhibitions. Reflections; Watercolors; 1994, The War Years on the Home Front; Show Time, 1945; Works of Art; WB Bus Romeling; Franke DeBevoise; Peaceable Kingdom. Kaleidoscope
Activities: Classes in museum studies; lect; tours; films; gift shop sells cards, jewelry, pottery

M **STATE UNIVERSITY OF NEW YORK COLLEGE AT ONEONTA,** Art Gallery & Sculpture Court, Fine Arts Ctr, 13820. Tel 607-436-3500; *Chmn Art Dept* Allen Farber
Open Mon - Fri 11 AM - 4 PM, Tues & Thurs 7 - 9 PM, Sat 1 - 4 PM. No admis fee. Art Gallery & Sculpture Court are major features of the Art Wing, separate fine arts & student galleries. Average Annual Attendance: 3384
Income: Financed by city & state appropriation
Collections: Paintings, sculpture
Exhibitions: Semi-annual student art exhibition

ORIENT

M **OYSTERPONDS HISTORICAL SOCIETY,** Museum, Village Lane, PO Box 844, 11957. Tel 516-323-2480; *Dir* Courtney Burns; *Pres* Fredrica Wachsberger; *VPres* Thomas Murray
Open July & Aug Wed, Thurs, Sat & Sun 2 - 5 PM, June & Sept weekends only. Admis adults $3, children $.50. Estab 1944 to discover, procure, & preserve material related to the civil & military history of Long Island, particularly the East Marion & Orient Hamlets. Mem: 500; dues family $30, individual $15; annual meeting in July
Income: $90,000 (financed by endowment, mem, grants & fundraising)
Collections: Early Indian artifacts, including arrowheads, baskets & clay vessels; 18th century furniture & decorative arts; late 19th century Victorian furniture; marine & portrait paintings; photographs; textile collection, including quilts, scarves, fans; tools, & equipment related to the agricultural & sea-related occupations of this area
Exhibitions: The Sea Around Us; Toys & Dolls; Indian Artifacts; 19th Century Boarding House; 18th Century Period Rooms
Publications: Griffin's Journal, book; Historical Orient Village, book; She Went A'Whaling, book; quarterly newsletter
Activities: Classes for adults & children; docent training; lect open to public; museum shop sells books, magazines, original art, reproductions & prints

OSSINING

M **MUSEUM OF OSSINING HISTORICAL SOCIETY,** 196 Croton Ave, 10562. Tel 914-941-0001; *Pres* George Pires; *Dir* Roberta Y Arminio
Open Mon, Wed & Sun 2 - 4 PM & by appointment. No admis fee. Estab 1931 to educate the pub in the history & traditions of the vicinity. East Gallery contains changing exhibitions & a portion of the permanent collection; West Gallery contains permanent collection. Average Annual Attendance: 2500. Mem: 497; dues patron $100, civic, commercial & contributing $25, family $15, individual $10, senior citizens & students $5
Income: Financed by mem & town appropriation
Library Holdings: AV — V-tapes 32
Special Subjects: Antiquities-Etruscan, Antiquities-Roman, Architecture, Art History, Conceptual Art, Flasks & Bottles, Folk Art, Graphic Design, Handicrafts, History of Art & Archaeology, Painting - Italian, Sculpture, Italian Art & Architecture
Collections: Costumes; textiles & quilts; slides & films of old Ossining; old photographs & daguerreotypes; Victorian dollhouse complete in minute detail, contains antique dolls, toys, miniatures, old school books & photographs; oil portraits; fine arts
Publications: Monthly brochure
Activities: Educ dept; class visits; special assignment guidance; lect open to public, 4 vis lectr per year; gallery talks; tours; competitions with awards; individual paintings & original objects of art lent to schools, banks & industry; sales shop sells books, magazines
L **Library,** 196 Croton Ave, 10562. Tel 914-941-0001; *Librn* John Drittler
Library Holdings: Vols 1000; Micro — Reels; AV — A-tapes, cassettes, lantern slides, slides, v-tapes 32; Other — Clipping files, exhibition catalogs, framed reproductions, memorabilia, original art works, photographs, prints, reproductions

OSTERBAY

SOCIETY OF AMERICAN HISTORICAL ARTISTS
For further information, see National and Regional Organizations

OSWEGO

M STATE UNIVERSITY OF NEW YORK AT OSWEGO, Tyler Art Gallery, Tyler Hall, 13126. Tel 315-341-2113; FAX 315-341-3394; *Dir* Barbara A Perry; *Asst Dir* Mindy Ostrow
Open Mon - Fri 9:30 AM - 4:30 PM, Sept - May; summer hours as posted. No admis fee. Estab 1969 to provide cultural stimulation & enrichment of art to the college community & to the residents of Oswego County. Two gallery spaces in Tyler Hall, the North Gallery is approx 2400 sq ft & the South Gallery is approx 1300 sq ft. Average Annual Attendance: 20,000
Income: Financed by University funds
Collections: Grant Arnold Collection of Fine Prints; Contemporary American Prints & Paintings
Exhibitions: Two galleries show a combined total of 14 exhibitions per school year
Publications: Brochures; occasional catalogs for exhibitions; posters
Activities: Lect open to public, 8-10 vis lect per year; concerts, gallery talks; lending collection contains individual & original objects of art; originates traveling exhibitions
L Penfield Library, 13126-3514. Tel 315-341-4232; FAX 315-341-3194; *Dir* Michael McLane
For lending & reference
Library Holdings: Vols 437,000; Per subs 1469; Micro — Fiche, reels; AV — A-tapes, cassettes, fs, motion pictures, rec, slides, v-tapes; Other — Framed reproductions, original art works, pamphlets, sculpture
Special Subjects: Advertising Design, Aesthetics, Art Education, Art History, Costume Design & Construction, Graphic Arts

OYSTER BAY

L PLANTING FIELDS FOUNDATION, Coe Hall at Planting Fields Arboretum, PO Box 58, 11771. Tel 516-922-0479; FAX 516-922-9226; *Dir* Lorraine Gilligan; *Archivist* Eugenia Clarke
Open Apr - Sept Mon - Fri 1 - 3:30 PM. Admis adults $2, senior citizens & children 6-12 $1. Archives estab 1979 for Coe family papers, architectural drawings, photos, Planting Fields Foundation documents. For reference only. Coe Hall, a Tudor revival mansion being restored to its 1920's appearance, contains 17th-20th century paintings
Income: Financed by endowment
Library Holdings: Vols 6000; AV — A-tapes, cassettes, fs, lantern slides, motion pictures, slides, v-tapes; Other — Clipping files, manuscripts, memorabilia, original art works, pamphlets, photographs, prints
Special Subjects: American Western Art, Architecture, Decorative Arts, Historical Material, Landscape Architecture, Painting - British, Painting - Dutch, Painting - European, Painting - Italian, Period Rooms, Photography, Porcelain, Portraits, Restoration & Conservation, Stained Glass
Activities: Classes for children; docent training; lect open to public, 5 vis lectr per year; concerts; guided tours of historic house

PELHAM

M PELHAM ART CENTER, 155 Fifth Ave, 10803. Tel 914-738-2525; FAX 914-738-2686; *Exec Dir* Alison Paul
No admis fee. Estab 1975 as a community art center. Average Annual Attendance: 20,000. Mem: 500; dues $25-$100; annual meeting in June
Income: $280,000 (financed by mem, tuition, earned income & gift shop sales)
Activities: Classes for adults & children; studio classes; docent programs; lect open to public, 2-3 vis lectr per year; scholarships & fels offered; retail store sells books & prints

PLATTSBURGH

M CLINTON COUNTY HISTORICAL ASSOCIATION, Clinton County Historical Museum, 48 Court St, 12901. Tel 518-561-0340; *Dir & Cur* Jane E Rupp
Open Tues - Fri Noon - 4 PM, Sat 1 - 4 PM, cl Sun & Mon. Admis adults $2, seniors $1.50, children $1. Estab in 1973 to preserve & publicize the history of Clinton County, New York. Five exhibition galleries including county history exhibit, military & naval exhibits, temporary exhibits. Average Annual Attendance: 4000. Mem: 450; dues $250, $100, $50, $25, $15, Business/Institution $25; annual meeting first Mon in Dec
Income: $70,000 (financed by mem, NYSCA & federal grants & county appropriation)
Collections: Glass & ceramics, paintings & prints, furniture & textiles collection; Military & Naval history; Redford Glass (19th Century handblown)
Exhibitions: McMasters Writing Prize for essays about history of Clinton, Essex & Franklin Counties
Publications: Antiquarian, annual magazine; North Country Notes, monthly newsletter
Activities: Lect open to the public, 10 vis lectr per year; gallery talks; tours; writing (historical-North Country Topics); individual paintings & original objects of art lent to other qualified museums; museum shop sells books, magazines, reproductions, prints & small collectibles

M STATE UNIVERSITY OF NEW YORK, SUNY Plattsburgh Art Museum, 12901. Tel 518-564-2813 Kent, 564-2288 Myers; FAX 518-564-7827; *Dir* Edward R Brohel
Open Tues - Wed & Fri 10 AM - 5 PM, Thurs 10 AM - 9 PM, Sun 2 - 5 PM, cl university holidays. No admis fee. Estab 1978
Collections: Rockwell Kent Collection, paintings, prints, drawings, sketches, proofs & designs, books; china; ephemera; Nina Winkle Sculpture Garden
Exhibitions: Sixteen exhibitions each year; antique & contemporary, all media
Publications: Exhibition catalogs; monthly exhibition announcements; semi-annual calendar of events
Activities: Programs for undergrad students, elementary & secondary schools & community groups in area; docent programs; lect open to public, 10 vis lectr per year; tours; competitions with awards; individual paintings lent

PLEASANTVILLE

M PACE UNIVERSITY GALLERY, 861 Bedford Rd, 10570. Tel 914-773-3694; FAX 914-773-3785; *Gallery Dir* Beth A Treadway
Open Sun - Fri 1 - 5 PM, cl Sat. No admis fee. Estab 1978 to exhibit the works of nationally known professional artists & groups, & to serve as a focal point for artistic activities within the university & surrounding communities. The gallery is located on the ground floor of the Arts Building & has a commanding view of the center of campus; it is both spacious & modern
Income: Financed by the university
Activities: Lect open to public, 8-10 vis lectr per year; gallery talks; tours

C THE READER'S DIGEST ASSOCIATION INC, World Headquarters, 10570. Tel 914-241-5797; FAX 914-244-7617; *Cur* Marianne Brunson Frisch
Art collection located throughout corporate headquarters; public viewing by appointment only
Collections: †Over 5000 works of art, French Impressionists & Post - Impressionists as well as 19th century & contemporary American artists & International artists; graphics; decorative arts; sculpture; painting; mixed media; works on paper

PORT CHESTER

L PORT CHESTER PUBLIC LIBRARY, Fine Arts Dept, One Haseco Ave, 10573. Tel 914-939-6710; *Dir* Robin Lettieri
Open Mon 9 AM - 9 PM, Tues & Wed 9 AM - 8 PM, Thurs - Sat 9 AM - 5 PM. Estab 1876 to circulate books, records, magazines, to the general public to provide reference services. Maintains an art gallery. A small gallery with about ten shows per year, mostly local artists. Circ 103,598. Average Annual Attendance: 2000
Income: $494,600 (financed by endowment, villages & state appropriations)
Purchases: $50,500
Library Holdings: Vols 73,861; Per subs 2000; Micro — Reels; AV — Fs, rec, slides; Other — Framed reproductions, pamphlets, prints
Exhibitions: Water colors, oils, acrylics, photographs
Activities: Educ dept; lect & films open to public; films; career seminars & workshops; individual paintings lent

PORT WASHINGTON

M LONG ISLAND GRAPHIC EYE GALLERY, 301 Main St, 11050. Tel 516-883-9668; *Pres* Hannah Ritter; *Treas* Ellen Brous
Open Wed - Sun Noon - 5 PM. No admis fee. Chartered 1974 as a non-profit educational gallery to educate the public in the understanding & appreciation of prints & works on paper to promote art techniques. Average Annual Attendance: 3500. Mem: 25; dues $500; open to professional artists & art instructors; monthly meetings
Income: Financed by mem & individual project grants
Collections: †Slide collection
Exhibitions: Annual Winter Show: Journeys-Group Show Group, individual & juried shows throughout the year
Activities: Educ dept; lect & demonstrations in print & other media open to public, 3-4 vis lectr per year; competitions with awards; scholarships offered; sales shop sells original art & prints

L PORT WASHINGTON PUBLIC LIBRARY, One Library Dr, 11050-2794. Tel 516-883-4400; FAX 516-944-6855; *Dir* Nancy Curtin
Open Mon, Tues, Thurs & Fri 9 AM - 9 PM, Wed 11 AM - 9 PM, Sat 9 AM - 5 PM, Sun 1 - 5 PM. No admis fee. Estab 1892. Circ 303,500
Income: Financed by state appropriation & school district
Library Holdings: Vols 128,000; Per subs 750; Micro — Cards, reels; AV — A-tapes, cassettes, fs, rec, v-tapes; Other — Clipping files, manuscripts, pamphlets, photographs, prints
Special Subjects: Drawings, Illustration, Manuscripts, Photography
Collections: Ernie Simon Collection of photographs & newspaper articles on the history of Port Washington; Sinclair Lewis Collection of books, manuscripts, photographs & ephemera; Mason Photograph Archive of photographic negatives spanning over 75 years of Port Washington social history; P W Play Troupe Archive of memorabilia covering the 60 year history of the oldest theatre group on Long Island; Collection of drawings by children's illustrator Peter Spier
Exhibitions: Lita Kelmenson (drawings & wood sculpture); Hajime Okubo (box constructions); Paul Wood (oil painting & watercolors); Photographers: Dency Ann Kane, Mariou Fuller, Christine Osinski
Publications: Monthly guide catalog

POTSDAM

M POTSDAM COLLEGE OF THE STATE UNIVERSITY OF NEW YORK, Roland Gibson Gallery, Pierrepont Ave, 13676. Tel 315-267-2250, 267-2481; *Dir* Dan Mills; *Cur* Diana Cooper
Open daily Noon - 5 PM. No admis fee. Estab 1967 to serve college & community as a teaching gallery. Gallery has 4800 square feet of exhibition space on three levels with security & environmental controls. Average Annual Attendance: 18,000. Mem: 200; dues $10-$100; annual meeting in Oct
Collections: †Contemporary Japanese, Italian & American art (painting, sculpture & prints); †contemporary drawing collection
Publications: Exhibition catalogs
Activities: Docent training; lect open to public, 10-12 vis lectr per year; concerts; gallery talks; tours; competitions; original objects of art lent to public institutions, art museums & art organizations; book traveling exhibitions 1-3 times per year; traveling exhibitions organized & circulated

M **POTSDAM PUBLIC MUSEUM,** Civic Ctr, Park St, 13676. Tel 315-265-6910; *Pres of Board* Louise Straub; *Dir* Betsy Travis
Open Tues - Sat 2 - 5 PM, cl Sun & Mon. No admis fee. Estab 1940 as an educational institution acting as a cultural & historical center for the Village of Potsdam & surrounding area. Educational services taken to area schools. Museum occupies a sandstone building, formerly a Universalist Church built in 1876. Maintains small reference library. Average Annual Attendance: 12,000
Income: Financed by village, town, state & federal appropriation
Collections: Burnap Collection of English Pottery; costumes of the 19th & 20th centuries; Mandarin Chinese hangings, china & costumes; photograph collection, artifacts & material on local history; pressed glass & art glass of the 19th & early 20th century
Exhibitions: Changing exhibitions
Publications: Newsletter, 3-4 times per year
Activities: Classes for adults & children; programs for schools; lect open to public, 8 vis lectr per year; concerts; tours

POUGHKEEPSIE

M **DUTCHESS COUNTY ARTS COUNCIL,** 39 Market St, 12601. Tel 914-454-3222; *Pres* Sherre Wesley; *Grants Coordr* Stephen Ladin; *Assoc Dir* Mary Koniz Arnold; *Bookkeeper* Lisa Fiorese
Open Mon - Fri 9 AM - 5 PM. No admis fee. Estab 1965 in mid-Hudson region as premiere location for arts cultural activities. Mem: 325; dues $25-$250; annual meeting in Jan
Income: $650,000 (financed by mem, county & state appropriation & Dutchess Arts Fund)
Publications: Artscene, quarterly newsletter; Arts in Education Quarterly
Activities: Coordinate arts-in-education programs in schools; lect open to public; technical assistance workshops; scholarships & fels offered

M **VASSAR COLLEGE,** The Frances Lehman Loeb Art Center, 124 Raymond Ave, 12604-6198. Tel 914-437-5235; FAX 914-437-7304; *Dir* James Mundy; *Cur* Francesca Consagra; *Registrar* Joann Potter; *Preparator* Bruce Bundock
Open Tues - Sat 10 AM - 5 PM, Sun Noon - 5 PM; cl Mon, Easter, Thanksgiving & the week between Christmas & New Year's. No admis fee. Estab 1864; collects Eastern & Western art of all periods. New mus opened in Nov 1993 in addition designed by Cesar Pelli. Mem: 1100; dues $35 & up; bi-annual meeting fall & spring
Income: Financed by Vassar College, endowment & mem
Collections: †Matthew Vassar collection of 19th century American paintings of Hudson River School & 19th century English watercolors; †Felix M Warburg Collection of medieval sculpture & graphics including Duerer & Rembrandt; †20th century art of all media including photography; †European paintings, sculpture & drawings ranging from the Renaissance to the 20th century, including Bacchiacca, Cezanne, Salvator Rosa, Claesz, Tiepolo, Robert, Corot, Cezanne, Delacroix, Gifford, Van Gogh, Tanner, Munch, Klee, Bourdelle, Laurent, Davidson, Gabo, Calder, Moore; †20th Century American & European paintings including Henri, Hartley, O'Keeffe, Bacon, Nicholson, Rothko, de Kooning, Hartigan, Weber; graphics ranging from Barocci to Rembrandt to Goya to Picasso, Matisse, Braque, Kelly, Grooms & Graves; photography from Anna Atkins, Cameron, Gilpin, Steichen, Abbott, Lange, Lynes & Linda Conner; †The Classical Collection includes Greek vases, Egyptian, Etruscan & Mycenaean objects, Roman glass, portrait busts, jewelry; other archaeological finds
Exhibitions: Recent Latin American Drawings; Works on Paper from Winston-Malbin Coll; Vanessa Bell; Nancy Graves
Publications: Occasional exhibition catalogues & biannual newsletter
Activities: Sales shop sells postcards, notecards, posters & exhibition catalogues
L **Art Library,** 124 Raymond Ave, 12604-6198. Tel 914-437-5790; Internet Home Page Address http://iberia.vassar.edu/art. *Librn* Thomas Hill
Open Mon - Thurs 8:30 AM - Midnight, Fri 8:30 AM - 10 PM, Sat 9 AM - 10 PM, Sun 10 AM - Noon, cl summer. Estab 1937. Circulation to students & faculty only
Library Holdings: Vols 45,000; Per subs 250; CD-ROMS; Micro — Fiche, reels; Other — Exhibition catalogs

PURCHASE

M **MANHATTANVILLE COLLEGE,** Brownson Art Gallery, Brownson Bldg, 2900 Purchase St, 10577. Tel 914-694-2200, Ext 331; FAX 914-694-6234; *Chmn* Randolph Williams; *Dean of Faculty* James B Bryan
Open 9 AM - 4:30 PM. No admis fee. Average Annual Attendance: 300 per wk
Income: Financed by endowment & tuition
Collections: Sculpture
Exhibitions: Leslie Lowinger, Graveyards & Other Places; Anthony & Ann Woiner, Exploring Spaces
Publications: Magazine, bimonthly; catalogs
Activities: Lect open to public, 5 vis lectr per year; concerts; gallery talks; scholarships; original objects of art lent; originate traveling exhibitions; sales shop sells books, magazines, reproductions & prints
L **Library,** 2900 Purchase St, 10577-0560. Tel 914-694-2200, Ext 274; FAX 914-694-6234; *Interim Dir* Debra Decorso
Library Holdings: Vols 250,000; Per subs 1100

C **PEPSICO INC,** Donald M Kendall Sculpture Garden, 700 Anderson Hill Rd, 10577. Tel 914-253-2900; *Former Chmn & Chief Exec Officer* Donald M Kendall; *Dir Art Prog* Katherine F Niles
Open Mon - Sun 9 AM - 5 PM. Estab 1970 to present sculpture of mus quality. Average Annual Attendance: 10,000
Collections: Forty-two large outdoor sculptures, works by Alexander Calder, Henry Moore, Louise Nevelson, David Smith, Arnaldo Pomodoro, Jacques Lipchitz, Henry Laurens, Auguste Rodin, Miro, Giacometti, Max Ernst, Jean DuBuffet, Tony Smith, George Segal, Claes Oldenburg, George Rickey, Richard Erdman & Barbara Hepworth

M **STATE UNIVERSITY OF NEW YORK AT PURCHASE,** Neuberger Museum of Art, 735 Anderson Hill Rd, 10577. Tel 914-251-6100; FAX 914-251-6101; *Dir* Lucinda H Gedeon; *Museum Mgr* Jay Block; *Registrar* Joan Hendricks; *Coordr Pub* Barbara Morgan; *Coordr Public Information* Patricia Greenhill; *Head Museum Educ* Eleanor Brackbill; *Membership Mgr* Jewel Hoogstoel; *Marketing Mgr* Nancy Drexler
Open Tues - Fri 10 AM - 4 PM, Sat & Sun 11 AM - 5 PM, cl Mon & major holidays. Suggested contribution $2. Estab 1968, opened May 1974 to serve university & residents of New York State & Connecticut. 78,000 sq ft facility designed by Johnson Burgee, with nine total galleries, five outside sculpture courts. Average Annual Attendance: 58,000. Mem: Dues sustaining $1000, patron $500, donor $250, contributing $100, family-dual $50, individual $35
Income: Financed by State University of New York, endowment fund, government grants, private foundations, donors & mem
Collections: African & ancient art; large scale sculpture; 3600 objects featuring 20th century European & American paintings, sculpture, drawings, prints, photographs & audio works
Exhibitions: Changing contemporary art exhibitions
Publications: Exhibition catalogues; brochures; quarterly calendars
Activities: Docent training; internships for Purchase College students; tours for children, adults & citizens with special needs; lect open to public, 10-12 vis lectr per year; concerts; gallery talks; tours; internships offered; original objects of art lent to other museums; book traveling exhibitions 2-3 per year; originate traveling exhibitions to other museums; sales shop sells books, magazines, prints, small gift items & cards
L **Library,** 735 Anderson Hill Rd, 10577-1400. Tel 914-251-6435; FAX 914-251-6437; *Dir* Lawrence E Randall; *Reference-Visual Arts Specialist* Martha C Smith
Library Holdings: Vols 255,000; Per subs 1000; Micro — Cards, fiche, reels; AV — A-tapes, cassettes, motion pictures, rec, slides, v-tapes; Other — Reproductions
Special Subjects: Afro-American Art, Art History, Drawings, Graphic Arts, Graphic Design, Painting - American, Painting - Dutch, Painting - European, Painting - Flemish, Painting - French, Painting - German, Painting - Italian, Photography, Prints, 20th Century American Art

RIVERHEAD

A **EAST END ARTS & HUMANITIES COUNCIL,** 133 E Main St, 11901. Tel 516-727-0900; FAX 516-727-0966; *Exec Dir* Patricia Berman
Open Mon - Fri 10 AM - 5 PM, Sat 12 - 5 PM. No admis fee. Estab 1972. Average Annual Attendance: 11,000. Mem: 900; dues $10 - $25
Income: Financed by public & private sector
Exhibitions: Neil Scholl, Muriel Rasserman, Beverly Livernoche & Pat Solan
Publications: East End Arts News, monthly; East End Calendar of Cultural Events
Activities: Classes for children; lect open to public; competitions with awards; gallery talks; tours; sales shop sells books, original art & crafts, hand crafted items

ROCHESTER

A **DEAF ARTISTS OF AMERICA INC,** * 302 N Goodman St, Ste 205, 14607. Tel 716-461-5464; FAX 716-461-5464; TTY 716-244-3450, Deaf Relay: 800-421-1220. *Exec Dir* Tom Willard
Estab 1985 to support & recognize America's deaf artists. Mem: 350; dues $25; biennial meeting in odd numbered years
Income: $35,000 (financed by mem, state appropriation, earned income)
Purchases: Assorted artwork
Collections: Permanent collection of artwork by deaf artists - all media included
Exhibitions: 1 exhibit per year
Publications: Directory of American Deaf Artists, annual; quarterly newsletter
Activities: Adult classes; workshops & conferences; lect open to public, 1-2 vis lectr per year

M **GEORGE EASTMAN HOUSE-INTERNATIONAL MUSEUM OF PHOTOGRAPHY & FILM,** 900 East Ave, 14607. Tel 716-271-3361; FAX 716-271-3970; *Chmn* Harris H Rusitzky; *Dir* Anthony Bannon; *Cur Film Coll* Paolo Cherchi Usai; *Controller* Paul J Piazza; *Cur Technology Coll* Todd Gustavson; *Mgr Information Technologies* Andrew Eskind; *Chief Cur Develop* Linda Gillim; *Chief Cur* Marianne Fulton; *Operations & Finance* Daniel Y McCormick
Open Tues - Sun. Admis adults $6.50, students & senior citizens $5, children 5-12 $2.50. Estab 1949 for photography exhibitions, research & educ. Restored landmark & gardens. Average Annual Attendance: 100,000. Mem: 3800; dues family $50, individual $40, students & senior citizens $25
Income: Financed by corp & individual gifts, foundation & government grants, earned income
Collections: Equipment (photographic); film; 19th & 20th century photography
Publications: Image, quarterly; books & catalogs
Activities: Classes for children; docent training; teacher workshops; school exhibition program; lect open to public; gallery talks; tours; scholarships offered; exten dept; lending collection contains photographs & original objects of art; book traveling exhibitions; traveling exhibitions organized & circulated; museum shop sells books, magazines & reproductions
L **Library,** 900 East Ave, 14607. Tel 716-271-3361; FAX 716-271-3970; *Archivist* David A Wooters; *Librn* Rachel Stuhlman
Open Tues by appointment only
Library Holdings: Vols 40,000; Per subs 375; Micro — Fiche, reels 75; AV — A-tapes, rec, slides; Other — Clipping files, exhibition catalogs, manuscripts, pamphlets, reproductions
Special Subjects: History & Aesthetics of Photography; Motion Pictures
Collections: Largest collection in the US of photographs, camera technology & Library dealing with the history & aesthetics of photography: 600,000 photographs including major collections of Edward Steichen, Alvin Langdon Coburn, Southworth & Howes, Louis Walton Sipley, Lewis Hine, Edward Muybridge & Nickolas Muray
Publications: Image, quarterly
Activities: Educ dept; docent training; Discovery Room for children

M LANDMARK SOCIETY OF WESTERN NEW YORK, INC, 133 S Fitzhugh St, 14608-2204. Tel 716-546-7029; FAX 716-546-4788; *Dir* Henry McCartney
Open Fri - Sun Noon - 4 PM. Admis adults $2, children under 14 $.25. Estab 1937. Mem: dues keystone $500, cornerstone $250, pillar $125, patron $75, family $35, active $25
Collections: Art, furnishings & decorative arts of the 1830s; furnishings & decorative arts of early 19th century
Publications: Bi-monthly newsletter; booklets; brochures; guides; postcards
Activities: Docent program; workshops; lect; tours
L Wenrich Memorial Library, 133 S Fitzhugh St, 14608-2204. Tel 716-546-7029; FAX 716-546-4788; *Asst Dir* Ann B Parks; *Res Coordr* Cynthia Howk
Open Tues - Fri 10 AM - 2 PM & by appointment. Estab 1970 to preserve landmarks in Western New York; information center containing drawings, photographs, slides, books & periodicals, as well as archives of local architecture & information on preservation & restoration techniques
Income: Financed by mem & special grants
Purchases: $900
Library Holdings: Vols 3000; Per subs 15; AV — Kodachromes, slides, v-tapes; Other — Clipping files, exhibition catalogs, manuscripts, original art works, pamphlets, photographs, prints
Special Subjects: Architecture, Decorative Arts, Furniture, Historical Material, Landscape Architecture, Landscapes, Restoration & Conservation, Architectural History, Historic Preservation, Local Architecture
Collections: Claude Bragdon Collection of Architectural Drawings; Historic American Buildings: Survey Drawings of Local Architecture; John Wenrich & Walter Cassebeer Collection of Prints & Watercolors
Exhibitions: Adaptive Use: New Uses for Old Buildings; The Architecture of Ward Wellington Ward; Rochester Prints, from the drawings of Walter Cassebeer
Publications: Newsletter, bi-monthly
Activities: Classes for adults & children; docent training; lect open to public; tours; originate traveling exhibitions to area schools, colleges, banks, community centers

M PYRAMID ARTS CENTER, 302 N Goodman St, 14607. Tel 716-461-2222; FAX 716-461-2223; *Dir* Elizabeth McDade
Open Thurs - Sun Noon - 5 PM. Admis $2 donation. Estab 1977 to hold exhibitions & performances, non-profit organization. Average Annual Attendance: 5000. Mem: 300; dues $48-$50
Income: Financed by the National Endowment to the Arts, The Appleman Foundation, The Village Gate Square, local businesses & our members
Exhibitions: Brazil: The Thinking Photography; Home ?; 7th Annual Members Exhibition; Upstate International
Activities: Educ dept; workshops with guest artists; lect open to public, 10 vis lectr per year; concerts; gallery talks; competitions; sales shop sells original art

A ROCHESTER HISTORICAL SOCIETY, 485 East Ave, 14607. Tel 716-271-2705; *Pres* Elizabeth G Holahan; *First VPres* David Hislop; *Cur* Nancy Schneiderman; *Cur* Meghan Lodge; *Treas* Clinton Steadman
Open Mon - Fri 10 AM - 4 PM. Admis adults $1.25, students & sr citizens $1, children under 12 $.50. Estab 1860, refounded 1888, to obtain & preserve relics & documents & publish material relating to Rochester's history. Headquaters on Woodside, Greek Revival Mansion built in 1839. Early Rochesterians portraits displayed throughout the house. Average Annual Attendance: 3000. Mem: 700; annual meeting in Spring
Income: Financed by mem
Collections: Rochester costumes, furnishings & portraits
Exhibitions: 19th century mansion with gardens
Publications: Genesee Valley Occasional Papers; The Rochester Historical Society Publication Fund Series, 25 volumes; Woodside's First Family, catalog
Activities: Lect open to public, 10 vis lectr per year; concerts; tours; individual paintings & original objects of art lent to museums & other institutions with adequate security

L ROCHESTER INSTITUTE OF TECHNOLOGY, Technical & Education Center of Graphic Arts & Imaging, 66 Lomb Memorial Dr, 14623-5604. FAX 716-475-7000; WATS 800-724-2536.
Center has been a leading provider of professional training for the graphic arts & imaging industries for more than 40 years. The T & E Center provides seminars & hands on workshops in traditional & leading edge technologies for graphic design & publishing software, image editing & compositing, digital photography & electronic prepress & publishing. In addition, introductory & advanced programs are also offered in printing production & technologies, business & production management, & Total Quality. T & E Center programs draw upon resources from RIT's School of Printing Management & Sciences, School of Photographic Arts & Sciences & the Center for Imaging Science as well as from industry to deliver practical training to today's graphic arts professional
Publications: T & E Update, monthly
Activities: Seminars for the graphic arts & imaging industries

M STRONG MUSEUM, One Manhattan Sq, 14607. Tel 716-263-2700; FAX 716-263-2493;
Internet Home Page Address http://www.rit.edu/-strwww. TDD 716-423-0746. *Pub Relations* Susan Trien
Open Mon - Sat 10 AM - 5 PM, Sun 1 - 5 PM. Admis adults $5, senior citizens & students with ID $4, children (3-16) $3, children under 3 free, mus members free, special reduced admis, greeting & group orientation & mus shop discount to booked groups of 20 or more. Accessible to people with disabilities; lectures may be sign interpreted with three days prior notice
Collections: 500,000 objects including dolls, furniture, glassware, miniatures & toys
Exhibitions: One History Place. (1997) Between 2 Worlds: African-American Identity & American Culture; Kid to Kid; Discovery Village; Can You Tell Me How to Get to Sesame Street? (1997-98) UnEARTHing the Secret Life of Stuff: Americans & the Environment; When Barbie Dated GI Joe: America's Romance with Cold War Toys
Activities: Family programs; Wed music; pre-school performance series

UNIVERSITY OF ROCHESTER
M Memorial Art Gallery, 500 University Ave, 14607-1415. Tel 716-473-7720; FAX 716-473-6266; TDD 716-473-6152. *Pres Board of Mgrs* Robert D Hursh; *Dir* Grant Holcomb; *Dir Develop* Peggy Hubbard; *Asst Dir Admin* Kim Hallatt; *Asst Dir Educ* Susan Dodge Peters; *Public Relations Mgr* Deborah Rothman; *Membership Mgr* Judie Van Bramer
Open Tues Noon - 9 PM, Wed - Fri 10 AM - 4 PM, Sat 10 AM - 5 PM, Sun Noon - 5 PM, cl Mon. Admis adults $5, senior citizens & students $4, children 6-18 $3, 5 & under, members & University of Rochester students free; $2 admis fee Tues 5 - 9 PM. Estab 1913 as a university art mus & pub art mus for the Rochester area. The original building is in an Italian Renaissance style. Average Annual Attendance: 160,000. Mem: 7200; dues $40 & up
Income: Financed by endowment, mem, grants, earned income & University support
Collections: Covers all major periods & cultural areas from Assyria & predynastic Egypt to the present, paintings, sculpture, prints, drawings, decorative arts; special strengths are medieval, 17th century Dutch painting, English Portraiture, 19th & early 20th century French painting, American art & American folk art
Exhibitions: Royal French Tapestries; Sacred Sand Painting of Tibet; The Studio Museum in Harlem
Publications: Gallery Notes, 6 times yr; Porticus, journal of the Memorial Art Gallery; exhibition catalogs
Activities: Studio art classes for adults & children; docent training; lect open to public; gallery talks; tours; exten dept serving Rochester area & surrounding nine counties; lending collection contains slides; book traveling exhibitions 4-6 per year; originate traveling exhibitions 10-12 per year; gallery store sells original art, fine crafts, prints, books & paper products
L Charlotte W Allen Library-Memorial Art Gallery, 500 University Ave, 14607. Tel 716-473-7720, Ext 3201; Elec Mail lbjh@db1.cc.rochester.edu. *Librn* Lucy Bjorklund Harper
Open Tues 1 - 8:30 PM, Wed - Fri 1 - 4 PM, Sun 12:30 - 4 PM, cl Sat & Mon. Estab as a research library
Income: Financed by endowment, mem & city appropriation
Library Holdings: Vols 25,000; Per subs 60; Auction catalogues; Micro — Reels; AV — Slides, v-tapes; Other — Clipping files, exhibition catalogs, manuscripts, memorabilia, pamphlets, photographs
Special Subjects: American Western Art, Architecture, Art Education, Art History, Decorative Arts, Drawings, Etchings & Engravings, Folk Art, Graphic Arts, History of Art & Archaeology, Laces, Landscapes, Painting - American, Painting - British, Painting - European
L Art Library, River Campus, 14627. Tel 716-275-4476; FAX 716-473-1906; *Librn* Stephanie J Frontz; *Slide Cur* Kim Kopatz
Open Mon - Thurs 9 AM - 10 PM, Fri 9 AM - 6 PM, Sat Noon - 5 PM, Sun 1 - 10 PM. Estab to support academic programs of Department of Art & Art History & other academic departments within the University. Small gallery is maintained by Art & Art History Department & Library
Library Holdings: Vols 40,000; Per subs 450; Micro — Fiche; AV — Kodachromes, lantern slides, motion pictures, slides; Other — Exhibition catalogs

M VISUAL STUDIES WORKSHOP, 31 Prince St, 14607. Tel 716-442-8676; FAX 716-442-1992; *Dir* Nathan Lyons; *Chmn Board of Trustees* William Edwards; *Coordr Exhib* James Wyman; *Coordr Book Distribution* Carise Skinner; *Coordr Summer Institute* Patti Healy
Open Mon - Fri 9 AM - 5 PM, Gallery open Tues - Sat Noon 5 PM. No admis fee. Estab 1969 to establish a center for the transmission & study of the visual image. Visual Studies Workshops produce & or present approximately 20 exhibitions per year encompassing contemporary & historical issues; subjects vary from photography, film, video, artists book works & related media. Average Annual Attendance: 300,000. Mem: 2300; dues $30
Income: $460,000 (financed by mem, state appropriation, federal & corporate resources & earned income)
Purchases: $5000
Special Subjects: Photography, Prints, Artist's Books
Collections: 19th & 20th century photographs, mechanical prints & artists books
Publications: Afterimage, monthly
Activities: Classes for adults; Summer Institute program with intensive short term workshops for artists & museum professionals; lect open to public, 15 vis lectr per year; gallery talks; tours (by appointment); original objects of art lent to institutions with proper exhibition facilities; lending collection contains 27,000 photographs of original artwork; traveling exhibitions organized & circulated to museums, colleges & universities; museum shop sells books, magazines, original art & prints
L Research Center, 31 Prince St, 14607. Tel 716-442-8676; FAX 716-442-1992; *Coordr* William Johnson
Open Mon & Tues 8:30 AM - 12:30 PM, Wed & Fri 8:30 AM - 2 PM, Thurs 6:30 - 9:30 PM. Estab 1971 to maintain a permanent collection for the study of the function & effect of the visual image. For reference only
Income: $80,000 (financed by grants)
Purchases: $5000
Library Holdings: Vols 19,000; Per subs 160; Posters; AV — A-tapes, cassettes, Kodachromes, lantern slides, motion pictures, slides, v-tapes; Other — Clipping files, exhibition catalogs, original art works, pamphlets, photographs, prints, reproductions
Special Subjects: Photography
Collections: Illustrated book collection; photographic print collection
Publications: Various publications
Activities: Internship programs; workshops; graduate museum studies program; visual studies; lect open to public; gallery talks; tours

ROME

A ROME ART & COMMUNITY CENTER, 308 W Bloomfield St, 13440. Tel 315-336-1040; FAX 315-336-1090; *Dir* Linda Finley
Open Mon - Sat 9 AM - 5 PM, Mon - Thurs 6:30 - 9 PM. No admis fee. Estab 1968 for art exhibits & classes. Three galleries. Average Annual Attendance: 30,000. Mem: 1000; dues family with 2 children $10, individual $5
Income: Financed by city appropriation, New York State Council on the Arts, Oneida County, United Arts Fund-Mohawk Valley, mem, donations & private foundations
Exhibitions: Various art & craft exhibitions every six weeks
Publications: Newsletter, bimonthly; community calendar, quarterly; class brochures, quarterly
Activities: Classes for adults & children; lect open to public, 20 vis lectr per year; tours; readings; concerts; weekly films; scholarships to gifted children

M ROME HISTORICAL SOCIETY MUSEUM, 200 Church St, 13440. Tel 315-336-5870; *Pres* Dr William Forbes; *Dir* Jon Austin; *First VPres* Randall Bright
Open Mon - Fri 9 AM - 4 PM & during special events, cl holidays. No admis fee. Estab 1936 as a historical mus & soc. 2 galleries for temporary exhibitions on specific topics of local interest. Average Annual Attendance: 11,500. Mem: 695; dues $10-$100; annual meeting in Aug
Income: Financed by mem, city appropriation, private foundations, federal & state grants
Collections: E Buyck; P F Hugunine; Forest Moses; Ann Marriot; Will Moses; Revolutionary War period paintings
Exhibitions: Variety of exhibitions examining local history using objects & 2-D materials
Publications: Annals & Recollections, quarterly; monthly newsletter
Activities: Classes for children; lect open to the public, 6 vis lectr per year; tours; museum shop sells books, prints & slides
L William E Scripture Memorial Library, 200 Church St, 13440. Tel 315-336-5870; FAX 315-336-5912; *Cur Coll* Barbara Schafer; *Cur Educ* Lisa Selander
Open Mon - Fri 9 AM - 4 PM. Estab 1936 for historical research of Rome & the Mohawk Valley
Library Holdings: Vols 3500; Micro — Reels; Other — Clipping files, manuscripts, pamphlets, photographs, prints
Special Subjects: Archaeology, Architecture, Crafts, Decorative Arts, Folk Art, Furniture, Historical Material, Manuscripts, Maps, Local history
Collections: Area paintings from the Revolutionary War period to the present; Frederick Hodges Journals; The Hathaway Papers; Local Malitia Records 1830-1840; La Vita: Local newspaper printed in Rome New York 1918-1950
Exhibitions: History of Rome

ROSENDALE

A WOMEN'S STUDIO WORKSHOP, INC, 722 Binnewater Lane, PO Box 489, 12472. Tel 914-658-9133; FAX 914-658-9031; Elec Mail wsw@mhv.net. *Exec Dir* Ann Kalmbach; *Prog Dir* Laura Moriarty; *Artistic Dir* Tana Kellner
Open Tues - Fri 10 AM - 5 PM. Estab 1974. Mem: 814; dues $25
Income: $200,000 (financed by sales, tuition & grants)
Publications: Artists' books, 5-7 per yr
Activities: Classes for adults & children; lect open to public, 45 vis lectr per year; tours; grants offered; exten dept; original objects of art lent; book traveling exhibitions, annually; originate traveling exhibitions; sales shop sells workshop products, books & handmade paper

ROSLYN

L BRYANT LIBRARY, 2 Paper Mill Rd, 11576. Tel 516-621-2240; FAX 516-621-7211, 621-5905; Elec Mail rnlinfo@lilrc.org. *Dir* Elizabeth McCloat; *Coordr Progs & Public Relations* Linda Locke
Estab 1878 as a public library. Gallery houses monthly exhibits, mostly paintings. Has been renamed the Heckscher Museum of Art at Bryant Library. Circ 272,894
Income: $2,700,000
Library Holdings: Vols 176,000; Per subs 465; Micro — Fiche, reels; AV — Cassettes 17,286, fs, v-tapes 3937; Other — Clipping files, manuscripts 11,933, pamphlets 1844, photographs 7697
Special Subjects: Architecture, Historical Material
Collections: William Cullen Bryant; Christopher Morley; local history of Roslyn, Long Island, New York
Publications: Bryant Library Calendar of Events, monthly; Bryant Library Newsletter, bi-monthly; The Bryant Library: 100 Years, 1878-1978, exhibit catalogue; W C Bryant in Roslyn, book; exhibit catalog
Activities: Lect open to public, 30-40 vis lectr per year; concerts

ROSLYN HARBOR

M NASSAU COUNTY MUSEUM OF FINE ART, One Museum Dr, 11576. Tel 516-484-9337; FAX 516-484-0710; *Dir & Chief Cur* Constance Schwartz; *Operations Mgr* Nicholas Doering; *Admin Asst* Christine Standridge; *Comptroller* Ann Gelles; *Registrar* Fernanda Bennett; *Coordr Young People's Prog* Jean Henning
Open Tues - Sun 11 AM - 5 PM. Admis adult $4, sr citizens $3, children $2. Estab 1989 to exhibit major exhibitions. Art mus housed in c 1900, three story Neo-Georgian brick mansion, former estate of Childs Frick, 9 galleries & 145 acres for sculpture park, formal gardens. Average Annual Attendance: 250,000. Mem: 3000; dues $40-$1000; annual meeting in Jan
Income: $900,000 (financed by mem, county appropriation, corporate & foundation grants, admis & special events)
Collections: 20th century American prints; drawings; outdoor sculpture; architectural blueprints & drawings relating to the museum building & property.
Publications: Catalogs for exhibitions
Activities: Classes for adults & children; docent training; lect open to public; gallery talks; tours; individual paintings lent; originate traveling exhibitions organized & circulated to the Gallery Association of New York State; sales shop sells art books, catalogs, crafts & other museum related items

SAINT BONAVENTURE

M SAINT BONAVENTURE UNIVERSITY, Regina A Quick Fine Art Center, 14778. Tel 716-375-2000; *Spec Coordr* Margaret Mead
Open Mon - Thurs 8 AM - midnight, Fri 8 AM - 5 PM, Sat 8 AM - 8 PM, Sun 10 AM - midnight. No admis fee. Estab 1856 to provide artistic surroundings for students. Average Annual Attendance: 4000
Income: Financed by university budget
Collections: Chinese porcelains; cloisonne; ivories, jade miniatures; paintings; porcelains & American Indian pottery;
Exhibitions: Rotating exhibitions
Publications: Art Catalog of Collection
Activities: Museum shop sells reproductions

SALAMANCA

M SENECA-IROQUOIS NATIONAL MUSEUM, 794-814 Broad St, 14779-1331. Tel 716-945-1738; FAX 716-945-1760; *Museum Dir* Judith Greene
Open 9 AM - 5 PM. Estab 1977
Collections: Archeological, anthropological & archival collections, including photography, audio; traditional & contemporary works
Exhibitions: Lands of Our Ancestors
Publications: SINM - Collection

SANBORN

M NIAGARA COUNTY COMMUNITY COLLEGE ART GALLERY, 3111 Saunders Settlement Rd, 14132. Tel 716-731-3271, Ext 390; *Gallery Dir* Monica Vacanti
Open Tues - Thurs 11 AM - 8 PM, Fri 9 AM - 4 PM. No admis fee. Estab 1973 for varied exhibits that will be of interest to students & the community. Gallery has 270 sq ft of area & approx 250 running ft. Average Annual Attendance: 9000
Income: $4500
Collections: Prints (contemporary)
Exhibitions: African Treasures; Faculty Exhibit; Spring Student Exhibit; Student Art Exhibit; Student Illustration Exhibit/SUNY Buffalo; Three Photographers Rural Vistas-Rediscovery of the American Landscape; paintings by Coniglie, Headrick, Hucke, Ram & Spurling; Yuppidreams in Darthvader Frames by Kim Yarwood (paintings); NCCC Student Exhibition; Architecture in Contemporary Prints; Dixon, Godsisz, Runca-NCC Alumni Exhibition (paintings, mixed media); Mary Roehm (architectural ceramics).
Publications: Catalogs
Activities: Classes for adults; dramatic programs; lect, 2-3 vis lectr per year; gallery talks

SARATOGA SPRINGS

M NATIONAL MUSEUM OF RACING, National Museum of Racing & Hall of Fame, 191 Union Ave, 12866. Tel 518-584-0400; FAX 518-584-4574; *Dir* Peter Hammell; *Cur* Field Horne
Open Mon - Sat 10 AM - 4:30 PM, Sun Noon - 4:30 PM. Admis adult $3, senior citizens & students $2, children under 12 must be accompanied by parents, Sun free. Estab 1950 as a mus for the collection, preservation & exhibition of all kinds of articles associated with the origin, history & development of horse racing. There are 10 galleries of sporting art. The handsome Georgian-Colonial design brick structure houses one of the world's greatest collections of equine art along with trophies, sculptures & memorabilia of the sport from its earliest days. Average Annual Attendance: 25,000. Mem: 1000; dues $35
Income: Financed through annual appeal, individual contributions, grants, shop sales & endowment
Collections: Oil paintings of thoroughbred horses, trophies, racing silks, bronzes, prints, racing memorabilia
Exhibitions: Student Art Show (annual); Treasures of the Track-Trophies; The Thrill of Excellence-Equine Paintings
Publications: Catalog; Hall of Fame booklets
Activities: Educ dept; lect open to public, 6 vis lectr per year; gallery talks; tours; competitions; museum shop sells books, magazines, original art, reproductions & prints
L Reference Library, 191 Union Ave, 12866. Tel 518-584-0400; FAX 518-584-4574; *Dir* Peter H Hammell
Open Mon - Sat 10 AM - 4:30 PM, Sun Noon - 4:30 PM. Estab 1970 as a reference library on thoroughbred racing. Open to researchers, students & authors by appointment
Library Holdings: Vols 3000; Other — Clipping files, exhibition catalogs, manuscripts, memorabilia, original art works, pamphlets, photographs
Special Subjects: Painting - American, Painting - British, Thoroughbred Racing

M SKIDMORE COLLEGE, Schick Art Gallery, N Broadway, 12866. Tel 518-584-5000, Ext 2370; FAX 518-584-3023; *Dir* David Miller; *Asst to Dir* Maureen Jones
Open Sept - May Mon - Fri 9 AM - 5 PM, Sat & Sun 1 - 3:30 PM; summer hours variable according to summer class schedules. No admis fee. Estab 1927 for educational enrichment of the college & community. Exhibitions are intended to bring awareness of both contemporary & historical trends in art. Average Annual Attendance: 12,000
Income: Financed through College
Collections: American & European Prints; Saratoga Springs Historical Collection
Exhibitions: Borne with a Silver Spoon: Metal Exhibition by Rosanne Raab; Art Faculty; Wolf Kahn Paintings; Series of videos produced by contemporary artists
Publications: Exhibition catalogs, occasionally
Activities: Lect open to public, 5-6 vis lectr per year; gallery talks; traveling exhibitions organized & circulated

L **Lucy Scribner Library**, Art Reading Area, N Broadway, 12866. Tel 518-584-5000, Ext 2618; *Fine & Performing Arts Librn* Jane Graves; *Visual Resource Assoc* Theresa Somaio
Open Mon - Sat 8 AM - 11 PM, Sun Noon - 11 PM. Estab 1925
Library Holdings: Vols 392,014; Per subs 1653; Micro — Cards; AV — Fs, Kodachromes, lantern slides, motion pictures, rec, slides 53,000; Other — Exhibition catalogs, memorabilia, original art works, photographs, prints 600, reproductions, sculpture
Collections: Anita Pohndorff Yates Collection of Saratoga History

SCHENECTADY

A **SCHENECTADY COUNTY HISTORICAL SOCIETY**, 32 Washington Ave, 12305. Tel 518-374-0263; *Pres* Robert Sager; *Coordr Exhib* Jo Mordecai
Open Mon - Fri 1 - 5 PM, 2nd Sat monthly 9 AM - 1 PM. Admis adults $2, children $1. Estab 1905, for the preservation of local historical materials. Three-story Victorian house has antique furniture & oil paintings from 18th century. Average Annual Attendance: 7500. Mem: 850; dues donor $50, family $25, individual $15; annual meeting 2nd Tues of Apr
Collections: Decorative arts; gun room; historical material; Indian artifacts; paintings; photographs; Schenectady artifacts from 18th century
Exhibitions: Temporary exhibitions from other museums
Publications: Monthly newsletter
Activities: Lect open to public, 20 vis lectr per year; tours; exten dept serves elementary schools; sales shop sells books & slides
L **Library**, 32 Washington Ave, 12305. Tel 518-374-0263; *Archivist Librn* Elsie Maddaus
Open Mon - Fri 1 - 5 PM, 2nd Sat each month 9 AM - 1 PM. Admis research $3, mus tour $2, members free. Estab 1905 to promote history & genealogy of the county & nearby counties. For reference only. Mem: 650; dues $15 & up; annual meeting in Apr
Library Holdings: Vols 4000; Micro — Fiche, reels; AV — A-tapes, cassettes, fs, motion pictures, slides; Other — Clipping files, manuscripts 16,000, memorabilia, pamphlets, photographs, reproductions
Special Subjects: Genealogy, Local History
Activities: Educ dept; some lect open to public & some to members only; tours; sales shop sells books

M **SCHENECTADY MUSEUM PLANETARIUM & VISITORS CENTER**, Nott Terrace Heights, 12308. Tel 518-382-7890; FAX 518-382-7893; *Dir* Bart A Rosselli; *Cur Exhibits* John Davis; *Cur Coll* Jennifer Drafen; *Cur Educ* Georgia Smolkis; *Public Information* Carol J Hudson
Open Tues - Fri 10 AM - 4:30 PM, Sat & Sun Noon - 5 PM. Mus only admis adults $3, children $1.50; mus & planetarium adults $5, children $2.50. Founded 1934, chartered by the New York State Regents in 1937 to increase & diffuse knowledge in appreciation of art, history, industry & science by providing collections, exhibits, lectures & other programs. Sales & rental gallery is maintained. Average Annual Attendance: 50,000. Mem: 2200; dues family $45, individual $30, student & senior citizens $15; annual meeting in Oct
Collections: Decorative arts; 19th & 20th century art; 19th & 20th century costumes & textiles; regional art; science & technology
Exhibitions: Electron City; Out of the Ordinary; Sense & Perception; Reptiles & Amphibians; Continuous Costume Exhibits
Publications: Annual Report; Museum Notes, bi-monthly; exhibition catalogues
Activities: Art & craft classes; Festival of Nations; Crafts Fair; Rock Festival; Haunted House; Museum Ball; docent training; lect open to public; concerts; gallery talks; tours; materials & exhibits lent to area schools, colleges & libraries; book traveling exhibitions 3-4 per year; museum shops sell books, original art, reproductions, prints & crafts
L **Hall of Electrical History**, Nott Terrace Heights, 12308. Tel 518-382-7890; *Dir* Bart A Roselli
For reference & technical information only, by appointment only
Collections: 1,500,000 photos & papers relating to the electrical industry from 1881 to present; 2000 artifacts

SENECA FALLS

M **SENECA FALLS HISTORICAL SOCIETY MUSEUM**, 55 Cayuga St, 13148. Tel 315-568-8412; *Acting Exec Dir* Frances Bardieri; *Pres* Rebecca Holden; *Educ Coordr* Frances Barbieri
Open Mon - Fri 9 AM - 5 PM. Admis adult $3, children & students $1.50. Estab 1896 as an educational institution dedicated to the preservation & interpretation of Seneca County. Victorian 23 room house with decorative arts collection. Average Annual Attendance: 9000. Mem: 400; dues family $25, single $15; annual meeting in Feb
Income: $85,000 (financed by endowment, mem, city, state & federal appropriation, United Way)
Collections: Local painters; central New York State folk art & crafts; Currier & Ives prints; nineteenth century decorative arts
Publications: Reprints of archival material
Activities: Classes for adults & children; docent training; school group programs; lect open to public, 8 vis lectr per year, concerts; gallery talks, tours; original objects of art lent to other institutions; sales shop sells books & reproductions

SETAUKET

M **GALLERY NORTH**, 90 N Country Rd, 11733. Tel 516-751-2676; FAX 516-751-0180; *Pres* Vinnie Fish; *VPres* James Lecky; *Dir* Louise Kalin; *Dir Asst* Carolyn Fell; *Treas* Janine Redlein
Open Tues - Sat 10 AM - 5 PM, Sun 1 - 5 PM. No admis fee. Estab 1965 to exhibit the work of contemporary Long Island artists & crafts people. Gallery is housed in Victorian building with 3 main exhibition rooms. Average Annual Attendance: 10,000. Mem: 150; dues $10 - $100; quarterly meetings
Income: $130,000 (financed by mem & sales)
Exhibitions: Eight changing exhibitions per yr; annual outdoor art show open to artists & crafts people
Activities: Lectures open to public; competitions with awards; sales shop sells crafts from local artists & imported crafts

SKANEATELES

M **JOHN D BARROW ART GALLERY**, 49 E Genesee St, 13152. Tel 315-685-5135
Open winter Thurs & Sat 2 - 4 PM; summer Mon - Sat 2 - 4 PM. No admis fee. Estab in 1900 to exhibit paintings of John D Barrow. Three rooms with unusual feature of tiered paintings built in a wainscoting
Income: Financed by donations
Activities: Lect open to public

A **SKANEATELES LIBRARY ASSOCIATION**, 49 E Genesee St, 13152. Tel 315-685-5135; *Pres* Robert Malone
Open Mon, Wed, Fri, Sat 10 AM - 5 PM, Tues & Thurs 10 AM - 8:30 PM, and by request. Estab 1900 to display paintings of John D Barrow. 2 rooms, one with single & one with triple wainscoting of paintings. Average Annual Attendance: 1150. Mem: Annual meeting 4th Thurs in Jan
Income: Financed by annual fundraising drive & endowments
Collections: Paintings by American artists; etchings by American & foreign artists; 300 paintings by John D Barrow, in separate wing; 19th century landscapes & portraits
Exhibitions: Occasional special exhibitions
Activities: Annual guided tours for 4th graders; docent training; occasional open lect; gallery talks; tours; paintings lent for one year on the condition that borrower pays for restoration; sales shop sells prints, postcards, calendars

SOUTHAMPTON

M **THE PARRISH ART MUSEUM**, 25 Jobs Lane, 11968. Tel 516-283-2118; FAX 516-283-7006; *Dir* Trudy Kramer; *Assoc Dir* Anke Jackson; *Cur* Alice Huei-Zu Yang; *Educ Dir* Kimberly Rhodes
Open Mon, Thurs, Fri & Sat 11 AM - 5 PM, Sun 1 - 5 PM, mid-June - mid-Sept Tues 11 AM - 5 PM, cl Wed. Admis $3, members free. Estab 1898 to exhibit, care for & research permanent collections & loaned works of art with empasis on american 19th & 20th century art. Three main galleries are maintained; total dimensions 4288 sq ft, 355 running feet. Average Annual Attendance: 70,000. Mem: 1500; dues $25-$1000 & up; annual meeting in Oct
Income: Financed by contributions & grants
Collections: †American paintings, 19th & 20th century; Dunnigan Collection of 19th century etchings; Japanese woodblock prints & stencils; Samuel Parrish Collection of Italian Renaissance panel
Exhibitions: (1997) The Kimono Inspiration: Art & Art-to-Wear in America; The Tenth Street Studio Building: Artists-Entrepreneurs from the Hudson River School to the American Impressionists; Alfonso Ossorio: Congregations, 1959-1969; Fairfield Porter from the Permanent Collection of the Parrish Art Museum. (1997-98) Collection in Context: selected Contemporary Photographs of Hands from the Collection of Henry Mendelssohn Buhl
Activities: Classes for adults & children; dramatic programs; docent training; lect open to public, 5 vis lectr per year; concerts; gallery talks; tours; competitions with prizes; exten dept serving area schools; individual paintings & objects of art lent to museums; traveling exhibitions organized & circulated; museum shop sells books, educational toys, gifts, posters
L **Aline B Saarinen Library**, 25 Jobs Lane, 11968. Tel 516-283-2118; FAX 516-283-7006; *Librn* Virginia Drucker
Open to staff members only. Reference library
Library Holdings: Vols 4200; Per subs 6; Other — Clipping files, exhibition catalogs, memorabilia
Special Subjects: Architecture, Art History, Drawings, Oriental Art, Painting - American
Collections: William Merritt Chase Archives; original documents, photographs, memorabilia, research materials pertaining to the life and work of Chase (1849-1916)

STAATSBURG

M **NEW YORK STATE OFFICE OF PARKS, RECREATION & HISTORICAL PRESERVATION**, Mills Mansion State Historical Site, Old Post Rd, PO Box 308, 12580. Tel 914-889-4100; FAX 914-889-8321; *Historic Site Mgr* Melodye Moore
Open May 26 - Oct 31, Wed - Sun 10 AM - 4:30 PM. No admis fee. Estab 1938 to interpret lifestyle of the very affluent segment of American society during the period 1890-1929. Average Annual Attendance: 10,000
Collections: Original furnishings, paintings, prints, decorative art objects and tapestries from Mr and Mrs Mills
Activities: Docent training; workshops; lectures open to the public; concerts; gallery tours; loans of paintings or original art objects have to be approved by New York State Office of Parks and Recreation, Division of Historic Preservation

STATEN ISLAND

M **JACQUES MARCHAIS MUSEUM OF TIBETAN ART CENTER OF TIBETAN ART**, Tibetan Museum, 338 Lighthouse Ave, 10306. Tel 718-987-3500 (main office); FAX 718-351-0402; *Asst Dir* Dorothy Reilly
Open Wed - Sun 1 - 5 PM. Admis adults $3, senior citizens $2.50, children under 12 $1. Estab 1946 for maintenance of library & museum in Buddhist philosophy, art & religion, with particular emphasis on Tibetan art & culture. Buildings planned for & collection amassed by Mrs Harry Klauber, (known professionally as Jacques Marchais) who ran an Oriental art gallery from 1938 until her death in 1948. Average Annual Attendance: 10,000. Mem: 300; dues $20 & up
Income: Financed by contributions, admis, mem, city, state & federal appropriations, gift shop sales, foundation & corporate grants
Purchases: Tibetan art & ethnographic materials; books on related subjects
Collections: †Jacques Marchais permanent collection of Tibetan and Buddhist Art

Publications: The Dalai Lama at the Jacques Marchais Tibetan Museum; Tibetan Museum Elementary School Teacher's Guide; Tibetan Museum Secondary School Teacher's Guide; Treasures of Tibetan Art: The Collections of the Jacques Marchais Museum of Tibetan Art

Activities: Educ programs are offered for school groups, adult groups, sr citizens & blind & visually impaired audiences, appointment required; dramatic programs, dance; poetry readings; lectures open to public, 20 vis lectr per year; concerts; gallery talks; tours; exten servs New York City; individual paintings & original objects of art lent to museums for special exhibits; museum shop sells books, Tibetan carpets, wooden masks, jewelry, music tapes, posters, textiles, gift ware & unique items from various Asian countries

M THE JOHN A NOBLE COLLECTION, 1000 Richmond Terrace, 10301. Tel 718-447-6490; *Dir* Erin Urban
Open weekdays 1 - 5 PM. No admis fee. Estab 1986 to present art & maritime history. Permanent installation of John A Noble's Houseboat Studio; art; gallery for changing exhibitions of prints & maritime history. Average Annual Attendance: 5000. Mem: 500; dues $25; annual meeting in Apr
Income: $100,000 (financed by mem, state & city appropriation)
Collections: Archives; †Art; Maritime Artifacts
Publications: Hold Fast!, quarterly newsletter
Activities: Classes for adults & children; lect open to public; lending collection contains 80 paintings & art objects

M ORDER SONS OF ITALY IN AMERICA, Garibaldi & Meucci Museum, 420 Tompkins Ave, 10305. Tel 718-442-1608; *Dir* Carol Quinby
Open Tues - Sun 9 AM - 5 PM. No admis fee. Estab 1956 to collect, preserve & interpret material pertaining to Italian culture. Average Annual Attendance: 3300. Mem: 125; dues $25
Income: $100,000 (financed by endowment, mem, city & state appropriation, Order Sons of Italy in America)
Collections: Bronzes; Coins; Decorative Arts; Medals; Paintings; Paper; Prints; Stamps
Exhibitions: Garibaldi, Champion of Liberty; Through the Golden Door, Lewis Hine (photos); Antonio Meucci, inventor, engineer & patriot
Activities: Classes for adults & children; lect open to public, 4 vis lectr per year

M SNUG HARBOR CULTURAL CENTER, Newhouse Center for Contemporary Art, 1000 Richmond Terrace, 10301. Tel 718-448-2500; FAX 718-442-8534; *Dir Visual Arts* Olivia Georgia
Open Wed - Sun Noon - 5 PM. Admis donation. Estab 1977 to provide a forum for regionally & nationally significant visual art. Average Annual Attendance: 50,000
Income: Financed by mem, city & state appropriation, corporate funds
Collections: Changing exhibits
Exhibitions: Outside The Frame: Performance Art 1950's to present; Neighborhoods: The Story of Staten Island; Woman's Art Caucus; Abstraction After the Fall: Abstract Art after 1970
Publications: Exhibition catalogs
Activities: Children's programs; docent programs; lect open to public, 3 vis lectr per year; retail store sells books, prints, original art, reproductions

M STATEN ISLAND INSTITUTE OF ARTS & SCIENCES, 75 Stuyvesant Pl, 10301. Tel 718-727-1135; FAX 718-273-5683; *Chmn Board* Jonathan Poznansky; *Pres & Chief Exec Officer* Hedy Hartman; *Cur History* Vince Sweeney
Open Mon - Sat 9 AM - 5 PM, Sun 1 - 5 PM. No admis fee, donations accepted. Estab 1881, inc 1906. Average Annual Attendance: 105,000. Mem: 750; dues $15 & up
Collections: †American paintings of the 19th & 20th centuries; Oriental, Greek, Roman & primitive art objects; †prints & small sculptures
Exhibitions: Decorative arts; design exhibitions in various media; major loan shows of paintings & prints; special exhibitions of graphic arts & of photography
Publications: Annual Reports; catalog
Activities: Fall & spring terms for adults & children classes; docent training; lect on art & science open to public; complete program of lectr, art & natural history for school children with annual registration of 47,000; 40 vis lectr per year; gallery talks; tours; competitions with awards; museum shop sells books, original art & reproductions
L Archives Library, 75 Stuyvesant PL, 10301. Tel 718-727-1135; FAX 718-273-5683; *Cur Archives & Library* Vince Sweeney
Library Holdings: Vols 30,000; Per subs 10
Collections: George W Curtis Collection of books, manuscripts & memorabilia; reference collection of 30,000 publications in science & art history; a choice collection of Staten Island newspapers from 1834-1934 on microfilm; letters, documents, journals, files of clippings & old photographs relating to the history of Staten Island & the metropolitan region
Publications: Proceeding of Staten Island Institute of Arts & Sciences

STONE RIDGE

M ULSTER COUNTY COMMUNITY COLLEGE, Muroff-Kotler Visual Arts Gallery, 12484. Tel 914-687-5000; *Chmn Prof* Allan L Cohan
Open Mon - Fri 10 AM - 3 PM, fall & spring semesters, cl summer. No admis fee. Estab 1963 as a center for creative activity. Gallery is maintained as an adjunct to the college's cultural & academic program; John Vanderlyn Hall has 40 x 28 ft enclosed space & is located on the campus. Average Annual Attendance: 3000
Income: Financed by college funds
Purchases: $750
Collections: Contemporary drawings, †paintings, photographs, prints, sculpture, historical works
Exhibitions: 6 exhibitions per year annual student show
Publications: Flyers announcing each exhibit, every four to six weeks
Activities: Lect open to public, 2-3 vis lectr per year; concerts

STONY BROOK

M THE MUSEUMS AT STONY BROOK, 1208 Rte 25A, 11790. Tel 516-751-0066; FAX 516-751-0353; *Pres* Deborah J Johnson; *Develop Assoc* Amanda Meyers
Open Wed - Fri 9 AM - 5 PM, Sat & Sun Noon - 5 PM. Admis adults $6, students & senior citizens $4, children 6-12 $3, under 6 & members free. Estab 1946 to make Long Island history & American Art available to pub. The Museums' 22 buildings, 13.5 acre complex include a History Mus, Art Mus, Carriage Mus, various period buildings, a mus store & the Hawkins-Mount House (currently not open to the pub). Average Annual Attendance: 50,000. Mem: 1000; dues $25-$5000
Collections: Paintings & drawings by †William Sidney Mount & other American Artists including †Shepard Alonzo Mount, †Henry S Mount, †William M Davis, †Edward Lange, †Charles H Miller; costumes; toys & dolls; decoys; textiles; carriages & carriage accoutrements; miniature rooms; American historical artifacts
Exhibitions: (1997) Shaking, Not Stired: Cocktail Shakers & Design; Out of the Ordinary; Community Taste & Values in Contemporary Fold Art. (1998) Stanford White on Long Island
Publications: Annual Report; Quarterly Newsletter; exhibition catalogs; brochures
Activities: Classes for adults & children; docent training; lect open to public, vis lectr varies; concerts; gallery talks; tours; individual paintings & original objects of art lent to qualifying institutions; originate traveling exhibitions to history & art museums; museum shop sells books, reproductions & prints
L Kate Strong Historical Library, 1208 Rte 25A, 11790. Tel 516-751-0066; FAX 516-751-0353; *Coll Mgr* Judy Estes; *Art Cur* Ita Berkow
Reference library & art mus open to researchers by appointment
Library Holdings: Vols 2194; Per subs 62; Trade catalogs; AV — Motion pictures, slides, v-tapes; Other — Exhibition catalogs, manuscripts, pamphlets, photographs
Special Subjects: Afro-American Art, American Indian Art, American Western Art, Architecture, Art Education, Art History, Ceramics, Coins & Medals, Collages, Commercial Art, Conceptual Art, Costume Design & Construction, Crafts, Decorative Arts, Display, American Art History
Collections: William Cooper, shipbuilder, 19th century, Sag Harbor; Israel Green Hawkins, Edward P Buffet, Hal B Fullerton; Archives: Papers of William Sidney Mount and family; Daniel Williamson & John Williamson, Stony Brook, Etta Sherry

M STATE UNIVERSITY OF NEW YORK AT STONY BROOK, University Art Gallery, 11794-5425. Tel 516-632-7240; *Dir* Rhonda Cooper
Open Tues - Fri Noon - 4 PM, Sat 5 - 8 PM. No admis fee. Estab 1967 to serve both the campus and the community by exhibiting professional artists. One gallery 41 x 73 with 22 ft ceiling; second space 22 x 73 ft with 12 ft ceilings. Average Annual Attendance: 2000 students & members of the community per show
Income: Financed by state appropriation
Exhibitions: (1997) Terry Netter; Text & Identity
Publications: Catalogues, five times a year
Activities: Lectures open to the public, bi-monthly, 4 - 6 vis lectrs per year; traveling exhibitions

SYRACUSE

M EVERSON MUSEUM OF ART, 401 Harrison St, 13202. Tel 315-474-6064; *Pres* David Nutting; *Dir* Sandra Trop; *VPres* Thomas Kennedy; *VPres* Carol Porter; *Dir* Ronald A Kuchta; *Cur* Thomas Piche Jr; *Develop Officer* Kristine Waelder; *Pub Information Officer* Linda M Herbert
Open Tues - Fri Noon - 5 PM, Sat 10 AM - 5 PM, Sun Noon - 5 PM, cl Mon. Admis $2 suggested donation. Estab 1896 to present free exhibitions by lending artists, chiefly American to serve as an educational element for the cultural & general community. The Syracuse China Center of the Study of American Ceramics provides 4022 sq ft of open storage for the museum's collection of 2000 pieces of American ceramics, ranging from Native American pots, circa AD 1000, to contemporary ceramic sculpture & vessel forms, also includes study collections of world ceramics, numbering 2000 objects. Average Annual Attendance: 80,000. Mem: 2000; dues general $35, senior citizens $25
Income: Financed by mem, county & state appropriation, New York Council on the Arts, gifts & grants
Collections: African Collection; †contemporary American ceramics; †contemporary American painting & sculpture; 17th, 18th & 19th century English porcelain; †traditional American painting & portraiture; video-tape collection; Cloud Wampler Collection of Oriental Art
Exhibitions: (1997) Art Explosion!; Life Cycles: The Charles E Burchfield Collection; Dale Chihuly: Seaforms
Publications: Art books; Quarterly bulletin; Educational materials; exhibition catalogs
Activities: Docent training; lect open to public, 10 vis lectr per year; concerts; gallery talks; tours; competitions; exten dept serves public schools of Syracuse; book traveling exhibitions 5 per year; originate traveling exhibitions; museum & sales shop selling books, magazines, original art, reproductions, prints, slides, ceramics, local & national arts & crafts

M LEMOYNE COLLEGE, Wilson Art Gallery, Le Moyne Heights, 13214-1399. Tel 315-445-4331; *Library Dir* James J Simonis; *Asst Prof Philosophy* Dr Donald Arentz; *Periodical Librn* Lynnette Stevens
Open Mon - Thurs 9 AM - 11 PM, Fri 9 AM - 9 PM, Sat & Sun 9 AM - 5 PM. No admis fee. Estab 1966. Average Annual Attendance: 1500
Income: Financed through the Faculty Art Gallery Committee
Collections: Paintings, etchings, prints & watercolors
Exhibitions: Hall Groat Watercolors; Student Show; Jappie King Black; Heinzerling
Activities: Individual painting & original objects of art lent

A **LIGHT WORK,** 316 Waverly Ave, 13244-3010. Tel 315-443-1300, 443-2450; FAX 315-443-9516; Elec Mail jjhoone@summon2.syr.edu; gfhesse@mailbox.syr.edu. *Dir* Jeffrey Hoone; *Assoc Dir* Gary Hesse; *Admin Asst* Mary Lee Hodgens; *Darkroom Mgr* Jon Freyer
Galleries open daily 10 AM - 10 PM, darkrooms Sun - Fri Noon - 8 PM. Galleries no admis fee, darkrooms carry semester lab fee. Estab 1973 to support artists working in the photographic arts. Light Work Gallery & Robert B Menschel Photography Gallery; maintains small reference library
Income: Financed by NEA, NYSCA & private contributions
Collections: Light Work Collection, photographic prints
Exhibitions: Temporary exhibitions held throughout the year
Publications: Contant Sheet, quarterly; Menschel Gallery exhibit catalogs, quarterly
Activities: Classes for adults; lect open to public, 4-8 vis lectr per year; gallery talks; competitions with awards; artist residence grants offered; original objects of art lent; lending collection contains 1500 photographs; book traveling exhibitions 1 per year; originate traveling exhibitions

SYRACUSE UNIVERSITY
M **Joe & Emily Lowe Art Gallery,** Shaffer Art Bldg, 13244-1230. Tel 315-443-4098; FAX 315-443-1303; *Dir* Edward A Aiken; *Registrar & Preparator* Bradley Hudson
Open Tues - Sun Noon - 5 PM. No admis fee. Estab 1952 to present art exhibitions to inform university & communities of central upstate New York areas of international heritage of art, new advances in contemporary art with emphasis on the discovery of regional values, outstanding local art including faculty & student work. Mus Training Program complements our exhibition program. 7134 sq ft of space normally divided into separate galleries by movable walls. Average Annual Attendance: 20,000
Income: Financed through University with additional outside grants
Publications: Exhibition catalogs each show
Activities: Private tours on request; originate traveling exhibitions organized & circulated
M **Art Collection,** Sims Hall, 13244-1230. Tel 315-443-4097; *Dir* Alfred T Collette; *Assoc Dir* Domenic J Iacono; *Cur* David Prince; *Preparator* Gary Wright
The Art Collection is housed in a temperature & humidity-controlled area of Sims Hall, adjacent to the Art Gallery. Used primarily for storage & care of the 35,000 object collection, this facility also includes a teaching display area to accommodate classes & individuals involved in research
Income: Financed by university funds & endowments
Purchases: WPA Federal Art Projects Prints, Contemporary American Prints
Collections: West African tribal art; Korean, Japanese & American ceramics; Indian folk art; Pre-Columbian & contemporary Peruvian ceramics; Scandinavian designs in metal, wood, clay & textiles; 20th century American works with an emphasis on the Depression & War years (prints & paintings); 19th century European Salon paintings; history of printmaking (emphasis on American artists); decorative arts; Mary Petty-Alan Dunn Center for Social Cartooning
Exhibitions: Whistler; German Expressionists; Artzybasheff (illustrator); Mary Petty, Bolton Brown, Meiji Photographs, Atget & Abbott photographs, modernist prints
L **Library,** Fine Arts Dept, 458 Bird Library, 13244-2010. Tel 315-443-2440; FAX 315-443-9510; Elec Mail bopar@syn.edu. *Fine Arts Librn* Randall Bond; *Architecture Librn & Dept Head* Barbara A Opar; *Music Librn* Carole Vidali; *Slide Coll Supv* Susan Miller
Open Mon - Thurs 8 AM - 10 PM, Fri 8 AM - 6 PM, Sat 10 AM - 6 PM, Sun Noon - 10 PM. Estab 1870 for reference & research in the history of art
Library Holdings: Vols 65,000; Per subs 335; Compact discs 4000; Picture file 27,000; Micro — Cards, fiche, prints, reels; AV — A-tapes, cassettes 1500, fs, motion pictures, rec 20,000, slides 350,000, v-tapes; Other — Exhibition catalogs 12,000, manuscripts, photographs
Collections: Manuscript Collections of many American artists

TARRYTOWN

C **CIBA-GEIGY CORPORATION,** Art Collection, 520 White Plains Rd, 10591. Tel 914-785-2035; FAX 914-785-2399; *Dir Corporate Art Services* Dorothy Munson
Estab 1959 to add color & warmth to interior of its new headquarters & to support promising artists. Collection displayed at various company facilities
Collections: †New York School of Painting, abstract expressionist, geometric & figurative art; Swiss Art
Exhibitions: Ciba Geigy Collects: Aspects of Abstraction, Figural Art of the New York School: Selections from the Ciba - Geigy Collection
Publications: Catalogues of collection & exhibition
Activities: Individual objects of art lent upon request to museums & educational institutions for limited periods; originate traveling exhibitions upon request to museums & educational institutions

M **HISTORIC HUDSON VALLEY,** 150 White Plains Rd, 10591. Tel 914-631-8200; FAX 914-631-0089; *Pres* John H Dobkin; *Cur* Kathleen E Johnson; *Dir Admin & Finance* Wadell Stillman; *Public Affairs* Burns Patterson; *Marketing* McKelden Smith
Open 10 AM - 5 PM, cl Thanksgiving Day, Christmas, New Year's Day & Tues Dec - Mar. Admis to Sunnyside, Philipsburg Manor & Van Cortland Manor adults $6 each property, senior citizens, juniors 6-17 $3 each property; Kykuit visitation program adults $18, reservations required; groups of 20 or more must make reservations in advance. Chartered 1951 as a nonprofit educational foundation. Owns & operates historic properties which are Sunnyside in Tarrytown, the home of author Washington Irving; Philipsburg Manor in North Tarrytown, A Dutch-American gristmill-farm site of the early 1700s; Van Cortlandt Manor in Croton-on-Hudson, a manorial estate of the Revolutionary War period; Montgomery Place in Annadale-on-Hudson- a 434 acre estate overlooking the Hudson River & Catskill Mountains. Historic Hudson Valley also operates the visitation program of Kykuit, the Rockefeller estate in North Tarrytown. Average Annual Attendance: 200,000
Collections: Memorabilia of Washington Irving, Van Cortlandt and Philipse families; 17th, 18th and 19th century decorative arts; Philipsburg Manor, Upper Mills, Four Centuries of History, A Decade of Restoration
Exhibitions: Union Church of Pocantico Hills; stained glass windows by Marc Chagall; Henri Matisse; 19th & 20th century toys; Candellight Tours
Publications: American Industrialization, Economic Expansion, & the Law; America's Wooden Age; Aspects of Early New York Society & Politics; Bracebridge Hall; Business Enterprise in Early New York; Diedrich Knickerbocker's A History of New York; An Emerging Independent American Economy: 1815-1875; The Family Collections at Van Cortlandt Manor; The Howe Map; The Hudson River 1850-1918, A Photographic Portrait; Life Along the Hudson; Life of George Washington; The Loyalist Americans; Material Culture of the Wooden Age; The Mill at Philipsburg Manor, Upper Mills, & a Brief History of Milling; Old Christmas; Party & Political Guidebook; A Portfolio of Sleepy Hollow Prints; Rip Van Winkle & the Legend of Sleepy Hollow; Six Publications related to Washington Irving; An American Treasure: The Hudson River Valley
Activities: Classes for adults and children; docent training; demonstrations of 17th and 18th century arts and crafts; lectures open to the public; guided tours; gallery talks; sales shop sells books, reproductions & slides
L **Library,** 150 White Plains Rd, 10591. Tel 914-631-8609; FAX 914-631-0089; *Librn* Kate Johnson; *Asst Librn* Claudia Dovman
Specialized reference library with particular emphasis on 17th, 18th and 19th century living in the Hudson River Valley
Library Holdings: Per subs 123; Micro — Reels; Other — Exhibition catalogs, manuscripts
Special Subjects: Washington Irving

M **LYNDHURST,** 635 S Broadway, 10591. Tel 914-631-4481; *Dir* Susanne Brendel-PanDich
Open May - Oct, Tues - Sun 10 AM - 5 PM, Nov - Apr, weekends only 10 AM - 5 PM. Admis adults $9, senior citizens $8, students $4, group rates by arrangement, free to National Trust members. A property of the National Trust for Historic Preservation as a National Historic Landmark. Lyndhurst is a Gothic revival castle designed in 1838 for General William Paulding by Alexander Jackson Davis, one of America's most influential 19th century architects. Comissioned by second owner, George Merritt, to enlarge the house. Davis, in 1865, continued the Gothic revial style in the additions. It was purchased in 1880 by Jay Gould & willed to his daughter, Helen. Later acquired by another daughter, Anna, Duchess of Talleyrand-Perigord, Lyndhurst was left to National Trust in 1961 Other highlights include a carriagehouse, stocked with period vehicles, stables, and the remains of private greenhouses. Windows attributed to L C Tiffany. The preservation of Lyndhurst is a composite of the contributions of the three families who lived in it. Property serves as a focal point for advancement of historic preservation. Through it are developed new relationships amoung cultural, community preservation groups and National Trust members in its area. Responds to community preservation needs by acting as a link between community and appropriate regional or headquarter offices of National Trust. Provides interpretive programs which are related to Lyndhurst's particular case study in historic preservation. The National Trust Restoration Workshop, located in a portion of the stable complex carries out restoration craft services for National Trust properties. Average Annual Attendance: 91,000
Income: Financed by admis fees, mem, private contributions, special events & federal appropriations
Collections: Collection of Gothic furniture designed by architect A J Davis in the 1830s & 1860s; 19th century furnishings & paintings; Tiffany glass
Exhibitions: Seasonal exhibitions
Activities: Summer outdoor concerts; antique & auto shows; Christmas programs; guided tours; individual paintings & original objects of art lent as requested for special exhibitions by museums & historical societies; museum shop sells books, reproductions, slides & gift items

TICONDEROGA

M **FORT TICONDEROGA ASSOCIATION,** PO Box 390, 12883. Tel 518-585-2821; FAX 518-585-2210; *Pres* Anthony D Pell; *Exec Dir* Nicholas Westbrook; *Cur* Christopher D Fox
Open daily early May - mid Oct 9 AM - 5 PM, July & Aug 9 AM - 6 PM. Admis adults $8, children $6. Estab 1909 to preserve & present the Colonial & Revolutionary history of Fort Ticonderoga. The Mus is in the restored barracks of the Colonial fort. Average Annual Attendance: 100,000. Mem: 1000; dues $20 & up
Income: Financed by admis fees, mus shop sales & donations
Collections: Artifacts; manuscripts; paintings
Exhibitions: Held in mid-May - mid-Oct
Publications: Bulletin of the Fort Ticonderoga Museum, semi-annual
Activities: Classes for adults & children; dramatic programs; docent training; lect open to public, 5 vis lectr per year; concerts; tours; original objects of art lent to qualified museums; museum shop sells books, magazines, reproductions, prints & slides
L **Thompson-Pell Research Center,** PO Box 390, 12883. Tel 518-585-2821; FAX 518-585-2210; *Exec Dir* Nicholas Westbrook; *Cur* Christopher D Fox
Open by appointment for reference only
Income: Financed by grants, contributions & earned income
Purchases: $30,000 per year
Library Holdings: Vols 12,000; Per subs 20; Micro — Fiche, reels; AV — A-tapes, cassettes, fs, Kodachromes, lantern slides, motion pictures, rec, slides, v-tapes; Other — Clipping files, exhibition catalogs, manuscripts, memorabilia, original art works, pamphlets, photographs, prints, reproductions, sculpture
Special Subjects: Archaeology, Bookplates & Bindings, Etchings & Engravings, Historical Material, Manuscripts, Maps, Painting - American, Painting - British, Portraits, Prints, Restoration & Conservation, Military History
Publications: The Bulletin of the Fort Ticonderoga Museum, annual; The Haversack, semi-annual newsletter

TROY

A RENSSELAER COUNTY COUNCIL FOR THE ARTS, RCCA: The Arts Center, 189 Second St, 12180. Tel 518-273-0552; FAX 518-273-4591; Internet Home Page Address http://crisny.org/-artscntr. *Pres* Raona Roy
Estab 1961, a regional center for the advancement of the arts in daily life. Though education, presentation, outreach, service advocacy; The Arts Center promotes a richer community through broad participation in the making & personal experience of art
Publications: Classes for adults & children

M RENSSELAER COUNTY HISTORICAL SOCIETY, Hart-Cluett Mansion, 1827, 59 Second St, 12180. Tel 518-272-7232; FAX 518-273-1264; Elec Mail rchs@crisny.org. *Pres* Jay F MacNulty; *Dir* Anne W Ackerson; *Cur* Stacy F Pomeroy Draper; *Educ Dir* Lorraine E Weiss
Open Feb - Dec Tues - Sat 10 AM - 4 PM. Admis donation for adults $2. Estab 1927 to promote historical research & to collect & exhibit materials of all kinds related to the history of the Rensselaer County area including books, papers, fine & decorative arts. The Hart-Cluett Mansion is an historic house mus with 11 furnished rooms. Average Annual Attendance: 13,000. Mem: 600; dues $35; annual meeting 2nd Mon in Sept
Income: $250,000 (financed by endowment & mem)
Collections: Three centuries of fine & decorative arts, including: ceramics; costumes; Elijah Galusha 19th century furniture; paintings by local artists including C G Beauregard, Joseph Hidley & Abel Buel Moore; portraits; quilts & coverlets; silver
Exhibitions: (1997) Re-Vision: Art Works with History
Publications: Annual report; quarterly newsletter
Activities: Classes for children; volunteer training; lect open to public; gallery talks; tours; book traveling exhibitions; traveling exhibitions organized & circulated; sales shop sells books, prints, original art & reproductions
L Library, 59 Second St, 12180. Tel 518-272-7232; *Cur* Stacy Pomeroy Draper
Open Tues - Sat 10 AM - 4 PM (mus), Tues - Fri 1 - 4 PM, Sat 10 AM - 4 PM (library). Two historic townhouse buildings; Hart-Cluett Mansion (1827); Carr Building. Average Annual Attendance: 10,000. Mem: 550; dues $35 & up; annual meeting in Sept
Income: Financed by endowment, mem, grants & events
Library Holdings: Vols 2000; Per subs 4; AV — A-tapes, fs, lantern slides, motion pictures, slides; Other — Clipping files, framed reproductions, manuscripts, memorabilia, photographs
Special Subjects: Architecture, Decorative Arts, Dolls, Furniture, Historical Material, Manuscripts, Maps, Painting - American, Period Rooms, Photography, Pottery, Local history
Activities: Classes for adults & children; docent training; lect open to public, 6 vis lectr per year; gallery talks; tours; book traveling exhibitions; museum shop sells books, reproductions & prints

M RENSSELAER NEWMAN FOUNDATION CHAPEL & CULTURAL CENTER, The Gallery, 2125 Burdett Ave, 12180. Tel 518-274-7793; *Pres* Michael Duffy; *Dir* William McQuiston; *Treas* Thomas Phelan; *Secy* Mairin Quinn
Open 9 AM - 11 PM. Estab 1968 to provide religion & culture for members of the Rensselaer Polytechnic Institute & Troy area, a broadly ecumenical service. Gallery maintained. Average Annual Attendance: 100,000
Income: $150,000 (financed by contributions)
Collections: Contemporary paintings, sculpture and needlework; liturgical vestments & artifacts; medieval sculpture
Exhibitions: Laliberte banners; Picasso traveling exhibition New York State Council on the Arts; Smithsonian Institution Traveling Exhibition; local one man shows
Publications: Sun and Balance, three times a year
Activities: Classes for adults & children; dramatic programs; lect open to public, 10 vis lectr per year; concerts; Poetry Series; Peace Fair; Festival of Religion & the Arts

M RUSSELL SAGE COLLEGE, Gallery, Schacht Fine Arts Ctr, 12180. Tel 518-270-2248; FAX 518-271-4545; *Gallery Dir* Harold Lohner
Open Mon - Fri 9 AM - 5 PM, Sun 2 - 5 PM. No admis fee. Estab 1970 for exhibition of contemporary art for college & public. Gallery is one room, with 150 running ft. Average Annual Attendance: 3000
Income: Financed by the college
Collections: Drawings (contemporary); paintings (contemporary); sculpture
Exhibitions: Faculty & student shows; paintings, drawings, sculpture from New York City galleries & area artists; photography; traveling exhibitions
Activities: Gallery talks; original objects of art lent on campus; lending collection contains original prints, paintings, sculpture; traveling exhibitions organized & circulated

UTICA

M MUNSON-WILLIAMS-PROCTOR INSTITUTE, Museum of Art, 310 Genesee St, 13502-4799. Tel 315-797-0000; FAX 315-797-5608; *Dir* Paul D Schweizer; *Museum Educator* Elaine DePalma-Sadzkoski; *20th Century Art Cur* Mary E Murray; *Decorative Arts Cur* Anna T D'Ambrosio; *Librn* Cynthia Barth
Open Tues - Sat 10 AM - 5 PM, Sun 1 - 5 PM, cl Mon & hol idays. No admis fee, donations accepted. Estab 1919 through an endowment granted a provisional charter by the Board of Regents of the University of the State of New York, changed to an absolute charter in 1941 & amended in 1948 to empower the institute to provide instruction at the college level in the field of fine arts. The institute became active in 1953 with the purpose of establishing & maintaining a gallery & collection of art to give instruction & to have an auxiliary library. It consists of a School of Art estab 1941; a Mus of Art opened in 1960; Fountain Elms, a house-mus was restored in 1960; a Meetinghouse opened in 1963 & a Performing Arts Division. Maintains reference library. Average Annual Attendance: 64,625. Mem: 3758; dues family $35, individual $25, senior citizens $20, student $15

Income: Financed by endowment, tuition & private contributions, voluntary donations at entrances
Purchases: 19th & 20th century American, European paintings, sculpture, graphic & decorative arts
Collections: †Arts of Central New York; †19th & 20th century European paintings & sculpture; Greek, Persian & Pre-Columbian art; †18th, 19th & 20th century American paintings, sculpture & decorative arts; †drawings & prints
Exhibitions: Next to Nature; Evolution of the American Chair; Rodney Ripps; Monotype of Maurice Prendergast; The Rivendell Collection; Side by Side by Cole: The Two Versions of Thomas Cole's Voyage of Life Series of Paintings; Filmmakers of Central New York; The Blue & the Gray: Stoneware of Oneida Country; The Painter's Music: The Musician's Art; Masters of Contemporary Polish Art; The Highway as Habitat; Splendors of the New World; Splendors of the Pre-Columbian Era; River of Gold; The Distinction of Being Different: Joseph P McHugh & the American Arts & Crafts Movement; Teenagers in Their Bedrooms; With Grace & Favour; Life Lines: American Master Drawings 1788-1962
Publications: Bulletin, monthly; exhibition catalogues
Activities: Classes for adults & children; docent training; lect open to public, 2 vis lectr per year; gallery talks; tours; scholarships & fels offered; museum shop sells books, magazines, prints, original art, reproductions
L Art Reference Library, 310 Genesee St, 13502. Tel 315-797-0000, Ext 23; FAX 315-797-5608; *Head Librn* Cynthia M Barth; *Asst Librn* Michael Schuyler
Open Tues - Fri 10 AM - 5 PM, Sat 2 - 5 PM. Estab 1940 to support School of Art, Mus of Art staff, Institute Mem & general pub; circulation only to members of the Institute. Circ 5000
Library Holdings: Vols 25,000; Per subs 60; AV — Fs; Other — Clipping files, exhibition catalogs, manuscripts, original art works, pamphlets
Special Subjects: Afro-American Art, American Western Art, Art History, Asian Art, Bookplates & Bindings, Carpets & Rugs, Ceramics, Crafts, Decorative Arts, Etchings & Engravings, Fashion Arts, Folk Art, Furniture, Glass, Graphic Arts, 19th & 20th Century Art, 19th Century Decorative Arts
Collections: Fountain Elms Collection; autographs, rare books & manuscripts, book plates
Publications: Bibliographies related to museum exhibitions; bibliographic instructional materials

M SCULPTURE SPACE, INC, 12 Gates St, 13502. Tel 315-724-8381; *Exec Dir* Gina Murtagh; *Studio Mgr* Jonathan Kirk
Open by appointment only. No admis fee. Estab 1975 to provide professional artists with studio space. Average Annual Attendance: 300
Income: $75,000
Publications: Sculpture Space News, semi-annual
Activities: Awards (funded residences); scholarships & fels offered

VALLEY COTTAGE

L VALLEY COTTAGE LIBRARY, Gallery, 110 Rte 303, 10989. Tel 914-268-7700; *Library Dir* Ellen Simpson; *Exhib Dir* Claudette Doran
Open Mon - Thurs 10 AM - 9 PM, Fri & Sat 10 AM - 5 PM. Estab 1959. 27 x 7, artificial & natural light
Publications: Focus, quarterly

VESTAL

M STATE UNIVERSITY OF NEW YORK AT BINGHAMTON, University Art Gallery, * Vestal Pky, 13901. Tel 607-777-2634; FAX 607-777-4000; *Dir* Lyn Gamwell; *Cur* Lucie Nelson; *Technical Dir* Matthew Zupnick
Open Tues - Fri 9 AM - 4:30 PM, Thurs evening 6 - 8 PM, Sat & Sun 1 - 4:30 PM, cl university holidays. Estab 1967
Income: $20,000 (financed by state appropriations)
Collections: Asian collection; †Teaching collection from Egyptian to contemporary art
Publications: Exhibit catalogs
Activities: Lect open to public; gallery talks; seminars; internships offered

WATERTOWN

M ROSWELL P FLOWER MEMORIAL LIBRARY, 229 Washington St, 13601. Tel 315-788-2352; FAX 315-788-2584; *Dir* Kenneth Hodosy
Open Sept - June Mon, Tues & Thurs 9:15 AM - 9 PM, Wed, Fri & Sat 9:15 AM - 5 PM, July & Aug Mon 9:15 AM - 9 PM, Tues - Fri 9:15 AM - 5 PM, cl Sat. Estab 1904. The library contains murals, paintings & sculptures scattered throughout the building. Circ 184,325
Income: $471,000 (financed by the City of Watertown)
Collections: New York State material & genealogy; United States military history
Exhibitions: Local Artists Guild; North Country Artist Guild
Activities: Lect open to public; concerts; library tours; film programs

M JEFFERSON COUNTY HISTORICAL SOCIETY, 228 Washington St, 13601. Tel 315-782-3491; *Dir* Fred H Rollins; *Cur Educ* Melissa Widrick; *Exec Secy* Elaine Norton; *Cur Coll* Elise Chan
Open Apr 1 - Dec 31 Tues - Fri 10 AM - 5 PM, Sat Noon - 5 PM. Admis $2 donation. Estab 1886. Average Annual Attendance: 12,000. Mem: 620; annual meeting in May
Income: $142,000 (financed by endowment, mem, county appropriation, grants, private foundations & gifts)
Collections: Tyler Coverlet Collection; Costume Collection; Kinne Water Turbine Collection; 19th century Furniture; Prehistoric Indian Arts, Jefferson County
Exhibitions: Fort Drum: A Historical Perspective
Publications: Bulletin, 1-2 times per yr; Museum Musings; 6 times per yr; Abraham Tuthill Catalog
Activities: Classes for adults & children; in-school local history programs; docent training; lect open to public, 2-6 vis lectr per year; tours; artmobile; lending collection includes; artifacts, 155 items; book traveling exhibitions 1-2 per year; originate traveling exhibitions; museum shop sells books, toys & other souvenir items

L **Library,** 228 Washington St, 13601. Tel 315-782-3491; *Dir* Fred H Rollins
Library Holdings: Vols 2211; Other — Clipping files, exhibition catalogs, framed reproductions, manuscripts, memorabilia, original art works, pamphlets, prints
Special Subjects: Architecture, Decorative Arts, Furniture, Glass, Historical Material
Publications: Museum Musings Newsletter, quarterly; Bulletin, annualy

WESTFIELD

L **PATTERSON LIBRARY & ART GALLERY,** 40 S Portage St, 14787. Tel 716-326-2154; FAX 716-326-2554; *Dir* Deborah Williams; *Arts Specialist* Korene Korol
Open Mon - Wed 9 AM - 8 PM, Thurs - Sat 9 AM - 5 PM. Estab 1896 (Octagon Gallery estab 1971) to provide opportunity for education & recreation through the use of literature, music, films, paintings & other art forms; Rotunda Gallery estab 1986. Octagon Gallery is 1115 sq ft with 11 ft ceilings & 100 ft running space. Circ 72,000. Average Annual Attendance: 14,000
Income: Financed by endowment & private sources
Library Holdings: Vols 34,000; Per subs 120; AV — A-tapes, cassettes 125, fs, motion pictures, rec, slides; Other — Framed reproductions, memorabilia, original art works, pamphlets, photographs 10,000, sculpture
Special Subjects: Glass plate negatives of local history, WW I posters, seashells, mounted birds
Exhibitions: Annual Westfield Revisited Exhibition
Activities: Classes for children; docent training; lect open to public, 2 vis lectr per year; concerts; gallery talks; tours; individual paintings & original objects of art lent to public; traveling exhibitions organized & circulated

WEST NYACK

M **ROCKLAND CENTER FOR THE ARTS,** 27 S Greenbush Rd, 10994. Tel 914-358-0877; *Exec Dir* Julianne Ramos , MFA
Open Mon - Fri 9 AM - 10 PM, Sat - Sun 9 AM - 4 PM. No admis fee. Estab 1947 to present excellence in the arts, education & services. 40 ft x 70 ft gallery space. Average Annual Attendance: 50,000. Mem: 3000; dues family $35, singles $20; annual meeting in Oct
Income: $400,000 (financed by mem, state appropriations, corporations, foundations & earned income)
Exhibitions: Troubled Waters American Socio-Political Art. Art of the Marketplace
Publications: Artline Newsletter; art school catalogues; exhibition catalogue
Activities: Classes for adults & children in visual, literary & performing arts; lect open to the public; performances in classical, jazz, folk music

WEST POINT

M **UNITED STATES MILITARY ACADEMY,** West Point Museum, 10996-5000. Tel 914-938-2203; Autovon 8-688-2203-3201. *Dir Museum* Michael E Moss; *Cur Weapons* Robert W Fisch; *Cur History* Michael J McAfee; *Cur Art* David Meschutt; *Museum Specialist* Walter J Nock; *Registrar* Pat A Dursi; *Cur Design* Richard Clark; *Museum Spec* Paul Ackermann
Open daily 10:30 AM - 4:15 PM. No admis fee. Estab 1854, supplementing the academic, cultural & military instruction of cadets; also disseminates the history of the US Army, the US Military Academy & the West Point area. Collections open to the public. Average Annual Attendance: 300,000
Purchases: $5000
Collections: Alexander M Craighead Collection of European & American Military Art; Jonas Lie Collection of Panama Canal Oils; Liedesdorf Collection of European Armor; Rindisbacher Watercolors; Sully Portrait Collection †cadet drawings from 1820-1940; European & American posters; extensive holdings from World War I & World War II, military & homefront subjects; †military artifacts including weapons, flags, uniforms, medals, etc; †military paintings & prints; paintings & prints of West Point
Exhibitions: The Toy Soldier: A Historical Review; Whisler & Others: Cadet Drawings from the 19th Century to World War I; Jonas Lie & the Building of the Panama Canal; The Land of Counterpane: Toy Soldiers; The US Cavalry in the Sest; Exhibition of Don Spulding's art & private collection; American & French Zouaves
Publications: Posters for Victory; The West Point Museum: A Guide to the Collections; The West Point Museum Bulletin, irregularly
Activities: Gallery talks; tours; individual paintings & original objects of art lent to accredited museums; book traveling exhibitions 2 per year to accredited museums; museum shop sells books, reproductions, prints & military souvenirs

WILLIAMSVILLE

A **BUFFALO SOCIETY OF ARTISTS,** 204 Seabrook Dr, 14221. Tel 716-631-3136; *Pres* Joyce Hill; *First VPres* Norine Spurling; *Second VPres* Bill Maggio; *Treas* Victor Shanchuk
Estab 1891 for practicing & exhibiting artists. Mem: 193; dues $20; annual meeting in May/June
Income: Financed by mem dues
Exhibitions: Annual Juried Exhibition
Activities: Lect open to public; competitions with awards

WOODSTOCK

A **CENTER FOR PHOTOGRAPHY AT WOODSTOCK INC,** 59 Tinker St, 12498. Tel 914-679-9957; FAX 914-679-6337; Elec Mail cpwphoto@aol.com. *Exec Dir* Colleen Kenyon
Open Noon - 5 PM, cl Mon & Tues. No admis fee. Estab 1977, a non-profit organization, an art & educ center, an artists space
Collections: Permanent collection contains 5000 photographic prints & art work which incorporates photography
Exhibitions: Eight shows per year

A **WOODSTOCK ARTISTS ASSOCIATION,** 28 Tinker St. 12948. Tel 914-679-2940; *Dir* Lisa Williams; *Head Archives* Linda Freaney
Open Thurs - Mon Noon - 5 PM. Estab 1922 to exhibit the work of artists of the region. Upstairs Gallery - Group member show; Downstairs Gallery - Solo exhibitions; exhibiting members must live within 25 miles of Woodstock. Average Annual Attendance: 10,000. Mem: 692; dues individual $35; meetings in May & Sept
Income: $40,000 (financed by endowment, mem, city appropriation)
Collections: The Permanent Collection of Woodstock Artists includes oils, prints & sculpture
Publications: Woodstock Art Heritage: The Permanent Collection of the Woodstock Artists Association (1987)
Activities: Concerts; gallery talks; tours; competitions with awards; museum shop sells books, gift items, original art, prints & reproductions

L **WAA Archives,** 28 Tinker St, 12948. Tel 914-679-2940; *Gallery Mgr* Lisa Williams; *Head Archivis* Linda Freaney
For reference only
Income: Financed by donations, endowments & mem
Library Holdings: Documents 50,000; Other — Clipping files, memorabilia, original art works, photographs, prints, sculpture
Special Subjects: Woodstock Artists, past-present

YONKERS

M **THE HUDSON RIVER MUSEUM OF WESTCHESTER,** 511 Warburton Ave, 10701. Tel 914-963-4550; FAX 914-963-8558; *Dir* Philip Verre; *Cur* Laura Vookles; *Dir Educ* Kathy Shiga-Gattullo; *Tech* John Matherly
Open Wed, Fri & Sat 1 - 5 PM, Thurs 10 AM - 9 PM, Sun Noon - 5 PM. Admis by voluntary contribution. Estab 1924 as a general mus of art, history & science
Income: $700,000 (financed by mem, city & county appropriation, state arts council, federal grants & donations)
Collections: 19th & 20th century American art, decorative arts, furniture, toys, dolls, costumes, accoutrement, silver, china, paintings, sculpture, photography
Publications: Bimonthly calendar of events; special exhibitions catalogs; annual report
Activities: Docent training; lect & special events open to public; concerts; gallery talks; tours; art lent to other museums for exhibition purposes; lending collection contains original art works, paintings, photographs, sculpture; book traveling exhibitions; traveling exhibitions organized and circulated to museums, college galleries - regional & national; museum shop sells books, inexpensive items for children

M **PHILIPSE MANOR HALL STATE HISTORIC SITE,** 29 Warburton Ave, PO Box 496, 10702. Tel 914-965-4027; FAX 914-965-6485; *Historic Site Mgr* Alix Sandra Schnee
Open by appointment only. No admis fee. Estab 1908 to preserve Georgian manor house owned by the Frederick Philipse family; to interpret Philipse Manor Halls architecture, its significance as the home of an American Loyalist & its importance as an example of 17th & 18th century Anglo-Dutch patterns in landholding & development. The State Historic Site is part of the New York State Office of Parks & Recreation; the Hall houses contemporary style exhibits of history, art & architecture hung against a backdrop of fine 18th & 19th century architectural carvings
Income: Financed by state appropriation
Collections: Cochran Portrait of Famous Americans; Cochran Collection of Windor Chairs
Exhibitions: Annual Christmas Exhibit
Activities: Lect open to public; concerts; tours; demonstrations; films

L **YONKERS PUBLIC LIBRARY,** Fine Arts Dept, 1500 Central Park Ave, 10710. Tel 914-337-1500, Ext 311; *Librn* Joanne Roche; *Librn* Barbara Sutherland
Open Mon - Thurs 10 AM - 9 PM, Fri & Sat 10 AM - 5 PM, Sun Noon - 5 PM, cl Sat & Sun during summer. Estab 1962 to serve the general pub with a special interest in the arts, especially the fine arts, performing arts & the decorative & applied arts. Circ printed material approx 22,000; recorded material approx 66,000
Income: $65,000 (financed by city appropriation & gifts)
Purchases: $65,000
Library Holdings: Vols 14,000; Per subs 82; Scores 3000; Micro — Fiche, reels; AV — A-tapes 3100, cassettes 1000, rec 15,000, v-tapes 200; Other — Clipping files, pamphlets 7000
L **Will Library,** 1500 Central Park Ave, 10710. Tel 914-337-1500; *Librn* Joanne Roche; *Librn* Barbara Sutherland
Library Holdings: Vols 126,000; Per subs 75
Exhibitions: Exhibits work by local artists & craftsmen

NORTH CAROLINA

ASHEVILLE

M **ASHEVILLE ART MUSEUM,** 2 S Pack Square, PO Box 1717, 28802. Tel 704-253-3227; FAX 704-257-4503; Elec Mail ashevilleart@main.nc.us. *Exec Dir* Pamela L Myers; *Assoc Dir Educ* Diane Dufilho; *Cur* Frank Thomson
Open July - Nov Tues - Sat 10 AM - 5 PM, Sun 1 - 5 PM. Admis adults $3, students & seniors $2.50, for museums at Pack Place adults $5.50, students & seniors $4.50, children $2-$3.50. Estab 1948 to provide art experiences to the Western North Carolina area through exhibitions. Six galleries maintained,. Average Annual Attendance: 50,000. Mem: 750; dues family $35, single $25; annual meeting July
Income: Financed by mem, United Arts Fund Drive & auxiliary
Purchases: Romane Bearden, James Chapin, Joseph Fiore, William Henry

Jackson, George Luks
Collections: 20th Century American Art; †studio glass
Exhibitions: (1997) Quiet Light: Isamu Noguchi's Akari Light Sculptures; Arts & Crafts: Style & Life; Ray Johnson: Black Mountain College to New York Correspondence School; The Velvet Years: Andy Warhol 1965-1967 (photographs by Stephen Shore)
Publications: Quarterly membership; newsletter, catalogues
Activities: Docent training; lect open to public; gallery talks; tours; competitions; original objects of art lent to other museums

M **G B GATE & SONS,** 28 Hendersonville Rd, 28803. Tel 704-277-7571; *Pres* Gayle B Tate; *Chmn* Hephziah M Tate
Open Mon - Fri 10 AM - 5 PM, Sat 10 AM - 2 PM. No admis fee. Estab 1967 to enhance careers of artists & craftsmen. Maintains reference library. Mem: dues $25; weekly meetings on Thurs
Collections: †American fine arts & crafts; †glass art; †jewelry; †paintings; †quilts; †sculpture; †wood work crafts
Activities: Classes for adults; lect open to public, 10 vis lectr per year; quarterly auctions; sales shop sells original art

A **SOUTHERN HIGHLAND CRAFT GUILD,** Folk Art Center, Riceville Rd Blue Ridge Pky, PO Box 9545, 28815. Tel 704-298-7928; FAX 704-298-7962; *Dir* Ruth Summers; *Educ Dir* Andrew Glasgow
Open Mon - Sun 9 AM - 5 PM, cl Thanksgiving, Christmas & New Year's. No admis fee. Estab 1930 to encourage wider appreciation of mountain crafts; raise & maintain standards of design & craftsmanship & encourage individual expression. Mem: 700; open to eligible craftsmen from Southern Appalachian Mountain Region upon approval of applicant's work by Standards Committee & Board of Trustees; dues group $40, single $20; annual meeting in Apr
Income: Financed by mem & merchandising
Publications: Highland Highlights; monthly newsletter
Activities: Workshops for adults & children; lect open to public & some for members only; gallery talks; tours; competitions

BREVARD

M **BREVARD COLLEGE,** Sims Art Center, 400 N Broad St, 28712. Tel 704-883-8292, Ext 2245; *Dir* Tim Murray
Open Mon - Thurs 8 AM - 10 PM, Fri 8 AM - 5 PM. No admis fee. Estab 1969 as Art Department with gallery. Center has three areas, 160 ft running space, & 1500 sq ft floor space
Income: Financed by departmental appropriation
Collections: Contemporary art; 1940-1970 paintings & watercolors; print & pottery collection
Exhibitions: Student & visiting artist exhibitions
Activities: Classes for adults; dramatic programs; college classes & continuing education; lect, 4 vis lectr per year; 4 gallery talks; competitions with cash awards; scholarships offered; lending collection contains books, cassettes, color reproductions, film strips, photographs, slides
L **James A Jones Library,** 28712-3306. Tel 704-884-8268; FAX 704-884-5424; *Library Dir* Michael M McCabe
Open Mon - Fri 8:30 AM - 5 PM. Estab 1934. For reference & circulation
Income: Financed by parent institution
Library Holdings: Vols 3400; Per subs 20; AV — Rec, v-tapes 400
Special Subjects: Art History, Painting - American, Photography
Publications: New book list, bi-monthly

CARY

M **NORTH CAROLINA NATURE ARTISTS ASSOCIATION (NCNAA),** 307 Electra Dr, 27513. Tel 919-481-2187; *Dir* Carl Regutti
Estab 1988 for wildlife art shows & education. Mem: 125; dues $15; quarterly meetings
Income: $10,000 (financed by mem & special projects)
Exhibitions: Sponsor 3 museum exhibitions per year throughout North Carolina; museums vary each year
Activities: Classes for adults & children; lect open to public; competitions

M **PAGE-WALKER ARTS & HISTORY CENTER,** 119 Ambassador Loop, PO Box 8005, 27512. Tel 919-460-4963; FAX 919-469-4344; *Supv* Robbie Stone
Open 10 AM - 5 PM. No admis fee. Estab 1992. Galleries housed in renovated historic hotel (circa 1868). Average Annual Attendance: 30,000. Mem: 300
Activities: Classes for adults & children; dramatic programs; docent training; lect open to public, 30 vis lectr per year; originate traveling exhibitions

CHAPEL HILL

UNIVERSITY OF NORTH CAROLINA AT CHAPEL HILL
M **Ackland Art Museum,** Campus Box 3400, 27599-3400. Tel 919-966-5736; FAX 919-966-1400; TDD 919-962-0837. *Dir* Gerald D Bolas; *Exhib Cur* Barbara Matilsky; *Educ Cur* Ray Williams
Open Tues - Sat 10 AM - 5 PM, Sun 1 - 5 PM, cl Mon & University holidays. No admis fee. Estab 1958 as an art mus which serves the members of the university community as well as the pub. The mus houses a permanent collection & presents a program of changing exhibitions. Average Annual Attendance: 30,000. Mem: 830; dues $500, $100, $45 & $25
Income: Financed by endowment, mem & state appropriation
Publications: Newsletter, fall & spring; The Ackland Art Museum (handbook)
Activities: Dramatic programs; docent training; lect open to public, 3 vis lectr per year; gallery talks; tours; exhibition catalogs available for sale
L **Joseph Curtis Sloane Art Library,** Hanes Art Ctr, Campus Box 3405, 27599-3405. Tel 919-962-2397; FAX 919-962-0722; *Art Librn* Philip Rees; *Libr Asst* Rachel Frew
Open Mon - Thurs 8 AM - 10 PM, Fri 8 AM - 5 PM, Sat 10 AM - 5 PM, Sun 2 - 10 PM

Income: Financed by state appropriation
Library Holdings: Vols 79,000; Micro — Fiche 14,500, reels 320; AV — V-tapes; Other — Exhibition catalogs, pamphlets
Special Subjects: Architecture, Art History, Painting - American, Painting - British, Painting - Dutch, Painting - Flemish, Painting - French, Painting - Italian

CHARLOTTE

M **DISCOVERY PLACE INC,** * 301 N Tryon St, 28202. Tel 704-372-6261; FAX 704-337-2670; *Chief Exec Officer* Freda Nicholson; *VPres Marketing* B G Metzler
Open Sept - May Mon - Fri 9 AM - 5 PM, June - Aug 9 AM - 6 PM, Sat 9 AM - 6 PM, Sun 1 - 6 PM. Admis adult $5.50, youth & senior citizens $4.50, children 3-5 with parent $2.75 & under 2 yrs free, no charge for members. Estab 1981 as a science museum with hands on concept of learning by doing. A small staff reference library is maintained. Average Annual Attendance: 600,000. Mem: 7000; dues family $50, senior citizen $30, student $25
Income: $2,500,000 (financed by city & county appropriations, fees & sales shop)
Collections: Arthropods; gems & minerals; Lepidoptera; †Pre-Columbian: Mayan, North American, Peruvian; †primitive art: African, Alaskan Eskimo, Oceania, South America; reptillia
Publications: Science Magazine, quarterly; activities bulletin, quarterly
Activities: Classes for adults & children; volunteer training program for demonstrators & guides; major programming for school lectures; tours; acceptable for internship from UNCC & Queens College; book traveling exhibitions 4 per year; originate traveling exhibitions that circulate to science museum collaborations; museum shop sells books, prints, shells, jewelry, school supplies & souvenirs; junior museum is primarily geared to pre-school and early elementary age children

M **LIGHT FACTORY,** 809 W Hill St, (ADP) PO Box 32815, 28232. Tel 704-333-9755; FAX 704-333-5910; Elec Mail tlf@webserve.net; Internet Home Page Address http://www.lightfactory.org. *Exec Dir* Bruce Lineker; *Asst Dir* Alice Sebrell; *Dir Educ* Betsy Bilger; *Dir Develop & Marketing* Monicah McGee
Open Wed & Fri 10 AM - 6 PM, Thurs 10 AM - 8 PM, Sat & Sun Noon - 6 PM. No admis fee. A non-collecting mus presenting the latest in photography, video & the internet. Year-round educ programs, community outreach & special events complement its changing exhibitions. Average Annual Attendance: 20,000. Mem: 4; dues $35-$1000
Exhibitions: (1997) 1996 Annual Members Show; 15th Annual Light Factory Art Auction; A Delicate Balance: six Israeli Photographers; Imogen Cunningham & Karl Blossfeld; Alfredo Jaar: Let There Be Light; Jennifer & Kevin McCoy: Small Appliances; North Carolina to Israel Photographic Projects; Caroline Vaughan; Fred Wilson: Collectibles
Publications: Exhibit catalogs
Activities: Classes for adults & children; lect open to public, 10 vis lectr per year; gallery talks; originate traveling exhibitions to museums & galleries nationally

M **MINT MUSEUM OF ART,** 2730 Randolph Rd, 28207. Tel 704-337-2000; FAX 704-337-2101; Elec Mail news2@mint.uncc.edu. *Chief Exec Officer & Pres* Bruce Evans; *Dir Admins* Mike Smith; *Dir Coll & Exhib* Charles Mo; *Asst Cur Coll* Anne Forcinito; *Registrar* Martha Mayberry; *VPres Develop & Marketing* Harry Creemers; *Dir Educ* Cheryl Palmer; *Dir Community Relations* Carolyn Mints
Open Tues 10 AM - 10 PM, Wed - Sat 10 AM - 5 PM, Sun Noon - 5 PM, cl Mon & holidays. Admis $4, seniors $3, students $2, children 12 & under & members free. Estab 1936 as an art mus in what was the first branch of the US mint erected in 1837. Mus houses seven changing galleries, 16 permanent galleries, Delhom Decorative Arts Gallery. Average Annual Attendance: 120,000. Mem: 5200; dues Mint Master $1000, benefactor $500, sustainer $250, patron $125, family $45, individual $30, senior citizen or student discounted
Income: Financed by endowment, mem & city appropriation, foundation & corporate giving
Collections: African art; decorative arts; historic pottery; 19th & 20th century European & American paintings; porcelain; pre-Columbian art; sculpture; Spanish Colonial art
Exhibitions: Ansel Adams; Antique Maps; Louis Orr Etchings; Processing the Image: The Art of Printmaking; Raised in Clay: The Southern Pottery Tradition; Victorian Silver 1860-1890
Publications: Mint Museum Newsletter and calendar of events, six times a year
Activities: Classes for adults; docent training; lect open to public, 25 vis lectr per year; concerts; gallery talks; tours; competitions; scholarships & fels offered; original objects of art lent to other museums; museum shop selling books, original art, prints, gifts, museum replicas, jewelry, cards
L **Library,** 2730 Randolph Rd, 28207. Tel 704-337-2000; FAX 704-337-2101; *Librn* Sara Wolf
Open Tues - Fri 10 AM - 5 PM. Open to the pub for reference only
Library Holdings: Vols 12,000; Per subs 100; Micro — Cards; AV — Slides, v-tapes; Other — Clipping files, exhibition catalogs, pamphlets
Special Subjects: Aesthetics, Afro-American Art, American Indian Art, Antiquities-Assyrian, Antiquities-Byzantine, Antiquities-Oriental, Antiquities-Persian, Antiquities-Roman, Art Education, Art History, Asian Art, Ceramics, Coins & Medals, Collages, Conceptual Art

L **PUBLIC LIBRARY OF CHARLOTTE & MECKLENBURG COUNTY,** 310 N Tryon St, 28202-2176. Tel 704-336-2801; FAX 704-336-2677; *Dir* Robert Cannon; *Assoc Dir* Judith Sutton; *Art Librn* Carolyn Hunter
Open Mon - Fri 9 AM - 9 PM, Sat 9 AM - 6 PM, Sun 2 - 6 PM, cl Sun June - Aug. Estab 1903 to provide free public library service to citizens of Mecklenburg County. Gallery contains 90 linear feet of wall space
Income: $10.9 million (financed by state & county appropriations)
Purchases: $713,068
Library Holdings: Vols 792,393; Maps 6865; AV — Cassettes, fs, motion pictures 2772, rec 27,869, slides 9261; Other — Prints 424, sculpture
Exhibitions: Local artists exhibit for one month

A **SPIRIT SQUARE CENTER FOR ARTS & EDUCATION,** 345 N College St, 28202. Tel 704-372-9664; FAX 704-377-9808; *Pres* Joe Golden, PhD; *VPres Arts & Educ* Dawn Womack; *Dir Visual Arts* Donna Devereaux
Open Tues - Sat Noon - 6 PM. Estab 1983. 5000 sq ft for six art galleries.
Average Annual Attendance: 20,000
Income: $3,000,000 (financed by mem, city & state appropriation & local arts drive)
Activities: Classes for adults & children; dramatic programs; docent training; lect open to the public, 18 vis lect per year; concerts; gallery talks; tours; scholarships; artmobile; museum shop sells books & original art

DALLAS

M **GASTON COUNTY MUSEUM OF ART & HISTORY,** 131 W Main St, PO Box 429, 28034-0429. Tel 704-922-7681; FAX 704-922-7683; *Pres* Robert Reagan; *Cur Educ* Cecilia Benoy
Open Tues - Fri 10 AM - 5 PM, Sat 1 - 5 PM, Sun 2 - 5 PM. No admis fee. Estab 1975, opened 1976 to promote the fine arts & local history in Gaston County, through classes, workshops & exhibitions; to preserve Historic Dallas Square; promote the history of the textile industry. The mus is located in an 1852 Hoffman Hotel; the Hands-On Gallery includes sculpture & weaving which may be touched; the two small galleries are on local history, with three galleries for changing & traveling exhibitions. Average Annual Attendance: 53,000. Mem: 715; dues $20-$1000; annual meeting in Nov, with quarterly meetings the first Thurs in Feb, May, Aug & Nov
Income: $345,000 (financed by mem & county appropriation)
Purchases: $1000 per yr for regional art
Collections: †Antique furniture; †contemporary sculpture; †documents; †19th - 20th century American art; objects of local history; †paintings by North Carolina artists living & dead photographs; †textile history
Publications: The Register Newsletter, quarterly
Activities: Classes for adults & children; docent training; lect open to public, 2 vis lectr per year; gallery talks, tours; exten dept serves Gaston County; individual paintings & original objects of art lent to qualified institutions; book traveling exhibitions 2 per year; sales shop sells books, magazines, original art, reproductions, prints, stationery, postcards, gifts & jewelry
L **Library,** 131 W Main St, PO Box 429, 28034. Tel 704-922-7681; FAX 704-922-7683;
Open to pub for reference use
Library Holdings: Vols 650; Per subs 13; AV — A-tapes, fs, slides; Other — Clipping files, exhibition catalogs, framed reproductions, memorabilia, pamphlets, photographs, prints

DAVIDSON

M **DAVIDSON COLLEGE VISUAL ARTS CENTER,** William H Van Every Jr & Edward M Smith Galleries, 315 N Main St, PO Box 1712, 28036-1712. Tel 704-892-2519; FAX 704-892-2691; Elec Mail penesbit@davidson.edu. *Dir* Perry L Nesbitt
Open Mon - Fri 10 AM - 5 PM, Sat & Sun 2 - 5 PM, cl holidays. No admis fee. Estab 1993 to provide exhibitions of educational importance. William H Van Every Jr Gallery-1400 sq ft; Edward M Smith Gallery-400 sq ft. Average Annual Attendance: 10,000
Income: $32,000
Collections: †Over 2500 works, mainly graphics, from all periods
Publications: Exhibition brochures & catalogs, 3-5 per year
Activities: Intern training; lect open to public, 5-7 vis lectr per year; gallery talks; tours; scholarships offered; individual paintings & original objects of art lent; book traveling exhibitions 1-3 per year
L **Library,** PO Box 1837, 28036. Tel 704-892-2331, 892-1837; *Librn* Dr Leland Park
Open to students & visitors
Library Holdings: Vols 200; Per subs 2

DURHAM

L **DUKE UNIVERSITY LIBRARY,** Hartman Center for Sales, Advertising & Marketing History, Box 90185, 27708-0185. Tel 919-660-5827; FAX 919-684-2855; Elec Mail hartman@mail.lib.duke.edu; gartrell@acpub.duke.edu; egg@mail.lib.duke.edu. *Dir* Ellen Gartrell; *Reference Archivist* Russell Koonts
Open Mon - Fri 9 AM - 5 PM, Sat 1 - 5 PM. Estab 1992. Open to academics, businesses, general public, for on-premises use. Fees charged for extended research by staff
Library Holdings: Vols 3000; Advertising Proofs & Tearsheets; Micro — Reels; AV — A-tapes, cassettes, fs, Kodachromes, motion pictures, slides, v-tapes; Other — Clipping files, memorabilia, original art works, photographs
Special Subjects: Advertising Design, Commercial Art, Historical Material, Illustration, Manuscripts
Collections: DMB&B Archives; Outdoor Advertising Association of America (OAAA) Archives; J Walter Thompson Co Archives; billboards; print advertising; TV commercials
Publications: Front & Center, semiannual newsletter

M **DUKE UNIVERSITY MUSEUM OF ART,** PO Box 90732, 27708-0732. Tel 919-684-5135; FAX 919-681-8624; *Dir* Michael P Mezzatesta; *Admin & Personnel Mgr* Lilian Antonovics; *Cur Pre-Colombian Art* Dorie Reents-Budet; *Cur Coll* Sarah Schroth; *Registrar* David Roselli
Open Mon - Fri 9 AM - 5 PM, Sat 11 AM - 2 PM, Sun 2 - 5 PM. No admis fee. Estab 1969 as a study mus with the collections being used & studied by various university departments, as well as by the pub school system & surrounding communities. The museum is located on the East Campus in a renovated two-story neo-Georgian building; gallery space includes part of the first floor & entire second floor with the space divided into eight major gallery areas. Average Annual Attendance: 30,000-35,000
Income: Financed by University

Collections: †African; Asian jade & porcelain; †Contemporary Russian; †Greek & Roman; Medieval decorative art & sculpture; paintings; †Pre-Columbian, ceramics & textiles
Publications: Exhibition catalogs 1-2 per year
Activities: Educ dept; lect open to public, 6-8 vis lectr per year; concerts; gallery talks; tours; individual paintings & original objects of art lent to other museums & galleries; originate traveling exhibitions to other museums; sales shop sells books, T-shirts
L **Lilly Art Library,** PO Box 90727, 27708. Tel 919-660-5994; FAX 919-660-5999; Elec Mail lslilly@acpub.duke.edu. *Librn & Art Bibliographer* Lee Sorensen
Open 8 AM - 2 AM. Estab 1930 to support the study of art at Duke University
Income: Financed by budget & endowment
Purchases: $64,000 excluding approval plan expenditure
Library Holdings: Vols 110,000; Per subs 416; Micro — Cards, fiche, reels; Other — Clipping files, exhibition catalogs, pamphlets 5125
Special Subjects: Afro-American Art, American Western Art, Architecture, Art History, Graphic Arts, History of Art & Archaeology, Judaica, Painting - American, Painting - British, Painting - Dutch, Painting - European, Painting - Flemish, Painting - French, Painting - German, Painting - Italian
Collections: Emphasis on European & American Art; Germanic-Language Historiography
Publications: Duke University Libraries, quarterly

M **DUKE UNIVERSITY UNION,** Duke University, 27708. Tel 919-684-2911; FAX 919-684-8395; *Union Dir* Brian Damiels; *Assoc Dir* Peter Coyle; *Asst Dir Programs* Beth Budd; *Specialist Ceramic Educ* Sharon Adams
Louise Jones Brown Gallery open Sun - Sat 7 AM - 1 AM; West Gallery & Hanks Gallery open Mon - Fri 8 AM - 5 PM; East Gallery open Sun - Sat 8 AM - midnight. No admis fee. Estab to bring to the university community exhibits of every type of graphic arts; to bring artists to campus for workshops. East Campus Gallery, room with waist high bookshelves in east campus library; West Gallery, exhibit walls & freestanding display cases in West Campus Library used for student work; Hanks Gallery & Louise Jones Brown Gallery, two galleries in Bryan Center (performing arts complex). Mem: 15; monthly meetings
Income: Financed by endowment, commission on exhibit works sold & student fees
Exhibitions: Professional & local artists, approx 3 monthly (1 in each gallery); plus Duke student artists in 1 gallery monthly
Activities: Classes for adults; lect open to public, 1 vis lectr per year; competitions; gallery talks

M **DURHAM ART GUILD INC,** 120 Morris St, 27701. Tel 919-560-2713; FAX 919-560-2713; *Gallery Dir* Laura Roselli
Open Mon - Sat 9 AM - 9 PM, Sun 1 - 6 PM. No admis fee. Estab 1948 to exhibit work of regional artists. 3600 sq ft gallery located in Arts Council Building. Average Annual Attendance: 10,000. Mem: 400; dues $25; annual meeting in June
Income: $50,000 (financed by mem, city & state appropriations)
Exhibitions: Exhibitions of work by regional artists, 8-10 per year; annual juried art shows
Publications: Juried Show Catalogue, annual; quarterly newsletter
Activities: Lect open to public, 3 vis lectr per year; competitions with awards; originate traveling exhibitions 2 per year

M **NORTH CAROLINA CENTRAL UNIVERSITY,** NCCU Art Museum, PO Box 19555, 27707. Tel 919-560-6211; FAX 919-560-5012; *Dir* Kenneth G Rodgers
Open Tues - Fri 9 AM - 5 PM, Sun 2 - 5 PM. No admis fee. Estab 1971 in a former black teaching institution with a collection of contemporary art, many Afro-American artists, reflecting diversity in style, technique, medium & subject. Three galleries are maintained; one houses the permanent collection & two are for changing shows. Average Annual Attendance: 10,500
Income: Financed by state appropriation
Collections: African & Oceanic; †Contemporary American with a focus on minority artists
Exhibitions: Joy of Living: Romare Bearden's Late Work. Carly Henry: Ancestral Home
Publications: Artis, Bearden & Burke: A Bibliography & Illustrations List; exhibition catalogs
Activities: Lect open to public; gallery talks; tours

FAYETTEVILLE

M **ARTS COUNCIL OF FAYETTEVILLE-CUMBERLAND COUNTY,** The Arts Center, 301 Hay St, PO Box 318, 28302-0318. Tel 910-323-1776; FAX 910-323-1727; Elec Mail artscncl@foto.infi.net. *Pres* Libby Seymour; *VPres* Deborah Mintz; *Artist Serv Dir* Anita Harris Alexander; *Community Outreach Dir* Jodi Schoenbrun; *Educ Dir* Karen Kostel
Open Mon - Thurs 8:30 AM - 5:30 PM, Fri 9 AM - 1 PM, Sat 1 - 5 PM. Estab 1973 to nurture, celebrate & advocate all of the arts. Maintains library. Average Annual Attendance: 60,000. Mem: 61 agencies; need board approval for non-profit agencies
Exhibitions: Annual Juried Art Competition; Annual Juried Photography Competition; Works by Regional Artists
Activities: Classes for adults & children; Urban Arts program; Arts Educ program; grants offered; originate traveling exhibitions

M **FAYETTEVILLE MUSEUM OF ART, INC,** 839 Stamper Rd, PO Box 35134, 28303. Tel 910-485-5121; *Dir* Tom Grubb; *Asst to Dir* Jessie Sova
Open Tues - Fri 10 AM - 5 PM, Sat & Sun 1 - 5 PM. No admis fee. Estab 1971 to promote in the area an active interest in the fine and applied arts; to establish and maintain a permanent collection. Front & main galleries are 996 sq ft, 143 ft wall space (231 ft wall space with temporary walls); maintains lending & reference library. Average Annual Attendance: 30,326. Mem: 600; dues $5000, $1500, $1000, $500, $250, $100, $50, $30; annual meeting in the spring
Income: $336,000 (financed by fundraisers, mem, grants & city)

Collections: American art of all media, with concentration on Southeastern artists; African Art
Exhibitions: James Beaman (paintings); Annual Competition for North Carolina Artists; Michael Northuis (paintings); Capital Art League
Publications: Annual competition catalogue; quarterly calendar
Activities: Classes for adults & children; docent training; lect open to public; concerts; gallery talks; tours; competitions; awards given; individual paintings & original objects of art lent to other museums & non-profit organizations; lending collection contains original art works, original prints, paintings, photographs, sculpture & slides; book traveling exhibitions 3 - 4 per year; museum shop sells pottery, notecards, jewelry, prints & educational items

GREENSBORO

M GREEN HILL CENTER FOR NORTH CAROLINA ART, 200 N Davie St, 27401. Tel 910-333-7460; FAX 910-275-2787; *Exec Dir & Cur* Jennifer W Moore; *Educ Dir* Mary Young; *Cur* Henry Link; *Pub Relations* Mary Pearson; *Admin Mgr* Sue Sur; *Shop Mgr* Julia Blocker; *Educ Asst* Kreta Graves
Open Tues - Sat 10 AM - 5 PM, Wed 10 AM - 7 PM, Sun 2 - 5 PM, cl Mon. No admis fee, donation suggested. Estab & incorporated 1974 as a non-profit institution offering exhibition & educational programming featuring the visual arts of North Carolina. Average Annual Attendance: 45,000. Mem: 600; dues $45-$2500
Income: Financed by mem, United Arts Council of Greensboro, Institute of Museum Services, North Carolina Arts Council
Exhibitions: Mass: Outdoor Sculpture Exhibition; Willie Little: Juke Joint
Publications: Catalogues; quarterly newsletter
Activities: Classes for adults & children; docent training; artists-in-the-schools program; lect open to public, 5-6 vis lectr per year; concerts; gallery talks; tours; competitions with awards; originate traveling exhibitions; museum shop sells books & original art

A GREENSBORO ARTISTS' LEAGUE, 200 N Davie St, 27401. Tel 910-333-7485; *Exec Dir* Sue Smith; *Cur* Peter Taylor
Open Tues, Thurs & Fri 10 AM - 5 PM, Wed Noon - 7 PM, Sat Noon - 5 PM, Sun 2 - 5 PM. No admis fee. Estab 1956 to encourage local artists to show & sell their works. Exhibitions gallery located in the Greensboro Cultural Center; twenty-five exhibitions per year; mostly one-person exhibitions & invitational group shows. Average Annual Attendance: 30,000. Mem: 500; dues patron $100, family/supportive $50, single $30, senior citizen/student $20; annual meeting last Tues in Jan
Income: $65,000 (financed by local arts council & mem)
Exhibitions: African American Arts Festival Celebration; All Members Exhibitions; Art Auction; Medical Friends of the Arts High School Senior Student Competition & Scholarship Awards
Publications: Bi-monthly newsletter
Activities: Classes & workshops for adults; lect open to public; concerts; gallery talks; tours; competitions with prizes; scholarships offered; exten dept; individual paintings lent; lending collection contains original art works, original prints, paintings & sculptures; originate traveling exhibitions 1 per year; sales shop sells original art & prints

M GREENSBORO COLLEGE, Irene Cullis Gallery, 815 W Market St, 27401. Tel 910-272-7102; *Assoc Prof* Robert Kowski
Open Mon - Fri 10 AM - 4 PM, Sun 2 - 5 PM. Estab to exhibit visual art by visiting professional artists, Greensboro College art students & others. Average Annual Attendance: 1500
Exhibitions: Scholastic High School Competition

M GUILFORD COLLEGE, Art Gallery, 5800 W Friendly Ave, 27410. Tel 910-316-2438; FAX 910-316-2950; Elec Mail hammondtn@rascal.guilford.edu. *Pres* Don McNeman; *Dir & Cur* Theresa Hammond
Open Mon - Fri 9 AM - 5 PM, Sun 2 - 5 PM during academic yr, cl holidays; Artium areas open Mon - Fri 8 AM - 8 PM, Sat & Sun 10 AM - 8 PM. No admis fee. Estab 1990. 5000 sq ft of exhibition space located in Hege Library
Collections: Contemporary American Crafts; Contemporary Polish etching & engraving; Renaissance & Barque Period Collection; 20th Century American Art
Activities: Lect open to public; gallery talks; tours; book traveling exhibitions 1-2 per year

M UNIVERSITY OF NORTH CAROLINA AT GREENSBORO, Weatherspoon Art Gallery, Spring Garden & Tate St, 27412. Tel 910-334-5770; FAX 910-334-5907;
Internet Home Page Address http://www.uncg.edu/wag/. *Dir* Ruth K Beesch; *Acting Adminr* Anne Willson; *Cur Coll* Douglas Dreishpoon; *Cur Educ* Pamela Hill; *Community Relations* Wendy Roach; *Registrar* Nora Kuper
Open Tues, Thurs & Fri 10 AM - 5 PM, Wed 10 AM - 8 PM, Sat & Sun 1 - 5 PM, cl Mon, University holidays & between academic sessions. No admis fee. Estab 1942. The gallery houses modern art; new facility, 46,000 sq ft. Average Annual Attendance: 23,000. Mem: 750; dues $25 & up; annual meeting in May
Collections: Asian Collection; Cone Collection: Matisse prints & bronzes; †Contemporary American paintings, drawings, prints & sculpture; Dillard Collection: Works on Paper
Exhibitions: (1997) Falk Visiting Artist: John Walker; Juried Senior Exhibition; Beth B; Marsden Hartley: Selected Works; Master of the Fine Arts Thesis Exhibition; Tobi Kahn: Metamorphases. (1997-98) Weatherspoon Collection Exhibition; UNCG Art Faculty Biennial Exhibition; Art on Paper 33rd Annual Exhibition. (1998) Inescapable Histories: Mel Chin Generating Our Century: New York Avant-Grade 1900-1910; Juried Senior Exhibition; Falk Visiting Artist Exhibition: Stephen Talasnik; Face-Off: The Portrait in Recent Art; Future Visions: A Forum on Public Art; The Everyday World: Selections from the Weatherspoon Collection
Publications: Art on Paper Catalogue, annually; exhibition catalogues, five per year; internal handouts, monthly; Matisse brochure; triannual member newsletter; Weatherspoon Art Gallery bulletin, biennially
Activities: Classes for adults; docent training; member programs; trips to national

exhibitions; lect open to public; gallery talks; tours; children's programs; exhibition-related performing arts; musicales; film & video; opening receptions & special events; volunteer opportunities & training; individual paintings & original objects of are are lent to other museums; originate traveling exhibitions; postcard reproductions sold at reception desk

GREENVILLE

M EAST CAROLINA UNIVERSITY, Wellington B Gray Gallery, Jenkins Fine Arts Ctr, 27858-4353. Tel 919-328-6336; FAX 919-328-6441; *Dir* Gilbert Leebrick
Open Mon - Sat 10 AM - 5 PM, Thurs evenings until 8 PM yr round, cl University holidays. No admis fee. Estab 1977, the Gallery presents 15 exhibitions annually of contemporary art in various media. Understanding of exhibitions is strengthened by educational programs including lectures, workshops, symposia & guided tours. The gallery is a large, modern 6000 sq ft facility with track lighting & modular moveable walls. Average Annual Attendance: 23,000
Income: Financed by state appropriation, Art Enthusiasts of Eastern Carolina, state & federal grants, corporate & foundation donations
Collections: African art 1000 works; Larry Rivers: The Boston Massacre - Color Lithographs
Exhibitions: (1997) 1st Annual Photography & Digital Imaging Competition; The American Tapestry Biannual & Tapestry Show; Shawn Jean Pere LaRochette & yel Luric
Publications: Anders Knuttson: Light Paintings; The Dream World of Minnie Evans; Jacob Lawrence: An American Master; exhibition catalogs
Activities: Lect open to public, 20 vis lectr per year; workshops & symposia; gallery talks; tours; competitions with prizes; scholarships offered; individual paintings & original objects of art lent; originate traveling exhibitions

L Art Library, Jenkins Fine Arts Ctr, 27858-4353. Tel 919-328-6785; *Librn* Tom Evans
Open daily 8 AM - 5 PM. Estab 1977 for Art School study of current & selected periodicals & selected reference books & slides. For lending & reference
Library Holdings: Vols 3500; Per subs 62; Micro — Cards, prints 30; AV — A-tapes, cassettes, fs, motion pictures, slides 80,000, v-tapes; Other — Exhibition catalogs, manuscripts, prints

A GREENVILLE MUSEUM OF ART, INC, 802 S Evans St, 27834. Tel 919-758-1946; *Exec Dir* Barbour Strickland; *Asst to Dir* Margaret Sloan; *Preparator* Christopher Daniels
Open Tues - Fri 10 AM - 5 PM, Sat & Sun 1 - 4 PM, cl Mon. No admis fee. Estab 1939, incorporated in 1956, to foster pub interest in art & to form a permanent collection. Six galleries 2000 sq ft including a children's gallery. Average Annual Attendance: 24,000. Mem: 600; dues $35 & higher; annual meeting in Spring
Income: $100,000 (financed by plus Foundation income for acquisition of art, contributions, mem, appropriations & grants)
Collections: †20th Centhry Contemporary paintings; drawings; graphics; †regional & national
Exhibitions: Exhibitions featuring work of regional artists; National traveling exhibits; Collection exhibits
Publications: Annual Report; A Visit to GMA, brochure; monthly exhibit announcements; quarterly members' newsletter
Activities: Classes for adults & children; demonstrations; dramatic programs; docent training; workshops; lect open to public, 8 vis lectr per year; gallery talks; tours; artmobile; individual paintings & original objects of art lent to museums & educational institutions; lending collection contains prints, paintings, sculpture & drawings; book traveling exhibitions 3-5 per year; museum shop sells books, original art, crafts & jewelry

L Reference Library, 802 S Evans St, 27834. Tel 919-758-1946; *Exec Dir* Barbour Strickland
Library Holdings: Vols 300; Per subs 150

HICKORY

M HICKORY MUSEUM OF ART, INC, 243 Third Ave NE, PO Box 2572, 28603. Tel 704-327-8576; FAX 704-327-7281; *Exec Dir* Arnold Cogswell Jr; *Asst Dir* Thomas Perryman; *Technical Advisor* Ladell Herman; *Dir Educ* Laurie Corral; *Registrar* Ellen Schwarzbek
Open Tues - Fri 10 AM - 5 PM, Sat & Sun 1 - 4 PM, cl Mon. No admis fee. Estab 1944 to collect & foster American art & serve the western Piedmont area as an exhibiting & training art center. Located in a renovated 1926 high school building; 10,000 sq ft gallery space for exhibition of permanent collection & traveling shows. Average Annual Attendance: 35,000. Mem: 1400; dues $40-$5000; annual meeting 1st Tues in May
Income: Financed by mem, donations, local United Arts Fund grants
Collections: Small European collection; very fine collection of 19th & 20th century American paintings; Oriental works; Pre-Columbian
Publications: Bi-monthly newsletter; calendar; exhibition catalogs
Activities: Classes for adults & children; dramatic programs; docent training; periodic art classes; films; lect open to public, 4 vis lectr per year; concerts; gallery talks; tours; competitions with awards; exten dept serves Catawba County & surrounding area; individual paintings & original objects of art lent to other museums & galleries; book traveling exhibitions twice a year; originate traveling exhibitions which circulate to qualifying museums & galleries; museum shop sells books, reproductions & gift items

L Library, PO Box 2572, 28603. Tel 704-327-8576; *Asst Dir* Thomas Perryman
Library Holdings: Vols 2000; Per subs 8; AV — Cassettes 50, motion pictures, slides 500, v-tapes; Other — Clipping files, exhibition catalogs, manuscripts, memorabilia, pamphlets, photographs, reproductions

HIGH POINT

M HIGH POINT HISTORICAL SOCIETY INC, Museum, 1859 E Lexington
Ave, 27262. Tel 910-885-6859; FAX 910-883-3284; *Exec Dir* Sherri Simon
Open Tues - Sat 10 AM - 4:30, Sun 1 - 4:30 PM. No admis fee. Estab 1970 to
preserve the history of High Point. Military History Gallery: Revolutionary War
up to Desert Storm; NC Pottery Gallery: Transportation/Communication/
Manufacturing Exhibits. Average Annual Attendance: 17,000. Mem: 275; dues
$25 - $150; annual meeting 4th Tues in May
Activities: Adult classes; docent programs; lect open to public, 14 vis lectr per
year; book traveling exhibitions 2-4 per year; originate traveling exhibitions 2 per
year; retail store sells books & prints

KINSTON

A COMMUNITY COUNCIL FOR THE ARTS, 400 N Queen St, PO Box 3554,
28501. Tel 919-527-2517; *Pres* John Shao; *Visual Arts Dir* Bill Dermody; *Admin
Asst* Andi Willis; *Bookkeeper* Odelle Taylor
Open Tues - Fri 9 AM - 5 PM, Sat 10 AM - 5 PM. No admis fee. Estab 1965 to
promote the arts in the Kinston-Lenoir County area. Maintains a library of art
magazines available for research by approval, five exhibition galleries & one sales
gallery. Mem: dues renaissance $1000, sustainer $500-$999, patron $250-$499,
donor $150-$249, sponsor $75-$149, family $40-$74, individual $25-$39
Income: Financed by county appropriations
Collections: Louis Orr engravings-history of North Carolina; Henry Pearson
Collection-donations of works by Henry Pearson & other leading modern artists;
permanent collection of over 250 works
Publications: Kaleidoscope, monthly newsletter
Activities: Classes for adults & children; concerts; tours; competitions with
awards; individual paintings & original objects of art lent; lending collection
contains original art works, original prints, paintings & sculpture; book traveling
exhibitions; sales shop sells books, original art, reproductions & gift items; Art
Center Children's Gallery

LEXINGTON

M DAVIDSON COUNTY MUSEUM OF ART, 224 S Main St, 27292. Tel 910-
249-2742; FAX 910-249-6302; *Pres* Gayle Burke; *VPres* Sandy Reynolds; *Exec
Dir* Mark Alley
Open Mon - Fri 10 AM - 4:30 PM, Sun 2 - 5 PM, two Sun a month. No admis
fee. Estab 1968 to expose & to educate the public in different art forms. Four
galleries - two main floor, 2 mezzanine floor in a Greek revival-style building
built in 1911; 1986 building was renovated into an arts center; children's museum
also called Chairs opened Nov 1996. Average Annual Attendance: 20,000. Mem:
400; dues $500 Benefactor, $250 Patron, $100 Donor, $50 Family, $25
individual, artists, student & senior citizen $15; annual meeting second week in
Oct
Income: $70,000 (financed by endowment, mem, city appropriation, sales)
Exhibitions: Katherine Skipper; Photography Invitational; Annual Members
Open; Spotlight
Publications: Davidson County Art Guild Newsletter, quarterly; annual yearbook
Activities: Adult & children's classes; docent programs; workshops;
demonstrations; museum trips; classes for senior citizens, mentally handicapped;
lect open to public, 4-6 lectr per year; gallery talks; tours; competitions with
awards

LOUISBURG

M LOUISBURG COLLEGE, Art Gallery, 501 N Main St, 27549. Tel 919-496-
2521; *Dir & Cur* William Hinton
Open Jan - Apr, Aug - Dec Mon - Fri 10 AM - 5 PM, cl holidays. No admis fee.
Estab 1957
Collections: American Impressionist Art; Primitive Art
Exhibitions: American Hieroglyphics; Mixed Media Sculpture by Gail Ritzer;
Who is Evelyn?; Photographic series by Louanne Watley; Franklin County Show
Activities: Arts festivals; lect; gallery talks; tours

MONROE

M UNION COUNTY PUBLIC LIBRARY UNION ROOM, 316 E Windsor St,
28112. Tel 704-283-8184; FAX 704-282-0657; *Dir* Pat Ryckman
Open Mon, Wed & Fri 9 AM - 6 PM, Tues & Thurs 9 AM - 8 PM, Sat 9 AM -
5 PM, Sun 2 - 5:30 PM. Gallery accommodates 25 large paintings & monthly
exhibits of local work or traveling exhibitions
Collections: North Carolina collection
Exhibitions: Various local artists exhibitions

MORGANTON

M BURKE ARTS COUNCIL, Jailhouse Galleries, 115 E Meeting St, 28655. Tel
704-433-7282; *Exec Dir* Gail Ross; *Pres* Ken Hanks
Open Mon - Fri 10 AM - 4 PM. No admis fee, gifts accepted. Estab 1977 to
provide high quality art shows in all media. 3 galleries in an old jail. Average
Annual Attendance: 2500. Mem: 500; dues from $15; annual meeting in May
Income: $55,000 (financed by mem, city & state appropriations, foundations &
grants)
Collections: Wachovia Permanent Collection
Exhibitions: Kaleidoscope Art Competition; 24-36 exhibitions annually
Publications: Burke County Artists & Craftsmen, every 3-4 years
Activities: Adult workshops; children's art classes; competitions with awards;
fundraisers; scholarships offered; individual paintings & original objects of art
lent to local businesses & corporations; lending collection contains books, original
art works, original prints, paintings, phono records, photographs & sculpture;
sales shop sells original art, prints, local & regional crafts

NEW BERN

M TRYON PALACE HISTORIC SITES & GARDENS, 610 Pollock St, 28563.
Tel 919-514-4900; FAX 919-514-4876; *Dir* Kay P Williams; *Communications
Specialist* Michele Raphoon; *Cur Interpretation* Hilarie M Hicks; *Cur Coll* Open;
Horticulturist Carleton B Wood; *Registrar* Nancy S Turner; *Historian* John R
Barden; *Conservator* Philippe Lafargue
Open Mon - Sat 9:30 AM - 4 PM, Sun 1:30 - 4 PM. Admis adults $12, children
$6. Estab 1959. Maintained are the historic house museums & galleries (Tryon
Palace, Dixon-Stevenson House, John Wright Stanly House & New Bern
Academy) with 18th & 19th century English & American furniture, paintings,
prints, silver, ceramic objects & textiles. Average Annual Attendance: 75,000
Income: Financed by state & private bequests
Collections: Paintings by William Carl Brown; Nathaniel Dance; Gaspard
Dughet; Thomas Gainsborough; Daniel Huntington; School of Sir Godfrey
Kneller; Claude Lorrain; Paul LaCroix; David Martin; Richard Paton; Matthew
William Peters; Charles Willson Peale; Charles Phillips; Alan Ramsay; Jan
Siberechts; Edward B Smith; E Van Stuven; Simon Preter Verelst; Richard
Wilson; John Wollaston; Graphics
Exhibitions: Temporary exhibitions on history & decorative arts, 3 per yr
Activities: Crafts demonstrations for adults & children; audio-visual orientation
program; annual symposium on 18th & 19th century decorative arts; interpretive
drama program; docent training; lect open to public, 10 vis lectr per year;
concerts; tours; scholarships offered; museum shop sells books, magazines,
reproductions, prints, slides & ceramics
L Library, 610 Pollock St, PO Box 1007, 28563. Tel 919-514-4900; FAX 919-514-
4876; *Librn* John Barden
For reference; open for use with permission
Income: Financed by state
Library Holdings: Vols 5000; Per subs 50; AV — Slides, v-tapes; Other —
Clipping files, pamphlets, photographs
Special Subjects: Archaeology, Architecture, Art History, Costume Design &
Construction, Decorative Arts, Historical Material, Interior Design, Landscape
Architecture, Painting - American, Painting - British, Period Rooms, Porcelain,
Portraits, Prints, Restoration & Conservation, Royal Governor William Tryon's
Inventory, bks, 18th Century Collection of Books, Decorative Arts
Collections: †18th & early 19th century decorative arts

NORTH WILKESBORO

M WILKES ART GALLERY, 800 Elizabeth St, 28659. Tel 910-667-2841; *Mgr*
Amanda Johnston; *Dir* Paula Koch
Open Tues - Fri 10 AM - 5 PM, Sat Noon - 4 PM, evenings for special events, cl
New Year's Day, Easter, Easter Mon, Thanksgiving, Labor Day, Memorial Day
& Christmas. No admis fee. Estab 1962 to take art to as many areas as possible.
Gallery is housed in a 1928 renovated structure; there are two galleries, one with
650 sq ft & one with 400 sq ft. Average Annual Attendance: 10,400. Mem: 400;
dues patron & corp $500, donor $250, sponsor $100, family $40; annual meeting
in May
Income: Financed by mem, local governments, state arts council & corporations
Collections: Contemporary paintings, graphics, sculpture, primarily of NC artists
Exhibitions: Artist League Juried Competition; Blue Ridge Overview (amateur
photography); temporary exhibitions Fall Harvest Competition; Northwest Artist
League Competition
Publications: Title of Exhibition, monthly brochures & catalogues; Wilkes Art
Gallery Newsletter, monthly
Activities: Classes for adults & children; docent training; arts festivals; films; art
& craft classes; lect open to public, 3 vis lectr per year; gallery talks; tours;
competitions with awards; concerts; individual paintings lent to medical center;
originate traveling exhibitions; sales shop sells, books, crafts, original art, pottery,
prints & reproductions

RALEIGH

ART LIBRARIES SOCIETY OF NORTH AMERICA
For further information, see National and Regional Organizations

A ARTSPACE INC, 201 E Davie St, 27601. Tel 919-821-2787; FAX 919-821-
0383; *Exec Dir* Margaret P Rader; *Facility Mgr* Angie Morris
Open Tues - Fri 9 AM - 6 PM, Sat 10 AM - 5 PM, Sun 1 -5 PM. No admis fee.
Estab 1986. Mem: Annual meeting in Apr
Income: $400,000 (financed by mem, city & state appropriation, rental income)
Exhibitions: Fantasy Art; Henley SE Spectrum; The Art is in the Mail; Holiday
Showcase; New Works; Get A Start in the Arts; Triangle Clay Show
Activities: Classes for adults & children; dramatic programs; docent programs;
artists business workshops; lect open to public, 6 vis lectr per year; competitions
with cash awards; scholarships & fels offered; book traveling exhibitions 2 per
year; originate traveling exhibition annually

ASSOCIATION OF AMERICAN EDITORIAL CARTOONISTS
For further information, see National and Regional Organizations

M CITY GALLERY OF CONTEMPORARY ART, 220 S Blount St, PO Box 66,
27601-0066. Tel 919-839-2077; FAX 919-831-2653; *Exec Dir* Denise Dickens;
Exec Asst & Cur Educ Colette Waters; *Develop Officer* Julia Waterfall; *Admin
Asst & Preparator* Joey Howard; *Photo* David Simonton
Open Tues - Sat 10 AM - 5 PM, cl Sun & Mon. Admis suggested donation $2.
Estab 1983 to support new & innovative works by regional, national &
international artists & designers; presents contemporary art & design
through a schedule of diverse exhibitions that explore aesthetic, cultural &
ideological issues. 8000 sq ft building in historic section of downtown Raleigh
with exhibition space of 5000 sq ft. Average Annual Attendance: 50,000. Mem:
700; dues small business $150, student $15; annual meeting in June
Income: Financed by mem, city & state appropriation, contributions &
foundations

Exhibitions: Six to eight exhibitions per year
Publications: Exhibition catalogues
Activities: Teacher workshops; mentoring program for adolescents; lect; performances; literary readings; film series; gallery talks; tours; video programs; internships for college & graduate students; book traveling exhibitions; originate traveling exhibitions; sales area sells catalogs, posters, postcards, T-shirts, caps, mugs & novelty items

A **CITY OF RALEIGH ARTS COMMISSION,** Municipal Building Art Exhibitions, 222 W Hargett St, PO Box 590, 27602. Tel 919-890-3477; FAX 919-890-3442; *Chmn* John Mabe; *Exec Dir* Martha Shannon; *Coordr* Beverly Ayscue
Open Mon - Fri 8:30 AM - 5:15 PM. Estab 1984 to showcase Raleigh-based artists/art collections in the local area. First & second floor lobbies of the Raleigh Municipal Building
Income: $4340 (financed by city & state appropriation)

M **NORTH CAROLINA MUSEUM OF ART,** 2110 Blue Ridge Rd, 27607. Tel 919-839-6262; FAX 919-733-8034; *Dir* Lawrence Wheeler; *Assoc Dir Admin* Hal McKinney; *Acting Chief Cur* John Coffey; *Dir Educ* Joseph F Covington; *Chief Designer* Stephanie Miller; *Chief Conservator* David Findley; *Registrar* Carrie Hedrick; *Librn* Dr Anna Dvorak; *Dir External Affairs* Georganne Bingham
Open Tues - Thurs, Sat 9 AM - 5 PM, Fri 9 AM - 9 PM, Sun 11 AM - 6 PM, cl Mon & holidays. No admis fee. Estab 1947, open to pub 1956, to acquire, preserve, & exhibit works of art for the educ & enjoyment of the people of the state & to conduct programs of educ, research & publications designed to encourage interest in & an appreciation of art. Average Annual Attendance: 265,000. Mem: 7900; dues $25 & up
Income: Financed by state appropriation
Collections: Ancient art; Mary Duke Biddle Education Gallery; European and American painting, sculpture & decorative arts; Samuel H Kress Collection; Pre-Columbian, African, Oceanic & New World art
Exhibitions: North Carolina Artists Exhibitions; wide range of temporary exhibitions
Publications: Bulletin, annual; Preview, trimestrial; exhibition & permanent collection catalogs
Activities: Classes for adults & children; docent training; lect open to public; concerts; gallery talks; tours; exten dept serving North Carolina;; originate traveling exhibitions to North Carolina museums & galleries; museum shop sells books, magazines, reproductions, prints and slides
L **Reference Library,** 2110 Blue Ridge Rd, 27607. Tel 919-839-6262; FAX 919-733-8034; *Librn* Dr Anna Dvorak
Open Tues - Fri 9 AM - 5 PM. Open to pub for reference
Income: Financed by State and NCMA Foundation
Purchases: $24,125
Library Holdings: Vols 30,000; Per subs 81; AV — Slides 25,000; Other — Clipping files, exhibition catalogs, pamphlets
Special Subjects: Decorative Arts, Fine Arts

A **NORTH CAROLINA MUSEUMS COUNCIL,** PO Box 2603, 27602. Tel 919-733-7450; FAX 919-733-1573; *Pres* Beverly Sanford; *VPres* Carl McIntosh; *Treas* Dusty Wescott
Estab 1963 to stimulate interest, support & understanding of museums. Mem: 250; dues individual $15; annual meeting in the fall
Income: Financed by mem
Publications: NCMC Newsletter, quarterly; North Carolina Museums Guide
Activities: Awards given

L **NORTH CAROLINA STATE UNIVERSITY,** Harrye Lyons Design Library, PO Box 7701, 27695-7701. Tel 919-515-2207; FAX 919-515-7330; *Librn* Caroline Carlton; *Librn Asst* Lynn Crisp; *Librn Asst* Dot Hunt; *Librn Asst* Sherry Johnson
Open Mon - Thurs 7:30 AM - 11 PM, Fri 7:30 AM - 10 PM, Sat 9 AM - 10 PM, Sun 1 - 11 PM. Estab 1942 to serve the reading, study, reference & research needs of the faculty, students & staff of the School of Design & the University campus, as well as off-campus borrowers. Primarily for lending. Circ 56,058
Income: Financed by state appropriation, private funds & mem
Purchases: $41,450
Library Holdings: Vols 40,747; Per subs 210; Trade literature, Vertical files; AV — A-tapes, motion pictures, slides, v-tapes; Other — Pamphlets
Special Subjects: Architecture, Art History, Furniture, Graphic Design, History of Art & Archaeology, Landscape Architecture, Urban & Product Design, Visual & Basic Design
Collections: File on measured Drawings of North Carolina Historic Sites; 458 maps & plans; 300 bibliographies compiled by the Design Library staff
Publications: Index to the School of Design, student publication book Vols 1-25
M **Visual Arts Center,** Cates Ave, PO Box 7306, 27695-7306. Tel 919-515-3503; FAX 919-515-6163; *Dir* Charlotte V Brown; *Registrar* Gregory Tyler
Galleries open Tues - Fri Noon - 8 PM, Sat & Sun 2 - 8 PM, except student holidays. No admis fee. Estab 1979 to collect, exhibit & provide changing exhibitions in the decorative & design arts. Two small shared spaces, 200 running ft, 18,000 sq foot mus opened 1992. 6000 ft exhibition galleries. Average Annual Attendance: 20,000. Mem: 200; dues $25-$1500; annual meeting in Apr
Income: $250,000 (financed by student fees)
Purchases: $10,000
Collections: †American, Indian, Asian & pre-Columbian textiles; †ceramics (fine, ironstone, porcelain, traditional); †furniture; †product design
Exhibitions: (1997) Simplicity, Order & Discipline: The Work of George Matsumoto from the North Carolina State University Libraries Special Collection; The Work of Eduard Catalano
Publications: Exhibit catalogs
Activities: Docent & self-guided tours; lect open to public, 6 vis lectr per year; gallery talks; tours; competitions; scholarships offered; individual paintings & original objects of art lent to museums; lending collection contains 50 framed reproductions; originate traveling exhibition

A **PORTRAITS SOUTH,** 105 S Bloodworth St, 27601. Tel 919-833-1630; FAX 919-833-3391; *Pres* Jac F ReVille; *Pres* Grayson ReVille
Estab 1980, agent for professional portrait artists. Mem: 100 represented artists
Publications: Newsletters for artists, twice a year
Activities: Book traveling exhibitions 100 per year; originate traveling exhibitions 100 per year

A **VISUAL ART EXCHANGE** (Formerly Wake Visual Arts Association), 325 Blake St (Mailing add: PO Box 744, 27602). Tel 919-828-7834; *Exec Dir* Aimee Flynn; *Pres* Wendy Painter
Open Tues - Fri 11 AM - 4 PM, Sat 10 AM - 3 PM. No admis fee. Estab 1980 to serve emerging & professional artists. Mem: 300; dues $45
Exhibitions: Holiday Show; New Show; Young Artist Show
Publications: Expressions, 10 per year
Activities: Classes for adults & children; lect open to public, 10 vis lectr per year; gallery talks; competitions with prizes; workshops; originate traveling exhibitions; sales shop sells original art

REIDSVILLE

M **NORTH CAROLINA STATE UNIVERSITY,** Chinqua-Penn Plantation House, Garden & Greenhouses, 2138 Wentworth St, 27320. Tel 910-349-4576; FAX 910-342-4863; *Pres* Susan Cline-Cordonier; *House Mgr* Vivian Forrester; *Supt of Grounds* Keith E Davis; *Admin Sec* Betty Citty
Open Wed - Sat 10 AM - 4 PM, Sun 1:30 - 4:30 PM, cl to the pub. Admis adults $6, senior citizens $5, children $2.50. Estab 1966 as part of University's total educational program to make the house with its collection & the gardens available to the pub. Average Annual Attendance: 30,000
Income: Financed by state appropriation & admis fee
Collections: Antique European Furniture; Oriental Art Objects; Botanical (growing)
Activities: Sales shop sells unique items from around the world & chinqua - Penn materials

RESEARCH TRIANGLE PARK

C **BURROUGHS WELLCOME COMPANY,** Art Collection, 3030 Cornwallis Rd, 27709. Tel 919-248-3000, Ext 4449; FAX 919-315-8375; *Sr VPres Corp Communications* Margret Dadess
Open 9 AM - 4 PM, groups only by prior arrangement. Estab 1979 to develop a meaningful collection of American Contemporary Art for enjoyment & enrichment for employees & communities. Collection displayed in Corporate Headquarters Building
Collections: Paintings & sculpture from permanent collection & on-loan from the Whitney Museum in New York City
Activities: Tours

ROCKY MOUNT

A **ROCKY MOUNT ARTS CENTER,** 1173 Nashville Rd, PO Box 4031, 27803-4031. Tel 919-972-1163, 972-1164; *Dir* Marlene Payne
Open Mon - Fri 8:30 AM - 5 PM, Sun 2 - 4 PM, cl Sat except for classes. No admis fee. Estab 1957 to promote the development of the creative arts in the community through educ, participation & appreciation of music, dance, painting, drama, etc; to provide facilities & guidance for developing talents & enriching lives through artistic expression & appreciation. Maintains the Hines Art Gallery. Average Annual Attendance: 25,000. Mem: 600; dues $20 & up; annual meeting in Oct
Income: Financed by City Recreation Department with supplemental support by mem
Exhibitions: Outdoor Art Exhibition in the Spring; Permanent collection & traveling shows change each month
Activities: Conducts art classes; year-round theatre program; classes for adults & children; lect open to public, 2-4 vis lectr per year; concerts; gallery talks; tours; competitions; book traveling exhibitions 5-6 per year

SALISBURY

M **HORIZONS UNLIMITED SUPPLEMENTARY EDUCATIONAL CENTER,** Art Gallery, 1637 Parkview Circle, 28144-2461. Tel 704-639-3004; FAX 704-633-8514; *Dir* Cynthia B Osterhus
Open Mon - Fri 8 AM - 4 PM. No admis fee. Estab 1968 to exhibit art work of pub schools, supplemented by exhibits of local artists from time to time during the school year; primary purpose is to supplement art educ activities in the pub schools. The center is comprised of two areas, one approximately 24 x 65 ft, the other 15 x 70 ft with an adjoining classroom for instruction & demonstrations. Average Annual Attendance: 4500
Income: Financed by mem, state & county appropriation & from local foundations
Collections: Planetarium; touch tank Rain Forest
Activities: Classes for adults & children; lect open to public, 5 vis lectr per year; gallery talks; tours; individual & original objects of art lent

M **WATERWORKS VISUAL ARTS CENTER,** One Water St, 28144. Tel 704-636-1882; *Chief Exec Officer & Exec Dir* Ronald L Crusan; *Asst Dir* Barbara Setzer
Open Tues - Sat 10 AM - 4 PM, Sun 1 - 4 PM. No admis fee. Estab 1977 for exhibition & instruction of visual arts. Four galleries with changing exhibitions. Average Annual Attendance: 30,000. Mem: 700
Income: $181,000 (financed by mem, city, county, appropriation, United Arts Fund, exhibition & educational corporate sponsors)
Publications: Charlotte Gallery Arts, catalogue; Salisbury Rennaisance, Understanding Abstract Art
Activities: Classes for adults & children; classes for special populations; classes for children in public housing; in-school programs; lect open to public, 5 vis lectr per year; gallery talks, tours; book traveling exhibitions; originate traveling exhibitions

SHELBY

A SHELBY ART LEAGUE, INC, PO Box 1708, 28151-1708. Tel 704-484-4023; *Pres* Hal Bryant; *VPres* Janet Berry; *Treas* Betsy Fonvielle
Estab 1974 to promote & sponsor visual art activities in the county. Utilizes exhibit galleries at Cleveland Community College in Shelby. These galleries are secure & having hanging systems & track lighting. Average Annual Attendance: 2000. Mem: 250; dues $25-$500; annual meeting in early Jan
Income: $13,000 (financed by mem & state appropriation)
Exhibitions: Cleveland County Adult Artists Exhibition; Cleveland County Student Artists Exhibition; Annual National Juried Artists Exhibition; Regional Photography Exhibition
Activities: Workshops; lect for members only, some open to public, 2-3 vis lectr per year; scholarships & fels offered

STATESVILLE

M ARTS & SCIENCE CENTER, 1335 Museum Rd, 28677. Tel 704-873-4734; *Exec Dir* Rita Rhodes; *Asst Dir* Diana Bromley
Open Tues - Sat 10 AM - 5 PM, Sun 2 - 5 PM. Admis non-members $1, children 5 & under free. Estab 1956 to aid the community in the promotion of art history & science. Bowles, Grier & Henkel Galleries features monthly changing exhibits; Artifacts Room features permanent displays. Average Annual Attendance: 22,000. Mem: 650; dues $15 & up; monthly meetings
Income: Financed by mem, CAFD (Cooperative Arts Fund Drive), grants & sponsorships
Collections: Collections entail †Ancient Arts, †Decorative Arts, †Fine Arts, †Natural History
Exhibitions: Annual Iredell Photography Club; Mitchell Community Art Students & Faculty; Statesville Artists' Guild & Mooresville Artists' Guild & Mooresville Artists Guild Sale & Show; Walking Trails & Pioneer Settlement
Activities: Art classes; classes for children; community booths; lect; gallery talks; tours; sponsors competitions with awards; individual & original objects of art lent to museums & responsible organizations; book traveling exhibitions, 2-3 per year, traveling educational trunks, annual NC Heritage Festival, annual Native American Evening with exhibits reflecting heritage

TARBORO

M EDGECOMBE COUNTY CULTURAL ARTS COUNCIL, INC, Blount-Bridgers House, Hobson Pittman Memorial Gallery, 130 Bridgers St, 27886. Tel 919-823-4159; FAX 919-823-6190; Elec Mail eccac@abaco.coastalnet.com. *Dir* Meade B Horne; *Educ* Eric A Greene; *Asst to Dir* Susan M Spain
Open Mon - Fri 10 AM - 4 PM, Sat - Sun 2 - 4 PM. Admis $2. Estab 1982, to present local culture as it relates to state & nation. Located in a restored 1810 plantation house, 5 rooms in period interpretation, 3 used as gallery space for 20th century art permanent & traveling exhibits
Income: $135,000 (financed by city & state appropriation, corporate & private donations)
Collections: Pittman Collection of oil, watercolors & drawings; American Collection of oils, watercolor & drawings; Decorative arts 19th century Southern
Exhibitions: Hobson Pittman retrospect; period rooms, 1810-1870
Publications: Around the House, monthly; Spotlight, quarterly
Activities: Classes for adults & children; docent programs; lect open to the public, 5 vis lectr per year; concerts; gallery talks; tours; exten dept lends out paintings; book traveling exhibitions, 6 times per year; originate traveling exhibitions, once per year; museum shop sells original art

WADESBORO

M ANSON COUNTY HISTORICAL SOCIETY, INC, 209 E Wade St, PO Box 732, 28170. Tel 704-694-6694; *Pres* Don Scarborough
Open Apr - Sept, 1st Sun of each month 2 - 4 PM & by appointment. No admis fee. Estab 1960 as a mus of 18th & 19th century furniture. Average Annual Attendance: 1000. Mem: 240; dues family $15, single $10; annual meeting in Nov
Income: $12,000 (financed by mem)
Collections: Collection of 18th & 19th century furniture
Publications: History of Anson County, 1750 - 1976

WASHINGTON

A BEAUFORT COUNTY ARTS COUNCIL, 108 Gladden St, PO Box 634, 27889-0634. Tel 919-946-2504; *Dir* Judy Jennette; *Gallery & Public Relations* Wanda Johnson; *Admin Asst* Mary Digrys
Open Mon - Fri 9 AM - 5 PM. No admis fee. Estab 1972
Collections: Aslando Suite by Jim Moon; Johannes Oertel Collection
Exhibitions: Printmaking (rotate exhibits every 2 months)
Activities: Book traveling exhibitions

WILMINGTON

M BATTLESHIP NORTH CAROLINA, Battleship Dr Eagle Island, PO Box 480, 28402. Tel 910-251-5797; FAX 910-251-5807; Elec Mail ncbb55@aol.com. *Dir* David R Scheu; *Asst Dir* Roger Miller; *Prom Dir* Mark Shore; *Cur* Kim Robinson Sincox; *Sales Dir* Leesa McFarlane
Open daily May 16 - Sept 15 8 AM - 8 PM, Sept 16 - May 15 8 AM - 5 PM. Admis adult $6, children between 6 & 11 $3, under 6 free. Estab 1961 as historic ship museum to memorialize the World War II dead of the state of North Carolina. Average Annual Attendance: 250,000
Income: Financed by admis, sales in gift shop & snack bar & rental functions
Collections: Artifacts associated with or appropriate to the ships bearing the

name North Carolina: BB-55 (1936-1947); CA-12 (1905-1930) & Ship-of-the-line (1818-1867); also artifacts associated with the memorial itself
Publications: Battleship North Carolina; Ship's Data 1
Activities: Lect open to public; scholarships offered; sales shop sells books, reproduction prints, slides, souveniers & post cards

M SAINT JOHN'S MUSEUM OF ART, 114 Orange St, 28401. Tel 910-763-0281; FAX 910-341-7981; *Dir* C Reynolds Brown; *Asst Dir* Pamela A Jobin; *Cur Educ* Tiffany Kitchen; *Cur & Registrar Colls* Anne Brennan
Open Tues - Sat 10 AM - 5 PM, Sun Noon - 4 PM. Admis $2. Estab 1962 to promote the visual arts in southeastern North Carolina. Average Annual Attendance: 50,000. Mem: 1250; dues $35-$1200
Collections: Mary Cassatt's color prints The Ten; 18th, 19th & 20th century North Carolina art; Jugtown Pottery
Exhibitions: 10-12 temporary exhibitions annually include art from all geographic regions & areas

WILSON

M BARTON COLLEGE, Barton Museum - Virginia Graves Gallery - Lula E Backley Gallery, 27893. Tel 919-399-6477; FAX 919-237-4957; *Dir & Chmn Art* J Chris Wilson
Open Mon - Fri 10 AM - 4:30 PM. No admis fee. Estab 1960 to provide art exposure for our students & community. Gallery is 50 x 50 ft. Average Annual Attendance: 3000
Income: Financed by college budget
Collections: Ceramics; recent drawings; painting; prints; sculpture; African masks
Exhibitions: National Scholastic Art Award Competition for Eastern North Carolina
Activities: Educ dept; lect open to public; gallery talks; tours
L Library, Whitehead & Gold Sts, College Station, 27893. Tel 919-399-6500; FAX 919-237-4957; *Dir* Shirley Gregory
For reference only
Library Holdings: Vols 2500; Per subs 94; AV — Kodachromes, v-tapes 50; Other — Exhibition catalogs, original art works, pamphlets, sculpture
Special Subjects: Art History

WINSTON-SALEM

A ARTS COUNCIL OF WINSTON-SALEM & FORSYTH COUNTY, 305 W Fourth St, Ste 1 C, PO Box 10935, 27101. Tel 910-722-2585; FAX 910-761-8286; *Pres & Exec Dir* David C Hudson; *Exhib Cur* Amy Fundenburke; *Dir Communications* Judy Sutherin
Open Mon - Fri 9 AM - 5 PM. Estab 1949 as a housing, coordinating, promoting & fundraising organization for 11 funded & 39 assoc member groups, including Assoc Artists, Sawtooth Center for Visual Design, the Winston-Salem Symphony Assoc, the Little Theatre, Southeastern Center for Contemporary Art & Children's Theatre Board; member groups are independently incorporated. Housing facilities include Hanes Community Center: theatre & rehearsal rooms, Sawtooth Building: art & craft studios & exhibition galleries. Mem: Annual meeting in May
Income: Financed by fund drives, pub & private grants & endowments

A ASSOCIATED ARTISTS OF WINSTON-SALEM, 226 N Marshall St, 27101. Tel 910-722-0340; *Exec Dir* Sue Kneppelt
Open Mon - Sat 9 AM - 9 PM. No admis fee. Estab 1956 to promote & conduct activities that support the awareness, educ, enjoyment & appreciation of visual fine art. The association rents the walls of the gallery from the Arts Council. Average Annual Attendance: 75,000. Mem: 400; dues $15-$40; regular programs
Income: $100,000 (financed by mem & Arts Council funds)
Exhibitions: One Southeastern regional show; two national shows; various member exhibitions
Publications: Exhibit catalogs; newsletter, bi-monthly
Activities: Membership programs; workshops; lect; demonstrations; lect open to public, 5 vis lectr per year; gallery talks; tours; competitions with awards; exten dept serves city; originate traveling exhibitions; gallery sells original art

M OLD SALEM INC, Museum of Early Southern Decorative Arts, 924 S Main St, PO Box 10310, 27108. Tel 910-721-7360; *Dir Research* Brad Rauschenberg; *Educ Coordr* Sally Gant; *Assoc Educ* Ruth Brooks; *Research Assoc* Martha Rowe; *Photographer Technician* Wes Stewart
Open Mon - Sat 10:30 AM - 5 PM, Sun 1:30 - 4:30 PM. Admis adult $5, children $3. Estab 1965 to bring to light the arts & antiquities produced in Maryland, Virginia, Kentucky, Tennessee, North & South Carolina & Georgia through the first two decades of the 19th century. Three galleries are furnished with Southern decorative arts or imported objects used in the South & fifteen period settings from Southern houses dating from 1690 to 1821. Average Annual Attendance: 25,000. Mem: 1250; dues $25 & up; annual meeting in Spring
Income: $225,000 (financed by endowment, mem, state appropriation & other funds)
Purchases: $50,000
Collections: †Southern decorative arts in general, & sepcifically furniture, paintings, silver, ceramics, metalwares, & woodwork of southern origin
Exhibitions: Ongoing Research in Southern Decorative Arts
Publications: Journal of Early Southern Decorative Arts, semiannually; catalog of the collection 1991, Museum of Early Southern Decorative Arts; The Luminary, newsletter, semiannually
Activities: Classes for adults & children; graduate Summer Institute; lect open to public, 15 vis lectr per year; gallery talks; scholarships offered; exten dept serves eight Southern States; individual paintings & original objects of art lent to museums & cultural institutions & with special permission from staff are available for special exhibits; lending collection contains 2000 original art works, 100 paintings, 18,000 photographs & 30,000 slides; originate traveling exhibitions; sales shop sells books, slides

L **Library**, PO Box 10310, 27108. Tel 910-721-7367; *Dir Research* Bradford L Rauschenberg; *Research Assoc* Martha Rowe
Open Mon - Sat 10:30 AM - 5 PM, Sun 1:30 - 4:30 PM. Estab 1965 to display & research early southern decorative arts through 1820
Library Holdings: Vols 5500; Per subs 1000; Computer data base index of early Southern Artists & Artisans; Micro — Fiche, prints, reels; AV — Slides; Other — Photographs
Special Subjects: Aesthetics, Afro-American Art, American Indian Art, Archaeology, Architecture, Art History, Carpets & Rugs, Ceramics, Costume Design & Construction, Crafts, Research of regional artists
Publications: Journal of Early Southern Decorative Arts, bi-annually; Luminary, bi-annually

M **REYNOLDA HOUSE MUSEUM OF AMERICAN ART,** Reynolda Rd, PO Box 11765, 27116. Tel 910-725-5325; FAX 910-721-0991; Elec Mail reynolda@ols.net. *Exec Dir* Nicholas B Bragg; *Assoc Dir Planning & Develop* Elizabeth L Morgan; *Asst Dir Prog* Marjorie J Northup; *Coordr Marketing & Pub Relations* Judith Smith; *Coordr Educ* Kathleen F B Hutton
Open Tues - Sat 9:30 - 4:30 PM, Sun 1:30 - 4:30 PM, cl Mon. Admis adults $6, senior citizens $5, students $3. Estab 1964 to offer a learning experience through a correlation of art, music & literature using the house & the collection of American Art as resources. Gallery located in the 40 rooms of the former R J Reynolds home. Average Annual Attendance: 45,000. Mem: 1200; board meeting in May & Nov
Income: Financed by endowment, annual fund, government & foundation grants, admis & earned income
Collections: Doughty Bird Collection; costume collection; †permanent collection of decorative arts, furniture, paintings, prints & sculpture
Exhibitions: William Sydney Mount; special exhibitions offered annually
Publications: Annual Report; Calendar of Events, 3 per year
Activities: Classes for adults and children; dramatic programs; docent training; lect open to public, 20 vis lectr per year; concerts; gallery talks; tours; individual paintings and original objects of art lent to specific museums with reciprocity agreement; lending collection contains original prints, paintings; museum shop sells slides of paintings
L **Library,** Reynolda Rd, PO Box 11765, 27116. Tel 910-725-5325; FAX 910-721-0991; *Librn* Ruth Mullen
Open to public
Library Holdings: Vols 2000; Per subs 19

M **SOUTHEASTERN CENTER FOR CONTEMPORARY ART,** 750 Marguerite Dr, 27106. Tel 910-725-1904; FAX 910-722-6059; *Pres* Morris Marley; *Dir* Susan L Talbott; *Asst Dir* Vicki Kopf; *Educ Coordr* Terri Dowell-Dennis; *Cur* Jeff Fleming; *Business Mgr* Susan Boone
Open Tues - Sat 10 AM - 5 PM, Sun 2 - 5 PM, cl Mon. Admis adults $3, students & senior citizens $2. Estab 1956 to indentify & exhibit the country's major contemporary artists of exceptional talent; to present educational programs for children & adults; to bring the viewing public in direct contact with artists & their art. Maintained are three indoor & outdoor exhibition areas. Average Annual Attendance: Average Annual Attendance: 50,000. Mem: 2000; dues varying categories; annual meeting May
Income: Financed by mem, local & state arts councils, grants, sales commissions & contributions
Exhibitions: Artist & the Community: Maya Lin; Tim Hawkinson; Joshua Neustein
Publications: Catalogs, 3-4 per yr; newsletter, quarterly
Activities: Classes for adults & children; dramatic programs; docent training; lect open to public; concerts; gallery talks; tours; scholarships; originate traveling exhibitions; museum shop sells books, original art, reproductions & contemporary crafts

C **WACHOVIA BANK OF NORTH CAROLINA,** 301 Church St, PO Box 3099, 27150-3099. Tel 910-770-6143; *Asst VPres* Linda G Cooper
Estab to support the arts & enhance the environment for customers & employees. Collection displayed throughout the 204 offices
Collections: Traditional & contemporary work, primarily by North Carolina & Southeastern United States artists

WAKE FOREST UNIVERSITY
L **A Lewis Aycock Art Slide Library & Print Collection,** PO Box 7232, Reynolds Sta, 27109-7232. Tel 910-759-5078, 759-5000; FAX 910-759-4691; *Cur Slides & Prints* Martine Sherrill
Open Mon - Fri 9 AM - 5 PM. Estab 1968. Circ 15,000 (slides)
Library Holdings: Per subs 19; Laserdisks; AV — Kodachromes, lantern slides, motion pictures, rec 128,088, slides 136,000, v-tapes; Other — Clipping files, exhibition catalogs, original art works, pamphlets, photographs, prints
Special Subjects: Afro-American Art, American Indian Art, Folk Art, History of Art & Archaeology, Islamic Art, Mexican Art, Oriental Art, Period Rooms, Pre-Columbian Art, Prints, Religious Art
Collections: Art Department Slide Collection; University Print Collection
M **Fine Arts Gallery,** Scales Fine Arts Ctr, PO Box 7232, Reynolds Sta, 27109-7232. Tel 910-759-5585; FAX 910-759-6014; Elec Mail faccinto@wfu.edu. *Dir* Victor Faccinto
Open Mon - Fri 10 AM - 5 PM, Sat & Sun 1 - 5 PM. No admis fee. Estab 1976 for international contemporary & historical exhibitions. 3500 sq ft of exhibition space in two separate galleries. Average Annual Attendance: 9000
Income: Financed by university
Collections: Contemporary Print Collection
Publications: Exhibit catalog
Activities: Lect open to public, 6 vis lectr per year
M **Museum of Anthropology,** Wingate Dr, PO Box 7267, 27109-7267. Tel 910-759-5282; FAX 910-759-5116; *Dir* Mary Jane Berman; *Cur* Beverlye Hancock; *Museum Educ* Kimberly Robertson; *Vol Coordr* Anne Gilmore; *Admin Secy* Myrna Mackin
Open Tues - Sat 10 AM - 4:30 PM. Estab 1968. Average Annual Attendance: 20,000. Mem: 200; dues $5-$100
Income: $19,586 (financed by mem & University)
Activities: Classes for adults & children; docent training; lect open to public, 3 vis lectr per year; gallery talks; traveling exhibitions 1 per year; museum shop sells jewelry, toys, books & masks

M **WINSTON-SALEM STATE UNIVERSITY,** Diggs Gallery, 601 Martin Luther King Jr Dr, 27110. Tel 910-750-2458; FAX 910-750-2459; *Dir* Brooke Davis Anderson; *Gallery Asst* Robin Leftwich
Open Tues - Sat 11 AM - 5 PM. No admis fee. Estab 1990 as a university exhibition space highlighting African & African-American Art. 7000 sq ft, state of the art gallery, flexible space. Average Annual Attendance: 10,000
Income: $150,000-$200,000 (financed by endowment, state appropriation, grants & donations)
Collections: African-American Art Collection
Exhibitions: African-American Quilts; Romare Bearden, John Biggers; Memory Juggs; Jacob Lawrence; Juan Logan; Alison Saar
Publications: Ashe Improvisation & Recycling In African-American Art Through African Eyes; Forget-Me-Not: The Art & Mystery of Memory Jugs; Model In The Mind
Activities: Classes for adults & children; lect open to public, 10-15 vis lectr per year; individual paintings & original objects of art lent; book traveling exhibitions 5 per year

NORTH DAKOTA

BELCOURT

M **TURTLE MOUNTAIN CHIPPEWA HISTORICAL SOCIETY,** Turtle Mountain Heritage Center, PO Box 257, 58316. Tel 701-477-6140; *Interim Dir* Alice Siroti
Open summer hrs Mon - Fri 8 AM - 4:30 PM, Sat & Sun 1 - 5 PM, winter hrs Mon - Fri 8 AM - 4:50 PM. No admis fee. Estab 1985 to promote & preserve culture. Small, well arranged, attractive gallery consisting of historical photos, memorabilia, artifacts, art works, beadwork, all pertaining to the Turtle Mountain Chippewa. Mem: 200; dues $10-$500; annual meeting in Aug
Income: $98,496 (financed by mem, sales, bazaars & promotions)
Collections: †Ancient tools & implements; †basketry; †beaded artifacts; †contemporary Indian crafts; †costumes; †memorabilia; †paintings; †pottery; †sculpture; †stones
Exhibitions: Paintings; Jingle Dress - Male Costume
Publications: Newsletter, twice a year
Activities: Lect open to public; competitions with prizes; originate traveling exhibition to high school juried art shows & tri-state museums; sales shop sells books, prints, original art & reproductions
L **Heritage Center Archives,** PO Box 257, 58316. Tel 701-477-6140; Estab 1986. For reference
Income: Financed by city appropriation
Library Holdings: Vols 200; Other — Clipping files, framed reproductions, manuscripts, memorabilia, original art works, pamphlets, photographs, prints, reproductions, sculpture
Special Subjects: American Indian Art, Archaeology, Art Education, Art History, Costume Design & Construction, Crafts, Display, Dolls, Drafting, Drawings, Embroidery, Ethnology, Fashion Arts, Film, Folk Art

DICKINSON

M **DICKINSON STATE UNIVERSITY,** Mind's Eye Gallery, 58601-4896. Tel 701-227-2312, 227-2342; *Dir* Lilly Veder; *Assoc Dir* Benni Privatsky
Open Mon - Thurs 8 AM - 10 PM, Fri 8 AM - 4 PM, Sat 1 - 4 PM, Sun 6 - 10 PM. No admis fee. Estab 1972 as a visual arts gallery presenting monthly exhibits representing the work of local, national & international artists. Gallery is a secure, large room approx 50 x 20 ft, with a 20 ft ceiling & approx 120 running ft of sheetrock display space. Average Annual Attendance: 5000
Income: Financed by North Dakota Council on the Arts, grants, students activities fees & mem
Purchases: $1000
Collections: Zoe Beiler paintings; contemporary graphics
Exhibitions: Bela Petheo; A Long Way to See: Photographs of North Dakota by Wayne Gudmundson; S U Art Faculty: Biennial Exhibit; Chambered Vessels Metalsmithing by Ellen Auyong; Early Dakota Quilting; North Dakota Centennial Juried Exhibition; Dakotas 100: International Competition of Works on Paper
Publications: Exhibit announcements
Activities: Lect open to public, 2-4 vis lectr per year; gallery talks; originate traveling exhibitions
L **Stoxen Library,** 291 Campus Dr, 58601. Tel 701-227-2135; FAX 701-227-2006; *Librn Dir* Bernnett Reinke; *Acquisition Dir* Jim Martz; *Public Servs Dir* Eileen Kopran; *Cataloging Dir* Lillian Sormson
Open Mon - Thurs 8 AM - 10 PM, Fri 8 AM - 4 PM, Sat 1 - 4 PM, Sun 6 - 10 PM. Open to college students & general pub
Library Holdings: Vols 4265; Per subs 20

FARGO

M **NORTH DAKOTA STATE UNIVERSITY,** Memorial Union Art Gallery, PO Box 5476, 58105. Tel 701-231-8239, 231-7900; *Dir* Barbara Hatfield
Open Sept - May Mon - Fri 10 AM - 5 PM. Sat & Sun 1 - 5 PM. Estab 1975 to educate through exposure to wide variety of artwork. 37 ft x 28 ft track lighting, gray carpet, attendent & security system
Income: $17,000 (financed by student activity fee allocation)
Collections: Permanent collection of contemporary work by American artists
Exhibitions: Contemporary works by American artists
Activities: Lect open to public, 3 vis lectr per year; gallery talks; book traveling exhibitions 5-7 per year to museums & galleries in North Dakota & Minnesota

M PLAINS ART MUSEUM, PO Box 2338, 58108-2338. Tel 701-293-0903; *Pres Board Dir* Fred Donath; *VPres Board Dir* Marjorie Ludwig; *Dir* Terry Jelsing; *Bus Mgr* Paula Stewart-Cyr; *Earned Income Dir* Dionne Merkens; *Dir Develop* Belinda Vogel; *Cur Art* Sally Steffenson; *Dir Educ* Jane Gudmundson
Estab 1965 to foster & promote a knowledge & love of art in the community & to provide a repository for the artistic heritage of this area; to operate & maintain an art gallery & mus, to promote the extension & improvement of educ in the arts; to provide facilities for the exhibition & conservation of the art in this area, past & present. Former International Harvestory Building (1908); 3 galleries for permanent collection & traveling exhibits. Maintains library. Mem: 500; annual meeting in Apr
Income: Financed by mem, NEH, NEA & foundations grants & charitable gaming, special events, state & business grants
Collections: Contemporary American, American Indian & West African; The Rolling Plains Art Gallery (traveling gallery); regional, national, international, fine arts, Woodland & Plain Indians
Exhibitions: Collection Revealed (a special exhibition from the permanent collection); Santos de Palo: Household Saints of Puerto Rico; Woven Vessels
Publications: Plains Art Museum, quarterly; exhibition checklist & catalogs with each exhibition
Activities: Classes for adults & children; docent training; lect open to public; concerts; gallery talks; tours; competitions with prizes; family art workshops; exten dept serves North Dakota, Minnesota, Montana, South Dakota & Manitoba; artmobile; book traveling exhibitions; originate traveling exhibitions circulated to galleries and museums in a 6 state area: ND, SD, MN, WI, IA, MT; museum shop sells books, magazines, original art, posters and prints, reproductions, t-shirts, jewelry, postcards and local craft items

FORT RANSOM

M SVACA - SHEYENNE VALLEY ARTS & CRAFTS ASSOCIATION, Bjarne Ness Gallery at Bear Creek Hall, 58033. Tel 701-973-4461, 973-4491; *Prog Coordr* Georgia Rusfvold
Open Sat, Sun & holidays 1 - 6 PM, June 1 - Sept 30. No admis fee, donations accepted. Estab 1966 to promote & encourage the arts in a rural setting. The Gallery is the former studio of the late Bjarne Ness. Average Annual Attendance: 2400. Mem: 180; dues couple $8; annual meeting in Oct
Income: Financed by mem, grants & Annual Festival
Collections: Paintings of Bjarne Ness; paintings & wood carvings by area artists in SVACA's Bear Creek Hall
Exhibitions: (1997) 29th Annual Arts & Crafts Festival
Activities: Classes for adults & children
L Library, RR 1, Box 21, 58033. Tel 701-973-4461;
Open to members for reference
Library Holdings: Vols 100; Per subs 3
Special Subjects: Arts & crafts

FORT TOTTEN

A FORT TOTTEN STATE HISTORIC SITE, Pioneer Daughters Museum, PO Box 224, 58335-0224. Tel 701-766-4441; *Co-Site Supv* Rhonda Greene; *Co-Site Supv* John Mattson
Open summer site 8 AM - 5 PM, museum May 16 - Sept 15 8 AM - 5 PM. Admis adult $5, children 6-15 $2, children 5 & under free. Estab 1931 to preserve & display local & state history. Average Annual Attendance: 14,000. Mem: 150; dues $40
Income: Financed by state appropriation, donations
Collections: Buildings of historic site, outdoor museum; Pioneer Artifacts;
Activities: Classes for adults & children; guided group tours; lect open to public; tours; competitions; originate traveling exhibitions; museum shop sells books & magazines; junior museum

GRAND FORKS

M NORTH DAKOTA MUSEUM OF ART, PO Box 7305, 58202-7305. Tel 701-777-4195; FAX 701-777-4425; *Dir & Head Cur* Laurel J Reuter; *Asst to Dir* Elliot Glassheim; *Events Coordr* Marsy Schroeder; *Office Mgr* Andrea Dobberman
Open Mon - Fri 9 AM - 5 PM, Thurs until 9 PM, Sat & Sun 1 - 5 PM. No admis fee. Estab 1971 as a contemporary art museum. In 1986 the museum moved into a renovated 1907 campus building. Average Annual Attendance: 50,000. Mem: 500; dues individual $25; annual meeting in June
Income: Financed by university, state & private endowments, gifts, mem & earned income
Collections: American, International & Native American art
Publications: Exhibition catalog
Activities: Dramatic programs; docent training; workshops; lect open to the public, 25 vis lectr per year; gallery talks; tours; book traveling exhibitions; originate traveling exhibitions for circulation to US museums & abroad; museum shop sells books, magazines, folk & ethnic art

M UNIVERSITY OF NORTH DAKOTA, Hughes Fine Arts Center, Dept of Visual Arts, Rm 127, 58202-7099. Tel 701-777-2257
Open 8:30 AM - 4:30 PM. Estab 1979 to augment teaching & offer another location to display art. 96 running ft of wall space. Average Annual Attendance: 1200
Collections: Collection chosen from Annual Print & Drawing Juried Exhibit
Activities: Lect open to public, 4-6 vis lectr per year; gallery talks; lending collection contains over 200 items; book traveling exhibitions 1 per year

MAYVILLE

M MAYVILLE STATE UNIVERSITY GALLERY, * 58257. Tel 701-786-2301, Ext 811; FAX 701-786-4748; *Dir* Dr Anthony Thine
Open Mon - Fri 9 AM - 5 PM
Exhibitions: Contemporary American & North Dakota artists; student exhibitions

MINOT

M MINOT ART ASSOCIATION, Minot Art Gallery, 2 Main St N, PO Box 325, 58702. Tel 701-838-4445; *Dir* Jeanne Rodgers
Open Jan - Dec, Wed - Sun 1 - 5 PM. Estab 1970 to promote means & opportunities for the educ of the pub with respect to the study & culture of the fine arts. Average Annual Attendance: 2500. Mem: 300; dues $15 - $1000, board meeting 2nd Wed of month
Income: Financed by endowment, mem, contributions & sales
Purchases: $500
Collections: Original art works; paintings; pottery; printmaking; sculpture; all done by local & national artists
Exhibitions: Art competitions; artfests; one-person exhibits; traveling art exhibits; exhibitions change monthly
Publications: Calendar of Exhibits; monthly newsletter
Activities: Classes for adults & children; gallery talks; tour; competitions; book traveling exhibitions 2-3 per year; traveling exhibitions organized & circulated

M MINOT STATE UNIVERSITY, Northwest Art Center, 500 University Ave W, 58707. Tel 701-857-3264; FAX 701-839-9633; Elec Mail olsonl.warp6.c5.misu.nodak.edu. *Dir* Linda Olson; *Chmn of Art Dept* Open
Open Mon - Fri 7 AM - 7 PM. No admis fee. Estab 1975 as a supplementary teaching aid, resource for Minot State University, Northwest & Central North Dakota. Two galleries 600 sq ft each, with movable pylons. Average Annual Attendance: 1000. Mem: 100
Income: $20,000 (financed by grants, mem & student fees)
Purchases: $2500
Collections: †Over 300 contemporary 2-D works on paper in all media on paper (printmaking, drawing, painting)
Exhibitions: America's 2000: Works on Paper Exhibition
Publications: Calendar of exhibits, annual; posters
Activities: Lect open to public, 3-5 vis lectr per year; concerts; gallery talks; tours; competitions; individual paintings & original objects of art lent; lending collection contains individual paintings, prints & drawings; book traveling exhibitions 18-20 per year

VALLEY CITY

M 2ND CROSSING ARTS CENTER, 200 Central Ave N, 58072. Tel 701-845-7206; *Office Mgr* Kleda Kuehne
Mem: 150; dues $15 and up
Income: $25,000 (financed by endowment, mem & grants)
Activities: Classes for adults & children; scholarships offered; original objects of art lent to campus offices

OHIO

AKRON

M AKRON ART MUSEUM, 70 E Market St, 44308-2084. Tel 330-376-9185; FAX 330-376-1180;
Internet Home Page Address http://www.winc/-aam. *Dir* Dr Mitchell Kahan; *Chief Cur* Dr Barbara Tannenbaum; *Dir Educ* Marcianne Herr; *Registrar* Arnold Tunstall; *Adminr* Carol Murphy; *Dir Development* Arlene Rossen
Open Tues - Fri 11 AM - 5 PM, Sat 10 AM - 5 PM, Sun Noon - 5 PM, cl Mon. No admis fee. Estab 1922 as a mus to exhibit & collect art. In 1981 opened new Akron Art Mus in restored & reconstructed 1899 National Register Historic Building; total of 10 galleries; two house the permanent collection & eight have changing exhibitions. Average Annual Attendance: 55,000. Mem: 2000; dues general $45; annual meeting in Sept
Income: $1,300,000 (financed by mem, endowment, corporate, foundation & government grants)
Collections: 20th Century American & European painting, photography & sculpture; Harry Callahan; Chuck Close; Richard Deacon; Walker Evans; Robert Frank; Philip Guston; Donald Judd; Philip Pearlstein; Elijah Pierce; Cindy Sherman; Nancy Spero; Thomas Struth; Mark Di Suvero; Andy Warhol; Carrie Mae Weems
Exhibitions: (1997) Fame & Misfortune: Andy Warhol's Portraits; Creative Communities: Art From Akron's Neighborhoods; A History of Women Photographers. (1997-98) Seventy-Fifth Anniversary Celebration of the Collection
Publications: Calendar, bi-monthly; exhibition catalogs; annual report
Activities: Educ dept; docent training; lect open to public, 6-8 vis lectr per year; concerts; gallery talks; tours; book traveling exhibitions 4 per year; originates traveling exhibitions; sales desk sells books & catalogues
L Martha Stecher Reed Art Library, 70 E Market St, 44308. Tel 330-376-9185; FAX 330-376-1180; *Educ Dir* Marcianne Herr; *Librn* Judy Perkins
Open for reference, not open to pub
Income: $3500
Library Holdings: Vols 10,000; Per subs 75; AV — A-tapes, cassettes, Kodachromes, slides, v-tapes 50; Other — Clipping files, exhibition catalogs, pamphlets
Special Subjects: Photography, Contemporary Art
Collections: Edwin Shaw Volumes, to accompany collection of American Impressionist Art

L AKRON-SUMMIT COUNTY PUBLIC LIBRARY, Fine Arts Division, 55 S
Main St, 44326. Tel 330-643-9035; FAX 330-643-9033; *Librn & Dir* Steven
Hawk; *Head of Fine Arts Div* Karla Steward
Open Mon - Thurs 9 AM - 9 PM, Fri 9 AM - 6 PM, Sat 9 AM - 5 PM, Sun 1 -
5 PM. Estab 1904 to serve the educational & recreational needs of the general
public of Summit & contiguous counties
Income: $75,000 (financed by fine arts div)
Library Holdings: Vols 50,000; Per subs 170; Micro — Fiche, reels; AV — A-
tapes, cassettes, motion pictures, rec, v-tapes; Other — Clipping files, exhibition
catalogs, original art works, pamphlets, sculpture
Special Subjects: Architecture, Art History, Ceramics, Costume Design &
Construction, Decorative Arts, Crafts, Drawings, Embroidery, Folk Art, Graphic
Arts, Glass, Illustration, Jewelry, Photography
Activities: Book traveling exhibitions 1-3 per year

M STAN HYWET HALL & GARDENS, INC, 714 N Portage Path, 44303. Tel
330-836-5533; FAX 330-836-2680; *Exec Dir* Harry Lynch; *Supt of Grounds* Carl
Ruprecht; *Dir Public Relations* Kelly A Kleinschmidt; *Dir Marketing* Linda Bass
Open Tues - Sat 10 AM - 4 PM, Sun 1 - 4 PM, cl Mon & major national
holidays. Admis adults $6, children 6 - 12 $3, children under 6 free. Incorporated
1957, Stan Hywet Hall is a house mus, serving as a civic & cultural center. All
restoration & preservation work is carefully researched to retain the original
concept of the property, which represents a way of life that is gone forever. The
mansion, the focal point of the estate, is a 65-room Tudor Revival manor house,
furnished with priceless antiques & works of art dating from the 14th century.
The property is the former home of Frank A Seiberling, (Akron rubber
industrialist & co-founder of Goodyear Tire & Rubber) & was completed in 1915.
There are 70 acres of formal gardens, meadow, woods & lagoons. Average
Annual Attendance: 175,000. Mem: 3100; dues $25 & up; annual meeting in
May
Income: $1,000,000 (financed by endowment, mem, admis, gifts, grants, rentals
& special events)
Collections: Antique furniture; china; crystal; paintings; porcelain; rugs; sculpture;
silver; tapestries
Exhibitions: Holiday Festival
Publications: Stan Hywet Hall and Gardens Annual Report, yearly; Stan Hywet
Hall Newsletter, monthly
Activities: Childrens programs; dramatic programs; docent training; lect open to
public; year round special events; concerts; exten dept serves libraries; original
objects of art lent to historical societies & museums; lending collection includes
5000 books & 250 slides; sales shop sells books, original art, slides & wide variety
of gift items

M SUMMIT COUNTY HISTORICAL SOCIETY, 550 Copley Rd, 44320-2398.
Tel 330-535-1120; *Dir* Stephen H Paschen; *Pres* Bill Bennett; *VPres* Jerry Young;
VPres Lynn Metzger
Open Tues - Sun 1 - 5 PM. Admis adults $3, children under 16 & senior citizens
$2. Estab 1926 for the collection, preservation & display of items of an historical
nature from Summit County. Average Annual Attendance: 3500. Mem: 900;
dues $20-$500; annual meeting in late Jan
Income: $150,000 (financed by endowment, mem, county appropriation)
Collections: 19th & 20th century costumes & accessories; 1810-1900 era
furniture; 19th century chinaware, glassware, silverware & pottery; 19th century
portraits; 19th & 20th century tools, household items & toys
Exhibitions: Coming Home-1865: Perkin's Stone Mansion
Publications: Old Portage Trail Review, monthly
Activities: Educ dept; docent training; awards; sales shop sells books, magazines,
crafts, souvenirs, toys, notepaper

UNIVERSITY OF AKRON
M University Galleries, 44325-7801. Tel 330-972-5950; FAX 330-972-5960; *Dir*
Andrew Borowic; *Asst Dir* Susan McKiernan; *Gallery Dir* Rod Bengston
Open Mon, Tues & Fri 10 AM - 5 PM, Wed & Thurs 10 AM - 9 PM. Estab
1974 to exhibit the work of important contemporary artists working in all regions
of the United States, as well as to provide a showcase for the work of artists
working within the university community. Two galleries: Emily H Davis Art
Gallery, 2000 sq ft of floor space; 200 running ft of wall space; Guzzetta Hall
Atrium Gallery, 120 running ft of wall space. Average Annual Attendance: 12,
000-15,000
Income: Financed by university funds & grants
Collections: Contemporary Photography; Southeast Asian Ceramics & Artifacts
Exhibitions: Geo Raicu, Your Generic Caution; Bill Yuksanovich, Beyond the
Mirrors Reflection. Andrew Borowiec Photographs
Publications: Catalogs & artists books in conjunction with exhibitions
Activities: Lect open to public; gallery talks; competitions; awards for Student
Show; scholarships & fels offered; book traveling exhibitions; originate traveling
exhibitions, circulation to other university galleries & small museums with
contemporary program

ASHLAND

M ASHLAND COLLEGE ARTS & HUMANITIES GALLERY, 401 College Ave,
44805. Tel 419-289-4142; *Chmn* Albert Goad
Open Tues - Sun 1 - 4 PM, Tues evenings 7 - 10 PM. No admis fee. Estab 1969.
Gallery maintained for continuous exhibitions
Collections: Mostly contemporary works, some historical, occidental & Oriental
Exhibitions: A Newbill: paintings & drawings; Audra Skoudas: paintings &
drawings; Annual Student Exhibition
Activities: Classes for children; dramatic programs; lect open to public; 2-3
gallery talks; tours & regular tours to leading art museums; concerts; scholarships;
original objects of art lent to Akron Art Institute and Cleveland Museum of Art

ASHTABULA

A ASHTABULA ARTS CENTER, 2928 W 13th St, 44004. Tel 216-964-3396;
FAX 216-964-3396; *Exec Dir* Beth Koski; *Admin Asst & Visual Arts & Exhibit
Coordr* Meeghan Humphery; *Business Mgr* Cindy Rimpela; *Theatre Coordr &
Public Relations Coordr* Darrell Lowe; *Technical Coordr* Charles Fike; *Pres*
Kathy Bobulsky; *Dance Coordr* Selagh Dubsky
Open Mon - Thurs 9 AM - 9 PM, Fri 9 AM - 7 PM, Sat 9 AM - 5 PM. No
admis fee. Estab 1953 as a non-profit, tax exempt art organization, to provide
high quality instruction. One major gallery area with smaller anex-fixed panels on
all walls. Average Annual Attendance: 5000. Mem: 1000; dues family $40,
individual $25; annual meeting in Oct
Income: Financed by mem, NEA, OAC, WSL, JTPA
Collections: Local & regional contemporary work, small international
contemporary print collection, regional wood sculpture (major portion of
collection represents local & regional talent)
Publications: Ashtabula Arts Center News, bimonthly; monthly exhibit
information
Activities: Classes for adults & children; dramatic program; lect open to public,
5-10 vis lectr per year; concerts; gallery talks; tours; competitions; cash awards;
scholarships & fels offered; exten dept serves Ashtabula County hospitals &
public buildings; individual paintings & original objects of art lent to schools &
public buildings; lending collection contains books, cassettes, color reproductions,
framed reproductions, original art works, original prints, paintings, phonorecords,
photographs, sculpture & slides; book traveling exhibitions; originate traveling
exhibitions

ATHENS

M OHIO UNIVERSITY, Kennedy Museum of American Art, Lin Hall, 45701-
2979. Tel 614-593-1304; FAX 614-593-1305; *Asst Dir Admin & Information*
Clair E Carpenter; *Registrar* Jennifer Kelly; *Asst Dir Exhib & Prog* Sally
Delgado; *Cur Native American Coll* John H Gerber
No admis fee
Collections: †Contemporary prints, some paintings, photographs & sculpture;
Southwest Native American Collection
Exhibitions: (1997) Ynez Johnston: A Retrospective; Paul Caponigro:
Meditations in Light
M Seigfred Gallery, School of Art, Seigfred Hall 528, 45701. Tel 614-593-4290;
FAX 614-593-0457; *Dir* Joe Bova
Open Tues - Fri 10 AM - 4 PM. No admis fee. Gallery is used for faculty
exhibitions, student exhibitions & vis artist shows
Collections: Student Works; Permanent collection
L Fine Arts Library, Alden Library, Park Place, 45701-2878. Tel 614-593-2663;
Art Librn Anne Braxton
Open Mon - Thurs 8 AM - midnight, Fri 8 AM - 10 PM, Sat 10 AM - 10 PM,
Sun Noon - midnight
Income: Financed by state appropriation
Library Holdings: Vols 65,000; Per subs 300; Micro — Fiche; Other — Clipping
files, exhibition catalogs, manuscripts, memorabilia, photographs, prints,
reproductions
Special Subjects: Photography, History of Photography
Collections: Research collection in history of photography; small collection of
original photographs for study purposes

BAY VILLAGE

A BAYCRAFTERS, INC, Huntington Metropark, 28795 Lake Rd, 44140. Tel 216-
871-6543; FAX 216-871-0452; *Dir* Sally Irwin Price
Open Mon - Fri 9 AM - 5 PM, weekends during shows. Estab 1948 for
advancement & enjoyment of arts & crafts in the area. Average Annual
Attendance: 30,000. Mem: 1800, dues $15 & $20
Exhibitions: Christmas Show; Emerald Necklace Juried Art Show; Juried Art
Show; Octoberfair; Renaissance Fayre; student competition; individual gallery
shows; floral juried art show; corporate juried art show
Publications: Bulletins & competition notices
Activities: Classes for adults & children; lect open to public, 9-12 vis lectr per
year; gallery talks; tours; sponsors two juried art shows for adults & one for
children; monetary prizes awarded; scholarships offered; originate traveling
exhibitions to local libraries; sales shop sells original art, reproductions, prints,
pottery & other crafts work from local & out-of-town artists

BEACHWOOD

M THE TEMPLE-TIFERETH ISRAEL, The Temple Museum of Religious Art,
26000 Shaker Blvd, 44122. Tel 216-831-3233; *Sr Rabbi* Benjamin Alon Kamin;
Museum Dir Claudia Z Fechter
Open daily 9 AM - 3 PM by appointment only. No admis fee. Estab 1950 for
the display & teaching of Judaica. Two galleries, each housed in a national
landmark temple. Average Annual Attendance: 10,000. Mem: 15,000; annual
meeting
Collections: Art & artifacts of Jewish synagogue & home; collection of antiquities
Activities: Classes for adults & children; lect open to public, 12 vis lectr per year;
gallery talks; tours; original objects of art lent to other professional institutions;
museum shop sells Judaic ritual objects
L Library, 26000 Shaker Blvd, 44122. Tel 216-831-3233; FAX 216-831-4216; *Dir*
Claudia Z Fechter
Two buildings
Library Holdings: Vols 40,000; Per subs 50; AV — A-tapes, cassettes, fs, rec, v-
tapes; Other — Clipping files, exhibition catalogs, framed reproductions,
manuscripts, memorabilia, original art works, pamphlets, photographs, prints,
reproductions, sculpture
Special Subjects: Archaeology, Architecture, Art History, Bookplates &
Bindings, Calligraphy, Drawings, Embroidery, Ethnology, Folk Art, Handicrafts,
Historical Material, Judaica, Painting - European, Painting - Israeli, Religious

Art, Antiquities, Children's Judaica
Collections: Permanent collection of silver, manuscripts & fabrics of Judaica over the last 200 years; pottery from antiquity
Exhibitions: In the Beginning - Jewish Birth Customs; The Loom & the Cloth: an exhibition of the fabrics of Jewish life; Abba Hillel Silver: a remembrance
Publications: The Loom and the Cloth: an exhibition of the fabrics of Jewish life

BEREA

M **BALDWIN-WALLACE COLLEGE,** Fawick Art Gallery, 275 Eastland Rd, 44017. Tel 216-826-2152; FAX 216-826-3640; *Dir* Dean Drahos
Open Mon - Fri 2 - 5 PM, cl weekends & holidays. No admis fee. The Art Gallery is considered to be a part of the art program of the department of art; its purpose is that of a teaching museum for the students of the college & the general public. Average Annual Attendance: 2500
Income: Financed through budgetary support of the college
Collections: Approx †200 paintings and sculptures by Midwest artists of the 20th century; approx †1900 drawings and prints from 16th - 20th century, with a concentration in 19th & 20th century examples
Exhibitions: A Home for Joe: Student & Restaurant Coffee Cups; Berea School Show
Publications: Exhibition catalogs are published for important exhibitions, 1 - 2 per year
Activities: Lect open to public; gallery talks; tours; competitions; individual paintings lent to schools; book traveling exhibitions

BOWLING GREEN

M **BOWLING GREEN STATE UNIVERSITY,** Fine Arts Center Galleries, Fine Arts Bldg, 43403-0211. Tel 419-372-8525; FAX 419-372-2544; Elec Mail jnathan@bgnet.bgsu.edu. *Exhib Prog Adminr* Jacqueline S Nathan
Open Tues - Sat 10 AM - 4 PM, Sun 2 - 5 PM, cl holidays. Estab 1964 to provide enrichment to School of Art program by furnishing research materials, exhibitions & related events; to provide for the growth of pub sensitivity to the visual arts. Three galleries located in the Fine Arts building have a combined total of approximately 9000 sq ft of exhibition space. Average Annual Attendance: 9500
Income: Financed by the University, state grants & donations
Collections: Contemporary prints
Activities: Lect open to public, 6-8 vis lectr per year; book traveling exhibitions; originate traveling exhibitions

BROOKLYN

M **BROOKLYN HISTORICAL SOCIETY,** 4442 Ridge Rd, 44144-3353. Tel 216-749-2804; *Pres* Barbara Stepic; *VPres* Edward Koschmann; *Treas* Helen Nedelka
Open Tues 10 AM - 2 PM, Sun 2 - 5 PM, cl holiday weekends & Sun in Jan, Feb & Mar, tours by appointment. No admis fee. Estab 1970 to preserve history of area. Wheelchair accessible to 1st floor. Maintains reference library. Average Annual Attendance: 1500. Mem: 150; dues life $100, couple $6, single $4; meetings last Wed of month, except July, Aug & Nov
Income: $10,000 (financed by fundraisers)
Collections: †China; †dolls; pre-1900 & 1920's furniture; †glass; †kitchenware; †old tools; †quilts & linens
Exhibitions: World War I & Brooklyn Airport
Activities: Classes for children; docent training; quilting & rug loom weaving demonstrations; lect open to public, 5 vis lectr per year; tours; sales shop sells handicrafts, rag rugs, quilted items, dried herb products

CANTON

M **CANTON MUSEUM OF ART,** 1001 Market Ave N, 44702. Tel 330-453-7666; FAX 330-452-4477; Elec Mail cartmuse@neo.lrwn.com. *Pres* Lee De Graff; *Treas* John Van-Able; *Exec Dir* Manuel J Albacete; *Business Mgr* Mrs Kenneth D Adams
Open Tues - Thurs 10 AM - 5 PM, 7 - 9 PM, Fri & Sat 10 AM - 5 PM, Sun 2 - 5 PM. No admis fee. Estab 1935, incorporated 1941. Nine modern gallery areas of varios sizes. Average Annual Attendance: 50,000. Mem: 1200; dues $15 and higher; annual meeting Fall
Collections: American, Italian & Spanish paintings; art objects; costumes; decorative arts; 18th & 19th century English & American portraiture; graphics; sculpture; 20th century regional art; Italian sculpture
Exhibitions: Approximately 25-40 traveling or collected exhibitions of commercial & industrial arts; painting; sculpture annually; French Music Hall Posters from 1890 to 1940's. (1997) Norman Rockwell's America. (1998) Nazi Olympics: Berlin 1936; Watercolorist: Joseph Raffael & Caroline Brady
Activities: Formally organized education programs for adults & children; docent training; lect open to public, 10 vis lectr per year; films; gallery talks; art festivals; competitions with awards; guided tours; scholarships offered; individual and original objects of art lent; book traveling exhibitions; originate traveling exhibitions; museum shop sells books, original art, prints
L **Art Library,** 1001 Market Ave N, 44702. Tel 330-453-7666; FAX 330-452-4477; Elec Mail cartmuse@neo.lrwn.com. *Exec Dir* Manuel J Albacete
Library Holdings: Vols 2500; Per subs 25; AV — A-tapes, slides, v-tapes 120; Other — Clipping files, exhibition catalogs, pamphlets, prints

CINCINNATI

A **CINCINNATI ART CLUB,** * 1021 Parkside Pl, 45202. Tel 513-241-4591; *Pres* Thomas Eckley
Open daily except Wed Sept - May, call for hours. No admis fee. Estab 1890, incorporated 1923 for purpose of advancing love & knowledge of fine art. Gallery contains a small collection of paintings by American artists; modern

building 100 ft x 50 ft. Average Annual Attendance: 3500. Mem: 300; open to all who show interest & appreciation of art; active members must be judged by proficiency of works; dues active $85, associate $75
Income: Financed by dues, rental of gallery, sales commissions, bequests
Collections: Small collection of works by former members
Exhibitions: Exhibition of members' work changed monthly. Annual Club Shows Sept, Jan, Spring (March-April) & Christmas Art Bazaar; juried annual show
Publications: Dragonfly Members Newsletter, monthly
Activities: Lect open for members only, 6-8 vis lectr demonstrations per year; competitions with awards; scholarships offered to Cincinnati Art Academy

A **CINCINNATI ARTISTS' GROUP EFFORT,** 1416 Main St, 45210. Tel 513-381-2437; *Pres* Jamey Ponte
Open Fri Noon - 8 PM, Sat Noon - 6 PM, Sun Noon - 4 PM. No admis fee. Estab 1978 as an artist-run alternative space exhibiting visual, media, & performance art. Store-front gallery on two floors in the gallery district of Cincinnati; permanent video screening facility. Average Annual Attendance: 15,000 gallery, 500,000 pub art viewers. Mem: 250; dues $20-$500; annual meeting in June
Income: $70,000 (financed by foundations, Ohio Arts Council, City of Cincinnati Arts Allocation, mem, & National Endowment for the Arts)
Publications: Artists' Pulp; catalogs, 2 Mid-Career
Activities: Lect open to public, 3-5 vis lectr per year; concerts; gallery talks; sales shop sells books, magazine & original art

M **CINCINNATI INSTITUTE OF FINE ARTS,** Taft Museum, 316 Pike St, 45202-4293. Tel 513-241-0343; FAX 513-241-7762; *Museum Dir* Phillip C Long; *Asst Dir Curatorial Affairs* David T Johnson; *Cur Educ* Abby S Schwartz; *Chmn Cincinnati Inst Fine Arts & Mus Comt* Raymond R Clark; *Admin Asst* Carolyn Rison; *Bus Mgr* Teri Haught; *Pub Affairs Mgr* Cate O'Hara; *Registrar* Susan M Hudson; *Chief Protection Serv* John Ring; *Asst Dir Admin & Develop* Carolyn McCoy
Open Mon - Sat 10 AM - 5 PM, Sun 1 - 5 PM, cl New Year's Day, Thanksgiving & Christmas. Admis adults $4, seniors & children $3. Estab 1927, a gift of Mr and Mrs Charles P Taft's art collection to the Cincinnati Institute of Fine Arts including the house and an endowment fund for maintenance. Active control was taken in 1931; museum opened in 1932. The historic house, built in 1820, is one of the finest examples of Federal architecture in this country & was designated a National Landmark. Its interior is decorated in the style of the period. An architectural formal (green) garden was opened in 1949. Maintains reference library. Average Annual Attendance: 60,000. Mem: 1300; dues $35-$5000
Income: $1,650,000 (financed by endowment & annual fine arts fund drive)
Collections: Furnishings include antique toiles and satins and a notable collection of Duncan Phyfe furniture; paintings including works by Rembrandt, Hals, Turner, Corot, Gainsborough, Raeburn; Whistler & other Old Masters; 200 notable Chinese Porcelains Kangxi, Yongzheng & Qianlong; 97 French Renaissance enamels; Renaissance jewelry & 16th-18th century watches from Europe
Exhibitions: Eight to ten exhibitions scheduled per year
Activities: Classes for adults & children, docent training; lect open to public, 10-15 vis lectr per year; chamber music; concerts; gallery talks; tours; scholarships offered; individual paintings & objects of art lent to accredited museums; lending collection contains paintings, sculptures, chinese ceramics, European decorative arts; book traveling exhibitions 2-3 per year; originate traveling exhibitions to accredited museums; museum shop sells books, reproductions, prints, slides, gifts, jewelry, porcelains & art kits

A **CINCINNATI INSTITUTE OF FINE ARTS,** 2649 Erie Ave, 45208. Tel 513-871-2787; FAX 513-871-2706; *Chmn Board & Pres* Raymond R Clark; *VChmn* Dudley S Taft; *Exec Dir* Mary McCullough-Hudson
Estab & incorporated in 1927 to provide for the continuance & growth of education & culture in the various fields of fine arts in the metropolitan community of Cincinnati. Mem: Annual meeting Oct
Income: Financed through endowments by Cincinnati Symphony Orchestra, Cincinnati Art Museum, Cincinnati Opera, Taft Museum, May Festival, Cincinnati Ballet, Contemporary Arts Center, Playhouse in the Park, Special Projects Pool & Annual Community Wide fine Arts Fund Drive
Publications: Quarterly calendar

M **CINCINNATI MUSEUM ASSOCIATION,** Cincinnati Art Museum, Eden Park, 45202-1596. Tel 513-721-5204; FAX 513-721-0129; *Dir* Barbara K Gibbs; *Dir Develop* Patricia Murdock; *Chief Cur & Cur Decorative Arts* Anita Ellis; *Cur Ed* Suzanne LeBlanc; *Cur Prints & Drawings* Kristin L Spangenberg; *Cur Classical, Near Eastern Art* Glenn E Markoe; *Cur Painting & Sculpture* John Wilson; *Cur Contemporary Art* Jean E Feinberg; *Assoc Cur Far Eastern Art* Ellen Avril; *Assoc Cur Photography & Design* Dennis Kiel; *Dir Marketing* Diane Smith; *Ed* Ann Cotter; *Head Exhibits & Registration* Mary Ellen Goeke; *Asst Cur Africa & Americas* Bill Mercer
Open Tues - Sat 10 AM - 5 PM, Sun Noon - 6 PM, cl Mon & Thanksgiving & Christmas. Admis adults $5, senior citizens & college students $4, children free, free to members, special rates for tour groups. Estab 1881 to collect, exhibit, conserve & interpret works of art from all periods & civilizations (range of 5000 years of major cultures of the world) paintings (European & American); world costumes, textiles; arts of Africa & the Americas; world prints, drawings & photographs; world sculpture, world decorative arts & period rooms. Exhibition galleries cover an area of approx 4 acres, occupying three floors, assembly areas & social center on ground level; altogether some 80 galleries given over to permanent collections, with additional galleries set aside for temporary exhibitions. Average Annual Attendance: 200,000. Mem: 12,500; dues $35 & up
Income: $6,500,000 (financed by endowment, mem, city appropriation, private donations, admis & Cincinnati Fine Arts Fund, mus shop earnings, federal, state, city & private grants)
Collections: Artists; art in Cincinnati: Egyption, Greek, Roman, Near and Far Eastern arts; musical instruments; paintings (European & American); world costumes, textiles; arts of Africa & the Americas; world prints, drawings & photographs; world sculpture; world decorative arts & period rooms

Publications: Catalogues for exhibitions & collections
Activities: Classes for adults & children; docent training; lect open to public, 12-18 vis lectr per year; gallery talks; tours; artmobile; book traveling exhibitions 4-6 per year; originate traveling exhibitions 2 per year; museum shop sells books & slides

L **Mary R Schiff Library,** Eden Park, 45202-1596. Tel 513-721-5204, Ext 223; FAX 513-721-0129; Elec Mail caml@ohionet.org. *Head Librn* Mona L Chapin
Open Tues - Fri 10 AM - 5 PM. Admis $5. Estab to satisfy research needs of museums staff, academy faculty & students. For reference
Income: Financed by endowment
Library Holdings: Vols 60,000; Per subs 150; Micro — Fiche; AV — V-tapes; Other — Clipping files, exhibition catalogs, manuscripts, memorabilia, pamphlets, photographs, prints, reproductions
Special Subjects: Afro-American Art, American Indian Art, American Western Art, Antiquities-Assyrian, Architecture, Art History, Commercial Art, Costume Design & Construction, Decorative Arts, Drawings, Folk Art, Furniture, History of Art & Archaeology, Mexican Art, Oriental Art
Collections: †Files on Cincinnati Artists, †Art in Cincinnati, †the Cincinnati Art Museum & the Art Academy of Cincinnati; encyclopedic collection covering 5000 years of art & art history

M **COLLEGE OF MOUNT SAINT JOSEPH,** Studio San Giuseppe, Art Dept, 5701 Delhi Pike, 45233-1670. Tel 513-244-4314; *Dir* Gerald Bellas
Open Mon - Fri 10 AM - 5 PM, Sat & Sun 1:30 - 4:30 PM, cl holidays. No admis fee. Estab 1962 to exhibit a variety of art forms by professional artists, faculty & students. Average Annual Attendance: 5000
Activities: Lect open to public; concerts; gallery talks; tours

L **Archbishop Alter Library,** 5701 Delhi Pike, 45233-1670. Tel 513-244-4216; FAX 513-244-4355; *Dir* Mark Cain
Estab 1920 to serve students of art department. Circ 1200
Library Holdings: Vols 97,863; Per subs 706; AV — A-tapes, fs, slides; Other — Exhibition catalogs, prints

M **CONTEMPORARY ARTS CENTER,** 115 E Fifth St, 45202. Tel 513-345-8400; FAX 513-721-7418; Elec Mail charles.desmarais@uc.edu. *Chmn* Dr Stanley Kaplan; *Pres* David Moffet; *VPres* Jenny Rosenthal Berliant; *Treas* Kenneth Butler; *Dir* Charles Desmarais; *Preparator* Kim Humphries; *Communications* Carolyn Krause
Open Mon - Sat 10 AM - 6 PM, Sun Noon - 5 PM. Admis adults $3.50, students & senior citizens $2, mem free. Estab 1939. The Center is a mus for the presentation of current developments in the visual & related arts. It does not maintain a permanent collection but offers changing exhibitions of international, national & regional focus. Average Annual Attendance: 65,000. Mem: 2000; dues from $20-$5000
Income: $1,100,000 (financed by endowment, fine arts fund drive, city state art council & federal groups, corporate sponsorship)
Exhibitions: Contemporary Center: (1997) Photo-Op: Tim Burton, Dennis Hopper, David Lynch, John Waters; Ode a Ma Mere: Works on a Theme by Louise Bourgeois; Sculptures by Robert Therrien; Center Board Room: Star Art Doodles; Vital Visions 1997
Publications: Catalogues of exhibitions, 1-2 per year
Activities: Classes for adults & children; docent training; performance programs; lect open to public, 8-12 vis lectr per year; concerts; gallery talks; programs for adults & children; tours; lending collection contains slides & videotapes; book traveling exhibitions 2-5 per year; originate traveling exhibitions organized & circulated; museum shop sells books, cards, reproductions & prints

L **Library,** 115 E Fifth St, 45202. Tel 513-721-0390, 345-8400 (admin office); FAX 513-721-7418; *Dir* Charles Desmarais; *Cur* David Brown
For in-house only
Library Holdings: Per subs 10; Other — Exhibition catalogs

M **HEBREW UNION COLLEGE - JEWISH INSTITUTE OF RELIGION,** Skirball Museum-Cincinnati Branch, 3101 Clifton Ave, 45220. Tel 513-221-1875; FAX 513-221-1842; *Dir* Marilyn F Reichert; *Cur* Judith S Lucas
Open Mon - Thurs 11 AM - 4 PM, Sun 2 - 5 PM. No admis fee. Estab 1913 to interpret Judaism to the general public through Jewish art & artifacts; also the archaeologic work of the college in Israel. 2450 sq ft of exhibition space; traveling exhibition gallery. Average Annual Attendance: 5000. Mem: 300; dues $35-$500
Income: Financed by endowment, donations & grants
Collections: Jewish ceremonial art; archaeologic artifacts; paintings, drawings & sculpture by Jewish artists; photography; textiles
Activities: Docent training; lect open to public; 1-2 vis lectr per year; tours; individual & original objects of art lent; museum shop sells books & Judaica subject matter

M **HILLEL FOUNDATION,** Hillel Jewish Student Center Gallery, 2615 Clifton Ave, 45220-2885. Tel 513-221-6728; FAX 513-221-7134; *Exec Dir* Rabbi Abie Ingber
Open Mon - Thurs 9 AM - 5 PM, Fri 9 AM - 3 PM. Estab 1982 to promote Jewish artists & educate students. Jewish artists in various media (exhibit & sale) & collection of antique Judaica from around the world. Listed in AAA guide
Collections: †Antique architectural Judaica from synagogues throughout the US; †Art in various media by living Jewish artists

L **PUBLIC LIBRARY OF CINCINNATI & HAMILTON COUNTY,** Art & Music Dept, 800 Vine St, Library Square, 45202-2071. Tel 513-369-6955; FAX 513-369-6067; Elec Mail artmusichead@plch.lib.oh.us, telnet: plchlib.oh.us; Internet Home Page Address http://plch.lib.oh.us. *Head Art & Music Dept* Anna Horton; *First Asst* Judy Inwood; *Dir & Treas* Robert Stonestreet
Open Mon - Fri 9 AM - 9 PM, Sat 9 AM - 6 PM, Sun 1 - 5 PM. Estab 1872 to provide the community with both scholarly & recreational materials in area of fine arts. Display cases in the department to exhibit collections
Income: $85,000 (financed by taxes, state & county appropriations)
Library Holdings: Vols 173,960; Per subs 660; Vertical file; Micro — Cards, fiche 29,188, prints, reels 1714; AV — A-tapes, cassettes, fs, lantern slides, motion pictures, rec, slides, v-tapes; Other — Clipping files 814,967, exhibition

catalogs 6151, memorabilia, original art works, pamphlets, photographs, prints 6125, reproductions
Special Subjects: Advertising Design, Aesthetics, Afro-American Art, American Indian Art, American Western Art, Antiquities-Assyrian, Archaeology, Art History, Calligraphy, Drawings, Folk Art, History of Art & Archaeology, Landscape Architecture, Mexican Art, Mixed Media, Painting - American, Photography, Pre-Columbian Art, Religious Art, Southwestern Art, American Art, Cincinnati & regional art, Picasso
Collections: Langstroth Collection, chromolithographs of 19th Century; †Plaut Collection, 20th century artist's books; †Valerio Collection, Italian art Film & recording center collection of videos, slides & audio tapes
Activities: Tours; sales shop sells books, reproductions, prints, tote bags, toys & stationery items

UNIVERSITY OF CINCINNATI

M **DAAP Galleries-College of Design Architecture, Art & Planning,** 5275 Aronoff, Mail Location 0016, 45221-0016. Tel 513-556-2839; FAX 513-556-3288; Elec Mail anne.timpano@uc.edu. *Dir* Anne Timpano
Open Mon - Fri 10 AM - 5 PM. No admis fee. Estab 1967 to preserve & maintain the University's art collection & to present quality contemporary & historical exhibitions of works by artists of local, regional & national reputation. Operates three exhibition facilities: Reed Gallery, Tangeman Gallery & Machine Shop Gallery. Gallery is maintained & presents quality contemporary & historical exhibitions of works by artists of local, regional & national reputation. Average Annual Attendance: 10,000
Income: Financed through university, grants & co-sponsorships
Collections: Art of the United States, Europe, Asia & the Americas
Publications: Fragments, catalogue
Activities: Lect open to public; concerts; performances; film & dance; gallery talks; tours; book traveling exhibitions 1-3 per year; originate small traveling exhibitions

L **Design, Architecture, Art & Planning Library,** Aronoff Ctr Design & Art 5480, 45221-0016. Tel 513-556-1320; FAX 513-556-3006; Elec Mail jane.carlin.@us.euc. *DAAP Librn* Jane Carlin
Open Mon - Thurs 8 AM - 10 PM, Fri 8 AM - 5 PM, Sat 9 AM - 5 PM, Sun 1 - 8 PM (Academic Year); summer hours vary. Estab 1925 to support the programs of the College of Design, Architecture, Art & Planning. Circ 42,000. Average Annual Attendance: 78,000
Purchases: $50,000
Library Holdings: Vols 72,000; Per subs 315; Artists' Book Collection; Micro — Fiche, reels 1000; AV — V-tapes; Other — Exhibition catalogs
Special Subjects: Art Education, Art History, Architecture, Graphic Design, Industrial Design, Interior Design, Collection of artists' publications

L **Visual Resource Center,** Aronoff Design & Art, 5480, PO Box 0016, 45221-0134. Tel 513-556-0279; FAX 513-556-3006; Elec Mail adrienne.varady@uc.edu. *Cur* Adrienne Varady
Library contains 210,000 slides
Library Holdings: AV — Slides; Other — Memorabilia

M **XAVIER UNIVERSITY,** Xavier Art Gallery, 3800 Victory Pky, 45207-7311. Tel 513-745-3811; FAX 513-745-4301; *Dir* Bernard L Schmidt; *Publicist* Jerome Pryor
Open Mon - Fri 1 - 4 PM. No admis fee. Estab 1987 as academic facility for students, faculty & community. Spacious galleries with white walls & hardwood floors; main gallery 21 x 50 ft, adjacent gallery 20 x 20 ft
Income: Privately financed
Exhibitions: Professional artists; qualified students of Xavier University; temporary exhibitions only
Activities: Classes for adults; lect open to public, 4-6 vis lectr per year; gallery talks; give awards; scholarships & fels offered

CLEVELAND

C **B P AMERICA,** 200 Public Square 4K, 44114. Tel 216-586-4592; FAX 216-586-4050; *Art Admin Consultant* Jane B Tesso
Estab to enhance quality of life in facilities & communities where the company has employees or operations
Collections: Contemporary American Art

L **CLEVELAND BOTANICAL GARDEN,** Eleanor Squire Library, 11030 East Blvd, 44106. Tel 216-721-1600; FAX 216-721-2056; Elec Mail jcb@en.com. *Dir* Brian Holley; *Asst Dir* Mark Druckenbrod; *Dir Information Serv* Joanna Bristol
Open Tues - Fri 9 AM - 5 PM, Sat Noon - 5 PM, Sun 1 - 5 PM. Estab 1930. Circulation to members only
Income: Financed by endowment
Library Holdings: Vols 16,000; Per subs 120; AV — A-tapes, cassettes, slides; Other — Clipping files, exhibition catalogs, original art works, pamphlets, photographs, prints, sculpture
Special Subjects: Landscape Architecture, Landscapes, Garden Design
Publications: The Bulletin, monthly

M **CLEVELAND CENTER FOR CONTEMPORARY ART,** 8501 Carnegie Ave, 44106. Tel 216-421-8671; FAX 216-421-0737; *Dir* Jill Snyder; *Chief Preparator & Registrar* Dann Witczak; *Dir of Sales* Rosalie Cohen; *Dir Develop* Marcie Goodman; *Dir Educ* Pam Esch
Open Tues - Fri 11 AM - 6 PM, Sat & Sun Noon - 5 PM, cl Mon. Admis adults $3, sr citizens & students $1, members free. Estab 1968 to enrich the cultural life of the community. Five galleries 20,000 sq ft, which change exhibits every 6-8 wks. Located in a renovated building which is part of the Cleveland Playhouse complex. Maintains reference library. Mem: 600; dues center circle $500; sustaining $129; contributing $50; family $35; single $25; student or artist $15
Income: $175,000 (financed by mem, state appropriation, federal & state agencies & local foundations)
Publications: Exhibition catalogues
Activities: Educ dept; docent training; lect open to public; 20 vis lectr per year; gallery talks; tours; individual & original objects of art lent to corporate members; originate traveling exhibitions; museum shop sells original art works, books, prints & reproductions

L **Library,** 8501 Carnegie Ave, 44106. Tel 216-421-8671; FAX 216-421-0737; *Dir* Jill Snyder
Reference Library. Mem: 900; dues $35
Library Holdings: Vols 2000; Per subs 10; AV — Slides; Other — Clipping files, exhibition catalogs, photographs

M **CLEVELAND INSTITUTE OF ART,** Reinberger Galleries, University Circle, 11141 East Blvd, 44106. Tel 216-421-7407; FAX 216-421-7438; *Gallery Dir* Bruce Checefsky; *Pres* Robert A Mayer
Open Mon 9:30 AM - 4 PM, Tues - Fri & Sat 9:30 AM - 9 PM, Sun 1 - 4 PM. No admis fee. Estab 1882 as a five-year, fully accredited professional college of art. Gallery is maintained with extensive exhibitions
Income: Financed by federal, state, local grants & private foundations
Exhibitions: (1997) Olga de Amaral: Monoliths & Other Landscapes; Still Time: Photographs by Sally Mann, 1971-91
Publications: Link (alumni magazine), quarterly; posters to accompany each exhibit; bi-annual school catalog
Activities: Classes for adults & children; lect open to public, 5-10 vis lectr per year; gallery talks; tours; book traveling exhibitions; originate traveling exhibitions

L **Jessica Gund Memorial Library,** 11141 East Blvd, 44106. Tel 216-421-7440; FAX 216-421-7439; *Library Dir* Cristine Rom; *Circulation Supvr* Lori Nofziger; *Technical Servs Librn* Hyosoo Lee; *Visual Resources-Reference Librn* Emily Tidball
Open Mon - Thurs 8 AM - 9:30 PM, Fri 8 AM - 5 PM, Sat 10 AM - 5 PM, Sun hrs vary. Estab 1882 to select, house & distribute library material in all media that will support the Institute's studio & academic areas of instruction
Income: Financed by tuition, gift, endowments
Library Holdings: Vols 42,000; Per subs 225; Artists' books 600; Micro — Fiche, prints; AV — A-tapes, cassettes, slides, v-tapes; Other — Clipping files, exhibition catalogs
Special Subjects: Advertising Design, Afro-American Art, Ceramics, Commercial Art, Crafts, Drawings, Enamels, Glass, Graphic Design, Interior Design, Metalwork, Photography, Pre-Columbian Art, Sculpture, Textiles, Art, Artists' Books, Artists' Books; Industrial Design
Activities: Library tours

A **Cleveland Art Association,** University Circle, 11141 East Blvd, 44106. Tel 216-421-7000; FAX 216-421-7438; *Pres* Caroline Oberndorf
Estab & inc 1916, re-incorporated 1950 as a non-profit organization, to unite artists & art lovers of Cleveland into a working body whose purpose it shall be to advance, in the broadest possible way, the art interest of the city. Mem: 140; dues $60, active mem
Income: $30,000 (financed through endowment, sales & dues)
Purchases: $12,000
Collections: Collection of art by Cleveland artists which includes ceramics, drawings, glass, paintings, prints & small sculpture
Exhibitions: Lending collection exhibited annually
Activities: Competitions; awards; scholarships offered; works of art lent to members for one-year period

M **CLEVELAND MUSEUM OF ART,** 11150 East Blvd, 44106. Tel 216-421-7340; FAX 216-421-0411;
Internet Home Page Address www.clemusart.com. *Pres* Michael J Horwitz; *Dir* Dr Robert P Bergman; *Dir Finance* Anthony M Gentile; *Cur Contemporary Art* Tom E Hinson; *Chief Cur Later Western Art* Henry Hawley; *Cur Textiles* Anne E Wardwell; *Chief Cur Asian Art* Michael R Cunningham; *Cur Indian & SE Asian Art* Stanislaw Czuma; *Chief Designer* Jeffrey Strean; *Cur Ancient Art* Arielle P Kozloff; *Cur Education* James A Birch; *Chief Cur Musical Arts* Karel Paukert; *Head Publications* Laurence Channing; *Mgr Marketing & Commission* William Prenezost; *Registrar* Mary Suzor; *Dir Development* Kate M Sellers
Open Tues, Thurs, Fri 10 AM - 6 PM, Wed 10 AM - 10 PM, Sat 9 AM - 5 PM, Sun 1 - 6 PM, cl Mon & four holidays. No admis fee. Estab & incorporated 1913; building opened 1916. Gallery addition in 1958; Educ Wing in 1971; New Library & Gallery addition in 1984. Average Annual Attendance: 500,000. Mem: 10,000; dues $25 & up; annual meeting in Dec
Income: $8,527,687 (financed by trust & endowment income, mem, gifts & grants)
Purchases: $6,757,978
Collections: Ancient Near Eastern, Egyptian, Greek, & Roman art; drawings & prints; European & American paintings, sculpture & decorative arts of all periods, with notable collections of medieval art, 18th-century French decorative arts & 17th-century European painting & 19th-century European & American painting; Islamic art; North American Indian, African & Oceanic art; Oriental art, including important collections of Chinese & Japanese painting & ceramics & Indian sculpture; photographs Pre-Columbian American art; textiles, especially from Egypt & medieval Persia
Exhibitions: (1997) Faberge in American 97; Thomas Eakins: The Rowing Pictures. (1997-98) When Silk Was Gold: Central Asian Chinese Textiles from the Cleveland & Metropolitan Museums of Art. (1998) Papal Treasures: Early Christian Renaissance, Baroque Art-From the Vatican Collection
Publications: Bulletin, 10 times per yr; News & Calendar, monthly; collection catalogs; exhibition catalogs
Activities: Classes for adults & children, studio workshops; teacher resource center; lect open to public, 14 vis lectr per year; concerts; gallery talks; tours; originate traveling exhibitions; museum shop sells books, reproductions & slides

L **Ingalls Library,** 11150 East Blvd, 44106. Tel 216-421-7340; FAX 216-421-0921; Elec Mail bm.cma@rlg.stanford.edu. *Librn* Ann B Abid; *Asst Librn Technical Serv* Elizabeth A Lantz; *Asst Librn Public Serv* Louis V Adrean; *Serials Librn* Kay Downey; *Asian Bibliographer* Yunah Sung; *Slide Librn* Sara Jane Pearman; *Systems Librn* Ken Feser
Estab 1916. Open to mus members, vis graduate students, faculty, curators
Library Holdings: Vols 215,000; Per subs 1000; Auction catalogues 50,000; Micro — Fiche, reels; AV — Lantern slides, slides 400,000; Other — Clipping files, exhibition catalogs, pamphlets, photographs, prints
Special Subjects: Art History, Asian Art, Decorative Arts, Etchings & Engravings, History of Art & Archaeology, Islamic Art, Oriental Art, Painting - American, Painting - British, Painting - Dutch, Painting - European, Painting - Flemish, Painting - French, Painting - German, Painting - Italian

A **Print Club of Cleveland,** 11150 East Blvd, 44106. Tel 216-421-7340; FAX 216-421-1994; *Pres* Caroline Oberndorf
Estab 1919 to stimulate interest in prints & drawings through educ, collecting & commissioning of new works & enhancement of the museum's collection by gifts & purchases. Mem: 250; dues $150 & up; annual meeting in Jan
Income: Financed by endowment, dues, sells prints from club inventory & sponsors annual fine print fair
Publications: The Print Club of Cleveland 1969-1994. Available at Museum Sales Desk, $19.94 plus postage
Activities: Lect open to public & members, 1-3 vis lectr per year; gallery talks; tours; awards

L **CLEVELAND PUBLIC LIBRARY,** Fine Arts & Special Collections Dept, 325 Superior Ave, 44114-1271. Tel 216-623-2848, 623-2818; FAX 216-623-7050; Elec Mail fine4@library.cpl.org, white1@library.cpl.org; Internet Home Page Address (FA)http://www.cpl.org/fahome.html; (SpCo)http://www.cpl.org/-spchome.html. *Dir* Marilyn Gell Mason; *Head Fine Arts & Special Colls Dept* Alice N Loranth; *Head Main Library* Joan Clark
Open Mon - Sat 9 AM - 6 PM, Sept - June Sun 1 - 5 PM. Estab 1869. Circ 5, 624,099
Income: $34,577,461
Library Holdings: Vols 190,092; Per subs 217; Folklore & Chess Archives; Original Documents; Special Collections-Rare Book vols 178,906 & per sub 425; CD's 18,595; Micro — Fiche 31,196, prints, reels 2008; AV — Cassettes 13,015, slides 457, v-tapes; Other — Clipping files, exhibition catalogs, manuscripts, pamphlets, photographs, prints
Special Subjects: Architecture, Art History, Decorative Arts, Oriental Art, Primitive Art, Archaeology of the Orient & Near East Egyptology
Collections: Cleveland Artist Original Graphics; Architectural plans, blue prints & drawings of five Cleveland buildings by Hubble & Benes architectural firm & other Cleveland Downtown buildings
Publications: Descriptive pamphlets of holdings; exhibit catalogs
Activities: Lect & collections open to public; tours available for groups; competitions; Sales shop sells books, reproductions, prints & gift items

L **CLEVELAND STATE UNIVERSITY,** Library & Art Services, Rhodes Tower 322, 44115. Tel 216-687-2492; *Supvr Art Serv* Pamela Eyerdam
Estab 1965 to house collection of visual arts
Purchases: $16,000
Library Holdings: Vols 15,000; Per subs 96; Color Reproductions; Micro — Cards, fiche, prints, reels; AV — A-tapes, cassettes, fs, motion pictures, rec, slides 65,000, v-tapes; Other — Clipping files, exhibition catalogs, original art works, pamphlets, photographs, prints, reproductions
Collections: 19th & 20th century European & American art; medieval art; Indian & West African art

M **Art Gallery,** 2307 Chester Ave, 44115. Tel 216-687-2103; FAX 216-687-2275; Elec Mail r.thurmer@csuohio.edu. *Dir* Robert Thurmer; *Asst Dir* Tim Knapp
Open Mon - Fri 10 AM - 4 PM. Admis free. Estab 1965 to present important art to University & Northeast Ohio community. 4500 sq ft floor space carpeted, 260 running ft wall space, 14 ft high track lighting, air conditioned, humidity controlled, motion detectors & closed circuit 24 hr surveillance by university police. Average Annual Attendance: 54,000
Income: $110,000 (financed by student fees & grants)
Collections: African; African American
Exhibitions: People's Art Show
Publications: Exhibition Catalog, 2-3 times per year
Activities: Educ dept; docent training; workshops; symposia; lect open to public, 24 vis lectr per year; competitions with awards; book traveling exhibitions; originate traveling exhibitions

M **NEW ORGANIZATION FOR THE VISUAL ARTS,** (NOVA), 4614 Prospect Ave, Ste 212, Prospect Park Bldg, 44103. Tel 216-431-7500; *Exec Dir* Janus Small; *Assoc Dir* Barbara Bachtell
Estab 1972 as a non-profit artists' service organization
Exhibitions: Jim Mersfelder Memorial Artists Advocacy Award (annual) Art Beat: Women Artists on Health & the Human Condition.

L **NORTHEAST OHIO AREAWIDE COORDINATING AGENCY (NOACA),** Information Resource Center, Atrium Office Plaza, 668 Euclid Ave, 44114-3000. Tel 216-241-2414, Ext 240; FAX 216-621-3024; *Information Specialist* Kenneth Goldberg
Open Mon - Fri 8 AM - 5 PM. Estab 1963, staff use only, public phone inquiries welcome
Library Holdings: Vols 7510; Per subs 165; AV — Fs; Other — Clipping files, exhibition catalogs, manuscripts, memorabilia, original art works, pamphlets, photographs, prints, reproductions
Special Subjects: Advertising Design, Commercial Art, Display, Furniture, Graphic Design, Industrial Design, Interior Design, Judaica, Maps, Metalwork, Photography, Restoration & Conservation
Collections: Architectural History; Presevation & Restoration; Urban Planning & Urban Design
Publications: Decision Maker; NOACA News; various reports related to planning, transportation & environmental issues; Seeking Grants in Times of Uncertainty

M **SAINT MARY'S ROMANIAN ORTHODOX CHURCH,** Romanian Ethnic Museum, 3256 Warren Rd, 44111. Tel 216-941-5550; *Pres* George Dobrea
Open Mon - Fri 8:30 AM - 4:30 PM, & on request. No admis fee. Estab 1960. Average Annual Attendance: 5000
Income: Financed by parish appropriation
Collections: Anisoara Stan Collection; O K Cosla Collection; Gunther Collection; Romanian art, artifacts, costumes, ceramics, painters, rugs, silver & woodwork; icons on glass & wood; books
Activities: Lect open to public; tours; individual paintings & original objects of art lent to other ethnic museums & faiths for exhibits; lending collection contains 100 original art works, 250 original prints, 50 paintings, sculpture, 2000 costumes, rugs & artifacts

M **SPACES,** 2220 Superior Viaduct, 44113. Tel 216-621-2314; FAX 216-621-2314; *Dir* Susan R Channing; *Assoc Dir* Julie Fehrenbach; *Gallery Mgr* Marilyn Ladd-Simmons
Open Tues - Sat 11 AM - 5 PM, Sun 1 - 5 PM. No admis fee. Estab 1978 to show innovative work by living artists. Single room, 6000 sq ft & 12 ft ceiling. Exhibitions, usually 6 artists per show, change monthly. Average Annual Attendance: 15,000. Mem: 300
Income: $250,000 (financed by mem, state appropriation & foundations)
Exhibitions: 6 exhibitions annually; Recent Immigrants; Group Exhibition
Publications: Exhibition catalogs, annual
Activities: Originate traveling exhibitions, one per year

M **WESTERN RESERVE HISTORICAL SOCIETY,** 10825 East Blvd, 44106. Tel 216-721-5722; *Exec Dir* Richard Ehrlich; *Business Mgr* Sally Adams; *Dir* Kermit J Pike
Mus open Tues - Sat 10 AM - 5 PM, Sun Noon - 5 PM. Admis adults $4, senior citizens & students $2, group rates available. Estab 1867 to discover, collect & preserve whatever relates to the history, biography, genealogy & antiquities of Ohio & the West. Average Annual Attendance: 85,000
Collections: Airplanes; automobiles; costumes; decorative, fine & domestic arts
Exhibitions: People at the Crossroads-Settling the Western Reserve, 1796- 1870; Chisholm Halle Custom Wing; Crawford Auto-Aviation collection
Publications: Books on Regional History; Western Reserve Historical Society News, bi-monthly
Activities: Classes for adults & children; docent training; lect open to public, 25 vis lectr per year; tours; gallery talks; awards; individual paintings & objects of art lent to qualified institutions; sales shop sells books, magazines, reproductions & prints
L **Library,** 10825 East Blvd, 44106. Tel 216-721-5722; FAX 216-721-5702; *Dir* Kermit J Pike
For reference only
Library Holdings: Vols 250,000; Per subs 100; Microfilm 40,000; Micro — Cards 200, fiche 2000, reels 25,000; AV — A-tapes, lantern slides, rec, slides; Other — Exhibition catalogs, manuscripts 5,000,000, pamphlets, photographs, prints
Special Subjects: Architecture, Decorative Arts, Folk Art, Maps, Photography, Prints

COLUMBUS

A **ACME ART CO,** 737 N High St, 43215. Tel 614-299-4003; *Artistic Dir* Margaret Evans
Open Wed - Sat 1 - 5 PM, or by appointment. No admis fee. Estab 1986 to provide programming that emphasizes emerging experimental & obscure art forms. Non profit gallery. Presents 12 major shows per year, in addition we also provide artist lectures fundraisers that involve & benefit both local artists & the gallery itself & performance & video programs. Average Annual Attendance: 150,000. Mem: 100
Income: $31,000 (financed by endowment, mem, Ohio Arts, Columbus Arts, Columbus Arts & private funding)
Exhibitions: Alan Crockett; John Sanborn; Bathroom Artists
Activities: Dramatic programs; lect open to public, 2-5 vis lectr per year

M **CAPITAL UNIVERSITY,** Schumacher Gallery, 2199 E Main St, 43209. Tel 614-236-6319; FAX 614-236-6490; *Dir* Dr Cassandra Lee Tellier; *Asst Dir* Jan Popp
Open Mon - Fri 1 - 5 PM, Sat & Sun 2 - 5 PM. No admis fee. Estab 1964 to provide the best available visual arts to the students; to serve the entire community with monthly traveling shows, community programming & permanent collections. Gallery is 16,000 sq ft, that includes six display galleries of permanent holdings, gallery area for temporary monthly exhibits, galleries, fabrication room, community reception room, lecture area seating 25. Average Annual Attendance: 7000
Income: Financed by foundation grants & individual gifts
Collections: †Ethnic Arts (including American Indian, Inuit, Oceanic); †American paintings, sculpture & graphics of 20th century; Period works from 16th - 19th century; †Major Ohio Artists; †Graphics; †Asian Art
Exhibitions: Seven individual & group visiting shows per year; individual exhibits include contemporary artists & loans from individuals & other museums
Activities: Lect open to public; gallery talks; competitions; individual paintings & original art objects lent by special request only; museum shop sells books, original art, glass, ceramics, handcrafted jewelry, cards & museum reproductions
L **Art Library,** 2199 E Main St, 43209. Tel 614-236-6615; FAX 614-236-6490; *Dir* Dr Albert Maag
Open to students, faculty, staff & for reference only to the pub
Library Holdings: Vols 5000; Per subs 15

L **COLUMBUS COLLEGE OF ART & DESIGN,** Packard Library, 107 N Ninth St, 43215-1758. Tel 614-224-9101; *Librn* Chilin Yu
Open Mon & Fri 8 AM - 5 PM, Tues - Thurs 8 AM - 9 PM. Estab 1879. Open to pub for reference only
Income: $279,000 (financed by tuition fees & grants)
Purchases: $71,000
Library Holdings: Vols 30,000; Per subs 200; AV — Cassettes, Kodachromes, lantern slides, rec, slides, v-tapes; Other — Clipping files, exhibition catalogs, original art works, pamphlets, photographs, reproductions, sculpture
Special Subjects: Advertising Design, American Indian Art, Architecture, Art History, Asian Art, Commercial Art, Decorative Arts, Drawings, Etchings & Engravings, Fashion Arts, Film, Folk Art, Goldsmithing, Graphic Arts, Graphic Design, History of Art & Archaeology, Illustration, Interior Design, Landscape Architecture, Mixed Media, Painting - American, Painting - European, Photography, Portraits, Pre-Columbian Art, Prints, Religious Art, Silversmithing, Theatre Arts, Video, Woodcarvings
Exhibitions: Students' work
Publications: Botticelli, annually
Activities: Classes for adults & children; lect open to public, 25 vis lectr per year; tours; competitions with awards; scholarships offered

M **COLUMBUS CULTURAL ARTS CENTER,** 139 W Main St, 43215. Tel 614-645-7047; *Dir* Jennifer Johnson
Open Mon - Fri 8:30 AM - 5 PM, Mon - Thurs 7 - 10 PM, Sat & Sun 1 - 5 PM. No admis fee. Estab 1978, visual arts facilities & gallery. Maintains small reference library. Average Annual Attendance: 50,000. Mem: 50; dues $25; annual meeting May 15
Income: Financed by city appropriation
Activities: Classes for adults & children; lect open to public, 58 vis lectr per year; concerts; gallery talks; tours; festivals; book traveling exhibitions 2 per year

L **COLUMBUS METROPOLITAN LIBRARY** (Formerly Public Library of Columbus & Franklin County), Humanities, Fine Art & Recreation Division, 96 S Grant Ave, 43215. Tel 614-645-2690; *Exec Dir* Larry Black; *Div Mgr* Suzanne Fisher; *Main Library Dir* Deb McWilliam
Open Mon - Thurs 9 AM - 9 PM, Fri & Sat 9 AM - 6 PM, Sun 1 - 5 PM school season. Estab 1873 to promote lifelong learning among residents of central Ohio by ensuring access to information, providing a diverse collection & advancing literacy by encouraging children & families to read
Income: Financed by state & county appropriation
Library Holdings: Vols 172,693; Per subs 2181; Catalogs; Micro — Reels; AV — A-tapes, cassettes, rec, slides, v-tapes; Other — Exhibition catalogs, original art works, pamphlets, photographs
Special Subjects: Architecture, Art History, Decorative Arts, Film, Photography, Theatre Arts, Antiques, Music, Television
Publications: Metroscene Main Library Magazine, bimonthly, Navel Events Newsletter, bimonthly
Activities: Summer reading for children; lect open to public; tours; exten dept serves Franklin County

M **COLUMBUS MUSEUM OF ART,** 480 E Broad St, 43215. Tel 614-221-6801; FAX 614-221-0226; *Dir* Irvin Lippman; *Sr Cur* Nanette Maciejunes; *Deputy Dir* Denny Griffith; *Registrar* Rod Bouc; *Dir Educ* Carole Genshaft
Open Tues - Fri & Sun 10 AM - 5:30 PM, Sat 10 AM - 5 PM, Thurs until 8:30 PM, cl Mon & holidays. Donations suggested, adults $3, children (6-17), senior citizens & students with valid ID $2. Estab 1878. Present main building constructed in 1931 in an Italianate palatial style; addition built in 1974; Sculpture Park & Garden added in 1979. Average Annual Attendance: 160,000. Mem: 7300; dues $50 family
Income: Financed by annual contributions, endowment, mem & pub support
Collections: 16th - 20th century European paintings, drawings & prints; 19th & 20th century American paintings, works on paper; 19th & 20th century European & American sculpture Chinese & Japanese ceramics; pre-Columbian sculpture
Exhibitions: (1997) The Paintings of Charles Burchfield: North by Midwest. (1998) African Intluencesin Contemporary Art: Artists of the Kwanzaa Playground Project
Publications: Exhibition & permanent collection catalogs; interpretive materials; monthly members calendar of events; three-month guide to programs & events; gallery handouts
Activities: Classes for adults & children; docent training; summer arts camp; lect open to public, 10 vis lectr per year; concerts; gallery talks; scholarships offered; exten dept serves Speaker Bureau & Docents-in-the-Schools; individual paintings & original objects of art lent to other museums & government buildings; lending collection contains color reproductions, slides & videos; originate traveling exhibitions; museum shop sells books
L **Resource Center,** 480 E Broad St, 43215. Tel 614-221-6801; FAX 614-221-8946; *Dir Educ* Carole Genshaft
Estab 1974 as a reference center for staff, mem, teachers & docents
Library Holdings: Vols 5000; Per subs 25; AV — Motion pictures, slides 15,000; Other — Clipping files, exhibition catalogs, pamphlets
Special Subjects: Antiquities-Oriental, Art Education, Art History, Eskimo Art, Folk Art, Oriental Art, Painting - American, Painting - Dutch, Painting - European, Painting - Flemish, Painting - French, Portraits, Pre-Columbian Art, American Coverlets

A **DIALOGUE INC,** PO Box 2572, 43216. Tel 614-621-3704; *Exec Ed* Lorrie Dirkse
Estab 1978 to promote the arts in the Midwest
Income: $160,000 (financed by endowment, state appropriation, advertising, subscriptions, private & pub donors)
Publications: Dialogue: Arts in the Midwest, bimonthly journal

A **OHIO HISTORICAL SOCIETY,** 1982 Velma Ave, 43211-2497. Tel 614-297-2300; FAX 614-297-2411;
Internet Home Page Address http://winslo.ohio.govjohswww/ohshome.html. *Dir* Gary Ness; *Chief Educ Division* Dr Amos Loveday; *Head Archaeology* Martha Otto; *Head Natural History* Carl Albrecht; *Head Historic Preservation* Amos Loveday
Open Mon - Sun 9 AM - 5 PM. No admis fee. Estab 1885, Ohio Historical Soc was chartered on this date, to promote a knowledge of history, natural history & archaeology, especially of Ohio; to collect & maintain artifacts, books & archives relating to Ohio's history. Main gallery covers over one acre of floor space & includes exhibits on history, natural history, archaeology; also houses a natural history demonstration laboratory & audiovisual theatre. Average Annual Attendance: 500,000. Mem: 12,000; dues individual $32; annual meeting in Sept
Income: Financed by endowment, mem, state appropriation & contributions
Collections: Archaeology; †artifacts; ceramics; †clothing; †furniture; †glassware; †paintings
Publications: Museum Echoes, newsletter, monthly; Ohio History, scholarly journal, quarterly; Timeline, popular journal, bi-monthly
Activities: Classes for adults & children; docent training; lect open to public; photographic competitions with awards; individual paintings & original art objects lent; lending collection to museum & art galleries; books traveling exhibitions; originate traveling exhibitions; sales shop sells books, magazines, reproductions, prints, slides and other souvenir items, post cards, jewelry

L **Archives-Library Division,** 1982 Velma Ave, 43211. Tel 614-297-2510; FAX 614-297-2546; *Division Chief & State Archivist* George Parkinson; *Head Collections* William G Myers; *Head Conservation* Vernon Will
Open Tues - Sat 9 AM - 5 PM. Estab 1885, to collect, preserve & interpret evidences of the past. For reference only. Average Annual Attendance: 13,000
Income: $1,100,000 (financed by state appropriation & private revenue)
Purchases: $80,000
Library Holdings: Vols 148,600; Per subs 300; Maps 5000; Micro — Reels 47,500; AV — A-tapes, cassettes 2500, fs, Kodachromes, lantern slides, motion pictures, rec, slides, v-tapes; Other — Exhibition catalogs, manuscripts 1000, memorabilia, pamphlets, photographs 50,000, prints, reproductions
Collections: †Broadsides; †Ohio government documents; †Ohio newspapers; †Temperance collection †maps; papers of early Ohio political leaders; †posters; †rare books; †trade catalogs; †photographs; †manuscripts
Publications: Ohio History (bi-annual); Timeline (bi-monthly)
Activities: Classes for adults & children; docent training

OHIO STATE UNIVERSITY
M **Wexner Center for the Arts,** N High St at 15th Ave, 43210-1393. Tel 614-292-0330; FAX 614-292-3369; *Dir* Sherri Geldin; *Cur Architecture* Mark Robbins; *Cur Media Arts* William Hurrigan; *Exhib Designer* Jim Scott; *Assoc Dir Public Affairs* Patrick McCusker; *Dir Performing Arts* Charles R Helm; *Dir Communications* Roger Addleman; *Dir Educ* Patricia Trumps; *Dir Admin* Timothy J Meager
Open Tues, Wed & Fri 10 AM - 6 PM, Thurs & Sat 10 AM -8 PM, Sun Noon - 5 PM, cl Mon. No admis fee. Estab 1989 to provide quality contemporary exhibitions for students & faculty, to promote interaction with the regional art community & to maintain & extend collection of contemporary art. Administers the permanent collection & exhibitions in 4 professionally equipped galleries & is the center for long-range planning in visual arts
Income: $5,700,000 (financed by operating funds from the university, program support from the Wexner Center Foundation & government foundation & corporate grants, earned income)
Collections: Contemporary Collection; Study Collection of graphic arts & manuscripts Wiant collection of Chinese art
Exhibitions: Solo Exhibits: Guillermo Kuitca: A Survey; Muntadas/Between the Frames: The Forum; Robert Frank: The Americans; Group Exhibits: House Rules; In the Spirit of Fluxus; Softworlds, Inc
Publications: Exhibition catalogs
Activities: Schools in gallery; lect open to public, 12 vis lectr per year; concerts; gallery talks; tours; invitational juried exhibitions; rent traveling exhibitions 1-5 per year; originate traveling exhibitions
L **Fine Arts Library,** 035L Wexner Ctr for the Arts, 27 W 17th Ave Mall, 43210. Tel 614-292-6184; FAX 614-292-6184; Elec Mail wyngaard.1@osu.edu. *Head Librn* Susan E Wyngaard; *Asst* Diana Druback; *Asst* Gretchen Donelson
Open Mon - Thurs 8 AM - 10 PM, Fri 8 AM - 5 PM, Sat Noon - 6 PM, Sun 2 - 10 PM, while classes are in session; vacation, 10 AM - 5 PM daily. Estab during 1930's to support teaching & research in art, art educ, design, history of art & photography. Average Annual Attendance: 200,000
Purchases: $120,000
Library Holdings: Vols 100,000; Per subs 350; Micro — Cards, fiche, reels; AV — Slides; Other — Exhibition catalogs, original art works
Special Subjects: Afro-American Art, American Indian Art, American Western Art, Architecture, Art Education, Asian Art, Ceramics, Crafts, Decorative Arts, Furniture, History of Art & Archaeology, Islamic Art, Latin American Art, Mosaics, Oriental Art, Art of the 1970's, 1980's & 1990's, Medieval & Renaissance, 19th Century French art, photography
L **Slide & Photograph Library,** 204 Hayes Hall, 108 N Oval Mall, 43210. Tel 614-292-0520; FAX 614-292-4401; *Cur* John J Taormina; *Assoc Cur* Janice Glowski; *Asst Cur* Mark Pompelia
Open Mon - Fri 8 AM - 5 PM. Estab 1925 to provide visual resources for instruction & research in history of art. Teaching - Reference Collection, restricted circulation
Income: Financed by state funds through State University System
Library Holdings: Vols 150; Per subs 3; AV — A-tapes 30, slides 270,000; Other — Exhibition catalogs, framed reproductions, original art works, photographs 230,000, prints, reproductions
Special Subjects: Asian Art, Islamic Art, Western Art
Collections: †Asian art & architecture; history of Western art & architecture; African art & architecture
L **Cartoon, Graphic & Photographic Arts Research Library,** 023L Wexner Ctr, 27 W 17th Ave Mall, OH 43210-1393. Tel 614-292-0538; FAX 614-292-6184; Elec Mail cartoons@osu.edu. *Cur* Lucy Shelton Caswell
Open Mon - Fri 9 AM - 5 PM, hrs vary between terms. Estab 1977
Income: Financed by state appropriation
Library Holdings: Micro — Reels; AV — Cassettes, motion pictures, rec, slides; Other — Clipping files, exhibition catalogs, manuscripts, memorabilia, original art works, photographs
Special Subjects: Cartoons, Illustration, Manuscripts, Photography, Posters
Collections: Cartoonist Collection, clippings, proofs & scrapbooks (hundreds of artists represented)
L **Human Ecology Library,** 1787 Neil Ave, 43210-1295. Tel 614-292-4220; *Librn* Leta Hendricks
Open Mon - Thurs 8 AM - 8 PM, Fri 8 AM - 5 PM, Sat 10 AM - 2 PM, Sun 1 - 3 PM
Library Holdings: Vols 23,000; Per subs 200; Micro — Fiche; AV — A-tapes, cassettes, fs, motion pictures, slides, v-tapes; Other — Exhibition catalogs, pamphlets
Special Subjects: Carpets & Rugs, Crafts, Decorative Arts, Embroidery, Fashion Arts, Folk Art, Furniture, Jewelry, Textiles
Collections: †Costumes; †Crafts; †Textiles & Clothing

COSHOCTON

M **JOHNSON-HUMRICKHOUSE MUSEUM,** 300 Whitewoman St, Roscoe Village, 43812. Tel 614-622-8710; FAX 614-622-8710, Ext 51; *Dir* Midge Derby
Open daily Noon - 5 PM May through Oct, 1 - 4:30 PM Nov through Apr, cl Mon, Thanksgiving, Christmas Eve, Christmas & New Year's Day. Admis adult $2, seniors $1.50, children 5-12 $1. Estab 1931, as a gift of two pioneer residents. Museum is located in historical Roscoe Village in a newly constructed building (1979) managed by the Library Board
Collections: American Indian baskets and bead work; Aztec, Toltec and Mayan pottery heads; Chinese and Japanese amber, brass, bronze, cloisonne, copper, embroideries, ivory, jade, lacquers, pewter ware, porcelains, prints, wood carvings; European glass, laces, pewter, porcelains, prints; Eskimo artifacts; material from Coshocton County Mound Builders; Miller-Preston bequest of furnishings and implements used by Coshocton County pioneer families
Exhibitions: Permanent collection exhibitions changed periodically; traveling exhibitions.
Activities: Educ dept; lect; gallery talks; museum shop sells books & collection-oriented items

CUYAHOGA FALLS

M **RICHARD GALLERY & ALMOND TEA GALLERY,** Divisions of Studios of Jack Richard, 2250 Front St, 44221. Tel 216-929-1575; *Dir* Jack Richard; *Agent* Jane Williams
Open Tues - Fri 11:30 AM - 5 PM, Sat 11 AM - 1:30 PM, Tues Eve 7 - 10 PM, cl Sun & Mon, other hours by appointment. No admis fee. Estab 1960, for exhibition of local, regional & national works of art. Average Annual Attendance: 12,000
Income: Financed privately
Collections: Ball; Brackman; Cornwell; Grell; Gleitsmann; Loomis; Terry Richard; †Oriental
Exhibitions: 50 Women Plus; student exhibits; Japanese Prints; members exhibits; 30 one-person exhibits; Pastel Exhibit; Age Old Masters; Brackman Masterpieces; Flowers, Flowers, Flowers; Great American Nude; Progress & Change in Paintings
Activities: Classes for adults & children; lect open to public, 5 vis lectr per year; gallery talks; tours; competitions with awards; scholarships offered; individual paintings & original objects of art lent; lending collection contains paintings, prints & cassettes; book traveling exhibitions; originate traveling exhibitions; sales shop sells books, magazines, original art, reproductions, prints & slides; frame shop
L **Library,** 2250 Front St, 44221. Tel 216-929-1575;
For reference & limited lending only
Library Holdings: Vols 1000; AV — Kodachromes, motion pictures, rec, slides, v-tapes; Other — Clipping files, framed reproductions, original art works, photographs, prints, reproductions

DAYTON

M **DAYTON ART INSTITUTE,** 456 Belmonte Park N, 45405-4700. Tel 937-223-5277; FAX 937-223-3140; *Dir* Alex Nyerges; *Sr Cur* Dominique Vasseur; *Cur Asian Art* Li Gian; *Dir Develop* James L Thortan; *Public Relations* Sara Weber; *Registrar* Edward Amatore
Open Tues - Sun Noon - 5 PM. Admis adults $2, senior citizens & students $1, children under 18 free. Estab 1919 for the pub benefit. Some of the galleries include: Ancient Gallery, Contemporary Gallery, European 16th-18th Century Gallery, Experiencenter Gallery, Print Corridor, Special Exhibitions Gallery & an Asian Wing & an American wing. Average Annual Attendance: 170,000. Mem: 3800; dues $3-$1000; annual meeting Sept
Income: $1,300,000 (financed by federal, state & local funds, mem dues, endowment & corporate grants)
Collections: †American Collection; European Art From Medieval Period to Present; Oriental Collection
Publications: Annual report; bulletin; Calendar of Events, bi-monthly; gallery guides & catalogs, periodically
Activities: Classes for adults & children; docent training; lect open to public, 3-6 per year; gallery talks; tours; concerts; annual Oktoberfest; annual style show; Guild Volunteer Organization; scholarships offered; book traveling exhibitions 6 per year; museum shop sells books, original art, toys & jewelry
L **Library,** 456 Belmonte Park N, 45405-4700. Tel 937-223-5277; FAX 937-223-3140; Elec Mail daytnart@ohionet.org. *Librn* Jane Dunwoodie; *Asst Librn* Kristina Sullivan; *Ref Librn* Alice Saidel
Open Mon, Wed & Fri 1 - 5 PM, Tues & Thurs 9 AM - Noon. Estab 1922. Open to the pub for art reference only
Income: Financed by Dayton Art Institute budget
Library Holdings: Vols 29,000; Per subs 103; Auction catalogs - from 1975-present; Micro — Fiche; AV — Slides; Other — Clipping files, exhibition catalogs, pamphlets
Special Subjects: Aesthetics, Afro-American Art, American Indian Art, American Western Art, Antiquities-Assyrian, Antiquities-Byzantine, Antiquities-Egyptian, Antiquities-Etruscan, Antiquities-Greek, Antiquities-Oriental, Antiquities-Persian, Antiquities-Roman, Archaeology, Architecture, Art Education
Collections: Louis J P Lott & Walter G Schaeffer, architectural libraries

M **PATTERSON HOMESTEAD,** 1815 Brown St, 45409. Tel 513-222-9724; *Dir* Mollie Lee Williams; *Staff Site Interpreter* Anne Lykins; *Meeting Room Hostess* Sharon Ness
Open Apr - Dec Tues - Fri 10 AM - 4 PM, Sun 1 - 4 PM, cl legal holidays. No admis fee. Estab 1953. Patterson Homestead is an 1816 Federal style farmhouse
Collections: Antique & period furniture, ranging from the hand-hewn to highly decorative Victorian Eastlake pieces, including Chippendale, Hepplewhite, Sheraton & American Empire styles; Oil Portraits of members of the Patterson family; Manuscript Collection
Exhibitions: Temporary exhibitions
Activities: Programs for children & grad students affiliated with Wright State Univ; docent program; lectures; tours

WRIGHT STATE UNIVERSITY
M **Dayton Art Institute**, 45435. Tel 513-873-2978; FAX 513-873-4082; *Curatorial Consultant* Eric Davis
Open Mon - Fri 10 AM - 4 PM, Sat & Sun Noon - 4 PM, cl holidays. No admis fee. Estab 1974, devoted to exhibitions of & research in contemporary art. Four galleries; multi-level contemporary building with 5000 sq ft & 500 running ft of wall space. Available also are areas outside on the campus & selected sites in Dayton. Average Annual Attendance: 25,000. Mem: 200; dues $25 & up
Income: Financed through the university & grants
Collections: Collection of Contemporary Art
Publications: Artist's books & exhibition catalogs, 2 per year
Activities: Classes for adults; lect open to public, 7-8 vis lectr per year; gallery talks; tours; individual paintings & art objects lent to faculty & administrative areas; lending collection contains original art works, original prints, paintings, photographs & sculpture; originate traveling exhibitions; sales desk sells catalogs, periodicals
L **Dept of Art & Art History Resource Center & Slide Library**, 45435. Tel 513-873-3567; FAX 513-873-4082, Ext 3567; *Slide Cur* Pat Robinow
Open Mon, Wed, Fri 9 AM - 5 PM, Tues & Thurs 10 AM - 2 PM. Estab 1970 to serve Wright State University & art professionals in the greater Dayton area. For lending & reference. Circ Approx 300 slides per week
Library Holdings: Vols 250; Per subs 15; Art school catalogs; AV — A-tapes, cassettes, slides, v-tapes; Other — Exhibition catalogs
Special Subjects: Architecture, Art History, Drawings, Etchings & Engravings, History of Art & Archaeology, Painting - American, Painting - British, Painting - Dutch, Painting - European, Painting - Flemish, Painting - French, Painting - German, Painting - Italian, Painting - Polish, Painting - Russian

DOVER

M **WARTHER MUSEUM INC**, 331 Karl Ave, 44622. Tel 330-343-7513; *Pres* David Warther; *General Mgr* Mark Warther
Open daily 9 AM - 5 PM. Admis $6. Estab 1936 to display carvings. Average Annual Attendance: 100,000
Income: $250,000 (financed by admis)
Collections: Carvings of American Railroad History; Carvings of ivory, ebony & walnut depicting the evolution of the steam engine
Exhibitions: Carvings of American Railroads by Ernest Warther
Activities: Retail store sells books, souvenirs, general gifts & handcrafted cutlery

FINDLAY

M **UNIVERSITY OF FINDLAY** (Formerly Findley College), Egner Fine Arts Center, 1000 N Main St, 45840. Tel 419-422-8313; FAX 419-424-4757; *Dir* Dale Brougher
Open Mon - Fri 9 AM - 4:30 PM. Estab in 1962 as an auxiliary to the college art department. Gallery is maintained
Income: Financed by endowment
Collections: †Contemporary prints; student works
Exhibitions: Contemporary Art & Crafts; annual Student Exhibition
Activities: Classes for adults & children; dramatic programs; lect open to public, 2-3 vis lectr per year; concerts; competitions with awards; scholarships offered; individual paintings & original objects of art lent, primarily to College offices

GALLIPOLIS

A **FRENCH ART COLONY**, 530 First Ave, PO Box 472, 45631. Tel 614-446-3834; *Dir* Mary Bea Sheets; *Cur* Janice M Thaler; *Cur* Saundra Koby; *Treasurer* Peggy Evans
Open Tues - Fri 10 AM - 3 PM, Sat & Sun 1 - 5 PM. No admis fee. Estab 1964 to promote the arts throughout the region. Mem: 325; dues $20 & up
Income: Financed by mem & donations
Exhibitions: Exhibits change monthly & include: International, Juried Festival, Ceramics, Watercolors, Oils & Mixed-Media
Publications: Newsletter, bi-monthly
Activities: Classes for adults & children; dramatic programs; community programs; creative writing; visual art programs & classes; lect open to public; concerts; tours; competitions; 10 - 12 purchase awards; book traveling exhibitions
L **Library**, 530 First Ave, PO Box 472, 45631. Tel 614-446-3834; *Dir* Mary Bea Sheets
Open Tues - Fri 10 AM - 3 PM, Sat & Sun 1 - 5 PM. Estab 1972 as small reference library dealing primarily with visual arts
Library Holdings: Vols 2000; Per subs 5; AV — Cassettes, lantern slides, slides; Other — Clipping files, exhibition catalogs, memorabilia, pamphlets, photographs, prints, reproductions
Special Subjects: Fine Arts

GAMBIER

M **KENYON COLLEGE**, Art Gallery, Olin Library, Kenyon College, 43022. Tel 614-427-5000; *Coordr* Ellen Sheffield
Open daily 8:30 AM - 8:30 PM, through school year only. No admis fee. Estab 1973 as teaching arm of the Art Department of Kenyon College
Income: Financed by college
Collections: Art collection and items of some historical importance
Activities: Lect open to public; gallery talks; tours; Honors Day cash awards

GRANVILLE

M **DENISON UNIVERSITY**, Art Gallery, Burke Hall of Music & Art, 43023. Tel 614-587-6255, 587-6596; FAX 614-587-5701; *Dir* Ankeney Weitz
Open Mon - Sun 1 - 4 PM. No admis fee. Estab 1946 for educational & exhibition purposes; one seminar room; storage for permanent collections173. Average Annual Attendance: 25,000
Income: Financed through University
Collections: American and European paintings, †prints, †drawings and sculpture; Burmese textiles, lacquerware and Buddhist sculpture; Chinese bronzes, robes and porcelains; Cuna Indian Molas, Uchus and ceremonial objects; American Indian pottery, baskets and rugs; African sculpture and basketry
Exhibitions: Burmese art on permanent display; faculty show; senior student shows; special exhibitions from permanent collection; visiting artists exhibitions
Activities: Lect open to public, 4-6 vis lectr per year; gallery talks; tours; exten dept; individual paintings & original objects of art lent to other museums
L **Art Dept Slide Library**, Cleveland Hall Annex, 43023. Tel 614-587-6480; *In Charge* Ann Watson
Open to students and faculty for reference only
Library Holdings: AV — Slides 95,000

HAMILTON

M **FITTON CENTER FOR CREATIVE ARTS**, 101 S Monument Ave, 45011-2833. Tel 513-863-8873; FAX 513-863-8865; *Exec Dir* Deby Sage; *Exhib* Nelly Bly Cogan; *Dir. ABCDE & SPECTRA +* Jackie Quay
No admis fee. Estab 1992 to reveal community excellence through the arts. Two large galleries with foyer on second floor. Large lobby display area on ground floor. One gallery with artificial light only, one with a view of great Miami River. Average Annual Attendance: 12,000. Mem: 900; dues $25 & up; annual meeting in the fall
Income: Financed by NEA, Ohio Arts Council, corporations, Hamilton Community Foundation & mem
Exhibitions: Angels & Other Delights; Feed the Body, Feed the Soul; Harper Harper Harper: Brett, Edie, Charley; Quilts
Publications: The Schooled Mind: Spectra+; quarterly newsletter; annual report
Activities: Classes for adults & children; dramatic programs; performing arts series; teacher workshops; lect open to public; competitions with prizes; scholarships offered; sales shop sells books, prints, original art & reproductions

JEFFERSON

M **DEZIGN HOUSE**, PO Box 284, 44047. Tel 216-294-2778; *Dir* Ramon J Elias; *Assoc* Margery M Elias
Open only to clients. Estab 1962 for the encouragement of original art. Private gallery
Income: Financed privately
Collections: Original American and European
L **Library**, PO Box 284, Jefferson, 44047. Tel 216-294-2778; *Dir* Ramon J Elias
Estab 1953. Open for private research only
Library Holdings: Vols 7000; Per subs 40; AV — Kodachromes 2000, rec; Other — Clipping files, exhibition catalogs, manuscripts, memorabilia, original art works, pamphlets, photographs, prints, sculpture
Special Subjects: North Eastern Ohio Art of the 60's

KENT

KENT STATE UNIVERSITY
M **School of Art Gallery**, 44242. Tel 330-672-7853; FAX 330-672-4729; *Dir* Dr Fred T Smith
Open Mon - Fri 10 AM - 4 PM, Sun 2 - 5 PM, cl school holidays. No admis fee. Estab 1950 as part of the instructional program at Kent State. One main gallery 2200 sq ft; two student galleries; Eells Gallery; Blossom Music Center. Average Annual Attendance: 22,000. Mem: 76; dues $10; annual meeting in June
Income: Financed by University, grants & fundraising
Collections: Michener Collection, contemporary prints & paintings; permanent collection sculpture, paintings, prints, crafts & photography, textiles
Exhibitions: Annual Invitational; faculty & student one-man & group exhibitions; traveling exhibitions from museums
Publications: Brochures; catalogs, 2-3 per year
Activities: Classes for students in museum preparation; lect open to public, 10-15 vis lectr per year; gallery talks; tours; competitions; individual paintings & original objects of art lent to offices on campus; book traveling exhibitions 3 per year

LAKEWOOD

A **BECK CENTER FOR THE CULTURAL ARTS**, 17801 Detroit Ave, 44107. Tel 216-521-2540; *Pres Board Trustees* Leroy B Parks Jr; *Dir Development* Linda J N Prosak
Open Mon - Fri 9 AM - 5 PM, Sat Noon - 6 PM, performance evenings 6 - 9 PM. No admis fee. Estab 1976 to present a wide variety of the fine & graphic arts including exhibits from the Cleveland Mus of Art. A cooperative art gallery, home to 73 artists, juried art shows & visual art programs. Average Annual Attendance: 50,000
Income: Financed by operating cost of the center
Collections: Contemporary pieces including acrylics, collages, etchings, oils, sculpture & watercolors
Exhibitions: Kwo, Miller, Thurmer (paintings & sculpture); Touching Stories, from Cleveland Mus of Art; Hungarian Art; Krabill (paintings)
Publications: Bulletins; Programs, every five weeks
Activities: Classes for adults & children; dramatic programs; docent training; lect open to public; concerts; gallery talks; tours; competitions with awards; exten dept serves youth in schools; sales shop sells original art, prints, jewelry & all art media

LIMA

M ARTSPACE-LIMA, 65-67 Town Square, PO Box 1948, 45802. Tel 419-222-1721; FAX 419-222-6587; *Exec Dir* Ellen Nelson; *Operations & Ed Dir* Nancy Lohr; *Gallery Coordr* Doug Drury; *Gallery Shoppe Coordr* Laura Wise
Open Mon - Fri 10 AM - 4 PM, Sat Noon - 4 PM, Sun 2 - 4 PM. Estab 1940 for the promotion of visual arts through educ & exhibition. Maintains resource center. Mem: 450; dues family $40, individual $30; annual meeting in Sept
Income: $10,000 (financed by mem, grants & fund raising events)
Publications: Perspectives, newsletter
Activities: Classes for adults & children; docent programs; teacher in-services; lect open to public, 6 vis lectr per year; concerts; gallery talks; tours; competitions with awards; scholarships & fels offered; individual paintings & original objects of art lent to local businesses, public school classrooms & art teachers; museum shop sells magazines, original art, reproductions, prints & children's art kits

MANSFIELD

A MANSFIELD FINE ARTS GUILD, Mansfield Art Center, 700 Marion Ave, 44903. Tel 419-756-1700; *Dir* H Daniel Butts III
Open Tues - Sat 11 AM - 5 PM, Sun Noon - 5 PM, cl Mon & national holidays. No admis fee. Estab 1945, incorporated 1956 to maintain an art center in which exhibitions, lectures, gallery talks, special programs, symposia & series of classes for adults & children are provided for the North Central Ohio area; maintained by mem, commission on sales & classes. Gallery dimensions 5000 sq ft with flexible lighting, movable walls, props, etc to facilitate monthly exhibition changes. Average Annual Attendance: 25,000. Mem: 1050; dues $15-$1000; annual meeting in Apr
Exhibitions: Changing exhibitions of member artists' work; traveling shows & locally organized one-man, group & theme exhibitions changing monthly throughout the year
Publications: Catalogs; class schedules; monthly newsletter
Activities: Classes for adults & children; lect open to public, 6 vis lectr per year; gallery talks mainly for school groups; competitions; scholarships offered
L Library, 700 Marion Ave, 44903. Tel 419-756-1700; *Art Dir* H Daniel Butts III
The library is basically a collection of monographs & studies of styles & periods for teacher & student reference
Library Holdings: Vols 500

MARIETTA

M MARIETTA COLLEGE, Grover M Hermann Fine Arts Center, 45750. Tel 614-376-4696; *Chmn* Valdis Garoza
Open Mon - Fri 8 AM - 10:30 PM, Sat & Sun 1 - 10:30 PM. No admis fee. Estab 1965. Gallery maintained. Average Annual Attendance: 20,000
Collections: Permanent collection of contemporary American paintings, sculpture & crafts; significant collection of African & pre-Columbian art
Activities: Lect open to public; competitions

M THE OHIO HISTORICAL SOCIETY, INC, Campus Martius Museum & Ohio River Museum, 601 Second St, 45750-2122. Tel 614-373-3750; *Mgr* John B Briley; *Asst Mgr* Kim McGrew
Open in Mar, Apr, Oct & Nov Wed - Sat 9:30 AM - 5 PM, Sun Noon - 5 PM, May - Sept Mon - Sat 9:30 AM - 5 PM, Sun & holidays Noon - 5 PM, cl Dec - Feb. Admis fee age 13 & up $4, ages 6-12 $1, members & children under 6 free. Estab 1929 as part of the Ohio Historical Society to collect, exhibit & interpret historical items, including art & manuscripts, pertaining to the history of Marietta, the Northwest Territory (Ohio portion) & in 1941 the Ohio River. Campus Martius Museum has 12,500 sq ft of exhibition space on three floors plus a two-story home, a portion of the original fort of 1790-95 enclosed within the building. The Ohio River Museum has approximately 4500 sq ft of exhibition space in three separate buildings connected by walkway. Average Annual Attendance: 30,000
Income: Financed by state appropriation, mem, grants, fund raising, admis & sales
Collections: Steamer W P Snyder Jr; Tell City Pilothouse, a replica of the 18th century flatboat decorative arts from 19th century Ohio; early Ohio paintings, prints, & photographs; items from early Putnam, Blennerhassett & other families; Ohio Company & Marietta materials; Ohio River landscapes
Exhibitions: (1997) New exhibits at Campus Martius deal with Ohio farmers migrating to the cities & Appalachian people moving to Ohio's urban centers
Activities: Classes for adults & children; tours; sales shop sells books, reproductions, prints, slides, crafts, & souvenir items

MASSILLON

M MASSILLON MUSEUM, 121 Lincoln Way E, 44646. *Dir* John Klassen; *Registrar* Margaret Vogt
Open Tues - Sat 9:30 AM - 5 PM, Sun 2 - 5 PM. No admis fee. Estab 1933 as a mus of art & history. The mus places emphasis on the Ohio area by representing the fine arts & crafts & the Massillon area with an historical collection. Average Annual Attendance: 24,000. Mem: 1254; dues $10 & higher
Income: Financed by local property tax
Collections: †Ceramics, china, costumes, drawings, furniture, †glass, †jewelry, †paintings, prints
Exhibitions: Monthly exhibitions
Publications: Pamphlet of activities & exhibitions, quarterly
Activities: Classes for adults & children; docent training; lect open to public, 3 vis lectr per year; gallery talks; tours; exten dept serves public schools; individual paintings & original objects of art lent to area museums; museum shop sells local arts & crafts

MAYFIELD VILLAGE

L MAYFIELD REGIONAL LIBRARY, 6080 Wilson Mills Rd, 44143. Tel 216-473-0350; FAX 216-473-0774; *Art Librn* Kenneth Neal
Open Mon - Thurs 9 AM - 9 PM, Fri & Sat 9 AM - 5:30 PM, Sun 1 - 5 PM (during school months). Estab 1972
Exhibitions: Original art works by local artists

MIDDLETOWN

A MIDDLETOWN FINE ARTS CENTER, AIM Bldg, 130 N Verity Pky, PO Box 441, 45042. Tel 513-424-2416; *Pres* Don Pelfrey; *Adminr* Peggy Davish
Open Mon 9 AM - 4 PM, Tues - Thurs 9 AM - 9 PM. No admis fee. Estab 1965 to offer exhibits & classes to the pub. Auditorium for large exhibits; gallery for small exhibits. Average Annual Attendance: 400-500. Mem: 596; dues minimum $12; annual meeting in July
Income: Funds generated through mem & donations
Exhibitions: 10-12 exhibitions per year including Annual Area Art Show; Annual Student Show; plus one & two-man invitational shows of regional artists
Publications: Brochures publicizing exhibitions; quarterly newsletters; schedule of classes
Activities: Classes for adults, children & the handicapped; lect open to public, 1-3 vis lectr per year; tours; competitions with awards; scholarships offered; individual paintings & original objects of art lent usually to businesses for display; lending collection contains books, original art works & paintings; book traveling exhibitions; sales shop sells pottery, jewelry & paintings produced at Center
L Library, 130 N Verity Pky, PO Box 441, 45042. Tel 513-424-2416
Open Tues - Thurs 9 AM - 9 PM, Mon 9 AM - 4 PM, Sat 9 AM - Noon, cl Sun. Estab 1963, to provide information and enjoyment for students and instructors. Library open for lending or reference. Circ 30
Income: Financed through annual budget & donations
Purchases: $150
Library Holdings: Vols 1500; Per subs 6; AV — Slides
Special Subjects: Art Education, Art History, Ceramics, Conceptual Art, Crafts, Decorative Arts, Drawings, Folk Art, Historical Material, Illustration, Photography, Portraits, Sculpture, Southwestern Art, Watercolors
Collections: All books pertain only to art subjects: Art history; ceramics; crafts; illustrations; references; techniques; theory

NEWARK

M LICKING COUNTY ART ASSOCIATION, Art Gallery, 391 Hudson Ave, PO Box 4277, 43058-4277. Tel 614-349-8031; *Pres* Leah Mitchell; *Admin Coordr* Bill Philabaum
Open Tues - San 1 - 4 PM; school tours by appointment. No admis fee. Estab 1967 to offer 12 monthly art exhibits of Ohio artists & promote visual arts. Three large rooms for monthly shows, also a youth gallery, members gallery and a permanent collection. Second building located at 19 North St adjoining, for art classes and houses a large kiln for ceramics. Average Annual Attendance: 6000. Mem: 300; dues $20; annual meeting in Dec
Income: Financed by mem, annual art auction & pending grants
Collections: Paintings
Exhibitions: Montly Member Exhibitions; Community Art Collection
Publications: Art Print, monthly newsletter
Activities: Classes for adults & children; docent training; lect open to public, 12 vis lectr per year; gallery talks; tours; competitions with prizes; fellowships; individual paintings & objects of art lent to public institutions & business; lending collection contains books, original art works, photographs

NORTH CANTON

L NORTH CANTON PUBLIC LIBRARY, Little Art Gallery, 185 N Main St, 44720. Tel 330-499-4712; *Library Dir* Eileen Flowers; *Chmn Art Committee* Virginia West; *Cur* Laurie G Fife
Open Mon - Thurs 10 AM - 9 PM, Fri 10 AM - 6 PM, Sat 9 AM - 5 PM. No admis fee. Estab 1936 to encourage & promote appreciation & educ of fine art, graphic arts, commercial art & other related subjects; also recognizes & encourages local artists by promoting exhibitions of their work. Circ 446. Average Annual Attendance: 5000. Mem: 175; dues $10, meetings in Sept, Nov & Apr
Income: Financed by city & state appropriation
Purchases: $500
Library Holdings: Vols 54,014; Per subs 180
Collections: †Original works by contemporary artists; †religious reproductions; †reproductions for juvenile; †reproductions for circulation
Exhibitions: Monthly exhibits; Stark County Competitive Artists Show
Activities: Classes for adults & children; lect open to public, 1 vis lectr per year; gallery talks; tours; competitions with awards; scholarships offered; individual paintings lent, lending collection contains color reproductions

OBERLIN

A FIRELANDS ASSOCIATION FOR THE VISUAL ARTS, 39 S Main St, 44074. Tel 216-774-7158; FAX 216-775-1107; *Exec Dir* Elizabeth Manderen; *Gallery Dir* Susan Jones; *Educ Dir* Open ; *Office Mgr* Laura Dellisanti
Gallery open Tues - Sat Noon - 5 PM, Sun 2 - 4 PM. No admis fee. Estab 1979 as a non-profit community art organization. Average Annual Attendance: 4000. Mem: 325; dues basic $30-$45, contributors up to $1000; annual meeting in Nov
Income: $25,000 (financed by grants, mem, fees, tuitions, commissions, contributions & the Ohio Arts Council)
Exhibitions: Monthly changing exhibits by Contemporary regional artists; Annual Juried Six-State Photography; Annual FAVA Members' Holiday Show
Activities: Classes for adults, teens & children; family workshops; lect open to public, 6 vis lectr per year; competitions with awards; scholarships for low income children; sales shop sells books, original art, reproductions & prints

INTERMUSEUM CONSERVATION ASSOCIATION
For further information, see National and Regional Organizations

M **OBERLIN COLLEGE,** Allen Memorial Art Museum, Main & Lorain Sts, 44074. Tel 216-775-8665; FAX 216-775-8799; *Dir* Anne F Moore; *Asst to Dir* Leslie Miller; *Registrar* Lucille Stiger; *Educ Coordr* Megan Burness; *Cur Western Art Before 1850* Marjorie Wieseman; *Cur Asian Art* Charles Mason; *Cur Modern Art* Amy Kurlander; *Museum Preparator* Michael Holubar
Open Tues - Sat 10 AM - 5 PM, Sun 1 - 5 PM, cl Mon. No admis fee. Estab 1917 to serve teaching needs of Oberlin College & provide cultural enrichment for Northern Ohio region. Original building was designed by Cass Gilbert, a new addition opened in 1977 & was designed by Venturi, Rauch & Assoc. Average Annual Attendance: 35,000. Mem: 525; dues Director's Circle $1000, supporting $500, contributing $100, family $50, individual $40, student & senior citizen $20, Oberlin College student $15
Income: Financed by endowment, mem & Oberlin College general fund
Collections: The collection which ranges over the entire history of art is particularly strong in the area of Dutch & Flemish paintings of the 17th century, European Art of the late 19th & early 20th centuries, contemporary American art, old masters & Japanese prints
Exhibitions: Frequent traveling exhibitions & special in-house exhibitions
Publications: Allen Memorial Art Museum Bulletin twice yearly; catalogues of permanent collections; exhibition catalogues
Activities: Classes for adults & children; docent training; lect open to public, 10 vis lectr per year; gallery talks; concerts; tours; travel programs; Original objects of art lent to other institutions for special exhibition; lending collection contains 250 original art works for lending to students on a semester basis; book traveling exhibitions 2-4 per year; traveling exhibitions organized & circulated; Museum shop & gallery shop sells books, prints, cards, slides, museum publications, uncommon objects, original arts & crafts
L **Clarence Ward Art Library,** Allen Art Bldg, Main & Lorain Sts, 44074. Tel 216-775-8635; Elec Mail jeffrey_weidman@qmgate.cc.oberlin.edu. *Art Librn* Dr Jeffrey Weidman
Open Mon - Thurs 8:30 AM - 5:30 PM & 7 - 11 PM, Fri 8:30 AM - 5:30 PM, Sat 1 - 6 PM, Sun 1 - 5 PM & 7 - 11 PM. Estab 1917 to serve the library needs of the art department, the Allen Memorial Art Museum & the Oberlin College community in the visual arts
Income: Financed by appropriations from Oberlin College Libraries
Library Holdings: Vols 75,000; Per subs 250; Auction sales catalogs 10,000; Other — Clipping files, pamphlets
Special Subjects: Advertising Design, Aesthetics, Afro-American Art, American Indian Art, American Western Art, Anthropology, Antiquities-Assyrian, Antiquities-Byzantine, Antiquities-Egyptian, Antiquities-Etruscan, Archaeology, Architecture
Collections: Jefferson & Arts Collections of early architectural books; †artists' books
Publications: Bibliographies & library guides
Activities: Classes for adults; tours

OXFORD

M **MIAMI UNIVERSITY,** Art Museum, Patterson Ave, 45056. Tel 513-529-2232; *Acting Dir* James Robeson; *Cur Coll* Edna Carter Southard; *Cur Educ* Bonnie C Mason; *Registrar* Beverly Bach; *Preparator* Mark DeGennaro
Open Tues - Sun 11 AM - 5 PM, cl Mon & university holidays. Estab 1972, Art Mus facility opened Fall 1978, to care for & exhibit University art collections, to arrange for a variety of traveling exhibitions & for the educational & cultural enrichment of the University & the region. Mus is maintained with exhibition space of 9000 sq ft, consisting of 5 galleries in contemporary building designed by Walter A Netsch, Skidmore, Owing & Merrill, Chicago; operates the McGuffey Mus, home of William Holmes McGuffey, a national historic landmark; accredited by the American Assoc of Museums. Average Annual Attendance: 50,000. Mem: 1000; dues $25 & up
Income: Financed by gift & state appropriation
Collections: Charles M Messer Leica Camera Collection; Ancient Art; Decorative Arts; International Folk Art, largely Middle European, Middle Eastern, Mexican, Central & South America; European & American paintings, prints & sculpture; African art; Chinese Art; Gandharan art; Native American Art; Oceanic Art; photography; textiles
Exhibitions: Twelve per year Looking Back: 20th Century American Art; From Puri to Bombay: Art of India
Publications: Brochures; catalogs approx 6-8 per year; quarterly newsletter
Activities: Programs for adults & children; docent training; lect open to public, 5-6 vis lectr per year; concerts; gallery talks; tours; individual paintings & original objects of art lent to qualified museums in US; book traveling exhibitions 2-3 per year; originate traveling exhibitions; museum shop sells books, magazines, original art, prints, notecards, jewelry & collectibles
L **Wertz Art & Architecture Library,** New Art Bldg, Rm 16, 45056. Tel 513-529-1904; Elec Mail olsonjd@muohio.edu. *Librn* Joann Olson
Open Mon - Thurs 9 AM - 10 PM, Fri 9 AM - 5 PM, Sat 1 - 5 PM, Sun 1 - 10 PM during academic year. Estab to support the programs of the Schools of Art & Architecture & related disciplines
Library Holdings: Vols 45,000; Per & serial subs 295; Micro — Fiche; Other — Exhibition catalogs
Special Subjects: Afro-American Art, American Indian Art, American Western Art, Architecture, Art Education, Decorative Arts, Folk Art, History of Art & Archaeology, Latin American Art, Marine Painting, Mexican Art, Oriental Art, Painting - American, Photography, Southwestern Art

PAINESVILLE

M **ARCHAEOLOGICAL SOCIETY OF OHIO,** Indian Museum of Lake County, Ohio, 391 W Washington St, 44077. Tel 216-352-1911; *Dir* Gwen G King; *Asst Dir* Ann Dewald
Open Mon - Fri 9 AM - 4 PM, Sat & Sun 1 - 4 PM, cl major holiday weekends. Admis donations suggested. Estab 1980 to educate & preserve arts & crafts of all cultures of Native Americans. Average Annual Attendance: 7000. Mem: 250; dues $18-$1000
Income: Financed by mem
Collections: Crafts & art of all cultures of Native Americans of North America; Prehistoric artifacts from 10,000 BC to 1650 AD of early Ohio area & Reeve Village Site, Lake County, Ohio
Activities: Classes for adults & children; docent training; lect open to public; tours; competitions with awards; museum shop sells books
L **Indian Museum Library,** 391 W Washington St, 44077. Tel 216-352-1911; *Dir* Gwen King
For reference
Income: Financed by mem
Library Holdings: Vols 700; Per subs 4
Special Subjects: American Indian Art, Archaeology, Eskimo Art

PORTSMOUTH

M **SOUTHERN OHIO MUSEUM CORPORATION,** Southern Ohio Museum & Cultural Center, 825 Gallia St, PO Box 990, 45662. Tel 614-354-5629; FAX 614-354-4090; *Admin Dir* Kay Bouyack; *Dir Planning* Sara Johnson
Open Tues & Fri 10 AM - 5 PM, Sat & Sun 1 - 5 PM. Admis adults $1, children $.75. Estab 1977 to provide exhibitions & performances. Museum facility is a renovated & refurbished neo-classical building, 21,000 sq ft, constructed in 1918 as a bank. Facility has two temporary exhibit galleries & a theatre. Average Annual Attendance: 30,000. Mem: 1000; dues family $25
Income: $200,000 (financed by endowment, mem & city appropriation)
Collections: Clarence Carter Paintings; watercolors & prints
Exhibitions: Contemporary & traditional arts, history, science or humanities
Publications: Annual report; exhibition catalogs
Activities: Classes for adults & children; dramatic programs; docent training; lect open to public, 5 vis lectr per year; exten dept serves county; book traveling exhibitions; originates traveling exhibitions; museum shop sells books, gift items, jewelry & prints

SALEM

A **G G DRAYTON CLUB,** 864 Heritage Lane, 44460. Tel 330-332-0959; *Pres* Patricia Bauman; *VPres* Thomas Bauman; *Treasurer* Jerry Wine
Estab 1979 to research Grace Drayton's art work. Mem: 80; dues $6 per yr
Income: $500 (financed by mem)
Collections: †Grace G Drayton Collection
Publications: International G G Drayton Association Newsletter, quarterly
Activities: Lect open to public

SPRINGFIELD

M **CLARK COUNTY HISTORICAL SOCIETY,** PO Box 2157, 45501. Tel 937-324-0657; *Pres* William Kinnison; *Exec Dir & Cur Museum* Floyd Barmann
Open Mon - Fri 10 AM - 4 PM; Sat 9 AM - 1 PM. Estab 1897 for collection & preservation of Clark County history & historical artifacts. Average Annual Attendance: 4000-5000. Mem: 600; dues patron $50, family $15, individual $10, senior citizen $7.50; annual meeting Nov
Income: $55,000 (financed by appropriation)
Collections: European Landscapes; Oil Paintings, mostly mid-late 19th century, of prominent Springfielders; artifacts
Publications: Newsletter, monthly; annual monograph
Activities: Monthly meetings & lect open to public; tours; restoration project: The David Crabill Homestead (1826), located at Lake Lagonda in Buck Creek State Park; individual paintings & original objects of art lent to museums; lending collection contains 150 original artworks, 50 original prints, 75 paintings & 2000 photographs; sales shop sells books
L **Library,** 818 N Fountain, 45504. Tel 937-324-0657; *Dir* Floyd Barmann; *Cur* Virginia Weygandt
Open Tues - Fri 10 AM - 4 PM. For reference only
Library Holdings: Vols 4000; Micro — Reels; Other — Clipping files, manuscripts, memorabilia, original art works
Collections: Photograph Collection

M **SPRINGFIELD MUSEUM OF ART,** 107 Cliff Park Rd, 45501. Tel 937-325-4673; FAX 937-325-4674; Elec Mail smoa@erinet.com; Internet Home Page Address spfld.museum.of.art.com. *Pres* Lorinda B Bartell; *First VPres* Steven Sharp; *Second VPres* Sara Landess; *Treas* W Staler; *Dir* Mark J Chepp
Open Tues - Fri 9 AM - 5 PM; Sat 9 AM - 3 PM; Sun 2 - 4 PM; cl Mon. No admis fee. Estab 1951 for educational & cultraul purposes, particularly the encouragement of the appreciation, study of, participation in & enjoyment of the fine arts. Average Annual Attendance: 30,000. Mem: 1000; dues benefactor $100, sustaining $50, family $35, individual $25; meetings third Tues in June
Income: $250,000 (financed by endowment, mem & tuition fees)
Collections: 19th & 20th Century Artists (mostly American, some French)
Exhibitions: (1997) Paintings from the Collection of the Clark County Historical Society; BuKang Kim: 1987-1997; How Great Thou Art; Sam Martineau: Recent Work; Annnual Springfield Museum of Art Faculty/Student Exhibition; Daniel Kaniess: Recent Work; Annual Members' Juried Exhibition; Deborah Morrissey-McGoff: 1987-1997; Historic Ohio Quilts from the Mina White Collection. (1997-98) The Western Ohio Watercolor Society Juried Exhibition. (1998) Archie Byron: Out of Print: British Printmaking 1946-1976; Annual Springfield Museum of Art Faculty & Student Exhibition; Elizabeth Hertz: Recent Works;

Annual Members' Juried Exhibition; Ohio Designer Craftsmen Annual Exhibition. (1998-99) The Western Ohio Watercolor Society Juried Exhibition
Publications: Newsletter, bi-monthly
Activities: Classes for adults & children; docent training; lect open to public, 6 vis lectr per year; tours; gallery talks; competitions with prizes; scholarships offered; individual paintings & original objects of art lent; book traveling exhibitions; originate traveling exhibitions; sales shop selling original art and prints
L **Library,** 107 Cliff Park Rd, 45501. Tel 937-325-4673; FAX 937-325-4674; *Dir* Mark Chepp
Open Tues - Fri 9 AM - 5 PM, Sat 9 AM - 3 PM, Sun 2 - 4 PM. Estab 1973 for art study. For reference only. Average Annual Attendance: 35,000
Income: Financed by endowment & mem
Library Holdings: Vols 4500; AV — Slides 400; Other — Clipping files, exhibition catalogs, pamphlets
Special Subjects: Art Education, Art History, Photography
Collections: Axel Bahnsen Photograph Collection
Activities: Lectures open to public; scholarships

SYLVANIA

L **LOURDES COLLEGE,** Duns Scotus Library, 6832 Convent Blvd, 43560. Tel 419-885-3211; FAX 419-882-3786; *Libr Dir* Sr Mary Thomas More
Estab 1949. Art pieces exhibited on walls of three academic bldgs; classroom & library
Library Holdings: Vols 66,600; Per subs 420; Micro — Fiche 11,134; AV — A-tapes, cassettes, fs, rec, slides, v-tapes; Other — Manuscripts, memorabilia, original art works, pamphlets, prints, reproductions, sculpture
Special Subjects: Afro-American Art, American Indian Art, American Western Art, Art Education, Art History, Asian Art, Calligraphy, Ceramics, Commercial Art, Crafts, Decorative Arts, Drawings, Enamels, Etchings & Engravings, Graphic Arts
Collections: †350 art pieces in library cataloged
Activities: Lect open to public; tours; scholarships & fels offered

TOLEDO

C **OWENS-CORNING CORPORATION,** Art Collection, One Owens Corning Pky, 43659. Tel 419-248-6179; *Cur* Penny McMorris
Open to pub by appointment only. Estab 1968 to create a pleasant & stimulating work environment for employees; to provide a focal point for contemporary art; supporting the arts both through purchase of works and display of the collection. Collection displayed in company offices in Toledo & other cities
Collections: Approximately 1000 works of art by contemporary American artists

A **SPECTRUM GALLERY,** Toledo Botanical Garden, 5403 Elmer Dr, 43615. Tel 419-531-7769; *Coordr* Pat Johnson
Open Mon - Fri Noon - 5 PM, Sat & Sun 1 - 4 PM, Dec Tues 1 - 5 PM, Sat & Sun 1 - 4 PM. No admis fee. Estab 1975 to encourage & support pub appreciation of fine art & to organize & promote related activities; promote mutual understanding & cooperation among artists, artist groups & the pub promote beautification of Toledo through use of art work. Clubhouse (3 galleries, sales room office & working studio) part of Artist Village in Toledo Botanical Garden; large adjacent Art Educ Center. Average Annual Attendance: 15,000-20,000. Mem: 175
Income: $20,000 (financed by mem & fund-raising events, sales of art, donations & art classes)
Exhibitions: Juried Membership Show; Crosby Festival of the Arts; Toledo Festival; spot exhibitions
Publications: Spectrum (newsletter), bi-monthly
Activities: Classes for adults & children; lect open to public, 4-5 vis lectr per year; competitions; traveling exhibitions organized & circulated; sales shop sells original art

A **TOLEDO ARTISTS' CLUB,** Toledo Botanical Garden, 5403 Elmer Dr, 43615. Tel 419-531-4079; *Office Mgr* Margie Carlile; *VPres* Betty Jean Jacobson
Open Mon - Fri 12 - 4 PM, Sat 9 AM - 1 PM. Estab 1943 to promote art in the area. New Clubhouse-Gallery opened at Crosby Gardens, Toledo in August 1979. Mem: 400-500; dues $15 (variable)
Income: Financed by mem & exhibitions
Exhibitions: Approximately 80 pieces of artwork exhibited each month in main gallery; includes paintings, pottery, sculpture, stained glass
Publications: Newsletter, monthly
Activities: Classes for adults and children; workshops; demonstrations; lect open to the public; competitions; jointly present Crosby Gardens Arts Festival in June with Crosby Gardens, Toledo Forestry Division & the Arts Commission of Greater Toledo; sales shop selling original art

A **TOLEDO MUSEUM OF ART,** 2445 Monroe St, 43620. Tel 419-255-8000; FAX 419-244-2217; *Dir* David Steadman; *First VPres* Helen Zeller; *Second VPres* Nathalie Davis; *Treas* Scott Heacock; *Assoc Coordr Exhib* Steve Frushour
Open 10 AM - 4 PM. No admis fee. Juried exhibition each spring of local artist. State of the art display gallery, 6000 sq ft, track lighting, environmentally controlled. Average Annual Attendance: 5000. Mem: 15 area clubs; dues $10; meetings first Sat after first Fri (Oct - May)
Income: Financed by mem, community contributions & exhibition entry charges
Collections: †Permanent collection
Exhibitions: Annual Exhibition
Publications: Annual Exhibit Catalogue
Activities: Competitions with cash awards; individual paintings & original objects of art lent to area civic & public institutions; lending collection contains original art works

M **TOLEDO MUSEUM OF ART,** 2445 Monroe St at Scottwood Ave, PO Box 1013, 43697. Tel 419-255-8000; Cable TOLMUSART. *Pres* David Welles Sr; *Dir* David W Steadman; *Deputy Dir* Roger M Berkowitz; *Registrar* Patricia Whitesides; *Asst to Dir* John S Stanley; *Chmn Museum Educ* Stef Stahl; *Chmn University Educ* Thomas Lingeman; *Cur Contemporary Art* Robert F Phillips; *Cur Ancient Art* Kurt T Luckner; *Cur Graphic Arts* Christine Swenson; *Mgr Performing Arts* Joyce Smar; *Public Information* Barbara Van Vleet; *Mgr Personnel* Robert Oates; *Cur 19th & 20th Century Glass* Davira Taragin; *Cur European Painting & Sculpture Before 1900* Lawrence Nichols
Open Tues - Sat 10 AM - 4 PM, Sun 1 - 5 PM, cl Mon & legal holidays; Collector's Corner open Tues - Sat 10 AM - 4 PM, Sun 1 - 4:30 PM. No admis fee. Estab & incorporated 1901; building erected 1912, additions 1926 & 1933. Mus contains Canaday Gallery, Print Galleries, Glass Gallery, School Gallery, Collector's Corner for sales & rental, a book store & an art supply store. Average Annual Attendance: 265,000. Mem: 9000; dues $35 & up
Collections: Ancient to modern glass; European paintings, sculpture & decorative arts; American paintings, sculpture & decorative arts; books & manuscripts; Egyptian, Greek, Roman, Near & Far East art, African art
Publications: American Paintings; Ancient Glass; Art in Glass; Corpus Vasorum Antiquorum I & II; European Paintings; Guide to the Collections
Activities: Classes for adults & children; lect; concerts; tours; book traveling exhibitions; originate traveling exhibitions
L **Library,** PO Box 1013, 43697. Tel 419-255-8000, Ext 280; FAX 419-255-4450; *Librn* Anne O Morris; *Asst Librn (Reference)* Diane Scoles; *Asst Librn (Technical)* Marilyn Czerniejewski
Open Mon - Thurs 10 AM - 9 PM, Fri 10 AM - 5 PM, Sat Noon - 4 PM; during university sessions, Sun 1 - 4:30 PM. Estab 1901 to provide resources for the museum's staff. Primarily for reference but does lend to certain groups of users
Library Holdings: Vols 60,000; Per subs 300; Micro — Fiche, reels 75; AV — A-tapes 250, slides, v-tapes; Other — Clipping files, exhibition catalogs 17,000
Special Subjects: Art History, Decorative Arts, Glass, Graphic Arts, Painting - American, Painting - European, Photography

VAN WERT

M **WASSENBERG ART CENTER,** 643 S Washington St, 45891. Tel 419-238-6837; *Dir* Michele L Smith; *Office Mgr* Kay R Sluterbeck
Open daily 1 - 5 PM, cl Mon. No admis fee. Estab 1961 to encourage the arts in the Van Wert area. Two large gallery areas, basement classroom; maximum exhibit 150 pieces. Average Annual Attendance: 1500. Mem: 350; dues individual $15, various other; annual meeting in Jan, date varies
Income: $20,000 (financed by endowment, mem, fundraisers)
Library Holdings: Vols 250; Per subs 6; AV — A-tapes, cassettes, fs, slides, v-tapes; Other — Original art works, prints, reproductions, sculpture
Collections: Wassenberg Collection; Prints & Original Art; All subjects/all media
Exhibitions: Annual June Art Exhibit; Annual Oct Photography Exhibit
Publications: Gallery Review, bi-monthly
Activities: Classes for adults & children; docent programs; lect open to public, some only to members; competitions; scholarships & fels offered; book traveling exhibitions 6-8 per year

VERMILION

M **GREAT LAKES HISTORICAL SOCIETY,** Island Seas Maritime Museum, 480 Main St, PO Box 435, 44089. FAX 216-967-1519; Elec Mail glhs1@aol.com. WATS 800-893-1485. *Exec Dir* William A O'Brien
Open daily 10 AM - 5 PM. Admis adults $5, seniors $4, youth $3, children under 6 free. Estab 1944 to promote interest in discovering and preserving material about the Great Lakes and surrounding areas. Maintains an art gallery as part of the Maritime History Museum. Average Annual Attendance: 20,000 & up. Mem: 2800; dues family $39; annual meetings in May & Oct
Income: $300,000 (financed by endowment, mem, sales from mus store & fundraising)
Collections: †Collection of Ship Models; †Marine Relics; †Paintings & †Photographs dealing with the history of the Great Lakes; paintings by Sprague, Shogren, LaMarre, Nickerson, Forsythe & Huntington
Exhibitions: Annual Model Boat Show Exhibition
Publications: Chadburn (newsletter), quarterly; Inland Seas, quarterly journal
Activities: Classes for adults & children; dramatic programs; docent training; boat building & lofting classes; lect open to public, 8 vis lectr per year; gallery talks; tours; competitions with prizes; individual painting lent to other museums; book traveling exhibitions 1 per year; originate traveling exhibitions; museum shop sells books, reproductions, prints, slides & videotapes

WELLINGTON

M **SOUTHERN LORAIN COUNTY HISTORICAL SOCIETY,** Spirit of '76 Museum, 201 N Main, PO Box 76, 44090. Tel 216-647-4367; *Pres* Dick Landis; *VPres* Phyllis Perkins; *Cur* Diane Stanley
Open Apr - Oct Sat & Sun 2:30 - 5 PM, groups of ten or more any time by reservation. No admis fee. Estab 1970 to memorialize Archibald M Willard who created the Spirit of '76, nation's most inspirational painting. Average Annual Attendance: 2000. Mem: 259; dues couple $10, individual $5; annual meeting in Apr
Income: $10,000 (financed by mem, gifts & gift shop)
Purchases: $10,000
Collections: Archibald M Willard Paintings; artifacts of local interest; memorabilia of Myron T Herrick
Publications: Quarterly newsletters
Activities: Sales shop sells books, reproductions, prints & miscellaneous items

WESTERVILLE

AMERICAN CERAMIC SOCIETY
For further information, see National and Regional Organizations

M **THE AMERICAN CERAMIC SOCIETY,** Ross C Purdy Museum of Ceramics, 735 Ceramic Pl, 43081. Tel 614-890-4700; FAX 614-899-6109; *Dir Communications* Mark Glasper; *Cur* William Gates; *Asst Cur* Yvonne Manring
No admis fee. Estab 1981 to display past, present & future of the ceramic industry. Mem: Annual meeting in Apr
Purchases: Ceramic hip implant, Rockingham pitcher & 30 piece ceramic tile collection
Collections: †Consists of over 2000 pieces representing a cross section of traditional & high-tech ceramics produced in the last 150 years; †commercial ceramics
Exhibitions: Traditional ceramic products such as brick, glass, dinnerware. High-tech displays include aerospace, bioceramics, automotive engines, sporting goods, military & environmental applications
Activities: Classes for children; docent programs; lending collection contains 2000 original objects of art
L **James I Mueller Ceramic Information Center,** 735 Ceramic Pl, 43081. Tel 614-890-4700; FAX 614-899-6109;
Estab 1954. For reference only; lending to members
Library Holdings: Vols 9782; Per subs 790; Micro — Fiche; AV — V-tapes; Other — Clipping files, photographs

WEST LIBERTY

M **PIATT CASTLES,** 10051 Rd 47, PO Box 497, 43357-0497. Tel 513-465-2821; Elec Mail macochee@logan.net. *Dir* Margaret Piatt; *Prog Mgr* James Nash
Open May - Sept daily 11 AM - 5 PM, Mar Sat & Sun Noon - 4 PM, Apr & Oct daily Noon - 4 PM. Admis adults $6, seniors & students $5, children 5-12 $3. Paintings & sculptures displayed throughout both homes - room like settings. Average Annual Attendance: 40,000
Collections: Early American family furnishings; European & Asian furnishings; Native American artifacts; Rare Art; Weapons
Publications: Brochures
Activities: Dramatic programs; docent training; tours

WILBERFORCE

AFRICAN AMERICAN ASSOCIATION
For further information, see National and Regional Organizations

M **OHIO HISTORICAL SOCIETY,** National Afro American Museum & Cultural Center, 1350 Brush Row Rd, PO Box 578, 45384-0578. *Dir* John E Fleming PhD; *Asst Dir* Vernon Courtney; *Cur* Floyd Thomas PhD; *Assoc Librn* Sue T Parker; *Educ Dir* Frank Eguargie PhD
Open Tues - Sun. Estab 1987. Maintains staff reference library
Collections: African American History & Literature
Exhibitions: Dolls; Photography

WILLOUGHBY

A **FINE ARTS ASSOCIATION,** School of Fine Arts, 38660 Mentor Ave, 44094. Tel 216-951-7500; FAX 216-975-4592; *Pres* Robert H Wigton; *Executive Dir* Charles Frank
Open Mon - Fri 9 AM - 8 PM, Sat 9 AM - 5 PM. No admis fee. Estab 1957 to bring arts education to all people regardless of their ability to pay, race or social standing. Main floor gallery houses theme, one-man & group monthly exhibitions; 2nd floor gallery houses monthly school exhibits. Average Annual Attendance: 70,000. Mem: 500; dues $25 and up; annual meeting Sept
Income: Financed by class fees and donations
Exhibitions: Monthly exhibitions, theme, one man & group; Annual juried exhibit for area artists
Activities: Classes for adults & children; dramatic programs; lect open to public, 10 vis lectr per year; gallery talks; tours; concerts; competitions with awards; scholarships

WOOSTER

M **THE COLLEGE OF WOOSTER,** Art Museum, University St, 44691. Tel 330-263-2495; FAX 216-263-2633; Elec Mail kzurko.acs.wooster.edu. WATS 800-321-9885. *Dir* Thalia Gouma-Peterson; *Cur* Kathleen McManus-Zurko
Open Mon - Fri 9 AM - Noon & 1 - 5 PM, Sun 2 - 5 PM. No admis fee
Income: Financed by college general fund & grants
Collections: John Taylor Arms Print Collection; African art; ancient & contemporary ceramics; Chinese snuff bottles & bronzes; Cypriote pottery; decorative arts; ethnographic materials; WWII posters
Exhibitions: Frequent traveling exhibitions & special in-house exhibitions. Average six yearly exhibitions drawn either from the collections or focusing on the work of contemporary American artists
Publications: Exhibition catalogs
Activities: Lect & receptions open to public

MIDWEST ART HISTORY SOCIETY
For further information, see National and Regional Organizations

M **WAYNE CENTER FOR THE ARTS,** 237 S Walnut St, 44691. Tel 330-264-8596; *Exec Dir* Roberta Looney; *Asst to Dir* Isabel Matson
Open Sun - Fri 2 - 5 PM. No admis fee. Estab 1944 to provide an opportunity for students, faculty & the local community to view original works of art. The gallery is housed in a former library; Main floor has large open areas & upper balcony more intimate exhibition space. Average Annual Attendance: 5000

Income: $20,000 (financed through college)
Collections: Chinese bronzes & porcelains; paintings; prints; tapestries; African artifacts; contemporary American ceramics
Exhibitions: Traveling & monthly exhibitions; Dr Bing Davis: African American Art; Edward S Curtis: Native American Photographs from the turn of the century
Publications: Exhibition catalogues, 2 per yr
Activities: Lect open to public, 10-15 vis lectr per year; gallery talks; book traveling exhibitions

M **WAYNE COUNTY HISTORICAL SOCIETY,** 546 E Bowman St, 44691. Tel 330-264-8856; *Pres* Paul Locher; *Treas* Rachel Fetzer; *Treas* Ethel Parker
Open Tues - Sun 2 - 4:30 PM, cl Mon & holidays. Admis adults $1, students $.50, under 14 free. Estab 1955 to discover, preserve & pass on the history of Wayne County. Main building built in 1815 is furnished partially as a home; one room school house, log cabin, building with model carpenter shop, model blacksmith shop, rebuilt 1890's general store to open spring 1995. Average Annual Attendance: 2000. Mem: 650; dues $10 - $200; annual meeting in Apr, quarterly meetings Jan, Apr, July, Oct
Income: Financed by mem, county commissioners
Collections: Memorabilia of Wayne County inhabitants, furnishings, artisans' tools
Publications: Baker's 1856 Map of Wayne Co, 1820 Tax Lists: Census, 1826 tax lists with details Wayne Co, Caldwell's Atlas of Wayne Co 1873 & 1897, Wayne Co Will Abstracts, Estates & Guardianships 1813 - 1852 Vol 1852 - 1900 Vol II, Wayne Co Abstracts of Naturalization 1812 - 1903, 75 years of Wayne Co marriages, History of Wayne Co, Wayne Co Burial Records, Early Land Records Wayne Co; quarterly newsletter
Activities: Dramatic programs; lect open to public, 5 vis lectr per year

WORTHINGTON

A **WORTHINGTON ARTS COUNCIL,** 777 High St, PO Box 612, 43085. Tel 614-431-0329; FAX 614-431-2491; *Exec Dir* Jeanne Earhart; *Visual Arts Coordr* Meredith Martin
Estab 1977 to encourage & stimulate the practice & appreciation of the arts by providing people opportunities in the community to participate in, experience & enjoy the arts so as to enrich the quality of daily life & further cultural growth of Worthington & to help the art & cultural organizations of the city grow & flourish
Activities: Lect open to public; concerts; performance series; scholarships offered

XENIA

A **GREENE COUNTY HISTORICAL SOCIETY,** 74 W Church St, 45385-2902. Tel 513-372-4606; *Exec Secy* Joan Baxter
Open Tues & Fri 9 AM - Noon & 1 - 3:30 PM. Admis adult $2. Estab 1929 to preserve the history of Greene County, OH. Average Annual Attendance: 2000. Mem: 450; dues individual $10, seniors $6; annual meeting in June
Income: Financed by mem, county appropriation & various fund raising activities
Collections: Clothing; Medical; Military; †Railroad (historic model)
Exhibitions: Conestoga Wagon; Log House & furnishings; Railroad; Victorian House & furnishings
Publications: Broadstone 1918 History Reprint; Next Stop... Xenia
Activities: Lect open to public, 12 vis lectr per year; sales shop sells books, note paper, materials relating to county

YELLOW SPRINGS

M **ANTIOCH COLLEGE,** Noyes & Read Galleries, 45387. Tel 513-767-7331; *Prof Art* Karen Shirley
Open Mon - Fri 1 - 4 PM. No admis fee. Estab 1972. Noyes Gallery to offer works to students & the community that both challenge & broaden their definitions of Art; Read Gallery is primarily a student gallery

YOUNGSTOWN

M **BUTLER INSTITUTE OF AMERICAN ART,** Art Museum, 524 Wick Ave, 44502. Tel 330-743-1107; FAX 330-743-9567; Elec Mail butler@cis.cisnet.com; Internet Home Page Address http://www.butlerart.com. *Dir* Dr Louis A Zona; *Assoc Dir* Clyde Singer; *Dir Educ* Carole O'Brien
Open Tues, Thur - Sat 11 AM - 4 PM; Wed 11 AM - 8 PM; Sun Noon - 4 PM. No admis fee. Estab 1919 & is the first museum building to be devoted entirely to American Art. Eighteen galleries containing 11,000 works of American artists. Average Annual Attendance: 212,000. Mem: 4000; dues $10-$3000; annual meetings in May
Income: Financed by endowment, grants & gifts
Collections: Comprehensive collection of American art covering three centuries; American Impressionism; the American West & Marine & Sports Art collections; Principle artists: Winslow Homer, Albert Bierstadt, Martin Johnson Heade, Georgia O'Keeffe, Charles Sheeler, Helen Frankenthaler, John S Sargent, J M Whistler, Mary Cassatt, Thomas Cole, Edward Hopper, Romare Bearden, Andy Warhol & Robert Motherwell †American Glass Bells, Miniatures of all the Presidents of the United States (watercolor)
Exhibitions: American Artists Celebrate the Eighth Art; Area Artists Annual; Charles Burchfield; Leo Castelli Collection (drawings & prints); The Complete Prints of Alfred Leslie; Nasjos Daphnis Color & Form: A Retrospective; Fireworks; Patrick Ireland: Gestures; Robert Motherwell: The Elegy Series; Philip Pearlstein, The Abstract Landscapes; Larry Rivers: Public & Private; Sounding the Depts; annual midyear show (national painting survey) Area Artists Annual; Youngstown State University Annual; one-person exhibitions
Publications: Exhibition catalogues; bi-monthly newsletter; bienniel report
Activities: Classes for children & adults; docent training; lect open to the public, 15 vis lectr per year; concerts; gallery talks; tours; competitions with awards;

individual paintings & original objects of art lent to qualified mus, institutions, world wide; book traveling exhibitions 10 per year; traveling exhibitions organized & circulated; museum shop sells books, original art, reproductions, prints, slides, crafts, jewelry, original pottery & art related materials
L **Hopper Resource Library,** 524 Wick Ave, 44502. Tel 330-743-1107, 743-1711
Open Tues, Thurs, Fri & Sat 11 AM - 4 PM, Wed 11 AM - 8 PM, Sun Noon - 4 PM. No admis fee. For reference only. Average Annual Attendance: 122,000. Mem: 3090
Income: Financed by endowment, grants & gifts
Library Holdings: Vols 1500; Per subs 10; AV — Kodachromes, slides; Other — Clipping files, exhibition catalogs, framed reproductions, memorabilia, pamphlets, photographs
Special Subjects: American Art

ZANESVILLE

A **ZANESVILLE ART CENTER,** 620 Military Rd, 43701. Tel 614-452-0741; FAX 614-452-0797; *Dir* Philip LaDouceur; *Secy & Registrar* Sara McCall; *Pres Board Trustees* Bill Plummer; *Cur Oriental Art* Mrs Willis Bailey; *Cur Glass* William Brown
Open Tues - Sun 1 - 5 PM; cl Mon & holidays. No admis fee. Estab 1936 to provide a pub center for the arts & crafts, permanent collections & temporary exhibitions, classes in arts & crafts, library of art volumes & a meeting place for art & civic groups. There are fifteen galleries for Old & Modern Masters' paintings, sculpture, prints, ceramics, glass, photography, children's art & gift art; handicapped facilities. Average Annual Attendance: 25,000. Mem: 350; dues $10 & up
Income: Financed by endowment & mem
Collections: †American, European & †Oriental Paintings, Sculptures, Ceramics, Prints, Drawings, & Crafts; †Children's Art; †Midwest & †Zanesville Ceramics & Glass
Exhibitions: Annual AAUW Children's Art Shows; Selections from Zanesville Art Center Permanent Collections; Bruce Evans' Kachinas; Bill Sailing's Life Size Wood Sculptures; Black History; Karl Kappes Retrospective; Artists Who Teach; Alan Cottrill Sculpture; Sall Emslie Plexiglass Boxes; 52nd Annual May Art & Craft Show; Marvin & Ann Trieuba Paintings & Hangings; Ken Frick Photos; Rosanna Moore Wood Carvings; Tom & Gail Turner Ceramics; Christiane Curry Small Paintings; Linda & Ken Shaffer Hangings & Paintings; Southeastern Ohio Watermedia Society Show; Ceramics of Today by Zanesville Art Center Permanent Collections; Ohio Watercolor Society Show; Gary Bryan Carved Painted Birds; Tom Haynes Collection Ancient Chinese Ceramics
Publications: Bulletin, tri-monthly
Activities: Classes for adults & children; docent training; lect open to public, 5 vis lectr per year; concerts; gallery talks; tours; competitions with awards; individual paintings lent to public institutions; lending collection contains art works, original prints, photographs sculptures, 6000 pieces of original art works & 2000 paintings; sales shop sells books & original art
L **Library,** 620 Military Rd, 43701. Tel 614-452-0741; FAX 614-452-0741; *Registrar & Librn* Sara McCall
Open Tues - Sun 1 - 5 PM, cl Mon & major holidays. Estab 1936 to provide fine arts & crafts information & exhibitions
Income: Financed by endowment, mem, trust funds & investments
Library Holdings: Vols 8000; Per subs 10; AV — Fs 20, Kodachromes 10,000, lantern slides, slides 10,000; Other — Clipping files, exhibition catalogs, framed reproductions 10, original art works, pamphlets, photographs, prints, reproductions, sculpture
Special Subjects: Midwest Glass & Ceramics
Publications: Bulletins; gallery brochures

OKLAHOMA

ANADARKO

M **NATIONAL HALL OF FAME FOR FAMOUS AMERICAN INDIANS,** PO Box 548, 73005. Tel 405-247-5555; *Dir & Exec VPres* Joe McBride; *Treas* George F Moran; *Secy* Carolyn N McBride
Open Mon - Sat 9 AM - 5PM, Sun 1 - 5 PM. No admis fee. Estab 1952 to honor famous American Indians who have contributed to the culture of America, including statesmen, innovators, sportsmen, warriors; to teach the youth of our country that there is a reward for greatness. An outdoor Museum in a landscaped area containing bronze sculptured portraits of honorees. Average Annual Attendance: 20,000. Mem: 250; dues life $100, Individual or Family $25; annual meeting Aug
Income: Finance by mem, city & state appropriation & donation
Purchases: $2500 - $20,000
Collections: †Bronze sculptured portraits & bronze statues of two animals important to Indian culture
Publications: Brochure
Activities: Dedication ceremonies for honorees in August; Sales shop sells books & postcards

M **SOUTHERN PLAINS INDIAN MUSEUM,** US Hwy 62, PO Box 749, 73005. Tel 405-247-6221; *Chief Cur* Rosemary Ellison
Open June - Sept Mon - Sat 9 AM - 5 PM; Sun 1 - 5 PM; Oct - May Tues - Sat 9 AM - 5 PM, Sun 1 - 5 PM; cl New Year's Day, Thanksgiving & Christmas. Estab 1947-48 to promote the development of contemporary native American arts & crafts of the United States. Administered & operated by the Indian Arts & Crafts Board, US Department of the Interior. Average Annual Attendance: 80,000
Income: Financed by federal appropriation
Purchases: Primarily dependent upon gifts
Collections: Contemporary native American arts & crafts of the United States;

Historic Works by Southern Plains Indian Craftsmen
Exhibitions: Historic Southern Plains Indian Arts; changing exhibitions by contemporary native American artists & craftsmen; continuing series of one-person exhibitions
Publications: One-person exhibition brochure series, quarterly
Activities: Gallery talks

ARDMORE

A **CHARLES B GODDARD CENTER FOR THE VISUAL & PERFORMING ARTS,** First & D St SW, PO Box 1624, 73402. Tel 405-226-0909; *Chmn* Lillian Williams; *Treas* John Snodgrass; *Dir* Mort Hamilton; *Admin Asst* Becky Jones
Open Mon - Fri 9 AM -4 PM, Sat & Sun 1 - 4 PM. No admis fee. Estab Mar 1970 to bring fine art programs in the related fields of music, art & theater to local community at minimum cost, gallery to bring traveling exhibitions to Ardmore. Four exhibit galleries. Average Annual Attendance: 35,000. Mem: 400; dues $10-$1000; monthly advisory board meetings, & monthly primary board meeting
Income: $200,000
Collections: †Western & Contemporary Art, paintings, sculpture, prints; †Small collection of Western Art & bronzes; †American Graphic Art; †photography
Exhibitions: Ardmore Art Exhibition; exhibits change monthly
Publications: Outlook, bi-monthly
Activities: Classes for adults & children in art, theatre & dance; docent training; dramatic programs; lect open to public, 5 vis lectr per year; concerts; gallery talks; competitions with awards; tours; individual paintings & original objects of art lent to qualified institutions-museums

BARTLESVILLE

M **FRANK PHILLIPS FOUNDATION INC,** Woolaroc Museum, State Hwy 123, Route 3 (Mailing add: PO Box 1647, 74003). Tel 918-336-0307; FAX 918-336-0084; *Dir* Dick Miller; *Cur Coll* Ken Meek
Open Tues - Sun 10 AM - 5 PM, cl Mon, Thanksgiving & Christmas. Admis 16 & older $2, children under 16 free. Estab 1929 to house art & artifacts of the Southwest. Mus dedicated by Frank Phillips. Gallery has two levels, 8 rooms upstairs & 4 rooms downstairs. Average Annual Attendance: 200,000
Income: Financed by endowment & revenues generated by admis fees & sales
Collections: American Indian artifacts; prehistoric artifacts; paintings, drawings, graphics, minerals, oriental material, sculpture, weapons
Publications: Woolaroc Story; Woolaroc, museum guidebook
Activities: Gallery talks; tours; lending collection contains transparencies to be used to illustrate educational publications; book traveling exhibitions; museum & sales shops sell books, magazines, original art, reproductions, prints, slides, Indian-made jewelry and pottery
L **Library,** State Hwy 123, Route 3 (Mailing add: PO Box 1647, 74003). Tel 918-336-0307; FAX 918-336-0084; *Dir* Robert R Lansdown
Circ Reference library open to employees only
Library Holdings: Vols 1000; AV — Kodachromes, slides; Other — Clipping files, exhibition catalogs, pamphlets, photographs

CLAREMORE

M **WILL ROGERS MEMORIAL & MUSEUM,** W Will Rogers Blvd, PO Box 157, 74018. Tel 918-341-0719; FAX 918-341-8246; *Dir* Joseph Carter; *Cur* Gregory Malak
Open daily 8 AM - 5 PM. No admis fee, donations accepted. Estab 1938 to perpetuate the name, works & spirit of Will Rogers. There are eight main galleries, diorama room, foyer & gardens. The large Jo Davidson statue of Will Rogers dominates the foyer; the north gallery includes photographs & paintings of Will Rogers & his ancestors (including a family tree, explaining his Indian heritage) & many other personal items; east gallery has saddle collection & other Western items; Jo Mora dioramas; additional gallery, research library & theatre; children's museum in basement. Average Annual Attendance: 350,000
Income: $750,000 (financed by state appropriation & private donations)
Collections: Borein Etchings; Bust by Electra Wagoner Biggs; Collections of Paintings by various artists commissioned by a calendar company with originals donated to Memorial; Count Tamburini Oil of Will Rogers; Jo Mora Dioramas (13); Large Equestrian Statue by Electra Wagoner Biggs; Mural by Ray Piercey; Original of Will Rogers by Leyendecker; Paintings of Will & his parents by local artists; original of Will Rogers by Charles Banks Wilson; 7-foot oil on canvas by Wayne Cooper of Will Rogers on horseback
Publications: Brochures and materials for students
Activities: Lect; films; assist with publishing project of Will Rogers works at Oklahoma State University; lending collection contains motion pictures, 50 photographs, 144 slides, 20 minute documentary of Will Rogers available to non-profit organizations; originate traveling exhibitions; museum shop selling books, magazines, reproductions of orginial photographs in sepiatone, slides, VHS tapes, Will Rogers & Oklahoma items
L **Media Center Library,** 1720 W Will Rogers Blvd, PO Box 157, 74018-0157. Tel 918-341-0719; FAX 918-341-8246; WATS 800-324-9455. *Dir* Joseph Carter; *Librn* Patricia Lowe; *Cur* Greg Malak
Reference library for research by appointment only
Library Holdings: Vols 2500; Per subs 15; Original writings on CD Rom; AV — A-tapes, cassettes, fs, Kodachromes, motion pictures, rec, slides, v-tapes; Other — Clipping files, framed reproductions, manuscripts, memorabilia, original art works, pamphlets, photographs 1500, prints, reproductions, sculpture
Collections: Will Rogers Collection

CUSHING

L LACHENMEYER ARTS CENTER, Art Resource Library, 700 S Little, PO Box 586, 74023-0586. Tel 918-225-7525; *Dir* Rob Smith
Open Mon, Wed & Fri 9 AM - 5 PM, Tues & Thurs 5 - 9 PM. Estab 1984
Income: Financed by endowment
Library Holdings: Vols 125

ENID

M PHILLIPS UNIVERSITY, Grace Phillips Johnson Art Gallery, 100 S University Ave, PO Box 2000, 73701. Tel 405-237-4433; *Cur Dir* Prof Mary Phillips
Open Tues - Fri 10 AM - 5 PM; Sat, Sun & holidays by appointment only, cl national holidays. No admis fee. Estab 1966
Collections: Decorative arts; historical material of the University; paintings, prints, sculpture
Exhibitions: Exhibitions from the collection; traveling exhibitions
Publications: Exhibition catalogs, bi-annual
Activities: Lect open to the public, 2 vis lectr per year; concerts; gallery talks; book traveling exhibitions

GOODWELL

M NO MAN'S LAND HISTORICAL SOCIETY MUSEUM, Sewell St, PO Box 278, 73939-0278. Tel 405-349-2670; FAX 405-349-2670; *Pres* Henry C Hitch, Jr; *VPres* Gerald Dixon; *Museum Dir* Dr Kenneth R Turner
Open Tues - Sat 9 AM - 5 PM, cl Sun, Mon & holidays. No admis fee. Estab 1934 to procure appropriate mus material with special regard to portraying the history of No Man's Land (Oklahoma Panhandle) & the immediate adjacent regions. The gallery is 14 ft x 40 ft (560 sq ft). Average Annual Attendance: 4000. Mem: 210; dues life 100, organization 100, individual $15
Income: Financed by state appropriation & donations
Collections: Duckett Alabaster Carvings; Oils by Pearl Robison Burrows Burns
Exhibitions: Nine exhibits each year by regional artists

LANGSTON

M LANGSTON UNIVERSITY, Melvin B Tolson Black Heritage Center, PO Box 907, 73050. Tel 405-466-2231; *Dir Library* Niambi Kamoche; *Cur* Bettie Black; *Asst Cur* Edward Grady
Open Mon, Wed & Fri 8 AM - 5 PM, Tues - Thurs 8 PM - 10 PM, Sun 2 - 10 PM. No admis fee. Estab 1959 to exhibit pertinent works of art, both contemporary & traditional; to serve as a teaching tool for students. Average Annual Attendance: 6000
Income: Financed by state appropriation
Collections: African American Art & Artifacts; Paintings & Photographs
Activities: Classes for adults; lect, 2 vis lectr per year; gallery talks; tours

LAWTON

M INSTITUTE OF THE GREAT PLAINS, Museum of the Great Plains, 601 Ferris, PO Box 68, 73502. Tel 405-581-3460; FAX 405-581-3458; *Dir* Steve Wilson; *Archaeologist* Joe Anderson; *Cur Anthropology* Joe Hayes; *Photo Lab Technician* Brian Smith; *Cur Spec Coll* Debby Baroff; *Cur Educ* Dorothy Logan; *Cur Exhib* John Hernandez
Open Mon - Fri 8 AM - 5 PM, Sat 10 AM - 5:30 PM, Sun 1:30 - 5:30 PM. Admis adult $2, child $1. Estab 1960 to collect, preserve, interpret & exhibit items of the cultural history of man in the Great Plains of North America. Galleries of the Mus of the Great Plains express a regional concept of interpreting the relationship of man to a semi-arid plains environment. 27,000 sq ft. Average Annual Attendance: 90,000. Mem: 700; dues $15
Income: Financed by endowment, city & state appropriations
Collections: Archaeological, ethnological, historical & natural science collections relating to man's inhabitance of the Great Plains; photographs relating to Plains Indians, agriculture, settlement, ranching
Exhibitions: History, archaeology & ethnological exhibits
Publications: Great Plains Journal, annual; Contributions to the Museum of the Great Plains 1-9, irregular; Museum Newsletter, irregular
Activities: Classes for adults & children; dramatic programs; docent training; lect open to public, 6 vis lectr per year; gallery talks; tours; lending collections contains framed reproductions, kodachromes, photographs & slides; originate traveling exhibitions; museum shop sells books, magazines, original art, reproductions, prints & slides
L Research Library, PO Box 68, 73502. Tel 405-581-3460; *Cur Spec Coll* Deborah Baroff
Open Mon - Fri 8 AM - 5 PM. Estab 1961 to provide research materials for the 10-state Great Plains region. Lending to staff only
Income: Financed by endowment, city & state appropriations
Library Holdings: Vols 30,000; Per subs 150; Documents 300,000; Micro — Reels; AV — Fs, Kodachromes, motion pictures, slides; Other — Clipping files, exhibition catalogs, manuscripts, memorabilia, original art works, pamphlets, photographs 22,000, prints
Special Subjects: Archaeology, Anthropology
Collections: Archives; photographic collections
Publications: Great Plains Journal, annual; Museum of the Great Plains Newsletter, irregularly

MUSKOGEE

M ATALOA LODGE MUSEUM, 2299 Old Bacone Rd, 74403-1597. Tel 918-683-4581, Ext 283; FAX 918-683-4588; *Dir* Thomas R McKinney
Open Mon - Fri 10 AM - 4:30 PM. Admis $2, group $1 per person. Estab to enhance Indian culture by having a collection of artifacts from various Indian tribes. Three large rooms. Average Annual Attendance: 2000
Income: Financed through Bacone College
Collections: Indian art; Indian crafts & artifacts; silverwork, weapons, blankets, dolls, beadwork, pottery, weaving & basketry
Activities: Tours; sales shop sells books, magazines, original art, reproductions, prints, ceramics, beadwork, silver smithing work, baskets & handcrafted items

M FIVE CIVILIZED TRIBES MUSEUM, Agency Hill, Honor Heights Dr, 74401. Tel 918-683-1701; FAX 918-683-3070; *Pres* Martin A Hagerstrand
Open Mon - Sat 10 AM - 5 PM, Sun 1 - 5 PM. Admis adults $2, senior citizens $1.75, students $1, children under 6 free. Estab 1966 to exhibit artifacts, relics, history, and traditional Indian art of the Cherokee, Chickasaw, Choctaw, Creek, and Seminole Indian Tribes. Average Annual Attendance: 30,000. Mem: 1000; dues vary; annual meeting in Mar
Income: $48,000 (financed by mem & admis)
Collections: †Traditional Indian art by known artists of Five Tribes heritage, including original paintings & sculpture; large collection of Jerome Tiger originals
Exhibitions: Four Annual Judged Exhibitions: Competitive Art Show; Students Competitive Show; Craft Competition; Masters' Exhibition
Publications: Quarterly newsletter
Activities: Docent training; lect open to public; gallery talks; tours; competitions with awards; individual paintings & original objects of art lent to other museums & special exhibits with board approval; lending collection contains original art works; museum shop selling books, original art, reproductions, prints, beadwork, pottery, basketry & other handmade items
L Library, Agency Hill, Honor Heights Dr, 74401. Tel 918-683-1701; *Exec Dir* Lynn Thornley
Open Mon - Sat 10 AM - 5 PM, Sun 1 - 5 PM by appointment only. Estab 1966 to preserve history, culture, traditions, legends, etc of Five Civilized Tribes (Cherokee, Creek, Choctaw, Chickasaw, and Seminole tribes). Maintains an art gallery
Income: Financed by museum
Library Holdings: Vols 3500; Per subs 5; Original documents; AV — Cassettes, lantern slides; Other — Clipping files, exhibition catalogs, framed reproductions, manuscripts, memorabilia, original art works, pamphlets, photographs, prints, reproductions, sculpture
Special Subjects: American Indian Art, Historical Material, Manuscripts, Maps
Publications: Newsletter, every three months

NORMAN

M FIREHOUSE ART CENTER, 444 S Flood, 73069. Tel 405-329-4523; *Exec Dir* Nancy McClellan
Open Mon - Fri 9 AM - 5 PM, Sat 10 AM - 4 PM. Estab 1971. 7-8 exhibits per year of contemporary work by local, state, regional & national artists. Average Annual Attendance: 5000. Mem: 450; dues family $25; annual meeting in Aug
Income: $60,000 (financed by mem, city & state appropriation, grants, donations, fundraising)
Exhibitions: Annual Christmas Gallery; Chocolate Art
Activities: Classes for adults & children; workshops; lect open to public, 2 vis lectr per year; gallery talks; competitions; scholarships & fels offered; retail store sells original art & prints

UNIVERSITY OF OKLAHOMA

M Fred Jones Jr Museum of Art, 410 W Boyd St, 73019. Tel 405-325-3272; FAX 405-325-7696; *Dir* Thomas R Toperzer; *Asst Dir & Acting Registrar* Gail Kana Anderson; *Mus Educator* Alyson Stanfield; *Preparator* James Meeks; *Mgr Admin & Operations* Becky Zurcher; *Supv Security* Joyce Cummin; *Community Relations Officer* Mary Jane Rutherford
Open Tues - Fri 10 AM - 4:30 PM, Thurs 10 AM - 9 PM, Sat & Sun Noon - 4:30 PM, cl Mon. Estab 1936 to provide cultural enrichment for the people of Oklahoma; to collect, preserve, exhibit & provide research in art of all significant periods. Approx 15,000 sq ft for permanent & temporary exhibitions on two indoor levels. Average Annual Attendance: 50,000. Mem: 360; dues $15-$100; meetings in Sept & Jan
Income: Financed by state, university allocation, foundation endowment & Board of Visitors
Purchases: Focus upon contemporary art
Collections: African sculpture; †American all media; Asian; †crafts; European all media; oceanic art; †photography; Kiowa Painting, Mexican Masks; Persian Manuscripts; small paintings from Permanent Collection; State Department Collection
Exhibitions: (1997) Through an Open Door: Selections from the Robert A Hefner Collection of Contemporary Chinese Oil Paintings; 83rd Annual School of Art Students Exhibition; School of Art MFA Thesis Exhibition; The Quiet Heresy: Biblical Themes in Contemporary Art 81st Annual School of Art Students Exhibition; Dan Klacz: New Work; MFA Thesis Exhibitions
Publications: Calender of activities; posters; announcements; exhibition catalogues
Activities: Docent training; lect open to public, 5-10 vis lectr per year; concerts; gallery talks; tours; competitions with prizes; originate traveling exhibitions; sales shop sells books, magazines, reproductions, jewelry, notecards & gifts
L Architecture Library, Gould Hall, 73019. Tel 405-325-5521; FAX 405-325-6637; Elec Mail qb6305@ou.edu. *Library Technician* Jane Travis
Library Holdings: Vols 17,000; Per subs 42
Special Subjects: Architecture, Interior Design, Landscape Architecture, Urban & Environmental Design

L **Fine Arts Library,** Catlett Music Ctr, Rm 007, 73019. Tel 405-325-4243; FAX 405-325-4243; Elec Mail jseifert@ou.edu. *Fine Arts Librn* Jan E Seifert
Open Mon - Thurs 8 AM - 9 PM, Fri 8 AM - 5 PM, Sat 10 AM - 3 PM, Sun 2 - 9 PM. Estab to provide instructional support to the academic community of the university & general service to the people of the state. Circ 6900
Income: Financed by state appropriation
Library Holdings: Vols 27,000; Per subs 50; Micro — Fiche, reels; AV — V-tapes

OKLAHOMA CITY

M **INDIVIDUAL ARTISTS OF OKLAHOMA,** One N Hudson, Ste 150, PO Box 60824, 73146. Tel 405-232-6060; *Dir* Shirley Blaschke
Open Tues - Sat 11 AM - 4 PM. No admis fee. Estab 1979 to promote Oklahoma artists of all disciplines. Average Annual Attendance: 7000. Mem: 400; dues $30; annual meeting in spring
Income: Financed by mem, state arts council & fundraising
Exhibitions: Monthly exhibits of 3 visual artists, including special photography gallery
Publications: Artzone, monthly newsletter
Activities: Lect open to public, 6 vis lectr per year; competitions; traveling exhibitions 1 per year; originate traveling exhibitions 1 per year

C **INTERNATIONAL INSTITUTE OF PIGEONS & DOVES,** PO Box 18476, 73154-0476. Tel 405-478-5155; *General Mgr* Johnnie L Blaine; *Facilities Mgr* Jim Davis; *Admin Asst* Dina Jones
Estab 1973 to preserve & display the rich heritage of domestic pigeons & doves & to foster the keeping of registered pigeons as a unique & rewarding hobby. Mem: 1000; dues $20
Income: Financed by mem
Purchases: Several pigeon art book collections
Activities: Classes for children; exten dept

M **NATIONAL COWBOY HALL OF FAME & WESTERN HERITAGE CENTER MUSEUM,** 1700 NE 63rd St, 73111. Tel 405-478-2250; FAX 405-478-4714; *Exec Dir* Ken Townsend; *Asst Dir* Bobby Weaver; *Art Dir* Ed Muno; *Coll Cur* Don Reeves; *Develop Dir* Bill Wyles; *Public Relations Dir* Linda Haller; *Chief Financial Officer* Denny Zimmerman
Open daily 8:30 AM - 6 PM summer; 9 AM - 5 PM winter, cl New Year's Day, Thanksgiving & Christmas Day. Admis adults $6, senior citizens $5, children 6-12 $3, children under 6 free; group rates available. Estab 1957, opened 1965 to preserve the American Western Heritage through art & artifacts. Two spacious galleries showcase exhibits from the Hall's nationally known contemporary western art collection, including Prix de West award winners from the National Academy of Western Art Exhibitions held here annually since 1973. Average Annual Attendance: 250,000. Mem: 8000; dues $35
Income: Financed by endowment, mem, grants & donations
Collections: Albert K Mitchell Russell-Remington Collection; †Contemporary Western Art; Fechin Collection; James Earle & Laura G Fraser Studio Collection; Schreyvogel Collection; Taos Collection; John Wayne Collection, kachinas, guns, knives & art; western art Great Western Performers Portrait Collection; Rodeo Portrait Collection
Exhibitions: Annual National Academy of Western Art & Western Heritage Awards (Prix de West Invitational); National Academy of Western Art Exhibit
Publications: Ketch Pen Magazine, biannual; Persimmon Hill Magazine, quarterly
Activities: Docent training; concerts; tours; scholarships & fels offered; originate traveling exhibitions, circulated to requesting agencies, universities, museums, galleries; gift shop sells books, magazines, reproductions & prints

M **OKLAHOMA CENTER FOR SCIENCE & ART,** Kirkpatrick Center, 2100 NE 52nd, 73111. Tel 405-424-5545 (Omniplex); 427-5461 (Kirkpatrick Center); 427-5461 (Air Space Museum); FAX 405-424-5106; *Pres* Marilyn Rippee; *Cur* Jim Eastep; *Coordr Indian Gallery* Barbara Jobe; *Coordr Sanamu African Gallery* Bruce Fisher; *Coordr Photography Hall Fame* Michael Harris; *Dir Air Space Museum* Don Finch
Open Mon - Sat 9 AM - 5 PM, Sun Noon - 5 PM. Admis adults $5, children & senior citizens $3, one price for entire center. Estab 1958 to focus on the inter-relationships between science, arts & the humanities & to supplement educational facilities offered in the pub schools in the areas of arts & sciences. The Kirkpatrick Center houses Omniplex, a hands-on science mus; mus shop; George Sutton bird paintings; Oklahoma Aviation & Space Hall of Fame & Mus; Center of American Indian Gallery; Sanamu African Gallery; Oriental Art Gallery; International Photography Hall of Fame; Oklahoma Zoological Society Offices; Kirkpatrick Planetarium; miiature Victorian house; antique clocks; US Navy Gallery; retired senior volunteer program; Oklahoma City Zoo offices. Average Annual Attendance: 350,000
Income: Financed by mem, private donations, Allied Arts Foundation, admis fees, & class tuition
Collections: European & Oriental Ivory Sculpture; Japanese Woodblock Prints; Oceanic art; Pre-Columbian & American Indian art; Sutton paintings; Traditional & Contemporary African art; 1,000 photographs in Photography Hall of Fame
Exhibitions: Changing exhibitions every six to ten weeks; Dinosaurs
Publications: Insights, quarterly; Omniplex Newsletter, monthly
Activities: Classes for adults & children; docent training; lect open to public; tours; book traveling exhibitions; museum shop sells books, prints, science related material, cards & jewelry

M **OKLAHOMA CITY ART MUSEUM,** 3113 Pershing Blvd, 73107. Tel 405-946-4477; FAX 405-946-7671; *Dir & Chief Cur* Carolyn Hill; *Cur Educ* Doris McGranahan; *Asst to Dir* Susie Bauer; *Registrar* Jayne Hazleton; *Adminr* Trish Knott; *Develop* Julia Kirt; *Develop Officer* Lynn Kickingbird
Open Tues - Sat 10 AM - 5 PM, Sun 1 - 5 PM, cl Mon & major holidays. Admis adults $3.50, students & sr citizens $2.50, children under 12 & members free. Estab 1989 with the merger of the Oklahoma Art Center & the Oklahoma Mus of Art. Five galleries, no permanent installations. Average Annual Attendance:

50,000. Mem: 1300; dues $25 - $5000; annual meeting in June
Income: Financed by mem, private contributions, grants & earned income
Collections: †19th-20th century American paintings including works by Bellows, Tiffany, Chase, Cropsey, Benton, Moran, Hassam; †20th century American paintings & graphics, including Henri, Marin, Kelly, Indiana, Francis, Davis, Warhol; American Sculpture by Bertoia, Bontecou, Calder, Lipton
Exhibitions: Ongoing: selections from the permanent collection of European & American painting
Publications: Calendar, bi-monthly, exhibition catalogs, posters, brochures, permanent collection catalogues
Activities: Studio classes for children; fine arts & crafts fairs; docent training; lect open to public, 10 vis lectr per year; gallery talks; tours; films; individual paintings & original objects of art lent to other accredited museums; lending collection contains original art works, original prints, paintings & photographs; book traveling exhibitions 2 per year; originate traveling exhibitions; museum shop sells books, cards, reproductions, prints, original art, jewelry, stationary

L **Library,** 3113 Pershing Blvd, 73107. Tel 405-946-4477; FAX 405-946-7671; *Dir & Cur* Carolyn Hill; *Cur Educ* Doris McGranahan; *Bus Mgr* Patricia Knott
Open Mon - Sat 10 AM - 5 PM, Thurs until 8 PM, Sun 1 - 5 PM. Admis general $3.50, senior citizens & students $2.50, children 12 & under free. Estab 1989 to bring a quality fine arts mus & related educational programming to Oklahoma. Library for reference only. Average Annual Attendance: 20,000. Mem: 1500
Income: Non-profit organization financed through private contribution
Library Holdings: Vols 6800; Per subs 15; AV — Slides, v-tapes; Other — Clipping files, exhibition catalogs
Special Subjects: Medieval Art, 19th Century French & American Paintings & Sculpture

M **OKLAHOMA CITY UNIVERSITY,** Hulsey Gallery-Norick Art Center, 2501 N Blackwelder, 73106. Tel 405-521-5226; FAX 405-557-6029; *Dir* Brunel Faris; *Admin Asst* Maria Amos
Open Mon - Fri 10 AM - 4 PM, Sat & Sun 1 - 5 PM. Admis free. Estab 1904 to educ in the arts. Gallery is 2200 sq ft with fabric covered walls & moveable display forms. Average Annual Attendance: 2000. Mem: 140
Income: Financed by endowment, mem & the University
Collections: †Oklahoma City University Art Collection; Art donated by individuals & organizations from Oklahoma
Exhibitions: Oklahoma City University Student Exhibit; Oklahoma High School Print & Drawing Exhibit; Annual exhibits change monthly
Publications: NAC Notes, quarterly; DepARTures, bi-annually
Activities: Classes for adults & children; docent training; lect open to public, 2-3 vis lectr per year; individual/paintings & original works of art lent to various departments of the Oklahoma City University campus

L **Reference,** 2501 N Blackwelder, 73106. Tel 405-521-5000 (Main), 521-5226 (Art Dept); FAX 405-557-6029; *Dir* Danelle Hall
For lending & reference
Income: Financed by endowment, donation & University
Library Holdings: Vols 207; AV — V-tapes; Other — Exhibition catalogs, original art works, photographs, prints, reproductions, sculpture

M **OKLAHOMA HISTORICAL SOCIETY,** State Museum of History, Wiley Post Historical Bldg, 2100 N Lincoln Blvd, 73105. Tel 405-521-2491; FAX 405-521-2492; *Pres Board Trustees* Marvin E Kroeker; *Exec Dir* J Blake Wade; *Publ* Mary Blochowiak; *Mus Div* Kathy Dickson; *Historical Sites* Dr William Lees; *Library Resources* Ed Shoemaker; *Preservation Dir* Melvena Heisch; *State Mus Dir* Bill Pitts; *Indian Archives & Mss* William Welge
Open Mon - Sat 8 AM - 5 PM, cl State holidays. No admis fee. Estab 1893 to provide an historical overview of the State of Oklahoma, from prehistory to the present, through interpretive exhibits, three dimensional artifacts, original art & photographs. Average Annual Attendance: 150,000. Mem: 3500; dues $15; annual meeting Apr
Income: Financed by state appropriations & mem; Soc depends on donations for additions to its collections
Collections: Anthropology; archaeology; historical artifacts; documents; American Indian art; Oklahoma art; Western art
Exhibitions: Permanent exhibits depicting pre-history, Oklahoma Indian Tribes' history, the Five Civilized Tribes' occupancy of Indian Territory, the land openings of the late 19th and early 20th centuries, statehood, and progress since statehood; special exhibits 2-3 times per yr
Publications: Mistletoe Leaves, monthly newsletter; The Chronicles of Oklahoma, Society quarterly; various brochures and reprints
Activities: Special presentations & films for children & adults; interpretive programs; self-guided tours; individual paintings & original objects of art lent to qualified museums; lending collection contains paintings, 19th century beadwork & Indian artifacts; originate traveling exhibitions; sales shop sells books, magazines

L **Library Resources Division,** 2100 N Lincoln Blvd, 73105. Tel 405-522-5225; FAX 405-521-2492; *Dir Library Resources Div* Edward C Shoemaker
Open Tues - Sat 9 AM - 5 PM, Mon 9 AM - 8 PM. Estab 1893 to collect & preserve historical materials & publications on Oklahoma history. For reference only
Library Holdings: Vols 64,946; Per subs 80; Micro — Fiche, reels 12,493; Other — Clipping files, pamphlets, photographs
Publications: Chronicles of Oklahoma, quarterly; Mistletoe Leaves, monthly newsletter

OKMULGEE

M **CREEK COUNCIL HOUSE MUSEUM,** Town Square, 74447. Tel 918-756-2324; *Acting Dir* Debbie Martin
Open Tues - Sat 9 AM - 5 PM. No admis fee. Estab 1867, first Council House built, present Council House erected in 1878 to collect & preserve artifacts from Creek history. Five rooms downstairs containing artifacts; four rooms upstairs showing art work, early time of Okmulgee; rooms of House of Warriors & House of Kings. Average Annual Attendance: 8000-10,000
Income: Financed by mem & city appropriation
Collections: †Creek Artifacts

Exhibitions: Annual Oklahoma Indian Art Market (juried competitions)
Activities: Seminars on Creek Culture & history; Annual Wild Onion Feast (traditional tribal foods); lect open to public, 5-10 vis lectr per year; gallery talks; artmobile; book traveling exhibitions; museum shop sells books, original art, reproductions, prints & Native American art & craft items
L **Library,** Town Square, 74447. Tel 918-756-2324; *Acting Dir* Debbie Martin
Open Tues - Fri 9 AM - 5 PM. Estab to collect Creek & related books & documents for research & historical purposes. For reference only
Library Holdings: Vols 250; Per subs 10; Micro — Reels; AV — A-tapes, motion pictures; Other — Clipping files, exhibition catalogs, framed reproductions, manuscripts, memorabilia, original art works, pamphlets, photographs, prints, sculpture

PONCA CITY

A **PONCA CITY ART ASSOCIATION,** 819 E Central, PO Box 1394, 74601. Tel 405-765-9746; *Office Mgr* Donna Secrest
Open Wed - Sun 1 - 5 PM. No admis fee. Estab 1947 to encourage creative arts, to furnish place & sponsor art classes, art exhibits & workshops. Mem: 600; dues $10 family; annual meeting third Tues in Apr
Income: $10,000 (financed by mem & flea market)
Collections: Permanent fine arts collection; additions by purchases & donations
Exhibitions: Eight per year
Publications: Association Bulletin, 6 per yr
Activities: Classes for adults & children; lect open to public; tours; competitions for members only with awards; scholarships offered; individual paintings lent to city-owned buildings; sales shop sells original art, reproductions & prints

M **PONCA CITY CULTURAL CENTER & MUSEUM,** 1000 E Grand Ave, 74601. Tel 405-767-0427; *Dir* La Wanda French
Open Mon, Wed - Sat 10 AM - 5 PM, Sun & holidays 1 - 5 PM; cl Tues, Thanksgiving, Christmas Eve & Christmas Day, New Year's Eve & New Year's Day. Admis adults $1. The Cultural Center & Mus, a National Historic House since 1976, houses the Indian Mus, the Bryant Baker Studio, the 101 Ranch Room, & the DAR Memorial Mus. The Indian Mus, established in 1936, places an emphasis on materials from the five neighboring tribes (Ponca, Kaw, Otoe, Osage, and Tonkawa) whose artistic use of beading, fingerweaving & ribbon-work are displayed throughout the Mus. The Bryant Baker Studio is a replica of the New York Studio of Bryant Baker, sculptor of the Pioneer Woman Statue, a local landmark, & the studio contains original bronze & plaster sculpture. The 101 Ranch Room exhibits memorabilia from the world renowned Miller Brothers' 101 Ranch, located south of Ponca City in the early 1900s. The mus is the former home of Ernest Whhtworth Marland, oilman & philanthropist & the tenth governor of Oklahoma. Average Annual Attendance: 25,000
Income: Financed by the City of Ponca City & donations
Collections: Bryant Baker original sculpture; 101 Ranch memorabilia; Indian ethnography and archeology of Indian tribes throughout the United States
Exhibitions: Smithsonian Indian Images; Indian costumes, jewelry, pottery, baskets, musical instruments & tools
Publications: Brochure
Activities: Tours; sales shop sells books, arrowheads, Indian arts & crafts
L **Library,** 1000 E Grand Ave, 74601. Tel 405-767-0427; *Dir* La Wanda French; *Asst* Roberta Gartrell
Open Mon, Wed - Sat 10 AM - 5 PM, Sun 1 - 5 PM, cl Tues. Primarily research library
Income: Financed by Ponca City
Library Holdings: Vols 230; Per subs 13
Special Subjects: Anthropology, Archaeology, Indian art

L **PONCA CITY LIBRARY,** Art Dept, 515 E Grand, 74601. Tel 405-767-0345; *Dir* Holly LaBossiere; *Head Technical Servs* Judi Anderson
Open Mon - Thurs 9 AM - 9 PM, Fri 9 AM - 6 PM, Sat 9 AM - 5 PM, Sun 2 - 5 PM, cl Sun in June, July & Aug. Estab 1904 to serve the citizens of Ponca City. Gallery maintained. Circ 150,000
Library Holdings: Vols 75,000; Per subs 250; AV — Cassettes; Other — Framed reproductions, original art works, pamphlets, photographs, sculpture
Collections: Oriental Art Collection; Sandzen Collection; paintings

SHAWNEE

M **SAINT GREGORY'S ABBEY & COLLEGE,** Mabee-Gerrer Museum of Art, 1900 W MacArthur Dr, 74801. Tel 405-878-5300; FAX 405-878-5198; *Dir* Melissa Owens; *Conservator* Bro Justin Jones, OSB; *Coll Mgr* Chris Owens
Open daily 1 - 4 PM, cl Mon. No admis fee. Estab 1904 to contribute to the cultural growth & appreciation of the general pub of Oklahoma as well as the student body of Saint Gregory's College. A new 16,000 sq foot gallery was completed in 1979. In 1990, 1500 sq ft was added which includes a new gallery, a multi-purpose room & theater. Collections are being enlarged by purchases & by gifts. Average Annual Attendance: 40,000
Income: Financed by endowment, Abbey, mem & foundation funds
Collections: †Artifacts from ancient civilization; African, Eqyptian, Roman, Grecian, Babylonian, Pre-Columbian North, South and Central American Indian, and South Pacific; †etchings, †engravings, †serigraphs and †lithographs; †oil paintings by American and European artists; †Native American; Icons: Greek, Russian & Balkan; Retablos from Mexico & New Mexico
Activities: Classes for adults & children; lect open to public, 4 vis lectr per year; gallery talks; tours; docent training; individual paintings & original objects of art lent to other museums

STILLWATER

M **OKLAHOMA STATE UNIVERSITY,** Gardiner Art Gallery, Dept of Art, Bartlett Ctr of the Studio Arts, 108 Bartlett Ctr. 74078-4085. Tel 405-744-9086; FAX 405-744-5767; *Dir* Nancy Wilkinson
Open Mon - Fri 8 AM - 5 PM. Sun 1 - 5 PM. No admis fee. Estab 1970 as a visual & educational extension of the department's classes & as a cultural service to the community & area. One gallery located on the ground floor in new annex behind the renovated building. 250 running ft of wall space, 12 ft ceiling. Average Annual Attendance: 5000
Income: Financed by college
Collections: 200 prints, mostly post World War II
Exhibitions: Exhibitions change every 3-4 weeks year round; faculty, student, invitational & traveling shows
Publications: Exhibition brochures; exhibition schedules
Activities: Book traveling exhibitions
L **Architecture Library,** 201A Architecture Bldg, 74078-0185. Tel 405-744-6047; *Architecture Librn* Tora Willamson
Open fall & spring semesters Mon - Thurs 8 AM - 5 PM & 7 - 10 PM, Fri 8 AM - 5 PM, Sun 1 - 5 PM, summer hrs vary. Estab 1976 to meet the combined needs of the faculty & students of the School of Architecture
Purchases: $14,000
Library Holdings: Vols 11,267; Per subs 50; Compact discs; AV — Slides
Special Subjects: Underground Housing

TAHLEQUAH

A **CHEROKEE NATIONAL HISTORICAL SOCIETY, INC,** PO Box 515, 74465. Tel 918-456-6007; FAX 918-456-6195; *Pres* Lowell Townson; *Admin* Mac Harris
Open Mon - Sat 10 AM - 5 PM, Sun 1 - 5 PM. Admis adult $2.50, children $1.25. Estab 1963 to commemorate & portray the history, traditions & lore of a great Indian tribe & to assist in improving local economic conditions. Maintains an art gallery, primarily Indian art. Average Annual Attendance: 130,000. Mem: 1500; dues $25 & up
Income: Financed by mem, admis & grants
Collections: Indian artists interpretations of Trails of Tears
Exhibitions: Trail of Tears Art Show, annually; Retrospective by famous Cherokee artist, annually; frequent one-artist shows
Publications: The Columns, quarterly
Activities: Lect open to public; competitions with cash awards; museum shop sells books, reproductions, prints & slides
L **Library,** PO Box 515, 74465. Tel 918-456-6007; *Librn* Robin Kichingbird
Open Mon - Sat 8 AM - 5 PM, Sun 1 - 5 PM. Estab 1976 to preserve remnants of Cherokee history & to educate the general pub about that cultural heritage; a respository of Indian art & documents. Maintains an art gallery with work by artists of several different tribes; heavy emphasis given to the Cherokee experience
Income: Financed by mem, admis & grants
Library Holdings: Vols 3000; Per subs 10; Archival materials in excess of 500 cu ft; Manuscripts; Micro — Reels 127; AV — A-tapes, cassettes, fs, Kodachromes, slides; Other — Clipping files, framed reproductions, manuscripts, memorabilia, original art works, pamphlets, photographs, prints, sculpture
Special Subjects: Cherokee history
Exhibitions: Annual Trail of Tears Art Show (Indian artists' interpretation of the Trail of Tears theme); Cherokee Artists Exhibition; rotating exhibitions; special exhibitions, periodically (primarily Indian artists)
Publications: Quarterly columns

TULSA

C **BANK OF OKLAHOMA NA,** Art Collection, PO Box 2300, 74192. Tel 918-588-6000; FAX 918-588-8692; *VPres Exec Committee* Scott Ellison
Open 8 AM - 5 PM. Estab 1968 to enhance work environment. Collection displayed on 7 floors of the Bank of Oklahoma Tower
Purchases: $15,000
Collections: Modern Art
Activities: Lect; tours; scholarships offered to University of Tulsa

M **GERSHON & REBECCA FENSTER MUSEUM OF JEWISH ART,** 1223 E 17th Pl, 74120. Tel 918-582-3732; *Exec Dir* Diana Aaronson
Open Tues - Fri 10 AM - 4 PM, Sun 1 - 4 PM. No admis fee. Estab 1966 to collect, preserve & interpret cultural, historical & aesthetic materials attesting to Jewish cultural history. Average Annual Attendance: 3000. Mem: 200; dues $35, annual meeting in Dec
Income: $45,000 (financed by endowment & mem)
Collections: Anti-semitica; archeology of old world; ethnographic materials; fine art by Jewish artists & on Jewish themes; ritual & ceremonial Judaica
Exhibitions: Permanent collections; quarterly exhibits; Oklahoma: The Land & the People Photographs by David Hapern Holocaust Exhibit
Publications: Fenster Museum News, quarterly
Activities: Classes for adults & children, docent training; lect open to public; gallery talks; tours; ividual paintings & originals objects of art lent to other museums & religious institutions

M **GILCREASE MUSEUM INSTITUTE OF AMERICAN HISTORY & ART,** 1400 Gilcrease Museum Rd, 74127. Tel 918-596-2700; FAX 918-596-2770; *Dir* J Brooks Joiner; *Asst to Dir & Dir Public Relations* Ken Busby
Open Tues - Sat 9 AM - 5 PM, Sun & holidays 11 - 5 PM, open Mon from Memorial Day - Labor Day, cl Christmas. No admis fee. Estab by the late Thomas Gilcrease as a private institution; acquired by the City of Tulsa 1954 (governed by a Board of Directors & City Park Board); building addition completed 1963 & 1987. Average Annual Attendance: 130,000. Mem: 3500; dues $30 & up
Income: Financed by city funds & fundraisers

Collections: American art from Colonial period to 20th century with emphasis on art of historical significance, sculpture, painting, graphics. Much of the work shown is of documentary nature, with emphasis on the Native American material & the opening of the Trans-Mississippi West. Art Collections include 10,000 paintings by 400 American artists; artifact collections include 250,000 objects including both prehistoric & historic materials from most of the Native American cultures in Middle & North America
Exhibitions: Special exhibitions periodically; rotating exhibits during fall, winter, spring seasons; Gilcrease Rendezvous; 8000 sq ft permanent exhibit of Art from Mexico
Publications: The Journal, bi-annual
Activities: Film program; lect on art & history; gallery tours; lect to school groups outside the museum
L **Library,** 1400 Gilcrease Museum Rd, 74127. Tel 918-596-2700; FAX 918-596-2770; *Cur Archival Colls* Sarah Erwin
Open daily, cl weekends & holidays. Library open for research by appointment, contains 90,000 books & documents, many rare books & manuscripts of the American frontier period, as well as materials concerning the Five Civilized Tribes
Income: Financed by city appropriation
Library Holdings: Vols 40,000; Per subs 10; Other — Exhibition catalogs, manuscripts, memorabilia, pamphlets, photographs
Special Subjects: American Indian Art, American Western Art, Historical Material, Manuscripts, Discovery & development of America; American Indian History

M **PHILBROOK MUSEUM OF ART,** 2727 S Rockford Rd, PO Box 52510, 74152-0510. Tel 918-749-7941; FAX 918-743-4230; *Dir* Marcia Manhart; *Dir Exhib & Coll* Christine Kallenberger; *Dir Annual Giving* Doris Frampton; *Hardman Cur* Richard Townsend; *Deputy Dir* David Singleton; *Dir Communictions* Cheryl Waldeck; *Museum Shop Mgr* Julia Barberia; *Preparator* Charles Taylor; *Dir Educ* Jeannette Lawson; *Dir Develop* Chica Sanderson; *Facility Coordr* Charisse Cooper; *Museum School Dir* Norman Nilsen
Open Tues - Sat 10 AM - 5 PM, Thurs 10 AM - 8 PM, Sun 11 AM - 5 PM. Admis adults $4, college students & senior citizens $2, high school students & younger free. Estab 1939 as a general art mus in an Italian Renaissance Revival Villa, the former home of philanthropist & oil baron Waite Phillips. Twenty-three acres of formal & natural gardens. Also contains a special exhibition gallery. Average Annual Attendance: 120,000. Mem: 4500; dues $25 & up; annual meeting in June
Income: Financed by endowment, mem, earned income, corporate & private gifts & pub grants
Collections: Laura A Clubb Collection of American & European Paintings; Clark Field Collection of American Indian Baskets & Pottery; Gillert Collection of Southeast Asian Ceramics; Gussman Collection of African Sculpture; Samuel H Kress Collection of Italian Renaissance Paintings & Sculpture; Roberta C Lawson Collection of Indian Costumes & Artifacts; Tabor Collection of Oriental Art; American Indian paintings & sculpture; European, early American & contemporary American oils, watercolors & prints; period furniture
Exhibitions: Paul Manship: Changing Taste in America; Baroque Gold & Jewelry from the Hungarian National Museum; From Elizabeth I to Elizabeth II: 400 Years of Drawing from the National Portrait Gallery, London; Glass from Ancient Craft to Contemporary Art: 1962 - 1992 & Beyond Design & World View: The Politics of Hopi Ceramics; SummerFaire; Gaston Lachaise: Sculpture & Drawings; Art of the Eye; Botticelli to Tiepolo: Three Centuries of Italian Painting; Festival of Trees
Publications: Bi-monthly bulletin; exhibition catalogs
Activities: Classes for adults & children; dramatic programs; docent training; lect open to public, 27 vis lectr per year; concerts; gallery talks; tours; scholarships offered; individual & original objects of art lent to museums, corporations & city government; book traveling exhibitions 3-5 per year; originate traveling exhibitions; museum shop sells books, magazines, original art, reproductions, prints, slides & gift items
L **Chapman Library,** 2727 S Rockford Rd, PO Box 52510, 74152-0510. Tel 918-748-5306; FAX 918-743-4230; Elec Mail lib__ty@centum.utulsa.edu. *Librn* Thomas E Young
Open Mon - Fri by appointment. Reference-resource center for the curatorial staff, teaching faculty, volunteers & mem
Library Holdings: Vols 12,000; Per subs 125; AV — Slides; Other — Clipping files, exhibition catalogs, pamphlets, reproductions
Special Subjects: American Indian Art, American Western Art, Art History, Decorative Arts, Folk Art, History of Art & Archaeology, Landscape Architecture, Oriental Art, Painting - American, Painting - European, Painting - Italian, Photography, Pottery, Pre-Columbian Art, Primitive Art
Collections: Roberta Campbell Lawson Library of source materials on American Indians

M **UNIVERSITY OF TULSA,** Alexandre Hogue Gallery, Art Dept, 600 S College Ave, 74104. Tel 918-631-2202; FAX 918-631-3423; *Dir* Steven Sumner
Open Mon - Fri 8:30 - 4:30 PM. No admis fee. Estab 1966 to display the works of regionally & nationally known artists. 176 running ft. Average Annual Attendance: 1000
Exhibitions: Annual Student Art Competition; National Scholastic Art Awards Scholarships & Competition
Activities: Lect open to public, 6 vis lectr per year; competition with awards; scholarships offered; individual paintings & original objects of art lent

WOODWARD

M **PLAINS INDIANS & PIONEERS HISTORICAL FOUNDATION,** Museum & Art Center, 2009 Williams Ave, PO Box 1167, 73801. Tel 405-256-6136; *Dir & Cur* Louise James; *Admin Asst* Kathy Smith
Open Tues - Sat 10 AM - 5 PM, Sun 1 - 4 PM, cl Mon. No admis fee. Estab 1957 to preserve local history & to support visual arts. Average Annual Attendance: 15,000. Mem: 450; dues $15 - $500; annual meeting Nov
Income: Financed by mem & trust fund
Collections: Early day artifacts as well as Indian material

Exhibitions: Juried contests for high school students & photographers; Fine Arts, Creative Crafts (guest artist featured each month in the gallery)
Publications: Below Devil's Gap (historical book); brochures; quarterly newsletter; Oklahoma's Northwest Territory Map; Woodward County Pioneer Families, 1907-57 (2 volumes)
Activities: Classes for adults & children; docent training; lect open to public, 3 vis lectr per year; tours; competitions with prizes; book traveling exhibitions 3 per year; museum shop sells books, magazines, original art & prints & Northwest Oklahoma artisans crafts

OREGON

ASHLAND

SOUTHERN OREGON STATE COLLEGE
M **Stevenson Union Gallery,** 1250 Siskiyou Blvd, 97520. Tel 541-552-6465; FAX 541-552-6440; *Dir* Phil Campbell; *Dir* Jeff Erickson
Open Mon - Fri 8 AM - 9 PM, Sat 9:30 AM - 2 PM. No admis fee. Estab 1972 to offer college & community high quality arts. Located on the third floor of Stevenson Union, the gallery is about 1200 sq ft. Average Annual Attendance: 20,000
Income: Financed by student fees
Collections: Small permanent collection of prints, paintings by local artists & a sculpture by Bruce West
Exhibitions: Ceramics, paintings, photography, prints, sculpture, faculty & student work. Annual Student Art Show; Installations, Alternative Works
Activities: Lect open to public, 3 vis lectr per year
M **Central Art Gallery,** 97520. Tel 541-552-6386; FAX 541-552-6429; *Gallery Dir* Carol Corrigan; *Chmn Dept Art* Cody Bustamante
Open Mon - Fri 8:30 AM - 5 PM
Income: Financed by Department of Art
M **Schneider Museum of Art,** 1250 Siskiyou Blvd, 97520. Tel 541-552-6245; FAX 541-552-6249; Elec Mail gmarkle@wpo.sosc.osshe.edu. *Dir* Greer Markle; *Preparator* Steve Fraizer; *Vol & Progs Coordr* Mary Gardiner; *Office Coordr* Karen Flynn
Open Tues - Sat 11 AM - 5 PM. Donations. Estab 1986. Average Annual Attendance: 20,000. Mem: 500; dues $30-$250; annual meeting in Oct
Income: Financed by endowment, mem, state appropriations & federal grants
Collections: Waldo Peirce-oils, watercolors & lithographs & a diverse collection of contemporary American art
Exhibitions: Andy Goldwothy: Stone Work, Chihuly Glass
Publications: Quarterly bulletin
Activities: Classes for adults & children; docent training; lect open to public, 3-4 vis lectr per year; book traveling exhibitions 3-4 per year; museum shop sells books & postcards

ASTORIA

M **COLUMBIA RIVER MARITIME MUSEUM,** 1792 Marine Dr, 97103. Tel 503-325-2323; FAX 503-325-2331; *Exec Dir* Jerry Ostermiller
Open daily 9:30 AM - 5 PM, cl on Thanksgiving & Christmas. Admis adults $5, senior citizens $4, children $2, children under 6 free. Estab 1962 as a maritime mus, to collect, preserve & interpret maritime history of Pacific Northwest. Maintains seven galleries of nautical history including works of art. Average Annual Attendance: 97,000. Mem: 2000; dues $15; annual meeting in Oct
Income: $500,000 (financed by admis, sales, mem & individual & corporate donations
Collections: †Maritime Paintings, †Prints & Photography; †Ship Models & †nautical artifacts; Lightship Columbia
Exhibitions: Rotating & temporary exhibit space in Great Hall; visiting vessels as available
Publications: The Quarterdeck, quarterly
Activities: Classes for adults; volunteer opportunities; docent training; lect open to public, 6 vis lectr per year; tours; competitions; outreach program to schools; individual paintings & original objects of art lent to accredited museums; museum shop sells books, limited edition prints, posters, reproductions, contemporary scrimshaw & jewelry
L **Library,** 1792 Marine Dr, 97103. Tel 503-325-2323; FAX 503-325-2331; *Cur* Anne Witty
Open by appointment only. Library for use on the premises; majority of contents are not relevant to art
Income: Financed by admis, trusts, mem dues & donations
Library Holdings: Vols 6000; Per subs 196; AV — Cassettes, motion pictures; Other — Clipping files, exhibition catalogs, manuscripts, original art works, pamphlets, photographs, prints, reproductions
Special Subjects: Drafting, Historical Material, Maps, Marine Painting, Scrimshaw, Maritime & Pacific Northwest history, ship models
Publications: The Quarterdeck, quarterly

BANDON

NATIONAL COUNCIL ON EDUCATION FOR THE CERAMIC ARTS (NCECA)
For further information, see National and Regional Organizations

BEND

M HIGH DESERT MUSEUM, 59800 S Hwy 97, 97702-7962. Tel 541-382-4754;
FAX 541-382-5256; *Pres* Arthur H Wolf; *VPres Operations* Jerry Moore;
Communications Dir Jack Cooper; *Exhibits Dir* Kevin Britz
Open daily 9 AM - 5 PM, cl Jan 1, Thanksgiving Day & Christmas. Admis
adults $6.25, senior citizens $5.75, youth 13-18 $5.75, children between 5-12 $3.
Estab 1974 to bring to life natural & cultural history of region. Brooks Gallery,
Spirit of the West Gallery & Nancy R Chandler Memorial Gallery. Average
Annual Attendance: 185,000. Mem: 5000; dues $25 & up; annual meeting in
Sept
Income: Financed by mem, donations, grants, admis & sales
Collections: Historical artifacts; Western art; wildlife sculpture, oils, watercolor,
photography; Sherry Sander, sculpture; Georgia Gerber, sculpture; Joe Halco,
sculpture; Rod Frederick, prints; Philip Hyde, photography
Exhibitions: (1997-98) Nature Photography; Rising from Tradition: Native
American Art
Publications: High Desert Quarterly; bi-annual exhibit catalogues
Activities: Classes for adults & children; docent programs; teacher in-service
training; lect open to public, 5-8 vis lectr per year; gallery talks; awards given;
book traveling exhibitions 1 per year; Museum shop sells books, magazines,
original art, reproductions, prints, slides, folk art, jewelry, educational games &
toys, nature items

CHILOQUIN

AMERICAN TAPESTRY ALLIANCE
For further information, see National and Regional Organizations

COOS BAY

M COOS ART MUSEUM, 235 Anderson Ave, 97420-1610. Tel 541-267-3901;
Pres Board Jean Macy; *VPres Board* Kathy Newhouse; *Admin* Helen G Scully
Open Tues - Fri 10 AM - 4 PM, Sat 1 - 4 PM, cl Sun & Mon. Admis donations
requested. Estab 1966 (relocated to an historic former Post Office Building in
downtown district) to bring contemporary art to Southwestern Oregon through
collections, exhibitions & educational programming. Five galleries with portable
furniture walls. Average Annual Attendance: 15,000. Mem: 800; dues family $30,
single $20; annual meeting first quarter of year
Income: $100,000 (financed by mem, fund raisers, memorials, contributions,
endowments & grants)
Collections: †Contemporary American Printmakers; †paintings, †photographs,
†sculpture
Exhibitions: Changing exhibits of painting, print, sculpture
Publications: Annual Museum Brochure; exhibit announcements, every 6 wks
Activities: Classes & workshops for adults & children; Artists-in-Education
Program for public schools; docent training; lect open to public; concerts; gallery
talks; tours; scholarships; rental/sales gallery & museum gift shop sells books,
original art prints, reproductions, prints, slides, Oregon handcrafted gift items &
educational items

COQUILLE

A COQUILLE VALLEY ART ASSOCIATION, HC 83 Box 625, 97423. Tel 541-
396-3294; *Pres* Pauline Sullivan; *VPres* Open; *Treas* Peggy James
Open Tues - Sun 1 - 4 PM, cl Mon & holidays. No admis fee. Estab 1950 to
teach art & art appreciation. Gallery maintained on main floor of Art Assoc
owned old refurbished schoolhouse. Mem: 120; dues $35 sr citizens $30; annual
meetings first Wed in Apr
Income: Financed by mem, annual bazaar
Exhibitions: Exhibits by local members, as well as by others throughout the state
Publications: Monthly newsletter
Activities: Classes for adults & children; lect open to public, 4-5 vis lectr per
year; gallery talks; tours; awards; scholarships offered; individual paintings lent to
banks, lobbies, automobile showrooms & music stores; traveling exhibitions
organized & circulated; sales shop sells original art, miniatures & handicraft
L Library, HC 83 Box 625, 97423. Tel 541-396-3294; *Pres* Pauline Sullivan

CORVALLIS

OREGON STATE UNIVERSITY
M Fairbanks Gallery, Fairbanks Hall, 97331-3702. Tel 541-737-5009; FAX 541-
737-2420; *Gallery Dir* Douglas Russell
Open Mon - Fri 8 AM - 5 PM, evenings & weekends during special events. No
admis fee. Estab 1933 to display work of contemporary artists. 160 linear ft. Set
in a cultural & conference center. Average Annual Attendance: 90,000
Income: Financed by state appropriation & grants
Collections: Goya to Rauschenberg; Japanese Print Collection; Wendel Black
Print Collection
Activities: Lect open to public; gallery talks
M Memorial Union Art Gallery, 97331. Tel 541-737-2416; 737-1566; FAX 541-
737-1565; *Dir* Michael Henthorne; *Asst Dir* Donald Johnson
Open daily 8 AM - 10 PM. Estab 1928. Average Annual Attendance: 50,000.
Mem: 15,000; annual meeting in May
Income: $70,000
Collections: William Henry Price Memorial Collection of Oil Paintings
Publications: Calendar & exhibition pamphlets
Activities: Educ program; lect; exten dept serving the State; individual paintings
lent to schools; material available to responsible galleries for fees; traveling
exhibitions organized & circulated
M Giustina Gallery, LaSells Stewart Ctr, 26th & Western Blvds, 97331. Tel 541-
737-2402, 737-5009; FAX 541-737-3187; *Gallery Dir* Douglas Russell
Open Mon - Fri 8 AM - 5 PM, additional hrs during special events at LaSells
Stewart Center. No admis fee. Estab 1981 to display work of contemporary
artists. Gallery is 4800 sq ft
Income: Financed by grants & state appropiation
Exhibitions: Exhibitions changing monthly

THE DALLES

A THE DALLES ART ASSOCIATION, The Dalles Art Ctr, 220 E Fourth &
Washington, 97058. Tel 541-296-4759
Open Tues - Sat 11 AM - 5 PM. No admis fee. Estab 1959 for presentation of
community arts activities. Gallery maintained. Average Annual Attendance:
4500. Mem: 250; dues corporate $250, patron $100, business $50, family $30,
individual $20, senior $15; meeting held first Thurs of each month
Income: Financed by dues, fund-raising events, grants, sponsorships
Exhibitions: Member & guest exhibits; state services exhibits
Publications: Bimonthly newsletter
Activities: Classes for adults & children; docent training; summer children's
program; lect open to public; competitions; gallery shop sells original art, jewelry,
pottery, basketry

EUGENE

M CITY OF EUGENE, HULT CENTER, Jacobs Gallery, One Eugene Ctr, 97401.
Tel 541-682-5087; FAX 541-682-5426; *Visual Arts Coordr* Suzanne Pepin;
Public Art Coordr Kirsten Jones
Open Mon - Fri 9 AM - 5 PM, Sat 11 AM - 4 PM. No admis fee. Estab 1982
for art appreciation & educ. Gallery in lower level of Hult Center for the
Performing Arts. Functions as a meeting & reception area, as well as a gallery
Income: $31,400 (financed by city appropriation, gallery sales commissions &
cost reimbursements from artists)
Exhibitions: Exhibits selected by committee of local artists, Hult Center
representative & Cultural Affairs Commission representative; Christopher
Burkett; Art in Education

M MAUDE I KERNS ART CENTER GALLERIES, 1910 E 15th Ave, 97403. Tel
541-345-1571; FAX 541-345-6248;
Internet Home Page Address http://www.premierelink.com/clients/mkac. *Exec
Dir* Deborah K Lauria; *Pres* Marvin Revoal
Open Mon, Fri & Sat 9 AM - 5 PM, Tues - Thurs 9 AM - 7 PM. Admis
suggested $2 donation. Estab 1950, the Center is a nonprofit educational
organization dedicated to promoting quality in the arts & crafts through classes,
exhibitions, workshops, community projects & special events. The center houses
3 galleries: Henry Korn Gallery, Brockelbank Gallery & Maude I Kerns Salon
Gallery. Features monthly shows of contemporary artists, the work of Maude
Kerns, Printmakers, Photo & Ceramics Co-ops. Average Annual Attendance: 12,
000. Mem: 500; dues family $36, individual $24; annual meeting in Jan/Feb
Income: $110,000 (financed by mem, class tuition, art sales, contributions, grants,
proceeds from annual outdoor fundraising festival)
Collections: Maude I Kerns Collection
Exhibitions: Every 6 weeks exhibits featuring individual theme & group shows by
Pacific Northwest artists Satellite gallery at LaVelle Vineyards, Elmira Oregon
Publications: Quarterly newsletter
Activities: Classes for adults & children; dramatic programs; volunteer program;
workshops; seminars; lect open to public; concerts; gallery talks; tours;
competitions; scholarships offered; exten dept

M LANE COMMUNITY COLLEGE, Art Dept Gallery, 4000 E 30th Ave, 97405.
Tel 503-747-4501; *Dir* Harold Hoy
Open Mon - Thurs 8 AM - 10 PM, Fri 8 AM - 5 PM. No admis fee. Estab 1970
as an educational gallery exhibiting works by National & Northwest artists
Income: Financed through county funds & state funds
Exhibitions: (1997) Painting by LCC Art Instructor Adam Grosowsky,
Metalsmithing by LCC Art Instructor Dan White; Works by the LCC Studio
Assistants; Annual LCC Juried Student Art Exhibition; 2nd Year Graphic Design
Student Graduation Show
Activities: Lect open to public, 9 vis lectr per year; gallery talks; competitions;
scholarships offered

UNIVERSITY OF OREGON
M Museum of Art, 1223 University of Oregon, 97403-1223. Tel 541-346-3027; Elec
Mail smcgough@oregon.uoregon.edu; lmfong@oregon.uoregon.edu. *Dir* David
Robertson; *Cur Educ* Laura Aaron-Sear; *Admin Asst* Ethel Weltman; *Registrar*
Lawrence Fong
Open Wed - Sun Noon - 5 PM, cl Mon, Tues & university holidays. No admis
fee. Estab 1930 to promote among university students & faculty & the general
pub an active & continuing interest in the visual arts of both Western & Oriental
cultures. Average Annual Attendance: 55,000. Mem: 600; dues $10-$500; annual
meeting in May
Income: $201,000 (financed by state appropriation, endowment income & private
donations)
Collections: African; Contemporary Northwest Collection; Greater Pacific Basin
Collection; Asian Art representing the cultures of China, Japan, Cambodia,
Korea, Mongolia, Tibet, Russia & American & British works executed in the
traditional Oriental manner; 19-20th century European & American
Exhibitions: La Verne Krause: Painter & Printmaker (1924 - 1987). Sculpture by
Auguste Rodin; Thomas Hart Benton on the Oregon Trail; Taking Pictures
Home: Oliver Gaglianti's Life Work in Photographs; Masters of Fine Arts
Exhibition
Publications: Exhibition catalog
Activities: Docent training; lect open to public, 5 vis lectr per year; gallery talks;
competitions with awards; individual paintings & original objects of art lent to
other museums that can provide suitable security & climate control; book
traveling exhibitions 2-3 per year; originate traveling exhibitions to other art
museums; sales shop sells books, slides, cards, gifts
M Aperture Photo Gallery - EMU Art Gallery, ERB Memorial Union, 97403. Tel
541-346-4373; FAX 541-346-4400; *Dir & Cur* Delta Smith; *Asst Dir* Frank
Geltner
Open Mon - Sat 7:30 AM - 11:30 PM, Sun Noon - 11:30 PM. No admis fee.
Estab 1981 to provide space for work of university community
Income: Financed by student fees
Collections: †Pacific Northwest Art
Exhibitions: Periodic art exhibitions on portable display boards in various rooms;
display in the art gallery of selections from the permanent collection
Activities: Classes for adults; craft workshops; lect

L **Architecture & Allied Arts Library,** 200 Lawrence Hall, 97403. Tel 541-346-3637; *Head Librn* Sheila M Klos; *Reference Librn* Kaia Stavig Esau; *Visual Resources Cur* Christine L Sundt
Open Mon - Thurs 8 AM - 11 PM, Fri 8 AM - 9 PM, Sat 10 AM - 9 PM, Sun 10 AM - 11 PM. Estab 1915 to provide resources for the courses, degree programs & research of the departments in the School of Architecture & Allied Arts. Primarily for lending
Income: Financed by state appropriation
Library Holdings: Vols 62,000; Per subs 340; Micro — Fiche; AV — Slides 275,000; Other — Exhibition catalogs, photographs 30,000
Special Subjects: Aesthetics, Architecture, Art History, Interior Design, Landscape Architecture, Arts Administration, Fine Arts, Historic Preservation

GRANTS PASS

M **ROGUE COMMUNITY COLLEGE,** Wiseman Gallery - Firehouse Gallery, 3345 Redwood Hwy, 97527. Tel 541-471-3500, 471-3525; FAX 541-471-3588; Elec Mail tdrake@rogue.cc.or.us. *Dir* Tommi Drake; *Dir Asst* Rita Grauer
No admis fee. Estab 1985 to present exhibits of high artistic content in a range of aesthetics which contribute to the educational environment & serve to inspire the community & to serve our community & students with an additional venue for fine art that will inspire, create & promote understanding of the arts & the part they play in our lives
Collections: African tools; Japanese woodblock prints; varied paintings
Exhibitions: El Dia de los Muertos; NW Women in Art
Publications: Exhibit brochures; quarterly catalogues; monthly postals
Activities: Classes for adults; docent training; lect open to public

KLAMATH FALLS

M **FAVELL MUSEUM OF WESTERN ART & INDIAN ARTIFACTS,** 125 W Main, PO Box 165, 97601. Tel 541-882-9996; *Pres & Cur* Gene H Favell; *VPres & Treas* Winifred L Favell; *Adminr* Bev Jackson
Open Mon - Sat 9:30 AM - 5:30 PM, cl Sun. Admis adults $4, sr citizens 65 & over $3, youth 6 - 16 years $2. Estab 1972 to preserve Western heritage as represented by Indian artifacts & contemporary western art. Gallery features contemporary western artists combined with art & artifacts displays. Average Annual Attendance: 20,000. Mem: Dues $75; annual meeting in Apr
Income: $250,000 (financed by admis, sales & owners)
Purchases: Paintings by: Grace Hudson, McCarthy, Arlene Hooker Fay & James Bama; 800 works of art by 300 artists
Collections: †Contemporary western art; †western Indian artifacts: pottery, stonework, baskets, bead and quiltwork; †miniature firearms
Publications: A treasury of our Western Heritage (book on cross section of museum collection)
Activities: Lect open to public; gallery talks; museum shop selling books, original art, reproductions, prints, slides

M **KLAMATH COUNTY MUSEUM,** 1451 Main St, 97601. Tel 541-883-4208; *Dir* Patsy McMillan
Open June - Sept daily 9 AM - 5:30 - PM, Oct - May Mon - Sat 8 AM - 4:30 PM. Admis by donation. Estab 1957 to tell the story of the Klamath Country & to preserve & exhibit related material. Average Annual Attendance: 20,000
Income: Financed by county appropriation
Collections: Indian & pioneer artifacts; four original Rembrandt etchings; Healey paintings; photograph document files
Publications: Museum Research Papers
Activities: Museum shop sells books, reproductions of photos & area souvenirs
L **Research Library,** 1451 Main St, 97601. Tel 541-883-4208; *Dir* Patsy McMillan
Open to the pub for reference Tues - Sat 9 AM - 4:30 PM by appointment. Admis research fee. Estab 1955 to collect, preserve, document & interpret the local history
Income: Financed by County General Fund
Library Holdings: Vols 10,000; Micro — Reels; AV — Motion pictures, slides; Other — Clipping files, manuscripts, original art works, pamphlets, photographs 5000
Collections: Modoc Indian Books, Documents & Manuscripts
Activities: Guided tours for 4th grade students; school kits lent to area schools; sales shop sells books, prints, paintings, ceramic & other miscellaneous items
M **Baldwin Hotel Museum Annex,** 31 Main St, 97601. Tel 503-883-4207; *Dir* Patsy McMillan
Open Tues - Sat 10 AM - 4 PM, June - Sept. Admis family $6, adults $3, students & senior citizens $2, under 3 free. A State & national historic landmark purchased by Klamath County in Jan 1978. Restoration of building began in Feb 1978 & it was dedicated as a mus by Oregon's Governor Robert Straub June 3, 1978. Opened to the pub Aug 19, 1978. May be viewed by tour only
Activities: Guided tours for 5th grade students; museum shop sells books & original art

A **KLAMATH FALLS ART ASSOCIATION,** Klamath Art Gallery, 120 Riverside Dr, PO Box 955, 97601. Tel 541-883-1833, 882-2958; *Pres* Peggy Gratzer
Open Thurs - Sun 1 - 4 PM & special occasions. No admis fee. Estab 1948 to provide art training for local residents. Gallery estab 1960 to provide display & teaching space for the Association's activities. Average Annual Attendance: 5000. Mem: 150; dues $15-$20; annual meeting in Sept
Income: Financed by mem, gallery sales, tuition
Collections: Ceramics; paintings; weaving (owned by members)
Exhibitions: Twelve annually; one membership show, remainder varies
Activities: Classes in painting, drawing, weaving; children's summer art classes; workshops; lect, vis lectr

MARYLHURST

M **MARYLHURST COLLEGE,** The Art Gym, 97036. Tel 503-636-8141; FAX 503-636-9526; *Dir* Terri M Hopkins
Open Tues - Sat Noon - 4 PM. No admis fee. Estab 1980. 3000 sq ft. Average Annual Attendance: 5000. Mem: 150; dues $15-$500
Income: $50,000 (financed by mem, city appropriation & college budget)
Collections: Contemporary Northwest Art
Exhibitions: Lee Kelly: 35 Years of Painting & Sculpture
Publications: Exhibition catalogs
Activities: Lect open to public, 3-5 vis lectr per year; book traveling exhibitions; originate traveling exhibitions

MEDFORD

A **ROGUE VALLEY ART ASSOCIATION,** Rogue Gallery & Art Center, 40 S Bartlett, 97501. Tel 503-772-8118; *Pres* Bill Jacobs; *Dir* Nancy Jo Mullen; *Admin Asst* Tamara Archibald
Open Tues - Fri 10 AM - 5 PM, Sat 11 AM - 3 PM, cl Sun & Mon, extended hours Wed until 6 PM. Estab 1960 to provide a full range of programs, exhibits & classes to the region. Gallery 6000 sq ft, 2200 sq ft, sales & rental space, 2000 sq ft & 200 running ft of sliding panels. Average Annual Attendance: 20,000. Mem: 671; dues $20-$500; annual meeting in Jan
Income: Financed by mem dues, grants, fund raising events
Collections: Contemporary Northwest prints
Publications: Newsletter, 6 per yr
Activities: Classes for adults & children; lect open to public, 2 vis lectr per year; gallery talks; tours; scholarships & fels offered; individual paintings lent through a rental program to members; lending collection contains art works, paintings, photographs & sculpture; book traveling exhibitions 2-3 per year; sales shop sells original art, crafts, books, prints, sculpture, pottery, jewelry, greeting cards

M **SOUTHERN OREGON HISTORICAL SOCIETY,** Jacksonville Museum of Southern Oregon History, 206 N Fifth St (Mailing add: 106 N Central Ave, PO Box 480, 97501). Tel 541-773-6536; FAX 541-776-7994; *Exec Dir* Brad Linder; *Develop Dir* Jerry Price; *Finance Dir* Maureen Smith; *Cur Coll* Mary Ames Sheret; *VIP Coordr* Dawna Curler; *Head Art & Media* Mike Leonard; *Membership Coordr* Susan Cox-Smith; *Cur Educ* Darlene Turner; *Cur Exhib* Greta Brunchwyler; *Prog Dir* Emila Chamberlin; *Oral Historian* Marjorie Edens
Open Sun & Tues Noon - 5 PM, Wed - Sat 10 AM - 5 PM (winter), Sun - Sat 10 AM - 5 PM (summer). Modest admis fee. Estab 1946 to preserve, promote & interpret the history of southern Oregon. Incl are the Peter Britt Gallery (19th century photography artifacts); Children's Mus (next door in old county jail, a hands-on mus, includes the Pinto Gallery of Bozo the Clown). The historic sites include the Cornelius C Beekman House (1876), Beekman Bank (1863), Catholic Rectory (circa 1861), US Hotel (1880). Average Annual Attendance: 114,194. Mem: 1810; dues $30; annual meeting in Nov
Income: Financed by mem, pub & private grants & county historical fund
Collections: Relate to the scope & diversity of human experience in Jackson County & the southern Oregon region
Exhibitions: (1997) Miner Baker Furniture Maker; The Art Work of Dorland Robertson; The Politics of Culture
Publications: Table Rock Sentinel, bimonthly; ArtiFACTS, monthly newsletter
Activities: Classes for adults & children; docent training; lect open to public; concerts; gallery talks; tours; sales shop sells books, magazines & reproductions; junior museum
L **Library,** 106 N Central Ave, Medford, 97501-5926. Tel 541-773-6536; FAX 541-776-7994; *Library Mgr* Carol Harbison-Samuelson; *Archivist & Historian* William Alley; *Library Archives Coordr* Jacquelyn Sundstrand
Open Tues - Sat 1 - 5 PM. Open to public for reference only
Income: Financed by mem & county tax
Library Holdings: Vols 4900; Per subs 30; Ephemera, art on paper; Micro — Fiche, reels; AV — Cassettes, fs, v-tapes; Other — Clipping files, exhibition catalogs, manuscripts, memorabilia, original art works, pamphlets, photographs, prints
Special Subjects: American Western Art, Anthropology, Archaeology, Architecture, Furniture, Gold, Historical Material, Maps, Painting - American, Photography, Portraits, Restoration & Conservation, Textiles, Watercolors, Historic preservation, museum techniques, Southern Oregon History
Publications: Southern Oregon History, quarterly

MONMOUTH

M **WESTERN OREGON STATE COLLEGE,** Campbell Hall Gallery, 345 Monmouth Ave, 97361. Tel 503-838-8340; *Head Art Dept* Diane Tarter
Open Mon - Fri 8 AM - 5 PM during scheduled exhibits. No admis fee. Estab to bring contemporary art work to the community & the college for study & visual understanding. Library maintained. Average Annual Attendance: 3000-4000
Income: $3000 (financed by state appropriation & student fees)
Collections: †Permanent collection
Exhibitions: Contemporary Northwest Visual Art; rotating faculty & student exhibits
Activities: Lect open to public, 3-5 vis lectr per year; gallery talks; tours; competitions with awards; lending collection contains 10,000 slides; originate traveling exhibitions

NORTH BEND

M **COOS COUNTY HISTORICAL SOCIETY MUSEUM,** 1220 Sherman, 97459. Tel 541-756-6320; *Dir* Ann Koppy
Open Tues - Sat 10 AM - 4 PM. Admis $1. Estab 1891 to collect, preserve & interpret history of Coos County. Average Annual Attendance: 7255. Mem: 400; dues $10-$250; annual meeting in June
Income: $31,100 (financed by endowment, mem, admis, sales & donations)
Collections: Maritime objects; Native American artifacts; photographs; tools/

implements of pioneer lifeways
Exhibitions: Pioneer Kitchen; Formal Parlor (c1900); rotating Exhibits; Maritime
Publications: Coos Historical Journal, annual; bimonthly newsletter
Activities: Lect open to public, vs lectr; lending collection contains 100 items; sales shop sells books

PORTLAND

L BASSIST COLLEGE LIBRARY, 2000 SW Fifth Ave, 97201. Tel 503-228-6528; *Pres* Gary Smith; *Librn* Nancy Thurston; *Librn* William Kownacki; *Provost* William Endsley
Open 7:30 AM - 6 PM, open some evenings. No admis fee. Estab 1964 to provide practical instruction in retail merchandising, interior design, display, fashion design, advertising & promotion, fashion history & textiles, industrial design. Average Annual Attendance: 200
Library Holdings: Vols 14,000; Per subs 120; AV — Slides; Other — Clipping files
Special Subjects: Art History, Costume Design & Construction, Fashion Arts, Furniture, Industrial Design, Interior Design, Textiles
Collections: Collection of Fashion & Costume History Books; Collection in Furniture & Interior Decoration Fields
Activities: Scholarships offered

M BLUE SKY, Oregon Center for the Photographic Arts, 1231 NW Hoyt St, 97209. Tel 503-225-0210; *Dir* Chris Rauschenberg; *Gallery Coordr* Kirsten Rian
Exhibitions: Monthly rotating exhibits

M CONTEMPORARY CRAFTS ASSOCIATION & GALLERY, 3934 SW Corbett Ave, 97201. Tel 503-223-2654; FAX 503-223-2659; *Exec Dir* Marlene Gabel; *Operations Mgr* Michelle Z Mosgrove
Open Tues - Sat 10 AM - 5 PM, Sun 1 - 5 PM, cl Mon. No admis fee. Estab 1937 to promote, exhibit & sell contemporary crafts. Gallery is maintained also as a consignment outlet & holds exhibits monthly. Average Annual Attendance: 30,000. Mem: 1000; dues $30
Income: $114,000 (financed by mem)
Collections: †Contemporary crafts in clay, glass, metal & wood
Publications: Contemporary Crafts News, quarterly
Activities: Artists-in-Educ Program; docent training; lect open to public, some for members only; 10-12 vis lectr per year; gallery talks; tours; competitions; artist-in-residence; originate traveling exhibitions; sales shop sells books, fine crafts, original art
L Library, 3934 SW Corbett Ave, 97201. Tel 503-223-2654; FAX 503-223-2659; *Acting Librn* Beulah Parisi
Open to members
Library Holdings: Vols 430; Per subs 260

L MULTNOMAH COUNTY LIBRARY, Henry Failing Art & Music Dept, 801 SW Tenth, 97205. Tel 503-248-5281; *Dir* Ginnie Cooper; *Head Art & Music Dept* Ella Seely
Open Mon - Thurs 10 AM - 8 PM, Fri & Sat 10 AM - 5:30 PM, Sun 1 - 5 PM. Estab 1864 as a pub library service to Multnomah County
Library Holdings: Vols 23,000; AV — Rec, slides; Other — Clipping files

M OREGON COLLEGE OF ART CRAFT, Hoffman Gallery, 8245 SW Barnes Rd, 97225. Tel 503-297-5544; FAX 503-297-9651; *Pres* Joe Wedding; *Chief Academic Officer* Jane Kyle
Open Mon - Thurs 7:30 AM - 9:30 PM, Fri 7:30 AM - 5 PM, Sat 8 AM - 5 PM, Sun 10 AM - 5 PM. No admis fee, except for special events & classes. Estab 1907 to teach seven disciplines in the arts & crafts. Hoffman Exhibition Gallery features national & international craftspeople. Maintains library. Average Annual Attendance: 1500. Mem: 600; dues $35 - $1000; annual meeting in June
Income: Financed by tuitions, endowment, mem, state appropriation & National Endowments of the Arts, Washington, DC
Special Subjects: Art History, Asian Art, Bookplates & Bindings, Calligraphy, Carpets & Rugs, Ceramics, Collages, Costume Design & Construction, Crafts, Decorative Arts, Embroidery, Enamels, Etchings & Engravings, Folk Art, Furniture, Glass
Collections: Permanent collection of historic, traditional craftwork
Exhibitions: Annual Juried Student Show; OP-ART: Eyeglasses by Jewelers; (1997) Sheri Simons: Agitation Cycle; Thesis Show; L L Balmuth: Tin Goddess; Nates From All Over (Messages from the Interior) by Artist/Curator Robert Hanson; Artist-in-Residence Exhibition; Since 1907: 90 Years of OCAC; The Holiday Show
Publications: Course schedules, quarterly; gallery announcements, 12 per year; newsletter to members, 2 per year; 2 year catalog; 2 year viewbook
Activities: Classes & workshops for adults; BFA & certificate program in crafts; lect open to public; gallery talks; tours; scholarships offered; sales shop sells books, magazines and original art
L Library, 8245 SW Barnes Rd, 97225. Tel 503-297-5544; FAX 503-297-9651; *Librn* Elizabeth Bilyeu
Open Mon - Thurs 9 AM - 6:30 PM, Fri 9 AM - 3:30 PM, Sat & Sun Noon - 5 PM. Estab 1979. Craft reference library for students & faculty & others interested in crafts
Library Holdings: Vols 5500; Per subs 90; AV — Slides, v-tapes; Other — Exhibition catalogs, original art works, pamphlets, photographs, prints
Special Subjects: Architecture, Ceramics, Drawings, Glass, Metalwork, Painting - American, Photography, Printmaking, Textiles, Art & Craft History, Books Arts, Ethnic/Pattern, Metals, Nature, Wood
Activities: Interlibrary loan services available

A OREGON HISTORICAL SOCIETY, 1200 SW Park Ave, 97205. Tel 503-306-5200; FAX 503-221-2035; *Exec Dir* Chet Orloff; *Deputy Dir* Barbara Abrans; *Cur of Coll* J D Cleaver; *Cur Coll* Carla Simon
Open Tues - Sat 10 AM - 5 PM, Sun Noon - 5 PM. Admis adults $6, students $1.50. Estab 1873, incorporated 1898, to collect, preserve, exhibit & publish materials pertaining to the Oregon country. Approx 20,000 sq ft of exhibit space;

Society maintains historic 1856 James F. Bybee House, Howell Territorial Park, Sauvie Island. Average Annual Attendance: 150,000. Mem: 8500; dues individual & family $25 - $49, senior $20, student $15; annual meeting Nov
Income: $3,363,000 biennially (financed by state appropriation, mem, grants, gifts & donations)
Collections: †Artifacts, †Manuscripts, †paintings, †photographs, collection by Oregon Country & Oregon State artists
Publications: Oregon Historical Quarterly; books; maps; pamphlets; newsletter
Activities: Seminars for adults; classes for children; docent training; dramatic programs; lect open to public, 15-20 vis lectr per year; concerts; gallery talks; tours; exten dept serves small museums statewide; individual collections & original objects lent to other museums; book traveling exhibitions 1-2 per year; originate traveling exhibitions to small museums regionwide; museum shop sells books, general merchandise, gift items, magazines
L Library, 1200 SW Park Ave, 97205. Tel 503-306-5200; FAX 503-221-2035; *Assoc Dir Coll* Louis Flannery; *Quarterly Ed* Rick Harmon; *Exhibits Coordr* Pat Kaczmarek; *Dir Image Coll* Susan Seyl; *Archival Dir* Khris White
Open Tues - Sat Noon - 5 PM. For reference only
Library Holdings: Vols 100,000; Per subs 620; Original documents; Micro — Cards, fiche, prints, reels; AV — A-tapes, cassettes, fs, lantern slides, motion pictures, rec, slides, v-tapes; Other — Clipping files, exhibition catalogs, framed reproductions, manuscripts, memorabilia, original art works, pamphlets, photographs, prints, reproductions, sculpture
Special Subjects: History of the Pacific Northwest & the Oregon Country; political & economic growth of Pacific Northwest; Northwest Exploration & voyages
Collections: 3500 separate manuscript collections containing 17,500,000 pieces; 1,500,000 historic photographs; 15,000 maps

M PORTLAND ART MUSEUM, 1219 SW Park Ave, 97205. Tel 503-226-2811; FAX 503-226-4842; Elec Mail admin@pam.org. *Exec Dir* John Buchanan; *Develop Dir* Lucy Buchanan; *Cur Asian Art* Donald Jenkins; *Cur Photo* Terry Toedtemeier; *Sr Cur American, Contemporary & European Art* Prudence Roberts; *Acting Cur Educ* Judy Schultz; *Registrar* Marc Pence; *Conservator* Sonja Sopher
Open Tues - Sun 10 AM - 5 PM. Admis adults $6, seniors & students $4.50, children 6-12 $1.50, members & children under 6 free. Estab 1892 to make a collection of works of art & to erect & maintain a suitable building in which the same may be studied & exhibited; to develop & encourage the study of art. Maintains reference library. Average Annual Attendance: 225,000. Mem: 13,000; dues $35 & up; annual meeting in Oct
Income: Financed by admis, endowment, grants, contributions & mem
Collections: †American painting, 19th & 20th centuries; Elizabeth Cole Butler Collection; Gebauer Collection of Cameroon Art; †Vivian & Gordon Gilkey Graphics Art Collection; Hirsch Collection of Oriental Rugs; Samuel H Kress Collection of Renaissance Painting & Sculpture; Mary Andrews Ladd Collection of Japanese Prints; Lawther Collection of Ethiopian Crosses; Lewis Collection of Classical Antiquities; †Alice B Nunn Collection of English Silver; †Oriental sculptures, paintings, bronzes, ceramics & other decorative arts; Persian & Hindu miniatures; Pre-Columbian Art; Rasmussen Collection of Northwest Coast Indian & Eskimo Arts; Evan H Roberts Memorial 19th & 20th Century Sculpture Collection; Margery H Smith Collection of Asian Art; †20th century photographs
Publications: Annual report; Art of Cameroon; Calendar, monthly; exhibition catalogs; Art in the Life of the Northwest Coast Indian; collection catalogs
Activities: Docent training; lect open to the public, 45-50 vis lectr per year; concerts; gallery talks; tours; awards; individual paintings & original objects of art lent; book traveling exhibitions 8-12 per year; originate traveling exhibitions; museum shop sells books & reproductions
L Rex Arragon Library, 1219 SW Park Ave, 97205. Tel 503-226-2811, Ext 215; FAX 503-226-4842; Elec Mail library@pam.org. *Library Dir* Dan Lucas
Estab 1892 to provide reference for mus staff, Pacific Northwest College of art students & pub
Library Holdings: Vols 25,000; Per subs 35; Northwest artist files; AV — A-tapes, cassettes, Kodachromes, lantern slides, motion pictures, rec, slides, v-tapes; Other — Exhibition catalogs, pamphlets, photographs
Special Subjects: Afro-American Art, American Indian Art, American Western Art, Art History, Asian Art, Folk Art, Islamic Art, Mexican Art, Oriental Art, Painting - American, Pre-Columbian Art, Southwestern Art, Northwest Coast Indian art & culture

A Northwest Film Center, 1219 SW Park Ave, 97205. Tel 503-221-1156; FAX 503-226-4842; *Dir* Bill Foster
Admis $5. Estab 1972 as a regional media arts center. Maintains film archive, circ film library, film & video exhibition program & classes. Average Annual Attendance: 40,000
Exhibitions: Annual Northwest Film & Video Festival; Best of the Northwest: New Work by Film & Video Artists in Oklahoma, Washington, Iowa, Montana & Alaska; Portland International Film Festival; Young Peoples Film Festival
Activities: Film screening program; courses in film and video; video/filmmaker-in-schools program; lect open to public, 24 vis lectr per year; competitions with awards; scholarships & fels offered; exten dept; originate traveling exhibitions

M PORTLAND CHILDREN'S MUSEUM, 3037 SW Second Ave, 97201. Tel 503-823-2227; FAX 503-823-3667; *Dir* John Houseman; *Educational Dir* Jon Ziady
Open daily 9 AM - 5 PM, cl some National Holidays. Admis $3.50. Estab 1949; sponsored jointly by Friends of the Children's Mus & the Portland Bureau of Parks & Recreation. Average Annual Attendance: 85,000. Mem: 2500; dues family $48
Income: Financed by city appropriation 50% & Friends of the Children's Mus 50%
Collections: Children's art; natural history, toys, dollhouses, miniatures; multicultural artifacts relating to children's culture
Exhibitions: Baby Room; Children's Cultural Center; Clay Shop; Grocery Store; Kid City Grocery Store, H2 Oh; 10 Best & 10 Worst Toys; rotating exhibitions quarterly
Publications: Museum Program Guide, quarterly
Activities: Hands-on art activities for children; docent training; lect; tours; book traveling exhibitions; museum shop sells books

M PORTLAND COMMUNITY COLLEGE, North View Gallery, 12000 SW 49th Ave, 97219. Tel 503-977-4269; FAX 503-977-4264; *Dir* Hugh Webb
Open Mon - Fri 8 AM - 5 PM. No admis fee. Estab 1970. Gallery's primary focus on contemporary Northwest artists, through solo shows, group invitations, installations & new genres. Average Annual Attendance: Over 20,000 in the Portland Metro area
Exhibitions: Contemporary art of the Northwest
Activities: Lect open to public; 4-6 vis lectr per year; scholarships & fels offered

PORTLAND STATE UNIVERSITY
M Littman Gallery, 725 SW Harrison, PO Box 751/SD, 97207. Tel 503-725-5656; FAX 503-725-5680; *Coordr* Theresa Tate
Open Mon - Fri Noon - 4 PM. No admis fee. Estab 1980 to exhibit art in variety of media, style & geographic distribution. Gallery space has 1500 sq ft
Exhibitions: 7-10 exhibitions annually
Activities: Lect open to public; gallery talks
M White Gallery, 1825 SW Broadway, Smith Center, PO Box 751, 97207. Tel 503-725-5656; FAX 503-725-5080; *Coordr* Theresa Tate
Open Mon - Fri 8 AM - 10 PM, Sat 9 AM - 7 PM. No admis fee. Estab 1970 as a student operated gallery exhibiting works by professional artists representing primarily photography
Collections: Permanent collection contains work by local professional artists with a few nationally recognized artists
Exhibitions: 4-5 exhibitions annually
Activities: Lect open to public; gallery talks; individual paintings & original objects of art lent to other schools or museums; lending collection contains original prints, paintings & sculpture

M REED COLLEGE, Douglas F Cooley Memorial Art Gallery, 3203 SE Woodstock Blvd, 97202-8199. Tel 503-777-7251; FAX 503-777-7798; Elec Mail Susan.Fillin-Yeh@Reed.edu. *Dir & Cur* Susan Fillin-Yeh
Open Tues - Sun Noon - 5 PM, Drawings Room open by appointment for study of works on paper. No admis fee. Estab 1989 to enhance the teaching of art, art history & the humanities. The program brings to the college & the community exhibitions of art from a variety of periods & traditions as well as significant contemporary art not otherwise available in the Northwest
Collections: Pre-20th century prints; 20th century prints, drawings, paintings, photographs & sculptures
Publications: Brochures; catalogues
Activities: Public openings; lectures; gallery talks

A REGIONAL ARTS & CULTURE COUNCIL (Formerly Metropolitan Arts Commission), Metropolitan Center for Public Arts, 309 SW Sixth, Ste 100, 97204. Tel 503-823-5111; FAX 503-796-3388; *Chmn* Chuck Clemans; *Dir* Bill Bulick
Open Mon - Fri 8 AM - 5 PM. No admis fee. Estab 1973, to promote and encourage programs to further the development and public awareness of and interest in the visual and performing arts
Income: Financed by city & county appropriation
Purchases: Visual Chronicle of Portland, one percent for Public Art projects
Collections: Works by local artists
Publications: Newsletter, biannual; Technical Assistance Newsletter, monthly
Activities: Competitions with awards; individual paintings & original objects of art lent

L UNIVERSITY OF PORTLAND, Wilson W Clark Memorial Library, 5000 N Willamette Blvd, PO Box 83017, 97283-0017. Tel 503-283-7111; Elec Mail kopp@uofport.edu. *Dir* James J Kopp; *Reference Librn* Pam Horan; *Technical Services Librn* Susan Hinken; *Spec Serv Librn* Michael Storwick
Open Mon - Thurs 8 AM - Noon, Fri 9 AM - 5 PM, Sat 9 AM - 4 PM, Sun 11 AM - midnight. Estab 1901 to support the university curriculum. Maintains an art gallery with a rotating exhibit. Circ 50,000
Income: Financed through the university
Collections: Rotating collections
Publications: Art Objects, holdings list

M UNIVERSITY OF PORTLAND, Buckley Center Gallery, 5000 N Willamette Blvd, 97203. Tel 503-283-7258; *Co-Dir* Michael Miller; *Co-Dir* Mary Margaret Dundore
Open Mon - Fri 8:30 AM - 8 PM, Sat 8:30 AM - 4 PM. Estab 1977
Exhibitions: Noel Thomas; Terry Waldron; Martha Wehrle

A WEST HILLS UNITARIAN FELLOWSHIP, 8470 SW Oleson Rd, 97223. Tel 503-246-3351, 244-1379; *Pres* Mindy Boyer; *VPres* Jeanette Parsons; *Office Admin* Doll Gardner
Open Mon - Fri 9 AM - Noon. No admis fee. Estab 1970 to give professional artists one or two-man shows in a lovely gallery space & to expose the congregation & pub to fine visual art. The entire sanctuary wall space is like a large gallery & the building is light, airy with a woodsy backdrop. Average Annual Attendance: 10,000
Income: $30,000 (financed by mem)
Collections: Paintings, wall sculptures by local artists
Publications: Bulletin, weekly; newsletter, monthly
Activities: Classes for adults & children; dramatic programs; lect open to public, 8 vis lectr per year; concerts; sales shop selling books

ROSEBURG

PASTEL SOCIETY OF OREGON
For further information, see National and Regional Organizations

SAINT BENEDICT

L MOUNT ANGEL ABBEY LIBRARY, 97373. Tel 503-845-3317; FAX 503-845-3500; *Head Librn* Paula Hamilton
Open 8:30 AM - 5 PM (school yr), 10:30 AM - 4:30 PM (summer & holidays). Estab 1882. The library serves Mount Angel Abbey, Mount Angel Seminary & the pub. It sponsors art exhibits in the foyer designed for this purpose & makes the auditorium available for concerts
Library Holdings: Vols 275,000; Per subs 1000; Micro — Fiche 10; Other — Framed reproductions 30, manuscripts, original art works 100, prints 30
Exhibitions: Local artists; Alvar Aalto

SALEM

A SALEM ART ASSOCIATION, 600 Mission St SE, 97302. Tel 503-581-2228; *Exec Dir* David Cohen
Open Tues - Fri Noon - 5 PM, Sat & Sun 1 - 5 PM. No admis fee. Estab 1919 to collect, preserve & interpret history & art. Sales gallery & exhibition galleries featuring contemporary art. Average Annual Attendance: 125,000. Mem: 1300; dues $25; annual meeting in Sept
Income: $335,000 (financed by sales, Salem Art Fair & Festival special fundraisers, admis, mem & donations)
Exhibitions: 10 exhibits yearly in 2 galleries
Activities: Classes for adults & children; lect open to public; gallery talks; sales shop sells original art
M Bush Barn Art Center, 600 Mission St SE, 97302. Tel 503-581-2228; *Exec Dir* David Cohen; *Exhib Dir* Saralyn Hilde
Open Tues - Fri 10 AM - 5 PM, Sat & Sun 1 - 5 PM. No admis fee. Estab 1965 to exhibit the best art of the past & the present. Houses the AN Bush Gallery & Corner Gallery which features 10 exhibitions each year & a sales gallery of Northwest art & crafts. Average Annual Attendance: 20,000
Exhibitions: Native American Abstract Design
Activities: Docent training; awards; scholarships offered; individual paintings rented to members only (2-D work only)
M Bush House, 600 Mission St SE, 97302. Tel 503-363-4714; *Bush House Cur* Jennifer Hagloch
Open Summer Tues - Sun Noon - 5 PM, Winter Tues - Sun 2 - 5 PM. Admis adults $2.50, senior citizens & students $2, children $1. Estab 1953 to preserve & interpret the Victorian Era of 1870-1900. Contains 16 room mansion with original furnishings. Average Annual Attendance: 10,000
Collections: Decorative Art, Furniture, books, documents & antiques, Victorian
Activities: Tours; museum shop sells books, post cards & brochures
L Archives, 600 Mission St SE, 97302. Tel 503-363-4714; *Cur* Jennifer Haglock
Library Holdings: Vols 150; AV — A-tapes, cassettes, motion pictures, v-tapes; Other — Clipping files, manuscripts, memorabilia, photographs
Collections: Bush family papers 1840-1950
Exhibitions: Victorian Historic House with furniture

M WILLAMETTE UNIVERSITY, George Putnam University Center, 900 State St, 97301. Tel 503-370-6267, ext 6394; *Dir* Scott Greenwood
Open Mon - Sun 8 AM - 11 PM. No admis fee. Estab 1970 to enrich the atmosphere of the University Center & to acquaint students, faculty & staff with various forms of art. Two separate areas are used: one area is a paneled wall; the other area is comprised of free standing art panels with surface area of approx 54 x 54 inches. Average Annual Attendance: 45,000
Income: Financed through the University
Exhibitions: Revolving exhibitions of several local artists & photographers
Activities: Lect; gallery talks

SPRINGFIELD

A EMERALD EMPIRE ART GALLERY ASSOCIATION, 421 N A St, 97477. Tel 541-726-8595; *Pres* Shirley Canning
Open Mon - Fri 11 AM - 4 PM. No admis fee. Estab 1957 to promote cultural arts in Springfield & surrounding areas. Downtown area is 3000 sq ft. Mem: 90; dues assoc mem $60, contributing members $25; monthly meetings 3rd Tues
Income: Financed by mem dues, commission on sales, fund raisers
Collections: Paintings donated by workshop teachers
Exhibitions: Exhibitions twice a year at local shopping malls & convention centers
Publications: Monthly Art League Bulletin
Activities: Classes for adults, material available to anyone; lect open to public; picture of the month award; competitions; individual paintings & original objects of art lent; traveling exhibitions organized & circulated; sales shop sells crafts, magazines & original art

PENNSYLVANIA

ALLENTOWN

M ALLENTOWN ART MUSEUM, Fifth & Courts Sts, PO Box 388, 18105-0388. Tel 610-432-4333; FAX 610-434-7409; *Pres Board Trustees* C Richard Wilson; *Dir* Peter F Blume; *Cur Educ* Lynn Berkowitz; *Assoc Dir* Cindy Orenstein; *Bus Mgr* Lisa Miller; *Registrar* Carl Schafer; *Sales Gallery* Sharon Yurkanin
Open Tues - Sat 11 AM - 5 PM, Sun Noon - 5 PM, cl Mon. Admis general $3.50, senior citizens $3, students $2, children 12 & under free. Estab 1939 to acquire, protect, display & interpret the visual arts from the past & present, world wide. Building & land cover three quarters of a city block; 28,000 sq ft wing was added in 1975 to more than double the space. Average Annual Attendance: 74,000. Mem: 2400; dues $15-$1000
Income: $850,000 (financed by endowment, mem, city, county & state

appropriation & contributions)
Purchases: American & European paintings; textiles; prints & drawings; photography
Collections: †American 18th, 19th & 20th century paintings, sculptures, prints & drawings; Chinese porcelains; English & American silver; Japanese Prints; Samuel H Kress Collection of European paintings & sculpture, c 1350-1750 (Bugiardini, Lotto, de Heem, Rembrandt, Ruisdael, Steen & others); Textile study room; 20th century photographs; Frank Lloyd Wright period room, 1912
Exhibitions: (1997) Needle Art of the Lehigh Valley; Dan Massad; IDEA; Judith Joy Ross; Charles Sheeler in Doylestown: American Modernism & the Pennsylvania Tradition; Salisbury School District; Winds of the Aegean: Greek Embroidery from the Collection; The James C Fuller Gem Collection & Materials of Nature/Nature of Materials; American Art; European Paintings & Sculpture
Publications: Calendar of events, quarterly; catalogs of major exhibitions; descriptive gallery handouts
Activities: Classes for adults & children; docent training; 3 family events each year; lect open to public; gallery talks; tours; competitions; concerts; museum shop sells books, jewelry & other art related games & stationery; Max Hess Junior Gallery

M **LEHIGH COUNTY HISTORICAL SOCIETY,** Hamilton at Fifth, PO Box 1548, 18105. Tel 610-435-9601; FAX 610-435-9812; *Exec Dir* Carol B Wickkiser; *Cur Coll* Andree Mey; *Coll Mgr* Colleen Curry; *Librn* June B Griffith; *Educ Cur* Sarah Nelson; *Dir Develop* David Voellinger; *Membership Coordr* Linda Buesgen; *Public Relations Coordr* Mary Rose Iuorno-Shirley; *Bus Mgr* Mary Erie
George Taylor House open June - Sept Sat & Sun 1 - 4 PM; Trout Hall Apr - Nov Tues - Sat Noon - 3 PM, Sun 1 - 4 PM; Lehigh County Mus Mon - Fri 9 AM - 4 PM, Sat & Sun 1 - 4 PM; Claussville, Lock Ridge, Saylor Cement, Haines Mill & Frank Buchman House May - Sept Sat & Sun 1 - 4 PM. No admis fee. Estab 1904 for collection, preservation & exhibition of Lehigh County history. Lock Ridge Furnace Mus 1868, Frank Buchman House 1892, Haines Mill Mus 1760, Lehigh County Mus 1814, Trout Hall 1770, George Taylor House 1768, Saylor Cement Industry Mus 1868, Troxell-Steckel House 1755, Claussville One-Room Schoolhouse 1893. Average Annual Attendance: 63,000. Mem: 1300; dues $15-$1000; annual meeting 3rd Wed in Apr
Income: $750,000 (financed by endowment, mem, tax-based support, foundations, corporate & business support)
Collections: American Indian items; decorative arts; local artworks; structures
Publications: Proceedings, biennial; Town Crier, quarterly newsletter
Activities: Workshops; lect open to public, 15 vis lectr per year; concerts; tours; individual paintings & original objects of art lent to museums; lending collection contains motion picture, filmstrip, original art works, original prints, paintings, 3000 photographs, 8000 decorative arts, tools & other objects; museum shop sells books, pamphlets & local souvenirs

L **Scott Andrew Trexler II Library,** Old Court House, Hamilton at Fifth (Mailing add: PO Box 1548, 18105). Tel 610-435-4664; FAX 610-435-9812; *Librn & Archivist* June B Griffiths; *Asst Librn* Carol M Herrity
Open Mon - Sat 10 AM - 4 PM. Estab 1974. For reference only
Income: $45,000
Purchases: $14,000
Library Holdings: Vols 10,000; Per subs 20; Micro — Reels 225; AV — A-tapes 10, cassettes 200, lantern slides 1000; Other — Framed reproductions, manuscripts 1000, memorabilia 1000, original art works, pamphlets, photographs 50,000, prints
Special Subjects: Genealogy, local & regional history
Collections: Allentown imprints; broadsides; Civil War; early German newspapers; fraktur; Native American materials; photographs
Publications: Proceedings, semi-annual; Town Crier

M **MUHLENBERG COLLEGE CENTER FOR THE ARTS,** Frank Martin Gallery, 2400 Chew St, 18104-5586. Tel 610-821-3466; FAX 610-821-3633; *Gallery Dir* Dr Lori Verderame
Open Tues - Fri 11 AM - 5 PM, Sat & Sun Noon - 5 PM, cl Mon. No admis fee. Estab 1976. The building was designed by architect Philip Johnson; the focal point of its design & function is a 220 ft glass-covered galleria which bisects the structure
Collections: Contemporary art; 1700 master prints; Rembrandt, Durer, Whistler, Goya, Pennell
Exhibitions: Three or more exhibitions each semester; three summer exhibitions
Publications: Exhibition catalogs

AMBLER

A **FUDAN MUSEUM FOUNDATION,** 1522 Schoolhouse Rd, 19002-1936. Tel 215-699-6448 (voice & FAX);
Estab 1988 to exhibit & teach Chinese museology in collaboration with the Shanghai Museum, Shanghai, China. Holds the complete material of the Gaoshan culture & currently building the American collection. Now contains the monoprints of Harry Bertoia
Income: Financed by university
Collections: Permanent collection of Chinese & American archaeology, history, anthropology, ethnography, arts, sciences, technology, industry & business
Activities: Originate traveling exhibitions

AUDUBON

M **AUDUBON WILDLIFE SANCTUARY,** Mill Grove, PO Box 7125, 19407. Tel 610-666-5593; *Adminr* D Roger Mower Jr; *Asst Adminr* L Alan Gehret
Open Tues - Sat 10 AM - 4 PM, Sun 1 - 4 PM. No admis fee. Estab 1951 to display the major artwork of John James Audubon, artist-naturalist, who made Mill Grove his first home in America 1803-06. This is a National Historic Landmark & features two original artworks by Audubon, plus examples of all his major publications. Average Annual Attendance: 20,000
Income: Financed by county appropriation

Collections: †Birds of America (double elephant folio, 4 vols, Audubon & Havell); †Birds of America (first ed Octavo, 7 vols, Audubon, Lithos by bowen); Quadrupeds of North America (Imperial size, 2 vols, Audubon & Bachmann); †Quadrupeds of North America (Octavo, 3 vols, Audubon, Lithos by Bowen)
Activities: Educ dept for children; lect open to public; gallery talks, tours; museum shop sells books & prints

BETHLEHEM

M **KEMERER MUSEUM OF DECORATIVE ARTS,** PO Box 1305, 18016-1305. Tel 610-868-6868; FAX 610-882-0460; *Pres* Nikki Vasiliadis; *Dir* Tony Hanna; *Dir Develop* Marie Sincavage; *Treas* Loretta Tubiello-Harr
Open Tues - Sun Noon - 5 PM. Admis adults $3. Estab 1954 for pub educ. Devoted to the display of antiques & historical & other objects illustrative of the growth of the museum's geographical area. Gallery on second floor of the south wing provides changing exhibits. Average Annual Attendance: 9000. Mem: 400
Income: $180,000 (financed by endowment & mem)
Collections: Bohemian Glass, Early Bethlehem Oil Paintings & Prints, 18th & 19th Century Furniture, Oriental Rugs, Pennsylvania German Frackturs, Victoriana, quilts & coverlets, locally made tall case clocks & tinware
Exhibitions: Changing gallery exhibitions; changing temporary museum; private collection exhibits
Publications: Newsletter, quarterly
Activities: Docent training; gallery talks; tours; competitions; museum shop sells books, reproductions, prints & decorative arts items

M **LEHIGH UNIVERSITY ART GALLERIES,** Chandler-Ullman Hall, 17 Memorial Dr E, 18015. Tel 610-758-3615; *Dir Exhib & Coll* Ricardo Viera; *Asst to Dir* Denise Beslanovits
Open Mon - Fri 9 AM - 10 PM, Sat 9 AM - Noon, cl Sun (DuBois Gallery), 9 AM - 5 PM, Sat 9 AM - Noon, Sun 2 - 5 PM (Ralph Wilson Gallery). Estab to bring diverse media & understanding to the Lehigh students & general pub of the Lehigh Valley area. Collection is maintained in two galleries: DuBois Gallery has four floors of approx 250 running ft of wall hanging space per floor; Ralph Wilson Gallery has two rooms of exhibition space; hall gallery consists of two corridors. Average Annual Attendance: 25,000 (per all galleries)
Income: Financed by endowment & gifts
Collections: Adler Collection of Paintings; Baker Collection of Porcelain; Berman Collection of Paintings & Outdoor Sculpture; Driebe Collection of Paintings; Grace Collection of Paintings; Kempsmith Collection of Sculpture and Graphics; photography collection; Ralph Wilsion Collection of Paintings & Graphics
Publications: Calendar, twice per year; exhibition catalogs
Activities: Classes for adults; lect open to public, 6 vis lectr per year; gallery talks; individual paintings & original objects of art lent to other schools & galleries; originate traveling exhibitions

M **MORAVIAN COLLEGE,** Payne Gallery, 1200 Main St, 18018. Tel 610-861-1675, 861-1680 (office); FAX 610-861-1682; *Chmn Art Dept* Dr Rudy Ackerman; *Dir* Les Reker; *Asst to Dir* David Leidich
Open Tues - Sun 11 AM - 4 PM. No admis fee. Estab 1982 to present historic & contemporary art to a diverse audience. Main floor & mezzanine have a combined total of 200 running ft. Average Annual Attendance: 15,000
Income: Financed by endowment & through the college
Purchases: Collection of paintings by W Elmer Schofield, Susan Eakins & Antonio Martino acquired
Collections: Collection of 18th, 19th & 20th century landscape paintings of Eastern Pennsylvania; Collection of contemporary paintings & prints
Publications: Exhibition catalogues
Activities: Lect open to the public, 8 vis lectr per year; competitions with awards; scholarships offered

BLOOMSBURG

M **BLOOMSBURG UNIVERSITY OF PENNSYLVANIA,** Haas Gallery of Art, Arts Dept All Science Hall, 17815. Tel 717-389-4646; FAX 717-389-4946; *Dir* Stewart Nagel; *Chmn Dept of Art* Kenneth Wilson
Open Mon - Fri 9 AM - 5 PM. No admis fee. Estab 1966 as an educational & cultural extension of the College's Department of Art. Gallery covers 2350 sq ft with track lighting & three dome skylights. Average Annual Attendance: 16,000
Income: Financed by community activities & grants
Collections: Permanent Collection
Exhibitions: Ten exhibitions annually in a variety of media
Publications: Exhibition catalogs & brochures, monthly
Activities: Lect open to public, 6-8 vis lectr per year; gallery talks; tours

BOALSBURG

M **COLUMBUS CHAPEL & BOAL MANSION MUSEUM,** * Business Rte 322, 16827. Tel 814-466-6210; *Dir* Jim Van Horn
Open June - Labor Day daily (except Tues) 10 AM - 5 PM, May, Sept & Oct 2 - 5 PM, weekends in Dec 1:30 - 5 PM. Admis adults $5, children $2. Estab 1952 as a nonprofit educational organization devoted to preservation of this unique American & international heritage & collection. Average Annual Attendance: 25,000
Income: Financed by admis
Collections: Chapel contains 16th & 17th century Spanish, Italian & Flemish art; furniture, china & glassware; mansion contains 18th & 19th century French, Spanish, Italian, Flemish & American art; weapons: American, French & German (1780-1920)
Activities: Sales shop sells books, slides & postcards

BRYN ATHYN

M ACADEMY OF THE NEW CHURCH, Glencairn Museum, 1001 Cathedral Rd, PO Box 757, 19009. Tel 215-947-9919; FAX 215-938-1056; *Pres* Daniel W Goodenough; *Dir* Stephen H Morley
Open Mon - Fri 9 AM - 5 PM by appointment, Sept - June Sun 2 - 5 PM. Admis adults $4, students & seniors $3, children $2. Estab 1878 to display, study & teach about works of art & artifacts which illustrate the history of world religions. Museum housed in Romanesque style building (1939), former home of Raymond & Mildred Pitcairn
Income: Financed by endowment
Collections: American Indian; †Ancient Near East; †Egypt; †Greece & Rome; Medieval sculpture, stained glass & treasury objects; †19th & 20th Century art by Swedenborgian artists; oriental rugs
Publications: Biannual newsletter
Activities: Programs for school groups; lectures open to the public, 3 vis lectr per year; concerts; gallery talks; tours; individual paintings & original art objects of art lent to institutions which provide satisfactory evidence of adequate security, insurance, fire protection

BRYN MAWR

L BRYN MAWR COLLEGE, Art & Archaeology Library, Thomas Library, 19010. Tel 610-526-5088; FAX 610-526-7480; *Head Librn* Eileen Markson; *Library Asst* Marshall Johnston
Open during academic year Mon - Thurs 9 AM - midnight, Fri 9 AM - 10 PM, Sat 10 AM - 5 PM, Sun 10 AM - midnight, summer Mon - Fri 9 AM - 5 PM. Estab 1931 to serve the needs of the general college program, the undergraduate majors & graduate students through the PhD degree in both history of art & Classical & Near Eastern archaeology. Non-circulating
Income: Financed by college funds
Library Holdings: Vols 90,000; Per subs 450; Micro — Fiche, reels; Other — Exhibition catalogs, pamphlets
Special Subjects: Early Christian and Byzantine, Italian Renaissance, Italian Baroque, Impressionism, Greek architecture and sculpture, Near Eastern archaeology, Aegean archaeology

BUTLER

L CENTER FOR HISTORY OF AMERICAN NEEDLEWORK, 6459 Old Route 8 (Mailing add: PO Box 359, Valencia, 16059-0359). Tel 412-586-5325; *Exec Dir* Mary Ann Geiger; *Exec Dir* N Brown; *Librn* Sally Pollifren
Open by appointment. Estab 1974
Income: Financed by mem & donations
Library Holdings: Vols 1500; AV — Slides, v-tapes; Other — Clipping files, memorabilia, pamphlets, photographs
Special Subjects: Carpets & Rugs, Costume Design & Construction, Crafts, Decorative Arts, Dolls, Embroidery, Fashion Arts, Folk Art, Handicrafts, Historical Material, Interior Design, Laces
Collections: Decorative needlework; doilies; needlework; vintage clothing
Exhibitions: Pot Holders; frequent exhibits of needlework
Publications: Newsletter, quarterly, patterns & anthologies

CARLISLE

M DICKINSON COLLEGE, Trout Gallery, High St, PO Box 1773, 17013-2896. Tel 717-245-1344; FAX 717-245-1937; *Dir* Peter M Lukehart; *Registrar & Exhib Preparator* Dwayne Franklin; *Community Outreach* Martha A Metz
Open Tues - Sat 10 AM - 4 PM. Estab 1983 as display & care facilities for college's art collection, serves college & community. Two floors with exhibition & permanent collection space
Income: $167,564 (financed by endowment, college & special grants)
Purchases: Auguste Rodin's St John the Baptist; Joseph Stella's Bold Flowers; African Art; Baselitz's Madchen mit Harmonika IV
Collections: Carnegie Collection of prints; Cole Collection of Oriental & decorative arts; Gerofsky Collection of African art; Potamkin Collection of 19th & 20th century work; 5000 Old Master & modern prints
Publications: Exhibition catalogues, 3 - 5 per year
Activities: Classes for adults & children; lect open to public, 4 - 8 vis lectr per year; book traveling exhibitions 2 - 4 per year; originate traveling exhibitions

CHADDS FORD

M BRANDYWINE RIVER MUSEUM, US 1, PO Box 141, 19317. Tel 610-388-2700; FAX 610-388-1197; *Dir* James H Duff; *Business Mgr* John Anderson; *Assoc Cur* Virginia O'Hara; *Cur Coll* Gene E Harris; *Dir Public Relations* Lucinda Laird; *Registrar* Jean A Gilmore; *Supv Educ* Mary Cronin; *Bookstore Mgr* Jean Young; *Librn* Ruth Bassett
Open daily 9:30 AM - 4:30 PM, cl Christmas. Admis adults $5, seniors & students $2.50. Estab 1971, devoted to the preservation, documentation & interpretation of art history in the Brandywine Valley, the history of American illustration, American still-life paintings & the relationship of regional art to the natural environment. Four galleries of permanent collections & special exhibitions, changing approx 5 times a year. Average Annual Attendance: 160,000. Mem: 4000; dues vary
Collections: †American illustration; †American still-life painting, drawing & sculpture, including a major Wyeth Family Collection; †art of the Brandywine Valley from early 19th century; †regional artists of the 20th century
Exhibitions: (1997) Of the Best Sort, But Plain; Quaker Quilts from the Delaware Valley; Ship Portrait & Marine Paintings of Alexander Charles Stewart. (1997-98) A Brandywine Christmas: Images of Snow White
Publications: The Catalyst, quarterly; Catalogue of the Collection; exhibition catalogs
Activities: Docent training; family programs; school programs; guided tours;

volunteer activities; individual paintings & original objects of art lent to other museums for exhibition purposes; book traveling exhibitions; traveling exhibitions, organized & circulated to other museums; museum shop sells books, reproductions, prints, gifts & cards

L Library, PO Box 141, 19317. Tel 610-388-2700; FAX 610-388-1197; *Librn* Ruth Bassett
Open daily 9:30 AM - 4:30 PM. For reference to staff & volunteers; by appointment to the pub
Purchases: $4000
Library Holdings: Vols 6500; Per subs 20; Artist memorabilia; Posters; Other — Clipping files, exhibition catalogs, manuscripts, pamphlets, photographs, reproductions
Special Subjects: The History of American illustration in books and periodicals; The History of Regional Art of the Brandywine Valley
Collections: Howard Pyle's published work; Other collections related to American illustration & American art history; Wyeth family memorabilia

CHESTER

M WIDENER UNIVERSITY, Art Museum, One University Pl, 19013. Tel 610-499-1189, 499-4000; *Acting Dir* Patricia Brant; *Asst to Dir* Rebecca Warda
Open Tues - Sat 10 AM - 4PM. Estab 1970
Income: Financed by endowment & university funding
Collections: 18th & 19th century Oriental art objects; 19th century European landscape & genre pictures; 20th century American paintings & sculpture
Publications: Exhibition catalog
Activities: Lect; guided tours

CLARION

M CLARION UNIVERSITY, Hazel Sandford Gallery, 16214. Tel 814-226-2412; FAX 814-226-2723; WATS 800-669-2000. *Dir* Diane Malley; *Chmn* Joe Thomas
Open Mon - Fri 8:30 AM - 4:30 PM. No admis fee. Estab 1970 for aesthic enjoyment & artistic educ of students. Gallery is 66 ft long, 17ft 3 inches wide; lit by some 50 adjustable spot lights; one side of gallery is glassed in; other side is fabric-covered panels & a dozen free standing panels, available for hanging. Average Annual Attendance: 4000. Mem: 85
Income: Financed by university dean
Purchases: Lidded basket by Chris Richard; High Country paintings & refrigerator by Norman Scott Quinn
Collections: Original paintings, drawings & prints, purchased from selected artists who have shown at gallery; sculpture & †ceramics; †photographs
Publications: Monthly announcements of shows
Activities: Lect open to public, 2-3 vis lectr per year; concerts; gallery talks; tours; competitions; individual paintings & original objects of art lent to departments on campus & other state colleges; lending collection contains original art works, original prints, paintings, photographs & sculpture; book traveling exhibitions

COLLEGEVILLE

M URSINUS COLLEGE, Philip & Muriel Berman Museum of Art, Main St, PO Box 1000, 19426-1000. Tel 610-409-3500; FAX 610-409-3664; *Dir* Lisa Tremper Barnes; *Colls Mgr* Nancy E Fago; *Admin Asst* Melanie Crossan
Open Tues - Fri 10 AM - 4 PM, Sat & Sun Noon - 4:30 PM. No admis fee. Estab 1987 to support the educational goals of Ursinus College & to contribute to the cultural life of the campus & regional community. Main gallery: 3200 sq ft; sculpture court; upper gallery 800 sq ft. Average Annual Attendance: 32,000. Mem: 250; dues minimum $50; annual meeting in June
Income: $150,000 (financed by endowment, mem, Ursinus College, government, foundation & corporate grants)
Purchases: $25,000
Collections: Philip & Muriel Berman Collection; Lynn Chadwick Sculpture Collection; 18th, 19th & 20th century European & American Art (drawings, paintings, prints & sculpture)
Exhibitions: Temporary exhibitions, 10 per year; selections from permanent collections on continuous view
Publications: Quarterly exhibition calendar; exhibitions catalogues; museum newsletter, 3 times a year
Activities: Lect open to public, 6 vis lectr per year; concerts; gallery talks; tours; individual paintings & original objects of art lent to museums & galleries for exhibition; book traveling exhibitions 4-6 per year; originate traveling exhibitions; sales shop sells books & prints

DOYLESTOWN

M BUCKS COUNTY HISTORICAL SOCIETY, Mercer Museum, 84 S Pine, 18901. Tel 215-345-0210; FAX 215-230-0823; *Chairperson* Grover J Friend; *Cur Coll* Cory Amsler
Open Mar - Dec, Mon, Wed - Sat 10 AM - 5 PM, Tues 10 AM - 9 PM, Sun Noon - 5 PM. Admis adults $5, senior citizens $4.50, students $1.50, under 6 free. Estab 1880. Inside this poured, re-inforced concrete building, four galleries wrap around a towering central court where different hand crafts are exhibited inside small cubicles. Additional artifacts hang from ceilings, walls and railings. A six story tower on each end completes the building. Average Annual Attendance: 55,000. Mem: 2400; dues $35 & up; annual meeting in Nov
Collections: Over 40,000 artifacts representing more than 40 early American crafts, their tools and finished products; large American folk art collection; the history and growth of our country as seen through the work of the human hand
Exhibitions: Continuous small changing exhibits.
Publications: Journal, bi-monthly; newsletter, monthly
Activities: Classes for adults & children; lect open to public; gallery talks; individual paintings & original objects of art lent; originate traveling exhibitions; museum shop sells books, reproductions, prints

L Spruance Library, 84 S Pine, 18901. Tel 215-345-0210; FAX 215-230-0823;
Librn Betsy Smith
Open Tues 1 - 9 PM, Wed - Fri 10 AM - 5 PM, cl July 4th, Thanksgiving,
Christmas & New Year's Day. No admis fee for BCHS members only. Open to
the pub for reference only
Library Holdings: Vols 20,000; Per subs 100; Archives; Micro — Reels; Other —
Clipping files, manuscripts, pamphlets, photographs
Special Subjects: Folk Art, Crafts and Early Industries of America

M JAMES A MICHENER ART MUSEUM, 138 S Pine St, 18901. Tel 215-340-
9800; FAX 215-340-9807; *Dir* Bruce Katsiff; *Assoc Dir* Judy Hayman; *Registrar*
Jackie Wampler; *Membership Coordr* Joan Welcker; *Assoc Cur Educ* Susan
Plumb; *Cur Exhib* Brian Peterson
Open Tues - Fri 10 AM - 4:30 PM, Sat & Sun 10 AM - 5 PM. Admis $5. Estab
1987. Average Annual Attendance: 70,000. Mem: 1800; dues $15-$500
Collections: American Art Collection, special focus on the arts in Bucks County,
Pennsylvania; 20th Century American Sculpture Collection
Activities: Classes for adults & children; docent training; museum trips; walking
tours; lect open to public, 10 vis lectr per year; gallery talks; tours; individual
paintings & original objects of art lent to museums & cultural institutions;
museum shop sells books, original art & prints

EASTON

M LAFAYETTE COLLEGE, Morris R Williams Center for the Arts, Art Gallery,
Hamilton & High St, 18042. Tel 610-250-5361, 250-5010; FAX 610-559-4042;
Elec Mail okayam@lafayette.edu. *Gallery Dir* Michiko Okaya; *Center Dir* H
Ellis Finger; *Asst Dir* Williams Center
Open Tues, Thurs & Fri 10 AM - 5 PM, Wed 10 AM - 8 PM, Sun 2 - 5 PM &
by appointment. No admis fee. Estab 1983 to present a variety of exhibitions for
enrichment of campus & community's exposure to visual arts. Versatile space
with movable panels & 160 running ft of wall space, climate control & track
lighting
Income: Financed by endowment, college program subsidy, government grants
Collections: 19th & 20th century American painting, prints & photographs
Exhibitions: Richard Anusziewicz; Tomie Avai & Lynne Yamamoto; Bill
Barrette; Ping Chong Performance Artist: In the Absence of Memory; The
Emperors Old Clothes: Ancient Andean Textiles; Grace Hartigan (paintings);
Kate Moran Grace Hartigan (paintings); William Tucker; Robert Watts: The
Emperors Old Clothes; Ancient Andean Textiles.
Publications: Annual exhibit catalogue; brochures; exhibit handouts
Activities: Lectures open to public

ELKINS

TEMPLE UNIVERSITY
M Tyler School of Art-Galleries, Tyler Gallery, Beech & Penrose Aves, 19027. Tel
215-782-2776; FAX 215-782-2799; *Dean* Rochelle Toner; *Dir Exhib* Don
DeSmett
Open Tues - Sat 10 AM - 5 PM. No admis fee. Track lighting. Average Annual
Attendance: 12,000
Income: Financed by state appropriation & grants
Exhibitions: A Day Without Art: Frank Moore & Anthony Vidi
Publications: Brochures, posters, announcements or exhibitions catalogs for
major shows
Activities: Lect open to public, 10-15 vis lectr per year; gallery talks; special
events
L Tyler School of Art Library, Beech & Penrose Aves, 19027. Tel 215-782-2849;
FAX 215-782-2799; *Librn* Andrea Goldstein
Open Mon - Thurs 8:30 AM - 9 PM, Fri 8:30 AM - 6 PM, Sat 9 AM - 5 PM,
Sun 1 - 9 PM. Estab 1935 to provide library services to students & faculty. Circ
27,254
Income: $118,368 (financed by appropriation from Central University Library)
Purchases: $32,600
Library Holdings: Vols 30,000; Per subs 100; Auction sale catalogs; Micro —
Fiche, reels; AV — Cassettes, v-tapes; Other — Exhibition catalogs, pamphlets,
prints
—**Slide Library,** Beech & Penrose Aves, 19027. Tel 215-782-2848; FAX 215-
782-2848; Elec Mail sliderm@vm.temple.edu. *Slide Cur* Kathleen Szpila; *Asst
Cur* Del Ramers
Library Holdings: AV — Slides 390,000
Special Subjects: Art History, Ceramics, Decorative Arts, Graphic Design,
Photography

EPHRATA

A HISTORICAL SOCIETY OF THE COCALICO VALLEY, 249 W Main St, PO
Box 193, 17522. Tel 717-733-1616; *Librn* Cynthia Marquet
Open Mon, Wed & Thurs 9:30 AM - 6 PM, Sat 8:30 AM - 5 PM. No admis fee.
Estab 1957. Average Annual Attendance: 1200. Mem: 450; dues family $25,
individual $15
Income: $35,000 (financed by endowment, mem, publications)
Collections: Pennsylvania German Folk Art
Publications: Journal of the Historical Society of the Cocalico Valley, annual
Activities: Classes for children; lect open to public, 10 vis lectr per year

ERIE

M ERIE ART MUSEUM, 411 State St, 16501. Tel 814-459-5477; FAX 814-452-
1744; Elec Mail erieartm@erie.net. *Pres* Kirk Steehler; *Dir* John Vanco; *Treas*
Tim Smyth
Open Tues - Sat 11 AM - 5 PM, Sun 1 - 5 PM. Admis $1.50 for non-members.
Estab 1898 for the advancement of visual arts. Galleries are located in historic
building. Average Annual Attendance: 40,000. Mem: Dues family $50,

individual $35
Income: $420,000 (financed through private donations, fundraising, mem &
grants)
Collections: Indian Bronze & Stone Sculpture; Chinese Porcelains, Jades,
Textiles; American Ceramics (historical & contemporary); Graphics (European,
American & Oriental); Photography; Paintings & Drawings (predominately 20th
century); Contemporary Baskets
Exhibitions: Annual Spring Show; Art of China & Japan; Art of India; Chicago
Works - Art from the Windy City; Early Color Photography; Paperthick: Forms
& Images in Cast Paper; A Peculiar Vision: The Work of George Ohr, the Mad
Potter of Biloxi; Frederick Hurten Rhead: An English Potter in America; The
Tactile Vessel - New Basket Forms; TECO - Art Pottery of the Prairie School
Publications: Four exhibition catalogues
Activities: Classes for adults & children; docent training; gallery talks; tours;
competitions; concerts; individual paintings & original objects of art lent to public
buildings, community centers, colleges; lending collection contains original art
works; traveling exhibitions organized & circulated; sales shop sells books & gifts.
Frame shop offers retail framing

M ERIE HISTORICAL MUSEUM (Formerly Gannon University), 356 W Sixth
St, 16507. Tel 814-871-5790
Open Tues - Sun 1 - 5 PM, extended summer hours. Admis adults $2, children
under 18 $1. Estab 1899 to display & collect regional & maritime history & art.
Mus is located in a Victorian mansion built in 1891-1892 & designed by Green &
Wicks of Buffalo, NY. Average Annual Attendance: 17,000
Income: Financed by university
Collections: Moses Billings (paintings); George Ericson-Eugene Iverd (paintings);
genre paintings; Native American pottery; Southwest & Northwest Coast baskets;
Victorian decorative arts; †Marx Toys
Exhibitions: Rotating exhibits of historical & art interest
Activities: Docent tours; lesson tours for students

FARMINGTON

A TOUCHSTONE CENTER FOR CRAFTS, RR 1, Box 60, 15437-9707. Tel 412-
329-1370; FAX 412-329-1371; Elec Mail tcc@hhs.net. *Registrar* Debbie Moore
Open Mon - Fri 9 AM - 5 PM. Estab 1972, dept estab 1972 to promote
excellence in the crafts. Average Annual Attendance: 5800. Mem: 300
Income: $170,000 (financed by mem, grants & donations)
Activities: Classes for adults & children; lect open to the public, 4 vis lectr per
year; scholarships offered

FRANKLIN CENTER

M FRANKLIN MINT MUSEUM, 19091. Tel 610-459-6168; *Cur* Judie Ashworth
Open Tues - Sat 9:30 AM - 4:30 PM, Sun 1 - 4:30 PM, cl Mon. No admis fee.
Estab 1973 to make available to the general public a location where the
collectibles created by The Franklin Mint can be viewed. Average Annual
Attendance: 55,000
Income: Financed by Franklin Mint funding
Collections: †Etchings & woodblock prints; †foreign coinage - coins minted for
19 foreign governments; †heirloom furniture; †medallic collecitons; †heirloom
dolls; †leather bound books ornamented in 22 karat gold; †porcelain, †crystal,
†bronze & †pewter art; precision dye-cast models
Exhibitions: Approximately 7 exhibits annually
Activities: Franklin Mint Gallery Store selling jewelry, medals, greeting cards &
collectibles

GLENSIDE

M BEAVER COLLEGE ART GALLERY, Church & Easton Rds, 19038. Tel 215-
572-2131; FAX 215-881-8795; *Gallery Dir* Paula Marincola
Open Mon - Fri 11 AM - 4:30 PM, June 1 - 4 PM. No admis fee. Estab 1969 to
show contemporary art generally. Gallery dimensions 20 x 50 ft. Average Annual
Attendance: 2000
Collections: Benton Spruance Print Collection
Publications: Brochures for major exhibitions, 3 per year
Activities: Lect open to public, 4 vis lectr per year; gallery talks; competitions
with awards

GREENSBURG

L SETON HILL COLLEGE, Reeves Memorial Library, College Ave, 15601. Tel
412-834-2200; FAX 412-834-4611; *Reference & Public Servs Librn* Denise
Sticha
For lending & reference. Circ 40,000
Library Holdings: Vols 101,000; Per subs 500; Micro — Cards; AV — A-tapes,
cassettes, fs, motion pictures, rec, slides, v-tapes; Other — Original art works,
pamphlets, sculpture

M WESTMORELAND MUSEUM OF AMERICAN ART, 221 N Main St,
15601-1898. Tel 412-837-1500; FAX 412-837-2921; Elec Mail
wma@westol.com;
Internet Home Page Address www.artspa.com/wma. *Chief Exec Officer & Dir*
Judith H O'Toole; *Cur* Barbara Jones; *Asst to Dir* Regina L Narad; *Dir External
Affairs & Chief Financial Officer* Sara Jane Lowry; *Dir Educ* Joan Guerin;
Preparator James Nelson; *Conservator* Christine Daulton; *Asst to Dir External
Affairs* Janet Carns; *Registrar* Douglas W Evans; *Dir Marketing & Public
Relations* Judith Ross
Open Wed - Sun 11 AM - 5 PM, Thurs 11 AM - 9 PM, cl Mon & Tues & major
holidays. No admis fee. Estab 1949 to operate & maintain a free pub art mus.
The mus houses five galleries for changing exhibitions; six galleries for permanent
collection. Average Annual Attendance: 28,665. Mem: 1400; dues $5-$1000 &
up

Income: Financed by endowment, grants & gifts
Collections: Extensive toy collection; 18th, 19th & early 20th century American decorative arts, furniture, paintings, sculpture & works on paper; 19th & early 20th century Southwestern Pennsylvania paintings
Exhibitions: Guy Pene du Bois: The Twenties at Home & Abroad; Pennsylvania: The Unspoiled Landscapes, paintings by Jim Salem; Western America: Landscapes & Portraits of Navive Americans
Publications: Viewer, quarterly newsletter
Activities: Classes for children; docent training; lect open to public, 4-6 vis lectr per year; gallery talks; tours; individual paintings & original objects of art lent to other museums & institutions accredited by AAM; lending collection contains original art works & paintings; book traveling exhibitions 1-2 per year; museum shop sells books, magazines, reproductions, slides, toys, postcards & notepaper
L **Art Reference Library,** 221 N Main St, 15601. Tel 412-837-1500; FAX 412-837-2921; *Dir* Judith H O'Toole
Open Tues - Sat 10 AM - 5 PM; Sun 1 - 5 PM, cl Mon & holidays. Estab 1949 for art reference. For reference only. Average Annual Attendance: 18,000
Purchases: $1200
Library Holdings: Vols 8000; Per subs 15; Other — Clipping files, exhibition catalogs, pamphlets
Special Subjects: American art

GREENVILLE

M **THIEL COLLEGE,** Sampson Art Gallery, 75 College Ave, 16125. Tel 412-588-7700, Ext 415; FAX 412-588-2021; *Dir* Ronald Pivovar; *Dir of Permanent Coll* Bill Mancuso
Open Mon - Fri 1 - 9 PM, Sat 11 AM - 5 PM, Sun 11 AM - 9 PM. No admis fee. Estab 1971 to provide students, faculty, college staff & the community with a gallery featuring a variety of exhibitions & give students an opportunity to show their work. Gallery has white walls, track floodlighting system, linoleum tile floor & one window wall. Average Annual Attendance: 1000
Income: $1000 (financed by college budget)
Exhibitions: Monthly exhibitions by students & faculty
Activities: Lect open to public; gallery talks

HARRISBURG

M **ART ASSOCIATION OF HARRISBURG,** School & Galleries, 21 N Front St, 17101. Tel 717-236-1432; FAX 717-236-6631; *Pres* Carrie Wissler-Thomas; *VPres* Terrie Hosey; *Dean* Kim Bowie; *Cur* Charles Hidley
Open Mon - Thurs 9 AM - 8 PM, Fri 9 AM - 4 PM, Sat 10 AM - 4 PM, Sun Noon - 3 PM. No admis fee. Estab 1926 to act as showcase for member artists and other professionals; community services offered. Building is historic Brownstone Building, former Governor's mansion (1817) & holds 2 floors of galleries, classrooms & a garden. Average Annual Attendance: 10,000. Mem: 800, dues $30 - $1000; annual meeting in May
Income: Financed by mem, tuitions, contributions, grants
Collections: Old area masters; member's work; Lavery & Lebret
Exhibitions: Annual International Juried Exhibition; Art School Annual; invitational shows; membership shows, 2 times per year; community shows in 9 locations - 36 total per year
Publications: Monthly exhibition announcements; newsletter, 6 times per year; quarterly school brochure
Activities: Classes for adults and children; lect open to public; competitions open to all states; monetary awards; concerts; gallery talks; tours; scholarships offered; sales shop sells original art & prints by member artists

A **DOSHI CENTER FOR CONTEMPORARY ART,** 441 Market St, 17101. Tel 717-233-6744; *Pres* Milt Friedly; *VPres* Ralph Zampogna
Open Mon - Fri Noon - 4 PM, Sat 2 - 5 PM, cl Sun. No admis fee. Estab 1972 as a non-profit gallery offering exposure to artists & enlightenment to the community. gallery is on street level. Average Annual Attendance: 6500. Mem: 242; dues benefactor $500, patron $100, donor $50, supporting $25; board meeting every second Wed every month
Income: $31,000 (financed by grants from Pennsylvania Council on the Arts, Allied Fund for the Arts, mem & corporate contributions)
Exhibitions: Five 2 person exhibitions; one 3 person exhibition; two juried competitive exhibitions; one 20th Anniversary retrospective; Annual Holiday Show
Activities: Student internships; lect open to public; gallery talks; tours; Maya Schock Educational Fund awarded; invitational cradft show & sale

A **PENNSYLVANIA ARTS ALLIANCE,** 1500 N Second St, 2nd Flr, 17102. Tel 717-234-0959; FAX 717-234-1501; Elec Mail paarts@aol.com. *Pres* Raymond M Flynt
Estab 1986 to develop & strengthen Pennsylvania arts at the local, state & federal levels by networking arts administrators, arts organizations, artists & volunteers & by providing technical assistance & professional training programs & services
Publications: Newsletter
Activities: Conferences & educational workshops

A **PENNSYLVANIA DEPARTMENT OF EDUCATION,** Arts in Education Program, 333 Market St, 8th Flr, 17126-0333. Tel 717-783-3958; FAX 717-787-7066; *Sr Adviser* Beth Cornell; *Dir Arts in Special Education Project* Lola Kearns; *Dir Governor's School for the Arts* Mary Klinedinst
The Arts in Education Program provides leadership & consultative & evaluative services to all Pennsylvania schools & arts educational agencies in arts program development & instructional practices. Infusion of arts processes into differentiated curriculums for all students is a particular thrust. The program offers assistance in designing aesthetic learning environments & consultation in identifying & employing regional & community resources for arts education

A **PENNSYLVANIA HISTORICAL & MUSEUM COMMISSION** (Formerly State Museum of Pennsylvania), Third & North Sts, PO Box 1026, 17108-1026. Tel 717-787-4980; *Dir* Anita D Blackaby; *Sr Cur Art Coll* N Lee Stevens
Open Tues - Sat 9 AM - 5 PM, Sun Noon - 5 PM, cl Mon. Estab 1945 to interpret the history & heritage of Pennsylvania. Mem: 3000; dues vary; annual meeting second Wed in Apr
Income: $13,000,000 for entire commission
Exhibitions: Art of the State, annual spring-summer juried statewide exhibition; Contemporary Artists Series; changing history exhibits
Publications: Pennsylvania Heritage, quarterly
Activities: Classes for adults & children; docent training; lect open to public; concerts; tours; exhibits; special events
M **State Museum of Pennsylvania,** PO Box 1026, 17108-1026. Tel 717-787-3362; FAX 717-783-1073; *Dir* Anita D Blackaby; *Sr Cur Art* N Lee Stevens; *Registrar* Richelle Rodgers
Open Tues - Sat 9 AM - 5 PM, Sun Noon - 5 PM; offices Mon - Fri 8:30 AM - 5 PM. Mus estab 1905. Average Annual Attendance: 200,000. Mem: 700; dues $35; annual meeting second Wed in Apr
Income: Financed by state & private funds
Collections: Anthropology; archaeology; art photography; ceramics; decorative arts; folk art; glass; Indian artifacts; paintings & sculpture; silver; textiles; works on paper; 1.2 million objects in all disciplines relating to Pennsylvania
Exhibitions: Art of the State, annual juried exhibition; Contemporary Artists Series
Publications: Books, brochures, quarterly calendar, quarterly newsletter
Activities: Classes for adults & children; docent training; lect open to public, 12 vis lectr per year; concerts; gallery talks; tours; awards; individual paintings & original objects of art lent to qualified & approved institutions; book traveling exhibitions 1-2 per year; originate traveling exhibitions; museum shop sells books, reproductions, prints & gift items
—**Brandywine Battlefield Park,** US Rte 1, Box 202, Chadds Ford, 19317-0202. Tel 610-459-3342; FAX 610-459-9586; *Adminr* Toni Collins; *Museum Educator* Helen Mahnke; *Educ Coordr* Richard Wolfe
Open 9 AM - 5 PM. Estab 1947 to commemorate Battle of the Brandywine, Sept 11, 1777. 2 historic Quaker farmhouses. Average Annual Attendance: 90,000. Mem: 95; dues $35; annual meeting in summer
Income: $295,000 (financed by endowment, mem & state appropriation)
Activities: Classes for children
L **Library,** PO Box 1026, Chadds Ford, 17108-1026. Tel 717-783-9898; FAX 717-787-4558, 787-4822; *Librn* Carol W Tallman
Open to the public for use on premises only, by appointment
Library Holdings: Vols 27,000; Per subs 200; Micro — Fiche, reels; AV — Motion pictures, v-tapes; Other — Clipping files, exhibition catalogs
Special Subjects: Archaeology, Decorative Arts, Historical Material, Fine Arts
M **Railroad Museum of Pennsylvania,** Rte 741, 00010145001, Strasburg, 17579. Tel 717-687-8628; FAX 717-687-0876; *Dir* Robert L Emerson; *Cur* George Deeming; *Office Mgr* Cheri S Garrett; *Prog Coordr* Robert McFadden
Open Mon - Sat 9 AM - 5 PM, Sun Noon - 5 PM, cl Mon Nov - Apr. Admis adults $6, senior citizens $5, children $4. Estab 1975 for preservation of significant artifacts appropriate to railroading. Maintains reference library. Average Annual Attendance: 150,000. Mem: 1100; dues $25; annual meeting in Oct
Income: $850,000 (financed by state appropriation & private fundraising)
Purchases: $45,000 (negative collection of the Baldwin Locomotive Works acquired)
Collections: Railroad Rolling Stock; locomotives & related artifacts including tools, maps, manuals, timetables, passes, uniforms, silverware & lanterns
Activities: Children programs; docent programs; lect open to public, 5-10 vis lectr per year; concerts; gallery talks; tours; scholarships offered; individual paintings & original objects of art lent; lending collection includes paintings & art objects; museum shop sells books, magazines, original art, reproductions, prints & slides

HAVERFORD

A **MAIN LINE ART CENTER,** Old Buck Rd & Lancaster Ave, 19041. Tel 610-525-0272; FAX 610-525-5036; *Exec Dir* Judy Herman; *Asst Dir* Tonya Weaver
Open Mon - Fri 10 AM - 4 PM, Sat 10 AM - 1 PM. No admis fee. Estab 1937 to develop and encourage the fine arts. Three large, well lit galleries, completely modernized to accommodate exhibits including sculptures, ceramics, paintings, crafts. Mem: 800; dues family $35, adult $25 & children $20; meetings once a month except Aug
Income: Financed by mem, tuition & fundraising
Exhibitions: Juried Exhibitions & Sale; membership exhibitions
Publications: Brochures, five times a year
Activities: Classes for adults, teens & children; gallery talks; trips; tours; competitions with awards; individual paintings & original objects of art lent to banks; lending collection contains original art works by children's & adult classes

HERSHEY

M **HERSHEY MUSEUM,** 170 W Hershey Park Dr, 17033. Tel 717-534-3439; FAX 717-534-8940; *Dir* David L Parke Jr
Open daily 10 AM - 5 PM, summer daily 10 AM - 6 PM. Admis adults $4.25, children 3-15 $2, 2 & under free. Estab 1933 to preserve & collect history of Hershey, Central Pennsylvania heritage (Pennsylvania Germans). Average Annual Attendance: 105,000. Mem: 1000; dues family $40
Collections: History of Hershey (the town, the business, & M S Hershey); 19th century Pennsylvania German Life-American Indian
Publications: Quarterly newsletter
Activities: Classes for adults & children; docent training; family programs; programs in schools; lect open to public; concerts; gallery talks; tours; museum shop sells books & craft items relating to museum collections; childrens' discovery room

HONESDALE

M WAYNE COUNTY HISTORICAL SOCIETY, Museum, 810 Main St, PO Box 446, 18431-0446. Tel 717-253-3240; *Pres* James Bader; *VPres* Grant Genzlinger; *VPres* Clinton Leet; *Treas* Bob Knash
Admis adults $3, children 12-18 $2, children under 12 free. Estab 1924 as a repository of artifacts, publications, archival & other items relating to Wayne County. Average Annual Attendance: 19,750. Mem: 675; dues $15; 4 meetings per year
Income: $55,000 (financed by dues, donations, sales & grants)
Collections: Artifacts of Wayne County History; Jennie Brownscomb (paintings)
Activities: School group tours; lect open to public, 4 vis lectr per year; tours; sales shop sells books, maps, t-shirts, train memorabilia

INDIANA

M INDIANA UNIVERSITY OF PENNSYLVANIA, Kipp Gallery, Sprowls Hall, 15705. Tel 412-357-2530; *Gallery Dir* Dr Vaughn Clay
Open Mon - Fri Noon - 4 PM; Sat & Sun 2 - 4 PM. No admis fee. Estab 1970 to make available a professional gallery program to Western Pennsylvania & to the university community. Versatile space with portable wall system, track lighting, secure, humidity controlled. Average Annual Attendance: 12,000
Income: Financed by Student Coop Assoc
Exhibitions: Student H Honors Exhibition; Marjorie Arnett/James Nestor; Chuck Olson/Paul Binai; Ceramic Invitational.
Activities: Lect open to public, 3-5 vis lectr per year; gallery talks; tours; traveling exhibitions organized & circulated; sales shop selling original art & prints

KUTZTOWN

KUTZTOWN UNIVERSITY
M Sharadin Art Gallery, 19530. Tel 610-683-4546, 683-4500; FAX 610-683-4547; *Gallery Dir* Dan R Talley
Open Tues - Fri 10 AM - 4 PM; Sat Noon - 4 PM, Sun 2 - 4 PM. No admis fee. Estab 1956 to make the best of the contemporary arts available to the town & college communities
Income: Financed by state & private appropriations
Collections: Approximately 400 works in prints, drawings & paintings
Publications: Brochure listing gallery shows; annual catalog
Activities: Artist-in-residence series; lectr program
L Rohrbach Library, 19530. Tel 610-683-4480; FAX 610-683-4483; *Dir Library Serv* Margaret Devlin; *Reference Librn* Margaret Apostolos
Open Mon - Thurs 7:45 AM - midnight, Fri 7:45 AM - 5 PM, Sat 9 AM - 5 PM, Sun 2 PM - midnight during school. Estab 1866. Circ 118,592
Library Holdings: Vols 414,000; Per subs 1926; Micro — Cards 17,331, fiche 1,201,000, prints 212,908, reels 35,000; AV — A-tapes, cassettes, fs, motion pictures, rec, slides; Other — Exhibition catalogs, pamphlets
Special Subjects: Art Education, Art History, Russian Art
Collections: Curriculum Materials; maps; Russian Culture

A NEW ARTS PROGRAM, INC, 173 W Main St, PO Box 82, 19530-0082. Tel 610-683-6440; FAX 610-683-6440; *Dir* James F L Carroll
Open Wed - Fri 1 - 5 PM, Sat 10 AM - 2 PM. Estab 1974 for artists to have consultation residencies, exhibitions, performance/presentations. Maintains reference library. Average Annual Attendance: 3500. Mem: 150; dues $25
Income: $95,000 (financed by mem, state appropriation, foundations, sales, mem & business)
Exhibitions: Eastern Pennsylvania Artist Salon Invitational (small works); NAP Video Festival
Publications: In & Out of Kutztown; NAP Text(s), biannual; Preview Flyers, semiannual; 71 Small Works on Paper
Activities: Two TV programs, monthly; lect open to public, 23 vis lectr per year; concerts; gallery talks; competitions with cash awards; museum shop sells prints

LANCASTER

M HERITAGE CENTER OF LANCASTER COUNTY MUSEUM, 13 W King St, 17603. Tel 717-299-6440; FAX 717-299-6916; *Exec Dir* Peter S Seibert; *Cur Education* Tricia Meley; *Cur* Wendel Zercher
Open May - Dec 10 AM - 4 PM. No admis fee. Estab 1976 to preserve & exhibit Lancaster County decorative arts. Five major galleries. Average Annual Attendance: 30,000. Mem: 800; dues vary; annual meeting third Wed in May
Income: Financed by endowment, mem, city appropriation, grants & fundraising efforts
Collections: †Lancaster County Decorative Arts & Crafts; furniture, silver, regional painting; folk art; architectural
Activities: Classes for adults & children; lect open to public, 9 vis lectr per year; tours; individual paintings & original objects of art lent to other museums; museum shop sells books & reproductions

A LANCASTER COUNTY ART ASSOCIATION, INC, 22 E Vine St, 17602. Tel 717-299-2788; *Pres* Anne F Fisher; *VPres* Jill Weidman; *Treas* Harry McCandless; *Office Mgr* Betty Ann Jones
Open Mon - Fri 10 AM - 2 PM, Sun 1 - 4 PM. No admis fee. Estab 1936, inc 1950, to increase appreciation of & participation in the fine arts. Average Annual Attendance: 10,000. Mem: 300; dues $35; general mem meeting the second Sun of the month, Sept - May
Income: Financed by dues, classes, contributions & volunteer service
Exhibitions: Monthly exhibitions for professional & non-professional members
Publications: Monthly newsletter; annual mem brochure
Activities: Classes for adults & children; lect open to public, 7-10 vis lectr per year; house tours; competitions with awards; scholarships offered

M LANCASTER MUSEUM OF ART (Formerly Community Gallery of Lancaster County), 135 N Lime St, 17602. Tel 717-394-3497; FAX 717-394-0101; *Pres* Timothy P Brown; *Dir* Ellen M Rosenholtz
Open Mon - Sat 10 AM - 4 PM, Sun Noon - 4 PM. No admis fee. Estab 1965 to present the best quality in art exhibits. Average Annual Attendance: 17,000. Mem: 1500; dues, various categories
Income: $120,000 (financed by mem, local business & county commissioners)
Exhibitions: (1997) Rob Evans: Paintings & Drawings; Selection 6: Selected Works from the Polaroid Collection; National Juried Exhibition: National Juried Exhibition; Leonard Ragouzeous: Paintings, Drawings & Prints; Art in Business I: Atomic Design; Trees Galore
Publications: Collage, quarterly newsheet
Activities: Docent training, art appreciation for 4-11 yr old children; lect; gallery talks; bus trips

M LANDIS VALLEY MUSEUM, 2451 Kissel Hill Rd, 17601. Tel 717-569-0401; FAX 717-560-2147; *Dir* Dr Caroline Stuckert; *Cur & Educ* Elizabeth Johnson; *Cur Coll* Susan Hanna
Open Mon - Sat 9 AM - 5 PM, Sun Noon - 5 PM, cl Mon & some holidays. Admis adults $7, senior citizens $6, children 6-17 $5, children under 6 free, group rates available. Estab 1925 to collect, preserve & interpret Pennsylvania rural life & Pennsylvania German culture, circa 1750 to 1900; farm implements, crafts, tools, domestic furnishings & folk art. The outdoor mus has 25 exhibit buildings, including restored 18th & 19th century structures & historical garden landscapes, as well as historical animal breeds. Average Annual Attendance: 57,000. Mem: 750; dues $35
Income: Financed by state appropriation & local support group
Collections: Baskets, books, ceramics & glass, farm equipment, Fraktur; ironware, musical instruments, Pennsylvania German furniture, textiles, toys & weapons
Publications: Newsletter, 4 times per year; Valley Gazette; special exhibit catalogs
Activities: Classes for children; tours; individual paintings & original objects of art lent; lending collection contains 30,000 books, 5000 ceramics & glass, 1800 textiles, 25,000 tools & equipment; museum shop sells books, original art, reproductions, prints, craft items and period reproductions
L Library, 2451 Kissel Hill Rd, 17601. Tel 717-569-0401; FAX 717-560-2147; *Dir* Dr Caroline M Stuckert
Open to staff, scholars by appointment for reference only
Library Holdings: Vols 12,000; Per subs 25
Special Subjects: Crafts, Decorative Arts, Embroidery, Folk Art, Furniture, Glass, Handicrafts, Historical Material, Local & Pennsylvania German culture

M ROCK FORD FOUNDATION, INC, Historic Rock Ford & Kauffman Museum, 881 Rock Ford Rd, PO Box 264, 17608-0264. Tel 717-392-7223; *Exec Dir* Heather Becker; *Dir Interpretive Serv* Diane L Kirstner
Open Apr - Oct Tues - Sat 10 AM - 4 PM, Sun Noon - 4 PM, cl Mon. Estab 1959 for preservation of General Edward Hand Mansion. Average Annual Attendance: 6000. Mem: 600; dues $15 - $100; annual meeting first Fri in Dec
Income: $120,000 (financed by mem, endowment, shop sales & special events)
Purchases: $10,000
Collections: †American furniture & decorative arts 1780 - 1802; Pennsylvania Folk Arts 1780 - 1850
Publications: Newsletter, semi-annual
Activities: Children's classes; docent programs; retail store sells books & reproductions

LENHARTSVILLE

L PENNSYLVANIA DUTCH FOLK CULTURE SOCIETY INC, Baver Genealogical Library, Folk Culture Ctr, 19534-0015. *Pres* Helen Kisthardt Kistler; *Exec Dir* Anna R Stein; *Librn & Treas* Florence Bauer
Reference library
Income: Financed by donations
Library Holdings: Vols 4000; Per subs 10; Micro — Reels; AV — A-tapes, cassettes, fs, rec, slides, v-tapes; Other — Clipping files, manuscripts, memorabilia, pamphlets, photographs, prints
Special Subjects: Calligraphy, Folk Art, Handicrafts, History of Art & Archaeology, Manuscripts, Posters, Textiles
Publications: News & Views, biannual

LEWISBURG

M BUCKNELL UNIVERSITY, Center Gallery, Elaine Langone Ctr, 17837. Tel 717-524-3792; FAX 717-524-3480; *Dir* Johann J K Reusch; *Asst Dir* Cynthia Peltier
Open Mon - Fri 11 AM - 5 PM, Sat & Sun 1 - 4 PM. No admis fee. Estab 1983. Gallery contains a study collection of 20 paintings and one sculpture of the Renaissance given by the Samuel H Kress Foundation. Average Annual Attendance: 9000
Income: Financed by endowment, tuition and gifts
Exhibitions: Organic Themes in Islamic Art; Black South African Art; Made in Pennsylvania: Antique Toys from the Lawrance Wilkinson Collection
Activities: Lect open to public, 5 vis lectr per year; concert; gallery talks; tours; competitions; individual paintings & original objects of art lent; book traveling exhibitions; originate traveling exhibitions

M FETHERSTON FOUNDATION, Packwood House Museum, 15 N Water St, 17837. Tel 717-524-0323; *Pres* Irving Williams; *Admnr* Joseph Dzwonchyk
Open Tues - Sat 10 AM - 5 PM, Sun 1 - 5 PM, last tour at 4 PM daily. Admis adults $4, senior citizens $3.25, students $1.75, under 6 free. Estab 1976 to serve the community as an educational institution. Average Annual Attendance: 4500. Mem: 200; dues life-time $1000, benefactor $500, patron $250, friend $100, family $35, individual $20, student $5
Income: Financed by endowment, admis, mem, mus shop & grants
Collections: Edith H K Fetherston Collection (paintings); †American Fine Arts; Central Pennsylvania artifacts; †Fine Period Clothing ranging from 1890's to

1960's; †1780-1940 decorative arts: ceramics, furniture, glass, metalwork, textiles
Exhibitions: Holiday Exhibit: Packwood House
Publications: Chanticleer, quarterly newsletter for members
Activities: Classes for adults & children; docent training; lect open to public; tours; competitions with awards; book traveling exhibitions; originate traveling exhibitions; museum shop sells books, original art, reproductions & local handcrafted items

LORETTO

M SOUTHERN ALLEGHENIES MUSEUM OF ART, Saint Francis College Mall, PO Box 9, 15940. Tel 814-472-6400; FAX 814-472-4131; *Dir* Michael M Strueber; *Cur* Dr Michael Tomor; *Asst Dir* Mary L Durbin; *Public Relations & Mem Coordr* Jane Gable; *Blair Art Extension Coordr* Noel Feeley; *Johnstown Art Extension Coordr* Madelon Sheedy
Open Tues - Fri 10 AM - 4 PM, Sat & Sun 1:30 - 4:30 PM. No admis fee. Estab & dedicated June 1976 to facilitate interest, understanding & the appreciation of the visual arts of the past, present & future through the exhibition of our permanent as well as temporary collections. Large open main gallery with flexible space, second floor graphics gallery. Average Annual Attendance: 10,000. Mem: 1000
Income: Financed by mem, business, corporate & foundation grants
Purchases: Contemporary American Art especially by living Pennsylvania artists are purchased for the permanent collection
Collections: †American paintings; 19th & 20th century drawings, †graphics & sculpture; 19th century ceramics & crafts
Exhibitions: Tri Annual-VI Soaphollow Furniture; Photography Exhibit
Publications: Exhibition catalogues
Activities: Classes for adults & children; intern program in cooperation with area colleges; lect open to public, 6 vis lectr per year; concerts; gallery talks; tours; exten dept serves Altoona, Johnstown & Hollidaysburg; individual paintings & original objects of art lent to other institutions on request for special exhibitions; lending collection contains 2000 lantern slides; book traveling exhibitions 1-3 per year; originate traveling exhibitions to art galleries
M Southern Alleghenies Museum of Art at Johnstown, Pasquerilla Performing Arts Ctr, Univ of Pittsburgh at Johnstown, Johnstown, 15904. Tel 814-269-7234; *Cur* Madelon Sheedy
Open Mon - Fri 10 AM - 4:30 PM, before & during all performing arts events. No admis fee. Estab 1982 to bring regional art to a wider audience & provide educational opportunities. Gallery 135 running ft. Average Annual Attendance: 38,500
Income: Financed by mem, city appropriation, private & foundation support, state & federal art agency funding
Activities: Classes for adults & children; dramatic training; docent programs; film series; workshops; lect open to public, 10 vis lectr per year; book traveling exhibitions 1 per year; originate traveling exhibitions

MEADVILLE

M ALLEGHENY COLLEGE, Bowman, Megahan & Penelec Galleries, Allegheny College, Box U, 16335. Tel 814-332-4365; FAX 814-333-8180; *Gallery Dir* Robert Raczka
Open Tues - Fri 12:30 - 5 PM, Sat 1:30 - 5 PM, Sun 2 - 4 PM, cl Mon. No admis fee. Estab 1971 as one of the major exhibition spaces in northwest Pennsylvania; the galleries present exhibits ranging from works of contemporary artists to displays relevant to other fields of study. Galleries are housed in three spacious rooms, white walls, terrazzo floor, 10 ft ceilings. Average Annual Attendance: 8000
Income: Financed by college funds & grants
Collections: †Alleghany College Permanent Collection; General David M Shoup Collection of Korean Pottery; Samuel Pees Collection of Contemporary Painting
Publications: Exhibition catalogs, 2 - 3 per year
Activities: Lect open to the public; gallery talks; tours; individual paintings & original objects of art lent to art galleries & museums; book traveling exhibitions

M CRAWFORD COUNTY HISTORICAL SOCIETY, Baldwin-Reynolds House Museum, 848 N Main St, 16335. Tel 814-724-6080; *Pres* John D Petruso; *1st VPres* David M Ellis; *Office Mgr* Barbara Finney
Open Wed - Sun 1 - 5 PM, Memorial Day - Labor Day & by appointment. Admis adults $3, students $1.50. Estab to preserve & interpret the history of the region. Art is hung in a period mansion. Average Annual Attendance: 3000. Mem: 500; annual meeting in June
Income: Financed by endowment, mem, city & county appropriations
Collections: Oil paintings - portraits; 1 Gouache 1812 Melling F; Photo portraits; Printer's proofs
Publications: Crawford County History (newsletter), semi-annually
Activities: Classes for children, docent training; tours

A MEADVILLE COUNCIL ON THE ARTS, Meadville Market House, PO Box 337, 16335. Tel 814-336-5051; *Exec Dir* Gwen Barboni
Open Tues - Fri 9 AM - 4:30 PM, Sat 9 AM - Noon. No admis fee. Estab 1975 for local arts information & programming; to create community arts center. Gallery has 50 ft of wall space. Average Annual Attendance: 2000. Mem: 500; dues businesses $25 - $250, individual $10 - $50; annual meeting Jan
Income: $50,000 (financed by mem & state appropriation)
Purchases: Yearly piece for permanent collection
Exhibitions: Annual October Evenings Exhibition; annual county wide exhibits; monthly gallery shows for local artists and crafters exhibits
Publications: Monthly calendar; monthly newsletter
Activities: Classes for adults & children; dramatic programs; lect open to public, 8-10 vis lectr per year; concerts; competitions with awards; scholarships offered

MERION

M BARNES FOUNDATION, 300 N Latch's Lane, 19066. Tel 610-667-0290; FAX 610-664-4026; *Pres Board of Trustees* Richard H Glanton; *Develop Officer* Laura Linton
Open Thurs 12:30 - 5 PM, Fri, Sat & Sun 9:30 AM - 5 PM. Admis $5, audio tour $5. Estab 1922 to educate in the appreciation of fine arts & horticulture. Average Annual Attendance: 100,000
Income: Financed by endowment
Collections: Permanent collection of post-impressionism & early French modern art. Includes works by Cezanne, Matisse & Renoir
Activities: Classes for adults; docent training; museum shop sells books, reproductions & prints

NAZARETH

M MORAVIAN HISTORICAL SOCIETY, Whitefield House Museum, 214 E Center St, 18064. Tel 610-759-5070; FAX 610-759-5070; *Exec Dir* Susan Dreydoppel
Open daily 1 - 4 PM, other times by appointment. Admis adults $2, children $1. Built in 1740 by George Whitefield, famous preacher, bought by the Moravians in 1741 & continued in use by various segments of the church. Now the seat of the Morvian Historical Soc (organized on Apr 13, 1857 to elucidate the history of the Moravian Church in America; not however, to the exclusion of the general history of the Morvian Church); used as a mus, which houses man unique & distinctive items pertaining to early Moraviana & colonial life. Average Annual Attendance: 7500. Mem: 500; dues $15 & up; annual meeting second Thurs in Oct
Income: Financed by endowment, mem & donation
Collections: Clothing & textiles; John Valentine Haidt Collection of Paintings; handwrought & cast bells; Indian & foreign mission artifacts; musical instruments; pottery & Stiegel glass; rare books; manuscripts
Publications: Transactions, biennial
Activities: Lect open to public, 1-2 vis lectr per year; concerts; gallery talks; library tours; original objects or art lent to recognized & approved museums; lending collection contains individual & original objects of art; originate travel exhibitions; museum shop sells books

NEW BRIGHTON

M MERRICK ART GALLERY, Fifth Ave & 11th St, PO Box 312, 15066. Tel 412-846-1130; *Dir & Educ Dir* Cynthia A Kundar; *Trustee* Robert S Merrick
Open Tues - Sat 10 AM - 4:30 PM; Sun 1 - 4:30 PM, cl Mon & holidays; reduced hours during summer. No admis fee; charge for docent tour. Estab 1880 to preserve & interpret the collection of paintings & other objects owned by Edward Dempster Merrick, the founder. Also to foster local art through classes & one-man shows. All galleries are on the second floors of two parallel buildings with a connecting bridge; there are three small rooms & one large one. Three rooms have clerestory monitors overhead. Average Annual Attendance: 6000. Mem: 415; dues $25, $15 & $10; annual meeting Jan or Feb
Income: Financed by endowment & mem
Collections: Most paintings date from the 18th & 19th century. American artists Emil Bott; Birge Harrison; Thomas Hill; A F King; Edward and Thomas Moran; E Poole; F K M Rehn; W T Richards; W L Sonntag; Thomas Sully; Charles Curran; John F Kensett; Andrew Melrose; Ralph A Blackelock; Asher B Durand; Worthington Whittredge. European artists Gustave Courbet; Hans Makart; Pierre Paul Prud'hon; Richard Westall; Franz Xavier; Winterhalter; Peter Baumgartner; Leon Herbo; Jaques Bertrand
Publications: Newsletter, bimonthly
Activities: Classes for adults & children; docent training; gallery talks; museum shop sells books

NEW CASTLE

M HOYT INSTITUTE OF FINE-ARTS, 124 E Leasure Ave, 16101. Tel 412-652-2882; FAX 412-657-8786; *Pres Board of Trustees* Francis E Bonadio; *Exec Dir* Kimberly Koller Jones
Open Tues - Sat 9 AM - 4 PM. No admis fee. Estab 1968 to encourage the development of the arts within the community. Average Annual Attendance: 27,000. Mem: 850; dues $100, $50, $20
Income: Financed by commission on sales of arts & crafts
Collections: National & regional artists
Exhibitions: Hoyt National Art Show
Publications: Newsletter, monthly
Activities: Classes for adults & children; dramatic programs; lect open to public; concerts; competitions

NEWTOWN

M BUCKS COUNTY COMMUNITY COLLEGE, Hicks Art Center, Fine Arts Dept, Swamp Rd, 18940. Tel 215-968-8425; *Chmn* Frank Dominguez; *Dir Exhib* Fran Orlando
Open Mon - Fri 8 AM - 10 PM, Sat 9 AM - 5 PM. No admis fee. Estab 1970 to bring outside artists to the community. Gallery covers 960 sq ft. Average Annual Attendance: 5000
Income: Financed by county and state appropriation
Exhibitions: Six exhibits each academic year, ending with student annual exhibit
Activities: Lect open to public, 8 vis lectr per year; competitions; artmobile

NEW WILMINGTON

M **WESTMINSTER COLLEGE**, Art Gallery, 16172. Tel 412-946-7266; *Dir* Kathy Koop
Open Mon - Sat 9 AM - 9 PM, Sun 1 - 9 PM. No admis fee. Estab 1854 to organize & present 7 exhibitions per season, to organize traveling exhibitions, publish art catalogs of national interest & to conduct visiting artists program. Average Annual Attendance: 15,000
Income: Financed by endowment, state & local grants
Collections: 19th & 20th century paintings; 20th century drawings & prints
Exhibitions: Seven exhibitions annually by regional & national artists
Publications: Catalogs; Westminster College Art Gallery, annually
Activities: Lect open to public, 4 vis lectr per year; gallery talks; traveling exhibitions organized & circulated

PAOLI

M **WHARTON ESHERICK MUSEUM**, PO Box 595, 19301-0595. Tel 610-644-5822; *Pres* Ruth E Bascom; *Dir* Robert Leonard; *Cur* Mansfield Bascom
Open Sat 10 AM - 5 PM, Sun 1 - 5 PM, by reservation only, weekdays groups only. Admis adults $6, children under 12 $3. Estab 1971 for the preservation and exhibition of the Studio and collection of sculptor Wharton Esherick (1887-1970), one of America's foremost artist/craftsmen. Esherick worked mostly in wood and is best known for his sculptural furniture. Studio is set high on hillside overlooking the Great Valley & is one of Wharton Esherick's monumental achievements. He worked forty years building, enlarging & altering it. A National Historic Landmark. Average Annual Attendance: 5000. Mem: 450; dues family $40, individual $25
Income: $90,000 (financed by mem, endowment, admis, sales & grants)
Collections: 200 pieces of the artist's work, including furniture, paintings, prints, sculpture in wood, stone and ceramic, utensils and woodcuts
Exhibitions: Annual Woodworking Competition; Excellence in Wood Craft Show
Publications: Brochures; catalog of Studio, collection & exhibit catalogues; Drawings by Wharton Esherick
Activities: Lect open to public; tours; competitions with awards; individual paintings and original objects of art lent to museums or exhibitions; originate traveling exhibitions to colleges, galleries & museums; museum shop sells books, magazines, prints, slides, posters, notecards, postcards & t-shirts

PHILADELPHIA

M **AFRO-AMERICAN HISTORICAL & CULTURAL MUSEUM**, 701 Arch St, 19106. Tel 215-574-0381; FAX 215-574-3110; *Exec Dir* Anne Edmunds; *Exhib Dir* Richard Watson; *Educ Dir* Pearl Robinson; *Pub Relations & Develpment Dir* Anthony Ng
Open Tues - Sat 10 AM - 5 PM, Sun Noon - 6 PM, cl New Years, Martin Luther King's Birthday, Memorial Day, July 4, Labor Day, Columbus Day, Thanksgiving, Christmas. Admis adults $3.50, senior citizens, children & students $1.75; group rates adults $1, children & students $.50. Estab 1976. Average Annual Attendance: 236,000. Mem: Dues patron $1500, friend $600, donor $150, sponsor $60, family $35, individual $25, student $5
Purchases: Bas relief in plaster by Henry O Tanner
Collections: African sculpture & artifacts; Afro-Americana; artifacts relating to Slave Trade, American Revolution, Black Church, Civil War, Reconstruction Period, Westward Movement, Harlem Renaissance, Civil Rights Movement, Black Scientists & Inventors; paintings, prints & sculpture by black artists; †archival documents; Chief Justice Robert N C Nix Sr Collection, legal writings & memorabilia; Negro Baseball Leagues Collection of photographs & documents
Publications: Annual report; brochure; exhibition catalog
Activities: Classes for adults & children; docent training; lect open to public; concerts; gallery talks; tours; awards; individual paintings & original objects of art lent; museum shop sells books, magazines, original art, reproductions, prints & African crafts

AMERICAN COLOR PRINT SOCIETY
For further information, see National and Regional Organizations

M **AMERICAN SWEDISH HISTORICAL FOUNDATION & MUSEUM**, 1900 Pattison Ave, 19145. Tel 215-389-1776; FAX 215-389-7701; *Dir* Ann Barton Brown
Open Tues - Fri 10 AM - 4 PM, Sat & Sun Noon - 4 PM, cl Mon & holidays. Admis adults $5, students $4, children under 12 free. Estab 1926 to preserve Swedish heritage in America and to promote continued cultural interchange between Scandinavia & USA. 14 galleries containing materials interpreting over 300 years of Swedish influence on American life. Average Annual Attendance: 15,000. Mem: 700; dues family $40, individual $35; annual meeting in Sept
Collections: †History and culture of Americans of Swedish descent
Exhibitions: Scandanavian history & culture; temporary exhibitions of paintings, arts & crafts by Scandanavian & Swedish-American artists
Publications: Newsletter, quarterly
Activities: Classes for adults & children; workshops; lect open to public, 5 vis lectr per year; gallery talks; tours; individual paintings & original objects of art lent to other museums; book traveling exhibitions; museum shop sells books, magazines, folk art & Swedish decorative arts
L **Library**, 1900 Pattison Ave, 19145. Tel 215-389-1776; FAX 215-389-7701; Elec Mail ashm@libertynet.org. *Exec Dir* Ann Barton Brown; *Cur Exhib* Margaretha Talerman
Open Tues - Fri 10 AM - 4 PM, Sat & Sun Noon - 4 PM. Admis adults $5, seniors & students $4, children under 12 free. Estab 1926 to create an awareness of Swedish & Swedish-American contribution to the US. 13 galleries with paintings, sculpture & artifacts. For reference only. Average Annual Attendance: 20,000. Mem: 750; dues $35; annual meeting in Sept
Library Holdings: Vols 15,000; Per subs 5; Micro — Reels; AV — Rec, slides; Other — Clipping files, exhibition catalogs, memorabilia
Special Subjects: Fredrika Bremer, John Ericsson, Jenny Lind, Rambo Research of genealogical and colonial material

L **ART INSTITUTE OF PHILADELPHIA LIBRARY**, 1622 Chestnut St, 19103. Tel 215-567-7080; FAX 215-246-3339; *Librn* Ruth Schachter
Open daily 9 AM - 9 PM. Estab 1966
Income: $88,000 (annual corporate budget)
Library Holdings: Vols 4000; Per subs 110; AV — A-tapes, cassettes, fs, Kodachromes, v-tapes; Other — Clipping files, exhibition catalogs, memorabilia, photographs
Special Subjects: Architecture, Art Education, Commercial Art, Fashion Arts, Graphic Arts, Graphic Design, History of Art & Archaeology, Illustration, Interior Design, Lettering, Painting - American, Photography, Posters

M **ATHENAEUM OF PHILADELPHIA**, 219 S Sixth St, 19106-3794. Tel 215-925-2688; FAX 215-925-3755; Elec Mail athena@libertynet.org; Internet Home Page Address http://www.libertynet.org/~athena/. *Dir* Roger W Moss; *Program Coordr* Eileen Magee; *Architectural Archivist* Bruce Laverty; *Circulation Librn* Ellen Batty; *Bibliographer* Open
Open Mon, Tues, Thurs & Fri 9 AM - 5 PM, Wed Noon - 8 PM. No admis fee. Estab 1814 to collect, preserve & make available original sources on American cultural history, 1814-1914. The fine & decorative arts are arranged in room settings. Average Annual Attendance: 25,000. Mem: 1200; annual meeting first Mon in Apr
Income: Financed by endowments, dues & fees
Collections: †Permanent study collection of American decorative arts, 1810-1850; 19th & 20th century architectural books; architectural drawings; trade catalogues
Exhibitions: HABS Peterson Prize for best set of drawings submitted to Historic American Buildings Survey
Publications: Annotations, quarterly newsletter; Athenaeum Architectural Archive; Annual Report; Bookshelf, six per year; Monographs, three to five per year
Activities: Lect open to public; concerts; gallery talks; tours; competitions with awards; fels for architectural research; originate traveling exhibitions to small historic site museums; sales shop sells books, prints & slides
L **Library**, 219 S Sixth St, 19106. Tel 215-925-2688; FAX 215-925-3755; *Circulation Librn* Ellen Batty
Open Mon - Fri 9 AM - 5 PM by appointment for reference only
Library Holdings: Vols 75,000; Per subs 50; Architectural drawings & related materials; Micro — Cards, fiche, reels; AV — Cassettes; Other — Manuscripts, original art works
Special Subjects: Architecture, Decorative Arts, Victorian Studies
Collections: Nineteenth century fiction and literary periodicals; trade materials relating to the building arts
Publications: Biographical dictionary of Philadelphia Architects, monograph

M **ATWATER KENT MUSEUM**, 15 S Seventh St, 19106. Tel 215-922-3031; FAX 215-922-0708; *Dir* Nancy Moses; *Chmn Board Dir* Fred Lindquist; *Cur Coll* Jeffrey Ray; *Cur Exhib* Patti Smith
Open Tues - Sun 9:30 AM - 5 PM, cl holidays. No admis fee. Estab 1938. The mus is dedicated to the history of Philadelphia. The main interpretive gallery covers the growth of Philadelphia from 1680-1880. Smaller galleries on William Penn, his life & times; The History of the city through maps; Municipal services: fire, police, gas & water. Average Annual Attendance: 63,000
Income: $200,000 (financed by endowment & city appropriation)
Collections: Artifacts of the colonial city; costumes; print & painting collection; manufactured & trade goods; maritime artifacts; toys & dolls; ceramics & glassware; urban archaeology
Exhibitions: Fairmount Park & the Fairmount Waterworks; Fine Art from the Atwater Kent Collections; Poetry of Motion-Eadweard Muybridge & Children's Action Toys; Sights for City Eyes; Travelling Neighborhood Exhibits;
Publications: Philadelphia: A City for All Centuries (in conjunction with KYW Newsradio)
Activities: Lect open to public, gallery talks, media events, tours; 500 original art works, 2500 original prints, 100 paintings available on loan to museums with adequate security systems; originate traveling exhibitions to community organizations & schools

A **BRANDYWINE WORKSHOP**, 730 S Broad St, 19146. Tel 215-546-3675; FAX 215-546-2825; Internet Home Page Address http://www.blackboard.com/brndywne. *Pres & Exec Dir* Allan L Edmunds; *Marketing & Develop Dir* Cindy Lee Hauger
Open Tues - Sat Noon - 5 PM. No admis fee. Estab 1972 to develop interest & talent in printmaking & other fine visual arts. Over 20,000 sq ft with 2 buildings in downtown Philadelphia. Facilities include offset lithography presses & computer/video technology lab & classrooms. Printed Image Gallery for professional exhibits of works on paper by contemporary artists of color. Tanner Gallery for Youth for Student exhibits. Average Annual Attendance: 2600-10, 000. Mem: 200; dues $25
Income: Financed by mem, city & state apppropriations, private corporations & foundations
Collections: †Contemporary fine art prints, including etchings, woodblocks, offset lithographs, silkscreens
Exhibitions: USA Artworks; Contemporary Print Images
Activities: Classes for adults & children; docent training; teacher in-service training; free computer/video clases for high school students; lect open to public, 6 vis lectr per year; gallery talks; tours; fels offered; original objects of art donated to historically black colleges, major museum collections, centers for research & Library of Congress; lending collection contains original prints; book traveling exhibitions 1 per year; originate traveling exhibitions; museum shop sells books, original art, prints, note cards, calendars, t-shirts, caps, tote bags & mugs

C **CIGNA CORPORATION**, CIGNA Museum & Art Collection, 1601 Chestnut St-TLP 7, 19192-2078. Tel 215-761-4907; FAX 215-761-5596; *Dir* Melissa Hough; *Cur* Sue Levy; *Registrar* Nancy Powell; *Adminr* Jean F Ronolich
Exhibits available by appointment Mon - Fri 9 AM - 5 PM. Estab 1925. Exhibits on company history, fire fighting history, Maritime history & American fine art
Income: Financed by company

Collections: Historical fire & marine art & artifacts 18th - 20th century American Art, two-dimensional works, ceramics, & sculpture
Exhibitions: Ships & the Sea
Publications: The Historical Collection of the Insurance Company of North America
Activities: Lect open to public; lending collection contains over 9000 pieces of historic fire & marine art & artifacts, 20th century American art & sculpture; loans are processed to qualifying institutions; book traveling exhibitions 1-3 per year; originate traveling exhibitions

M **CLAY STUDIO,** 139 N Second St, 19106. Tel 215-925-3453; FAX 215-925-7774; *Exec Dir* James Clark; *Gen Mgr* Kathryn Narrow
Open Tues - Fri noon - 6 PM, Sat & Sun Noon - 5 PM. Estab 1974. Two galleries with exhibits changing monthly of various ceramic artwork of solo, group & historical shows. Average Annual Attendance: 24,000
Collections: Ceramic Arts
Exhibitions: Annual Fellowship Artist Solo Show; The Forum Exhibition; Annual Resident Artist Group Show; Annual Holiday Show. Rookwood Ceramics; 1991 - Pueblo Pottery. Contemporary East European Ceramics Architectural Clay
Activities: Classes for adults & children; lect open to public, 4 - 6 vis lectr per year; gallery talks; tours; spring jurying for group & solo exhibition & one year residency program; scholarships; exten dept serves Philadelphia & suburbs; sales shop sells books, magazines, original art

M **CLIVEDEN,** 6401 Germantown Ave, 19144. Tel 215-848-1777; FAX 215-438-2892; *Exec Dir* Jennifer Esler; *Office Mgr* Anne Marie Duffy; *Cur Coll* Elizabeth Laurent
Open Apr - Dec Thurs - Sun Noon - 4 PM, cl Easter, July 4th, Thanksgiving & Christmas. Admis adults $6, students $4. 18th Century house museum. Average Annual Attendance: 7000. Mem: 350
Collections: 18th Century house museum with decorative arts, furniture, paintings, collections site related only, no acquisitions
Activities: Classes for children; docent training; guided tours for individuals & groups; museum shop sells books, reproductions, prints, gift items

A **THE COMMUNITY EDUCATION CENTER,** 3500 Lancaster Ave, 19104. Tel 215-387-1911; *Exec Dir* Naomi Nelson
Open Mon - Fri 9 AM - 5 PM. No admis fee. Estab 1973 to support emerging talent. 35 ft x 60 ft room, 14 ft ceilings. Average Annual Attendance: 1000. Mem: dues family $30, single $20
Income: $180,000 (financed by mem, city & state appropriation, foundation, corporate & private donars)
Activities: Classes for adults & children; lect open to public, 4 vis lectr per year

A **CONSERVATION CENTER FOR ART & HISTORIC ARTIFACTS,** 564 S 23rd St, 19103. Tel 215-545-0613; FAX 215-735-9313; Elec Mail ccaha@shrsys.hslc.org. *Dir* Linda V Ellsworth
Estab 1977 as a nonprofit regional conservation laboratory serving cultural, educational & research institutions as well as private individuals & organizations throughout the United States. Maintains small reference library
Income: Financed by earned income

M **FABRIC WORKSHOP & MUSEUM,** 1315 Cherry St, 5th Flr, 19107-2026. Tel 215-568-1111; FAX 215-568-8211; Elec Mail fw&m@libertynet.org. *Dir* Marion Boulton Stroud; *Public Relations Dir* Aaron Igler
Open Mon - Fri 9 AM - 6 PM, Sat 10 AM - 4 PM. Estab 1977 devoted to experimental fabric design & silkscreen printing by nationally recognized & emerging artists representing all mediums, incl painting, sculpture, ceramics, architecture & theater. Invites artists to collaboratively explore new directions for their work, while furthering the use of fabric as an integral medium for contemporary art
Collections: Extensive permanent collection of unique contemporary art (over 2300 artworks)
Exhibitions: Ongoing series of exhibitions including print multiples, monoprints, sculptural objects, installation pieces, performance costumes, furniture & functional objects, along with preliminary objects & paintings for artists projects & related sculptures & ceramics
Publications: An Industrious Art; exhibit catalogs
Activities: Classes for adults & children; high school & college apprentice training programs; workshops; lect open to public, study tours; print demonstrations; museum sales shop sells unique, artist-designed functional objects & workshop publications

A **FAIRMOUNT PARK ART ASSOCIATION,** 1616 Walnut St, Ste 2012, 19103-5313. Tel 215-546-7550; FAX 215-546-2363; *Pres* Charles E Mather III; *VPres* William P Wood; *VPres* Henry W Sawyer III; *Exec Dir* Penny Balkin Bach; *Asst Dir* Laura S Griffith; *Treas* Theodore T Newbold
Estab 1872 for the purpose of acquiring sculpture for the City of Philadelphia. Mem: 350; dues $25 - $100; annual meeting May
Income: Financed by mem, grants & endowment

M **FOUNDATION FOR TODAY'S ART,** Nexus Gallery, 137 N Second St, 19106. Tel 215-629-1103; *Gallery Dir* Anne Raman; *Foundation Dir & Trustee* Suzanne Horvitz; *Trustee* Vivian Golden; *Trustee* Alexandra Lerner
Open Tues & Fri Noon - 6 PM, Sat & Sun Noon - 5 PM. No admis fee. Estab 1975, artist-run space for contemporary art, featuring experimental-emerging artists, new directions-new media; national/international exchanges; cultural outreach programs. Two contemporary galleries, each 750 sq ft. Average Annual Attendance: 5000. Mem: 25; dues $35 per month; monthly meetings; half of exhibits feature member artists selected for experimental & creative approach to both traditional & new media with demonstrated level of consistency & commitment; the other half feature non-member artists & invited curators
Income: Financed by mem, state, federal & foundation grants
Activities: Lect open to public, 5 or more vis lectr per year; concerts; gallery talks; tours upon request; internships offered

FREE LIBRARY OF PHILADELPHIA
L **Art Dept,** Logan Square, 19103. Tel 215-686-5403; FAX 215-563-3628; *Library Pres & Dir* Elliot Shelkrot; *Head Librn, Art Dept* William Lang
Open Mon - Wed 9 AM - 9 PM, Thurs - Fri 9 AM - 5 PM, Sat 9 AM - 5 PM, Sun 1 - 5 PM, cl Sun June - Aug. Estab 1891, art department estab 1896, to serve the citizens of the City of Philadelphia. Non-circulating, reference & research collection
Income: Financed by endowment, city & state appropriations
Purchases: $71,000
Library Holdings: Vols 60,000; Per subs 220; Vertical files 40,000; Micro — Fiche, reels; Other — Clipping files, exhibition catalogs, pamphlets
Collections: 18th & 19th century architectural pattern books; John Frederick Lewis Collection of books on fine prints & printmaking; 368 original measured drawings of colonial Philadelphia buildings, Philadelphia Chapter, American Institute of Architects
Exhibitions: Rotating exhibitions
L **Print & Picture Dept,** 1901 Vine St, 19103-1189. Tel 215-686-5405; *Head* Deborah Litwack
Open Mon - Fri 9 AM - 5 PM. Estab 1954 by combining the Print Department (estab 1927) & the Picture Collection
Collections: (non-circulating) †Americana (1200); Hampton L Carson Collection of Napoleonic prints (3400); †graphic arts (2000); †greeting and tradesmen's cards (27,000); †John Frederick Lewis Collection of portrait prints (211,000); †Philadelphiana (8000); Rosenthal Collection of American Drawings (900); †Benton Spruance lithographs (450) (circulating) †picture collection of pictures in all media and universal in subject coverage (1,000,000)
Exhibitions: Benton Spruance Prints; Portraits from the Lewis Collection
L **Rare Book Dept,** 1901 Vine St, 19103-1189. Tel 215-686-5416; FAX 215-563-3628; Elec Mail refrbd@library__phila.gov. *Head* Martha Repman; *Asst Head* Cornelia King; *Ref Librn* Karen Lightner
Open Mon - Fri 9 AM - 5 PM. No admis fee. Estab 1949. Average Annual Attendance: 3000
Special Subjects: Illustration, Manuscripts
Collections: †American Sunday-School Union; †Early American children's books including Rosenbach Collection of Early American Children's books (1682-1836); Elisabeth Ball Collection of Horn books; †Borneman & Yoder Collection of Pennsylvania German Fraktur; Hampton L Carson Collecttion of legal prints; Frederick R Gardner Collection of Robert Lawson original drawings; †Kate Greenaway; †Grace Clark Haskell Collection of Arthur Rackham; John Frederick Lewis Collection of cuneiform tablets & seals, Medieval & Renaissance manuscripts & miniatures, Oriental manuscripts & miniatures (mostly Mughul, Rajput & Persian); Thornton Oakley Collection of †Howard Pyle & His Schnool, books & original drawings; †Beatrix Potter, including H Bacon Collamore Collection of original art; Evan Randolph Collection consisting of angling prints from the 17th to the 20th century & prints of Philadelphia from 1800-1950; †original drawings, paintings, prints & other illustrative material relating to the works of Dickens, Goldsmith, Poe & Thackeray
Activities: Individual paintings & original objects of art lent to other institutions for exhibition not to exceed 3 months; lending collection contains books, original artworks & paintings

M **GERMANTOWN HISTORICAL SOCIETY,** 5501 Germantown Ave, 19144-2691. Tel 215-844-0514; FAX 215-844-2831; *Exec Dir* Barbara Silberman
Open Tues & Thurs 10 AM - 4 PM, Sun 1 - 5 PM. Admis $5. Estab 1900 as an educational center. Average Annual Attendance: 5000. Mem: 600; dues $25; annual meeting first Sun in Nov
Income: $100,000 (financed by endowment, mem, city & state appropriations, foundations & corporations)
Collections: African-American history; genealogy; German immigration; local history; Wissahickon natural area
Publications: The Germantown Crier, semiannual
Activities: Classes for adults & children; lect open to public, 4 vis lectr per year; individual paintings & original objects of art lent to institutions meeting professional standards; museum shop sells books, magazines, reproductions & prints
L **Library,** 5501 Germantown Ave, 19144-2697. Tel 215-844-0504; FAX 215-844-2831; *Reference Librn* Anne Dempsey
Open Tues & Thurs 10 AM - 4 PM, Sun 1 - 5 PM. Estab 1878. For reference only
Income: Financed by contributions, foundation grants & pub funding
Library Holdings: Vols 3000; Micro — Fiche, reels; AV — A-tapes, cassettes, Kodachromes, lantern slides, motion pictures, rec, slides, v-tapes; Other — Clipping files, exhibition catalogs, framed reproductions, manuscripts, memorabilia, original art works, pamphlets, photographs, prints, reproductions
Special Subjects: Architecture, Crafts, Decorative Arts, Dolls, Etchings & Engravings, Film, Furniture, Historical Material, Landscapes, Manuscripts, Maps, Painting - American, Period Rooms, Photography, Portraits, Genealogy
Exhibitions: Orientation to Germantown Historical Society & other sites; on-going, others vary

M **GIRARD COLLEGE,** Stephen Girard Collection, 2101 S College Ave, 19121. Tel 215-787-2602; FAX 215-787-2710; *Head* Joseph T Devlin; *Asst Head* Mary Catherine Snyder
Open Wed & Thurs 10 AM - 2 PM. No admis fee. Estab 1848. The basic plan & structured details of Founder's hall were dictated by Girard in his will. America's most outstanding example of Greek Revival architecture, the huge Corinthian temple-form building was designed by a twenty-nine year old Philadelphian, Thomas Ustick Walter, who later planned & drew the wings & dome of the US Capitol at Washington. Average Annual Attendance: 1500
Income: Financed by endowment
Collections: Furniture, silver, porcelain, paintings, marble busts & statues which belonged to Stephen Girard (1750 - 1831) founder of Girard College
Exhibitions: Continuous display in room settings

M **HIGH WIRE GALLERY,** 137 N Second St, 19106. Tel 215-829-1255; Elec Mail malcor@aol.com. *Pres* Jeff Waring; *VPres* Peter Kenny; *Treas* Marge Peterson
Open Wed - Fri Noon - 6 PM, Sat & Sun Noon - 5 PM. No admis fee. Estab 1985 as an independent co-operative arts & performance space. Exhibitions of plastic arts & poetry, dance, music & performance in the heart of Philadelphia's Old City arts district. Average Annual Attendance: 30,000. Mem: 24; mem qualification-juried review; dues $540; meetings 1st Mon each month
Income: $13,000 (financed by mem & donation)
Exhibitions: Members Solo Exhibitions; Poets & Prophets (poetry series); This Not That (open art forum); musical & dance performances
Activities: Lect open to public; weekly public art forums; lending collection contains individual paintings & original objects of art

A **HISTORICAL SOCIETY OF PENNSYLVANIA,** 1300 Locust St, 19107-5699. Tel 215-732-6200; FAX 215-732-2680; Elec Mail hsppr@aol.com. *Pres* Susan Stitt; *VPres Coll* Jonathan Cox; *Dir Develop* Carroll Anne Sheppard; *VPres Interpretation* Cynthia Little; *Business Mgr* James McCann
Open Tues, Thurs, Fri & Sat 10 AM - 5 PM, Wed 1 - 9 PM, cl Sun & Mon. Admis $5, students $2 to library. Estab 1824 to collect & preserve documentary records relating primarily to 18th century national US history, 19th century regional Pennsylvania & 20th century Delaware Valley history. Mem: 2230; dues $35; meetings 5 times per yr
Income: $1,500,000 (financed by endowment, mem dues & contributions)
Collections: Unmatched collection of more than 15 million manuscripts, archives, graphics, paintings, furniture household & personal effects form pre-Revolution through 1990; more than 1000 paintings & miniatures by early American artists Birch, Copley, Inman, Neagle, Peale, Stuart, Sully, Wright & others
Publications: Guide to the Manuscript Collections of the Historical Society of Pennsylvania; Pennsylvania Magazine of History & Biography, quarterly
Activities: Workshops for adults; conferences on history & historical research; orientations to documentary collections

M **INDEPENDENCE NATIONAL HISTORICAL PARK,** 313 Walnut St, 19106. Tel 215-597-9373; FAX 215-597-5556; Elec Mail inde_curatorial@nps.gov. *Supt* Martha Aikens; *Chief Museum Branch* Karie Diethorn
Open daily 9 AM - 5 PM. No admis fee. Estab 1948 to preserve & protect for the American people, historical structures, properties & other resources of outstanding national significance & associated with the Revolution & growth of the Nation. Seventeen pub buildings with 54 period rooms & 38 on-site exhibits. Maintains reference library. Average Annual Attendance: 4,500,000
Income: Financed by federal agency
Collections: †18th century American period furnishings; decorative arts; American portraits from 1740-1840
Activities: Classes for adults & children; docent training; lect open to public, 6 vis lectr per year; tours; individual paintings & original objects or art lent to qualified professional institutions; museum shop sells books, magazines, reproductions, prints & slides

L **Library,** 120 S Third St, 19106. Tel 215-597-8047; *Archivist & Library Mgr* Karen Stevens; *Librn Technician* Andrea Ashby
Open to pub Mon - Fri 8 AM - 4:30 PM
Library Holdings: Vols 9500; Per subs 12; Research notecard file; Micro — Fiche, reels; AV — A-tapes, cassettes, Kodachromes, motion pictures, rec, slides, v-tapes; Other — Clipping files, exhibition catalogs, manuscripts, pamphlets, photographs
Collections: Decorative arts of Philadelphia & Pennsylvania for the 18th century

M **INDEPENDENCE SEAPORT MUSEUM** (Formerly Philadelphia Maritime Museum), 211 S Columbus Blvd & Walnut St, 19106-3100. Tel 215-925-5439; Elec Mail seaport@libertynet.org. *Pres* John S Carter; *Acting Cur* Mark Isaksen; *Librn* Michael DeAngelo; *Educator* William Ward
Open Tues - Sat 10 AM - 5 PM, Sun 1 PM - 5 PM. Admis adults $2.50, children $1. Estab 1960 to preserve & interpret the maritime heritage of the Bay & River Delaware & the Ports of Philadelphia. Gallery 1, The Sea Around Us, general maritime history; Gallery 3, changing exhibits; Gallery 4 changing exhibits. Average Annual Attendance: 41,5000. Mem: 965; dues $35 minimum; annual meeting May
Income: Financed by endowment, mem & federal, private & corporate gifts
Collections: †Paintings by major American marine artists; Philadelphia Views; †19th-20th century maritime prints
Exhibitions: (1997) From Dreams to Reality The SS US
Publications: Annual Report; books & catalogs, intermittently; Spindrift, quarterly newsletter
Activities: Classes for adults & children; lect for members only, 10 vis lectr per year; concerts; gallery talks; competitions; individual paintings & original objects of art lent to recognized non-profit museums with adequate facilities & pertinent need, six months only; museum shop sells books

L **Library,** 211 S Columbus Blvd & Walnut St, 19106-3100. Tel 215-925-5439; *Librn* Michael DeAngelo
Open Tues - Fri 10 AM - 4:30 PM & 1st Sat each month 10 AM - 4 PM. Open to members & scholars, for reference only
Library Holdings: Vols 12,000; Per subs 100; Boat plans 9000, Rare books & maps; Micro — Fiche, reels; AV — Cassettes 150, Kodachromes, lantern slides, motion pictures, slides 2000; Other — Exhibition catalogs, manuscripts, original art works, pamphlets, photographs 25,000, prints
Special Subjects: Traditional Small Craft Plans, Maritime Art and History Reference Works; Shipbuilders of the Delaware River, Maritime History of Philadelphia
Collections: Photographic file of Birch prints; photographic file of ships built by New York Shipbuilding Corp; art reference books on marine artists

A **INSTITUTE OF CONTEMPORARY ART,** 118 S 36th St, 19104-3289. Tel 215-898-7108; FAX 215-898-5050; *Dir* Patrick T Murphy; *Asst Dir* Judith Tannenbaum
Open daily (except Mon) 10 AM - 5 PM, Wed evenings until 7 PM, cl holidays. Estab 1963 to provide a continuing forum for the active presentation of advanced development in the visual arts. Gallery space devoted to exhibiting contemporary art in all media. Average Annual Attendance: 80,000. Mem: 600; dues $30, $75, $150, $300 & up
Income: Approx $700,000 (financed by endowment, mem & grants)
Exhibitions: ICA Street Sights 1 & 2; Masks, Tents, Vessels & Talismans; Paul Thek; Processions; Urban Encounters; Art Architecture Audience; Drawings: The Pluralist Decade; Made in Philadelphia 4 & 5; Machineworks; Vito Acconci; Alice Aycock; Dennis Oppenheim; Robert S Zakanitch; Photography: A Sense of Order; The East Village Scene; Laurie Anderson; Siah Armajani; David Salle; Robert Kushner
Publications: Annual newsletter; calendar of events; exhibition catalogs
Activities: Lect open to public, 5-10 vis lectr per year; concerts; gallery talks; tours; traveling exhibitions organized & circulated; sales shop sells original art & catalogs

M **LA SALLE UNIVERSITY,** Art Museum, 20th & Olney Ave, 19141. Tel 215-951-1221; *Dir* Daniel Burke; *Cur* Caroline Wistar
Open Tues - Fri 11 AM - 4 PM, Sun 2 - 4 PM; cl Mon. No admis fee. Estab 1975 for educational purposes and to house the collection begun in 1965, also as support for the art history program and as a service to the community. Average Annual Attendance: 11,000. Mem: 60; dues $5 - $1000
Income: Financed by endowment, university budget, grants, public & private donations
Collections: †15th - 20th century paintings, drawings, watercolors, Old Master & those of 1 9th & 20th centuries prints; †Western, European & American art, with a few pieces of sculpture & decorative art; †rare illustrated 15th - 20th century Bibles; portrait prints
Exhibitions: Two special exhibitions are held each semester
Publications: La Salle Art Museum Guide to the Collection
Activities: Classes for adults; lectures open to public, 2-3 vis lectr per year; concerts; gallery talks; tours; individual paintings & original objects of art lent to museums

L **LIBRARY COMPANY OF PHILADELPHIA,** 1314 Locust St, 19107. Tel 215-546-3181, 546-8229; FAX 215-546-5167; Elec Mail jg24@libertynet.org. *Librn* John C Van Horne; *Asst Librn* James Green; *Cur Prints* Sarah Weatherwax; *Chief Reference* Philip Lapsansky; *Chief Conservation* Jennifer L Woods
Open Mon - Fri 9 AM - 4:45 PM. No admis fee. Estab 1731 for the purpose of scholarly research. For reference only. Average Annual Attendance: 2500. Mem: 850; dues $40; annual meeting first Mon in May
Income: Financed by endowment, mem, city appropriation, state & federal grants
Library Holdings: Vols 450,000; Per subs 160; Micro — Cards; AV — Fs; Other — Exhibition catalogs, framed reproductions, memorabilia, original art works, pamphlets, photographs, sculpture
Special Subjects: Afro-American Art, Architecture, Art History, Bookplates & Bindings, Cartoons, Coins & Medals, Drawings, Etchings & Engravings, Fashion Arts, Historical Material, History of Art & Archaeology, Judaica, Landscape Architecture, Landscapes, Manuscripts, Maps, Marine Painting, Painting-American, Painting-European, Portraits
Collections: †American Printing; †Philadelphia prints, watercolors, drawings and photography; collection of Americana
Publications: Annual Report; Occasional Miscellany, 2-4 times per year; exhibition catalogues
Activities: Lect open to public; gallery talks; tours; fels offered; individual & original objects of art lent to museums, libraries & cultural institutions; sale of books & publications

L **LUTHERAN THEOLOGICAL SEMINARY,** Krauth Memorial Library, 7301 Germantown Ave, 19119-1794. Tel 215-248-4616; FAX 215-248-4577; Elec Mail lutthelib@ltsp.edu. *Dir Library* David J Wartluft; *Head Public Serv* Darren Poley; *Head Technical Servs* Lois Reibach; *Cur Archives* John E Peterson
Open Mon - Fri 9 AM - 5 PM, during academic sessions, Mon - Thurs 5 - 10 PM. Estab 1906
Library Holdings: Vols 185,000; Per subs 570; AV — A-tapes, cassettes, fs, Kodachromes, lantern slides, rec, slides, v-tapes; Other — Manuscripts, memorabilia, original art works, reproductions
Special Subjects: Architecture, Religious Art
Collections: Liturgical arts; Modern Prints; Rentschler Coll of Last Supper Art; Schreiber Coll of Numismatic Art on Martin Luther & the Reformation
Exhibitions: 20 Religious Artists

M **MOORE COLLEGE OF ART & DESIGN,** Goldie Paley Gallery, 20th & the Parkway, 19103. Tel 215-568-4515, Ext 1119; FAX 215-568-5921; Elec Mail galmoore@libertynet.org. *Gallery Dir* Elsa Longhauser
Open Tues - Fri 10 AM - 5 PM, Sat Noon - 4 PM. No admis fee. Estab 1984 to display contemporary art, architecture, photography & design. Gallery is housed in moderate exhibition space with flexible panels to accommodate current exhibit. Average Annual Attendance: 5000. Mem: 175; dues $50-$2500
Income: Financed by endowment, government & foundation grants, individual & corporate donation
Exhibitions: William Daley; Hanne Darboven; Marlene Dumas; Terry Fox; Viola Frey; Dan Graham Exhibit; Josef Hoffman; Jean-Frederic Schnyder; Pat Ward Williams Annual exhibition curated from the Levy Registry of Philadelphia area artists
Publications: Bulletins, irregularly; Catalogs for major exhibitions
Activities: Educ dept; one-day family workshops; lect open to public, 10 vis lectr per year; concerts; gallery talks; tours; book signings; films; performances; book traveling exhibitions 1 per year; originate traveling exhibitions to other university galleries & small exhibition spaces in large museums throughout US & Canada

L **Library,** 20th & The Parkway, 19103. Tel 215-568-4515, Ext 1204; FAX 215-568-8017; *Library Dir* Judy Donovan; *Catalog Librn* Kristin Bayrus; *Slide Cur* Helen F McGinnis; *AV Specialist* George Stewart
Open Mon - Thurs 8 AM - 10 PM, Fri 8 AM - 6 PM, Sat 8:30 AM - 5 PM, Sun 1 - 5 PM, for student use; pub use Mon - Fri 8:30 AM - 4:30 PM & by appointment. Estab to serve Moore staff & students. For lending & reference
Purchases: $37,000
Library Holdings: Vols 36,186; Per subs 230; Picture files; AV — A-tapes,

cassettes, fs, lantern slides, motion pictures, rec, slides 117,000, v-tapes; Other — Clipping files, exhibition catalogs, manuscripts, memorabilia, reproductions
Special Subjects: Women in the Visual Arts
Collections: Sartain Family Collection; Bookworks Artists Books Collection

M **MUSE ART GALLERY,** 60 N Second St, 19106. Tel 215-627-5310; *Dir* Sissy Pizzollo
Open Wed - Sun 11 AM - 5 PM. Estab 1970 to make women artists more visible. Average Annual Attendance: 2500. Mem: 15; qualifications: professional exhibiting or emerging artist; dues $600; monthly meetings
Income: Financed by mem, sales commissions, Pennsylvania State Council of the Arts & private contributions
Exhibitions: Members & community oriented exhibitions
Publications: Catalogues; MUSE Gallery and Her Own Space
Activities: Art consultant program; lect open to public, 2 vis lectr per year; poetry readings; competitions; originate international traveling exhibitions; original art for sale

M **THE MUSEUM AT DREXEL UNIVERSITY,** Chestnut & 32nd Sts, 19104. Tel 215-895-2424, 895-2423; *Dir* Ivy Strickler
Open Mon - Fri 10 AM - 4 PM, cl Sat, Sun & holidays. No admis fee. Estab 1891; Picture Gallery 1902. Main Gallery contains the John D Lankenau & the Anthony J Drexel Collections of German & French paintings, sculpture & decorative arts of the 19th century & a changing exhibition gallery. Average Annual Attendance: 10,000
Income: Financed by Drexel University
Collections: 19th century sculpture, academic European painting, decorative arts & costumes; ceramics; hand printed India cottons; decorative arts of China, Europe, India & Japan
Exhibitions: Annual Student Art Show; Regional Artists
Activities: Lect open to public, 8-10 vis lectr per year; concerts; gallery talks; book traveling exhibitions

M **PAINTED BRIDE ART CENTER,** The Gallery at the Painted Bride, 230 Vine St, 19106. Tel 215-925-9914; *Exec Dir* Gerry Givnish; *Dir* A M Weaver; *Dir Development* Patricia Robinson
Open Wed - Sun Noon - 6 PM. No admis fee. Estab 1968, forum for work outside traditional channels to present interdisciplinary work. Average Annual Attendance: 25,000. Mem: 350
Collections: Contemporary Art & Theater
Activities: Lect open to public, 2 vis lectr per year; gallery talks

M **PENNSYLVANIA ACADEMY OF THE FINE ARTS,** Museum of American Art, 118 N Broad St, 19102. Tel 215-972-7600; FAX 215-972-5564; Internet Home Page Address http://www.pafa.org/-pafa. *Chmn Board* Charles L Andes; *Pres* Gresham Riley; *VPres Develop* Theodore Greene; *VPres Finance Admin* Maureen Brusca; *Dir Annual Giving & Mem* Melissa Sly; *Public Information Officer* Chuck McDevitt; *Cur* Sylvia Yount; *Museum Registrar* Gale Rawson; *Museum Shop Mgr* Mark DeLelys; *Paintings Conservator* Mark F Bockrath
Open Mon - Sat 10 AM - 5 PM, Sun 11 AM - 5 PM. Admis adults $5.95, senior citizens & students $4.95, children under 12 $3.95, members & children under 5 free. Estab 1805 by Charles Willson Peale to cultivate collecting, training & development of the fine arts in America. The Academy Building, opened in 1876, was restored for the American Bicentennial. Considered the masterpiece of its architect, Philadelphian Frank Furness, its style is called, alternatively, polychrome picturesque & High or Gothic Victorian. It was designated a Registered National Historic Landmark in 1975. The School Gallery features faculty & student exhibitions. Average Annual Attendance: 75,000. Mem: 2200; dues $40-$10,000
Income: Financed by endowment, mem, city & state appropriations, contributions & federal grants
Purchases: Shadow by Jennifer Bartlett; Second Small Quarter by Mel Bochner; Pink Chinese Scissors by Jim Dine; Study for Political Prisoner by Sidney Goodman; Vanquished by Bill Jensen; Dream Series No 5, The Library by Jacob Lawrence; Let us Celebrate by Ree Morton; For M W & the Pure Desire by William T Wiley
Collections: American contemporary works; 18th, 19th & early 20th century American paintings, sculpture, drawings & prints, including Allston, West, the Peale Family, Stuart, Sully, Rush, Neagle, Mount, Eakins, Cassatt, Homer, Hopper, Hassam, Carles, Bellows, Henri, Beaux, Pippin
Exhibitions: (1997) Annual Student Exhibition & Graduate Thesis Exhibition; The Pennsylvania Academy at Port Auen; Reconstruction: William Christenberry's Art; The Unbroken Line: 100 Years of the Fellowship, 1897-1997; Kate Moran; The People's Choice
Publications: Annual report; Calendar of Events; exhibition & school catalogues; quarterly newsletter
Activities: Classes for adults & children; docent training; lect open to public, 50 vis lectr per year; concerts; gallery talks; tours; competitions with awards; scholarships offered; exten dept serves senior citizens; original objects of art lent to other institutions, the White House, the Governor of Pennsylvania & embassies abroad; book traveling exhibitions 2-3 per year; originate traveling exhibitions; museum shop sells books, magazines, reproductions, prints, slides, ceramics, games, stationery, jewelry, toys & pottery

L **Library,** 1301 Cherry St. . Tel 215-972-7600, Ext 3256; FAX 215-569-0153; Elec Mail pafine@hslc.org. *Librn* Aurora Deshauteurs
Open Mon - Thurs 9 AM - 7 PM, Fri 9 AM - 5 PM, Sat 10 AM - 1 PM, open to pub, cl during school vacations. Estab 1805, the library serves students of painting, sculpture, printmaking & research in American Art. Open to pub for reference
Income: Financed by school funds
Library Holdings: Vols 13,500; Per subs 82; AV — Slides, v-tapes; Other — Clipping files, exhibition catalogs

L **Archives,** Broad & Cherry Sts, 19102. Tel 215-972-7600; *Archivist* Cheryl Leibold
Open weekdays by appointment only; mail inquires welcome
Library Holdings: Artifacts; AV — A-tapes, fs, Kodachromes, lantern slides,

slides, v-tapes; Other — Clipping files, exhibition catalogs, manuscripts, memorabilia, pamphlets, photographs
Special Subjects: History of Penn Academy
Collections: Charles Bregler's Thomas Eakins Collection, consisting of more than 1000 art objects & documents
Publications: Brochure about the archives; Index to Annual Exhibitions, 3 vols

A **Fellowship of the Pennsylvania Academy of the Fine Arts,** c/o Museum of American Art of the Pennsylvania Academy of the Fine Arts, 118 N Broad St, 19102. Tel 215-972-7600, Ext 3507; *Pres* Rodger Lapelle; *Exec VPres* Ruth C Davis; *VPres* Margaret Engman; *VPres* William Greenwood; *Treas* William Cunningham
Estab 1897 to provide opportunities for creative incentive & sharing in responsibilities for the development of facilities & activities in the field of art for its members & to maintain relations with the students of the Pennsylvania Academy of the Fine Arts. Mem: 3500; dues resident $30, nonresidents $20, students $15; meetings held Sept, Nov, Feb & May
Income: $20,000 (financed by mem & investments)
Purchases: $1000 (art collection & operating expenses)
Collections: Paintings and sculpture
Exhibitions: Annual Fellowship Show; Juried Members Exhibition
Publications: Perspective magazine, 3 times yr
Activities: Classes; lect; awards; films; workshops; auctions; picnic; ball; individual paintings & original objects of art lent to schools, libray & other public institutions; lending collection contains originial art works, original prints, paintings, photographs, sculpture, slides; originate traveling exhibitions

A **PHILADELPHIA ART ALLIANCE,** 251 S 18th St, 19103. Tel 215-545-4305; FAX 215-545-0767; *Pres* Carole Price Shanis; *Adminr* Diane Brubaker; *VPres Admin* John K Hunter
Galleries open Tues - Sun 11 AM - 5 PM, cl Mon. No admis fee. Estab 1915, a unique, educational & cultural organization catering to all the arts: music, drama, painting, sculptue, prints, design, literary arts, illustation, architecture, photography. Average Annual Attendance: 80,000. Mem: 1600; both artist & non-artist categories are available; dues $25 - $1000; annual meeting in May
Income: Financed by mem
Collections: †Contemporary paintings; original antique furnishings
Exhibitions: Juried visual exhibitions
Publications: The Art Alliance Bulletin, published 6 times a year, Sept to July;
Activities: Classes for adults & children; lect open to public; concerts; gallery talks; tours; originate traveling exhibitions; book traveling exhibitions

A **PHILADELPHIA ART COMMISSION,** 1600 Arch St, 19102. Tel 215-686-2851, 686-1776; *Pres* Thora Jacobson; *Exec Dir* William J Burke
Open 8:30 AM - 5 PM. No admis fee. Estab 1911 under Philadelphia Home Rule Charter as the Art Jury, later retitled Art Commission. An Art Ordinance passed in 1959 provides for art work in city buildings and on city owned property. The Art Commission reviews architectural designs and art work covering all media for municipal locations or other locations in which municipal funds are expended. The Art Commission's files are open to inspection by anyone since the information contained therein qualifies as public information. As indicated, the material deals solely with art proposals and architectural designs. Designs cover all buildings, major highways, and bridges. Mem: 9; between 20 and 24 meetings annually
Income: Financed by city appropriation

M **PHILADELPHIA COLLEGE OF TEXTILES & SCIENCE,** Paley Design Center, 4200 Henry Ave, 19144. Tel 215-951-2860; FAX 215-951-2662; Elec Mail mangellij@laurel.texsci.edu. *Dir* Anne R Fabbri; *Asst to Dir* Jennifer L Mangelli; *Museum Shop Dir* Deborah T Mangel
Open Tues - Fri 10 AM - 4 PM, Sat & Sun Noon - 4 PM. No admis fee; free guided tour by reservation. Estab 1978 to promote knowledge & appreciation of textiles & their design. Three galleries; small library of textile & costume subjects available to scholars & members. Average Annual Attendance: 12,000. Mem: Dues $20
Income: Financed by PCT&S & grants from the PCA & private foundations
Collections: Costumes - 18th to 20th centuries; historic & contemporary textiles 1st - 20th centuries, International; Manufacturers' fabric swatches 19th & 20th centuries, American & Western European; manuscripts, records, textile fibers, tools & related materials
Exhibitions: (1997) 1 Screen, 2 Souls, 4 Hands; Philadelphia Furniture Makers; Bridging Worlds: Visiting Artists' Jacquard Project; Complexity & Contradiction: Postmodernism in Philadelphia Photography; Log Cabin Quilts: New Quilts from an Old Favorite
Publications: The Art of the Textile Blockmaker; Florabunda: The Evolution of Floral Design on Fabrics; Flowers of the Yayla, Yoruk Weaving of the Toros Mountains; The Philadelphia System of Textile Manufacture 1884 - 1984
Activities: Museum shop sells unique works by craft artists in jewelry, pottery, glass, wood, paper & textiles; annual holiday crafts market

M **PHILADELPHIA MUSEUM OF ART,** 26th & Parkway, PO Box 7646, 19101-7646. Tel 215-763-8100; FAX 215-236-4465; Internet Home Page Address http://pma.libertynet.org/. *Chmn Board* Philip Berman; *Pres* Robert Montgomery Scott; *The George D Widener Dir* Anne d'Harnoncourt; *VPres Operations* Walter Taylor Jr; *VPres Development* Alexander Q Aldridge; *VPres Finance* John Sergovic; *VPres External Affairs* Cheryl McClemey-Brooker; *McNeil Cur American Art* Darrel Sewell; *Sr Cur Prints, Drawings & Photographs* Innis Shoemaker; *Cur Drawings* Ann Percy; *Cur Educ* Danielle Rice; *Registrar* Irene Taurins; *Public Relations Mgr* Sandra Horrocks; *Special Exhibitions Coordr* Suzanne Wells
Open Tues - Sun 10 AM - 5 PM, Wed 10 AM - 8:45 PM. Admis adults $6, senior citizens, students & children over 5 $3, Sun 10 AM - 1 PM free. Estab 1876 as an art mus & for art educ; known as Pennsylvania Mus of Art until the present name was adopted in 1938. Buildings owned by the City, opened 1928; wings 1931 & 1940; fashion galleries 1949, 1951 & 1953; Gallatin & Arensberg Collections 1954; Far Eastern Wing 1957; decorative arts galleries 1958; Charles Patterson Van Pelt Auditorium 1959; Nepalese-Tibetan Gallery 1960; new galleries of Italian & French Renaissance Art 1960; American Wing, galleries of

contemporary painting, sculpture & decorative arts & special exhibitions galleries 1976; Alfred Stieglitz Center of Photography 1978; print & drawing gallery 1979; 19th century decorative arts galleries 1980 & 1981. Mus contains 200 galleries. Average Annual Attendance: 600,000. Mem: 25,000; dues $20-$1000; annual meeting Oct

Income: $26,000,000 (financed by endowment, mem, city & state appropriations, grants, bequests & auxiliary activities)

Collections: †Indian sculpture & miniature painting & the installation of 16th century South Indian temple; †Chinese & Southwest Asian sculpture, ceramics & decorative arts from the Crozier, Crofts, Williams, McIlhenny, Thompson & other collections, with installations of a Ming period Chinese palace hall & temple & a Ch'ing scholar's study; †Japanese scroll paintings, prints & decorative arts, with installations of a tea house & a 14th century temple; Himalayan sculpture & painting; Middle Eastern tile, miniatures & decorative arts from the White & other collections; Oriental carpets from the McIlhenny, Williams & other collections; Pre-Columbian sculpture & artifacts from the Arensberg Collections; †Medieval & Renaissance sculpture, painting & decorative arts from the Foulc, Barnard & other collections; installations of a Gothic chapel, Romanesque cloister, French Renaissance choir screen & period rooms; Barbarini-Kress Foundation tapestry series; Kienbusch Collection of Arms & Armor; †French, Dutch, English & Italian painting & decorative arts of the 14th-19th centuries, from the †Wilstach, Elkins, McFadden, Tyson, John G Johnson, McIlhenny, Coxe-Wright & other collections; †Italian, Dutch & French drawings from the Clark & other collections; †French & English 17th & 18th century decorative arts from the Rice, Bloomfield-Moore & other collections, with period rooms; †French & English art-nouveau decorative arts; †costume & textiles from all periods of western & eastern art, including the Whitman sampler collection; †American collections include painting, sculpture & decorative arts from the colonial era to the present, with period rooms, Philadelphia furniture & silver, Tucker porcelain, Lorimer Glass Collection & the Geesey Collection of Pennsylvania German folk art; †20th century painting, sculpture & works on paper from the Gallatin, Arensberg, Tyson, White, Stern, Stieglitz, Zigrosser, Greenfield, Woodward & other collections; †Ars Medica Collection of prints on the subject of sickness & healing from all periods of western art; †Alfred Stieglitz Center Collection of Photography; †20th century decorative arts

Exhibitions: Design 1900-1940; European Sculpture & Decorative Art: Acquisitions by David DuBon, 1958-1985; The Quest for Eternity: Chinese Ceramic Sculpture from the People's Republic of China; Double You (and X, Y, Z) Videodisc Installation by Peter d'Agostino; Twelve Photographers Look at Us; Claude Monet; Federal Philadelphia, 1785-1825: The Athens of the Western World; Recent Acquisitions of Prints, Drawings & Photographs; Miro; Richard Misrach: The American Desert; Duchamp Centennial Celebration; Paul Klee; The Henry P McIlhenny Collection

Publications: Bulletin, quarterly; exhibitions catalogs; members' magazine, semi-annually; monthly calendar

Activities: Classes for adults, children & families; guide training; symposia; lect open to public; concerts; gallery talks, films; tours; traveling exhibitions organized & circulated; museum shops sells books, magazines, reproductions, prints, slides, jewelry, needlework & postcards; art sales & rental gallery

M **Rodin Museum of Philadelphia,** 22nd & Benjamin Franklin Pky, 19101. Tel 215-763-8100; Cable PHILMUSE. *Cur of Pre-1900 European Painting & Sculpture* Joseph Rishel; *Assoc Cur* Christopher Riopelle

Open Tues - Sun 10 AM - 5 PM, cl holidays. Admis by donation. Estab 1926. Rodin Mus of Philadelphia houses one of the largest collections outside of Paris of works by the major late 19th Century French sculptor, Auguste Rodin. Average Annual Attendance: 30,000

Collections: Collection includes many of the most famous sculptures created by Rodin, as well as drawings, prints, letters, books & a variety of documentary material

Activities: Classes for adults & children; docent training; concerts; gallery talks; tours; individual sculptures & drawings lent to museums for exhibitions; museum shop sells books, reproductions, slides, cards & memorabilia; audio tour

M **Mount Pleasant,** Fairmount Park, 19101. Tel 215-684-4019; *Cur American Decorative Arts* Jack Lindsey; *Mgr Vol Services* Caroline T Gladstone; *Admin Asst* Deborah W Troemner

Open daily except Mon, cl major holidays. Admis adults $1, children $.50. Historic house built in 1761; an outstanding example of the Georgian style in 18th century building & woodcarving; installed with period furnishings

Collections: †Period furnishings from the Museum represent the elegant way of life in Philadelphia in the 1760's

Activities: Tours

M **Cedar Grove,** Cedar Grove Mansion Fairmount Park, Lansdowne Dr, 19101. Tel 215-684-4013, 878-2123

Open Tues - Sun 10 AM - 5 PM, cl Mon. Admis adults $1, children $.50. This Quaker farmhouse built as a country retreat in 1748 was moved stone by stone to Fairmount Park in 1928 & restored with the furnishings of the five generations of Quakers who lived in it

Collections: The furniture was given with the house & reflects changes in styles through the 17th, 18th & 19th centuries

Activities: Tours

M **John G Johnson Collection,** Parkway & 26th, PO Box 7646, 19101-7646. Tel 215-684-7616; FAX 215-763-8955; *Cur* Joseph Rishel; *Asst Cur* Katherine Crawford Luber; *Adjunct Cur* Carl B Strehlke

Open Tues - Sun 10 AM - 5 PM. Admis to Philadelphia Mus of Art $6. Upon his death in 1917, prominent Philadelphia lawyer, John Graver Johnson left his extensive collection intact to the city of Philadelphia; since 1933 the collection has been housed in the Philadelphia Mus of Art; administration & trusteeship of the collection is maintained separately from the other collections in the mus

Income: Financed by trust established by John G Johnson, contributions city of Philadelphia & Philadelphia Mus of Art

Collections: Early & later Italian Renaissance paintings; French 19th century paintings; northern European schools of Flanders, Holland & Germany in the 15th, 16th & 17th centuries

Exhibitions: In house exhibitions featuring works from permanent collection; (1997) A Show of Sienese Painting; Yon Van Iycke-Comparing the Two St Francis

Publications: Several catalogs for various parts of the collection including Catalog of Italian Paintings & Catalog of Flemish & Dutch Paintings

Activities: Special lect & related activities; occasional lending of collection to significant exhibitions

M **Samuel S Fleisher Art Memorial,** 709-721 Catharine St, 19147. Tel 215-922-3456; FAX 215-922-5327; *Pres* Edward B Putnam; *Dir* Thora E Jacobson

Open during exhibitions Mon - Fri 11 AM - 5 PM, Mon - Thurs 6:30 - 9:30 PM, Sat 1 - 3 PM. No admis fee. Estab 1898 as a free art school & sanctuary (Mus of Religious Art). Permanent collections are housed in an Italian Romanesque Revival building; Gallery is used for school-related exhibitions & for special shows of contemporary artists. Average Annual Attendance: 8000. Mem: 2800; mem contribution $25 per term

Income: $650,000 (financed by estate income, mem, materials fees, grants & gifts)

Collections: Medieval & Renaissance religious paintings & sculpture; 18th-19th century Portuguese liturgical objects; 17th-20th century Russian icons; some sculpture

Exhibitions: Challenge Series, annual schedule of four exhibitions featuring work by Philadelphia area artists; annual student, faculty, adult & childrens' exhibitions; occasional special subject exhibitions

Activities: Classes for adults & children; lect open to public, 4 vis lectr per year; concerts; gallery talks; tours; competitions; sales shop sells art materials & books

L **Library,** PO Box 7646, 19101. Tel 215-684-7650; FAX 215-236-0534; Elec Mail aktownsend@aol.com. *Librn* Allen Townsend; *Slide Librn* Mary Wassermann; *Assoc Librn* Gina Kaiser

Open Wed - Fri 10 AM - 4 PM. Estab 1876 as a research source for mus staff & mus members, graduate students & university faculty. For reference only

Library Holdings: Vols 132,000; Per subs 570; Micro — Fiche, reels; AV — Slides; Other — Clipping files, exhibition catalogs, pamphlets

Special Subjects: Art History, Decorative Arts, Drawings, Etchings & Engravings, Painting - American, Painting - European, Photography, Prints, Silver, Textiles, 20th century art

L **Slide Library,** 26th St & Benjamin Franklin Pkwy, PO Box 7646, 19101-7646. Tel 215-684-7658; FAX 215-236-0534; *Slide Librn* Mary Wassermann

Provides slides to museum staff, not open to public

Library Holdings: AV — Slides 150,000

Special Subjects: Architecture, Art History, Decorative Arts, Furniture, Glass

A **Women's Committee,** PO Box 7646, 19101-7646. Tel 215-684-7931, Ext 448; FAX 215-236-8320; *Pres* Lynn Gadson; *Exec Dir* Nancy G O'Meara

Open Mon - Fri 9 AM - 5 PM. Estab 1883, inc 1915; takes an active interest in the mus. Organization sponsors Art Sales & Rental Gallery, park houses & mus guides, The Philadelphia Mus of Art Craft Show, classes for blind artists & tours for the deaf

Income: Financed by fund raising events

A **PHILADELPHIA SKETCH CLUB, INC,** 235 S Camac St, 19107. Tel 215-545-9298; *Pres* Betty McDonald

Call for hours. No admis fee. Estab 1903 to provide a showcase for artist members & juried & invited shows. Gallery is on second floor of the Club House, 30 ft x 40 ft, skylighted, also used six times a week for life & still-life classes. Average Annual Attendance: 3500. Mem: 135; applicants must be proposed by two members & show portfolio of their artwork to Board of Directors; dues $100; meetings 10 times per year

Income: Financed by endowment & mem

Collections: Permanent collection is from past & present members, oils, watercolors, etchings; fourty-four Thomas Anshutz Portraits; J Pennell Lithographs

Publications: The Portfolio, (bulletin), monthly

Activities: Classes for adults & life classes; lect open to public, 9 vis lectr per year; gallery talks; tours; competitions with cash awards; individual paintings & original objects of art lent to art museums who have exhibitions of PSC past members; lending collection contains 100 books, 100 original art works, photographs, sculptures, documents & letters of past members; Philadelphia area Art College Students Scholarship Competition

A **PLASTIC CLUB,** Art Club, 247 S Camac St, 19107. Tel 215-545-9324; *Pres* Michael Runcevich; *VPres* Ellen Davenport; *Treas* Hilda Schoenwetter; *House Chmn* Hannah Kohn

Open Mon & Thurs 10 AM - 2 PM, Wed 10 AM - 3 PM. No admis fee. Estab 1897 to promote wider knowledge of art and to advance its interest among artists. Two historic homes provide space for exhibits & a studio. Average Annual Attendance: 200 at lectures, 400 at exhibits & receptions. Mem: 80; must qualify for mem by submitting three framed paintings or other works of art to be juried; dues $40; association members (non-exhibiting) $25; annual meeting in May

Income: Financed by mem, donations, gifts & money-making projects

Exhibitions: Monthly exhibitions of paintings by members & invited artists. Open Works on Paper; Open Show All Media

Publications: Calendar of Events, 3 times a year; newsletter, 3 times a year

Activities: Classes for adults; lect open to public, 20 vis lectr per year; gallery talks; competitions with awards; scholarships & fels offered; individual paintings & objects of art lent to hospitals, banks & public buildings; lending collection contains original art works, original prints, paintings, sculpture & crafts, such as jewelry; sales shop sells original art, prints & craft items

M **PLEASE TOUCH MUSEUM,** 210 N 21st St, 19103. Tel 215-963-0667, 567-5551; FAX 215-963-0424; *Exec Dir* Nancy D Kolb; *Educ Prog Specialist* Cynthia Kreilick; *Dir Research & Child Develop* Mary Sykes; *Dir Exhibits* Aaron Goldblat; *Dir Develop & Marketing* Laura Campbell; *Dir Visitor Servs* Joan Wilder; *Dir Finance* James Hall

Open daily 9 AM - 4:30 PM, summer 9 AM - 6 PM, cl Thanksgiving, Christmas & New Year's Day. Admis $6.50. Estab 1976 & accredited by American Assoc of Museums (1986) to provide a developmentally appropriate mus for young children, their parents & teachers. Gallery spaces are small-scaled, objects are accessible; two-tiered interpretation for adults coming with children (arts, crafts, ethnic materials & childlife exhibits). Average Annual Attendance: 170,000. Mem: 2500; dues family units $55

Income: $1,600,000 (financed by earned income: admis, store receipts, program fees; contributions, mem, governmental appropriations, foundations, corporate support & individuals)

Collections: Art works by contemporary artists, sculpture, environmental,

paintings & crafts; †cultural artifacts from around the world: costumes, playthings, musical instruments, objects from daily life; Materials from the natural sciences; †contemporary American toys, artifacts & archives documenting American childhood
Exhibitions: Foodtastic Journey; Future-Sendak at Please Touch Museum; Growing Up; Move It; Nature's Nursery; Studio PTM
Publications: Annual report; The Please Touch Museum Cookbook; quarterly newsletter; thematic exhibition catalog, biannual
Activities: Workshops for adults & children; theater programs; docent training; work with area colleges, universities & art schools; coop programs; lect open to public, 3 vis lectr per year; concerts; competitions with awards; original objects of art lent; lending collection contains art works, sculpture & artifacts concerning childhood; originate traveling exhibitions; museums shop sells books, posters, toys & educational materials

A PRESBYTERIAN HISTORICAL SOCIETY, 425 Lombard St, 19147. Tel 215-627-1852; *Dir* Frederick J Heuser; *Mgr Cataloging Servs* Barbara Schnur
Open Mon - Fri 8:30 AM - 4:30 PM. No admis fee. Estab May 1852 to collect & preserve official records & memorabilia of the Presbyterian Church USA, its predecessors & affiliates. Portraits displayed in the Reading Room, Mus Room, Mackie Room, Board Room & hallways. Six Alexander Stirling Calder statues representing American Presbyterian personalities who played a significant role in the history of the Church are displayed outside in front of the building. Average Annual Attendance: 1900. Mem: 1275; dues $20; annual meeting first Fri Mar
Income: Financed by mem & General Assembly
Collections: †Paintings & sculptures; †church plates; †relics; †silver & pewter communionware
Publications: American Presbyterians: Journal of Presbyterian History, quarterly
Activities: Tours
L Library, 425 Lombard St, 19147. Tel 215-627-1852; *Dir Libr Servs* Richard Bater
Open to the pub for reference
Collections: Jackson Collection; National Council of Churches Collection; Scotch-Irish Society Archives; Shane Collection

THE PRINT CENTER
For further information, see National and Regional Organizations

A PRINTS IN PROGRESS, 34 W Coulter, 19144. Tel 215-849-9579; FAX 215-849-9627; *Exec Dir* Michele Grant
Open Mon - Fri 9AM - 5 PM. Estab 1960 to provide inner city children with hands-on quality visual arts experiences using a neighborhood-based approach. 300 sq ft with 12 ft ceilings. Average Annual Attendance: 1000 (classes)
Income: $250,000 (financed by endowment, city & state appropriation, businesses, foundations, individual contributions, art sales & classes)
Exhibitions: Ongoing exhibitions of art work by students
Activities: Classes for adults & children; 1-5 day adult workshops; vis artists programs; lect open to public; scholarships & fels offered; exten dept serves five Philadelphia neighborhoods; originate traveling exhibitions to libraries, parks, art centers, galleries & other public facilities; sales shops sells original art, various handmade objects made by children

M THE ROSENBACH MUSEUM & LIBRARY, 2010 DeLancey Pl, 19103. Tel 215-732-1600; *Dir* Stephen K Urice; *Cur Art Coll* Constance Kimmerle
Open daily 11 AM - 4 PM except Mon, open to scholars Mon - Fri 9 AM - 4:45 PM by appointment; cl Aug & national holidays. Admis adults $3.50, students $2.50, groups of 8 or more $3 per person; exhibits $2.50. Estab 1953 as a nonprofit corporation
Collections: 18th century English antiques & silver, paintings, prints & drawings, porcelain, rugs & objets d'art; rare books & manuscripts, consisting of British & American literature, Americana & book illustrations; 260,000 manuscripts; 30,000 books, Marianne Moore Archive; Maurice Sendak Archive
Exhibitions: Jean Baptiste Le Prince: Drawings; Marianne Moore: Vision into Verse; Rosenbach Abroad: In persuit of books in private collections
Publications: A Selection from Our Shelves; Fantasy Sketches; The Rosenbach Newsletter; exhibition catalogs
Activities: Lect open to public, 3 vis lectr per year; gallery talks; tours; individual paintings & original objects of art lent to museum & libraries with proper environmental & security systems; originate traveling exhibitions; museum shop sells books & reproductions

M ROBERT W RYERSS LIBRARY & MUSEUM, 7370 Central Ave, 19111. Tel 215-745-3061, 685-0599; *Supv* Amy Freitag
Library Open Fri - Sun 10 AM - 5 PM, mus Fri 11 AM - 4 PM & Sat & Sun 1 - 4 PM or by appointment. No admis fee. Estab 1910. House (Historic Register) left to City complete with contents in 1905; three period rooms; three other museum rooms with art objects - predominately Victorian. Average Annual Attendance: 20,000. Mem: 75; dues $5; meeting first Mon every month
Income: Financed by endowment, city appropriation, volunteer fund-raising & trust fund
Collections: Static collection; export china, ivory, paintings, period rooms, prints, sculpture, weapons
Activities: Tours; lending collection contains 12,000 books
L Library, 7370 Central Ave, 19111. Tel 215-745-3061, 685-0599; *Supv* Amy Freitag; *Librn* Ermioni Rousseas
Open Fri - Sun 10 AM - 5 PM. Estab 1910. Victoriana Collection available to scholars by appointment only
Library Holdings: Vols 20,000; Per subs 40; AV — Cassettes, fs, slides; Other — Framed reproductions, memorabilia, original art works, photographs, prints, sculpture
Collections: Victoriana

M UNIVERSITY OF PENNSYLVANIA, Arthur Ross Gallery, 220 S 34th St, 19104-6303. Tel 215-898-4401; FAX 215-573-2045; *Dir* Dilys Winegrad; *Coordr* Lucia I Dorsey
Open Tues - Fri 10 AM - 5 PM, Sat & Sun Noon - 5 PM. No Admis fee. Estab 1983 to make art accessible to campus community & the general pub. One large

high-ceilinged room & an entrance room with approx 1700 sq ft of exhibition space. Average Annual Attendance: 10,000. Mem: 54; dues $100; annual meeting
Income: $290,000 (financed by endowment, grants, gifts, in-kind contributions)
Collections: University art collection of paintings, prints, photographs, books, manuscripts, textiles & sculpture
Publications: Exhibition catalogues
Activities: Lect open to public, 2-3 vis lectr per year; gallery talks; tours; book traveling exhibitions 1 per year; originate traveling exhibitions to other university galleries & museums

UNIVERSITY OF PENNSYLVANIA
L Fisher Fine Arts Library, 220 S 34th St, 19104-6308. Tel 215-898-8325; FAX 215-573-2066; *Librn* Alan E Morrison
Library Holdings: Vols 100,000; Per subs 500
M Museum of Archaeology & Anthropology, 33rd & Spruce Sts, 19104. Tel 215-898-4000; FAX 215-898-0657; *Dir* Dr Jeremy A Sabloff; *Assoc Dir* Dr Stephan Epstein; *American History Arch Assoc Cur* Dr Robert L Schuyler; *American Sections Cur* Dr Robert Sharer; *Near East Section Assoc Cur* Dr Richard Zettler; *Babylonian Section Cur* Dr Erle Leichty; *Egyptian Section Cur* Dr David Silverman; *European Section Assoc Cur* Dr Bernard Wailes; *Mediterranean Section Cur* Dr Donald White; *Physical Anthropology Cur* Dr Francis E Johnston
Open Tues - Sat 10 AM - 4:30 PM, Sun 1 - 5 PM, cl Mon & Sun from Memorial Day - Labor Day. Admis adults $5 donation, students & senior citizens $2.50 donation, children under 6, members, University of Pennsylvania faculty, staff & students free. Estab 1887 to investigate the origins & varied developments of human cultural achievements in all times & places; to preserve & maintain collections to document these achievements & to present to the pub the results of these investigations by means of permanent exhibits, temporary exhibitions & special events. Average Annual Attendance: 200,000. Mem: 3300; dues individual $35, Loren Eiseley Assoc $1000
Income: $5,000,000 (financed by endowment, mem, state appropriation & University)
Collections: Archaeological & ethnographic artifacts relating to the Old & New World; the classical civilization of the Mediterranean, Egypt, Mesopotamia, Iran, Southeast Asia & the Far East, North, Middle & South America, Oceania; Africa; physical anthropology
Exhibitions: Tutavoh; Learning the Hopi Way; Symbolic Heat; Gender, Health & Worship among the Tamils of South India & Sri Lanka. Ancient Greek World. Living in Balance: The Universe of The Hopi, Zuni, Navajo & Apache
Publications: Expedition Magazine, quarterly; Museum Applied Science Center for Archaeology Journal; Museum Monographs; exhibition catalogues
Activities: Classes for adults & children; docent training; lect open to public, 20 vis lectr per year; concerts; gallery talks; tours; exten dept servs Pennsylvania Commonwealth; objects of art lent to libraries & instructional centers in the state; lending collection contains motion pictures, original art works & slides; traveling exhibitions organized & circulated; museum shop sells books, magazines, reproductions, slides, jewelry & craft items
L Museum Library, 3260 South St, 19104-6324. Tel 215-898-7840; FAX 215-573-2008; *Dir* Lisa Harowitz
Library Holdings: Vols 110,000; Per subs 800; Microforms 70,000; Micro — Fiche, reels; AV — Fs; Other — Pamphlets
Special Subjects: Anthropology, Archaeology, Egyptology, Mayan Studies

M UNIVERSITY OF THE ARTS, Broad & Pine Sts, 19102. Tel 215-875-1116; FAX 215-875-5467; *Pres* Peter Solmssen; *Provost* Virginia Red; *Dir Exhib* Leah Douglas
Open Sept - May Mon, Tues, Thurs & Fri 10 AM - 5 PM, Wed 10 AM - 9 PM, Sat & Sun Noon - 5 PM, June - Aug Mon - Fri 10 AM - 5 PM. No admis fee. College contains two galleries: Rosenwald - Wolf Gallery & Haviland - Strickland Building Galleries. Temporary exhibitions which relate to the University's diverse instruction. The galleries present high quality contemporary exhibitions which attract national & international artists to the campus. Major exhibitions are accompanied by catalogs, symposia & lectures
Income: Financed by city, state & federal appropriations, private & corporate support
Exhibitions: Contemporary & 20th century work in visual arts & design
Publications: Catalogs & brochures accompany major gallery exhibitions
Activities: Lect; opening receptions; tours; slide presentations; gallery talks; workshops
L Albert M Greenfield Library, 320 S Broad St, 19102. Tel 215-875-1111; FAX 215-875-2296; *Library Dir* Stephen Bloom; *Access Servs & Visual Resources Librn* Martha Hall; *Assoc Dir* Carol Homan Graney; *Reference Librn* Sara MacDonald; *Music Librn* Dr Mark Germer
Open Mon - Thurs 8:30 AM - 10:30 PM, Fri 8:30 AM - 5 PM, Sat Noon - 5 PM, Sun 5 - 9 PM. Estab 1876 to support the academic programs of the School. Lending to university patrons only
Library Holdings: Vols 96,000; Per subs 495; Picture files 110,000; Reproduction files; Micro — Fiche, prints, reels 450; AV — A-tapes 450, cassettes 450, Kodachromes, rec 15,000, slides 160,000, v-tapes 625; Other — Clipping files, exhibition catalogs, photographs, prints, reproductions
Special Subjects: Theatre Arts, Dance, Design, Music, Visual Arts

L WILLET STAINED GLASS STUDIOS, 10 E Moreland Ave, 19118. Tel 215-247-5721; FAX 215-247-2951; *Pres* E Crosby Willet; *Librn* Helen H Weis
Open Mon - Fri 8 AM - 4:30 PM by appointment. Estab 1890 as the largest stained glass studio in the United States. For reference only
Activities: Individual paintings & original objects of art lent; lending collection contains photographs, Kodachromes & motion pictures; traveling exhibitions organized & circulated

WOMEN'S CAUCUS FOR ART
For further information, see National and Regional Organizations

M WOODMERE ART MUSEUM, 9201 Germantown Ave, 19118. Tel 215-247-0476; FAX 215-247-2387; *Dir* Dr Michael W Schantz; *VPres* Joly W Stewart; *VPres* James C Weaver; *VPres* John Affleck; *Treas* Richard Carbonaro
Open Tues - Sat 10 AM - 5 PM, Sun 1 - 5 PM, cl holidays. No admis fee. Estab 1940; founded by Charles Knox Smith, in trust for benefit of the pub. A large addition in 1965 provides additional gallery & studio space. Average Annual Attendance: 20,000. Mem: 1300; dues $30 & higher; annual meeting in Jan
Income: Financed by endowments, gifts, grants & mem fees
Purchases: Philadelphia art, past & present
Collections: Contemporary American †paintings, †sculpture & †graphics; European porcelains & furniture; European & American sculpture; Oriental rugs, furniture, procelains; Smith Collection of European & American paintings
Exhibitions: 12 current exhibitions annually; prizes awarded in Members' Annual Juried & Special Exhibitions
Activities: Classes for adults & children; docent training; lect open to public, 3 vis lectr per year; concerts; gallery talks; tours; competitions with prizes; individual paintings & original objects of art lent to other museums & galleries; museum shop sells books, gifts, jewelry & original art
L Library, 9201 Germantown Ave, 19118. Tel 215-247-0476; FAX 215-247-2387; *Cur Educ* Meri Adelman
Reference only
Library Holdings: Micro — Cards; Other — Clipping files, exhibition catalogs

PITTSBURGH

A ASSOCIATED ARTISTS OF PITTSBURGH, 937 Liberty Ave, 15222. Tel 412-263-2710; *Exec Dir* Frances A Frederick
Open Tues - Sat 10 AM - 5:30 PM, Sun 1 - 5 PM, cl Mon. Estab 1910 to give exposure to member artists & for educ of the area in the field of art. An art gallery is maintained. Average Annual Attendance: 25,000. Mem: 568 (must be juried into the group); dues $45
Income: Financed by mem
Publications: The First 75 Years
Activities: Lect open to public; competitions with awards; originate traveling exhibitions in conjunction with Vira I Heinz endowment, Arts on Tour

M JOHN P BARCLAY MEMORIAL GALLERY, 526 Penn Ave, 15222. Tel 412-263-6600; *Dir* Nancy Ruttner; *Resource Center Dir* Susan Moran
Open Mon, Tues & Thurs 9 AM - 8 PM, Wed & Fri 9 AM - 5 PM, Sat 9 AM - 4 PM. No admis fee. Estab 1921 as an art school & proprietary trade school
Exhibitions: Local art group shows; local artists; loan exhibitions; student and faculty members; technical art exhibits
Publications: Brochures; Catalog; School Newspaper
Activities: Classes for adults & teens; lect open to public, 2-4 vis lectr per year; scholarships offered
L Resource Center, 526 Penn Ave, 15222. Tel 412-263-6600; *Resource Center Dir* Susan Moran
Open Mon - Fri 7:30 AM - 3 PM, Mon, Tues & Thurs 6 - 10 PM. Estab 1971 to supply our students with readily available reference materials. Circ Approx 2600
Purchases: $1295
Library Holdings: Vols 5674; Per subs 208; Micro — Fiche; AV — Cassettes, fs, rec, slides; Other — Clipping files, exhibition catalogs, framed reproductions, memorabilia, pamphlets
Special Subjects: Architecture, Art History, Commercial Art, Crafts, Fashion Arts, Graphic Arts, Interior Design, Mixed Media, Photography

M CARNEGIE INSTITUTE, Carnegie Museum of Art, 4400 Forbes Ave, 15213. Tel 412-622-3131; FAX 412-622-3112; *Dir & Cur Contemporary Arts* Richard Armstrong; *Asst Dir* Michael J Fahlund; *Chmn Mus Art Board* Milton Fine; *Cur Architecture* Christopher Monkhouse; *Cur Decorative Arts* Sarah C Nichols; *Cur Educ* Marilyn M Russell; *Cur Film & Video* William D Judson; *Cur Fine Art* Louise W Lippincott; *Chief Conservator* William A Real; *Head Publ* Gillian Belnap; *Registrar* Cheryl A Saunders; *Exhib Coordr* Jack W Schlechter; *Dir Marketing* Doris Carson Williams; *Media Relations Mgr* Elisa Behnk; *Head Publ* Marcia Whitehead; *Media Relations Mgr* Elisa Behnk
Open Tues - Sat 10 AM - 5 PM, Sun 1 - 5 PM, cl Mon (except July & Aug) & major holidays. Admis by suggested contribution adults $5, senior citizens $4, children & students $3, members free. Estab 1895, incorporated 1926. Original building 1896-1907. Average Annual Attendance: 700,000. Mem: 27,400; dues $40 & up
Income: Financed by endowment, mem, city, county & state appropriation & other funds
Collections: †American & European paintings & sculpture, especially Impressionist & Post-Impressionist; †Contemporary International Art; Japanese woodblock prints; †American & European decorative arts; Antiquities; Asian Art; African Art; †Films; †Video tapes; †Photographs, †Prints & Drawings
Publications: Annual report; Carnegie Magazine, six times per year; catalogue of permanent collection; exhibition catalogs
Activities: Classes for adults & children; lect open to public, concerts; gallery talks; tours; film & video programs; inter-museum loans; originate traveling exhibitions; museum shop sells books, periodicals, posters, reproductions, slides, textiles, jewelry, ceramics & postcards
L Library, 4400 Forbes Ave, 15213. Tel 412-622-3100; FAX 412-622-6278; *Dir* Robert B Croneberger
Open to staff & mus docents for reference only
Library Holdings: Vols 3,000,000; Per subs 4000; Micro — Cards; AV — Cassettes, motion pictures, rec, slides, v-tapes; Other — Clipping files, exhibition catalogs, manuscripts, memorabilia, pamphlets, photographs

L CARNEGIE LIBRARY OF PITTSBURGH, Music & Art Department, 4400 Forbes Ave, 15213. Tel 412-622-3105; FAX 412-621-1267; Elec Mail logank@clpgh.org;
Internet Home Page Address http://www.clpgh.org/clp/musicart/. *Head* Kathryn Logan; *Asst Head* Kirby Dilworth; *Staff Librn* Heather Brodhead; *Staff Librn* Kaarin Van Ausdal; *Staff Librn* Catherine Tack; *Staff Librn* Yale Fineman
Open Mon - Thurs 9 AM - 9 PM, Fri & Sat 9 AM - 5:30 PM, Sun 1 - 5 PM, cl Sun during summer. Estab 1930 to provide reference & circulating materials on

all aspects of art
Income: Financed by city, state & county appropriation
Library Holdings: Vols 65,000; Per subs 85; Micro — Reels; AV — Slides, v-tapes; Other — Clipping files, exhibition catalogs, pamphlets, reproductions
Special Subjects: Architecture, Art History, Decorative Arts, Studio Arts
Collections: Architecture; archival materials; costume; †Pittsburghiana; Western Pennsylvania Architectural Survey Archival Materials

CARNEGIE MELLON UNIVERSITY
M Forbes Gallery, * 4825 Forbes Ave, 15213. Tel 412-268-2081; *Co-Dir* Shaunach Talley; *Co-Dir* Gretchen Dematera
Open Wed 3 - 6 & 7 - 9 PM, Thurs & Fri Noon - 6 PM & Thurs evening 7 - 9 PM, Sat Noon - 6 PM, Sun Noon - 3 PM. Estab 1969 to offer exhibition space to students, & an opportunity to learn about gallery management through practice. Gallery is approximately 20 x 40 ft plus small back room space. Average Annual Attendance: 750
Income: $5000 (financed by university fundings)
Exhibitions: Weekly senior art student exhibitions
L Hunt Library, * 4909 Frew St, 15213-3890. Tel 412-268-2444; FAX 412-268-3890; *Fine Arts Librn* Henry Pisciotta; *University Librn* Charles B Lowrey
Open Mon - Thurs 8 AM - 3 AM, Fri 8 AM - midnight, Sat 9 AM - midnight, Sun Noon - 3 AM. Estab 1912. The Fine Arts Library is on the 4th floor of the Hunt Library, supports College of Fine Arts program & is open to the pub
Income: Financed by University Libraries general operating funds & endowments
Library Holdings: Vols 54,900; Per subs 4000; Architectural drawings; Compact discs; Electronic datafiles; Micro — Reels; AV — A-tapes, rec, slides 120,700, v-tapes; Other — Clipping files, exhibition catalogs, reproductions
Special Subjects: Architecture, Design, Modern Art
Collections: Architectural Archives; Swiss Poster Collection, Thomas Gonda Poster Collection
Exhibitions: Pittsburgh Architectural Drawings
M Hunt Institute for Botanical Documentation, Frew St, 15213-3890. Tel 412-268-2434; FAX 412-268-5677; *Dir* Robert W Kiger; *Asst Dir* Terry D Jacobsen; *Cur Art* James J White; *Librn* Charlotte Tancin; *Bibliographer* Gavin D R Bridson; *Archivist* Anita L Karg
Open Mon - Fri 9 AM - Noon & 1 - 5 PM. No admis fee. Estab 1961 for the study of botany, history of botany, botanical art & illustration
Collections: †Botanical Art Collection, Archives, Library
Exhibitions: Botanical Watercolors; Poisonous Plants; Orchids from the Hunt Institute Collection
Publications: Huntia, irregular; Bulletin, semi-annually; exhibition catalogues, reference works, monographs
Activities: Retail store sells books, posters & cards

M CHATHAM COLLEGE, Art Gallery, Woodland Rd, 15232. Tel 412-365-1106, 365-1100; FAX 412-365-1505; *Dir* Michael Pestel
Open Tues - Sun 2 - 5 PM, cl Mon. No admis fee. Estab 1960 as an art gallery in a small liberal arts college, serving both the college & community by mounting exhibitions of high quality. Gallery is 100 running ft, is located in Jennie King Mellon Library & is fitted with track lighting. Average Annual Attendance: 1500
Income: Financed by college
Exhibitions: Linda Benglis; Don Reitz; Idelle Weber; Jerry L Caplan
Activities: Lect open to public, 2 vis lectr per year; gallery talks; scholarships offered; individual paintings & original objects of art lent

C FISHER SCIENTIFIC COMPANY, Fisher Collection of Alchemical & Historical Pictures, 2000 Park Lane, 15275-1126. Tel 412-490-8300; FAX 412-490-8982, 490-8313; *Dir* John Pavlik
Open Mon - Fri 9 AM - 4 PM. Estab 1917 to preserve for scientists a record of their professional ancestors. To maintain paintings & other graphics regarding science history, especially chemistry, for the pub. Collection is housed in two small rooms & a hallway with 4000 sq ft of wall space, housed within Fisher Scientific Company's headquarters. Average Annual Attendance: 1000
Collections: Permanent collection consists of oil paintings, engravings & etchings dealing with science history, especially alchemy; works executed by 17th century Dutch & Flemish artists: D Teniers, Hellemont, Wyck & Heerschopp; Louis Pasteur Special Collection, books, artworks, letters

M THE FRICK ART & HISTORICAL CENTER, Frick Art Museum, 7227 Reynolds St, 15208. Tel 412-371-0600; FAX 412-371-6140; *Vis Serv Mgr* Sue Martin; *Asst Cur & Registrar* Nadine Grabania
Open Tues - Sat 10 AM - 5:30 PM, Sun Noon - 6 PM. No admis fee. Estab 1970 as an art mus for pub enjoyment & educ. Average Annual Attendance: 35,000
Income: Financed by endowment
Collections: Italian, French Renaissance; bronzes, Chinese porcelains, furniture, sculpture, tapestries
Publications: Exhibit catalogues
Activities: Classes for adults & children; dramatic programs; docent training; studio workshops; family programs; lect open to public, 5-12 vis lectr per year; concerts; gallery talks; tours; competitions with awards; scholarships & fels offered; book traveling exhibitions 4-6 per year; originate traveling exhibitions; museum shop sells books, catalogues, color reproductions, photographs, posters, post cards

M MANCHESTER CRAFTSMEN'S GUILD, 1815 Metropolitan St, 15233. Tel 412-322-1773; FAX 412-321-2120; *Exec Dir* William Strickland Jr; *Asst Exec Dir* Nancy Brown; *Dir Performing Arts* Marty Ashby; *Dir Ceramic Arts* Joshua Green; *Dir Photography* Lonnie Graham
Estab 1968 to present photography & ceramic art of regional & nationally recognized artists
Exhibitions: Chris Gustin. Ben Fernandez; Angelia Pozo; Chris Johnson & Suzanne Lacy
Activities: Classes for adults & children; lect open to public, 10 vis lectr per year; sales shop sells original art

M **MATTRESS FACTORY,** 500 Sampsonia Way, 15212. Tel 412-231-3169; FAX 412-322-2231; *Exec Dir* Barbara Luderowski; *Cur* Michael Olijnyk
Open Tues - Sat 10 AM - 5 PM, Sun 1 - 5 PM. No admis fee. Estab 1978 as a research & development residency program featuring site-specific installations. Average Annual Attendance: 22,000
Collections: Permanent collection of William Anastasi, Jene Highstein, Rolf Julius, Winifred Lutz, James Turrell, Allan Wexler & Bill Woodrow
Exhibitions: Permanent collection & changing exhibitions of site-specific installations

C **MELLON BANK CORPORATION,** One Mellon Bank Ctr, 15258. FAX 412-234-4775; *Art Dir* Brian J Lang
Collections: 18th & 19th century British drawings & paintings; American historical prints; 19th century American & Pennsylvanian paintings; contemporary American & British paintings; contemporary works on paper; textiles

A **PITTSBURGH CENTER FOR THE ARTS,** 6300 Fifth Ave, Mellon Park, 15232. Tel 412-361-0873; FAX 412-361-8338; Elec Mail pcat@cmu.edu. *Exec Dir* Bob Grote
Open Mon - Sat 10 AM - 5:30 PM, Sun Noon - 5 PM. No admis fee, suggested donation. Estab 1944, inc 1947 to support artists & educate public about & through art. Galleries maintained for monthly contemporary exhibitions, group & one-person shows. Headquarters for non-profit organizations in the creative arts consists of sixteen resident and two affiliated member groups, gallery lodged in converted mansion. Average Annual Attendance: 150,000. Mem: 6500; dues vary; patron members; annual meeting in Nov
Income: Financed by school tuition, mem, commission on art sales & contributions
Exhibitions: (1997) Altered Environments; Fiberarts International; Hiroshi Sugimoto; Le Mauvement Quotidien
Publications: For the Arts, regional magazine with PCA listings; artists directory; class schedule; exhibition catalogs; monthly calender
Activities: Arts & crafts classes for adults and children; dramatic programs; docent training; workshops; vocational & teacher training; summer art camps; lect open to public; concerts; gallery talks; tours; awards; annual holiday art sales; scholarships & fels offered; exten dept serves western Pennsylvania; originate traveling exhibitions; sales shop sells original art

L **PITTSBURGH HISTORY & LANDMARKS FOUNDATION,** James D Van Trump Library, Landmarks Bldg, Rm 450, Station Square, 15219. Tel 412-471-5808; FAX 412-471-1633; *Pres* Arthur P Ziegler, Jr; *Exec Dir* Louise Sturgess
Open Mon - Fri 9 AM - 5 PM. Estab 1964 to preserve the architectural legacy & historic neighborhoods of Allegheny County. Reference for members only. Mem: 2200; dues $5
Library Holdings: Vols 4700; Per subs 17; Architectural & engineering drawings; Other — Clipping files, original art works, photographs, prints
Special Subjects: Architecture, Drawings, Landscape Architecture, Allegheny County History & Architecture, Civil Engineering, Historic Preservation
Collections: Paintings: Aaron Gorson, Otto Kuhler, Edward B Lee, William C Wall
Activities: Classes for adults & children; dramatic programs; docent training; lect open to public, 2 vis lectr per year; tours; competitions with prizes; museum shop sells books, reproductions, prints & slides

C **PNC BANK,** Art Collection, One PNC Plaza, 249 Fifth Ave, 15265. Tel 412-762-2000; *Art Dir* Heather Simple
Estab 1970 to enhance offices. Collection displayed at PNC Building
Collections: Eclectic media & periods
Activities: Awards to local groups only; individual objects of art lent

C **ROCKWELL INTERNATIONAL CORPORATION TRUST,** 625 Liberty Ave, 15222-3123. Tel 412-565-5803, 565-2000; FAX 412-565-7156;
Income: Financed by contributions & grants
Collections: Paintings by a wide variety of artists

A **SILVER EYE CENTER FOR PHOTOGRAPHY,** 1015 E Carson St, 15203. Tel 412-431-1810; FAX 412-431-5777; *Exec Dir* Jody Guy
Open Tues - Sat Noon - 5 PM. No admis fee. Average Annual Attendance: 5000. Mem: 260; dues $35-$750
Income: Financed by government, corporations, foundations & individuals
Exhibitions: Rotating exhibits of national & international photography, 2 national photo competitions per year
Publications: Members quarterly newsletter
Activities: Classes for children; outreach public school program; lect open to public, 1-5 vis lectr per year; gallery talks; lending collection contains books & videos

UNIVERSITY OF PITTSBURGH

M **University Art Gallery,** 15260. Tel 412-648-2400; FAX 412-648-2792; *Acting Dir* Matthew Roper; *Admin* Linda Hicks
Open Tues - Sat 10 AM - 4 PM, Sun 2 - 5 PM, cl Mon. No admis fee. Estab 1970 to provide exhibitions for the university community & the community at large & to provide students with gallery experience. Gallery comprised of 350 running ft in five areas. Average Annual Attendance: 4000
Income: Financed through the University
Collections: †Drawings, †paintings, †prints & †sculpture
Publications: Exhibition catalogs, 3 per year
Activities: Original objects of art lent; lending collection contains original art works, original prints, paintings, photographs, sculptures & drawings; originate traveling exhibitions

L **Henry Clay Frick Fine Arts Library,** Henry Clay Frick Fine Arts Bldg, 15260. Tel 412-648-2410; FAX 412-648-7568; Elec Mail frickart@vms.cis.pitt.edu. *Librn* Ray Anne Lockard
Open Mon - Thurs 9 AM - 9 PM, Fri & Sat 9 AM - 5 PM, Sun Noon - 7 PM. Estab 1928 to support the teaching activities of the Departments of History Art & Architecture & Studio Arts. For reference only

Library Holdings: Vols 75,000; Per subs 250; Micro — Fiche 15,000, reels; AV — Slides; Other — Clipping files, exhibition catalogs, pamphlets
Special Subjects: Art History, Graphic Arts, Sculpture, Architectural History, Medieval, Renaissance & Modern Art
Collections: Facsimile mss

C **WESTINGHOUSE ELECTRIC CORPORATION,** Art Collection, 11 Stanwix St, 15222. Tel 412-642-5904; *Corporate Art Cur* Barbara Antel
Open by appointment 8:15 AM - 5:15 PM. Estab 1970 to create pleasant working environment for employees. Collection displayed in headquarters building; a working collection used by the employees
Collections: 1600 pieces: contemporary international paintings & prints, ethnic artifacts, antique posters, primarily 1965 to present
Activities: Individual paintings & original objects of art lent to museums & galleries

READING

M **ALBRIGHT COLLEGE,** Freedman Gallery, 13th & Burn Sts, 19602. Tel 610-921-2381, Ext 7171; FAX 610-921-7530; *Dir* Christopher Youngs
Open Tues, Wed & Fri Noon - 6 PM, Thurs Noon - 8 PM, Sat & Sun 2 - 4 PM, also by appointment. No admis fee. Estab 1976 to present primarily contemporary art in a context of teaching. Large Gallery: 40 ft x 50 ft; Small Gallery: 20 ft x 24 ft. Average Annual Attendance: 18,000. Mem: 220; dues Director Circle $1000, supporter $500, contributor $100, family $40, dues $25, Albrightan $15
Income: $150,000 (financed by endowment, college, mem & grants)
Collections: Contemporary Painting, Prints, Sculpture, Photography
Publications: Exhibit catalogues
Activities: Lect open to public, 4-6 vis lectr per year; gallery talks; tours; Freedman Gallery Student Award; produce video-tapes on exhibitions, these include interviews with artists & commentary, tapes are available for rent; film series; individual paintings & original objects of art lent to galleries & museums; originate traveling exhibitions; sales shop sells catalogues, prints, t-shirts

A **BERKS ART ALLIANCE,** Wyomissing Institute of Art Bldg, 1100 Belmont St, 19610. Tel 610-376-1576, 775-9444; *Pres* Christiane David
Estab 1941 to maintain active art center in Reading & Berks county. Mem: 150; dues $12; annual meetings 2nd Tues of odd months
Income: Financed by dues & auction; commissions from members shows
Exhibitions: Three annual membership shows, plus solo or two-persons shows of a two week period each; juried show
Publications: Palette, every other month
Activities: Life or costume drawing workshop Thurs morning; open painting workshop Thurs afternoon; life drawing workshop Thurs evening; three day seminars by professional artists; sponsors annual trip to American Watercolor Society Show in New York

M **READING PUBLIC MUSEUM,** 500 Museum Rd, 19611-1425. Tel 610-371-5850; *Dir & Cur Fine Arts* Dr Robert Metzger
Open Tues, Thurs - Sat 11 AM - 5 PM, Wed 11 AM - 8 PM, Sun Noon - 5 PM. Admis suggested adults $3, children $2. Estab 1904 to promote knowledge, pleasure & cultivation of the arts & sciences. Ground floor: oil painting gallery. First floor: natural & social sciences exhibits. Second floor: permanent & temporary art exhibitions. Average Annual Attendance: 160,000. Mem: 600; dues $40; annual meeting in May
Income: $750,000 (financed by government)
Collections: American & European paintings; Natural Science; 19th Century Paintings; Old Masters Gallery; Pennsylvania-German Room; World History
Exhibitions: American Beauty Photographs by David Graham; Spectrums of Seasons, Jimmie Ernst; Retrospective Exhibits
Publications: Catalogue of selections from Permanent Collection
Activities: Classes for children; docent training; lect open to public & members, 10 vis lectr per year; concerts; gallery talks; tours; competitions with purchase awards; individual paintings & original objects of art lent to AAM accredited museums; lending collection contains 6000 original prints, 750 paintings, 100 photographs & 100 sculpture; museum shop sells books, reproductions, gift items, prints & slides

L **Library,** 500 Museum Rd, 19611-1425. Tel 610-371-5850; *Dir* Dr Robert Metzger
Open Mon - Fri 9 AM - 4 PM. For reference only
Library Holdings: Vols 15,000; Per subs 31; Original documents; AV — A-tapes, cassettes, fs, Kodachromes, lantern slides, v-tapes; Other — Clipping files, exhibition catalogs, manuscripts, memorabilia, pamphlets, prints, reproductions
Collections: American Bureau of Ethnology Collection

SCRANTON

M **EVERHART MUSEUM,** Nay Aug Park, 18510. Tel 717-346-7186; *Chmn Trustees* James J Walsh; *Dir* Daniel K Perry; *Cur Art* Dr Josephine Dunn
Open Tues - Fri 10 AM - 5 PM, Sat & Sun & summer holidays Noon - 5 PM, cl major holidays. No admis fee. Estab & incorporated 1908, a gift to the city by Dr Isaiah F Everhart; building enlarged 1928-29. Average Annual Attendance: 52,000. Mem: 1400; dues $15 & up
Income: Financed by endowment, city, state & county appropriations & mem
Collections: African Art; American Folk Art; American Indian objects; European & American painting, prints & sculpture; Dorflinger Glass; Oceanic Art; Oriental Art
Exhibitions: 5-6 exhibtions per year & permanent collections
Publications: Newsletter, 4 times per yr; annual report; exhibition catalogs
Activities: Classes for children; gallery talks; tours; educational programs for schools & other groups by appointment; planetarium demonstrations; book traveling exhibitions; originate traveling exhibitions & circulate to other museums; sales shop sells gifts & crafts

SELINSGROVE

M SUSQUEHANNA UNIVERSITY, Lore Degenstein Gallery, 514 University Ave, 17870-1001. Tel 717-372-4058; FAX 717-372-2745; *Dir* Dr Valerie Livingston
Open Tues - Sat 1 - 4 PM, Wed Noon - 4 PM & 7 - 9 PM. No admis fee. Estab 1993 to exhibit, interpret, collect & preserve objects of art & material culture through a rich & diverse exhibition program of inquiry supporting academic investigations & contributing to the cultural life of central Pennsylvania. Gallery offers a schedule of changing exhibitions focusing its program on historic, contemporary, regional, national & decorative art. Sponsors lectures & opening receptions
Collections: American Painting
Exhibitions: Intimate Perceptions: Aesthetic Considerations of Photography through the Microscope
Activities: Docent training; lect open to public, 3-4 vis lectr per year; book traveling exhibitions 2-3 per year; originate traveling exhibitions

SEWICKLEY

M INTERNATIONAL IMAGES, LTD, The Flatiron Bldg, 514 Beaver St, 15143. Tel 412-741-3036; FAX 412-741-8606; *Pres* Elena Kornetchuk; *Dir Exhib* Charles M Wiebe; *Gallery Assoc* Janet Caldarelli
Open Tues - Fri 9:30 AM - 5:30 PM, Sat 10 AM - 4 PM

SHIPPENSBURG

M SHIPPENSBURG UNIVERSITY, Kauffman Gallery, 1871 Old Main Dr, 17257. Tel 717-532-1530; FAX 717-532-1273; *Dir* William Q Hynes; *Secy* Veronica Mowery
Open Mon - Fri 9 AM - 4 PM, Wed evenings 6 - 9 PM. No admis fee. Estab 1972 to bring art to the college community. Average Annual Attendance: 1500
Income: Financed by Student Association funds & university
Exhibitions: Scholastic Art Awards - Area 6; SU Student Art Exhibits; changing exhibitions every month
Activities: Lect open to the public, 4 vis lectr per year; gallery talks

STROUDSBURG

M MONROE COUNTY HISTORICAL ASSOCIATION, Elizabeth D Walters Library, 537 Ann St, 18360. Tel 717-421-7703; FAX 717-421-9199; *Dir* Janet Mishkin
Open Tues - Fri 10 AM - 4 PM, Sun 1 - 4 PM, cl Sat. Admis fee $2. Estab 1921 for research. Average Annual Attendance: 5000. Mem: 400; dues $15; annual meeting 3rd Sat in Jan
Income: $80,000 (financed by endowment, mem, state appropriation & county)
Collections: Decorative Arts; Furniture; Indian Artifacts; Textiles
Exhibitions: Period Room; Toy Room
Publications: Fanlight Newsletter, quarterly
Activities: Lect open to public, 5 vis lectr per year; museum shop sells books

SWARTHMORE

L SWARTHMORE COLLEGE, Friends Historical Library of Swathmore College, 500 College Ave, 19081-1399. Tel 610-328-8496; FAX 610-328-7329; Elec Mail mchijio1@cc.swarthmore.edu. *Dir* Dr J William Frost; *Cur* Mary Ellen Chijioke; *Cur Peace Collection* Wendy Chmielewski
Open Mon - Fri 8:30 AM - 4:30 PM, Sat 9 AM - Noon; cl Sat when college not in session. Estab 1871 to preserve & make available to the pub material by & about Quakers & their concerns, records of non-sectarian peace organizations & papers of peace movement leaders
Income: $375,000 (financed by endowment & college)
Purchases: $15,000
Library Holdings: Vols 55,000; Per subs 584; charts; Maps; Original documents; Posters; Micro — Reels; AV — A-tapes, cassettes, Kodachromes, lantern slides, motion pictures, rec, slides, v-tapes; Other — Clipping files, manuscripts, memorabilia, original art works, pamphlets, photographs, prints, sculpture
Collections: Quaker paintings; Quakers as subject in art; †Meeting House Picture Collection; †portraits, group pictures, †residence pictures, †silhouettes & sketches of individual Friends; †Swarthmore College pictures; Swarthmore College Peace Collection consists primarily of archival material, records of non-sectarian peace organizations in the United States and 59 foreign countries, papers of peace leaders including Jean Addams, Emily Greene Balch, Elihu Burritt, A J Muste, †Wilhelm Sollmann and others; †1400 peace posters and war posters
Exhibitions: John Greenleaf Whittier, 1807 - 1892. Lucretia Mott Bi-centennial: The Nineteenth Struggle for Peace, Racial Justice & Women's Rights
Publications: Collection guides; exhibit catalogs
Activities: Annual Honorary Curators & Lippincott lect

UNION DALE

A ART EXCHANGE, Main St, PO Box 21, 18470. Tel 717-679-9000; Elec Mail artexc@epix.net;
Internet Home Page Address http://artexc.org. *Dir* Robert Stark
Estab 1970 to provide opportunities for community participation in the creative voices & forms of expression within the region, to bring to the community the art forms of other cultures & people, to support local & regional artists in the documentation & exhibition of their work; & to be a vigorous advocate for the development of the visual, verbal, performing, & craft arts within the community & region. Maintains reference library

UNIVERSITY PARK

PENNSYLVANIA STATE UNIVERSITY
M Palmer Museum of Art, 16802. Tel 814-865-7672; FAX 814-863-8608; *Dir* Jane Keene Muhlert; *Cur* Dr Glenn Willumson; *Registrar* Ok Hi Lee; *Exhib Designer* Ronald Hand; *Asst Dir* Dr Mary F Linda; *Cur Ed* Dr Patrick J McGrady
Open Tues - Sat 10 AM - 4:30 PM, Sun Noon - 4 PM, cl Mon & major holidays. No admis fee. Estab 1972 to promote a program of changing exhibitions; a window to the world for the university & surrounding communities. Mus is now a ten gallery post-modernist structure designed by Charles W Moore renovated & expanded in 1992 to accomodate continuous display of the permanent collection as well as changing exhibitions that are national & international in scope. Average Annual Attendance: 60,000
Income: Financed by state appropriation
Collections: American & European painting, drawings, graphics & sculpture with some emphasis on Pennsylvania artists; limited material in Ancient, African & Near Eastern areas; Kehl & Nina Markley Collection of Ancient Peruvian Ceramics; Dr Helen Adolf Collection of Austrian Academic Paintings; Asian paintings, sculpture, prints & decoratives art (ceramics, jade & cloisonne); John C O'Connor & Ralph M Yeager Collection of Pennsylvania Prints from the late 18th to the early 20th Century; Professor Francis E Hyslop Jr Collection of American & European prints; Tonkin Collection of Chinese export porcelain, Chinese jade carvings, paintings & watercolors releated to the Oriental Trade
Publications: Brochures; exhibition catalogs; posters; quarterly newsletter
Activities: Lect open to public, 18 vis lectr per year; concerts; gallery talks; tours; symposia; museum shop sells books, original art & reproductions
L Arts Library, Pattee Library E 405, 16802. Tel 814-865-6481; Elec Mail lls@psulias.psu.edu. *Arts & Architecture Librn* Loanne Snavely; *Music Librn* Amanda Maple; *Electronic Text Librn* Steven Ellis
Open Mon - Thurs 8 AM - midnight, Fri & Sat 8 AM - 9 PM, Sun Noon - midnight. Estab 1957 to support the academic programs of the College of Arts & Architecture & the Division of Art & Music Educ; to provide information on the arts to members of the university & community
Income: Financed through University Libraries
Library Holdings: Vols 85,000; Per subs 610; Compact discs; Electronic texts; Micro — Cards, fiche; AV — Cassettes, rec, v-tapes; Other — Exhibition catalogs, prints
Special Subjects: Art Education, Asian Art, Prints, Byzantine, Medieval, Baroque and Renaissance art and architecture history, history of printmaking, illuminated manuscripts
Collections: †Fine Print Collection (original prints)
M HUB Galleries, 312 Hub, 16802. Tel 814-865-2563; FAX 814-863-0812; Elec Mail aqsl@psu.edu. *Dir* Ann Shields
Open daily Noon - 8 PM, cl Mon. No admis fee. Estab 1976 to provide life-enriching visual arts experiences to the University & community. Browsing gallery; Art Alley Panels & Cases; HUB gallery (formal). Average Annual Attendance: 25,000
Exhibitions: Annual Children's Art Exhibit
Activities: Book traveling exhibitions 7 per year
L Architecture Library, Engineering Unit C, 16802. Tel 814-863-0511; Elec Mail lls@psulias.psu.edu. *Arts & Architecture Librn* Loanne Snavely; *Architecture Asst* Linda Zimmers
Open Mon - Thurs 8 AM - 11 PM, Fri & Sat 8 AM - 9 PM, Sun Noon - 11 PM. Estab 1978 to support the academic programs of the Department of Architecture & Department of Landscape Architecture to provide information on architecture & landscape architecture to members of the university & community
Income: Financed through university libraries
Library Holdings: Vols 18,000; Per subs 150; Other — Exhibition catalogs
Special Subjects: Architecture, Landscape Architecture

WARREN

M CRARY ART GALLERY INC, 511 Market St, 16365. Tel 814-723-4523; *Pres & Chief Exec Officer* Ann Lesser; *VPres* Adele Tranter
Open by appointment. No admis fee. Estab 1977 for art appreciation & educ & to exhibit the work of Clare J Crary, Gene Alden Walker & guest artists. The gallery was contructed in 1962 as a private dwelling on the general plan of a Roman Villa. There are 6 gallery rooms, one housing a permanent exhibit of Crary photographs. The others will accomodate fine art exhibits of the works of other artists
Income: $28,000 (financed by endowment)
Collections: Photographs by Clare J Crary; Oils by Gene Alden Walker; drawings, etchings, oils, acrylics by various artists; 19th Century Japanese wood-block prints-Ukiyo-E
Exhibitions: Watercolors by Anne F Fallin, NWS, AWS.
Activities: Gallery talks; tours; book traveling exhibitions

WASHINGTON

M WASHINGTON & JEFFERSON COLLEGE, Olin Art Gallery, E Wheeling St, Olin Art Ctr, 15301. Tel 412-223-6084, 223-6110; *Gallery Dir* Paul B Edwards
Open Mon - Sun Noon - 7 PM during school yr. No admis fee. Estab 1980 to provide college & community with art shows. Flexible lighting, air conditioned gallery. Average Annual Attendance: 6000
Income: Financed by college
Purchases: Over $3000 annually during National Painting Show
Collections: Art dept collection; college historical collection; National Painting Show collection
Exhibitions: Monthly exhibits
Publications: Exhibition catalogs
Activities: Lect open to public; concerts; gallery talks; competitions with awards;; individual paintings & original objects of art lent to students, faculty & staff; lending collection contains 200 original art works, 100 original prints, 300 paintings, 200 photographs & 4 sculpture; book traveling exhibitions 1 - 2 per year

WAYNE

A **WAYNE ART CENTER,** 413 Maplewood Ave, 19087. Tel 610-688-3553; *Dir* Nancy Campbell
Open Mon - Fri 9:30 AM - 4 PM. No admis fee. Estab 1930 as a community art center. Two galleries offer rotating exhibits of work by local artists. Average Annual Attendance: 2000. Mem: 400; dues $20; annual meeting May
Income: $60,000 (financed by mem, grants, corporations & Pennsylvania Council on the Arts)
Exhibitions: 10-12 changing exhibitions per year
Activities: Classes for adults & children; gallery talks; competitions

WEST CHESTER

A **CHESTER COUNTY HISTORICAL SOCIETY,** 225 N High St, 19380. Tel 610-692-4800; FAX 610-692-4357; *Exec Dir* Roland H Woodward; *Mus Cur* Margaret Bleecker Blades
Estab 1893 for the acquisition & preservation of property & information of historic value or interest to the people of Chester County. Maintains reference library. Average Annual Attendance: 35,000. Mem: 2500; dues family $35, individual $25
Income: Financed by endowment & mem
Collections: Museum houses regional collections of furniture, from ca 1690 to early 20th century through Victorian; ceramics, needlework, glassware, pewter, textiles, clocks, iron, dolls & costumes
Exhibitions: Chester County Furniture; decorative arts (permanent installation); changing interpretive exhibits on county history, agriculture & industries
Publications: Chester County History, occasionally; Newsletter, bi-monthly
Activities: Docent training; lect open to public; tours; individual paintings and original objects of art lent to other museums; museum shop selling books, reproductions and prints

WHITEHALL

NATIONAL SOCIETY OF PAINTERS IN CASEIN & ACRYLIC, INC
For further information, see National and Regional Organizations

WILKES-BARRE

M **WILKES UNIVERSITY,** Sordoni Art Gallery, 150 S River St, 18766. Tel 717-824-4651, Ext 4325; FAX 717-829-2434; *Dir* Stanley I Grand; *Asst Dir* Nancy L Krueger
Open Mon - Wed & Fri - Sun Noon - 5 PM, Thurs 5 - 9 PM. No admis fee. Estab 1973 to encourage the fine arts in the Wilkes-Barre & the northeastern Pennsylvania areas. The Gallery has one exhibition space, 30 x 40 ft, with adjustable flats for hanging. Average Annual Attendance: 20,000. Mem: 600; dues $15 - $1000
Income: Financed by mem, foundation endowment & Wilkes University
Collections: Nineteenth century European sculpture & paintings; 20th century American paintings & prints; mining photography collection
Exhibitions: They consist of loan exhibitions from other college galleries, independent galleries, major museums & loan services; group & one-person exhibits feature established modern masters & contemporary artists
Publications: Calendar of Events, bimonthly; scholarly catalogs; illustrated brochures; posters
Activities: Gallery talks; tours; loans to other universities & museums; book traveling exhibitions; originate traveling exhibitions to schools & museums

WILLIAMSPORT

M **LYCOMING COLLEGE GALLERY,** 17701. Tel 717-321-4242, 368-1140; FAX 717-321-4090; *Coordr* Deborah Caulkins; *Co-Dir* Roger Shipley
Open Mon - Thurs 8 AM - 11 PM, Fri 8 AM - 4:30 PM, Sat 10 AM - 5 PM, Sun 1 - 11 PM. No admis fee. Estab 1980 to bring quality art work to the students & faculty as well as to the interested community. The new gallery, 30 x 60 ft, is located in the College Library. Average Annual Attendance: 5000
Income: Financed by school budget
Collections: †Paintings & prints of 19th & 20th century artists
Exhibitions: One-man shows of regional artists & alumni of the Department
Activities: Gallery talks; tours; individual paintings lent; book traveling exhibitions; originate traveling exhibitions

YORK

A **HISTORICAL SOCIETY OF YORK COUNTY,** 250 E Market St, 17403. Tel 717-848-1587; FAX 717-848-1589; *Exec Dir* Patrick A Foltz; *Cur Coll* Janet Deranian; *Head Librn* June Lloyd
Open Mon - Sat 9 AM - 5 PM, Sun 1 - 4 PM, Historic Houses Mon - Sat 10 AM - 4 PM, Sun 1 - 4 PM, cl all major holidays. Estab 1895 to record, preserve, collect & interpret the history of York County & Pennsylvania. Restoration Properties: General Gates House (1751); Golden Plough Tavern (1741) & Bobb Log House (1812), 157 W Market; Bonham House (1875), 152 E Market. Maintains reference library. Average Annual Attendance: 50,000. Mem: 2000; dues $25 & up; annual meeting in Apr
Income: $500,000 (financed by endowment, gifts & mem)
Library Holdings: Vols 32,000; Per subs 30; Micro — Reels; AV — A-tapes, motion pictures, slides; Other — Clipping files, exhibition catalogs, manuscripts, memorabilia, pamphlets, photographs
Collections: Fraktur & other Pennsylvania decorative arts & furnishings; Works by Lewis Miller & other local artists; James Shettel Collection of theater & circus material; Horace Bonham artworks
Exhibitions: Six galleries featuring various subjects of regional interest; historic houses

Publications: The Kentucky Rifle; Lewis Miller Sketches & Chronicles; monthly newsletter; The Philadelphia Chair, 1685-1785; William Wagner-Views of York in 1830
Activities: Classes for adults & children; summer internship program; lect; guided tours; concerts; museum shop sells books, reproductions & prints

L **Library,** 250 E Market St, 17403. Tel 717-848-1589; *Librn* June Lloyd
Open to the public, cl Sun. For reference only
Library Holdings: Vols 25,000; Per subs 50; Maps; Vertical files 156; Micro — Reels; AV — A-tapes, cassettes, slides, v-tapes; Other — Clipping files, manuscripts, memorabilia, pamphlets, photographs
Special Subjects: Architecture, Folk Art

L **MARTIN MEMORIAL LIBRARY,** 159 E Market St, 17401. Tel 717-846-5300; *Dir* William H Schell; *Adult Servs* Rebecca Shives
Open Mon - Fri 9 AM - 5:30 PM, Sat 9 AM - 5 PM. No admis fee. Estab 1935
Library Holdings: Vols 100,000; Per subs 200; Mounted pictures; AV — Cassettes, motion pictures, rec; Other — Pamphlets
Publications: Annual Reports; Bulletin, monthly; Martin Memorial Library Historical Series; occasional bibliographies of special collections
Activities: Programs for adults and children; lect; concerts

RHODE ISLAND

BRISTOL

L **ROGER WILLIAMS UNIVERSITY,** Architecture Library, One Old Ferry Rd, 02809-2921. Tel 401-254-3625; FAX 401-254-3565; *Architecture Librn* Elizabeth Peck Learned; *Asst Slide Cur* Susan Travis; *Circulation Asst* Mary Masley
Estab 1987
Library Holdings: Vols 15,000; Per subs 200; Micro — Fiche, reels; AV — Slides 50,000, v-tapes 100; Other — Clipping files, pamphlets
Special Subjects: Architecture, Drafting, Furniture, Historical Material, Industrial Design, Interior Design, Landscape Architecture, Maps, Restoration & Conservation, Historic Preservation
Collections: †Architecture; †historic preservation

KINGSTON

A **SOUTH COUNTY ART ASSOCIATION,** 2587 Kingstown Rd, 02881. Tel 401-783-2195; *Pres* Brie Taylor; *VPres* Peg Gregory; *Recording Secy* Gail Ambrose; *Treas* Cheslie Carpenter; *Cur & Caretaker* Jane Auger
Open Wed - Sun 1 - 4 PM during exhibitions. No admis fee. Estab 1929 to promote an interest in art & to encourage artists & to support, in every way, the aesthetic interests of the community. Average Annual Attendance: 400; applicants for membership must submit three paintings and be accepted by a committee; dues lay member & artist $15; annual meeting Oct
Collections: No large permanent collection; paintings by early members, usually not on display
Publications: Newsletter, 3-4 annually
Activities: Classes for adults & children; lect open to public, 4 vis lectr per year; gallery talks; competitions with awards; scholarships; original objects of art lent to other art associations; lending collection contains books, lantern slides, sculpture, original art works & slides

M **UNIVERSITY OF RHODE ISLAND,** Fine Arts Center Galleries, c/o Department of Art, 02881-0820. Tel 401-874-2131; FAX 401-874-2729; *Galleries Dir* Judith Tolnick
Open Main Gallery Tues - Fri Noon - 4 PM & 7:30 - 9:30 PM, Sat 1 - 4 PM, Photography Gallery Tues - Fri Noon - 4 PM, Sat 1 - 4 PM, Corridor Gallery, Mon - Fri 9 AM - 5 PM. No admis fee. Estab 1970 to expose university & Southern New England communities to contemporary & historical art. Average Annual Attendance: 15,000
Income: Financed through University
Exhibitions: 18-20 ongoing exhibitions per yr
Publications: Catalogs, occasionally; brochures/wall text for each exhibit
Activities: Educ dept; classes for adults; lect open to the public, 20 vis lectr per year; concerts; gallery talks; sponsor competitions; book traveling exhibitions 2 times per year; originate traveling exhibitions to university museums & galleries nationally

NEWPORT

M **NAVAL WAR COLLEGE MUSEUM,** Coasters Harbor Island, 02841-1207. Tel 401-841-4052; FAX 401-841-3804; *Dir* Anthony S Nicolosi; *Sr Cur* Robert Cembrola
Open Mon - Fri 10 AM - 4 PM, Sat & Sun Noon - 4 PM, June - Sept. Estab 1978. Themes: history of naval warfare, history of Navy in Narragansett Bay. 7000 sq ft on two floors of Founder Hall, a National Historic Landmark. Average Annual Attendance: 17,000
Income: Financed by Federal Navy & Naval War College Foundation, Inc
Exhibitions: Sea Power According to Alfred Thayer Mahan; Nay-Newport Articles & Art Exhibit, annual
Publications: Exhibition catalogs
Activities: Staff talks on themes & exhibits; lect open to public, 2 vis lectr per year; gallery talks; tours; retail store sells books, reproductions, prints, clothing, & costume jewelry

M **NEWPORT ART MUSEUM,** 76 Bellevue Ave, 02840. Tel 401-848-8200; FAX 401-848-8205; *Dir* Judith Sobel; *Dir Admin* Christine Callahon; *Art School Dir* Judy Hambleton; *Grants & Membership* Ruth Taylor
Open summer Mon - Sat 10 AM - 5 PM, Sun & most holidays 1 - 5 PM, winter Tues - Sat 10 AM - 4 PM, Sun & most holidays 1 - 4 PM, cl Christmas, New Year's Day & Thanksgiving. Admis adults $4, senior citizens & students $3, children 12 & under free. The Griswold House, designed by Richard Morris Hunt for John N A Griswold in 1862 - 1863, has been the home of the Art Museum since 1916. Retaining some of the original interior decor of the era, the building is listed in the National Register of Historic Places. Cushing Memorial Gallery was built in 1920, commissioned from the firm of Delano & Aldrich, by friends & associates of Howard Gardiner Cushing. Buildings contain 6 galleries exhibiting contemporary visual arts, historic & regional exhibits. Average Annual Attendance: 30,000. Mem: 1750; dues $40 & up; annual meeting in Sept
Income: Financed by donations, endowment, mem, classes & admis
Collections: †Drawings, †Paintings, †Photographs, †Prints, †Sculpture
Exhibitions: Changing exhibitions, all media. (1997) Red Grooms: A Personal Art History; Winslow Homer in Everyday Life; Wood Engravings
Publications: News, quarterly members' newsletters
Activities: Day & evening classes for adults & children; docent training; lect open to public & some for members only, 25 vis lectr per year; concerts; gallery talks; tours; awards; scholarships offered; exten dept serves area schools; individual paintings & original objects of art lent to other museums; book traveling exhibitions, 1 - 2 per year; originate traveling exhibitions

A **NEWPORT HISTORICAL SOCIETY,** 82 Touro St, 02840. Tel 401-846-0813; FAX 401-846-1853; *Pres* Bradford A Becken; *Exec Dir* Dr Daniel Snydacker
Open Tues - Fri 9:30 AM - 4 PM, Sat 9:30 AM - Noon; summer, Sat 9:30 AM - 4:30 PM, cl Sun & Mon. No admis fee. Estab 1853 to collect & preserve items of historical interest pertaining to the city. Maintains gallery & also owns & exhibits the first Seventh Day Baptist Church in America (1729); the Wanton-Lyman-Hazard House (1675), the first home to be restored in Newport; the Friends Meeting House (1699), site of the annual New England Quakers Meeting for over 200 years & Mus of Newport History. Maintains reference library. Average Annual Attendance: 20,000. Mem: 1250; dues $30 & up; annual meeting in May
Income: Financed by endowment, mem, state appropriation & other contributions
Collections: Artifacts, china, Colonial silver, dolls, glass, furniture, Newport scenes & portraits, pewter & toys, photographs
Exhibitions: Numerous changing exhibits
Publications: Newport History, quarterly; Newport Historical Society Newsletter, 6 times per yr
Activities: Classes for adults & children; dramatic programs; docent training; walking tours; harbor tours by boat; lect open to public, 8-10 vis lectr per year; tours; competitions with awards; exten dept serves SE New England; individual paintings & original objects of art lent to educational institutions only; originate traveling exhibitions

L **Library,** 82 Touro St, 02840. Tel 401-846-0813; *Librn* Bertram Lippincott III
Open Tues - Fri 9:30 AM - 4:30 PM, Sat 9 AM - Noon, summers, Sat 9:30 AM - 4:30 PM. Estab 1853 to provide resource materials. For reference only
Library Holdings: Vols 9000; Per subs 10; Micro — Fiche, reels; AV — A-tapes, Kodachromes, slides, v-tapes; Other — Clipping files, exhibition catalogs, manuscripts, memorabilia, original art works, pamphlets, photographs, prints, sculpture
Special Subjects: Architecture, Art History, Ceramics, Costume Design & Construction, Decorative Arts, Dolls, Furniture, Historical Material, Landscape Architecture, Maps, Painting - American, Period Rooms, Pewter, Restoration & Conservation, Silver, Silversmithing, Stained Glass, Textiles, Genealogy

L **REDWOOD LIBRARY & ATHENAEUM,** 50 Bellevue Ave, 02840-3292. Tel 401-847-0292; FAX 401-841-5680; Elec Mail robertba@dsl.rhilinetl.gov. *Acting Dir* Marilyn D Curtis
Open Mon - Sat 9:30 AM - 5:30 PM. Estab 1747 as a general library
Income: Financed by endowment & mem
Library Holdings: Vols 150,000; Per subs 175; AV — Rec
Collections: Approximately 150 paintings, largely portraits; approximately 40 sculptures; approximately 50 pieces of furniture & other decorative arts items; those on display include portraits by Washington Allston, Robert Feke, G P A Healy, Charles Willson Peale, Rembrandt Peale, John Smibert, Gilbert Stuart, Thomas Sully; many paintings by Charles Bird King, historical & classical busts, & early Newport furniture
Activities: Group tours by prior arrangement

M **ROYAL ARTS FOUNDATION,** Belcourt Castle, 657 Bellevue Ave, 02840-4280. Tel 401-846-0669; Internet Home Page Address http://www.belcourt.com.
Open Feb - May Sat - Sun & holidays 10 AM - 3 PM; Memorial Day - Mid Oct daily 9 AM - 5 PM; Mid Oct - Nov daily 10 AM - 4 PM, cl Jan. Admis adult $7.50, senior 65+ & college undergraduate $6, student (ages 13-18) $5, child (ages 6-12) $3. Estab 1957. 60-room private residence of the Tinney family open to visitors under the auspices of the Royal Arts Foundation. Average Annual Attendance: 30,000. Mem: annual meeting in Jan
Income: $300,000 (financed by admis fees)
Activities: Lect open to public, 4 vis lectr per year; guided & specialty tours; sales shop sells books

PAWTUCKET

M **OLD SLATER MILL ASSOCIATION,** Slater Mill Historic Site, 67 Roosevelt Ave, PO Box 696, 02862. Tel 401-725-8638; FAX 401-722-3040; *Cur* Louis Hutchins; *Cur* Karin Conopash
Open May - Nov Tues - Sun 10 AM - 5 PM, Nov - Dec 20 & Mar - May Sat & Sun 1 - 5 PM. Estab 1921. Wilkinson Gallery for temporary exhibits including history, art & craft shows. Three permanent galleries in historic buildings. Average Annual Attendance: 35,500. Mem: dues $35; annual meeting in June
Income: $225,000 (financed by endowment, mem & city appropriation)
Collections: Machine tools; manuscripts; photographs; textiles; textile machinery
Publications: Quarterly flyer
Activities: Adult classes; docent programs; lect open to public, 2-3 vis lectr per year; traveling educ programs; book traveling exhibitions 4 per year; sales shop sells books, prints, slides & photographs

A **RHODE ISLAND WATERCOLOR SOCIETY,** Slater Memorial Park, Armistice Blvd, 02861. Tel 401-726-1876; *Pres* Allen Hall; *VPres* Lois Hebner; *Treas* Barbara LaPierre; *Asst Treas* Mary Gene Plante
Open Tues - Sat 10 AM - 4 PM, Sun 1 - 5 PM; cl Mon. No admis fee. Estab 1896 to encourage & promote the advancement of watercolor painting. Large carpeted upper & lower tiled gallery. Lower level gallery open for classes & exhibitions. Mem: 249; dues $60; annual meeting May; must submit work for jurying for mem
Income: Financed by dues, commissions, contributions & programs
Collections: Paintings & drawings by early members; prints & paintings by contemporary members
Exhibitions: Annual Exhibition of Member's work; Annual Christmas Exhibition; Annual Open Graphics Show; Annual Open Juried Watermedia Show; Annual New Members Show; 12 or more member exhibitions per year
Activities: Classes for adults; workshops; 6 lect & demonstrations per year, open to members & guests; competitions with prizes; sales shop sells wrapped matted paintings from bins

PROVIDENCE

BROWN UNIVERSITY

M **David Winton Bell Gallery,** 64 College St, 02912. Tel 401-863-2932; Elec Mail richard_benefield@brown.edu. *Dir* Jo-Ann Conklin; *Adminr* Richard Benefield
Open Sept - May Mon - Fri 11 AM - 4 PM, Sat & Sun 1 - 4 PM, cl major holidays. No admis fee. Estab 1971 to present exhibitions of interest to the university & community. The gallery is modern, covers 2625 sq ft, 14 ft ceilings & has track lighting. Average Annual Attendance: 14,000
Income: Financed by endowment & university funds
Collections: Substantial print collection of historical & modern masters; selected color field paintings & modern sculpture
Publications: Exhibition catalogs
Activities: Lect open to public; art work lent to exhibitions mounted by museums & galleries; permanent collection contains 5000 original prints & photographs, over 100 modern paintings & sculptures; originates traveling exhibitions

M **Annmary Brown Memorial,** 21 Brown St, PO Box 1905, 02912. Tel 401-863-1994; *Supv* Carole Cramer
Open Mon - Fri 9 AM - 5 PM. Estab 1907 to offer representatives of schools of European & American painting. There are three galleries which house the art collection of the founder & his wife, & portraits of the Brown family. Average Annual Attendance: 3000
Exhibitions: World War II: Archival Photos, book, newspapers & memorabilia
Activities: Lect open to public, 10-20 vis lectr per year; concerts; tours

L **Art Slide Library,** 02912. Tel 401-863-3218; *Cur* Norine Duncan; *Assoc Cur* Karen Bouchard
Open Mon - Fri 8:30 AM - 5 PM. Circ 30,000
Income: $185,000 (financed by university funds)
Library Holdings: Vols 550; Micro — Fiche; AV — Slides; Other — Exhibition catalogs, photographs, reproductions
Special Subjects: Architecture, Art History, Asian Art, Decorative Arts, Drawings, Etchings & Engravings, Folk Art, Industrial Design, Ivory, Landscapes, Manuscripts, Metalwork, Mosaics, Photography, Portraits, Religious Art, Antiquities, Paintings, Sculpture, Stained Glass, Watercolors

M **Haffenreffer Museum,** 300 Tower St, 02809-4050. FAX 401-253-1198; *Dir* Shepard Krech III; *Deputy Dir & Cur* Barbara A Hail; *Assoc Cur & Coll Mgr* Thierry Gentis
Open June, July & Aug Tues - Sun 11 AM - 5 PM, academic yr Sat & Sun 11 AM - 5 PM. Admis adults $2. Estab 1955 to educate Brown University Students & the general pub through anthropological research on humankind, about cultural differences & human similarities & to serve its constituencies with excellence. Average Annual Attendance: 15,000. Mem: 250; dues $20-$100; annual meeting in May
Collections: Worldwide material culture-artifacts, costumes, pottery, tools, sculpture, etc
Exhibitions: Passionate Hobby-North American Gallery-a collection of objects of native North Americans
Activities: Classes for adults & children; docent training; lect open to public, 8 vis lectr per year; gallery talks; tours; artmobile; book traveling exhibitions 1 per year; originate traveling exhibitions; museum shop sells books, magazines, original art, reproductions, prints, slides & objects related to the collections

A **PROVIDENCE ART CLUB,** 11 Thomas St, 02903. Tel 401-331-1114; FAX 401-521-0195; *Pres* Robert F Venditto
Open Mon - Fri 10 AM - 4 PM, Sat Noon - 3 PM, Sun 3 - 5 PM. No admis fee. Estab 1880 for art culture & to provide exhibition space for artists. Galleries maintained in two 18th century buildings on historic Thomas street in Providence. Average Annual Attendance: 4000. Mem: 615; to qualify, artists' work must pass a board of artists; personal qualifications for non-artists; dues non-artist $388, artist $276; annual meeting first Wed in June
Income: Financed by endowment & mem
Collections: Small permanent collection of paintings & sculpture by Club members since 1880
Exhibitions: Eighteen shows a season of which two-three are juried open shows
Publications: Newsletter for members
Activities: Lect for members & guests; gallery talks; competitions with awards; scholarships offered

M **PROVIDENCE ATHENAEUM,** 251 Benefit St, 02903. Tel 401-421-6970; FAX 401-421-2860; *Exec Dir* Gary Mason; *Asst Dir* Lee Teverow
Open Mon - Fri 8:30 AM - 5:30 PM, Sat 9:30 AM - 5:30 PM, Sun 1 - 5 PM, cl Sat & Sun mid June - Labor Day. No admis fee. Estab 1753 to provide cultural services, information, rare & current materials in an historic setting. Maintains a rare book library. Mem: Estab 1367; dues $25-$100 annual meeting in the Fall
Income: $303,544 (financed by endowment & mem)
Purchases: $40,000
Collections: Strength in the 19th century
Exhibitions: Exhibitions vary each month; local artists' works shown
Publications: The Athenaeum Bulletin, summer; Annual Report, Fall

Activities: Dramatic programs; film programs; lect open to public; tours; festivals; concerts; day trips; original objects of art lent to bonafide institutions, libraries or societies; lending collection contains books, periodicals, records, videotapes, cassettes; sales shop sells Audubon prints in limited editions, stationery, t-shirts & Athenaeum cookbooks

L **Library**, 251 Benefit St, 02903. Tel 401-421-6970; FAX 401-421-2860; *Dir* Gary Mason; *Asst Dir* Lee Teverow; *Head Adult Services* Risa Gilpin
Open Mon - Fri 8:30 AM - 5:30 PM, Sat 9:30 AM - 5:30 PM, Sun 1 - 5 PM, cl Sat & Sun mid June - Labor Day. Estab 1753 to provide cultural services, information rare & current materials in a historic setting. Circ 106,000
Library Holdings: Vols 161,486; Per subs 133; Posters; AV — A-tapes, cassettes, rec, v-tapes; Other — Clipping files, exhibition catalogs, manuscripts, memorabilia, original art works, pamphlets, photographs, prints, sculpture
Special Subjects: Art History, Architecture History, Biography, Voyage and Travel, Literature, Fiction and Children's
Collections: 19th century Robert Burns collection; 19th century library - rare book library; Audubon, Old Fiction, Holder Borde Bowen collection
Activities: Docent training; childrens programs; film programs; festivals; readings & lectr; tours; trips

L **PROVIDENCE PUBLIC LIBRARY,** Art & Music Services, 225 Washington St, 02903. Tel 401-455-8036; FAX 401-455-8080; Elec Mail susanwn@dsl.rhilinet.gov. *Coordr* Susan R Waddington; *Specialist* Margaret Chevian
Open Oct - May, Mon - Thurs 9 AM - 8 PM, Fri, Sat 9 AM - 5:30 PM, Sun 1 - 5 PM, summer hours vary. Estab 1878 to serve needs of the public
Income: $2,700,000 (financed by endowment, city and state appropriations and federal funds)
Library Holdings: Vols 43,000; Per subs 85; Posters; AV — Rec, v-tapes; Other — Clipping files, framed reproductions, original art works, photographs, prints
Special Subjects: Advertising Design, Architecture, Cartoons, Ceramics, Commercial Art, Costume Design & Construction, Crafts, Decorative Arts, Drawings, Furniture, Graphic Design, Handicrafts, Illustration, Interior Design, Landscape Architecture, Painting - American, Painting - British, Photography, Pottery, Sculpture, Silversmithing, design
Collections: †Nickerson Architectural Collection; art & music books

M **RHODE ISLAND COLLEGE,** Edward M Bannister Gallery, 600 Mount Pleasant Ave, 02908. Tel 401-456-9765; FAX 401-456-8379; Elec Mail domalley@grog.ric.edu. *Dir* Dennis M O'Malley
Open Tues - Sat 11 AM - 4 PM, Thurs evenings 6 - 9 PM, cl holidays. No admis fee. Estab 1977 to provide the Rhode Island community with a varied & progressive exposure to the visual arts, to offer to the college community, with its liberal arts perspective, access to top quality exhibits, artists & workshops. Gallery consists of one room, 25 x 60 ft separated by supports; a 12 ft ceiling on one side & an 8 ft ceiling on the other, as well as moveable walls & partitions used in two person shows, lighting is incandescent track light, approx 60 track fixtures. Average Annual Attendance: 5000
Income: Financed by state appropriation
Purchases: Works of artists exhibited at the gallery
Collections: Teaching collection of works purchased from exhibiting artists
Publications: Brochures; semiannual calendars; monthly exhibit announcements

A **RHODE ISLAND HISTORICAL SOCIETY,** 110 Benevolent St, 02906. Tel 401-331-8575; FAX 401-351-0127; *Dir* Albert T Klyberg; *Ed, Nathanael Green Papers* Dennis Conrad; *Museum Cur* Linda Eppich; *Dir Educ* Daniel Romani; *Public Relations* William Greene
Open Tues - Fri 9 AM - 5 PM, Sun 1 - 4 PM. Admis adults $2, students $1. Estab 1822 to preserve, collect & interpret Rhode Island historical materials, including books, manuscripts, graphics, films, furniture & decorative arts. Mem: 2500; dues $35; annual meeting in Sept
Income: Financed by endowment, mem & city & state appropriation
Exhibitions: Changing exhibitions on Rhode Island history & decorative arts
Publications: American Paintings in the Rhode Island Historical Society, (catalogue); The John Brown House Loan Exhibition of Rhode Island Furniture; Nathanael Green Papers; Rhode Island History, quarterly; Roger Williams Correspondence; occasional monographs; newsletter, bimonthly
Activities: Classes for adults & children; children's tours; film programs; lect open to public, 4-6 vis lectr per year; concerts; gallery talks; tours; lending collection contains 10,000 prints for reference and copying; traveling exhibitions organized & circulated locally

M **John Brown House,** 52 Power St, 02906. Tel 401-331-8575; *Cur* Linda Eppich
Open Tues - Sat 10 AM - 4:30 PM, Sun Noon - 4 PM, cl weekdays Jan & Feb except by appointment. Estab 1942, the 1786 house carefully restored & furnished with fine examples of Rhode Island heritage. Average Annual Attendance: 11,500
Collections: Carrington Collection of Chinese export objects; McCrollis Collection of Antique Dolls; †furniture by Rhode Island Cabinetmakers, some original to the house; †portraits, †china, †glass, †pewter & †other decorative objects; Rhode Island furniture, silver, porcelain, paintings, textiles
Activities: Classes for children; docent training; lect open to public, 10 vis lectr per year; tours; museum shop sells books, reproductions, prints & slides

M **Aldrich House,** 110 Benevolent St, 02906. Tel 401-331-8575
Open Mon - Sat 11 AM - 4 PM, Sun 1 - 4 PM. Admis adults $2, senior citizens & students $1. Estab 1974. Galleries for changing exhibitions of Rhode Island artists & history
Income: Financed by endowment, state & local funds, grants (state & federal) & admis rates

L **Library,** 121 Hope St, 02906. Tel 401-331-8575; FAX 401-751-7930; *Dir* Madeleine Telseyan
Open Tues - Sat 9 AM - 5 PM, June, July & Aug Mon 1 - 9 PM, Tues - Fri 9 AM - 5 PM. No admis fee. Estab 1822 to collect, preserve & make available materials relating to state's history & development. Small exhibit area at library, also galleries at John Brown & Aldrich houses. Average Annual Attendance: 9000. Mem: 3000; dues individual $30; annual meetings in Sept
Income: $700,000 (financed by endowment, mem & state appropriation)
Library Holdings: Vols 150,000; Per subs 2600

Collections: †5000 manuscripts collections dating from 17th century; †Rhode Island Imprints, 1727-1800; †Rhode Island Broadsides; †Providence Postmaster Provisional Stamps; †Rhode Island Post Office Covers; †genealogical sources, all state newspapers, maps, films, TV news films and movies, graphics, architectural drawings; †150,000 reference volumes; †200,000 photographs; business archives; oral history tapes
Exhibitions: Rhode Island photography
Publications: Rhode Island History, quarterly
Activities: Classes for adults & children; docent training; lect open to public, 12 vis lectr per year; concerts; gallery talks; tours; awards; individual paintings lent; originate traveling exhibitions to educational and governmental institutions; museum shop sells books & prints

M **RHODE ISLAND SCHOOL OF DESIGN,** Museum of Art, 224 Benefit St, 02903-2723. Tel 401-454-6500; FAX 401-454-6556; *Museum Dir* Doreen Bolger; *Museum Shop Mgr* Anne Meretta
Open Tues, Wed, Fri, Sat 10:30 AM - 5 PM, Thurs Noon - 8 PM. Admis adults $2, children 5 - 18 $.50, children under 5 free. Estab 1877 to collect & exhibit art for general educ of RISD students & the pub. Present buildings opened in 1897, 1906, 1926 & 1990. Average Annual Attendance: 100,000. Mem: 3500
Income: Financed by endowment, mem, state & federal appropriation, private & corporate contributions
Collections: Lucy Truman Aldrich Collection of European porcelains & Oriental textiles; †Ancient Oriental & ethnographic art; †American painting; †contemporary graphic arts; †Nancy Sayles Day Collection of modern Latin American art; †English watercolors; †15th - 18th century European art; †19th & 20th century French art from Romanticism through Surrealism; †Albert Pilavin Collection of 20th century American Art; Pendleton House collection of 18th century American furniture & decorative arts; Abby Aldrich Rockefeller collection of Japanese prints
Exhibitions: Neoteric Jewelry; Romanticism & Revival: 19th Century American Art from Permanent Collection; Expressionist Visions: Prints & Drawings from the Museum's Collection; Form, Pattern & Function: Design in American Indian Art; Edward W Curtis Photogravures: Selections from the North American Indian. (1997) Art in a Box, Exhibition & Auction
Publications: Gallery guides for select exhibits; catalogs
Activities: Classes for adults & children; docent training; lect open to public; gallery talks; concerts; tours; outreach programs serve schools, nursing homes & hospital children's ward in the area; traveling exhibitions organized & circulated; museum shop sells books, original art, reproductions, prints, jewelry, posters & postcards

L **Library,** 2 College St, 02903-2784. Tel 401-454-6365; FAX 401-454-6226; Elec Mail cterry@risd.edu. *Dir* Carol Terry
Open to the public for reference
Library Holdings: Vols 92,000; Per subs 395; Artists' books; Compact discs; Postcards; Posters; Micro — Fiche; AV — Rec, slides 144,000, v-tapes 1000; Other — Clipping files 446,000, exhibition catalogs, photographs, reproductions 19,000
Special Subjects: Architecture, Fine & Applied Arts & Design

SAUNDERSTOWN

M **GILBERT STUART MEMORIAL, INC MEMORIAL ASSOCIATION, INC,** Museum, 815 Gilbert Stuart Rd, 02874. Tel 401-294-3001; *Cur* John Thompson; *Cur* Deborah Thompson; *Pres* George Gardiner
Open Apr - Nov weekends 11 AM - 4:30 PM, call ahead on weekdays as hours are subject to caretaker availability. Admis $3, children 6-12 $1. Designated 1966 as a national historic landmark, the furnished birthplace of America's foremost portrait painter, the home was built 1751. Average Annual Attendance: 4000. Mem: 300; dues $15 & up; annual meeting in July
Income: Financed by endowment, admis fees & grants
Activities: Guided tours of the home

WAKEFIELD

M **HERA EDUCATION FOUNDATION,** Hera Gallery, 327 Main St, Box 336, 02880-0336. Tel 401-789-1488; *Dir* Patti Candelari
Open Wed - Fri 1 - 5 PM, Sat 10 AM - 4 PM. No admis fee. Estab 1974 as a women's cooperative gallery exhibiting the work of members & non-members. 30 ft x 40 ft in dimension with 9 ft ceiling. Average Annual Attendance: 200
Income: Financed by mem, contributions, grants & scholarships
Activities: Lect open to public, 4-6 vis lectr per year; juried competition with cash award; symposia; critique group; sales shop sells books & art

WARWICK

M **COMMUNITY COLLEGE OF RHODE ISLAND,** Art Department Gallery, Knight Campus, 400 East Ave, 02886. Tel 401-825-2220; FAX 401-825-2282; *Chairwoman* Rebecca Clark
Open Mon - Sat 11 AM - 4 PM. No admis fee. Estab 1972. Maintains reference library. Average Annual Attendance: 1000
Exhibitions: Exhibitions are changed bi-monthly
Activities: Lect open to public; original objects of art lent; lending collection contains 300 color reproductions, 20 filmstrips, 10,000 Kodachromes, motion pictures & clippings & small prints

M **Flanagan Valley Campus Art Gallery,** Louisquisset Pike, Lincoln, 02865. Tel 401-333-7154; FAX 401-825-2265; *Dir & Librn* Tom Morrissey
Open Mon - Fri 10 AM - 2 PM. No admis fee. Estab 1974. 26 sq ft space with track lighting. Average Annual Attendance: Over 5000
Exhibitions: Exhibitions are changed bi-monthly
Activities: Lect open to public, 10 vis lectr per year; concerts; gallery talks; tours; competitions with awards; exten dept; individual paintings & original objects of art lent; originate traveling exhibitions

WESTERLY

M **WESTERLY PUBLIC LIBRARY,** Hoxie Gallery, 44 Broad St, 02891. Tel 401-596-2877; FAX 401-596-5600; *Dir* Regan Robinson
Open Mon - Wed 8 AM - 9 PM, Thurs & Fri 8 AM - 5 PM, Sat 8 AM - 3 PM. Estab 1892 as a memorial to soldiers of the Civil War & to provide a library & activities center for the community. Art gallery maintained, 30 x 54 ft, 16 ft ceiling, with incandescent track lighting
Income: Financed by endowment, city & state appropriation
Exhibitions: Ten - twelve exhibitions scheduled per year
Publications: First Westerly Coloring Book; Life's Little Pleasures; Westerly Photographys 1890-1910
Activities: Lect open to public; library tours

SOUTH CAROLINA

AIKEN

M **AIKEN COUNTY HISTORICAL MUSEUM,** 433 New Berry St SW, 29801. Tel 803-642-2015; *Dir* Carolyn Miles
Open Tues - Fri 9:30 AM - 4:30 PM, Sat & Sun 2 - 5 PM. Admis donations requested. Open 1970 to document local history. Average Annual Attendance: 7500. Mem: 350; mem open to residents; dues $10 & up; annual meeting in Oct
Income: $71,000 (financed by endowment, mem, county subsidy)
Purchases: All donations
Collections: Agricultural-implements; Dairy-implements; log cabins; military; Savannah River Site (nuclear); Schools-furniture & winter items; Winter Colony-furniture
Exhibitions: Selections from permanent collection
Activities: Children's classes; docent programs; book traveling exhibitions 10 per year; retail store sells books & prints

ANDERSON

A **ANDERSON COUNTY ARTS COUNCIL,** 405 N Main St, 29621. Tel 864-224-1483; FAX 864-224-8864; *Exec Dir* Kimberly Spears; *Admin Dir* Judy Swain
Open Mon - Fri 9 AM - 5 PM, Sun 2 - 5 PM, cl holidays. No admis fee. Estab 1972 as a non-profit institution, serving as a clearinghouse for individuals & organizations interested in the promotion of visual, literary & performing arts. Gallery rotates exhibits monthly, featuring locally, regionally & nationally known artists. Average Annual Attendance: 10,000. Mem: 550; dues $1000, $500, $100, $50, $25, $18, $10, $5; annual meeting last Tues of Sept
Income: Financed by mem, foundations, donations, county appropriation & grants
Publications: Calendar of events; newsletter, bi-monthly
Activities: Classes for adults & children; gallery talks; tours

CHARLESTON

M **CAROLINA ART ASSOCIATION,** Gibbes Museum of Art, 135 Meeting, 29401. Tel 803-722-2706; *Pres Board* Charlton DeSaussure; *Dir* Paul C Figueroa; *Registrar* India Hopper; *Cur Educ* Shellie Williams; *Public Information* Hanna Goss; *Bus Mgr* Barbara Smith; *Cur Coll* Angela Mack
Open Tues - Sat 10 AM - 5 PM, Sun & Mon 1 - 5 PM; cl national holidays. No admis fee. Estab 1858 as an art gallery & mus. Beaux-Arts style building erected in 1905, renovated in 1978; gallery is 31,000 sq ft. Average Annual Attendance: 60,000. Mem: 2500; dues $35 & up; annual meeting 3rd Mon in Oct
Income: $1,300,000 (financed by endowment, mem, city & county appropriation, grants & contributions)
Purchases: Contemporary & historical paintings, sculpture, prints, drawings & photographs
Collections: Colonial & Federal Portraits; Contemporary American Paintings & Prints; Japanese Woodblock Prints; Miniature Portraits; American art related to Charleston
Exhibitions: Approx 25 per yr
Publications: Bulletins, quarterly; books; exhibit catalogs
Activities: Classes for adults & children; docent training; lect open to public, 5 vis lectr per year; gallery talks; tours; exten dept serves tri-county area; individual paintings & original objects of art lent to museums; lending collection includes framed reproductions & original prints; originate traveling exhibitions; museum shop sells books, reproductions, prints, original crafts & jewelry
L **Library,** 135 Meeting, 29401. Tel 803-722-2706; *Dir* Paul C Figueroa; *Pres Board* Charlton DeSaussure
Open to scholars for reference only, by appointment
Income: Financed by public & private support
Library Holdings: Vols 3709; Per subs 26; AV — Kodachromes, rec, v-tapes; Other — Clipping files, exhibition catalogs, manuscripts, original art works, pamphlets, photographs, sculpture
Special Subjects: Oriental Art, American Art, History of Charleston art & architecture

M **CHARLESTON MUSEUM,** 360 Meeting St, 29403. Tel 803-722-2996; FAX 803-722-1784; *Dir* Dr John R Brumgardt; *Pres* Hugh C Lane Jr; *Cur Historic Archaeology* Martha Zierden; *Cur History* Christopher Loeblein; *Cur Historic Houses* Karen King; *Cur Natural History* Albert E Sanders; *Registrar* Jan Hiester; *Cur Ornithology* Dr William Post; *Archivist* K Sharon Bennett
Open daily 9 AM - 5 PM. Admis adults $3, children $1.50. Estab 1773 as a mus & library to diffuse knowledge of history, decorative arts, art, natural history, anthropology & technology; also to preserve houses & monuments. It is the oldest mus in the United States. Average Annual Attendance: 20,000. Mem: 550;

dues $15 & up; annual meeting in Feb
Income: $530,000 (financed by mem, city & county appropriations, admis & sales)
Collections: Ceramics, decorative arts, furniture, glass, maps, photos, prints & textiles, art of northern BC
Publications: Bi-monthly newsletter
Activities: Tours for adults & children; docent training; lect, 8 per year; concerts; sales shop sells books, magazines & prints related to collections
L **Library,** 360 Meeting St, 29403. Tel 803-722-2996; FAX 803-722-1784; *Librn* K Sharon Bennett; *Asst Archivist* Mary Giles
Open daily 9 AM - 5 PM by appointment only. Estab 1773 as an educational institution, collects, preserves & uses artifacts of natural history, history, anthropology & decorative arts
Income: Financed by city & county appropriations & mem
Library Holdings: Vols 5000; Per subs 120; Maps; AV — Rec; Other — Clipping files, exhibition catalogs, manuscripts, memorabilia, pamphlets, photographs, prints
Special Subjects: Decorative Arts, Natural History
Publications: Quarterly newsletter

M **Heyward-Washington House,** 87 Church St, 29401. Tel 803-722-0354; *House Adminr* Morris Loflin
Open daily 10 AM - 5 PM; Sun 1 - 5 PM. Admis adults $3, children $1.50. Built 1772; home of Thomas Heyward, Jr; purchased by the Mus in 1929. Mus is furnished with Charleston-made furniture of the period; a National Historic Landmark
Collections: House furnishings
Activities: Daily tours

M **Joseph Manigault House,** 350 Meeting St, 29403. Tel 803-723-2926; *House Adminr* Anne Fox
Open Mon - Sat 9 AM - 5 PM, Sun 1 - 5 PM. Admis adults $6, children 3-12 $3. Estab 1773 to preserve & interpret Charleston natural & social history. Early history, revolutionary war, civil war natural history, children's educational room. Average Annual Attendance: 160,000. Mem: 2200; dues varies
Collections: Charleston silver; †furniture & textiles; local natural history & animals; paleontological fossils
Activities: Classes for adults & children; lect open to public, 10 vis lectr per year; gallery talks; tours; individual paintings & original objects of art lent to accredited museums; museum shop sells books, reproductions & slides

M **CITY OF CHARLESTON,** City Hall Council Chamber Gallery, 80 Broad St, 29401. Tel 803-724-3799; *Cur* Lynda Heffley
Open Mon - Fri 8:30 AM - 5 PM. No admis fee. Estab 1818 to preserve for the citizens of Charleston a portrait collection of the city's history. A unique collection of American portraits housed in the 2nd oldest city council chamber in continuous use in the US. Average Annual Attendance: 20,000
Collections: Washington Trumbull, 1791; J Monroe Samuel Morse, 1819; A Jackson John Vanderlyn, 1824; Zachary Taylor James Beard, 1848; Marquis de Lafayette Charles Fraser, 1825; Pierre Beauregard George Healy, 1861; C Gaddsen-R Peale; portraits by Jarvis, Savage, John Blake White, James Earle, G Whiting Flagg
Publications: Catalogue of paintings & sculpture

M **COLLEGE OF CHARLESTON,** Halsey Gallery, School of the Arts, 66 George St, 29424-0001. Tel 803-953-5680; *Gallery Dir* Mark Sloan
Open Mon - Sat 11 AM - 4 PM. No admis fee. Estab 1978 as a college gallery with focus on contemporary art. Two floors in modern building located in Schools of the Arts building, includes director's office & storage space. Average Annual Attendance: 5000
Income: $15,000 (financed by state appropriation)
Publications: Periodic catalogs & gallery guides
Activities: Lect open to public, 6 - 8 vis lectr per year; juried student competitions

M **TRADD STREET PRESS,** Elizabeth O'Neill Verner Studio Museum, 38 Tradd St, 29401. Tel 803-722-4246; *Pres* David Verner Hamilton; *Secy* Daphne vom Baur
Open 10 AM - 5 PM. No admis fee. Estab 1970 to exhibit works of Elizabeth O'Neill Verner. Average Annual Attendance: 31,200
Income: Financed by endowment
Collections: †Works of Elizabeth O'Neill Verner
Exhibitions: Collected works of Elizabeth O'Neill Verner
Activities: Educ dept provides cultural presence, historic perspective programs; lectures open to public; sales store sells books, prints, original art, reproductions

CLEMSON

CLEMSON UNIVERSITY
M **Rudolph E Lee Gallery,** Lee Hall, 29634. Tel 803-656-3883; FAX 803-656-0204; *Dir* David Houston
Open Mon - Fri 9 AM - 4:30 PM, Sun 2 - 5 PM, cl Sat. No admis fee. Estab 1956 to provide cultural & educational resources; to collect, preserve, interpret & display items of historical, educational & cultural significance. Average Annual Attendance: 20,000
Income: Financed by state appropriation
Collections: †Clemson Architectural Foundation Collection; Contemporary American Paintings & Graphics
Publications: Exhibition Bulletin, annually; Posters on Exhibits, monthly
Activities: Lect open to public, 12-15 vis lectr per year; gallery talks; tours; exten dept servs southeast United States; individual paintings & original objects of art lent to museums, universities; lending collection contains original prints, paintings, sculpture; originate traveling exhibitions
L **Emery A Gunnin Architectural Library,** Lee Hall, 29634-0501. Tel 864-656-3932; FAX 864-656-0204; *Branch Head* Deborah Babel; *Media Resources Cur* Phyllis Pivorun
Mon - Thurs 8 AM - 10 PM, Fri 8 AM - 5 PM, Sat 1 - 5 PM, Sun 2 - 10 PM. For reference only. Average Annual Attendance: 74,000
Library Holdings: Vols 25,899; Per subs 218; AV — A-tapes, cassettes, motion

pictures, slides 84,000, v-tapes; Other — Exhibition catalogs, pamphlets
Special Subjects: Aesthetics, Archaeology, Art History, Ceramics, Conceptual Art, Constructions, Crafts, Decorative Arts, Drafting, Drawings
Collections: Rare Book Collection; South Carolina City & Regional Planning Documents

M **Fort Hill Plantation,** Tilman Hall, Rm 103, 29634-5605. Tel 864-656-3311, 656-2475; FAX 864-656-1026; *Dir Historic Houses & Cur* Will Hiott
Open Mon - Fri 10 AM - 5 PM, Sat 10 AM - 5 PM, Sun 2 - 5 PM, cl holidays & Christmas week. A historic house mus located in the home of John C Calhoun. Restoration of the house & furnishings are an on-going project of the John C Calhoun Chapter of the United Daughters of the Confederacy & Clemson University
Income: Financed by Clemson University
Collections: Flemish paintings; family portraits; period rooms & furnishings of original family heirlooms & memorabilia
Publications: Fort Hill, brochure
Activities: Lect; guided tours

COLUMBIA

M **COLUMBIA MUSEUM OF ART,** 1112 Bull St, 29201. Tel 803-799-2810; *Dir* Salvatore G Cilella; *Pres* Cary K Smith; *VPres* Charlie Cole; *Registrar* Cynthia Connor; *Admin Asst* Ruth Hisaw; *Cur Coll* Kevin Tucker; *Cur Coll* William Bodine; *Dir External Affairs* Bonnie Adams; *Dir Marketing & Public Relations* Suzanne Flowers; *Develop & Membership* Christine Minkler
Open Tues - Fri 10 AM - 5 PM, Sat & Sun 12:30 PM - 5 PM. Admis free. Estab 1950 to extend & increase art understanding, to assist in the conservation of a valuable cultural heritage & to recognize & assist contemporary art expression. Library for reference only. Average Annual Attendance: 100,000. Mem: 2100; dues family $35 & up, single $20; annual meeting in Jan
Income: $900,000 (financed by mem, city & county appropriation)
Purchases: Works of art on paper, Southeastern artists & textiles
Collections: Kress Collection of Renaissance Paintings; Scotese Collection of Graphics; European and American paintings and decotative art; South Carolina dispensary bottles; Spanish Colonial Collection; textiles; South Carolina collection of paintings & graphics; †decorative arts & textiles
Exhibitions: Adornment in Africa: Treasures of the Continent; British Watercolors; Chinese Porcelain; Roycroft Exhibit; White House Photographs; exhibits from the permanent collection
Publications: Annual report; Columbia Museum Magazine, quarterly; exhibition folders & catalogues; monthly member calendars
Activities: Classes for adults & children; docent training; lect open to public, 6 vis lectr per year; concerts; gallery talks; tours; exten dept serving Metropolitan area; originate traveling exhibitions; museum shop sells books, original art, reproductions, prints, ceramics, glass, jewelry

L **Library,** 1112 Bull St, 29201. Tel 803-799-2810; FAX 803-343-2150; *Librn* Elizabeth Rich
Open Tues - Fri 10 AM - 5 PM, Sat - Sun 1 - 5 PM. Open to members & pub for reference only
Income: $10,000 (financed by mus)
Library Holdings: Vols 13,000; Per subs 50; Vertical files; AV — A-tapes, cassettes, v-tapes; Other — Clipping files, exhibition catalogs, memorabilia, pamphlets
Special Subjects: Reference relating to the permanent collection, plus general art sources

A **Columbia Art Association,** 1112 Bull St, 29201. Tel 803-799-2810; *Pres* Carrie Smith; *Dir* Salvatore G Cilella
Open Tues - Sat 10 AM - 5 PM, Sun 1 - 5 PM. No admis fee. Estab 1949 to provide exhibitions & educ programs to the pub. Average Annual Attendance: 110,000. Mem: 3000; dues $15-$140; annual meeting in Jan
Collections: †American fine, decorative & design arts of 16th century to present, †Works on Paper, †Furniture, †Paintings & Sculpture, †Textiles; Kress Collection of Rennaisance & Baroque Art
Activities: Classes for adults & children; docent training; lect open to public, 3 vis lectr per year; concerts; gallery talks; tours; exten dept serves central South Carolina; individual paintings & original objects of art lent; book traveling exhibitions 6-8 per year; museum shop sells books, original art, reproductions & prints

A **SOUTH CAROLINA ARTS COMMISSION,** 1800 Gervais St, 29201. Tel 803-734-8696; *Exec Dir* Suzette Surkmer; *Head Media* Susan Leonard; *Visual Arts Dir* Harriett Green; *Equipment Coordr* Rick Dalton
Open 9 AM - 5 PM. No admis fee. Estab 1967 to promote & develop the arts in Southeast
Income: $225,000 (financed by state & federal income)
Purchases: Films, videotapes, video/film equipment
Collections: †State Art Collection
Exhibitions: Film/Video artists exhibitions
Publications: Independent Spirit, media arts newsletter, 3 times a yr
Activities: Educational programming; lect open to public, 4 vis lectr per year; concerts; gallery talks; competitions with awards; artists' workshops; grants-in-aid & fels offered; exten dept serves state; art mobile; individual paintings & original objects of art lent to galleries & museums; lending collection contains lantern slides, 235 original art works, paintings, photographs, sculpture, slides, 100 books & 125 motion pictures; book traveling exhibitions; originate traveling exhibitions, circulates to 6 sites in the Southeast

L **Media Center,** 1800 Gervais St, 29201. Tel 803-734-8696; *Dir* Susan Leonard
Library Holdings: AV — A-tapes, cassettes, motion pictures, slides, v-tapes
Special Subjects: Film

M **SOUTH CAROLINA STATE MUSEUM,** 301 Gervais St, PO Box 100107, 29202-3107. Tel 803-737-4921; FAX 803-737-4969; *Exec Dir* Overton G Ganong; *Dir Coll & Interpretation* Rodger Stroup; *Dir Exhibits* Mike Fey; *Dir Public Information & Marketing* Tut Underwood; *Exec VPres* Patty Cooper; *Chief Cur Art* Polly Laffitte
Open Mon - Sat 10 AM - 5 PM, Sun 1 - 5 PM. Estab 1973. Four large floors in a renovated textile mill with exhibits in art, history, natural history & science &

technology. Average Annual Attendance: 250,000. Mem: 6500; annual meeting in June
Income: Financed by admis, state appropriations, store revenue & supplement state money
Collections: †Art - all media; Cultural History; Natural History; Science & Technology
Exhibitions: Art - South Carolina/Kentucky Exchange; History - The Palmetto State Goes Tower: WW II & South Carolina; Natural History - Fossil Collectors & Collections
Publications: Annual report; Images, quarterly
Activities: Docent programs; lect open to public; lending collection contains 500 paintings; book traveling exhibitions 10 per year; originate traveling exhibitions 4 per year; retail store sells books & slides

M **UNIVERSITY OF SOUTH CAROLINA,** McKissick Museum, 29208. Tel 803-777-7251; Internet Home Page Address http://cal.sc.edu/mcrs/index.html. *Dir* Lynn Robertson; *Chief Cur* Jay Williams; *Bus Mgr* Maria Ballard; *Cur Education Museum* Craig Kridel; *Cur Educational Servs* John Wright; *Cur of Exhib* Alice R Bauknight; *Cur Folk Art & Research* Dr Jane Przbysz
Open Mon - Fri 9 AM - 4 PM, Sat 10 AM - 5 PM, Sun 1 PM - 5 PM, cl July 4th, Labor Day, Thanksgiving & day after, Dec 25, Jan 1. No admis fee. Estab 1976 to centralize the university's mus collections. Contains 4 major gallery areas for temporary & changing exhibitions in art, science & history. Average Annual Attendance: 65,000
Income: Financed by state appropriation & donations
Purchases: Southern Folk Art
Collections: Bernard Baruch Collection of 18th Century Silver; Movietonews News Reels; James F Byrnes Collection; Howard Gemstone Collection; Richard Mandell: Art Nouveau Collection; Colburn Gemstone Collection; university memorabilia; southeastern folk art; minerals, fossils, rocks & meteorites; contemporary art works
Exhibitions: Students & Faculty Art. (1997) Juke Joint USC History; Knowing Nature
Publications: Exhibition catalogs; Calendar of events (quarterly)
Activities: Docent training; lect open to public, 4-5 vis lectr per year; concerts; gallery talks; tours; competitions; slide-tape programs & classes for students & senior citizens; community outreach to senior citizens groups & children's hospital wards; originate traveling exhibitions

L **Art Library,** Sloan College, Rm 200A, 29208. Tel 803-777-4236; *Instructional Media Specialist* Linda D Morgan
Open Mon - Fri 8 AM - 4 PM. Estab as a major teaching resource for the Art Department
Library Holdings: Vols 3000; Per subs 17; Slide-tape Programs; AV — Cassettes, motion pictures, slides 96,000, v-tapes; Other — Clipping files, exhibition catalogs, manuscripts, pamphlets, photographs
Special Subjects: Decorative Arts, Museology

C **WACHOVIA BANK OF SOUTH CAROLINA,** 1426 Main St, 29226. Tel 803-765-3000; *Exec VPres* Charles T Cole, Jr
Estab 1971 to recognize & promote artists who have or have had a connection with South Carolina. Collection displayed in offices throughout South Carolina
Collections: Contemporary South Carolina art
Activities: Sponsor purchase awards for selected competitions in the state; individual objects of art lent to museums for display; originate traveling exhibitions, have carried-out two statewide tours from collection, work was displayed in a number of cities at museums, libraries, court houses & banks

FLORENCE

M **FLORENCE MUSEUM OF ART, SCIENCE & HISTORY,** 558 Spruce St, 29501. Tel 803-662-3351; *Dir* Dana Parker; *Pres* Rebecca H Crawford; *VPres* William S Dowis, Jr
Open Tues - Sat 10 AM - 5 PM, Sun 2 - 5 PM, cl Mon & major holidays. No admis fee. Estab 1924 (incorporated in 1936) as a general mus of art, natural science & history of South Carolina, with emphasis on the region know as the Pee Dee & to acquaint the pub with fine art. Changing art exhibitions, main galleries. Average Annual Attendance: 19,000. Mem: 450; dues benefactor $1000, patron $500, donor $250, sustaining $100, sponsor $50, family $30, individual $15
Income: $80,000 (financed by mem, county & city appropriation & donations)
Collections: Permanent Collection includes: African, Asian, Southwestern American Indians, Catawba Indian Collections; Greek & Roman Archaeological material; historical artifacts; works of local Black artist particularly William H Johnson; works of local & regional artists; Museum Permanent Collection, Regional Artists
Exhibitions: The Miniature Art Competition
Publications: Florence Museum newsletter, quarterly
Activities: Classes for adults & children; docent training; lect open to public; gallery talks; self-guided tours; art competitions with prizes; book traveling exhibitions

GREENVILLE

M **BOB JONES UNIVERSITY,** Museum & Art Gallery, 29614. Tel 803-242-5100; FAX 803-233-9829; *Chmn of the Board* Bob Jones; *Dir* Joan C Davis; *Staff Supvr* Janice Churdar; *Asst Dir* John Nolan
Open Tues - Sun 2 - 5 PM, cl Mon, Dec 20 - 25, New Year's Day, July 4 & Commencement Day in May. No admis fee. Estab 1951 to show how universal the Word of God is in its appeal to human hearts in every generation. Average Annual Attendance: 23,000
Income: Financed by university & gifts
Collections: Bowen Collection of Biblical antiquities & illustrative material from Palestine, Syria, Lebanon, Egypt & Jordan; Religious art by the Old Masters from the 13th-19th centuries including Benson, Botticelli, Cranach the Elder, G David, Murillo, Rembrandt, Ribera, Rubens, Solimena del Piombo, Tintoretto, Titian, Van Leyden, Veronese, Zurbaran; Revealed Religion by Benjamin West, 7

paintings; furniture; sculpture
Publications: Catalogs; illustrated booklets
Activities: Tours for school & adult groups by appointment; individual paintings lent to other galleries in the US & abroad; sales shop sells reproductions, prints & slides

M GREENVILLE COUNTY MUSEUM OF ART, 420 College St, 29601. Tel 864-271-7570; FAX 864-271-7579; *Exec Dir* Thomas W Styron; *Head Collections Management & Security* Claudia Beckwith; *Pub Relations Officer* Angela Murphy
Open Tues - Sat 10 AM - 5 PM, Sun 1 - 5 PM, cl Mon. No admis fee. Estab 1958 for the collection & preservation of American Art. Four major galleries devoted to permanent collections of American art from the colonial to the contemporary, changing & traveling exhibitions. Average Annual Attendance: 100,000. Mem: 1000; dues $30 - $1000; annual meeting in May
Income: Financed by mem, donations & county appropriation
Purchases: Acquisitions include works by Louis Remy Mignot, Gari Melchers & Elaine de Kooning
Collections: Limited to American art with emphasis on Southern-related works before World War II & contemporary American art
Exhibitions: Telling Tales: 19th-century Narrative Painting From the Collection of the Pennsylvania Academy of the Fine Arts; Messengers of Tyle: Itinerancy & Taste in Southern Portraiture, 1790-1861; Homecome: William H Johnson & Afro-America. 1938-1946
Publications: Museum News, bi-monthly; exhibition catalogs; quarterly events calendars
Activities: Classes for adults & children; docent training; Museum School of Art; lect open to public, 6-10 vis lectr per year; gallery talks; tours; exten dept serves Greenville County schools; lending collection contains slides; museum shop sells books, original art, slides, prints, children educational toys, regional crafts & cards

C LIBERTY LIFE INSURANCE COMPANY, 2000 Wade Hampton Blvd, PO Box 789, 29602-0789. Tel 864-609-8111; *Chmn* Francis M Hipp
Open during normal business hrs by appointment. Estab 1978 to collect textile art selections from various cultures & historical periods. Collection displayed throughout corporate headquarters
Collections: Limited edition prints, graphics & silkscreens; textile art works from around the world
Publications: The Liberty Textile Collection
Activities: Individual paintings & original objects of art lent to regional & national museums & galleries

GREENWOOD

M GREENWOOD MUSEUM (Formerly The Museum), 106 Main St, PO Box 3131, 29648. Tel 864-229-7093; *Pres* Jack Jennings; *Admin* Paula McKinley
Open Tues - Fri 9 AM - 5 PM, Sat & Sun 2 - 5 PM, cl Mon. No admis fee. Estab 1967 for educational purposes. Average Annual Attendance: 9000. Mem: 220; dues $25; meetings in Jan, Mar, May & Nov
Income: Financed by mem, contributions & grants
Collections: Frank E Delano Gallery of African animal mounts & rare African works of art by the now extinct Katanga Tribe; bone, wood & ivory carvings; chinaware; crystals; glassware; limited art works; photographs
Exhibitions: Individual artists; Siebozs; Bruce; South Carolina arts & crafts; South Carolina Watercolor Society
Activities: Lect open to public; book traveling exhibitions; sales shop sells original art

HARTSVILLE

M CECELIA COKER BELL GALLERY, Coker College, Gladys C Fort Art Bldg, 29550. Tel 803-383-8152; *Dir* Larry Merriman
Open Mon - Fri 10 AM - 4 PM. No admis fee. Estab 1983 to serve campus & community. 30 ft x 40 ft self-contained, movable partitions, track light, security system. Average Annual Attendance: 5000
Income: $3300
Collections: American prints
Exhibitions: Area artists; annual student juried show; senior students show; vis artists; national, international exhibitions
Publications: Collection catalog
Activities: Classes for adults; lect open to public, 2 vis lectr per year; gallery talks; student juried competitions with awards

MURRELLS INLET

M BROOKGREEN GARDENS, 1931 Brookgreen Dr, 29576. Tel 803-237-4218; FAX 803-237-1014; *Pres* Lawrence Henry; *VPres Academic Affairs & Cur* Robin Salmon
Open 9:30 AM - 4:45 PM, cl Christmas. Admis adults $6.50, 6-12 years $3, under 6 free. Estab 1931 to exhibit the flora & fauna of South Carolina & to exhibit objects of art. The outdoor mus exhibits American sculpture, while smaller pieces are shown in the Small Sculpture Gallery & Indoor Galleries. Average Annual Attendance: 180,000. Mem: 3000; dues $35-$5000
Income: Financed by endowment, mem, gifts, grants & admis
Collections: †Collection of American representative, sculpture, †pieces by sculptors
Exhibitions: Permanent Collection
Publications: Brookgreen Journal, quarterly; Brookgreen Newsletter, quarterly; Brookgreen Gardens Sculpture, catalogue
Activities: Classes for adults & children; docent training; workshops; lect open to public, 4 vis lectr per year; concerts; gallery talks; tours; awards; museum shop sells books, magazines, postcards, pamphlets, prints, slides & sculpture

L Library, 1931 Brookgreen Dr, 29576. Tel 803-237-4218; FAX 803-237-1014; *VPres & Cur* Robin Salmon
For reference only to staff
Library Holdings: Vols 2200; Per subs 50; Architectural & engineering drawings & prints; Maps; Micro — Reels; AV — A-tapes, cassettes, fs, Kodachromes, motion pictures, slides, v-tapes; Other — Clipping files, exhibition catalogs, framed reproductions, manuscripts, memorabilia, pamphlets, photographs, prints
Special Subjects: American sculpture, local history, plants & animals of the Southeast
Publications: Brookgreen Journal, quarterly; Brookgreen Newsletter, quarterly; Brookgreen Calendar of Events, three times per year; Brookgreen Gardens Annual Report

ROCK HILL

M MUSEUM OF YORK COUNTY, 4621 Mount Gallant Rd, 29732-9905. Tel 803-329-2121; FAX 803-329-5249; Elec Mail myco@infoave.net. *Exec Dir* Van W Shields
Open 9 AM - 5 PM. Admis $2. Estab 1948. Spring, Alternative & Lobby galleries (changing art exhibits). Average Annual Attendance: 50,000. Mem: 1248; dues vary
Income: $1,383,225 (financed by mem, admis & county appropriation)
Collections: African animals - mounted specimens; African art & ethnography; local art; local history & archaeology; local natural history specimens
Exhibitions: (1997) Animals As Architects; Southern Light & Color; VG Animals; VG Books; VG Santas; Visible Spectrum; Tod Warner Animals; Stans African Halls (African peoples & natural history); Halls of Western Hemisphere; Come See Me, local artist competition; Student Art, local jr & sr high school students competition; Southern Visions, photography - Southeast
Publications: Quarterly, bi-monthly; Teacher's Guide, annual
Activities: Classes for adults & children; docent programs; lect open to public, 10 vis lectr per year; competitions with purchase awards; exten dept servs county; book traveling exhibitions 5 per year; retail store sells books & prints

L Staff Research Library, 4621 Mount Gallant Rd, 29732-9905. Tel 803-329-2121; FAX 803-329-5249; *Cur Coll* Janis Wilkins
For research
Income: Financed by departmental budgets
Library Holdings: AV — A-tapes, cassettes, v-tapes; Other — Exhibition catalogs, pamphlets
Special Subjects: American Indian Art, Anthropology, Archaeology, Art Education, Crafts, Ethnology, Photography, Primitive Art, Restoration & Conservation, African Art, Museum Studies, Travel & Adventure

M WINTHROP UNIVERSITY GALLERIES, 701 Oakland Ave, 29733. Tel 803-323-2493; FAX 803-323-2333; *Dir* Tom Stanley
Open Mon - Fri 8:30 AM - 4:30 PM. No admis fee. Housed within Rutledge Building, Department of Art & Design of the School of Visual & Performing Arts at Winthrop College. Presents temporary visual art & design exhibitions for the enhancement of academic achievement & understanding within the college community. Gallery is 3500 sq ft. Average Annual Attendance: 15,000
Income: Financed by state appropriation
Exhibitions: Student Exhibitions; South Carolina State Art Collection; one-person shows; invitational exhibitions in photo, drawing, painting, printmaking, textiles, design, ceramics & glass
Activities: Classes for adults; lect open to public; concerts; gallery talks; scholarships & fels offered; originate traveling exhibitions

SPARTANBURG

A ARTS PARTNERSHIP OF GREATER SPARTANBURG, INC, Spartanburg Arts Center, 385 S Spring St, 29306. Tel 803-542-2787; FAX 803-948-5353; *Pres & Chief Operating Officer* Everett G Powers; *Arts Educ Dir* Mrs Danny R Hughes; *Dir Develop* Mary Smith; *Organization Servs & Outreach Dir* George Loudon
Open Mon - Fri 9 AM - 5:30 PM. No admis fee. Estab 1968 to coordinate & develop all cultural activities in the area. Mem: Annual meetings in May
Income: $1,200,000 (financed by pub, private & corporate donations & project grants)
Exhibitions: Changing exhibits
Publications: Membership Brochure, annual; Spartanburg Arts Calendar, quarterly
Activities: Artist residences in schools; performances in school; David W Reid Award for Achievement in the Arts; scholarships offered; book traveling exhibitions 10 per year; sales shop sells books, original art & prints

M CONVERSE COLLEGE, Milliken Art Gallery, 580 E Main, 29302. Tel 864-585-6421, Ext 251; FAX 864-596-9158; *Dir* Jim Creal
Open Mon - Fri 11 AM - 4 PM, cl holidays. No admis fee. Estab 1971 for educational purposes. A brick & glass structure of 40 x 60 ft; movable panels 4 x 6 ft for exhibition of work, 16 panels, 12 sculpture stands. Average Annual Attendance: 2400
Income: Financed by endowment
Exhibitions: Invitational exhibits of regional artists; annual juried student show; senior exhibit
Activities: Educ dept; lect open to public, 5-6 vis lectr per year; gallery talks; tours

M SPARTANBURG COUNTY MUSEUM OF ART, 385 S Spring St, 29306. Tel 864-582-7616; FAX 864-948-5353; *Exec Dir* Scott M Brown; *Exhibits Coordr* Theresa Mann; *Art School Dir* Scott Cunningham; *Colors Dir* Laura Baker
Open Mon - Sat 10 AM - 5 PM, Sun 2 - 4 PM (or by appointment). No admis fee. Estab 1969 to promote the works of contemporary artists in the southeastern United States. Gallery is located in the Spartanburg County Arts Center & contains both a permanent sales section & a changing exhibit area. Average Annual Attendance: 7000. Mem: 250; dues $25-$500
Income: Financed by endowment & mem

Collections: †Contemporary Southeastern Artists
Exhibitions: Annual Juried Exhibit
Publications: Quarterly newsletter
Activities: Classes for adults & children; lect open to public, 2 vis lectr per year; gallery talks; tours; competitions with awards; individual paintings & original objects of art lent to local government & qualified businesses; sales shop sells original art & fine crafts

M **UNIVERSITY OF SOUTH CAROLINA AT SPARTANBURG,** Art Gallery, Horace C Smith Bldg, 800 University Way, 29303. Tel 864-503-5556; *Gallery Dir* Katie Hicks
Open daily 10 AM - 4 PM. No admis fee. Estab 1982, primarily as a teaching gallery. Contemporary art displayed. 800 sq ft of carpeted wall space with windows along one wall, located across from Performing Art Center
Income: $1200 (financed by Student Affairs Office of University)
Exhibitions: Recent Paintings by Tom Stanley; Annual Student Art Exhibition
Publications: Exhibition announcements
Activities: Lect open to public, 4-6 vis lectr per year; competitions; book traveling exhibitions 5 per year; originate traveling exhibitions 1 per year

M **WOFFORD COLLEGE,** Sandor Teszler Library Gallery, 429 N Church St, 29303-3663. Tel 864-597-4300; FAX 864-597-4329; *Dir* Oakley H Coburn
Open daily 8 AM - Noon. Estab 1969 to support educational & cultural activities of the college. Gallery located within college library. Average Annual Attendance: 100,000
Collections: Hungarian Impressionist
Exhibitions: US, regional & international works in all media
Activities: Book traveling exhibitions, 1-2 per year

SUMTER

M **SUMTER GALLERY OF ART,** 421 N Main St, PO Box 1316, 29151. Tel 803-775-0543; *Exec Dir* Priscilla Haile
Open Tues - Fri Noon - 5 PM, Sat & Sun 2 - 5 PM, cl Easter, Thanksgiving & Christmas. No admis fee. Estab 1970 to bring to area exhibits of works of recognized artists, to provide an outlet for local artists for showing & sale of their work, & to serve as a facility where visual art may become a part of life & educ of the people, particularly children of this community. The Gallery is the 1850 home of the late Miss Elizabeth White, well-known artist of Sumter, which was deeded to the gallery in 1977 under the terms of her will. Presently using hall, four downstairs rooms, back studio & rooms upstairs. Average Annual Attendance: 8500. Mem: 460; dues commercial patron & patron $100, family $40, individual $25; annual meeting in May
Income: $100,000 (financed by mem, earned income, exhibit sponsors, donations, County Council)
Collections: Approximately sixty paintings, etchings & drawings of Elizabeth White given to the gallery by trustees of her estate
Exhibitions: Annual Young People's Exhibit; Individual & group exhibits of paintings, sculpture, collages, photography & crafts by recognized artists primarily from Southeast; Touchable exhibit for the blind & visually impaired
Publications: Newsletter, 3 times a year
Activities: Classes for adults & children; lect open to public; competitions, awards given; gallery gift shop primarily sells works by South Carolinian artists. Also on sale art to wear including jewelry

WALTERBORO

M **SOUTH CAROLINA ARTISANS CENTER,** 334 Wichman St, 29488. Tel 803-549-0011; *Exec Dir* Mary Hunt
Open Mon - Sat 10 AM - 7 PM, Sun 1 - 6 PM. No admis fee. Estab 1994 to provide a showcase & market for the handcrafted work of the state's leading artisans. Housed in restored nine-room Victorian cottage; 2800 sq ft retail facility. Average Annual Attendance: 26,000
Exhibitions: Sweetgrass Baskets
Publications: Hands On, newsletter every 2 months
Activities: Classes for adults & children; demonstrations; workshops; lect open to public; sales shop sells books, original art & original crafts

SOUTH DAKOTA

ABERDEEN

M **DACOTAH PRAIRIE MUSEUM,** Lamont Gallery, 21 S Main St, PO Box 395, 57402-0395. Tel 605-626-7117; FAX 605-626-4010; *Cur Educ* Sherri Rawstern; *Cur Exhib* Michael Keneally; *Dir* Sue Gates
Open Tues - Fri 9 AM - 5 PM, Sat & Sun 1 - 4 PM. No admis fee. Estab 1969 to preserve the heritage of the peoples of the Dakotas; to maintain & develop exhibits that educate people about the heritage of the Dakotas. Average Annual Attendance: 30,000
Income: Financed by county funds
Collections: Sioux & Arikara Indian artifacts; local & regional artists; photography
Exhibitions: (1997) Dakota Artists: Arthur Amoitte; Laurel Mehrer; Randy Smith; Charlene Ward
Publications: Annual Report; Dacotah Prairie Times, 3 per year
Activities: Classes for adults & children; gallery talks; tours; individual paintings & original objects of art lent to museums, art centers & some materials to schools; book traveling exhibitions 12 per year; museum shop sells books, magazines, prints, original art & reproductions

L **Ruth Bunker Memorial Library,** 21 S Main St, PO Box 395, 57402-0395. Tel 605-626-7117; FAX 605-626-4010; *Dir* Sue Gates; *Cur Coll* Jennifer Hudson
Open Tues - Fri 9 AM - 5 PM, Sat & Sun 1 - 4 PM, cl national holidays. Estab 1980 to store books, archives, maps, blueprints, etc. Reference only
Income: Financed by county funds
Library Holdings: Vols 2300; AV — A-tapes, slides; Other — Clipping files, exhibition catalogs, manuscripts, original art works, pamphlets, photographs, prints, reproductions, sculpture
Exhibitions: Exhibits of regional & national art
Publications: Annual report; quarterly newsletter
Activities: Special classes; lect open to public; gallery talks; tours; book traveling exhibitions; originate traveling exhibitions in midwest

M **NORTHERN STATE UNIVERSITY,** Northern Galleries, 1200 S Jay St, 57401. Tel 605-626-2596; FAX 605-626-2263; Elec Mail mulvaner@wolf.northern.edu. *Gallery Dir* Rebecca Mulvaney
Open 8 AM - 5 PM. No admis fee. Estab 1902 to support University program. Four galleries. Lincoln professional secure setting. Union - student area. Two hallway locations. Average Annual Attendance: 3000
Income: $6000 (financed by state appropriation)
Collections: Drawings, painting, photography, prints, sculpture
Activities: Educ dept; lect open to public, 3 vis lectr per year; gallery talks; tours; competitions with prizes; individual paintings & original objects of art lent to regional locations; lending collection contains framed reproductions, original prints, paintings, photographs; book traveling exhibitions 2 per year

BROOKINGS

M **SOUTH DAKOTA STATE UNIVERSITY,** South Dakota Art Museum, Medary Ave at Harvey Dunn St, 57007. Tel 605-688-5423; *Dir* Lynda K Clark; *Cur Marghab Coll* Cora Sivers; *Exhib Cur* Francine Marcel
Open Mon - Fri 8 AM - 5 PM, Sat 10 AM - 5 PM, Sun 1 - 5 PM. No admis fee. Estab 1969 as the state center for visual arts with various programs. The facility was designed by Howard Parezo, AIA, Sioux Falls, & occupies 112 x 90 foot site. There are seven galleries & a 147 seat auditorium. Average Annual Attendance: 81,000. Mem: 400
Income: Financed by state appropriation, endowment, gifts & grants
Collections: American Art; Harvey Dunn Paintings; Oscar Howe Paintings; MarghabLinens; Native American Art; Native American Tribal Art
Exhibitions: (1997) The Harvey Dunn Painting Oscer Howe, Paul Gobel Illustrations - Marghab Linens; Native American Tribal Art
Publications: Exhibition catalogues; newsletter; brochures
Activities: Docent training; lect open to public, 6-10 vis lectr per year; gallery talks; tours; artmobile; individual paintings & original objects of art lent to professionally run museums with excellent facilities; traveling exhibitions; museum shop sells books, original art, reproductions, prints, slides, cassettes, CD's cards & stationary

L **Jeannette Lusk Library Collection,** Medary Ave at Harvey Dunn St, 57007. Tel 605-688-5423;
Open to the pub for lending through the main library
Library Holdings: Vols 2000; AV — Slides, v-tapes; Other — Exhibition catalogs
Special Subjects: Archives of South Dakota Art

CRAZY HORSE

M **CRAZY HORSE MEMORIAL,** Indian Museum of North America & Native American Educational & Cultural Center, Ave of the Chiefs, 57730-9506. Tel 605-673-4681; FAX 605-673-2185; *Chief Executive Officer & Chmn Board* Ruth Ziolkowski; *Museum & Center Dir* Anne Ziolkowski
Open dawn - dusk. Admis memorial $15 per car, mus & center free. Memorial estab 1947, mus estab 1974, Center estab 1995, for preservation of the culture of the North American Indian. Three wings. Average Annual Attendance: 1,100, 000
Income: Financed by Crazy Horse Memorial Foundation
Collections: North American Indian Artifacts; Mountain Sculpture/Carving Displays; Pioneer memorabilia; Paintings & Sculptures
Exhibitions: Art shows on Life of Crazy Horse (adults & students)
Publications: Memorial: Progress; Mus: Indian Museum of North America; Crazy Horse Coloring Book
Activities: Classes for adults & children; lect open to public, 6 vis lectr per year; concerts; tours; scholarships offered; book traveling exhibitions; retail store sells books, prints, magazines, slides, original art, reproductions

CUSTER

M **GLORIDALE PARTNERSHIP,** National Museum of Woodcarving, Hwy 16 W, PO Box 747, 57730. Tel 605-673-4404; *Co-owner* Dale E Schaffer; *Co-owner* Gloria Schaffer
Open May - Oct, Mon - Fri 8 AM - 9 PM, cl Oct - May. Admis adult $5.50, sr citizens $5, children 6 - 14 $3, group rates available. Estab 1972 in order to elevate the art of woodcarving. Average Annual Attendance: 74,000
Income: $200,000 (financed by mus admis)
Purchases: $100,000 for gallery & gift shop
Collections: †Wooden Nickel Theater; †36 scenes by original animator of Disneyland; †carving studio
Exhibitions: Area woodcarvers & artists
Activities: Scholarships & fels offered; exten dept serves Custer Community School; museum & sales shop sells books, original art, reproductions, prints, slides

DEADWOOD

M **HOUSE OF ROSES,** Senator Wilson Home, 15 Forest Ave, 57732. Tel 605-578-1879; *Pres* Harry Lehman; *VPres* Michael Bockwoldt
Open daily 9 AM - 6 PM. Admis by donation. Estab 1976 to offer a Victorian home tour. Twenty-seven rooms open to public. Average Annual Attendance: 2000
Collections: †Antique Victorian furniture; †old prints
Activities: Lect open to public, 2-5 vis lectr per year; concerts; gallery talks; tours; competitions with awards; museum shop sells antiques

FLANDREAU

A **MOODY COUNTY HISTORICAL SOCIETY,** PO Box 25, 57028. Tel 605-997-3191; *Pres* Dale Johnson; *Dir* Chris Roelfsema-Hummel
Open Tues - Thurs 9 AM - 1 PM, Fri 1 - 4 PM, Memorial Day - Labor Day, Sun & holidays 2 - 5 PM. No Admis fee. Estab 1965 to promote understanding of history. Average Annual Attendance: 900. Mem: 400; dues family $10, single $5; annual meeting first Sun after Labor Day
Income: $12,000 (financed by county & city appropriation, donations & mem)
Collections: County artifacts, census records on microfilm, newspapers, photographs (available for reproduction), postcards
Activities: Lect open to public, 7 vis lectr per year; tours; competitions with prizes; contests; Sales shop sells note papers, silver teaspoons, centennial museum plates

MITCHELL

A **OSCAR HOWE ART CENTER,** 119 W Third Ave, PO Box 1161, 57301. Tel 605-996-4111; *Dir* Alan Lerdahl
Open Sept - May Tues - Sat 10 AM - 5 PM, June - Aug Tues - Sat 9 AM - 6 PM, Sun 1 - 5 PM. Admis adult $1 (June - Aug only), children under 12 free. Estab 1971 to promote Native American artists, local & regional artists. Center is housed in a former Carnegie Library building constructed in 1902 and designated as a National Historic Site
Income: Financed by private & pub funds
Collections: †19 paintings by Sioux artist & South Dakota artist laureate, Oscar Howe
Exhibitions: Young Artists Competition; Formal Images: Photographic Exhibit; Joseph Broghammer & Mark Anderson: Pastel Images & Bronze Sculpture; South Dakota Traditional Folk Art; Wild Life Exhibit; Mitchell Area Juried Art Competition; James Munce; Calligraphy: Diane Grupp; Book Art: Richard Zauft; Native American Art; Red Cloud Indian Art
Activities: Classes for adults & children; docent training; lect open to public; concerts; gallery talks; tours; competitions with awards; scholarships offered; individual paintings & original objects of art lent to other galleries; lending collection contains paintings; book traveling exhibitions; Garret museum shop sells original art work of regional artists including pottery, watercolors, weaving, oils & acrylics, books, Indian beadwork & reproductions of Oscar Howe paintings, magazines & prints

PINE RIDGE

M **HERITAGE CENTER, INC,** Red Cloud Indian School, PO Box 100, 57770. Tel 605-867-5491; *Pres* C Jumping Bull; *VPres* John Paul; *Dir* C M Simon
Open Mon - Fri 9 AM - 5 PM. Estab 1974 to exhibit Indian art & culture. Mus has four galleries of American & Canadian Native American art. Mainly paintings & sculpture. Average Annual Attendance: 9000
Income: Financed by donations & grants
Collections: †Native American paintings & prints; †Native American sculpture; †star quilts & tribal arts
Exhibitions: Selections from permanent collection; Eskimo prints; Northwest coast prints; Annual Red Cloud Indian Art Show
Activities: Tours; awards; scholarships offered; individual paintings & original objects of art are lent to other museums & art centers; book traveling exhibitions 4-6 per year; originate traveling exhibitions; museum shop sells books, original art, reproductions

RAPID CITY

M **INDIAN ARTS & CRAFTS BOARD,** Sioux Indian Museum, PO Box 1504, 57709. Tel 605-348-0557; FAX 605-348-6182; *Cur* Paulette Montileaux
Open June - Sept, Mon - Sat 9 AM - 5 PM, Sun 1 - 5 PM; Oct - May, Tues - Sat 10 AM - 5 PM, Sun 1 - 5 PM; cl New Year's Day, Thanksgiving, Christmas. No admis fee. Estab 1939 to promote the development of contemporary native American arts & crafts of the United States. Average Annual Attendance: 80,000
Income: Financed by federal appropriation
Collections: Contemporary native American arts & crafts of the United States; Historic works by Sioux craftsmen
Exhibitions: Continuing series of one-person exhibitions
Publications: One-person exhibition brochure series, bimonthly
Activities: Lect; tours; sales shop sells original arts & crafts

M **RAPID CITY ARTS COUNCIL,** Dahl Fine Arts Center, 713 Seventh St, 57701. Tel 605-394-4101; Elec Mail rbrennan@artswire.org. *Exec Dir* Ruth Brennan; *Admin Asst* Diane Bullard; *Cur* Grete Bodogaard
Open Mon - Sat 9 AM - 5 PM, Sun 1 - 5 PM. No admis fee. Estab 1974 to promote, educate & serve the arts. The art center contains 3 galleries: Cyclorama Gallery, a 200 ft oil mural of American history; Central Gallery, touring & invitational exhibitions; Dakota Art Gallery for juried original works for sale. Average Annual Attendance: 45,000. Mem: Annual meeting fourth Mon in July
Income: $200,000 (financed by earned income, city appropriation, rentals, grants & contributions)
Purchases: $151,000

Collections: Grace & Abigail French Collection, oils & watercolors; Hazel Schwentker Collection, watercolors, inks & washes; contemporary original prints; contemporary original work by regional artists
Exhibitions: New Eyes: Visions of Young Lakota Photographers
Publications: The French Sisters; Public Art in Rapid City
Activities: Classes for adults & children; dramatic programs; docent training; Tours; individual paintings & original objects of art lent; lending collection contains original art works & original prints; originate traveling exhibitions to museums, galleries, colleges & art centers; sales shop sells original art & reproductions

SIOUX FALLS

A **AMERICAN INDIAN SERVICES,** 100 W Sixth St, Ste 102, 57104. Tel 605-334-4060; FAX 605-334-8415; WATS 800-658-4797. *Exec Dir* Shirley Bordeaux
Estab 1979. Maintains reference library. Mem: Member federally recorded tribe, proof of decendency
Income: Financed by mem, state appropriation & individual donations
Activities: Local school shows

A **AUGUSTANA COLLEGE,** Center for Western Studies, PO Box 727, 57197. Tel 605-336-4007; *Exec Dir* Arthur R Hustboe; *Development Dir* Dean A Schueler; *Secy* Phyllis Harmsen; *Cur & Managing Ed* Harry F Thompson
Open 8 AM - 5 PM. No admis fee. Estab 1970 for collection & preservation of historic material for the promotion of South Dakota & its Western artists. Artists of the Plains Gallery, original oils, watercolors, bronzes & prints by regional artists. Average Annual Attendance: 500-750. Mem: 400; dues $30 & up; annual meeting in Dec
Income: Financed by endowment, mem, gifts, grants & book sales
Collections: South Dakota Art; historical manuscripts; photos; art by regional artists
Exhibitions: 3-4 exhibits per year featuring South Dakota Artists
Publications: An Illustrated History of the Arts in South Dakota; Poems & Essays of Herbert Krause; Yanktonai Sioux Water Colors: Cultural Remembrance of John Saul
Activities: Classes for adults; docent training; lect open to public, 10 vis lectr per year; tours; competitions with awards; individual paintings & original objects of art lent to other offices on campus; book traveling exhibitions 6-8 per year; originate traveling exhibitions oganized & circulated; museum shop sells books, original art, prints and slides, beadwork & silver jewelry

L **Center for Western Studies,** 57197-0001. Tel 605-336-4007; *Dir* Arthur R Huseboe; *Cur & Managing Ed* Harry F Thompson; *Development Dir* Dean A Schueler; *Secy* Phyllis Harmsen
Open daily 8 AM - 5 PM. For reference only
Library Holdings: Vols 30,000; Per subs 15; Micro — Reels; AV — A-tapes, slides; Other — Clipping files, memorabilia, original art works, pamphlets, photographs, prints, sculpture
Special Subjects: American Indian Art, American Western Art, Archaeology, Bronzes, Display, Ethnology, Furniture, Historical Material, Manuscripts, Maps, Painting - American, Photography, Prints, Sculpture, Western Americana
Collections: Historical manuscripts, photos art by regional artists
Publications: The Country Railroad Station in America by H Roger Grant & Charles Bohi; other titles in book & catalog, available on request; newsletter; Center for Western Studies Newsletter (bi- annually)

M **CIVIC FINE ARTS CENTER,** 235 W Tenth St, 57104. Tel 605-336-1167; FAX 605-332-2615; *Dir* Kent Ahrens; *Asst to Dir* Paul Groeneveld; *Prog Asst* Darren Garanoes; *Develop Officer* Cathie Rodman
Open Tues - Sat 10 AM - 5 PM, Sun 1 - 5 PM, cl major holidays. No admis fee. Estab 1961 as a contemporary mus. Four galleries: two permanent & two for special exhibitions. Average Annual Attendance: 60,000. Mem: 1250; dues $15; annual meeting in June
Collections: Historical & contemporary interest, monthly 2D work; National Printmakers collection
Exhibitions: Exhibition galleries
Publications: Monthly newsletter
Activities: Classes for adults & children; lect open to public, 3 vis lectr per year; concerts; gallery talks; tours; individual paintings & original art lent; museum shop sells books, magazines, original art, prints, reproductions, pottery & cards

L **Library,** 235 W Tenth St, 57102. Tel 605-336-1167; *Dir* Kent Ahrens
Open to members only
Library Holdings: Vols 320
Publications: Art News

SPEARFISH

M **BLACK HILLS STATE UNIVERSITY,** Ruddell Gallery, 1200 University, 57799. Tel 605-642-6104, Ext 6111, 642-6852; *Dir* Jim Knutsen
Open Mon - Fri 8 AM - 4 PM, Sat & Sun by appointment. Estab 1936 to encourage art expression & greater appreciation in the Black Hills area. Work of the art center is promoted jointly by Black Hills State College Art Department & the Student Union. Average Annual Attendance: 1500. Mem: 500; dues $5 & up
Activities: Classes for adults; programs held each semester; summer workshop; lect open to public, 3 vis lectr per year; competitions with awards; individual paintings & original objects of art lent to other colleges & universities; sales shop sells original art

L **Library,** 1200 University, 57799. Tel 605-642-6833; *Library Dir* Edmunbd Erickson
Library Holdings: Vols 300; AV — Motion pictures; Other — Reproductions
Collections: Carnegie gift library containing 1000 prints and 150 books

VERMILLION

M UNIVERSITY OF SOUTH DAKOTA ART GALLERIES, W M Lee Ctr for the Fine Arts, 57069. Tel 605-677-5481; FAX 605-677-5988; Elec Mail jday@charlie.usd.edu. *Dir* John A Day
Open Mon - Fri 10 AM - 4:30 PM; Sat & Sun 1 - 5 PM. No admis fee. Estab 1965. Primary mission is educational, serving specifically the needs of the college & augmenting the university curriculum as a whole. There are two galleries. One is a changing gallery 50' x 50' located in the Fine Arts Center. The second houses the university collection of Works by Oscar Howe, a native American painter. This facility is approximately 30' x 20'. Average Annual Attendance: 15, 000
Income: $60,000 (financed by state appropriation & student fee allotment)
Purchases: $4000
Collections: †60 Works by Oscar Howe; †variety of media by contemporary artists
Publications: Catalogues for major exhibitions
Activities: Lect open to public; gallery talks; tours; competitions, awards given; exten dept serves 150 miles in general region; individual paintings & original objects of art lent to professional museums & galleries; book traveling exhibitions 2 per year; originate traveling exhibitions

YANKTON

M YANKTON COUNTY HISTORICAL SOCIETY, Dakota Territorial Museum, * 610 Summit St, PO Box 1033, 57078. Tel 605-665-3898; *Pres* Dr Brooks Ranmey; *VPres* Dr Willis Stauage; *Dir & Cur* Donald J Binder
Open Memorial Day - Labor Day 1 - 5 PM. No admis fee, contributions accepted. Estab 1961 as an historical museum. Average Annual Attendance: 6000. Mem: 200; dues $5; annual meeting in Jan
Income: $20,000 (financed by city & county appropriation)
Collections: Paintings by Louis Janousek; sculptures by Frank Yaggie

TENNESSEE

CHATTANOOGA

L CHATTANOOGA-HAMILTON COUNTY BICENTENNIAL LIBRARY, Fine Arts Dept, 1001 Broad St, 37402. Tel 423-757-5316; *Head of Dept* Barry Bradford
Open Mon - Sun Sept - May, Mon - Sat June - Aug. No admis fee. Estab 1888, dept estab 1976
Income: Financed by city, county & state appropriation
Library Holdings: AV — A-tapes, cassettes, motion pictures, v-tapes; Other — Clipping files
Special Subjects: Art History, Film, Furniture, Historical Material, Painting - American, Painting - British, Pre-Columbian Art
Collections: Collection of books, cassette tapes, †compact discs, †music books, phono records, 16mm film & †video VHS tapes

M HOUSTON MUSEUM OF DECORATIVE ARTS, 201 High St, 37403. Tel 423-267-7176; *Dir* Amy Frierson
Open Apr - Oct Mon - Sat 9:30 AM - 4 PM, Sun Noon - 4 PM, cl Nov - Mar & major holidays. Admis $5. Estab 1961, incorporated 1949. Average Annual Attendance: 8000. Mem: 700; dues $1000, $250, $100, $50, $35, $15; annual meeting in May
Income: Financed by mem, dues, annual grant from Allied Arts, Inc, profits from antiques show & admis fees
Collections: Coverlet Collection; Early American furniture; rare collection of glass (5000 pitchers, 600 patterns of pressed glass, all types of art glass, steins & Tiffany glass); ceramics, dolls, porcelains
Exhibitions: Annual Antique Show
Publications: Always Paddle Your Own Canoe: The Life, Legend & Legacy of Ann Safley Houston; Fabulous Houston; Houston Museum of Decorative Arts Coverlet Collection
Activities: Classes for adults & children; docent training; lect open to public, 6 - 8 vis lectr per year; tours; museum shop sells books, reproductions, decorative art objects & items reflective of pieces in permanent collection

M HUNTER MUSEUM OF AMERICAN ART, 10 Bluff View, 37403. Tel 423-267-0968; FAX 423-267-9844; *Dir* Cleve K Scarbrough; *Prog Coordr* Eileen Henry; *Chief Preparator* John Hare; *Cur Coll* Ellen Simak; *Cur Educ* Elizabeth Whitaker; *Accounting Mgr* Linda Tate
Open Tues - Sat 10 AM - 4:30 PM; Sun 1 - 4:30 PM; cl Mon. Admis adults $5, children $2.50, under 3 free. Estab 1924, chartered in 1951 to present a visual arts program of high quality, maintain a fine collection of American art & to carry out a vigorous educational program in the community & the schools. The permanent collection of American art is housed in the George Thomas Hunter Mansion constructed in 1904 & a contemporary addition was opened in 1975 with 50,000 sq ft of space in four major gallery areas, a classroom wing & an auditorium. Average Annual Attendance: 55,000. Mem: 1900; dues grand benefactor $5000, benefactor $2500, member $1000, patron $500, sponsor $250, donor $100, advocate $75, general $35, advantage hunter $25, student & senior citizens $15
Collections: American paintings, later 18th century to present, including works by Bierstadt, Benton, Burchfield, Cassatt, Durand, Hassam, Henri, Inness, Marsh, Miller, Twachtman, Whistler & others; contemporary works including Beal, Bechtle, Fish, Frankenthaler, Golub, Goodman, Johns, LeWitt, Park, Pearlstein, Rauschenberg, Schapiro, Stackhouse, Wesselman, Wonner & Youngerman; contemporary American prints; sculpture by Calder, Hunt, Nevelson, Segal, Snelson & others; glass by Chihuly, Littleton, Morris, Zinsky
Exhibitions: Suzy Frelinghuysen & George L K Morris, American Abstract

Artists: Aspects of their Work & Collection; The American West: Legendary Artists of the Frontier, the John F Eulich Collection of American Western Art; Robert Henri: Nebraska's Favorite Son; Charles Burchfield's Spirituality; Clearly Art: Pilchuck's Glass Legacy
Publications: Brochures & announcements; bulletin, quarterly; A Catalogue of the American Collection, Hunter Museum of Art, 1985, 300-page illustrated focus on pieces in the permanent collection
Activities: Classes for adults & children; docent training; lect open to public, approximately 7 vis lectr per year; gallery talks; concerts; tours; individual paintings are lent to other museums; book traveling exhibitions 18-20 per year; originate traveling exhibitions which circulate to qualified galleries & museums; museum shop sells books, reproductions, gift items, jewelry
L Reference Library, 10 Bluff View, 37403. Tel 423-267-0968
Open Tues - Sat 10 AM - 4:30 PM, Sun 1 - 4:30 PM, cl Mon, open to public by appointment. Estab 1958
Library Holdings: Vols 1500; Per subs 8; Micro — Cards; AV — Cassettes, motion pictures, slides; Other — Clipping files, exhibition catalogs, memorabilia, original art works, pamphlets, photographs, prints, sculpture
Special Subjects: Architecture, American Art

M UNIVERSITY OF TENNESSEE AT CHATTANOOGA, George Ayers Cress Gallery of Art, Fine Arts Ctr, 37043. Tel 615-755-4178; *Gallery Coordr* George Cress
Open Mon - Fri 9 AM - 4 PM, cl university holidays. No admis fee. Estab 1949 to provide teaching gallery for art department, campus & community. Average Annual Attendance: 5000
Collections: Graphics; paintings; students work
Activities: Gallery talks; individual paintings & original objects of art lent to various campus areas; lending collection contains original prints & paintings; temporary and traveling exhibitions

CLARKSVILLE

M AUSTIN PEAY STATE UNIVERSITY, Margaret Fort Trahern Gallery, Art Department, PO Box 4677, 37044. Tel 615-648-7348; *Dir* Bettye Holte
Open Mon - Fri 9 AM - 4 PM. No admis fee. Estab 1962 as a university community service to exhibit a variety of visual media from regional professionals & university art majors. Average Annual Attendance: 8000
Income: Financed by university appropriations
Collections: Larson Drawing Collection; †Graphics & sculpture; watercolors
Exhibitions: Average 10-12 per year
Publications: Announcements of shows & artist biographies, monthly; biennial drawing competition/exhibition catalog
Activities: Lect open to public, 8 vis lectr per year; gallery talks; tours; competitions with awards; scholarships offered
L Art Dept Library, 37040. Tel 615-648-7333; FAX 615-648-5997; *Gallery Cur* Bettye Holte; *Slide Librn* Dixie Webb
Open Mon - Fri 8:30 AM - 4 PM. Estab 1974. Large single unit space with storage. Average Annual Attendance: 4,000
Library Holdings: AV — Fs, motion pictures, slides, v-tapes; Other — Clipping files, exhibition catalogs, original art works, photographs, prints, reproductions, sculpture
Special Subjects: Advertising Design, Afro-American Art, Art Education, Art History, Asian Art, Decorative Arts, Drawings, Etchings & Engravings, Folk Art, Graphic Arts, Islamic Art, Latin American Art, Mexican Art, Painting - American, Sculpture
Collections: †Larson Drawing Collection
M Harned Gallery, PO Box 4677, 37044. *Dir* Bettye S Holte
Exhibitions: Changing exhibits of the University permanent collection

COOKEVILLE

A CUMBERLAND ART SOCIETY INC, Cookeville Art Gallery, 186 S Walnut, 38501. Tel 615-526-2424; *Pres* Romola Drost
Open Mon - Fri & Sun 1 - 4 PM. No admis fee. Estab 1961 to promote arts in the community & area. A new building with adequate gallery & studio space. The gallery is carpeted & walls are finished with wallscape & track lighting. Average Annual Attendance: 3000. Mem: 100; dues $20, renewal $15, students $10; meetings twice annually
Income: $5500 (financed by mem, city & state appropriations)
Exhibitions: Changing exhibits, monthly
Activities: Classes for children & adults; lect open to public, 6 vis lectr per year; gallery talks; tours; competitions with awards

HENDERSONVILLE

A HENDERSONVILLE ARTS COUNCIL, 252 E Main St, 252 E Main Street, 37077-0064. Tel 615-822-0789; *Exec Dir* Emma Dye
Open 9 AM - 3 PM. Estab 1975 to promote & educate through the arts. Galleries are located in 200 yr old home. Average Annual Attendance: 10,000
Exhibitions: Monthly changing exhibits
Publications: News d'Art, quarterly
Activities: Classes for adults & children; dramatic programs

JOHNSON CITY

EAST TENNESSEE STATE UNIVERSITY
M Carroll Reece Museum, 37614. Tel 423-929-4392, 929-4283; FAX 423-439-6340; Elec Mail whiteb@etsu-tn.edu. *Museum Dir* Dr Jean Speer; *Museum Registrar* Margaret S Carr; *Installation Supv* Harold Stewart; *Cur* Blair White; *Slide Cur* Nancy Earnest
Open Mon - Sat 9 AM - 4 PM, Sun 1 - 5 PM. No admis fee. Estab 1965 to enhance the cultural & educational advantages of the University & the people of upper East Tennessee. The purpose of Friends of the Reece Museum is to

acquire fine arts works for the permanent collection. Average Annual Attendance: 23,500. Mem: 200; dues President's trust $10,000 plus, President's partners $500, Century Club $100-$499, supporting $25, family $15, individual $10, student $1

Income: Financed through the state of Tennessee

Collections: Frontier Exhibit, an exhibit of historical Tennessee household & farming items, includes a log cabin & conestoga wagon; Marks Collection of Pre-Columbian Art; Music From the Past, a collection of early musical instruments; Old Master & contemporary prints; Printshop of the Past; Reece Room, an exhibition of memorabilia of former United States Congressman from Tennessee, B Carroll Reece; John Steele Collection of Contemporary Prints; contemporary paintings; historical material

Exhibitions: Photographs/Appalachian Serpent & Firehandlers; Page Coleman: Recent Works; Prints from the Permanent Collection; Senior Art Competition-Wining Entries; Pace Editions: Contemporary Prints from the Pace Gallery; Southern Voices: English in the American South; First Tennessee Bank Show/Johnson City Arts Council Competition & Exhibition; Ending of World War II, exhibit; Peggy Root & T B Root, paintings; Annual Alumni Exhibit; Annual Holiday Exhibit

Publications: CRM Newsletter, quarterly

Activities: Lect, 6 vis lectr per year; concerts; gallery talks; tours; competitions with awards; scholarships offered; individual paintings & original objects of art lent to inner administrative offices on campus; lending collection contains 354 original prints, 25 paintings, 400 original art works, 6 sculpture & 1000 slides; book traveling exhibitions; originate traveling exhibitions; rotating exhibitions at Kingsport University Center

M Elizabeth Slocumb Galleries, Department of Art & Design, PO Box 70708, 37614-0708. Tel 423-439-7078; FAX 423-439-4393; *Dir Exhib* Ann Ropp; *Gallery Asst* Gail Vollrath

Open Mon - Fri 9 AM - 4 PM. No admis fee. Estab 1950 to augment all the programs & areas of instruction within the Art Department & to foster interest in various modes of artistic expression in the campus at large. Average Annual Attendance: 5000

Collections: A small teaching collection of prints, paintings, ceramics, weaving, wood, photographs & graphic designs & a camera collection

Exhibitions: Appreciating Rising Talent Juried Competition 14-18 year olds; MFA & BFA Candidate Exhibitions

Publications: Catalogs; posters

Activities: Lect open to public; gallery talks; tours; competitions; scholarships & fels offered; originate traveling exhibitions

L C C Sherrod Library, Art Collection, PO Box 70665, 37614-0665. Tel 615-929-5308, 929-5309; FAX 615-461-7026; *Dir* F Borchuck

Open Mon - Thurs 8 AM - midnight, Fri 8 AM - 6 PM, Sat 9 AM - 6 PM, Sun 1 PM - midnight

Income: Financed by the state

Library Holdings: Vols 449,250; Per subs 3808

Special Subjects: Drawings, Photography, Sculpture, Painting

Collections: Appalachian Culture & Arts; photographs archives; videotape archives

KINGSPORT

A ARTS COUNCIL OF GREATER KINGSPORT, Renaissance Center Main Gallery, 1200 E Center St, 37660-4946. Tel 423-392-8420; FAX 423-392-8422; *Pres* Lillian Agel; *Dir* Marilyn Schieferdecker

Open Mon - Fri 8 AM - 5 PM. No admis fee, charge for special events. Estab 1968 to promote & present all the arts to all the people in area; this includes performing arts, visual arts & classes. One gallery with monthly shows. Average Annual Attendance: 20,000. Mem: 400; dues $20-$500

Income: $150,000 (financed by mem & grants)

Publications: Newsletter, bimonthly

Activities: Classes for adults & children; lect open to public, 3 vis lectr per year; concerts; competitions with awards; scholarships; originate traveling exhibitions through Southern Arts Federation

KNOXVILLE

M BECK CULTURAL EXCHANGE CENTER, 1927 Dandridge Ave, 37915. Tel 423-524-8461; *Chief Exec Officer* Robert J Booker

Open Tues - Sat 10 AM - 6 PM. No admis fee. Estab 1975 to encourage, collect, preserve & display local Black history. Average Annual Attendance: 5000. Mem: 400; dues $10; annual meeting in Sept

Income: $90,000 (financed by mem, city, county & state appropriations)

Exhibitions: Federal Judge William H Hastie Room; Library of Books & Recordings; oral histories; weekly newspapers of the local Black experience; Senior Citizens Storywriting Contest

Activities: Classes for adults & children; school & community presentations; docent programs; competitions with cash awards; traveling slide presentations

M KNOXVILLE MUSEUM OF ART, 1050 World's Fair Park Dr, 37916. Tel 423-525-6101; FAX 423-546-3635; *Chmn* Jim Smith; *Dir* Richard I Ferrin; *Treas* Jim Shelby

Open Tues, Wed, Thurs & Sat 10 AM - 5 PM, Fri 10 AM - 9 PM, Sun Noon - 5 PM. No admis fee. Estab 1961 as a nonprofit private corporation. Grand opening was held in 1990. Located on the former World's Fair site downtown. New state-of-the-art 53,000 sq ft facility. Maintains reference library. Average Annual Attendance: 140,000. Mem: 3400; dues from $35-$1000

Income: Financed by mem, contributions, sponsorships, foundations & local, state & federal grants

Collections: American Art during & after the 1960's in paintings, photography, sculpture & works on paper

Exhibitions: (1997) Six Centuries of European Painting: Masterworks from the Sarah Campbell Blaffer Foundation Collection; Selections from the Contemporary Collection of the Hunter Museum of Art; Awakening the Spirts: Sculpture by Bessie Harvey; Red Grooms (sculpture) English Silver 1770-1834: Masterpieces by Matthew Bougton from the Collection of James C Codell, Jr.

Defying Gravity: Paintings by Robert Longo; Threads of the World: Selections from the Colleection of Mary Ewing

Publications: Bi-monthly calendar; exhibition catalogs; newsletter

Activities: Classes for adults & children; dramatic programs; docent training; jazz classes; school outreach; lect open to public, 5-10 vis lectr per year; concerts; gallery talks; tours; competitions; exten dept serves East Tennessee region; individual paintings & original objects of art lent to other art museums; lending collection contains 5000 books, cassettes, color reproductions, motion pictures, original art works, original prints, paintings, photographs, sculptures & slides; book traveling exhibitions 10-15 per year; originate traveling exhibitions; museum shop sells books, magazines, reproductions, prints, jewelry, accessories (apparel); greeting cards, calendars, toys, t-shirts & art-related gifts

UNIVERSITY OF TENNESSEE

M Frank H McClung Museum, 1327 Circle Park Dr, 37996-3200. Tel 423-974-2144; FAX 423-974-3827; *Dir* Jefferson Chapman; *Exhib Coordr* Andrew W Hurst; *Cur Coll* Elaine A Evans

Open Mon - Fri 9 AM - 5 PM, Sun 2 - 5 PM. No admis fee. Estab 1961 to collect, maintain & interpret paintings, works of art, items of natural history & historical objects with emphasis placed on the Tennessee area. A major purpose is to provide research materials for students & faculty of the university. Average Annual Attendance: 20,000

Income: Financed by city & state appropriations

Collections: Eleanor Deane Audigier Art Collection; Frederick T Bonham Collection (18th - 20th Century furniture, art objects); Lewis-Kneberg Collection (Tennessee archaeology); Grace Moore Collection (memorabilia of her career 1920 - 1940); Malacology Collection (marine species & fresh water North American mollusks)

Exhibitions: Museum Animals: Wildlife paintings by Guy Coheleach & other animal art; Behind the Great House: Architecture of Plantation Slavery; With Care They Made These, tribal styles in Plains Indian Art

Activities: Lect open to public; gallery talks; tours; competitions; exten dept serves the Southwest; original objects of art lent to members of university & educational organizations; lending collection contains prints & photographs

M Eleanor Dean Audigier Art Collection, Frank H McClung Museum, 1327 Circle Park Dr, 37916. Tel 423-974-2144; FAX 423-974-3827; *Dir* Jefferson Chapman; *Cur* Elaine A Evans; *Exhibits Coordr* Andrew W Hurst

Open Mon - Fri 9 AM - 5 PM, Sat 10 AM - 3 PM, Sun 2 - 5 PM. No admis fee. Estab 1961. Average Annual Attendance: 19,600

Income: Financed by state appropriations, supplemental income from mem sponsorships

Collections: †The Audigier Collection Greco-Roman objects; 19th Century copies of Italian Renaissance paintings, furniture & sculpture; personal jewelry; early 20th century decorative arts objects

Exhibitions: The Decorative Experience: Selections from the Audigier Collection

Activities: Lect open to public; tours; individual & original objects of art lent

M Ewing Gallery of Art and Architecture, University of Tennessee, 1715 Volunteer Blvd, 37996-2410. Tel 423-974-3200; FAX 423-974-3198; *Dir* Sam Yates; *Registrar* Cindy Spangler

Open Mon - Thurs 8:30 AM - 8 PM, Fri 8:30 AM - 4:30 PM, Sun 1 - 4 PM. Estab 1981 to provide quality exhibitions focusing on contemporary art & architecture. Gallery consists of 3500 sq ft exhibition space. Average Annual Attendance: 6000

Collections: †Contemporary American prints, paintings & drawings; Japanese prints

Activities: Lect open to public, 12 vis lectr per year; gallery talks; tours; sponsor competitions; scholarships offered; lending collection contains individual & original objects of art; originate traveling exhibitions

A Visual Arts Committee, 305 University Ctr, 37996. Tel 423-974-5455; FAX 423-974-9252; *Prog Advisor* Berri Cross

Open Mon - Fri 7:30 AM - 10:30 PM, Sat 7 AM - 10 PM, Sun 1 - 6 PM. No admis fee. Estab to provide cultural arts for the students of the university. Two major galleries: Gallery Concourse has 300 running ft. Average Annual Attendance: 20,000

Income: Financed by student activities fees

Collections: †Dunford Collection; †Marion Heard Collection of Crafts

Exhibitions: 10 exhibits per year; student shows & traveling shows

Activities: Lect open to public, 6 vis lectr per year; originate traveling exhibitions

MARYVILLE

C FIRST TENNESSE BANK, 101 W Broadway, PO Box 9720, 37802-9720. Tel 423-977-5100; FAX 423-977-5196; *In Charge of Art Coll* Ann McEntire

Estab to provide community interest in the arts; to aid participating artists; to enhance lobby. Supports local artists & art forms on displays that lend an interest to the community

Collections: Paintings by local artists in a variety of media

Activities: Sponsors Wildlife Artist Guy Coheleach

M MARYVILLE COLLEGE, Fine Arts Center Gallery, 502 E Lamar Alexder Pky, 37804-5907. Tel 423-981-8150, 981-8000; FAX 423-981-8010; *Chmn* Daniel Taddie

Open Mon - Fri during school year. No admis fee

Library Holdings: Vols 1300

Collections: †Print collection

Activities: Gallery programs in connection with circulating exhibitions; art movies, four times a year; originate traveling exhibitions 10-12 during college year

MEMPHIS

AUTOZONE
For further information, see National and Regional Organizations

A **CENTER FOR SOUTHERN FOLKLORE,** 209 Beale St, 38103. Tel 901-525-3655; FAX 901-525-3945; *Exec Dir* Judy Peiser
Open Mon & Thurs 10 AM - 8 PM, Fri & Sat 10 AM - Noon, Sun 1 AM - 8 PM. Admis $2. Estab 1972 as a non-profit organization which archives, documents & presents folk art, culture & music through film, photography, exhibits & lectues. Mem: 800; dues $25
Income: $350,000 (financed by mem, state appropriation & national endowment)
Collections: African - American Quilt; Contemporary Slides - Folk Art & Culture; Folk Art; Historical & Contemporary Photographs
Exhibitions: WDIA Radio; Rockabilly; Memphis Music
Activities: Classes for adults & children; cultual tourism; lect open to public; lending collection contains 50 paintings & art objects; retail store sells books, magazines & original art

M **THE DIXON GALLERY & GARDENS,** 4339 Park Ave, 38117. Tel 901-761-5250; FAX 901-680-0721; *Dir* Joseph Czestochowski; *Cur Coll* Sheila K Tabakoff; *Registrar* Deborah Bass; *Vol Coordr* Jane Faquin; *Museum Shop Mgr* Joanne Glasgow
Open Tues - Sat 10 AM - 5 PM, Sun 1 - 5 PM, cl Mon. Admis adults $5, students & senior citizens $4, children 2-11 years $1. Estab 1976 as a bequest to the pub from the late Margaret & Hugo Dixon. Their Impressionist Art Collection & their Georgian-style home & gardens, situated on 17 acres of landscaped woodland, serve as the museum's foundation. Two wings added in 1977 & 1986 house the developing permanent collection & accommodate loan exhibitions. Formal & informal gardens, a camellia house & greenhouses are located on the site. Average Annual Attendance: 160,000. Mem: 5700; dues corporate patron $1000 & up, patron $500, donor $250, sponsor $125, family $60, dual $55, individual $45, student $20
Income: Financed by endowment & contributions
Collections: French Impressionist painting; Barbizon, Post-Impressionist & related schools; 18th century British paintings; Georgian period furniture & decorative arts; the Warda Stevens Stout Collection of 18th century German porcelain; 18th & 19th centuries works by Pierre Bonnard, Eugene Boudin, Theodore Earl Butler, A F Cals, Jean-Baptiste Carpeaux, Mary Cassatt, Marc Chagall, William Merritt Chase, John Constable, J B C Corot, Kenyon Cox, Henri-Edmond Cross, Charles Francois Daubigny, Edgar Degas, Julien Dupre, Sir Jacob Epstein, Henri Fantin-Latour, Jean-Louis Forain, Thomas Gainsborough, Paul Gauguin, Edmond Grandjean, Francesco Guardi, Paul Guigou, Armand Guillaumin, Henri Joseph Harpignies, William James, Johan Jongkind, S V E Lepine, Maximilien Luce, Albert Marquet, Paul Mathey, Henri Matisse, Claude Monet, Berthe Morisot, Henriette A Oberteuffer, Ludovic Piette, Camille Pissarro, Sir Henry Raeburn, J F Raffaelli, Auguste Renoir, Sir Joshua Reynolds, Henri Rouart, Paul Signac, Alfred Sisley, Allen Tucker, J M W Turner, Horatio Walker and Richard Wilson
Publications: Exhibition catalogues; quarterly newsletter
Activities: Classes for adults; workshops; docent training; lect open to public; concerts; gallery talks; tours; film series; individual paintings & original objects of art lent to museums & galleries; lending collection contains original paintings, prints, sculpture & porcelain; museum shop sells art & garden books, prints, jewelry, notecards & garden items
L **Library,** 4339 Park Ave, 38117. Tel 901-761-5250; FAX 901-682-0943; *Dir* Joseph S Czestochowski; *Asst Dir* Katherine Lawrence; *Cur Coll* Sheila K Tabakoff; *Registrar* Deborah Bass
Open Tues - Sat 10 AM - 5 PM, Sun 1 - 5 PM. Open to members during mus hours, for reference only
Income: $8000 (financed by mem, corporate & private sponsorship & the Hugo Dixon Foundation)
Library Holdings: Per subs 15; Micro — Cards; Other — Clipping files, exhibition catalogs, pamphlets, photographs
Special Subjects: Ceramics, Decorative Arts, Painting - French, Pewter, 18th century German Porcelain, 19th century French art; gardens
Collections: †19th Century French Porcelain
Publications: Quarterly newsletter

C **FIRST TENNESSEE NATIONAL CORP,** First Tennessee Heritage Collection, 165 Madison Ave, 38103. Tel 901-523-4382, 523-4291; FAX 901-523-4354; *Chmn* Ralph Horn; *Communication Specialist* Kathie Alexander; *Tours* Leslie Lee
Mus open Mon - Thurs 8:30 AM - 4 PM, Fri 8:30 AM - 5 PM. Estab 1979 to depict Tennessee's heritage & history through art. Gallery, with over 150 original works, is located in First Tennessee's corporate headquarters. Average Annual Attendance: 20,000
Income: Financed by corporation
Purchases: $75,000
Collections: Engravings, etchings, lithographs, murals, paintings, sculpture, watercolors
Exhibitions: Permanent collection
Activities: Educ dept; scout program; book traveling exhibitions 3 per year

M **MEMPHIS BROOKS MUSEUM OF ART,** 1934 Poplar Ave, 38104. Tel 901-722-3525, 722-3500; FAX 901-722-3522; *Dir* E A Carlean Jr; *Cur Educ* Patty Blandon-Lawrence; *Registrar* Kip Peterson; *Shop Mgr* Lillian Trotter; *Chief Preparator* Elbert L Sharp III; *Asst Preparator* Paul Tracy; *Chief Financial Officer* Jesse Gresham; *Account Mgr* Jim Thompson; *Librn* Janelle Schieffer; *Dir Facility Servs & Security* Charles Beagle
Open Tues - Sat 10 AM - 5 PM; Sun 1 - 5 PM. No admis fee. Estab 1912 to exhibit, preserve & elucidate works of art. The original building was opened in 1916 with additions in 1955 and 1973. Maintained by the city of Memphis, Public Service Department. Average Annual Attendance: 125,000. Mem: 3156; dues $35 & up
Income: $1,000,000 (financed by city appropriation & Friend's Foundation)
Collections: American Paintings & Sculpture, 18th-20th centuries; Dutch &

Flemish Paintings, 16th-18th centuries: Eastern & Near-Eastern Decorative Arts Collection (Han, Tang & Ching Dynasty); English Paintings, 17th-19th centuries; French Paintings, 16th-19th centuries; †International Collection of Paintings & Sculpture, 19th & 20th centuries; Kress Collection of Italian Paintings & Sculptures, 13th-18th centuries; Dr Louis Levy Collection of American Prints; Mid-south Collection of 20th century paintings & sculptures; glass, textile & porcelain collection
Exhibitions: (1997) Turner Watercolors From Manchester. (1997-98) Unseen Splendors: The Romanoff Diamonds & Treasures of the Russian Collection; Discovery & Deceit: Archaeology & The Forgens Craft
Publications: Bimonthly newsletter
Activities: Classes for adults & children; docent training; outreach program & studio art activities for student groups; lect open to public, 9 vis lectr per year; concerts; gallery talks; tours; competitions; awards; individual paintings & original objects of art lent; book traveling exhibitions 7-10 per year; originate traveling exhibitions; museum shop sells books, reproductions, prints, slides, museum replicas, jewelry & regional pottery
L **Library,** 1934 Poplar Ave, 38104. Tel 901-722-3500; *Lirn* Janelle Schieffed
Open Wed & Fri 10 AM - 4 PM & by appointment. Reference only
Library Holdings: Vols 5166; Per subs 24; Other — Clipping files 2910, exhibition catalogs 1705

MEMPHIS COLLEGE OF ART
L **G Pillow Lewis Memorial Library,** 1930 Poplar Ave, 38104. Tel 901-726-4085; *Pres* Jeffrey D Nesin; *Dean* Alonzo Davis; *Librn* Lloyd Ostby
Open Mon - Thurs 8 AM - 9 PM, Fri 8 AM - 6 PM, Sat 9 AM - 4 PM, Sun 1 - 6 PM, summer hrs Mon - Fri 8 AM - 5 PM. No admis fee. Estab 1936 as an adjunct educational program. The Standing Committee on Exhibitions arranges visiting shows
Library Holdings: Vols 14,500; Per subs 110; AV — Slides; Other — Clipping files, exhibition catalogs, prints, reproductions
Special Subjects: Art Education, Art History, Bookplates & Bindings, Calligraphy, Drawings, Graphic Arts, Graphic Design, History of Art & Archaeology, Illustration, Jewelry, Metalwork, Mixed Media, Photography, Pottery, Printmaking
Collections: Jacob Marks Memorial Collection; works by college graduates
Exhibitions: Juried student shows; one & two-person faculty shows; senior exhibition; summer student show; traveling exhibitions
Publications: Exhibition catalogs
Activities: Classes for adults, children & undergraduate college students; lect; guided tours; films; competitions; book traveling exhibitions
L **Library,** 1930 Poplar Ave, 38104. Tel 901-726-4085; *Librn* Lloyd Ostby; *Slide Cur* Bette Ray Callow
Open Mon - Thurs 8 AM - 9 PM, Fri 8 AM - 6 PM, Sat 9 AM - 4 PM, Sun 1 - 6 PM
Library Holdings: Vols 14,500; Per subs 110; Original prints; AV — Slides 30,000; Other — Reproductions
Special Subjects: Art History, Bookplates & Bindings, Illustration, Industrial Design, Jewelry, Metalwork, Photography, Pottery, Printmaking, Sculpture, Textiles, Woodcarvings

L **MEMPHIS-SHELBY COUNTY PUBLIC LIBRARY & INFORMATION CENTER,** Dept of Art, Music & Films, 1850 Peabody, 38104. Tel 901-725-8837, 725-8830; FAX 901-725-8814; *Dir* Judith Drescher; *Deputy Dir* Sallie Johnson; *Sr Mgr Humanities* Gary Johnson
Open Mon - Thurs 9 AM - 9 PM, Fri & Sat 9 AM - 6 PM, Sun 1 - 5 PM. Estab 1895 to serve the reference, informational, cultural & recreational needs of residents of Memphis-Shelby County. Turner-Clark Gallery exhibits promising & established local & regional artists of various media
Income: Financed by city & state appropriation
Library Holdings: Vols 63,000; Per subs 245; AV — Cassettes 800, motion pictures 3000, rec 35,000, v-tapes 3000

M **MISSISSIPPI RIVER MUSEUM AT MUD-ISLAND,** 125 N Front St, 38103. Tel 901-576-7230; FAX 901-576-6666; *River Museum Mgr* Susan Elliott
Open Apr 5 - May 25 Tues - Sun 10 AM - 5 PM, May 26 - Sept 1 daily 10 AM - 8 PM, Sept 2 - Oct 31 Tues - Sun 10 AM - 5 PM. Admis adults $4, children 3-11 & seniors $3. Estab 1978 to interpret the natural & cultural history of the Mississippi River Valley. Maintains reference library. Average Annual Attendance: 150,000
Income: $350,000 (financed by city appropriation)
Collections: 2-D & 3-D pieces that interpret the natural & cultural history of the lower Mississippi River
Activities: Classes for children; dramatic program; docent training; lect open to public; gallery talks; tours; competitions with prizes; book traveling exhibitions 3-5 per year; originate traveling exhibitions; museum shop sells books, magazines, reproductions & prints

A **NUMBER INC,** PO Box 12226, 38182-0226. Tel 901-722-5905; *Exec Ed* Deborah Gordon
Estab 1987 to give exposure to contemporary visual arts & artistic communities
Income: Financed by grants & contributions
Exhibitions: 10th Anniversary Slide Installations; X Marks the spot (work with University of Memphis Art Museum)
Publications: Independent Visual Arts Journal

M **RHODES COLLEGE,** Jessie L Clough Art Memorial for Teaching, Clough Hall, 2000 N Parkway, 38112. Tel 901-726-3833; FAX 901-726-3727; *Cur* Marina Pacini
Open Mon - Fri 8:30 AM - 5 PM. Estab 1951 for the study of fine & decorative arts
Collections: Japanese & woodblock prints; Asian & European textiles
Exhibitions: Selections from the Jessie L Clough Art Memorial for Teaching

UNIVERSITY OF MEMPHIS (Formerly Memphis State University)

M **Art Museum,** Communication & Fine Arts Bldg, 38152. Tel 901-678-2224; FAX 901-678-5118; *Dir* Leslie L Luebbers

Open Tues - Sat 9 AM - 5 PM year round except between changing exhibits. No admis fee. Estab 1981 to sponsor programs & mount temporary exhibitions to expand knowledge about all periods of art with a special emphasis on contemporary art. Mus has 7000 sq ft of exhibition space including two permanent exhibits of ancient Egypt & traditional African art. Average Annual Attendance: 30,000. Mem: 200

Income: Financed by state appropriation, pub & private support

Collections: Egyptian Hall: antiquities from 3500 BC - 7th century AD; Neil Nokes Collection of African Art, traditional West African masks & sculpture; Print Collection: contemporary prints; collection of over 250 prints, an overview

Exhibitions: Changing exhibition schedule

Publications: AM Edition Newsletter, quarterly

Activities: Classes for adults & children; lect open to public, 5 vis lectr per year; tours; competitions with awards; scholarships offered; permanent collections lent to other institutions with proper facilities; lending collections contain 1200 original art works, slides & VHS tapes

L **Visual Resource Collection,** 220 Jones Hall, 38152. Tel 901-678-2938; FAX 901-678-2735; *Visual Resources Coll Cur* Lynn Cunningham

Open Mon - Fri 8 AM - 4:30 PM. Estab 1967 to provide slides for Art Faculty, University Faculty, & some outside organizations. Circ 127,000

Income: Financed by the university

Library Holdings: Vols 218; Per subs 160; AV — A-tapes, cassettes, fs, rec, slides, v-tapes; Other — Clipping files, exhibition catalogs, original art works, prints, reproductions, sculpture

Special Subjects: Afro-American Art, American Indian Art, American Western Art, Antiquities-Assyrian, Antiquities-Byzantine, Antiquities-Egyptian, Antiquities-Etruscan, Antiquities-Greek, Antiquities-Oriental, Antiquities-Persian, Antiquities-Roman, Archaeology, Architecture, Art Education, Art History

Collections: 35 mm slides of history of Western art, †photography, non-Western art

MORRISTOWN

A **ROSE CENTER & COUNCIL FOR THE ARTS,** PO Box 1976, 37816. Tel 423-581-4330; *Dir* Bill Cornrich

Estab 1976 to promote, implement, & sustain historical, educational, & cultural activities & projects of both local & national importance; to preserve & maintain Rose School as a museum & cultural center. Art gallery, historic gallery, children's touch mus, historical classroom-exhibits remain same, never change. Average Annual Attendance: 25,000. Mem: 450

Income: Financed by endowment, mem, city appropriation & state appropriation

Activities: Sales shop sells books & crafts; lect open to public; school programs

MURFREESBORO

M **MIDDLE TENNESSEE STATE UNIVERSITY,** Baldwin Photographic Gallery, PO Box 305, 37132. Tel 615-898-2085; FAX 615-898-5682; Elec Mail tjimison@frank.mtsu.edu. *Cur* Tom Jimison

Open Mon - Fri 8 AM - 4:30 PM, Sat 8 AM - Noon, Sun 6 - 10 PM. No admis fee. Estab 1970 for the exhibition of outstanding photographers & beginners. Gallery has 193 running ft of display area. Average Annual Attendance: 30,000

Income: Financed by the university

Collections: Ansel Adams; Shelby Lee Adams; Richard Avedon; Harold Baldwin; Harry Callahan; Marrie Camhi; Geri Della Rocea de Candal; Barbara Crane; Jim Ferguson; Dore Gardner; Philip Gould; Tom Jimison; Builder Levy; Minor White & others; Jim Norton; April Ottey; John Pfahl; Walter Rosenblum; John Schulze; Aaron Sisking; Marianne Skogh; H H Smith; Michael P Smith; Jerry Velsman; Ed Weston by Cole; Jack Wilgus; Sean Wilkinson; Kelly Wise

Publications: Lightyear, annually

Activities: Original objects of art lent to responsible organizations; lending collection contains photographs; book traveling exhibitions 3 per year; originate traveling exhibitions to university galleries

NASHVILLE

M **BOARD OF PARKS & RECREATION,** The Parthenon, Centennial Park, West End Ave (Mailing add: Metro Postal Service, Centennial Park Office, 37201). Tel 615-862-8431; FAX 615-880-2265; Elec Mail parthenon@nashville.org. *Dir* Wesley M Paine; *Asst Dir* Gary Pace; *Museum Store Mgr* Timothy Cartmell

Open Tues - Sat 9 AM - 4:30 PM, Apr - Sept Sun 12:30 - 4:30 PM, cl Sun, Mon & legal holidays. Admis adult $2.50, children (4-17) & senior citizens $1.25. Estab 1897 to offer Nashville residents & tourists quality art for viewing & sale in a Historical setting of significance & beauty. Central Gallery, changing exhibit gallery & James M Cowan Gallery of American Art. Average Annual Attendance: 160,000

Income: Financed by city & county taxes & donations

Collections: Cowan Collection, sixty three paintings by 19th & 20th century American artists, donated by James M Cowan; †Century III Collection, sixty two art works, purchased from area artists, juried by John Canaday in celebration of Nashville's bicentennial

Exhibitions: Exhibitions change monthly

Publications: The Cowan Catalog, Century III Catalog

Activities: Co-sponsor, with Tennessee Art League of Annual Central South Exhibition, juried show with awards given; sales shop sells books, magazines, souvenirs, prints & slides

M **CHEEKWOOD-TENNESSEE BOTANICAL GARDENS & MUSEUM OF ART,** 1200 Forrest Park Dr, 37205-4242. Tel 615-356-8000; FAX 615-353-2156; *Pres* Jane Jerry; *Dir* Open; *Registrar* Elizabeth Cunningham; *Preparator* Todd McDaniel; *Cur Coll & Exhib* Christine Kreyling; *Cur Coll & Exhib* Celia Walker; *Public Information* Angelia Hartline; *Dir Educ* Donna Glassford

Open Mon - Sat 9 AM - 5 PM, Sun Noon - 5 PM, cl Thanksgiving, Christmas Eve, Christmas, New Year's Eve & New Year's Day. Admis adults $5, children 7-17 $2, children under 7 free. Estab 1957 to collect, preserve & interpret American art, with special emphasis on artists of the region. Mus opened to pub in 1960 in a Georgian-style mansion built in 1929 by Mr & Mrs Leslie Chreek. Originally adapted for mus use in 1960, the site underwent further renovation & adaptation in 1980. Galleries contain 12,000 sq ft of exhibition space, divided almost equally between installation of permanent collection & temporary, special exhibitions. Three galleries are used for temporary exhibitions. Mary Cheek Hill Gallery houses the Thompson Snuff & Medicine Bottle Collection; adjoining gallery houses the Collection of Worcester Porcelain; other permanent collection gallery installations include: Painters in Middle Tennessee, 1825-1925, An American Gallery & William Edmondson, Sculptor & John A & Margaret Hill Gallery of American Western Art. Average Annual Attendance: 170,000. Mem: 8700; dues supporting $100, family $50, individual $35, senior (65 & over) $35; annual meeting 3rd Wed in June

Income: Financed by mem, admis, corporate & foundation grants, private gifts, several fundraising events

Collections: †American paintings & sculpture, 1750-1950; †Mid-state Tennessee paintings & sculpture, 1750-1950; †sculpture; †graphic art, all periods & schools; Oriental snuff & medicine bottles; †Worcester Porcelain, 1750-1825; †Shefields Silver, 19th & 20th Century Landscape Collection; Tennessee paintings; †William Edmundson

Exhibitions: Upper Stallworth Gallery: Nashville Collects; National Contemporary Painting Competition. Facing the Past: 19th Century Portraits from the Collection of the Pennsylvania Academy of Fine Arts; New Works Fellowships: Northern Telecom; Red Grooms: Watercolors; Ultra Realistic Sculpture by Marc Sijan; National contemporary Painting Competition. Lower Stallworth Gallery: Nashville Collects; National Contemporary Painting Competition. The Biltmore Estate: A Centennial Celebration 1895-1995; Imperial Russian Porcelain from the Raymond F Piper Collection; The John A & Margaret Hill Collection; National Contemporary Painting Competition; Hill Gallery/Works on Paper: Lasting Impressions: Drawings by Thomas Hart Benton; Light Boxes: Transparencies by Connie Sullivan; Discovery Room; Loggia Gallery: American Art through the 19th Century; American Art of the 20th Century; American Impressionism; Old Sheffield Plate from the Caldwell & Speights Collections; Selections from the Gift of Dr & Mrs Benjamin Caldwell; About Face; Pre-Columbian Pottery Grounds: Henry Moore in a Sheep Meadow, by Red Grooms

Publications: Brochures, catalogues, checklists, monographs, monthly newsletter, posters

Activities: Classes for adults & children; dramatic programs; docent training; workshops; poetry readings; lect open to public, 8-10 vis lectr per year; concerts; gallery talks; tours; competitions with awards; individual paintings & original objects of art lent to museums; lending collection contains original art works, paintings & sculpture; book traveling exhibitions 10 per year; originate traveling exhibitions organized & circulated to museums & cultural institutions; museum shop sells books, slides, posters; junior museum

L **Museum of Art Library,** 1200 Forrest Park Dr, 37205. Tel 615-353-2140; FAX 615-353-2730; *Librn* Virginia Khouri

Open to staff & members for reference

Library Holdings: Vols 5000; Per subs 58

Special Subjects: Afro-American Art, American Western Art, Architecture, Art History, Decorative Arts, Folk Art, Graphic Arts, History of Art & Archaeology, Painting - American, Photography, Pre-Columbian Art, Printmaking, Prints, Restoration & Conservation, Sculpture

L **Botanic Hall Library,** 1200 Forrest Park Dr, 37205. Tel 615-353-2148; FAX 615-353-2156; *Librn* Ida Galehouse

M **FISK UNIVERSITY,** University Galleries, 1000 17th Ave N, 37208-3051. Tel 615-329-8720; FAX 615-329-8711; *Dir* Kevin Grogan

Open Tues - Fri 10 AM - 5 PM, Sat & Sun 1 - 5 PM; cl Mon & university holidays. Admis voluntary donation. Estab 1949 as an educ resource center for the Fisk & Nashville communities & for the promotion of the visual arts. Van Vechten Gallery houses the library, temporary exhibits & art offices; The Aaron Douglas Gallery in the library houses selections from the permanent collection of African Art. Average Annual Attendance: 24,000

Income: Financed through the university, state appropriations, grants & private donations

Collections: Cyrus Baldridge Drawings; Carl Van Vechten Photographs; Alfred Stieglitz Collection of Modern Art; †Afro-American Collection; European & American prints & drawings; †Traditional African Art Collection

Publications: Fisk Art Report, annually

Activities: Lect open to public, 4-6 vis lectr per year; gallery talks; tours; individual paintings & original objects of art lent to institutions, organizations, community groups; lending collection contains original art work, original prints, paintings, photographs & sculptures; book traveling exhibitions; traveling exhibitions organized & circulated; sales shop sells books & reproductions

L **Florine Stettheimer Library,** 1000 17th Ave N, 37208. Tel 615-329-8720; *Dir* Kevin Grogan

Open Tues - Fri 10 AM - 5 PM, Sat & Sun 1 - 5 PM, cl Mon. Estab 1949. Publications are used by students & instructors for research

Library Holdings: Vols 1100; AV — A-tapes, fs, Kodachromes, lantern slides, motion pictures, slides; Other — Clipping files, exhibition catalogs, original art works, pamphlets, photographs, reproductions

M **GENERAL BOARD OF DISCIPLESHIP, THE UNITED METHODIST CHURCH,** The Upper Room Chapel & Museum, 1908 Grand Ave, PO Box 189, 37212. Tel 615-340-7207; FAX 615-340-7006; *Upper Room Cur* Kathryn Kimball

Open Mon - Fri 8 AM - 4:30 PM. No admis fee, contributions encouraged. Estab 1953 as a religious mus reflecting universal Christianity. Average Annual Attendance: 70,000

Income: Self supporting

Collections: Bibles from 1577; 2/3 Lifesize Woodcarving of da Vinci's Last Supper; †Navtivity Scenes; Ukranian Eggs; Furniture; Illuminated Manuscripts; Oriental rugs; Porcelain

Exhibitions: Woodcarving; Porcelains; Furniture; Manuscripts from 1300-1800s; Paintings-copies from several masterworks of Raphael, da Vinci, Ruebens

Publications: Upper Room Devotional Guide, every 2 months; books; magazines

Activities: Retail store sells books, magazines, slides, post cards of woodcarving

A **TENNESSEE HISTORICAL SOCIETY,** War Memorial Bldg, Ground Flr, 37243. Tel 615-741-8934; FAX 615-741-8937; *Exec Dir* Ann Toplovich
Open Mon - Fri 8 AM - 5 PM, cl national holidays. No admis fee. Estab 1849 to preserve & interpret the history of all Tennesseans. Average Annual Attendance: 700, does not include museum attendance. Mem: 2800; dues John Haywood Society $250, sustaining $50, regular $25; annual meeting in May
Income: Financed by mem dues, grants & gifts
Collections: Art, decorative art & artifacts related to Tennessee culture, history & pre-history The Tennessee State Museum holds the entire collection belonging to the Society in trust
Publications: News in Tennessee History, seasonal, Tennessee Historical Quarterly
Activities: Lect provided, 7 vis lectr per year;; individual painting & original works of art lent; sales shop sells books, magazines & reproductions

M **TENNESSEE STATE MUSEUM,** Polk Cultural Ctr, 505 Deaderick, 37243-1120. Tel 615-741-2692; FAX 615-741-7231; *Exec Dir* Lois Riggins-Ezzell; *Dir Admin* Evadine McMahan; *Dir Coll* Dan Pomeroy; *Dir Spec Projects* Leigh Hendry; *Dir Exhib* Philip Kreger; *Dir Educ* Patricia Rasbury; *Public Relations Mgr* Paulette Fox; *Coordr Tennessee State Museum Foundation* Neil Rausmussen
Open Sun 1 - 5 PM, Tues - Sat 10 AM - 5 PM, cl Mon, Christmas, Easter, Thanksgiving, New Year's Day. Estab 1937 to preserve & interpret the historical artifacts of Tennessee through mus exhibits & statewide outreach & educational programs. A military history mus in the War Memorial Building depicts Tennessee's involvement in modern wars (Spanish-American to World War II). Exhibits highlight life in Tennessee from early man through 1920. Gallery houses changing art & history exhibits. Maintains small reference library. Average Annual Attendance: 200,000. Mem: 1500; dues $20 & up
Income: Financed by state appropriation
Purchases: Tennessee related early 19th century paintings & prints; 19th century Tennessee made silver; 19th century Tennessee made firearms
Collections: Objects relating to Tennessee history from pre-historic times to the present, Tennessee Historical Society; portraits & paintings of & by prominent Tennesseans; contemporary Tennessee related artists works
Publications: Exhibition catalogues; quarterly newsletter
Activities: Docent training; exten dept serving statewide; individual paintings & original objects of art; book traveling exhibitions; originate traveling exhibitions; museum shop sells books, Tennessee crafts, items relating to the collection; junior museum
L **Library,** 505 Deaderick, 37219. Tel 615-741-2692; FAX 615-741-7231; *Dir Coll* Dan Pomeroy
Income: Financed by State Appropriation
Library Holdings: Vols 1700; Per subs 15; AV — Slides, v-tapes; Other — Exhibition catalogs, pamphlets, photographs
Special Subjects: American Indian Art, Ceramics, Coins & Medals, Costume Design & Construction, Crafts, Decorative Arts, Dolls, Flasks & Bottles, Folk Art, Glass, Handicrafts, Historical Material, Jewelry, Laces, Painting - American

C **UNITED STATES TOBACCO MANUFACTURING COMPANY INC,** Museum of Tobacco Art History, 800 Harrison St, 37203. Tel 615-271-2349; FAX 615-271-2285; *Museum Cur* David Wright
Open Mon - Sat 9 AM - 4 PM. Estab 1982 to preserve & dipslay art objects related to tobacco history. Outstanding collection of tobacco-related antiques including Meerschaum pipes, tobacco containers, snuff boxes, cigar store figures, advertising art, antique pipes from America, Europe, Africa & Asia. Average Annual Attendance: 15,000
Income: Financed by Corporate Mus
Purchases: Corporate Museum
Collections: †Advertising Art; Antique Pipes; Cigar Store Figures; †Tobacco Containers
Exhibitions: Meerschaum Masterpieces: The Premiere Art of Pipes
Activities: Tours; original objects of art lent to museums; book traveling exhibitions 1 per year; sales shop sells books, prints, reproductions

M **VANDERBILT UNIVERSITY,** Fine Arts Gallery, 23rd & West End Ave, PO Box 1801 B, 37235. Tel 615-322-0605; FAX 615-343-1382; *Dir* Joseph S Mella; *Asst Art Cur* Kathryn M Hannen
Open Mon - Fri 1 - 4 PM; Sat & Sun 1 - 5 PM, cl holidays and some university vacations. No admis fee. Estab collection 1956, gallery 1961, to provide exhibitions for the university & Nashville communities, & original art works for study by Vanderbilt students. The gallery is housed in the Old Gym, built in 1880 & listed in the National Register of Historic Places
Income: Financed by university resources
Collections: Herman D Doochin Collection of Asian Art; Anna C Hoyt Collection of Old Master Prints; former Peabody College Art Collection including Kress Study Collection of Italian Renaissance Paintings; Harold P Stern Collection of Oriental Art; †Vanderbilt Collection of Western, Eastern, Ancient & Modern Cultures
Activities: Individual paintings & original objects of art lent to museums & galleries; book traveling exhibitions 2-3 per year; originate traveling exhibitions
L **Arts Library,** 419 21st Ave S, 37203. Tel 615-322-6284; Elec Mail boyer@library.vanderbilt.edu. *Librn* Yvonne Boyer
Library Holdings: Vols 55,000; Per subs 300; Micro — Fiche, reels; AV — Fs, motion pictures; Other — Clipping files, exhibition catalogs, pamphlets, reproductions 6000
Special Subjects: Afro-American Art, American Indian Art, American Western Art, Anthropology, Archaeology, Decorative Arts, Ethnology, Folk Art, History of Art & Archaeology, Landscape Architecture, British 18th & 19th century landscape painting & the Norwich School

A **VISUAL ARTS ALLIANCE OF NASHVILLE,** PO Box 40244, 37204-0244. Tel 615-321-4966; FAX 615-822-4642; *Dir* Marnie McNamara; *Pres* Joseph Mella; *VPres* Jane Braddock
Estab 1991 to promote visual arts & artists locally, statewide & regionally through educ, exhibitions & advocacy. Average Annual Attendance: 10,000. Mem: 322; dues $20; meeting first Tues each month

Income: $35,000 (financed by mem, grants, donations, fundraising)
Publications: Newsletter
Activities: Classes for children at-risk; lect open to public; competitions with prizes

A **WATKINS INSTITUTE COLLEGE OF ART & DESIGN,** 601 Church St, 37219. Tel 615-242-1851; FAX 615-242-4278; *Dean Academic Affairs* Dr David Hinton; *Art Dir* Madeline Reed
Open Mon - Thurs 9 AM - 9 PM, Fri 9 AM - 1:30 PM, cl Sat & Sun, Christmas, New Years, July 4, Labor Day, Thanksgiving Day. No admis fee. Estab 1885 as an adult educ center for art, interior design, adult evening high school & courses of a general nature
Income: Financed by rent from business property
Collections: All-State Artist Collection (oldest collection of Tennessee art in the state); this is a purchase-award collection of oil, pastels, watercolors, graphics and sculpture; several other collections of lesser value
Exhibitions: Six or eight exhibitions per year
Publications: Art brochure; quarterly catalogue listing courses
Activities: Classes for adults & children; lect open to public, 6-8 vis lectr per year; competitions; individual paintings lent to schools; original objects of art lent; traveling exhibitions organized & circulated
L **Library,** 601 Church St, 37219. Tel 615-242-1851; FAX 615-242-4278; *Librn* Christie Harris
Open 9 AM - 8:30 PM. Estab 1885
Library Holdings: Vols 12,000; Per subs 15; AV — Fs, slides, v-tapes

OAK RIDGE

A **OAK RIDGE ART CENTER,** 201 Badger, PO Box 7005, 37831-7005. Tel 423-482-1441; *Pres* Cleva Marrow; *Dir* Leah Marcum-Estes
Open Tues - Fri 9 AM - 5 PM, Sat - Mon 1 - 4 PM. No admis fee. Estab 1952 to encourage the appreciation & creation of the visual arts. Two galleries house temporary exhibitions & permanent collection exhibitions, one rental gallery, classrooms & library. Average Annual Attendance: 50,000. Mem: 500; dues $25; meetings 2nd Mon of month
Income: $30,000 (financed by mem)
Collections: †The Mary & Alden Gomez Collection; Contemporary Regional Works; European Post World War II
Exhibitions: Open Show, Juried Competition (all media)
Publications: Vison, monthly bulletin
Activities: Classes for adults & children; docent training; forums; workshops; lect open to public, 6-8 vis lectr per year; recorded concerts; gallery talks; tours; competitions with awards; scholarships offered; individual paintings & original objects of art rented to individuals & businesses on semi-annual basis; lending collection contains original art works, VCR tapes, 2000 books & 1000 slides; sales shop sells original art
L **Library,** 201 Badger Rd, PO Box 7005, 37831-7005. Tel 423-482-1441; *Dir* Leah Marcum-Estes
Open to members for lending & reference
Library Holdings: Vols 2000; AV — A-tapes, fs, slides, v-tapes; Other — Exhibition catalogs, memorabilia, original art works
Special Subjects: Pottery
Publications: Monthly newsletter

SEWANEE

M **UNIVERSITY OF THE SOUTH,** University Gallery, 735 University Ave, 37375. Tel 615-598-1384; FAX 615-598-1145; *Gallery Dir* Steven Michael Vroom
Open Tues - Sun Noon - 5 PM, cl holidays & non-university sessions. No admis fee. Estab 1938 to provide exhibits of broad scope to coincide with art classes. One large space with balcony, one main entry door, carpeted walls, trac lighting. Average Annual Attendance: 3000-5000
Exhibitions: Monthly exhibitions during school year, 3 per semester; changing shows
Activities: Lect open to public, 1 - 3 vis lectr per year; gallery talks; tours; Individual paintings & original objects of art lent to professors & administration

TEXAS

ABILENE

M **MCMURRY UNIVERSITY,** Ryan Fine Arts Center, Sayles Blvd, PO Box 8, 79697. Tel 915-691-6310, 691-6200; *Dept Chmn & Gallery Dir* Kathy Walker-Millar
Open Mon - Fri 8 AM - 5 PM, cl Sat & Sun. No admis fee. Estab 1970 when building was completed. Large room overlooking larger sculpture garden. Average Annual Attendance: 2500
Income: Financed by college art budget
Collections: Artists represented include Picasso, Adolph Dehn, Frelander
Exhibitions: Lynn Lown: Photography; Beth Thomas: Ceramics; Beatrice Proctor: Paintings & Watercolors
Publications: Art Through the Ages (color reproductions & slides to accompany text)
Activities: Classes for adults; lect open to public; gallery talks; competitions; individual paintings & original objects of art lent to college offices

M **MUSEUMS OF ABILENE, INC,** 102 Cypress, 79601. Tel 915-673-4587; FAX 915-675-5993; *Exec Dir* John Collins; *Develop Dir* Mary Gill; *Cur Exhib & Coll* Jana Hallmark Smith; *Cur Edu* Annette Musgrave
Open Tues - Sat 10 AM - 5 PM, Thurs 10 AM - 8:30 PM, cl Mon. Admis adults

$2, children $1. Estab 1937 as an art & history educ institution. Contemporary, neutral spaces. Average Annual Attendance: 48,000. Mem: 1200; dues $40 & up
Income: Financed by mem, grants, fund-raising events & sponsors
Collections: †American Paintings & Prints; †Local History; †T&P Railway Collection
Exhibitions: Regular schedule of temporary & long-term exhibitions, including contemporary art
Publications: Annual report; brochures; quarterly newsletter
Activities: Classes for adults & children; docent training; lect open to public, 2-5 vis lectr per year; gallery talks; tours; competition with prizes; individual paintings & original works of art lent to other museums; lending collection contains original art works, original prints, paintings, photographs, sculptures, slides; book traveling exhibitions 2-3 per year; museum shop sells books, magazines, reproductions, prints, slides, games, toys, crafts, note cards & decorative arts

ALBANY

M **OLD JAIL ART CENTER,** Rte 1, Box 1, 76430. Tel 915-762-2269; FAX 915-762-2260; Elec Mail ojac@camalott.com. *Chair* Glenn Picquet; *VChair* Pat Jones; *Treas* James H Cotter; *Registrar* Wilma Jo Mitchell
Open Tues - Sat 10 AM - 5 PM, Sun 2 - 5 PM. No admis fee. Estab 1980 to collect & display contemporary art of US & Europe. Four galleries in old 1877 jail. 8 additional galleries plus Stasney Center for Educ. Courtyard for outdoor sculpture. Average Annual Attendance: 30,000. Mem: 636; dues $25; annual meetings in Fall
Income: $200,000
Collections: Antique Furniture & Pre-Columbian; Sculpture; †Paintings & graphics; Photography; †Oriental pottery & Chinese tomb figures
Exhibitions: Paintings from the Permanent collection; Terra Cotta tomb figures - the Tang collection; The Cross: The Bill Bomar Collection of Crosses
Publications: Exhibit catalogs; The Art Record, newsletter, bi-annual
Activities: Classes for adults & children; dramatic programs; docent training; lect for members only, 2 vis lectr per year; scholarships offered; individual paintings & original objects of art lent; lending collection contains 400 paintings & some sculpture; book traveling exhibitions annually; originate traveling exhibitions; sales shop sells books, reproductions, notecards, plus other items
L **Green Research Library,** Rte 1, Box 1, 76430. Tel 915-762-2269; *Registrar* Jo Mitchell
Open Tues - Sat 10 AM - 5 PM, Sun 2 - 5 PM. Estab 1984. For reference only
Library Holdings: Vols 2000; Per subs 4
Special Subjects: American Indian Art, American Western Art, Antiquities-Egyptian, Antiquities-Greek, Architecture, Art Education, Art History, Asian Art, Drawings, History of Art & Archaeology, Illustration, Mexican Art, Oriental Art, Photography, Sculpture

AMARILLO

A **AMARILLO ART ASSOCIATION**
Amarillo Art Center, 2200 S Van Buren, PO Box 447, 79178. Tel 806-371-5050; FAX 806-373-9235; *Dir & Cur* Patrick McCracken; *Cur Educ* Mark Morey; *Admin Asst* Jena McFall; *Admin Asst* Jackie R Smith; *Coll Mgr* Reba Jones
Open Tues - Fri 10 AM - 5 PM, Thurs until 9:30 PM, Sat & Sun 1 - 5 PM. No admis fee. Estab 1972 for visual arts. Gallery 100, 90 x 30 ft, atrium area 45 ft; Gallery 200 & 203, 90 x 32 ft, 11 ft ceiling; Gallery 305 & 307, each 32 x 28 ft, 10 ft ceiling. Average Annual Attendance: 60,000. Mem: 1800; dues $50-$5000, family $35, single $25
Income: Financed by mem, college, endowment sponsorship program & exhibition underwriting
Collections: †Contemporary American drawings, paintings, prints & sculpture
Publications: Annual Report; brochures, as needed; Calendar of Events, bimonthly; catalogs on exhibits
Activities: Classes for adults & children; docent training; lectr open to public, 2 vis lectr per year; gallery talks; tours; individual paintings & original objects of art lent to qualified institutions; originate traveling exhibitions; museum shop sells books, original art, reproductions, prints, posters, crafts
L **Library,** 2200 S Van Buren, PO Box 447, 79178. Tel 806-371-5050; FAX 806-373-9235; *Librn* Dru Scamahorn
For reference only
Library Holdings: Vols 1500; Per subs 18

ARLINGTON

M **UNIVERSITY OF TEXAS AT ARLINGTON,** Center for Research & Contemporary Arts, 700 W Second St, Rm 335, 76019. Tel 817-272-3110; FAX 817-272-2805; *Dir* Dalton Maroney
Open Mon - Thurs 9 AM - 4 PM, Tues 5 - 9 PM, cl Sat & major holidays. No admis fee. Estab 1975 on completion of Fine Arts Complex. The Gallery serves the entire university; exhibitions are contemporary. Main Gallery is air-cooled, carpeted, fabric wall covered with incandescent light. Average Annual Attendance: 15,000
Income: $56,000 (financed by state appropriation & private gifts)
Collections: Very small collection mainly American & Contemporary
Exhibitions: UTA Art Faculty Exhibit; A Video Invitational, Selected Work by Steiva Vasulka; Bill Viola; & Tom Giebink; A Photo Invitational, Selected Work by Geanna Merola; Gary Monroe; & Lew Thomas; A Small Sculpture Invitational, Selected Work by Nancy Chambers; Thelma Coles; Nick DeVries; Joe Havel; Leslie Leuppe; Randy Long; Marjorie Schick; & Pat Tillman Graduating Art Senior Exhibition; Companeras: An International Exhibition of Contemporary Latina Art; Blood Relatives: Selection of Large Scale Dry Brush Drawings by Ummarid Eltharong; Johann Eyfells & Vignir Johannsson (sculpture); Eric Holt & Darryl Pottorf (sculpture). Modern Metals: Objects of Contemplation; Harmony Hammond: Farm Ghosts (drawings, paintings & prints); Annual Juried All Student Exhibition
Activities: Undergraduate course on museum techniques; lect open to public, 3 vis lectr per year; catalogs on sale

AUSTIN

M **AUSTIN CHILDREN'S MUSEUM,** 1501 W Fifth, 78703. Tel 512-472-2499; FAX 512-472-2499; *Dir* Deborah Edward
Open Wed - Sat 10 AM - 5 PM, Sun Noon - 5 PM. Admis $2.50, children under 2 free. Estab 1983 to provide hands on exhibits & activities for children & families focusing on everyday science & technology & the human body. Offers a variety of hands-on exhibits for children of all ages
Collections: Mexican Folk Art
Exhibitions: City Scape; Looking Lens; Play Scape; Sound Tracks; Studio Stage; Weather; Whole Foods Market

M **AUSTIN MUSEUM OF ART AT LAGUNA GLORIA** (Formerly Laguna Gloria Art Museum), 3809 W 35th St, PO Box 5568, 78703. Tel 512-458-8192; *Chief Exec Officer* Sidney Mallory; *Dir Prog* Judith Sims; *Dir Development* Tara Holley; *Dir Public Information* Laurie Seale; *Dir Admin* Jack Nokes; *Cur* Peter Mears
Open Tues - Sat, 10 AM - 5 PM, Thurs 10 AM - 9 PM, Sun 1 - 5 PM. No admis fee. Three galleries downstairs, one upstairs. Average Annual Attendance: 90,000. Mem: 4000; dues $1000 - $25; annual meeting September
Income: Financed by City of Austin, Fiesta, mem, annual fund, grants, Art School, corporate donations & special events
Special Subjects: 20th Century American Art
Exhibitions: Changing exhibitions of 20th Century American Art, its roots & antecedents
Publications: Calendar, bi-monthly; Estate-Planning, quarterly
Activities: Art School classes for adults & children; cultural & educational programs in conjunction with exhibitions; museum guides program; art after school

M **CITY OF AUSTIN PARKS & RECREATION,** O Henry Museum, 409 E Fifth St, 78701. Tel 512-472-1903; FAX 512-472-7102; *Cur* Valerie Bennett
Open Wed - Sun Noon - 5 PM. No admis fee. Estab 1934 to preserve O Henry's works. The 1891 historic home of the famous short story writer. The home exhibits artifacts & memorabilia relating to the author. Average Annual Attendance: 10,000. Mem: 30; dues $25; annual meeting in Jan
Income: $62,000 (financed by mem, city appropriations & programs)
Activities: Classes for adults & children; lect open both to members only & to public, 1 vis lectr per year; book traveling exhibitions 1 per year; originate traveling exhibitions 1 per year; museum shop sells books

M **CITY OF AUSTIN PARKS & RECREATION DEPARTMENT,** Dougherty Arts Center Gallery, 1110 Barton Springs Rd, 78704. Tel 512-397-1455; FAX 512-397-1460; *Gallery Preparator* Julie Butridge; *Visual Arts Mgr* Martha Peters
Open Mon - Thurs 9 AM - 9:30 PM, Fri 9 AM - 5:30 PM, Sat 10 AM - 2 PM, cl Sun. No admis fee. Estab to preserve & enrich the cultural life of the city. 1800 sq ft of space in a multi-use arts facility available to organizations & artists in the Austin area
Income: Financed by city appropriation
Exhibitions: Rotating schedule presented by local artists & art organizations (all media & subject matter); (1997) Austin Community College Fine Arts Students

A **MEXIC-ARTE MUSEUM,** 419 Congress Ave, PO Box 2632, 78768. Tel 512-480-9373; FAX 512-480-8626; *Exec Dir* Sylvia Orozco
Open Mon - Sat 10 AM - 6 PM. Estab 1984 to help develop the arts by production & presenting high quality exhibits, performances & programs. Average Annual Attendance: 100,000
Collections: Graphic prints from workshop of popular graphics from Mexico; Contemporary art work in all disciplines with a focus on culturally diverse communities
Activities: Children's hands-on activities; panel discussions; lect open to public; gallery talks; awards; original objects of art lent to other arts facilities; lending collection contains 564 photographs; museum shop sells books, magazines, reproductions, folk art

M **ELISABET NEY MUSEUM,** 304 E 44th, 78751. Tel 512-458-2255; FAX 512-472-2174; *Dir* Mary Collins Blackmon
Open Wed - Sat 10 AM - 5 PM, Sun Noon - 5 PM. No admis fee. Estab 1911 to preserve & exhibit the studio & works of German-Texas portrait sculptor, Elisabeth Ney (1833-1907). Administered by the city of Austin. One of five 19th-century American sculpture studios to survive with its contents. Average Annual Attendance: 17,000
Income: $100,000 (financed by city appropriation)
Collections: Portrait sculptures of 19th-century European & Texas notables by Elisabet Ney in plaster & marble, tools, furnishings & personal memorabilia
Activities: Docent training; children's programs; monthly special events; lect; concerts; gallery talks
L **Library,** 304 E 44th, 78751. Tel 512-458-2255; FAX 512-972-2174; *Dir* Mary Collins Blackmon
Open Wed - Sat 10 AM - 5 PM, Sun Noon - 5 PM. Estab 1908 to collect background material on subjects relevant to the museum's history & period. For reference only
Library Holdings: Vols 330; Per subs 7; Letters; AV — Slides; Other — Clipping files, exhibition catalogs, manuscripts, memorabilia, original art works, pamphlets, photographs
Special Subjects: Art Education, Art History, Bronzes, Furniture, Historical Material, Manuscripts, Portraits, Sculpture, 19th Century Sculpture; Elizabet Ney
Exhibitions: A Life in Art; Elizabet Ney in Austin
Publications: SURSUM, collected letters of Elizabet Ney
Activities: Classes for adults & children; dramatic programs; docent training; AV programs; lect open to public, 3-5 vis lectr per year; concerts; gallery talks; tours; exten dept serves Austin area school systems

M **SAINT EDWARD'S UNIVERSITY,** Fine Arts Exhibit Program, 3001 S Congress Ave, 78704. Tel 512-448-8400; FAX 512-448-8492; *Dir* Stan Irvin
Open Mon - Fri 8 AM - 6 PM, Sun 1 - 5 PM. No admis fee. Estab 1961 to present for the university population & general pub a monthly schedule of

exhibits in the visual arts, as a means of orientation toward established & current trends in art styles in terms of their historical-cultural significance & aesthetic value, through teaching exhibitions, artfilms, pub & private collections from distributing & compiling agencies, museums, galleries & artists. Average Annual Attendance: 10,000
Exhibitions: Annual art student & faculty exhibitions
Activities: Classes; lect, 1 vis lectr per year; tours; literature

A **TEXAS FINE ARTS ASSOCIATION,** 3809-B W 35th St, 78703. Tel 512-453-5312; FAX 512-459-4830; *Dir* Sandra Gregor; *Office Mgr* Leslie Cox; *Art on Tour Coordr* Kelly Tankersley; *Develop Asst* Elaine Wolff
Open Mon - Fri 8:30 AM - 5:30 PM. No admis fee. Estab 1911 to promote the growth, development & appreciation of contemporary visual arts & artists in Texas. Average Annual Attendance: 20,000. Mem: 1300; dues $25
Income: $300,000 (financed by endowment, mem, government grants & earned income)
Exhibitions: Two annual national juried survey exhibitions, one of which is New American Talent; an all media exhibition; the 2nd exhibition has a different theme each year; curated exhibitions & an annual exhibition auction
Publications: Exhibition catalogs; quarterly newsletter
Activities: Lect open to public, 3 vis lectr per year; originate traveling exhibitions

M **UMLAUF SCULPTURE GARDEN & MUSEUM,** 605 Robert E Lee Rd, 78704. Tel 512-445-5582; FAX 512-445-5583; *Exec Dir* Nelie Plourde; *Business Mgr* Claire Sarantakes; *Vol Coordr* Ann Herbert
Open Thurs, Sat & Sun 1 - 4:30 PM, Fri 10 AM - 4:30 PM, Sat 10 AM - 4:30 PM (June - Aug). Admis general $2, student $1. Estab 1991 to educate the community to the value of art, specifically sculpture with programs designed to enrich the artistic experience. Average Annual Attendance: 23,000
Income: Financed by endowment, garden rentals for weddings, receptions & parties
Collections: Charles Umlauf Collection (sculptures & drawings); original drawings & paintings; sculptures in exotic woods, terra cotta, cast stone, bronze, alabaster & marble in detailed realism & abstractions
Publications: Garden Grapevine, Newsletter bi-annual
Activities: Classes for children; docent training; sculpture workshops for special needs students; lect open to public, 6-8 vis lectr per year; concerts; gallery talks; tours; original objects of art lent to other museums that fit borrowing criteria; museum shop sells books, postcards, notecards, mugs & t-shirts

UNIVERSITY OF TEXAS AT AUSTIN
L **Fine Arts Library,** Fine Arts Bldg 3-200, 23rd & Trinity, 78713-8916. Tel 512-495-4480, 495-4481; FAX 512-495-4490; Elec Mail marcia@mail.utexas.edu. *Head Librn* Marcia M Parsons; *Art Librn* Laura Schwartz
Open Mon - Thurs 8 AM - 11 PM; Fri 8 AM - 5 PM; Sat 10 AM - 5 PM; Sun 2 - 11 PM. Estab 1948 to support teaching & research in Fine Arts fields including PhD level in art history & to the master's level in art educ & studio art. For lending. Circ 300,000
Income: Financed by state appropriation
Library Holdings: Vols 220,000; Per subs 900; Compact discs 12,000; Micro — Fiche 24,000, reels 4500; AV — A-tapes, cassettes, rec 38,000, v-tapes 900; Other — Exhibition catalogs
M **Archer M Huntington Art Gallery,** College of Fine Arts, 23rd & San Jacinto Sts, 78712-1205. Tel 512-471-7324; FAX 512-471-7023; *Dir* Ms Jessie O Hite; *Dir Public Relations & Develop* Barbara Vejvoda; *Cur Latin American Art* Dr Mari Carmen Ramirez; *Cur Prints & Drawings* Jonathan Bober; *Cur Educ* Susan Sternberg; *Cur Exhib* Patricia Hendricks
Open Mon - Sat 9 AM - 5 PM, Sun 1 - 5 PM. No admis fee. Estab 1963 to serve the students & faculty of the university & the general pub. Galleries in the art building house temporary exhibitions; galleries in the Harry Ransom Center house the permanent collections. Average Annual Attendance: 90,000. Mem: 650; dues $40 & up
Collections: †Greek and Roman art; †19th & 20th century American paintings, including James and Mari Michener Collection of 20th Century American Art and the C R Smith Collection of Western American Painting; contemporary Australian paintings; †20th century Latin American art; †prints and drawings from all periods
Exhibitions: Durer's Engraved Passion; 56th Annual Art Faculty Exhibition. Augustus Vincent Tack: Landscape of the Spirit; Prints & Drawings; Acquisitions, 1993-94; Art Students Exhibition; Print Study Exhibition, spring; Master of Fine Arts Exhibition; The Early Prints of Efvard Munch; 57th Annual Art Faculty Exhibition; Print Study Exhibition. Internaternationalism & Painting in the Sixties: Australia, Latin America & the United States
Publications: Exhibition catalogues; children's publications
Activities: Classes for adults & children; docent training; lect open to public, 5-15 vis lectr per year; concerts; gallery talks; tours; symposia; vis artists; film & video series; scholarships & fels offered; exten dept serves Texas & the region; individual paintings & original objects of art lent to educational exhibiting organizations (universities & college museums); originate traveling exhibitions to other university art museums & city museums; museum shop sells books, reproductions
L **Harry Ransom Humanities Research Center,** 21st & Guadalupe, PO Box 7219, 78713-7219. Tel 512-471-8944; FAX 512-471-9646; Elec Mail info@hrc.utexas.edu. *Dir* Thomas F Staley, PhD; *Assoc Dir* Sally Leach, MLIS; *Registrar* Debra Armstrong Morgan
Open 9 AM - 5 PM. Library estab 1957 for reference only. Average Annual Attendance: 11,000
Income: Financed by endowment, mem, city & state appropriation
Library Holdings: Vols 1,000,000; Other — Manuscripts, photographs, prints
Activities: Docent training; lect open to public, 8 vis lectr per year; gallery talks; tours; scholarships & fels offered; individual paintings & original objects of art lent
L **Architecture & Planning Library,** Battle Hall 200, 78713-8916. Tel 512-495-4620; Internet Home Page Address http://www.lib.utexas.edu/libs/apl/archlib.html. *Head Librn* Janine Henri; *Cur. Architectural Drawings Coll* Beth Dodd
Estab 1925

Library Holdings: Vols 50,000; Per subs 189; Architectural drawings 140,000; Micro — Fiche 7770, reels 405; AV — A-tapes, cassettes, fs, lantern slides, slides 591, v-tapes; Other — Clipping files, exhibition catalogs, manuscripts, memorabilia, original art works, pamphlets, photographs 14,082
Special Subjects: Architecture, Carpets & Rugs, Constructions, Decorative Arts, Drafting, Furniture, Historical Material, Interior Design, Landscape Architecture, Period Rooms, Restoration & Conservation, Stained Glass, Tapestries, City & Regional Planning, Urban Design

A **WOMEN AND THEIR WORK,** 1710 Lavaca, 78701. Tel 512-477-1064; FAX 512-477-1090; *Dir* Chris Cowden; *Operations Mgr* Kim Cook; *Publicity & Gallery Dir* Cynthia Noe
Open Mon - Fri 10 AM - 5 PM, Sat & Sun 1 - 5 PM. Estab 1976 to promote recognition & appreciation of women's art. Average Annual Attendance: 7500. Mem: 175; dues $25
Income: $140,000 (financed by endowment, members, city & state appropriation, private foundations & corporations)
Collections: Ties That Bind: Photography; Cuban Film Posters; Red River Women's Press Posters
Publications: Membership Report, quarterly
Activities: Workshops & symposia; lect open to public, 3-4 vis lectr per year; competitions with awards; book traveling exhibitions; originate traveling exhibitions, circulate to Dallas, Snyder, Houston, Victoria, & San Antonio

BANDERA

M **FRONTIER TIMES MUSEUM,** PO Box 1918, 78003. Tel 210-796-3864; *Pres* Pat D'Spain
Open Mon - Sat 10 AM - 4:30 PM, Sun 1 - 4:30 PM. Admis adults $1.50, children under 12 years $.25 (free when accompanied by teachers). Estab 1933 to preserve records, photographs & artifacts of the American West with emphasis on the local Texas hill country area. Average Annual Attendance: 12,000. Mem: 25; Board of Directors meets 4 times a yr
Income: $20,000 (financed by endowment, $8000 from F B Doane Foundation)
Collections: F B Doane Collection of Western Paintings; Louisa Gordon Collection of Antiques, including bells from around the world; J Marvin Hunter Collection of Photographs, Artifacts, Memorabilia of American West and the Texas Hill Country; Photograph Collection; many rare items
Exhibitions: Artist of the Month
Activities: Tours; museum shop sells books, Indian dolls, arrowheads, bolos & wildlife posters

BEAUMONT

M **ART MUSEUM OF SOUTHEAST TEXAS,** 500 Main St, 77701. Tel 409-832-3432; *Exec Dir* Jeffery York; *Registrar* Margaret Fehrenbacher; *Cur Educ* Cullen Lutz; *Admin Asst* Patsy Brittain; *Public Relations* Camilla Viator
Open Mon - Sat 9 AM - 5 PM, Sun Noon - 5 PM, cl major holidays. No admis fee. Estab 1950 as a non-profit institution to serve the community-through the visual experience & its interpretation as an instrument for educ, cultural enrichment & aesthetic enjoyment. The mus has 2400 sq ft of exhibition space, four galleries. Average Annual Attendance: 65,000. Mem: 820; dues individual $25; annual meeting in Sept
Income: Financed by endowment, mem, city appropriation, Kaleidoscope, grants, mus shop & contributions
Collections: 19th & 20th century American folk art, painting, sculpture, graphics & photography
Publications: Quarterly newsletter
Activities: Classes for adults & children; docent training; lect open to public, 9 vis lectr per year; slide lect; gallery talks; tours; sponsors competitions with awards; scholarships offered; individual paintings & original objects of art lent to other institutions; traveling exhibitions organized & circulated; museum shop sells books, original art & reproductions
L **Library,** 500 Main St, 77701. Tel 409-832-3432; FAX 409-832-8508; *Educ Cur* Cullen Lutz
Open Mon - Fri 10 AM - 5 PM. Open to staff & docents for reference only; oublic for reference only
Library Holdings: Vols 3400; Per subs 6; AV — A-tapes, slides; Other — Exhibition catalogs
Collections: 19th & 20th century American art; videos on various artists, tours of museums throughout the world
Publications: Quarterly newsletter; exhibition catalogs

A **THE ART STUDIO INC,** 720 Franklin, 77701. Tel 409-838-5393; *Dir* Greg Busceme; *Asst Dir* Terri Fox
Open Mon - Fri 10 AM - 5 PM, Sat by appointment. No admis fee. Estab 1983 to provide workspace for area artist/community outreach. One gallery 60 x 30 for exhibitions; one sales gallery; 2-D & 3-D work specializing in ceramics. Mem: 1700; dues $15-$250
Income: $70,000 (financed by mem, individual contributions & private foundations)
Collections: Permanent ceramic collection of local & international artists' work
Publications: Issue
Activities: Classes for adults & children; juvenile & adult probation programs; dramatic programs; lect open to public; concerts; gallery talks; tours; scholarships & fels; exten dept serves Juvenile Probation Dept; artmobile; retail store sells original art

M **BEAUMONT ART LEAGUE,** 2675 Gulf St, 77703. Tel 409-833-4179; *Office Mgr* Sharon Day; *Pres* Robin Adame; *VPres* Dale Miller; *Treas* Sandy Laurette
Open Tues - Fri 10 AM - 4 PM. No admis fee. Estab 1943 to promote fine art through exhibitions & art educ. Two spacious galleries with color corrected lighting & spot lights. Average Annual Attendance: 2500. Mem: 325; dues $10, $20, $30, $35, $60, $100, $500; annual meeting in May
Income: $26,000 (financed by mem, donations & fundraising)
Purchases: Five paintings through purchase awards from juried competition

Collections: Permanent collection of paintings, photography & sculpture (88 pieces)

Exhibitions: Portrait Show; 3-D Show; Neches River Festival Exhibition; Gulf Coast Educators; Photography 1993-Juried Competition Tri-State Plus

Publications: Newletters, 10 per year; class schedules, 4 per year; show entry forms & invitations

Activities: Classes for adults & children; lect open to public, 1-2 vis lectr per year; competitions with awards; lending collection contains books

M **MAMIE MCFADDIN WARD HERITAGE HISTORIC FOUNDATION INC,** 1906 McFaddin Ave, 77701. Tel 409-832-1906; FAX 409-832-3483; *Dir* Bradley C Brooks; *Cur of Coll* Jessica Foy; *Adminr* Matthew White; *Buildings & Grounds Supv* Kenneth Sanderfer

Open Tues - Sat 10 AM - 4 PM, Sun 1 - 4 PM, cl Mon. Admis adults $3, senior citizens $1.50, children under 12 not admitted. Estab 1982 to preserve, publish, exhibit & present knowledge of the period. Historic house mus with original collections of decorative arts of the period 1890-1950 as left by original owners; 17 rooms, 12,800 sq ft wood frame Beaux Arts Colonial Home with carriage house. Average Annual Attendance: 10,000

Income: $700,000 (financed by endowment)

Collections: American-made furniture; Continental European ceramics; Oriental rugs; period glass; period silver & porcelain

Publications: Brochure; souvenir booklet; Viewpoints, quarterly

Activities: Classes for adults; docent training; lect open to public, 4-6 vis lectr per year; museum shop sells magazines, reproductions, prints & slides

L **McFaddin-Ward House,** 1906 McFaddin Ave, 77701. Tel 409-832-1906; FAX 409-832-3483; *Dir* Bradley C Brooks

Open Tues - Sat 10 AM - 4 PM, Sun 1 PM - 4 PM. Admis adults $3. Estab 1982 for staff & docent study. For reference only. Average Annual Attendance: 10,000

Income: Foundation funded

Library Holdings: Vols 700; Per subs 100; AV — A-tapes, slides, v-tapes; Other — Clipping files, memorabilia, pamphlets, photographs

Special Subjects: Decorative arts, 1890-1950

Collections: Decorative arts

Activities: Classes for adults & children; docent training; lect open to public, 3 vis lectr per year; museum shop sells books, magazines, slides

BROWNSVILLE

M **BROWNSVILLE ART LEAGUE MUSEUM,** 230 Neale Dr, 78520. Tel 210-542-0941; *Dir* Gerda Settle; *Office Mgr* Rebecca Welsh

Open Mon - Fri 9:30 AM - 3 PM, Sun 1 - 5 PM, cl Thanksgiving & Christmas. No admis fee, donations requested. Estab 1935, mus opened 1977 to offer cultural advantages to lower Rio Grande Valley. Permanent collection on rotating basis housed in the Clara Ely Gallery, 90 x 14 ft; loan exhibitions & members; work in Octavia Arneson Gallery, a 90 x 26 ft gallery; students work in the Ruth Young McGonigle Gallery. Average Annual Attendance: 3000. Mem: 150; dues $75 family, $60 active; meetings 1st Thurs of each month

Income: Financed by donations

Collections: Paintings by Marc Chagall, H A DeYoung, M Enagnit, William Hogarth, Augustus John, Dale Nichols, Fredric Taubes, Hauward Veal, James McNeil Whistler, N C Wyeth, Milford Zornes

Exhibitions: RGB arts & crafts

Publications: Brush Strokes, six per year

Activities: Classes for adults & children; workshops by vis artists; lect open to public; tours; individual paintings lent to schools; originate traveling exhibitions

CANYON

M **PANHANDLE-PLAINS HISTORICAL SOCIETY MUSEUM,** 2401 Fourth Ave, 79015. Tel 806-656-2244; FAX 806-656-2250; *Dir* Walter R Davis II; *Cur Art* Michael R Grauer

Open Mon - Sat 9 AM - 5 PM, Sun 2 - 6 PM, cl New Years Day, Thanksgiving, Christmas. No admis fee. Estab 1921 to preserve history of the region, including all phases of history, fine arts & natural sciences. Five galleries for American, European, Texas & Frank Reaugh art & changing exhibitions. Average Annual Attendance: 125,000. Mem: 1000; dues contributing $1000, life $500, annual $20, student $10; annual meeting May

Income: $500,000 (financed by state)

Collections: Over 1300 paintings by 19th & early 20th century American Painters; 16th-19th century European painters

Exhibitions: Exhibitions rotate & change

Publications: Panhandle-Plains Historical Review, annually

Activities: Classes for adults & children; dramatic programs; docent training; outreach programs for public schools; lect open to public, 5 vis lectr per year; gallery talks, tours; individual paintings & original objects of art lent to museums only, lending collection includes 1300 paintings; book traveling exhibitions 1 per year; museum shop sells books, reproductions, prints, slides

L **Research Center,** 2401 Fourth Ave, 79015. Tel 806-656-2261; FAX 806-656-2250; *Archivist & Librn* Lisa Shippee Lambert

For reference only

Library Holdings: Vols 2000; Per subs 40; Micro — Cards, fiche, prints, reels; AV — A-tapes, cassettes, Kodachromes, lantern slides, motion pictures, rec, slides, v-tapes; Other — Clipping files, exhibition catalogs, framed reproductions, manuscripts, memorabilia, pamphlets, photographs, reproductions

Special Subjects: American Indian Art, American Western Art, Anthropology, Antiquities-Egyptian, Antiquities-Oriental, Archaeology, Architecture, Art Education, Art History, Carpets & Rugs, Cartoons, Ceramics, Commercial Art, Crafts, Decorative Arts

COLLEGE STATION

M **TEXAS A&M UNIVERSITY,** J Wayne Stark University Center Galleries, PO Box J-3, 77844. Tel 409-845-8501; FAX 409-862-3381; Elec Mail uart@dante.tamu.edu. *Dir Art Exhib* Open; *Registrar Art* Catherine A Hastedt

Open Tues - Fri 9 AM - 8 PM, Sat - Sun Noon - 6 PM. No admis fee. Estab 1974 to bring art exhibits of state & national significance to Texas A & M University

Income: Financed by university funds

Collections: Paintings by Texas artists

Activities: Docent training; lect open to public; gallery talks; tours; individual paintings & original objects of art lent to qualified exhibitors & to publishers for use in books or catalogues

A **Visual Arts Committee,** Memorial Student Ctr, PO Box J-1, 77844-9081. Tel 409-845-9252; *Chmn* Clyde Brown; *Gallery Coordr* Patrick Jones; *Public Relations* Kelly Aceves; *Develop* Carie Jenson; *Finance* Holly Walters; *Cultural Travel* John Brannan

Open daily 9 AM - 8 PM, Sat & Sun 11 AM - 8 PM. No admis fee. Estab 1989. Gallery is 12 x 30 ft with lighting; windows to interior hallway for partial viewing after hours. Mem: 30

Income: Financed by student service fees allotment, donations & art sales

Exhibitions: Annual Juried Student Competition

Publications: Exhibition brochures

Activities: Lect open to public, 1 vis lectr per year; gallery talks; tours; sponsor competitions; book traveling exhibitions 7-8 per year

COLORADO CITY

M **COLORADO CITY HISTORICAL MUSEUM,** 340 E Third St, 79512. Tel 915-728-8285; *Pres* A W Rowe

Open Tues - Sat 2 - 5 PM, cl Mon. No admis fee

Income: Financed by city appropriation

COMMERCE

M **TEXAS A&M UNIVERSITY - COMMERCE** (Formerly East Texas State University), University Gallery, 75429. Tel 903-886-5455; FAX 903-886-5987; Elec Mail linda__west@tamu-commerce.edu. *Dir* Barbara Frey; *Asst Dir* Kay Ellis

Open Mon - Fri Noon - 5 PM. No admis fee. Estab 1979 to provide exhibitions of interest to the University & local community. Gallery 37 x 30 ft; running ft 206, sq ft 1460; track lighting; floor electrical outlets, climate control, security system. Average Annual Attendance: 3000

Income: Financed by state appropriation

Collections: Collection of Student Work

Exhibitions: Annual Department of Art Christmas Sale; Faculty Art Show; Graduating Senior's Show; Roger Lolombik, one person exhibition; The Lotton Exchange, Austin College; The One Show Traveling Exhibition; Rethinking the Natural; Student Art Association Members' Show; Thomas Seawell: Paper & Clay Works; ETSU Student Awards Show; Society of Illustrators Travelling Exhibition; ETSU; ETSU Graduating Seniors Show

Activities: Classes for children; lect open to public, 5-10 vis lectr per year; gallery talks; tours; scholarships offered; individual paintings & original objects of art lent to regional citizens & University facilities

CORPUS CHRISTI

M **ART COMMUNITY CENTER,** Art Center of Corpus Christi, 100 Shoreline, 78401. Tel 512-884-6406; *Dir* Alley Snow; *Admin Asst* Kemper Lengel

Open Tues - Sun 10 AM - 4 PM. No admis fee. Estab 1972 to promote & support local artists. Average Annual Attendance: 7500. Mem: 700; dues $10-$25; annual meeting in June

Income: $75,000 (financed by city appropriation, exhibit fees & sales commissions)

Exhibitions: Monthly exhibits by member groups; Annual Dimension Show; Gulf of Mexico Symposium

Activities: Adult classes; lect open to public; competitions with awards; retail store sells books, prints, original art

M **ART MUSEUM OF SOUTH TEXAS,** 1902 N Shoreline Dr, 78401. Tel 512-884-3844; FAX 512-884-8646; *Dir* William Otton; *Adminr* Marilyn Smith; *Educator* Deborah Fullerton-Ferrigno

Open Tues - Fri 10 AM - 5 PM; Sat & Sun Noon - 5 PM, cl Mon, New Year's, Christmas, Thanksgiving. Admis fee. Estab 1960 as a non-profit organization offering a wide range of programs to the South Texas community in an effort to fulfill its stated purpose to stimulate & encourage the fullest possible understanding & appreciation of the fine arts in all forms with particular interest in the region. A large central area, the Great Hall & a small gallery. The sky-lighted Upper Gallery on the second floor level has over 1900 sq ft of space. Average Annual Attendance: 70,000. Mem: 900; dues $15-$5000

Income: $900,000 (financed by mem, city & state appropriations, school district)

Exhibitions: Rediscovering The Landscape of the Americas; Sarah Campbell Blaffer Found French

Publications: Exhibition catalogs

Activities: Classes for adults & children; docent training; filmstrips; lect open to public, 10 vis lectr per year; concerts; gallery talks; tours; competitions; book traveling exhibitions; museum shop sells books, magazines, original art & artifacts related to exhibits

L **Library,** 1902 N Shoreline Dr, 78401. Tel 512-884-3844; *Cur Educ* Deborah Fullerton-Ferrigno

Open Tues - Fri 10 AM - 5 PM. Estab 1965, to provide reference information for visitors to mus & docent students. For reference only

Income: $2723

Purchases: $2100

Library Holdings: Vols 8000; Per subs 40; AV — A-tapes, cassettes, Kodachromes, slides, v-tapes; Other — Clipping files, exhibition catalogs, pamphlets, photographs, reproductions

Special Subjects: 19th & 20th century American Art History

M BILLIE TRIMBLE CHANDLER ARTS FOUNDATION, Asian Cultures Museum & Educational Center, 1824 N Mesquite St, 78401. Tel 512-993-3963; FAX 512-993-3965; *Exec Dir* Nancy W Stevens; *Educ Dir* Catherine LaCroix
Open Tues - Sat Noon - 6 PM, cl News Years, Easter, Memorial Day, July 4, Labor Day, Thanksgiving & Christmas. Admis adults $4, seniors & military $3, children (5-15) $2.50, children under 5 free. Estab 1973. Exhibits artifacts from Japan, Korea, China, India & Philippines
Income: Financed by private donations & grants
Collections: Buddhist decorative arts; oriental & decorative arts including Hakata dolls, porcelains, metal ware, cloisonne & lacquerware; oriental fan collection
Publications: Quarterly newsletter
Activities: Educ dept; gallery talks; sales shop sells general gift items of Asian origin

M DEL MAR COLLEGE, Joseph A Cain Memorial Art Gallery, 101 Baldwin, 78404-3897. Tel 512-886-1216; FAX 512-886-1511; *Dir* William E Lambert
Open Mon - Thurs 9 AM - 4 PM, Fri 9 AM - Noon. No admis fee. Estab 1932 to teach art & provide exhibition showcase for college & community. Gallery consists of 1750 sq ft plus other smaller areas. Average Annual Attendance: 3300
Income: Financed by state appropriation & private donations
Collections: Purchases from Annual National Drawings and Small Sculpture Show
Exhibitions: 31st Annual Exhibition
Activities: Originate traveling exhibitions

M TEXAS A&M UNIVERSITY-CORPUS CHRISTI, Weil Art Gallery, Ctr for the Arts, 6300 Ocean Dr, 78412. Tel 512-994-2314; FAX 512-994-6097; *Dir* Jim Edwards
Open Mon - Fri, cl school holidays. No admis fee. Estab 1979 to provide high quality art exhibitions to the university & the pub. Average Annual Attendance: 10,000
Income: Financed by private & state funding
Purchases: Corpus Christi Star, Vernon Fisher
Collections: The Lee Goodman Collection
Exhibitions: Contemporary Texas & Mexican Artists
Publications: Exhibition catalogs
Activities: Classes for adults & children; dramatic programs; docent training; lect open to public; gallery talks; tours; scholarships offered; exten dept serves regional & local communities

CORSICANA

L NAVARRO COLLEGE, Gaston T Gooch Library & Learning Resource Center, 3200 W Seventh Ave, 75110-4818. Tel 903-874-6501; FAX 903-874-4636; Elec Mail dbeau@nav.cc.tx.us. *Dir* Dr Darrell Beauchamp
Open Mon - Thurs 8 AM - 9 PM, Fri 8 AM - 5 PM, Sun 5 - 8 PM. No admis fee. Estab 1996 to inform & educate regarding the US Civil War. Open viewing of documents in cases
Income: Financed by endowment
Purchases: $1,000,000
Special Subjects: Advertising Design, American Indian Art, Art History, Commercial Art, Drafting, Historical Material, Intermedia, Woodcarvings
Collections: Samuels Hobbit Collection, woodcarvings; †Pearce Civil War Documents Collection; Reading Indian Artifacts Collection; †Roe & Ralston Law Library, documents
Exhibitions: Civil War Documents & Memorabilia; Native American Artifacts; Woodcarvings of Artist Ludwig Kleninger

DALLAS

A DALLAS HISTORICAL SOCIETY, Hall of State, Fair Park, PO Box 150038, 75315. Tel 214-421-4500; *Dir* Andy Wolber
Open Mon - Sat 9 AM - 5 PM, Sun 1 - 5 PM. No admis fee. Estab 1922 to collect & preserve materials relative to the history of Texas & Dallas. The Hall of State is an example of Art-Deco architecture; exhibition space totals 5000 sq ft. Average Annual Attendance: 130,000. Mem: 2000; dues $50; annual meeting in Apr
Income: Financed by mem & city appropriation
Collections: Texas/Dallas Gallery; Dallas Fashion Gallery
Publications: Dallas Historical Society Register, newsletter quarterly; Dallas Rediscovered: A Photographic Chronicle of Urban Expansion; When Dallas Became a City: Letters of John Milton McCoy, 1870-1881; A Guide to Fair Park, Dallas
Activities: In-class programs; dramatic programs; docent training; summer children's workshops; gallery talks; tours; awards; exten dept; individual & original objects of art lent; book traveling exhibitions 4 per year; originate traveling exhibitions
L Research Center Library, Hall of State, Fair Park, PO Box 150038, 75315. Tel 214-421-4500; *Librn* Gaylon Polatti
For reference only
Library Holdings: Vols 1600; Per subs 20; Archives, pages 2,000,000; Micro — Cards, reels; AV — Cassettes, fs, motion pictures, rec, slides, v-tapes; Other — Clipping files, exhibition catalogs, framed reproductions, memorabilia, original art works, pamphlets, photographs, prints, reproductions, sculpture
Collections: R M Hayes Photographic Collection of Texas Historic Sites; J J Johnson & C E Arnold Photographs of Turn-of-the-Century Dallas; Frank Reaugh Paintings; Allie Tennant Papers; Texas Centennial Papers; WWI & WWII posters; Texas Centennial posters
Exhibitions: All Together; WWI Posters of the Allied Nations; Fair Park Moderne: Art & Architecture of the 1936 Texas Centennial Exposition
Publications: Exhibit catalogs

M DALLAS MUSEUM OF ART, 1717 N Harwood, 75201. Tel 214-922-1200; FAX 214-954-0174; *Dir* Jay Gates; *Assoc Cur American Art* Eleanor Jones; *Cur Textiles* Carol Robbins; *Cur Decorative Arts* Charles Venable; *Assoc Cur Contemporary Art* Annegreth Nill; *Assoc Cur Ancient Art* Dr Anne R

Bromberg; *Publications* Ginger Reeder; *Registrar* Kimberly Bush
Open Tues, Wed & Fri 11 AM - 4 PM, Sat & Sun 11 AM - 5 PM, Thurs 11 AM - 9 PM, cl Mon. No admis fee. Estab 1903 to purchase and borrow works of art from all periods for the aesthetic enjoyment and education of the public. Fifteen galleries for permanent collection; five for temporary exhibition. Average Annual Attendance: 350,000. Mem: 22,000; dues $30 - $10,000; annual meeting May
Income: $7,200,000 (financed by endowment, mem & city appropriation)
Purchases: $1,000,000
Collections: †European and American painting and sculpture; †ancient Mediterranean, Pre-Columbian, African, Oceanic and Japanese art; †decorative arts; †drawings; †prints; American furniture
Publications: Newsletter, bimonthly; annual report; president's newsletter; exhibition catalogs; Dallas Museum of Art Bulletin quarterly
Activities: Classes for adults & children; docent training; lect open to public, 10 vis lectr per year; concerts; gallery talks; tours; exten dept serving Dallas County; artmobile; individual paintings & original objects of art lent to other museums; book traveling exhibitions; originate traveling exhibitions; museum shop sells books, magazines, original art, reproductions, prints and slides
L Mildred R & Frederick M Mayer Library, 1717 N Harwood St, 75201. Tel 214-922-1277; Elec Mail Muatowns@amigos.org. *Head* Allen Townsend; *Cataloger* Catherine Zisk; *Reader Servs Librn* Darin Marshall
For reference only
Income: Financed by city & private endowment
Library Holdings: Vols 25,000; Per subs 105; Artist File; Other — Exhibition catalogs
Special Subjects: Art History, Decorative Arts, African & Contemporary Art

M DALLAS VISUAL ART CENTER, 2917 Swiss Ave, 75204. Tel 214-821-2522; FAX 214-821-9103; *Exec Dir* Katherine Wagner; *Asst Dir* Cheryl Mick; *Admin Coordr* Jen Wu; *Develop Coordr* Allison Moore; *Events Coordr* Charlotte Richardson
Open Mon - Fri 9 AM - 5 PM, Tues 9 AM - 9 PM, Sat Noon - 4 PM. No admis fee. Estab 1981 to provide exhibition, educ & information opportunities for visual arts & art appreciators in North Texas. 5 galleries totalling 24,000 sq ft, large windows, natural light; track lighting; third gallery long uninterrupted auditorium walls with no natural light. Average Annual Attendance: 50,000. Mem: 800; dues $35 & up; mem open to artists & art appreciators
Income: Financed by donations, grants, facility use fees, mem & fundraising
Exhibitions: Annual Critic's Choice Competition; various art exhibitions throughout the year open to the public with both private & public openings
Publications: D-Art Newsletter, monthly; exhibition programs & catalogues
Activities: Classes for adults & children; docent training; lect open to public, 12 vis lectr per year; gallery talks; competitions

L J ERIE JOHNSON LIBRARY (Formerly Dallas Public Library), Fine Arts Division, 1515 Young St, 75201-9987. Tel 214-670-1643; *Div Head* Roger Carroll; *Music Librn* John Elfers; *Art Librn* Ruth Games
Open Mon - Thurs 9 AM - 9 PM; Fri & Sat 9 AM - 5 PM; Sun 1 AM - 5 PM. Estab 1901 to furnish the citizens of Dallas with materials and information concerning the arts
Income: Financed by city appropriation, federal & state aid, Friends of the Library, endowment
Purchases: $84,960
Library Holdings: Vols 52,662; Per subs 500; Micro — Fiche, reels; AV — A-tapes, fs, rec, slides; Other — Clipping files, exhibition catalogs, manuscripts, memorabilia, original art works, pamphlets, photographs, prints, reproductions
Collections: W E Hill Collection (history of American theater); Lawrence Kelly Collection of Dallas Civic Opera Set and Costume Designs; Manuscript Archives (music); Margo Jones Theater Collection; original fine print collection; John Rosenfield Collection (art and music critic); Interstate Theatre Collection; USA Film Festival Files; Local Archival Material in Film, Dance, Theatre & Music

M MIRACLE AT PENTECOST FOUNDATION (Formerly Biblical Arts Center), Biblical Arts Center, 7500 Park Lane, PO Box 12727, 75225. Tel 214-691-4661; FAX 214-691-4752;
Internet Home Page Address www.biblicalarts.org. *Dir* Ronnie L Roese
Open Tues - Sat 10 AM - 5 PM, Sun 1 - 5 PM, cl New Years Day, Thanksgiving, Christmas Eve & Christmas Day. Admis adults $3.75, senior citizens $3, children 6-12 $2, exhibition galleries free. Estab 1966
Collections: Joseph Boggs Beale's Biblical Illustrations; founder's collection of oriental art; Torger Thompson's Miracle at Pentecost painting & Miracle at Pentecost pilot painting
Publications: Books, Creation of a Masterpiece, Videotape, Pentecost: Gift from God
Activities: Educ programs; docent training; tours; individual paintings & original objects of art lent; museum shop sells books, reproductions, prints, slides

A SOCIETY FOR PHOTOGRAPHIC EDUCATION, PO Box 222116, 75222-2116. Tel 817-272-2845; FAX 817-272-2846; *Exec Dir* Lee Hutchins
Estab 1963. Open to all with an interest in photography. Average Annual Attendance: 1000. Mem: 1700; dues $55; annual meeting in Mar
Income: $180,000 (financed by mem)
Exhibitions: Photograph Exhibitions
Publications: Exposure, biannual; SPE Newsletter, quarterly; annual membership directory & resource guide
Activities: Eight regional conferences each fall

SOUTHERN METHODIST UNIVERSITY
L Hamon Arts Library, Owen Arts Ctr, 75275-0356. Tel 214-768-2894; FAX 214-768-1800; *Art Librn* Kathryn A Jackson; *Dir* Tinsley Silcox
Open Mon - Thurs 8 - Midnight, Fri 8 AM - 6 PM, Sat 9 AM - 5 PM, Sun 1 PM - Midnight. No admis fee. Estab to support educational curriculum of art & art history department of university. Open to the pub for reference & research
Library Holdings: Vols 80,000; Per subs 269; Music scores; Micro — Fiche, reels; AV — A-tapes, cassettes, v-tapes 20,000; Other — Exhibition catalogs, pamphlets
Special Subjects: Antiquities-Byzantine, Antiquities-Egyptian, Antiquities-Etruscan, Antiquities-Greek, Antiquities-Roman, Architecture, Art History, Ceramics, Coins & Medals, Costume Design & Construction, Decorative Arts, Etchings & Engravings, Fashion Arts, Film, Folk Art

M **Meadows Museum,** Meadows School of the Arts, Owens Art Center, 75275. Tel 214-768-2614; FAX 214-692-3272; *Dir* John L Lunsford; *Cur Educ* Maria Teresa Garcia; *Registrar* Dan Rockwell; *Asst to Dir* Jack Powers; *Admin Asst* Christine Moore; *Membership & Spec Events* Marilyn Spencer
Open Mon, Tues, Fri & Sat 10 AM - 5 PM, Thurs 10 AM - 8 PM, Sun 1 - 5 PM, cl Wed. Donations accepted. Estab 1965 to preserve & study the art of Spain. Average Annual Attendance: 44,000
Income: Financed by endowment
Collections: Paintings: Fernando Yanez de la Almedina (active 1505-1531); Saint Sebastian (1506); Juan de Borgona (active 1508-1514); Juan Carreno de Miranda (1614-1685); The Flaying of Saint Bartholomew (1666); Bartolome Esteban Murillo (1618-1682); The Immaculate Conception (ca 1655); Jacob Laying the Peeled Rods Before the Flocks of Laban (ca 1665); Jusepe de Ribera (1591-1652); Portrait of a Knight of Santiago (ca 1630-40); Diego Rodriguez de Silva y Velazquez (1599-1660); Sibyl With Tabula Rasa (ca 1644-1648); Francisco de Goya (1746-1828); The Madhouse at Saragossa (1794); Joan Miro (1893-1983); Queen Louise of Prussia (1929); Pablo Picasso (1881-1973); Still Life in a Landscape (1915); Antoni Tapies Grand Noir (Great Black Relief) (1973); Sculpture: Alejo de Vahia (active ca 1480-1510); Pieta (1490-1510); Juan Martinez Montanes (1568-1649); Saint John the Baptist (ca 1630-1635); Anonymous (Follower of Pedro de Mena); Saint Anthony of Padua Holding the Christ Child (ca 1700)
Exhibitions: (1997) Jerry Bywaters: A Force in Texas Art
Publications: Exhibition Catalogue
Activities: Classes for children; docent training; outreach program; lect open to public; concerts; tours; gallery talks; internships & apprenticeships offered; individual paintings & original objects of art lent to other museums & galleries in US & Europe for scholarly exhibitions; traveling exhibitions organized & circulated; sales shop sells slides, catalogs & postcards

C **THE SOUTHLAND CORPORATION,** Art Collection, 2711 N Haskell, PO Box 711, 75221-0711. Tel 214-828-7434, 828-7011; *Cur* Richard Allen
Collections: 19th & 20th Century Paintings, Sculpture, Photography & Works on Paper

DENTON

M **TEXAS WOMAN'S UNIVERSITY ART GALLERY,** PO Box 425469, 76204. Tel 817-898-2530; FAX 817-898-2496; *Dir* Gary Washmon
Open Mon - Fri 9 AM - 4 PM, Sat & Sun upon request. No admis fee. Fine Arts Building consists of two galleries, each consisting of 3000 sq ft. Average Annual Attendance: 4000
Income: Financed by Art Department & student activities fees
Exhibitions: Departmental galleries have approximately twelve exhibits per school year
Activities: Concerts; gallery talks; tours; competitions with awards; scholarships offered

M **UNIVERSITY OF NORTH TEXAS,** Art Gallery, Art Bldg, Mulberry at Welch, PO Box 5098, 76203-5098. Tel 817-565-4316; FAX 817-565-4717; *Gallery Dir* Diana Block
Open Mon & Tues Noon - 8 PM, Wed - Sat Noon - 5 PM, cl Thanksgiving. No admis fee. Estab 1960 as a teaching gallery directed to students of University of North Texas, the Denton Community & Dallas/Fort Worth area. The gallery covers 193 running ft of exhibition wall sapce, approx 10 ft high, which may be divided into smaller spaces by the use of semi-permanent portable walls; the floor is carpeted-terrazzo. Average Annual Attendance: 10,000
Income: Financed by state appropriation
Collections: †Voertman Collection (student purchases); †permanent collection
Exhibitions: (1997) Xenology: Immigrant Instruments works by Krzysztof Wodiczko; Chris Marker Films; Annual Voertman Student Competition; Suiting the Modern Woman
Publications: Exhibition announcements
Activities: Lect open to public, 4-8 vis lectr per year; tours; competitions; individual paintings & original objects of art lent to the university offices; originate traveling exhibitions to other universities & museums

L **Visual Resources Collection,** School of Visual Arts, 76203. Tel 817-565-4019; Elec Mail graham@art.unt.edu. *Visual Resources Cur* Ann Graham
Open during school term Mon - Fri 7:45 AM - 9 PM. Estab to provide art slides for instruction. For reference only
Income: Financed by state taxes
Purchases: $6000
Library Holdings: Interactive CD 25; Laserdiscs 10; AV — Cassettes, fs, lantern slides, slides 110,000, v-tapes 200

L **Willis Library,** PO Box 5188, 76203-5188. Tel 817-565-3245; FAX 817-565-2599; *Dir* Donald Grose
Open Mon - Thurs 7:30 AM - midnight; Fri 7:30 AM - 9 PM; Sat 9 AM - 9 PM, Sun 1 PM - midnight. Estab 1903 to support the academic programs & faculty & student research
Income: Financed by state appropriation
Library Holdings: Vols 50,000; Per subs 186; AV — Fs, motion pictures, slides; Other — Exhibition catalogs
Special Subjects: Advertising Design, Art Education, Art History, Fashion Design, Medieval - 20th Century Art
Collections: Art auction sales catalogs & information

EDINBURG

M **HIDALGO COUNTY HISTORICAL MUSEUM,** 121 E McIntrye, 78539. Tel 210-383-6911; FAX 210-381-8518; *Exec Dir* Mrs Shan Rankin; *Asst Dir & Cur Exhibits* Tom Fort; *Cur Archaeology & Coll* David Mycue; *Develop* Lynne Beeching; *Educ* Oliver Franklin; *Public Relations* Jackie Nirenberg
Open 9 AM - 5 PM. Admis $1, $.25. Estab 1967. Average Annual Attendance: 15,000. Mem: 500; dues $20-$1000
Income: $280,000 (financed by endowment, mem, county & city appropriation, fundraising)

Purchases: $450,000 (building)
Exhibitions: Regional Emphasis: Early Spanish Settlement; Mexican American War; Civil War; Ranching; Steamboat Era; Bandit Wars; Hanging Tower; Early Agriculture; Home Front; World War II
Publications: Exhibition catalogs
Activities: Children's classes; docent programs; lect open to public, 15-20 vis lectr per year; sales store sells books

EL PASO

M **BRIDGE CENTER FOR CONTEMPORARY ART,** 1112 E Mandell St, 79902. Tel 915-532-6707; FAX 915-532-6746; *Exec Dir* Richard Baron; *Prog Coordr* Mona Pennypacker; *Asst Dir & Educ Coordr* Sandra Troyer-Kern
Estab 1986; incorporated 1987. A multi-disciplinary arts center which focuses only on contemporary leading edge arts. It is the only contemporary arts center within 250 miles of the El Paso/Juarez/Las Cruces area. 4000 sq ft including a window of art exhibition space viewed from outside the building, available to local artists. Average Annual Attendance: 35,000
Exhibitions: Six to ten art exhibitions presented in the Bridge galleries each year
Activities: Classes for adults & children; senior citizen programs; Arts in the Schools Program; Gang-Intervention visual arts workshops; lect open to public; ongoing reading series-Puente Negro Series & Regional Reading Series; sales shop sells regional books, gifts & independent press

M **EL PASO MUSEUM OF ART,** 1211 Montana, 79902-5588. Tel 915-541-4040; FAX 915-533-5688; *Dir* Becky Duval Reese; *Chief Cur* Stephen Vollmer; *Registrar* Open
Open Tues, Wed, Fri & Sat 9 AM - 5 PM, Thurs 9 AM - 9 PM, Sun 1 - 5 PM, cl Mon. No admis fee. Estab 1960 as a cultural & educational institution. Three galleries house a permanent display of the Kress Collection; 4 galleries are used for changing exhibitions. Average Annual Attendance: 80,000. Mem: 700; dues $15-$5000
Income: Financed by mem & city appropriation
Collections: Kress Collection of Renaissance & Baroque Periods; 19th & 20th century American painting; contemporary American & Mexican; Mexican Colonial paintings; works on paper, American & European
Publications: Artline (newsletter), quarterly
Activities: Classes for adults & children; dramatic programs; docent training; lect open to public, 30 vis lectr per year; concerts; gallery talks; tours; individual paintings & original objects of art lent to other museums & institutions on request; book traveling exhibitions 6 per year; originate traveling exhibitions to accredited museums & university galleries; museum shop sells books, magazines, original art, reproductions & prints

L **Library,** 1211 Montana, 79902-5588. Tel 915-541-4040; FAX 915-533-5688; *Dir* Becky Duval Reese; *Cur* Stephen Vollmer; *Cur Educ* Paul Kennedy
Open to the pub & mem for reference only
Library Holdings: Vols 1500; Per subs 8; Micro — Cards; AV — Kodachromes, slides; Other — Exhibition catalogs
Special Subjects: Aesthetics, Afro-American Art, American Indian Art, American Western Art, Art History, Latin American Art, Mexican Art, Painting - American, Painting - European, Painting - Flemish, Painting - French, Painting - German, Painting - Italian, Painting - Spanish, Photography, Contemporary Art, Samuel H Kress Collection, Renaissance Art
Collections: Samuel H Kress Collection

M **Wilderness Park Museum,** 4301 Transmountain Rd, 79999. Tel 915-755-4332; FAX 915-533-5688; *Admin Dir* Carlos Madrigal
Open Tues - Sun 9 AM - 5 PM. No admis fee. Estab 1977 as an archaeological mus to show man's adaptation to a desert environment. Mus contains replica of Olla Cave & Mogollon cliff dwelling. Average Annual Attendance: 27,000
Income: Financed by city appropriation
Collections: Five dioramas depict life styles & climate changes of Paleo Indians including the hunting & gathering era & the Hueco Tanks site; Pre-Columbian (Casas Grandes) & Mogollon archaeological artifacts; Hopi, Apache, Tarahumara artifact collections
Activities: Slide lect demonstrations at schools & civic organizations; lect open to public; book traveling exhibitions annually; sales shop sells books, original art, reproductions, prints & slides

M **UNIVERSITY OF TEXAS AT EL PASO,** Glass Gallery, University Ave at Wiggins Rd, 79968. Tel 915-747-5181; *Dir* Mark Alexander
Open Tues - Fri 10 AM - 4:30 PM, Sat 10 AM - 4 PM. No admis fee. University established 1916, Department of Art established 1940. Average Annual Attendance: 50,000
Income: Financed by city and state appropriation
Collections: The permanent collection reflects the nature & culture of the region
Publications: Exhibition catalogs
Activities: Classes for adults & children; lect open to public, 2-4 gallery talks per year; tours; competitions; extension work offered through university extension service to anyone over high school age; fees vary

FORT WORTH

C **BANK ONE FORT WORTH,** 500 Throckmorton, PO Box 2050, 76102. Tel 817-884-4000; FAX 817-870-2454; *Property Mgr* Lew Massey
Estab 1974 to enhance the pub areas of bank lobby & building; to provide art for offices of individual bank officers. Collection displayed throughout bank building, offices & public space
Collections: Alexander Calder sculpture; more than 400 pieces of drawings, graphics, paintings, prints, sculpture & tapestries, focusing on art of the Southwest, including artists throughout the nation & abroad
Activities: Tours for special groups only; sponsor two art shows annually; provide cash prizes; scholarships offered

M AMON CARTER MUSEUM, 3501 Camp Bowie Blvd, PO Box 2365, 76107. Tel 817-738-1933; FAX 817-377-8523; *Pres* Ruth Carter Stevenson; *Dir* Rick Stewart; *Cur Paintings & Sculpture* Barbara McCandless; *Cur Photographic Coll* Tom Southall; *Registrar* Melissa Thompson; *Public Affairs* Ruth Ann Rugg; *Ed* Nancy Stevens
Open Tues - Sat 10 AM - 5 PM, Sun Noon - 5 PM, cl Mon. No admis fee. Estab 1961 for the study & documentation of nineteenth & early twentieth century American art through permanent collections, exhibitions & publications. Main gallery plus ten smaller galleries. Average Annual Attendance: 160,000
Income: Financed by endowment, grants & contributions
Collections: American paintings & sculpture; print collection; photographs
Publications: Monthly Calendar of Events, bi-annual Program & active publication program in American art & history
Activities: Classes for adults; dramatic programs; docent training; lect open to public, some for members only; concerts; gallery talks; tours; competitions; individual paintings & original objects of art lent to national art museums; lending collection contains original art works, original prints, paintings, photographs & sculpture; book traveling exhibitions 2-3 per year; originate traveling exhibitions to national art museums; museum shop sells books
L Library, 3501 Camp Bowie Blvd, 76107-2062. Tel 817-738-1933; FAX 817-738-4066;
Internet Home Page Address http://www.cartermuseum.org. *Librn* Milan R Hughston; *Asst Librn* Sam Duncan; *Archivist* Paula Stewart
Open Mon - Fri 10 AM - 5 PM. Estab 1961. By appointment only
Library Holdings: Vols 30,000; Per subs 130; Micro — Fiche 100,000, reels 7000; Other — Clipping files, exhibition catalogs, pamphlets
Special Subjects: American Western Art, Bronzes, Drawings, Graphic Arts, Painting - American, Photography, Prints
Collections: Western Americana; exhibition catalogs (including the Knoedler Library on fiche); American art, history & photography; Laura Gilpin Library of photographic books, pamphlets & periodicals; New York Public Library artist files and print files on microfiche

M FORT WORTH ART ASSOCIATION, Modern Art Museum of Fort Worth, 1309 Montgomery, 76107. Tel 817-738-9215; FAX 817-735-1161; *Dir* Marla Price; *Chief Cur* Michael Auping; *Asst to Dir External Affairs* Robert Bowen; *Membership & Spec Events* Suzanne Woo; *Registrar* Andrea Karnes; *Educ Coordr* Ann Farmer; *Librn* Laura Martinez; *Admin Asst to Dir* Amy Riley; *Admin Asst to Cur* Susan Colegrove; *Information Asst* Carri Ann Wantuchowicz; *Assoc Registrar & Asst Cur* Christine Berry; *Head Design & Installation* Tony Wright; *Design & Installation* Bill LeSueur; *Bus Mgr* James B Corser III; *Computer Systems Mgr* Jim Colegrove; *Bookstore Mgr* Francie Allen; *Asst Bookstore Mgr* Keith Lymon; *Educ Coordr* Terri Thornton; *Museum Asst* Sarah Duckett; *Building Engineer* Scott Grant; *Asst Building Engineer* Chris Huls; *Museum Store Mgr* Mary Beth Ebert; *Asst Museum Store Mgr* Lorri Wright; *Sales Assoc* Jessica Brandrup; *Sales Assoc* Jennifer Fridge; *Sales Assoc* Becki Vavrek
Open Tues - Fri 10 AM - 5 PM, Sat 11 AM - 5 PM, Sun Noon - 5 PM, cl Mon & holidays. No admis fee. Estab 1892, the oldest art mus in Texas. Five large galleries on the main floor. Average Annual Attendance: 80,000. Mem: 1200; dues $1000, $100, $25
Income: Financed by mem, city appropriations, grants & private donations
Collections: Works by modern & contemporary masters, notably Picasso, Kandinsky, Still, Rothko, Judd, Marden, Dine, Rauschenberg, Oldenburg, Lichtenstein, Warhol, Hodgkin, Avery, Scully & Motherwell; 20th Century Art from all countries, paintings, sculpture, drawings & prints
Exhibitions: Fay's Fairy Tales: William Wegman's Cinderella & Little Red Riding Hood; Duane Hans on (sculptor); Drawing Rooms: Jonathan Borofsky, Sol Lewitt, Richard Serra; History & Memory: Paintings by Christopher Brown; The Studio Museum in Harlem: 25 Years of African-American Art; Robert Rauschenberg: Sculpture; Howard Hodgkin; Arshile Gorky: The Breakthrough Years; Mark Rothko: Works on Paper; Nancy Graves: A Sculpture Retrospective; Jasper Johns: A Print Retrospective; Ellsworth Kelly: Works on Paper (1997) Kiki Smith
Publications: Bi-monthly calendar
Activities: Classes for adults & children; docent training; lect open to public & for members only, 20 vis lectr per year; gallery talks; tours; originate traveling exhibitions organized & circulated; museum shop sells books, magazines & reproductions
L Library, 1309 Montgomery, 76107. Tel 817-738-9215; FAX 817-735-1161; *Librn* Laura Martinez
Estab 1971 as a reference library for mus staff
Income: $4348 (financed by trust)
Purchases: $4348
Library Holdings: Vols 6000; Per subs 25; Other — Clipping files, exhibition catalogs, pamphlets, photographs
Special Subjects: Afro-American Art, Architecture, Art Education, Art History, Ceramics, Collages, Conceptual Art, Etchings & Engravings, Glass, Intermedia, Landscape Architecture, Landscapes, Metalwork, Mexican Art, Mixed Media, 20th Century Art

L FORT WORTH PUBLIC LIBRARY, Fine Arts Section, 300 Taylor St, 76102. Tel 817-871-7739; FAX 817-871-7734; *Arts Unit Mgr* Thelma Stone; *Librn* Elmer Sackman; *Art Asst* Mary Flowers
Open Mon - Thurs 9 AM - 9 PM, Sat 10 AM - 6 PM, Sun Noon - 6 PM. No admis fee. Estab 1902
Income: Financed by appropriation
Library Holdings: Articles, Books, Music scores, Pamphlets & programs, Sheet music, Special clipped picture files; Micro — Fiche; AV — Cassettes, rec, v-tapes; Other — Clipping files, original art works, pamphlets, photographs, prints
Special Subjects: Bookplates & Bindings, Cartoons, Sheet Music
Collections: Hal Coffman Collection of original political cartoon art; Nancy Taylor Collection of bookplate; historic picture & photograph collection autographed by various celebrities; rare books
Exhibitions: Antiques, crafts, prints, original photographs & original works
Publications: Bibliographies; catalogs; monthly Focus
Activities: Tours

M KIMBELL ART FOUNDATION, Kimbell Art Museum, 3333 Camp Bowie Blvd, 76107. Tel 817-332-8451; FAX 817-877-1264; *Pres* Kay Fortson; *Dir* Dr Edmund P Pillsbury; *Asst Dir Academic Affairs* Nancy Edwards; *Chief Conservator* Claire Barry; *Cur Educ* Linda Powell; *Chief Cur* Joachim Pissarro; *Assoc Dir Admin* Barbara White; *Public Affairs Asst Dir* Wendy Gottlieb; *Asst Dir Marketing & Development* Jo Vecchio; *Registrar* Anne Adams; *Librn* Chia-Chun Shih
Open Tues - Thurs & Sat 10 AM - 5 PM, Fri Noon - 8 PM, Sun Noon - 5 PM, cl Mon, July 4, Thanksgiving, Christmas & New Year's. No admis fee. Open to public 1972 for the collection, preservation, research, publication & public exhibition of art of all periods. Average Annual Attendance: 400,000. Mem: 15,000; dues $30-$500
Income: Financed by endowment
Collections: Highly selective collection of European paintings & sculpture from Renaissance to early 20th century; Mediterranean antiquities; African sculpture; Asian sculpture, paintings & ceramics; Pre-Columbian sculpture & ceramics
Exhibitions: (1997) Georges de La Tour & His World; Monet & the Mediterranean. (1997-98) Treasures of the Tervuren Museum; Qing Porcelain from the Percival David Foundation of Chinese Art. (1998) Renoir's Portraits: Impressions of an Age
Publications: In Pursuit of Quality: The Kimbell Art Museum/An Illustrated History of the Art & Architecture; Light is the Theme: Louis I Kahn & the Kimbell Art Museum; biannual calendar; exhibition catalogues
Activities: Classes for adults & children, hearing impaired & sight impaired; docent training; lect open to public; gallery talks; tours; original objects of art & individual paintings lent to other museums organizing important international loan exhibitions; book traveling exhibitions; originate traveling exhibitions to other museums; museum shop sells books, magazines, reproductions, slides, art related videotapes, puzzles, posters
L Library, 3333 Camp Bowie Blvd, 76107. Tel 817-332-8451; FAX 817-877-1264; *Librn* Chia-Chun Shih
Open Tues - Thurs 10 AM - 5 PM, Fri 1 - 5 PM. Estab 1967 to support museum staff, docents & research in area. For reference use of curatorial staff
Library Holdings: Vols 36,000; Per subs 135; Micro — Fiche 20,500, reels; AV — Motion pictures, slides; Other — Exhibition catalogs
Collections: Western art from ancient to early 20th century, Oriental, Pre-Columbian & African art; Witt Library on microfiche

M SID W RICHARDSON FOUNDATION, Collection of Western Art, 309 Main St, 76102. Tel 817-332-6554; FAX 817-332-8671; *Dir* Jan Brenneman
Open Tues & Wed 10 AM - 5 PM, Thurs & Fri 10 AM - 8 PM, Sat 11 AM - 8 PM, Sun 1 - 5 PM, cl Mon & major holidays. No admis fee. Estab 1982 to enable downtown visitors & workers to view the paintings in a metropolitan setting. Average Annual Attendance: 40,000
Income: Financed by the Sid W Richardson Foundation
Collections: Frederic Remington, Charles M Russell & others (over 100 western art paintings)
Exhibitions: Permanent exhibit of 55 paintings by Frederic Remington & Charles M Russell
Publications: Remington & Russell, The Sid Richardson Collection
Activities: Classes for adults & children; outreach program; gallery talks; tours; museum shop sells books, prints, postcards, note cards & posters

M TEXAS CHRISTIAN UNIVERSITY, Moudy Exhibition Hall, Dept of Art & Art History, Campus Box 298000, 76129. Tel 817-921-7643; FAX 817-921-3703; Elec Mail rwatson@gamma.is.tcu.edu. *Dir* Ronald Watson
Open Mon 11 AM - 6 PM, Tues - Fri 11 AM - 4 PM, Sat & Sun 1 - 4 PM. No admis fee. Estab to present the best art possible to the student body; to show faculty & student work. Gallery consists of one large room, 30 x 40 ft, with additional movable panels. Average Annual Attendance: 10,000
Income: Financed by college funds
Collections: Japanese 18th Century Prints & Drawings; Contemporary Graphics
Exhibitions: Semi-Annual One-Person Retrospective & student exhibitions
Publications: Exhibition notes, mailers & posters
Activities: Classes for adults; lect open to public, 15 vis lectr per year; gallery talks; competitions

M UNIVERSITY OF NORTH TEXAS HEALTH SCIENCE CENTER FORTH WORTH, Atrium Gallery, 3500 Camp Bowie Blvd, 76109-2699. Tel 817-735-2000; *Art Show Coordr* Judy Sager
Open Mon - Fri 8 AM - 5 PM, Sat 9 AM - 5 PM, Sun 1 - 5 PM. Estab 1986 as a non-profit, pub service gallery. Three-story pub service gallery in North Texas featuring international groups like The Sea & works in all media by a variety of artists. Average Annual Attendance: 4000
Income: Financed by state appropriation
Exhibitions: Annual 12-County High School Art Competition; changing monthly exhibits
Activities: Teacher workshops; competitions with prizes

GAINESVILLE

L NORTH CENTRAL TEXAS COLLEGE (Formerly Cooke County College Library), Art Dept, 1525 W California St, 76240. Tel 817-668-7731, Ext 237; FAX 817-668-6049; *Dir Library Servs* Patsy Wilson
Open Mon - Thur 8 AM - 9:30 PM, Fri 8 AM - 4:30 PM, Sun 2 - 5 PM. Estab 1924 to serve the needs of the administration, faculty & students. Circ 500
Purchases: $1500
Library Holdings: Vols 43,000; Per subs 325; Micro — Cards, fiche; AV — A-tapes, cassettes, fs, Kodachromes, lantern slides, motion pictures, rec, slides, v-tapes; Other — Clipping files, pamphlets, prints, reproductions

GALVESTON

L ROSENBERG LIBRARY, 2310 Seally Ave, 77550. Tel 409-763-8854; FAX 409-763-0275; *Exec Dir* Nancy M Smith; *Head Spec Coll* Casey Greene; *Rare Books Librn* Anna Peebler; *Museum Cur* Lise Darst
Open Mon - Sat 9 AM - 5 PM; cl Sun & national holidays. No admis fee. Estab 1904 to provide library services to the people of Galveston, together with lectures, concerts, exhibitions. Library includes the Harris Art Gallery, The James M Lykes Maritime Gallery, The Hutchings Gallery, together with miscellaneous art & historical exhibit galleries & halls. Mem: 800; dues $7.50-$100; annual meeting in Apr
Income: $1,387,480 (financed by endowment, city & state appropriation)
Purchases: $125,778
Library Holdings: Vols 250,000; Per subs 500
Collections: †Contemporary American graphics; †historical artifacts relating to Texas, 15th century to present; Lalique crystal; 19th century American & European paintings & sculptures; 19th century Japanese art; photographic reference collection; †maritime history, maps & charts; incunabula; †Russian icons, 15th - 20th centuries; †works by Texas artists
Exhibitions: Approx 14 per year; numerous one-man shows
Activities: Lect open to public, 5 vis lectr per year; tours; competitions with awards; exten dept serves Galveston County; material available to individuals & organizations; libraries lending collection contains 7071 photographs, 18,527 color reproductions, 708 motion pictures, 311 film strips, 615 framed pictures, 10 sculptures; 3600 items lent in average year; originate traveling exhibitions

HOUSTON

A ART LEAGUE OF HOUSTON, 1953 Montrose Blvd, 77006. Tel 713-523-9530; *Pres* Jon Jenkins; *Exec Dir* Linda Haag Carter
Open Mon - Fri 9 AM - 5 PM, Sat 11 AM - 3 PM. No admis fee. Estab 1948 to promote pub interest in art & the achievements of Houston area artists. Gallery maintained for monthly exhibits. Average Annual Attendance: 7500-10,000. Mem: 700; dues $20-$1000; annual meeting in May/June
Income: $300,000 (financed by grants, mem & fundraising functions)
Exhibitions: Dimension Houston; Membership Exhibits; Student Exhibits; Regional exhibitions
Publications: Annual membership roster; exhibition catalogs; newsletter, 6 times per year
Activities: Classes for adults & children; lect open to public, 6 vis lectr per year; competitions with prizes; workshops, gallery talks; tours; scholarships & fels offered; exten dept for exhibitions & classes for the detainees at Harris County Juvenile Detention Center; individual paintings lent to other art leagues; sales shop sells calendars, craft items, original art, print reproductions

M CONTEMPORARY ARTS MUSEUM, 5216 Montrose, 77006-6598. Tel 713-284-8250; FAX 713-284-8275;
Internet Home Page Address http://riceinfo.rice.edu/projects/cam/. *Dir* Marti Mayo; *Asst Dir* Mike Reed; *Sr Cur* Dana Friis-Hansen; *Assoc Cur* Lynn Herbert; *Registrar* Terry Andrews; *Public Relations Dir* Susan Schmaeling
Open Tues, Wed, Fri & Sat 10 AM - 5 PM, Thurs 10 AM - 9 PM, Sun Noon - 5 PM. No admis fee. Estab 1948 to provide a forum for art with an emphasis on the visual arts of the present & recent past, to document new directions in art through changing exhibitions & publications, to engage the public in a lively dialogue with today's art & to encourage a greater understanding of contemporary art through educational programs. One large gallery of 10,500 sq ft and a smaller gallery of 1500 sq ft. Average Annual Attendance: 40,000. Mem: 1800; dues $30 or more
Income: $1,300,000
Exhibitions: Agnes Martin; Liz Phillipps; Works by Lorna Simpson; Robin Utterback: Paintings 1989-92; Meg Webster: Garden & Sculpture; Krzysztof Wodiczko: Public Address; On The Road: Selections from the Permanent Collection of the Museum of Contemporary Art, San Diego; 3-D Rupture. Pieter Laurens Mol. Elvis & Marilyn: 2 x Immortal; Art Guys: Schmart Guys
Publications: Exhibition catalogs; quarterly calendar; annual report
Activities: Classes for adults & children; lect open to public, 5-6 vis lectr per year; gallery talks; tours; museum shop sells books, magazines & prints

M DIVERSE WORKS, 1117 E Freeway, 77002. Tel 713-223-8346; FAX 713-223-4608; Elec Mail info@diverseworks.org. *Exec Dir* Emily Todd; *Performing Arts Dir* Loris Bradley; *Coordr* Jennifer King
Open Wed - Sat Noon - 6 PM. No admis fee. Estab 1983 to present work by contemporary artists working in all arts media & residencies. Average Annual Attendance: 30,000
Income: $450,000 (financed by individual & foundation contributions, federal & city funds, earned income)
Exhibitions: 10-15 exhibitions a year of Texas & National Artists; 40 exhibitions per year of dance, music, performance & theatre
Activities: Lect open to public, 20 vis lectr per year; concerts; tours

M HOUSTON BAPTIST UNIVERSITY, Museum of American Architecture and Decorative Arts, 7502 Fondren Rd, 77074. Tel 713-995-3311; *Dir* Lynn Miller
Open Tues - Fri 10 AM - 4 PM, Sun 2 - 5 PM, cl holidays & summer. No admis fee. Estab 1969 to depict social history of Americans & diverse ethnic groups who settled in Texas. Small reference library maintained. Average Annual Attendance: 9000. Mem: 125; dues $25
Collections: Theo Redwood Blank Doll Collection; Schissler Antique Miniature Furniture Collection; furniture & decorative arts
Activities: Docent training; lect open to public, 2-4 vis lectr per year; tours

A HOUSTON CENTER FOR PHOTOGRAPHY, 1441 W Alabama, 77006. Tel 713-529-4755; FAX 713-529-9298; *Pres* Joan Morgenstern; *Exec Dir* Jean Caslin; *Operations Mgr* Ann Lancaster; *Assoc Dir* Michael G DeVoll; *Coordr Marketing & Development* Linda Renner; *Membership Asst* Adele Horne; *Prog Coordr* Thuy M Tran
Open Wed - Fri 11 AM - 5 PM, Sat - Sun Noon - 5 PM. No admis fee. Estab

1981. Maintains reference library. Mem: 1200; dues $35 & up
Income: $175,000 (financed by endowment, mem, city & state appropriation, NEA & private gifts)
Exhibitions: Windows on Houston, juried competition for Houston area photographers with an exhibition at Houston Intercontinental Airport
Publications: Spot, tri-annual; bi-monthly newsletter
Activities: Classes for adults & children; outreach program; lect open to public; gallery talks; tours; competitions; fels; book traveling exhibitions; originate traveling exhibitions to museums & non-profit galleries

L HOUSTON PUBLIC LIBRARY, Fine Arts & Recreation Dept, 500 McKinney, 77002. Tel 713-236-1313; FAX 713-247-3302; Elec Mail far_dept@jesse.hpl.lib.tx.us. *Mgr, Fine Arts & Recreation* John Harvath; *Asst Mgr* Scott Skelton
Open Mon - Fri 9 AM - 9 PM, Sat 9 AM - 6 PM, Sun 2 - 6 PM. Estab 1848 as a private library for the Houston Lyceum & opened to the pub in 1895. Monthly exhibits, including art shows are spread throughout the Central Library Building. Circ 154,281
Income: Financed by endowment, city appropriation, federal & state aid (LSA & LSCA), Friends of the Library
Purchases: $232,740
Library Holdings: Vols 159,979; Per subs 375; Auction catalogs; Compact discs; Exhibition posters; Portrait file; Sheet music collection; AV — Rec, slides; Other — Clipping files, exhibition catalogs, framed reproductions, pamphlets, reproductions, sculpture
Special Subjects: Decorative Arts, Oriental Art
Activities: Lect open to public; tours; lending collection contains 20,000 printings, photographs, sculpture, compact discs

M MENIL COLLECTION, 1515 Sul Ross, 77006. Tel 713-525-9400; FAX 713-525-9444; *Pres* Dominique De Menil; *Dir* Paul Winkler; *Financial Dir* Miles R Glaser; *Dir Develop* Judith M Gibbs; *Cur* Bertrand Davezac; *Consulting Cur* Walter Hopps; *Assoc Cur* Susan Davidson; *Chief Conservator* Carol Mancusi-Ungaro; *Paper Conservator* Elizabeth Lunning; *Librn* Philip T Heagy; *Registrar* Julia Addison Bakke; *Exhib Coordr* Deborah Brauer
Open Wed - Sun 11 AM - 7 PM. No admis fee. Estab to organize & present art exhibitions. Average Annual Attendance: 175,000
Income: Financed by private foundation
Collections: Antiquities from the Paleolithic to the pre-Christian eras; Art of Africa; Medieval & Byzantine art; Oceanic & Pacific Northwest tribal cultures; 20th century drawings, paintings, photographs, prints & sculpture
Publications: Exhibition catalogues
Activities: Lect open to public; originate traveling exhibitions; museum shop sells books & exhibitions posters

M MIDTOWN ART CENTER, 3414 La Branch, 77004. Tel 713-521-8803; *Dir* Lindi Yeni
Estab 1982 as a multi-cultural, multi-disciplinary art center serving grassroots artists
Exhibitions: Frank Fajardo's Works; local artist exhibitions throughout the year

M MUSEUM OF FINE ARTS, HOUSTON, 1001 Bissonnet, PO Box 6826, 77265. Tel 713-526-1361; FAX 713-639-7399; Telex 77-5232; Cable MUFA HOU. *Dir* Peter C Marzio; *Chmn Board* Alfred C Glassell Jr; *Assoc Dir & Sr Cur* David Warren; *Cur Decorative Arts* Katherine Howe; *Assoc Dir Spec Projects* Janet Landay; *Cur Photo* Anne Tucker; *Cur Bayou Bend* Michael Brown; *Registrar* Charles Carrol; *Asst Cur Africa, Oceania & the Americas* Anne Louise Schaffer; *Assoc Dir Develop* Margaret Skidmore; *Assoc Dir Finance & Admin* Gwen Goffe; *Cur European Art* George Shackelford; *Assoc Cur 20th Century Art* Allison Greene; *Eduction Dir* Beth Schneider; *Cur Prints & Drawings* Barry Walker
Open Tues - Sat 10 AM - 5 PM, Thurs evening until 9 PM, Sun 12:15 - 6 PM. Estab 1924 as an art mus containing works from prehistoric times to the present. Exhibition space totals 75,000 sq ft. Average Annual Attendance: 375,000. Mem: 10,000; dues $35; annual meeting in May
Collections: †African, Oceanic, Pre-Columbian & American Indian art objects; †American & European graphics, paintings & sculpture; †European & American decorative arts including Bayou Bend Collection of American Decorative Arts; major collection of Impressionist & Post-Impressionist paintings; †Medieval & Early Christian work; †Oriental art; †Western Americana; †antiquities; †photography; Lillie & Hugh Roy Cullen Sculpture Garden
Exhibitions: Arms & Armor from the State of Syria; Benin: Royal Art of Africa; Imperial Austria: Treasures of Art; The Lure of Italy; Kenneth Noland: The Concentric Circle Paintings; The Royal Tombs of Sipan, Peru; Two Lives: Georgia O'Keefe & Alfred Stieglitz
Publications: Bulletin, semi-annual; calandar of events, bimonthly; catalogs of exhibitions
Activities: Classes for adults & children; docent training; lect open to public, 25 vis lectr per year; concerts; gallery talks; tours; individual paintings & original objects of art lent to other art institutions; originate traveling exhibitions; museum shop sells books, magazines, prints & slides

L Hirsch Library, 1001 Bissonnet, PO Box 6826, 77265-6826. Tel 713-639-7325; FAX 713-639-7399; Elec Mail hirsch@mfah.org. *Librn* Jeannette Dixon; *Archivist* Lorraine Stuart; *Image Librn* Marty Stein; *Art Reference Librn* Jacqueline Allen; *Library Asst* Jon Evans
Open Tues, Wed & Fri 10 AM - 5 PM, Thur 10 AM - 9 PM, Sat Noon - 5 PM, cl Sun. For reference only. Average Annual Attendance: 7000
Income: Financed by Hirsch Endowment
Library Holdings: Vols 38,000; Per subs 299; Archival Records; Artists' Ephemera Files; Museum Files; Micro — Fiche, reels; AV — Slides, v-tapes; Other — Exhibition catalogs, pamphlets
Special Subjects: Afro-American Art, American Indian Art, Art Education, Art History, Asian Art, Costume Design & Construction, Decorative Arts, Fashion Arts, Film, Furniture, Glass, Gold, History of Art & Archaeology, Jewelry, Latin American Art, Fine Arts
Collections: Costumes

RICE UNIVERSITY
L Alice Pratt Brown Library of Art, Architecture & Music, Fondren Library MS 44, 6100 S Main St, 77005-1892. Tel 713-527-4832, 527-4800; FAX 713-285-5258; *Art Librn* Jet M Prendeville; *Music Librn* Paul Orkiszewski
Open Mon - Thurs 8:30 AM - 11 PM, Fri 8:30 AM - 10 PM, Sat 11 AM - 10 PM, Sun 2 - 11 PM. Estab 1964 combined art, architecture, music collections in the Alice Pratt Brown Library estab 1986
Income: $130,300 (financed by Rice Univ)
Library Holdings: Vols 87,027; Per subs 493; Scores; AV — Cassettes, rec; Other — Exhibition catalogs 6000
Special Subjects: Architecture, Art History, Film, Photography, Classical Archaeology
M Art Gallery, 6100 S Main MS 21 (Mailing add: 77251). Tel 713-527-8011, Ext 3470, 3502, 527-6069 (Gallery); *Dir* Kimberly Davenport; *Coordr* Jaye Anderton
Open Tues - Sat Noon - 5 PM & Thurs til 9 PM during academic yr. No admis fee. Estab 1971 as an extension of the teaching activities in the Department of Art & Art History. Gallery is administered by a member of the faculty. Average Annual Attendance: 8000
Income: $12,000 (financed by Rice University, gifts & grants)
Purchases: Prints, master & contemporary
Collections: African, †Pre-Columbia, †prints, †photos
Exhibitions: Annual Student Exhibition
Publications: Exhibit catalogs
Activities: Lect & panel discussions, symnposia & performances are free & open to public; gallery talks; tours; lending from permanent Rice Art Collection; book traveling exhibitions; originate traveling exhibitions

C TRANSCO ENERGY COMPANY INC, Transco Gallery, 2800 Post Oak Blvd, 77056. Tel 713-439-4401; FAX 713-439-2440; *Admin VPres* T W Spencer; *Art Cur* Sally Sprout
Gallery open Mon - Fri 8 AM - 6 PM. Estab 1974 to enhance atmosphere for employees. Collection displayed within office spaces & hallways; annual amount of art contributions & grants $250,000; suports Mus of Fine Arts, Houston Ballet, Houston Symphony, Grand Opera, Business Committee for the Arts, Pub Library, Pub Television, Combined Arts Corporation Campaign, Houston Business Committee For the Arts & various Houston Cultural Arts Council projects
Purchases: Financed by art budget
Collections: †2000 original works, mostly on paper by living contemporary artists; †American master watercolors including artists: Homer, Sargent, LaFarge, Demuth, Burchfield, Wyeth & Bricher
Publications: Catalog of American Master Watercolors; exhibit catalogs
Activities: Competitions with awards; loans of original prints, drawings & watercolors to non-profit institutions for exhibition purposes may be arranged; book traveling exhibitions to museums in Transco's marketing areas in United States

M UNIVERSITY OF HOUSTON, Sarah Campbell Blaffer Gallery, Entrance 16 off Cullen Blvd, 77204-4891. Tel 713-743-9521; FAX 713-743-9525; *Dir* Don Bacigalupi PhD; *Asst Dir* Nancy Hixon; *Coordr Develop* Ellen Efsic; *Coordr Public Information & Membership* Thuy Tran; *Coordr Educ* Amy Trachtenberg-Patent; *Adminr* Rusty Campbell
Open Tues - Fri 10 AM - 5 PM; Sat - Sun 1 - 5 PM; cl major holidays & between exhibitions. No admis fee. Estab 1973 to present a broad spectrum of visual arts, utilizing the interdisciplinary framework of the University, to the academic community and to the rapidly increasing diverse population of greater Houston. Main gallery is 6000 sq ft, ceiling height varies from 10-25 ft; Mezzanine gallery is 1500 sq ft. Average Annual Attendance: 27,000-40,000
Income: Financed by state appropriation, university, local funds, grants, gifts
Exhibitions: Robert Helm, 1981-1993. Darkness & Light; Student Exhibition; Master of Fine Arts Thesis Exhibition
Publications: Exhibition catalogues
Activities: Outreach school programs; workshops; videos; docent training; lect open to public; concerts; gallery talks; tours; competitions with awards; book traveling exhibitions 4-5 per year; originate traveling exhibitions 1 per year to various art museums; sales shop selling books
L William R Jenkins Architecture & Art Library, 77204-4431. Tel 713-743-2340; *Librn* Margaret Culbertson; *Asst* Yolanda Rodriguez
Open Mon - Thurs 8 AM - 8 PM, Fri 8 AM - 5 PM, Sat 1 - 5 PM. For reference only
Income: Financed by state appropriation
Library Holdings: Vols 65,000; Per subs 230; Micro — Fiche 15,683, reels 182; Other — Pamphlets
Special Subjects: Architecture, Art History, Photography

INGRAM

A HILL COUNTRY ARTS FOUNDATION, Duncan-McAshan Visual Arts Center, Hwy 39, PO Box 176, 78025. Tel 210-367-5121; *Art Dir* Betty Vernon; *Theatre Dir* Susan Balentine
Gallery open Mon - Fri 10 AM - 4 PM, Sat 1 - 4 PM. No admis fee except for special events. Estab 1958 to provide a place for creative activities in the area of visual arts & performing arts; also to provide classes in arts, crafts & drama. Art Gallery maintains a small reference library; 1800 sq ft. Average Annual Attendance: 30,000. Mem: 600; dues $25 & up; annual meeting first Sat in Dec
Income: Financed by endowment, mem, benefit activities, donations & earned income
Collections: 50 pieces contemporary paintings, prints, photographs & sculpture
Exhibitions: The Fifth Annual National Juried Quilt Exhibition; The Ninth Annual Juried Kerrville Art Club Exhibition; Confluence: the 22nd Annual National Juried Painting & Sculpture Exhibition; Youth Art Show; The HCAF Art Faculty Exhibition; Invitational Group Show: Women View Art in Healing; Counterpoint: the 26th Annual National Drawing, Printmaking & Photography Exhibition; Fall Festival of the Arts Gallery Exhibition; Selections from the HCAF Permanent Collection of Art
Publications: Spotlight, quarterly newsletter
Activities: Classes for adults & children; dramatic programs; lect open to public, 1 vis lectr per year; national juried competitions with awards; scholarships offered; sales shop sells books, prints, T-shirts & gifts

IRVING

M IRVING ARTS CENTER, Main Gallery & New Talent Gallery, 333 N MacArthur Blvd, 75062. Tel 972-252-7558; FAX 972-570-4962; Elec Mail iac@airmail.net. *Exec Dir* Richard E Huff; *Cur* Marcie J Inman
Open Mon - Fri 9 AM - 5 PM, Sat 10 AM - 5 PM, Sun 1 - 5 PM. No admis fee. Estab 1990
Income: Financed by hotel/motel occupancy tax
Publications: Artimes, monthly
Activities: Classes for children; lect open to public, 3 vis lectr per year; book traveling exhibitions 2 per year

KERRVILLE

M COWBOY ARTISTS OF AMERICA MUSEUM, 1550 Bandera Hwy, PO Box 1716, 78029. Tel 210-896-2553; FAX 210-896-2556; *Dir* Natalee Nunn
Open Mon - Sat 9 AM - 5 PM, Sun 1 - 5 PM. Admis adults $3, children 6-18 $1. Estab 1983 to display contemporary art of American West. Average Annual Attendance: 45,000. Mem: 1000; dues $30-$10,000
Income: $650,000 (financed by mem dues, contributions, entrance fees & sales in mus shop)
Collections: Western American Realism Art by members of The Cowboy Artists of America
Publications: Visions West: History of the Cowboy Artists Museum, newsletter, quarterly
Activities: Classes for young serious art students; docent programs; lect open to public, 4 vis lectr per year; original objects of art lent to other museums; book traveling exhibitions 2 per year; originate traveling exhibitions; museum shop sells books, magazines, original art, reproductions & prints
L Library, PO Box 1716, 78029. Tel 210-896-2553; FAX 210-896-2556; *Librn* Nan Stover
For reference only
Income: Financed by donations & mem
Library Holdings: Vols 2500; Per subs 10; Micro — Cards; AV — Slides; Other — Clipping files, exhibition catalogs, framed reproductions, manuscripts, memorabilia, original art works, pamphlets, photographs, prints
Special Subjects: American Western Art, Art History, Bronzes, Historical Material, Illustration, Painting - American, Printmaking, Prints, Western Art, History of Range Cattle Industry

KINGSVILLE

M TEXAS A&M UNIVERSITY, Art Gallery, Art Dept, Box 157, 78363. Tel 512-593-2619, 593-2111; *Dir* Dr Richard Scherpereel
Open Mon - Fri 9 AM - 4 PM. No admis fee. Estab to exhibit art work of students, as well as visitors. Average Annual Attendance: 3000
Income: Financed by state appropriations
Exhibitions: Student Art Exhibits

LONGVIEW

M LONGVIEW ART MUSEUM, 102 W College, 75601. Tel 903-753-8103; *Dir* M Shannon Gilliland
Open Tues - Sat 10 AM - 5 PM, Sun 1 - 4 PM. No admis fee. Estab 1970 for the encouragement of art through a program of exhibition of professional quality work, educ & participation of all interested persons. East Gallery 40 x 60 ft, overhead lights; West Gallery smaller but similar; galleries between are rooms that were once a private home, plus two class rooms. Average Annual Attendance: 20,000. Mem: 800; dues patron $500, sponsor $200, contributing $100, family $40; Board of Trustees monthly meetings
Income: Financed by mem & guild projects
Purchases: Contemporary Southwestern artists work
Collections: †Regional Artists Collection formed by purchases from Annual Invitational Exhibitions over the past 35 years; work by contemporary Texas artists
Exhibitions: Permanent collection & 6-8 temporary exhibitions of a variety of art styles & periods
Publications: Exhibition catalogs
Activities: Classes for adults & children; docent training; day at museum with artist in residence for all 4th grade students; graduate course, Art for Elementary Teachers, offered by Univ of Texas-Tyler extension department; lect open to public, 4-6 vis lectr per year; talks; competitions with cash awards; individual paintings & original objects of art lent; lending collection contains books, cassettes, film strips; book traveling exhibitions; originate traveling exhibitions; museum shop sells prints, museum quality crafts & gifts
L Library, 102 W College, 75601. Tel 903-753-8103; *Dir* M Shannon Gilliland
Open Mon - Sat 10 AM - 4 PM, cl holidays. Estab 1970 for the enjoyment of members & pub
Income: Financed by mem, guild fundraising, local & state grants
Library Holdings: Vols 300; AV — V-tapes; Other — Clipping files, exhibition catalogs
Collections: Work by contemporary Texas artists
Exhibitions: Permanent collection & 6-8 temporary exhibitions of a variety of art styles & periods
Publications: Exhibit catalogues
Activities: Classes for adults & children; docent training; day at museum; films & slide shows when available with exhibition

LUBBOCK

A LUBBOCK ART ASSOCIATION, INC, 4215 University Ave, PO Box 93125, 79493-3125. Tel 806-766-75?? *Pres* Conny Martin; *VPres* Deidre Trotter; *Treas* Amy Haggard
Open Mon - Fri 9 AM - 5 PM, Sat & Sun 1 - 5 PM. No admis fee. Estab 1951 to promote art in Lubbock-South Plains. Located in beautiful Municipal Garden & Art Center near arboretum & is 54 x 64 ft. Average Annual Attendance: 100,000. Mem: 200; dues $18; meeting second Thurs every month
Income: Financed by mem
Collections: Regional & nationally known artists; works representing professional quality in graphics, painting, sculpture & crafts
Exhibitions: Classic; Membership show; permanent collection; special one & three-person exhibitions; state level invitationals
Publications: Bi-monthly newsletter
Activities: Workshops for adults; lect open to public, 4 vis lectr per year; gallery talks; competitions with awards; scholarships offered; lending collection contains 1000 books; book traveling exhibitions; originate traveling exhibitions

M TEXAS TECH UNIVERSITY, Museum, Fourth & Indiana Aves, Box 43191, 79409-3191. Tel 806-742-2442; *Exec Dir* Gary Edson; *Assoc Dir Operations* David K Dean; *Registrar* Henry Crawford; *Cur Anthropology* Dr Eileen Johnson; *Cur Clothing & Textile* Mei Wan Campbell; *Cur Natural Science Research Lab* Dr Robert Baker; *Cur Vertebrate Paleontology* Dr Sankar Chatterjee; *Coll Mgr (Sciences)* Stephen Williams; *Coll Mgr (Anthropology)* Nicola Ladkin
Open Main Building Tues - Sat 10 AM - 5 PM, Thurs 10 AM - 8:30 PM, Sun 1 - 5 PM, cl Mon; Ranching Heritage Center Mon - Sat 10 AM - 5 PM, Sun 1 - 5 PM; Moody Planetarium Tues - Fri, Thurs 2 PM - 7:30 PM, Sat & Sun 2 - 3:30 PM. Estab 1929 for pub service, research & teaching. Mus Complex Theme: collect, preserve & interpret knowledge about the Southwest & other regions as related by natural history, heritage & climate. Two permanent galleries for art; five temporary galleries in Main Building. Average Annual Attendance: 200,000. Mem: 2500; dues WTMA $15 & $25, RHA $20; annual meetings WTMA in Feb & RHA in Sept
Income: Financed by state appropriations, West Texas Mus Assoc, Ranching Heritage Assoc; private donations; local, regional, national research grants
Collections: Archaeology; ceramics; contemporary paintings; ethnology; graphics; history
Exhibitions: Fourteen Acre Outdoor Museum of 30 Historic Ranch Structures display history of Southwest ranching; changing exhibitions of art, sciences, photography & history; permanent exhibitions of anthropology, archaeology & history; Paleo/indian aracheological site, Lubbock Lake Landmark
Publications: Museum Digest, quarterly; Ranch Record, quarterly; Museum Journal; Occasional Papers; MuseNews, semi-annual; Museology, annually
Activities: Classes for adults & children; docent training; lect open to public, 10 vis lectr per year; concerts; gallery talks; tours; scholarships offered; individual paintings & original objects of art lent to other museums; book traveling exhibitions 10 per year; originate traveling exhibitions; two museum shops sell books, magazines, reproductions, prints & slides
L Art Dept Visual Resource Center, Box 42081, 79409-2081. Tel 806-742-2887; FAX 806-742-1971; Elec Mail ubprw@ttacs.ttu.edu. *Visual Resource Cur* Philip Worrell
Income: $9000 (financed by State legislature appropriations, private donations & grants)
Library Holdings: Vols 3000; Per subs 50; AV — Fs, slides 80,000, v-tapes; Other — Exhibition catalogs
Special Subjects: Advertising Design, Aesthetics, American Indian Art, American Western Art, Antiquities-Assyrian, Antiquities-Byzantine, Antiquities-Egyptian, Antiquities-Etruscan, Antiquities-Greek, Antiquities-Oriental, Antiquities-Roman, Architecture, Art Education, Art History, Ceramics, Commericial Art, Crafts, Eskimo Art

LUFKIN

A MUSEUM OF EAST TEXAS, 503 N Second St, 75901. Tel 409-639-4434; *Exec Dir* J P McDonald; *Admin Asst* Claudine Lovejoy; *Cur Educ* Christine Hanning
Open Tues - Fri 10 AM - 5 PM, Sun 1 - 5 PM, cl Thanksgiving & Christmas. No admis fee. Estab 1975 by the Lufkin Service League to bring the fine arts to East Texas & to cultivate an interest in regional history. Average Annual Attendance: 12,000. Mem: 500; dues benefactor $5000, guarantor $1000, patron $500, sustainer $250, sponsor $150, family $60, individual $25 & $20
Exhibitions: East Texas Art
Publications: Bi-monthly newsletter
Activities: Classes for adults & children; docent training; trips; film series; lect open to public; gallery talks; tours; competitions with awards; book traveling exhibitions

MARFA

M CHINATI FOUNDATION, One Cavalry Row, PO Box 1135, 79843. Tel 915-729-4362; FAX 915-729-4597; *Dir* Marianne Stockebrand PhD; *Assoc Dir* Rob Weiner; *Acting Adminr* Ellen Moriarty
Open Thurs - Sat 1 - 5 PM. donations. Estab 1986. Average Annual Attendance: 10,000. Mem: 320
Income: $300,000 (financed by mem, grants & donations)
Collections: Carl Andre Collection of poems; John Chamberlain Collection of 23 sculptures; Donald Judd Collection, 100 mill aluminum sculptures & 15 concrete outdoor works; Ilya Kabakov Collection, mixed media installation; Claes Oldenburg Collection of aluminum/fiberglass outdoor work
Exhibitions: Permanent installation: six buildings of work in fluorescent light by Dan Flavin
Publications: Art in the Landscape, 1997; Chinati Foundation Handbook, 1997; Chinati Foundation Newsletter, annual
Activities: Classes for children; docent training; artist residencies; lect open to public, 7 per biennial symposium; sales shop sells books & prints

MARSHALL

M HARRISON COUNTY HISTORICAL MUSEUM, Old Courthouse, Peter Whetstone Sq, 75670. Tel 903-938-2680; *Pres* Martha Robb; *Dir* Open
Open Sun & Mon 1:30 - 5:00 PM, Tues - Sat 9 AM - 5 PM, cl wk before Christmas. Admis adults $2, students $1, children under 6 free, groups of 10 or more half price. Estab 1965, housed in a 1901 courthouse. Average Annual Attendance: 3000. Mem: 475; dues couples $15, individual $10
Income: Financed by mem, donations, admis & endowment
Collections: Cut & Pressed Glass; 400 BC - 1977 Ceramics; Hand-painted China; Historical Material; Religious Artifacts; etchings; jewelry; paintings; porcelains; portraits; Pioneer implements; transportation
Publications: Historical Newsletter, monthly
Activities: Guided tours; genealogical records researched; competitions with awards

M MICHELSON MUSEUM OF ART, 216 N Bolivar, PO Box 8290, 75671. Tel 903-935-9480; FAX 903-935-1974; *Dir* Linda Austin; *Educ Coordr* Laurie Krushenisky
Open Tues - Fri Noon - 5 PM, Sat & Sun 1 - 4 PM, cl Mon & holidays. Admis adults $2, children & groups $1, members free. Estab 1985 to exhibit works of Leo Michelson & special exhibits. Two galleries, one exhibits permanent collection of works by Leo Michelson, second gallery contains traveling exhibits. Average Annual Attendance: 8000. Mem: 400; dues $15 & up
Income: $75,000 (financed by mem, city & state appropriations)
Collections: Leo Michelson, Russian/American 1887 - 1978
Exhibitions: Leo Michelson (1887-1978 Russian/American); Japanese Woodblock Prints: Sweet Briar College; East Texas Fine Arts Association Citation Winners; Texas Watercolor Society 45th Juried Traveling Exhibit; Christmas in Toyland. London Brass Rubbings; Cross Cultural Legacies: An Exhibition of Ten WY'MN Artists; Marshall PTA Cultural Arts School Exhibit Winners; Marshall Schools Faculty Art Exhibit; Hoover Watercolor Society 37th Juried Traveling Exhibit
Activities: Classes for adults & children; docent programs; lect open to public; gallery talks; tours; book traveling exhibitions 4 per year

MCALLEN

M MCALLEN INTERNATIONAL MUSEUM, 1900 Nolana, 78504. Tel 210-682-1564; FAX 210-686-1813; Elec Mail mim@hiline.net. *Exec Dir* Terry R Melton; *Exhib Dir* Vernon G Weckbacher; *Educ Dir* Suzanne E Alvarez; *Public Relations* Berry Fritz; *Cur Colls* Vernon Weckbacher; *Develop Dir* Amy Seitz
Open Tues - Sat 9 AM - 5 PM, Sun 1 - 5 PM, cl holidays. Admis adults $1, students $.25. Estab 1969 to exhibit arts & sciences. One folk art gallery, two for traveling exhibits & a science hall. Maintains reference library. Average Annual Attendance: 65,000. Mem: 800; dues $25 & up
Income: Financed by mem, city appropriation & other funds
Collections: †Local, state & regional artists; †Mexican folk art; 20th century prints - US & European Canton Collection of old European oil paintings; †original prints; natural sciences
Exhibitions: Monsters in the Backyard; That's Life, sculpture & ceramics; continuous traveling exhibits for one to two month duration
Publications: Bulletins & brochures periodically; Newsletter, monthly
Activities: Classes for adults & children; docent training; art & craft demonstrations; lect open to public, 30 vis lectr per year; concerts; gallery talks; tours; competitions; individual paintings & original works of art lent to museums; traveling exhibitions organized & circulated; museum shop sells books, reproductions, prints, slides, museum related science kits
L Library, 1900 Nolana, 78504. Tel 210-682-1564, 682-5661; FAX 210-686-1813; Elec Mail mim@hiline.net. *Cur Colls* Vernon Weckbacher
Open to staff, volunteers & researchers for reference only
Library Holdings: Vols 2100; Per subs 10; AV — Slides; Other — Photographs
Special Subjects: Art Education, Art History, Folk Art, Painting - American, Painting - European, Photography, Pottery, Prints, Textiles, Watercolors, Woodcarvings, Woodcuts

MIAMI

M ROBERTS COUNTY MUSEUM, Hwy 60 E, PO Box 306, 79059. Tel 806-868-3291; *Dir* Cecil Gill; *Cur* Jane Bright
Open Tues - Fri 10 AM - 5 PM, weekends by appointment, cl Mon & holidays. No admis fee. Estab 1979. Average Annual Attendance: 3000
Collections: Locke Collection of Indian artifacts; Mead Collection of mammoth bones & fossils; Historical Museum of early Miami
Activities: Lect open to public; tours; museum shop sells books, shirts, jewelry & keychains

MIDLAND

M MUSEUM OF THE SOUTHWEST, 1705 W Missouri, 79701-6516. Tel 915-683-2882, 570-7770; FAX 915-570-7077; *Dir* Thomas W Jones; *Asst to Dir* Enid Davis; *Planetarium Dir* Steve Schmidt
Open Tues - Sat 10 AM - 5 PM, Sun 2 - 5 PM, cl Mon. No admis fee. Incorporated 1965 as an art & history mus with a separate planetarium providing various science exhibits; children's mus. Average Annual Attendance: 100,000. Mem: 800; dues $20-$1000; board meeting third Wed monthly
Income: Financed by mem, contributions & grants
Collections: †Art & archaeological materials of the Southwest; †Indian art collection; permanent art collection
Exhibitions: The Collection; The Search for Ancient Plainsmen: An Archaeological Experience; Under Starr Skies: Defining the Southwest; (1997) Texas Realists: Contemporary Artists Series Mike Hill (drawings), Kermit Oliver (paintings), David S Gibson (photography), Susan Davidoff (drawings), Richard Wood (paintings); Student Art Festival; Texas Watercolor Society; Texas Abstract: New Painting in the Nineties; Wanderlust: Works by Eight

Contemporary Photographers. (1997-98) Selections from the Mari & James A Michener Collection of Twentieth Century American Paintings
Publications: Annual Report; Museum Bulletin, bimonthly
Activities: Classes for adults & children; docent training; arts & crafts classes; video showings; lect open to public & for members only, 204 vis lectr per year; concerts; gallery talks; tours; individual paintings lent to other museums; book traveling exhibitions 6-8 per year; museum shop sells books, jewelry, gifts & original clothing
L **Library,** 1705 W Missouri, 79701-6516. Tel 915-683-2882; *Planetarium Dir* Steve Schmidt
Open Tues - Sat 10 AM - 5 PM, Sun 2 - 5 PM. No admis fee. Estab 1965. Average Annual Attendance: 20,000. Mem: 795; dues $15-$1000
Income: Financed by foundations, county & private donations
Purchases: Fine arts & cultural anthropology material from the US Southwest
Library Holdings: Vols 400; Per subs 15; Other — Clipping files, exhibition catalogs
Collections: †Southwestern material
Publications: Catalog; quarterly bulletin

NACOGDOCHES

M **STEPHEN F AUSTIN STATE UNIVERSITY,** SFA Gallery, PO Box 13041, 75962. Tel 409-468-1131; FAX 409-468-2938; *Dir* Eloise Adams
Open Tues - Sat Noon - 5 PM, Sun 10 AM - 3 PM. No admis fee. Estab as a teaching gallery & to bring in art from outside this area for our students & the East Texas community. One room approx 56 x 22 ft, plus storage. Average Annual Attendance: 5000
Income: Financed by state educ funds & private contributions
Collections: Student works; Donation of Prints & Mulitiples from Martin Ackerman Foundation
Exhibitions: Art Furniture; Figurative Art from the George Adams Gallery - New York; Bill Hawes/Recent Work; Human Condition; Texas Clay II; Works by Leonard Baskin
Activities: Classes for children; workshops; lect open to public; gallery talks; museum trips; competitions with awards

ODESSA

M **ELLEN NOEL ART MUSEUM OF THE PERMIAN BASIN** (Formerly Art Institute for the Permian Basin), 4909 E University Blvd, 79762-8144. Tel 915-368-7222, 550-3811; FAX 915-368-9226; *Dir* Marilyn Bassinger; *Asst Cur* Letha Hooper; *Office Mgr* Gina Hood
Open Tues - Sat 10 AM - 5 PM, Sun 2 - 5 PM, cl Mon. No admis free. Estab 1985 to increase public awareness & appreciation of art through exposure & education. Average Annual Attendance: 18,000. Mem: 475; dues $25 & up; annual meeting in Apr
Income: $210,000 (financed by mem, grants, donations & fund raisers)
Collections: Jeff Parker Collection of contemporary US paintings & sculpture; Italian contemporary bronzes from the Meadows Foundation
Exhibitions: (1007) L'Ancien Regime, French paintings from the Sarah Campbell Blaffer Foundation Collection
Activities: Classes for adults & children; docent training; gallery walks; workshops; demonstrations; lect open to public, 2-3 vis lectr per year; concerts; competitions; scholarships offered; exten dept; lending collection, contains paintings; museum shop sells art related books, prints, video, stationary & educational toys

M **PRESIDENTIAL MUSEUM,** 622 N Lee, 79761. Tel 915-332-7123; *Exec Dir* Carey Behrends; *Cur* Timothy Hewitt
Open Tues - Sat 10 AM - 5 PM. No admis fee. Estab 1965 & dedicated to the study & understanding of constitutional government & the election process culminating in the Presidency. Average Annual Attendance: 23,000. Mem: 244; dues $500 - $25
Income: Financed by Ector County & Presidential Mus board of trustees
Collections: Campaign memorabilia; original signatures; portraits
Exhibitions: Long-term exhibitions on the presidency & first ladies; special temporary exhibitions
Publications: News & Views, 4 times per yr; library newsletter, 4 times per yr
Activities: Lect open to public, 4 vis lectr per year; concerts; gallery talks; tours; awards; individual paintings & original objects of art lent to qualified museums & other cultural organizations; lending collection includes books, 3-D objects & memorabilia; book traveling exhibitions vary; originate traveling exhibitions to circulate to qualified museums; museum shop sells books, magazines, children's games & toys
L **Library of the Presidents,** 622 N Lee, 79761. Tel 915-332-7123; *Exec Dir* Carey Behrends
For reference only
Library Holdings: Vols 4500; Per subs 15; AV — A-tapes, cassettes, rec, slides, v-tapes; Other — Clipping files, exhibition catalogs, pamphlets
Special Subjects: Cartoons, Coins & Medals, Decorative Arts, Flasks & Bottles, Folk Art, Historical Material, Photography, Restoration & Conservation, Material related to the presidency

ORANGE

M **NELDA C & H J LUTCHER STARK FOUNDATION,** Stark Museum of Art, 712 Green Ave, PO Box 1897, 77630. Tel 409-883-6661; FAX 409-883-3530; *Chmn* Nelda C Stark; *VChmn* Eunice R Benckenstein; *Dir* David Hunt; *Registrar* Jennifer Stafford; *Exhibits Cur* Janis Ziller Becker; *Gift Shop Mgr* Gina Carline; *Rights & Reproductions Coordr* Laura Bowler; *Librn* Nell Horton
Open Wed - Sat 10 AM - 5 PM, Sun 1 - 5 PM. No admis fee. Estab 1978 to preserve & display the Stark collection of art & promote interests in subjects relative to the same through exhibitions, publications & educational programs. Five galleries & lobby, 18,000 sq ft of total exhibition area. Average Annual Attendance: 10,000

Income: Financed by endowment
Collections: Art relating to American West 1830-1965, special emphasis on artist explorers, illustrators & New Mexico artists; Native American Art (Plains, Southwest Northwest Coast, decorative arts, glass)
Publications: Exhibition catalogs
Activities: Museum shop sells books, exhibit catalogs, postcards & prints

PANHANDLE

M **CARSON COUNTY SQUARE HOUSE MUSEUM,** Fifth & Elsie Sts, PO Box 276, 79068. Tel 806-537-3524; FAX 806-537-5628; *Exec Dir* Dr Paul Katz; *Office Mgr* Laquita Hurt; *Registrar* Georgia Lane; *Dir Educ* James Hinkley; *Admin Asst* Sharon Maples
Open Mon - Sat 9 AM - 5 PM, Sun 1 - 5 PM, cl Thanksgiving, Christmas Eve, Christmas & New Years. No admis fee. Estab 1965 as a general mus with art galleries, area & State & National historical displays; Wildlife building & displays; Historic house, listed in National Register of Historic Places. Two enclosed security controlled art galleries, an educ center & art gallery. Average Annual Attendance: 30,000
Income: Financed by endowments, income & pub contributions
Collections: Paintings of area pioneers by Marlin Adams; sculpture & bronze by Jim Thomas, Grant Speed & Keith Christi; Kenneth Wyatt paintings; Ben Carlton Mead & Harold Bugbee paintings; †contemporary Native American art, Native American beadwork, Acoma pottery; costumes; antiques
Exhibitions: (1997) Regional Photographs 1905-1915; Pastel Society; Old Masters from the Sarah Campbell Blaffer Collection; Amarillo Fine Arts Association; Panoramic Photographs of the Panhandle
Publications: A Time To Purpose, county history book; Land of Coronado, coloring book; The Square House Cook Book; Voices of the Square House, poems
Activities: Classes for adults & children; dramatic programs; docent training; lect open to public, 1 vis lectr per year; concerts; gallery talks; tours; museum shop sells books, reproductions, prints & museum related gift items

SAN ANGELO

M **ANGELO STATE UNIVERSITY,** Houston Harte University Center, PO Box 11027, 76909. Tel 915-942-2062; FAX 915-942-2229; *Chmn Art Committee* Shannon Shields; *Dir* Phil Martin; *Program Dir* Rick E Greig
Open Mon - Fri 8 AM - 7:30 PM, Sat & Sun 2 - 5 PM. No admis fee. Estab 1970 to provide entertainment & informal educ for the students, faculty & staff. Gallery is maintained
Income: $3000 (financed by city & state appropriations)
Collections: Wax drawings done by Guy Rowe for illustration of the book In Our Image by Houston Harte
Exhibitions: Historical artifacts; modern drawings; photography; pottery; weaving; children, students and faculty exhibitions
Activities: Lect open to public, 2 vis lectr per year; gallery talks; tours; concerts; dramatic programs; competitions

M **SAN ANGELO ART CLUB,** Helen King Kendall Memorial Art Gallery, * 119 W First St, 76903. Tel 915-653-4405; *Pres* Harlon Dempsey
Open Wed 9:30 AM - 3:30 PM, Sat & Sun 2 - 5 PM. No admis fee. Club estab 1928 & gallery estab 1948 to promote the visual fine arts in San Angelo. Average Annual Attendance: 1500. Mem: 100; dues $20; meeting first Mon each month
Income: $8000 (financed by Memorial Endowment Fund)
Collections: Paintings by George Biddle, Gladys Rockmore Davis, Xavier Gonzales, Iver Rose & Frederick Waugh, Hazel Janick Karl Albert, Joseph Sharp, Willard Metcalf, Robert Woods, Dwight Holmes
Exhibitions: Monthly exhibits from area artists
Publications: Splashes, monthly newsletter
Activities: Classes for adults & children; tours; competitions with awards; individual paintings & original objects of art lent to libraries, churches & businesses

M **SAN ANGELO MUSEUM OF FINE ARTS,** 704 Burgess, PO Box 3092, 76902. Tel 915-658-4084; FAX 915-659-2407; *Pres* Heidi Curry; *VPres* Frank Rose; *Dir* Howard J Taylor; *Asst Dir & Registrar* Valerie C Bluthardt; *Develop Coordr* Samantha Miller; *Children's Art Museum Adminr* Kimberly Herbert
Open Tues - Sat 10 AM - 4 PM, Sun 1 - 4 PM, cl Mon & major holidays. Admis adults $2, students & senior citizens $1, members & children under 6 free. Estab 1981 to provide quality visual arts exhibits & stimulating programs for educational & cultural growth. Mus housed in 1868 Quartermaster building on grounds of Ft Concho. Interior adapted for art mus with 3 lower level galleries & one on the mezzanine. Total exhibition space is 3800 sq ft. Average Annual Attendance: 56,000
Income: $450,000 (financed by endowment, sales & admis
Collections: American crafts (1945-present), particularly ceramic & fiber art; American paintings & sculpture of all eras; Mexican & Mexican-American art of all eras; Selected European, Oriental & African art; Texas art (1942-present)
Exhibitions: San Angelo National Ceramic Competition; Annual Fiber Art Exhibit; Vistas Series Living Texas artists exhibitions
Publications: Exhibit catalogs
Activities: Classes for adults & children; programs; docent training; lect open to public; competitions with awards; exten dept serves 14 counties in W Texas; book traveling exhibitions, 15 per year; originate traveling exhibitions; museum shop sells books, magazines, original art, reproductions, prints, educational toys, paper goods; Children's Art Museum located at 36 E Twohig

SAN ANTONIO

L CENTRAL LIBRARY (Formerly San Antonio Public Library), Dept of Fine Arts, Art, Music & Films Dept, 600 Soledad St, 78205-1208. Tel 210-207-2500; FAX 210-271-9497; *Dir* June Garcia; *Asst Dir* Nancy Gandara; *Dept Head* Mary A Wright
Open Mon - Fri 9 AM - 9 PM, Sat 9 AM - 6 PM. Estab to provide art reference & lending materials to the residents of Bexar County. Art gallery is maintained. Also serves as a major resource center to regional libraries in South Texas
Income: Financed by city, state & federal appropriation
Purchases: $250,000
Library Holdings: Micro — Fiche, reels; AV — A-tapes, cassettes, fs, motion pictures, rec, slides, v-tapes; Other — Clipping files, exhibition catalogs, memorabilia, pamphlets, photographs, reproductions
Exhibitions: Monthly exhibit of local artists work
Activities: Classes for children; dramatic programs; lect open to public, 2 vis lectr per year; concerts; gallery talks; tours; competitions with awards; exten dept; lending collection contains 320,000 books, 400 video cassettes, 10,000 audio cassettes, 15,000 motion pictures; book traveling exhibitions

A CENTRO CULTURAL AZTLAN, 803 Castroville Rd, Ste 402, 78237. Tel 210-432-1896; FAX 210-432-1899; *Exec Dir* Malena Gonzalez-Cid; *Arts Prog Dir* Ramon Vasquez Y Sanchez
Estab 1977 to support & strengthen Chicano/Latino culture & identity. Expression Fine Art Gallery mounts 10 art exhibits per year to showcase visual artists
Exhibitions: Annual Lowrider Car Exhibition
Publications: ViAztlan, quarterly journal of contemporary arts & letters
Activities: Guest lectr; reading recitals

M CONTEMPORARY ART FOR SAN ANTONIO BLUE STAR ART SPACE (Formerly Blue Star Art Space Contemporary Art for San Antonio), 116 Blue Star, 78204. Tel 210-227-6960; FAX 210-229-9412; *Dir* Jeffrey Moore; *Assoc Dir* Heather Edwards; *Admin Asst* Anet Alaniz
Open Wed - Sun Noon - 6 PM. Estab 1986 to advance & celebrate quality contemporary art produced in San Antonio & to present challenging, regional, national & international exhibitions & programs. 11,000 sq ft warehouse. Average Annual Attendance: 12,000
Income: Financed by endowment, mem, city & state grants
Collections: Contemporary multimedia painting, prints, sculpture, photographs
Exhibitions: H X W X Depth
Activities: Educ program for school children; lect open to public; book traveling exhibitions 6 per year

A COPPINI ACADEMY OF FINE ARTS, 115 Melrose Pl, 78212. Tel 210-824-8502; *Pres* Kathy Olsen; *Gallery Mgr* Sally Gatlin
Open Fri & Sun 1 - 5 PM or by appointment. No admis fee. Estab 1945 to foster a better acquaintance & understanding between artists & patrons; to encourage worthy accomplishment in the field of art & to serve as a means of public exhibition for the work of active members. Upstairs gallery donated by founder Dr Pompeo Coppini to the academy for exhibition of works. Mem: 210; dues $20 per annum; annual meeting third Sun of Nov
Income: Financed by mem
Collections: Oil paintings by Rolla Taylor; sculpture by Waldine Tauch & Pompeo Coppini; paintings
Exhibitions: Annual May Garden Show. Monthly changing exhibits in upper gallery by members
Publications: Coppini News Bulletin, monthly newsletter distributed to members
Activities: Educ dept; lect open to public, 6 vis lectr per year; gallery talks; tours; competitions; scholarships offered; individual paintings & original objects of art lent; originate traveling exhibitions
L Library, 115 Melrose Pl, 78212. Tel 210-824-8502; *Pres* Kathy Olsen
Library Holdings: Vols 200; Per subs 50; AV — Slides, v-tapes; Other — Clipping files, original art works, photographs, sculpture

A GUADALUPE CULTURAL ARTS CENTER, 1300 Guadalupe St, 78207. Tel 210-271-3151; *Exec Dir* Pedro A Rodriguez; *Visual Arts Dir* Kathy Vargas; *Xicano Music Prog Dir* Juan Tejeda; *Literature Prog Dir* Byrce Milligan; *Dance Prog Dir* Belinda Menchaca; *Theater Arts Prog Dir* Jorge Pina
Estab 1979, non-profit, multi-disciplinary arts organization dedicated to the development, preservation & promotion of Latino arts & to facilitating a deeper understanding & appreciation of Chicano/Latino & Native American cultures. Center manages the beautifully restored, historic Guadalupe Theatre, a 410 seat, handicapped accessible, multi-purpose facility that houses the Theater Gallery, a large auditorium, a proscenium stage & equipment for theatrical & cinematic presentations
Income: $1,500,000
Exhibitions: Annual Tejano Conjunto Festival; Annual Performing Arts Series; Annual San Antonio Inter-Americas Bookfair. David Zamora Casas (paintings); The Art You Love to Hate (velvet painting by Jennifer Heath); Ninth Annual Juried Women's Art Exhibit; Statewide exhibit in conjunction with Chicano art: Resistance & Affirmation; CARA Exhibit; Attempted Not Known; Student Exhibit; Agnes Chavez; Hecho a Mano/Made by Hand (annual fine arts & crafts market)
Activities: Visual arts program; classes & workshops; creative dramatics classes; dance program; media program

M MARION KOOGLER MCNAY ART MUSEUM, 6000 N New Braunfels Ave, PO Box 6069, 78209-6069. Tel 210-824-5368, 824-5369; FAX 210-824-0218; Internet Home Page Address www.mcnayart.org. *Pres* Tom Semmes; *Dir* William J Chiego; *Cur Educ* Rose M Glennon; *Cur Tobin Theatre Coll & Library* Linda Hardberger; *Coll Mgr* Heather Hornbuckle; *Librn* Ann Jones; *Develop Dir* Dianne Garrett Powell; *Public Relations* Steven Bennett; *Chief Preparator* Edward Hepner; *Controller* Kathann El-A-Min; *Museum Store Mgr* Barbara Bowie; *Dir Emeritus* John P Leeper; *Assoc Cur Prints & Drawings* Lyle Williams
Open Tues - Sat 10 AM - 5 PM, Sun Noon - 5 PM, cl Mon, Jan 1, July 4, Thanksgiving & Christmas. No admis fee, donations appreciated; occasional

charge for temporary exhibits. Estab 1954 for the encouragement & development of modern art. 30,000 vol art history reference library; 23 acres of gardens; 300-seat auditorium; McNay Mus Store; handicap accessibility. Average Annual Attendance: 92,000. Mem: Dues benefactor $5000, sponsor $2500, sustaining patrons $1000, patron $500 sustaining $150, family $60, individual $35
Income: Financed by endowment, mem & private gifts
Collections: Modern art, 19th & 20th century European & American painting, sculpture & graphics; Oppenheimer Collection of late medieval & early Renaissance sculpture & paintings; Southwest religious art & Native American decorative arts; Tobin Theatre Arts Collection related to opera, ballet & musical stage
Exhibitions: (1997) Ruckus Rodeo by Red Grooms; Pop & Beyond: Printmaking Since 1960; Designing for the Top Twenty Operas: Barvissino; Selections from the Mary & Sylvan Collection; Berman: Works in Progress; Joseph Sudek: The Pigment Prints, 1947-1954; Carl Embrey: A Retrospective; The New Stagecraft: Setting an American Style, 1915-1949; Recycling Reality: Surrealist Sculpture; The Nightmare Before Christmas; The Art of Enchantment: Children's Book Illustrators; San Jose & Miz Harrie: Texas Tiles with a Mission; Collectors Gallery XXXI. (1997-98) Small Paintings by Arthur Dove, 1942-43. (1998) Georgia O'Keeffe & Texas
Publications: Annual report; exhibition catalogues & brochures; Impressions, quarterly newsletter
Activities: Docent training; lect open to public, 8 vis lectr per year; concerts; gallery talks; tours; individual paintings & original objects of art lent to other museums; book traveling exhibitions 4 per year; originate traveling exhibitions; museum shop sells books & original art
L Reference Library, 6000 N New Braunfels St, 78209. Tel 210-824-5368; *Librn* Ann Jones
Open to the pub Tues - Sat 10 AM - 5 PM. Estab 1970 as an adjunct to the mus. For reference only. Circ non-circulating
Income: Financed by endowment & gifts
Library Holdings: Vols 30,000; Per subs 224; Micro — Fiche; AV — V-tapes; Other — Clipping files, exhibition catalogs
Special Subjects: Fine Arts

A SAN ANTONIO ART LEAGUE, 130 King Williams St, 78204. Tel 210-223-1140; *Pres* Nancy M Bacon
Open Mon - Fri 10 AM - 4 PM. No admis fee. Estab 1912 as a pub art gallery for San Antonio & for the promotion of a knowledge & interest in art by means of exhibitions. 4 rooms & large hall capable of hanging 150 paintings. Mem: 700; dues $15-$300; meetings monthly Oct - May
Income: Financed by mem & fundraising projects
Collections: Crafts, paintings, prints & sculpture
Exhibitions: 63rd Annual Artist Exhibition
Publications: Exhibiton catalogs; monthly calendar of events
Activities: Educ dept; lect open to public, 3 vis lectr per year; gallery talks; tours; paintings & original art objects lent
L Library, 130 King Williams St, 78204. Tel 210-223-1140; *Pres* Nancy M Bacon
For reference only
Library Holdings: Vols 350

M SAN ANTONIO MUSEUM OF ART, 200 W Jones Ave, 78215. Tel 210-978-8100; FAX 210-978-8118; *Dir* Douglas Hyland; *Sr Cur* Marion Oettinger; *Cur Western Antiquities* Gerry Scott III; *Cur Contemporary Art* Beverly Adams; *Dir Operations* Dan Walton; *Dir Development* Lila Cockrell; *Chief Financial Officer* Sandra Ferguson; *Cur Educ* Tracy Baker White; *Registrar* Rachel Lewanbowski
Open Mon & Wed - Sat 10 AM - 5 PM, Tues 10 AM - 9 PM, Sun Noon - 5 PM. Admis adult $4, senior citizen & student $2, child 4-11 $1.75, under 3 free; free for all Tues 3 - 9 PM. Estab 1981, a renovation project, the Brewery was originally chartered in 1883. Anheuser-Busch Brewing Assoc of St Louis, during the early 1900's replaced the original wooden structures with a castle-like brick complex. Twin towers, housing glass elevators, can be seen for miles; 110,000 sq ft of exhibition space. Average Annual Attendance: 127,825
Collections: American photography since 1920; contemporary & modern art; †18th-20th century paintings & sculpture; European & American paintings & decorative art; Greek & Roman antiquities; Mexican folk art; Pre-Columbian art; Spanish colonial art
Exhibitions: Permanent: Asian Art Galleries; The Genius of Irish Silver; Greek & Roman Antiquities; Latin American Folk Art; Mummies: The Egyptian Art of Death
Publications: Exhibition catalogues, 2-4 per yr
Activities: Docent training; artists-in-residency; teacher workshops; parent-child classes; lect open to public, 10-20 vis lectr per year; concerts; gallery talks; tours; individual paintings & original objects of art lent to other art institutions for special exhibitions; originate traveling exhibitions to other art museums; museum shop sells books, reproductions & general art-interest merchandise

A SOUTHWEST CRAFT CENTER, Emily Edwards & Ursuline Sales Gallery, 300 Augusta St, 78205. Tel 210-224-1848; FAX 210-224-9337; *Dir* Paula Owen; *Ursuline Gallery Mgr* Laura Pitts
Open Mon - Sat 10 AM - 5 PM. Estab 1963, shop estab 1968; an alternative art worksite for children and adults. Ursuline Gallery sells crafts by a variety of local, regional & national artists. Emily Edwards Gallery hosts exhibits of nationally-recognized artists. Average Annual Attendance: 2000. Mem: 100; dues $35 & up; annual meeting in May
Income: Financed by mem, National Endowment for the Arts, Texas Commission on the Arts, City of San Antonio Arts & Cultural Affairs Department
Exhibitions: Eight exhibitions per year. Student show, plus seven one to three person shows by nationally recognized artists. One show by young San Antonio artist during Contemporary Art Month in July
Publications: Opening Invitations; handouts for all exhibitions including photo of artists, curator's essay, exhibition checklist
Activities: Classes for adults & children; arts workshop programs with vis artists; lect open to public, 30 vis lectr per year; tours; performances; scholarships offered; sales shop sells magazines, etc

M SPANISH GOVERNOR'S PALACE, 115 Plaza de Armas, 78205. Tel 210-224-0601; *Museum Asst* Nora Ward; *Museum Aide* Gildardo Lopez
Open Mon - Sat 9 AM - 5 PM, Sun 10 AM - 5 PM. Admis adults $1, children under 14 $.50. Estab 1749. Average Annual Attendance: 62,000
Income: $66,000 (financed by city appropriation)
Collections: Spanish-colonial furnishings, paintings, earthenware, brass & copper pieces from 16th - 17th century
Publications: Spanish Governor's Palace brochure
Activities: Museum shop sells slides & postcards

M THE UNIVERSITY OF TEXAS, Institute of Texan Cultures, 801 S Bowie at Durango Blvd, 78205-3296. Tel 210-458-2300; FAX 210-458-2205; *Exec Dir* Rex Ball; *Librn* Stephen Green; *Photo Archivist* Tom Shelton; *Dir Prog* Judith York; *Dir Marketing* Lynn Catalina
Open Tues - Sun 9 AM - 5 PM, cl Mon. Estab 1968. Maintains reference library. Average Annual Attendance: 350,000. Mem: 400; dues $50
Income: $4,500,000 (financed by endowment, mem, state appropriation, gifts & sales)
Collections: Ethnic culture including Anglo, Belgian, Black, Chinese, Czech, Danish, Dutch, English, Filipino, French, German, Greek, Hungarian, Indian, Irish Italian, Japanese, Jewish, Lebanese, Mexican, Norwegian, Polish, Scottish, Spanish & Swedish (all Texans); one room school house, barn, windmill, fort & log house
Publications: Texican, quarterly
Activities: Classes for adults & children; dramatic programs; docent programs; lect open to public; concerts; gallery talks; tours; festivals; book traveling exhibitions 2-3 per year; originate statewide traveling exhibitions; sales shop sells books, prints, magazines & slides, original art, reproductions & international gift items

M WITTE MUSEUM, 3801 Broadway, 78209. Tel 210-820-2111; FAX 210-820-2109; *Pres & Exec Dir* Linda K Johnson
Open Mon - Sat 10 AM - 5 PM, Sun Noon - 5 PM; winters until 6 PM. Admis adults $4, children 4 - 11 $1.75, children 3 & under free; group discount rates; Tues free from 3 - 9 PM. Estab 1926 by Ellen Schulz (later Quillin). Historical building located on the edge of the 450 acre Brackenridge Park on the banks of the San Antonio River & ancient Indian encampment area. Three restored historic homes on the grounds--the Ruiz, Navarro & Twohig houses. Average Annual Attendance: Over 208,000
Collections: Yena Collection
Exhibitions: Ancient Texans: Rock Art & Lifeways along the Lower Pecos; Art for History's Sake; H-E-B Science Treehouse Sounds of South Texas; Texas Wild: Ecology Illustrated (1997) Thundering Hooves II; Fiesta: Order of the Alamo. (1998) Children of Children (photography); Whodunit?; Cabeza de Vaca
Activities: Classes for adults & children; dramatic programs; docent training; lect open to public; concerts; gallery talks; tours; camp-ins; family days; volunteer training; hands-on activities; book traveling exhibitions

SHERMAN

M AUSTIN COLLEGE, Ida Green Gallery, 900 N Grand Ave, 75090-4440. Tel 903-813-2251; FAX 214-813-3199; *Chair* Timothy Tracz
Open 9 AM - 5 PM weekdays. No admis fee. Estab 1972 to serve campus and community needs. Selected exhibitions of contemporary art by regional & national artists. Average Annual Attendance: 7000
Income: Financed by endowment
Purchases: Occasional purchases of outdoor sculpture
Collections: Prints
Exhibitions: Monthly, except summer
Activities: Classes for adults & children; lect open to public; 20 vis lectr per year; gallery talks; tours; competitions; scholarships offered

TYLER

M TYLER MUSEUM OF ART, 1300 S Mahon Ave, 75701. Tel 903-595-1001; FAX 903-595-1055; *Dir* Wendell Ott; *Cur Educ* Susan LeFure
Open Tues - Sat 10 AM - 5 PM, Sun 1 - 5 PM. No admis fee. Estab 1968 as a mus of 19th & 20th century art. Two galleries are 40 x 60 ft with 20 ft ceilings; one gallery covers 25 x 45 ft. Average Annual Attendance: 18,000. Mem: 720; dues $25-$10,000
Income: $239,000 (financed by endowment, mem & auction)
Collections: 200 works: large regional photography collection; sculpture; paintings; artists represented: Connell, Allen, Fisher, Blackburn, Munoz & Carter
Activities: Docent training; lect open to public; concerts; gallery talks; tours; musical performances; films; individual paintings & originial art objects lent; originate traveling exhibitions; sales shop sells books
L Reference Library, 1300 S Mahon Ave, 75701. Tel 903-595-1001; FAX 903-595-1055; *Dir* Wendell Ott; *Cur Educ* Susan Lefevre; *Public Relations & Marketing* Robert Owen
Open Tues - Sat 10 AM - 5 PM, Sun 1 - 5 PM. No admis fee. Open for reference only. Average Annual Attendance: 20,000
Income: $236,000 (financed by private donations, grants & city appropriation)
Library Holdings: Vols 1500; Per subs 6; AV — Slides, v-tapes; Other — Clipping files, exhibition catalogs
Collections: 19th & 20th century Contemporary art
Exhibitions: (1997) Alain Galaup/Sister City Artist from Metz FR
Activities: Classes for adults & children; docent training; artists travel to schools for hands on projects with all age groups; concerts; gallery talks; tours

VERNON

M RED RIVER VALLEY MUSEUM, 4600 College Dr W, PO Box 2004, 76385-2004. Tel 817-553-1848; *Exec Dir* Ann G Huskinson; *Clerical Hostess* Carole Hanna
Open Tues - Sun 1 - 5 PM. No admis fee, donations accept. Estab 1963 to provide for & preserve local heritage while maintaining national exhibits in the arts, history & science programs. One gallery with one hundred linear ft of hanging space. Average Annual Attendance: 8000
Income: Financed by contributions, local government & donations
Collections: Electra Waggoner Biggs Sculpture Collection; J H Ray Indian Artifacts; Taylor Dabney Mineral Collection Bill Bond Wild Game Trophies
Publications: Museum Newsletter, quarterly
Activities: Classes for children; lect open to public; gallery talks; tours; book traveling exhibitions; museum shop sells books, brochures, collectors items

WACO

M THE ART CENTER OF WACO, 1300 College Dr, 76708. Tel 817-752-4371; *Dir* Joseph L Kagle Jr; *Dir Educ* Kate Miller
Open Tues - Sat 10 AM - 5 PM, Sun 1 - 5 PM. No admis fee. Estab 1972 to provide a variety of exhibitions for appreciation & classes for participation. Former residence of William Cameron, now renovated & contains one large main gallery & a small adjacent gallery, also additional exhibition space on the second floor. Average Annual Attendance: 20,000. Mem: 1100; dues $30-$1500
Income: $200,000 (financed by endowment, mem & grants)
Collections: Contemporary regional art
Exhibitions: Edmund Kinzinger; Robert Wilson; Art View 1993; Karl Umlauf; Dixie Friend Gay; Leon Lank Leonard; Chelsey Smith
Publications: Catalogs; exhibit brochures; newsletter
Activities: Classes for adults & children; docent training; lect open to public, 2-3 vis lectr per year; gallery talks; tours; competitions; exten dept serves ethnic minorities & low socio-economic groups; originates traveling exhibitions; museum shop sells books, reproductions & gift items
L Library, 1300 College Dr, 76708. Tel 817-752-4371; *Dir* Joseph Kagle
Open 10 AM - 5 PM Tues - Sat, 1 - 5 PM Sun. Estab 1976 as a non-circulating reference source for staff, faculty & patrons of the Art Center
Income: $2000
Purchases: $650
Library Holdings: Vols 1000; Per subs 18; Other — Exhibition catalogs
Special Subjects: Architecture, Crafts, Photography, Regional Art

BAYLOR UNIVERSITY
M Martin Museum of Art, PO Box 97263, 76798-7263. Tel 817-755-1867; FAX 817-755-1765; Elec Mail heidi_hornik@baylor.edu. *Dir* Dr Heidi Hornik
Open Tues - Fri 10 AM - 5 PM, Sat Noon - 5 PM, cl Sun & Mon. No admis fee. Estab 1967 as a teaching arm of the university to serve the area. Gallery contains one large room with storage & preparation room. Average Annual Attendance: 7000
Income: Financed through the art dept
Purchases: Contemporary American Art
Collections: †Contemporary painting & sculpture; graphics; local artists; prints; sculpture from Sepik River area, New Guinea, African
Activities: Lect open to public, 4 vis lectr per year; gallery talks
L Armstrong Browning Library, Eighth & Speight Sts, PO Box 97152, 76798-7152. Tel 817-755-3566; *Dir* Mairi C Rennie; *Cur Manuscripts* Rita S Humphrey; *Cur Books & Printed Material* Cynthia A Burgess
Open to visitors Mon - Fri 9 AM - Noon & 2 - 4 PM, Sat 9 AM - Noon; open for research Mon - Fri 8 AM - 5 PM, Sat 9 AM - Noon. Estab 1918 to provide a setting for the personal possessions of the Brownings & to have as complete as is possible a collection for the use of Browning scholars. Gallery is maintained. Average Annual Attendance: 16,000. Mem: dues individual $25
Income: Financed by endowment & private university
Library Holdings: Vols 15,000; Per subs 25; Original documents; Micro — Reels; AV — A-tapes, cassettes, fs, motion pictures, rec, slides; Other — Clipping files, manuscripts, memorabilia, original art works, pamphlets, photographs, prints, reproductions, sculpture
Special Subjects: Robert & Elizabeth Barrett Browning, Victorian Era of Literature
Collections: Kress Foundation Gallery Collection of Portraits; Meynell; Pen Browning photograph collection of prints; portraits of Robert Browning & Elizabeth Barrett Browning; portraits of donors; Julia Margaret Cameron, photographs; Forster; Lytton; Armstrong
Publications: Armstrong Browning Library Newsletter, semi-annual; Baylor Browning Interests, irregular; Studies in Browning & His Circle, annual; More Than Friend, The Letters of Robert Browning to Katherine Dekay Bronson; Robert Browning's Flowers; EBB at the Mercy of Her Publishers
Activities: Lect open to public, 2 vis lectr per year; tours; exhibits; scholarships offered; book traveling exhibitions

M TEXAS RANGER HALL OF FAME & MUSEUM, Interstate 35 & the Brazos River, Fort Fisher Park (Mailing add: PO Box 2570, 76702-2570). Tel 817-750-8631; FAX 817-750-8629; *Dir & Supt* Byron Johnson
Open 9 AM - 5 PM daily (winter), 9 AM - 5 PM daily (summer). Admis adults $3.50, children (6 & up) $1.50, 10 or more adults $2.50, 10 or more children $1
Collections: Texas Ranger items; Western history; paintings & sculpture
Activities: Lect; research on Texas Rangers
L Moody Texas Ranger Memorial Library, PO Box 2570, 76702-2570. Tel 817-750-8631; FAX 817-750-8629; *Librn & Archivist* Christina Stopka
For reference only
Income: Financed by City of Waco
Library Holdings: Vols 1511; Micro — Reels; AV — Cassettes, v-tapes; Other — Clipping files, manuscripts, memorabilia, photographs
Special Subjects: Texas History, Texas Rangers (law enforcement agency)

WAXAHACHIE

M ELLIS COUNTY MUSEUM INC, 201 S College, PO Box 706, 75168. Tel 214-937-0681; *Cur* Shannon Simpson
Open Tues - Sat 10 AM - 5 PM, Sun 1 - 5 PM, cl Mon. Estab 1969 to collect & maintain artifacts relating to County's history. Average Annual Attendance: 10,000-12,000. Mem: 275; dues business & family $20, individual $10, sr citizens $5; annual meeting last Mon in July
Income: $40,000 (financed by annual fundraiser)
Collections: Decorative Arts, Clothing, Furniture; Folding Fans; Photographs, Memorabilia; Technological Implements; Weaponry
Exhibitions: Artifacts relating to county's history
Activities: Retail store sells books, prints

WICHITA FALLS

M WICHITA FALLS MUSEUM & ART CENTER, Two Eureka Circle, 76308. Tel 817-692-0923; FAX 817-696-5358; *Dir* Carole Borgman
Open Tues - Sat 10 AM - 5 PM, Sun 1 - 5 PM. Admis fee varies with exhibits. Estab 1964 for the purpose of serving the community. Two galleries house art exhibits, 2 galleries house science exhibits. Average Annual Attendance: 60,000. Mem: 1000; dues $25-$1000
Income: Financed by endowment, mem, city appropriation & schools
Collections: †American prints
Publications: Events calendar, Sept, Jan, May
Activities: Classes for adults & children; dramatic programs; docent training; lect open to public; concerts; tours; competitions; lending collection has original prints; originate traveling exhibitions; museum shop sells books, prints, crafts & jewelry

WIMBERLEY

M PIONEER TOWN, Pioneer Museum of Western Art, 7A Ranch Resort, 333 Wayside, 78676. Tel 512-847-3289; FAX 512-847-6705; *Dir* Raymond L Czichos
Open Memorial Day - Labor Day 10 AM - 8 PM daily, rest of the year: Sat 10 AM - 5 PM, Sun 1 - 5 PM, cl Oct - Feb. Admis $2. Estab 1956 as a village & art museum
Collections: Remington Bronze Collection; Jack Woods Collection (sculpture); contemporary Western artists; sculpture & metalwork

UTAH

BRIGHAM CITY

M BRIGHAM CITY MUSEUM-GALLERY, 24 N Third W, PO Box 583, 84302. Tel 801-723-6769; FAX 801-723-5011; *Dir* Larry Douglass; *Chmn* Colleen H Bradford
Open Tues - Fri 11 AM - 6 PM, Sat 1 - 5 PM, cl Sun & Mon. No admis fee. Estab 1970 to document local history & serve as a state-wide art collection. Average Annual Attendance: 13,000
Income: Financed by Brigham City Corporation
Collections: Crystal & glass; 19th century clothing, artifacts & furniture folk art; fibers; ceramics; painting; printmaking
Activities: Educ dept for research, & oral histories; lect open to public; gallery talks; tours; awards; monthly rotating exhibits of art & varied collections

CEDAR CITY

M SOUTHERN UTAH UNIVERSITY, Braithwaite Fine Arts Gallery, 351 W Center St, 84720. Tel 801-586-5432; FAX 801-865-8012; Elec Mail museums@suu.edu. *Dir* Lydia Johnson
Open Mon - Fri 1 - 7 PM. No admis fee. Estab 1976 to provide a quality visual arts forum for artists' work and the viewing public. The gallery has 2000 sq ft of space with 300 linear ft of display surface; it is equipped with facilities for two & three-dimensional media with electronic security system. Average Annual Attendance: 10,000. Mem: 100; dues $50-$75
Income: Financed by city and state appropriations and private donations
Collections: 18th, 19th & 20th century American art
Publications: Exhibition announcements, quarterly; newsletter, quarterly
Activities: Gallery talks; tours; competitions; book traveling exhibitions 6 per year

FILLMORE

M UTAH DEPARTMENT OF NATURAL RESOURCES, DIVISION OF PARKS & RECREATION, Territorial Statehouse, 50 W Capital Ave, 84631. Tel 801-743-5316; FAX 801-743-4723; *Park Mgr* Gordon Chatland; *Cur* Carl Camp
Open June 1st - Sept 1st 8 AM - 8 PM, remainder of year 9 AM - 6 PM, cl Sun. Admis $5 per vehicle, $2 per person. Estab 1930, as a mus for pioneer relics. Restored by the state & local Daughters of Utah Pioneers; owned & operated by Utah State Division of Parks & Recreation. Average Annual Attendance: 25,000
Income: Financed by state appropriations
Collections: Charcoal & pencil sketches; paintings by Utah artists; photograph prints collection; pioneer portraits in antique frames; silk screen prints; furniture arranged in household settings
Activities: Educ dept; lect; gallery talks; tours; museum shop sells books, postcards, kids toys, old time toys & candy

LOGAN

M NORA ECCLES HARRISON MUSEUM OF ART, Utah State Univ, 84322-4020. Tel 801-797-0163; FAX 801-797-3423; *Dir & Chief Cur* Steven W Rosen; *Assoc Cur* Rose M Milovich; *Staff Asst* Cheryl E Sampson
Open Tues, Thurs & Fri 10:30 AM - 4:30 PM, Wed 10:30 AM - 9 PM, Sat & Sun 2 - 5 PM. No admis fee. Estab 1983. Over 10,000 sq ft of exhibition area, half devoted to permanent exhibits & half to temporary shows. Average Annual Attendance: 25,000. Mem: 120; dues $10 - $500; annual meeting 2nd Tues of May
Purchases: $120,000
Collections: †Native American art; †20th century American art, with emphasis on Western US artists; †20th century American ceramics
Publications: Exhibition catalogs; Insight, newsletter, three times per yr
Activities: Lect open to public & to members only, 5 vis lectr per year; scholarships & fels offered; book traveling exhibitions 3-4 per year; originate traveling exhibitions; museum shop sells books & magazines

OGDEN

A ECCLES COMMUNITY ART CENTER, 2580 Jefferson Ave, 84401. Tel 801-392-6935; FAX 801-392-5295; *Dir* Sandy Havas; *Gift Shop Mgr* Arlene Muller
Open 9 AM - 5 PM Mon - Fri, 10 AM - 4 PM Sat, cl Sun & holidays. No admis fee. Estab 1959 to serve as focal point for community cultural activities & to promote cultural growth. Maintains an art gallery with monthly exhibits. Average Annual Attendance: 25,000. Mem: 400; dues $25-$100; annual meeting in Nov
Income: $100,000 (financed by mem, state appropriation & fund raising)
Collections: †Utah Artists (historic & contemporaries)
Exhibitions: Paintings by Carlin, Ji, Leek, Preece, Brown-Wagner, Songer South; Chris Gittins (ceramics); woodcuts & wood engravings from Utah State University; 5th Statewide Black & White Competition; 19th Statewide Competition, Ogden Collects; Utah Quilt Show; Weber School District Student Show; Westcoast Watercolor Society
Publications: Newsletter, quarterly
Activities: Classes for adults & children; lect open to public; concerts; competition with awards; gallery talks; tours;; individual paintings & original art works lent to galleries, government offices, hospitals & businesses; book traveling exhibitions; sales shop sells original art, reproductions, prints, ceramics, jewelry & artist produced cards

OGDEN UNION STATION

M Myra Powell Art Gallery, 2501 Wall Ave, 84401. Tel 801-629-8444; *Exec Dir* Bob Geier
Open Mon - Sat 10 AM - 5 PM. No admis fee. Estab 1979 to acquaint more people with the visual arts & to heighten awareness of art. 12.5 ft x 113 ft; 39 panels 6 ft x 4 ft
Income: Financed by endowment
Collections: Non-objective painting, Indian Design, Landscape, Navajo Sand Painting, Alumin Sculpture
Activities: Lect open to public; competitions with awards; scholarships & fels offered; individual paintings & original objects of art lent
M Union Station Museums, 2501 Wall Ave, 84401. Tel 801-629-8444, 629-8533; *Exec Dir* Bob Geier; *Museum Coordr* Evelyn Moritz
Open Mon - Sat 10 AM - 6 PM, Sun 1 - 5 PM (Memorial Day - Labor Day). Admis adults $2, senior citizens $1.50, children under 12 $1. Estab 1976 to serve as a cultural & civic center for Ogden, Utah. Average Annual Attendance: 40,000. Mem: Dues $15-$1000; meetings 1st Tues of month
Income: Financed by endowment, mem, city appropriation
Collections: Railroad memorabilia
Exhibitions: 1930s & 1940s memorabilia; Browning Firearms; Browning Classic Cars; Wattis-Dumke Model Railroad; Gem & Mineral Display; Myra Powell Gallery; Utah State Railroad Museum
Publications: The Inside Track, annual newsletter
Activities: Museum shop sells books & reproductions

PARK CITY

A KIMBALL ART CENTER, 638 Park Ave, PO Box 1478, 84060. Tel 801-649-8882; FAX 801-649-8889; *Dir* Gary Sanders
Open Mon - Sun 10 AM - 6 PM. Estab 1976 for monthly gallery shows & workshops in arts & crafts, fine arts. Main gallery has movable walls & is 80 x 180 ft, Badami gallery measures 17 x 20 ft. Average Annual Attendance: 250,000. Mem: 600; dues $35; meeting in Feb
Income: $700,000 (financed by endowment, mem & contributions)
Exhibitions: Twenty-four exhibits annually in various styles & mediums
Activities: Classes for adults & children; docent training; lect open to public, 6 vis lectr per year; gallery talks; tours; competitions; opening receptions with exhibiting artists; annual art festival; book traveling exhibitions; sales shop sells original art, reproductions & prints

PRICE

M COLLEGE OF EASTERN UTAH, Gallery East, 451 E Fourth N, 84501. Tel 801-637-2120, Ext 264; FAX 801-637-4102; *Dir* James L Young; *Chmn* Brent Haddock
Open Mon - Fri 8:30 AM - 5 PM. No admis fee. Estab 1976 to provide an educational & aesthetic tool within the community. 2300 sq ft; maintains reference library. Average Annual Attendance: 15,000
Income: $1600 (financed by school appropriation)
Collections: Broad collection of contemporary prints & painting
Exhibitions: Changing exhibits
Activities: Classes for adults; docent training; lect open to public, 4-5 vis lectr per year; gallery talks; tours; competitions with awards; scholarships offered; traveling exhibits organized & circulated to colleges

PROVO

BRIGHAM YOUNG UNIVERSITY

M **B F Larsen Gallery,** Harris Fine Arts Ctr F-303, 84602. Tel 801-378-2881; FAX 801-378-5964; *Actg Dir* Todd Frye
Open 9 AM - 5 PM. No admis fee. Estab 1965 to bring to the University students & faculty a wide range of new experiences in the visual arts. B F Larsen Gallery is a three story atrium shaped gallery with exhibition areas in center floor & upper levels; Gallery 303 is large room with foyer & single entrance-exit; total exhibition space 15,260 sq ft. Average Annual Attendance: 55,000 Gallery 303; 100,000 Larsen
Income: Financed by university
Exhibitions: Invitational exhibits; exhibits by students & faculty, curated exhibits of contemporary artists & circulating exhibits
Activities: Lect open to public; competitions; monetary & certificate awards; individual paintings & original objects of art lent to university executive, faculty & university library; book traveling exhibitons monthly

L **Harold B Lee Library,** 84602. Tel 801-378-4005; FAX 801-378-6708; *Dir Libraries* Sterling Albrecht; *Fine Arts Librn* Christiane Erbolato-Ramsey
Open Mon - Sat 7 AM - Midnight. Estab 1875 to support the university curriculum
Income: Financed by endowment, mem & Latter-day Saints church funds
Library Holdings: Vols 3,677,805; Per subs 16,487; Micro — Fiche, reels; AV — A-tapes, cassettes, fs, motion pictures, slides; Other — Memorabilia, pamphlets, photographs 12,000, prints
Collections: George Anderson Collection of early Utah photographs; 15th & 16th century graphic art collection; C R Savage Collection; Vought indexed & mounted art reproduction collection
Activities: Tours

M **Museum of Art,** North Campus Dr, 84602. Tel 801-378-8256; FAX 801-378-8222; Elec Mail moadmin@byu.edu. *Dir* Dr Campbell Grey; *Assoc* Michael Sparr; *Head Cur* Linda Gibbs; *Head Exhib Develop* Paul Anderson
Open Mon - Sat 9 AM - 9 PM. No admis fee. Estab 1993 to educate patrons & community. 11 galleries including Asian, instruments, study & general purpose sculpture garden. Average Annual Attendance: 100,000
Collections: †American art-Hudson River School of American Impressionism; †Asian art; †musical instruments; †Utah art
Exhibitions: CCA Christensenj Mormon Panorama; 150 Years of American Painting; Out of Print-Prints by 25 Utah Artists
Publications: Expressions, quarterly newsletter
Activities: Classes for children; docent programs; academic & public programs; lect open to public, 12 vis lectr per year; lending collection contains 14,000 items, including individual paintings & original objects of art; book traveling exhibitions 6 per year; museum shop sells books, magazines, original art, prints, reproductions & slides

L **Fritz B Burns Library,** North Campus Dr, 84602. *Dir* Dr Campbell Grey
For lending & reference
Library Holdings: Vols 2000; Per subs 15; AV — A-tapes, cassettes, Kodachromes, rec, slides, v-tapes; Other — Clipping files, exhibition catalogs, pamphlets

SAINT GEORGE

M **DIXIE COLLEGE,** Southwestern Utah Art Gallery, 225 S 700 East, 84770. Tel 801-652-7500; FAX 801-656-4000; *Dir* Don Hinton
Open 8 AM - 6 PM. No admis fee. Estab 1960 to serve southwestern Utah as a visual arts exhibit center. Gallery is located in Fine Arts Center. Average Annual Attendance: 10,000-15,000
Income: Financed by state appropriation & 30% of sales from monthly shows
Collections: Early & contemporary Utah painters
Exhibitions: Dixie Annual Invitational (regional)
Activities: Classes for adults; dramatic programs; lect open to public, vis lectr; gallery talks

SALT LAKE CITY

M **CHURCH OF JESUS CHRIST OF LATTER-DAY SAINTS,** Museum of Church History & Art, 45 N West Temple, 84150-1003. Tel 801-240-2299; FAX 801-240-5342; *Dir* Glen Leonard; *Operation Mgr* Steven Olsen
Open Mon - Fri 9 AM - 9 PM, Sat, Sun & holidays 10 AM - 7 PM, cl Easter, Thanksgiving, Christmas & New Year's Day. No admis fee. Estab 1869 to disseminate information & display historical memorabilia, artifacts & art to the vis pub. Assists in restorations & furnishing of Church historic sites. Average Annual Attendance: 300,000
Income: Financed by Church
Collections: †Mostly 19th & 20th century Morman art & historical artifacts: †portraits, paintings, drawings, sculpture, prints, American furniture, china, pottery, glass; †Morman quilts & handwork; †decorative arts; †clothing & textiles; architectural elements & hardware; † Oceanic & American Indian pottery, basketry & textiles
Exhibitions: Permanent Installations: Presidents of the Church; Portraits of Church Leaders; Western Themes; Masterworks of Mormon art; Latter-day Saint History International Art Competition, every 3 years
Publications: Exhibition catalogs; brochures; Image of Faith: Art of the Latter-day Saints (1995)
Activities: Docent training; seminars; gallery demonstrations; school outreach; lect open to public; gallery talks tours; individual paintings & original objects of art lent; museum shop sells books, reproductions, prints, slides & posters

L **Art Library,** 45 N West Temple, 84150. Tel 801-240-4604; FAX 801-240-5342; Reference library
Library Holdings: Vols 2200; Per subs 25; Micro — Fiche, reels; AV — A-tapes, cassettes, motion pictures, slides, v-tapes; Other — Clipping files, exhibition catalogs, memorabilia, original art works, pamphlets, photographs, sculpture
Special Subjects: Latter-day Saints art, artists, history & historic sites

A **SALT LAKE ART CENTER,** 20 S W Temple, 84101. Tel 801-328-4201; FAX 801-322-4323; *Pres* Scott Pickett; *Dir* Ric Colliar
Open Tues - Sat 10 AM - 5 PM, Fri 10 AM - 9 PM, Sun 1 - 5 PM, cl Mon. No admis fee. Estab 1931 to educate the community in the visual arts through exhibitions & classes. Center has one large gallery of 5000 sq ft; one small gallery of 2000 sq ft; sales shop of 1000 sq ft, one permanent collection gallery of 2500 sq ft. Average Annual Attendance: 60,000. Mem: 1250; dues family $30, individual $20; annual meeting in Nov
Income: $400,000 (financed by mem, city & state appropriation, earned income, gifts & private & corporate contributions)
Purchases: $70,000 Bolotowsky Sculpture
Collections: Utah artists (1930-Present)
Exhibitions: 200 Years of American Art, Santa Barbara Museum of Art Collection; Art of the Muppets; Santa Fe Collection of Southwester Art; Retrospectives of Utah Artists: V Douglas Snow, Bonnie Sucec & Avard Fairbanks; Rembrandt Etchings, Brigham Young University Collection; Lost & Found: An Archaeological Composition
Publications: Bulletin, quarterly
Activities: Classes for adults & children; studio & lect courses; lect open to public, 20 vis lectr per year; concerts; gallery talks; tours; competitions with awards; originate traveling exhibitions; sales shop sells books, original art, reproductions & prints

L **SALT LAKE CITY PUBLIC LIBRARY,** Fine Arts/Audiovisual Dept and Atrium Gallery, 209 E Fifth S, 84111. Tel 801-524-8200; FAX 801-524-8272; *Dir* Nancy Tessman; *Head Fine Arts & Audiovisual Dept* Carolyn Dickinson
Open Mon - Thurs 9 AM - 9 PM, Fri - Sat 9 AM - 6 PM. Estab 1898. Maintains an art gallery with monthly exhibitions
Income: Financed by endowment & city appropriation
Library Holdings: Vols 400,000; Picture files; AV — Fs, rec, slides, v-tapes; Other — Clipping files, exhibition catalogs, framed reproductions, original art works, reproductions
Special Subjects: Film, Contemporary art, photography
Collections: Art of Western United States; Utah Artists; American & European Works on Paper
Publications: Brochures accompanying individual exhibitions; Permanent Art Collection Catalogue
Activities: Films; gallery talks; tours; demonstrations; slide presentations; individual paintings & original objects of art lent to museums & non-profit galleries; originate traveling exhibitions

M **UNIVERSITY OF UTAH,** Utah Museum of Fine Arts, 101 Art & Architectural Ctr, 84112. Tel 801-581-7332; FAX 801-585-5198;
Internet Home Page Address www.utah.edu/umfa. *Dir & Cur Coll* E F Sanquinetti; *Asst Dir* Allison South; *Gallery Supt & Preparator* David Hardy; *Registrar* David Carroll; *Cur Educational Serv* Bernadette Brown; *Membership & Vol Coordr* Tonya Todd; *Assoc Cur Educ* Virginia Catherall
Open Mon - Fri 10 AM - 5 PM, Sat & Sun 2 - 5 PM. No admis fee. Average Annual Attendance: 110,000. Mem: 1,000; dues family $35, single $20
Income: Financed by university & private gifts
Collections: Winifred Kimball Hudnut Collection; Natacha Rambova Egyptian Collection; Marion Sharp Robinson Collection; Trower & Michael Collections of English, American & Peruvian Silver; Bartlett Wicks Collection; English 17th & 18th century furniture & pictures; Egyptian antiquities; French 18th century furnishings & tapestries; graphics, contemporary works; Italian Renaissance paintings & furniture; objects from the Buddhist culture; African Art; Indonesian Art; Oceanic Art, American Indian Art; North Western Coastal Art
Activities: Classes for adults; docent training; lect open to public, some members only; concerts; gallery talks; tours; paintings & art objects lent; originate traveling exhibitions

L **Owen Library,** Art & Architecture Ctr, 84112. Tel 801-581-3840; *Dir* Paul Davis
Open Mon - Fri 10 AM - 5 PM. Estab 1978 as a reference library for art students
Library Holdings: Vols 2000; Per subs 40; AV — Cassettes, Kodachromes, slides, v-tapes; Other — Clipping files, exhibition catalogs, manuscripts, memorabilia, original art works, pamphlets

L **Marriott Library,** 84112. Tel 801-581-8558; *Fine Arts Librn* Myron Patterson; *Sr Libr Specialist, Fine Arts Dept* Dorothy Greenland
Open Mon - Thurs 8 AM - 11 PM, Fri 8 AM - 11 PM, Sat 9 AM - 5 PM, Sun 1 - 11 PM. Estab 1967 to serve the students & faculty of the University with research materials & specialized services. For lending & reference
Income: Financed by state appropriation
Purchases: $60,000 per yr for fine arts books
Library Holdings: Vols 2,000,000; Per subs 17,000; AV — Slides; Other — Clipping files, exhibition catalogs, prints, reproductions
Special Subjects: Advertising Design, Aesthetics, Afro-American Art, American Indian Art, American Western Art, Folk Art, Furniture, Glass, Graphic Arts, Graphic Design, Painting - American, Painting - British, Painting - Dutch, Painting - European, Painting - Flemish

M **UTAH ARTS COUNCIL,** Chase Home Museum of Utah Folk Art, 617 E South Temple, 84102. Tel 801-533-5760; FAX 801-533-4202; *Chmn* Robert Olpin; *Exec Dir* Bonnie Stephens; *Folk Arts Coordr* Carol Edison
Open mid Apr - Oct Noon - 5 PM, spring & fall weekends only, daily during the summer. Estab 1986 to showcase folk art in the State Art Collection. Four small galleries, one small reception area & two hallways for display in a 19th century two-story farmhouse. Average Annual Attendance: 20,000
Income: Financed by state & federal appropriations
Library Holdings: Vols 600; Per subs 5; AV — A-tapes, cassettes, motion pictures, rec, slides; Other — Clipping files, pamphlets, photographs, prints
Collections: †Ethnic; †Familial; †Occupational; †Religious; †Regional with a emphasis on traditional work by living folk artists
Exhibitions: Annual exhibit of Utah folk art
Activities: Lect open to the public; concerts; group tours; originates traveling exhibitions; sales shop sells books

A **UTAH LAWYERS FOR THE ARTS,** 170 S Main St, Ste 1500, 84101. Tel 801-521-3200; FAX 801-328-0537; *Pres* James W Stewart
Estab 1983 to provide pro bono legal services. Mem: 36; mem open to attorneys & law students; $30 annual fee, $15 student fee
Income: Financed by mem
Publications: Art/Law News, quarterly newsletter

A **UTAH TRAVEL COUNCIL,** Council Hall, Capitol Hill, 84114. Tel 801-538-1030; FAX 801-538-1399; *Dir* Dean Reeder; *Asst Dir* Spence Kinard; *Asst Dir* Ruth Kurzbauer; *Travel Publications Specialist* Janice Carpenter; *Media Dir* Dave Porter; *Travel Develop Specialist* Open
Open 8 AM - 5 PM; Sat & Sun 10 AM - 5 PM. No admis fee. Constructed in 1866 & served as seat of government for 30 years; reconstructed on Capitol Hill & presented to Utah state in 1963; contains small mus of pioneer & historic items, paintings & furniture
Income: Financed by legislative appropriation
Publications: Brochures; two newsletters
Activities: Lending collection contains motion pictures, photographs, transparencies for public use, videos on travel opportunities in Utah; originate traveling exhibitions

SPRINGVILLE

M **SPRINGVILLE MUSEUM OF ART,** 126 E 400 South, 84663. Tel 801-489-2727; *Dir* Dr Vern G Swanson; *Asst Dir* Dr Sharon R Gray
Open Tues - Sat 10 AM - 5 PM, Wed 10 AM - 9 PM, Sun 3 - 5 PM, cl Mon & holidays. No admis fee. Estab 1903 for the collection & exhibition of Utah fine arts & as educational resource. Built in Spanish Moraccan style in 1937. One of the largest museums in the mountain west, it has eleven galleries with 25,000 sq ft of exhibit space; maintains a photographic art reference library for Utah art history. Average Annual Attendance: 130,000. Mem: 350; dues family $30, individual $20, student $10; annual meeting in Apr
Income: $350,000 (financed by donations, bookstore, mem, city & state appropriations)
Purchases: $10,000-$50,000 of fine art per year
Collections: Artwork by Cyrus Dallin & John Hafen; 20th Century American Realism, Soviet Realism; Utah artists from 1850 to present of all styles
Exhibitions: Annual Spring Salon Utah Invitational Fine Art; High Schools of Utah Show; Annual Utah Autumn Exhibit
Publications: Exhibition catalogs, quarterly bulletin
Activities: Docent programs; children's programs; lect open to public, 6 vis lectr per year; concerts; gallery talks; tours; competitions with awards; individual paintings & original objects of art lent to professional, governmental & educational institutions & museums; lending collection contains paintings & sculpture; originate traveling exhibitions to Utah Arts Council, other museums & to schools; museum shop sells books, magazines, reproductions, prints & catalogues

VERMONT

BENNINGTON

M **BENNINGTON MUSEUM,** Bennington Museum, W Main St, 05201. Tel 802-447-1571; FAX 802-442-8305; *Exec Dir* Steven Miller; *Cur Coll* Deborah Anne Federhen; *Registrar* Ruth Levin; *Museum Shop Mgr* Judith Rodman; *Membership & Public Relations Coordr* Mary Ellen Mason
Open Nov 1 - May 31 9 AM - 5 PM, June 1 - Oct 31 9 AM - 6 PM. Admis family $12, adults $5, students & senior citizens $4.50, children under 12 free. Estab 1875 as resource for history and fine and decorative arts of New England. Local historical mus with 10 galleries, Grandma Moses Schoolhouse Mus. Average Annual Attendance: 50,000. Mem: 740; dues $20-$1500; annual meeting in May
Income: $486,385
Collections: Bennington pottery; Bennington flag; American blown & pressed glass; American painting & sculpture; American furniture & decorative arts; dolls & toys; Grandma Moses paintings; rare documents
Exhibitions: Vermont Samplers & Needlework Pictures
Publications: Exhibition catalogs
Activities: Classes for adults & children; docent training; lect open to public, 4 vis lectr per year; gallery talks; tours; individual paintings & original objects of art lent to other qualifying institutions; originate traveling exhibitions to other northern New England museums; museum shop sells books, original art, reproductions, prints

L **Library,** W Main St, 05201. Tel 802-447-1571; FAX 802-442-8305; *Librn* Tyler Resch
Open by appointment only. For reference only
Library Holdings: Vols 5000; Per subs 10; Micro — Reels; AV — Lantern slides, slides, v-tapes; Other — Clipping files, exhibition catalogs, manuscripts, memorabilia, pamphlets, photographs
Special Subjects: Art History, Ceramics, Coins & Medals, Decorative Arts, Flasks & Bottles, Folk Art, Furniture, Glass, Historical Material, Portraits, Pottery, Sculpture, Silver, Textiles, American Decorative Arts, New England Genealogy

BRATTLEBORO

M **BRATTLEBORO MUSEUM & ART CENTER,** Union Railroad Sta, PO Box 662, 05302-0662. Tel 802-257-0124; *Pres* Paul Stone; *Dir* Mara Williams
Open May 15 - Nov 1 Tues - Sun Noon - 6 PM. Admis adults $3, senior citizens & college $2, children & members free. Estab 1972 to present art & historical exhibition programs integrated through an annual theme. The museum is located in a railroad station built in 1915, now a registered historic site. Four galleries with changing exhibitions & one permanent gallery of Estey organs. Average Annual Attendance: 20,000. Mem: 700; dues family $40, individual $25; annual meeting in Mar
Income: $185,000 (financed by mem, donations, town, state & federal appropriations)
Exhibitions: Estey Organ Exhibit
Publications: Built Landscapes; Gardens of the Northeast; Seeing Japan
Activities: Docent training; programs for school groups; week-long artist-in-residence program; lect open to public, 20 vis lectr per year; concerts; gallery talks; originate traveling exhibitions

BROOKFIELD

M **MUSEUM OF THE AMERICAS,** 05036. Tel 802-276-3386; *Dir* Earle W Newton
Open daily 2 - 5 PM. Admis donations requested. Estab 1971 to gather materials in support of Anglo-Americqan & Hispanic-American studies. 4000 sq ft gallery
Income: Financed by endowment & gifts
Collections: Anglo-American 16th-19th century paintings; English mezzotints; Hispanic-American decorative arts; Hogarth prints & paintings; Latin American folk art; maps of the colonies; Pre-Columbian artifacts
Exhibitions: English Faces: 1500-1800; World of William Hogarth: Paintings & Engravings English Faces: 1500 - 1800
Activities: Classes for adults in prospect; lect open to public; concerts; individuals paintings lent; lending collection contains 5000 books, 1000 video cassettes, 300 paintings; museum shop sells books

L **Library,** 05036. Tel 802-276-3386; *Dir* Earle W Newton
For reference only
Income: Financed by endowment & gifts
Library Holdings: Vols 5000; Per subs 10; AV — V-tapes; Other — Clipping files, original art works
Special Subjects: Etchings & Engravings, Historical Material, Latin American Art, Maps, Mexican Art, Painting - American, Painting - British, Portraits, Pre-Columbian Art
Collections: Anglo-American & Latin American art & history

BURLINGTON

M **UNIVERSITY OF VERMONT,** Robert Hull Fleming Museum, 05405. Tel 802-656-0750, 656-2090; FAX 802-656-8059; *Dir* Ann Porter; *Cur* Janie Cohen; *Bus Mgr* Anna Seyller; *Bus Mgr* Janet Daignault; *Exhib Designer & Preparator* Merlin Acomb; *Museum Educator* Chris Fearon; *Registrar* Darcy Coates
Call 802-656-2090 for hours. No admis fee. Estab 1873 as a fine arts mus for the area & a teaching facility for the University. Permanent gallery of 18th & 19th century American Art; permanent gallery of European painting; ethnographic gallery of rotating exhibitions. Mus also contains a reference library. Average Annual Attendance: 30,000. Mem: 700; dues Fleming Soc $1000, benefactor $500-$999, patron $250-$499 supporting $100-$249 contributing $50-$99, family $30, individual $20, student $10
Income: Financed by mem, university appropriations & grants
Collections: American, European, Pre-Columbian & Oriental art including paintings, sculpture, decorative arts & artifacts; costumes; ethnographic collection, especially native American; prints & drawings of various periods
Exhibitions: American historic & contemporary; Asian; Ethnographic; Medieval & Ancient; European; Egyptian
Publications: Exhibition catalogs; newsletter-calendar, 3 per yr
Activities: Classes for adults & children; docent training; lect open to public, 20 vis lectr per year; concerts; gallery talks; tours; community outreach serves all Vermont; individual paintings & original objects of art lent to museum community; book traveling exhibitions; originate traveling exhibitions; museum shop sells books, magazines, reproductions, prints & Vermont crafts

M **Francis Colburn Gallery,** Williams Hall, 05405. Tel 802-656-2014; FAX 802-656-8429
Open Sept - May 9 AM - 5 PM. No admis fee. Estab 1975
Exhibitions: Student, faculty & visiting artist works

L **Wilbur Room Library,** Robert Hull Fleming Museum, 05405. Tel 802-656-0750; FAX 802-656-8059
Open Wed 1 - 4 PM. Estab for Mus staff & volunteers & use by university & community. Books & materials related to Fleming Mus collections. For reference only
Library Holdings: Vols 1000; Other — Clipping files, exhibition catalogs, pamphlets
Special Subjects: Asian Art, Decorative Arts, Painting - American

FERRISBURGH

A **ROWLAND EVANS ROBINSON MEMORIAL ASSOCIATION,** Rokeby Museum, RR 1, Box 1540, 05456-9711. Tel 802-877-3406; *Dir* Jane Williamson
Open May - Oct Thurs - Sun 11 AM - 3 PM, open by appointment only remainder of yr. Estab 1963 to exhibit & interpret lives & works of the Robinson family. Robinson family (prolific artists) art is displayed throughout the house. Work of Rachael Robinson Elmer (1878 - 1919), student at Art Students League, is most prominent. She & her father, Rowland E Robinson (1833 - 1900), were published artists. Average Annual Attendance: 1300. Mem: 250; dues family $25, individual $15, senior citizen & student $10; annual meeting in mid-May
Income: Financed by mem, contributions & grants
Collections: Art, oils & watercolor sketches; books & manuscripts; 17th - 20th century furnishings; textiles & costumes
Publications: Messenger
Activities: Classes for children; docent training; lect open to public; museum shop sells books & prints

GLOVER

M BREAD & PUPPET THEATER MUSEUM, Rte 122, Rd 2, 05839. Tel 802-525-6972; *Mgr* Elka Schumann; *Artist* Peter Schumann
Open June - Oct daily 10 AM - 5 PM. No admis fee. Estab 1975 to exhibit & promote the art of puppetry. Average Annual Attendance: 25,000
Income: $10,000 (financed by donations, sales of publications & art & by the Bread & Puppet Theater)
Collections: Puppets; giant puppets; masks; graphics
Publications: Bread & Puppet Museum, The Radicality of Puppetry
Activities: Museum shop sells books, prints, original art, posters & postcards

JERICHO

A JERICHO HISTORICAL SOCIETY, The Old Red Mill, PO Box 35, 05465. Tel 802-899-3225
Open Mon - Sat 10 AM - 5 PM, cl winter. No admis fee. Estab 1978
Income: Financed by mem & contributions
Collections: Milling Machinery (video tape); Slides of Snow Flakes & Ice Crystals (video tape)
Exhibitions: Machinery, permanent exhibit

LUDLOW

M BLACK RIVER HISTORICAL SOCIETY, Black River Academy Museum, High St, PO Box 73, 05149. Tel 802-228-5050; *Dir* Georgia L Brehm
Open Noon - 4 PM, summer only. Estab 1972. 3-story brick building built in 1889. Average Annual Attendance: 1200. Mem: 200; dues family $15, single $10
Income: $25,000 (financed by endowment)
Collections: School memorabilia, farming implements, domestic items - 19th century, furnishings, clothing
Publications: History of Ludlow, VT, J Harris (monograph)
Activities: Dramatic programs; concerts; tours on holidays; Traveling exhibitions 2 per year; museum shop sells books

MANCHESTER

A SOUTHERN VERMONT ART CENTER, PO Box 617, 05254. Tel 802-362-1405, 362-4823; *Pres* Charles M Ams III; *Dir* Christopher Madkour; *Dir Public Relations* Margaret Donovan
Open Tues - Sat 10 AM - 5 PM, Sun Noon - 5 PM, cl July 4th. Admis adults $3, students $.50, free admis Sun. Estab 1929 to promote educ in the arts & to hold exhibitions of art in its various forms. 10 galleries; sculpture garden. Average Annual Attendance: 20,000. Mem: Dues $30 - $45; annual meeting in Sept
Income: Financed by mem & contributions
Collections: Contemporary American sculptors & painters; loan collection
Exhibitions: Annual exhibitions for members; Fall Show; one-man & special exhibitions
Publications: Annual catalog & brochures
Activities: Classes for adults & children in painting, drawing, graphic arts, photography, sculpture & pottery; concerts; scholarship & fels offered
L Library, PO Box 617, 05254. Tel 802-362-1405;
Library Holdings: Vols 500

MIDDLEBURY

M MIDDLEBURY COLLEGE, Museum of Art, Ctr for the Arts, 05753-6177. Tel 802-443-5000; *Dir* Richard H Saunders; *Asst Dir* Emmie Donadio; *Preparator Designer* Ken Pohlman
Open Tues, Wed & Fri 10 AM - 5 PM, Thurs 10 AM - 8 PM, Sat & Sun Noon - 5 PM, cl Mon & holidays. No admis fee. Estab 1968 as a teaching collection. Now also presents loan exhibitions, work by individuals & groups, student exhibits. In 1992 moved to new Middlebury College Center for the Arts, designed by Malcolm Holzman of Hardy, Holzman & Pfeiffer Associates
Income: Financed through College, Friends of Art, grants
Collections: †Drawings; †paintings; photographs; †prints; †sculpture;
Exhibitions: The Artist as Native: Reinventing Regionalism; Danny Lyon Photo-Film, 1959-1990; The Crayon & The American Landscape; Richard Stankiewicz: Sculpture in Steel; American Abstraction from the Addison Gallery of American Art; Czech & Slovak Photography: 1918-1992; Fabulous Pictures: Contemporary Russian Images of Folk & Fairy Tales; Faster than a Speeding Bullet: Photographs of Harold Edgerton; Cravings, Casts & Replicas: Nineteenth-Century Sculpture from Europe & America in New England Collections; Horatio Greenough: The Unknown Drawings
Publications: Annual Report; Friends of Art Newsletter; gallery brochure; exhibition catalogues
Activities: Lect open to public, 10-12 vis lectr per year; book traveling exhibitions 6-7 per year; originate traveling exhibitions

M SHELDON MUSEUM, One Park St, 05753. Tel 802-388-2117; *Dir* Elizabeth W Fitzsimmons
Open June - Oct Mon - Fri 10 AM - 5 PM, Sat 10 AM - 4 PM, winter hours Mon - Fri 10 AM - 5 PM. Admis adults $3.50, senior citizens & students $3, children $.50. Estab 1882 for the preservation of furniture, portraits, decorative arts, artifacts & archival material of Middlebury & Addison Counties. Nine rooms arranged as a 19th century Vermont home; art gallery. Average Annual Attendance: 3500. Mem: 650; dues $20 & up
Collections: China; furniture; glass; †historical material; landscapes; pewter; portraits; prints
Exhibitions: Changing exhibits in the Cerf Gallery; permanent exhibits of 19th Century home & furnishings
Publications: Marble in Middlebury; Walking History of Middlebury; annual report; quarterly newsletter
Activities: Classes for children; lect; guided tours; out-reach program to county schools; museum shop sells books, prints, crafts & toys

M VERMONT STATE CRAFT CENTER AT FROG HOLLOW, One Mill St, 05753. Tel 802-388-3177; FAX 802-388-5020; Elec Mail vsccfrog@sover.net. *Exec Dir* Susan Farrow; *Gallery Dir* Anne Majusiak; *Sales Mgr* Beth McCoy; *Public Relations* Kirt Zimmer
Open Mon - Sat 9:30 AM - 5 PM, Sun afternoon spring - fall. No admis fee. Estab 1971 to provide craft educational, informational & marketing services to school children, adults & professionals. Sales gallery exhibits the work of over 250 juried Vermont crafts people, also hosts yearly exhibition schedule featuring the work of noted crafts people world wide. Average Annual Attendance: 120, 000. Mem: 900; dues $25-$250; annual meeting in Nov; exhibiting members are juried into the gallery
Income: Financed by mem, federal & state grants, fundraising activities, consignment receipts & tuition
Collections: Vermont Crafts
Publications: Information services bulletin; calendar; show announcements; course brochures
Activities: Classes for adults & children; craft demonstrations; professional workshops for crafts people; pottery facility; resident potter studios; lect open to public, 4 vis lectr per year; tours; original objects of fine craft lent to Vermont State Senate office in Washington; traveling exhibitions organized & circulated; gallery shop sells books, Vermont crafts

MONTPELIER

M VERMONT HISTORICAL SOCIETY, Museum, 109 State St, 05609-0901. Tel 802-828-2291; FAX 802-828-2199; Elec Mail jcalder@vhs.state.vt.us. *Dir* Gainor Davis; *Cur* Jacqueline Calder; *Librn* Paul Cannahan; *Educ Dir* Sarah Roover
Open Tues - Fri 9 AM - 4:30 PM, Sat 9 AM - 4 PM, Sun Noon - 4 PM, cl Mon; call for holiday hours. Admis adults $3, seniors & students $2. Estab 1838 to collect, preserve and make available for study items from Vermont's past. Average Annual Attendance: 22,000. Mem: 2600; dues $30-$600; annual meeting in Aug or Sept
Income: Financed by endowment, mem, state appropriation & contributions
Special Subjects: Historical Material, Manuscripts, Geneology
Collections: Collection of fine arts, decorative arts, tools & equipment and work of Vermont artists
Exhibitions: Tourists Accommodated: Visiting Vermont (1895-1995); All the Precious Past
Publications: Vermont History, 2 times per year; Vermont History News, bi-monthly
Activities: Lect open to the public; fellowships offered; museum shop sells books, prints, gifts & postcards
L Library, 109 State St, 05609-0901. Tel 802-828-2291; FAX 802-828-3638; Elec Mail vhs@vhs.state.vt.us;
Internet Home Page Address http://www.state.vt.us/vhs. *Dir* Gainor B Davis
Open 9 AM - 4:40 PM. Admis donation. Estab 1838. Reference Library
Purchases: $4900
Library Holdings: Vols 150,000; Micro — Reels; AV — A-tapes, cassettes, motion pictures, v-tapes; Other — Manuscripts, pamphlets, photographs
Special Subjects: Advertising Design, Archaeology, Architecture, Bookplates & Bindings, Ceramics, Coins & Medals, Costume Design & Construction, Crafts, Decorative Arts, Dolls, Embroidery, Flasks & Bottles, Folk Art, Furniture, Glass, Handicrafts, Historical Material, Interior Design, Landscape Architecture, Landscapes, Manuscripts, Vermont History

M T W WOOD GALLERY & ARTS CENTER, College Hall, Vermont College, 05602. Tel 802-828-8743; FAX 802-828-8855; Elec Mail twwood@norwich.edu. *Dir & Cur* Megan Smith
Open Tues - Sun Noon - 4 PM. Admis $2 non-members. Estab 1895 by 19th century genre & portrait artist T W Wood to house & exhibit a portion of his works. Gallery acts as archive for information about T W Wood. 3 gallery spaces: 2700 sq ft, 800 sq ft, 500 sq ft, 15 ft high ceilings; in newly renovated 1870 College Hall on Vermont College campus. Average Annual Attendance: 10,000. Mem: 200; dues $35-$100
Income: Financed by endowment, city appropriation, grants, mem
Collections: Oil paintings, watercolors, prints by T W Wood, A B Durand, J G Brown, A Wyant, Edward Gay; 100 works from the 1920s & 30s, some by WPA painters Reginald Marsh, Louis Boucher, Paul Sample, Joseph Stella; early 19th century American portraits
Publications: Monograph on the Wood Collection
Activities: Classes for children; docent training; lect open to public, 25 vis lectr per year; concerts; gallery talks; tours; state-wide competitions; individual paintings & original objects of art lent to local organizations, businesses & other museums with appropriate security systems; lending collection includes original prints & photographs; museum shop sells crafts, magazines, reproductions, prints, postcards, & posters

RUTLAND

M NEW ENGLAND MAPLE MUSEUM, Rte 7 in Pittsford, PO Box 1615, 05701. Tel 802-483-9414; *Pres* Thomas H Olson; *Cur & Mgr* Dona Olson; *Shop* Jean Lyon
Open daily 8:30 AM - 5:30 PM. Admis adults $1.50, senior citizens $1.25, children between 6 - 12 $.50. Estab 1977 to present the complete history of maple sugaring. Average Annual Attendance: 20,000
Income: $200,000 (financed by gift shop sales & admis)
Purchases: $1000 per yr, mainly maple sugaring antiques
Collections: Oil paintings on maple sugaring by Paul Winter; oil murals on early maple sugaring by Vermont artist Grace Brigham
Exhibitions: Permanent collection
Activities: Museum shop sells books, reproductions, slides

A RUTLAND AREA ART ASSOCIATION, INC, Chaffee Art Center, 16 S Main St, 05701. Tel 802-775-0356; *Pres* Jess Anderson
Open daily 10 AM - 5 PM July - Oct, 11 AM - 4 PM Nov - June, cl Tues. No admis fee, donations appreciated. Estab & incorporated 1961 to promote &

maintain an educational & cultural center in the central Vermont region for the area artists, photographers, craftsmen & others in the art field. Average Annual Attendance: 10,000. Mem: 200; juried artists; dues $30; annual meeting in Jan
Income: Financed by mem, special funding, contributions, grants, foundations & activities
Exhibitions: Annual Members Exhibit, juried; Art-in-the-Park outdoor festivals; one-man & invitational exhibits
Publications: Calendar of events, annually; exhibition posters
Activities: Classes for adults & children; lect open to public, 4 vis lectr per year; concerts; tours; competition with awards; scholarships offered; individual printings lent to local banks & corporations; sales shop sells original art & prints

SAINT JOHNSBURY

M FAIRBANKS MUSEUM & PLANETARIUM, Main & Prospect Sts, 05819. Tel 802-748-2372; FAX 802-748-3347; *Dir* Charles C Browne
Open Mon - Sat 10 AM - 4 PM, Sun 1 - 5 PM, extended summer hours. Admis families $6, adults $2.50, students & senior citizens $2, children $1.25, group rates available. Estab 1889 as a center for exhibits, special exhibitions & programs; special exhibitions & programs on science, technology, the arts & the humanities. Art gallery for special exhibitions & work of regional artists. Average Annual Attendance: 70,000. Mem: 600; dues $30; monthly meeting
Income: $330,000 (financed by admis income, grants, endowment, mem & municipal appropriations)
Collections: Hudson River School, primarily oil paintings; 19th century American & European art; Extensive natural science, history & anthropology collections
Exhibitions: The Orchid Photographs of William Balch; Shadowbirds: Photographs of William Burt
Publications: Exhibit catalogs; quarterly newsletter
Activities: Classes for adults & children; docent training; lect open to public; concerts; gallery talks; exten dept serving Northeast Vermont; artmobile; individual paintings & original objects of art lent to other accredited museums; lending collection contains 500 nature artifacts, 50 original art works, 10 paintings & 500 photographs; book traveling exhibitions; museum shop sells books, magazines, original art, reproductions, prints, slides, science kits, kites & crafts; junior museum

M SAINT JOHNSBURY ATHENAEUM, 30 Main St, 05819. Tel 802-748-8291; FAX 802-748-8086; *Exec Dir* Perry Viles; *Cur* Sallee Lawrence
Open Mon & Wed 10 AM - 8 PM, Tues, Thurs & Fri 10 AM - 5:30 PM, Sat 9:30 AM - 4 PM. No admis fee. Estab 1873 & maintained as a 19th century gallery; given to the townspeople by Horace Fairbanks. It is the oldest art gallery still in its original form in the United States; a one-room addition to the public library building; maintains general library. Average Annual Attendance: 8000
Income: Financed by endowment, town appropriation & annual giving
Collections: 19th century American landscape paintings of the Hudson River School (Bierstadt, Colman, Whittredge, Cropsey, Gifford, Hart brothers); copies of masterpieces; sculpture
Exhibitions: Permanent Collection
Publications: Art Gallery Catalogue
Activities: Docent training; lect open to public; tours; sales shop sells reproductions, art card-reproductions & posters

SHELBURNE

M SHELBURNE MUSEUM, Rte 7, 05482. Tel 802-985-3346, Ext 390; FAX 802-985-2231; *Dir* Brian Alexander; *Dir Coll* Eloise Beil; *Registrar* Pauline Mitchell
Open Mid-May - mid-Oct 10 AM - 5 PM. Admis adults $15, children $6, special group & student rates. Estab 1947 as Mus of the American Spirit to collect, preserve & exhibit American fine, decorative & utilitarian arts, particular emphasis on Vermont. 37 buildings on 45 acres. Average Annual Attendance: 160,000
Income: Financed primarily by admis & fundraising from members
Collections: American paintings, folk art, decoys, architecture, furniture, quilts & textiles, dolls, sporting art & sculpture, ceramics, tools, sleighs & carriages, toys, farm & home implements; seven period houses; European material: Impressionist & Old Master paintings; English furniture & architectural elements; Native American ethnographic artifacts; Sidewheeler Ticonderoga, railroad memorabilia including steam train, circus material & carousel animals
Exhibitions: (1997) Pictorial Quilts
Activities: Classes for children; docent training; lect open to public, 5 vis lectr per year; concerts; gallery talks; tours; exten dept serves Vermont; book traveling exhibitions annually; museum shop sells books, reproductions, prints, slides & original art
L Library, Rte 7, 05482. Tel 802-985-3346, Ext 390; FAX 802-985-2331; *Dir* Brian Alexander; *Dir Coll* Eloise Beil
Open to pub by appointment
Library Holdings: Vols 6000; Per subs 40; AV — A-tapes, cassettes, fs, Kodachromes, motion pictures, rec, slides, v-tapes; Other — Clipping files, exhibition catalogs, manuscripts, memorabilia, pamphlets, photographs, prints

SPRINGFIELD

A SPRINGFIELD ART & HISTORICAL SOCIETY, 9 Elm St, PO Box 313, 05156-0313. Tel 802-885-2743; *Pres* Frederick Richardson; *Dir* Robert McLaughlin
Open Tues, Wed & Fri 10 AM - 4 PM, Thurs 1 - 5 PM & 7 - 9 PM. No admis fee. Estab 1956 for the purpose of presenting history, art & classes in the arts to the community. Gallery located in a Victorian mansion built in 1867 & is maintained for monthly exhibits. Average Annual Attendance: 1200. Mem: 140; dues $50, $20 & $10; annual meeting in Sept
Income: $15,000 (financed by endowment & mem)
Collections: Primitive portraits by H Bundy, Aaron D Fletcher & Asahel Powers; Richard Lee, pewter; Bennington pottery; paintings by local artists; toys,

costumes, sculpture, crafts
Exhibitions: Historical exhibits: costumes; toys; photography; fine arts
Publications: Annual schedule of events & monthly notices
Activities: Classes for adults & children; lect open to the public, 4 vis lectr per year; concerts; gallery talks; competitions; scholarships & fels offered; individual paintings lent; lending collection contains original art work, paintings, photographs, sculpture, slides; sales shop sells books, original art, slides

M Miller Art Center, 9 Elm St, PO Box 313, 05156. Tel 802-885-2415; *Pres* Frederick Richardson; *Cur* Amanda Page
Open daily 10 AM - 4 PM. No admis fee. Estab 1958 to preserve & present art & history of region. Gallery I-changing exhibits; gallery II-pewter, pottery; gallery III-historic artifacts; gallery IV-changing exhibits; gallery V-member gallery-artworks. Average Annual Attendance: 2000. Mem: 250; dues friend $50, family $25, single $15; annual meeting 3rd Tues in Oct
Income: $20,000 (financed by endowment, mem, fundraising, gifts, grants)
Purchases: $500
Collections: Bennington Pottery; 19th century Dolls & Toys, Paintings; 18th century Pewter; 18th & 19th century Textiles
Exhibitions: Springfield Student Art Show. Quilts; The Children's Room (Early Toys & Textiles)
Activities: Classes for adults & children; docent training; lect open to public, 6 vis lectr per year; competitions with prizes; sales shop sells books & prints

VIRGINIA

ALEXANDRIA

A ART LEAGUE, 105 N Union St, 22314. Tel 703-683-2323, 683-1780; FAX 703-683-5786; *Pres* Kathy O'Day; *VPres* Jamie Brooks; *Exec Dir* Cora Rupp; *Asst Executive Dir* Maria Simonsson; *Asst Dir* Linda Hafer; *Gallery Dir* Marsha Staiger; *School Dir* Geri Gordon; *Treas* Marge Alderson
Open Mon - Sat 10 AM - 5 PM, Sun Noon - 5 PM. No admis fee. Estab 1953 to promote & maintain standards of art through mem juried exhibitions & a large school which teaches all facets of the fine arts & some high skill crafts. Eleven rooms in the Torpedo Factory Art Center in Old Town Alexandria, Virginia; four gallery rooms & seven classrooms plus annex. Average Annual Attendance: 500,000. Mem: 1100; dues $45; annual meeting in June
Exhibitions: Monthly juried shows for members
Activities: Classes for adults & children; lect open to public, 15 vis lectr per year; gallery talks; tours; sponsors competitions with awards; sales shop sells art supplies

ART SERVICES INTERNATIONAL
For further information, see National and Regional Organizations

M GALLERY WEST LTD, 205 S Union St, 22314. Tel 703-549-7359; *Dir* Craig Snyder
Open Noon - 6 PM, cl Wed & Thurs. Estab 1979 to showcase artists in the Washington DC metro area. Average Annual Attendance: 3100. Mem: 30; dues $720; meeting first Mon night of each month
Income: $45,000 (financed by mem & commission on sales of art)
Collections: All media
Exhibitions: Solo & group shows

A NORTHERN VIRGINIA FINE ARTS ASSOCIATION, The Athenaeum, 201 Prince St, 22314. Tel 703-548-0035; FAX 703-768-7471; *Dir* Mary Gaissert Jackson; *Ballet Headmistress* Virginia Britton
Open Wed - Sat 11 AM - 3 PM, Sun 1 - 4 PM, cl Mon, Tues & holidays. No admis fee. Estab 1964 to promote education, appreciation, participation & pursuit of excellence in all forms of art & crafts; to enrich the cultural life of the metropolitan area & Northern Virginia. Main gallery space on main floor, with additional area available. Average Annual Attendance: 35,000. Mem: 950; dues $25
Income: Financed by mem & fund raisers
Exhibitions: Annual Joint Art League/Athenaeum Multi-media Juried show. Five Virginia Photographers: Sally Mann, E Gowen & Others. Thomas Hart Benton. Washington Color School: Stars & Stripes
Publications: Quarterly newsletter
Activities: Classes for adults & children; dramatic programs; docent training; lect open to public, 1-7 vis lectr per year; gallery talks; tours; competitions with awards; concerts; scholarships offered

ARLINGTON

M ARLINGTON ARTS CENTER, 3550 Wilson Blvd, 22201-2348. Tel 703-524-1494; *Dir* Carol Sullivan
Open Tues - Fri 11 AM - 5 PM, Sat & Sun 1 - 5 PM. No admis fee. Estab to present new work by emerging & established artists from the region (Virginia, Maryland, Washington DC, West Virginia, Pennsylvania, Delaware)

L ARLINGTON COUNTY DEPARTMENT OF PUBLIC LIBRARIES, Fine Arts Section, 1015 N Quincy St, 22201. Tel 703-358-5990; FAX 703-358-5962; *Head* Jayne McQuade
Open Mon - Thur 9 AM - 10 PM, Fri & Sat 9 AM - 5 PM, Sun 1 - 9 PM. Estab 1935 to serve needs of an urban-suburban population in all general subjects
Income: Financed by county & state appropriations
Library Holdings: Vols 2500; Total holdings: 20,000
Exhibitions: Local artists, crafts people & photographers have exhibitions at the central library each month. Six branch libraries also have special exhibits of similar nature
Publications: Monthly almanac of programs, library activities & exhibit
Activities: Lect open to public, 10 vis lectr per year; workshops; film shows; extended learning institute video-tapes from Northern Virginia Community College available

BLACKSBURG

VIRGINIA POLYTECHNIC INSTITUTE & STATE UNIVERSITY

M **Armory Art Gallery,** 201 Drapper Rd, 24061-0103. Tel 703-231-4859, 231-5547; FAX 703-231-7826; *Head Art Chair* David Crane; *Gallery Dir* Ray Kass
Open Mon - Fri Noon - 5 PM, Sat Noon - 4 PM. No admis fee. Estab 1969 to serve needs of art department as a teaching gallery as well as to meet community needs in an area where there are few large art centers & museums. Gallery is located in same building as Art Department; exhibition area is approx 16 x 40 ft. Average Annual Attendance: 2000 plus student use
Income: Financed through special university budget
Exhibitions: Special invited exhibitions & exhibitions by Virginia artists, students & visiting artists
Publications: Exhibition calendar; gallery announcements
Activities: Docent training to college students; lect open to public, 3 vis lectr per year; gallery talks; individual paintings & original objects of art lent to faculty & staff offices on campus, as well as library & continuing educ center; originate traveling exhibitions

M **Perspective Gallery,** Squires Student Ctr, Virginia Tech, 24061-0138. Tel 703-231-5431; FAX 703-231-5430; *Art Dir* Thomas F Butterfield
Estab 1969 to provide exhibits on the local & national level for the students, faculty & the college community. Average Annual Attendance: 50,000
Income: Financed by university unions & student activities
Exhibitions: Beatific Visions: Germana; English Silver: Masterpieces by Omar Ramsden; Enchanted Echoes, An installation by Truman Capone; Vessel & Wall, Recent Works by Janet Niewald & David Crane; Maryann Harman, Recent Paintings
Activities: Lect open to public; competitions

L **Art & Architecture Library,** 301 Cowgill Hall, 24061. Tel 703-231-9271; Elec Mail apburr@vtvm1.bitnet. *Librn* Annette Burr
Open Mon - Thurs 8 AM - 11 PM, Fri 8 AM - 5 PM, Sat 1 - 5 PM, Sun 2 - 11 PM. Estab 1928 to provide service to the College of Architecture & Urban Studies & the other divisions of the university. Circ 55,000
Income: Financed by state appropriation & gifts
Purchases: $69,500
Library Holdings: Vols 65,000; Per subs 300; Micro — Fiche, reels; AV — Cassettes, slides 65,000, v-tapes; Other — Clipping files, exhibition catalogs, pamphlets
Special Subjects: Architecture, Art, Building Construction, Urban Affairs & Planning
Publications: New Acquisitions List - Architecture Library, monthly

BROOKNEAL

M **PATRICK HENRY MEMORIAL FOUNDATION,** Red Hill National Memorial, Rte 2, PO Box 127, 24528. Tel 804-376-2044; *Exec Dir* James M Elson; *Admin Asst* Patrick Schroeder
Estab 1944 to preserve & develop a memorial to Patrick Henry. 1 room with Rothermel painting as focal point. Average Annual Attendance: 7000. Mem: dues $10 & up; annual meeting in May
Income: $168,000 (financed by endowment, mem, county & state appropriation)
Exhibitions: Patrick Henry Before the Virginia House of Burgesses by P F Rothermel; Patrick Henry Memorabilia
Publications: Quarterly newsletter
Activities: Classes for adults & children; docent programs; lect open to public; exten dept provides lending collection; retail store sells books, prints, slides

CHARLES CITY

M **SHIRLEY PLANTATION,** 501 Shirley Plantation Rd, 23030. Tel 804-829-5121; FAX 804-829-6322; *Owner* Charles Hill Carter Jr
Open daily 9 AM - 5 PM, cl Christmas Day. Admis adults $7.50, senior citizens $6.50, AAA $6, youths 13-21 $5, children 6-12 $3.75, group rates. Estab 1613 to show the history of one distinguished family from colonial times to the present. Oldest Virginia Plantation continuous home to the Hill Carter Family, currently 10th & 11th generations. Average Annual Attendance: 40,000
Income: $136,000 (financed by admis fees)
Collections: Original portraits; silver & furniture: English & American
Activities: Individual paintings & original objects of art lent occasionally for exhibitions staged by such organizations as Virginia Museum & Colonial Williamsburg; museum shop sells books, reproductions, brass, silver, porcelain, prints & slides

M **WESTOVER,** 7000 Westover Rd, 23030. Tel 804-829-2882; *Owner* Mrs B C Fisher; *Mgr* F S Fisher
Grounds & garden open daily 9 AM - 6 PM. Admis $2, children $.50; house interior not open. Built about 1730 by William Byrd II, Founder of Richmond, the house is considered an outstanding example of Georgian architecture in America, with steeply sloping roof, tall chimneys in pairs at both ends, elaborate Westover doorway, a three story central structure with two end wings. The path from the Caretakers House to the house is lined with tulip poplars over 100 years old; former kitchen is a separate small brick building. East of the house (open to visitors) is the Necessary House, an old icehouse & a dry well with passageways leading under the house to the river. The Westover gates of delicate ironwork incorporate initials WEB; lead eagles on the gateposts, fence column topped with stone finials cut to resemble pineapples, beehives, & other symbolic designs. Long estab boxwood garden with tomb of William Byrd II. Members of his family, & Captain William Perry, who died Aug 1637, are buried in old church cemetery one-fourth mile west of house

CHARLOTTE

A **ARTS & SCIENCE COUNCIL,** 227 W Trade St, Ste 250, 28202. Tel 704-372-9667; Elec Mail 704-372-8210. *Pres* Michael Marsicano; *Sr VPres Resource Management* Hellena M Tidwell; *Sr VPres Admin* Laura Smith; *Public Relations Dir* Scott Bedford
Estab 1958 to provide planning, oversight & funding required to ensure & support a vibrant, culturally diverse arts & science community in Mecklenburg County
Income: Financed by city appropriation & fundraising
Activities: Grants offered

CHARLOTTESVILLE

M **THOMAS JEFFERSON MEMORIAL FOUNDATION,** Monticello, PO Box 316, 22902. Tel 804-984-9801; FAX 804-977-7757; Elec Mail monticello@va.pubnix.com. *Pres* Daniel P Jordan
Open Mar - Oct Mon - Sun 8 AM - 5 PM, Nov - Feb Mon - Sun 9 AM - 4:30 PM, cl Christmas. Admis adults $8, children 6-11 & school groups $3. Monticello is owned & maintained by the Thomas Jefferson Memorial Foundation, a non-profit organization founded in 1923. The home of Thomas Jefferson, designed by him & built 1769-1809, contains many original furnishings & art objects
Collections: †Jeffersonian furniture; †memorabilia; †art objects & manuscripts
Activities: Museum shop sells books, reproductions & slides

M **SECOND STREET GALLERY,** 201 Second St NW, 22902. Tel 804-977-7284; *Dir* Sarah Sargent; *Pres Board of Dirs* Theresa Murt; *Treas* William Chapman
Open Tues - Sat 10 AM - 5 PM, Sun 1 - 5 PM. No admis fee. Estab 1973 as an alternative arts space to present emerging & accomplished contemporary artists from regional & national localities, to increase the appreciation of contemporary art in Virginia region, & to increase the dialogue between artists & the community. One gallery 24 ft x 32 ft. Average Annual Attendance: 15,000. Mem: 300; dues family $500, contributing $100, individual $35
Income: Financed by individual, corporate & foundation contributions, grants from the Virginia Commision for the Arts, The National Endowment for the Arts & special fund raising activities
Exhibitions: M T Landis (paintings); Jeanette Montgomery-Barron (photographs); Laurel Quarberg, site specific installations
Publications: Laurel Quarberg, Returning the Favor, catalogue; The Second Glance, quarterly newsletter
Activities: Lect; tours; literary readings; workshops

UNIVERSITY OF VIRGINIA

M **Bayly Art Museum,** Rugby Rd, 22903. Tel 804-924-3592, 924-7458 (Tours); FAX 804-924-6321; *Dir* Anthony Hirschel; *Cur* Suzanne Foley; *Dir Educ* Jane Anne Young; *Registrar* Jean Collier; *Cur Works on Paper* Stephen Margulies; *Adminr* Susan Howell; *Dir Develop* Claire Holman Thompson; *Preparator* Rob Browning
Open Tues - Sun 1 - 5 PM, cl Mon. No admis fee, donations accepted. Estab 1935 to make original works of art available to the university community & to the general pub. Average Annual Attendance: 26,000. Mem: 1400; dues director's circle $2500, benefactor $1000, patron $500, sponsor $250, fellow $100, donor $60, member $35, senior citizens $15, student free
Income: Financed by mem, state appropriation & gifts
Purchases: Paintings by Gaspard Duguet (1660), Van den Bosch (mid 17th century), St Jerome in His Study; Roman coins; Indian Paintings; sculptures & manuscript pages; contemporary paintings, drawings, prints & photographs; African & Chinese objects
Collections: †American art; †European & American Art in the age of Jefferson; †Old Master prints; †East Asian art; †contemporary art; †American Indian art; †Ocean Art; †prints, drawings, photographs, Roman Coins
Exhibitions: The Big Picture: Contemporary Painting & Sculpture from the Permanent Collection; Inult Art from the Canadian Arctic: Prints & Sculpture; Suitable to a Woman: images of Women from the Age of Jefferson; The Made Landscape: City & County in 17th Century Dutch Prints; The Luminous Line: Four-Hundred Years of Western Printmaking; Images of Ancestors: Ties That Bind; Shifting Ground: Urban & Pastoral landscape Photographs, 1860-1993; The Loophole of Retreat, an Installation by Ellen Driscoll: ARTS Board 1995 Exhibition; Constance Stuart Larrabee: Selections from the WW II Photojournal; Multiple Exposure: The Group Portrait in Photography. Lowell Nesbitt (1933-1993): Paintings, Prints & Drawings in the Permanent Collection; Signs & Symbols: African Images in African-American Quilts; John Douglas Woodward; Movement & Meaning: Images of Dance in Early Modernist Art; Frank Benson: Paintings & Prints; Sally Mann Photographs; Astor Collection
Publications: Thomas Jefferson's Academical Village: The Creation of an Architectural Masterpiece; Masterpieces of Renaissance & Baroque Printmaking: A Decade of Collecting; Leon Kroll: A Spoken Memoir; John Barber: Selections from the archives; exhibition brochures; Newsletter
Activities: Educ programs for adults, students, children; docent training; lect open to public, 10 vis lectr per year; gallery talks; fels & internships offered; original works of art lent; museum shop sells books & cards

L **Fiske Kimball Fine Arts Library,** Bayly Dr, 22903. Tel 804-924-7024; FAX 804-982-2678; Elec Mail jsr8s@virginia.edu. *Librn* Jack Robertson; *Asst Librn & Public Services* Lynda White; *Coordr Digital Image Center* Christie Stephenson
Open school year Mon - Thurs 8 AM - 11 PM, Fri 8 AM - 5 PM, Sat 9 AM - 6 PM, Sun 1 - 11 PM. Estab 1970; combination of existing art & architecture libraries to provide a research facility providing printed, microform, audio visual & electronic materials for the art, architecture & drama curriculum. Fifty percent of collection is noncirculating. Circ 115,000
Income: $212,000
Library Holdings: Vols 127,000; Per subs 285; Micro — Fiche, reels; AV — A-tapes, cassettes, fs, Kodachromes, slides 171,000; Other — Exhibition catalogs, manuscripts, photographs
Special Subjects: Archaeology, Architecture, Art History, Film, Photography, Drama, Landscape Architecture, Planning and Urban Design

Collections: Francis Benjamin Johnson Photographs of Virgina Architecture;
Rare books
Publications: Bibliography of the Arts: Including Fine & Decorative Arts,
Architecture, Design & the Performing Arts, updated quarterly; Guide To
Souices, irregular serial; Notable Additions to the library collection, quarterly
Activities: Lect; tours

CHRISTIANSBURG

A BLACKSBURG REGIONAL ART ASSOCIATION, 302 Rolling Hills Dr,
24073. Tel 540-381-1018; *Pres* Leslye Bloom; *Membership Chmn* Barbara
Barlow
Estab 1950, affiliated with the Virginia Mus of Fine Arts, dedicated to the
encouragement & enjoyment of the arts. Mem: Dues including mem to the
Virginia Mus, family $12, individual $8
Income: Financed by mem & patron contributions
Collections: †Collection of paintings by contemporary artists who have exhibited
in Blacksburg
Activities: Dramatic programs; lect open to public, 3-5 vis lectr per year;
concerts; competitions; artmobile; originate traveling exhibitions

COURTLAND

M WALTER CECIL RAWLS MUSEUM, PO Box 310, 23837. Tel 804-653-2821;
FAX 804-653-9374; *Dir* Bruce Bumbalough; *Asst Dir* Beverly Worsham
Open Mon, Wed & Thurs 9 AM - 8:30 PM, Tues & Fri 9 AM - 5 PM, Sat 9 AM
- 3 PM. Estab 1958 to promote the arts in the city of Franklin & the counties of
Isle of Wight, Southampton, Surry & Sussex. Main gallery is 45 by 50 ft, 12 ft
high with track lighting. Average Annual Attendance: 3000. Mem: 248; dues
$14, $17, $30; annual meeting in April, Board of Trustees meet monthly
Income: $17,500 (financed by endowment & mem)
Collections: Antique glass & silver; †Southeastern Virginia Artists; drawings,
paintings, lithographs
Exhibitions: Annual Regional Photography Exhibition ; Annual Student Art
Show; regular; regular group exhibitions by area artists
Publications: R M A Bulletin
Activities: Classes for adults & children; Chamber concert series; sponsor annual
4 county art show; awards; paintings & art objects lent to museums & libraries

DANVILLE

M DANVILLE MUSEUM OF FINE ARTS & HISTORY, 975 Main St, 24541.
Tel 804-793-5644; FAX 804-799-6145; *Pres* James Nevin; *Dir* Nancy Perry;
Museum Shop Mgr Deborah Howard; *Public Affairs Mgr* Doris Jones; *Bus Mgr*
Betty Jones
Open Tues - Fri 10 AM - 5 PM, Sat & Sun 2 - 5 PM. No admis fee. Estab 1974.
Mus has two galleries: 27 x 35 ft with track lighting; two smaller galleries: 24 x
17 ft with track lighting. Average Annual Attendance: 20,000. Mem: 779;
meetings in Mar & Sept
Income: Financed by mem, city & state appropriation & grants
Collections: 19th & 20th century decorative arts including furniture, silver,
porcelain; Victorian American paintings & works on paper 1932 - present;
emphasis on works by contemporary Southern & Mid Atlantic Artists; American
Costume Collection including 2 locally made crazy quilts; historic artifacts &
documents pertaining to the history of Danville;
Exhibitions: Rotating schedule of art & history exhibitions; Survey shows
highlighting historic & modern artists in movement; Historic exhibit includes
restored period rooms, a Victorian parlor, bedroom & library; Civil War artifacts;
Artifacts from the wreck of the Old 97; (1997) Artist of the Month Exhibition.
(1998) Danville During the Civil War Years Exhibition
Publications: Last Capital of the Confederacy, book; Activities Report, quarterly
newspaper; Record of Davis' government in Danville, Last week of Civil War
Activities: Classes for adults & children; dramatic programs; docent training; lect
open to public, 6 vis lectr per year; concerts; gallery talks; tours; original objects
of art lent to other museums or galleries; museum shop sells books, original art &
reproductions

FAIRFAX

C MOBIL CORPORATION, Art Collection, 3225 Gallows Rd, 22037. Tel 703-
846-3043, 846-3000; *Art Consultant* Ivan Chermayeff; *Art Consultant* Lori
Shepherd; *Art Cur* Pamela Maslansky
Collections: Primarily works of young artists; paintings, drawings; watercolors;
original prints; sculpture

FORT MONROE

M HEADQUARTERS FORT MONROE, DEPT OF ARMY, Casemate Museum,
Bldg 20, Bernard Rd, PO Box 51341, 23651-0341. Tel 757-727-3935; FAX 757-
727-3886; AUTOVON 680-3935. *Dir* Dennis Mroczkowski; *Exhibit Specialist*
Chuck Payne; *History Specialist* Kathy Rothrock; *Archivist* David J Johnson
Open daily 10:30 AM - 4:30 PM. No admis fee. Estab 1951 to depict history of
Fort Monroe. Average Annual Attendance: 65,000. Mem: 200; dues one-time-
only fee based on plateaus: annual meeting in mid Jan
Income: Financed by federal appropriation
Collections: Jack Clifton Paintings; Remington Drawings; Zogbaum Drawings;
Artillery Implements; Military Posters
Exhibitions: Civil War Artifacts; Coast Artillery Guns in Action
Publications: Exhibition catalogs
Activities: Docent training; lect provided upon request to local organizations;
tours; individual paintings & original objects of art lent to other federal agencies;
originate traveling exhibitions 3 per year; museum shop sells books,
reproductions, prints, slides, original art, coffee cups, civil war games, pewter
soldiers & cannons

FREDERICKSBURG

MARY WASHINGTON COLLEGE

M Belmont, The Gari Melchers, 224 Washington St, 22405. Tel 703-899-4860; *Dir*
David Berreth; *Cur* Joanna D Catron
Open Mar - Nov, daily 10 AM - 5 PM, Sun 1 - 5 PM, Dec - Feb, daily 10 AM -
4 PM, Sun 1 - 4 PM. Admis adults $4, adult groups, senior citizens & groups $3,
children between 6 & 18, school & scout groups $1. Estab 1975 to exhibit,
preserve & interpret the works of art & memorabilia of the late American artist
Gari Melchers, in his former estate & studio. Studio consists of three gallery
rooms, a work room & storage rooms. Average Annual Attendance: 13,000
Income: $250,000 (financed by endowment & state appropriation)
Collections: †Over six hundred works of art, paintings, drawings & etchings by
Gari Melchers; †Over 1000 sketches & studies by Gari Melchers; †Paintings &
drawings by Berthe Morisot, Franz Snyders, Puvis de Chavannes & others;
†Furnishings from Europe & America
Publications: Exhibition catalogs
Activities: Docent training; aesthetics tours for school groups; outreach programs
for school & nursing homes; lect open to public; gallery talks; tours; individual
paintings & original objects of art lent

M Ridderhof Martin Gallery, College Ave at Seacobeck St, 22401-5358. Tel 540-
654-2120, Ext 1013; FAX 540-899-4373; *Dir* Forrest McGill; *Preparator* Carol
Kramer
Open Mon, Wed & Fri 10 AM - 4 PM, Sat & Sun 1 - 4 PM. No admis fee.
Estab 1956 for educ in art history & cultural history. Average Annual
Attendance: 3000
Collections: Asian art of all periods; 20th Century American art
Exhibitions: American Painting; Alfred Levitt: An Artist's Centennial. The
Stories of Gods & Goddesses: Mythological Themes in Western Art; Phyllis
Ridderhof Martin: Unseen Works & Margaret Sutton: Drawings of the 1940s
Publications: Booklets; catalogs
Activities: Classes for adults; lect open to public, 10 vis lectr per year; book
traveling exhibitions 2 per year; originate traveling exhibitions 1 per year

M JAMES MONROE MUSEUM, 908 Charles St, 22401. Tel 540-654-1043; FAX
540-654-1106; *Cur* Lee Langston-Harrison
Open Mar 1 - Oct 31 daily 9 AM - 5 PM, Nov 1 - Feb 28 daily 10 AM - 4 PM,
cl Thanksgiving, Dec 24, 25, 31 & Jan 1. Admis adults $3, children 6-18 $1.
Estab 1927 to keep in memory the life & service of James Monroe & of his
contribution to the principles of government, to preserve his treasured
possessions for present & future generations. Open to the pub in 1928; owned by
Commonwealth of Virginia & under the control of Mary Washington College; a
National Historic Landmark. Average Annual Attendance: 25,000
Collections: Louis XVI furniture purchased by the Monroes in France in 1794 &
later used by them in the White House; portraits; sculpture; silver; china; jewelry;
books; documents
Exhibitions: Images of a President: Portraits of James Monroe; Time Pieces:
Monroe's Fascination with Clocks & Watches; From Washington to Carter:
Presidential Paraphanelia at the J M Museum
Publications: Images of a President: Portraits of James Monroe, catalog Library
of James Monroe, catalog
Activities: Docent training; workshops; lect open to public; gallery talks; tours;
scholarships offered; exten dept serves Mary Washington College University of
VA area; museum shop sells books, magazines, reproductions, prints, slides,
history related objects & exclusive items from local crafts people

L James Monroe Memorial Library, 908 Charles St, 22401. Tel 540-654-1043;
FAX 540-654-1106; *Cur* Lee Langston-Harrison; *Dir Planning & Prog* John N
Pearce
Open daily 9 AM - 5 PM. Estab 1927 as a presidential mus & library. Open to
pub; archival resources available by appointment only. Average Annual
Attendance: 20,000
Income: Financed by state allocations & revenues
Library Holdings: Vols 10,000; Documents; Letters; Other — Manuscripts
27,000
Special Subjects: Monroe, Jefferson, Carter, Minor, Hoes, Virginia manuscripts

GLEN ALLEN

M COUNTY OF HENRICO, Meadow Farm Museum, 3400 Mountain Rd
(Mailing add: PO Box 27032, Richmond, 23273). Tel 804-672-5520; *Historic
Preservation Supv* Susan Hanson; *Coll Mgr* Kimberly Sicola
Open Tues - Sun Noon - 4 PM. Admis adults $1, children under 12 $.50. Estab
1981 to exhibit works of 20th century American folk artists. 20 ft by 20 ft, AV
room. Average Annual Attendance: 50,000
Income: Financed by Henrico County
Collections: 19th & 20th Century folk art
Publications: Exhibition flyers, annually
Activities: Children's classes; lect open to public, 4 vis lectr per year; tours;
individual paintings & original objects of art lent to Virginia Beach Art Center;
lending collection contains original art works, paintings & sculptures; sales shop
sells books & reproductions

L Library, 3400 Mountain Rd (Mailing add: PO Box 27032, 23273). Tel 804-672-
5520;
For reference only
Library Holdings: Vols 100; Per subs 10; AV — A-tapes, Kodachromes, slides, v-
tapes; Other — Clipping files, exhibition catalogs, photographs

GREAT FALLS

INDUSTRIAL DESIGNERS SOCIETY OF AMERICA
For further information, see National and Regional Organizations

HAMPTON

A CITY OF HAMPTON, Hampton Arts Commission, 4205 Victoria Blvd, 23669.
Tel 804-722-2787; *Dir* Michael P Curry; *Admin Asst* Evelyn McDonald; *Admin
Secy* Tricia Waldon
Open year round Tues - Fri 10 AM - 6 PM, Sat - Sun 1 - 5, cl major holidays.
No admis fee. Created in December, 1987, housed in the Charles H Taylor Arts
Center
Income: Financed by municipal funds & contributions
Exhibitions: Regional artists presented at Charles H Taylor Arts Center,
monthly; special events art shows; performances by international artists presented
at Ogden Hall
Activities: Classes for adults & children; dramatic programs; workshops;
demonstrations; lect open to public; concerts; gallery talks; tours; competitions
with awards

M HAMPTON UNIVERSITY, University Museum, 23668. Tel 804-727-5308;
FAX 804-727-5084; *Dir* Jeanne Zeidler
Open Sept - May Mon - Fri 8 AM - 5 PM, Sat & Sun Noon - 4 PM. No admis
fee. Estab 1868 as a mus of Traditional art & artifacts from African, Asian,
Oceanic & American Indian cultures & contemporary & traditional Afro-
American Art. Average Annual Attendance: 36,000
Income: Financed by college funds
Collections: African, Asian, Oceanic & American Indian Art; Contemporary &
traditional Afro-American Art
Activities: Educ dept; lect open to public; gallery talks; group tours by
appointment; individual paintings & original objects of art lent to other museums
& art galleries with appropriate security; lending collection includes 900 paintings
& 800 sculputes

HARRISONBURG

M JAMES MADISON UNIVERSITY, Sawhill Gallery, Duke Hall, 22807. Tel
703-568-6407; *Gallery Dir* Stuart C Downs
Open Sept - Apr, Mon - Fri 10:30 AM - 4:30 PM, Sat & Sun 1:30 - 4:30 PM,
May - Aug call for summer schedule & hours. No admis fee. Estab 1967 to
schedule changing exhibitions for the benefit of students and citizens of this area.
One-room gallery of 1040 sq ft with movable panels. Average Annual
Attendance: 10,000-12,000
Income: Financed by state appropriation, and is part of operation in Art
Department budget
Collections: Sawhill Collection, mainly artifacts from classical civilizations;
Staples Collection of Indonesian Art; small group of modern works
Exhibitions: One person exhibitions. Holography by D E Tyler; Philip Pearlstein:
Personal Selections, Faith Ringgold, Alan Shields, Ken Tyler, Jerry Vellsmann
Activities: Competitions

LEESBURG

M OATLANDS, INC, 20850 Oatlands Plantation Lane, 20175. Tel 703-777-3174;
FAX 703-777-4427; *Mgr* Linda Glidden
Open Mar - Dec, Mon - Sat 10 AM - 5 PM, Sun 1 - 5 PM, cl Thanksgiving Day.
Admis adults $5, senior citizens & youths (7-18) $4, under 12 free; special events
at special rates, group rates by arrangement, free to National Trust members
except during special events. Oatlands is a Classical Revival Mansion constructed
by George Carter, son of Robert (Councillor) Carter (circa 1800-06). It was
partially remodeled in 1827 when the front portico with hand carved Corinthian
capitals was added. Confederate troops were billeted here during part of the Civil
War. The home remained in possession of the Carters until 1897. In 1903 Mr &
Mrs William Corcoran Eustis, of Washington DC, bought Oatlands. Their
daughters gave the property to the National Trust for Historic Preservation; the
property is protected by preservation easements which help insure the estates
continuing role as a center for equestrian sports & cultural events which are
produced by Oatlands & various groups. Average Annual Attendance: $50,000
Income: $600,000 (financed by grants, endowments, admis, fundraising events &
shop sales)
Collections: Carter & Eustis Collection of Furniture Greek-Revival ornaments
adorn interior
Exhibitions: Annual needlework Show; Christmas at Oatlands; semi annual
Antique Show
Publications: Oatlands Column, quarterly newsletter
Activities: Special events

LEXINGTON

WASHINGTON & LEE UNIVERSITY
M Gallery of DuPont Hall, 24450. Tel 540-463-8861; *Dir* Kathleen Olsen
Open Mon - Fri 9 AM - 5 PM, Sat 11 AM - 3 PM, Sun 2 - 4 PM. No admis fee.
Estab 1929 in separate gallery as teaching resource of art. One room, 30 x 60 ft,
is maintained for temporary exhibits; also maintained one storeroom. Average
Annual Attendance: 40,000
Income: Financed through the university
Exhibitions: Annual faculty show; annual student show; monthly exhibitions;
traveling exhibitions
Publications: Exhibition catalogs
Activities: Lect open to public, 5 vis lectr per year; gallery talks; tours; book
traveling exhibitions 3 per year
L Leyburn Library, 24450. Tel 540-463-8644, 463-8662; FAX 540-463-8964; Elec
Mail warren.y@wlu.edu. *Head Librn* Barbara J Brown; *Art Librn* Yolanda
Warren
Open for reference to students, scholars, public; this library is part of the main
university library
Library Holdings: Vols 450,000; Per subs 35; AV — Slides 40,000; Other —
Sculpture 4000
Special Subjects: Aesthetics, Antiquities-Oriental, Art History, Asian Art,
Oriental Art, American Art of 18th & 19th centuries
Collections: Rare books, 17th - early 20th centuries
Activities: Lect open to public, 2 vis lectr per year; gallery talks

M Lee Chapel & Museum, 24450. Tel 540-463-8768; *Dir* Robert C Peniston; *Dir*
Robert C Peniston
Open mid-Apr - mid-Oct Mon - Sat 9 AM - 5 PM, Sun 2 - 5 PM, mid-Oct -
mid-Apr Mon - Sat 9 AM - 4 PM, Sun 2 - 5 PM. No admis fee. Estab 1868 as a
part of the university. It is used for concerts, speeches & other events. Mus is
used also to display the paintings, collections & personal items of the Washington
& Lee families. The Lee Chapel is a National Historic Landmark. Average
Annual Attendance: 55,00
Income: Financed through the university
Collections: Custis-Washington-Lee Art Collection; Lee archives; Lee family
crypt; Lee's office; recumbent statute of General Lee by Valentine
Publications: Brochure
Activities: Sales shop sells books, prints, souvenirs

LYNCHBURG

L JONES MEMORIAL LIBRARY, 2311 Memorial Ave, 24501. Tel 804-846-
0501; *Dir* Edward Gibson
No admis fee. Estab 1907. For reference
Income: $180,000 (financed by endowment & donations)
Purchases: $5000
Library Holdings: Vols 20,000; Per subs 45; Architectural drawings; Other —
Clipping files, exhibition catalogs, manuscripts, memorabilia, original art works,
photographs, sculpture
Special Subjects: Architecture, Drawings, Historical Material
Collections: †Lynchburg Architectural Archives

A LYNCHBURG FINE ARTS CENTER INC, 1815 Thomson Dr, 24501. Tel
804-846-8451; FAX 804-846-3806; *Exec Dir* Mary Brumbaugh
Open Mon - Fri 9 AM - 5 PM; other hours depending upon programs. No
admis. Estab 1958 to promote interest in and appreciation and talent for art,
music, dramatic literature and other fine arts. Mem: Annual meeting in June
Income: Financed by corporate & private donation, earned income from
programs & performances
Exhibitions: Eighteen per year including Area Photography Juried Show & Area
Art Juried Show
Publications: Facets, monthly newspaper
Activities: Classes for adults & children; dramatic programs; dance, theater,
music & visual arts workshops; lect open to public, 2-3 vis lectr per year;
concerts; gallery talks; tours; competitions with cash awards; scholarships; exten
dept serving youth

M RANDOLPH-MACON WOMAN'S COLLEGE, Maier Museum of Art, 2500
Rivermont Ave, 24503. Tel 804-947-8136; FAX 804-947-8726; *Exec Dir* Sarah
Cash; *Dir Colls & Progs* Ellen Schall Agnew; *Museum Educator* Doni
Guggenheimer
Open Sept - May Tues - Sun 1 - 5 PM, cl Mon. No admis fee. American Art
Collection established 1920 to promote scholarship through temporary
exhibitions & a permanent collection. Building currently housing collection built
in 1952. 5 galleries contain more than 75 paintings from the permanent
collection by American artists. One gallery is used for the 6 to 8 temporary
exhibitions displayed each academic year
Income: Financed by endowment
Purchases: Joseph Cornell (collage); Jamie Wyeth (watercolor); John Frederick
Peto (oil); Jennifer Bartlett (work on paper)
Collections: Extensive collection of 19th & 20th Century American paintings
European & American graphics
Exhibitions: Realism in a Post Modern World: Selections from the Sydney &
Frances Lewis Collection; Jennifer Bartlett; Joan Mitchell
Publications: Annual exhibition catalogue; biannual newsletter
Activities: Dramatic programs; lect open to public, 5 vis lectr per year; concerts;
gallery talks; tours; objects of art lent; originate traveling exhibitions

MASON NECK

M GUNSTON HALL PLANTATION, 10709 Gunston Rd, 22079. Tel 703-550-
9220; FAX 703-550-9480; *Dir* Thomas A Lainhoff; *Asst Dir* Ross G Randall
Open daily 9:30 AM - 5 PM, cl Thanksgiving, Christmas, New Years Day.
Admis adults $5, students (6-15) $1.50. Estab 1950 to acquaint the pub with
George Mason, colonial patriot & his 18th century house & gardens, covering
555 acres. Owned & operated by the Commonwealth of Virginia. Average
Annual Attendance: 50,000. Mem: 2200
Income: Financed by state appropriation & admis fee
Collections: 18th century English & American decorative arts, furniture &
paintings; 18th & 19th century family pieces
Activities: Classes for children; docent training; lect open to public, 8-12 vis lectr
per year; tours; individual paintings & original objects of art lent to other
museums; sales shop sells books, reproductions; Childrens Touch Museum
located in basement
L Library, 10709 Gunston Rd, 22079. Tel 703-550-9220; FAX 703-550-9480; *Dir*
Thomas Lainhoff; *Cur* Susan Borchardt
Open Mon - Fri 9:30 AM - 5 PM, cl Thanksgiving, Christmas & New Years
Day. Estab 1950 to recreate an 18th Century Virginia gentlemen's library as a
research source plus acquiring a working reference collection on George Mason,
early Virginia history & the decorative arts
Income: Financed by endowment
Library Holdings: Vols 11,000; Per subs 50; Original documents; Micro —
Fiche, reels; AV — Cassettes, fs, motion pictures; Other — Exhibition catalogs,
manuscripts, memorabilia, pamphlets, photographs, reproductions
Special Subjects: Archaeology, Architecture, Decorative Arts, Furniture,
Historical Material, Manuscripts, Period Rooms, Pewter, Porcelain, Portraits,
Prints, Restoration & Conservation, Silver, Textiles, Mason Family, Early
Virginiana
Collections: Robert Carter Collection; Pamela C Copeland Collection; Elizabeth
L Frelinghuysen Collection; Mason-Mercer Rare Book Collection

MIDDLETOWN

M **BELLE GROVE PLANTATION,** PO Box 137, 22645. Tel 540-869-2028; FAX 540-869-9638; *Pres* Peter J Cook; *Exec Dir* Elizabeth McClung
Open Apr - Oct Mon - Sat 10 AM - 4 PM, Sun 1 - 5 PM, Nov - Mar by appointment. Admis adults $2.50, senior citizens $2, students $1.25, special rates. Open to the pub in 1967, it is preserved as an historic house & is the property of the National Trust for Historic Preservation & managed by Belle Grove, Inc, an independent local nonprofit organizaiton. It serves as a local preservation center & resource for the interpretation of regional culture in the Shenandoah Valley. Built in 1794 for Major Issac Hite, Jr, a Revolutionary War officer & brother-in-law of James Madison, Belle Grove was designed with the help of Thomas Jefferson. During the Battle of Cedar Creek in 1864, the house served as headquarters to General Phillip Sheridan. The property is a working farm & Belle Grove maintains an active prog of events for the vis pub
Exhibitions: Four Portraits by Charles Peal Polk: Colonel James Madison, Nelly Conway Madison, Major Isaac Hite, Mrs Isaac Hite
Activities: Seminars on various subjects in museum field offered through the year

MOUNT VERNON

M **MOUNT VERNON LADIES' ASSOCIATION OF THE UNION,** PO Box 110, 22121. Tel 703-780-2000; FAX 703-799-8698; *Regent* Mrs Robert E Lee IV; *Resident Dir* James C Rees; *Cur* Christine Meadows; *Librn* Dr Barbara McMillan
Open to the public every day in the year from 9 AM: entrance gate closes Mar 1 - Oct 1 at 5 PM, Oct 1 - Mar 1 at 4 PM. Admis annual pass $12, adults $8, $7. 50 for groups of 12 or more children or groups of 20 or more adults, student groups $4.50, adults over 62 $7.50, children 6-11 $4, children under 6 free. The home of George Washington, purchased in 1858 from his great-grand-nephew by the Mount Vernon Ladies Assoc of the Union, which maintains it. The estate includes spinning house, coach house, various quarters, restored flower & kitchen gardens; also the tomb of George & Martha Washington. George Washington: Pioneer Farm - a four acre site with a reconstruction of his sixteen sided treading barn. Average Annual Attendance: 1,000,000. Mem: Semi-annual meeting Oct & Apr
Income: Financed by admis fees & donations
Collections: Mansion is fully furnished with original & period furniture, silver, portraits & prints; large collection of original Washington memorabilia, manuscripts & books
Publications: Annual Report; The Gardens & Grounds at Mount Vernon; George Washington, A Brief Biography; The Last Will & Testament of George Washington; The Maxims of Washington; Mount Vernon; The Mount Vernon Coloring Book; The Mount Vernon Cookbook; The Mount Vernon Gardens; Mount Vernon Handbook; Nothing More Agreeable: Music in George Washington's Family; George Washington: Citizen - Soldier
Activities: Sales shop sells books, reproductions, prints, slides, coloring books, t-shirts, food & Christmas items

L **Library,** George Washington Pky S, PO Box 110, 22121. Tel 703-799-8639; *Librn* Barbara McMillan; *Library Asst* Rebecca Case
Open by appointment only
Special Subjects: Archaeology, Architecture, Decorative Arts, Furniture, Historical Material, Landscape Architecture, Manuscripts, Painting - American, Painting - British, Period Rooms, Portraits, Printmaking, Prints, Restoration & Conservation, Textiles
Collections: American Revolution; 18th Century Agriculture; Mount Vernon; Virginia slavery; Washington family; George Washington
Publications: Annual report

M **WOODLAWN PLANTATION,** PO Box 37, 22121. Tel 703-780-4000; FAX 703-780-8509; *Dir* Susan Olsen
Open 9:30 AM - 4:30 PM, except Thanksgiving, Christmas & News Years. Admis adults $6, senior citizens & students $4, group rates by arrangement. Land originally part of Mount Vernon. Built in 1800-05 for George Washington's granddaughter upon her marriage to Lawrence Lewis, Washington's nephew. It was designed with central pavilion & flanking wings by Dr William Thornton, winner of the architectural competition for the design of the United States Capitol. A group of Quakers, a pioneer anthropologist, a playwright & Senator Oscar W Underwood of Alabama were among Woodlawn's residents after the Lewises. In 1951 the foundation's trustees decided that the visiting public would be better served if Woodlawn was administered by the National Trust. The mansion furnishings are largely from the Federal & early Empire periods & include Lewis family furniture. Average Annual Attendance: 47,500. Mem: 350; dues $35
Exhibitions: Needlework Exhibit; Formal Rose Teas; Antiques & Crafts Fair; Civil War Days; Fall Festival of Needlework; Fall Quilt Show; A Woodlawn Christmas in December
Publications: Friends of Woodlawn Newsletter, quarterly; Welcome to Woodlawn, booklet
Activities: Classes for adults & children; dramatic programs; docent training; special events; lect open to public, 6 vis lectr per year; concerts, tours; individual paintings & original objects of art lent to qualified museums; lending collection consists of original prints, paintings, furnishings & textiles; museum shop sells books, reproductions, prints, antiques, foods, toys

M **FRANK LLOYD WRIGHT POPE-LEIGHEY HOUSE,** 9000 Richmond Hwy, 22309. Tel 703-780-3264; *Dir* Susan Olsen
Open Mar - Dec, daily 9:30 AM - 4:30 PM. Frank Lloyd Wright's Pope-Leighey House is a property of the National Trust for Historic Preservation, located on the grounds of Woodlawn Planation. This residence was designed in 1939 by Frank Lloyd Wright for his clients, the Loren Pope Family. Built of cypress, brick and glass, the Usonian structure contains such features as a flat roof, radiant heat, indirect lighting, carport & custom furniture, all designed by Frank Lloyd Wright, as an example of architecture for the average-income family. Threatened by construction of an interstate highway in 1964, Mrs Marjorie Folsom Leighey, second owner, presented the property to the National Trust for Historic Preservation. It was then moved to the Woodlawn grounds
Exhibitions: Christmas at Pope-Leighey House & annual candlelight tour
Publications: Brochure and paperback history of house
Activities: Classes for adults & children; docent training; lect open to public, 6 vis lectr per year; tours

NEWPORT NEWS

M **THE MARINERS' MUSEUM,** 100 Museum Dr, 23606-3759. Tel 804-596-2222; Elec Mail info@mariner.org;
Internet Home Page Address http://mariner.org. WATS 800-581-7245. *Pres* John B Hightower; *VPres Finance & Admin* Larry Dobrinsky; *VPres Public Affairs & Publications* Karen Wible; *VPres Facilities Management* John Cannup; *VPres Develop* Marguerite K Vail
Open daily 10 AM - 5 PM, cl Thanksgiving Day & Christmas Day. Admis adults $6.50, students $3.25 (ID required for students 18 & older), children ages 5 & under free, discounts offered for active duty military, AAA members & senior citizens, group rate for party of 10 or more. Estab 1930 as an educational, non-profit institution accredited by the American Assoc of Museums, preserves & interprets maritime history & other maritime artifacts. Costumed interpreters & film Mariner, help maritime history come alive. Located in a 550 acre park which features the 5 mile Noland Trail. Mus has twelve permanent galleries, including Age of Exploration & Chesapeake galleries; paintings & decorative arts; Crabtree Collection of miniature ships; collection of International Small Craft; Great Hall of Steam; William F Gibbs: Naval Architect Gallery. Maintains reference library. Average Annual Attendance: 100,000. Mem: 1600
Collections: Crabtree Collection of miniature ships; thousands of marine artifacts; over 1000 paintings; over 1000 ship models; ceramics, scrimshaw, small craft
Exhibitions: (1997) The Art of the Shipcarver; Sun Ships: Photographs by Barry Winiker; The Weapons of War; Under the Black Flag-Life Among the Pirates; The Culture of the Sea: One Hundred Photographs from the Mariners Museum
Publications: Mariners' Museum Pipe, quarterly newsletter; Mariners' Museum Annual, annual journal
Activities: Classes for adults & children; docent training; lect open to members, 6 vis lectr per year; concerts; gallery talks; tours; competitions with awards; scholarships & fels offered; individual paintings & original objects of art lent to museums; collection contains 120 motion pictures, 2000 original art works, 8000 original prints, 1300 paintings; museum shop sells books, magazines, reproductions, prints, slides, jewelry & other maritime related items

L **Library,** 100 Museum Dr, 23606-3759. Tel 804-595-0368; FAX 804-591-8212; *Librn* Benjamin Trask; *Asst to Librn* Kathryn B Braig; *Archivist* Roger T Crew Jr
Open Mon - Sat 9 AM - 5 PM, cl Sun. Estab 1930. For reference only
Income: Financed by endowment
Library Holdings: Vols 75,000; Per subs 150; Original documents; Other — Clipping files, exhibition catalogs, manuscripts, memorabilia, pamphlets, photographs 350,000, prints
Special Subjects: Anthropology, Art History, Crafts, Decorative Arts, Drafting, Eskimo Art, Flasks & Bottles, Handicrafts, History of Art & Archaeology, Manuscripts, Maps, Marine Painting, Painting - American, Painting - British, Painting - Dutch, Maritime and Naval history

A **PENINSULA FINE ARTS CENTER,** 101 Museum Dr, 23606. Tel 804-596-8175; FAX 804-596-0807; *Pres* Harriet Storm; *VPres* Frank Corbett; *VPres* C Frederick Westfall; *VPres* Angie Allison; *Exec Dir* Lisa Swenson
Open Tues - Sat 10 AM - 4 PM, Sun 1 - 4 PM. No admis fee. Estab 1962 to promote an appreciation of the fine arts through changing monthly exhibitions with works from the Virginia Mus, other institutions & outstanding artists, both emerging & estab. Three galleries maintained with changing exhibitions. Mem: 850; dues family (incl mem) $30, individual $25
Income: Financed by mem
Exhibitions: Juried exhibition; Art as in Vocation; Master Enamalist-Invitational
Publications: Art class schedules; newsletter to members, quarterly; notification of special events
Activities: Classes for adults & children; lect open to public, 8 vis lectr per year; gallery talks; competitions; cash awards & certificates of distinction; gallery shop sells books, original art & crafts

NORFOLK

M **CHRYSLER MUSEUM OF ART,** 245 W Olney Rd, 23510-1587. Tel 757-644-6201, 622-2787 (Art Info Line); FAX 757-664-6201; *Dir* Dr William J Hennessey; *Chief Cur* Jeff Harrison; *Vol Spec Events* Ronda Baucom; *Cur American Art* Nick Clark; *Cur Photo* Brooks Johnson; *Dir Educ* Ann D Vernon; *Public Relations Mgr* Rick Salzberg; *Pres Board of Trustees* Harry T Lester; *Head Librn* Steven A Eichner
Open Tues - Sat 10 AM - 4 PM, Sun 1 - 5 PM, cl Mon. Admis adults $4, seniors & students $2, children under 5 free; Wed contributions only. Mus originates from a memorial assoc estab in 1901 to house a collection of tapestries & paintings donated in memory of & by Irene Leache. The Norfolk Soc of Arts was founded in 1917, which raised funds throughout the 1920's to erect a building to permanently hold the collection. A Florentine Renaissance style building, named the Norfolk Mus of Arts & Sciences, opened to the pub in 1933. The Houston Wing, housing the Mus Theatre & Lounge, was added in 1956, the Centennial Wing in 1976 & another wing to house the library & additional galleries was opened in 1989. The building has been designated the Chrysler Mus since 1971, when a large portion of the collection of Walter P Chrysler, Jr was given to Norfolk. Mus contains 140,000 sq ft. Average Annual Attendance: 200,000. Mem: 3500; dues benefactor $10,000, fellow $5000, sponsor $2500, director's circle $1000, patron $500, friend $250, sustaining $100, associate $60, family $35, individual $25, student & senior citizens $20, corporate mem also available
Income: Financed by municipal appropriation & state appropriations as well as federal grants
Collections: African artists; American art from 18th century primitives - 20th century Pop Art; Bernini's Bust of the Savior; Francoise Boucher, The Vegetable Vendor; Mary Cassatt, The Family; Thomas Cole, The Angel Appearing to the

Shepherds; Decorative arts including furniture, silver, gold, enameled objects & Worcester porcelain; 18th century English paintings; 14th-18th century Italian paintings; 15th-18th century Netherlandish & German works; Gaugin's Loss of Virginity; Bernice Chrysler Garbish & Edgar William Garbish Native American paintings; Institute of Glass; Matisse, Bowl of Apples on a Table; Near & Far East Artists; Oriental artists; photography collection including Alezander Gardner, Lewis W Hine, Walker Evans, Ansel Adams, W Eugene Smith & contemporaries Joel Meyerowitz & Sheila Metzner; Pre-Columbian artists; Reni, The Meeting of David & Abigail; 16th - 20th century French paintings; works from Spanish school
Exhibitions: (1997) Land of Paradox; The Decorative Art of Louis Comfort Tiffany; The Art of the Silversmith: Silver from the Permanent Collection; With This Ring: A Portrait of Marriage by Mary Kalergis. (1997-98) Contemporary Art from the Permanent Collection Master Drawings from the Chrysler Museum; Images of Childhood: the World of Children in the Chrysler Museum; Frank Lloyd Wright; Daguerrean Masters; Light Images 1990 (photography); Fantasy in Fabric: The Artist as Couturier; 30th Irene Leach Memorial Exhibition
Publications: Monthly members' newsletter; exhibition catalogues; Annual Report
Activities: Educ program; family programs; docent training; teacher workshops; outreach information packages; lect open to public, 20 vis lectr per year; concerts; gallery talks; tours; competitions (juried); exten dept operates three historic home; individual paintings & original objects of art lent to accredited museums; book traveling exhibitions; originate traveling exhibitions organized & circulated; museum shop sells books, original art, reproductions, prints, slides, glass, gold & silver jewelry, ceramics, stationary, postcards & toys
L **Jean Outland Chrysler Library,** 245 W Olney Rd, 23510-1587. Tel 757-664-6200; FAX 757-664-6201; *Library Asst* Steven A Eichner
Estab 1918 to collect materials in support of the collections of the Chrysler Mus. Open to the pub for reference only
Income: Financed partially by endowment
Library Holdings: Vols 60,000; Per subs 200; Auction catalogs; Micro — Fiche; AV — V-tapes; Other — Clipping files, exhibition catalogs
Special Subjects: Art History, Decorative Arts, Glass, Photography, Pre-Columbian Art, American Art, Western European Art
Activities: Lect open to public

M **HERMITAGE FOUNDATION MUSEUM,** 7637 N Shore Rd, 23505. Tel 804-423-2052; FAX 804-423-1604; *Dir* Philip R Morrison; *Asst to Dir* Patricia Kirby; *Pres of Bd* W Marshall Jr; *Admin Asst* Jean Turmel
Open daily 10 AM - 5 PM, Sun 1 - 5 PM, cl New Years Day, Thanksgiving Day, Christmas Day. Admis adults $4, children 6-18 $1. Estab 1937 to disseminate information concerning arts & maintain a collection of fine art materials. Mansion on 12 acre site houses major collections as well as two small changing exhibition galleries. Average Annual Attendance: 20,000. Mem: 400; dues $30; meeting four times per yr
Income: $110,000 (financed by endowment & mem)
Collections: English oak & teakwood woodcarvings; Major collection of decorative arts from various periods & countries; Oriental collection of Chinese bronzes & ceramic tomb figures, lacquer ware, jades & Persian rugs; Spanish & English furniture; individual paintings & original objects of art lent to institutions; lending collection contains original art works, paintings, records & sculpture
Exhibitions: American Illustrator; Art on Paper; Isabel Bishop; Bernard Chaet (paintings); Contemporary American Graphics; Currier & Ives; Export Porcelain from a Private Collection; Freshwork (Virginia photographers); Alexandra Georges (photographs); The Photographs of Wright Morris; Henry Pitz (one man show); student exhibitions from summer workshops
Activities: Classes for adults & children; dramatic programs; lect open to public & auxiliary lect for members only, 10-12 vis lectr per year; concerts; tours; scholarships offered; individual paintings & original objects of art lent to institutions; lending collection contains 750 original art works, 300 paintings, 150 records & 50 sculpture; book traveling exhibitions; originate traveling exhibitions
L **Library,** 7637 N Shore Rd, 23505. Tel 804-423-2052; FAX 804-423-1604; *Dir* Philip R Morrison
Open to students for reference only
Library Holdings: Vols 800

M **MACARTHUR MEMORIAL,** MacArthur Sq, 23510. Tel 757-441-2965; FAX 757-441-5389; Elec Mail macmem@norfolk.infi.net. *Cur* Jeffrey Acosta; *Admin Asst* Janice Stafford Dudley; *Archivist* James W Zobel
Open Mon - Sat 10 AM - 5 PM, Sun 11 AM - 5 PM, cl Thanksgiving, Christmas, New Years Day. No admis fee. Estab 1964 to memorialize General Douglas MacArthur. Located in the 1850 Court House which was rebuilt in 1962; nine galleries contain memorabilia. Average Annual Attendance: 70,000
Income: $427,630 (financed by city appropriation & the General Douglas MacArthur Foundation)
Collections: Objects d'art, murals, portraits, photographs
Activities: Concerts; gallery talks; tours; research assistance grants & fellowships offered; individual paintings and original objects of art lent to museums; museum shop sells books, reproductions, prints, slides
L **Library & Archives,** MacArthur Sq, 23510. Tel 804-441-2965; FAX 804-441-5389; *Archivist* James W Zobel
Open 8:30 AM - 5 PM. Estab 1964. Average Annual Attendance: 75,000
Income: Financed by the City of Norfolk & the General Douglas MacArthur Foundation as part of the MacArthur Memorial Museum
Library Holdings: Vols 4000; Original documents; Micro — Fiche, reels; AV — A-tapes, cassettes, motion pictures, rec, slides, v-tapes; Other — Clipping files, framed reproductions, manuscripts
Special Subjects: Douglas MacArthur, Philippine Insurrection, Philippines, World War I, World War II
Collections: Brigadier General Bonner F Fellers Collection (papers); Major General Courtney Whitney Collection (papers)
Activities: Classes for adults & children; lect open to public, 2-3 vis lectr per year; tours; competitions with prizes; scholarships offered

M **OLD DOMINION UNIVERSITY,** Gallery, 765 Granbe St, 23501. Tel 804-683-4047, 683-2843; FAX 804-683-5923; *Dir* David Johnson; *Art Chmn* Michael Fanivza
Open Fri - Sun 11 AM - 4 PM. No admis fee. Estab 1972 for the exhibition of contemporary work; also estab as a pub forum for contemporary artists, with student exposure. Average Annual Attendance: 3000
Income: Financed by endowment & city appropriation
Library Holdings: Vols 7000; Per subs 40
Exhibitions: Monthly exhibitions during academic year
Activities: Lect open to public, 10 vis lectr per year; gallery talks; tours; competitions; exten dept
L **Elise N Hofheimer Art Library,** Fine & Performing Arts Ctr, Rm 109, 23529. Tel 804-683-4059; Elec Mail clv100u@mozart.fpa.odu.edu. *Art Librn Asst* Clayton Vaughan
Open Mon - Thurs 8 AM - 9 PM, Fri 8 AM - 5 PM, Sat 1 - 5 PM, Sun 1 - 6 PM. Open to students & faculty; open to the public for reference
Income: Financed by state, gifts & grants
Library Holdings: Vols 11,000; Per subs 36; Micro — Cards, fiche, prints, reels; AV — A-tapes, fs, rec, slides, v-tapes; Other — Clipping files, exhibition catalogs, framed reproductions, manuscripts, memorabilia, original art works, pamphlets, photographs, prints, reproductions

PETERSBURG

M **THE CITY OF PETERSBURG MUSEUMS,** 15 W Bank St, 23803. Tel 804-733-2401; *Dir* Suzanne Savery
Open Mon - Sun 10 AM - 5 PM, cl holidays. Admis adults $3, senior citizens, children & groups $2. Estab 1972 as a system of historic house museums. Seven historic sites dating from 1770-1839. Average Annual Attendance: 85,000
Collections: †City of Petersburg photographs & manuscripts; †Military-Civil War; †19th century decorative arts
Activities: Classes for adults & children, dramatic programs; docent training; lect open to public, 4 vis lectr per year; concerts; gallery talks; tours; individual paintings & original objects of art lent to other museums; book traveling exhibitions 4 per year; museum shop sells books, reproductions, prints & slides

PORTSMOUTH

M **PORTSMOUTH MUSEUMS,** Art Center, 420 High St, 23704. Tel 757-393-8543, 393-8983; FAX 757-393-5228; *Dir* M E Burnell; *Museum Coordr* Albert Harris; *Cur Art* Gayle Paul; *Cur Asst* Cooper Carter
Open Tues - Sat 10 AM - 5 PM, Sun 1 - 5 PM, cl Mon. Admis $5 to tour four municipal museums, general fee $1. Estab 1974 to offer a wide variety of the visual arts to the citizens of Tidewater area & beyond. Average Annual Attendance: 60,000. Mem: 1200; dues corporate director's circle $5000, corporate benefactor $2500, corporate patron $1000, corporate friend $500, corporate associate $250, contributing $100, sponsoring $50, family $35, individual $25
Income: $204,193
Purchases: $1500
Collections: Contemporary drawings & paintings, primarily by American artists
Publications: Quarterly newsletter
Activities: Classes for adults & children; workshops; lect open to public, 16 vis lectr per year; gallery talks; tours; outreach program; book traveling exhibitions, 6 per year; museum shop sells books, prints & gifts related to exhibitions & holidays

PULASKI

M **FINE ARTS CENTER FOR THE NEW RIVER VALLEY,** 21 W Main St, PO Box 309, 24301. Tel 540-980-7363; *Exec Dir* Michael B Dowell
Open 10 AM - 5 PM. No admis fee. Estab 1978 to foster & furnish activities, programs & facilities to increase understanding of the arts. Gallery area 800 sq ft, classroom area 1800 sq ft. Average Annual Attendance: 16,000. Mem: 550; dues $10-$550; annual meeting in Mar
Income: $80,000 (financed by mem, city & state appropriation & business sponsorship)
Purchases: $80,000 (building in 1988)
Collections: Permanent collection established by donated pieces of art, sculpture & original paintings
Exhibitions: Monthly exhibits of regional artists work
Publications: Centerpiece, monthly newsletter; Rainbow of Arts, childrens quarterly newsletter
Activities: Classes for adults & children; dramatic programs; docent programs; scholarships & fels offered; artmobile serves New River Valley; lending collection; retail store sells books, prints, original art, local craft items

RESTON

NATIONAL ART EDUCATION ASSOCIATION
For further information, see National and Regional Organizations

NATIONAL ASSOCIATION OF SCHOOLS OF ART & DESIGN
For further information, see National and Regional Organizations

RICHMOND

A **AGECROFT ASSOCIATION,** Agecroft Hall, 4305 Sulgrave Rd, 23221. Tel 804-353-4241; FAX 804-353-2151; *Exec Dir* Richard W Moxley; *Cur Educ* Alice Young; *Cur* Mary Anne Caton
Open Tues - Fri 10 AM - 4 PM, Sat & Sun 12:30 - 5 PM. Admis adults & seniors $4.50, students $2.50, group rates by prior arrangements. Estab 1969 to exhibit 15th century Tudor Manor house brought over from Lancashire, England

in 1926 & rebuilt in Richmond. Furnished with period objects of art. Average Annual Attendance: 20,000

Income: Financed by endowment & admis

Purchases: 1560 portrait of William Dauntesey

Collections: 16th & early 17th century furniture & objects of art depicting Elizabethan lifestyle, when Agecroft Hall was at its pinnacle

Exhibitions: Permanent exhibit of British memorabilia 1890 - present

Activities: Classes for adults; docent training; lect open to public; concerts; gallery talks; specialized tours; museum shop sells books & reproductions

M **Museum,** Agecroft Hall, 4305 Sulgrave Rd, 23221. Tel 804-353-4241; FAX 804-353-2151; *Cur Coll* Mary Anne Caton; *Cur Educ* Alice D Young

Open Tues - Sat 10 AM - 4 PM, Sun 12:30 - 5 PM. Admis adults $4.50, seniors $4, students $2.50, children under 6 free. Estab 1969 to interpret the material, culture & social history of England (1580-1640). Revival residence, rebuilt from 16th century English house, 7 period rooms & 2 exhibit galleries. Maintains reference library. Average Annual Attendance: 21,000

Activities: Classes for adults & children; dramatic programs; quarterly living history events; workshops; lect open to public, 10-12 vis lectr per year; concerts; gallery talks; tours; original objects of art lent to Folger Shakespeare Library in Washington, DC; lending collection contains 3000 books, paintings, phono records, photographs & 500 decorative art holdings; musuem shop sells books, original art, reproductions, textiles, games, jewelry

A **ARTS COUNCIL OF RICHMOND, INC,** 1435 W Main St, 23220. Tel 804-355-7200; FAX 804-355-7367; *Pres* Charles Chambliss; *Exec Dir* Stephanie Micas

Open Mon - Fri 9 AM - 5 PM. Estab 1949 to promote & support the arts & to provide arts programs & services to enhance the quality of city living

Income: Financed by grants, contributions & city appropriation

Publications: Arts Spectrum Directory, annually

Activities: Management seminars; downtown arts festival, children's festival for the arts; Public Art Program including art at airport

A **ASSOCIATION FOR THE PRESERVATION OF VIRGINIA ANTIQUITIES,** 204 W Franklin St, 23220. Tel 804-648-1889; FAX 804-775-0802;

Estab 1889 to acquire & preserve historic buildings, grounds & monuments in Virginia. APVA owns & administers 36 properties in Virginia. Among the properties: Jamestown Island; Water Reed Birthplace, Gloucester County; Bacon's Castle & Smith's Fort Plantation, Surry County; John Marshall House, Richmond; Scotchtown, Hanover County; Mary Washington House, Hugh Mercer Apothecary Shoe & Rising Sun Tavern, St James Cottage, Fredericksburg; Smithfield Plantation, Blacksburg; Farmers Bank, Petersburg; Cape Henry Lighthouse & Lynnhaven House, Virginia Beach; Dora Armistead House, Williamsburg; Holly Brook, Eastville. Hours & admis vary according to location. Mem: 6000; dues individual $20; annual meeting in spring

Income: Financed by mem, endowment fund donations & grants

Collections: Decorative arts; 17th - 19th century furniture, glass, ceramics, metalwork & textiles

Publications: Discovery (magazine) annually; newsletter, quarterly

Activities: Lect open to public; individual paintings & objects of art lent to other non-profit preservation organizations' exhibits; sales shop sells books, reproductions, prints & slides, magazines, gifts, Virginia handicrafts

L **Library,** 204 W Franklin St, 23220. FAX 804-648-1889; *Cur* Elizabeth Kostelny

Open by appointment only. For reference use only

Library Holdings: Vols 3000; Per subs 12; AV — Slides; Other — Clipping files, exhibition catalogs, pamphlets, photographs

Special Subjects: Architecture, Decorative Arts, Historical Material, Restoration Technology & Archaeology

M **John Marshall House,** 818 E Marshall St, 23219. Tel 804-648-7998; *Site Coordr* Melissa J Haines

Open Oct - Dec Tues - Sat 10 AM - 4:30 PM, Apr - Sept Tues - Sat 10 AM - 5 PM. Admis adults $3, seniors 55 & up $2.50, children 7-12 $1.25. Historical house mus built in 1790. Portrays John Marshall's life (1790-1835) in this historic Richmond home & his contribution to the nation. Average Annual Attendance: 8000

Collections: Decorative arts; period furniture 1790-1835

Exhibitions: Marshall family pieces including his judicial robe

Activities: Lect open to public, some for members only; tours; individual paintings & original objects of art lent to Supreme Court Historical Society; retail store sells books, prints & Marshall items

C **CRESTAR BANK,** Art Collection, 919 E Main St, 23219. Tel 804-782-5000; *Pres* Richard Tilgham

Estab 1970. Collection displayed in banks and offices; separate gallery used for new exhibit each month

Collections: Contemporary Art

Activities: Competitions with awards

A **HAND WORKSHOP ART CENTER,** 1812 W Main St, 23220. Tel 804-353-0094; FAX 804-353-8018; *Dir* Thomas Kendall; *Prog Dir* Barbara Hill

Open Mon - Sat 10 AM - 4 PM, Sun 1 - 4 PM. No admis fee. Estab 1963 as a non-profit center for the visual arts committed to preservation of craft traditions & to promote artistic excellence through educational programs, gallery exhibitions & artists services

Exhibitions: Annual Richmond Craft & Design Show; Juried Exhibitions. (1997) Two Traditional Potters: Winnie Owens-Hart & Rob Barnard; Sculptural Books; In Memory of This Earth

Publications: Exhibition catalogs

Activities: Classes for adults & children; lect open to public; talks; tours; competitions with awards; scholarships offered for children only; originates traveling exhibitions; sales shop sells magazines

M **NATIONAL SOCIETY OF THE COLONIAL DAMES,** Wilton House Museum, 215 S Wilton Rd, 23226. Tel 804-282-5936; *Adminr* Jim Hollomon

Open Tues - Sat 10 AM - 4:30 PM, Sun 1:30 AM - 4:30 PM, cl Mon. Admis $3. 50. Estab 1935. Average Annual Attendance: 3500

Collections: †18th & 19th century furniture; †18th century decorative arts

Activities: Classes for children; docent training; lect open to public, 5-7 vis lectr per year; tours

C **NATIONS BANK,** Art Collection, Nations Bank Ctr, 1111 E Main St, 23219. Tel 804-553-5000; *In Charge* Shelby Duncan

Certain areas open to pub 9 AM - 5 PM, or by appointment with tour guides. Estab 1974 to support the arts (mostly Virginia artists), to enhance bank surroundings & as an investment. Collection displayed on 2nd floor (monthly exhibits); permanent collection in reception areas & offices throughout 24 floors

Collections: Contemporary works of art in different media, mostly local & Virginia artists & some known artists

Activities: Tours by appointment; sponsored employee art exhibit; individual objects of art lent; monthly exhibits by local, employee & Virginia artists; paintings on loan by local gallery

M **1708 GALLERY,** 103 E Broad St, PO Box 12520, 23241. Tel 804-643-7829; *Dir* Sally Bowring

Open Sept - June Tues - Fri 11 AM - 5 PM, Sat & Sun 1 - 5 PM. No admis fee. Estab 1978 to offer an alternative presentation space to emerging & professional artists. Two ground floor, artist-run galleries are devoted to the presentation of contemporary art. Average Annual Attendance: 10,000. Mem: 50; mem open to professional artists; dues 1st & 2nd yr $25, 3rd & 4th yr $20, 5th yr pledge; monthly meetings

Income: $85,000 (financed by endowment, mem, state appropriation, grants, gifts from corporations & foundations)

Activities: Educ dept; mentor program; lect open to public, 9 vis lectr per year; performance art series, 6 events per season; concerts; competitions; paintings & original objects of art lent to Wella Corp & Contenental Cable Vision; originate traveling exhibitions

M **UNIVERSITY OF RICHMOND,** Marsh Art Gallery, George M Modlin Ctr for the Arts, 23173. Tel 804-289-8276; FAX 804-287-6006; *Elec Mail* rwaller@richmond.edu. *Dir* Richard Waller

Open Tues - Sun 1 - 5 PM, cl fall break, Thanksgiving wk, semester break & spring break. No admis fee

Exhibitions: Annual Juried Student Exhibition; Looking at the Seventies: The Meyer Schapiro Portfolio from the I Webb Surrat, Jr Print Collection; Pygmalion & Galatea: Poem/Sculpture/Installation by Mark Rhodes

Publications: Exhibition catalogues

Activities: Originate traveling exhibitions

M **VALENTINE MUSEUM,** 1015 E Clay St, 23219-1590. Tel 804-649-0711; FAX 804-643-3510; *Elec Mail* valmus@rmond.mindspring.com. *Dir* William Martin

Open Mon - Sat 10 AM - 5 PM, Sun Noon - 5 PM. Admis adults $5, students $4, children 7-12 $3. Estab 1892 as a mus of the life & history of Richmond. Average Annual Attendance: 60,000. Mem: 500; dues individual $30

Income: Financed by endowment, mem, city & state appropriation & gifts

Collections: Conrad Wise Chapman (oils, almost entire life works); William James Hubard (drawings & oils); William Ludwell Sheppard (drawings & watercolors); Edward Virginius Valentine (sculpture); outstanding collection of Southern photographs; candlesticks, ceramics, costumes, glass, jewelry, lace, paintings, photographs, prints, sculpture, local history, regional art and decorative arts; neo classical wall paintings

Publications: Valentine Newsletter, quarterly

Activities: Classes for adults & children; docent training; dramatic programs; lect open to the public; concerts; tours; exten dept serving city & area counties; originate traveling exhibitions; museum & sales shops sell books, original art, reproductions, prints, slides & silver; Family Activity Center

L **Library,** 1015 E Clay St, 23219-1590. Tel 804-649-0711; FAX 804-643-3510; *Librn* Teresa Roane

Open to the pub by appointment only; non-lending, reference library

Library Holdings: Vols 10,000; Per subs 20; Other — Clipping files, exhibition catalogs, manuscripts, memorabilia, original art works, pamphlets, photographs 50,000, prints 600, reproductions

Special Subjects: Photography, Local History, Tobacco, Virginia Art

VIRGINIA COMMONWEALTH UNIVERSITY

M **Anderson Gallery,** 907 1/2 W Franklin St, 23824-2514. Tel 804-828-1522; FAX 804-828-8585; *Actg Dir* Chuck Bleick; *Admin* Wendy Wallace; *Mgr* Leon Roger; *Registrar* Leslie Brothers

Open Tues - Fri 10 AM - 5 PM, Sat & Sun 1 - 5 PM, cl Mon except by appointment. Estab 1930, re-opened 1970 as the showcase for the contemporary arts in Richmond; to expose the university & community to a wide variety of current artistic ideas & expressions. Gallery is situated on campus in a four-story converted stable. There are seven galleries with a variety of exhibition spaces. Average Annual Attendance: 20,000. Mem: 200; dues $25

Collections: †Contemporary prints & paintings; cross section of prints from the 15th to 20th century covering most periods; vintage & contemporary photography

Exhibitions: Messages: words & images; Jud Fine; Paul Rotterdam; Future Histories; Larry Miller; Masters of Contemporary Drawing; Francesc Torres; Rita Myers; Suzan Etkin; Thomas Florschuetz; Clemens Weiss; Abstraction in Contemporary Photography; Lorna Simpson; Rainer Gross; Anonymity & Identity; Barbara Ess; Dushi Drozdik; Brian Weil

Publications: Catalogs; newsletters; posters & brochures

Activities: Lect open to public, 10 vis lectr per year; concerts; gallery talks; competitions; lending collection contains original art works, original paintings & photographs; originate traveling exhibitions; museum shop sells books, magazines, original art & miscellaneous items

L **School of The Arts Library,** 325 N Harrison St, 23284-2519. Tel 804-828-1683; FAX 804-828-6469; *Elec Mail* jboone@saturn.vcu.edu. *Dir* Jeanne Boone

Open Mon - Thurs 9 AM - 6 PM, Fri 9 AM - 5 PM. Estab in 1960's to currently support the teaching program & the 16 departments of the School of the Arts, as well as the university at large, other institutions & the community

Income: Financed by state appropriation & fees from various depts within the School of the Arts

Library Holdings: Per subs 13; AV — Slides 450,000

Special Subjects: Architecture, Art Education, Art History, Ceramics, Commercial Art, Costume Design & Construction, Fashion Arts, Film, Graphic Arts, Graphic Design, Interior Design, Jewelry, Photography, Printmaking, Sculpture

Collections: †Exhibition Catalogs; in-house photography from books, catalogs, clippings, magazines & post cards

L VIRGINIA DEPT HISTORIC RESOURCES, Research Library, 221 Governor St, 23219. Tel 804-786-3143; *Archivist* Suzanne Durham
Open daily 8:30 AM - 4:30 PM. Estab 1966. For reference only
Library Holdings: Vols 4500; Per subs 20; Maps; AV — Kodachromes, slides, v-tapes; Other — Clipping files, manuscripts, photographs
Special Subjects: Anthropology, Archaeology, Architecture, Decorative Arts, Historical Material, History of Art & Archaeology, Maps
Collections: Archaeology; Architecture; Ethnography; History

A VIRGINIA HISTORICAL SOCIETY, 428 North Blvd, PO Box 7311, 23221. Tel 804-358-4901; FAX 804-355-2399; *Dir* Dr Charles F Bryan Jr; *Assoc Dir* Robert Strohm; *Asst Dir* James Kelly
Open Mon - Sat 10 AM - 5 PM, Mus Sun 1 - 5 PM. Admis $3, students $2, members free. Estab 1831 for collecting, preserving & making available to scholars research material relating to the history of Virginia, its collections include extensive holdings of historical portraiture. Seven galleries feature changing & permanent exhibits drawn from public & private collections throughout Virginia. Average Annual Attendance: 40,000. Mem: 5000; dues $35
Income: Financed by endowment & mem
Collections: †Books; †Manuscripts; Museum Collection; †Portraits
Publications: Bulletin, quarterly; Virginia Magazine of History & Biography, quarterly
Activities: Classes for adults & children; docent training; teacher recertification; lect open to public, 15 vis lectr per year; gallery talks; William Rachel Award; individual paintings & original objects of art lent; lending collection contains paintings, original prints, sculptures, 125,000 books & 100,000 photographs; Museum shop sells books, prints
L Library, 428 North Blvd, PO Box 7311, 23221-0311. Tel 804-358-4901; FAX 804-355-2399; *Dir* Charles F Bryan
Open Mon - Sat 9 AM - 5 PM. Estab 1831 for the study of Virginia history. For reference only
Income: Financed by endowment, mem, state appropriation & private donations
Library Holdings: Vols 125,000; Per subs 300; Micro — Fiche, reels; AV — Fs; Other — Clipping files, exhibition catalogs, manuscripts, memorabilia, original art works, pamphlets, photographs 100,000, prints, reproductions, sculpture
Special Subjects: 17th & 18th Century English Architecture
Publications: Bulletin, quarterly; Virginia Magazine of History & Biography, quarterly
Activities: Lect open to members, 3 vis lectr per year

M VIRGINIA MUSEUM OF FINE ARTS, 2800 Grove Ave, 23221-2466. Tel 804-367-0844; FAX 804-367-9393; Elec Mail ddale@vmfa.state.va.us. *Pres* W Taylor Reveley III; *Dir* Katharine C Lee; *Deputy Dir* Carol Amato; *Assoc Dir Exhib/Prog Div* Richard Woodward; *Registrar* Lisa Hancock; *Develop Dir* David Bradley; *Fellowship Coordr* David Pittman; *Statewide Exhib Coordr* Eileen Mott
Open Tues - Sun 11 AM - 5 PM, cl Mon. Suggested donation $4. Estab 1934; theater opened 1955; South wing added 1970. Participating in the museum's programs are the Fellows of the Virginia Mus, who meet yearly to counsel the mus on its future plans; the Council, which sponsors & originates speciail programs; the Collectors' Circle, a group of Virginia art lovers which meets four times a year to discuss various aspects of collecting; the Corporate Patrons, state & local business firms who lend financial support to mus programs. Average Annual Attendance: 1,250,000. Mem: 16,500; dues $15 & higher; annual meeting in May
Income: Financed by state agency
Collections: Lady Nancy Astor Collection of English China; Branch Collection of Italian Renaissance Paintings, Sculpture & Furniture; Ailsa Mellon Bruce Collection of 18th Century Furniture & Decorative Arts; Mrs Arthur Kelly Evans Collection of Pottery & Porcelain; Arthur & Margaret Glasgow Collection of Flemish & Italian Renaissance Paintings, Sculpture & Decorative Arts; Nasli & Alice Heeramaneck Collection of Art of India, Nepal, Kashmir & Tibet; T Catesby Jones Collection of 20th Century European Paintings & Drawings; Dr & Mrs Arthur Mourot Collection of Meissen Porcelain; The John Barton Payne Collection of Paintings, Prints & Portuguese Furniture; Lillian Thomas Pratt Collection of Czarist Jewels by Peter Carl Faberge; Adolph D & Wilkins C Williams Collection of Paintings, Tapestries, China & Silver; archaic Chinese bronzes; archaic Chinese jades; comprehensive collections of early Greek vases (8th century to 4th century BC); representative examples of the arts from early Egypt to the present time, including paintings, sculpture, furniture and objects d'art
Exhibitions: Approximately 50 crated exhibitions of original art
Publications: Virginia Museum Calendar, bi-monthly; brochures; catalogues for special exhibitions & collections; programs
Activities: Classes for adults & children in painting, drawing, graphics, ceramics & weaving; workshops; demonstrations; docent training; lect open to public, 20 vis lectr per year; concerts; gallery talks; tours; concerts; drama productions; fels offered (10 - 15 per year) to Virginia artists; originate traveling exhibitions throughout the state of Virginia; museum shop sells books, magazines, original art, reproductions, prints & slides
L Library, 2800 Grove Ave, 23221-2466. Tel 804-367-0827, 367-0858; FAX 804-367-0886, 367-9393; *Librn* Susanne Freeman
Open Tues - Sat 11 AM - 5 PM, summer Tues - Fri 11 AM - 5 PM. Estab 1954 for art history research. For reference only
Income: Financed by private funds
Library Holdings: Vols 60,000; Per subs 130; Auction catalogs; Micro — Reels; AV — Slides, v-tapes; Other — Clipping files, exhibition catalogs, manuscripts, pamphlets, photographs
Special Subjects: Art History, Crafts, Decorative Arts, Painting - American, Sculpture, Art Nouveau, Art Deco, Classical Art
Collections: Weedon Collection; Hayes Collections; Strauss Collection; Oriental art

ROANOKE

M ART MUSEUM OF WESTERN VIRGINIA, Ctr in the Square, One Market Sq, 2nd Flr, 24011-1436. Tel 540-342-5760; FAX 540-342-5798; *Chief Cur & Admin Dir* Mark Scala; *Spec Events Dir* Sheryl Perry; *Asst Cur Colls & Exhibit* Carissa South; *Registrar* Mary LaGue; *Marketing Dir* Jeanne Fishwick
Open Tues - Sat 10 AM - 5 PM, Sun 1 - 5 PM. Admis by donation. Estab 1951 as a general art mus with a focus on art of the South. Mus is located in a downtown cultural complex called Center in the Square. There are three major rotating galleries, one permanent collection gallery, studio classrooms, educational gallery & lecture hall. Average Annual Attendance: 100,000. Mem: 1500; dues $20 & up; annual meeting in May
Income: Financed by mem earned income, donations & endowment
Collections: Contemporary American Paintings, Sculpture & Graphic Arts; Folk Art; Japanese Prints & Decorative Arts; 19th Century American Paintings; Regional Art
Exhibitions: Hunt Slonem, In the Realm of the Spirit; Gari Melchers (portraits & landscapes); William Eggleston (photographs); Gregory Henry (paintings & sculpture); Art in Bloom; Roanoke City Art Show; Steven Bickley (sculpture); Cartoon Magic; Ray Kass (watercolors); Edward Beyer (painting & prints). Fritz Bultman: From Mardi Gras to Manhattan; The American Spirit: 19th Century Masterpieces from the Maslo Collection; James Harold Jennings Art World
Publications: Annual Report; Docent Guild newsletter; exhibition catalogs; quarterly newsletter
Activities: Classes for adults & children; docent training; lect open to the public; gallery talks; tours; individual paintings lent to qualified museums; museum store selling books, original art, prints, reproductions, handmade crafts including jewelry & children's items

A ARTS COUNCIL OF THE BLUE RIDGE, 20 E Church Ave, 24011. Tel 703-342-5790; FAX 703-342-5720; *Exec Dir* Susan Jennings; *Prog Educ Coordr* Patricia Cronin; *Dir Operations & Member Services* Heather Smith; *Bookkeeper* Lynn Schleupner
Open Tues - Fri 9 AM - 3 PM. Estab 1976 as a liaison serv between the public & cultural & arts organizations; aids in artist registry & grant assistance. Maintains reference library
Income: Financed by mem, city & state appropriation industrial & corporate donations & foundations
Publications: Cultural education resource guide; cultural directory artists; registry; newsletter

SPRINGFIELD

L VICANA (VIETNAMESE CULTURAL ASSOCIATION IN NORTH AMERICA) LIBRARY, 6433 Northana Dr, 22150-1335. Tel 703-971-9178; FAX 703-719-5764; *Pres* Nguyen Ngoc Bich ; *Librn* Dao Thi Hoi
Open by special arrangement. No admis fee. Estab 1982
Library Holdings: Vols 1500; AV — A-tapes, cassettes, fs, rec, v-tapes; Other — Clipping files, exhibition catalogs, framed reproductions, pamphlets, photographs
Special Subjects: Aesthetics, Art Education, Art History, Asian Art, Ceramics, Crafts, Ethnology, Folk Art, Handicrafts, Historical Material, History of Art & Archaeology, Oriental Art
Collections: Historical collection-Vietnamese, English, French; slides of Vietnamese life; Vietnamese cultural artifacts

STAUNTON

A STAUNTON FINE ARTS ASSOCIATION, Staunton Augusta Art Center, One Gypsy Hill Park, 24401. Tel 540-885-2028; *Exec Dir* Penny Warren
Open Mon - Fri 9 AM - 5 PM. No admis fee. Estab 1961 for art exposure & educ to area residents. Average Annual Attendance: 5000. Mem: 550; dues $50
Income: $106,000 (financed by mem, city & state appropriations)
Exhibitions: Annual Art in the Park; Christmas Art for Gifts; Summer Studio; Virginia Artist Craft Invitational; Virginia Museum Teams Exhibit; Youth Art Month
Activities: Classes for adults & children; lect open to public; book traveling exhibitions 8 per year

M WOODROW WILSON BIRTHPLACE & MUSEUM, 20 N Coalter St, PO Box 24, 24402-0024. Tel 540-885-0897; FAX 540-886-9874; *Dir Coll* Patricia Hobbs
Open daily 9 AM - 5 PM Mar - Nov, 10 AM - 4 PM Dec - Feb, cl Thanksgiving, Christmas & New Year's Day. Admis adults $6, AAA discount & senior citizens $5.50, students age 13 & up or with ID $4, children 6-12 $2, children under 6 free. Estab 1938 for the interpretation & collection of life & times of Woodrow Wilson. Collection is housed in the 1846 Presbyterian Manse which was the birthplace of Woodrow Wilson. Mem: 700; dues $25 & up
Collections: Historical Material pertinent to the Wilson family; decorative arts, furniture, manuscripts, musical instruments, paintings, photographs, prints & drawings, rare books, textiles
Exhibitions: (1997) Valley Collects: Images of Staunton-The Wilson Years, images of Staunton from 1856 When Wilson was born to 1912 when he visited his birthplace as president-elect
Publications: Brochures; guides; newsletter, quarterly; pamphlets
Activities: Classes for children; lect open to public; tours; internships offered; original objects of art lent to museums & libraries; lending collection contains original art work & sculpture; sales shop sells books, magazines, reproductions, prints & slides
L Library, 20 N Coalter St, PO Box 24, 24402-0024. Tel 540-885-0897; *Librn* Jean Smith
Income: Financed by endowment, admis & grants
Library Holdings: Vols 2000; Other — Pamphlets, photographs
Special Subjects: Wilsoniana; World War I; diplomatic history
Exhibitions: Women's History; Black History; Wedding Customs
Publications: Wilson Newsletters, quarterly

STRASBURG

M **STRASBURG MUSEUM,** E King St, 22657. Tel 540-465-3428; *Pres* David Nelson
Open May to Oct, daily 10 AM - 4 PM. Admis adults $1, children $.50. Estab 1970 to present the past of a Shenandoah Valley community & to preserve the pottery-making tradition of Strasburg. The mus is housed in the former Southern Railway Depot, which was originally built as a steam pottery. Average Annual Attendance: 4000. Mem: 133; dues $3; annual meeting in Mar
Income: Financed by mem, admis fees & gifts
Collections: Artifacts & exhibits, farm & railroad crafts, pottery
Activities: Classes for adults & children in pottery making; museum shop selling books original art, pottery & other local crafts

SWEET BRIAR

L **SWEET BRIAR COLLEGE,** Martin C Shallenberger Art Library, 24595. Tel 804-381-6138; FAX 804-381-6173; *Dir* John G Jaffe; *Asst Dir* Patricia Wright; *Public Serv* Lisa N Johnston; *Bibliographic Instruction & Branch Librn* Alicia D Grant; *Serials Librn* Liz Linton
Estab 1961, when it was separated from the main library, the library serves an undergraduate community. The Art Library is now located in the Pannell Fine Arts Center
Income: Financed by college funds
Library Holdings: Vols 12,500; Per subs 60; Micro — Fiche; AV — Cassettes, Kodachromes, lantern slides; Other — Exhibition catalogs, original art works, pamphlets, prints
Special Subjects: Aesthetics, Afro-American Art, American Indian Art, American Western Art, Antiquities-Assyrian, Folk Art, Furniture, Glass, Gold, Graphic Arts, Painting - American, Painting - Australian, Painting - British, Painting - Canadian, Painting - Dutch

M **Art Gallery,** 24595. Tel 804-381-6248; FAX 804-381-6173; *Dir* Rebecca Massie-Lane
Open Tues - Thurs 7:30 - 9:30 PM - Sun Noon - 5 PM. Estab 1985 to support the educational mission at Sweet Briar College through its exhibits, collections & educational programs. Average Annual Attendance: 4000. Mem: 215; dues $25; annual meeting in Apr
Collections: American & European drawings & prints; Japanese Woodblock prints, 18th & 19th century
Exhibitions: Rotating exhibits from permanent collection plus traveling exhibits
Activities: Docent training; lect open to the public, 4 vis lectr per year; concerts; gallery talks; tours; individual paintings are lent to other museums; originate traveling exhibitions; bookshop sells books, magazines & reproductions

M **VIRGINIA CENTER FOR THE CREATIVE ARTS,** Camp Gallery, PO Box VCCA, 24595. Tel 804-946-7236; FAX 804-946-7239; Elec Mail vcca@sbc.edu. *Acting Dir* Craig Pleasants; *Admissions Coordr* Sheila Gully Pleasants
Open by appointment. No admis fee. Estab 1971 as a residential retreat for writers, composers & visual artists. Facilities include 23 studios, a gallery, a darkroom, a printing press, a library, private bedrooms in a modern residence. Breakfast & dinner served in diningroom, lunch is delivered to studios. Access to Sweet Briar College facilities. Average Annual Attendance: 300 professional writers, composers & visual artists
Income: $434,000 (financed by endowment, artists' fees, donations & grants)
Collections: Books, fiction & non-fiction; donated paintings by Fellows; donated poetry by Fellows; donated sculpture by Fellows
Exhibitions: exhibitions are in the summers, no proposals accepted
Publications: Annual newsletter; Notes From Mt San Angelo
Activities: Scholarships offered

VIRGINIA BEACH

A **VIRGINIA BEACH CENTER FOR THE ARTS,** 2200 Parks Ave, 23451. Tel 804-425-0000; FAX 804-425-8186; *Interim Dir* Jim Spruance; *Dir Educ* Betsy Gough-DiJulio
Open Mon - Sat 10 AM - 5 PM, Sun 1 - 5 PM. Admis adults $2, children $1. Estab 1952, as a non-profit organization serving citizens of the greater Hampton Roads area with exhibits & programming in the visual arts. Exhibition space 800 sq ft student gallery & 5600 sq ft main gallery. Average Annual Attendance: 50,000. Mem: 1500, dues family $50 & up, single $30; annual meeting in Sept
Income: Financed by mem, pub grants, private donations, various fundraising events
Collections: Best-in-Show winners from Boardwalk Art Show
Exhibitions: 12 exhibitions per year covering all media
Publications: ArtLetter, monthly; exhibition catalogues
Activities: Classes & workshops for adults & children; dramatic programs; docent training; film series; performing arts; lect open to public; 15 vis lectr per year; concerts; gallery talks; tours; scholarships & fels offered; exten dept serves municipal employees; museum shop sells books, original art, reproductions, prints, crafts, jewelry, wearable art

WILLIAMSBURG

M **COLLEGE OF WILLIAM & MARY,** Joseph & Margaret Muscarelle Museum of Art, 23187. Tel 757-221-2710; FAX 757-221-2711; Elec Mail bgkelm@facstaff.wm.edu. *Dir* Bonnie G Kelm PhD; *Cur* Ann Madonia; *Registrar* Melissa Liks; *Educator* Rachel Strawn; *Preparator* Fred Rich; *Asst to Dir* Cindy Sharkey
Open Mon - Fri 10 AM - 4:45 PM, Sat - Sun Noon - 4 PM. Estab 1983. Average Annual Attendance: 60,000. Mem: 1000; dues $20 & up
Income: Financed by endowments, state appropriations & donations
Collections: African Art; Asian Art; Native American Art; 16th - 20th century American & European works on paper, paintings & sculpture
Publications: Calendar, three times a year; exhibition catalogues
Activities: Classes for adults & children; docent training; lect open to public;

concerts; gallery talks; tours; scholarships & fels offered; individual paintings & original objects of art lent to special exhibitions organized by other museums; originate traveling exhibitions that circulate to other museums, art centers, colleges; sales shop sells books, prints, catalogues, postcards & other items

M **COLONIAL WILLIAMSBURG FOUNDATION,** PO Box 1776, 23187-1776. Tel 757-229-1000; FAX 757-220-7286; *Pres* Robert Wilburne; *VPres Coll & Museums* Graham S Hood; *Dir Colonial Williamsburg Journal* Wayne Barrett; *Dir Marketing Communications* Susan M Stuntz
Open 9 AM - 5 PM; DeWitt Wallace Decorative Art Gallery open 10 AM - 6 PM. Estab 1927 the worlds largest outdoor mus, providing first hand history of 18th-century English colony during period of subjects becoming Americans. The colonial area of this 18th century capital of Virginia, encompassing 173 acres with nearly 500 homes, shops, taverns, pub buildings, dependencies, has been carefully restored to its original appearance. Included are 90 acres of gardens & greens. The work was initiated by the John D Rockefeller, Jr. There are more than 40 exhibition homes, pub buildings & craft shops where guides & craftsmen in colonial costumes show vistors the arts & decoration as well as the way of life of pre-Revolutionary Virginia. Incl are the historic Burton Parish Church, the Governors Palace, Capitol, the Courthouse of 1770, Bassett Hall (local residence of the Rockefellers), the Wallace Gallery & Carter's Grove plantation. The exhibition properties include 225 furnished rooms. Average Annual Attendance: 1,000,000
Income: Financed by admis, gifts & grants, real estate, products, restaurants & hotels
Collections: †18th-Century English & American Painting; †English Pottery & Porcelains; †English & Early American Silver; †Collections of American & English furnishings, with frequent additions, include representative pieces, rare English pieces in the palace; †exceptionally fine textiles & rugs; extensive collection of primary & secondary materials relating to British North America, the Colonial Period & the early National Period
Publications: The foundation publishes many books on a wide range of subjects; Colonial Williamsburg, quarterly journal
Activities: Classes & tours for adults & children; lect open to public, 30 vis lectr per year; concerts; gallery talks; special focus tours; individual paintings & original objects of art lent; museum shop sells books, magazines, original art, reproductions, prints & slides

A **Visitor Center,** PO Box 1776, 23187-1776. Tel 757-220-7645; *Dir* William Pfeifer
Estab 1927. Outside the historic area this modern center houses graphic exhibits of the restoration & colonial life. Continuous showings of a full-color, vista vision film, Williamsburg: The Story of a Patriot
Publications: Books & brochures on Williamsburg & colonial life; gallery book of the Folk Art Collection
Activities: Limited grant-in-aid program for researchers; slide lect; annual events including Antiques Forum; Garden Symposium; regular performance of 18th century dramas, organ recitals & concerts

L **John D Rockefeller, Jr Library,** 313 First St, PO Box 1776, 23187-1776. Tel 757-220-7422; FAX 757-565-8902; Elec Mail eackert@widomaker.com; Internet Home Page Address http://www.history.org. *Dir* Susan Berg; *Office Mgr* Inge Flester; *Decorative Arts Librn* Susan Shames; *Reference Librn* Del Moore; *Circulation Library Asst* Lois Danuser; *Spec Coll Librn & Assoc Cur Rare Books & Manuscripts* Gail Greve; *Assoc Cur Architecture Coll* George Yetter; *Technical Servs Librn* Mary Haskell; *Cataloger* Julie Conlee; *Acquisitions Librn* Annette Parham; *Acquisitions Library Asst* Beth Martin; *Visual Resources Librn* Marianne Carden; *Visual Resources Editorial Librn* Cathy Grosfils; *Visual Resources Library Asst* Laura Arnette
Open Mon - Fri 10 AM - 5 PM, cl major holidays
Library Holdings: Vols 65,000; Per subs 500; Architectural drawings 65,000; Compact discs-Music 100; Negatives 250,000; Micro — Fiche, reels 6000; AV — Fs, slides 250,000, v-tapes 1000; Other — Clipping files 100, manuscripts 45,000, photographs 125,000
Special Subjects: Archaeology, Architecture, Decorative Arts, Colonial History, Historic Trade
Collections: 18th Century Arts & Trades; Historical Preservation in America; History of the Restoration of Colonial Williamsburg
Publications: Annual reports; exhibit catalogs

M **Abby Aldrich Rockefeller Folk Art Center,** 307 S England St, PO Box 1776, 23187-1776. Tel 757-220-7670; *Dir* Carolyn Weekley
Open Mon - Sun 10 AM - 6 PM. Admis adult $8, children $5. Estab 1939 for research, educ & the exhibition of some of the country's leading collections of American folk art of the 18th, 19th & 29th centuries. 18 galleries of American folk art. Average Annual Attendance: 200,000
Collections: Decorative usefulwares, decoys, painted furniture, paintings, sculptures, signs & textiles
Exhibitions: (1997) Covered in Glory; Meet the Makers; Flying Free: 20th Century Self-Taught Art from the Collection of Ellin & Baron Gordon; Painted Furniture. (1998) Folk Arts of the South. (1998-99) The Kingdoms of Edward Hicks
Publications: Exhibition catalogs
Activities: Docent training; lect open to public; tours; paintings & sculpture lent to other museums; book traveling exhibitions; originate traveling exhibitions; museum shop sells books, reproductions, prints & slides

—**Abby Aldrich Rockefeller Folk Art Center Library,** 307 S England St, PO Box 1776, 23187-1776. Tel 757-220-7668; FAX 757-565-8915; *Librn* Anne Motley
Open to serious scholars of folk art for reference by appointment
Library Holdings: Vols 4500; Bound per 120 linear ft (20 titles); Micro — Fiche; AV — Fs, rec, slides, v-tapes; Other — Clipping files, exhibition catalogs, manuscripts, memorabilia, pamphlets, photographs, prints
Special Subjects: Decorative Arts, Folk Art
Collections: 19th century children's books

M **DeWitt Wallace Decorative Arts Gallery,** 325 Francis St, PO Box 1776, 23187-1776. Tel 757-229-1000; FAX 757-565-8804; *Mgr* Donald Thomas
Open daily 10 AM - 6 PM. Admis adults $8.50. Estab 1985. The Wallace Gallery is a contemporary bi-level mus featuring an introductory gallery, an upper level balcony of the central court which presents works from the

permanent collection, study galleries which are organized by specific media & changing special exhibition galleries

Collections: English and American decorative arts from 1600-1830
Exhibitions: Permanent: Selected Masterworks from the Colonial Williamsburg Collection; study galleries present English & American furniture, ceramics, metals, prints & textiles. (1997) Almost a Deception...John Singleton Copley & Company in Williamsburg; Artistry & Ingenuity; Lock, Stock & Barrel; The Owl & the Pussycat; Revolution in Taste; Ruffles & Flourishes; Medicine in 18th Century Williamsburg. (1997-98) Furniture of the American South; Virginia Samplers: Young Ladies & Their Needle Wisdom; King George III & American Natural History: Mark Catesby's Watercolours from the Royal Library, Windsor Castle
Activities: Lect open to public; tours; slide & video presentations; musical events

M JAMESTOWN-YORKTOWN FOUNDATION, Rte 1020 & Colonial Pky, 23187-1607. Tel 804-887-1776; FAX 804-887-1306; *Dir* Sam Wagner; *Cur* Brent Pharp
Open daily 9 AM - 5 PM, cl Christmas & New Year's. Admis adults $5.75, children $2.75, senior citizen & group discounts. Estab 1976 to interpret the history of the American Revolution. Average Annual Attendance: 100,000. Mem: 260; dues $25-$5000; annual meeting in Apr
Income: $700,000 (financed by admis & state appropriation)
Purchases: $20,000
Collections: Gen John Steele collection of furniture, silver, paintings; †paintings by Oscar DeMejo; †varied series of prints, paintings & art works on theme of Revolution; 18th century Revolutionary War artifacts
Exhibitions: The Town of York; Yorktown's Sunken Fleet; The Road to Revolution, Witnesses to Revolution
Publications: Series of biographies of Revolutionary Virginia leaders
Activities: Classes for adults & children; dramatic programs; school programs; lect open to public, 2-5 per year; craft shows; book traveling exhibitions 1-2 per year; sales shop sells books, magazines, original art, reproductions, prints, slides & craft items

WASHINGTON

BAINBRIDGE ISLE

A BAINBRIDGE ISLAND ARTS COUNCIL, 261 Madison Ave S, 98110. Tel 206-842-7901; *Dir* Nancy Frye
Estab 1986
Income: Financed by city & state appropriations & donations
Activities: Artist grants offered

BELLEVUE

M BELLEVUE ART MUSEUM, 301 Bellevue Sq, 98004. Tel 206-454-3322; FAX 206-637-1799; Elec Mail elissa@bellevuearts.org. *Dir & Cur* Diane Douglas; *Chief Finance Officer* C William Edwards; *Public Relations & Marketing Coordr* Michael McGrann; *Develop Coordr* Marlynn Littauer; *Develop Asst* Elissa Waldstead; *Develop Officer* Susan Anderson; *Assoc Cur* Michael Crane; *Vol Coordr* Melissa Alexander; *Store Mgr* Nora Smids; *Educ Coordr* Beverly Silver
Open Mon & Tues 10 AM - 8 PM, Wed - Sat 10 AM - 6 PM, Sun 11 AM - 6 PM. Admis adults $3, senior citizens & students $2, children under 12 free; free every Tues. Estab 1975 to bring visual arts to Bellevue East King County area. Maintains 6000 sq ft for changing & temporary exhibitions. Average Annual Attendance: 48,000-60,000. Mem: 1450; dues family $40
Income: $850,000 (financed by mem, private contributions, store sales, grants, fundraising events, arts & crafts fair)
Collections: Contemporary Northwest art & crafts
Exhibitions: Annual Pacific Northwest Arts Fair; exhibitions of local, regional & national significance, with an emphasis on Northwest art & crafts
Publications: Annual report; quarterly newsletter; exhibition catalogs; posters; membership brochures
Activities: Workshops for adults & children; docent training; lect open to public, 8-12 vis lectr per year; films; symposia; hands-on activities for children; awards through art & craft juries; museum store sells books, prints, jewelry, reproductions, cards & papers

A NORTHWEST WATERCOLOR SOCIETY, PO Box 905, 98004. Tel 206-842-0168; *Pres* Beverly A Taylor; *VPres* Cathy Woo; *Treas* Barbara Pitts
Estab 1939. Mem: 800; dues $30; monthly meetings Sept-May
Income: Financed by mem
Exhibitions: Annual National Show; Waterworks-Juried Members Show
Publications: Hot Press Newsletter, bimonthly
Activities: Lect open to public, 6-8 vis lectr per year; workshops; competitions with awards; scholarships offered

BELLINGHAM

M WESTERN WASHINGTON UNIVERSITY, Viking Union Gallery, 516 High St (Mailing add: 202 Viking Union, 98225-9106). Tel 360-650-6534; *Gallery Dir* Susan Musi; *Asst Gallery Dir* Mark Shetabi; *Advisor* Lisa Rosenberg; *Cur* Paul Brower
Open Mon - Sat 11 AM - 4 PM. No admis fee. Estab 1899 to provide a wide variety of gallery exhibits in a visible campus gallery. Average Annual Attendance: 7000
Income: $7000 (financed by student activity fees)
Exhibitions: Exhibitions change every month
Activities: Book traveling exhibitions 2 per year

M Western Gallery, Fine Arts Complex, 98225-9068. Tel 360-650-3963; FAX 360-650-6878; *Dir* Sarah Clark-Langager, PhD
Open Mon - Fri 10 AM - 4 PM, Sat Noon - 4 PM when university is in session. No admis fee. Old gallery estab 1950, new gallery estab 1989 to exhibit contemporary art. Rotating exhibitions on contemporary art, 6 per yr. Average Annual Attendance: 15,000. Mem: dues Friends of Gallery Group $25 & up
Income: Financed by state appropriation
Collections: †Outdoor Sculpture Collection WWU (contemporary sculpture since 1960); American drawings & prints
Exhibitions: (1997) Rediscovering Landscape of Americas
Publications: Outdoor Sculpture Collection brochures
Activities: Lect open to public, 3 vis lectr per year; gallery talks; audio tour of outdoor sculpture collection; Wed noon hour discussions; original objects of art lent; book traveling exhibitions 3 per year; originate traveling exhibitions 3 per year

M WHATCOM MUSEUM OF HISTORY AND ART, 121 Prospect St, 98225. Tel 360-676-6981; FAX 360-738-7409; *Dir* Mary Pettus; *Deputy Dir* John Olbrantz; *Educ Coordr* Richard Vanderway; *Cur Coll* Janis Olson; *Public Relations* Mark Rensink; *Business Mgr* Gladys Fullford
Open Tues - Sun Noon - 5 PM, cl Mon & holidays. No admis fee, donations accepted. Estab 1940 to collect, preserve & use, through exhibits, interpretation & research, objects of historic or artistic value & to act as a multi-purpose cultural center for the Northwest Washington area providing presentations in all aspects of the arts. Nine galleries plus permanent history exhibit spaces. Average Annual Attendance: 100,000. Mem: 1000; dues family $60, individual $35; annual meeting in Feb; open to pub
Income: Financed by private & pub funds
Collections: Contemporary Northwest Arts; Darius Kinsey & Wilbur Sandison Historic Photograph Collection; Northwest Native American Artifacts; Regional Historic Photographs & Artifacts; H C Hanson Naval Architecture Collection
Exhibitions: (1997) Frank Okada: The Poetics of Abstraction; Trashformations: Recycled Materials in Contemporary American Art & Design; Transfromations: Views of the Klondike; Ross Palmer Beecher; 17th Annual Northwest International Art Competition; The Mideke Legacy. (1997-98) Rick Bartow; First Nations; Contemporary Northwest Coast Indian Art
Publications: Art & Events Calendar, quarterly; Exhibit catalogs; History texts
Activities: Classes for adults & children; docent training; lect open to public; concerts; gallery talks; tours; competitions; awards; originate traveling exhibitions; museum shop sells books, original art & reproductions; junior museum located at 227 Prospect St
L Library, 121 Prospect St, 98225. Tel 360-676-6981; *Public Relations Coordr* Mark Rensauk
Open to pub by appointment only. For reference only
Library Holdings: Vols 500

CHEHALIS

M LEWIS COUNTY HISTORICAL MUSEUM, 599 NW Front Way, 98532. Tel 360-748-0831; *Dir* Paulette Kotter
Open Tues - Sat 9 AM - 5 PM, Sun 1 - 5 PM. Donations. Estab 1979 to preserve Lewis County history. Displays of a parlor, kitchen, logging displays. Average Annual Attendance: 14,000. Mem: 600; annual meeting Jan
Income: $55,000 (financed by endowment, mem & county funds)
Collections: Local Indian History; Photographic Collection of Lewis County; Obits of County Residents; Oral History
Exhibitions: (1997) Weaving/Spinning - Fiber To Form; Children's Hands-on Area
Publications: The Log
Activities: Classes for adults, docent training; lect open to public, 3-5 vis lectr per year; traveling exhibitions 6 per year; originate traveling exhibitions 10 per year; museum shop sells books, prints, magazines, reproductions
L Library, 599 NW Front Way, 98532. Tel 360-748-0831; *Dir* Paulette Kotter
Library Holdings: Vols 150; Other — Clipping files, manuscripts, memorabilia, pamphlets, reproductions
Special Subjects: Dioramas, Display, Dolls, Fashion Arts, Flasks & Bottles, Furniture, Historical Material, Manuscripts, Maps, Period Rooms, Photography, Pottery, Restoration & Conservation, Textiles

CLARKSTON

A VALLEY ART CENTER INC, 842 Sixth St, PO Box 65, 99403. Tel 509-758-8331; *Exec Dir* Pat Rosenberger; *Co-Chmn* Gloria Teats; *Treas* Richard Schutte
Open Mon - Fri 9 AM - 4 PM & by appointment. No admis fee, donations accepted. Estab 1968 to encourage & instruct in all forms of the visual arts & to promote the cause of art in the community. A portion of the center serves as the gallery; wall space for display of paintings or other art; showcases for collections & artifacts. Average Annual Attendance: 5000-7000. Mem: 175; dues $10; annual meeting in Jan
Income: Financed by mem & class fees
Exhibitions: Annual Heritate Show; Annual Western Bronze Show; Lewis-Clark Art Association Show; Kaleidoscope of Prize Winning Art
Publications: Newsletter, semi-annually
Activities: Classes for senior citizens, adults & children; lect open to public, 4 vis lectr per year; gallery talks; tours; competitions with awards; scholarships offered; individual paintings & original objects of art lent to local businesses & individuals, including artists; lending collection contains books, original prints, paintings, records & photographs; sales shop sells books, original art, prints, pottery & soft goods

COUPEVILLE

A **COUPEVILLE ARTS CENTER,** PO Box 171, 98239. Tel 360-678-3396; FAX 360-678-7420; Elec Mail cac@whiabey.net. *Dir* Judy Lynn
Open Mon - Fri 9 AM - 5 PM. No admis fee. Estab 1989 for arts educ. Average Annual Attendance: 1400. Mem: 450; dues vary; annual meeting in Jan
Collections: Paintings & photography donated by NFS faculty & students
Publications: Biannual catalog of visual arts workshops
Activities: Classes for adults & children; scholarships offered; sales shop sells prints

ELLENSBURG

M **CENTRAL WASHINGTON UNIVERSITY,** Sarah Spurgeon Gallery, 400 E Eighth Ave, 98926-7564. Tel 509-963-2665; FAX 509-963-1918; *Dir Art Gallery* James Sahlstrand
Open Mon - Fri 8 AM - 5 PM. No admis fee. Estab 1970 to serve as university gallery & hold regional & national exhibits. The gallery is a large, single unit. Average Annual Attendance: 20,000
Income: Financed by state appropriations
Publications: Catalogs for all National shows
Activities: Lect open to public; competitions

M **GALLERY ONE,** 408 1/2 N Pearl St, 98926. Tel 509-925-2670; *Dir* Eveleth Green; *Asst Dir* Edith Connolly
Open Mon - Sat 11 AM - 5 PM. No admis fee. Estab 1968 to offer quality artistic & educational experience to all ages. 5 rooms for exhibits & 3 sales rooms. Average Annual Attendance: 60,000. Mem: 350; dues $200-$500; meeting 4th Wed each month
Income: $120,000 (financed by sales & mem)
Exhibitions: John Lucas (oil paintings); Kenneth Olson (oil/enamel paintings & watercolors); Jason Sheldon (wood sculpture)
Activities: Occasional classes for adults & children; lect open to public, 2 vis lectr per year; competitions with awards; individual paintings are lent; lending collection contains original artworks, paintings & sculptures; sales shop sells original art, prints, arts & crafts

A **WESTERN ART ASSOCIATION,** 416 N Pearl, PO Box 893, 98926. Tel 509-962-2934; Elec Mail waa@ellensburg.com. *Exec Dir* Diane Legere
Open 10 AM - 5 PM. Estab 1972 to promote western art, artifacts & heritage. Average Annual Attendance: 8000-10,000. Mem: 275; dues family $40, individual $25; annual meeting in Oct
Income: $125,000 (financed by mem, Annual National Western Art Show & Auction)
Publications: Brushstrokes, semiannual newsletter
Activities: Lect open to public; competitions with prizes; scholarships & fels offered; individual paintings & original objects of art lent; originate traveling exhibitions 1 per year; sales shop sells prints & original art

GOLDENDALE

M **MARYHILL MUSEUM OF ART,** 35 Maryhill Museum Dr, 98620. Tel 509-773-3733; FAX 509-773-6138; Elec Mail maryhill@gorge.net. *Dir* Josie E DeFalla; *Registrar* Betty Long; *Cur Education* Colleen Schafroth; *Business Mgr* Patricia Perry; *Public Relations Officer* Lee Musgrave
Open daily 9 AM - 5 PM Mar 15 - Nov 15. Admis adults $5, students (6-16) $1.50, under six free. Estab 1923 as a museum of art. Chateau-style mansion with 3 stories of galleries on 26 acres of parklands plus full scale Stonehenge nearby; cafe & museum shop. Average Annual Attendance: 80,000. Mem: 600; dues $20 individual, $35 family
Collections: American Indian artifacts; antique & modern chessmen; European & American paintings; Mary, Queen of Romania furniture & memorabilia; regional historic photographics; Rodin sculpture & drawings; Russian icons; World War II costumed French fashion mannequins, decorative arts
Publications: Brochure, souvenir & exhibition booklets
Activities: Classes for adults & children, performing arts programs, docent training; lectr open to public, 4 vis lectr per year; concerts; gallery talks; tours; competitions with awards; lending collection contains individual paintings & original objects of art; book traveling exhibitions, 4 annually; originate traveling exhibitions to national & international museums; museum shop sells gift items & publications on collections

ISSAQUAH

A **NORTHWEST PASTEL SOCIETY (NPS),** 1420 NW Gilman Blvd, No 2732, 98027-7001. Tel 206-391-0777; Elec Mail rebraeutigam@worldnet.att.net. *Pres* Peggy Braeutigam
Estab 1988 to promote, encourage & foster creative painting with pastels, encourage pastel artists in their artistic growth & success, promote a fellowship of pastel artists & to promote public awareness about pastel. Mem: dues $25
Exhibitions: Open juried international exhibitions & member exhibitions
Publications: Bimonthly newsletter

KENNEWICK

A **ARTS COUNCIL OF THE MID-COLUMBIA REGION,** 5 N Morain (Mailing add: PO Box 730, Richland, 99352). Tel 509-735-4612; FAX 509-783-8142; Elec Mail arts_council@tcfn.org. Arts Hotline - Modem 509-543-2900. *Exec Dir* Barbara Gurth
Open Mon - Fri 10:30 AM - 5 PM, Sat 11 AM - 3 PM. Estab Apr 1968 to advocate the arts in the Mid-Columbia Region. Average Annual Attendance: 17,000. Mem: 300; dues $35
Income: $130,000 (financed by city, corporate & private mem)
Publications: Calendar & Newsletter, monthly
Activities: Educ programs; lect open to the public, 5 vis lectr per year; gallery talks; tours; book traveling exhibitions 1 per year

OLYMPIA

M **EVERGREEN STATE COLLEGE,** Evergreen Galleries, 98505. Tel 360-866-6000, Ext 6488; *Dir* Peter Ramsey
Exhibitions: Contemporary West Coast art; functional & sculptured ceramics

M **STATE CAPITOL MUSEUM,** 211 W 21st Ave, 98501. Tel 360-753-2580; FAX 360-586-8322; *Dir* Derek R Valley; *Cur Exhib* Susan Torntore
Open Tues - Fri 10 AM - 4 PM, Sat & Sun Noon - 4 PM, cl Mon. No admis fee. Estab 1941 to interpret history of the State of Washington & of the capital city. The one-room gallery presents changing monthly shows. Average Annual Attendance: 40,000. Mem: 400; dues family $12, individual $6; annual meeting in June
Income: Financed by city & state appropriation & local funds
Collections: Etchings by Thomas Handforth; Winslow Homer Woodcuts; Northwest Indian serigraphs; small collection of paintings by Washington artists
Publications: Museum Newsletter, bi-monthly; Museum Calender; every other month: lists all scheduled events
Activities: Classes for adults & children; dramatic programs; docent training; lect open to the public; concerts; gallery talks; tours; individual paintings & original objects of art lent to State offices; lending collection contains original prints, paintings; originate traveling exhibitions; sales shop sells books & slides

PORT ANGELES

M **PORT ANGELES FINE ARTS CENTER,** 1203 E Lauridsen Blvd, 98362. Tel 360-457-3532; *Dir* Jake Seniuk; *Asst Dir* Barbara Slavik
Open Thurs - Sun 11 AM - 5 PM. Donations accepted. Estab 1986. 1950's NW contemporary semi-circular home designed by Paul Hayden Kirk, converted to gallery. Changing shows of contemporary art in all media. Panoramic views & integration of natural surroundings in gallery space via many glass walls
Income: $90,000 (financed by endowment, mem, grants & corporate gifts)
Collections: Esther Webster Art Collection, miscellaneous donated works
Exhibitions: Chihuly Baskets (glass); Charles Stokes Retrospective (paintings)
Publications: On Center, quarterly
Activities: Classes for children; docent programs; lect open to public, 6 vis lectr per year; concerts; readings; sales shop sells books, handicrafts, original art & reproductions

PORT TOWNSEND

A **CENTRUM FOUNDATION,** Fort Worden State Park, PO Box 1158, 98368-0958. Tel 360-385-3102; FAX 360-385-2470;
Internet Home Page Address http://www.olympus.net/centrum. WATS 800-733-3608. *Dir Prog* Peter McCracken
Estab 1973 to assist those who seek creative & intellectual growth & to present visual, literary & performing arts to the pub
Income: Financed by donations, fees & grants
Activities: Resident workshops for children; Thinking Classroom program; workshops for seniors 55 & older; lect; artist in residence program

PULLMAN

M **WASHINGTON STATE UNIVERSITY,** Museum of Art, 99164-7460. Tel 509-335-1910 (office), 335-6607 (information); FAX 509-335-6635 (pause) 51910; Elec Mail artmuse@wsu.edu. *Dir* Patricia Watkinson; *Admin Mgr* Kierstie Nelson; *Coordr Exhib & Coll* Alan Shipman
Open Mon - Fri 10 AM - 4 PM, Tues 10 AM - 10 PM, Sat & Sun 1 - 5 PM. No admis fee. Estab 1973 to contribute to the humanistic & artistic educational purpose & goal of the university for the direct benefit of the students, faculty & surrounding communities. Gallery covers 5000 sq ft & is centrally located on campus. Average Annual Attendance: 28,000. Mem: 400; dues $35-$1000; annual meeting in the spring
Income: Financed by the state of Washington, private & pub grants & contributions
Collections: Late 19th century to present-day American art, with particular strength in the areas of the Ash Can School & Northwest regional art; contemporary American & British prints
Exhibitions: A Different War: Vietnam in Art; Americans in Glass; The American Eight from permanent collection; The Art of Architecture; Arts of Kenya; A Song to the Creator; Milton Avery: Outside Japan; British Landscape Photography; British Prints; Clearly Art: Robert Helm, 1981-93; Contemporary American Potter; Contemporary Metals; Diverse Directions: The Fiber Arts; Drawing on Death; Form & Figure; Fabric Traditions of Indonesia; Gaylen Hansen: The Paintings of a Decade; Historic Vision: Early Photography as Document; Eikoh Hosoe: META; Imperial Robes from the Ch'ing Dynasty; Living With the Volcano: Artists of Mt St Helens; The Master Weavers; Noritake Art Deco Porcelains; Philip Pearlstein; Paintings to Watercolor; Arnulf Rainer; Swords of the Samurai; Annual faculty & student exhibitions
Publications: Annual special exhibition catalog
Activities: Docent training; lect open to public, 4 vis lectr per year; gallery talks; tours; competitions; originate traveling exhibitions

RICHLAND

A **ALLIED ARTS ASSOCIATION,** Allied Arts Center & Gallery, 89 Lee Blvd, 99352. Tel 509-943-9815; *Pres* Diana Schlauder; *Admin Asst* Nancy Shade
Open Tues - Sat 11 AM - 5 PM. No admis fee. Estab 1947 to stimulate interest in various forms of visual art. 4532 sq ft. Consists of the Townside Gallery, Motyka Room, Parkside Gallery & an Educational Wing. Mem: 400; dues $10; annual meeting in Nov
Income: $80,000
Activities: Classes for adults & children; docent programs; conferences; lect open to public; scholarships & fels offered; sales shop sells original art, prints, pottery & fine crafts

SEATTLE

A ALLIED ARTS OF SEATTLE, INC, 105 S Main St, Rm 201, 98104. Tel 206-624-0432; FAX 206-624-0433; *Pres* Clint Pehrson
Open Mon - Fri 9 AM - 4 PM. No admis fee. Estab 1954 to promote & support the arts & artists of the Northwest & to help create the kind of city that will attract the kind of people who support the arts. Mem: 1000; dues $10 - $250 depending on category; annual meeting Jan
Income: $70,000 (financed by mem & fundraising events)
Exhibitions: Access Book Cover for Disabled Artists; Competition for Art a La Carte
Publications: Allied Arts Newsletter, 10 times per year; Access: The Lively Arts, directory of arts organizations in Puget Sound, biannual; Art Deco Seattle; Image of Imagination: Terra-Cotta Seattle
Activities: Self-guided tours; tour of artists' studios; competitions; awards; scholarships offered

A CENTER ON CONTEMPORARY ART, 65 Cedar St, 98121. Tel 206-728-1980; *Dir* Susan Purves; *Asst Dir* Bradley Thompson
Open Tues - Sat 11 AM - 6 PM, Sun Noon - 4 PM. Admis $2, members free. Estab 1980 to serve as a catalyst & forum for the advancement & understanding of contemporary art. Average Annual Attendance: 40,000. Mem: 1000; dues $15-$100
Exhibitions: Nirvana: Capitalism & the Consumed Image; Square Painting
Publications: Bimonthly newsletter
Activities: Lect open to public, 3 vis lectr per year; concerts; gallery talks; competitions with awards, five $1000 for new annual artist; book traveling exhibitions; museum shop sells items depending on exhibit

M CORNISH COLLEGE OF THE ARTS, Fisher Gallery, 710 E Roy St, 98102. Tel 206-323-1400; FAX 206-726-5055; *Dept Chair* Greg Skinner; *Admin Asst* Sally Johnson; *Gallery & Events Coordr* Susan Olds
Open Tues - Fri Noon - 6 PM, Sat Noon - 4 PM. No admis fee. Estab 1975 to support & enhance the visual arts curricula & reflect current trends in art. Gallery is 36 x 22 ft & has a lite-trak system, double door entry, 1200 ft of free wall space, 10 ft ceilings & tile floor
Income: Financed through institution
Exhibitions: Temporary one-person & group exhibitions
Publications: Gallery mailers
Activities: Classes for adults interested in part-time study; dramatic programs; lect open to public; gallery talks; competitions; traveling exhibitions organized & circulated

L Cornish Library, 710 E Roy St, 98102. Tel 206-323-1400, Ext 5040; FAX 206-726-5055; *Librn* Ronald G McComb
Open to students & faculty; primarily for lending
Library Holdings: Vols 12,000; Per subs 90; AV — Rec 9000, slides 20,000, v-tapes; Other — Exhibition catalogs 1000
Special Subjects: Design
Activities: Lending collection contains 1500 books, 2000 phono records, 20,000 slides, 150 video tapes & 1100 compact discs

A CORPORATE COUNCIL FOR THE ARTS, 1420 Fifth Ave, Ste 475, 98101. Tel 206-682-9270; FAX 206-447-0954; *Pres* Peter Donnelly
Open 8:30 AM - 5 PM. Estab 1968 as a clearinghouse for corporate contributions to the arts, to monitor budgeting of art agencies & assess ability of business to provide funding assistance. Gallery not maintained. Mem: 300; minimum contribution of $500 to qualify for mem; annual meeting in Sept
Income: $1,012,000 (financed by mem)
Publications: Annual Report; brochures; periodic membership reports
Activities: Annual fundraising event & campaign

M FRYE ART MUSEUM, 704 Terry Ave, PO Box 3005, 98114. Tel 206-622-9250; FAX 206-223-1707; Elec Mail fry@arteaol.com. *Pres & Dir* Richard West
Open Tues - Sat 10 AM - 5 PM, Thurs 10 AM - 9 PM, Sun Noon - 5 PM, cl Mon, Thanksgiving, Christmas & New Year's Day. No admis fee. Estab 1952 to display & preserve the Frye Art Collection. 10 galleries with over 12,000 sq ft of exhibition space; 142 seat auditorium with stage (ceramics/sculpture & painting/drawings), studios (for classes) & art workshops. Maintains reference library. Average Annual Attendance: 60,000
Income: $1,200,000 (financed by endowment)
Collections: American masters from the Colonial period to American representational prints of today; Munich School paintings; Northwest regional art & Alaskan paintings; 19th & 20th century American, German & French paintings Hoch, Jongkind, Kaulbach, Koester, Lenbach, Leibl, Liebermann, Lier, Llermitte, Manet, Gabriel Max, Monticelli, Slevogt, Soren, Stuck, Thoma, Willroider, Winterhalter, Uhde, Ziem, Zugel, Zumbusch
Exhibitions: Selections from the Frye Collection; (1997) Prints of Roy Partridge; Melissa Weinman: Saints' Stories; Art From Currier Gallery; Michael Flanagan; Czech & Slovak Photography; American Society of Marine Artists; American Masters; Petroglyphy & Pictographs; Art of Vaslor Nisinsky
Publications: Frye Vues, monthly
Activities: Classes for adults & children; lect open to public; concerts; gallery talks; tours; book traveling exhibitions

L Library, 704 Terry Ave, 98114. Tel 206-622-9250; FAX 206-223-1707; *Exec Dir* Richard West
Open Mon - Sat 10 AM - 5 PM, Sun Noon - 5 PM. No admis fee. Estab 1950. For reference only. Average Annual Attendance: 48,000
Income: $850,000 (financed by private funds)
Purchases: American 19th Century & Alaskan Paintings; Russian Collection of Paintings
Library Holdings: Vols 3000
Activities: Classes for adults & children; lect open to public; concerts; gallery talks; tours; awards

A GLASS ART SOCIETY, 1305 Fourth Ave, Ste 711, 98101-2401. Tel 206-382-1305; FAX 206-382-2630; Elec Mail glasartsoc@aol.com. *Exec Dir* Penny Berk
Estab 1971 to encourage excellence & to advance the appreciation, understanding & development of the glass arts worldwide.

M HENRY GALLERY ASSOCIATION, Henry Art Gallery, 15th Ave NE & NE 41st St, PO Box 353070, 98195. Tel 206-543-2280; FAX 206-685-3123; Elec Mail hartg@u.washington.edu. *Dir* Richard Andrews; *Sr Cur* Sheryl Conkelton; *Deputy Dir* Claudia Bach; *Educ Dir* Tamara Moats; *Cur Coll* Judy Sourakli
Estab 1927 for modern & contemporary art. Average Annual Attendance: 80,000. Mem: 1700; dues $25-$2500; annual meeting in the summer
Income: $1,300,000 (financed by endowment, mem, state appropriation & grants)
Collections: Mixed Media, paintings, prints, photography, sculpture & textiles
Exhibitions: (1997) Chris Burden: Sculpture; Selections from the Permanent Collection
Publications: Exhibition Catalogue, annually
Activities: Classes for adults & children; docent training; film series; lect open to public; 10 vis lectr per year; book traveling exhibitions 3 per year; originate traveling exhibitions; sales shop sells books, magazines, original art, prints, reproductions, slides

A KING COUNTY ARTS COMMISSION, Smith Tower, Rm 1115, 506 Second Ave, 98104-2311. Tel 206-296-8671; FAX 206-296-8629; Elec Mail jimkelly@metrokc.gov. *Exec Dir* Jim Kelly; *Arts Coordr* Charlie Ratheum; *Arts Coordr* Michael Killoren
Open Mon - Fri 8:30 AM - 4:30 PM. Estab 1967 to provide cultural arts opportunities to the citizens of King County. The Arts Commission purchases & commissions many works of art for public buildings; annual grant program for organizations & artists in all artistic disciplines, also multi-cultural & disabled arts population; operates touring program of performing arts events in county locations. Mem: 16; 1 meeting per month
Income: $1,300,000 million (financed by county government, plus one percent for commissioned art in county construction projects)
Purchases: Occasional works commissioned for public art
Collections: †King County art collection
Publications: The ARTS, bimonthly newsletter; The Touring Arts Booklet biennially; public art brochure; guide to programs, annually
Activities: Workshops; performances

M LEGACY LTD, 1003 First Ave, 98104. *Pres* Mardonna Austin-Mckillop
No admis fee. Estab 1933 for the collection & sale of Northwest Coast Indian contemporary & historic material
Exhibitions: Annual in-house special exhibits of historic contemporary Northwest Coast Indian & Eskimo art, ongoing exhibits of same
Activities: Sales shop sells books, magazines & prints

A 911 ARTS MEDIA CENTER, 117 Yale Ave N, 98109. Tel 206-682-6552; FAX 206-682-7422; *Dir* Karen Hirsch
Open Mon - Fri 10 AM - 6 PM. No admis fee. Estab 1981 as a film & video post-production center. Exhibition space. Average Annual Attendance: 15,000. Mem: 350; dues $40
Income: Financed by earned income, grants including McArthur Foundation, NEA, WASAC, SAC, KCAC
Collections: †Artists' video tapes
Publications: Film & video calendar, bimonthly
Activities: Workshops in film video making, video editing, grant writing & internet

A PRATT FINE ARTS CENTER, Gallery, 1902 S Main St, 98144-2206. Tel 206-328-2200; FAX 206-328-1260; *Exec Dir* Gregory Robinson; *Develop Dir* Patricia Warren; *Educ Dir* Kristin Tollefson; *Operations Dir* Damian Murphy
Open daily 9 AM - 6 PM. No admis fee. Estab 1976. Average Annual Attendance: 3000
Exhibitions: Rotating monthly exhibits (glass, jewelry, painting, prints, metal, mixed media, sculpture)
Publications: Quarterly class & exhibit brochure
Activities: Classes for adults & children; lect open to public, 6 vis lectr per year

C SAFECO INSURANCE COMPANY, Art Collection, Safeco Plaza, T-8, 98185. Tel 206-545-6100; FAX 206-545-5730; *Art Cur* Julia Anderson
Gallery open Mon - Fri 8 AM - 4:30 PM for employees & invited guests, by appointment only. Coll estab 1973 to support the work of both established & emerging Northwest artists through purchase. Small exhibition space with adjacent auditorium in mezzanine space. Average Annual Attendance: 18,000
Income: $100,000 (financed by company)
Purchases: Northwest Artists & glass artists associated with Pilchuck Glass School
Collections: Works in all media by artists of the Pacific Northwest
Publications: Checklists & essays for some exhibitions
Activities: Lect open to public; by appointment; individual paintings & original objects of art lent to non-profit museums; lending collection contains original art work, original prints, paintings, photographs & sculptures; originate traveling exhibitions

M SEATTLE ART MUSEUM, PO Box 22000, 98122-9700. Tel 206-625-8900; *Chmn* Herman Sarkowsky; *Pres Board* Belle Maxwell; *Dir* Mimi Gates; *Asst Dir Finance & Admin* Jeff Eby; *Public Relations Mgr* Jackie Thompson-Dodd
Open Tues - Sat 10 AM - 5 PM, Thurs 10 AM - 9 PM, Sun Noon - 5 PM. Admis adults $2, students & senior citizens $1, children under 6 with adult, members & Thurs free. Estab 1906, incorporated 1917, building opened 1933; gift to the city from Mrs Eugene Fuller & Richard Eugene Fuller, for recreation, educ & inspiration of its citizens. Average Annual Attendance: 300,000. Mem: 10,000; dues $12 & up
Collections: LeRoy M Backus Collection of Drawings and Paintings; Manson F Backus Collection of Prints; Norman Davis Collection (with emphasis on classical art); Eugene Fuller Memorial Collection of Chinese Jades from Archaic through 18th Century; Eugene Fuller Memorial Collection (with special emphasis on Japan, China, India, & including Egypt, Ancient Greece & Rome, European, Near Eastern, primitive & contemporary Northwest art); Alice Heeramaneck Collection of Primitive Art; Henry & Marth Issacson Collection of 18th Century European Porcelain; H Kress Collection of 14th - 18th Century European Paintings; Thomas D Stimson Memorial Collection (with special emphasis on Far

Eastern art); Extensive Chinese & Indian Collection; 18th Century Drawing Room (furnished by the National Society of Colonial Dames of American in the State of Washington); major holdings in Northwest art, including Tobey, Callahan, Graves as well as all contemporary art, especially American artists Gorky, Pollock, Warhol & Lichtenstein; selected highlights on Asian collection on permanent display (with special emphasis on on Japanese screens, paintings, sculpture and lacquers); Katherine C White Collection of African Art
Publications: Annual Report; Japanese Paintings from the Sanso Collection; Johsel Namking: An Artist's View of Nature; Newsletter, 10 per year; Northwest Traditions; Song of the Brush
Activities: Docent training; film programs; double lecture course under the Museum Guild; adult art history classes; lect open to public, 12 vis lectr per year; tours; program for senior citizens; museum shop sells books, gifts & jewelry
L **Library,** PO Box 22000, 98122-9700. Tel 206-625-8900; *Librn* Elizabeth de Fato
For reference only
Library Holdings: Vols 15,000; Per subs 50; AV — Slides 75,000; Other — Exhibition catalogs 3000

M **SHORELINE HISTORICAL MUSEUM,** 749 N 175th St, PO Box 7171, 98133. Tel 206-542-7111; *Pres* Carolyn Edmonds; *VPres* Bob Phelps; *Treas* Margaret Boyce; *Dir* Vicki Stiles
Open Tues - Sat 10 AM - 4 PM. Admis by donation. Estab 1976 to preserve local history. Average Annual Attendance: 5000. Mem: 360; dues family $25, annual $10, pioneer $5; annual meeting third Wed in Nov
Income: $35,000 (financed by mem, donations, room rentals & fundraising)
Exhibitions: School room; home room; vintage radios; vintage clothing; blacksmith shop; transportation exhibit; post office; country store; other rotating exhibits
Publications: Newsletter, 5 times a year
Activities: Classes for children; docent training; lect open to public; tours; original objects of art lent; sales shop sells books, prints, postcards & area photo cards

UNIVERSITY OF WASHINGTON
M **Henry Art Gallery,** 15th Ave NE & NE 41st St, 98195. Tel 206-543-2281; FAX 206-685-3123; *Dir* Richard Andrews; *Asst Dir* Joan Caine; *Sr Cur* Chris Bruce; *Cur Coll* Judy Sourakli; *Public Information Dir* Claudia Bach; *Bookstore Mgr* Paul Cabarga; *Cur Educ* Tamara Moats
Open Tues - Sun 11 AM - 5 PM, Thurs evenings 5 - 7 PM, cl Mon. Estab 1923. 8 galleries, 6000 sq ft of exhibition space. Average Annual Attendance: 100,000. Mem: 1250; dues $20 & up
Collections: 19th century American landscape painting; contemporary West Coast ceramics; works on paper, prints, drawings & photographs; 20th century Japanese folk pottery; Elizabeth Bayley Willis Collection of Textiles from India; western & ethnic textiles; 19th & 20th century western dress (formerly Costume & Textile Study Center)
Publications: Books, exhibition catalogues; monographs
Activities: Educ dept; lect open to public; gallery talks; tours; originate traveling exhibitions to museums in the United States & abroad; museum shop sells books & prints
L **Architecture & Urban Planning Library,** 334 Gould Hall, Box 355730, 98195. Tel 206-543-4067; *Librn* Betty L Wagner
Estab 1923
Library Holdings: Vols 45,000; Per subs 300; Micro — Fiche 5246; Other — Exhibition catalogs, memorabilia, pamphlets 1684
Special Subjects: Architecture, Landscape Architecture, Building Construction, Urban Planning
L **Libraries,** Special Collections & Preservation Div, PO Box 352900, 98195-2900. Tel 206-543-1929; FAX 206-543-1931; Elec Mail speccoll@u.washington.edu. *Librn* Gary Menges; *Photog & Graphics Librn* Richard Engeman
Library Holdings: Architectural plans, drawings & renderings 63,137
Special Subjects: Native American Art, Pacific Northwest
Collections: Book arts collection
L **Art Library,** 101 Art Bldg, PO Box 353440, 98195-3440. Tel 206-543-0648; Elec Mail art@lib.washington.edu. *Librn* Connie Okada
Open Mon - Thurs 8 AM - 9 PM, Fri 8 AM - 5 PM, Sat 1 - 5 PM, Sun 1 - 5 PM. Estab 1940 to provide resources for the instructional & research programs of the School of Art & serves as the Art Library for the university community
Income: Financed by state appropriation
Library Holdings: Vols 43,000; Per subs 402; Micro — Fiche; Other — Clipping files, exhibition catalogs, reproductions
Special Subjects: Art History, Ceramics, Graphic Design, Industrial Design, Photography, Printmaking, Sculpture, Fiber Arts, General Art, Metal Design
—**Art Slide Library,** 120 Art Bldg, DM-10, PO Box 353440, 98195-3440. Tel 206-543-0649; FAX 206-685-1657; Elec Mail jcmills@u.washington.edu. *Dir Visual Servs* Jeanette C Mills
Slide library is a teaching collection that is only available to University of Washington faculty, staff & students
Library Holdings: AV — Slides 275,000
Collections: Asian & Tribal Art, slides; Western Art History
M **Thomas Burke Memorial Washington State Museum,** 98195. Tel 206-543-5590; *Dir* Dr Karl Hutterer; *Cur Asian & Pacific Ethnology* Miriam Kahn; *Cur Native American Art* Robin Wright; *Asst Dir* Roxana Augusztiny; *Cur Vertebrate Paleontology* John Rensberger; *Cur Birds* Sievert Rohwer; *Cur Invertebrate Paleontology* Peter Ward; *Cur Archaeology* Julie Stein; *Dir Public Prog* Scott Freeman; *Cur New World Ethnology* James Nason; *Cur Mammalogy* G James Kenagy; *Cur Fishes* Theodore Pietsch
Open daily 10 AM - 5 PM, Thurs 10 AM - 8 PM. Admis general $3, senior citizens & students $2, children 6-18 $1.50. Estab 1885 for research & exhibitions. Average Annual Attendance: 60,000. Mem: 1200; dues $15-$500 & up
Income: Financed by state, endowment, gifts, self-generated revenues
Collections: Natural & cultural history of Washington State, the Pacific Northwest & the Pacific Rim
Publications: Contributions & Monograph series
Activities: Classes for adults & children; docent training; lect open to public, 4-8 vis lectr per year; tours; circulates study collection; museum store sells books, native art, jewelry & cards

M **WING LUKE ASIAN MUSEUM,** 407 Seventh Ave S, 98104. Tel 206-623-5124, 623-5190 (tour desk); FAX 206-623-4559; *Dir* Ron Chew; *Co-Pres* Gloria Wakayama; *Co-Pres* Helen Kay; *VPres* Alma Kimura; *Treas* Ross Ohashi; *Secy* Julie O'Neil; *Coll Cur* Ruth Vincent; *Educ Coordr* Charlene Mano; *Special Events Coordr* Alina Hua; *Videographer* John Pai; *Develop Dir* Diane Wah; *Exhibit Coordr* Cassie Chinn; *Volunteer Coordr* Laura Shapiro; *Communications Mgr* Debbie Louie; *Membership Coordr* Jennie Pu
Open Tues - Fri 11 AM - 4:30 PM, Sat & Sun Noon - 4 PM. Estab 1966 to preserve & present the history, art & culture of Asian Pacific Americans & to bridge Asians, Asian Pacific Americans & Americans of other backgrounds. Permanent Asian Pacific American exhibit spanning 200 yrs of community history in Washington State & changing exhibit gallery used for Asian Pacific American historical, cultural & art exhibitions. Average Annual Attendance: 70, 000. Mem: 1000; dues $30; annual meeting in Jan
Income: $500,000 (financed by endowment, mem, annual art auction, local & state commissions & grants for exhibits)
Collections: †Asian folk art, textiles & household items; Asian-American historical artifacts & photographs
Exhibitions: (1997) A Bridge Home: Music in the Lives of Asian Pacific Americans. (1997-98) Asian Pacific American Immigration Exhibit. (1998) Welcoming the New: Celebrating Asian New Years in America
Publications: Publishes exhibit catalogs
Activities: Classes for adults & children; docent training; lect open to public, 20 vis lectr per year; book readings; panel presentation; tours; annual Asian American artist award; Exten dept serves teacher educ; artifacts lent to accredited scholars & institutions for study, research, publishing & exhibition; lending collection contains 2800 pieces; book one traveling exhibition; originate traveling exhibitions that circulate to community colleges, libraries, & museums
L **Library,** 407 Seventh Ave S, 98104. Tel 206-623-5124; *Cur Coll* Ruth Vincent
Library Holdings: Vols 5000; AV — Slides 150, v-tapes; Other — Clipping files, photographs

SPOKANE

M **EASTERN WASHINGTON STATE HISTORICAL SOCIETY,** Cheney Cowles Museum, 2316 W First Ave, 99204. Tel 509-456-3931; FAX 509-456-7690; *Dir* Glenn Mason; *Cur Art* Barbara Racker; *Deputy Dir* Larry Schoonover; *Archivist* Karen De Seve
Open Tues - Fri & Sat 10 AM - 5 PM, Wed 5 - 9 PM, Sun 1 - 5 PM. Admis $4. Estab 1916 to collect & preserve Pacific Northwest History, art & American Indian materials. 2 temporary galleries totaling 3500 sq ft, 350 running ft. Maintains reference library. Average Annual Attendance: 90,000. Mem: 1565; dues $25-$35
Income: Financed by mem, state appropriations & private sector support
Collections: American Indian, regional history, Northwest modern contemporary art; Historic house of 1898 by architect Kirtland K Cutter, interior designed & decorated with period furnishings; 19th & 20th century American & European art; representative works of Pacific Northwest artists
Exhibitions: Behind the Red White & Blue; Pop Art & Its Legacy; Posters, Propaganda & Pride
Publications: Museum Notes, six per year; exhibition catalogs
Activities: Classes for adults & children; docent training; lect open to public, 100 vis lectr per year; gallery talks; tours; individual paintings & original objects of art lent to professional non-profit institutions nationally; lending collection contains books, original art works; original prints, paintings, sculptures & 135,000 photographs; book traveling exhibitions; traveling exhibitions organized & circulated; museum shop sells books, original art & gift items
L **Library,** 2316 W First Ave, 99204. Tel 509-456-3931, Ext 113; FAX 509-456-7690; *Dir* Glen Mason; *Deputy Dir* Larry Schoonover; *Cur Art* Barbara Racker; *Archivists* Karen De Seve
For reference & research only by staff
Library Holdings: Vols 800; Per subs 18; AV — A-tapes, cassettes, fs, lantern slides, slides, v-tapes; Other — Clipping files, exhibition catalogs, manuscripts, memorabilia, original art works, pamphlets, photographs, prints, sculpture
Special Subjects: American Indian Art, Architecture, Historical Material, Manuscripts, Maps, Photography
Collections: Inland Empire history

M **GONZAGA UNIVERSITY,** Jundt Art Museum, Ad Art Gallery, 502 E Boone Ave, PO Box 1, 99258-0001. Tel 509-328-4220, Ext 3211; FAX 509-324-5718; *Dir & Cur* J Scott Patnode; *Asst Cur* Midge Collins
Open Mon - Fri 10 AM - 4 PM, Sat Noon - 4 PM, through academic yr. No admis fee. Estab 1971 to service the Spokane Community, art department & general university population at Gonzaga University; Jundt Gallery estab 1995. Jundt Gallery 2720 sq ft. Arcade Gallery 1120 sq ft. Average Annual Attendance: 30,000
Income: Financed by parent institution
Purchases: Jacob Lawrence, Wayne Thiebaud & Sylvia Wald prints
Collections: Dale Chihuly Glass Installation (Chandelier); †Rodin Sculpture Collection; †Contemporary & old master print collection; †glass; †prints; student art collection
Exhibitions: (1997) Selections from the permanent collection photographs by Robert Doisneau; Las (in)Visibles: Women Artist of Uruguay; Dan Murphy: Ceramics & The Student Annual: senior thesis
Activities: Educ dept; docent training; lect open to public, 6 vis lectr per year; gallery talks; tours; student purchase awards; individual paintings lent to museums, art centers & university galleries; lending collection contains paintings, photographs, sculptures & 3000 original prints; book traveling exhibitions 3 per year

L **SPOKANE PUBLIC LIBRARY GALLERY,** 906 W Main St, 99201. Tel 509-626-5300; *Dir* Daniel Walters; *Mgr Community Relations* Dolly Richendrfer
Open Mon - Thurs 10 AM - 9 PM, Fri & Sat 10 AM - 6 PM. Estab 1894 basically to meet citizens educ, information, recreation & cultural lifelong learning needs through a variety of programs & facilities. Gallery maintained for special exhibitions
Library Holdings: Original documents; Micro — Fiche, prints, reels; AV — A-

tapes, cassettes, fs, Kodachromes, motion pictures, rec, slides, v-tapes; Other — Clipping files, exhibition catalogs, manuscripts, memorabilia, original art works, pamphlets, photographs
Collections: AV; childrens' & young adult; fiction; genealogy; non-fiction; northwest; periodicals; rare books
Publications: Previews, monthly
Activities: Classes for adults & children; dramatic programs; lect open to public; concerts

TACOMA

M TACOMA ART MUSEUM, 1123 Pacific Ave, 98402. Tel 206-272-4258; FAX 206-627-1898; *Exec Dir* Chase W Rynd; *Sr Cur & Cur Exhib* Barbara Johns; *Cur Educ* Gary LaTurner
Open Tues, Wed, Fri & Sat 10 AM - 5 PM, Thurs 10 AM - 7 PM, Sun Noon- 5 PM. Admis general $3, students & senior citizens $2, children 6-12 yrs $1, under 6 & Tues free. Estab 1891. Mus features traveling exhibitions & an interactive art gallery. Average Annual Attendance: 65,000. Mem: 1900; dues $12-$2500
Income: $1,000,000 (financed by contributions, grants, mem & carried income)
Collections: †American & French paintings; American sculpture; Chinese Textiles; 19th & 20th Century American Art; European & Asian Works of art; European Impressionism; Japanese Woodblock prints, Northwest Art
Exhibitions: Catalin Masters - Spanish Artists, Dali, Piccasso; (1997) 25 years at 12th & Pacific-French Impressionist American, Artists, Japanese Woodblock works
Publications: Annual Report; Quarterly Bulletin; exhibit catalogs
Activities: Classes for adults & children; docent training; lect open to public, 10 vis lectr per year; gallery talks; tours; biennial competition with awards; individual paintings & original objects of art lent to other professional museums; museum shop sells books, original art, reproductions, prints, cards, jewelry, concerts & films
L Reference Library, 1123 Pacific Ave, 98402. Tel 206-272-4258; *Librn* Sadie Uglow
Open to the pub for reference only
Income: Financed by mem, donations & grants
Library Holdings: Vols 2526; Per subs 30; Micro — Cards; Other — Clipping files, exhibition catalogs, pamphlets
Special Subjects: Japanese woodcuts
Collections: Unique collection of research material on Japanese woodcut
Publications: Monthly bulletins

M TACOMA ARTS COMMISSION, Commencement Art Gallery, 902 Commerce, 98402-4407. Tel 206-593-4331; FAX 206-591-5232; Internet Home Page Address http://www.halcyon.com/aart. *Gallery Coordr* Benjamin Meeker
Open Tues - Sat 11 AM - 5 PM. Estab 1993. Average Annual Attendance: 6000
Income: Financed by city appropriation
Exhibitions: South Sounds. (1997) Wendi Bruovik, Russel Card, Shirley Halverson, Ron Hinson, Chris Kirages, Kathleen McMahon, Earl Olsen, Thomas Shader, Jill Stutzman, John Tylzak
Publications: Sightings, bimonthly magazine
Activities: Classes for adults & children; open workshops; lect open to public, 11 vis lectr per year; competitions with prizes

L TACOMA PUBLIC LIBRARY, Handforth Gallery, 1102 Tacoma Ave S, 98402. Tel 206-591-5666; FAX 206-627-1693; *Dir* David Domkoski
Open Mon - Thurs 9 AM - 9 PM, Fri & Sat 9 AM - 6 PM. Estab 1952 to extend library services to include exhibits in all media in the Thomas S Handforth Gallery. Circ 1,237,000
Income: Financed by city appropriation
Library Holdings: Vols 800,000; Per subs 1600; Audio compact discs; Micro — Reels; AV — A-tapes, cassettes, motion pictures, rec, v-tapes; Other — Clipping files, exhibition catalogs, framed reproductions, memorabilia, original art works, pamphlets, photographs, prints
Special Subjects: Manuscripts, Photography, Genealogy, Northwest
Collections: Art book; city, county, federal & state documents; rare books
Exhibitions: Monthly changing exhibits
Activities: Classes for children; dramatic programs; lect open to public, 3-4 vis lectr per year; originate traveling exhibitions

M UNIVERSITY OF PUGET SOUND, Kittredge Art Gallery, 1500 N Warner, 98416. Tel 206-756-3348; FAX 206-756-3500; *Dir* Greg Bell
Open Mon - Fri 10 AM - 4 PM, Sun 2 - 4 PM. No admis fee. Estab 1961 for showing of student & professional works. Exhibition space consists of 2 galleries: Fireplace Gallery with 100 ft of running wall space & Kittredge Gallery with 160 ft of running wall space; track lighting; security alarms. Average Annual Attendance: 6200
Collections: †Abby Williams Hill, painter of Northwest scenes from 1880s to 1930s
Exhibitions: David Gilhooly (ceramics); Katherine Levin-Lau (painting); Caroline Law (sculpture); Patricia Bellan-Gillen (paintings); Pamela Gazale (sculpture); Dan Webb (sculpture); Student Senior Exhibition
Publications: Monthly show bulletins
Activities: Classes for adults & children; lect open to public, 4 vis lectr per year; gallery talks; individual paintings & original works of art lent to professional art museums & historical museums; lending collection contains original prints, paintings & ceramic works

M WASHINGTON STATE HISTORY MUSEUM, 1911 Pacific Ave, 98402. Tel 206-272-3500; FAX 206-272-9518; *Dir* David Nicandri
Open Tues - Fri 10 AM - 4 PM, Sat & Sun Noon - 4 PM, cl holidays. Admis adults $2, senior citizens $1.50, students $1, members & children under 6 free. Estab 1891 to research, preserve & display the heritage of Washington State. Soc owns three buildings; art gallery under the direction of the Soc; two floors of exhibits (Washington State, Native American Artifacts, temporary special exhibits). Average Annual Attendance: 125,000. Mem: 3000; dues $25 & up;

annual meeting in August
Income: Financed by mem, state appropriations & gifts
Collections: Pre-historic relics; †Indian & Eskimo artifacts, baskets, clothing, utensils; Oriental items; †Washington-Northwest pioneer relics; archives
Exhibitions: Train Exhibit (permanent)
Publications: History Highlights (newsletter), quarterly; Columbia (popular historical journal), quarterly
Activities: Classes for adults & children; docent training; lect open to public, 15 vis lectr per year; tours; interpretative programs; concerts; dramatic programs with awards; scholarships offered; individual paintings & original objects of art lent to comparable museums & cultural institutions; lending collection contains natural artifacts, photographs & sculpture; traveling exhibitions organized & circulated; museum shop sells books, magazines, reproductions, prints, postcards & stationery
L Special Collections Div, 315 N Stadium Way, 98403. Tel 206-593-2830; *Cur Spec Coll* Ed Nolan; *Asst Cur Photo* Elaine Miller; *Asst Cur Manuscripts* Joy Werlink
Open Tues, Wed & Thurs by appointment. No admis fee. Estab 1941 for research in Pacific Northwest history. For reference only
Income: Financed by mem, state appropriations & gifts
Library Holdings: Vols 12,000; Micro — Reels; Other — Clipping files, manuscripts 2,500,000, memorabilia, pamphlets, photographs 500,000, prints 30,000
Collections: Asahel Curtis Photograph Collection

WALLA WALLA

A CARNEGIE ART CENTER, * 109 S Palouse, 99362. Tel 509-525-4270; *Dir* Christine Bishop
Open Tues - Sat 11 AM - 4:30 PM, June - Aug 11 AM - 3 PM. No admis fee. Estab 1970 in 1905 Carnegie Library, built of Kansas brick & paneled with oak, incorporated 1971 as a non-profit educ organization. Average Annual Attendance: 12,000. Mem: 500; dues life $1500 or more, individual $15
Income: Financed by endowments, dues, contributions, art sales & rentals & gift shop
Exhibitions: 10 exhibitions annually
Activities: Classes for adults & children; docent training; lect open to public; gallery talks; tours; competitions with awards; scholarships offered; individual paintings lent; book traveling exhibitions; sales shop sells books, original art, reproductions, prints, pottery & handcrafted gifts

WENATCHEE

M CHELAN COUNTY PUBLIC UTILITY DISTRICT, Rocky Reach Dam, US 97A Chelan Hwy, PO Box 1231, 98807-1231. Tel 509-663-812i; FAX 509-664-2874; 509-663-7522 (Visitor Center). *Chief Exec Officer & General Mgr* Sonny Smart
Open 8 AM - dusk. No admis fee. Estab 1961 as a landscape ground & exhibit galleries. History of Electricity & Edisonia, Geology, Anthopology - Local Indian & Pioneer History. Average Annual Attendance: 100,000
Income: Financed by Hydro Electric revenue
Collections: Electrical artifacts; Indian Artifacts (Central Columbia River Region); Nez Perce Indian Portraits
Exhibitions: Monthly art exhibits
Activities: Educ dept; teacher seminars; seasonal tours; science camp

M NORTH CENTRAL WASHINGTON MUSEUM, Gallery, 127 S Mission, 98801. Tel 509-664-3340; *Pres* Lloyd Berry; *Dir* Keith Williams; *Cur* Mark Behler; *Dir Public Relations* Mary Tomsen; *Art Gallery Coordr* Terri White
Open Mon - Fri 10 AM - 4 PM, Sat & Sun 1 - 4 PM, cl holidays. Admis families $5, adult $3, children 6-12 $1, mem free. Estab 1939 to preserve & present history & the arts. Gallery program offers exhibits of regional, national & international importance. Average Annual Attendance: 32,000. Mem: 700; dues $25; annual meeting in Mar
Collections: International Ceramics Collection; 19th Century Japanese Woodblock Prints; local historical collections
Exhibitions: Rotating art exhibits; rotating historical exhibits; permanent history exhibits, including Pioneer Living & Apple Industry Exhibit
Publications: The Confluence, quarterly; The Correction, quarterly
Activities: Classes for adults & children; docent training; lect open to public; concerts; gallery talks; tours; educ dept serves local public schools; original objects of art lent; book traveling exhibitions annually; originate traveling exhibitions; museum shop sells books, magazines, original art

M WENATCHEE VALLEY COLLEGE, Gallery 76, 1300 Fifth St, 98801. Tel 509-664-2521; *Coordr* Kathy Wagers
Open Mon - Fri 10 AM - 2 PM, Wed & Thurs evenings 7 - 9 PM. Donation accepted. Estab 1976 to serve a rural, scattered population in North Central Washington State, which without Gallery 76, would not have access to a non-sales gallery. Non-profit community art gallery housed in Sexton Hall on Wenatchee Valley College Campus. Average Annual Attendance: 3150. Mem: 235; dues $15-$100; annual meeting in Feb
Income: $18,000 (financed by mem, grants, donations, fundraising events, art auction, Casino Night)
Collections: Oil Painting, Stephen Tse
Exhibitions: Members Invitational; Aerial photos by Mark Abrahmson; Juried Art Exhibit; Students Art Exhibit
Publications: Annual Brochure
Activities: Lect open to public; 1-2 vis lectr per year; gallery talks; tours; Invitational Exhibit for North Central Washington Artists; Juried art exhibit (national); sales shop, located in another building, sells & rents original art

YAKIMA

A ALLIED ARTS GALLERY OF THE YAKIMA VALLEY, 5000 W Lincoln Ave, 98908. Tel 509-966-0930; *Pres* Pat Balleaw; *Exec Dir* Elizabeth Miller
Open Mon - Fri 9 AM - 5 PM. No admis fee. Estab 1962 to encourage, promote & coordinate the practice & appreciation of the arts among the people of Yakima Valley. General gallery shows changing monthly exhibits. Average Annual Attendance: 20,000. Mem: 600; dues $25 - $500; annual meeting in Sept
Income: Financed by mem
Exhibitions: Monthly exhibits by local and area artists; annual juried exhibit
Publications: Artscope (arts calendar) monthly
Activities: Classes for adults & children; dramatic programs; lect open to public, 1-3 vis lectr per year; concerts; gallery talks; tours; competitions with awards; sales shop sells original art
L Library, 5000 W Lincoln Ave, 98908. Tel 509-966-0930; *Exec Dir* Elizabeth Miller
Library Holdings: Vols 400

WEST VIRGINIA

CHARLESTON

M SUNRISE MUSEUM, INC, Sunrise Art Museum & Sunrise Science Museum, 746 Myrtle Rd, 25314. Tel 304-344-8035; FAX 304-344-8038; *Dir* Ross McGire; *Chief Cur* Richard Ambrose; *Prog Dir* Andrea Ambrose; *Cur/Registrar* Kelli Burns; *Science Educator* Chuck English
Open Wed - Sat 11 AM - 5 PM, Sun Noon - 5 PM, cl Mon, Tues & national holidays. Admis adults $3, students, teachers & senior citizens $2, children under 3 free. Estab 1960. Sunrise is located on a 16 acre estate containing two stone mansions & a carriage/natural trail. The Colonial Revival Sunrise Mansion, built in 1905, houses science mus & planetarium. The Georgian Torquilstone Mansion, built in 1928, houses the art museum. Average Annual Attendance: 70,000. Mem: 1500; dues Benefactors' Circle $1000, patron $500, supporting $250, contributing $100, participating $50, family $40, double $30, individual $20; annual meeting in mid-Apr
Income: $1,000,000 (financed by endowment, mem, earned income, corporate & business contributions)
Collections: 17th through 20th century American paintings, prints, decorative arts & sculpture
Exhibitions: Numerous regional & international exhibits held throughout the year
Publications: Art Museum Bulletin, monthly newsletter
Activities: Classes for adults & children; docent training; guided tours; planetarium programs; individual & original objects of art lent to other museums & public institutions; museum shop sells books, prints & variety of scientific, educational & decorative gift items including jewelry

HUNTINGTON

M HUNTINGTON MUSEUM OF ART, 2033 McCoy Rd, 25701. Tel 304-529-2701; FAX 304-529-7447; *Dir* Mary Anne Pennington; *Sr Cur* G Eason Eige; *Chief Cur* Louise Polan; *Dir Education* Ed Pauley; *Development Officer* Open; *Registrar* Daniel Silosky; *Public Relations* Julie Brown Marsh; *Comptroller* Kathy Saunders
Open Tues - Sat 10 AM - 5 PM, Sun Noon - 5 PM; cl Mon. No admis fee. Estab 1952 to own, operate & maintain an art museum for the collection of paintings, prints, bronzes, porcelains & all kinds of art & utility objects; to permit the study of arts & crafts & to foster an interest in the arts. Three building complex on 52-acre site includes ten galleries, two sculpture courts, seven studio workshops, a 10,000 volume capacity library, 300 seat auditorium, two & one-half miles of nature trails, an observatory with Celestron-14 telescope & an amphitheatre. Average Annual Attendance: 75,000. Mem: Mem dues vary; annual meeting in June
Income: Financed by endowment, mem, city, state & county appropriations
Collections: American & European Paintings & Prints; American Decorative Arts; Georgian silver; firearms; historical and contemporary glass; Turkish prayer rugs
Exhibitions: By the People, American Folk & Self-Taught Art; Mark Rothko: The Spirit of the Myth; Sources of Joy & Laughter: Art of the Children's Book
Publications: Exhibit catalogs; quarterly newsletter
Activities: Classes & workshops for adults & children; docent training; public lectures; concerts; theatre productions; gallery talks; tours; individual paintings & original objects of art lent to museums; traveling exhibitions organized & circulated; museum shop sells books, original art, reproductions, prints & crafts; Junior Art Museum

MARTINSBURG

M ASSOCIATES FOR COMMUNITY DEVELOPMENT, Boarman Arts Center, 208 S Queen St, 25401. Tel 304-263-0224; *Pres Board Dir* Dorothea McMillan; *VPres Board Dir* Stewart Borger; *Adminr* Judy Peyton
Open Mon - Fri 10 AM - 5 PM. No admis fee. Estab 1987 to exhibit the work of local & regional artists & craftsmen. Mem: 200; dues $20-$1000; quarterly meetings
Income: $88,000 (financed by mem, city appropriation, state appropriation & exhibit sponsors)
Exhibitions: Changing exhibits featuring a variety of arts & crafts including photography, sculpture, oil, acrylic, watercolor by local artisans Cubert L Smith Retrospective. Media Gathering, works of 10 local artists. Annual Black History & Youth Art Month Exhibits
Publications: Boarman Newsletter, quarterly; annual brochure; show invitations, 7 per year

Activities: Classes for adults & children; artist-in-residence; lect open to public, 4 vis lectr per year; competitions with awards; scholarships & fels offered; book traveling exhibitions 1 per year; sales shop sells books, prints, original art & handcrafts

MORGANTOWN

WEST VIRGINIA UNIVERSITY
L Evansdale Library, PO Box 6105, 26506-6105. Tel 304-293-5039; FAX 304-293-7330; Elec Mail kkey@wvnet.edu. *Head Librn* Jo Ann Calzonetti; *Art Reference Librn* Kathleen Key
Library Holdings: Vols 260,000; Per subs 2250
Special Subjects: Art Education, Art History, Landscape Architecture
M Laura & Paul Mesaros Galleries, Creative Arts Ctr, PO Box 6111, 26506-6111. Tel 304-293-2140, Ext 138; FAX 304-293-5731; Elec Mail kolson@wvu.edu. *Cur* Kristina Olson
Open Mon - Sat Noon - 9:30 PM, cl Sun & university holidays. No admis fee. Estab 1867
Collections: Costumes; music; paintings; theatre
Activities: Lect; gallery talks; tours; concerts; drama; competitions; temporary traveling exhibitions

PARKERSBURG

A PARKERSBURG ART CENTER, 220 Eighth Street, PO Box 131, 26101. Tel 304-485-3859; *Dir & Exhib Coordr* Pat Lawrence; *Cur Educ* Wendy Ross
Open Tues - Fri 10 AM - 4 PM, Sat & Sun 1 - 4 PM. No admis fee. Estab 1938 for the operation & maintenance of an art center & mus facility for the appreciation & enjoyment of art, both visual & decorative, as well as art history, crafts & other related educational or cultural activities. Main gallery 43 x 27 ft & upper gallery 38 x 27 ft, completely carpeted, airconditioned & climate controlled. Average Annual Attendance: 25,000. Mem: 500; dues corporate or patron $250, sustaining $100, individual $20; annual meeting in June
Income: $160,000 (financed by endowment, mem & state appropriation)
Collections: Advice of Dreams (oil by Beveridge Moore); Amish: African Artifacts; Patrick Henry Land Grant Document; The Hinge (watercolor by Rudolph Ohrning); Parmenides (sculpture by Beverly Pepper)
Exhibitions: West Virginia Watercolor Society; David Hostetler; Artists & Models-Portraits from the Hirschorn; Architecture-Wright, Sullivan, Fuller; Symbols of Faith/Islamic Prayer Rugs; American Impressionism
Publications: Calendar of events, bimonthly; annual report; exhibition catalogs
Activities: Classes for adults & children; docent training; workshops; outreach program, Arts-in-the-parks; lect open to public. 8 vis lectr per year; concerts; gallery talks; tours; competition with awards; book traveling exhibitions; originate traveling exhibitions
L Art Center, 220 Eighth St, 26101. Tel 304-485-3859; *Exec Dir* Pat Lawrence; *Educ Coordr* Wendy Ross
Open Tues - Fri 10 AM - 4 PM, Sat - Sun 1 - 4 PM, cl Mon. Estab 1938, main gallery 2000 sq ft, upper gallery 1400 sq ft. Open to the pub. Average Annual Attendance: 20,000. Mem: 400; dues $30; annual meeting in June
Income: Financed by grants, mem, united arts fund drive, fund-raising
Library Holdings: Vols 500; Per subs 3; AV — Slides, v-tapes; Other — Clipping files, exhibition catalogs, reproductions
Special Subjects: Art Education, Art History, Crafts, Decorative Arts, Drawings, Graphic Arts, Interior Design, Landscape Architecture, Marine Painting, Mixed Media, Painting - American, Photography, Pottery, Prints, Stained Glass
Collections: Collection of Amish items: Buggy, Clothes, Quilts, Photo Essay
Activities: Outreach: Art in the parks, Video Library; 5 vis lectr per year; American Realistim: A Nation Competition (painting; cash/purchase); lend to qualified museums; lending collection contains books, prints, natural artifacts, original art, original prints & phonorecords

ROMNEY

L HAMPSHIRE COUNTY PUBLIC LIBRARY, 153 W Main St, 26575. Tel 304-822-3185; *Librn* Brenda Riffle; *Children's Prog Specialist* Kathy Puhalla
Open Mon - Sat 10 AM - 5 PM. No admis fee. Estab 1942. 7 Display cases changed every month. Average Annual Attendance: 30,000. Mem: 8469
Income: $57,000
Purchases: $8000
Library Holdings: Vols 30,000; Per subs 96; Micro — Reels; AV — Cassettes, fs, motion pictures, rec, v-tapes; Other — Clipping files, exhibition catalogs, framed reproductions, memorabilia, original art works, pamphlets, photographs, prints
Exhibitions: Children's art; private collections of rocks, antiques, displays of items of other countries; various local artists collection; weaving
Activities: Lect open to public; concerts; tours; competitions with awards; individual paintings lent

WHEELING

OGLEBAY INSTITUTE
A Stifel Fine Arts Center, 1330 National Rd, 26003. Tel 304-242-7700; Estab 1930 to present art exhibitions & to provide the opportunity for long-life learning in the fine arts fields. Three galleries located in the Stifel Mansion occupy the center of the facility on both floors
Exhibitions: A Celebration of Mt de Chantal: Tradition with a Vision
Publications: Exhibition catalogues, 7 per year
Activities: Classes for adults & children; docent training; lect open to public; concerts
M Mansion Museum, Oglebay Park, 26003. Tel 304-242-7272; FAX 304-242-4203; *Exec Dir* Dr Frederick A Lambert; *Dir* John A Artzberger; *Cur Colls & Educ* Holly McCluskey
Open Mon - Sat 9:30 AM - 5 PM, Sun & holidays 1 - 5 PM. Admis $3.50, 55 & over $3, students $2.50, children under 12 free with paying adults. Estab &

incorporated 1930 to promote educational, cultural & recreational activities in Wheeling Tri-State area. Building & ground are the property of the city; an exhibition wing adjoins the main house; annual Christmas decorations. Average Annual Attendance: 83,394. Mem: 1430; dues $15 & up

Collections: †Early 19th century china; †early glass made in Wheeling & the Midwest; period rooms; †pewter

Exhibitions: Current exhibits of art & other allied subjects change periodically; decorative arts

Activities: Antique show & sales; antique classes; gallery talks; self-guided & prearranged group tours

L **Library,** Oglebay Park, 26003. Tel 304-242-7272; FAX 304-242-4203; *Dir* John A Artzberger

Open by appointment only. Founded 1934. Highly specialized on the early history of the area

Library Holdings: Vols 800; Documents bound 100, Maps, VF 4; Micro — Prints 20; AV — Slides

Special Subjects: Decorative Arts, Historical Material

Collections: Brown Collection of Wheeling History, photographs; Wheeling City Directories; Wheeling & Belmont Bridge Company Papers

WISCONSIN

APPLETON

M **LAWRENCE UNIVERSITY,** Wriston Art Center Galleries, PO Box 599, 54912. Tel 414-832-6621; FAX 414-832-7362; Elec Mail nadine.wasserman@lawrence.edu. *Cur* Nadine Wasserman; *Gallery & Coll Asst* Pamela O'Donnell

Open Tues - Fri 10 AM - 4 PM, Sat Noon - 4 PM, cl Sun & Mon. Estab 1950 for teaching & community exhibitions. Wriston Art Center opened Spring 1989. Three exhibitions galleries for changing exhibits of contemporary & historical shows

Collections: Ottilia Buerger Collection of Ancient Coins; Pohl Collection-German Expressionism; American regionalist art; graphics; Japanese prints & drawings

Activities: Lect open to public, 3-6 vis lectr per year; individual paintings & original works of art lent for exhibitions in other museums

BELOIT

M **BELOIT COLLEGE,** Wright Museum of Art, 700 College St, 53511. Tel 608-363-2677; FAX 608-363-2718; *Dir* Henry Moy; *Registrar* Tom Skwerski

Open Mon - Fri 9 AM - 5 PM, Sat & Sun 11 AM - 4 PM. No admis fee. Estab 1893; Wright Art Hall built 1930 to house the collection for the enrichment of the college & community through exhibition of permanent collection & traveling & temporary art exhibitions of cultural & aesthetic value. A Georgian building architecturally styled after the Fogg Mus in Cambridge, Massachusetts. Three galleries on main floor, on a large center court; Art Department shares other floors in which two student galleries are included. Average Annual Attendance: 20,000

Purchases: 17th - 20th century graphics; Asian decorative arts

Collections: European & American (paintings, sculpture & decorative arts); Fisher Memorial Collection of Greek Casts; graphics, emphasis on German Expressionist & contemporary works; Gurley Collection of Korean Pottery, Japanese Sword Guards, Chinese Snuff Bottles & Jades; Morse Collection of Paintings & Other Art Objects; Neese Fund Collection of Contemporary Art; Oriental; Pitkin Collection of Oriental Art; Prints by Durer, Rembrandt, Whistler & others; sculpture of various periods; 19th century photographs

Publications: Exhibition catalogs

Activities: Classes; supportive programs; docent training; lect open to public; gallery talks; tours; traveling exhibitions organized & circulated

A **Friends of the Beloit College Museums,** 700 College St, 53511. Tel 608-363-2677; FAX 804-363-2718;

Estab 1972, to support the Beloit College Museums. Mem: 200; dues $10; annual meetings in Sept

Publications: Friends of the Beloit College Museums newsletter, quarterly

Activities: Lect open to public, 10 vis lectr per year

CEDARBURG

A **WISCONSIN FINE ARTS ASSOCIATION, INC,** Ozaukee Art Center, W62 N718 Riveredge Dr, 53012. Tel 414-377-8230; *Pres* Lon Horton

Open Tues - Sun 1 - 4 PM. No admis fee. Estab 1971. Historical landmark with cathedral ceiling. Average Annual Attendance: 10,000. Mem: 600; dues business patron $500, patron $200, sustaining $100, associate sustaining $50, family $30, individual $22, student $10; annual meeting in Oct

Collections: Paintings, sculpture, prints, ceramics

Exhibitions: Ozaukee County Show; Harvest Festival of Arts

Publications: Monthly newsletter

Activities: Classes for adults and children; docent training; lectures open to public, 2 vis lectr per year; concerts; gallery talks; tours; competitions with awards; arts festivals

EAU CLAIRE

M **UNIVERSITY OF WISCONSIN-EAU CLAIRE,** Foster Gallery, Fine Arts Ctr, 54702-5008. Tel 715-836-2328; FAX 715-836-4882; *Dir* Thomas Wagener

Open Mon - Fri 10 AM - 4:30 PM, Sat & Sun 1 - 4:30 PM. No admis fee. Estab 1970 to show finest contemporary art in all media. State University Gallery in Fine Arts Center. Average Annual Attendance: 23,000

Income: Funded by state appropriation

Purchases: Tim High: Rebel Earth/Ramath Ieh; Bill Pearson: Trout Quarte

Collections: Eau Claire Permanent Art Collection; †20th Century Artists

Exhibitions: American Indian Arts Festival; Annual Juried Student Art Show; Mental/Visual/Manual; Metalia; Midwest Photography Inntational; Outsider Art

Activities: Lect open to public, 10-12 vis lectr per year; competition with awards; book traveling exhibitions 3-4 per year

GREEN BAY

M **NEVILLE PUBLIC MUSEUM,** 210 Museum Pl, 54303. Tel 414-448-4460; FAX 414-448-4458; *Dir* Ann L Koski

Open Tues, Thurs & Sat 9 AM - 4 PM, Wed 9 AM - 9 PM, Sun Noon - 4 PM. No admis fee, donations accepted. Estab 1915 as Green Bay Pub Mus; names changed 1926, estab to interpret the collections & educate through exhibits, educational programming, research & publications. 3 art galleries presently in use, largest 3000 sq ft. Maintains reference library. Average Annual Attendance: 75,000. Mem: 1000; dues $25; annual meeting in May

Income: Financed by county appropriation & private donations

Collections: David Belasco Collection of Victoriana, antique furniture, †china, †glass, costumes & †accessories; †contemporary & historical paintings; †drawings; †prints & sculpture

Exhibitions: Juried exhibitions

Publications: Musepaper, 6 times per yr

Activities: Classes for adults & children; docent training; lect open to public, 5 vis lectr per year; concerts; gallery talks; tours; competitions with awards; individual paintings & original objects of art lent to other museums; book traveling exhibitions 1 per year; traveling exhibitions organized and circulated; museum shop sells books, magazines, original art, reproductions, prints, gifts & cards

L **Library,** 210 Museum Pl, 54303. Tel 414-448-4460; FAX 414-448-4458; *Recorder* Louise Pfotenhauer

Open to the public for reference by appt only

Library Holdings: Vols 5000; Per subs 20; Micro — Fiche, reels; AV — A-tapes, Kodachromes, motion pictures, slides, v-tapes; Other — Clipping files, exhibition catalogs, memorabilia, pamphlets, photographs

M **UNIVERSITY OF WISCONSIN, GREEN BAY,** Lawton & Weidner, 2420 Nicolet Dr, 54311. Tel 414-465-2916; FAX 414-465-2890; *Dir* Tomas Gallaty

Open Tues - Sun Noon - 4 PM, cl Mon. No admis fee. Estab 1974 to show changing exhibitions of contemporary & 20th century art & recent ethnic art. Gallery is 2000 sq ft. Average Annual Attendance: 5000

Income: $5000

Collections: Contemporary ethnic art

Publications: Exhibition catalogs

Activities: Lect open to public, 2-3 vis lectr per year; competitions; book traveling exhibitions; originates traveling exhibitions

GREENBUSH

M **WADE HOUSE & WESLEY W JUNG CARRIAGE MUSEUM,** Historic House & Carriage Museum, W 7747 Plank Rd, PO Box 34, 53026. Tel 414-526-3271; FAX 414-526-3626; *Dir* Jeffrey Schultz; *Cur Interpretation* Sally Wood; *Cur Coll* Gina Sacchetti

Open May 1 - Oct 31 9 AM - 5 PM. Admis adult $5, sr citizen $4.50, child $2. Estab 1953 to educate public concerning 1850s Wisconsin Yankee town life. Average Annual Attendance: 25,000-30,000

Income: $125,000 (financed by state appropriation, admis fees)

Collections: Wisconsin made Carriages; 1850-1870 Household Furnishings

Exhibitions: 1850s Historic House Tour

Activities: Classes for adults & children; docent training; lect open to public, 5-8 vis lectr per year; tours; museum shop sells books, reproductions & prints

KENOSHA

M **KENOSHA PUBLIC MUSEUM,** 5608 Tenth Ave, 53140. Tel 414-652-4140; *Dir* Paula Touhey; *Cur Educ* Nancy Mathews; *Cur Exhib & Coll* Daniel Joyce

Open Mon - Fri 9 AM - 5 PM, Nov - Apr Sat 9 AM - Noon, Sun 1 - 4 PM, May Oct Sat 9 AM - 4 PM. No admis fee. Estab 1935 to promote interest in general natural history & regional art. The gallery has 8000 sq ft of permanent exhibition space & 1000 sq ft for temporary exhibits. Average Annual Attendance: 50,000. Mem: 1500; dues $10; annual meeting in April

Income: $300,000 (financed by city appropriation)

Purchases: $2200

Collections: †African Art; †Historic Wisconsin Pottery; Ivory Carvings; Oriental Art; Regional Artists; Regional Natural History individual paintings lent on yearly basis to municipal & county offices to be displayed in public areas; lending collections contains cassettes, color reproductions, filmstrips, framed reproductions, motion pictures, nature artifacts & slides

Exhibitions: (1997) Impressions of Wildlife Scott Schiller; Kenosha Art Association Show Wooly Mammoth found in Kenosha County

Publications: Newsletter, bi-monthly; Wisconsin Folk Pottery Book

Activities: Classes for adults & children; dramatic programs; docent training; lect open to public, 12 vis lectr per year; gallery talks; tours; competitions; individual paintings lent on yearly basis to municipal & county offices to be displayed in public areas; lending collection contains cassettes, color reproductions, filmstrips, 30 framed reproductions, 280 motion pictures, nature artifacts & slides; museum shop sells crafts, ethnic jewelry, earrings, Oriental boxes & toys

KOHLER

C KOHLER CO, Art Collection, 444 Highland Dr, 53044. Tel 414-457-4441; FAX 414-459-1656;
Estab 1973. Items from collection displayed in Kohler Co general office, Kohler Design Center & Village of Kohler
Income: Financed by Kohler Co
Collections: Original ceramic art pieces created in Kohler Co facilities by resident artists in the Art Industry Program

LAC DU FLAMBEAU

A DILLMAN'S BAY PROPERTIES, Dillman's Creative Arts Foundation, 3305 Sand Lake Lodge Lane, Box 98, 54538. Tel 715-588-3143; FAX 715-588-3110; *Pres* Dennis Robertson; *VPres* Sue Robertson
Open 24 hrs. No admis fee. Estab 1987 to offer educational experience. Display on Dillman Lodge walls, hallway, studios & rack in gift shop. Average Annual Attendance: 3000
Publications: Annual brochure & video
Activities: Classes for adults & children; lect open to public, 100 vis lectr per year; scholarships & fels offered; exten dept serves Bermuda, Tahiti & Carribean; lending collection contains books; book traveling exhibitions 12-15 per year; originate traveling exhibitions 12-15 per year; sales shop sells books, original art & prints
L Tom Lynch Resource Center, 3305 Sand Lake Lodge Lane, Box 98, 54538. Tel 715-588-3143; FAX 715-588-3110; *Pres* Dennis Robertson
Library Holdings: Vols 500; AV — A-tapes 20, v-tapes 20; Other — Exhibition catalogs, framed reproductions 20, original art works 100, prints 4000, reproductions 100

M LAC DU FLAMBEAU BAND OF LAKE SUPERIOR CHIPPEWA INDIANS, George W Brown Jr Ojibwe Museum & Cultural Center, 603 Peace Pipe, PO Box 804, 54538. Tel 715-588-3333; *Acting Dir* Gregg Guthrie; *Archivist & Cur* Marcus Guthrie
Open May - Oct Mon - Sat 10 AM - 4 PM & Nov - Apr Mon - Fri 10 AM - 2 PM. Admis $2. Estab 1988 to collect, preserve & exhibit the cultural history of the Lac du Flambeau Ojibwe. Main floor: Four seasons exhibit featuring the economic cycle of the traditional ways of the Ojibwe Indian people plus numerous objects of the Ojibwe. Average Annual Attendance: 6500
Income: $100,000 (financed by Tribal appropriation)
Purchases: Various historical, cultural objects, photos & documents
Collections: Manuscripts, documents & photography of the Lac du Flambeau Band of the Lake Superior Ojibwes; Objects of the cultural history of The Lake Superior Ojibwes
Exhibitions: Various exhibits of the cultural ways of the Lac du Flambeau Ojibwes
Activities: Classes for adults; lect open to public, 6 vis lectr per year; individual paintings lent; gift shop sells books, art & craft objects

LA CROSSE

M VITERBO COLLEGE ART GALLERY, 815 S Ninth St, 54601. Tel 608-796-3675, 796-3000 (Main), 796-3754; FAX 608-796-3736; *Dir* Tim Crane
Open Mon - Fri 10 AM - 5 PM. Estab 1964 to exhibit arts & crafts which will be a valuable supplement to courses offered. Gallery is located in the center of the Art Department; 100 running feet; soft walls; good light
Income: Financed by school appropriation
Collections: Mrs Lynn Anna Louise Miller, Collection of the contemporary United State primitive; Peter Whitebird Collection of WPA project paintings
Activities: Classes for adults; dramatic programs; lect open to public; gallery talks

MADISON

M EDGEWOOD COLLEGE, DeRicci Gallery, 855 Woodrow, 53711. Tel 608-257-4861; FAX 608-257-1455; *Pres* Dr James Ebben; *Art Dept Chmn* David Smith
Open Mon - Fri 9 AM - 5 PM. Estab 1965 to serve local artists & provide educational opportunity for students. Large room; carpeted walls. Average Annual Attendance: 5000
Collections: Edgewood College Collection
Exhibitions: Old Bergen Art Guild; Local Artists

M MADISON ART CENTER, 211 State St, 53703. Tel 608-257-0158; FAX 608-257-5722; *Elec Mail* mac@itis.com. *Dir* Stephen Fleischman; *Registrar* Marilyn Sohi; *Bus Mgr* Michael Paggie; *Dir Develop & Community Relations* Kathy Paul; *Membership & Program Liaison* Barbara Banks; *Technical Servs Supvr* Mark Verstegen; *Cur Exhib* Toby Kamps; *Gallery Shop Mgr* Leslie Genszler; *Cur Educ & Public Programming* Sheri Castelnuovo; *Publicist* David Lantz; *Gallery Operations Mgr* Jim Kramer
Open Tues - Thurs 11 AM - 5 PM, Fri 11 AM - 9 PM, Sat 10 AM - 9 PM, Sun 1 - 5 PM. No admis fee, donations accepted. Estab 1969 to promote the visual arts. Galleries on 3 levels in civic center complex. Average Annual Attendance: 98,500. Mem: 1800; dues $25 & up; annual meeting in May
Income: $1,062,000 (financed by mem, grants, gifts & earned revenue)
Purchases: $15,000
Collections: Emphasis on contemporary Americans; large print & drawing collection (Japanese, European, Mexican & American); paintings; sculpture
Exhibitions: Louisa Chase; Julia Fish; Martin Kersels; David Nash; Claes Oldenburg; Printed Stuff; Ursula von Rydingsvard; Wisconsin Triennial
Publications: Catalogs; posters & announcements usually accompany each exhibition
Activities: Docent training; lect open to public, 10 vis lectr per year; tours; competitions; films; originate traveling exhibitions; sales shop sells books, magazines, original art, reproductions & prints

M STATE HISTORICAL SOCIETY OF WISCONSIN, State Historical Museum, 30 N Carroll St, 53703-2707. Tel 608-264-6555; FAX 608-262-5554; *Dir* George Vogt; *Assoc Dir* Robert Thomasgard; *Museum Adminr* William Crowley; *Chief Cur* Paul Bourcier; *Cur Art Coll* Douglas Kendall; *Cur Visual Materials* Nicolette Bromberg; *Cur Antropology* David Wooley; *Cur Costumes & Textiles* Leslie Bellais
Open Tues - Sat 10 AM - 5 PM, Sun Noon - 5 PM, cl Mon. No admis fee. Estab 1846, mus added 1854; organized to promote a wider appreciation of the American heritage, with particular emphasis on the collection, advancement & dissemination of knowledge of the history of Wisconsin & of the Middle West. Average Annual Attendance: 100,000. Mem: 6000; dues $22.50 & up
Income: Financed by state appropriation, earnings, gifts & federal grants
Collections: American Historical & ethnographic material; iconographic collection; ceramics, coins, costumes, dolls, furniture, paintings, prints, photographs, & slides
Exhibitions: Frequent special exhibitions; four annual gallery changes
Publications: Wisconsin Magazine of History, quarterly
Activities: Docent training; lect open to public; individual paintings & original objects of art lent to other museums & individuals for educational purposes; book traveling exhibitions; sales shop sells books, magazines, reproductions, slides & post cards
L Archives, 816 State St, 53706-1488. Tel 608-264-6460; FAX 608-264-6486; Internet Home Page Address www.wisc.edu/shs-archives/arche.heml. *Archivist* Peter Gottlieb
Open Mon - Fri 8 AM - 5 PM, Sat 9 AM - 4 PM
Library Holdings: Original documents; Maps; AV — Motion pictures; Other — Photographs, prints

M STEEP & BREW GALLERY, 544 State St, 53703. Tel 608-256-2902; *Dir* Mark Duerr
Open Mon - Thurs 8 AM - 10 PM, Fri & Sat 9 AM - 11 PM, Sun 11 AM - 8 PM. Estab 1985 as a gallery showing emerging & experimental local artists. Store front street level gallery with 1700 sq ft of space
Income: $4000 (financed by exhibition fees & commission on sales)
Purchases: Ray Esparsen, Theron Caldwell Ris, Randy Arnold
Exhibitions: Ray Esparsen, Theron Caldwell Ris, David Auquirre, Doris Litzer, Terry Gottesfeld, Douglas Isaac Busch, Mark Duerr, Anita Jungi, Dennis Carroll, Woody Holliman
Activities: Concerts; gallery talks

UNIVERSITY OF WISCONSIN-MADISON

M Wisconsin Union Galleries, 800 Langdon St, 53706. Tel 608-262-5969; FAX 608-262-8862; *Dir* Ted Crabb; *Art Coordr* Margaret Tennessen
Open 10 AM - 8 PM. No admis fee. Estab 1907 to provide a cultural program for the members of the university community. Owns two fireproof buildings with three separate galleries 1700 sq ft: Memorial Union, 800 Langdon; Union South, 227 N Randal Ave. Average Annual Attendance: 125,000. Mem: 50,000 faculty, alumni & townspeople, plus 45,000 students; dues $45; annual meeting in Nov
Purchases: $1500
Collections: Oil & watercolor paintings, photographs, prints & sculptures, mostly by Wisconsin artists
Publications: A Reflection of Time: The WI Union Art Collection
Activities: Informal classes in arts & crafts; dramatic programs; docent training; lect open to public, 5 vis lectr per year; films; gallery talks; competitions with prizes; book traveling exhibitions 4 per year
M Elvehjem Museum of Art, 800 University Ave, 53706. Tel 608-263-2246; FAX 608-263-8188; *Dir* Russell Panczenko; *Assoc Dir* Corinne Magnoni; *Ed* Patricia Powell; *Registrar* Lucille Stiger; *Cur Educ* Anne Lambert
Open Mon - Sun 9 AM - 5 PM, cl holidays. No admis fee. Estab 1962, building opened 1970 to display, preserve & build a general art collection of high quality for the study & enjoyment of students, community & state. Three levels, 12 galleries covering 25,000 sq ft of exhibition space. Average Annual Attendance: 100,000. Mem: 1800; dues $20-$1000
Income: Financed by endowment, mem, state appropriation & private sources
Purchases: Vary according to income
Collections: Ancient Egyptian & Greek pottery, sculpture, glass and coins; Joseph E Davies Collection of Russian Icons, Russian & Soviet Paintings; Vernon Hall Collection of European Medals; Indian sculpture; Medieval painting & sculpture; Renaissance painting & sculpture; Edward Burr Van Vleck Collection of Japanese Prints; Ernest C & Jane Werner Watson Collection of Indian Miniatures; 16th - 20th century prints - †general collection; 17th - 20th century European painting, sculpture, furniture & decorative arts; 18th, 19th & 20th century American painting, sculpture & furniture
Exhibitions: Six to eight temporary exhibitions per year in all media from varied periods of art history; UW-Madison Dept Art Exhibition; James Rosenquist: Time Dust, Complete Graphics: 1962-1992; Ansel Adams to Andy Warhol: Portraits & Self Portraits
Publications: Annual bulletin; calendar, bimonthly; special exhibition catalogs
Activities: Docent training; lect open to public; concerts; gallery talks; tours; individual paintings & original objects of art lent to other museums; book traveling exhibitions 2-4 per year; originate traveling exhibitions; sales shop sells books, magazines & reproductions
L Kohler Art Library, 800 University Ave, 53706. Tel 608-263-2256, 263-2258; Elec Mail bunce@macc.wisc.edu. *Dir* William Bunce; *Pub Serv* Beth Abrahams
Open Mon - Thurs 8 AM - 9:45 PM, Fri 8 AM - 4:45 PM, Sat & Sun 1 - 4:45 PM. Estab 1970 to support the teaching & research needs of the Art & Art History Departments & the Elvehjem Mus of Art. For lending. Circ 34,000. Average Annual Attendance: 73,000
Income: Financed by state appropriation & private funding
Library Holdings: Vols 130,000; Per subs 300; Micro — Fiche 21,000, reels 400; AV — Cassettes 50, v-tapes; Other — Clipping files, exhibition catalogs
Activities: Tours

MANITOWOC

M RAHR-WEST ART MUSEUM, Park St at N Eighth, 54220. Tel 414-683-4501; FAX 414-683-5047; *Dir* Richard Quick; *Asst Dir* Daniel Juchniewich
Open Mon, Tues, Thurs & Fri 10 AM - 4 PM, Wed 10 AM - 8 PM, Sat & Sun 11 AM - 4 PM, cl holidays. No admis fee. Estab 1950 as an art center to serve the city of Manitowoc. Transitional gallery in new wing built 1975; period rooms in Victorian Rahr Mansion built c 1981; a Registered Historic home; American art wing built in 1986. Ruth West Gallery 48' x 63'; Corridor Gallery, for changing exhibits; Permanent Collections Gallery. Average Annual Attendance: 26,000. Mem: 500; dues $15-$100
Income: $250,000 (financed by mem & city appropriation)
Collections: 19th & 20th Century American Paintings & Prints; Schwartz Collection of Chinese Ivories; contemporary art glass; porcelain; works by Francis, Johns Lichtenstein & O'Keeffe
Exhibitions: Monthly changing exhibitions
Activities: Lect open to public, 10 vis lectr per year; concerts; gallery talks; tours; scholarships offered; book traveling exhibitions 10 per year; museum shop sells reproductions
L Library, 610 N Eighth St, 54220. Tel 414-683-4501; FAX 414-683-5047; *Dir* Richard Quick; *Asst Dir* Dan Juchniewich
Open to the public for reference only
Library Holdings: Vols 1500; AV — Fs; Other — Exhibition catalogs
Special Subjects: Art reference

MARSHFIELD

M NEW VISIONS GALLERY, INC, 1000 N Oak, Marshfield Clinic, 54449. Tel 715-387-5562; *Dir* Ann Walsbrot
Open Mon - Fri 9 AM - 5:30 PM, Sat 10 AM - 4 PM. No admis fee. Estab 1975 for the education, awareness & appreciation of visual arts. 1500 sq ft exhibition space, track lighting, moveable display panels, sculpture stands. Average Annual Attendance: 75,000. Mem: 300; dues $10-over $1000
Income: $90,000 (financed by mem, earned income, fundraising & gifts)
Collections: Australian Aboriginal Art Collection; Haitian Painting Collection; West African Art Collection; original prints
Exhibitions: (1997) Emerging Talents; New Visions' Culture & Agriculture; Annual Marshfield Art Fair; Art Nouveau; Traces; Ecoterns; Multiple Impressions. (1998) Eastern Exposure
Publications: Brochures, every 6 wks; catalogs
Activities: Classes for adults & children; docent training; lect open to public, 2-5 vis lectr per year; gallery talks; tours; competitions with awards; lending collection contains books; book traveling exhibitions 1-3 annually; originate traveling exhibitions; museum shop sells gifts producted by artists or craft studios, jewelry, pottery & cards

MENOMONIE

M UNIVERSITY OF WISCONSIN-STOUT, J Furlong Gallery, 54751. Tel 715-232-2261; Elec Mail in%bloedorng@uwstout.edu. *Cur* Gene Bloedhorn
Open Mon - Fri 10 AM - 4 PM, Tues 6 - 9 PM, Sat Noon - 3PM. No admis fee. Estab 1966 to serve university & local community with exhibits of art. A single room gallery; track lighting. Average Annual Attendance: 1500
Income: Financed by state appropriation
Collections: African Art; paintings including works by Warrington Colescott, Roy Deforest, Walter Quirt, George Rouault & Raphael Soyer; drawings; prints; sculpture
Exhibitions: Changing exhibits
Activities: Classes for children; gallery talks; individual paintings & original objects of art lent to faculty, staff & campus offices

MEQUON

M CONCORDIA UNIVERSITY WISCONSIN, Fine Art Gallery, 12800 N Lake Shore Dr, 53092. Tel 414-243-5700; FAX 414-243-4351; *Academic Dean* Dr David Eggebrecht; *Gallery Dir* Prof Gaylund Stone
Open Sun Tues, Wed, Thurs 1 - 4 PM, Tues 7 - 9 PM. No admis fee. Estab 1972 to exhibit work of area & national artists as an educational arm of the college. Average Annual Attendance: 1000
Income: Financed through college budget
Collections: Russian bronzes & paintings; graphics include Roualt, Altman & local artists; John Wiley Collection; American landscape; religious art

MILWAUKEE

M CHARLES ALLIS ART MUSEUM, 1801 N Prospect Ave (Mailing add: 1630 E Royall Pl, 53202). Tel 414-278-8295; *Acting Admin Dir* Susan Modder
Open Wed - Sun 1 - 5 PM, Wed evenings 7 - 9 PM. Estab 1947 as a house-mus with 850 art objects from around the world & spanning 2500 years, collected by Charles Allis, first president of the Allis-Chalmers Company & bequeathed to the people of Milwaukee. The mus is part of the Milwaukee County War Memorial Complex. Average Annual Attendance: 40,000. Mem: 700; dues $5 - $100; annual meetings in Oct
Income: $170,000 (financed by endowment & Milwaukee County appropriation)
Collections: Chinese, Japanese & Persian ceramics; Greek & Roman antiques; 19th century French & American paintings; Renaissance bronzes
Publications: Exhibition catalogs
Activities: Docent training; lect open to public, vis lectr; concerts; gallery talks; tours; film series

M ALVERNO COLLEGE GALLERY, 3401 S 39th St, PO Box 343922, 53234-3922. Tel 414-382-6000; FAX 414-382-6004; *Fine Arts Mgr* Cate Deicher
Open Mon - Fri 11 AM - 3 PM, Sun 1 - 3 PM, by appointment. No admis fee. Estab 1954 for the aesthetic enrichment of community & the aesthetic educ of students
Income: $2000
Exhibitions: First Photos Collection; Senior Show; Juried Student Exhibition; Form Figure & Function-Jeffrey Naska
Activities: Docent training; lect open to public, 4 vis lectr per year; concerts; gallery talks; tours; competitions with awards; book traveling exhibitions 1-2 per year

AMERICAN SOCIETY FOR AESTHETICS
For further information, see National and Regional Organizations

L ASCENSION LUTHERAN CHURCH LIBRARY, 1236 S Layton Blvd, 53215. Tel 414-645-2933; *Librn* Lorraine Pike
Open Sun 8:30 - 11 AM & upon request. Estab 1954
Income: Financed by church budget, donations & bequests
Library Holdings: Vols 13,000; Per subs 30; AV — A-tapes, cassettes, fs, v-tapes 40; Other — Framed reproductions
Special Subjects: Crafts, Decorative Arts, Embroidery, Religious Art, Renaissance Art
Collections: Classic Art, framed pictures, organ music

C BANC ONE WISCONSIN CORP, * 111 E Wisconsin Ave, 53202. Tel 414-765-3000; FAX 414-765-0553; *In Charge Art Coll* Cathy Voss; *Gallery Coordr* Kelly Skinezelewski
Estab to encourage Wisconsin art & artists; to enhance the environment of marine personnel. Collection displayed in offices, conference rooms & corridors of headquarters of bank holding company
Collections: Acrylics, batik, bronze sculpture, lithographs, oils, wall sculpture, watercolors by Wisconsin artists
Activities: Invitational competitions in 1965, Wisconsin Renaissance in 1976; cash & purchase awards sponsored for college university & community art exchange; individual objects of art lent

M CARDINAL STRITCH COLLEGE, Layton Honor Gallery, 6801 N Yates Rd, 53217. Tel 414-352-5400; FAX 414-351-7516; *Dir* Barbara Manger
Open Mon - Fri 10 AM - 4 PM, Sat & Sun 1 - 4 PM. No admis fee. Estab 1947 to encourage creative art in each individual
Income: Financed by endowment, city & state appropriations & tuition
Exhibitions: Acquisitions from distant lands, children's art, professor's works, senior graduating exhibitions, well-known area artists; Clay, an exhibit of ten of Wisconsin's outstanding ceramic artists; Concerning the Narrative, prints, painting & sculpture; Two Views, photography; student exhibit; Global Awareness Exhibit; Ray Gloeckler, Wisconsin woodblock artist; Joanna Poehlmann, book artist; Student Show
Activities: Classes for adults & children; lect open to public, 2-4 vis lectr per year; gallery talks; tours; individual paintings & original objects of art lent to galleries, libraries & educational institutions

M MARQUETTE UNIVERSITY, Haggerty Museum of Art, PO Box 1881, 53201-1881. Tel 414-288-7290; FAX 414-288-5415; *Dir* Curtis L Carter; *Registrar* Allison Smith; *Cur Educ Public Prog* Beth McGaffey; *Admin Asst* Shelly Goldsmith; *Communications Asst* Michelle Muhoney; *Asst Dir Adminstration & Cur* James Scarborough; *Preparator Asst* Jason Rohlf; *Curatorial Asst* Paula Schulze
Open Mon - Wed & Fri 10 AM - 4:30 Pm, Thurs 10 AM - 8 PM, Sat 10 AM - 4:30 PM, Sun Noon - 5 PM. No admis fee. Serves educational & aesthetic purposes in the university community & the region. Presents the balance of art including Old Master to contemporary art in all media from the past to present. Modern building with security & climate control. Average Annual Attendance: 40,000. Mem: 500
Income: Financed through private contributions & the university
Collections: †Old Master, †Modern, †Contemporary paintings; †prints, photography; decorative arts; tribal arts
Exhibitions: British Artists from 16th-20th Century; Sarah Buckrodt (large scale seashores); Robert Dunn: Dance Findings (video dance); Rudolf Koppitz 1884-1936; Matter-Surrealist Art 1940-1990; O'Neal Collection (drawings); Gary Schneider (photographs)
Publications: Exhibit catalogs
Activities: Docent training; lect open to public, 6-10 vis lectr per year; concerts; gallery talks; tours; awards; individual paintings & original objects of art lent to museums; originate traveling exhibitions; museum shop sells books, reproductions & prints

M MILWAUKEE ART MUSEUM, 750 N Lincoln Memorial Dr, 53202. Tel 414-224-3200; FAX 414-271-7588; *Pres Bd Trustees* Allen L Samson; *Dir* Russell Bowman; *Admin Dir* Christopher Goldsmith; *Dir Educ* Barbara Brown-Lee; *Dir Marketing* Fran Serlin-Cobb; *Registrar* Leigh Albritton; *Dir Communications* Polly Scott
Open Tues, Wed, Fri & Sat 10 AM - 5 PM, Thurs Noon - 9 PM, Sun Noon - 5 PM, cl Mon. Admis adults $4, students, handicapped & senior citizens $2.50, children under 12 with adult free. Estab 1888 to create an environment for the arts that will serve the people of the greater Milwaukee community. Large flexible galleries, including a sculpture court & outdoor display areas. Fine arts & decorative arts are mixed to create an overview of a period, especially in the fine American Wings; small galleries provided for specific or unique collections. Average Annual Attendance: 150,000. Mem: 11,000; dues $45, senior citizens & students $25; annual meeting in May
Income: Financed by endowment, mem, county & state appropriations & fund drive
Collections: 19th & 20th Century American & European Art, including the Bradley & Layton Collections: The American Ash Can School & German Expressionism are emphasized; All media from Ancient Egypt to Modern America; The Flagg Collection of Haitian Art; a study collection of Midwest Architecture—The Prairie Archives; The von Schleinitz Collection of 19th Century German Painting, Mettlach Steins, & Meissen Porcelain
Exhibitions: 100 Years of Wisconsin Art; Second Benefit Art Auction Exhibition; Early Needlework from Milwaukee Collection; William Wegman;

The Centennial Collection; Jennifer Barlett: Recent Work; Richard Misrach: The American Desert; Focus: American Folk Art from the Permanent Collection; The Velvet Line: Drypoint Prints from Milwaukee Collections; The Detective's Eye: Investigating the Old Masters; Objects of Bright Pride: Northwest Coast Indian Art from The American Museum of Natural History; Currents 14: Ross Bleckner; Joseph Albers Photographs; The Modern Poster: Selections from The Museum of Modern Art; Really Big Prints; Currents 15; Sounding the Depths: 150 Years of American Seascape; Renaissance & Baroque Bronzes; recent acquisitions

Publications: Exhibitions & program brochure, 3 per year; numbers calendar, bi-monthly

Activities: Classes for adults & children; docent training; lect open to public, 4-6 vis lectr per year; concerts; gallery talks; tours; competitions; films; scholastic art program; originate traveling exhibitions; museum shop sells books & magazines

L Library, 750 N Lincoln Memorial Dr, 53202. Tel 414-224-3200; FAX 414-271-7588; Elec Mail schultz@mam.org. *Librn* Rebecca Schultz
Open Tues & Wed 10 AM - 4 PM, Thurs Noon - 4 PM
Library Holdings: Vols 24,000; Per subs 60; Vertical files, 60 drawers
Special Subjects: Afro-American Art, American Indian Art, American Western Art, Architecture, Costume Design & Construction, Decorative Arts, Folk Art, Furniture, Islamic Art, Latin American Art, Oriental Art, Painting - German, Porcelain, Pre-Columbian Art, Southwestern Art, 19th Century German painting
Collections: Prairie Archives material (architecture & decorative arts of the Frank Lloyd Wright period) gift of Jacobson; von Schleinitz bequest of material on Meissen porcelain & 19th Century German painting

L MILWAUKEE INSTITUTE OF ART DESIGN, Library, 273 E Erie St, 53202. Tel 414-276-7889; FAX 414-291-8077; *Dir Library Services* Nancy Lundgren
Open Mon & Thurs 7:45 AM - 9 PM, Fri 7:45 AM - 4 PM, Sun 3 - 7 PM. Estab 1974 as an Art & Design Library for the art school
Income: Financed by institution & private grants
Library Holdings: Vols 18,500; Per subs 72; Postcards 2440; AV — Slides 32,000, v-tapes 45; Other — Clipping files, exhibition catalogs 3000, pamphlets, reproductions
Special Subjects: Advertising Design, Decorative Arts, Graphic Design, Industrial Design, Interior Design, Photography, Fine Art
Collections: Member of Switch Consortium
Publications: MIAD Acquisitions List, quarterly

L MILWAUKEE PUBLIC LIBRARY, Art, Music & Recreation Dept, 814 W Wisconsin Ave, 53233. Tel 414-286-3000; FAX 414-286-2137; *City Librn* Kathleen Huston; *Supvr Central Servs* Venora McKinney; *Coordr Fine Arts* Ruth Ruege
Open Mon - Thurs, 9 AM - 8:30 PM, Fri & Sat 8:30 AM - 5:30 PM. No admis fee. Estab 1897. Circ 125,000
Income: $47,000 (financed by budgeted funds & endowments)
Library Holdings: Vols 2,300,000; Auction catalogs, Compact discs, Original documents, Theatre programs; Micro — Fiche, reels; AV — Cassettes, rec, v-tapes; Other — Clipping files, exhibition catalogs, manuscripts, memorabilia, pamphlets, photographs, prints
Special Subjects: Architecture, Art History, Coins & Medals, Costume Design & Construction, Crafts, Decorative Arts, Landscape Architecture, Photography, City Planning, Folklore, Music, Philately, Recreation
Collections: Record Collection
Exhibitions: Bi-monthly changing exhibits in Wehr-McLenegan Gallery

M MILWAUKEE PUBLIC MUSEUM, 800 W Wells St, 53233. Tel 414-278-2700; FAX 414-278-6100; *Dir* Open; *Deputy Operations Dir* James Krivitz; *Marketing Coordr* Debra Zindler; *Museum Librn* Judy Turner; *Dir Audio-Visual* Sharon Kayne Chaplock
Open Mon Noon - 8 PM, Tues - Sun 9 AM - 5 PM. Admis family $10, adults $4, senior citizens with county ID & children 4-17 $2. Estab 1883 as a natural history mus. Vihlein Hall & Gromme Hall are two rooms used to display traveling, temporary & in-house collections. Average Annual Attendance: 413,000. Mem: 7400
Collections: All major sub-disciplines of anthropology, including botany, geology-paleontology; invertebrate & vertebrate zoology; decorative, fine & folk arts; film, photographs & specimen collection
Activities: Classes for children (school groups only); lect open to public & members; vis lectr annually; sales shop sells pottery, jewelry, stationery, ornaments, models, games, dolls

M MOUNT MARY COLLEGE, Tower Gallery, 2900 Menomonee River Pky, 53222. Tel 414-258-4810; *Chmn* Sr Angelee Fuchs
Open Mon - Fri 8 AM - 4:30 PM, Sat & Sun 1 - 4 PM. No admis fee. Estab 1940 to provide both students & local community with exposure to art experiences & to provide artists, both estab professionals & aspirants with a showplace for their work
Income: Financed by private funds
Collections: Antique furniture, 16th Century & Victorian period; contemporary print collection; watercolors by Wisconsin artists
Exhibitions: Ralph Carvan Oils

UNIVERSITY OF WISCONSIN
M University Art Museum, * 3253 N Downer Ave, PO Box 413, 53201. Tel 414-229-6509; *Dir* Michael Flanagan; *Assoc Cur* Open
Open Tues - Fri 10 AM - 4 PM, Wed 10 AM - 8 PM, Sat & Sun 1 - 4 PM, cl holidays & Sun. No admis fee. Estab 1982 to function as university museum; also oversees operations of art history gallery & fine arts galleries
Income: Financed by state appropriation
Collections: †Large graphic collection, primarily 20th century; †19th & 20th century painting, sculpture, drawings and photography; Oriental art; Ethiopian Art & Artifacts; 18th & 19th Century English Regency Prints; Greek & Russian icons & religious objects; Renaissance through 18th century sculptures, paintings & drawings
Exhibitions: Permanent, temporary & traveling exhibitions. UWM Art Museum Story Tellers - The Expressionist Narrative. Humor & High Adventure:

Caricature, Cartoons & the Comics; Contemporary South African Print Makers
Publications: Catalogs; checklists; handouts
Activities: Classes for children; lect open to public, 4 - 5 vis lectr per year; gallery talks; concerts; tours; inter-museum loans; paintings & original works of art lent; book traveling exhibitions 2 - 3 per year; originate traveling exhibitions 1 - 2 per year

M Union Art Gallery, * 2200 E Kenwood Blvd, 53211. Tel 414-229-6310; *Dir* Patricia Kozik
Open Mon, Tues, Wed 11 AM - 4 PM, Thurs 11 AM - 7 PM, cl Sat & Sun. No admis fee. Estab 1971 to provide space for student art, primarily undergraduate, to be shown in group exhibits established by peer selection and apart from faculty selection. Average Annual Attendance: 13,000
Exhibitions: 4 exhibitions per semester
Activities: Concerts; competitions with awards; sale shop sells original art

A WALKER'S POINT ARTISTS ASSOC, Gallery 218, 218 S Second St, 53204. Tel 414-277-7800; *Pres* Judith Hooks
Open Wed 11 AM - 4 PM, Thurs & Fri 5 - 9 PM, Sat & Sun Noon - 5 PM, appointments welcome. No admis fee. Estab 1991 to provide opportunities for local artists. Warehouse type space, wood floor, white walls, 1500 sq ft plus office, extra exhibit space. Maintains reference library. Average Annual Attendance: 1500. Mem: 45; dues $35; four meetings annually
Income: Financed by mem & sales
Exhibitions: Annual Juried Show; group shows; solo shows; monthly exhibits of contemporary original art by area artists
Publications: WPAA Newsletter
Activities: Lect open to mem, 1 vis lectr per year; competitions with prizes; poetry readings; museum shop sells books, prints & magazines

NEENAH

M BERGSTROM MAHLER MUSEUM, 165 N Park Ave, 54956. Tel 414-751-4658; *Executive Dir* Alex Vance; *Cur* Jan Smith
Open Tues - Fri 10 AM - 4:30 PM, Sat & Sun 1 - 4:30 PM. No admis fee. Estab 1959 to provide cultural & educational benefits to the pub. Average Annual Attendance: 29,000
Income: $200,000 (financed by endowment, state & county appropriations & gifts)
Collections: Over 1900 contemporary & antique paperweights; Victorian Glass Baskets; Mahler Collection of Germanic Glass; paintings; sculpture
Exhibitions: Monthly exhibitions in varied media
Publications: Museum Quarterly; Glass Paperweights of Bergstrom - Mahler Museum Collection Catalogue; Paul J Stankard: Poetry in Glass
Activities: Classes for adults & children; docent training; lect open to public; concerts; gallery talks; tours; individual paintings & original objects of art lent to museums; museum shop sells glass paperweights & glass items, original art

L Library, 165 N Park Ave, 54956. Tel 414-751-4658; *Cur* Jan Smith
Open to the pub for reference only
Library Holdings: Vols 2000; Per subs 10; AV — Slides
Special Subjects: Art History, Glass

NEW GLARUS

M CHALET OF THE GOLDEN FLEECE, 618 Second, 53574. Tel 608-527-2614; *Cur* Phyllis Richert
Open May - Oct 10 AM - 4:30 PM. Admis adults $3, students 6-17 $1. Estab 1955. Authentic Swiss style chalet which was once a private residence; collection from around the world. Average Annual Attendance: 5000
Income: Financed by admis fees & village of New Glarus
Collections: Swiss wood carvings & furniture; antique silver & pewter samplers; prints; exceptional glass & china
Activities: Lect open to public; tours

OSHKOSH

M OSHKOSH PUBLIC MUSEUM, 1331 Algoma Blvd, 54901. Tel 414-424-4731; FAX 414-424-4738; *Pres Board* Elizabeth Wyman; *Dir* Bradley Larson; *Prog Coordr* Paul Poeschl; *Registrar* Joan Lloyd; *Cur* Debra Daubert; *Staff Artist* Don Oberweiser
Open Tues - Sat 9 AM - 5 PM, Sun Noon - 5 PM. No admis fee. Estab 1924 to collect & exhibit historical, Indian & natural history material relating to the area & fine & decorative & folk arts. 1908 converted home with new wing, Steiger Memorial Wing, opened in 1983 for additional exhibition space. Mus housed in city owned mansion near university campus. Average Annual Attendance: 60,000. Mem: 300; dues $10
Income: Financed by city appropriation
Collections: †American Artists: archeology; firearms; †Indian Artifacts; †Local & Wisconsin History; †Natural History; Pressed Glass; period textiles
Exhibitions: Monthly changing exhibits; permanent exhibits; Annual Art Fair
Publications: Introductions to the Art & Artists Exhibited
Activities: Classes for adults & children; offers museology & graduate history internship; lect open to public; competitions with purchase awards; individual paintings & original objects of art lent to museums; book traveling exhibitions 1 per year; originate traveling exhibitions; museum shop sells books & reproductions

L Library, 1331 Algoma Blvd, 54901. Tel 414-424-4732; FAX 414-424-4738; *Archivist* Linda Mittlestadt
Open Tues - Sat 9 AM - 5 PM; Sun 1 - 5 PM. Estab 1923. Research for mus exhibits & general pub. For reference only
Income: Financed by city & county appropriations
Purchases: $2000
Library Holdings: Vols 2500; Per subs 5; Maps; AV — A-tapes, cassettes, fs, Kodachromes, lantern slides, motion pictures, rec, slides, v-tapes; Other — Clipping files, exhibition catalogs, memorabilia, original art works, pamphlets, photographs, prints
Special Subjects: Archaeology, Art Reference, Wisconsin, Upper Midwest
Publications: Exhibition catalogs
Activities: Lect open to public, 2-4 vis lectr per year

A PAINE ART CENTER & ARBORETUM, 1410 Algoma Blvd, 54901. Tel 414-235-6903; FAX 414-235-6303; *Exec Dir* Jill Donabauer; *Bus Mgr* Mohammed Mohabali; *Dir Vol Servs* John Nieman; *Cur Horticulture* Ciel Anderson; *Cur Educ* Julie Toth; *Cur Educ* Jane Nicholson
Open Tues - Fri 11 AM - 4 PM, Sat & Sun 1 - 4 PM, cl national holidays. Admis $3, students free. Estab 1947 as a non-profit corporation to serve the needs of the upper midwest by showing fine & decorative arts & horticulture. Average Annual Attendance: 30,000. Mem: 900; dues contributing $50, general $35, senior citizens $15
Income: Financed by endowment, mem & donations
Collections: American glass; †decorative arts; icons; †19th & 20th century American paintings & sculpture; †19th century English & French paintings; period rooms; oriental rugs; American silver; †arboretum contains displays of native & exotic trees, shrubs & herbacious plants
Exhibitions: Temporary exhibitions drawn from sources, coast to coast
Publications: Exhibition catalogues; bi-monthly newsletter; class schedules
Activities: Classes for adults & children; docent training; lect open to public, 3-6 vis lectr per year; concerts; gallery talks; tours; individual paintings & original objects of art lent to other museums & institutions; traveling exhibitions organized & circulated; sales shop sells books, reproductions & jewelry

L George P Nevitt Library, 1410 Algoma Blvd, 54901. Tel 414-235-6903; *Librn* Corinne H Spoo
Open Mon - Fri 11 AM - 4 PM upon request. Estab primarily for staff use as an art reference but also open to pub by appointment. For reference only. Mem: 542; dues $25; annual meeting in Apr
Library Holdings: Vols 5200; AV — Cassettes, Kodachromes, slides; Other — Clipping files, exhibition catalogs, memorabilia, original art works, pamphlets, photographs
Special Subjects: Architecture, Art History, Asian Art, Ceramics, Decorative Arts, Drawings, Etchings & Engravings, Goldsmithing, History of Art & Archaeology, Interior Design, Oriental Art, Painting - American, Period Rooms, Photography, Sculpture, English Furniture
Exhibitions: American Realism: The Urban Scene; Creative Plays; American Pottery from New Orleans Museum of Art; Romar Bearden as Printmaker

M UNIVERSITY OF WISCONSIN OSHKOSH, Allen R Priebe Gallery, 800 Algoma Blvd, 54901. Tel 414-424-2222; *Dir* Jeff Lipschutz
Open Mon - Fri 10:30 AM - 3 PM, Mon - Thurs 7 - 9 PM, Sat & Sun 1 - 4 PM. No admis fee. Estab 1971 for the purpose of offering exhibits which appeal to a wide range of people. Gallery is 60 x 40 with additional wall space added with partitions, a skylight along back ceiling. Average Annual Attendance: 15,000
Income: Financed by student allocated monies & Dept of Art
Purchases: $1500
Collections: Works Progress Administration Collection; †prints & drawings
Activities: Classes for adults & children; lect open to public, 2-4 vis lectr per year; gallery talks; tours; competitions with awards; individual paintings & original objects of art lent to University staff & area museums

PLATTEVILLE

M UNIVERSITY OF WISCONSIN - PLATTEVILLE, Harry Nohr Art Gallery, One University Plaza, 53818. Tel 608-342-1398; FAX 608-342-1478; *Bus Mgr for the Arts* Susan Davis
Open Mon - Fri 11 AM - 4 PM, Mon - Thurs evenings 5 - 8 PM, Sat & Sun 1 - 4 PM. No admis fee. Estab 1978. Average Annual Attendance: 9000
Income: Financed by student fees & state funds
Activities: Lect open to public, 4 vis lectr per year; gallery talks; tours; competitions with awards; book traveling exhibitions

PORT WASHINGTON

COALITION OF WOMEN'S ART ORGANIZATIONS
For further information, see National and Regional Organizations

RACINE

A WUSTUM MUSEUM ART ASSOCIATION, 2519 Northwestern Ave, 53404. Tel 414-636-9177; FAX 414-636-9231; *Pres* Serge E Logan; *VPres* Roger Hoff; *Treas* Neil Vail; *Dir* Bruce W Pepich
Open daily 1 - 5 PM, Mon & Thurs 1 - 9 PM. No admis fee. Estab 1941 to foster & aid the establishment & development to pub art galleries & museums, programs of educ & training in the fine arts & to develop pub appreciation & enjoyment of the fine arts. Estab 1846 Italianate farmhouse, 2 stories, 6-room classroom addition, 13 acres of parkland, Boerner-designed formal gardens. Maintains library. Average Annual Attendance: 50,000. Mem: 650; dues $20 & up; annual meeting in May
Income: $500,000 (financed by mem, grants & fundraising)
Collections: 300 works WPA; 20th century works on paper, studio glass, ceramics, fibers; 19th century African jewerly, metals, artists books, paintings
Exhibitions: Watercolor Wisconsin (annual); Wisconsin Photography (triennial); Annual Nationwide Thematic Show (summer); Area Arts
Publications: Exhibit brochures & catalogs; Vue, quarterly newsletter
Activities: Classes for adults & children; docent training; outreach for local school children; gang intervention programs; lect open to public, 6-10 vis lectr per year; gallery talks; tours; competitions with awards; individual paintings & original art objects lent to museums; lending collection contains books, nature artifacts, original art works; original prints & paintings; book traveling exhibitions; originate traveling exhibitions; museum shop sells books & original art, gifts & collectibles

M Charles A Wustum Museum of Fine Arts, 53404. Tel 414-636-9177; FAX 414-636-9231; *Dir* Bruce W Pepich
Open Sun - Sat 1 - 5 PM & Mon & Thurs 5 - 9 PM. No admis fee. Estab 1940 to serve as cultural center for greater Racine community. Mus contains six galleries located in 1856 Wustum homestead & 1996 addition. Average Annual Attendance: 40,000

Income: $500,000 (financed by endowment, city & county appropriations, private gifts & programs)
Purchases: $500-$1000
Collections: Contemporary Wisconsin Watercolors; WPA Project paintings & prints; †contemporary graphics; †works on paper, †ceramic sculpture, †glass sculpture, all post-1850 & primarily American
Activities: Classes for adults & children; docent training; lect open to public, 2-3 vis lectr per year; gallery talks; tours; competitions with awards; film programs; individual paintings & original object of art lent to other institutions; lending collection contains 1500 original art works, 500 original prints, 300 paintings, 200 photographs & 250 sculptures; book traveling exhibitions; originate traveling exhibitions; museum shop sells books, original art, stationery, arts & crafts

L Wustum Art Library, 2519 Northwestern Ave, 53404. Tel 414-636-9177; *Dir* Bruce W Pepich; *Librn* Nancy Elsmo
Open Sun - Sat 1 - 5 PM, Mon & Thurs 1 - 9 PM. Estab 1941 to provide mus visitors & students with exposure to art history & instructional books. For reference only to pub, members may check out books
Income: $2500
Library Holdings: Vols 1500; Per subs 12; AV — V-tapes; Other — Exhibition catalogs, pamphlets
Special Subjects: Photography, Porcelain, Pottery, Printmaking, Prints, Sculpture, Textiles, Watercolors, Woodcarvings, 20th Century Art & Architecture
Publications: Quarterly catalogues

RHINELANDER

L RHINELANDER DISTRICT LIBRARY, 106 N Stevens St, 54501-3193. Tel 715-369-1070; FAX 715-369-1076; *Dir* Robert Toth
Estab 1903
Income: $1200 (financed by endowment)
Purchases: $1600
Library Holdings: Vols 1500; AV — V-tapes
Special Subjects: American Western Art, Architecture, Art History, Asian Art, Calligraphy, Etchings & Engravings, Folk Art, Painting - American, Painting - Dutch, Painting - European, Painting - Flemish, Painting - French, Painting - German, Painting - Italian, Photography
Collections: †Architecture; †arts & crafts; †books & videos; †Bump Art Collection; †European & American Artists; †photography

RICHLAND CENTER

M FRANK LLOYD WRIGHT MUSEUM, AD German Warehouse, 300 S Church St, 53581. Tel 608-647-2808; *Co-owner Mgr* Harvey W Glanzer; *Co-owner & Creative Dir* Beth Caulkins
Open by request May - Nov, call ahead. Admis $5. Estab 1915. Warehouse is a red brick structure topped by a mayan concrete frieze. It employs a structural concept known as the Burton Spider-web system. Interior grid of massive concrete columns provide structural support for floors & roof. Elimination of interior walls allows maximum freedom of interior space. Gift shop on first & lower level, mus & gallery on second floor
Exhibitions: Large 8 ft x 8 ft Photographic Murals of Wright's Work

RIPON

M RIPON COLLEGE ART GALLERY, 300 Seward St, 54971. Tel 414-748-8110; *Chmn* Evelyn Kain
Open Mon - Fri 9 AM - 4 PM. No admis fee. Estab 1965 to provide student body with changing exhibits. Average Annual Attendance: 4000
Collections: Paintings, print, sculpture, multi-media
Exhibitions: Henry Gernhardt exhibit
Activities: Individual paintings lent to schools

RIVER FALLS

M UNIVERSITY OF WISCONSIN, Gallery 101, Cascade St, 54022. Tel 715-425-3236; *Gallery Dir* Michael Padgett
Open Mon - Fri 9 AM - 5 PM & 7 - 9 PM, Sun 2 - 4 PM. No admis fee. Estab 1973 to exhibit artists of regional & national prominence & for educational purposes. Maintains one gallery. Average Annual Attendance: 21,000
Income: $5000 (financed by state appropriation & student activities funds)
Collections: †National & International Artists; †Regional Artists; WPA Artists
Activities: Lect open to public; gallery talks; originate traveling exhibitions

SHEBOYGAN

A SHEBOYGAN ARTS FOUNDATION, INC, John Michael Kohler Arts Center, 608 New York Ave, PO Box 489, 53082-0489. Tel 414-458-6144; FAX 414-458-4473; *Dir* Ruth DeYoung Kohler; *Cur* Alison Ferris; *Mgr Community Develop* Mary Jo McBrearty
Open weekdays 10 AM - 5 PM, Thurs 10 AM - 9 PM, weekends Noon - 5 PM. No admis fee. Estab 1967 as a visual & performing arts center focusing on contemporary American crafts & works which break barriers between art forms. Contains five exhibition galleries, the largest being 60 ft x 45 ft, theatre, four studio-classrooms, library, sales gallery. Average Annual Attendance: 135,000. Mem: 200; dues family $35, individual $25, student $15; contributing mem
Income: Financed by mem, grants, corporate-foundation donations, sales gallery, ticket sales
Collections: †Contemporary Ceramics; †Contemporary Visionary Art; Historical Decorative Arts
Publications: Biennial Report; Exhibition Checklist 6-10 annually; Exhibition Catalogues, 2-4 annually; Newsletter, bi-monthly
Activities: Classes for adults & children; dramatic programs; docent training;

artists-in-residence programs; demonstrations; lect open to public, 18-20 vis lectr per year; concerts; gallery talks; tours; competitions with awards; scholarships & fels offered; individual paintings & original objects of art lent to other arts institutions which meet the loan requirements, lending collection includes 6000 original art works & 100 paintings; book traveling exhibitions; originate traveling exhibitions which circulate to museums & artists organizations; sales shop sells magazines, original art, slides, postcards & notecards

STEVENS POINT

M **UNIVERSITY OF WISCONSIN-STEVENS POINT,** Carlsten Art Gallery, Fine Arts Bldg, 54481-3897. Tel 715-346-4797; Elec Mail swoods @ uwsp.edu. *Dir* Suzanne Woods
Open Mon - Fri 10 AM - 4 PM, Sat & Sun 1 - 4 PM, Thurs 7 - 9 PM. No admis fee
Exhibitions: Tom Bamberger; Juried Student Exhibition; Drawing on the Figure; BFA Exhibition

STURGEON BAY

M **DOOR COUNTY,** Miller Art Center, 107 S Fourth Ave, 54235. Tel 414-746-0707 (office), 743-6578 (gallery); *Adminr* Bonnie Oehler; *Cur* Deborah Rosenthal
Open Mon - Sat 10 AM - 5 PM, Mon - Thurs evenings 7 - 9 PM. No admis fee. Estab 1975. Gallery is 35 x 50 ft, plus mezzanine, 2 new gallery spaces being added - 24 ft x 35 ft. Average Annual Attendance: 14,000. Mem: 225; dues associate $20, active $5; annual meeting second Thurs in Nov
Income: Financed by endowment, mem & county funds
Collections: †Permanent collection contains over 250 paintings; emphasis on paintings, prints & drawings by 20th century Wisconsin artists
Exhibitions: 9 Photographers from Lake Michigan's Shores; Jack Anderson & Phil Austin; Salon of High School Art; Wildlife Biennial Invitational exhibit VI; Wearable Art Invitational Exhibit; 18th Juried Annual; Very Special Arts Wisconsin
Activities: Classes for adults & children; lect open to public, 4 vis lectr per year; concerts; gallery talks; tours; competitions with awards; individual paintings lent to other museums & art centers; lending collection contains 250 original art works; sales shop sells books & reproductions

SUPERIOR

M **DOUGLAS COUNTY HISTORICAL SOCIETY,** Fairlawn Mansion & Museum, 906 E Second St, 54880. Tel 715-394-5712; *Exec Dir* Rachael E Martin; *Coll Mgr* Joseph Korman; *Vol Coordr* Kari Bostrom
Open 9 AM - 5 PM. Admis adults $5, seniors & students $4, children 6-12 $3. Estab 1854 to promote education of religious history. 1890's historic house, period rooms. Average Annual Attendance: 15,000. Mem: 158; dues corporation $100, family $30, individual $15, junior historian $5; annual meeting in Apr
Income: $105,000 (financed by endowment, mem, city & county appropriations, grants, catering & gift shop sales)
Purchases: 1847 sideboard originally used in historic house
Collections: David Barry Photography Collection; †Chippewa Indian Artifacts; Railroad, Shipping, Logging, Farming & Mining Tools (from area); †1890's Period Furniture & Furnishings
Exhibitions: David Barry Photographs; Chippewa Indian Artifacts; Railroad, Shipping, Logging, Farming & Mining in Area
Activities: Dramatic programs; docent training; lect open to public, 12 vis lectr per year; tours; competitions; scholarships offered; museum shop sells books, Victorian & Indian items
L **Archives,** 906 E Second St, 54880. FAX 715-394-2043; *Exec Dir* Rachael E Martin; *Coll Mgr* Joseph Korman; *Vol Coordr* Kari Bostrom
Admis adults $5, seniors & students $4, children 6-12 $3. For reference
Income: $105,000 (financed by endowment, mem, city & county appropriations, gift shop, catering & grants)
Library Holdings: Documents; Maps; Scrapbooks; AV — A-tapes, cassettes, fs, lantern slides, motion pictures, rec, slides, v-tapes; Other — Clipping files, framed reproductions, manuscripts, memorabilia, original art works, pamphlets, photographs, prints
Special Subjects: American Indian Art, Archaeology, Architecture, Crafts, Decorative Arts, Dolls, Folk Art, Historical Material, Maps, Marine Painting, Painting - American, Period Rooms, Reproductions, Restoration & Conservation, Textiles
Activities: Dramatic programs; docent training; lect open to public; tours; scholarships offered; museum shop sells books, Victorian & Indian items

WAUSAU

M **LEIGH YAWKEY WOODSON ART MUSEUM, INC,** 700 N 12th St, 54403-5007. Tel 715-845-7010; FAX 715-845-7103; Elec Mail lywam@lywam.com. *Pres* John A Slayton; *Dir* Robert A Kret; *Cur of Exhib* Andrew J McGivern; *Cur Coll* Jane Weinke; *Assoc Dir* Marcia M Theel; *Cur Educ* Michael Nelson
Tues - Fri 9 AM - 4 PM, Sat & Sun Noon - 5 PM. No admis fee. Estab 1973 for acquisition of a creditable permanent collection of bird-theme art; program of changing exhibits; art educ. 7750 net sq ft of exhibition space; galleries on three floors; parquet & carpeted floors; 628 running ft in galleries. Average Annual Attendance: 45,000. Mem: 275; mem $250
Income: $850,000 (financed by mem & private foundation)
Collections: Contemporary & historic wildlife theme paintings & sculptures with birds as the main subject; Historical period pieces of Royal Worcester porcelain; 19th & 20th century art glass
Exhibitions: Birds In Art; Beyond the Lens: Compositions by Art Wolfe; Natural Wonders; Naturally Drawn; Only Owls
Publications: Birds in Art, annually; Wildlife: The Artist's View, triennially; exhibition catalogs; Vista, quarterly newsletter

Activities: Docent programs; lect open to public; gallery talks; tours; competitions for participation in exhibitions; individual paintings & original objects of art lent to recognized museums & art centers; book traveling exhibitions 6-8 per year; originate traveling exhibitions, circulation to established museums, art centers, galleries & libraries
L **Art Library,** 700 N 12th St, 54403. Tel 715-845-7010; *Cur Educ* Michael Nelson
Open by appointment. Estab 1976. For reference only
Income: $1500
Purchases: $1500
Library Holdings: Vols 2500; Per subs 20; AV — A-tapes, cassettes, fs, motion pictures, slides 5000, v-tapes 50; Other — Exhibition catalogs 1000, pamphlets
Special Subjects: Aesthetics, Architecture, Art Education, Art History, Decorative Arts, Glass, Painting - American, Porcelain, Birds, Wildlife art

WEST BEND

M **WEST BEND ART MUSEUM,** 300 S Sixth Ave, PO Box 426, 53095. Tel 414-334-9638, 334-1151; FAX 414-334-8080; *Pres* Sharon Ziegler; *Exec Dir* Thomas D Lidtke; *Asst Dir* Cheryl Ann Parker; *Librn* Linda Goetz
Open Wed - Sat 10 AM - 4:30 PM, Sun 1 - 4:30 PM, cl Mon & Tues. No admis fee. Estab 1961 as an art museum & exhibition space for regional & national shows. The large colonial style building contains eight gallery exhibit rooms & three art classrooms. Average Annual Attendance: 14,000. Mem: 600; dues $10-$30; annual meeting first Tues in Apr
Income: Financed by endowment, mem & donations
Purchases: $10,000
Collections: Carl von Marr Collection; Wisconsin Art History 1850-1950
Exhibitions: Monthly exhibitions, 10 - 12 per yr
Publications: Carl Von Marr, American-German Artist (1858-1936); Bulletin, monthly
Activities: Classes for adults and children; docent training; lect open to public; travelogues; tours; Art Aware an educational outreach (art appreciation) service to local schools; book traveling exhibits, 1-3 per year; originate traveling exhibitions; museum shop sells books, reproductions, prints from collection
L **Library,** 300 S Sixth Ave, 53095. Tel 414-334-9638; FAX 414-334-8080; *Exec Dir* Thomas D Lidtke
Open Mon - Sat 10 AM - 4:30 PM, Sun 1 - 4:30 PM. No admis fee. Estab 1960 to preserve & collect the work of Carl von Marr & Early Wisconsin art history. Building of colonial architecture houses, 2 large permanent collection rooms, 2 changing exhibition spaces. Mem: 600; dues family $30
Library Holdings: Vols 2000; Per subs 6; AV — Cassettes, slides, v-tapes; Other — Clipping files, exhibition catalogs, original art works, photographs
Special Subjects: Architecture, Art Education, Art History, Decorative Arts, Drawings, Folk Art, Photography, Printmaking, Textiles, Woodcarvings
Collections: Car von Marr Collection; Doll House Collection (1850-1952); Wisconsin Art History (1850-1950) Collection
Publications: Carl Von Marr (catalogue)
Activities: Classes for adults & children; docent training, educational out-reach to public schools, art history; lect open to public; concerts; gallery talks; tours; individual paintings lent to other museums or galleries for cultural shows; lending collection contains books, cassettes, paintings, slides; originate traveling exhibitions; museum shop sells reproductions, prints, note cards, sweat shirts & post cards

WHITEWATER

M **UNIVERSITY OF WISCONSIN-WHITEWATER,** Crossman Gallery, Ctr of the Arts, 800 W Main St, 53190. Tel 414-472-1207, 472-5708; *Dir* Michael Flanagan
Open Mon - Fri 10 AM - 5 PM & 7 - 9 PM, Sat 1 - 4 PM, cl Sun. No admis fee. Estab 1965 to provide professional exhibits. 47 ft x 51 ft, 3 walls gray carpeted. Average Annual Attendance: 5000
Income: $7000 (financed by segregated student fee appropriation)
Collections: American Folk Art Collection; Regional Art Collection
Exhibitions: (1997) Spinners & Weavers Exhibition Bindley Ceramic Collection; Color Photo Invitational Exhibition; Presswork National Women Printmakers
Activities: Classes for adults & children; student training in gallery management

WYOMING

BIG HORN

M **BRADFORD BRINTON MEMORIAL MUSEUM & HISTORIC RANCH,** 239 Brinton Rd, PO Box 460, 82833. Tel 307-672-3173; FAX 307-672-3258; *Dir & Chief Cur* Kenneth L Schuster; *Office & Sales Mgr (May-Sept)* Marge Johnson; *Office & Sales Mgr (Oct-Apr)* Tessa Dalton; *Cur* Dorothy Savage; *Asst Cur* Charles B Faust
Open May 15 - Labor Day daily 9:30 AM - 5 PM. Admis adults $3, students over 6 & sr citizens over 62 $2. Estab 1961 to show a typical Gentlemen's Working ranch as established in the late 19th century. Two galleries and house museum are maintained. Average Annual Attendance: 12,000
Income: $150,000 (financed by endowment)
Collections: Plains Indians Artifacts; Western American Art by Frederic Remington & Charles M Russell; American art & a few pieces of European art, largely of the 19th & 20th century; china; furniture; silver
Exhibitions: (1997) In Celebration of Hans Kleiber; James F Jackson: In Paint & On Leather
Publications: Monographs on artists in the collection from time to time
Activities: Educ dept; lect open to public, 4 vis lectr per year; tours; museum shop sells books, magazines, original art, reproductions, prints, slides, American Indian jewelry & crafts

CASPER

M NICOLAYSEN ART MUSEUM & DISCOVERY CENTER, Childrens Discovery Center, 400 E Collins Dr, 82601. Tel 307-235-5247; FAX 307-235-0923; *Dir* Karen Mobley; *Educ Cur* Val Martinez; *Registrar* John Hyden
Open Tues - Sun 10 AM - 5 PM, Thurs till 8 PM. Admis fee adults $2, children $1, family $5, members free, 1st & 3rd Thurs 4-8 PM free. Estab 1967 to exhibit permanent collection, nationwide traveling exhibits & provide school tours, art classes & workshops. Two galleries, 2500 sq ft and 500 sq ft. Average Annual Attendance: 25,000. Mem: 790; dues individual $30, family $50, annual meeting third Tues in May
Income: $235,000 (financed by mem, grants & fundraising events)
Collections: Carl Link Drawings; †Artists of the Region
Exhibitions: Twenty per year.
Publications: Historic Ranches of Wyoming
Activities: Classes for adults & children; docent training; lect open to public, 5-10 vis lectr per year; concerts; gallery talks; competitions with cash awards; individual paintings & original objects of art lent to qualified exhibiting institutions; lending collection contains 2500 original art works; book traveling exhibitions; originate traveling exhibitions; children's museum
L Museum, 400 E Collins Dr, 82601. Tel 307-235-5247; FAX 307-235-0923; *Dir* Karen Mobley; *Discovery Center Coordr* Val Martinez; *Registrar* John Hyden
Open Tues - Sun 10 AM - 5 PM, Thurs till 8 PM. Admis fee family $5, adults $2, children under 12 $1, members free. Estab 1967 to collect & exhibit regional contemporary art. 8000 sq ft including 6 small and 1 large gallery. Computer controlled temerature & humidity. Hands on discovery center for children. Average Annual Attendance: 60,000. Mem: 700; dues $50; annual meeting 3rd Tues May
Income: $235,000 (financed by donations & fundraising events)
Library Holdings: Vols 66; Per subs 8; AV — Slides; Other — Exhibition catalogs, pamphlets
Collections: Carl Link Collection; Regional Contemporary Pottery
Activities: Classes for children; dramatic programs; lect open to public, 2000 lectr per year; gallery talks; tours; juried regional competitions; book traveling exhibitions 1-2 per year; museum shop sells books, original art, prints, pottery, glass, jewelry & cards

CHEYENNE

M DEPARTMENT OF COMMERCE, Wyoming Arts Council Gallery, 2320 Capitol Ave, 82002. Tel 307-777-7742; FAX 307-777-5499; *Visual Arts Prog Mgr* Liliane Francuz
Open Mon - Fri 8 AM - 9 PM. Estab 1990 to exhibit work of artists living & working in Wyoming. Average Annual Attendance: 3500
Exhibitions: 4-6 exhibits annually, work of artists living & working in Wyoming
Publications: All Arts Newsletter
Activities: Lect open to public

M WYOMING STATE MUSEUM, State Art Gallery, 2301 Central Ave, 82002. Tel 307-777-7022; FAX 307-777-6005;
No admis fee. Estab 1969 to collect, preserve & to exhibit the work of Wyoming & Western artists. Average Annual Attendance: 50,000
Income: Financed by state appropriation
Collections: Wyoming artists, historical & contemporary including Historical Hans Kleiber, William Gollings, M D Houghton, Cyrenius Hall, William H Jackson, J H Sharp
Exhibitions: Regional & Wyoming contemporary art, western art
Activities: Educ dept; lect open to public, 9 vis lectr per year; gallery talks; tours; individual paintings & original objects of art lent to institutions belonging to AAM, Colo-Wyo Association of Museums (CWAM) & Mount Plains Museums Association; museum shop sells books, original art, reproductions, prints & gift merchandise

CLEARMONT

M UCROSS FOUNDATION, Big Red Barn Gallery, 2836 US Hwy 14-16 E, 82835. Tel 307-737-2291; FAX 307-737-2322; *Exec Dir* Sharon Dynak; *Prog Coordr* Aurele Sheehan
Open 9 AM - 5 PM. No admis fee. Estab 1981. A renovated barn gallery on the grounds of an artists' & writers' residency program
Exhibitions: Quilts by Linda Behar; 4-6 group & solo shows a year
Publications: Ucross newsletter, annually
Activities: Sales shop sells books

CODY

A BUFFALO BILL MEMORIAL ASSOCIATION, Buffalo Bill Historical Center, 720 Sheridan Ave, 82414. Tel 307-587-4771; FAX 307-587-5714; Elec Mail bbhc@wave.park.wy.us. *Chmn* Mrs Henry H R Coe; *Acting Dir* B Byron Price; *Librn* Frances Clymer; *Cur Whitney Gallery* Sarah Boehme; *Cur Plains Indian Museum* Emma Hanson; *Cur Cody Firearms Museum* Howard M Madaus; *Cur Buffalo Bill Museum* Paul Fees; *Dir Educ* Joy Comstock; *Dir Public Relations* Scott Hagel; *Registrar* Joanne Patterson; *Assoc Dir* Wally Reber
Open May & Sept 8 AM - 8 PM, Oct & Apr 8 AM - 5 PM, Mar & Nov 10 AM - 3 PM, June - Aug 7 AM - 10 PM. Admis Adults $8, senior citizens $6.25 & special group rate. Estab 1917 to preserve & exhibit art, artifacts & memorabilia of the Old West; to operate Buffalo Bill Mus, Plains Indian Mus, Whitney Gallery of Western Art & Cody Firearms Mus. Average Annual Attendance: 250,000. Mem: Dues $25
Income: Financed by admis & private funds
Exhibitions: Seasons of the Buffalo; The Kriendler Mezzanine of Contemporary Western Art (permanent collection); Heart Mountain Relocation Center: Both Sides of the Fence; Frederic Remington Catalog Raisonne
Publications: Annual exhibition catalogues; quarterly newsletter
Activities: Classes for adults & children; docent training; lect open to public; gallery talks; tours; scholarships offered; individual paintings & original objects of art lent to other institutions; book traveling exhibitions; originate traveling exhibitions around the US; museum shop sells books, original art, reproductions, prints, slides, jewelry, collectible items, Indian crafts & Kachina dolls

M Buffalo Bill Historical Center, 720 Sheridan Ave, 82414. Tel 307-587-4771; FAX 307-587-5714; Elec Mail bbhc@wave.park.wy.us. *Dir Communications* Scott Hagel
Open June - Sept 7 AM - 8 Pm, Oct 8 AM - 5 PM, Nov - Apr 10 AM - 2 PM, May Thurs - Mon 8 AM - 8 PM. Admis adults $8, senior citizens $6.50, students 13-21 $4, youth 6-12 $2, under 5 free. Estab 1927, is one of the largest western heritage centers. four museums in one complex; Buffalo Bill Mus, Whitney Gallery of Western Art, Cody Firearms Mus, Plains Indian Mus. Average Annual Attendance: 250,000. Mem: 3200
Collections: Western American art includes Catlin, Bierstadt, Miller, Remington, Russell & others
Exhibitions: It Never Failed Me: The Arms & Art of the Remington Arms Co; 21st Annual Plains Indian Seminar
Publications: Exhibition catalogs
Activities: Classes for adults & children; dramatic programs; docent training; art & ethnology programs; lect open to public, 10 vis lectr per year; gallery talks; tours; scholarships offered; individual paintings & original objects of art lent to other recognized museums; museum shop sells books, magazines, original art, reproductions & prints
L Harold McCracken Research Library, PO Box 1000, 82414. Tel 307-587-4771; FAX 307-587-5714; *Acting Librn* Frances Clymer
Open 9 AM - 4 PM. Estab 1980 for research in Western history & art. Open to the pub for reference only
Library Holdings: Vols 15,000; Per subs 45; Micro — Fiche, reels; AV — Cassettes, fs, Kodachromes, motion pictures, slides, v-tapes; Other — Clipping files, exhibition catalogs, manuscripts, memorabilia, original art works, pamphlets, photographs, prints, reproductions
Special Subjects: Firearms, Plains Indians, Western Art, History & Geology
Collections: WHD Koerner Archives; †Buffalo Bill Cody Archives; †Photo Collections; †Rare Books
Activities: Classes for children; docent training; lect open to public, 10 vis lectr per year; gallery talks; tours

A CODY COUNTRY ART LEAGUE, 836 Sheridan Ave, 82414. Tel 307-587-3597; *Pres* Shirley Barhaug
Open for exhibitions & workshops year around. No admis fee. Estab 1964 for promotion of artistic endeavor among local & area artists; also established for exhibits, displays & sales. Average Annual Attendance: 15,000. Mem: 130; dues $25; annual meeting in Dec
Income: Financed by endowment, mem, grants from Wyoming Council on the Arts, yearly auction & sponsors
Activities: Classes for adults & children; dramatic programs; films; workshops; lect open to public, 2-3 vis lectr per year; competitions; sales shop sells original art & prints

JACKSON

M NATIONAL MUSEUM OF WILDLIFE ART, 2820 Rungius Rd, PO Box 6825, 83002. Tel 307-733-5771; FAX 307-733-5787; Elec Mail nmwa@sisna.com. *Exec Dir* Daniel Provo; *Cur* Maria Hajic; *Dir Develop* Laine Goodman
Open 10 AM - 5 PM. Admis $4. Estab 1987 devoted to North American Wildlife Art; collection spans 150 years. Facility hass 12 galleries, cafe, gift shop, 2 classrooms & 200 seat auditorium; galleries house travelling exhibits & permanent collections. Average Annual Attendance: 130,000. Mem: Annual dues $25 individual
Income: Financed by endowment, mem & admis
Exhibitions: Special Grand Opening exhibits
Publications: NWAM newsletter, quarterly
Activities: Classes for adults & children; docent training; lect open to public, 100 vis lectr per year; concerts; gallery talks; tours; competitions; individual paintings & original objects of art lent to the Cowboy Hall of Fame, The Gilcrease Institute & Denver Art Museum; museum shop sells books, prints, magazines
L Library, 2820 Rungius Rd, PO Box 6825, 83002. Tel 307-733-5771; FAX 307-733-5787; Elec Mail nmwa@sisna.com. *Cur* Maria Hajic
Library Holdings: Vols 1000; AV — A-tapes, motion pictures, v-tapes; Other — Pamphlets

LARAMIE

M UNIVERSITY OF WYOMING, University of Wyoming Art Museum, 2111 Willett, PO Box 3807, 82071-3807. Tel 307-766-6622; FAX 307-766-3520; *Dir* Charles Guerin; *Cur Educ* Maria Cocchiarelli; *Registrar* E K Kim; *Cur Museum & Progs* Susan Moldenhauer
Open Tues - Fri 10 AM - 5 PM, Sat 11 AM - 5 PM, Sun 10 AM - 3 PM. Estab 1968 to serve as an art resource center for faculty, students & the general public. Exhibition space consists of 8 galleries & outdoor sculpture court. Average Annual Attendance: 120,000. Mem: 500; dues $10 & up
Income: Financed by state appropriation & friends organization
Collections: 19th & 20th Century American & European paintings, prints, sculpture & drawings
Exhibitions: Special exhibits from the permanent collections as well as traveling exhibitions on a regular basis during the year; faculty shows; student shows
Publications: Exhibition catalogs
Activities: Lect open to public, 6 vis lectr per year; gallery talks; tours; individual paintings and original objects of art lent to other museums; lending collection contains 5000 original art works, 3000 original prints and 2000 paintings; originates traveling exhibitions

MOOSE

A GRAND TETON NATIONAL PARK SERVICE, Colter Bay Indian Arts Museum, PO Drawer 170, 83013. Tel 307-739-3594; *District Naturalist* Mike Nicklaus
Open May 8 AM - 5 PM, June - Sept 8 AM - 8 PM, cl Oct - Apr. No admis fee. Estab 1972
Collections: David T Vernon Indian Arts Collection
Exhibitions: Native American Guest Artist's Demonstration Program; David T Vernon Indian Arts Collection

ROCK SPRINGS

A COMMUNITY FINE ARTS CENTER (Formerly Sweetwater Community Fine Arts Center), Halseth Gallery, 400 C St, 82901. Tel 307-362-6212; FAX 307-352-6657; *Dir* Gregory Gaylor; *Asst to Dir* Kari Jensen
Open Mon - Sat 10 AM - Noon, 1 PM - 5 PM, 6 PM - 9 PM, Mon, Wed, Thurs, Fri & Sat are in operation on alternating basis, call for specific hours. No admis fee. Estab 1966 to house permanent art collection and hold various exhibits during the year; Halseth Gallery houses permanent art collection. Average Annual Attendance: 8000
Income: Financed by endowment, city appropriation, county funds & school district No 1
Collections: Own 452 pieces of original art including Norman Rockwell, Grandma Moses, Raphael Soyer among others
Publications: Calendar of events; catalogue brochure
Activities: Classes for adults & children; art painting workshops for children & students; lect open to public, 1-2 vis lectr per year; concerts; gallery talks, tours; competitions; Best of Show; artmobile; individual painting & original objects of art lent to established museums & art galleries

SUNDANCE

M CROOK COUNTY MUSEUM & ART GALLERY, PO Box 63, 82729. Tel 307-283-3666; FAX 307-283-1091; *Dir* Cheryl McLaughlin
Open Mon - Fri 8 AM - 5 PM, cl holidays. No admis fee. Estab to preserve & display Crook County history, display County artists & provide a showcase for county residents' collections
Income: Financed by County appropriation
Collections: Furniture, pictures, Western historical items
Publications: Brochure
Activities: Tours for school children

PACIFIC ISLANDS

PAGO PAGO, AMERICAN SAMOA

M JEAN P HAYDON MUSEUM, PO Box 1540, 96799. FAX 011-684-633-2059; Tel 011-684-633-4347. *Chmn Board Trustees* Fagafaga D Langkilde; *Exec Dir & Cur* Foailoilo Lauvao
Open Mon - Fri 10 AM - 4 PM, Sat 10 AM - Noon. No admis fee. Estab 1971 to establish, maintain, acquire & supervise the collection, study preservation, interpretation & exhibition of fine arts objects & such relics, documents, paintings, artifacts & other historical & related materials as well as evidence that illustrate the history of the Samoan Islands & the culture of their inhabitants, particularly of American Samoa. New extension of the mus is an art gallery displaying local artists work & student arts. Average Annual Attendance: 67,000
Income: Financed by city or state appropriations and grants from NEA
Collections: Natural Sciences; Polynesian Artifacts; †Samoan Village Life; †US Navy History; †paintings, †drawings, †slides, †photographs, †artifacts
Exhibitions: Traditional Folk Art
Activities: Classes for adults & children; dramatic programs; lect open to public, 3 vis lectr per year; artmobile; duplicate but not original objects of art lent to schools & individuals; lending collection contains books, paintings & photographs; museum & sales shop sells books, reproductions, prints, handicrafts & postcards

PUERTO RICO

OLD SAN JUAN

M MUSEO DE LA AMERICAS, Cuartel de Ballaja, 2nd Flr, PO Box 3126, 00902. Tel 787-724-5052; *Dir* Ricardo E Alegria; *Sub Dir* Maria Angela Lopez Vilella; *Registrar* Marlene Hernandez Casillas; *Public Relations* Maria de Lourdes Morales Cruz; *Staff Supv* Maria del Carmen Rodriguez
Open 10 AM - 4 PM. Estab 1991 for popular arts of the Americas. Old Spanish style military quarters. Tall ceilings in show rooms. Mem: 84; dues $15 minimum
Income: Financed by endowment & mem
Exhibitions: Loiza: Herencia Negra; Popular arts of the Americas: Antonio Frasconi, Zooisla, Fotoseptiembre
Publications: Boletin Informativo Museo de las Americas, semiannual
Activities: Classes for children; lect open to public, 6 vis lectr per year; book traveling exhibitions 3 per year; originate traveling exhibitions; museum shop sells books & prints

PONCE

M MUSEO DE ARTE DE PONCE, Ponce Art Museum, The Luis A Ferre Foundation Inc (Mailing add: Avenida de las Americas, PO Box 9027, 00732-9027). Tel 787-848-0505, 840-1510; FAX 787-841-7309; *Exec Dir* Dr Carmen Fischler; *Emeritus Dir* Dr Rene Taylor; *Registrar* Hiromi Shiba; *Conservator* Lidia Quigley
Open daily 10 AM - 5 PM. Admis adults $4, children under 12 $2, student with ID $1. Estab 1959 to exhibit a representative collection of European paintings & sculpture; Puerto Rican & Latin American art. Seven hexagonal galleries on upper floor; three rectangular galleries on lower floor. Average Annual Attendance: 80,000. Mem: 700; dues single $30, double $50
Income: Financed by endowment, mem & government
Collections: African, Latin American, Pre-Columbian & Puerto Rican Santos Art; 19th century art, contemporary art, 14th - 18th century paintings & sculpture
Exhibitions: El Paisaje Puertorriqueno; Arquitectura Barroca y Moderna; Ceramica del Grupo Manos Auspiciador; Grabados de Jose Luis Cuevas y Actualidad Grafica Panamericana; Colectiva Juan Ramon Velazquez, Carmelo Sobrino y Joaquin Reyes; El Puerto Rico que nunca fue; Artistas Puertorriquenos residentes en NY; Juan Ramon Jimenez y los ninos; Francisco Oller: A Realist Impressionist; Diaspora Puertorriquena; Fashion in Puerto Rico XV to XIX Century; Jaime Suarez; 25 Years of Puerto Rican Painting; Fernando Botero; Actos Compulsivos: Arnaldo Roche; Ponce Carnival Masks
Activities: Educ dept; tours; individual paintings & original objects of art lent to other museums & government offices; book traveling exhibitions 1-2 per year; originate traveling exhibitions; museum shops sells books & reproductions
L Library, Avenida de las Americas, PO Box 9027, 00732-9027. Tel 787-848-0505, 840-1510; FAX 787-841-7309; *Exec Dir* Carmen Fischler
Closed for reference with the exception of special permission
Library Holdings: Vols 4000; Other — Exhibition catalogs

SAN JUAN

M ATENEO PUERTORRIQUENO, PO Box 1180, 00902. Tel 809-722-4839; FAX 809-725-3873; *Pres* Eduardo Morales-Coll
Open Mon - Fri 9 AM - 5 PM, cl Sun & holidays. No admis fee. Estab 1876 & is the oldest cultural institution in Puerto Rico. Mem: dues $25; annual meeting in June
Collections: Decorative arts; drawings; historical material; prints; Puerto Rican paintings; sculpture
Exhibitions: Temporary exhibitions, monthly
Publications: Cuadernos (publications on general topics); Revista Ateneo, every 4 months
Activities: Classes for adults; dramatic programs; lect; gallery talks; guided tours; films; concerts; recitals; competitions with prizes; dramas; individual paintings & original objects of art lent to other cultural institutions; book traveling exhibitions 1 per year
L Library, PO Box 1180, 00902. Tel 809-722-4839; FAX 809-725-3873; *Pres* Eduardo Morales-Coll
Library Holdings: Vols 15,000

INSTITUTE OF PUERTO RICAN CULTURE

M Escuela de Artes Plasticas Galleria, PO Box 1112, 00902-1112. Tel 809-725-8120; FAX 809-725-8111; *Dir* Marimar Benites
Open daily 8 AM - 4 PM. Exposition of drawing, painting & art work of the students of visual school
Collections: †Permanent collection of student art work
A Instituto de Cultura Puertorriquena, Apartado 9024184, 00902-4148. Tel 809-724-0700; FAX 809-724-8993; *Dir* Dr Luis A Diaz Hernandez
Open Mon - Sun 8 AM - Noon & 1 - 5 PM. No admis fee. Estab 1955 to stimulate, promote, divulge & enrich Puerto Rico's cultural & historical heritage. The institute has created 16 museums around the island & has five more in preparation, including museums of historical collections, art museums & archaeological museums
Income: Financed by endowment & state appropriation
Collections: Puerto Rican art, archaeology & historical collections
Publications: Revista del Institute de Cultura Puertorriquena, quarterly
Activities: Educ dept; lect open to public; gallery talks; concerts; tours; competitions; exten dept serves cultural centers around the Island; artmobile; individual paintings & original objects of art lent to government agencies, universities & cultural centers; lending collection contains motion pictures, original art works; original prints, paintings, photographs; originates traveling exhibition; sales shop sells books, records & craft items; junior museum
M Dr Jose C Barbosa Museum & Library, Calle Dr Barbosa, No 16, Bayamtu, 00928. Tel 809-786-8115, 724-0700; *In Charge* Alexis Boscas
Open 9 AM - 5 PM. No admis fee. The house where patriot Jose Celso Barbosa was born & raised, restored to its original status as representative of a typical Puerto Rican family home of the 19th century. Contains a small library geared to children's books
Income: Financed by state appropriations
Collections: Furniture, personal objects & documents belonging to Dr Barbosa, including medical instruments, manuscripts & books
M Centro Ceremonial de Caguana, HC-03, Box 13660, Utuado, 00641-9728. Tel 809-894-7325; *Dir* Angel Perez
Open daily 8:30 AM - 5 PM. No admis fee. Caguana Indian Ceremonial Park & Mus includes the ceremonial center of the Taino Indians in Caguana, Utuado, a small town in the center of the Island, constituting the most important archeological find of the Caribbean & the most outstanding exposition of Indian primitive engineering. The plazas & walks where the Indians held their ceremonies, celebrations & games were restored & excavated to form an archaeological park. Numerous petroglyphs are exhibited in the monoliths bordering the plazas & a mus exhibits Indian objects found during the excavations at the site
Income: Financed by state appropriations

M **Museo de Arte Religioso Porta Coeli,** Ramas No 2 St, San German, 00683. Tel 809-892-5845; FAX 809-725-5608; *Adminr* Guido Barletta
Open 8:30 AM - 5 PM. No admis fee. In the first years of the 17th century the Dominican monks constructed a convent in the town of San German, with a chapel they called Porta Coeli, the convent has now disappeared, but the chapel has been restored as a valuable example of missionary architecture in America
Income: Financed by state appropriations
Collections: Paintings & sculptures from between the 11th & 19th century obtained from different churches in the island

M **Museo del Grabado Latinoamericano,** Calle San Sebastian, Plaza San Jose, PO Box 4184, 00905. Tel 809-724-1844, 724-0700
Open 8:30 AM - 4:30 PM. No admis fee. Houses representative samples of graphic art of past & contemporary Puerto Rican artists along with outstanding works of Latin American graphic engravers. Collection of prized works from the San Juan Biennial of Latin American Graphics
Income: Financed by state appropriations
Collections: Grafics; works from Orozco, Matta, Tamayo, Martorell, Alicea, Cardillo, Nevarez, Hernandez Acevedo

M **Museo y Parque Historico de Caparra,** Carretera 2, PO Box 4184, 00902-4184. Tel 809-781-4795; *Dir* Jose Bartelo
Open 8:30 AM - 4:30 PM. No admis fee. Contains ruins of Caparra, first nucleus of colonization in Puerto Rico, founded by Ponce de Leon in 1508 & 1509, now excavated & transformed into a park memorial plaques indicating the historic significance. While the restoration & excavation was being conducted, numerous objects related to the period were discovered, which are now on exhibit
Income: Financed by state appropriations
Collections: Cannons, flags, pistols, ceramics

L **Library,** Avenida Ponce de Leon 500, Puerta de Tierra, 00901. Tel 809-725-7405; FAX 809-722-9097;
Open for reference to pub, investigators & students
Library Holdings: Vols 120,000; AV — A-tapes, cassettes, fs, Kodachromes, lantern slides, motion pictures, slides, v-tapes; Other — Clipping files, exhibition catalogs, framed reproductions, manuscripts, memorabilia, original art works, pamphlets, photographs, prints, reproductions, sculpture
Collections: Pre-Columbian Archaeological Collection

M **LA CASA DEL LIBRO MUSEUM,** Cristo 255, 00901. Tel 809-723-0354; *Dir* Maria Teresa Arraras
Open Tues - Sat 11 AM - 4:30 PM. No admis fee. Estab 1955 as a mus-library devoted to the history & arts of the book & related graphic arts. Average Annual Attendance: 14,000. Mem: 350; dues $25 & up
Income: Financed by donations & state appropriation
Collections: Bibliography of graphic arts; binding; book illustration; calligraphy; early printing, especially 15th & 16th Century Spanish; modern fine printing; papermaking
Exhibitions: Gallery has displays on the first floor relating to printing and other arts of the book, such as: Editions of the Quixote, Spanish Incunables, Sevilla y El Libro Sevillano, Espana 1492, Homenajea Nebrija, Conversosy Sefarditas
Activities: Visits from school groups; students of library science & workers in graphic arts; material available, no fees; gallery talks; original objects of printing arts, material must be used on premises; originate traveling exhibitions; museum shop sells books, posters & cards

M **UNIVERSITY OF PUERTO RICO,** Museum of Anthropology, History & Art, PO Box 21908, 00931-1908. Tel 809-764-0000; *Dir* Luis Cruz Hernandez; *Cur Archaeology* Diana Lopez; *Cur Art* Flavia Marichal; *Archaeologist* Luis A Chanlatte; *Admin Asst* Ruth Rodriguez
Open Mon - Fri 9 AM - 9 PM, Sat & Sun 8 AM - 3:30 PM, cl national holidays. No admis fee. Estab 1940
Purchases: Puerto Rican graphics; paintings of past & contemporary Puerto Rican artists
Collections: Archaeology; Puerto Rican paintings of the past & present; sculpture
Exhibitions: Temporary exhibitions from the collection & from museum loans
Activities: Provide concerts; gallery talks; tours; individual paintings & original objects of art lent to organizations & museums; originate traveling exhibitions; sales shop sells books & reproductions

National and Regional Organizations In Canada

O **CANADIAN CONFERENCE OF THE ARTS,** 189 Laurier Ave E, Ottawa, ON K1N 6P1. Tel 613-238-3561; FAX 613-238-4849; Elec Mail cca@mail.culturenet.ca. *National Dir* Keith Kelly; *Librn* Sharon Griffiths
Estab 1945 as a national non-profit assoc to strengthen pub & private support to the arts & enhance the awareness of the role & value of the arts. Mem: 1223; dues individuals $25 & GST organizations based on budget; annual meeting in May
Income: Financed by mem, grants & contracts
Publications: Handbook Series: Directory of the Arts, Who Teaches What, policy papers & reports; Proscenium, quarterly
Activities: Awards-Diplome d'Honneur to persons who have contributed outstanding service to the arts in Canada; Financial Post Awards: in collaboration with The Council for Business & the Arts in Canada, encourages the corporate sector's involvement with the visual & performing arts in Canada & recognizes those corporations whose involvement is already at a high & productive level; Imperial Oil reward for Excellence in Arts Journalism; Rogers Communications Inc Media Award

O **CANADIAN CRAFTS COUNCIL,** Conseil Canadien de l'Artisanat, * 189 Laurier Ave E, Ottawa, ON K1N 6P1. Tel 613-235-8200; FAX 613-235-7425; *Pres* Jean Kares; *VPres* Ross Bradley; *VPres* Megan Broner; *Exec Dir* Peter H Weinrich
Open Mon - Fri 8:30 AM - 4:30 PM. Estab 1974 to encourage the highest quality Canadian crafts & improve standards of craftsmen through educ & information. Mem: 31 associations; annual meeting in Sept
Income: $350,000 (financed by mem & federal appropriation)
Collections: Cooperating with National Museum of Civilization
Publications: Bulletin, members only
Activities: Educ dept; lect open to pub; originate traveling exhibitions

O **CANADIAN MUSEUMS ASSOCIATION,** Association des Musees Canadiens, 280 Metcalfe St, Ste 400, Ottawa, ON K2P 1R7. Tel 613-567-0099; FAX 613-233-5438; *Pres* Candace Stevenson; *Exec Dir* John G McAvity
Estab 1947 to advance pub mus services in Canada, to promote the welfare & better administration of museums & to foster a continuing improvement in the qualifications & practices of mus professions. Mem: 2300; dues $50-$2000; annual meeting in May/June
Income: Financed by mem & government grants
Publications: Muse, quarterly; Museogramme, monthly; Official directory of Canadian Museums, occasional
Activities: Correspondence course in introductory museology; bursary program; travel grants

O **CANADIAN SOCIETY FOR EDUCATION THROUGH ART,** 1487 Parish Lane, Oakville, ON L6M 2Z6. Tel 905-847-0975; FAX 905-847-0975; *Secy General* Dr A Wilson
Estab 1955; voluntary association founded in Quebec City. Members dedicated to the advancement of art education, the publication of current thinking & action in art education & the promotion of higher standards in the teaching of art. Average Annual Attendance: 400. Mem: 700; dues professional $65 (CN)
Income: Financed by mem
Collections: Historical Canadian Art; Children's Art
Publications: Canadian Review of Art Education, 1-2 times per year; Journal, 1-2 times per year; newsletter, quarterly; special publications
Activities: Workshops; research; lect open to public; gallery talks; tours; awards; scholarships offered

O **CANADIAN SOCIETY OF PAINTERS IN WATERCOLOUR,** 258 Wallace Ave, Ste 102, Toronto, ON M6P 3M9. Tel 416-533-5100; *Pres* Margaret Squire; *Adminr* Shirley Barrie
Estab 1926 to promote watercolour painting in Canada. AIRD Gallery, MacDonald Block, Queen's Park - shared on a rotating basis with five other societies. Average Annual Attendance: 30,000. Mem: 165 & 125 associates; dues $100; annual meeting in May. Mem qualifications: recommendation by members &/or chosen for annual open exhibition plus election at annual meeting
Income: $30,000 (financed by members dues, associates, commissions on sale of work & book sales)
Collections: Diploma Collection at Art Gallery of Peel, Brampton, Ontario
Exhibitions: Annual Open Juried Exhibition; Members' Exhibitions; International Exchanges International Waters with AWS & RWS; Open Waters, annual
Publications: Aquarelle; Tri-annual newsletter
Activities: Lect open to members; competitions with awards; originate traveling exhibitions across Canada to galleries; internationally to fellow arts organizations; national watercolor weekend of demonstrations & discussions

O **THE METAL ARTS GUILD,** 80 Spadina Ave, Ste 303, Toronto, ON M5V 2J3. Tel 416-504-8453; *Adminr* Camille Anderson
Estab 1946. Gallery with changing exhibits
Exhibitions: Traveling 50th Anniversary Show at venues across Canada & one US venue
Publications: Magazine, 3 times per year

O **ORGANIZATION OF SASKATCHEWAN ARTS COUNCILS (OSAC),** 1102 Eighth Ave, Regina, SK S4R 1C9. Tel 306-586-1250; FAX 306-586-1550; *Exec Dir* Dennis Garreck; *Visual Arts Coordr* Donna Kriekle; *Performing Arts Coordr* Nan Carson; *Performing Arts Coordr* Nancy Martin; *Performing Arts Coordr* Karen Mondor
Estab 1969 to tour exhibitions of Saskatchewan artists work & tour performers from across Canada, US & of international stature. Mem: 60; meetings in June & Oct
Library Holdings: Vols 175; Per subs 10; AV — A-tapes, cassettes, Kodachromes, rec, slides, v-tapes; Other — Clipping files, exhibition catalogs, manuscripts, pamphlets, reproductions
Activities: Classes for adults & children; dramatic programs; docent training; lectures open to public; exten dept serves lending collection

O **PROFESSIONAL ART DEALERS ASSOCIATION OF CANADA,** 80 Spadina Ave, Ste 307, Toronto, ON M5V 2J3. Tel 416-703-0061; FAX 416-703-0063; Elec Mail padacadm@sympatico.ca. *Pres* Fela Grunwald; *VPres* David Tuck; *Treas* Ian Muncaster; *Exec Adminr* Asha Croggon
Estab 1966 for the promotion of art & artists of merit in Canada. Mem: 59, members must have five years in operation plus approved reputation, general exhibitions, financial integrity; dues $500; annual meeting May
Income: Financed by mem & appraisal fees
Publications: Benefits of donation brochure; general information brochure; membership directory; print brochure
Activities: Scholarships offered

O **QUICKDRAW ANIMATION SOCIETY,** 209 Eighth Ave SW, Ste 300, Calgary, AB T2P 1B8. Tel 403-261-5767; *Pres* Kevin Kurytnik
Open Tues - Sat 10 AM - 4:30 PM. Estab 1984 to promote study of animation & provide equipment for the production of independent animated film. Mem: 30; dues $20; annual meeting in Apr
Income: $50,000 (financed by endowment, mem & state appropriation)
Purchases: $5000
Exhibitions: Animated film festivals
Publications: Pegbar, quarterly
Activities: Classes for adults & children; lect open to public, 1 vis lectr per year; competitions with awards; lending collection contains books, videotapes, equipment for use in animated film

O **ROYAL ARCHITECTURAL INSTITUTE OF CANADA,** 55 Murray St, Ste 330, Ottawa, ON K1N 5M3. Tel 613-241-3600; FAX 613-241-5750; *Chief Admin Officer* Tim Kehoe
Open 9 AM - 5 PM. Estab 1908 to promote a knowledge & appreciation of architecture & of the architectural profession in Canada & to represent the interests of Canadian architects. Mem: 3000; mem open to architectural graduates; dues $214
Publications: RAIC Directory, annually
Activities: Lect open to public; awards given; scholarships offered
L **Library,** 55 Murray St, K1N 5M3. Tel 613-241-3600
Library Holdings: Vols 200
Special Subjects: Architecture

O **ROYAL CANADIAN ACADEMY OF ARTS,** 401 Richmond St W, Ste 375, Toronto, ON M5V 3A8. Tel 416-408-2718; FAX 416-408-2718; *Pres* Ernest Annau; *VPres* Don Vaughan
Estab 1880 to better the visual arts field in Canada through exhibitions, assistance to young artists & to museums. Mem: 550; honor soc; mem open to visual artists who demonstrated excellence in their own medium; dues $200; annual meeting in Apr
Income: Nonprofit assoc financed by mem & donations
Exhibitions: Special exhibitions of the History of the Royal Canadian Academy 1880-1980; national, multi-disciplined, juried exhibition
Publications: Passionate Spirits: A History of the Royal Canadian Academy of Arts 1880-1980; limited edition of original prints
Activities: Originate traveling exhibitions

O **SASKATCHEWAN ARTS BOARD,** 3475 Albert St, Regina, SK S4S 6X6. Tel 306-787-4056; FAX 306-787-4199; *Exec Dir* Valerie Creighton
Open 8 AM - 4:30 PM. Estab 1948 as an autonomous agency for promotion & development of the arts in Saskatchewan; Board is composed of 7-15 appointed members whose major concern at the present time is the support & development of professionals & professional standards within the province
Income: Financed by annual provincial government grant
Collections: †Permanent collection containing over 1000 works by Saskatchewan artists & artisans only, dating from 1950 to present; part of collection hangs in the Saskatchewan Centre of the Arts, Regina
Publications: Annual Report; brochures for Saskatchewan School of the Arts classes; services & programs brochure

Activities: Programs include individual & group assistance grants; workshop assistance; aid for exhibitions; community assistance for the performing arts; script reading service; play-script duplication subsidy; community artists program; consultative services; operates Saskatchewan School of the Arts at Echo Valley Centre, summer classes for young people are offered in a wide variety of crafts, visual & performing arts

O **SCULPTOR'S SOCIETY OF CANADA,** * 2 First Canadian Pl, 130 King St W, Toronto, ON M5R 3A8. Tel 416-214-0389; *Pres* Andrew Pawlowski; *Treas* Herman Falke
Estab 1928 to promote the art of sculpture, to present exhibitions (some to travel internationally), to educate the public about sculpture. Mem: 108; to qualify for mem, sculptors must submit photos of work for jury approval; dues $45; 2 general meetings per yr, exec committee meetings, 6 per yr
Income: $10,000 (financed by mem, provincial appropriation & sales commission)
Collections: 150 pieces representing all sculpture media
Exhibitions: Sculptures for the Eighties; McMichael Canadian Collection; Member Show; Canadian National Exhibition
Publications: Exhibition catalogues
Activities: Workshops

O **SIAS INTERNATIONAL ART SOCIETY,** 253-52152 Range Rd 210 (Mailing add: PO Box 3039, Sherwood Park, AB T8A 2A6). Tel 403-922-5463; *Managing Dir* Dr Klaus Bous; *Assoc Dir* Horacio Venancio; *Assoc Dir* Doria Venancio
Admis fee $25. Estab 1986 to promote unity of art, science & humanity & to promote interrealism

Collections: †Prem Bio chemistry of Canada; †SIAS International Art Society; Ernst Fuchs, Wolfgang Hutter, Rud Hausner (engravings); Claus Cumpel (oil paintings)
Publications: Creativity from the Sub conscious; The Art of Claus Cumpel (monograph)

L **Library,** PO Box 3039, T8A 2A6. Tel 403-922-5463;
Income: $56,000 (financed by mem & sponsors)
Library Holdings: Vols 981; Per subs 11; AV — Cassettes, motion pictures, rec, slides, v-tapes; Other — Manuscripts, original art works, photographs, prints, reproductions
Special Subjects: American Indian Art, Art Education, Etchings & Engravings, Film, Graphic Arts, Manuscripts, Mixed Media, Painting - European, Painting - German, Photography, Portraits, Religious Art, Reproductions, Woodcuts

O **SOCIETY OF CANADIAN ARTISTS,** 1435 Woodvine Ave, Toronto, ON M4C 4G8. Tel 416-429-3592; *Pres* George Sanders; *Shows* Elizabeth Elliott; *Treas* Margaret Nurse
Estab in 1957 as the Soc of Cooperative Artists & operated the first cooperative gallery in Toronto. In 1967 the name was changed to the Soc of Canadian Artists and the gallery moved to larger premises. In 1968 the members elected to give up the gallery and concentrate on organizing group art shows for members in galleries across Canada. Mem: 120, mem by jury, open to artists throughout Canada
Income: Financed by mem, community fundraisings and commissions
Publications: Two Decades, members' biographical catalog; quarterly newsletter
Activities: Sponsorship of art conferences & workshops; promotion of Canadian artists; originate traveling exhibitions

Museums, Libraries and Associations In Canada

ALBERTA

BANFF

M BANFF CENTRE, Walter Phillips Gallery, PO Box 1020, Sta 14, T0L 0C0. Tel 403-762-6281; FAX 403-762-6659; *Dir & Cur* Catherine Crowston; *Admin Coordr* Heather Klassen; *Preparator* Mimmo Maiolo
Open Tues - Sun Noon - 5 PM, cl Mon. No admis fee. Estab 1977 to serve the community & artists in the visual arts program at The Banff Centre, School of Fine Arts. Contemporary exhibits are presented. Gallery is 15.24 x 21.34 m with 60.96 m of running space. Average Annual Attendance: 20,000
Income: Financed by provincial & public funding
Collections: Walter J Phillips Collection; permanent collection of artwork in various media by artists making a significant contribution to contemporary art
Publications: Exhibition catalogs
Activities: Lect open to public; concerts; gallery talks; tours; original objects of art lent to other galleries & museums; book traveling exhibitions 1 per year; originate traveling exhibitions to Canadian & international galleries
L Centre for the Arts Library, PO Box 1020, Sta 14, T0L 0C0. Tel 403-762-6265; FAX 403-762-6266; *Dir* Bob Foley; *Managing Librn* Patrick Lawless
Open daily 9 AM - 9 PM. For reference only
Library Holdings: Vols 32,000; Per subs 200; Micro — Fiche; AV — Cassettes, rec 11,000, slides 27,000, v-tapes 1100; Other — Exhibition catalogs
Special Subjects: Aesthetics, Architecture, Art Education, Conceptual Art, Costume Design & Construction, Film, Furniture, Intermedia, Painting - American, Painting - Canadian, Photography, Pottery, Primitive Art

M PETER & CATHARINE WHYTE FOUNDATION, Whyte Museum of the Canadian Rockies, 111 Bear St (Mailing add: PO Box 160, T0L 0C0). Tel 403-762-2291; FAX 403-762-8919; Elec Mail wmcr@banff.net. *Pres* Bernadette MacDonald; *Dir* E J Hart; *Assoc Dir* Douglas Leonard; *Art Cur* Katherine Lipsett; *Archives* Donald Bourdon
Open winter Tues - Sat 1 - 5 PM, Thurs 1 - 9 PM, summer 10 AM - 6 PM, Archives open Mon 1 - 5 PM, Sat mornings by appointment only. Admis adults $3, students & senior $2, children under 12 free. Estab 1968 to preserve & collect materials of importance in the Canadian Rocky Mountain regions; to exhibit, publish & make material available for research study & appreciation. Gallery consists of three main areas: the 2 large main galleries & the Elizabeth Rummel Room upstairs. Average Annual Attendance: 50,000. Mem: 600; dues $25
Income: Financed by endowment, federal & provincial special activities grants, private fundings, admis & sales
Collections: †Historical & contemporary art by artists of the Canadian Rockies; art relating to or influenced by the region
Exhibitions: Approximately 20 per year: local, regional, national & international interest; ceramics, paintings, photographs, sculpture, textiles both historic & contemporary
Publications: The Cairn, 3 times per year; gallery calendars, tri-annual
Activities: Classes for adults & children; dramatic training; lect open to public, 20 vis lectr per year; concerts; gallery talks; tours; films; individual paintings & original objects of art lent to certified museums & art galleries; book traveling exhibitions; originate travel exhibitions to other certified museums & art galleries; sales shop sells books, reproductions, note cards

CALGARY

M ALBERTA COLLEGE OF ART & DESIGN, Illingworth Kerr Gallery, 1407 14th Ave NW, T2N 4R3. Tel 403-284-7632; FAX 403-289-6682; Elec Mail ron.moppett@acad.ab.ca. *Dir & Cur* Ron Moppett; *Asst Cur* Richard Gordon; *Technician* Mark Dicey
Open Tues - Sat 10 AM - 6 PM. No admis fee. Estab 1958 as an academic-didactic function plus general visual art exhibition service to pub. Two galleries: 425 sq meters of floor space; 125 meters running wall space; full atmospheric & security controls. Average Annual Attendance: 20,000
Collections: †Permanent collection of ceramics, graphics, paintings, photography, student honors work
Exhibitions: Contemporary art in all media by regional, national & international artists
Publications: Exhibition catalogs; posters
Activities: Lect open to public, 20 vis lectr per year; gallery talks; individual paintings & objects of art lent to other galleries; lending collection contains original art works; book traveling exhibitions 3-4 per year
L Luke Lindoe Library, 1407 14th Ave NW, T2N 4R3. Tel 403-284-7631; FAX 403-289-6682; Elec Mail christine.sammon@acad.ab.ca. *Library Dir* Christine E Sammon
Open Mon - Thurs 8:15 AM - 10 PM, Fri 8:15 AM - 4:30 PM, Sat 11 AM - 5

PM. Estab 1972 to support both college academic & studio programs. Circ 45,000. Mem: $15 annual fee for community borrowers
Purchases: $50,000
Library Holdings: Vols 21,000; Per subs 80; AV — Cassettes, fs, lantern slides, motion pictures, slides 98,000, v-tapes; Other — Clipping files, exhibition catalogs, reproductions
Special Subjects: Advertising Design, Aesthetics, Antiquities-Assyrian, Architecture, Art Education, Art History, Commercial Art, Drawings, Etchings & Engravings, Glass, Goldsmithing, Illustration, Metalwork, Painting - American, Photography
Activities: Lect open to public, 25 vis lectr per year; concerts; gallery talks; competitions; individual & original objects of art lent to galleries

A ALBERTA SOCIETY OF ARTISTS, 5151 Third St SE,Ste 147, T2H 2X6. Tel 403-640-4542; *Pres* Elizabeth Allen
Estab 1926 as an association of professional artists designed to foster and promote the development of visual and plastic fine arts primarily within the province. Mem: Approx 100; dues $15; annual meeting May
Publications: Highlights (newsletter), bimonthly

M CALGARY CONTEMPORARY ARTS SOCIETY, Triangle Gallery of Visual Arts, 800 Macleod Trail SE, Ste 104, T2G 2M3. Tel 403-262-1737; FAX 403-262-1764; *Gallery Mgr* Alan Duffy
Open Mon - Fri 11 AM - 5 PM, Sat Noon - 4 PM. Estab 1988 to exhibit contemporary art in all media & provide extension programs for pub. 3500 sq ft adjacent to municipal hall. Average Annual Attendance: 17,000. Mem: 500; dues $15; annual meeting in Nov
Income: $150,000 (financed by mem, city & state appropriation, corporate & private donations, fundraising events)
Collections: Artist circle, donated works
Exhibitions: Alberta Glass, Irene McCaugherty, retrospective, Calgary Aboriginal exhibition, sculpture; Children's Christmas Show
Publications: Update, monthly newsletter; exhibition brochures & catalogs
Activities: Docent training; workshops; lect open to public, 20-30 vis lectr per year; performances; exten servs provides paintings & art rentals; book traveling exhibitions 3-6 times a year

L CALGARY PUBLIC LIBRARY, Arts & Recreation Dept, 616 Macleod Trail SE, T2G 2M2. Tel 403-260-2780; FAX 403-262-5929; *Mgr Arts & Recreation* Gail Anderson
Open Mon - Thurs 9 AM - 9 PM, Fri & Sat 9 AM - 5 PM. Estab to provide information & recreational materials for the general public
Purchases: $80,000
Library Holdings: Vols 85,000; Per subs 250; AV — Motion pictures, rec; Other — Clipping files, exhibition catalogs
Special Subjects: American Indian Art, American Western Art, Architecture, Art History, Crafts, Fashion Arts, Film, Graphic Arts, Painting - Canadian, Photography, Theatre Arts, Video
Collections: Clipping files on local artists

M GLENBOW MUSEUM, 130 Ninth Ave SE, T2G 0P3. Tel 403-268-4100; FAX 403-265-9769; Elec Mail glenbow.lexicom.ab.ca. Telex 03-825523. *Chmn Board* Sherrold Moore; *Pres* Dr R Janes; *VPres Coll* Patricia Ainslie; *Cur Art* Cathy Mastin; *Cur Cultural History* Sandra Morton Weizman; *Cur Ethnology* Gerald Conaty; *VPres Prog Exhib* Donna Livingstone; *Mgr Mus Shop* Connie Smith; *Pub Relations* John Gilchrist
Open Tues - Sun 9 AM - 5 PM, cl Mon, Summer, open daily. Admis adults $5, students & sr citizens $3.50, children under 7 with adult free. Estab 1966 for art, books, documents, Indian & pioneer artifacts that lead to the preservation & better understanding of the history of western Canada. Mus has three exhibition floors; 93,000 sq ft of exhibition space. Average Annual Attendance: 200,000. Mem: 5000; dues family $35, individual $25, sr citizen $15, student $10
Income: $6,800,000 (financed by endowment, provincial & federal appropriation)
Purchases: $100,000
Collections: †Art: Representative collections of Canadian historical & contemporary art; large collection of natural history illustration & works of art on paper; †Ethnology: Large collection of material relating to Plains Indians; representative holdings from Africa, Australia, Oceania, Central & South America, Inuit & Northwest Coast; †Library & Archives: Western Canadian historical books, manuscripts & photographs
Exhibitions: (1997) The Canadian Cowboy. (1997-98) Communities. (1998) Youth
Publications: Chautauqua in Canada; Max Ernst; Four Modern Masters; exhibition catalogs
Activities: Classes for adults & children; dramatic programs; docent training; lect open to public; gallery talks; tours; exten dept; individual paintings & original objects of art lent to public museums & galleries; lending collection contains 15,000 works on paper, 5000 paintings, sculpture & 5000 items of decorative art; book traveling exhibitions 25 per year; originate traveling exhibitions; museum shop sells books, magazines, reproductions & prints

L Library, 130 Ninth Ave SE, T2G 0P3. Tel 403-268-4197; FAX 403-232-6569; Elec Mail glenbow@lexicom.ab.ca. *Archivist* Doug Cass; *Librn* Lindsay Moir
Open for reference
Income: Financed by endowment & government of Alberta
Library Holdings: Vols 90,000; Per subs 500; Micro — Cards, fiche, reels; Other — Clipping files, exhibition catalogs, pamphlets
Special Subjects: Illustration, Manuscripts, Maps, Painting - British, Painting - Canadian, Printmaking, Prints, Textiles
Collections: †Western Canadian Art

M MUSEUM OF MOVIE ART, 3600 21st St NE, No 9, T2E 6B6. Tel 403-250-7588; FAX 403-250-7589; Elec Mail 103075.526@compuserve.com. *General Mgr* Sol Candel
Open Tues - Fri 9:30 AM - 5:30 PM. No admis fee. Estab 1950. Average Annual Attendance: 1000
Purchases: $58,000
Collections: Consolidated Theatre Services; Federal Estate (Gaiety Theatre)
Publications: Catalogue
Activities: Retail store sells prints & original movie posters

M MUTTART PUBLIC ART GALLERY, 1221 Second St SW, T2R 0W5. Tel 403-266-2764; FAX 403-264-8077; Internet Home Page Address http://www.ffa.ucalgary.ca.muttart/. *Dir & Cur* Kathryn Burns; *Mgr Develop & Marketing* Sherry Robertson; *Treas* Marilyn Olson
Open Mon - Wed & Fri Noon - 5 PM, Thurs 2 - 8 PM, Sat 10 AM - 5 PM. No admis fee. Estab 1978 to exhibit the works of emerging & estab western Canadian artists. Top floor of the restored Memorial Park Library (old Carnegie Library). Average Annual Attendance: 90,000. Mem: 500; dues family $30, individual $20, students & seniors $15; annual meeting in Apr
Income: $550,000 (financed by mem, city & provincial appropriation, grants, private donations & corporate funds)
Exhibitions: (1997) The Sound of Art; To Co-Existence of Opposites; New Artists/New Works; Off The Wall Accompanying Exhibition; Travelling Exhibition Summer Showcase; Symbols of Humanity; Impact of Technology; Joane Cardinal-Schubert: Two Decades/The Muttart: Two Decades; Educators' Choice: Character & Identity; Christmas Salon Show & Sale
Publications: Quarterly exhibit catalogues; quarterly newsletter; semiannual exhibition brochures
Activities: Classes for adults & children; professional development; lect open to public, 10 vis lectr per year; gallery talks; tours; family days; art appreciation club; exten dept serves city of Calgary; book traveling exhibitions 6 per year; originate traveling exhibitions to Southern Alberta; sales shop sells books, t-shirts & cards

C NOVA CORPORATION OF ALBERTA, NOVA Garden Court Gallery, 801 Seventh Ave SW, T2P 3P7. Tel 403-290-6000; Telex 038-21503.
Open Mon - Fri 8 AM - 6 PM. Estab 1982 to provide employees & general public exposure to a variety of art. Coporate gallery space used for both in-house & outside group temporary exhibitions
Collections: †Mostly contemporary art prints & paintings, with emphasis on Canadian artists
Exhibitions: Canadian Association of Photographers & Illustrators in Communication Show; John Snow Exhibition
Activities: Individual paintings lent; book traveling exhibitions

C PETRO-CANADA, Corporate Art Programme, PO Box 2844, T2P 3E3. Tel 403-296-6019; FAX 403-296-4990; *Art Cur* Pauline Lindland
Estab 1984 for encouragement of Canadian art
Income: $120,000 (financed by corporation)
Collections: †1600 Two-dimensional works in all media by contemporary Canadian artists

QUICKDRAW ANIMATION SOCIETY
For further information, see National and Regional Organizations

C SHELL CANADA LTD, 400 Fourth Ave SW, PO Box 100, Sta M, T2P 2H5. Tel 403-691-3111; FAX 403-691-3099; *Coordr Coll* Myrna Ichelson
Collections: Works of contemporary Canadian artists with media concentrations in painting, sculpture, graphics, photography, mixed media & works on paper

M UNIVERSITY OF CALGARY, The Nickle Arts Museum, 2500 University Dr NW, T2N 1N4. Tel 403-220-7234; FAX 403-282-4742; Elec Mail nickle@acs.ucalgary.ca;
Internet Home Page Address http://www.ucalgary.ca/-nickle. *Dir* Ann Davis; *Curatorial Asst (Art)* Elizabeth Clark; *Curatorial Asst (Numismatics)* Geraldine Russell; *Curatorial Asst (Art)* Christine Sowiak
Open Tues - Fri 10 AM - 5 PM, Sat & Sun 1 - 5 PM, cl Mon & holidays. Admis adults $2, children & senior citizens $1, students of institutions of higher learning, children under 6 & Tues free. Estab 1970, an Alberta pioneer, Samuel C Nickle, gave the University a gift of one million dollars & the mus was opened in 1979. His son, Carl O Nickle, presented the University with an immensely valuable collection of some 10,000 ancient coins, covering over 1500 years of human history which is housed in the Numismatics dept of the mus. Mus houses the permanent collection of the University; exhibitions are presented on a continuous basis in the gallery on the main floor (15,000 sq ft). A smaller numismatic gallery displays a permanent collection. The smaller Teaching Gallery on the second floor (1500 sq ft) is used for small exhibitions, lectures, films & seminars. Average Annual Attendance: 25,000. Mem: 200; dues $10-$40
Income: Financed by state appropriation through the University, donations, earned income & grants
Purchases: $15,000
Collections: Ceramics; †contemporary paintings; †drawings; †photography, †prints; sculpture; †watercolors
Exhibitions: Local, national & international exhibitions are presented on a continuous basis
Publications: Exhibition catalogs

Activities: Classes for adults; university museology program; lect open to public, 10-20 vis lectr per year; gallery talks; individual paintings & original objects of art lent to other museums & art galleries; book traveling exhibitions 3-6 per year; originate traveling exhibitions; museum shop sells books, magazines, original art, reproductions, prints, jewerly, crafts, gift items & exhibition catalogues

L Faculty of Environmental Design, 2500 University Dr, ES 951, T2N 1N4. Tel 403-220-6815; *Dir* Ann Davis
Open Mon - Fri 9:30 AM - 4:30 PM. Estab 1973 as a resource facility for students & faculty in 4 program areas: architecture, urban planning, industrial design & environmental science. Small gallery for display of student works & traveling exhibitions; workshop; photo lab facilities
Library Holdings: Vols 500; Per subs 30; Drawings; Models; AV — A-tapes, cassettes, slides, v-tapes; Other — Manuscripts, memorabilia
Special Subjects: Architecture, Interior Design, Industrial Design

CZAR

M SHORNCLIFFE PARK IMPROVEMENT ASSOC, Prairie Panorama Museum, PO Box 60, T0B 0Z0. Tel 403-857-2155; *Cur* Helena Lawrason
Open Sun 2 - 6 PM, other days by appointment. Estab 1963 for the enjoyment of the public. Average Annual Attendance: 580
Income: Finances by government grant &donations
Collections: Indian artifacts, clothing, tools, dolls, books; Salt & Pepper Collection
Activities: Classes for children

EDMONTON

A ALBERTA FOUNDATION FOR THE ARTS, Beaver House, 5th Flr, 10158 103rd St, T5J 0X6. Tel 403-427-9968; FAX 403-422-0398; *Chmn* John C Osler; *Exec Dir* Clive Padfield; *Arts Develop Officer* Ross Bradley
Open Mon - Fri 8:15 AM - 4:30 PM. No admis fee. Estab 1972 to collect & to exhibit art works produced by Alberta artists; to provide financial assistance to Alberta public, institutional & commercial art galleries, art groups & organizations for programs & special projects
Income: Financed by Alberta Lotteries
Collections: Alberta Foundation for the Arts Collection
Exhibitions: Exhibits are provided through a consortium of Alberta public galleries. The programs vary from year to year & from region to region Spaces & Places; Little by Little
Publications: Annual Report; exhibition catalogs
Activities: Acquisition of art works by Alberta artists; exhibition program in and outside Canada; Jon Whyte Memorial Prize, Tommy Banks Award; scholarships & fels offered; individual paintings & original objects of art lent to public government buildings; book traveling exhibitions; sales shop sells books

DEPARTMENT OF COMMUNITY DEVELOPMENT
M Provincial Museum of Alberta, 12845 102nd Ave, T5N 0M6. Tel 403-453-9100; FAX 403-454-6629; *Dir* Dr Philip H R Stepney; *Asst Dir Exhibits & Visitor Servs* Don Clevett; *Asst Dir Natural History & Coll Admin* Dr Bruce McGillivray; *Asst Dir Operations* Tim Willis; *Asst Dir Archaelogy & Ethnology* Dr Jack Ives
Open summer 9 AM - 8 PM, winter Tues - Sun 9 AM - 5 PM. cl Mon. Admis fee. Estab 1967 to preserve & interpret the human & natural history of the Alberta region. Four major exhibit areas divided equally into human & natural history under broad themes of settlement history, archaelogy & anthropology, natural history & habitats. Average Annual Attendance: 325,000. Mem: 1200; dues $12-$19; annual meeting in June
Income: $3,900,000 (financed by provincial government, mus shop, facility rentals, programs, special exhibits)
Purchases: $54,000
Collections: Archaeological, †ethnographical; †fine & decorative arts; folk life; †geology; historical; invertebrate zoology; mammalogy; palaeontology; †ornithology: †vascular & non vascular plants
Exhibitions: Approx 10 feature exhibits
Publications: Occasional papers; occasional series; publ series; exhibit catalogs; teacher guides
Activities: Classes for children; dramatic programs; docent training; lect open to public, 6-20 vis lectr per year; gallery talks; tours; exten dept serves western Canada; individual paintings & original objects of art lent to other museums; originate traveling exhibitions to members of Alberta Exhibit Network; other museums in Canada, occasional exhibits in Japan; museum shop sells books, children's articles, jewelry, logo pins, original art, reproductions, prints, slides & t-shirts

L Provincial Archives of Alberta, 12845 102nd Ave, T5N 0M6. Tel 403-427-1750; FAX 403-427-4646; *Provincial Archivist* David Leonard; *Sr A-V Archivist* Marlena Wyman
Open Mon - Fri 9 AM - 4:30 PM, Tues & Wed evening until 9 PM, Sat 9 AM - 1 PM. Estab 1967 to identify, evaluate, acquire, preserve, arrange & describe & subsequently make available for pub research, reference & display those diversified primary & secondary sources that document & relate to the overall history & development of Alberta. For reference only
Income: Financed by provincial appropriation
Purchases: $73,000
Library Holdings: Vols 10,000; Per subs 100; Original documents; Micro — Fiche, reels; AV — A-tapes, cassettes, motion pictures, rec, slides; Other — Clipping files, manuscripts, original art works, pamphlets, photographs, prints
Special Subjects: Ethno-culture, Genealogy, Immigration, Land Settlement, Local History, Religious Archives
Exhibitions: Several small displays each year highlighting recent accessions or historical themes; periodic major exhibitions
Publications: Exhibition catalogues; guides to collections; information leaflets; occasional papers

M **EDMONTON ART GALLERY,** 2 Sir Winston Churchill Sq, T5J 2C1. Tel 403-422-6223; FAX 403-426-3105; *Exec Dir* Vincent J Varga
Open Mon, Tues & Sat 10:30 AM - 5 PM, Thurs & Fri 10:30 AM - 8 PM, Sun & holidays 11 AM - 5 PM, cl New Year's & Christmas. Admis adults $3, senior citizens & students, $1.50, members & children 12 & under free. Estab 1924 to collect & exhibit paintings, sculptures, photographs & other works of visual art & to teach art appreciation. Gallery covers 45,000 sq ft; exhibition area 20,000 sq ft. Average Annual Attendance: 180,000. Mem: 2000; dues $40
Income: $2,000,000 (financed by donations, fees, mem, municipal, provincial & federal grants)
Purchases: $119,000
Collections: †Contemporary Canadian art; †contemporary & historical photography; †contemporary international art; †historical Canadian art; historical European & American art
Exhibitions: 29 in-house exhibitions & 23 extension shows
Publications: Outlook magazine, quarterly; exhibition catalogues
Activities: Classes for adults & children; docent training; lect open to public, 3-5 vis lectr per year; gallery talks; tours; exten dept serves Province of Alberta; individual paintings & original objects of art lent to other public institutions & galleries; lending collection contains 4000 works of art-painting, drawings, prints, sculptures & photographs; book traveling exhibitions; traveling exhibitions organized & circulated; museum shop sells books, magazines, original art, reproductions, prints, jewelry, novelties & craft items
L **Library,** 2 Sir Winston Churchill Sq, T5J 2C1. Tel 403-422-6223; FAX 403-426-3105; *Exec Dir* Vincent J Varga
Open Tues. Estab 1924. Maintained by volunteer staff. Reference library open to researchers only
Library Holdings: Vols 10,000; Per subs 38; Micro — Fiche, reels; AV — Cassettes, slides 17,000; v-tapes 150; Other — Clipping files, exhibition catalogs, sculpture 70,000
Special Subjects: Art History, Painting - American, Painting - Canadian, Portraits, Printmaking, Religious Art, Sculpture, Video, Watercolors, Woodcuts, Canadian Art History, Western Canada
Publications: Outlook Magazine, quarterly
Activities: Classes for adults & children; docent training; lect open to public; concerts; gallery talks; tours; original objects of art lent to members & non-members; originate traveling exhibitions circulating to Alberta & other Canadian areas; museum shop sells books, magazines, prints, jewelry, toys, handicrafts

L **EDMONTON PUBLIC LIBRARY,** Foyer Gallery, 7 Sir Winston Churchill Sq, T5J 2V4. Tel 403-496-7000; *Coordr* Sherri Ritchie
Open Mon - Fri 9 AM - 9 PM, Sat 9 AM - 6 PM, Sun 1 - 5 PM. Foyer Gallery has 120 running ft with 420 sq ft of floor space
Exhibitions: Twelve exhibitions per year

A **LATITUDE 53 SOCIETY OF ARTISTS,** 10137 104th St, T5J 0Z9. Tel 403-423-5353; *Pres* Nick Dobson; *Gallery Adminr* Jain Kurany
Open Tues - Fri 10 AM - 5 PM, Sat 11 AM - 5 PM, cl Sun & Mon. No admis fee. Estab 1973 to encourage & promote the artistic endeavours of contemporary artists & to build a public awareness of current & experimental cultural developments. Visual, installations, performance & fibre art. Resource center for grants & contracts. Average Annual Attendance: 2000. Mem: 300; dues $20; annual meeting third Mon in Oct
Income: $165,000 (financed by grants, donations, public & private funding, mem & fundraising events)
Publications: Exhibition catalogues
Activities: Lect open to public, 8 vis lectr per year; concerts; gallery talks; tours; book traveling exhibitions 10 per year; originate traveling exhibitions for other art centers

M **UKRAINIAN CANADIAN ARCHIVES & MUSEUM OF ALBERTA,** 9543 110th Ave, T5H 1H3. Tel 403-424-7580; *Pres* Khrystyna Jendyk; *Spec Project Dir* Alexandra Makar
Open Tues - Fri 10 AM - 5 PM, Sat Noon - 5 PM, cl Mon & Sun. No admis fee. Estab 1941
Collections: Drawings, historical material, national costumes, paintings, prints, sculpture & textiles
Activities: Guided tours; displays

FORT SASKATCHEWAN

L **FORT SASKATCHEWAN MUNICIPAL LIBRARY,** 10011 102nd St, T8L 2C5. Tel 403-998-4275
Open winter Mon, Tues & Thurs Noon - 9 PM, Wed & Fri 10 AM - 6 PM, Sat & Sun 1 - 5 PM, cl Sun in summer. Estab 1980 as a gallery available for local artists & for interested citizens. Exhibit Room has 78 running ft of exhibition space & a floor space of approximately 731 sq ft
Income: Financed by town grant, provincial grant, fees & fines
Library Holdings: Vols 50,000; Per subs 100

GRANDE PRAIRIE

M **PRAIRIE ART GALLERY,** 10209 99th St, T8V 2H3. Tel 403-532-8111; FAX 403-539-9522; *Dir & Cur* Laura Van Hauen; *Educator* John Kerl; *Technician* Carrie Klukas; *Admin Asst* Rachelle Himer
Open Mon - Fri 10 AM - 6 PM, Sat & Sun 1 - 5 PM. No admis fee. Estab 1975 for exhibitions. Maintains reference library. Average Annual Attendance: 36,000. Mem: 285; dues presidents council $400, patron $399, supporter $60-$99, family $40, individual $25; annual meeting in Mar
Income: $360,000 (financed by mem, city appropriation, provincial & federal government grants)
Collections: Alberta Art; Contemporary Western Canadian Art
Activities: Classes for adults & children; docent training; lect open to public, 8 vis lectr per year; gallery talks; tours; competitions with prizes; scholarships offered; exten dept serves Northwest Quadrant of Alberta; individual paintings & original objects of art lent to commercial companies, public institutions & individuals; lending collection contains books, original art works, original prints, paintings; book traveling exhibitions 10 per year; originate traveling exhibitions; sales shop sells books, jewelry, exhibition catalogues, crafts

LETHBRIDGE

A **ALLIED ARTS COUNCIL OF LETHBRIDGE,** Bowman Arts Center, 811 Fifth Ave S, T1J 0V2. Tel 403-327-2813; FAX 403-327-6118; *Pres* Birthe Perry; *Exec Dir* Shirley Wyngaard
Open Mon - Fri 10 AM - 9 PM, Sat & Sun 1 - 5 PM. No admis fee. Estab 1958 to encourage & foster cultural activities in Lethbridge, to provide facilities for such cultural activities & to promote the work of Alberta & western Canadian artists. Average Annual Attendance: 20,000. Mem: 300; dues $15; annual meeting in Feb
Income: $67,000 (financed by mem & city appropriation, Alberta Culture granting & fundraising)
Exhibitions: Local & regional exhibitions: Children's art, fabric makers, painters, potters; one-man shows: Paintings, photography, prints, sculpture, silversmithing; provincial government traveling exhibits
Publications: Calendar of Arts, weekly
Activities: Classes for adults & children; dramatic programs; concerts; competitions; scholarships offered; traveling exhibitions organized & circulated; sales shop sells original art

M **CITY OF LETHBRIDGE,** Sir Alexander Galt Museum, c/o City of Lethbridge, 910 Fourth Ave S, T1J 0P6. Tel 403-320-3898 (mus), 329-7302 (archives); *Mus Supv* M Cecile McCleary; *Display Artist* Brad Brown
Open daily July & Aug, cl statutory holidays Sept - June. No admis fee. Estab 1964 to promote the study of human history in southern Alberta. Five Galleries; One gallery is for community use; 800 sq ft & 100 ft running wall space. Average Annual Attendance: 25,000
Income: $247,000
Collections: Historical artifact collection; Archives Collection--photos, manuscripts, books, tapes, films
Activities: Children's classes; docent programs; lect open to public, 10 vis lectr per year; tours; book traveling exhibitions 8 per year; originate traveling exhibitions to area schools, institutions, fairs; museum shop sells books & locally handcrafted items

L **LETHBRIDGE COMMUNITY COLLEGE,** Buchanan Library, 3000 College Dr S, T1K 1L6. Tel 403-320-3352; FAX 403-320-1461; *Mgr Library Servs* Kathy Lea; *Info Servs Librn* Fran Noone
Open Mon - Thurs 8 AM - 10 PM, Fri 8 AM - 5 PM, Sat 1 - 5 PM, Sun 1 - 6:30 PM. No admis fee. Estab 1978 in memory of the Hon W A Buchanan & Mrs Buchanan. Gallery consists of 183.41 running ft of wall space in the Buchanan Library
Collections: Canadian Perspectives Collection

L **LETHBRIDGE PUBLIC LIBRARY,** Art Gallery, 810 Fifth Ave S, T1J 4C4. Tel 403-380-7340; FAX 403-329-1478; *Librn* Duncan Rand
Open Mon - Fri 9:30 AM - 9 PM, Sat 9:30 AM - 5 PM, Sun 1:30 - 5:30 PM. No admis fee. Estab 1974 to expand human experience, to encourage people to look at art as well as read & attend library programs. Theatre gallery 4000 sq ft wall space for each exhibit, 150 linear ft wall space. Average Annual Attendance: 8000
Library Holdings: Vols 193,243; Per subs 500
Activities: Lect open to public, 8-10 vis lectr per year; tours; lending collection contains 250,000 books, 250,000 cassettes, CDs & talking books; book traveling exhibitions 6 per year; Originate traveling exhibitions

M **SOUTHERN ALBERTA ART GALLERY,** 601 Third Ave S, T1J 0H4. Tel 403-327-8770; FAX 403-328-3913; *Pres* Garry Kaye; *VPres* Eric Hillman; *Dir & Cur* Joan Stebbins; *Pub Prog Cur* Anine Vonkeman
Open Tues - Sat 10 AM - 5 PM, Mon 3 - 8 PM, Sun 1 - 5 PM. No admis fee. Estab 1975 to present historical & contemporary art programs designed to further the process of art appreciation. Three gallery spaces contained in historical Lethbridge building remodelled as art gallery. Average Annual Attendance: 30,000. Mem: 325; dues family $35, single $20; meeting Feb 15
Income: Financed by mem, city, provincial & federal appropriation
Collections: Buchanan Collection of City of Lethbridge containing mid-20th Century Canadian work & various international pieces
Exhibitions: Historical and contemporary art changing monthly
Publications: Exhibition catalogues; quarterly newsletter
Activities: Classes for children; docent training; professional development series; lect open to public, numerous vis lectr per year; gallery talks; tours; artmobile; originate traveling exhibitions; sales shop sells magazines & reproductions
L **Library,** 601 Third Ave S, T1J 0H4. Tel 403-327-8770; FAX 403-328-3913; *Librn* Carol Busse
Reference library by appointment only
Library Holdings: Vols 4000; Per subs 12; AV — A-tapes, cassettes, fs, slides, v-tapes; Other — Clipping files, exhibition catalogs, manuscripts, pamphlets 3200, reproductions
Special Subjects: Eskimo Art, Painting - Canadian
Activities: Classes for children; lect open to public, 25 - 30 vis lectr per year; concerts; gallery talks; tours; video competitions; exten dept serves southern & central Alberta; lending collection contains 520 books, 22 cassettes, fs, 56 videos (in house viewing only)

M **UNIVERSITY OF LETHBRIDGE,** Art Gallery, 4401 University Dr, T1K 3M4. Tel 403-329-2690; FAX 403-382-7115; *Gallery Dir & Cur* Jeffrey Spalding; *Asst Cur* Victoria V Baster; *Chief Preparator* Adrian G Cooke; *Registrar* Lucie E Linhart; *Gift Adminr* Pam Clark
Open Mon - Fri Noon - 4:30 PM. No admis fee. Estab 1968 for pub service & the teaching mechanism. 29 ft x 42 ft gallery; Visual Arts Study Centre, 8:30 - 4:30 PM Mon - Fri, where any work from the collection will be made available for viewing
Income: Financed by university & government appropriations
Collections: †Permanent Collection consists of 19th century art (primarily Canadian), 20th century international art; Inuit
Exhibitions: Exhibitions with exception of the Annual BFA show are curated from the permanent collection; Faculty & Staff Exhibitions; approximately 10

shows per yr
Activities: Lect open to public, 10-15 vis lectr per year; tours; individual paintings & original objects of art lent to public & commercial galleries & corporations

MEDICINE HAT

M MEDICINE HAT MUSEUM & ART GALLERY, 1302 Bomford Crescent SW, T1A 5E6. Tel 403-527-6266 (mus), 526-0486 (gallery); FAX 403-528-2464; *Dir* Tom Willock
Open June - Aug Mon - Fri 9 AM - 5 PM, winter hours Mon - Fri 10:30 AM - Noon & 1 - 5 PM, cl News Year's, Good Friday & Christmas. Admis donations are welcomed. Estab 1951. Gallery has 2425 sq ft on main floor. Average Annual Attendance: 13,000
Collections: Pioneer artifacts of city & the district; Indian artifacts
Activities: School programs; films; gallery talks

L MEDICINE HAT PUBLIC LIBRARY, 414 First St SE, T1A 0A8. Tel 403-527-5528; FAX 403-527-4595; *Chief Librn* Bruce Evans; *Asst Chief Librn* Erin T Doyle
Open Mon - Thurs 10 AM - 9 PM, Fri & Sat 10 AM - 5:30 PM, Sun 1 - 5:30 PM. Library has a display area for traveling and local art shows. 600 sq ft room with track lighting and alarm system
Library Holdings: Vols 140,441; Per subs 297; Compact discs 1340; Phono discs 213; Talking books 725; Micro — Reels 22; AV — Cassettes 3161, motion pictures 476, rec, v-tapes 1653; Other — Clipping files, original art works 38, pamphlets 22, prints, sculpture
Exhibitions: Glenbow Museums (about 4 displays a year); Art loans from Alberta Foundation for the Arts
Activities: Dramatic programs; lect open to public, 10 vis lectr per year; concerts

MUNDARE

A BASILIAN FATHERS, PO Box 379, T0B 3H0. Tel 403-764-3887; *Dir* Father Larry Huculak
Open daily Mon - Fri 10 AM - 4 PM, weekends July - Aug 1 - 5 PM. Donations accepted. Estab 1902 to serve the people in their church, Mus estab 1953
Income: Financed by donations, government grants
Collections: Arts & Crafts; Historical Church Books; Ukrainlan Folk Art
L Library, PO Box 379, T0B 3H0. Tel 403-764-3887; *Dir* Father Larry Huculak
Library Holdings: Vols 650

RED DEER

M RED DEER & DISTRICT MUSEUM & ARCHIVES, 4525 47A Ave, PO Box 800, T4N 5H2. Tel 403-343-6844; FAX 403-342-6644; *Dir* Wendy Martindale; *Interpretive Prog Coordr* Rod Trentham; *Exhibits Coordr* Diana Anderson
Open daily Noon - 5 PM, Sat, Sun & holidays 1 - 5 PM, Mon - Thurs evenings 7 - 9 PM, summer Mon - Thurs 10 AM - 9 PM, Fri 10 AM - 5 PM. No admis fee. Estab 1978 to present the human history of the region through an on-going series of exhibitions & interpretive programs. Stewart Room has 64 running ft of exhibition space; Volunteer's Gallery has 124 running ft of exhibition space; Donor's Gallery has 160 running ft of exhibition space; 2500 sq ft total area of circulating exhibition space; 4100 sq ft of permanent exhibition space. Average Annual Attendance: 60,000. Mem: 1000; dues family $15, individual $10
Income: Financed by municipal, provincial & federal grants
Collections: Bower Collection of archaeological specimens from Central Alberta; Central Alberta human history; Inuit carving, prints & related material; Swallow Collection of Inuit & Indian Art; permanent art collection
Exhibitions: Programs featuring local, international, national & provincial artists; Alberta Community Art Clubs Association; Alberta Wide Juried Exhibition; Central Alberta Photographic Society Annual Exhibit; Red Deer College Student Show
Activities: Educ dept; museo-kits; concerts; gallery talks; tours; museum shop sells books, magazines, original art, prints, coloring books, learning tools, souvenirs, postcards, stationery & gifts

SHERWOOD PARK

SIAS INTERNATIONAL ART SOCIETY
For further information, see National and Regional Organizations

STONY PLAIN

M MULTICULTURAL HERITAGE CENTRE, 5411 51st St, T7Z 1X7. Tel 403-963-2777; *Exec Dir* Judy Unterschultz; *Cur Oppertshauser House* Ellen Green
Open Mon - Sat 10 AM - 4 PM, Sun 10 AM - 6:30 PM. No admis fee. Estab 1974 to provide exposure to high quality art with priority given to local Alberta artists, to develop an appreciation for good art, to provide exposure for upcoming artists. Gallery has 1200 sq ft of exhibition space; Multicultural Heritage Centre also consists of Opertshauser Gallery on same site. Average Annual Attendance: 102,000. Mem: 300; dues individual $20, family $30; annual meeting Jan
Income: Financed by Government grants, fees for children & adult programs, commissions from handicraft sales, art rental fees, Homesteaders Kitchen & bingos
Collections: Area history; family histories; photographs
Exhibitions: 14 exhibitions per yr
Publications: Monthly newsletter
Activities: Classes for adults & children; gallery talks; tours; competitions; sales shop sells handicrafts; Homesteader's Kitchen serves ethnic fare

VANCE

A WESTERN CANADA ART ASSOCIATION INC, Whyte Museum of Canadian Rockies, PO Box 160, T0L 0C0. Tel 403-762-2291; FAX 403-762-8919; *Pres* Kathryn Lipsett
Estab 1970 as art lobby & support assoc. Mem: 100
Income: Financed by mem
Publications: Wagon, annual
Activities: Seminars; competitions with awards

BRITISH COLUMBIA

BURNABY

M BURNABY ART GALLERY, 6344 Deer Lake Ave, V5G 2J3. Tel 604-291-9441; FAX 604-291-6776; *Pres Board Trustees* Barry Gilson; *Dir & Cur* Karen Henry; *Asst Cur* Grace Thomson; *Preparator* Bob Macintyre
Open Tues - Fri 9:30 AM - 4:30 PM, weekends & holidays 12:30 - 4:30 PM, cl Christmas. Admis $2. Estab 1967 to collect & exhibit Canadian art, with continually changing exhibitions of prints, paintings, sculpture & other art forms. Gallery is housed in Ceperley Mansion in Deer Lake Park. Average Annual Attendance: 25,000. Mem: 250; dues sponsor $100, sustaining $50, family $40, single $25, senior citizen & student $10; annual meeting in June
Income: Financed by municipal, provincial & federal grants, public & private donations
Collections: 20th Century prints including contemporary artists; Works on paper
Exhibitions: (1997) Cultural Imprints: Contemporary works by First Nations Artists; Art's Alive in the Schools '96 Crossing Cultures; Video-Reviewing the Mosiac; Print Revival: From the Permanent Collection; Tracing Cultures I: External Recall; Marianna Schmidt Collection; Ken Webb Fine Art Printing (Calgary) Collection; Cheryl Sourkes: Photo Installation; Tracing Cultures II: Banko Djuras & Taras Polataiko; Tracing Culture III: Zainub Verjee: Through the Soles of My Mothers Feet; Tracing Culture IV; Day Without Art (video)
Publications: Catalogues & brochures to accompany exhibitions; quarterly members bulletin
Activities: Docent training; film series; workshops for schools; lect open to public; concerts; gallery talks; tours; exten dept serves BC; individual paintings & original objects of art lent to other exhibition centers; lending collection contains 600 original prints, 50 paintings, 25 sculpture & drawings; museum shop sells books, magazines, original art, prints, crafts & pottery by local & other artists

M SIMON FRASER UNIVERSITY, Simon Fraser Gallery, V5A 1S6. Tel 604-291-4266; FAX 604-291-3029; *Dir* Dr E M Gibson; *Registrar* Janet Menzies
Open Mon 1 - 7 PM, Tues - Fri 10 AM - 4 PM, cl Sat & Sun. No admis fee. Estab 1971 to collect, conserve & display original works of art, principally contemporary Canadian. Gallery is 150 to 310 running ft, 1200 sq ft. Permanent works are installed throughout the university campus. Average Annual Attendance: 10,000
Income: Financed by pub university appropriations, government grants & corporate donations
Collections: Simon Fraser Collection, including contemporary & Inuit graphics; international graphics
Publications: Bi-annual report
Activities: Individual paintings & original objects of art loaned to University faculty & staff on campus
L W A C Bennett Library, V5A 1S6. Tel 604-291-3869; FAX 604-291-3023; *Librn* Theodore C Dobb
Reference material available in Fine Arts Room & University Archives
Library Holdings: Vols 1,000,000; Per subs 11,500; CD-ROM; Compact discs; Micro — Cards, fiche, reels; AV — A-tapes, fs, rec, slides, v-tapes; Other — Clipping files, exhibition catalogs, manuscripts, pamphlets

CHILLIWACK

A CHILLIWACK COMMUNITY ARTS COUNCIL, 45899 Henderson Ave, V2P 2X6. Tel 250-792-2069; FAX 250-792-2640; *General Mgr* Rod Hudson
Open 9 AM - 4 PM. Estab 1959 as Arts Council, Arts Centre estab 1973 to encourage all forms of art in the community. Mem: 5000; dues organizational $7.50, individual $5; annual meeting Sept
Income: Financed by endowment, mem & grants
Collections: Twenty-six Salish Weavings
Exhibitions: Local artists' exhibitions, including oils, pottery, prints, weaving, wood carving & other fabric arts
Publications: Arts Council Newsletter, 11 per year
Activities: Classes for adults & children; dramatic programs; concerts; scholarships offered

COQUITLAM

A PLACE DES ARTS, 1120 Brunette Ave, V3K 1G2. Tel 250-664-1636; *Dir* Gillian Elliot
Open Mon - Thurs 9 AM - 10 PM, Fri 9 AM - 9 PM, Sat 9 AM - 5 PM. No admis fee. Estab 1972 as a cultural, community crafts & resource center, an art school & gallery. Average Annual Attendance: 50,000
Income: Financed by municipal grant
Exhibitions: Bi-weekly shows of artists & craftsmen throughout the year
Publications: Program (12 weeks), every three months
Activities: Special educ dept serving retarded young adults, school children, senior citizens & women's groups; satellite courses within the school of the district on request; classes for adults & children; dramatic programs; music program; lect open to public; concerts; gallery talks; scholarships offered

DAWSON CREEK

M SOUTH PEACE ART SOCIETY, Dawson Creek Art Gallery, 101-816 Alaska Ave, V1G 4T6. Tel 604-782-2601; *Pres* Carrie Schafer; *Dir* Ellen Cores; *Treas* Sheilagh Glibbery
Open winter Tues - Sat 10 AM - 5 PM, summer daily 9 AM - 5 PM. Estab 1961 to promote art appreciation in community. Art Gallery in elevator annex in NAR Park. NAR Park includes museum & Tourist Information Office. Average Annual Attendance: 65,000. Mem: 100; dues $25; annual meeting third Thurs of Mar
Income: $130,000 (financed by municipal building & annual sponsorship, commission from sales, provincial cultural grant, federal grant Canada council)
Exhibitions: Approximately 15-18 per year, local & traveling
Activities: Classes for adults & children; lect open to public, 3 vis lectr per year; gallery talks; individual paintings lent to members, businesses, private homes; lending collection contains color reproductions, slides, 145 books & 350 original prints; book traveling exhibitions 4 per year; sales shop sells original art

KAMLOOPS

M KAMLOOPS ART GALLERY, 207 Seymour St, V2C 2E7. Tel 250-828-3543; FAX 250-828-0662; *Dir & Cur* Jann L M Bailey; *Bus Mgr* Shelley Whittaker; *Registrar* Trish Keegan; *Admin Asst* Nancy Owens; *Communications & Pub Prog* Krina Forbes
Open Tues - Sat 10 AM - 5 PM, cl Mon & Sun. Admis fee $2. Estab 1978. Two exhibition galleries, 200 running ft & 100 running ft, also children's gallery. Average Annual Attendance: 30,000. Mem: 400; mem fee $100; dues family $40, individual $25, senior citizens $15; annual meeting in May
Income: $500,000 (financed by mem, city & province appropriation, government & fundraising)
Purchases: $20,000
Collections: Contemporary Canadian Art; Canadian Prints & Drawings; photography; sculpture
Exhibitions: Monthly National & International Exhibitions
Publications: Newsletter, 5 times a year; exhibition catalogs
Activities: Classes for adults & children; lect open to public, 10-12 vis lectr per year; lending collection contains 600 primarily works on paper; sale shop sells books, magazines, prints & regional crafts

KELOWNA

M KELOWNA MUSEUM, 470 Queensway Ave, V1Y 6S7. Tel 604-763-2417; FAX 604-763-5722; *Pres* Don Best; *Dir & Cur* Ursula Surtees; *Asst Cur* Dan Bruce; *Asst Cur* Wayne Wilson
Open summer Mon - Sat 10 AM - 5 PM, Sun 2 - 5 PM, winter Tues - Sat 10 AM - 5 PM. No admis fee. Estab 1936 as a community museum where traveling exhibits are received & circulated. 12,000 sq ft of display plus storage, workshop & archives; permanent galleries: Natural History, Local History, Ethnography, two exhibit galleries. Average Annual Attendance: 35,000. Mem: 200; dues $25; annual meeting in Mar
Income: Financed by mem, city & state appropriation
Collections: †Coins & medals; †decorative arts; †enthnography; †general history; †Kelowna History; †natural history
Exhibitions: Changing exhibitions every 4-6 weeks
Publications: The Games Grandpa Played, Early Sports in BC; Nan, A Childs Eye View of Okanagan; Lak-La-Hai-Ee Volume III Fishing; A Short History of Early Fruit Ranching Kelowna; Sunshine & Butterflies
Activities: Classes for adults & children; lect open to public, 6 vis lectr per year; tours; gallery talks; individual paintings & original objects of art lent to qualified museums; book traveling exhibitions 7-8 per year; originate traveling exhibitions; museum shop sells books, original art, reproductions, prints
L Library, 470 Queensway Ave, V1Y 6S7. Tel 604-763-2417; FAX 604-763-5722;
Library Holdings: Micro — Fiche, prints; AV — Cassettes, motion pictures, slides, v-tapes; Other — Clipping files, manuscripts, original art works, photographs, prints
Collections: Photograph Collection

NANAIMO

M MALASPINA COLLEGE, Nanaimo Art Gallery & Exhibition Centre, 900 Fifth St, V9R 5S5. Tel 250-755-8790; FAX 250-741-2214; *Cur* Pamela Speight; *Adminr* Marc-Andre Boies-Manseau; *Educ Office* Cathy Gibson
Open 10 AM - 5 PM, Sun Noon - 5 PM. No admis fee. Estab 1976 for art, cultural, historical & scientific programs. Two Galleries: gallery I is 1300 sq ft with 11 ft ceilings; gallery II is 775 sq ft with 10 ft ceilings
Income: Financed by mem, earned gallery shop, city & state appropriations; schools & school districts
Exhibitions: Art, Cultural, Historical & Scientific exhibits Street Banner Painting Competition
Publications: Madrona, newsletter, 6 per year
Activities: Children's classes; docent programs; lect open to public, 2-3 vis lectr per year; competitions with awards; book traveling exhibitions 10-12 per year; sales shop sells books & prints

PRINCE GEORGE

M PRINCE GEORGE ART GALLERY, 2820 15th Ave, V2M 1T1. Tel 604-563-6447; FAX 604-563-3211; Elec Mail pgag@vortex.netbistro.com. *Pres* Bonnie Chappell; *VPres* Paul Zanette; *Dir & Cur* George Harris; *Treas* Ron Epp; *Marketing & Develop Officer* Melanie Kroeker; *Admin Asst* Robert Wyma; *Exhibition Technician* Annette Schroeter
Open Tues - Sat 10 AM - 5 PM, Sun 1 - 4 PM, cl Mon. Admis by donation. Estab 1970 to foster development of arts & crafts in the community; to foster & promote artists. Old Forestry Building, 2 floors, art rental section; two 1000 sq ft galleries, offices, storages space & small foyer. Average Annual Attendance: 10, 000. Mem: 385; dues business $55, family $20, single $15; annual meeting in Feb
Income: Financed by provincial & municipal grants, private donations
Collections: Original paintings by British Columbia artists
Exhibitions: Exhibitions held every 6-8 weeks, primarily Canadian Artists; Annual fundraiser
Publications: Quarterly newsletter
Activities: Classes for adults; docent training; lect open to public, 6-10 vis lectr per year; gallery talks; tours for school children; exten dept serves regional district; individual paintings & original objects of art rented to members; book traveling exhibitions 2 per year; sales shop sells original paintings, drawings, pottery, handicrafts, prints, cards

PRINCE RUPERT

M MUSEUM OF NORTHERN BRITISH COLUMBIA, Ruth Harvey Art Gallery, McBride St & First Ave, PO Box 669, V8J 3S1. Tel 250-624-3207; FAX 250-627-8009; *Pres* Wes Baker; *Dir & Cur* Robin Weber
Open Sept - May Mon - Sat 10 AM - 5 PM, June - Aug Mon - Sat 9 AM - 9 PM, Sun 9 AM - 5 PM. Admis by donation. Estab 1924, new building opened 1958, to collect, maintain & display the history of the north coast, particularly of the Prince Rupert area. One main hall has two small side galleries & a third gallery is the mus art gallery. Average Annual Attendance: 60,000. Mem: 199; dues $10; annual meeting in May
Income: $250,000 (financed primarily by municipality & province)
Collections: †Contemporary North Coast First Nations; †historical collections; †native First Nations collections; natural history; †photographs
Exhibitions: A continually changing display program; fine arts exhibitions from large galleries; local artists shows
Activities: Educ dept; lect open to public, 3-4 vis lectr per year; gallery talks; tours; competitions; book traveling exhibitions; museum shop sells books, native art, original art, reproductions, prints & souvenirs
L Library, McBride St and First Ave, PO Box 669, V8J 3E7. Tel 250-624-3207; FAX 250-627-8009; *Dir & Cur* Robin Weber; *Cur* Susan Marsden
Open June - Aug Mon - Sat 9 AM - 9 PM, Sun 9 AM - 5 PM, Sept - May Mon - Sat 10 AM - 5 PM, cl Sun & holidays. No admis fee. Small reference library for staff & researchers
Income: $280,000 (financed by city, province, donations & gift shop)
Library Holdings: Vols 1000; Per subs 10; Archival materials; AV — V-tapes; Other — Clipping files, exhibition catalogs, manuscripts, pamphlets, photographs
Special Subjects: Painting - Canadian, Primitive Art, Prints, Restoration & Conservation, Textiles, Concentration on British Columbia pre-modern history
Exhibitions: Monthly exhibitions
Publications: Curator's log; quarterly newsletter
Activities: Educ dept

REVELSTOKE

A REVELSTOKE ART GROUP, 315 W First St, PO Box 2655, V0E 2S0. Tel 250-837-3067; *Pres & Dir* Rene Terlinden; *VPres* Suzanne Grieve; *Treas* Tom Atherton
Open May - Aug Tues - Sat 10 AM - 8 PM. Estab 1949 to promote & stimulate interest in art by studying art, artists methods & work, developing local interest & interchanging ideas. Average Annual Attendance: 2500. Mem: 30; dues $5; annual meeting in Apr
Income: $2200 (financed by art show commissions, donations & raffles)
Purchases: $460
Collections: Centennial collection contains 50 watercolours, acrylics & oils by Sophie Atkinson, Art Phillips, Mel Abbott, Mary Wells
Exhibitions: Landscapes by Jack Davis; Weaving & Pottery by Local Artisans; Sr Citizens' Paintings; Snowflake Porcelain Painters; Works by members of the Revelstoke Art Group; Annual fall art show
Activities: Classes for adults & children; lect open to public, 3 vis lectr per year; competitions; original objects of art lent to Selkirk Health Clinic, Moberly Manor & Royal Bank; sales shop sells original art

RICHMOND

A RICHMOND ARTS CENTRE, 7700 Minoru Gate, V6Y 1R9. Tel 604-231-6440; FAX 604-231-6423; Elec Mail artscentre@city.richmond.bc.ca. *Coordr* Jane Wheeler
Open Mon - Fri 9 AM - 9 PM, Sat & Sun 10 AM - 5 PM. No admis fee. Estab 1967 to provide stimulation & nourishment to the arts in the community
Income: Financed by city appropriation
Publications: Newsletter, monthly
Activities: Classes for adults & children in visual & dramatic arts, ballet & jazz; special events & festivals

SOOKE

M SOOKE REGION MUSEUM & ART GALLERY, 2070 Phillips Rd, PO Box 774, V0S 1N0. Tel 250-642-6351; FAX 250-642-7089; *Exec Dir* Terry Malone
Open winter Tues - Sun 9 AM - 5 PM, summer daily 9 AM - 5 PM. Admis donation. Estab 1977 to advance local history & art. Exhibit changes monthly featuring a different local artist or artist group, or segment of mus collection.
Average Annual Attendance: 30,000
Collections: Fishing, Logging & Mining Artifacts; Native Indian Crafts (post & pre-contact); Pioneer Implements
Exhibitions: Polemaker's Shack; Moss Cottage; Wreck of Lord Western
Activities: Children classes; docent training; lect open to public, 4 vis lectr per year; tours; competitions with awards; retail store sells books & original art

SURREY

M SURREY ART GALLERY, 13750 88th Ave, V3W 3L1. Tel 604-501-5580; FAX 604-501-5581; *Cur* Liane Davison; *Asst Cur* Carol Prokof; *Cur Programs* Ingrid Kolt
Open Tues - Thurs 9 AM - 9 PM, Mon & Fri 9 AM - 4:30 PM, Sat & Sun 10 AM - 5 PM, cl statutory holidays. Admis by donation. Estab 1975. Average Annual Attendance: 50,000
Income: Financed by city & provincial appropriation, special private foundations grants & federal grants per project application
Purchases: $4200
Collections: Contemporary Canadian Art, mostly works on paper
Publications: Exhibition catalogues; Surrey Arts Center, bi-monthly calendars
Activities: Classes for children, docent training; lect open to public, 6 vis lectr per year; concerts; gallery talks; tours; individual paintings & original objects of art lent to other institutions; book traveling exhibitions 1 or more per year; originates traveling exhibitions; sales shop sells original art, locally made jewelry, arts & crafts, glasswork, woodwork & cards
L Library, 13750 88th Ave, V3W 3L1. Tel 604-501-5580; FAX 604-501-5581; Elec Mail artgallery@city.bc.ca. *Cur Exhib & Coll* Liane Davison; *Cur Prog* Ingrid Kolt
Open Mon - Fri 9 AM - 5 PM, weekends 10 AM - 5 PM, some evenings 5 - 9 PM. Admis by donation. Estab 1975 for exhibitions & educ in contemporary art. Reference library for staff & docents only. Average Annual Attendance: 50,000
Purchases: $300
Library Holdings: Vols 550; Per subs 20; Micro — Cards; AV — Slides; Other — Clipping files, exhibition catalogs
Collections: Contemporary public art since 1975
Exhibitions: 17 exhibitions per year
Activities: Classes for adults & children; docent training; lect open to public; concerts; gallery talks; tours; exten dept serves city of Surrey; individual paintings & original objects of art lent to public art museum; lending collection contains paintings & sculptures; book traveling exhibitions 1-2 per year; originate traveling exhibitions; museum shop sells books, original art & prints

VANCOUVER

M THE CANADIAN CRAFT MUSEUM, 639 Hornby St, V6C 2G3. Tel 604-687-8266; FAX 604-684-7174; *Cur* Ron Kong; *Admin Dir* Gioranni Festa; *Admin Asst* Annette Wooff; *Museum Shop Mgr* Cherryl Masters
Open Mon - Wed, Fri & Sat 10 AM - 5 PM, Sun & holidays Noon - 5 PM. Admis adults $4, students & senior citizens $2, group rates for 10 or more, members & children 12 & under free. Estab 1980 dedicated to presenting excellence in Canadian & international craft, craftmanship & design, both contemporary & historical. Main floor 3500 sq ft, mezzanine 350 sq ft. Average Annual Attendance: 30,000. Mem: 550; dues affinity $200, group & family $50, individual $35, senior couple $30, senior/student $20, craft artists $18.50, non-resident $15; annual meeting in May
Income: $350,000 (financed by mem, city & state appropriations & fundraising)
Collections: †Permanent collection
Exhibitions: (1997) Canada China Applied Arts
Publications: Exhibit catalogues; CraftWards Newsletter, quarterly
Activities: Lect open to public; gallery talks; docent-led group & school tours; contemporary & historical craft lect; craft workshops for adults & children; occasional craft demonstrations; book traveling exhibitions; museum shop sells exhibit catalogues, quality one-of-a-kind & production Canadian crafts

A COMMUNITY ARTS COUNCIL OF VANCOUVER, 837 Davie St, V6Z 1B7. Tel 250-683-4358; FAX 250-683-4394; *Exec Dir* Susan Hull; *Admin Asst* Raj Sihota
Open 9 AM - 5 PM. No admis fee. Estab 1946 as a soc dedicated to the support of arts, with a wide range of inerest in the arts; to promote standards in all art fields including civic arts; also serves as a liaison centre. Exhibition Gallery shows works of semi-professional & emerging artists; 2200 sq ft on two levels, street level entrance. Mem: 500; dues $15; annual meeting in Sept
Income: Financed by British Columbia Cultural & Lotteries Fund, City of Vancouver, mem & donations
Exhibitions: Two shows per month
Publications: Arts Vancouver Magazine, 4 issues per year
Activities: Lect open to public; performances; workshops; concerts; gallery talks; competitions; scholarships & fels offered

M CONTEMPORARY ART GALLERY SOCIETY OF BRITISH COLUMBIA, 555 Hamilton St, V6B 2R1. Tel 604-681-2700; FAX 604-683-2710; Elec Mail cag@axionet.com. *Dir & Cur* Keith Wallace; *Prog Coordr* Sylvia Blessin; *Financial Mgr* Dennis Kulpas
Open Tues - Sat 11 AM - 5 PM. No admis fee. Estab 1971 as an exhibition space for regional, national & international contemporary art. The Gallery has a 1000 sq ft exhibition area. Average Annual Attendance: 6000. Mem: 400; dues $26.75
Income: Financed by Federal Government, British Columbia Cultural Fund, city

of Vancouver, mem fees & fundraising
Collections: City of Vancouver Art Collection; Contemporary Gallery Society of B C Art Collection
Publications: Exhibition brochure & catalogs
Activities: Lect open to public, 8 vis lectr per year; gallery talks; individual paintings & original objects of art lent to civic agencies; lending collection contains 3400 works
L Art Library Service, 555 Hamilton St, V6B 2R1. Tel 604-681-2700; FAX 604-683-2710; Elec Mail cag@axionet.com. *Dir & Cur* Keith Wallace; *Prog Coordr* Sylvia Blessin
Open Tues - Sat 11 AM - 5 PM. Estab 1971 for pub enhancement, the Gallery provides this service to the pub agencies for free; commercial agencies pay a fee. Circ 3000
Income: Financed by British Columbia Cultural Fund, Vancouver Civic Cultural Grant, federal grant, consulting, sales
Library Holdings: AV — Slides; Other — Pamphlets
Publications: Brochures; exhibit catalogs

M EMILY CARR INSTITUTE OF ART & DESIGN, The Charles H Scott Gallery, 1399 Johnston St, V6H 3R9. Tel 604-844-3809; FAX 604-844-3801; *Cur* Greg Bellerby; *Admin Asst* Kate Miller
Open daily Noon - 5 PM. No admis fee. Estab 1980 to provide mus quality exhibitions & publications of critically significant visual art. 3000 sq ft gallery with all environmental & security safeguards. Average Annual Attendance: 30,000
Income: $95,000 (financed by provincial appropriation)
Exhibitions: Social Process - Collective Action, Mary Kelly 1970-75
Publications: Exhibition catalogues
Activities: Tours upon request; book traveling exhibitions 1-2 per year; originate traveling exhibitions; sales shop sells exhibition catalogues
L Library, 1399 Johnston St, V6H 3R9. Tel 604-844-3840; FAX 604-844-3801; *Library Dir* Sheila Wallace; *Librn* Donna Zwierciadlowski
Open May - Aug Mon - Fri 8:30 AM - 5 PM, Sept - Apr Mon - Thurs 8:30 Am - 8 PM, Fri & Sat 8:30 AM - 5 PM
Income: Financed by government funding
Library Holdings: Vols 16,500; Per subs 165; Micro — Fiche; AV — A-tapes, rec, slides 115,500, v-tapes 1175; Other — Clipping files, exhibition catalogs
Special Subjects: Film, Painting - American, Painting - Canadian, Painting - European, Printmaking, Photography, Posters, Pottery, Pre-Columbian Art, Primitive Art, Prints, Sculpture, Video, Woodcarvings, Electronic Communication Design

UNIVERSITY OF BRITISH COLUMBIA

M Fine Arts Gallery, 1825 Main Mall, V6T 1Z2. Tel 604-822-2759; FAX 604-822-6689; *Dir & Cur* Scott Watson; *Prog Coordr* Mary Williams
Open Sept - Apr Tues - Fri 10 AM - 5 PM, Sat Noon - 5 PM. No admis fee. Estab 1948, The gallery has a mandate to encourage projects conceived for its special content. Our programming emphasizes contemporary art & also projects which serve to further understanding of the history of Avant-Garde. Gallery covers 27,000 sq ft. Average Annual Attendance: 15,000
Income: Financed by departmental funds
Exhibitions: Rotating exhibitions
Publications: Announcements; exhibition catalogues
Activities: Lect open to public, 2 vis lectr per year; gallery talks; originate traveling exhibitions
L Fine Arts Library, 1956 Main Mall, V6T 1Z1. Tel 604-822-2720, 822-3943; FAX 604-822-3893; Telex 04-53296. *Head Librn* Hans Burndorfer; *Reference Librn* Diana Cooper; *Reference Librn* Peggy McBride
Open Mon - Thurs 8 AM - 11 PM, Fri 8 AM - 5 PM, Sat Noon - 5 PM, Sun Noon - 8 PM. Estab 1948 to serve students & faculty in all courses related to fine arts, architecture, planning, dance, costume & design
Library Holdings: Vols 180,000; Dial incongraphic index, Marburg index; Micro — Fiche, prints, reels; Other — Clipping files, exhibition catalogs, pamphlets, reproductions
Special Subjects: Canadian Art, Fashion Design & Planning
Publications: Fine Masters Theses, updated annually; Starts Here (short introductory bibliographies), produced as needed
Activities: Lectr; tours
M Museum of Anthropology, 6393 NW Marine Dr, V6T 1Z2. Tel 604-822-5087; FAX 604-822-2974; *Dir & Prof* Michael M Ames; *Designer & Technician* Skooker Broome; *Cur & Ethnology/Media* Pam Brown; *Conservator* Miriam Clavir; *Asst Coll Mgr* Allison Cronin; *Designer/Exhib* David Cunningham; *Mgr Admin* Anne-Marie Fenger; *Cur Ethnology* Marjorie Halpin; *Cur Art & Pub Programmes* Rosa Ho; *Curatorial Asst Archaeology* Joyce Johnson; *Cur Ethnography* Michael Kew; *Dir Communications* Kersti Krug; *Designer Graphics* Bill McLennan; *Cur Archaeology* Michael Blake; *Admin Asst* Salma Mawani; *Cur Ethnology & Ceramics* Carol Mayer; *Research Assoc Conservation* Darrin Morrison; *Col Mgr* Ann Stevenson; *Mgr Admin* Moya Waters; *Prog Coordr & Dir Asst* Jennifer Webb
Open Tues 11 AM - 9 PM, Wed - Sun 11 AM - 5 PM. Admis family $15, adults $6, senior citizens, students & children $3.50, group rates for 10 or more, Tues free 5 - 9 PM. Estab 1947 to develop a high quality institution that maximizes pub access & involvement while also conducting active programs of teaching, research & experimentation. Average Annual Attendance: 170,000. Mem: 1000; dues family $50, individual student/senior couple $30, student & senior citizens $20
Collections: Ethnographic areas around the world, especially the northwest coast of British Columbia; European ceramics; museum journals; oriental art & history
Activities: Classes for adults & children; volunteer training; lect open to public, 20-30 vis lectr per year; tours; competitions with awards; exten dept; original objects of art lent to institutions for special exhibits; book traveling exhibitions; originate traveling exhibitions; museum shop sells books, original art, reproductions, prints, slides, postcards, note cards & t-shirts

M VANCOUVER ART GALLERY, 750 Hornby St, V6Z 2H7. Tel 604-682-4668; FAX 604-682-1086; *Pres* Garth Thurber; *Dir* Alf Boquski; *Chief Cur* Diana Augaitis; *Sr Cur* Ian Thom; *Head Marketing Develop* Janet Meredith; *Head Mus Servs* Nancy Kirkpatrick; *Conservator* Monica Smith; *Exhib Coll* Helle Viirlaid; *Registrar* Christine Nielsen
Open Mon, Wed, Fri & Sat 10 AM - 5 PM, Thurs 10 AM - 9 PM, Sun Noon - 5 PM, cl Tues, Christmas & New Year's Day. Admis adults $5, students with cards & senior citizens $2.50, children under 12 free, Thurs evening pay-what-you-can. Estab 1931 to foster the cultural development of the community & a pub interest in the arts. Gallery moved in 1983 into a reconstructed 1907 classical courthouse which had been designed by Francis Rattenbury. The building contains 41,400 net sq ft of gallery space. Complex contains a total gross area of 164,805 sq ft. Average Annual Attendance: 200,000. Mem: 4000; dues family $55, individual $39, senior family $27, student & senior citizen $22
Income: Financed by city, provincial & federal government grants, private & corporate donations
Collections: Emily Carr; 5000 works, including drawings, film, objects, paintings, photographs, prints, sculpture, videotape & watercolors, mostly 20th century Canadian works
Publications: Annual Report; Calendar, 5 times per annum; Exhibition Catalogues
Activities: Classes for adults & children; docent training; lect open to public; gallery talks; tours; individual paintings & original objects of art lent to museums who comply with security & climate control standards; originate traveling exhibitions; gallery shop sells books, magazines, reproductions, postcards, posters, native Indian art, jewelry, goods in leather, paper & wood by local artisans
L Library, 750 Hornby St, V6Z 2H7. Tel 604-662-4709; FAX 604-682-1086; Elec Mail casiegel@vanartgallery.bc.ca. *Librn* Cheryl A Siegel
Open Sun, Mon, Wed - Fri 1 - 5 PM. Estab 1931 to serve staff, docents, students & the public. For reference only
Library Holdings: Vols 35,000; Per subs 120; Other — Clipping files, memorabilia, pamphlets, photographs
Collections: Fine arts specializing in Canadian & contemporary art

L VANCOUVER CITY ARCHIVES, 1150 Chestnut St, V6J 3J9. Tel 604-736-8561; FAX 604-736-0626; *Dir* Sue M Baptie; *Records Mgr* John K Chang
Open Mon - Fri 9:30 AM - 5:30 PM, cl weekends & legal holidays. No admis fee. Estab 1933
Income: Financed by city appropriation
Library Holdings: Charts; Civic Records; Drawings; Maps; Paintings; Other — Manuscripts, prints
Exhibitions: Temporary exhibitions
Activities: Lect open to public; tours

M VANCOUVER MUSEUM COMMISSION, Vancouver Museum, 1100 Chestnut St, V6J 3J9. Tel 604-736-4431; FAX 604-736-5417; *Interim Dir* Hendrik Slegtenhorst
Estab 1894 as a civic mus reflecting the history & natural history of the area & its peoples. Mem: dues family $30, adult $20
Exhibitions: History Gallery; Urbanarium: City Life
Activities: Classes for children; docent programs; lect open to public
L Vancouver Museum Library, 1100 Chestnut St, V6J 3J9. *Dir* Wilma Wood
For reference
Library Holdings: Vols 9000; Per subs 30; AV — A-tapes, cassettes, v-tapes; Other — Clipping files, exhibition catalogs, pamphlets
Special Subjects: American Indian Art, Anthropology, Archaeology, Asian Art, Decorative Arts, Eskimo Art, Folk Art, Historical Material, Mexican Art, Oriental Art

M VANCOUVER PUBLIC LIBRARY, Fine Arts & Music Div, 350 W Georgia St, V6B 6B1. Tel 604-665-3388; FAX 604-665-2265; *Head Librn* John Cull
Open Mon - Wed 10 AM - 9 PM, Thurs, Fri & Sat 10 AM - 6 PM, cl Sun. Estab 1960; Library estab 1903
Library Holdings: Vols 110,000; Per subs 500; AV — Cassettes, lantern slides, slides, v-tapes 5000; Other — Clipping files, exhibition catalogs, pamphlets, photographs, prints

VERNON

M VERNON ART GALLERY, 3228 31st Ave, V1T 9G9. Tel 250-545-3173; FAX 604-545-9096; *Dir* Susan Brandoli; *Art Educ* Jude Clarke; *Gift Shop Coordr* Linda McConnell
Open Mon - Thurs 10 AM - 5 PM, Fri 10 AM - 9 PM, Sat Noon - 4 PM. No admis fee. Estab 1967 for the collection & exhibition of art work by Okanagan, national & international artists. Two gallery spaces professionally designed & measures 5500 sq ft, also reception area, gift shop & administrative/kitchen area. Average Annual Attendance: 27,000. Mem: 420; dues family $30, individual $20, senior citizens & students $15
Income: Financed by mem, city appropriation & grants
Collections: Permanent collection consists of ceramics, paintings, prints, sculpture and serigraphs
Exhibitions: 20 exhibits annually
Publications: Art Quarterly
Activities: Classes for adults & children; docent training; lect, 3 vis lectr per year; gallery talks; concerts; tours; performances; competitions; book traveling exhibitions 3-4 per year; originate traveling exhibitions; museum shop sells books, magazines, original art, reproductions & local crafts

VICTORIA

M ART GALLERY OF GREATER VICTORIA, 1040 Moss St, V8V 4P1. Tel 604-384-4101; FAX 604-361-3995; *Pres* Robert Gill; *Dir* Patricia A Bovey; *Asst Dir & Chief Cur* Nicholas Tuele; *Cur Asian Art* Barry Till; *Educ Officer* Nancy Klazek; *Financial Officer* Linda Mary Giles
Open Mon, Tues, Wed, Fri, Sat 10 AM - 5 PM, Thurs 10 AM - 9 PM, Sun 1 - 5 PM. Admis nonmembers $4, students $2, children under 12 free. Estab 1949. Six

modern galleries adjoin 19th Century Spencer Mansion-Japanese Garden. Average Annual Attendance: 56,500. Mem: 3000; dues family $30, individual $20, student & non-resident $10; annual meeting 2nd wk of June
Income: $700,000 (financed by mem, city, federal & provincial grants)
Collections: Chinese, Indian, Persian & Tibetan Art; Contemporary Canadian, American & European; European Painting & Decorative Arts from 16th-19th centuries; Japanese Art from Kamakura to Contemporary; Primitive Arts
Exhibitions: Approx 35 exhibitions in 6 exhibition halls, changing every 6 weeks
Publications: Membership newsletter, 6 times a year
Activities: Classes for adults & children; docent training; gallery in the schools program; workshops; lect open to public, 12 vis lectr per year; concerts; tours; gallery talks; exten dept serves BC; individual paintings & original objects of art lent to museums & local public buildings; lending collections contains cassettes, original art works, sculpture, scrolls, 4800 books, 5000 original prints, 2000 slides; book traveling exhibitions 5-20 per year; originate traveling exhibitions; sales shop sells books, magazines, reproductions, stationery, jewelry, pottery, ornaments, glass & prints
L Library, 1040 Moss St, V8V 4P1. Tel 250-384-4101; FAX 250-361-3995; Elec Mail aggv@pinc.com. *Librn* Mrs J M Paige
Open Mon - Sat 10 AM - 5 PM, Sun 1 - 5 PM. Estab 1951. For reference only. Average Annual Attendance: 100,000
Income: $1000
Purchases: $1000
Library Holdings: Vols 4800; Per subs 46; Micro — Fiche; AV — Slides; Other — Clipping files, exhibition catalogs, pamphlets, reproductions
Special Subjects: Asian Art, Canadian Art
Activities: Classes for adults & children; docent training; lect open to public, 20 vis lectr per year; concerts; gallery talks; tours; awards; museum shop sells books, magazines, slides, contemporary ceramics

L BRITISH COLUMBIA INFORMATION MANAGEMENT SERVICES, 865 Yates St (Mailing add: 655 Belleville St, V8V 1X4). Tel 604-387-5885; FAX 604-387-2072; Elec Mail access@bcars.gs.gov.bc.ca; Internet Home Page Address http://www.bcars.gs.gov.bc.ca/bcars.html. *Provincial Archivist* John A Bovey
Open Mon - Fri 9:30 AM - 4:45 PM. Estab 1893 to collect & preserve all records relating to the historical development of British Columbia
Income: Financed by provincial appropriation
Library Holdings: Vols 70,380; Per subs 100; Original documents; Maps; Micro — Reels; AV — A-tapes; Other — Clipping files, exhibition catalogs, manuscripts, original art works, pamphlets, photographs
Special Subjects: British Columbia history
Publications: Art reproductions

A BRITISH COLUMBIA MUSEUMS ASSOCIATION, 514 Government St, V8V 4X4. Tel 250-387-3315; FAX 250-387-1251; *Exec Dir* Gregory Evans
Open Mon - Fri 8:30 AM - 4:30 PM. Estab 1956 supports museums & art galleries of British Columbia
Activities: Training in museum methods

M CRAIGDARROCH CASTLE HISTORICAL MUSEUM SOCIETY, 1050 Joan Crescent, Sta B, V8S 3L5. Tel 250-592-5323; FAX 250-592-1099; Elec Mail Express: can-cdc; Internet: uf308. *Exec Dir* Bruce W Davies; *Registrar & Technician* Delphine Castle; *Cur* Kristine Webster; *Vol Coordr* Bill Blore
Open daily. Admis $6. Estab 1959 for conservation & restoration of house. Average Annual Attendance: 120,000. Mem: 500; dues $20; annual meeting in the spring
Income: $450,000 (financed by programmes & visitation)
Collections: †Historical objects pertaining to the years 1890-1908; 5000 objects used to furnish an historical turn of the century mansion
Publications: Castle Quarterly, newsletter
Activities: Classes for children; docent training; lect open to public, 5 vis lectr per year; gallery talks; tours; individual paintings & original objects of art lent to other qualified cultural institutions; lending collection contains books, original art works, prints & paintings; museum shop sells books, magazines, original art, reproductions, souvenirs

A OPEN SPACE, * 510 Fort St, V8W 1E6. Tel 604-383-8833; FAX 604-380-1999; *Dir* Sue Donaldson
Open Tues - Sat 12 - 5 PM, cl Mon & Sun. No admis fee. Estab 1971; Open Space is a member of ANNPAC, the national body of artist-run center in Canada; dedicated to exhibiting contemporary art as well as performance programs & symposium. Maintains reference library. Gallery has 3000 sq ft, 220 running ft with full light grid controlled to level for works of art & for performance programs. Average Annual Attendance: 10,000. Mem: 230; dues $20
Income: $80,000 (financed by federal & provincial appropriations, city grants, donations & mem fees)
Exhibitions: 10-12 contemporary visual art exhibitions per year
Publications: B C Photos 1978, Photos 1979; Secession Excerpts from the Literature of Photography, periodic; Stereo Bookwork
Activities: Lect open to public, 10-20 vis lectr & symposium per year; concerts; gallery talks; awards for music composers of British Columbia; book traveling exhibitions 1 per year

M UNIVERSITY OF VICTORIA, Maltwood Art Museum and Gallery, PO Box 3025, V8W 3P2. Tel 250-721-8298; FAX 250-721-8997; *Dir & Cur* Martin Segger; *Pres* Dr David F Strong; *VPres* Dr Don Rowlatt; *Chmn of Board* Dr S Scully; *Secy-Registrar* B Jackson
Open Mon - Fri 9 AM - 1 PM, Sun Noon - 4 PM. No admis fee. Estab 1963 to collect, preserve & exhibit the decorative arts, maintain teaching collections for the university. Gallery has 3000 sq ft of environmentally controlled exhibition space, three galleries programmed, loan exhibits & from collection permanent exhibit. Maintains reference library. Average Annual Attendance: 100,000
Income: $200,000 (financed by endowment & state appropriation)
Purchases: $25,000
Collections: †Maltwood Collection of Decorative Art; †contemporary art

(Canadian); Ethnographic & design art
Exhibitions: Permanent collections, continuing and rotating
Activities: Lect open to public, 10 vis lectr per year; gallery talks; tours; individual paintings lent to offices & public spaces on campus; lending collection contains 3000 original prints, 1000 paintings & sculpture; book traveling exhibitions 5 per year; originate traveling exhibitions

WHITE ROCK

M ARNOLD MIKELSON MIND & MATTER GALLERY, 13743 16th Ave, V4A 1P7. Tel 604-536-6440, 536-6460; *Dir* Mary Mikelson; *Asst Dir* Myra Mikelson; *Mgr* Arnold Mikelson; *Asst Mgr* Sapphire Mikelson
Open Noon - 6 PM or by appointment. No admis fee. Estab 1965. 2000 sq ft gallery on three acres, upper flr mus, main flr continues exhibitions of Canadian artists. Average Annual Attendance: 15,000
Income: Funded by the Mikelson Family
Collections: Showcase wood sculpture by the late Arnold Mikelson
Exhibitions: Metal art, modern landscape, painting, stone sculpture, wildlife, wood sculpture
Activities: Lect open to public, 25-30 lectr per year; museum shop sells original art

MANITOBA

BOISSEVAIN

M MONCUR GALLERY, PO Box 1241, R0K 0E0. Tel 204-534-6422; FAX 204-534-6399; *Chmn* Shannon Moncur; *VChmn* Anna Grace Diehl; *Secy Treas* Gerald May
Open 8 AM - 5 PM. No admis fee. Estab 1986. Average Annual Attendance: 500-1000
Income: $8000 (financed by city & state appropriation)
Collections: Aboriginal artifacts dating back 10,000 years collected in the Turtle Mountain area

BRANDON

A THE ART GALLERY OF SOUTHWESTERN MANITOBA, 638 Princess Ave, R7A 0P3. Tel 204-727-1036; FAX 204-726-8139; *Dir* Glenn Allison
Open Mon - Sat 9 AM - 5 PM, Sun 2 - 5 PM. No admis fee. Estab 1960 to promote & foster cultural activities in western Manitoba. Average Annual Attendance: 2400. Mem: 700; dues $6 - $20; annual meeting May
Income: Financed by mem, city & provincial appropriations & federal grants
Exhibitions: Exhibitions of regional, national & international significance
Publications: Bulletin, every 2 months
Activities: Classes for adults & children; lect open to public, 2 vis lectr per year; gallery talks; tours; competitions; individual paintings & original objects of art lent to members; lending collection contains original art works, original prints, paintings, weaving
L Centennial Library - Arts Complex, R7A 0P3. Tel 204-727-6648; FAX 204-726-8139; *Chief Librn* Kathy Thornborough
Open to members
Library Holdings: Vols 78,000

CHURCHILL

M ESKIMO MUSEUM, 242 La Verendrye, PO Box 10, R0B 0E0. Tel 204-675-2030; FAX 204-675-2140; *Dir* Bishop Reynald Rouleau; *Cur* Lorraine Brandson; *Asst Cur* Anne Gould
Open Mon - Sat 9 AM - Noon & 1 - 5 PM, Sun 1 - 4 PM. No admis fee. Estab 1944 to depict the Eskimo way of life through the display of artifacts. Mus has large single display room. Average Annual Attendance: 10,000
Income: Administered & funded by the Roman Catholic Episcopal Corporation of Churchill Hudson Bay
Collections: †Contemporary Inuit carvings; ethnographic collections; prehistoric artifacts; wildlife specimens
Publications: Carved From the Land by Lorraine Brandson 1994; The Churchill Eskimo Museum by Jeannine Veisse
Activities: Films & slide shows for school groups upon request; tours upon request; original objects of art lent to special exhibits & galleries; museum shop sells books, original art, art cards, postcards & northern theme clothing (t-shirts, sweatshirts & caps)
L Library, 242 La Verendrye, PO Box 10, R0B 0E0. Tel 204-675-2030; FAX 204-675-2140; *Cur* Lorraine Brandson
Estab mainly for Arctic Canada material
Purchases: $200
Library Holdings: Vols 500; Other — Clipping files, exhibition catalogs, photographs
Special Subjects: Archaeology, Crafts, Eskimo Art, Ethnology, Handicrafts, Restoration & Conservation, European exploration of Arctic Canada

DAUPHIN

M DAUPHIN & DISTRICT ALLIED ARTS COUNCIL, 104 First Ave NW, R7N 1G9. Tel 204-638-6231; *Adminr* Nina Crawford
Open 10 AM - 3 PM. Estab 1973 to provide a home for the arts in the Dauphin District. Average Annual Attendance: 20,000. Mem: dues assoc $25, family $15, individual $5; annual meeting in Mar
Income: $100,000 (financed by mem, town appropriation, provincial

appropriation, donations)
Publications: Arts council newsletter, quarterly
Activities: Classes for adults & children; dramatic programs; lending collection contains paintings & art objects; book traveling exhibitions 12 per year; originate traveling exhibitions

PORTAGE LA PRAIRIE

A PORTAGE AND DISTRICT ARTS COUNCIL, Portage Arts Centre, 160 Saskatchewan Ave W, R1N 0M1. Tel 204-239-6029; FAX 204-239-1472; *Acting ExecDir* Darlene Robinson; *Adminr* Ilene Jackson
Open Tues - Sat 11 AM - 5 PM, Fri 11 AM - 9 PM. Financed by donations. Estab 1976 to enhance artistic awareness in the individual & the community. 1240 sq ft (146 running ft) exhibition area, hanging system - chain & hook, sculpture stands, display stands, shelves & cases. Average Annual Attendance: 5000. Mem: 350; dues group $50, family $40, individual $20, child $10
Income: Financed by commission on sale of art, mem, fees, government grants, ticket sales, fundraising events & donations
Exhibitions: Country Vision; Exhibition from Winnipeg Art Gallery; Sold! To the Highest Bidder; Mennonite Artists; Music & Arts Festival - Visual Arts; Hosting Central Region Juried Art Show at Portage Community Centre; For the Love of It; Habitual Perfection; Central Region Juried Art Show Tour; Lovers & Friends; Dufresne - Watercolors; Mauws - Photography; Rural Manitoba - Winnipeg Art Gallery; Smith - Mixed Media; Hart - Papier-mache. Photographs by Les Green, Oils by Nick Plaseski; Common Ground; Against Wind & Weather: The Barns in Canadian Art; A Few of My Favourite Things-Water Colours by Eileen Korponay; For the Love of It-Portage & District Art Council Student Show; Central Region Juried Art Show Tour; Watercolours by Lynn Sissons; Our Daily Bread-Oils by Stephen Lowe; Staying Young-Oils & Watercolours by Fay Jelly; Water Colorours by Terry Kleemola; Faces of Africa-Watercolours by Ray Dirks; As we See It-Oils by Nell Owens, Mixed Media by Karen Braden, Pottery by Gabriele Neuschwander; Under the Umbrella-Christmas Art & Craft Sale; Portage & District Art Council Show
Publications: Newsletter, Sept - June
Activities: Classes for adults & children; lect open to public, 6 vis lectr per year; concerts; gallery talks; tours; scholarships & fels offered; individual paintings & original objects of art rented to members, private individuals & businesses; lending collection contains books & color reproductions; sales shop sells handcrafted pottery, stained glass, jewelry, stationery, books, original art, prints, photo cards & quilting

WINNIPEG

L CRAFTS GUILD OF MANITOBA, INC, Library, 183 Kennedy St, R3C 1S6. Tel 204-943-1190; *Librn* Moira Wilson
Open to members only. For lending & reference
Income: $1500 (financed by mem)
Library Holdings: Vols 1500; Per subs 22
Special Subjects: Carpets & Rugs, Ceramics, Crafts, Dolls, Embroidery, Eskimo Art, Glass, Handicrafts, Pottery, Textiles
Collections: Crafts

A MANITOBA ASSOCIATION OF ARCHITECTS, 137 Bannatyne Ave, 2nd Flr, R3B 0R3. Tel 204-925-4620
Open Mon - Fri 9 AM - 5 PM. Estab 1906 as a Provincial Architectural Registration Board & professional governing body. Mem: 350; dues $375; annual meeting in Mar
Income: Financed by annual mem dues
Publications: Columns, quarterly

M MANITOBA HISTORICAL SOCIETY, Dalnavert Museum, 61 Carlton St, R3C 1N7. Tel 204-943-2835; *Pres Manitoba Historical Society* Teline Kear; *Chmn Management Comt* Bill Fraser; *Cur* Timothy Worth; *Cur Asst* Nancy Anderson
Open summer 10 AM - 6 PM, winter Noon - 5 PM, cl Mon & Fri. Admis adults $3, senior citizens & students $2, children $1.50. Estab 1975 to preserve & display the way of life of the 1895 well-to-do family. Average Annual Attendance: 9000
Income: $40,000 (financed by mem, city & state appropriation & private donation)
Collections: Home furnishings of the 1895 period: clothing, decorative arts material, furniture, household items, paintings & original family memorabilia
Activities: Classes for children; docent training; lect open to public, 6 vis lectr per year; sales shop sells books, postcards & tourist material

A MANITOBA SOCIETY OF ARTISTS, 504 Daer Blvd, R3K 1C5. Tel 204-837-1754; *Pres* Les Dewar
Estab 1901 to further the work of the artist at the local & community levels. Mem: 60; dues $20; annual meeting Oct
Income: Financed by mem & commission on sales
Exhibitions: Annual competition & exhibition open to all residents of Manitoba
Activities: Educ aspects include teaching by members in rural areas & artist-in-residence work in public schools; workshops; lect open to public; gallery talks; tours; competitions with awards; scholarships offered; originate traveling exhibitions

L PROVINCIAL ARCHIVES OF MANITOBA, 200 Vaughan St, R3C 1T5. Tel 204-945-3971; Elec Mail gourecs@mbnet.mb.ca, hbca@mb.sympatico.ca. *Provincial Archivist* Peter Bower
Open mid-May - Labour Day Mon - Fri 9 AM - 4 PM, mid-Sept - mid-May Tues - Sat 9 AM - 4 PM. No admis fee. Estab 1952 to gain access to Manitoba's documentary heritage; to preserve the recorded memory of Manitoba
Income: Financed by provincial appropriation through the Minister of Culture, Heritage & Recreation
Collections: Hudson's Bay Company Archives; Documentary & archival paintings, drawings, prints & photographs relating to Manitoba
Activities: Individual paintings & original objects of art lent to public institutions with proper security; book traveling exhibitions

M UKRAINIAN CULTURAL & EDUCATIONAL CENTRE, 184 Alexander Ave E, R3B 0L6. Tel 204-942-0218; FAX 204-943-2857; *Exec Dir* Eernie Cicierski; *Educ Exten Coordr* Andrea Balas; *Cur* Shawna Balas; *Archivist* Zenon Hluszok
Open Tues - Sat 10 AM - 4 PM; Sun 2 - 5 PM, cl Mon. No admis fee. Estab as the largest Ukrainian cultural resource centre & repository of Ukrainian historical & cultural artifacts in North America. Mem: 2000; dues $15, annual meeting June
Income: $216,328 (financed by province of Manitoba, federal government, donations, mem, trust fund, fundraising events)
Collections: Ukrainian Folk Art; †folk costumes; †embroidery; †weaving; †pysanky (Easter eggs); †woodcarving; †ceramics; coins, postage stamps and documents of the Ukrainian National Republic of 1918-1921; works of art by Ukrainian, Ukrainian-Canadian and Ukrainian-American artists: †prints, †paintings, †sculpture; archives: †Ukrainian immigration to Canada, †music collections
Publications: Visti Oseredok/News from Oseredok, members' bulletin, 2-3 times per yr
Activities: Classes for adults & children; traveling workshops; lect open to public; gallery talks; tours; competitions; scholarships offered; individual paintings & original objects of art lent to educational institutions, galleries & museums; lending collection contains color reproductions, framed reproductions, motion pictures, phonorecords, 40,000 photographs, 2000 slides; book traveling exhibitions annually; originate traveling exhibitions; sales shop sells books, original art, reproductions, prints, folk art, phonorecords, cassettes
M Gallery, 184 Alexander Ave E, R3B 0L6. Tel 204-942-0218; FAX 204-943-2857; *Gallery Cur* Shawna Balas
Mem: Dues family & organization $25, individual $15, student & senior citizen $5
Collections: 18th Century Icons; Contemporary Graphics (Archipenko, Gritchenko, Trutoffsky, Krycevsky, Hluschenko, Pavlos, Kholodny, Hnizdovsky, Mol, Levytsky, Shostak, Kuch); Contemporary Ukrainian; †Canadian Collection
Exhibitions: Works by visiting Ukrainian, Canadian, American and European artists; permanent collection
L Library & Archives, 184 Alexander Ave E, R3B 0L6. Tel 204-942-0218; FAX 204-943-2857; *Librn* Larisa Tolchinska
For reference only; lending to members
Library Holdings: Vols 30,000; Ukranian newspapers & periodicals; AV — Cassettes, motion pictures, rec, slides, v-tapes; Other — Clipping files, exhibition catalogs, pamphlets, photographs
Special Subjects: Ukrainian Studies
Publications: Visti, annual newsletter

M UNIVERSITY OF MANITOBA, Gallery III, School of Art, R3T 2N2. Tel 204-474-9322; FAX 204-275-3148; *Dir* Dale Amundson
Open Mon - Fri Noon - 4 PM. No admis fee. Estab 1965. Gallery III estab 1965 to provide exhibitions of contempory art & activities on the university campus; exhibitions open to the public. Average Annual Attendance: 20,000
Collections: †Contemporary Canadian & American painting, prints & sculpture; Fitzgerald Study Collection
Exhibitions: Exhibitions of Canadian, European & American Art, both contemporary & historical; special exhibitions from other categories; annual exhibitions by the graduating students of the School of Art
Publications: Exhibition catalogues
Activities: Discussion groups; workshops; lect open to public, 3-6 vis lectr per year; gallery talks; individual paintings & original objects of art lent; book traveling exhibitions, 2-4 per year; originate traveling exhibitions
M Faculty of Architecture Exhibition Centre, Architecture II Bldg, R3T 2N2. Tel 204-474-9558; FAX 204-275-7198; *Co-Dir* Dr George Fuller; *Co-Dir & Prof* Herb Enns
Open Mon - Fri 8:30 AM - 4:30 PM, weekend by special arrangements. Estab 1959 with the opening of the new Faculty of Architecture Building to provide architectural & related exhibitions for students & faculty on the University campus. 760 sq ft, secured climate controlled; over 900 linear ft of hanging space. Average Annual Attendance: 7500
Income: Financed by endowments, grants & private sponsorships
Collections: An extensive collection of drawings, prints, paintings, sculpture, ceramics, furniture & textiles (tapestries)
Exhibitions: Exhibitions from a diversity of private & public sources; annual exhibitions by the students in the Faculty of Architecture
Activities: Lect open to public, 6 vis lectr per year; gallery talks; symposia; individual paintings & original objects of art lent to recognized institutions; lending collection contains original art works, original prints, paintings, photographs, sculptures, furniture, textiles & ceramics
L Architecture & Fine Arts Library, 206 Russell, R3T 2N2. Tel 204-474-9216; FAX 204-269-8357; Telex 07-587721. *Head Librn* Mary Lochhead
Open Mon - Thurs 8:30 AM - 9 PM, Fri 8:30 AM - 5 PM, Sat & Sun Noon - 5 PM. Estab 1916 to serve the needs of students & faculty in the areas of architecture, fine arts, landscape architecture, environmental design, city & regional planning, graphic design, interior design & photography. Circ 100,000
Income: Financed primarily by provincial government
Library Holdings: Vols 63,000; Per subs 430; Product catalogs 5000; Micro — Fiche 560, reels 210; AV — A-tapes 75, slides 107,000, v-tapes 90; Other — Clipping files, pamphlets, photographs, reproductions 776
Special Subjects: Architecture, Interior Design, Landscape Architecture, Photography, City & Regional Planning, Design, Environmental Studies, Fine Arts, Sculpture

M UPSTAIRS GALLERY, 266 Edmonton St, R3C 1R9. Tel 204-943-2734; FAX 204-943-7726; *Dir & Owner* Faye Settler
Open Mon - Sat 9:30 AM - 5:30 PM, cl Sun. Estab 1966
Collections: Contemporary & early 20th Century Canadian paintings, prints & drawings; Inuit Eskimo sculpture, prints, drawings & wall hangings

M WINNIPEG ART GALLERY, 300 Memorial Blvd, R3C 1V1. Tel 204-786-6641; FAX 204-788-4998; *Dir* Michel V Cheff; *Mgr Financial Operations* Judy Murphy; *Educ Mgr* Claudette Lagimodiene; *Assoc Dir. Curatorial Servs* Tom Smart; *Communications Mgr* Christopher Brown

Open Tues, Thurs - Sun 10 AM - 5 PM, Wed 10 AM - 9 PM. Admis family $5, adult $3, senior citizen & student $2, children under 12 free. Estab 1912, incorporated 1963. Rebuilt & relocated 1968, opened 1972, to present a diversified, quality level program of art in all media, representing various cultures, past & present. Building includes 9 galleries as well as displays on mezzanine level, sculpture court & main foyer. Average Annual Attendance: 142,000. Mem: 4400; dues family $50, individual $35, student & senior citizen couples $30, senior citizens $20; annual meeting in Aug
Income: $3,500,000 (financed by endowment, mem, city, state & federal appropriation)
Collections: Canadian art; contemporary Canada; contemporary Manitoba; decorative arts; Inuit art; European art; Gort Collection; Master prints & drawings; modern European art; †photography
Exhibitions: The changing exhibition includes contemporary & historical works of art by Canadian, European & American artists
Publications: Tableau (calendar of events), monthly; exhibition catalogs
Activities: Classes for adults & children; docent training; lect open to public, 10 vis lectr per year; concerts; gallery talks; tours; exten dept serves Manitoba, Canada, United States & Europe; individual paintings & original objects of art lent to centres & museums; book traveling exhibitions 4 per year; originate traveling exhibitions; museum shop sells books, magazines, original art, reproductions & prints
L Clara Lander Library, 300 Memorial Blvd, R3C 1V1. Tel 204-786-6641, Ext 237; FAX 204-788-4998; *Librn* Catherine Shields
Open Tues - Fri 11 AM - 4:30 PM. Estab 1954 to serve as a source of informational & general interest materials for members & staff of the Winnipeg Art Gallery & to art history students. Circ 1500
Income: Financed by mem, city & provincial appropriations
Purchases: $10,000
Library Holdings: Vols 23,000; Per subs 60; Original documents; AV — Slides 10,000; Other — Clipping files 10,000, exhibition catalogs, manuscripts, memorabilia, pamphlets
Special Subjects: Canadian Art, Inuit Art
Collections: Archival material pertaining to Winnipeg Art Gallery; Rare Books on Canadian & European Art; George Swinton Collection on Eskimo & North American Indian art & culture

NEW BRUNSWICK

CAMPBELLTON

M GALERIE RESTIGOUCHE GALLERY, 39 Andrew St, PO Box 674, E3N 3H1. Tel 506-753-5750; FAX 506-759-9601; Elec Mail rgaleri@nbnet.nb.ca. *Chmn* Nathalie Godin
Open Mon - Fri 9 AM - 5 PM, Sat & Sun 1 - 5 PM. No admis fee. Estab 1975 for exhibitions & activities. Building has 4800 sq ft; Exhibition hall is 1500 sq ft, small gallery 400 sq ft; 230 running feet. Average Annual Attendance: 25,000. Mem: 185; dues $15
Income: $100,000 (financed by federal, provincial & city appropriations, by Friends of the Gallery & by private donations)
Exhibitions: Hands on Signs
Publications: Exhibitions catalogues; Restigouche Gallery brochure
Activities: Classes for adults & children; art & craft workshops; lect open to public, 10 vis lectr per year; concerts; gallery talks; tours; traveling exhibitions exten service; originate traveling exhibitions

FREDERICTON

M BEAVERBROOK ART GALLERY, 703 Queen St, PO Box 605, E3B 5A6. Tel 506-458-8545; FAX 506-459-7450;
Internet Home Page Address http://www.discribe.ca/bag/. *Dir* Ian G Lumsden; *Cur* Tom Smart; *Educ & Communications Officer* Caroline Walker; *Cur* Tom Smart
Open Sept - June Tues - Fri 9 AM - 5 PM, Sat 10 AM - 5 PM, Sun Noon - 5 PM. Admis adults $3, seniors $2, students $1, children under 6 free. Estab 1959 to foster & promote the study & the pub enjoyment & appreciation of the arts. Major galleries upstairs: British, Canadian & High Galleries & Pillow Porcelain Room. East wing galleries: Hosmer, Pillow-Vaughan Gallery, Sir Max Aitken Gallery & Vaulted Corridor Gallery. Downstairs galleries: exhibition gallery & Foyer Gallery. Average Annual Attendance: 45,000. Mem: 800; dues family $40, individual $30
Income: $670,000 (financed by endowment & private foundation)
Purchases: $330,000
Collections: Hosmer-Pillow-Vaughan collection of Continental European fine & decorative arts from the 14th to 19th century; Works by Dali, Constable, Gainsborough, Hogarth, Cornelius Krieghoff, Reynolds, Sutherland & Turner; 16th-20th century English paintings; 18th & early 19th century English porcelain; 19th & 20th century Canadian New Brunswick paintings
Exhibitions: William Blake & His Contemporaries: Prints & Drawings from the National Gallery of Canada; Chris Cran: Ileads; Fallout: Chernobyl Through the Eyes of Soviet Children; Terry Graff-Ectopia; The Nan Gregg Gift; Light, Air & Colour: American Impressionist Paintings from the Collection of the Pennsylvania Academy of the Fine Arts William Blake & his Contemporaries: Prints & Drawings from the National Gallery of Canada; The Nan Gregg Gift; Fallout: Chernobyl Through the Eyes of Soviet Children; Light, Air & Colour: American Impressionist Paintings from the Collection of the Pennsylvania Academy of the Fine Arts; Studio Watch: Sarah Petit - Modern Times; Chris Cran: Ileads; Tauromaquia: Goya - Picasso; Studio Watch: Terry Graff - Ectopia; Fred Ross & the Tradition of Figurative Painting in Saint John; Dan Steeves: Through the Looking Glass: Self Portraits of Leslie Poole
Publications: Annual report; Calendar of Events; exhibition catalogs; Tableau announcing gallery's program

Activities: Classes for adults & children; docent training; lect open to the public; gallery talks; tours; films; exten dept serving New Brunswick as well as the rest of Canada; individual paintings lent to recognized art galleries & museums which operate as educational institutions; collection contains 1575 original art works, sculpture; book traveling exhibitions; originate traveling exhibitions; sales shop sells books, magazines, reproductions, exhibition catalogs, Christmas cards, postcards, hasty-notes & gift items

L **Library,** 703 Queen St, E3B 5A6. Tel 506-458-8545; FAX 506-459-7450; *Librn* Barry Henderson
Open to gallery personnel only, for reference
Library Holdings: AV — V-tapes; Other — Exhibition catalogs
Special Subjects: Painting - British, Painting - Canadian, Painting - European
Publications: Auction Catalogs

A **NEW BRUNSWICK COLLEGE OF CRAFT & DESIGN,** PO Box 6000, E3B 5H1. Tel 506-457-2305; FAX 506-457-7352; *Principal* Janice Gillies, BSc
Open Mon - Fri 8:15 AM - 4:30 PM. No admis fee. Estab 1938 to educate students as professional crafts people & designers. Maintains reference library
Income: Financed by provincial government
Exhibitions: Student & staff juried shows; periodic vis exhibitions
Publications: Provincial Craft Directory
Activities: Classes for adults & children; lect open to public, 10 vis lectr per year; awards; lending collection contains original art works, video tapes, slides & 3000 books

L **Library,** PO Box 6000, E3B 5H1. Tel 506-453-2305; FAX 506-457-7352; *Principal* Janice Gillies
A very small but growing library which is primarily for students & craftsmen
Income: Financed by government & book donations
Library Holdings: Vols 3000; Per subs 50; AV — Fs, slides, v-tapes; Other — Exhibition catalogs, pamphlets
Special Subjects: Advertising Design, Aesthetics, American Indian Art, Antiquities-Egyptian, Antiquities-Greek, Antiquities-Oriental, Antiquities-Roman, Architecture, Art Education, Art History, Asian Art, Calligraphy, Carpets & Rugs, Ceramics, Commercial Art
Publications: Computerized catalogue

M **ORGANIZATION FOR THE DEVELOPMENT OF ARTISTS,** Gallery Connexion, Justice Bldg, Queen St (Mailing add: PO Box 696, E3B 5B4). Tel 506-454-1433; FAX 506-454-1401; Elec Mail conney@nbnet.nb.ca. *Coordr* Sarah Maloney
Open Tues - Fri Noon - 4 PM, Sun 2 - 4 PM. Estab 1984 to show contemporary experimental work. Maintains a reference library. Average Annual Attendance: 2600. Mem: 70; dues full member $30, associate $20, students $15; annual meeting in Oct
Income: $31,371 (financed by mem, provincial appropriation & Canada Council)
Publications: Connexionews, monthly
Activities: Lect open to public, 6-10 vis lectr per year; book traveling exhibitions 6-10 per year; originate traveling exhibitions 1 per year

M **UNIVERSITY OF NEW BRUNSWICK,** UNB Art Centre, Memorial Hall, Bailey Ave, PO Box 4400, E3B 5A3. Tel 506-453-4623; FAX 506-453-4599; *Dir* Marie Maltais
Open winter Mon - Fri 8:30 AM - 4:30 PM, Sun & holidays 2 - 4 PM, summer Mon - Fri 9 AM - 4 PM, Sun & holidays Noon - 4 PM. No admis fee. Estab 1940 to broaden the experience of the university students & serve the city & province. Two galleries, each with approx 100 running ft of wall space; display case. Average Annual Attendance: 5000
Income: Financed by provincial university & grants for special projects
Purchases: $7000
Collections: Chiefly New Brunswick Artists; some Canadian (chiefly printmakers)
Publications: Chiefly New Brunswick Artists; Canadian artists
Activities: Classes for adults; lect open to public, 4 vis lectr per year; gallery talks; tours; individual paintings & original objects of art lent to public but secure areas on this campus & the university campus in Saint John & reproductions to students; lending collection contains framed reproductions, original prints, paintings, photographs, sculptures & slides; book traveling exhibitions 4 per year; originate traveling exhibitions provincially to national

HAMPTON

M **KINGS COUNTY HISTORICAL SOCIETY AND MUSEUM,** PO Box 5001, E0G 1Z0. Tel 506-832-6009; FAX 506-832-6007; *Pres* Stephen Cripps; *Cur* A Faye Pearson; *Treas* Julie Hughes; *Genealogist* Harvey Dalling; *Co-Genealogist* Ernest Friars
Open Mon - Fri 10 AM - 5 PM. Admis adults $2, children $1. Estab 1968 to preserve loyalist history & artifacts. Maintains small reference library. Average Annual Attendance: 1400. Mem: 262; dues society $15 & $ 20; annual meeting in Nov
Income: $2250 (financed by provincial & student grants, dues, fairs & book sales)
Collections: Coin; dairy; glass; 1854 brass measures; jewelry; quilts
Exhibitions: School exhibitions; Women's Institute; Christmas Fair
Publications: Newsletters, 7 per year
Activities: Lect open to public, 7 vis lectr per year; tours; originate traveling exhibitions; sales shop sells books

MONCTON

M **RADIO-CANADA SRC CBC,** Galerie Georges Goguen, 250 Archibald St, PO Box 950, E1C 8N8. Tel 506-853-6666;
Estab 1972 for maritime artist. Gallery size 15 x 25, track lighting. Average Annual Attendance: 300
Exhibitions: (1997) Roland Diagle (mixed media); Rene Herbert (paintings); Corinne Gallant (photography); Ronald Price (paintings); Donald Savoie (photography)

M **GALERIE D'ART DE L'UNIVERSITE DE MONCTON,** 85th Edific Clement Cormier, E1A 3E9. Tel 506-858-4088; FAX 506-858-4043; *Dir* Luc Charette; *Secy* Necol LaBlanc; *Technician* Paul Bourque
Open Mon - Fri 10 AM - 5 PM, Sat - Sun 1 - 5 PM. No admis fee. Estab 1965 to offer outstanding shows to the university students & to the pub. 400 linear ft wall space, 3500 sq ft vinyl plywood walls, controlled light, temperature, humidity systems, security system. Average Annual Attendance: 13,000
Income: $100,000 (financed through university)
Collections: Artists represented in permanent collection: Bruno Bobak; Alex Colville; Francis Coutellier; Tom Forrestall; Georges Goguen; Hurtubise; Hilda Lavoie; Fernand Leduc; Rita Letendre; Toni Onley; Claude Roussel; Romeo Savoie; Pavel Skalnik; Gordon Smith
Activities: Classes for children; dramatic programs; lect open to public, 10 vis lectr per year; concerts; gallery talks; tours; individual paintings & original objects of art lent to university personnel & art galleries & museums; lending collection contains 500 reproductions, 300 original art works, 180 original prints, 30 paintings, 20 sculpture

SACKVILLE

M **MOUNT ALLISON UNIVERSITY,** Owens Art Gallery, York St, E0A 3C0. Tel 506-364-2574; FAX 506-364-2575; Telex 014-2266. *Dir* Gemey Kelly; *Fine Arts Conservator* J Tisdale; *Fine Arts Technician* R Ibbitson
Open Mon - Fri 10 AM - 5 PM, Tues evenings 7 - 10 PM, Sat & Sun 1 - 5 PM, cl university holidays. No admis fee. Estab 1895, rebuilt 1972. Building includes five gallery areas; conservation laboratory. Average Annual Attendance: 11,000
Income: Financed by Mount Allison University, Government, Corporate & Private Assistance
Collections: Broad collection of graphics, paintings, works on paper; 19th & 20th century Canadian, European & American Art
Publications: Exhibition catalogs
Activities: Lect open to public, 7 vis lectr per year; gallery talks; tours; individual paintings lent to other galleries & museums; book traveling exhibitions 10-12 per year; originate traveling exhibitions

M **STRUTS GALLERY,** 5 Lorne St, E0A 3C0. Tel 506-536-1211; *Dir* Gregory Elgstrand
Open Noon - 5 PM. No admis fee. Estab 1982. Average Annual Attendance: 1500. Mem: Open to professional artist, associate or student; dues professional $35, associate/student $15; annual meeting in Oct
Income: $40,000 (financed by mem, Canada Council, Province of New Brunswick)
Exhibitions: Show work by contemporary living artists & a broad range of experimental art works
Activities: Lect open to public, 2-5 vis lectr per year

SAINT ANDREWS

M **ROSS MEMORIAL MUSEUM** (Formerly Henry Phipps & Sarah Juliette/Ross Memorial Museum), 188 Montague St (Mailing add: PO Box 603, E0G 2X0). Tel 506-529-1824; FAX 506-529-3383; *Dir* Margot Magee Sackett
Open late June - mid Oct, cl Sun, cl Sun & Mon in the fall. Admis by donation. Estab 1980. 1 small gallery. Average Annual Attendance: 8000
Collections: Jacqueline Davis China Collection; Mowat Loyalist Collection; New Brunswick Furniture Collection; Ross Decorative Art Collection; Van Horne Collection
Exhibitions: Special summer exhibit
Activities: Classes for children; lect open to public; individual paintings & original objects of art lent to museums; originate traveling exhibitions

A **SUNBURY SHORES ARTS & NATURE CENTRE, INC,** Gallery, 139 Water St, PO Box 100, E0G 2X0. Tel 506-529-3386; FAX 506-529-4779; *Pres* Mary Blather; *Dir* Lois Fenety
Open Mon - Sat 10 AM - 4 PM, cl Sun. No admis fee. Estab 1964, to function as a link for & harmonize views of scientists, artists & industrialists. Gallery maintained, 200 running ft, fire & burglar protection, security during hours, controllable lighting & street frontage. Average Annual Attendance: 5000. Mem: 500; dues family $40, individual, students & senior citizens $25; annual meeting in Aug
Income: Financed by endowment, mem, grants, revenue from courses & activities, including special projects
Exhibitions: Exhibits change frequently throughout the year
Publications: Brochure, summer annually; Sunbury Notes, quarterly
Activities: Lect open to public, 10-15 vis lectr per year; gallery talks; scholarships offered; museum shop sells books, original art, reproductions & prints

L **Library,** 139 Water St, PO Box 100, E0G 2X0. Tel 506-529-3386; *Dir* Lois Fenety
Open to pub; primarily for reference
Income: Financed by mem
Library Holdings: Vols 600; Per subs 10; Other — Exhibition catalogs

SAINT JOHN

M **NEW BRUNSWICK MUSEUM,** 277 Douglas Ave, E2K 1E5. Tel 506-643-2300; FAX 506-643-6081; *Dir* Dr Frank Milligan; *Assoc Dir* Jane Fullerton; *Controller* Judith Brown; *Chief Cur* Gary Hughes; *Mgr Temporary Exhibits* Regina Mantin; *Mgr Marketing & Develop* Zita Longobardi; *Natural Sciences-Zoology* Dr Donald McAlpine; *Educ Officer Natural Science* Dr Randy Miller; *Cur Canada & International Art* Andrea Kirkpatrick; *Cur New Brunswick Art* Peter Larocque; *Natural Sciences-Botany* Stephen Clayden
Open Mon - Fri 9 AM - 9 PM, Sat 10 AM - 6 PM, Sun Noon - 5 PM. Admis families $12, adults $5.50, seniors $4.50, students $3, children 3 & under free. Estab 1842 to collect, conserve, exhibit & interpret the Human & Natural history of New Brunswick in relation to itself & to the outside world. Twelve major galleries for permanent exhibits, three galleries for changing temporary exhibits;

62,000 sq ft gallery space. Average Annual Attendance: 75,000. Mem: 700; dues $15-$100

Income: $1,600,000 (financed by municipal, federal & provincial appropriations)
Collections: 3 galleries: Canadian Art, International Art; New Brunswick Art; Oriental arts; Russian Silver (Faberge pre-Revolution); social history
Publications: Courier, quarterly newsletter
Activities: Classes for children; docent training; lect open to public; gallery talks; tours; competitions sponsored in schools; scholarships & fels offered; individual paintings & original objects of art lent to museums & galleries; book traveling exhibitions; originate traveling exhibitions organized & circulated nationally & internationally; museum shop sells books & gifts

L **Library,** 277 Douglas Ave, E2K 1E5. Tel 506-643-2322; FAX 506-643-2360; *Head* Gary Hughes
Open to the pub for reference only
Library Holdings: Vols 20,000; Per subs 75; Micro — Fiche, reels; Other — Clipping files, exhibition catalogs, manuscripts
Special Subjects: Aesthetics, Afro-American Art, American Indian Art, American Western Art, Anthropology, Antiquities-Assyrian, Archaeology, Architecture, Art Education, Art History, Bookplates & Bindings, Bronzes, Calligraphy, Carpets & Rugs, Cartoons

NEWFOUNDLAND

CORNER BROOK

M **MEMORIAL UNIVERSITY OF NEWFOUNDLAND,** Sir Wilfred Grenfell College Art Gallery, University Dr, A2H 6P9. Tel 709-637-6357; FAX 709-637-6383; Elec Mail coneill@beothuk.swgc.mun.ca. *Dir & Cur* Colleen O'Neill
Open Tues - Sun 11 AM - 5 PM. No admis fee. Estab 1988. 2000 sq ft, 170 running ft, white walls, neutral carpet. Average Annual Attendance: 6000. Mem: 300
Income: $100,000 (financed by university & Canada Council)
Collections: †Drawings, paintings, †photography & †prints (mainly contemporary Canadian)
Exhibitions: Changing contemporary exhibitions every 7 weeks
Publications: Exhibition catalogues
Activities: Docent programs; lect open to public, 8 vis lectr per year; lending collection; book traveling exhibitions 3 per year; originate traveling exhibitions 1 per year; sales shop sells catalogues

SAINT JOHN'S

M **MEMORIAL UNIVERSITY OF NEWFOUNDLAND,** Art Gallery of Newfoundland & Labrador, Arts & Culture Centre, PO Box 4200, A1C 5S7. Tel 709-737-8210; FAX 709-737-2007; Elec Mail aghl@morgan.ucs.mun.ca. *Dir* Patricia Grattan; *Supv of Operations* Edward Cadigan; *Educ & Exhib Cur* Caroline Stone; *Secy* Judy Tucker; *Registrar* Brian Murphy; *Admin Staff Specialist* Wanda Mooney; *Develop Mgr* Rita Gardiner
Open Tues - Sun Noon - 5 PM, Thurs, Fri & Sat evenings 7 - 10 PM, cl Mon. No admis fee. Estab 1961 to display contemporary Canadian art, with an emphasis on Newfoundland work & provide visual art educational programs. Four galleries with 130 running ft each. Average Annual Attendance: 30,000
Income: Financed through the university, federal funding & revenue generation
Collections: Post 1960 Canadian art
Exhibitions: Contemporary art
Publications: Catalogs of in-house exhibitions
Activities: Classes for children; workshops; lect open to public; concerts; gallery talks; tours; individual paintings & original objects of art lent to other institutions; lending collection contains books, catalogs & 1500 slides; book traveling exhibitions; originate traveling exhibitions

M **NEWFOUNDLAND MUSEUM,** 285 Duckworth St, A1C 1G9. Tel 709-729-2329; *Dir* Mike Clair; *Exhib Officer* Allan Clarke
No admis fee. Estab 1878 as the Athenaeum for the preservation of Provincial Heritage. The Newfoundland Mus now houses collections & exhibitions reflecting the 7000 year history of Newfoundland & Labrador. Branches at The Murray Premises Mus, St John's & The Newfoundland Seamen's Mus at Grand Bank & The Mary March Mus at Grand Falls. Average Annual Attendance: 80,000
Income: Financed by federal & provincial appropriations
Collections: Beothuk, Thule, Maritime Archaic, pre-Dorset, Dorset, Naskapi, Montagnais and Micmac artifacts; history material; maps; naval and military; 19th century Newfoundland domestic artifacts, maritime, natural history, mercantile; 18th - 20th century Newfoundland material, outport furniture, textiles, navigational instruments, ship portraits, watercolors, prints, drawings
Exhibitions: Rotating exhibits
Publications: Museum Notes; exhibition catalogues; technical bulletins; Archeology in Newfoundland & Labrador, Natural History Curatorial Reports; annual report
Activities: Classes for children; docent training; lect open to public, 12 vis lectr per year; tours; book traveling exhibitions; originate traveling exhibitions

L **Library,** 285 Duckworth St, A1C 1G9. Tel 709-729-2460; FAX 709-729-2179; *Public Programming Asst* Karen Walsh
Open to researchers for reference
Special Subjects: Military history
Collections: Mercury Series of National Museums in Archaeology, Ethnology, Restoration; National Historic Parks & Sites Reports

NOVA SCOTIA

DARTMOUTH

M **DARTMOUTH HERITAGE MUSEUM,** 100 Wyse Rd, B3A 1M1. Tel 902-464-2300; FAX 902-464-8210; *Dir* Dr Richard Henning Field; *Cur* Betty Ann Aaboe-Milligan
Open summer Mon - Fri 9 AM - 4 PM, Sat & Sun 1 - 4:30 PM, winter Mon - Sat 1 - 4:30 PM, Sun 2 - 5 PM. No admis fee. Estab 1968 to collect & preserve the history & heritage of the City of Dartmouth. Average Annual Attendance: 15,000
Income: Financed by city appropriation & provincial funds
Collections: Local history collection including art, archival, textile/costume & general social history material
Exhibitions: Twenty-four exhibitions scheduled per year
Activities: Classes for adults & children; gallery talks; tours; exten dept serves historic houses

L **SOCIETY FOR THE PROTECTION & PRESERVATION OF BLACK CULTURE IN NOVA SCOTIA,** Black Cultural Center for Nova Scotia, 1149 Main St, B2Z 1A8. Tel 902-434-6223; FAX 902-434-2306; *Cur* Henry Bishop; *Prog Coordr* Robert Ffrench
Open 9 AM - 5 PM. Admis $2. Estab 1984. For reference only. Average Annual Attendance: 10,000
Income: Financed by provincial & federal government
Library Holdings: Vols 3000; AV — A-tapes, cassettes, lantern slides, rec, slides, v-tapes; Other — Clipping files, framed reproductions, manuscripts, memorabilia, original art works, pamphlets, prints, reproductions
Publications: Newsletter Preserver
Activities: Lect open to public; school tours; presentations; sales shop sells books

HALIFAX

M **ART GALLERY OF NOVA SCOTIA,** 1741 Hollis at Cheapside, PO Box 2262, B3J 3C8. Tel 902-424-7542; FAX 902-424-7359; *Dir* Bernard Riordon; *Deputy Dir & Head Programming* Virginia Stephen; *Mgr Coll & Gallery Services* Judy Dietz; *Exhib Cur* Susan Foshay; *Mgr Develop & Pub Relations* Denise Rooney; *Fine Arts Conservator* Laurie Hamilton; *Admin Officer* Suzanna Tingley
Open Tues - Fri 10 AM - 5 PM, Sat & Sun Noon - 5 PM; Summer hours: June - Aug Thurs 10 AM - 9 PM. Admis family $5.50, adult $2.50, student & senior $1.25, group of 10 or more $2, children under 12 & members free, Tues free sponsored by Sprint Canada Inc. Estab 1975 to replace the Nova Scotia Mus of Fine Arts, dedicated to serving the pub by bringing the visual arts & people together in an environment which encourages exploration, dialogue & enjoyment. Seventeen galleries, for permanent collection & temporary exhibitions. Average Annual Attendance: 80,000. Mem: 2000; dues life members $2000, family $40, individual $30, senior couple $20, artist $15, senior individual $15, young member/student $10
Income: Financed by Nova Scotia Dept of Educ & Culture, Dept of Canadian Heritage, The Canada Council, municipal governments, private foundations & individual & corporate supporters
Collections: Canadian Historical & Contemporary Art Collection drawings, paintings, prints, sculpture, ceramics & international art; Nova Scocia Folk Art Collection; Nova Scotian Collection
Exhibitions: (1997) Guido Molinari, A Retrospective; The Illuminated Life of Maud Lewis, An Exhibition of Works by the Nova Scotian Folk Artist (1903-1970); The Huntington Folk Art Exhibition; Rene Marcil, A Life Apart; Mary Pratt: The Substance of Light; Mermaid's Magic; Dawn MacNutt-All The Ancients Walk Inside US; Nova Scotia Collects: Tony Sauliner; Contemporary Paperworks; Math & Art Exhibition
Activities: Classes for adults & children; docent training; lect open to public, 20 vis lectr per year; gallery talks; tours, family Sundays, family weekends; Black Tie Gala; Pick of the Month; exten dept serves Canada; artmobile; individual paintings & original objects of art lent to Province & Government House; lending collection contains original art works, framed reproductions, original prints, paintings & sculpture; book traveling exhibitions 6-8 per year; originate traveling exhibitions 10-15 per year; museum & sales shop sells books, jewelry, magazines, original art, pottery, prints, reproductions, slides, crafts & also rental service

M **DALHOUSIE UNIVERSITY,** Art Gallery, 6101 University Ave, B3H 3J5. Tel 902-494-2403, 494-2195; FAX 902-494-2890; *Dir* Mern O'Brien; *Registrar & Preparator* Michele Gallant; *Adjunct Cur* Susan Gibson Garvey; *Office Mgr* Denise Hoskin
Open Tues - Fri 11 AM - 5 PM, Tues 7 - 10 PM, Sat & Sun 1 - 5 PM, cl Mon. No admis fee. Estab 1943 to collect, preserve, interpret & display works of art, primarily of Canadian origin. Dalhousie Art Gallery is located in the Dalhousie Arts Centre and open to university community and local area; it contains 400 running ft of wall space & 4000 sq ft floor space. Average Annual Attendance: 16,000
Income: Financed by university supplemented by government grants
Collections: †Canadian works on paper
Publications: Annual Report; Calendar of Events, 3 times per yr
Activities: Classes for children; docent training; lect open to public, 12 vis lectr per year; concerts; gallery talks; tours; exten dept serves regional & national area; individual paintings & original objects of art lent to professional galleries & campus areas; book traveling exhibitions; originate traveling exhibitions; sales shop sells gallery publications

M **MOUNT SAINT VINCENT UNIVERSITY,** Art Gallery, 166 Bedford Hwy, B3M 2J6. Tel 902-457-6788, 457-6160; FAX 902-457-2447; *Dir Art Gallery* Ingrid Jenkner; *Office Mgr* Traci Scanlan
Open Mon - Fri 9 AM - 5 PM, Sat, Sun & holidays 1 - 5 PM, Tues until 9 PM. No admis fee. Estab 1970 & operating throughout the year with continuously-changing exhibitions of local, regional, national & international origin in the area of visual culture. Gallery situated on the main floor & mezzanine. Average

Annual Attendance: 15,000
Income: Financed by university funds
Purchases: Judith Mann; Peter Barss; Susanne MacKay, Herself; Felicity Redgrave, Peggy's Rocks; Carol Fraser, Nocturne
Collections: The Art Gallery is custodian of a collection of pictures, ceramics & pottery of the late Alice Egan Hagen of Mahone Bay, noted Nova Scotia potter & ceramist; †works by Atlantic region artists; women artists
Publications: Gallery News, 4 times per yr; exhibition catalogs
Activities: Workshops; lect open to public, 12 vis lectr per year; concerts; gallery talks; tours; competitions; individual paintings & original objects of art lent to other galleries; lending collection contains videotapes; book traveling exhibitions 6 per year; originate traveling exhibitions

A **NOVA SCOTIA ASSOCIATION OF ARCHITECTS,** 1361 Barrington St, B3J 1Y9. Tel 902-423-7607; FAX 902-425-7024; *Exec Dir* Diane Scott-Stewart
Estab 1932 to license & regulate architects of Nova Scotia. Mem: 200; annual meeting in Feb
Publications: Newsletter, monthly

M **NOVA SCOTIA COLLEGE OF ART AND DESIGN,** Anna Leonowens Gallery, 5163 Duke St, B3J 3J6. Tel 902-494-8223; FAX 902-425-3997; *Pres* Alice Mansell; *Dir* Jessica Kerrin
Open Tues - Sat 11 AM - 5 PM, Mon evenings 6 - 8 PM. Estab for educational purposes. One small & two large galleries
Income: Financed by state appropriations & tuition
Exhibitions: 100 exhibitions per yer
Publications: Ten books; exhibition catalogs, occasionally
Activities: Lect open to public; gallery talks; scholarships offered

L **Library,** 5163 Duke St, B3J 3J6. Tel 902-494-8196; FAX 902-425-2420; Elec Mail ilga@nscad.ns.ca. *Dir* Ilga Leja; *Dir of Non-Print Coll* Mary Snyder
Open Mon - Fri 8:30 AM - 9 PM, Sat & Sun 1 - 5 PM. Circ 30,000
Income: Financed by state appropriation & student fees
Purchases: $51,000
Library Holdings: Vols 28,000; Per subs 250; Micro — Fiche, reels; AV — A-tapes, cassettes, fs, rec, slides, v-tapes; Other — Exhibition catalogs, pamphlets
Special Subjects: Contemporary art

M **NOVA SCOTIA MUSEUM,** Maritime Museum of the Atlantic, 1675 Lower Water St, B3J 1S3. Tel 902-424-7490; FAX 902-424-0612; *Cur* Gerry Lunn
Open June 1 - Oct 15 9:30 AM - 5:30 PM, Sun 1 - 5:30 PM, Oct 16 - May 31 9:30 AM - 5:00 PM. Admis adults $4.50, children 5-17 $1, under 5 free. Estab 1948 to interpret maritime history of eastern coast of Canada. Average Annual Attendance: 140,000
Income: Financed by state appropriations
Collections: Halifax Explosion; Historical Marine Painting display; Lawrence Family memorabilia; small craft, ship models, ship portraits, uniforms, marine artifacts; Titantic artifacts
Activities: Lect open to public, 20 vis lectr per year; gallery talks; individual paintings & original objects of art lent to other institutions; sales shop sells books

M **ST MARY'S UNIVERSITY,** Art Gallery, B3H 3C3. Tel 902-420-5445; FAX 902-420-5561; *Dir & Cur* J R Leighton Davis; *Asst Dir & Cur* Gordon Laurin; *Performing Arts Coordr* Cathryn Ellis
Open Tues - Thurs 1 - 7 PM, Fri 1 - 5 PM, Sat & Sun Noon - 5 PM, cl Mon. Estab 1970 to present a variety of exhibitions & performances of both regional & national interest & by contemporary artists. Average Annual Attendance: 12,000
Income: Financed by provincial appropriation
Collections: Works on paper by contemporary Canadian artists
Publications: Exhibit catalogues, 1-2 times per year
Activities: Adult drawing classes; lect open to public, 3-4 vis lectr per year; concerts; gallery talks; tours; individual paintings & original objects of art lent; exten dept serves university; book traveling exhibitions 2-3 per year; originate travelling exhibitions; circulated to the Atlantic Provinces of Canada

A **VISUAL ARTS NOVA SCOTIA,** 1809 Barrington St, Ste 901, B3J 3K8. Tel 902-423-4694; FAX 902-422-0881; Elec Mail vans@fox.nstn.ca. *Exec Dir* Andrew Terris
Open 9:30 AM - 4:30 PM. Estab 1976 as a non-profit arts service organization to foster the development, awareness & understanding of the visual arts in Nova Scotia. Encourages the production, exhibition & appreciation of works by Nova Scotia's visual artists. Maintains slide registry, video library & archives. Mem: Over 500; dues corporate $50, couple, group or gallery $30, individual $20, student $10
Income: $125,000 (financed by mem & provincial appropriation)
Exhibitions: FAR & WIDE, the VANS 20th Anniversary Exhibition; biennial juried exhibitions, annual open exhibitions & occasional regional exhibitions
Publications: Visual Arts News, quarterly
Activities: PAINTS (Professional Artists in the Schools); internships offered

WOLFVILLE

M **ACADIA UNIVERSITY ART GALLERY,** c/o Beveridge Arts Centre, B0P 1X0. Tel 902-542-2201; FAX 902-542-4727; *Dir* Franziska Kruschen Leiter; *Secy* Marjorie Gee Baird
Estab 1978, art dept 1928, to exhibit contemporary & historical art particularly from the Atlantic region. Average Annual Attendance: 15,000
Income: $65,000 (financed by endowment & University funds)
Purchases: $15,000 (works by Atlantic region artists)
Collections: Contemporary & Historical Paintings, Drawings & Prints
Activities: Lectures open to public; 4 vis lectr per year; book traveling exhibitons 8 per year; originate travel exhibitions 4 per year

YARMOUTH

M **YARMOUTH COUNTY HISTORICAL SOCIETY,** Yarmouth County Museum, 22 Collins St, B5A 3C8. Tel 902-742-5539; FAX 902-749-1120; Elec Mail ycn0056@ycn.library.ns.ca. *Pres* Dick Robicheau; *Cur* Eric Ruff; *Archivist* Laura Bradley
Open Jun 1 - Oct 15 9 AM - 5 PM, Sun 1 - 5 PM, Oct 10 - May 31 2 - 5 PM, cl Mon. Admis adults $2.50, students $1, children $.50. Estab 1958 to display artifacts & paintings relating to Yarmouth's past. Located in former Congregational Church built in 1893. Average Annual Attendance: 14,000. Mem: 400; dues $17; meetings first Fri each month
Income: $100,000 (financed by mem, admis & state appropriation)
Purchases: $500
Collections: Gen historical coll; paintings of & by Yarmouthians; coll of ship portraits of Yarmouth vessels & vessels commanded by Yarmouthians; gen & marine artifacts; marine drawings & portraits
Exhibitions: Various local exhibits
Publications: Monthly newsletter
Activities: Lect open to public, 12 vis lectr per year; concerts; gallery talks; tours; Heritage Awards; museum shop sells books, prints

ONTARIO

ALMONTE

M **MISSISSIPPI VALLEY CONSERVATION AUTHORITY,** Mill of Kintail Museum, RR 1 (Mailing add: PO Box 268, Lanark, K0G 1K0). Tel 613-256-3610; *Cur* Carol Munden
Open May 15 - Oct 15 Wed - Sun & holidays 11:30 AM - 4:30 PM. Admis family $2.50, adults $1, senior citizens & children $.50. Estab 1952 as a private mus, publicly owned since 1973 by Mississippi Valley Conservation Authority as a memorial to Dr R Tait McKenzie, Canadian sculptor, physical educator, surgeon & humanitarian. Average Annual Attendance: 7500
Income: Financed by provincial government grant
Collections: 70 Original Athletic, Memorial & Monumental Sculptures, nearly all in plaster; 600 Pioneer Artifacts, mostly collected by Dr McKenzie
Activities: Classes for children; gallery talks; tours; sales shop sells books, reproductions, postcards & gift notes

ATIKOKAN

L **QUETICO PARK,** John B Ridley Research Library, Quetico Park, P0T 1C0. Tel 807-929-2571; FAX 807-929-2123; Elec Mail aallison@atikokan.lakeheadu.ca. *Librn* Andrea Allison
Open year-round by appointment. Estab 1986. For reference only
Income: Financed by endowment
Purchases: $1500
Library Holdings: Vols 1700; Per subs 20; AV — Cassettes 300, slides 15,000, v-tapes 100; Other — Photographs 8000
Special Subjects: Archaeology, Natural History, Wilderness
Collections: Natural history & cultural history displays on Quetico Park including archaeology, fur trade & voyageur history

BANCROFT

M **ALGONQUIN ARTS COUNCIL,** Art Gallery of Bancroft, PO Box 1360, K0L 1C0. Tel 613-332-1542; FAX 613-332-2119; *Dir* Heather Rennie; *Assoc Cur* Bill Tomlinson
Open July & Aug Noon - 5 PM, Sept - June Wed - Sat Noon - 5 PM. Admis by donation. Estab 1980 to foster the fine arts in the area. Gallery is located in an historic railway station. Average Annual Attendance: 7000. Mem: 15; dues $15; annual meeting in Sept
Income: $16,500 (financed by mem, grants from the Ontario Arts Council & fundraising)
Collections: Murray Schafer: Sound Sculptures; †miscellaneous glass, fabric, †paintings
Exhibitions: 12 exhibitions per year
Publications: The News BAG, newsletter monthly
Activities: Classes for children; lect open to public, 3 vis lectr per year; sales shop sells books, prints, original art, crafts, pottery blown & stained glass, wood carvings & photographs

BELLEVILLE

M **GLANMORE, HASTINGS COUNTY MUSEUM,** 257 Bridge St E, K8N 1P4. Tel 613-962-2329, 962-6340; *Cur* Rona Rustige; *Educ* Christine Zaporzan
Open summer Tues - Sun 10 AM - 4:30 PM, winter Tues - Sun 1 - 4:30 PM. Admis $3. Estab 1973 to collect & interpret history of Hastings County & 1890s nat historic site. Historic House with art gallery dedicated to local artist Manley McDonald, also extensive collection of Victorian paintings, notably Horatio Henry Couldery, Bertram & Cecelia Couldery, copies of Gainsborough, Constable, Uens & Wilkie. Average Annual Attendance: 8000
Income: Financed by city & county appropriation
Collections: Couldery European Art Collection (Cloisonne, paintings & furniture, typical of upper class turn of the century tastes); Hastings County Collections; Dr Paul Lamp Collection; Phillips-Burrows-Faulkner Collection
Exhibitions: Permanent collection of Manley McDonald Originals & Beverly McDonald Originals & Couldery Originals; artists, photographers (1997) Seeds in Disguise; Washing Machines
Activities: Classes for adults & children; docent training; internships; student

placements; education kits lent to schools & groups; lect open to public; tours; exten dept serves Hastings County; individual paintings & original objects of art lent to museums, galleries & City Hall; lending collection contains history artifacts & slides; book traveling exhibitions, annually; museum shop sells books & reproductions artifacts

BRACEBRIDGE

M **MUSKOKA ARTS & CRAFTS INC,** Chapel Gallery, 15 King St, PO Box 376, P1L 1S7. Tel 705-645-5501; FAX 705-645-0385; *Cur* Elene J Freer
Open 10 AM - 5 PM. Admis donations accepted. Estab 1963, museum estab 1989. Average Annual Attendance: 10,000. Mem: 340; dues $20-$30; annual meeting in Oct
Publications: Newsletter, 12 per year
Activities: Classes for adults & children; lect open to public, 4 vis lectr per year; scholarships offered

BRAMPTON

M **ART GALLERY OF PEEL,** Peel Heritage Complex, 9 Wellington St E, L6W 1Y1. Tel 905-454-5441; *Cur* David Somers
Open Tues - Fri 10 AM - 4:30 PM, Thurs 6 - 9 PM, Sat & Sun Noon - 4:30 PM. Estab 1968 to collect works relevant to Region of Peel & to promote visual art & artists. Average Annual Attendance: 18,000. Mem: 200; dues corporate $100, family $25, individual $20; annual meeting in Feb
Collections: Permanent art collection of Canadian Artists; Caroline & Frank Armington print collection
Exhibitions: Eight exhibits per year (all mediums); Annual Open Juried Show; Regional Artists
Publications: Caroline & Frank Armington: Canadian Painter - Etchers in Paris
Activities: Classes for children; docent training; lect open to public, 1-2 vis lectr per year; gallery talks; tours; competitions with prizes; exten dept serves Southern Ontario; individual paintings & original objects of art lent to public buildings & other institutions; originate traveling exhibitions to libraries & other galleries; sales shop sells books, reproductions & prints
L **Library,** 9 Wellington St E, L6W 1Y1. Tel 905-454-5441; FAX 905-451-4931; *Cur* David Somers; *Asst Cur* Judy Daley
Reference only
Library Holdings: Vols 550; Per subs 3; Other — Clipping files, exhibition catalogs

BRANTFORD

M **BRANT HISTORICAL SOCIETY,** Brant County Museum, 57 Charlotte St, N3T 2W6. Tel 519-752-2483; *Dir* Susan Twist; *Asst Cur* Anne Byard
Open Sept - Apr Wed - Fri 10 AM - 4 PM, Sat 1 - 4 PM, July - Aug Wed - Fri 10 AM - 4 PM, Sat & Sun 1 - 4 PM. Admis adults $2, students & seniors $1.50, children $1.25, under 6 free. Estab 1908 to preserve, interpret & display Brant County history. Average Annual Attendance: 8000. Mem: 210; dues patron $25, family $20, single $15
Income: Financed by mem, provincial, county & city grants & fundraising
Collections: Early Indian history; historical figures; portraits & paintings; Brant County history
Publications: Annual brochure; Brant County, the Story of its People, vol I & II; Grand River Navigation Company Newsletter, quarterly
Activities: Classes for children; docent training; lect open to public; tours; museum shop sells books, reproductions & prints
L **Library,** 57 Charlotte St, N3T 2W6. Tel 519-752-2483;
Library Holdings: Vols 500
Collections: First editions of history & archaeology; old Bibles available for research on premises under supervision of curator; rare books

M **GLENHYRST ART GALLERY OF BRANT,** 20 Ava Rd, N3T 5G9. Tel 519-756-5932; FAX 519-756-5910; *Dir* Stephen Robinson
Open Tues - Fri 10 AM - 5 PM, Sat & Sun 1 - 5 PM. No admis fee. Estab 1957 as a non-profit pub arts center serving the citizens of Brantford & Brant County. Situated on 16 picturesque acres, the gallery is housed in a Heritage Building. Average Annual Attendance: 18,000. Mem: 761; dues benefactors $250 & up, patrons $100-$250, family $25, individual $15, student & senior citizen $10; annual meeting in Mar
Income: Financed by mem, municipal, provincial & federal appropriations & local foundations
Collections: Contemporary Canadian graphics/works on paper; historical works by R R Whale & descendants
Activities: Classes for adults & children; lect open to public, 2 vis lectr per year; tours; individual paintings lent to public art galleries & museums; originate traveling exhibitions
L **Library,** 20 Ava Rd, N3T 5G9. Tel 519-756-5932; FAX 519-756-5910; *Educ Prog Coordr* Kelly Harrington
Open to pub for reference; works from permanent collection are circulated
Library Holdings: Vols 140
Special Subjects: Art Education, Art History, Folk Art, History of Art & Archaeology, Painting - Canadian, Primitive Art, Printmaking, Prints, Tapestries, Textiles
Activities: Lect open to public, 8 vis lectr per year; gallery talks; juried shows; art rental & sales service

BUCKHORN

M **THE GALLERY ON THE LAKE, BUCKHORN,** Hwy 36, Box 10, K0L 1J0. Tel 705-657-3296; FAX 705-657-8766; WATS 800-461-1787.
Open 9 AM - 5 PM. No admis fee. Estab 1976. Retail art gallery featuring landscape & wildlife art originals, limited edition & decorator prints, sculpture, jewelry, pottery, art supplies
Activities: Museum shop sells prints, original art, reproductions & giftware

BURLINGTON

M **BURLINGTON ART CENTRE,** 1333 Lakeshore Rd, L7S 1A9. Tel 905-632-7796; FAX 905-632-7796; Elec Mail infobac@burlingtonartcentre.on.ca; Internet Home Page Address http://www.burlingtonartcentre.on.ca. *Exec Dir* Ian D Ross; *Dir Programs* George Wale; *Cur Coll* Jonathan Smith
Open Mon - Thurs 9 AM - 10 PM, Fri - Sat 9 AM - 5 PM, Sun Noon - 5 PM. No admis fee. Estab 1978. Maintains reference library, main gallery, F R Perry Gallery; permanent collection corridor courtyard. Average Annual Attendance: 65,000. Mem: 1200; dues $30-$65; annual meeting in Mar
Income: $999,950 (financed by mem, city appropriation, province appropriation, earned revenues, fund raising, donations & sponsorship)
Purchases: $10,000
Collections: †Contemporary Canadian Ceramic Art
Activities: Classes for adults & children; docent training; hands-on programs; lect open to public, 2 vis lectr per year; tours; Exten dept; original objects of art lent; book traveling exhibitions 1 per year; originate traveling exhibitions 20 per year; museum shop sells original art & jewelry

CAMBRIDGE

L **CAMBRIDGE PUBLIC LIBRARY AND GALLERY,** 20 Grand Ave N, N1S 2K6. Tel 519-621-0460; FAX 519-621-2080; *Chief Librn* Greg Hayton; *Coordr Cultural Servs* Mary Misner
Open Mon - Thurs 9:30 AM - 8:30 PM, Fri & Sat 9:30 AM - 5:30 PM; Sept - May open Sun 1 - 5 PM. No admis fee. Estab 1969. Gallery on second floor with 2000 sq ft, 250 linear ft. Average Annual Attendance: 25,000
Income: Financed by provincial appropriation, federal & private
Library Holdings: Vols 150,000; Per subs 100
Collections: Regional Artists
Publications: Bi-monthly newsletter
Activities: Classes for adults & children; lect open to public, 10 vis lectr per year; concerts; gallery talks; tours; competitions with awards; individual paintings & original objects of art lent; originate traveling exhibitions

CHATHAM

A **CHATHAM CULTURAL CENTRE,** Thames Art Gallery, 75 William St N, N7M 4L4. Tel 519-354-8338; FAX 519-334-4170; *Dir* Doug Jackson; *Mus Cur* David Benson
Open daily 1 - 5 PM. No admis fee. Estab 1963 to operate as a regional arts centre, to advance knowledge & appreciation of & to encourage, stimulate & promote interest in the study of culture & the visual & performing arts. Gallery maintained; designated National Exhibition Centre for the presentation of visual art works & museum related works, to the public of this country. Average Annual Attendance: 100,000. Mem: 600; dues family $28, single $17
Income: Financed by mem, city & state appropriation & National Museum Grants
Collections: Local Artists; Historical Photographs
Publications: At the Centre, 5 per year
Activities: Classes for adults & children; dramatic programs; docent training; lect open to public, 9 vis lectr per year; concerts; gallery talks; tours; juried fine art shows; individual & original objects of art lent to accredited galleries & museums; lending collection contains 2100 slides

CORNWALL

M **CORNWALL GALLERY SOCIETY,** Regional Art Gallery, 164 Pitt St Promenade, K6J 3P4. Tel 613-938-7387; FAX 613-938-9619; Elec Mail crag@cnwl.igs.net. *Dir* Sylvie Lizotte
Open Mon - Sat 10 AM - 5 PM. No admis fee. Estab 1982 to promote interest in & study of visual arts. Main gallery has 3 display walls measuring 44.5 ft, 30 ft & 10 ft 9 inches; walls 12 ft; Gallery Shoppe where local art is sold. Average Annual Attendance: 10,000. Mem: 200; dues $25; annual meeting in June
Income: $190,000 (financed by mem & city appropriation)
Collections: Contemporary Canadian Art
Exhibitions: Annual Juried Exhibition; changing exhibits from Canadian artists, on a monthly basis
Publications: Triannual newsletter
Activities: Classes for adults & children; individual paintings lent; museum shop sells original art

DON MILLS

C **ROTHMANS, BENSON & HEDGES,** Art Collection, 1500 Don Mills Rd, M3B 3L1. Tel 416-449-5525; FAX 416-449-4486; *Dir Corp Affairs* John MacDonald
Open to public. Estab 1967. Collection displayed at head office
Collections: Contemporary Canadian art from last decade
Activities: Awards for Toronto Outdoor Art Exhibition each year; individual objects of art lent to traveling or special exhibitions; originate traveling exhibitions to all major public galleries in Canada

GANANOQUE

M **GANANOQUE HISTORICAL MUSEUM,** * 5 King St, K7G 2T8. Tel 613-382-4024; *Pres* Cliff Weir; *Cur* Lynette McClellan
Open Mon - Sat 11 AM - 5 PM. Admis adults $1, children under 12 $.50. Estab 1964 to preserve local history. Average Annual Attendance: 2500
Collections: China Collection; Military & Indian Artifacts; Victorian Dining Room, Parlour & Bedroom; glass; portraits & photographs pertaining to local history; Victorian kitchen
Activities: Book traveling exhibitions

GUELPH

M MACDONALD STEWART ART CENTRE, 358 Gordon St, N1G 1Y1. Tel 519-837-0010; FAX 515-767-2661; *Dir* Judith Nasby; *Cur* Nancy Campbell; *Prog Coordr* Steve Robinson
Open Tues - Sun Noon - 5 PM, Thurs 5 - 9 PM. No admis fee. Estab 1978 by University of Guelph, city, county & board of educ to collect & exhibit works of art; maintain & operate a gallery & related facilities for this purpose fulfilling a pub role in city & county. 30,000 sq ft building comprising galleries, lecture room, studio, meeting rooms, resource centre, gift shop & rental service. Restored & renovated in 1980. Average Annual Attendance: 25,000. Mem: 600; dues family $30, individual $20, senior & student $10; annual meeting Sept-Oct
Income: Financed by university, city, county, board of educ, provincial & federal grants, mem & donations
Purchases: Canadian art
Special Subjects: Donald Forster Sculpture Park
Collections: †Historical & contemporary Canadian art; historical & contemporary international prints; †Inuit Collection; †contemporary sculpture; outdoor sculpture (Donald Forster Sculpture Park)
Publications: Catalogue of permanent collection of University of Guelph 1980; exhibition catalogues, 6 per yr; quarterly newsletter
Activities: Classes for adults & children; docent training; parent/child workshops; lectures open to public; gallery talks; school & group tours; competitions; awards; exten dept serves Wellington County & other Canadian public galleries, also have circulated in US & Europe; individual paintings lent to institutions & public galleries; art rental to gallery members; lending collection contains 500 original paintings, 400 prints, photographs & 50 sculptures; book traveling exhibitions 4-6 per year; originate traveling exhibitions 1 -2 per year for museums in Canada & abroad; sales shop sells books, magazines, reproductions, toys, pottery, textiles, jewelry & catalogues

HAILEYBURY

M TEMISKAMING ART GALLERY, PO Box 1090, P0J 1K0. Tel 705-672-3706; FAX 705-672-5966; *Dir* Maureen Steward
Open daily 2 - 8 PM. Admis free. Estab 1980 to educate. Average Annual Attendance: Annual meeting Jan
Income: Financed by mem & city appropriation
Activities: Classes for adults & children; lect open to public, 5 vis lectr per year

HAMILTON

M ART GALLERY OF HAMILTON, 123 King St W, L8P 4S8. Tel 905-527-6610; FAX 416-577-6940; *Dir* Ted Pietrzak; *Sr Cur* Ihor Holubizky; *Head Learning Servs* Jennifer Kaye; *Community Relations* Liz Mitchell
Open Wed - Sat 10 AM - 5 PM, Thurs 5 - 9 PM, Sun 1 - 5 PM. Admis adults $4, students $3, children free. Estab Jan 1914 to develop & maintain a centre for the study & enjoyment of the visual arts; new gallery opened Oct 1977. Building is 76,000 sq ft, 24,000 sq ft of exhibition space. Average Annual Attendance: 35,000. Mem: 1200; dues family $50, single $30; annual meeting first Tues in June
Income: Earned revenue financed by endowment, mem, city & provincial appropriation & federal grants
Collections: Complete graphics of Karel Appel; Canadian fine arts; American, British & European fine arts; historical, modern & contemporary collection
Exhibitions: Twenty-two exhibitions scheduled per year
Publications: Art Gallery of Hamilton Bulletin, 3 times per year
Activities: Classes for adults & children; docent training; lect open to public, 18 vis lectr per year; concerts; gallery talks; tours; exten dept; individual paintings & original objects of art lent to other galleries & museums; lending collection contains 7500 art works; originate traveling exhibitions; museum shop sells books, magazines & reproductions
L Muriel Isabel Bostwick Library, 123 King St W, L8P 4S8. Tel 905-527-6610; FAX 416-577-6940; *Sr Cur* Ihor Holubizky; *Librn* Helen Hadden
Open to gallery members & researchers for reference
Library Holdings: Vols 3000; Per subs 14; Other — Clipping files, exhibition catalogs, photographs
Special Subjects: Art History, Mixed Media, Oriental Art, Painting - American, Painting - European, Portraits, Printmaking, Prints, Restoration & Conservation, Sculpture
Collections: References on Canadian art history; exhibition catalogues

M DUNDURN CASTLE, Dundurn Castle, 610 York Blvd, L8R 3H1. Tel 905-546-2872; FAX 905-546-2875; Elec Mail can.dc.ha@immedia.ca. *Cur* Bill Nesbitt; *Cur Asst* Don Patterson; *Cur Asst* Elizabeth Wakeford
Open June 1 - Labor Day daily 10 AM - 4 PM, Labor Day - June, cl Mon, booked tours mornings, open to public Noon - 4 PM, cl Christmas & New Year's Day. Admis family $16, adults $6, senior citizens $5.50, students $5, children $2.50, discounts on group rates for over 20 people. Dundurn, the home of Sir Allan Napier MacNab; Hamilton's Centennial Project was the restoration of this historic house; built in 1832-35, it was tenured by MacNab until his death in 1862. The terminal date of the furnishings is 1855. Approximately 43 rooms are shown; two-room on-site exhibit area. Average Annual Attendance: 70,000
Income: Financed by city of Hamilton, owner & operator
Collections: Regency & mid-Victorian furnishings depicting the lifestyle of an upper class gentleman living in upper Canada in the 1850s; restored servants quarters
Exhibitions: Historical Crafts Fair, Harvest Home-baking & preserving competitions; Victorian Christmas
Activities: Classes for adults & children; docent training; lect open to public; concerts; gallery talks, tours; individual paintings & original objects of art lent; museum shop sells books, reproductions, prints & slides, tea room & food service facilities

M MCMASTER UNIVERSITY, Museum of Art, University Ave, 1280 Main St W, L8S 4L6. Tel 905-525-9140, Ext 23081; FAX 905-527-4548; *Dir & Cur* Kim G Ness; *Registrar* Geraldine Loveys; *Preparator* Jennifer Petteplace; *Exhib Asst* Colin Wiginton; *Asst to Dir & Special Prog Officer* Jane Zatylny
Open Tues - Fri 11 AM - 6 PM, Thurs 7 - 9 PM, Sun Noon - 5 PM, cl Mon & Sat. Admis fee $2 suggested. Estab 1967 to provide the university & pub with exhibitions of historical & contemporary art from Canada & other countries. Five galleries incandescent lighting throughout; display cases; sculpture stands. Average Annual Attendance: 25,000
Income: $12,400 (financed by university & private endowment, corporate & individual support)
Purchases: $15,000
Collections: Levy Collection, impressionist & post-impressionist, paintings & early Dutch panels; †American & †Canadian Art; †European paintings, prints & drawings; †Expressionist Prints
Exhibitions: Douglas Clark: North America (photographic installations; Summa show; Thematic Exhibitions from the permanent collection)
Publications: The Art Collection of McMaster University
Activities: Classroom facilities; lect open to public; concerts; gallery talks; Individual paintings and original objects of art lent to National Gallery of Canada, Art Gallery of Ontario & other Canadian institutions
L Library, University Ave, 1280 Main St W, L8S 4L6. Tel 905-525-9140, Ext 23081; FAX 905-527-4548; *Head Information* Rose Anne Prevec
Open Tues - Fri 11 AM - 6 PM, Thurs evenings 7 - 9 PM, Sun Noon - 5 PM. Houses reference materials on art gallery management, exhibition & sales catalogues
Library Holdings: Vols 3000; Serial titles
Publications: Exhibition Catalogues, artist files, auction catalogues

JORDAN

M JORDAN HISTORICAL MUSEUM OF THE TWENTY, 3082 Main St, L0R 1S0. Tel 905-562-5242, 562-4849; *Cur* Helen Booth
Open May - Oct daily 1 - 5 PM. Admis $1. Estab 1953 to preserve the material & folklore of the area known as The Twenty, Mile Creek vicinity. Average Annual Attendance: 10,000. Mem: 100; dues $5; annual meeting Feb
Income: Financed by admis, provincial grants, municipal grants, internal fund raising activities & donations
Collections: Archives; furniture; historical material & textiles
Exhibitions: Special annual exhibits; Pioneer Day
Activities: Classes for children; special displays as requested by the community; Pioneer Day first Sat after Canadian Thanksgiving holiday; lect open to public, 1 vis lectr per year; individual paintings & original objects of art lent; sales shop sells books, original art, prints, pottery, textiles & local craft items

KINGSTON

M QUEEN'S UNIVERSITY, Agnes Etherington Art Centre, K7L 3N6. Tel 613-545-2190; FAX 613-545-6765; *Dir* Dr David McTavish; *Assoc Dir & Cur* Dorothy Farr; *Cur Contemporary Art* Jan Allen; *Educ Officer* Jeri Harmsen; *Projects Mgr* Patricia Howorth
Open year round Tues - Fri 10 AM - 5 PM, Sat & Sun 1 - 5 PM. No admis fee. Estab 1957 to provide the services of a pub art gallery & mus for the community & region. Gallery has approximately 8000 sq ft of display space, in four separate areas, showing a balanced program of exhibitions of contemporary & historical, national, international & regional art. Average Annual Attendance: 25,000. Mem: 870; dues $12-$150; annual meeting in May (Gallery Association)
Income: $1,081,000 (financed by endowment, city & provincial appropriation, University & Canada Council funds)
Purchases: $100,000
Collections: African Art; Canadian Dress Collection; †Canadian Paintings, Prints, Sculpture, Historical & Contemporary; Decorative Objects; †Ethnological Collection; †European Graphics; European 17th Century; †Old Master Paintings; Quilts; Silver
Exhibitions: About 30 exhibitions mounted each year
Publications: Currents, bimonthly; annual report; exhibition publications & catalogues; studies
Activities: Docent training regarding tours for school & other groups; lect open to public, 10 vis lectr per year; gallery talks; tours; individual paintings rented by Gallery Association Art Rental to private individuals & businesses; rental collection contains original prints & paintings; originate traveling exhibitions
L Art Library, Ontario Hall, K7L 3L6. Tel 613-545-2841; FAX 613-545-6819; Elec Mail lawj@qucdn.queensu.ca. *Librn* Jane Law
Open to students, faculty & staff; open to public for reference only
Library Holdings: Vols 42,000; Per subs 140; Reference bks; Micro — Fiche 1400, reels 300; Other — Exhibition catalogs 12,000, photographs
Special Subjects: Art History, Art Conservation, British, Canadian & European Art

M ST LAWRENCE COLLEGE, Art Gallery, King & Portsmouth, PO Box 6000, K7L 5A6. Tel 613-544-5400, Ext 1283; *Gallery Dir* David Gordon; *Dept Coordr* Terry Pfliger
Open Noon - 4 PM. No admis fee. College estab 1968, mus estab 1973 to augment the creative art program with shows, visiting artists. Average Annual Attendance: 4000

KITCHENER

M KITCHENER-WATERLOO ART GALLERY, 101 Queen St N, N2H 6P7. Tel 519-579-5860; FAX 519-578-0740; *Dir* Brad Blain
Open Tues - Sat 10 AM - 5 PM, 1 hr before Center performances, Sun 1 - 5 PM, cl Mon. Admis contribution adults $2, students & senior citizens $1, members free. Estab 1956, the Kitchener-Waterloo Art Gallery is a pub institution interested in stimulating an appreciation of the visual arts & dedicated to bringing to the community exhibitions, art classes, lectures, workshops & special

events. Average Annual Attendance: 75,492. Mem: 756; dues business $100, family $40, individual $30, senior citizens & students $15
Income: Financed by government grants, foundation grants, corporate & individual donations, special events, mem dues, voluntary admis & sales of publication
Collections: Canadian; Homer Watson Collection
Publications: Calendar, quarterly; exhibition catalogs, quarterly
Activities: Art classes for adults & children; lect open to public; tours; scholarships offered; exten dept serves Waterloo region; book traveling exhibitions; sales shop sells books, original art, reproductions

L **Eleanor Calvert Memorial Library,** 101 Queen St N, N2H 6P7. Tel 519-579-5860; FAX 519-578-0740; *Dir* Brad Blain
Estab 1972 for pub art reference & lending to members
Library Holdings: Vols 4500; Per subs 25; AV — Cassettes, slides; Other — Clipping files, exhibition catalogs, pamphlets
Special Subjects: Canadian artists biographical material

M **HOMER WATSON HOUSE & GALLERY,** 1754 Old Mill Rd, N2P 1H7. Tel 519-748-4377; FAX 519-748-6808; *Cur/Adminr* Gretchen McCulloch; *Prog Coordr* Astero Kalogeropoulos; *Mgr* Faith Hieblinger
Open Tues - Sun Noon - 4:30 PM. No admis fee. Estab 1981 as Homer Watson Memorial. Three galleries for contemporary art - total of 155 running ft. Average Annual Attendance: 6000. Mem: 165; dues family $25, individual $15; annual meeting 2nd Tues in June
Income: $140,000 (financed by mem, city appropriation, workshops & classes)
Purchases: $6000
Collections: †Watson Family Artifacts; †Homer Watson Paintings
Exhibitions: Contemporary art-regional & provincial artists
Activities: Classes for adults & children; lect for members only, 1 vis lectr per year

KLEINBURG

M **MCMICHAEL CANADIAN ART COLLECTION,** 10365 Islington Ave, L0J 1C0. Tel 905-893-1121; FAX 905-893-2588; *Chmn Bd Trustees* Joan Goldfarb; *Dir & CEO* Barbara Tyler
Open Nov 1 - Mar 31 Tues - Sun 11 AM - 4:30 PM, Apr 1 - Oct 31 daily 10 AM - 5 PM. Admis family $8, adults $4, students & senior citizens $2, children under 5 free, Wed free
Collections: Focus of the collection is the works of art created by Indian, Inuit & Metis artists, the artists of the Group of Seven & their contemporaries & other artists who have made or make a contribution to the development of Canadian Art
Exhibitions: Temporary exhibitions lasting from 1 to 3 months
Publications: Permanet collection catalogue; exhibition catalogues; quarterly newsletters
Activities: Comprehensive educ programme at the elementary & secondary school levels; guided group tours by appointment; exten programme & temporary exhibition programme; programmes for kindergarten & special interest groups
L **Library/Archives,** Islington Ave, L0J 1C0. Tel 905-893-1121; FAX 905-893-2588; *Librn & Archivist* Linda Morita
Open by appointment
Library Holdings: Vols 5000; Per subs 30; Archival material; Micro — Fiche; AV — A-tapes, cassettes, slides, v-tapes; Other — Clipping files, exhibition catalogs, manuscripts, memorabilia, original art works, pamphlets, photographs, reproductions
Special Subjects: Art History, Landscapes, Painting - Canadian, Printmaking, Prints, Canadian Art, Inuit & First Nations Art & Culture

LINDSAY

M **THE LINDSAY GALLERY,** 190 Kent St W, K9V 2Y6. Tel 705-324-1780; FAX 705-324-2051; *Pres* Valerie Konyer
Open Mon - Fri 10 AM - 5 PM, Sat 1 - 5 PM. Estab 1976. 600 sq ft of converted house for main gallery & separate room 100 sq ft. Average Annual Attendance: 10,500. Mem: 400; family $20, individual $15, senior citizens $10, student $5; annual meeting in Feb
Income: $76,000 (financed by mem, city & province appropriation, corporate sponsorship)
Purchases: $50,000 (200 drawings by Ernest Thompson Seton)
Collections: †Historical & contemporary Canadian; Ernest Thompson Seton Collection
Publications: Quarterly bulletin
Activities: Classes for adults & children; lect open to public, 10 vis lectr per year; book traveling exhibitions 1-2 times per year

LONDON

M **LONDON REGIONAL ART & HISTORICAL MUSEUMS,** 421 Ridout St N, N6A 5H4. Tel 519-672-4580; FAX 519-660-8397; *Exec Dir* Ted Fraser; *Cur Contemporary Art* James Patten; *Dir Finance & Personnel* Brenda Fleming; *Asst Cur Mus* Michael Baker; *Exec Asst* Gloria Kerr; *Technician Mus Coll & Exhib* Linda Berko; *Coordr Pub Progs* Chris Aldred; *Publicity & Promotion Coordr* Ruth Anne Murray; *Graphic Designer* Robert Ballantine; *Accounts Receivable & Donations Clerk* Colleen Ross; *Tour Coordr & Secy* Heidi Sara; *Visitor Services Coordr* Elaine Laszlo
Open Tues - Sun & holidays Noon - 5 PM. No admis fee. Estab 1940. New bldg open 1980 containing 26,500 sq ft of exhibition space, 150 seat auditorium. Mem: 3310; family $50, individual $30, senior citizens & students $15; annual meeting in Jan
Income: $1,201,900 (financed by city, province, mem & donations, community)
Collections: Permanent Collection stresses regional & local artists, who have become internationally & nationally recognized such as Jack Chambers, Greg Curnoe, F M Bell-Smith & Paul Peel; Hamilton King Meek Memorial Collection; F B Housser Memorial Collection; The Moore Collection; a collection of

historical art & artifacts, primarily of London & region
Exhibitions: Works of art - international, national & regional; programs of multi-media nature, including performing arts, exhibitions of historical artifacts & art
Publications: Exhibition catalogues
Activities: Classes for adults & children; docent training; lect open to public, some for members only; concerts; gallery talks; tours; individual paintings & objects of art lent; book traveling exhibitions; originate traveling exhibitions; gallery shop sells books, jewelry magazines, original art, prints & reproductions

M **UNIVERSITY OF WESTERN ONTARIO,** McIntosh Gallery, N6A 3K7. Tel 519-661-3181; FAX 519-661-3292; Elec Mail mci.amk@uwoadmin.uwo.ca. *Dir* Arlene Kennedy; *Cur* Catherine Elliot Shaw; *Installations Officer & Registrar* David Falls
Open Tues - Thurs Noon - 7 PM, Fri - Sun Noon - 4 PM, cl Mon. No admis fee. Estab 1942. Three galleries with a total of 2960 sq ft. Average Annual Attendance: 14,000. Mem: 155
Income: Financed by endowment, mem, provincial appropriation, special grants & University funds
Collections: Canadian Art
Exhibitions: 12 to 14 exhibitions per year
Publications: Newsletter, bimonthly; exhibition catalogues
Activities: Docent training; lect open to public, 6-10 vis lectr per year; gallery talks; tours; individual paintings & original objects of art lent to galleries; lending collection contains books, cassettes, framed reproductions, original art works & prints, paintings, photographs & sculpture; book traveling exhibitions 1-3 per year; originate traveling exhibitions
L **D B Weldon Library,** 1151 Richmond St, N6A 3K7. Tel 519-661-3162; *Dir* Catherine Quinlan
Open to all university staff, faculty & students for research & borrowing. Open to the public for in-house research
Library Holdings: Vols 45,000; Per subs 129; Micro — Fiche, reels; Other — Clipping files, exhibition catalogs, pamphlets
Special Subjects: American Western Art, Antiquities-Byzantine, Antiquities-Etruscan, Antiquities-Greek, Antiquities-Roman, Archaeology, Art History, Carpets & Rugs, Decorative Arts, Eskimo Art, History of Art & Archaeology, Maps, Metalwork, Painting - American, Painting - Canadian, Applied Art, Canadian Art, Medieval & Byzantine Art, Western Art

MIDLAND

M **HURONIA MUSEUM,** Little Lake Park, L4R 4P4. Tel 705-526-2844; FAX 705-527-6622; *Dir* James Hunter; *Photographer & Cur* Bill Smith; *Educ* Natalie Quealey
Open Mon - Sat 9 AM - 5 PM, Sun 10 AM - 5 PM. Admis adult $4, student $3. Estab 1947 to collect art of Historic Huronia. Several large galleries dealing with local contemporary artists, historical regional artists, design exhibit on Thor Hansen & other designers. Average Annual Attendance: 20,000. Mem: dues $25; annual meeting last Thurs in May
Income: $400,000 (financed by endowment, mem, admis, sales, fundraising, grants)
Purchases: $10,000 (Ted Lord Art Collection)
Collections: †Mary Hallen Collection (watercolors); †Franz Johnson Collection (oils, watercolors); †Ted Lord Collection (paintings, prints, watercolors); †Bill Wood Collection (etchings, oils, watercolors); General Collection (carvings, oil, watercolors)
Exhibitions: A Photographic History of the Georgian Bay Lumber Co 1871-1942
Publications: Exhibition catalogues, annual
Activities: Children's classes; docent programs; lect open to public, 10 vis lectr per year; gallery talks; tours; competitions with awards; lending collection contains paintings to other institutions who put together exhibitions; originate traveling exhibitions 5 per year; museum shop sells books, prints, magazines, slides, original art, reproductions

MISSISSAUGA

M **ART GALLERY OF MISSISSAUGA,** 300 City Centre Dr, L5B 3C1. Tel 905-896-5088; FAX 905-615-4167; *Exec Dir* Fred Troughton; *Cur* Stuart Reid
Open Mon - Fri 9 AM - 6 PM, Sat & Sun Noon - 4 PM. No admis fee. Estab 1987. Average Annual Attendance: 18,000. Mem: 320; dues $15-$1000; annual meeting in Apr
Income: Financed by mem, city appropriation, federal & provincial government
Purchases: $50,000
Collections: Permanent collection
Exhibitions: 11 exhibitions per year, 5 week average per exhibition
Publications: Brush Up
Activities: Lect open to public, 3-5 vis lectr per year; individual paintings & original objects of art lent; book traveling exhibitions 1 per year

M **ERINDALE COLLEGE, UNIVERSITY OF TORONTO AT MISSISSAUGA,** Blackwood Gallery, 3359 Mississauga Rd N, L5L 1C6. Tel 905-828-3789; FAX 905-828-5474; Elec Mail nhazelgr@credit.erin.utoronto.ca. *Cur* Nancy Hazelgrove
Open Mon - Fri Noon - 4:30 PM. No admis fee. Estab 1973 to educate the public & display artists works. Gallery has four walls with various dividers & floor space of 36 x 60 ft. Average Annual Attendance: 2000
Collections: Acrylics, drawings, oils, pen sketches & prints, sculpture, water colour
Exhibitions: (1997) Art & Art History Student Exhibition; Anne O'Callaghan (mixed media works); Scott Childs (sculpture); Tim Noonan (prints); Paperbacked-Paperbound 6th Annual Juried Members Exhibition
Publications: Blackwood Bulletin, annual
Activities: Classes for children; lect open to public, 2-3 vis lectr per year; gallery talks; tours; competitions with awards; individual paints & original objects of art lent in house & to public art galleries; book traveling exhibitions

L MISSISSAUGA LIBRARY SYSTEM, 301 Burnhamthorpe Rd W, L5B 3Y3. Tel 905-615-3500; FAX 905-615-3625; *Chief Librn* Don Mills
Open: Hours vary according to branch. No admis fee. Outlet for local artists at branch galleries; present more widely recognised artists at Central & Burnhamthrope Galleries. Total of eleven galleries in system, 90 running ft each, often multi-purpose rooms
Collections: Permanent collection of 135 paintings and prints by Canadian artists, emphasis on prints (all framed)
Publications: Link News Tabloid Format, quarterly
Activities: Lect open to public; competitions with cash prizes; lending collection contains books & motion pictures; book traveling exhibitions
L Central Library, Art Dept, 301 Burnhamthorpe Rd W, L5B 3Y3. Tel 905-615-3600; FAX 905-615-3625; *Dir Pub Serv* Barbara Quinlan
Open Mon - Fri 9 AM - 9 PM, Sat 9 AM - 5 PM, Sept - June Sun 1 - 5 PM
Income: $7,000,000 (financed by Municipal & Provincial funds)
Library Holdings: Vols 22,700; Per subs 29; AV — Cassettes, fs, lantern slides, motion pictures, slides, v-tapes; Other — Clipping files, exhibition catalogs, original art works, pamphlets, prints
Special Subjects: Canadian prints
Activities: Lect open to public; competitions with awards

NORTH YORK

M JEWISH COMMUNITY CENTRE OF TORONTO, The Koffler Gallery, 4588 Bathurst St, M2R 1W6. Tel 416-636-1880; FAX 416-636-1536; *Dir* Diane Uslaner; *Educ Coordr* Michelle Pittini; *Asst Cur* John Massier
Open Sun - Thurs 10 AM - 4 PM, Wed 5-8 PM, Fri 9 AM - Noon. Estab 1976. Average Annual Attendance: 12,000. Mem: 250
Income: $35,000 (financed by mem)
Collections: Clay, Glass
Publications: Catalogues & exhibitions brochures
Activities: Classes for adults & children; docent training; lect open to public; 7 artist talks per year; book traveling exhibitions 1-3 per year; originate traveling exhibitions 1 per year; gallery shop sells original glass, ceramics & jewelry produced by Canadian crafts people

M YORK UNIVERSITY, Art Gallery of York University, Ross Bldg N1, 4700 Keele St, M3J 1P3. Tel 416-736-5169; FAX 416-736-5985; Elec Mail agyu@yorku.ca;
Internet Home Page Address http://www.yorku.ca/admin/agyu. *Dir & Cur* Loretta Yarlow; *Asst Cur* Jack Liang; *Admin Asst* Marie SilverThorne
Open Tues - Fri 10 AM - 4 PM, Wed 10 AM - 8 PM, Sun Noon - 5 PM, cl July & Aug. Admis donations welcomed. Estab 1970 to maintain a program of exhibitions covering a broad spectrum of the contemporary visual arts. Gallery is 3600 sq ft, exhibition space 2800 sq ft, including program space & support space 750 sq ft. Average Annual Attendance: 15,000
Income: Financed by university, federal, provincial & municipal grants & private donations
Collections: Approx 750 works including ethnographical items & artifacts, approx 550 of the works are by Canadian artists. Current emphasis & expansion of outdoor sculpture collection
Exhibitions: (1997-98) Robert Therrien; Roy Arden, Becky Singleton; Alison Wilding; Rodney Graham; Luc Tuymans; Pierre Dorion & Marie Jose Burki
Publications: Exhibit catalogs
Activities: Lect open to public, 3-4 vis lectr per year; gallery talks; tours; individual paintings & original objects of art lent for major shows or retrospectives to other members of the University & faculty for their offices; book traveling exhibitions; originate traveling exhibitions
L Fine Arts Phase II Slide Library, 4700 Keele St, Rm 274, M3J 1P3. Tel 416-736-5534; FAX 416-736-5447; *Cur* M Metraux; *Slide Librn* Marie Holubec; *Slide Librn* Lillian Heinson
Income: Financed through university
Library Holdings: AV — Slides 250,000
Collections: Bazin Library; T A Heinrich Collection; Rare Books Library

M YORK UNIVERSITY, Glendon Gallery, Glendon Col York Univ, 2275 Bayview Ave, M4N 3M6. Tel 416-487-6721; FAX 416-487-6779; Elec Mail gallery@erda.glendon.yorku.ca. *Dir & Cur* Sylviane de Roquebrune; *Admin Asst* Tiffany Moore
Open Mon - Fri 10 AM - 4:30 PM, Sun 1 - 4 PM. Estab 1977, focus on contemporary visual arts. 107.2 ft of running wall space, dark hardwood flooring, natural sunlight & halogen track lighting; ground floor of Glendon Hall. Average Annual Attendance: 4000. Mem: 150; dues family $25, individual $15, student $6; annual meeting end of June
Income: $141,868 (financed by mem, York University & granting agencies)
Exhibitions: (1997) Susan Shantz: Recent Works (sculpture); Michele Karch Ackerman: Lost Girls (mixed-media)
Publications: Bilingual exhibition catalogue
Activities: Classes for children; lect open to public, 5 vis lectr per year; gallery talks; tours; book traveling exhibitions

OAKVILLE

CANADIAN SOCIETY FOR EDUCATION THROUGH ART
For further information, see National and Regional Organizations

OAKVILLE GALLERIES
M Centennial Gallery and Gairloch Gallery, 1306 Lakeshore Rd E, L6J 1L6. Tel 905-844-4402; FAX 905-844-7968; *Pres Board* J MacDonald; *Dir* Francine Perinet; *Cur Contemporary Art* Marnie Fleming; *Installations & Registrar* Rod Demerling; *Spec Projects Officer* Kristina Sparkes; *Office Mgr* Marilyn Barnes; *Develop Officer* Marlene Klassen; *Adjunct Cur* Richard Rhodes
Centennial Gallery open Tues - Thurs Noon - 9 PM, Fri & Sat Noon - 5 PM, Sun 1 - 5 PM; Gairloch Gallery open Tues - Sun 1 - 5 PM. Estab Centennial 1967, Gairloch 1972, to exhibit contemporary visual arts. Average Annual Attendance: 48,000. Mem: 500

Collections: Contemporary Canadian painting, sculpture, photographs, drawing & prints; contemporary outdoor sculpture
Exhibitions: Monthly exhibits
Publications: Exhibition catalogues
Activities: Classes for children; docent training, volunteer committee; lect open to public; gallery talks; tours; originate traveling exhibitions

L SHERIDAN COLLEGE OF APPLIED ARTS AND TECHNOLOGY, Trafalgar Campus Library, 1430 Trafalgar Rd, L6H 2L1. Tel 905-845-9430, Ext 2488; *Reference Technician* Susan Platt
Open daily 8:30 AM - 4:30 PM. Estab 1970 to serve the students & faculty of the Faculty of Arts
Library Holdings: Vols 8851; Per subs 96; Micro — Fiche; AV — Slides 27,809; Other — Clipping files, exhibition catalogs
Special Subjects: Art History, Crafts, Graphic Design, Illustration, Photography, Animation, Computer Animation Design, Computer Graphics

OSHAWA

M THE ROBERT MCLAUGHLIN GALLERY, Civic Centre, L1H 3Z3. Tel 905-576-3000; *Dir* Joan Murray; *Chief Adminr* Sally Bowers
Open Tues, Wed & Fri 10 AM - 5 PM, Thurs 10 AM - 9 PM, Sat & Sun Noon - 4 PM, cl Mon. No admis fee. Estab Feb 1967 as The Art Gallery of Oshawa, in May 1969 as the Robert McLaughlin Gallery. R S McLaughlin Gallery 77 x 38 x 15 ft; Isabel McLaughlin Gallery 77 x 38 x 13 ft; Alexandra Luke Gallery (no 1) 62 x 48 x 9 1/2 ft; Alexandra Luke Gallery (no 2) 46 x 27 x 13 ft; E P Taylor Gallery 23 x 37 x 9 ft; General Motors Gallery 25 x 37 x 9 ft; Corridor Ramp (Isabel McLaughlin Gallery) 48 x 8 x 10 ft; Corridor (Alexandra Luke) 68 x 5 1/2 x 8 ft with Foyer & Director's Office. Average Annual Attendance: 26,598. Mem: 500; dues family $35, single $25, student & senior citizens $10; annual meeting in May
Income: Financed by membership, city appropriation, Canada Council, Ministry Culture & Recreation, Wintario & Ontario Arts Council
Collections: Canadian 19th & 20th century drawings, paintings, prints & sculpture; †major collection of works by Painters Eleven
Publications: Annual Report; bi-monthly bulletin; Calendar of Events, annually; exhibition catalogs
Activities: Classes for adults and children; docent training; lect open to public, 6 vis lectr per year; gallery talks; tours; scholarships & fels offered; original objects of art lent to schools, institutions & industries; lending collection contains cassettes, 300 color reproductions, framed reproductions, original art works, 10,000 slides & 3000 books; sales shop sells books, reproductions, prints & local crafts
L Library, Civic Centre, L1H 3Z3. Tel 905-576-3000; FAX 905-576-9774; *Librn* Patricia Claxton-Oldfield
Open Tues, Wed & Fri 10 AM - 5 PM, Thurs 10 AM - 9 PM, Sat & Sun Noon - 4 PM. Admis donations accepted. Open to gallery members
Library Holdings: Vols 3000; AV — A-tapes, cassettes, slides, v-tapes; Other — Clipping files, exhibition catalogs, manuscripts, pamphlets, photographs
Special Subjects: Research of Painters Eleven and 19th and 20th Century works
Collections: †Canadian contemporary art books

OTTAWA

A THE CANADA COUNCIL, Conseil des Arts du Canada, 350 Albert St, PO Box 1047, K1P 5V8. Tel 613-237-3400; FAX 613-566-4390; WATS 800-263-5588. *Chmn* Donna M Scott; *Dir* Rock Carrier
Estab 1957 to foster & promote the arts. The Council provides a wide range of grants & services to professional Canadian artists & art organizations in dance, media arts, music, opera, theatre, writing, publishing & the visual arts. Also Arts Awards Service, Explorations Program, Art Bank & Touring Office
Income: Financed by Parliament of Canada, endowment fund & private individuals
Activities: Prizes awarded; grants & fels offered

CANADIAN CONFERENCE OF THE ARTS
For further information, see National and Regional Organizations

CANADIAN CRAFTS COUNCIL, Canadien de l'Artisanat
For further information, see National and Regional Organizations

M CANADIAN HERITAGE - PARKS CANADA (Formerly Environment Canada - Canadian Parks Service), Laurier House, Rideau Canal, 335 Laurier Ave E, K1N 6R4. Tel 613-692-2581, 992-8142; FAX 613-992-9233; *Area Mgr* Peter Minnelli
Open Oct - Mar Tues - Sat 10 AM - 5 PM, Sun 2 - 5 PM; Apr - Sept Tues - Sat 9 AM - 5 PM, Sun 2 - 5 PM. No admis fee. Estab 1951. This is a historic house & former residence of Two Prime Ministers, Sir Wilfrid Laurier & the Rt Honorable William Lyon Mackenzie King & contains furniture & memorabilia belonging to a third Prime Minister, Lester Pearson. The house is primarily furnished in the style of its last occupant, the Rt Honorable William Lyon Mackenzie King, with space given to the Laurier Collection. The Lester Pearson study was installed in 1974. Average Annual Attendance: 30,000
Income: Financed by federal government & trust fund
Publications: Main Park Brochure provided to visitors
Activities: Guided tours

M CANADIAN MUSEUM OF CONTEMPORARY PHOTOGRAPHY, One Rideau Canal, PO Box 465, Sta A, K1N 9N6. Tel 613-990-8257; FAX 613-990-6542; *Acting Dir* Martha Hanna; *Nat & International Prog Mgr* Anne Jolicoeur; *Assoc Cur* Pierre Dessureault; *Prog Mgr* Maureen McEvoy
Open Thanksgiving Tues - Apr 30 Wed & Thurs 11 AM - 8 PM. Fri, Sat & Sun 11 AM - 5 PM, May 1 - Thanksgiving Mon, Tues, Fri, Sat & Sun 11 AM - 5 PM. Wed 4 - 8 PM, Thurs 11 AM - 8 PM. No admis, donations accepted. Estab 1985 as an affiliate of the National Gallery of Canada. Reconstructed railway tunnel houses 354 sq metres of exhibition galleries

specially lit for photography, a theatre designed for flexible programming, a boutique & a research centre; exhibitions change quarterly. Mem: 300; dues based on sliding scale
Income: Financed by federal government & National Gallery of Canada
Collections: 158,000 images by Canadian photographers
Exhibitions: Over 40 exhibitions, solo & group, are available for loan
Publications: Exhibition catalogues; quarterly newsletter
Activities: Family programmes; teacher workshops; educational exhibitions; interpreter training; didactic printed materials; evaluation studies; lect open to public, 10-12 vis lectr per year; gallery talks; tours for adults & children; original objects of art lent to other museums & galleries for use in exhibitions; book traveling exhibitions 1-2 per year; originate traveling exhibitions to other museums, art galleries or spaces that meet conservation requirements across Canada & abroad; museum shop sells books, prints, photo related jewelry, children's gifts & postcards

M **CANADIAN MUSEUM OF NATURE,** Musee Canadien de la Nature, Metcalfe & McLeod Sts, PO Box 3443, Sta D, K1P 6P4. Tel 613-364-4042; FAX 613-998-1065; *Head Library & Archives* Arch W L Stewart; *Temporary Exhib* Monique Horth
Open Sept - Apr daily 10 AM - 5 PM & Thurs 10 AM - 8 PM, May - Sept daily 9:30 AM - 5 PM & Sun, Mon & Thurs 9:30 AM - 8 PM, cl Christmas. Admis family $12, adult $4, students $3, senior citizens & children 6 - 16 $2, children under 6 free. Estab 1842 to disseminate knowledge about the natural sciences, with particular but not exclusive reference to Canada. Average Annual Attendance: 300,000
Collections: †Prints; †Paintings, †Sculpture
Exhibitions: Evergreen (Natiional nature-related exhibition, annual); 15 exhibitions by various artists
Activities: Lect; film series; demonstrations & workshops dealing with natural history subjects; exten dept; individual paintings & original objects of art lent to other museums on the traveling exhibition circuit; lending collection contains 600 original prints & paintings, 150 photographs, 400 sculputres; book traveling exhibitions; originate traveling exhibitions

CANADIAN MUSEUMS ASSOCIATION, Association des Musees Canadiens
For further information, see National and Regional Organizations

M **CANADIAN WAR MUSEUM,** 330 Sussex Dr, K1A 0M8. Tel 819-776-8600, 776-8623; *Dir* V J H Suthren
Open daily, cl Christmas. Estab 1880 to collect, classify, preserve & display objects relevant to Canadian military history. Average Annual Attendance: 225, 000
Income: Financed by government funds
Collections: Uniforms & accoutrements; medals & insignia; equipment; vehicles; art; archives; photographs; weapons
Exhibitions: Victory 1 - Liberation of Western Europe, For Services Rendered - Valour decorations won by Canadians
Activities: Educ dept; lect & film presentations open to public; tours; artwork lent to other museums & galleries, educational institutions, national exhibition centers; lending collection contains 13,000 books; sales shop sells books, reproductions, prints, slides, shirts, caps, spoons, plastic models, films & postcards

M **CANADIAN WILDLIFE & WILDERNESS ART MUSEUM,** PO Box 98, Sta D, K1P 6C3. Tel 613-237-1581; FAX 613-237-1581; Elec Mail cawa@intranet.ca;
Internet Home Page Address http://intranet.ca/cawa/. *Dir* Gary Slimon; *Asst to Dir* Cody Sadler
Open Mon - Sun 10 AM - 5 PM. Admis $3. Estab 1987. Mem: Dues $50-$1000; annual meeting in Jan
Income: Financed by endowment, mem, state appropriation, mus proceeds
Collections: Wildlife & wilderness paintings, sculpture, carvings & decoys
Publications: Brochure; newsletter
Activities: Classes for children; 'how-to' seminars; lect open to public, 4 vis lectr per year; individual paintings & original objects of art lent to museums with similar mandates; lending collection contains original art work paintings & sculpture; book traveling exhibitions 1 per year; originate traveling exhibitions; museum shop sells books, magazines, prints, slides

L **Library,** PO Box 98, Sta D, K1P 6C3. *Dir* Gary Slimon; *Co-Dir* Cody Sadler
Library mainly for research for member artists
Library Holdings: Magazines; AV — Slides; Other — Exhibition catalogs

NATIONAL ARCHIVES OF CANADA

L **Visual & Sound Archives,** 344 Wellington St, K1A 0N3. Tel 613-995-7539, 996-7766, 992-5170; FAX 613-995-6226; Elec Mail jburant@archives.ca. *National Archivist* Jean-Pierre Wallot; *Dir* Betty Kidd; *Dir & Custodian Holdings* Brian Carey; *Chief Coll Consultation* Robert Grandmaitre; *Documentary Art Acquisition* Jim Burant; *Descriptive Servs Section* Gerald Stone; *Photo Acquisition* Jerry O'Brien
Open daily 9 AM - 4:45 PM. Estab 1905 to acquire & preserve significant Canadian archival material in the area of visual media, including paintings, watercolours, drawings, prints, medals, heraldry, posters & photography relating to all aspects of Canadian life, to the development of the country, to provide suitable research services, facilities to make this documentation available to the pub by means of exhibitions, publications & pub catalogue
Income: Financed by federal appropriation
Purchases: $80,000
Library Holdings: Vols 4000
Special Subjects: American Indian Art, Coins & Medals, Drawings, Etchings & Engravings, Landscapes, Miniatures, Painting - British, Painting - Canadian, Painting - Italian, Photography, Portraits, Posters, Prints, Reproductions, Watercolors, 18th & 19th century paintings, prints & drawings of Canadian views & subjects; 19th & 20th century Canadian photography
Collections: †1400 paintings; †20,000 watercolours & drawings; †90,000 prints; †30,000 posters; †14,000 medals; †7000 heraldic design & seals; 55,000 caricatures; 17 million photographs
Publications: Catalog of publications available on request

M **NATIONAL GALLERY OF CANADA,** 380 Sussex Dr, PO Box 427, Sta A, K1N 9N4. Tel 613-990-1985; FAX 613-990-9824; Elec Mail info@gallery.ca; info@beaux-arts.ca;
Internet Home Page Address http://national.gallery.ca; http://musee.beaux-arts.ca. *Dir* Dr Shirley L Thomson; *Chief Cur* Dr Colin Bailey; *Asst Dir Exhib & Installations* Daniel Amadei; *Asst Dir Communications & Marketing* Helen Murphy; *Cur Canadian Art* Charles Hill; *Asst Cur Later Canadian Art* Denise Leclerc; *Asst Cur Later Canadian Art* Pierre Landry; *Asst Cur Early Canadian Art* Victoria Baker; *Asst Cur Early Canadian Art* Rene Villeneuve; *Assoc Cur Canadian Prints & Drawings* Rosemarie Tovell; *Asst Cur Inuit Art* Marie Routledge; *Cur Contemporary Art* Diane Nemiroff; *Assoc Cur Film & Video* Jean Gagnon; *Asst Cur Contemporary Art* Janice Seline; *Cur European Art* Catherine Johnston; *Assoc Cur European Art* Michael Pantazzi; *Cur 20th Century Art* Brydon Smith; *Cur Prints & Drawings* Mimi Cazort; *Assoc Cur European & American Prints & Drawings* Douglas Schoenherr; *Acting Cur Photo Coll* Ann Thomas
Open Sept - May Wed - Sat 10 AM - 5 PM, Thurs 10 AM - 8 PM, May - Sept daily 10 AM - 6 PM, Thurs 10 AM - 8 PM. No admis fee to the permanent collection. Fee for special exhibitions. Founded 1880 under the patronage of the Governor-General, the Marquess of Lorne & his wife the Princess Louise; first inc 1913 & charged with the develop & care of the nat coll & the promotion of art in Canada. On May 21 1988, the first permanent home of National Gallery of Canada opened to the pub & to critical & popular acclaim. Overlooking the Ottawa river & steps away from Parliament Hill, the gallery is a landmark in the Capital's skyline. Light, spacious galleries & quiet courtyards lead the visitors on a voyage of discovery of Canada's exceptional art coll. Average Annual Attendance: 500,000. Mem: 3000; dues $50
Purchases: $3,000,000
Collections: Over 45,000 works in entire coll, over 1200 on display in permanent coll galleries; contemporary Inuit artists work; historical & contemporary Canadian art; media arts in the world over 600 titles, totalling more than 10,000 hours of video & film; 19,000 photography works; 20th century American art; western European art 14th-20th centuries
Exhibitions: Exhibitions from permanent coll, private & pub sources are organized & circulated in Canada & abroad
Publications: Annual report (incorporating annual review, with current acquisition lists); catalogues of permanent coll; CD-Rom on the Canadian coll; documents in the history of Canadian Art; exhibition books & catalogues; masterpieces in the National Gallery of Canada
Activities: Classes for adults & children; docent training; workshops for physically & mentally challenged; lect open to public, 50 vis lectr per year; concerts; gallery talks; tours; scholarships offered; individual paintings & original objects of art lent to art museums & galleries in Canada & abroad, subject to the same environmental conditions (other conditions apply); book traveling exhibitions 1-2 per year; originate traveling exhibitions; museum shop sells books, magazines, reproductions

L **Library,** 380 Sussex Dr, PO Box 427, Sta A, K1N 9N4. Tel 613-998-8949; FAX 613-990-9818; *Chief Librn* Murray Waddington; *Head Systems & Cataloging* Nancy Sprules; *Head Reader Serv* Peter Trepanier; *Head Archives* Cyndie Campbell
Estab 1918 to support the research & information requirements of gallery personnel; to make its collections of resource materials in the fine arts available to Canadian libraries & scholars; to serve as a source of information about Canadian art & art activities in Canada. For reference only
Library Holdings: Vols 200,000; Per subs 1100; Auction catalogues; Illustrated books; Rare books; Micro — Cards, fiche, reels; AV — A-tapes, cassettes, fs, Kodachromes, lantern slides, motion pictures, rec, slides, v-tapes; Other — Clipping files, exhibition catalogs, manuscripts, memorabilia, pamphlets, photographs
Special Subjects: Aesthetics, Architecture, Art History, Drawings, Eskimo Art, Film, Graphic Arts, Painting - Canadian, Printmaking, Video, Canadian art, post-medieval Western art with special emphasis on drawings, painting, prints, photography & sculpture
Collections: Art Documentation; Canadiana
Publications: Artists in Canada; Reference Database (CHIN)
Activities: Library tours

M **NATIONAL MUSEUM OF SCIENCE & TECHNOLOGY,** 1867 St Laurent Blvd, PO Box 9724, Sta T, K1G 5A3. Tel 613-991-3044; FAX 613-990-3654; *Dir* Dr G Sainte-Marie
Open daily 9 AM - 5 PM, Thurs to 8 PM, cl Mon during winter. Admis adults $4, senior citizens & students $3, children 6-15 $1. Estab 1967 to foster scientific & technological literacy throughout Canada by establishing & maintaining a collection of scientific & technological objects
Collections: Canada & Space Trains
Exhibitions: Leonardo Di Vinci; Data on the Move; All Family; All Different
Activities: Educ dept

M **NATIONAL MUSEUM OF SCIENCE & TECHNOLOGY CORPORATION,** National Aviation Museum, Rockcliffe Airport, K1G 5A3. Tel 613-993-2010; FAX 613-990-3655; Elec Mail aviation@istar.ca;
Internet Home Page Address http://www.aviation.nmstc.ca. *Dir* C Terry; *Cur* A J (Fred) Shortt
Open May 1 - Labour Day daily 9 AM - 5 PM, Thurs 9 AM - 9 PM, after Labour Day - Apr 30 Tues - Sun 10 AM - 5 PM, Thurs 10 AM - 9 PM, cl Mon. Admis adults $5, seniors & students with ID $4, children 6-15 $1.75, families with children under 16 $10, children under 6, members & Thurs evenings free. Estab 1960 to illustrate the evolution of the flying machine & the important role aircraft played in Canada's development. Average Annual Attendance: 250,000. Mem: 2000; dues $20-$80
Collections: 118 aircraft plus thousands of aviation related artifacts
Activities: Educ Dept; sales shop sells books, magazines & prints

L **OTTAWA PUBLIC LIBRARY,** Fine Arts Dept, 120 Metcalfe St, K1P 5M2. Tel 613-236-0301; FAX 613-567-4013; *Dir* Barbara Clubb; *Admin Dir* Jean Martel
Open Mon - Thurs 10 AM - 9 PM, Fri 10 AM - 6 PM, Sat 9:30 AM - 5 PM, Sun 1 - 5 PM (winters). Estab 1906 to serve the community as a centre for

general & reliable information; to select, preserve & administer books & related materials in organized collections; to provide opportunity for citizens of all ages to educate themselves continuously
Income: $8,808,600 (financed by city, province, other)
Library Holdings: Vols 12,000; Per subs 85; Micro — Fiche, reels; AV — Cassettes, fs; Other — Clipping files, pamphlets
Exhibitions: Monthly exhibits highlighting local artists, craftsmen, photographers & collectors
Activities: Lect open to public; library tours

ROYAL ARCHITECTURAL INSTITUTE OF CANADA
For further information, see National and Regional Organizations

OWEN SOUND

M OWEN SOUND HISTORICAL SOCIETY (Formerly Marine & Rail Heritage Museum), Marine & Rail Heritage Museum, 1165 First Ave W, N4K 4K8. Tel 519-371-3333; *Pres* Ken Carr; *Acting Cur* Orris Hull
Open May - Oct 10 AM - 4:30 PM. Estab 1985 for the preservation of Owen Sound's marine, rail & industrial history
Income: Financed by mem, donations & government grant
Collections: Charts, timetables, railway artifacts & models; Corvette HMCS Owen Sound artifacts; Dug-out & Birchback canoes; house flags of Marine Transport Coys; lifeboat from the Paul Evans; marine & railway uniforms; patterns from local foundry in production of propellers & shipbuilding; scale models of ships that sailed the Great Lakes
Activities: Lect open to public, 6 vis lectr per year; children's competition with prizes; lending collection contains books; museum shop sells books, hasti-notes, postcards, railway caps & trivets

M TOM THOMSON MEMORIAL ART GALLERY, 840 First Ave W, N4K 4K4. Tel 519-376-1932; FAX 519-376-3037; *Dir* Brian Meehan; *Educ* David Huff
Open Sept - June Tues - Fri 11 AM - 5 PM, Wed 7 - 9 PM, Sat & Sun Noon - 5 PM; July & Aug Mon - Sat 10 AM - 5 PM, Sun Noon - 5 PM. No admis fee. Estab 1967 to collect & display paintings by Tom Thomson, a native son & Canada's foremost landscape artist; to educate the public. Paintings by Tom Thomson on permanent display, plus 2 galleries of changing exhibitions. Average Annual Attendance: 30,000. Mem: 300; dues family $25, individual $15, senior citizens & students $10
Income: Financed by city appropriation & provincial grants & fundraising
Collections: Tom Thomson; Historic & Contemporary Canadian Artists; Group of Seven
Publications: Bulletin, six per year; exhibition catalogs 3 per year
Activities: Classes for adults & children; docent training; lect open to public; gallery talks; tours; films; competitions with awards; concerts; exten dept serves city buildings; art rental & sales library; museum shop sells books, reproductions, prints & postcards
L Library, 840 First Ave W, N4K 4K4. Tel 519-376-1932; FAX 519-376-3037; *Dir* Brian Meehan; *Educ* David Huff
Open for reference of Canadian Art only
Library Holdings: Vols 400; Per subs 6; Other — Exhibition catalogs
Collections: Files on Tom Thomson

PETERBOROUGH

M ART GALLERY OF PETERBOROUGH, 2 Crescent St, K9J 2G1. Tel 705-743-9179; FAX 705-743-8168; *Dir* Illi-Maria Tamplin; *Prog Asst* Dominick Hardy; *Secy* Vera Novacek
Open Tues - Sun 1 - 5 PM, Thurs 1 - 9 PM. No admis fee. Estab 1973. Gallery situated along a lake & in a park; new extension added & completed June 1979. Average Annual Attendance: 18,600. Mem: 1000; dues sustaining $25, family $20, individual $15, sr citizens $12, student $8; annual meeting June
Income: Financed by mem, fundraising & provincial, federal, municipal grants
Collections: European and Canadian works of art
Exhibitions: Mark Gomes, Joey Morgan, Susan Schelle, Nancy Paterson, Ron Bolt; French Photography - New Directions
Publications: Catalogues on some exhibitions; Bulletin of Events, monthly; pamphlets on artists in exhibitions
Activities: Classes for adults & children; dramatic programs; docent training; workshops; art program to public schools; lect open to public; gallery talks; tours; individual paintings & original objects of art lent to other galleries; lending collection contains 250 original art works; sales shop sells books, magazines, crafts

SAINT CATHARINES

M NIAGARA ARTISTS' CENTRE, 2 Bond St, L2R 4Y9. Tel 905-641-0331; FAX 905-641-0331; *Artistic Dir* Tobey Anderson
Open Tues - Fri Noon - 5 PM, Sat Noon - 4 PM. Estab 1969. Average Annual Attendance: 6100. Mem: 135; mem open to volunteers for exhibits & fundraisers; dues $15-$50; annual meeting mid-July
Income: $120,000 (financed by mem, Ontario government, federal government & sponsorship)
Publications: NAC News, monthly
Activities: Lect open to public

A RODMAN HALL ARTS CENTRE, 109 St Paul Crescent, L2S 1M3. Tel 905-684-2925; FAX 905-682-4733; *Pres* A Kurcz; *VPres* C Day; *Dir* David Aurandt; *Cur Educ* Debra Attenborough
Open Tues - Fri 11 AM - 5 PM, Sat & Sun 1 - 5 PM. Estab 1960, art gallery, cultural centre & visual arts exhibitions. Four galleries in an 1853, 1960 & 1975 addition. 1975 - A1 - National Museums of Canada. Maintains reference library. Average Annual Attendance: 45,000. Mem: 800; dues tax receipt $75 or more, family $40, individual $25; annual meeting in Sept

Income: Financed by mem, city, province & government of Canada
Collections: American graphics & drawings; †Canadian drawings, †paintings, †sculpture & †watercolours; international graphics & sculpture
Exhibitions: Monthly exhibitions featuring painting, photographs, sculpture & other art
Publications: Catalogue - Lord and Lady Head Watercolours; monthly calendar; Rodmon Hall Arts Center (1960-1981)
Activities: Classes for adults & children; dramatic programs; docent training; workshops; films; lect open to public, 6 vis lectr per year; concerts; gallery talks; tours; individual paintings & original objects of art lent to city hall & other art galleries; book traveling exhibitions 16 per year; book traveling exhibitions 5 per year; museum shop sells books, original art, gifts, pottery, glassware & jewerly
L Library, 109 St Paul Crescent, L2S 1M3. Tel 905-684-2925; FAX 905-682-4733; *Librn* Debra Attenborough
Open Tues - Fri 9 AM - 5 PM. Estab 1960. Reference library
Library Holdings: Vols 3500; Per subs 7; Micro — Cards; AV — Cassettes, slides, v-tapes; Other — Clipping files, exhibition catalogs, pamphlets, photographs, reproductions

SAINT THOMAS

M ST THOMAS ELGIN ART GALLERY, 301 Talbot St, N5P 1B5. Tel 519-631-4040; *Exec Dir* Rick Nixon; *Admin* Diane Dobson
Open Wed - Sun Noon - 5 PM, Thurs Noon - 9 PM, cl Mon & Tues. Admis donation suggested. Estab 1969. Mem: 658; dues senior citizens $15, family $30, single $20; annual meeting in June
Income: $120,000 (financed by endowment, mem, province appropriation & earned revenues)
Purchases: $20,000
Collections: †Fine Art Works by Canadian Artists
Publications: Exhibition catalogues, semi-annually; gallery newsletter 6 per year
Activities: Classes for adults & children; docent training; school programs; lect open to public, 10 vis lectr per year; scholarships offered; exten dept servs provide lending collection of 500 paintings & art objects; book traveling exhibitions 5 per year; originate traveling exhibitions; sales shop sells books & original art

SARNIA

L GALLERY LAMBTON, 150 N Christina St, N7T 7W5. Tel 519-336-8127; *Cur* David Taylor
Open Mon - Fri 9 AM - 9 PM, Sat 9 AM - 5:30 PM, Sun Oct - May 2 - 5 PM. No admis fee. Estab 1961, a collection of Canadian paintings instituted in 1919 & administered by the Women's Conservation Art Assoc of Sarnia. The Collection was turned over to the Sarnia Library Board in 1956 & additions are being made from time to time. 3500 sq ft; also small display area of 300 sq ft in newly renovated Lawrence House, a Victorian home. Average Annual Attendance: 35,000
Income: Financed by municipal & provincial appropriations
Purchases: Canadian works of art
Collections: †Canadian Paintings; Eskimo Carvings; a Collection of Old Photographs of Sarnia & Lambton County; sculpture
Exhibitions: Twelve to fifteen shows a year, either traveling from other galleries or initiated by the Sarnia Art Gallery
Publications: Exhibition catalogues
Activities: Classes for adults & children; lect open to public; gallery talks; tours; competitions with awards; films; bus trips; workshops; individual paintings & original objects of art lent; book traveling exhibitions 6-7 per year; junior museum located at Lawrence House

SCARBOROUGH

M CITY OF SCARBOROUGH, Cedar Ridge Creative Centre, 225 Confederation Dr, M1G 1B2. Tel 416-396-4026; FAX 416-396-4026; *Mgr* Todd Davidson
Open 9 AM - 9 PM. No admis fee. Estab 1985 as a gallery & teaching studio. 3-interconnecting rooms & solarium with oak panelling. 18' x 22', 18' x 28', 16' x 26'. Average Annual Attendance: 1300. Mem: Annual dues $10 (it entitles member to rent gallery for one week for $39)
Exhibitions: Contemporary Art Show
Activities: Classes for adults & children; one day workshops in arts & crafts; lect open to public, 2 vis lectr per year

SIMCOE

M EVA BROOK DONLY MUSEUM, 109 Norfolk St S, N3Y 2W3. Tel 519-426-1583; *Cur* William Yeager
Open Sept - May Wed - Sun 1 - 5 PM, May - Sept Mon - Fri 10 AM - 5 PM, Sat & Sun 1 - 5 PM. Admis general $1. Estab 1946 to display & aid research in the history of Norfolk County. Average Annual Attendance: 7000. Mem: 600; dues $15-$25; annual meeting in Jan
Income: Financed by endowment, mem, city & provincial appropriation
Collections: Large Collection of important Early Documents & Newspapers, 370 paintings of historic Norfolk by W E Cantelon; Displays of artifacts of the 19th century Norfolk County; historical materials
Exhibitions: Concerned mainly with focusing new light on some aspects of the permanent collection; 1860's Victorian Home; Glorious Old Norfolk: 300 years of Norfolk History; Changing Exhibitions
Activities: Lect open to public, 15 vis lectr per year; tours; book traveling exhibitions 3 per year; museum shop sells books, crafts & candy
L Library, 109 Norfolk St S, N3Y 2W3. Tel 519-426-1583; *Cur* William Yeager
Reference & a photograph collection for display
Library Holdings: Vols 2000; Micro — Fiche, reels; AV — Cassettes, slides; Other — Clipping files, manuscripts, memorabilia, original art works, photographs, prints

A **LYNNWOOD ARTS CENTRE,** 21 Lynnwood Ave, PO Box 67, N3Y 4K8. Tel 519-428-0540; *Chmn* Kathy Olsson; *Dir* Rod Demerling; *Office Mgr* Bettianne Engell
Open Tues - Fri 9 AM - 5 PM, Sat & Sun 1 - 5 PM. No admis fee. Estab 1973 to provide a focal point for the visual arts in the community. Built in 1851 - Greek Revival Architecture; orange brick with ionic columns & is a National Historic Site. Average Annual Attendance: 20,000. Mem: 800; dues family $15, individual $10, student & senior citizen $5; annual meeting in Jan
Income: $140,000 (financed by mem, patrons-private & commercial, Ministry of Citizenship & Culture, Ontario Arts Council, Town of Simcoe, Regional Municipality of Haldimand-Norfolk)
Collections: †Contemporary Canadian Art
Exhibitions: Changing monthly exhibitions
Publications: Bi-monthly Newsletter
Activities: Classes for adults & children; docent training; lect open to public, 15 lectr per year; concerts; gallery talks; tours; seminars; juried art exhibitions (every two years) with purchase awards; individual paintings & original objects of art lent to members; museum shop sells books, hand-crafted items, prints & reproductions

STRATFORD

M **STRATFORD ART ASSOCIATION,** The Gallery Stratford, 54 Romeo St N, PO Box 1, N5A 6S8. Tel 519-271-5271; FAX 519-271-1642; *Dir* Robert Freeman; *Pres Bd Trustees* Ian Fisher
Open Sept - May Sun, Tues - Fri 1 - 5 PM, Sat 10 AM - 5 PM; summer hours June - Sept Tues - Sun 9 AM - 6 PM; business hours weekdays 9 AM - 5 PM. Admis $4, senior citizens & students $3.50, children under 12 free. Estab 1967 as a non-profit permanent establishment open to the pub & administered in the pub interest for the purpose of studying, interpreting, assembling & exhibiting to the pub. Average Annual Attendance: 25,000. Mem: 700; annual meeting in Mar
Income: $348,743 (financed by mem, city appropriation, provincial & federal grants & fundraising)
Collections: †Works of art on paper
Exhibitions: Changing exhibits, geared to create interest for visitors to Stratford Shakespearean Festival; during winter months geared to local municipality
Publications: Catalogs; calendar of events
Activities: Classes for adults & children; docent training; lect open to public; gallery talks; tours; scholarships offered; traveling exhibitions organized & circulated; sales shop sells books, glass, Inuit, jewelry, northwest Indian, pottery & silk

SUDBURY

LAURENTIAN UNIVERSITY
M **Museum & Art Centre,** 453 Ramsey Rd, P3E 2Z7. Tel 705-675-1151, Ext 1400; FAX 705-674-3065; *Dir & Cur* Pierre Arpin
Open Tues - Sun Noon - 5 PM, cl Mon, mornings by appointment. Admis fee voluntary. Estab 1968 to present a continuous program of exhibitions, concerts & events for the people of Sudbury & the district. Gallery has two floors of space: 124 running ft in one & 131 running ft in the second gallery & 68.5 running ft in third gallery. Average Annual Attendance: 15,000. Mem: 400; dues family $26.75, single $16.05, student & senior citizen $8.56; annual meeting in June
Income: Financed by endowment, mem, city & provincial appropriation, government & local organizations
Collections: Canadian coll dating from the late 1800s & early 1900s to contemporary. The Group of Seven, Eskimo sculptures & prints as well as works of historical Canadian artists comprise the coll; Indian works from northern Ontario
Exhibitions: (1997) Go Figure: Dennis Geden; Secondary School Art
Publications: Communique, every eight weeks
Activities: Lect open to public, 10 vis lectr per year; concerts; gallery talks; tours; lending collection contains 1300 original art works & 8300 slides; book traveling exhibitions 2-4 per year; museum shop sells magazines, catalogues, postcards, posters, prints & gift items
L **Art Centre Library,** 453 Ramsey Rd, P3E 2Z7. Tel 705-675-1151, Ext 1400; FAX 705-674-3065; *Dir* Pierre Arpin
Open Winter daily 9 AM - 4:30 PM, Summer daily 8:30 AM - 4 PM. Estab 1977. For reference only
Library Holdings: Vols 5000; Per subs 78; Micro — Cards; AV — Cassettes, lantern slides, slides 8300, v-tapes; Other — Clipping files, exhibition catalogs, pamphlets, photographs

TORONTO

M **ART GALLERY OF ONTARIO,** 317 Dundas St W, M5T 1G4. Tel 416-977-0414; FAX 416-979-6646; *Dir* Maxwell Anderson; *Chief Cur* Matthew Teitelbaum; *Controller* Tom Lewis; *Mgr Marketing* Frank Comella; *Head Develop* Sean St Michael
Open Tues - Sun 11 AM - 5:30 PM, Wed evening until 9 PM, cl Mon. Admis adults $3.50, students $1.50, senior citizens $1.50, Fri, members, accompanied children under 12 & Wed evenings free. Estab 1900 to cultivate & advance the cause of the visual arts in Ontario; to conduct programmes of educ in the origin, development, appreciation & techniques of the visual arts; to collect & exhibit works of art & displays & to maintain & operate a gallery & related facilities as required for this purpose; to stimulate the interest of the pub in matters undertaken by the Gallery. Average Annual Attendance: 400,000. Mem: 28,000; dues supporting $100, family $60, individual $45; annual meeting in June
Income: Financed by mem, provincial, city & federal appropriations & earned income
Purchases: $1,000,000
Collections: American & European Art (16th century to present); Canadian Historical & Contemporary Art; Henry Moore Sculpture Center, Prints & Drawings
Publications: Ago News, eleven times per year; annual report; exhibition catalogs

Activities: Classes for adults & children; docent training; lect open to public; 35 vis lectr per year; concerts; gallery talks; tours; exten dept organizes traveling exhibitions, circulated throughout the Province, Canada & United States; individual paintings & original objects of art loaned; lending coll includes 60 cassettes, fs, educational v-tapes & 100,000 slides; originate traveling exhibitions; sales shop sells books, magazines, reproductions, prints, slides & jewelry; art rental shop for members to rent original works of art
L **Edward P Taylor Research Library & Archives,** 317 Dundas St W, M5T 1G4. Tel 416-979-6642; FAX 416-979-6602; *Chief Librn* Karen McKenzie; *Deputy Librn* Larry Pfaff; *Information Systems Librn* Donald Rance
Open Wed - Fri 1 - 4:45 PM. Estab 1933 to collect printed material for the documentation & interpretation of the works of art in the Gallery's collection, to provide research & informational support for the Gallery's programmes & activities; to document the art & artists of Ontario, Toronto & Canada
Income: Financed by parent institution, donations, grants
Library Holdings: Vols 100,000; Per subs 650; Auction catalogs; Micro — Fiche, reels; Other — Clipping files, exhibition catalogs, manuscripts, pamphlets, photographs, reproductions
Special Subjects: Art History, Conceptual Art, Eskimo Art, Etchings & Engravings, Graphic Arts, Landscapes, Latin American Art, Marine Painting, Mixed Media, Painting - American, Painting - British, Painting - Canadian, Painting - Dutch, Painting - Flemish, Painting - French, Canadian, American & European Art from the Renaissance to the present, concentrating mainly on drawing, engraving, painting & sculpture
Collections: †Canadian Illustrated Books; Alan Garrow Collection of British Illustrated Books & Wood Engravings of the 1860s; Canadian Book-Plates; †International Guide Books; Robert D McIntosh Collection of Books on Sepulchral Monuments

M **ART METROPOLE,** 788 King St W, M5V 1N6. Tel 416-703-4400; FAX 416-703-4404; *Dir* A A Bronson; *Distribution Coordr* Ann Dean; *Asst Cur* Roger Bywater
Open Wed - Fri 10 AM - 6 PM, Sat Noon - 5 PM. Estab 1974 to document work by artists internationally working in non-traditional & multiple media
Activities: Sales shop sells books, artists video & multiples

A **ARTS AND LETTERS CLUB OF TORONTO,** 14 Elm St, M5G 1G7. Tel 416-597-0223; *Pres* Ezra Schabas
Admis by appointment. Estab 1908 to foster arts & letters in Toronto. Mem: 550; annual meeting May
Collections: Club Collection - art by members & others; Heritage Collection - art by members now deceased
L **Library,** 14 Elm St, M5G 1G7. Tel 416-597-0223; *Librn* Ann Schabas
Open to club members & researchers for reference
Library Holdings: Vols 2500; Per subs 40; AV — A-tapes, cassettes, Kodachromes, motion pictures, slides, v-tapes; Other — Clipping files, exhibition catalogs, manuscripts, memorabilia, original art works, prints, sculpture
Special Subjects: Architecture, Sculpture, Theatre Arts, Literature, Music, Paintings, Canadian Art

M **A SPACE,** 401 Richmond St W, Ste 110, M5V 3A8. Tel 416-979-9633; FAX 416-979-9683; Elec Mail aspace@interlog.com. *Prog Dir* Ingrid Mayrhofer; *Admin Dir* Bill Huffman
Open Tues - Fri 11 AM - 6 PM, Sat Noon - 5 PM. No admis fee. Estab 1971. 1000 sq ft of gallery space & hardwood floors. Maintains reference library. Average Annual Attendance: 6000. Mem: 150; dues $20; 4 meetings yearly
Income: $171,000 (financed by endowment, mem, city & state appropriation)
Publications: Addendum-A Space Community Newsletter, quarterly
Activities: Lect open to public, 5 vis lectr per year; concerts; gallery talks; tours; originate traveling exhibitions; museum shop sells books

M **BAYCREST CENTRE FOR GERIATRIC CARE,** Irving E & Ray Kanner Heritage Museum, 3560 Bathurst St, M6A 2E1. Tel 416-785-2500, Ext 2802; FAX 416-785-2378; *Coordr* Pat Dinkinson
Open 9 AM - 9 PM. No admis fee. Estab 1973
Collections: †Judaica: ceremonial objects, domestic artifacts, memorabilia, books, photos, documents & works on paper

CANADIAN SOCIETY OF PAINTERS IN WATERCOLOUR
For further information, see National and Regional Organizations

M **GEORGE R GARDINER MUSEUM OF CERAMIC ART,** 111 Queen's Park, M5S 2C7. Tel 416-586-8080; FAX 416-586-8085; *Cur* Meredith Chilton
Open Mon - Sat 10 AM - 5 PM, Sun 11 AM - 5 PM, Tues evenings until 8 PM. Admis adults $6, sr citizens, students & children $3.25. Estab 1984 as the only specialized museum of ceramics in North America. Museum houses one of the world's greatest collections of European ceramic art from the early 15th century to the turn of the 19th century. The earlier museum merged operations with the Royal Ontario Museum in 1984 & visitors now pay one fee to visit both facilities
Collections: English delftware; European porcelain; Italian maiolica; Pre-Columbian pottery
Activities: Classes for adults & children; docent programs; lect open to public; book traveling exhibitions 2 per year; retail store sells books, original art & modern ceramics

A **LYCEUM CLUB AND WOMEN'S ART ASSOCIATION OF CANADA,** 23 Prince Arthur Ave, M5R 1B2. Tel 416-922-2060; *Pres* Lynn Cumine
Open to pub for scheduled exhibitions & lectures. Estab 1886 to encourage women in the arts; branches in Ontario, Hamilton, St Thomas & Peterborough. Mem: 115; dues $125, qualifications: interest in the arts, nominated & seconded by members; annual meeting in Apr
Collections: Canadian Art Collection
Activities: Classes for adults; lect open to public, 10 vis lectr per year; concerts; competitions with awards; scholarships given to Ontario College of Art, Royal Conservatory of Music, National Ballet School, University of Toronto Faculty of Music; individual paintings & original objects of art lent

L Library, 23 Prince Arthur Ave, M5R 1B2. Tel 416-922-2060; *Librn* D M Johnston
Library Holdings: Vols 1000
Special Subjects: Extensive Canadiana

M THE MARKET GALLERY OF THE CITY OF TORONTO ARCHIVES, 95 Front St E, M5E 1C2. Tel 416-392-7604; FAX 416-392-0572; *Cur* Pamela Wachna; *Cur* Gillian Reddyhoff
Open Wed - Fri 10 AM - 4 PM, Sat 9 AM - 4 PM, Sun Noon - 4 PM, cl Mon & Tues. Admis free. Estab 1979 to bring the art & history of Toronto to the public. Average Annual Attendance: 25,000
Collections: †City of Toronto Fine Art Collection (oil, watercolor, prints & sculpture)
Exhibitions: Various exhibitions on Toronto's history, featuring the city's archival collections are presented on an on-going basis. (1997) Topics on Toronto's architectural history, such as the Don Jail & St James Cathedral
Publications: Exhibit catalogs
Activities: Classes for children; gallery talks; tours; exten dept servs other institutions; paintings lent

METAL ARTS GUILD
For further information, See National and Regional Organizations

METROPOLITAN TORONTO LIBRARY BOARD
L Main Reference, 789 Yonge St, M4W 2G8. Tel 416-393-7131; FAX 416-393-7229; *Libr Bd Dir* Frances Schwenger; *Asst Dir Reference Div* Dora Dempster; *Mgr* Lesley Bell
Open Mon - Thurs 9 AM - 9 PM, Fri 9 AM - 6 PM, Sat 9 AM - 5 PM, Sun Oct 15 - end of Apr 1:30 - 5 PM. Estab 1959 for public reference
Income: Financed by city appropriation
Library Holdings: Vols 50,000; Per subs 450; Micro — Fiche, reels; Other — Clipping files, exhibition catalogs, photographs, prints, reproductions
Special Subjects: Decorative Arts, Canadian Fine Arts, Costume Design
Collections: Postcards, scenic & greeting; †printed ephemera; †private presses with emphasis on Canadian; 834,000 picture clippings; theatre arts & stage design

A ONTARIO ASSOCIATION OF ART GALLERIES, 489 King St W, Ste 306, M5V 1K4. Tel 416-598-0714; FAX 416-598-4128; Elec Mail oaag@interlog.com. *Pres* Dorothy Farr; *VPres* Catherine Elliot Shaw; *Exec Dir* Anne Kolisnyk
Open 9 AM - 5 PM. Estab in 1968 as the provincial nonprofit organization representing pub art galleries in the province of Ontario. Institutional mem includes approx 84 pub art galleries, exhibition spaces & arts related organizations. Mem is also available to individuals. Gallery not maintained. Mem: 83; annual meeting in June
Income: Financed by mem, Ontario Arts Council, Ontario Ministry of Culture, Tourism & Recreation, Department of Canadian Heritage
Publications: Context, bimonthly newsletter
Activities: Professional development seminars & workshops; awards; active job file & job hot-line

M ONTARIO COLLEGE OF ART & DESIGN, OCAD Gallery, 291 Dundas St W, M5T 1G1. Tel 416-977-6000, 977-5311, Ext 262; FAX 416-977-0235; *Cur* Christine Swiderski
Open Tues - Sat 11 AM - 5 PM. Estab 1970 for faculty & student exhibitions & to exhibit outside work to benefit the college. Average Annual Attendance: 15,000
Income: Financed by College
Exhibitions: Exhibiting student works, rotate every 3 weeks
Publications: Invitations; small scale catalogs
Activities: Dramatic programs; Concerts; competitions; individual paintings & original objects of art lent; traveling exhibitions organized & circulated
L Dorothy H Hoover Library, 100 McCaul St, M5T 1W1. Tel 416-977-5311, Ext 255; FAX 416-977-0235; Elec Mail jpatrick@hookup.net. *Dir* Jill Patrick
Open Mon - Thurs 8:30 AM - 7:45 PM, Fri 8:30 AM - 5 PM. Estab to support the curriculum
Income: Financed through the College
Purchases: $100,000
Library Holdings: Vols 30,000; Per subs 225; Pictures 40,000; Vertical files 43,000; Micro — Fiche, reels; AV — Cassettes 620, fs, Kodachromes, lantern slides, motion pictures 75, rec, slides 85,000, v-tapes 1000; Other — Clipping files, exhibition catalogs, pamphlets
Special Subjects: Advertising Design, Art History, Commercial Art, Conceptual Art, Decorative Arts, Drawings, Graphic Arts, Graphic Design, Jewelry, Mixed Media, Contemporary Art & Design

M ONTARIO CRAFTS COUNCIL, The Craft Gallery, Chalmers Bldg, 35 McCaul St, M5T 1V7. Tel 416-977-3551; FAX 416-977-3552; *Pres* Oz Parsons; *Exec Dir* Sarah Lupmanis; *Cur* Dale Barrett; *Mgr Resource Centre* Jane Moore
Open Mon - Fri 9 AM - 5 PM, Sat 10 AM - 5 PM, Sun Noon - 5 PM. Admis $2. Estab 1976 to foster crafts & crafts people in Ontario & is the largest craft organization in Canada. Has over 100 affiliated groups. Maintains an art gallery. Average Annual Attendance: 8000. Mem: 3500; dues $50; annual meeting in June
Income: Financed by mem & provincial appropriation, The Guild Shop, fundraising & publications
Exhibitions: Ontario Crafts Regional Juried Exhibition; bimonthly exhibitions in craft gallery
Publications: Ontario Craft; bimonthly magazine; shows list, annual
Activities: Lect open to public; gallery talks; tours; competitions with awards; scholarships offered; book traveling exhibitions 1 per year; sales shop sells books, original craft, prints, Inuit art, sculpture & prints
L Craft Resource Centre, 35 McCaul St, M5T 1V7. Tel 416-977-3551; FAX 416-977-3552; *Information Officer* Kathleen Morris; *Information Officer* Jane Mallory; *Information Officer* Dale Barret; *Information Officer* Carol-Ann Casselman
Open Wed - Sun Noon - 5 PM. No admis fee. Estab 1976. A comprehensive, special library devoted exclusively to the field of crafts. It is a primarily mem-

funded not-for-profit organization & is available as an information service to the general pub & Ontario crafts Council members. Has an extensive portfolio registry featuring Canadian craftspeople. For reference only. Average Annual Attendance: 6000. Mem: 4000; dues $40; annual meeting in June
Library Holdings: Vols 3000; Per subs 350; Portfolios of craftspeople 530; AV — Slides 100,000, v-tapes; Other — Clipping files, exhibition catalogs, manuscripts
Special Subjects: Enamels, Glass, Metalwork, Pottery, Fibre, Leather, Wood
Publications: Annual Craft Shows in Ontario; Business Bibliography; Crafts in Ontario; Craftspersons Guide to Good Business; Directory of Suppliers of Craft Materials; Shops & Galleries; Starting Your Own Craft Business; The Photography of Crafts; The Trials of Jurying: A Guide for Exhibition Organizers & Jurors
Activities: Educ dept; tours; competitions with awards; scholarships & fels offered; slide rental; publishing; sales shop sells books, magazines, contemporary Canadian crafts

A Artists in Stained Glass, 35 McCaul St, M5T 1V7. *Pres* Sue Obata; *Ed* Virginia Smith
Estab 1974 to encourage the development of stained glass as a contemporary art form in Canada. Maintains slide file library through the Ontario Crafts Council. Mem: 130; dues $25-$70; annual meeting in Nov
Income: $6000 (financed by mem & state appropriation)
Publications: Flat Glass Journal, quarterly; Leadline, occasionally
Activities: Classes for adults; lect open to public, 5 vis lectr per year

A THE PHOTON LEAGUE OF HOLOGRAPHERS, 401 Richmond St W, Ste B03, M5V 3A8. Tel 416-599-9332, 203-7243; *Dir* C Abrams
Open Noon - 5 PM. Estab 1985 for holography production. The Photon League is committed to providing affordable access to a professional level holography facility, education about holography through workshops, encouragement & support of artistic production & dialogue in the field of holography. As a resource center, The Photon League organizes & curates exhibitions, maintains an archive of holographic work & fosters the exploration of relevant technologies. Holography studio includes: 50 mw Helium Neon laser, 3 mw Helium Neon laser, 2 mw Helium Neon laser, 8 x 16 ft floating table, darkroom, computer controlled stereogram, optics & mounts. Mem: 30; dues international $75, core $60, student $20, associate $15
Income: Financed by mem
Publications: Quarterly newsletter
Activities: Classes for adults & children; artist-in-residence; workshops; panel discussions; open house; discussion group; lect open to public; lending collection contains original objects of art; sales shop sells holograms & T-shirts

PROFESSIONAL ART DEALERS ASSOCIATION OF CANADA
For further information, see National and Regional Organizations

ROYAL CANADIAN ACADEMY OF ARTS
For further information, see National and Regional Organizations

M ROYAL ONTARIO MUSEUM, 100 Queen's Park, M5S 2C6. Tel 416-586-5549; FAX 416-586-5863; *Chmn Board of Trustees* Elizabeth Samuel; *Secy Board of Trustees* Robert Barnett; *Dir* Dr John McNeill; *VPres Coll & Research* David Preudergast; *Assoc VPres Exhibits & Marketing* Florence Silver; *VPres Bus Affairs & Operations* Mike Shoreman; *Dir Human Resources* Elsebeth Riccardi; *Exhib Dir* Stanley Rahmi; *Acting Dir Human Resources* Barbara Wade; *Dir Exhib Prog* Margo Welch
Open daily 10 AM - 6 PM, Tues & Thurs evenings until 8 PM, cl Labor Day in Sept to Victoria Day in May. Admis families $13, adults $6, senior citizens, students & children $3.25. Estab 1912 & includes 20 curatorial departments in the fields of fine & decorative arts, archaeology & the natural & earth sciences. Average Annual Attendance: 1,000,000. Mem: 35,000; dues individual $65
Income: $25,000,000 (financed by federal grants, provincial grants, mus income, mem, bequests, grants & donations)
Collections: Extensive Far Eastern collection
Publications: Rotunda, quarterly magazine; numerous academic publications; gallery guides; exhibition catalogs; publications in print
Activities: Classes for adults & children; throughout the school year, prebooked classes receive lessons in the museum. Unconducted classes can also be arranged with the museum at a cost of $3 per student; lect open to public with vis lectr, special lect for members only; concerts; gallery talks; tours; competitions; outreach dept serves Ontario; individual paintings & original objects of art lent to museums & galleries; originate traveling exhibitions; museum shop sells books, magazines, reproductions, prints & slides
L Library & Archives, 100 Queen's Park, M5S 2C6. Tel 416-586-5595; FAX 416-586-5863; *Head Librn* Julia Matthews
Estab 1960 for curatorial research
Library Holdings: Vols 60,000; Per subs 390; Micro — Fiche, reels; Other — Exhibition catalogs
Special Subjects: Archaeology, Decorative Arts, Furniture, Textiles, Antiquities, Canadiana, Museology
M Dept of Western Art & Culture, 100 Queen's Park, M5S 2C6. Tel 416-586-5524; FAX 416-586-5516; *Dept Head* Dr Howard Collinson
Open Mon - Sat 10 AM - 5 PM, Sun 1 - 5 PM. No admis fee. Estab 1951 to collect, exhibit & publish material on Canadian historical paintings & Canadian decorative arts. Canadiana Gallery has three galleries: first gallery has six rooms showing English Colonial, French, Maritime, Ontario & German-Ontario furniture, also silver, glass, woodenware; second gallery has ceramics, toys, weathervanes, religious carving, early 19th century Quebec panelled room; third is a picture gallery for changing exhibitions. Average Annual Attendance: 35,000
Collections: Canadian 18th & 19th centuries decorative arts - ceramics, coins & medals books, †furniture, †glass, guns, silver, woodenware; 16th-18th centuries exploration; †portraits of Canadians & military & administrative people connected with Canada; 18th & 19th centuries topographic & historical Canadian views; 19th century travels
Publications: William Berczy; D B Webster Brantford Pottery; Canadian Watercolors & Drawings; The William Eby Pottery, Conestogo, Ontario 1855 - 1970; English Canadian Furniture of the Georgian Period; An Engraver's Pilgrimage: James Smillie Jr in Quebec, 1821-1830; Georgian Canada: Conflict & Culture, 1745 - 1820; Printmaking in Canada: The Earliest Views & Portraits
Activities: Classes for children; lect; gallery talks; exten dept serves Ontario; original objects of art lent to institutions

L RYERSON POLYTECHNICAL INSTITUTE, Library, 350 Victoria St, M5B 2K3. Tel 416-979-5031; FAX 416-979-5215; *Chief Librn* Richard M Malinski
Open Mon - Thurs 8:30 AM - 10:30 PM, Fri 8:30 AM - 5 PM, Sat 9 AM - 5 PM, Sun 10 AM - 6 PM. Estab 1948 to meet the needs of the students
Income: Financed by provincial appropriation & student fees
Purchases: $27,200
Library Holdings: Vols 17,000; Per subs 180; Micro — Fiche, prints, reels; AV — A-tapes, cassettes, fs, motion pictures, rec, slides, v-tapes; Other — Clipping files, pamphlets
Special Subjects: Architecture, Fashion Arts, Interior Design, Photography, Film, Theatre Arts, Graphic Arts, Media Arts

SCULPTOR'S SOCIETY OF CANADA
For further information, see National and Regional Organizations

SOCIETY OF CANADIAN ARTISTS
For further information, see National and Regional Organizations

M STEPHEN BULGER GALLERY, 700 Queen St W, M6J 1E7. Tel 416-504-0575; FAX 416-504-8929; *Dir* Stephen Bulger; *Asst Dir* Tonja Brown
Open Tues - Sat 11 AM - 6 PM. Estab 1995
Collections: Canadian & International Photography Collection
Activities: Lect open to public; occasional gallery talks; sales shop sells books, prints & supplies

C TORONTO DOMINION BANK, Toronto Dominion Ctr, PO Box 1, M5K 1A2. Tel 416-982-8473; FAX 416-982-6335; *Cur Art* Natalie Ribkoff
Contemporary Art Collection is available for viewing by appointment only. The Inuit Gallery is open Mon - Fri 8 AM - 6 PM, Sat & Sun 10 AM - 4 PM. The Contemporary Art Collection is shown throughout branch offices in Canada & internationally; the Inuit Art Collection has its own gallery in the Toronto-Dominion Centre
Collections: The Inuit Collection consists of a selection of prints, as well as stone, bone & ivory carvings; the Contemporary Collection is an ongoing project focusing on the art of emerging & mature Canadian artists, including original prints, paintings, sculpture & works on paper

A TORONTO HISTORICAL BOARD, Historic Fort York, 100 Garrison Rd (Mailing add: 205 Yonge St, M5B 1N2). Tel 416-392-6907; FAX 416-392-6917; *Cur* Carl Benn
Open end of May - end Sept Tues - Sun 9:30 AM - 5 PM, Oct - mid May 9:30 AM - 4 PM, Sat & Sun 10 AM - 5 PM. Admis adults $5, senior citizens & youth 13-18 years $3.25, children $3. Estab 1934 to tell the story of the founding of Toronto & the British Army in the 19th century. Average Annual Attendance: 55,000
Income: Financed by city appropriation
Collections: 19th century British Military; Original War of 1812 Buildings; Original War of 1812 Uniforms; Original War of 1812 Weapons
Activities: Classes for adults & children; lect open to public; sales shop sells books, prints & reproductions

M TORONTO SCULPTURE GARDEN, 115 King St E, PO Box 65, M4T 2L7. Tel 416-485-9658; *Dir* Rina Greer
Open 8 AM - dusk. No admis fee. Estab 1981. Outdoor park featuring exhibitions of site-specific work commissioned for the site
Publications: Exhibition brochures

UNIVERSITY OF TORONTO
M Justina M Barnicke Gallery, 7 Hart House Circle, M5S 1A1. Tel 416-978-2453, 978-8398; FAX 416-978-8387; Elec Mail judi.schwartz@utoronto.ca. *Dir* Judith Schwartz
Open Mon - Fri 11 AM - 7 PM, Sat & Sun 1 - 4 PM. No admis fee. Estab 1919 to promote young Canadian artists, as well as present a historical outlook on Canadian art. Gallery has modern setting & total wall space of 350 running ft; outdoor quadrangle is available for summer sculpture shows. Average Annual Attendance: 12,000
Income: Financed by Hart House
Purchases: Canadian art
Collections: †Canadian Art (historical & contemporary)
Exhibitions: Temporary exhibitions of historical & contemporary Canadian art
Publications: The Hart House Collection of Canadian Paintings by Jeremy Adamson
Activities: Classes for adults; docent training; lect, 8 vis lectr per year; concerts; gallery talks; tours; individual paintings & original objects of art lent; originate traveling exhibitions
L Fine Art Library, Sidney Smith Hall, 100 St George St, M5S 3G3. Tel 416-978-5006; FAX 416-978-1491; *Librn* A Retfalvi
Open Mon - Fri 10 AM - 5 PM. Estab 1936 for reference only
Income: Financed by state appropriation & Department of Fine Art
Library Holdings: Vols 20,000; Other — Exhibition catalogs 19,000, photographs 90,000
Special Subjects: Archaeology, Art History
Collections: Catalog materials including †temporary, †permanent, †dealer catalogs; †photographic archives in various fields of Western art
Publications: Canadian Illustrated News (Montreal); Index to Illustrations, quarterly

A VISUAL ARTS ONTARIO, 439 Wellington St W, 2nd Flr, M5V 1E7. Tel 416-591-8883; FAX 416-591-2432; *Exec Dir* Hennie L Wolff; *Coordr Art Placement* Andrew Cripps; *Reprography Coordr* Andrienne Trent; *Bookkeeper* Frima Yolleck
Open Mon - Fri 9 AM - 5 PM. Estab 1974, Visual Arts Ontario is a non-profit organization dedicated to furthering the awareness & appreciation of the visual arts. Mem: 3000; dues 2 year $35, 1 year $20
Income: Financed by mem, fundraising, municipal, provincial & federal grants, attendance at events
Collections: Resource Center; Slide Registry of Ontario artists

Publications: Agenda, quarterly newsletter; Art in Architecture: Art for the Built Environment in the Province of Ontario; The Guidebook to Competitions & Commissions; Visual Arts Handbook
Activities: Workshops for professional artists; lect open to public; seminars & conferences; special projects; individual paintings & original objects of art lent to Ontario Government Ministries & corporations; art rental programme; colour reprography programmes; originate traveling exhibitions
L Library, 439 Wellington St W, 2nd Flr, M5V 1E7. Tel 416-591-8883; FAX 416-591-2432; *Exec Dir* Hennie Wolff
Resource library open to pub for reference
Income: Financed by government, private funds, mem fees & programme revenues
Library Holdings: Archival material, current art periodicals

WATERLOO

M ENOOK GALLERIES, 29 Young St E, PO Box 335, N2J 4A4. Tel 519-884-3221; *Dir* H Norman Socha; *Cur* Laura Napran
Open Tues - Sat 11 AM - 5 PM. No admis fee. Estab 1981 to promote awareness of Native art
Income: Financed by sales
Collections: Benjamin Chee/Chee Collection; David General Collection; Kiakshuk Collection; Doug Maracle Collection; Native American, Indian & Eskimo/Inuit Art; Papua New Guinea artifacts; graphics, paintings & sculptures
Exhibitions: (1997) Cape Dorset Graphics; Aspects of the Feminine
Publications: Visions of Rare Spirit
Activities: Lect open to public, 2 vis lectr per year; book traveling exhibitions 2 per year; originate exhibitions for international art galleries & universities on contemporary Native art, 4 per year; retail store sells sculpture, prints, original art & reproductions

M THE SEAGRAM MUSEUM, 57 Erb St W, N2L 6C2. Tel 519-885-1857; FAX 519-746-1673; *Exec Dir* T G Tyssen; *Cur* Anne Chafe
Open Jan 2 - Apr 30 Tues - Sun 10 AM - 6 PM, May 1 - Dec 31 daily 10 AM - 6 PM. No admis fee. Estab 1980 as a pub, non-profit mus for educ in history & technology of the wines & spirits industry & related subjects. Permanent & temporary exhibitions, industrial artifacts & decorative & fine art related to wines & spirits; restaurant. Average Annual Attendance: 100,000
Income: Financed by annual donation
Collections: Historic glass, vessels & accessories for liquor service; bottles; fine art; industrial objects; sculpture; tools
Publications: 2000 Years of Tradition: The Story of Canadian Whiskey, monograph; quarterly newsletter
Activities: Classes for adults & children; programs on feature exhibitions; workshops; school programs; lect open to public; tours; special programs; gallery talks; originate traveling exhibitions to other museums; museum shop sells books, reproductions, art glass, pottery, textiles & giftware
L Library, 57 Erb St W, N2L 6C2. Tel 519-885-1857; FAX 519-746-1673; *Registrar & Researcher* Sean Thomas
Estab 1971
Library Holdings: Vols 6000; Per subs 30; AV — Motion pictures 100, slides 5000, v-tapes 200; Other — Clipping files, manuscripts, memorabilia, pamphlets, photographs 2000
Special Subjects: Advertising Design, Decorative Arts, Drawings, Etchings & Engravings, Flasks & Bottles, Glass, Porcelain, Prints, Restoration & Conservation, Engravings, industrial artifacts, tools, wines & spirits

UNIVERSITY OF WATERLOO
M Art Gallery, 200 University Ave W, N2L 3G1. Tel 519-885-1211, Ext 3575; FAX 519-746-4982; *Cur* Joseph Wyatt
Open Mon - Fri 11 AM - 4 PM, Sun 2 - 5 PM, cl Sun July & Aug. No admis fee. Estab 1962
Collections: Contemporary Canadian Art
Exhibitions: Hamilton Museum's Polish-Canadian Series
L Dana Porter Library, 200 University Ave W, N2L 3G1. Tel 519-885-1211, Ext 5763; FAX 519-747-4606; Telex 069-5259. *Univ Librn* Murray Shepherd; *Spec Coll Librn* Susan Bellingham; *Reference & Coll Develop Librn - Fine Arts & Archit* Michele Sawchuk
Open Mon - Thurs 8 AM - 11 PM, Fri 8 AM - 10 PM, Sat 11 AM - 10 PM, Sun 11 AM - 11 PM. Estab 1958 to provide access to information appropriate to the needs of the academic community
Income: $244,311 (financed by mem)
Library Holdings: Vols 26,770; Per subs 160; Micro — Fiche, reels; AV — Rec; Other — Clipping files, exhibition catalogs
Special Subjects: Etchings & Engravings, Printmaking
Collections: The Dance Collection (monographs, periodicals & pamphlets from 1535 to date relating to the history of dance-ballet); B R Davis Southy Collection; Euclid's Elements & History of Mathematics; Eric Gill Collection; Lady Aberdeen Library of Women; George Santayana Collection; Private Press Collection; Rosa Breithaupt Clark Architectural History Collection
Publications: Library publishes four bibliographic series: Bibliography, Technical Paper, Titles & How To
Activities: Undergraduate curriculum in architecture, art history & studio

M WILFRID LAURIER UNIVERSITY, Robert Langen Gallery, N2L 3C5. Tel 519-884-0710, Ext 2714; *Pres* Dr Lorna Marsden; *Cur & Mgr* T Hranka
Open Mon - Sat 10 AM - 7 PM. No admis fee. Estab 1969 to exhibit for the students, staff & faculty. The gallery has its own space in the John Aird Building & has 18 x 50 ft rectangular space incl various modular mounts. Average Annual Attendance: 50,000
Purchases: $16,000
Collections: 2000 pieces of original art works & prints
Exhibitions: Student, staff & faculty show; the gallery mounts 10 exhibitions each year, mostly shows by artists in local area
Publications: Buried Treasure (75th Anniversary of WLU 1986)
Activities: Classes for adults; docent training; lect open to public, 1-5 vis lectr per year; gallery talks; competitions; individual paintings & original works of art lent to campus offices & public areas; originate traveling exhibitions

WINDSOR

M ART GALLERY OF WINDSOR, 3100 Howard Ave, N8X 3Y8. Tel 519-969-4494; FAX 519-969-3732; *Pres* Murray C Temple; *Dir* Nataley Nagy; *Bus Mgr* Ken Ferguson; *Cur* Robert Kaskell; *Cur* Helga Pakasaar; *Information Coordr* Dee Douglas; *Registrar* Janine Butler; *Admin Asst* Diane Lane
Open Tues - Fri 10 AM - 7 PM, Sat 10 AM - 5 PM, Sun Noon - 5 PM, cl Mon. No admis fee. Estab 1943 for collection & exhibition of works of art, primarily Canadian, for the study & enjoyment of the Windson-Detroit area. Average Annual Attendance: 70,000. Mem: 1800; president's club $1000 & up, director's circle $500-$999, advocate $250-$499, supporter $100-$249, gallery friend $50-$99, family $45, single $25, student $20; annual meeting in Mar
Income: $1,300,000 (financed by mem, city appropriation & federal & provincial grants)
Collections: †Primarily Canadian drawings, paintings, prints & sculpture 18th century to present; †Inuit prints & sculpture: non-Canadian paintings & sculpture
Exhibitions: Approx 30 exhibitions a year, besides installation of permanent collection, of mostly Canadian historic & contemporary art works, paintings & graphics
Publications: Quarterly bulletin & catalogues for exhibitions organized by this gallery, 6 times a year
Activities: Docent training; lect open to public, 20 vis lectr per year; gallery talks; tours; book traveling exhibitions approximately 20 per year; originate traveling exhibitions; museum shop sells Canadian handicrafts, original art, reproductions & prints; Education Gallery
L Reference Library, 3100 Howard Ave, N8X 3Y8. Tel 519-969-4494; FAX 519-969-3732; *Librn* Janine Butler
Open Tues, Wed, Fri & Sun 1 - 4 PM, Thurs 1 - 7 PM. Estab 1966. Reference for staff, members & public
Income: Financed by mem
Library Holdings: Vols 2500; Per subs 30; Catalogs & museum bulletins; AV — V-tapes; Other — Clipping files, exhibition catalogs, pamphlets

WOODSTOCK

M CITY OF WOODSTOCK, Woodstock Art Gallery, 447 Hunter St, N4S 4G7. Tel 519-539-6761; FAX 519-539-2564; *Cur* Anna-Marie Larsen; *Educ Officer* Brenda Irvine; *Gallery Asst* Jo-Anne Bendit; *Installation Officer* Michael Shea
Open Tues - Fri 11 AM - 5 PM, Sat 10 AM - 5 PM, Sun 1 - 5 PM, cl Sun Oct - May. No admis fee. Estab 1967 as a community art gallery. Moved into neo-Georgian building (c1913) in 1983. Four gallery spaces: Carlyle Gallery (313 sq ft); Verne T Ross Gallery (464 sq ft); Nancy Rowell Jackman Gallery (323) sq ft); East Gallery (1303.75 sq ft). Average Annual Attendance: 18,500. Mem: 400; dues, life member $300, corporate $50, family $30, individual $20, senior citizen, children & students $15
Income: Financed by City of Woodstock, Ministry of Citizenship & Culture, Ontario Arts Council, mem & donations
Collections: 290 works collection of Canadian Art, concentrating on Florence Carlyle contemporary Canadian regional artists
Publications: Newsletter 4 times per year; educational handouts on current exhibitions; monthly bulletin
Activities: Classes for adults & children; dramatic programs; lect open to public, 6-8 vis lectr per year; concerts; gallery talks; tours; competitions with awards; scholarships offered; art rental paintings are leased to residents of Oxford County & business firms; lending collection contains paintings; originate traveling exhibitions to circulate southwestern Ontario & Toronto vicinities; gift shop sells cards, wrapping & writing paper, pottery, jewelry, weaving

PRINCE EDWARD ISLAND

CHARLOTTETOWN

M CONFEDERATION CENTRE ART GALLERY AND MUSEUM, 145 Richmond St, C1A 1J1. Tel 902-628-6111; FAX 902-566-4648; *Dir* Terry Graff; *Registrar* Kevin Rice
Open Tues - Sat 11 AM - 6 PM, Sun 2 - 5 PM, Mid June - Oct 10 AM - 8 PM, cl Mon. Estab 1964 as a coll devoted to Canadian art & fine crafts. Average Annual Attendance: 100,000. Mem: 500; group $25, family $25, individual $15
Income: Financed by federal, provincial, city & private sector
Collections: 19th & 20th century Canadian paintings, drawings & decorative arts; paintings & drawings by Robert Harris
Exhibitions: Twenty-five exhibitions including special exhibition each July & Aug to coincide with summer festival
Publications: Arts Atlantic, quarterly subscription
Activities: Lect open to public; tours; concerts; lending collection contains paintings, 7000 kodachromes, fs, slides; originate traveling exhibitions; junior museum
L Library, 145 Richmond St, C1A 1J1. Tel 902-368-4642; *Dir* Don Scott; *Registrar* Kevin Rice
Open for reference
Library Holdings: Vols 3500; Per subs 20; AV — A-tapes 30, fs 60, slides 5000; Other — Photographs

QUEBEC

AYLMER

A CANADIAN ARTISTS' REPRESENTATION-LE FRONT DES ARTISTES CANADIENS, 21 Forest, J9H 4E3. Tel 819-682-4183; *Dir* Greg Graham
Open daily 9 AM - 4 PM. Estab 1968, Canadian Artists' Representation-Le Front des Artistes Canadiens is an assoc of professional artists whose mandate is the improvement of the financial & professional status of all Canadian artists through research & pub educ. CARFAC is a national organization run by artists for artists, mem works on three levels: local, provincial & national. Mem: 1200; open to practicing professional artists; dues $20-$250; annual meeting in May
Income: Financed by endowment & mem
Publications: ArtAction, 3 issues per year; Canadian Visual Artist; Taxation Information for Canadian Visual Arts
Activities: Lect open to public, 1 vis lectr per year

DORVAL

A DORVAL CULTURAL CENTRE, 1401 Lakeshore Dr, H9S 2E5. Tel 514-633-4170; FAX 514-633-4177; *Coordr* Danyelle Brodeur
Open Tues - Thurs 2 - 5 PM & 7 - 9 PM, Fri - Sun 2 - 5 PM. No admis fee. Estab 1967 to promote culture and art. Maintains an art gallery
Income: Financed by city appropriation
Publications: Calendar, biannually
Activities: Classes for adults and children; dramatic programs; lect open to public; gallery talks; tours

HULL

M CANADIAN MUSEUM OF CIVILIZATION, 100 Laurier St, PO Box 3100, Sta B, J8X 4H2. Tel 819-776-7000; FAX 819-776-8300; *Exec Dir* Dr George MacDonald; *Managing Dir* Joe Geurts; *Dir Exhib* Sylvie Morel
Open Jan 2 - Apr 30 9 AM - 5 PM, cl Mon, May 1 - June 30 daily 9 AM - 5 PM, July 1 - Sept 5 daily 9 AM - 6 PM, Sept 6 - Oct 10 daily 9 AM - 5 PM, Oct 11 - Dec 31 9 AM - 5 PM, cl Mon. Admis adults $4.50, youth & seniors $3, children 15 & under free, free on Thurs 5 - 8 PM, special group rates when scheduled three weeks in advance. Estab 1989 to promote among all Canadians the advancement of intercultural understanding & make known the cultural legacy with special, but not exclusive, reference to Canada. The Canadian Mus of Civilization was formerly known as the National Mus of Man. It is located on a 24-acre site in Hull, Quebec, on the Ottawa River, directly opposite Parliament Hill. The building has 1,076,430 sq ft & designed in two distinct structures: the Glacier Wing, the pub exhibition wing with over 177,611 sq ft of display space & the Canadian Shield Wing, housing the collections (3.5 million artifacts), plus conservation labs & administration; children's mus; Cineplus-Imax/Omnimax 295 seat theatre. Average Annual Attendance: Victorial Memorial Mus Building 493, 470
Collections: Archaeological Collection; Ethnological Collection; Folk Culture Collections; Historical Collection; Military History Collection
Exhibitions: Permanent exhibitions: XWE NAL MEWX Coast Salish-First Nations of the South Coast of British Columbia; From Time Immemorial: Tsimshian Prehistory; Folk Art in Canada: Land & People; On the Cutting Edge: The Arthur Pascal Collection of Woodworking Hand Tools.
Publications: Several series of publications & periodicals, 500 titles published in-house in last six years
Activities: Classes for adults & children; dramatic programs; docent training; lect open to the public, several vis lectr per year; exten dept; original artifacts lent to museums & other institutions meeting specifications regarding security, environment, etc; originate traveling exhibitions; The Boutiques stock a vast range of gift & educational articles; Kidshoppe; Bookstore/Collector's shop offers selection of books & fine crafts including folk art pieces & Native artwork; Postscriptum, philatelist's boutique

M LA GALERIE MONTCALM LA GALERIE D'ART DE LA VILLEDE HULL, 25 rue Laurier Maison du Citoyen, J8X 4C8. Tel 819-595-7488; FAX 819-595-7425; *Dir Serv Arts Culture* Jacqueline Tardif; *Coordr Expositions* Louise Parisien; *Dir* Jacqueline Tardif
No admis fee. Estab 1981, to present the art of local artists & national exhibitions, multi-disciplinary. One gallery, 2505 sq ft, three other secondary areas. Average Annual Attendance: 25,000
Income: $145,500 (financed by public & private enterprises)
Collections: City of Hull (permanent collection); heritage artifacts; paintings; photographs; prints; sculpture
Exhibitions: Hull & His Area in Paintings; Exhibition of the Permanent Collection
Publications: Exhibition catalogs
Activities: Classes for children; workshops; lect open to public, 1560 vis lectr per year; concerts; gallery talks; tours of the permanent collection; competitions with awards; retail store sells books, prints, original art

JOLIETTE

M MUSEE D'ART DE JOLIETTE, 145 Wilfrid-Corbeil St, PO Box 132, J6E 3Z3. Tel 514-756-0311; FAX 514-756-6511; *Pres* Anand Swaminadhan; *VPres* Rene Despres; *Dir* France Gascon
Open Tues - Sun Noon - 5 PM July & Aug, Wed - Sun Noon - 5 PM winter. Admis adults $4, senior citizens $3, students $2. Estab 1967 for educational purposes; preservation of the collections; save local patrimony. 3 rooms of temporary exhibitions; Sacred Art Gallery; European Medieval Renaissance Gallery; Canadian Art Gallery; Permanent Collection room tells story of the collection. Average Annual Attendance: 15,000. Mem: 600; dues family $30, individual $20; annual meeting in Oct

Income: $450,000 (financed by endowment, municipal & provincial government grants)
Collections: †Canadian art; European art; sacred art of Quebec; painting & sculpture
Exhibitions: 12 exhibitions per year
Publications: Catalog & pamphlet entitled Le Musee d'Art de Joliette; catalogs of temporary exhibits
Activities: Classes for children; lect open to public; concerts; gallery talks; tours; films; originate traveling exhibitions 3 per year; sales shop sells books, magazines, postcards & reproductions
L **Library,** 145 Wilfrid-Corbeil St, PO Box 132, J6E 3Z3. Tel 514-756-0311; FAX 514-756-6511; *Dir* France Gascom
Estab 1976. Open with reservations only for art reference
Purchases: $200-$250
Library Holdings: Vols 1000; Per subs 5; AV — Slides; Other — Exhibition catalogs, photographs, sculpture
Special Subjects: History of art, well-known artists
Collections: Art Journal; Great Masters; History of Painting; Larousse Mensuel

JONQUIERE

M **INSTITUT DES ARTS AU SAGUENAY,** Centre National D'Exposition a Jonquiere, 4160 du Vieux Pont, CP 605, Succursale A, G7X 7W4. Tel 418-546-2177; FAX 418-546-2180; *Dir* Jacqueline Caron
Open daily 10 AM - 5 PM, Wed & Thurs until 9 PM. Estab 1979 as an art exposition. 3 galleries. Average Annual Attendance: 20,000. Mem: 150; open to all interested in Au Milieu Des Arts; dues $20; annual meeting in June
Income: $350,000 (financed by endowment, mem, city & state appropriation)
Activities: Classes for adults & children; concerts; gallery talks; tours; fellowships offered; book traveling exhibitions 3-5 per year

KAHNAWAKE

M **KATERI TEKAKWITHA SHRINE,** CP 70, J0L 1B0. Tel 514-632-6030; FAX 514-632-5116; *Dir* Louis Cyr
Open daily 9 AM - Noon & 1 - 5 PM. No admis fee. Estab as a mission in 1667
Collections: Archives, Canadian church silver, historic chapel, old paintings
Publications: Kateri

LENNOXVILLE

M **BISHOP UNIVERSITY,** Artists' Centre, J1M 1Z7. Tel 819-822-9600, Ext 2687; FAX 819-822-9661; *Gallery Coordr* Carole Bherer
Open May - July Tues - Fri 1 - 4:30 PM, Sat 1 - 4 PM, Sept - Apr Tues - Sun 1 - 4:30 PM, also Thurs 7 - 9 PM. No admis fee. Estab 1992 to serve the University Community & the entire Eastern Townships by displaying regional, national & international art work. 162m2 exhibition space located adjacent to the Foyer of Centennial Theatre

MONTREAL

C **ALCAN ALUMINIUM LTD,** 1188 Sherbrooke St W, H3A 3G2. Tel 514-848-8000; FAX 514-848-8115; *Cur* JoAnn Meade
Estab 1982 to enhance new offices in which they are installed to enrich the lives of those who work there. Collection displayed in reception areas and private offices
Collections: International arts & crafts from regions where Alcan operates
Publications: Artluminium catalogue
Activities: Lect; individual objects of art lent for special exhibits upon request

L **ARTEXTE INFORMATION & DOCUMENTATION CENTRE,** 460 Sainte Catherine Ouest, Rm 508, H3B 1A7. Tel 514-874-0049; FAX 514-874-0316; *Dir* Nicole Cloutier; *Librn* Danielle Leger
Open Tues - Sat 12 AM - 5:30 PM & by appointment, cl Sun & Mon. Institution estab 1980, libr estab 1982. Documentation of contemporary visual arts, from 1965 - present with particular emphasis on Canadian art, for reference only.
Mem: 125; dues $25 & up
Income: $400,000 (financed by mem, city & state appropriation, donations)
Purchases: $22,300 ($11,500 in donated documents)
Library Holdings: Vols 2000; Per subs 100; Other — Clipping files 7200, exhibition catalogs 10,500, memorabilia, pamphlets, photographs
Special Subjects: Ceramics, Collages, Conceptual Art, Drawings, Eskimo Art, Mixed Media, Painting - Canadian, Photography, Printmaking, Sculpture, Artist Books, Copy Art, Installation, Performance, Public Art
Publications: Catalogue of catalogues, annual
Activities: Distribution service

L **CANADIAN CENTRE FOR ARCHITECTURE,** Library, 1920 Baile St, H3H 2S6. Tel 514-939-7000; FAX 514-939-7020; Elec Mail ref@cca.oc.ca. *Dir* Phyllis Lambert; *Assoc Dir* Robert Spiekler; *Asst Dir Museum Serv* Wendy Owens; *Chief Cur* Nicholas Olsberg; *Assoc Librn* Rosemary Haddad
Estab 1979. For reference only
Special Subjects: Architecture, Landscape Architecture, Landscape Design, Urban Planning

M **CHATEAU RAMEZAY MUSEUM,** 280 Notre-Dame E, H2Y 1C5. Tel 514-861-7182; FAX 514-861-8317; *Dir* Andre Delisle
Open Tues - Sun 10 AM - 4:30 PM, cl Mon. Admis adults $5, students $3. Estab 1895 in residence of Claude de Ramezay (1705), governor of Montreal. Average Annual Attendance: 60,000. Mem: 150; dues life $1000, individual $40
Collections: Canadian drawings, furniture, paintings, prints & sculpters; 18th, 19th & 20th century collections; Indian collections
Activities: Classes for children; docent training; lect open to public & some for members only, 6 vis lectr per year; gallery talks; tours; sales shop sells books, reproductions, prints & slides

L **Library,** 280 Notre-Dame E, H2Y 1C5. Tel 514-861-7182; *Librn* Judith Berlyn
Library Holdings: Vols 2200
Special Subjects: Canadian History

M **CONCORDIA UNIVERSITY,** Leonard & Bina Ellen Art Gallery, 1400 de Maisonneuve Blvd W, H3G 1M8. Tel 514-848-4750; FAX 514-848-4751; *Dir & Cur* Karen Antaki; *Admin Asst* Jenny Calder-Lacroix
Open Mon - Fri 11 AM - 7 PM, Sat 11 AM - 5 PM. No admis fee. Estab 1962 for exhibitions of Canadian art, to provide a venue for a variety of significant touring exhibitions chosen from within the region & across Canada; to display the permanent collection, all with the idea of providing an important cultural arena both for the university & public alike. One gallery, 4111 sq ft with 328 running ft, located in University Library Pavillian. Average Annual Attendance: 66,000
Income: Financed by university & governmental funds
Purchases: Historic, modern & contemporary Canadian art
Collections: †Modern & Contemporary Canadian Art Collection
Exhibitions: Edge & Image; ChromaZone; John MacGregor: A Survey; The Photographs of Professor Oliver Buell (1844-1910); Goodridge Roberts: The Figure Works; Figure Painting in Montreal 1935-1955; Sickert, Orpen, John & their Contemporaries at the New English Art Club; Robert Bordo: New York + Montreal; Conservation: To Care for Art; Undergraduate Student Exhibition; Recent Acquisitions to the Collection: Selections from the Concordia Collection of Art; Michael Jolliffe: Paintings; Phillip Guston: Prints; John Arthur Fraser: Watercolours; Brian Wood: Drawings & Photographs; Barbara Astman: Floor pieces; K M Graham: Paintings & Drawings 1971-1984; Robert Flaherty: Photographs; Work by Selected Fine Art Graduates: A 10th Anniversary Celebration; Joyce Wieland: A Decade of Painting; Francois Baillarge (1759-1830): A Portfolio of academic drawings; Faculty of Fine Arts Biennial; Murray MacDonald & R Holland Murray: Recent Sculptures; Jean Paul Lemieux: Honoured by the University; The Figurative Tradition In Quebec; Contemporary Works on Paper; Undergraduate Student Exhibition; Selections from the Concordia Collection of Art; Canadian Pacific Poster Art 1881-1955; Shelagh Keeley: Drawings; Bernard Gamoy: Paintings; Harold Klunder:Paintings; Marcel Bovis: Photographs; Neerland Art Quebec: an exhibition by artists of Dutch descent in Quebec; Canada in the Nineteenth Century: The Bert & Barbara Stitt Family Collection; Posters from Nicaragua; Betty Goodwin: Passages; Ron Shuebrook: Recent Work; Louis Muhlstock: New Themes & Variations 1980-1985; John Herbert Caddy 1801-1887; Expressions of Will: The Art of Prudence Heward; Riduan Tomkins: Recent Paintings; Undergraduate Student Exhibition; Selections from the Concordia Collection of Art; Concordia: The Early Years of Loyola & Sir George Williams; Porcelain: Traditions of Excellence; Francois Houde: Glass Work; Shelley Reeves: Relics; Pre-Columbian Art from the Permanent Collection; Josef Albers: Interaction of Color; Brian McNeil: Ironworks; Robert Ayre: The Critic & the Collection; Claude-Philppe Benoit: Interieur, jour; A Decade of Collecting: A selection of Recent Acquisitions; Contemporary Montreal Sculpture & Installation from the Canada Council Art Bank: A Twentieth Anniversary Celebration; First Impressions: Views of the Natural History of Canada 1550-1850; Local Developments: 20th century Montreal Area Art from the Collection of the Universite de Montreal; Montreal Photo Album: Photographs from Montreal Archives; Joanne Tod: The (Dis) Order of Things; Undergraduate Student Exhibition; Temporal Borders: Image & Site; Faculty Exhibition; Alex Colville: Selected Drawings; Selections from the Permanent Collection; From the Permanent Collection: A Selection of Recent Acquisitions; Chris Cran; Tom Dean; Undergraduate Student Exhibition; Nina M Owens (1869-1959); In Habitable Places
Publications: Exhibition catalogues
Activities: Lect open to public, 3 vis lectr per year; originate traveling exhibitions

L **CONSEIL DES ARTS TEXTILES DU QUEBEC (CATQ),** Centre de Documentation, 811A Ontario St E, H2L 1P1. Tel 514-524-6645; FAX 514-525-2621; *Pres* Carole Gauron
Open Mon - Wed 9 AM - 5 PM. Estab 1980. For reference only
Income: $43,500 (financed by endowment & mem)
Purchases: $1100
Library Holdings: Vols 800; Per subs 17; Artist CV (textile); AV — Cassettes 10, slides 1000, v-tapes 13
Publications: Textile bulletin, 8-10 issues per year

A **GUILDE CANADIENNE DES METIERS D'ART QUEBEC,** Canadian Guild of Crafts Quebec, 2025 Peel St, H3A 1T6. Tel 514-849-6091; FAX 514-849-7351; *Managing Dir* Nairy Kalemkerian
Open Tues - Fri 9 AM - 5:30 PM, Sat 10 AM - 5 PM. Estab 1906 to promote, encourage & preserve arts & crafts of Canada. Permanent Collection Gallery of Eskimo & Indian Art; Exhibition Gallery. Average Annual Attendance: 30,000. Mem: 107; dues $30 & up; annual meeting in Mar/Apr
Collections: †Permanent collection of Eskimo and Indian Arts and Crafts; Audio Video tapes
Exhibitions: Fine craft exhibitions every 5 weeks except Jan & Feb
Activities: Educ dept; lect open to public; gallery talks; tours; awards; individual paintings & original objects of art lent to accredited institutions; lending collection includes prints; sales shop sells books, original art, reproductions, prints & Canadian crafts

M **INTERNATIONAL MUSEUM OF CARTOON ART,** 5788 Notre Dame de Grace Ave, H4A 1M4. Tel 514-489-0527; *Pres* Peter Adamakos; *VPres* Mark Scott
Estab 1988 to foster pub appreciation of cartoon arts & research. Mounts exhibitions & screenings in museums & universities across North America. Special events vary. Maintains reference library
Income: Financed by government & corporate sponsorships
Collections: Artifacts, novelties, posters & publicity, toys, clippings; films & tapes; original artwork; publications of all types relating to the cartoon arts
Exhibitions: The Art of Animation; The Hollywood Cartoon; Homage to Walt Disney
Activities: Classes for adults; lect open to public, vis lectr varies per year; book traveling exhibitions 5 per year; originate traveling exhibitions; sales shop sells books, magazines, original art, various posters & merchandise

L **JARDIN BOTANIQUE DE MONTREAL,** Bibliotheque, 4101 Sherbrooke St
E, H1X 2B2. Tel 514-872-1824; FAX 514-872-3765; *Botanist & Librn* Celine
Arseneault
Estab 1931. For reference
Library Holdings: Vols 14,000; Per subs 400; Posters 300; AV — Cassettes 100,
slides 100,000, v-tapes 200; Other — Photographs
Special Subjects: Asian Art, Landscape Architecture, Botany, Garden History,
Horticulture, Japanese Art

M **LA CENTRALE POWERHOUSE GALLERY,** 460 Sainte Catherine Quest, Rm
506, H3B 1A6. Tel 514-871-0268; FAX 514-871-9830; *Coordr* Elaine Frigon;
Coordr Manon B Thibault
Open Wed - Sun Noon - 5 PM. No admis fee. Estab 1973 to promote &
broadcast the work of women artists in all domains. Gallery has 1500 sq ft.
Mem: 35; dues $20; annual meeting in Sept
Income: $120,000 (financed by mem, grants from federal, provincial & city
governments, corporate & private donations)
Exhibitions: Ten exhibitions per year; a mixture of local & other parts of the
country, occasionally American
Publications: Exhibit catalogues
Activities: Lect open to public, 2-3 vis lectr per year; concerts; gallery talks;
originate traveling exhibitions to Canadian Art Centers; sales shop sells
catalogues & t-shirts

A **LA SOCIETE DES DECORATEURS-ENSEMBLIERS DU QUEBEC,**
Interior Designers Society of Quebec, 354 Notre Dame W, Rm 200, H2Y 1T9.
Tel 514-284-6263; FAX 514-284-6112; *Pres* Denis Chouinard; *Dir* Sylvie
Champeau
Open 9 AM - 5 PM. Estab 1935 as a nonprofit professional association. Mem:
483; dues $320
Exhibitions: Traveling exhibitions in the Province of Quebec
Publications: Journal magazine, monthly; News Bulletin, 10 issues per year
Activities: Education Committee to improve the level of teaching in interior
design; lect for members only, 5-8 vis lectr per year; book traveling exhibitions

M **LE MUSEE MARC-AURELE FORTIN,** 118 St Pierre, H2Y 2L7. Tel 514-845-
6108; *Dir* Rene Buisson; *Asst to Dir* Marcelle Trudeau
Open 11 AM - 5 PM, cl Mon. Admis $4, seniors $2. Estab 1984. Average
Annual Attendance: 15,000. Mem: 400; dues $27
Income: $100,000 (financed by endowment, mem & sales of reproductions)
Purchases: $45,000
Exhibitions: Marc-Aurele Fortin; Professional Book-Binding
Activities: Lect open to public

M **MCCORD MUSEUM OF CANADIAN HISTORY,** 690 Sherbrooke St W,
H3A 1E9. Tel 514-398-7100; *Exec Dir* Claude Benoit; *Cur Costume* Jacqueline
Beaudoin-Ross; *Head Exhib* Elizabeth Kennell; *Registrar* Nicole Vallieres; *Cur
Ethnology* Morra McCaffrey; *Cur Decorative Arts* Conrad Graham; *Archivist*
Pamela Miller
Open Tues - Sun 10 AM - 5 PM, Thurs to 9 PM, cl Mon. Admis family $8,
adults $5, sr citizens $3, student $2, children under 12 free. Estab 1919 as a
museum of Canadian Ethnology & Social History
Publications: Exhibition catalogs & monographs; guides to collections for
children
Activities: Book traveling exhibitions 2 per year; originate traveling exhibitions to
other museological institutions in Canada

MCGILL UNIVERSITY (Formerly National Gallery of Canada)
L **Blackader-Lauterman Library of Architecture and Art,** 3459 McTavish St, H3A
1Y1. Tel 514-398-4743; FAX 514-398-6695; Elec Mail berger@lib1.lan.mcgill.ca.
Librn Mrs M Berger; *Reference Librn* Mrs J Lowenstein; *Cur* Mrs I Murray
Open winter 9 AM - 7 PM, summer 9 AM - 5 PM. Estab 1922 to establish a
special collection of architectural material
Library Holdings: Vols 86,000; Per subs 355; Drawings 211,431; Other —
Exhibition catalogs, pamphlets, photographs 25,000
Special Subjects: Baroque, Byzantine Art, Dutch Art Renaissance & Northern
Renaissance, Medieval Art, 19th & 20th century Canadian architecture
Collections: †Canadian Architecture Collection
Publications: The Libraries of Edward & W S Maxwell in the Collection of the
Blacker-Lauterman; Moshe Safdie: Buildings & Projects, 1967-1992

M **MAISON SAINT-GABRIEL MUSEUM,** 2146 Dublin Place, H3K 2A2. Tel
514-935-8136; FAX 514-935-5695; *Dir* Therese Cloutier
Group tours Tues - Sat 1:30 & 3 PM, Sun 1:30, 2:30 & 3:30 PM. Admis $4.
Estab 1966
Collections: †Antique Tools, Embroidery, Paintings & Sculpture; †Furniture,
Crafts & †Upholstery of 18th & 19th centuries located in a 17th century house
Exhibitions: From Root Cellar to Attic; Laces & Embroideries

M **MONTREAL MUSEUM OF FINE ARTS,** PO Box 3000, Sta H, H3G 2T9. Tel
514-285-1600; FAX 514-844-6042; *Dir* Pierre Theberge; *Chief Conservator* Mrs
Mayo Graham; *Cur Non-Canadian Decorative Arts* Robert Little; *Cur Prints &
Drawings* Marle Claude Mirandette; *Cur Contemporary Art* Pierre Theberge; *Cur
Old Masters* Mitchell Merling; *Dir Communications* Danielle Sauvage; *Dir
Admin* Paul Lavallee; *Registrar* Elaine Tolmatch; *Cur Early Canadian Art*
Rosalina Pepall
Open Tues - Sun 10 AM - 5 PM, cl Mon. Admis adults $4, students 12-16 $2,
children under 12 $1, handicapped, senior citizens & members free. Estab 1860
as an art assoc for the exhibition of paintings; mus estab 1916. Average Annual
Attendance: 275,000. Mem: 15,000; dues $30 & up; annual meeting Sept
Income: Financed by endowment, mem & provincial appropriation
Collections: Collection of African art by Fr Gagnon; Chinese, Near Eastern,
Peruvian, Inuit primitive art; Saidye and Samuel Bronfman Collection of
Contemporary Canadian art; European decorative arts; French, Spanish, Dutch,
British, Canadian and other schools; Japanese incense boxes; The Parker Lace
Collection; Harry T Norton Collection of ancient glass; Lucile Pillow Collection
of porcelain; decorative arts, painting, sculpture from 3000 BC to the present

Exhibitions: Rotating exhibitions
Publications: Collage (a calendar of events)
Activities: Docent training; lect open to public; concerts; gallery talks; tours;
exten dept serving Quebec & other provinces; individual paintings & original
objects of art lent to art galleries & cultural centers; museum shop sells books,
original art, reproductions, prints, slides
L **Library,** CP 3000, Succursale H, H3G 2T9. Tel 514-285-1600; FAX 514-285-
5655; *Librn* Joanne Dery
Open 11 AM - 4:45 PM, cl Mon. Estab 1882 for a reference & research centre
for art students, specialists & visitors. Open for reference to students, scholars,
teachers, researchers & general public
Income: Financed by endowment & mem
Library Holdings: Vols 70,287; Per subs 745; Art sales catalogs 51,122;
Institutional archives 8552; Vertical files 14,976; Micro — Fiche; AV — A-tapes,
slides 40,496; Other — Clipping files, exhibition catalogs, manuscripts,
pamphlets, photographs
Special Subjects: Art History, Decorative Arts, Drawings, Painting - Canadian,
Sculpture
Collections: Canadiana
Publications: Collage, bi-monthly; Annual report

M **MUSEE D'ART CONTEMPORAIN DE MONTREAL,** 185 Saint Catherine St
W, H2X 1Z8. Tel 514-847-6226; FAX 514-847-6913; *Dir* Marcel Brisebois;
Cur-in-Chief Paulette Gagnon; *Traveling Exhib Officer* E Meren Garcia
Open Tues, Thurs - Sun 11 AM - 6 PM, Wed 11 AM - 9 PM. Admis adults $6.
Estab 1964. Conservation & information about contemporary art are the most
important aspects of the mus; also to present contemporary artists to the general
pub. Building is a medium-sized four-story, art mus, with an exhibition area of
2800 sq meters divided in eight galleries & a Multimedia room. Average Annual
Attendance: 150,000
Income: Financed by provincial grants
Collections: Contemporary Art - †Canadian, international & †Quebecois:
drawings, engravings, installations, paintings, photographs, sculptures, videos
Publications: Catalogs of exhibitions
Activities: Classes for adults & children; lect open to public, 15 vis lectr per year;
concerts; gallery talks; tours; competitions; exten dept serving Quebec province;
originate traveling exhibitions; sales shop sells books & magazines
L **Mediatheque,** 185 Saint Catherine St W, H2X 1Z8. Tel 514-847-6906; FAX 514-
864-9844; *Librn* Michelle Gauchier
Open Tues, Wed, Thurs & Fri 11 AM - 4:30 PM. Estab 1965. For reference only
Income: Partially financed by Quebec Government
Purchases: $22,000
Library Holdings: Vols 30,015; Per subs 359; AV — A-tapes 250, cassettes,
Kodachromes, motion pictures, rec, slides 40,000, v-tapes 325; Other — Clipping
files 8332, exhibition catalogs 25,644, framed reproductions, photographs
Special Subjects: Art History, Etchings & Engravings, Graphic Arts, Mixed
Media, Contemporary Visual Arts
Collections: Archives of Paul-Emile Borduas (Painter 1905-1960); about 12,500
items including writings, correspondence, exhibition catalogs, etc

M **MUSEE DE LA BASILIQUE NOTRE-DAME,** 424 St Sulpice St, H2Y 2V5.
Tel 514-842-2925; FAX 514-842-3370; *Pastor & Dir* Ivanhoe Poirier
Open Sat, Sun & Holidays 9 AM - 4:30 PM. Admis adults $1, students and
adults over 65 $.50. Estab 1937 as an historical and religious museum. Average
Annual Attendance: 10,000 - 15,000
Activities: Concerts; tours; individual paintings & original objects of art lent to
other museums; lending collection contains framed reproductions, nature
artifacts, original art works, original prints & paintings; sales shop sells religious
artifacts

A **SAIDYE BRONFMAN CENTRE FOR THE ARTS CENTRE,** 5170 Cote
Sainte Catherine Rd, H3W 1M7. Tel 514-739-2301; FAX 514-739-9340; *Exec
Dir* Alain Danciger; *Asst Dir* Alain Danciger; *Cur* Regine Basha; *Asst Dir* Katia
Meir
Open Mon - Thurs 9 AM - 9 PM, Fri 9 AM - 2 PM, Sun 10 AM - 5 PM, cl Sat.
No admis fee. Estab 1967 as a non-profit cultural centre for the promotion &
dissemination of the arts. 3000 sq ft gallery. Average Annual Attendance: 90,000
Income: Financed by mem & government grant
Exhibitions: Ten plus major exhibitions per year, special interest in
contemporary art, local, national & international
Publications: Exhibition catalogs
Activities: Classes for adults & children; lect open to public, 12 vis lectr per year;
gallery talks; tours; competitions with awards; book traveling exhibitions;
originate traveling exhibitions; sales shop sells books & magazines

M **SAINT JOSEPH'S ORATORY,** Museum, 3800 Queen Mary Rd, H3V 1H6. Tel
514-733-8211; FAX 514-733-9735; *Dir* Jean-Pierre Aumont; *Artistic Cur* Father
Andre Bergeron
Open daily 10 AM - 5 PM. Admis contributions welcomed. Shrine founded
1904, estab 1953 as art mus. St Joseph's Oratory is also a Montreal landmark,
the highest point in this city (856 ft above sea level), a piece of art - architecture
- with a history, style, etc of its own
Collections: Ancient & Contemporary Art; Nativity Scenes from around the
world
Exhibitions: Christmas Exhibition; Sacred Art Exhibition
Activities: Concerts; films
L **Library,** 3800 Queen Mary Rd, H3V 1H6. Tel 514-733-8211, Ext 2341; *Librn*
Pierre Germin
Open daily 10 AM - 5 PM. Open to pub for use on the premises & for
interlibrary loan
Library Holdings: Vols 100,000; Other — Photographs

A **SOCIETE DES MUSEES QUEBECOIS,** * 870 Mainsouneuve E St, T-4410
(Mailing add: CP8888, Succursale Centre Ville, UQAM, H3C 3P8). Tel 514-987-
3264; FAX 514-987-8210; Elec Mail can-smq@immedia.ca. *Dir* Sylvie Gagnon
Open daily 9 AM - Noon & 1 - 5 PM. Estab 1958. Mem: 800; annual meeting in
Oct

Income: $900,000 (financed by pub grants & sponsorships)
Publications: Musees, 4 times a year; bulletin, 10 times a year
Activities: Classes for museum works; lect open to public; museum shop sells books & magazines

L **Association of Museums,** * 870 Mainsonneuve E St (Mailing add: CP 8888, Succursale Centre Ville, UQAM, H3C 3P8). Tel 514-987-3264; Elec Mail can-smq@immedia.ca. *Exec Dir* Sylvie Gagnon
Income: $700,000
Library Holdings: Per subs 20; AV — Fs; Other — Pamphlets
Publications: Musees, magazine; books, 1 per year

M **DAVID M STEWART MUSEUM,** The Fort, St Helen's Island, PO Box 1200, Sta A, H3C 2Y9. Tel 514-861-6701; FAX 514-284-0123; *Dir* Bruce D Bolton; *Cur* Guy Vadeboncoeur
Open summer daily 10 AM - 6 PM. Estab 1955 to exhibit artifacts relating to Canada's history. Located in an old British Arsenal, built between 1820-24; galleries cover theme chronologically & by collection. Average Annual Attendance: 75,000. Mem: 100; dues $30; annual meeting in May
Income: $2,000,000 (financed by grants & self generated sources)
Collections: Firearms; Kitchen & Fireplace, dating from 16th century; prints; maps, navigation & scientific instruments
Publications: Exhibition catalogs
Activities: Classes for children; during summer months 18th century military parades by La Compagnie Franche de la Marine & the 78th Fraser Highlanders; museum shop sells books, reproductions, prints & slides

L **Library,** The Fort, St Helen's Island, PO Box 1200, Sta A, H3C 2Y9. Tel 514-861-6701; FAX 514-284-0123; *Librn* Eileen Meillon
Open Mon - Fri 9 AM - 5 PM. Estab 1955 as an 18th century administrator's library. Library of rare books open to researchers & members for reference
Library Holdings: Vols 8156; Per subs 50; Maps 704; AV — Slides; Other — Original art works, photographs, prints 3501, reproductions
Special Subjects: Cookbooks, Exploration, History pre 1763, Military, New France, Science
Publications: Exhibition catalogs

C **UNITED WESTURNE INC,** Art Collection, Ville Saint Laurent, 505 Locke St, H4T 1X7. Tel 514-342-5181; FAX 514-342-5181; *Chmn* Herbert Chervrier
Estab 1977. Mem: 250; dues $15
Collections: Sculptures, mixed media, works on canvas, works on paper
Publications: Selections from the Westburne Collection
Activities: Individual paintings & original objects of art lent

L **UNIVERSITE DE MONTREAL,** Bibliotheque d'Amenagement, 5620 Darlington, H3T 1G2. Tel 514-343-6009, 343-7177; FAX 514-343-5698; *Chef de Bibliotheque* Marc Joanis
Estab 1964
Purchases: $100,000
Library Holdings: Vols 40,000; Per subs 615; Micro — Fiche; AV — A-tapes, fs, rec, slides 44,000, v-tapes; Other — Clipping files, exhibition catalogs, photographs
Special Subjects: Architecture, Industrial Design, Landscape Architecture, urban studies
Collections: †Rare books; †History of Landscape Architecture

L **UNIVERSITE DU QUEBEC,** Bibliotheque des Arts, CP 8889, Succursale, H3C 3P3. Tel 514-987-6134; FAX 514-987-0262; *Dir* Daphne Dufresne; *Serials Librn* Marthe Fournier
Library Holdings: Vols 65,000; Per subs 500; AV — Slides; Other — Clipping files, exhibition catalogs
Special Subjects: Advertising Design, Architecture, Art Education, Eskimo Art, Painting - American, Pre-Columbian Art, Primitive Art, Religious Art, Restoration & Conservation, Sculpture, Silver, Video, Watercolors, Woodcarvings, Woodcuts

POINTE CLAIRE

A **POINTE CLAIRE CULTURAL CENTRE,** Stewart Hall Art Gallery, Stewart Hall, 176 Bord du Lac, H9S 4J7. Tel 514-630-1254; FAX 514-630-1259; *Dir Cultural Serv* Claire Cote; *Art Gallery Dir* Ingeborg Hiscox; *Prog Dir* Susan Stokley
Open Mon & Wed 2 - 5 PM & 7 - 9 PM, Tues, Thurs & Fri 2 - 5 PM, Sat & Sun 1 - 5 PM, cl Sat after June 24 & Sun after June 1 for summer. No admis fee. Estab 1963. Gallery is 25 x 120 ft. Average Annual Attendance: 11,000. Mem: Policy & Planning Board meets 6 times per year
Income: Financed by endowment & city appropriation
Purchases: Contemporary Canadian Art for city of Pointe Claire permanent collection
Collections: Permanent collection of contemporary Canadian art
Exhibitions: Approximately ten per year, local, provincial, national and international content
Publications: Bulletins; schedules of classes, study series, social events, approximately 30 per year
Activities: Classes for adults & children; dramatic programs; resident workshops in pottery, weaving & photography; lect open to the public, 4 vis lectr per year; gallery talks; lending collection contains framed reproductions, original prints, paintings & crafts; sells framed reproductions for young people & adults in Art Lending Service

QUEBEC

L **LES EDITIONS INTERVENTION, INTER-LE LIEU,** Documentation Center, 345 Du Pont, G1K 6M4. Tel 418-529-9680; FAX 418-529-6933; *Coordr* Richard Martel; *Coordr* Yvan Pageau
Open 10 AM - 4 PM. Estab 1978. For reference, possible lending & magazine exchanges
Special Subjects: American Indian Art, Architecture, Conceptual Art,

Constructions, Mixed Media, Photography, Video, Installation, Mail Art, Multi disciplinary, Multimedia, Performance Art, Visual Poetry
Publications: Inter, Art Actuel, 3 per year
Activities: Lect open to public, 3 vis lectr per year

M **L'UNIVERSITE LAVAL,** Ecole des Arts Visuels, Edifice La Fabrique, 255 Charest E, G1K 7P4. Tel 418-656-7631; FAX 418-656-7807; *Dir* David Taylor
Open Mon - Fri 8:30 AM - 7 PM. No admis fee. Estab 1970
Collections: Art color slides, decorative arts, graphics, paintings, sculpture
Exhibitions: Temporary exhibitions, changing monthly
Activities: Originate traveling exhibitions organized & circulated

L **Library,** Edifice La Fabrique, 255 Charest E, G1K 7P4. Tel 418-656-3344; FAX 418-656-7897; *Dir General Library System* Claude Bonnelly; *Dir Art* Madeleine Robin
Open to the pub for use on the premises; original prints & works of art available for study
Library Holdings: Vols 25,000

M **MUSEE DES AUGUSTINES DE L'HOTEL DIEU DE QUEBEC,** 32 rue Charlevoix, G1R 5C4. Tel 418-692-2492; *Dir Mus* Sr Nicole Perron; *Guide* Jacques St-Arnaud
Open Tues - Sat 9:30 AM - Noon & 1:30 - 5 PM, Sun 1:30 - 5 PM. No admis fee, donations appreciated. Estab 1958 in the Monastere des Augustines (1695). The Hotel Dieu relives three centuries of history of the French Canadian people. Average Annual Attendance: 11,000
Collections: Antique furniture; embroideries; medical equipment 17th-20th century; objects from everyday life, models & several other unique works; paintings; silver & pewter artifacts
Activities: Original objects of art lent to museums

L **Archive,** 32 rue Charlevoix, G1R 5C4. Tel 418-692-2492, Ext 247; FAX 418-692-2668; *Archivist* Sr Marie-Paule Couchon; *Dir Mus* Sr Nicole Perron
Religious & medical books available for research upon special request
Library Holdings: Vols 4000

M **MUSEE DU QUEBEC,** Parc des Champs-de-Bataille, G1R 5H3. Tel 418-643-2150; FAX 418-646-3330; *Dir* John R Porter; *Dir Develop* Helene Riberin; *Conservator Early Art* Mario Beland; *Conservator Modern Art* Pierre L'Allier; *Conservator Contemporary Art* Michel Martin; *Head Educative Serv & Cur* Didier Prioul; *Pub Relations* Lise Boyer; *Publ* Pierre Murgia; *Dir Admin* Gaetan Chouinard; *Prints & Drawings* Denis Martin; *Prints & Drawings* Michele Grandbois; *Dean Communications* Suzanne LeBlanc
Open (June 1 - Sept 8) daily 10 AM - 6 PM, (Sept 9 - May 31) Tues - Sun 11 AM - 6 PM, cl Mon. Admis $5.75. Estab 1933 under Government of Province of Quebec. 12 galleries, 1 restaurant, 1 theatre. Average Annual Attendance: 200,000
Income: Financed by Quebec government appropriation
Purchases: $60,000
Collections: Quebec art from 18th century to present; Design, drawings, goldsmith's work, paintings, photography, sculpture, tapestry works
Exhibitions: Rotating exhibitions
Publications: Exhibit catalogs
Activities: Classes for adults & children; lect open to public; concerts; gallery talks; tours; exten dept serves province of Quebec; individual paintings lent to government; museum shop sells books, magazines, original art, reproductions & postcards; junior museum

L **Bibliotheque des Arts,** Parc des Champs-de-Bataille, G1R 5H3. Tel 418-643-7134; *Chief Librn* L Allard; *Asst Librn* N Gastonguay; *Asst Librn* Richard St-Gelais; *Asst Librn* M Audet; *Asst Librn* Lena Doyon
Open Tues - Fri 1 - 5 PM. Estab 1933
Income: $150,000 (financed by Quebec government appropriation)
Purchases: $35,000
Library Holdings: Vols 35,000; Per subs 200; CD-Rom; Micro — Fiche, reels; AV — Slides 58,000, v-tapes; Other — Clipping files, exhibition catalogs, photographs 18,000
Special Subjects: Quebecois art; Canadian art; American art; English art; French art

M **MUSEE DU SEMINAIRE DE QUEBEC,** 9 rue de l'Universite, CP 460 Haute-Ville, G1R 4R7. Tel 418-692-2843; FAX 418-692-5206; *Dir* Andre Juneau; *Registrar* Sonia Mimeault; *Cur* Yves Bergeron; *Asst to Cur* Jean-Pierre Pare
Open daily from June 1 - Sept 30 10 AM - 5:30 PM, Oct 1 - May 31 Tues - Sun 10 AM - 5 PM, free on Tues. Admis family $6, adult $3, sr citizen $2, student $1.50, under 16 $1, under 12 free. Mem: dues $25
Income: Financed by Ministere des Affaires Culturelles, Gouvernement du Quebec, Gouvernement Federal
Collections: †18th & 19th centuries Canadian paintings; †17th & 18th centuries European paintings; †Ethnology; †Gold & Silver Objects; †Scientific Instruments; †Sketches & Prints; †Sculpture; †Coins & Medals; †Zoology
Activities: Classes for adults & children; lect open to public; concerts; gallery talks; tours; scholarships & fels offered; sales shop sells books, magazines, prints & slides

M **VU CENTRE D'ANIMATION ET DE DIFFUSION DE LA PHOTOGRAPHIE,** 523 Saint Zallirsaast, G1K 3A9. Tel 418-640-2585; *Dir* Gaetan Gosselin; *Coordr* Alain Belanger
Open Thurs - Sun 1 - 5 PM. Estab 1982. Gallery contains exhibition area, studio & darkroom. Average Annual Attendance: 15,000. Mem: 200
Income: $200 (financed by endowment, mem, city appropriation & special events)
Activities: Classes for adults; workshop; lect open to public, 5 vis lectr per year; book traveling exhibitions annually; originate traveling exhibitions

RIMOUSKI

M **LE MUSEE REGIONAL DE RIMOUSKI,** Centre National d'Exposition, 35 W St Germain, G5L 4B4. Tel 418-724-2272; FAX 418-725-4433; *Dir Mus* Francois Lachapelle; *Animatric* Yves Landry; *Conservatrice en Art Contemporain* Carl Johnson
Open Sept - June Wed - Sun Noon - 5 PM, Thurs Noon - 9 PM. Admis family $10, adults $4, students & senior citizens $3, children 5 & under free. Estab 1972 for the diffusion of contemporary art, historic & scientific exhibitions; to present local, national & international exhibitions & organize itinerant exhibitions. An old church, built in 1823, now historical monument, completely restored inside with three floors of exhibitions. Average Annual Attendance: 15,000. Mem: 400; dues $40; annual meeting in May or June
Income: $237,000 (financed by federal, provincial & municipal appropriation)
Publications: L'Esprit des lieux; L'Artiste au jardin; Messac; Opera, Les Nuits de Vitre; Cozic; exhibit catalogs
Activities: Classes for children; school programs; lect open to public, 5 vis lectr per year; concerts; gallery talks; tours; originate traveling exhibitions; museum shop sells magazines
L **Library,** 35 W St Germain, G5L 4B4. Tel 418-724-2272; FAX 418-725-4433; Open to pub for reference
Library Holdings: Vols 2500; Documents 800; Other — Exhibition catalogs, pamphlets, reproductions, sculpture

SAINT-LAURENT

M **MUSEE D'ART DE SAINT-LAURENT,** 615 Sainte Croix Ave, H4L 3X6. Tel 514-747-7367; FAX 514-747-8892; *Pres* Jean Royer; *VPres* Georgette Berube
Open Tues - Sun 12:30 - 5 PM. Admis family $10, adult $5, senior citizen & student $4, child $3. Estab 1962 to didactic exhibitions of traditional arts & crafts of Quebec. Mus situated in a Gothic chapel of the Victorian period, built in 1867 in Montreal & moved in Saint-Laurent in 1930. Besides its permanent collection, the mus presents periodical exhibitions illustrating various aspects of the Quebec cultural heritage
Collections: Traditional & folk art of French Canada from 17th - 19th century: ceramics, crafts, furniture, metalworks, paintings, sculpture, religious art, silver, textiles, tools & wood-carving
Exhibitions: Album: Email au Quebec: 1949 - 1989; La dentelle au fil des ans; Album: Un musee dans une eglise
Publications: Album: Images Taillees du Quebec; Album: Les eglises et le tresor de Saint Laurent; Album: Les cahiers du musee: Hommage a Jean Palardy; Les cahiers du musee: Premiere biennale de la reliure du Quebec; La main et l'outil; monthly calendar
Activities: Lect open to public; concerts; gallery talks; tours

SEPT-ILES

M **MUSEE REGIONAL DE LA COTE-NORD,** 500 boul Laure, G4R 1X7. Tel 418-968-2070; FAX 418-964-3213; *Dir & Cur* Guy Tremblay, PhD; *Animator & Educ* Francine Levesque; *Technician* Sophie Levesque; *Secy* Caroline Cornier
Estab 1975. Protects, preserves, studies & exhibits the heritage of the Cote-Nord region, with particular emphasis on fishing, hunting, mining & archaeological activity. Average Annual Attendance: 22,000. Mem: 260; annual meeting in June
Income: Financed by mem, city & state appropriation
Collections: †Archaeology; †art; †ethnology; †history
Activities: Classes for adults & children; docent programs; lect open to public; book traveling exhibitions 2 per year; sales shop sells books & prints

SHAWINIGAN

A **SHAWINIGAN ART CENTER,** 2100 des Hetres, CP 400, G9N 6V3. Tel 819-539-1888; FAX 819-539-2400; *Dir* Robert Y Desjardins
Open Thurs - Sun 2:30 - 4:30 PM & 7 - 9:30 PM. No admis fee. Estab 1967. Gallery is maintained. Average Annual Attendance: 50,000
Income: Financed by city appropriation
Collections: Oils; pastels; watercolors; polyesters; reproductions; copper enameling; inks; sculpture; tapestries
Activities: Classes for adults & children; dramatic programs; concerts; lending collection contains original art works, original prints, paintings, sculpture, slides; sales shop sells original art

SHERBROOKE

M **UNIVERSITY OF SHERBROOKE,** Art Gallery, J1K 2R1. Tel 819-821-7748; FAX 819-820-1361; *Dir* Johanne Brouillet
Open Mon - Fri 12:30 - 5 PM, Sat & Sun 1 - 5 PM. No admis fee. Estab 1964 to introduce pub to the best art work being done in Canada & to place this work in a historical (European) & geographical (American) context. Gallery has three exhibition areas totalling 12,800 sq ft on university campus & serves the community. Average Annual Attendance: 30,000
Income: $300,000 (financed by state & city appropriation & university funds)
Collections: 90 per cent Contemporary Graphics & Paintings Quebec & 10 per cent international
Publications: Monthly bulletin; catalogue
Activities: Lect open to public, 20 vis lectr per year; gallery talks; lending collection contains books, cassettes, color reproductions, Kodachromes, original prints, paintings, photographs, sculpture, slides & videos

SUTTON

M **EBERDT MUSEUM OF COMMUNICATIONS,** Heritage Sutton, 30A Main St, J0E 2K0. Tel 514-538-2649, 538-2544; *Cur* Edmund Eberdt
Admis $1.50. Estab 1965 to educate. Average Annual Attendance: 2000. Mem: 160; dues $10
Income: $20,000 (financed by mem, city & state appropriation)
Collections: †History, art & †communications collection; 2300 historic objects
Activities: Lect open to public; museum shop sells books

TROIS RIVIERES

A **CENTRE CULTUREL DE TROIS RIVIERES,** 376 Ire des Soijes, CPC 368, G9A 5H3. Tel 819-372-4614; FAX 819-372-4632; *Dir* Francois Lahaye
Open 9 AM - Noon, 1:30 - 5 PM & 7 - 10 PM. Estab 1967
Income: Financed by city appropriation
Activities: Classes for adults & children; dramatic programs

M **FORGES DU SAINT-MAURICE NATIONAL HISTORIC SITE,** 10,000 des Forges Blvd, G9C 1B1. Tel 819-378-5116; FAX 819-378-0887; *Supt* Carmen D Le Page
Estab 1973 as the first iron & steel industry in Canada 1729-1883. 50 acres of land-2 main exhibition centers. The ironmaster's house & the blast furnace. Average Annual Attendance: 50,000

M **GALERIE D'ART DU PARC-MANOIR DE TONNANCOUR,** Manoir de Tonnancour, 864 rue des Ursulines, CP 871, G9A 5J9. Tel 819-374-2355; FAX 819-374-1758; *Dir* Christiane Simoneau
No admis fee. Estab 1972 to promote visual arts. Non-profit organization; 10-12 exhibitions in visual arts per year & permanent history exhibition. Average Annual Attendance: 19,000
Income: Financed by city appropriation & government
Activities: Classes for adults & children; book traveling exhibitions 1 per year; originate traveling exhibitions; museum shop sells original art & reproductions

VAUDREUIL

M **MUSEE REGIONAL DE VAUDREUIL-SOULANGES,** 431 Avenue Chaud, J7V 2N3. Tel 514-455-2092; *Dir* Daniel Bissonnette
Open Mon - Fri 10 AM - 5 PM, Sat & Sun 1 - 5 PM. Admis adults $3, children $1.50. Estab 1953, non-profit organization subsidized by the Direction des Musees et Centres d'Exposition of the Ministere des Affaires culturelles du Quebec. The collection consists of artifacts & artists production that have & still illustrate the traditional way of life in the counties of Vaudreuil & Soulanges, the surroundings & the Province of Quebec. Mus has four rooms for permanent collection & one for temporary & traveling exhibitions. A documentation centre is open for searchers & students & an animator will receive groups on reservation for a commented tour. Average Annual Attendance: 10,000. Mem: 300; dues $20; annual meeting in Apr
Income: Financed by endowment
Collections: Edison Gramophone 1915; antique pottery; historic documents & material; farming; furniture, paintings, portraits, sculpture & woodworking
Publications: Musee de Vaudreuil Catalog (selectif); Vaudreuil Soulanges, Western Gateway of Quebec
Activities: Classes for children; concerts; original objects of art lent
L **Library,** 431 Avenue Chaud, J7V 2N3. Tel 514-455-2092; *Dir* Daniel Bissonnette
Reference only
Library Holdings: Vols 2500; AV cylinders 600; Other — Photographs

SASKATCHEWAN

ALBERTA

M **IMHOFF ART GALLERY,** 5011 49th Ave, T9V 0T8. Tel 306-825-6184; *Cur* Barbara McKeand
Open 8 AM - 6 PM. Admis adults $2.75, students $2, children $1.50. Estab to exhibit 200 paintings done by Berthold Imhoff, who died in 1939

ESTEVAN

M **ESTEVAN NATIONAL EXHIBITION CENTRE INC,** 118 Fourth St, S4A 0T4. Tel 306-634-7644; *Dir* Sallie Pierson; *Educ Coordr* Bill Wilkinson
Open Mon - Fri 9 AM - 5 PM, Sat & Sun 1 - 3:30 PM. No admis fee. Estab 1978 to receive, display & interpret objects & collections, that would increase the communities access to culture. Two galleries; one 16 x 30 ft, the other 26 x 65 ft. Average Annual Attendance: 16,000
Income: $150,000 (financed by provincial & city appropriation & private sector fundraising)
Collections: Saskatchewan artists print series; Saskatchewan painting collection
Publications: Annual Report; newsletter, 6 times per year
Activities: Classes for adults & children; lect open to public, 4 vis lectr per year; children's & regional art show competitions; awards of merit; exten dept serves area within a 30 mile radius; book traveling exhibitions 13-18 per year; originate traveling exhibitions; sales shop sells souvenirs

LLOYDMINSTER

A BARR COLONY HERITAGE CULTURAL CENTRE, c/o City of
Lloydminster, 5011 49th Ave, S9V 0T8. Tel 306-825-6184, 825-5655; FAX 306-
825-7170; *Cur* Barbara McKeand
Open daily May - Sept 10 AM - 8 PM, Sept - May Wed - Sun 1 - 6 PM. Admis
family $5.75, adults $2.75, senior citizens & students $2, children 12 & under $1.
50, school tours $.50. Estab 1963 to promote & support appreciation for & educ
about local history & the arts. The center is comprised of 4 exhibit galleries
(1000 sq ft), a mus bldg (24,000 sq ft) & classroom teaching space
Income: Financed by donations & city appropriations
Collections: Antique Museum; Fuchs' Wildlife; Imhoff Paintings; Berghammer
Art Collection; over 5000 artifacts related to the Barr Colonists, the first settlers
of the area
Activities: Gallery talks; tours; traveling exhibitions

MOOSE JAW

M MOOSE JAW ART MUSEUM & NATIONAL EXHIBITION CENTRE, Art
& History Museum, Crescent Park, S6H 0X6. Tel 306-692-4471; FAX 306-694-
8016; *Cur* Heather Smith; *Bus Mgr* Nancy Dougherty
Open Tues - Sun Noon - 5 PM, Tues & Wed 7 - 9 PM, cl Mon. No admis fee.
Estab 1966 for preservation, educ, collection & exhibitions. Gallery has 4304 sq
ft with movable walls, Mus has 3970 sq ft, Discovery Centre has 1010 sq ft.
Average Annual Attendance: 30,000. Mem: 190; dues family $25, individual $15
Income: $260,000 (financed by city, province & national appropriations & self-
generated revenues)
Purchases: $260,000
Collections: †450 Canadian Historical & Contemporary Art Collection; †4200
Human History Artifacts Collection
Publications: Annual catalogs; bi-annual newsletter
Activities: Classes for adults & children; docent training; school tours; lect open
to public, 10-15 vis lectr per year; gallery talks; tours; individual paintings &
original objects of art lent to other professional public institutions that meet
appropriate environmental standards; book traveling exhibitions 5-10 per year;
originate traveling exhibitions; museum shop sells books, magazines &
reproductions

NORTH BATTLEFORD

M ALLEN SAPP GALLERY, One Railway Ave, PO Box 460, S9A 2Y6. Tel 306-
445-1760; FAX 306-445-0411; *Cur* Dean Bauche
Open Wed - Sun 1 - 5 PM. Estab 1989. 8000 sq ft gallery built in 1916 contains
state of the art equipment incl high tech audiovisual presentation equipment.
Average Annual Attendance: 12,000. Mem: 100
Income: $10,000
Collections: The Gonor Collection, paintings, photos, slides
Publications: gallery catalog, biennally
Activities: Lect open to public, 5 vis lectr per year; sales shop sells books,
original art, prints

PRINCE ALBERT

M JOHN M CUELENAERE LIBRARY, Grace Campbell Gallery, 125 12th St E,
S6V 1B7. Tel 306-763-8496; FAX 306-763-3816; *Head Librn* Eleanor Acorn
Open Mon - Fri 9 AM - 9 PM, Sat 9 AM - 5:30 PM, Sun 1 - 5 PM. No admis
fee. Estab 1973. Gallery is 100 linear ft
Income: Financed by city appropriation

REGINA

ORGANIZATION OF SASKATCHEWAN ARTS COUNCILS (OSAC)
For further information, see National and Regional Organizations

L REGINA PUBLIC LIBRARY, Art Dept, PO Box 2311, S4P 3Z5. Tel 306-777-
6070; FAX 306-352-5550; *Chief Librn* Ken Jensen
Open Mon - Thurs 9:30 AM - 9 PM, Fri 9:30 AM - 6 PM, Sat 9:30 AM - 5 PM,
Sun 1:30 - 5 PM, cl holidays. No admis fee. Estab 1947. Also operates Sherwood
Village Branch Gallery
Library Holdings: Vols 10,230; Per subs 60; Micro — Fiche; AV — A-tapes,
cassettes, fs, motion pictures, slides, v-tapes; Other — Clipping files, exhibition
catalogs 4000, original art works, pamphlets, photographs, prints
Special Subjects: Saskatchewan Art and Artists; Folk Art
M Dunlop Art Gallery, 2311 12th Ave, PO Box 2311, S4P 3Z5. Tel 306-777-6040;
FAX 306-777-6221; *Elec Mail* dunlop@rpl.regina.sk.ca. *Dir & Cur* Helen
Marzolf; *Cur* Vera Lemecha; *Preparator & Technician* Darcy Zink; *Cur Asst*
Joyce Clark; *Clerical Asst* Bev Antal
Open Mon - Thurs 9:30 AM - 9 PM, Fri 9:30 AM - 6 PM;, Sat 9:30 AM - 5
PM, Sun 1:30 - 5 PM, cl holidays. No admis fee. Estab 1947 to exhibit, collect,
interpret, catalogue & preserve works of art of contemporary & historical value
for the citizens of Regina & Saskatchewan; to make available information about
art, artists & the art community to the citizens of Regina, Saskatchwan &
Canada; to stimulate interest in the art history & cultural development of Regina,
Saskatchewan, Canada & the world. 130-seat film theater with stage, preview
room, meeting rooms, library van, woodworking shop, collections & services of
the Regina library. Maintains resource centre. Average Annual Attendance:
100,000
Income: Financed by city appropriation, provincial & federal grants
Purchases: $10,000
Collections: †Permanent collection of Saskatchewan art; Inglis Sheldon-Williams
Collection; †Art Rental Collection 205 works of historical & contemporary art
including paintings, sculpture & graphic art by Saskatchewan artists; rental
collection, 226 works of historical & contemporary paintings & graphic art by
Canadian artists

Exhibitions: 18 exhibitions per year
Publications: At the Dunlop Newsletter, quarterly; brochures; exhibition catalogs
Activities: Lect open to public, 6 vis lectr per year; gallery talks; tours;
competitions; individual paintings & original objects of art lent through an art
rental coll available to the pub & works from permanent coll lent to other
galleries; lending coll contains original art works, original prints & drawings; book
traveling exhibitions; originate traveling exhibitions; sales shop sells books,
magazines, cards, catalogues & posters

SASKATCHEWAN ARTS BOARD
For further information, see National and Regional Organizations

C SASKPOWER, Gallery on the Roof, 2025 Victoria Ave, S4P 0S1. Tel 306-566-
2553; FAX 306-566-2548; *Graphics Supv* Shirley Fehr
Open Mon - Fri 1 PM - 9 PM, Sun & holidays 1 PM - 5 PM. Estab 1963 to give
local artists & art groups exposure. Gallery approx 100 ft of wall space adjoining
the observation deck that overlooks the city. Average Annual Attendance:
100,000
Publications: Brochure, monthly; exhibition brochures

UNIVERSITY OF REGINA
M MacKenzie Art Gallery, 3475 Albert St, S4S 6X6. Tel 306-522-4242; FAX 306-
569-8191;
Internet Home Page Address http://www.uregina.ca/-macken//. *Bus Mgr*
Sudeep Bhargava; *Coordr Communications* Bonnie Schaffer
Open Mon, Tues, Fri, Sat & Sun 11 AM - 6 PM, Wed & Thurs 11 AM - 10 PM.
No admis fee. Estab 1953 to preserve & expand the collection left to the gallery
by Norman MacKenzie & to offer exhibitions to the city of Regina; to offer
works of art to rural areas through the Outreach Program. Eight discreet galleries
totalling approx 1500 running ft of exhibition space. Average Annual
Attendance: 100,000. Mem: 1079; dues $35; annual meeting in June
Income: $1,000,000 (financed by federal & provincial governments, University of
Regina & city of Regina & private funds)
Collections: †Contemporary Canadian & American work; †contemporary
Saskatchewan work; 19th & early 20th century works on paper; a part of the
collection is early 20th century replicas of Eastern & Oriental artifacts & art
Exhibitions: Changing exhibitions from the permanent collection & traveling
exhibitions
Publications: Exhibition catalogues; staff publications of a professional nature;
Vista, quarterly
Activities: Docent training; community programme of touring exhibitions in
Saskatchewan; interpretive programs; lect open to public, 8-10 vis lectr per year;
concerts; gallery talks; tours; films; exten dept serves entire province; originate
traveling exhibitions nation-wide; gallery shop sells books, magazines,
reproductions, cards & catalogues
   —MacKenzie Art Gallery Resource Centre, 3475 Albert St, S4S 6X6. Tel
306-522-4242; FAX 306-569-8191
Open Mon, Tues, Fri, Sat & Sun 11 AM - 7 PM, Wed & Thurs 11 AM - 10 PM.
Estab 1970 to offer the community a resource for art information, both historical
& current. For reference only
Special Subjects: Saskatchewan Art, historical & contemporary
Collections: Regional press clippings from 1925
Exhibitions: Between Abstraction & Representation, George Glenn; Jana
Sterbak; Jan Gerrit Wyels 1888-1973; The Asymmetric Vision; Philosophical
Intuition & Original Experience in the Art of Yves Gaucher; Peace Able
Kingdom, Jack Severson; Artists With Their Work; Ryan Arnott; Grant
McConnell; Memory in Place
Publications: Exhibition catalog
Activities: Film program, twice a month
   —Slide Library, Fine Arts Dept, S4S 0A2. Tel 306-585-5879; FAX 306-585-
5744; *Elec Mail* finearts@max.cc.uregina.ca. *Cur* Pat Matheson
Estab for the instruction of art history
Library Holdings: AV — A-tapes, slides 90,000, v-tapes
Special Subjects: 20th century art
Collections: †Prehistoric - contemporary, eastern & western art
L Fine Arts Library, College Ave, S4S 0A2. Tel 306-585-5826; *Fine Arts Librn*
Linda Winkler
Open (semester) Mon - Fri 8:30 AM - 5 PM & 7 AM - 10 PM, Sat & Sun 1 - 5
PM, (summer) Mon - Fri 8:15 AM - 4:30 PM, cl during Noon hour. Estab 1969
to service the students of music & the visual arts. For both lending & reference
Library Holdings: Vols 14,000; Per subs 55; Micro — Fiche, reels; AV — A-
tapes, cassettes, rec; Other — Clipping files, exhibition catalogs, pamphlets

SASKATOON

M MENDEL ART GALLERY & CIVIC CONSERVATORY, 950 Spadina
Crescent E, PO Box 569, S7K 3L6. Tel 306-975-7610; FAX 306-975-7670; *Dir*
Terry Fenton; *Bus Mgr* Richard Moldenhauer; *Admin Asst* Judy Koutecky; *Asst
Cur* George Moppett; *Asst Cur* Dan Ring; *Extension Coordr* Dan Ring; *Gallery
Store Supvr* Michael Gibson; *Communications Coordr* Karen Eckhart; *Registrar*
Sylvia Tritthardt; *Pub Relations* Noreen Neu
Open daily 9 AM - 9 PM, cl Christmas Day. No admis fee. Estab 1964 to
exhibit, preserve, collect & interpret works of art; to encourage the development
of the visual arts in Saskatoon; to provide the opportunity for citizens to enjoy &
understand & to gain a greater appreciation of the fine arts. Average Annual
Attendance: 200,000. Mem: 700; dues $30, senior citizens & students $10
Income: $2,000,000 (financed by grants, gift shop, mem, donations & other
sources)
Collections: Regional, National and International Art
Exhibitions: (1997) The Plain Truth: Western Canadian; Photographers &
Filmmakers. (1998) LandScape
Publications: Exhibition catalogues; Folio, gallery newsmagazine
Activities: Classes for adults & children; gallery theatre; dramatic programs; lect
open to public; gallery talks; tours; exten dept; individual paintings & original
objects of art lent to other galleries; lending collection contains 3000 paintings,
500 photographs, 300 sculptures; originate traveling exhibitions; gallery shop sells
books, magazines, original Inuit art, reproductions, prints & craft items, all with
an emphasis on Canadian handcrafts

L Reference Library, 950 Spadina Crescent E, PO Box 569, S7K 3L6. Tel 306-975-7610; FAX 306-975-7670; *Librn* Frances Bergles
For staff use; open to pub by appointment
Library Holdings: Vols 10,057; Per subs 43; AV — A-tapes, cassettes, fs, rec, slides, v-tapes; Other — Clipping files, exhibition catalogs, pamphlets, photographs
Special Subjects: Canadian art, Saskatchewan art

L NUTANA COLLEGIATE INSTITUTE, Memorial Library and Art Gallery, 411 11th St E, S7N 0E9. Tel 306-683-7580; FAX 306-683-7587; *Principal* Michael LeClaire; *VPrincipal* George Rathwell
Open daily 8 AM - 4 PM, summer 9 AM - 3 PM. No admis fee. Estab 1919 to promote an appreciation for art; a memorial to students who lost their lives in the two world wars. Maintains an art gallery
Library Holdings: Vols 8000; Per subs 35; Micro — Reels; AV — A-tapes, cassettes, fs, Kodachromes, motion pictures, rec, slides, v-tapes; Other — Clipping files, exhibition catalogs, original art works, pamphlets
Collections: Paintings & wood cuts by Canadian artists

M PHOTOGRAPHERS GALLERY, 12 23rd St E, 2nd Flr, S7K 0H5. Tel 306-244-8018; FAX 306-665-6568; *Dir* Monte Greenshields; *Prog Coordr* Brenda Barry Byrne; *Admin Asst* Jeff Gee
Open Mon - Sat Noon - 5 PM. Admis $2 (optional). Estab 1970, incorporated 1973 to encourage the development of photography as a creative visual art. Main gallery is 650 sq ft, & workshop gallery is 250 sq ft. Average Annual Attendance: 8000. Mem: 100; dues $25; annual meeting first Sun in May
Income: $196,000 (financed by mem, province appropriation, federal grants & fundraising)
Collections: Permanent Collection of 901 Contemporary Canadian photographs
Exhibitions: 8 main gallery exhibitions per year; 8 workshop gallery exhibitions per year
Publications: Backflash, quarterly magazine; members monthly newsletter
Activities: Classes for adults; lect open to public, 12 vis lectr per year; tours; exten dept; worshops throughout the province; portable darkrooms travel with instructors; book traveling exhibitions; originate traveling exhibitions to public galleries in Canada; sales shop sells books, postcards, tee shirts
L Library, 12 23rd St E Saskatoon, 2nd Flr, S7K 0H5. Tel 306-244-8018; *Dir* Monte Greenshields
Open Mon - Sat Noon - 5 PM. Estab 1970. For references
Library Holdings: Vols 1500; Per subs 10; AV — A-tapes, cassettes, slides; Other — Clipping files, exhibition catalogs, manuscripts, pamphlets, reproductions

A SASKATCHEWAN ASSOCIATION OF ARCHITECTS, 200-642 Broadway Ave, S7N 1A9. Tel 306-242-0733; FAX 306-664-2598; *Exec Dir* Margaret Topping
Estab 1911. Mem: 111; dues $550; annual meeting in Feb
Income: Financed by mem
Publications: Columns, quarterly newsletter
Activities: Book prize given to architectural technology student at Saskatchewan Technical Institute, Moose Jaw (4 twice a year)

M SASKATCHEWAN CRAFT GALLERY, 813 Broadway Ave, S7N 1B5. Tel 306-653-3616; FAX 306-244-2711; *Exhib Coordr* Terry Schwalm; *Exhib Coordr* Leslie Potter
Open 1 - 5 PM. No admis fee. Estab 1975 to support, promote, exhibit & develop excellence in Saskatchewan craft. 900 sq ft. Average Annual Attendance: 14,000. Mem: 385; dues $50; annual meeting in May
Income: $429,000 (financed by mem, city appropriation, provincial grants)
Exhibitions: 8 exhibitions yearly.
Publications: The Craft Factor, 3 per year
Activities: Classes for adults; lect open to public, 8 vis lectr per year; gallery talks; tours; open juried competition with award for residents; book traveling exhibitions 2 per year; originate traveling exhibitions to provincial galleries

M UNIVERSITY OF SASKATCHEWAN, Gordon Snelgrove Art Gallery, 3 Campus Dr, S7N 5A4. Tel 306-966-4208; *Gallery Cur* Gary Young
Open Mon - Fri 9 AM - 4:30 PM, Sat 11 AM - 5 PM. No admis fee. Estab approx 1960 for the educ of students & local pub. Gallery covers approx 3000 sq ft of floor space, 300 running ft of wall space. Average Annual Attendance: 12, 000
Income: Financed by provincial & federal government appropriations & university funds
Collections: Contemporary art from western & midwestern Canada
Exhibitions: Constantly changing exhibitions of art works; internationally organized & traveling shows
Publications: Show announcements, every three weeks; catalogues for selected exhibits
Activities: Individual paintings & individual objects of art lent to recognized regional exhibition centres for one time presentation or tour; lending collection contains 150 original art works, 75 original prints, 150 paintings, 100,000 slides; originate traveling exhibitions on a limited basis
M Diefenbaker Canada Centre, University of Saskatchewan, 101 Diefenbaker Pl, S7N 5B8. Tel 306-966-8382; FAX 306-966-6207; *Dir* Bruce Shepard; *Archivist* Joan Champ; *Educ Liaison* Lee Brodie; *Technician* G Burke
Open Mon & Fri 9:30 AM - 4:30 PM, Tues, Wed & Thurs 9:30 AM - 8 PM, Sat, Sun & holidays 12:30 - 5 PM. Admis donations requested. Estab 1979 to explore Canada's evolution with its citizens & their visitors. Its focus is Canada's citizenship, leadership & the country's international role. Average Annual Attendance: 25,000

Income: Financed by pub foundations, donations & endowments
Collections: Priministal papers of the Rt Honourable J G Diefenbaker & related papers
Exhibitions: Canadian Politics focuses upon the country during the 10th decade of the Confederacy; international & national regional travel exhibits; Prime Ministers office & the Canadian Cabinet room
Activities: Study of modern Canadian history; reference service; curriculum-based programs on Canadian law, politics & government; Conferences; seminars; public events; book traveling exhibitions, 30 plus per year; retail store sells books, prints, slides, jewelry, scarfs, gifts

SWIFT CURRENT

M SWIFT CURRENT NATIONAL EXHIBITION CENTRE, 411 Herbert St E, S9H 1M5. Tel 306-778-2736; FAX 306-778-2194; *Dir & Cur* Kim Houghtaling; *Educ Coordr* Laurie Spearing; *Admin Asst* Wendy Muri
Open 2 - 5 PM & 7 - 9 PM. No admis fee. Estab 1974 to exhibit temporary art exhibitions. 1876 sq ft. Average Annual Attendance: 18,000
Income: $120,000 (financed by city & state appropriation & federal grant)
Exhibitions: Ima Uhtoff; Swift Current Photo Works; Nuclear Visions; Pulling People Together by Betty Meyers; History Abstract Art in Saskatchewan
Activities: Classes for adults & children; docent training; film series; lect open to public, 3-6 vis lectr per year; book traveling exhibitions; originate traveling exhibitions

WEYBURN

M WEYBURN ARTS COUNCIL, Allie Griffin Art Gallery, 45 Bison Ave N, PO Box 1178, S4H 2L5. Tel 306-848-3278; *Cur* Helen Mamer
No admis fee. Estab 1964 to showcase art & craft work by Weyburn artists, Saskatchewan artists from various large & small communities, nationally known artists & artisans as well as international exhibitions on tour from lending galleries
Exhibitions: Exhibits works from the Weyburn permanent collection at regular intervals throughout each year
Activities: Tours; original objects of art lent to offices in city owned buildings; lending collection contains original art works & paintings

YUKON TERRITORY

DAWSON CITY

M DAWSON CITY MUSEUM & HISTORICAL SOCIETY, PO Box 303, Y0B 1G0. Tel 403-993-5291; FAX 403-993-5839; *Dir* Mac Swackhammer; *Registrar* Susan Parsons; *Exhib Coordr* Sally Robinson
Open 10 AM - 6 PM May - Sept, winter hrs 9 AM - 5 PM. Admis Adult $3.50, senior citizens & students $2.50. Estab 1959 to collect, preserve & interpret the history of the Dawson City area. Two long term, two changing exhibition spaces featuring Dawson & Klondike gold fields. Average Annual Attendance: 20,000. Mem: 250; dues $15-$250; annual meeting in Apr
Income: $300,000 (financed by mem, state appropriation, grants)
Collections: 30,000 piece collection including archives, cultural, enthnographic, household, industrial, paleontology, photographs
Exhibitions: Gold Rush; Railway; natural history; mining; Han People
Publications: Newsletter, quarterly
Activities: Docent programs; lect open to public, 600 vis lectr per year; book traveling exhibitions; originate traveling exhibitions 2 per year; museum shop sells books, original art, prints & reproductions
L Resource Room Library, PO Box 303, Y0B 1G0. Tel 403-993-5291; FAX 403-993-5839; Elec Mail Envoy (Express) CAN-DCM. *Dir & Cur* Mac Swackhammer
For reference
Library Holdings: Vols 3500; AV — Cassettes, lantern slides, slides; Other — Clipping files, photographs
Special Subjects: Furniture, Glass, Gold, Historical Material, Industrial Design, Manuscripts, Maps, Mixed Media, Photography, Restoration & Conservation, Scrimshaw, Gold Rush, Han People, Klondike, Mining

WHITEHORSE

A YUKON HISTORICAL & MUSEUMS ASSOCIATION, PO Box 4357, Y1A 3T5. Tel 403-667-4704
Open Wed - Fri 9:30 - 3:30 PM. No admis fee. Estab 1977 as a national organization to preserve & interpret history. Mem: 180; dues individual $20, annual meeting in Oct
Income: Financed by mem, donations & fundraising
Publications: Newsletters, tour booklet, Yukon Exploration by G Dawson
Activities: Lect open to public, 4 or more vis lectr per year; tours; competitions with awards; lending collection contains books, photographs, audio equipment (oral history taping); originate traveling photo exhibitions to Yukon communities; sales shop sells books, t-shirts, heritage pins & reproductions of old Canadian expedition maps

II ART SCHOOLS

Arrangement and Abbreviations

Art Schools in the U.S.

Art Schools in Canada

ARRANGEMENT AND ABBREVIATIONS
KEY TO ART ORGANIZATIONS

ARRANGEMENT OF DATA

Name and address of institution; telephone number, including area code.

Names and titles of key personnel.

Hours open; admission fees; date established and purpose; average annual attendance; membership.

Annual figures on income and purchases.

Collections with enlarging collections indicated.

Exhibitions.

Activities sponsored, including classes for adults and children, dramatic programs and docent training; lectures, concerts, gallery talks and tours; competitions, awards, scholarships and fellowships; lending programs; museum or sales shops.

Libraries also list number of book volumes, periodical subscriptions, and audiovisual and micro holdings; subject covered by name of special collections

ABBREVIATIONS AND SYMBOLS

Acad—Academic
Admin—Administration, Administrative
Adminr—Administrator
Admis—Admission
A-tapes—Audio-tapes
Adv—Advisory
AM—Morning
Ann—Annual
Approx—Approximate, Approximately
Asn—Association
Assoc—Associate
Asst—Assistant
AV—Audiovisual
Ave—Avenue
Bldg—Building
Blvd—Boulevard
Bro—Brother
C—circa
Cert—Certificate
Chap—Chapter
Chmn—Chairman
Circ—Circulation
Cl—Closed
Col—College
Coll—Collection
Comt—Committee
Coordr—Coordinator
Corresp—Corresponding
Cr—Credit
Cur—Curator
D—Day
Den—Denominational
Dept—Department
Develop—Development
Dipl—Diploma
Dir—Director
Dist—District
Div—Division
Dorm—Dormitory
Dr—Doctor, Drive
E—East, Evening
Ed—Editor

Educ—Education
Elec Mail—Electronic Mail
Enrl—Enrollment
Ent—Entrance
Ent Req—Entrance Requirements
Est, Estab—Established
Exec—Executive
Exhib—Exhibition
Exten—Extension
Fel(s)—Fellowships
Fri—Friday
Fs—Filmstrips
Ft—Feet
FT—Full Time Instructor
GC—Graduate Course
Gen—General
Grad—Graduate
Hon—Honorary
Hr—Hour
HS—High School
Hwy—Highway
Inc—Incorporated
Incl—Including
Jr—Junior
Lect—Lecture(s)
Lectr—Lecturer
Librn—Librarian
M—Men
Maj—Major in Art
Mem—Membership
Mgr—Manager
Mon—Monday
Mss—Manuscripts
Mus—Museums
N—North
Nat—National
Nonres—Nonresident
Per subs—Periodical subscriptions
PM—Afternoon
Pres—President
Prin—Principal
Prof—Professor

Prog—Program
PT—Part Time Instructor
Pts—Points
Pub—Public
Publ—Publication
Pvt—Private
Qtr—Quarter
Rd—Road
Rec—Records
Reg—Registration
Req—Requirements
Res—Residence, Resident
S—South
Sat—Saturday
Schol—Scholarship
Secy—Secretary
Sem—Semester
Soc—Society
Sq—Square
Sr—Senior, Sister
St—Street
Ste—Suite
Sun—Sunday
Supt—Superintendent
Supv—Supervisor
Thurs—Thursday
Treas—Treasurer
Tues—Tuesday
Tui—Tuition
TV—Television
Undergrad—Undergraduate
Univ—University
Vis—Visiting
Vol—Volunteer
Vols—Volumes
VPres—Vice President
V-tapes—Videotapes
W—West, Women
Wed—Wednesday
Wk—Week
Yr—Year(s)

* No response to questionnnaire
† Denotes collection currently being enlarged
A Association
C Corporate Art Holding
L Library
M Museum
O Organization

ALABAMA

AUBURN

AUBURN UNIVERSITY, Dept of Art, 101 Biggin Hall, 36849-5125. Tel 334-844-4373; FAX 334-844-4024; *Head* Robert F Lyon; *Dean* Gordon C Bond
Estab 1928; pub; D; enrl 300
Ent Req: HS dipl, ACT, SAT
Degrees: BFA 4 yr, MFA 2 yr
Tuition: Res—$750 per quarter; nonres—$2250 per quarter
Courses: †Ceramics, †Drawing, †Graphic Design, †Illustration, †Painting, †Printmaking, †Sculpture
Summer School: Complete 10 wk program

BAY MINETTE

JAMES H FAULKNER COMMUNITY COLLEGE, Art Dept, 1900 US Hwy 31 S, 36507. Tel 334-937-9581; Elec Mail 334-580-2253. *Div Chmn of Music* Milton Jackson, MM; *Div Chmn of Art* Walter Allen, MFA
Estab 1965; pub; D & E; scholarships; SC 4, LC 3; enrl D 35, E 40, non-maj 57, maj 18
Ent Req: HS dipl
Degrees: AA 2 yrs
Tuition: Res—undergrad $29.50 per cr hr; nonres $46 per cr hr; campus res—room & board $1215
Courses: †Art History, †Drawing, History of Art & Archaeology, †Painting, †Printmaking, †Sculpture, †Commercial Design
Summer School: Dir, Milton Jackson. Courses—Art Appreciation

BIRMINGHAM

BIRMINGHAM-SOUTHERN COLLEGE, Art Dept, 900 Arkadelphia Rd, PO Box A-21, 35254. Tel 205-226-4928; *Chmn Div Fine & Performing Arts* Michael Flowers; *Prof* Bob Tucker; *Prof* Bob Shelton; *Prof* Lloyd Slone; *Assoc Prof* Steve Cole. Instrs: FT 5
Estab 1946; den; D; financial aid awarded, some leadership scholarships available on variable basis; SC 22, LC 8, interim term courses of 4 or 8 wk, 4 req of each student in 4 yr period; enrl 500, maj 50
Ent Req: HS dipl, ACT, SAT scores, C average
Degrees: AB, BS, BFA, BM and BME 4 yr
Tuition: $2800 per term
Courses: Aesthetics, Art Appreciation, Art Education, Art History, Collages, Constructions, Design, Drawing, Film, Graphic Design, History of Art & Archaeology, Mixed Media, Painting, Photography, Printmaking, Sculpture, Video
Adult Hobby Classes: Enrl 30; 8 wk term. Courses—Art History, Basic Drawing, Basic Painting
Children's Classes: Enrl approx 20. Laboratory for training teachers
Summer School: Enrl 100; 8 wk beginning June 11 & Aug 10. Courses—Art History, Design, Drawing, Painting, Sculpture

SAMFORD UNIVERSITY, Art Dept, 800 Lakeshore Dr, 35229. Tel 205-870-2849; *Chmn* Dr Lowell C Vann. Instrs: FT 3, PT 11
Estab 1841; pvt; D; scholarships; SC 24, LC 4
Ent Req: HS dipl, ent exam, ACT, SAT
Degrees: BA, BS & AB 4 yr
Tuition: $3500 per sem
Courses: Advertising Design, Ceramics, Commercial Art, Costume Design & Construction, Drawing, Graphic Arts, Graphic Design, Handicrafts, History of Art & Archaeology, Interior Design, Painting, Photography, Sculpture, Stage Design, Teacher Training, Theatre Arts
Adult Hobby Classes: Enrl 45; tuition $381 for 3 cr hr. Courses—Appreciation, Studio Arts
Children's Classes: Enrl 10; 2 wk summer session. Courses—Introduction to Art
Summer School: Dir, Lowell Vann. Enrl 30, 2 five week terms. Courses—Appreciation, Studio Arts

UNIVERSITY OF ALABAMA AT BIRMINGHAM, Dept of Art, Univ Sta, 1113 Humanitic Bldg, 900 13th St S, 35294-1260. Tel 205-934-4941; FAX 205-934-4941, 975-6639; *Chmn Dept* Sonja Rieger; *Prof* John W Dillon; *Prof* John Schnorrenberg, PhD; *Assoc Prof* James Alexander, MFA; *Assoc Prof* Janice Kluge, MFA; *Assoc Prof* Heather McPherson, PhD; *Asst Prof* Gary Chapman; *Asst Prof* Marie Weaver; *Asst Prof* Katherine Meiver, PhD; *Instr* Barbara Morgan, MFA; *Instr* Alan Atkinson, PhD. Instrs: FT 9, PT 2
Estab 1966, dept estab 1974; pub; D & E; scholarships; SC 27, LC 34, GC 10; enrl D 212, E 78, maj 100, grad 18

Ent Req: HS dipl, ACT, SAT
Degrees: BA
Tuition: Res—undergrad $58 per sem hr, grad $116 per sem hr; nonres—undergrad $63 per sem hr, grad $126 per sem hr
Courses: Art Appreciation, Art Education, Art History, Ceramics, Drawing, Graphic Design, Illustration, Mixed Media, Painting, Photography, Printmaking, Sculpture, †Art Studio
Adult Hobby Classes: Enrl 208; tuition $35-$60. Courses—Calligraphy, Drawing & Sketching, Experience of Art, Painting
Children's Classes: Enrl 60; tuition $20-$30. Courses—Drawing & Sketching, Painting, Sculpture
Summer School: Enrl 107; tuition as above for term of 11 wks beginning June 7. Courses—range over all fields and are about one half regular offerings

BREWTON

JEFFERSON DAVIS COMMUNITY COLLEGE, Art Dept, 220 Alco Dr, 36426. Tel 334-867-4832; *Instructor* Larry Manning
Estab 1965; pub; D & E; SC 10, LC 1; enrl D 700, E 332, maj 25
Ent Req: HS dipl or equiv
Degrees: AA & AS
Tuition: Res—$300 per yr, $25 per cr hr; nonres—$600 per yr
Courses: Art History, Ceramics, Drawing, Handicrafts, Painting, Photography, Basic Design, Introduction to Art
Summer School: Enrl 200. Courses—Ceramics, Drawing, Introduction to Art

DECATUR

JOHN C CALHOUN STATE COMMUNITY COLLEGE, Department of Fine Arts, Hwy 31 N, PO Box 2216, 35609-2216. Tel 205-306-2698; FAX 205-306-2889; *Dept Chair* Frances Moss, EdD; *Instr* Helen C Austin, PhD; *Instr* Janice Gibbons, MFA; *Instr* William Godsey, MA; *Instr* Jimmy Cantrell, EDS; *Instr* Joan Goree, MA; *Instr* Joyce Lowman, MA; *Instr* William Provine, MBA
Estab 1963; pub; D & E; scholarships; SC 46, LC 8; enrl D 80, E 22, non-maj 29, maj 70, others 3
Ent Req: HS dipl, GED
Degrees: AS, AA and AAS 2 yrs
Tuition: $29 per cr hr
Courses: Art Education, Art History, †Commercial Art, †Drawing, †Film, †Graphic Design, Illustration, Lettering, †Painting, †Photography, Printmaking, †Video
Summer School: Courses are selected from regular course offerings

FLORENCE

UNIVERSITY OF NORTH ALABAMA, Dept of Art, PO Box 5006, 35632-0001. Tel 205-760-4384; FAX 205-760-4329; *Prof* Fred Owen Hensley, MFA; *Prof* Elizabeth M Walter, PhD; *Asst Prof* Chiong-Yiao Chen, MFA; *Asst Prof* John D Turner, MFA; *Asst Prof* Duane L Phillips, MFA; *Asst Prof* Ronald Shady, MFA; *Asst Prof* Wayne Sides, MFA; *Instr* Michele Fabiano, MA. Instrs: FT 8
Estab 1830, dept estab approx 1930; pub; D; scholarships; SC 39, LC 10; enrl D 5380, non-maj 550, maj 125
Ent Req: HS dipl, or GED, ACT
Degrees: BFA, BS & BA 4 yr
Tuition: $951 per sem in state, $1020 out of state; campus res—room & board $1590
Courses: Advertising Design, Art Appreciation, Art Education, Art History, Ceramics, Design, Drawing, Graphic Arts, Graphic Design, History of Art & Archaeology, Illustration, Lettering, Painting, Photography, Printmaking, Sculpture
Summer School: Dir, Dr Elizabeth Walter. Enrl 50; tuition $951 for 8 wk term beginning June 5. Courses—Computer Graphics, Painting

HUNTSVILLE

UNIVERSITY OF ALABAMA IN HUNTSVILLE, Dept of Art & Art History, Roberts Hall, Rm 313, 35899. Tel 205-890-6114; *Chmn Art & Art History Dept* Michael Crouse, MFA; *Asst Prof* Mark Marchlinski, MFA; *Asst Prof* David Stewart, PhD; *Asst Prof* Dan Younger, MFA; *Asst Prof* Carol Farr, PhD
Estab 1969 (as independent, autonomous campus), dept estab 1965; pub; D & E; scholarships; SC 46, LC 14; enrl D 150
Ent Req: HS dipl, ACT
Degrees: BA 4 yr
Courses: Advertising Design, Art Education, Art History, Commercial Art, Drawing, Graphic Arts, Illustration, Mixed Media, Painting, Photography, Printmaking, Sculpture, Commercial Design, Screen Printing, Typography
Adult Hobby Classes: Tuition $411 per 3 hr course. Courses—Computer Graphics, other miscellaneous workshops offered through Div of Continuous Educ
Summer School: Dir, Glenn T Dasher. Tuition $411 for 3 hr for term of 10 wks beginning mid-June. Courses—Vary from summer to summer, part of the 46 studio classes & some art history offered

JACKSONVILLE

JACKSONVILLE STATE UNIVERSITY, Art Dept, 700 Pelham Rd N, 36265. Tel 205-782-5626; FAX 205-782-5419; *Head* Charles Groover
Estab 1883; pub; D & E; scholarships; SC 22, LC 8, GC 4; enrl D 8000, E 24, non-maj 70, maj 100, grad 11, others 15
Ent Req: HS dipl, ACT
Degrees: BFA, BA 4 yr
Tuition: $660 per sem
Courses: Art Appreciation, Art History, Calligraphy, Ceramics, Commercial Art, Drawing, Graphic Arts, Graphic Design, History of Art & Archaeology, Painting, Photography, Printmaking

LIVINGSTON

UNIVERSITY OF WEST ALABAMA (Formerly Livingston University), Division of Fine Arts, Sta 10, 35470. Tel 205-652-3400 (main), 652-3510 (arts); *Chmn* Jason Guynes
Estab 1835; pub; scholarships; enrl 1800
Degrees: BA, BS, BMus, MEd, MSc
Courses: Art Education, Art History, Ceramics, Display, Drawing, Graphic Arts, Industrial Design, Painting, Art Appreciation, Art for the Teacher, Crafts, Design, Mechanical Drawing, Metal Work, Woodworking

MARION

JUDSON COLLEGE, Division of Fine Arts, PO Box 120, 36756. Tel 334-683-6161; FAX 334-683-5147; *Chmn* Dr Roger Walworth
Estab 1838; den, W; D & E; scholarships, loans, grants; SC 23, LC 6; enrl 450
Ent Req: HS grad, adequate HS grades & ACT scores
Degrees: BA 3-4 yr
Tuition: $1375 per sem
Courses: Commercial Art, Design, Drawing, Painting, Sculpture, Elementary Art, Perspective Drafting, Pottery, Special Courses
Adult Hobby Classes: Enrl 5. Courses—Painting, Studio Drawing
Children's Classes: Drawing, Painting

MOBILE

SPRING HILL COLLEGE, Fine Arts Dept, 4000 Dauphin St, 36608. Tel 334-380-4000; *Chmn* Barbara Starr, MA; *Asst Prof* Ruth Belesco, MFA; *Asst Prof* Thomas Loehr, MFA; *Asst Prof* Stephen Campbell
Estab 1830; dept estab 1965; den; D & E; SC 21, LC 3; enrl D 163, non-maj 128, maj 35
Ent Req: HS dipl, ACT, CEEB, SAT
Degrees: BA
Tuition: Undergrad $6210 per 12-18 cr hrs; campus res—room $275-$1700 , board $650-$1200 per sem
Courses: Advertising Design, Aesthetics, Art Appreciation, Art Education, Art History, Ceramics, Commercial Art, Costume Design & Construction, Design, Drawing, †Art Business, †Therapy, †Textile Printing
Adult Hobby Classes: Enrl 15. Courses—wide variety
Summer School: Enrl 15. Courses—wide variety

UNIVERSITY OF SOUTH ALABAMA, Dept of Art & Art History, 172 Visual Arts Bldg, 36688. Tel 334-460-6335; FAX 334-414-8294; *Chmn & Printmaker* John H Cleverdon; *Graphic Design* Clint Orr; *Printmaker* Sumi Putman; *Art Historian* Robert Bantens; *Art Historian* Janice Gandy; *Art Historian* Philippe Oszuscik; *Painting & Drawing* Lee Hoffman; *Ceramisist* Lloyd Pattern; *Sculptor* James Conlon; *Graphic Design* Larry Simpson
Estab 1963; dept estab 1964; pub; D & E; SC 32, LC 25; enrl maj & 150
Ent Req: HS dipl, ACT
Degrees: BA, BFA and BA(Art History) 4 yrs
Tuition: Undergrad $52 per cr hr; grad $68 per cr hr
Courses: Art Appreciation, Art Education, Art History, Ceramics, Drawing, Graphic Design, Illustration, Painting, Photography, Printmaking, Sculpture
Summer School: Chmn, John H Cleverdon. Courses—Art Appreciation, Art History, Ceramics, Drawing, Graphic Design, Painting

MONROEVILLE

ALABAMA SOUTHERN COMMUNITY COLLEGE, Art Dept, PO Box 200, 36461. Tel 334-575-3156; *Chmn* Dr Margaret H Murphy
Sch estab 1965; dept estab 1971; pub; D & E; SC 6, LC 1; enrl D 25, E 8, non-maj 23, maj 3
Ent Req: HS dipl, GED
Degrees: AA & AS 2 yrs
Tuition: Res—undergrad $2950 per cr hr
Courses: Art Appreciation, Drafting, †Drawing, †Painting, Stage Design, Theatre Arts

MONTEVALLO

UNIVERSITY OF MONTEVALLO, College of Fine Arts, Art Department, 35115. Tel 205-665-6000; *Chmn* Sandra Jordan; *Dean* L Frank McCoy
Estab 1896; pub; D & E; scholarships, Work Study; SC 35, LC 10, GC 7; enrl Maj 120, others 2800
Ent Req: ACT
Degrees: BA, BS, BFA, BM, MA, MM
Tuition: $490 per sem
Courses: Advertising Design, Art Appreciation, Art Education, Art History, Ceramics, Commercial Art, Design, †Drawing, †Graphic Arts, †Graphic Design, †Painting, †Photography, †Printmaking, †Sculpture
Children's Classes: Enrl 20; tuition $30 per 10 wk term. Courses—General Studio
Summer School: Dir, Sandra Jordan. Enrl 1000; two 5 wk sessions beginning June 5 & July 5

MONTGOMERY

ALABAMA STATE UNIVERSITY, Art Dept, 915 S Jackson, 36101. Tel 334-229-4474; FAX 334-229-4920; *Act Dept Chmn* Dr William Colvin
Degrees: BA, BS
Tuition: Res—undergrad $750 per sem; nonres—undergrad $1500 per sem
Courses: Advertising Design, Art Appreciation, Art History, Calligraphy, Ceramics, Design, Drawing, Handicrafts, Printmaking, Photography, Printmaking, Stage Design, Graphics

AUBURN UNIVERSITY AT MONTGOMERY, Dept of Fine Arts, 36193. Tel 334-244-3377; *Head Dept* Joseph Schwarz, PhD; *Dean School Liberal Arts* Robbie Walker; *Prof* Philip Coley, MFA; *Prof* Richard Mills, MFA; *Assoc Prof* Mark Benson, PhD; *Assoc Prof* Susan Hood, PhD; *Asst Prof* Sue Jensen, MFA
Estab 1972; pub; D & E; scholarships; SC 18, LC 5, GC 4; enrl D 400, non-maj 200, maj 125
Ent Req: HS dipl
Degrees: BA
Tuition: Res—$675 per qtr; non res—$2025 per qtr
Courses: Art Education, Art History, Ceramics, Drawing, Graphic Arts, Graphic Design, Painting, Photography, Sculpture
Adult Hobby Classes: Courses—Ceramics, Painting
Summer School: Head, Joseph Schwarz. Tuition $675. Courses—same as above

HUNTINGDON COLLEGE, Dept of Art, 1500 E Fairview Ave, 36106-2148. Tel 334-265-0511, Ext 454; *Chmn* Christopher Payne, MFA
Estab 1973; E; enrl 119
Tuition: $5800 per yr
Courses: Art Appreciation, Art Education, Art History, Ceramics, Design, Drawing, Graphic Design, Painting, Photography, Printmaking, Teacher Training, Theatre Arts, Art in Religion
Adult Hobby Classes: Enrl 119; tuition $80 per hr. Courses—Art Appreciation, Beginning Drawing, Ceramics, Painting
Summer School: Enrl 329; tuition $800 per term for 6 hrs in Art. Courses—Ceramics, Drawing, Painting, Photography

NORMAL

ALABAMA A & M UNIVERSITY, Art & Art Education Dept, PO Box 26, 35762. Tel 205-851-5516; *Head Dept* William L Boyd; *Assoc Prof* Jimmie Dawkins, MFA; *Assoc Prof* William W Nance, MFA; *Assoc Prof* Oscar Logan, PhD; *Asst Prof* Allen Davis
Estab 1875, dept estab 1966; pub; D & E; scholarships; SC 18, LC 3; enrl non-maj 430, maj 35, grad 10
Ent Req: HS dipl
Degrees: BS (Commercial Art & Art Education), MS, MEd (Art Educ)
Tuition: Res—undergrad $850 per sem, grad $103 per sem; nonres—undergrad $1700 per sem, grad $206 per sem
Courses: †Advertising Design, Art Appreciation, †Art Education, †Commercial Art, Drawing, Graphic Arts, Jewelry, Painting, Photography, Printmaking, Sculpture, Weaving, Fibers, Glass Blowing
Adult Hobby Classes: Enrl 10 - 15; tuition $89 per sem. Courses offered in all areas
Children's Classes: Enrl 15 - 20; tuition $89 per sem. Courses offered in all areas
Summer School: Dir, Dr Clifton Pearson. Enrl 50; tuition $426 for 8 wk sem. Courses—Art Education, Art History, Ceramics

TROY

TROY STATE UNIVERSITY, Dept of Art & Classics, 36082. Tel 334-670-3391; FAX 334-670-3390; *Dean School of Fine Arts* Dr John M Long; *Chmn* Peter Howard; *Asst Prof* Pamela Allen; *Asst Prof* S L Shillabeer. Instrs: FT 5
Estab 1957. University has 2 other campuses; pub; scholarships; SC 23, LC 11
Ent Req: HS grad, ent exam
Degrees: BA and BS (Arts & Sciences), MS
Tuition: Res—undergrad $20 per cr hr, grad $22.50 per cr hr; in- state $465 12-18 cr hrs; out-of-state $690 12-18 cr hrs
Courses: Art Education, †Art History, Commercial Art, Drawing, Graphic Arts, Handicrafts, Jewelry, Lettering, Painting, Photography, Silversmithing, Teacher Training, Museology, Pottery
Adult Hobby Classes: Courses—Basketry, Crafts, Matting & Framing
Children's Classes: Enrl 30. Courses—Summer Workshop
Summer School: Dir, Robert Stampfli. Enrl 100; tuition $600 for June 12-Aug 11 term. Courses—Art Appreciation, Art Education, Art History, Drawing, Painting

TUSCALOOSA

STILLMAN COLLEGE, Stillman Art Gallery & Art Dept, 3601 15th St, PO Box 1430, 35403. Tel 205-349-4240, Ext 8860; *Prof* R L Guffin, MFA; *Asst Prof* Keyser Wilson, MFA
Estab 1876, dept estab 1951; pvt den; D; SC 8, LC 2; enrl D 73, non-maj 73
Ent Req: HS dipl, ent exam
Tuition: $5200 per yr; campus res—room & board $3100 per yr
Courses: Art Education, Art History, Ceramics, Commercial Art, Design, Drawing, Mixed Media, Painting, Sculpture, Afro-American Art History

UNIVERSITY OF ALABAMA, Art Dept, PO Box 870270, 35487-0270. Tel 205-348-5967; Elec Mail wbaker@woodsquad.as.ua.edu. *Chmn Dept* W Lowell Baker
Estab 1831, dept estab 1919; pub; D & E; scholarships; SC 43, LC 12, GC 18; enrl D 750, maj 200, grad 30
Ent Req: HS dipl, ACT
Degrees: BA and BFA 4 yr, MFA 3 yr, MA (art) 2 yr
Tuition: Res—undergrad & grad $905 per sem; nonres—undergrad & grad $2243 per sem; campus res available
Courses: Advertising Design, Aesthetics, Art Appreciation, Art History, Ceramics, Commercial Art, Constructions, Costume Design & Construction, Design, Display, Drafting, Drawing,

Fashion Arts, Graphic Arts, Graphic Design, History of Art & Archaeology, Intermedia, Interior Design, Mixed Media, Museum Staff Training, Painting, Photography, Printmaking, Sculpture, Stage Design, Textile Design, Theatre Arts
Children's Classes: Enrl 70; tuition $52-$70 for 5 wk term. Courses—Discoveries, Drawing, Explorations, Photography, 3-D Design
Summer School: Tuition $358.31 per sem. Courses—Art History, Ceramics, Foundation, Graphic Design, Painting, Photography, Printmaking, Sculpture

TUSKEGEE

TUSKEGEE UNIVERSITY, Liberal Arts & Education, 36088. Tel 334-727-8913; *Dept Chmn* Uthman Abdur-Rahman; *Instr* Carla Jackson-Reese
Estab 1881; pvt
Courses: Art Appreciation, Art Education, Design Foundation

ALASKA

ANCHORAGE

UNIVERSITY OF ALASKA ANCHORAGE, Dept of Art, College of Arts and Sciences, 3211 Providence Dr, 99508. Tel 907-786-1783; FAX 907-786-1799; *Chmn* Christine Erikson. Instrs: FT 11, PT 15
Pub; D & E; scholarships; SC 43, LC 7-9; enrl College of Arts & Sciences FT 1310
Ent Req: Open enrl
Degrees: BA in art, BFA 4 yr
Tuition: Res—$55 per cr, $660 for 12 or more cr; nonres—$55 per 3 cr, $1980, 9 or more cr
Courses: †Art Education, †Ceramics, †Drawing, Graphic Design, Illustration, †Painting, †Photography, †Printmaking, †Sculpture
Adult Hobby Classes: Same as regular prog
Summer School: Dir, Dennis Edwards. One term of 10 wks beginning May or two 5 wk sessions. Courses—Art Appreciation, Art Education, Native Art History, Photography & various studio courses

FAIRBANKS

UNIVERSITY OF ALASKA-FAIRBANKS, Dept of Art, Fine Arts Complex, Rm 310, PO Box 755640, 99775-5640. Tel 907-474-7530; Elec Mail fyart@aurora.alaska.edu. *Dept Head* Kesler Woodward; *Prof* Glen C Simpson; *Prof* Arthur W Brody; *Assoc Prof* Barbara Alexander; *Asst Prof* Wendy Croskrey; *Asst Prof* Todd Sherman; *Asst Prof* Larry Vienneau; *Asst Prof* Alvin Amason; *Vis Asst Prof* Tom Rohr
Estab 1963; pub; D & E; scholarships; SC 28, LC 4; enrl D 293, E 50, maj 45
Ent Req: HS dipl
Degrees: BA, BFA
Tuition: Res—$200 per sem; nonres $780 per sem
Courses: Art History, Ceramics, †Drawing, †Painting, †Printmaking, †Sculpture, Computer Art, Metalsmithing, Native Art
Children's Classes: Enrl 50. Courses—Ceramics, Drawing, Design, Metalsmithing, Painting, Sculpture. Under the direction of the downtown center
Summer School: Dir, J Henricks. Enrl 65; 6 wk term. Courses—Ceramics, Drawing, Printmaking, Sculpture

ARIZONA

DOUGLAS

COCHISE COLLEGE, Art Dept, 4910 Hwy 80, 85607-9724. Tel 520-364-7943, Ext 225; *Instr Dept Head* Monte Surratt; *Instr* Manual Martinez. Instrs: PT 7
Estab 1965, department estab 1965; pub; D & E; scholarships; SC 12, LC 2; enrl D 280, E 225, maj 20
Ent Req: HS dipl, GED
Degrees: AA 2 yrs(Painting & Sculpture)
Tuition: Res—$26 per unit per sem; nonres—$39 per 1-6 units; $158 per over 6 units sem
Courses: Art History, Ceramics, Drawing, Jewelry, Painting, Photography, Printmaking, Sculpture, Art, Appreciation, Color & Design, Commercial Design, Special Topics in Art
Adult Hobby Classes: Courses—Painting

FLAGSTAFF

NORTHERN ARIZONA UNIVERSITY, School of Art & Design, 86011. Tel 520-523-4612; FAX 520-523-3333; *Dir* Dr Joel Eide; *Prof* Dr D Bendel, EdD; *Prof* Dr Ronald Piotrowski, EdD; *Assoc Prof* J Cornett, MFA; *Assoc Prof* J O'Hara, MFA; *Assoc Prof* B Horn, MFA; *Assoc Prof* C Piotrowski; *Asst Prof* A Bakovych, MA
Estab 1899; pub; D & E; scholarships; SC 56, LC 19, GC 8-10; enrl D 400, E 100, non-maj 342, maj 300, grad 30
Ent Req: HS dipl, ACT
Degrees: BA & BS 4 yr, MA(Art Educ)
Tuition: Res—undergrad $947 per sem; nonres—undergrad $278 per cr hr, $3340 per sem (12 cr hr); campus res available
Courses: Art History, Ceramics, Interior Design, Jewelry, Painting, Printmaking, Sculpture, †Fashion Merchandising, †Fine Arts, †Metalsmithing
Adult Hobby Classes: Most of the above studio areas
Children's Classes: Enrl 80; tuition $5 for 5 Sat. Courses—Ceramics, Drawing, Painting, Puppetry
Summer School: Dir, Richard Beasley. Enrl 150; tuition $46 per cr. Courses—Most regular courses

HOLBROOK

NORTHLAND PIONEER COLLEGE, Art Dept, 1200 E Hermosa Dr, PO Box 610, 86025. Tel 520-524-6111; FAX 520-524-2772; *Dir* Pat Wolf, MS. Instrs: FT 2, PT 60
Estab 1974; pub; D & E; SC 28, LC 2
Degrees: AA, Assoc of Applied Sci 2 yr
Tuition: Res—$20 per sem, nonres—$1125 per sem
Courses: Art History, Calligraphy, Ceramics, Commercial Art, Drawing, Graphic Arts, Art Appreciation, Design, Painting, Photography, Lettering, Printmaking, Sculpture, Textile Design, Weaving, Crafts
Adult Hobby Classes: Courses—Same as above
Summer School: 4 wk session in June

MESA

MESA COMMUNITY COLLEGE, Dept of Art & Art History, 1833 W Southern Ave, 85202. Tel 602-461-7524, 461-7000 (main); *Chmn Art Dept* Sarah Capawana; *Instr* Carole Drachler, PhD; *Instr* Jim Garrison, MA; *Instr* Linda Speranza; *Instr* Darlene Swain, MFA; *Instr* Robert Galloway
Estab 1965; pub; D & E; schol; SC 10, LC 8; enrl D 667, E 394
Ent Req: HS dipl or GED
Degrees: AA 2 yrs
Tuition: Res—$34 per cr hr, nonres—out of state $150 per cr hr, out of county $121 per cr hr, audit $25 per hr
Courses: †Advertising Design, Art Appreciation, †Art History, †Ceramics, †Drawing, Film, Interior Design, Jewelry, †Painting, †Photography, Weaving, Crafts

PHOENIX

GRAND CANYON UNIVERSITY, Art Dept, 3300 W Camelback Rd, 85017. Tel 602-249-3300, Ext 2840; *Art Dept Chair* Tim Kimmerman; *Res Artist* Esmeralda Delaney, MFA; *Instr* Arlene Besore, BFA; *Instr* Greg Osterman, BS
Estab 1949; den; D & E; scholarships; SC 23, LC 10; enrl D 106, E 25, non-maj 75, maj 30
Ent Req: HS dipl
Degrees: BA & BS
Tuition: Res—undergrad $8860 per yr, $268 per hr; nonres—undergrad $8860 per yr, $268 per hr; campus res available
Courses: Aesthetics, Art History, Ceramics, †Drawing, †Jewelry, †Graphic Design, †Mixed Media, †Painting, †Photography, †Printmaking, †Sculpture, †Teacher Training, Professional Artist Workshop
Children's Classes: Enrl 31; tuition $25. Courses—Ceramics, Composition, Drawing, Sculpture

PHOENIX COLLEGE, Dept of Art & Photography, 1202 W Thomas Rd, 85013. Tel 602-285-7276, 285-7280 (Mercer); *Chmn* Joan Ritsch; *Coordr, Photograph Dept* John Mercer. Instrs: FT 5, PT 22
Estab 1920; pub; scholarships
Ent Req: HS dipl
Degrees: AA & AG 2 yrs
Tuition: Res—undergrad $34 per cr hr
Courses: Art Education, Ceramics, Commercial Art, Drawing, Painting, Photography, Sculpture, Basic Design, Computer Design, Computer Graphics
Adult Hobby Classes: Enrl 500; tuition $22.50 for 16 wks. Courses—Full range incl Computer Art
Summer School: Dir, John Mercer. Enrl 100; two 5 wk sessions. Courses—Intro to Art, Western Art

PRESCOTT

YAVAPAI COLLEGE, Visual & Performing Arts Division, 1100 E Sheldon, 86301. Tel 520-445-7300, 776-2312 (Karyn), 776-2006 (Kelly); *Chmn* Richard Marcusen, MFA; *Instr* Edward V Branson, MA; *Instr* Beth LaCour, MFA; *Instr* Glen L Peterson, EdD; *Instr* Vincent Kelly, MA; *Instr* Dr Will Fisher; *Instr* Roy Breiling
Estab 1966, dept estab 1969; pub; D & E; scholarships; SC 50, LC 50; enrl D 1650, E 1563
Ent Req: HS dipl
Degrees: AA 2 yr
Courses: Advertising Design, Art History, Ceramics, Drawing, Graphic Design, Painting, Sculpture
Adult Hobby Classes: Enrl open; tuition per course. Courses offered through Retirement College
Children's Classes: Enrl open; tuition $15 per course. Courses—Ceramics, Drawing, Painting
Summer School: Dir, Donald D Hiserodt. Enrl open; tuition $12 per sem hr for term of 6 wks beginning June 4. Courses—Ceramics, Drawing, Jewelry, Painting, Photography, Printmaking

SCOTTSDALE

SCOTTSDALE ARTISTS' SCHOOL, 3720 N Marshall Way, PO Box 8527, 85252-8527. Tel 602-990-1422; FAX 602-990-0652; WATS 800-333-5707. *Exec Dir* Ruth Kaspar
Estab 1983; D & E; scholarships; enrl 2500
Courses: Drawing, Painting, Printmaking, Sculpture

TEMPE

ARIZONA STATE UNIVERSITY
—School of Art, 85287-1505. Tel 602-965-3468; FAX 602-965-8338; *Dir* Julie Codell, PhD
Estab 1885; pub; D & E; scholarships & fels; SC 88, LC 70, GC 116; enrl D 44,500, maj 960, grad 175
Ent Req: HS dipl, ACT
Degrees: BA & BFA 4 yrs, MFA 3 yrs, MA 2 yrs, EdD 3 yrs
Tuition: Res—undergrad & grad $764 per sem; nonres—undergrad & grad $3467 per sem; campus res—room & board $4110
Courses: Art Education, Art History, Ceramics, Drawing, Graphic Design, Intermedia, Jewelry, Painting, Photography, Printmaking, Sculpture, Fibers, Computer Art, Video Art
Children's Classes: Enrl 390. Courses—Studio
Summer School: Dir, Julie Codell. Enrl 500; tuition $93 per sem hr. Courses—Varies
—College of Architecture & Environmental Design, 85287. Tel 602-965-8169; FAX 602-965-0894; *Dean* John Meunier; *Dir Archit* Michael Underhill, McPUD; *Dir Design* Robert L Wolf, MFA; *Chmn Planning* Frederick Steiner
Estab 1885, college estab 1949; pub; D & E; enrl lower div 212, upper div 466, grad 135
Ent Req: HS dipl, SAT
Degrees: BA, MA
Tuition: Res—$914 per sem; nonres—$3717 per sem
Courses: Architecture, Interior Design, Mixed Media, Photography, Graphics, History, Sketching
Summer School: Courses—lower & upper div courses primarily in Design, Graphics, History, Sketching and Rendering

THATCHER

EASTERN ARIZONA COLLEGE, Art Dept, 600 Church St, 85552. Tel 520-428-8233; FAX 520-428-8462; *Instr* James Gentry; *Instr* Richard Green, PhD. Instrs: PT 14
Estab 1888, dept estab 1946; pub; D & E; scholarships; SC 25, LC 3; enrl D 105, E 202, maj 30
Ent Req: HS dipl or GED
Degrees: AA & AAS 2 yrs
Tuition: Res—$314 per sem; nonres—$1960 per sem
Courses: Advertising Design, Art Appreciation, Art History, Calligraphy, Ceramics, Design, Drawing, Photography, Printmaking, Sculpture, Silversmithing, Stage Design, Weaving, Airbrush, Fibers, Gem Faceting, Lapidary, Life Drawing, Stained Glass, Wood Carving

TUCSON

TUCSON MUSEUM OF ART SCHOOL, 140 N Main Ave, 85701. Tel 520-624-2333; FAX 520-624-7202; *Dir Educ* Judith D'Agostino. Instrs: PT 30
Estab 1924; pvt; D & E; scholarships; SC 42, LC 2; enrl D & E 1139
Ent Req: None
Tuition: Varies per course; no campus res
Courses: Art Appreciation, Art History, Ceramics, Collages, Constructions, Design, Drawing, Intermedia, Mixed Media, Painting, Photography, Printmaking, Sculpture, Theatre Arts, Docent Training
Adult Hobby Classes: Enrl 300; tuition $120-180 for 12 wks. Courses—Ceramics, Design, Drawing, Painting, Printmaking, Sculpture
Children's Classes: Ceramics, Drawing, Painting, Photography, Primary Art, Sculpture
Summer School: Dir, Judith D'Agostino. Enrl 800; tuition $60 half day, $145 full day per wk. Courses—Ceramics, Design, Drama, Drawing, Painting, Photography, Printmaking, Puppetry, Sculpture

UNIVERSITY OF ARIZONA, Dept of Art, Art Bldg, Rm 108, PO Box 210002, 85721. Tel 520-621-1251, 621-7570; *Foundations, Dept Head* Andrew W Polk III; *Regents Prof* Robert Colescott, MA; *Prof Jewelry & Metalsmithing* Michael Croft, MFA; *Prof Painting & Drawing* Peggy Bailey Doogan; *Prof Sculpture* Moira Geoffrion, MFA; *Prof Emerita* Judith Golden, MFA; *Prof Art Educ* Dwaine Greer, PhD; *Prof Painting & Drawing* Harmony Hammond, MA; *Prof Painting & Drawing* Chuck Hitner, MFA; *Prof Photography* Harold Jones, MFA; *Prof Fibers* Gayle Wimmer, MFA; *Prof Painting & Drawing* Bruce McGrew, MFA; *Prof Art History* Lee Parry, PhD; *Prof Painting & Drawing* Barbara Rogers, MA; *Assoc Prof Art History* Keith McElroy, PhD; *Prof Graphic Design-Illustration* Jackson Boelts, MFA; *Assoc Prof Graphic Illustration* Jerold Bishop, MFA; *Assoc Prof Drawing & Printmaking* Rosemarie Bernardi, MFA; *Assoc Prof Ceramics* Aurore Chabot, MFA; *Assoc Prof Sculpture* John Heric, MFA; *Assoc Prof* Bart Morse, MFA; *Assoc Prof Painting & Drawing* Barbara Penn, MFA; *Assoc Prof Printmaking* Andrew Polk, MFA; *Assoc Prof Photography* Ken Shorr, MFA; *Assoc Prof Graphic Design-Illustration* David Christiana, MFA; *Asst Prof Art History* Pia Cuneo, PhD; *Assoc Prof Art Educ* Lynn Galbraith, PhD; *Asst Prof Art History* Paul Ivey, PhD; *Asst Prof Gallery Management* Sheila Pitt, MFA; *Asst Prof Art History* Julie Plax, PhD; *Assoc Prof Painting & Drawing* Alfred Quiroz, MFA; *Asst Prof New Genre* Joyan Saunders, MFA; *Assoc Prof Art History* Stacie Widdifield, PhD; *Assoc Prof Art History* Jane Williams, PhD; *Asst Prof Graphic Design-Illustration* Ellen McMahon; *Asst Prof Art History* Sarah Moore, PhD; *Assoc Prof Art History* Mikelle Omari; *Assoc Prof Art Educ* Elizabeth Garber
Estab 1891, dept estab 1893; pub; D; scholarships; SC 30, LC 21, GC 32; enrl D 3094, maj 600, grad 100
Ent Req: Res—undergrad $919 per 7 units; grad $942 per 7 units per sem; campus res available
Degrees: BFA(Studio), BFA(Art Educ) and BA(Art History) 4 yrs, MFA(Studio) and MA(Art History or Art Educ) 2-3 yrs
Tuition: Res—undergrad $770 per 7 units, 1-6 units $80 per sem hr; grad $1922 per 7 units per sem; campus res—available
Courses: Advertising Design, †Art Education, †Art History, †Ceramics, †Drawing, †Graphic Design, †Illustration, †Painting, †Photography, †Printmaking, †Sculpture, Teacher Training, Video, Weaving, Printmaking, Sculpture, Fibers, New Genre
Summer School: Presession & two sessions offered. Request catalog (available in April) by writing to: Summer Session Office, Univ of Arizona, Tucson, AZ 85721

ARKANSAS

ARKADELPHIA

OUACHITA BAPTIST UNIVERSITY, Dept of Art, OBU Box 3785, 71998-0001. Tel 501-245-5564; Elec Mail halabyr@obu.edu. *Chmn* Dr Raouf Halaby; *Dean School Fine Arts* Charles Wright; *Instr* Malde Jones; *Instr* Sandy McDowell
Estab 1886, dept estab 1934; den; D; scholarship; SC 11, LC 2
Ent Req: HS dipl, ACT
Degrees: BA, BSE, BS and BME 4 yr
Tuition: $3495 per sem
Courses: Art Education, Art History, Ceramics, Commercial Art, Drawing, Handicrafts, History of Art & Archaeology, Illustration, Jewelry, Painting, Sculpture, Teacher Training, †Theatre Arts, Public School Arts
Summer School: Dir, Jim Berryman. Enrl 550; tuition $50 sem hr; two terms of 5 wks beginning June 1

CLARKSVILLE

UNIVERSITY OF THE OZARKS, Dept of Art, 415 College Ave, 72830. Tel 501-754-3839; *Prof* Blaine Caldwell; *Asst Prof* Nancy Farrell
Estab 1836, dept estab 1952; den; D; schol; SC 9, LC 2; enrl D 83, non-maj 8, maj 17
Ent Req: HS dipl, ACT
Degrees: BA & BS 4 yr
Tuition: Res—undergrad $2500 per sem
Courses: Design, Sculpture, Art Appreciation
Summer School: Drawing, History of Contemporary Art, Sculpture, Watercolor

CONWAY

UNIVERSITY OF CENTRAL ARKANSAS, Art Dept, 72032. Tel 501-450-3113; Elec Mail kenb@ccl.uca.edu. *Chair* Dr Kenneth Burchett; *Prof* Patrick Larsen; *Prof* Robert C Thompson; *Prof* Helen Phillips; *Assoc Prof* Gayle Seymour; *Assoc Prof* Roger Bowman; *Assoc Prof* Andrew Cohen; *Assoc Prof* Cathy Caldwell; *Assoc Prof* Bryan Massey; *Assoc Prof* Lyn Brands Wallace; *Asst Prof* Jeff Young. Instrs: FT 11, PT 6
Estab 1908; pub; scholarships; SC 26, LC 16
Ent Req: HS dipl
Degrees: BFA, BA
Tuition: Res $1196 12 hrs & up; nonres—additional fee $986, summer term res—$111 per cr hr; nonres—$222 per cr hr
Courses: Art Appreciation, †Art Education, †Art History, †Ceramics, Design, Drawing, †Graphic Design, †Painting, †Printmaking, †Sculpture, Advanced Studio, Color, Crafts, Figure
Summer School: Dir, Kenneth Burchett. Tuition $72 per sem hr. Courses—various

FAYETTEVILLE

UNIVERSITY OF ARKANSAS, Art Dept, 116 Fine Arts Bldg, 72701. Tel 501-575-5202; FAX 501-575-2062; Elec Mail artdept@vafsysb.uark.edu. *Dept Chairperson* Michael Peven; *Prof Emeritus* Neppie Conner, MFA; *Prof* Myron Brody, MFA; *Prof* Ken Stout, MFA; *Assoc Prof* Robert Ross, MFA; *Assoc Prof* Donald Harington, MA; *Asst Prof* Lynn Jacobs, PhD; *Asst Prof* Walter D Curtis, MFA; *Asst Prof* Kristin Musgnug, MFA; *Asst Prof* John Newman, MFA; *Asst Prof* Jacqueline Golden, MFA; *Asst Prof* Marilyn Nelson, MFA. Instrs: FT 13
Estab 1871; pub; D & E; SC 34, LC 16, GC 20; enrl D 14,000, non-maj 950, maj 115, grad 15
Ent Req: HS dipl, ent exam, GED
Degrees: MFA 60 cr hours & BA 4 yrs
Tuition: Res—$774 per sem; nonres—$1950 per sem; campus res—available
Courses: Art Appreciation, †Art Education, †Art History, Ceramics, Design, Drawing, Graphic Design, Jewelry, Painting, Photography, Printmaking, Sculpture
Adult Hobby Classes: Enrl 100; tuition res $500 & nonres $1256 per sem. Courses—Ceramics, Painting, Sculpture
Summer School: Dir, M Peven. Enrl 150; 6 wk session. Courses—Ceramics, Drawing, Painting, Photography, 2-D Design, 3-D Design

HARRISON

NORTH ARKANSAS COMMUNITY-TECHNICAL COLLEGE, Art Dept, Pioneer Ridge, 72601. Tel 501-743-3000, Ext 311; FAX 501-743-3577; *Chmn Div of Communications & Arts* Bill Skinner
Estab 1974, dept estab 1975; pub; D & E; SC 7, LC 1; enrl in art dept D 80, E 30-40, non-maj 45, maj 35
Ent Req: HS dipl
Degrees: AA 2 yrs
Tuition: County res—$31 per cr hr; non-county res—$40 per cr hr; nonres—$78 per cr hr
Courses: Art Appreciation, Commercial Art, Costume Design & Construction, Drafting, Drawing, Graphic Design, Painting, Elementary Art Education
Adult Hobby Classes: Various courses offered each sem through Continuing Education Program
Summer School: Enrl 20-30; tuition $30-$35 for term of 6-8 wks beginning June 1. Courses—open; Art Workshop on Buffalo National River

HELENA

PHILLIPS COUNTY COMMUNITY COLLEGE, Dept of English & Fine Arts, PO Box 785, 72342. Tel 501-338-6474; *Art Instr* Stanley Cobb
Estab 1966; pub; D & E; scholarships; SC 8, LC 1; enrl 55
Ent Req: HS dipl, ent exam, GED
Degrees: AA and AAS 2 yr
Tuition: $35-$40 12 sessions
Courses: Pottery

LITTLE ROCK

THE ARKANSAS ARTS CENTER, Museum School, PO Box 2137, 72203. Tel 501-372-4000; FAX 501-375-8053; *Chief Cur* Townsend Wolfe; *Dir Museum School* Michael Preble, MA; *Instr* Maribeth Anders, BA; *Instr* Gayle Batson, BA; *Instr* Virginia Baltosser, BA; *Instr* Angela Cummings, BA; *Instr* Patsy Daggett; *Instr* Rick Hall; *Instr* Sharon Struthers; *Instr* Jackie Kaucher; *Instr* Shep Miers, MFA; *Instr* Bob Ocken; *Instr* Billy Peebles; *Instr* Selma Blackburn; *Instr* Nancy Wilson, MA; *Instr* Jean Mross; *Instr* Dominique Simmons, BA; *Instr* Rick Hall; *Instr* Gary Hufford; *Instr* Lou Tobian; *Instr* Kevin Kresse; *Instr* Martha Jordon. Instrs: 25
Estab 1960, dept estab 1965; pub; D & E; scholarships; SC 62, LC 3; enrl D 350, E 300 children & adults
Ent Req: Open to anyone age 2 through adult
Tuition: 10 wk course for adults $95-$125; 10 wk course for children $65-$75
Courses: Aesthetics, Art Appreciation, Art History, Ceramics, Drawing, History of Art & Archaeology, Jewelry, Mixed Media, Painting, Photography, Sculpture, Jewelry, Lettering, Mixed Media, Painting, Photography, Sculpture, Teacher Training, Glass Fusing, Stained Glass, Woodworking
Adult Hobby Classes: Enrl 1265; tuition $95-$125 for 10 wk term
Children's Classes: Enrl 1373; tuition $65-$75 for 10 wk term. Courses—Theater Arts, Visual Arts
Summer School: Same as above

UNIVERSITY OF ARKANSAS AT LITTLE ROCK, Fine Arts Galleries, 2801 S University, 72204. Tel 501-569-3182; FAX 501-569-8775; *Chmn* Jane Brown. Instrs: FT 12, PT 5
Estab 1928; pub; D & E; scholarships; SC, LC; enrl Univ sem 10,200, dept sem 1100
Ent Req: HS grad
Degrees: BA 4 yr, MA(studio), MA(art history)
Tuition: $1131 per sem
Courses: Art Appreciation, Art Education, †Art History, Ceramics, Commercial Art, Design, Drawing, Graphic Design, Illustration, Painting, Photography, Printmaking, Sculpture, Pottery, †Studio Art
Summer School: Dean, Deborah Baldwin. Enrl 250; tuition $584 per sem. Courses—Art Appreciation, Art Education, Art History, Studio Art

MAGNOLIA

SOUTHERN ARKANSAS UNIVERSITY, Dept of Art, 100 E University, 71753-5000. Tel 501-235-4242; FAX 501-235-5005; *Chmn* Jerry Johnson, MFA; *Asst Prof* Steven Ochs, MFA; *Instr* Ralph Larmann, MFA
Estab 1909; pub; D & E; scholarships; SC 18, LC 4; enrl D 240, non-maj 260, maj 40
Ent Req: HS dipl
Degrees: BA & BSE 4 yr
Tuition: Res—undergrad $1080 per yr; nonres—undergrad $1250 per yr
Courses: Advertising Design, Art Appreciation, Art Education, Art History, †Ceramics, Commercial Art, Design, Drafting, Drawing, Graphic Arts, †Graphic Design, †Painting, †Printmaking, †Sculpture
Adult Hobby Classes: Classes & courses open to all at regular tuition rates
Children's Classes: Enrl 30; tuition $30. Courses—Kinder Art
Summer School: Dir, Jerry Johnson. Enrl 60. Courses—Art, Fine Arts

MONTICELLO

UNIVERSITY OF ARKANSAS AT MONTICELLO, Fine Arts Dept, PO Box 3607, 71655. Tel 501-460-1060; *Chmn* Dr Paul C Denny Jr
Scholarships
Degrees: BA
Tuition: Res—undergrad $705 per sem, $82.75 per cr hr; waiver from MI, LA, TX
Courses: Art Appreciation, †Art Education, Ceramics, Design, Drawing, Graphic Arts, History of Art & Archaeology, Mixed Media, Painting, Printmaking
Summer School: Dir, Paul Denny, Jr. Enrl 25; tuition $65 per cr hr for June-July. Courses—Art Appreciation, Art Education

PINE BLUFF

UNIVERSITY OF ARKANSAS AT PINE BLUFF, Art Dept, N University Dr, 71601. Tel 501-543-8236, 543-8238; *Dept Chmn* Henri Linton
Scholarships
Degrees: BS
Tuition: Undergrad—$840 per sem nonres— $1944 per sem
Courses: Art Appreciation, Art Education, Art History, Calligraphy, Ceramics, Design, Drawing, Handicrafts, Painting, Photography, Printmaking, Sculpture, Textile Design, Weaving

RUSSELLVILLE

ARKANSAS TECH UNIVERSITY, Dept of Art, 72801. Tel 501-968-0244; *Head Dept* Ron Reynolds, MA; *Assoc Prof* Gary Barnes, MFA; *Asst Prof* John Mori, MFA; *Assoc Prof* John Sullivan, MFA
Estab 1909; pub; D & E; scholarships; SC 28, LC 5, GC 1; enrl D 200, non-maj 130, maj 88
Ent Req: Ent req HS dipl, ACT, SAT
Degrees: BA 4 yr
Tuition: Res—undergrad $951 per sem, $84 per cr hr, grad $86 per cr hr; nonres—undergrad $1902 per sem, $168 per cr hr, grad $172 per cr hr; no campus res
Courses: Advertising Design, Architecture, Art Education, Art History, Ceramics, Display, Drawing, Graphic Arts, Illustration, Industrial Design, Lettering, Painting, Printmaking, Teacher Training, †Fine Arts, Intro to Art, Packaging Design
Adult Hobby Classes: Drawing, Oil Painting, Watercolor
Summer School: Head Dept, Ron Reynolds. Enrl 30-50; tuition res $84 per cr hr, nonres $168 per cr hr; terms of 6 wks beginning June 8 & July 12. Courses—Art Education, Art History, Ceramics, Design, Drawing, Painting

SEARCY

HARDING UNIVERSITY, Dept of Art, PO Box 2253, 72149-0001. Tel 501-279-4000, Ext 4426; *Chmn Dept* Don D Robinson, MA; *Prof* Faye Doran, EdD; *Prof* Paul Pitt, MFA; *Assoc Prof* John Keller, PhD; *Asst Prof* Daniel Adams, MFA; *Instr* Janie Giles; *Lectr* Beverly Austin
Estab 1924; pvt; D; schol; SC 27, LC 9, GC 7; enrl D 103, non-maj 25, maj 103
Ent Req: HS dipl, ACT
Degrees: BA, BS and BFA 4 yrs, MEd 5-6 yrs
Tuition: $227.50 per sem hr; campus res—room & board $3184 per yr
Courses: Advertising Design, Aesthetics, Architecture, Art Appreciation, Art Education, Art History, Ceramics, Design, Drafting, Drawing, Graphic Arts, Graphic Design, Interior Design, Jewelry, Painting, Printmaking, Sculpture, Silversmithing, Teacher Training, Weaving, †Art Therapy, Color Theory, Computer Graphics, 2-D Design
Summer School: Dir, Dr Dean Priest. Enrl 1000; tuition per sem hr for two 16 wk sessions beginning August. Courses—Vary depending upon the demand, usually Art Education, Art History, Ceramics, Drawing, Graphic Design, Interior Design, Painting

SILOAM SPRINGS

JOHN BROWN UNIVERSITY, Art Dept, 2000 W University, 72761. Tel 501-524-3131, Ext 182; *Head Dept* Charles Peer; *Asst Prof* David Andrus
Estab 1919; pvt; D; scholarships; SC 9, LC 3
Ent Req: HS grad
Degrees: AS(Art)
Tuition: $2700 yr, $1350 per sem, $112.50 per sem hr; campus res—room & board $2100
Courses: Art Appreciation, Art Education, Drawing, Painting, Composition, Design & Color, Crafts (copper tooling, enameling, jewelry, macrame, mosaic, pottery, weaving)

STATE UNIVERSITY

ARKANSAS STATE UNIVERSITY, Dept of Art, PO Box 1920, 72467. Tel 501-972-3050; FAX 501-972-3932; Elec Mail csteele@aztec.astate.edu. *Chmn* Curtis Steele, MFA; *Prof* Evan Lindquist, MFA; *Prof* William Allen, PhD; *Prof* Steven L Mayes, MFA; *Prof* Tom Chaffee, MFA; *Prof* William Rowe, MFA; *Prof* John Keech, MFA; *Assoc Prof* Roger Carlisle, MFA; *Assoc Prof* Curtis Steele; *Assoc Prof* Debra Satterfield, MFA; *Assoc Prof* John J Salvest, MFA; *Asst Prof* Dr Paul Hickman, PhD; *Instr* Gayle Ross, MFA; *Instr* Penelope Miller, PhD. Instrs: FT 13
Estab 1909, dept estab 1938; pub; D & E; scholarships; SC 33, LC 10, GC 34; enrl D 300, E 100, non-maj 800, maj 132, grad 10
Ent Req: HS dipl
Degrees: BFA, BSE 4 yr, MA
Tuition: Res—$975 per sem, $82 per sem hr; nonres—$2520 per sem $211 per sem hr; campus res—room & board $1270 per sem
Courses: Art Appreciation, †Art Education, †Art History, Ceramics, Drawing, †Graphic Design, Illustration, Intermedia, Painting, Photography, †Studio Art
Adult Hobby Classes: 20; tuition $82 per sem hr. Courses—Art History, Ceramics, Drawing, Painting
Summer School: Dir, Curtis Steele. Enrl 100; tuition res—$490; nonres—$1260 per 5 wk term. Courses—Art History, Drawing, Painting, Photography, Sculpture

WALNUT RIDGE

WILLIAMS BAPTIST COLLEGE, Dept of Art, 60 W Fulbright, 72476. Tel 501-886-6741; *Asst Prof Art* Dr David Midkiff
Den; D & E; scholarships
Tuition: Res—$1976 per yr; campus res available
Courses: Art Education, Ceramics, Conceptual Art, Drawing, Painting, Theatre Arts
Summer School: Dir, Dr Jerrol Swaim. Tuition $925 for 12-16 hrs, &75 per hr

CALIFORNIA

ANGWIN

PACIFIC UNION COLLEGE, Art Dept, 94508. Tel 707-965-6311; *Chmn* Thomas Morphis
Scholarships
Degrees: AS, BA, BS
Tuition: $4320 per qtr for 12-17 cr
Courses: Art History, Ceramics, Design, Drawing, Graphic Design, Illustration, Painting, Photography, Printmaking, Sculpture, Stained Glass
Summer School: Dir, Gary Gifford. Courses—Art History, Photography

APTOS

CABRILLO COLLEGE, Visual & Performing Arts Division, 6500 Soquel Dr, 95003. Tel 408-479-6464; *Chmn* Dan Martinez. Instrs: FT 12, PT 22
Estab 1959; pub; D & E; scholarships; SC 46, LC 7
Ent Req: HS dipl
Degrees: AA 2 yr
Tuition: $50 for 6 or more units
Courses: Art History, Ceramics, Design, Drawing, Handicrafts, Jewelry, Painting, Photography, Sculpture, Textile Design, Color

ARCATA

HUMBOLDT STATE UNIVERSITY, College of Arts & Humanities, 95521. Tel 707-826-3624; *Chmn* James Crawford; *Instr* M D Benson; *Instr* M Bravo; *Instr* C DiCostanza; *Instr* M Isaacson; *Instr* R Johnson; *Instr* E Land-Weber; *Instr* D M LaPlantz; *Instr* L B Marak; *Instr* D Mitsanas; *Instr* J Crawford; *Instr* L Price; *Instr* S Ross; *Instr* E S Sundet; *Instr* W H Thonson; *Instr* M Morgan; *Instr* W Anderson; *Instr* A M Scott; *Instr* D Anton; *Instr* T Stanley
Estab 1913; pub; D & E; scholarships; SC 35, LC 11, GC 11
Degrees: BA 4 yr, BA with credential 5 yr
Tuition: Res—$1820 per yr; campus res available
Courses: Ceramics, Drawing, Graphic Design, Jewelry, Painting, Photography, Printmaking, Sculpture, Teacher Training
Children's Classes: Children's Art Academy
Summer School: Dir, Dick Swanson. Enrl 24; tuition $75 per unit for 6 weeks

AZUSA

AZUSA PACIFIC UNIVERSITY, College of Liberal Arts, Art Dept, 901 E Alosta, PO Box 7000, 91702-7000. Tel 818-969-3434; FAX 818-969-7180; *Chmn Dept* Susan Ney, MA; *Assoc Prof* James Thompson, EdD; *Asst Prof* William Catling, MFA; *Asst Prof* Dave McGill, MFA
Estab 1915, dept estab 1974; den; D & E; scholarships; SC 16, LC 3; enrl maj 60
Ent Req: HS dipl, state test
Degrees: BA(Art) 4 yrs
Tuition: $6000 per sem
Courses: Advertising Design, Art Education, Art History, Ceramics, Drawing, Graphic Arts, Illustration, Painting, Printmaking, Teacher Training
Summer School: Dir, S Ney; Enrl varies; Courses—varies

BAKERSFIELD

BAKERSFIELD COLLEGE, Art Dept, 1801 Panorama Dr, 93305. Tel 805-395-4011; FAX 805-395-4241; Elec Mail bwaters@kern.cc.ca.us. *Chmn* Albert Naso
Estab 1913; pub; D & E; SC 16, LC 4; enrl D 6000, maj 150-200
Ent Req: Ent exam, open door policy
Degrees: AA 2 yr
Tuition: Calif res—$5 per unit (max 5 and a half); 6 or more units $50; nonres—$85 per unit (max 15); no charge for units in excess of maximum
Courses: Advertising Design, Art Appreciation, Art History, Ceramics, Design, Drawing, Jewelry, Lettering, Painting, Photography, Printmaking, Sculpture, Glassblowing
Adult Hobby Classes: Enrl 100-150. Courses—Ceramics, Painting, Photography
Summer School: Dir, Al Naso. Enrl 100; tuition $13 per unit for 6 wk term. Courses—Art Appreciation, Ceramics, Drawing

CALIFORNIA STATE UNIVERSITY, BAKERSFIELD, Fine Arts Dept, 9001 Stockdale Hwy, 93311. Tel 805-664-3093; FAX 805-665-6901; *Chmn* Dr Jeffrey Mason. Instrs: FT 13
Scholarships
Degrees: BA
Tuition: Res—$396 0-6 units; $618 6 or more units per qtr; nonres $2055 per qtr
Courses: Art Education, Art History, Ceramics, Design, Drawing, Painting, Photography, Printmaking, Sculpture

BELMONT

COLLEGE OF NOTRE DAME, Dept of Art, 1500 Ralston Ave, 94002. Tel 415-595-3595; *Head Dept* Terry St John. Instrs: FT 2, PT 6
Estab 1951; den; D & E; scholarships; SC 18, LC 12; enrl D 200, E 70, maj 50
Ent Req: HS dipl, ent exam
Degrees: BA 3 1/2 - 4 yrs, BFA
Courses: Advertising Design, Art Education, Art History, Drawing, Graphic Design, Graphic Design, Interior Design, Painting, Photography, Printmaking, Sculpture, Color, Composition, Etching, Gallery Techniques, Lithography, 2-D & 3-D Design
Summer School: Dir, Lisa Baker. Upper division courses as in regular program plus special art education workshops; 6 wk term

BERKELEY

UNIVERSITY OF CALIFORNIA, BERKELEY
—**College of Letters & Sciences-Art Dept,** 238 Kroeber Hall, 94720-1800. Tel 510-642-2582; FAX 510-643-0884; *Chmn* Charles Altieri; *Prof* Ann Healy; *Prof* Mary O'Neal, MFA; *Prof* Richard Shaw. MFA; *Prof* Katherine Sherwood, MFA; *Prof* Wendy Sussman, MFA
Estab 1915; pub; D; scholarships
Degrees: BA, MFA(sculpture & painting)
Tuition: Res—undergrad $2173.25 per sem, grad $2193.25 per sem; nonres—undergrad $6022.75 per sem, grad $6042.75 per sem
Courses: Drawing, Painting, Sculpture, Art Theory
—**College of Environmental Design,** 370 Wurster Hall, 94720. Tel 510-642-5577; *Dean Environmental Design* Harrison Fraker; *Chmn Architecture* Don Lynlyndon; *Chmn City & Regional Planning* Michael Southworth; *Chmn Landscape Architecture* Michael Lowry
Pub; D & E; scholarships
Degrees: BA, MA, MSC, PhD
Tuition: Res—undergrad $2173 per sem, grad $2193 per sem; nonres—undergrad $6022.75 per sem, grad $6042.75 per sem
Courses: Design, Drawing

BURBANK

WOODBURY UNIVERSITY, Dept of Graphic Design, 7500 Glen Oaks Blvd, 91510-7846. Tel 818-767-0888; FAX 818-504-9320; *Chmn Graphic Design* Bill Keeney; *Chmn Interior Design* Linda Pollari; *Chmn Fashion Design* Hoda Meisamy
Estab 1884; pvt; D & E; scholarships; SC 56, LC 18
Ent Req: HS dipl
Degrees: BS 4 yrs, MRA 2 yrs, BArc 5 yrs
Tuition: $3150 per qtr
Courses: Advertising Design, Architecture, Art History, Commercial Art, Costume Design & Construction, Design, Display, Fashion Arts, Graphic Design, Illustration, Interior Design, Photography, Textile Design, †Interior Design, †Fashion Design
Summer School: Regular session

CARSON

CALIFORNIA STATE UNIVERSITY, DOMINGUEZ HILLS, Art Dept, LCH-A111 College of Arts & Sciences, 1000 E Victoria St, 90747. Tel 310-243-3310; *Chmn* Dr Louise Ivers
Estab 1960; pub; D & E; scholarships; SC 35, LC 25; enrl maj 130
Ent Req: 2.0 GPA
Degrees: BA 4 yr
Tuition: Res—undergrad $565 per sem for 6.0 units or less, $898 per sem for more than 6 units; tuition includes several fees
Courses: Art History, Design, Studio Art
Children's Classes: Tuition $36 - $55 per unit for 4 - 8 wk term. Courses—Crafts
Summer School: Dir, Dr Louise H Ivers. Enrl 40; tuition $36 - $55 per unit for 4 - 8 wk term. Courses—Crafts, Experiencing Creative Art

CHICO

CALIFORNIA STATE UNIVERSITY, CHICO, Art Dept, First & Normal, 95929-0820. Tel 916-898-5331; FAX 916-898-4171; Elec Mail vpatrick@oavax.csuchico.edu. *Chmn* Vernon Patrick; *Graduate Advisor, Instr & Prof* Michael Bishop, EdD; *Instr* Sheri Simons; *Instr* Marion Epting, MFA; *Instr* David Hoppe, MFA; *Instr* James Kuiper, MFA; *Instr* Yoshio Kusaba, PhD; *Instr* Jean Gallagher, BA; *Instr* Manuel Lucero, MA; *Instr* James McManus, MFA; *Instr* Dolores Mitchell, PhD; *Instr* Vernon Patrick, MFA; *Instr* Cameron Crawford; *Instr* Michael Simmons, EdD; *Instr* Sharon Smith, EdD; *Instr* Karen VanDerpool, MFA; *Instr* Stephen Wilson, MFA
Estab 1887; pub; D & E; SC 39, LC 29, GC 29; enrl non-maj & maj 1704, grad 59
Ent Req: Ent exam and test scores
Degrees: BA 4 yr, BFA 4 yr, MA 1 1/2 yr minimum
Tuition: Res—$280 per sem for less than 6 cr hrs, $439 per sem for over 6 cr hrs; nonres— $189 per unit
Courses: Aesthetics, Art Appreciation, Art Education, †Art History, †Ceramics, Design, Display, †Drawing, †History of Art & Archaeology, Intermedia, †Interior Design, Mixed Media, Museum Staff Training, †Painting, Photography, †Printmaking, †Sculpture, Teacher Training, †Weaving, Glass
Summer School: Chmn, Vernon Patrick. Enrl 50. Courses—Varies

CLAREMONT

CLAREMONT GRADUATE SCHOOL, Dept of Fine Arts, 251 E Tenth St, 91711. Tel 909-621-8071; *Chmn* Roland Reiss, MA; *Prof* Karl Benjamin, MA; *Prof* Michael Brewster, MFA; *Prof* Connie Zehr, BFA; *Vis Instr* Coleen Sterritt, MFA; *Vis Instr* David Amico, MFA; *Vis Instr* Ann Bray, MFA; *Vis Instr* John Millei, BA; *Vis Instr* Gary Lang, MFA
Estab 1925; priv; D; scholarships; SC 43 LC 7 GC50; enrl non-maj 1, maj 56, grad 53
Ent Req: BA, BFA or Equivalent
Degrees: MA 1 yr, MFA 2 yr
Tuition: Grad $19,000 per yr; $600 per unit fewer than 12; campus res available
Courses: Aesthetics, Art History, †Drawing, †Film, Graphic Arts, Intermedia, Mixed Media, †Painting, †Photography, †Printmaking, †Sculpture, Installation, Newmedia, Performance

PITZER COLLEGE, Dept of Art, 1050 N Mills Ave, 91711. Tel 909-621-8000, Ext 3176; *Prof Ceramics* David Furman; *Photography* Stephen Cahill; *Drawing* Kathryn Miller
Estab 1964; pvt; D; scholarships; SC 8, LC 6; enrl Sept-June maj 19, grad 10 (Claremont Grad School)

Ent Req: HS dipl, various criteria, apply Dir of Admis
Degrees: BA 4 yr
Tuition: Res—$15,784 (including campus res)
Courses: Art History, Ceramics, Constructions, Drawing, Film, History of Art & Archaeology, Mixed Media, Photography, Sculpture, Video, Environments, Weaving

POMONA COLLEGE, Dept of Art & Art History, 333 N College Way, 91711-6322. Tel 909-607-2221; FAX 909-621-8403; *Chmn Art & Art History Dept & Assoc Prof* Judson Emerick, PhD; *Prof* Enrique Martinez Celaya, MFA; *Prof* George Gorse; *Prof* Norman Hines, MFA; *Assoc Prof* Sheila Pinkel, MFA; *Assoc Prof* Frances Pohl, PhD; *Asst Prof* Mercedes Teixido
Estab 1889; pvt; D; scholarships; SC 15, LC 25; enrl D 330 maj 37
Ent Req: HS dipl
Degrees: BA 4 yrs
Tuition: Res—undergrad $7850 per sem. $22,455 with room & board
Courses: †Art History, Ceramics, Drawing, Graphic Design, Painting, Photography, Sculpture, Art Studio

SCRIPPS COLLEGE, Millard Sheets Art Center, 1030 Columbia, 91711. Tel 909-621-8000, Ext 2973; *Chmn Dept* Bruce Coats
Estab 1928; dept estab 1933; pub; D; scholarships; enrl D 580, non-maj 480, maj 100
Ent Req: HS dipl
Degrees: BA
Courses: Architecture, Art History, Ceramics, Drawing, Film, Mixed Media, Painting, Printmaking, †Sculpture, Fiber Arts, Typography

COALINGA

WEST HILLS COMMUNITY COLLEGE, Fine Arts Dept, 300 Cherry Lane, 93210. Tel 209-935-0801, Ext 328; FAX 209-935-5655; *Instr* Ron Mitchell
Estab 1935; pub; D & E; SC 15, LC 2; enrl D 625, E 1250, non-maj 25, maj 10
Degrees: AA 2 yrs
Tuition: Res—undergrad $13 per unit; campus res available
Courses: Art History, †Ceramics, Design, †Drawing, Fashion Arts, †Illustration, Lettering, †Museum Staff Training, †Painting, Printmaking, Sculpture

COMPTON

COMPTON COMMUNITY COLLEGE, Art Dept, 1111 E Artesia Blvd, 90221. Tel 310-637-2660; *Chmn* David Cobbs; *Prof* Verneal De Silvo. Instrs: FT 1
Estab 1929; pub; D & E; schol; SC 16, LC 6; enrl D 3500, E 2000, maj 18
Ent Req: HS dipl, 18 yrs of age
Degrees: AA 2 yr
Tuition: Res—$13 per unit
Courses: Advertising Design, Drafting, Drawing, History of Art & Archaeology, Lettering, Painting, Photography, Theatre Arts, Afro-American Art, Art Appreciation, Showcard Writing
Summer School: Courses—Art Appreciation

CORONADO

CORONADO SCHOOL OF FINE ARTS, 176 C Ave, PO Box 180156, 92178-0156. Tel 619-435-8541; *Dir* Monty Lewis
Estab 1944; pvt; SC, LC; enrl D 50, E 25
Degrees: Dipl 3-4 yr
Tuition: Full-time $275 for 4 wks, part-time $125-$200 for 4 wks
Courses: Advertising Design, Art History, Commercial Art, Graphic Arts, Illustration, Painting, Sculpture, Fine Arts, Mural Decoration
Children's Classes: Enrl 15; tuition $25 for Sat morning classes
Summer School: Dir, Monty Lewis. Enrl 75; tuition $160 per 4 wk; watercolor seminar $95 per 4 wk, $160 per 8 wk

COSTA MESA

ORANGE COAST COLLEGE, Division of Fine Arts, 2701 Fairview, 92628. Tel 714-432-5629; *Division Dean* Edward R Baker. Instrs: FT 35, Adjunct 80
Estab 1946; pub; D & E; scholarships; SC 225, LC 25; enrl D 4000, E 3500, maj 750
Ent Req: Ent exam
Degrees: AA 2 yr
Tuition: Undergrad $13 per unit, grad $50 per unit
Courses: Advertising Design, Art Appreciation, Art History, Ceramics, Commercial Art, Design, Display, Drawing, Drawing, Film, Graphic Arts, Graphic Design, Illustration, Interior Design, Jewelry, Lettering, Mixed Media, Painting, Photography, Printmaking, Sculpture, Stage Design, Theatre Arts, Video, Advertising Design, †Art, †Computer Graphics, †Display & Visual Presentation, †Music
Summer School: Eight wk session. Courses—same as regular session

CUPERTINO

DE ANZA COLLEGE, Creative Arts Division, 21250 Stevens Creek Blvd, 95014. Tel 408-864-8832; *Dean Creative Arts* David Trend; *Instr* William Geisinger; *Instr* Michael Cole; *Instr* Lee Tacang; *Instr* Charles Walker; *Instr* Michael Cooper
Estab 1967; dept estab 1967; pub; D & E; scholarships
Ent Req: 16 yrs of age
Degrees: Certificates of Proficiency, AA 2 yrs
Courses: Aesthetics, Art History, Ceramics, Drafting, Drawing, Film, Graphic Arts, Graphic Design, Lettering, Painting, Photography, Printmaking, Sculpture, Theatre Arts, Video, Stage Design
Adult Hobby Classes: Tuition varies per class. Courses—Bronze Casting, Calligraphy, Museum Tours,
Children's Classes: Computer art camp
Summer School: Courses—Drawing, Painting, Printmaking

CYPRESS

CYPRESS COLLEGE, Fine Arts Division, 9200 Valley View St, 90630. Tel 714-826-2220, Ext 139; *Chairperson* Charlene Felos; *Fine Arts Mgr* Barbara Russell
Estab 1966; pub; D & E; scholarships; enrl D 13,200
Ent Req: HS dipl
Degrees: AA 2 yrs
Tuition: $13 per unit up to 5 units; nonres $114 per unit; foreign $118 per unit plus enroll fee $13
Courses: Advertising Design, Art Appreciation, Art History, Ceramics, Commercial Art, Design, Drawing, Goldsmithing, Graphic Arts, Graphic Design, Instrumental Music, Vocal Music
Adult Hobby Classes: Adults may take any classes offered both day & extended; also offer adult education classes
Summer School: Extended Day Coordinator, Dr Evelyn Maddox

DAVIS

UNIVERSITY OF CALIFORNIA, DAVIS, Art Dept, 95616-8528. Tel 916-752-0105; FAX 916-752-0795; *Dir Art History* Jeffrey Ruda; *Prin Staff Asst* Jerrie Wright. Instrs: FT 17
Estab 1952; pub; D; scholarships; SC 28, LC 35; enrl maj 130, others 900
Degrees: BA 4 yrs, MA(Art History), MFA(Art Studio)
Tuition: Res—$1311; nonres—$4109 per quarter
Courses: Art History, Drawing, Painting, Photography, Printmaking, Sculpture, Video, Ceramic Sculpture, Criticism

EL CAJON

GROSSMONT COLLEGE, Art Dept, Div of Communications & Fine Arts, 8800 Grossmont College Dr, 92020. Tel 619-465-1700; *Dean* Dr Linda Mann. Instrs: FT 7, PT 16
Estab 1961; pub; D & E; schol; SC 22, LC 5; enrl total 1000
Ent Req: None
Degrees: AA
Tuition: Res—$13 per unit, $10 house free (mandatory)
Courses: Art History, Ceramics, Drawing, Painting, Photography, Sculpture, Art History
Summer School: Dir, Suda House. Enrl 100; tuition res $10 per unit for 6 - 8 wks. Courses—Art History, Drawing, Photography

EUREKA

COLLEGE OF THE REDWOODS, Arts & Languages Dept Division, 7351 Tompkins Hill Rd, 95501-9300. Tel 707-445-6700; FAX 707-441-5916; *Dean* Lea Mills. Instrs: FT 4, PT 8
Estab 1964; pub; D & E; scholarships; SC 15, LC 3 per sem; enrl 8330, maj 160
Ent Req: HS grad
Degrees: AA & AS 2 yrs
Tuition: Nonres—$123 per unit plus $13 enrollment fee per unit
Courses: Ceramics, Drawing, Photography, Weaving, Art Fundamentals, Fabrics, Jewelry Making
Summer School: Tuition $20 per unit

FRESNO

CALIFORNIA STATE UNIVERSITY, FRESNO, Art & Design, 5225 N Backer Ave, Mail-Stop No 65, 93740-8001. Tel 209-278-4240, 278-2516; *Chmn* Pat Hennings. Instrs: FT 19
Estab 1911, dept estab 1915; pub; D; scholarships; SC 45, LC 9, GC 4; enrl 1000
Ent Req: HS dipl, SAT or ACT
Degrees: BA 4 yrs, MA 2 yrs
Tuition: Res—undergrad $748 per sem; nonres—$4438 per sem; campus res available
Courses: Art Education, Art History, Ceramics, Drawing, Film, Painting, Photography, Printmaking, Sculpture, Teacher Training, Crafts, Metalsmithing
Adult Hobby Classes: Tuition $35 unit. Courses—various
Summer School: Courses—Ceramics

FRESNO CITY COLLEGE, Art Dept, 1101 E University Ave, 93741. Tel 209-442-4600; FAX 209-485-3367; *Dean* Anthony Cantu
Estab 1910, dept estab 1955; pub; D & E; SC 13, LC 3; enrl D 14,000, E 2000
Ent Req: None, open door policy
Degrees: AA 2 yrs
Tuition: Res—$13 first unit, then $5 reg fee per unit up to maximum of $50; nonres—$96 per unit
Courses: Art Appreciation, Art History, Ceramics, Drawing, Painting, Printmaking, Sculpture, Fiber Art, Gallery Practices, Interaction of Color
Adult Hobby Classes: Ceramics, Design, Drawing, Painting, Sculpture
Summer School: Art Appreciation, Art History, Ceramics

FULLERTON

CALIFORNIA STATE UNIVERSITY, FULLERTON, Art Dept, 92634-9480. Tel 714-773-3471; FAX 714-773-3005; *Dean School of Arts* Jerry Samuelson, MA; *Chmn Dept* Darryl J Curran
Estab 1957, dept estab 1959; pub; D & E; scholarships; SC 62, LC 27, GC 12; enrl grad 140, undergrad 700
Ent Req: HS dipl, SAT or ACT
Degrees: BA, BFA, MA, MFA
Tuition: Res—undergrad & grad $356 for 0 - 6 units, $554 for 7 or more units; nonres—undergrad & grad $246 per unit plus $356 or $554; no campus res
Courses: Art Education, †Art History, †Ceramics, Collages, Conceptual Art,

Constructions, Design, Display, †Drawing, †Graphic Design, †Illustration, Intermedia, †Jewelry, Lettering, Mixed Media, Museum Staff Training, †Painting, †Photography, †Printmaking, Restoration & Conservation, †Sculpture, Silversmithing, †Textile Design, Video, †Weaving, Environmental Design, Fibers, Glass, Museum Studies, Wood
Summer School: Enrl 60; tuition $125 per unit. Courses—Art History, Printmaking

FULLERTON COLLEGE, Division of Fine Arts, Art Dept, 321 E Chapman Ave, 92632-2095. Tel 714-992-7000; FAX 714-447-4097; *Chmn Division Fine Arts* Terrence Blackley
Estab 1913; pub; D & E; scholarships
Ent Req: HS dipl, ent exam
Degrees: AA 2 yr
Tuition: Nonres—$104 per unit; no campus res
Courses: Art History, Ceramics, Display, Drawing, Graphic Arts, Graphic Design, Illustration, Jewelry, Museum Staff Training, Painting, Photography, Printmaking, Sculpture, Textile Design, Weaving, Computer Graphics, Woodworking

GILROY

GAVILAN COLLEGE, Art Dept, 5055 Santa Teresa Blvd, 95020. Tel 408-847-1400; FAX 408-848-4801; *Chmn* Tony Ruiz; *Prof* John Porter; *Prof* Silva Riof-Metcalf; *Prof* Jane Rekedael; *Prof* Richard Young; *Prof* Morrie Roison. Instrs: FT 2, PT 3
Estab 1919; pub; D & E; SC 12, LC 2; enrl D 150, E 75, maj 30
Ent Req: HS dipl or 18 yrs of age
Degrees: AA 2 yrs
Tuition: Res—undergrad $13 per unit; nonres—undergrad $120 per unit
Courses: Ceramics, Drawing, Painting, Sculpture, Teacher Training, Theatre Arts, Art of the Americans, History of Art & Architecture
Summer School: Courses—Ceramics, Drawing, Painting

GLENDALE

GLENDALE COMMUNITY COLLEGE, Visual & Performing Arts Division, 1500 N Verdugo Rd, 91208. Tel 818-240-1000; FAX 818-549-9436; *Chmn Division* Kathleen Burke-Kelly; *Prof* Kenneth Gray; *Prof* Joan Watanabe; *Prof* Andrew Georgias, MFA; *Assoc Prof* Robert Kibler, MA; *Instr* Susan Sing, MA; *Instr* Annabelle Aylmer; *Instr* Daniel Stearns; *Instr* Guido Girardi
Estab 1927; pub; D & E; SC 25, LC 7; enrl D 4100, E 3900, nonmaj 800, maj 200
Ent Req: HS dipl, ent exam
Degrees: AA 2 yrs
Tuition: None
Courses: †Advertising Design, †Art History, Ceramics, Costume Design & Construction, Design, Drawing, Illustration, Lettering, Painting, †Photography, Sculpture, Stage Design, Theatre Arts, †2-D & 3-D Art
Summer School: Superintendent, Dr John Davitt

GLENDORA

CITRUS COLLEGE, Art Dept, 1000 W Foothill, 91740. Tel 818-914-8862, 914-8526; *Art Dept Chmn* Tom Tefft
Estab 1915; pub; D & E; scholarships; SC 26, LC 7; enrl D 400, E 175, non-maj 400, maj 175
Ent Req: HS dipl
Degrees: AA and AS 2 yrs
Tuition: Nonres—$76 per unit
Courses: Advertising Design, Art Appreciation, Art History, Ceramics, Commercial Art, Design, Drafting, Drawing, Graphic Design, Illustration, Painting, Photography, Sculpture, Computer Art
Children's Classes: Animation, Art Appreciation, Art History, Clay Sculpture, Computer Art, Design, Figure Drawing, Graphic Design, Watercolor
Summer School: Dir, Tom Tefft. Enrl 80; 6 wk term beginning June 1. Courses—Art History, Ceramics

HAYWARD

CALIFORNIA STATE UNIVERSITY, HAYWARD, Art Dept, 94542. Tel 510-885-3111; FAX 510-885-2281; Elec Mail jpetrillo@csuhayward.edu. *Chmn* James Perrizo
Estab 1957; pub; D & E; SC 30, LC 12; enrl 9900
Ent Req: HS dipl, ent exam, ACT
Degrees: BA 4 yr
Tuition: Res—undergrad $865.50 per yr; nonres—undergrad $3024 per yr
Courses: Art Appreciation, Art History, Ceramics, Design, Drawing, Graphic Arts, Graphic Design, History of Art & Archaeology, Intermedia, Museum Staff Training, Painting, Photography, Printmaking, Sculpture, Theatre Arts, Computer Graphics
Adult Hobby Classes: Courses offered through Continuing Education Dept

CHABOT COLLEGE, Humanities Division, 25555 Hesperian Blvd, 94545. Tel 510-786-6600; FAX 510-782-9315; *Chmn* Elliott Charnow. Instrs: FT 21, PT 50
Estab 1961; pub; D & E; scholarships; SC 27, LC 5
Ent Req: HS dipl
Degrees: AA 2 yr
Tuition: None to res; nonres—$110 per unit, $13 per sem unit; no campus res
Courses: Advertising Design, Ceramics, Costume Design & Construction, Drafting, Drawing, History of Art & Archaeology, Illustration, Lettering, Painting, Sculpture, Stage Design, Theatre Arts, Cartooning
Summer School: Dir, Robert Hunter. Enrl 72-100; tuition $2-$100 per 6 wks. Courses—Art History, Drawing, Introduction to Art, Sculpture, Watercolor

HOLLYWOOD

HOLLYWOOD ART CENTER SCHOOL, 2027 N Highland Ave, 90068. Tel 213-851-1103; *Dir* Mona Lovins
Estab 1912; pvt; D & E; SC 6; enrl D 40, E 12
Ent Req: HS dipl, submission of art work
Degrees: 3 yr cert
Courses: Commercial Art, Illustration, Interior Design, Fashion Design, Fine Art

HUNTINGTON BEACH

GOLDEN WEST COLLEGE, Visual Art Dept, 15744 Golden West St, 92647. Tel 714-895-8358; *Dean* David Anthony; *Chmn & Instr* Roger Camp, MA, MFA; *Instr* H Clemans, MA; *Instr* P Donaldson, MFA; *Instr* D Ebert, MA; *Instr* C Glassford; *Instr* A Jackson; *Instr* K Hauser Mortenson; *Instr* N Tornheim
Estab 1966; pub; D & E; scholarships; SC 12, LC 6; enrl D 13,820, E 9339
Ent Req: HS dipl
Degrees: AA 2 yrs
Tuition: Nonres—undergrad $104 per unit
Courses: †Advertising Design, Art History, Calligraphy, Ceramics, Display, †Drafting, Drawing, Illustration, Interior Design, Jewelry, Lettering, Mixed Media, Painting, Photography, Printmaking, Sculpture, Silversmithing, Stage Design, †Theatre Arts, Video
Summer School: Ceramics, Drawing, Painting, Photography, Sculpture

IDYLLWILD

IDYLLWILD ARTS ACADEMY (Formerly Idyllwild School of Music & The Arts), PO Box 38, 92549. Tel 909-659-2171; FAX 909-659-5463; *Chmn Dance* Jean-Marie Martz; *Chmn Theater* Jude Levinson; *Visual Arts Chmn* Greg Kennedy; *Chmn Music* Laura Melton; *Humanities Chmn* Ned Barrett; *Chmn Math & Science* Jerry McCampbell
Estab 1950; pvt; Idyllwild Arts Academy is a 14 wk summer program beginning in mid-June with courses in the arts for all ages; scholarships
Degrees: Not granted by the Idyllwild Campus, university credits earned through USC-LA Campus; documentation provided to high schools for credit
Tuition: Boarding students $20,750 per yr; day students $10,375 per yr
Courses: Ceramics, Painting, Photography, Printmaking, Sculpture, Fiber, Papermaking
Adult Hobby Classes: Enrl open; tuition $165 per wk
Children's Classes: Enrl open; tuition $90-$120 per wk, $65 for half day program. Day & Residential Children's Arts Program; also Youth Ceramics

IMPERIAL

IMPERIAL VALLEY COLLEGE, Art Dept, * PO Box 158, 92251. Tel 619-352-8320; *Chmn Dept Humanities* Open; *Asst Prof Art* Nannette Kelly
Scholarships
Degrees: AA
Courses: Art Appreciation, Art History, Ceramics, Drawing, Painting

IRVINE

CITY OF IRVINE, Fine Arts Center, 14321 Yale Ave, 92714. Tel 714-724-6880; *Supv* Toni Pang; *Educ Coordr* Tim Jahns, MA; *Cur* Dori Rawlins. Instrs: FT 3
Estab 1980; pub; D & E; SC 35; enrl D 600, E 600
Tuition: Res—undergrad $20 - $150 per course
Courses: Art Appreciation, Calligraphy, Ceramics, Drawing, Handicrafts, Jewelry, Mixed Media, Painting, Sculpture, Teacher Training
Children's Classes: Enrl 400. Tuition varies. Courses—Arts
Summer School: Enrl 40. Tuition varies. Courses—Arts

UNIVERSITY OF CALIFORNIA, IRVINE, Studio Art Dept, School of The Arts, 92697-2775. Tel 714-824-6648; FAX 714-824-5297; *Dean* Stephen Barker
Estab 1965; pub; D; scholarships; SC 24, LC 2, GC 4
Ent Req: HS dipl
Degrees: BA(Studio Art) 4 yr, MFA(Art)
Tuition: Res—undergrad $4324.50 per yr, grad $5082 per yr; nonres—undergrad $7699 per yr, grad $12,781 per yr
Courses: Ceramics, Drawing, History of Art & Archaeology, Painting, Photography, Sculpture, Video, Digital Imaging, Installation, Mural Painting
Summer School: Ceramics, Drawing, Painting

KENTFIELD

COLLEGE OF MARIN, Dept of Art, 835 College Ave, 94904. Tel 415-485-9480; *Chmn* Ted Grier
Estab 1926; pub; D & E; SC 48, LC 8; enrl D 5000
Ent Req: HS dipl, ent exam
Degrees: AA, AS 2 yrs
Tuition: Res—undergrad $13 per unit; nonres—undergrad $129 per unit
Courses: Architecture, Art History, Ceramics, Drawing, Interior Design, Jewelry, Painting, Photography, Printmaking, Sculpture, Textile Design, Architectural Design, Art Gallery Design Management, Color Theory, History of Art & Architecture
Adult Hobby Classes: Enrl 400. Courses—Calligraphy, Drawing, Illustration, Jewelry, Painting, Printing
Children's Classes: College for Kids
Summer School: Ceramics, Drawing, Painting, Sculpture

LAGUNA BEACH

ART INSTITUTE OF SOUTHERN CALIFORNIA, 2222 Laguna Canyon Rd, 92651. Tel 714-497-3309; FAX 714-497-4399;
Estab 1962; pvt; D & E
Tuition: $9800 per yr
Courses: Art History, Ceramics, Drawing, †Graphic Arts, †Graphic Design, †Painting, Photography, Printmaking, Sculpture, Fine Arts, Visual Communication
Adult Hobby Classes: 15 wk semesters. Courses—Studio & Lecture courses
Children's Classes: 15 wk semesters. Courses—Studio & Lecture courses
Summer School: Pres, Patricia Caldwell. Two 5 wk sessions. Courses—Studio & Lecture courses

LA JOLLA

UNIVERSITY OF CALIFORNIA, SAN DIEGO, Visual Arts Dept, 9500 Gilman Dr, 92093-0327. Tel 619-534-2860; *Dept Chmn* Louis Hock
Estab 1967; pub; D & E; scholarships; SC 55, LC 30, GC 15; enrl Maj 350, grad 40
Ent Req: HS dipl
Degrees: BA(Studio Art, Art History/Criticism, & Media) 4 yrs, MFA(Studio or Art Criticism) 2-3 yrs
Tuition: Res—undergrad $1400 per qtr; nonres—undergrad $3966 per qtr
Courses: Art Criticism/Film Criticism
Summer School: Dir, Mary Walshok

LA MIRADA

BIOLA UNIVERSITY, Art Dept, 13800 Biola Ave, 90639. Tel 562-903-4807; FAX 562-903-4748; *Chmn Dept* Barry A Krammes; *Assoc Prof* Dan Callis; *Assoc Prof* Roger Feldman
Estab 1908, dept estab 1971; pvt; D & E; scholarships; SC 17, LC 4; enrl D 55, maj 55
Ent Req: HS dipl, SAT or ACT
Degrees: BA 4 yrs
Tuition: Undergrad—$11,954 per yr; grad—Masters $272 per unit, Dr $499 per unit
Courses: Aesthetics, Art Appreciation, Art Education, Art History, Ceramics, Design, Graphic Arts, Graphic Design, Illustration, Mixed Media, Occupational Therapy, Painting, Photography, Printmaking, Sculpture, Teacher Training, Video
Summer School: Dir, Barry A Krammes. six week courses. Courses—vary

LANCASTER

ANTELOPE VALLEY COLLEGE, Art Dept, Division of Fine Arts, 3041 W Ave K, 93536. Tel 805-943-3241; FAX 805-943-5573; *Dean Fine Arts Div* Dr Dennis White; *Prof* Robert McMahan, MFA; *Prof* Richard Sim, MFA; *Prof* Pat Hinds, MFA; *Asst Prof* Cynthia Minet
Estab 1929; pub; D & E
Degrees: AA 2 yrs
Tuition: Nonres—undergrad $108 per unit
Courses: Art History, Ceramics, Drawing, Graphic Arts, Jewelry, Painting, Photography, Sculpture, Color & Design, Computer Graphics

LA VERNE

UNIVERSITY OF LA VERNE, Dept of Art, 1950 Third St, 91750. Tel 909-593-3511, Ext 4274, 4282, 4273, 4763; *Sculpture* George Stone; *Painting* Toella-Jean Mahoney; *Photography* Gary Colby
Estab 1891; pvt; D & E; scholarships; SC 12, LC 8; enrl D 125, E 60, maj 12
Ent Req: HS dipl
Degrees: BA(Art) 4 yrs
Tuition: $7325 per sem; $9625 per sem room & board
Courses: Drawing, History of Art & Archaeology, Painting, Photography, Sculpture, Theatre Arts, Contemporary Art Seminar
Summer School: Terms of 3 and 4 wks

LONG BEACH

CALIFORNIA STATE UNIVERSITY, LONG BEACH
—Art Dept, 1250 Bellflower Blvd, 90840. Tel 310-985-4376; FAX 310-985-1650; *Chmn* Jay Kzapil; *Dean* Wade Hobgood. Instrs: FT 40, PT 36
Estab 1949; pub; scholarships; SC 164, LC 26, GC 23, for both locations; enrl 5356 for both locations
Ent Req: HS grad, ent exam, SAT
Degrees: BA, BFA, MA, MFA
Tuition: Res—$580 per sem; nonres—$246-$580 per unit, $875.50 per sem
Courses: Art History, Ceramics, Drawing, Painting, †Painting, †Printmaking, †Sculpture, †Textile Design, Bio Medical Art, †Crafts (furniture), †General Art, †Jewelry-Metalsmithing, Museum Studies
Children's Classes: Ceramics, Drawing, Painting
Summer School: Dean, Dr Donna George. Tuition $77 per unit for sessions beginning June 7 & 23. Courses—Art History, Ceramics, Drawing, Painting, Special Topics
—Design Dept, 1250 Bellflower Blvd, 90840. Tel 310-985-5089; FAX 310-985-2284; *Chmn* Charles Leinbach; *Dean* Wade Hobgood. Instrs: FT 10, PT 9
Estab 1949; pub; SC 164, LC 26, GC 23 for both locations; enrl 5356 for both locations
Ent Req: HS grad, ent exam
Degrees: BF, BFA, BS, MA, MFA
Tuition: Res—$580 per sem, nonres—$246-$580 per unit, $875.50 per sem
Courses: Design, Industrial Design, Interior Design, Perspective, Rapid Visualization
Summer School: Dean, Dr Donna George

LONG BEACH CITY COLLEGE, Dept of Art, 4901 E Carson St, 90808. Tel 310-938-4319; *Head Dept Art* Larry White; *Instr* Joseph Hooten, MA; *Instr* Marcia Lewis, MFA; *Instr* Linda King, MFA; *Instr* Carol Roemer, PhD; *Instr* Rodney Tsukashima, MA; *Instr* Harvey Stupler, MA; *Instr* Mike Daniel, MFA
Pub; D & E; scholarships; SC 13, LC 2; enrl D 400, E 200, non-maj 450, maj 150
Ent Req: HS dipl, ent exam
Degrees: AA & cert 2 yrs
Tuition: $10 per unit
Courses: Art History, Ceramics, Commercial Art, Drawing, Illustration, Jewelry, Lettering, Mixed Media, Painting, Photography, Printmaking, Sculpture, Weaving, Computer Art & Design, Studio Crafts
Adult Hobby Classes: Enrl 1500; tuition $13 per unit sem. Courses—Art History, Ceramics, Computer Graphics, Drawing, Jewelry, Painting, Photography, Printmaking, Sculpture
Summer School: Tuition $13 for 6 wk sem. Courses—same as above

LOS ALTOS HILLS

FOOTHILL COLLEGE, Fine Arts & Communications Div, 12345 El Monte Rd, 94022. Tel 415-949-7777; *Dean* Alan Harvey
College has three campuses; scholarships
Degrees: AA, cert
Tuition: Res—undergrad & grad $9 per unit; nonres—grad &78 per unit
Courses: Advertising Design, Art Appreciation, Art History, Ceramics, Design, Drawing, Photography, Film, Illustration, Painting, Printmaking, Sculpture, Stage Design, Textile Design, Computer Graphics

LOS ANGELES

THE AMERICAN FILM INSTITUTE, Center for Advanced Film & Television, 2021 N Western Ave, 90027. Tel 213-856-7628; FAX 213-467-4578; *Dir CAFTS* Frank Pierson; *Dir Educ & Training* Debra Henderson
Estab 1969 to aid in the development & collaberation of making films; scholarships
Tuition: $15,000
Courses: Film, Video, †Cinematography, †Directing, †Editing, †Producing, †Production Design & Screen Writing
Adult Hobby Classes: Non degree evening & weekend classes

ART IN ARCHITECTURE, 7917 1/2 W Norton Ave, 90046. Tel 213-654-0990, 656-2286; *Dir* Dr Joseph L Young
Estab 1955; pvt; D; scholarships; SC 4, LC 4, GC 4; enrl D 6, E 7, non-maj 2, maj 8, grad 3
Ent Req: Art school diploma, ent exam
Tuition: $4000 for annual nine month program
Courses: Architecture, Calligraphy, Collages, Design, Drafting, Drawing, Graphic Arts, History of Art & Archaeology, Intermedia, Lettering, Mixed Media, Painting, Photography, Printmaking, Sculpture, Stage Design, †History of Art in Architecture

BRENTWOOD ART CENTER, 13031 Montana Ave, 90049. Tel 310-451-5657; FAX 310-395-5403; *Dir* Edward Buttwinick, BA. Instrs: 25
Estab 1971; D & E; SC 40; enrl D 400, E 100
Tuition: $100-$225 per month per class
Courses: Design, Drawing, Mixed Media, Painting, Sculpture
Adult Hobby Classes: Enrl 300; tuition $175-$225 per month. Courses—Basic Drawing, Design, Life Drawing, Mixed Media, Painting, Sculpture
Children's Classes: Enrl 300; tuition $100-$180 per month. Courses—Cartooning, Drawing, Mixed Media, Painting, Sculpture
Summer School: Dir, Ed Buttwinick. Enrl 400; tuition $300-$500 for nine wk prog. Courses—Drawing, Mixed Media, Painting, Sculpture

CALIFORNIA STATE UNIVERSITY, LOS ANGELES, Art Dept, 5151 State University Dr, 90032. Tel 213-343-4010; FAX 213-343-4045; *Chmn* Joe Soldate, MFA
Estab 1947; pub; D & E; scholarships; SC 85, LC 12, GC 9; enrl D 2500 (Art), non-maj 324, grad 47 (per quarter)
Ent Req: HS dipl, ent exam
Degrees: BA(Art), MA(Art), MFA(Art)
Tuition: Res-undergrad & grad $474 per quarter; nonres-undergrad & grad $164 per unit; campus res available
Courses: Advertising Design, Architecture, †Art Appreciation, Art Education, Art History, Calligraphy, †Ceramics, †Commercial Art, Costume Design & Construction, Design, Display, †Drawing, Graphic Arts, History of Art & Archaeology, †Illustration, †Interior Design, Jewelry, Lettering, Painting, †Photography, Printmaking, Sculpture, Silversmithing, †Teacher Training, †Textile Design, Weaving, †Art Therapy, Costume Design, †Design Theory, Enameling, Exhibition Design, Fashion Illustration, Textiles, Weaving, †Computer Graphics

LOS ANGELES CITY COLLEGE, Dept of Art, 855 N Vermont Ave, 90029-9990. Tel 213-953-4240; *Chmn* Lee Whitton; *Assoc Dean* Phyllis Muldavin; *Prof* Dennis Elmore, MA; *Prof* Raoul De La Sota, MA; *Prof* Gloria Bohanon, MFA; *Prof* Lee Whitten, MA; *Assoc Prof* Gay Johnson. Instrs: PT 9
Estab 1929; pub; D & E; scholarships; SC 48, LC 8; enrl D 450, E 150, non-maj approx 2/3, maj approx 1/3
Ent Req: HS dipl & over 18 yrs of age
Degrees: AA 2 yr
Tuition: Res—undergrad $13 per unit, 10 or more units $100; nonres—$125 per unit plus $13 per sem
Courses: †Advertising Design, †Art History, Ceramics, †Commercial Art, Display, Drawing, †Graphic Design, †Painting, Printmaking, Sculpture, Life Drawing
Adult Hobby Classes: Enrl 2090; tuition approx $20 per class of 8 wks. Courses—Ceramics, Design, Drawing, Painting, Perspective, Printmaking, Sculpture
Summer School: Chmn, Phyllis Muldavin. Enrl 250; tuition $50 for term of 6 wks beginning July. Courses—basic courses only

LOYOLA MARYMOUNT UNIVERSITY, Art & Art History Dept, Communications & Fine Arts, Loyola Blvd & W 80th St, 90045. Tel 310-338-2700, 338-3054; FAX 310-338-1948; *Prof* Rudolf Fleck, MFA; *Prof* Michael Brodsky; *Prof* Susan Robinson, PhD; *Assoc Prof* Carm Goode, MFA; *Assoc Prof* Katherine Harper, PhD; *Asst Prof* Jane Brucker, MFA. Instrs: FT 8, PT 9
Estab as Marymount Col in 1940, merged with Loyola Univ 1968; pvt; D; scholarships; SC 37, LC 21
Ent Req: HS dipl
Degrees: BA 4 yrs
Tuition: $8580 annual tuition; campus res available
Courses: Advertising Design, Aesthetics, Art Appreciation, Art History, Calligraphy, Ceramics, Design, Drawing, Graphic Arts, Graphic Design, Illustration, Jewelry, Lettering, Painting, Photography, Printmaking, Sculpture, Silversmithing, Computer Animation, Computer Graphics
Adult Hobby Classes: Animation, Ceramics, Computer Graphics, Jewelry, Sculpture, Stained Glass
Summer School: Dir, Dr Joanne Fisher. Courses— Ceramics, Computer Graphics, Drawing, Jewelry, Mixed Media, Photography

MOUNT SAINT MARY'S COLLEGE, Art Dept, 12001 Chalon Rd, 90049. Tel 310-476-2237, Ext 250; *Chmn & Prof* Norman Schwab
Estab as Chalon Campus in 1925, also maintains Doheny Campus estab 1962; den; D & E; scholarships; enrl D 60, non-maj 31, maj 29
Ent Req: HS dipl
Degrees: BA and BFA 4 yrs
Tuition: $12,914 per yr; campus res—room & board available
Courses: †Art Education, †Art History, Ceramics, †Collages, †Conceptual Art, †Constructions, Drawing, †Graphic Arts, †Graphic Design, †Illustration, †Intermedia, †Mixed Media, Painting, Photography, †Printmaking, Sculpture, †Textile Design, Fiber Design

OCCIDENTAL COLLEGE, Dept of Art History & Visual Arts, 1600 Campus Rd, 90041. Tel 213-259-2749; FAX 213-259-2958; *Chmn* Dr Eric Frank. Instrs: FT 7, PT 2
Estab 1887; pvt; D; scholarships & grants according to need; SC 19, LC 25, GC 5; enrl maj 40, others 300
Ent Req: HS dipl, col transcript, SAT, recommendations
Degrees: BA 4 yr
Tuition: $19,000 campus res available
Courses: †Art Education, †Art History, †Drawing, †Painting, †Sculpture, †Graphics, †Theory & Criticism
Adult Hobby Classes: Fundamentals

OTIS SCHOOL OF ART & DESIGN, Fine Arts, 2401 Wilshire Blvd, 90057. Tel 213-251-0500; FAX 213-480-0059; *Chmn* Linda Burnham; *Pres* Neil Hoffman
Estab 1918; pvt; scholarships; SC 150, LC 48, GC 9; enrl D 820, E 209, maj 600, grad 20
Degrees: BFA 4 yrs, MFA 2 yrs
Tuition: $6570 per sem
Courses: Ceramics, Graphic Design, Illustration, Photography, †Architecture Design, †Communication Design, Environmental Art, †Environmental Design, †Fashion Design, Fine Arts, †Glass, Metal & Surface Design
Adult Hobby Classes: Enrl 820; tuition $234 per cr
Children's Classes: Enrl 200; tuition $500 4 wks
Summer School: Continuing educ & pre-college programs

SOUTHERN CALIFORNIA INSTITUTE OF ARCHITECTURE, 5454 Beethoven St, 90066. Tel 310-574-1123; FAX 310-574-3801; *Dir* Michael Rotondi
Degrees: BArch, MArch
Tuition: Undergrad—$5810 per sem
Courses: Architecture
Adult Hobby Classes: Dir, Rose Marie Rabin. Summer term only
Summer School: Dir, Gary Paige. Enrl 30; tuition $1000 for 12-15 wk term beginning July. Courses—Foundation Program in Architecture

UNIVERSITY OF CALIFORNIA, LOS ANGELES
—Dept of Art, 1300 Dickson Art Ctr, 405 Hilgard Ave, 90095. Tel 310-825-3281; FAX 310-206-6676; *Chmn* Mary Kelly
Scholarships & fels
Degrees: BA, MA, MFA
Tuition: Res—undergrad $1252 per qtr, grad $1420 per qtr; nonres—undergrad $3819.50 per qtr, grad $3987 per qtr
Courses: Ceramics, Drawing, Painting, Photography, Printmaking, Sculpture, Modernism, New Genres, Survey of Critical Thought
—Dept of Design, 1300 Dickson Art Ctr, 405 Hilgard Ave, 90095. Tel 310-825-9007; FAX 310-206-6676; *Acting Chmn* William Hutchinson
Degrees: BA, MA, MFA
Tuition: Res—undergrad $1252 per quarter, grad $1420 per quarter; nonres—undergrad $3819.50 per quarter, grad $3987 per quarter
Courses: Ceramics, Graphic Design, Industrial Design, Interior Design, Video, Computer Imagery, Fiber Textile
—Dept Art History, 100 Dodd Hall, 405 Hilgard Ave, 90095. Tel 310-825-2530; FAX 310-206-6905; *Dept Chmn* A Bidler
Scholarships & fels
Degrees: BA, MA, PhD
Tuition: Res—undergrad $1252 per quarter, grad $1420 per quarter; nonres—undergrad $3819.50 per quarter, grad $3987 per quarter
Courses: †Art History

UNIVERSITY OF JUDAISM, Dept of Continuing Education, 15600 Mulholland Dr, 90077. Tel 310-476-9777; FAX 310-471-1278; *Dir* Jack Shechter, MA
Sch estab 1947; den; SC 14, LC 6
Degrees: Units in continuing education only
Tuition: $144 per sem, reg fee $9
Courses: Art History, Calligraphy, Drawing, Interior Design, Painting, Photography, Sculpture, Book Illustration, History of Jewish Art, Picture Book Making for Children, Tile Painting
Adult Hobby Classes: Enrl 8; tuition $127 per sem
Summer School: Courses offered

UNIVERSITY OF SOUTHERN CALIFORNIA, School of Fine Arts, Watt Hall 104, University Park, 90089-0292. Tel 213-740-2787; FAX 213-740-8938; *Dean* Dr Lynn Matteson; *Prof* Jud Fine; *Prof* Robbert Flick; *Prof* Ron Rizk; *Prof* Ruth Weisberg; *Prof* Jay Willis; *Prof* Dr Susan Larsen-Martin; *Prof* Dr John Pollini; *Assoc Prof* Dr Eunice Howe; *Assoc Prof* Margaret Lazzari; *Assoc Prof* Dr Carolyn Malone; *Assoc Prof* Bob Alderette; *Assoc Prof* Margit Omar; *Assoc Prof* David Bunn; *Asst Prof* Dr Glenn Hartcourt; *Adjunct Prof* Dr John Bowlt; *Adjunct Assoc Prof* Dr Selma Holo; *Adjunct Asst Prof* Hisako Asano; *Adjunct Asst Prof* Dr Shelley Bennett; *Adjunct Asst Prof* Leslie Bowman; *Adjunct Asst Prof* Dr Kenneth Hamma; *Adjunct Asst Prof* Edward Maeder; *Adjunct Asst Prof* Dr Marion True
Estab 1887, school estab 1979; pvt; D & E; scholarships; SC 78, LC 11, GC 23; enrl non-maj 600, maj 250, grad 50
Ent Req: HS dipl, SAT, GRE
Degrees: BA & BFA 4 yrs, MFA 2-3 yrs, MA 2 yrs, MA with Museum Studies Option 3 yrs, PhD 4 yrs minimum
Tuition: $529 per unit
Courses: Art History, Ceramics, History of Art & Archaeology, Museum Staff Training, Painting, Photography, Printmaking, Sculpture, Computer Graphics
Summer School: Dir, L Matteson. Enrl 75; tuition $529 per unit for 6 wks. Courses—Art History, Studio

MALIBU

PEPPERDINE UNIVERSITY, SEAVER COLLEGE, Dept of Art, Culture Art Ctr, 90263. Tel 310-456-4155; *Instr* Avery Falkner; *Prof* Bob Privitt; *Prof* Joe Piesentin; *Adjunct Prof* Susan Wulfeck; *Instr* Sonya Sorrell
Scholarships
Tuition: Apartment $26,100; campus res—room & board $25,850 per yr
Courses: Art Appreciation, Art Education, Art History, Ceramics, Design, Drawing, Graphic Arts, Jewelry, Painting, Sculpture, Monotypes
Summer School: Enrl 20; tuition $235 per unit. Courses—Jewelry, Mixed Media, Monotypes, Painting

MARYSVILLE

YUBA COLLEGE, Fine Arts Division, 2088 N Beale Rd, 95901. Tel 916-741-6700, 741-6984; *Assoc Dean* Michael Moyers. Instrs: FT 2
Estab 1927; pub; D & E; scholarships; SC 23, LC 2; enrl total 1437, maj 493
Ent Req: HS grad or 18 yrs of age
Degrees: AA 2 yr
Tuition: Res—$13 per unit per sem; nonres—$120 per unit
Summer School: Dean & Assoc Dean Community Educ, Cal Gower. Courses—Ceramics, Drawing

MENDOCINO

MENDOCINO ART CENTER, 45200 Little Lake St, PO Box 765, 95460. Tel 707-937-5818; WATS 800-653-3328. *Exec Dir* Elaine Beldin-Reed
Estab 1959; pvt; D & E; SC 24, LC 6; enrl D 24
Ent Req: Mutual interview, ceramics ROP 2 yr prog
Courses: Calligraphy, †Ceramics, Drawing, Graphic Design, Jewelry, Lettering, Painting, Printmaking, Sculpture, Silversmithing, Textile Design, Weaving, Silkscreen
Summer School: Dir, Elaine Beldin-Reed. Enrl 6-15; tuition $175-$250 for 1 wk term. Courses—Acting, Ceramics, Fine Art, Jewelry, Weaving

MERCED

MERCED COLLEGE, Arts Division, 3600 M St, 95348. Tel 209-384-6000; *Pres* Jan Moser; *Chmn* Robert Harvey
Estab 1964; pub; D & E; scholarships; SC 50, LC 10; enrl D 4741, E 3187, non-maj 3700, maj 4228
Ent Req: 18 yrs & older
Degrees: AA & AS 2 yr
Tuition: Res—undergrad $13 per unit; nonres—undergrad $107 per unit
Courses: Art History, Calligraphy, Ceramics, Drawing, Illustration, Painting, Photography, Sculpture, Theatre Arts
Summer School: Dir, Dr Ron Williams, Dean of Arts & Sciences. Tuition res—undergrad $13 for 7 wk term beginning June 21

MODESTO

MODESTO JUNIOR COLLEGE, Arts Humanities & Communications Division, 435 College Ave, 95350. Tel 209-575-6067; FAX 209-575-6086; *Division Dean* Robert Gauvreau; *Instr* Richard Serroes; *Instr* Doug Smith; *Instr* Terry L Hartman, MA; *Instr* Daniel W Petersen, MA; *Instr* Jerry M Reilly, MFA; *Instr* J Gary Remsing, MA. Instrs: FT 259, PT 385
Estab 1921, div estab 1964; pub; D & E; scholarships; enrl 16,024 total
Ent Req: Grad of accredited high school, minor with California High School Proficiency Cert & parental permission, 11th & 12th graders with principal's permission, persons 18 or older who are able to profit from the instruction
Degrees: AA and AS 2 yrs
Tuition: Res—$6 health fee; nonres—$87 per sem unit to maximum of $1044 per sem plus health fee; no campus res
Courses: Advertising Design, Architecture, Art History, Ceramics, Display, Drafting, Drawing, Film, Jewelry, Lettering, Painting, †Photography, Printmaking, Sculpture, Silversmithing, Theatre Arts, Enameling, Lapidary
Adult Hobby Classes: Courses—Arts & Crafts, Lapidary
Summer School: Dir, Dudley Roach. Tuition $6 health fee. Courses—a wide variety offered

MONTEREY

MONTEREY PENINSULA COLLEGE, Art Dept, Div of Creative Arts, 980 Fremont St, 93940. Tel 408-646-4200; *Chairperson Div Creative Arts* Pat Boles; *Chairperson Dept Art* Gary Quinonez; *Instr* Tobin Keller; *Instr* Richard Janick; *Instr* Jane Miller; *Instr* Joyce Clark; *Instr* Don Santos; *Instr* Anita Benson; *Instr* Bonnie Britton; *Instr* Skip Kadish; *Instr* Cathy Hendig; *Instr* Michael Martin; *Instr* Tim Craighead; *Instr* Don Fritz; *Instr* Paul Roehl; *Instr* Vi Ly; *Instr* Reid Winfrey; *Instr* Pam Mura Kami; *Instr* Susan Kingsley; *Instr* Carol Holoday; *Instr* Alevis Zeitler Estab 1947; pub; D & E; scholarships; SC 17, LC 8; enrl D 1343, E 623, maj 160
Ent Req: HS dipl, 18 yrs or older
Degrees: AA & AS 2 yrs
Tuition: Res—$50; nonres—$28 per unit; no campus res
Courses: Art Appreciation, †Ceramics, Collages, Design, Drafting, †Drawing, Graphic Design, History of Art & Archaeology, Illustration, Intermedia, †Jewelry, Mixed Media, †Painting, †Photography, †Sculpture, Silversmithing, Video, Weaving, †Commercial Graphics, †Studio Art
Summer School: Dir, Thorne Hacker. Term of 6 wks beginning June. Courses are limited

MONTEREY PARK

EAST LOS ANGELES COLLEGE, Art Dept, 1301 Brooklyn Ave, 91754. Tel 213-265-8650, 265-8842; *Dept Chmn* Carson Scott. Instrs: FT 5
Estab 1949; pub; D & E; SC 43, LC 10; enrl D 486, E 160, maj 646
Degrees: AA 2 yr
Tuition: $13 per unit
Courses: †Advertising Design, †Art History, †Ceramics, Design, Display, †Drawing, Graphic Arts, Graphic Design, Lettering, Mixed Media, †Painting, †Art Fundamentals, †Art Graphic Communications, †Computer Graphics, †Electronic Publishing, †Life Drawing
Children's Classes: Enrl 60. Courses—Ceramics, Direct Printing Methods, Drawing, Painting
Summer School: Dir, Carson Scott. Enrl 50; tuition $13 per unit for 6 wk term. Courses—Art 201, Beginning Drawing, Beginning 2-D Design

NAPA

NAPA VALLEY COLLEGE, Art Dept, 2277 Napa Vallejo Hwy, 94558. Tel 707-253-3000; *Dir* Jan Molen; *Prof* Jay Golik; *Prof* Caroyln Broodwell
Tuition: $13 per unit up to 5 units
Courses: Art Appreciation, Art History, Ceramics, Design, Drawing, Painting, Photography, Printmaking, Sculpture
Adult Hobby Classes: Courses offered
Children's Classes: Courses offered
Summer School: Courses—Painting, Ceramics, Drawing

NORTHRIDGE

CALIFORNIA STATE UNIVERSITY, NORTHRIDGE, Dept of Art-Two Dimensional Media, College of Arts, Media at Communications, 18111 Nordhoff St, 91330-8300. Tel 818-677-1200; *Dept Chmn* Joe Lewis; *Chmn General Studies* Mark Jurey; *Chmn Art History* Donald Strong; *Chmn Art 3-D Media* Joe Arimitsu. Instrs: 48
Estab 1956; pub; D & E; SC 13, GC 5; enrl D & E 2231, grad 101
Ent Req: HS dipl, GRE, SAT
Degrees: BA 4-5 yrs, MA
Tuition: Nonres—$189 per unit
Courses: Art Education, †Art History, Calligraphy, Ceramics, Drawing, †Graphic Design, Illustration, Industrial Design, †Interior Design, Lettering, Painting, Photography, Printmaking, Sculpture, Textile Design, Airbrush, Animation, Typography, Packaging Graphics, Reproduction Graphics, Computer Graphics
Summer School: Dir, Art Weiss. Tuition $92 per unit for 6 wks beginning June 1. Courses—Beginning Design, Drawing, Graphic Design, Illustration Painting
—Dept of Art, 18111 Nordhoff St, 91330. Tel 818-677-2242; FAX 818-677-3046; Estab 1958, dept estab 1971; pub; D & E; scholarships & fels; SC 1, LC 30, grad 10; enrl grad 81, undergrad 650
Ent Req: HS dipl, SAT, subject to GPA
Degrees: BA(Art) 4 yrs, MA(Art) & MFA(Studio Art) 5 yrs
Tuition: $936 annually
Courses: †Art Education, †Art History, Calligraphy, Design, Drawing, Graphic Arts, †Graphic Design, History of Art & Archaeology, Illustration, Industrial Design, Lettering, Mixed Media, Painting, Photography, Printmaking, Animation, Fiber & Fabric, Wood Design
Adult Hobby Classes: Courses available through Continuing Educ Extension Prog

NORWALK

CERRITOS COMMUNITY COLLEGE, Art Dept, 11110 Alondra Blvd, 90650. Tel 310-860-2451; *Instr Dean Fine Arts* Dr Ella White
Estab 1956; pub; D & E; SC 36, LC 6
Ent Req: HS dipl or 18 yrs of age
Degrees: AA 2 yrs
Tuition: Res—$13 per unit; nonres—$114 per unit
Courses: Calligraphy, Ceramics, Commercial Art, Display, Drawing, Graphic Arts, Graphic Design, History of Art & Archaeology, Jewelry, Museum Staff Training, Printmaking, Sculpture, 2-D & 3-D Design
Summer School: Drawing, Painting, History, Design, Ceramics, Calligraphy

OAKLAND

CALIFORNIA COLLEGE OF ARTS & CRAFTS, 5212 Broadway, 94618. Tel 510-653-8118; *Pres* Lorne Buchman; *Interior Architecture Design* Mark Jensen; *Wood & Furniture Design* Donald Fortescue; *Textiles* Lia Cook; *Photography* Larry Sultan; *Ceramics* Viola Frey; *Printmaking* Charles Gill; *General Studies* Martin VanBuren; *Film-Video* David Heintz; *Sculpture* Linda Fleming; *Graduate Studies* Lewis DeSoto; *Glass* Clifford Raine; *Drawing* Vince Perez; *Art History* Marc LeSueur; *Graphic Design* Michael Vanderbyl; *Jewelry & Metal Arts* Marilyn DaSilva; *Painting* Mary Snowden; *Ethnic Art Studies* Opal Palmer Adisa; *Architecture* David Meckel
Estab 1907; pvt; D & E; scholarships; SC 24, LC 58, GC 5; enrl D 1100, non-maj 50, maj 979, grad 77
Ent Req: HS dipl, Portfolio, SAT or ACT recommended, C grade-point average, 2 letters of recommendation
Degrees: BArch 5 yrs, BFA 4 yrs, MFA 3 yrs
Tuition: $7475 per sem; campus res available
Courses: Aesthetics, †Architecture, Art History, †Ceramics, †Drawing, †Fashion Arts, †Film, Graphic Arts, †Graphic Design, Handicrafts, Illustration, †Industrial Design, †Interior Design, †Jewelry, Mixed Media, †Painting, †Photography, †Printmaking, †Sculpture, †Textile Design, †Video, Weaving, †Ethnic Studies, †Fine Arts, †General Crafts, †Glass, †Interior Architectural Design, †Metal Arts, †Textiles, †Woodwork & Furniture Design
Children's Classes: Enrl 100; tuition $575 for July 10-28 term. Courses—Architecture, Drawing, Graphic Design, Painting, Sculpture
Summer School: Enrl 150; tuition $590 for July 7-25 term. Courses—Architecture, Ceramics, Drawing, Fashion Design & Illustration, Graphic Design, Painting, Photography, Sculpture

HOLY NAMES COLLEGE, Art Dept, 3500 Mountain Blvd, 94619. Tel 510-436-1000, Ext 1458; *Chmn Dept* Rick Patrick. Instrs: FT 2, PT 4
Estab 1917; pvt; D & E; scholarships; SC 24, LC 4
Ent Req: HS dipl
Degrees: BA and BFA 4 yrs
Tuition: $405 per unit
Courses: Art History, Calligraphy, Ceramics, Drawing, Jewelry, Painting, Photography, Printmaking, Sculpture

LANEY COLLEGE, Art Dept, 900 Fallon St, 94607. Tel 510-464-3221; FAX 510-464-3240; *Chmn* David Bradford; *Asst Dean* Fran White. Instrs: FT 8, PT 9
Estab 1962; pub; D & E; SC 52, LC 8; enrl D 1400, E 450
Ent Req: HS dipl
Degrees: AA 2 yrs
Tuition: Res—undergrad $13 per unit, grad $50 per unit
Courses: †Ceramics, †Commercial Art, Design, Drawing, †Graphic Arts, Graphic Design, Handicrafts, History of Art & Archaeology, Lettering, †Painting, †Sculpture, Illustration, Cartooning, Color & Design, Etching, Lithography, Portraiture, Relief Printing, Silkscreen, Advertising Design and Architectural Design Courses available through the Architectural Design Dept; Photography Courses available through the Photography Dept
Summer School: Chmn, David Bradford. Enrl 250; tuition $10 per unit for 6 wk term

MERRITT COLLEGE, Art Dept, 12500 Campus Dr, 94619. Tel 510-436-2431; *Dir* Helmut Schmitt
Degrees: AA
Tuition: Undergrad—$13 per unit; grad—$50 per unit
Courses: Art History, Ceramics, Design, Illustration, Painting, Sculpture, Life Drawing
Adult Hobby Classes: Dir, Helmut Schmitt
Summer School: Dir, Helmut Schmitt. Enrol 120; tuition $5 per unit; six week courses. Courses—Life Drawing, Painting

MILLS COLLEGE, Art Dept, 5000 MacArthur Blvd, PO Box 9975, 94613. Tel 510-430-2117; FAX 510-430-3314; *Chmn* Joanne Bernstein; *Prof Art Hist* Moiro Roth, PhD; *Prof Hist* Mary-Ann Lutzker, PhD; *Asst Prof* Hung Liu, MFA; *Asst Prof* Anna Valentina Murch, MFA; *Asst Prof* Catherine Wagner, MA
Estab 1852; pvt; D; scholarships; SC 23, LC 22, GC 20; enrl grad 16-20
Ent Req: HS dipl, SAT, Advanced Placement Exam for undergrads
Degrees: BA 4 yrs, MFA 2 yrs
Tuition: $15,260 per yr; campus res—room & board $6480
Courses: Aesthetics, Art History, Ceramics, Drawing, Mixed Media, Painting, Photography, Sculpture, 3-D Design

OCEANSIDE

MIRACOSTA COLLEGE, Art Dept, 1 Barnard Dr, 92056. Tel 619-757-2121; *Dir* Kristina Nugent, MA; *Instr* Erik Growborg, MA; *Instr* Susan Delaney; *Instr* Leslie Nemour, MA
Estab 1934; pub; D & E; scholarships; SC 12, LC 4; enrl maj 200
Ent Req: HS dipl
Degrees: AA and AS normally 2 yrs
Tuition: Res—no fee; nonres—$1272 per yr; no campus res
Courses: Aesthetics, †Architecture, Art Appreciation, Art Education, †Art History, Ceramics, Collages, Conceptual Art, Constructions, †Costume Design & Construction, Design, †Drafting, Drawing, Film, †Graphic Design, History of Art & Archaeology, Interior Design, Landscape Architecture, Mixed Media, †Painting, †Photography, †Printmaking, †Sculpture, †Stage Design, Teacher Training, †Theatre Arts, Computer Art, Figure Drawing, Figure Painting, Figure Sculpture
Children's Classes: Enrl 200; tuition small fees. Courses—Art, Theater
Summer School: Enrl 2000; tuition $15. Courses—Various subjects

ORANGE

CHAPMAN UNIVERSITY, Art Dept, 333 N Glasell, 92666. Tel 714-997-6729; FAX 714-997-6744; *Chmn* Wendy Salmond, PhD; *Prof* Jane Sinclair, MFA; *Prof* Richard Turner, MFA; *Prof* Sharon Corey, MFA; *Prof* Denise Weyhrich, MFA; *Prof* Stephen Berens, MFA; *Prof* David Kiddie, MFA
Estab 1918, branch estab 1954; den; D & E; scholarships; SC 20, LC 15; enrl D 245, non-maj 200, maj 50
Ent Req: HS dipl, ACT, SAT or CLEP
Tuition: $460 per unit; campus res—room & board $5346 per yr
Courses: Advertising Design, Art History, Ceramics, Drawing, Film, Graphic Design, Illustration, Painting, Photography, Sculpture, Computer Graphics
Children's Classes: Courses—workshops in connection with art education classes
Summer School: Courses—Introductory Art, Ceramics

ORINDA

JOHN F KENNEDY UNIVERSITY, Graduate School for Holistic Studies, 12 Altarinda Rd, 94563. Tel 510-254-0105, 253-2232; *Dir Admis & Records* Ellena Bloedorn
Estab 1964; pvt; E; enrl E 34, grad 34
Ent Req: BA from regionally accredited institution
Degrees: MA 2 yr
Tuition: Res—grad $264 per cr hr; nonres—grad $264 per cr hr
Courses: Museum Staff Training, Arts & Consciousness, Museum Studies

OROVILLE

BUTTE COLLEGE
—Dept of Fine Arts, 3536 Butte Campus Dr, 95965. Tel 916-895-2404; FAX 916-895-2346; *Dean Instruction* Frederick E Allen, MFA; *Chmn* David Cooper; *Ceramic Coordr* Idie Adams; *Prof* John R Wilson, MA; *Vis Prof* Ruben Heredia; *Prof* Will Stule; *Prof* Geoff Fricker
Estab 1968; pub; D & E; scholarships; SC 21, LC 4; enrl D 3988, E 4194
Ent Req: HS dipl or 18 yrs or older
Degrees: AA
Tuition: Res—$13 per unit; nonres—$125 per unit
Courses: Ceramics, Graphic Arts, Commercial Photography, Fine Arts
—Dept of Performing Arts, 3536 Butte Campus Dr, 95965. Tel 916-895-2581; *Assoc Dean* Roger Ekins
Degrees: Transfer major
Tuition: Res—$13 per unit; nonres—$125 per unit
Courses: Acting, Adaptive Dramatics, Set Design & Construction, Theater Arts Appreciation, Theater for Children

PALM DESERT

COLLEGE OF THE DESERT, Art Dept, 43-500 Monterey Ave, 92260. Tel 619-773-2574; FAX 619-776-7310; *Chmn* John Norman. Instrs: FT 3, PT 10
Estab 1962; pub; D & E; scholarships; SC 10, LC 3; enrl D 150, E 150, maj 15
Ent Req: HS dipl, ent exam
Degrees: AA 2 yrs
Tuition: $13 per unit; no campus res
Courses: Art History, Ceramics, Design, Drawing, Painting, Photography, Printmaking, Sculpture, Advertising Art, Introduction to Art, Oriental Brush Painting
Summer School: Six wk session. Courses—Art History, Ceramics, Painting, Sculpture

PASADENA

ART CENTER COLLEGE OF DESIGN, 1700 Lida St, PO Box 7197, 91109. Tel 818-396-2200; FAX 818-405-9104; *Pres* David R Brown, MA; *Communication Design Chmn* James Miho, BFA; *Fine Arts Dept Chmn* Laurence Drieband, MFA; *Film Dept Chmn* Robert Peterson, BFA; *Photography Dept Chmn* Tim Bradley, BFA; *Transportation Design Chmn* Ron Hill, BS; *Liberal Arts, Sciences & Graduate Studies Chmn* Richard Hertz, PhD; *Computer Graphics Chmn* Robert Hennigar, MFA; *Illustration Chmn* Philip Hays, BFA; *Product Design Chmn* C Martin Smith, BFA; *Environmental Design Chmn* Patricia Oliver, MArch
Estab 1930; pvt; D & E; scholarships; SC 168, LC 82, GC 22; enrl D 1200, E 200, non-maj 200, maj 1200, grad 60
Ent Req: HS dipl, ACT, SAT if no col background, portfolio required, at least 12 samples of work in proposed maj
Degrees: BFA, BS, MFA, MS
Courses: †Advertising Design, Aesthetics, Architecture, Art History, Calligraphy, Collages, Commercial Art, Conceptual Art, Design, Drafting, Drawing, Fashion Arts, †Film, Graphic Arts, †Graphic Design, History of Art & Archaeology, †Illustration, Intermedia, Interior Design, Mixed Media, †Painting, †Photography, Printmaking, Video, †Advertising Illustration, †Critical Theory, †Environmental Design, †Fashion Illustration, †Graphic Packaging, New Media, †Product Design, †Transportation Design
Adult Hobby Classes: Enrl 550, tuition $255 per cr for 14 wk term. Courses—Advertising, Computer Graphics, Film, Fine Arts, Graphics, Illustration, Industrial Design, Liberal Arts & Sciences, Photography
Children's Classes: Enrl 230; tuition $125 per class for 10 wks; Sat classes for high school

PASADENA CITY COLLEGE, Art Dept, 1570 E Colorado Blvd, 91106. Tel 818-578-7238; FAX 818-585-7123; *Div Dean* Dr Linda Malm; *Acting Area Head Design* Eric Peterson; *Acting Area Head Art* Suzanne Bravender, MA; *Acting Area Head Photography* Michael Mims, MA; *Acting Area Head History* Sandra Haynes, MA; *Acting Area Head Jewelry* Kay Yee, MA; *Acting Area Head Ceramics* Phil Cornelius, MA
Estab 1902, dept estab 1916; pub; D & E; scholarships; SC 50; enrl D 2000, E 1200,

non-maj 3200, maj 400
Ent Req: HS dipl
Degrees: AA 2 yrs
Tuition: $13 per unit
Courses: Advertising Design, Art History, Ceramics, Commercial Art, Drawing, Graphic Arts, Graphic Design, Illustration, Jewelry, Lettering, Painting, Photography, Printmaking, Sculpture, Film Art, Filmmaking, Product Design
Adult Hobby Classes: Enrl 3000; tuition $10 per unit, BA $50 per unit
Summer School: Dir, Linda Malm. Enrl 500; tuition $13 per unit for two wk sessions. Courses—Art History, Ceramics, Cinema, Design, Jewelry, Photography, Studio Arts

POMONA

CALIFORNIA STATE POLYTECHNIC UNIVERSITY, POMONA, Art Dept, College of Environmental Design, 3801 W Temple Blvd, 91768. Tel 909-869-3508; FAX 909-869-4939; *Chair* Dr Maren Henderson, PhD; *Prof* Stanley Wilson, MFA; *Prof* Yoram Makow, MA; *Prof* Charles Fredrick, MFA; *Prof* Joe Hannibal, MFA; *Prof* Eileen Fears, MFA; *Assoc Prof* Sandra Rowe, MFA; *Assoc Prof* Babette Mayor, MFA
Estab 1966; pub; D & E; SC 66, LC 15; enrl D approx 300, E approx 50, non-maj 470, maj 300
Ent Req: HS dipl, plus testing
Degrees: BA 4 yrs
Tuition: $297 per qtr 6 or more units, $187 per qtr 5 units or less; campus res $4245 per yr
Courses: †Advertising Design, †Art Education, †Art History, †Ceramics, †Drafting, †Drawing, †Graphic Arts, †History of Art & Archaeology, †Illustration, †Lettering, Museum Staff Training, †Painting, †Teacher Training, Textile Design, †Studio Crafts
Adult Hobby Classes: Courses offered through Office of Continuing Education
Summer School: Tuition same as above for regular 10 wk quarter. Courses—usually lower division

PORTERVILLE

PORTERVILLE COLLEGE, Dept of Fine Arts, 100 E College, 93257. Tel 209-781-3130, Ext 257, 323; *Chmn* Tom Howell. Instrs: FT 2, PT 6
Estab 1927; pub; D & E; SC 18, LC 3; enrl D 300, E 78, non-maj 320, maj 58
Ent Req: HS dipl or over 18 yrs of age
Degrees: AA and AS 2 yrs
Tuition: Nonres—$107 per unit
Courses: Art History, Ceramics, Drawing, Design, Handicrafts, Jewelry, Painting, Photography, Sculpture, Textile Design, Theatre Arts, Airbrush, color, weaving
Adult Hobby Classes: Courses—Jewelry, Weaving
Summer School: Dir, Nero Pruitt. Enrl 700 Term of 6 wks beginning June 13. Courses—Ceramics, Jewelry, Weaving

QUINCY

FEATHER RIVER COMMUNITY COLLEGE, Art Dept, PO Box 1110, 95971. Tel 916-283-0202; *Chmn* Jack Greenspan
Scholarships
Tuition: Res—$13 per unit; nonres—$125 per unit
Courses: Art Appreciation, Art History, Ceramics, Design, Drawing, Painting, Sculpture, Textile Design, Weaving

RANCHO CUCAMONGA

CHAFFEY COMMUNITY COLLEGE, Art Dept, 5885 Haven Ave, 91737. Tel 909-987-1737; *Dept Chmn* Jan Raithel
E; scholarships offered
Degrees: AA
Tuition: Nonres—$55 per unit
Courses: Art History, Ceramics, Design, Drawing, Graphic Arts, Graphic Design, Illustration, Interior Design, Mixed Media, Museum Staff Training, Painting, Photography, Sculpture, Theatre Arts
Summer School: Dir, Byron Wilding. Enrl 200; tuition $13 for 6 wk courses. Courses—Art History, Ceramics, Design, Drawing, Graphic Computer Design

REDDING

SHASTA COLLEGE, Art Dept, Fine Arts Division, PO Box 496006, 96049. Tel 916-225-4761; FAX 916-225-4830; *Dir Division Fine Arts* Kathleen Kistler
Estab 1950; pub; D & E
Ent Req: HS dipl
Degrees: AA 2 yr
Tuition: Res—$13 per unit; nonres—$106 per unit
Courses: Art History, Ceramics, Commercial Art, Drawing, Jewelry, Painting, Printmaking, Sculpture
Summer School: Dir, Dean Summer Prog. Enrl 150; tuition same as regular sem

REDLANDS

UNIVERSITY OF REDLANDS, Dept of Art, 1200 E Colton Ave, 92374. Tel 909-793-2121; *Chmn* John Brownfield
Estab 1909; pvt; D & E; scholarships and fels; SC 18, LC 12; enrl 1500
Ent Req: HS grad, ent exam
Degrees: BA and BS 4 yr, MA, ME, MAT
Tuition: $16,500 per yr with food & housing $23,000
Courses: Art History, Ceramics, Drawing, Graphic Arts, Painting, Teacher Training, Ethnic Art

RIVERSIDE

CALIFORNIA BAPTIST COLLEGE, Art Dept, 8432 Magnolia Ave, 92504. Tel 909-689-5771, Ext 270; *Chmn* Mack Branden
Scholarships
Degrees: BA
Tuition: $300 per unit
Courses: Art Appreciation, Art History, Ceramics, Design, Drawing, Painting, Printmaking, Sculpture

LA SIERRA UNIVERSITY, Art Dept, 4700 Pierce, 92515. Tel 909-785-2170; *Chmn & Prof* Luis Ramirez; *Prof* Susan Patt; *Prof* Roger Churches; *Instr* Jan Inman; *Instr* Richard McMillan
Estab 1905; den; D & E; SC 29, LC 8, GC 1; enrl D 2354
Ent Req: HS dipl, SAT
Degrees: BA, BS 4 yrs
Tuition: Res—$3580 per quarter; nonres—$3580 per quarter; campus res—room & board $1195
Courses: Art History, Calligraphy, †Ceramics, Drawing, †Graphic Design, Illustration, Lettering, Occupational Therapy, †Painting, †Photography, †Printmaking, †Sculpture, Computer Graphics
Adult Hobby Classes: Enrl 35 per wk; tuition $330 per wk for 4 wk term. Courses—Watercolor Workshop
Summer School: Chmn, Roger Churches. 6 wk, 2-4 units. Courses—Art in the Elementary & Secondary School

RIVERSIDE COMMUNITY COLLEGE, Dept of Art & Mass Media, 4800 Magnolia Ave, 92506. Tel 909-222-8000; FAX 909-222-8033; *Chmn* Charles Richard; *Chmn* Jo Dierdorff
Estab 1917; pub; D & E; SC 20, LC 3; enrl D 910, E 175
Ent Req: HS dipl or over 18 yrs of age
Degrees: AA 2 yrs
Tuition: Res—undergrad $13 per unit, nonres—$114 per unit
Courses: Advertising Design, Art Appreciation, Art History, Ceramics, Design, Drawing, Painting, Printmaking, Sculpture, Teacher Training, 3-D Design
Summer School: Term of 6 wks beginning June 21. Courses—Art for Elementary Teachers, Art History, Ceramics, Drawing, Painting, Sculpture

UNIVERSITY OF CALIFORNIA, RIVERSIDE

—Dept of the History of Art, 92521. Tel 909-787-1012, 787-4627; FAX 909-787-2331; *Chmn & Assoc Prof* Steven F Ostrow, PhD; *Prof* Jonathan W Green, MA; *Prof* Francoise Forster-Hahn, PhD; *Prof Emeriti* Derioksen M Brinkerhoff, PhD; *Prof Emeriti* Thomas O Pelzel, PhD; *Assoc Prof* Conrad Rudolph, PhD; *Asst Prof* Ginger C Hsu, PhD; *Asst Prof* Amelia G Jones, PhD; *Asst Prof* Patricia M Morton, PhD; *Asst Prof* Regina Stefaniak, PhD
Estab 1954; pub; D; LC 18, GC 5; enrl maj 13, grad 13
Ent Req: HS dipl, res grad-point average 3.1, nonres grade-point average 3.4
Degrees: BA, MA
Tuition: Res—undergrad $1364, grad $1603; nonres—undergrad $3930, grad $4163
Courses: Art History, History of Photography
—Dept of Art, 92521. Tel 909-787-4634; *Chmn* John Divola; *Prof* James S Strombotne, MFA; *Assoc Prof* Erika Sudeburg; *Asst Prof* Uta Barth; *Lectr* Gordon L Thorpe, MA
Estab 1954; pub; D; SC 14, LC 2; enrl maj 48
Ent Req: HS dipl
Degrees: BA, MA, MFA
Tuition: Res—undergrad $1364 per qtr, grad $1603; nonres—undergrad $3930 per qtr, grad $4163
Courses: Drawing, Painting, Photography, Printmaking, Video

ROCKLIN

SIERRA COMMUNITY COLLEGE, Art Dept, Liberal Arts Division, 5000 Rocklin Rd, 95677. Tel 916-624-3333; *Dean Humanities* Bill Tsuji; *Instr* Jim Adamson, MA; *Instr* Pam Johnson; *Instr* Dottie Brown
Estab 1914; pub; D & E; SC 18, LC 4; enrl D & E approx 9000
Ent Req: English Placement Test
Degrees: AA
Tuition: Res—undergrad $13 per unit; nonres—$125 per unit
Courses: Art Education, Art History, Ceramics, Drawing, Painting, Photography, Printmaking, Sculpture
Summer School: Ceramics, Painting

ROHNERT PARK

SONOMA STATE UNIVERSITY, Art Dept, 1801 E Cotati Ave, 94928. Tel 707-664-2151, 664-2364; FAX 707-664-2505; *Art Chmn* William Guynn; *Interim Chair* Michael Schwager
Estab 1961, dept estab 1961; pub; D & E; SC 38, LC 17; enrl D 6000
Ent Req: HS dipl, SAT, eligibility req must be met
Degrees: BA & BFA
Tuition: Res—$1101 regular fee per sem; nonres—$1101 regular fee plus $246 per unit; payment plan available; regular campus res available
Courses: Art Education, Art History, Ceramics, Drawing, Painting, Photography, Printmaking, Sculpture, Teacher Training, Papermaking
Adult Hobby Classes: Various classes offered through Extended Educ
Summer School: Various classes offered through Extended Educ

SACRAMENTO

AMERICAN RIVER COLLEGE, Dept of Art, 4700 College Oak Dr, 95841. Tel 916-484-8011, 484-8433; *Instr* Ken Magri, MA; *Instr* Betty Nelsen, MA; *Instr* Gary L Pruner, MA; *Instr* Pam Maddock, MA; *Instr* Tom J Brozovich, MA; *Instr* James Kaneko
Estab 1954; pub; D & E; scholarships; SC 50, LC 12; enrl D 10,000, E 10,000, non-maj 5000
Ent Req: HS dipl
Degrees: AA 2 yrs or more
Tuition: Nonres—$600 per sem or $40 per unit
Courses: Art Appreciation, Art History, Ceramics, Commercial Art, Design, Drawing, Film, Graphic Arts, Graphic Design, Illustration, Interior Design, Jewelry, Lettering, Painting, Photography, Printmaking, Sculpture, Gallery Management
Summer School: Dir, Rick Ida. Enrl 120; tuition $13 per unit June-Aug. Courses—Ceramics, Design, Drawing, Introduction to Art, Photography

CALIFORNIA STATE UNIVERSITY, SACRAMENTO, Dept of Art, 6000 J St, 95819-6061. Tel 916-278-6166; FAX 916-278-7287; *Chmn* Lita Whitesel. Instrs: FT 20
Estab 1950; pub; D; scholarships; SC 40, LC 18, GC 12; enrl maj 585
Ent Req: HS dipl, ent exam
Degrees: BA 4 yr, MA
Tuition: Res—$597 (0-6 units), $930 (7 plus units); nonres—$843 per unit
Courses: Art Education, Art History, Ceramics, Drawing, Jewelry, Painting, Printmaking, Sculpture, Arts with Metals, Computer Art
Summer School: Enrl 225; 3 & 6 wk sessions

SACRAMENTO CITY COLLEGE, Art Dept, 3835 Freeport Blvd, 95822. Tel 916-558-2551; *Dir Humanities & Fine Arts* Larry Hendricks; *Instr* Laureen Landau, MFA; *Instr* F Dalkey; *Instr* Darrell Forney; *Instr* George A Esquibel, MA; *Instr* B Palisin; *Instr* I Shaskan
Estab 1927, dept estab 1929; pub; D & E; SC 17, LC 9; enrl D 880, E 389
Ent Req: HS dipl
Degrees: AA 2 yrs
Tuition: Res—undergrad $13 per unit, grad $50 per unit; nonres—undergrad $120 per unit
Courses: Ceramics, Commercial Art, Drawing, Jewelry, Painting, Photography, Sculpture, Theatre Arts, Modern Art, Technology
Summer School: Dir, George A Esquibel. Courses—Art History, Design, Drawing, Oil-Acrylic, Watercolor

SALINAS

HARTNELL COLLEGE, Art & Photography Dept, 156 Homestead Ave, 93901. Tel 408-755-6905; FAX 408-759-6052; *Dean Fine Arts* Dr Daniel A Ipson. Instrs: FT 6, PT 13
Estab 1922; pub; D & E; SC 14, LC 3; enrl D 350 E 160, major 30
Ent Req: HS dipl
Degrees: AA 2 yr
Tuition: None; no campus res
Courses: Ceramics, Drafting, Drawing, Graphic Arts, History of Art & Archaeology, Painting, Photography, Sculpture, Stage Design, Theatre Arts, Video, Weaving, Foundry, Gallery Management, Metalsmithing
Summer School: Enrl 150; tuition free; begins approx June 15. Courses—Art Appreciation, Ceramics, Drawing, Film Making, Photography

SAN BERNARDINO

CALIFORNIA STATE UNIVERSITY, SAN BERNARDINO, Visual Arts, 5500 University Pky, 92407. Tel 909-880-5802; *Chmn Dept* William D Warehall; *Gallery Dir* Richard M Johnston; *Instr* Roger Lintault, MFA; *Instr* Joe Moran, MFA; *Instr* Leo Doyle, MFA; *Instr* Don Woodford, MFA; *Instr* Billie Sessions; *Instr* Julius Kaplan, PhD; *Instr* George McGinnis; *Instr* Sant Khalsa, MFA; *Instr* Mary Goodwin, PhD; *Instr* Peter Holliday, PhD
Estab 1965; pub; D & E; scholarships; enrl D 13,000, maj 190
Ent Req: HS dipl, SAT
Degrees: BA 4 yr, MA 2 yr
Tuition: Res—undergrad $645 per 15 units; nonres—undergrad $126 per unit; campus res—room & board $3195 per yr
Courses: †Advertising Design, Art Education, †Art History, †Ceramics, Drawing, †Painting, †Photography, †Printmaking, †Sculpture, †Furniture Design, Glassblowing, Glasscasting

SAN BERNARDINO VALLEY COLLEGE, Art Dept, 701 S Mount Vernon Ave, 92410. Tel 909-888-6511; *Head Dept* David Lawrence. Instrs: FT 5, PT 7
Estab 1926; pub; D & E; scholarships; enrl D 750, E 400, maj 230
Ent Req: HS dipl or 18 yrs of age
Degrees: AA and AS 2 yrs
Tuition: Res—undergrad $13 per unit; nonres—$120 per unit
Courses: Architecture, Art History, Ceramics, Commercial Art, Drafting, Drawing, Film, Lettering, Painting, Photography, Sculpture, Theatre Arts, Advertising Art, Basic Design, Computer Graphics, Designs in Glass, Glass Blowing, Life Drawing

SAN DIEGO

SAN DIEGO MESA COLLEGE, Fine Arts Dept, 7250 Mesa College Dr, 92111-0103. Tel 619-627-2829; *Chmn* Beate Berman-Enn; *Instr* Barbara Blackmun, PhD; *Instr* Ross Stockwell, MA; *Instr* Anita Brynolf, MA; *Instr* Hiroshi Miyazaki, MA; *Instr* Georgia Laris, MA; *Instr* John Conrad; *Instr* Richard Lou
Estab 1964; pub; D & E; scholarships; SC 29, LC 7; enrl D 10,000, E 29,000, maj 300
Ent Req: HS dipl or age 18
Degrees: AA 2 yrs
Tuition: Res—$10 per unit; nonres—$75 per unit; no campus res

Courses: Art History, Ceramics, Drawing, Handicrafts, Jewelry, Art Education, Painting, Photography, Sculpture, Book Arts, Crafts, Graphic Communications, Gallery Studies, Studio Arts
Summer School: Dir, John Conrad. Enrl 200; tuition & courses same as regular sem

SAN DIEGO STATE UNIVERSITY, School of Art, Design & Art History, 5500 Campanile Dr, 92182-4805. Tel 619-594-6511; FAX 619-594-1217; *Dir* Fredrick Orth, MFA; *Studio Graduate Coordr* Richard Burkett, MFA; *Art History Graduate Coordr* Ida K Rigby, PhD
Estab 1897; pub; D & E; scholarships; SC 140, LC 35, GC 30; enrl maj 900
Ent Req: HS dipl
Degrees: BA 4 yrs, MA, MFA
Tuition: Campus res—room & board
Courses: †Art History, †Ceramics, Commercial Art, Conceptual Art, †Drawing, Fashion Arts, Goldsmithing, †Graphic Design, Handicrafts, History of Art & Archaeology, Intermedia, †Interior Design, †Jewelry, Mixed Media, †Painting, †Printmaking, †Sculpture, †Silversmithing, †Textile Design, †Weaving, †Environmental Design, †Furniture Design †Gallery Design
Summer School: Dir, F J Orth. Tuition $128 per cr hr June-Aug. Courses— Art History, Ceramics, Drawing, Graphic Design, Painting, Sculpture

UNIVERSITY OF SAN DIEGO, Art Dept, 5998 Alcala Park, 92110. Tel 619-260-4600; FAX 619-260-4619, Ext 4486; *Chmn* Sally Yard. Instrs: FT 4
Estab 1952; pvt; D & E; scholarships; SC 19, LC 7; enrl univ 5300, maj 50
Ent Req: HS dipl, SAT
Degrees: BA 4 yrs
Tuition: $465 per unit
Courses: †Art History, †Ceramics, †Drawing, †Painting, †Photography, †Printmaking, †Sculpture, †Art in Elementary Education, †Art Management, †Design, †Enameling, †Exhibition Design, †Museum Internship, †Weaving
Summer School: Tuition $230 per unit for terms of 3 wk, 6 wk beginning June 1; 2 courses offered

SAN FRANCISCO

ACADEMY OF ART COLLEGE, Fine Arts Dept, 625 Sutter, 94108. Tel 415-274-2229; *Pres* Elisa Stephens; *Dir Advertising* John Heaphy; *Dir Illustration* Melissa Marshall, BFA; *Co Chair Fine Art* Craig Nelson; *Co Chair Fine Art* William Maughan; *Dir Photography* Bob Turner; *Co Chair Interior Design* David Davis. Instrs: FT 2, PT 8
Estab 1929; pvt; D & E; scholarships; SC 200, LC 100; enrl D 2000, E 150, grad 20
Ent Req: HS dipl
Degrees: BFA 4 yrs, MFA 2 yrs
Tuition: Res—undergrad $6000 per yr, $250 per unit, grad $6600 per yr, $275 per unit; campus res available
Courses: Advertising Design, Aesthetics, Architecture, Art History, Ceramics, Collages, Commercial Art, Design, Drawing, Fashion Arts, Film, Graphic Arts, Graphic Design, Illustration, Industrial Design, Interior Design, Jewelry, Mixed Media, Painting, Photography, Printmaking, Sculpture, Video
Adult Hobby Classes: Enrl 75; tuition $350 per unit. Courses—Basic Painting, Ceramics, Portrait Painting, Pottery
Summer School: Term of 6 wks beginning June 23. Courses—Commercial & Fine Art

CITY COLLEGE OF SAN FRANCISCO, Art Dept, 50 Phelan Ave, 94112. Tel 415-239-3157; *Chairperson* Raymond Holbert
Estab 1935; pub; D & E; SC 45, LC 10; enrl col D 15,000, E 11,000
Degrees: AA 2 yrs
Tuition: $13 per unit
Courses: Art History, Ceramics, Drawing, Graphic Design, Illustration, Industrial Design, Jewelry, Lettering, Painting, Sculpture, Basic Design, Metal Arts, Mixed Media, Printmaking, Visual Communication
Summer School: Courses—same as regular yr

SAN FRANCISCO ART INSTITUTE, Admissions Office, 800 Chestnut St, 94133. Tel 415-771-7020; *Dir Admissions* Tim Robison
Estab 1871; pvt; D & E; scholarships; SC 80, LC 22, GC 11; enrl non-maj 44, maj 4538 grad 143
Ent Req: HS dipl or GED
Degrees: BFA 4 yrs, MFA 2 yrs
Tuition: $12,400 per yr, $6200 per sem; no campus res
Courses: †Ceramics, Film, Painting, Photography, Printmaking, Sculpture, †Performance/Video
Adult Hobby Classes: Tuition $290 for 4-11 wk session (per course).
Courses—Variety of studio courses year round
Children's Classes: Enrl 40; tuition 8 wk session. Courses—Variety of studio courses, summers
Summer School: Dir, K Reasoner. Tuition 2-8 wk sessions $1800 course. Courses—Variety of studio courses

SAN FRANCISCO STATE UNIVERSITY, Art Dept, 1600 Holloway, 94132. Tel 415-338-2176; FAX 415-338-6537; *Chmn* Sylvia Walters; *Dean* Morrison Keith. Instrs: FT 25, PT 10
Estab 1899; pub; D; SC 80, LC 20, GC 15; enrl D 450, maj 450, grad 80
Ent Req: HS dipl
Degrees: BA 4 yrs, MFA 3 yrs, MA 2 yrs
Tuition: Nonres—$189 per unit; campus res available
Courses: Art Education, Art History, Ceramics, Painting, Photography, Printmaking, Sculpture, Textile Design, Conceptual Design, Mixed Emphasis
Summer School: Not regular session. Self-supporting classes in Art History, Ceramics, Photography, Printmaking

SAN JACINTO

MOUNT SAN JACINTO COLLEGE, Art Dept, 1499 N State St, 92583. Tel 909-654-8011, Ext 1531; *Dept Chair* John Seed, MA; *Instr* Carolyn Kaneshiro, MA; *Instr* Max DeMoss; *Instr* Gary Cominotto; *Instr* Sandra Robinson; *Instr* Anita Rodriguez
Estab 1964; pub; D & E; SC 8, LC 2; enrl D 250, E 420, non-maj 400, maj 50
Ent Req: HS dipl
Degrees: AA & AS
Tuition: $12 per unit
Courses: Art History, Ceramics, Painting, Sculpture, Basic Design
Children's Classes: Studio courses
Summer School: Courses—Drawing

SAN JOSE

SAN JOSE CITY COLLEGE, School of Fine Arts, 2100 Moorpark Ave, 95128. Tel 408-298-2181, Ext 3815; *Interim Dean Humanities & Social Science* Jim Potterson; *Interim Pres* William Kester; *Instr* Judith Bell
Estab 1921; pub; D & E; SC 7, LC 2; enrl D 320, E 65
Ent Req: HS dipl or 18 yrs of age or older
Degrees: AA 2 yrs
Tuition: Res—$13 per unit; nonres—$126 per unit
Courses: Art History, Ceramics, Drawing, Painting, Photography, Theatre Arts, Color, Expressive & Representational Drawing, Life Drawing, 2-D & 3-D Design

SAN JOSE STATE UNIVERSITY, School of Art & Design, One Washington Square, 95192-0089. Tel 408-924-4320; FAX 408-924-4326; *Dir* Robert Milnes, PhD; *Art Educ Coordn* Adrienne Kraut, DED; *Art Educ Coordr* Pamela Sharp, PhD; *Assoc Chair, Art History* Bruce Radde, PhD; *Assoc Chair, Studio* David Middlebrook, MFA; *Assoc Chair, Design* Lanning Stern, MFA; *Assoc Chair, Art History* William Gaugler, PhD; *Graduate Prog Coordr* Paul Staiger, MFA
Estab 1857, dept estab 1911; pub; D & E; scholarships; SC 90, LC 28, GC 25; enrl D 4529, maj 1400, grad 94
Ent Req: ACT & grade point average, SAT
Degrees: BA(Art), BA(Art History) 4 yrs, BS(Graphic Design), BS(Industrial Design), BS(Interior Design) & BFA(Art) 4 1/2 yrs, MA(Art), MA(Art History), MA(Design), MA(Multimedia) & MA(Computers in Fine Arts) 1 yr, MFA(Pictorial Arts), MFA(Photography), MFA(Spatial Arts) & MFA(Computers in Fine Arts) 2 yrs
Tuition: Res—$502 - $778 per sem; non-res—$502 - $778 per sem plus $246 per unit
Courses: †Art Education, †Art History, Ceramics, Drawing, †Graphic Design, Illustration, †Industrial Design, †Interior Design, Jewelry, Photography, Printmaking, Sculpture, Teacher Training, †Crafts (Jewelry, Textiles)
Summer School: Interim Dean Continuing Educ, Paul Bradley. Tuition $160 per unit for three summer sessions of 3 & 6 wks; 3 wk Jan session. Courses-Vary according to professors available & projected demand

SAN LUIS OBISPO

CALIFORNIA POLYTECHNIC STATE UNIVERSITY AT SAN LUIS OBISPO, Dept of Art & Design, 93407. Tel 805-756-1148; *Prof* C W Jennings, MFA; *Prof* Robert Reynolds, MAE; *Prof* Robert Densham, MFA; *Prof* Clarissa Hewitt, MFA; *Prof* Robert D Howell, MA; *Prof* John Mendenhall, MA; *Prof* Keith Dills, PhD; *Prof* Eric B Johnson, MFA; *Prof* Henry Wessels, MFA; *Prof* Joanne Ruggles, MFA; *Prof* Mary La Porte, MFA; *Prof* George Jercich, MFA; *Prof* Sky Bergman, MFA; *Prof* Jean Wetzel, PhD. Instrs: FT 14
Estab 1901, dept estab 1969; pub; D & E; scholarships; SC 40, LC 12; enrl D 1000, E 100, non-maj 1100, maj 220
Ent Req: HS dipl, portfolio review
Degrees: BS(Applied Art & Design) 4 yrs
Tuition: Res—undergrad $2220 per yr; nonres—undergrad $4029 per yr; campus res—room & board $3120 per yr
Courses: Advertising Design, Art History, Ceramics, Drawing, Graphic Arts, Graphic Design, Painting, Photography, Printmaking, Sculpture, Design History, Glass, Metalsmithing
Summer School: Chair, Eric B Johnson. Enrl 215; tuition $740 for term June 20-Sept 2. Courses—Basic b/w Photography, Ceramics, Fundamentals of Drawing, Intermediate Drawing

CUESTA COLLEGE, Art Dept, PO Box 8106, 93403-8106. Tel 805-546-3199; *Chmn Fine Arts Div & Instr* Bob Pelfrey; *Instr* Guyla Call Amyx; *Instr* Marian Galczenski
Estab 1964; pub; D & E; scholarships; enrl in col D 3200, E 3082
Ent Req: HS dipl or Calif HS Proficiency Exam
Degrees: AA and AS
Tuition: Nonres—$85 per unit
Courses: Art History, Ceramics, Display, Drawing, Graphic Design, Painting, Printmaking, Sculpture, Video, Camera Art
Summer School: Chmn Div Fine Arts, Barry Frantz. Courses—Drawing, Art History

SAN MARCOS

PALOMAR COMMUNITY COLLEGE, Art Dept, 1140 W Mission Rd, 92069. Tel 619-744-1150, Ext 2302; FAX 619-744-8123; *Chmn* Val Sanders, MA; *Assoc Prof* Harry E Bliss, MFA; *Assoc Prof* G D Durrant, MA; *Assoc Prof* Jay Shultz; *Assoc Prof* Frank Jones, MFA; *Assoc Prof* Anthony J Lugo, MA; *Assoc Prof* Barry C Reed, MFA; *Assoc Prof* James T Saw, MA; *Assoc Prof* Louise Kirtland Boehm, MA; *Assoc Prof* Michael Steirnagle; *Assoc Prof* Steve Miller
Estab 1950; pub; D & E; scholarships; SC 31, LC 4; enrl D 775, E 200
Ent Req: Art exam
Degrees: AA 2 yr
Tuition: $13 per unit

Courses: Art History, †Ceramics, Collages, †Commercial Art, †Drawing, Graphic Arts, Graphic Design, Handicrafts, Illustration, †Jewelry, Lettering, †Painting, †Printmaking, Sculpture, †Silversmithing, Design Composition, Glassblowing, Life Drawing, Stained Glass
Summer School: Courses—basic courses except commercial art and graphic design

SAN MATEO

COLLEGE OF SAN MATEO, Creative Arts Dept, 1700 W Hillsdale Blvd, 94402. Tel 415-574-6288; FAX 415-358-6842; *Dir Fine Arts* Grace Sonner
Pub; D & E
Degrees: AA 2 yr
Tuition: Res—$13 per unit, nonres—$113 per unit; no campus res
Courses: †Architecture, Art History, Ceramics, †Commercial Art, Design, Drafting, Drawing, †Film, Graphic Arts, Graphic Design, Painting, Photography, Printmaking, Sculpture, Video, †General Art

SAN PABLO

CONTRA COSTA COMMUNITY COLLEGE, Dept of Art, 2600 Mission Bell Dr, 94806. Tel 510-235-7800; FAX 510-236-6768; *Dept Head* Paul Pernish
Estab 1950; pub; D & E; SC 10, LC 16; enrl D 468, E 200
Ent Req: HS dipl or 18 yrs old
Degrees: Cert of Achievement 1 yr, AA and AS 2 yrs
Tuition: Res—$13 per unit; nonres—$114 per unit; no campus res
Courses: Art History, Ceramics, Drawing, Painting, Photography, Sculpture, Silkscreen
Summer School: Assoc Dean Continuing Educ, William Vega. Enrl 50; tuition free for term of 8 wks beginning June 26. Courses—Art, Art Appreciation

SAN RAFAEL

DOMINICAN COLLEGE OF SAN RAFAEL, Art Dept, 50 Acacia Ave, 94901. Tel 415-457-4440; FAX 415-485-3205; *Chmn* Edith Bresnahan
Scholarships
Degrees: BA, MA 4 yr
Tuition: Undergrad—$6395 per sem
Courses: Advertising Design, Art Appreciation, Art Education, Art History, Calligraphy, Ceramics, Design, Drawing, Handicrafts, Painting, Photography, Printmaking, Sculpture, Stage Design, Textile Design, Theatre Arts, Weaving, Pottery

SANTA ANA

RANCHO SANTIAGO COLLEGE, Art Dept, 1530 W 17th St, 92706. Tel 714-564-5600; FAX 714-564-6379; *Dean of Fine & Performing Arts* Thom Hill, MA; *Art Instr* Gene Isaacson; *Instr* Estelle Orr, MFA; *Instr* George E Geyer, MA; *Instr* Patrick Crabb, MA; *Instr* Frank Molner, MA; *Instr* Mayde Herberg; *Instr* Sharon Ford, MA; *Instr* Carol Miura
Estab 1915, dept estab 1960; pub; D & E; scholarships; SC 21, LC 5; enrl D 280, E 160, maj 57
Ent Req: HS dipl
Degrees: AA 2 yrs
Tuition: Res—$13 per unit; nonres—$114 per unit
Courses: Advertising Design, Architecture, Art History, Ceramics, Commercial Art, Display, Drawing, Graphic Arts, Graphic Design, Handicrafts, Interior Design, Jewelry, Museum Staff Training, Painting, Sculpture, Computer Graphics, Glass Blowing
Adult Hobby Classes: Ceramics, Stained Glass
Summer School: Dir, Dean Thom Hill. Enrl 3000; tuition free for term of 6-8 wks beginning early June. Courses—Art Concepts, Ceramics, Design, Drawing, Painting

SANTA BARBARA

SANTA BARBARA CITY COLLEGE, Fine Arts Dept, 721 Cliff Dr, 93109-2394. Tel 805-965-0581; FAX 805-963-7222; *Chmn* Ed Inks
Scholarships
Degrees: AA
Tuition: Res—undergrad $107 per yr
Courses: Advertising Design, Architecture, Art Appreciation, Art History, Calligraphy, Ceramics, Design, Drawing, Fashion Arts, Film, Handicrafts, Industrial Design, Interior Design, Jewelry, Painting, Printmaking, Sculpture, Stage Design, Textile Design, Weaving, Cartooning, Glassblowing

UNIVERSITY OF CALIFORNIA, SANTA BARBARA, Dept of Art Studio, 93106. Tel 805-893-3138; FAX 805-893-7206; *Chmn Dept* Richard Ross
Estab 1868, dept estab 1950; pub; D; scholarships; SC 32, LC 17, GC 7; enrl D 431, grad 60
Ent Req: HS dipl
Degrees: BA 4 yrs, MFA 2 yrs, PhD 7 yrs
Tuition: Res—undergrad $1459 per qtr; nonres—$4026 per qtr
Courses: Art Education, Ceramics, Drawing, Painting, Photography, Printmaking, Sculpture

SANTA CLARA

SANTA CLARA UNIVERSITY, Art Dept, Alameda & Bellomy, 95053. Tel 408-554-4594; FAX 408-554-2343; *Chmn* Robert K Detweiler, MFA; *Assoc Prof* Susan Felter, MFA; *Assoc Prof* Sam Hernandez, MFA; *Sr Lect* Gerald P Sullivan, SJ; *Asst Prof* Eric Apfelstadt, PhD; *Lectr* Kathleen Maxwell, PhD
Estab 1851, dept estab 1972; pvt; D; SC 9, LC 14; enrl D 700, non-maj 650, maj 50
Ent Req: HS dipl

Degrees: BA(Fine Arts)
Tuition: $5150 per quarter; campus res—room & board $2260 per quarter
Courses: †Art History, Ceramics, Drawing, Painting, Photography, Printmaking, Sculpture, Computer Art, Etching, Intro to Studio Art
Summer School: Dir, Dr Philip Boo Riley. Enrl 15 per class; 5 & 10 wk terms. Courses—Ceramics, Intro to Art History, Painting, Watercolor

SANTA CRUZ

UNIVERSITY OF CALIFORNIA, SANTA CRUZ, Board of Studies in Art, E104 Baskin Visual Arts, 1156 High St, 95064. Tel 408-459-0111; *Chmn* Joyce Brodsky
Pub; D; SC per quarter 11, LC per quarter 3; enrl D approx 7000, maj 80
Ent Req: HS dipl
Degrees: BA 4 yrs
Tuition: Res—$1463.40 per qtr; nonres—$2566 per qtr
Courses: Aesthetics, Ceramics, Drawing, Graphic Arts, History of Art & Archaeology, Painting, Photography, Sculpture, Stage Design, Theatre Arts, Book Arts, Intaglio Printmaking, Lithography, Metal Sculpture, Women Artists

SANTA MARIA

ALLAN HANCOCK COLLEGE, Fine Arts Dept, 800 S College Dr, 93454. Tel 805-922-6966, Ext 3252; *Head* Harold Case. Instrs: FT 10, PT 20
Estab 1920. College has three other locations; pub; D & E; scholarships; SC 24, LC 4; enrl D 800, E 220, maj 115
Ent Req: HS dipl, over 18 and educable
Degrees: AA 2 yrs
Tuition: Nonres—$114 per unit
Courses: Art Appreciation, Art History, Ceramics, Costume Design & Construction, Design, Drawing, †Film, †Graphic Arts, Graphic Design, History of Art & Archaeology, Painting, †Photography, Sculpture, †Theatre Arts, †Video, Art Appreciation, Dance, Life Drawing, Music, Silk Screen, Video Production
Adult Hobby Classes: Enrl 100. Courses—Drawing, Watercolor
Children's Classes: Enrl 20. Courses—Drawing
Summer School: Enrl 230; term of 6-8 wks beginning June. Courses—Animation, Art, Computer Graphics, Dance, Drama, Electronic Music, Film, Video, Graphics, Music, Photography

SANTA ROSA

SANTA ROSA JUNIOR COLLEGE, Art Dept, 1501 Mendocino Ave, 95401. Tel 707-527-4011; FAX 707-527-8416; *Chmn* Kevin Fletcher; *Instr* Will Collier, MA
Estab 1918, dept estab 1935; pub; D & E; scholarships; SC 40, LC 8; enrl D approx 800, E approx 1000
Ent Req: HS dipl
Degrees: AA 2 yrs
Tuition: Res—undergrad $13 per unit; nonres—undergrad $117 per unit; campus res available
Courses: Art Appreciation, Art History, Ceramics, Drawing, Graphic Design, Jewelry, Lettering, Painting, Photography, Printmaking, Sculpture, Weaving, Bronze Casting, Etching, Layout, Poster Design, Pottery, Principles of Color, Silkscreen, 3-D Design
Summer School: Chmn Dept, Maurice Lapp. Term of 6 wks beginning June 20. Courses—Art History, Ceramics, Design, Drawing, Jewelry, Painting, Printmaking, Sculpture, Watercolor

SARATOGA

WEST VALLEY COLLEGE, Art Dept, 14000 Fruitvale Ave, 95070. Tel 408-741-2014; FAX 408-741-2059; *Chmn* Morry Roizen. Instrs: FT 8, PT 5
Estab 1964; pub; D & E; SC 51, LC 12; enrl D 1260, E 801
Ent Req: HS dipl or 18 yrs of age
Degrees: AA, 2 yrs
Tuition: Res fee under $50; no campus res
Courses: Aesthetics, †Ceramics, Commercial Art, Costume Design & Construction, †Design, †Drawing, †Graphic Arts, †History of Art & Archaeology, †Jewelry, Museum Staff Training, †Painting, †Sculpture, Stage Design, Theatre Arts, Weaving, †Etching, †Furniture Design, †Lithography, †Metal Casting, †Occupational Work Experience, †Papermaking, Stained Glass
Adult Hobby Classes: Tuition varies. Courses—many classes offered by Community Development Dept

SONORA

COLUMBIA COLLEGE, Fine Arts, 11600 Columbia College Dr, 95370. Tel 209-588-5115, 588-5150; FAX 209-588-5104; *Instr* Dale Bunse
Estab 1968; pub; D & E; SC 50, LC 4; enrl D 100, E 75, non-maj 90, maj 10
Ent Req: HS dipl or over 18 yrs old
Degrees: AA 2 yrs
Tuition: Nonres—$58 per unit; no campus res
Courses: Art History, Calligraphy, Ceramics, Drafting, Drawing, Film, History of Art & Archaeology, Painting, Photography, Sculpture, Theatre Arts, Video
Summer School: VPres Instruction, Joan Barrett. Courses—Ceramics, Watercolor

SOUTH LAKE TAHOE

LAKE TAHOE COMMUNITY COLLEGE, Art Dept, One Col Dr, 96150. Tel 916-541-4660, Ext 228; *Chmn Art Dept* David Foster, MA; *Painting Instr* Phyllis Shafer, MFA
Estab 1975; pub; D & E; scholarships; SC 22, LC 6; enrl D 375, E 150, non-maj 300, maj 75
Ent Req: HS dipl

Degrees: AA 2 yrs
Tuition: Undergrad $7 per unit, grad $33 per unit
Courses: Art Appreciation, Art History, Ceramics, Design, Drawing, Painting, Photography, Printmaking, Sculpture, Theatre Arts, Color, Design, Watercolor Painting
Summer School: Dir, David Foster. Enrl 100; tuition undergrad $7 per unit, grad $33 per unit. Courses—Art History, Bronze Casting, Ceramics, Design, Intro to Art, Life Drawing, Painting, Photography, Raku Pottery, Sculpture, Watercolor

STANFORD

STANFORD UNIVERSITY, Dept of Art, Cummings Art Bldg, 94305-2018. Tel 415-723-3404; *Chmn Dept Art* Richard Vinograd. Instrs: FT 19
Estab 1891; pvt; D; scholarships; SC 48, LC 63, GC 37 (seminars); enrl 3200, maj 70, grad 40
Ent Req: HS dipl
Degrees: BA 4 yrs, MA 1 yr, MFA 2 yrs, PhD 5 yrs
Tuition: $20,490 per yr; campus res—room & board $7105 per yr
Courses: Art History, Drawing, Painting, Photography, Printmaking, Sculpture
Adult Hobby Classes: Offered through Stanford Continuing Education
Children's Classes: Enrl 250. Courses—Offered through Museum
Summer School: Dir, Paul V Turner. Enrl 100; eight wk term. Courses—Art History, Drawing, Painting, Photography, Printmaking

STOCKTON

SAN JOAQUIN DELTA COLLEGE, Art Dept, 5151 Pacific Ave, 95207. Tel 209-474-5209; *Chmn* Bob Tellander
Estab 1935; pub; D & E; SC 12, LC 2; enrl D 7000, E 6000, Maj 100
Ent Req: HS dipl
Degrees: AA 2 yrs
Tuition: Res—undergrad $10 per unit, with BA $50 per unit; nonres—$115 per unit; no campus res
Courses: Advertising Design, †Architecture, Art Appreciation, Art History, Calligraphy, Ceramics, Collages, Commercial Art, Costume Design & Construction, Design, Drafting, Drawing, Fashion Arts, Film, Graphic Arts, Graphic Design, History of Art & Archaeology, Interior Design, Landscape Architecture, Lettering, Painting, Photography, Printmaking, Sculpture, Stage Design, Textile Design, Theatre Arts, Video
Summer School: Dir, Dr Phillip N Laughlin. Enrl 8000; Six week session. Courses—Same as regular sessions

UNIVERSITY OF THE PACIFIC, College of the Pacific, Dept of Art & Art History, 3601 Pacific Ave, 95211. Tel 209-946-2241; *Chmn* Lucinda Kasser. Instrs: FT 9
Estab 1851; pvt; scholarships; 37 (3 unit) courses & 14 (4 unit) courses available over 4 yrs, independent study; enrl maj 55-70
Ent Req: HS grad with 20 sem grades of recommending quality earned in the 10th, 11th and 12th years in traditional subjects, twelve of these grades must be in acad subj
Degrees: BA & BFA
Tuition: $17,900 per yr, $779 per unit (9-11 units), $615 per unit (1/2-8 1/2 units); campus res—$5526
Courses: Art Education, †Art History, Ceramics, Design, Drawing, Graphic Arts, †Graphic Design, Illustration, Lettering, Painting, Photography, Printmaking, Sculpture, †Arts Administration, Commercial Design, Computer Art, †Studio Art
Summer School: Two 5 wk sessions

SUISUN CITY

SOLANO COMMUNITY COLLEGE, Division of Fine & Applied Art, 4000 Suisun Valley Rd, 94585. Tel 707-864-7000; *Div Dean* Richard Ida; *Instr* Jan Eldridge; *Instr* Kate Delos; *Instr* Marc Lancet; *Instr* Marilyn Tannebaum; *Instr* Ray Salmon; *Instr* Rod Guyer; *Instr* Brice Bowman; *Instr* Marc Pondone; *Instr* Debra Bloomfield; *Instr* Vern Grosowsky; *Instr* Christine Rydell; *Instr* Al Zidek; *Instr* Bruce Blondin
Estab 1945; pub; D & E; SC 16, LC 5; enrl D 255, E 174, maj 429
Ent Req: HS dipl
Degrees: AA 2 yrs
Tuition: Res—$13 per unit; nonres—$122 per unit
Courses: Art History, Ceramics, Commercial Art, Drawing, Illustration, Lettering, Painting, Photography, Printmaking, Sculpture, Fashion Illustration, Form & Composition, Fundamentals of Art, Papermaking, Raku, Silkscreen, Survey of Modern Art, †3-D Art
Adult Hobby Classes: Tuition varies per class. Courses—Cartooning, Jewelry Design, Stained Glass
Summer School: Dean summer session, Dr Don Kirkorian

TAFT

TAFT COLLEGE, Art Department, 29 Emmons Park Dr, 93268. Tel 805-763-4282; *Chmn* Sonja Swenson-Wolsey
Estab 1922; pub; D & E; scholarships; SC 67, LC 6; enrl 1500 total
Ent Req: HS grad or 18 yrs old
Degrees: AA 2 yrs
Tuition: $107 per unit (7-14 units), $114 per unit for out-of-state
Courses: Architecture, †Art History, Ceramics, Commercial Art, Conceptual Art, †Drafting, Drawing, Graphic Arts, Graphic Design, †History of Art & Archaeology, Illustration, Painting, †Photography, Sculpture, Basic Design
Adult Hobby Classes: Courses—Ceramics, Graphic Arts, Jewelry, Painting, Photography
Summer School: Dean, Don Zumbro. Term of 6-8 wks. Courses—vary

THOUSAND OAKS

CALIFORNIA LUTHERAN UNIVERSITY, Art Dept, 60 W Olson Rd, 91360. Tel 805-493-3356; *Chmn* Joel Edwards; *Prof* Larkin Higgins; *Prof* Gerald Shattum; *Lectr* Craig Leese
Estab 1961; pvt; D & E; scholarships; SC 12, LC 7; enrl D 110, non-maj 46, maj 40
Ent Req: HS dipl, SAT or ACT, portfolio suggested
Degrees: BA 4 yr; MA(Educ) 1 - 2 yr
Tuition: Res—undergrad $7500 per yr, $3750 per sem, $230 per unit; campus res—room & board $2900 per year
Courses: Art Education, Art History, Ceramics, Design, Drawing, Graphic Design, Painting, Photography, Printmaking, Sculpture, Stage Design, Teacher Training, Theatre Arts, Medical Illustration
Summer School: Dean, Jonathan Boe. Tuition $270 per unit for term June-July, July-Aug. Courses—Art Education, Design, Drawing, Painting, Pottery, Sculpture

TORRANCE

EL CAMINO COLLEGE, Division of Fine Arts, 16007 Crenshaw Blvd, 90506. Tel 310-660-3715; FAX 310-715-7734; Elec Mail rquadham@admin.elcamino.cc.ca.us. *Dean Div* Dr Roger Quadhamer. Instrs: FT 33, PT 61
Estab 1947; pub; D & E; scholarships; SC 46, LC 6; enrl D 1700, E 900, non-maj 2378, maj 222
Ent Req: HS dipl
Degrees: AA 2 yrs
Tuition: None; no campus res
Courses: Art Appreciation, Drawing, Graphic Arts, Jewelry, Museum Staff Training, Painting, Photography, Printmaking, Sculpture
Children's Classes: Enrl 30. Courses—Exploration of Children's Art
Summer School: Enrl 400; tuition $13 per unit. Courses—Art Appreciation, Drawing, Painting

TUJUNGA

MCGROARTY CULTURAL ART CENTER, 7570 McGroarty Terrace, 91042. Tel 818-325-5285, 352-0865; *Co-Dir* Isabella Barone; *Co-Dir* Susan Cheyno. Instrs: PT 24
Estab 1953; pub; D & E; scholarships; SC 40, LC 1; enrl D 600, E 200
Tuition: Adults $2.50 per hr for 8 wk session; children & teens $1.50 per hr for 8 wk session
Courses: Ceramics, Painting, Sculpture, Chinese Brush Painting, Dance, Holiday Art, Life Drawing, Piano, Quilting, Stained Glass, Tai Chi Chuan
Children's Classes: Ceramics, Creative Drama, Dance, Guitar, Literature & Art, Music for Little People, Painting, Piano, Putting on a Play, Visual Arts

TURLOCK

CALIFORNIA STATE UNIVERSITY, Art Dept, 801 W Monte Vista Ave, 95382. Tel 209-667-3431; FAX 209-667-3333; *Chmn Dept* John Barnett, MFA; *Prof* Hope Werness, PhD; *Prof* C Roxanne Robbin; *Prof* James Piskoti, MFA; *Prof* David Olivant, MFA; *Prof* Richard Savini, MFA
Estab 1963, dept estab 1967; pub; D & E; scholarships; SC 27, LC 6, GC 4; enrl D 400, E 50, non-maj 350, maj 85, grad 20
Ent Req: HS dipl
Degrees: BA 4 yrs; Printmaking Cert Prog, Special Masters Degree Prog
Tuition: Res—undergrad & grad $851 per sem, $57 winter terms; nonres—undergrad & grad are same as res plus $246 per unit; limited campus res
Courses: Art History, †Drawing, Painting, †Printmaking, †Sculpture, Teacher Training, †Painting, †Photography, †Printmaking, †Sculpture, Teacher Training, †Gallery Management
Summer School: Dir, J Barnett

VALENCIA

CALIFORNIA INSTITUTE OF THE ARTS, School of Art, 24700 McBean Pkwy, 91355. Tel 805-255-1050; FAX 805-259-5871; *Pres* Dr Steven D Lavine; *Dean* Thomas Lawson. Instrs: FT 30
Estab 1970; pvt; scholarships; enrl D 270
Ent Req: Portfolio
Degrees: BFA 4 yrs, MFA
Tuition: $15,400 per yr; campus res available
Courses: Aesthetics, Architecture, Art History, Collages, †Conceptual Art, Constructions, Drawing, Film, Graphic Arts, †Graphic Design, Intermedia, Mixed Media, †Painting, Photography, Printmaking, †Sculpture, †Video, Post Studio, Visual Communication, Critical Theory

COLLEGE OF THE CANYONS, Art Dept, 26455 N Rockwell Canyon Rd, 91355. Tel 805-259-7800, Ext 392; *Head Dept* Joanne Julian, MFA; *Instr* Robert Walker, MFA; *Instr* Deborah Horewitz, MFA; *Instr* Philip Morrison, MFA; *Instr* Janice Metz, BA; *Instr* Barbara Ketwin; *Instr* Colleen Sterritt
Estab 1970, dept estab 1974; pub; D & E; SC 11, LC 4; enrl D 300, E 300, maj 50
Ent Req: Must be 18 yrs of age
Degrees: AA & AS 2 yrs
Tuition: Res—$13 per unit; nonres—$110 per unit; non res foreign—$120 per unit
Courses: Advertising Design, Art History, Drawing, Illustration, Painting, Photography, Printmaking, Sculpture, Computer Graphics, 3-D Design
Adult Hobby Classes: Tuition $10 plus lab fees usually another $10 per sem
Children's Classes: Classes offered in continuing educ under child development

VAN NUYS

LOS ANGELES VALLEY COLLEGE, Art Dept, 5800 Fulton Ave, 91401-4096. Tel 818-781-1200, Ext 358, 431; FAX 818-785-4672; *Chmn* Sam Goffredo
Degrees: AA, cert
Tuition: Undergrad—$13 per unit; nonres—$13 per unit
Courses: Advertising Design, Art History, Ceramics, Design, Drawing, Painting, Photography, Printmaking, Sculpture
Summer School: Beginning Design I, Drawing

VENICE BEACH

EASTERN COMMUNITY COLLEGE, Dept of Art, 101 Clubhouse, Ste 2, 90291. Tel 213-826-5696; *Head Dept* Ginger Kerns; *Instr* Donald Bumper
Estab 1955, dept 1970; pub; D & E; scholarships; SC 12, LC4; enrl D 130, E 222, non-maj 317, maj 35
Ent Req: HS dipl, Non-res Act
Degrees: AA 2 yrs
Tuition: Res - undergrad $317 per sem
Courses: Advertising Design, Art Education, Leather
Adult Hobby Classes: Enrl 100; tuition $2 per sem cr hr. Courses vary

VENTURA

VENTURA COLLEGE, Fine Arts Dept, 4667 Telegraph Rd, 93003. Tel 805-642-3211, Ext 1381; *Chmn* Myra Toth. Instrs: FT 7, PT 24
Estab 1925; pub; D & E; SC 50, LC 15; enrl D 500, E 500, maj 300
Ent Req: HS dipl or 18 yrs of age
Degrees: AA and AS
Tuition: Res—$13 per unit to 90 units; nonres— $114 per unit, foreign students $128 per unit; no campus res
Courses: Advertising Design, Art Appreciation, Art History, †Ceramics, †Commercial Art, Drawing, Fashion Arts, Graphic Arts, Graphic Design, Illustration, Painting, †Photography, Sculpture, Textile Design, Fiber Design
Adult Hobby Classes: Enrl 500; tuition same as regular session. Courses—Art, Ceramisc, Photography
Summer School: Dir, Tom Roe. Enrl 200; tuition same as regular courses, 6 - 8 wk term. Courses—Ceramics, Color & Design, Drawing, Life Drawing, Photography

VICTORVILLE

VICTOR VALLEY COLLEGE, Art Dept, 18422 Bear Valley Rd, 92392. Tel 619-245-4271; FAX 619-245-9745; *Chmn* John Foster; *Instructional Aide* Tom Williams; *Instructional Aide* Brian Clements
Estab 1961, dept estab 1971; pub; D & E; scholarships; SC 20, LC 5; enrl D 125, E 125, non-maj 200, maj 50
Ent Req: HS dipl
Degrees: AA 2 yrs
Courses: Art History, Commercial Art, Design, Drawing, Graphic Design, History of Art & Archaeology, Painting, Photography
Adult Hobby Classes: Enrl 100; tuition $10 per 6 wks
Summer School: Dir, John F Foster. Enrl 75; tuition $13 per cr hr. Courses—Art Concepts, Art History, Design, Drawing, Photography

VISALIA

COLLEGE OF THE SEQUOIAS, Art Dept, Fine Arts Division, 915 S Mooney Blvd, 93277. Tel 209-730-3700; FAX 209-730-3894; *Chmn Art Dept* Barbara Strong; *Chmn Fine Arts Div* Marlene Tabor; *Instr* Ralph Homan, MA; *Instr* Gene Maddox. Instrs: PT 12
Estab 1925, dept estab 1940; pub; D & E; scholarships; SC 12, LC 4; enrl D 60, E37, maj 10
Ent Req: HS dipl, must be 18 yr of age
Degrees: AA 2 yr
Tuition: Res—$15 per unit
Courses: Advertising Design, Architecture, Art Appreciation, Art Education, Art History, Calligraphy, Ceramics, Commercial Art, Costume Design & Construction, Display, Drafting, Drawing, Fashion Arts, Film, Graphic Arts, Graphic Design, History of Art & Archaeology, Illustration, Industrial Design, Lettering, Painting, Photography, Printmaking, Sculpture, Stage Design, Textile Design, Theatre Arts, Video, Gallery Staff Training
Adult Hobby Classes: Ceramics, Painting, Photography
Summer School: Dir, Marlene Taber. Courses—Drawing, Painting

WALNUT

MOUNT SAN ANTONIO COLLEGE, Art Dept, 1100 N Grand Ave, 91789. Tel 909-594-5611; FAX 909-468-3937; *Chmn* Ronald B Ownbey. Instrs: FT 14, PT 10
Estab 1945; pub; D & E; SC 24, LC 5; enrl D 2254, E 852, maj 500
Ent Req: Over 18 yrs of age
Degrees: AA and AS 2 yrs
Tuition: Non-district res—$13 per unit; nonres—$114 per unit
Courses: Advertising Design, Ceramics, Commercial Art, Drafting, Drawing, Graphic Arts, Art History, Illustration, Lettering, Painting, Photography, Printmaking, Sculpture, Theatre Arts, Fibers, Life Drawing, Metals & Enamels, Woodworking
Summer School: Enrl art 50; term of 6 wks beginning June 16. Courses—Ceramics, Drawing

WEED

COLLEGE OF THE SISKIYOUS, Art Dept, 800 College Ave, 96094. Tel 916-938-5257; FAX 916-938-5227; *Area Dir* James Witherell
Estab 1957; pub; D & E; scholarships; SC 15, LC 2; enrl D 1200, maj 20
Degrees: AA 2 yrs
Tuition: $13 unit to res, $114 unit to out-of-state & foreign
Courses: Art History, Ceramics, Collages, Constructions, Drafting, Drawing, Graphic Arts, History of Art & Archaeology, Painting, Photography, Printmaking, Sculpture, Life Drawing

WHITTIER

RIO HONDO COLLEGE, Visual Arts Dept, 3600 Workman Mill Rd, 90601-1699. Tel 562-908-3472; FAX 562-908-3446; Elec Mail carlson07@aol.com. *Dean* Lance Carlson. Instrs: FT 41, PT 65
Estab 1962; pub; D & E; SC 18, LC 3; enrl D & E 19,000, non-maj 2100, maj 200
Ent Req: HS dipl
Degrees: AA 2 yrs
Tuition: $50; no campus residence
Courses: Advertising Design, Aesthetics, Architecture, Art Appreciation, Art History, Ceramics, Commercial Art, Conceptual Art, Design, Display, Drafting, Drawing, Graphic Arts, Graphic Design, History of Art & Archaeology, Illustration, Lettering, Painting, Photography, Theatre Arts
Adult Hobby Classes: Courses—Calligraphy, Printmaking, Oriental Brush Painting, Tole & Decorative Painting
Summer School: Enrl 3468; tuition $5 per unit for term of 6 wks beginning June 23

WHITTIER COLLEGE, Dept of Art, 13406 Philadelphia St, 90601. Tel 310-693-0771; FAX 310-698-4067; *Chmn* Dr David Sloan. Instrs: FT 2, PT 2
Estab 1901; pvt; D & E; scholarships and fels; SC 12, LC 12; enrl 552-560 per sem
Ent Req: HS dipl, accept credit by exam CLEP, CEEBA
Degrees: BA 4 yrs
Tuition: Off campus $16,828 per yr; on campus $22,527 per yr
Courses: Art Education, Art History, Ceramics, Drawing, Painting, Printmaking
Adult Hobby Classes: Tuition $5. Courses—Classes for special students
Children's Classes: Tuition $5. Courses—Classes for special students
Summer School: Dir, Robert W Speier. Enrl 25; tui $140 per credit 1-7 credits, $125 per credit 7-up credits, May 31-June 17, June 20-July 29, Aug 1-Aug 19. Courses—Water Soluble Painting, Color & Basic Drawing

WILMINGTON

LOS ANGELES HARBOR COLLEGE, Art Dept, 1111 Figueroa Pl, 90744. Tel 310-522-8200; FAX 310-834-1882; *Chmn Humanities & Fine Arts* Robert H Billings, MA; *Assoc Prof* John Cassone, MA; *Asst Prof* Nancy E Webber, MFA; *Instr* DeAnn Jennings, MA; *Instr* Jay McCafferty, MA
Estab 1949; pub; D & E; SC 48, LC 11; enrl D 10,000, E 4200
Ent Req: HS dipl
Degrees: AA 2 yrs
Tuition: Res—undergrad $13 per unit; nonres—$119 per sem
Courses: Architecture, Art History, Ceramics, Drawing, Fashion Arts, Painting, Photography, Printmaking, Stage Design, Theatre Arts
Summer School: Art Dept Chmn, DeAnn Jennings. Courses—Art Fundamentals, Art History and Photography

WOODLAND HILLS

PIERCE COLLEGE, Art Dept, 6201 Winnetka, 91371. Tel 818-347-0551, Ext 475, 719-6475, 710-4369; *Art Dept Chmn* John D Kuczynski; *Prof* H C Pinkston, MFA; *Assoc Prof* Constance Moffatt, PhD; *Asst Prof* A Nancy Snooks, MFA; *Instr* Paul C Nordberg, AA
Estab 1947, dept estab 1956; pub; D & E; scholarships; SC 35, LC 3; enrl D & E 23,000
Ent Req: HS dipl 18 yrs and over
Degrees: AA 60 units
Tuition: Res—$13 per unit; nonres—$125-$130 per unit plus enrl fee
Courses: Advertising Design, Architecture, Art Appreciation, Art History, Ceramics, Design, Drawing, Graphic Arts, Graphic Design, Jewelry, Fine Art
Adult Hobby Classes: Offered through Community Services Dept
Children's Classes: Offered through Community Services Dept
Summer School: Dir, Paul Whelan

COLORADO

ALAMOSA

ADAMS STATE COLLEGE, Dept of Visual Arts, 81102. Tel 719-589-7823; FAX 719-589-7522; *Head Dept* Charlotte Nichols, MFA
Estab 1924; pub; D & E; scholarships; SC 43, LC 6, GC 5; enrl D 450, non-maj 200, maj 50, grad 12
Ent Req: HS dipl, ACT & SAT
Degrees: BA 4 yrs, MA 1-1/2 yrs
Tuition: Res—undergrad $726 per sem, grad $876 per sem; nonres—$2622 per sem, grad $3144 per sem; campus res—room & board $975-$1430
Courses: Art Education, Art History, Ceramics, Design, Drawing, Painting, Photography, Sculpture, Metalsmithing
Adult Hobby Classes: Enrl 60; tuition $69 per sem hr
Summer School: Dir, Gary Peer. Tuition res—$71 per cr hr, nonres—$251 per cr hr. Courses—Art Education, Art History, Ceramics, Design, Drawing, Metals, Painting, Photography, Sculpture

BOULDER

UNIVERSITY OF COLORADO, BOULDER, Dept of Fine Arts, Sibell-Wolle Fine Arts Bldg N196A, Campus Box 318, 80309. Tel 303-492-6504; *Chmn* Merrill Lessley; *Assoc Chmn* Suzanne Foster. Instrs: FT 28, PT 15
Estab 1861; pub; D & E; scholarships; SC 55, LC 53, GC 67; enrl D 2000, E 90, non-maj 1340, maj 430, grad 50, others 100
Ent Req: HS dipl
Degrees: BA or BFA(Art History & Studio Arts) 4 yrs, MA(Art History) 2 yrs, MFA(Studio Arts) 2 yrs
Tuition: Res—undergrad $1135 per sem; grad $1507 per sem for 9-15 hrs; nonres—undergrad $6669 per sem; grad $6570 per sem; campus res—room & board $1350-$1559 per sem, $2700-$3118 per yr
Courses: Art History, Ceramics, Drawing, Painting, Photography, Printmaking, Sculpture, Media Arts
Summer School: Enrl 20-25 per course; tuition $540 res, $1920 nonres for term of 5 weeks beginning in June. Courses—Art History, Drawing, Painting, Photography, Printmaking, Sculpture, Special Topics, Watermedia

COLORADO SPRINGS

COLORADO COLLEGE, Dept of Art, 14 E Cashe La Poudre, 80903. Tel 719-389-6000; FAX 719-389-6882; *Chmn* Carl Reed; *Prof* James Trissel, MFA; *Assoc Prof* Gale Murray, PhD; *Prof* Bougdon Swider; *Assoc Prof* Edith Kirsch, PhD
Estab 1874; pvt; D; scholarships; SC 20, LC 20; enrl D 1800, maj 40
Ent Req: HS dipl or equivalent & selection by admis committee
Degrees: BA & MAT 4 yr
Tuition: Undergrad $17,142 per yr
Courses: Art History, Drawing, Graphic Design, Painting, Photography, Printmaking, Sculpture, 3-D Design, Art Studio
Summer School: Dean, Elmer R Peterson. Tuition $260 per unit for term of 8 wks beginning June 19. Courses—Architecture, Art Education, Photography

UNIVERSITY OF COLORADO-COLORADO SPRINGS, Fine Arts Dept, 1420 Austin Bluffs Pky, PO Box 7150, 80933-7150. Tel 719-262-3000; FAX 719-262-3146; *Chmn* Louis Cicotello, MFA; *Prof* Lin Fife, MFA; *Prof* Julia Hoerner, MFA; *Asst Prof* Kathryn Andrus-Walck, PhD; *Asst Prof* John Peters-Campbell, PhD
Estab 1965, dept estab 1970; pub; D & E; SC 18 LC 16; enrl maj 63
Ent Req: HS dipl, res-ACT 23 SAT 1000, non-res ACT 24 SAT 1050
Degrees: BA Studio 4 yr, BA (Art History) 4 Yr
Tuition: Res—undergrad $67 per sem hr; nonres—undergrad $215 per sem hr
Courses: Aesthetics, Architecture, Art Appreciation, Art History, Collages, Drawing, Mixed Media, Painting, Photography, Sculpture, †Art, Computer Art
Summer School: Dir, Louis Cicotello. Enrl 30. Courses—Art History, Beginning Studio, General/Survey

DENVER

COLORADO INSTITUTE OF ART, 200 E Ninth Ave, 80203. Tel 303-837-0825; FAX 303-860-8520; *Pres* David Zorn; *Dir Educ* Larry Horn
Estab 1952; pvt; D & E; scholarships; SC all; enrl D 1200, non-maj 600, maj 600
Ent Req: HS dipl
Degrees: Assoc 2 yr
Tuition: Undergrad—$2870 per qtr; photography $2870
Courses: Interior Design, Photography, Video, †Fashion Illustration, †Fashion Merchandising, Music & Video Business
Adult Hobby Classes: Evening career training; 1 yr diploma. Courses—Nine week avocational workshops in fine arts & photography
Summer School: Commercial art prep school for post-secondary students only

METROPOLITAN STATE COLLEGE OF DENVER, Art Dept, Box 59, PO Box 173362, 80217-3362. Tel 303-556-3090; FAX 303-556-4094; *Chmn* Susan Josepher, PhD
Estab 1963, dept estab 1963; pub; D & E; scholarships; SC 52, LC 8; enrl D 650, E 325, maj 500
Ent Req: HS dipl or GED
Degrees: BFA 4 yrs
Courses: †Advertising Design, Aesthetics, Art Appreciation, Art Education, †Art History, †Ceramics, †Design, †Drawing, Graphic Arts, Graphic Design, Illustration, †Jewelry, †Painting, †Photography, †Printmaking, †Sculpture, Video, Electronic Media
Summer School: Same as regular session

REGIS UNIVERSITY, Fine Arts Dept, 3333 Regis Blvd, 80221. Tel 303-458-3576, 458-4286; *Head Div* Richard Stephenson. Instrs: FT 4, PT 10
Estab 1880; pvt; D & E; SC 8, LC 4
Ent Req: HS dipl, ent exam
Degrees: BA, BS & BFA 4 yrs
Tuition: $6350 per sem
Courses: Drawing, Graphic Design, Painting, Photography, Sculpture, Theatre Arts, Computer Art, †Music, †Studio Art
Summer School: Ceramics, Glass, Jewelry, Printmaking, Weaving

ROCKY MOUNTAIN COLLEGE OF ART & DESIGN, 6875 E Evans Ave, 80224. Tel 303-753-6046; FAX 303-759-4970; WATS 800-888-2787. *Dir* Steven M Steele; *Financial Aid* Bob Lyons; *Academic Dean* Lisa Steele; *Admis* Rex Whisman. Instrs: FT 6, PT 40
Estab 1963; pvt; D & E; scholarships; enrl D 350
Ent Req: Enrl 425; tuition $3090 for 14 wk term. Courses—Same as regular sem
Degrees: AA & BA
Tuition: $2805 per trimester for all full time students; $187 per cr for all part-time students; no campus res
Courses: Advertising Design, Aesthetics, Art History, Calligraphy, Commercial Art, Conceptual Art, Constructions, Design, Display, Drafting, Drawing, Film, Graphic Arts, †Graphic Design, †Illustration, Intermedia, †Interior Design, Lettering, Mixed

Media, †Painting, Photography, †Sculpture, Textile Design, Theatre Arts, †Environmental, †Graphic Design
Adult Hobby Classes: Enrl 425; tuition $3090 for 14 wk term. Courses—Same as regular semester
Summer School: Enrl 425; tuition $3090 for 14 wk term; Courses—Same as regular semester

UNIVERSITY OF COLORADO AT DENVER, Dept of Fine Arts, Campus Box 177, PO Box 173364, 80217-3364. Tel 303-556-4891; *Acting Co-Chair* Jerry Johnson, MFA; *Acting Co-Chair* Charles Moone, MFA; *Prof* Ernest O Porps, MFA; *Asst Prof* Lorre Hoffman, MFA; *Asst Prof* Stephanie Grilli, PhD; *Asst Prof* Debra Goldman, MFA; *Asst Prof* Karen Mathews, PhD
Estab 1876, dept estab 1955; pub; D & E; schol; SC 21, LC 13, GC 11; enrl maj 168
Ent Req: HS dipl, ACT or SAT, previous academic ability and accomplishment
Degrees: BA and BFA 4 yrs
Tuition: Res—undergrad $958 per sem, $116 per cr hr; nonres—undergrad $5032 per sem
Courses: †Art History, †Drawing, †Painting, †Photography, †Sculpture, †Creative Arts, †Studio Arts
Summer School: Tuition same as regular sem, term of 10 wk beginning June 12. Courses—Art History, Studio Workshops

UNIVERSITY OF DENVER, School of Art & Art History, 2121 E Asbury, 80210. Tel 303-871-2846; FAX 303-871-4112; WATS 800-876-3323. *Dir* Bethany Kriegsman; *Asst Dir* Sheelagh Dytri
Pvt; D; scholarships; SC 44, LC 33, GC 50; enrl D 450, non-maj 170-200, maj 176, grad 40
Ent Req: HS dipl
Degrees: BA & BFA 4 yrs, MFA 2 yrs, MA 4 qtrs; honors program
Tuition: $422 per qtr hr; campus res available
Courses: Art History, Ceramics, Drawing, Graphic Design, Painting, Photography, Printmaking, Museum Studies

DURANGO

FORT LEWIS COLLEGE, Art Dept, 1000 Rim Dr, 81301-3999. Tel 970-247-7243; FAX 970-247-7520; *Chmn & Prof* Gerald Wells, MFA; *Assoc Prof* Laurel Covington-Vogl, MFA; *Assoc Prof* David Hunt, MA; *Prof* Mick Reber
Estab 1956; pub; D & E; scholarships; SC 30, LC 6; enrl D 600, non-maj 450, maj 150
Ent Req: HS dipl, SAT
Degrees: BA & BS
Tuition: Campus res available
Courses: Aesthetics, Art History, Ceramics, Drawing, Drawing, Handicrafts, Illustration, Industrial Design, Intermedia, Jewelry, Southwest Art
Summer School: Dean, Ed Angus. Enrl 1000. Courses—Art Education, Ceramics, Drawing, Mural Design, Painting

FORT COLLINS

COLORADO STATE UNIVERSITY, Dept of Art, 80523. Tel 970-491-6774; *Chmn* Phil Risbeck. Instrs: 34
Estab 1870, dept estab 1956; pub; D; scholarships; SC 55, LC 13, GC 5; enrl D 547, non-maj 860, maj 547, grad 22
Ent Req: HS dipl, portfolio if by transfer
Degrees: BA(Art History & Art Education) and BFA 4 yr, MFA 60 hrs
Tuition: Res—undergrad $2855 per yr, $1428 per sem, $93 per cr hr; grad $3193 per yr, $1597 per sem; nonres—undergrad $9791 per yr, $4896 per sem; grad $10, 187 per yr, $5094 per sem
Courses: Advertising Design, Aesthetics, Art Appreciation, †Art Education, †Art History, †Ceramics, †Drawing, Goldsmithing, Graphic Arts, †Graphic Design, History of Art & Archaeology, Illustration, Jewelry, †Painting, †Photography, †Printmaking, †Sculpture, Silversmithing, Teacher Training, Textile Design, Weaving, †Fibers, †Metalsmithing, †Pottery
Children's Classes: Continuing education art offerings not on regular basis
Summer School: Dir, James T Dormer. Enrl 700; tuition $77 per cr. Courses—most regular session courses

GOLDEN

FOOTHILLS ART CENTER, INC, 809 15th St, 80401. Tel 303-279-3922; FAX 303-279-9470; *Exec Dir* Carol Dickinson, MA. Instrs: PT 10
Estab 1968; pvt; D & E (winter and spring)
Ent Req: None
Tuition: $100 & up for 6-10 wk class
Courses: Drawing, Painting, Photography, Sculpture
Adult Hobby Classes: Enrl limited; 8-10 wk class. Courses—Pottery, Printmaking

GRAND JUNCTION

MESA COLLEGE, Art Dept, PO Box 2647, 81502. Tel 303-248-1020; *Chmn* Michael Gerlach
Estab 1925; pub; D & E; scholarships; SC 23, LC 5; enrl D 538, E 103
Ent Req: HS dipl, GED
Degrees: AA, BA
Tuition: Res—undergrad $907 per sem; nonres—undergrad $2698 per sem
Courses: Art Education, Art History, Ceramics, Drawing, Painting, Printmaking, Sculpture, Exhibitions & Management, Metalsmithing

GREELEY

AIMS COMMUNITY COLLEGE, Visual & Performing Arts, PO Box 69, 80632. Tel 970-330-8008; FAX 970-330-5705; *Chmn Div Communications & Humanities* Susan Cribelli; *Dir Visual & Performing Arts* Alysan Broda
Tuition: Res—$23.50 per cr hr; $42 per cr hr for in-state, out-of-district; nonres—$127 per cr hr for out-of-state
Courses: Art Appreciation, Art History, Ceramics, Design, Drawing, Fashion Arts, Interior Design, Jewelry, Painting, Photography, Sculpture, Textile Design, Weaving
Children's Classes: Courses offered
Summer School: Courses offered

UNIVERSITY OF NORTHERN COLORADO, Dept of Visual Arts, 80639. Tel 970-351-2143; FAX 970-351-2290; *Chmn* Richard Munson. Instrs: FT 10
Estab 1889; pub; D & E
Ent Req: HS dipl
Degrees: BA 4 yr
Tuition: Res—undergrad $957 per sem, grad $4208 per sem; nonres—undergrad $1132 per sem, grad $4479 per sem; campus—room & board available upon request
Courses: Art Education, Art History, Ceramics, Drawing, Graphic Design, Graphic Arts, Jewelry, Painting, Photography, Printmaking, Sculpture, Fiber Art, Papermaking, Photo Communications
Summer School: Courses—Comparative Arts Program in Florence, Italy, Study of the Indian Arts of Mesa Verde, Mesa Verde workshop & on campus courses, Workshops in Weaving & Ceramics in Steamboat Springs, Colorado

GUNNISON

WESTERN STATE COLLEGE OF COLORADO, Dept of Art & Industrial Technology, 81231. Tel 303-943-0120; *Chmn* Charles Tutor. Instrs: FT 7, PT 3
Estab 1911; pub; D & E; scholarships; SC 29, LC 7, GC 8; enrl 2550
Ent Req: HS dipl, special exam
Degrees: BA & BFA, 4 yr
Tuition: Res—$1407 per yr; nonres—$6153 per yr
Courses: Art Appreciation, Art Education, Art History, Calligraphy, Ceramics, Commercial Art, Conceptual Art, Drawing, Goldsmithing, Graphic Arts, Graphic Design, History of Art & Archaeology, Jewelry, Mixed Media, Painting, Photography, Printmaking, Sculpture, Textile Design, Weaving, Design, Indian Art, Introduction to Art, Studio Art, Weaving
Summer School: 4 & 8 wk courses. Courses—Drawing, Painting, Photography

LA JUNTA

OTERO JUNIOR COLLEGE, Dept of Arts, 1802 Colorado Ave, 81050. Tel 719-384-8721; *Head Dept* Timothy F Walsh
Estab 1941; pub; D & E; scholarships; SC 12, LC 3; enrl 776
Ent Req: HS grad
Degrees: AA & AAS 2 yr
Courses: Art History, Drawing, Painting, Creative Design
Adult Hobby Classes: Enrl 60; tuition $47.50 per cr, non-credit courses vary. Courses—Art, Drawing, Painting

LAKEWOOD

RED ROCKS COMMUNITY COLLEGE, Arts & Humanities Dept, 13300 W Sixth Ave, 80228. Tel 303-988-6160; FAX 303-914-6666; *Instr Pottery* James Robertson; *Art Instr* Susan Arndt
Tuition: $60 per sem cr hr
Courses: Art Appreciation, Art History, Ceramics, Design, Drawing, Painting, Photography, Printmaking, Sculpture, Electronic Studio
Summer School: Enrl 80; tuition $99 per 3 cr course per 10 wks. Courses—Ceramics, Drawing, Design, Watercolor

PUEBLO

UNIVERSITY OF SOUTHERN COLORADO, BELMONT CAMPUS, Dept of Art, 2200 Bonforte Blvd, 81001. Tel 719-549-2816; *Chmn* Carl Jensen; *Assoc Prof* Robert Hench, MA; *Assoc Prof* Charles Marino; *Asst Prof* Carl Jensen, MFA; *Asst Prof* Robert Wands, MA; *Asst Prof* Nick Latka, MFA; *Instr* Laura Audrey
Estab 1933; pub; D & E; scholarships; SC 66, LC 19, GC 2; enrl D 700, E 50, non-maj 600, maj 150
Ent Req: HS dipl, GED, Open Door Policy
Degrees: BA and BS 4 yrs
Tuition: Res—undergrad & grad $662 18 hr sem; nonres—$2624 18 hr sem; campus res—available
Courses: Art History, Ceramics, Collages, Commercial Art, Drawing, Graphic Design, Illustration, Painting, Photography, Printmaking, Sculpture, Teacher Training, Video, Computer Animation, Computer Imaging, Exhibition Design
Summer School: Dir, Ed Sajbel. Enrl 125; tuition resident $40 per cr hr, nonres $150 per cr hr. Courses—Art Education, Art History, Ceramics, Introduction to Art, Painting

SALIDA

DUNCONOR WORKSHOPS, 432 H St, PO Box 416, 81201-0416. Tel 719-539-7519; *Head* Harold O'Connor
Estab 1976; pvt; D; SC; enrl D 34
Ent Req: Professional experience
Courses: Design, Goldsmithing, Jewelry, Silversmithing
Adult Hobby Classes: Enrl 24; tuition $450 per wk. Courses—Jewelry Making
Summer School: Enrl 34; tuition $450 per wk. Courses—Jewelry Making

STERLING

NORTHEASTERN JUNIOR COLLEGE, Dept of Art, 100 College Dr, 80751. Tel 970-522-6600, Ext 671; *Instructional Dir, Humanities & Human Servs* Peter L Youngers, MFA
Estab 1941; pub; D & E; schol; SC 16, LC 2; enrl D 103, E 23, non-maj 73, maj 30, others 23
Ent Req: HS dipl, GED
Degrees: AA 2 yr
Tuition: Res— $901 per sem; non res—$2331 per sem
Courses: Art Education, Art History, Ceramics, Display, Drawing, Handicrafts, Lettering, Mixed Media, Painting, Printmaking, Sculpture, Teacher Training
Adult Hobby Classes: Enrl 100; tuition $8 per cr hr. Courses—Basic Crafts, Ceramics, Drawing, Macrame, Painting, Stained Glass
Summer School: Dir, Dick Gritz. Courses—vary each yr

VALE

COLORADO MOUNTAIN COLLEGE, Visual & Performing Arts, 1310 W Haven Dr, 81657. Tel 970-476-4040; *Dir* Jim Olson
Estab 1971 for summers only; enrl 1500 per summer
Tuition: Res—$60 per cr hr; nonres—$185 per cr hr; res—room & board $150 per wk
Courses: Ceramics, Drawing, Painting, Photography, Children's Art, Enameling, Foundry Fibers & Surface Design

CONNECTICUT

BRIDGEPORT

HOUSATONIC COMMUNITY & TECHNICAL COLLEGE, Art Dept, 900 Lafayette Blvd, 06604. Tel 203-579-6443, 579-6400; FAX 203-579-6993; *Prog Coordr* Ronald Abbe, MFA; *Faculty* David Kintzler, MFA; *Faculty* Michael Stein, MFA
Estab 1967, dept estab 1968; pub; D & E; SC 15, LC 5; enrl maj 100
Ent Req: HS dipl
Degrees: AA 2 yr
Tuition: Res—$57 per cr; nonres—$2296 per sem
Courses: Art Education, Art History, Ceramics, Collages, Constructions, Drafting, Drawing, Graphic Design, Mixed Media, Painting, Photography, Sculpture, Teacher Training, Computer Graphics
Adult Hobby Classes: Varied
Summer School: Dir, James Link. Courses—Same as regular session

UNIVERSITY OF BRIDGEPORT, School of Arts, Humanities & Social Sciences, University & Iranistan, 06602. Tel 203-576-4239, 576-4709; FAX 203-576-4653; *Dir* Thomas Julius Burger; *Assoc Prof* Donald McIntyre, MFA; *Assoc Prof* Jim Lesko, MFA; *Assoc Prof* Sean Nixon, MFA; *Asst Prof* Ketti Kupper, MFA
Estab 1927, dept estab 1947; pvt; D & E; scholarships; SC 38, LC 24, GC 15; enrl D 1150, E 200, non-maj 1070, maj 260, GS 22
Ent Req: Portfolio for BFA candidates only, college boards
Degrees: BA, BS & BFA 4 yr
Tuition: Res—undergrad $6010 per sem
Courses: Advertising Design, Art History, Ceramics, †Graphic Design, †Illustration, †Industrial Design, †Interior Design, Painting, Photography, Printmaking, Sculpture, Theatre Arts, Weaving
Adult Hobby Classes: Enrl open; Courses—most crafts
Summer School: Chmn, Sean Nixon. Details from chairperson (203-576-4177)

DANBURY

WESTERN CONNECTICUT STATE UNIVERSITY, School of Arts & Sciences, 181 White St, 06810. Tel 203-837-8410; FAX 203-837-8526; *Interim Dean* Dr Carol Hawkes. Instrs: FT 7
Estab 1903; pub; D & E; scholarships; SC 30, LC 3-6, GC 5; enrl D 100
Ent Req: HS dipl
Degrees: BA (graphic communications) 4 yr
Tuition: Res—$1693 per sem; nonres—$4157 per sem
Summer School: Courses—same as regular session

FAIRFIELD

FAIRFIELD UNIVERSITY, Visual & Performing Arts, N Benson Rd, 06430-5195. Tel 203-254-4000; FAX 203-254-4119; *Dean* Dr Orin Grossman; *Chmn* Dr Catherine Schwab
Scholarships
Tuition: $7500 per sem
Courses: Art History, Design, Drawing, Video, Painting, Photography, Printmaking, Sculpture, Art of Film, Film Production, History of Film, Visual Design
Adult Hobby Classes: Enrl 2000; tuition $330 per 3 cr. Courses—Full Fine Arts curriculum
Summer School: Dir, Dr Vilma Allen. Enrl 2000. Semester June - August

SACRED HEART UNIVERSITY, Dept of Art, 5151 Park Ave, 06432-1000. Tel 203-371-7737; *Prof* Virginia F Zic, MFA. Instrs: 8
Estab 1963, dept estab 1977; pvt; D & E; scholarships; SC 26, LC 5; enrl D 300, E 100, non-maj 225, maj 70
Ent Req: HS dipl
Degrees: BA 4 yrs
Tuition: $6106 per sem; campus res—available
Courses: Advertising Design, Art History, Design, Drawing, †Graphic Design, History of Art & Archaeology, †Illustration, †Painting, Computer Design
Summer School: Prof, Virgina Zic. Courses—Art History

FARMINGTON

TUNXIS COMMUNITY COLLEGE, Graphic Design Dept, 271 Scott Swamp Rd, 06032. Tel 203-677-7701; *Acting Acad Dean* Dr John Carey; *Graphic Design Coordr* Stephen A Klema, MFA; *Instr* William Kluba, MFA
Estab 1970, dept estab 1973; pub; D & E; SC 15, LC 4; enrl non-maj 40, maj 90
Ent Req: HS dipl
Degrees: AS, AA(Graphic Design, Visual Fine Arts)
Tuition: $300 per sem
Courses: Drawing, Graphic Design, Illustration, Painting, Photography, Color, Computer Graphics, Typography, 2-D & 3-D Design
Summer School: Dir Community Services, Dr Kyle. Courses—Computer Graphics, Drawing, Painting, Photography

GREENWICH

CONNECTICUT INSTITUTE OF ART, 581 W Putnam Ave, 06830. Tel 203-869-4430; FAX 203-869-0521; *Dir* Michael Propersi; *Pres* August Propersi; *VPres* Joann Propersi; *Asst Dir* Linda MacDonald
Estab 1954; pvt; D & E; scholarships; SC 7, LC 2; enrl D 60, E 40
Ent Req: HS dipl, portfolio, interview
Degrees: Dipl, 2 yrs
Tuition: $7200 per yr; no campus res
Courses: Advertising Design, Commercial Art, Conceptual Art, Drawing, Graphic Design, Illustration, Lettering, Painting, Airbrushing, Fine Art, Production, Studio Skills

HAMDEN

PAIER COLLEGE OF ART, INC, * 20 Graham Ave, 06514. Tel 203-287-3030; FAX 203-287-3021; *Pres* Jonathan Paier. Instrs: FT 36, PT 11
Estab 1946; pvt; D & E; scholarships; SC 10, LC 6 GC 1; enrl D 185, E 130
Ent Req: HS grad, presentation of portfolio, transcript of records, recommendation
Degrees: BFA & AFA programs offered
Tuition: Res—undergrad $8610 per yr
Courses: Advertising Design, Architecture, Art Education, Art History, Calligraphy, Conceptual Art, Design, Drafting, Drawing, Graphic Arts, †Graphic Design, History of Art & Archaeology, †Illustration, †Interior Design, Lettering, †Painting, †Photography, Printmaking, Textile Design, Fine Arts
Summer School: Dir, Dan Paier. Enrl 50; tuition $200 per sem hr, one 5 wk term beginning July. Courses—CADD, Fine Arts, Graphic Design, Illustration, Interior Design, Photography

HARTFORD

CAPITOL COMMUNITY TECHNICAL COLLEGE, Humanities Division & Art Dept, 61 Woodland St, 06105. Tel 860-520-7800; FAX 860-520-7906; *Prof* Ronald Buksbaum; *Prof* Thomas Werle
Degrees: AA & AS 2 yr
Tuition: $760 per sem
Courses: Art History, Ceramics, Design, Drawing, Painting, Printmaking, Sculpture, Figure Drawing
Summer School: Courses offered

TRINITY COLLEGE, Dept of Fine Arts, 300 Summit St, 06106. Tel 860-297-2330; *Assoc Prof of Fine Arts & Dir of Studio Arts* Robert Kirschbaum, MFA; *Prof* Alden R Gordon, PhD; *Assoc Prof* Jean Cadogan, PhD; *Assoc Prof* Michael Fitzgerald; *Asst Prof* Kathleen Curren, PhD; *Visiting Prof* Robert C Morris, MFA; *Visiting Assoc Prof* Nathan Margalit, MFA; *Visiting Asst Prof* Mary Lewis, PhD; *Visiting Asst Prof* Jacqueline Metheny, MFA
Estab 1823, dept estab 1939; pvt; D; scholarships; SC 20, LC 22; enrl D 400, non-maj 350, major 50
Ent Req: HS dipl
Degrees: MA
Tuition: Res—undergrad $15,120 per yr; campus res—room $2710, board $1760
Courses: Design, Drawing, History of Art & Archaeology, Painting, Printmaking, Sculpture, †Studio Arts

MANCHESTER

MANCHESTER COMMUNITY COLLEGE, Fine Arts Dept, 60 Bidwell St, PO Box 1046, 06040. Tel 860-647-6272; FAX 860-647-6214; *Prof* John Stevens. Instrs: PT 4
Estab 1963, dept estab 1968; pub; D & E; enrl D & E 300, non-maj 240, maj 60
Ent Req: HS dipl, portfolio for visual fine arts prog
Degrees: AA & AS 2 yrs
Tuition: 3 cr courses $88 per cr hr
Courses: Art History, Calligraphy, Ceramics, Drawing, Film, Graphic Arts, Lettering, Painting, Photography, Printmaking, Sculpture, Basic Design, History of Film, Sign Painting

MIDDLETOWN

MIDDLESEX COMMUNITY TECHNICAL COLLEGE, Fine Arts Division, 100 Training Hill Rd, 06457. Tel 860-343-5800; *Head of Dept* Charles Eckert
Degrees: AS
Tuition: Res—$88 per cr hr; nonres—$185 per cr hr
Courses: Art History, Ceramics, Design, Drawing, Painting, Sculpture

WESLEYAN UNIVERSITY, Art Dept, Ctr for the Arts, Wesleyan Station, 06459-0442. Tel 860-685-2000; FAX 860-685-2061; *Chmn* Jonathan Best; *Prof* John T Paoletti, PhD; *Prof* David Schorr, MFA; *Prof* Jeanine Basinger; *Prof* Clark Maines, PhD; *Prof* J Seeley, MFA; *Prof* Jonathan Best, PhD; *Prof* John Frazer, MFA; *Prof*

Joseph Siry, PhD; *Adjunct Prof* Ellen D'Oench, PhD; *Assoc Prof* Peter Mark, PhD; *Assoc Prof* Jeffrey Schiff; *Assoc Prof* Tula Telfair; *Assoc Prof* Elizabeth Milroy, PhD; *Adjunct Assoc Prof* Phillip Wagoner, PhD; *Adjunct Assoc Prof* Mary Risley Emeeita, MFA; *Asst Prof* Martha Amez
Estab 1831, dept estab 1928; pvt; D; SC 30, LC 25; enrl in school D 3604, maj 94, undergrad 2667
Ent Req: HS dipl, SAT
Degrees: BA 4 yrs
Tuition: Campus res available
Courses: Drawing, History of Art & Archaeology, Mixed Media, Painting, Photography, Printmaking, Sculpture, Film History, Film Production, History of Prints, Printroom Methods & Techniques, Typography
Summer School: Dir, Barbara MacEachern. Enrl 576; Term of 6 wks beginning July 5. Courses—grad courses in all areas

NEW BRITAIN

CENTRAL CONNECTICUT STATE UNIVERSITY, Dept of Art, 1615 Stanley St, 06050. Tel 860-832-3200; FAX 203-832-2634; *Chmn Dept* Dr M Cipriano. Instrs: FT 14, PT 15
Estab 1849; pub; D & E; SC 36, LC 8, GC 20; enrl D 200, E 150, non-maj 1000, maj 200, grad 200
Ent Req: HS dipl
Degrees: BA(Graphic Design), BA(Fine Arts) & BS(Art Educ) 4 yrs
Courses: Art Education, Art History, Ceramics, Display, Drawing, Graphic Arts, Graphic Design, Handicrafts, Jewelry, Lettering, Painting, Photography, Printmaking, Sculpture, Teacher Training, Ceramic Sculpture, Color Theory, Curatorship, Fibre Sculpture, Fine Arts, Gallery Management, Serigraphy (Silk Screen), Stained Glass
Children's Classes: Enrl 30, 5-17 yr olds; tuition $90 per 30 wks. Courses—Crafts, Fine Arts
Summer School: Dean Continuing Educ, P Schubert. Enrl 200; tuition $150 per cr hr for term of 5 wks. Courses—Crafts, Design, Drawing, Fine Arts

NEW CANAAN

GUILD ART CENTER, 1037 Silvermine Rd, 06840. Tel 203-866-0411, 966-6668; FAX 203-966-2763; *School Dir* Anne Connell
Estab 1949; pvt; D & E; SC 60, LC 1; enrl 560
Ent Req: None
Degrees: None
Tuition: No campus res
Courses: Advertising Design, Art History, Ceramics, Drawing, Illustration, Painting, Photography, Printmaking, Sculpture, Computer Graphics, Sogetsu Ikebana, Youth Programs in Art
Adult Hobby Classes: Enrl 550-600; tuition $6 per studio hr for sem of 14 wks. Courses offered
Children's Classes: Enrl 80-100; tuition $6 per studio hr for sem of 14 wks. Courses offered
Summer School: Tuition $6 for 8 wk prog. Courses—Same as above

NEW HAVEN

ALBERTUS MAGNUS COLLEGE, Art Dept, 700 Prospect St, 06511. Tel 203-773-8546; FAX 203-773-3117; *Dir* Jerry Nevins, MFA; *Instr* Beverly Chieffo, MA
Estab 1925, dept estab 1970; pvt; D & E; scholarships; SC 20, LC 9; enrl D 120, non-maj 60, maj 40
Ent Req: HS dipl, SAT, CEEB
Degrees: BA, BFA 8 sem
Tuition: Res—undergrad $10,990 per yr, part-time $520 per cr; campus res—room & board $5500 per yr
Courses: Aesthetics, Art Education, Art History, Ceramics, Collages, Design, Drawing, History of Art & Archaeology, Mixed Media, Painting, Photography, Printmaking, Sculpture, Teacher Training, Art Therapy, Fabric Design & Construction, Weaving
Adult Hobby Classes: Courses offered
Summer School: Dir, Elaine Lewis. Courses—vary

SOUTHERN CONNECTICUT STATE UNIVERSITY, Dept of Art, 501 Crescent St, 06515-1355. Tel 203-392-6653; FAX 203-392-6655; *Dept Head* Keith Hatcher. Instrs: FT 17, PT 12
Estab 1893; pub; D & E; SC 40, LC 18, GC 20; enrl D 315, GS 100
Ent Req: HS dipl, SAT
Degrees: BS, MS(Art Educ), BA(Art History) & BA, BS(Studio Art) 4 yrs
Tuition: Res—$1916 per yr, grad $200, undergrad $186 per cr hr, nonres—$1842 per yr, $81 per cr hr; out-of-state $6200 per yr; campus res available
Courses: Art Education, Art History, Ceramics, Graphic Design, Jewelry, Painting, Photography, Printmaking, Teacher Training, Metalsmithing#Stained Glass
Summer School: Dir, Keith Hatcher. Enrl 320; tuition undergrad $133 per cr hr, grad 144 per cr hr for 2 - 5 wk terms. Courses—Art History, Crafts, Drawing, Graphic Design, Painting, Photography, Printmaking, Sculpture, Stained Glass

YALE UNIVERSITY
—School of Art, 180 York St, PO Box 208242, 06520-8242. Tel 203-432-2600; FAX 203-432-7158; *Dean* Richard Benson; *Prof* Rochelle Feinstein, MFA; *Prof* Tod Papageorge, MA; *Prof* William Bailey, MFA; *Prof* Richard Lytle, MFA; *Prof* Sheila de Bretteville, MFA; *Prof* Robert Reed, MFA
Estab 1869; pvt; D; scholarships; GC 118
Ent Req: BFA, BA, BS or dipl from four year professional art school & portfolio
Degrees: MFA 2 yrs
Tuition: $14,600 per yr
Courses: Drawing, Graphic Design, Painting, Photography, Printmaking, Sculpture
Summer School: 8 wk undergrad courses in New Haven, 3 cr each; 5 wk Graphic Design Prog in Brissago, Switzerland; 8 wk Fel Prog in Norfolk

—**Dept of the History of Art,** PO Box 208272, 06520-8272. Tel 203-432-2668; FAX 203-432-7462; *Chmn* Mary Miller; *Dir Grad Studies* Creighton Gilbert; *Dir Undergrad Studies* Mimi Yiengpruksawan. Instrs: FT 27, PT 2
Estab 1940; pvt; D; scholarships, fels and assistantships
Ent Req: For grad prog—BA & foreign language
Degrees: PhD(Art History) 6 yr
Tuition: $15,920 per yr
Courses: †Art History
—**School of Architecture,** 06520-8242. Tel 203-432-2296, 432-2288; FAX 203-432-7175; *Dean* Fred Koetter
Estab 1869; pvt; scholarships; enrl 142 maximum
Ent Req: Bachelor's degree, grad record exam
Degrees: MEd 2 yr, MArchit 3 yr
Tuition: $17,990 per yr
Courses: Aesthetics, Architecture, Art History, Design, Drawing, Landscape Architecture, Photography

NEW LONDON

CONNECTICUT COLLEGE
—**Dept of Art,** 270 Mohegan Ave, 06320-4196. Tel 860-439-2740; FAX 860-439-5339; *Chmn* Tim McDowell; *Prof* Peter Leibert; *Prof* David Smalley; *Prof* Barkley L Hendricks; *Prof* Maureen McCabe; *Asst Prof* Pamela Marks; *Asst Prof* Andrea Wollensak; *Asst Prof* Ted Hendrickson
Estab 1911; pvt; D; scholarships; SC 20, LC 34
Ent Req: HS dipl, ent exam
Degrees: BA 4 yrs
Tuition: $15,175 per yr; campus res—room & board $4800
Courses: Advertising Design, †Art History, Ceramics, Collages, Design, Drawing, Graphic Arts, History of Art & Archaeology, Illustration, Mixed Media, Painting, Photography, Printmaking, Sculpture, Video, Mixed Media, Painting, Photography, Printmaking, Sculpture, Video, Computer Art, Computer Design
Adult Hobby Classes: Acting Dir, Ann Whitlach
Summer School: Acting Dir, Ann Whitlach. Courses—Vary
—**Dept of Art History,** 270 Mohegan Ave, 06320. Tel 860-439-2740; FAX 860-439-2700; *Chmn* Barbara Zabel; *Prof* Nancy Rash; *Assoc Prof* Robert Baldwin; *Asst Prof* Daniel Abramson
Estab 1911, dept estab 1972; pvt; D & E
Ent Req: HS dipl, SAT
Degrees: BA 4 yrs
Tuition: $17,000 per yr
Courses: Art History

OLD LYME

LYME ACADEMY OF FINE ARTS, 84 Lyme St, 06371. Tel 860-434-5232; *Pres* Henry E Putsch, MA; *Acad Dean* Sharon Hunter, MA
Estab 1976; pvt; D & E; scholarships & fels; SC 42, LC 6; enrl 196
Ent Req: HS dipl, portfolio
Degrees: BFA 4 yr
Tuition: $5800 per yr, $241.66 per cr
Children's Classes: Enrl 30; tuition $60 for 6 wk term
Summer School: Enrl 200; tuition $241.66 per cr

STORRS

UNIVERSITY OF CONNECTICUT, Dept of Art & Art History, 875 Coventry Rd, Box U-99, 06269-1099. Tel 203-486-3930; FAX 860-486-3869; Elec Mail dkelly@fwearts.sfa.uconn.edu. *Head Dept* David C Kelly. Instrs: FT 24, PT 10
Estab 1882, dept estab 1950; pub; D; scholarships; SC 43, LC 32, GC 15; enrl D 1600, maj 280
Ent Req: HS dipl, SAT
Degrees: BA(Art History), BFA(Studio) 4 yrs, MFA 2 yrs
Tuition: Res—undergrad $4036 per yr, grad $2484 per yr; nonres—undergrad $12,306 per yr, grad $6455 per yr; campus res available
Courses: †Art History, Drawing, †Graphic Design, †Illustration, †Painting, †Photography, †Printmaking, †Sculpture
Summer School: Dir, Matthew McLoughlin. Enrl 100; tuition $105 per cr hr; 3 wk studio sessions. Courses—Computer Graphics, Drawing, Painting, Photography

VOLUNTOWN

FOSTER CADDELL'S ART SCHOOL, Northlight, 47 Pendleton Hill Rd, 06384. Tel 860-376-9583; *Head Dept* Foster Caddell, PSA
Estab 1958; D & E; enrl D 75, E 50
Tuition: $750 per course; no campus res
Courses: †Drawing, †Painting, †Teacher Training, †Pastel
Adult Hobby Classes: Enrl 40; tuition $2000. Courses—Drawing, Painting

WEST HARTFORD

SAINT JOSEPH COLLEGE, Dept of Fine Arts, 1678 Asylum Ave, 06117. Tel 860-232-4571; FAX 203-231-8396; *Chmn Dept* Dorothy Bosch Keller. Instrs: FT 1, PT 2
Estab 1932; pvt; W; D & E; scholarships & fels; SC 5, LC 7; enrl D 104
Ent Req: HS dipl, CEEB
Degrees: BA, BS and MA 4 yr
Tuition: $19,000 (24-36 cr) incoming freshman
Courses: Architecture, Art Appreciation, †Art History, Drawing, History of Art & Archaeology, Painting, Creative Crafts, Fundamental of Design, Egyptian Art, Greek Art, Art of Ireland, History of American Antiques, American Architecture, History of American art, History of Women Artists, Victorian Antiques, Impressionism, Renaissance
Summer School: Chmn, D Keller. Enrl 400; tuition $250 per cr hr. Maj in art history offered

UNIVERSITY OF HARTFORD, Hartford Art School, 200 Bloomfield Ave, 06117. Tel 860-768-4391, 768-4393; FAX 860-768-5296; *Dean* Stuart Schar, MFA; *Assoc Dean* Stephen Keller, MA; *Asst Dean* Tom Bradley, MA; *Prof* Lloyd Glasson, MFA; *Prof* Frederick Wessel, MFA; *Prof* Peter McLean, MFA; *Assoc Prof* Gilles Giuntini, MFA; *Assoc Prof* Christopher Horton, MAT; *Assoc Prof* Jim Lee, MFA; *Assoc Prof* Patricia Sutton, MA; *Assoc Prof* Ellen Carey, MFA; *Assoc Prof* Walter Hall, MFA; *Assoc Prof* John Rohlfing, MFA; *Assoc Prof* Mary Frey, MFA; *Assoc Prof* Stephen Brown, MFA; *Assoc Prof* Alex White, MFA; *Asst Prof* Douglas Anderson, MA; *Asst Prof* Eve Olitski, MFA; *Asst Prof* Mark Snyder, MFA; *Asst Prof* Hirokazu Fukawa; *Asst Prof* Susan Wilmarth-Rabineau; *Asst Prof* Gene Gort, MFA; *Asst Prof* Lisa Stinson, MFA
Estab 1877; pvt; Enrl 60-100; tuition $80 for 6 wks. Courses—Ceramics, Drawing, Illustration, Portfolio, Printmaking; scholarships; SC 70, LC 5, GC 32; enrl D 375, E 100, non-maj 125, maj 375, grad 20
Ent Req: HS dipl, SAT
Degrees: BFA 4 yr, MFA 2 yr
Tuition: undergrad $15,600 per yr, $7800 per sem, $255 evenings; campus res—room $4700, board $1710
Courses: Architecture, †Art History, †Ceramics, †Conceptual Art, †Drawing, †Graphic Design, †Illustration, †Painting, †Photography, †Printmaking, †Sculpture, †Video, Glass
Adult Hobby Classes: Day and evening classes
Children's Classes: Enrl 60-100; tuition $80 for 6 wks. Courses—Drawing, Portfolio, Preparation, other Studio Areas
Summer School: Dir, Tom Bradley, Enrl 70-100; tuition $255 per cr for 8 wks. Courses—Ceramics, Drawing, Graphic Design, Painting, Photography, Printmaking, Sculpture

WEST HAVEN

UNIVERSITY OF NEW HAVEN, Dept of Visual & Performing Arts & Philosophy, 300 Orange Ave, 06516. Tel 203-932-7101; *Chmn* Michael G Kaloyanides; *Coordr of Arts* Jerry Zinser. Instrs: FT 2, PT 8
Estab 1927, dept estab 1972; pvt; D & E; SC 30, LC 5; enrl D 350, E 110
Ent Req: HS dipl
Degrees: BA & BS 4 yrs, AS 2 yrs
Tuition: $5300 per sem
Courses: †Advertising Design, Art History, Calligraphy, Ceramics, Commercial Art, Constructions, Drawing, Graphic Arts, Graphic Design, History of Art & Archaeology, Illustration, Interior Design, Mixed Media, Painting, Photography, Printmaking, Sculpture, Dimensional Design, Film Animation, Interaction of Color
Summer School: June 12th - July 20th. Courses—Ceramics, Drawing, History of Art, Painting, Photography, Sculpture

WILLIMANTIC

EASTERN CONNECTICUT STATE UNIVERSITY, Fine Arts Dept, 83 Windham St, 06226. Tel 860-465-5000; FAX 860-456-5508; *Chmn* Imna Arrowo; *Asst Prof* Lula Blocton. Instrs: FT 4, PT 4
Estab 1881; pub; D & E; scholarships; enrl D 300, E 75, maj 40
Ent Req: HS dipl
Degrees: BA(Fine Arts) & BS(Art) 4 yrs
Tuition: Res—$1542 per sem; nonres—$4006 per sem
Courses: Art History, Ceramics, Drawing, Graphic Arts, Interior Design, Jewelry, Painting, Sculpture, Enameling, Weaving
Summer School: Dir, Owen Peagler. Courses—Art & Craft Workshop

WINSTED

NORTHWESTERN CONNECTICUT COMMUNITY COLLEGE, Fine Arts Dept, Park Pl E, 06098. Tel 860-738-6300; FAX 860-379-4995; *Prof* Richard Fineman; *Prof* Charles Dmytriw; *Prof* Janet Nesteruk
Tuition: $88 per cr hr
Courses: Advertising Design, Art Appreciation, Art History, Ceramics, Design, Drawing, Graphic Arts, Painting, Photography, Printmaking, Sculpture, Video

DELAWARE

DOVER

DELAWARE STATE COLLEGE, Dept of Art & Art Education, 1200 N Dupont Hwy, 19904. Tel 302-739-5182; FAX 302-739-5182; *Art Dept Chmn* Arturo Bassolos. Instrs: FT 4
Estab 1960; pub; D & E; scholarships; SC 13, LC 9; enrl 50-60 maj
Ent Req: HS dipl or GED, SAT or ACT
Degrees: BS(Art Educ), BS(General Art) & BS(Art Business)
Tuition: Boarding: in-state $3121 sem, out-of-state $4737 sem
Courses: Art Appreciation, Art History, Jewelry, †Art Education, Ceramics, Commercial Art, Drawing, Interior Design, Lettering, Painting, Photography, Printmaking, Sculpture, Teacher Training, Design, Fibers, Independent Study, Senior Exhibition (one man show & research)
Adult Hobby Classes: Courses—same as above
Summer School: Courses—same as above

NEWARK

UNIVERSITY OF DELAWARE, Dept of Art, Main St & N College Ave, 19716. Tel 302-831-2244; *Chmn* Martha Carothers; *Coordr Sculpture* Joe Moss, MA; *Coordr Photography* John Weiss, MFA; *Coordr Ceramics* Victor Spinski, MFA; *Coordr Printmaking* Rosemary Lane, MFA; *Coordr Jewelry* Anne Graham, MFA; *Coordr Drawing & Painting* Steven Tanis, MFA; *Coordr Foundations* Robert Straight, MFA; *Coordr Fibers* Vera Kaminsky, MFA; *Coordr Illustration* Charles Rowe; *Coordr Visual Communication* Ray Nichols; *Grad Coordr* Carry Holmes
Estab 1833; pub; D & E; SC 62, LC 2, GC 12, non-maj 600, maj 400, grad 30
Ent Req: Portfolio, BFA prog & graphic design prog (both sophomore yr)
Degrees: BA, BS & BFA 4 yrs, MFA 2 yrs, MA 1 yr
Tuition: Res—undergrad $1845 per yr, grad $89 per cr hr, res—grad $5110 per sem; nonres—undergrad $3900, grad $217 per cr hr, nonres—grad $1950 per sem; campus res—room & board $2254, nonres—room & board $2354
Courses: Advertising Design, Art Education, Ceramics, Drawing, Graphic Design, Illustration, Jewelry, Painting, Photography, †Printmaking, †Sculpture, Fibers
Adult Hobby Classes: Courses—various

REHOBOTH BEACH

REHOBOTH ART LEAGUE, INC, 12 Dodds Lane, 19971. Tel 302-227-8408; FAX 302-227-4121; *Dir* Nancy O'Brien
Estab 1938; pvt; D; SC 7; enrl D 400, others 400
Ent Req: Interest in art
Courses: Calligraphy, Ceramics, Drawing, Painting, Photography
Adult Hobby Classes: Enrl 150. Courses—Ceramics, Drawing, Painting, Pottery
Children's Classes: Courses—Art Forms

DISTRICT OF COLUMBIA

WASHINGTON

AMERICAN UNIVERSITY, Dept of Art, 4400 Massachusetts Ave NW, 20016. Tel 202-885-1670; FAX 202-686-2828; *Chmn Dept* Don Kimes; *Prof* C Stanley Lewis; *Prof* Mary Carrard; *Prof* Norma Broude, PHD; *Prof* M Oxman; *Assoc Prof* M Hirano; *Assoc Prof* C Ravenal; *Assoc Prof* Ron Haynie; *Assoc Prof* Charlotte Story; *Assoc Prof* Deborah Kahn; *Assoc Prof* Michael Graham; *Asst Prof* Helen Langa
Estab 1893, dept estab 1945; pvt; D & E; scholarships; SC 19, LC 14, GC 26; enrl D & E 1520, maj 191, grad 65
Ent Req: HS dipl
Degrees: BA, BFA(Studio Art), BA(Design), BA(Art History) 4 yrs, MA(Art History) 18 months, MFA(Painting, Sculpture, Printmaking) 2 yrs
Tuition: Undergrad $8757 per sem, grad $5643 per sem
Courses: Art History, Ceramics, Drawing, Graphic Design, Painting, Printmaking, Sculpture
Summer School: Design, Studio & Art History

CATHOLIC UNIVERSITY OF AMERICA
—School of Architecture & Planning, 20064. Tel 202-319-5188; FAX 202-319-5728; *Dean* Gregory K Hunt; *Assoc Dean* James O'Hear III, MArchit; *Dir Grad Studies* Joseph Miller, BArchit; *Prof* Seymour Auerbach, MArchit; *Prof* Ernest Forest Wilson, PhD; *Prof* W Dodd Ramberg, BArchit; *Assoc Prof* Julius S Levine, MCP; *Prof* George T Marcou, MArchit; *Assoc Prof* Theodore Naos, MArchit; *Assoc Prof* Thomas Walton; *Assoc Prof* John V Yanik; *Vis Asst Prof* Ann Cederna; *Vis Asst Prof* Neal Payton; *Asst Prof* J Ronald Kabriel, MArchit; *Asst Prof* Richard Loosle
Estab 1887, dept estab 1930; den; D & E; SC 6, LC 4 per sem, GC 15 per sem; enrl D 240, maj 240, grad 95
Ent Req: HS dipl and SAT for undergrad, BS or BA in Archit or equivalent plus GPA of 2.5 in undergrad studies for grad
Degrees: BArchit & BS(Archit) 4 yr, MArchit 4 yr
Tuition: $6915 per sem
Courses: Architecture, Drafting, Landscape Architecture, Photography, Graphics, History and Theory of Architecture, Urban Design, Planning, Technology, Practice
Children's Classes: Session of 3 wks. Courses—High School Program
Summer School: Dir, Richard Loosle. Enrl 100, term of 5-9 wks May-Aug. Courses—Computers, Construction & Documents, Design Studio, Environmental Systems, Graphic, History & Theory of Architecture, Photography, Structures
—Dept of Art, 20064. Tel 202-319-5282; *Chmn Dept* John Winslow; *Prof* Thomas Nakashima; *Assoc Prof* Thomas Rooney; *Asst Prof* Robert Ross
Estab 1930; den; D & E; scholarships; SC 17, LC 9, GC 20; enrl D 48, maj 38, grad 10
Ent Req: HS dipl and SAT for undergrad, BA-BFA; MAT, GRE for grad
Degrees: MFA(Painting) 2 yrs
Tuition: FT $6278 per sem; PT $480 per cr hr
Courses: Aesthetics, Architecture, †Art History, Costume Design & Construction, Design, Film, †Painting, Photography, Printmaking, †Sculpture, Stage Design, Teacher Training, Theatre Arts, Video
Summer School: Chmn, John Winslow. Term of 8 wks beginning June. Courses—Drawing, Ceramics, Painting, Special Independent Courses

CORCORAN SCHOOL OF ART, 500 17th St NW, 20006-4899. Tel 202-639-1800; FAX 202-628-3186; *Dean* Samuel Hoi; *Assoc Dean of Faculty* Rona Slade, BA; *Assoc Dean of Students* Susan Moran; *Chmn Fine Arts* Nancy Palmer, MFA; *Chmn Academic Studies* Bernard Welt; *Chmn Ceramics* Robert Epstein, MFA; *Chmn Printmaking* Georgia Deal; *Chmn Sculpture* F L Wall; *Chmn Photography* Claudia Smigrod, MA; *Chmn Graphic Design* Johan Severtson, BFA
Estab 1890; pvt; D & E; scholarships; SC 84, LC 42; enrl D 300 maj, E 750 non-maj
Ent Req: HS dipl, SAT or ACT, portfolio & interview
Degrees: BFA 4 yrs

Tuition: $9980 per yr, $425 per 3 cr hr course; campus—res dorm $2700 per yr
Courses: Art Appreciation, Art History, Ceramics, Design, Drawing, Illustration, Interior Design, Landscape Architecture, Painting, Photography, Printmaking, Sculpture, Video, Airbrush, Animation, Business & Law for the Artist, Computer Art, †Fine Arts, Furniture, History of Photography, Philosophy, Typography
Adult Hobby Classes: Enrl 750 per sem; tuition $360-$960 for 15 wks.
Courses—Art History, Ceramics, Color & Design, Computer Graphics, Drawing, Furniture, Interior Design, Landscape Design, Painting, Photography, Printmaking, Sculpture
Children's Classes: Enrl 70, tuition $110 per 5 wk session, Saturday ages 6-10; $330-$370 per 13 wk session, Saturday ages 10-15. Courses—General Studio ages 15-18. Courses—Ceramics, Computer Art, Drawing, Painting, Photography, Portfolio Prep Workshop, Screenprinting
Summer School: Dean, Samuel Hoi. Enrl 400; Adult—tuition $350-$960 for 6 wks beginning June. Courses—Art History, Ceramics, Computer Graphics, Drawing, Illustration, Interior Design, Landscape Design, Painting, Photography, Printmaking, Sculpture, Watercolor. HS (ages 15-18)—tuition $390-$690 for 5 wks beginning June. Courses—Ceramics, Drawing, Painting, Photography, Portfolio Prep, Pre-College. Children's Workshops (ages 6-10)—tuition $10 for 5 day session beginning June

GEORGETOWN UNIVERSITY, Dept of Art, Music & Theatre, Walsh 196, 20057. Tel 202-687-7010; FAX 202-687-3048; *Gallery Dir* John Morrell, MFA; *Chmn* Elizabeth Prelinger, PhD; *Prof* Donn Murphy, PhD; *Assoc Prof* Peter Charles, MFA; *Assoc Prof* Alison Hilton, PhD; *Assoc Prof* B G Muhn, MFA; *Assoc Prof* Carra Ferguson, PhD; *Assoc Prof* Cynthia Schneider, PhD
Estab 1789, dept estab 1967; pvt; D; SC 8, LC 6; enrl D 600 (includes non-maj), maj 12 per yr
Ent Req: HS dipl
Degrees: BA 4 yrs
Tuition: campus res available
Courses: †Art History, †Drawing, Graphic Arts, †Painting, †Printmaking, †Sculpture, Theatre Arts, Music History
Adult Hobby Classes: Continuing Education Dir, Phyllis O'Callaghan
Summer School: Dir, Michael Collins. Courses offered

GEORGE WASHINGTON UNIVERSITY, Dept of Art, Smith Hall of Art, 801 22nd St NW, 20052. Tel 202-994-6085; FAX 202-994-8657; *Chmn* Lilien Robinson; *Prof* Douglas H Teller, MFA; *Prof* J Franklin Wright Jr, MFA; *Prof* Arthur Hall-Smith, MFA; *Prof* Constance C Costigan, MFA; *Prof* Jerry L Lake, MFA; *Prof* Turker Ozdogan, MFA; *Assoc Prof* H I Gates, MFA; *Assoc Prof* Barbara Von Barghahn, PhD; *Assoc Prof* Jeffrey C Anderson, PhD; *Assoc Prof* D Michael Hitchcock, PhD; *Assoc Prof* W T Woodward, MFA; *Assoc Prof* Samuel B Molina, MFA; *Assoc Prof* Jeffrey L Stephanic, MFA; *Assoc Prof* Kim Hartswick, PhD; *Asst Prof* David Bjelajac, PhD
Estab 1821, dept estab 1893; pvt; D & E; scholarships; SC 103, LC 74, GC 68; enrl D 1350, GS 196
Ent Req: HS dipl, ent exam
Degrees: BA 4 yr, MA 2-2 1/2 yr, MFA 2 yr, PhD 4 yr
Tuition: $575 per cr hr
Courses: †Art History, †Ceramics, †Drawing, †Design, †Graphic Arts, †Painting, †Photography, †Sculpture, †American Art, †Classical Art & Archaeology, †Contemporary Art, †Medieval Art, †Renaissance & Baroque Art, †Visual Communications
Summer School: Chmn, Melvin P Lader. Enrl 150; tuition $403 per cr hr for two 6 wk sessions. Courses— Art History, Ceramics, Drawing, Painting, Photography, Sculpture, Visual Communications

MOUNT VERNON COLLEGE, School of Art & Design, 2100 Foxhall Rd NW, 20007. Tel 202-625-4552; *Assoc Dean* Joseph Wnuk
Estab 1875; pvt; D & E; scholarships; SC 16
Degrees: AA and BA
Courses: Aesthetics, Art History, Ceramics, Design, Drafting, Drawing, Graphic Arts, †Graphic Design, †Interior Design, Painting, Photography, Printmaking, Sculpture, Textile Design, Theatre Arts, Arts & Humanities, Historical Preservation, †History of Decorative Art, †Studio Art
Adult Hobby Classes: Graphic Design, History of Decorative Art, Interior Design, Studio Art
Summer School: Dir, Dr Sharon Fechter. Enrl 40, 8 wks, June-July. Courses—History of Decorative Art, Interior Design, Studio Arts

TRINITY COLLEGE, Art Program, 125 Michigan Ave NE, 20017. Tel 202-884-9280, 884-9296; FAX 202-939-5000; *Head Dept* Dr Yvonne Dixon; *Assoc Prof* Dr Rebecca Easby; *Adjunct Prof* Gordon Kray; *Adjunct Prof* Gene Markowski; *Lectr* Sara Stout; *Lectr* Ann Betts Burton; *Lectr* Sarah Stout
Estab 1897; den; D & E; scholarships; SC 8, LC 2-3; enrl D 120, maj 12
Ent Req: HS dipl, SAT or ACT, recommendation
Degrees: BA 4 yr
Tuition: $11,080 per yr, $363 per cr hr; campus res—room & board $17,510
Courses: Art History, Design, Drawing, Film, Graphic Design, History of Art & Archaeology, Lettering, Painting, Photography, Printmaking, Sculpture, Documentary, Photography, Photojournalism
Summer School: Dir, Susan Ikerd. Courses—Vary

UNIVERSITY OF THE DISTRICT OF COLUMBIA, Dept of Mass Media, Visual & Performing Arts, 4200 Connecticut Ave NW, MB-10-01, 20008. Tel 202-274-7402; *Prof* Charles A Young; *Prof* Meredith Rode, MFA; *Coordr* Manon Cleary, MFA; *Prof* David Lanier, MFA; *Prof* Yvonne Carter, MFA; *Asst Prof* Walter Lattimore, MFA; *Asst Prof* George Smith, MS; *Asst Prof* Rufus Wells, BFA
Estab 1969; pub; D & E; SC 65, LC 21; enrl D 616, E 99, non-maj 405, maj 112
Ent Req: HS dipl, GED
Degrees: AA(Advertising Design) 2 yrs, BA(Studio Art) and BA(Art Educ) 4 yrs
Tuition: Res—undergrad $300 per sem; non-res—undergrad $1200 per sem; no campus res
Courses: †Advertising Design, †Art Education, Art History, Ceramics, Conceptual Art, Drawing, Graphic Arts, Graphic Design, Handicrafts, Illustration, Lettering, Mixed Media, Museum Staff Training, †Painting, Photography, †Printmaking, Sculpture
Summer School: C A Young. Enrl 200. Courses—Art History, Ceramics, Drawings, Painting, Photography

FLORIDA

BELLEAIR

FLORIDA GULF COAST ART CENTER, INC, 222 Ponce de Leon Blvd, 34616.
Tel 813-584-8634; FAX 813-586-0782; *Exec Dir* Ken Rollins; *Cur Educ* Elaine
Georgilas; *Registrar* Devon Larsen
Estab 1949; pvt; D & E; enrl D 315
Ent Req: None
Degrees: None
Courses: Ceramics, Drawing, Goldsmithing, Jewelry, Mixed Media, Painting,
Photography, Sculpture, Metalsmithing
Children's Classes: After school & summer programs

BOCA RATON

FLORIDA ATLANTIC UNIVERSITY, Art Dept, 33431. Tel 407-367-3870; *Chmn*
Dr Kathleen Russo. Instrs: FT 8
Estab 1964; pub; D & E; scholarships; SC 25, LC 8, GC 6; enrl D 1600, maj 220,
grad 7, special students 7
Degrees: BFA & BA 4 yrs
Tuition: Res—$57.77 per cr hr; nonres—$216.42 per cr hr; grad res—$108.18 per cr
hr; nonres—$361.20 per cr hr
Courses: Advertising Design, Aesthetics, Art Appreciation, Art Education, †Art
History, Ceramics, Costume Design & Construction, Design, Drafting, Graphic Arts,
Graphic Design, Jewelry, Museum Staff Training, Painting, Photography,
Printmaking, Sculpture, Stage Design, Teacher Training, Theatre Arts, Video,
Applied Art, History of Architecture, Silkscreen & Etching, Studio Crafts, Weaving
Adult Hobby Classes: Courses offered through continuing education
Summer School: Courses offered

LYNN UNIVERSITY, Art & Design Dept, 3601 N Military Trail, 33431. Tel 407-
994-0770, Ext 101; *Prof* Ernest Ranspach, MFA; *Prof* Winslow Wedin
Scholarships offered
Degrees: AA, BFA, BS & Design
Tuition: $6350 per yr
Courses: Advertising Design, Art Appreciation, Art History, Design, Drafting,
Drawing, Interior Design, Painting, Photography, Stage Design, Textile Design,
Corporate Identity Rendering Techniques, Environmental Design, Graphics,
Portfolio & Exhibition

BRADENTON

MANATEE COMMUNITY COLLEGE, Dept of Art & Humanities, PO Box 1849,
34206. Tel 941-755-1511, Ext 4251; FAX 813-755-1511, Ext 4251; *Chmn* John W
James, MA; *Prof* Edward Camp, MFA; *Prof* Sherri Hill, MFA; *Prof* Priscilla
Stewart, MA; *Prof* Joe Loccisano. Instrs: FT 5, PT 4
Estab 1958; pub; D & E; scholarships; SC 22, LC 5; enrl D 310, E 90, maj 75
Ent Req: HS dipl, SAT
Degrees: AA & AS 2 yrs
Tuition: Res—undergrad $24 per cr hr; nonres—undergrad $52 per cr hr
Courses: Art Appreciation, Art History, Ceramics, Costume Design & Construction,
Drawing, Film, Graphic Arts, Graphic Design, Interior Design, Lettering, Painting,
Photography, Printmaking, Sculpture, Stage Design, Theatre Arts, Video, Art
Appreciation, 2-D & 3-D Design, Color Fundamentals, Figure Drawing
Adult Hobby Classes: Enrl 200; average tuition $30 per class. Courses—Ceramics,
Drawing, Oil Painting, Photography, Watercolor
Summer School: Pres, Cortez Francis. Enrl 100; tuition $20.50 per cr hr for term of
6 wks. Courses—Art Appreciation, Ceramics, Intro Art Studio, Photography

CORAL GABLES

UNIVERSITY OF MIAMI, Dept of Art & Art History, PO Box 248106, 33124-
4410. Tel 305-284-2542; FAX 305-284-2115; *Chmn* Darby Bannard; *Assoc Chmn*
Marion Jefferson, PhD; *Prof* Christine Federighi, MFA; *Prof* Gerald G Winter,
MFA; *Assoc Prof* Paula Harper, PhD; *Assoc Prof* Edward Ghannam, MFA; *Assoc
Prof* Perri Lee Roberts, PhD; *Assoc Prof* Carlos Aquirre, MFA; *Assoc Prof* Brian
Curtis, MFA; *Assoc Prof* Tom Gormley; *Assoc Prof* J Tomas Lopez; *Asst Prof*
William Betsch, PhD; *Asst Prof* Lise Drost, MFA
Estab 1925, dept estab 1960; pvt; D; scholarships; SC 81, LC 15, GC 25; enrl D
975, non-maj 800, maj 230, grad 33
Ent Req: HS dipl, SAT
Degrees: BA & BFA 4 yrs, MA(Art History) & MFA 2 yrs
Tuition: Res & nonres—undergrad $18,220 per yr, $9110 per sem, $742 per cr hr
Courses: Art History, Ceramics, Graphic Design, Illustration, Painting, Photography,
Printmaking, Sculpture, Computer Imaging
Adult Hobby Classes: Tuition $160 for 8 wk term. Courses—Bronzecasting, Digital
Imaging, Drawing, Glassblowing, Handbuilding, Painting, Photography, Wheel
Throwing

DANIA

SOUTH FLORIDA ART INSTITUTE OF HOLLYWOOD, 35 SW First Ave,
33004. Tel 954-920-2961; *Dir* Elwin Porter
Estab 1958; pvt; D & E; scholarships; SC 30, LC 2, GC 2; enrl D 230, E 20
Ent Req: Portfolio
Degrees: Cert fine arts & cert 2 & 4 yrs
Tuition: $900 per yr, no campus res
Courses: Design, Drawing, Painting, Sculpture, Abstraction, Anatomy, Clay
Modeling, Color Theory, Composition, Life Sketching
Adult Hobby Classes: Enrl 100. Courses—Fine Arts, Graphic Design
Children's Classes: Enrl 30; tuition $45 per 8 wks. Courses—Painting, Drawing,
Sculpture
Summer School: Dir, Elwin Porter. Courses—Most of above

DAYTONA BEACH

DAYTONA BEACH COMMUNITY COLLEGE, Dept of Fine Arts & Visual Arts,
PO Box 2811, 32120-2811. Tel 904-255-8131; FAX 904-947-3134; *Dean* Dr Frank
Wetta; *Prof* Denis Deegan, MFA; *Prof* Pamela Griesinger, MFA; *Prof* Gary
Monroe, MFA; *Prof* Eric Breitenbach, MS; *Prof* Patrick Van Duesen, BS; *Prof* Dan
Biferie, MFA; *Prof* Bobbie Clementi; *Prof* Jacques A Dellavalle; *Prof* John Wilton
Estab 1958; pub; D & E; scholarships; SC 15, LC 3; enrl D 250, E 50, maj 30
Ent Req: HS dipl or GED
Degrees: 2 year program offered
Tuition: Res—$35.80 per sem hr; nonres—$134.23 per sem hr
Courses: Ceramics, Design, Drawing, Painting, Printmaking, Sculpture,
Cinematography, Papermaking
Summer School: Courses offered

DE LAND

STETSON UNIVERSITY, Art Dept, 32720. Elec Mail favis@suvaxl.stetson.edu;
khansen@suvax1.stetson,edu. *Head Dept* Roberta Favis. Instrs: FT 3
Estab 1880; den; scholarships; SC 5, LC 5; enrl 200
Ent Req: Col boards
Degrees: 4 yr
Courses: Art History, Ceramics, Drawing, Mixed Media, Painting, Printmaking,
Sculpture, Teacher Training
Summer School: Dir, Roberta Favis

DUNEDIN

DUNEDIN FINE ARTS & CULTURAL CENTER, 1143 Michigan Blvd, 34698.
Tel 813-738-1892; FAX 813-736-0796; Elec Mail dfac@gte.net. *Dir* Nancy
McIntire; *Instr* Chris Still; *Instr* Kitty Johnson; *Instr* Susan Huskey; *Instr* Betty
Welch; *Instr* Brooke Allison; *Instr* Ira Burhans
Estab 1975; pub; D & E & weekends; scholarships; SC 20-25, LC 5-10; enrl approx
900
Tuition: Members $38-$75 per class; nonmembers $48-$85 per class; no campus res
Courses: Calligraphy, Collages, Drawing, Jewelry, Painting, Photography,
Printmaking, Sculpture, Arts for the Handicapped, Batik, Children's Art, Clay, Fine
Crafts, Pastel, Pottery
Children's Classes: Tuition $25-$35 per quarter. Courses—Fine Arts, Drama
Summer School: Dir, Carla Crook. Enrl approx 250; tuition $15-$45 for two 5 wk
sessions beginning June. Courses—Visual Arts

FORT LAUDERDALE

ART INSTITUTE OF FORT LAUDERDALE, 1799 SE 17th St, 33316. Tel 954-
527-1799; FAX 305-728-8637; WATS 800-275-7603. *Dir Admis* Eileen Northrop;
Dir Educ Wallace Lewis; *Dir Visual Communications* Linda Weeks; *Dir Photo* Ed
Williams; *Dir Interior Design* Bill Kobrynich, AA; *Asst Chmn Advertising Design*
Lorna Hernandez; *Dir Music & Video Bus* Ed Galizia; *Dir Fashion Design* June
Fisher
Estab 1968; pvt; D & E; scholarships; enrl D 1900, maj 1900
Ent Req: HS dipl
Degrees: AS(technology)
Tuition: Res—undergrad $2980 per qtr
Courses: Advertising Design, Art History, Conceptual Art, Display, Drafting,
Drawing, †Fashion Arts, Graphic Arts, Graphic Design, Illustration, †Interior
Design, Lettering, Mixed Media, Painting, †Photography, Video, Fashion Design
Summer School: Same as regular semester

FORT MYERS

EDISON COMMUNITY COLLEGE, Dept of Fine & Performing Arts, 8099
College Pkwy SW, 33906-6210. Tel 813-489-9300, 489-9482; *Head Dept Fine &
Performing Arts* Edith Pendleton; *Instr of Art* Robert York; *Music Instr* Dr Dennis
Hill; *Music Instr* Dr Glenn Cornish; *Music Instr* Dr T Defoor; *Theatre Arts Instr*
Richard Westlake. Instrs: FT 1, PT 5
Estab 1962; pub; D & E; scholarships
Ent Req: HS dipl
Degrees: AA & AS 2 yrs
Tuition: Res—$22 per cr hr; nonres—$49 per cr hr
Courses: Art Appreciation, Art History, Ceramics, Design, Drawing, Jewelry,
Painting, Photography, Printmaking, Sculpture, 3-D Design, Intro to Computer
Imaging
Adult Hobby Classes: Enrl 20. Courses—any non-cr activity of interest for which a
teacher is available

FORT PIERCE

INDIAN RIVER COMMUNITY COLLEGE, Fine Arts Dept, Virginia Ave,
33450. Tel 561-462-4391, 462-4700; *Chmn Fine Arts* David Moberg; *Asst Dean of
Arts & Sciences* Raymond Considine; *Dir* Open ; *Instr* Anthony Allo
Estab 1960; pub; D & E; scholarships; SC 10, LC 10
Ent Req: HS dipl
Degrees: AA & AS 2 yrs
Tuition: Res—$22 per unit; nonres—$44 per unit
Courses: Advertising Design, Art Education, Art History, Ceramics, Display,
Drafting, Drawing, Graphic Arts, Painting, Printmaking, Sculpture, Acting, General
Art, Intro to Drama, Landscape, Music Theory, Portrait, Vocal Ensemble
Summer School: Dir, Jane Howard. Enrl 80. Courses—Gifted students in the arts

GAINESVILLE

UNIVERSITY OF FLORIDA, Dept of Art, 302, FAC Complex, 32611. Tel 352-392-0211; FAX 904-392-8453; *Chmn* John E Catterall; *Distinctive Serv Prof* Kenneth A Kerslake, MFA; *Prof* Jack C Nicholson, MFA; *Prof* Robert C Skelley, MFA; *Grad Research Prof* Jerry Velsmann; *Prof* Robert Westin; *Prof* Joseph Sabatella; *Prof* John A O'Connor, MFA; *Prof* Evon Streetman, MFA; *Prof* John L Ward, MFA; *Prof* Marcia Isaacson, MFA; *Assoc Prof* Barbara Barletta, PhD; *Assoc Prof* Jerry Cutler, MFA; *Assoc Prof* Richard Heipp, MFA; *Asst Prof* Craig Roland; *Assoc Prof* David Kremgold, MFA; *Assoc Prof* Robin Poynor, PhD; *Assoc Prof* John Scott, PhD; *Assoc Prof* Nan Smith, MFA; *Assoc Prof* David Stanley, PhD; *Assoc Prof* Donald Murray; *Assoc Prof* Merle Flannery; *Assoc Prof* Karen Valdes; *Assoc Prof* Muheeva Spence; *Asst Prof* Kevin Daniels; *Asst Prof* Craig Freeman; *Asst Prof* Robert Mueller; *Asst Prof* Jan Schall; *Asst Prof* Celesk Roberga; *Asst Prof* Brian Slawson; *Asst Art Prof* Louise Rothman. Instrs: FT 22
Estab 1925; pub; D & E; scholarships; SC 40, LC 26, GC 11; enrl maj 200 upper div, grad 16
Ent Req: HS dipl, SAT, ACT, TOEFL, SCAT or AA degree (transfers must have 2.0 average) GRE
Degrees: BAA & BFA 4 yrs, MA 2 yrs, MFA 3 yrs
Tuition: Res—undergrad $37.29 per cr hr, grad $64.58 per cr hr; nonres—undergrad $124.44 per cr hr, grad $189.53 per cr hr; campus res—$800 per yr with air conditioning
Courses: †Art Education, †Art History, †Ceramics, †Drawing, †Graphic Design, Lettering, †Painting, †Photography, †Printmaking, †Sculpture, Electronic Media
Summer School: Limited classes

JACKSONVILLE

FLORIDA COMMUNITY COLLEGE AT JACKSONVILLE, SOUTH CAMPUS, Art Dept, 11901 Beach Blvd, 32216. Tel 904-646-2031; FAX 904-646-2396; *Faculty Coordr Fine Arts* Larry Davis; *Gallery Dir* Bob Pina; *Prof* Eleanor Allen; *Prof* Derby Ulloa; *Prof* Ron Wetherell. Instrs: FT 5
Estab 1966; pub; D & E; scholarships; SC 14, LC 6; enrl D 150, E 75
Ent Req: HS dipl
Degrees: AA & AS 2 yrs
Tuition: Res—$18 per cr hr; nonres—$26 per cr hr; no campus res
Courses: Ceramics, Drawing, Graphic Design, History of Art & Archaeology, Painting, Photography, Sculpture, Batik, Blockprinting, Computer Graphics, Experimentations, Serigraphy
Adult Hobby Classes: Enrl 75-80; for term of 6 wks beginning June. Courses—Art Appreciation, Crafts, Drawing, Painting, Photography
Summer School: Courses—Ceramics, Design, Drawing, Painting, Printmaking, Sculpture

JACKSONVILLE UNIVERSITY, Dept of Art, College of Fine Arts, 2800 University Blvd N, 32211. Tel 904-744-3950; *Dean* Jesse G Wright; *Dir Dance* Violet Angeles Hollis; *Art Chair* Joun J Turnock
Estab 1932; pvt; D & E; scholarships; SC 47, LC 13; enrl D 403, maj 80
Ent Req: HS dipl, ent exam
Degrees: BFA, BA, BS & BAEd, 4 yr; MAT
Tuition: $4800 per sem 12-16 cr hrs
Courses: †Art Education, †Art History, Ceramics, Drawing, Painting, Photography, Sculpture, †Computer Art & Design, †Studio Art, †Visual Communication, Hotglass
Adult Hobby Classes: Enrl 10. Courses vary
Children's Classes: Courses offered June-July
Summer School: Tuition $180 per sem hr. Courses—Basic Art

UNIVERSITY OF NORTH FLORIDA, Dept of Communications & Visual Arts, 4567 St Johns Bluff Rd S, 32224. Tel 904-646-2650; *Chmn* Robert H Bulle, MFA; *Prof* Louise Freshman Brown, MFA; *Assoc Prof* David S Porter, MFA; *Assoc Prof* Robert L Cocaougher, MFA; *Assoc Prof* Charles Charles MA; *Assoc Prof* Paul Ladnier, MFA; *Asst Prof* Debra E Murphy
Estab 1970; pub; D & E; scholarships; enrl maj 385
Ent Req: AA
Degrees: BA 2 yr, BFA
Tuition: Res—undergrad $16.50 per sem hr, grad $22 per qtr hr; nonres—undergrad $51.50 per qtr hr, grad $62 per qtr hr
Courses: Advertising Design, Aesthetics, Art Appreciation, Art History, †Ceramics, Commercial Art, Conceptual Art, Design, †Drawing, Graphic Arts, Graphic Design, †History of Art & Archaeology, Illustration, Lettering, Mixed Media, †Painting, †Photography, Printmaking, †Sculpture, †Video, Broadcasting, Computer Images, Digital Photography, Electronic Multi-Media
Summer School: Various courses offered on demand

KEY WEST

FLORIDA KEYS COMMUNITY COLLEGE, Fine Arts Div, 33040. Tel 305-296-9081, 296-1520 (Box Office); FAX 305-292-5155; *Chmn Fine Arts Div* G Gerald Cash
Scholarships
Degrees: AA, AS
Tuition: Res—$39.65 per cr hr; nonres—$147.60 per cr hr
Courses: Art Appreciation, Art Education, Art History, Calligraphy, †Ceramics, Commercial Art, Costume Design & Construction, Design, Display, Drafting, Drawing, Film, Graphic Arts, Graphic Design, Handicrafts, Jewelry, Mixed Media, Painting, †Photography, Printmaking, Sculpture, Stage Design, †Theatre Arts, †Fine Arts, Jewelry Making, Voice
Adult Hobby Classes: Enrl 150; Sept-Apr. Courses—Acting, Costume Design, Theatre Production (Lighting, Stagecraft, Design)

LAKE CITY

LAKE CITY COMMUNITY COLLEGE, Art Dept, Rte 19 Box 1030, 32055. Tel 904-752-1822, Ext 256; *Dir* Charlie Carroll. Instrs: FT 1, PT 2
Estab 1962; pub; D & E; SC 9, LC 2; enrl D 160, maj 10
Ent Req: HS dipl
Degrees: AA 2 yrs
Courses: Ceramics, Drawing, Handicrafts, Jewelry, Painting, Sculpture, Composition, Weaving

LAKELAND

FLORIDA SOUTHERN COLLEGE, Art Dept, 111 Lake Hollingsworth Dr, 33801. Tel 941-680-4224; *Chmn Dept* Downing Barnitz, MFA; *Asst Prof* Gale L Doak, MA; *Asst Prof* Allyson Sheckler, PhD; *Asst Prof* Beth M Ford, MA
Estab 1885; den; D; scholarships; SC 20, LC 6, maj 34
Ent Req: HS dipl
Degrees: AB & BS 128 hr
Courses: †Art Education, Art History, Ceramics, Drawing, Graphic Arts, Handicrafts, Lettering, Painting, Photography, Sculpture, Teacher Training, Theatre Arts, Weaving, Advertising Design, Ancient & Medieval Art, †Art Communication, Design (19th & 20th century art), Graphic Illustration, Renaissance & Baroque Art, †Studio Art
Adult Hobby Classes: Courses—Graphics, Oil Painting
Summer School: Dean, Dr Ben F Wade. Tuition $126 per hr, two terms of 4 wks beginning June & July. Courses—Art Humanities, Drawing, Painting

LAKE WORTH

PALM BEACH COMMUNITY COLLEGE, Dept of Art, 4200 S Congress Ave, 33461-4796. Tel 561-439-8142; Cable FLASUNCOM. *Art Prog Leader* W Patrick Slatery
Estab 1935; pub; D & E; scholarships; SC 20, LC 5; enrl D 15,000 maj 400
Ent Req: HS dipl or over 25
Degrees: AA and AS 2 yr
Tuition: $36.50 per cr hr
Courses: Advertising Design, Architecture, Art Appreciation, Art History, Ceramics, Commercial Art, Design, Drawing, Fashion Arts, Graphic Arts, Graphic Design, Handicrafts, History of Art & Archaeology, Illustration, Intermedia, Interior Design, Jewelry, Painting, Photography, Printmaking, Sculpture, Stage Design, Theatre Arts, Weaving, Architectural Drawing, †Basic Design, Enameling, †Etching, Graphic Arts, Lithography, Screen Printing, Technical Photo Courses, Technical Printing, Typography
Adult Hobby Classes: Courses—Ceramics, Jewelry, Painting, Photography, Picture Frame Making, Printmaking, Weaving
Summer School: Dir, Richard Holcomb. Enrl 300; tuition $36.50 per cr hr. Courses—Art Appreciation, Ceramics, Crafts, Design, Drawing, History of Art, Photography

MADISON

NORTH FLORIDA COMMUNITY COLLEGE, Dept Humanities & Art, 100 Turner Davis Dr, 32340. Tel 904-973-2288; *Chmn* Frances S Adleburg; *Instr* William F Gardner Jr
Scholarships
Degrees: AA
Tuition: Res—$33 per sem hr; nonres—$126 per sem hr
Courses: Art History, Ceramics, Design, Drawing, Painting, Sculpture

MARIANNA

CHIPOLA JUNIOR COLLEGE, Dept of Fine & Performing Arts, 3094 Indian Circle, 32446. Tel 904-718-2277; *Dean Fine Arts Div* Sarah Clemmons
Estab 1947; pub; D & E; scholarships; SC 14, LC 2; enrl D 60
Ent Req: HS dipl
Degrees: AA 2 yr
Tuition: Res—$37.34 per sem hr; nonres—$143.38 per sem hr
Courses: Art History, Ceramics, Drawing, Painting, Stage Design, Theatre Arts, 2-D & 3-D Design, Crafts, Color Picture Comp, Purpose of Arts
Summer School: Dir, Dr Donald A Dellow. Enrl 300; tuition res—$37.34 per sem hr, nonres—$143.38 per sem hr. Courses—varied

MIAMI

FLORIDA INTERNATIONAL UNIVERSITY, Visual Arts Dept, University Park Campus Bldg DM-382, 33199. Tel 305-348-2897, 348-2000 (main); *Chmn* Clive King; *Prof* William Maguire; *Prof* James M Couper; *Prof* Ellen Jacobs; *Assoc Prof* Richard Duncan; *Assoc Prof* William J Burke; *Assoc Prof* R F Buckley; *Assoc Prof* Manuel Torres; *Assoc Prof* Ed del Valle; *Assoc Prof* Mirta Gomez; *Assoc Prof* Sandra Winters; *Asst Prof* Barbara Watts; *Gallery Dir & Lecturer* Dahlia Morgan; *Instr & Art Historian* Juan Martinez; *Instr & Art Historian* Carol Damiam; *Instr & Art Historian* Kate Kretz; *Instr & Art Historian* Nora Heimann
Estab 1972, dept estab 1972; pub; D & E; scholarships; SC 20, LC 12, GC 18; enrl D 320, E 100, non-maj 225, maj 175, grad 20
Ent Req: 1000 on SAT, 3.0 HS grade point average
Degrees: BFA
Tuition: Res—undergrad $59.34 per cr hr; nonres—undergrad $234.27 per cr hr; res—grad $114.99 per cr hr; nonres $385.73 per cr hr
Courses: Art History, Ceramics, Drawing, Jewelry, Painting, Photography, Printmaking, Sculpture, Glass Blowing
Summer School: Dir, Clive King. Enrl 160; tuition $55 per sem hr for term of 6.5 wks beginning May 13 & June 28

INTERNATIONAL FINE ARTS COLLEGE, 1737 N Bayshore Dr, 33132. Tel 305-373-4684; *Dir & Chmn of Visual Arts* Marcel Lissek; *Pres College* Edward Porter; *Dean* Maryse Levy
Estab 1965, dept estab 1966; pvt; D; SC 6; enrl D 180, maj 110
Ent Req: HS dipl
Degrees: AA
Tuition: $8975 acad yr for Fashion majors & Commerical Art; $9975 calendar yr for Interior Design; $11,940 acad yr for Computer Graphics
Courses: †Commercial Art, Computer Graphics, Fashion Design, Fashion Merchandise

MIAMI-DADE COMMUNITY COLLEGE, Visual Arts Dept, 11011 SW 104th St, 33176. Tel 305-237-2281; *Chmn* Robert Huff
Estab 1960, dept estab 1967; pub; D & E; scholarships; SC 14, LC 4; enrl E 300, non-maj 150, maj 150
Ent Req: Open door
Degrees: AA & AS 2 yr
Tuition: Res—$41.25 per cr; nonres—$145 per cr
Courses: Ceramics, Commercial Art, Design, Drawing, Jewelry, Painting, Photography, Printmaking, Sculpture, Art in The Elementary School, Metals
Adult Hobby Classes: Courses by demand
Summer School: Dir, Robert Huff. Courses vary

NEW WORLD SCHOOL OF THE ARTS, 25 NE Second St (Mailing add: 300 NE Second Ave, 33132-2297). Tel 305-237-3620; FAX 305-237-3794; Elec Mail nwsapost.mel@mdcc.edu. *Dean Visual Arts* Dr Mel Alexenberg; *Asst Dean* Louise Romeo
Estab 1987; pub; D; SC 43, LC 6; enrl D 249, maj 249
Ent Req: HS dipl, entrance exam, portfolio review
Degrees: AA 2 yr, BFA 4 yr
Tuition: Lower Division: res—undergrad $30 per cr hr; non res—undergrad $135 per cr hr; Upper Division: res—undergrad $57 per cr hr; non res—undergrad $220 per cr hr
Courses: Advertising Design, Art Education, Art History, †Ceramics, Collages, Conceptual Art, Design, †Drawing, †Graphic Design, †Illustration, Intermedia, Mixed Media, †Painting, †Photography, †Printmaking, Restoration & Conservation, †Sculpture, Theatre Arts, Cyberarts
Summer School: scholarships

MIAMI SHORES

BARRY UNIVERSITY, Dept of Fine Arts, 11300 NE Second Ave, 33161. Tel 305-899-3426, 899-3000; *Chmn Fine Arts Dept* Derna Ford; *Dean* Dr Laura Aimesto. Instrs: FT 4
Estab 1940; pvt; D & E; scholarships; SC 33, LC 12; enrl D 300, E 60, maj 30
Ent Req: HS dipl, portfolio for BFA
Degrees: BA, BFA, BFA(Educ) 4 yrs
Tuition: $5645 per sem
Courses: Advertising Design, Art Appreciation, Art Education, Art History, Ceramics, Collages, Commercial Art, History of Art & Archaeology, Mixed Media, †Photography, Sculpture, Theatre Arts, Video, Costume Design & Construction, Design, Drawing, Graphic Design, Jewelry, Painting, Photography, Stage Design, Teacher Training
Summer School: Dir, Dr Laura Aimesto. Tuition $155 per cr hr for 6 wk terms. Courses—Ceramics, Drawing, Photography, Watercolor

NICEVILLE

OKALOOSA-WALTON COMMUNITY COLLEGE, Dept of Fine & Performing Arts, 100 College Blvd, 32578. Tel 904-678-5111; FAX 904-729-5215; *Chmn* Cliff Herron; *Instr* Walter B Shipley, MA; *Instr* Arnold Hart; *Instr* David Owens
Estab 1964, dept estab 1964; pub; D & E; scholarships; SC 26, LC 3; enrl D 2000, E 1000, maj 80
Ent Req: HS dipl
Degrees: AA 2 yrs
Tuition: Res—$114.60 per sem; nonres—$40 per cr hr; campus res available
Courses: Architecture, Art History, Ceramics, Costume Design & Construction, Drafting, Drawing, Graphic Arts, Handicrafts, Interior Design, Jewelry, Painting, Photography, Printmaking, Sculpture, Silversmithing, Stage Design, Teacher Training, Theatre Arts, Weaving, Acting, 2-D & 3-D Design, Ethics, Humanities, Philosphy, Religion
Adult Hobby Classes: Enrl 15 per class. Courses—Antiques, Interior Decorating, Painting, Photography, Pottery, Vase Painting, others as needed
Summer School: Dir, Dr James Durham. Term of 6 or 12 wks beginning May 2 & June 18. Courses—same as regular sessions

OCALA

CENTRAL FLORIDA COMMUNITY COLLEGE, Humanities Dept, 3001 SW College Rd, PO Box 1388, 34478-1388. Tel 352-237-2111, Ext 293; *Dean* Ira Holmes
Estab 1957; pub; D & E; SC 5, LC 1; enrl 3500, non-maj 85, maj 15
Ent Req: HS dipl
Degrees: AA & AS 2 yr
Tuition: Res—$38.44 per cr hr; nonres—$137.68 per cr hr
Courses: Art History, Ceramics, Design, Drawing, Painting, Printmaking, Sculpture
Adult Hobby Classes: Ceramics, Commercial Art; Design, Drawing, Painting
Summer School: Two 6 wk terms

ORLANDO

UNIVERSITY OF CENTRAL FLORIDA, Art Dept, 4000 Central Florida Blvd, PO Box 161342, 32816-0342. Tel 407-823-2676; FAX 407-823-6470; *Chmn* Robert Reddy; *Asst Chmn* Charles Wellman
Scholarships
Degrees: BA, BFA, cert
Tuition: Res—undergrad $57 per sem hr; nonres—undergrad $221 per sem hr
Courses: Art History, Ceramics, Design, Graphic Design, Painting, Photography, Printmaking, Sculpture, Fibers & Fabrics
Summer School: Tuition same as above. Courses—vary

VALENCIA COMMUNITY COLLEGE - EAST CAMPUS, Art Dept, 701 N Econlachachee Trail, 32825. Tel 407-299-5000, Ext 2270; FAX 407-293-8839; *Chmn* Rickard Rietveld
Estab 1967, dept estab 1974; pub; D & E; scholarships; SC 16, LC 5; enrl D 6858
Ent Req: HS dipl
Degrees: AA and AS 2 yrs
Tuition: $36.75 per cr
Courses: Art History, Design, Drawing, Visual Arts Today
Summer School: Same as for regular academic yr

PALATKA

FLORIDA SCHOOL OF THE ARTS, Visual Arts, 5001 Saint Johns Ave, 32177-3897. Tel 904-328-1571, 312-4072 (Barrineau); *VPres Student Servs* Annette W Barrineau; *Coordr Graphic Design* Phil Parker, BFA; *Dir Galleries* David Ouellette, MFA
Estab 1974, dept estab 1974; pub; D; scholarships; SC 35, LC 10; enrl D 85, maj 85
Ent Req: HS dipl, recommendation, review, interview
Degrees: AA 2 yrs, AS 2 1/2 yrs
Tuition: Res—$38.90 per hr; nonres—$145.95 per hr
Courses: Advertising Design, Art History, Commercial Art, Display, Drafting, Drawing, Graphic Arts, †Graphic Design, Illustration, Lettering, Mixed Media, †Painting, Photography, †Printmaking, †Stage Design, †Theatre Arts

PANAMA CITY

GULF COAST COMMUNITY COLLEGE, Division of Visual & Performing Arts, 5230 W Hwy 98, 32401-1058. Tel 904-769-1551; *Dir* Rosemarie O'Bourke; *Assoc Prof* Sharron Barnes, MA; *Assoc Prof* Roland L Hockett, MS
Estab 1957; pub; D & E; SC 5, LC 2; enrl D 300, E 70, non-maj 330, maj 40
Ent Req: HS dipl
Degrees: AA 2 yrs
Tuition: Res—undergrad $36.30 per cr hr; nonres—undergrad $144.16 per cr hr
Courses: Art History, Ceramics, Design, Drawing, Illustration, Lettering, Photography
Adult Hobby Classes: Macrame, Painting, Weaving

PENSACOLA

PENSACOLA JUNIOR COLLEGE, Dept of Visual Arts, 1000 College Blvd, 32504. Tel 904-484-2550; FAX 904-484-2564; *Head Dept* Allan Peterson. Instrs: FT 9, PT 5
Estab 1948; pub; D & E; scholarships; enrl maj 180
Ent Req: HS dipl
Degrees: AS & AA 2 yrs
Tuition: Res—$40.20 per cr hr; nonres—$144.20 per cr hr; no campus res
Courses: Advertising Design, Art History, Ceramics, Drawing, Graphic Arts, Illustration, Mixed Media, Painting, Photography, Printmaking, Sculpture, †Art Studio, Crafts, Design, Pottery
Adult Hobby Classes: Enrl 600. Courses—Drawing, Painting
Summer School: Dir, Allan Peterson. Enrl 300; tuition $30.30 per cr. Courses—same as regular session

UNIVERSITY OF WEST FLORIDA, Dept of Art, 11000 University Pkwy, 32514. Tel 904-474-2045; FAX 904-474-3247; *Chmn* Jim Jipson, MFA; *Prof* William A Silhan, EdD; *Assoc Prof* Henry J Heuler, MFA; *Assoc Prof* Robert Marshman, MFA; *Assoc Prof* Duncan E Stewart, MA; *Asst Prof* Deb Davis, MFA; *Asst Prof* Stephen K Haworth, MFA; *Asst Prof* Suzette J Doyon-Bernard, PhD
Estab 1967; pub; D & E; scholarships; SC 20, LC 10; enrl D 600, E 300, non-maj 500, maj 175
Ent Req: AA degree or 60 sem hrs credit
Degrees: BA & BFA 4 yr
Tuition: Res—undergrad $57.84 per sem hr; nonres—undergrad $57.52 per sem, grad $1976 per sem; campus res—room $4134 two sem
Courses: Aesthetics, †Art Education, †Art History, Calligraphy, Design, Graphic Design, Handicrafts, †History of Art & Archaeology, Illustration, Intermedia, †Jewelry, Mixed Media, Museum Staff Training, Painting, Photography, Printmaking, Sculpture, Teacher Training, Video, BFA, Studio Art
Summer School: Dir, Jim Jipson. Enrl 400; 2 sessions. Courses—Ceramics, Drawing, Painting, Photography, Printmaking, Sculpture

SAINT AUGUSTINE

FLAGLER COLLEGE, Visual Arts Dept, 74 King St, 32084. Tel 904-829-6481; *Chmn* Robert Hall; *Prof* Enzo Torcoletti, MFA; *Assoc Prof* Don Martin
Estab 1968; pvt; D & E; SC 29, LC 7; enrl 1000, maj 100
Ent Req: HS dipl
Degrees: BA 4 yr
Tuition: $4750 for 2 sem
Courses: Advertising Design, Art Education, Art History, Commercial Art, Drawing, Graphic Design, Illustration, Jewelry, Painting, Photography, Sculpture, Teacher Training, Air Brush, Visual Arts, Visual Communications
Summer School: Academic Affairs, William Abare. Tuition $180 per hr for terms of 7 wks beginning May. Courses—Airbrush, Art, Ceramics, Computer Illustration

SAINT PETERSBURG

ECKERD COLLEGE, Art Dept, 4200 54th Ave S, 33711. Tel 813-867-1166; FAX 813-866-2304; *Chmn* Tom Bunch; *Prof* James Crane; *Assoc Prof* Margaret Rigg; *Asst Prof* Arthur Skinner
Scholarships
Degrees: BA
Tuition: $8667 full-time per sem
Courses: Art Education, Art History, Calligraphy, Ceramics, Design, Drawing, Painting, Photography, Printmaking
Adult Hobby Classes: Enrl 25. Courses—Ceramics, Drawing, Painting
Summer School: Dir, Cheryl Gold. Enrl 150

SAINT PETERSBURG JUNIOR COLLEGE, Humanities Dept, 6605 Fifth Ave N, PO Box 13489, 33710. Tel 813-341-3600, 341-4614; *Acting Dir* Dr Jonathan Steele
Estab 1927. College has four campuses; pub; D & E; scholarships; SC 13, LC 3; enrl D 7031, E 2478
Ent Req: HS dipl
Degrees: AA & AS 2 yr
Tuition: Res—$39.78 per cr hr; nonres—$142.26 per cr hr; no campus res
Courses: Advertising Design, Ceramics, Design, Drawing, Painting, Photography, Theatre Arts, Art History Survey, Survey in Crafts
Summer School: Courses—Same as regular session

SARASOTA

FRIENDS OF THE ARTS & SCIENCES, Hilton Leech Studio Workshops, PO Box 15766, 34277-1766. Tel 941-924-5770; *Exec Dir* Connie Shannon
Estab 1946, dept estab 1963; pvt; SC 16; enrl D 200, E 10
Courses: Collages, Drawing, Fashion Arts, Mixed Media, Painting, Photography
Adult Hobby Classes: Enrl 200. Courses—Drawing, Painting, Photography
Summer School: Enrl 80. Courses—Photography, Watercolor

NEW COLLEGE OF THE UNIVERSITY OF SOUTH FLORIDA, Fine Arts Dept, Humanities Division, 5700 N Tamiami Trail, 34243. Tel 813-359-4360, 359-5605; *Chmn Humanities Div* Steven Miles. Instrs: FT 4
Estab 1963; D; SC 6, LC 5; enrl D 150-200, maj 15
Ent Req: Ent exam, SAT
Degrees: BA(Fine Arts) 3 yrs
Tuition: Res—undergrad $52.70 per cr hr, grad $104.62 per cr hr; nonres—undergrad $216.11 per cr hr, grad $357.64 per cr hr
Courses: †Aesthetics, †Art History, Ceramics, †Drawing, †Painting, †Printmaking, †Sculpture, †Color Theory, Design, Life Drawing, Stained Glass

RINGLING SCHOOL OF ART & DESIGN, 2700 N Tamiami Trail, 34234. Tel 941-351-5100; FAX 941-359-7517; *Pres* Thomas E Linehan; *Dean Admis* Jim Dean. Instrs: 31
Estab 1931; pvt; scholarships; enrl 830
Ent Req: HS dipl or equivalency, portfolio
Degrees: BFA, 4 yrs
Tuition: $600 per sem; campus res—room & board $3150
Courses: †Graphic Design, †Illustration, †Interior Design, †Photography, Painting, Sculpture, †Computer Animation, †Fine Arts
Adult Hobby Classes: Enrl 150; tuition $40 per 7 wk session

TALLAHASSEE

FLORIDA A & M UNIVERSITY, Dept of Visual Arts, Humanities & Theatre, 32307. Tel 904-599-3831; *Dir* Ronald O Davis; *Chair* Jan DeCosmo; *Prof* Kenneth Falana; *Prof* Ronald F Yarbedra; *Assoc Prof* Yvonne Tucker
Estab 1887; pub; D & E; scholarships; enrl D 5887, non-maj 5800, maj 87
Ent Req: HS dipl, ent exam
Degrees: BS & BA with Fine Arts Cert
Tuition: Res—$62.10 per sem hr; nonres $236.94 per sem hr
Courses: Art Education, Art History, Ceramics, Design, Drawing, Textile Design, Metals, Plastic, Wood
Summer School: Enrl 125; tuition same as regular session for term of 9 & 7 wks beginning June. Courses—Arts, Ceramics, Design, Drawing, Metal & Plastics, Textile Design, Wood

FLORIDA STATE UNIVERSITY
—Art Dept, 220 Fine Arts Bldg, 32306. Tel 904-644-6474; FAX 904-644-8977; *Chmn Studio Art* Roald Nasgaard; *Prof* Trevor Bell; *Prof* James Roche, MFA; *Prof* Ed Love, MFA; *Prof* George C Blakely, MFA; *Prof* Robert Fichter, MFA; *Assoc Prof* Ray Burggraf, MFA; *Assoc Prof* George Bocz, MEd; *Assoc Prof* Janice E Hartwell, MFA; *Assoc Prof* Charles E Hook, MFA; *Assoc Prof* Mark Messersmith, MFA; *Assoc Prof* Paul Rutkovsky, MFA; *Assoc Prof* Terri Lindbloom; *Asst Prof* Susan Cannell, MFA
Estab 1857, dept estab 1911; pub; D & E; scholarships & fels
Ent Req: HS dipl, C average & upper 40 percent of graduating class, SAT
Degrees: BA, BFA, BS, MFA
Tuition: Res—$59.93 per cr hr; nonres—$223.34 per cr hr
Courses: Drawing, Graphic Design, Illustration, Painting, Photography, Printmaking, Sculpture, †Studio Art
Summer School: Term of 13 wks; two terms of six & a half wks
—Art Education Dept, 32306-3014. Tel 904-644-5473; FAX 904-644-5067; *Chmn* Sally McRorie; *Prof* Jessie Lovano-Kerr, PhD; *Prof* Tom Anderson, PhD; *Prof* Charles Dorn; *Assoc Prof* Betty J Troeger, PhD; *Asst Prof* June Eyestone, PhD
Estab 1857, dept estab 1948; pub; D & E; scholarships
Ent Req: HS dipl
Degrees: BA(Art Educ) 4 yr, MA(Art Therapy) & MA(Arts Admin), 1-2 yr, EDS degree
Tuition: Res
Courses: †Art Education, Teacher Training, Arts Administration, Art Therapy, Special Population
Summer School: Studio Art & Art History Emphasis

—Art History Dept (R133B), 220D Fine Arts Bldg, 32306-3058. Tel 904-644-1250; FAX 904-644-8977; *Chmn* Paula Gerson; *Dean School Visual Arts* Jerry L Draper, PhD; *Prof* Francois Bucher, PhD; *Prof* Robert M Neuman, PhD; *Prof* Jehnne Teilhet-Fisk; *Assoc Prof* Cynthia J Hahn, PhD; *Assoc Prof* Lauren Weingarden, PhD; *Assoc Prof* Karen Bearor, PhD; *Asst Prof* Jack Freiberg, PhD
Estab 1857, dept estab 1948; pub; D & E; scholarships
Ent Req: HS dipl
Degrees: MA(Art History) 2 1/2 yr, PhD(Art History) 3 yr
Tuition: Res—$59.93 per cr hr; nonres—$223.34 per cr hr
Courses: Art Appreciation, †Art History, History of Art & Archaeology, Arts Administration

TALLAHASSEE COMMUNITY COLLEGE, Art Dept, 444 Appleyard Dr, 32304. Tel 904-488-9200; *Div Dir* Sam Cunningham. Instrs: PT 4
Estab 1966; pub; D & E; scholarships; SC 13, LC 2; enrl D 350 per sem, E 150 per sem
Ent Req: HS dipl
Degrees: AA 2 yrs
Tuition: $16 per sem hr
Courses: Art History, Design, Drawing, Painting, Photography, Color Theory, History & Appreciation of Cinema, Silk Screen, Art Appreciation
Summer School: Dir, Dr Cunningham. Tuition $36 per sem hr for 10 wk term. Courses—Basic Photo, Drawing Techniques, Freehand Drawing, Silkscreen

TAMPA

HILLSBOROUGH COMMUNITY COLLEGE, Fine Arts Dept, Ybor Campus, PO Box 5096, 33675-5096. Tel 813-253-7685; *Chmn & Dean* Diana Fernandez; *Prof* Steve Holm; *Assoc Prof* David Dye; *Assoc Prof* Suzanne Crosby
Scholarships
Degrees: AA
Tuition: Res—$34 per cr hr; nonres—$130.50 per cr hr
Courses: Art Appreciation, Art History, Ceramics, Design, Drawing, Painting, Photography, Printmaking, Sculpture, Weaving

UNIVERSITY OF SOUTH FLORIDA, Art Dept, College of Fine Arts, 4202 E Fowler Ave, 33620-7350. Tel 813-974-2360; FAX 813-974-9226; *Chmn* Wallace Wilson. Instrs: FT 26
Estab 1956; pub
Ent Req: HS grad, 14 units cert by HS, ent exam
Degrees: BA(Art) minimum 120 sem hrs, MFA 60 sem hrs, MA(Art History) 40 sem hrs
Tuition: Res—undergrad $29 per cr hr, grad $47 per cr hr; nonres—undergrad $80 per cr hr, grad $137 per cr hr
Courses: Art History, Ceramics, Drawing, Painting, Photography, Sculpture, Printmaking, Cinematography

UNIVERSITY OF TAMPA, Dept of Art, Dept Art, 401 W Kennedy Blvd, 33606. Tel 813-253-3333, Ext 217; *Dept Chmn* Jack King. Instrs: FT 3
Estab 1930; pvt; D & E; scholarships; SC 17, LC 8
Degrees: 4 yrs
Tuition: $265 per cr hr 1-8 hrs
Courses: Art Education, Art History, Ceramics, Design, Drawing, Graphic Design, Painting, Photography, Printmaking, Sculpture, Arts Management, Computer Graphics
Summer School: Art courses offered

TEMPLE TERRACE

FLORIDA COLLEGE, Division of Art, 119 N Glen Arven Ave, 33617. Tel 813-988-5131; FAX 813-899-6772; *Faculty* Julia Gibson
Scholarships offered
Degrees: BA
Tuition: $1850 per sem
Courses: Art Appreciation, Art Education, Art History, Design, Drawing, Painting, Photography, Sculpture

WINTER HAVEN

POLK COMMUNITY COLLEGE, Art, Letters & Social Sciences, 999 Ave H NE, 33881. Tel 941-297-1025; FAX 941-297-1037; *Dir* Hugh B Anderson; *Prof* Gary Baker, MFA; *Prof* Bob Morrisey, MFA
Estab 1964; pub; D & E; scholarships; SC 10, LC 1; enrl D 175, E 50
Ent Req: HS dipl
Degrees: AA & AS 2 yrs
Tuition: Res—undergrad $34.82 per cr hr; nonres—undergrad $130.46 per cr hr, no campus res
Courses: Advertising Design, Art Appreciation, Ceramics, Design, Drawing, Film, Interior Design, Painting, Photography, Printmaking, Sculpture, Theatre Arts
Adult Hobby Classes: Enrl 60; tuition res—$36.13 per cr hr, non res—$135.46 per cr hr. Courses—Calligraphy, Ceramics, Christmas Crafts, Drawing, Interior Design, Jewelry, Painting

WINTER PARK

ROLLINS COLLEGE, Dept of Art, Main Campus, 1000 Holt Ave, 32789. Tel 407-646-2498; FAX 407-628-6395; *Chmn* Robert Lemon Jr, PhD
Estab 1885; pvt; D & E; scholarships; SC 11, LC 10; enrl D & E 250
Degrees: BA 4 yr
Tuition: Res—$10,881
Courses: Aesthetics, Art History, Drawing, Painting, Sculpture, Art History Survey, Design, Humanities Foundation, Principles of Art
Adult Hobby Classes: Selected Studio & History courses
Summer School: Selected Art History & Appreciation courses

GEORGIA

AMERICUS

GEORGIA SOUTHWESTERN STATE UNIVERSITY, Dept of Fine Arts, 800 Wheatley St, 31709-4693. Tel 912-931-2204; FAX 912-931-2927; *Chmn* Dr Duke Jackson
Scholarships
Degrees: BA, BSEd, BSA, cert
Tuition: Res—$593 per qtr; nonres—$948 per qtr
Courses: Ceramics, Drawing, Graphic Design, Jewelry, Painting, Photography, Printmaking, Sculpture, Textile Design, Glassblowing

ATHENS

UNIVERSITY OF GEORGIA, FRANKLIN COLLEGE OF ARTS & SCIENCES, Lamar Dodd School of Art, Visual Arts Bldg, Jackson St, 30602-4102. Tel 706-542-1511; *Dean* Wyatt Anderson; *Dir* Evan R Firestone; *Undergrad Coordr* Tom Polk; *Grad Coordr & Chmn Art Educ* William Squires; *Art History* Andrew Ladis; *Ceramics* Ted Saupe; *Drawing & Painting* Arthur Rosenbaum; *Drawing & Painting* Bill Johansen; *Fabric Design* Glen Kaufman; *Graphic Design* Kenneth Williams; *Interior Design* John Huff; *Jewelry & Metalwork* Gary Noffke; *Scientific Illustration* Gene Wright; *Sculpture* Horace Farlowe; *Printmaking* Tom Hammond; *Photography* Stephen Scheer
Opened 1801, chartered 1875; scholarships & grad assistantships
Ent Req: HS dipl, SAT
Degrees: BA, BFA, BSEd, MA, MFA, MAE, EdS, EdD, PhD
Tuition: Res—undergrad $898 per quarter, grad $933 per quarter; nonres—undergrad $2625 per quarter, grad $2746 per quarter
Courses: Art Appreciation, †Art Education, †Art History, Calligraphy, †Ceramics, †Graphic Design, Illustration, †Interior Design, †Jewelry, Lettering, Mixed Media, †Painting, †Photography, †Printmaking, †Sculpture, Silversmithing, †Textile Design, Weaving, Scientific Illustration
Summer School: Dir, Evan R Firestone

ATLANTA

ART INSTITUTE OF ATLANTA, 3376 Peachtree Rd NE, 30326. Tel 404-266-1341; *Head Visual Communications & Graphic Arts* Ann Critchfield
The Institute has the following departments: Visual Communications, Photography, Interior Design & Fashion Merchandising; scholarships offered
Degrees: AA
Courses: Advertising Design, Commercial Art, Design, Display, Drawing, Graphic Arts, Interior Design, Lettering, Mixed Media, Painting, Photography, Video, Cartooning, Fashion, Photo Design, Portrait

ATLANTA AREA TECHNICAL SCHOOL, Visual Communications Class, 1560 Stewart Ave SW, 30310. Tel 404-756-3700; FAX 404-756-0932; *Head Dept* Judy Cent
Estab 1967; pub; D; SC 13; enrl D 25, E 25
Ent Req: HS dipl, ent exam
Degrees: AA in conjunction with the Atlanta Metro Col
Tuition: $296 per quarter
Courses: Advertising Design, Commercial Art, Graphic Arts, Photography, Video, Print Production Art

ATLANTA COLLEGE OF ART, 1280 Peachtree St NE, 30309. Tel 404-733-5001; *Pres* Ellen Meyer, MFA; *Acad Dean* Mark Salmon, PhD; *Dir Student Life* Zach Zuehlke, MA; *Visual Studies Chmn* William Nolan, MFA; *Electronic Arts Head* Enrique Lecuna; *Electronic Arts (Video)* Scott Vogel, MFA; *Drawing Chmn* Larry Anderson, MFA; *Sculpture Chmn* Scott Gilliam, MFA; *Printmaking Chmn* Norman Wagner, MA; *Acting Communication Design Chmn* Mark Rokfalusi; *Photography Chmn* Elizabeth Turk, MFA; *Painting Chmn* Tom Francis, MFA; *Interior Design Chmn* Allan Hing, MFA; *Prof* Anthony Greco, MFA; *Assoc Prof* Michael Brekke, MFA; *Assoc Prof* Curtis Patterson, MFA; *Assoc Prof* Fred Gregory, MFA; *Assoc Prof* Corrine Colarusso, MFA; *Prof* Marcia R Cohen, MA; *Prof* Martin Emanuel, MFA; *Assoc Prof* Daniel Zins, PhD; *Asst Prof* Harriette Gressom, PhD; *Asst Prof* J Mark Rokfalusi; *Assoc Prof* Robert Stewart; *Vis Prof* Cynthia Graham, PhD; *Vis Instr* Patti Hastings, BFA
Estab 1928; pvt; D & E; scholarships; SC 168, LC 46; enrl D 422, E 450, non-maj 450, maj 422
Ent Req: HS dipl, ent exam, SAT, portfolio of art work
Degrees: BFA 4 yrs
Tuition: $11,150 per 12-18 cr hr
Courses: †Advertising Design, †Drawing, †Graphic Design, †Illustration, †Intermedia, †Interior Design, †Sculpture, †Video, Mixed Media, †Painting, †Photography, †Printmaking, †Sculpture, †Video, †Communication Designs, †Computer Arts & Graphics
Adult Hobby Classes: Dir, Rick Fisher. MA. Enrl 400 - 500; tuition $130 per course for 10 wk term
Children's Classes: Enrl 30 - 50; tuition $90 for 10 wk term. High School (15 - 18) - Enrl 40; tuition $110 for 10 wk term
Summer School: Dir, Rick Fisher. Enrl 400; tuition $130 for 2 five wk terms. Children's Classes—Enrl 50; tuition $100 for 5 wks. Courses—Drawing, Painting, Art & Theatre Camp. Summer Visual Studies Program for High School students enrl 30 - 50; tuition $1175 for 3 wk term. BFA Program: Dir Xena Zed. Enrl 95; tuition $775 per course for 7 wk term. Courses—Curriculum Courses

CLARK-ATLANTA UNIVERSITY, School of Arts & Sciences, 240 James P Brawley Dr SW, 30314. Tel 404-880-8730, 880-8000; *Chmn Dept* Christopher Hickey
Estab 1869, dept estab 1964; pvt; D; SC 8, LC 8; enrl D 198, non-maj 240, maj 30
Ent Req: HS dipl
Degrees: BA (Art, Art Educ, Fashion Design) 4 yrs, Honors Program
Tuition: $8108 per yr
Courses: Art Education, Art History, Design, Drawing, Graphic Design, Illustration, Painting, Photography, Printmaking, Sculpture, Fashion Design

EMORY UNIVERSITY, Art History Dept, 30322. Tel 404-727-6282; *Chmn* Judith Rohrer, PhD; *Prof* Clark V Poling, PhD; *Assoc Prof* Dorinda Evans, PhD; *Assoc Prof* Elizabeth Carson Pastan, PhD; *Assoc Prof* Bonna D Wescoat, PhD; *Assoc Prof* Sidney L Kasfir, PhD; *Assoc Prof* Rosemary Gay Robins, PhD; *Asst Prof* David H Brown, PhD; *Assoc Prof* Rebecca Stone-Miller, PhD; *Assoc Prof* Marc J Gotlieb, PhD; *Asst Prof* Sarah McPhee, ABD; *Asst Prof* James S Meyer, PhD; *Asst Prof* Eric Varner, PhD; *Lectr* Nancy Marshall, MFA; *Lectr* Katherine Mitchell, MFA; *Lectr* Dorothy Fletcher, MA; *Lectr* William A Brown, MFA; *Lectr* Julia Kjelgaard, MFA; *Lectr* Eycke Strickland; *Lectr* Linda Armstrong, MFA
Estab 1847; pvt; D; scholarships; SC 27, LC 26, GC 18; enrl non-maj 240, maj 80, grad 41
Ent Req: HS dipl, ent exam, SAT
Degrees: BA(Art History) & PhD(Art History)
Tuition: $19,870 per yr; campus res available
Courses: †Art History, Ceramics, Drawing, Film, History of Art & Archaeology, Museum Staff Training, Painting, Photography, Sculpture, Video
Summer School: Dir, Elizabeth Pastan. Enrl 51; tuition $621 per cr hr, 2 six wk sessions. Courses—Drawing, History of Art Abroad, Photography, Video, Sculpture, Studio Art, Various seminars in Europe (variable 8 cr hr)

GEORGIA INSTITUTE OF TECHNOLOGY, College of Architecture, 247 Fourth St, 30332-0155. Tel 404-894-3880; FAX 404-894-2678; Elec Mail t.galloway@arch.gatech.edu. *Dean* Thomas D Galloway, PhD
Estab 1885, dept estab 1908; pub; D; scholarships; SC 41; enrl D 904, maj 904, grad 165
Ent Req: HS dipl, CEEB
Degrees: BS(Architecture), BS(Industrial Design) and BS(Building Construction) 4 yr, M(Architecture) and MCP 2 yr
Tuition: Res—$726 per quarter; nonres—$2106 per quarter
Courses: †Architecture, Art Appreciation, Art History, Commercial Art, Conceptual Art, Design, Drawing, Graphic Arts, Graphic Design, †Industrial Design, Intermedia, Interior Design, Landscape Architecture, Mixed Media, Painting, Printmaking, Building Construction, City Planning
Summer School: Dir, Micha Bandini. Enrl 150; tuition same. Courses—vary

GEORGIA STATE UNIVERSITY, School of Art & Design, University Plaza, 30303-3083. Tel 404-651-2257; FAX 404-651-1779; *Dir School* John McWilliams. Instrs: FT 28, PT 8
Estab 1914; pub; D; scholarships; SC 80, LC 16; enrl maj 450, others 300
Ent Req: HS dipl, ent exam, college board, interview
Degrees: BFA, BA(Art) and BA(Art History) 4 yrs, MA(Art History), MAEd (Art Education), MFA (Studio), MFA
Tuition: Res—$36.40 per cr hr; nonres—$124.80 per cr hr
Courses: Art Education, Art History, Ceramics, Drawing, Graphic Design, Illustration, Interior Design, Jewelry, Painting, Photography, Printmaking, Sculpture, Textile Design, Weaving, Metalsmithing
Children's Classes: Enrl 10-15, 8-10 wk term
Summer School: Dir, Larry Walker. Enrl 350-400; tuition $36.40 per cr hr for 6-8 wk term. Courses—Art Education, Art History, Studio

AUGUSTA

AUGUSTA COLLEGE, Dept of Fine Arts, 2500 Walton Way, 30904. Tel 706-737-1453, Ext 2200; *Chmn* Clayton Shotwell; *Asst Prof* Eugenia Comer; *Asst Prof* Janice Williams, MFA; *Asst Prof* James Rosen, MFA; *Asst Prof* Michael Schwartz; *Instr* Brian Rust, MFA; *Scholar in Art* Morris Eminent; *Scholar in Art* Philip Morsberger
Estab 1925, dept estab 1965; pub; D & E; scholarships; SC 46, LC 4, GC 1; enrl D 150, E 30, non-maj 10, maj 140, GS 5
Ent Req: HS dipl, SAT
Degrees: AA, BA & BFA
Tuition: Res—undergrad $600 per quarter; nonres—undergrad $1893 per quarter; no campus res
Courses: †Ceramics, †Drawing, †Photography, †Mixed Media, †Painting, †Printmaking, †Sculpture
Adult Hobby Classes: Enrl 25; tuition $30-$60 per 10 sessions. Courses—Painting

BARNESVILLE

GORDON COLLEGE, Dept of Fine Arts, 419 College Dr, 30204. Tel 770-358-5301; FAX 770-358-3031; *Dir* Ric Thurman; *Instr* Marlin Adams; *Instr* Kevin Grass
Scholarships
Degrees: AA
Tuition: Res—$358 per qtr; nonres—$1039 per qtr
Courses: Art Appreciation, Ceramics, Design, Drawing, Graphic Design, Illustration, Painting, Photography, Printmaking, Introduction to Art, Survey Art History

CARROLLTON

STATE UNIVERSITY OF WEST GEORGIA (Formerly West Georgia College), Art Dept, 30018. Tel 770-836-6521; FAX 770-836-4392; *Chmn* Bruce Bobick
Estab 1906; pub; D; scholarships; SC 36, LC 12, GC 16; enrl maj 124
Ent Req: HS dipl, ent exam
Degrees: BFA, AB(Studio, Art Educ), MEd 4 yrs
Tuition: Res—$1704 per yr, PT $37 per quarter hr; nonres—$1462 per quarter, PT $112 per quarter hr; campus res—$400 - $440 per quarter
Courses: Art Appreciation, †Art Education, Art History, †Ceramics, Design, Drawing, †Graphic Design, †Interior Design, Lettering, †Painting, †Photography, †Printmaking, †Sculpture, Textile Design, Papermaking
Summer School: Dir, B Bobick. 8 wk sem. Courses - Art Education, Art History, Art Appreciation, Art Education, Ceramics, Design, Drawing, Painting, Papermaking, Printmaking, Sculpture

CLEVELAND

TRUETT-MCCONNELL COLLEGE, Fine Arts Dept & Arts Dept, 100 Alumni Dr, 30528. Tel 706-865-2134; FAX 706-865-0975; *Prof* Dr David N George; *Instr* Susan Chapman
Estab 1946; den; D & E; SC 10, LC 2; enrl D 700, non-maj 98, maj 15
Ent Req: HS dipl, SAT
Degrees: AA and AS 2 yr
Tuition: $670 per quarter
Courses: Aesthetics, Art History, Ceramics, Drawing, Graphic Design, Handicrafts, Painting, Sculpture, 3-D Design
Children's Classes: Enrl 21; tuition $20. Courses—Children's Art

COCHRAN

MIDDLE GEORGIA COLLEGE, Dept of Art, 31014. Tel 912-934-6221; FAX 912-934-3199; *Chmn* W Hal Lunsford. Instrs: FT 2
Estab as Junior College Unit of University of Georgia; Pub; D & E; SC 6; enrl D 270, E 45
Ent Req: HS dipl, GED
Degrees: AA 2 yr
Tuition: $348 per qtr; campus res—$360 per qtr; board (5 day) $455, (7 day) $480 per qtr
Courses: Art Appreciation, Art Education, Commercial Art, Drawing, Lettering, Painting, Fine Art, Hands-on Art, Understanding Art

COLUMBUS

COLUMBUS STATE UNIVERSITY, Dept of Art, Fine Arts Hall, 4225 University Ave, 31907-5645. Tel 706-568-2047; FAX 706-568-2084; *Chmn* Jeff Burden
Estab 1958; pub; D & E; scholarships; SC 30, LC 7, GC 28; enrl D 300, E 50, maj 130, grad 20
Ent Req: HS dipl, ent exam
Degrees: BS(Art Educ), BFA(Art) & MEd(Art Educ) 4 yr
Tuition: Res—$615 per quarter; nonres—$1908 per quarter
Courses: Art Appreciation, Art Education, Art History, Ceramics, Design, Drawing, Graphic Arts, Graphic Design, Painting, Photography, Printmaking, Sculpture, Textile Design, Critical Analysis, Intaglio
Adult Hobby Classes: Enrl 200. Courses—various subjects
Children's Classes: Enrl 200. Courses—various subjects
Summer School: Enrl 200; term of one quarter. Courses—various

DAHLONEGA

NORTH GEORGIA COLLEGE, Fine Arts Dept, 30597. Tel 706-864-1423; FAX 706-864-1429; *Chmn* Robert L Owens
Scholarships
Degrees: BA, BS, MEd
Tuition: $652 per 12 cr hrs
Courses: Art Appreciation, †Art Education, Art History, Calligraphy, †Ceramics, Design, †Drawing, Handicrafts, Painting, †Photography, Printmaking, †Sculpture, Textile Design, Weaving
Adult Hobby Classes: Enrl 15; tuition $30. Courses—Weaving, Watercolor
Children's Classes: Enrl 10; tuition $30. Courses—Children's Art
Summer School: Dir, Robert L Owens. Enrl 20. Courses—Art Appreciation

DECATUR

AGNES SCOTT COLLEGE, Dept of Art, 141 E College Ave, 30030-3797. Tel 404-638-6245; FAX 404-638-5369; *Chmn* Donna Sadler
Estab 1889; pvt; D; scholarships; SC 13, LC 15; enrl non-maj 200, maj 23
Degrees: BA 4 yr
Tuition: Res—undergrad $12,960 yr; nonres—undergrad $12,960 yr; campus res—room & board $5450
Courses: Aesthetics, Art History, Drawing, Graphic Arts, Painting, Printmaking, Sculpture

DEMOREST

PIEDMONT COLLEGE, Art Dept, PO Box 10, 30535. Tel 706-778-3000, Ext 390; FAX 706-778-2811; *Dept Head* Cheryl Goldsleger
Scholarships
Degrees: BA
Tuition: Res—undergrad $250 per cr
Courses: Art Appreciation, Art Education, Art History, Ceramics, Drawing, Graphic Design, Painting, Photography, Printmaking, Sculpture

GAINESVILLE

BRENAU UNIVERSITY, Art Dept, One Centennial Circle, 30501. Tel 770-534-6240; FAX 770-534-6262; *Dir* Mary Jane Taylor, MAEd; *Asst Prof* Neal Smith-Willow; *Asst Prof* Lynn Jones; *Asst Prof* Gene Westmacott
Estab 1878; pvt; D & E; scholarships; enrl maj 75
Ent Req: HS dipl
Degrees: BA & BS 4 yrs
Tuition: $15,471 per yr
Courses: Advertising Design, Art History, Ceramics, Commercial Art, Drawing, Graphic Design, Interior Design, Painting, Photography, Printmaking, Sculpture, †Art Management, Silkscreen, †Studio
Summer School: Dir, Dr John Upchurch. Enrl 150; tuition $575 for 2 wks. Courses—Dance, Music, Theatre, Visual Art

LA GRANGE

LA GRANGE COLLEGE, Lamar Dodd Art Center Museum, 30240. Tel 706-812-7211; FAX 706-812-7212; *Dept Head* John D Lawrence. Instrs: FT 3, PT 1
Estab 1831; pvt; D & E; scholarships; SC 11, LC 2; enrl maj 40
Ent Req: HS dipl, ent exam
Degrees: BA 4 yr
Tuition: Undergrad $2625 per qtr; campus res—room & board $3820 per qtr
Courses: Art Education, Art History, Ceramics, Drawing, Graphic Design, Painting, Photography, Printmaking, Sculpture, Textile Design, Art History Survey, Batik
Summer School: Dir, Luke Gill. Enrl 200; tuition $250 per course. Courses—Art History, Ceramics, Drawing, Photography

MACON

MERCER UNIVERSITY, Art Dept, 1400 Coleman Ave, 31207. Tel 912-752-2591; *Assoc Prof* Samuel L Hutto. Instrs: FT 4
Estab 1945; den; D; SC 9, LC 7, GC 2; enrl maj 25
Ent Req: HS dipl
Degrees: BA 4 yr
Tuition: Res—$2805 per qtr; nonres—$3387 per qtr; campus res—room and board $2196
Courses: Art Education, Art History, Ceramics, Drawing, Photography, Printmaking, Sculpture
Adult Hobby Classes: Evening classes
Summer School: Dir, JoAnna Watson. 2 terms, 5 wks each beginning June 23. Courses—Art Education, Ceramics, Crafts, Drawing, Painting, Photography, Sculpture

WESLEYAN COLLEGE, Art Dept, 4760 Forsyth Rd, 31210-4462. Tel 912-477-1110; FAX 912-757-4030; *Chmn* Art Werger, MFA; *Asst Prof* Lebe Bailey; *Asst Prof* Robin Starbuck
Estab 1836; den; D & E; scholarships; SC 38, LC 10; enrl D 159, non-maj 13, maj 45, others 12
Ent Req: HS dipl, SAT, GPA
Degrees: BFA 4 yrs
Tuition: $8100 per yr; $13,500 per yr incl room & board
Courses: Advertising Design, Art Education, Art History, Ceramics, Commercial Art, Drawing, Graphic Arts, Graphic Design, Illustration, Painting, Photography, Printmaking, Sculpture, Stage Design, Teacher Training, Theatre Arts, Elementary School Arts & Crafts, Special Topics in Art, Visual Arts
Summer School: Art History Survey, Ceramics, Graphic Design, Illustration, Painting, Photography, Printmaking, Sculpture

MILLEDGEVILLE

GEORGIA COLLEGE, Art Dept, 31061. Tel 912-453-4572; *Chmn* Dorothy D Brown
Scholarships
Courses: Art Appreciation, †Art Education, Art History, Ceramics, Design, Drawing, Handicrafts, Jewelry, Painting, Printmaking, Sculpture, Textile Design, Weaving
Adult Hobby Classes: Courses offered
Summer School: Courses offered

MOUNT BERRY

BERRY COLLEGE, Art Dept, 30149. Tel 706-236-2219; FAX 706-802-6738; *Chmn* T J Mew, PhD; *Asst Prof* Jere Lykins, MEd
Estab 1902, dept estab 1942; pvt; D & E; scholarships; SC 24, LC 9; enrl D 122, non-maj 38, maj 84, others 7
Ent Req: HS dipl, SAT, CEEB, ACT
Degrees: BA, BS 4 yrs
Tuition: Res—undergrad $6500 yr; nonres—undergrad $6600 yr; campus res—available
Courses: Aesthetics, Art Education, Art History, Calligraphy, †Ceramics, Collages, Conceptual Art, Constructions, Drawing, Film, Graphic Arts, History of Art & Archaeology, Printmaking, Sculpture, Teacher Training, Video, Ecological Art
Summer School: Dir, Dr T J Mew. Courses—Same as above

MOUNT VERNON

BREWTON-PARKER COLLEGE, Visual Arts, Hwy 280, 30445. Tel 912-583-2241, Ext 306; FAX 912-583-4498; *Dir* E W Addison, MFA
Estab 1906, dept re-estab 1976; pvt; den; D & E; SC 10, LC 4; enrl in dept D 19, non-maj 4, maj 15
Ent Req: HS dipl
Degrees: AA(Visual Arts) 2 yrs
Tuition: $1500, 12-16 units
Courses: Art History, Drawing, Painting, Photography, Printmaking, Sculpture, Art Media & Theory, 2-D & 3-D Design, Art for Teachers
Adult Hobby Classes: Same courses as above, on and off campus classes
Summer School: Same courses as above

ROME

SHORTER COLLEGE, Art Dept, 315 Shorter Ave, 30165. Tel 706-291-2121; FAX 706-236-1515; *Prof* Steve Frazier; *Prof* Brian Taylor
Estab 1873, dept estab 1900; den; D; scholarships; SC 5; enrl D 250, non-maj 230, maj 20
Ent Req: HS dipl
Degrees: AB(Art) and BS(Art Ed) 4 yr
Tuition: $5300 per qtr

Courses: Art Appreciation, Art Education, Art History, †Ceramics, Commercial Art, Design, †Drawing, Graphic Arts, Graphic Design, Illustration, †Mixed Media, †Painting, Printmaking, †Sculpture, Theatre Arts, Color Theory
Children's Classes: Enrl 20; tuition varies

SAVANNAH

ARMSTRONG ATLANTIC STATE UNIVERSITY, Art & Music Dept, 11935 Abercorn St, 31419-1997. Tel 912-927-5325; FAX 912-921-5492; *Chmn* Dr Jim Anderson
Scholarships
Tuition: $107 per cr hr
Courses: Art Appreciation, Art Education, Art History, Ceramics, Design, Drawing, Handicrafts, Jewelry, Painting, Photography, Printmaking, Sculpture, Weaving
Adult Hobby Classes: Courses—Ceramics, Painting, Watercolors
Children's Classes: Enrl 30. Two wk session. Courses—Computer Art, Printing, Sculpture

SAVANNAH STATE UNIVERSITY, Dept of Fine Arts, PO Box 20059, 31404. Tel 912-356-2248; FAX 912-353-3159; *Dir* Terrance A Anderson; *Asst Prof* Farnese Lumpkin, MA; *Asst Prof* Clara Aguero, MA; *Asst Prof* Roland C Wolff
Estab 1880s, dept estab 1950s; pub; D; SC 13, LC 3
Ent Req: HS dipl
Degrees: BFA
Tuition: Res—$600, nonres—$1250; campus res available
Courses: Art History, Ceramics, Calligraphy, Graphic Design, Interior Design, Painting, Photography, Sculpture, Textile Design, Weaving, Basic Design, Color Theory, Computer Design, Advertising & Editorial Illustration
Summer School: Dir, Dr Luetta Milledge. Enrl 60; tuition $180. Courses—on demand

STATESBORO

GEORGIA SOUTHERN UNIVERSITY, Dept of Art, PO Box 8032, 30460. Tel 912-681-5918, 681-5358; *Head Dept* Richard Tichich, MFA; *Prof* Thomas Steadman; *Assoc Prof* Jessica Hines; *Assoc Prof* Dr Jane R Hudak; *Assoc Prof* Henry Iler; *Assoc Prof* Dr Bruce Little; *Assoc Prof* Onyile B Onyile; *Assoc Prof* Elizabeth Peak; *Assoc Prof* Dr Roy B Sonnema; *Asst Prof* Patricia Walker; *Asst Prof* Marie Cochran; *Temporary Asst Prof* Greg Carter; *Temporary Asst Prof* Patricia Carter; *Temporary Asst Prof* Micheal Obershan; *Temporary Asst Prof* Iris Sandkulher; *Temporary Instr* Julie Mcguire
Pub; D & E
Ent Req: HS dipl
Degrees: BA & BSEd 4 yr
Tuition: Res—undergrad $40 per qtr hr (1-11 hrs); nonres—undergrad $120 per qtr hr (1-11 hrs); campus res—room & board $515
Courses: Art Education, Art History, Ceramics, Commercial Art, Constructions, Drawing, Graphic Arts, Graphic Design, Lettering, Mixed Media, Painting, Photography, Printmaking, Sculpture, Teacher Training
Adult Hobby Classes: Enrl 40; tuition $35 per 10 wks. Courses—Painting, Photography
Children's Classes: Offered in Laboratory School & Sat Program

THOMASVILLE

THOMAS COLLEGE, Humanities Division, 1501 Mill Pond Rd, 31792. Tel 912-226-1621; *Div Chmn* Pat Carmoney; *Asst Prof of Art* John Cone
Scholarships offered
Degrees: AA
Tuition: $60 per quarter cr hr
Courses: Art Appreciation, Art Education, Drawing, Painting
Adult Hobby Classes: Enrl 30; 2 terms (quarters) per yr. Courses—Art Structure
Children's Classes: Courses offered on demand
Summer School: Enrl 60; summer quarter. Courses—same as regular yr

TIFTON

ABRAHAM BALDWIN AGRICULTURAL COLLEGE, Art & Humanities Dept, 2802 Moore Hwy, ABAC Sta, 31794. Tel 912-386-3236, 386-3250; *Chmn* Dr Oscar Patton
Degrees: Cert
Courses: Art Appreciation, Art History, Design, Drawing, Painting

VALDOSTA

VALDOSTA STATE UNIVERSITY, Dept of Art, N Patterson St, 31698. Tel 912-333-5835; FAX 912-245-3799; Elec Mail lmilbran@grits.valdosta.peachnet edu.. *Head Dept* Dr J Stephen Lahr. Instrs: FT 8
Estab 1911; pub; D; scholarships; SC 25, LC 10, GC 9; enrl 400, maj 95, total 7500
Ent Req: SAT
Degrees: BA, BFA & BFA (Art Ed) 4 yr
Tuition: Res—$447 12 hrs or more per qtr, $37 per hr; nonres—$1341 12 hrs or more, $112 per hr; plus other fees
Courses: Advertising Design, Aesthetics, Art Appreciation, †Art Education, Art History, Calligraphy, Ceramics, Collages, Commercial Art, Constructions, Design, Display, Drawing, Graphic Arts, Graphic Design, Handicrafts, History of Art & Archaeology, Illustration, Intermedia, Lettering, Mixed Media, Painting, Photography, Printmaking, Sculpture, Teacher Training, Textile Design, Weaving, Computer Graphics, Portfolio Preparation
Summer School: Dir, L Milbrandt. Enrl 70; tuition res—$40 per qtr hr for 4 or 8 wk term. Courses—Art Appreciation, Computer Graphics, Design

YOUNG HARRIS

YOUNG HARRIS COLLEGE, Dept of Art, One College St, PO Box 68, 30582. Tel 706-379-3112; *Chmn* Richard Aunspaugh. Instrs: FT 2
Estab 1886; den; D; scholarships; SC 6, LC 4; enrl D 450, maj 25
Degrees: AFA 2 yr
Tuition: $6360 per yr
Courses: Art History, Design, Drawing, Painting, Sculpture

HAWAII

HONOLULU

HONOLULU ACADEMY OF ARTS, The Art Center at Linekona, 1111 Victoria St, 96814. Tel 808-532-8742; FAX 808-532-8787; *Cur* Carol Khewhok. Instrs: FT 3, PT 1
Estab 1946; pvt
Ent Req: 16 yrs of age with talent
Courses: Ceramics, Drawing, Painting, Printmaking, Etching, Lithography
Adult Hobby Classes: Tuition $130 per sem. Courses—Ceramics, Drawing, Jewelry, Painting, Printmaking, Watercolors, Weaving
Children's Classes: tuition $95 for 11 wks. Courses—Drawing, Exploring Art, Painting

HONOLULU COMMUNITY COLLEGE, Commercial Art Dept, 874 Dillingham Blvd, 96817. Tel 808-845-9211; FAX 808-845-9173; *Dept Head* Sandra Sanpei; *Instr Commercial Art* Michel Kaiser; *Instr Graphic Arts* Romolo Valencia, BA
College maintains three art departments: Commercial Art, Art & Graphic Arts; pub; D & E; SC 20, LC 2; enrl D 150 majors
Ent Req: 18 yrs of age, English & math requirements, motivation, interest in learning, willingness to work
Degrees: AS 2 yr
Tuition: Res—$250 plus $20 per cr hr; nonres—$1470 plus $124 per cr hr
Courses: Advertising Design, Commercial Art, Drafting, Drawing, Graphic Arts, Graphic Design, Illustration, Lettering, Painting, Photography, Printmaking, Textile Design

UNIVERSITY OF HAWAII, Kapiolani Community College, 4303 Diamond Head Rd, 96816. Tel 808-734-9282; FAX 808-734-9151; *Chmn* Delmarie Klobe. Instrs: FT 4, PT 4
Estab 1965; pub; D & E; scholarships; SC 11, LC 5; enrl D 4800, E 500
Ent Req: Ent exam
Degrees: AA and AS 1-2 yr
Tuition: No campus res
Courses: Art Appreciation, Art History, Ceramics, Conceptual Art, Design, Drawing, History of Art & Archaeology, Painting, Photography, Sculpture, Computer Graphics
Adult Hobby Classes: Enrl 15 per class; tuition depends on number of units. Courses—Art Appreciation, Art History, Ceramics, Color Theory, Computer Graphics, Conceptual Art, Design
Summer School: Dir, Jim Jefferies. Tuition res—$65 per cr, non res—$130 per cr for term of 6 wks. Courses—Art Appreciation

UNIVERSITY OF HAWAII AT MANOA, Dept of Art, 2535 The Mall, 96822. Tel 808-956-8251; FAX 808-956-9043; *Chmn* Robert Jay. Instrs: FT 26, PT 25
Estab 1907; pub; D & E; scholarships; SC 64, LC 34; enrl maj 450, grad 40
Ent Req: HS dipl or GED and SAT or ACT
Degrees: BA(Art History), BA(Studio) and BFA 4 yr
Tuition: Res—undergrad $615 per sem, $52 per cr hr; grad $730 sem, $61 per cr hr; non res—undergrad $1840 per sem, $154 per cr hr; grad $2190 per sem, $183 per cr hr, plus fees; campus res limited
Courses: Aesthetics, Art Appreciation, Art History, Calligraphy, Ceramics, Design, Drawing, Film, Graphic Arts, Graphic Design, History of Art & Archaeology, Intermedia, Jewelry, Mixed Media, Museum Staff Training, Painting, Photography, Printmaking, Sculpture, Textile Design, Video, †Fiber Arts, Glass
Adult Hobby Classes: Drawing, Painting, Sculpture
Summer School: Dean, Victor Kobayashi. Tuition $55 per cr hr, non res $110 per cr hr, plus fees. Courses—Art History (Western, Asian & Pacific), Ceramics, Drawing, Design, Fiber, Glass, Painting, Photography, Printmaking, Sculpture

KAHULUI

MAUI COMMUNITY COLLEGE, Art Program, 310 Kaahumanu Ave, 96732. Tel 808-244-9181; *Div Chmn* Dorothy Pyle. Instrs: FT 1, PT 3
Estab 1967; pub; D & E; scholarships; SC 8, LC 2; enrl 2600
Ent Req: Ent exam
Degrees: AS 2 yr
Tuition: Res—$150; nonres—$800
Courses: Advertising Design, Architecture, †Ceramics, Display, †Drawing, Graphic Arts, Graphic Design, †History of Art & Archaeology, Jewelry, †Painting, †Photography, Sculpture, †Textile Design, †Weaving, †Batik, Copper Enameling, History of Architecture, Welding
Adult Hobby Classes: Enrl 200. Courses—Art, Art History, Ceramics, Drawing, Intro to Visual Art, Painting

LAIE

BRIGHAM YOUNG UNIVERSITY, HAWAII CAMPUS, Division of Fine Arts, 55 220 Kulanui, 96762. Tel 808-293-3211; FAX 808-293-3645, 293-3900; *Chmn* Dr Preston K Larson
Scholarships
Degrees: BA
Tuition: Church mem $1025 per sem; non church mem $1535 per sem
Courses: †Ceramics, †Painting, †Printmaking, †Sculpture, Polynesian Handicrafts
Summer School: Dir, V Napua Tengaio. Tuition $60 per cr, 2 four wk blocks.
Courses—Ceramics, Polynesian Handicrafts

LIHUE

KAUAI COMMUNITY COLLEGE, Dept of Art, 3-1901 Kaumualii, 96766. Tel 808-245-8284; *Faculty* Wayne A Miyata, MFA; *Faculty* Waihang Lai, MA. Instrs: FT 2, PT 1
Estab 1965; pub; D & E; scholarships; SC 6, LC 2; enrl D 965, E 468
Ent Req: HS dipl
Degrees: AA and AS 2 yr
Tuition: Res—$17 per cr hr; nonres—$104 per cr hr
Courses: Art History, Ceramics, Drawing, Painting, Photography, Oriental Brush Painting
Summer School: Term of 6 wk beginning June and July

PAHOA

KALANI HONUA INSTITUTE FOR CULTURAL STUDIES, Conference Ctr, RR2 Box 4500, 96778-9724. Tel 808-965-7828; FAX 808-965-9613; *Exec Dir* Richard Koob, MFA; *Registrar* Donna Perry, BA; *Arts Instr* Arthur Johnson, BA; *Personnel Mgr* Delton Johnson, BA
Estab 1980, sch estab 1982; pvt; D & E; scholarships offered; SC 3; enrl D 4000, E 4000, all non-maj
Tuition: $6 - $15 per 1 - 1 1/2 hr class; campus res—$15 - $80 per night
Courses: Costume Design & Construction, Design, Drawing, History of Art & Archaeology, Illustration, Painting, Photography, Textile Design, Theatre Arts, Weaving
Adult Hobby Classes: Enrl 3500; tuition approx $300 per wk. Courses—Dance, Drawing, Music, Yoga
Children's Classes: Enrl 500; tuition approx $200 per wk

PEARL CITY

LEEWARD COMMUNITY COLLEGE, Arts & Humanities Division, 96-045 Ala Ike, 96782. Tel 808-455-0228; *Dean* Dr Mark Silliman
Estab 1968; pub; D & E; scholarships; SC 11, LC 3; enrl D 400, E 100
Ent Req: Over 18 yrs of age
Degrees: AA & AS 2 yrs
Tuition: Res—$32 per cr hr; nonres—$213 per cr hr
Courses: Art History, Ceramics, Costume Design & Construction, Drawing, Graphic Arts, Painting, Photography, Printmaking, Sculpture, Theatre Arts, Aspects of Asian Art, 2-D Design, 3-D Design
Summer School: Enrl 100; Term of 7 wks beginning June 12th. Courses—vary

IDAHO

BOISE

BOISE STATE UNIVERSITY, Art Dept, 1910 University Dr, 83725. Tel 208-385-1230; FAX 208-385-1243; *Chmn* Dr Gary Orsine
Estab 1932; pub; D & E; scholarships; SC 51, LC 8, GC 4; enrl D 2539, maj 550, GS 14
Ent Req: HS dipl
Degrees: BA, BFA, BA(Educ), BFA(Educ), BA(Graphic Design), BFA(Graphic Design) 4 yr, MA(Art Educ) 4 yr
Courses: Architecture, Art Appreciation, †Art Education, Art History, Calligraphy, Ceramics, Collages, Design, Drawing, Goldsmithing, †Graphic Design, †Illustration, Interior Design, Jewelry, Lettering, Mixed Media, Painting, Photography, Printmaking, Sculpture, Silversmithing, Teacher Training, †General Art
Adult Hobby Classes: Enrl 500; tuition $74 per cr hr for 16 wks. Courses—Basic Design, Introduction to Art
Children's Classes: Enrl 125; tuition $10 per child for 5 Saturdays. Courses—Variety of art projects
Summer School: Dir, Bill Jensen. Enrl 200; tuition $74 per cr hr for 5 wks. Courses—Art History, Basic Design, Ceramics, Drawing, Elementary School Art Methods, Introduction to Art, Special Topics, Watercolor

COEUR D'ALENE

NORTH IDAHO COLLEGE, Art Dept, 1000 W Garden Ave, 83814. Tel 208-769-3300; FAX 208-769-3431; *Dept Chmn* Allie Vogt; *Instr* Lisa Lynes, MA; *Instr* Joe Jonas
Tuition: Res—$402 per sem; nonres—$900 per sem
Courses: Art Appreciation, Art History, Ceramics, Design, Drawing, Graphic Design, Illustration, Painting, Photography, Sculpture, Stage Design, Weaving, Letter Form, Life Drawing, Portfolio, Professional Advertising

LEWISTON

LEWIS-CLARK STATE COLLEGE, Art Dept, 500 Eighth Ave, 83501-2691. Tel 208-746-2341; *Prof* Ray P Esparsen, MFA. Instrs: FT 1
Estab 1893; pub; D & E; scholarships; SC 10, LC 1; enrl D 89, E 43
Ent Req: HS dipl or GED, ACT
Degrees: BA and BS 4 yrs
Tuition: Res—undergrad $600 per yr; nonres—undergrad $2300 per yr; PT (up to 7 cr) $40 per cr; campus res—room and board $1870 double room, $2070 single room
Courses: Art Education, Drawing, Graphic Arts, Painting, Stage Design, Teacher Training, Theatre Arts, Video, Composition, Independent Study
Adult Hobby Classes: Discipline Coordr, Robert Almquist, MFA

MOSCOW

UNIVERSITY OF IDAHO, College of Art & Architecture, 83844-2471. Tel 208-885-6851; FAX 208-885-9428; *Dept Chmn* Jill Dacey; *Prof* George T Wray; *Prof* Bryon Clerk; *Prof* Frank Crank; *Prof* Lynne Haagenson; *Prof* Williard L'Hote; *Prof* William Doelle; *Prof* Karen Watts
Estab 1923; pub; D & E; scholarships; SC 30, LC 6, GC 8; enrl D 450 (Art and Architecture), non-maj 345 (Architecture), maj 85 (Art), GS 18 (Art)
Ent Req: HS dipl
Degrees: BA, BS, BFA, MFA, MAT
Tuition: Campus res—available
Courses: Art History, Ceramics, Graphic Design, Painting, Photography, Printmaking, Sculpture, Textile Design, Mosaic Art, Visual Art
Summer School: Dir, Frank Cronk. Enrl 40; tuition $43 per cr hr per 8 wks. Courses—vary

NAMPA

NORTHWEST NAZARENE COLLEGE, Art Dept, 63 Holly, 83686. Tel 208-467-8011; *Art Head* Dr Mary Shaffer; *Prof* Don Davis. Instrs: FT 3
Den; D & E; scholarships; SC 12, LC 5; enrl D 200, E 40, maj 24
Ent Req: HS dipl
Degrees: AA 2 yr, BA 4 yr
Tuition: Undergrad $283 per cr hr; grad $110 per cr hr
Courses: Art Education, Ceramics, Drawing, Graphic Design, History of Art & Archaeology, Illustration, Painting, Printmaking, Sculpture, Teacher Training, Crafts for Teachers
Adult Hobby Classes: Crafts, Painting
Summer School: Courses—Art Education

POCATELLO

IDAHO STATE UNIVERSITY, Dept of Art, 1010 S Fifth, PO Box 8004, 83209. Tel 208-236-2361, 236-2484; FAX 208-236-4741; *Chmn* Gail Dial; *Faculty* Doug Warnock; *Faculty* Dr Miles E Friend, PhD; *Faculty* Scott Evans, MFA; *Faculty* Tony Martin, MFA; *Faculty* Rudy Kovacs, MFA; *Faculty* Robert Granger, MFA
Estab 1901; pub; D & E; scholarships; SC 32, LC 6, GS 22; enrl maj 75, GS 15, total 500
Ent Req: HS dipl, GED, ACT
Degrees: BA, BFA and MFA 4 yr
Tuition: Nonres—$850 per yr; campus res—$1260 per yr
Courses: Art Education, Art History, Ceramics, Drawing, Painting, Printmaking, Sculpture, Design, Metals, Weaving
Adult Hobby Classes: Enrl 20; tuition $45 for 6 wk term. Courses—Drawing, Landscape Painting
Children's Classes: Enrl 20; tuition $40 for 8 wk term. Courses—Vary
Summer School: Dir, Gail Dial. Enrl 75. Courses—Art History, Ceramics

REXBURG

RICKS COLLEGE, Dept of Art, 83460. Tel 208-356-2913; *Chmn* Richard Bird; *Instr* Scott Franson; *Instr* Kelly Burgner; *Instr* Vince Bodily; *Instr* Gerald Griffin; *Instr* Mathew Geddes; *Instr* Leon Parson; *Instr* Gary Pearson
Estab 1888; pvt; D & E; schol; SC 23, LC 1; enrl D 123, maj 123
Ent Req: HS dipl
Degrees: AAS, AAdv Design and AFA 2 yrs
Tuition: $920
Courses: Art Appreciation, Art Education, Art History, Ceramics, Drawing, †Graphic Design, Illustration, Painting, †Photography, †Fine Art, Typography
Adult Hobby Classes: Enrl 150. Courses—Art History, Introduction to Visual Arts
Summer School: Dir, Jim Gee. Enrl 370; tuition $60 per cr hr. Courses—Art History, Ceramics, Drawing, Graphic Design, Illustration, Photography

SUN VALLEY

SUN VALLEY CENTER FOR THE ARTS & HUMANITIES, Dept of Fine Art, PO Box 656, 83353. Tel 208-726-9491; FAX 208-726-2344; *Dir* Sally Brock; *Visual Arts Dir* Marcelle Marsh; *Visual Arts Dir* Gary Riley; *Performing Arts* Dick Hilmer; Estab 1971
Adult Hobby Classes: Calligraphy, Ceramics, UFE Drawing
Children's Classes: Enrl vary per sem. Courses—Ceramics, Musical Theatre Workshop
Summer School: Dir, Roberta Heinrich. Tuition $100-$200 per wk. Courses—Ceramics, Mixed Media, Painting from Nature, Photography, Watercolor

TWIN FALLS

COLLEGE OF SOUTHERN IDAHO, Art Dept, PO Box 1238, 83303. Tel 208-733-9554, Ext 344; FAX 208-736-3014; WATS 800-680-0274. *Chmn* LaVar Steel, MS; *Assoc Prof* Michael Green, MFA; *Assoc Prof* Russell Hepworth
Estab 1965; pub; D & E; scholarships; SC 26, LC 2; enrl D 3000, E 2000, non-maj 50, maj 45
Ent Req: HS dipl, ACT
Degrees: Dipl or AA
Tuition: Res—undergrad $550 per yr; nonres—undergrad $1350 per yr; campus res—room & board
Courses: Art History, Ceramics, Design, Drawing, Lettering, Mixed Media, Painting, Photography, Printmaking, Sculpture, Theatre Arts, Papermaking
Adult Hobby Classes: Enrl 100; tuition $35 per class. Courses—Photography, Pottery, Printmaking
Children's Classes: Enrl 50; tuition $20 per class. Courses—Crafts, Drawing, Photography, Pottery
Summer School: Dir Jerry Beck. Courses—Art General, Crafts, Drawing, Papermaking, Pottery

ILLINOIS

AURORA

AURORA UNIVERSITY, Art Dept, 347 S Gladstone Ave, 60506. Tel 630-844-5519; *Prof* Stephen Lowery, MFA
Estab 1893, dept estab 1979; pvt; D & E; SC 7, LC 3; enrl D 116, E 55, non-maj 171
Ent Req: HS dipl
Degrees: BA 4 yrs
Tuition: $10,800 per yr; campus res—$4134 per yr
Courses: Art Appreciation, Art History, Design, Drawing, Graphic Design, Painting, Photography, Sculpture, 2-D Design, 3-D Design

BELLEVILLE

BELLEVILLE AREA COLLEGE, Art Dept, 2500 Carlyle Rd, 62221. Tel 618-235-2700; *Dept Head* Wayne Shaw
Estab 1948; pub; D & E; scholarships; SC 36, LC 9; enrl D 4000, E 3500, maj 200
Ent Req: HS dipl
Degrees: AA and AS 2 yrs
Tuition: $450 per sem
Courses: Advertising Design, Art Appreciation, Art Education, Art History, Calligraphy, Ceramics, Commercial Art, Design, Drawing, Film, Graphic Arts, Graphic Design, History of Art & Archaeology, Jewelry, Lettering, Painting, Photography, Printmaking, Sculpture, Theatre Arts, Video
Summer School: Dir, Wayne Shaw. Tuition $30 per hr for 8 wks. Courses—Art History, Ceramics, Drawing, Photography

BLOOMINGTON

ILLINOIS WESLEYAN UNIVERSITY, School of Art, PO Box 2900, 61702-2900. Tel 309-556-1000 (information), 556-3077 (school of art), 556-3134 (Dir); *Dir* Miles Bair, MA; *Instr* Marie Dutka, MFA; *Instr* Rimas VisGirda, MFA; *Instr* Timothy Garvey, PhD; *Instr* Kevin Strandberg, MFA; *Instr* Sherri McElroy, MS
Estab 1855, school estab 1946; pvt; D; scholarships; enrl non-maj 150, maj 60
Ent Req: HS dipl, SAT or ACT
Degrees: BA, BFA and BFA with Teaching Cert 4 yrs
Tuition: $15,410, room & board & tuition $19,910
Courses: Art History, Ceramics, Drawing, Graphic Design, Painting, Photography, Printmaking, Sculpture

CANTON

SPOON RIVER COLLEGE, Art Dept, 61520. Tel 309-647-4645; FAX 309-647-6498; *Dir* Dr Sue Spencer; *Instr* Tracy Snowman
College maintains three campuses; scholarships
Degrees: AA
Tuition: $14 per cr hr
Courses: Ceramics, Design, Drawing, Painting, Sculpture

CARBONDALE

SOUTHERN ILLINOIS UNIVERSITY, School of Art & Design, 62901-4301. Tel 618-453-4315; FAX 618-453-7710; *Dir* Robert Paulson, MFA; *Undergrad Admissions* Joyce Jolliff; *Grad Studies* Michael O Onken, MA; *Two-Dimensional Area Head* Ed Shay; *Sculpture Area Head* Thomas Walsh, MFA; *Crafts Area Head* Bill H Boysen, MFA; *Academic Area Head* Roy E Abrahamson, EdD; *Design Area Head* Larry S Briggs, BFA; *Asst Dir* Harris Deller, MFA; *Prof* M Joan Lintault, MFA; *Prof* Richard Mawdsley, MFA; *Assoc Prof* Aldon Addington, MFA; *Assoc Prof* W Larry Busch, MS; *Assoc Prof* Joel B Feldman, MFA; *Assoc Prof* Gretel Chapman, PhD; *Assoc Prof* George Mavigliano, MA; *Assoc Prof* James E Sullivan, MA; *Assoc Prof* Ann O Saunders, MFA; *Assoc Prof* Larry S Briggs, BFA; *Assoc Prof* Robert B Croston, MS; *Asst Prof* Richard Archer, MS; *Asst Prof* Jed Jackson
Estab 1874; pub; D & E; scholarships; SC 100, LC 24, GC 28; enrl D 1304, E 338, non-maj 400, maj 350, grad 60, others 400
Ent Req: HS dipl, upper 50 percent of class, ACT
Degrees: BA, BFA & BS 4 yrs, MFA 3 yrs
Tuition: Res—undergrad & grad $1125 per sem, $75 per cr hr; nonres—undergrad &

grad $3375 per sem, $225 per cr hr; campus res—available
Courses: Advertising Design, Aesthetics, Architecture, †Art History, †Art Education, †Ceramics, Collages, †Commercial Art, Conceptual Art, Constructions, Drafting, Drawing, Fashion Arts, Goldsmithing, Graphic Arts, Graphic Design, Industrial Design, Jewelry, Lettering, Mixed Media, Museum Staff Training, Painting, Printmaking, Sculpture, Silversmithing, †Teacher Training, Textile Design, †Art for Elementary Education, †Blacksmithing, †Fibers, †Foundry, †Glassblowing, †Weaving
Adult Hobby Classes: Drawing, Jewelry, Painting
Children's Classes: Enrl 150; tuition $30 per 4-6 wk term. Courses—Ceramics, Drawing, Fibers, Jewelry, Mask-Making, Painting, Papermaking, Printing, Sculpture, 3-D Design
Summer School: Enrl 500; tuition $75 per hr for term of 4-8 wks beginning June. Courses—selection from regular courses
—College of Technical Careers, 62901. Tel 618-453-8863; *Prog Representative* David White. Instrs: 5
Art Dept Estab 1960; pub; D; enrl D 65, maj 65
Ent Req: HS dipl, ent exam
Degrees: AAS 2 yr, BS 4 yr
Tuition: Res—undergrad$75.00 per cr hr; nonres—undergrad $225.00 per cr hr
Courses: Drawing, Graphic Design, Air Brush & Photo Retouching

CARLINVILLE

BLACKBURN COLLEGE, Dept of Art, 700 College Ave, 62626. Tel 217-854-3231, Ext 235; FAX 217-854-3713; *Chmn* James M Clark, MFA; *Prof* Christina Downey. Instrs: FT 2, PT 2
Estab 1837; pvt; D & E; scholarships; SC 14, LC 7; enrl maj 15
Ent Req: HS grad
Degrees: BA 4 yrs
Tuition: $6500 per yr; room & board $2700
Courses: †Art History, Ceramics, Drawing, Painting, Printmaking, †Teacher Training, Theatre Arts, Art Studio

CHAMPAIGN

UNIVERSITY OF ILLINOIS, URBANA-CHAMPAIGN, College of Fine & Applied Arts, 61820. Tel 217-333-1661; *Dean* Kathleen F Conlin, PhD. Instrs: FT 268, PT 150
Estab 1931; pub; D; fels; enrl underg 2000, grad 750
Ent Req: HS grad, ent exam
Degrees: Bachelors 4 yrs, Masters, Doctorate
Tuition: Res—undergrad $1674 per sem, grad $1994 per sem; nonres—undergrad $3800 per sem, grad $4760 per sem
Adult Hobby Classes: Scheduled through University Extension
Children's Classes: Sat; summer youth classes
Summer School: courses offered
—School of Art & Design, 143 Art & Design Bldg, 408 E Peabody Dr, Urbana, 61820. Tel 217-333-0855; FAX 217-244-7688; *Dir School* Theodore Zernich; *In Charge Art Educ* Christine M Thompson, EdD; *In Charge History* Katherine Manthorne, PhD; *In Charge Ceramics* Ron Kovatch, MFA; *In Charge Graphic Design* Thomas Kovacs, MFA; *In Charge Industrial Design* Andrzej Wroblewski, MFA; *In Charge Painting* Sarah Krepp, MFA; *In Charge Photography* Bea Nettles, MFA; *In Charge Printmaking* Dennis Rowan, MFA; *In Charge Glass & Sculpture* William Carlson, MFA; *In Charge Metals* Billie Theide, MFA
Estab 1867, dept estab 1877; pub; D & E; scholarships; SC 119, LC 72, GC 77; enrl maj 563, grad 137, others 15
Ent Req: HS dipl, ACT, SAT, CLEP
Degrees: BFA 4 yrs, MA 2 yrs, MFA 2-3 yrs, EdD & PhD 5 yrs
Tuition: Res—undergrad $3550 per yr, $1775 per sem; res—grad $3990 per yr, $1995 per sem; nonres—undergrad $9850 per yr, $4925 per sem, nonres—grad $10, 344 per yr, $5172 per sem; campus res—room & board $4408 for double for undergrad or grad per yr
Courses: Art Education, Art History, Ceramics, Graphic Design, Industrial Design, Jewelry, Painting, Photography, Printmaking, Sculpture, Glass, Metals
Adult Hobby Classes: Enrl 150; tuition varies. Courses—Art History, Art Education, Studio
Children's Classes: 220; tuition $60 per sem. Courses—Creative Arts for Children
Summer School: Dir, Robin Douglas. Courses—foundation & lower division courses with some limited offerings & independent study at upper division & graduate levels

CHARLESTON

EASTERN ILLINOIS UNIVERSITY, Art Dept, FAA 216, 61920. Tel 217-581-3410; *Dept Chmn* William Hubschmitt, PhD; *Prof* Suzan Braun, MFA; *Prof* Garret DeRuiter, MFA; *Prof* Carl Emmerich, EdD; *Prof* Melinda Hegarty, MFA; *Prof* Walter Sorge, EdD; *Prof* Jerry McRoberts, PhD; *Assoc Prof* Paul Bodine, MA; *Prof* Charles Nivens, MFA; *Assoc Prof* Mary Leonard-Cravens, MFA; *Assoc Prof* Janet Marquardt-Cherry, MFA; *Assoc Prof* Denise Rehm-Mott, MFA; *Assoc Prof* Jeff Boshart, MFA; *Asst Prof* Katherine Bartel, MFA; *Asst Prof* Patricia Belleville, PhD; *Asst Prof* David Griffin, MFA; *Asst Prof* Albert Grivetti, MFA; *Asst Prof* Eugene Harrison; *Asst Prof* Hongyu Ji, MFA; *Asst Prof* Dwain Naragon, MFA. Instrs: FT 20, PT 4
Estab 1895, dept estab 1930; pub; D & E; scholarships; SC 45, LC 24, GC 29; enrl non-maj 1700, maj 225, grad 15
Ent Req: HS dipl, ACT, grad - MAT or GRE
Degrees: BA 4 yrs, MA 1 yr, Specialist Educ 2 yrs
Tuition: Res—undergrad $1026 per sem, $2052 per yr, $85.50 per hr, grad $1083 per sem, $2166 per yr, $90.25 per sem hr; nonres—undergrad $3078 per sem, $6156 per yr, $256.50 per hr, grad $3249 per sem, $6498 per yr, $270.75 per sem hr; Campus res—available
Courses: Art Appreciation, †Art Education, Art History, Ceramics, Drawing, †Graphic Design, Jewelry, Painting, Printmaking, Sculpture, Studio Art
Summer School: Dept Chmn, William Hubschmitt, PhD. Enrl 200; tuition undergrad $1026, grad $1083 for 8 wk term beginning in June. Courses—Same as regular session

CHICAGO

AMERICAN ACADEMY OF ART, 332 S Michigan Ave, 60604-4302. Tel 312-461-0600; FAX 312-294-9570; *Dir* John Balester; *Dir Educ* Wendy Schmidt. Instrs: FT 17, PT 22
Estab 1923; pvt; D & E; scholarships; SC 13; enrl D 396, E 462
Ent Req: HS dipl, portfolio
Degrees: AA 2-3 yrs
Tuition: $5190 per sem, $10,380 per yr
Courses: †Advertising Design, Aesthetics, Art History, Commercial Art, Design, †Drawing, †Graphic Design, History of Art & Archaeology, †Illustration, †Painting, †Electronic Design
Adult Hobby Classes: Enrl 100; tuition $250 for 9 wk session, 1 class per wk. Courses—Commercial Illustration, Computer Imaging & Design, Desktop Publishing, Life Drawing, Oil Painting, Photography, Watercolor Painting
Children's Classes: Enrl 20; tuition $200 for 9 wk session, 1 class per wk. Courses—Art Adventure-Chileren & Preteens, Drawing & Going Beyond, Seeing, The Play's the Thing
Summer School: Dir, Donna M Meeks. Enrl 30; tuition $2595 for 9 wk session, full-time. Courses—Desktop Publishing, Graphic Design, Oil Painting

CITY COLLEGES OF CHICAGO
—Daley College, Art & Architecture Dept, 7500 S Pulaski Rd, 60652. Tel 312-735-3000; *Chmn* Lee Hautt; *Prof* A Lerner; *Prof* T Palazzolo; *Prof* C Grenda; *Prof* M Rosen; *Prof* D Wiedemann
Estab 1960; enrl 5500
Tuition: Undergrad—$600
Courses: Architecture, Art Appreciation, Art History, Ceramics, Design, Drawing, Handicrafts, Painting, Photography, Weaving
—Kennedy-King College, Art & Humanities Dept, 6800 S Wentworth Ave, 60621. Tel 312-602-5000; *Chmn* Dr Thomas Roby
Estab 1935; enrl 9010
Degrees: AA, AS
Tuition: In-county res—$39.50 per cr hr; out-of-county res—$118.85 per cr hr; out-of-state res—$146.95 per cr hr
Courses: Art Appreciation, Ceramics, Painting, Photography, Humanities
—Harold Washington College, Art & Humanities Dept, Rm 406, 30 E Lake St, 60601. Tel 312-553-6065; *Chmn Humanities* James Mack
Estab 1962; enrl 8000
Degrees: AA, AS
Tuition: In-county res—$39.50 per cr hr; out-of-county res—$118.85 per cr hr; out-of-state res—$146.95 per cr hr
Courses: Art Appreciation, Ceramics, Painting, Photography, Printmaking, Humanities
—Malcolm X College, Art and Humanities Dept, 1900 W Van Buren St, 60612. Tel 312-850-7324; FAX 312-850-3323; *Chmn Humanities* Mark Schwertley; *Asst Prof* Barbara J Hogu
Estab 1911; enrl 5000
Degrees: AA
Tuition: In-county res—$39.50 per cr hr; out-of-county res—$79.35 per cr hr
Courses: Art Appreciation, Drawing, Freehand Drawing, Individual Projects
—Olive-Harvey College, Art and Humanities Dept, 10001 S Woodlawn Ave, 60628. Tel 312-568-3700; FAX 312-291-6304; *Chmn Humanities* Richard Reed
Estab 1957; enrl 4700
Degrees: AA, Liberal Arts
Tuition: In-county res—$39.50 per cr hr; out-of-county res—$118.85 per cr hr; out-of-state res—$146.95 per cr hr
Courses: Art Appreciation, Ceramics, Painting, Photography, Arts & Crafts, Color Photography, Visual Arts Photography
—Truman College, Art & Humanities Dept, 1145 W Wilson Ave, 60640. Tel 312-878-1700; FAX 312-907-4479; *Chmn Humanities* Dr Michael Swisher
Estab 1956; enrl 3800
Degrees: AA, AS
Tuition: In-county res—$39.50 per cr hr; out-of-county res—$118.85 per cr hr; out-of-state res—$146.95 per cr hr
Courses: Ceramics, Painting, Photography
—Wright College, Art Dept, 3400 N Austin Ave, 60634. Tel 312-481-8800; *Chmn* James Mack. Instrs: FT 3
Estab 1934; pub; D & E; SC 15, LC 8; enrl D 3000, E 2500
Ent Req: HS dipl
Degrees: AA, AS
Tuition: In-county res— $39.50 per cr hr; out-of-county res—$118.85 per cr hr; out-of-state res—$146.95 per cr hr
Courses: Ceramics, Drawing, Painting, Photography, Sculpture, Lettering, Painting, Arts & Crafts, Visual Arts
Adult Hobby Classes: Enrl 400; tuition $15 per course for 6 or 7 wks. Courses—Drawing, Fashion, Painting, Watercolor
Summer School: Dir, Roy LeFevour. Enrl 24; 8 wk session. Courses—Vary

COLUMBIA COLLEGE, Art Dept, 600 S Michigan Ave, 60605. Tel 312-663-1600; FAX 312-987-9893; *Chmn Art & Photo Depts* John Mulvany, MFA; *Coordr Graphics* Marlene Lipinski, MFA; *Coordr Interior Design* Tony Patano, BFA; *Coordr Fine Arts* Tom Taylor, BFA; *Coordr Illustration* Fred Nelson; *Coordr Fashion Design* Dennis Brozynski; *Coordr Pkg Designs* Kevin Henry; *Architectural Studies & Graduate Studies* Joclyn Oats
Estab 1893; pvt; D & E; scholarships; SC 43, LC 17
Ent Req: HS dipl
Degrees: BA 4 yrs, MA (photog)
Tuition: Res—undergrad $3655 per sem, $250 per cr hr; no campus res
Courses: Advertising Design, Architecture, Art Education, Art History, Calligraphy, Ceramics, Commercial Art, Drafting, Drawing, Fashion Arts, Film, Graphic Arts, Graphic Design, Handicrafts, Illustration, Industrial Design, Interior Design, Jewelry, Mixed Media, Painting, Printmaking, Sculpture, Silk Screen, Typography
Summer School: Dir, John Mulvany

CONTEMPORARY ART WORKSHOP, 542 W Grant Pl, 60614. Tel 773-472-4004; *Dir* Lynn Kearney, BA; *Sculpture* Paul Zakoian, MA
Estab 1950. Twenty artists studios are available to artists for a modest fee on a month to month basis; D & E
Ent Req: None, studio artists are juried
Degrees: None, we offer an apprentice program in sculpture
Tuition: $110 for 10 wks
Courses: Sculpture
Adult Hobby Classes: Tuition $110 for 10 wks. Courses—Sculpture
Summer School: Dir, Paul Zakoian. Tuition $110 for 10 wks. Summer courses—Sculpture

DEPAUL UNIVERSITY, Dept of Art, College of Liberal Arts & Sciences, 2323 N Seminary, 60614. Tel 312-362-8194; FAX 312-362-5684; *Chmn Dept* Stephen Luecking, MFA; *Gallery Dir* Robert Tavani, MFA; *Prof* Robert Donley, MFA; *Assoc Prof* Simone Zurawski, PhD; *Assoc Prof* Elizabeth Lillehoj, PhD; *Assoc Prof* Bibiana Swarez, MFA; *Asst Prof* Jenny Morlan, MFA; *Asst Prof* Paul Jaskot, PhD; *Asst Prof* Mark Pohlad, PhD
Estab 1897, dept estab 1965; pvt; D; scholarships; SC 20, LC 12; enrl D 150 art maj
Ent Req: HS dipl, SAT or ACT
Degrees: BA(Art) 4 yrs
Tuition: All tuition fees are subject to change, contact admissions office for current fees; campus res available
Courses: †Advertising Design, Aesthetics, Architecture, Art Appreciation, †Art History, Ceramics, Design, †Drawing, Film, Graphic Arts, †Graphic Design, Illustration, Intermedia, Mixed Media, †Painting, †Photography, †Printmaking, †Sculpture, †Video, Computer Graphics, Studio Art
Summer School: Chmn, Stephen Luecking

HARRINGTON INSTITUTE OF INTERIOR DESIGN, 410 S Michigan, 60605-1496. Tel 312-939-4975; FAX 312-939-8005; *Dean* Robert C Marks
Estab 1931; pvt; D & E; scholarships; enrl D 220, E 209
Ent Req: HS dipl, interview
Degrees: AA & BA(interior design)
Tuition: $9920 per yr, $4960 per sem; campus res—room & board $4420
Courses: Interior Design
Adult Hobby Classes: Enrl 209; tuition $2322 per sem, 3 yr part-time prog. Courses—Interior Design

THE ILLINOIS INSTITUTE OF ART (Formerly Ray College of Design), 350 N Orleans, Ste 136-L, 60654. Tel 312-280-3500; FAX 312-280-3528; *Pres* Sondra VanDyke; *Dean* Bruce Dempsey; *Interior Design Dept Head* Mary Morro; *Dept Head* Dennis Glenn; *Illustration Dept Head* Bruno Surdo; *Campus Dir* David Ray; *Dept Head* Cheryl Zuhn; *Dept Head* Madeleine Slutsky
Estab 1916; pvt; D; SC 7; enrl D 450
Ent Req: HS dipl, portfolio review
Degrees: BA, AAS
Tuition: $8280 per yr, $4140 per sem; no campus res
Courses: †Advertising Design, Architecture, Art History, Commercial Art, Costume Design & Construction, Design, Display, Drafting, Drawing, Fashion Arts, Graphic Arts, Graphic Design, †Illustration, †Interior Design, Jewelry, Landscape Architecture, Painting, †Photography, †Fashion Design, Fashion Illustration, †Fashion Merchandising
Adult Hobby Classes: Enrl 150; tuition $190 per cr hr for 15 wk courses. Courses—Advertising Design, Fashion Design, Fashion Merchandising, Interior Design
Summer School: Pres, Sandra VanDyke. Enrl 125; tuition $110 per cr for 8 wks beginning 4th wk of June. Courses—Advertising Design, Display, Fashion Design, Fashion Merchandising, Illustration, Interior Design, Photography

ILLINOIS INSTITUTE OF TECHNOLOGY
—College of Architecture, Crown Hall Bldg, 3360 S State St, 60616. Tel 312-567-3262; FAX 312-567-8871; *Dean* Donna Robertson; *Assoc Dean* Peter Beltemacchi; *Assoc Dean* Dirk Denison. Instrs: FT 23
Estab 1895 as Armour Institute, consolidated with Lewis Institute of Arts & Sciences 1940; pvt; enrl 345
Degrees: BA 5 yr, MA 3 yr
Tuition: $15,000 per yr
Courses: Architecture
Summer School: Term June 15 through August 8
—Institute of Design, 10 W 35th St, 13th Flr, 60616. Tel 312-808-5300; FAX 312-808-5322; *Dir* Patrick Whitney. Instrs: FT 12, PT 5
Estab 1937; pvt; D; scholarships; enrl D 150
Degrees: BS 4 yr, MD, PhD(Design)
Tuition: Undergrad $7275 per sem, grad $7500 per sem
Courses: Industrial Design, Photography, Visual Communications

LOYOLA UNIVERSITY OF CHICAGO, Fine Arts Dept, 6525 N Sheridan Rd, 60626. Tel 773-508-2820; FAX 773-508-2282; *Chmn Fine Arts Dept* Eugene Geimzer, MFA; *Prof* Ralph Arnold, MFA; *Prof* Juliet Rago, MFA; *Assoc Prof* James Jensen, MFA. Instrs: PT 20
Estab 1870, dept estab 1970; den; D & E; SC 25, LC 17
Degrees: BA 4 yr
Tuition: $4620 per yr, $2310 per sem, $123 per hr; campus res—room & board $1460-$1540 per sem
Courses: Art History, Ceramics, Drawing, Jewelry, Painting, Photography, Printmaking, Sculpture, Art Therapy, Medical Illustration, Visual Communications
Summer School: Dir, Dr Mark Wolff. Courses—Art Appreciation, Art History, Ceramics, Drawing, Painting, Photography

NORTHEASTERN ILLINOIS UNIVERSITY, Art Dept, 5500 N St Louis, 60625. Tel 312-583-4050, Ext 3324; *Chmn* La Verne Ornelas
Estab 1869; pub; D & E; scholarships; SC 44, LC 22; enrl total 10,200, maj 175, grad 1583, others 798
Ent Req: HS dipl, GED, upper half high school class or higher ACT
Degrees: BA 4 yrs
Courses: Art History, Ceramics, Commercial Art, Drawing, Graphic Arts, Jewelry, Painting, Photography, Printmaking, Sculpture

NORTH PARK COLLEGE, Art Dept, 3225 W Foster, 60625. Tel 773-244-5622; FAX 773-583-0858; *Chmn Dept* Neale Murray, MA; *Prof* Gayle V Bradley-Johnson, MA. Instrs: PT3
Estab 1957; den; D & E; scholarships; SC 18, LC 5; enrl D 40
Ent Req: HS dipl
Degrees: BA 4 yrs
Tuition: Res— & nonres—undergrad $13,990; campus res—room & board $4610
Courses: Advertising Design, Aesthetics, Art Education, Art History, Calligraphy, Ceramics, Commercial Art, Drawing, Illustration, Painting, Photography, Printmaking, Sculpture, Teacher Training
Summer School: Enrl 25; tuition $200 course for term of 8 wks beginning June 12.
Courses—Ceramics, Drawing, Painting, Sculpture

SAINT XAVIER UNIVERSITY, Dept of Art, 3700 W 103rd St, 60655. Tel 312-779-3300; FAX 312-779-9061; *Chmn* Jayne Hileman, MFA; *Assoc Prof* Mary Ann Bergfeld, MFA; *Assoc Prof* Brent Wall, MFA; *Assoc Prof* Michael Rabe, PhD; *Assoc Prof* Cathie Ruggie Saunders, MFA; *Assoc Prof* Monte Gerlach, MS
Estab 1847, dept estab 1917; pvt; D & E; scholarships; SC 35, LC 15; enrl D 50, E 5, maj 55, others 250
Ent Req: HS dipl
Degrees: BA & BS 4 yrs
Tuition: Undergrad—$2500 per sem, $399 per cr hr; campus res—room & board $4985 per yr
Courses: Art Education, Art History, Ceramics, Drawing, Film, Graphic Design, Illustration, Painting, Photography, Printmaking, Sculpture, Teacher Training, Video, Art Business
Adult Hobby Classes: Enrl 15-20; tuition $20-$40 per course. Courses—Drawing, Calligraphy, Painting, Photography
Summer School: Dir, Richard Venneri. Tuition $242 per cr hr for term of 6 wks beginning June 1. Courses—Various studio courses

SCHOOL OF THE ART INSTITUTE OF CHICAGO, 37 S Wabash, 60603. Tel 312-899-5100; FAX 312-263-0141; *Pres* Tony Jones; *Undergrad Div Chmn* Lisa Wainwright; *Grad Div Chair* Frank Dubose; *Dir Admis* Anne Morley; *Prof* Leah Bowman; *Prof* Barbara Crane; *Prof* Theodore Halkin; *Prof* Ken Josephson; *Prof* Richard Keane; *Prof* Robert Loescher; *Prof* Richard Loving; *Prof* Ray Martin; *Prof* Bill Farrell; *Prof* Ray Yoshida; *Prof* John Kurtich; *Prof* Frank Barsotti; *Prof* Catherine Bock; *Prof* Joseph Cavalier; *Prof* Tom Jaremba; *Prof* Michael Miller; *Prof* Joyce Neimanas; *Prof* Angela Paterakis; *Prof* Anthony Phillips; *Prof* Don Seiden; *Prof* Robert Skaggs; *Prof* Robert Snyder. Instrs: FT 80, PT 160
Estab 1866; pvt; D 1600; E 600; scholarships; SC 280, LC 90, GC 50; enrl maj 1400, non-maj 800
Ent Req: Portfolio; recommendations
Degrees: BFA 4 yrs, MFA 2 yrs, Grad Cert(Art History) 1 yr, MA(Art Therapy) 1 yr, MA(Modern Art History, Theory & Criticism) 2 yr
Tuition: Res—undergrad $5250 per sem, grad $5400 per sem
Courses: †Art Education, †Art History, †Ceramics, †Drawing, †Fashion Arts, †Film, †Graphic Arts, †Painting, †Photography, †Printmaking, †Sculpture, †Textile Design, †Video, †Weaving, Art Therapy, Book Arts, †Fiber, Interior Architecture, †Performance, †Sound, †Visual Communications
Adult Hobby Classes: Tuition $360 non cr course, $669 1 1/2 cr course. Courses—Varies, see summer session
Children's Classes: Tuition $240 non cr course. Courses—Drawing, Exploring the Arts Workshop, Multi-Media, Open Studio
Summer School: Dir, E W Ross. Enrl 200 (degree), 121 (non-degree); tuition undergrad $1338 per 3 cr hr for 4 & 8 wk term, grad $1455 for 8 wk seminar & courses. Courses—Art Education & Therapy, Art & Technique, Art History, Ceramics, Drawing, Fashion Design, Fiber, Filmmaking, Interior Architecture, Painting, Performance, Photo, Printmaking, Theory & Criticism, Sculpture, Sound, Video & Visual Communications

TEXTILE ARTS CENTRE, 916 W Diversey, 60614
Estab 1986; pub; D; SC 118, LC 10; enrl D 256, E 480
Tuition: Res—undergrad $60-$250 per class
Courses: Fashion Arts, †Textile Design, Weaving, Fiber
Adult Hobby Classes: Enrl 500. Courses—Fiber Techniques
Children's Classes: Enrl 35. Courses—Fiber Techniques
Summer School: Enrl 100. Courses—Fiber Techniques

UNIVERSITY OF CHICAGO, Dept of Art History & Committee on Art & Design, 5540 S Greenwood, 60637. Tel 773-702-0278; FAX 773-702-5901; Elec Mail ctoakle@midway.uchicago.edu. *Chmn* Joel Snyder
Estab 1892; pvt; D; scholarships; SC, LC and GC vary; enrl maj 11, grad 104, others 3
Ent Req: Through college of admissions
Degrees: BA 4 yrs, MA 1 yr, PhD 4-6 yrs
Tuition: $18,930

UNIVERSITY OF ILLINOIS AT CHICAGO, College of Architecture, 929 W Harrison St, M/C 033, Rm 303, 60607-7038. Tel 312-996-3351, Art & Design 996-3337; FAX 312-996-5378; *Dean* Dr Ellen Baird; *Dir School Archit* Katerina Ruedi; *Dir School Art & Design* Judith Kirshner; *Performing Arts Interim Chair* Luigi Salerni. Instrs: FT 80, PT 28
Estab 1946; pub; D; scholarships; SC 79, LC 10, GC 3; enrl D 579, non-maj 325, maj 579, grad 17
Ent Req: 3 units of English plus 13 additional units, rank in top one-half of HS class for beginning freshman, transfer students 3.25 GPA
Degrees: BA(Design), BA(Studio Arts), BA(Art Educ), BA(History of Archit & Art), BA(Music), BA(Theatre), BArchit, MFA(Studio Art or Design), MArchit, MA(Theatre)
Tuition: Res—freshmen & sophomores $930, jrs & srs $1012, grad $1154 per qtr; nonres—freshmen & sophomores $2110, jrs & srs $2356, grad $2714 per qtr; no campus res
Courses: †Architecture, †Art History, †Art Education, Ceramics, Drawing, †Film, †Industrial Design, †Painting, †Photography, †Printmaking, †Sculpture, †Video, †Communications Design, †Comprehensive Design, †Studio Arts, †Urban Planning & Policy

Children's Classes: Enrl 50; tuition $5. Courses—Saturday school in connection with art education classes
Summer School: Dir, Morris Barazani. Tuition res undergad $229, nonres undergrad $547 for term of 8 wks beginning June

UNIVERSITY OF ILLINOIS, CHICAGO, HEALTH SCIENCE CENTER, Biomedical Visualizations, College of Associated Health Professions, 1919 W Taylor St, Rm 211, 60612. Tel 312-996-7337; *Head* Walter Panko; *Assoc Prof* Raymon Evenhouse; *Assoc Prof* Mary Rasmussen
Estab 1963; pub; D; scholarships
Ent Req: Bachelors degree
Degrees: Master of Associated Medical Sciences in Biocommunication Arts
Tuition: Res—$1154 per qtr; nonres—$2714 per qtr
Courses: Medical Illustration

CHICAGO HEIGHTS

PRAIRIE STATE COLLEGE, Art Dept, 202 S Halsted, 60411. Tel 708-756-3110; FAX 708-755-2587; *Dept Chmn* Michael Henrey. Instrs: FT 4, PT 30
Estab 1958; pub; D & E; SC 24, LC 6; enrl dept 600, maj 200
Ent Req: HS dipl, ACT
Degrees: AA 2 yrs
Tuition: $48 per cr hr, out of district $109 per cr hr, out of state $145 per cr hr
Courses: Advertising Design, Art Appreciation, Art Education, Commercial Art, Design, †Drawing, †Graphic Design, Illustration, †Interior Design, Jewelry, Painting, †Photography, Airbrush, Computer Graphics, Life Drawing, Materials Workshop, Package Design, Production Processes, Sign Painting, Stained Glass, Typography, Video Graphics
Summer School: Dir, John Bowman. Tuition $48 per cr hr for term of 8 wks. Courses—Art History, Drawing, Graphic Design, Interior Design, Painting, Photography

DECATUR

MILLIKIN UNIVERSITY, Art Dept, 1184 W Main St, 62522. Tel 217-424-6227; *Chmn Art Dept* James Schietinger, MFA. Instrs: FT 3, PT 3
Estab 1901, dept estab 1904; pvt; D & E; scholarships; SC 47, LC 3; enrl D 1700, non-maj 25, maj 110
Ent Req: HS dipl, ACT
Degrees: BA & BFA 4 yrs
Tuition: $9200 per yr; campus res—room & board $2600 yr
Courses: Art Appreciation, Art Education, Art History, Ceramics, Commercial Art, Drawing, Graphic Arts, Graphic Design, Illustration, Painting, Photography, Printmaking, Sculpture, Teacher Training, Computer Graphics
Summer School: Dir Special Prog, Gerald Redford. Enrl 400; tuition $164 per cr hr for 7 wk term beginning June 13. Courses—Ceramics, Drawing, Painting

DE KALB

NORTHERN ILLINOIS UNIVERSITY, School of Art, 60115. Tel 815-753-1473; FAX 815-753-7701; *Chmn, School of Art* Richard M Carp, PhD; *Asst Chmn* Jerry D Meyer, PhD; *Grad Coordr* Carmen Armstrong, EdD; *Dir Coordr* Dorothea Bilder, MFA; *Div Coordr* John DeLillo, MA; *Div Coordr* Ron Mazanowski V, MFA; *Div Coordr* Jeff Kowalski, PhD; *Div Coordr* Stanley Madeja, PhD
Estab 1895; pub; D & E; scholarships; SC 127, LC 59, GC 98, other 15; enrl D 5000, maj 800, grad 160
Ent Req: HS dipl, ACT, SAT
Degrees: BA, BFA, BSEd 4 yrs, MA, MS 2 yrs, MFA 3 yrs, EdD 3 yrs
Tuition: Res—$4138 per yr; nonres—$10,208 per yr; campus res available
Courses: Advertising Design, Art Education, Art History, Ceramics, Design, Drawing, Graphic Arts, Graphic Design, Illustration, Interior Design, Painting, Photography, Sculpture, Teacher Training, Art Gallery Studies, †Art Therapy, Cinematography, †Computer Graphics/Design, †Jewelry/Metalwork, †On-Loom/Off-Loom Construction, Television Graphics, †Visual Communications
Summer School: Dir, Richard M Carp. Tuition res—$115.48 per cr hr, nonres—$288.78 per cr hr. Courses—Vary

DES PLAINES

OAKTON COMMUNITY COLLEGE, Art & Architecture Dept, 1600 E Golf Rd, 60016. Tel 847-635-1600; FAX 847-635-1987; *Chmn & Prof* James A Krauss, MA; *Prof* Robert A Stanley, MS; *Prof* Les Jacobs; *Assoc Prof* Peter Hessemer, MFA; *Assoc Prof* Bernard K Krule, MS
Degrees: AA
Tuition: Res district—$35 per cr hr; nonres district—$128 per sem hr
Courses: Architecture, Art Appreciation, Art History, Ceramics, Design, Drawing, Painting, Photography, Printmaking, Sculpture, Weaving
Summer School: Dir, James A Krauss. Enrl 90; tuition $17 cr for 8 wk term. Courses—Design I, Photography, Ceramics, Field Study, Painting

EAST PEORIA

ILLINOIS CENTRAL COLLEGE, Dept of Fine Arts, One College Dr, 61635. Tel 309-694-5011; FAX 309-694-5735; *Chmn* Jeff Hoover; *Instr* Wayne Forbes, MFA; *Instr* Fred Hentchel, MFA; *Instr* Robert Majeske, MFA; *Instr* Marlene Miller, MFA; *Instr* Stan Adams, MA; *Instr* Christie Cirone, BA
Estab 1967, dept estab 1967; pub; D & E; SC 27, LC 3; enrl D 800, E 400, maj 272
Ent Req: HS dipl
Degrees: Assoc(Arts & Sciences) 2 yrs, Assoc(Applied Science)
Tuition: $40 per sem hr; no campus res
Courses: †Advertising Design, Art Education, Art History, Ceramics, †Commercial Art, Drawing, †Graphic Arts, †Graphic Design, Illustration, Interior Design, Jewelry, Lettering, Painting, Photography, Printmaking, Sculpture, Color, Design
Adult Hobby Classes: Tuition $28 per cr hr. Courses—Drawing, Painting
Summer School: Chmn Fine Arts, Kenneth Camp. Tuition $28 per cr hr. Courses—Drawing, Introduction to Art, Photography, Sculpture

EDWARDSVILLE

SOUTHERN ILLINOIS UNIVERSITY AT EDWARDSVILLE, Dept of Art & Design, PO Box 1774, 62026-1764. Tel 618-692-3071; FAX 618-692-3096; *Chmn Dept* Robin Brown; *Head Art History* Pamela Decoteau; *Head Printmaking* Robert R Malone, MFA; *Head Drawing* Dennis L Ringering; *Head Fiber & Fabric* Laura Strand; *Head Ceramic* Daniel J Anderson; *Art Educ* Joseph A Weber, PhD; *Photography & Graphic Design* Robin Brown; *Head Painting* Jane Barrow; *Head Sculpture* Thomas D Gipe
Estab 1869, dept estab 1959; pub; D & E; scholarships; SC 65, LC 26, GC 45; enrl D 250, E 75, maj 200, grad 50
Ent Req: HS dipl, ACT, portfolio req for BFA & MFA
Degrees: BA, BS & BFA 4 yrsm NFA 3 yrs, MS 2 yrs
Tuition: Res—undergrad & grad $1245 per yr, $415 per qtr, $197 for 5 hrs, $295 for 6-11 hrs, $415 for 12 hrs or more; nonres—for 12-up hrs undergrad & grad $3129 per yr, $1041 per qtr, $458 for 5 hrs, $713 for 6-11 hrs, $1041 for 12 hrs or more; campus res available
Courses: Aesthetics, †Art Education, Art History, †Ceramics, †Drawing, †Graphic Design, History of Art & Archaeology, Jewelry, Mixed Media, †Painting, Photography, †Printmaking, †Sculpture, Silversmithing, †Teacher Training, Fiber Art
Summer School: Chmn, Don F Davis. Term of 8 wks beginning June 21.
Courses—full curriculum

ELGIN

ELGIN COMMUNITY COLLEGE, Fine Arts Dept, 1700 Spartan Dr, 60123. Tel 847-697-1000; *Dean* Dr Marisa Reyes; *Instr* Roger Gustafson; *Instr* Sue Peterson; *Instr* John Grady; *Instr* Howard Russo
Scholarships
Degrees: AA
Tuition: In district—$40 per cr hr; res—$76.51 per cr hr; nonres—$180.91 per cr hr
Courses: Art Appreciation, Art History, Ceramics, Design, Drawing, Jewelry, Painting, Photography, Printmaking, Sculpture

JUDSON COLLEGE, Division of Fine Arts, 1151 N State St, 60123. Tel 847-695-2500; FAX 847-695-8014; *Chmn* Del Rey Loven
Pvt; D; scholarships; SC 15, LC 10; enrl D 481
Ent Req: HS dipl, ent exam, ACT, or SAT
Degrees: BA 4 yrs
Tuition: $14,368 per yr; campus res available
Courses: Aesthetics, Art Education, Art History, Ceramics, Drawing, Graphic Arts, Graphic Design, History of Art & Archaeology, Painting, Printmaking, Stage Design, Textile Design, Photography

ELMHURST

ELMHURST COLLEGE, Art Dept, 190 Prospect, 60126. Tel 630-617-3542; FAX 630-279-4100; *Chmn* Richard Paulsen; *Prof* John Weber, MFA; *Asst Prof* Lynn Hill
Estab 1871; den; D & E; scholarships; SC 13, LC 8; enrl D 1927, E 1500, maj 33
Ent Req: HS dipl, ACT or SAT
Degrees: BS, BA & BM 4 yrs
Tuition: $5488 per term
Courses: Art Education, Design, †Painting, †Photography, †Printmaking, †Sculpture, †Art-business, Electronic Imaging
Summer School: Dir, Joan Lund. Enrl 1379; tuition $160 per cr hr for courses of 4, 6 & 8 weeks. Courses in selected program

EVANSTON

NORTHWESTERN UNIVERSITY, EVANSTON
—Dept of Art Theory & Practice, 1859 Sheridan Rd, Rm 216, 60208-2207. Tel 847-491-3741; FAX 708-491-5090; *Chmn Art Dept* William Conger. Instrs: FT 4, PT 3
Estab 1851; pvt; scholarships & fels; SC 15, LC 8, GC 5; enrl 300-500
Degrees: AB 4 yrs, MFA
Tuition: $11,475
Courses: Practice of Art
Summer School: Courses—Introductory & graduate level independent study
—Dept of Art History, 244 Kresge Hall, 1859 Sheridan Rd, 60208-2208. Tel 847-491-3230; *Chmn Dept* Sandra Hindman; *Prof* Larry Silver, PhD; *Prof* Nancy J Troy; *Assoc Prof* Hollis Clayson, PhD; *Assoc Prof* Whitney Davis, PhD; *Asst Prof* Michael Leja; *Lectr* Ikem Okoye
Estab 1851; pvt; D; scholarships; LC 36, GC 15; enrl maj 60, grad 40
Ent Req: HS dipl, SAT or ACT
Degrees: PhD
Tuition: $5468 per qtr
Courses: Architecture, †Art History, Architecture of Ancient Rome, 20th Century Art, Introduction to African Art, Medieval Art, Renaissance Art
Summer School: Dir Louise Love. Courses—vary in Western Art History

FREEPORT

HIGHLAND COMMUNITY COLLEGE, 2998 W Pearl City Rd, 61032. Tel 815-235-6121; FAX 815-235-6130; *Dir* Tom Meyers. Instrs: FT 1, PT 5
Estab 1962; pub; D & E; scholarships; SC 6, LC 1; enrl 126
Ent Req: HS dipl, ent exam
Degrees: AS, AA, ABA, AAS 2 yrs
Tuition: In-district $38 per cr hr; out-of-district $116.08 per cr hr; out-of-state $147. 50 per cr hr
Courses: Art History, Design, Drawing, Graphic Design, Painting, Printmaking, Sculpture, Art Materials & Processes, Fabrics, History of Modern Art, Introduction to Art, Pottery, Metals & Jewelry
Adult Hobby Classes: Enrl 278. Courses—Basic Drawing, Oil, Charcoal, Printmaking, Sculpture, Pottery, Handweaving & Related Crafts, Rosemaking,

Macrame, Needlepoint
Children's Classes: Occasional summer workshops for high school and elementary school students
Summer School: Courses same as above

GALESBURG

KNOX COLLEGE, Dept of Art, 2 E South St, 61401. Tel 309-343-0112, Ext 7423 (Art); *Chmn* Frederick Ortner; *Asst Prof* Lynette Lombard
Scholarships
Degrees: BA 4yrs
Tuition: $17,571 per yr, room & board $4662 per yr
Courses: Art History, Ceramics, Design, Drawing, History of Art & Archaeology, Painting, Photography, Printmaking, Sculpture

GLEN ELLYN

COLLEGE OF DUPAGE, Humanities Division, Lambert Rd at 22nd St, 60137. Tel 708-858-2800; FAX 708-858-9845; *Assoc Dean Liberal Arts* Ed Storke; *Asst Prof* Charles Boone, MFA; *Prof* Richard Lund, MFA; *Prof* John A Wantz, MA; *Coordr Commercial Art* Peter Bagnuolo, AAS; *Asst Prof* Anita Dickson, AAS; *Asst Prof* Lynn Mackenzie, MA; *Asst Prof* Fred Brunez, MFA; *Asst Prof* Jennifer Hereth, MFA; *Asst Prof* Kathleen Karmal, MFA
Estab 1966; pub; D & E; SC 24, LC 5
Ent Req: Completion of application
Degrees: AA(Art) & AAS(Interior Design, Fashion Design, Commercial Art) 2 yrs
Tuition: DuPage County res—$29 per cr hr, other Illinois res—$83 per cr hr; nonres—$107 per cr hr; no campus res
Courses: Aesthetics, Architecture, Art History, Ceramics, Commercial Art, Costume Design & Construction, Design, Drafting, Drawing, Fashion Arts, Graphic Arts, Illustration, Interior Design, Jewelry, Landscape Architecture, Painting, Photography, Printmaking, Sculpture, Textile Design, Theatre Arts, Book Arts, Computer Art, Fiber Arts, Papermaking
Children's Classes: Ceramics, Drawing, Painting
Summer School: Tuition $19 per hr for term of 3, 5 or 10 wks. Courses—Vary

GODFREY

LEWIS & CLARK COMMUNITY COLLEGE, Art Dept, 5800 Godfrey Rd, 62035. Tel 618-466-3411, Ext 279; *Chmn Div Communications & Humanities* William Gardner; *Coordr* Mary Griesell. Instrs: FT 2, PT 3
Estab 1970, formerly Monticello College; pub; D & E; scholarships; SC 13, LC 2; enrl D 1800, E 600, maj 40
Ent Req: HS dipl, ent exam, open door policy
Degrees: AA 2 yrs
Tuition: $34.50 per cr hr; no campus res
Courses: Art History, Ceramics, Drawing, Painting, Printmaking, Sculpture, Weaving, Advanced Drawing, Basic Design, Fibers
Adult Hobby Classes: Enrl 30; tuition variable. Courses—Antiques, Interior Design, Introduction to Drawing & Painting
Summer School: Enrl 15; tuition $17 per sem hr for 8 wks. Courses—Introduction to Visual Arts

GRAYSLAKE

COLLEGE OF LAKE COUNTY, Art Dept, 19351 W Washington St, 60030. Tel 847-223-6601, Ext 377; FAX 847-548-3383; *VPres Curriculum & Educ Affairs* Russell O Peterson; *Dean* Sandria Rodriguiz
Estab 1969, dept estab 1969; pub; D & E; SC 22, LC 5; enrl D 250, E 250, non-maj 500, maj 100
Ent Req: HS dipl, SAT
Degrees: AA & AS 2 yrs
Tuition: In-district—$41 per cr hr; out-of-district—$176.56 per cr hr; nonres—$220.38 per cr hr
Courses: Art Appreciation, Art Education, Art History, Ceramics, Costume Design & Construction, Drafting, Drawing, Fashion Arts, Landscape Architecture, Mixed Media, Painting, Photography, Printmaking, Sculpture, Stage Design, Theatre Arts, 2-D & 3-D Design
Adult Hobby Classes: Advertising, Ceramics, Drawing, Lettering, Mixed Media, Portrait, Stained Glass
Summer School: Dir, Russ Hamm. Courses—same as above

GREENVILLE

GREENVILLE COLLEGE, Division of Language, Literature & Fine Arts, Dept of Art, 315 E College Ave, 62246. Tel 618-664-1840, Ext 311; FAX 618-664-1373; *Dept Head* Guy M Chase, MFA
Estab 1892, dept estab 1965; pvt; D & E; SC 16, LC 4; enrl D 135, non-maj 105, maj 30
Ent Req: HS dipl
Degrees: BA 4 yrs, BS 4 1/2 yrs
Tuition: $10,310 per yr; campus—room & board $4330 per yr
Courses: †Art Education, Art History, Calligraphy, †Ceramics, †Drawing, †Graphic Arts, †Graphic Design, Handicrafts, History of Art & Archaeology, Lettering, †Painting, Photography, †Sculpture, †Teacher Training
Summer School: Registrar, Tom Morgan. Tuition $424 or $848 for term of 8 wks beginning June. Courses—Introduction to Fine Arts

JACKSONVILLE

MACMURRAY COLLEGE, Art Dept, 447 E College Ave, 62650. Tel 217-479-7000; FAX 217-479-7086; *Chmn Art Dept* Larry Calhoun
Estab 1846; den; scholarships; SC 29, LC 6
Degrees: 4 yr degrees
Tuition: $9620; campus res—room & board $3750
Courses: Advertising Design, Ceramics, Drawing, Painting, Teacher Training, Photography. Sculpture

JOLIET

COLLEGE OF SAINT FRANCIS, Fine Arts Dept, Division of Humanities and Fine Arts, 500 N Wilcox St, 60435. Tel 815-740-3360; FAX 815-740-4285; *Dept Head* Dr K M Kietzman
Estab 1950; pvt; D & E; SC 6, LC 3; enrl D 150, maj 25
Ent Req: HS grad, ent exam
Degrees: BA(Creative Arts with Art Specialization or Art Educ)
Tuition: Full-time $49.05 per cr hr, part-time $270 per cr hr
Courses: Ceramics, Photography, Silversmithing, Advanced Drawing & Painting, Applied Studio, Basic Design, Fabrics, Special Topics, Textiles
Children's Classes: Courses—Art in variety of media
Summer School: Term of 6 wks beginning June

JOLIET JUNIOR COLLEGE, Fine Arts Dept, 1215 Houbolt Rd, 60431. Tel 815-729-9020, Ext 2232; FAX 815-744-5507; *Chmn Dept* Jerry Lewis, MM; *Instr* James Dugdale, MA; *Instr* Joe Milosevich, MFA; *Instr* Steve Sherrell
Estab 1901, dept estab 1920; pub; D & E; scholarships; SC 15, LC 4; enrl D 10,000, maj 120
Ent Req: HS dipl, ent exam
Degrees: AA 2 yrs
Tuition: $31 per sem cr for res of Ill Dist 525; $113.86 per sem cr for res outside Ill Dist 525; no campus res
Courses: Art Appreciation, Art History, Ceramics, Drawing, Graphic Arts, Interior Design, Jewelry, Painting, Silversmithing, Weaving, 2-D & 3-D Design
Summer School: Dir, Jerry Lewis, MM. Courses—Same as winter school

KANKAKEE

OLIVET NAZARENE UNIVERSITY, Dept of Art, 60901. Tel 815-939-5229, 939-5172; FAX 815-939-5112; *Prof* William Greiner. Instrs: FT 1, PT 1
Estab 1907, dept estab 1953; den; D & E; scholarships; SC 14, LC 4; enrl D 100, non-maj 80, maj 21
Ent Req: HS dipl
Degrees: MBA, BS & BA 4 yrs, MEd & MTheol 2 yrs
Tuition: $1940 per yr, $970 per sem, $81 per sem hr; campus res—room & board
Courses: †Art Education, Art History, †Ceramics, Drawing, Film, Graphic Arts, Graphic Design, Lettering, †Painting, Photography, Printmaking, Sculpture, Teacher Training, Textile Design
Summer School: Dean, Dr Don Royal. Courses — Ceramics, Drawing, Harpbuilding, Intro to Fine Arts

LAKE FOREST

BARAT COLLEGE, Dept of Art, 700 E Westleigh Rd, 60045. Tel 847-234-3000; FAX 847-615-5000; *Chmn Art Dept* Irmfriede Lagerkvist. Instrs: FT 6, PT 4
Estab 1858; den; W; D; scholarships; SC 32, LC 16; enrl maj 58
Ent Req: HS dipl, ent exam
Degrees: BA & BFA 4 yrs
Tuition: $5280 per sem; campus res—housing $2250
Courses: Ceramics, Drawing, History of Art & Archaeology, Illustration, Painting, Photography, Printmaking, Sculpture, Theatre Arts, Fibers, 3-D Design, Weaving
Summer School: Ceramics, Fibers, History of Art, Painting, Photography, 2-D Design

LAKE FOREST COLLEGE, Dept of Art, 555 N Sheridan Rd, 60045. Tel 847-234-3100; FAX 847-735-6291; *Chmn* Anne Roberts; *Prof Emeritus* Karen Lebergoh; *Prof Emeritus* Chris Reed; *Lectr* Katheryn Field; *Lectr* Christine Bell; *Lectr* Mary Lawton, PhD
Estab 1857; pvt; D & E; scholarships; SC 8, LC 21; enrl D 1050 (sch total), maj 38
Ent Req: HS dipl, SAT, CEEB or ACT
Degrees: BA 4 yrs
Tuition: Res—undergrad $17,072 per yr, $8395-$8677 per sem; nonres—undergrad $13,895 per yr, $6855-$7040 per sem; $1715 per course; campus res—room & board $3362 per yr
Courses: Aesthetics, Architecture, Art Appreciation, Art Education, Art History, Drawing, Film, Graphic Design, History of Art & Archaeology, Painting, Photography, Computer Assisted Design
Adult Hobby Classes: Enrl 5-15. Courses—Photography
Summer School: Dir, Arthur Zilversmit. Enrl 200; tuition $990 per 4 sem hrs for 7 wks. Courses—Photography

LINCOLN

LINCOLN COLLEGE, Art Dept, 300 Keokuk St, 62656. Tel 217-732-3155; FAX 217-732-8859; *Assoc Prof* E J Miley; *Assoc Prof* Bob Stefl
Estab 1865; pvt; D & E; scholarships; SC 35, LC 5; enrl maj 200
Ent Req: HS dipl
Degrees: AA
Tuition: $8750 per yr; campus res—$4000 per yr
Courses: Art History, Ceramics, Drawing, Illustration, Painting, Photography, Stage Design, Textile Design, Theatre Arts
Children's Classes: Courses offered through summer
Summer School: Dir, Dr Joe DiLillo. Courses—Art of France, Theatre of England, Introduction to Fine Arts (New York)

LISLE

ILLINOIS BENEDICTINE UNIVERSITY, Fine Arts Dept, 5700 College Rd, 60532. Tel 630-829-6250; FAX 630-960-4805; *Chair* Dr Lee Bash
Estab 1887, dept estab 1978; den; D & E; enrl Full time 1150, grad 915
Ent Req: HS dipl, ACT, SAT
Degrees: BA, BS, MS & MBA 4 yrs
Tuition: Undergrad $9300 per yr; campus res available
Courses: Art Appreciation, Art History, Calligraphy, Design, Drawing, Lettering, Painting, Printmaking
Summer School: Dir, Philip Bean, PhD

MACOMB

WESTERN ILLINOIS UNIVERSITY, Art Dept, 32 Garwood Hall, 61455-1396. Tel 309-298-1549; FAX 309-298-2605; *Dean College Fine Arts* James M Butterworth; *Chmn Art Dept* Edmond Gettinger, MFA; *Instr* F G Jones, MFA; *Instr* D J Kelly, MFA; *Instr* G P Stengel, MFA; *Instr* A G Mullin, MFA; *Instr* J E Neumann, MFA; *Instr* S M Parker, MFA; *Instr* G W Potter, MFA; *Instr* A Schindle, MFA; *Instr* L C Schwartz, PhD; *Instr* D E Crouch, MFA; *Instr* J Clough, MFA; *Instr* M Gill, EdD; *Instr* J Gregory, PhD; *Instr* M Mahoney, MFA; *Instr* J Rose, MFA
Estab 1900, dept estab 1968; pub; D & E; scholarships; SC 40, LC 30, GC 50; enrl maj 200
Ent Req: HS dipl
Degrees: BA 4 yrs, BFA
Tuition: Res—undergrad $2810 per yr
Courses: Advertising Design, Art Education, Art History, Ceramics, Commercial Art, Conceptual Art, Drawing, Graphic Design, Illustration, Jewelry, Painting, Printmaking, Sculpture, Foundry Casting, Metal Working
Children's Classes: Dir, J Rose, MFA. HS Summer Arts Prog
Summer School: Dir, E Gettinger. Enrl 65; 8 wk session. Courses—Art Appreciation, Studio

MOLINE

BLACK HAWK COLLEGE, Art Dept, 6600 34th Ave, 61265. Tel 309-796-1311, Ext 3218; *Chmn Dept* Philip H Johnson, MS; *Assoc Prof* William Hannan; *Asst Prof* Jeanne Tamisiea
Estab 1962; pub; D & E; scholarships; SC 17, LC 4; enrl D 300, E 100, non-maj 300, maj 60
Ent Req: HS dipl
Degrees: AA & AAS(Commercial Art) 2 yrs
Tuition: Res—undergrad $48 per cr hr; nonres—undergrad $196 per cr hr; outside district res—undergrad $109 per cr hr; no campus res
Courses: Advertising Design, Art History, Calligraphy, Ceramics, Drawing, Graphic Design, Jewelry, Painting, Photography, Printmaking, Sculpture, Art Appreciation
Adult Hobby Classes: Calligraphy, Drawing, Painting, Stained Glass, Photography
Summer School: Chmn, Philip H Johnson. Enrl 20; tuition $45 per cr hr for term of 6 wks beginning June 7. Courses—Art Appreciation, Photography

MONMOUTH

MONMOUTH COLLEGE, Dept of Art, McMichael Academic Hall, 61462. Tel 309-457-2311; FAX 309-734-7500; *Chmn Dept* Harlo Blum. Instrs: FT 2, PT 1
College estab 1853; pvt; D; scholarships, grants; SC 16, LC 4
Ent Req: 15 units incl English, history, social science, foreign language, mathematics & science, SAT or ACT
Degrees: BA
Tuition: $6600 per sem
Courses: Art History, Drawing, Painting, Photography, Printmaking, Sculpture, Ceramics, Advanced Special Topics, Contemporary Art, Independent Study, Secondary Art Methods, Senior Art Seminar, Open Studio

MOUNT CARROLL

CAMPBELL CENTER FOR HISTORIC PRESERVATION STUDIES, 203 E Seminary St, PO Box 66, 61053. Tel 815-244-1173; FAX 815-244-1619; *Dir* Mary Wood Lee
Estab 1979; D; scholarships
Tuition: Campus res available
Courses: Collections Care, Conservation, Historic Preservation

NAPERVILLE

NORTH CENTRAL COLLEGE, Dept of Art, 30 N Brainard St, 60566. Tel 630-637-5542; FAX 630-637-5121; *Chmn* Barry Skurkis, MA; *Prof Emeritus* Diane Duvigneaud, MFA; *Prof Emeritus* Vytas O Virkau, MFA; *Adjunct Prof* Joan Bredendick, MFA; *Adjunct Prof* Dale Wisniewski, MA; *Adjunct Prof* Edward Herbeck, MFA; *Asst Prof* Kathryn Baxa, MFA; *Asst Prof* Thomas Rowlands, PhD
Estab 1861; pvt; D & E; scholarships; SC 16, LC 5; enrl non-maj 3000, maj 35
Ent Req: HS dipl, SAT or ACT
Degrees: BA 4 yrs
Tuition: Res & nonres—undergrad $9096 per yr, $3032 per term, $160-$1890 part time per term; non-degree—$135-$2394 per term; campus res—room & board $3528 per yr
Courses: Aesthetics, Art Education, Art History, Ceramics, Design, Drawing, Handicrafts, History of Art & Archaeology, Painting, Photography, Printmaking, Sculpture, Teacher Training, Theatre Arts, Figure Drawing, Studio Survey, Advanced Studio
Adult Hobby Classes: Enrl 3800. Courses offered through Continuing Education
Children's Classes: Enrl 500; tuition $45-$50 per term of 8 wks. Courses—Art, Beginning Art, Ceramics, Drawing
Summer School: Dir, B Roth. Enrl 1000; tuition $1136 per course. Courses—Ceramics, Drawing, Painting

NORMAL

ILLINOIS STATE UNIVERSITY, Art Dept, CVA 119, 61790-5620. Tel 309-438-5621; *Chmn* Ron Mottram. Instrs: FT 40; 6 vis profs per yr
Estab 1857; pub; D & E; scholarships; SC 50, LC 35, GC 40; enrl D 20,000, non-maj 100, maj 500, grad 40
Ent Req: HS dipl, SAT or ACT
Degrees: BA & BS 4 yrs, BFA 5 yrs, MA, MS, MFA
Tuition: Res—undergrad & grad $2430 per yr, $1215 per sem, $75 per hr; nonres—undergrad $6030 per yr, $3015 per sem, $225 per hr, grad $2454 per yr, $1227 per sem
Courses: †Art Education, †Art History, †Ceramics, †Drawing, Film, †Graphic Design, Mixed Media, †Painting, †Photography, †Sculpture, Art Foundations, †Art Therapy, †Fibers, †Glass, †Intaglio, †Lithography, †Metalwork & Jewelry Design
Summer School: 8 wk term beginning in June

OGLESBY

ILLINOIS VALLEY COMMUNITY COLLEGE, Division of Humanities & Fine Arts, 815 N Orlando Smith Ave, 61348-9691. Tel 815-224-2720, Ext 491; *Chmn* Samuel J Rogal, MA; *Instr* David Bergsieker, MFA; *Instr* Dana Collins, MFA
Estab 1924; pub; D & E; scholarships offered; SC 14, LC 2; enrl D 120, E 44, non-maj 156, maj 8
Degrees: AA 2 yrs
Tuition: $37 per sem hr
Courses: Art Education, Art History, Ceramics, Drawing, Graphic Design, Painting, Photography, Sculpture, Weaving
Summer School: Dir, Samuel J Rogal. Tuition $17 per hr

PEORIA

BRADLEY UNIVERSITY, Dept of Art, Heuser Art Ctr, 61625. Tel 309-677-2967; FAX 309-677-3505; *Chair* James Ludwig. Instrs: FT 10, PT 4
Pvt; undergrad scholarships, grad assistantships & grad scholarships; enrl maj 121, others 500
Ent Req: HS grad
Degrees: BA, BA, BS, BFA 4 yrs, MA, MFA
Tuition: $7990 per yr
Courses: Art History, Ceramics, Drawing, Graphic Arts, Graphic Design, Illustration, Painting, Photography, Printmaking, Sculpture, †Art Metal
Summer School: Chair, James Hansen. Enrl 39; tuition $281 per cr hr for courses June-Aug. Courses—Ceramics, Drawing, Graphic Design, Independent Study, Painting, Printmaking

QUINCY

QUINCY UNIVERSITY, Dept of Art, 1800 College Ave, 62301-2699. Tel 217-222-8020, Ext 5371; FAX 217-228-5354; *Prof Art* Robert Lee Mejer. Instrs: FT 3, PT 2
Estab 1860, dept estab 1953; SC 21, LC 13; enrl maj 25, total enrl 1715, E 150
Ent Req: HS grad, ACT or SAT ent exam
Degrees: BA, BS & BFA 4 yrs
Tuition: $5620 per sem; campus res—$875 per sem
Courses: Aesthetics, Art Appreciation, Art History, Ceramics, Commercial Art, Design, Drawing, Teacher Training, Weaving, Illustration, Jewelry, Mixed Media, Painting, Photography, Printmaking, Sculpture, Art Seminars, Modern Art, Non-Western Art, 2-D & 3-D Design, Weaving
Summer School: Dir, Robert Lee Mejer. Tuition $190 per sem hr, optional jr yr abroad

RIVER GROVE

TRITON COLLEGE, School of Arts & Sciences, 2000 N Fifth Ave, 60171. Tel 708-456-0300; *Chmn* Norman Weigo. Instrs: FT 5, PT 6
Estab 1965; pub; D & E; SC 17, LC 3; enrl D 650, E 150, maj 138, adults and non-cr courses
Ent Req: HS dipl, some adult students are admitted without HS dipl, but with test scores indicating promise
Degrees: AA 2 yrs
Tuition: No campus res
Courses: Advertising Design, Art History, Ceramics, Commercial Art, Drawing, Graphic Arts, Graphic Design, Illustration, Lettering, Painting, Printmaking, Sculpture, Theatre Arts, Recreational Arts & Crafts
Adult Hobby Classes: Enrl 550. Courses—Candle Making, Continuing Education Classes, Crafts, Drawing, Ceramics, Jewelry, Quilting, Painting, Plastics, Stained Glass, Sculpture, Theatre Arts
Summer School: Dir, Norm Wiegel. Enrl 100; tuition $27 per cr hr. Courses—Selection from regular classes offered

ROCKFORD

ROCKFORD COLLEGE, Dept of Fine Arts, Clark Arts Ctr, 5050 E State St, 61108. Tel 815-226-4000; *Chmn Dept Fine Arts* Robert N McCauley. Instrs: FT 4, PT 2
Estab 1847, dept estab 1848; pvt; D & E; scholarships; SC 20, LC 3-4; enrl D 750, E 700, non-maj 135, maj 45
Ent Req: HS dipl, SAT or ACT
Degrees: BA, BFA and BS 4 yrs, MAT 2 yrs
Tuition: $8630 per yr
Courses: Art History, Ceramics, Drawing, Painting, Photography, Printmaking, Sculpture, Papermaking
Summer School: Dir, Dr Winston McKean. Courses—Art History, Fine Arts (Studio), Stage Design

ROCK VALLEY COLLEGE, Dept of Art, 3301 N Mulford Rd, 61114. Tel 815-654-4250; FAX 815-654-5359; *Pres* Carl Jacobs; *Prof* Cheri Rittenhouse. Instrs: FT 2, PT 3
Estab 1964, dept estab 1965; pub; D & E; SC 10, LC 4; enrl D 158, non-maj 70, maj 27
Degrees: AA, AS & AAS 2 yrs
Courses: Art Education, Art History, Commercial Art, Drawing, Painting, Printmaking, Color Theory, Design

ROCK ISLAND

AUGUSTANA COLLEGE, Art & Art History Dept, 61201. Tel 309-794-7231; FAX 309-794-7678; *Chmn Dept* C C Goebel. Instrs: FT 6, PT 2
Estab 1860; den; D & E; scholarships & fels; SC 8, LC 9, LabC 3; enrl 2000
Ent Req: HS grad plus exam
Degrees: 4 yr degree
Tuition: $3984 per term
Courses: †Art Education, †Art History, Ceramics, Design, Drawing, Graphic Arts, Painting, Photography, Printmaking, Sculpture, Teacher Training, Textile Design, Video, Weaving, †Studio Art
Children's Classes: Enrl 175; tuition $38 for 8 wk term. Courses—Calligraphy, Clay, Drawing, Mixed Media, Painting, Sculpture, Weaving
Summer School: Provost, Douglas Nelson. Enrl 100; tuition $298 per sem hr for 5 wk term. Courses—Drawing, Fabric Design, Painting, Photography, Weaving

SOUTH HOLLAND

SOUTH SUBURBAN COLLEGE, Art Dept, 15800 S State St, 60473. Tel 708-596-2000; *Chmn* Open ; *Dean* Linda Uzureau
Degrees: AA, AAS
Tuition: $45 per cr hr
Courses: †Advertising Design, Art Appreciation, Art History, Calligraphy, Ceramics, Design, Drawing, Illustration, Jewelry, Painting, Printmaking, Sculpture, Illustration
Summer School: Dir, Dr Fred Hanzelin. Enrl 65; tuition $32 per academic hr. Courses - Art History, Ceramics, Design, Drawing, Nature of Art

SPRINGFIELD

SPRINGFIELD COLLEGE IN ILLINOIS, Dept of Art, 1500 N Fifth, 62702. Tel 217-525-1420; *Head Dept* Jeff Garland; *Instr* Marianne Stremsterfer, BA; *Instr* John Seiz, MA; *Instr* Jim Allen, MA; *Instr* Lisa Manuele, BA
Estab 1929, dept estab 1968; pvt; D & E; SC 12, LC 4; enrl D 27, E 6, non-maj 11, maj 16
Ent Req: HS dipl, ACT
Degrees: AA 2 yrs
Tuition: $2850 per sem
Courses: Art History, Ceramics, Design, Drawing, History of Art & Archaeology, Painting, Photography, Printmaking, 2-D & 3-D Design, Weaving
Adult Hobby Classes: Enrl 125; tuition $125 per cr hr. Courses—Art History, Ceramics, Design, Drawing, Photography
Children's Classes: Enrl 20; tuition $30 for 2 wks in summer. Courses—Art for Children 6 - 9 yrs, 10 - 14 yrs
Summer School: Dir, Dorothy Shiffer. Tuition $125 per cr hr

UNIVERSITY OF ILLINOIS AT SPRINGFIELD (Formerly Sangamon State University), Visual Arts Program, Shepherd Rd, 62794-9243. Tel 217-786-6790; FAX 217-786-7280; *Assoc Prof* Bob Dixon, MFA & MS; *Asst Prof* Mauri Formigoni, MFA
Estab 1969, dept estab 1974; pub; D & E; scholarships; SC 24, LC 10
Ent Req: 2 yrs col educ
Degrees: BA(Creative Arts) 2 yrs
Tuition: Res—$85 per cr hr, $88 per cr hr PT; nonres—undergrad $255 per cr hr, grad $264 per cr hr
Courses: †Advertising Design, Aesthetics, Art History, †Ceramics, Constructions, †Drawing, †Painting, †Photography, †Printmaking, †Sculpture, Theatre Arts, Video

SUGAR GROVE

WAUBONSEE COMMUNITY COLLEGE, Art Dept, Rte 47 at Harter Rd, 60554. Tel 630-466-4811; *Chmn* Ed Forst
Estab 1967; pub; D & E; scholarships; SC 8, LC 3; enrl D approx 275, E approx 200, maj 25
Ent Req: HS dipl, open door policy for adults without HS dipl
Degrees: AA, AS and AAS 2 yrs
Tuition: $39 per sem hr
Courses: Art Education, Art History, Ceramics, Drawing, Painting, Teacher Training, Theatre Arts
Adult Hobby Classes: Enrl 250; tuition $33 per sem hr. Courses—Ceramics, Interior Design, Painting
Children's Classes: Enrl 50; tuition $30 per course. Courses—Dramatics, Experience in Art, Photography
Summer School: Dean External Services, Dr Ken Allen. Enrl 50; tuition $20.50 per sem hr for term of 8 wks beginning June 6. Courses—as per regular session

UNIVERSITY PARK

GOVERNORS STATE UNIVERSITY, College of Arts & Science, Art Dept, 60466. Tel 708-534-5000; FAX 708-534-7895; *Div Chmn* Sonny Goldenstein
Scholarships; enrl 175
Degrees: BA, MA
Tuition: Undergrad $79.25 per cr hr, grad $83.50 per cr hr
Courses: Art History, Ceramics, Drawing, History of Art & Archaeology, Jewelry, Mixed Media, Painting, Photography, Printmaking, Sculpture, Art Studio, Electronic Arts
Summer School: Dir, Mary Bookwalter. Enrl 150; tuition $79.25 per cr hr for May-Aug term. Courses—Art History, Art Studio

VILLA PARK

THE CREATIVE SOLUTIONS (Formerly School of Airbrush Arts), 1330 S Villa Ave, 60181-3467. Tel 630-834-7333; FAX 630-832-0897; *Dir* Dennis D Goncher, MFA
Estab 1982; pvt; D & E
Ent Req: For vocational status HS dipl or portfolio or professional status, no entrance requirements for avocational status
Degrees: Dipl in Airbrush painting 120 hrs, photo-retouching 160 hrs, photorestoration 160-200 hrs
Tuition: $450 per class
Courses: Airbrush Painting, Photo-Retouching, Photo Restoration
Summer School: Dir, Dennis D Goncher. Enrl 16 per class; tuition $450 for 40 hrs per class. Courses—Airbrush Painting, Photo-Retouching, Photo-Restoration

WHEATON

WHEATON COLLEGE, Dept of Art, 501 E College, 60187. Tel 630-752-5050; *Chmn* Dr E John Walford. Instrs: FT 5
Estab 1861; pvt; D & E; scholarships; SC 24, LC 13; enrl 2250, maj 38, grad 350
Ent Req: HS dipl
Degrees: BA 4 yrs
Tuition: $6550 per sem; room & board $2275 per sem
Courses: Aesthetics, Art Education, Ceramics, Drawing, Film, Graphic Arts, Graphic Design, History of Art & Archaeology, Painting, Photography, Printmaking, Sculpture, Video, Television Production, Theory & Techniques

WINNETKA

NORTH SHORE ART LEAGUE, 620 Lincoln, 60093. Tel 708-446-2870; *Pres* Rita Price
Estab 1924; pvt; D & E; SC 28; enrl D 310, E 84
Tuition: 16 wks, 3 hrs a session; no campus res
Courses: Drawing, Graphic Arts, Graphic Design, Jewelry, Painting, Critique, Stitchery

INDIANA

ANDERSON

ANDERSON UNIVERSITY, Art Dept, 1100 E Fifth St, 46012-3462. Tel 317-641-4320; FAX 317-641-3851; *Chmn* M Jason Knapp
Estab 1928; pvt; D & E; scholarships; SC 30, LC 3; enrl non-maj 15, maj 60
Ent Req: HS dipl, ent exam plus recommendation
Degrees: BA 4 yrs
Tuition: Undergrad $13,820 per yr
Courses: Advertising Design, Art Education, †Art History, Ceramics, Commercial Art, Drawing, †Graphic Arts, Graphic Design, History of Art & Archaeology, Illustration, Jewelry, Lettering, Museum Staff Training, †Painting, †Photography, Printmaking, Sculpture, †Stage Design, Teacher Training, Glass
Summer School: Dir, Robert Smith

BLOOMINGTON

INDIANA UNIVERSITY, BLOOMINGTON, Henry Radford Hope School of Fine Arts, 47405. Tel 812-855-7766; *Dir* Jeffrey Wolin; *Prof* Robert Barnes; *Prof* Bruce Cole; *Prof* Thomas Coleman; *Prof* Molly Faries; *Prof* Louis Hawes; *Prof* William Itter; *Prof* Jerry Jacquard; *Prof* Eugene Kleinbauer; *Prof* Gina Dabrowski; *Prof* Crista Erickson; *Prof* John Goodheart; *Prof* Roy Sieber; *Prof* Bonnie Sklarski; *Prof* Budd Stalnaker; *Prof* Joan Sterrenburg; *Prof* Barry Gealt; *Assoc Prof* Sarah Burns; *Assoc Prof* Randy Long; *Assoc Prof* Eleanor Scheifele; *Assoc Prof* Wendy Calman; *Assoc Prof* John Turner; *Assoc Prof* Patrick McNaughton; *Assoc Prof* Wolf Rudolph; *Assoc Prof* Shehira Davezac; *Assoc Prof* Janet Kennedy; *Assoc Prof* Jeffrey Wolin; *Assoc Prof* Georgia Strange; *Assoc Prof* Susan Nelson; *Assoc Prof* James Reidhaar; *Assoc Prof* Ed Bernstein; *Asst Prof* Randy Long; *Asst Prof* Eve Mansdorf; *Asst Prof* Tim Mather; *Asst Prof* Karen Ros; *Asst Prof* Yolanda McKay; *Asst Prof* Dale Newkirk; *Asst Prof* John Ciofalo; *Asst Prof* Michelle Facos; *Asst Prof* Molly Faries
Estab 1911; pub; D; scholarships; SC 55, LC 100, GC 110; enrl maj undergrad 300, grad 135 (45 Art History, 90 Studio), others 5600
Ent Req: Admis to the Univ
Degrees: BA, BFA, 4 yrs, MA, MFA, PhD
Tuition: Res—undergrad $1581 per sem, grad $133.35 per cr hr; nonres—undergrad $5175 per sem, grad $388.40 per cr hr
Courses: Art History, Ceramics, Graphic Design, Jewelry, Photography, Printmaking, Sculpture, Painting & Drawing, Printed Textiles, Woven Textiles
Summer School: Dir, John Goodheart. Tuition res—undergrad $71 per cr hr, grad $93 per cr hr; nonres—undergrad $222.15 per cr hr, grad $266.60 per cr hr. Courses—Art History, Ceramics, Drawing, Painting, Photography

CRAWFORDSVILLE

WABASH COLLEGE, Art Dept, 301 W Wabash Ave, 47933. Tel 317-362-1400, Ext 386; *Chmn* Gregory Huebner; *Prof* Doug Cowish
Estab 1832, dept estab 1950; pvt; D; scholarships; SC 16, LC 7; enrl D 80, non-maj 70, maj 10
Ent Req: HS dipl, SAT
Degrees: BA 4 yrs
Tuition: $14,525 per yr; campus res—room & board $4620
Courses: Aesthetics, Art History, †Ceramics, Display, †Drawing, †History of Art & Archaeology, †Painting, †Photography, Printmaking, †Sculpture, 2-D & 3-D Design

DONALDSON

ANCILLA COLLEGE, Art Dept, PO Box One, 46513. Tel 219-936-8898; FAX 219-935-1773; *Act Dept Head* Charles Duff
Estab 1936, dept estab 1965; pvt; D & E; SC 9-12, LC 2
Ent Req: HS dipl
Degrees: AA, AAA(Applied Arts) 2 yrs
Tuition: $89 per sem hr
Courses: Aesthetics, Art Appreciation, Calligraphy, Ceramics, Design, Photography, Drawing, Lettering, Graphic Design, Enameling
Children's Classes: Enrl 12; tuition $40 for 6 sessions; Courses—Crafts for Children, Drawing and Painting for Children. Classes on Saturday

EVANSVILLE

UNIVERSITY OF EVANSVILLE, Art Dept, 1800 Lincoln Ave, 47722. Tel 812-479-2043; FAX 812-479-2101; Elec Mail lm23@evansville.edu. *Dept Head & Prof* Les Miley, MFA; *Asst Prof* William Richmond, MFA; *Asst Prof* William Brown, MFA; *Instr* Tracy Steiner, MFA; *Instr* Daryl Wepfer, MA; *Instr* Suzanne Aiken, MA; *Instr* Janice Greene, MA; *Instr* James Goodridge, MA
Estab 1854; pvt; D & E; scholarships; SC 20, LC 10; enrl D 2600, maj 70
Ent Req: HS dipl
Degrees: BA(Art History), BS(Art Educ, Art & Assoc Studies), BFA, BA(Art) 4 yrs
Tuition: $12,990
Courses: Art Appreciation, †Art Education, †Art History, †Ceramics, Design, Drawing, †Graphic Design, Jewelry, †Painting, Photography, Printmaking, †Sculpture, †Painting, †Printmaking, †Sculpture, †Art & Associated Studies, Life (figure) Drawing
Summer School: Tuition $210 5 wk sessions. Courses—Art Appreciation, Ceramics, Photography

UNIVERSITY OF SOUTHERN INDIANA, Art Dept, 8600 University Blvd, 47712. Tel 812-464-8600; FAX 812-464-1960; *Chmn* Dr Margaret Skoglond; *Prof* Dr Hilary Braysmith; *Asst Prof* Leonard Dowhie Jr, MFA; *Instr* Eric Braysmith. Instrs: FT 5, PT 1
Estab 1969; pub; D & E; scholarships; SC 27, LC 4; enrl D 150, E 30, maj 90
Ent Req: HS dipl
Degrees: BS (Art Educ), BA (Art) 4 yrs
Tuition: Res—$72.25 per cr hr; nonres—$176 per cr hr
Courses: Art History, Graphic Design, Painting, Ceramics, Photography, Printmaking, Sculpture, Contemporary Art
Adult Hobby Classes: Enrl 25. Courses—Silkscreen

FORT WAYNE

INDIANA-PURDUE UNIVERSITY, Dept of Fine Arts, 2101 Coliseum Blvd E, 46805-1499. Tel 219-481-6705; *Chmn* Leslie P Motz; *Assoc Prof* Hector Garcia, MFA; *Assoc Prof* Donald Kruse, BS; *Assoc Prof* Anne-Marie LeBlanc, MFA; *Assoc Prof* Norman Bradley, MFA; *Assoc Prof* Audrey Ushenko, PhD; *Asst Prof* Dennis Krist, BFA; *Asst Prof* John Hrehov, MFA; *Asst Prof* Nancy McCroskey, MFA
Estab 1920, dept estab 1976; pub; D & E; scholarships; SC 96, LC 5; enrl non-maj 60, maj 235
Degrees: AB, AS, BFA 4 yrs
Tuition: Res—$89.40 per cr hr; nonres—$213.95 per cr hr; no campus res
Courses: Art History, †Ceramics, †Drawing, †Graphic Arts, Illustration, †Painting, †Photography, †Printmaking, †Sculpture, †Crafts, †Computer Design, †Metalsmithing
Children's Classes: Enrl 75; tuition $60 for 11 wks. Courses—Ceramics, Drawing, Painting, Sculpture

SAINT FRANCIS COLLEGE, Art Dept, 2701 Spring St, 46808. Tel 219-434-3235; FAX 219-434-3194; *Head Dept* Maurice A Papier, MS; *Assoc Prof* Sufi Ahmad, MFA; *Assoc Prof* Rick Cartwright, MFA; *Asst Prof* Karen Thompson, BFA; *Instr* Lawrence Endress, MAT; *Instr* Jenny Sanders, MS; *Instr* Tom Keesee, MFA; *Instr* Alan Nauts, BA
Estab 1890; den; D & E; scholarships; SC 22, LC 6, GC 14; enrl D 100, maj 100
Ent Req: HS dipl, class rank in HS, SAT
Degrees: AA(Commercial Art) 2 yrs, BA & BS(Art or Art Educ) 4 yrs, MA(Art Educ) 1 yr
Tuition: Undergrad $9820 per sem hr, grad $320 per sem hr; campus res—room & board $4070 per yr
Courses: Advertising Design, †Art Education, Art History, Calligraphy, Ceramics, †Commercial Art, Display, Drawing, Fashion Arts, Graphic Arts, Graphic Design, Illustration, Lettering, Painting, Photography, Printmaking, Sculpture, †Teacher Training, Computer Graphics
Children's Classes: Enrl 60; tuition $65 per sem. Courses—General Art Instruction grades K - 8
Summer School: Dir, M Papier. Enrl 150; two 6 wk sessions. Courses—Art Appreciation, Computer Graphics, Drawing, Painting

FRANKLIN

FRANKLIN COLLEGE, Art Dept, 501 E Monroe, 46131. Tel 317-738-8279; FAX 317-736-6030; *Chmn Dept* Michael Swanson. Instrs: FT 2, PT 2
Estab 1834; den; D; scholarships; SC 9, LC 4; enrl 900
Ent Req: HS grad
Degrees: BA 4 yrs
Tuition: $13,200 per yr
Courses: Art History, Design, Drawing, Painting, Sculpture, Basic Design

GOSHEN

GOSHEN COLLEGE, Art Dept, 1700 S Main St, 46526. Tel 219-535-7592; FAX 219-535-7660; WATS 800-348-7422. *Chmn* Marvin Bartel, EdD; *Prof* Abner Hershberger, MFA; *Assoc Prof* Judy Wenig-Horswell, MFA; *Asst Prof* John Mishler, MFA
Estab 1950; den; D & E; scholarships; enrl D 145, E 25, non-maj 60, maj 50
Ent Req: HS dipl, top half of class
Degrees: AB(Art) and AB(Art) with Indiana Teaching Cert
Tuition: $8310 per yr, $3760 per trimester, $295 per hr, campus res—room & board $3180 yr
Courses: Aesthetics, Architecture, Art Appreciation, †Art Education, Art History, †Ceramics, Commercial Art, Design, Drafting, Drawing, Graphic Design, †Jewelry, †Painting, Photography, †Printmaking, Sculpture, Silversmithing, Stage Design, †Teacher Training, †Theatre Arts, Video, Architectural Drawing
Summer School: Acad Dean, John Nyce. Tuition $520 for term of 3 1/2 wks beginning end of Apr, ending in late July. Courses—Drawing, Raku, Screenprinting, Watercolor; Florence, Italy Tour

GREENCASTLE

DEPAUW UNIVERSITY, Art Dept, 46135. Tel 317-658-4340; *Chmn* Catherine Fruhan; *Prof* David Herrold; *Asst Prof* Mitch Murback
Estab 1837, dept estab 1877; pvt den; D; SC 14, LC 9, GC 18; enrl D 300, E 20 (Art Dept), non-maj 25%, maj 75%, grad 20
Ent Req: HS dipl, upper half of high school graduating class
Degrees: BA & BM 4 yrs
Tuition: $4100 per sem; campus res—room & board $1607.50
Courses: Art Education, Art History, Ceramics, Drawing, Painting, Photography, Printmaking, Studio Arts

HAMMOND

PURDUE UNIVERSITY CALUMET, Dept of Communication & Creative Arts, 2233 171st St, 46323. Tel 219-989-2393; FAX 219-989-2008; *Head* William Robinson
Estab 1946; pub; D & E; scholarships; SC 1-4, LC 1-2, GC 1
Ent Req: HS dipl
Tuition: Res—$90.25 per cr hr; nonres—$199.50 per cr hr
Courses: Architecture, Art Education, Ceramics, Drawing, Film, Painting, Teacher Training, Theatre Arts, Video, Photography
Summer School: Dir, Michael R Moore. Enrl 60; tuition $90.25 per cr hr for res; $159.50 nonres. Courses—vary

HANOVER

HANOVER COLLEGE, Dept of Art, PO Box 108, 47243. Tel 812-866-7000; FAX 812-866-7114; *Chmn Dept* James W Shaffstall, MFA
Estab 1827, dept estab 1967; pvt; D; scholarships; SC 16, LC 4; enrl D 960
Ent Req: HS dipl
Degrees: BS and BA 4 yrs
Tuition: $12,080 per yr (includes everything except personal & books)
Courses: Advertising Design, Aesthetics, Art Education, Art History, Ceramics, Collages, Commercial Art, Constructions, Drawing, Film, Graphic Arts, Graphic Design, Jewelry, Painting, Photography, Printmaking, Sculpture, Stage Design, Teacher Training, Theatre Arts, Video, Fiber, Glass Blowing, Stained Glass

HUNTINGTON

HUNTINGTON COLLEGE, Art Dept, 2303 College Ave, 46750. Tel 219-356-6000; FAX 219-356-9448; *Dean* Gerald D Smith; *Asst Prof* W Kenneth Hopper; *Asst Prof* Rebecca L Coffman
Estab 1897; den; D & E; SC 5, LC 3
Ent Req: HS dipl, SAT & two recomendations
Tuition: $9950 per year; campus res available
Courses: Art Appreciation, †Art Education, Art History, Ceramics, Drawing, †Graphic Design, Painting, Painting, Photography, Arts & Crafts, Computer Graphics, Fine Arts
Summer School: Dean, Dr G D Smith. Tuition $180 per sem hr beginning May 21. Courses—same as above

INDIANAPOLIS

INDIANA UNIVERSITY-PURDUE UNIVERSITY, INDIANAPOLIS, Herron School of Art, 1701 N Pennsylvania St, 46202. Tel 317-920-2416; FAX 317-920-2401; *Dean* Robert Shay; *Assoc Dean* Valerie Eickmeier; *Coordr Fine Arts* Robert Eagerton; *Coordr Visual Communications* Paula Differding; *Coordr Art History* Sam Roberson; *Coordr Foundation* Phil Tennant; *Coordr Art Educ* Cindy Borgman
Estab 1902; pub; D & E; SC 112, LC 16, GC 20; enrl D 523, non-maj 395, grad 80
Degrees: BFA and BAE 4 yrs, MAE 5 yrs
Tuition: Res—undergrad $102.15 per cr hr, grad $138.75 per cr hr; nonres—undergrad $313.50 per cr hr, grad $400.25 per cr hr; no campus res
Courses: Art Education, Art History, Ceramics, Drawing, Graphic Arts, Graphic Design, Illustration, Mixed Media, Painting, Photography, †Printmaking, †Sculpture, Teacher Training, †Fine Arts, Furniture Design, †Visual Communications, Computer Graphics
Children's Classes: Enrl 150; tuition $125 (partial scholarships) for 10 wk term, Saturday art classes for jr & sr HS students
Summer School: Dir, Robert Shay. Enrl 450; tuition res—$80.50, nonres—$242.60 per cr hr, two 6 wk sessions. Courses—Art Appreciation, Art History, Ceramics, Drawing, Painting, Printmaking, Sr HS workshop

MARIAN COLLEGE, Art Dept, 3200 Cold Spring Rd, 46222. Tel 317-929-0123; FAX 317-929-0263; *Chmn & Instr* Mark Hall, MFA; *Instr* Richard Patterson, MFA; *Instr* Sam Smith; *Instr* Mary Ellen Reed, BFA; *Instr* Roberta Williams, MA
Estab 1938; den; D & E; scholarships; SC 21, LC 6; enrl D 60. E 30, non-maj 20, maj 30
Ent Req: HS dipl, SAT
Degrees: AA 2 yrs, BA 4 yrs
Tuition: Undergrad—$4995 per sem; campus res—room & board $1916 per sem
Courses: Art History, Ceramics, Design, Drawing, Graphic Design, Interior Design, Painting, Photography, Sculpture, Stage Design, Theatre Arts, Art Therapy, Crafts

UNIVERSITY OF INDIANAPOLIS, Art Dept, 1400 E Hanna Ave, 46227. Tel 317-788-3253; *Chair* Dee Schaad, MFA; *Prof* Earl Snellenberger, MFA
Estab 1902; den; D & E; scholarships; SC 24, LC 7, GC 7; enrl D 400, E 160, maj 70, grad 5
Ent Req: HS dipl, SAT, upper half of HS class
Degrees: BA and BS 4 yrs
Tuition: Commuter $9820 pr yr; campus res—room & board $3700 per yr
Courses: Advertising Design, Art Appreciation, Art Education, Art History, Ceramics, Commercial Art, Design, Drawing, Graphic Arts, History of Art & Archaeology, Jewelry, Lettering, Occupational Therapy, Painting, Photography, Printmaking, Sculpture, Teacher Training, †Art Therapy
Children's Classes: Enrl 20; free for 10 wk session. Courses—Drawing
Summer School: Dir, Dee Schaad. Enrl 60; $104 per cr hr. Courses—Art Appreciation, Ceramics, Computer, Photography, Printmaking

MARION

INDIANA WESLEYAN UNIVERSITY, Art Dept, 4201 S Washington St, 46953. Tel 317-674-6901; FAX 317-677-2333; *Head Dept* Ardelia Williams, MA; *Asst Prof* Robert Curfman, MA; *Instr* Rodney Crossman, BS Ed; *Instr* Ron Mazellen, MA; *Instr* Nathan Clement, BS; *Instr* Randi Gunyon, ME
Estab 1890, dept estab 1969; den; D & E; scholarships; SC 32, LC 11; enrl D 35, non-maj 5, maj 30
Ent Req: HS dipl
Degrees: BS(Art Educ)
Tuition: $10,260 per yr; campus res—available
Courses: †Advertising Design, Art Appreciation, Art Education, Art History, Ceramics, Commercial Art, Drawing, Graphic Arts, Graphic Design, Illustration, Jewelry, Painting, Photography, Printmaking, Sculpture, Silversmithing, †Teacher Training, Weaving, Batik, Pre-Art Therapy, Stained Glass, Studio Administration, Studio Practicum, †Visual Arts Education
Summer School: Dir, Ardelia Williams. Enrl 20; tuition $657 for 5 wks 3 cr hr. Courses—Air Brush, Ceramics, Weaving

MUNCIE

BALL STATE UNIVERSITY, Dept of Art, 2000 University Ave, 47306. Tel 317-285-5838; FAX 317-285-3790; *Chmn* Thomas Spoerner, EdD. Instrs: FT 21
Estab 1918; pub; D & E; scholarships; SC 82, LC 25, GC 30; enrl non-maj 386, maj 341, grad 15
Ent Req: HS dipl
Degrees: BS & BFA 4 yrs, MA 1 yr
Tuition: Res—undergrad $4594 per sem, grad $1666 per sem; nonres—undergrad $4224 per sem, grad $4296; campus res available
Courses: Art Appreciation, †Art Education, Art History, †Ceramics, †Drawing, †Graphic Design, Jewelry, †Painting, †Photography, †Printmaking, †Sculpture, Silversmithing, †Metals
Adult Hobby Classes: Enrl 15; tuition $102 per cr hr
Children's Classes: Enrl 75; tuition $30 per child. Courses—General Art Activities
Summer School: Enrl 5000; tuition $1008 for term of 5 wks beginning May

NEW ALBANY

INDIANA UNIVERSITY-SOUTHEAST, Fine Arts Dept, 4201 Grant Line Rd, 47150. Tel 812-941-2342; FAX 812-941-2529; *Coordr & Assoc Prof* Brian H Jones, MFA; *Assoc Prof* John R Guenthler, MFA; *Assoc Prof* Susan M Moffett, MFA; *Assoc Prof* Debra Clem
Estab 1945, dept estab 1966; pub; D & E; SC 25, LC 2; enrl D 150, E 35, non-maj 100, maj 50
Ent Req: HS dipl
Degrees: BA 4 yrs
Tuition: Res—undergrad $78.95 per cr hr; nonres—undergrad $204.65 per cr hr
Courses: Advertising Design, Art Appreciation, Art Education, Art History, Ceramics, Drawing, Painting, Printmaking
Adult Hobby Classes: Enrl 35; tuition $25 per sem. Courses—Crafts, Watercolor
Summer School: Enrl 60; term of two 6 wk sessions beginning May 15 & July 5. Courses—Same as above

NORTH MANCHESTER

MANCHESTER COLLEGE, Art Dept, 604 College Ave, 46962. Tel 219-982-5000; FAX 219-982-6868; *Chmn Dept* James R C Adams, MFA; *Prof* Stephen Batzka, BA
Estab 1889; den; D & E; scholarships; SC 15, LC 3; enrl D 45, maj 15
Ent Req: HS dipl
Degrees: AA 2 yrs, BA and BS 4 yrs
Tuition: Res—undergrad $16,400-$16,700 per yr, incl room & board
Courses: Advertising Design, Art Education, †Art History, Ceramics, Drawing, Film, Graphic Arts, Handicrafts, History of Art & Archaeology, Lettering, Painting, Photography, Printmaking, Sculpture, Teacher Training, Textile Design, Camera Techniques
Adult Hobby Classes: Tuition $35 per sem hr. Courses—Camera Techniques, Sculpture

NOTRE DAME

SAINT MARY'S COLLEGE, Dept of Art, 46556. Tel 219-284-4000, Ext 4631; FAX 219-284-4716; *Chmn* Marcia R Rickard
Estab 1844; pvt, W; D & E; scholarships, fels; SC 21, LC 10; enrl maj 50
Ent Req: CEEB, standing, recommendations, others
Degrees: BA and BFA 3 1/2-5 yrs
Tuition: $13,494 per yr
Courses: Art Appreciation, Art Education, Art History, Ceramics, Drawing, Display, Graphic Arts, History of Art & Archaeology, Painting, Photography, Printmaking, Sculpture, Teacher Training, Textile Design, Computer Media, Holography, Fibers, Photo Silkscreen
Summer School: Dir, Johnson Bowles. Enrl 25; tuition $800 (includes room & board) for 2 wk session. Courses—Ceramics, Drawing, Painting, Photography, Printmaking

UNIVERSITY OF NOTRE DAME, Dept of Art, Art History & Design, 132 O'Shaughnessy Hall, 46556. Tel 219-631-7602; FAX 219-631-6312; *Chmn* William Kremer. Instrs: FT 15, PT 8
Estab 1855; pvt; D; scholarships; SC 38, LC 8, GC 20; enrl maj 100
Ent Req: Upper third HS class, ent exam
Degrees: BA, BFA 4 yrs, MA, MFA
Tuition: Undergrad $12,390, grad $12,270 per yr; campus res—available
Courses: Drawing, †Art History, †Ceramics, †Graphic Design, †Industrial Design, †Painting, †Photography, †Printmaking, †Sculpture, Fibers
Summer School: Enrl 30-50; $93 per cr hr plus general fee for 7 wk term. Courses—Art History, Ceramics, Photography, Studio Workshops

OAKLAND CITY

OAKLAND CITY COLLEGE, Division of Fine Arts, 143 N Lucretia St, 47660. Tel 812-749-4781, Ext 274; FAX 812-749-1233; *Div Chair Arts & Science* Margaret Harper; *Assoc Prof* Joseph E Smith, MFA; *Assoc Prof* Carol Spitler; *Assoc Prof* Jean Cox; *Asst Prof* Donna Hazelwood. Instrs: FT 4, PT 1
Estab 1961; den; D & E; scholarships; SC 10, LC 5; enrl maj 35
Ent Req: HS dipl, SAT
Degrees: AA 2 yrs, BA & BS 4 yrs
Tuition: Undergrad $242 per cr hr
Courses: Art Appreciation, Art Education, Art History, Ceramics, Design, Drawing, Painting, Sculpture, Teacher Training, Weaving, Crafts
Summer School: Two 5 wk terms. Courses—Ceramics, Painting, plus others

RICHMOND

EARLHAM COLLEGE, Art Dept, 701 National Rd W, PO Box 148, 47374. Tel 317-983-1200, 983-1410; *Chmn Dept* Dick Rodgers
Estab 1847; den; D; scholarships; SC 10, LC 7; enrl maj 10
Ent Req: HS dipl
Degrees: BA 4 yrs
Courses: Art History, Ceramics, Drawing, Film, Painting, Photography, Printmaking, Theatre Arts

INDIANA UNIVERSITY-EAST, Humanities Dept, 2325 Chester Blvd, 47374. Tel 317-973-8200; FAX 317-973-8237; *Chmn* Dr Judith Worman-Royer
Tuition: Res—$78.95 per cr hr; nonres—$204.65 per cr hr
Courses: Art Appreciation, Art Education, Art History, Drawing, Handicrafts, Painting, Photography, Sculpture

SAINT MARY-OF-THE-WOODS

SAINT MARY-OF-THE-WOODS COLLEGE, Art Dept, 3301 Saint Mary's Rd, 47876. Tel 812-535-5151, 535-5279; FAX 812-535-4613; *Area Coordr* Donna Foy. Instrs: FT 2, PT 1
Estab 1840; den; D; scholarships; SC 15, LC 4; enrl maj 14
Ent Req: HS dipl, SAT or ACT
Degrees: BA & BS 4 yrs
Tuition: $10,800 per yr
Courses: †Art Education, Art History, †Ceramics, Drawing, †Graphic Design, †Painting, Photography, Printmaking, Teacher Training, Fiber Arts

SAINT MEINRAD

SAINT MEINRAD COLLEGE, Humanities Dept, 47577. Tel 812-357-6501; *Chmn* Dr George Mason
Estab 1854; pvt; D & E; SC 3, LC 3; enrl D 36, E 30
Ent Req: Admis & reg in the school
Tuition: $6950 per yr
Courses: Advertising Design, Aesthetics, Ceramics, Drawing, Graphic Design, History of Art & Archaeology, Painting, Theatre Arts
Adult Hobby Classes: Enrl 30. Courses—Ceramics, Painting

SOUTH BEND

INDIANA UNIVERSITY SOUTH BEND, Fine Arts Dept, 1700 Mishawaka Ave, 46615. Tel 219-237-4134; *Chmn* Robert W Demaree, Jr; *Prof* Alan Larkin, MFA; *Adjunct Asst Prof* Linda Crimson, MFA; *Adjunct Asst Prof* Anthony Droega
Estab 1964; pub; D & E; SC 18, LC 6; enrl non-maj 300, maj 40
Ent Req: HS dipl
Degrees: AA(Fine Arts) 2 yr, BA & BFA(Fine Arts) 4 yr
Tuition: Res—undergrad $88.60 per cr hr, grad $116.25 per cr hr; nonres—undergrad $242.35 per cr hr, grad $281.80
Courses: Art Education, Art History, Drawing, Graphic Design, Painting, Printmaking, Sculpture
Summer School: Chmn, Anthony Droege. Tuition same as regular session; two 6 wk summer sessions. Courses—Art Appreciation, Drawing, Painting

TERRE HAUTE

INDIANA STATE UNIVERSITY
—**Dept of Art,** Fine Arts 108, 47809. Tel 812-237-3697; FAX 812-237-4369; *Chmn* Adrian R Tio. Instrs: FT 19, PT 3
Estab 1870; pub; D & E; SC 66, LC 45, GC 61; enrl D 2432, E 311, maj 180, grad 40
Ent Req: HS dipl, top 50% of class with C average
Degrees: BA(Art History) & BFA(Studio Art) 4 yr, MA(Art History) & MFA(Studio Art) 2 yr
Tuition: Res—$16.88 per cr hr (18 hr); nonres—$41.40 per cr hr (18 hr)
Courses: Art Education, Art History, Ceramics, Drawing, Graphic Design, Mixed Media, Painting, Photography, Printmaking, Sculpture, Metalry, Papermaking, Studio Furniture, Wood Sculpture
Summer School: Dir, Dr Louis Jensen. Tuition res—undergrad $88, grad $105 per cr hr; nonres—undergrad $209, grad $235 per cr hr for term of two 5 wks beginning June. Courses—variety of studio & lecture courses

UPLAND

TAYLOR UNIVERSITY, Art Dept, 500 W Read Ave, 46989-1001. Tel 317-998-2751, Ext 5322; FAX 317-998-4910; *Chmn* Lon D Kaufmann. Instrs: FT 3, PT 4
Estab 1846, dept estab 1968; pvt; D & E; scholarships; SC 12, LC 7; enrl D 175, E 10, non-maj 250, maj 36
Ent Req: HS dipl, SAT, recommendations
Degrees: BA and BS 4 yr
Tuition: $15,175 incl tuition, room & board
Courses: †Art Education, Art History, Ceramics, Drawing, Graphic Arts, Jewelry, Mixed Media, Painting, Photography, Printmaking, Sculpture, †Art Studio, Computer Assisted Design, †Computer Graphic Arts

VINCENNES

VINCENNES UNIVERSITY JUNIOR COLLEGE, Art Dept, 1002 N First St, 47591. Tel 812-888-4318; FAX 812-888-5868; Elec Mail ajenorze@vunet.vino.edu. *Chmn* Andrew Jendrzejewski; *Prof* Amy DeLap; *Prof* Jim Pearson; *Assoc Prof* Steve Black; *Assoc Prof* Deborah Hagedorn; *Assoc Prof* John Puffer; *Assoc Prof* Bernard Hagedorn; *Asst Prof* Kevin Hughes
Scholarships
Degrees: AA, AS
Tuition: Res—$77.70 per cr hr; nonres—$188 per cr hr
Courses: Art Appreciation, †Art Education, Art History, Ceramics, †Commercial Art, Costume Design & Construction, †Design, Drafting, Drawing, Graphic Arts, †Graphic Design, Illustration, Intermedia, Painting, Photography, Printmaking, Sculpture, †Fine Art

WEST LAFAYETTE

PURDUE UNIVERSITY, WEST LAFAYETTE, Dept of Visual & Performing Arts, Div of Art & Design, 1352 CA-1 Bldg, 47907-1352. Tel 317-494-3058; *Chmn Div* D L Sigman; *Head Dept* D Y Ichiyama. Instrs: FT 32
Estab 1869; pub; D & E; scholarships; SC 50, LC 22, GC 22; enrl maj 523, other 2390
Degrees: BA 4 yrs, MA
Tuition: Res—$1260 per sem; nonres—$4095 per sem
Courses: Aesthetics, Architecture, Art Appreciation, Art Education, Art History, Ceramics, Costume Design & Construction, Design, †Drawing, †Graphic Design, History of Art & Archaeology, Illustration, †Industrial Design, †Interior Design, †Jewelry, †Painting, †Photography, †Printmaking, †Sculpture, †Silversmithing, Stage Design, Teacher Training, †Textile Design, Theatre Arts, †Weaving, †Visual Communications Design, †Metals, †Textiles
Summer School: Courses offered

WINONA LAKE

GRACE COLLEGE, Dept of Art, 200 Seminary Dr, 46590. Tel 219-372-5268; *Head Dept* Art Davis, MA; *Assoc Prof* Gary Nietcr, MA
Estab 1952, dept estab 1971; pvt; D & E; scholarships; SC 12, LC 3; enrl maj 45, non-maj 80
Ent Req: HS dipl, SAT
Degrees: 4 yr Art Major, 4 yr Art Educ Major, 4 yr Graphic Art and 2 yr assoc
Tuition: $266 per cr hr; campus res available
Courses: Art Appreciation, Art Education, Art History, Ceramics, Commercial Art, Drawing, Graphic Arts, Graphic Design, History of Art & Archaeology, Illustration, Painting, Photography, Printmaking, Typography, 2-D Design, 3-D Design

IOWA

AMES

IOWA STATE UNIVERSITY, Dept of Art & Design, 158 College of Design Bldg, 50011-3092. Tel 515-294-6724; FAX 515-294-2725; *Chmn Dept* Nancy Polster; *Assoc Chair* Timothy J McIlrath; *Coordr Drawing & Painting* Lu Bro, MFA; *Coordr Crafts* Priscilla Sage, MFA; *Coordr Graphic Design* Lisa Fontaine, MFA; *Coordr Art Educ* Dennis Dake, MA; *Coordr Visual Studies* Donna Friedman, MFA; *Coordr Art History* Gary Tartakov, PhD; *Coordr Interior Design* Shirlee Singer, MA
Estab 1858, dept estab 1920; pub; D & E; scholarships; SC 45, LC 15, GC 6; enrl non-maj 1000, maj 750, grad 50
Ent Req: HS dipl

Degrees: BA, BFA(Graphic Design, Craft Design, Interior Design, Drawing, Painting, Printmaking & Visual Studies), MA(Art & Design & Art Education), MFA(Graphic & Interior Design)
Tuition: Res—undergrad $1235 per sem; nonres—undergrad $4142 per sem; campus res available
Courses: Art Education, Art History, Calligraphy, Ceramics, Design, Drawing, Graphic Design, Illustration, Intermedia, Interior Design, Jewelry, Mixed Media, Painting, Photography, Printmaking, Silversmithing, Teacher Training, Textile Design, Weaving, †Surface Design, †Wood Design
Summer School: Dir, Prof Nancy Polster. Term of 8 wks. Courses—Art Education, Art History, Design, Drawing, Painting

BOONE

DES MOINES AREA COMMUNITY COLLEGE, Art Dept, Boone Campus, 1125 Hancock Dr, 50036. Tel 515-432-7203; FAX 515-432-6311; *Chmn* Lee McNair
Estab 1927, dept estab 1970; pub; D & E; SC 3, LC 2; enrl D 100, E 60
Ent Req: HS dipl
Degrees: AA 2 yrs
Tuition: Res—$49.65 per cr hr
Courses: Art Appreciation, Art History, Drawing, Painting, Stage Design, Teacher Training, Theatre Arts, Life Drawing

CEDAR FALLS

UNIVERSITY OF NORTHERN IOWA, Dept of Art, Col of Humanities and Fine Arts, 50614-0362. Tel 319-273-2077; FAX 319-273-7333; *Head Dept* William W Lew, PhD; *Prof* Steve Bigler, MFA; *Prof* Felipe Echeverria, MFA; *Prof* Vera Jo Siddens, MA; *Prof* Roy Behrens, MFA; *Assoc Prof* Charles Adelman, PhD; *Assoc Prof* Crit Streed, MFA; *Assoc Prof* Allan Shickman, MA; *Assoc Prof* Matthew Sugarman, MFA; *Assoc Prof* Richard Colburn, MFA; *Assoc Prof* Thomas Stancliffe, MFA; *Assoc Prof* Kee-Ho Yuen, MFA; *Assoc Prof* Jeff Byrd, MFA; *Assoc Prof* JoAnn Schnabel, MFA; *Asst Prof* Philip Fass, MFA; *Asst Prof* Paula Eubanks, EdD; *Asst Prof* Grace Deniston, PhD; *Asst Prof* Osie Johnson Jr, MFA
Estab 1876, dept estab 1945; pub; D & E; scholarships; SC 65, LC 20, GC 31; enrl 13,000, non-maj 150, maj 250, grad 10
Ent Req: HS dipl, ACT
Degrees: BA and BFA 4 yrs, MA 1 yr
Tuition: Res—undergrad $1235 per sem, grad $1466 per sem; nonres—$3344 per sem, grad $3615 per sem; campus res—room & board $3264 per yr
Courses: Art Appreciation, Art Education, Art History, Ceramics, Commercial Art, Design, Drawing, Goldsmithing, Graphic Arts, Graphic Design, History of Art & Archaeology, Illustration, Jewelry, Mixed Media, Painting, Photography, Printmaking, Sculpture, Silversmithing, Teacher Training, Performance Art
Summer School: Head Dept, William Lew, PhD. Enrl 235

CEDAR RAPIDS

COE COLLEGE, Dept of Art, 52402. Tel 319-399-8564; *Chmn* John Beckelman, MFA; *Prof* Robert Kocher, MA; *Assoc Prof* David Goodwin, MFA; *Asst Prof* Lucy Goodson, MFA; *Lectr* Dennis Weller; *Lectr* Kahleen Carracio; *Asst Prof* Peter Thompson, MFA
Estab 1851; pvt; D & E; scholarships; SC 15, LC 8; enrl D 1200
Ent Req: HS dipl, SAT, ACT or portfolio
Degrees: BA 4 yr
Tuition: $8000; campus res—room & board $7920 per yr
Courses: Advertising Design, Aesthetics, Architecture, †Art Appreciation, †Art Education, †Art History, Calligraphy, †Ceramics, †Collages, Commercial Art, Conceptual Art, Constructions, Costume Design & Construction, Design, Drafting, †Drawing, Film, Graphic Design, History of Art & Archaeology, Illustration, Lettering, Mixed Media, †Painting, †Photography, †Printmaking, †Sculpture, †Teacher Training, Video

KIRKWOOD COMMUNITY COLLEGE, Dept of Fine Arts, 6301 Kirkwood Blvd SW, 52406. Tel 319-398-5537; *Head Dept* Rhonda Kekke; *Prof* Doug Hall, MFA; *Prof* Rick Hintze, MFA; *Asst Prof* Helen Gruenwald, MA
Estab 1966; pub; D & E; SC 18, LC 6; enrl D 180, E 50
Ent Req: HS dipl
Degrees: AA 2 yr
Tuition: $55 per cr hr; no campus res
Summer School: Tuition $35 per cr hr. Courses—Art History, Art Appreciation, Ceramics, Design, Drawing, Lettering, Painting, Photography, Printmaking, Sculpture

MOUNT MERCY COLLEGE, Art Dept, 1330 Elmhurst Dr NE, 52402. Tel 319-363-8213; FAX 319-363-5270; *Chmn Dept* Robert Naujoks, MFA; *Prof* Charles Barth, PhD; *Prof* Jane Gilmor, MFA
Estab 1928, dept estab 1960; pvt; D & E; scholarships; SC 20, LC 6; enrl D 150, E 35, non-maj 150, maj 35
Ent Req: HS dipl, ACT
Degrees: BA 4 yr
Tuition: $11,370 per yr, $5685 per sem; $320 per cr hr; campus res—room & board $3800
Courses: †Art Education, Art History, Ceramics, Design, Drawing, †Graphic Design, Jewelry, Painting, Photography, Printmaking, Sculpture, Computer, Fiber Arts, New Genres, †Studio Art, Textiles, Travel Study
Summer School: Dir, Dr Jean Sweat. Enrl 500; tuition $960 per 3 hr course, two 5 wk sessions. Courses—Art Appreciation, Ceramics, Graphic Design, Microcomputer, Photography

CENTERVILLE

INDIAN HILLS COMMUNITY COLLEGE, Dept of Art, Centerville Campus, N First St, 52544. Tel 515-856-2143, Ext 210; *Head Dept* Richard H Dutton, MA; *Instructor* Mark McWhorter, MA
Estab 1932, dept estab 1967; pub; D & E; scholarships; SC 10; enrl D 70, E 30, non-maj 50, maj 14
Ent Req: HS dipl or equal, open door
Degrees: AA 2 yr
Tuition: Res $50 per cr hr; nonres—$65 per cr hr
Courses: Art History, Ceramics, Drawing, Painting, Sculpture, Art Appreciation, Arts & Crafts, Design
Adult Hobby Classes: Enrl 20; tuition $45 per sem hr. Courses—Ceramics, Design, Drawing, Painting, Watercolor
Summer School: Dir, Dick Sharp. Courses—Art Appreciation, Ceramics, Design, European Art Tours, Painting

CLINTON

EASTERN IOWA COMMUNITY COLLEGE, Art Dept, 1000 Lincoln Blvd, 52732. Tel 319-242-6841; FAX 319-242-7868; *Instr* Curt Pefferman
Scholarships
Degrees: AA
Tuition: Res—$51 per sem hr; nonres—$76.50 per sem hr (without fees); Res—$56.50 per sem hr; nonres—$82 per sem hr (includes fees)
Courses: Art Appreciation, Art History, Design, Drawing, Painting, Photography, Printmaking

MOUNT SAINT CLARE COLLEGE, Art Dept, 400 N Bluff, 52732. Tel 319-242-4023; *Head Dept* Dr Robert Engelson
Estab 1928, dept estab 1940; den; D & E; scholarships; SC 5, LC 1; enrl non-maj 80, maj 8
Ent Req: HS dipl
Degrees: AA 2 yr
Tuition: Res—undergrad $10,980 per yr
Courses: Art Appreciation, Calligraphy, Ceramics, Design, Drawing, Computer Art, Computer Graphics, Desktop Publishing, Fiber Art, Fiber Sculpture, 2-D & 3-D Design
Summer School: Art Appreciation, Calligraphy, Painting

COUNCIL BLUFFS

IOWA WESTERN COMMUNITY COLLEGE, Art Dept, 2700 College Rd, PO Box 4C, 51502. Tel 712-325-3200; FAX 712-325-3424; *Chmn* Frances Parrott; *Prof Art* Nick J Chiburis
Enrl 2000
Courses: Art Appreciation, Art History, Ceramics, Design, Drawing, Painting, Photography, Sculpture

CRESTON

SOUTHWESTERN COMMUNITY COLLEGE, Art Dept, 1501 W Townline Rd, 50801. Tel 515-782-7081; FAX 515-782-3312; Elec Mail jackson@swcc.cc.ia.us. *Dir Art Dept* Dale Jackson
Estab 1966; pub; D & E; scholarships; SC 6, LC 3; enrl D 550, E 200, non-maj 40, maj 15, others 15
Ent Req: HS dipl
Degrees: AA 2 yrs
Courses: Art Appreciation, Art Education, Art History, Ceramics, Design, Drawing, Graphic Design, Painting, Photography, Teacher Training, Computer Graphics
Adult Hobby Classes: Enrl 10-30; tuition $30 per sem. Courses—Per regular session
Summer School: Workshops in arts science

DAVENPORT

SAINT AMBROSE UNIVERSITY, Art Dept, 518 W Locust St, 52803. Tel 319-333-6000; FAX 319-333-6243; *Chmn* Kristin Quinn; *Faculty* Janet Seiz, MA
Estab 1892; den; D & E; scholarships; SC 17, LC 12; enrl D 450, E 40, maj 55
Ent Req: HS dipl
Degrees: BA 4 yrs
Tuition: $325 per cr hr; campus res—available
Courses: Advertising Design, Art Education, Calligraphy, Ceramics, Commercial Art, Drawing, Graphic Arts, Graphic Design, History of Art & Archaeology, Illustration, Lettering, Painting, Photography, Printmaking, Sculpture, Teacher Training
Summer School: Tuition $244 per sem hr. Courses—vary

TEIKYO MARYCREST UNIVERSITY, Art & Computer Graphics Dept, 1607 W 12th St, 52804. Tel 319-326-9532; FAX 319-326-9250; Elec Mail garfield@tmu1.mcrest.edu. *Chmn* Dr Alan Garfield; *Assoc Prof* Bruce Walters; *Asst Prof* Lane Hall
Estab 1939; den; D & E; scholarships; SC 35, LC 15, GC 13; enrl D 446, E 129, maj 68, grad 56
Ent Req: HS dipl
Degrees: BA 3-4 yrs, MA
Tuition: Tuition $2070 per sem; campus res—room & board $995 per sem
Courses: Advertising Design, Aesthetics, Art Education, Ceramics, Commercial Art, Drafting, Drawing, Fashion Arts, Graphic Design, History of Art & Archaeology, Museum Staff Training, Painting, Photography, Sculpture, Stage Design, Teacher Training, Theatre Arts, †Computer Graphics, Computer Art & Design
Adult Hobby Classes: Tuition $300 per cr hr; Weekend College Courses—2-D & 3-D Animation, Art Appreciation, Desktop Publishing, Drawing, Composition, Masterpieces of Art, Painting
Summer School: Dir, Dr A Garfield. Courses - Independent Study, Painting, Readings, Computer Graphics

DECORAH

LUTHER COLLEGE, Art Dept, 700 College Dr, 52101. Tel 319-387-1113; FAX 319-387-2158; *Head Dept* Kute Murtensen. Instrs: FT 3, PT 2
Estab 1861; den; D; scholarships; SC 13, LC 5; enrl D 160
Ent Req: HS dipl or ent exam
Degrees: BA 4 yr
Tuition: $16,800 per yr
Courses: †Aesthetics, †Art Education, †Ceramics, †Drawing, Graphic Arts, †History of Art & Archaeology, †Lettering, †Painting, †Printmaking, †Stage Design, †Teacher Training, †Theatre Arts, Art Management, Fibers, Spinning, Hand Made Paper, Computer Art
Children's Classes: Enrl 50; Courses offered spring & fall
Summer School: Academic Dean, A Thomas Kraalsel. Enrl 200 June & July. Courses—Drawing, Invitation to Art

DES MOINES

DRAKE UNIVERSITY, Art Dept, 25th & University Ave, 50311. Tel 515-271-2863; *Chmn Dept* Jules Kirschenbaum. Instrs: FT 10, PT 8
Estab 1881; pvt; D & E; scholarships; SC 64, LC 15, GC 33; enrl D 140, maj 140, grad 10
Ent Req: 2 pt average in HS or previous col
Degrees: BA, BFA, MFA
Tuition: $6710 per sem
Courses: †Art Education, Costume Design & Construction, Design, †Drawing, †Graphic Design, †History of Art & Archaeology, †Interior Design, †Painting, †Printmaking, †Sculpture, Silversmithing, Stage Design, Teacher Training, Theatre Arts
Summer School: Dir, T Westbrook. 4-5 wk sessions. Courses—Art History, Drawing, Painting

GRAND VIEW COLLEGE, Art Dept, 1200 Grandview Ave, 50316. Tel 515-263-2800; FAX 515-263-2974; *Dept Head* Dennis Kaven
Scholarships
Degrees: BA, cert
Tuition: Res—$4910 per sem
Courses: Drawing, Jewelry, Painting, Photography, Printmaking, Textile Design, Theatre Arts, Art Therapy, Computer Graphics

DUBUQUE

CLARKE COLLEGE, Dept of Art, 1550 Clarke Dr, 52001. Tel 319-588-6300; FAX 319-588-6789; *Chmn* Carmelle Zserdin, BVM
Estab 1843; den; D & E; scholarships; SC 15, LC 4; enrl maj 50, others 900
Ent Req: HS grad, 16 units and Col Ent Board
Degrees: BFA(studio) & BA(studio & art history)
Tuition: $11,730
Courses: Aesthetics, †Art Education, Art History, Calligraphy, †Ceramics, Conceptual Art, Design, †Drawing, Graphic Design, Mixed Media, †Painting, Photography, †Printmaking, †Sculpture, Stage Design, †Teacher Training, †Theatre Arts, Book Arts
Adult Hobby Classes: Enrl varies; 3, 4, 7 & 15 wk terms
Children's Classes: Enrl 10 per camp; tuition $60 per wk, summers
Summer School: Dir, David Nevins. 3-4 wk term. Courses—Varies from year to year

LORAS COLLEGE, Dept of Art, PO Box 22-178, 52004-0178. Tel 319-588-7117; FAX 319-588-7292; *Chmn* John Hoffman; *Prof* Roy Haught; *Assoc Prof* Thomas Jewell Vitale; *Instr* Tom Gibbs
Degrees: MA (Art Educ &Studio Arts), BA
Tuition: $11,205 per yr
Courses: Art Appreciation, †Art Education, †Art History, Design, Drawing, Painting, Printmaking, Sculpture, †Fibers, †Studio Art
Summer School: Dir, John Hess. Enrl $170 per course

ESTHERVILLE

IOWA LAKES COMMUNITY COLLEGE, Dept of Art, 300 S 18th St, 51334. Tel 712-362-2604; FAX 712-362-8363; *Prof* Richard William, MA; *Instr* Wayne Hollis, MA; *Instr* David Goughnour, MA
Estab 1967; pub; D & E; scholarships; SC 26, LC 1
Ent Req: HS dipl
Degrees: AA, AS(Commercial Art) 2 yrs
Tuition: Res—undergrad $832 per sem; nonres—undergrad $1392 per sem
Courses: Advertising Design, Art History, Calligraphy, Ceramics, Commercial Art, Drawing, Graphic Arts, Graphic Design, Illustration, Mixed Media, Painting, Photography, Computer Graphics, Commercial Studio Portfolio Preparation
Summer School: Courses—Internships in Commercial Art

FOREST CITY

WALDORF COLLEGE, Art Dept, 50436. Tel 515-582-8210; FAX 515-582-8194; *Chair* Kristi Carlson. Instrs: FT 1, PT 1
Estab 1903; den; D; scholarships; SC 4; enrl D 80, maj 15
Ent Req: HS dipl, ACT or SAT
Degrees: AA, AC and AAS 2 yr
Tuition: $5212 per sem
Courses: Art Appreciation, Design, Drawing, Painting, Photography, Printmaking

FORT DODGE

IOWA CENTRAL COMMUNITY COLLEGE, Dept of Art, 330 Ave M, 50501. Tel 515-576-7201; *Assoc Prof* Maureen Seamonds; *Instr* Rusty Farrington
Pub; D & E; scholarships; SC 4, LC 2; enrl D 120, E 15, non-maj 153, maj 20
Ent Req: HS dipl
Degrees: AA 2 yr
Tuition: Res— $825-$1650 per 15 cr hr; nonres—$2475 per cr hr; campus res—room & board $2860 per yr
Courses: Art History, Painting, Studio Art
Adult Hobby Classes: Enrl 50; tuition $25 for 6 wk session. Courses—Cartooning, Drawing, Printmaking
Summer School: Dir, Rusty Farrington. Enrl 45; tuition $53 per cr hr

GRINNELL

GRINNELL COLLEGE, Dept of Art, Fine Arts Ctr, PO Box 805, 50112-0806. Tel 515-269-3064, 269-3085; FAX 515-269-4420; *Chmn Dept & Instr* J Anthony Crowley; *Instr* Merle W Zirkle
Estab 1846, dept estab 1930; pvt; D; scholarships; SC 9, LC 9; enrl D 150, non-maj 125, maj 25
Ent Req: HS dipl, SAT or ACT
Degrees: BA 4 yrs
Tuition: Res—undergrad $15,688 per yr; campus res—room & board
Courses: Art Education, Art History, Ceramics, Design, Drawing, Jewelry, Painting, Printmaking, Sculpture

INDIANOLA

SIMPSON COLLEGE, Art Dept, 701 NC, 50125. Tel 515-961-1561; FAX 515-961-1498; *Chmn Dept* Janet Heinicke
Estab 1860, dept estab 1965; pvt; D & E; scholarships; SC 3, LC 3; enrl D 120, maj 20
Ent Req: HS dipl, ACT or SAT
Degrees: BA and BM 4 yrs
Tuition: Res—undergrad $8815 per yr; campus res—room $1380 and board $1695
Courses: †Art Education, Art History, Commercial Art, Design, Drawing, History of Art & Archaeology, Photography, Printmaking, Sculpture, Teacher Training, Art Therapy, Art Management, †Commercial Design, Museum Education
Adult Hobby Classes: Enrl 500; tuition $165 per sem hr. Courses—Art Education, Art Methods
Summer School: Dir, Dr Jill Rossiter

IOWA CITY

UNIVERSITY OF IOWA, School of Art & Art History, 120 N Riverside Dr, 52242. Tel 319-335-1771; FAX 319-335-1774; *Dir* Dorothy Johnson; *Prof Foil Stamping* Virginia Myers; *Prof Metalsmithing & Jewelry* Chunghi Choo. Instrs: FT 38, PT 3
Estab 1847, school estab 1911; pub; D & E; scholarships; SC 60, LC 55, GC 55; enrl D 681, maj 508, grad 173
Ent Req: HS dipl, ACT or SAT, upper rank in HS
Degrees: BA and BFA 4 yr, MA, MFA, PhD
Tuition: Res—undergrad $1235 per sem; nonres—$4534 per sem
Courses: Aesthetics, †Art Education, †Art History, †Calligraphy, †Ceramics, Conceptual Art, †Design, †Drawing, †Graphic Design, Industrial Design, †Intermedia, Interior Design, †Jewelry, †Painting, †Photography, †Printmaking, †Sculpture, †Silversmithing, Teacher Training, †Video, †Multimedia
Summer School: Dir, Dorothy Johnson. Enrl undergrad 195, grad 115; tuition res—undergrad $1030, grad $1467; nonres—undergrad $3780, grad $4726 for term of 8 wks, beginning June 10. Courses—Full range of Art Education, Art History, Studio Courses

IOWA FALLS

ELLSWORTH COMMUNITY COLLEGE, Dept of Fine Arts, 1100 College Ave, 50126. Tel 515-648-4611; FAX 515-648-3128; *Chmn* Greg Metzon
Estab 1890; pub; D & E; SC 10, LC 1; enrl in dept D 20-25
Ent Req: HS dipl, ACT
Degrees: AA 2 yrs
Tuition: Res $900 per yr, $55 per cr hr; nonres—undergrad $1800 per yr, $110 per cr hr; campus res—room & board $1900
Courses: †Advertising Design, Art Appreciation, Art History, Ceramics, Commercial Art, Design, Drawing, Graphic Arts, Graphic Design, Illustration, Mixed Media, Painting, Photography, Sculpture
Adult Hobby Classes: Enrl 12; tuition $20 per 20 hrs. Courses—Pottery
Summer School: Dir, Dr Del Shepard. Enrl 14; tuition $40 per sem hr for 4 weeks. Courses—Art Interpretation

LAMONI

GRACELAND COLLEGE, Fine Arts Dept, 700 College Ave, 50140. Tel 515-784-5000; *Dept Coordr* James Mai; *Assoc Prof* Wayne Allison; *Asst Prof* Steve Greenquist
Estab 1895, dept estab 1961; pvt den; D; scholarships; SC 30, LC 10; enrl D 180, maj 52, others 4
Ent Req: HS dipl
Degrees: BA and BS 4 yrs
Tuition: 10,230 per yr
Courses: Art Appreciation, †Art Education, Art History, Ceramics, Design, Drawing, †Graphic Design, Illustration, †Painting, Photography, †Printmaking, †Sculpture, Color Theory, †Commercial Design, Computer Graphic Design
Summer School: Dir, Dr Velma Ruch

LEMARS

TEIKYO WESTMAR UNIVERSITY, Art Dept, 1002 Third Ave SE, 51031. Tel 712-546-7081, Ext 2570; *Art Prog Dir* Randy Strathman-Becker; *Instr* Anne Lubben. Instrs: FT 1
Estab 1890; pvt; D; enrl 700, maj 22
Ent Req: ACT, SAT or PSAT
Degrees: BA, BMEd and BAS 4 yr
Tuition: $4060 per yr
Courses: Aesthetics, Architecture, Art Appreciation, Art Education, Art History, Ceramics, Design, Drawing, Graphic Arts, History of Art & Archaeology, Mixed Media, Painting, Printmaking, Sculpture, Art Philosophy & Criticism, Business World of Art, Design, Foundations of Art, Synthetic Media & Color
Adult Hobby Classes: JANUS Continuing Education for Retired Persons
Summer School: Dir, Randy Strathman-Becker. Tuition $600-$700 for 4-6 wk term. Courses—Painting, Printmaking, Sculpture

MASON CITY

NORTH IOWA AREA COMMUNITY COLLEGE, Dept of Art, 500 College Dr, 50401. Tel 515-423-1264, Ext 242, 307; *Instr* Peggy L Bang; *Instr* Carol Faber
Estab 1964; pub; D & E; scholarships; SC 4, LC 2; enrl D 240, E 100, maj 30
Ent Req: HS dipl
Degrees: AA 2 yr
Tuition: Res— $800 per 15 cr hrs; nonres—$1200 per 15 cr hr
Courses: Art Education, Art History, Ceramics, Drawing, Painting, Photography, Computer Graphic Design, 2-D Design
Adult Hobby Classes: Enrl 30. Courses—Crafts, Painting
Summer School: Dir, Carol Faber. Enrl 30; tuition $46 per cr for 6 wk term. Courses—Essence of Art, Drawing

MOUNT PLEASANT

IOWA WESLEYAN COLLEGE, Art Dept, 601 N Main, 52641. Tel 319-385-8021; *Chmn* Don R Jones; *Assoc Prof* Ann Klingensmith; *Adjunct* Adam Tilson
Estab 1842; den; scholarships; SC 10, LC 4; enrl maj 32
Degrees: BA 4 yr
Tuition: Res—undergrad $16,000 per yr incl room & board
Courses: Art Education, Art History, Ceramics, Design, Drawing, Graphic Arts, Painting, Photography, Printmaking, Introduction to Art, Secondary Art, Special Problems, Twentieth Century Art History

MOUNT VERNON

CORNELL COLLEGE, Art Dept, Armstrong Hall, Fine Arts, 600 First St W, 52314. Tel 319-895-4000; FAX 319-895-4492; *Head Dept* T Plaut. Instrs: FT 4
Estab 1853; den; D; scholarships; SC 30, LC 12; enrl 1000
Ent Req: HS dipl
Degrees: BA, BSS and BPhil 4 yr
Tuition: $15,248 per yr
Courses: Art History, Ceramics, Collages, Design, Drawing, Painting, Photography, Sculpture, Textile Design, Weaving, Fiber Design, Weaving

ORANGE CITY

NORTHWESTERN COLLEGE, Art Dept, 51041. Tel 712-737-7003; *Chmn* John Kaericher, MFA; *Asst Prof* Rein Vanderhill, MFA; *Prof* Nella Kennedy, MA
Estab 1882; dept estab 1965; den; D & E; scholarships; SC 25, LC 3-4; enrl D 200, non-maj 175, maj 23-25
Ent Req: HS dipl
Degrees: BA 4 yr
Tuition: Campus residency available
Courses: Art Education, Art History, Ceramics, Design, Drawing, Painting, Photography, Printmaking, Sculpture

OSKALOOSA

WILLIAM PENN COLLEGE, Art Dept, 201 Trueblood Ave, 52577. Tel 515-673-1001; FAX 515-673-1396; *Chmn* Ron Lofgren
Estab 1876; pvt; D & E; scholarships; SC 5, LC 5; enrl D 120
Ent Req: HS dipl, ACT, PSAT or SAT
Degrees: BA
Tuition: $10,290 per sem
Courses: Art Education, Ceramics, Costume Design & Construction, Drafting, Drawing, History of Art & Archaeology, Industrial Design, Interior Design, Teacher Training
Adult Hobby Classes: Enrl 500; tuition $120 per hr. Courses—Crafts
Summer School: Dir, Dr Howard Reitz. Tuition $120. Courses—Ceramics, Elementary Art Methods

OTTUMWA

INDIAN HILLS COMMUNITY COLLEGE, OTTUMWA CAMPUS, Dept of Art, 525 Grandview, 52501. Tel 515-683-5111, 683-5149; FAX 515-683-5184; WATS 800-726-2585. *Dept Head* Richard Dutton; *Dir of Arts & Sciences* Dana Grove; *Instr* Mark McWhorter
Estab 1932; pub; D & E; scholarships; SC 3, LC 2; enrl D 73, E 5
Ent Req: HS dipl, GED, ACT or SAT
Degrees: AA, AAS and AAA 2 yrs
Tuition: Res—$44 per sem cr hr; nonres—$66 per sem cr hr (res acquired after 90 days)
Courses: Art History, Ceramics, Design, Drawing, Painting, Crafts

Adult Hobby Classes: Enrl 10-20; tuition $35 per sem cr hr. Courses—Ceramics, Painting, Watercolor
Children's Classes: Enrl 15-20. Courses—General Workshops, Painting, Ceramics
Summer School: Dir, Dana Grove. Enrl 120; 6 wk session. Courses—Liberal Arts

PELLA

CENTRAL UNIVERSITY OF IOWA, Art Dept, 812 University, 50219. Tel 515-628-5261; *Chmn* J Vruwink, MFA; *Asst Prof* Dr Valerie Hedquist; *Asst Prof* J D DeJong, MA
Estab 1853; pvt; D & E; scholarships; SC 20, LC 6; enrl D 180, non-maj 140, maj 40
Ent Req: HS dipl, ACT
Degrees: BA 4 yrs
Tuition: $8517 per yr; campus res—room & board $3285
Courses: Art History, Ceramics, Drawing, Painting, Glassblowing, Modern Art, Primitive Art, Studio Art
Children's Classes: Enrl 40; part of Elementary School Art Program

SIOUX CITY

BRIAR CLIFF COLLEGE, Art Dept, 3303 Rebecca St, 51104. Tel 712-279-5321, Ext 5452; *Chairperson* William J Welu, MFA; *Instr* Mary Ann Lonergan, MA
Estab 1930; den; D & E; scholarships; SC 7, LC 7; enrl D 250, non-maj 150, maj 30
Ent Req: HS dipl, ACT
Degrees: BA and BS 4 yr
Tuition: $3650 per term, $365 per hr; campus res—room & board $3840 per yr
Courses: Art Appreciation, Art Education, Art History, Calligraphy, Ceramics, Collages, Drawing, Intermedia, †Mixed Media, †Painting, †Sculpture, †Teacher Training, Art 1, 2, 3 & 4 (major studio areas & independent study), Critical Seminar, Design
Summer School: Dir, Dr Sean Warner. Enrl 30-40; tuition $195 per cr hr for 5 wk term. Courses—Contemporary Art History, Elementary Art Education, Pottery

MORNINGSIDE COLLEGE, Art Dept, 1501 Morningside Ave, 51106. Tel 712-274-5212; *Chmn* John Bowitz. Instrs: FT 3
Pvt; D & E; scholarships; SC 17, LC 4; enrl D 161, maj 40
Ent Req: HS dipl
Degrees: BA and BS (Art Educ) 4 yrs
Tuition: $10,686 per yr
Courses: Advertising Design, Collages, Commercial Art, Conceptual Art, Design, Illustration, Mixed Media, Stage Design, Theatre Arts, Video
Children's Classes: Enrl 40; tuition $25 for 5 wk summer term. Courses—Ceramics, Photography
Summer School: Dir, John Bowitz. Enrl 50; tuition $120 per cr, May, June, July. Courses—Drawing, Photography, Teaching Methods

SIOUX CITY ART CENTER, 225 Nebraska St, 51101. Tel 712-279-6272; *Interim Dir* Janet Brown; *Instr* Open
Estab 1938; pvt; D & E; scholarships; SC 14-20, LC 1-2; enrl D 100, E 400
Tuition: $25-$70 members; $5-$7 workshops
Courses: †Art Education, †Art History, †Ceramics, †Drawing, †Mixed Media, †Painting, †Photography
Adult Hobby Classes: Enrl 60, tuition $25-$30 for 3-6 wk terms. Courses—Drawing, Painting, Pottery, Studio, Printmaking
Children's Classes: Enrl 900; tuition $25-$27 for 6 wk term. Courses—Clay, Drawing, Mixed Media, Painting, Photography

WAVERLY

WARTBURG COLLEGE, Dept of Art, 222 Ninth St NW, 50677. Tel 319-352-1200; WATS 800-553-1797. *Dept Head* Thomas Payne, MFA; *Prof Emeritus* Arthur C Frick, MS; *Asst Prof* Aida Frick, MA; *Asst Prof* Edward Charney, MFA
Estab 1852; den; D & E; scholarships; SC 18, LC 4; enrl D 135, non-maj 110, maj 25
Ent Req: HS dipl, PSAT, ACT & SAT, foreign students TOEFL and upper 50 percent of class
Degrees: BA(Art), BA(Art Educ) 4 yrs
Tuition: Res—undergrad $10,250 per yr, $550 PT; campus res—room $1410 - $1550, board $1770; general fee $110
Courses: Advertising Design, Art Appreciation, Art Education, Art History, Design, Drawing, Graphic Design, Painting, Photography, Printmaking, Sculpture, Computer Graphic Design, Metal Design
Summer School: Dir, Dr Edith Waldstein. Enrl 20; tuition $550 per course for 3 wk term. Courses—Drawing, Independent Study, Painting

KANSAS

ATCHISON

BENEDICTINE COLLEGE, Art Dept, 1020 N Second St, 66002. Tel 913-367-5340; FAX 913-367-6102; *Chmn* Dan Carrell. Instrs: FT 1
Estab 1971; den; D; SC 15, LC 3; enrl D 145, non-maj 123, maj 22
Ent Req: HS dipl, ent exam
Tuition: Campus res— room & board $3850
Courses: Art Education, Art History, Calligraphy, Ceramics, Drawing, Graphic Arts, Painting, Photography, Printmaking, Sculpture, Teacher Training

BALDWIN CITY

BAKER UNIVERSITY, Dept of Art, 618 Eighth St, 66006. Tel 913-594-6451;
FAX 913-594-2522; *Chmn* Walter J Bailey; *Assoc Prof* Inge Balch; *Assoc Prof*
Collene Z Gregoire
Estab 1858; pvt; D; scholarships; SC 11, LC 3; enrl D 105, maj 28
Ent Req: HS dipl, provision made for entrance without HS dipl by interview &
committee action
Degrees: AB (Art) 4 yrs
Tuition: $8620 per yr
Courses: Art Education, Ceramics, Drawing, Graphic Arts, History of Art &
Archaeology, Painting, Printmaking, Sculpture, Teacher Training, Textile Design

COFFEYVILLE

COFFEYVILLE COMMUNITY COLLEGE, Art Dept, 11th & Willow, 67337. Tel
316-251-7700, Ext 2091; FAX 316-251-7798; *Head Dept* Michael DeRosa
Estab 1923, dept estab 1969; pub; D & E; scholarships; SC 8, LC 2; enrl D 75, E 60,
non-maj 25, maj 110
Ent Req: HS dipl
Degrees: AA
Tuition: Res—undergrad $30 per cr hr; nonres—undergrad $78 per cr hr; campus
res—$1100
Courses: Art Appreciation, Art Education, Art History, Ceramics, Design, Drawing,
Handicrafts, Painting, Photography, Printmaking, Sculpture, Theatre Arts, Video
Adult Hobby Classes: Enrl 15-20; 3 month sem. Courses—Crafts
Children's Classes: Enrl 15; tuition $60 for 2 wks. Courses—Clay, Sculpture
Summer School: Dir, Michael DeRosa. Enrl 25; 2 month session.
Courses—Ceramics I, Drawing I

COLBY

COLBY COMMUNITY COLLEGE, Visual Arts Dept, 1255 S Range, 67701. Tel
913-462-3984; FAX 913-462-4600; *Dir* Kathy Gordon
Estab 1965, dept estab 1966; pub; D & E; scholarships; SC 18, LC 8; enrl D 141, E
210, maj 18
Ent Req: HS dipl
Degrees: AA 2 yrs
Tuition: Res—$26 per cr hr; nonres—$74 per cr hr
Courses: Painting, Color Structure & Design, Figure Drawing: Advanced, Problems
in Drawing
Adult Hobby Classes: Enrl 10-20; tuition $15 per hr
Summer School: Enrl 5-20; Term of 4 wks beginning June 1. Courses—Drawing,
Jewelry, Watercolor

EL DORADO

BUTLER COUNTY COMMUNITY COLLEGE, Art Dept, 901 S Haverhill Rd,
67042. Tel 316-321-2222; FAX 316-322-3318; *Dean* Larry Patton; *Instr* Peter
Johnson, MFA
Estab 1927, dept estab 1964; pub; D & E; scholarships; SC 13, LC 1; enrl D 168, E
57
Ent Req: HS dipl, ACT, EED
Degrees: AA 2 yr
Tuition: Res—$35 per cr hr; nonres—$80 per cr hr
Courses: Art History, Ceramics, Drawing, Interior Design, Painting, Printmaking,
Silversmithing

EMPORIA

EMPORIA STATE UNIVERSITY, Division of Art, 66801. Tel 316-341-5246;
Chmn Donald Perry
Estab 1863, dept estab early 1900's; pub; D & E; scholarships; SC 42, LC 15, GC
30; enrl D 700, E 25, maj 120, grad 25
Ent Req: HS dipl, HS seniors may enroll in regular classes
Degrees: BFA, BSE, BS(Art Therapy) 4 yr, MS(Art Therapy)
Tuition: Res—undergrad $917 per sem; nonres—undergrad $2967 per sem; campus
res available
Courses: Art Education, Art History, Ceramics, Commercial Art, Display, Drawing,
Graphic Arts, History of Art & Archaeology, Illustration, Interior Design, Jewelry,
Mixed Media, Painting, Photography, Printmaking, Sculpture, Silversmithing,
Teacher Training, Weaving, Introduction to Graphic Design, Metals
Summer School: Acting Chair, Donald Perry. Enrl 150; tuition res $55 per hr,
nonres $140 per hr for term beginning June 11. Courses—most of the regular classes

GARDEN CITY

GARDEN CITY COMMUNITY COLLEGE, Art Dept, 801 Campus Dr, 67846.
Tel 316-276-7611; FAX 316-276-9630; *Chmn Human & Fine Arts* Larry Fowler
Degrees: AA
Tuition: Res—undergrad $26 per cr hr
Courses: Art Appreciation, Art History, Ceramics, Design, Drawing, Handicrafts,
Interior Design, Jewelry, Painting, Photography, Printmaking, Stage Design, Stained
Glass

GREAT BEND

BARTON COUNTY COMMUNITY COLLEGE, Fine Arts Dept, RR No 3,
67530. Tel 316-792-2701; *Instr* Steve Dudek, MFA; *Instr* Marcia Polenberg, MFA
Estab 1965, dept estab 1969; pub; D & E; scholarships
Ent Req: HS dipl or GED
Degrees: AA

Tuition: Res—undergrad $28 per cr hr; campus residence available
Courses: Advertising Design, Architecture, Art Appreciation, Art Education, Art
History, Ceramics, Commercial Art, Conceptual Art, Constructions, Design,
Drafting, Drawing, Goldsmithing, Graphic Arts, Graphic Design, History of Art &
Archaeology, Illustration, Interior Design, Jewelry, Occupational Therapy, Painting,
Photography, Printmaking, Sculpture, Silversmithing, Stage Design, Teacher
Training, Theatre Arts, Weaving
Adult Hobby Classes: Enrl 50-300; tuition $38 per cr hr. Courses—Ceramics,
Computer Graphics, Design, Drawing, Graphic Design, Jewelry, Painting, Photo
Children's Classes: Enrl 30-200; tuition $25 per class for 4 days. Courses—Various
summer classes
Summer School: Dir, Steve Dudek. Enrl 30-60; tuition $38 per hr for 8 wks.
Courses—Art Education, Art Media, Ceramics, Drawing, Painting, Photo

HAYS

FORT HAYS STATE UNIVERSITY, Dept of Art, 600 Park St, 67601. Tel 913-
628-4247; *Chmn* Gary Coulter; *Prof* Jim Hinkhouse, MFA; *Prof* Kathleen Kuchar;
Prof Merlene Lyman; *Prof* Frank Nichols, MFA; *Prof* Michael Jilg, MFA; *Assoc*
Prof Joanne Harwick, MFA; *Assoc Prof* Chaiwat Thumsujarit, MFA; *Assoc Prof*
Zoran Stevanov, PhD; *Asst Prof* Martha Holmes, MA; *Asst Prof* Linda Ganstrom;
Asst Prof Alan Schoer; *Asst Prof* Leland Powers; *Instr* Adelle Rich
Estab 1902, dept estab 1930; pub; D & E; scholarships; SC 66, LC 19, GC 28; enrl
D 742, non-maj 555, maj 286, grad 36, others 7
Ent Req: HS dipl
Degrees: BA & BFA 4 yrs, AA & MFA 2 - 3 yrs
Tuition: Res—undergrad $44.50 & grad $51.25 per cr hr; nonres—undergrad $100.
52 & grad $107.25 per cr hr; campus res—room & board: double $600, single $839
(20 meals included)
Courses: Advertising Design, Art Appreciation, †Art Education, †Art History,
†Ceramics, Commercial Art, Design, †Drawing, †Graphic Design, †Handicrafts,
Illustration, Intermedia, †Interior Design, †Jewelry, Lettering, Mixed Media,
†Painting, †Photography, †Printmaking, †Sculpture, †Silversmithing, †Teacher
Training, Textile Design, †Art Therapy
Summer School: Enrl 157; tuition res—undergrad $41.75 per cr hr, grad $45;
nonres—undergrad $91.25 per cr hr, grad $94.75 per cr hr for term of 8 wks
beginning June 6. Courses—Studio Courses & Workshops

HESSTON

HESSTON COLLEGE, Art Dept, PO Box 3000, 67062-3000. Tel 316-327-8164;
FAX 316-327-8300; *Head Dept* John Blosser, MFA
Estab 1915; den; D & E; scholarships; SC 9, SC 1; enrl non-maj 50, maj 5
Ent Req: HS dipl
Degrees: AA 2 yr
Tuition: $8100 annual tuition; campus res available
Courses: Art Appreciation, Art History, Ceramics, Design, Drawing, Graphic
Design, Painting, Photography, Printmaking, Sculpture, Theatre Arts, Design

HUTCHINSON

HUTCHINSON COMMUNITY JUNIOR COLLEGE, Visual Arts Dept, 600 E
11th St, 67501. Tel 316-665-3500, Ext 3503; *Prof* Dee Connett; *Prof* Roy Swanson;
Color & Graphic Instr Nancy Masterson; *Ceramics & Sculpture Instr* Jerri Griffin;
Art History Instr Teresa Preston; *Instr* John Eberly
Estab 1928; pub; D & E; scholarships; SC 17, LC 4; enrl D 215, E 41, non-maj 180,
maj 81
Ent Req: HS dipl
Degrees: AA 2 yrs
Tuition: $27 per cr hr; campus res—room & board $2300 per yr
Courses: Art Appreciation, Art Education, Art History, Ceramics, Commercial Art,
Drawing, Graphic Arts, Graphic Design, Jewelry, Painting, Printmaking, Sculpture,
Silversmithing, Stage Design, Teacher Training, Theatre Arts, Video, Computer
Graphics Design
Summer School: Dir, Dee Connett. Tuition $27 per hr for 6 wk session.
Courses—Art Appreciation, Art Education

IOLA

ALLEN COUNTY COMMUNITY COLLEGE, Art Dept, 1801 N Cottonwood,
66749. Tel 316-365-5116; *Dept Head* Steven R Greenwall, MFA
Estab 1965; pub; D & E; scholarships; SC 5, LC 2; enrl D 700, E 1000, non-maj 40,
maj 10
Ent Req: HS dipl or GED
Degrees: AA, AS & AAS 2 yr
Tuition: Res—$42 per cr hr
Courses: Ceramics, Commercial Art, Drawing, Painting, Photography, Sculpture, Art
Appreciation, Art Fundamentals, 2-D & 3-D Design
Summer School: Courses—all courses

LAWRENCE

HASKELL INDIAN NATIONS UNIVERSITY, Art Dept, 155 Indian Ave,
66046. Tel 913-749-8431, Ext 252; *Instr* B J Wahnee, MA
Estab 1884, dept estab 1970; pub; D; SC 14, LC 1; enrl in dept D, non-maj 90, maj
10
Ent Req: HS dipl or GED, at least 1/4 Indian, Eskimo or Aleut and receive agency
approval
Degrees: AA and AAS 2 yrs
Tuition: Government funded for native Americans only; campus res available
Courses: Art Appreciation, Art History, Ceramics, Design, Drawing, Jewelry,
Painting, Sculpture, Textile Design

UNIVERSITY OF KANSAS, School of Fine Arts, 66045. Tel 913-864-3421; FAX 913-864-4404; *Dean* Peter G Thompson; *Assoc Dean Grad Studies* Carole Ross
Pub; scholarships & fels; enrl 1300
Degrees: BA, BAE, BFA, BS, MFA 4-5 yr
—Dept of Art, 66045. Tel 913-864-4401; FAX 913-864-4404; *Chmn* Judith McCrea. Instrs: FT 19
Estab 1885; SC 50, GC 25; enrl maj 150
Tuition: Res—undergrad $899 per sem, grad $1088 per sem; nonres— $2985 per sem
Courses: †Drawing, †Painting, †Printmaking, †Sculpture
Summer School: Dir Robert Brawley. Enrl 60; Tuition $57 for 8 wks. Courses—Life Drawing, Intro to Drawing I & II, Painting I-IV
—Dept of Design, 66045. Tel 913-864-4401; *Chmn* Joe Zeller. Instrs: FT 25, PT 5
Estab 1921; SC 83, LC 32, GC 26; enrl maj 550, grad 30
Tuition: Res—undergrad $899 per sem, grad $1088 per sem; nonres—undergrad $2985 per sem, grad $3198 per sem
Courses: †Art Education, †Ceramics, †Graphic Design, †Illustration, †Industrial Design, †Interior Design, †Jewelry, Photography, †Textile Design, †Weaving, Design, Weaving, Textile Printing & Dyeing, Visual Communications
Summer School: Term of 4-8 wks beginning June
—Kress Foundation Dept of Art History, Spencer Museum of Art, Rm 209, 66045. Tel 913-864-4713; FAX 913-864-5091; Elec Mail arthist@lark.cc.ukans.edu. *Prof* Linda Stone-Ferrier; *Prof Emeritus* Chu-tsing Li PhD; *Prof* Charles Eldredge, PhD; *Prof & Asian Grad Advisor* Marsha Weidner; *Assoc Prof* Edmund Eglinski, PhD; *Asst Prof* David Cateforts, PhD; *Asst Prof* John Teramoto, PhD; *Asst Prof* Marie Aquilino, PhD; *Lectr* Roger Ward; *Museum Dir* Andrea Norris, PhD; *Asst Prof* William Samonides, PhD; *Asst Prof* John Pultz, PhD; *Asst Prof* Patricia Darish, PhD
Estab 1866, dept estab 1953; pub; D & E; scholarships; LC 30, GC 10; enrl D 900, E 40, maj 50, grad 70
Ent Req: HS dipl
Degrees: BA, BFA, BGS, MA, PhD
Tuition: Res—undergrad $63 per hr, grad $94 per hr; nonres—undergrad $265, grad $309
Courses: Art History, Photography, African Art, American Art, Chinese Art, Japanese Art, Western Europen Art
Summer School: Enrl 80. Intro courses—Art History, Asian Art History & Modern Art History. Classes in Great Britain & Rome
—Dept of Art & Music Education & Music Therapy, 311 Bailey Hall, 66045. Tel 913-864-4784; FAX 913-864-5076; *Chmn Dept* Joe Zeller; *Asst Prof* Denise Stone, PhD; *Asst Prof* Patricia Villanueve; *Asst Prof* Elizabeth Kowalchek
Estab 1865, dept estab 1969; pub; D & E; scholarships; GC 12; enrl D 535, maj 123, grad 123, others 289
Ent Req: HS dipl, ent exam
Degrees: BAE 5 yrs, MA 1-6 yrs, PhD 3-6 yrs
Tuition: Res—undergrad $899 per sem, $74 per cr hr, grad $1088 per sem, $86 per cr hr; nonres—undergrad $2985 per sem, $213 per cr hr, grad $3198 per sem, $227 per cr hr
Courses: Visual Arts Education
Summer School: Term of 8 wks beginning June

LEAVENWORTH

SAINT MARY COLLEGE, Art Program, 4100 S Forth St Trafficway, 66048-5082. Tel 913-682-5151; FAX 913-758-6140; *Prog Dir* Susan Nelson, MFA; *Asst Prof* Jason Burrell, MFA
Estab 1923; pvt; D & E; scholarships; SC 25, LC 5; enrl non-maj 80, maj 10
Ent Req: HS dipl
Degrees: BA, BS 4 yr
Tuition: Res—$6975 per sem
Courses: Advertising Design, Art Appreciation, Art Education, Art History, Ceramics, Commercial Art, Design, Drawing, Graphic Design, Illustration, Painting, Photography, Printmaking, Computer Graphics
Summer School: Dir, Susan Nelson. Enrl 10-15 per class; tuition $325 per cr hr for 3 wk workshops. Courses—Basic Photography, Ceramics, Drawing

LIBERAL

SEWARD COUNTY COMMUNITY COLLEGE, Art Dept, 1801 N Kansas, PO Box 1137, 67905. Tel 316-624-1951; FAX 316-629-2691; *Chmn Humanities* John Loucks
Estab 1969; pub; D & E; scholarships; SC 23, LC 5; enrl D 650, E 900
Ent Req: HS dipl
Degrees: AA 2 yrs
Tuition: Res—$25 per cr hr; nonres—$68 per cr hr
Courses: Art Education, Art History, Ceramics, Costume Design & Construction, Drawing, History of Art & Archaeology, Painting, Photography, Sculpture, Stage Design
Summer School: Dir, Jon Ulm. Term of 6 wks beginning June 1. Courses varied & subject to change

LINDSBORG

BETHANY COLLEGE, Art Dept, 421 N First St, 67456. Tel 913-227-3311, Ext 145 & 147; FAX 913-227-2860; *Head Art Dept* Caroline Kahler, MA; *Prof* Mary Kay, MFA; *Asst Prof* Frank Shaw, MFA; *Asst Prof* Jennifer Torres, MFA
Den; D; scholarships; SC 19, LC 3; enrl D 195, non-maj 200, maj 40
Ent Req: HS dipl
Degrees: BA 3-4 yr
Courses: Art Appreciation, †Art Education, Art History, †Ceramics, Design, †Drawing, Jewelry, †Occupational Therapy, †Painting, †Photography, Printmaking, †Sculpture, Silversmithing, †Teacher Training, Theatre Arts, Art Therapy, Studio Concentration
Summer School: Acad Dean, Amanda Golbeck

MANHATTAN

KANSAS STATE UNIVERSITY
—Art Dept, 322 Willard Hall, 66506. Tel 913-532-6605; *Head Dept* Anna Holcomb; *Prof* Yoshiro Ikedo, MFA; *Emeritus Prof* Oscar V Larmer, MFA; *Prof* Elliott Pujol, MFA; *Assoc Prof* Rex Replogle, MFA; *Emeritus Assoc Prof* John Vogt, MFA; *Assoc Prof* Gary Woodward, MFA; *Assoc Prof* Lou Ann Culley, PhD; *Assoc Prof* James C Munce; *Assoc Prof* Duane Noblett, MFA; *Assoc Prof* Margo Kren, MFA. Instrs: FT 23, PT 3, 13 Area Coordrs
Estab 1863, dept estab 1965; pub; D & E; scholarships & fels; SC 45, LC 19, GC 7; enrl D 1940, E 60, non-maj 1800, maj 200, grad 15
Ent Req: HS dipl
Degrees: BS(Art Educ) jointly with Col Educ, BA & BFA 4 yrs, MFA 60 sem cr
Tuition: Res—undergrad $775 per sem, grad $800 per sem; nonres—undergrad $2200 per sem; grad $2015 per sem; campus res available, out-of-state tuition waived plus reduction of fees with GRA & GTA appointments
Courses: Advertising Design, Aesthetics, †Art Education, †Art History, †Ceramics, Design, Drawing, Graphic Arts, †Graphic Design, Illustration, †Jewelry, Lettering, †Painting, Printmaking, †Sculpture, †Teacher Training, Weaving, Fibers, Pre-Art Therapy
Summer School: Dir, Anna Holcomb. Enrl 150; tuition res $37 per cr hr, nonres $118 per cr hr for term of 4 to 8 wks beginning June. Courses—most of above, varies from summer to summer
—College of Architecture & Design, Seaton Hall, 66506. Tel 913-532-5950; FAX 913-532-6722; *Dean* Dennis Law; *Assoc Dean* Ray Weisenburger. Instrs: FT 53
Estab 1904; enrl 800
Degrees: BA, MA(Archit, Regional Planning & Interior Archit)
Tuition: Res—$1042.55 per sem; nonres—$3774.55 per sem
Courses: Architecture, Art History, Landscape Architecture, Architectural Programming, Building Construction, Landscape Design
Adult Hobby Classes: Dean, Lane L Marshall. Courses—Graphic Delineation, Preservation
Children's Classes: Courses—Special Design Program in June
Summer School: Dean, Lane L Marshall. 8 wks from June 4. Courses—Design Discovery Program, Design Studio

MCPHERSON

MCPHERSON COLLEGE, Art Dept, 1600 E Euclid, PO Box 1402, 67460. Tel 316-241-0731, Ext 234; *Chmn* Wayne Conyers; *Asst Prof* Christin Caskey
Estab 1887; den; D & E; scholarships; SC 14, LC 5; enrl D 150, maj 10, others 140
Ent Req: HS dipl, ACT
Degrees: AB 4 yr
Tuition: Res & nonres—undergrad $3975 per sem
Courses: †Art Education, Art History, Ceramics, Drawing, †Interior Design, Lettering, Museum Staff Training, Painting, Printmaking, Teacher Training, Textile Design
Adult Hobby Classes: Offered in summer
Children's Classes: Offered in summer
Summer School: Dir, Dr Constance Nichols. Term of 10 wks beginning end of May. Courses—Varied Liberal Arts

NORTH NEWTON

BETHEL COLLEGE, Dept of Art, 67117. Tel 316-283-5223; FAX 316-284-5286; *Chmn* Merrill Kraball; *Assoc Prof* Gail Lutsch, MFA
Estab 1888, dept estab 1959; den; D; scholarships; SC 11, LC 3; enrl D 240, non-maj 215, maj 25
Ent Req: HS, ACT
Degrees: BA(Art) 4 yrs
Tuition: $4270 per sem; campus res—room & board $1790 per sem
Courses: Art Education, Art History, Ceramics, Drawing, Graphic Arts, Graphic Design, Painting, Photography, Printmaking, Sculpture, Crafts
Adult Hobby Classes: Enrl 15; tuition $40 per 6 wk session. Courses—Ceramics, Drawing, Painting
Summer School: Courses—Drawing, Painting

OTTAWA

OTTAWA UNIVERSITY, Dept of Art, 1001 S Cedar St, 66067-3399. Tel 913-242-5200; FAX 913-242-7429; *Chmn* Frank J Lemp. Instrs: FT 1
Estab 1865; pvt; D; scholarships; SC 16, LC 5; enrl D 35, maj 5
Ent Req: HS grad, SAT, ACT
Degrees: BA 4 yrs
Courses: Art Education, Art History, Ceramics, Drawing, Graphic Arts, Painting, Photography, Arts Management
Children's Classes: Enrl 15. Courses—Art Foundation, Ceramics
Summer School: Dir, Dr Ed Morrissey. Tuition $89 per cr hr for 8 wk session. Courses—Life Drawing, Painting

OVERLAND PARK

JOHNSON COUNTY COMMUNITY COLLEGE, Visual Arts Program, 12345 College Blvd, 66210. Tel 913-469-3690; FAX 913-469-4409; *Dir* George Thompson; *Instr* Stuart Beals, BA; *Instr* Ron Hicks, MS; *Instr* John Larry Thomas; *Instr* Thomas Tarnowski, MFA; *Instr* Zigmunds Priede, MFA; *Dir Art Gallery* Bruce Hartman, MFA
Estab 1969; pub; D & E; scholarships; SC 30, LC 4; enrl D 200, E 100
Ent Req: HS dipl or equivalent
Degrees: AA 2 yr
Tuition: Res—$34 per sem cr hr; nonres—$100 per sem cr hr; no campus res
Courses: Art Education, Art History, Ceramics, Commercial Art, Drawing, Illustration, Lettering, Painting, Photography, Printmaking, Sculpture, Silversmithing, Layout, Life Drawing, Preparation of Portfolio, Silkscreen, 2-D &

3-D Design, Weaving, Visual Communications, Visual Technology
Adult Hobby Classes: All fine arts areas
Children's Classes: Accelerated fine arts for gifted children ·
Summer School: Dir, Dr Landon Kirchner. Enrl 95; tuition $25.50 per cr hr for term of 8 wks beginning June 5. Courses—Ceramics, Design, Drawing, Painting, Photogrpahy, Sculpture, Silversmithing

PITTSBURG

PITTSBURG STATE UNIVERSITY, Art Dept, 1701 S Broadway St, 66762-7512. Tel 316-235-4302; FAX 316-232-7515; *Chairperson* Larrie J Moody, PhD; *Prof* Alex Barde, MFA; *Prof* Robert P Russell, MFA; *Prof* Marjorie K Schick, MFA; *Assoc Prof* Malcolm E Kucharski, MFA; *Asst Prof* Dena L Hawes, MFA; *Asst Prof* Dennis Raverty, PhD; *Asst Prof* Barbara Parker-Bell, MA
Estab 1903, dept estab 1921; pub; D & E; scholarships; SC 50, LC 24, GC 22; enrl D 600, E 50, non-maj 300, maj 90, grad 30
Ent Req: HS dipl
Degrees: BFA & BSed 4 yr, MA 36 hr
Tuition: Res—undergrad $938 & grad $1090 per sem, $68 per sem hr; nonres—undergrad $2988 & grad $2834 per sem, undergrad $205 per sem hr, grad $238 per sem hr, Campus res—room & board available
Courses: †Art Education, Ceramics, Commercial Art, Design, Drawing, Jewelry, Painting, Photography, Printmaking, Sculpture, Teacher Training, Weaving, †Art Therapy, Crafts
Adult Hobby Classes: Enrl 20; Courses—Printing
Children's Classes: Enrl 40; tuition varies for 6 wk term
Summer School: Dir, Larrie J Moody. Enrl 200; tuition res—undergrad $66 per cr hr; grad $90 per cr hr; nonres—undergrad $199 per cr hr, grad $231 per cr hr, for term of 8 wks beginning June 5th. Courses—Art Education, Ceramics, Crafts, Drawing, Painting, Printmaking

PRATT

PRATT COMMUNITY COLLEGE, Art Dept, 348 NE SR 61, 67124. Tel 316-672-5641; Ext 228; FAX 316-672-5288; 800-794-3091, Ext 228. *Chmn* Gene Wineland, MFA
D & E; scholarships; SC 12, LC 1
Ent Req: HS dipl
Degrees: AA and AS
Tuition: Res—$39 per cr hr; nonres—$68 per cr hr
Courses: Art Appreciation, Ceramics, Design, Drawing, Graphic Design, Illustration, Painting, Photography, Printmaking, Elementary School Arts, Introduction to Art
Adult Hobby Classes: Enrl 6-12 per class; tuition $39 per cr hr. Courses—Ceramics, Drawing, Painting
Summer School: Graphic Design, Illustration, Introduction to Art

SALINA

KANSAS WESLEYAN UNIVERSITY, Art Dept, 100 E Claflin, 67401. Tel 913-827-5541; FAX 913-827-0927; *Chmn* Dr Jack Faver
Estab 1886; den; scholarships; SC 8, LC 3; enrl maj 15, others 500 for two sem
Degrees: AB 4 yr
Courses: †Art Education, Art History, †Advertising Art, †Arts Management, †Art Studio
Summer School: Enrl 125; for term of 8 wks beginning June

STERLING

STERLING COLLEGE, Art Dept, Eighth & Washington, PO Box 98, 67579. Tel 316-278-2173; *Chmn* George William Forst
Estab 1876; den; D & E; scholarships; SC 16, LC 2; enrl D 410
Ent Req: HS dipl
Degrees: AB & BS
Tuition: $4798 per sem
Courses: Ceramics, Costume Design & Construction, Drawing, Graphic Arts, Graphic Design, Painting, Fibers, 2-D Color Design, 3-D Design
Adult Hobby Classes: Enrl 25; tuition $20. Courses—all areas
Children's Classes: Art Education

TOPEKA

WASHBURN UNIVERSITY OF TOPEKA, Dept of Art & Theatre Arts, 1700 SW College, 66621. Tel 913-231-1010; FAX 913-231-1089; *Art & Theatre Arts Chmn* John Hunter. Instrs: FT 4, PT 5
Estab 1900; pub; SC 11, LC 5; enrl maj 60, others 280
Ent Req: HS dipl
Degrees: AB and BFA 4 yr
Tuition: Res—$90 per cr hr; nonres—$171 per cr hr
Courses: Art Appreciation, Art History, Ceramics, Design, Drawing, Painting, Photography, Printmaking, Sculpture, Computers, Computer Graphic Design, Etching, Lithography, Silkscreen
Children's Classes: Tuition $35 for ten 1 1/2 hr sessions

WICHITA

FRIENDS UNIVERSITY, Art Dept, 2100 University Ave, 67213. Tel 316-261-5800; FAX 316-263-1092; *Chmn* Ted Krone
Estab 1898; den; D & E; scholarships; SC 18, LC 4; enrl D 329, E 37
Ent Req: HS dipl
Degrees: MA 6 yrs, BA & BS 4 yrs
Tuition: $4258 per sem, $284 per cr hr; campus res—room & board $1140-$1386 per sem

Courses: †Art Education, Photography, Printmaking, Sculpture, Silversmithing, Teacher Training, †Computer Graphics, †Fine Arts 2 & 3-D
Adult Hobby Classes: Courses—Drawing, Jewelry, Painting
Summer School: Courses of 6 wks beginning June 5th

WICHITA CENTER FOR THE ARTS, 9112 E Central, 67206. Tel 316-634-2787; FAX 316-634-0593; *Exec Dir* Sally Luallen; *Dir Educ & Exhib* Betty Roberts; *Dir Performing Arts* Charlotte Sanderson. Instrs: 35
Estab 1920; pvt; D & E; scholarships; enrl 300
Tuition: $45 - $180 per class
Courses: Art Education, Art History, Ceramics, Drawing, Mixed Media, Painting, Photography, Printmaking, Sculpture, Teacher Training, Enameling, Pottery, 3-D Design, Weaving
Adult Hobby Classes: Enrl 150; tuition $40 for 6 wk term. Courses—Performing Arts, 2-D & 3-D Design
Children's Classes: Enrl 150; tuition $40. Courses—Performing Arts, 2-D & 3-D Design
Summer School: Dir, Glenice L Matthews. Enrl 300; tuition $45-$55 for 6 wk term. Courses—same as regular sessions

WICHITA STATE UNIVERSITY, School of Art & Design, College of Fine Arts, 67208. Tel 316-978-3555; *Chmn* Donald Byrum; *Graduate Coordr* Ronald Christ
Estab 1895, dept estab 1901; pub; D & E; scholarships; enrl D 1149, E 194, non-maj 78, maj 285, grad 51, others 2
Ent Req: HS dipl
Degrees: BAE, BA & BFA 4 yr, MFA 2 yr, MA 1 yr
Tuition: Res—undergrad $79.30 per cr hr, grad $109.05 per cr hr; nonres—undergrad $276.05 per cr hr, grad $320.05 per cr hr
Courses: †Art Education, †Art History, †Ceramics, Drawing, †Graphic Design, Illustration, Lettering, †Painting, Photography, †Printmaking, †Sculpture, Teacher Training
Summer School: Tuition as above for term of 8 wks

WINFIELD

SOUTHWESTERN COLLEGE, Art Dept, 100 College St, 67156. Tel 316-221-4150, Ext 270; *Prof* Michael Wilder, PhD
Estab 1885; pvt & den; D & E; scholarships; SC 12, LC 4
Ent Req: HS dipl
Degrees: BA 4 yr
Tuition: $4280 per 16 hrs
Courses: Art Education
Adult Hobby Classes: Design, History of Art, Life Drawing, Painting
Summer School: Dir, Rick L Peters. Enrl 15-20; term May 27-June 20. Courses—Art History, Design, Drawing, Painting, Sculpture

KENTUCKY

BARBOURVILLE

UNION COLLEGE, Art Dept, 310 College St, 40906. Tel 606-546-4151; FAX 606-546-2215; *Dept Head* Dr Betty Stroud
Den; D & E
Ent Req: HS dipl
Degrees: BA, BS and MA (Educ) 4 yr
Tuition: $3900 per sem
Courses: Art Education, Art History, Drawing, Painting, Teacher Training, Theatre Arts, Art Appreciation, Art Fundamentals, Recreational Arts and Crafts

BEREA

BEREA COLLEGE, Art Dept, 40404. Tel 606-986-9341, Ext 5530; *Chmn* Robert Boyce, PhD; *Prof* Neil DiTeresa, MA; *Prof* Walter Hyleck, MFA; *Assoc Prof* William Morningstar, MFA; *Assoc Prof* Jeannine Anderson, MFA; *Asst Prof* Christopher Pierce, MFA; *Asst Prof* Jeanette Klein
Estab 1855, dept estab 1936; pvt; D; scholarships; SC 14, LC 8; enrl C 1500, D 324, maj 71
Ent Req: HS dipl (preference given to students from Southern Appalachian region)
Degrees: BA 4 yr
Tuition: None; campus res—room and board $1812
Courses: Art Appreciation, †Art Education, †Art History, †Ceramics, Design, †Drawing, †Painting, Photography, †Printmaking, †Sculpture, †Textile Design, Weaving

BOWLING GREEN

WESTERN KENTUCKY UNIVERSITY, Art Dept, Ivan Wilson Ctr for Fine Arts, Room 441, 42101. Tel 502-745-3944; *Chmn* Leo Fernandez. Instrs: FT 10, PT 5
Pub; D; SC 49, LC 21; enrl maj 187
Ent Req: HS dipl
Degrees: BA & BFA 4 yrs, MA(Art Educ)
Tuition: $950 per sem; nonres—$2480.50
Courses: †Art Education, Art History, †Ceramics, Drawing, Graphic Design, †Painting, Photography, †Printmaking, †Sculpture, Design, †Weaving
Summer School: Dir, Leo Fernandez. Enrl 100; tuition res $61 per cr hr, nonres $172 per cr hr. Courses—Lecture & Studio Art Courses

CAMPBELLSVILLE

CAMPBELLSVILLE COLLEGE, Fine Arts Division, One University Dr, 42718. Tel 502-465-8158, Ext 6268; *Div Head* Robert Gaddis; *Asst Prof* Tommy Clark; *Asst Prof* Linda Cundiff; *Instr* Russell Mobley; *Instr* Dr Wesley Roberts; *Instr* Dr Jim Moore; *Instr* Nevalyn Moore; *Instr* Dr Kenneth Martin; *Instr* Dr Mark Bradley
Estab 1906, dept estab 1967; den; D & E; scholarships; SC 26, LC 5; enrl D 35, E 10, non-maj 12, maj 22, others 8 minors
Ent Req: HS dipl, ACT
Degrees: BA, BS, BM & BChM 4 yr, AA, AS & ASSW 2 yr
Tuition: $3030 per sem
Courses: Art Appreciation, Art Education, Art History, Ceramics, Collages, Commercial Art, Constructions, Design, Drawing, Graphic Design, Jewelry, Lettering, Painting, Photography, Printmaking, Sculpture, Stage Design, Teacher Training, Theatre Arts, Elementary School Art, Secondary School Art
Adult Hobby Classes: Enrl 15; tuition $50 per audit hr. Courses—Understanding Art, courses above as auditors
Summer School: Term of 8 wks. Courses—Art Appreciation, Art Education, Drawing, Painting

CRESTVIEW HILLS

THOMAS MORE COLLEGE, Art Dept, 333 Thomas More Pky, 41017. Tel 606-341-5800, Ext 3420; FAX 606-344-3345; *Chmn* Rebecca Bilbo; *Assoc Prof* Barbara Rauf, MFA
Estab 1921; pvt; D & E; SC 12, LC 4; enrl D 12, E 5, maj 17
Ent Req: HS dipl
Degrees: BA, BES, BS, AA & AES
Tuition: $247 per cr hr 1-7 hrs, $278 per cr hr 8-11 hrs
Courses: Aesthetics, Art Education, Art History, Ceramics, Design, Drawing, Painting, Photography, Printmaking, Sculpture, Teacher Training, Theatre Arts, Arts Management, Figure Drawing, Anatomy, Perspective, Color
Summer School: Dir, Dr Raymond Hebert. Courses—various

GEORGETOWN

GEORGETOWN COLLEGE, Art Dept, 400 College St & Mulberry St, PO Box 201, 40324. Tel 502-863-8106; FAX 502-868-8888; *Chmn* Charles James McCormick. Instrs: FT 2
Estab 1829; den; D; scholarships & grants; SC 14, LC 6; enrl 1150
Ent Req: HS transcript, ACT
Degrees: BA 4 yrs
Tuition: Res—$1480 per term; nonres—$1525 per term; sem curriculum; May interterm
Courses: Art Appreciation, Art Education, Art History, Design, Drawing, Graphic Design, Illustration, Painting, Photography, Printmaking, Sculpture, Teacher Training, Electronic Imaging (computer)
Summer School: Two 4 1/2 wk sem 6-7 hrs each. Courses—Art Education, Art Humanities, Studio Classes

HIGHLAND HEIGHTS

NORTHERN KENTUCKY UNIVERSITY, Art Dept, 41099. Tel 606-572-5421; FAX 606-572-6501; *Chmn* Barbara Houghton. Instrs: FT 8, PT 12
Estab 1968; pub; D & E; scholarships; SC 31, LC 10
Ent Req: HS grad, ACT scores
Degrees: BA(Art Educ), BFA(Studio Art), BA(Graphic Design)
Tuition: Res—grad $94 per sem hr; nonres—undergrad $208 per sem hr; res—undergrad $76 per sem hr
Courses: Art Appreciation, †Art Education, Art History, Ceramics, Drawing, †Graphic Design, Painting, Photography, Printmaking, Sculpture
Adult Hobby Classes: Enrl 350; tuition $50-$100 for a period of 5-10 wks. Courses — Various Art & Crafts
Summer School: Dir, Howard Storm. Enrl 90; tuition $47 per sem hr for sessions. Courses — Art Appreciation, Drawing

LEXINGTON

TRANSYLVANIA UNIVERSITY, Studio Arts Dept, 300 N Broadway, 40508. Tel 606-233-8246, 233-8115; *Prog Dir* Dan S Selter, MFA; *Prof* Jack Girard, MFA; *Assoc Prof* Florence Thorne, MFA; *Instr* Nancy Wolsk, MA
Estab 1780; pvt; D & E; scholarships; SC 20, LC 3; enrl D 105, E 14, maj 18
Ent Req: HS dipl
Degrees: BA
Tuition: $15,000
Courses: Art Appreciation, Art Education, Art History, Ceramics, Collages, Costume Design & Construction, Design, Drawing, Film, Graphic Arts, Mixed Media, Painting, Photography, Sculpture, Stage Design, Teacher Training, Theatre Arts
Adult Hobby Classes: Enrl 5 - 10; tuition $40-$80 per 3-5 wk sessions
Children's Classes: Enrl 5-10; tuition $40-$60 per 3-5 wk sessions
Summer School: Dir, Jack Girard. Enrl 5-20; tuition $650 per course. Courses—Black & White Photographics, Ceramics, Painting, Survey

UNIVERSITY OF KENTUCKY, Dept of Art, College of Fine Arts, 207 Fine Arts Bldg, 40506-0022. Tel 606-257-8151; FAX 606-257-3042; *Chmn* Jack Gron; *Dean* Rhoda-Gale Pollack. Instrs: FT 20, PT 20
Estab 1918; pub; scholarships and grad assistantships; SC 23, LC 19, GC 6; enrl maj 200, others 1500
Degrees: BA, BFA, MA & MFA 3 yr
Tuition: Res—undergrad $1297, grad $1407 per sem; nonres—undergrad $3557, grad $3887 per sem, Pt res—undergrad $101 per cr hr,—grad $144 per cr hr, nonres—undergrad $289 per cr hr—grad $420 per cr hr
Courses: †Art Education, †Art History, Ceramics, Drawing, Graphic Design,

Painting, Photography, Printmaking, Sculpture, Film, Video, †Studio Art, Fibers
Children's Classes: Saturday classes for children
Summer School: Dir, Robert James Foose. Tuition res—$70 per cr hr, nonres—$210 per cr hr. Courses—varied

LOUISVILLE

JEFFERSON COMMUNITY COLLEGE, Fine Arts, 109 E Broadway, 40202. Tel 502-584-0181, Ext 2289; *Coordr Fine Arts* Wes Lites; *Asst Prof* J Barry Motes. Instrs: PT 6
Estab 1968; pub; D & E; scholarships; SC 11, LC 6; enrl D 4774, E 4172
Ent Req: HS dipl
Degrees: AA & Assoc in Photography 2 yrs
Tuition: $350 per sem
Courses: †Advertising Design, Aesthetics, Art Education, Art History, †Commercial Art, Display, Drawing, Graphic Arts, Graphic Design, Mixed Media, Painting, †Photography, Sculpture, †Theatre Arts
Summer School: Dean, Dr Pat Ecker. Tuition $30 per cr hr. Courses—Art Appreciation, Drawing, Photography

UNIVERSITY OF LOUISVILLE, Allen R Hite Art Institute, Department of Fine Arts, Belknap Campus, 40292. Tel 502-852-6794; *Chmn* James T Grubola, MFA; *Prof* Henry J Chodkowski, MFA. Instrs: FT 21, PT 18
Estab 1846, dept estab 1935; pub; D & E; scholarships; SC 35, LC 71, GC 26; enrl D 1000, E 90, non-maj 800, maj 400, grad 29
Ent Req: HS dipl, CEEB
Degrees: MA 1 to 2 yrs, PhD 3 yrs, BA & BS 4 yrs, BFA 5 yrs
Tuition: Res—$99 per hr, nonres—$280.50 per hr
Courses: Advertising Design, Aesthetics, Architecture, Art Appreciation, †Art Education, †Art History, Calligraphy, Ceramics, Collages, Conceptual Art, Constructions, Design, Drafting, Drawing, Graphic Arts, Graphic Design, Handicrafts, History of Art & Archaeology, †Interior Design, Lettering, Mixed Media, Museum Staff Training, Painting, Photography, Printmaking, Sculpture, Teacher Training, Weaving, †Fiber
Summer School: Dir, James T Grubola. Enrl 100 for May-June & June-Aug. Courses—Various Art & Art History Classes

MIDWAY

MIDWAY COLLEGE, Art Dept, 512 E Stephens St, 40347-1120. Tel 606-846-4421, Ext 5809; FAX 606-846-5349; *Instr* Kate Davis-Rosenbaum; *Instr* Wayne Gebb; *Instr* Steve Davis-Rosenbaum. Instrs: FT 2
Den, W; D; scholarships; SC 7, LC 3; enrl 55
Ent Req: HS dipl, ACT
Degrees: 2 yr
Tuition: $3650 per sem
Courses: Art Education, Ceramics, Drawing, Painting, Sculpture, Textile Design, Basic Design, Historical Furniture, Art in the Child's World

MOREHEAD

MOREHEAD STATE UNIVERSITY, Art Dept, Claypool-Young Art Bldg 211, 40351. Tel 606-783-2221, 783-2193; *Chmn* Robert Franzini
Estab 1922; pub; D & E; scholarships; SC 40, LC 16, GC 28; enrl D 900, E 20, non-maj 800, maj 180, GS 55, others 145
Ent Req: HS dipl, ACT
Degrees: BA 4 yr, MA 1 yr
Tuition: Res—undergrad $760 per sem, grad $830 per sem; nonres—undergrad $2100 per sem, grad $2310 per sem
Courses: Advertising Design, Art Education, Ceramics, Commercial Art, Conceptual Art, Drawing, Graphic Design, Illustration, Mixed Media, Painting, Photography, Printmaking, Sculpture, Textile Design, Video, Computer Art
Adult Hobby Classes: Courses—Ceramics, Crafts, Oil Painting, Watercolor Painting, Weaving
Summer School: Dir, T Sternal. Enrl 600; 2-4 wk sessions. Courses—Wide Variety

MURRAY

MURRAY STATE UNIVERSITY, Dept of Art, College of Fine Arts and Communication, PO Box 9, 42071-0009. Tel 502-762-3784; FAX 502-762-3920; *Chmn* Richard Dougherty; *Prof* Karen W Boyd, MFA; *Prof* Fred Shepard, MFA; *Prof* Robert W Head, MFA; *Prof* Dale Leys, MFA; *Prof* Paul Sasso, MFA; *Prof* Jerry Speight, MFA; *Assoc Prof* Michael Johnson, MFA; *Assoc Prof* Camille Douglas, PhD; *Assoc Prof* Steve Bishop, MFA; *Asst Prof* Peggy Schrock, PhD; *Asst Prof* Susan Dixon, PhD; *Asst Prof* Harvey Arche, MFA; *Asst Prof* Andrew Gillham, MFA; *Gallery Dir* Albert Sperath
Estab 1925, dept estab 1931; pub; D & E; scholarships; SC 117, LC 15, GS 48; enrl non-maj 475, maj 200, grad 13
Ent Req: HS dipl, ACT, portfolio required for grad students
Degrees: BA, BS & BFA 4 yr, MA(Studio) 1 1/2 - 2 yrs
Tuition: Res—undergrad $1600 per yr, $800 per sem, $60 per hr, grad $1740 per yr, $870 per sem, $89 per hr; nonres—udergrad $4280 per yr, $2140 per sem, $173 per cr hr, grad $4700 per yr, $2350 per sem, $252 per hr; campus res—room & board $1170 per yr
Courses: Art Appreciation, Art Education, Art History, Ceramics, Drawing, Graphic Design, History of Art & Archaeology, Jewelry, †Painting, †Photography, †Printmaking, †Sculpture, Silversmithing, Teacher Training, Textile Design, †Weaving, Surface Design, Wood Design
Children's Classes: Summer art workshops for HS students
Summer School: Dir, Dale Leys. Enrl 40-80; tuition res—undergrad $67 per hr, grad $99 per hr; nonres—undergrad $193 per hr, grad $282 per hr for short sessions of 5 wk 7 1/2 wk or 10 wk terms

OWENSBORO

BRESCIA COLLEGE, Dept of Art, 717 Frederica St, 42301. Tel 502-685-3131; FAX 502-686-4266; *Chmn* Sr Mary Diane Taylor. Instrs: FT 4
Estab 1950; den; D & E; scholarships; SC 47, LC 10; enrl 960, maj 30
Ent Req: HS dipl, placement exam, ACT, GED
Degrees: AA(Photograph) 2 yr, BA in art & art education 4 yr
Tuition: $225 per cr hr
Courses: Art Education, Art History, Calligraphy, †Ceramics, Drawing, †Graphic Design, Painting, Printmaking, †Black & White Photography, †Color Photography, 2-D & 3-D Design, Museology
Adult Hobby Classes: Tuition $110 per cr hr, sr citizens free. All regular courses offered
Summer School: Dir, Sr Mary Diane Taylor. Tuition $110 per cr hr for 6 wk term. Courses according to demand

KENTUCKY WESLEYAN COLLEGE, Dept Art, 3000 Frederica St, 42302. Tel 502-926-3111, Ext 250; FAX 502-926-3196; *Chmn* William Kolok, MFA
Dept estab 1950; den; scholarships; SC 11, LC 4; enrl maj 40
Degrees: BA 4 yr
Tuition: Res—$8000 per yr, $250 per cr hr
Courses: Design, Painting, Arts & Crafts
Summer School: Enrl 60. Courses—Art for the Elementary Schools, Art Survey

PIKEVILLE

PIKEVILLE COLLEGE, Humanities Division, 214 Sycamore St, 41501. Tel 606-432-9200; FAX 606-432-9238; *Chmn* Dr Brigitte LaTrespo; *Gallery Dir* Janice Ford
Estab 1889; pvt den; D & E; SC 16, LC 5
Ent Req: SAT, ACT
Degrees: BA & BS 4 yrs
Tuition: $2825 annual tuition
Courses: †Art Education, Art History, Ceramics, Drawing, History of Art & Archaeology, Painting, Printmaking, Sculpture, †Teacher Training
Summer School: Courses—vary

PIPPA PASSES

ALICE LLOYD COLLEGE, Art Dept, 100 Purpose Rd, 41844. Tel 606-368-2101, Ext 5606; FAX 606-368-2125; *Instr* Mike Ware. Instrs: FT 1
Estab 1922; pvt; D & E; scholarships; SC 6, LC 1
Ent Req: HS dipl, ent exam
Degrees: BS & BA 4 yrs
Tuition: $3800 per yr; no tuition for 76 mountain counties
Courses: Art Appreciation, †Art for Elementary Education, Art History Survey No 2, Pottery
Children's Classes: Enrl 10-20; tuition free. Courses—Drawing, Painting, Sculpture

RICHMOND

EASTERN KENTUCKY UNIVERSITY, Art Dept, Campbell 309, 40475. Tel 606-622-1629; FAX 606-622-1020; Elec Mail arthale@acs.eku.edu. *Chmn* Dr Gil R Smith
Estab 1910; pub; D; SC 30, LC 6, GC 6
Ent Req: HS grad
Degrees: BA, BFA & MA(Educ) 4 yrs
Tuition: Res—$626 per yr; nonres—$1780 per yr
Courses: Art Appreciation, Art History, †Ceramics, †Design, Drawing, †Painting, †Sculpture, †Metals
Adult Hobby Classes: Non-credit courses offered
Summer School: Chmn, E Carroll Hale. Tuition same as regular sem

WILLIAMSBURG

CUMBERLAND COLLEGE, Dept of Art, 7523 College Station Dr, 40769-1386. Tel 606-549-2200, Ext 4265 & 4416; FAX 606-539-4490; *Chmn* Kenneth R Weedman
Estab 1889; den; D & E; scholarships; SC 20, LC 10; enrl D 1614, E 60, maj 30
Ent Req: HS dipl, ACT test
Degrees: BA and BS 4 yr
Tuition: $3549 per sem
Courses: Aesthetics, Art Appreciation, Art Education, Art History, Design, Drawing, Film, Painting, Printmaking, Sculpture, Stage Design, Teacher Training, Theatre Arts, Video, Computer Imaging

WILMORE

ASBURY COLLEGE, Art Dept, One Macklem Dr, 40390. Tel 606-858-3511, Ext 239; FAX 606-858-3921; *Art Dept Head* Rudy Medlock; *Div Head Music & Art* Dr Ronald W Holz; *Instr* Clifford Davis. Instrs: FT 13
Estab 1892; pvt; D & E; scholarships; SC 30, LC 6; enrl D 1150, maj 65, others 250
Ent Req: HS dipl
Degrees: AB & BS 4 yr
Tuition: $12,000 per yr incl tuition, room & board
Courses: Aesthetics, †Art Education, Art History, Ceramics, Drawing, Graphic Design, Handicrafts, Lettering, †Mixed Media, †Painting, †Photography, †Printmaking, †Sculpture, Teacher Training, Batik, †Weaving
Summer School: Dir, Rudy Medlock. Enrl 8 - 12; tuition $650.50 for term June 9 - July 9. Courses—Art Appreciation, Ceramics, Drawing, Painting, Stained Glass

LOUISIANA

ALEXANDRIA

LOUISIANA STATE UNIVERSITY AT ALEXANDRIA, Dept of Fine Arts & Design, Student Ctr, Hwy 71 S, 71302. Tel 318-473-6449; *Prof Art* Roy V deVille, MA
Estab 1960; pub; D; scholarships; enrl D 200, E 50, non-maj 300, maj 15
Ent Req: HS dipl, entrance exam, state exam & ACT
Degrees: Fine Arts Assoc 2-3 yr
Children's Classes: Enrl 50; tuition $189 per course. Courses—Painting, Pottery
Summer School: Enrl 150; tuition $120 per cr. Courses—Art Appreciation, Art History, Painting, Pottery

BATON ROUGE

LOUISIANA STATE UNIVERSITY, School of Art, 123 Art Bldg, 70803. Tel 504-388-5411; *Dir* Michael Daugherty, MFA; *Prof* Richard Cox, PhD; *Prof* Mark Zucker, PhD; *Prof* Patricia Lawrence, PhD; *Prof* Melody Guichet, MFA; *Prof* A J Meek, MFA; *Prof* Christopher Hentz, MFA; *Prof* Ed Pramuk, MA; *Prof* Robert Warrens, MFA; *Prof* Kimberly Arp, MFA; *Prof* Robert Hausey, MFA; *Prof* Gerald Bower, MFA; *Prof* Marchita Mauck, PhD; *Assoc Prof* Michael Book, MFA; *Asst Prof* Gregory Elliot, MFA; *Asst Prof* Paul Dean; *Asst Prof* Herb Goodman, MFA; *Asst* Larry Livaudais; *Asst* Rosa Sanchez; *Asst* Lynne Jodderell; *Asst* Susan Ryan; *Asst* Chris Siefert
Estab 1874, dept estab 1935; pub; D & E; scholarships
Ent Req: HS dipl, ACT scores
Degrees: BFA 4 yr, MFA 3
Tuition: Res—undergrad $1330, grad $1166 per sem; nonres—undergrad $2980 per sem, grad $2988 per sem
Courses: †Art History, †Ceramics, Drawing, †Graphic Design, †Painting, †Printmaking, †Sculpture
Summer School: Tuition res—$273, nonres—$653 for 8 wk course

SOUTHERN UNIVERSITY A & M COLLEGE, School of Architecture, Southern Branch, PO Box 11947, 70813. Tel 504-771-3015; FAX 504-771-4709; *Interim Dean* Mohommed Udein
Estab 1956; pub; D & E; scholarships; SC 14; enrl D 250, non-maj 7, maj 162
Ent Req: HS dipl
Degrees: BA 5 yrs
Tuition: Res—undergrad $1114 per sem, grad $1023 per sem
Courses: Architecture, Art Education
Summer School: Dir, E D Van Purnell. Term of 8 wks beginning June. Courses—Architectural Design, Construction Materials & Systems, Graphic Presentation, Structures

GRAMBLING

GRAMBLING STATE UNIVERSITY, Art Dept, PO Box 1184, 71245-3090. Tel 318-274-2274; *Chmn* Thomas O Smith
Tuition: Res—$1044 per sem; nonres—$2019 per sem
Courses: Art Appreciation, †Art Education, Art History, Ceramics, Design, Drawing, Handicrafts, Illustration, Painting, Printmaking, Sculpture, Teacher Training

HAMMOND

SOUTHEASTERN LOUISIANA UNIVERSITY, Dept of Visual Arts, SLU 765, 70402. Tel 504-549-2193; *Chmn* C Roy Blackwood, MFA; *Prof* Ronald Kennedy, MFA; *Assoc Prof* Barbara Tardo, MA; *Assoc Prof* Gail Hood, MFA; *Asst Prof* Dr Catherine Schieve; *Asst Prof* Gary Keown; *Asst Prof* Don Marshall; *Instr* David Gibson; *Instr* Lynda Katz, MFA; *Instr* Alexander Stolin; *Instr* Hasmig Vartanian
Estab 1925; pub; D & E; scholarships; SC 25, LC 4, GC 2; enrl D 109, E 75, maj 122
Ent Req: HS dipl, ACT
Degrees: BA(Educ), BA(Humanities), BA(Cultural Resource Management) 4 yrs
Tuition: $598 per 12 hr load
Courses: Art Education, Art History, Ceramics, Drawing, Painting, Photography, Printmaking, Sculpture, Teacher Training
Summer School: Dir, C Roy Blackwood. Enrl 150; 8 wk term. Courses—Art Education, Art Survey for Elementary Teachers

LAFAYETTE

UNIVERSITY OF SOUTHWESTERN LOUISIANA, College of the Arts, USL Box 43850, 70504. Tel 318-482-6224; FAX 318-482-5907; *Dean* Gordon Brooks. Instrs: FT 68, PT 7
Estab 1900; pub; scholarships; enrl univ 16,000
Degrees: BArchit & BFA 4-5 yrs
Tuition: $700 per sem
Courses: †Advertising Design, †Architecture, †Art Education, †Ceramics, †Photography, †Choreographic Design, †Fine Arts, †Interior Architecture
Adult Hobby Classes: Enrl 20-30; tuition $300
Children's Classes: Enrl 70; tuition $75 for 10 day sessions. Courses—Ceramics, Clays
Summer School: Dir, Gordon Brooks. Enrl 300; study aboard program in Paris, France & London, England. Courses—Ceramics, Computer Art, Design, Drawing, Film & Video Animation, Painting, Photography

LAKE CHARLES

MCNEESE STATE UNIVERSITY, Dept of Visual Arts, Ryan St, MSU Box 92295, 70609. Tel 318-475-5060; FAX 318-475-5927; *Chmn* Bill R Iles. Instrs: FT 9
Estab 1950, dept estab 1953; pub; D & E; scholarships; SC 24, LC 4, GC 1; enrl D 85, E 15, non-maj 215, maj 85
Ent Req: HS dipl
Degrees: BA (Art Educ) and BA (Studio Arts) 4 yrs
Tuition: $679 per sem
Courses: †Advertising Design, Art Appreciation, †Art Education, Art History, †Ceramics, †Drawing, Graphic Arts, Graphic Design, Mixed Media, †Painting, †Photography, †Printmaking, Survey crafts course
Adult Hobby Classes: Enrl 50; tuition $254 per sem (3 hrs). Courses—Art History & Ceramics
Summer School: Dir, Bill Iles. Enrl 100; tuition $254 per 3 hrs. Courses—Basic Design, Beginning Drawing, Ceramics, Printmaking, Photography

MONROE

NORTHEAST LOUISIANA UNIVERSITY, Dept of Art, 700 University Ave, Stubbs 141, 71209. Tel 318-342-1375, 342-5252; *Head Dept* Ronald J Alexander, MFA; *Instr* Brian Fassett; *Instr* Richard Hayes; *Instr* Dr Randy Miley; *Instr* Gary Ratcliff; *Instr* Robert Ward; *Instr* Cynthia Kee; *Instr* Susan Mingledorff; *Instr* James Norton; *Instr* Joni Noble; *Instr* Linda Ward
Estab 1931, dept estab 1956; pub; D & E; scholarships; SC 28, LC 4, GC 9; enrl non-maj 300, maj 125, GS 3
Ent Req: HS dipl
Degrees: BFA 4 yrs, MEd
Tuition: Res—$168 per unit
Courses: Advertising Design, Art Appreciation, Ceramics, Drawing, Painting, Photography, Printmaking, Sculpture, Analytical Perspective, Block Printing, Figure Drawing, Silkscreen, Survey Class, 3-D Design
Adult Hobby Classes: Enrl 20. May 31 - July 2. Courses—Art 411
Summer School: Dir, Ronald J Alexander. Enrl 30; tuition $168 from May 25 - July 3 & July 5 - Aug 11. Courses—Art Appreciation, Art Education, Drawing, Painting

NATCHITOCHES

NORTHWESTERN STATE UNIVERSITY OF LOUISIANA, Dept of Art, 71497. Tel 318-357-4476; FAX 318-357-5567; *Head Dept* Rivers Murphy, MFA; *Asst Prof* Nolan Bailey, MA
Estab 1885; pub; D & E; SC 67, LC 17, GC 36; enrl maj 93, grad 16
Degrees: BA & BS 4 yrs, MA 2 yrs, special prog for advanced students MA in Art
Tuition: Res—undergrad $1033.50; nonres—undergrad $2143.50
Courses: †Advertising Design, †Art Education, Art History, Ceramics, Commercial Art, Drawing, Painting, Printmaking, Sculpture, Fiber Arts, Professional Photography, Stained Glass, Stringed Instrument Construction
Adult Hobby Classes: Courses—most of above

NEW ORLEANS

DELGADO COLLEGE, Dept of Fine Arts, 615 City Park Ave, 70119. Tel 504-483-4511; FAX 504-483-4954; *Chmn Fine Arts* Lisette Copping
Dept estab 1967. College has 2 campuses; pub; D & E; scholarships; SC 12-20, LC 12-20; enrl D 150, E 65, maj 60
Ent Req: HS dipl, 18 yr old
Degrees: AA and AS 2 yrs
Tuition: Res—$558 per sem; nonres—$1338 per sem
Courses: Art Appreciation, Art History, Ceramics, Drawing, History of Art & Archaeology, Painting, Sculpture, Jewelry

LOYOLA UNIVERSITY OF NEW ORLEANS, Dept of Visual Arts, 6363 Saint Charles Ave, 70118. Tel 504-865-2011, 861-5456; FAX 504-861-5457; *Chmn* William M Grote
Den; D & E; scholarships; SC 9, LC 3; enrl D 150, E 45, maj 28
Ent Req: HS dipl, ent exam
Degrees: BSA 4 yrs
Tuition: $4785 per yr, 12 - 20 hrs
Courses: Art History, Ceramics, Design, Drawing, Painting, Photography, Printmaking, Sculpture, Teacher Training, Computer Graphics
Summer School: Chmn, John Sears. Enrl 40; term of 6 wks beginning in June. Courses—Drawing, Painting, Printmaking, Sculpture

SOUTHERN UNIVERSITY IN NEW ORLEANS, Fine Arts & Philosophy Dept, 6400 Press Dr, 70126. Tel 504-286-5000, 286-5267; FAX 504-286-5131; *Acting Chmn* Ron Bechet; *Prof* Sara Hollis, MA; *Prof* Eddie J Jordan, EdD; *Asst Prof* Gary Oaks, MFA; *Music* Roger Dickerson; *Music* Valeria King; *Humanities* Dr Elmore DeGrange
Estab 1951, dept estab 1960; pub; D & E; BA 4 yrs; enrl D 21, E 26, non-maj 700, maj 47
Ent Req: HS dipl
Degrees: BA 4 yrs, BS(Art Educ) 4 yrs, BS(Music Educ) 4 yrs
Tuition: Res—undergrad $831 per 12 cr hrs, grad $1713 per 12 cr hrs, $1200 per 9 cr hrs
Courses: Art Education, Art History, Ceramics, Commercial Art, Drawing, Painting, Photography, Printmaking, Sculpture, Video, African Art, African & American Art, Crafts
Adult Hobby Classes: Courses offered
Summer School: Courses offered

TULANE UNIVERSITY
—School of Architecture, 6823 Saint Charles Ave, 70118. Tel 504-865-5389; FAX 504-862-8798; *Dean* Donald Gatzke. Instrs: FT 24, PT 12
Estab 1907; pvt; enrl 320
Degrees: BA, MA(Archit)
Tuition: $9380 per sem
Courses: Design, Theory, Life Drawing, Structures, Technology, History, Computer Graphics, Frank Lloyd Wright's Architecture

—Sophie H Newcomb Memorial College, Woldenberg Art Ctr, 1229 Broadway, 70118. Tel 504-865-5327; FAX 504-862-8710; *Chmn* Jeremy Jernegan; *Prof* Arthur Okazaki; *Prof* Caecilia W Davis; *Prof* Arthur E Kern; *Prof* Elizabeth Boone; *Prof* Theresa Cole; *Assoc Prof* Gene H Koss; *Assoc Prof* Marilyn R Brown; *Asst Prof* Ronna Harris; *Asst Prof* Jeremy Jerenigan; *Asst Prof* Barry Bailey
Estab 1886; pvt; D & E; scholarships; SC 33, LC 25, GC 29; enrl D 817 per sem, E 37 per sem
Ent Req: HS dipl, CEEB, interview, review of work by chmn & or faculty (optional)
Degrees: BA, BFA, BA(Art Biology), MA, MFA
Tuition: $26,000 incl room & board per yr
Courses: Ceramics, Drawing, Painting, Photography, Printmaking, Sculpture, †Photography, †Printmaking, †Sculpture, American Art, Glass Blowing, Pre-Columbian Art
Adult Hobby Classes: Art History, Ceramics, Drawing, Glass, Painting, Photography, Printmaking, Sculpture
Children's Classes: Offered through the Dept of Educ
Summer School: Dean, Richard Marksbury. Courses—Art History, Ceramics, Drawing, Glass, Painting, Photography, Sculpture

UNIVERSITY OF NEW ORLEANS-LAKE FRONT, Dept of Fine Arts, 70148. Tel 504-280-6493; *Prof* Doyle J Gertjejansen, MFA; *Prof* Richard A Johnson, MFA; *Prof* Joseph Howard Jones, MFA; *Prof* Harold James Richard, MFA; *Prof* Marcia E Vetroco, PhD; *Assoc Prof* Thomas C Whitworth, MFA; *Assoc Prof* Annette E Fournet, MFA; *Assoc Prof* Cheryl A Hayes, MFA; *Asst Prof* Christopher Saucedo, MFA; *Asst* Lawrence Jenkins; *Asst Prog* Jeffrey Prente
Estab 1958, dept estab 1968; pub; D & E; SC 29, LC 24, GC 34; enrl D 16,000 (university), non-maj 3000, maj 150, grad 20
Ent Req: HS dipl
Degrees: BA 4 yrs, MFA 60 hrs
Tuition: Res—undergrad & grad $1181 per sem FT, nonres—undergrad $2577 per sem FT, grad $2577 per sem FT, res grad & undergrad $1396 9 cr hrs, campus res available
Courses: †Art History, Drawing, †Graphic Arts, Graphic Design, †Painting, †Photography, †Printmaking, †Sculpture
Adult Hobby Classes: Ceramics, Design, Drawing, Painting, Photography
Children's Classes: Design, Drawing, Painting, Sculpture
Summer School: Tuition $600 for term of 6 wks beginning June Courses—Art Fundamentals, Art History, Drawing, Graphic Design, Graphics, Painting, Photography, Sculpture

XAVIER UNIVERSITY OF LOUISIANA, Dept of Fine Arts, 7325 Palmetto St, 70125. Tel 504-483-7556; *Chmn* Charles E Graves; *Prof* John T Scott, MFA; *Assoc Prof* Absalon Jackson; *Asst Prof* Open
Estab 1926, dept estab 1935; den; D & E; scholarships; SC 48, LC 10; enrl D 50, E 12, non-maj 10, maj 52
Ent Req: HS dipl, SAT or ACT, health cert, C average at least
Degrees: BA, BA (Art Ed), BFA, BS & MA
Tuition: $3450 per sem
Adult Hobby Classes: Courses—Creative Crafts

PINEVILLE

LOUISIANA COLLEGE, Dept of Art, 71359. Tel 318-487-7262; FAX 318-487-7337; *Chair* Ted Barnes; *Prof* Bob Howell
Den; scholarships; LC, Lab C; enrl maj 24
Ent Req: HS grad
Degrees: BA 4 yrs, 49 hrs of art req plus 78 hrs acad for degree
Tuition: Res—$187 per sem hr
Courses: Advertising Design, Art Appreciation, †Art Education, Art History, Ceramics, Design, Drawing, †Graphic Design, Illustration, Painting, Photography, Printmaking, †Studio Arts
Adult Hobby Classes: Courses offered through Continuing Education
Summer School: Limited courses

RUSTON

LOUISIANA TECH, School of Art, 3175 Tech Sta, 71272. Tel 318-257-3909; FAX 318-257-4890; *Interim Dir* Robert Berguson. Instrs: FT 8, PT 4
Estab 1904; pub; D; scholarships; SC 98, LC 8, GC 87; enrl maj 652, others 538
Ent Req: HS dipl
Degrees: Degrees BA & MA 4 yrs, BArchit 5 yrs
Tuition: Res—undergrad $754 per sem; Nonres—undergrad $1254 per sem
Courses: †Architecture, †Ceramics, †Drawing, †Graphic Design, †Interior Design, †Painting, †Photography, †Printmaking, †Sculpture, †Studio Art
Summer School: Summer program in Rome & on campus

SHREVEPORT

CENTENARY COLLEGE OF LOUISIANA, Dept of Art, Centenary Blvd, 71104. Tel 318-869-5261; FAX 318-869-5730; Elec Mail ballen@bata.centenary.edu. *Chmn Dept & Prof* Bruce Allen, MFA; *Lectr* Neil Johnson, BA; *Lectr* Laura Noland; *Lectr* Ann Roberts, MLA; *Lectr* Graham Mears; *Lectr* Judy Godfrey, MA
Estab 1825, dept estab 1935; den; D & E; scholarships; SC 22, LC 8; enrl D 125 per sem
Ent Req: HS dipl, SAT or ACT
Degrees: BA 4 yrs
Tuition: $3775 per sem, $270 per hr; campus res—room & board $3200 per yr
Courses: Aesthetics, Art Education, Art History, Ceramics, Drafting, Drawing, Graphic Arts, Painting, Printmaking, Sculpture, Teacher Training

THIBODAUX

NICHOLLS STATE UNIVERSITY, Dept of Art, 70310. Tel 504-448-4597; FAX 504-448-4927; *Art Dept Head* Dennis Sipiorski. Instrs: FT 8
Estab 1948; pub; D & E; scholarships; SC 73, LC 6; enrl D 100, non-maj 20, maj 80, others 20
Ent Req: HS dipl, ACT
Degrees: BA 4 yrs
Tuition: $824.55 for 12 hrs or more per sem
Courses: Art Appreciation, Art Education, Art History, Ceramics, Design, Drawing, Graphic Design, Illustration, Painting, Photography, Printmaking, Sculpture, Applied Design, Rendering, Water Media

MAINE

AUGUSTA

UNIVERSITY OF MAINE AT AUGUSTA, Division of Fine & Performing Arts, 46 University Dr, University Heights, 04330. Tel 207-621-3000; FAX 207-621-3293; *Chmn* Joshua Nadel, MFA; *Prof* Philip Paratore, MFA; *Prof* Robert Katz, MFA; *Prof* Karen Gilg, MFA; *Prof* Tom Hoffman; *Prof* Lizabeth Libbey; *Prof* Bill Moseley; *Prof* Mark Polishook; *Prof* Roger Richman; *Prof* Donald Stratton; *Prof* Charles Winfield; *Assoc Prof* Brooks Stoddard
Estab 1965, dept estab 1970; pub; D & E; SC 20, LC 8; enrl D 50, E 40, non-maj 40, maj 60
Ent Req: HS dipl
Degrees: AA(Architural Studies) 2 yrs
Tuition: Res—$3840 per yr, $94 per cr hr; nonres—$9000 per yr, $229 per cr hr
Courses: Advertising Design, Art History, Ceramics, Drawing, Graphic Arts, Mixed Media, Painting, Photography, Sculpture, Paper Making
Summer School: Provost, Richard Randall. Enrl 30-50; tuition $52 per cr hr for term of 7 wks beginning last wk in June. Courses - Drawing, Painting, Sculpture

BRUNSWICK

BOWDOIN COLLEGE, Art Dept, Visual Arts Ctr, 04011. Tel 207-725-3697; FAX 207-725-3123; *Chmn* Mark Wethli, MFA; *Dir Art History* Clifton C Olds, PhD; *Emeritus Prof* Philip C Beam, PhD; *Prof* Susan Wegner; *Prof* Larry D Lutchmansingh, PhD; *Prof* Thomas B Cornell, AB; *Prof* Anne Harris, MFA; *Prof* Linda Docherty, PhD; *Lectr* John McKee, MA; *Vis Instr* Christopher Glass, PhD; *Vis Instr* John Bisbee
Estab 1794; pvt; D & E; scholarships; SC 15, LC 18; enrl maj 54
Ent Req: HS dipl
Degrees: AB 4 yrs
Tuition: $9325 per yr, campus res—room & board $3375
Courses: Art History, Visual Arts

DEER ISLE

HAYSTACK MOUNTAIN SCHOOL OF CRAFTS, PO Box 518, 04627-0518. Tel 207-348-2306; *Dir* Stuart J Kestenbaum. Instrs: FT 36
Estab 1951; pvt; D, Summer school; scholarships; enrl D 75
Tuition: $480 for 2 wk session, $630 for 3 wk session
Courses: Ceramics, Graphic Arts, Basketry, Blacksmithing, Fabric, Glassblowing, Metalsmithing, Papermaking, Quiltmaking, Stained Glass, Woodworking, Weaving
Summer School: Dir, Stu Kestenbaum. Enrl 80; tuition $630 for 3 wks. Courses—Basketry, Blacksmith, Fabric Arts, Glassblowing, Graphics, Metalsmithing, Papermaking, Quiltmaking, Woodworking

GORHAM

UNIVERSITY OF SOUTHERN MAINE, Art Dept, 37 College Ave, 04038. Tel 207-780-5460; FAX 207-780-5759; *Chmn* Michael Shoughnessy
Estab 1878, dept estab 1956; pub; D & E; SC 9, LC 2; enrl maj 200
Ent Req: HS dipl, portfolio
Degrees: BA, BFA
Tuition: Res—undergrad $101 per cr hr; nonres—undergrad $286 per cr hr
Courses: Art Education, Art History, Ceramics, Design, Drawing, Film, Museum Staff Training, Painting, Photography, Printmaking, Sculpture, Philosophy of Art; Problems in Art
Children's Classes: Enrl 15; tuition $475 res $375 commuter 1 wk in the summer. Courses—Drawing, Painting, Photography & Sculpture
Summer School: Dir, John Labrie. Enrl 125; same as general tuition May 15-Aug 30. Courses—Art Education, Art History, Ceramics, Design, Drawing, Painting, Photography, Printmaking, Sculpture

LEWISTON

BATES COLLEGE, Art Dept, Liberal Arts College, 04240. Tel 207-786-6258; *Chmn* Rebecca Corrie. Instrs: FT 4, PT 4
Estab 1864, dept estab 1964; pvt; D; scholarships; SC 13, LC 19; enrl 1450 total
Degrees: BA 4 yr
Tuition: $22,850 per yr (comprehensive fee)
Courses: Aesthetics, Art History, Ceramics, Drawing, History of Art & Archaeology, Painting, Printmaking, †Studio Art

ORONO

UNIVERSITY OF MAINE, Dept of Art, 5712 Carnegie Hall, 04469-5712. Tel 207-581-3245; FAX 207-581-3276; *Chair* Laurie E Hicks; *Prof* Michael H Lewis, MFA; *Prof* James Linehan, MFA; *Prof* Susan Groce, MFA; *Prof* Deborah DeMoulpied, MFA; *Assoc Prof* Ronald Ghiz, MFA; *Assoc Prof* David Decker, MA; *Asst Prof* Owen Smith, PhD; *Asst Prof* Michael Grillo, PhD; *Asst Prof* Nina Sutcliffe, MA
Estab 1862, dept estab 1946; pub; D & E; scholarships; SC 24, LC 24; enrl D 135, maj 135
Ent Req: HS dipl, 3 CEEB tests
Degrees: BA 4 yrs
Tuition: Res—undergrad $112 per cr hr; nonres—undergrad $317 per cr hr; campus res—room & board $4842 per yr
Courses: Aesthetics, Art Appreciation, †Art Education, †Art History, Design, Drawing, Graphic Design, History of Art & Archaeology, Mixed Media, Painting, Photography, Printmaking, Sculpture, Teacher Training, †Studio Art
Children's Classes: Chair, Laurie E Hicks, PhD
Summer School: Acting Dir, Jim Toner. Tuition $105 per cr hr, 3-8 wk courses. Courses—Art Education, Art History, Basic Drawing, Basic Painting, Computer Graphics, Photography, Printmaking

PORTLAND

MAINE COLLEGE OF ART, 97 Spring St, 04101. Tel 207-775-3052; *Pres* Roger Gilmore; *Dean* George Smith; *Instr* Edwin P Douglas, MFA; *Instr* John Eide, MFA; *Instr* Allen R Gardiner; *Instr* Regina Kelley, MFA; *Instr* John T Ventimiglia, MFA; *Instr* Mark Johnson, MFA; *Instr* Tim McCreight, MFA; *Instr* George LaRou; *Instr* Johnnie Ross, MFA; *Instr* Gan Xu, Ph; *Instr* Joan Uraneck, MFA; *Instr* Jonathan Aldrich, MA
Estab 1882; pvt; D & E; scholarships; SC 37, LC 9; enrl D 300, E 250, maj 300, others 160 HS, 75 children (4th-9th grades)
Ent Req: HS dipl, portfolio
Degrees: BFA 4 yr (under Maine law, and academically advanced high school senior may take the freshman yr at Maine College of Art for both HS & Maine College of Art credit)
Tuition: $13,860 per yr; campus res available
Courses: †Advertising Design, Aesthetics, Art Education, Art History, †Ceramics, Commercial Art, Design, Drawing, Goldsmithing, Graphic Arts, †Graphic Design, History of Art & Archaeology, Illustration, Intermedia, †Jewelry, †Painting, †Photography, †Printmaking, †Sculpture, Silversmithing, Art in Service, Computer Arts, †Metalsmithing, †Self-Designed Major
Adult Hobby Classes: Enrl 250; tuition $260 per 1 cr course plus lab fee $10-$25. Courses—Apparel Design, Cartooning, Ceramics, Design, Drawing, Electronic Imaging, Graphic Design, Illustration, Jewelry, Landscape Design, Metalsmithing, Painting, Photography, Printmaking, Sculpture, Textile Design
Children's Classes: Enrl 75; tuition $165 per class. Courses—Ceramics, Drawing, Graphic Design, Metalsmithing, Photography, Printmaking, Sculpture
Summer School: Dir, Maria Gallace. Enrl 400; tuition $240 per cr for term of 1-6 wks beginning June 23, 1997. Courses—Art History, Ceramics, Computer Imaging, Drawing, Graphic Design, Jewelry & Metalsmithing, Painting, Photography, Printmaking, Sculpture, Watercolor, 2 & 3-D Design

ROCKPORT

MAINE PHOTOGRAPHIC WORKSHOPS, 2 Central St, 04856. Tel 207-236-8581; FAX 207-236-2558; *Founder & Dir* David H Lyman
Scholarships; enrl 1200
Degrees: AA
Tuition: Workshops $600
Courses: Film, Editorial, Fine Art & Commercial Photography, Television & Video, Writing
Adult Hobby Classes: Enrl 1000
Summer School: Dir, David H Lyman. Enrl 2000; tuition $250-$600 for 1 wk workshop. Courses—Directing, Editing, Film, Video, Writing

WATERVILLE

COLBY COLLEGE, Art Dept, 04901. Tel 207-872-3233; *Prof* Harriett Matthews, MFA; *Prof* David Simon; *Prof* David Lubin, PhD; *Prof* Michael Marlais, PhD; *Prof* Abbott Meader; *Assoc Prof* Sonia Simon; *Asst Prof* Kenneth Gauza; *Asst Prof* Scott Reed
Estab 1813, dept estab 1944; pvt; D & E; scholarships; SC 12, LC 17; enrl D 500, non-maj 425, maj 75
Ent Req: HS dipl
Degrees: BA 4 yrs
Tuition: $27,900 per yr incl room & board
Courses: Art History, Drawing, Painting, Photography, Printmaking, Sculpture, History of Architecture

MARYLAND

BALTIMORE

BALTIMORE CITY COMMUNITY COLLEGE, Dept of Fine Arts, Main Bldg, Rm 243, 2901 Liberty Heights Ave, 21215. Tel 410-462-7605; *Chmn* Peter Ashley; *Assoc Prof* David Bahr, MFA; *Asst Prof* Sally De Marcos, MEd. Instrs: FT 7, PT 20
Estab 1947; pub; D & E; scholarships; enrl D & E 9800, non-maj 505, maj 388
Ent Req: HS dipl or HS equivalency, ent exam

Degrees: AA 2 yrs
Tuition: Res—undergrad $47 per cr hr; nonres—undergrad $125 per cr hr
Courses: Advertising Design, Art Education, Art History, Ceramics, Commercial
Art, Drawing, Graphic Arts, †Graphic Design, Jewelry, Painting, †Photography,
Printmaking, Sculpture, Textile Design, †Fashion Design, Fashion Illustration,
†Fashion Merchandising
Adult Hobby Classes: Tuition res $56 per cr; nonres $168 per cr. Courses—same as
above
Summer School: Dir, Dr Stephen Millman. Enrl 2655. Courses - Ceramics, Crafts,
Design, Drawing, Fashion Design, Painting

COLLEGE OF NOTRE DAME OF MARYLAND, Art Dept, 4701 N Charles St,
21210. Tel 410-435-0100; WATS (Md) 800-435-0200; all other 800-435-0300.
Chmn & Assoc Prof Domenico Firmani, PhD; *Prof* Linelle LaBonte, MFA; *Prof*
Kevin Raines, MFA; *Instr* Sally Meride, BFA
Pvt; D & E; scholarships; SC 32, LC 13; enrl D 680, non-maj 480, maj 45
Ent Req: HS dipl, SAT
Degrees: BA 4 yrs
Tuition: Res—undergrad $11,180 per yr, $5590 per sem; campus res—room & board
$5620 per yr
Courses: Advertising Design, Art Education, †Art History, Commercial Art, Design,
Drawing, †Graphic Arts, Graphic Design, Illustration, †Museum Staff Training,
Painting, †Photography, Printmaking, Sculpture, Teacher Training, †Studio
Adult Hobby Classes: Enrl 55; tuition $150 per cr (1-9 cr). Courses offered in
Weekend College & Continuing Education Programs
Summer School: Dir, Bernadette Brenner. Enrl 35; tuition $95 per cr.
Courses—Calligraphy, Drawing, History of Art Surveys, Painting, Photography,
Printmaking, Sculpture, Teacher Training

COPPIN STATE COLLEGE, Dept Fine & Communication Arts, 2500 W North
Ave, 21216. Tel 410-383-5806; FAX 410-383-9606; *Chmn* Dr Judith Willner. Instrs:
FT 1, PT 2
Scholarships; SC 6, LC 7; enrl D 350, E 45
Degrees: BS, MA & Doc in Art Education
Tuition: Res—$1896 per yr; nonres—$3364 per yr
Courses: Advertising Design, Art Education, Art History, Calligraphy, Ceramics,
Drawing, Film, Graphic Design, Lettering, Painting, Photography, Printmaking,
Sculpture, Teacher Training, Theatre Arts

GOUCHER COLLEGE, Art Dept, 1021 Dulaney Valley Rd, 21204. Tel 410-337-
6000, 337-6235; FAX 410-337-6405; *Chmn* Karen Acker
Estab 1885; pvt; D; scholarships; SC 38, LC 18; enrl D 970, non-maj 558, maj (art)
29
Ent Req: HS dipl, SAT, achievement tests (CEEB), American College Testing
Program
Degrees: MA 4 yrs, MA (Dance Movement Therapy) 2 yrs
Tuition: $7794 per sem
Summer School: Dir, Fontaine M Belford. Enrl 160; Term of 4 wks beginning June
12 and July 10. Courses—(Art) Dance, Fibers Workshop, Nature Drawing
Workshop, Photography, Pottery Workshop, Theatre

JOHNS HOPKINS UNIVERSITY
—**Dept of the History of Art,** 3400 N Charles St, 21218. Tel 410-516-7117; FAX
410-516-5188; *Chmn* Dr Herbert L Kessler. Instrs: FT 5, PT 3
Estab 1947; pvt; D & E; scholarships; LC; enrl 10-20 in advanced courses, 80-100 in
introductory courses
Degrees: Scholarships & fels
Tuition: $16,750 per yr
Courses: Art History, History of Art & Archaeology
—**School of Medicine, Dept of Art as Applied to Medicine,** 1830 E Monument St,
Ste 7000, 21205. Tel 410-955-3213; FAX 410-955-1085; *Dir Dept* Gary P Lees,
MS; *Dir Emerita* Rancie W Crosby, MLA; *Assoc Prof* Timothy H Phelps, MS;
Assoc Prof Leon Schlossberg; *Asst Prof* Howard C Bartner, MA; *Asst Prof* Brent A
Bauer, MA; *Asst Prof* Elizabeth Blumenthal; *Asst Prof* Neil Hardy, BFA; *Asst Prof*
Dale R Levitz, MS; *Asst Prof* Raymond Lund; *Asst Prof* Corrine Sandone, MA;
Instr Norman Barker; *Instr* Paul S Calhoun; *Instr* David Rini; *Instr* J Robert
Duckwall; *Lectr* Nancy L Held; *Lectr* Anne R Altemus; *Lectr* Joseph Dieter Jr
Univ estab 1876, School Medicine estab 1893, dept estab 1911; pvt; D; scholarships;
SC 13, LC 5, GC 18
Ent Req: Baccalaureate degree
Degrees: MA
Tuition: $18,800 per yr
Courses: Display, Drawing, Graphic Design, Illustration, Intermedia, Mixed Media,
Painting, Photography, Sculpture, Video, Anatomical Sketching, Cells & Tissue,
Surgical Illustration

MARYLAND INSTITUTE, College of Art, 1300 W Mt Royal Ave, 21217. Tel
410-669-9200; *Pres* Fred Lazarus IV. Instrs: FT 45, PT 55
Estab 1826; pvt; D & E; scholarships; enrl D 1107, E 554, Sat 280
Ent Req: HS grad, exam
Degrees: BFA & MFA 4 yrs
Tuition: $12,300 per yr; campus res—$3700
Courses: Ceramics, Drawing, Graphic Design, Illustration, Interior Design, Painting,
Photography, Printmaking, Sculpture, Teacher Training, Computer Graphics, Fibers
& Wood
Adult Hobby Classes: Evenings & Saturdays, cr-non cr classes
Children's Classes: Saturdays & Summer classes
Summer School: Dir Continuing Studies, M A Marsalek. Enrl 1066; tuition $400
per sem per class for Continuing Studies
—**Hoffberger School of Painting,** 1300 W Mt Royal Ave, 21217. Tel 410-225-2255;
FAX 410-225-2408; *Dir* Grace Hartigan
Fel awarded annually for study at the grad level; enrl limited to 14
Tuition: $14,950
—**Rinehart School of Sculpture,** 1300 W Mt Royal Ave, 21217. Tel 410-225-2255;
FAX 410-225-2408; *Dir* Norman Carlberg
Tuition: $14,950
Adult Hobby Classes: Enrl 748; tuition $200 per cr
Children's Classes: Enrl 174; tuition $170 per class

—**Mount Royal School of Art,** 21217. Tel 410-225-2255; *Faculty* Babe Shapiro;
Faculty Salvatore Scarpitta
Enrl 79
Degrees: MAT 2 yrs
Tuition: $14,950
Courses: Aesthetics, Art Education, Art History, Calligraphy, †Ceramics, †Drawing,
History of Art & Archaeology, Intermedia, †Mixed Media, Painting, Photography,
†Sculpture, Teacher Training, Video, Studio Art
—**Graduate Photography,** 1300 W Mount Royal Ave, 21217. Tel 410-225-2306; *Dir*
Will Larson
Degrees: MFA 2 yrs
Tuition: Res—grad $15,950 per yr
Courses: History of Photography
—**Art Education Graduate Studies,** 1300 W Mount Royal Ave, 21217. Tel 410-225-
2306; *Dir* Dr Karen Carroll
Degrees: MFA 2 yrs
Tuition: Res—grad $15,950 per yr
Courses: Art Education, Teacher Training

MORGAN STATE UNIVERSITY, Dept of Art, 1700 E Coldspring Lane, 21239.
Tel 410-319-3021, 319-3333 (main); *Dept Chmn* Dr Nathan Carter. Instrs: FT 7
Estab 1867, dept estab 1950; pub; D & E; scholarships; SC 28, LC 11, GC 17; enrl
D 340, E 50, non-maj 250, maj 140, GS 11
Ent Req: HS dipl
Degrees: BA(Art & Music Performance) & BS(Art Educ)
Tuition: Res—$1563 per sem; nonres—$3644 per sem
Courses: Architecture, Art Education, Art History, Ceramics, Design, Drawing,
Graphic Arts, Graphic Design, Illustration, Painting, Photography, Sculpture,
†Theatre Arts, 3-D Design
Children's Classes: Enrl 20; tuition $10 per sem. Courses—Painting, Printmaking,
Sculpture
Summer School: Dir, Dr Beryl W Williams. Term of 6 wks beginning June & July.
Courses—Art Appreciation, Art Education, Basic Design, Photography

SCHULER SCHOOL OF FINE ARTS, 5 E Lafayette Ave, 21202. Tel 410-685-
3568; *Dir* Hans C Schuler
Estab 1959; pvt; D & E; SC 9, GC 3; enrl D 50, E 30, grad 2
Degrees: 4 yrs
Tuition: $2910 per yr, part-time students pay by schedule for sem
Courses: Drawing, Painting, Sculpture
Children's Classes: Tuition $400-$550 (summer - ages 14 and over).
Courses—Drawing, Painting, Sculpture
Summer School: Dir, Hans C Schuler. Enrl 30; tuition $400 for term of 6 wks
beginning June, $550 for 6 hrs per day, 6 wks. Courses—Drawing, Oil Painting,
Sculpture, Watercolor

UNIVERSITY OF MARYLAND, BALTIMORE COUNTY, Visual Arts Dept,
5401 Wilkens Ave, Rm 111, 21250. Tel 410-455-2150; FAX 410-455-1070; *Chmn*
David Yager; *Assoc Prof* Jerry Stephany; *Assoc Prof* Vin Grabill; *Assoc Prof* Daniel
Bailey; *Assoc Prof* Ruth Leavitt; *Asst Prof* Carol Fastuca; *Asst Prof* Hillary Kapan;
Asst Prof Franc Nunoo-Quarcoo; *Asst Prof* Alan Rutberg; *Asst Prof* Hollie
Lavenstein
Estab 1966; pub; D & E; SC 27, LC 12, GC 4; enrl in dept D 485, non-maj 375, maj
110
Ent Req: HS dipl, SAT
Degrees: BA 4 yrs
Tuition: Res—$681 per sem; nonres—$1879 per sem
Courses: Advertising Design, Aesthetics, †Art History, Calligraphy, Ceramics,
Collages, Commercial Art, Conceptual Art, †Drawing, †Film, Graphic Arts,
†Graphic Design, †History of Art & Archaeology, Intermedia, Lettering, Mixed
Media, †Painting, †Photography, Printmaking, †Video
Summer School: Dir, David Yager. Six wk term. Courses—Drawing, Film, History,
Photography, Video

BEL AIR

HARFORD COMMUNITY COLLEGE, Fine & Applied Arts Division, 401
Thomas Run Rd, 21015. Tel 410-836-4000; FAX 410-836-4198; *Prof* Paul Labe.
Instrs: FT 5, PT 10
Estab 1957; pub; D & E; SC 17, LC 4; enrl FT 1000, PT 1000
Ent Req: HS dipl
Degrees: AA 2 yrs
Tuition: Res—undergrad $60 per cr hr; nonres—undergrad $94 (out of county),
$165 (out of state) per cr hr
Courses: Architecture, Art History, Ceramics, †Commercial Art, Design, Drawing,
Graphic Arts, Graphic Design, History of Art & Archaeology, Illustration, †Interior
Design, Mixed Media, Painting, †Photography, Printmaking, Sculpture, Video,
Digital Imaging, Digital Media, †Fine Art
Summer School: Div Chair, Paul Labe

BOWIE

BOWIE STATE UNIVERSITY, Fine Arts Dept, MLK Bldg, Rm 236, Jericho Park
Rd, 20715. Tel 301-464-3000, 464-7286, 464-7510; *Chmn* Clarence Knight; *Coordr
Gallery Dir* Robert Ward. Instrs: FT 8
Estab 1865, dept estab 1968; pub; D; SC 7, LC 3; enrl D 1600, E 350, non-maj 180,
maj 45
Ent Req: HS dipl
Degrees: BA(Art) 4 yrs
Tuition: Res—undergrad $1257 per sem, grad $111 per cr hr; nonres—$2344.50 per
sem
Courses: Art History, Ceramics, Design, Drawing, Painting, Photography, Sculpture,
African & American History, Cinematography, Computer Graphics, Crafts,
Graphics, Museum & Gallery Study
Summer School: Dir, Dr Ida Brandon. Courses—Ceramics, Media Workshop

CATONSVILLE

CATONSVILLE COMMUNITY COLLEGE, Art Dept, 800 S Rolling Rd, 21228.
Tel 410-455-4429, 455-4422; *Chmn Dept* Dr W C Zwingelberg
Estab 1957; pub; D & E; scholarships; SC 26, LC 6; enrl D 600, E 400, non-maj
200, maj 300, applied arts maj 350
Ent Req: HS dipl
Degrees: Cert & AA 2 yrs
Tuition: In-county $54 per cr hr; in-state $97 per cr hr; nonres--$157 per cr hr
Courses: †Advertising Design, Art Education, Art History, Ceramics, Commercial
Art, Drawing, Graphic Design, Illustration, Interior Design, Painting, †Photography,
Sculpture
Adult Hobby Classes: Chmn Dept, Dr Dian Fetter
Summer School: Same as above

COLLEGE PARK

UNIVERSITY OF MARYLAND
—**Dept of Art History,** 1211-B Art-Sociology Bldg, 20742. Tel 301-405-1479; FAX
301-314-9652; *Chmn* Dr William L Pressly. Instrs: FT 15, PT 1
Estab 1944; pub; D; scholarships; SC 39, LC 37, GC 22; enrl 2000 per sem, maj
100, grad 20
Ent Req: 3.0 grade average
Degrees: BA, MA, PhD
Tuition: Res—$1740 per sem; nonres—$4642 per sem
Courses: Art History
Adult Hobby Classes: Enrl 500 per yr. Courses—Art History
Summer School: Dir, Dr Melvin Bernstein. Enrl 350; tuition $56 per cr hr for term
of 6 wks. Courses—Art History
—**Department of Art,** 1211-E Art-Sociology Bldg, 20742-1311. Tel 301-405-1442;
Chmn Stephanie Pogue. Instrs: FT 20, PT 3
Estab 1944; pub; D; scholarships; SC 39, LC 37, GC 22; enrl 850 per sem, maj 170,
grad 20
Ent Req: 3.0 grade average
Degrees: BA, MFA
Tuition: Res—$1740 per sem; nonres—$4642 per sem
Courses: Design, Mixed Media, Photography, Printmaking, 2-D & 3-D Drawing,
Artist Survival, Art Theory, Lithography, Papermaking
Summer School: Dir, Dr Melvin Berstein. Two six-week sessions. Courses—Design,
Drawing, Painting, Printmaking, Sculpture

CUMBERLAND

ALLEGANY COMMUNITY COLLEGE, Art Dept, Willow Brook Rd, 21502. Tel
301-724-7700; FAX 301-724-6892; *Chmn* James D Zamagias
Estab 1966; pub; D & E; scholarship; SC 6, LC 1; enrl Enrl D 30, E 9
Ent Req: HS dipl
Degrees: AA 2 yrs
Tuition: Res—undergrad $64 per cr hr; nonres—undergrad $107 per cr hr
Courses: Ceramics, Drawing, Painting, Survey of Art History, 2-D & 3-D Design
Adult Hobby Classes: Courses offered
Summer School: Dir, James D Zamagias. Term of 6 wks beginning July.
Courses—Painting, 2-D Design

EMMITSBURG

MOUNT SAINT MARY'S COLLEGE, Visual & Performing Arts Dept, 21727. Tel
301-447-6122, Ext 5308; FAX 301-447-5755; *Chmn* Daniel C Nusbaum; *Prof*
Walter Nichols, MA; *Prof* Kurt E Blaugher, PhD; *Prof* Robert Terentieff, MS; *Prof*
John J Zec, MM
Estab 1808; pvt; D & E; scholarships; SC 9, LC 10; enrl D 1200, maj 12
Ent Req: HS dipl, SAT
Degrees: BA and BS 4 yrs
Tuition: $14,400 per yr, $7200 pr sem; campus res available
Courses: Art History, Drawing, Painting, Sculpture, Theatre Arts

FREDERICK

HOOD COLLEGE, Dept of Art, 401 Rosemont Ave, 21701-8575. Tel 301-663-
3131; FAX 301-694-7653; *Chmn* Dr Anne Derbes; *Assoc Prof* Elaine Gates, MFA;
Assoc Prof Fred Bohrer
Estab 1893; pvt, W; D; SC 18, LC 16; enrl D 700, maj 60
Ent Req: HS dipl
Degrees: BA 4 yrs
Tuition: $13,960 per yr, $20,000 incl room & board
Courses: Five Areas of Concentration: Studio Arts, Art History, Art Therapy,
Secondary Art Eduction, Visual Communications
Summer School: Dir, Dr Patricia Bartlett. Tuition by course for term of 6 wks, June-
Aug. Courses—Internships and Independent Studies, Photography, Watercolor and
Sketching, Woodcut

FROSTBURG

FROSTBURG STATE UNIVERSITY, Dept of Visual Arts, E College Ave, 21532-
1099. Tel 301-687-4797; FAX 301-689-4737; WATS 800-687-8677. *Head Dept*
Dustin Davis
Estab 1898; pub; D; scholarships; SC 25, LC 5; enrl D 230, maj 150, GS 13
Ent Req: HS dipl
Degrees: BFA(Art Educ Certification) 4 yr
Tuition: Res—$3544 per yr; nonres—$7530 per yr; campus res—room & board
$4260-$5260 per yr
Courses: Art Appreciation, Art Education, Art History, Ceramics, Drawing, Graphic
Design, Painting, Photography, Printmaking, Sculpture, Teacher Training, Art
Criticism, Art Therapy, Crafts, 2-D & 3-D Design, Visual Imagery

HAGERSTOWN

HAGERSTOWN JUNIOR COLLEGE, Art Dept, 11400 Robinwood Dr, 21742.
Tel 301-790-2800, Ext 221; FAX 301-739-0737; *Coordr* Ben Culbertson
Estab 1946; pub; D & E; SC 10, LC 4; enrl D 110, E 66
Degrees: AA, 2 yrs
Tuition: Washington County res—$61 per cr hr; out-of-county—$87 per cr hr;
nonres—$114 per cr hr
Courses: Art Appreciation, Art History, Ceramics, Drawing, Painting, Photography,
Sculpture, Video, Art Methods, Basic Design
Summer School: Courses - Art & Culture, Basic Drawing, Painting, Photography,
Special Studies in Ceramics, Parent & Child Art Studio

LARGO

PRINCE GEORGE'S COMMUNITY COLLEGE, Art Dept, English & Humanities
Div, 301 Largo Rd, 20772. Tel 301-322-0966; FAX 301-808-0960; *Chmn* Judith
Andraka
Estab 1958, dept estab 1967; pub; D & E; scholarships; SC 18, LC 2; enrl D 220, E
140, maj 11
Ent Req: HS dipl, CGP test
Degrees: AA
Courses: Advertising Design, Art Appreciation, Art History, Ceramics, Design,
Drawing, Graphic Arts, Graphic Design, Illustration, Jewelry, Lettering, Mixed
Media, Painting, Photography, Printmaking, Sculpture, Advertising Illustration, Art
Survey, Computer Graphics
Summer School: Dean, Dr Robert Barshay. Courses—Drawing, Intro to Art,
Painting, Photography

PRINCESS ANNE

UNIVERSITY OF MARYLAND EASTERN SHORE, Art & Technology Dept,
11931 Art Shell Plaza, UMES, 21853. Tel 410-651-6488, 651-2200; *Coordr Art
Education* Ernest R Satchell
Tuition: Res—$3235.50 incl room & board per sem; nonres—$5565.50
Courses: Art Appreciation, Art Education, Art History, Calligraphy, Ceramics,
Drawing, Handicrafts, Jewelry, Painting, Photography, Printmaking, Sculpture

ROCKVILLE

MONTGOMERY COLLEGE, Dept of Art, 51 Manakee St, 20850. Tel 301-279-
5115; FAX 301-251-7640; *Chmn* Ed Ashlstrom; *Prof* Orest S Poliszczuk
Estab 1946, dept estab 1966; pub; D & E; scholarships; SC 25, LC 7
Ent Req: HS dipl
Degrees: AA 2 yrs
Tuition: Res—$109 per sem hr; out-of-state—$153 per sem hr
Courses: †Advertising Design, †Architecture, Art Appreciation, †Art Education,
†Art History, Ceramics, †Commercial Art, Design, Drawing, Film, Goldsmithing,
†Illustration, †Interior Design, Jewelry, Lettering, Painting, †Photography,
Printmaking, Sculpture, Video, Color, Crafts, Computer Graphics, Enameling,
Metalsmith, Printing
Summer School: Dir Robert S Cohen. Tuition $35 per sem hr. Courses—Ceramics,
Color, Crafts, Design, Drawing, Painting, Printmaking

SAINT MARY'S CITY

SAINT MARY'S COLLEGE OF MARYLAND, Art Dept, 20686. Tel 301-862-
0200, 862-0225; FAX 301-862-0958; *Dept Chmn & Assoc Prof* Lisa Scheer, MFA;
Assoc Prof Jeffrey Carr, MFA; *Assoc Prof* Sandra L Underwood, PhD; *Asst Prof*
Sue Johnson, MFA
Estab 1964; pub; D & E; scholarships; SC 14, LC 16; enrl D 155, E 43, non-maj
128, maj 70
Ent Req: HS dipl, SAT scores
Degrees: BA
Tuition: Res—undergrad $11,225 per yr; nonres—undergrad $14,775 per yr; campus
res—room & board $5220
Courses: Art History, Drawing, Painting, Photography, Printmaking, Sculpture
Adult Hobby Classes: Art History, Drawing, Mixed Media, Painting, Photography,
Printmaking, Sculpture
Summer School: Tuition $104 per cr

SALISBURY

SALISBURY STATE UNIVERSITY, Art Dept, College & Camden Ave, 21801.
Tel 410-543-6270; FAX 410-543-3002; *Chmn* Kent N Kimmel, PhD; *Assoc Prof*
John R Cleary, MFA; *Asst Prof* Ursula M Ehrhardt, MA; *Asst Prof* Dean A
Peterson
Estab 1925, dept estab 1970; pub; D & E; scholarships; SC 26, LC 7, GC 1; enrl
non-maj 500, maj 111, grad 2
Ent Req: HS dipl, SAT verbal & math, ACT
Degrees: BA & BFA 4 yrs,
Tuition: Res—undergrad $1804 spring sem only (room & board $1375 single, $1275
double); nonres—undergrad $3459 spring sem only; part-time res—undergrad $105
per sem cr hr, grad $140 per sem cr hr; part-time nonres—undergrad $190 per sem
cr hr, grad $210 per sem cr hr
Courses: †Advertising Design, Art Appreciation, Art Education, Art History,
Ceramics, Commercial Art, Design, History of Art & Archaeology, Painting,
Photography, Sculpture, †European Field Study, †Independent Study, †Principles of
Color, †Visual Communications
Summer School: Dean, Dr Darrel Hagar. Courses—various art educ & studio
courses

SILVER SPRING

MARYLAND COLLEGE OF ART & DESIGN, 10500 Georgia Ave, 20902. Tel 301-649-4454; FAX 301-649-2940; *Pres* Wesley E Paulson; *Dean* Edward Glynn; *Prof* John Meza, MFA; *Asst Prof* Karen Jelenfy, MFA; *Asst Prof* Chris Medley, MFA
Estab 1955; pvt; D & E; scholarships; enrl Degree Prog 83, Enrichment & Special Students 175
Ent Req: HS dipl, SAT verbal scores, letter of recommendation, portfolio interview
Degrees: AA 2 yrs
Tuition: $5751 per yr, $1917 per quarter, $145 per cr hr; no campus res
Courses: Advertising Design, Art History, Ceramics, Commercial Art, Conceptual Art, Design, Advertising Design, Drawing, Graphic Arts, Graphic Design, Illustration, Intermedia, Lettering, Painting, Photography, Printmaking, Sculpture, Computer Graphics
Adult Hobby Classes: Enrl 1000; tuition $80-180 for 6-10 wks. Courses—Computer, Design, Drawing, Painting, Photography, Printmaking, Sculpture, Watercolor
Children's Classes: Enrl 1200; tuition $80-100 for 1-8 wks. Courses—Cartooning, Ceramics, Computer, Design, Drawing, Painting, Photography, Printmaking, Sculpture
Summer School: Dir, David Gracyalny. Enrl 1000; tuition $80-250 for 1-9 wks. Courses—Cartooning, Ceramics, Computer, Design, Drawing, Painting, Photography, Printmaking, Sculpture, Watercolor

TOWSON

TOWSON STATE UNIVERSITY, Dept of Art, 8000 York Rd, 21204. Tel 410-830-2142; *Dept Chmn* Dan Brown. Instrs: FT 20, PT 19
Estab 1866; pub; D & E
Ent Req: HS grad
Degrees: BA, BS, MEd(Art Educ) 4 yr & MFA; spring sem Florence, Italy, Feb-May
Tuition: Res—undergrad $1227 per sem; nonres—undergrad $2272 per sem
Courses: Art Education, Art History, Ceramics, Drawing, Graphic Arts, Jewelry, Painting, Sculpture, Textile Design, Enameling, Weaving, Wood & Metal
Adult Hobby Classes: Enrl 60
Summer School: Dir, Jim Flood. Enrl 25; 2 five wk sessions. Courses—Art History, Studio

WESTMINSTER

WESTERN MARYLAND COLLEGE, Dept of Art & Art History, 2 College Hill, 21157-4390. Tel 410-857-2595; *Dept Head* Sue Bloom; *Prof* Wasyl Palijczuk; *Assoc Prof* Michael Losch. Instrs: FT 4, PT 2
Estab 1867; independent; D & E; scholarships; SC 15, LC 12, GC 6; enrl D 1213, maj 40-60, grad 15
Ent Req: HS dipl, ent exam, SAT
Degrees: BA, BS & MEd 4 yrs
Tuition: $7255 per sem
Courses: Ceramics, Drawing, Graphic Design, †History of Art & Archaeology, Jewelry, Lettering, Painting, Photography, Printmaking, Sculpture, †Teacher Training, Computer Graphics, Design
Summer School: Two 5 wk terms beginning June 21. Courses—Art History, Ceramics, Painting, Printmaking, Sculpture, Weaving

MASSACHUSETTS

AMHERST

AMHERST COLLEGE, Dept of Fine Arts, Box 2249, 01002-5000. Tel 413-542-2365; FAX 413-542-7917; *Chmn* Joel Upton. Instrs: FT 10
Estab 1822; pvt; D; scholarships; SC 15, LC 15
Ent Req: HS dipl
Degrees: BA 4 yrs
Tuition: $27,460 comprehensive fee for yr
Courses: Aesthetics, Art History, Drawing, Painting, Photography, Printmaking, Sculpture, Anatomy, 3-D Design

UNIVERSITY OF MASSACHUSETTS, AMHERST
—College of Arts & Sciences, Department of Art, 01003-2510. Tel 413-545-1902; *Chmn Dept* Hanlyn Davies. Instrs: FT 36
Estab 1958; pub; SC 50, LC 19, GC 20; enrl maj undergrad 430, grad 85
Ent Req: HS grad, portfolio & SAT required, 16 units HS
Degrees: BA, BFA, MFA
Tuition: Res—$9670 incl room & board; nonres—$11,920 tuition only
Courses: Ceramics, Design, Drawing, Painting, Photography, Printmaking, Sculpture, Computer Art
Summer School: Dir, Angel Ramirez. Enrl 150-250; tuition $175 per 3 cr course, 2 six wk sessions. Courses—Architectural Drawing, Drawing, Painting, Photography
—Art History Program, 317 Bartlett Hall, 01003-0505. Tel 413-545-3595; FAX 413-545-3880; *Chmn* Bill Odel; *Emeritus Prof* Jack Benson, PhD; *Prof* Paul Norton, PhD; *Prof* Mark Roskill, PhD; *Prof* Walter B Denny, PhD; *Prof* Craig Harbison, PhD; *Assoc Prof* Kristine Haney, PhD; *Assoc Prof* Laetitia La Follette, PhD
Estab 1947; prog estab 1958; pub; D & E; scholarships & fels; LC 36, GC 16; enrl D 1735, non-maj 1369, maj 105, grad 40
Ent Req: HS dipl & transcript, SAT
Degrees: BA, MA
Tuition: Res—$9670 per yr incl room & board; nonres—$11,920 tuition only
Courses: Aesthetics, Architecture, †Art History, History of Art & Archaeology, Museum Staff Training, American Art to 1860, Ancient Art, Greek & Roman Art &

Architecture, Islamic Art, Renaissance to Modern Art, Survey
Adult Hobby Classes: All courses available through Continuing Education
Summer School: Enrl 15 per course. Tuition $30 per cr & $42 service fee for term of 6 wks beginning June 2 & July 14. Courses—Introduction to Art, Modern Art
—Dept of Landscape Architecture & Regional Planning, 109 Hills N, 01003. Tel 413-545-2255; FAX 413-545-1772; *Dept Head* Meir Gross; *Asst Dept Head* Merle Willman, PhD
Estab 1903; pub; D; SC 6, LC 5; enrl 35
Ent Req: Res-undergrad $702 per sem, graduate $73.25 pr cr hr up to $879
Degrees: MA(Archit, Regional Planning & Landscape Design)
Tuition: Res—$115.75 per cr, $1389 per sem; nonres—$357 per cr, $4283 per sem
Courses: Drafting, Drawing, Landscape Architecture, Aspects of Design Environment, Drawing & Measuring, Environmental Policy & Planning, Site Planning, Studio Landscape
Summer School: Planning & design short courses

AUBURNDALE

LASELL COLLEGE, Art & Interior Design Program, 1844 Commonwealth Ave, 02166. Tel 617-243-2000; FAX 617-243-2389; *Dir* Andre S Van De Putte
Estab 1851; pvt; W; D & E; scholarships
Ent Req: HS dipl
Degrees: AA and AS 2 & 4 yrs
Tuition: Res—undergrad $11,475 per yr
Courses: Ceramics, Drawing, Interior Design, Jewelry, Painting, Photography, Art for Child Study, Design & Color, Portfolio, 3-D Design

BEVERLY

ENDICOTT COLLEGE, Art Dept, 376 Hale St, 01915. Tel 508-927-0585; FAX 508-232-3100; WATS 800-325-1114. *Head Dept* J David Broudo, EdM
Estab 1939; pvt; W; D; scholarships; enrl 250, non-maj 15, maj 235
Ent Req: HS dipl
Degrees: BS 4 yr, AA & AAS 2 yrs
Tuition: Res—$16,200 per yr (incl rm & board); non—$7200 per yr
Courses: Advertising Design, Art History, †Ceramics, †Commercial Art, Drafting, Drawing, Fashion Arts, Graphic Arts, Illustration, †Interior Design, Jewelry, Painting, †Photography, Printmaking, Sculpture, Silversmithing, Weaving, †Apparel Design, †Fibers, †Metal, †Fine Arts Management
Adult Hobby Classes: Enrl 200. Tuition $90 per cr. Courses—Varies as to interest
Summer School: Dir, Ralph Carrivono. Tuition $90 per cr. Courses—Majority of day courses

MONSERRAT COLLEGE OF ART, 23 Essex St, 01915. Tel 508-922-8222; FAX 508-922-4268; *Pres* John Raimo; *Dean* Barbara Moody; *Foundation Dept* George Creamer; *Painting* George Gabin; *Printmaking* Ethan Berry; *Illustration* Elissa Della-Piana; *Sculpture* Claire Lieberman; *Graphic Design* John McVey; *Gallery Dir* Barbara O'Brien
Estab 1970; pvt; D & E; scholarships; SC 58, LC 13; enrl D 315, E 250
Ent Req: Personal interview and portfolio review
Degrees: BFA 4 yr dipl granted
Tuition: $10,272 per yr, $5136 per sem, $1284 per course; campus res available
Courses: Advertising Design, Art Education, Art History, Conceptual Art, Design, Drawing, †Graphic Design, Illustration, Mixed Media, †Painting, †Photography, †Printmaking, †Sculpture, Video
Adult Hobby Classes: Enrl 400. Courses—Drawing, Graphic Design, Painting, Photography, Printmaking
Children's Classes: Enrl 150; summer sessions. Courses—Drawing & Painting
Summer School: Dir, Doug Williams. Enrl 40; Pre-College Prog in July & Aug. Courses—Life Drawing, Painting & Illustration, Printmaking

BOSTON

ART INSTITUTE OF BOSTON, 700 Beacon St, 02215. Tel 617-262-1223; FAX 617-437-1226; *Pres* Stan Trecker, MA; *Chmn Design Dept* Geoffry Fried, MFA; *Chmn Illustration Dept* David Schuster; *Chmn Fine Arts Dept* Anthony Apesos, MFA; *Chmn Photography Dept* Christopher James, MFA; *Chmn Found Dept* Nathan Goldstein, MFA; *Chmn Liberal Arts* Robert Wauhkonen, MA
Estab 1912; pvt; D & E; scholarships; SC 80, LC 20; enrl D 400, E 250
Ent Req: HS dipl, portfolio and interview
Degrees: BFA
Tuition: Res—$7150 per yr, $3575 per sem
Courses: Art Education, Art History, Ceramics, Commercial Art, Conceptual Art, Design, Drawing, Graphic Arts, Graphic Design, History of Art & Archaeology, Illustration, Painting, Photography, Printmaking, Sculpture, Video, Computer Graphics, Typography
Adult Hobby Classes: Enrl 200; tuition $180 per cr. Courses—Continuing education offers most of the above typically 2-3 cr each
Summer School: Dir, Naomi Kadinoff. Enrl 250; tuition $180 per cr term of 8 wks beginning June 15. Courses—most of above

BOSTON CENTER FOR ADULT EDUCATION, 5 Commonwealth Ave, 02116. Tel 617-267-4430; FAX 617-247-3606; *Exec Dir* Mary McTique
Estab 1933; pvt; SC 26, LC 2; enrl D 2300, E 20,000
Ent Req: Open to all over 17
Tuition: $57 for 2 hr art or craft studio course; no campus res
Courses: Advertising Design, Architecture, Art Appreciation, Art History, Calligraphy, Ceramics, Drawing, Graphic Design, Interior Design, Painting, Photography, Printmaking, Video, Weaving, Sculpture, Theatre Arts, Clay Sculpture, Crafts, Studio Crafts, Stained Glass, Wood Carving
Summer School: Same as winter program

BOSTON UNIVERSITY, School of Visual Arts, 855 Commonwealth Ave, 02215. Tel 617-353-3371; *Dir* Hugh O'Donnell; *Prof* Joseph Ablow; *Prof* Lloyd Lillie; *Prof* John Moore; *Assoc Prof* Alston Purvis; *Assoc Prof* Edward Leary; *Assoc Prof* Nicolas Edmonds; *Assoc Prof* Isabel McIlvain Shedd
Estab 1869, sch estab 1954; pvt; D; scholarships; SC 38, LC 12, GC 15; enrl 395, non-maj 75, maj 260, grad 60
Ent Req: Ent req HS dipl, portfolio
Degrees: BFA 4 yrs, MFA 2 yrs
Tuition: $19,000 per yr; campus res—room & board $5700 per yr
Courses: Art Education, Art History, Design, Drawing, Graphic Design, Painting, Photography, Printmaking, Sculpture, Teacher Training, Studio Teaching (grad level), Typographic Design
Adult Hobby Classes: Enrl 215; tuition $2072 (4 cr) 15 wk term.
Courses—Drawing, Graphic Design, Painting, Sculpture

BUTERA SCHOOL OF ART, 111 Beacon St, 02116. Tel 617-536-4623; FAX 617-262-0353; *Pres* Joseph L Butera, MFA; *Dir* Charles Banks; *Head Commercial Art* Hal Trafford; *Head Sign Painting* Jim Garballey
Estab 1932; pvt; D & E; enrl D 100, E 60
Ent Req: HS dipl, portfolio
Degrees: 2 yr and 3 yr dipl progs
Tuition: $9800-$10,200 per yr; independent dormitories available
Courses: Advertising Design, Art Education, Art History, Calligraphy, Commercial Art, Drawing, Fashion Arts, Graphic Arts, Graphic Design, Illustration, Lettering, Painting, Sign Painting

EMMANUEL COLLEGE, Art Dept, 400 The Fenway, 02115. Tel 617-735-9794; FAX 617-735-9877; *Chmn Art Dept* Ellen M Glavin, SND; *Prof* Theresa Monaco, MFA; *Prof* C David Thomas, MFA; *Assoc Prof* Kathleen A Soles, MFA; *Adjunct Instr* Karen Saltalamacchia, MA
Estab 1919, dept estab 1950; pvt; D & E; scholarships; SC 30, LC 11; enrl D 300, E 50, non-maj 200, maj 80
Ent Req: HS dipl, SAT
Degrees: BA & BFA 4 yrs
Tuition: $10,966 full time or $1372 per course; campus res—room & board $5528 per yr
Courses: †Art Education, †Art History, Ceramics, Drawing, †Graphic Arts, Graphic Design, Mixed Media, †Painting, †Printmaking, Sculpture, Teacher Training, †Art Therapy
Adult Hobby Classes: Enrl 300; tuition $193 per cr. Courses—Art Educ, Art History, Art Theory, In Studio Art
Summer School: Dir, Dr Jacquelyn Armitage. Enrl 230; tuition $143 per cr hr for term of 6 wks in June-Aug

MASSACHUSETTS COLLEGE OF ART, 621 Huntington Ave, 02115. Tel 617-232-1555; FAX 617-566-4034; *Pres* William O'Neil, PhD; *Sr VPres* Betty Bachsbaum, PhD; *Dean Grad & Continuing Educ* Pat Doran; *Chmn Fine Arts, 2D Dean* Nimmer, MFA; *Chmn Fine Arts, 3-D* Marilyn Pappas; *Chmn Design* Margaret Hickey, BArch; *Chmn Art* Christy Park; *Chmn Media* Abelardo Morell; *Chmn Critical Studies* Virginia Allen; *Co-Chmn Design* Marilyn Gabarro
Estab 1873; pub; D & E; SC 400, GC 50; enrl D 1100, E 1000, grad 100
Ent Req: HS transcript, college transcript, SAT, statement of purpose, portfolio
Degrees: BFA 4 yrs, MFA 2 yrs, MSAE 2 yrs
Tuition: Res—$1463 per yr; nonres—$6422 per yr; New England Regional Program $2195
Courses: Art Education, Art History, Ceramics, Film, Graphic Design, Illustration, Industrial Design, Intermedia, Painting, Photography, Printmaking, Sculpture, Video, Architectural Design, Fashion Design, Fibers, Film Making, Freshman Artistic Seminars, Glass, Metals
Adult Hobby Classes: Enrl 1000; tuition $65 per cr hr. Courses—All areas
Children's Classes: Enrl 150; tuition $45 for 10 wks. Courses—All areas
Summer School: Dir Continuing Educ. Enrl 900; tuition $65 per cr hr. Courses—all areas

MOUNT IDA COLLEGE
—Chamberlayne School of Design & Merchandising, 777 Dedham St, 02159. Tel 617-969-7000, Ext 236; *School Dir* Phyllis Misite; *Lectr* M Crowe, MFA
Estab 1892, dept estab 1952; pvt; D & E; enrl D 253, E 38, maj 253
Ent Req: HS dipl
Degrees: AA, BA
Tuition: $17,866 per yr incl room & board
Courses: Fashion Arts, Interior Design, Drawing, Fashion Arts, Graphic Arts, Illustration, Interior Design, Jewelry, Painting, Sculpture, Textile Design, Merchandising
Summer School: Dir Susan Holton. 12 wks beginning June 1. Courses—same as regular academic yr

THE NEW ENGLAND SCHOOL OF ART & DESIGN AT SUFFOLK UNIVERSITY, 81 Arlington St, 02116. Tel 617-536-0383; FAX 617-536-0461; *Pres* William Davis; *Dir Admis* Anne Blevins; *Chmn Dept Graphic Design* Laura Golly; *Chmn Fine Arts* Audrey Goldstein
Estab 1923; pvt; D & E; scholarships; enrl D 200, E 250, maj 200
Ent Req: HS dipl, portfolio
Degrees: Certificate, Dipl, BFA
Tuition: Res—undergrad $320 per cr hr, Dipl $290 per cr, cert $250 per cr; nonres—undergrad $12,046 per yr, Dipl $10,980 per yr, $6023 per sem
Courses: Advertising Design, Art History, Drafting, Drawing, Graphic Arts, †Graphic Design, Illustration, †Interior Design, Painting, Photography, Printmaking, Computer Graphics, †Fine Arts
Adult Hobby Classes: Enrl 275; tuition $366 per cr for 10 wk term. Courses—Fine Arts, Interior Design, Graphic Design, Computer Graphics
Summer School: Dir, Felicia Onksen. Enrl 275; tuition $366 per cr for 10 wk term. Courses—those above

NORTHEASTERN UNIVERSITY, Dept of Art & Architecture, 239 Ryder Hall, 02115. Tel 617-373-2347; FAX 617-373-8535; *Chmn* Elizabeth Cromley; *Prof* Mardges Bacon, PhD; *Assoc Prof* Samuel Bishop, MFA; *Assoc Prof* T Neal Rantoul, MFA; *Asst Prof* Mira Cantor, MFA; *Asst Prof* Dianne Pitman, PhD; *Asst Prof* Edwin Andrews, MFA
Estab 1898, dept estab 1952; pvt; D & E; scholarships; enrl D 1200, E 1200, non-maj 1500, maj 380
Ent Req: HS dipl
Degrees: BA & BS 4 yrs
Tuition: Freshmen $4460 per acad qtr; upperclassmen $5775 per acad qtr; campus res available
Courses: Advertising Design, Aesthetics, Architecture, Art History, Design, Drafting, Drawing, Film, Graphic Arts, Graphic Design, Illustration, Mixed Media, Painting, Photography, Printmaking, Video, †History of Art & Architecture, Architectural Design, Computer Aided Design, Media Design
Adult Hobby Classes: Enrl 180; tuition $116 per 12 wk quarter cr. Courses—same as full-time program
Summer School: Chmn, Peter Serenyi. Enrl 240. Tuition & courses—same as above

SCHOOL OF FASHION DESIGN, 136 Newbury St, 02116. Tel 617-536-9343; *Head Art Dept* Richard Alartoski
Estab 1934; pvt; D & E; scholarships; enrl D approx 100, E approx 200
Ent Req: HS dipl
Degrees: No degrees, 2 yr cert or 3 yr dipl
Tuition: Res—$6500 per yr; school approved res
Courses: Costume Design & Construction, Drawing, Fashion Arts, Illustration, Textile Design, Theatre Arts
Adult Hobby Classes: Enrl 100; tuition $650 per 3 cr course. Courses—Fashion Design
Summer School: Dir, R F Alartosky. Enrl 100; tuition $650 per 3 cr course of 15 wks. Courses—Fashion Design

SCHOOL OF THE MUSEUM OF FINE ARTS, 230 The Fenway, 02115. Tel 617-267-6100, 267-1219; FAX 617-424-6271; *Dean* Deborah H Dluhy, PhD
Estab 1876; pvt; D & E; scholarships; SC 139, LC 16; enrl D 700, E 1000, grad 50, others 24
Ent Req: HS dipl, HS and col transcripts, portfolio
Degrees: Dipl, BFA, BFA plus BA or BS, BSEd, MFA, MAT (all degrees in affiliation with Tufts University)
Tuition: Dipl $12,250 per yr; BFA varies on ratio of academics & studies taken in any given year; MFA $23,000 for the degree
Courses: Art Education, Art History, Ceramics, Drawing, Film, Graphic Arts, Graphic Design, Illustration, Jewelry, Mixed Media, Painting, Photography, Printmaking, Sculpture, Video, Performance
Adult Hobby Classes: E & Saturday classes; enrl 1378; tuition $450-750 per 15 wk sem, 1.5 cr or 3 cr per course. Courses—Artists' Books, Ceramics, Drawing, Electronic Arts, Film/Animation, Graphic Design, Jewelry, Mixed Media, Painting, Papermaking, Photography, Printmaking, Sculpture, Stained Glass, Video
Summer School: Dir, Donald Grey. Enrl 717; 3 terms of 1-8 wks beginning 2nd wk in June. Courses—same as adult education courses

UNIVERSITY OF MASSACHUSETTS - BOSTON, Art Dept, Harbor Campus, 100 Morrissey Blvd, 02125-3393. Tel 617-287-5730; FAX 617-287-5757; *Chmn* Anne McCauley; *Emeritus Prof* Ruth Butler, PhD; *Emeritus Prof* Hal Thurman; *Assoc Prof* Wilfredo Chiesa; *Assoc Prof* Melissa Shook; *Assoc Prof* Ronald Polito; *Assoc Prof* Nancy Stieber; *Assoc Prof* Pamela Jones-Rothwell; *Asst Prof* John Gianvito; *Asst Prof* Sam Walker; *Asst Prof* Victoria Weston
Sch estab 1965, dept estab 1966; pub; D & E; SC 18, LC 32; enrl D 900, E 100, maj 200
Ent Req: Entrance exam
Degrees: BA
Tuition: Res—$1300 per sem; nonres—$3600 per sem
Courses: Art History, Constructions, Drawing, Film, Intermedia, Painting, Photography, Printmaking, Video, Film History

BRADFORD

BRADFORD COLLEGE, Creative Arts Division, 320 S Main St, 01835. Tel 508-372-7161; *Chmn* Peter Waldron, MFA; *Prof* Marc Mannheimer, MFA; *Prof* Richard Newman, MFA; *Assoc Prof* Mary Lee Karlins, MFA; *Assoc Prof* Scott Stroot, MFA; *Assoc Prof* Dr Frederick Schuetze; *Asst Prof* Rita Berkowitz, BA; *Asst Prof* Marvin Sweet, MFA; *Asst Prof* Fred Evers, MFA
Estab 1803; pvt; D & E; scholarships; SC 20, LC 12; enrl D 300
Ent Req: HS dipl
Degrees: BA(Creative Arts) 4 yrs
Tuition: Res—$12,415 per yr; nonres—$425 per cr; campus res—room $5950 per yr
Courses: Advertising Design, Aesthetics, Art Appreciation, Art History, Ceramics, Collages, Costume Design & Construction, Design, Drawing, Film, Painting, Theatre Arts, Color & Composition, 2-D & 3-D Design, Psychology of Art, Weaving

BRIDGEWATER

BRIDGEWATER STATE COLLEGE, Art Dept, School and Summer Sts, 02325. Tel 508-697-1200; FAX 508-279-6128; *Chmn* John Heller, MFA; *Prof* John Droege, MFA; *Prof* Joan Hausrath, MFA; *Prof* William Kendall, MFA; *Prof* Stephen Smalley, EdD; *Prof* Roger Dunn, PhD; *Prof* Robert Ward; *Assoc Prof* Mercedes Nunez; *Assoc Prof* Dorothy Pulsifer
Estab 1840; pub; D & E; SC 35, LC 10, GC 35; enrl D 500, E 100, non-maj 440, maj 100, grad 10
Ent Req: HS dipl, SAT
Degrees: BA 4 yrs
Tuition: Res—undergrad $125.81 per cr hr, grad $140.60 per cr hr
Courses: Art Education, Art History, Ceramics, Drawing, Goldsmithing, Graphic Arts, Graphic Design, Handicrafts, Jewelry, Painting, Printmaking, Sculpture, Silversmithing, †Studio Art
Adult Hobby Classes: Enrl 100. Courses—Same as day courses; rotational
Summer School: Dir, Dorothy Pulsifer. Enrl 40. Courses—Same as above

CAMBRIDGE

HARVARD UNIVERSITY, Dept of Fine Arts, Sackler Museum, 485 Broadway, 02138. Tel 617-495-2377; FAX 617-495-1769; *Chmn Dept* I Kalavrezou. Instrs: FT 24
Estab 1874; pvt; scholarships; LC 26 incl GC 12; enrl undergrad 88, grad 100
Courses: Art History

LESLEY COLLEGE, Arts Institute, 29 Everett St, 02138. Tel 617-868-9600; FAX 617-349-8150; WATS 800-999-1959. *Prog Dir* Dr Julia Byers
Scholarships
Tuition: $5400 annual tuition
Courses: Art Appreciation, Art Education, Art History, Ceramics, Design, Drawing, Handicrafts, Painting, Photography, Printmaking, †Art Therapy
Summer School: Dir, Paolo J Knill. Enrl 80; 6 wk

MASSACHUSETTS INSTITUTE OF TECHNOLOGY
—**School of Architecture and Planning,** 77 Massachusetts Ave, Rm 7-231, 02139. Tel 617-253-4401; FAX 617-253-9417; *Dean* William J Mitchell; *Assoc Dean* Bernard Frieden; *Head Dept* Stanford Anderson; *Urban Studies & Planning* Bish Sanyal. Instrs: FT 62
Estab 1865; pvt; scholarships; SC, LC, GC; enrl 600
Degrees: MA, PhD(Building Technol); Media Arts & Sciences
Tuition: $20,100 per yr
Courses: History of Art & Architecture
—**Center for Advanced Visual Studies,** 265 Massachusetts Ave, NS2-157, 02139. Tel 617-253-4415; FAX 617-253-1660; *Dir* Steve Benton
Estab dept 1967; pvt; D & E; SC 9, LC 1, GC 5; enrl D & E 250, non-maj 240, grad 10
Ent Req: BA degree
Degrees: MS(Visual Studies)
Tuition: $10,050 per term
Courses: †Video, Art & Technology, Environmental Art
Summer School: Art Workshop

CHESTNUT HILL

BOSTON COLLEGE, Fine Arts Dept, 02167. Tel 617-552-4295; *Chmn* John Michalczyk. Instrs: FT 11, PT 20
Degrees: BA offered
Courses: Art History, Ceramics, Drawing, Film, Painting, Photography, Sculpture, Studio Art

PINE MANOR COLLEGE, Visual Arts Dept, 400 Heath St, 02167. Tel 617-731-7157; FAX 617-731-7199; *Div Chmn* Robert Owczarek
Estab 1911; pvt; D; SC 25, LC 25; enrl D 80
Ent Req: HS dipl
Degrees: AA & AS 2 yrs, BA 4 yrs
Tuition: Res—undergrad $15,190 per acad yr; campus res—room & board $6460 per acad yr
Courses: Architecture, †Art History, Costume Design & Construction, Drafting, Drawing, Graphic Arts, Interior Design, Museum Staff Training, Painting, Printmaking, Sculpture, Stage Design, Theatre Arts, Visual Arts
Adult Hobby Classes: Studio courses 25, lecture courses 25
Summer School: Dir, Dr Eva I Kampits

CHICOPEE

OUR LADY OF ELMS COLLEGE, Dept of Fine Arts, 291 Springfield St, 01013. Tel 413-594-2761; FAX 413-592-4871; *Chmn Dept* Nancy Costanzo
Estab 1928, dept estab 1950; pvt; D & E; scholarships; SC 14, LC 6; enrl D 210, non-maj 193, maj 17
Ent Req: HS dipl, Col Ent Exam (Verbal and Math)
Degrees: BA 4 yrs
Tuition: Res—$16,565 per yr on campus, $11,004 per yr commuter
Courses: Art Education, Photography, Art History, Calligraphy, Ceramics, Drawing, Painting, Printmaking, Sculpture

DOVER

CHARLES RIVER SCHOOL, Creative Arts Program, 56 Centre St, PO Box 339, 02030-0339. Tel 508-785-0068, 785-8250; FAX 508-785-8291; *Dir* Toby Dewey
Estab 1970; pvt summer school; D
Ent Req: None
Tuition: $1070 per 4 wks
Courses: Photography, Textile Design, Art, Dance, Drama, Media, Music, Sports, Writing
Summer School: Dir, Talbot Dewey Jr. Art Program

FRAMINGHAM

DANFORTH MUSEUM OF ART SCHOOL, 123 Union Ave, 01702. Tel 508-620-0050; *Dir* Beverly Snow
Pvt; scholarships
Ent Req: None
Tuition: Varies per course; museum members receive a tuition reduction
Courses: Art History, Calligraphy, Ceramics, Drawing, Graphic Arts, Interior Design, Jewelry, Painting, Photography, Printmaking, Sculpture, Weaving
Adult Hobby Classes: Enrl 100 - 200; tuition varies per 9 wk sessions. Courses—Arts, Crafts, Photography
Children's Classes: Enrl 100 - 200; tuition varies per 8 wk session. Courses—Art Multi-Media, Ceramics
Summer School: Enrl 100-150; tuition varies per 2 wk courses. Courses—Same as above

FRAMINGHAM STATE COLLEGE, Art Dept, 100 State St, 01702. Tel 508-620-1220, 626-4011 (Sullivan); *Chmn* Eugene Sullivan; *Prof* Dr Brucia Witthoft, PhD; *Assoc Prof* John Anderson; *Asst Prof* Sachiko Beck; *Asst Prof* Barbara Milot; *Asst Prof* Marc Cote
Estab 1839, dept estab 1920; pub; D & E; scholarships; SC 20, LC 10, GC 10; enrl D 3000, E 2500, maj 124
Ent Req: HS dipl, portfolio review
Degrees: BA 4 yrs
Tuition: Res $878 per yr nonres $2957; campus res—room & board $1800 per yr
Courses: †Art History, Museum Studies, †Studio Art
Adult Hobby Classes: Art History, Studio Art
Summer School: Dir, James Brown. Tuition $170 per course for term of 8 wks. Courses—Art History, Studio

FRANKLIN

DEAN COLLEGE, Visual Art Dept, 99 Main St, 02038. Tel 508-541-1795; FAX 508-541-8726; *Div Chmn* Nancy Kerr; *Asst Prof* Lyn Stangland-Cameron, MFA; *Instr* Margaret Fitzpatrick, MFA
Estab 1865, dept estab 1960; pvt; D & E; Scholarships; SC 10, LC 4; enrl D 220, E 30, non-maj 180, maj 30
Ent Req: HS dipl
Degrees: AA, AS 2 yrs
Tuition: $9155 per yr; campus res—room & board $5700
Courses: Art Appreciation, Art History, Ceramics, Constructions, Design, Drawing, Film, Graphic Arts, Graphic Design, History of Art & Archaeology, Painting, Photography, Printmaking, Sculpture, Theatre Arts, Fundamentals of Color, †Graphics, †Introduction to Visual Art, †Survey of Art - Greek through Renaissance, †Survey of Modern Art & Architecture, †2-D Design, †3-D Design
Adult Hobby Classes: Enrl 10-25 per class; tuition $125 per cr hr for 14 wk term. Courses—Ceramics, Fundamental Drawing, Introduction to Visual Art, Photography I
Summer School: Dir, Jay Evans. Enrl 10-25 per class; tuition $125 for 4-6 wk term. Courses—Fundamental Drawing, Introduction to Visual Art, Photography I

GREAT BARRINGTON

SIMON'S ROCK COLLEGE OF BARD, Visual Arts Dept, 84 Alford Rd, 01230. Tel 413-528-0771; FAX 413-528-7365; *Chmn Studio Arts Dept* William Jackson; *Instr* Arthur Hillman, MFA. Instrs: PT 2
Estab 1966; pvt; D & E; scholarships; SC 14, LC 4
Ent Req: Personal interview
Degrees: AA 2-3 yrs, BA 4 yrs
Tuition: $16,900 per yr; campus res—room $2740, board $2880
Courses: Aesthetics, Art History, Ceramics, Drawing, Graphic Design, Illustration, Intermedia, Jewelry, Painting, Photography, Printmaking, Sculpture, Artist & the Book, Introduction to the Arts, Microcomputer Graphics, 2-D Design, 3-D Design

GREENFIELD

GREENFIELD COMMUNITY COLLEGE, Art, Graphic Design & Media Communication Dept, One College Dr, 01301. Tel 413-774-3131; *Head Art Dept* Tom Boisvert; *Instr* John Bross, MFA; *Instr* Pamela Sacher, MA; *Instr* Penne Krol, MFA; *Instr* Tom Young, MFA; *Art Historian* Keith Hollingworth; *Instr* Ron Kim
Estab 1962; maintains a small gallery; pub; D & E; scholarships; SC 16; enrl in school D 1400, E 400, maj 110
Ent Req: HS dipl
Degrees: AA, AS 2 yrs
Tuition: Res—$36 per day, $52 per evening; nonres—$188 per cr, $54 per cr to VT & NH res
Courses: †Advertising Design, †Art History, †Commercial Art, Display, †Drawing, Graphic Arts, Graphic Design, Illustration, †Painting, †Photography, †Printmaking, Video, Media Communication
Adult Hobby Classes: Enrl 85; tuition $38 per cr. Courses—Design, Drawing, Photography & Non-credit workshops
Children's Classes: Enrl 50; no tuition during Spring & Fall. Courses—Talented & Gifted Program
Summer School: Dir, Bob Keir. Tuition $38 per cr for a 7 wk term. Courses—Color, Design, Drawing Workshop, Photography

HOLYOKE

HOLYOKE COMMUNITY COLLEGE, Dept of Art, 303 Homestead Ave, 01040. Tel 413-538-7000; FAX 413-534-8975; *Chmn* John Field
Estab 1946; pub; D & E; scholarships; SC 7, LC 4; enrl D 115, E 20, maj 50
Ent Req: HS dipl, portfolio
Degrees: AA 2 yrs
Tuition: Res—$600.50 per sem; nonres— $1344 per sem plus $198 student fee
Courses: Art Education, Drawing, Graphic Arts, Graphic Design, History of Art & Archaeology, Painting, Photography
Summer School: Dir, William Murphy. Courses—Per regular session, on demand

LONGMEADOW

BAY PATH COLLEGE, Dept of Art, 588 Longmeadow St, 01106. Tel 413-567-0621; FAX 413-567-9324; *Dir Humanities* Irene Herden; *Instr* Carole Guthrie
Estab 1947; pvt; W; D & E; SC 18, LC 2; enrl D 660, E 400, maj 10
Ent Req: HS dipl
Degrees: AFA 2 yr
Tuition: $320 per cr, $10,200 comprehensive tuition
Courses: Ceramics, Drawing, Graphic Arts, Handicrafts, History of Art & Archaeology, Painting
Adult Hobby Classes: Enrl 300; tuition $80 per 8 wk course. Courses - Drawing, Painting, Watercolor

LOWELL

UNIVERSITY OF MASSACHUSETTS LOWELL, Dept of Art, 01854. Tel 508-934-3851, 934-3494; FAX 508-934-3034; *Chmn Dept* Fred Faudie; *Prof* Brenda Pinardi, MFA; *Assoc Prof* James Veatch, EdM; *Assoc Prof* James Coates, MFA; *Prof* Arno Minkkinen
Estab 1975 (merger of Lowell State College and Lowell Technological Institute); pub; D & E; enrl D 1200, E 25, non-maj 450, maj 150
Ent Req: HS dipl, SAT
Degrees: BA(Art), BFA 4 yrs
Tuition: Res—undergrad $4000 per yr, $2000 per sem; nonres—undergrad $10,000 per yr, $5000 per sem; campus res—room & board $2366 per yr
Courses: †Art History, †Studio Art
Adult Hobby Classes: Enrl 15 - 20 per course; tuition $135. Courses—Art Appreciation, Drawing, Painting, Survey of Art
Summer School: Dir, Jackey Malone. Enrl 10-15; tuition $135 per cr for 3 weeks. Courses—Art Appreciation, Drawing, Photography, Survey of Art I & II, Seminars in Italy, Greece, Finland, France

MEDFORD

TUFTS UNIVERSITY, Dept of Art & Art History, 11 Talbot Ave, 02155. Tel 617-627-3567; FAX 617-627-3890; *Chmn Art & Art History* Andrew McClellan; *Prof* Miriam Balmuth, PhD; *Prof* Madeline H Caviness, PhD; *Prof* Margaret H Floyd, PhD; *Prof* Judith Wechsler, PhD; *Assoc Prof* Eric Rosenberg, PhD; *Asst Prof* Ikumi Kaminishi, PhD; *Asst Prof* Eva Hoffman, PhD; *Asst Prof* Jodi Magness, PhD; *Adjunct Prof* Barbara E White, PhD; *Adjunct Prof* Lucy Der Manuelian, PhD; *Lectr* Steven Nelson
Pvt; D
Ent Req: HS dipl
Degrees: BA, BS, BFA, MA, MFA; certificate in museum studies
Tuition: $22,992 per yr, room, board & fees
Courses: †Art History, Calligraphy, Ceramics, Design, Drawing, Film, Graphic Arts, Graphic Design, Illustration, Jewelry, Lettering, Mixed Media, Museum Staff Training, History of Architecture, Studio, Museum Studies, Metal Working, Interdisciplinary Studio Art
Adult Hobby Classes: Courses offered
Summer School: Dir, Andrew McClellan. Enrl 100; tuition $990 for 6 wks. Courses—Boston Architecture, Modern Art, Survey, Museum History

NORTHAMPTON

SMITH COLLEGE, Art Dept, Hillyer Hall, Rm 112, 01063. Tel 413-584-2700; FAX 413-585-3119; *Chmn Art Dept* Dwight Pogue; *Prof* Marylin Rhei, PhD; *Prof* Helen Searing; *Prof* Elliot Offner, MFA; *Assoc Prof* Craig Felton, PhD; *Assoc Prof* A Lee Burns, MFA; *Assoc Prof* Caroline Houser, PhD; *Assoc Prof* Martha Armstrong; *Asst Prof* Brigitte Buettner; *Asst Prof* N C Christopher Couch; *Asst Prof* Barbara Kellum; *Asst Prof* Dana Leibsohn; *Asst Prof* Gary Niswonger; *Asst Prof* John Moore; *Lecturer* Richard Joslin, MArchit; *Lectr* Ruth Mortimer, MS. Instrs: FT 17
Estab 1875, dept estab 1877; pvt; W; D; scholarships; SC 24, LC 34; enrl maj 170
Ent Req: HS dipl, col board exam
Degrees: BA 4 yrs
Tuition: $20,000 per yr incl room & board
Courses: Architecture, Art History, Calligraphy, Drafting, Drawing, Graphic Arts, Graphic Design, History of Art & Archaeology, Landscape Architecture, Painting, Photography, Printmaking, Sculpture, Color, Design with Computer, Woodcut

NORTH DARTMOUTH

UNIVERSITY OF MASSACHUSETTS DARTMOUTH, College of Visual & Performing Arts, 285 Old Westport Rd, 02747. Tel 508-999-8564; FAX 508-999-8901; *Dean Col* Michael D Taylor, PhD; *Chmn Music Dept* Eleanor Carlson, DMA; *Chmn Art Educ* Dante Vena, PhD; *Chmn Fine Art* Anthony J Miraglia, MFA; *Chmn Design* Harvey Goldman, MFA; *Chmn Art History* Magali M Carrera, PhD; *Coordr Gallery* Lasse Antonsen, MA. Instrs: FT 38, PT 15
Estab 1895, col estab 1948; pub; D & E; scholarships; SC 75, LC 41, GC 7; enrl D 700
Ent Req: HS dipl, SAT, open admis to qualified freshmen
Degrees: BFA and BA 4 yr, MFA and MAE 2-5 yrs
Tuition: Res—undergrad $4151 per yr, grad $10,400 per yr; nonres—undergrad $4784 per yr, grad $10,733 per yr; campus res room & board $4128 per yr
Courses: Art Education, Art History, Ceramics, Design, Illustration, Jewelry, Painting, Photography, Printmaking, Sculpture, Textile Design, Electronic Imaging
Adult Hobby Classes: Enrl 175; tuition $365 for 14 wk session. Courses—13 including Art History, Ceramics, Jewelry
Children's Classes: Enrl 35; tuition $95 for 9 wk session. Courses—Children's Theater
Summer School: Dir, Dean R Waxler. Enrl 240; tuition $365 for 5 wk session. Courses—15 including Art History, Crafts

NORTON

WHEATON COLLEGE, Art Dept, 26 E Main St, 02766. Tel 508-285-7722; FAX 508-285-2908; *Chmn Dept* Tim Cunard. Instrs: FT 6, PT 3
Estab 1834; pvt; scholarships; SC 6, LC 18; enrl 1307
Degrees: BA (art history) 4 yr, BFA(Studio Art)
Tuition: $19,740 per yr, incl room & board $25,990 per yr
Courses: †Art History, Drawing, Painting, Photography, Printmaking, Sculpture, 2-D & 3-D Design

PAXTON

ANNA MARIA COLLEGE, Dept of Art, Sunset Lane, PO Box 114, 01612. Tel 508-849-3441; *Chmn Dept* Alice Lambert. Instrs: FT 2, PT 4
Estab 1948; pvt; D & E; scholarships; SC 15, LC 12; enrl D 397, maj 32
Ent Req: HS dipl, ent exam
Degrees: 4 yr
Tuition: $7875 per sem
Courses: †Advertising Design, Aesthetics, †Art Education, Art History, Ceramics, Drawing, Lettering, Painting, Photography, Sculpture, †Teacher Training, Weaving, †Art Therapy, Enameling, Macrame, Modeling, Rug Design, Silk Screen, Stitchery, †Studio Art
Summer School: Dir, Ann McMorrow. Two sessions beginning May.

PITTSFIELD

BERKSHIRE COMMUNITY COLLEGE, Dept of Fine Arts, 1350 West St, 01201. Tel 413-499-4660; FAX 413-447-7840; *Chmn Dept* Mark Milloff; *Instr* Benigna Chilla, MFA
Estab 1960, dept estab 1961; pub; D & E; scholarships; SC 16, LC 4; enrl D 72, E 75, non-maj 12, maj 72
Ent Req: HS dipl
Degrees: AA 2 yrs
Tuition: Res—$80 per cr hr; nonres—$230 per cr hr
Courses: Art History, Drawing, Mixed Media, Painting, Photography, Printmaking, Applied Graphics, 2-D Design, 3-D Design, Primitive Art, 20th Century Art
Adult Hobby Classes: Continuing education evening classes, some may be applied to degree program
Summer School: Enrl 75; tuition $35 per cr hr for term of 7 wks beginning June. Courses—Design, Drawing, Painting, Photography

PROVINCETOWN

CAPE COD SCHOOL OF ART, 48 Pearl St, 02657. Tel 508-487-0101; *Dir* Lois Griffel
Estab 1899; pvt summer school; D
Ent Req: None
Courses: Drawing, Painting, Plein Air Painting in Landscape, Still Life, Portraits
Adult Hobby Classes: Enrl 20 per workshop; tuition $275 for 5 days. Courses—Oil Painting, Pastel Painting, Portrait Painting, Watercolor Painting
Children's Classes: Enrl 20; tuition $275 for 5 days (ages 12-18). Courses—Oil Painting for Beginners
Summer School: Dir, Lois Griffel. Courses—Oil Painting, Pastel Painting, Portrait Painting, Watercolor Painting

QUINCY

QUINCY COLLEGE, Fine Arts Dept, 34 Coddington St, 02169. Tel 617-984-1611; FAX 617-984-1779; *Chmn Humanities Div* Deann Elliott
Degrees: AA, AS and Certificate offered
Tuition: $925 per sem
Courses: Drawing, Painting, Photography, Development to American Film

SALEM

SALEM STATE COLLEGE, Art Dept, 352 LaFayette St, 01970. Tel 508-741-6222; FAX 508-741-6126; *Chmn Dept* Ingrida Raudzens, MA; *Prof* Elissa Ananian, MAT; *Prof* N E Wagman, MEd; *Prof* John Volpacchio, MFA; *Prof* Frank Quimby, MEd; *Prof* Patricia Johnston, PhD; *Prof* Mark Raudzens, MFA; *Prof* Richard Lewis, MFA; *Prof* Ruth Trussell, MFA
Estab 1854; pub; D & E; scholarships; SC 19, LC 8, GC 5; enrl maj 167
Ent Req: HS dipl
Degrees: BA 4 yrs
Tuition: Res—$1408 per yr; nonres—$5542 per yr; campus res available
Courses: †Art Education, †Art History, Ceramics, †Graphic Design, Illustration, Jewelry, Mixed Media, †Painting, †Photography, †Printmaking, Sculpture, Multimedia Design, 3-D Studio
Summer School: Pres, Dr Nancy D Harrington

SOUTH HADLEY

MOUNT HOLYOKE COLLEGE, Art Dept, 01075. Tel 413-538-2200; FAX 413-538-2167; *Chmn* John Varriano; *Asst Chmn* Nancy Campbell
Estab 1858; pvt; W; D & E; scholarships; SC 13, LC 32; enrl D 409, maj 52
Ent Req: SAT, college boards
Degrees: BA
Tuition: Res—undergrad $19,300 per yr
Courses: Drawing, Painting, Printmaking, Sculpture
Adult Hobby Classes: Continuing education program leading to BA

SPRINGFIELD

SPRINGFIELD COLLEGE, Dept of Visual & Performing Arts, 263 Alden St, 01109. Tel 413-748-3540; FAX 413-748-3764; *Chmn Dept* William Blizard, MA; *Assoc Prof* Ron Maggio, MFA; *Asst Prof* Martin Shell, MFA; *Asst Prof* Chris Haynes; *Asst Prof* Simone Alter-Muri, Ed; *Asst Prof* Cynthia Noble, MA; *Asst Prof* Leslie Abrams; *Instr* Paula Hodecker, MFA; *Instr* Charles Abel; *Instr* Holly Murray, MFA; *Instr* Ruth West, MFA; *Instr* John Moriarty; *Instr* Ross Fox; *Instr* Catherine Lydon
Estab 1885, dept estab 1971; pvt; D & E; scholarships; SC 30, LC 6; enrl D 335, E 10, non-maj 300, maj 50
Ent Req: HS dipl, SAT, portfolio

Degrees: BA, BS 4 yr, MS(Art Therapy) 2 yr
Tuition: $11,900 per yr
Courses: Advertising Design, Aesthetics, Art Appreciation, Art Education, Art History, Ceramics, Collages, Conceptual Art, Constructions, Costume Design & Construction, Design, Drawing, Graphic Arts, Graphic Design, History of Art & Archaeology, Illustration, Intermedia, Teacher Training, Mixed Media, Museum Staff Training, Painting, Photography, Printmaking, Restoration & Conservation, Sculpture, Stage Design, Theatre Arts, Video, †Art Therapy, †Computer Graphics, Computer Graphics Animation, Arts Management
Summer School: Dir, Diane Erickson. Enrl 200; 3 or 6 wk term beginning May 30. Courses—Art Therapy, Drawing, Painting, Photography, Pottery, Sculpture

TRURO

TRURO CENTER FOR THE ARTS AT CASTLE HILL, INC, Castle Rd, PO Box 756, 02666. Tel 508-349-7511; *Dir* Mary Stackhouse; *Instr* Alan Dugan; *Instr* Douglas Huebler; *Instr* Sidney Simon; *Instr* Paul Bowen; *Instr* Anna Poor; *Instr* Ethel Edwards. Instrs: over 45 other nationally known instructors
Estab 1972; pvt summer school; D & E; scholarships; SC 50, LC 3, GC 30; enrl 590
Ent Req: None
Tuition: $150 for one wk; no campus res
Courses: Ceramics, Collages, Conceptual Art, Drawing, Painting, Printmaking, Photography, Sculpture, Bronze Foundry, Literature, Writing
Summer School: Dir, Mary Stackhouse. Enrl 500-550; tuition $150 per workshop. Courses—Clay, Drawing, Painting, Photography, Printmaking, Sculpture, Woodwork, Writing

WALTHAM

BRANDEIS UNIVERSITY, Dept of Fine Arts, PO Box 9110, 02254-9110. Tel 617-736-2655; *Chmn* Susan Lichtman. Instrs: FT 12
Estab 1948; pvt; D; scholarships; SC 10, LC 28; enrl 2800
Ent Req: HS dipl, college board ent exam
Degrees: BS 4 yr
Tuition: $19,380 per yr
Courses: Art History, Drawing, Painting, Sculpture, Design
Summer School: Dir, Sanford Lotlor. Enrl 10-12 per course; tuition $585 per course for 4 week term. Courses—Introduction to History of Art II, Survey of Western Architecture

WELLESLEY

WELLESLEY COLLEGE, Art Dept, 02181. Tel 617-283-2042; FAX 617-283-3647; *Chmn* Margaret Carroll; *Prof* Peter J Fergusson, PhD; *Prof* James F O'Gorman, PhD; *Prof* James W Rayen, MFA; *Prof* Richard W Wallace, PhD; *Prof* Miranda Marvin, PhD; *Prof* Anne Clapp, PhD; *Prof* Carlos Dorrien; *Prof* Lilian Armstrong; *Assoc Prof* Bunny Harvey, MFA; *Assoc Prof* Alice T Friedman, PhD; *Asst Prof* Anne Higonnet; *Asst Prof* Patricia Berman
Estab 1875, dept estab 1886; pvt; D; SC 19, LC 46; enrl D 1233
Ent Req: HS dipl
Degrees: BA
Tuition: $16,690 per yr; campus res—room $2860 & board $3025
Courses: †Architecture, †Art History, Drawing, Graphic Arts, Painting, Photography, Printmaking, Sculpture, †Studio Art

WEST BARNSTABLE

CAPE COD COMMUNITY COLLEGE, Art Dept, Humanities Division, Route 132, 02668. Tel 508-362-2131; FAX 508-362-8638; *Coordr Art* Robert McDonald, MFA; *Prof* Sara Ringler, MFA; *Prof* Marie Canaves
Estab 1963, dept estab 1973; pub; D & E; SC 14, LC 7; enrl in school D 2000, E 3000, maj 60
Ent Req: HS dipl
Degrees: AA and AS 2 yrs
Tuition: Res—$950 per yr, nonres—$5052 per yr
Courses: Art History, Drafting, Drawing, Graphic Design, Illustration, Mixed Media, Painting, Stage Design, Theatre Arts, Video, Life Drawing, Visual Fundamentals
Adult Hobby Classes: Enrl 100 - 150; tuition $225 per 3 cr. Courses—Art History, Drawing, Graphic Design, Watercolor
Summer School: Dir, Dean Peter Birkel. Enrl 100 - 200; tuition $225 per 3 cr for 8 wk term beginning June 23. Courses—Art History, Drawing, Graphic Design, Visual Fundamentals

WESTFIELD

WESTFIELD STATE COLLEGE, Art Dept, Western Ave, 01086. Tel 413-568-3311, Ext 300; *Chmn* Barbara Keim
Estab 1972; pub; D & E; scholarships
Ent Req: HS dipl & portfolio review
Degrees: BA (Fine Arts) 4 yrs
Courses: Art Appreciation, Art Education, Art History, Commercial Art, Design, Drawing, Illustration, Lettering, Mixed Media, Printmaking, Sculpture, Teacher Training, Anatomy, Computer Graphics, Practicum
Adult Hobby Classes: Enrl 100. Courses—Design Fundamentals, Studio Courses
Summer School: Dept Chmn, P Conant. Courses—Design Fundamentals, Studio Courses

WESTON

REGIS COLLEGE, Dept of Art, 235 Wellesley St, 02193. Tel 617-768-7000; FAX 617-768-8339; *Chmn* Sr Marie de Sales Dinneen
Estab 1927, dept estab 1944; den; D & E; scholarships; SC 12, LC 12; enrl D 250, non-maj 200, maj 50
Ent Req: HS dipl, SAT, various tests
Degrees: AB 4 yr
Tuition: $11,410 annual tuition
Courses: †Art History, Ceramics, Drawing, Illustration, Painting, Art Therapy, Computer Design, Coordinating Seminars, Enameling, Etching, †Introduction to Art, Silk Screen, Stained Glass, Weaving, Woodcut, Graphic Techniques

WILLIAMSTOWN

WILLIAMS COLLEGE, Dept of Art, 01267. Tel 413-597-2377 (Art History Office), 597-3578 (Art Studio Office); FAX 413-597-3498 (Art History Office), 597-3693 (Art Studio Office); *Chmn Art History* Zirka Filipczak, PhD; *Chmn Studio Art* Aida Laleian, MFA; *Dir Grad Prog* Charles Haxthausen, PhD. Instrs: FT 12, PT 12
Estab 1793, dept estab 1903; pvt; D; scholarships; SC 14, LC 40, GC 10; enrl 2000, maj 85, grad 29
Ent Req: HS dipl
Degrees: BA 4 yrs, MA(History of Art) 2 yrs
Tuition: $21,759 per yr; campus res—room & board $6140 per yr
Courses: Architecture, Art History, Drawing, Painting, Photography, Printmaking, Sculpture, Video

WORCESTER

ASSUMPTION COLLEGE, Dept of Art & Music, 500 Salisbury St, 01615-0005. Tel 508-752-5615, Ext 206; *Chmn* Michelle Graveline, DMA; *Prof* Dona Lamothe; *Assoc Prof* Nancy Flanagan, MFA; *Assoc Prof* Michelle Granelina; *Asst Prof* Mary Ann Powers
Estab 1904, dept estab 1976; den; D & E; scholarships; enrl D 600, E 25
Ent Req: HS dipl
Degrees: BA 4 yr
Tuition: $13,700 per yr; campus res available
Courses: Aesthetics, Architecture, Art Education, Art History, Drawing, Graphic Arts, History of Art & Archaeology, Painting, Printmaking, Theatre Arts

CLARK UNIVERSITY, Dept of Visual & Performing Arts, 950 Main St, 01610. Tel 508-793-7113; *Chmn* Gerald Castonguay; *Dir Studio Art Prog* Donald W Krueger, MFA; *Dean Admissions* Richard Pierson. Instrs: FT 4, PT 10
Estab 1887; pvt; D & E; scholarships; SC 50, LC 24; enrl Maj 100, non-maj 450, other 20
Ent Req: HS dipl, portfolio, CEEB, achievement tests, SAT & ACH
Tuition: BFA & BA $7906 per yr, diploma $4000 per yr; campus res room & board $2610 per yr
Courses: Aesthetics, Ceramics, Drawing, †Graphic Design, †Illustration, †Painting, †Photography, Printmaking, Arts Management, Art Therapy, Environmental Art, †History of Art & Architecture, Visual Design, Visual Studies
Adult Hobby Classes: Offered through Clark University College of Professional and Continuing Education
Summer School: Offered through Clark University College of Professional and Continuing Education

COLLEGE OF THE HOLY CROSS, Dept of Visual Arts, 01610. Tel 508-793-2237; *Chair&Assoc Prof* Joanne Ziegler, PhD; *Gallery Dir* Ellen Lawrence; *Prof* Virginia C Raguin, PhD; *Assoc Prof* Father John Reboli; *Assoc Prof* Susan S Schmidt, MFA; *Asst Prof* Sarah Slavick; *Asst Prof* Sharon McComell; *Asst Prof* Stephen Burt; *Asst Prof* Robert Parke-Harrison; *Lectr* Ellen Lawrence
Estab 1843, dept estab 1954; pvt; D; SC 12, LC 15; enrl D 485, maj 25
Ent Req: HS dipl, SAT, ATS
Degrees: BA 4 yr
Courses: Aesthetics, Architecture, †Art History, Drawing, Graphic Arts, Graphic Design, History of Art & Archaeology, Painting, Photography, Printmaking, Sculpture, †Studio

WORCESTER CENTER FOR CRAFTS, 25 Sagamore Rd, 01605. Tel 508-753-8183; FAX 508-797-5626; *Exec Dir* Maryon M Attwood
Estab 1856; pvt; D & E; scholarships; SC 33, LC varies; enrl D & E 280, non-maj 30, maj 12
Ent Req: Portfolio review for two year professional prog, no req for adult educ
Tuition: $4,300 per yr, 2 year program; adult educ $105 per 10 wk session; no campus res
Courses: Calligraphy, †Ceramics, Goldsmithing, †Jewelry, Photography, †Silversmithing, Textile Design, Weaving, Enameling, †Fibre, Furniture Restoration, Stained Glass, †Wood Working
Adult Hobby Classes: Enrl 12-14 per class; four 10 wk sessions, Courses—Ceramics, Enamel, Furniture Refinishing, Photography, Stained Glass, Weaving & Fibre, Wood Working, Metal Working
Children's Classes: Enrl 10-14 per class; tuition $100 per 12 wks. Courses—Clay, Wood, Photography, Enameling, Baskets
Summer School: Enrl 150 adults & children, also children's summer camp

WORCESTER STATE COLLEGE, Visual & Performing Arts Dept, 486 Chandler, 01602. Tel 508-793-8000; FAX 508-793-8191; *Chmn* Dr Ellen Kosmere
Estab 1874; pub; D & E; SC 18, LC 9; enrl D & E 725
Ent Req: HS dipl, col board exams, completion of systems application form
Degrees: BA and BS 4 yrs
Tuition: Res—$1326.50 per sem; nonres—$3393.50
Courses: Art Education, Art History, Collages, Drafting, Drawing, Graphic Design, Handicrafts, Intermedia, Mixed Media, Painting, Printmaking, Sculpture, Environmental Design, History of Urban Form
Summer School: Usually 5-8 courses & workshops

MICHIGAN

ADRIAN

ADRIAN COLLEGE, Art & Design Dept, 110 S Madison, 49221. Tel 517-265-5161, Ext 454; Elec Mail pbenio@adrian.edu. *Chmn Art Dept* Pauleve Benio, MFA; *Prof* Michael Cassino, MFA; *Prof* Norman Knutson, MFA; *Asst Prof* Nancy Van Over, MA; *Asst Prof* Barbara Lock, MA; *Instr* Louise Kleinsmith, MA
Estab 1859, dept estab 1962; den; D & E; scholarships; SC 27, LC 6; enrl in dept D 250, E 50, non-maj 200, maj 70
Ent Req: HS dipl
Degrees: BA, BA with teaching cert & BFA
Tuition: $3126 per sem, $145 per sem hr; $854 per yr for room, $1260 per yr for board
Courses: Art Education, Ceramics, Design, Drawing, Fashion Arts, Graphic Design, Interior Design, Painting, Printmaking, Arts Management, Pre-Art Therapy
Children's Classes: Enrl 45; tuition $60-$100 for 6 wks. Courses—Ceramics, Mixed Media
Summer School: Dir, Pi Benio. Enrl 15; May term, summer term June-July. Courses—Advanced Study, Art Education, Design, Drawing

SIENA HEIGHTS COLLEGE, Studio Angelico-Art Dept, 1247 Siena Heights Dr, 49221. Tel 517-264-7860; FAX 517-264-7704; *Chmn Dept* Thomas Venner, MFA; *Prof* David Van Horn, MFA; *Assoc Prof* Joseph Bergman, MFA; *Assoc Prof* John Wittershiem, MFA; *Assoc Prof* Christine Reising, MFA; *Assoc Prof* Deborah Danielson, MFA; *Instr* Donna Milbauer, BFA; *Instr* Lois DeMots, MA
Estab 1919; pvt; D & E; scholarships; SC 56; enrl D 200, maj 96, grad 25
Ent Req: HS dipl
Degrees: BA & BFA 4 yrs
Tuition: Undergrad & grad $260 per cr hr; campus res—room & board $2100 per yr
Courses: Aesthetics, Architecture, Art Appreciation, Art Education, Art History, †Ceramics, Collages, †Drawing, †Graphic Arts, Jewelry, Mixed Media, †Painting, †Photography, †Printmaking, †Sculpture, Silversmithing, †Metalsmithing
Summer School: Dir, Thomas Venner. Enrl 20-40; tuition $240 cr hr, May 15-June 15. Courses—Bookmaking, Graphics, Metalsmithing, Mixed Media, Paris Study, Photography

ALBION

ALBION COLLEGE, Dept of Visual Arts, 611 E Porter St, 49224. Tel 517-629-0246; *Chmn Dept Visual Arts & Assoc Prof* Douglas Goering, MFA; *Prof* Douglas Goering, MFA; *Asst Prof* Lynne Chytilo, MFA; *Asst Prof* Billie Wicker, MA
Estab 1835; den; D & E; scholarships; SC 32, LC 8
Ent Req: HS dipl
Degrees: BA and BFA 4 yrs
Tuition: $13,868 per yr
Courses: Art History, Ceramics, Drawing, Film, Painting, Photography, Printmaking, Sculpture, Stage Design, Teacher Training, Theatre Arts
Summer School: Acad Dean, Dr Daniel Poteet. Tuition $131 per sem hr for term of 7 wks beginning May 15

ALLENDALE

GRAND VALLEY STATE UNIVERSITY, Art & Design Dept, 49401. Tel 616-895-3486; FAX 616-895-3106; *Chmn* J David McGee PhD; *Prof* Chester Alkema; *Prof* Donald Kerr; *Prof* Daleene Menning; *Assoc Prof* Ed Wong-Ligda; *Assoc Prof* Beverly Seley; *Assoc Prof* Rosalyn Muskovitz; *Assoc Prof* Dellas Henke; *Asst Prof* Lorelle Thomas; *Asst Prof* Richard Weis; *Asst Prof* Gary Sampson; *Asst Prof* Elona van Gent
Estab 1960; pub; D & E; scholarships; SC 15, LC 12, GC 1; enrl D 80, E 40
Ent Req: HS dipl or equivalent, portfolio
Degrees: BA(Studio), BS(Studio), BFA 4 yrs
Tuition: Res—undergrad $1093 per sem, $96 per cr hr; nonres—undergrad $2420 per sem, $220 per cr hr; campus res—room & board $3500 - $3970
Courses: Advertising Design, Art Appreciation, Art Education, Art History, Ceramics, Drawing, Graphic Design, Illustration, Jewelry, Painting, Printmaking, Sculpture
Summer School: Courses—Introduction to Art, Art for the Classroom Teacher, Workshops; Drawing and Painting at Aix-en-Provence, France

ALMA

ALMA COLLEGE, Clack Art Center, 614 W Superior, 48801. Tel 517-463-7220, 463-7111; FAX 517-463-7277; *Chmn* Carie Parks-Kirby, MFA; *Asst Prof* C Sandy Lopez-Isnardi
Estab 1886; pvt; D & E; scholarships; SC 10, LC 3; enrl D 200, maj 32
Degrees: BA, BFA
Tuition: $13,690; campus res—room & board $4905
Courses: Ceramics, Drawing, Graphic Design, History of Art & Archaeology, Jewelry, Museum Staff Training, Painting, Photography, Printmaking, Sculpture, Weaving, Advertising Design, Aesthetics, Art Education, Art History, Illustration, Mixed Media, Computer Graphics, Foreign Study, Scientific Illustration

ANN ARBOR

UNIVERSITY OF MICHIGAN, ANN ARBOR
—**School of Art & Design,** 2000 Bonisteel Blvd, Rm 2055, 48109-2069. Tel 313-764-0397; FAX 313-936-0469; *Dean* Allen Samuels. Instrs: FT 35, PT 13
Estab 1817, sch estab 1974; pub; D & E; scholarships; SC 50, LC 6, GC 15; enrl non-maj 533, maj 490, grad 50
Ent Req: HS dipl, portfolio exam
Degrees: BA, BFA, MA, MFA

Tuition: Res—$5200 per yr; nonres—$16,000 per yr
Courses: Graphic Design, Industrial Design, Photography, Printmaking, Sculpture, Jewelry, Mixed Media, Painting, Photography, Printmaking, Sculpture, Silversmithing, Textile Design, Jewelry Design, Metal Work, Scientific Illustration
Summer School: Interim Dean, Allen Samuels. Enrl varies; tuition res $799, nonres $3000 for term of spring & summer, spring May 1 to June 30, summer July 1 to Aug 30. Courses—2 & 3 wk intensive workshops offered
—**Dept of History of Art,** 48109. Tel 313-764-5400; *Chmn* Margaret Root; *Dir Kelsey Museum* Elaine K Gazda; *Adjunct Prof* Milo Beach; *Cur* Marshall Wu; *Dir Museum Art* William Hennessey; *Prof* Ilene H Forsyth; *Prof Emeritus* Richard Edwards; *Prof Emeritus* Marvin Eisenberg; *Prof* Diane Kirkpatrick; *Prof* R Ward Bissell; *Prof Emeritus* Nathan T Whitman; *Prof* Joel Isaacson; *Prof* Victor H Miesel; *Prof* John G Pedley; *Prof* Walter M Spink; *Prof* Margaret Root; *Assoc Prof* Thelma Thomas; *Assoc Prof* Virginia C Kane; *Assoc Prof* Martin Powers; *Assoc Prof* Patricia Simons; *Assoc Prof* John Humphrey; *Asst Prof* Yasser Tabbaa; *Assoc Prof* Sharon Patton; *Assoc Prof* Celeste Brusati; *Assoc Prof* Anatole Sonkevitch; *Asst Prof* Rebecca Zurier; *Asst Prof* Nii Quarcoopome; *Asst Prof* Jonathan Reynolds; *Asst Prof* Elizabeth Sears; *Asst Prof* Matthew Biro; *Instr* Eleanor Mannikka. Instrs: FT 16
Dept estab 1910; pub; scholarships & fels; enrl maj 75, grad 60
Degrees: BA, MA, PhD
Tuition: Res—undergrad $2095 per term, grad $3608 per term; nonres—undergrad $6947, grad $7424
Courses: †Art History, Museology
Summer School: Chairman, Diane Kirkpatrick. Enrl 77; tuition res $379 per cr, nonres $803 per cr

BATTLE CREEK

KELLOGG COMMUNITY COLLEGE, Visual & Performing Arts Dept, 450 North Ave, 49017. Tel 616-965-3931, Ext 2555; FAX 616-965-4133; *Chmn* Wyhomme Mathews; *Art Instr* Martin Hubbard; *Art Instr* Peter Williams. Instrs: FT 9, PT 18
Estab 1962; pub; D & E; scholarships; enrl D 2200, E 2000, maj 60
Ent Req: None
Degrees: AA 2-4 yr
Courses: †Advertising Design, †Architecture, †Art Education, †Art History, †Ceramics, †Commercial Art, Design, Drafting, †Drawing, †Graphic Arts, †Graphic Design, †Illustration, †Industrial Design, †Mixed Media, †Painting, †Photography, †Sculpture, Stage Design, Teacher Training, Theatre Arts
Adult Hobby Classes: Courses—all areas
Summer School: Courses—Basic Art & Appreciation

BENTON HARBOR

LAKE MICHIGAN COLLEGE, Dept of Art, 2755 E Napier Ave, 49022. Tel 616-927-3571, Ext 5180; *Instr* Ken Schaber, MFA
Estab 1943; pub; D & E; scholarships; SC 10, LC 5; enrl 3377 total
Ent Req: Open door policy
Degrees: AA 2 yrs
Tuition: Res—$45 per sem hr; nonres—out of district $55 per sem hr, out of state $65 per sem hr; no campus res
Courses: Art Appreciation, Art Education, Art History, Ceramics, Design, Drawing, Occupational Therapy, Painting, Photography, Printmaking, Sculpture, Weaving, 2-D & 3-D Design

BERRIEN SPRINGS

ANDREWS UNIVERSITY, Dept of Art, Art History & Design, 49104. Tel 616-471-3279; *Prof* Steve Hansen; *Prof* Gregory Constantine; *Assoc Prof* Charyl Jetter; *Assoc Prof* D L May; *Asst Prof* Peter Erhard. Instrs: FT 4
Estab 1952; den; D & E; SC 18, LC 5; enrl enrl 130, maj 20
Ent Req: HS grad
Degrees: BS(Art Educ), BA 4 yrs, BFA 4 yrs
Tuition: Tuition, room & board $5177 per quarter
Courses: Art Education, Art History, Ceramics, Drawing, Graphic Design, Painting, Photography, Printmaking, Sculpture, European Study
Summer School: Classes June 14-Aug 6

BIG RAPIDS

FERRIS STATE UNIVERSITY, Visual Communication Dept, 119 S State St, 49307. Tel 616-592-2426; *Dept Head* Kaaren Denyes. Instrs: 10
Scholarships
Degrees: AAS & BS
Tuition: Res—undergrad $1706 per sem; nonres—undergrad $3455.50 per sem
Courses: Advertising Design, Art History, Conceptual Art, Design, Drawing, Film, †Graphic Arts, †Graphic Design, Illustration, Intermedia, Lettering, Mixed Media, Painting, Photography, Printmaking, Video, Air Brush, Concept Development, Creative Writing, Figure Drawing, Production Art, Rendering, Typography
Adult Hobby Classes: Enrl 400; tuition $46.50 per cr hr
Summer School: Dir, Karl Walker. Enrl 3195, tuition $557 per qtr

BIRMINGHAM

BIRMINGHAM-BLOOMFIELD ART ASSOCIATION, 1516 S Cranbrook Rd, 48009. Tel 810-644-0866; *Exec Dir* Janet E Torno. Instrs: PT 75
Estab 1956; pub; D & E; SC 90-100, LC 4; enrl 3000 total
Tuition: $0-$300 per term, no campus res
Courses: Advertising Design, Aesthetics, Architecture, Art Appreciation, Art History, Calligraphy, Ceramics, Collages, Commercial Art, Design, Drawing, Fashion Arts, Goldsmithing, Graphic Arts, Graphic Design, Handicrafts, History of Art & Archaeology, Illustration, Intermedia, Jewelry, Lettering, Mixed Media, Painting, Printmaking, Sculpture, Silversmithing, Textile Design, Weaving, Glass,

Surface Design
Adult Hobby Classes: Enrl 3000-3500; tuition $0-$300 for 3-39 hrs.
Courses—Crafts, Drawing, Painting, Pottery, Sketching
Children's Classes: Enrl 500; tuition $75-$100.
Summer School: Dir, J Torno. Enrl 4-500; 2 wk term. Program on abbreviated basis

BLOOMFIELD HILLS

CRANBROOK ACADEMY OF ART, 1221 N Woodward, PO Box 801, 48303-0801. Tel 810-645-3300; FAX 313-646-0046; *Dir* Gerhardt Knodel; *Co-Head 2-D Design Dept* Laurie Makela; *Co-Head 2-D Design Dept* P Scott Makela; *Interim Head Fiber Dept* Margo Mensing; *Head Metalsmithing Dept* Gary Griffin; *Head Painting Dept* Beverly Fishman; *Head Photo Dept* Carl Toth; *Head Ceramics Dept* Tony Hepburn; *Head Archit Dept* Peter Lynch; *Head Printmaking Dept* Steve Murakishi; *Head Sculpture Dept* Heather McGill; *Head 3-D Design Dept* Peter Stathis
Estab 1932; pvt; scholarships; enrl 140
Ent Req: Portfolio
Degrees: MFA & MArchit 2 yrs
Tuition: $15,100 per yr; campus res—room & board $2000 (single), $1200 (double)
Courses: Architecture, Ceramics, Design, Painting, Photography, Printmaking, Sculpture, Fiber, Metalsmithing

DEARBORN

HENRY FORD COMMUNITY COLLEGE, Art Dept, 5101 Evergreen Rd, 48128. Tel 313-845-9634; *Chmn* Martin Anderson. Instrs: FT 6, PT 40
Estab 1938; pub; D & E; scholarships; SC 25, LC 9; enrl D 3500, E 7500, maj 600
Ent Req: HS dipl
Degrees: AA 2 yrs
Tuition: Res—$45 per cr hr; nonres—$71 per cr hr, plus lab fees; drive in campus
Courses: Art Appreciation, Art History, †Ceramics, Drawing, †Graphic Design, †Interior Design, Jewelry, †Painting, Photography, Printmaking, Sculpture, Textile Design, 2-D Design, 3-D Design
Children's Classes: Ceramics, Jewelry, Painting/Drawing, Sculpture
Summer School: Dir, Martin W Anderson. Tuition res-$30 per cr hr, nonres $42. Courses—Art Appreciation, Art History, Ceramics, Color Photography, Directed Study, Drawing, Black & White Photography, 2-D Design

DETROIT

CENTER FOR CREATIVE STUDIES, College of Art & Design, 201 E Kirby, 48202. Tel 313-872-3118; *Pres* Richard L Rogers; *Chmn Graphic Design* Lothar Hoffman; *Chmn Industrial Design* Clyde Foles; *Chmn Photography* Carlos Diaz; *Chmn Fine Arts* Aris Koutroulis; *Chmn Crafts* Herb Babcock; *Chmn Academic Studies* Dr Dorothy Kostuch; *Chmn Illustration* Nelson Greer; *Chmn Art Direction* Larry Fleming
Estab 1926; pvt; D & E; scholarships; enrl D 950, E 250, others 200
Ent Req: HS dipl & portfolio
Degrees: BFA 4 yrs
Tuition: $8900 yr, $4450 per sem
Courses: Advertising Design, Aesthetics, Art Appreciation, Art History, Calligraphy, Ceramics, Commercial Art, Design, Display, Drafting, Drawing, Film, Goldsmithing, †Graphic Arts, Graphic Design, History of Art & Archaeology, Illustration, †Industrial Design, Interior Design, Jewelry, Lettering, Mixed Media, Painting, Photography, Printmaking, Sculpture, Silversmithing, Textile Design, Video, Weaving, Crafts, Fine Arts, Glass
Adult Hobby Classes: Enrl 281. Courses—Computer Technology, Crafts, Fine Arts, Graphic Communication, Industrial Design, Photography
Children's Classes: Enrl 59. Courses—Art, Music
Summer School: Dir Acad Affairs, Clyde Foles. Enrl 230; tuition $392 per cr hr. Courses—Computer Technology, Crafts, Fine Arts, Industrial Design, Photography

MARYGROVE COLLEGE, Visual & Performing Arts Div, 8425 W McNichols Rd, 48221. Tel 313-862-8000, Ext 290; *Chmn Div* David Vandegrift, MFA; *Prof* Rose DeSloover; *Prof* Virginia Jones, DED; *Assoc Prof* Jean Louise Leahy; *Assoc Prof* David Vandegrift, MFA; *Assoc Prof* James Lutomski, MFA
Estab 1910; pvt; D & E; SC 37, LC 20, GC 5; enrl D 150, E 25, non-maj 60, maj 50, grad 5
Ent Req: Interview with portfolio
Degrees: BA & BFA 4 yrs
Tuition: Res—undergrad $319 per cr hr, grad $312 per cr hr; campus res available
Courses: Advertising Design, Art Education, Art History, †Ceramics, Commercial Art, Constructions, †Drawing, †Graphic Arts, Graphic Design, Lettering, Mixed Media, †Painting, Photography, †Printmaking, †Teacher Training
Adult Hobby Classes: Enrl 65; tuition $35-$90 per course. Courses—Drawing, Painting, Photography
Children's Classes: Enrl 100; tuition $20-$50 per course. Courses—Ceramics, Painting, Photography
Summer School: Dean Continuing Educ, Sr Andrea Lee, PhD. Enrl 40, tuition $86 per cr hr for term of two 6 wk terms. Courses—Basic courses, graduate and undergraduate

UNIVERSITY OF DETROIT MERCY, School of Architecture, 4001 W McNichols, PO Box 19900, 48219-0900. Tel 313-993-1532; FAX 313-993-1512; *Prof* John C Mueller; *Dean* Stephan P Vogel
Estab 1877; school estab 1964; pvt; D & E; scholarships; SC 14, LC 36; enrl D 200, maj 200
Ent Req: HS dipl, B average
Degrees: BArch 5 years
Tuition: $6108 per 12-18 cr per sem, $303 per 1-11 cr
Courses: Architecture, Design

WAYNE STATE UNIVERSITY, Dept of Art & Art History, School of Fine, Performing & Communication Arts, 150 Community Arts Bldg, 48202. Tel 313-577-2980; *Chmn* Marian Jackson. Instrs: FT 25, PT 20
Tuition: Res—undergrad $971 for 12 cr hrs, grad $944 for 8 cr hrs; nonres—undergrad $2105 for 12 cr hrs, grad $1990 for 8 cr hrs
Courses: Advertising Design, Art History, Ceramics, Design, Drawing, Industrial Design, Painting, Photography, Printmaking, Sculpture, Fibers, Interiors, Metals
Summer School: Tuition same as regular sem for 7 wks. Courses—Art History, Ceramics, Design, Drawing, Fibers, Painting, Photography, Sculpture

DOWAGIAC

SOUTHWESTERN MICHIGAN COLLEGE, Fine & Performing Arts Dept, 58900 Cherry Grove Rd, 49047. Tel 616-782-5113; *Chmn* Dr William Skoog, DA; *Instr* David R Baker, MFA; *Instr* Camille Riner, MFA; *Instr* Patty Bunner, MFA; *Instr* Jonathan Korzun, MA; *Instr* Wendy Willis, MM
Estab 1964; pub; D & E; scholarships; SC 13, LC 3; enrl D 200, E 100, non-maj 200, maj 100
Ent Req: HS dipl
Degrees: AA & AS
Tuition: Res—undergrad $44 per hr; nonres—undergrad $56 per hr; foreign & out of state $68 per hr
Courses: Advertising Design, Architecture, Ceramics, Commercial Art, Drafting, Drawing, Graphic Arts, Lettering, Painting, Photography, Printmaking
Adult Hobby Classes: Art Appreciation, Ceramics, Painting, Photography
Summer School: Dir, Marshall Bishop. Enrl 1000; 7 wk terms

EAST LANSING

MICHIGAN STATE UNIVERSITY, Dept of Art, 113 Kresge Art Ctr, 48824-1119. Tel 517-355-7610; FAX 517-432-3938; *Chmn* Linda O Stanford. Instrs: FT 30
Estab 1855; pub; D & E; scholarships; SC 77, LC 45, GC 25; enrl D 2500, non-maj 1500, maj 450, grad 60
Ent Req: HS dipl
Degrees: BA & BFA 4 yrs, MA 1 yr, MFA 2 yrs
Tuition: Res—undergrad $133-$148 per cr hr, grad $204 per cr hr; nonres—undergrad $361-$374 per cr hr, grad $411 per cr hr; campus res—room & board $1914
Courses: Art Appreciation, Art Education, Art History, Ceramics, Collages, Conceptual Art, Constructions, Design, Drawing, Graphic Design, History of Art & Archaeology, Jewelry, Mixed Media, Painting, Photography, Printmaking, Sculpture, Teacher Training, Video
Adult Hobby Classes: Tuition $10 per session. Courses—History of Art & Studio Art
Children's Classes: Enrl 150; tuition $20 for 16 wks. Courses—Computer, Drawing, Painting, Photography, Sculpture
Summer School: Dir, L O Stamford

ESCANABA

BAY DE NOC COMMUNITY COLLEGE, Art Dept, 2001 N Lincoln Rd, 49829. Tel 906-786-5802, Ext 174; *Chmn* Larry Leffel; *Instr* Mary Hoback
Scholarships offered
Tuition: County res—$51 per sem cr hr; non-county res—$69.75 per sem cr hr; non-state res—$111.50 per sem cr hr
Courses: Art History, Design, Drawing, Painting, Sculpture

FARMINGTON HILLS

OAKLAND COMMUNITY COLLEGE, Art Dept, * Orchard Ridge Campus, 27055 Orchard Lake Rd, 48334-4579. Tel 810-471-7667, 471-7796; FAX 810-471-7544; *Secy* Eve Dillon
Degrees: AA and ASA offered
Tuition: District res—$46 per cr hr; non-district—$78 per cr hr; non-state—$109 per cr hr
Courses: Advertising Design, Art Appreciation, Art History, Calligraphy, Ceramics, Design, Drawing, Fashion Arts, Handicrafts, Photography, Sculpture

FLINT

CHARLES STEWART MOTT COMMUNITY COLLEGE, Art Area, School of Arts & Humanities, 1401 E Court St, 48502. Tel 810-762-0443; *Assoc Dean* Doug Hoppa; *Instr* Jessie Sirna, MA; *Instr* Samuel E Morello, MFA; *Instr* Catherine Smith, MFA; *Instr* Thomas Nuzum, MFA; *Instr* William O'Malley, MAEd; *Instr* Jim Gould; *Instr* Jim Bakken; *Instr* Thomas Bohnert
Estab 1923; pub; D & E; enrl D & E 250, maj 250
Ent Req: HS dipl or 19 yrs old
Degrees: AA 2 yrs
Tuition: District res—$54.85 per cr hr; state res—$79.10 per cr hr; nonres—$105.50 per cr hr; no campus res
Courses: Art Education, Art History, Ceramics, Drafting, Drawing, Film, Graphic Design, Jewelry, Painting, Printmaking, Sculpture, Teacher Training
Adult Hobby Classes: Classes offered through cont education division
Summer School: Coordr, Thomas Bohnert. Tuition same as above; 7.5 wk sessions, first May 15 - July 1, second July 1 - Aug 15. Courses—vary

GRAND RAPIDS

AQUINAS COLLEGE, Art Dept, 1607 Robinson Rd SE, 49506. Tel 616-459-8281, Ext 3401; FAX 616-459-2563; WATS 800-678-9593. *Chmn Dept* Ron Pederson, MFA; *Prof* James S Karsina, MFA; *Assoc Prof* Sr Marie Celeste Miller, PhD; *Assoc Prof* Steve Schousen, MFA; *Asst Prof* Dana Freeman, MFA; *Sr Lectr* Kurt Kaiser, MFA
Estab 1940, dept estab 1965; pvt; D & E; scholarships; SC 28, LC 9; enrl $12,534 per yr; campus res—room & board $4198 per yr
Ent Req: HS dipl
Degrees: BA and BFA 4 yrs
Tuition: $11,208 per yr; campus res—room & board $4124 per yr
Courses: Art History, †Drawing, †Painting, †Photography, Printmaking, †Sculpture
Adult Hobby Classes: Art History, Design, Drawing, Painting, Photography, Printmaking, Sculpture

CALVIN COLLEGE, Art Dept, 3201 Burton SE, 49546. Tel 616-957-6326; FAX 616-957-8551; *Chmn Dept* Charles Young; *Prof* Chris Stoffel Overvoorde, MFA; *Prof* Carl J Huisman, MFA; *Prof* Helen Bonzelaar, PhD; *Prof* Charles Young, PhD; *Assoc Prof* Franklin Spevers, MS; *Assoc Prof* Anna Greidanus Probes, MFA; *Asst Prof* Henry Whikhuizen, MA
Estab 1876, dept estab 1965; den; D & E; scholarships; SC 16, LC 4, GC 5; enrl maj 130, grad 4, others 4
Ent Req: HS dipl, SAT or ACT
Degrees: BA(Art, Art Educ, Art History) & BFA(Art), MAT
Tuition: $5828 per sem, $440 per sem hr; campus res—room & board $4160 per yr
Courses: Advertising Design, Aesthetics, Architecture, Art Appreciation, Art Education, Art History, Ceramics, Design, Drawing, Graphic Arts, Graphic Design, History of Art & Archaeology, Jewelry, Painting, Photography, Printmaking, Sculpture, †Teacher Training, Photography, Printmaking, Sculpture, †Teacher Training, Art Therapy
Summer School: Courses vary

GRAND RAPIDS COMMUNITY COLLEGE, Art Dept, 143 Bostwick NE, 49503. Tel 616-771-3942; *Chmn* Lynn Asper; *Instr* Nancy Cluse. Instrs: FT 6, PT 4
Estab 1920; pub; D & E; scholarships; SC 17, LC 2; enrl D 250, E 75, maj 60
Ent Req: HS dipl or ent exam
Degrees: AA 2 yrs
Tuition: Res—$51; nonres—$75; out-of-state—$91; no campus res
Courses: Art Appreciation, Art Education, Art History, Ceramics, Drawing, Graphic Design, Painting, Printmaking, Teacher Training, Architecture Rendering, Color & Design, Life Drawing, 20th Century Art
Summer School: Term of 8 wks beginning June. Courses—Art History & Appreciation, Drawing, Pottery

KENDALL COLLEGE OF ART & DESIGN, 111 Division Ave N, 49503-3194. Tel 616-451-2787; *Pres* Oliver Evans; *Chmn Foundation Fine Arts* Margaret Vega, MFA; *Chmn Design Studies* Bruce Mulder; *Chmn Art History & Liberal Arts* Robert Sheardy, MA. Instrs: FT 42, PT 14
Estab 1928; pvt; D & E; scholarships; SC 64, LC 27, AH 9; enrl 700
Ent Req: HS dipl, ACT, SAT
Degrees: BFA 4 yrs
Tuition: $4998 per sem
Courses: †Advertising Design, Art History, Design, Drafting, Drawing, Graphic Design, †Illustration, †Industrial Design, †Interior Design, Lettering, Mixed Media, Painting, Photography, Printmaking, Sculpture, Textile Design, Video, Weaving, †Broadcast Video, †Environmental Design, †Furniture Design, †Fine Arts
Adult Hobby Classes: Courses—Drawing, Painting, Calligraphy, Photography (Airbrush), Interiors, Advertising, Furniture Detailing
Children's Classes: Calligraphy, Commercial Art, Drawing, Painting
Summer School: Full semester, May - July; same program as regular session

HANCOCK

SUOMI INTERNATIONAL COLLEGE OF ART & DESIGN, Fine Arts Dept, 601 Quincy St, 49930. Tel 906-482-5300; *Chmn Dept* Jon Brookhouse, MA; *Instr* Elizabeth Leifer, MA; *Instr* Patti Pawlicki; *Instr* Phyllis McIntyre; *Instr* Tom Gattis
Estab 1896, dept estab 1974; pvt; D & E; SC 5; enrl D 24, E 30, non-maj 18, maj 12
Ent Req: HS dipl, open door policy
Degrees: AA 2 yrs, BFA, BA 4 yrs
Tuition: $7000 per sem; campus res available
Courses: Ceramics, Design, Drawing, Graphic Arts, Painting, Photography, Printmaking, Sculpture, Weaving, Fiber, Product Design, Visual Communications

HILLSDALE

HILLSDALE COLLEGE, Art Dept, 338 College St, 49242. Tel 517-437-7341, Ext 2371; FAX 517-437-3923; *Dir* Samuel Knecht, MFA; *Asst Prof* Tony Frudakis, MFA
Estab 1844; pvt; scholarships; SC 12, LC 5; enrl D 1000, non-maj 150, maj 15
Ent Req: HS dipl, SAT
Degrees: BA & BS 4 yrs
Tuition: $12,110 per yr, $6055 per sem; campus res available
Courses: Art Education, Art History, Ceramics, Drawing, Painting, Photography, Sculpture, Teacher Training
Summer School: Dir, Dr Kay Cosgrove. Courses—Vary

HOLLAND

HOPE COLLEGE, Art Dept, 49423. Tel 616-395-7500; FAX 616-395-7499; Elec Mail mayer@hope.cit.hope.edu. *Chmn* William Mayer, MFA; *Prof* Delbert Michel, MFA; *Prof* John M Wilson, PhD; *Prof* Bruce McCombs, MFA; *Assoc Prof* Carol Anne Mahsun, PhD; *Asst Prof* Steve Nelson, MFA; *Instr* Judy Hillman, BS
Estab 1866, dept estab 1962; den; D & E; scholarships; SC 18, LC 12; enrl D 185, E 61, non-maj 488, maj 26

Ent Req: HS dipl, CEEB-SAT or ACT
Degrees: BA and BM 4 yrs
Tuition: $7110 per sem
Courses: †Art Education, †Art History, †Ceramics, Design, †Drawing, †Painting, †Photography, †Printmaking, †Sculpture, 2-D & 3-D Design
Summer School: Registrar, John Huisken. Tuition $70 per cr hr. Courses—Vary from year to year

INTERLOCHEN

INTERLOCHEN ARTS ACADEMY, Dept of Visual Art, 49643. Tel 616-276-7408; *Acad Visual Arts Chmn* Jean Parsons, MFA; *Instr* Jason Novetsky; *Instr* Wayne Brill, BS; *Instr* John Church, MFA
Pvt; D; scholarships; enrl 440, non-maj 30, maj 40
Ent Req: Portfolio, HS dipl
Tuition: $18,875 per yr, includes room & board
Courses: Art History, Ceramics, Drawing, Jewelry, Painting, Photography, Printmaking, Sculpture, 2-D & 3-D Design, Fibers, Metalsmithing
Summer School: Dir, Carlene Perebrine. Enrl 1300; tuition $3550. Interlochen Arts Camp, formerly National Music Camp Courses & same as above

IRONWOOD

GOGEBIC COMMUNITY COLLEGE, Fine Arts Dept, E 4946 Jackson Rd, 49938. Tel 906-932-4231, Ext 283; *Chmn* Jeannie Milakovich
Estab 1932; pub; D & E; scholarships; SC 14, LC 3; enrl D 37, E 32, non-maj 65, maj 4
Ent Req: HS dipl or equivalent
Degrees: AA 2 yrs
Tuition: In-district $32; out-of-district/state $45
Adult Hobby Classes: Courses—Painting
Summer School: Dean Instruction, Dale Johnson. Courses—Ceramics, Ceramic Sculpture, Drawing, Painting

KALAMAZOO

KALAMAZOO COLLEGE, Art Dept, 1200 Academy St, 49006. Tel 616-337-7047; Elec Mail fischer@kzoo.edu. *Chmn Dept* Billie Fischer, PhD; *Prof* Marcia J Wood, MFA; *Prof* Bernard Palchick, MFA; *Prof* David Curl, EdD; *Prof* Tom Rice, MFA
Estab 1833, dept estab approx 1940; pvt; D; scholarships; SC 14, LC 10; enrl (school) 1200, non-maj 250 (dept), maj 20, others 5
Ent Req: HS dipl, SAT, ACT, class rank
Degrees: BA 4 yrs
Tuition: $13,800 per yr; campus res available
Courses: Aesthetics, Art History, Ceramics, Drawing, Painting, Photography, Printmaking, Sculpture, Teacher Training

KALAMAZOO INSTITUTE OF ARTS, KIA School, 314 S Park St, 49007. Tel 616-349-7775; *Dir KIA School* Denise Lisiecki, MA; *Head Photography Dept* James Riegel; *Head Weaving Dept* Midge Lewis; *Head Jewelry Dept* Tom Turner, BFA; *Head Children's Prog* Anne Mane Forrest; *Head Children's Prog* Leslie Hoff
Estab 1924; pvt; D & E; scholarships; SC 29; enrl D 530, E 490
Tuition: $109-$129 depending upon membership; no campus res
Courses: Ceramics, Design, Drawing, Jewelry, Painting, Photography, Sculpture, Courses for the Handicapped, Weaving
Children's Classes: Enrl 400; tuition $108-$148 for one yr. Courses—Varied
Summer School: Dir, Denise Lisiecki. Enrl 250; tuition $108-$148 June - Aug. Courses—Full schedule

KALAMAZOO VALLEY COMMUNITY COLLEGE, Humanities Dept, 6767 W O Ave, PO Box 4070, 49003-4070. Tel 616-372-5000; *Dept Chair Humanities* Martin Obed; *Coordr Technical Communications* Karen Matson; *Instr* Arleigh Smyrnios, MA
Estab 1968; pub; E; SC 12; enrl D & E 500
Degrees: AA and AS
Tuition: In-county—$38 per cr hr; out-of-county—$74 per cr hr; nonres—$107 per cr hr
Courses: Advertising Design, Aesthetics, Art Appreciation, Art Education, Calligraphy, Ceramics, Commercial Art, Design, Drafting, Drawing, Graphic Design, Illustration, Lettering, Painting, Photography, Teacher Training, Electronic Publishing, Illustration Media, Illustrator, Pagemaker, Photoshop, 2-D Design
Adult Hobby Classes: Courses—Same as regular session
Children's Classes: Courses—Ceramics
Summer School: Enrl 1125; tuition $38 per cr hr for 8 wk term. Courses—Ceramics, Design, Drawing, Watercolor

WESTERN MICHIGAN UNIVERSITY, Dept of Art, 1201 Oliver St, 49008. Tel 616-387-2436; *Chmn Dept* Phillip VanderWeg. Instrs: FT 22
Estab 1904, dept estab 1939; pub; D & E; scholarships; SC 60, LC 9, GC 8; enrl non-maj 200, maj 500, grad 20
Ent Req: HS dipl, ACT
Degrees: BA, BS & BFA 4 yrs, MA 1 yr, MFA 2 yrs
Tuition: Res—undergrad $77.50 - $87.25 per cr hr, grad $111.50 per cr hr; nonres—undergrad $250 per cr hr, grad $276 per cr hr; campus res—room & board $3827
Courses: †Art Education, Art History, †Ceramics, Drawing, †Graphic Design, †Jewelry, †Painting, †Photography, †Printmaking, †Sculpture, †Metalsmithing
Adult Hobby Classes: Chairperson Dept
Summer School: Chairperson dept. Enrl 250; tuition same per hr as academic yr for one 8 wk term beginning May. Courses—same as above

LANSING

LANSING COMMUNITY COLLEGE, Art Program, 315 N Grand Ave, PO Box 40010, 48901-7210. Tel 517-483-1476; FAX 517-483-9781; *Assoc Prof* Jack Bergeron, MA; *Assoc Prof* Sharon Wood, MFA; *Asst Prof* Lily Liu, BFA; *Asst Prof* Francia Trosty, MFA; *Instr* John Washingon, BS; *Instr* Constance Peterson. Instrs: FT & PT 60
Pub; D & E; scholarships; SC 80, LC 10; enrl D 758, E 506, non-maj 400, maj 560, others 304
Ent Req: HS dipl
Degrees: AA 2 yrs
Tuition: Res—$26 per cr hr; nonres—$42 per cr hr; out-of-state- $58 per cr hr; no campus res; $59 International
Courses: Advertising Design, Commercial Art, Design, Drawing, Fashion Arts, Graphic Arts, †Graphic Design, †Illustration, Lettering, Painting, Printmaking, Computer Graphics Animation, Computer Graphics Commercial Art
Adult Hobby Classes: Enrl 60; duration 16 wks. Courses—Handmade Paper, Watercolor, Sketching
Summer School: Dir, Jack Bergeron. Enrl 250. Courses—Same as Fall & Spring sem

LIVONIA

MADONNA UNIVERSITY, Art Dept, 36600 Schoolcraft Rd, 48150. Tel 313-432-5300; *Chmn Art Dept* Ralph F Glenn; *Prof* Sr M Angeline, PhD; *Instr* Anthony Balogh, MA; *Instr* Gerry Panyard; *Instr* Douglas Semiven; *Instr* Marjorie Chellstrop; *Commercial Art* George Toth; *Sculptor* Donald Gheen
Estab 1947; pvt; D & E; SC 17, LC 3; enrl D 43, E 22, maj 17
Ent Req: HS dipl, portfolio
Degrees: AA 2 yrs, AB 4 yrs
Tuition: $160 per sem hr
Courses: Advertising Design, Art History, Calligraphy, Ceramics, Commercial Art, Drawing, Lettering, Painting, Photography, Printmaking, Sculpture, Teacher Training
Adult Hobby Classes: Enrl 25; tuition $70 per 10 wk course. Courses—Painting
Summer School: Dir, Sr Mary Angeline

SCHOOLCRAFT COLLEGE, Dept of Art & Design, 18600 Haggerty Rd, 48152. Tel 313-462-4400; FAX 313-462-4538; *Chmn Dept of Art & Design* Robert Dufort; *Prof* Lincoln Lao, MFA; *Prof* Stephen Wroble, MA
Estab 1964; pub; D & E; scholarships & fels; SC 13, LC 4; enrl D 300, E 150, maj 100
Ent Req: Ent exam
Degrees: AAS & AA 2 yrs
Tuition: Res—In District $50 per cr hr; nonres—$73 per cr hr; no campus res
Courses: Ceramics, Design, Drawing, Film, Graphic Arts, Jewelry, Painting, Photography, Printmaking, Sculpture, Computer Aided Art & Design, History of Art & Design
Adult Hobby Classes: Enrl 200; tuition res—$35 per cr, non-res—$53 per cr, out of state res—$78 per cr. Courses—Acrylic Painting, Ceramics, Drawing, Jewelry, Macrame, Photography, Stained Glass
Children's Classes: Enrl 40; tuition same as above. Courses—Talented & Gifted Program
Summer School: Design, Drawing, Printmaking, Watercolor

MARQUETTE

NORTHERN MICHIGAN UNIVERSITY, Dept of Art & Design, 49855. Tel 906-227-2194, 227-2279; *Head Dept* Michael J Cinelli; *Prof* Thomas Cappuccio; *Prof* John D Hubbard; *Prof* Marvin Zehnder; *Prof* William C Leete; *Prof* James Quirk; *Prof* Diane D Kordich; *Prof* Dennis Staffne; *Prof* Dale Wedig; *Assoc Prof* Eileen Roberts; *Asst Prof* Jane Milkie
Estab 1899, dept estab 1964; pub; D & E; scholarships; SC 30, LC 20, GC 18
Ent Req: HS dipl, ACT
Degrees: BS, BFA, BA 4 yrs, MAE
Tuition: Res—undergrad $90.05 per cr hr, grad $117.40 per cr hr; nonres—undergrad $168.40 per cr hr, grad $168.40 per cr hr; campus res—room & board $4141 per yr
Courses: †Art Education, †Art History, †Ceramics, †Drawing, †Film, Graphic Design, Illustration, Industrial Design, Jewelry, Painting, Photography, Printmaking, Sculpture, Silversmithing, Video, Weaving, Computer Graphics, Electronic Imaging
Children's Classes: Enrl 40; tuition $25 for 8 wk term
Summer School: Dir, Michael J Cinelli. Enrl 15-20; 6 wk terms

MIDLAND

ARTS MIDLAND GALLERIES & SCHOOL, 1801 W St Andrews, 48640. Tel 517-631-3250; *Dir* B B Winslow. Instrs: FT 15
Estab 1971; pvt; D & E; SC 12-20, LC 2; enrl D & E 250
Tuition: $85-$120 member-nonmember status
Courses: Calligraphy, Ceramics, Design, Mixed Media, Painting, Photography, Printmaking, Sculpture, Weaving, Metalsmithing, Papermaking, Stained Glass
Adult Hobby Classes: Enrl 200; tuition $85-$120 per sem
Children's Classes: Enrl 50; tuition $50-$65 per sem

NORTHWOOD UNIVERSITY, Alden B Dow Creativity Center, 3225 Cook Rd, 48640-2398. Tel 517-837-4478; FAX 517-837-4468; *Exec Dir* Carol B Coppage
Available to those with innovative ideas or specific projects

MONROE

MONROE COUNTY COMMUNITY COLLEGE, Humanities Division, 1555 S Raisinville Rd, 48161. Tel 313-384-4153; FAX 313-384-4160; *Secy* Peggy Faunt. Instrs: FT 2
Degrees: AFA offered
Tuition: Res—$3450 per sem cr hr; nonres—$52 per sem cr hr
Courses: Illustration, Art Appreciation, Art History, Ceramics, Design, Drawing, Painting, Printmaking, †Art for Elementary Teachers

MOUNT PLEASANT

CENTRAL MICHIGAN UNIVERSITY, Dept of Art, 48859. Tel 517-774-3025; *Chmn Dept* Richard Janis. Instrs: FT 17, PT 2
Estab 1892; pub; D & E; scholarships & fels; SC 50, LC 9; enrl for univ 17,000
Ent Req: HS dipl
Degrees: BA, BFA & BAA 4 yrs, MA, MFA
Tuition: Res—undergrad $95.50 per cr hr, grad $131.35 per cr hr; nonres—undergrad $249.05 per cr hr, grad $260.60 per cr hr
Courses: Aesthetics, Art Education, Art History, Ceramics, Drawing, Graphic Design, Jewelry, Painting, Photography, Printmaking, Sculpture, Art Appreciation, Art Criticism, Fiber Design, Metalsmithing

MUSKEGON

MUSKEGON COMMUNITY COLLEGE, Dept of Creative & Performing Arts, 221 S Quarterline Rd, 49442. Tel 616-773-9131, Ext 324; *Chmn* Lee Collet
Estab 1926; pub; D & E; scholarships; SC 18, LC 6; enrl D 280, E 60
Ent Req: HS dipl
Degrees: AA 2 yrs
Tuition: County res—$45 per cr hr; state res—$64.50 per cr hr; nonres—$79.50 per cr hr
Courses: Art Education, Art History, Ceramics, Costume Design & Construction, Drawing, Film, Interior Design, Painting, Printmaking, Sculpture, Stage Design, Teacher Training, Theatre Arts
Adult Hobby Classes: Enrl 50; tuition variable, 6 wk term. Courses—Cartooning, Interior Design, Stained Glass, Watercolor
Children's Classes: Enrl 30; 6 wk term, 6 sessions. Courses—Beginning Art, Pottery

OLIVET

OLIVET COLLEGE, Art Dept, 320 S Main, 49076. Tel 616-749-7000; *Chmn* Gary Wertheimer; *Prof* Donald Rowe; *Instr* Susan Rowe, MFA
Estab 1844, dept estab 1870; pvt; D & E; scholarships; SC 17, LC 8, GC 10; enrl D 610, non-maj 50, maj 20, grad 2
Ent Req: HS dipl
Degrees: BS and BM 4 yrs, MA 1 yr
Tuition: $11,030 per yr, part-time $315 per hr; campus res—room & board $3680 per yr
Courses: Art History, †Commercial Art, †Design, †Drawing, †Painting, †Printmaking, †Sculpture

PETOSKEY

NORTH CENTRAL MICHIGAN COLLEGE, Art Dept, 1525 Howard St, 49770. Tel 616-348-6651, 348-6600; *Chmn* Douglas Melvin, MA
Degrees: AA offered
Tuition: Res—$42 per cr hr; nonres—$55 per cr hr; out-of-state—$68 per cr hr
Courses: Art Education, Art History, Drawing, Painting, Photography, Printmaking, Sculpture, Stained Glass
Adult Hobby Classes: Courses offered
Summer School: Courses offered

PONTIAC

CREATIVE ART CENTER, 47 Williams St, 48341. Tel 810-333-7849; FAX 810-333-7841; *Exec Dir* Carol Paster
Estab 1968; pub; D & E; scholarships; SC 15; enrl 200
Ent Req: Open enrollment
Tuition: Varies; no campus res
Courses: Ceramics, Drawing, Painting, Photography, Sculpture
Children's Classes: Courses—Dance, Drawing, Music, Painting, Sculpture
Summer School: Three wk session. Courses—Creative Writing, Dance, Drama, Visual Arts

PORT HURON

SAINT CLAIR COUNTY COMMUNITY COLLEGE, Jack R Hennesey Gallery, Art Dept, 323 Erie St, PO Box 5015, 48061-5015. Tel 810-984-3881; *Dean* Anita Gliniecki
Estab 1923; pub; D & E; scholarships; SC 30, LC 5; enrl D 60
Ent Req: HS dipl
Degrees: AA and AAS 2 yrs
Tuition: In-county—$40 per cr hr; out-of-county—$63 per cr hr; nonres—$87 per cr hr
Courses: Advertising Design, Architecture, Art Appreciation, Art Education, Art History, Ceramics, Design, Drawing, Graphic Arts, Graphic Design, Illustration, Industrial Design, Jewelry, Lettering, Mixed Media, Painting, Photography, Printmaking, Sculpture, Theatre Arts, Weaving, †Pottery
Adult Hobby Classes: Courses—Drawing, Painting, Pottery

ROCHESTER

OAKLAND UNIVERSITY, Dept of Art & Art History, 48309-4401. Tel 810-370-3375; *Chmn Dept* Janice C Schimmelman, PhD; *Prof* John B Cameron, PhD; *Prof* Carl F Barnes Jr; *Assoc Prof* Susan Wood, PhD; *Assoc Prof* Bonnie Abiko, PhD; *Lectr* Lisa Ngote, MA; *Lectr* Andrea Eis, MFA; *Lectr* Paul Webster, MFA; *Lectr* Stephen Goody, MFA; *Lectr* Brenda Lawrence, MFA; *Lectr* Lisa Baylis Ashby, MA
Estab 1957, dept estab 1960; pub; D & E; scholarships; SC 3, LC 9
Ent Req: HS dipl
Degrees: BA 4 yrs
Tuition: Res—undergrad $101.75 per cr hr, grad $189 per cr hr; nonres—undergrad $299.75 per cr hr, grad $418.50 per cr hr; campus res—room & board $600 per sem
Courses: †Art History, Studio Art

SCOTTVILLE

WEST SHORE COMMUNITY COLLEGE, Division of Humanities & Fine Arts, 3000 N Stiles Rd, 49454. Tel 616-845-6211; *Chmn* Sharon Bloom; *Assoc Prof* Rebecca Mott, MA; *Instr* Teresa Soles; *Instr* Todd Reed, BA; *Instr* Judy Peters. Instrs: PT 3
Pub; D & E; scholarships; SC 18, LC 10; enrl non-maj 250, maj 10
Ent Req: HS dipl
Degrees: AA 2 yrs
Tuition: Res—$43 per cr hr; nonres—$67 per cr hr; out-of-state—$82 per cr hr; no campus res
Courses: †Art History, Ceramics, Drafting, Drawing, Graphic Design, Mixed Media, Painting, Photography, Printmaking, Sculpture, Stage Design, †Theatre Arts
Adult Hobby Classes: Art Workshops & Studio, Crafts, Photography
Summer School: Painting, Pottery

SOUTHFIELD

LAWRENCE TECHNOLOGICAL UNIVERSITY, College of Architecture, 21000 W Ten Mile Rd, 48075-1058. Tel 810-204-4000, Ext 2800; FAX 810-204-2900; *Dean* Neville Clouten
Degrees: BArchit, BS(Archit), BS(Interior Archit)
Tuition: $250 per sem freshmen & sophomore, $260 per sem Jr & Sr, $300 per sem for BA Archit
Courses: †Architecture, †Interior Architecture
Summer School: Dir, Harold Linton. Enrl 75; tuition $250. Courses—Pre-College Architecture

SPRING ARBOR

SPRING ARBOR COLLEGE, Art Dept, 106 E Main, Sta 19, 49283. Tel 517-750-1200, Ext 1364; *Dir* Paul Wolber, MA; *Division Dir Music Arts* Bill Bippes, MFA
Estab 1873, dept estab 1971; pvt den; D & E; scholarships; SC 17, LC 6; enrl D 200, E 20, non-maj 20, maj 32
Ent Req: HS dipl
Degrees: AA(Commercial) 2 yrs, BA 4 yrs
Tuition: $4700 per sem, campus res—room & board $850-$1025
Courses: Advertising Design, Commercial Art, †Drawing, †Graphic Arts, †Illustration, †Painting, †Printmaking, †Sculpture, †Teacher Training

TRAVERSE CITY

NORTHWESTERN MICHIGAN COLLEGE, Art Dept, 1701 E Front St, 49686. Tel 616-922-1325; *Chmn Dept* Stephen Ballance, MA; *Instr* Doug Domine, BFA; *Instr* Jill Hinds; *Art Historian* Jackie Shinners, MFA
Estab 1951, dept estab 1957; pub; D & E; scholarships; SC 40, LC 4; enrl non-maj 400, maj 75
Ent Req: HS dipl
Degrees: AA 2 yrs
Tuition: $49.25 per billing hr per sem in-district $81.50 per billing per sem in-state, $91 per billing hr per sem out-of-state; maritime classes $81.50 per billing in-state, $99.75 per billings out-of-state; campus res room & board
Courses: Advertising Design, Art Education, Art History, Commercial Art, Drawing, Goldsmithing, Graphic Arts, Graphic Design, Illustration, Jewelry, Lettering, Painting, Photography, Printmaking, Silversmithing, Textile Design, Life Drawing, Perspective, Pottery, Publication Design, Reproduction Techniques, Typography
Adult Hobby Classes: Enrl 50; tuition $23. Courses - Drawing, Life Drawing, Painting, Pottery, Printmaking
Summer School: Dir, Stephen Ballance. Enrl 100 tuition $49.25 per billing hr in-district, $81.50 per billing hr other for 5, 8, 10 wk terms. Courses—Design, Drawing, Photography, Pottery

TWIN LAKE

BLUE LAKE FINE ARTS CAMP, Art Dept, Rte 2, 49457. Tel 616-894-1966; FAX 616-893-5120; *Chmn* Carol Tice
Tuition: $610 for 12 days & camp res
Courses: Ceramics, Drawing, Illustration, Painting, Sculpture, Weaving, Fibre Arts, Wheel-Work, 2D-3D

UNIVERSITY CENTER

DELTA COLLEGE, Art Dept, Humanities Division, 48710. Tel 517-686-9000, Ext 9101; *Chmn Dept* Russel Thayer; *Assoc Prof* John McCormick, MFA; *Assoc Prof* Larry Butcher, MA; *Instr* Linda Menger; *Instr* Randal Crawford
Estab 1960; pub; D & E; scholarships; SC 21, LC 5; enrl D 550, E 100, maj 190
Ent Req: Open door policy
Degrees: AA 2 yrs

Tuition: Res—in district $54.75 per cr hr, out of district $70 per cr hr; nonres—$100 per cr hr; $20 registration fee per sem
Courses: Art Education, Art History, Ceramics, Commercial Art, Drawing, Graphic Design, Interior Design, Painting, Photography, Printmaking, Sculpture

SAGINAW VALLEY STATE UNIVERSITY, Dept of Art & Design, 7400 Bay Rd, 48710. Tel 517-790-4390; *Chmn Dept* Matthew Zivich, MFA; *Prof* Barron Hirsch, MFA; *Assoc Prof* Hideki Kihata, MFA; *Adjunct Instr* Bruce Winslow, MFA; *Adjunct Instr* David Littell, MFA; *Adjunct Instr* Marlene Pellerito; *Adjunct Instr* Paul Kowaski, BFA; *Adjunct Instr* Sara B Clark, MFA
Estab 1960, dept estab 1968; pub; D & E; scholarships; SC approx 20, LC approx 15; enrl D 200, E 50, maj 65
Ent Req: HS dipl
Degrees: BA(Art) 4 yrs or less
Tuition: $62.50 per cr hr; campus res available
Courses: Advertising Design, Art Appreciation, Art Education, Art History, Ceramics, Commercial Art, Design, Drafting, Drawing, Graphic Arts, Graphic Design, Handicrafts, Illustration, Lettering, Occupational Therapy, Painting, Photography, Printmaking, Sculpture, Stage Design, Teacher Training, Theatre Arts
Summer School: Courses vary

WARREN

MACOMB COMMUNITY COLLEGE, Art Dept, Division of Humanities, 14500 E Twelve Mile Rd, 48093. Tel 810-445-7000, 445-7354; *Prof* David Barr, MA; *Prof* James Pallas, MFA
Estab 1960, dept estab 1965; pub; D & E; scholarships; SC 14, LC 6
Ent Req: HS dipl, ent exam
Degrees: AA 2 yrs
Tuition: Res—in county $38 per hr, in state $61 per hr; nonres—$74 per hr
Courses: Art History, Ceramics, Design, Drawing, Painting, Photography, Sculpture

YPSILANTI

EASTERN MICHIGAN UNIVERSITY, Dept of Art, 114 Ford, 48197. Tel 313-487-1268, 487-0192; FAX 313-481-1095;
Internet Home Page Address http://www.art.acad.emich.edu. *Head Dept* Dr Roy E Johnston
Estab 1849, dept estab 1901; pub; D & E; scholarships; SC 55, LC 18; enrl undergrad maj 420, non-maj 800, grad 100
Ent Req: HS dipl
Degrees: BA(Art History), BFA(Studio Art), BS & BA(Art Educ) 4 yrs, MA(Art Educ), MA(Studio) & MFA 2 yrs
Tuition: Undergrad $91 per cr, grad $101 per cr
Courses: Art Education, †Art History, †Ceramics, †Drawing, †Graphic Design, †Jewelry, †Painting, †Photography, †Printmaking, †Sculpture, †Textile Design
Children's Classes: Enrl 40; tuition $35 for 8-10 classes offered on Sat for Art talented & gifted
Summer School: Term of 7 1/2 wks, major & non-major courses

MINNESOTA

BEMIDJI

BEMIDJI STATE UNIVERSITY, Visual Arts Dept, 1500 Birchmont Dr, 56601. Tel 218-755-3735; *Chmn* Marley Kaul; *Prof* Kyle Crocker, PhD; *Assoc Prof* Mary-Ann Papanek-Miller, MFA; *Asst Prof* John Holden, MFA; *Asst Prof* Steve Sundahl, MFA; *Asst Prof* Jaineth Skinner, MFA
Estab 1918; pub; D & E; scholarships; SC 54, LC 17, GC individual study
Ent Req: HS dipl, ACT, SAT, PSAT, or SCAT
Degrees: BA, BS(Teaching) and BS(Tech Illustration, Commercial Design), BFA
Tuition: Res—undergrad $36.30 per quarter hr, grad $52 per quarter hr; nonres—undergrad $62.30 per quarter hr, grad $75 per quarter hr; campus residency available
Courses: Advertising Design, Art Appreciation, Art Education, Art History, Ceramics, Design, Drawing, Graphic Arts, Graphic Design, Jewelry, Painting, Printmaking, Sculpture, Teacher Training, Crafts
Adult Hobby Classes: Tuition res—$46.70 per qtr hr. Courses—Graphic Design, Elementary Art Concepts & Methods, Secondary Art Concepts & Methods
Summer School: Dir, M Kaul. Enrl 250; tuition res—undergrad $46.70 per qtr hr, nonres—undergrad $101.40 per qtr hr. Courses—Art, Ceramics, History, Metals, Painting, Printmaking, 3-D Design

BLOOMINGTON

NORMANDALE COMMUNITY COLLEGE, 9700 France Ave S, 55431. Tel 612-832-6000; *Instr* E L Gleeman, MA; *Instr* D R Peterson, BFA; *Instr* Marilyn Wood, MFA
Tuition: $42.75 per cr
Courses: Art Appreciation, Art History, Ceramics, Design, Drawing, Jewelry, Painting, Photography, Sculpture
Adult Hobby Classes: Courses offered
Summer School: Courses offered

BROOKLYN PARK

NORTH HENNEPIN COMMUNITY COLLEGE, Art Dept, 7411 85th Ave N, 55445. Tel 612-424-0775, 424-0814, 424-0722; FAX 612-424-0929; *Interim Asst Dean* Robert Alexander. Instrs: FT 6
Estab 1964; pub; D & E; scholarships; SC 15, LC 4; enrl D 500, E 100, maj 200, others 100
Ent Req: HS dipl. ent exam
Degrees: AA & AAS 2 yr
Tuition: In-state $41.75 per cr; out-of-state $83.50 per cr
Courses: Art History, Drawing, Graphic Design, Illustration, Jewelry, Painting, Photography, Printmaking, Contemporary Crafts, Exhibition Design, Introduction to Art, Metalsmithing, 2-D & 3-D Design, Typography, Visual Communications
Adult Hobby Classes: Enrl 30-100. Courses—Painting, Photography, Video
Summer School: Two 5 week sessions. Enrl 700; Courses—Drawing, Introduction of Art, Photography, Fundamentals of Color, Painting

COLLEGEVILLE

SAINT JOHN'S UNIVERSITY, Art Dept, Box 2000, 56321. Tel 320-363-2011, 363-5036; *Chmn* Gordon Goetemann; *Prof* Bela Petheo, MFA; *Assoc Prof* James Hendershot, MFA; *Assoc Prof* Bro Alan Reed, MFA; *Assoc Prof* Sr Baulu Kuan; *Asst Prof* Hugh Witzmann, MFA; *Asst Prof* Sr Dennis Frandrup
Estab 1856, joint studies with College of Saint Benedict; pvt; scholarships; SC 20, LC 15
Ent Req: HS dipl
Degrees: BA, BS
Tuition: Approx $10,000 for all 4 yrs; campus res—room & board $4000
Courses: Art History, Ceramics, Drawing, Jewelry, Painting, Photography, Printmaking, Sculpture
Adult Hobby Classes: Occasional adult education classes

COON RAPIDS

ANOKA RAMSEY COMMUNITY COLLEGE, Art Dept, 11200 Mississippi Blvd NW, 55433. Tel 612-422-3522; FAX 612-422-3341; *Dean* Brenda Robert; *Instr* Robert E Toensing, MFA
Scholarships
Degrees: AA offered
Tuition: $42.75 per cr hr
Courses: Advertising Design, Art Appreciation, Art Education, Ceramics, Design, Drawing, Film, Jewelry, Painting, Photography, Sculpture, Glassblowing

DULUTH

UNIVERSITY OF MINNESOTA, DULUTH, Art Dept, 317 Humanities Bldg, 10 University Dr, 55812. Tel 218-726-8225; FAX 218-726-8503; Elec Mail art@ub.d.umn.edu. 800-232-1339, Ext 8225 (Admissions). *Head Dept* Gloria D Brush; *Prof* Thomas Kerrigan, MFA; *Prof* Thomas F Hedin, PhD; *Prof* Leif Brush, MFA; *Prof* Dean R Lettenstrom, MFA; *Assoc Prof* James H Brutger, MA; *Assoc Prof* Robyn Roslak, PhD; *Assoc Prof* James Klueg, MFA; *Asst Prof* Robert Repinski, MFA; *Asst Prof* Gunnar Swanson, MFA; *Asst Prof* Janice Anderson, MFA
Pub; D & E; scholarships; SC 30, LC 6, GC 10; enrl D 200, E 50, maj 200, grad 12
Ent Req: HS dipl
Degrees: BFA, BA 4 yrs, MA
Tuition: Averages $50 per cr hr; campus res available
Courses: Advertising Design, Art Appreciation, Art Education, Art History, Calligraphy, Ceramics, Commercial Art, Constructions, Design, Drawing, Film, Graphic Arts, Graphic Design, History of Art & Archaeology, Illustration, Intermedia, Jewelry, Lettering, Mixed Media, Museum Staff Training, Painting, Photography, Printmaking, Sculpture, Silversmithing, Teacher Training, Weaving, Fibers, †Studio Major
Adult Hobby Classes: 10 wk courses. Courses—Studio Arts, Graphic Design
Summer School: Dir, T Anderson. 5 wk summer sessions. Courses—Art Appreciation, Art Education, Ceramics, Drawing, Graphic Design, Jewelry & Metals, Painting, Photography, Prints

ELY

VERMILION COMMUNITY COLLEGE, Art Dept, 1900 E Camp St, 55731. Tel 218-365-7273; WATS 800-657-3608. *Instr* Victoria Hutson
Estab 1922, dept estab 1964; pub; D & E; SC 13, LC 5; enrl D 63, E 15, non-maj 65, maj 13
Ent Req: HS dipl
Degrees: AA 2 yr
Tuition: $40.75 per cr
Adult Hobby Classes: Tuition $40.75 per cr. Courses—Drawing, Introduction, Painting

FERGUS FALLS

LUTHERAN BRETHREN SCHOOLS, Art Dept, 815 W Vernon Ave, 56537. Tel 218-739-3371, 739-3376; Elec Mail 218-739-3372. *Head Dept* Gaylen Peterson
Estab 1900; den; D & E; SC 1, LC 1; enrl D 20
Ent Req: HS dipl, questionnaire
Tuition: $1900 per sem; campus res—room & board $1000 per sem
Courses: Drawing

GRAND MARAIS

GRAND MARAIS ART COLONY, 55604. Tel 218-387-2737; *Adminr* Jay Andersen; *Faculty* Elizabeth Erickson; *Faculty* Hazel Belvo; *Faculty* Gerald Korte; *Faculty* Joyce Lyon
Estab 1947; D & E; scholarships; SC 4; enrl D 200
Ent Req: Open
Tuition: $200 per wk
Courses: Drawing, Painting, Pastels, Personal Creativity
Adult Hobby Classes: Enrl 200; tuition same as above; 15 wks of 1 - 2 wk workshops. Courses—Drawing, Painting,
Children's Classes: Enrl 50; tuition $70 for 1 full wk. Courses—Drawing, Mixed Media, Painting
Summer School: Dir, Jay Andersen. Courses—Drawing, Painting, Watercolor

HIBBING

HIBBING COMMUNITY COLLEGE, Art Dept, 1515 E 25th St, 55746. Tel 218-262-6700; *Instr* Bill Goodman; *Instr* Theresa Chudzik
Scholarships
Degrees: AA & AAS 2 yrs
Tuition: Res—undergrad $43 per cr hr
Courses: Art Appreciation, Ceramics, Design, Drawing, Painting, Photography, Sculpture, Stage Craft, Introduction to Theatre

MANKATO

BETHANY LUTHERAN COLLEGE, Art Dept, 734 Marsh St, 56001. Tel 507-386-5364; FAX 507-386-5376; *Head of Dept* William Bukowski
Estab 1927, dept estab 1960; den; D; scholarships; SC 2, LC 2; enrl D 36, non-maj 40, maj 18
Ent Req: HS dipl, ACT
Degrees: AA 2 yr, dipl
Tuition: $3800 per sem
Courses: Art History, Ceramics, Design, Drawing, Painting, Art Appreciation, Art Structure
Summer School: Dir, William Bukowski. Enrl 20; tuition $130 for 2 wk - 1 1/2 days

MANKATO STATE UNIVERSITY, Art Dept, PO Box 8400, 56002-8400. Tel 507-389-6412; WATS 507-389-5887. *Chmn* Robert Finkler, MFA. Instrs: FT 15
Estab 1868, dept estab 1938; pub; D & E; scholarships; SC 42, LC 28, GC 54; enrl D 3000 (total), E 500, non-maj 1000, maj 200, grad 25
Ent Req: HS dipl
Degrees: BA, BFA and BS 4 yr, MA and MS 1-1 1/2 yr
Tuition: Res—$59 per quarter hr, grad $85.10 per quarter hr; nonres—$129.25 per quarter hr
Courses: Art Education, Art History, Ceramics, Drawing, Graphic Arts, Painting, Photography, Printmaking, Sculpture, Fibers
Summer School: Tuition same as above

MINNEAPOLIS

ART INSTRUCTION SCHOOLS, Education Dept, 3309 Broadway St NE, 55413. Tel 612-362-5060; FAX 612-362-5500; *Dir* Judith Turner
Estab 1914; pvt
Courses: Fundamentals of Art and Specialized Art
Adult Hobby Classes: Enrl 5000; tuition $1495 - $2000. Courses—Fundamentals of Art, Specialized Art

AUGSBURG COLLEGE, Art Dept, 2211 Riverside Ave, 55454. Tel 612-330-1285; FAX 612-330-1649; Elec Mail anderso3@augsburg.edu. *Chmn* Kristin Anderson. Instrs: FT 3, PT 4
Estab 1869, dept estab 1960; den; D & E; scholarships; SC 15, LC 6; enrl D 200, maj 60, others 1500
Ent Req: HS dipl
Degrees: BA 4 yrs
Tuition: $10,853 per yr; campus res—room & board $4022
Courses: Art Education, Art History, Calligraphy, Ceramics, Drawing, Handicrafts, History of Art & Archaeology, Painting, Photography, Sculpture, Stage Design, Teacher Training, Theatre Arts, Communications Design, Environmental Design
Adult Hobby Classes: Enrl 1200; tuition $780 per course. Courses—Art History, Calligraphy, Ceramics, Communications Design, Drawing, Environmental Design, Painting, Publication Design
Summer School: Enrl 350; term of six or four wks beginning end of May

MINNEAPOLIS COLLEGE OF ART & DESIGN, 2501 Stevens Ave S, 55404. Tel 612-874-3700; FAX 612-874-3704; *Pres* John S Slorp, MFA; *Chmn Fine Arts* Hazel Belvo, MFA; *Acting Visual Studies* Rebecca Alm; *Liberal Arts* Anedith Nash; *Chmn Media Arts* Thomas De Biaso; *Dir Continuing Studies* Brian Szott. Instrs: FT 58, PT 19
Estab 1886; pvt; D & E; scholarships; SC 78, LC 23; enrl D 585, E 490
Ent Req: HS dipl or GED
Degrees: BFA 4 yr
Tuition: $14,710 annual tuition; campus—res available
Courses: Advertising Design, Art History, Drawing, Film, Graphic Arts, Illustration, Painting, Photography, Printmaking, Sculpture, Video, Computer Graphics, Critical Studies, Design Theory & Methods, Liberal Arts, Packaging & Product Design, Performance Arts
Adult Hobby Classes: Continuing Studies
Children's Classes: Courses offered
Summer School: Dir of Continuing Studies & the Gallery, Brian Scott. Courses—Drawing, Graphic Design, History of Art & Design, Liberal Arts, Painting, Papermaking, Photography, Printmaking, Sculpture, Video

UNIVERSITY OF MINNESOTA, MINNEAPOLIS

—**Art History,** 27 Pleasant St SE, 108 Jones Hall, 55455. Tel 612-624-4500; Elec Mail asher@maroon.tc.umn.edu. *Chmn* Frederick Asher, PhD; *Prof* Norman Canedy, PhD; *Prof* Karal Ann Marling, PhD; *Prof* Robert Poor, PhD; *Assoc Prof* John Steyaert, PhD; *Assoc Prof* Michael Stoughton, PhD; *Assoc Prof* Robert Silberman, PhD; *Assoc Prof* Catherine Asher, PhD
Pub; D & E; scholarships & fels; LC 28, GC 59; enrl res 108 per quarter, nonres 216 per quarter, maj 68, grad 52
Ent Req: HS dipl, ent exam, GRE required for grad school
Degrees: BA 4 yrs, MA 2 yrs
Tuition: Res—$58.93 per cr, nonres—$173.84 per cr
Courses: †Art History
Adult Hobby Classes: Enrl 200; qtr system. Courses—Ancient & Modern Art History, Asian Art History
Summer School: Dir, Frederick Asher. Enrl 270; tuition $46 per cr for terms June 11 - July 16 & July 18 - Aug 21

—**Dept of Art,** 216 21st Ave S, 55455. Tel 612-625-8096; FAX 612-625-7881; *Chmn Dept* Wayne Potratz, MA; *Prof* Curtis Hoard, MFA; *Prof* Karl Bethke, MFA; *Prof* Robert Poor, PhD; *Prof Emeritus* Warren MacKenzie; *Prof Emeritus* Malcolm Myers, MFA; *Prof* Thomas Rose, MA; *Prof* Herman Rowan, MFA; *Prof* Mary Diane Katsiaficas, MFA; *Prof* Clarence Morgan, MFA; *Assoc Prof* Thomas Cowette, BFA; *Assoc Prof* David Feinberg, MFA; *Assoc Prof* Gary Hallman, MFA; *Assoc Prof* Lynn Gray, MFA; *Assoc Prof* James Henkel, MFA; *Assoc Prof* Guy Baldwin, MFA; *Assoc Prof* Jerald Krepps, MFA; *Assoc Prof* Thomas Lane, MFA; *Assoc Prof* Susan Lucey, MFA; *Assoc Prof* William Roode, MFA; *Assoc Prof* Joyce Lyon, MFA; *Assoc Prof* Victory Caglioti, BS
Estab 1851, fine arts estab 1939; pub; D & E; scholarships; SC 39, LC 7; enrl D 1000, E 560, maj 325, grad 55
Ent Req: HS dipl, PSAT, ACT
Degrees: BA, BFA, MFA
Tuition: Res—undergrad $74 per cr hr, grad $183.60 per cr hr; nonres—undergrad $218 per cr hr, grad $435 per cr hr
Courses: Ceramics, Drawing, Painting, Photography, Printmaking, Sculpture, Neon, Papermaking, Silkscreening
Adult Hobby Classes: Tuition $160-$166 for 4 cr for 10 wk term. Courses—same as above
Children's Classes: Summers Honors College for HS students
Summer School: Dir, Carol Ann Dickinson. Enrl 20; tuition $500 for June 16 - July 2 term. Courses—same as above
Split Rock Arts Program, 306 Wesbrook Hall, 77 Pleasant St SE, 55455-0216. Tel 612-624-6800; FAX 612-625-2568; Elec Mail srap@mail.cee.umn.edu. *Dir* Andrea Gilats; *Prog Assoc & On-Site Dir* Phyllis Campbell; *Prog Assoc* Vivien Oja
Estab 1984; scholarships
Tuition: $375 plus; campus res—$162-$246 per wk
Courses: Ceramics, Collages, Design, Drawing, Handicrafts, Jewelry, Mixed Media, Painting, Printmaking, Sculpture, Textile Design, Weaving, Basketry, Bookmaking, Fabric Art, Quiltmaking
Summer School: Enrl 550; tuition $375 per wk. Courses—Creativity Enhancement, Creative Writing, Fine Crafts, Visual Arts

MOORHEAD

CONCORDIA COLLEGE, Art Dept, 901 S Eighth, 56562. Tel 218-299-4623; FAX 218-299-3947; *Chmn* Duane Mickelson, MFA; *Assoc Prof* David Boggs, MFA; *Asst Prof* Jennie Couch, MFA; *Asst Prof* Heidi Allen, MFA; *Asst Prof* Robert Meadows-Rogers, PhD; *Asst Prof* Susan Pierson Ellingson, PhD; *Instr* Barbara Anderson, MA; *Instr* John Borge, BA
Estab 1891; pvt; D; scholarships; SC 10, LC 5; enrl D 300, maj 80, total 2900
Ent Req: HS dipl, character references
Degrees: BA and BM 4 yrs, independent studio work, work-study prog and special studies
Tuition: $14,400 per yr, $7900 per sem, student association dues $80; campus res—room $1600 & board $2200
Courses: †Art Education, †Art History, Ceramics, Drawing, Graphic Design, Painting, Photography, Printmaking, Sculpture, Figure Drawing, 2-D Foundations, 3-D Foundations, Macintosh Computer Design Lab, Senior Project, †Studio Art
Summer School: Dir, Cherie Hatlem. Enrl 40; tuition $1200 for term of 4 wks beginning May 15 & June 12. Courses—Art Education, Art History, Drawing, Graphic Design, Painting, Printmaking, Travel Seminar, 2-D Foundation

MOORHEAD STATE UNIVERSITY, Dept of Art, 1104 Seventh Ave S, 56563. Tel 218-236-2011; *Chmn* Allen Sheets, MFA; *Prof* Lyle Laske, MFA; *Prof* P J Mousseau, MFA; *Prof* Donald B McRaven Jr, MFA; *Prof* P R Szeitz, MFA; *Prof* Carl Oltvedt; *Prof* Timothy Ray, MFA; *Prof* Deborah Broad, MFA; *Prof* Robert Tom, MFA; *Asst Prof* Kathleen Enz Finken, MA; *Asst Prof* Patrick Fahey, PhD
Estab 1887; pub; D & E; scholarships; SC 47, LC 20, GC 11; enrl D 4520, maj 175, grad 2
Ent Req: HS dipl
Degrees: BA, BS 4 yr, BFA 5 yr, MS additional 1 1/4 yr
Courses: Advertising Design, Art Education, Art History, Ceramics, Collages, Constructions, Drawing, Graphic Arts, Graphic Design, Illustration, Mixed Media, Painting, Photography, Printmaking, Sculpture, Teacher Training, Theatre Arts
Summer School: Tuition per cr hr for term of 5 wks beginning June. Courses—Basic Drawing, Ceramics, Elements of Art Design, Glass, Graphic Design, Illustration, Painting, Photography, Printmaking

MORRIS

UNIVERSITY OF MINNESOTA, MORRIS, Humanities Division, 600 E Fourth St, 56267. Tel 320-589-2211, 589-6251; *Chmn* C F Farrell Jr; *Coordr* Frederick Peterson, PhD
Estab 1960, dept estab 1963; pub; D; scholarships; SC 16, LC 8; enrl D 195, non-maj 150, maj 45
Ent Req: Top 50% in HS, ACT or PSAT
Degrees: BA 4 yrs
Tuition: Res—undergrad $1065.50 per qtr; nonres—undergrad $3439.50 per qtr; campus res—room & board $1461 per qtr
Courses: †Art History, Teacher Training, †Studio Art

NORTHFIELD

CARLETON COLLEGE, Dept of Art & Art History, One N College St, 55057. Tel 507-646-4341, 646-4000 (main); *Chmn* Fred Hagstrom
Estab 1921; pvt; scholarships; SC 30, LC 20; enrl maj 42, others 550
Degrees: 4 yr
Tuition: $25,410 (comprehensive)
Courses: †Art History, †Studio Art

SAINT OLAF COLLEGE, Art Dept, 1520 Saint Olaf Ave, 55057-1098. Tel 507-646-3248; *Chmn* Wendell Arneson; *Museum Dir* Karen Helland; *Prof* Malcolm Gimse, MFA; *Assoc Prof* Jan Shoger, MFA; *Asst Prof* Irve Dell; *Asst Prof* Meg Ojala; *Asst Prof* Ron Gallas; *Asst Prof* Steve Edwins; *Asst Prof* Mathew Rohn; *Asst Prof* John Saurer; *Asst Prof* Katherine Smith-Abbott; *Asst Prof* Mary Griep; *Asst Prof* Judy Yourman; *Instr* Patricia Olson
Estab 1875, dept estab 1932; den; D & E; scholarships
Ent Req: HS dipl, SAT
Degrees: BA 4 yr
Tuition: $15,700 per yr; campus res—$3850 per yr
Courses: Advertising Design, Aesthetics, †Architecture, Art Appreciation, †Art Education, †Art History, Calligraphy, Ceramics, Commercial Art, Design, Drafting, Drawing, Film, Graphic Arts, Graphic Design, History of Art & Archaeology, Illustration, Intermedia, Interior Design, Landscape Architecture, Mixed Media, Painting, Photography, Printmaking, Sculpture, Stage Design, Teacher Training, Theatre Arts, Video, †Animation, †Art Studio
Adult Hobby Classes: Dir, Susan Hammerski
Summer School: Dir, Susan Hammerski. Enrl 300; two 5 wk sessions. Courses—Art History, Studio

NORTH MANKATO

SOUTH CENTRAL TECHNICAL COLLEGE (Formerly Albert Lea - Mankato Technical College), Commercial & Technical Art Dept, 1920 Lee Blvd, 56003. Tel 507-389-7200; *Instr* Robert Williams; *Instr* Kevin McLaughin
Estab 1969; pub; D; scholarships; enrl D 20
Ent Req: Portfolio
Degrees: AA 2 yr
Courses: Advertising Design, Calligraphy, Commercial Art, Conceptual Art, Drafting, Drawing, Fashion Arts, Graphic Arts, Graphic Design, Illustration, Lettering, Mixed Media, Desktop Publishing, Multi-Media
Adult Hobby Classes: Enrl 200; tuition $36.35 per cr. Courses—Adobe Illustrator, Photoshop, Quark XPress

ROCHESTER

ROCHESTER COMMUNITY & TECHNICAL COLLEGE, Art Dept, 851 30th Ave SE, 55904-4999. Tel 507-285-7215 (Pres), 285-7210 (main); *Instr* James Prom, MS; *Instr* Pat Kraemer, MS; *Instr* Terry Dennis
Estab 1920s; pub; D & E; scholarships; SC 17, LC 4; enrl D & E 4000, maj 50
Ent Req: State req
Degrees: AAS, AA
Tuition: Res—$46.95 tuition & fees; nonres—$88.55 except in reciprocal states
Courses: Advertising Design, Art Appreciation, Art History, †Ceramics, Design, †Drawing, †Graphic Design, Interior Design, Jewelry, †Painting, Photography, Printmaking, Sculpture, Stage Design, Theatre Arts, Weaving, Craft Design Series, Fibers
Adult Hobby Classes: All areas, cr & non cr for variable tuition. Courses—Cartooning, & others on less regular basis
Summer School: Dir, A Olson. Art workshops are offered for at least one session each summer

SAINT CLOUD

SAINT CLOUD STATE UNIVERSITY, Dept of Art, 720 Fourth Ave S, KVAC, Room 111, 56301. Tel 320-255-4283, 255-0121; *Assoc Prof* Virginia Bradley. Instrs: FT 13, PT 6
Pub; D & E; SC 65, LC 15, GC 20; enrl maj 300, grad 30
Ent Req: HS dipl
Degrees: BA, BFA, BS, MA(Studio Art) 4 yrs
Tuition: Res—undergrad $42.35 per cr hr, grad $62.90 per cr hr; nonres—undergrad $83.80 per cr hr, grad $83.80 per cr hr
Courses: Art Education, Ceramics, Drawing, Design, Graphic Design, Art History, Jewelry, Painting, Photography, Sculpture, Teacher Training, Textile Design, Printmaking, Weaving
Summer School: Two terms

SAINT JOSEPH

COLLEGE OF SAINT BENEDICT, Art Dept, 56374. Tel 320-363-5036; *Chmn* Gordon Goetemann; *Prof* Bela Petheo, MFA; *Assoc Prof* Sr Baulu Kuan, MA; *Assoc Prof* James Hendershot; *Assoc Prof* Bro Alan Reed; *Assoc Prof* Sr Dennis Frandrup, MFA; *Asst Prof* Andrea Shaker; *Instr* Robert Wilde; *Instr* Ann Salisbury
Estab 1913; joint studies with St John's University, Collegeville, MN; pvt; D & E; scholarships; SC 21, LC 15; enrl D 1893, maj 70
Ent Req: HS dipl, SAT, PSAT, ACT
Degrees: BA(Art) & BA(Art History) 4 yr, internships & open studio
Tuition: $18,508 comprehensive
Courses: †Art History, †Ceramics, †Drawing, Jewelry, Mixed Media, †Painting, †Photography, †Printmaking, †Sculpture

SAINT PAUL

BETHEL COLLEGE, Dept of Art, 3900 Bethel Dr, 55112. Tel 612-638-6400; FAX 612-638-6001; *Prof* Wayne L Roosa, PhD; *Prof* Stewart Luckman, MFA; *Prof* George Robinson, BFA; *Asst Prof* Karen Berg-Johnson, MFA; *Assoc Prof* Kirk Freeman; *Prof* Dale R Johnson, MFA
Estab 1871; den; D & E; scholarships; SC 30, LC 7; enrl non-maj 100, maj 75
Ent Req: HS dipl, SAT, ACT, PSAT or NMSQT, evidence of a standard of faith & practice that is compatible to Bethel lifestyle
Degrees: BA(Art Educ), BA(Art History) & BA(Studio Arts) 4 yr
Tuition: $13,180 per sem; campus res—room $17,870
Courses: †Art Education, †Art History, †Ceramics, †Drawing, †Graphic Design, †Painting, †Photography, †Printmaking, †Sculpture, 2-D Design, 3-D Design

COLLEGE OF SAINT CATHERINE, Art & Art History Dept, 2004 Randolph, 55105. Tel 612-690-6636, 690-6000; *Chmn* Ann Jennings. Instrs: FT 4, PT 8
Pvt, W; D; scholarships; enrl 65
Ent Req: HS dipl
Degrees: BA(Art) 4 yr
Tuition: $1528 per course sem
Courses: Art Education, Art History, Calligraphy, Ceramics, Drawing, Graphic Arts, Graphic Design, History of Art & Archaeology, Illustration, Jewelry, Mixed Media, Museum Staff Training, Painting, Photography, Printmaking, Restoration & Conservation, Sculpture, Pottery, Publication Design, Typography, †Studio Art
Adult Hobby Classes: Special Workshops
Summer School: Enrl 30. Courses—Art Education, Art History, Art Studio

COLLEGE OF VISUAL ARTS (Formerly College of Associated Arts), 344 Summit Ave, 55102. Tel 612-224-3416; FAX 612-224-8854; *Pres* Chris R Kabella; *Prof* Philip Ogle, MFA; *Assoc Prof* Maria Santiago, MFA; *Assoc Prof* Glenn Biegon, MFA; *Asst Prof* Karen Wirth
Estab 1924; pvt; D; scholarships; SC 30, LC 8; enrl D 220, maj 134
Ent Req: HS dipl, portfolio, essay
Degrees: BFA 4 yr
Tuition: $8960 per yr
Courses: †Advertising Design, Aesthetics, Art Appreciation, Art History, Commercial Art, Conceptual Art, Design, †Drawing, Graphic Design, †Illustration, Lettering, †Painting, Photography, Printmaking, †Sculpture, Typography
Summer School: Enrl 150; tuition $85-$210. Courses—Summer Kids Art Adventure, Summer Teen Visual Arts Sampler

CONCORDIA COLLEGE, Art Dept, Fine Arts Division, 275 N Syndicate St, 55104. Tel 612-641-8494; *Chmn* Keith Williams; *Prof* Karla Ness; *Prof* Win Bruhl
Estab 1897, dept estab 1967; den; D & E; scholarships; SC 14, LC 3; enrl D 84, E 20, others 35
Ent Req: HS dipl
Degrees: BS and BA 4 yrs
Tuition: $1150 per qtr
Courses: Aesthetics, Art Education, Art History, Ceramics, Drawing, Jewelry, Painting, Photography, Printmaking, Sculpture, Teacher Training, Theatre Arts
Summer School: Courses—Art Educ Methods, Art Fundamentals

HAMLINE UNIVERSITY, Dept of Art & Art History, 55104. Tel 612-641-2296, Ext 2415; FAX 612-659-3066; *Head Dept* Leonardo Lasansky, MFA; *Prof* Michael Price, MFA; *Prof* Keli Rylance, PhD; *Prof* Clifford Garten, MFA; *Prof* Barbara Kreft; *Adjunct Asst Prof* Michelle Nordtorp-Madson, PhD; *Vis Prof* Deborah Sigel
Estab 1854; pvt; D & E; scholarships; SC 13, LC 13; enrl non-maj 70, maj 35
Ent Req: HS dipl
Degrees: BA 4 yrs
Tuition: $14,182 per yr; campus res—room & board $4536 per yr
Courses: Art Education, †Art History, †Ceramics, Drawing, Museum Staff Training, †Painting, †Printmaking, †Sculpture, Design
Summer School: Dir, Deirdre Kramer

MACALESTER COLLEGE, Dept of Art, 1600 Grand Ave, 55105. Tel 612-696-6279; *Head Dept* Stanton Sears
Estab 1946; den; D; scholarships; SC 9, LC 8; enrl 20
Degrees: BA(Art) 4 yrs
Tuition: Res—undergrad $17,580 per yr; campus res—room & board $5275 per yr
Courses: Art Appreciation, Ceramics, Design, Drawing, Painting, Printmaking, Sculpture, American Art, Art of the Last Ten Years, Classical Art, Far Eastern Art, Fibers, Medieval Art, Principles Art, Renaissance Art, Tribal Art, Senior Seminar, Women in Art

UNIVERSITY OF MINNESOTA, Dept of Design, Housing & Apparel, 1985 Buford Ave (Mailing add: 240 McNeal Hall, 55108-6136). Tel 612-624-9700; FAX 612-624-2750; *Head Dept* Dr Becky L Yust
Pub; D & E; SC 57, LC 54, GC 25; enrl D 877 (spring quarter 92), grad 75
Ent Req: HS dipl; math requirement
Degrees: BS, MS, MA & PhD yrs
Tuition: Res—undergrad lower division $76.45 per cr, upper division $86.65 per cr, grad $705 per 3 cr hr; nonres—undergrad lower division $1359 per 3 cr hr, upper division $255.60
Courses: Art History, †Costume Design & Construction, Drawing, Handicrafts, †Interior Design, Textile Design, †Applied Design, Costume History, Decorative Arts, †Housing, †Textiles Clothing, Weaving Off-Loom, †Retail Merchandising
Summer School: Courses—vary each yr

UNIVERSITY OF SAINT THOMAS, Dept of Art History, 2115 Summit Ave, Loras Hall, Mail LOR 302, 55105-1096. Tel 612-962-5560, 962-5000; *Chmn* Mark Stansbury O'Donnell; *Prof* Dr Mary T Swanson
Estab 1885, dept estab 1978; den; D & E; scholarships; SC 25, LC 8; enrl D 2847, E 275, maj 40
Ent Req: HS dipl
Degrees: BA 4 yrs
Tuition: $1508 full sem cr
Courses: Art Education, †Art History, Calligraphy, Ceramics, Drawing, Graphic Arts, Graphic Design, Jewelry, Painting, Photography, Printmaking, Sculpture, Teacher Training
Summer School: Dir, Dr Verome Halverson. Courses—Introduction to Art History

SAINT PETER

GUSTAVUS ADOLPHUS COLLEGE, Art & Art History Dept, Schaefer Fine Arts Ctr, 800 W College Ave, 56082-1498. Tel 507-933-8000, 933-7019; *Chmn* Stanley Shetka. Instrs: FT 5, PT 2
Estab 1876; den; D; scholarships; SC 27; enrl 2300 total, 750 art, maj 50
Ent Req: HS grad, ent exam
Degrees: BA 4 yr
Tuition: $15,825 per yr (comprehensive fee); PT $1400 per course
Courses: Art Appreciation, †Art Education, †Art History, Ceramics, Design, Drawing, Painting, Photography, Printmaking, Sculpture, Teacher Training, Basic Design, Bronze Casting, †Studio Art
Summer School: Independent Study prog for three 4 wk periods during June, July or Aug

WHITE BEAR LAKE

CENTURY COLLEGE (Formerly Lakewood Community College), Humanities Dept, 3401 Century Ave N, 55110. Tel 612-779-3200; FAX 612-779-3417; *Instr* Kenneth Maeckelbergh; *Instr* Lew Schnellman; *Instr* Mel Sundby; *Instr* Karin McGinness; *Instr* Ken Hoff
Scholarships
Tuition: Res—$47.42 per quarter cr; nonres—$89.42 per cr hr
Courses: Art Appreciation, Art History, Calligraphy, Ceramics, Design, Drawing, Painting, Photography, Printmaking, Sculpture, Stage Design, American Art, Art Therapy
Adult Hobby Classes: Enrl 6000; tuition varies. 39 courses offered
Children's Classes: Enrl 500; tuition under $100 each course. 30 courses offered
Summer School: Dir, Dr Ron Leatherbarrow. Tuition $47.42 per cr, two 5 wk sessions

WILLMAR

WILLMAR COMMUNITY COLLEGE, Art Dept, 2021 15th Ave NW, PO Box 797, 56201. Tel 320-231-5102; FAX 320-231-6602; *Coordr Art Gallery* Sheryl Paulson; *Coordr Art Gallery* Bob Matson. Instrs: FT 1, PT 1
Estab 1962-63; pub; D & E; SC 8, LC 3; enrl D 50, maj 15
Ent Req: HS dipl
Degrees: AA & AS 2 yrs
Tuition: Res—$40.75 per cr hr; nonres—$81.50 per cr hr
Courses: Art Education, Ceramics, Display, Drawing, Graphic Arts, Graphic Design, History of Art & Archaeology, Painting, Teacher Training, Introduction to Studio Practices, Structure
Adult Hobby Classes: Courses—Ceramics, Design, History of Art, Painting

WINONA

SAINT MARY'S UNIVERSITY OF MINNESOTA, Art & Design Dept, 700 Terrace Heights, 55987. Tel 507-457-1593; FAX 507-457-6967; WATS 800-635-5987; Internet: http://www.rroberts@rex.mnsmc.edu. *Head Dept* Roderick Robertson, MFA; *Assoc Prof* Margaret Mear, MFA; *Assoc Prof* Karen Kryszko, MFA
Estab 1912, dept estab 1970; den; D; scholarships; SC 20, LC 6; enrl in school D 1240
Ent Req: HS dipl
Degrees: BA 4 yrs
Tuition: $9630 per yr; campus res—room & board $3250 per yr
Courses: Advertising Design, Art Appreciation, Art Education, Art History, Ceramics, Commercial Art, Costume Design & Construction, Design, Drafting, Drawing, †Graphic Design, History of Art & Archaeology, Illustration, Jewelry, Lettering, Museum Staff Training, Painting, Photography, Printmaking, Sculpture, Stage Design, Teacher Training, Theatre Arts, Computer Design, †Electronic Publishing, †Studio Arts

WINONA STATE UNIVERSITY, Dept of Art, 55987. Tel 507-457-5395; FAX 507-457-5086; *Chmn* Dominic Ricciotti; *Prof* Judy Schlawin, MS; *Assoc Prof* Seho Park, PhD; *Asst Prof* Ann Plummer, MFA; *Assoc Prof* Don Schmidlapp, MFA
Estab 1860; pub; D & E; scholarships
Degrees: BA and BS
Tuition: Res—undergrad $35 per cr hr; nonres—undergrad $83 per cr hr; plus student fees; campus res—room & board $2500 per yr single occupancy, double occupancy $2032
Courses: Art Education, Art History, Ceramics, Drawing, Graphic Design, Interior Design, Lettering, Painting, Printmaking, Sculpture, Weaving
Summer School: Courses offered

MISSISSIPPI

BLUE MOUNTAIN

BLUE MOUNTAIN COLLEGE, Art Dept, Box 296, 38610. Tel 601-685-4771, Ext 62; *Chmn Dept* William Dowdy, MA
Estab 1873, dept estab 1875; den; D & E; scholarships; SC 16, LC 2; enrl D 28, E 12, non-maj 20, maj 8, others 12
Ent Req: HS dipl
Degrees: BA & BS(Educ) 4 yr
Tuition: $3932 per yr; campus res—room & board $6092
Courses: Art History, Commercial Art, Drawing, Painting
Adult Hobby Classes: Enrl 12; tuition $42 per sem hr. Courses—Drawing, Painting
Summer School: Dir, William Dowdy. Enrl 20

BOONEVILLE

NORTHEAST MISSISSIPPI JUNIOR COLLEGE, Art Dept, 101 Cunningham, 38829. Tel 601-728-7751, Ext 229; *Chmn* Jerry Rains; *Instr* Terry Anderson; *Instr* Judy Tucci. Instrs: FT 2, PT 1
Estab 1948; pub; D & E; scholarships; SC 6, LC 3; enrl D 2800, maj 30
Ent Req: HS dipl, ent exam
Degrees: 2 yr Associate degrees in art educ, fine arts and interior design
Tuition: res—$435 per sem; nonres—$830 per sem; foreign countries—$2385 per sem
Courses: Advertising Design, Aesthetics, Art Education, Art History, Ceramics, Design, Drafting, Drawing, Painting, Teacher Training, Theatre Arts
Adult Hobby Classes: Watercolor

CLARKSDALE

COAHOMA COMMUNITY COLLEGE, Art Education & Fine Arts Dept, 3240 Friars Pt Rd, 38614. Tel 601-627-2571; *Chmn* Henry Dorsey
Degrees: AA
Tuition: In district—$700 per yr; res—$2511.70 per yr; outside district $1100 per yr; outside state $2100 per yr; out of district boarding $2911.70 per yr, out of state boarding $3911.70 per yr
Courses: Art Appreciation, Art Education, Art History, Drawing, Handicrafts, Intro to Art
Adult Hobby Classes: Enrl 15-32; tuition $27.50 per sem hr. Courses—Art & Music Appreciation

CLEVELAND

DELTA STATE UNIVERSITY, Dept of Art, PO Box D-2, 38733. Tel 601-846-4720; *Chmn* Collier B Parker; *Prof* Dr Carolyn Rea Stone, Ph D; *Prof* Sam Glenn Britt, MFA; *Prof* William Carey Lester Jr, MFA; *Prof* Ron Koehler, MFA; *Assoc Prof* Mary Anne Ross, BFA; *Asst Prof* Kim Rushing; *Asst Prof* Marcella Small; *Asst Prof* Margaret Rutledge; *Asst Prof* Patricia L Brown; *Instr* Molly Rushing; *Instr* Joe Abide
Estab 1924; pub; D & E; scholarships; SC 42, LC 10, GC 30; enrl maj 116
Ent Req: HS dipl
Degrees: BA & BFA
Tuition: Res—undergrad $2294 per yr, $1147 per sem; nonres—undergrad & grad $3591 per yr, $2444 per sem
Courses: †Advertising Design, Aesthetics, †Art Education, Art History, Calligraphy, Ceramics, †Commercial Art, Costume Design & Construction, Drawing, Fashion Arts, Graphic Arts, †Graphic Design, Handicrafts, Illustration, †Interior Design, Lettering, Mixed Media, †Painting, Printmaking, †Sculpture, Teacher Training, Textile Design, Clay, Computer Graphics, Fibers
Summer School: Tuition & living expenses $488 per term, June 2 - July 3 or July 7 - August 8. Courses—Art for Elementary, Ceramics, Drawing, Internship in Commercial Design, Introduction to Art, Painting, Sculpture

CLINTON

MISSISSIPPI COLLEGE, Art Dept, PO Box 4205, 39058. Tel 601-925-3231; *Head Art Dept* Ruth Glaze, PhD. Instrs: FT 4, PT 2
Estab 1825, dept estab 1950; den; HS grad; scholarships and student assistantships; SC 22, LC 3; enrl maj 80, others 300
Ent Req: BA, BE(Art), MA(Art) and ME(Art) 4 yr, Freshman Art merit
Tuition: Undergrad $187 per cr hr, grad $200 per cr hr
Courses: †Art Education, Art History, Ceramics, Drawing, †Graphic Design, †Interior Design, †Painting, †Sculpture, Foundry Casting
Adult Hobby Classes: Enrl 50; tuition $35 for 5 weeks. Courses—Calligraphy, Drawing, Flower Arranging, Painting
Summer School: Dir, Dr Sam Gore. Tuition $1200 for two 6-wk terms. Courses—Ceramics, Drawing, Painting, Printmaking

COLUMBUS

MISSISSIPPI UNIVERSITY FOR WOMEN, Division of Fine & Performing Arts, PO Box W-70 MUW, 39701. Tel 601-329-7341; *Head Dept* Dr Sue S Coates; *Prof* David Frank; *Prof* Thomas Nawrocki, MFA; *Prof* Lawrence Feeny, MFA; *Asst Prof* Robert Gibson; *Asst Prof* John Alford
Estab 1884; pub; D & E; scholarships; SC 49, LC 8; enrl D 263, E 39, non-maj 45, maj 72
Ent Req: HS dipl, ACT, SAT
Degrees: BA, BS and BFA 4 yrs
Tuition: Res—undergrad $1119.50 per sem; nonres—undergrad $2228 per sem
Courses: †Art Education, Art History, Calligraphy, Ceramics, Commercial Art, Conceptual Art, Graphic Design, †Interior Design, Illustration, Lettering, Mixed Media, †Painting, Photography, †Printmaking, Sculpture, Stage Design, Teacher Training, †Theatre Arts, Weaving, Architectual Construction & Materials
Adult Hobby Classes: Enrl 45; tuition $25 per hr. Courses—Drawing, Painting, Weaving
Summer School: Tuition $66 per hr for term of 5 wks beginning June 1 & July 6. Courses—Vary according to demand

DECATUR

EAST CENTRAL COMMUNITY COLLEGE, Art Dept, PO Box AA, 39327. Tel 601-635-2121; *Head Dept* J Bruce Guraedy, MEd
Estab 1928, dept estab 1965; pub; D & E; scholarships; SC 10, LC 8; enrl D 160, E 52, non-maj 100, maj 10
Ent Req: HS dipl, GED
Degrees: AA and AS 2 yr
Tuition: Res—$3000 per yr, $1500 per sem; nonres—$6700 per yr, $1850 per sem;

campus res available
Courses: Advertising Design, Art Appreciation, Art Education, Art History, Ceramics, Collages, Design, Drafting, Drawing, Fashion Arts, Handicrafts, Illustration, Industrial Design, Interior Design, Landscape Architecture, Mixed Media, Painting, Printmaking, Sculpture, Stage Design, Theatre Arts
Adult Hobby Classes: Enrl 15; tuition $100 per sem for 10 wks. Courses—Beginning Painting, Drawing, Painting
Children's Classes: Kid's College & pvt lessons available
Summer School: Acad Dean, Dr Phil Sutphin. Enrl 300 - 400; tuition $50 per sem hr for term of 10 wks. Courses—vary according to student demand

ELLISVILLE

JONES COUNTY JUNIOR COLLEGE, Art Dept, 900 S Court St, 39437. Tel 601-477-4148, 477-4000; *Chmn Fine Arts* Jeff Brown
Estab 1927; pub; D; scholarships; SC 12, LC 4; enrl D 100, E 12, maj 15, others 12
Ent Req: HS dipl
Degrees: AA 2 yrs
Tuition: Res—$410 per sem; $40 per cr hr; nonres—$925 per sem; $42 per cr hr
Adult Hobby Classes: Enrl 20. Courses—Painting
Summer School: Dir, B F Ogletree. Term of 4 wks beginning June. Courses—same as regular session

GAUTIER

MISSISSIPPI GULF COAST COMMUNITY COLLEGE-JACKSON COUNTY CAMPUS, Art Dept, PO Box 100, 39553. Tel 601-497-9602; *Chmn Fine Arts Dept* Martha Richardson, MA; *Head Visual Arts* Patt Odom, MA; *Instr* Kevin Turner
Pub; D & E; scholarships; SC 9, LC 2; enrl D 90, E 8, non-maj 62, maj 28
Degrees: AA, 2 yrs
Tuition: Res—$440; out-of-state—$510
Courses: Art Appreciation, Ceramics, Design, Drawing, Painting, Sculpture, Teacher Training, Allied Art, Introduction Art, Pottery
Adult Hobby Classes: Courses—Ceramics, Art Appreciation, Drawing, Painting
Children's Classes: Enrl 30; tuition $35. Courses—Drawing, Painting, Pottery
Summer School: Dir, Patt Odom. Courses—Art Appreciation, Ceramics, Introductory Art, Art Educ

HATTIESBURG

UNIVERSITY OF SOUTHERN MISSISSIPPI, Dept of Art, College of the Arts, PO Box 5033, 39406. Tel 601-266-4972; FAX 601-266-6379; *Chmn* Harry Ward; *Coordr Art Educ* Tom Brewer. Instrs: FT 11, PT 3
Estab 1910; pub; D & E; scholarships; SC 64, LC 41, GC 34; enrl non-maj 35, maj 120, grad 5
Ent Req: HS dipl
Degrees: BA, BFA, MAE
Tuition: Res—undergrad $1188 per sem; nonres—$980 fee; res—grad $127 per sem hr; campus residency available
Courses: Art Education, Ceramics, Drawing, Graphic Design, Painting, Sculpture, Graphic Design, Handicrafts, Illustration, Interior Design, Jewelry, Lettering, Mixed Media, Painting, Photography, Printmaking, Sculpture, Teacher Training, Textile Design, Weaving
Adult Hobby Classes: Enrl 20-50; 16 wk sem. Courses—Ceramics, Drawing, Painting, Sculpture
Children's Classes: Classes offered by Office of Lifelong Learning. Courses—Painting
Summer School: Dir, Jerry Walden. Enrl 60; 5 & 10 wk sessions. Courses—as above

ITTA BENA

MISSISSIPPI VALLEY STATE UNIVERSITY, Fine Arts Dept, 14000 Hwy 82 W, PO Box 61, 38941-1400. Tel 601-254-9041, Ext 3484; *Head* Sandra Scott
Estab 1952; pub; D & E
Ent Req: HS dipl
Degrees: BA & BS
Tuition: Res—undergrad $2094.50 per sem; out-of-state—$3074.50
Courses: Art History, Ceramics, Drawing, Graphic Arts, Illustration, Painting, Photography, Printmaking, Art Appreciation, Arts & Crafts, Color Fundamentals, Public School Art, 2 & 3-D Design, Typography, Visual Communications
Summer School: Courses—Art Appreciation, Public School Art

JACKSON

BELHAVEN COLLEGE, Art Dept, 1500 Peachtree St, 39202. Tel 601-968-5950, 968-5928 (main); *Chmn* Bruce Bezaire
Estab 1883, dept estab 1889; den; D & E; scholarships; LC 3; enrl D 650, E 200, maj 30
Ent Req: HS dipl
Degrees: BA
Courses: Art History, Drawing, Graphic Arts, Painting, Photography, Printmaking
Summer School: Dir, Dr Dewey Buckley

JACKSON STATE UNIVERSITY, Dept of Art, Lynch at Dalton St, 39217. Tel 601-968-2040; FAX 601-968-7022; *Chmn* Dr A D Macklin
Estab 1949; pub; D; scholarships; SC 16, LC 7, GC 1; enrl D 486, maj 57
Ent Req: HS dipl
Degrees: BA & BS(maj in Art) 4 yrs
Tuition: $99 per cr hr 1-11 hrs; $1190 per sem 12-19 hrs; campus res available
Courses: Art History, Ceramics, Commercial Art, Drawing, Graphic Arts, Painting, Studio Crafts
Adult Hobby Classes: Athenian Art Club activities
Summer School: Dir, Dr A D Macklin. Enrl 300; tuition $95. Courses—Art Appreciation, Painting

MILLSAPS COLLEGE, Dept of Art, 1701 N State St, 39210. Tel 601-974-1000, 974-1432; *Chmn* Elise Smith; *Assoc Prof* Lucy Millsaps, MA; *Asst Prof* Collin Asmus; *Instr* Skip Allen, BFA; *Instr* Ray Holloway
Estab 1913, dept estab 1970; priv; D & E; scholarships; LC 4; enrl non maj 100, maj 20
Ent Req: HS dipl, SAT combined 1100 average
Degrees: BA 4 yr
Tuition: $1132 per yr; campus res—room & board $4501
Courses: Aesthetics, Architecture, Art History, Calligraphy, Ceramics, Design, Drawing, History of Art & Archaeology, Lettering, Museum Staff Training, Painting, Photography, Printmaking, Sculpture, Stage Design, Teacher Training, Textile Design, Theatre Arts, Weaving
Adult Hobby Classes: Tuition $35 per class
Children's Classes: Limited courses

LORMAN

ALCORN STATE UNIVERSITY, Dept of Fine Arts, 39096. Tel 601-877-6271, 877-6100; *Chmn* Joyce Bolden, PhD; *Instr* John Buchanan
Estab 1871, dept estab 1973; pub; D & E; SC 9, LC 3
Ent Req: HS dipl, ACT
Tuition: Res—$1194.50 per yr; nonres—$2445.50; meals—res $2309; nonres—$3560 per sem
Courses: Art Appreciation, Art Education, Ceramics, Drawing, Painting
Adult Hobby Classes: Drawing, Graduate Level Art Education, Painting
Summer School: Enrl 40 for term of 10 wks beginning May 28. Courses—Art Education, Fine Arts

MISSISSIPPI STATE

MISSISSIPPI STATE UNIVERSITY, Art Dept, PO Box 5182, 39762. Tel 601-325-2970, 325-2323 (main), 325-2224 (admis), 325-6900 (art dept); *Head* Brent Funderburk; *Prof* Paul Grootkerk, PhD; *Assoc Prof* Jack Bartlett, MFA; *Assoc Prof* Linda Seckinger, MFA; *Assoc Prof* Marita Gootee, MFA; *Asst Prof* Robert Long, MFA; *Asst Prof* Jamie Mixon; *Asst Prof* Anna Chupa; *Asst Prof* Bill Woodward; *Gallery Dir* Eden Brown; *Instr* Scott Belz; *Instr* Mickey Luck; *Instr* Anne Hauger; *Lect* Bart Galloway
Estab 1879, dept estab 1971; pub; D; scholarships; SC 23, LC 6; enrl D 750, non-maj 650, maj 150
Ent Req: HS dipl
Degrees: BFA 4 yrs
Tuition: In-state $1315.50; out-state $2725.50; campus res—room & board $2065.50 per yr
Courses: Art History, Ceramics, Commercial Art, Drawing, Painting, Photography, Printmaking, Sculpture
Adult Hobby Classes: Enrl 40; tuition $1700 per yr. Courses—Drawing, Fundamentals, Painting

MOORHEAD

MISSISSIPPI DELTA COMMUNITY COLLEGE, Dept of Fine Arts, PO Box 668, 38761. Tel 601-246-6322; *Chmn* Joseph R Abrams III; *Coordr* Jean Abrams; *Instr* Evelyn Kiker
Estab 1926; pub; D & E; SC 11, LC 2; enrl D 68, E 29, maj 28
Ent Req: HS dipl, ent exam
Degrees: AA & AS(Commercial Art) 2 yrs
Tuition: Res—undergrad $920 per yr
Courses: Advertising Design, Ceramics, Commercial Art, Drawing, Graphic Arts, Painting, Art Appreciation
Adult Hobby Classes: Enrl 29. Courses—Ceramics, Painting

POPLARVILLE

PEARL RIVER COMMUNITY COLLEGE, Art Dept, Division of Fine Arts, Sta A, PO Box 5007, 101 Highway 11 N, 39470. Tel 601-795-1230; FAX 601-795-6815; *Chmn* James A Rawls; *Instr* Charleen A Null. Instrs: FT 1, PT 2
Estab 1921; pub; D & E; scholarships; enrl D 85 - 100, non-maj 65 - 75, maj 20 - 25, E 20 - 40, non-maj 20 - 30, maj 10 - 20
Ent Req: HS dipl or ACT Score & GED
Tuition: Res—$425 per sem; out of state $1025; campus res available
Courses: Art Appreciation, Art Education, Art History, Calligraphy, Design, Drafting, Drawing, Handicrafts, Interior Design, Painting, Photography, Teacher Training, Elementary Art Education, Introduction to Art

RAYMOND

HINDS COMMUNITY COLLEGE, Dept of Art, 39154. Tel 601-857-3274; FAX 601-857-3392; *Chmn* Russell Schneider. Instrs: FT 4
Estab 1917; pub; D & E; scholarships; SC 5, LC 2; enrl D 400, E 75, maj 60
Degrees: AA 2 yr
Tuition: Res—$510 per sem (12-19 hrs), nonres—$1613 per sem (12-19 hrs); campus res available
Courses: Advertising Design, Ceramics, Commercial Art, Display, Drawing, Graphic Design, Painting
Adult Hobby Classes: Courses offered
Children's Classes: Courses offered
Summer School: Dir, Russell F Schneider. Enrl 24; tuition $165 for 8 wk term. Course—Art Appreciation

TOUGALOO

TOUGALOO COLLEGE, Art Dept, 500 W County Line Rd, 39174. Tel 601-977-7700; *Co-Chmn* Johnnie Mae Gilbert, MAE; *Assoc Prof* Bruce O'Hara, MFA
Estab 1869, dept estab 1968; pvt; D; scholarships; SC 14, LC 4; enrl D 650, non-maj 420, maj 12
Ent Req: HS dipl
Degrees: BA and BS 4 yrs
Tuition: Res—undergrad average $5115 per yr
Courses: Advertising Design, Art Appreciation, Art Education, Art History, Commercial Art, Design, Drawing, History of Art & Archaeology, Painting, Photography, Printmaking, Teacher Training, African American Art, American & Contemporary Art, Photojournalism

UNIVERSITY

UNIVERSITY OF MISSISSIPPI, Dept of Art, 38677. Tel 601-232-7193; FAX 601-232-5013; *Chmn* Margaret Gorove, MFA; *Prof* Charles M Gross, MFA; *Prof* Ron Dale, MFA; *Prof* Jere H Allen, MFA; *Assoc Prof* John L Winters, MFA; *Assoc Prof* Tom Dewey II, PhD; *Assoc Prof* Tom Rankin, MFA; *Assoc Prof* Paula Temple, MFA; *Assoc Prof* Betty Crouther, PhD; *Assoc Prof* Gregory Shelnutt; *Asst Prof* John Hull, MFA; *Asst Prof* Aileen Ajootian, PhD; *Asst Prof* Stephen Larson, MFA. Instrs: FT 13, PT 6
Dept estab 1949; pub; D; merit scholarships and out-of-state tuition waivers; SC 470, LC 265, GC 48; enrl D 735, non-maj 350, maj 260, grad 15
Ent Req: HS dipl
Degrees: BA 4 yr, BFA 4 yr, MFA 2 yr, MA 1 yr
Tuition: Res—undergrad $998 per sem, $83 per cr hr, grad $998 per sem $111 per cr hr; nonres—undergrad $2683 per sem, $201 per cr hr, grad $2683 per sem, $137 per cr hr; campus res—room $800-$966
Courses: †Art Education, †Art History, †Ceramics, Drawing, Graphic Arts, †Graphic Design, Illustration, †Interior Design, †Painting, †Printmaking, †Sculpture
Summer School: Dir, G Walton. Two 5 wk sessions beginning June. Courses—Art Education, Art History, Ceramics, Design, Drawing, Painting, Printmaking, Sculpture

MISSOURI

BOLIVAR

SOUTHWEST BAPTIST UNIVERSITY, Art Dept, 1601 S Springfield, 65613. Tel 417-326-1651; *Chmn* Wesley A Gott, MFA; *Adjunct Prof* Diane Callahan, BFA
Sch estab 1876, dept estab 1974; den; D & E; scholarships; SC 30, LC 3; enrl D 150, E 20, maj 35
Ent Req: HS dipl
Degrees: BS & BA
Tuition: Res—undergrad $3854 per yr; nonres—undergrad $3854 per yr; campus res—room & board $2563 per academic yr
Courses: †Art Education, Art History, †Ceramics, †Commercial Art, Costume Design & Construction, †Drawing, †Graphic Arts, Graphic Design, Interior Design, †Painting, †Photography, †Printmaking, †Sculpture, Stage Design, †Teacher Training, Theatre Arts
Adult Hobby Classes: Enrl 10; tuition $35 per hr for 15 weeks. Courses—Drawing, Painting, Photography
Summer School: Enrl 600; tuition $161 per hr for 4 wk term beginning in June, also a 4 wk term beginning in July. Courses—Drawing, Painting, Photography

CANTON

CULVER-STOCKTON COLLEGE, Art Dept, 63435-1299. Tel 217-231-6367, 231-6368; FAX 217-231-6611; Elec Mail croyer_culver.edu, jjorgen@culver.edu. *Gallery Dir* Catherine M Royer; *Prof* Albert Beck; *Assoc Prof* Joe Harris; *Assoc Prof* Joseph Jorgensen; *Lectr* John Nelson; *Lectr* Kevin Dingman
Estab 1853; pvt; D; scholarships; SC 16, LC 6; enrl 1030, maj 40
Ent Req: HS dipl, ACT or Col Board Ent Exam
Degrees: BFA & BA(Visual Arts), BS(Art Educ) & BS(Arts Management) 4 yrs
Tuition: $350 per cr hr
Courses: Art Appreciation, †Art Education, Art History, †Ceramics, Drawing, †Graphic Design, History of Art & Archaeology, Jewelry, †Painting, †Photography, Printmaking, †Sculpture, Teacher Training, Textile Design
Summer School: Reg, Barbara Conover. Tuition $150 per cr hr. Courses—Various studio workshops

CAPE GIRARDEAU

SOUTHEAST MISSOURI STATE UNIVERSITY, Dept of Art, One University Plaza, 63701. Tel 573-651-2143, 651-2000; *Chmn* Sarah Riley
Estab 1873, dept estab 1920; pub; D & E; scholarships; SC 28, LC 10, GC 18; enrl D 1300
Ent Req: HS dipl
Degrees: BS, BS(Educ) & BA 4 yrs, MAT
Tuition: Res—$2550 per sem, $85 per cr hr; nonres—$4680 per sem, $156 per cr hr
Courses: Advertising Design, Art History, Ceramics, Commercial Art, Drawing, Graphic Design, Illustration, Lettering, Painting, Printmaking, Sculpture, Silversmithing, Color Composition, Design Foundation, Fiber, Perceptive Art, Screen Printing, 3-D Design, Typography, Video Art Graphic
Summer School: Chmn, Sarah Riley

COLUMBIA

COLUMBIA COLLEGE, Art Dept, 1001 Rogers, 65216. Tel 573-875-8700, 875-7520; *Chmn* Ed Collings; *Instr* Sidney Larson, MA; *Instr* Ben Cameron; *Instr* Thomas Watson, MFA; *Instr* Richard Baumann; *Instr* Michael Sledd. Instrs: FT 5, PT 2
Estab 1851; den; D; scholarships; SC 55, LC 13; enrl D 180, non-maj 80, maj 115
Ent Req: HS dipl or equivalent, ACT or SAT, also accept transfer students
Degrees: AA 2 yrs, BA, BS and BFA 4 yrs
Tuition: Res—$3583 per sem; nonres—$5201
Courses: Art History, Ceramics, Drawing, Fashion Arts, Graphic Arts, Graphic Design, Illustration, Painting, Photography
Adult Hobby Classes: Enrl 15; tui $75 per cr. Courses—Arts & Crafts, Photography
Summer School: Evening Studies Dir, Dr John Hendricks. Enrl 20; tui $75 per cr hr

STEPHENS COLLEGE, Art & Fashion Dept, PO Box 2012, 65215. Tel 573-442-2211, Ext 173; *Instr* Robert Friedman; *Instr* Rosalind Kimball-Moulton
Estab 1833, dept estab 1850; pvt; D & E; scholarships; SC 25, LC 6; enrl D 800, maj 3, others 10
Ent Req: SAT or ACT, recommendations, interview
Degrees: BA 3-4 yrs, BFA 3 1/2-4 yrs
Tuition: $14,830 per yr; campus res—room & board $5540
Courses: Advertising Design, Art Education, Art History, Ceramics, Commercial Art, Costume Design & Construction, Drawing, †Fashion Arts, Film, Graphic Arts, Graphic Design, Illustration, Occupational Therapy, †Painting, †Photography, †Printmaking, †Sculpture, †Stage Design, Teacher Training, †Theatre Arts, †Video
Children's Classes: Tuition $900 per yr; Stephens Child Study Center, grades K-3, preschool; includes special creative arts emphasis

UNIVERSITY OF MISSOURI
—Art Dept, A 126 Fine Arts, 65211. Tel 573-882-3555; FAX 314-884-6807; *Chmn* William Berry. Instrs: FT 12, PT 3
Estab 1901, dept estab 1912; pub; D & E; SC 76, LC 1, GC 53; enrl non-maj 1600 per sem, maj 180, grad 34
Ent Req: HS dipl
Degrees: BA, BFA, MFA, MeD, PhD, EDD
Tuition: Res—undergrad $113.05 per cr hr, grad $139.91 per cr hr; nonres—undergrad $373.95 per cr hr, grad $385.11 per cr hr
Courses: Ceramics, Design, Drawing, Jewelry, Painting, Photography, Printmaking, Sculpture, Fibers, Introduction to Art
Summer School: Chmn, Oliver A Schuchard. Enrl 175; tuition $161 for term of 8 wks beginning June 12. Courses—Art Education, Ceramics, Design, Drawing, Fibers, Intro to Art, Jewelry, Painting, Photography, Printmaking, Sculpture, Watercolor
—Art History & Archaeology Dept, 109 Pickard Hall, 65211. Tel 573-882-6711; FAX 314-884-4039; *Chmn* Howard Marshall; *Prof* Osmund Overby, PhD; *Prof* Norman Land, PhD; *Prof* William R Biers, PhD; *Prof* Patricia Crown, PhD; *Assoc Prof* Marcus Rautman, PhD; *Asst Prof* Anne Rudloff Stanton, PhD; *Asst Prof* John Klein, PhD
Estab 1839, dept estab 1892; pub; D; scholarships; LC 42, GC 18; enrl maj 48, grad 39
Ent Req: HS dipl, SAT, GRE for grad students
Degrees: BA 4 yrs, MA 2-3 yrs, PhD 4 yrs
Tuition: Res—grad $103 per cr hr; nonres—grad $288 per cr hr; campus res available
Courses: Art History, †History of Art & Archaeology, Museum Staff Training, Classical Archaeology, Historic Preservation
Summer School: Courses offered

FERGUSON

SAINT LOUIS COMMUNITY COLLEGE AT FLORISSANT VALLEY, Liberal Arts Division, 3400 Pershall Rd, 63135. Tel 314-595-4375; *Chmn Div* Jim Gormley
Estab 1962; pub; D & E; SC 36, LC 4; enrl maj 70
Ent Req: HS dipl, ent exam
Degrees: AA, AAS 2 yr
Tuition: District res—$31, non district res—$41, non state res—$52
Courses: Advertising Design, Art History, Ceramics, Commercial Art, Drawing, Illustration, Lettering, Painting, Photography, Printmaking, Sculpture, Air Brush, Electronic Certificate, Transfer Art, Typography
Summer School: Enrl 270; tuition $20.50 per cr hr for term beginning June 9. Courses—Design, Drawing, Figure Drawing, Lettering, Painting

FULTON

WILLIAM WOODS-WESTMINSTER COLLEGES, Art Dept, 200 W 12th, 65251. Tel 573-592-4372; *Chmn* Paul Clervi; *Instr* Terry Martin, MA; *Instr* Jeff Ball, MA; *Instr* Tina Mann, MA; *Instr* Bob Elliott, MA; *Instr* Sharon Kilfoyle; *Instr* Ken Greene, BA
Estab 1870; pvt; D; scholarships; SC 54, LC 6; enrl maj 71
Ent Req: HS dipl, SAT or ACT
Degrees: BA, BS & BFA 4 yr
Tuition: Res—$9800 per yr (incl room & board); campus res—room & board $3700
Courses: Aesthetics, Art Education, Art History, Ceramics, Collages, Commercial Art, Costume Design & Construction, Drawing, Handicrafts, History of Art & Archaeology, Illustration, Interior Design, Jewelry, Painting, Photography, Printmaking, Sculpture, Silversmithing, Stage Design, Teacher Training, Theatre Arts, Weaving, Art Therapy

HANNIBAL

HANNIBAL LA GRANGE COLLEGE, Art Dept, 2800 Palmyra, 63401. Tel 573-221-3675; *Chmn* James Stone; *Instr* Bob Greenlee; *Instr* Richard Griffen; *Instr* Bill Krehmeier; *Instr* Dorothy Hahn
Scholarships
Degrees: AA, BA(Art)
Tuition: $3025 per sem (12-17 hrs)
Courses: Advertising Design, Art Appreciation, Art Education, Art History, Calligraphy, Ceramics, Commercial Art, Design, Drawing, Handicrafts, Lettering, Mixed Media, Painting, Photography, Printmaking, Sculpture, Textile Design, Cartooning
Summer School: Dean, Dr Woodrow Burt. Term 2-4 wk & one 8 wk. Courses—vary

JEFFERSON CITY

LINCOLN UNIVERSITY, Dept Fine Arts, 820 Chestnut St, 65102-0029. Tel 573-681-5280; *Chmn* James Tatum; *Instr* Jane Carol. Instrs: FT 1, PT 4
Estab 1927; pub; enrl maj 35, others 100
Degrees: BS(Art) & BS(Art Educ) 4 yr
Tuition: Res—undergrad $75 per cr hr
Courses: Art Education, Art History, Teacher Training, Applied Art, Studio Art
Summer School: Courses—same as above

JOPLIN

MISSOURI SOUTHERN STATE COLLEGE, Dept of Art, 3950 Newman Rd, 64801. Tel 417-625-9563; *Dept Head* Jim Bray; *Prof* V A Christensen; *Prof* Jon H Fowler; *Prof* Garry J Hess; *Prof* David Noblett; *Prof* Robert Schwieger; *Adjunct Prof* Alice Knepper
Estab 1937; pub; D & E; scholarships; SC 22, LC 3; enrl D 425, E 83, non-maj 360, maj 105, others 10
Ent Req: HS dipl
Degrees: BA & BSE 4 yrs
Tuition: Res—undergrad $70 per cr hr
Courses: †Art Education, †Graphic Design, †Jewelry, †Painting, †Printmaking, †Sculpture, Jewelry, Painting, Printmaking, Sculpture, Studio Crafts
Summer School: Art Appreciation, Studio Course

KANSAS CITY

AVILA COLLEGE, Art Division, Dept of Humanities, 11901 Wornall Rd, 64145. Tel 816-942-8400, Ext 2289; FAX 816-942-3362; *Chmn* Daniel Larson; *Coordr* Susan Lawlor; *Instr* George Christman; *Instr* Sharyl Wright; *Instr* Brian Klapmeyer; *Instr* Kelly Mills; *Instr* Nancy Premer; *Instr* Lisa Sugimoto; *Artist in Residence* Sr Margaret Reinhart
Estab 1948; den; D & E; scholarships; SC 35, LC 4; enrl D 140, E 20, non-maj 120, maj 40
Ent Req: HS dipl, SAT and PSAT
Degrees: BA 4 yrs
Tuition: $2975 per sem
Courses: Art Appreciation, Art Education, Art History, Ceramics, Commercial Art, Design, Drawing, Graphic Arts, Graphic Design, Illustration, Painting, Photography, Printmaking, Sculpture, Teacher Training
Adult Hobby Classes: Courses offered

KANSAS CITY ART INSTITUTE, 4415 Warwick Blvd, 64111. Tel 816-561-4852; FAX 816-561-6404; *Pres* Kathleen Collins, MFA; *Chmn Ceramics* Cary Esser, MFA; *Chmn Design* Sherry Sparks; *Chmn Painting & Printmaking* Warren Rosser; *Chmn Photo* Patrick Clancy, MFA; *Chmn Sculpture* Karen McCoy; *Chmn Found* Steve Whitacre, MFA; *Chmn Liberal Arts* Milton Katz, PhD; *Chmn Fiber* Jane Lackey, MFA
Estab 1885; D & E; scholarships; maj areas 7, LC 104 in liberal arts; enrl D 517, maj 517
Ent Req: HS dipl, portfolio interview
Degrees: BFA 4 yrs
Tuition: $15,820 per yr, $7910 per sem, $630 per cr hr; campus res—room $4470 per yr (double occupancy)
Courses: Art History, †Ceramics, Commercial Art, †Design, Drawing, Film, Graphic Arts, Graphic Design, Interior Design, Mixed Media, †Photography, †Printmaking, †Sculpture, †Video, †Textile
Adult Hobby Classes: 250; tuition $630 per cr hr for 12 wk term
Summer School: Dir, Christopher Leitch. Tuition $1500 2 sessions 1-3 wk; 1-2 wk; 3 wk term. Courses—Liberal Arts, Studio

MAPLE WOODS COMMUNITY COLLEGE, Dept of Art & Art History, 2601 NE Barry Rd, 64156. Tel 816-437-3000; *Head Dept* Jennie Frederick. Instrs: PT 6
Estab 1969; pub; D & E; scholarships; SC 12, LC 2; enrl D 125, E & Sat 80
Ent Req: HS dipl or GED
Degrees: AA 2 yrs
Tuition: District res—$133 per cr hr
Courses: Art Education, Art History, Ceramics, Commercial Art, Drawing, Painting, Photography, Printmaking, Sculpture, Art Fundamentals
Adult Hobby Classes: Enrl 30; tuition same as above. Courses same as above
Children's Classes: Summer classes; enrl 30; tuition $30 for 6 wks
Summer School: Dir, Helen Mary Turner. Tuition same as above for 8 wks beginning June 1. Courses—Ceramics, Drawing, Painting

PENN VALLEY COMMUNITY COLLEGE, Art Dept, 3201 SW Trafficway, 64111. Tel 816-759-4000; FAX 816-759-4050; *Div Chmn Humanities* Eleanor Bowie
Scholarships offered
Degrees: AA
Tuition: District res—$43 per sem hr; non-district res—$71 per sem hr; non-state res—$102 per sem hr
Courses: Advertising Design, Art History, Calligraphy, Ceramics, Design, Drawing, Fashion Arts, Film, Painting, Photography, Printmaking, Sculpture, Video, Animation, Art Fundamentals, Cartooning, Computer Graphics

UNIVERSITY OF MISSOURI-KANSAS CITY, Dept of Art & Art History, 5100 Rockhill Rd, 64110-2499. Tel 816-235-1501; FAX 816-235-5507; *Chmn* Dr Frances Connelly. Instrs: FT 10, PT 7
Estab 1933; pub; D & E; scholarships; enrl maj 138
Ent Req: Contact Admis Office
Tuition: Res—freshman & sophomore $68.10 per cr hr, jr & sr $74.40, grad $88.40; nonres—freshman & sophomore $187.80 per cr hr, jr & sr $206.90, grad $226
Courses: Art Appreciation, †Art History, Drawing, Graphic Design, Intermedia, Painting, Photography, Printmaking, Computer Art
Summer School: Dir, B L Dunbar. Enrl 65; 8 wk term. Courses—Art History, Drawing, Painting, Photography, Printmaking

KIRKSVILLE

TRUMAN STATE UNIVERSITY (Formerly Northeast Missouri State University), Art Dept, Division of Fine Arts, 63501. Tel 816-785-4417; *Head Div Fine Arts* Robert L Jones
Estab 1867; pub; D & E; scholarships; SC 27, LC 8; enrl D 220, non-maj 45, maj 155
Ent Req: HS dipl
Degrees: BFA(Visual Comminications, Studio) 4 yrs, BA(Liberal Arts) 4 yrs, BA(Art History) 4 yrs
Tuition: Res—undergrad $125 per sem hr, grad $133 per sem hr; nonres—undergrad $225 per sem hr, grad $241 per sem hr
Courses: †Art History, †Ceramics, †Painting, †Photography, †Printmaking, †Sculpture, Visual Communications, Fibers
Summer School: Enrl 80-100; term of two 5 wk sessions beginning June & July

LIBERTY

WILLIAM JEWELL COLLEGE, Art Dept, 500 College Hill, 64068. Tel 816-781-7700, Ext 5414; *Chmn* David B Johnson, MFA; *Instr* Nano Nore, MFA; *Instr* Rebecca Koop, BFA
Estab 1849, dept estab 1966; pvt (cooperates with the Missouri Baptist Convention); D & E; scholarships; enrl D 120, E 35-40, maj 30
Degrees: BA & BS 4 yrs
Tuition: $14,400 (incl room & board)
Courses: Art Appreciation, Art History, Calligraphy, Ceramics, Design, Drawing, Painting, Photography, Printmaking, Sculpture, Computer Graphic
Adult Hobby Classes: Enrl 10 - 15; tuition $120 per 14 wk sem.
Courses—Calligraphy, Drawing, Illustration, Painting, Photograhy
Children's Classes: Enrl 10 - 15; tuition $30 - $40 for a 6 wk session.
Courses—Ceramics, Drawing, Painting, Photography
Summer School: Dir, Dr Steve Schwegler. Enrl 10 - 15; tuition $120 per cr hr for 8 wk term. Courses—Calligraphy, Drawing, Painting ,

MARYVILLE

NORTHWEST MISSOURI STATE UNIVERSITY, Dept of Art, 800 University Dr, 64468. Tel 816-562-1314; *Chmn* Lee Hageman, MFA; *Assoc Prof* Philip Laber, MFA; *Assoc Prof* George Rose, MFA; *Assoc Prof* Robert Sunkel, MFA; *Assoc Prof* Kenneth Nelsen, MFA; *Asst Prof* Russell Schmaljohn, MS; *Asst Prof* Kim Spradling, PhD; *Asst Prof* Paul Falcone, MFA
Estab 1905, dept estab 1915; pub; D & E; scholarships; SC 74, LC 19; enrl D 475, E 25, non-maj 350, maj 150
Ent Req: HS dipl
Degrees: BFA, BSE & BA 4 yrs
Tuition: Res—$71 per hr; nonres—$124.50 per hr; campus res—room & board $1500-$1800 per sem
Courses: Art Appreciation, Art Education, Art History, Ceramics, Commercial Art, Drawing, Graphic Design, Jewelry, Painting, Photography, Printmaking, Sculpture, Computer Graphics, Metalsmithing
Summer School: Chmn Dept Art, Lee Hageman. Two wk short courses varying from summer to summer; cost is hourly rate listed above. Courses—Art Education, Ceramics, Jewelry, Painting, Photography, Watercolor

NEOSHO

CROWDER COLLEGE, Art & Design, 601 La Clede Blvd, 64850. Tel 417-451-4700, Ext 306; *Div Chmn* Glenna Wallace; *Chmn* Janie Lance. Instrs: FT 1, PT 5
Estab 1964; Pub; D & E; scholarships; enrl D 1000, E 300, maj 20, others 250
Ent Req: HS grad or equivalent
Degrees: AA & AAS 2 yrs
Tuition: District res—$36 per cr hr; out-of-district res—$54 per cr hr; out-of-state—$73 per cr hr
Courses: Art Appreciation, Art History, Design, Drawing, Graphic Design, Jewelry, Painting, Sculpture, Ceramic Design, Fibers Design
Summer School: Dean of Col, Jackie Vietti. Term of 8 wks beginning in June. Courses—Varied academic courses

NEVADA

COTTEY COLLEGE, Art Dept, 1000 W Austin, 64772. Tel 417-667-8181; *Dean* Harold Ross; *Instr* L Bruce Holman, PhD; *Instr* Patricia McLoone, MFA; *Instr* Joann Morgan, PhD. Instrs: FT 3
Estab 1884; pvt; W; D; scholarships; SC 15, LC 4; enrl maj 12-15, total 369
Ent Req: HS grad, AC Board
Degrees: AA 2 yrs
Tuition: $6100 comprehensive fee (includes room & board)
Courses: Art Appreciation, Art History, Ceramics, Design, Drawing, Illustration, Painting, Photography, Printmaking, Graphic Arts, Handicrafts, Jewelry, Painting, Photography, Printmaking, Weaving, Metals

PARKVILLE

PARK COLLEGE, Dept of Art, 8700 NW River Park Dr, 64152. Tel 816-741-2000; *Chmn* Alex Kutchins
Estab 1875; pvt; D & E; scholarships; SC 13, LC 4; enrl D 50, non-maj 40, maj 20
Ent Req: HS dipl, ACT
Degrees: BA, 4 yrs
Tuition: Res—undergrad $118 per cr hr; campus res—room & board available
Courses: Advertising Design, Art Education, Art History, Ceramics, Drawing, Graphic Design, History of Art & Archaeology, Painting, Photography, Sculpture, Teacher Training, 3-D Design
Summer School: Chmn, Alex Kutchins. Tuition $118 per cr hr for 8 wk term. Courses—Ceramics, Printmaking, varied curriculum

POINT LOOKOUT

COLLEGE OF THE OZARKS, Dept of Art, 65726. Tel 417-334-6411, Ext 4255; *Prof* Anne Allman, PhD; *Prof* Jayme Burchett, MFA; *Assoc Prof* Donald Barr, MA; *Assoc Prof* Jeff Johnston, MFA
Estab 1906, dept estab 1962; pvt; D & E; scholarships; SC 22, LC 4; enrl D 200, E 25, non-maj 180, maj 40
Ent Req: HS dipl, ACT
Degrees: BA & BS 4 yr
Tuition: No fees are charged; each student works 960 hrs in on-campus employment
Courses: †Art Education, †Ceramics, †Drawing, †Painting, Graphic Design, Fibers

SAINT CHARLES

LINDENWOOD COLLEGE, Art Dept, 209 S Kings Hwy, 63301. Tel 314-949-4862, 949-2000; *Chmn Dept* Elaine Tillinger. Instrs: FT 4, PT 4
Estab 1827; pvt; D & E; scholarships; SC 24, LC 16; enrl D 200, E 30, maj 40
Ent Req: HS dipl, ent exam
Degrees: BA, BS, BFA 4 yrs, MA
Tuition: Res—undergrad $14,000 per yr
Courses: Art Education, Art History, Ceramics, Design, Drawing, Graphic Arts, Sculpture, Painting, Photography, Printmaking, Teacher Training, Computer Art

SAINT JOSEPH

MISSOURI WESTERN STATE COLLEGE, Art Dept, 4525 Downs Dr, 64507-2294. Tel 816-271-4200, Ext 422; *Chmn Dept* William Eickhorst, EdD; *Prof* Jim Estes, MFA; *Assoc Prof* John Hughes, MFA; *Assoc Prof* Jean Harmon, MFA; *Asst Prof* Allison Sauls, PhD
Estab 1969; pub; D & E; scholarships; SC 25, LC 8; enrl D 355, E 100, non-maj 120, maj 130
Ent Req: HS dipl, GED, ACT
Degrees: BS(Art Educ), BA & BS(Commercial Art) 4 yrs
Tuition: Res—$465 per sem; nonres—$875 per sem; campus residence available
Courses: Advertising Design, Aesthetics, Art Appreciation, Art Education, Art History, Ceramics, Commercial Art, Design, Drawing, Graphic Arts, Graphic Design, History of Art & Archaeology, Illustration, Painting, Photography, Printmaking, Sculpture, Commercial Art, Teacher Training, Computer Art, Tools & Techniques
Summer School: Chmn, Art Dept, William S Eickhorst. Tuition res—$130 for 5 or more cr hrs, nonres—$240 for 5 or more cr hrs; term of 8 wks beginning June 1. Courses—Art Education, Ceramics, Introduction to Art, Photomedia, Painting

SAINT LOUIS

FONTBONNE COLLEGE, Art Dept, 6800 Wydown Blvd, 63105. Tel 314-889-1431; *Chmn Dept* Catherine Connor-Talasek, MFA
Estab 1923; pvt; D & E; scholarships; SC 10, LC 2, GC 6; enrl non-maj 10, maj 46, grad 12, others 5
Ent Req: HS dipl, portfolio
Degrees: BA and BFA 4 yrs, MA 1 yr, MFA 2 yrs
Courses: Aesthetics, Art Appreciation, Art Education, Art History, †Ceramics, Commercial Art, Design, †Drawing, Graphic Design, History of Art & Archaeology, Illustration, Interior Design, †Photography, Printmaking, †Sculpture, Teacher Training, Weaving
Adult Hobby Classes: Tuition $180 per cr. Courses—Art History, Ceramics, Drawing, Painting, Photography, Sculpture
Summer School: Dir, C Connor-Talasek. Enrl 75; tuition $780 for 6 wk term. Courses—Ceramics, Drawing, Modern Art, Painting, Printmaking

MARYVILLE UNIVERSITY OF SAINT LOUIS, Art Division, 13550 Conway Rd, 63141-7299. Tel 314-529-9300, 529-9381 (art div); FAX 314-542-9085; *Art Division Chmn* Steven Teczar, MFA; *Prof* Cherie Fister; *Prof* Nancy Rice, MFA; *Prof* Les Armantrout; *Prof* R Jaffe; *Asst Prof* John Baltrushunas; *Adjunct Instr* Geof Wheeler; *Adjunct Instr* Dayne Sislen; *Adjunct Instr* Clay Pursell; *Adjunct Instr* Peggy Carothers; *Adjunct Instr* Mark Weber; *Adjunct Instr* Esley Hamilton; *Adjunct Instr* Elizabeth Metcalfe; *Adjunct Instr* Jeanne Merson; *Adjunct Instr* Nancy Bridwell; *Adjunct Instr* Carol A Felberbaum, IES; *Adjunct Instr* Ken Worley; *Adjunct Instr* Frank McGuire; *Adjunct Instr* Carole Lasky, PhD; *Adjunct Instr* Robert Acree, BA; *Adjunct Instr* Beth Baile, MA; *Adjunct Instr* Ken Mohr; *Adjunct Instr* Bob Moskowitz, MFA; *Adjunct Instr* Ron Nuetzel, BFA; *Adjunct Instr* Evann Richards, BFA; *Adjunct Instr* Bettina Braun, MA; *Adjunct Instr* Michael Lyss; *Instr* Les Addison, MA
Estab 1872, dept estab 1961; pvt; D & E; scholarships; SC 74, LC 6; enrl D 140, E 30, non-maj 60, maj 110
Ent Req: HS dipl, ACT or SAT
Degrees: BA, BFA, cert(Interior Design)
Tuition: $8200 per yr, $5140 per sem; $293 per cr hr; campus res—room & board $2450 per yr
Courses: Advertising Design, †Aesthetics, Architecture, †Art Appreciation, †Art

Education, †Art History, †Calligraphy, †Ceramics, †Commercial Art, Conceptual Art, Constructions, †Design, †Drafting, Drawing, Film, †Graphic Arts, †Graphic Design, History of Art & Archaeology, Illustration, †Interior Design, †Mixed Media, †Painting, †Photography, †Printmaking, †Sculpture, †Teacher Training, †Art Studio, †Auto CAD, †Color Theory, †Fibers & Soft Sculpture, †Furniture Design, †2-D & 3-D Design, †Handmade Book, †Painting the Figure, †Stone - Carving
Adult Hobby Classes: Enrl & tuition vary. Courses—Art & Architectural History, Art in St Louis, Drawing, Interior Design, Painting, Photography
Children's Classes: Enrl 115; tuition $150 (1 cr) & 100 (no cr) for 10 wk session. Courses—Ceramics, Cartooning, Drawing, Painting, Photography, Printmaking, Watercolor
Summer School: Dir, Dan Ray. Enrl 60; tuition same as regular year. Courses—Photography, Art Appreciation, Art History, Auto CAD, Drawing, Painting

SAINT LOUIS COMMUNITY COLLEGE AT FOREST PARK, Art Dept, 5600 Oakland Ave, 63110-1393. Tel 314-644-9350; FAX 314-644-9752; *Chmn* Mark Weber; *Asst Prof* Evann Richards, BA; *Instr* Joe C Angert, MA; *Instr* Allen Arpadi, BA. Instrs: PT 14
Estab 1962, dept estab 1963. College maintains three campuses; pub; D & E; scholarships; SC 36, LC 6; enrl D 200, E 100, non-maj 75, maj 75
Ent Req: HS dipl
Degrees: AA & AAS 2 yrs
Tuition: College Res—$40 per cr hr; nonres—$50 per cr hr; nonres out-of-state—$61 per cr hr
Courses: Advertising Design, Art Appreciation, Art Education, †Art History, Ceramics, Commercial Art, Design, Drawing, Film, †Graphic Design, Illustration, Lettering, †Painting, †Photography, Color, Commercial Photography, Computer-Assisted Publishing
Adult Hobby Classes: Courses—Drawing, Painting, Photography, Printmaking, Sculpture, Video
Summer School: Chmn, Leon Anderson. Enrl 100; tuition $40 per cr hr. Courses—Same as those above

SAINT LOUIS COMMUNITY COLLEGE AT MERAMEC, Art Dept, 11333 Big Bend Blvd, 63122. Tel 314-984-7500, 984-7628; *Chmn Dept* David Durham, BFA; *Instr* F Robert Allen, MFA; *Instr* John Ferguson; *Instr* Kay Hagan, MA; *Instr* Ruth Hensler, MFA; *Instr* Peter Hoell, BFA; *Instr* John Nagel, BA; *Instr* Patrick Shuck, MFA; *Instr* Keith Lamb, MA; *Instr* Ronald Thomas, MFA; *Instr* Yvette Woods, BFA
Estab 1964; D & E; scholarships; SC 15, LC 2
Ent Req: HS dipl
Degrees: AA 2 yrs
Tuition: Res—$40 per cr hr; nonres—$50 per cr hr; non campus res
Courses: Advertising Design, Art History, Ceramics, Commercial Art, Drawing, Illustration, Interior Design, Painting, Photography, Printmaking, Sculpture
Summer School: Chmn Dept, David Durham. Tuition $40 per cr hr for term of wks beginning June 11. Courses—Art Appreciation, Ceramics, Design, Drawing, Photography

SAINT LOUIS UNIVERSITY, Fine & Performing Arts Dept, 221 N Grand, 63103. Tel 314-977-3030; *Chmn* Dr Cindy Stollhans
Scholarships
Degrees: BA
Tuition: Undergrad $6400 full-time per term, $455 part-time per hr
Courses: Art History, Design, Drawing, Painting, Photography, Sculpture, Approaching the Arts, †Studio Art
Summer School: Courses—Drawings, Painting, Studio Art

UNIVERSITY OF MISSOURI, SAINT LOUIS, Dept of Art & Art History, 8001 Natural Bridge, 63121. Tel 314-516-5975, 516-6969; *Chmn* Ruth Bohan, PhD; *Prof* Janet Berlo, PhD; *Prof* Thomas Patton, MFA; *Assoc Prof* Ken Anderson, MFA; *Assoc Prof* Yael Even, PhD; *Assoc Prof* W Jackson Rushing, PhD; *Assoc Prof* Jeanne Morgan Zarucchi, PhD; *Asst Prof* Judith Mann, PhD; *Asst Prof* Terry Suhre, MFA; *Asst Prof* Dan Younger, MFA; *Lectr* Juliana Yuan, MA
Estab 1963; pub; D & E; scholarships; SC 62, LC 44; enrl maj 80
Ent Req: HS dipl
Degrees: BA(Art Hist)
Tuition: Res—undergrad $121 per cr hr; nonres—undergrad $361.70 per cr hr
Courses: Art Education, †Art History, Design, †Drawing, †Graphic Design, Illustration, †Painting, †Photography

WASHINGTON UNIVERSITY
—School of Art, One Brookings Dr, Campus Box 1031, 63130. Tel 314-935-6500; FAX 314-935-4862; Elec Mail jdeal@art.wustl.edu. *Dean School* Joe Deal, MFA; *Assoc Dean School* Jeffrey C Pike
Estab 1853; pvt; D; scholarships & fels; SC 62, LC 10, GC 31; enrl 390, non-maj 50, maj 300, grad 40
Ent Req: HS dipl, SAT or ACT, portfolio
Degrees: BFA 4 yrs, MFA 2 yrs
Tuition: $16,750 per yr, $8375 per sem, $700 per cr hr; campus res—room & board available
Courses: †Advertising Design, Aesthetics, Architecture, Art Appreciation, Art Education, Art History, †Ceramics, Costume Design & Construction, Design, Drawing, †Fashion Arts, Graphic Arts, †Graphic Design, History of Art & Archaeology, †Illustration, Mixed Media, Occupational Therapy, †Painting, †Photography, †Printmaking, †Sculpture, Stage Design, Theatre Arts, Video, †Fashion Design, †Glass Blowing
Adult Hobby Classes: Enrl 120; tuition $185 per cr hr. Courses—Calligraphy, Design, Drawing, Fashion, Graphic Communications, Painting, Printmaking, Wood Furniture & Workshops
Summer School: Dir, Libby Reuter. Enrl 80; tuition $185 - $285 per cr for term beginning June 9 - Aug 1. Courses—Computer Graphics, Drawing, Fashion Design, Graphic Design, High School Workshop, Photography. Santa Reparata, Florence, Italy, enrl 32; tuition $855 June 2 - June 25. Courses—On-site Drawing, Photography, Printmaking

—School of Architecture, One Brookings Dr, PO Box 1079, 63130. Tel 314-935-6200; FAX 314-935-8520; *Dean School* Cynthia Weese, FAIA
Estab 1910; pvt; D; scholarships; SC 28, LC 58, GC 42; enrl 300, maj 200, grad 100
Degrees: BA(Arch), MArch, MA(UD)
Tuition: $18,350 per yr, $765 per cr hr
Courses: †Architecture, Design, Drawing, Interior Design, Landscape Architecture, Photography
Adult Hobby Classes: Enrl 43; tuition $175 per unit. Certificate degree program, Bachelor of Technology in Architecture
Summer School: Tuition varies. Courses—Advanced Architectural Design, Fundamentals of Design, Structural Principles

SPRINGFIELD

DRURY COLLEGE, Art & Art History Dept, 900 N Benton Ave, 65802. Tel 417-873-7263, 873-7879; *Chmn Dept* Thomas Parker. Instrs: FT 6, PT 9
Estab 1873; den; scholarships; SC 12, LC 5; enrl 2246
Degrees: 4 yrs
Tuition: Res—undergrad $8730 per yr, $290 per cr hr
Courses: Architecture, Art History, Ceramics, Commercial Art, Photography, Teacher Training, Weaving, Studio Arts
Adult Hobby Classes: Enrl 25-35; tuition $74 per cr hr. Courses—Studio Art & History of Art
Children's Classes: Summer Scape, gifted children. Courses—Architecture, Design, Photography
Summer School: Dir, Sue Rollins. Enrl 292; tuition $110 per cr hr June-Aug for 9 wk term. Courses—Art History, Ceramics, Drawing, Painting, Photography

SOUTHWEST MISSOURI STATE UNIVERSITY, Dept of Art & Design, 901 S National, 65804-0089. Tel 417-836-5111; *Head Dept* Dr James K Hill. Instrs: FT 25, PT 5
Estab 1901; D & E; scholarships; SC 31, LC 10; enrl maj 400, others 2100
Ent Req: HS dipl, ent exam
Degrees: BFA, BS(Educ, Educ Comprehensive) & BA 4 yrs
Tuition: Res—$876; nonres—$1692; campus res—$1315 or $1512 per sem
Courses: Art Education, Art History, Ceramics, Drawing, Graphic Design, Jewelry, Painting, Printmaking, Sculpture, Silversmithing, Bronze Casting, Computer Graphics, Fibers, Metals/Jewelry
Adult Hobby Classes: Tuition $68 per cr hr for 1 & 2 wk sessions. Courses—Computer Graphics, Photography, Watercolor
Summer School: Dean, David Belcher. Enrl 17,000; special workshops available during summer session; tuition $79 per cr hr for 5 & 8 week sessions. Courses—Selected from above curriculum

UNION

EAST CENTRAL COLLEGE, Art Dept, PO Box 529, 63084. Tel 314-583-5195; *Chmn* John Morris. Instrs: FT 2, PT 1
Estab 1968; pub; D & E; scholarships; SC 8, LC 8; enrl D 370, E 120, maj 40
Ent Req: HS dipl, ent exam
Degrees: AA & AAS 2 yrs
Tuition: In-district—$21 per cr hr; out-of-district—$26 per cr hr; nonres—$38 per cr hr
Courses: Art Appreciation, Art Education, Art History, Design, Drawing, Handicrafts, History of Art & Archaeology, Lettering, Painting, Photography, Printmaking, Sculpture, Teacher Training, Art Appreciation, Business of Art, Figure Drawing
Adult Hobby Classes: Enrl 121; tuition $21-$38 per semester. Courses—Painting
Children's Classes: Tuition $25 for 4 wk summer term. Courses—Art, Drawing, Sculpture, Painting
Summer School: Tuition $21 per cr hr for 8 wk term. Courses—Art Appreciation, Art History

WARRENSBURG

CENTRAL MISSOURI STATE UNIVERSITY, Art Dept, Art Ctr 120, 64093. Tel 816-543-4481; FAX 816-543-8006; *Chair Dept* Jerry Miller, EdD; *Prof* Kathleen Desmond, EdD; *Prof* Richard D Monson, MFA; *Prof* Margaret Peterson, MFA; *Prof* John R Haydu, MFA; *Assoc Prof* Harold M Reynolds, EdD; *Assoc Prof* LeRoy McDermott, PhD; *Assoc Prof* Andrew Katsourides, MFA; *Assoc Prof* Chris Willey, MFA; *Assoc Prof* John W Lynch, MFA; *Asst Prof* George Sample, MSEd; *Asst Prof* John Owens, MFA; *Asst Prof* Neva Wood, MFA
Estab 1871; pub; D & E; scholarships; SC 40, LC 14, GC 10; enrl D 300, maj 300
Ent Req: HS dipl, Missouri School & Col Ability Test, ACT
Degrees: BA, BSE, & BFA 4 yrs, MA 1 yr
Tuition: Res—$84 per cr hr; nonres— $168 per cr hr; campus res—room & board varies
Courses: †Art Education, Art History, †Commercial Art, Drawing, Graphic Arts, Illustration, †Interior Design, Painting, Sculpture, Teacher Training, †Studio Art
Summer School: Chair Dept, Jerry L Miller. Term of 8 wks beginning first wk in June. Courses—Ceramics, Drawing, Grad Studio Courses, Painting

WEBSTER GROVES

WEBSTER UNIVERSITY, Art Dept, 470 E Lockwood Blvd, 63119-3194. Tel 314-968-7171; *Chmn* Tom Lang; *Assoc Prof* Leon Hicks, MFA; *Asst Prof* Carol Hodson; *Asst Prof* Jeffrey Hughes, PhD; *Asst Prof* Brad Loudenback; *Asst Prof* Jeri Au; *Lectr* Bill Kreplin, MFA; *Artist-in-Residence* Gary Passanise
Estab 1915; dept estab 1946; pvt; D & E; scholarships; SC 60, LC 15; enrl 1100, maj 100
Ent Req: HS dipl, SAT or ACT
Degrees: BA & BFA 4 yrs
Tuition: $280 per cr hr; campus res available
Courses: †Art Education, †Art History, †Ceramics, Collages, Conceptual Art,

†Drawing, Film, †Graphic Design, †Painting, †Photography, †Printmaking, †Sculpture, †Teacher Training, †Papermaking
Adult Hobby Classes: Tuition $175 per cr hr for 16 wk sem. Courses—Art, Photography, Watercolor
Summer School: Assoc Dean Fine Arts, Peter Sargent. Tuition $175 per cr hr for term of 6 or 8 wks beginning June. Courses—Introductory Photography, Sculpture Workshop: Bronze

MONTANA

BILLINGS

MONTANA STATE UNIVERSITY-BILLINGS, Art Dept, 1500 N 30th St, 59101-0298. Tel 406-657-2324; FAX 406-657-2187; *Head* John Pollock. Instrs: FT 7, PT 11
Estab 1927; pub; scholarhships
Ent Req: HS dipl
Degrees: AA, BS(Educ), BSEd(Art), BA(Lib Arts & Studio)
Tuition: Res—$174.50 per cr hr; nonres—$323.45 per cr hr
Courses: Art Appreciation, †Art Education, Art History, Ceramics, Display, Drawing, Painting, Photography, Printmaking
Summer School: Tuition res $174.50 per cr, nonres $323.45 per cr for two 6 wk sessions from May 13-June 17 & June 19-July 24. Courses—Art Appreciation, Ceramics, Drawing, Painting, Sculpture

ROCKY MOUNTAIN COLLEGE, Art Dept, 1511 Poly Dr, 59102. Tel 406-657-1094, 657-1040 (main), 657-1000 (admis); *Chmn* James Baken
Estab 1878, dept estab 1957; pvt; D; scholarships; SC 12, LC 5; enrl 112, non-maj 40, maj 30, others 5
Ent Req: HS dipl, ACT
Degrees: BA & BS 4 yrs
Tuition: $10,099 per yr; campus res—room & board $3882 per yr for double
Courses: Art Education, Art History, Ceramics, Drawing, Graphic Design, Painting, Photography, Sculpture, Teacher Training
Adult Hobby Classes: Enrl 100; tuition $20 for 5 wks. Courses—Crafts, Painting, Picture Framing

BOZEMAN

MONTANA STATE UNIVERSITY, *Interim Dir Art* Richard Helzer
—School of Art, 213 Haynes Hall, 59717. Tel 406-994-4501; *Dir Art* Willem Volkersz. Instrs: 14
Estab 1893; pub; D; scholarships; SC 38, LC 19, GC 13; enrl maj 250, grad 15
Ent Req: HS dipl 2.5 GPA or ACT score of 20
Degrees: BA, MFA
Tuition: Res—$1426 per yr, nonres—$3456 per yr
Courses: Ceramics, Graphic Design, Painting, Printmaking, Sculpture, Metals
Summer School: Dir, Richard Helzer. Enrl 65; tuition res—$760, nonres—$1178 for 12 wk term. Courses—Art History, Ceramics, Drawing, Graphic Design, Metals, Painting, Printmaking, Sculpture, Special Workshops
—School of Architecture, Cheever Hall, Rm 160, 59717. Tel 406-994-4255; FAX 406-994-6696; *Dir Archit* Clark Llewellyn. Instrs: FT 13, PT 1
Pub; scholarships; LabC 31, LC 39; enrl maj 400
Degrees: BA(Archit)
Tuition: Res—$1426 per yr; nonres—$3456 per yr
Courses: Architecture, Interior Design, Architectural Graphics, Computer Applications in Architecture, Construction Drawings & Specifications, Environmental Controls, Introduction to Design, Professional Practice, Structures
Summer School: Dir, Thomas R Wood. Enrl 35; tuition $358 for 4 wks, $381.75 for 8 wks

DILLON

WESTERN MONTANA COLLEGE, Art Dept, 710 S Atlantic, 59725. Tel 406-683-7342; FAX 406-683-7493; *Chmn Dept* Barney Brienza. Instrs: FT 3
Estab 1897; pub; D & E; scholarships; SC 15, LC 6, GC 21
Ent Req: HS dipl
Degrees: BS 4 yrs, MA
Courses: Art Education, Art History, Ceramics, Commercial Art, Drawing, Graphic Arts, Graphic Design, Handicrafts, Jewelry, Lettering, Painting, Weaving, Blacksmithing, Glass Blowing, Stained Glass
Adult Hobby Classes: Enrl 100; fees & duration vary. Courses—Blacksmithing, Jewelry, Oil Painting, Stained Glass, Watercolor
Summer School: Dir, Sue Jones. Enrl 350; 15 wk term. Courses—Art Methods, Blacksmithing, Bookmaking, Ceramics, Drawing, Glassblowing, Graphics, Oil Painting, Travel Study, Watercolor

GREAT FALLS

COLLEGE OF GREAT FALLS, Humanities Division, 1301 20th St S, 59405. Tel 406-761-8210; *Div Chmn* Lydon Marshall; *Prof* Mirle E Freel Jr. Instrs: FT 1, PT 2
Estab 1933; den; D & E; scholarships; SC, Lab C, LC; enrl approx 1250
Degrees: 4 yrs
Tuition: $3900 per yr
Courses: Art Education, Ceramics, Design, Drawing
Summer School: General art classes

HAVRE

MONTANA STATE UNIVERSITY-NORTHERN, Humanities & Social Sciences, PO Box 7751, 59501. Tel 406-265-3751, 265-3700; *Art Dept Chmn* Steve Sylvester
Estab 1929; pub; D & E; scholarships; SC 15, LC 5, GC 9; enrl D 425, grad 7
Ent Req: HS dipl
Degrees: AA 2 yrs, BS(Educ) and BA 4 yrs, MSc(Educ)
Tuition: Res—$3827 per sem; nonres—$4900 per sem
Courses: Art Education, Ceramics, Commercial Art, Drafting, Drawing, Graphic Arts, Painting, Sculpture
Adult Hobby Classes: Enrl 60. Courses—Classroom and Recreational Art, Watercolor Workshop
Summer School: Dir, Dr Gus Korb. Enrl 1390; two 5 wk sessions. Courses—Art Education, Art Methods K-12, Art Therapy

MILES CITY

MILES COMMUNITY COLLEGE, Dept of Fine Arts & Humanities, 2715 Dickinson St, 59301. Tel 406-232-3031; *Head Dept* Sydney R Sonneborn; *Instr* Fred McKee, MFA
Estab 1937, dept estab 1967; pub; D & E; scholarships; SC 17, LC 1; enrl D 36, E 23, non-maj 55, maj 4
Ent Req: HS dipl, ACT
Degrees: AA 2 yrs, cert
Tuition: Res—$1392 per yr; nonres—$1992 per yr; campus res available
Courses: Art Appreciation, Ceramics, Design, Graphic Arts, Graphic Design, Jewelry, Painting, Photography
Adult Hobby Classes: Enrl 39; tuition $58 per cr hr. Courses—Crafts, Jewelry Making, Painting, Photography, Pottery
Children's Classes: Kids Kamp-2 wks in summer

MISSOULA

UNIVERSITY OF MONTANA, Dept of Art, 59812. Tel 406-243-4181; FAX 406-243-4968; *Chmn* Steven Connell, MFA; *Prof* James Todd, MFA; *Prof* Marilyn Bruya, MFA; *Prof* Beth Lo, MFA; *Prof* David James, MFA; *Asst Prof* Barbara Tilton; *Asst Prof* Rafael Chacon; *Asst Prof* Mary Ann Bonjorni; *Asst Prof* Martin Fromm
Pub; D & E; scholarships; SC 28, LC 20, GC 10; enrl D 850, E 30
Ent Req: HS dipl
Degrees: BA & BFA 4 yrs, MA & MFA
Tuition: Res—$1242 per sem (12-21 cr hrs); nonres—$3366 per sem (12-21 cr hrs)
Courses: Art Appreciation, Art Education, †Art History, †Ceramics, †Drawing, History of Art & Archaeology, Mixed Media, †Painting, †Photography, †Printmaking, †Sculpture, Art Criticism and Social History of Art
Summer School: Dir, Steven Connell. Enrl 25 per class; Courses—Various regular & experimental classes

NEBRASKA

BELLEVUE

BELLEVUE COLLEGE, Art Dept, 1000 Galvin Rd S, 68005. Tel 402-291-8100; *Chmn* Dr Joyce Wilson, PhD
Scholarships
Degrees: BA, BFA, BTS(Commercial Art)
Tuition: Undergrad—$115 per cr hr, grad $250 per cr hr
Courses: Advertising Design, Aesthetics, Art History, Ceramics, Commercial Art, Design, Drawing, History of Art & Archaeology, Painting, Photography, Printmaking, Sculpture, Art Management, Life Drawing, Papermaking

BLAIR

DANA COLLEGE, Art Dept, 2848 College Dr, 68008. Tel 402-426-7206, 426-9000; *Chmn* Dr Milton Heinrich; *Prof* Jim Olsen; *Prof* Starla Stensaas
Scholarships
Degrees: BA, BS
Tuition: $4565 per sem
Courses: Advertising Design, Art Appreciation, Art Education, Art History, Ceramics, Commercial Art, Drawing, Jewelry, Painting, Photography, Printmaking, Sculpture, Teacher Training, Theatre Arts

CHADRON

CHADRON STATE COLLEGE, Dept of Art, Speech & Theatre, 1000 Main St, 69337. Tel 308-432-6317; FAX 308-432-3561; *Chmn* Richard Bird, MFA; *Prof Dr* Noel Gray; *Prof* Vince Haazen
Estab 1911, dept estab 1935; pub; D & E; scholarships; SC 20, LC 6, GC 2; enrl 4000, D 3000, off-campus 1000, non-maj 200, maj 35
Ent Req: HS dipl
Degrees: BSE & BA 4 yrs
Tuition: Res—undergrad $55.50 per hr, grad $69 per hr; nonres—undergrad $110 per hr, grad $137.50 per hr; campus res—room & board $1491
Courses: Art Education, Art History, Ceramics, Drawing, Graphic Arts, Jewelry, Painting, Photography, Sculpture, †Teacher Training, Weaving
Adult Hobby Classes: Enrl 30. Tuition varies. Courses vary
Summer School: Dir, Donald Green, PhD. Enrl 30; tuition same as above. Courses—usually 2 - 4 courses on semi-rotation basis

COLUMBUS

CENTRAL COMMUNITY COLLEGE - PLATTE CAMPUS, Business & Arts Cluster, PO Box 1027, 68602-1027. Tel 402-564-7132; *Head Dept* Ellen Lake; *Instr* Richard Abraham, MA; *Instr* Kathleen Lohr, MA
Estab 1969, dept estab 1971; pub; D & E; scholarships; SC 8, LC 1; enrl D 100, E 20, non-maj 77, maj 43
Ent Req: HS dipl
Degrees: AA 2 yrs
Tuition: Res—$41 per cr hr; nonres—$57.90 per cr hr; campus res
Courses: Art History, Ceramics, †Commercial Art, Design, Drafting, Drawing, Graphic Arts, Handicrafts, Interior Design, Mixed Media, Painting, Photography, Printmaking, Stage Design, Textile Design, Theatre Arts, Air Brush, Color Theory, Life Drawing
Summer School: Dir, Richard D Abraham. Enrl 25; tuition $41 per hr for term of 7 wks beginning June. Courses—Drawing, Painting

CRETE

DOANE COLLEGE, Dept of Art, 1014 Boswell Ave, 68333. Tel 402-826-2161, 826-8273; *Head Dept* Richard Terrell
Estab 1872, dept estab 1958; pvt; D; scholarships; SC 6, LC 5; enrl 150, non-maj 140, maj 10
Ent Req: HS dipl
Degrees: BA 4 yrs
Tuition: $10,295 per yr, includes room & board
Courses: Art Education, Art History, Ceramics, Drawing, Film, Graphic Design, Painting, Printmaking, Sculpture, Stage Design

HASTINGS

HASTINGS COLLEGE, Art Dept, Seventh & Turner, 68902-0269. Tel 402-463-2402; FAX 402-463-3002; *Chmn Dept* Gilbert L Neal; *Dir Pub Relations* Joyce Ore. Instrs: FT 3, PT 2
Estab 1925; den; scholarships; SC 16, LC 5; enrl maj 50, others 350
Ent Req: HS grad
Degrees: BA 4 yrs
Tuition: $4688 per sem; campus res—room & board $1636 per sem
Courses: Art Education, Art History, Ceramics, Design, Drawing, Painting, Printmaking, Sculpture, Color, Glass Blowing
Summer School: Dean, Dwayne Strasheim. Enrl 25; tuition res $187 per cr hr for 6 wks beginning June

KEARNEY

UNIVERSITY OF NEBRASKA, KEARNEY, Dept of Art & Art History, 68849. Tel 308-865-8353; *Chmn* Dr John Dinsmore, MFA; *Prof* Keith Lowry, MFA; *Prof* Larry D Peterson, EdD; *Prof* Raymond W Schultze, MFA; *Prof* Gary E Zaruba, EdD; *Prof* Jack Karraker, MFA; *Prof* Al Kraning, MFA; *Assoc Prof* Jake Jacobson; *Assoc Prof* Marsha Hewitt, MFA; *Assoc Prof* Tom Dennis, MFA; *Asst Prof* James M May, MA; *Asst Prof* Richard Schuessler. Instrs: FT 13, PT 11
Estab 1905; pub; D & E; scholarships; SC 20, LC 12, GC 18; enrl D 870, E 22, non-maj 1400, maj 250, grad 25
Ent Req: HS dipl, SAT or ACT recommended
Degrees: BFA, BA, BA(Art History), BA(Educ), 4 yrs, MA(Educ-Art)
Tuition: Res—$60.75 per cr hr; nonres—$110.50 per cr hr
Courses: Aesthetics, Art Education, Art History, Ceramics, †Drawing, †Painting, Photography, †Printmaking, †Sculpture, †Teacher Training, Computer Graphics, Fibers, Glass Blowing, Visual Communication & Design
Summer School: Chmn, John Dinsmore. Enrl 250; tuition undergrad $60.75 per hr, grad $75.25 per hr. Courses—Aesthetics, Computer Graphics, Drawing, Painting, Special Problems in Art History

LINCOLN

NEBRASKA WESLEYAN UNIVERSITY, Art Dept, 5000 St Paul, 68504. Tel 402-465-2273; FAX 402-465-2179; *Chmn* Dr Donald Paoletta; *Assoc Prof* John Clabaugh; *Asst Prof* Lisa Lockman; *Vis Prof* Susan Horn; *Vis Prof* Brad Krieger
Estab 1888, dept estab 1890; pvt; D & E; scholarships; SC 22, LC 4; enrl non-maj 300, maj 50
Ent Req: HS dipl, ent exam
Degrees: BA, BFA & BS 4 yrs
Tuition: $5142 per sem
Courses: Art Education, Art History, Ceramics, Design, Drawing, Jewelry, Painting, Photography, Printmaking, Sculpture, Silversmithing
Adult Hobby Classes: Enrl 30; tuition $142 per sem hr. Degree Program
Summer School: Enrl 30; tuition $142 per sem hr per 8 wks. Courses—Paintings, Paste-up, Special Projects

UNIVERSITY OF NEBRASKA-LINCOLN, Dept of Art & Art History, 207 Nelle Cochrane Woods Hall, 68588-0114. Tel 402-472-2631; FAX 402-472-9746; *Chmn Dept* Joseph M Ruffo, MFA; *Chmn Graduate Committee* David Routon. Instrs: FT 20, PT 15
Estab 1869, dept 1912; pub; D & E; scholarships; SC 71, LC 27, GC 45; enrl D 1950, E 175, non-maj 600, maj 400, grad 25
Ent Req: HS dipl
Degrees: BA, BFA & BFA(Educ) 4 yrs, MFA 2-3 Yrs
Tuition: Res—undergrad $53.50 per cr hr, grad $67.75; nonres—$145.50 per cr hr
Courses: Advertising Design, †Art History, †Ceramics, †Drawing, †Graphic Arts, †Graphic Design, †Illustration, Mixed Media, †Painting, †Photography, †Printmaking, †Sculpture, Book Art, Papermaking, †2-D & 3-D Design
Summer School: Dir, L Grobsmith. Enrl 250; two 5 wk sessions beginning June & Aug. Courses—Art History, Ceramics, Drawing, Painting, Photography, Printmaking, Special Problems & Topics

NORFOLK

NORTHEAST COMMUNITY COLLEGE, Dept of Liberal Arts, 801 E Benjamin Ave, PO Box 469, 68702-0469. Tel 402-371-2020, Ext 480; *Chmn Dept* Larry Godel; *Instr* Julie Noyes, MA; *Instr* Harry Lindner, MA
Estab 1928; pub; D & E; scholarships; SC 5, LC 5; enrl D 150, E 50, non-maj 100, maj 50
Ent Req: HS dipl
Degrees: AA 2 yrs
Tuition: Res—$414 per sem, $32 per cr hr; nonres—$37 per cr hr; campus res—room & board $1044-$1332
Courses: Art Education, Art History, Drawing, Graphic Design, Painting, Photography
Adult Hobby Classes: Oil Painting
Summer School: Chmn Dept, Patrick Keating. Tuition same as regular yr. Courses—Photography

OMAHA

COLLEGE OF SAINT MARY, Art Dept, 1901 S 72nd St, 68124. Tel 402-399-2400; *Chmn Dept* Tom Schlosser
Estab 1923; pvt, W; D & E; scholarships; SC 11, LC 5; enrl D 620, maj 18, special 2
Ent Req: HS dipl
Degrees: BA and BS 4 yrs
Tuition: $4825 per sem, full-time; $20 per cr hr, part-time
Courses: Art History, Ceramics, Design, Painting, Photography, Sculpture, Teacher Training, Computer Graphics, Women in Art
Adult Hobby Classes: Enrl 587; tuition $133 per cr hr. Evening & weekend college offer full range of general education classes
Summer School: Dir, Dr Vernon Lestrud. Enrl 572; tuition $133 per cr hr. Full range of studio & history general education classes

CREIGHTON UNIVERSITY, Fine & Performing Arts Dept, 2500 California Plaza, 68178. Tel 402-280-2509; *Chmn&prof* Dr Roger Aikin, PhD; *Asst Prof* Michael Flecky, MFA; *Instr* Alan Klem, MFA; *Instr* Valerie Roche, ARAD; *Instr* John Thein, MFA; *Instr* Gail Dunning; *Instr* Carole Seitz; *Instr* Bob Bosco, MFA; *Instr* Bill Hutson; *Instr* Elaine Majors; *Instr* Bill Vandest; *Artist-in-Res* Littleton Alston
Estab 1878, dept estab 1966; den; D & E; scholarships; SC 87, LC 16; enrl 888, non-maj 850, maj 38, cert prog 24
Ent Req: HS dipl, regular col admis exam
Degrees: BA & BFA 4 yrs
Tuition: $600 average per yr; campus res available
Courses: Advertising Design, Art Appreciation, Art Education, Art History, Ceramics, Design, Drawing, History of Art & Archaeology, Painting, Photography, Printmaking, Sculpture, Teacher Training, †Theatre Arts, Color Theory, Intaglio, Lithography, Studio Fundamentals, 3-D Design
Adult Hobby Classes: Advertising, Art History, Ceramics, Design, Life Drawing, Painting, Photography

UNIVERSAL TECHNICAL INSTITUTE, Commercial Art Division, 902 Capitol Ave, 68102. Tel 402-345-2422; *Chmn* Mike Abdouch
Scholarships
Degrees: Dipl offered
Courses: Commercial Art, Computer Graphics
Adult Hobby Classes: Enrl 60; tuition $7950. Courses—Commercial Art

UNIVERSITY OF NEBRASKA AT OMAHA, Dept of Art & Art History, 60th & Dodge Sts, 68182. Tel 402-554-2420, 554-2800; *Chmn Dept* Dr Martin Rosenberg; *Prof* Sidney Buchanan, MA; *Prof* Peter Hill, MFA; *Prof* Frances T Thurber, MA; *Assoc Prof* Henry Serenco, MFA; *Assoc Prof* Gary Day, MFA; *Assoc Prof* Dr Martin Rosenberg; *Assoc Prof* James Czarnecki; *Asst Prof* Bonnie O'Connell; *Asst Prof* Thomas Majeski
Estab 1908, dept estab 1910; pub; D & E; scholarships; SC 32, LC 22, GC 10; enrl D 550, E 100
Ent Req: HS dipl
Degrees: BA & BFA 4 yrs
Tuition: Res—undergrad $62.50 per cr hr, grad $78 per cr hr; nonres—undergrad $168 per cr hr, grad $188 per cr hr; no campus res
Courses: †Art Education, †Art History, †Ceramics, †Drawing, †Painting, †Printmaking, †Sculpture, Paper Making
Summer School: Chmn Dept, Dr Martin Rosenberg. Tuition same as above for term of 5 wks. Courses—Vary

PERU

PERU STATE COLLEGE, Art Dept, PO Box 10, 68421. Tel 402-872-2271, 872-3815; Elec Mail perry@nscs.peru.edu. *Prof* Kenneth Anderson; *Prof* Peggy Jones
Scholarships
Degrees: BA, BAEd, BS, MA
Tuition: Res—$375 per sem; nonres—$630 per sem
Courses: Art Appreciation, Art Education, Art History, Ceramics, Design, Drawing, Lettering, Painting, Photography, Printmaking, Sculpture, Stage Design, Figure Drawing, Independent Art Study
Summer School: Tuition $50 per hr for 5 wks. Courses—Art Appreciation

SCOTTSBLUFF

WESTERN NEBRASKA COMMUNITY COLLEGE, Division of Language & Arts, 1601 E 27th St, 69361. Tel 308-635-3606; *Chmn Div Language* Paul Jacobson; *Chmn Art* Ziya Sever, MA
Estab 1926; pub; D & E; scholarships; SC 8, LC 3; enrl D 60, E 150, non-maj 50, maj 10
Ent Req: HS dipl
Degrees: AA & AS 2 yrs

Tuition: Res—$36.50 per cr hr; nonres—$41 per cr hr; campus res available
Courses: Art Education, Art History, Drawing, Painting, Photography, Theatre Arts, Music Education, History of Film
Adult Hobby Classes: Enrl 150; tui $15 per course. Courses—Carving, Drawing, Macrame, Pottery, Sculpture, Stained Glass, Watercolor & Oil Painting, Weaving

SEWARD

CONCORDIA COLLEGE, Art Dept, 800 N Columbia, 68434. Tel 402-643-3651; *Head Dept* William R Wolfram, MFA; *Prof* Donald Dynneson, MFA; *Prof* Reinhold P Marxhausen, MFA; *Prof* Richard Wiegmann, MFA; *Prof* Lynn Soloway, MFA; *Prof* Jim Bockelman, BA
Estab 1894; den; D & E; scholarships; SC 8, LC 4; enrl non-maj 30, maj 40
Ent Req: HS dipl
Degrees: BS, BA 4 yr
Tuition: $150 per cr hr; campus res available
Courses: Advertising Design, Art Education, Ceramics, Commercial Art, Drawing, Graphic Design, Illustration, Painting, Printmaking, Sculpture
Summer School: Tuition $90 per cr hr for term of 2 1/2 wks beginning June 6

WAYNE

WAYNE STATE COLLEGE, Art Dept, 1111 Main St, 68787. Tel 402-375-7359; *Div Chmn* Dr Jay O'Leary; *Prof* Ray Replogle; *Prof* Pearl Hansen; *Prof* Wayne Anderson; *Prof* Marlene Mueller; *Prof* Vic Reynolds
Estab 1910; pub; scholarships; SC 21, LC 8; enrl maj 65, others 700, total 4000
Ent Req: HS grad
Degrees: BA, BFA, MA & MS
Tuition: Res—$33 per cr hr; nonres—$54 per cr hr
Courses: Art History, Commercial Art, Design, Drafting, Drawing, Graphic Arts, Handicrafts, Jewelry, Painting, Sculpture, †Teacher Training
Summer School: Three sessions

YORK

YORK COLLEGE, Art Dept, Ninth & Kiplinger St, PO Box 442, 68467. Tel 402-362-4441, Ext 218; *Asst Prof* Paul M Shields
Sch estab 1956, dept estab 1962; pvt; D; scholarships; SC 6, LC 1; enrl D 26, non-maj 20, maj 10
Ent Req: HS dipl, ACT
Degrees: AA 2 yrs
Tuition: Res—undergrad $2893 per sem
Courses: Art Appreciation, Art History, Drawing, Painting, Commercial Design, 2-D & 3-D Design

NEVADA

INCLINE VILLAGE

SIERRA NEVADA COLLEGE, Visual & Performing Arts Dept, 800 College Dr (Mailing add: PO Box 4269, 89450). Tel 702-831-1314; *Chmn & Dir Summer Arts Prog* Ken Rowe; *Gallery Dir* Russell Dudley
Estab 1969; pvt; D & E; scholarships; SC 75, LC 8; enrl D 260, E 40, maj 26
Ent Req: HS dipl, 2.5 grade point avg
Degrees: BA & BFA 4 yr
Tuition: res—undergrad $315 per sem; nonres—$315 per sem; campus—room & board
Courses: Art Appreciation, Art Education, Art History, †Ceramics, Design, †Drawing, †Film, Goldsmithing, Graphic Arts, Jewelry, Mixed Media, †Painting, †Photography, †Printmaking, Sculpture, Silversmithing, Teacher Training, †Textile Design, †Theatre Arts
Adult Hobby Classes: Enrl 80; tuition $60 per cr. Courses—Calligraphy, watercolor
Children's Classes: Enrl 60. Courses—Ceramics, painting
Summer School: Dir, Carol Sphar, PhD. Enrl 220; tuition $250 per cr, $60 per unit non credit. Courses—Studio Arts

LAS VEGAS

UNIVERSITY OF NEVADA, LAS VEGAS, Dept of Art, 4505 S Maryland Pky, Box 455002, 89154-5002. Tel 702-895-3237; *Chmn* Lee Sido; *Asst Prof* Cathie Kelly; *Instr* Thomas J Holder; *Instr* Bill Leaf; *Instr* Jim Pink; *Instr* Pasha Rafat
Estab 1955; pub; D & E; scholarships; SC 32, LC 18; enrl all courses 551, maj 95
Ent Req: HS dipl, ACT
Degrees: BA and BFA 4 yrs, MFA
Tuition: Res—$2375 per sem, $58.50 per cr hr; campus res—room & board varies per sem
Courses: Art History, Ceramics, Conceptual Art, Drawing, Film, Intermedia, Painting, Photography, Printmaking, Sculpture
Adult Hobby Classes: Courses—Drawing, Fiber, Painting, Photography
Summer School: Dir, Thomas Holder. Enrl varies; tuition $41 per cr hr for 5 wk session. Courses—Ceramics, Drawing, Fiber, Painting, Printmaking

RENO

UNIVERSITY OF NEVADA, RENO, Art Dept, 89557-0007. Tel 702-784-6682; *Chmn Dept* Ed W Martinez. Instrs: FT 10
Estab 1940; pub; scholarship; SC 20, LC 6, GC 5; enrl maj 120, others 800
Ent Req: HS grad and 16 units
Degrees: BA 4 yr
Courses: †Art Education, †Art History, †Ceramics, †Drawing, Graphic Design, †Painting, †Photography, †Printmaking, †Sculpture
Adult Hobby Classes: Evening division in all areas
Summer School: Courses in all studio areas

NEW HAMPSHIRE

DURHAM

UNIVERSITY OF NEW HAMPSHIRE, Dept of Arts & Art History, Paul Creative Arts Ctr, 30 College Rd, 03824-3538. Tel 603-862-2190, 862-1234, 862-1360; FAX 603-862-2191; *Chmn* Dan Valenza; *Prof* David Andrew, PhD; *Prof* Melvin Zabarsky, MFA; *Prof* Michael McConnell; *Prof* Carol Aronson, MFA; *Assoc Prof* David Smith, PhD; *Assoc Prof* Maryse Searls-McConnel, MFA; *Assoc Prof* Mara Witzling, PhD; *Assoc Prof* Chris Enos, MFA; *Assoc Prof* Craig Hood, MFA; *Assoc Prof* Scott Schnepf, MFA; *Assoc Prof* Grant Drumheller; *Asst Prof* Jennifer Moses
Estab 1928, dept estab 1941; pub; D & E; scholarships; SC 60, LC 20; enrl non-maj 1000, maj 175, grad 5, others 60
Ent Req: HS dipl, portfolio
Degrees: BFA & BA(Studio Arts & Art History) 4 yrs, MAT 5 yrs
Tuition: Res—$3550; nonres—$11,180; campus res available
Courses: Architecture, Art Education, Art History, Ceramics, Drawing, Painting, Photography, Printmaking, Sculpture

HANOVER

DARTMOUTH COLLEGE, Dept of Art History, 6033 Carpenter Hall, 03755-3570. Tel 603-646-2306; Elec Mail elizabeth.w.alexander@dartmouth.edu. *Chmn* Kathleen Corrigan. Instrs: FT 7
Estab 1906; pvt; SC 16, LC 26; enrl in col 4000, maj 46
Degrees: AB 4 yr
Tuition: $5743 per term; operating 4 terms on yr-round basis
Courses: †Art History, 3-D Design

HENNIKER

NEW ENGLAND COLLEGE, Art & Art History, 24 Bridge St, 03242. Tel 603-428-2211; FAX 603-428-7230; *Prof* David F MacEachran, MFA; *Prof* Farid A Haddad, MFA; *Prof* Doris A Birmingham; *Assoc Prof* Marguerite Walsh, MFA
Also has campuses in Arundel, West Sussex England; scholarships
Degrees: BA
Courses: Aesthetics, †Art History, Ceramics, Design, Drawing, Graphic Arts, Graphic Design, Mixed Media, †Painting, †Photography, Printmaking, Sculpture, Stage Design, Theatre Arts, Video

MANCHESTER

NEW HAMPSHIRE INSTITUTE OF ART (Formerly Manchester Institute of Arts & Sciences), 148 Concord St, 03104. Tel 603-623-0313; *Pres* Dr Andrew Svedlow
Estab 1898; pvt; credit and adult educ courses; SC 16; enrl 1000
Ent Req: None
Degrees: BFA
Tuition: $6000 per yr
Courses: Aesthetics, Art Appreciation, Art Education, Art History, Calligraphy, †Ceramics, Collages, Design, Fashion Arts, Handicrafts, History of Art & Archaeology, Illustration, Jewelry, Mixed Media, †Painting, †Photography, Printmaking, Sculpture, Silversmithing, Theatre Arts, Weaving
Adult Hobby Classes: Enrl 400; tuition $150-$250 for 12-15 wks. Courses—Art History, Ceramics, Drawing, Fiber Arts, Painting, Photography, Printmaking, Sculpture
Children's Classes: Enrl 75; tuition $75-$125 for 6-12 wks. Courses—Artful Hands
Summer School: Courses—Same as in Fall & Spring

NOTRE DAME COLLEGE, Art Dept, 2321 Elm St, 03104. Tel 603-669-4298; *Dean* Carolyn Hill; *Asst Prof* Frank Oehlschlaeger, MA; *Assoc Prof* Jean Landry; *Asst Prof* Harry Umen, MFA; *Lectr* Al Jaeger. Instrs: 2
Estab 1950, dept estab 1965; pvt; D & E; scholarship; SC 20, LC 6; enrl non-maj 15, maj 125
Ent Req: HS dipl
Degrees: BA(Fine Arts), BA(Commercial Art & Art Educ) 4 yr
Tuition: Undergrad $9990; campus res—room & board $4900
Courses: Advertising Design, Architecture, Art Education, Ceramics, Commercial Art, Drawing, Graphic Design, Illustration, Painting, Photography, Printmaking, Sculpture, Teacher Training, Visual Arts, Women in Art, Primitive Art, History of Modern Art, American Art, 19th Century Art, Western Art and Culture, Basic Design
Adult Hobby Classes: Enrl 110; tuition $109 per cr
Summer School: Dir, Janet Clark. Tuition $109 per cr. Courses—Art History, Ceramics, Computer Graphics, Drawing, Sculpture

SAINT ANSELM COLLEGE, Dept of Fine Arts, 03102-1310. Tel 603-641-7370; FAX 603-641-7116; *Chmn* Katherine Hoffman. Instrs: FT 3
Estab 1889; pvt; D & E; scholarships; SC 2, LC 9; enrl 1500
Ent Req: HS dipl, relative standing, SAT, interview
Degrees: BA 4 yr
Tuition: $13,700 per yr
Courses: Aesthetics, Architecture, †Art History, Design, Drawing, Film, Graphic Arts, Graphic Design, Mixed Media, Painting, Photography, Printmaking, Sculpture, Teacher Training, Theatre Arts, Mixed Media, Painting, Photography, Printmaking, Sculpture, †Fine Arts
Summer School: Dir, Dennis Sweltland. Courses—Vary

NASHUA

NASHUA CENTER FOR ARTS, * 120 Main St, 03060. Tel 603-883-1506; FAX 603-882-7705; *Dir* Robert Daniels. Instrs: PT 25-30
Estab 1958; pub; D & E; SC, LC
Ent Req: None
Degrees: None, nonaccredited
Courses: Ceramics, Drawing, Painting, Photography, Sculpture, Theatre Arts
Adult Hobby Classes: Tuition varied. Courses—Acting, Drawing, Figure Life, Oil Painting, Pottery, Silk Screen, Watercolor
Children's Classes: Tuition varied. Courses—Acting, Drawing, Painting, Pottery, Preschool Art, Silk Screen
Summer School: Tuition varied; 8 wk term from Sept-June. Courses—Cartooning, Computers, Pottery, Watercolor

RIVIER COLLEGE, Art Dept, 420 Main St, 03060. Tel 603-888-1311, Ext 276; *Co-Chmn* Sr Marie Couture, MA; *Co-Chmn* Sr Theresa Couture, MFA
Estab 1933, dept estab 1940; pvt; D & E; scholarships; SC 100, LC 25; enrl D 50,E 40, non-maj 20, maj 70
Ent Req: HS dipl, SAT, certain HS equivalencies, preliminary evidence of artistic ability, slide portfolio
Degrees: AA 2 yrs, BA, and BFA 4 yrs
Tuition: $5085 per sem, $339 per cr; part-time $339 per cr; evening $171 per cr; campus res—$2500 room & board per sem
Courses: Aesthetics, †Art Education, Art History, Calligraphy, Ceramics, Conceptual Art, Constructions, Display, Drawing, Film, †Graphic Design, Illustration, Jewelry, Lettering, Mixed Media, †Painting, Photography, Printmaking, Sculpture, Teacher Training, Textile Design, Art Therapy, Computer Graphics, Design History, Design Internship, Design Portfolio, Film Graphics, Loom Weaving, Stitchery
Adult Hobby Classes: Enrl 60; tuition $171 per cr for 15 wk term. Courses—Variety of fine arts & design studio courses
Children's Classes: Enrl 24. Courses—Pre-college summer art program
Summer School: Dir, Rose Arthur, PhD. Tuition $132 per cr for 6 wks. Courses—Master Workshops in Basic Design, Drawing, Etching, Graphic Design, Painting, Sculpture

NEW LONDON

COLBY-SAWYER COLLEGE, Dept of Fine & Performing Arts, 100 Main St, 03257. Tel 603-526-3000, 526-3662, Ext 3662 (Chair); FAX 603-526-2135; *Prof* Martha Andrea, MFA; *Prof* John Bott, MFA; *Assoc Prof* Loretta Barnett, MFA; *Asst Prof* Jon Keenan; *Asst Prof* Jane Petrillo; *Asst Prof* Jerry Bliss, MFA. Instrs: FT 6
Estab 1837; pvt; W; D; scholarships; SC 10, LC 25; enrl 775
Degrees: BA, BFA(Art & Graphic Design), Arts Management (student designed major)
Tuition: Res—undergrad $21,480 yr, $10,740 sem; nonres—undergrad $15,530 per yr
Courses: Advertising Design, Aesthetics, Art Appreciation, Art History, †Ceramics, †Design, †Drawing, Graphic Arts, †Graphic Design, Illustration, Museum Staff Training, †Painting, †Photography, †Printmaking, †Sculpture, Acting, American Art, Contemporary Art since 1945, Creative Expression, Dance, European Trips to France & Italy, Life Drawing, Music, Origins of Modern Art, Stage Craft, Theatre Design, Theatre History, Women in Art
Adult Hobby Classes: Acad Dean, Dan Meerson, PhD. Continuing educ classes

PETERBOROUGH

SHARON ARTS CENTER, RR 2, Box 361, 03458. Tel 603-924-7256; *Dir* A Marshall Lawton. Instrs: PT 30
Estab 1947; pvt; D & E; scholarship; SC 20; classes yr round
Ent Req: None
Tuition: $85 members, $105 non-members
Courses: Calligraphy, Ceramics, Drawing, Graphic Arts, Jewelry, Lettering, Painting, Photography, Printmaking, Textile Design, Basketry, Batik, Patchwork & Applique, Pottery, Stained Glass, Sumi-E, Weaving
Adult Hobby Classes: Enrl 600. Courses—Visual & Tactile Arts
Children's Classes: Enrl 100. Courses—Visual & Tactile Arts
Summer School: Dir, Pamela Miley. Courses—Visual & Tactile Arts

PLYMOUTH

PLYMOUTH STATE COLLEGE, Art Dept, 03264. Tel 603-535-2201; *Head Dept* Robert Morton. Instrs: FT 11
Estab 1871; pub; D & E; scholarships; SC 17, LC 8; enrl D 3050, maj 90
Ent Req: HS grad, references, health record, transcript, SAT, CEEB, ACT
Degrees: BS, BFA & BA 4 yrs
Tuition: Res—$2590 per sem; nonres—$7870 per sem; room & board $4024
Courses: Architecture, Art Appreciation, †Art Education, †Art History, †Ceramics, Design, †Drawing, †Graphic Design, Illustration, Museum Staff Training, †Painting, †Photography, †Printmaking, †Sculpture, †Teacher Training
Adult Hobby Classes: Dir, Gail Carr. Enrl 50. Courses—Vary
Children's Classes: Courses available
Summer School: Courses vary

RINDGE

FRANKLIN PIERCE COLLEGE, Dept of Fine Arts & Graphic Communications, College Rd, PO Box 60, 03461. Tel 603-899-4000; FAX 603-899-4308; *Co-Chmn* Robert Diercks
Estab 1962; pvt; D & E; scholarships; SC 20, LC 2
Ent Req: HS dipl
Degrees: BA(Fine Arts), BA(Graphic Design)
Tuition: $14,850; campus res—$2680 double room, $2250 board
Courses: Art Education, Art History, Ceramics, Commercial Art, Design, Drawing, Graphic Design, Illustration, Painting, Photography, Printmaking, Sculpture, Stage Design, Teacher Training, Color Photography
Summer School: Color Photography, Landscape Painting

NEW JERSEY

BLACKWOOD

CAMDEN COUNTY COLLEGE, Dept of Art, College Dr, PO Box 200, 08012. Tel 609-227-7200; *Academic Dean* Dr Kaczorowski; *Prof* L Dell'Olio; *Prof* J Rowlands; *Prof* W Marlin
Estab 1966; scholarships; SC 12, LC 10; enrl 100
Ent Req: HS dipl or equivalent
Degrees: AA 2 yrs
Tuition: In county—$17 per cr hr; res—$19 per cr hr; nonres—$65 per cr hr
Courses: Art History, Ceramics, Design, Drawing, Painting, Sculpture, Art Therapy, Computer Graphics
Adult Hobby Classes: Special sessions
Children's Classes: Special sessions
Summer School: Courses available

CALDWELL

CALDWELL COLLEGE, Art Dept, 9 Ryerson Ave, 07006-6195. Tel 201-228-4424, Ext 254; *Chmn* Judith Croce. Instrs: FT 3, PT 6
Estab 1964; pvt; W; D; scholarships; SC 24, LC 12; enrl maj 76, dept 90
Ent Req: HS grad, ent exam, art portfolio
Degrees: BA 3-4 yr, BFA 4-5 yr
Tuition: Full time $10,050 per yr, $179 per cr hr; part-time $258 per cr hr
Courses: Art Education, Art History, Calligraphy, Ceramics, Drawing, Painting, Photography, Sculpture, Art Therapy, Visual Communications

CAMDEN

RUTGERS UNIVERSITY, CAMDEN, Art Dept, Fine Arts Ctr, 311 N Fifth St, 08102. Tel 609-225-6176; *Chmn* John Giannatti. Instrs: FT 6, PT 8
Pub; D; SC 24, LC 13; enrl art D 450, maj 75
Ent Req: HS dipl, must qualify for regular col admis, portfolio
Degrees: BA(Art) 4 yrs
Tuition: Res—$117.75 per cr; nonres—$240.25 per cr
Courses: Art History, Graphic Arts, Graphic Design, Painting, Printmaking, Sculpture, Computer Graphics, Museum Studies
Summer School: Chmn, William M Hoffman. Three sessions beginning May 20. Courses—Varies

DOVER

JOE KUBERT SCHOOL OF CARTOON & GRAPHIC ART, INC, 37 Myrtle Ave, 07801. Tel 201-361-1327; FAX 201-361-1844; *Pres* Joe Kubert; *Instr* Phillip Blaisdell; *Instr* Hy Eisman; *Instr* Irwin Hasen; *Instr* Douglas Compton; *Instr* Michael Chen; *Instr* Jose Delbo; *Instr* Kum Demulder; *Instr* Jim McWeeney; *Instr* Judy Mates; *Instr* Greg Webb; *Instr* John Troy
Estab 1976; pvt; D & E; scholarships; SC all, LC all; enrl D 200, E 100
Ent Req: HS dipl, interview, portfolio
Degrees: 3 yr dipl
Tuition: $92.50 per yr; campus res—room $2925 per yr
Courses: Commercial Art, Design, Graphic Arts, Illustration, Lettering, Painting, Video, Cartoon Graphics, Cinematic Animation
Adult Hobby Classes: Enrl 100; tuition $200 per 12 wks. Courses—Basic & Advanced Paste-Ups & Mechanicals, Cartoon Workshop, Computer Graphic/ Animation Workshop
Children's Classes: Enrl 20; tuition $15 per class. Courses—Saturday Cartoon Sketch Class
Summer School: Courses—same as regular session

EDISON

MIDDLESEX COUNTY COLLEGE, Visual Arts Dept, 155 Mill Rd, PO Box 3050, 08818. Tel 908-906-2589; FAX 908-906-2510; *Chmn* Jay Siegfried Scholarships
Degrees: AA
Tuition: County $57,50 per cr hr; out-of-county $115; out-of-state $115 per cr hr
Courses: Art Appreciation, Art Education, Art History, Ceramics, Drawing, Painting, Printmaking, Sculpture, Stage Design, Art Foundation, Art Fundamentals (2-D & 3-D Design), Art Industry & Communication
Adult Hobby Classes: Courses offered
Summer School: Dir, Warren Kelerme. Courses—Art History, Ceramics, Drawing, Painting

GLASSBORO

ROWAN COLLEGE OF NEW JERSEY, Dept of Art, 201 Mullica Hill Rd, 08028-1701. Tel 609-256-4000; FAX 609-863-6553; *Chmn Dept* George Neff
Estab 1925; pub; D & E; enrl D 6100, E 5000, maj 300, grad 5-
Ent Req: HS dipl, ent exam, portfolio and SAT
Degrees: BA 4 yrs, MA
Tuition: Res—$124.35 per cr hr; nonres—$215.35 per cr hr
Courses: Advertising Design, Art Appreciation, Art Education, Ceramics, Drawing, Illustration, Jewelry, Sculpture, Theatre Arts, Art History Survey, Batik, Computer Art, Enameling, Fiber Arts, Metaltry, Puppetry, Theatrical Design
Children's Classes: Enrl 30. Courses—Crafts, Drawing, Mixed Media, Painting
Summer School: Dir, Dr George Neff. Enrl 100; tuition $107 per cr hr res grad & $67 per cr hr res undergrad for 8 wk term. Courses—Art History, Computer Art, Drawing, Jewelry, Painting, Printing, Print Making

HACKETTSTOWN

CENTENARY COLLEGE, Humanities Dept, 400 Jefferson St, 07840. Tel 908-852-1400, Ext 2265; *Assoc Prof* Carol Yoshimine-Webster, MFA; *Assoc Prof* Richard Wood, MFA; *Asst Prof Interior Design* Elena Kays, MA; *Instr* Elizabeth Desabritas
Estab 1874; pvt; scholarships; SC 11, LC 2; enrl maj 70, others 367, total 678
Degrees: BFA(Art & Design), AA(Interior Design), BFA(Interior Design), BS(Communications)
Tuition: Res—$18,348; nonres—$12,608, $230 per cr hr
Adult Hobby Classes: Tuition $98 per cr. Courses—Graphic Arts, Interior Design
Summer School: Dir, Larry Friedman. Tuition $98 per cr. Courses—Graphic Art, Interior Design

JERSEY CITY

JERSEY CITY STATE COLLEGE, Art Dept, 2039 Kennedy Blvd, 07305. Tel 201-200-3214, Ext 3241; FAX 201-200-3238; *Chmn* Denise Mullen, MFA; *Prof Dr* Elaine Foster, EdD; *Prof* Harold Lemmerman, EdD; *Prof* Anneke Prins Simons, PhD; *Prof* Ben Jones, MFA; *Prof Dr* Eleanor Campulli, EdD; *Assoc Prof* Marguarite LaBelle, MA; *Assoc Prof* Mary Campbell, MFA; *Assoc Prof* Jose Rodeiro, PhD; *Assoc Prof* Charles Plosky, MFA; *Assoc Prof* Herbert Rosenberg, MFA; *Assoc Prof* Raymond Statlander, MFA; *Asst Prof* Sr Joan Steans, MFA; *Asst Prof* Mauro Altamura, MFA; *Asst Prof* Winifred McNeill, MFA; *Asst Prof* Tom Reiss, MFA; *Asst Prof* Ellen Quinn, MFA; *Asst Prof* Karen Santry, MFA. Instrs: PT 15
Estab 1927, dept estab 1961; pub; D & E; scholarships; SC 61, LC 19, GC 31; enrl D 350, E 60, GS 60
Ent Req: HS dipl or equivalent
Degrees: BA & BFA 128 sem hrs, MA, MFA 60 sem hrs, grad assistantship
Tuition: Res—undergrad $80 per cr, grad $146 per cr; nonres—undergrad $106 per cr; grad $172 per cr; campus res available
Courses: Advertising Design, Aesthetics, Art Appreciation, Art Education, Art History, Ceramics, Conceptual Art, Design, Drawing, Graphic Design, Illustration, Jewelry, Lettering, Mixed Media, Painting, †Photography, Printmaking, Sculpture, Industrial Design, Intermedia, Interior Design, Jewelry, Lettering, Mixed Media, Painting, Photography, Printmaking, Sculpture, Art Therapy, †Communication Design, †Crafts, Digital Imaging, Fashion Illustration, †Fine Arts, History of Art, Metalsmithing, †Teacher Certification

SAINT PETER'S COLLEGE, Fine Arts Dept, 2641 Kennedy Blvd, 07306. Tel 201-915-9238; *Chmn* Jon D Boshart, PhD
Estab 1872, dept estab 1963; D & E; scholarships; SC 4, LC 13; enrl D 2000, E 900, maj 10
Ent Req: HS dipl
Degrees: BA, BA in Cursu Classico, BS 4 yrs
Tuition: $401 per cr hr
Courses: Advertising Design, Aesthetics, Architecture, Art Appreciation, †Art Education, †Art History, Commercial Art, Drawing, History of Art & Archaeology, Painting, Photography, Restoration & Conservation, Sculpture, Mixed Media, †Painting, Photography, Sculpture, Teacher Training
Adult Hobby Classes: Tuition $401 per sem. Courses—Art History, Dance, Studio
Summer School: Dir, Dr Boshart. Tuition $1203 per 3 cr, one 3 wk session & two 5 wk sessions. Courses—Art History, Electives, Dance, Drawing, Film History, Introduction to Visual Arts, Painting

LAKEWOOD

GEORGIAN COURT COLLEGE, Dept of Art, 900 Lakewood Ave, 08701-2697. Tel 908-364-2200, Ext 348; FAX 908-905-8571; *Head Dept* Sr Mary Christina Geis, MFA; *Prof* Geraldine Velasque, EdD; *Prof* Sr Mary Phyllis Breimayer, MA; *Asst Prof* Suzanne Pilgram, MFA; *Asst Prof* Sr Joyce Jacobs, MA; *Asst Prof* Vincent Hart; *Lectr* Nicholas Caivano, MFA; *Lectr* Eva Bousard-Hui, EdD
Estab 1908, dept estab 1924; pvt; D & E; scholarships; SC 18, LC 11; enrl 240, non-maj 150, maj 90
Ent Req: HS dipl, col board scores, portfolio
Degrees: BA 4 yr
Tuition: Undergrad $10,332, $287 per cr; campus res—room & board 7 day $4450, 5 day $4300
Courses: Advertising Design, †Art Education, †Art History, Calligraphy, Ceramics, Commercial Art, Drafting, Drawing, Fashion Arts, Handicrafts, Illustration, Jewelry, Lettering, Painting, Photography, Sculpture, Teacher Training, Textile Design, Weaving, †Art (studio & art history), Color & Design, Computer Graphics
Summer School: Dir, Linda Capuano. Tuition $287 per cr for term of 12 wks beginning May 17. Courses—Art History

LAWRENCEVILLE

RIDER COLLEGE, Dept of Fine Arts, 2083 Lawrenceville Rd, 08648. Tel 609-896-5168; *Chmn* Patrick Chmel. Instrs: FT 3
Estab 1966; pvt; D & E; SC 9, LC 4; enrl D 3500, E 5169, maj 35
Ent Req: HS dipl
Degrees: BA(Fine Arts) 4 yrs
Tuition: $13,250 per yr; campus res available
Courses: Drawing, Graphic Arts, Graphic Design, Painting
Summer School: Dir John Carpenter. Tuition $123 per cr. Courses—Drawing, Art & Society

LINCROFT

BROOKDALE COMMUNITY COLLEGE, Art Dept, 765 Newman Springs Rd, 07738. Tel 908-842-1900; *Chmn* Ed Stein
Degrees: AA
Tuition: County res—$62 per cr hr; non-county res—$124 per cr hr; non-state res—$248 per cr hr
Courses: Ceramics, Design, Drawing, Jewelry, Painting, Printmaking

LIVINGSTON

ART CENTRE OF NEW JERSEY, Riker Hill Art Pk Bldg 501, PO Box 2063, 07039. Tel 201-675-7411; *Pres* Tim Maher; *First VPres* Alden Baker; *Second VPres* Salomon Kadoche; *Treas* Louis de Smet
Estab 1924 as an art school & presently is a venue for workshops, art events, lectures, etc;
Adult Hobby Classes: Workshops

MADISON

DREW UNIVERSITY, Art Dept, College of Liberal Arts, 36 Madison Ave, 07940. Tel 201-408-3331, 408-3000; FAX 201-408-3768; *Chmn Dept* Sara Henry, PhD; *Prof* Livio Saganic, MFA; *Asst Prof* Michael Peglau, PhD; *Adjunct Asst Prof* Donna Page, MFA; *Adjunct Asst Prof* Frank Bosco, MFA; *Adjunct Asst Prof* Harvey Stein, MBA; *Adjunct Asst Prof* Tim Cassidy, MA
Estab 1928; pvt; D & E; scholarships; SC 17, LC 10; enrl D 275, E 12, maj 35, minors 6
Ent Req: HS dipl
Degrees: BA 4 yrs
Tuition: $10,860 per yr
Courses: Aesthetics, Art History, Ceramics, Design, Drawing, History of Art & Archaeology, Painting, Photography, Printmaking, Sculpture, Theatre Arts, Art Therapy, Computer Graphics
Summer School: Dir, Ron Ross. Enrl 40; tuition $100. Courses—Ceramics, Color Photography, Watercolor

MAHWAH

RAMAPO COLLEGE OF NEW JERSEY, School of Contemporary Arts, 505 Ramapo Valley Rd, 07430-1680. Tel 201-529-7368; *Dir* Shalom Gorewitz; *Prof Art History* Carol Duncan, PhD; *Prof* Judith Peck, EdD; *Prof Painting* W Wada, MFA; *Prof* Jay Wholley, MFA; *Assoc Prof Architecture* Newton LeVine, MCRP; *Assoc Prof Photo* David Freund, MFA
Estab 1968; pub; D & E; SC 53, LC 15; enrl D 800, E 50, non-maj 750, maj 100
Ent Req: HS dipl, SAT
Degrees: BA
Tuition: Res—undergrad $32 per cr hr; nonres—undergrad $50 per cr hr; campus res available
Courses: Architecture, Art Appreciation, Art History, Commercial Art, Conceptual Art, Design, Drawing, Film, Graphic Arts, Graphic Design, Intermedia, Painting, Photography, Printmaking, Sculpture, Stage Design, Video, Computer Art
Summer School: Dir, Shalom Gorewitz. Tuition $71.50 cr hr, $91.50 out of state. Courses—Computer Graphics, Photography

MERCERVILLE

JOHNSON ATELIER TECHNICAL INSTITUTE OF SCULPTURE, 60 Ward Ave Extension, 08619. Tel 609-890-7777; FAX 609-890-1816; Elec Mail lrn2sculpt@aol.com. *Pres* James Barton, MFA; *Acad Dir* James E Ulry, MFA; *Dir* Dona Warner, BFA; *Acad Asst* E Gyuri Hollosy, MFA
Estab 1974; pvt; D & E; scholarships; SC 12; enrl apprentices 20, interns 2
Ent Req: HS dipl, portfolio review
Degrees: The Atelier is a non degree granting institution with a two year apprenticeship program in sculpture
Tuition: $4800 per academic yr, $400 monthly
Courses: Restoration & Conservation, Sculpture, Ceramic Shell, Foundry, Metal Chasing, Modeling & Enlarging, Moldmaking, Patina, Sand Foundry, Structures, Wax Working & Casting

MONTCLAIR

MONTCLAIR ART MUSEUM, Art School, Education Dept, 3 S Mountain Ave, 07042. Tel 201-746-5555; FAX 201-746-9118; *Dir* Ellen Harris; *Registrar* Randolph Black; *Cur Coll* Gail Stavitsky; *Cur Educ* Twig Johnson; *Cur Asst* Mara Sultan; *Prog Coordr* Meryl Hillsberg. Instrs: FT 18
Art school estab 1924; pvt; D & E; scholarships; SC 17; enrl D 300 per term, E 100 per term
Tuition: Children $120-$140 for 11 sessions; adults $135-$175 for 8 sessions
Courses: Art Education, Collages, Drawing, Mixed Media, Painting, Printmaking, Sculpture, Chinese Print, Portraiture

Adult Hobby Classes: Enrl 300; tuition $135-$175, duration 8 wks.
Courses—Anatomy, Drawing, Painting, Pastels, Portraiture, Still Life, Watercolor
Children's Classes: Enrl 90; tuition $120-$140 per 8 wk sem. Courses—Mixed Media

MORRISTOWN

COLLEGE OF SAINT ELIZABETH, Art Dept, 2 Convent Rd, 07960-6989. Tel 201-605-7000; *Chmn Dept* Sr Ann Haarer
Estab 1899, dept 1956; den, W; D & E; scholarships; SC 17, LC 4; enrl D 250, maj 27
Ent Req: HS dipl, ent exam
Degrees: BA 4 yrs
Tuition: $10,900 per yr; campus res available
Courses: Sculpture, Teacher Training, Color and Design, Leather Work, Sand Casting, Stitchery
Summer School: Dir, Sr Alberta Jaeger. Courses—Art Education, Painting

NEWARK

NEWARK SCHOOL OF FINE & INDUSTRIAL ART, 460 Lyons Ave, 07112. Tel 201-705-3880; *Dir* Elaine C Sopka. Instrs: D PT 42, E PT 28
Estab 1882; pub; scholarships; enrl D 300, E 300
Tuition: City res—$750 per yr; nonres—$1500 per yr
Courses: Advertising Design, Illustration, Interior Design, Painting, Sculpture, Textile Design, Fashion
Adult Hobby Classes: Enrl D 150, E 75; tuition res $750, nonres $1500; Sept-Apr. Courses—Advertising, Fashion, Fine Arts, Illustration, Interior Design, Textile Design
Children's Classes: Ages 10-18

RUTGERS UNIVERSITY, NEWARK, Dept of Visual & Performing Arts, University Heights, 110 Warren St Bradley Hall, 07102. Tel 201-648-5119; FAX 201-648-1392; WATS 800-648-5600. *Chair* Annette Juliano; *Deputy Chair* Frank D'Astolfo. Instrs: FT 6
Pub; D; scholarships; enrl D 486, maj 100
Ent Req: HS dipl, or as specified by col and univ
Degrees: BA 4 yrs, BFA(Design)
Courses: Art Appreciation, Art Education, Art History, Ceramics, Design, Drawing, Graphic Design, History of Art & Archaeology, Illustration, Painting, Photography, Printmaking, Sculpture, Stage Design, Teacher Training, Theatre Arts, Computer Graphics
Summer School: Dir, Annette Juliano. Enrl 100. Courses—Art History, Ceramics, Drawing, Painting, 2-D Design, 3-D Design

NEW BRUNSWICK

INSTITUTE FOR ARTS & HUMANITIES EDUCATION, New Jersey Summer Arts Institute, 100 Jersey Ave, Ste B-104, 08901. Tel 908-220-1600; FAX 908-220-1515; *Admin Dir* Jacqueline Ruble; *Exec Dir* Carol Dickert
Estab 1980; pvt; D & E; scholarships; enrl 130
Ent Req: Audition, master class, portfolio, interview
Tuition: Campus res avail $2500 (summer only)
Courses: Advertising Design, Aesthetics, Architecture, Art Appreciation, Art Education, Art History, Ceramics, Collages, Conceptual Art, Costume Design & Construction, Design, Display, Drawing, Fashion Arts, Film, Graphic Arts, Graphic Design, History of Art & Archaeology, Illustration, Intermedia, Jewelry, Mixed Media, Painting, Photography, Printmaking, Sculpture, Stage Design, Teacher Training, Textile Design, Theatre Arts, Video, Weaving

RUTGERS, THE STATE UNIVERSITY OF NEW JERSEY
—**Mason Gross School of the Arts,** Livingston Arts Dept, PO Box 270, Berrue Circle Livingston Campus, 08903. Tel 908-445-9078; *Dean* Marilyn Sombille; *Dir Visual Arts* Warren Ewing; *Assoc Dean* Charles Woolfolk; *Dir Graduate Prog* Toby MacLennan; *Dir Undergrad Prog* Emma Amos; *Prof* Judith Brodsky; *Prof* Geoffrey Hendricks; *Prof* Lauren Ewing, MFA; *Prof* Raphael Ortiz; *Prof* Melvin Edwards, BFA; *Prof* John Goodyear, MDesign; *Prof* Gary Kuehn, MFA; *Prof* Emma Amos, MA; *Prof* Joan Semmel, MFA; *Assoc Prof* Lloyd McNeill, MFA; *Assoc Prof* Toby MacLennan; *Assoc Prof* Diane Neumaiere; *Assoc Prof* Robert T Cooke, MFA; *Assoc Prof* Phil Orenstein; *Asst Prof* Michael Eisenmenger; *Asst Prof* Ardele Lister; *Asst Prof* Sheena Calvert; *Asst Prof* Martin Ball; *Asst Prof* Lynne Allen
Estab 1766, school estab 1976; pub; D; scholarships; SC 24, LC 9, GC 33; enrl MFA prog 60, BFA prog 450
Ent Req: HS dipl, portfolio
Degrees: BHA, BFA, MFA
Tuition: Res—undergrad $3600 per yr, grad $2590; nonres—undergrad $7400 per yr, grad $3797
Courses: Ceramics, Film, Mixed Media, Painting, Photography, Printmaking, Sculpture, Video, Computer Arts, Critical Studies, Event and Performance, Seminars and Museum Internship
Summer School: Dir, Mark Berger. 4 wk courses. Courses—Computer Art, Drawing, Fundamentals, Figure Drawing, Painting Studio, Seminar on Contemporary Art, Studio Fundamentals
—**Graduate Program in Art History,** Voorhees Hall, Hamilton St, 08903. Tel 908-932-7041, 932-7819; FAX 908-932-1261; *Dir Prog* Joan Marter; *Prof* Matthew Baigell; *Prof* Sarah McHam; *Prof* Jack J Spector, PhD; *Prof* Rona Goffen; *Prof* Martin Eidelberg, PhD; *Prof* Tod Marder; *Prof* Jocelyn Small; *Assoc Prof* John F Kenfield, PhD; *Assoc Prof* Archer Harvey; *Assoc Prof* Sarah Brett-Smith; *Assoc Prof* Angela Howard; *Assoc Prof* Catherine Puglisi, PhD; *Assoc Prof* Elizabeth McLachlan; *Asst Prof* David Underwood; *Asst Prof* James Small
Estab 1766, grad prog estab 1971; pub; D; scholarships & fels; grad courses 15; enrl grad students 97
Ent Req: BA
Degrees: MA 2 yrs, PhD 4 yrs
Tuition: Res—undergrad $191 per cr hr, grad $2315 per sem; nonres—$282 per cr

hr, grad $3394 per sem
Courses: Architecture, Art History, History of Art & Archaeology, Museum Staff Training
Summer School: Intro to Art Hist, 19th & 20th century Art

OCEAN CITY

OCEAN CITY ART CENTER, 1735 Simpson Ave, 08226. Tel 609-399-7628; *Exec Dir* Eunice Bell; *Instr* Ruth Veasey; *Instr* Bethany Bonner
Estab 1974; pvt; D & E; scholarship; SC 14, LC 1; enrl D 1, E 8
Ent Req: None
Tuition: Varies
Courses: Calligraphy, Ceramics, Drawing, Mixed Media, Painting, Photography, Sculpture, Dance, Pottery
Summer School: Same classes offered during summer plus workshops & demonstrations

PARAMUS

BERGEN COMMUNITY COLLEGE, Visual Art Dept, 400 Paramus Rd, 07652. Tel 201-447-7100; *Dean Humanities* Michael Redmond
Scholarships offered
Degrees: AA
Tuition: In county—$57.60 per cr; nonres—$119.70 per cr hr
Courses: Art Appreciation, Art History, Ceramics, Design, Drawing, Graphic Design, Handicrafts, Interior Design, Lettering, Painting, Photography, Printmaking, Sculpture, Animation, Art Anatomy, Color Theory, Commercial Illustration, Craft Design, Fundamentals Art

PATERSON

PASSAIC COUNTY COMMUNITY COLLEGE, Division of Humanities, One College Blvd, 07505-1179. Tel 201-684-6800; *VPres* Steve Rose; *Prof* Mark G Bialy
Estab 1969; pub; D & E; SC 4, LC 3; enrl D 100, E 25
Ent Req: HS dipl, New Jersey basic skills exam
Degrees: AA 2 yrs
Tuition: $59.50 per cr hr
Courses: Advertising Design, Aesthetics, Art Appreciation, Art History, Commercial Art, Design, Drawing

PEMBERTON

BURLINGTON COUNTY COLLEGE, Humanities & Fine Art Div, Rte 530, Pemberton & Browns Mills Rd, 08068. Tel 609-894-9311, Ext 7290; *Division Chmn* Frank Nappo
Degrees: AA
Tuition: County res—$160.50 per cr hr; non-county res—$58.60 per cr hr; non-state res—$120.50 per cr hr
Courses: Art Appreciation, Art Education, Art History, Calligraphy, Ceramics, Design, Drawing, Film, Handicrafts, Painting, Photography, Sculpture, Theatre Arts, Video

PRINCETON

PRINCETON UNIVERSITY
—**Dept of Art & Archaeology,** 105 McCormick Hall, 08544-1018. Tel 609-258-3782; FAX 609-258-0103; *Chmn Dept&Prof* John Wilmerding, PhD; *Chmn Prog Chinese & Japanese Art & Archaeology* Wen Fong, PhD; *Chmn Prog in Classical Archaeology* William A P Childs, PhD; *Prof* T Leslie Shear Jr, PhD; *Prof* Yoshiaki Shimizu, PhD; *Prof* Peter Bunnell, MFA; *Prof* R J Clark, PhD; *Prof* Slobodan Curcic, PhD; *Prof* Dorothea Dietrich, PhD; *Prof* Robert Bagley; *Prof* John Pinto, PhD; *Prof* Hugo Meyer, PhD; *Prof* Thomas Kaufmann, PhD; *Prof* Pat Brown, PhD; *Prof* Deborah Kahn, PhD; *Prof* Mary Vidal, PhD; *Prof* James Marrow, PhD; *Prof* Todd Porterfield
Estab 1783; pvt; scholarships; LC 16, GC 9; enrl 761, maj 70, grad 50
Degrees: PhD
Tuition: $26,000 per yr
Courses: Photography, Archaeology, Early Chinese Art, Greek Archaeology, Italian Renaissance Art & Architecture, Later Japanese Art
—**School of Architecture,** 08544. Tel 609-258-3741; *Dean* Ralph Lerner. Instrs: FT 16
Estab 1919; pvt; D; scholarships and fels; SC 6, LC 13, GC 6, seminars 17; enrl undergrad 120, grad 50
Ent Req: HS dipl
Degrees: BA, MA, PhD
Tuition: $26,000 per yr
Courses: Acoustics & Lighting, Building & Science Technology, Environmental Engineering, History of Architectural Theory, Modern Architecture, Urban Studies

RANDOLPH TOWNSHIP

COUNTY COLLEGE OF MORRIS, Art Dept, 214 Center Grove Rd, 07869. Tel 201-328-5000; *Chmn & Prof* Charles Luce
Estab 1970; pub; D & E; SC 15, LC 3; enrl maj 263
Ent Req: HS dipl
Degrees: AA(Humanities/Art) 2 yrs, AAS(Photography Technology) 2 yrs
Tuition: $70.30 per cr; out-of-county $131.45; out-of-state $177.15
Courses: Advertising Design, Art History, Ceramics, Drawing, Painting, Photography, Printmaking, Sculpture, Color & Design, Major Styles & Historical Periods, Modern Art
Summer School: Two 5 week day sessions, one evening session

SEWELL

GLOUCESTER COUNTY COLLEGE, Liberal Arts Dept, 1400 Tanyard Rd, 08080. Tel 609-468-5000; *Head* John Henzy
Estab 1967; pub; D & E; scholarships; SC 6, LC 6
Ent Req: HS dipl
Tuition: Res—$56 per cr hr; nonres—$206 per cr hr
Courses: Art History, Ceramics, Drawing, Graphic Arts, Jewelry, Mixed Media, Painting, Sculpture, Arts & Crafts for Handicapped, General Design
Summer School: Dir, Dr Mossman

SHREWSBURY

GUILD OF CREATIVE ART, 620 Broad St, Rte 35, 07702. Tel 908-741-1441; *Pres* Otis Arnts
Tuition: $130 per 10 wks
Courses: Design, †Drawing, Handicrafts, Painting, Stage Design
Adult Hobby Classes: Enrl 185; tuition $130 for 10 wk term. Courses—Design, Drawing, Painting
Children's Classes: Enrl 100; tuition $65 for 10 wk term. Courses—Design, Life Drawing, Painting
Summer School: Oil & Acrylic Painting, Watercolor

SOUTH ORANGE

SETON HALL UNIVERSITY, College of Arts & Sciences, 400 S Orange Ave, 07079. Tel 201-761-9459, 761-9460; FAX 201-275-2368; *Chmn* Petra Chu; *Prof* Julius Zsako, PhD; *Assoc Prof* Barbara Cate; *Assoc Prof* Peter Rosenblum, MA; *Assoc Prof* Jeanette Hile, MA; *Asst Prof* Alison Dale; *Asst Prof* Anthony Triano; *Asst Prof* Charlotte Nichols, PhD; *Asst Prof* Arline Lowe. Instrs: FT 10, PT 9
Estab dept 1968; pvt; D & E; scholarships & fels; SC 8
Degrees: BA 4 yr, MA
Tuition: $11,000 per sem, $375 per cr hr
Courses: Art Education, Art History, Commercial Art, Drawing, Graphic Design, Illustration, Mixed Media, Painting, Printmaking, Sculpture, Advertising, Chinese Brush Painting, Fine Art, Music Art
Summer School: Dir, Petra Chu. Enrl 200; May-July. Courses—Art, Art History, Fine Arts

TEANECK

FAIRLEIGH DICKINSON UNIVERSITY, Fine Arts Dept, Becton Hall, 1000 River Rd, 07666. Tel 201-692-2801; FAX 201-692-2773; *Prof* David A Hanson; *Assoc Prof* Joan Taylor, MA; *Assoc Prof* Marie Roberts, MFA
Estab 1942, dept estab 1965; pvt; D & E; scholarships offered; SC 37, LC 9
Ent Req: HS dipl, SAT
Degrees: Degrees BA (Art & Fine Arts)
Tuition: Res—undergrad $367 per cr, room & board; nonres—undergrad $367 per cr hr; campus res available
Courses: Advertising Design, Art Appreciation, Art History, Calligraphy, Ceramics, Commercial Art, Design, Drawing, History of Art & Archaeology, Illustration, †Graphic Design, Lettering, Mixed Media, Painting, Photography, Printmaking, Sculpture, Bio & Wildlife Illustration, Computer Animation, Computer Graphics, Desktop Publishing

TOMS RIVER

OCEAN COUNTY COLLEGE, Humanities Dept, College Dr, 08754-2001. Tel 908-255-4000, Ext 375; FAX 908-255-0444; *Dean Humanities* Dr Martin Novelli; *Coordr* Joseph Conrey; *Prof* Patricia Kennedy, MS; *Prof* Lisa Horning; *Prof* Howard Unger, EdD; *Prof* John R Gowen; *Prof* Charles Read; *Prof* Arthur Waldman
Estab 1964, dept estab 1964; pub; D & E; scholarships; SC 19, LC 3; enrl D 1500, E 1500, maj 67
Ent Req: HS dipl
Degrees: AA in Liberal Arts with concentration in Fine Art & AAS(Visual Communication Technology) 2 yrs
Tuition: Res—undergrad $1066 per yr, PT $41; nonres—undergrad $1196 per yr, PT $46; no campus res
Courses: Advertising Design, Aesthetics, Art History, Calligraphy, Ceramics, Commercial Art, Conceptual Art, Costume Design & Construction, Drawing, Film, Graphic Arts, Graphic Design, Handicrafts, Lettering, Painting, Photography, Printmaking, Sculpture, Stage Design, Theatre Arts
Summer School: Enrl 175; tuition $34 for term of 5 wks or 6 wks beginning June. Courses—Arts & Humanities, Basic Drawing, Ceramics, Computer Graphics, Crafts, Photography

TRENTON

COLLEGE OF NEW JERSEY (Formerly Trenton State College), Art Dept, Pennington Rd, 08650-4700. Tel 609-771-2652; FAX 609-771-2610; *Chmn Dept* Ruane Miller, MFA; *Prof* Bruce Rigby, MFA; *Prof* Joseph Shannon, EdD; *Assoc Prof* Kenneth Kaplowitz, MFA; *Assoc Prof* Charles Kumnick, MFA; *Assoc Prof* Lois Fichner-Rathus, PhD; *Assoc Prof* Marcia Taylor, PhD, MAATR; *Assoc Prof* Wendell Brooks, MFA; *Assoc Prof* Elizabeth Mackie, MFA; *Assoc Prof* Christina Craig, EdD; *Asst Prof* Philip Sanders, MA; *Asst Prof* Mark Lehman, MFA; *Asst Prof* Johanna Jacob, MFA; *Asst Prof* Charles McVicker, BPA; *Asst Prof* Guy Norman, BS; *Asst Prof* William Nyman, MFA; *Asst Prof* Jeffrey Otto; *Instr* Diane Laird, MA. Instrs: FT 17, PT 18
Estab 1855; pub; D & E; scholarships; SC 40, LC 10, GC 11; enrl non-maj 5200, maj 300
Ent Req: HS dipl
Degrees: BA & BFA 4 yr
Tuition: Res—$4446; nonres—$7032

Courses: Advertising Design, Art Appreciation, †Art Education, Art History, Ceramics, Design, Display, Drafting, Drawing, †Graphic Design, History of Art & Archaeology, Illustration, Intermedia, †Interior Design, Jewelry, Lettering, Mixed Media, Painting, Photography, Printmaking, Sculpture, Silversmithing, Teacher Training, Computer Animation, Computer Graphics, †Fine Arts
Summer School: June & July five wk sessions, Governor's School of the Arts (July)

MERCER COUNTY COMMUNITY COLLEGE, Arts & Communication/ Engineering Technology, 1200 Old Trenton Rd, PO Box B, 08690. Tel 609-586-4800, Ext 350; FAX 609-586-2318; *Dean* David S Levin, PhD; *Cur* Henry Hose; *Prof* Mel Leipzig, MFA; *Prof* Frank Rivera, MFA; *Instr* Michael Welliver. Instrs: FT 10, PT 13
Estab 1902, dept estab 1967; pub; D & E; scholarships; SC 44, LC 6; enrl E 350, maj 261
Ent Req: HS dipl
Degrees: AA & AAS 2 yrs
Tuition: Res—grad $69
Courses: †Advertising Design, †Architecture, Art Education, Art History, †Ceramics, Commercial Art, Design, Drawing, Film, Graphic Arts, Graphic Design, History of Art & Archaeology, Illustration, †Painting, †Photography, Printmaking, †Sculpture, †Theatre Arts, Video
Adult Hobby Classes: Enrl 448. Tuition varies. Courses—Caligraphy, Ceramics, Drawing, Painting, Photography, Stained Glass
Children's Classes: Enrl 1000. Tuition varies. Courses—Drawing, Maskmaking, Painting, Printmaking, Soft Sculpture
Summer School: Dir, R Serofkin. Enrl 712 (camp college); 2 - 4 wk sessions. Dir, M Dietrich. Enrl 22; 4 wks. Courses—Architecture. Dir, M K Gitlick. Enrl 160; Arts Camp 2 - 4 wk sessions. Also regular cr courses

UNION

KEAN COLLEGE OF NEW JERSEY, Fine Arts Dept, Morris Ave, 07083. Tel 908-527-2307; *Chmn* Jack Cornish; *Gallery Dir* Alec Nicolescu; *Coordr Interior Design* Asher Derman, PhD; *Coordr Art Educ* Michael DeSiano; *Coordr Art History* Virginia Stotz, MA; *Coordr Studio Prog* Michael Metzger, MFA. Instrs: FT 31
Estab 1855; pub; D & E; scholarships; SC 58, LC 37, GC 24; enrl FT 383, PT 236, maj 656, grad 37
Ent Req: HS dipl, portfolio interview for art maj
Degrees: BA 4 yrs, BFA 4, MA(Art Educ)
Tuition: Res—undergrad $89.65 per cr hr, grad $168.15 per cr hr; nonres—undergrad $207 per cr hr, grad $145 per cr hr
Courses: Advertising Design, Aesthetics, †Art Education, †Art History, Ceramics, †Commercial Art, Display, Drafting, Drawing, Film, Graphic Arts, Graphic Design, Illustration, †Interior Design, Jewelry, Lettering, Museum Staff Training, Occupational Therapy, Painting, Photography, Printmaking, Sculpture, Textile Design, Furniture Making
Summer School: Asst Dir, George Sisko. Tuition $43 per cr for term of 6 wks beginning June 26. Courses—Art History, Art in Education, Ceramics, Drawing, Introduction to Art, Introduction to Interior Design, Jewelry, Life Drawing, Painting, Printmaking, Sculpture, Watercolor

UPPER MONTCLAIR

MONTCLAIR STATE UNIVERSITY, Fine Arts Dept, Normal Ave, 07043. Tel 201-655-4000; *Dean* Geoffrey Newman; *Chmn* Dr Anne Betty Weinshenker. Instrs: FT 18, PT 4
Estab 1908; pub; scholarship; SC 35, LC 18; enrl maj 250, grad maj 200
Ent Req: HS grad and exam, interview, portfolio
Degrees: BA 4 yr, BFA 4 yr, MA
Tuition: Res—undergrad $94.50 per cr, grad $163.50 per cr; nonres—grad $203 per cr
Courses: Art Education, Art History, Ceramics, Drawing, Film, Graphic Design, Illustration, Jewelry, Painting, Photography, Printmaking, Sculpture, Textile Design, Metalwork, TV as Art
Summer School: Life Drawing, Painting, Photography, Sculpture

VINELAND

CUMBERLAND COUNTY COLLEGE, Humanities Div, College Dr, PO Box 517, 08360. Tel 609-691-8600; *Coordr* Nancy Kozak
Tuition: County res—$737 per sem; out-of-county res—$122.50 per cr hr; out-of-state res—$245 per cr hr
Courses: Art Appreciation, Art History, Drawing, Painting, Photography, Video, Multi-media

WAYNE

WILLIAM PATERSON COLLEGE, Art Dept, Div of Fine and Performing Arts, 300 Pompton Rd, 07470. Tel 201-595-2401; *Chmn* Charles J Magistro. Instrs: FT 24, PT 8
Dept estab 1958; pub; scholarships; SC 9, LC 9; enrl maj 420, grad 105, E non-maj 170
Degrees: BA 4 yr, BFA, MA
Tuition: Res—undergrad $73, grad $131
Courses: †Art History, †Ceramics, †Design, †Drawing, †Graphic Design, †Illustration, †Painting, †Photography, †Printmaking, †Sculpture, †Textile Design, Computer Graphics, Computer Illustration
Summer School: Dir, Alan Lazarus. Enrl 150; tuition $65 per cr, $90 out of state. Courses—Art History, Drawing, Painting, Photography

WEST LONG BRANCH

MONMOUTH UNIVERSITY, Dept of Art & Design, 400 Cedar Ave, 07764. Tel 908-571-3428; *Chmn* Vincent Dimattio; *Prof* Pat Cresson; *Assoc Prof* Arie van Everdingen, MFA; *Assoc Prof* Martin Ryan, MA; *Assoc Prof* Alfred Provencher; *Asst Prof* Edward Jankowski, MFA
Estab 1933; pvt; D & E; scholarship; SC 25, LC 8; enrl in dept D 108, E 6, non-maj 80, maj 108, audits 6
Ent Req: HS dipl, portfolio for transfer students
Degrees: BA(Art), BFA & BA(Art Educ) 4 yr
Tuition: Res—$17,770 with room & board
Courses: †Art Education, Art History, †Ceramics, Drawing, Graphic Arts, Handicrafts, History of Art & Archaeology, †Painting, Photography, Printmaking, †Sculpture, Teacher Training, Appreciation of Art, Metalsmithing
Adult Hobby Classes: Courses—Painting
Summer School: Art Appreciation, Ceramics, Independent Study, Painting, Sculpture

NEW MEXICO

ALBUQUERQUE

UNIVERSITY OF NEW MEXICO
—College of Fine Arts, Fine Arts Ctr, 87131-1396. Tel 505-277-2111; FAX 505-277-0708; *Dean Colls* Dr Thomas A Dodson
Estab 1935; pub
Degrees: BFA, MA, MAFA, PhD(Art)
Tuition: $78.50 per cr hr, $35.57 (12-15 hrs) per cr hr
Courses: Ceramics, Drawing, Jewelry, Painting, Photography, Printmaking, Sculpture, Dance, Music, Theater
Adult Hobby Classes: Wide variety of courses offered
Summer School: Arts of the Americas Program, wide variety of courses offered
—Dept of Art & Art History, 87131-1401. Tel 505-277-5861; FAX 505-277-5955; *Chmn* Elen Feinberg
Estab 1889; pub; D & E; scholarships & fels; SC 190, LC 43, GC 73; enrl E 511, non-maj 230, maj 227, grad 116
Ent Req: HS dipl
Degrees: BA & BFA 4 yrs, MA 2 yrs, MFA 3 yrs, PhD 3 yrs
Tuition: Res—undergrad $1554 per yr, $777 per sem, grad $1684 per yr, $842 per sem; nonres—undergrad $5520 per yr, $2760 per sem, grad $5656 per yr, $2828 per sem
Courses: Aesthetics, Architecture, Art Appreciation, Art History, Ceramics, Conceptual Art, Design, Drawing, Film, Graphic Arts, History of Art & Archaeology, Landscape Architecture, Mixed Media, Painting, Photography, Printmaking, Sculpture, Video, Metalwork
Children's Classes: Offered through Art Educ Dept
Summer School: Tuition res $78.50 per cr hr, 6-9 hrs $471. Two 4 wk terms & one 8 wk term beginning June 11. Courses—same as above
—Tamarind Institute, 108 Cornell Dr SE, 87106. Tel 505-277-3901; FAX 505-277-3920; Elec Mail mdevon@unm.edu. *Dir* Marjorie Devon; *Tamarind Master Printer & Studio Mgr* Bill Lagattuta; *Educ Dir* Jeffrey Sippel
Fels
Degrees: Cert as Tamarind Master Printer 2 yrs
Tuition: $60.75 per cr hr
Courses: †Lithography
Summer School: 4 wk prog; campus res available. Courses—Various lithographic techniques

VERY SPECIAL ARTS NEW MEXICO, Enabled Arts Center, 2015 Yale Blvd SE, PO Box 7784, 87194. Tel 505-245-8545; FAX 505-843-8262; *Exec Dir* Beth Rudolph; *Dir Enabled Arts Center* Deborah Marshibini; *Exhib Coordr* Richard Garriot-Stejskal
Estab 1992; pvt; D; enrl D 30-40
Ent Req: 14 years or older
Courses: Art Appreciation, Ceramics, Collages, Drawing, Mixed Media, Painting, Printmaking, Sculpture

FARMINGTON

SAN JUAN COLLEGE, Art Dept, 4601 College Blvd, 87402. Tel 505-326-3311, Ext 281, 599-0281; *Dept Chmn* Bill Hatch. Instrs: FT 1, PT 3
Scholarships
Degrees: AA
Tuition: Res—$15 per cr hr; nonres—$25 per cr hr
Courses: Art Appreciation, Art Education, Art History, Calligraphy, Ceramics, Design, Drawing, Film, Graphic Design, Jewelry, Painting, Photography, Printmaking, Sculpture

HOBBS

NEW MEXICO JUNIOR COLLEGE, Arts & Sciences, 5317 Lovington Hwy, 88240. Tel 505-392-4510; *Dean* Steve McCleery; *Instr* Dale Short; *Instr* Lawrence Wilcox, MFA; *Instr* George Biggs
Estab 1965; pub; D & E; scholarships; SC 5, LC 1; enrl D 75, E 25, non-maj 95, maj 5
Ent Req: HS dipl, GED or special approval
Degrees: AA 2 yrs
Courses: Advertising Design, Ceramics, Drawing, Goldsmithing, Interior Design, Jewelry, Painting, Photography, Printmaking, Collage, Color & Design
Adult Hobby Classes: Drawing, Painting, Portraiture, Watercolor
Children's Classes: Drawing, Painting
Summer School: Dean, Steve McLeary. Enrl 30; term of 8 wks beginning June 10. Courses—Ceramics, Printmaking

LAS CRUCES

NEW MEXICO STATE UNIVERSITY, Art Dept, Dept 3572, PO Box 30001, 88003. Tel 505-646-1705; *Dept Head* Joshua Rose, MFA; *Prof* Louis Ocepek, MFA; *Prof* Spencer Fidler, MFA; *Prof* John Moffitt, PhD; *Assoc Prof* Amanda Jaffe, MFA; *Asst Prof* Doug DuBois; *Asst Prof* William Green; *Asst Prof* Julia Barello, MFA; *Asst Prof* Rachel Stevens, MFA
Estab 1975; pub; D & E; scholarships & fels; SC 52, LC 25, GC 53; enrl maj 150, grad 28
Ent Req: HS dipl
Degrees: BA & BFA 4 yrs, MFA 3 yrs, MA(Studio) & MA(Art Hist) 2 yrs
Tuition: Res—$854 per sem; nonres—$2819 per sem
Courses: Art Appreciation, Art History, Ceramics, Design, Drawing, Graphic Arts, Graphic Design, Illustration, Jewelry, Mixed Media, Painting, Photography, Printmaking, Sculpture, Silversmithing, †Metal Arts

LAS VEGAS

NEW MEXICO HIGHLANDS UNIVERSITY, Dept of Communications & Fine Arts, 87701. Tel 505-454-3238; *Dir* Drake Bingham; *Prof* Catherine Clinger; *Prof* Birgitte Brigmann; *Asst Prof* David Lobdell
Estab 1898; pub; D & E; scholarships; SC 24, LC 8, GC 12; enrl non-maj 55, maj 51, grad 4
Ent Req: HS dipl, ACT, Early Admis Prog, GED
Degrees: BA 4 yrs, MA 1 yr
Tuition: Res—$732 per sem; nonres—$2826 per sem; campus res available
Courses: Art Education, Art History, Calligraphy, Ceramics, Drawing, Graphic Arts, Jewelry, Lettering, Painting, Photography, Printmaking, Sculpture, Silversmithing, Stage Design, Teacher Training, Theatre Arts
Adult Hobby Classes: Courses—Ceramics, Painting, Weaving
Summer School: VPAA, Gilbert D. Riveva. Tuition sames as winter school. Courses—Mainly studio plus core curriculum, depending upon staffing

PORTALES

EASTERN NEW MEXICO UNIVERSITY, Dept of Art, Sta 19, 88130. Tel 505-562-2778; *Chmn* Greg Erf; *Asst Prof* Greg Senn, MFA; *Asst Prof* Mary Finneran, MFA
Estab 1932; pub; D & E; scholarships; SC 44, LC 6, GC 25; enrl D 507, E 150, maj 110
Ent Req: HS dipl, GED, ACT
Degrees: AA 2 yrs, BS, BA & BFA 4 yrs
Tuition: Res—$759 per sem; nonres—$2793 per sem
Courses: †Advertising Design, Art Education, Art History, Calligraphy, †Ceramics, †Commercial Art, †Drawing, †Graphic Arts, Graphic Design, Illustration, †Jewelry, Lettering, †Painting, Photography, †Sculpture, †Teacher Training, Theatre Arts, Video
Summer School: Chmn, Greg Erf. Terms of 8 & 16 wks beginning June 4. Courses—Ceramics, Commercial Art, Crafts, Drawing, Lettering, Photography

RUIDOSO

CARRIZO LODGE, Carrizo Art & Craft Workshops, PO Drawer A, 88345. Tel 505-257-9131; FAX 505-257-5621; Instrs: PT 75
Estab 1956; pvt; D; SC 150; enrl 300 summer school; 200 fall school; 200 spring school
Ent Req: Art interest
Tuition: $185 to $300 for 1 wk workshop; campus res—room & board $125-$325 for 1 wk, 4 day meal plan $35
Courses: Mixed Media, Painting, Photography, Sculpture, Creative Writing

SANTA FE

COLLEGE OF SANTA FE, Art Dept, 1600 Saint Michael's Dr, 87501. Tel 505-473-6011; *Chmn* Richard L Cook, MA; *Prof* Ronald Picco, MFA; *Asst Prof* Robert Sorrell, MFA; *Asst Prof* David Schienbaum, MFA; *Instr* Ralph Pardington, MFA; *Asst Prof* Richard Fisher; *Adjunct Assoc* Steve Fitch, MFA; *Adjunct Assoc* Linda Swanson, MFA; *Adjunct Assoc* Gail Rieke, MFA; *Adjunct Assoc* Terrence McKay, MA; *Adjunct Assoc* Shelley Horton-Trippe, MFA; *Adjunct Assoc* Katrinal Lasko, BFA; *Adjunct Assoc* Don Messec, MFA; *Gallery Dir* Rhae Burden, MFA
Estab 1947, dept estab 1986; pvt; D & E; scholarships; SC 35, LC 10; enrl D 350, non-maj 250, maj 95, non-degree 30
Ent Req: HS dipl or GED
Degrees: BA & BFA (Visual Arts)
Tuition: $2625 per sem, $250 per sem hr; campus res—room & board $2200 per yr
Courses: Aesthetics, Art Appreciation, Art Education, †Art History, Ceramics, Collages, Conceptual Art, Constructions, †Drawing, Film, Intermedia, Mixed Media, Museum Staff Training, †Painting, †Photography, †Printmaking, †Sculpture, Theatre Arts, Video, Art, †Art Studio, Art Therapy, Psychology
Children's Classes: Enrl 20-25; tuition $500-$750 for 3 wk term. Courses—General Studio Art
Summer School: Dir, Richard Cook. Tuition $372 per sem hr for term of 4-12 wks beginning May 13. Courses—Art History, Drawing, Lifecasting, Painting, Photography, Printmaking, Sculpture

INSTITUTE OF AMERICAN INDIAN ARTS MUSEUM, 108 Cathedral Pl, 87501. Tel 505-988-6281; FAX 505-988-6273; *Dir* Fred Nahwooksi; *Cur Coll* Manuelita Lovato
Estab 1962; pvt; D; scholarships; SC 18, LC 11; enrl 263
Ent Req: HS dipl
Degrees: AA (Fine Arts) 2 yrs
Tuition: $300 per hr non-Indian, free to native Americans
Courses: Art Appreciation, Art History, Costume Design & Construction, Drawing, History of Art & Archaeology, Lettering, Museum Staff Training, Painting,

Photography, Printmaking, Restoration & Conservation, Sculpture, Silversmithing, Traditional Indian Techniques, 2-D & 3-D Design
Summer School: Dir, Jon Wade. Enrl 150; tuition $60 per cr hr, free to Native Americans. Courses—Arts, Creative Writing, Museum Training

SANTA FE ARTS INSTITUTE, PO Box 4607, 87502-4607. Tel 505-983-6157; FAX 505-983-1162; *Dir* Kerry J Benson
Estab 1985; pvt; D & E; scholarships; SC 12
Ent Req: Portfolio review
Tuition: $1000 per two sessions
Courses: Collages, Mixed Media, Painting, Photography, Sculpture, Video, Installation, Video Art
Adult Hobby Classes: Installation & Video Art, Master classes in Printing, Mixed Media, Sculpture

SOUTHWEST ART LEAGUE SEMINARS, Art Horizons Ltd, 812 Camino Acoma, 87505. Tel 505-982-9981, 983-4825; *Dir* Maurice Loriaux, PhD
Estab 1971; D & E; enrl all seminars are limited to 21 delegates
Ent Req: Intermediate proficiency in painting—watercolor, oil, acrylics, all styles
Tuition: $519 per 6 day seminar includes room & board
Courses: All media

SILVER CITY

WESTERN NEW MEXICO UNIVERSITY, Dept of Expressive Arts, 1000 W College Ave, 88062. Tel 505-538-6614; FAX 505-538-6155; *Chmn* Dr Brian Saunders; *Prof* Gloria Maya, MFA; *Prof* Anthony Howell, MFA; *Prof* Claude Smith, MFA; *Prof* Michael Metcalf, MFA; *Artist-in-Residence* Ruben Gonzalez
Pub; D & E; scholarships; SC 10, LC 7; enrl D 211, non-maj 196, maj 15
Ent Req: HS dipl
Degrees: BA & MA, 4 yrs
Tuition: Res—$48 per cr hr; $743 for 12-18 cr hrs; nonres—$2727 for 12-18 cr hrs; campus res available
Courses: Advertising Design, Art Appreciation, Art Education, Art History, †Ceramics, Costume Design & Construction, Design, Drawing, Graphic Arts, Occupational Therapy, †Painting, Photography, †Printmaking, †Sculpture, Stage Design, Teacher Training, Theatre Arts, Weaving, †Sculpture, Silversmithing, Teacher Training, Textile Design, Fiber Arts
Adult Hobby Classes: Ceramics, Fiber, Lapidary
Summer School: Enrl 80-100; tuition $257 for 4-6 cr hr more credits from June 1-July 3 or July 5-Aug 9. Courses—Art Appreciation, Ceramics, Clay Workshop, Elementary Art Methods, Painting & Drawing Workshop, Printmaking, Special Art Tours in New Mexico & Europe

NEW YORK

ALBANY

COLLEGE OF SAINT ROSE, Dept of Art, 432 Western Ave, 12203. Tel 518-454-5111; FAX 518-438-3293; *Chmn* Karene Faul, MFA; *Prof* Patricia Clahassey, EdD; *Assoc Prof* Paul Mauren; *Assoc Prof* Kristine Herrick, MFA; *Asst Prof* Scott Brodie, MFA; *Asst Prof* Lucy Bodwitch, PhD; *Asst Prof* Jessica Loy; *Asst Prof* Deborah Zlotsky, MFA; *Asst Prof* Thomas Santelli, MFA
Estab 1920, dept estab 1970, pvt, D & E; scholarships; SC 21, LC 7, GC 8; enrl non-maj 200, maj 120, GS 20
Ent Req: HS dipl, SAT or ACT, rank in top 2/5 of class
Degrees: BS(Art, Art Educ, Graphic Design, Studio Art), MS(Art Educ)
Courses: Aesthetics, Art Education, Art History, Design, Drawing, Graphic Design, Illustration, Painting, Photography, Printmaking, Sculpture, Studio Art, Typography
Adult Hobby Classes: Enrl 20; tuition $250 per cr hr. Courses—Some continuing education courses each sem
Summer School: Dir Karene Faul. Enrl 80; two 5 wk courses from May 19-June 27 & June 30-Aug 8. Courses—Ceramics I & II, Grad Screenprint, Photo I & II

JUNIOR COLLEGE OF ALBANY, Fine Arts Division, 140 New Scotland Ave, 12208. Tel 518-445-1778; *Chairperson* Terrence Tiernan
Estab 1957, dept estab 1970; pvt; D & E; scholarships; SC 43, LC 16 (Art); enrl D 700 (total), 200 (art), E 823 (total)
Ent Req: HS dipl, references, records, SAT
Degrees: AAS 2 yrs
Tuition: $7700 per yr
Courses: Art History, Ceramics, Collages, Design, Drafting, Drawing, Graphic Design, Illustration, Intermedia, Interior Design, Lettering, Mixed Media, Painting, Photography, Printmaking, Sculpture, Printmaking, Fine Arts, Fine Arts Illustration, Studio Studies
Children's Classes: Summer courses for High School students
Summer School: Dir, Dierdra Zarrillo. Enrl 60.

STATE UNIVERSITY OF NEW YORK AT ALBANY, Art Dept, 1400 Washington Ave, 12222. Tel 518-442-4020; *Chair Dept* Roberta Bernstein; *Prof* Edward Mayer, MFA; *Prof* Thom O'Connor, MFA; *Assoc Prof* Mark Greenwold; *Assoc Prof* Arthur Lennig; *Assoc Prof* Robert Cartmell, MFA; *Assoc Prof* Phyllis Galembo; *Assoc Prof* Roberta Bernstein, PhD; *Assoc Prof* Marja Vallila, MFA; *Assoc Prof* JoAnne Carson; *Assoc Prof* David Carbone; *Asst Prof* Sarah Cohen; *Asst Prof* Rachel Dressler
Estab 1848; pub; D & E; scholarships; SC 43, LC 20, GC 33; enrl D 750, E 400, non-maj 600, maj 150, grad 45
Ent Req: HS dipl
Degrees: BA 4 yr, MA 1.5 yr, MFA 2 yr
Tuition: Res—undergrad $1325 per sem, $105 per cr hr, grad $2000 per sem, $168 per cr hr; nonres undergrad $3275 per sem; $274 per cr hr, grad $3658 per sem, $308 per cr hr; campus res—room & board $1930 per sem

Courses: †Art History, Drawing, History of Art & Archaeology, Painting, Photography, Printmaking, Sculpture, Plastics
Adult Hobby Classes: Courses in all studio areas
Summer School: Dir, Michael DeRensis. Enrl 350; term of 3-6 wks beginning July 1

ALFRED

NEW YORK STATE COLLEGE OF CERAMICS AT ALFRED UNIVERSITY, School of Art & Design, 2 Pine St, 14802. Tel 607-871-2412; FAX 607-871-2490; *Interim Dean* Mario Prisco. Instrs: FT 25
Estab 1900; scholarships; enrl maj undergrad 400, grad 25. Two yrs of foundation study & two yrs of upper level study
Degrees: BFA and MFA 4 yrs
Tuition: Res—$10,676 out-of-state $7704 in-state per yr, grad $11,466 per yr
Courses: Art Education, Ceramics, Drawing, Graphic Design, Painting, Photography, Printmaking, Sculpture, Video, Glass Arts, Wood
Summer School: Dean's Office, School Art & Design. Tuition 4 cr $840.
Courses—Art History, Ceramics, Glass, Painting, Sculpture

AMHERST

DAEMEN COLLEGE, Art Dept, 14226-3592. Tel 716-839-8241; FAX 716-839-8516;
Internet Home Page Address http://www.daemon.edu. *Chmn Dept* James Allen, MFA; *Assoc Prof* Dennis Barraclough; *Part-time Assoc Prof* Carol Townsend, MFA; *Asst Prof* Donna Stanton, MFA; *Instr* Jane Marinsky, BFA
Estab 1947; pvt; D & E; scholarships; SC 50; enrl D 1800, non-maj 1740, maj 60
Ent Req: HS dipl, art portfolio
Degrees: BFA(Drawing, Graphic Design, Illustration, Painting, Printmaking, Sculpture), BA(Art), & BS(Art Educ) 4 yrs
Tuition: Undergrad—$4975 per sem, $335 per cr hr; campus res—room & board $2600
Courses: Advertising Design, Aesthetics, Art Appreciation, Art Education, Art History, Ceramics, Collages, Design, Drawing, Graphic Design, Illustration, Mixed Media, Painting, Photography, Printmaking, Sculpture, Textile Design, Weaving, Computer Art
Summer School: Dean, Charles Reedy

ANNANDALE-ON-HUDSON

BARD COLLEGE, Milton Avery Graduate School of the Arts, 12504. Tel 914-758-7481, 758-6822; *Dir Prog* Arthur Gibbons; *Instr* Lydia Davis; *Instr* Ann Lauterbach; *Instr* Alan Cote; *Instr* Peggy Ahwesh; *Instr* Nicholas Maw; *Instr* Jessica Stockholder; *Instr* Jean Feinberg; *Instr* Regina Granne; *Instr* Stephen Shore; *Instr* Anne Turyn; *Instr* Lynne Tillman; *Instr* Peter Hutton
Estab 1981; pvt; scholarships; enrl 70
Degrees: MFA
Tuition: $4250
Courses: Film, Painting, Photography, Sculpture, Music, Writing
Summer School: A student will normally be in res for three summers terms, earning 13 credits per term; eight credits are awarded for the Master's project, for a total of 60; 13 independent study credits are awarded towards a degree

BARD COLLEGE, Center for Curatorial Studies Graduate Program, 12504-5000. Tel 914-758-7598, 758-7597; *Dir* Norton Batkin; *Registrar* Marcia Acita
Prog estab 1994; pvt; D; scholarships; GC 10; enrl grad 13
Ent Req: BA, BFA or equivalent
Degrees: Master's 2 yr
Tuition: Non res—grad $9740 per yr
Courses: Aesthetics, Art History, †Museum Staff Training

AURORA

WELLS COLLEGE, Dept of Art, Rte 90, 13026. Tel 315-364-3440, 364-3266; *Div Chmn* Bill Roberts
Estab 1868; pvt; W; D; scholarships; SC 19, LC 20; enrl D 500 (total), non-maj 122, maj 18
Ent Req: HS dipl, cr by exam programs
Degrees: BA 4 yrs
Tuition: Res—undergrad $14,900 per yr; campus res available
Courses: Aesthetics, †Art History, †Ceramics, †Drawing, †Painting, Photography, Printmaking, Teacher Training, †Theatre Arts

BAYSIDE

QUEENSBOROUGH COMMUNITY COLLEGE, Dept of Art & Photography, 222-05 56th Ave, 11364. Tel 718-631-6395; *Chmn* Lola B Gellman, PhD; *Prof* John Hawkins, MFA; *Prof* Paul Tschinkel, MFA; *Prof* Kenneth Walpuck, PhD; *Assoc Prof* Robert Rogers, MFA; *Asst Prof* Heinz Wipfler, MA; *Asst Prof* Jules Allen
Estab 1958; dept estab 1968; pub; D & E; scholarships; SC 21, LC 14; enrl D 9000, E 4000
Ent Req: HS dipl, placement exams
Degrees: AA, AS and AAS
Tuition: Res—undergrad $1050 per sem, $85 per cr; nonres—undergrad $1338 per sem, $104 per cr; no campus res
Courses: Advertising Design, Art History, Ceramics, Design, Drawing, Illustration, Painting, †Photography, Printmaking, Sculpture, Video, Artist Apprenticeships, Arts Internships, Arts for Teachers of Children, Color Theory
Summer School: Dir, Bob Rogers. Courses—Drawing, Photography, Sculpture

BELLPORT

INTERNATIONAL COUNCIL FOR CULTURAL EXCHANGE (ICCE), 5 Bellport Lane, 11713. Tel 516-286-5228; *Prog Coordr* Stanley I Gochman PhD
Estab 1982; pvt
Courses: Art History, Drawing, History of Art & Archaeology, Painting
Summer School: Tuition $3334 for 3 wk session. Courses—Landscape, Painting, Studio Art

BINGHAMTON

STATE UNIVERSITY OF NEW YORK AT BINGHAMTON, Dept of Art History, PO Box 6000, 13902-6000. Tel 607-777-2111; FAX 607-777-4466; *Chmn Dept* Barbara Abou-El-Haj
Estab 1950; pub; D; scholarships; SC 18, LC 32, GC 63; enrl 679, non-maj 400, maj 82, grad 45
Ent Req: HS dipl, Regents Scholarship, ACT or SAT
Degrees: BA 4 yrs, BFA 4 yrs, MA 1-2 yrs, PhD varies
Tuition: Res—undergrad $1325 per sem, grad $2000 per sem; nonres—undergrad $3225 per sem, grad $3658 per sem
Courses: †Art History, Drawing, Film, Graphic Design, Painting, Printmaking, Video, †Cinema, †Studio Art
Summer School: Dir, Donald Bell. Tuition same as academic yr, 3 separate sessions during summer. Courses—Art History, Drawing Workshop, Sculpture Foundry

BROCKPORT

STATE UNIVERSITY OF NEW YORK COLLEGE AT BROCKPORT, Dept of Art, Tower Fine Arts, 14420-2985. Tel 716-395-2209; FAX 716-395-2588; *Chmn* Jennifer Hecker; *Prof* Tom Markusen; *Prof* William Stewart; *Assoc Prof* Wolodymry Pylyshenko; *Asst Prof* Beth Blake; *Asst Prof* Dr Hafez Chehab; *Lectr* Nancy Leslie. Instrs: FT 9, PT 10
Pub; D; scholarships; SC 33, LC 29(Art History); enrl 8188, maj 100, grad 2000, grad 30
Ent Req: HS dipl, ent exam
Degrees: BA, BS & BFA 4 yrs
Tuition: Res—$2650; nonres—$3600, grad $4000
Courses: Art Appreciation, Art History, Ceramics, Design, Drawing, Jewelry, Painting, Photography, Sculpture, Artists Books
Adult Hobby Classes: Tuition $105 per cr hr for 13 wk term. Courses—Ceramics, Drawing, Methods, Museum & Gallery Studies, Painting, Photography, Sculpture, 2-D & 3-D Design
Summer School: Dir, Dr Kenneth O'Brien

BRONX

BRONX COMMUNITY COLLEGE, Music & Art Dept, 181 St & University Ave, 10453. Tel 718-289-5100; *Chmn* Peter Schira
Degrees: Cert, AS, AAS
Tuition: $1050 per sem
Courses: Art Appreciation, Art History, Ceramics, Commercial Art, Design, Drawing, Painting, Photography, Printmaking, Modern Art
Adult Hobby Classes: Enrl 25; tuition $45 for 7 wks. Courses—Calligraphy, Drawing

HERBERT H LEHMAN COLLEGE, Art Dept, 250 Bedford Park Blvd W, 10468. Tel 718-960-8256; FAX 718-960-7203; *Chmn* Herbert R Broderick; *Prof* Richard Ziemann, MFA; *Prof Emeritus* Ursula Meyer, MA; *Assoc Prof* Arvn Bose; *Asst Prof* Salvatore Romano; *Asst Prof* David Gillison, MFA
Estab 1968; pub; D & E; scholarship; SC 18, LC 29, GC 31; enrl non-maj 100, major 50, grad 15
Ent Req: HS dipl, ent exam
Degrees: BA & BFA 4 yrs, MA, MFA & MA 2 yrs
Tuition: Res—$1100 per sem, $92 per cr, nonres—$2400 per sem, $202 per cr; no campus res available
Courses: †Art History, †Graphic Arts, †Painting, †Sculpture
Summer School: Dean, Chester Robinson. Enrl 45; tuition $35 & $40 per cr for 6 wk term beginning June 28. Courses—Art History, Drawing, Painting

MANHATTAN COLLEGE, School of Arts, Manhattan College Pky, 10471. Tel 718-862-7345; *Chmn Fine Arts Dept* John F Omelia, PhD
Estab 1853; pvt den; D; scholarships; LC 8; enrl D 3000
Ent Req: HS dipl
Degrees: BA 4 yrs
Tuition: Res—undergrad $14,890 per yr, $275 per cr; nonres—undergrad $9640 per yr; campus res—room & board $2500 per yr
Courses: Art History, Ceramics, Drawing, Film, Graphic Arts, Graphic Design, History of Art & Archaeology, Painting, Photography, Printmaking, Sculpture

BRONXVILLE

CONCORDIA COLLEGE, 171 White Plains Rd, 10708. Tel 914-337-9300; FAX 914-395-4500; *Dir Art Dept* Serdar Arat; *Asst Prof* Ellen F Halter, MA
Estab 1881; pvt; D; scholarships; SC 4, LC 2
Ent Req: HS dipl, SAT or ACT
Degrees: BA and BS 4 yrs
Tuition: $4995
Courses: Art Education, Art History, Ceramics, Drawing, Handicrafts, History of Art & Archaeology, Painting, Photography, Sculpture, Teacher Training
Adult Hobby Classes: Courses—Painting

SARAH LAWRENCE COLLEGE, Dept of Art History, One Meadway, 10708. Tel 914-337-0700; *Instr* Abigail Child, MFA; *Instr* Nancy Bowen, MFA; *Instr* Dave Gearey, BA; *Instr* Gary Burnley, MFA; *Instr* Mary Delahoyd, MA; *Instr* Joseph C Forte, PhD; *Instr* David Castriota, PhD; *Instr* U Schneider, MFA; *Instr* Kris Phillips, MFA; *Instr* Susanna Heller, BFA; *Instr* Joel Sternfeld, BA; *Instr* Marsha Pels, MFA; *Instr* Mira Schor, MFA; *Instr* Terry Koshel, MFA; *Instr* Mary Patierno, BA; *Instr* Patricia Karetzky, PhD; *Instr* Suzanne Boorsch, MA; *Instr* Mac Griswold, BA; *Instr* Sandra Sider, PhD. Instrs: FT 1, PT 9
Estab 1926; pvt; D; scholarships
Ent Req: HS dipl
Degrees: BA 4 yrs
Tuition: $17,280 per yr
Courses: Drawing, Painting, Printmaking, Art History, Photography, Sculpture, Filmmaking, Visual Fundamentals
Summer School: Center for Continuing Education

BROOKLYN

BROOKLYN COLLEGE, Art Dept, Bedford Ave & Ave H, 11210. Tel 718-951-5181; FAX 718-951-4728; *Chmn* Michael Mallory
Scholarships
Degrees: BA, BFA, MA, MFA
Tuition: Res—undergrad $92 - $100 per cr hr, grad $145 per cr hr; non res—grad $250 per cr hr
Courses: Aesthetics, Art History, Calligraphy, Ceramics, Collages, Design, Drawing, Graphic Arts, Graphic Design, History of Art & Archaeology, Intermedia, Mixed Media, Museum Staff Training, Painting, Photography, Printmaking, Sculpture, Computer Graphics
Adult Hobby Classes: Enrl 50. Courses—Studio Art
Summer School: Enrl 100-150; two summer sessions. Courses—Art History, Computer Graphics, Studio Art

KINGSBOROUGH COMMUNITY COLLEGE, Dept of Art, 2001 Oriental Blvd, 11235. Tel 718-368-5000; *Chmn* Thomas I Nonn, PhD
Estab 1965, dept estab 1972; pub; D & E; SC 10, LC 8; enrl maj 135
Ent Req: HS dipl
Degrees: AS 2 yrs
Courses: Art History, Ceramics, Design, Drawing, Graphic Arts, Graphic Design, Illustration, Jewelry, Mixed Media, Painting, Printmaking, Sculpture, Communication Design
Adult Hobby Classes: Overseas travel courses
Summer School: Courses—Art

LONG ISLAND UNIVERSITY, BROOKLYN CAMPUS, Art Dept, University Plaza, 11201. Tel 718-488-1051; *Chmn* Liz Rudey. Instrs: FT 3, PT 15
Pvt; D & E; scholarships; SC 5, LC 3
Ent Req: HS dipl, ent exam
Degrees: BA & BS 4 yrs
Tuition: $408 per cr
Courses: Art History, Calligraphy, Ceramics, Drawing, Painting, Printmaking, Sculpture, Arts Management, Media Arts, Medical-Scientific Illustration, Teaching Art to Children, Visual Experience
Adult Hobby Classes: Courses—Teaching Art to Children
Summer School: Dir, Liz Audey. Term of two 6 wk sessions. Courses—Ceramics, Drawing, Painting

NEW YORK CITY TECHNICAL COLLEGE OF THE CITY UNIVERSITY OF NEW YORK, Dept of Art & Advertising Design, 300 Jay St, 11201. Tel 718-260-5175; FAX 718-260-5995; *Chmn* Joel Mason
Estab 1949; pub; D & E; scholarships; SC 16, LC 3; enrl D 350, E 125
Ent Req: HS dipl
Degrees: AAS 2 yrs
Tuition: $705 per sem
Courses: †Advertising Design, Commercial Art, Drawing, Graphic Design, Illustration, Lettering, Painting, Printmaking, Packaging, Paste-ups, Type Specing
Summer School: Computer Graphics, Design, Illustration, Lettering, Life Drawing, Paste-up, Photography, Video Design

PRATT INSTITUTE
—**School of Art & Design,** 200 Willoughby Ave, 11205. Tel 718-636-3600, 636-3619; FAX 718-636-3410; *Dean* William Fasolino
Pub; enrl 3700
Degrees: BFA & BID 4 yr, MA, MF, MFA & MPF 2 yr
Tuition: Undergrad $6987 per sem, grad $505 per cr hr
Courses: †Art Education, †Art History, †Ceramics, †Drawing, †Film, †Graphic Design, †Illustration, †Industrial Design, †Interior Design, †Painting, †Photography, †Printmaking, †Sculpture, †Video, †Computer Graphics
Adult Hobby Classes: Enrl 195. Various courses offered
Children's Classes: Morning classes
Summer School: Dean, Vieri Salvadori. Enrl for high school students only; tuition $400 per 4 cr. Courses—Computer Graphics, Fine Arts, Foundation Art
—**School of Architecture,** 200 Willoughby Ave, 11205. Tel 718-636-3404; *Dean* Thomas Hanrahan
Degrees: BArchit 5 yr, MArchit
Tuition: $13,975 per yr
Courses: Architecture, Art History, Landscape Architecture, Design, History of Architecture, Materials, Structures, Construction documents in professional practice

PROMOTE ART WORKS INC (PAWI), Job Readiness in the Arts-Media-Communication, 123 Smith St (Mailing add: PO Box 154, New York, 10012-0003). Tel 718-797-3116; FAX 718-797-3116; Elec Mail laziza4@gramercy.ios.com.
Estab 1993; pub; scholarships
Ent Req: Interview process
Adult Hobby Classes: Tuition $50 per hr. Courses—Video Editing
Children's Classes: Tuition $15 per class. Courses—Dance, Drama, Movement
Summer School: Tuition $15 per class. Courses—Art, Science

BROOKVILLE

C W POST CENTER OF LONG ISLAND UNIVERSITY, School of Visual & Performing Arts, 720 Northern Blvd, 11548. Tel 516-299-2000, 299-2395 (visual & performing arts); *Chmn* Jerry Zimmerman; *Dean Visual & Performing Arts* Lynn Croton; *Prof* Marilyn Goldstein; *Prof* Howard LaMarcz; *Prof* Robert Yasuda; *Prof* Jerome Zimmerman; *Assoc Prof* David Henley; *Assoc Prof* Jacqueline Frank; *Assoc Prof* Frank Olt; *Assoc Prof* Joan Powers; *Asst Prof* John Fekner; *Asst Prof* Richard Mills; *Asst Prof* Carol Huebner-Venezia; *Asst Prof* Donna Tuman; *Asst Prof* Vincent Wright

Dept estab 1957; pvt; D & E; scholarships; SC 70, LC 15, GC 40; enrl D 2000, E 450, non-maj 2000, maj 250, grad 150, others 50
Ent Req: HS dipl, portfolio
Degrees: BA(Art Educ), BA(Art Hist), BA(Studio), BS(Art Therapy) & BFA(Graphic Design) 4 yrs, MA(Photography), MA(Studio), MS(Art Educ) & MFA(Art, Design or Photography) 2 yrs
Tuition: Full-time grad $6845 per 12 cr hrs, $427 per cr hr; part-time $408 per sem cr
Courses: †Advertising Design, Aesthetics, †Art Education, †Art History, Ceramics, Collages, Commercial Art, Conceptual Art, Constructions, Drawing, Film, Graphic Arts, Graphic Design, Handicrafts, Illustration, Intermedia, Jewelry, Lettering, Mixed Media, Painting, Photography, Printmaking, Sculpture, Stage Design, Teacher Training, Theatre Arts, Video, Computer Graphics, Fine Arts, Weaving
Adult Hobby Classes: Courses—Varied
Summer School: Prof, Howard LaMarcz. Duration 3-5 wk sessions. Courses—varied

BUFFALO

STATE UNIVERSITY COLLEGE AT BUFFALO, Fine Arts Dept, 1300 Elmwood Ave, 14222. Tel 716-878-6014; FAX 716-878-4231; *Chmn* Peter Sowiski. Instrs: FT 16
Estab 1875, dept estab 1969; pub; D & E; SC 34, LC 17, GC 6; enrl maj 300 (art) 50 (BFA) 12 (art history)
Ent Req: HS dipl
Degrees: BA(Art), BA(Art History) & BFA 4 yrs
Tuition: Res—undergrad $3400 per sem, room & board $5455; nonres—undergrad $8300 per sem, room & board $5256
Courses: †Art History, †Drawing, †Painting, †Photography, †Printmaking, †Sculpture, †Papermaking
Summer School: Dir, Gerald Accurso. Tuition res—$45 per cr hr, nonres—$107 per cr hr for 10 wk term beginning June 2. Courses—Art History, Studio

UNIVERSITY AT BUFFALO, STATE UNIVERSITY OF NEW YORK, Fine Arts Dept, 202 Centre for the Arts, 14260-6010. Tel 716-645-6878; FAX 716-645-6970; *Chmn* Paul McKenna. Instrs: FT 16, PT 17
Estab 1846; pub; D & E; scholarships, fels; SC, LC, GC; enrl D 400, E 150, grad 30
Ent Req: HS dipl, portfolio, for all undergraduate students
Degrees: BFA(Studio Art), BA & MFA(Fine Art)
Tuition: Res—undergrad $1700 per sem, $137 per cr hr, grad $2550 per sem, $213 per cr hr; nonres—undergrad $4150 per sem, $346 per cr hr, grad $4208 per sem, $351 per cr hr; campus res—single $1907 per sem, double $1562 per sem, three-person $1436 per sem (rates vary depending on campus location)
Courses: Drawing, †Illustration, †Painting, †Photography, †Printmaking, †Sculpture, †Communications Design, †Computer Art
Summer School: Dean, George Lopos. Enrl 100; tuition res $137 per cr hr, nonres $346 per cr hr for 3-6 wk term. Courses— Computer Art, Drawing, Foundations, Illustration Workshop, Painting, Photo Workshop, Printmaking

VILLA MARIA COLLEGE OF BUFFALO, Art Dept, 240 Pine Ridge Rd, 14225. Tel 716-896-0700, Ext 363; FAX 716-896-0705; *Chmn* Brian R Duffy, MFA; *Assoc Prof* Carol B Wells, MS; *Instr* Carole C Gates, MS; *Instr* Roberley Bell, MFA; *Instr* Daniel V Calleri; *Instr* Barbara P Wojciechowski; *Instr* Bonnie Scheller
Estab 1961; pvt; D & E; scholarships; SC 27, LC 3; enrl D 450, E 100, maj 170
Ent Req: HS dipl of equivalency
Degrees: AA, AAS & AS 2 yrs
Tuition: $3000 per sem
Courses: Advertising Design, Art History, Design, Drafting, Drawing, Graphic Arts, Graphic Design, Interior Design, Lettering, Painting, Photography, Printmaking, Sculpture, Textile Design, Advertising Graphics, Color Photo, Commercial Design, Computer-aided Design, Etching, History of Interior Design, History of Photography, Mechanical Systems & Building Materials, Rendering & Presentation, Serigraphy, Studio Lighting, 3-D Design, View Camera Techniques
Adult Hobby Classes: Courses - Drawing, Painting, Photography
Summer School: Enrl 10-20. courses—a variety of interest courses, including drawing, painting and photography

CANANDAIGUA

FINGER LAKES COMMUNITY COLLEGE, Visual & Performing Arts Dept, 4355 Lake Shore Dr, 14424. Tel 716-394-3500; FAX 716-394-5005; *Chmn* Elaine Lomber; *Prof* Thomas F Insalaco, MFA; *Prof* Wayne Williams; *Asst Prof* John Fox, MFA. Instrs: FT 5
Estab 1966; pub; D & E; SC 14, LC 2; enrl D 60, non-maj 700, maj 50
Ent Req: HS dipl
Degrees: AA & AAS 2 yrs
Tuition: Res—$890 per sem; nonres—$1780 per sem
Courses: Advertising Design, Art History, Ceramics, Commercial Art, Drawing, Graphic Arts, Graphic Design, Illustration, Painting, Photography, Printmaking, Sculpture, Stage Design, Theatre Arts
Summer School: Courses—Per regular session

CANTON

ST LAWRENCE UNIVERSITY, Dept of Fine Arts, 13617. Tel 315-379-5192; *Chmn* Betsy Rezelman, PhD; *Prof* J Michael Lowe, MFA; *Prof* Guy Berard, MFA; *Prof* Roger Bailey, MFA; *Assoc Prof* Elizabeth Kahn, PhD; *Assoc Prof* Dr Dorothy LiMouze; *Assoc Prof* Faye Serio
Estab 1856; pvt; D; SC 16, LC 13; enrl maj 40
Ent Req: HS dipl
Degrees: BA
Tuition: $20,410 per yr; campus res—room & board $6110
Courses: Art History, Ceramics, Drawing, Painting, Photography, Printmaking, Sculpture, Teacher Training
Summer School: Dir, Donna Fish

CAZENOVIA

CAZENOVIA COLLEGE, Center for Art & Design Studies, 13035. Tel 315-655-9446, Ext 162; FAX 315-655-2190; *Prof* Kohn Aistars, MFA; *Prof* Josef Ritter, MFA; *Prof* Scott Ottaviano, MFA; *Assoc Prof* Jeanne King, MFA; *Assoc Prof* Anita Fitzgerald, MS; *Assoc Prof* Constance Roy, MA; *Assoc Prof* Jo Buffalo; *Assoc Prof* Charles Goss, MFA; *Asst Prof* Kim Waale, MFA; *Asst Prof* Anita Welych, MFA; *Asst Prof* Karen Steen, MFA
Estab 1824; pvt; D & E; scholarships; SC 21, LC 3
Ent Req: HS dipl
Degrees: AA, AS, AAS, BS, & BPS 2 yr & 4 yr progs
Tuition: Res—$8592 per yr, $187 per cr hr; campus res—room & board $4388
Courses: †Advertising Design, Ceramics, Drawing, Drafting, †Illustration, †Interior Design, Lettering, Painting, Photography, Printmaking, Advertising Layout, †Advanced Studio Art, Basic Design, Fashion Design, Typography, Rendering, Residential Interiors, Office & Mercantile Interiors
Adult Hobby Classes: Enrl 200; tuition $84 per cr. Courses—large variety
Summer School: Dir, Marge Pinet. Enrl 100; tuition $1650 for 5 wk term. Courses—Variety

CHAUTAUQUA

CHAUTAUQUA INSTITUTION, School of Art, PO Box 1098, 14722. Tel 716-357-6233; FAX 716-357-9014; *Dir Art School* Don Kimes; *Instr* Stanley Lewis; *Instr* William Daley; *Instr* Frank Martin; *Instr* Polly Martin; *Instr* Chris Semergieff; *Instr* Barbara Goodstein; *Instr* Josette Urso; *Instr* Barbara Grossman; *Instr* Jackie Hayden; *Instr* George Rose; *Instr* Libby Kowalski; *Instr* Shari Mendelson; *Instr* David Lund; *Instr* Ed Smith; *Instr* Steffi Franks; *Instr* Piper Shepard
Estab 1874; pub; D (summers only); scholarships; SC 40, LC 20; enrl D 500
Tuition: $2610-$2770 full cost for 8 wk term
Courses: Ceramics, Drawing, Painting, Printmaking, Sculpture
Adult Hobby Classes: Enrl 300; tuition $75 per wk; Courses—same as above
Children's Classes: Young artists programs, ages 6 - 17
Summer School: Dir, Don Kimes. Enrl 55; tuition $2200 beginning June 26 - Aug 18

CLAYTON

THOUSAND ISLANDS CRAFT SCHOOL & TEXTILE MUSEUM, 314 John St, 13624. Tel 315-686-4123; *Dir* Lisa La Rue. Instrs: PT 27
Estab 1964; D & E; SC 21; enrl D 210, E 10
Degrees: No degrees but transfer credit
Tuition: $158-$185 for 1 wk course
Courses: Ceramics, Drawing, Fashion Arts, Handicrafts, Jewelry, Mixed Media, Painting, Sculpture, Weaving, Basketry, Bird Carving, Country Painting, Decoy Carving, Fiber Arts, Pottery, Quilting, Spinning
Children's Classes: Drawing, Painting, Pottery, Weaving
Summer School: July 3-Aug 25. Courses—Country Painting, Decoy Carving, Painting on Silk, Pottery, Quilting, Sculpture, Watercolor Painting, Weaving

CLINTON

HAMILTON COLLEGE, Art Dept, 13323. Tel 315-859-4269; FAX 315-859-4632; *Chmn* Deborah Pokinski; *Instr* Rand Carter; *Instr* Robert Palusky, MFA; *Instr* William Salzillo, MFA; *Instr* Robert Muirhead, MFA; *Instr* John McEnroe, PhD; *Instr* Scott MacDonald, PhD; *Instr* Laurie Gant, MFA; *Slide Librn* Jacqueline Medina
Pvt; D; enrl non-maj 850, maj 50
Ent Req: HS dipl, SAT
Degrees: AB
Tuition: $21,700 per yr, room $5450
Courses: †Art History, Ceramics, Mixed Media, Painting, Photography, Sculpture, Video

COBLESKILL

STATE UNIVERSITY OF NEW YORK, AGRICULTURAL & TECHNICAL COLLEGE, Art Dept, Rte 7, 12043. Tel 518-234-5011; FAX 518-234-5333; *Chmn Art Dept* Charles C Matteson, MA
Estab 1950; pub; D & E; SC 2, LC 2; enrl D 95
Ent Req: HS dipl
Degrees: AA & AS 2 yrs
Tuition: Res—undergrad $1325 per sem; nonres—undergrad $1950 per sem; campus res—room & board $2380-$2460 per yr
Courses: Art Education, Art History, Drawing, Painting, Sculpture, Teacher Training, Theatre Arts
Adult Hobby Classes: Enrl 4000 per yr; tuition $9 per course. Courses—large variety of mini-courses

CORNING

CORNING COMMUNITY COLLEGE, Division of Humanities, One Academic Dr, 14830. Tel 607-962-9271; *Prof* John M Runyon, MFA; *Prof* Margaret Brill, MA; *Assoc Prof* Horst Werk, MFA. Instrs: FT 3
Estab 1958, dept estab 1963; pub; D & E; SC 8, LC 6
Ent Req: HS dipl, SAT
Degrees: AA, AS, AAS 2 yrs
Tuition: $1100 per sem
Courses: Architecture, Art Appreciation, Art History, Ceramics, Design, Drawing, History of Art & Archaeology, Jewelry, Painting, Photography, Silversmithing, Silkscreen
Adult Hobby Classes: Enrl 18; $73 sem
Summer School: Dir, Betsy Brune

CORTLAND

STATE UNIVERSITY OF NEW YORK, COLLEGE AT CORTLAND, Art Dept, PO Box 2000, 13045. Tel 607-753-4316; FAX 607-753-5999; *Chmn* Fred Zimmerman; *Cur D* Jo Schaffer, MA; *Gallery Dir* Janet Steck, MAT; *Prof* John Jessiman, MFA; *Assoc Prof* Libby Kowalski; *Prof* Steven Barbash, MFA; *Prof* George Dugan, MFA; *Assoc Prof* James Thorpe, MFA; *Assoc Prof* Charles Heasley; *Asst Prof* Barbara Wisch, PhD; *Asst Prof* Allen Mooney, MFA
Estab 1868, dept estab 1948; pub; D & E; scholarships; SC 40, LC 10; enrl D 5600 (total), 1200 (art), maj 80
Ent Req: HS dipl, all college admissions standards based on high school average or scores from SAT, ACTP or Regent's tests
Degrees: BA 4 yrs
Tuition: Res—undergrad $1450 per yr; nonres—undergrad $3100 per yr; other college fee & activity assessment $87 per yr; campus res—$1400 per yr(room) and $972 per yr(board)
Courses: Aesthetics, Art Appreciation, Art Education, Art History, Ceramics, Conceptual Art, Design, Drawing, Graphic Arts, Graphic Design, History of Art & Archaeology, Painting, Photography, Printmaking, Sculpture, Stage Design, Video, Weaving, Arts Management, Design, Lithography, Weaving
Summer School: Two terms of 5 wks beginning June 26. Courses—Art History, Studio

ELMIRA

ELMIRA COLLEGE, Art Dept, 14901. Tel 607-735-1800, 735-1804 (Acad Affairs); *Chmn* Dr Michael Clark; *Prof* James Cook; *Prof* Doug Holtgrewe; *Asst Prof* Leslie Kramer, MFA; *Asst Prof* Edwin Christenson; *Asst* John Diamond-Nigh; *Asst* Jan Kather
Estab 1855; pvt; D & E; scholarships; SC 26, LC 15, GC 8; enrl D 250, E 125, maj 35, grad 6
Ent Req: HS dipl
Degrees: AA, AS, BA, BS & MEduc
Tuition: $17,550 per yr; $3500 for room, $2380 for board; $100 house fee
Courses: †Art Education, †Art History, †Ceramics, †Drawing, †Painting, †Photography, †Printmaking, †Sculpture, †Video
Adult Hobby Classes: Tuition $180 - $265 per cr hr. Courses—Art History, Ceramics, Drawing, Landscape Painting & Drawing, Painting, Photography, Video
Summer School: Dir, Lois Webster. Tuition undergrad $180 cr hr, grad $265 per cr hr. Courses—Art History, Ceramics, Drawing, Landscape Painting & Drawing, Painting

FARMINGDALE

STATE UNIVERSITY OF NEW YORK AT FARMINGDALE, Advertising Art Design Dept, * Broadhollow Rd, Rte 110, 11735-1021. Tel 516-420-2181; FAX 516-420-2034; *Dept Chmn* William J Steedle
Degrees: AAS
Tuition: $1515 Spring sem, $1575 Fall sem
Courses: †Advertising Design, Design, Drawing, Illustration, Lettering, Painting, Photography, Printmaking, Airbrush, Computer Art, Computer Graphics, Electronic Publishing, Layout, TV Graphics
Adult Hobby Classes: Tuition $45 per credit hr. Courses same as above
Summer School: Dir, Francis N Pellegrini. Tuition $45 per cr; June-Aug. Courses—Advertising, Art History, Design, Drawing, Lettering, Mechanical Art, Production

FLUSHING

QUEENS COLLEGE, Art Dept, 65-30 Kissena Blvd, 11367. Tel 718-997-5770, 997-5411; *Chmn* Marvin Hoshine
Degrees: BA, BFA, MA, MFA, MSEd
Tuition: Res—undergrad $2120 per sem, $100 per cr hr; nonres— $2525 per sem, $210 per cr hr
Courses: Advertising Design, Architecture, Art Appreciation, Art Education, Art History, Calligraphy, Ceramics, Design, Drawing, Illustration, Painting, Photography, Printmaking, Sculpture
Summer School: Courses held at Caumsett State Park

FOREST HILLS

FOREST HILLS ADULT CENTER, 6701 110th St, 11375. Tel 718-263-8066; *Principal* Elma Fleming
Degrees: Cert
Tuition: $70 plus materials for 7 wk course
Courses: Art Appreciation, Calligraphy, Drawing, Handicrafts, Painting, Quilting

FREDONIA

STATE UNIVERSITY COLLEGE AT FREDONIA, Dept of Art, 14063. Tel 716-673-3537; *Elec Mail* lundem@fredonia. *Chmn* Mary Lee Lunde
Estab 1867, dept estab 1948; pub; D & E; scholarships; SC 30, LC 18; enrl D 650, E 70, non-maj 610, major 140
Ent Req: Ent req HS dipl, GRE, SAT, portfolio review all students
Degrees: BA 4 yrs, BFA 4 yrs
Courses: Art History, †Ceramics, Drawing, †Painting, †Photography, Printmaking, †Sculpture, Video

GARDEN CITY

ADELPHI UNIVERSITY, Dept of Art & Art History, 11530. Tel 516-877-4460; *Chmn* Harry Davies; *Prof* Richard Vaux; *Assoc Prof* Yvonne Korshak; *Prof* Thomas MacNulty; *Asst Prof* Dale Flashner; *Asst Prof* Peter Chametzky. Instrs: FT 8, PT 18
Estab 1896; pvt; D & E; scholarships; SC 40, LC 20, GC 20; enrl D 700, E 100, maj 130, grad 60
Ent Req: HS dipl; portfolio required for undergrad admission, required for grad
Degrees: BA 4 yrs, MA 1 1/2 yrs
Tuition: $4650 per sem; campus res available
Courses: †Advertising Design, Aesthetics, Art Education, Art History, Calligraphy, Ceramics, Design, Drawing, Graphic Arts, Graphic Design, History of Art & Archaeology, Jewelry, Lettering, Mixed Media, Painting, Photography, Printmaking, Sculpture, Teacher Training
Summer School: Tuition—same as regular session; two 4 wk summer terms also 2 wk courses. Courses—Crafts, Drawing, Painting, Sculpture, Photography

NASSAU COMMUNITY COLLEGE, Art Dept, One Education Dr, 11530. Tel 516-572-7162; *Prof* John Fink; *Prof* Dr Russell Housman; *Prof* Stanley Kaplan; *Prof* Salli Zimmerman; *Prof* Robert Carter; *Prof* Robert Lawn; *Prof* Edward Fox; *Adjunct Prof* Charles Reina
Estab 1959, dept estab 1960; pub; D & E; scholarships; SC 22, LC 5; enrl D & E 20,000
Ent Req: HS dipl
Degrees: AA 2 yrs, cert in photography & advertising design 1 yr
Tuition: $78 per cr hr
Courses: Art History, Ceramics, Painting, Drawing, Fashion Arts, Painting, Photography, Printmaking, Sculpture, Advertising Art, Arts & Crafts
Summer School: Two 5 wk terms

GENESEO

STATE UNIVERSITY OF NEW YORK COLLEGE AT GENESEO, Dept of Art, College of Arts & Science, 14454. Tel 716-245-5814; *Chmn* Carl Shanahan. Instrs: FT 8, PT 3
Estab 1871; pub; D & E; Scholarships; SC 35, LC 7; enrl D 1000, E 1150, maj 115
Ent Req: HS dipl, ent exam
Degrees: BA(Art) 3-4 yrs
Tuition: $2105 per yr
Courses: Art History, Ceramics, Drawing, Graphic Arts, Jewelry, Painting, Photography, Sculpture, Textile Design, Computer Art, Photolithography, Wood Design, 2-D & 3-D Design
Summer School: Enrl 180; tuition undergrad $45.85 per hr, grad $90.85 per hr for two 5 wk sessions & a 3 wk session. Courses vary

GENEVA

HOBART & WILLIAM SMITH COLLEGES, Art Dept, Houghton House, 14456-3397. Tel 315-781-3487; FAX 315-781-3560; *Chmn* Dan Ewing. Instrs: FT 6
Estab 1822; pvt; D; scholarships; SC 15, LC 8; enrl D 1800
Ent Req: HS dipl, ent exam
Degrees: BA & BS 4 yrs
Tuition: $27,255; room & board $6315
Courses: †Architecture, †Art History, Drawing, Mixed Media, Painting, Photography, Printmaking, Sculpture, †Studio Art

HAMILTON

COLGATE UNIVERSITY, Dept of Art & Art History, 309 Charles A Dana Arts Ctr, 13346. Tel 315-824-7633, 824-1000; FAX 315-824-7787; *Chmn* John Knecht, MFA; *Prof* Eric Van Schaack, PhD; *Prof* Jim Loveless, MFA; *Assoc Prof* Judith Oliver, PhD; *Assoc Prof* Robert McVaugh, PhD; *Assoc Prof* Lynn Schwarzer, MFA; *Asst Prof* Padma Kaimal, MA; *Asst Prof* Mary Ann Calo; *Asst Prof* Daniella Dooling; *Asst Prof* Carol Kinne
Estab 1819, dept estab 1905; pvt; D; scholarships; SC 22, LC 23; enrl D 941, maj 50
Ent Req: HS dipl, CEEB or ACT
Degrees: BA 4 yrs
Tuition: $13,595 per yr; campus res—room & board $4540
Courses: Art History, Drawing, Mixed Media, Painting, Photography, Printmaking, Sculpture, Combined Media, Motion Picture Productions

HEMPSTEAD

HOFSTRA UNIVERSITY
—Department of Fine Arts, Calkins Hall, Rm 118, 107 Hofstra University, 11550-1090. Tel 516-463-5474; *Chmn* Warren Insield. Instrs: FT 11
Estab 1935, dept estab 1945; pvt; D & E; scholarships; LC 20, GC 16; enrl D 1610, maj 100, grad 10
Ent Req: HS dipl
Degrees: BA, BFA, MA
Tuition: Undergrad $5215 per sem
Courses: Art History, Drawing, Graphic Arts, Jewelry, Painting, †Jewelry, †Painting, †Photography, †Sculpture, Appraisal of Art and Antiques
Summer School: Dean, Deanna Chitayat. Courses—Art History, Fine Arts

HERKIMER

HERKIMER COUNTY COMMUNITY COLLEGE, Liberal Arts & Public Service Division, 100 Reservoir Rd, 13350. Tel 315-866-0300, Ext 200; *Chmn* Richard Friedrich; *Prof* Guido Correro, MA; *Instr* James Bruce Schwabach, MFA
Estab 1966; pub; D & E; SC 8, LC 4; enrl D 329 (total), maj 16
Ent Req: HS dipl, SAT or ACT
Degrees: AA, AS & AAS 2 yrs
Tuition: Res—undergrad $940 per sem, $70 per cr hr; nonres—undergrad $2350 per sem; no campus res
Courses: Art Appreciation, Art History, Drawing, Painting, Photography, Theatre Arts, Video
Adult Hobby Classes: Enrl 40 credit, 100 non-credit; tuition $33 per cr hr.
Courses—Art Appreciation, Calligraphy, Pastels, Portraits, Photography
Children's Classes: Enrl 40; tuition varies. Courses—Cartooning Workshop, Introduction to Drawing
Summer School: Dir, John Ribnikac. Enrl 40. Courses—Same as regular session

HOUGHTON

HOUGHTON COLLEGE, Art Dept, One Willard Ave, 14744. Tel 716-567-2211; *Head Art Dept* Ted Murphy
Estab 1883; den; D & E; scholarship; SC 8, LC 6
Degrees: AA & AS 2 yrs, BA & BS 4 yrs
Tuition: $4995 per sem
Courses: Ceramics, Drawing, Graphic Design, Painting, Photography, Printmaking, Sculpture

ITHACA

CORNELL UNIVERSITY
—**Dept of Art,** College of Architecture, Art & Planning, 14853. Tel 607-255-3558; FAX 607-255-3462; *Dean College* Anthony Vidler; *Chmn Dept* Jean Locey; *Prof* Steve Poleskie, BS; *Prof* Jack L Squier, MFA; *Assoc Prof* Zevi Blum, BArchit; *Assoc Prof* Stanley J Bowman; *Assoc Prof* Jean Locey, MFA; *Assoc Prof* Greg Page, MFA; *Assoc Prof* Elisabeth Meyer, MFA; *Assoc Prof* Roberto Bertoia; *Assoc Prof* Barry Perlus; *Asst Prof* W Stanley Taft; *Asst Prof* Kay Walking Stick; *Asst Prof* Gail Scott White
Estab 1868, dept estab 1921; pvt; D; scholarships; SC 25, LC 1, GC 4; enrl maj 118, grad 13
Ent Req: HS dipl, HS transcript, SAT
Degrees: BFA, MFA
Tuition: Res—$3870 per sem; nonres—$7450 per sem
Courses: Drawing, Painting, Photography, Printmaking, Sculpture
Summer School: Dir, Stanley Taft. Tuition $375 per cr for term of 3 & 6 wks beginning June 27
—**Dept of the History of Art,** College of Arts and Sciences, 35 Goldwin Smith Hall, 14853. Tel 607-255-4905; *Prof* Robert G Calkins, PhD; *Prof* Stanley J O'Connor, PhD; *Prof* Andrew Ramage, PhD; *Prof* Martie W Young, PhD; *Assoc Prof* Judith E Bernstock, PhD; *Assoc Prof* Hal Foster, PhD; *Assoc Prof* Peter I Kuniholm, PhD; *Assoc Prof* Claudia Lazzaro, PhD; *Assoc Prof* Laura L Meixner, PhD; *Asst Prof* Karen-edis Barzman, PhD
Estab 1939; pvt; D; scholarships; LC 64, GC 12; enrl D 1300, maj 40, grad 18, others 5
Ent Req: HS dipl, SAT, grad admission requires GRE
Degrees: BA, PhD
Tuition: Res—$3870 per sem; nonres—$7450 per sem
Courses: Art History, Classical Art & Architecture, 1940-1990 Art, Gothic Art & Architecture
Summer School: Dean, Glenn Altschuler. Tuition $410 per cr hr.
Courses—Introductory
—**New York State College of Human Ecology,** Dept of Design and Environmental Analysis, 14853-4401. Tel 607-255-2168; FAX 607-255-0305; *Chmn Dept* William R Sims. Instrs: FT 12
Scholarships
Degrees: BS, MA, MS, MPF
Tuition: Res—$3870 per sem; nonres—$7450 per sem
Courses: Interior Design, Facilities Planning & Management, Human Factors & Management

ITHACA COLLEGE, Fine Art Dept, 101 Ceracche Ctr, 14850-7277. Tel 607-274-3330; *Chmn* Harry McCue, MFA; *Assoc Prof* Raymond Ghirardo; *Assoc Prof* Susan Weisend; *Assoc Prof* Joy Adams; *Asst Prof* Carl Johnson
Estab 1892, dept estab 1968; pvt; D & E; scholarships; SC 10; enrl non-maj 200, maj 40
Ent Req: HS dipl, SAT scores, review of portfolio
Degrees: BA and BFA 4 yrs
Tuition: $18,547 per yr; campus res—available
Courses: Art History, Drawing, Painting, Printmaking, Sculpture, Computer Art, Figure Drawing, Silkscreen, 2-D Design
Summer School: Chmn, Harry McCue. Enrl 10-20. Courses—Introduction to Drawing & Computer Art

JAMAICA

SAINT JOHN'S UNIVERSITY, Dept of Fine Arts, 8000 Utopia Pky, 11439. Tel 718-990-6161; FAX 718-990-1907; *Chmn* William Ronalds
Pvt; D; scholarships; SC 24, LC 9; enrl D 1300, maj 100
Ent Req: HS dipl, ent exam, portfolio review
Degrees: BFA & BS 4 yrs
Tuition: $312 per cr hr, $4700 per sem (12-18 cr)
Courses: †Graphic Design, †Photography, Saturday Scholarship Program, †Fine Arts
Adult Hobby Classes: Enrl 100; tuition $0 senior citizens. Courses—Drawing, Painting, Figure
Children's Classes: Enrl 300; tuition $0 advanced placement art. Courses—Airbrush, Cartoon
Summer School: Dir, Joyce Lawlor. Enrl 150-200; Courses—Drawing, Painting, Watercolor

YORK COLLEGE OF THE CITY UNIVERSITY OF NEW YORK, Fine & Performing Arts, 94-20 Guy Brewer Blvd, 11451. Tel 718-262-2400; *Coordr Fine Arts* Elena Borstein; *Prof* Jane Schuler, PhD; *Assoc Prof* Phillips Simkin, MFA; *Assoc Prof* Ernest Garthwaite, MA; *Assoc Prof* Arthur Anderson, MFA
Estab 1968; pub; D & E; enrl 4303
Ent Req: HS dipl
Degrees: BA 4 yrs
Tuition: Res—$1050 per sem, $100 per cr; nonres—$1338 per sem, $210 per cr; no campus res
Courses: Art Education, Art History, Drawing, Graphic Arts, Painting, Photography, Printmaking, Sculpture, Computer Graphics
Summer School: Dean, Wallace Schoenberg. Enrl $20 per course; tuition $47 per cr for term of 6 wks beginning late June. Courses—Art History, Drawing, Painting

JAMESTOWN

JAMESTOWN COMMUNITY COLLEGE, Arts & Humanities Division, 525 Falconer St, 14701. Tel 716-665-5220, Ext 394; FAX 716-665-9110; *Div Chmn* Bill Disbro. Instrs: FT 7, PT 12
Estab 1950, dept estab 1970; pub; D & E; SC 11, LC 1; enrl D 310, E 254
Ent Req: Open
Degrees: AA 60 cr hrs
Tuition: Res—$70 per cr hr; non res—$140 per cr hr
Courses: Ceramics, Drawing, Painting, Photography, Sculpture, Stage Design, Theatre Arts, Video, Computer Graphics, Design, Introduction to Visual Art, Survey of Visual Arts
Summer School: Dir, Dr Wade Davenport. Enrl 50-75; tuition res $77 per cr hr; non res $140 per cr hr, 2 terms of 6 wks beginning in May. Courses—Ceramics, Drawing, Painting, Photography

LOCH SHELDRAKE

SULLIVAN COUNTY COMMUNITY COLLEGE, Division of Commercial Art & Photography, 1000 Leroy Rd, PO Box 4002, 12759. Tel 914-434-5750, Ext 215; *Chmn Art Dept* Robert Glatt; *Prof* L Jack Agnew, MEd; *Assoc Prof* Earl Wertheim, BS; *Prof* Thomas Ambrosino, BPS; *Instructional Asst* Bernie Kroop, BPS
Estab 1962, dept estab 1965; pub; D & E; SC 24; enrl D 200, maj 180
Ent Req: HS dipl or equivalent
Degrees: AA, AS & AAS 2 yrs
Tuition: Res—undergrad $1000 per sem, $70 per cr; nonres—undergrad $1950 per sem, $155 per cr
Courses: Advertising Design, Commercial Art, Design, Drawing, Graphic Arts, Graphic Design, Photography, Computer Graphics
Summer School: Assoc Dean of Faculty for Community Services, Allan Dampman

LOUDONVILLE

SIENA COLLEGE, Dept of Creative Arts, 515 Loudon Rd, 12211. Tel 518-783-2300; FAX 518-783-4293; *Chmn* Greg Zoltowski
Tuition: $5400 per sem, $210 per cr hr
Courses: Aesthetics, Art Appreciation, Art History, Drawing, Graphic Design, History of Art & Archaeology, Mixed Media, Painting, Printmaking, Theatre Arts, Music
Adult Hobby Classes: Enrl 35; tuition $315 per cr hr for 15 wks.
Courses—Introduction to Visual Arts
Summer School: Enrl 35; tuition $315 per cr hr for 7 wk term. Courses—Intro to Visual Arts

MIDDLETOWN

ORANGE COUNTY COMMUNITY COLLEGE, Art Dept, 115 South St, 10940. Tel 914-343-1121; *Chmn Dept* Richard Heppner
Estab 1950, dept estab 1950; pub; D & E; scholarships; SC 12, LC 5; enrl D 135, maj 60
Ent Req: HS dipl
Degrees: AA 2 yrs, AAS(Visual Comm Graphics)
Tuition: $1050; no campus res
Courses: Art History, Design, Drawing, Painting, Photography, Sculpture, Color, Computer Graphic Design

NEW PALTZ

STATE UNIVERSITY OF NEW YORK COLLEGE AT NEW PALTZ
—**Art Studio Dept,** SAB 106, 12561-2499. Tel 914-257-3830; FAX 914-257-3859; *Chmn Art Studio & Art Educ* Francois DeSchamps. Instrs: 33
Pub
Degrees: BA, BS(Visual Arts), BFA, MA, MS, MFA
Tuition: res—$1500.50 per sem; nonres—$3450 per sem
Courses: Ceramics, Graphic Design, Painting, Photography, Printmaking, Sculpture, Metal
Summer School: Dir, Patricia C Phillips. Courses—Art Education
—**Art Education Program,** SAB 204, 12561. Tel 914-257-3850; *Dir* Kristin Rauch. Instrs: 3
Degrees: BA, MA
Tuition: res—$1500.50 per sem; nonres—$3450.50 per sem
Courses: Drawing, Painting, Photography, Printmaking, Sculpture
Summer School: Dir, Robert Davidson. 8 wk sem

NEW ROCHELLE

COLLEGE OF NEW ROCHELLE SCHOOL OF ARTS & SCIENCES, Art Dept, School of Arts and Sciences, 10805. Tel 914-654-5274; *Chmn* Susan Canning, PhD; *Prof* William C Maxwell; *Assoc Prof* Mary Jane Robertshaw, MFA; *Asst Prof* Cristina de gennaro; *Asst Prof* Emily Stein, MFA
Estab 1904, dept estab 1929; pvt; scholarships; SC 52, LC 14, GC 21; enrl D 150, non-maj 45, maj 105, grad 98
Ent Req: HS dipl, SAT or ACT scores, college preparatory program in high school
Degrees: BA, BFA and BS 4 yrs
Tuition: $9300 per yr; campus res— room and board $4320 per yr
Courses: Art Education, Art History, Ceramics, Collages, Design, Drawing, Film, Graphic Design, Intermedia, Interior Design, Jewelry, Mixed Media, Painting, Photography, Printmaking, Sculpture, Teacher Training, Weaving, †Art Therapy, Computer Graphics, Fiber Arts, Metalwork
Summer School: Dir, Jean Carlson. Enrl 400; tuition $180-$255 per cr for two terms of 5 wks beginning June. Courses—Compute Graphics, Drawing, Painting, Photography & special workshops

NEW YORK

AESTHETIC REALISM FOUNDATION, 141 Greene St, 10012-3201. Tel 212-777-4490; FAX 212-777-4426; *Class Chmn Aesthetic Realism* Ellen Reiss; *Exec Dir* Margot Carpenter
Estab 1973, as a not for profit educational foundation to teach Aesthetic Realism, the philosophy founded by American poet & critic Eli Siegel (1902-1978), based on his historic principle: All beauty is a making one of opposites, and the making one of opposites is what we are going after in ourselves
Courses: Art History, Drawing, Theatre Arts, Art Criticism, Music, Poetry, Singing
Children's Classes: Learning to Like the World

AMERICAN ACADEMY IN ROME, 7 E 60th St, 10022. Tel 212-751-7200; FAX 212-751-7220; *Chmn* Michael I Sovern; *Pres* Adele Chatfield Taylor; *Exec VPres* Wayne Linker
Estab 1894, chartered by Congress 1905; consolidated with School of Classical Studies 1913; Dept of Musical Composition estab 1921; scholarships
Summer School: 28 fellowships

ARTIST STUDIO CENTERS, INC, 1651 Third Ave, 10128. Tel 212-348-3102; *Dir* James E Youngman
Estab 1956; pvt; D & E
Tuition: $105-$405 per month
Courses: Constructions, Drawing, Painting, Sculpture, Crafts all Media, Moldmaking, Sculpture Installation & Mounting, Sculpturing of Clay-Stone-Wax & Wood
Adult Hobby Classes: Enrl 70; tuition $4200 per yr for full time. Part time available. Courses—Moldmaking, Painting, Sculpture
Summer School: Dir, Jim Youngman. Courses—Painting, Sculpture

ART STUDENTS LEAGUE OF NEW YORK, 215 W 57th St, 10019. Tel 212-247-4510; *Instrs* FT 65
Estab 1875; pvt; scholarships; LC; enrl D 1200, E 600, Sat 500 (adults and children)
Ent Req: None
Tuition: $125 month full-time, $63 part-time
Courses: Drawing, Graphic Arts, Illustration, Painting, Sculpture
Children's Classes: Classes on Saturday
Summer School: Enrl 800, beginning June

BERNARD M BARUCH COLLEGE OF THE CITY UNIVERSITY OF NEW YORK, Art Dept, 46 E 26th St (Mailing add: 17 Lexington Ave, PO Box 281, 10010). Tel 212-802-2287, 802-6590; *Chmn* Mimi D'Aponte
Estab 1968; pub; D & E; SC 26, LC 16; enrl D 2000, E 500
Ent Req: HS dipl
Degrees: BA, BBA and BSEd 4 yrs, MBA 5 yrs, PhD
Tuition: Res—$1100 per sem, $92 per cr hr; nonres—$2400 per sem, $202 per cr hr
Courses: Advertising Design, Art History, Ceramics, Drawing, History of Art & Archaeology, Illustration, Painting, Photography, Sculpture, Computer Graphics
Summer School: Courses - Art History Survey, Ceramics, Crafts, Drawing, Painting, Photography

THE CHILDREN'S AID SOCIETY, Visual Arts Program of the Greenwich Village Center, 219 Sullivan St, 10012. Tel 212-254-3074; FAX 212-420-9153; *Dir* Risa Young
Estab 1854, dept estab 1968; D & E; scholarships; SC 7; enrl D 200, E 175
Tuition: Adults $175 per sem; children $150 per sem; no campus res
Courses: Ceramics, Collages, Drawing, Handicrafts, Jewelry, Painting, Photography, Comic Book Art, Enameling, Pottery, Puppet Making, Woodworking
Adult Hobby Classes: Enrl 95; tuition $60-$75 per sem. Courses—Cabinetmaking, Ceramics, Drawing, Enameling, Painting, Photography, Pottery
Children's Classes: Enrl 325; tuition $32-$42 per sem. Courses—Dance, Drawing, Enameling, Mixed Media, Painting, Photography, Puppet Making, Woodwork, Theatre & Mime
Summer School: Dir, H Zaremben & Allen M Hart

CITY COLLEGE OF NEW YORK, Art Dept, 138th St & Convent Ave, 10031. Tel 212-650-7000; *Chair* Elizabeth O'Connor; *Deputy Chair* Sylvia Netzer; *Dir Grad Studies* Michi Itami; *Supervisor Art Education* Joan Price, EdD; *Dir Museum Studies* Harriet F Senie
Estab 1847; pub; D & E; scholarships; SC 45, LC 29; enrl D 1043, E 133, maj 100, grad 122
Ent Req: HS dipl, entrance placement exams
Degrees: BA, MA, MFA
Tuition: Res—undergrad $650 per sem, $46 per cr hr, grad $950 per sem, $81 per cr hr; nonres—undergrad $937.50 per sem, $76 per cr hr, grad $1337.50 per sem, $116 per cr hr
Courses: Advertising Design, Aesthetics, Architecture, Art Appreciation, Art Education, Art History, Ceramics, Design, Drawing, Graphic Arts, Graphic Design,

History of Art & Archaeology, Intermedia, Interior Design, Mixed Media, Museum Staff Training, Painting, Photography, Printmaking, Sculpture
Adult Hobby Classes: Courses—Advertising & Design, Art History, Ceramics, Drawing, Graphics, Museum Studies, Painting, Photography, Sculpture

CITY UNIVERSITY OF NEW YORK, PhD Program in Art History, Grad School & Univ Ctr, 33 W 42nd St, 10036. Tel 212-642-2865; FAX 212-642-2845; *Distinguished Prof* Janet Cox-Rearick; *Distinguished Prof* Jack Flam; *Prof* Laurie Schneider Adams; *Prof* Rosemarie Haag Bletter; *Prof* Anna Chave; *Prof* George Corbin; *Prof* Rosalind Krauss, PhD; *Prof* William H Gerdts; *Prof* Mona Hadler; *Prof* Eloise Quinones Keber; *Prof* Diane Kelder; *Prof* Susan Koslow; *Prof* Gail Levin; *Prof* Patricia Mainardi; *Prof* Michael Mallory; *Prof* Marlene Park; *Prof Emeritus* Robert Pincus-Witten; *Prof Emeritus* Milton Brown; *Prof* Sally Webster; *Assoc Prof* Carol Armstrong; *Assoc Prof* Jane Roos
Estab 1961, prog estab 1971; pub; D; scholarships; LC 9, GC 8; enrl D 230
Ent Req: BA or MA in Art History
Degrees: PhD
Tuition: Res—$1675 per sem, $145 per cr hr; nonres—$2925 per sem, $250 per cr hr
Courses: Art History, African, Oceanic, Native American & Pre-Columbian Art & Architecture, Renaissance & Baroque Art & Architecture

COLUMBIA UNIVERSITY
—**Graduate School of Architecture, Planning & Preservation,** 400 Avery Hall, 1172 Amsterdam Ave, 10027. Tel 212-854-3414; FAX 212-864-0410; *Dean Architectural Planning* Bernard Tschumi; *Chmn Div Urban Design* Stan Allen; *Chmn Div Urban Planning* Sig Guava. Instrs: FT 31, PT 32
Estab 1881; pvt; scholarships & fels; enrl 400
Ent Req: Bachelor's degree in appropriate area of study
Degrees: MPlanning & MPreservation 2 yr, MArchit 3 yr
Tuition: $18,000
Courses: Architecture, Architecture & Urban Design, Historic Preservation, Urban Planning
—**Dept of Art History & Archaeology,** 826 Schermerhorn Hall, 10027. Tel 212-854-4505; FAX 212-854-7329; Telex 749-0397. *Chmn* Allen Staley; *Dir Grad Studies* Esther Pasztorri
Pvt
Degrees: MA, MPhil, PhD
Tuition: $18,000 per yr
Courses: Aesthetics, Architecture, Art Appreciation, Art History, History of Art & Archaeology, Classical Art & Archaeology, Far Eastern Art & Archaeology, History of Architecture, History of Western Art, Near Eastern Art & Archaeology, Primitive & Pre-Columbian Art & Archaeology, History & Theory of Art History
—**Columbia College,** 208 Hamilton Hall, 10027. Tel 212-854-2522; *Dean* Austin Quigley
Pvt, M; scholarships & fels
Degrees: BA & BS 4 yr
Tuition: $20,000 per yr
Courses: Art and Archaeology of South Eastern Asia, Asian Art and Archaeology, Classical Art and Archaeology, History of Western Art, Near Eastern Art and Archaeology, Primitive and Pre-Columbian Art and Archaeology
—**School of the Arts, Division of Visual Arts,** 310 Dodge Hall, 116th St & Broadway, 10027. Tel 212-854-2829, 854-4065; FAX 212-854-1309; *Chmn* Alan Hacklin; *Admin Asst* Jana Ragsdale; *Instr* Archie Rand; *Instr* Reeva Potoff; *Instr* Stuart Diamond; *Instr* Jonathan Kessler; *Instr* Nancy Bowen; *Instr* Gregory Amenoff; *Instr* David Chow; *Instr* Suzanne Joelson; *Instr* Elena Sistro; *Instr* Pier Consragra; *Instr* Suzanne Winkler; *Instr* Michael Board
Estab 1754, div estab 1945; pvt; D & E; scholarships
Ent Req: Special students required to have studied at the college level in an institution of higher learning, non-degree students are permitted to register for one or more courses in the division
Degrees: BA
Tuition: Undergrad $18,624 per yr, grad $19,000 per yr
Courses: Drawing, Painting, Printmaking, Sculpture
Summer School: Enrl 25. Two sessions per summer. Courses—Drawing & Painting
—**Barnard College,** Dept of Art History, 3009 Broadway, 10027. Tel 212-854-2118; *Chmn* Benjamin Buchloh
Estab 1923; pvt; W; scholarships; enrl maj 29, total 1930
Degrees: AB 4 yrs
Tuition: $16,228 per yr; campus res available
Courses: Art History, Drawing, Painting
—**Teachers Col Program in Art & Art Educ,** Teachers College, 525 W 120th St, 10027. Tel 212-678-3000, 678-3361; FAX 212-678-4048; *Dean* Karen Zumwalt; *Dir* Judith Burton
Estab 1888; pvt; scholarships, assistantships & fels; GC; enrl 225
Ent Req: Bachelor's degree & Portfolio review
Degrees: EDD, EDDCT, EDM, MA
Tuition: $520 per cr hr
Courses: Art Appreciation, Ceramics, Design, Drawing, Painting, Photography, Printmaking, Sculpture, Art Education, Artistic-Aesthetic Development, Crafts, Curriculum Design, Historical Foundations, Museum Studies, Painting Crafts, Philosophy of Art, Teacher Education
Adult Hobby Classes: Enrl 35; tuition $150 per 10 wk session

COOPER UNION, School of Art, Cooper Sq, 10003. Tel 212-353-4200; FAX 212-353-4345; *Dean* Robert Rindler, MED. Instrs: FT 10, PT 60
Estab 1859; pvt; D & E; scholarships
Ent Req: HS dipl, ent exam
Degrees: BFA 4 yr
Adult Hobby Classes: Extended Studies Prog
Children's Classes: Enrl 200. Courses—Pre College Art & Architecture for HS students
Summer School: Dir, Stephanie Hightower. Enrl 100. Courses—Same as above

EDUCATION ALLIANCE, Art School, 197 E Broadway, 10002. Tel 212-475-6200; FAX 212-982-0938; *Dir* Mischa Galperin
Scholarships offered
Degrees: Cert
Tuition: Varies per course
Courses: Ceramics, Drawing, Mixed Media, Painting, Photography, Sculpture, Metal Sculpture
Adult Hobby Classes: Enrl 150; 15 wk term; Courses—Painting, Drawing, Sculpture, Metal Sculpture, Ceramics, Photography, Photo Silk Screen
Children's Classes: Enrl 20; 30 wk term. Courses—Mixed Media
Summer School: Dir Clare J Kagel. Enrl 60; tuition by the course for 10 wk term. Courses—Painting, Sculpture

FASHION INSTITUTE OF TECHNOLOGY, Art & Design Division, Seventh Ave at 27th St, 10001-5992. Tel 212-760-7665; FAX 212-760-7160; *Dean* Mark Karlen; *Chmn Interior Design* Susan Forbes; *Chmn Fashion Design* Rose Rosa; *Chmn Advertising Design* Jerry McDaniel; *Chmn Fine Arts* M Frauenglass; *Chmn Illustrations* Jane Weller; *Chmn Photo* James Collier; *Chmn Display Design* G Murray; *Chmn Jewelry Design* Anthony Lent
Estab 1951; pub; D & E; scholarships; SC 317, LC 26; enrl D 4011, E 7004
Ent Req: HS dipl, ent exam
Degrees: AAS 2 yr, BFA 4 yr
Tuition: Res—undergrad $1200 per sem; nonres—undergrad $2825 per sem; campus res—room & board $4412 per yr
Courses: †Advertising Design, Art History, †Display, History of Art & Archaeology, †Illustration, †Interior Design, †Jewelry, Painting, †Photography, Printmaking, †Restoration & Conservation, Sculpture, Silversmithing, †Textile Design, Weaving, Accessories Design, Toy Design
Adult Hobby Classes: Part-time Studies
Summer School: VPres Student Affairs, Stayton Wood. Enrl 4589; tuition $78-$200 per course for term of 3, 5 & 7 wks beginning June. Courses—Same as above

HARRIET FEBLAND ART WORKSHOP, 245 E 63rd St, Ste 1803, 10021. Tel 212-759-2215; *Dir* Harriet FeBland; *Instr* Bernard Kassoy; *Instr* John Close
Estab 1962; pvt; D & E; SC 6, LC 1, GC 2; enrl D 85, others 25
Ent Req: Review of previous work, paintings or sculpture
Tuition: $750 per 15 wk class, $250 for 5 wk 1 hr critique session
Courses: Collages, Constructions, Drawing, Painting
Adult Hobby Classes: Enrl 65; $750 per sem (15 wk each sem). Courses—Advanced Painting, Assemblage, Construction, Drawing
Summer School: Workshops for 2 to 3 wks are given at various universities in US & England

FORDHAM UNIVERSITY, Art Dept, Arts Division, Lincoln Ctr, 113 W 60th St, 10023. Tel 212-636-6000; *Div Chmn* William Conlon. Instrs: FT 7
Estab 1968; pvt; D & E; scholarships; SC 18, LC 25; enrl D 900, E 1750, maj 56
Ent Req: HS dipl
Degrees: BA 4 yrs
Tuition: Undergrad—$365 per cr hr, grad $390 per cr hr; campus res available
Courses: Aesthetics, Costume Design & Construction, Drawing, Graphic Arts, History of Art & Archaeology, Painting, Photography, Sculpture, Stage Design, Teacher Training, Theatre Arts
Summer School: Dir, Dr Levak. Four terms per summer for 5 wks each

GREENWICH HOUSE POTTERY, 16 Jones St, 10014. Tel 212-242-4106; *Dir* Elizabeth Zawada; *Asst Dir* Lynne Lerner. Instrs: 26
Estab 1902, dept estab 1948; pvt; D & E; scholarships; SC 32; enrl D 200, E 94
Ent Req: None
Degrees: None
Tuition: $200 per sem; no campus res
Courses: Art History, Ceramics, Drawing, Sculpture, Glazing Chemistry
Adult Hobby Classes: Enrl 200; tuition $170 per 12 wk term. Courses—Pottery Wheel, Handbuilding, Sculpture
Children's Classes: Enrl 50; tuition $55 and $65 for 12 wk term. Creative technique instruction
Summer School: Dir, Susan B Wood. Enrl 40; tuition $160 per 4 wk term

HENRY STREET SETTLEMENT ARTS FOR LIVING CENTER, 466 Grand St, 10002. Tel 212-598-0400; FAX 212-505-8329; *Dir* Barbara Tate
Estab 1895; pvt; D; scholarships; enrl D 60, E 60
Ent Req: None
Tuition: $45-$175 per course
Courses: Calligraphy, Ceramics, Drawing, Graphic Arts, Mixed Media, Painting, Printmaking, Sculpture
Adult Hobby Classes: Courses—Crafts, Drawing, Painting, Pottery
Children's Classes: Courses—Arts & Crafts, Cartooning, Drawing, Experimental Art, Painting, Pottery, Printmaking

HUNTER COLLEGE, Art Dept, 695 Park Ave, 10021. Tel 212-772-4000; FAX 212-772-4458; *Chmn Art Dept* Sanford Wurmfeld; *Dean* Carlos Hortas. Instrs: FT 29
Estab 1890, dept estab 1935; pub; D & E; SC 20-25, LC 10, GC 14-20; enrl D 250 (including evening), maj 250, GS 250
Ent Req: HS dipl
Degrees: BA & BFA 4 yrs
Tuition: Res—$1225 per sem, $100 per cr hr; nonres—$2525 per sem, $210 per cr hr
Courses: Art History, Drawing, Painting

JOHN JAY COLLEGE OF CRIMINAL JUSTICE, Dept of Art, Music & Philosophy, 899 Tenth Ave, 10019-1029. Tel 212-237-8325; *Chmn* Patrick Collins; *Prof* Marlene Park, PhD; *Prof* Laurie Schneider, PhD; *Assoc Prof* Helen Ramsaran, MFA; *Lectr* Irene Gordon, AB. Instrs: FT 4, PT 3
Estab 1964, dept estab 1971; pub; D & E; SC 5, LC 6; enrl D 180, E 180
Ent Req: HS dipl
Degrees: BA and BS 4 yr
Tuition: Res—undergrad $1475 per sem, $125 per cr; nonres—undergrad $3400 per sem, $285 per cr
Courses: Art History, Drawing, Painting, Sculpture

LOWER EAST SIDE PRINTSHOP, 59-61 E Fourth St, 6th Flr, 10003. Tel 212-673-5390; FAX 212-979-6493; Elec Mail lesp@ingress.com. *Exec Dir* Dusica Kirjakovic
Estab 1968; pvt; E; scholarships; SC 4; enrl E 32
Tuition: $180 per 3 month session
Adult Hobby Classes: Enrl 81; tuition up to $200 for 8 wks. Courses—Printmaking

MANHATTAN GRAPHICS CENTER, 481 Washington St, 10013. Tel 212-219-8783; *Pres* John Kirby; *VPres* Randolph Huebsch
Estab 1986; D & E
Courses: Photography, Printmaking
Adult Hobby Classes: Enrl 10; tuition $30 per wk. Courses—Etching, Lithography, Monotype, Silkscreen, Woodcut

MARYMOUNT MANHATTAN COLLEGE, Fine & Performing Arts Dept, 221 E 71st St, 10021. Tel 212-517-0400; FAX 212-517-0413; *Chmn* Mary Fleischer; *Prof* Bill Bordeau. Instrs: FT 12
Degrees: BA & BFA
Tuition: $10,700 per yr, $315 per cr hr
Courses: Advertising Design, Art Appreciation, Ceramics, Design, Drawing, Illustration, Museum Staff Training, Painting, Photography, Printmaking

NATIONAL ACADEMY SCHOOL OF FINE ARTS, 5 E 89th St, 10128. Tel 212-996-1908; FAX 212-426-1711; *Dir* Charles O'Connor. Instrs: 35
Estab 1826; pvt; D, E & weekends; scholarships; SC 16; enrl 500
Ent Req: None
Tuition: $2700
Courses: Drawing, Painting, Printmaking, Sculpture, Anatomy, Composition-Portraiture, Drawing the Classical Orders, Life Sketch Class, Methods & Techniques, Painting Materials, Perspective
Adult Hobby Classes: Enrl 500; tuition $200 per class, $825 per sem, $1230 per yr. Courses—Drawing, Painting, Printmaking, Sculpture & related subjects
Children's Classes: Enrl 25; tuition varies per workshop intensive or master class. Courses ages 9-16 & older—Drawing & Painting
Summer School: Dir, Edward P Gallagher, Adminr, Ellen Lee Klein. Enrl 150.Courses—Drawing, Painting, Printmaking, Sculpture

NEW SCHOOL FOR SOCIAL RESEARCH, Adult Education Division, 66 W 12th St, 10011. Tel 212-229-5600; FAX 212-929-2456; *Dean* Elizabeth Dickey
Tuition: $450 per course
Courses: Advertising Design, Art Appreciation, Art History, Calligraphy, Ceramics, Design, Drawing, Fashion Arts, Film, Jewelry, Painting, Photography, Printmaking, Sculpture, Textile Design, Fine Art, Cartooning, Glassblowing
Adult Hobby Classes: Enrl 1500; tuition $220 per course. Courses—All fine arts
Children's Classes: Summer Program for Young Adults
Summer School: Dir, Wallis Osterholz. Enrl 500; 6 wk term. Courses—All fine arts

NEW YORK ACADEMY OF ART, Graduate School of Figurative Art, 111 Franklin St, 10013. Tel 212-966-0300; FAX 212-966-3217; *Pres* Bruce W Ferguson; *Dir* Barbara S Krulik; *Assoc Dean* David Davidson; *Chmn* Martha Mayer Erlebacher; *Instr* Edward Schmidt; *Instr* Harvey Citron; *Instr* Randolph Melick; *Instr* Eric Fischl; *Instr* Vincent Desiderio
Scholarships
Degrees: MFA 2 yrs, part-time MFA 4 yrs
Tuition: Full-time $13,000 per yr
Courses: Art History, †Drawing, History of Art & Archaeology, †Painting, †Sculpture, Anatomy
Adult Hobby Classes: Enrl 150; tuition $350-$400 per course for 12 wk term. Courses—Anatomy, Drawing, Painting, Sculpture
Summer School: Dir, David Davidson. Enrl 150; tuition $225 per course for 8 wk term. Courses—Anatomy, Drawing, Painting, Sculpture

NEW YORK INSTITUTE OF PHOTOGRAPHY, 211 E 43rd St, 10017. Tel 212-867-8260; FAX 212-867-8122; *Dean* Charles DeLaney; *Dir* Donald Sheff
Estab 1910; Correspondence course in photography approved by New York State and approved for veterans; enrl 10,000
Degrees: Cert of graduation
Tuition: $748
Courses: Still Photography

NEW YORK SCHOOL OF INTERIOR DESIGN, 170 E 70th St, 10021. Tel 212-472-1500; FAX 212-472-3800; *Pres* Inge Heckel
Estab 1916; pvt; D & E; scholarships; enrl D 700
Ent Req: HS dipl, application & interview
Degrees: AAS, BFA
Tuition: $5850 per sem; no campus res
Courses: Architecture, Art History, Drafting, Drawing, †Interior Design, Color, Space Planning, Design Materials
Summer School: Assoc Dean, Ethel Rompilla. Enrl 500; tuition $425 per cr

NEW YORK STUDIO SCHOOL OF DRAWING, PAINTING & SCULPTURE, 8 W Eighth St, 10011. Tel 212-673-6466; FAX 212-777-0996; *Dean* Graham Nickson; *Prog Dir* Ro Lohin; *Instr* Robert Bordo; *Instr* Garth Evans; *Instr* Bruce Gagnier; *Instr* Elena Sisto; *Instr* Charles Cajori; *Instr* Riley Brewster; *Instr* Ruth Miller; *Instr* Mathew Radford; *Instr* Mercedes Matter; *Instr* Glenn Goldberg; *Instr* Jake Berthol; *Instr* Carole Robb; *Instr* Hugh O'Donnell
Estab 1964; pvt; D; scholarships; SC 13, LC 2; enrl D 80
Ent Req: HS dipl, portfolio of recent work
Tuition: $3300 per sem; campus res—available
Courses: Drawing, Painting, Sculpture
Adult Hobby Classes: Enrl 40; tuition $185 per 16 wks. Courses—Drawing (from the model)
Summer School: Program Dir, Ofra Shemesh. Enrl 60; tuition $1200 for term of 8 wks beginning June. Courses— Drawing, Painting, Sculpture

NEW YORK UNIVERSITY, Institute of Fine Arts, One E 78th St, 10021. Tel 212-772-5800; FAX 212-772-5807; *Dir* James R McCredie
Pvt; D & E; scholarships & fels; enrl grad 400
Tuition: $1700 per course
Courses: History of Art & Archaeology, Conservation and Technology of Works of Art; Curatorial Staff Training
—Dept of Art & Art Professions, 34 Stuyvesant St, 10003. Tel 212-998-5700; FAX 212-995-4320; *Chmn* Leonard Lehrer, MFA; *Dir Undergraduate Studies* Judith S Schwartz, PhD; *Prof* Angiola R Churchill, EdD; *Prof* David W Ecker, EdD; *Prof* Marilynn G P Karp, PhD; *Prof* Laurie Wilson, PhD; *Assoc Prof* Carlo Lamagna, MA; *Assoc Prof* Peter Campus, BS; *Assoc Prof* Judith Reiter Weissman, PhD; *Assoc Prof* John Torreano, MFA; *Artist-in-Residence* N Krishna Reddy; *Artist-in-Residence* Gerald Pryor, MA. Instrs: FT 10, PT 72
Pvt; D & E; scholarships and fels; undergrad SC 26, LC 13, grad SC 40, LC 25; enrl maj undergrad 115, grad 230
Ent Req: Col board ent exam, 85 HS average, portfolio, interview
Degrees: BS, MA, EdD, DA, PhD
Tuition: $520 per cr
Courses: †Art Education, Ceramics, Collages, †Drawing, †Intermedia, Jewelry, Mixed Media, †Painting, †Photography, †Printmaking, †Sculpture, Teacher Training, Video, Arts Administration, Art Therapy, Computer Art, Costume Studies, Dealership & Collecting Folk Art, Studio Art
Summer School: Tuition $470 per cr. Four summer sessions 3-wk period, four days a wk; International Overseas Prog in Studio Arts in Venice, Italy; three summer prog, two summers abroad & one in New York (8 wks each summer) - Arts Administration in Utrecht & Berlin

PACE UNIVERSITY, Theatre & Fine Arts Dept, Pace Plaza, 10038. Tel 212-346-1352; *Chmn* Dr Lee Evans
Estab 1950; pvt; D & E; scholarships; SC 4, LC 20; enrl D 200, E 150, 700-800 per yr art only
Ent Req: HS dipl, ent exam
Degrees: 4 yr, Art History Major
Tuition: $6355 per sem, $398 per cr hr; campus res—available
Courses: Art History, Drawing, Graphic Design, Modern Art, Oriental Art, Studio Art
Adult Hobby Classes: Courses same as above
Summer School: Two summer sessions. Courses—Studio Art

PARSONS SCHOOL OF DESIGN, 66 Fifth Ave, 6th Flr, 10011. Tel 212-229-8910; *Dean* Charles S Olton, PhD
Estab 1896; pvt (see also Otis Art Institute of Parsons School of Design, Los Angeles, California); D & E; scholarships; SC 200, LC 400, GC 25; enrl D 1800, E 4000, GS 25, other 40
Ent Req: HS dipl, portfolio
Degrees: AAS, BFA, BBA, MA, MFA & MArch
Tuition: $15,030 per yr, $510 per cr; campus res—room & board $7000
Courses: †Advertising Design, Aesthetics, Architecture, †Art Education, Art History, Calligraphy, †Ceramics, †Commercial Art, Fashion Arts, Graphic Design, History of Art & Archaeology, Illustration, Industrial Design, Interior Design, Jewelry, Painting, Photography, Sculpture, †Textile Design, †Fine Arts, †History of Decorative Arts, Lighting Design, Marketing & Fashion Merchandising, Product Design
Adult Hobby Classes: Enrl 4200; tuition $374 per cr for term of 12 wks.
Courses—Advertising, Computer Graphics, Fashion Design, Fine Arts, Floral Design, Illustration, Interior Design, Lighting Design, Marketing & Merchandising, Product Design, Surface Decoration, Theatre Design
Summer School: Dir, Francine Goldenhar. Tuition $4000 for term of 4-6 wks.
Courses—Art, Art History, Design

PRATT INSTITUTE, Pratt Manhattan, 295 Lafayette St, 10012. Tel 212-925-8481; FAX 212-941-6397; *Chmn* Elliott Gordon
Estab 1892; pvt; D; scholarships
Ent Req: HS dipl, portfolio, interview
Degrees: AOS, 2 yrs
Tuition: $504 per cr; campus res available
Courses: Advertising Design, Art History, Commercial Art, Design, Graphic Design, Illustration, Computer Graphics

SCHOOL OF VISUAL ARTS, 209 E 23rd St, 10010. Tel 212-592-2000, Div Continuing Educ 592-2050; FAX 212-725-3587; *Chmn* Silas H Rhodes; *Pres* David Rhodes
Estab 1947; pvt; scholarships; enrl FT 2541, PT 2316
Ent Req: HS transcript, portfolio review, SAT or ACT test results, interview, 2 letters of recommendation
Degrees: BFA, MFA, teachers' cert (K-12) in Art Educ
Tuition: $13,000 plus fees per yr
Courses: †Advertising Design, †Art Education, Art History, Ceramics, Commercial Art, Conceptual Art, Design, Display, Drafting, Drawing, †Film, Graphic Arts, †Graphic Design, History of Art & Archaeology, †Illustration, Intermedia, †Interior Design, Mixed Media, †Painting, †Photography, †Printmaking, †Sculpture, Silversmithing, Teacher Training, †Video, †Animation, †Cartooning, †Computer Art
Adult Hobby Classes: Enrl 2353; tuition $165 per cr for 12 wks/sem.
Courses—Advertising & Graphic Design, Art Education, Art History, Art Therapy, Computer Art, Craft Arts, Film & Video, Fine Arts, Humanities Sciences, Illustration & Cartooning, Interior Design, Photography
Children's Classes: Enrl 195; tuition $150/course-8wks/sem. Courses—Cartooning, Design, Drawing, Film, Interior Design, Painting, Photography, Portfolio Preparation, Sculpture
Summer School: Dir, Joseph Cipri. Enrl 2148 tuition $165 per cr/10 wks.
Courses—Same as adult education classes, Archaeology in Greece, Painting in Barcelona

SCHOOL OF VISUAL ARTS, 209 E 23rd St, 10010-3994. Tel 212-592-2144; FAX 212-592-2095; *Dir* Francis Di Tommaso; *Asst Dir* Meg Asaro; *Gallery Mgr* Lane Twitchell
Estab 1947; pvt; D & E; enrl D 2473, E 11,500, grad 287

Ent Req: HS dipl, SAT or ACT
Degrees: BFA 4 yr, MFA 2 yr
Tuition: Res—undergrad $13,000 per yr; nonres—undergrad $13,000 per yr; res—grad $14,700 per yr; nonres—grad $14,700; campus res—room & board $5500 per yr
Courses: †Advertising Design, Aesthetics, Art Appreciation, †Art Education, Art History, Calligraphy, Ceramics, Collages, †Commercial Art, Conceptual Art, Constructions, Costume Design & Construction, Design, Display, Drawing, †Film, Graphic Arts, †Graphic Design, History of Art & Archaeology, †Illustration, Intermedia, †Interior Design, Lettering, Mixed Media, †Painting, †Photography, Printmaking. Sculpture, Teacher Training, †Video
Adult Hobby Classes: Enrl 350; tuition $330 per class
Summer School: Enrl 3500; tuition $330 per class

SCULPTURE CENTER GALLERY & SCHOOL, 167 E 69th St, 10021. Tel 212-737-9870, 879-3500; FAX 212-861-7439; *Dir* Michael Cochran; *Gallery Dir* Marion Griffith
Estab 1933; pvt; D & E; scholarships
Tuition: $100 to $200 per course
Courses: Sculpture, Sculpture (stone, wood, welding, plaster molds, bronze casting)
Adult Hobby Classes: Enrl 102; tuition $50-$300 per month during June - Aug.
Courses same as regular sem
Children's Classes: Enrl 16; tuition $45 per month. Courses—Sculpture (clay, wood, stone & plaster)
Summer School: Dir, G L Sussman. Enrl 100; tuition $50 - $300. Courses—Same as reg session plus special seminars

SKOWHEGAN SCHOOL OF PAINTING & SCULPTURE, 200 Park Ave S, Ste 1116, 10003-1503. Tel 212-529-0505; FAX 212-473-1342; *Exec Dir Develop & Admin* Cecilia C Clarke; *Exec Dir Prog* Tom Finkelpearl. Instrs: 10
Estab 1946; nine wk summer residency prog for independent work; fels; enrl 65
Ent Req: Proficient in English, 19 years of age & slide portfolio
Degrees: Credits recognized for transfer, no degrees
Tuition: $5200 includes room & board
Courses: No academic work; individual critiques only
Summer School: Enrl 65; 9 wk summer res prog in Maine for independent work.
Contact admin office at 200 Park Ave S, No 116, New York, NY 10003

WOOD TOBE-COBURN SCHOOL (Formerly Tobe-Coburn School), 8 E 40th St, 10016. Tel 212-686-9040; FAX 212-686-9171; *Pres* Sandi Gruninger. Instrs: FT 7, PT 10
Estab 1937; pvt; D; scholarships; 2 yr course, 16 months, for HS grad; 1 yr course, 9-12 months, for those with 15 or more transferable college sem cr, classroom study alternates with periods of work in stores or projects in fashion field; enrl 250
Degrees: AOS(Occupational Studies)
Tuition: $5060 per yr
Courses: Display, Fashion Arts, Fabrics, Fashion Design, Fashion Merchandising, Marketing & Management

NIAGARA FALLS

NIAGARA UNIVERSITY, Fine Arts Dept, De Veaux Campus, 14109. Tel 716-285-2090; *Chmn* Sharon Watkinson
Tuition: $3750 per sem
Courses: Art Appreciation, Art History, Ceramics, Drawing, Painting
Adult Hobby Classes: Enrl 150; tuition $85 per sem. Courses—Ceramics, Painting
Summer School: Dir, L Centofanti. Enrl 25; tuition $185 per sem hr.
Courses—Ceramics

OAKDALE

DOWLING COLLEGE, Dept of Visual Arts, Idle Hour Blvd, 11769. Tel 516-244-3099; FAX 516-589-6644; *Div Coordr* Dr Stephen Lamia; *Instr* Filomena Romano; *Instr* Panchita Carter; *Instr* Siobhan Conaty; *Instr* Marina Delaney; *Instr* Patricia Pickett; *Instr* Felicitas Wetter; *Instr* Mary Abell; *Instr* Ellen Goldin; *Instr* Seung Lee; *Instr* Colin Lee; *Instr* Anthony Grimaldi; *Instr* Elissa Iberti; *Instr* Woody Hughes; *Instr* Kathy Levine; *Instr* Christina Staudt
Pvt; D & E; enrl D 1100, E 500
Ent Req: HS dipl
Degrees: BA(Visual Art), BS and BBA 4 yrs
Tuition: $339 per cr hr
Courses: Advertising Design, Art History, Calligraphy, Ceramics, Costume Design & Construction, Design, Drawing, Goldsmithing, Graphic Arts, Graphic Design, History of Art & Archaeology, Illustration, Jewelry, Lettering, Painting, Photography, Printmaking, Sculpture, Textile Design, Art Criticism, Life Drawing, 2-D & 3-D Design

OLD WESTBURY

NEW YORK INSTITUTE OF TECHNOLOGY, Fine Arts Dept, Wheatley Rd, 11568. Tel 516-686-7543; *Chmn & Assoc Prof* Peter Voci; *Prof* John Murray; *Prof* Valdis Kupris, MFA; *Prof* Faye Fayerman, MFA; *Assoc Prof* Albert Prohaska, MA; *Assoc Prof* Nieves Micas; *Asst Prof* Felix Zbarsky; *Asst Prof* Lev Poliakov; *Asst Prof* Jaduiga Przybylak; *Asst Prof* Gary Viskupic; *Asst Prof* Domenic Alfano; *Adjunct Asst Prof* Steven Woodburn, MFA; *Instr* Walter Leighton, MFA; *Instr* James DeWoody, MFA; *Instr* Ruben Cruz, MA; *Instr* Martin Clements, MA
Estab 1910, dept estab 1963; pvt; D; scholarships; SC 11, LC 85; enrl D 427, non-maj 100, maj 327
Ent Req: HS dipl, portfolio review
Degrees: BFA 4 yr
Tuition: $310 per cr; no campus res
Courses: †Advertising Design, Aesthetics, †Architecture, Art Appreciation, †Art Education, Art History, Calligraphy, Graphic Arts, †Graphic Design, Illustration, †Interior Design, Lettering, Mixed Media, Painting, Photography, Printmaking, Sculpture, Computer Graphics
Summer School: Tuition $80 per cr for term of 8 wks. Courses—Drawing, Interior Design, Painting, Sculpture

STATE UNIVERSITY OF NEW YORK COLLEGE AT OLD WESTBURY,
Visual Arts Dept, PO Box 210, 11568. Tel 516-876-3000, 876-3056, 876-3135 (acad
affairs); *Chmn* Christine Griffin
Estab 1968, Dept estab 1969; pub; D & E; SC 10, LC 10; enrl D & E 277
Ent Req: HS dipl, skills proficiency exam, GED, special exception - inquire through
admissions
Degrees: BA & BS(Visual Arts) 4 yr
Tuition: Res—$1800 per sem, $137 per cr
Courses: Collages, Conceptual Art, History of Art & Archaeology, Mixed Media,
Painting, Photography, Printmaking, Sculpture, Video, TV Production/Editing

ONEONTA

HARTWICK COLLEGE, Art Dept, 13820. Tel 607-431-4825; *Chmn* Katharine
Kreisher, MFA; *Prof* Phil Young, MFA; *Prof* Roberta Griffith, MFA; *Asst Prof* Dr
Elizabeth Ayer; *Asst Prof* Terry Slade, MFA; *Assoc Prof* Dr Fiona Dejardin; *Asst
Prof* Gloria Escobar, MFA. Instrs: FT 7, PT 8
Estab 1797; pvt; D; scholarships; enrl 1500, non-maj 1433, maj 67
Ent Req: HS dipl, SAT or ACT, recommendation from teacher or counselor &
personal essay, $35 fee
Degrees: BA 4 yr
Tuition: $14,350 per yr; campus res—$4450
Courses: †Art History, Ceramics, Drawing, Graphic Design, Painting, Photography,
Printmaking, Sculpture, Teacher Training, †Studio
Summer School: High sch arts workshop, 3 wks in July

STATE UNIVERSITY OF NEW YORK COLLEGE AT ONEONTA, Dept of Art,
Ravine Pky, 13820. Tel 607-436-3500; *Chmn* Alan Farber; *Instr* Nancy Callahan;
Instr Andrea Modica, MFA; *Instr* Daniel Young; *Instr* Yolanda Sharpe
Estab 1889; pub; D & E; SC 31, LC 22; enrl D 660, E 35, maj 123, 25-30 at
Cooperstown Center
Ent Req: Ent req HS dipl, regents scholarship exam, SAT & ACT
Degrees: Degrees BA(Studio Art, Art History) other programs include: one leading
to MA(Museum History, Folk Art) in conjunction with the New York State
Historical Association at Cooperstown, NY 13326 (Daniel R Porter III, SUNY Dir);
a 3-1 program in conjunction with the Fashion Institute of Technology in New York
City, with 3 years at Oneonta as a Studio Art major leading to a BS degree and/or 1
year at FIT leading to a AAS(Advertising & Communications, Advertising Design,
Apparel Production & Management, Fashion Buying & Merchandising, Fashion
Design, Textile Design, and/or Textile Technology
Tuition: Res—$1325 per sem; nonres—$3275 per sem
Courses: Art History, Ceramics, Drawing, Painting, Computer Art, Images of
Women in Western Art, 2-D Design, 3- D Design, Visual Arts
Adult Hobby Classes: Offered only on a subscription basis at normal tuition rates
through the Office of Continuing Education
Summer School: Dir, Dr Robert Nichols. Enrl 40-50. Tuition same as in regular
session for two 4 & 5 wk terms beginning June and July. Courses—Studio

ORANGEBURG

DOMINICAN COLLEGE OF BLAUVELT, Art Dept, 470 Western Hwy, 10962.
Tel 914-359-7800; FAX 914-359-2313; *Chmn* Sr Margaret J Gillis; *Dir Dept Arts &
Science* William Hurst
Degrees: BS & BA 4 yr
Tuition: $4155 per sem, $277 per cr
Courses: Art Education, Art History, Drawing, Painting
Adult Hobby Classes: Enrl 40; tuition $117 per cr. Courses—Art History, Painting
Summer School: Dir, S Florence Dwyer. Enrl 35; tuition $117 per cr.
Courses—History of Art, Watercolor

OSSINING

ADAMY'S CONCRETE & CAST PAPER WORKSHOPS, 11-1 Woods Brooke
Circle, 10562-2025. Tel 914-941-1157; FAX 914-941-2986;
Internet Home Page Address http://www.together.net/~lewis/gpa.html. *Dir* George
E Adamy, MBA. Instrs: FT 1, PT 1
Estab 1968; pvt; D & E; SC 13, LC 2, GC 13; enrl D 20, E 30
Tuition: From $30 per hr (open-ended sessions) to $225 for 10 sessions of advanced
courses. Individual arrangements for special projects or commissions, & for lect &
demonstrations at other schools, museums, art organizations; no campus res
Courses: Collages, Museum Staff Training, †Sculpture, †Teacher Training, Plastics,
Polyadam Concrete & H-M (Hand-Made) Paper Casting & Construction
Adult Hobby Classes: Courses offered
Children's Classes: Courses offered
Summer School: Courses offered

OSWEGO

STATE UNIVERSITY OF NEW YORK COLLEGE AT OSWEGO, Art Dept, 125
Tyler Hall, 13126. Tel 315-341-2111; FAX 315-341-3394; *Chmn* Sewall Oertling.
Instrs: FT 18
Estab 1861; pub; D & E; SC 31, LC 9; enrl maj 150, grad 10
Ent Req: HS dipl, SAT or NYS regents scholarship exam
Degrees: BA 4 yr, BFA 4 yr, MA 2 yr
Tuition: Res—$1325 per sem, $105 per cr hr; nonres—$3275 per sem, $274 per cr
hr
Courses: Aesthetics, †Art History, †Ceramics, †Drawing, †Graphic Arts, †Graphic
Design, Museum Staff Training, †Painting, †Photography, †Printmaking, Jewelry/
Metalsmithing
Summer School: Dir, Lewis C Popham III. Tuition state grad res $90.85 per cr hr,
non-grad res $45.85 per cr hr, grad nonres $156.85 per cr hr, non-grad nonres $107.
85 per cr hr

PLATTSBURGH

CLINTON COMMUNITY COLLEGE, Art Dept, Lake Shore Rd, Rte 9 S (Mailing
add: 136 Clinton Point Dr, 12901). Tel 518-562-4200; FAX 518-561-8261; *Chmn*
Bonnie Black
Degrees: AS & AA 2 yr
Tuition: Res—$76 per cr hr; nonres—$152 per cr hr
Courses: Art Appreciation, Design, Drawing, Painting, Photography, Sculpture

STATE UNIVERSITY OF NEW YORK AT PLATTSBURGH, Art Dept, Myers
Fine Arts Bldg, 101 Broad St, 12901. Tel 518-564-2179; FAX 518-564-7827; *Chmn*
Rick Mikkelson, MFA. Instrs: FT 9, PT 4
Estab 1789; dept estab 1930; pub; D & E; scholarships; SC 30, LC 10; enrl D 700,
maj 120
Ent Req: HS dipl, EOP
Degrees: BA & BS 4 yr
Tuition: $2650 per yr; campus res available
Courses: †Art History, †Ceramics, †Design, †Drawing, †Graphic Arts, †Graphic
Design, Illustration, Lettering, Mixed Media, †Painting, †Photography,
†Printmaking, †Sculpture, †Computer Graphics

PLEASANTVILLE

PACE UNIVERSITY, Dyson College of Arts & Sciences, Fine Arts Dept, Bedford
Rd, 10570. Tel 914-773-3675; *Assoc Dean Arts & Science* Ruth Anne Thompson;
Chmn John Mulgrew, MA; *Prof* Barbara Friedman, MFA; *Prof* Janetta Benton,
PhD; *Prof* Linda Gottesfeld, MFA; *Prof* Roger Sayre, MFA. Instrs: FT 5, PT 12
Pvt; D & E; SC 4, LC 4
Ent Req: HS dipl
Degrees: AA & BS
Tuition: Full-time—$5900 per sem; part-time—$380 per cr hr; campus res available
Courses: Aesthetics, Architecture, Art Appreciation, Art History, Ceramics,
Commercial Art, Design, Drawing, Graphic Arts, Graphic Design, History of Art &
Archaeology, Illustration, Industrial Design, Interior Design, Painting, Photography,
Printmaking, Sculpture, Teacher Training, Theatre Arts, Typography
Summer School: Dir, Prof John Mulgrew. Courses—Art History, Ceramics,
Drawing, Painting

POTSDAM

STATE UNIVERSITY OF NEW YORK COLLEGE AT POTSDAM, Dept of Fine
Arts, 13676. Tel 315-267-2251; *Chmn & Prof* James Sutter, MFA; *Prof* Arthur
Sennett, MFA; *Prof* John Riordan; *Prof* Michelle Van Parys, MFA; *Asst Prof* Tracy
Watts, PhD
Estab 1948; pub; D & E
Ent Req: HS dipl, SAT, portfolio review recommended
Degrees: BA 4 yrs, special program Empire State studio sem in New York City
Tuition: Res—undergrad lower div $1300 per yr, $615 per sem, $35.85 per cr hr;
nonres—undergrad lower div $2120 per yr; no grad students; campus res—$675
room & $560 (10 meals per wk) per sem
Courses: †Art History, †Ceramics, Drawing, †Painting, Photography, †Printmaking,
†Sculpture
Adult Hobby Classes: Enrl 15; tuition $30 for 10 weeks. Courses—Pottery
Children's Classes: Enrl 30; tuition $20 for 6 weeks. Courses—General Art
Workshop
Summer School: Dir, Joe Hildreth. Enrl 50-60; tuition $180 for 4 cr class of 5
weeks. Courses—Ceramic Survey, Intro to Studio Art

POUGHKEEPSIE

DUTCHESS COMMUNITY COLLEGE, Dept of Visual Arts, 53 Pendell Rd,
12601. Tel 914-431-8000; *Dir* Eric Somers
Estab 1957; pub; D & E; scholarships; SC 24, LC 22; enrl D 660, E 340, maj 100
Ent Req: HS dipl
Degrees: AAS (Commercial Art)
Tuition: $900 per sem, $73 per cr hr
Courses: Painting, Photography, Glass, Leather, Metal, Plastic, Weaving, Wood

VASSAR COLLEGE, Art Dept, 125 Raymond Ave, 12601. Tel 914-437-5220; FAX
914-437-7187; *Chmn* Nicholas Adams; *Prof* E A Carroll; *Prof* Susan D Kuretsky;
Assoc Prof Peter Charlap; *Assoc Prof* Peter Huenink; *Assoc Prof* Karen Lucic;
Assoc Prof Brian Lukacher; *Assoc Prof* Molly Nesbit; *Asst Prof* Eve D'Ambra; *Asst
Prof* Andrew Watsky. Instrs: FT 10, PT 7
Estab 1861; pvt; D; scholarships; SC 8; enrl maj 90, others 2400
Ent Req: HS grad, ent exam
Degrees: BA(Art History) 4 yr
Tuition: $18,920 per yr; campus res—room & board $5950
Courses: Architecture, Art History, Drafting, Drawing, Painting, Printmaking,
Sculpture

PURCHASE

MANHATTANVILLE COLLEGE, Art Dept, 2900 Purchase St, 10577. Tel 914-
694-2200, Ext 5331; FAX 914-694-2386; *Head Dept* Randolph Williams
Estab 1841; pvt; D & E; scholarships; SC 25, LC 10, GC 7; enrl D 180, non-maj 90,
maj 90, grad 10
Ent Req: HS dipl, portfolio, interview
Degrees: BA and BFA 4 yrs, MAT 1 yr, special prog MATA (Masters of Art in
Teaching Art)
Tuition: $14,700 per yr; room & board $6550
Courses: Advertising Design, Art Education, Art History, Ceramics, Commercial
Art, Conceptual Art, Constructions, Design, Drawing, Graphic Arts, Graphic
Design, Illustration, Lettering, Painting, Photography, Printmaking, Sculpture,
Teacher Training, Book Design, Metal Sculpture
Summer School: Dir, Donna Messina. Two sessions June & July. Courses—Art
History, Ceramics, Computer Graphics, Drawing, Painting, Sculpture

STATE UNIVERSITY OF NEW YORK COLLEGE AT PURCHASE
—Division of Visual Arts, 735 Anderson Hill Rd, 10577-1400. Tel 914-251-6750;
FAX 914-251-6793; *Dean* Ken Strickland; *Asst Dean* John Esser. Instrs: FT 18, PT 18
Estab 1974; pub; scholarships; enrl 3600, maj 400
Degrees: BFA 4 yr, MFA 2 or 3 yr
Tuition: Res—undergrad $2650 per yr; nonres—$6550 per yr
Courses: Art History, Drawing, Graphic Design, Painting, Printmaking,
Photography, Art of the Book, Design in Wood, Media, 3-D Design
Adult Hobby Classes: Enrl 450-500
Children's Classes: Enrl 50; summer session art program
Summer School: Dir, Laura Evans. Enrl 400; 6 wk sessions
—Art History Board of Study, 735 Anderson Hill Rd, 10577-1400. Tel 914-251-
6550; *Coordr* Jane Kromm; *Prof* Irving Sandler, PhD; *Assoc Prof* Paul Kaplan, PhD;
Asst Prof Elizabeth Guffey
Estab 1971, dept estab 1977; pub; D & E; scholarships; enrl 2500, maj 50
Ent Req: HS dipl, essay on application, grades, test scores
Degrees: BA & BALA 4 yrs
Tuition: Res—$2650 per yr; nonres—$6550 per yr
Courses: Art History

RIVERDALE

COLLEGE OF MOUNT SAINT VINCENT, Fine Arts Dept, 6301 Riverdale Ave,
10471-1093. Tel 718-549-8000; FAX 718-601-6392; *Prof* Enrico Giordana, BFA;
Prof Richard Barnett
Estab 1911; pvt; D & E; scholarships; SC 22, LC 10; enrl D 950, E 50
Ent Req: HS dipl and SAT
Degrees: BA, BS and BS(Art Educ) 4 yrs
Tuition: $11,790 per yr
Courses: Art History, Ceramics, Design, Drawing, Painting, Photography
Summer School: Dir Continuing Education, Dr Marjorie Connelly. Courses—vary
each summer

ROCHESTER

MONROE COMMUNITY COLLEGE, Art Dept, 1000 E Henrietta Rd, 14623. Tel
716-292-2000; FAX 716-427-2749; *Prof* George C McDade, MA; *Assoc Prof* Bruce
R Brown, MFA; *Assoc Prof* Joe Hendrick; *Assoc Prof* Juliana F Williams; *Asst Prof*
Charles W Haas, MFA
Estab 1961; pub; D & E; SC 16, LC 4
Ent Req: HS dipl
Degrees: Assoc in Arts 2 yrs, Assoc in Science 2 yrs, Assoc in Applied Science 2
yrs
Tuition: $1345 per nine months
Courses: Art History, Ceramics, †Commercial Art, Drafting, Drawing, Graphic Arts,
Graphic Design, Handicrafts, Illustration, Jewelry, Lettering, Painting, Printmaking,
Sculpture, Textile Design, Theatre Arts, Video, Weaving
Adult Hobby Classes: Tuition $36 per hr. Courses—Batik, Ceramics, Jewelry,
Leatherwork, Macrame, Rugmaking, Soft Sculpture, Weaving
Summer School: Dir, George C McDade

NAZARETH COLLEGE OF ROCHESTER, Art Dept, 4245 East Ave, 14618. Tel
716-586-2525, Ext 521; FAX 716-586-2452; *Head Dept* Ron Netsky; *Prof* Kathy
Calderwood, BFA; *Prof* Maureen Brilla, MFA; *Prof* Lynn Duggan, MFA; *Assoc
Prof* Roger J Adams; *Asst Prof* Karen Trickey, MSEd; *Asst Prof* Mitchell Messina;
Asst Prof Judy Natal
Estab 1926, dept estab 1936; pvt; D & E; scholarships; SC 40, LC 15, GC 6; enrl D
180, E 74, non-maj 50, maj 200, grad 48
Ent Req: HS dipl
Degrees: BA and BS 4 yrs
Tuition: Undergrad $5425 per sem, $316 per cr hr; board $3580 per yr
Courses: †Art Education, †Art History, Ceramics, Drawing, †Graphic Arts, Jewelry,
Painting, Photography, Printmaking, Sculpture, Textile Design, Art Therapy,
Computer Graphics
Summer School: 6 wks beginning July 5th. Courses—Grad & undergrad

ROBERTS WESLEYAN COLLEGE, Art Dept, 2301 Westside Dr, 14624. Tel 716-
594-9471; *Dir* Loren Baker; *Prof* Willard Peterson; *Assoc Prof* Douglas Giebel
Scholarships
Degrees: BA(Fine Art), BA(Studio Art), BS(Studio Art), BS(Art Education)
Tuition: $4511 per sem
Courses: Art Appreciation, Art Education, Art History, Ceramics, Design, Drawing,
Graphic Design, Jewelry, Lettering, Painting, Photography, Printmaking, Sculpture,
Weaving

ROCHESTER INSTITUTE OF TECHNOLOGY
—College of Imaging Arts & Sciences, One Lomb Memorial Dr, 14623. Tel 716-
475-2646; FAX 716-475-6447; *Dean Col* Dr Margaret Lucas; *Assoc Dean Col* Carol
Sack; *Asst Dir* Steve Loar; *Asst Dir Admin* Becky Eddy; *Dir* Dr Tom Morin
Degrees: BFA, MFA
Tuition: Undergrad $333 per cr, grad $432 per cr
Courses: Illustration, Jewelry, Computer Graphics, Metals
Adult Hobby Classes: Courses offered
Children's Classes: One wk summer workshop for juniors in HS
Summer School: 5 wk sessions, 2 1/2 wk sessions, & special one wk workshops
—School of Art & Design, College of Fine & Applied Arts, One Lomb Memorial
Dr, 14623. Tel 716-475-2646; FAX 716-475-6447; *Chmn Fine Arts & Prof* Luvon
Sheppart; *Chmn Graphic Design & Prof* Mary Anne Begland; *Chmn Industrial,
Interior & Packaging Design* Toby Thompson; *Chmn Foundation Studies & Assoc
Prof* Joyce Hertzson; *Chmn Crafts* Michael White; *Prof* Kener E Bond Jr, BEd; *Prof*
Frederick Lipp, MFA; *Prof* R Roger Remington, MS; *Prof* Joanne Szabla, PhD; *Prof*
James E Thomas, MFA; *Prof* Lawrence Williams, MFA; *Prof* Philip W Bornarth;
Prof Barbara Hodik, PhD; *Prof* James Ver Hague; *Prof* Robert A Cole, MS; *Prof*
Robert Heischman, UCFA; *Prof* Craig McArt, MFA; *Prof* William Keyser, MFA;
Prof Doug Sigler, MFA; *Prof* Robert Schmitz, MFA; *Prof* Richard Hirsch, MFA;

Prof Richard Tanner, MS; *Prof* Michael Taylor, MFA; *Prof* Mark Stanitz, MA; *Prof*
Len Urso, MFA; *Prof* Max Lenderman; *Prof* Albert Paley; *Prof* Wendell Castle,
MFA; *Prof* Robert C Morgan, PhD; *Prof* James H Sias, MA; *Prof* Robert Wabnitz,
Dipl & Cert; *Assoc Prof* Edward C Miller, MFA; *Assoc Prof* Bruce Sodervick,
MFA; *Assoc Prof* Joseph A Watson, MFA; *Assoc Prof* Robert M Kahute, MFA;
Assoc Prof Steve Loar, MA; *Asst Prof* Heinz Klinkon, BFA; *Asst Prof* Doug
Cleminshaw, MFA; *Asst Prof* Elizabeth Fomin, MFA; *Asst Prof* Glen Hintz, MFA;
Asst Prof Thomas Lightfoot, PhD. Instrs: FT 47, PT 19
Estab 1829; pvt; enrl 1000
Ent Req: HS grad, ent exam, portfolio
Degrees: BFA, MFA
Tuition: Undergrad $333 per cr, grad $425 per cr
Courses: Drawing, Illustration, Jewelry, History of Art & Archaeology, †Illustration,
†Industrial Design, †Interior Design, †Jewelry, Sculpture, †Silversmithing, †Textile
Design, †Weaving, Computer Graphics, Glass Blowing, Stained Glass
Adult Hobby Classes: Crafts, Design, Painting
Summer School: Enrl 250; tuition undergrad $260 per cr, grad $330 per cr for 8 wk
term beginning June. Courses—Ceramics, Computer Graphics, Glass, Graphic
Design, Metal, Painting, Printmaking, Textiles, Wood, Industrial, Interior, Packaging
Design, Art History, 2-D and 3-D Design
—School of Photographic Arts & Sciences, One Lomb Memorial Dr, Rochester,
14623-5604. Tel 716-475-2716; FAX 716-475-5804; *Dir* Elaine O'Neil, MS; *Assoc
Dir* Nancy Stuart, AB; *Chmn Imaging & Photographic Technology* Andrew
Davidhazy, MEd; *Chmn Fine Arts Photo* Ken White; *Chmn Film/Video* Howard
Lester; *Chmn Biomedical Photo Communications* Michael Peres; *Chmn American
Video Institute* John Ciampa, JD; *Chmn Photographic Processing & Finishing
Management* James Rice, BS; *Prof* John E Karpen, MFA; *Prof* Weston D Kemp,
MFA; *Prof* Lothar K Engelmann, PhD; *Prof* Russell C Kraus, EdD; *Prof* David J
Robertson, MFA; *Assoc Prof* Owen Butler, BFA; *Assoc Prof* Kerry Coppin; *Assoc
Prof* Jeff Weiss; *Assoc Prof* Patti Ambroge; *Assoc Prof* Bradley T Hindson, BA;
Assoc Prof Alan Vogel; *Assoc Prof* Robert Kayser, BS; *Assoc Prof* James Reilly,
MA; *Assoc Prof* Guenther Cartwright, BA; *Assoc Prof* Howard Lester, MFA; *Assoc
Prof* Howard LeVant, BS; *Assoc Prof* Elliott Rubenstein, MA; *Assoc Prof* Erik
Timmerman, BS; *Assoc Prof* Douglas F Rea, MFA; *Assoc Prof* Steve Diehl, BS;
Assoc Prof Mark Haven, BA; *Assoc Prof* John Retallack, BA; *Assoc Prof* Nancy
Stuart, MS; *Asst Prof* Ken White; *Asst Prof* Tom Lopez; *Asst Prof* Stephanie
Maxwell; *Asst Prof* Bruce Lane; *Asst Prof* Adrianne Carrageorge; *Asst Prof* Lorett
Falkner; *Asst Prof* Deni Defenbaugh; *Asst Prof* Sabrine Susstrink; *Asst Prof* Kaleen
Moriority; *Asst Prof* Jack Holm; *Asst Prof* Glen Miller; *Asst Prof* William
Osterman, MFA; *Asst Prof* Martha Leinroth, MFA; *Lectr* Dan Larken
Enrl 900
Degrees: AA, BA, MA
Tuition: Undergrad $333 per cr, grad $425 per cr
Courses: Film, Photography, Video, Advertising, Biomedical Photography, Film
Studies, Photographic Communications, Photographic Technology, Processing &
Finishing
Summer School: Courses—Photography, Film/Video, Motion Picture Workshops,
Narrative/Documentary/Editorial workshop, Nature Photography
—School of Printing, College of Imaging Arts & Sciences, One Lomb Memorial
Dr, 14623. Tel 716-475-2728; FAX 716-475-7029; *Dir* Harold Gaffin; *Chmn Design
Composition Division* Emery E Schneider, BS & MEd; *Coordr Grad Prog* Joseph L
Noga, MS; *Paul & Louise Miller Prof* Robert G Hacker, BS; *Prof* Barbara Birkett,
BS; *Prof* Miles F Southworth, BS; *Assoc Prof* William H Birkett, BS; *Assoc Prof*
Clifton T Frazier, BS; *Assoc Prof* Herbert H Johnson, BS; *Assoc Prof* Archibald D
Provan, BS; *Assoc Prof* Werner Rebsamen, dipl; *Asst Prof* Robert Y Chung, BA;
Asst Prof Hugh R Fox, AB & JD; *Asst Prof* David P Pankow, BA & MA
School has 25 laboratories, occupying 125,000 sq ft. More than 70 courses are
offered; enrl 700
Degrees: BS, MS
Tuition: Undergrad $333 per cr, grad $425 per cr
Courses: Printmaking, Color Separation, Flexography, Gravure, Ink & Color,
Introduction to Book Production, Newspaper Design, Systems Planning, Typography
& Design
Summer School: Graphic Arts, Layout & Printing, Reproduction Photography, Ink
& Color, Newspaper & Magazine Design, Hand Papermaking, Web Offset, Gravure,
Lithography, Printing Plates, Typography, Bookbinding
—School of Art & Design & School for American Craft, 73 Lomb Memorial Dr, PO
Box 9887, 14623. Tel 716-475-2732, 475-6447; *Dean* Dr Margaret Lucas; *Dir*
Thomas Morin
Degrees: BS, BFA, MS, MST
Tuition: Undergrad $333 per cr, grad $425 per cr
Courses: Ceramics, Furniture & Wood Working, Glass, Metals, Textiles
Adult Hobby Classes: Extensive seminar schedule
Summer School: scholarships

UNIVERSITY OF ROCHESTER, Dept of Art & Art History, 424 Morey Hall,
14627. Tel 716-275-9249; *Chmn* Michael Ann Holly. Instrs: FT 10, PT 5
Estab 1902; scholarships; SC 25, LC 25; enrl maj 15, others 600
Degrees: MA, PhD(Visual & Cultural Studies)
Tuition: $19,630 per yr
Courses: Art History, Painting, Photography, Sculpture
Summer School: Enrl 40; tuition & duration vary. Courses—Beginning Photography

SANBORN

NIAGARA COUNTY COMMUNITY COLLEGE, Fine Arts Division, 3111
Saunders Settlement Rd, 14132. Tel 716-731-3271, 731-4101, Ext 480; *Chmn* Paul
Seland. Instrs: FT 15, PT 14
Estab 1965; pub; D & E; SC 12, LC 4; enrl D 400, E 120, maj 140
Ent Req: HS dipl
Degrees: AS(Fine Arts) 2 yrs
Tuition: In state $1125 per sem; out of state $1687.50 per sem
Courses: Art Education, †Drawing, †Graphic Design, Illustration, †Painting,
Photography, Sculpture, Art Therapy, Visual Art

SARATOGA SPRINGS

SKIDMORE COLLEGE, Dept of Art & Art History, N Broadway, 12866. Tel 518-584-5000; *Chmn* Doretta M Miller. Instrs: FT 20
Estab 1911; pvt; scholarships; SC 32, LC 18; enrl maj 350, 2000 total
Ent Req: HS grad, 16 cr, ent exam, portfolio
Degrees: BA & BS 4 yrs
Courses: Art History, Ceramics, Design, Drawing, Graphic Design, Painting, Photography, Printmaking, Sculpture, Computer Imaging, Design, Jewelry/Metalsmithing, Weaving
Summer School: Dir, Regis Brodie. Enrl 194 for two 6 wk sessions.
Courses—Advanced Studio & Independent Study, Art History, Ceramics, Drawing, Etching, Jewelry, Lettering, Painting, Photography, Sculpture, 2-D Design, Vidio, Watercolor, Weaving

SCHENECTADY

UNION COLLEGE, Dept of Visual Arts, Arts Bldg, 12308. Tel 518-388-6714; *Chmn Visual Arts* Walter Hatke. Instrs: FT 10
Estab 1795; pvt; D; scholarships; SC 14, LC 4; enrl maj 35
Ent Req: HS dipl, ent exam
Degrees: BA with emphasis in music, art or theatre arts 4 yr
Tuition: $13,500 per yr
Courses: Art History, Drawing, Painting, Photography, Printmaking, Sculpture, Stage Design, Theatre Arts, 3-D, †Visual Arts
Adult Hobby Classes: Enrl 30; tuition $1390 & lab fee for 10 wks.
Courses—Drawing, Photography
Children's Classes: Enrl 15; tuition $250 wk for 3 one wk sessions
Summer School: Dean, Jane Zacek. Enrl 30; tuition $1390 & lab fee for 6 wks.
Courses—Art History, Drawing, 3-D, Painting, Photography, Printmaking

SEA CLIFF

STEVENSON ACADEMY OF TRADITIONAL PAINTING, 361 Glen Ave, 11579. Tel 516-676-6611; *Head Dept* Alma Gallanos Stevenson. Instrs: FT 2
Estab 1960; pvt; E; SC 3, LC 5; enrl 95
Ent Req: Interview
Tuition: $325 per 10 wk sem, one evening per wk
Courses: Drawing, Illustration, Painting, Artistic Anatomy, Basic Form
Summer School: Enrl 57; tuition $250 per term of 8 wks beginning June-July.
Courses—Artistic Anatomy, Drawing, Painting

SELDEN

SUFFOLK COUNTY COMMUNITY COLLEGE, Art Dept, 533 College Rd, 11784. Tel 516-451-4110; *Dept Head* Arthur Kleinfelder. Instrs: FT 6, PT 6
Degrees: AFA
Tuition: Res—$79 per cr; nonres—$158 per cr
Courses: Art Appreciation, Art History, Ceramics, Design, Drawing, Painting, Printmaking
Adult Hobby Classes: Enrl 200; tuition $15 per hr. Courses—Photography, Interior Design
Summer School: Dir, Maurice Flecker. Tuition res $60 per cr for 6-8 wk sessions.
Courses—Painting, Sculpture, 2-D Design, Life Drawing, Printmaking & Ceramics

SOUTHAMPTON

SOUTHAMPTON COLLEGE OF LONG ISLAND UNIVERSITY, Arts & Media Division, 11968. Tel 516-287-8427; FAX 516-287-8435; *Div Dir* R Marc Fasanella; *Prof* Yosh Higa, MGA; *Assoc Prof* Roy Nicholson; *Assoc Prof* Neill Slaughter; *Assoc Prof* P Kudder-Sullivan; *Asst Prof* Catherine Bernard, PhD; *Asst Prof* Jerry Domatob, PhD
Estab 1963; pvt; D & E; scholarships; SC 36, LC 17, GC 11; enrl D 398, E 20, non-maj 100, maj 280, grad 20, others 18
Ent Req: HS dipl and portfolio review
Degrees: BFA, BS(Art Educ), BA(Fine Arts), 4 yrs, MA Educ
Tuition: $5150 per sem; campus res—room & board $2340 per sem
Courses: Advertising Design, Aesthetics, Art Appreciation, †Art Education, Art History, Calligraphy, Ceramics, Collages, Commercial Art, Conceptual Art, Constructions, Design, Drafting, Drawing, Film, Graphic Arts, †Graphic Design, History of Art & Archaeology, Illustration, Jewelry, Lettering, Mixed Media, Museum Staff Training, †Painting, †Photography, Printmaking, Sculpture, Stage Design, Theatre Arts, Communications Arts, Computer Graphics, Public Relations
Adult Hobby Classes: Courses—Drawing, Painting, Photography, Various Crafts
Children's Classes: 8 wk summer children's prog
Summer School: Dir, Jon Fraser. Tuition $325 per cr hr for three 4 wk sessions.
Courses—Master Workshop in Art & various other courses

SPARKHILL

SAINT THOMAS AQUINAS COLLEGE, Art Dept, 125 Rte 340, 10976. Tel 914-359-9500, Ext 211; FAX 914-359-8136; *Prof* Carl Rattner, MFA; *Assoc Prof* George Jones; *Instr* Sr Adele Myers, MFA; *Instr* Sr Elizabeth Slenker, MFA
Estab 1952, dept estab 1969; pvt; D & E; scholarships; enrl D 1100, maj 50
Ent Req: HS dipl
Degrees: BA and BS 4 yrs
Tuition: $6450 per yr; campus res—available
Courses: Advertising Design, Art Education, Ceramics, Commercial Art, Drawing, Jewelry, Painting, Photography, Printmaking, Sculpture, Teacher Training, Textile Design, Theatre Arts, Video, Art Therapy
Summer School: Dir, Dr Joseph Keane. Tuition $210 for 3 cr course.
Courses—Varies 3-6 art courses including Ceramics, Painting, Photography

STATEN ISLAND

COLLEGE OF STATEN ISLAND, Performing & Creative Arts Dept, 2800 Victory Blvd, 10314. Tel 718-982-2000; FAX 718-982-2537; *Dir* Eugene Matta
Degrees: BA & MA(Cinema Studies), BS(Art), BS(Photography)
Tuition: Res—undergrad $1225 per sem, grad $1800 per sem
Courses: Advertising Design, †Architecture, †Art Appreciation, Art Education, †Art History, †Design, †Drawing, †Film, †Museum Staff Training, †Painting, †Photography, †Printmaking, Sculpture, Video
Summer School: Courses offered

WAGNER COLLEGE, Performing & Visual Arts Dept, Howard Ave, 10301. Tel 718-390-3192, 390-3100; FAX 718-390-3467; *Chmn* Richard W Gaffney
Estab 1948; den; D & E; SC 20, LC 6; enrl maj 35, others 2000
Ent Req: HS grad
Degrees: BA(Art), BS(Art Admin)
Tuition: Res—undergrad campus res $13,500 per yr; campus res—room & board $5000
Courses: Advertising Design, Art History, Ceramics, Drawing, Graphic Arts, Mixed Media, Painting, Photography, Printmaking, Sculpture, Crafts Design, 3-D Design, 2-D Design
Summer School: Two sessions of 4 wks

STONE RIDGE

ULSTER COUNTY COMMUNITY COLLEGE, Dept of Visual Arts, Cottekill Rd, 12484. Tel 914-687-5066; *Head Dept* Allan Cohen, MFA; *Prof* John A Locke III, MFA; *Prof* Peter Correia, MS; *Instr Asst* Susan Jeffers, BFA. Instrs: PT 5
Estab 1963; pub; D & E; SC 17, LC 6; enrl D 540, E 120, non-maj 590, maj 70
Ent Req: HS dipl
Degrees: AA 2 yrs, AS 2 yrs
Tuition: Res—undergrad $1185 per yr; nonres—undergrad $2370 per yr; no campus res
Courses: Advertising Design, Aesthetics, Art History, Drawing, †Graphic Design, Painting, Photography, Theatre Arts, Computer Art, Computer Assisted Graphic Design, Desk-Top Publishing, Life Drawing & Anatomy, 3-D Design, 2-D Design
Summer School: Dir, Allen Cohen. Enrl 30 - 50; tuition $198 per 3 sem hrs for 6 wks. Courses—Computer Art, Drawing, Painting, Photography

STONY BROOK

STATE UNIVERSITY OF NEW YORK AT STONY BROOK, Art Dept, 11794-5400. Tel 516-632-7250; FAX 516-632-7261; *Chmn* James Rubin, PhD; *Prof* Jacques Guilmain, PhD; *Prof* Donald B Kuspit, PhD; *Prof* Nina Mallory, PhD; *Prof* Howardena Pindell, MFA; *Prof* Toby Buonagurio, MA; *Prof* Michele H Bogart, PhD; *Prof* Anita Moskowitz, PhD; *Assoc Prof* Michael Edelson; *Asst Prof* Barbara Frank, PhD; *Asst Prof* Dan Monk, PhD; *Asst Prof* Zaihab Bahrani, Phd; *Asst Prof* Martin Levine, MFA
Estab 1957; pub; D; SC 33, LC 39; enrl D 1850
Ent Req: HS dipl, SAT
Degrees: BA(Art History) & BA(Studio Art), MA(Art History & Criticism), MFA(Studio Art), PhD(Art History & Criticism)
Tuition: Res—grad $5100 per yr; nonres—grad $8416 per yr
Courses: †Art History, Ceramics, Conceptual Art, Design, Drawing, History of Art & Archaeology, Painting, Photography, Printmaking, Sculpture, Printmaking, Sculpture, Studio Art
Summer School: Tuition res—undergrad $45 per cr hr, grad $90 per cr hr; nonres—undergrad $107 per cr hr, grad $156 per cr hr for term of 6 wks (two sessions). Courses vary in areas of Art Education, Art History & Criticism, Studio Art

SUFFERN

ROCKLAND COMMUNITY COLLEGE, Graphic Arts & Advertising Tech Dept, 145 College Rd, 10901. Tel 914-574-4251; FAX 914-356-1529; *Discipline Coordr* Emily Harvey
Estab 1965; pub; D & E; SC plus apprenticeships; enrl D 900, E 300, maj 200
Ent Req: Open
Degrees: AAS 2 yrs
Tuition: Res—$85.50 per sem hr; nonres—$171 per sem hr
Courses: Advertising Design, Art Appreciation, Art History, Drawing, Graphic Arts, Graphic Design, Lettering, Painting, Photography, Sculpture, Art Therapy, Color Production, Electric Art, Alternative Processes in Photography, Lithography, Portfolio Workshop, Serigraphy Printing
Adult Hobby Classes: Enrl 528; tuition varies. Courses—Ceramics, Crafts
Summer School: Dir, Emily Harvey. Enrl 180; June - Aug. Courses—Computer Graphics, Drawing, Overseas Program, Painting, Sculpture

SYRACUSE

LE MOYNE COLLEGE, Fine Arts Dept, Le Moyne Heights, 13214-1399. Tel 315-445-4100, 445-4147; *Chmn & Prof* Jacqueline Belfort-Chalat; *Adjunct Asst Prof* Barry Darling; *Adjunct Asst Prof* Charles Wollowitz; *Adjunct Instr* Charles Aho, MA; *Adjunct Instr* William West
Pvt; D; SC 4, LC 1; enrl non-maj 350
Ent Req: HS dipl, SAT or ACT
Degrees: BS & BA 4 yrs
Tuition: $9620 per yr, $224 per cr hr; campus res—room & board $4260 per yr
Courses: Art History, Drawing, Graphic Arts, Painting, Sculpture
Adult Hobby Classes: Dir Continuing Learning, Norbert Henry
Summer School: Dir Continuing Learning, Norbert Henry

SYRACUSE UNIVERSITY

—College of Visual & Performing Arts, School of Art & Design, 203 Crouse College, 13244-1010. Tel 315-443-2507; FAX 315-443-1935; *Dean* Donald M Lantzy, MFA; *Dir* Tom Sherman. Instrs: FT 60, PT 52
Estab 1873; pvt; D & E; scholarships; SC 200, LC 25, GC 100; enrl D 1200
Ent Req: HS dipl, portfolio review
Degrees: BID 5 yrs, BFA 4 yrs, MFA, MID & MA(Museum Studies) 2 yrs
Tuition: Undergrad $13,480 per yr; grad $406 per cr; campus res available
Courses: †Advertising Design, Art Education, †Art History, †Ceramics, Drawing, †Film, †Illustration, †Industrial Design, †Interior Design, †Painting, †Printmaking, †Sculpture, †Video, †Art Photography, †Computer Graphics, †Communications Design, †Metalsmithing, Papermaking, †Surface Pattern Design, †Museum Studies Program
Adult Hobby Classes: Vice Pres, Thomas Cummings. Enrl 155; tuition undergrad $276 per cr. Courses—same as above
Children's Classes: Enrl 80; tuition $50 per sem. Courses—general art
Summer School: Dean, Thomas O'Shea. Tuition undergrad $408 per cr, grad $456 per cr. Courses—same as above
—Dept of Fine Arts (Art History), 308 Bowen Hall, 13244-1200. Tel 315-443-4148, 443-4186; *Prof* Gary Radke, PhD; *Prof* David Tatham, PhD; *Prof* Meredith Lillich, PhD; *Prof* Wayne Franits PhD; *Prof* Laurinda Dixon, PhD; *Prof* Mary Marien, PhD; *Prof* Peg Weiss, PhD; *Prof* Bert Winther, PhD
Estab 1870, dept estab 1946; pvt; D & E; scholarships; LC 25, GC 15; enrl non-maj 900, maj 82, grad 46
Ent Req: HS dipl, SAT
Degrees: BA, MA
Tuition: Grad $456 per cr
Courses: Art History, Arts & Ideas, Baroque, Italian Medieval Art, Music

TARRYTOWN

MARYMOUNT COLLEGE, Art Dept, Neperhan Rd, 10591. Tel 914-631-3200; *Chmn* David Holt; *Prof* Bianca Haglich, RSHM; *Assoc Prof* Maria Chamberlin-Hellman; *Assoc Prof* Scott Ageloff; *Asst Prof* Carla Johnson
Estab 1918; pvt; D & E; schol; SC 42, LC 15; enrl D 806, Weekends 337
Ent Req: HS dipl, CEEB
Degrees: BA and BS 4 yrs
Tuition: Res—undergrad $10,350 per yr; nonres—undergrad $10,350 per yr; PT student $325 per hr; campus res—room board $5990 per yr
Courses: Advertising Design, Art Education, Art History, Ceramics, Drawing, Fashion Arts, Film, Handicrafts, Illustration, Interior Design, Mixed Media, Painting, Photography, Printmaking, Sculpture, Stage Design, Teacher Training, Textile Design, Theatre Arts, Weaving, Stitchery
Adult Hobby Classes: Changing lect series - continuing education
Summer School: Dir, Loretta Donovan. Tuition $165 per cr. Courses—Changing Studio & Art History courses

TROY

EMMA WILLARD SCHOOL, Arts Division, 285 Pawling Ave, 12180. Tel 518-274-4440, Ext 231; FAX 518-274-0923; *Div Chmn* Christine Leith
Estab 1814, dept estab 1969; pvt; D & E; scholarships
Tuition: $19,600 incl room & board
Courses: Art Appreciation, Art History, Ceramics, Drawing, Jewelry, Photography, Printmaking, Theatre Arts, Advanced Studio Art, Dance, Music, Visual Arts Foundation, Weaving

RENSSELAER POLYTECHNIC INSTITUTE

—School of Architecture, 110 Eighth St, 12180-3590. Tel 518-276-6466; FAX 518-276-3034; *Dean* Alan Balfour. Instrs: FT 18, PT 18
Estab 1929; pvt; D; scholarships; enrl 275
Degrees: BA(Archit, MA(Archit), MS(Lighting)
Tuition: Undergrad $17,745 per yr; grad $525 per cr hr
Courses: Design, History, Practice, Structure, Studio
Summer School: Architectural Design
—Dept of Art, School of Humanities and Social Science, 12180-3590. Tel 518-276-4778; *Chmn* Neil Rolnick, PhD
Scholarships & fels
Degrees: MFA (Electronic Arts) 2 1/2 - 3 yrs
Tuition: $12,250 annual tuition
Courses: Drawing, Painting, Sculpture, Video, Animation, Computer Music, Computer Graphics, Installation, Performance

RUSSELL SAGE COLLEGE, Visual & Performing Arts Dept, Schacht Fine Arts Ctr, 12180. Tel 518-270-2000; FAX 518-271-4545; *Chmn* Dr Richard Jones; *Dir Creative Arts* Marion Terenzio
Pvt, W; enrl 20-40 per class
Ent Req: HS grad
Degrees: Fine arts and divisional maj in Music, Art and Drama 4 yrs
Tuition: Res—undergrad $6175 per sem, $415 per cr hr; campus res—room & board $2822 per sem
Courses: †Arts Management, †Creative Arts Therapy, 2-D Design

UTICA

MOHAWK VALLEY COMMUNITY COLLEGE, Advertising Design & Production, 1101 Sherman Dr, 13510. Tel 315-792-5400; *Pres* Michael L Schafer, PhD; *Head Dept* Ronald Labuz, PhD; *Assoc Prof* James O'Looney, MS; *Assoc Prof* Henry Godlewski, BS; *Asst Prof* Larry Migliori; *Asst Prof* E Duane Isenberg, MA; *Asst Prof* Jerome Lalonde; *Asst Prof* Robert Duffek, BA; *Asst Prof* Robert Clarke, BFA; *Instr* Thomas Maneen; *Instr* Alex Piejko, BFA; *Instr* Kathleen Partridge, BFA; *Instr* Kenneth Murphy, BA; *Instr* Natalie Buda, MFA; *Instr* Christine Miller, MFA. Instrs: FT 16, ADJ 14
Estab 1947, dept estab 1955; pub; D & E; scholarships; SC 18 (over 2 yr period), LC 6 (over 2 yr period); enrl D 450, E varies, maj 450

Ent Req: HS dipl
Degrees: AAS 2 yrs
Tuition: $2000 per yr; campus res—available
Courses: †Advertising Design, Aesthetics, Art Appreciation, Art History, †Design, Drawing, Graphic Arts, Graphic Design, †Handicrafts, History of Art & Archaeology, Illustration, Lettering, Painting, †Photography, Textile Design, Weaving, Computer Graphics
Adult Hobby Classes: Enrl 440; tuition $1000 per 15 wks sem. Courses—Air Brush, Design, Illustration, Painting, Photography, Sketching, Watercolor
Summer School: Dir, Ronald Labuz. Enrl 40; tuition $200 per course. Courses—Drawing, Design, Photography

MUNSON-WILLIAMS-PROCTOR INSTITUTE, School of Art, 310 Genesee St, 13502. Tel 315-797-0000; *Dir* Clyde E McCulley, EdD; *Instr* Bryan McGrath, MFA; *Instr* James McDermid, MFA; *Instr* Francis Fiorentino, MFA; *Instr* Marjorie Salzillo, MFA; *Instr* Keith Sandman, MFA; *Instr* Lisa Gregg-Wightman, MA; *Instr* Alfred Wardle, BS
Estab 1941; pvt; scholarships; enrl adults 1900, children 533
Degrees: Dipl 2 yrs
Tuition: Nonres—undergrad $5000 per sem; res—$2500
Courses: Ceramics, Drawing, Painting, Photography, Printmaking, Sculpture, Dance, Metal Arts, Pottery, Humanities, 2-D & 3-D Design, Color Theory
Adult Hobby Classes: Enrl 805. Courses—Dance, Design, Drawing, Jewelry, Painting, Photography, Pottery, Printmaking, Sculpture
Children's Classes: Enrl 423. Courses - Dance, Drama, Drawing, Painting, Pottery
Summer School: Dir, Clyde E McCulley. Enrl 413, tuition $65 - $110 for 4 wk term. Courses—Dance Drawing, Jewelry Making, Painting, Photography, Pottery

UTICA COLLEGE OF SYRACUSE UNIVERSITY, Division of Humanities, Burrstone Rd, 13502. Tel 315-792-3057; FAX 315-792-3292; *Assoc Dean Humanities* Frank Bergmann
Estab 1946, school of art estab 1973; pvt; D; scholarships; SC 20, LC 7; enrl School of Art D 94, Utica College maj 14
Degrees: BS(Fine Arts) 4 yrs
Tuition: $14,206 per yr
Courses: Art History, †Ceramics, Design, Drafting, Drawing, Film, Graphic Arts, Occupational Therapy, †Painting, Photography, †Sculpture, Stage Design, Theatre Arts, Video

WATERTOWN

JEFFERSON COMMUNITY COLLEGE, Art Dept, Outer Coffeen St, 13601. Tel 315-786-2200; FAX 315-788-0716; *Pres* John Deans. Instrs: FT 1
Estab 1963; pub; D & E; SC 2, LC 1; enrl 850
Degrees: AA, AS & AAS 2 yr
Tuition: $888 per sem, $74 per cr hr
Courses: Art Appreciation, Art History, Ceramics, Photography, Sculpture, Computer-Aided Art & Design, Film Appreciation, Snow Sculpture, 2-D Studio
Summer School: Pres, John T Henderson

WEST NYACK

ROCKLAND CENTER FOR THE ARTS, 27 S Greenbush Rd, 10021. Tel 914-358-0877; FAX 914-358-0971; *School Dir* Petra Ludwig, MFA; *Exec Dir* Julianne Ramos, MFA
Estab 1947; pub; D & E; scholarships; SC 100; enrl D 1000, E 500
Courses: Calligraphy, Ceramics, Drawing, Handicrafts, Painting, Printmaking, Theatre Arts, Weaving, Creative Writing, Tai Chi
Adult Hobby Classes: Enrl 300; tuition $170 - $200 for twelve 3 hr sessions. Courses—Ceramics, Fine Arts & Crafts, Writing
Children's Classes: Enrl 300; tuition $110 for ten 1 1/2 hr sessions. Courses—same as above
Summer School: Dir, Lucy Brody. Enrl 100 children & 200 adults; tuition average $120 per 6 wks. Courses—same as above

WHITE PLAINS

WESTCHESTER COMMUNITY COLLEGE, Westchester Art Workshop, County Ctr, 196 Central Ave, 10606. Tel 914-684-0094; FAX 914-684-0608; *Dir* Wayne Kartzinel; *Prog Dir* Abre Chen. Instrs: 75
Estab 1926; pub; D & E; scholarships; SC 90 per sem, 5 sem per yr; enrl D 650, E 550, others 700 (credits given for most courses)
Ent Req: No special req
Degrees: AA, AS & AAS
Tuition: $98 per cr; no campus res
Courses: Art Appreciation, Calligraphy, Ceramics, Commercial Art, Design, Drawing, Goldsmithing, Graphic Arts, Graphic Design, Illustration, Jewelry, Mixed Media, Painting, Photography, Printmaking, Sculpture, Silversmithing, Video, Weaving, Art Foundation, Art Therapy, Computer Art Animation, Faux Finishes, Lost Wax Casting, Portrait Painting, Quilting, Stained Glass
Adult Hobby Classes: 100; $98 per cr Sept-May
Children's Classes: Enrl 150; tuition $132 for 12 wks. Courses—Cartooning, Ceramics, Drawing, Jewelry, Mixed Media, Painting
Summer School: 700; tuition $98 per cr. Courses—same as above

WOODSTOCK

WOODSTOCK SCHOOL OF ART, INC, PO Box 338, Rte 212, 12498. Tel 914-679-2388; FAX 914-679-2388; *Dir* Paula Nelson; *Instr* Mary Anna Goetz; *Instr* Deane Keller; *Instr* Anna Contes; *Instr* Karen O'Neil; *Instr* Kate Mcgloughlin; *Instr* Franklin Alexander; *Instr* Eric Angeloch; *Instr* Richard Segalman; *Instr* Roger Bischoff; *Instr* Zhang Hong Nian; *Instr* Richard McDaniel; *Instr* Peter Clapper; *Instr* Elizabeth Mowry; *Instr* Nancy Summers; *Instr* Robert Angeloch; *Instr* John Bradford; *Instr* Statts Fasoldt; *Instr* Ron Netsky; *Instr* Pablo Shine; *Instr* Lois

Woolley; *Instr* Pia Oste-Alexander
Estab 1968, dept estab 1981; pvt; D & E; Cert, fels & Artist Residency Prog; SC 19, LC 8; enrl D 330, E 15
Tuition: $90-$230 per month
Courses: Collages, Drawing, Painting, Printmaking, Sculpture
Summer School: Dir, Paula Nelson. Enrl 220; tuition $230 per wk.
Courses—Collage, Drawing, Etching, Landscape, Lithography, Monotype, Painting, Pastel, Portrait, Sculpture, Watercolor

NORTH CAROLINA

ASHEVILLE

UNIVERSITY OF NORTH CAROLINA AT ASHEVILLE, Dept of Art, One University Heights, 28804. Tel 704-251-6559; *Chmn* S Tucker Cooke, MFA
Estab 1927, dept estab 1965; pub; D & E; scholarships; SC 20, LC 5; enrl 3277, maj 69
Ent Req: HS dipl, ent exam
Degrees: BA, BFA 4-5 yrs
Tuition: Res—$892 per sem; nonres—$4072 per sem; campus res available
Courses: Art Education, Art History, Ceramics, Drawing, Intermedia, Mixed Media, Painting, Photography, Printmaking, Sculpture, Life Drawing, 2-D & 3-D Design
Adult Hobby Classes: Contact Educ Dept 704-251-6420
Summer School: Dir, S Tucker Cooke. Courses vary

BOONE

APPALACHIAN STATE UNIVERSITY, Dept of Art, 28608. Tel 704-262-2000; *Chmn* Thomas Sternal
Estab 1960; pub; D; scholarships; SC 38, LC 10, GC 12; enrl D 1000, maj 350, grad 45
Ent Req: HS dipl, ent exam
Degrees: BA, BS & BFA (graphic design, art educ, studio art, art marketing & production) 4 yrs
Tuition: Res—$774 per sem; nonres—$3296 per sem
Courses: Art Appreciation, Art History, Graphic Arts, Fibers
Summer School: Dir, L F Edwards. Enrl 300; term of 2, 4 & 6 wks beginning May-Aug. Courses—per regular session

BREVARD

BREVARD COLLEGE, Division of Fine Arts, 400 N Broad St, 28712. Tel 704-883-8292; FAX 704-884-3790; *Chmn* Virginia Tillotson; *Prof* Timothy G Murray, MACA; *Prof* Virginia Tillotson. Instrs: PT 2
Estab 1853; den; D & E; scholarships; SC 12, LC 2
Ent Req: HS dipl
Degrees: AFA 2 yrs
Tuition: Res—undergrad $8050 per yr; nonres— $12,425 per yr
Courses: Art History, Ceramics, Drawing, Film, Graphic Arts, Graphic Design, Painting, Photography, Printmaking, Sculpture, Theatre Arts, 2-D Design, 3-D Design
Summer School: Courses vary

CHAPEL HILL

UNIVERSITY OF NORTH CAROLINA AT CHAPEL HILL, Art Dept, Hanes Art Ctr, 27599-3405. Tel 919-962-2015; FAX 919-962-0722; *Chmn* Mary C Sturgeon, PhD; *Asst Chmn Studio Art* Beth Grabowski; *Prof* Mary Sheriff, PhD; *Prof* Jaroslav Folda, PhD; *Prof* Marvin Saltzman, MA; *Prof* Beth Grabowski, MFA; *Prof* R Kinnaird; *Prof* Arthur S Marks, PhD; *Prof* Dennis Zaborowski; *Assoc Prof* James Gadson, MFA; *Prof* Jerry Noe, MFA; *Assoc Prof* Jim Hirschfield, MFA; *Assoc Prof* Carol Mavor; *Asst Prof* Helen Hills; *Asst Prof* Dorothy Verkerk; *Asst Prof* Yun-Dong Nam ; *Asst Prof* Michael Harris
Estab 1793, dept estab 1936; pub; D; scholarships; SC 15, LC 15, GC 10; enrl D 100 undergrad, 55 grad
Ent Req: HS dipl, SAT
Degrees: BA & BFA 4 yr, MFA & MA(Art History) 2 yr, PhD(Art History) to 6 yr
Tuition: Res—undergrad $693 per sem, grad $693 per sem; nonres—undergrad $4959 per sem, grad $4959; campus res—available
Courses: Architecture, †Art History, Ceramics, †Drawing, History of Art & Archaeology, †Mixed Media, †Painting, †Sculpture
Summer School: Dir, Beth Grabowski. Courses—Various Art History & Studio Courses

CHARLOTTE

CENTRAL PIEDMONT COMMUNITY COLLEGE, Visual & Performing Arts, PO Box 35009, 28235. Tel 704-330-2722; *Chmn* Frank Williams
Degrees: AS, AA & AAS 2 yrs
Tuition: Res—undergrad $13.25 per cr hr; nonres—$107.50 per cr hr
Courses: Advertising Design, Architecture, Art Appreciation, Art History, Calligraphy, Ceramics, Design, Drawing, Fashion Arts, Handicrafts, Interior Design, Jewelry, Painting, Photography, Printmaking, Sculpture, Stage Design, Weaving, Cartooning, Stained Glass

QUEENS COLLEGE, Fine Arts Dept, 1900 Selwyn Ave, 28274-0001. Tel 704-337-2213; *Fine Arts Chmn* David Evans. Instrs: FT 3, PT 1
Estab 1857; den; scholarships; SC 19, LC 7
Degrees: Granted
Tuition: $12,310 annual tuition
Courses: Art History, Ceramics, Commercial Art

UNIVERSITY OF NORTH CAROLINA AT CHARLOTTE, Dept of Visual Arts, 9201 University City Blvd, Rm 153, 28223. Tel 704-547-2473; *Chmn* Dr Sally Kovach; *Prof* Eric Anderson; *Prof* Edwina Bringle; *Prof* Dean Butchovitz; *Prof* Michael Kampen; *Prof* Rod MacKillop; *Prof* Martha Strawn; *Prof* Ron Taylor; *Prof* Winston Trite; *Prof* Joan Tweedy; *Prof* Eldered Hudson; *Prof* Lili Bezner; *Prof* Linda Kroff; *Prof* Susan Brenner; *Prof* Rita Dibert; *Instr* Heather Hoover; *Instr* Sister Aguilo; *Instr* Jane Butckovitz; *Instr* Betsy Bilger; *Instr* Patti Elder; *Instr* Leslie Malone; *Instr* Tony Swider; *Instr* Frances Hawthorne; *Instr* Ann Kluttz; *Instr* Esther Kurti; *Instr* Karen Van Vleet
Estab 1965, dept estab 1971; pub; D & E; SC 54, LC 26; enrl D 785, non-maj 500, maj 430
Ent Req: HS dipl, SAT, Col Boards
Degrees: BCA 4 yrs, K - 12 Art Educ Cert 4 yrs
Tuition: res—$574.50; nonres—$3101.50; room & board per sem $1216 - $1720.52
Courses: Advertising Design, Art Appreciation, Art Education, Art History, Ceramics, Commercial Art, Conceptual Art, Design, Drawing, Graphic Arts, Graphic Design, Illustration, Intermedia, Jewelry, Mixed Media, Museum Staff Training, Painting, Printmaking, Sculpture, Teacher Training, Textile Design, Video, Computer-Aided Design, Fibers, Visual Communications & Design
Summer School: Dir, Dr Sally Kovach. Enrl 120; tuition res—$384, nonres—$2912; two 5 wk sessions, one 3 wk session. Courses—Art Appreciation, Art History, Ceramics, Computer Art, Drawing, Fiber, Jewelry, Painting, Photography, Printmaking

CULLOWHEE

WESTERN CAROLINA UNIVERSITY, Dept of Art, Belk Bldg, 28723. Tel 704-227-7210; *Head Dept* Robert Godfrey; *Assoc Prof* Lee P Budahl, PhD; *Prof* James E Smythe, MFA; *Prof* Joan Byrd; *Prof* Jon Jicha, MFA; *Assoc Prof* Cathryn Griffin, MFA; *Assoc Prof* James Thompson; *Asst Prof* Marya Roland, MFA; *Asst Prof* Matt Liddle, MA; *Asst Prof* Lois Petrovich-Mwaniki
Estab 1889, dept estab 1968; pub; D & E; scholarships; SC 51, LC 12; enrl non-maj 1200 per sem, maj 150
Ent Req: HS dipl, SAT & C average in HS
Degrees: BFA, BA & BSE 4 yrs, MA, art honors studio
Tuition: Res—undergrad and grad $830 per yr, $425 per sem; nonres—undergrad and grad $3697 per yr, $1848.50 per sem; campus res—room & board $1600 per yr
Courses: Art Appreciation, Art Education, Art History, Ceramics, Conceptual Art, Drawing, Graphic Design, Intermedia, Jewelry, Mixed Media, Painting, Photography, Printmaking, Sculpture, Silversmithing, Weaving, Book Arts
Summer School: Dir, Dr Pauline Christenson. Courses—Art History, Studio Courses in Ceramics, Drawing, Experimental Studio, Fibers, Metalsmithing, Painting, Sculpture

DALLAS

GASTON COLLEGE, Art Dept, 201 Hwy 321 S, 28034. Tel 704-922-6343, 922-6344; *Dept Chmn* Gary Freeman
Estab 1965; pub; D & E; SC 22, LC 3; enrl D 140, E 50, maj 50
Ent Req: HS dipl
Degrees: AA & AFA 2 yrs, cert 1 yr
Tuition: Res—$13.25 per quarter cr hr; nonres—$107.50 per quarter cr hr
Courses: Drawing, Illustration, Jewelry, Painting, Printmaking, Sculpture, 2-D & 3-D Design, Color Design, Computer Graphics, Commercial Art Fundamentals, Fabrication & Casting, Pottery
Adult Hobby Classes: Ceramics, Jewelry, Macrame, Weaving
Summer School: Dir, Franklin U Creech. Enrl 20; term of 11 wks beginning June. Courses—Design, Drawing, Painting, Pottery, Sculpture

DAVIDSON

DAVIDSON COLLEGE, Art Dept, 102 N Main St, 28036. Tel 704-892-2000; FAX 704-892-2691; *Chmn* Herb Jackson, MFA; *Prof* Larry L Ligo, PhD; *Prof* Russell Warren, MFA; *Assoc Prof* Shaw Smith, PhD; *Asst Prof* Nina Serebrennikov; *Asst Prof* Cort Savage
Estab 1837, dept estab 1950; pvt & den; D; scholarships; SC 12, LC 9; enrl non-maj 300, maj 18
Ent Req: Col Boards, HS transcripts
Degrees: BA & BS 4 yrs
Tuition: $19,500 per yr (comprehensive fee); campus res—room & board fee included in tuition
Courses: Aesthetics, Art History, Collages, Conceptual Art, Drawing, Graphic Design, History of Art & Archaeology, Painting, Printmaking, Sculpture, Theatre Arts

DOBSON

SURRY COMMUNITY COLLEGE, Art Dept, PO Box 304, 27017. Tel 910-386-8121; FAX 910-386-8951; *Dean* John Collins; *Instr* Archie Bennett; *Instr* William Sanders; *Instr* Abbe Rose Cox
Tuition: Res—$13.25 per cr hr; nonres—$107.50 per cr hr
Courses: Art Appreciation, Art History, Commercial Art, Design, Drawing, Handicrafts, Painting, Printmaking, Sculpture

DURHAM

DUKE UNIVERSITY, Dept of Art & Art History, PO Box 90764, 27708-0764. Tel 919-684-2224; FAX 919-684-3200; *Chair* Annabell Wharton, PhD; *Prof* Caroline Bruzelius, PhD; *Assoc Prof* Richard Powell; *Assoc Prof* Vernon Pratt, MFA; *Assoc Prof* Hans J Van Miegroet, PhD; *Assoc Prof* Kristine Stiles, PhD; *Adjunct Prof* Michael Mezzatesta, PhD; *Adjunct Assoc Prof* Dorie Reents-Budet, PhD; *Asst Prof* Stanley Abe, PhD; *Asst Prof* Sarah Cormack, PhD; *Asst Prof Practice* William Noland, BA; *Asst Prof Practice* Merrill Shatzman

Pvt; D; SC 19, LC 41, GC 12; enrl D 1850, maj 134
Ent Req: HS dipl & ent exam
Degrees: MA 4 yrs
Tuition: Campus res—available
Courses: Art History, Design, Drawing, Painting, Printmaking, Sculpture
Summer School: Dir, Paula E Gilbert. Two 6 wk sessions offered

NORTH CAROLINA CENTRAL UNIVERSITY, Art Dept, 1801 Fayetteville St,
PO Box 19555, 27707. Tel 919-560-6391, 6012; *Chmn* Melvin Carver, MPD; *Prof*
Lana Henderson, Phd; *Prof* Acha Debla; *Prof* Rosie Thompson; *Prof* Isabell Levitt,
MFA; *Prof* Norman Pendergraft, MA; *Prof* John Hughley, EDD; *Prof* Michelle
Patterson
Estab 1910, dept estab 1944; pub; D & E; SC 30, LC 11; enrl D 120, E 30, non-maj
1678, maj 120
Ent Req: HS dipl, SAT
Degrees: In Art Educ, Visual Communications & Studio Art 4 yrs
Tuition: Res—undergrad $421.50 yr; nonres—undergrad $1800 yr; campus
res—$2041.50-$2854.50 per yr
Courses: †Advertising Design, †Art Education, Art History, Calligraphy, Ceramics,
Commercial Art, Drawing, Graphic Arts, Handicrafts, Illustration, Jewelry,
Lettering, Painting, Printmaking, Sculpture, Teacher Training, Engineering Graphics,
Stained Glass, Studio Arts
Children's Classes: Saturday school

ELIZABETH CITY

ELIZABETH CITY STATE UNIVERSITY, Dept of Art, 1704 Weeksville Rd,
27909. Tel 919-335-3632, 335-3346 (Art Dept); *Chmn* Jenny C McIntosh, PhD
Estab 1891, dept estab 1961; pub; D & E; scholarships; SC 27, LC 18, advance courses in
Studio and History of Art; enrl D 2003, E 455, non-maj 1928, maj 75
Ent Req: HS dipl, portfolio
Degrees: BA 4 yrs
Tuition: Res—$368 per yr; nonres—$3740 per yr
Courses: Art History, Painting, Photography, Sculpture, Teacher Training, Art
Studio general
Summer School: Dir, James Townes. Enrl 950. Courses—same as regular session

FAYETTEVILLE

FAYETTEVILLE STATE UNIVERSITY, Fine Arts & Humanities, 1200
Murchison Rd, 28301-4298. Tel 910-486-1111, 486-1571; FAX 910-486-1572; *Head
Div Fine Arts & Humanities* Dr Robert G Owens
Estab 1877; pub; D & E; enrl D 60, E 20
Ent Req: HS dipl, ent exam
Degrees: BA & BFA 4 yr
Tuition: Res—$1382 per sem, $96 per cr hr; nonres—$3624 per sem, $906 per cr hr
Courses: Advertising Design, Aesthetics, Art Education, Ceramics, Drawing,
Graphic Arts, Handicrafts, History of Art & Archaeology, Lettering, Painting,
Photography, Sculpture, Weaving, Leather Craft
Summer School: Dir, Dr Beeman C Patterson. Courses—Art in Childhood
Education, Arts & Crafts, Drawing, Photography, Survey of Art

METHODIST COLLEGE, Art Dept, 5400 Ramsey St, 28311-5400. Tel 910-630-
7000; FAX 910-822-1289; *Chmn* Silvana Foti-Soublet, MFA. Instrs: FT 2, PT 1
Estab 1960; den; D & E; scholarships; SC 6, LC 4; enrl D 650, maj 22
Ent Req: HS dipl, SAT
Degrees: BA & BS 4 yrs
Tuition: Res—undergrad $9400 per yr, $13,150 incl room & board
Courses: Art Education, Art History, Design, Drawing, Painting, Photography,
Printmaking, Sculpture, Papermaking
Summer School: 3 terms, 3 wk early session, 5 wk main session, 6 wk directed
study. Courses—Art Appreciation, Painting, Sculpture, others as needed

GOLDSBORO

GOLDSBORO ART CENTER, Community Arts Council, 901 E Ash St, 27530.
Tel 919-736-3300; FAX 919-736-3335; *Exec Dir* Alice Strickland
Estab 1971; pub; D & E; scholarships; SC 25; enrl D 150, E 60, others 210
Tuition: $35 per class
Courses: Drawing, Painting, Pottery, Spinning
Adult Hobby Classes: Enrl 75; tuition $19 for 11 wk term. Courses— Calligraphy,
Oil Painting, Pottery, Watercolors
Children's Classes: Enrl 50; tuition $15 for 6 wk term. Courses—Discovering Art,
Drawing, Painting, Pottery

WAYNE COMMUNITY COLLEGE, Liberal Arts Dept, Caller Box 8002, 27533.
Tel 919-735-5151; FAX 919-736-3204; *Chmn* Marion Wessell; *Instr* Patricia
Turlington
Degrees: AA, AS, AAS & AFA 2 yr
Tuition: Res—$194.50 per qtr, $13.25 per cr hr; nonres—$1514 per qtr, $107 per cr
hr
Courses: Art Appreciation, Art History, Design, Drawing
Adult Hobby Classes: Courses offered

GREENSBORO

GREENSBORO COLLEGE, Dept of Art, Division of Fine Arts, 815 W Market St,
27401. Tel 910-272-7102; *Prof* Robert Kowski, MFA; *Asst Prof* Ray Martin, MFA
Estab 1838; pvt den; D; scholarships; SC 15, LC 4; enrl D 200, non-maj 50, maj 20
Ent Req: HS dipl
Degrees: BA
Tuition: Res & nonres—undergrad $9550 per yr; campus res—room & board $4040
per yr
Courses: Art Appreciation, †Art Education, Art History, Ceramics, Design,

Drawing, †Painting, Photography, Printmaking, †Sculpture, Stage Design, †Theatre
Arts
Adult Hobby Classes: Enrl 40; tuition $225 per cr hr. Courses—Art History
Summer School: Dir, Dr John Drayer. Tuition $138 per cr hr for two 5 wk sessions.
Courses—Art Appreciation, Art History

GUILFORD COLLEGE, Art Dept, 5800 W Friendly Ave, 27410. Tel 910-292-
5511; FAX 910-316-2951; *Chmn* Roy Nydorf
Estab 1837, dept estab 1970; den; D & E; scholarships; enrl 35 maj
Ent Req: HS dipl, entrance examination
Degrees: BA 4 yr, BFA 4 yr
Tuition: $7090 per sem
Courses: Art History, Ceramics, Design, Drawing, History of Art & Archaeology,
Painting, Photography, Printmaking, Sculpture

NORTH CAROLINA AGRICULTURAL & TECHNICAL STATE UNIVERSITY,
Art Dept, 312 N Dudley St, 27411. Tel 910-334-7993; *Chmn* Dr Timothy O Hicks.
Instrs: FT 4, PT 1
Estab 1930; pub; SC 29, LC 7; enrl maj 100
Tuition: $800 per sem
Courses: Art Education, Art History, Ceramics, Commercial Art, Drawing, Graphic
Arts, Painting, †Art Design, Crafts, 3-D Design, 2-D Design
Summer School: Dir, Dr Ronald Smith. Courses—Crafts, Public School Art, Art
History, Art Appreciation

UNIVERSITY OF NORTH CAROLINA AT GREENSBORO, Art Dept, 162
McIver Bldg, 27412. Tel 910-334-5248; *Head* K Porter Aichele. Instrs: FT 22
Dept estab 1935; pub; SC 22, LC 6, GC 8; enrl D 1000, non-maj 750, maj 200, grad
63
Ent Req: HS grad, ent exam
Degrees: BA, BFA, MEd & MFA 4 yr
Tuition: Res—undergrad $846; nonres—$7888
Courses: Art History, Ceramics, Drawing, Painting, Photography, Printmaking,
Sculpture, Teacher Training, Fibers
Summer School: Dir, Dr John Young. Enrl 225; beginning May - June and July -
Aug. Courses—Art History, Drawing, Etching, Fibers, Jewelry, Moldmaking-Metal
Casting, Painting, Photography, Picture Composition, Sculpture, Watercolor

GREENVILLE

EAST CAROLINA UNIVERSITY, School of Art, E Fifth St, 27858-4353. Tel 910-
328-6665; FAX 910-328-6441; *Dean* Michael Dorsey. Instrs: FT 38, PT 3
Estab 1907; pub; scholarships; SC 155, LC 28, GC 142; enrl maj 650
Ent Req: HS dipl, 20 units, Col Board Exam
Degrees: BA, BFA, MA & MFA, MAEd
Tuition: Campus res—available
Courses: Advertising Design, Art Appreciation, Art Education, Art History,
Ceramics, Commercial Art, Design, Drawing, Goldsmithing, Graphic Arts, Graphic
Design, History of Art & Archaeology, Illustration, Mixed Media, Painting,
Printmaking, Sculpture, Silversmithing, Textile Design, Weaving, Color & Design,
†Frabric Design, Computer-Aided Art & Design, †Wood Design, †Metal Design,
†Environmental Design, Interdisciplinary 3-D Design, Work Experience in the
Visual Arts & Design, Independent Study
Summer School: Dir, Phil Phillips. Enrl 200; two 5 wk terms. Courses—Foundation
& Survey

HICKORY

LENOIR RHYNE COLLEGE, Dept of Art, Seventy Ave & Eighth St NE, 28603.
Tel 704-328-1741; FAX 704-328-7338; *Chmn Dept* Dr Larry Yoder; *Asst Prof*
Douglas Burton, MA; *Asst Prof* Robert Winter, PhD
Estab 1892, dept estab 1976; den; D & E; scholarships; SC 5; enrl D 1200, E 350
Ent Req: HS dipl
Degrees: AB & BS 4 yrs
Tuition: Res—undergrad $5490 per sem; res—room & board $7870 per sem
Courses: Aesthetics, Art Appreciation, Art Education, Art History, Ceramics,
Drawing, Painting, Photography, Printmaking, Sculpture
Adult Hobby Classes: Courses on Tues & Thurs evenings
Children's Classes: Summer courses for gifted & talented
Summer School: Dir, Dr James Lichtenstein. Enrl 900; tuition $175 per sem hr for
2-5 wk terms beginning June. Courses—Art Appreciation, Art Education, Ceramics,
Painting

HIGH POINT

HIGH POINT COLLEGE, Fine Arts Dept, University Sta, 833 Montlieu Ave,
27262-3598. Tel 910-841-9000; FAX 910-841-5123; *Chmn* Dr Cheryl Harrison
Estab 1924, dept estab 1956; pvt den; D & E; scholarships; SC 16, LC 6; enrl non-
maj 950, maj 10
Ent Req: HS dipl, SAT
Degrees: AB & BS 4 yrs
Tuition: Res—undergrad $4150 per sem; nonres—undergrad $6175 per sem; campus
res available
Courses: Advertising Design, Aesthetics, †Art Education, Art History, Ceramics,
Drawing, History of Art & Archaeology, Interior Design, Painting, Printmaking,
Sculpture, Stage Design, Teacher Training, †Theatre Arts, Crafts
Summer School: Dean, W H Bearce. Enrl 200; two 5 wk sessions. Courses—Art
Education, Crafts, Design, Interior Design

JAMESTOWN

GUILFORD TECHNICAL COMMUNITY COLLEGE, Commercial Art Dept, PO
Box 309, 27282. Tel 910-454-1126, Ext 2580; FAX 910-819-9022; *Head*
Norman D Faircloth, MEd Art; *Instr* Awilda Feliciano, BFA; *Instr* Frederick N
Jones, MFA; *Instr* Scott Burnette, BA; *Instr* F Eugene Stafford, BFA; *Instr* Matilda
Kirby-Smith, MA; *Instr* Margaret Reid, MFA
Estab 1964; pub; D & E; scholarships; SC 20, LC 4; enrl D 130, E 60
Ent Req: HS dipl, English & math placement
Degrees: AAS 2 yrs
Tuition: Res—undergrad $13.25 per hr; nonres—undergrad up to $107.50 per hr
Courses: †Advertising Design, Art History, Commercial Art, Drafting, Drawing,
Graphic Arts, Illustration, Lettering, Photography, Computer Graphics
Adult Hobby Classes: Courses—Variety of subjects
Summer School: 9 wk term. Courses—Various

KINSTON

LENOIR COMMUNITY COLLEGE, Dept of Visual Art, PO Box 188, 28502-
0188. Tel 919-527-6223; *Prof* Larry Shreve
Degrees: AA, AS & AFA
Tuition: Res—$13.25 per cr hr; nonres—$107.50 per cr hr
Courses: Ceramics, Commercial Art, Design, Drawing, Illustration, Painting,
Photography, Printmaking, Introduction to Art
Summer School: Dir, Gerald A Elliott. Enrl 32; tuition $51 for 12 cr hrs.
Courses—Lecture & Studio Art

LAURINBURG

SAINT ANDREWS PRESBYTERIAN COLLEGE, Art Program, 28352. Tel 910-
277-5000, Ext 5264; *Chmn Dept Humanities & Fine Arts* Mel Bringle; *Chmn Art
Dept&Instr* Stephanie McDavid. Instrs: FT 2
Estab 1960; den; D; scholarships; SC 14, LC 2; enrl D 852, maj 20 - 30
Ent Req: HS dipl, SAT, 2.6 grade point average, 12 academic units
Degrees: BA, MS & BM 4 yrs or 32 courses
Tuition: $11,440 per yr
Courses: Art Appreciation, Art Education, Art History, Design, Drawing, Painting,
Photography, Printmaking, Sculpture, Video, Painting, Sculpture, Computer
Graphics
Summer School: Studio courses offered

LEXINGTON

DAVIDSON COUNTY COMMUNITY COLLEGE, Humanities Div, Old
Greensboro Rd, PO Box 1287, 27293-1287. Tel 910-249-8186; *Chmn* Dr Ron
Oakley; *Instr* Katherine Montgomery, MFA. Instrs: FT 2, PT 3
Estab 1963; dept estab 1966; pub; D & E; scholarships; SC 14, LC 4; enrl D 100, E
30, non-maj 195, maj 30
Ent Req: HS dipl
Degrees: AFA, AS & AA 2 yrs
Tuition: Res—undergrad $193.50 per qtr, $13.25 per cr hr; no campus res available
Courses: Art Education, Design, Art History, Drafting, Handicrafts, Painting,
Photography, Printmaking, Sculpture, Independent Studio
Adult Hobby Classes: Courses—Variety taught through continuing educ

MARS HILL

MARS HILL COLLEGE, Art Dept, 28754. Tel 704-689-1396; Elec Mail
rcary@mhc.edu. *Chmn* Richard Cary, PhD
Estab 1856, dept estab 1932; pvt and den; D & E; scholarships; SC 9, LC 6; enrl D
120, non-maj 100, maj 20
Ent Req: HS dipl, ent exam
Degrees: BA 4 yrs
Tuition: Undergrad $5900 per yr, $9100 per yr incl room & board
Courses: †Advertising Design, Aesthetics, †Art Education, †Art History, Ceramics,
†Graphic Arts, †Painting, Photography, †Printmaking, Sculpture, †Teacher Training,
†Theatre Arts
Summer School: Enrl 450; tuition $65 per cr hr for 5 wk term.
Courses—Introduction to the Arts & Photography

MISENHEIMER

PFEIFFER COLLEGE, Art Program, Hwy 52, 28109. Tel 704-463-7343; FAX
704-463-1363; *Dir* James Haymaker. Instrs: FT 1
Estab 1965; den; D; scholarships; SC 4, LC 4; enrl D 100
Ent Req: HS dipl
Courses: Art Education, Art History, Ceramics, Drawing, Painting, Sculpture

MOUNT OLIVE

MOUNT OLIVE COLLEGE, Dept of Art, 634 Henderson St, 28365. Tel 919-658-
2502; FAX 919-658-7180; *Chmn* Larry Lean
Estab 1951; den; D & E; scholarships; SC 5, LC 3
Degrees: AA and AS
Tuition: Res—undergrad $7450 per yr campus res available
Courses: Art Appreciation, Art History, Design, Drawing, Painting, American Art,
Arts Administration, Arts & Crafts
Summer School: Tuition $180 for session beginning May 19. Courses—Art
Appreciation

MURFREESBORO

CHOWAN COLLEGE, Division of Art, 200 Jones Dr, 27855. Tel 919-398-4101,
Ext 267; *Head Div* Beth Micheals, MFA; *Prof* Elizabeth Vick, MFA; *Prof* Stanley A
Mitchell, MA
Estab 1848, dept estab 1970; den; scholarships; SC 18, LC 3; enrl maj 64
Ent Req: HS dipl, SAT recommended
Degrees: AA 2 yrs
Tuition: Room & board $9500 per yr; commuter—$4950 per yr, $2475 per sem
Courses: Advertising Design, Art Appreciation, Art Education, Art History,
Ceramics, Commercial Art, Drawing, Illustration, Lettering, Painting, Figure
Drawing
Summer School: Dir, Doug Eubank. Enrl 10; tuition $165 per sem hr for term of 6
wks beginning June 8. Courses—Art Appreciation, Ceramics, Drawing, Painting

PEMBROKE

UNIVERSITY OF NORTH CAROLINA AT PEMBROKE (Formerly Pembroke
State University), Art Dept, PO Box 1510, 28372. Tel 910-521-6000, Ext 6216;
Chmn Dept Paul VanZandt. Instrs: FT 4, PT 3
Estab 1887; pub; scholarships; SC 30, LC 12; enrl maj 60
Ent Req: CEEB scores, HS record, scholastic standing in HS grad class,
recommendation of HS guidance counselor & principal
Degrees: BA & BS 4 yrs
Tuition: $474 per sem
Courses: †Art Education, Art History, †Ceramics, Commercial Art, Design,
Drawing, Handicrafts, Jewelry, †Painting, Photography, †Printmaking, †Sculpture
Summer School: Variety of courses

PENLAND

PENLAND SCHOOL OF CRAFTS, Penland Rd, 28765-0037. Tel 704-765-2359;
FAX 704-765-7389; *Dir* Ken Botnick; *Asst Dir* Geraldine Plato; *Asst Dir* Dana
Moore; *Develop Dir* Jean Dreyer
Estab 1929; pvt; D (summer, spring & fall classes); scholarships; SC 10-20; enrl D
approx 100
Ent Req: Age 18, special fall and spring sessions require portfolio and resume
Degrees: None granted but credit may be obtained through agreement with East
Tennessee State Univ & Western Carolina Univ
Tuition: $225 - $275 per wk for term of 2 - 3 wks; campus res—room & board $130
- $330 per wk
Courses: Ceramics, Graphic Design, Jewelry, Photography, Printmaking, Sculpture,
Weaving, Basketry, Blacksmithing, Book Arts, Clothing Construction, Crochet,
Dyeing, Enameling, Felting, Fibers, Glass, Marbling, Metalsmithing, Papermaking,
Quilting, Spinning, Woodworking
Summer School: Dir, Ken Botnick. Tuition varies for 1, 2 & 2-1/2 wk courses
between June & Sept; 8 wk concentrations-spring & fall. Courses—Basketry, Book
Arts, Clay, Drawing, Fibers, Glass, Iron, Metal, Paper, Photography, Printmaking,
Sculpture, Surface Design, Wood

RALEIGH

MEREDITH COLLEGE, Art Dept, Gaddy-Hamrick Art Ctr, 3800 Hillsborough St,
27607-5298. Tel 919-829-8332; FAX 919-829-2347; *Chmn* Rebecca Bailey
Estab 1898; den; W; D & E; scholarships; SC 15, LC 5; enrl D 490, E 130, maj 85,
others 30
Ent Req: HS dipl
Degrees: AB 4 yrs
Tuition: Res—undergrad $3360 per sem, $190 per cr hr; campus res—room & board
$2310 per yr
Courses: Advertising Design, Art Appreciation, Art Education, Art History,
Calligraphy, Ceramics, Costume Design & Construction, Design, Drawing, Graphic
Design, Handicrafts, Computer Graphics
Adult Hobby Classes: Courses—Art History, Ceramics, Drawing, Fibers, Graphic
Design, Painting, Photography, Sculpture
Summer School: Dir, John Hiott. Courses—vary

NORTH CAROLINA STATE UNIVERSITY AT RALEIGH, School of Design,
PO Box 7701, 27695-7701. Tel 919-515-8310; FAX 919-515-7330; *Dean* Marvin J
Malecha; *Head Landscape Architecture Dept* Arthur Rice; *Head Architecture Dept*
Christos Saccopoulos; *Head Design & Technology Dept* Percy Hooper; *Head
Graphic Design Dept* Meredith Davis. Instrs: FT 38, PT 5
Estab 1948; pub; enrl Architecture 251, Art & Design 60, Graphic Design 118,
Industrial Design 135, Landscape Architecture 94
Ent Req: Col board, ent exam
Degrees: BEnv(Design in Architecture, Design, Graphic & Industrial Design,
Landscape Architecture, MArch), MGraphic Design, MLandscape Arch, 4-6 yrs
Tuition: Res—$1100; nonres—$5366
Courses: Architecture, Design, Graphic Design, Industrial Design, Landscape
Architecture, Product Design, Visual Design
Summer School: Courses—Undergrad: Architecture, Graphic Design, Industrial
Design, Landscape Architecture

PEACE COLLEGE, Art Dept, 15 E Peace St, 27604. Tel 919-508-2000; FAX 919-
508-2326; *Head Dept* Carolyn Parker; *Chmn Division Fine Arts, Language,
Literature* Dr E P DeLuca; *Instr* M M Baird
Estab 1857; pvt; D; SC 8, LC 2; enrl D 500
Ent Req: HS dipl, SAT
Degrees: AA & AFA 2 yrs
Tuition: $5560 per yr
Courses: Art Education, Art History, Drawing, Fashion Arts, History of Art &
Archaeology, Painting, Theatre Arts, Color & Design

SAINT MARY'S COLLEGE, Art Dept, 900 Hillsborough St, 27603. Tel 919-828-2521; FAX 919-832-4831; *Chmn Dept* Ellen Anderson
Estab 1842; pvt den; D; scholarships; SC 11, LC 2; enrl D 150
Ent Req: HS dipl, SAT or PSAT
Degrees: AA & AAS
Tuition: Res—undergrad $7025 per yr; campus res available
Courses: Art History, Ceramics, Drawing, Graphic Arts, Painting, Printmaking, Stage Design, Theatre Arts
Adult Hobby Classes: Tuition $25-$50 for 6 week courses. Courses - Drawing, Painting
Summer School: Dean of the College, Robert J Miller. Enrl varies; tuition $250 for term of 3-5 wks beginning May or June

ROCKY MOUNT

NORTH CAROLINA WESLEYAN COLLEGE, Dept of Visual & Performing Arts, 3400 N Wesleyan Blvd, 27804-8630. Tel 919-985-5100; FAX 919-977-3701; *Chmn Dept* Michael McAllister; *Instr* Everett Mayo Adelman; *Instr* Michele A Cruz Scholarships
Tuition: Grad $7250 per yr
Courses: Advertising Design, Architecture, Art Appreciation, Art Education, Visual Communication
Adult Hobby Classes: Enrl 1055; tuition $125 per sem hr. Courses—Art Appreciation, American Architecture

STATESVILLE

MITCHELL COMMUNITY COLLEGE, Visual Art Dept, E Broad St, 28677. Tel 704-878-3310; *Chmn* Donald Everett Moore, MA. Instrs: FT 2, PT 1
Estab 1852, dept estab 1974; pub; D & E; scholarships; SC 12-15, LC 5; enrl D 85, E 40, non-maj 100, maj 25
Ent Req: HS dipl, HS transcripts, placement test
Degrees: AA & AFA 2 yrs
Tuition: Nonres—undergrad in state $315 yr; $75 per quarter, $19 per course part-time, out of state $2943 yr; no campus res available
Courses: Art History, †Ceramics, Drawing, Intermedia, †Painting, Printmaking, †Sculpture, Color Theory
Adult Hobby Classes: Enrl 100; tuition $50 per 10 wks. Courses—Continuing education courses in art & crafts available

SYLVA

SOUTHWESTERN COMMUNITY COLLEGE, Commercial Art & Advertising Design Dept, 447 College Dr, 28779. Tel 704-586-4091, Ext 233; *Head Dept* Bob Clark, MS; *Instr* Roger Stephens, MA. Instrs: FT 2, PT 2
Estab 1964, dept estab 1967; pub; D; scholarships; SC 19, LC 14; enrl D 40, maj 40
Ent Req: HS dipl
Degrees: AAS
Tuition: Res—undergrad $185.50 quarterly; nonres—undergrad $1505 quarterly; no campus res
Courses: Advertising Design, Art Appreciation, Art History, Commercial Art, Conceptual Art, Design, Drafting, Drawing, Graphic Arts, Graphic Design, History of Art & Archaeology, Illustration, Lettering, Occupational Therapy, Photography, Computer Graphics
Adult Hobby Classes: Enrl 30, tuition $35 per class hr

WHITEVILLE

SOUTHEASTERN COMMUNITY COLLEGE, Dept of Art, PO Box 151, 28472. Tel 910-642-7141, Ext 237; FAX 919-642-5658; *Instr* David McCormick
Estab 1965; pub; D & E; SC 18, LC 7
Ent Req: HS dipl or 18 yrs old
Degrees: AFA 2 yrs
Tuition: Res—undergrad $104.50 per qtr, part time $8.75 per hr; nonres—undergrad $899.25 per quarter, part time $81.25 per hr
Courses: Art History, Ceramics, Drawing, Painting, Printmaking, Sculpture, Pottery
Adult Hobby Classes: Tuition res—$25 per course
Summer School: Dir, Christa Balogh

WILKESBORO

WILKES COMMUNITY COLLEGE, Arts & Science Division, PO Box 120, 28697. Tel 910-838-6100; FAX 910-838-6277; *Dir* Blair Hancock; *Instr* William Moffett
Estab 1965, dept estab 1967; pub; D & E; scholarships; SC 2, LC 2; enrl D 1600, E 800
Ent Req: HS dipl
Degrees: AA, AFA
Tuition: Res—$13.25 per cr hr; nonres—$107.50 per cr hr; no campus res
Courses: Art History, Costume Design & Construction, Drafting, Drawing, Painting, Photography, Sculpture, Theatre Arts, Art Travel Courses
Summer School: Dir, Bud Mayes

WILMINGTON

UNIVERSITY OF NORTH CAROLINA AT WILMINGTON, Dept of Fine Arts - Division of Art, 601 S College Rd, 28403-3297. Tel 962-395-3415; FAX 919-395-3550; *Chmn* Anthony F Janson, PhD; *Prof* Ann Louise Conner, MFA; *Prof* Donald Furst, MFA; *Assoc Prof* Stephen Lequire, MFA; *Assoc Prof* Kemille Moore, PhD; *Asst Prof* Margaret Worthington
Estab 1789, dept estab 1952; pub; D & E
Ent Req: HS dipl, ent exam

Degrees: BCA 4 yrs
Tuition: $267 per sem
Courses: Art Appreciation, Art History, Ceramics, Design, Drawing, Painting, Printmaking, Sculpture
Adult Hobby Classes: Courses—Drawing, Painting
Summer School: Dir, David Miller. Two 5 wk sessions. Courses—Varied

WILSON

BARTON COLLEGE, Art Dept, College Sta, 27893. Tel 919-399-6477; *Chmn* Chris Wilson, MFA; *Prof* Edward Brown, MFA; *Assoc Prof* Jennifer Reitmeyer, MFA; *Asst Prof* John Hancock, BFA; *Instr* Lora Stutts, MFA
Estab 1903, dept estab 1950; pvt; D & E; scholarships; SC 15, LC 8; enrl D 60, E 5, non-maj 68, others 8 (PT)
Ent Req: HS dipl, ent exam
Degrees: BS, BA & BFA 4 yrs
Tuition: Undergrad—$5730 yr, $2866 per sem; campus res—room & board $2000 yr
Courses: Advertising Design, Art Education, Art History, †Ceramics, †Commercial Art, Display, †Drawing, †Graphic Design, †Illustration, Museum Staff Training, †Painting, Photography, †Printmaking, †Sculpture, †Teacher Training, Textile Design, Theatre Arts
Adult Hobby Classes: Tuition $120 per sem hr. Courses—any adult can audit any studio class
Summer School: Dir, Thomas Marshall. Enrl 30; 2 four-wk sessions. Courses— Art Appreciation, Crafts (ceramics, paper making, stained glass, wearing), Drawing

WINGATE

WINGATE UNIVERSITY, Division of Fine Arts, PO Box 159, 28174. Tel 704-233-8000; WATS 800-755-5550. *Chmn Div* Martha Asti
Estab 1896, dept estab 1958; den; D & E; scholarships; enrl D & E 1500
Ent Req: HS grad
Degrees: BA(Art), BA(Art Education) 4 yrs
Tuition: $2880 average per sem, campus res—available
Courses: Art Appreciation, Art History, Ceramics, Drawing, Film, Painting, Photography, Printmaking, Sculpture, Art Methods, Composition, Gallery Tours, Metalsmithing, Sketching, 3-D Design
Summer School: Pres, Dr Jerry McGee. Term of 4 wks beginning first wk in June. Courses—all regular class work available if demand warrants

WINSTON-SALEM

SALEM COLLEGE, Art Dept, PO Box 10548, 27108. Tel 910-721-2600, 721-2683; *Asst Prof* Tom Hutton; *Asst Prof* Geoff Bates; *Asst Prof* Penny Griffin; *Instr* John Hutton; *Instr* Carann Graham
Den, W; D; scholarships; enrl D 642, maj 44
Ent Req: HS Dipl
Degrees: BA 4 yrs
Tuition: Res—$15,060 per yr includes room & board; nonres—$9270 per yr includes room & board
Courses: Art Education, Art History, Ceramics, Drawing, Graphic Arts, Painting, Sculpture

SAWTOOTH CENTER FOR VISUAL ART, 226 N Marshall St, 27101. Tel 910-723-7395; *Executive Dir* James H Sanders III. Instrs: PT 75
Estab 1943 as Community School of Craft & Art; SC
Degrees: Non-degree
Tuition: $25 - $125 per 10 wk course
Courses: Calligraphy, Ceramics, Drawing, Graphic Arts, Handicrafts, Jewelry, Mixed Media, Painting, Photography, Printmaking, Silversmithing, Teacher Training, Textile Design, Weaving, Stained Glass
Adult Hobby Classes: Enrl 2000; tuition $38-$125 for 5-10 wk term. Courses—All visual arts & craft mediums
Children's Classes: Enrl 3000, tuition $19-60, for 5 wks. Courses—35 different media oriented courses
Summer School: Courses offered

WAKE FOREST UNIVERSITY, Dept of Art, PO Box 7232, 27109. Tel 910-759-5310; *Chmn* Robert Knott, PhD; *Gallery Dir* Victor Faccinto; *Prof* Harry B Titus; *Prof* Margaret Supplee Smith; *Assoc Prof* David Faber; *Assoc Prof* Page Laughlin; *Assoc Prof* Bernadine Barnes; *Vis Asst Prof* David Finn; *Instr* Alix Hitchcock
Estab 1834, dept estab 1968; pvt; D; scholarships; SC 14, LC 28; enrl D 350, non-maj 300, maj 50
Ent Req: HS dipl, SAT
Degrees: BA 4 yrs
Tuition: Undergrad—$18,000 yr, $9000 per sem, $475 per cr; campus res—room & board $5200
Courses: †Art History, †Drawing, †Painting, †Printmaking, †Sculpture
Summer School: Dir, Lu Leake. Enrl 25; tuition $205 per cr. Courses—Independent Study, Intro to Visual Arts, Practicum, Printmaking Workshop

WINSTON-SALEM STATE UNIVERSITY, Art Dept, 601 Martin Luther King Junior Dr, 27110. Tel 910-750-2000; *Interim Chmn* Arcenia Davis
Estab, 1892, dept estab 1970; pub; D & E; SC 10, LC 7; enrl D 65, nonmaj 275, maj 65
Ent Req: HS Dipl
Degrees: BA 4 yr
Tuition: Res—$631 per sem; nonres—$3497 per sem
Courses: Art Education, Art History, Drawing, Graphic Arts, Painting, Sculpture
Summer School: Courses offered

NORTH DAKOTA

BISMARCK

BISMARCK STATE COLLEGE, Fine Arts Dept, 1500 Edwards Ave, 58501. Tel 701-224-5471; *Chmn* Ervin Ely; *Instr* Richard Sammons; *Instr* Tom Porter; *Instr* Marietta Turner; *Instr* Michelle Lindblom; *Instr* Dan Rogers; *Instr* Carol Cashman; *Instr* Barbara Cichy
Degrees: AA 2 yrs
Tuition: Res—undergrad $904.32 per sem; nonres—undergrad $2200.08 per sem
Courses: Art Appreciation, Ceramics, Drawing, Design, Handicrafts, Jewelry, Lettering, Painting, Photography, Printmaking, Sculpture, Elementary Art, Gallery Management, Introduction to Understanding Art

DICKINSON

DICKINSON STATE UNIVERSITY, Dept of Art, Div of Fine Arts and Humanities, 58601. Tel 701-227-2312, 227-2339; *Chmn* David Solheim; *Prof* Katrina Callahan-Dolcater, MFA; *Asst Prof* Lily Pomeroy, MA; *Asst Instr* Mary Huether, BA
Estab 1918, dept estab 1959; pub; D & E; scholarship; SC 36, LC 8; enrl D approx 150 per quarter, non-maj 130, maj 20
Ent Req: HS dipl, out-of-state, ACT, minimum score 18 or upper-half of class
Degrees: BA, BS and BCS 4 yr
Tuition: Res—undergrad $1300 per yr, $741 per sem, $54.13 per sem hr, $69 extension per sem hr; nonres—undergrad $2917 per yr, $1977 per sem, $1417 per yr for the following states MN, SD, MT, MB & SK, $879 per sem hr; campus res—room & board $1750 double occupancy per yr
Courses: Advertising Design, †Art Education, Art History, †Ceramics, Costume Design & Construction, Display, Drawing, Graphic Design, Handicrafts, Intermedia, Jewelry, Lettering, Painting, Photography, Printmaking, Sculpture, Stage Design, Teacher Training, Theatre Arts, Color
Adult Hobby Classes: Enrl 15 - 25; tuition $213.40 & up for 16 wks.
Courses—Photography

FARGO

NORTH DAKOTA STATE UNIVERSITY, Division of Fine Arts, State Univ Sta, PO Box 5691, 58105. Tel 701-237-7932; *Dir* Taylce Harding, DM; *Assoc Prof* Wayne Tollefson; *Asst Prof* Kimble Bromley, MFA; *Lectr* David Swenson, MFA; *Lectr* Jaime Penuel, BFA; *Lectr* Kent Kapplinger
Estab 1889, dept estab 1964; pub; D & E; scholarships; SC 21; enrl D 225, E 60, non-maj 250, maj 30
Ent Req: HS dipl
Degrees: BA & BS 4 yr
Tuition: Res—undergrad $77.50 per cr hr; nonres—$207 per cr hr; campus res available
Courses: †Architecture, Art Appreciation, Art History, †Ceramics, †Painting, †Photography, †Printmaking, †Sculpture, †Theatre Arts

GRAND FORKS

UNIVERSITY OF NORTH DAKOTA, Visual Arts Dept, PO Box 7099, 58202. Tel 701-777-2257; Elec Mail mcelroye@badlands.nodak.edu. *Chmn* J McElroy-Edwards. Instrs: D FT 11
Estab 1883; pub; scholarships; SC 30, LC 4, GC 14; enrl maj 90, others 1000
Degrees: BFA, BA, BSEd, MFA
Tuition: Campus res—available
Courses: Aesthetics, Art Appreciation, †Art Education, Art History, †Ceramics, Design, Drawing, Goldsmithing, History of Art & Archaeology, †Jewelry, Lettering, †Painting, †Photography, †Printmaking, †Sculpture, Silversmithing, †Teacher Training, †Weaving, †Fibers, †Metalsmithing
Adult Hobby Classes: Enrl 800-1000; tuition $2428 per yr. Courses—Various studio art & art history
Summer School: Dir, J McElroy-Edwards. Enrl 100; tuition one half cash of regular sem. Courses—Varies every summer

JAMESTOWN

JAMESTOWN COLLEGE, Art Dept, PO Box 6003, 58401. Tel 701-252-3467; *Chmn* Sharon Cox. Instrs: FT 21
Pvt; D; scholarship; SC 13, LC 4; enrl 146, maj 14
Ent Req: HS dipl
Degrees: BA and BS 4 yr, directed study and individual study in advanced studio areas, private studios
Tuition: $6000 per yr; campus res—available
Courses: Art Appreciation, Art Education, Art History, Ceramics, Commercial Art, Drawing, Graphic Arts, History of Art & Archaeology, Painting, Printmaking, Sculpture, Theatre Arts, †2-D Design; Art Business; Fine Arts
Summer School: Term of 6 wks beginning June

MINOT

MINOT STATE UNIVERSITY, Dept of Art, Division of Humanities, 58701. Tel 701-858-3000; *Chmn Div Humanities* Walter Piehl. Instrs: FT 3, PT 1
Estab 1913; pub; scholarships; SC 30; enrl per quarter 200, maj 40
Degrees: BA & BS 4 yr
Tuition: Res—undergrad $980 per qtr, $81 per cr hr; nonres—undergrad $2466.50 per qtr, $205 per cr hr; campus res available
Courses: Advertising Design, Art History, Ceramics, Drawing, Handicrafts, Jewelry, Painting, Photography, Printmaking, Sculpture, Design, Silk Screen, Weaving
Summer School: Courses—same as above

VALLEY CITY

VALLEY CITY STATE COLLEGE, Art Dept, 101 College St, 58072. Tel 701-845-7598; *Co-Chair* Linda Whitney; *Co-Chair* Richard Thorn. Instrs: FT 2, PT 3
Estab 1890, dept estab 1921; pub; D & E; scholarships; SC 20, LC 3; enrl D 1300, E 200, non-maj 120, maj 30
Ent Req: HS dipl, ACT
Degrees: AA 2 yr, BS & BA 4 yr
Courses: Art Appreciation, Art Education, Art History, Ceramics, Design, Drawing, Mixed Media, Painting, Printmaking, Theatre Arts
Adult Hobby Classes: Enrl 20; tuition $21 per quarter. Courses—Drawing

WAHPETON

NORTH DAKOTA STATE COLLEGE OF SCIENCE, Dept of Graphic Arts, 800 N Sixth St, 58076-0002. Tel 701-671-2401; *Dept Head* Arlyn Nelson
Estab 1903, dept estab 1970; pub; D & E
Degrees: AA 2 yr
Tuition: Res—$1701 per yr; nonres—$4293 per yr
Courses: Drafting, Graphic Design, Lettering, Painting, Layout Design & Image Assembly
Adult Hobby Classes: Enrl 15; tuition $30. Courses—Calligraphy, Drawing, Painting
Summer School: Dir, Mary Sand. 2 wk term, 3 hrs per day. Courses—Teacher's Art Workshop

OHIO

ADA

OHIO NORTHERN UNIVERSITY, Dept of Art, 525 S Main St, 45810. Tel 419-772-2000; *Chmn* Bruce Chesser
Pvt; D; scholarships; SC 30, LC 8; enrl maj 30
Ent Req: HS dipl, ent exam
Degrees: BA and BFA 4 yrs
Tuition: Freshman $5530 per qtr; senior $4740 per qtr
Courses: Art Education, Art History, Ceramics, Drawing, Graphic Arts, Jewelry, Lettering, Painting, Sculpture, Teacher Training
Adult Hobby Classes: Enrl 10-15; tuition $48 for 6 wks. Courses—Ceramics, Watercolor Painting
Summer School: Dir, Bruce Chesser. Enrl 10. Courses - Ceramics, Drawing, Watercolor Painting

AKRON

UNIVERSITY OF AKRON, School of Art, * 44325. Tel 330-972-8257; FAX 330-972-5960; *Dept Head* Andrew Borowiec
Estab 1926; pub; D & E; scholarships; SC 25, LC 7, GC 8; enrl D 943, E 129, non-maj 493, maj 450
Ent Req: HS dipl
Degrees: AA 2 yr, BA, BS & BFA 4 yr
Tuition: Res—undergrad $1328 per yr, grad $110 per cr; nonres—undergrad $108 per cr, grad $110 per cr; campus res—available
Courses: †Art History, †Ceramics, †Commercial Art, †Drawing, †Graphic Design, Illustration, †Interior Design, †Jewelry, †Painting, †Photography, †Printmaking, †Sculpture, Textile Design, Weaving, †Art Studio, Computer, †Metalsmithing
Adult Hobby Classes: Tuition $45 - $75 for 5 - 6 wks. Courses—Art History, Ceramics, Drawing, Painting, Photography
Children's Classes: Tuition $354 for 2 wks. Courses—Visual Literacy (high school students)
Summer School: Dir, Bud Houston. Enrl 400; tuition $354 per course for term of 5 wks. Courses—Art History, Computer, Drawing, Graphics, Photography, Painting

ALLIANCE

MOUNT UNION COLLEGE, Dept of Art, 1972 Clark Ave, 44601. Tel 216-821-5320; FAX 216-821-0425; *Chmn* Joel Collins, MFA
Estab 1846; pvt; D; scholarships; SC 27, LC 6; enrl D 150, non-maj 125, maj 25
Ent Req: HS dipl, SAT
Degrees: BA
Tuition: Undergrad—$12,250 per yr; campus res available
Courses: Aesthetics, Art Education, Art History, Drawing, Painting, Printmaking, Sculpture, Teacher Training

ASHLAND

ASHLAND UNIVERSITY, Art Dept, College Ave, 44805. Tel 419-289-5130; *Chmn* Albert W Goad. Instrs: FT 4
Estab 1878; den; D & E; scholarship; enrl D 1460, maj 32, minors 12
Ent Req: HS dipl
Degrees: BA, BS 4 yr
Tuition: $9067 per yr
Courses: †Advertising Design, Art Appreciation, Art Education, †Ceramics, †Commercial Art, Constructions, Costume Design & Construction, Design, Drawing, Fashion Arts, Computer Art, available through affiliation with the Art Instititue of Pittsburgh: Fashion Illustration, Interior Design, Photography/Multi-media, Visual Communication

ATHENS

OHIO UNIVERSITY, School of Art, College of Fine Arts, 45701. Tel 614-593-4288; *Dean* Jim Stewart. Instrs: FT 32, PT 5
Estab 1936; pub; D & E; scholarships & fel; SC 88, LC 30, LGC 29, SGC 50; enrl maj 573, others 1718
Ent Req: Secondary school dipl, portfolio
Degrees: BFA, MA & MFA 4-5 yrs
Tuition: Res—undergrad $1184 per qtr, grad $1430 per qtr; nonres—undergrad $2543 per qtr, grad $2789 per qtr
Courses: †Art Education, †Art History, †Ceramics, Drawing, †Graphic Design, †Illustration, †Painting, †Photography, †Printmaking, †Sculpture, †Art Therapy, Fibers, Glass, †Studio Arts, †Visual Communication
Summer School: Two 5 wk sessions June-July & July-Aug; 8 qtr hr maximum per session; SC, LC, GC

BEREA

BALDWIN-WALLACE COLLEGE, Dept of Art, * 95 E Bagley Rd, 44017. Tel 216-826-2900; *Chmn Div* Harold D Cole; *Head Dept* Dean Drahos
Estab 1845; den; D & E; SC 23, LC 12; enrl 1900, maj 65
Degrees: AB 4 yrs
Tuition: $6153 per yr; campus res—available
Courses: Art Education, Art History, Ceramics, Drawing, Painting, Photography, Printmaking, Sculpture, Design & Color
Summer School: Tuition $89 per cr hr

BOWLING GREEN

BOWLING GREEN STATE UNIVERSITY, School of Art, Fine Arts Bldg, 43403. Tel 419-372-2786; FAX 419-372-2544; *Dir* Lou Krueger; *Assoc Dir* Janet Ballweg; *Dir Grad Studies* Dennis Wojtkiewicz; *Chmn Design Studies* Ronald Jacomini; *Chmn 3-D Studies* Shawn Morin; *Chmn 2-D Studies* Robert Mazur; *Chmn Art Educ* Rosalie Politsky; *Chmn Art History* Willard Misfeldt, PhD; *Gallery Dir* Jacqueline Nathan
Estab 1910, dept estab 1946; pub; D & E; scholarships & fels; SC 53, LC 14, GC 33; enrl D 2460, E 150, non-maj 995, maj 629, grad 33, others 40
Ent Req: ACT (undergrad), GRE (grad)
Degrees: BA, BS & BFA 4 yrs, MA 1 yr, MFA 2 yrs
Tuition: Res—undergrad $1404 per sem, grad $171 per cr hr, FT $1825 per sem; nonres—undergrad $3500 per sem
Courses: Advertising Design, †Art Education, †Art History, †Ceramics, Design, †Drawing, †Graphic Design, Jewelry, †Painting, †Photography, †Printmaking, †Sculpture, †Silversmithing, Weaving, †Computer Art, †Fibers, †Glass, †Jewelry/Metals
Children's Classes: Enrl 120; tuition $40 per 10 wk sem of Sat mornings
Summer School: Dir, Thomas Hilty. Enrl 300; tuition $1192 for 8 wk & 5 wk session. Couses—Art History, Drawing, Jewelry, Photography, Printmaking, Sculpture, Special Workshops, Watercolor

CANTON

CANTON MUSEUM OF ART, 1001 Market Ave N, 44702. Tel 330-453-7666; FAX 330-452-4477; *Dir* Manuel J Albacete; *Cur Exhibits & Registrar* Lynnda Arrasmith; *Cur Educ* Laura Kolinski; *Bus Mgr* Bebo Adams
Pub; D & E; scholarships; SC 28; enrl D 322, E 984, others 1306
Tuition: Children $35; Adults $75
Adult Hobby Classes: Enrl 150-200; tuition $75 for 12 wks. Courses—Drawing, Jewelry, Painting, Pottery
Children's Classes: Enrl 100; tuition $25-$50 for 6-12 wks. Courses—Clay, Drawing, Mask Making, Mixed Media, Painting, Puppetry
Summer School: Enrl 100; tuition $25-$45 for 6-12 wks. Courses—Clay, Drawing, Mask Making, Mixed Media, Painting, Puppetry

KENT STATE UNIVERSITY, STARK CAMPUS, School of Art, 6000 Frank Ave NW, 44720. Tel 330-499-9600; FAX 216-494-6121; *Coordr* Jack McWhorter. Instrs: FT 2, PT 3
Estab 1946, dept estab 1967; pub; D & E; scholarships; SC 20, LC 6; enrl D 174, E 13, non-maj 50, maj 40
Ent Req: HS dipl, ACT
Degrees: AA
Tuition: Res—undergrad $1442.70 per sem, $131.25 per hr
Courses: †Art Education, †Art History, Ceramics, Conceptual Art, Drawing, Film, †Graphic Design, †Industrial Design, †Painting, †Printmaking, †Sculpture, Weaving, Stained Glass
Adult Hobby Classes: Enrl varies; tuition $175 per course for 16 wks sem. Courses—same as regular classes
Summer School: 6 & 8 wk sessions. Courses—same as regular classes

MALONE COLLEGE, Dept of Art, Division of Fine Arts, 515 25th St NW, 44709. Tel 330-471-8100; *Chmn Fine Arts* Sandra Carnes; *Assoc Prof* Dr Susan Armstrong; *Asst Prof* Timothy Young; *Asst Prof* Barbara Drennen
Estab 1956; den; D & E; scholarships; SC 20, LC 2; enrl D 75, maj 30
Ent Req: HS dipl, ent exam
Degrees: BA & BS(Educ) 4 yrs
Tuition: $270 per sem hr; campus res—available
Courses: Art Appreciation, †Art Education, Art History, Ceramics, Commercial Art, †Drawing, History of Art & Archaeology, Jewelry, †Painting, Printmaking, Sculpture, Stage Design, Teacher Training, Applied Design, Graphic Communications, History and Criticism of Art

CHILLICOTHE

OHIO UNIVERSITY-CHILLICOTHE CAMPUS, Fine Arts & Humanities Division, 571 W Fifth St, PO Box 629, 45601. Tel 614-774-7200; FAX 614-774-7214; *Assoc Prof* Dennis Deane, MFA; *Assoc Prof* Margaret McAdams, MFA
Estab 1946; D & E; scholarships
Ent Req: HS dipl, ACT or SAT
Tuition: Res—$52 per hr; nonres—$114 per hr
Courses: Art Appreciation, Art Education, Art History, Ceramics, Design, Drawing, Film, Graphic Design, History of Art & Archaeology, Painting, Photography, Teacher Training

CINCINNATI

ACA COLLEGE OF DESIGN, 2528 Kemper Lane, 45206. Tel 513-751-1206; FAX 513-751-1209; *Pres* Marion Allman; *Instr* Roy Waits; *Instr* Dan Devlin; *Instr* Doug Best; *Instr* Cyndi Mendell; *Instr* Tom Greene; *Instr* Philip Desch
Estab 1976; priv; D; scholarships
Ent Req: HS dipl, portfolio, interview
Degrees: Commercial Art AD 2 yr
Tuition: $5980 per yr, additional $2000 second yr for computer graphics major
Courses: Advertising Design, Commercial Art, Design, Graphic Design, Illustration, Computer Graphics
Adult Hobby Classes: Enrl 60-75. Courses—Computer Graphics, Design
Summer School: Dir, Ennis Jones. Enrl 60-75. Courses—Computer Graphics for professional artists

ANTONELLI INSTITUTE OF ART & PHOTOGRAPHY, 124 E Seventh St, 45202. Tel 513-241-4338; FAX 513-241-9396; *Dept Head Commercial Arts* James Slouffman; *Co-Dir* Christy Connelly; *Dept Head Fashion Merchandise* Connie Crossley; *Dir Coll* Carla Wasko; *Head International Design* Joseph Miller; *Instr* Kelly Tow. Instrs: FT 5, PT 12
Estab 1947; pvt; D & E; enrl D 200
Ent Req: HS dipl, review of portfolio
Tuition: Undergrad—$3495 Commercial Art & Interior Design, $3995 Photography
Courses: †Commercial Art, †Interior Design, †Photography, †Fashion Merchandise
Adult Hobby Classes: Courses offered
Summer School: Courses offered

ART ACADEMY OF CINCINNATI, 1125 St Gregory St, 45202. Tel 513-721-5205; FAX 513-562-8778; *Chmn* Anthony Batchelor; *Chmn* Stewart Goldman, BFA; *Dir* Gregory A Smith; *Prof* Mark Thomas; *Chmn* Gary Gaffney, MFA; *Instr* Lawrence W Goodridge, MFA; *Instr* Kenn Knowlton, MS; *Instr* Calvin Kowal, MS; *Instr* Larry May, MFA; *Instr* Diane Smith-Hurd, MA; *Instr* Jay Zumeta, MA; *Instr* April Foster, MFA; *Instr* Rebecca Seeman, MFA
Estab 1887; pvt; D & E; scholarships; enrl 220
Ent Req: HS grad
Degrees: Cert, BS collaboration with Univ of Cincinnati, BFA offered at the Academy, 4-5 yr
Tuition: $9000 for 4 yr prog
Courses: Advertising Design, Aesthetics, Art Education, Art History, Commercial Art, Conceptual Art, Constructions, Design, Drawing, Graphic Arts, Graphic Design, Illustration, Museum Staff Training, Painting, Photography, Printmaking, Sculpture, †Communication Design
Adult Hobby Classes: Enrl 2000. Courses—Design, Drawing, Illustration, Painting, Photography, Sculpture
Children's Classes: Enrl 500; tuition $100 per class. Courses—Drawing, Painting, 3-D Design

CINCINNATI ACADEMY OF DESIGN, 2181 Victory Pky, Ste 200, 45206. Tel 513-961-2484; *Dean Educ* Michael C McGuire; *Instr* David Schlosser; *Registrar* Tonya Emmons
Tuition: $5500 per yr, $2750 per sem
Courses: Advertising Design, Calligraphy, Commercial Art, Drawing, Fashion Arts, Illustration, Lettering, Painting, Color Composition, Finished Art, Keyline, Layout, Letterhead, Life Class Mediums, Logotype, Magic Marker, Mediums, Package Design, Perspective, TV Storyboard, others

COLLEGE OF MOUNT SAINT JOSEPH, Art Dept, 5701 Delhi Rd, 45233-1670. Tel 513-244-4420; FAX 513-244-4222; Elec Mail dan_mader@mail.msj.edu; Internet Home Page Address http://www.msj.edu. WATS 800-654-9314. *Chmn* Daniel Mader, MA; *Prof* Sharon Kesterson; *Assoc* Beth Belknap, MDES; *Asst Prof* Loyola Walter, MFA; *Asst Prof* Gerry Bellas, MFA; *Instr* Robert Voigt, BA
Estab 1920; den; D & E; scholarships; SC 35, LC 4; enrl 203 maj
Ent Req: HS dipl, national testing scores
Degrees: AA 2 yr, BA and BFA 4 yr
Tuition: Res—undergrad $11,300 per yr; campus res—room & board $4950 per yr
Courses: †Art Education, Art History, †Ceramics, †Drawing, †Graphic Design, †Interior Design, †Jewelry, Lettering, †Painting, †Photography, †Printmaking, †Sculpture, †Fabrics Design, †Pre-Art Therapy
Adult Hobby Classes: Enrl 1000; tuition $290 per cr hr
Summer School: Chairperson, Daniel Mader, MA. Enrl 100; tuition $290 per cr hr

UNIVERSITY OF CINCINNATI, School of Art, 839c DAAP, ML 0016, 45221. Tel 513-556-2962; FAX 513-556-2887; *Dir* Wayne Enstice; *Chmn Art History & Prof* Lloyd Engelbrecht, PhD; *Chmn Fine Arts & Prof* Linda Einfalt, PhD; *Dir MFA Prog* Kimberly Burleigh; *Prof Fine Arts* Frank Herrmann, MFA; *Prof Fine Arts* Benjamin Britton, MFA; *Prof Fine Arts* Denise Burge, MFA; *Prof Fine Arts* Roy Cartwright, MFA; *Prof Fine Arts* Tarrence Corbin, MFA; *Prof Fine Arts* James Duesing, MFA; *Prof Fine Arts* Don Kelley, MFA; *Prof Fine Arts* Patricia Renick, MFA; *Prof Fine Arts* Beverly Semmens, MFA; *Prof Fine Arts* Jane Alden Stevens, MFA; *Prof Fine Arts* John Stewart, MFA; *Prof Fine Arts* Gerald Stratton, BA; *Prof Fine Arts* Martin Tucker, MFA; *Prof Fine Arts* Jim Williams, MFA; *Prof Fine Arts* Derrick Woodham, ARCA; *Prof Art History* George Stricevic, PhD; *Prof Art History* Kristi Nelson, PhD; *Prof Art History* Jonathan Riess, PhD; *Prof Art History* Theresa Leininger-Miller, PhD; *Prof Art History* Jo Face, MA

Estab 1819, dept estab 1946; pub; D & E; scholarships
Ent Req: HS dipl - top 3rd class rank, transfers to Fine Arts, portfolio optional & MFA, portfolio required
Degrees: BA(Art History) 4 yr, 5 yr with teaching certification, BFA(Fine Arts) 4 yr, 5 yr with teaching certification, MA(Art History) 2 yr, MA(Art Educ) 2 yr, MFA 2 yr
Tuition: Res—undergrad $1384, $115 per cr hr, grad $1815, $182 per cr hr; nonres—undergrad $3488, $290 per cr hr, grad $3461, $347 per cr hr; campus res available
Courses: Art Education, Art History, Ceramics, Conceptual Art, Drawing, Photography, Printmaking, Sculpture, Teacher Training, Painting, Photography, Printmaking, Sculpture, Teacher Training, Textile Design, Video, Weaving, Electronic Arts, Fiber Arts
Adult Hobby Classes: Art Education, Art History
Children's Classes: Enrl 25; tuition $60 for 10 wks. Courses—Intro to Life Drawing
Summer School: Dir, Wayne Enstice. Enrl 200. Courses—Art Education, Art History, Fine Arts

XAVIER UNIVERSITY, Dept of Art, 3800 Victory Pky, 45207-7311. Tel 513-745-3811; FAX 513-745-4301; *Chmn* Bernard L Schmidt, MFA; *Prof* Marsha Karagheus-Murphy, MFA; *Prof* Suzanne Chauteau, MFA; *Prof* Jerome Pryor, DEd; *Prof* Ann Beiersdorfer, MA
Estab 1831, dept estab 1935; pvt; D & E; scholarships; SC 17, LC 20; enrl D 403, E 349, non-maj 349, maj 54
Ent Req: HS dipl, SAT or ACT
Degrees: BA 4 yr, BFA 4 yr
Tuition: Res—undergrad $2270 per yr; nonres—$300 per cr hr
Courses: Advertising Design, Aesthetics, Art Appreciation, Art Education, Art History, Ceramics, Collages, Commercial Art, Constructions, Costume Design & Construction, Design, Display, Drawing, Film, Graphic Arts, Graphic Design, History of Art & Archaeology, Illustration, Intermedia, Mixed Media, Occupational Therapy, Painting, Printmaking, Sculpture, Teacher Training, Textile Design, Theatre Arts, Weaving, Art Therapy, History of Art, Humanities
Summer School: Art Appreciation, School Art

CLEVELAND

CASE WESTERN RESERVE UNIVERSITY, Dept of Art History & Art, Mather House, 44106-7110. Tel 216-368-4118; FAX 216-368-4681; *Chmn* Jenifer Neils, PhD; *Prof* Walter Gibson, PhD; *Prof* Edward J Olszewski, PhD; *Prof* Ellen G Landau, PhD; *Asst Prof* David Steinberg, PhD; *Asst Prof* Tim Shuckerow, MA; *Asst Prof* Catherine Scallen
Estab 1875; pvt; D; scholarships; SC 24, LC 55, GC 73; enrl D 644, grad 75
Ent Req: HS transcript, SAT or ACT, TOEFL for foreign students
Degrees: BA, BS, MA and PhD
Tuition: $6417 per sem; campus res available
Courses: Architecture, †Art Education, †Art History, Ceramics, Costume Design & Construction, †History of Art & Archaeology, Jewelry, †Museum Staff Training, Painting, Photography, †Teacher Training, Textile Design, Weaving, Enameling, Medical Illustration
Summer School: June & July. Courses—Art Education, Art History, Art Studio, Museum Studies

CLEVELAND INSTITUTE OF ART, 11141 E Blvd, 44106. Tel 216-421-7000; FAX 216-421-7438; *Pres* Robert A Mayer; *Prof* Tina Cassara; *Prof* Michael Holihan; *Prof* Hugh Greenlee; *Prof* Paul St Denis; *Prof* Lawrence Krause; *Prof* Carl Floyd; *Prof* Kenneth Dingwall; *Assoc Prof* Eugene Powlowski; *Assoc Prof* Robert Palmer; *Assoc Prof* Brent Young; *Assoc Prof* William Brouillard; *Assoc Prof* Richard Hall
Estab 1882; pvt; D & E; scholarships; SC 90, LC 38; enrl D 483, E 266, non-maj 169, maj 300, others 23
Ent Req: HS dipl SAT, ACT and transcript, portfolio
Degrees: BFA 5 yrs, BS & MEd (educ with Case Western Reserve Univ) 4 yrs
Courses: Aesthetics, Art Education, Art History, †Ceramics, †Drawing, †Film, †Graphic Arts, †Illustration, †Industrial Design, †Jewelry, †Painting, †Photography, †Printmaking, †Sculpture, †Silversmithing, †Enameling, †Fiber, †Glass, †Interior Design, †Medical Illustration
Adult Hobby Classes: Enrl 266; tuition varies per course. Course—Calligraphy, Ceramic, Crafts, Design, Drawing, Fiber & Surface Design, Graphic Design, Painting, Printmaking, Sculpture, Silversmithing, Watercolor
Children's Classes: Enrl 210; tuition varies per course. Courses—Art Basics, Ceramic Sculpture, Crafts, Design, Drawing, Painting, Portfolio Preparation, Printmaking, Photography
Summer School: Dir, William Jean. Courses—Ceramics, Design, Drawing, Jewelry & Metalsmithing, Photography, Printmaking, Sculpture, Watercolor

CLEVELAND STATE UNIVERSITY, Art Dept, 2307 Chester Ave (Mailing add: 1983 E 24th St, 44115). Tel 216-687-2040; FAX 216-687-2275; *Chmn & Prof* John Hunter, PhD; *Prof* Thomas E Donaldson, PhD; *Prof* Gene Kangas, MFA; *Prof* Walter Leedy Jr, PhD; *Prog* Marvin H Jones, MA; *Prof* Kenneth Nevadomi, MFA; *Prof* Masumi Hayashi, MFA; *Assoc Prof* George Mauersberger, MFA; *Assoc Prof* Kathy Corhnew Nasara, PhD; *Assoc Prof* Laurel Lampela, PhD; *Assoc Prof* Richard Schnider, MA
Estab 1972; pub; D & E; scholarships; SC 26, LC 32
Ent Req: HS dipl
Degrees: BA 4 yr
Tuition: Res—undergrad $95.60 per cr hr
Courses: †Art Education, †Art History, †Ceramics, †Drawing, †Painting, †Photography, †Printmaking, †Sculpture, Computer Graphics, Introduction of Art & Basic Design
Summer School: Chmn, John Hunter. Tuition & courses same as regular schedule

CUYAHOGA COMMUNITY COLLEGE, Dept of Art, * 2900 Community College Ave, 44115. Tel 216-987-4525; *Prof* David Haberman, MFA; *Prof* Gerald Kramer, MFA; *Instr* Marilyn Fzalay; *Instr* Megan Sweeney
Estab 1963. College maintains four campuses; pub; D & E; scholarships; SC 15, LC 4; enrl D 150, E 80, maj 50

Ent Req: HS dipl
Degrees: AA yrs
Tuition: County res—$31.50 per cr hr; out-of-county—$41.75 per cr hr; nonres—$83.50 per cr hr
Courses: Art Appreciation, Art Education, Art History, Calligraphy, Ceramics, Graphic Design, Occupational Therapy, Painting, Photography, Printmaking, Sculpture, Stage Design, Teacher Training, Theatre Arts, Video
Summer School: Courses—various

JOHN CARROLL UNIVERSITY, Dept of Art History & Humanities, University Heights, 44118. Tel 216-397-1886; *Chmn* Dr Charles Scillia
Estab 1886, dept estab 1965; pvt; D & E; SC 3, LC 30; enrl D 400, non-maj 350, maj-humanities 30, art hist 14
Ent Req: HS dipl, SAT
Degrees: BA Art History 4 yrs, BA Humanities 4 yrs
Tuition: Res—undergrad $353 per cr hr, grad $363 per cr hr; campus res—MBA $475 per cr hr
Courses: Art History, Modern History

COLUMBUS

CAPITAL UNIVERSITY, Fine Arts Dept, 2199 E Main St, 43209. Tel 614-236-6011; *Chmn* Gary Ross. Instrs: FT 3
Degrees: BA, BFA
Tuition: $6525 per sem, grad $235 per cr hr; room & board $2000 per sem
Courses: Advertising Design, Art Education, Art History, Ceramics, Design, Drawing, Jewelry, Painting, Photography, Sculpture, Theatre Arts, Weaving, Stained Glass

COLUMBUS COLLEGE OF ART & DESIGN, Fine Arts Dept, 107 N Ninth St, 43215. Tel 614-224-9101; *Dean* Lowell Tolstedt. Instrs: 68
Estab 1879; pvt; approved for Veterans; D & E; scholarships
Ent Req: HS grad, art portfolio
Degrees: BFA 4 yr
Tuition: $9700 per yr
Courses: Advertising Design, Fashion Arts, Graphic Arts, Illustration, Industrial Design, Interior Design, Painting, Sculpture, Fine Arts, Packaging Design, Retail Advertising
Children's Classes: Saturday sessions 9 - 11:30 AM

OHIO DOMINICAN COLLEGE, Art Dept, 1216 Sunbury Rd, 43219. Tel 614-253-2741, 251-4580; *Dept Chmn* William Vensel
Estab 1911; den; D & E; scholarships; SC and LC 709 per sem; enrl D 139, E 105, maj 17
Ent Req: HS dipl
Degrees: BA 4 yrs, also secondary educ cert or special training cert, K-12
Tuition: $8100 per yr, $4050 per sem, $254 per cr hr
Courses: Textile Design, Theatre Arts, Video

OHIO STATE UNIVERSITY
—**School of Architecture,** 190 W 17th Ave, 43210. Tel 614-292-1012; FAX 614-292-7106; *Dir* Jerrold Voss, AICP. Instrs: FT 43, PT 23
Estab 1899; pub; scholarships; enrl Archit 450, Landscape Archit 170, City & Regional Planning 65
Degrees: BS(Archit), MA, PhD
Tuition: Res—$1200 per qtr; nonres—$3000 per qtr
Courses: Design, Landscape Architecture, City Planning, History of Architecture
Adult Hobby Classes: Enrl limited; Tuition $170-$469.
Summer School: Dir, Robert Liveson. Enrl 50-70; tuition $170-$469 for 10 wks. Courses—Architecture 200, 202, 341, 441, 844
—**College of the Arts,** 425 Mendenhall Lab, 125 S Oval Mall, 43210-1308. Tel 614-292-5171; *Dean Col* Donald Harris
Univ estab 1870, col estab 1968; pub; D & E; scholarships; SC 106, LC 192, GC 208; enrl D 3678, E varies, non-maj 2300, maj 893, grad 150
Ent Req: HS dipl
Degrees: BA, MA, PhD
Tuition: Res—$1200 per qtr; nonres—$3000 per qtr
Courses: Art History, †Stage Design, †Teacher Training, †Theatre Arts, †Weaving, Art, Dance, Music
Adult Hobby Classes: Courses—art experiences in all media for local adults
Children's Classes: Enrl 300 per quarter; fees $36 per quarter; Saturday School. Courses—art experiences in all media for local children
Summer School: Same as regular session
—**Dept of Art,** 146 Hopkins Hall, 128 N Oval Mall, 43210. Tel 614-292-5072; FAX 614-292-1674; *Chmn* Georg Heimdal. Instrs: FT 36, PT 34
SC 56, LC 6, GC 30
Degrees: BA, BFA, MFA
Tuition: Res—undergrad $993 per quarter, grad $1322 per quarter; nonres—undergrad $2764 per quarter, grad $3426 per quarter
Courses: †Ceramics, †Drawing, †Mixed Media, †Painting, †Photography, †Printmaking, †Sculpture, †Glass
Adult Hobby Classes: Offered through CAP (Creative Art Program)
—**Dept of Art Education,** Hopkins Hall 340, 128 N Oval Mall, 43210-1363. Tel 614-292-7183; *Chmn Dept* James Hutchens; *Prof* Arthur Efland; *Assoc Prof* Judith Koroscik, PhD; *Assoc Prof* Louis Lankford, PhD; *Assoc Prof* Terry Barrett, PhD; *Asst Prof* Pat Stuhr, PhD
Estab 1907; pub; D & E; scholarships; SC 6, LC 10, GC 16; enrl maj 95, grad 115
Ent Req: HS dipl
Degrees: BA, MA, PhD
Tuition: Res—$1200 per qtr; nonres—$3000 per qtr
Courses: Art Appreciation, Computer Graphics, Ethnic Art, History of Art
Children's Classes: Enrl 1000; tuition $25 for 7 wks; Courses—Variety of studio activities
Summer School: Chmn Dept, Michael J Parsons, PhD

—**Dept of Industrial Interior & Visual Communication Design**, 380 Hopkins Hall, 128 N Oval Mall, 43210. Tel 614-292-6746; FAX 614-292-0217; *Chmn* Jim Kaufman. Instrs: FT 11, PT 5
Scholarships: SC 35, LC 10, GC 10
Degrees: BS, MS
Tuition: Res—$1200 per quarter; nonres—$3000 per quarter
Courses: 3-D Computer Modeling, Manufacturing Materials & Processes, Research Problems & Design, Visual Thinking Design Methodology, †Design Development, †Design Education, †Design Management
Summer School: Advanced Typography
—**Dept of the History of Art**, 100 Hayes Hall, 108 N Oval Mall, 43210. Tel 614-292-7481; FAX 614-292-4401; *Chmn Dept* Mark Fullerton
Estab 1871, dept estab 1968; pub; D & E; scholarships & fels; LC 56, GC 29; enrl D 854, non-maj 700, maj 71, grad 73
Ent Req: HS dipl
Degrees: BA, MA 2 yrs, PhD 4-6 yrs
Courses: †Art History, History of Art & Archaeology
Summer School: Enrl 250; tuition same as regular session for term of ten wks beginning June. Courses—vary each yr

CUYAHOGA FALLS

CUYAHOGA VALLEY ART CENTER, 2131 Front St, 44221. Tel 330-928-8092; *Pres* Bill Bryant; *Instr* Eugene Bell; *Instr* Robert Putka; *Instr* Sandra Dennison; *Instr* Dino Massaroni; *Instr* Jack Lieberman; *Instr* Beth Lindenberger; *Instr* Tony Cross; *Instr* Dave Everson; *Instr* Wanda Montgomery
Estab 1934; pub; D & E; SC 23; enrl 200
Ent Req: None, interest in art
Degrees: None
Tuition: $75 members for 10 wks, $90 nonmembers; no campus res
Courses: Ceramics, Collages, Drawing, Painting, Special Workshops
Adult Hobby Classes: Enrl 100. Courses—Drawing, Painting, Pottery
Children's Classes: Enrl 25; tuition $50 for members, $60 for nonmembers per 10 wks. Courses—Ceramics, Painting
Summer School: Courses—same as regular session

STUDIOS OF JACK RICHARD CREATIVE SCHOOL OF DESIGN, 2250 Front St, 44221. Tel 330-929-1575; *Dir* Jack Richard. Instrs: FT 3
Estab 1960; pvt; D & E; scholarships; SC 4, LC 10; enrl D 50-60, E 50-60
Courses: Aesthetics, Art Education, Design, Drawing, Illustration, Occupational Therapy, Painting, Photography, Sculpture, Color, Mural
Adult Hobby Classes: Enrl 200-300 per session; tuition $11 per class. Courses—Design, Drawing, Painting
Children's Classes: Saturday mornings
Summer School: Dir, Jane Williams. Enrl 90; tuition $10 - $12 per class for term of 8 wks beginning June. Courses—Design, Drawing, Painting

DAYTON

SINCLAIR COMMUNITY COLLEGE, Division of Fine & Performing Arts, 444 W Third St, 45402. Tel 937-226-2540; FAX 513-449-5192; Elec Mail abierley@midas.sinclair.edu. *Chmn Fine Arts* Sally A Struthers, PhD
Estab 1973; pub; D & E; scholarships; enrl 3900
Ent Req: HS dipl, ent exam
Degrees: AA 2 yrs
Tuition: County res—$29 per cr hr; non-county res—$39 per cr hr; out of state—$59 per cr hr; no campus res
Courses: Advertising Design, Ceramics, Commercial Art, Drawing, Graphic Arts, Painting, Sculpture, Theatre Arts
Summer School: Dir, Sally Struthers. Enrl 300; tuition $31 per cr hr for 5 or 10 wk term. Courses—Art Appreciation, Ceramics, Computer Photography, Drawing, Printing, Studio Art

UNIVERSITY OF DAYTON, Visual Arts Dept, 300 College Park, 45469-1690. Tel 513-229-3237; *Chmn* Sean Wilkinson, MFA; *Assoc Prof* Fred Niles, MFA; *Assoc Prof* Mary Zahner, PhD; *Assoc Prof* Beth Edwards, MFA; *Assoc Prof* Tim Wilbers, MFA; *Assoc Prof* Peter Gooch, MFA; *Assoc Prof* Terri Hitt, MFA; *Asst Prof* Roger Crum, PhD; *Asst Prof* Karen Kettering, MA; *Asst Prof* Gary Marcinowski, MFA; *Asst Prof* Jayne Matlock, MFA; *Asst Prof* Jeff Murphy, MFA; *Asst Prof* Joel Whitaker, MFA
Estab 1850; pvt; D & E; scholarships; SC 15, LC 8; enrl D 225, E 75-100, non-maj 100, maj 200
Ent Req: HS dipl
Degrees: BA, BFA
Tuition: $6585 per term; campus res available
Courses: †Art Education, †Art History, Ceramics, Drawing, Illustration, Mixed Media, †Painting, †Photography, †Printmaking, †Sculpture, Teacher Training, †Visual Communication Design
Summer School: Tuition $410 per cr hr

WRIGHT STATE UNIVERSITY, Dept of Art & Art History, Colonel Glenn Hwy, 45435. Tel 513-873-2896; *Chmn* Linda Caron; *Prof* Thomas Macaulay, MFA; *Prof* Jerry McDowell, MA; *Prof* Ron Geibert, MFA; *Assoc Prof* David Leach, MFA; *Assoc Prof* Carol Nathanson, PhD; *Assoc Prof* Diane Fitch, MFA; *Assoc Prof* Ernest Koerlin, MFA; *Asst Prof* Kimberly Vito, MFA
Estab 1964, dept estab 1965; pub; D & E; scholarships; SC 67, LC 16, GC 8; enrl D 516, E 43, non-maj 80, maj 150
Ent Req: HS dipl
Degrees: BA(Studio Art), BA(Art History), BFA 4 yr
Tuition: Res—undergrad $961 per quarter; nonres—undergrad $1922 per quarter
Courses: Art History, Drawing, Painting, Printmaking, Sculpture
Summer School: Dir, Linda Caron. Enrl 65; tuition res $961, nonres $1922 per 5-10 wk session. Courses—Drawing, Painting, Photography, Printmaking, Sculpture

DELAWARE

OHIO WESLEYAN UNIVERSITY, Fine Arts Dept, 43015. Tel 614-368-3600; FAX 614-368-3299; *Chmn* Justin Kronewetter, MFA; *Prof* Marty J Kalb, MA; *Prof* Carol Neuman de Vegvar, PhD; *Assoc Prof* James Krehbiel, MFA; *Assoc Prof* Rinda Metz, MFA; *Assoc Prof* Cynthia Cetlin, MFA; *Asst Prof* Joh Quick
Estab 1842, dept estab 1864; pvt; D & E; scholarships & fels; enrl D 1925, non-maj 1805, maj 120
Ent Req: HS dipl, SAT or ACT
Degrees: BA and BFA 4 yrs
Tuition: Res—$18,346 per yr; Campus res—room & board $24,222 per yr
Courses: Aesthetics, Art Education, Art History, Ceramics, Drawing, Graphic Design, Jewelry, Painting, Photography, Printmaking, Sculpture, Teacher Training, Computer Graphics
Summer School: Dean, Richard Fusch. Tuition $1125 for 6 wks. Courses—Varies

ELYRIA

LORAIN COUNTY COMMUNITY COLLEGE, Art Dept, 1005 N Abbe Rd, 44035. Tel 216-365-4191; *Chmn* Robert Beckstrom
Tuition: County res—$46 per cr hr; out-of-county res—$56 per cr hr; out-of-state res—$117 per cr hr
Courses: Art Appreciation, Ceramics, Design, Drawing, Painting, Photography, Printmaking, Sculpture, Textile Design

FINDLAY

UNIVERSITY OF FINDLAY, Art Dept, 1000 N Main St, 45840. Tel 419-422-8313, Ext 4729; *Dean College & Liberal Arts* Dr Dale Brougher. Instrs: FT 2, PT 6
Estab 1882; pvt; D & E; scholarships; SC 21, LC 4; enrl maj 30
Ent Req: HS dipl
Degrees: AA 2yr, BA & BS 4 yr
Tuition: $5900 per sem (12-17 sem hrs)
Courses: Advertising Design, Aesthetics, Art Education, Art History, Ceramics, Collages, Drawing, Graphic Design, Painting, Photography, Printmaking, Sculpture, Teacher Training
Adult Hobby Classes: Enrl 10-20. Courses—Ceramics
Children's Classes: Courses—Ceramics, Drawing
Summer School: Dir, Ed Erner

GAMBIER

KENYON COLLEGE, Art Dept, 43022. Tel 614-427-5459; *Prof* Martin Garhart; *Prof* Barry Gunderson, MFA; *Prof* Eugene J Dwyer, PhD; *Prof* Gregory P Spald, MFA; *Assoc Prof* Kay Willens; *Assoc Prof* Melissa Dabakis; *Assoc Prof* Janis Bell; *Assoc Prof* Claudia Esslinger, MFA; *Gallery Dir* Ellen Sheffield
Estab 1824, dept estab 1965; pvt; D; scholarships; SC 15, LC 10; enrl D 450, non-maj 250, maj 60
Ent Req: HS dipl
Degrees: BA and BFA
Tuition: Res—undergrad $19,240 per yr; campus res required
Courses: †Art History, Drawing, Painting, Photography, Printmaking, Sculpture

GRANVILLE

DENISON UNIVERSITY, Dept of Art, PO Box M, 43023. Tel 614-587-0810; FAX 614-587-6417; *Prof* Michael Jung, MFA; *Prof* George Bogdanovitch, MFA; *Assoc Prof* L Joy Sperling, PhD; *Assoc Prof* Karl Sandin, PhD; *Assoc Prof* David Jokinen, MFA; *Asst Prof* Ronald Abram, MFA; *Asst Prof* Ankeney Weitz, PhD; *Instr* Kok Yong, MA
Estab 1831, dept estab 1931; pvt; D; scholarships; SC 24, LC 16; enrl D 800, maj 65, double maj 35
Ent Req: HS
Degrees: BA, BFA, BS 4 yr
Tuition: Res—undergrad $18,570 per yr; campus res—double room & board $5160 per yr
Courses: Aesthetics, Architecture, †Art History, †Ceramics, Drawing, Graphic Arts, Graphic Design, History of Art & Archaeology, Mixed Media, Museum Staff Training, †Painting, Photography, †Printmaking, Restoration & Conservation, †Sculpture

HAMILTON

FITTON CENTER FOR CREATIVE ARTS, 101 S Monument Ave, 45041-2833. Tel 513-863-8873; FAX 513-863-8865; *Exec Dir* Rick H Jones; *Arts in Common Dir* Deby Sage; *Exhibitions* Nelly Bly Cogan
Estab 1992; pub; D & E; scholarships; SC 50, LC 2; enrl D & E 400
Courses: Aesthetics, Art Appreciation, Art Education, Art History, Drawing, Fashion Arts, Film, Graphic Arts, Graphic Design, Handicrafts, Illustration, Industrial Design, Intermedia, Painting, Photography

MIAMI UNIVERSITY, Dept Fine Arts, 1601 Peck Blvd, 45011. Tel 513-529-6026; *Art Coordr* Phil Joseph; *Prof* Edward Montgomery
Scholarships
Tuition: $126 per cr hr
Courses: Advertising Design, Art Appreciation, Art Education, Art History, Calligraphy, Drawing, Painting, Printmaking, Sculpture
Adult Hobby Classes: Enrl 25-30. Courses—Painting, Printmaking
Summer School: Courses—Drawing

HIRAM

HIRAM COLLEGE, Art Dept, Dean St, 44234. Tel 330-569-5304; *Chmn* Linda Bourassa. Instrs: FT 3, PT 2
Estab 1850; pvt; D; scholarships; SC 20, LC 14; enrl D 400
Ent Req: HS dipl
Degrees: AB 4 yr
Tuition: $15,600 per acad yr
Courses: Aesthetics, Art Education, Art History, Ceramics, Drawing, Painting, Photography, Printmaking, Sculpture, Teacher Training, †Studio Art
Summer School: Enrl 15-20 per course; 6-7 wks. Courses—Art History, Ceramics, Film Studies, Photography

HURON

BOWLING GREEN STATE UNIVERSITY, Art Dept, Firelands Col Div of Humanities, 901 Rye Beach Rd, 44839. Tel 419-433-5560; *Asst Prof Art* David Sapp. Instrs: FT 1, PT 3
Estab 1907, col estab 1966; pub; D & E; scholarships; SC 12, LC 3; enrl D 1200
Ent Req: HS dipl, SAT
Degrees: AA 2 yr
Tuition: Res—undergrad $1435 per sem, $141 per cr hr
Courses: Art Education, Art History, Drawing, History of Art & Archaeology, Painting, Photography, Teacher Training, Theatre Arts, Enameling
Summer School: Term of 5 wks beginning June 18. Courses—Art Education, Studio Courses

KENT

KENT STATE UNIVERSITY, School of Art, 44242. Tel 330-672-2192; FAX 330-672-4729; *Dir* William Quinn; *Asst Dir* Joseph Fry; *Div Coordr Design* J Charles Walker, MFA; *Div Coordr Fine Art* Paul O'Keefe; *Div Coordr Art History* Fred T Smith; *Div Coordr Crafts* Kirk Mangus; *Grad Coordr* Frank Susi. Instrs: FT 43, PT 6
Estab 1910; pub; D & E; scholarships; SC 105, LC 35, GC 50; enrl non-maj 600, maj 600, grad 100
Ent Req: HS dipl, ACT
Degrees: BFA, BA 4 yrs, MA 1 - 2 yrs, MFA 2 - 3 yrs
Tuition: Res—undergrad $1650 per sem, grad $1915 per sem; nonres—undergrad $3285 per sem, grad $3713 per sem, $309.82 per cr hr; campus res—room & board $1601 per sem
Courses: Art Appreciation, †Art Education, †Art History, Calligraphy, †Ceramics, Design, †Drawing, †Graphic Design, History of Art & Archaeology, †Illustration, †Jewelry, Lettering, Mixed Media, Museum Staff Training, †Painting, Photography, †Printmaking, †Sculpture, Silversmithing, Teacher Training, Textile Design, †Weaving, Arts Therapy, Enameling, †Glass Blowing, Neon
Children's Classes: Enrl 150; tuition $15 per 6 wk session, two 6 wk sessions, fall & spring
Summer School: Dir, William Quinn. Enrl 500; tuition $137.50 per cr hr, 5 or 10 wk term. Courses—approx 30 - 35

MARIETTA

MARIETTA COLLEGE, Art Dept, 45750. Tel 614-376-4643; FAX 614-376-4529; *Chmn* Valdis Garoza; *Prof* Ron Wright. Instrs: FT 2
Estab 1835; pvt; grants in aid & student loans; SC 20, LC 7; enrl maj 75, total col 1600
Degrees: BA(Studio, Art History, Art Education & Graphic Design)
Tuition: $6185 per sem
Courses: Advertising Design, Art Appreciation, Art Education, Art History, Calligraphy, Ceramics, Commercial Art, Design, Drawing, Painting, Printmaking, Carving in Wood & Stone, Computer Graphic, Design, Jewelrymaking, Life Drawing, Lithography & Silkscreen, Modeling & Casting, Stained Glass

MENTOR

LAKELAND COMMUNITY COLLEGE, Visual Arts Dept, Rt 306 at I-90, 44060. Tel 216-953-7028; *Chmn & Dir of Humanities Div* Dr Larry Aufderheide; *Prof* Richard Parsons, MA; *Prof* Walter Swyrydenko, MA; *Instr* John Merchant, BA
Estab 1967, dept estab 1968; D & E; scholarships; enrl D & E 350
Ent Req: HS dipl
Degrees: AA with concentration in Art 2 yrs, AA Technology degree in Graphic Arts
Tuition: Res—undergrad $601.50 per qtr; in-county res—$40.10 per cr hr; out-of-county res—$49.20 per cr hr
Courses: Advertising Design, Art Appreciation, Art History, Calligraphy, Ceramics, Commercial Art, Conceptual Art, Drawing, †Graphic Arts, Graphic Design, Illustration, Intermedia, Jewelry, Lettering, Painting, Photography, Printmaking, Sculpture
Summer School: Courses—Ceramics, Drawing, Jewelry, Painting, Sculpture

MOUNT VERNON

MOUNT VERNON NAZARENE COLLEGE, Art Dept, Martinsburg Rd, 43050. Tel 614-397-1244; *Chmn* Jim Hendrickx; *Instr* John Donnelly
Estab 1968, dept estab 1970; den; D & E; scholarships; SC 20, LC 5; enrl D 1052, non-maj 1032, maj 20
Ent Req: HS dipl & grad of upper 2/3, ACT
Degrees: BA; Sr project required for graduation
Tuition: Res, nonres, undergrad $276 per cr hr per term
Courses: Aesthetics, Art Education, Art History, Ceramics, Design, Drafting, Drawing, Painting, Photography, Printmaking, Sculpture, Art in the Western World, Design Fundamentals, Graphic Communication, Selected Topics, Senior Project

NEW CONCORD

MUSKINGUM COLLEGE, Art Department, Johnson Hall, 43762. Tel 614-826-8315, 826-8211; *Chmn* James Wallace; *Prof* Gaile Gallatin; *Lectr* Laura Waters. Instrs: FT 3
Estab 1837; pvt; D; scholarships; SC 13, LC 6; enrl D 300, maj 15
Ent Req: HS dipl, ent exam, specific school standards
Degrees: BA and BS 4 yr
Tuition: $13,240 per yr; room & board $3914
Courses: Art History, †Art Education, Ceramics, Design, Drawing, Graphic Arts, Painting, Photography, Sculpture, Teacher Training
Adult Hobby Classes: Enrl 60. Courses—Art Educ
Children's Classes: Enrl 10. Courses—Ceramics

OBERLIN

OBERLIN COLLEGE, Dept of Art, 87 N Main St, 44074. Tel 216-775-8181; FAX 216-775-8969; *Chmn* William Hood, PhD; *Prof* Richard Spear, PhD; *Prof* John Pearson, MFA; *Prof* Athena Tacha, PhD; *Assoc Prof* Susan Kane, PhD; *Assoc Prof* Patricia Mathews, PhD; *Assoc Prof* Jeffrey Hamburger, PhD; *Asst Prof* Robert Harrist, PhD; *Asst Prof* Sarah Schuster, MFA; *Asst Prof* Johnny Coleman, MFA; *Asst Prof* Nanette Yannuzzi Macias, MFA; *Asst Prof* Lynn Lukkas, MFA
Estab 1833, dept estab 1917; pvt; D; scholarships; SC 28, LC 38, advanced undergrad & grad courses 13; enrl D approx 1200, non-maj 500, maj 100, grad 5
Ent Req: HS dipl, SAT
Degrees: BA 4 yr
Tuition: Undergrad and grad $15,600 per yr; campus res—room and board $4890
Courses: Art History, Drawing, History of Art & Archaeology, Painting, Photography, Sculpture, Interactive Media, Silkscreening

OXFORD

MIAMI UNIVERSITY, Art Dept, New Art Bldg, 45056. Tel 513-529-2900; *Dean School Fine Arts* Hayden B May; *Chmn* Jerry W Morris
Estab 1809, dept estab 1929; pub; D & E; scholarships; SC 49, LC 35, GC 20; enrl D 2309, non-maj 1890, maj 419, grad 32
Ent Req: HS dipl, class rank, ACT or SAT
Degrees: BFA and BS(Art) 4 yrs, MFA 2 yrs, MA(Art or Art Educ) and MEd(Art Educ) 1 yr
Tuition: Res—$4286 with room & board; nonres—$6844 with room & board
Courses: Advertising Design, Architecture, †Art Education, Art History, Calligraphy, †Ceramics, Collages, Commercial Art, Display, †Drawing, Graphic Arts, †Graphic Design, History of Art & Archaeology, Illustration, †Jewelry, Lettering, Museum Staff Training, †Painting, Photography, †Printmaking, †Sculpture, †Silversmithing, †Teacher Training, †Textile Design, Stitchery, Weaving
Children's Classes: Enrl 70; tuition $5 per sem. Courses—General Art
Summer School: Dir, Peter Dahoda. Courses—varied workshops

PAINESVILLE

LAKE ERIE COLLEGE, Fine Arts Dept, 391 W Washington St, 44077. Tel 216-352-3361, Ext 4745; *Prof* Paul Gothard. Instrs: FT 2, PT 1
Estab 1856; pvt; SC 20, LC 7; enrl 800 total
Ent Req: Col board exam
Degrees: BA & BFA 4 yrs
Tuition: Res—undergrad $330 per cr hr
Courses: Art Education, Art History, †Ceramics, Drawing, †Painting, †Photography, †Printmaking, Sculpture, Design, Introductory Art
Summer School: Courses vary

SAINT CLAIRSVILLE

OHIO UNIVERSITY-EASTERN CAMPUS, Dept Comparitive Arts, 43950. Tel 614-695-1720; *Prof* David Miles
Degrees: BA & BS 4 yrs
Tuition: Res—undergrad $86 per cr hr, grad $178 per cr hr; nonres—undergrad $220 per cr hr, grad $347 per cr hr
Courses: Art Appreciation, Art Education, Design, Drawing, Photography

SPRINGFIELD

SPRINGFIELD MUSEUM OF ART, 107 Cliff Park Rd, 45501. Tel 513-325-4673; *Dir* Mark Chepp. Instrs: PT 20
Estab 1951; pvt; D & E; scholarships; D 600
Tuition: No campus res
Courses: Ceramics, Drawing, Jewelry, Painting, Photography, Sculpture
Adult Hobby Classes: Enrl 287; tuition varies
Children's Classes: Enrl 286; tuition $39 per qtr. Courses—vary

WITTENBERG UNIVERSITY, Art Dept, Koch Hall, N Wittenberg Ave, PO Box 720, 45501. Tel 513-327-6231; *Chmn* Jack Osbun, MFA; *Prof* Don Dunifon, MFA; *Prof* George Ramsay; *Assoc Prof* Ann Terry, MFA; *Assoc Prof* Jack Mann
Estab 1842; pvt den; D & E; scholarships; SC 30, LC 17; enrl D 350, non-maj 270, maj 80
Ent Req: HS dipl, class rank, transcript, SAT or ACT test results, recommendations & if possible, a personal interview
Degrees: AB & BFA 4 yr
Tuition: Nonres—undergrad $15,948 per yr; campus res—room $2190, board $2214
Courses: †Art Education, †Art History, †Ceramics, Drawing, Graphic Arts, Graphic Design, †Illustration, Interior Design, Jewelry, †Painting, Photography, †Printmaking, †Sculpture, †Teacher Training
Summer School: Provost, William Wiebenga. Enrl 400; tuition $250 for term of 7 wks beginning June 14. Courses—Art in the Elementary School, Fundamental of Art, Painting

SYLVANIA

LOURDES COLLEGE, Art Dept, 6832 Convent Blvd, 43560. Tel 419-885-3211; FAX 419-882-3987; *Chmn Fine Arts* Sr Sharon Havelak
Estab 1958; pvt, den; D & E; scholarships; SC 12, LC 9; enrl D 70, E 30, non-maj 60, maj 35
Ent Req: HS dipl, ACT or SAT
Degrees: AA, BA, BIS
Tuition: $250 per cr hr; no campus res
Courses: Aesthetics, Art Appreciation, Art History, Calligraphy, Ceramics, Design, Drawing, Occupational Therapy, Painting, Printmaking, Sculpture, Weaving, Art Therapy, Copper Enameling, Fiber Arts
Adult Hobby Classes: Enrl 40; tuition $3-$35 per 1-5 classes. Courses - Same as above & others through Life-Long Learning Center
Children's Classes: Enrl 95; tuition $50 for 10 wks. Courses—Ceramics, Drawing, Painting
Summer School: Dir, Sr Sharon Havelak. Enrl 30; tuition $250 per cr for 10 wk term. Courses—Art History, Studio Courses

TIFFIN

HEIDELBERG COLLEGE, Dept of Art, 310 E Market St, 44883. Tel 419-448-2125; *Chmn* Brian Haley
Estab 1850; pvt; D; scholarships; SC 22, LC 9; enrl 200, maj 24
Ent Req: HS dipl, each applicant's qualifications are considered individually
Degrees: AB 4 yrs, independent study, honors work available
Tuition: $18,890 per yr
Courses: Advertising Design, Aesthetics, Art Education, Ceramics, Commercial Art, Display, Drawing, Graphic Arts, Graphic Design, History of Art & Archaeology, Illustration, Jewelry, Lettering, Museum Staff Training, Painting, Sculpture, Stage Design, Teacher Training, Textile Design, Chip Carving, Copper Enameling, Metal Tooling, Mosaic
Summer School: Term of 6 wks beginning June. Courses—Materials & Methods in Teaching, Practical Arts

TOLEDO

UNIVERSITY OF TOLEDO, Dept of Art, University Art Bldg, 620 Grove Place, 43620. Tel 419-530-8300; FAX 419-530-8337; *Chmn* Tom Lingeman; *Prof* Duane Bastian, PhD; *Prof* David Guip, PhD; *Prof* Diana Attie, MS; *Prof* Linda Ames-Bell, MFA; *Prof* Peter Elloian, MFA; *Assoc Prof* Carolyn Autry, MFA; *Assoc Prof* Marc Gerstein, PhD; *Assoc Prof* Rex Fogt, MFA; *Assoc Prof* Alan Melis, MFA. Instrs: FT 13, PT 12
Estab 1919; D & E; scholarships; Same as regular session
Ent Req: HS dipl
Degrees: BA, BFA, BEd 4 yr; MEd (Art Educ) 2 yr
Tuition: Res—undergrad $999 per quarter or $83.25 per cr hr, grad $1269 per quarter or $105.83 per cr hr; nonres—undergrad $2177 per quarter or $181.43 per cr hr, grad $2517 per quarter or $209 per cr hr
Courses: Advertising Design, Art Education, †Art History, †Ceramics, Design, †Drawing, †Painting, †Photography, †Printmaking, †Sculpture, †Metalsmithing
Summer School: Courses offered from those above

WESTERVILLE

OTTERBEIN COLLEGE, Art Dept, 43081. Tel 614-823-1258; FAX 614-823-1118; *Chmn* Jo Anne Stickhweh
Pvt; scholarships; SC 11, LC 4; enrl D 1400, maj 32
Ent Req: HS dipl
Degrees: BA 4 yrs
Tuition: Res—undergrad $11,502 per yr; campus res—room & board $4107
Courses: Art Education, Art History, Ceramics, Drawing, Graphic Design, Painting, Photography, Computer Art

WILBERFORCE

CENTRAL STATE UNIVERSITY, Dept of Art, * 45384. Tel 513-376-6610; *Chmn* Willis Davis. Instrs: FT 6
Estab 1856; D; SC 20, LC 8; enrl D 175, maj 50, others 130
Ent Req: HS dipl
Degrees: BA and BS 4 yr
Courses: Advertising Design, Art Education, Art History, Ceramics, Drawing, Graphic Arts, Lettering, Painting, Sculpture, Teacher Training, Studio
Summer School: Chmn, Willis Bing Davis. Enrl maj 50, others 200; term of 12 wks beginning June 16, two sessions. Courses—Art for the Elementary Teacher, Art History, Black Artists, Ceramics, Introduction to Art, Painting, Sculpture

WILBERFORCE UNIVERSITY, Art Dept, 1055 N Bickett Rd, 45384. Tel 513-376-2911; *Advisor* James Padgett, MFA
Estab 1856, dept estab 1973; pvt; D; scholarships; SC 22, LC 5
Ent Req: HS dipl
Degrees: BA, BS & BA(Educ) 4 yrs
Tuition: $6670 per yr
Courses: Commercial Art, Printmaking, Sculpture, Teacher Training, Fine Arts
Summer School: Courses offered

WILLOUGHBY

SCHOOL OF FINE ARTS, Visual Arts Dept, 38660 Mentor Ave, 44094. Tel 216-951-7500; *Dir* Charles M Frank; *Visual Arts Coordr* Robert Raack
Estab 1957; pvt; D & E; scholarships; enrl D 85, E 195
Tuition: $35-$170 per class; no campus res
Courses: Ceramics, Drawing, Intermedia, Mixed Media, Painting, Photography
Adult Hobby Classes: Tuition $35-$170 for one 6 wk session & two 16 wk sessions. Courses—Ceramics, Drawing, Painting
Children's Classes: Enrl 240; tuition $35-$170 for one 6 wk session & two 16 wk sessions. Courses—Ceramics, Drawing, Painting
Summer School: Dir, Doris Foster. Enrl 210; tuition $25-$71 for term of 6 wks beginning mid-June. Courses—same as above

WILMINGTON

WILMINGTON COLLEGE, Art Dept, 251 Ludovic St, 45177. Tel 513-382-6661; *Prof* Terry Inlow; *Asst Prof* Hal Shunk
Scholarships
Degrees: BA
Tuition: $10,230 per yr
Courses: Art Education, Art History, Ceramics, Design, Drawing, Handicrafts, Painting, Photography, Printmaking, Sculpture, Stage Design

WOOSTER

COLLEGE OF WOOSTER, Dept of Art, University St, 44691. Tel 330-263-2388; FAX 330-263-2633; Elec Mail dwarner@acs.wooster.edu. WATS 800-321-9885. *Chmn* Linda Hults, PhD; *Prof* Walter Zurko, MFA; *Prof* George Olson, MFA; *Prof* Thalia Gouma-Peterson, PhD; *Asst Prof* Garth Amandson, MFA; *Slide Cur* Linda Kammer; *Admin Asst* Donna Warner
Estab 1866; pvt; D & E; SC 13, LC 19; enrl D 1800, maj 40
Ent Req: HS dipl
Degrees: BA 4 yr
Tuition: $23,230 per yr (board & room included)
Courses: Architecture, Art Education, †Art History, Ceramics, Drawing, History of Art & Archaeology, Mixed Media, Painting, Photography, Printmaking, Sculpture, Studio Art
Adult Hobby Classes: Available through student activities board. Enrl 12-20; tuition varies
Summer School: Dir, Dr Pamela Frese

YELLOW SPRINGS

ANTIOCH COLLEGE, Visual Arts Dept, 45387. Tel 513-767-7331; FAX 513-767-6470; *Prof* David Lapalombara, MFA; *Prof* Daniel Hignite; *Prof* Karen Shirley, MFA
Estab 1853; pvt; D & E; SC 48, LC 10; enrl D 665 per quarter, non-maj 100, maj 50
Ent Req: HS dipl
Degrees: BA
Tuition: $21,628 per yr (tuition, fees, room & board)
Courses: Art Education, Ceramics, †Drawing, Film, Painting, Photography, Printmaking, †Sculpture, Stage Design, Theatre Arts, Video

YOUNGSTOWN

YOUNGSTOWN STATE UNIVERSITY, Art Dept, One University Plaza, 44555. Tel 330-742-3000; *Chmn* Susan Russo
Estab 1908, dept estab 1952; pub; D & E; SC 44, LC 26, GC 8; enrl D & E 1250, maj 300, grad 15
Ent Req: HS dipl
Degrees: AB, BFA & BS 4 yrs
Tuition: Res—$81 per cr hr; nonres—$1810 per sem
Courses: †Art Education, †Art History, †Ceramics, †Commercial Art, Drawing, Graphic Arts, †Graphic Design, Illustration, Interior Design, Jewelry, Lettering, Museum Staff Training, †Painting, Photography, †Printmaking, †Sculpture, †Teacher Training
Adult Hobby Classes: Courses—Calligraphy, Ceramics, Drawing, Painting, Photography, Weaving
Summer School: Two 5 wk sessions beginning June. Courses—same as above

OKLAHOMA

ADA

EAST CENTRAL UNIVERSITY, Art Dept, 74820. Tel 405-332-8000, Ext 356; *Chmn* Robert Sieg, MFA; *Prof* Roger Huebner, MFA; *Instr* Marc Etier, MFA; *Instr* Brad Jessop; *Instr* Marybeth Coleman, BFA; *Instr* Alan Burris, BA
Estab 1909; pub; D & E; scholarships; SC 22, LC 10, GC 8; enrl D 222, E 105, non-maj 103, maj 80, grad 3, others 36
Ent Req: HS dipl, ATC
Degrees: BA & BA(Educ) 4 yr, MEd 33 hrs, post grad work, pub sevice prog
Tuition: Res—lower $40.39 cr hr, upper $41.25 cr hr; non res—lower $68.75 cr hr, upper $75.97 cr hr
Courses: Aesthetics, Art Appreciation, Art Education, Art History, Ceramics, Design, Drawing, Graphic Arts, Handicrafts, History of Art & Archaeology, Mixed Media, Painting, Photography, Printmaking, Sculpture, Teacher Training, Wood Design
Adult Hobby Classes: Enrl 25 average. Courses—Drawing, Painting, Silk Screen
Summer School: Dir, Robert Sieg. Tuition lower $49.69, upper $50.50. Courses—Art Education, Drawing, Painting, Sculpture

ALTUS

WESTERN OKLAHOMA STATE COLLEGE, Art Dept, 2801 N Main, 73521. Tel 405-477-2000; FAX 405-521-6154; *Chmn* Jerry Bryan
Scholarships
Degrees: AA, AS, AT
Tuition: Res—undergrad $27.80 per hr; nonres—undergrad $49.25 hr
Courses: Advertising Design, Art Appreciation, Art History, Ceramics, Design, Drawing, Handicrafts, Jewelry, Painting, Photography, Printmaking, Sculpture, Stage Design, Video, Weaving

BETHANY

SOUTHERN NAZARENE UNIVERSITY, Art Dept, 6729 NW 39th Expressway, 73008. Tel 405-789-6400; *Head Dept* Nila West Murrow
Estab 1920; den; D & E; scholarships; SC 13, LC 7; enrl D 51, E 6, non-maj 38, maj 13
Ent Req: HS dipl, ACT
Tuition: Res—undergrad $158 per hr, grad $190 per hr; campus res available
Courses: Aesthetics, Art Education, Art History, Commercial Art, Drawing, Painting, Printmaking, Sculpture, †Teacher Training, Crafts, Pottery
Children's Classes: Enrl 55; tuition $115 one wk summer art camp (grades 3 - 12). Courses—Drawing, Pottery, Watercolor & various crafts
Summer School: Dir, Nila Murrow. Same as children's classes

CHICKASHA

UNIVERSITY OF SCIENCE & ARTS OF OKLAHOMA, Arts Dept, 73018. Tel 405-224-3140, Ext 301; *Prof* Kent Lamar. Instrs: FT 3, PT 2
Estab 1909; pub; D; scholarship; SC 26, LC 3; enrl maj 84, others 180
Degrees: 124 hr req for grad
Tuition: Res—undergrad $43 per hr, grad $44 per hr; nonres—undergrad $99.45 per hr, grad $108.50 per hr
Courses: Ceramics, Design, Drawing, Jewelry, Painting, Photography, Printmaking, Sculpture, Teacher Training, Pottery & Modeling
Adult Hobby Classes: Enrl 30; tuition $43 per hr. Courses—Ceramics, Drawing, Graphics Design, Stained Glass
Summer School: Enrl 60; tuition $43 per hr for 10 wk course. Courses—Ceramics, Jewelry, Painting, Sculpture

CLAREMORE

ROGERS STATE COLLEGE, Art Dept, 1701 W Will Rogers Blvd, 74017-3252. Tel 918-341-7510; *Dir* Gary E Moeller, MFA
Estab 1971; pub; D & E; scholarships; SC 22, LC 3; enrl D 126, E 60, non-maj 146, maj 82
Ent Req: HS dipl, ACT
Degrees: AA & AS 2 yr
Tuition: Res—$40 per hr; nonres—$160 per hr; campus res available
Courses: Art History, Ceramics, Drawing, Lettering, Painting, Photography, Printmaking, Sculpture, †Fine Arts, †Graphic Technology
Children's Classes: Tuition $35 per hr. Courses—Children's Art
Summer School: Tuition $35 per hr for term of 8 wks beginning June 5th. Courses—Advanced Ceramics, Art Appreciation, Drawing, Graphic Technology, Painting

DURANT

SOUTHEASTERN OKLAHOMA STATE UNIVERSITY, Art Dept, Sta A, 74701. Tel 405-924-0121; FAX 405-924-7313; *Chmn* Brad Cushman; *Asst Prof* Paul Pfrehm
Estab 1909; pub; scholarships; enrl 330
Ent Req: HS dipl, col exam
Degrees: BA & BAEduc 4-5 yrs, MEd
Tuition: Res—lower div $55 per hr, upper div $54 per hr, grad div $54 per hr; nonres—lower div $93.70 per hr, upper div $120 per hr, grad div $150 per hr
Courses: Art Appreciation, Art Education, Art History, Ceramics, Design, Drawing, Graphic Arts, Jewelry, Painting, Printmaking, Sculpture, Applied Design, Crafts
Adult Hobby Classes: Enrl 20; 12 wk term. Courses—Ceramics, Drawing, Jewelry, Painting
Summer School: Dir, Susan H Allen. Enrl 130; tuition same as above. Courses—Art Appreciation, Ceramics, Drawing, Design, Fundamentals, Painting, Printmaking, Special Studies

EDMOND

UNIVERSITY OF CENTRAL OKLAHOMA, Dept of Visual Arts & Design, 100 N University Dr, 73034-0180. Tel 405-341-2980, Ext 5201; FAX 405-341-4964; *Chmn* William L Hommel, PhD
Estab 1890; pub; D & E; scholarships; enrl maj 280, grad 20, dept 1168, school 13, 086
Ent Req: HS dipl, health exams, IQ test, scholarship tests
Degrees: BA, BS and MEduc 3-4 yrs
Courses: Art Education, Art History, Ceramics, Commercial Art, Design, Graphic Design, Jewelry, Museum Staff Training, Painting, Photography, Sculpture, Weaving, African Art, Art in America, Arts & Crafts, Etching & Lithography, Figure Drawing, Metal Design, Studio Art
Summer School: Chmn, William L Hommel PhD. Enrl 276; tuition $40.39 per cr hr lower div, $41.20 per cr hr upper div. Courses—Art Appreciation, Art History, Ceramics, Computer Graphics, Design, Drawing, European Study Tour. Fibers, Figure Drawing, Jewelry, Painting, Sculpture

ENID

PHILLIPS UNIVERSITY, Dept of Art, University Sta, PO Box 200, 73702. Tel 405-237-4433; *Chmn* Mary Phillips, MFA
Estab 1907, dept estab 1909; den; D & E; scholarships; SC 20, LC 6; enrl D 45, E 18, non-maj 20, maj 25, others 18
Ent Req: HS dipl
Degrees: MBA & ME 5 yrs, BA, BS & BFA 4 yrs
Tuition: Res & nonres—undergrad $247 per hr; campus res—room & board $3000
Courses: †Advertising Design, Art Appreciation, †Art Education, Art History, Calligraphy, †Ceramics, Commercial Art, Design, Drawing, Graphic Arts, History of Art & Archaeology, Lettering, Painting, Photography, Sculpture, Teacher Training, Pre-Art Therapy
Adult Hobby Classes: Enrl 18; tuition $125 per course
Summer School: Enrl 15; tuition $227 for term of one cr hr. Courses vary

LAWTON

CAMERON UNIVERSITY, Art Dept, 2800 W Gore Blvd, 73505. Tel 405-581-2450, 581-2200; *Chmn* Jack Bryan
Estab 1970; pub; D & E; scholarships; SC 22, LC 5; enrl D 417, E 90, maj 60
Ent Req: HS dipl
Degrees: BA 4 yrs
Tuition: Res—undergrad $46.65 per hr, grad $58.65 per hr; nonres—undergrad $117.65 per hr, grad $141.40 per hr; campus res—room & board $643 per sem
Courses: Art Appreciation, Art Education, †Art History, Ceramics, Drawing, Design, Graphic Arts, Graphic Design, †Mixed Media, Painting, Photography, †Printmaking, †Sculpture, Color, Crafts
Summer School: Courses—Art Education, Ceramics, Drawing, Graphics, Mixed Media, Painting, Photography, Printmaking

MIAMI

NORTHEASTERN OKLAHOMA A & M COLLEGE, Art Dept, 74354. Tel 918-542-8441, 540-6354; FAX 918-542-9759; *Chmn* Jack Rucker. Instrs: FT 2, PT 1
Estab 1919; pub; D & E; scholarships; SC 12, LC 3
Ent Req: HS dipl
Degrees: AA 2 yr
Tuition: Res—$27.30 per hr; nonres—$76.55; campus res available
Courses: Advertising Design, Art Appreciation, Art Education, Calligraphy, Ceramics, Commercial Art, Costume Design & Construction, Design, Display, Drawing, Fashion Arts, Graphic Arts, Lettering, Painting, Photography, Sculpture, Stage Design, Theatre Arts, Video

NORMAN

UNIVERSITY OF OKLAHOMA, School of Art, 520 Parrington Oval, Rm 202, 73019. Tel 405-325-2691; FAX 405-325-1668; *Dir* Dr Andrew Phelan
Estab 1911; pub; scholarships; SC 27, LC 22, GC 12; enrl maj 400, others 1200
Degrees: BFA, BA(Art History), MA(Art History) & MFA
Courses: Art Appreciation, Art Education, †Art History, †Ceramics, †Drawing, †Film, †Graphic Design, Jewelry, Museum Staff Training, †Painting, †Photography, Printmaking, Sculpture, Video, Metal Design, Product Design

OKLAHOMA CITY

OKLAHOMA CHRISTIAN UNIVERSITY OF SCIENCE & ARTS, Dept of Art & Design, PO Box 11000, 73136-1100. Tel 405-425-5556; FAX 405-425-5547; *Chmn* Michael J O'Keefe, MFA; *Assoc Prof* Cherry Tredway, PhD; *Asst Prof* David Crismon, MFA; *Adjunct Prof* Rick Barnes, MFA; *Adjunct Prof* John Finney, MFA; *Adjunct Prof* Gayle Canada, MFA; *Med Adjunct Prof* Annette Pate, MEd; *Adjunct Prof* Skip McKinstry; *Adjunct Prof* Donna Watson, PhD
Scholarships
Tuition: $2125 per trimester (12-16 hrs)
Courses: †Advertising Design, Art Appreciation, †Art Education, Art History, Design, Drawing, Graphic Design, Illustration, †Interior Design, Painting, Photography, Printmaking, Stage Design, Computer Graphics

OKLAHOMA CITY UNIVERSITY, Norick Art Center, 2501 N Blackwelder, 73106. Tel 405-521-5226; FAX 405-557-6029; *Chmn* Jack R Davis. Instrs: FT 3, PT 13
Estab 1904; den; D & E; scholarships offered; SC 44, LC 26; enrl maj 62
Degrees: 4 yr
Tuition: $4025 per sem
Courses: †Advertising Design, Art History, Ceramics, Collages, †Commercial Art, Design, Drawing, †Graphic Design, History of Art & Archaeology, Illustration, History of Art & Archaeology, Illustration, Lettering, Mixed Media, Museum Staff Training, Occupational Therapy, Painting, Photography, Printmaking, Sculpture, Teacher Training, Airbrush, Art Marketing, Computer Graphics
Adult Hobby Classes: Summer workshops
Children's Classes: Enrl 120; tuition $95 for 2 wks in summer. Courses—Drawing, Painting, Printmaking, Sculpture
Summer School: Chmn, Jack Davis. Enrl 15; tuition $270 per cr hr for two 6 wk sessions May to July, July to August. Courses—Ceramics, Drawing, Painting, Sculpture

OKMULGEE

OKLAHOMA STATE UNIVERSITY, Graphic Arts Dept, 1801 E Fourth, 74447.
Tel 918-756-6211; *Head Dept* Gary Borchert; *Instr* Paul A Gresham, MFA; *Instr*
Bill Welch, BS. Instrs: FT 5, PT 1
Estab 1946, dept estab 1970; pub; D & E; scholarships; SC 12, LC 1; enrl D 130, E
18
Ent Req: HS dipl or 18 yrs of age
Degrees: 2 yr Associate, degree granting technical school
Tuition: Res—$43.97 per cr hr; out-of-state $111.67 per cr hr
Courses: Advertising Design, †Art History, Commercial Art, Drafting, Drawing,
Graphic Arts, †Graphic Design, Illustration, Jewelry, Lettering, Photography,
†Studio
Summer School: Tuition same as above per trimester beginning June 1st to last of
Sept

SHAWNEE

OKLAHOMA BAPTIST UNIVERSITY, Art Dept, 500 W University, 74801. Tel
405-275-2850, Ext 2345; *Chmn* Steve Hicks, MFA; *Asst Prof* Janie Wester, MA;
Asst Prof Nelle Agee, MEd; *Instr* Gloria Duncan, MA; *Instr* Julie Blackstone, MA
Estab 1910; den; D; scholarships; SC 7, LC 3, grad 2; enrl D 100, non-maj 75, maj
25, grad 2
Ent Req: HS dipl, SAT-ACT
Degrees: BA & BFA 4 yrs
Tuition: Res—undergrad $1615 per sem, $110 per hr; nonres—undergrad $1300;
campus res—room & board $1000 per academic yr
Courses: Art Appreciation, Art Education, Art History, Calligraphy, Ceramics,
Design, Drawing, History of Art & Archaeology, Painting, Photography,
Printmaking, Teacher Training, Weaving, Fibers

SAINT GREGORY'S COLLEGE, Dept of Art, 1900 W MacArthur Dr, 74801. Tel
405-878-5100; *Chmn* Shirlie Bowers Wilcoxson, BFA
Estab 1898, dept estab 1960; den; D & E; SC 6; enrl D 325
Ent Req: HS dipl, ACT or SAT
Degrees: AA 2 yrs
Tuition: $2319.50 per sem
Courses: Art History, Ceramics, Commercial Art, Drawing, Mixed Media, Sculpture
Adult Hobby Classes: Courses—Ceramics, Drawing, Sculpture

STILLWATER

OKLAHOMA STATE UNIVERSITY, Art Dept, 108 Bartlett Ctr for the Studio
Arts, 74078. Tel 405-744-6016; FAX 405-744-5767; *Dept Head* Nancy B Wilkinson,
PhD
Estab 1890, dept estab 1928; pub; D & E; scholarships; SC 20, LC 4; enrl D 850, E
60, non-maj 810, maj 210
Ent Req: HS dipl
Degrees: BA, BA(Art Hist), BFA, 4 yr
Courses: Advertising Design, Art Appreciation, Art History, Ceramics, Commercial
Art, Design, Display, Drawing, Goldsmithing, Graphic Arts, Graphic Design,
Illustration, Jewelry, Lettering, Painting, Printmaking, Sculpture, Silversmithing
Adult Hobby Classes: Enrl 169; tuition $950 per sem. Courses—Lecture, Studio
Summer School: Dept Head, Nancy B Wilkinson, PhD

TAHLEQUAH

NORTHWESTERN STATE UNIVERSITY, 74464. Tel 918-456-5511, Ext 2705;
Dean Arts & Letters Dr Thomas Cottrill, EdD; *Instr* Jerry Choate, MFA;
Instr R C Coones, MFA; *Instr* Dr Kathleen Schmidt, EdD
Estab 1889; pub; D & E; scholarships; enrl non-maj 50, maj 30, grad 10
Ent Req: HS dipl
Degrees: BA & BA(Educ) 4 yr
Tuition: Res—undergrad $48.89 per hr, grad $49.70 per hr; nonres—undergrad $68.
75 per hr, grad $85.54; campus res available
Courses: Art Education, Art History, Ceramics, Commercial Art, Costume Design &
Construction, Drafting, Drawing, Graphic Arts, Lettering, Painting, Photography,
Printmaking, Sculpture, Stage Design, Teacher Training, Theatre Arts
Adult Hobby Classes: Enrl 20; tuition $20.85 per cr hr for 1 sem. Courses—Indian
Art
Summer School: Dir, Tom Cottrill. Courses—Art Education, Fundamentals of Art

TULSA

ORAL ROBERTS UNIVERSITY, Fine Arts Dept, 7777 S Lewis, 74171. Tel 918-
495-6611; FAX 918-495-6033; *Chmn* Stu Branston; *Assoc Prof* Douglas Latta,
MFA; *Adjunct Prof* Dorothea Heit; *Adjunct Prof* Brian Pohl; *Vis Prof* Don Wilson,
photography; *Instr* Greg Stiver, MTA
Estab 1965; pvt; D & E; scholarships; SC 22, LC 3; enrl D 287, maj 100, others 87
Ent Req: HS dipl, SAT
Degrees: BA(Art Educ), BA & BS(Commercial Art), BA(Studio Art) &
BS(Broadcast Design) 4 yrs
Tuition: Res & nonres—undergrad $280 per hr, $2975 per sem 12 - 18.5 hrs; campus
res—room & board $1658
Courses: Advertising Design, Art Appreciation, Art Education, Art History,
Calligraphy, Ceramics, Commercial Art, Design, Constructions, Drawing, Graphic
Arts, Graphic Design, Handicrafts, Art History, Illustration, Intermedia, Interior
Design, Jewelry, Lettering, Mixed Media, Painting, Photography, Printmaking,
Sculpture, Teacher Training, †Studio Art, †Broadcast Design

TULSA JUNIOR COLLEGE, Art Dept, 909 S Boston, 74119. Tel 918-595-7000;
FAX 918-595-7118; *Instr* William Derrevere, MA; *Instr* Dwayne Pass, MFA. Instrs:
PT 8
Estab 1970; pub; D & E; scholarships; SC 16, LC 7; enrl non-maj 40, maj 160

Ent Req: HS dipl
Degrees: AA 2 yrs
Tuition: Campus residency available
Courses: Art Appreciation, Art History, Design, Goldsmithing, Graphic Arts,
Jewelry, Painting, Printmaking, Silversmithing, Health & Safety for Artists &
Craftsmen
Adult Hobby Classes: Special prog of art courses & crafts courses
Summer School: Art Appreciation, Color & Design, Drawing, Painting

UNIVERSITY OF TULSA, School of Art, 600 S College Ave, 74104. Tel 918-631-
2000, Ext 2202; FAX 918-631-3423; *Dir* Stephen Sumner
Estab 1898; pvt; scholarships; SC 20, LC 13, GC 22; enrl maj 160, others 400
Degrees: BA, BFA, MA, MFA and MTA 4 yrs
Tuition: Res—$5200 per yr; campus res available
Courses: †Art Education, †Ceramics, †Commercial Art, †Painting, †Printmaking,
†Sculpture
Adult Hobby Classes: Courses offered through Continuing Education

WEATHERFORD

SOUTHWESTERN OKLAHOMA STATE UNIVERSITY, Art Dept, 100 Campus
Dr, 73096. Tel 405-772-6611, Ext 3756, 774-3756; FAX 405-772-5447; *Chmn* Dr R
Park Lang
Estab 1901, dept estab 1941; pub; D & E; scholarships; SC 35, LC 8, GC 43; enrl D
5000
Ent Req: HS dipl
Degrees: BA(Art), BA(Art Educ) and BA(Commercial Art) 4 yr
Tuition: Res—undergrad $38.65 per hr, grad $39.50 per hr; nonres—undergrad $97.
20 per hr; grad $106.25; campus res available
Courses: Advertising Design, Art Education, Art History, Ceramics, Commercial
Art, Drawing, Graphic Arts, Graphic Design, Illustration, Jewelry, Lettering, Mixed
Media, Painting, Sculpture, Teacher Training
Adult Hobby Classes: Tuition $40.30 for 16 wk term. Courses—Native American
Art, Painting, Stained Glass
Summer School: Dir, Dr R Park Lang. Enrl 90-120; 8 wk term. Courses—Art
Survey, Drawing, Painting

OREGON

ALBANY

LINN BENTON COMMUNITY COLLEGE, Fine & Applied Art Dept, * 6500
SW Pacific Blvd, 97321. Tel 541-917-4999; FAX 541-967-6550; *Chmn* Doris Litzer;
Instr John Aikman; *Instr* Rich Bergeman; *Instr* Judith Rogers; *Instr* Jason Widmer;
Instr Sandra Zimmer
Estab 1968; pub; D & E; SC 14, LC 2; enrl D 2000, E 4000
Ent Req: Open entry
Degrees: AA, AS & AAS 2 yrs
Tuition: Res—$700 per yr
Courses: †Advertising Design, Art History, Ceramics, Display, Drafting, Drawing,
†Graphic Arts, †Graphic Design, Handicrafts, Illustration, Lettering, Painting,
Photography, Sculpture, Textile Design, Theatre Arts
Adult Hobby Classes: Painting, Tole Painting, Watercolor

ASHLAND

SOUTHERN OREGON STATE COLLEGE, Dept of Art, 1250 Siskiyou Blvd,
97520. Tel 503-552-6386; *Chmn Dept Art* Cody Bustamante
Estab 1926; pub; D & E; scholarships; SC 53, LC 17, GC 18; enrl D 120, E 30, non-
maj 700, maj 100
Ent Req: HS dipl, SAT or ACT
Degrees: BFA, BA or BS(Art) 4 yrs
Tuition: Res—undergrad $3147 per yr; nonres—undergrad $8847 per yr; campus res
available
Courses: Advertising Design, Architecture, Art Appreciation, Art Education, Art
History, Ceramics, Collages, Commercial Art, Conceptual Art, Constructions,
Design, Drawing, Graphic Arts, Graphic Design, Illustration, Intermedia, Mixed
Media, Museum Staff Training, Painting, Photography, Printmaking, Sculpture,
Video, Computer Art, Fibers
Adult Hobby Classes: Various courses
Children's Classes: Summer classes
Summer School: Dir, Kevin Talbert. Enrl 210; 4 - 8 wk term. Courses—various

BEND

CENTRAL OREGON COMMUNITY COLLEGE, Dept of Art, 2600 NW College
Way, 97701. Tel 541-382-6112, 383-7700; FAX 541-385-5978; *Prof* Douglas
Campbell-Smith, MA
Estab 1949; pub; D & E; scholarships; enrl in col D 2025, E 2000
Ent Req: HS dipl
Degrees: AA, AS, Cert
Tuition: In-district—$32 per cr hr; out-of-district—$42 per cr hr; out-of-state—$112
per cr hr; campus res available
Courses: Calligraphy, Ceramics, Drawing, Painting, Photography, Printmaking, Stage
Design, Theatre Arts
Adult Hobby Classes: Enrl 1500-2000; tuition, duration & courses offered vary
Summer School: Dir. John Weber. Enrl 300-400; tuition $32 per course for a term
of 8 wks beginning June 23. Courses—General courses

COOS BAY

COOS ART MUSEUM, 235 Anderson Ave, 97420. Tel 541-267-3901; *Dir* Helen Scully
Estab 1966; pvt; D & E; SC 7; enrl D 15, E 100
Tuition: Varies
Courses: Painting, Rose Maling
Adult Hobby Classes: Enrl 100; tuition for 10 wks, non-mem $23, mem $20
Children's Classes: Tuition varies depending on courses & membership status
Summer School: Tuition same as above

SOUTHWESTERN OREGON COMMUNITY COLLEGE, Visual Arts Dept, 1988 Newmark, 97420. Tel 503-888-7322; *Div Dir* Bob Bower; *Prof* Melanie Schwartz, MFA; *Prof* Carol Vernon, MA
Estab 1962, dept estab 1964; pub; D & E; scholarships; SC 11, LC 1; enrl D 420, E 300, non-maj 250, maj 170
Degrees: AA 2 yrs
Tuition: Res—undergrad $540 per quarter; nonres—undergrad $1476 per quarter; campus res—$295 per month
Courses: Art History, Calligraphy, Ceramics, Design, Drawing, Painting, Printmaking, Sculpture, Computer Art, Handmade Paper
Adult Hobby Classes: Tuition $396 per qtr. Courses—Art History, Ceramics, Drawing, Handmade Paper & Prints, Painting
Children's Classes: Only as occasional workshops
Summer School: Dean Instruction, Phill Anderson. Tuition varies.
Courses—Ceramics, Painting & Composition, Watercolor

CORVALLIS

OREGON STATE UNIVERSITY, Dept of Art, 97331-3702. Tel 541-737-4745; *Chmn* David Hardesty, MFA; *Prof* Harrison Branch, MFA; *Prof* Clinton Brown, MFA; *Prof* Berkley Chappell, MFA; *Prof* James Folts, MS; *Prof* Elizabeth Pilliod; *Prof* Theodore Wiprud, MFA; *Prof* Henry Sayre, PhD; *Assoc Prof* Shelley Jordon, MFA; *Assoc Prof* Barbara Loeb, PhD; *Asst Prof* Andrea Marks, MFA; *Asst Prof* Yuji Hiratsuka, MFA; *Asst Prof* John Bowers, MFA; *Asst Prof* John Maul, MFA; *Sr Research Assoc* Douglas Russell, BA
Estab 1868, dept estab 1908; pub; D & E; scholarships; SC 63, LC 16, GC 271; enrl non-maj 2000, maj 275, grad 10
Ent Req: HS dipl
Degrees: BA, BS, BFA & MAIS
Tuition: Res—undergrad $875 per quarter; res—grad $1200 per quarter; nonres—undergrad $2302 per quarter; nonres—grad $1922 per quarter; campus res available
Courses: Art History, Drawing, Graphic Design, Painting, Photography, Printmaking, Sculpture, 2-D & 3-D Design, Visual Appreciation
Summer School: Dir, John Maul. Enrl 75; 3 wk session beginning 3rd wk in June. Jumpstart-Preschool Visual Arts Workshop for HS students

EUGENE

MAUDE I KERNS ART CENTER SCHOOL, 1910 E 15th Ave, 97403. Tel 541-345-1571; FAX 541-345-6248;
Internet Home Page Address http://www.premierelink.com/clients/mkac. *Exec Dir* Deborah Lauria
Estab 1951; pvt; D & E; scholarships; SC 45; enrl D & E 450
Tuition: $20-$60 per class per quarter
Courses: Calligraphy, Ceramics, Design, Drawing, Graphic Design, Handicrafts, Jewelry, Photography, Printmaking, Sculpture, Textile Design, Weaving, Glass Blowing, Lampworking, Leaded Glass
Adult Hobby Classes: Enrl 100. Courses—Per regular session
Children's Classes: Enrl 200; tuition $75. Courses—Ceramics, Drawing & other special workshops
Summer School: Courses varied

LANE COMMUNITY COLLEGE, Art & Applied Design Dept, 4000 E 30th Ave, 97405. Tel 541-747-4501, Ext 2409; Instrs: FT 10
Estab 1964, dept estab 1967; pub; D & E; scholarships; SC 42, LC 4; enrl D 300, E 75, non-maj 240, maj 60
Ent Req: HS dipl
Degrees: AA, AAS 2 yrs
Tuition: Res—$34 per cr hr; out-of-state $116 per cr hr; international student $116
Courses: Art Appreciation, Art History, Ceramics, Commercial Art, Conceptual Art, Design, Drawing, Graphic Arts, Graphic Design, History of Art & Archaeology, Illustration, Jewelry, Lettering, Painting, Printmaking, Sculpture, Silversmithing, Textile Design, Weaving, Metal Casting, 2-D & 3-D Design, Air Brush
Adult Hobby Classes: Enrl 250, tuition $56 for 30 hrs & fees. Courses—Art Appreciation, Calligraphy, Ceramics, Chinese Brush Painting, Doll Making, Drawing, Jewelry, Oil Painting, Papermaking, Sculpture, Stained Glass, Watercolor
Summer School: Dir, R Seymour. Enrl 205; tuition $34 per cr hr for 8 wks.
Courses—Art Appreciation, Drawing, Independent Study, Sculpture, Watercolor

UNIVERSITY OF OREGON, Dept of Fine & Applied Arts, 5232 University of Oregon, 97403-5232. Tel 503-346-3610; FAX 503-346-3660; *Assoc Prof* L Alpert. Instrs: FT 20, PT 10
Pub; D; scholarships; enrl D 1475, non-maj 350, maj 1050
Degrees: BA, BS 4 yrs, BFA 5 yrs, MFA 2 yrs minimum after BFA or equivalent
Tuition: Res—undergrad $1163 per term; grad $1945 per term; nonres—undergrad $3874 per term; grad $3332; campus res available
Courses: Ceramics, Drawing, Jewelry, Painting, Photography, Printmaking, Sculpture, Computer Graphics, Fibers, Metalsmithing, Visual Design
Summer School: Dir, Ron Trebon. Tuition res—undergrad $1009, grad $1194; nonres—undergrad $1309, grad $1419 for term of 8 wks beginning June.
Courses—Ceramics, Computer Graphics, Drawing, Fibers, Jewelry, Metalsmithing, Painting, Photography, Printmaking, Sculpture, Visual Design

FOREST GROVE

PACIFIC UNIVERSITY IN OREGON, Arts Div, Dept of Art, 2043 College Way, 97116. Tel 503-359-2216; *Chmn* Garry Mueller, MFA; *Prof* Jan Shield, MFA; *Instr* Patricia Cleyne, MFA
Estab 1849; D & E; scholarships
Ent Req: HS dipl, SAT or ACT, counselor recommendation, transcript of acad work
Degrees: BA, MA(Teaching)
Tuition: $13,000 per yr; campus res—room & board $3200
Courses: Art Appreciation, Art Education, Art History, Ceramics, Collages, Design, Drawing, Film, Goldsmithing, Illustration, Intermedia, Jewelry, †Occupational Therapy, Painting, Photography, Printmaking, Sculpture, Silversmithing, †Communications, Computer Graphics
Children's Classes: Enrl 15. Courses—Childrens Art (children of faculty & staff)
Summer School: Dean, Willard Kniep. Enrl 7-15; 3 terms over summer.
Courses—Varies

GRESHAM

MOUNT HOOD COMMUNITY COLLEGE, Visual Arts Center, * 26000 SE Stark St, 97030. Tel 503-667-7309; FAX 503-667-7389; *Assoc Dean* Eric Sankey
Scholarships
Degrees: AA
Courses: Art Education, Art History, Calligraphy, Ceramics, Design, Drawing, Film, Graphic Design, Illustration, Jewelry, Painting, Printmaking, Sculpture
Adult Hobby Classes: Tuition $30 per cr. Courses—All studio courses
Summer School: Dir, Eric Sankey. Enrl 60 - 90; two 5 wk sessions.
Courses—Calligraphy, Ceramics, Drawing, Watercolor

LA GRANDE

EASTERN OREGON STATE COLLEGE, Arts & Humanities Dept, Division of Humanities and Fine Arts, 1410 L Ave, 97850-2899. Tel 541-962-3672; FAX 503-962-3596; *Dean Art* Sandra Elston; *Assoc Prof Art* Judd R Koehn, MFA; *Asst Prof Art* Thomas Dimond; *Asst Prof* Terry Gloeckler
Estab 1929; pub; D & E; SC 32, LC 8, GC 2
Ent Req: HS dipl
Degrees: BA & BS in Art, BA & BS in Secondary Educ with Endorsement in Art, BA & BS in Elementary Educ with Specialization in Art 4 yrs
Tuition: Res—$922 per term; campus res available
Courses: Aesthetics, Art Education, Art History, Calligraphy, Ceramics, Design, Drawing, Jewelry, Lettering, Painting, Photography, Glassblowing, Life Drawings
Adult Hobby Classes: Dir, Dr Werner Bruecher
Summer School: Dir, Dixie Lund. Enrl 400. Term of 4-8 wks. Courses—Two or three per summer, beginning level

MARYLHURST

MARYLHURST COLLEGE, Art Dept, 97036. Tel 503-636-8141; FAX 503-636-9526; *Chmn* Kay Slusarenko; *Asst Chmn* Paul Sutinen; *Instr* Rodd Ambroson; *Instr* Kelcey Beardsley; *Instr* Christopher Rauschenberg; *Instr* Dennis Cunningham; *Instr* Margaret Shirley; *Instr* Sr Patricia Stebinger; *Instr* Bonnie Bruce; *Instr* Fernanda D'Agostino; *Instr* Michael Bowley; *Instr* Karen O'Malley; *Instr* Barbara Eiswerth; *Instr* Rich Rollins; *Instr* Terri Hopkins; *Instr* Martha Pfanschmidt; *Instr* Denise Roy; *Instr* JoAnn Thomas
Scholarships; enrl 110
Ent Req: HS dipl or equivalent
Degrees: BA, BFA, MA (Art Therapy)
Tuition: $159 per cr
Courses: Art History, Design, Drawing, Interior Design, Mixed Media, Museum Staff Training, Painting, Photography, Printmaking, Sculpture, Art Therapy Program, History of Photography
Summer School: Chmn, Kay Slusarenko. Enrl 100; tuition $189 per cr for 10 wk term. Courses—Drawing, Independent Studies, Interior Design, Painting, Photography, Printmaking, Sculpture

MCMINNVILLE

LINFIELD COLLEGE, Art Dept, 97128. Tel 503-434-2275; *Chmn Dept* Connie Waltz
Estab 1849, dept estab 1964; pvt; D; scholarships; SC 16, LC 2; enrl non-maj 250, maj 35
Ent Req: HS dipl
Degrees: BA 4 yr, ME 2 yr
Tuition: $8600 per yr
Courses: Art Education, Art History, Ceramics, Drawing, Mixed Media, Painting, Photography, Printmaking, Sculpture, Teacher Training

MONMOUTH

WESTERN OREGON STATE COLLEGE, Creative Arts Division, Visual Arts, 97361. Tel 503-838-8000; FAX 503-838-8144; *Chmn Creative Arts* Dr Myra Brand; *Assoc Prof* Kim Hoffman. Instrs: FT 8, PT 2
Estab 1856; pub; D & E; scholarships; SC 72, LC 21, GC 27; enrl total 3600
Degrees: BA and BS 4 yr
Tuition: Res—undergrad $940 per term, grad $887 per term; nonres—undergrad $2603 per term, grad $2383 per term
Courses: Art Education, Art History, Ceramics, Drawing, Graphic Design, Painting, Printmaking, Sculpture, Art Theory, Design, Individual Studies

ONTARIO

TREASURE VALLEY COMMUNITY COLLEGE, Art Dept, * 650 College Blvd, 97914. Tel 541-889-6493, Ext 270; *Chmn* Robert Armstrong; *Instr* Mike Lundstrom; *Instr* Carson Legree
Estab 1961; pub; D & E; scholarships; SC 14, LC 1; enrl D 50, E 35, non-maj 10, maj 15
Ent Req: Placement testing
Degrees: AS & AA 2 yrs
Tuition: Res—$312 per quarter; nonres—$380 per quarter; out-of-country—$900 per quarter; campus res available
Courses: Art History, Drawing, Painting, Sculpture
Summer School: Chmn, Robert M Jackson. Tuition $190 for term of 8 wks beginning June 22. Courses—Ceramics, Drawing, Painting

OREGON CITY

CLACKAMAS COMMUNITY COLLEGE, Art Dept, 19600 S Molalla Ave, 97045. Tel 503-657-8400, Ext 2540; *Chmn* Les Tipton
Tuition: Res—$32 per cr hr, nonres—$112 per cr hr
Courses: Advertising Design, Art History, Calligraphy, Ceramics, Design, Drawing, Jewelry, Painting, Sculpture

PENDLETON

BLUE MOUNTAIN COMMUNITY COLLEGE, Fine Arts Dept, 2411 NW Carden Ave, PO Box 100, 97801. Tel 541-276-1260; *Chmn* Bruce Guiwits
Estab 1962, dept estab 1964; pub; D & E; SC 8, LC 2; enrl D 255, E 72
Degrees: AA, 2 yrs
Tuition: Res—undergrad $30 per cr hr; nonres—undergrad $90 per cr hr
Courses: Art History, Ceramics, Drawing, Jewelry, Lettering, Painting

PORTLAND

LEWIS & CLARK COLLEGE, Dept of Art, 0615 SW Palatine Hill Rd, 97219. Tel 503-768-7390; FAX 503-768-7401; *Chmn Dept* Stewart Buettner; *Prof* Phyllis Yes; *Assoc Prof* Michael Taylor; *Asst Prof* Sherry Fowler; *Asst Prof* Theodore Vogel; *Visiting Lect* Robert B Miller; *Visiting Lect* Bruce West
Dept estab 1946; pvt; D; scholarships; SC 10, LC 2
Ent Req: HS dipl
Degrees: BS and BA 4 yr
Tuition: Res—undergrad $15,800 per yr, grad $338 per sem
Courses: Art History, Ceramics, Drawing, Graphic Arts, History of Art & Archaeology, Jewelry, Painting, Printmaking, Sculpture, Weaving

OREGON SCHOOL OF ARTS & CRAFTS, 8245 SW Barnes Rd, 97225. Tel 503-297-5544; *Pres* Paul Magnusson, PhD; *Admis Counselor* Valorie Hadley. Instrs: Ft 10, PT 13
Estab 1906; pvt; D & E; scholarships; SC & LC 60; enrl D 225, E 250
Ent Req: Portfolio review
Degrees: Cert in Art, 3 yr
Tuition: $8280 full-time certificate program; no campus res
Courses: †Ceramics, †Drawing, †Jewelry, †Textile Design, Book Arts, Wood
Adult Hobby Classes: Enrl 1300; tuition $195 noncr hr $295 per 1.5 cr hrs for 10 wk term. Courses—Aesthetics, Book Arts, Ceramics, Drawing, Fibers, Metals, Photography, Writing, Wood
Summer School: Dir, Valorie Hadley. Enrl 215; tuition $240 for 1 wk workshop. Courses—same as above

PACIFIC NORTHWEST COLLEGE OF ART, 1219 SW Park Ave, 97205. Tel 503-226-4391, 226-0462; FAX 503-226-3587; Elec Mail pncainfo@pnca.edu. *Pres* Sally Lawrence; *Dir Admis* Colin Page; *Instr* Richard Kraft; *Instr* William Moore; *Instr* Paul Missal; *Instr* Betsy Lindsay; *Instr* Robert Hanson; *Instr* Frank Irby; *Instr* Anne Johnson; *Instr* Jim Hicks; *Instr* Chris Gander; *Instr* Tom Fawkes; *Instr* Gordon Gilkey; *Instr* Judy Cooke. Instrs: FT 19, PT 24
Estab 1909; pvt; D & E; scholarships; SC 54, LC 15; enrl D 258, PT 47, E 249
Ent Req: HS dipl, portfolio
Degrees: BFA 4 yr
Tuition: $10,072 per yr, $5036 per sem; no campus res
Courses: Art History, †Ceramics, †Drawing, †Graphic Design, †Illustration, †Painting, †Photography, †Printmaking, †Sculpture, †General Fine Arts
Adult Hobby Classes: Enrl 546; tuition $215 per 12 wk term. Courses—Ceramics, Graphic Design, Illustration, Life Drawing, Painting, Photography, Printmaking, Sculpture & other art-related courses
Children's Classes: Enrl 132; tuition $125 per 12 wk term. Courses—Ceramics, Drawing, Painting, Printmaking, Sculpture
Summer School: Dir, Greg Ware. Enrl 500; tuition $210 per 12 wk term. Courses—Wide range of Visual Arts

PORTLAND COMMUNITY COLLEGE, Visual & Performing Arts Division, PO Box 19000, 97280-0990. Tel 503-244-6111, Ext 4263; *Div Dean* Mary Stupp-Greer
Estab 1961, dept estab 1963; pub; D & E; SC 40, LC 5; enrl D 864, E 282
Ent Req: None
Degrees: AA 2 yrs
Tuition: $28 per cr hr, 1-12 hrs; $364 per cr hr, 13-19 hrs
Courses: Art History, Calligraphy, Ceramics, Drawing, Graphic Design, Painting, Photography, Sculpture, Stage Design, Theatre Arts, Printing Tech
Adult Hobby Classes: Tuition varies per quarter. Courses—various
Children's Classes: Courses offered
Summer School: Dept Chmn, Mary Stupp-Greer. Enrl 400; Term of 8 wks beginning June. Courses—same as regular session

PORTLAND STATE UNIVERSITY, Dept of Art, PO Box 751, 97207. Tel 503-725-3515; FAX 503-725-4541; *Dept Chmn&Prof* Mary Constans, MA; *Prof* James Hibbard, MFA; *Prof* Melvin Katz, Cert; *Prof* Michihiro Kosuge, MFA; *Prof* Leonard B Kimbrell, PhD; *Prof* Craig Cheshire, MFA; *Assoc Prof* Claire Kelly-Zimmers, MA; *Assoc Prof* Jane Kristof, PhD; *Assoc Prof* Lisa Andrus, PhD
Estab 1955; pub; D & E; scholarships; enrl E 2000, non-maj 1300, maj 600, grad 30, others 70
Ent Req: HS dipl
Degrees: BS & BA(Art) 4 yr, MFA (Painting, Ceramics, Sculpture) 2 yr
Tuition: Res—undergrad $1020 per qtr; nonres—undergrad $3036 per qtr; campus res available
Courses: Architecture, Art History, †Ceramics, †Drawing, †Graphic Design, †Painting, Printmaking, †Sculpture, †Applied Design
Summer School: Enrl 4-500; term of 8-12 wks beginning June 28. Courses—vary. Two centers, one in Portland and one at Cannon Beach: The Haystack Program

REED COLLEGE, Dept of Art, 3203 S E Woodstock Blvd, 97202-8199. Tel 503-771-1112; FAX 503-788-6691; *Chmn Art History&Humanities* William J Diebold; *Prof Art* Michael Knutson; *Prof Art History & Humanities* Peter W Parshall; *Assoc Prof Art History* William J Diebold; *Asst Prof Art History & Humanities* Hsingyuan Tsao; *Asst Prof Art* Geraldine Ondrizek. Instrs: FT 5
Estab 1911; pvt; D; scholarships; SC 7, LC 5; enrl D 1150, E 15
Degrees: BA 3-5 yr
Tuition: $14,520 annual tuition; campus res—available
Courses: Aesthetics, Architecture, †Art History, Ceramics, †Conceptual Art, †Drawing, Graphic Arts, †History of Art & Archaeology, †Painting, Photography, Printmaking, Restoration & Conservation, †Sculpture, History of Art & Architecture, Humanities, Theory
Adult Hobby Classes: Courses offered & MA degree
Summer School: Courses offered

ROSEBURG

UMPQUA COMMUNITY COLLEGE, Fine & Performing Arts Dept, PO Box 967, 97470. Tel 541-440-4600, Ext 692; *Chmn Fine & Performing Arts* Marie Rasmussen; *Instr* Ted Isto; *Instr* Robert Bell; *Instr* Walt O'Brien
Estab 1964; pub; D & E; scholarships; SC 5, LC 2; enrl D 190, E 90, maj 18
Ent Req: HS dipl
Degrees: AA 2 yr
Tuition: Res—$496 per term (12 hrs); out of district $1500
Courses: Art History, Calligraphy, Ceramics, Drawing, Painting, Photography, Printmaking, Sculpture, Theatre Arts, Basic Design
Adult Hobby Classes: Enrl 195; tuition $45 & lab fee for 10 weeks. Courses—Calligraphy, Ceramics, Drawing, Painting, Photography, Printmaking, Sculpture

SALEM

CHEMEKETA COMMUNITY COLLEGE, Dept of Humanities & Communications, 4000 Lancaster Dr NE, 97309. Tel 503-399-5184; FAX 503-399-5214; *Dir* Bernie Knab; *Instr* Robert Bibler, MFA; *Instr* Lee Jacobson, MFA; *Instr* Donna Reid, PhD
Estab 1969, dept estab 1975; pub; D & E; SC 9, LC 3; enrl D 125, E 75
Ent Req: None
Degrees: AA 2 yr
Tuition: Res—$23 per cr hr, $210 per quarter; nonres—$83 per cr hr
Courses: Art Appreciation, Art History, Ceramics, Design, Drawing, Film, Graphic Design, Painting, Photography, Printmaking, Sculpture, Art as a Profession
Adult Hobby Classes: Enrl 150-200; tuition $33 per cr hr
Summer School: Dir, B Knob. Tuition varies, 8 wk term

SHERIDAN

DELPHIAN SCHOOL, 20950 SW Rock Creek Rd, 97378. Tel 503-843-3521; FAX 503-843-4158; *Headmaster* Greg Ott; *Dir Educ Consulting* Bruce Wiggins
Degrees: Cert
Courses: Art Education, Calligraphy, Drawing, Handicrafts, Painting, Sculpture

PENNSYLVANIA

ALLENTOWN

CEDAR CREST COLLEGE, Art Dept, * 100 College Dr, 18104-6196. Tel 610-437-4471; *Chmn* Nelson R Maniscalco, MFA; *Prof* Ryland W Greene; *Asst Prof* Pat Badt; *Prof* William Clark; *Instr* Andrew Hall. Instrs: FT 3, PT 2
Estab 1867; pvt; D & E; scholarships; SC 11, LC 4; enrl 750
Ent Req: HS dipl, CEEB
Degrees: BA, BS, Interdisciplinary Fine Arts Maj (art, theatre, music, dance, creative writing), 4 yr
Tuition: Res—$14,000 per yr
Courses: Aesthetics, Art Education, Art History, Ceramics, Drawing, Jewelry, Painting, Sculpture, Theatre Arts, Comparative Study of Art, Metal Forming
Summer School: Courses—Ceramics, Jewelry-Metalsmithing

MUHLENBERG COLLEGE, Dept of Art, 2400 Chew St, 18104-5586. Tel 610-821-3243, 821-3100; *Chmn* Jadviga Da Costa Nunes, PhD; *Dir* Lori Verderame, PhD; *Assoc Prof* Scott Sherk, MFA; *Asst Prof* Raymond S Barnes, MFA; *Asst Prof* Joseph Elliott, MFA
Estab 1848; den; D & E; SC 16, LC 12; enrl D 320, non-maj 284, maj 36
Ent Req: HS dipl, SAT, 3 achievemnt tests & English Composition Acievement

required
Degrees: BA 4 yrs
Tuition: Res—$21,540 per yr with room & board
Courses: Art History, †Art History, Ceramics, Drawing, Graphic Arts, History of Art & Archaeology, Museum Staff Training, Painting, Photography, Printmaking, Sculpture, †Studio Arts
Adult Hobby Classes: Courses—Art History, Drawing, Painting, Photography, Photo-Journalism
Summer School: Courses—same as adult educ courses

BETHLEHEM

LEHIGH UNIVERSITY, Dept of Art & Architecture, 17 Memorial Dr E, 18015. Tel 610-758-3610; *Chmn* Ivan Zacnic; *Prof* Ricardo Viera, MFA; *Prof* Thomas Peters, PhD; *Prof* Lucy Gans, MFA; *Adjunct Prof* Anne Priester, PhD; *Assoc Prof* Richard Redd, MFA; *Assoc Prof* Berrisford Boothe, MFA; *Asst Prof* Bruce Thomas, PhD; *Asst Prof* Anthony Viscardi, M Arch. Instrs: FT 10, PT 4
Estab 1925; pvt; D & E; SC 22, LC 16; enrl D & E 100
Ent Req: HS dipl, SAT, CEEB
Degrees: BA 4 yrs
Tuition: $8350 per sem; campus res available
Courses: †Architecture, Art History, Drawing, Graphic Design, Painting, Photography, Printmaking, Sculpture, Computer Aided Design
Summer School: Dir, James Brown. Courses—Architectural Design, Art History, Graphic Design Workshop, Color

MORAVIAN COLLEGE, Dept of Art, Church Street Campus, 18018. Tel 610-861-1680; FAX 610-861-1682; *Chmn Dept* Rudy S Ackerman, DEd; *Assoc Prof* Les Reker, MFA; *Photographer in Residence* Jeffrey Hurwitz; *Spec Appointment* Sharon Cross, BFA; *Ceramist-in-Residence* Renzo Faggioli, Master Craftsman
Estab 1742, dept estab 1963; pvt; D & E; scholarships; SC 15, LC 8; enrl D 350, E 15, non-maj 1200, maj 100
Ent Req: HS dipl
Degrees: BA and BS 4 yrs
Tuition: $8250 per yr
Courses: †Advertising Design, †Art Education, †Art History, †Ceramics, Commercial Art, Design, †Drawing, Graphic Arts, Graphic Design, History of Art & Archaeology, Jewelry, Museum Staff Training, †Painting, †Photography, †Sculpture, Silversmithing, Teacher Training
Summer School: Dir, Dr Linda Heindel. Enrl 110; tuition $410 per course beginning June. Courses—Same as above

NORTHAMPTON COMMUNITY COLLEGE, Art Dept, 3835 Green Pond Rd, 18017. Tel 610-861-5300, Ext 5485; FAX 610-861-5373; *Prog Coordr* Gerald Rowan; *Asst Prof* Andrew Szoke
Estab 1967; pub; D & E; scholarships; SC 12, LC 8; enrl D 100, E 350
Ent Req: HS dipl, portfolio
Degrees: AAS(Advertising), cert in photography
Tuition: Res—$62 per cr hr; nonres—$128 per cr hr
Courses: Advertising Design, Architecture, Art History, Ceramics, Drafting, Drawing, Fashion Arts, Graphic Arts, Graphic Design, Handicrafts, History of Art & Archaeology, Illustration, Interior Design, Lettering, Painting, Photography, Printmaking, Sculpture, Color & Spacial Concepts, Computer Graphics, Pottery, 3-D Materials
Adult Hobby Classes: Courses—Art, Photography

BLOOMSBURG

BLOOMSBURG UNIVERSITY, Dept of Art, Old Science Hall, 17815. Tel 717-389-4646; FAX 717-389-4946; *Chmn* Dr Christine Sperling; *Prof* Stewart Nagel, MFA; *Prof* Robert Koslosky, PhD; *Assoc Prof* Barbara J Strohman, MFA; *Assoc Prof* Karl Beamer, MFA; *Assoc Prof* Carol Burns; *Assoc Prof* Vera Ziditz-Ward; *Asst Prof* Charles Thomas Walter, PhD; *Asst Prof* Gary F Clark, MA
Estab 1839, dept estab 1940; pub; D & E; scholarships; SC 7, LC 12; enrl D 1800, E 200, maj 75
Ent Req: HS dipl
Degrees: BA(Art Studio) and BA(Art History) 4 yrs, MA(Art Studio), MA(Art Hist)
Tuition: Res—tuition & campus res—room & board $5978; nonres—tuition & campus res—room & board $7868
Courses: Art History, Ceramics, Painting, Photography, Printmaking, Sculpture, Computer Graphics, Crafts, General Design, Weaving
Children's Classes: Enrl 20; tuition $30 per 8 sessions
Summer School: Dean, Michael Vavrek. Enrl 200. Courses—Art History, General Studio

BLUE BELL

MONTGOMERY COUNTY COMMUNITY COLLEGE, Art Dept, 340 De Kalb Pike, 19422. Tel 215-641-6477, 641-6551, 641-6328; *Coordr* Frank Short; *Assoc Prof* Roger Cairns, MFA; *Assoc Prof* Michael Smyser. Instrs: FT 6, PT 8
Pub; D & E; scholarships; LC 3; enrl D 250
Ent Req: HS dipl
Degrees: AA Fine Arts, AAS Commercial Art
Tuition: Count res—undergrad $62 per cr hr; nonres—undergrad $988 per sem, $127 per cr hr; out-of-state $192 per cr hr
Courses: Advertising Design, Art Education, Art History, Ceramics, †Commercial Art, Drawing, Film, Graphic Design, Illustration, Painting, Photography, Printmaking, Sculpture, Teacher Training, Theatre Arts, Video, †Fine Art, Typography
Summer School: Dir, Michael Smyser. Enrl 66; tuition $35 per cr. Courses—Ceramics, Drawing, Painting, Photography

BRYN MAWR

BRYN MAWR COLLEGE, Dept of the History of Art, 101 N Merion Ave, 19010. Tel 610-526-5000; FAX 610-526-7479; *Chmn Dept* David Cast; *Prof* Steven Levine; *Prof* Phyllis B Bober, PhD; *Prof* Gridley McKim-Smith, PhD; *Asst Prof* Christiane Hertel. Instrs: FT 5, PT 1
Estab 1913; pvt, W (men in grad school); scholarships and fel; LC 10, GC 8; enrl maj 15, grad 30, others 250
Degrees: BA 4 yr, MA, PhD
Tuition: $18,165 per yr; campus res—room & board $6750
Courses: Art History

HARCUM JUNIOR COLLEGE, Illustrations & Graphic Design Dept, * 19010. Tel 610-526-6048, Ext 215; *Dir* Nancy Shill; *Prof* Katherine Little; *Instr* Lane Heise. Instrs: FT 1, PT 5
Estab 1915; pvt, W; D & E; scholarships; SC 7, LC 1; enrl D 40, E 8, maj 10
Ent Req: HS dipl
Degrees: AA 2 yr
Tuition: $7704 per yr
Courses: Commercial Art, Drawing, Fashion Arts, Graphic Design, History of Art & Archaeology, Lettering, Painting, Sculpture

CALIFORNIA

CALIFORNIA UNIVERSITY OF PENNSYLVANIA, Dept of Art, 250 University, 15419. Tel 412-938-4000, 938-4182; *Dept Chmn* Richard Mieczinkowski
Estab 1852, dept estab 1968; pub; D & E; SC 20, LC 5; enrl maj 137
Ent Req: SAT
Degrees: Cert(Art Educ), BA 4 yrs
Courses: Advertising Design, Aesthetics, Art Appreciation, Art Education, Art History, Ceramics, Commercial Art, Costume Design & Construction, Design, Drawing, Fashion Arts, Graphic Arts, Handicrafts, Illustration, Interior Design, Jewelry, Mixed Media, Painting, Printmaking, Sculpture, Stage Design, Textile Design, Weaving, Stained Glass
Adult Hobby Classes: Enrl 25 per class. Courses—Pottery, Stained Glass
Summer School: Chmn, Richard Grinstead. Term of 5 or 10 wks beginning June

CARLISLE

DICKINSON COLLEGE, Fine Arts Dept, Weiss Ctr for the Arts, PO Box 1773, 17013-2896. Tel 717-245-1344; FAX 717-245-1937; *Chmn* Barbara Diduk; *Assoc Prof* Ward Davenny, MFA; *Asst Prof* Melinda Schlitt, PhD; *Asst Prof* Peter Lukehart, PhD; *Instr* Michael Guv
Estab 1773, dept estab 1940; pvt; D; SC 7, LC 11; enrl 550, non-maj 500, maj 50
Ent Req: HS dipl, SAT
Degrees: BA and BS 4 yrs
Tuition: Res—undergrad $16,645 per yr, campus res available
Courses: Art History, Ceramics, Drawing, History of Art & Archaeology, Painting, Photography, Printmaking, Sculpture, †Studio Major
Summer School: Dir, Stephen MacDonald. Tuition $835 per course for term of 6 wks beginning May. Courses—per regular session

CHELTENHAM

CHELTENHAM CENTER FOR THE ARTS, 439 Ashbourne Rd, 19012. Tel 215-379-4660; *Exec Dir* Gerard Brown; *Asst to Exec Dir* Lisa Muller; *Pub Relations Dir* Robin K Garland; *Dir Admis* Lauretta Sall
Estab 1940; Scholarships; enrl 3600
Courses: Ceramics, Drawing, Jewelry, Painting, Printmaking, Sculpture, Theatre Arts, Video, Pottery, Stained Glass, Theater Classes

CHEYNEY

CHEYNEY UNIVERSITY OF PENNSYLVANIA, Dept of Art, * 19319. Tel 610-399-2286; *Chmn* J Hank Hamilton Jr
Estab 1937; pub; D & E; scholarships; SC 16, LC 4
Ent Req: HS dipl, ent exam
Degrees: BA 4 yrs
Tuition: Res—$3289 per sem; nonres—$4936 per sem
Courses: Drawing, Handicrafts, Painting, Sculpture

CLARION

CLARION UNIVERSITY OF PENNSYLVANIA, Dept of Art, 16214. Tel 814-226-2291; *Chmn* Dr Joe Thomas; *Asst Prof* Charles H Dugan, MFA; *Asst Prof* James Flahaven; *Asst Prof* Gary Greenberg; *Asst Prof* Christopher Lambl
Estab 1867; pub; D & E; scholarships; SC 13, LC 7; enrl D & E 925 per sem, maj 25
Ent Req: HS dipl
Degrees: BFA(Art)
Tuition: Res—undergrad $1543 per sem, $129 per cr; nonres—undergrad $3922 per sem, $327 per cr
Courses: Art Appreciation, Art Education, Art History, †Ceramics, Design, Drawing, Graphic Arts, Graphic Design, Handicrafts, History of Art & Archaeology, Jewelry, †Painting, Photography, †Sculpture, Textile Design, Weaving, †Fabric, Fiber, 3-D Design, Commercial Design
Adult Hobby Classes: Enrl 20; tuition $55-$65 for 9-12 wk course. Courses—Calligraphy, Ceramics, Drawing, Painting
Summer School: Dir, Dr Randall Potter. Tuition $76 per cr hr for 2-5 wk sessions. Courses—various

EASTON

LAFAYETTE COLLEGE, Dept of Art, Williams Ctr for the Arts, 18042-1768. Tel 610-250-5356, 5357, 5358, 5359 & 5360; *Dept Head* Ed Kerns. Instrs: FT 4, PT 4
Estab 1827; pvt; D & E; SC 8, LC 12; enrl D 300, E 250, non-maj 1, maj 17
Ent Req: HS dipl, ent exam, selective admis
Degrees: BS and AB 4 yr
Tuition: $17,500 per yr
Courses: Art History, Drawing, Graphic Design, Painting, Photography, Printmaking, Sculpture, History of Architecture, 2-D & 3-D Design
Summer School: Graphic Design, Painting, Photography

EAST STROUDSBURG

EAST STROUDSBURG UNIVERSITY, Fine Arts Center, Fine Arts Bldg, 18301. Tel 717-422-3759; *Chmn* Terry Flatt; *Asst Prof* Dr Herb Weigand
Estab 1894; pub; D & E; SC 17, LC 6, grad 1; enrl D 45
Ent Req: HS dipl, HS equivalency
Degrees: BA in Fine Arts
Tuition: Res—undergrad $1192 per sem, grad $1845 per sem; nonres—undergrad $4301 per sem, grad $3074 per sem; campus res available
Courses: Aesthetics, Art Education, Art History, Calligraphy, Ceramics, Design, Drawing, Handicrafts, Lettering, Painting, Printmaking, Sculpture, American Art Communication Graphics, Graphics
Summer School: Tuition res—grad $89 per cr hr

EDINBORO

EDINBORO UNIVERSITY OF PENNSYLVANIA, Art Dept, Doucette Hall, 16444. Tel 814-732-2406; *Chairperson* Dr Connie Mullineaux; *Chmn Crafts* Bernard Maas; *Fine Arts Representative* Ben Gibson; *Gallery Dir* William Cox. Instrs: FT 34, PT 2
Estab 1857; pub; D & E; scholarships; SC 86, LC 30, GC 20; enrl D 400 art maj, non-maj 6000, grad 30
Ent Req: HS dipl, SAT
Degrees: BSEd, BFA and BA 4 yrs, MA 1 yr, MFA 2 yrs
Tuition: Res—$5512, $129 per cr hr; nonres—$7546, $327 per cr hr
Courses: Advertising Design, Art Education, Art History, Ceramics, Film, Goldsmithing, Handicrafts, History of Art & Archaeology, Jewelry, Mixed Media, †Painting, †Photography, †Printmaking, †Sculpture, †Silversmithing, †Teacher Training, †Textile Design, Video, Weaving, †Communications Graphics
Summer School: Chmn, Ian Short. Tuition $129 per cr for two 5 wk sessions

ERDENHEIM

ANTONELLI INSTITUTE, Professional Photography, Commercial Art & Interior Design, 300 Montgomery Ave, 19038. Tel 215-836-2222; FAX 215-275-5630; *Pres* Joseph B Thompson; *Dir* Thomas D Treacy, EdD; *Instr* James Donato, MBA
Estab 1938; pvt; D & E; enrl D 150, E 25
Ent Req: HS dipl
Tuition: $4800 per sem (photography), $4000 per sem (all others); campus res—room $1600 per sem
Courses: Advertising Design, Architecture, Art History, Commercial Art, Design, Drafting, Drawing, Film, Graphic Arts, Graphic Design, History of Art & Archaeology, Illustration, Intermedia, Interior Design, Lettering, Photography, Video
Adult Hobby Classes: Workshops as scheduled
Summer School: Workshops

ERIE

MERCYHURST COLLEGE, Dept of Art, Glenwood Hills, 16546. Tel 814-824-2000; FAX 814-825-0438; *Dept Chmn* Thomas Hubert. Instrs: FT 6, PT 4
Estab 1926, dept estab 1950; pvt; D & E; scholarships; SC 45, LC 12; enrl D 80, E 20, maj 100
Ent Req: HS dipl, col boards, portfolio review
Degrees: BA 4 yr
Courses: Aesthetics, Art Education, Art History, Ceramics, Drawing, Graphic Design, Jewelry, Painting, Photography, Printmaking, Sculpture, Airbrush Painting, Art Foundations, Art Therapy, Child Art, Contemporary Art Theories, Creative Arts for Adolescents & Childrren, Fabrics, Fibers, Internship, Independent Study, Individualized Studio, Senior Seminar, Teaching Internship, 3-D Design

FACTORYVILLE

KEYSTONE JUNIOR COLLEGE, Fine Arts Dept, College Ave (Mailing add: PO Box 50, LaPlume, PA 18440-0200). Tel 717-945-5141; *Chmn Fine Arts* Karl O Neuroth, MEd; *Prof* William Tersteeg; *Assoc Prof* Clifton A Prokop, MFA; *Instr* Rochelle Campbell; *Instr* Mark Webber, MFA
Estab 1868, dept estab 1965; pvt; D & weekends; scholarships; SC 15, LC 2; enrl D 155, weekenders 15, non-maj 100, maj 55
Ent Req: HS dipl, SAT
Degrees: AFA 2 yrs
Tuition: Res—$8060 per yr; campus res—room & board $5240
Courses: Art History, Ceramics, Drawing, Painting, Photography, Printmaking, Sculpture, Color, Intro to Commercial Design, Life Drawing, 3-D Design, 2-D Design

FARMINGTON

TOUCHSTONE CENTER FOR CRAFTS, RD1, Box 60, 15437. Tel 412-329-1370; Estab 1983; D; scholarships; enrl D 500
Tuition: $100-$250 per wk; campus housing available
Courses: Ceramics, Design, Fashion Arts, Handicrafts, Illustration, Jewelry, Painting, Photography, Printmaking, Sculpture, Silversmithing, Textile Design, Video, Weaving
Adult Hobby Classes: Enrl 400; tuition $100-$250 per wk. Courses—Blacksmithing, Clay, Fibre, Glass, Metal, Painting, Photography, Printmaking, Wood
Children's Classes: Enrl 100. Courses—Art

GETTYSBURG

GETTYSBURG COLLEGE, Dept of Visual Arts, PO Box 2452, 17325. Tel 717-337-6121; Elec Mail atrevely@gettysburg.edu. *Chmn* Dr Amelia M Trevelyan; *Prof* Norman Annis; *Prof* Alan Paulson; *Assoc Prof* James Agard; *Asst Prof* Carol Small; *Asst Prof* Jeanne Thrane; *Instr* Lisa Dorrill; *Instr* Jim Ramos; *Instr* Brent Blair; *Instr* Lynn Hanley; *Instr* John Winship
Estab 1832, dept estab 1956; pvt; D; SC 10, LC 15; enrl D 300
Ent Req: HS dipl, ent exam
Degrees: BA 4 yrs
Tuition: $21,000 annual tuition; campus res available
Courses: Architecture, †Art History, Ceramics, Design, Drawing, Film, History of Art & Archaeology, Museum Staff Training, Painting, Printmaking, Sculpture, America Indian Art, Art of Cinema, 2-D & 3-D Design, Gallery Training

GLENSIDE

BEAVER COLLEGE, Dept of Fine Arts, Easton & Church Rds, 19038. Tel 215-572-2900; *Chmn* Robert Mauro, MFA; *Asst Prof* Bonnie Hayes, MA, ABD; *Assoc Prof* Betsey Batchelor, MFA; *Assoc Prof* Paula Winokur, MFA; *Asst Prof* Judith Taylor; *Asst Prof* Scott Rawlins, MFA; *Asst Prof* Carol Sarraullo. Instrs: PT 7
Estab 1853; pvt; D & E; scholarships; SC 43, LC 14; enrl in Col D FT 625, PT 115, non-maj in dept 30, maj in dept 140
Ent Req: HS dipl, SAT, ACT, optional portfolio review
Degrees: BA and BFA 4 yrs, MA(Educ) 1 yr
Tuition: $13,690 per yr, $6845 per sem, $1040 per 4 cr course; campus res—room & board $5750
Courses: Art Education, Art History, Ceramics, Design, Drawing, Goldsmithing, Graphic Design, History of Art & Archaeology, Interior Design, Jewelry, Painting, Photography, Printmaking, Silversmithing, †Art Therapy
Summer School: Chmn, Robert Mauro. Enrl approx 30; tuition $1040 per cr hr for term of 7 wks. Courses—Drawing, Painting, Visual Fundamentals

GREENSBURG

SETON HILL COLLEGE, Dept of Art, 15601. Tel 412-834-2200, Ext 399; *Chmn* Maureen Vissat, MA; *Prof* Josefa Filkosky, MFA; *Prof* Stuart Thompson, PhD; *Assoc Prof* Raymond DeFazio; *Dir Gallery & Instr* Carol Brode
Estab 1918, dept estab 1950; den; D & E; scholarships; SC 40, LC 8; enrl D 300, maj 100, minor 15, pt 10
Ent Req: HS dipl, review portfolio
Degrees: BA, BFA 4 yr
Tuition: $11,090 per yr; campus res—room & board $4180 per yr
Courses: †Art Education, †Art History, Calligraphy, †Ceramics, Design, Drafting, †Drawing, Film, Graphic Arts, †Graphic Design, Illustration, †Interior Design, †Interior Design, Jewelry, †Painting, †Photography, †Printmaking, †Sculpture, Fabrics, 3-D Design, Metalsmithing
Adult Hobby Classes: Enrl 25; tuition $208 per cr for 14 wk sem. Courses— Art History, Photography, Design
Summer School: Dir, M Raak. Enrl 20. Courses—Art in Elementary Educ, Design, Photography

GREENVILLE

THIEL COLLEGE, Dept of Art, 75 College Ave, 16125. Tel 412-589-2094, 589-2000; *Chmn Dept* Ronald A Pivovar, MFA
Estab 1866, dept estab 1965; pvt; D & E; scholarships; SC 14, LC 11; enrl D 105, non-maj 65, maj 40
Ent Req: HS dipl, interviews
Degrees: BA 4 yrs
Tuition: $16,455 includes room & board, $178 per cr hr
Courses: Art History, Ceramics, Drawing, Graphic Arts, Jewelry, Painting, Printmaking, Sculpture, Stage Design, Theatre Arts
Adult Hobby Classes: Classes offered
Summer School: Asst Acad Dean, Richard Houpt. Term of 4 wks beginning June 3. Courses--Art History, Extended Studies, Drawing

HARRISBURG

HARRISBURG AREA COMMUNITY COLLEGE, Division of Communication & the Arts, One HACC Dr, 17110. Tel 717-780-2420; *Chmn* Michael Dockery, PhD; *Instr* Ronald Talbott, MFA
Estab 1964; pub; D & E; SC 15, LC 5; enrl D 500, E 100, maj 100
Ent Req: HS dipl
Degrees: AA 2 yrs
Tuition: Res—undergrad $55.25 per cr hr; out-of-district—undergrad $110.50 per cr hr; out-of-state $185.95 per cr hr; no campus res
Courses: Art History, Ceramics, Commercial Art, Drafting, Drawing, Film, Graphic Arts, Handicrafts, Jewelry, Painting, Photography, Printmaking, Sculpture, Stage Design, Theatre Arts
Adult Hobby Classes: Courses—Calligraphy, Drawing, Painting, Photography, Pottery
Children's Classes: Courses—Calligraphy, Creative Dramatics
Summer School: Dir, Michael Dockery. Courses vary

HAVERFORD

HAVERFORD COLLEGE, Fine Arts Dept, 3070 Lancaster Ave, 19041-1392. Tel 610-896-1000, 896-1267 (Art Dept); FAX 610-896-1495; *Chmn* William E Williams, MFA; *Prof* R Christopher Cairns; *Prof* Charles Stegeman
Estab 1833, dept estab 1969; pvt; D, M; scholarships; enrl maj 12
Ent Req: HS dipl, programs in cooperation with Bryn Mawr College, Fine Arts Program
Degrees: BA 4 yrs
Tuition: $16,960 annual yr; campus res—$5700 room & board
Courses: Drawing, Graphic Arts, History of Art & Archaeology, Painting, Photography, Sculpture

MAIN LINE ART CENTER, Old Buck Rd & Lancaster Ave, 19041. Tel 610-525-0272; *Admin Exec Dir* Judy S Herman; *Instr* James Toogood; *Instr* Carol Cole, BA; *Instr* Elizabeth Meyer, MFA; *Instr* Robert Finch, BFA; *Instr* Ginny Kendall; *Instr* Carol Kardon; *Instr* Bonnie Mettler, BFA; *Instr* Francine Shore, BFA; *Instr* Carson Fox; *Instr* Sallee Rush, BFA; *Instr* Chris Fox, MA; *Instr* Mimi Oritsky, MFA; *Instr* Val Rossman; *Instr* Robin Tedesco, MFA; *Instr* Scott Wheelock; *Instr* Amy Sarner-Williams, BA; *Instr* Martha Kent Martin, BFA; *Instr* Patrick Arnold, BFA; *Instr* Lisa Learner, MFA; *Instr* Maryann Matlock-Hinkle, MFA; *Instr* Lydia Lehr, MFA; *Instr* Ann Simon; *Instr* Kathie Regan-Dalzell, BA; *Instr* Aurelia Viguers, BFA; *Instr* Nury Vicens, MFA; *Instr* Susanna T Saunders, BA
Estab 1937; pvt; D & E; scholarships; SC 45; enrl D 300, E 250
Courses: Art History, Calligraphy, Ceramics, Collages, Drawing, Jewelry, Mixed Media, Painting, Photography, Printmaking, Sculpture, Silversmithing, Textile Design, Batik, Faux Painting, Tie-dyeing
Children's Classes: Enrl 1500, Courses—General Arts, Pottery
Summer School: Admin Dir, Judy S Herman. Tuition varies, classes begin mid-June. Courses—same as above

HUNTINGDON

JUNIATA COLLEGE, Dept of Art, Moore St, 16652. Tel 814-643-4310, Ext 3683; *Chmn Dept* Karen Rosell. Instrs: FT 3, PT 1
Estab 1876; pvt; D; scholarships; SC 12, LC 3; enrl 1100, maj 40
Ent Req: HS dipl
Degrees: BA 4 yrs
Tuition: Campus res
Courses: Aesthetics, Ceramics, Drawing, History of Art & Archaeology, Painting, Photography, Theatre Arts, Arts Management, Computer Graphics, Museum Studies
Summer School: Dir, Jill Pfrogner, Courses —Art History, Ceramics, Studio Art

INDIANA

INDIANA UNIVERSITY OF PENNSYLVANIA, Dept of Art & Art Education, 114 Sprowls Hall, 15705. Tel 412-357-2530; FAX 412-357-7899; *Chmn* Dr A G DeFurio; *Instr* Paul Ben'zvi; *Instr* Sandra Burwell; *Instr* Ronald Ali; *Instr* Vaughn Clay; *Instr* Susan Paulnisano; *Instr* P Parker Boerner; *Instr* Donn Hedman; *Instr* Brenda Mitchell; *Instr* Thomas Lacey; *Instr* Chris Weiland; *Instr* Robert Hamilton; *Instr* Robert Slenker; *Instr* Jean Slenker; *Instr* James Nestor
Estab 1875, dept estab 1875; pub; D & E; scholarships & assistantships; SC 26, LC 21, GC 30; enrl D 250, non-maj 1700, maj 270, grad 30
Ent Req: HS dipl, SAT, portfolio review
Degrees: BS(Art Educ), BA(Art History & Humanities with Art Concentration), BFA(Studio Art Concentration) 4 yr, MA 2 yr & MFA
Tuition: Res undergrad $2478 per yr, grad $2478 per yr; nonres—undergrad $4512 per yr, grad $4512 per yr; campus res—room & board $1340 per yr
Courses: Art Appreciation, Art Education, Art History, Ceramics, Design, Drawing, Goldsmithing, Graphic Design, Jewelry, Painting, Printmaking, Sculpture, Silversmithing, Weaving, Art Studio, Computer Graphics, Fiber Arts, Papermaking, Woodworking
Adult Hobby Classes: Enrl 60; Courses—Ceramics, Drawing
Summer School: Dir, Anthony G DeFurio. Enrl 140; tuition regular acad sem cr cost. Courses—Art Appreciation, Art History, Special Workshops, Studios

JOHNSTOWN

UNIVERSITY OF PITTSBURGH AT JOHNSTOWN, Dept of Fine Arts, 450 Schoolhouse Rd, 15904. Tel 814-269-7000; FAX 814-269-2096; *Chmn* Carroll Grimes
Estab 1968; pub, pvt; D & E; SC 4, LC 10; enrl D 120, maj 3
Ent Req: HS dipl, SAT
Degrees: BA 4 yrs
Tuition: Campus res available
Courses: Aesthetics, Art Education, Art History, †Commercial Art, Drawing, Film, History of Art & Archaeology, Painting, Photography, Stage Design, Theatre Arts
Summer School: Enrl 30. Courses—Contemporary Art

KUTZTOWN

KUTZTOWN UNIVERSITY, College of Visual & Performing Arts, 19530. Tel 610-683-4500; FAX 610-683-4547; *Dean* Dr Arthur W Bloom, PhD
Institution estab 1860, art dept estab 1929; pub; D & E; scholarships; SC 284, LC 40, GC 8; enrl D 943, maj 10
Ent Req: HS dipl
Degrees: BFA 4 yr, BS(Art Educ) 4 yr, MA(Educ)
Tuition: Res—undergrad & grad $1830; nonres—undergrad $3266, grad $2040; campus res—$2447 per yr
Courses: †Advertising Design, Aesthetics, Art Appreciation, †Art Education, †Art History, †Ceramics, †Commercial Art, Design, Drafting, †Drawing, Graphic Arts, †Graphic Design, History of Art & Archaeology, Illustration, †Jewelry, Mixed Media, †Painting, Photography, †Printmaking, Sculpture, Silversmithing, Textile Design, Weaving
Adult Hobby Classes: Stage Costume Design
Children's Classes: Young at Art
Summer School: Regular sessions 5 wks. Courses—Art Ed, Studio

LANCASTER

FRANKLIN & MARSHALL COLLEGE, Art Dept, PO Box 3003, 17604. Tel 717-291-4199; FAX 717-291-3969; *Chmn Dept* James Peterson; *Instr* Carol Hickey; *Instr* Linda Cunningham
Estab 1966; pvt; D & E; scholarships; SC 10, LC 17; enrl in col D 1900, E 580
Ent Req: HS dipl, SAT
Degrees: BA 4 yr
Tuition: Res—$24,940 per yr
Courses: Architecture, Art History, Drawing, History of Art & Archaeology, Painting, Printmaking, Sculpture, Basic Design

PENNSYLVANIA SCHOOL OF ART & DESIGN, 204 N Prince St, 17603. Tel 717-396-7833; FAX 717-396-1339; *Pres* Mary Colleen Heil
Estab 1982; pvt; D & E; scholarships; SC 160, LC 9; enrl D 200, E 150, non-maj 60, maj 140
Ent Req: HS Dipl
Degrees: Dipl, 3 yr
Tuition: Res—undergrad $6700 per yr, $225 per cr hr; non res—undergrad $6700 per yr
Adult Hobby Classes: Enrl 350; tuition $260 per cr. Courses—Computer Design, Studio
Children's Classes: Enrl 125; tuition $150 per cr, 20 contact hrs. Courses—Figure Drawing, Studio
Summer School: Dir, Tracy Beyl. Enrl 50; tuition youth $150 20 contact hrs, adult $260 per cr for 30 hrs. Courses—Computer, Studio

LEWISBURG

BUCKNELL UNIVERSITY, Dept of Art, 17837. Tel 717-524-1307; *Head Dept* William Lasansky, MFA; *Prof* Janice Mann, PhD; *Prof* Neil Anderson, MFA; *Prof* James Turnure, PhD; *Prof* Christiane Andersson, PhD; *Prof* Jody Blake, PhD
Estab 1846; pvt; D; scholarships; SC 19, LC 20, GC 30; enrl D 500, non-maj 450, maj 50, grad 2
Ent Req: HS dipl
Degrees: BA 4 yrs
Tuition: $16,560 per yr; campus res—room $2170, board $1940
Courses: Art History, Drawing, Graphic Arts, History of Art & Archaeology, Painting, Printmaking, Sculpture
Summer School: Dir, Lois Huffines. Enrl 426; term of 3 or 6 wks beginning June 14. Courses—Lectures, Studio

LOCK HAVEN

LOCK HAVEN UNIVERSITY, Dept of Fine Arts, Sloan Fine Arts Ctr, 17745. Tel 717-893-2151, 893-2011, 893-2143; FAX 717-893-2432; *Chmn* Dr Mohinder Gill. Instrs: FT 4
Scholarships
Degrees: BA
Tuition: Res—$3086 per 2 sem, $129 per cr hr; nonres—$7844 per 2 sem, $327 per cr hr
Courses: Art Appreciation, Art Education, Art History, Ceramics, Drawing, Jewelry, Painting, Photography, Printmaking, Sculpture, Stage Design, Textile Design, Weaving, Arts & Crafts, 2-D Design, 3-D design
Summer School: Courses offered

LORETTO

ST FRANCIS COLLEGE, Fine Arts Dept, 15940. Tel 814-472-3216; FAX 814-472-3044, 472-3000; *Chmn* Charles Olsen, MFA
Scholarships
Tuition: $340 per cr hr; campus res—room & board $5440
Courses: Art Appreciation, Art History, Design, Drawing, Museum Staff Training, Painting, Photography, Weaving, Culture & Values, Exploration of Arts, Independent Study, Modern Art

MANSFIELD

MANSFIELD UNIVERSITY, Art Dept, Allen Hall, 16933. Tel 717-662-4500; FAX 717-662-4114; *Chmn Dept* Dr Harold Carter; *Assoc Prof* Dale Witherow, MFA; *Assoc Prof* Tom Loomis, MA; *Assoc Prof* Sam Thomas, MEd; *Asst Prof* Stan Zujkowski, MS; *Asst Prof* Dr Bonnie Kutbay
Estab 1857; pub; D; scholarships; SC 26, LC 18; enrl D 700, maj 90
Ent Req: HS dipl, SAT
Degrees: BA(Studio Art), BA(Art History) & BSE(Art Educ) 4 yr, MEd(Art Educ)
Tuition: Res—$800 per sem, $1600 per yr; nonres—$2868 per yr, $1434 per sem; campus residency available
Courses: Advertising Design, Art Appreciation, †Art Education, †Art History, Ceramics, Drawing, Goldsmithing, Jewelry, Painting, Printmaking, Sculpture, Silversmithing, Weaving, Color & Design, Computer Art, Fibers, Studio Crafts, Visual Studies in Aesthetic Experiences
Adult Hobby Classes: Enrl 10. Courses—Art History, Studio Art, Graduate Level Art Education
Children's Classes: Instr, Dr Harold Carter. Enrl 100, tuition $10 for 10 wks, fall sem. Courses—Elementary Art Education
Summer School: Term of 5-6 wks beginning May 27. Courses—Ceramics, Drawing, Fibers, Graduate Courses, Painting, Printmaking, Sculpture, Studio Courses

MEADVILLE

ALLEGHENY COLLEGE, Art Dept, 520 N Main St, 16335. Tel 814-332-4365; Elec Mail name@alleg.edu. *Chair Art Dept* George Roland
Estab 1815, dept estab 1930; pvt; D; scholarships; SC 17, LC 7; enrl 550, maj 30
Ent Req: HS dipl, ent exam
Degrees: BA and BS 4 yr
Tuition: Tuition $13,760; tuition, room & board $17,890
Courses: Art History, Ceramics, Costume Design & Construction, †Drawing, Film, Mixed Media, †Painting, †Photography, †Printmaking, †Sculpture, Stage Design, Theatre Arts, †Video
Summer School: Dir, A Geffen. Enrl 40. Courses—Art History, Studio Art

MEDIA

DELAWARE COUNTY COMMUNITY COLLEGE, Communications & Humanities House, 901 S Media Line Rd, 19063. Tel 610-359-5000 Ext 5391; *Assoc Dean* Rosina Fieno; *Prof* John Botkin, MFA; *Prof* Al DeProspero, EdM; *Instr* Judith Wisniewfki, BFA; *Instr* Lisa Woollman; *Instr* Gail Fox
Estab 1967; pub; D & E
Degrees: AS, AA and AAS 2 yrs
Tuition: District res—$51.50 per cr hr; non-district res—$114.50 per cr hr; non-state res—$114.50 per cr hr; no campus res
Courses: Art Education, Art History, Drawing, Graphic Design, Illustration, Painting, Photography, Printmaking, Theatre Arts, Advertising, Cmputer Graphics, Desk Top Publishing, 2-D & 3- D Design, Production Techniques, Typography
Adult Hobby Classes: Enrl varies; tuition varies. Courses—Calligraphy, Crafts, Drawing, Graphic Design, Interior Design, Needlepoint, Photography, Stained Glass, Sketching, Woodcarving
Summer School: Tuition res $27 per cr hr, nonres $81 per cr hr for term of 6 wks. Courses—Drawing, Painting

MIDDLETOWN

PENN STATE HARRISBURG, Humanities Division, 777 W Harrisburg Pike, 17057-4898. Tel 717-948-6189; FAX 717-948-6008; *Prof* Irwin Richman, PhD; *Assoc Prof* Troy Thomas, PhD; *Head Humanities* William J Mahar. Instrs: PT 10
Estab 1965; pub; D & E; scholarships; SC 7, LC 15; enrl D & E 60, grad 40
Ent Req: 2 yrs of col or CLEP
Degrees: BHumanities 2 yrs, MA
Tuition: Res—undergrad 12 or more crs per sem $2594, undergrad 11 or fewer crs $217 per cr, grad 12 or more crs per sem $2901, grad 11 or fewer crs $244 per cr; nonres—undergrad 12 or more crs per sem $5670, undergrad 11 or fewer crs $469 per cr, grad 12 or more crs per sem $5974, grad 11 or fewer crs $499 per cr
Courses: Aesthetics, Architecture, Art Education, Art History, Drawing, Graphic Design, History of Art & Archaeology, Mixed Media, Painting, Photography, Theatre Arts, Video

MILLERSVILLE

MILLERSVILLE UNIVERSITY, Art Dept, Breidenstine Hall, 17551. Tel 717-872-3298; FAX 717-871-2004; *Chmn* R Gordon Wise, EdD
Estab 1855, dept estab 1930; pub; D & E; SC 65, LC 10, GC 64; enrl maj 330, grad 20
Ent Req: HS dipl
Degrees: BA(Art), BS(Art Educ), BFA 4 yr, MEd(Art Educ) 1 yr
Tuition: Res—$3224 per yr; nonres; nonres—$8168 per yr
Courses: Advertising Design, Aesthetics, Art Appreciation, Art Education, Art History, Calligraphy, Ceramics, Commercial Art, Design, Drawing, Goldsmithing, Graphic Arts, Graphic Design, Illustration, Jewelry, Lettering, Painting, Photography, Printmaking, Sculpture, Silversmithing, Teacher Training, Art Crafts, Computer Art, †Visual Communication
Summer School: Dir, R Gordon Wise. Enrl 200; term of 5 wks, two sessions beginning June & July. Courses—Art, Art Education, Art History

MONROEVILLE

COMMUNITY COLLEGE OF ALLEGHENY COUNTY, BOYCE CAMPUS, Art Dept, 595 Beatty Rd, 15146. Tel 412-733-4342; *Prof* Bruno Sorento, MFA; *Prof* Jeanne Moffatt Connors, MEd
Pub; D & E; SC 13, LC 1; enrl D 200, E 40, non-maj 140, maj 60
Ent Req: HS dipl
Degrees: AS 2 yrs
Tuition: In County—$1020 per sem; out of county—$2040 per sem; out of state & foriegn—$3060 sem
Courses: Art History, Ceramics, Collages, Constructions, Drawing, Graphic Arts, Mixed Media, Painting, Photography, Printmaking, Sculpture, Color & Design
Adult Hobby Classes: Ceramics, Color & Design, Drawing, History of Art, Mixed Media, Painting, Photography, Printmaking
Children's Classes: Enrl varies. Courses—Drawing, Painting
Summer School: Tuition $68 per cr. Courses—Vary

NANTICOKE

LUZERNE COUNTY COMMUNITY COLLEGE, Commercial Art Dept, Prospect St & Middle Rd, 18634. Tel 717-735-8300, 829-7319; *Coordr* Susan Sponenberg, BFA; *Instr* Mike Molnar; *Instr* George Schelling; *Instr* Sam Cramer
Estab 1967; pub; D & E; SC 20, LC 7; enrl D 140, E 60, non-maj 5, maj 60
Ent Req: HS dipl
Degrees: 2 year programs offered
Courses: Art History, Drawing, Graphic Arts, †Graphic Design, Illustration, Mixed Media, Painting, Photography, Airbrush, Color & Design, Color Photography, †Computer Graphics, Life Drawing, Phototypesetting, Typography

Adult Hobby Classes: Enrl 10; tuition $53 per cr for 15 wk term. Courses—Selected from above offerings
Summer School: Dir, Susan Sponenberg. Enrl 40; tuition $53 per cr for 15 wk term. Courses—Selected from above offerings

NEW KENSINGTON

PENNSYLVANIA STATE UNIVERSITY AT NEW KENSINGTON, Depts of Art & Architecture, 3550 Seventh St Rd, 15068. Tel 412-339-5466, 339-5456; *Assoc Prof Art* Bud Gibbons. Instrs: FT 2
Estab 1968; pub; D; scholarships; SC 3-4, LC 1 per sem
Ent Req: Col boards
Degrees: 2 yr (option for 4 yr at main campus at University Park)
Tuition: Res—undergrad $2404, $193 per cr hr; nonres—undergrad $3700, $309 per cr hr
Courses: Art Education, Art History, Ceramics, Design, Drawing, Painting, Theatre Arts, Music
Adult Hobby Classes: Courses—Ceramics, Painting, Theater for Children
Children's Classes: Courses—Art, Drama, Music Workshops
Summer School: Dir, Joseph Ferrino. Enrl 100; 8 wk term. Courses—Art, Drama, Music, Workshops

NEWTOWN

BUCKS COUNTY COMMUNITY COLLEGE, Fine Arts Dept, Swamp Rd, 18940. Tel 215-968-8421; *Chmn Dept* Frank Dominguez; *Instr* Jon Alley; *Instr* Robert Dodge; *Instr* Jack Gevins; *Instr* Alan Goldstein; *Instr* Catherine Jansen; *Instr* Diane Lindenheim; *Instr* Marlene Miller; *Instr* Charlotte Schatz; *Instr* Helen Weisz; *Instr* Mark Sfirri; *Instr* Milt Sigel; *Instr* Gwen Kerber; *Instr* John Mathews
Estab 1965; pub; D & E; enrl D & E 9200 (school)
Ent Req: HS dipl
Degrees: AA
Courses: Art History, Ceramics, Design, Drawing, Graphic Design, Jewelry, Painting, Photography, Printmaking, Sculpture, Glass, Woodworking

NEW WILMINGTON

WESTMINSTER COLLEGE, Art Dept, 16172. Tel 412-946-8761, 946-6260; *Chmn* Peggy Cox. Instrs: 3
Estab 1852; den; D; scholarships; enrl maj 30, total 1100
Degrees: BS & BA(Fine Arts, Educ) 4 yrs
Tuition: $16,275 with room & board
Children's Classes: Enrl 20

PHILADELPHIA

ART INSTITUTE OF PHILADELPHIA, 1622 Chestnut St, 19103. Tel 215-567-7080; WATS 800-275-2474. *Pres* Stacey Savchuk; *Dir Admis* James Palermo; *Registrar* Dianne Runyon. Instrs: FT 40, PT 65
Estab 1966; pvt; D & E; scholarships; SC 30, LC 8; enrl D 1125, E 72
Ent Req: HS dipl, portfolio
Degrees: AST 2 yr
Tuition: $2875-$2980 per qtr
Courses: Advertising Design, Art History, Design, Graphic Design, Illustration, †Interior Design, Lettering, Mixed Media, †Photography, Weaving, Computer Graphics, †Fashion Merchandising, †Fashion Illustration

DREXEL UNIVERSITY, Nesbitt College of Design Arts, Nesbitt Hall, 33rd & Market Sts, 19104. Tel 215-895-2386; FAX 215-895-4917; *Dean* J Michael Adams; *Head Dept Interiors & Graphic Studies* Marjorie Kriebel; *Head Dept Fashion & Visual Studies* David Raizman; *Head Dept Architecture* Paul Hirschorn, MArch. Instrs: FT 19, PT 38
Estab 1891; pvt; scholarships; SC 39, LC 9; enrl undergrad $550, grad 50
Ent Req: Col board exam
Degrees: BS 4 yr (cooperative plan for BS), BArch 2 yr undergrad & 4 yr part time program, MS
Tuition: Freshmen $11,000; Sophmore - Sr $13,100 plus $560 general fee
Courses: Advertising Design, †Architecture, Advertising, Art History, Calligraphy, Commercial Art, Conceptual Art, Costume Design & Construction, Design, Display, Drawing, †Fashion Arts, †Film, †Graphic Arts, †Graphic Design, Illustration, †Interior Design, Lettering, Mixed Media, Painting, Photography, Printmaking, Sculpture, Stage Design, Textile Design, Theatre Arts, †Video, Design & Merchandising, †Fashion Design
Summer School: Dir, J Michael Adams. Enrl 220; term of 11 wks

SAMUEL S FLEISHER ART MEMORIAL, 709-721 Catharine St, 19147. Tel 215-922-3456; FAX 215-922-5327; *Dir* Thora E Jacobson; *Asst Dir* Nancy Wright; *Instr* Mac Fisher; *Instr* Frank Gasparro; *Instr* Tom Gaughan; *Instr* Gabriel Martinez; *Instr* Louise Clement
Estab 1898; administered by the Philadelphia Museum of Art; pvt; E; scholarships; LC 1; enrl E 2000
Ent Req: None
Degrees: None
Courses: Art Appreciation, Ceramics, Drawing, Jewelry, Painting, Photography, Printmaking, Sculpture, Folk Arts
Adult Hobby Classes: Enrl 850; tuition free Sept-May. Courses—Ceramics, Drawing, Painting, Photography, Printmaking, Sculpture
Children's Classes: Enrl 425; tuition free Sept-May. Courses—Drawing, Painting, Papermaking, Sculpture
Summer School: Ceramics, Drawing, Landscape Painting, Painting, Photography, Printmaking, Sculpture

HUSSIAN SCHOOL OF ART, Commercial Art Dept, 1118 Market St, 19107. Tel 215-981-0900; FAX 215-864-9115; *Pres* Ronald Dove. Instrs: FT 1, PT 28
Estab 1946; pvt; D; enrl 150
Ent Req: HS dipl, portfolio interview
Degrees: AST
Tuition: No campus res
Courses: †Advertising Design, Art Appreciation, Commercial Art, Drawing, Graphic Design, †Illustration, Lettering, Mixed Media, Painting, Photography, Printmaking, Airbrush, Computer Graphics, Fine Art
Adult Hobby Classes: Courses offered
Summer School: Summer workshop in Advertising Design, Computer Graphics, Drawing & Illustration

LA SALLE UNIVERSITY, Dept of Art, * 20th St & Olney Ave, 19141. Tel 215-951-1126; *Chmn Dept Fine Arts* Dr Charles White; *Prof* James Lang, MFA; *Asst Prof* Beverly Marchant
Estab 1865; dept estab 1972; den; D & E; SC 2; enrl D 4, maj 2
Ent Req: HS dipl
Degrees: BA 4 yr
Tuition: $10,000 per yr; campus res—available
Courses: Art History, Painting, Printmaking
Summer School: Selected courses offered

MOORE COLLEGE OF ART & DESIGN, 20th & The Parkway, 19103-1179. Tel 215-568-4515; FAX 215-568-8017; *Pres* Barbara Gillette Price; *Dean* Gretchen Garner; *Chmn 2-D Fine Arts* Vivian Woloritz; *Chmn 3-D Fine Arts* Charles Fahlen; *Chmn Fashion Design* Janice Lewis; *Chmn Liberal Arts* Jill Furst; *Chmn Illustration* Millie Ivins; *Chmn Interior Design* Curtis Estes; *Chmn Textile Design* Deborah Warner; *Chmn Basic Arts* David Bowman
Estab 1848; pvt; D; scholarships; enrl D 400, non-maj 25, maj 375
Ent Req: HS dipl, portfolio, SAT
Degrees: BFA 4 yr, Certification in Art Education
Tuition: Res—$20,026 per yr includes room & board; part-time students $600 per cr
Courses: Aesthetics, Art Education, †Art History, Ceramics, Design, Display, Drawing, Fashion Arts, Film, Graphic Arts, †Graphic Design, History of Art & Archaeology, †Illustration, †Interior Design, Jewelry, Mixed Media, Sculpture, Teacher Training, †Textile Design, Weaving, †Textile Design, †2-D & 3-D Design
Adult Hobby Classes: Tuition $250 per 3 hr class, 1 cr each, once per wk; 10 wk term. Courses—CADD, Computer Seminars, Desktop Publishing, Drawing, Fashion Design Studio, Illustration, Interior Design, Jewelry Making, Life Drawing, Millinery, Oil Painting, Print Design
Children's Classes: Enrl 500; tuition $30, registration $165 per class; Oct - Dec & Feb - Apr on Sat. Courses—General Art

PENNSYLVANIA ACADEMY OF THE FINE ARTS, 118 N Broad St, 19102. Tel 215-972-7600; FAX 215-569-0153; *Dir* Frederick S Osborne; *Pres* Gresham Riley
Estab 1805; pvt; D & E; scholarships; SC 15, LC 4
Ent Req: HS dipl, portfolio & recommendations
Degrees: Cert, 4 yrs; BFA Coordinated prog with Univ Pennsylvania or Univ of the Arts 5 yr, MFA(Painting), MFA(Printing) & MFA(sculpture) 2 yrs, Post-Baccalaurcate prog 1 yr
Tuition: Nonres—undergrad $4215 per sem, MFA $13,375 per yr, Post-Baccalaurcate $10,430 per yr; no campus res
Courses: Drawing, Painting, Printmaking, Sculpture, Anatomy, Perspective
Adult Hobby Classes: Enrl 310; tuition $330 per class for 5 wk term. Courses—Drawing, Painting, Printmaking, Sculpture
Children's Classes: Enrl 200; tuition $110 one wk session. Courses—Theme Camps
Summer School: Dir, Angela G Walker. Enrl 320; tuition $330 per class for 1 wk workshop 6 wk classes. Courses—Drawing, Painting, Printmaking, Sculpture

PHILADELPHIA COLLEGE OF TEXTILES & SCIENCE, School of Textiles, 4201 Henry Ave, 19144. Tel 215-951-2751; *Pres* Dr James Gallagher
Estab 1884; pvt; scholarships; enrl D 1600, E 1100
Degrees: BS 4 yrs
Tuition: $10,844 per yr
Courses: Interior Design, Chemistry & Dyeing, Fashion Apparel Management, Fashion Design, Fashion Merchandising, Knitted Design, Print Design, Textile Engineering, Textile Quality Control & Testing, Weaving Design
Summer School: Dir, Maxine Lentz

PHILADELPHIA COMMUNITY COLLEGE, Dept of Art, 1700 Spring Garden St, 19130. Tel 215-751-8771; *Dir Div Liberal Arts* Dr Sharon Thompson; *Prof* Diane Burko, MFA; *Prof* Robert Paige, MFA; *Assoc Prof* Valerie Seligsohn, MFA; *Assoc Prof* Madeline Cohen, PhD; *Assoc Prof* Dan Evans, MA; *Asst Prof* Meiling Hom, MFA; *Asst Prof* Karen Aumann, BFA; *Asst Prof* Michael Saluato, MA
Estab 1967; pub; D & E; SC 10, LC 6; enrl D 80 art maj
Ent Req: HS dipl, portfolio
Degrees: AA 2 yr
Tuition: $69 per cr hr, approx $1500 per yr; no campus res
Courses: Art History, Ceramics, Drawing, Graphic Design, Painting, Photography, Computer Graphics, Design, 2-D Design, 3-D Design, Transfer Foundation Program
Summer School: Dir, Bob Paige. Tuition $61 per cr. Courses—Art History, Ceramics, Design, Drawing, Painting

SAINT JOSEPH'S UNIVERSITY, Dept of Fine & Performing Arts, 5600 City Ave, 19131. Tel 610-660-1000, 660-1840; *Chmn* Dennis Weeks; *Chmn Head Music* Lewis Gordon, DMA; *Lectr* Peg Schofield, MFA; *Lectr* Jeff Blake; *Lectr* Betsy Anderson, MA
Estab 1851, prog estab 1975; den; D & E; scholarships; SC 15, LC 4; enrl D 200, E 20
Ent Req: HS dipl
Tuition: $12,750 per yr; campus res—room & board $6300
Courses: Advertising Design, Aesthetics, Art Education, Architecture, Art Appreciation, Art Education, Art History, Ceramics, Drawing, Film, History of Art & Archaeology, Painting, Photography, Stage Design, Theatre Arts, Music History
Adult Hobby Classes: Enrl 30 per sem; tuition $175 per cr hr. Courses—same as above
Children's Classes: Chmn, Rev Dennis McNally, SJ, PhD. Enrl 60; tuition $175 per cr hr, 3 cr for 6 wk term. Courses—Art History, Drawing, Photography

TEMPLE UNIVERSITY, Tyler School of Art, Beech & Penrose Aves, Elkins Park, 19027. Tel 215-782-2715; *Dean* Rochelle Toner, MFA; *Chmn Painting, Drawing, & Sculpture* Susan Moore, MFA; *Chmn Graphic Arts & Design* Allen Koss, MFA; *Chmn Crafts* Jon Clark, MFA; *Chmn Art History* Philip Betancourt, PhD; *Chmn Univ Art & Art Educ* Marilyn Holsing
Dept estab 1935; pvt; D & E; scholarships; enrl 700
Ent Req: HS dipl, SAT, portfolio
Degrees: BA(Art History & Studio Art), BS(Art Educ), BFA, MA(Art History), MEd(Art Educ), MFA & PhD(Art History)
Tuition: Res—undergrad $5624 per yr, grad $7110 per yr; nonres—undergrad $9860 per yr, grad $9000 per yr
Courses: †Art Education, †Art History, †Ceramics, Drawing, Film, †Graphic Design, †History of Art & Archaeology, Illustration, †Painting, †Photography, †Printmaking, Sculpture, Video, Weaving, Computers, †Fibers Fabric Design, Foundry, Handmade Cameras, Metals, Papermaking, Performance Art, †Glass, Animation,
Children's Classes: Courses—Computer & Studio, also programs for HS students

UNIVERSITY OF PENNSYLVANIA, Graduate School of Fine Arts, 19104-6311. Tel 215-898-8321; FAX 215-898-9215; *Dean* Gary Hack; *Prof* Patricia Conway
Estab 1874; pvt; scholarships & fels; GC
Ent Req: Ent exam
Tuition: Grad $8792 per sem; campus res available
Courses: Landscape Architecture, Architectural Design, Fine Arts
Summer School: Dir, Adele Santos. Tuition $2500 per 6 wks. Studio courses in Paris, Venice & India
—**Dept of Architecture,** 207 Meyerson Hall, 19104-6311. Tel 215-898-5728; FAX 215-898-9215; *Chmn* David Leatherbarrow; *Chmn Grad Group* Joseph Rykwert. Instrs: FT 7, PT 25
Enrl 180
Degrees: MA 3 yrs, PhD 4 - 5 yrs
Tuition: $16,546 per yr
Courses: Architectural Design and Construction
Summer School: Chmn, Adele Santos. Enrl 70; tuition $1200 per 3 cr course (4-6 wks duration). Courses—Summer studios (only upper level students)
—**Dept of Landscape Architecture & Regional Planning,** Meyerson, Rm 119, 19104-6311. Tel 215-898-6591; FAX 215-573-3770; *Chmn* John Dixon Hunt. Instrs: FT 6, PT 5
Scholarships; LC 7, Design Courses 4; enrl 68
Degrees: MLA 2 - 3 yrs, MRP 2 yrs, Cert & joint degrees available
Tuition: Res—full-time $21,990 per yr
Courses: Computation - GIS & CAD, Design Studio, Field Ecology, History & Theory, Regional Planning Studio, Workshop Series
—**Graduate School of Fine Arts,** Dept of Fine Arts, 205 S 34th St, Rm 100 Morgan 6312, 19104-6311. Tel 215-898-8374; FAX 215-898-2915; *Chmn&Adj Prof* Hitoshi Nakazato; *Prof* Robert Slutzky; *Lectr* Arlene Gostin; *Lectr* Diane Lachman; *Lectr* Laura Lichtenstein; *Lectr* Barbara Grossman; *Lectr* Diane Keller; *Lectr* John Boyce; *Lectr* Nick Vidnovic; *Lectr* Becky Young; *Lectr* Scot Kaylor; *Lectr* Jacalyn Brookner. Instrs: FT 7, PT 3
SC 21, LC 5, GC; enrl 65
Degrees: BFA 4 yrs, MFA 3 yrs
Tuition: $16,546 per yr
Courses: Painting, Printmaking, Sculpture, Color

UNIVERSITY OF THE ARTS, Philadelphia College of Art & Design, 320 S Broad St, 19102. Tel 215-875-4800 (Univ), 875-1100 (PCAD); FAX 215-875-1100 (PCAD);
Internet Home Page Address http://www.uarts.edu. *Pres* Peter Solmssen, JD; *Provost* Virginia Red, MM; *Dean, College of Art & Design* Stephen Tarantal, MFA; *Dean, College of Performing Arts* Stephen Jay, MM; *Dir of Admis* Barbara Elliot; *Chmn Crafts* Jeanne Jaffe, MFA; *Chmn Graphic Design* Chris Myers, MFA; *Chmn Illustration* Phyllis Purves-Smith, MFA; *Chmn Industrial Design* Anthony Guido, BS; *Chmn Fine Arts Dept* Lois Johnson, MFA; *Chmn Photography, Media Arts, Film & Animation* Alida Fish, MFA; *Co-Chmn Foundation Prog* Robert McGovern, BFA; *Co-Chmn Foundation Prog* Michael Rossman, MFA; *Chmn Educ Art* Janis Norman, PhD; *Chmn Museum Educ* Anne El-Omami, PhD; *Dir Continuing Studies* Barbara Lippman, BA; *Dir Pre-College Prog* Erin Elman; *Dir Graduate Prog* Carol Moore, MFA; *Graduate Prog* Mary Phelan, MA; *Graduate Prog* Charles Burnette, PhD; *Graduate Prog* Jane Bedno, BA
Estab 1876; pvt; D & E; scholarships; enrl Undergrad 760, grad 120
Ent Req: HS dipl, portfolio, SAT
Degrees: BFA 4 yrs, BS, MA, MFA, MID, Mat certificates
Tuition: $13,850 per yr; campus res—room $3980 per yr
Courses: Aesthetics, Art Education, Art History, Calligraphy, †Ceramics, Collages, Conceptual Art, Constructions, Drawing, †Film, Goldsmithing, †Graphic Design, †Illustration, †Industrial Design, Intermedia, Jewelry, Lettering, Mixed Media, †Museum Staff Training, †Painting, †Photography, †Printmaking, †Sculpture, Silversmithing, †Teacher Training, †Textile Design, Weaving, Animation, †Book Arts, Electronic Media, Museum Exhibition Planning & Design, Wood
Adult Hobby Classes: Evening & weekend prog enrl 1400; $360 per cr. Courses—Ceramics, Computer Graphics, Creative Writing, Design, Fine Arts, Illustration, Jewelry & Metalsmithing, Photography, Printmaking, Sculpture, Woodworking
Children's Classes: Saturday school; enrl 400; tuition $215 per course & $15 materials. Courses—Acting, Bookmaking, Ceramics, Comix, Creative Writing, Dance, Drawing, Figure Drawing, Graphic Design, Illustration, Jewelry, Musical Theater, Painting, Photography, Sculpture
Summer School: Dir, Erin Elman. Enrl 200; tuition $1400-$1800; term of 2-6 wks. Courses—Acting, Crafts, Design, Fine Arts, Jazz Performing, Media Arts, Musical Theater

PITTSBURGH

ART INSTITUTE OF PITTSBURGH, 526 Penn Ave, 15222. Tel 412-263-6600;
Pres Dr Dennis Fantaski
Estab 1921; pvt; scholarships; enrl 2300
Ent Req: HS grad
Degrees: AA 2 yrs, dipl
Tuition: $2875-$2980 (6-9 qtrs)
Courses: Fashion Arts, Industrial Design, Interior Design, Photography, Computer Animation Multimedia, Desktop Publishing, Layout & Production Art, Music & Video Business, Retailing, Residential Planning, Visual Communications

CARLOW COLLEGE, Art Dept, 3333 Fifth Ave, 15213. Tel 412-578-6000, 578-6003; *Chmn Dept* Richard Devlin; *Assoc Chmn* Suzanne Steiner. Instrs: FT 1, PT 3
Estab 1945; den; D & E; scholarships; SC 17, LC 6; enrl 800, maj 35
Ent Req: HS dipl and transcript, col boards
Degrees: BA, Certificate Art Education
Tuition: Res—undergrad $321 per cr hr, grad $341 per cr hr, $5066 12-17 cr
Courses: Art Education, Ceramics, Drawing, Painting, Printmaking, Sculpture, Teacher Training, American Art, Art Therapy, Fiber Arts, Survey of Art, Twentieth Century Art, 2-D Design
Summer School: Acad Dean, Sr Elizabeth McMillan. Enrl approx 40; two summer sessions 4 wks each. Courses—Fiber Arts, Ceramics

CARNEGIE MELLON UNIVERSITY, College of Fine Arts, 5000 Forbes Ave, Rm 100, 15213. Tel 412-268-2000, Ext 2349 (dean's office), Ext 2409 (art); *Dean* Martin Prekop; *Assoc Dean* Barbara Anderson; *Assoc Dean* Craig Vogel
Estab 1905; pvt; scholarships & fels
Ent Req: Col board ent exam plus auditions or portfolio
Degrees: 4-5 yr, MFA in Stage Design available in Dept of Drama
Tuition: Undergrad $19,400 per yr; campus res available
Summer School: Term of 6 wks. Courses—includes some pre-college courses
—**Dept of Architecture,** 5000 Forbes Ave, Rm 201, 15213. Tel 412-268-2354; *Head* Vivian Loftness. Instrs: FT 22, PT 20
Enrl 295
Degrees: BArch, MS, PhD
Tuition: Undergrad $19,400 per yr
Courses: Architecture
Summer School: Dir, John Papinchak. tuition $2094 per 6 wks
—**Dept of Design,** MMCH 110, 5000 Forbes Ave, 15213. Tel 412-268-2828; *Head* Richard Buchanan. Instrs: FT 14, PT 4
Enrl 200
Degrees: BFA 4 yrs
Tuition: Res—undergrad $19,400 per yr
Courses: Graphic Design, Industrial Design
Adult Hobby Classes: Calligraphy
Summer School: Design Studio
—**Dept of Art,** 15213-3890. Tel 412-268-2409; FAX 412-268-7817; *Head* Byran Rogers; *Assoc Dept Head Admin Affair* Mary Schmidt; *Assoc Dept Head Acad Affairs* John Sturgeon. Instrs: FT 28, PT 2-6
Scholarships; enrl 215
Degrees: BFA & MFA
Tuition: Undergrad & grad $19,400 per yr
Courses: Aesthetics, Art History, Ceramics, Conceptual Art, Constructions, Drawing, Mixed Media, Painting, Printmaking, Sculpture, Video, †Art, Computer
Children's Classes: Enrl 100; tuition $525 for 9 months. Courses—same as undergrad prog
Summer School: Dir, Janice Hart. Enrl 50; tuition $2870 for 6 wks. Courses—same as undergrad prog

CHATHAM COLLEGE, Fine & Performing Arts, Woodland Rd, 15232. Tel 412-365-1100; *Chmn* Dr Spinelli ; *Dir* Dr Margaret Ross; *Asst Prof* Michael Pestel. Instrs: FT 2, PT 2
Estab 1869; pvt; W; SC 17, LC 7
Ent Req: HS grad
Degrees: BA 4 yrs
Tuition: $13,500 (incl res fees); $6750 per sem
Courses: Aesthetics, Art Appreciation, Art Education, †Art History, Conceptual Art, Constructions, Design, Drawing, Film, History of Art & Archaeology, Mixed Media, †Painting, Photography, Printmaking, †Sculpture, Independent Study, Introduction to Art, Tutorial

LA ROCHE COLLEGE, Division of Graphics, Design & Communication, 9000 Babcock Blvd, 15237. Tel 412-367-9300; *Chmn* Martha Fairchild-Shepler, MFA; *Prof* Tom Bates; *Prof* Martha Fairchild MFA; *Assoc Prof* George Founds; *Instr* Diane Foltz, PhD; *Instr* Wendy Bechwith, MArchit; *Instr* Grant Dismore, MFA; *Instr* Devvrat Nagar, BArchit; *Interior Design* Crispan Zuback; *Interior Design* Carolyn Freeman; *Graphic Design* Rosemary F Gould. Instrs: PT 15
Estab 1963, dept estab 1965; pvt; D & E; SC 25, LC 15; enrl D & E 200, non-maj 20, maj 180
Ent Req: HS dipl
Degrees: BA and BS 4 yr
Tuition: $4422 per sem
Courses: Advertising Design, Aesthetics, Art History, Ceramics, Commercial Art, Display, Drawing, †Graphic Arts, †Graphic Design, Illustration, Industrial Design, †Interior Design, Lettering, Painting, Photography, Sculpture, Airbrush Illustration, Communication, Computer Graphics, Fashion Design, †Multimedia Design, Package Design, 3-D Design
Summer School: Dir of Admissions, Marianne Shertzer. Tuition $170 per cr

POINT PARK COLLEGE, Performing Arts Dept, 201 Wood St, 15222. Tel 412-392-3450; FAX 412-391-1980; *Chmn* Shirley Barasch
Degrees: BA & BFA
Tuition: $4300 per sem
Courses: Architecture, Art Appreciation, Art History, †Film, †Interior Design, †Photography, †Stage Design, †Fashion Illustration, Theatre Design, †Visual Arts

UNIVERSITY OF PITTSBURGH, 15260
—**Henry Clay Frick Dept History of Art & Architecture,** 15260. Tel 412-648-2400; FAX 412-648-2792; *Chmn* Anne Weis
Estab 1787, dept estab 1927; pvt; D & E; scholarships; LC 35, GC 20; enrl D 750, E 250, grad 50
Ent Req: HS dipl, BA, GRE for grad work
Degrees: BA 4 yrs, MA 2 yrs, PhD
Tuition: Res—grad $3095; nonres—grad $6190
Courses: Art History, History of Art & Archaeology
Summer School: Dir, Anne Weis. Enrl 150; 7 wks, 2 sessions
—**Dept of Studio Arts,** 104 Frick Fine Arts Bldg, 15260. Tel 412-648-2430; FAX 412-648-2792; *Chmn* Michael Morrill. Instrs: FT 6, PT 4-7
Estab 1968; pub; D; SC 29; enrl 1500
Degrees: BA
Tuition: Res—$4048 per yr; nonres—$8620 per yr
Courses: Design, Drawing, Graphic Design, Painting, Sculpture, Print Etching
Adult Hobby Classes: Enrl 120; tuition res—$113 per cr, nonres—$226 per cr for 15 wk term . Courses—Design, Color, Drawing, Sculpture
Summer School: Dir, Kenneth Batista. Enrl 60; tuition res $113 per cr, nonres—$226 per cr, 7 1/2 wks each. Courses—Design, Color, Drawing, Sculpture

RADNOR

CABRINI COLLEGE, Dept of Fine Arts, 610 King of Prussia Rd, 19087-3699. Tel 215-902-8380; FAX 215-902-8539; *Chmn Dept* Adeline Bethany, EdD. Instrs: FT 2, PT 3
Estab 1957; den; D & E; scholarships; SC 11, LC 4
Ent Req: HS dipl, statisfactory average & rank in secondary school class, SAT, recommendations
Degrees: BA(Arts Administration, Fine Arts & Graphic Design), BS & BSED
Tuition: $11,660 per yr; campus res—room & board $6700
Courses: Art Education, Ceramics, Drawing, Graphic Design, History of Art & Archaeology, Painting, Teacher Training, Computer Publication Design, Design & Composition
Adult Hobby Classes: Courses offered
Summer School: Dir, Dr Midge Leahy. Term of 6 wks beginning May & July. Courses—Color Theory, Drawing, Elem Art Methods, Mixed Media, Painting

READING

ALBRIGHT COLLEGE, Dept of Art, 13th & Exeter Sts, PO Box 15234, 19612-5234. Tel 610-921-7715; FAX 610-921-7530; *Chmn* Tom Watcke
Estab 1856, dept estab 1964; SC 14, LC 7; enrl D 322, E 41, non-maj 340, maj 14, others 20
Ent Req: HS dipl, SAT
Degrees: BA 4 yrs
Tuition: $11,800 per yr; campus res—room $1970, board $1650
Courses: Art History, Ceramics, Constructions, Drawing, Fashion Arts, Film, History of Art & Archaeology, Interior Design, Mixed Media, †Painting, Photography, Printmaking, †Sculpture, Theatre Arts
Adult Hobby Classes: Enrl 40; tuition $110 per cr. Courses—Drawing, Photography
Children's Classes: Enrl 25-35; tuition $35-$50 per course. Courses—Crafts, Drawing
Summer School: Chmn, Bert Brouwer. Enrl 30 - 50; 2 terms of 4 wks beginning in June & July. Courses—Art History, Drawing, Painting

ROSEMONT

ROSEMONT COLLEGE, Division of the Arts, 1400 Montgomery Ave, 19010. Tel 610-527-0200; *Chmn Div* Tina Walduier Bizzarro; *Assoc Prof* Patricia Nugent, MFA; *Assoc Prof* Michael Willse, MFA; *Asst Prof* Amy Orr, MFA; *Lectr* Peter Lister; *Lectr* Janice Merendino, BFA; *Lectr* David Tafler, MFA; *Lectr* James Victor. Instrs: FT 4, PT 7
Estab 1921; pvt, W (exchange with Villanova Univ, Cabrini College, Eastern College, The Design Schools); D; scholarships; enrl total col 600, art 200, grad approx 17
Ent Req: HS dipl, SAT
Degrees: BFA (Studio Art), BA (Art History, Studio Art), Teacher certificate in Art K-12
Tuition: $11,200 annual tuition; campus res available
Courses: Aesthetics, Art Education, Ceramics, Drawing, Graphic Arts, Painting, Photography, Printmaking, Sculpture, Teacher Training, American Indian Art, Art Criticism, Creativity & the Marketplace, Fibres History, Studio Art
Summer School: Dir, Tina Walduier Bizzarro

SCRANTON

ICS LEARNING SYSTEMS
—**School of Interior Design,** 925 Oak St, 18515. Tel 717-342-7701, Ext 341; *Dir Educ Serv* Connie Dempsey. Instrs: FT 1
Estab 1890, dept estab 1969; pvt; enrl 4200
Ent Req: HS dipl
Tuition: $689
Courses: Interior Decorating
Adult Hobby Classes: Interior Decorating
—**School of Art,** 925 Oak St, 18515. Tel 717-342-7701, Ext 341; *Dir Educ Serv* Connie Dempsey. Instrs: FT 1, PT 2
Estab 1890; pvt; enrl 4900
Ent Req: HS dipl
Tuition: $399-$499 per yr
Courses: Drawing, Painting
Adult Hobby Classes: Drawing, Painting

LACKAWANNA JUNIOR COLLEGE, Fine Arts Dept, 501 Vine St, 18509. Tel 717-961-7827; *Chmn* John De Nunzio
Degrees: AA
Tuition: $795 per cr, $585 per 3 cr
Courses: Fine Arts, Survey Class

MARYWOOD COLLEGE, Art Dept, 2300 Adams Ave, 18509. Tel 717-348-6211, 348-6278; *Chmn* Matt Pouse. Instrs: FT 12, PT 15
Estab 1926; pvt; D & E; scholarships; SC 28, LC 7, GC 12; enrl maj 240, grad 80
Ent Req: HS dipl, portfolio & interview
Degrees: BA(Art Educ), BA(Arts Admin), BS(Educ with concentration in Art), BFA(Drawing & Painting, Illustration, Advertising Graphics, Photography, Ceramics, Sculpture, Interior Design), MA(Studio Art, Art Educ, Art Therapy), MFA(Painting, Ceramics, Weaving)
Tuition: Grad MA $305, MFA $315 per cr, undergrad $300 per cr
Courses: †Advertising Design, †Art Education, Art History, Calligraphy, †Ceramics, Drawing, Fashion Arts, †Graphic Arts, †Illustration, †Interior Design, Jewelry, Mixed Media, †Painting, †Photography, Printmaking, †Sculpture, Textile Design, Theatre Arts, †Weaving, †Art Therapy, Contemporary Learning Theories, Fabrics, Metalcraft, Serigraphy, Tapestry
Adult Hobby Classes: Enrl 50; tuition varies for non-cr 10 wk term.
Courses—Ceramics, Drawing, Painting, Photography
Children's Classes: College for Kids, enrl 50. Courses—Computer Graphics, Drawing, Painting, Sculpture
Summer School: Graduate degree programs only

SHIPPENSBURG

SHIPPENSBURG UNIVERSITY, Art Dept, * Huber Art Ctr, 871 Old Main Dr, 17257-2299. Tel 717-532-1530; FAX 717-532-1273; *Chmn Art Dept* William Hynes; *Asst Prof* Bill Davis, MFA; *Asst Prof* George Waricher, MEd; *Asst Prof* Michael Campbell, MFA
Estab 1871, dept estab 1920; pub; D & E; scholarships; SC 17, LC 6; enrl D 400, E 100, non-maj 600, grad 15, continuing educ 20
Ent Req: HS dipl, Portfolio review
Degrees: BA(Art)
Tuition: Res—$1314 per sem, nonres—$2446 per sem; campus res—room & board $1451 per sem
Courses: Art History, Ceramics, Drawing, Painting, Printmaking, Sculpture, Arts & Crafts, Enamelling
Adult Hobby Classes: Sr citizen tuition waived in regular classes if space is available
Summer School: Dir, William Hynes. Tuition $110 per cr hr for terms of 3 - 5 wks beginning May 18. Lectr & Studio courses

SLIPPERY ROCK

SLIPPERY ROCK UNIVERSITY OF PENNSYLVANIA, Dept of Art, 16057. Tel 412-738-0512; FAX 412-738-4485; *Chmn Dept* Glen Brunken. Instrs: FT 9
Pub; D & E; SC 27, LC 3; enrl maj 70
Ent Req: HS dipl
Degrees: BA(Art), BFA(Art) 4 yr
Tuition: in-state res—$1543 per sem (12-18 hrs), $129 per cr; out-of-state—$3922 per sem, $327 per cr
Courses: Art History, Ceramics, Drawing, Painting, Photography, Printmaking, Sculpture, Textile Design, Art Synthesis, Metalsmithing
Summer School: Tuition $129 per cr hr

SWARTHMORE

SWARTHMORE COLLEGE, Dept of Art, 500 College Ave, 19081-1397. Tel 610-328-8116, 328-8000; *Chmn Dept Art & Assoc Prof* Randall L Exxon, MFA; *Prof* T Kaori Kitao, PhD; *Prof* Constance Cain Hungerford, PhD; *Assoc Prof* Brian A Meunier, MFA; *Assoc Prof* Maribeth Graybill; *Asst Prof* Syd Carpenter
Estab 1864, dept estab 1925; pvt; D; scholarships; SC 14, LC 33; enrl non-maj 500, maj 25
Ent Req: HS dipl, SAT, CEEB
Degrees: BA 4 yrs
Tuition: $19,124 per yr; campus res—room & board $6776 per yr
Courses: Aesthetics, Architecture, Art History, Ceramics, Drawing, History of Art & Archaeology, Landscape Architecture, Mixed Media, Painting, Photography, Printmaking, Sculpture, Stage Design, Theatre Arts, Art, History, History of Architecture, History of Cinema, Philosophy, Theatre Program, Urban History

UNIVERSITY PARK

PENNSYLVANIA STATE UNIVERSITY, UNIVERSITY PARK
—School of Visual Arts, 210 Patterson Bldg, 16802. Tel 814-865-0444; FAX 814-863-8664; *Dir School of Visual Arts* James Stephenson, MA
Estab 1855, col estab 1963; pub; D & E; SC 282, LC 99, GC 104
Ent Req: HS dipl and GPA, SAT
Degrees: MA, MED, MFA, MS & MS(Art Educ)
Tuition: Res—$2483 per sem; nonres—$3725 per sem
Courses: Art Education, Ceramics, Drawing, Graphic Design, Painting, Photography, Printmaking, Sculpture, Metals
Adult Hobby Classes: Tuition varies. Courses—informal, vary with demand
Summer School: Enrl 1565; tuition same. Courses—regular session
—Dept of Art History, 229 Arts II Bldg, 16802. Tel 814-865-6326; *Dept Head* Craig Zabel; *Prof* Roland E Fleischer, PhD; *Prof* George L Mauner, PhD; *Assoc Prof* Jeanne Chenault Porter, PhD; *Assoc Prof* Elizabeth B Smith, PhD; *Assoc Prof* Elizabeth J Walters, PhD; *Asst Prof* Carolyn Smyth; *Grad Officer* Roland E Fleischer
Estab 1855, dept estab 1963; pub; D & E; scholarships; LC 50, GC 36; enrl D 56, maj 51, grad 27, others 10
Ent Req: HS dipl

Degrees: BA, MA, PhD
Tuition: Res—$2483 per sem; nonres—$3725 per sem
Courses: Aesthetics, †Art History, History of Art & Archaeology, Ancient Roman, Buroque, Byzantine & Early Christian Colonial America, Rennaisance, Surveys
Adult Hobby Classes: Classes offered through Continuing Education
Summer School: Courses same as regular session, but limited

VILLANOVA

VILLANOVA UNIVERSITY, Dept of Art & Art History, 800 Lancaster Ave, 19085. Tel 610-519-4610; *Chmn* Bro Richard Cannuli; *Prof* George Radan; *Asst Prof* Dr Mark Sullivan
Estab 1842, dept estab 1971; pvt; D & E; SC 25, LC 6; enrl D 35, maj 35
Ent Req: HS dipl, SAT
Degrees: BFA 4 yrs; courses taught in conjunction with Rosemont College
Tuition: Res—undergrad $15,300 per yr; campus res—room & board $6850 per yr
Courses: †Aesthetics, Art Education, Art History, Drawing, Painting, Theatre Arts, Archaeology, Conservation
Adult Hobby Classes: Enrl 20-30; tuition $585 per course in 14 wk sem.
Courses—Calligraphy, Drawing
Summer School: Held in Siena, Italy. Courses—Art History, Language, Studio Art

WASHINGTON

WASHINGTON & JEFFERSON COLLEGE, Art Dept, Olin Art Ctr, 15301. Tel 412-222-4400, 223-6110; *Chmn Art Dept* Paul B Edwards, MA; *Prof* Hugh H Taylor, MA; *Asst Prof* Patricia Maloney, MFA; *Adjunct Prof* John Yothers, MA; *Adjunct Prof* James McNutt; *Adjunct Prof* Kathleen Madigan
Estab 1787, dept estab 1959; pvt; D & E; scholarships; SC 14, LC 8; enrl D 162, E 18, non-maj 139, maj 23, others 15
Ent Req: HS dipl, SAT, achievement tests
Degrees: BA 4 yr
Tuition: $17,190 per yr; campus res—room & board $4215 per yr
Courses: Art Appreciation, Art Education, Art History, Ceramics, Design, Drawing, Lettering, Painting, Photography, Printmaking, Restoration & Conservation, Sculpture, Teacher Training, Framing & Matting, Gallery Management, Photography
Summer School: Dir, Dean Dlugos. Enrl 250, two 4 wk sessions, June-Aug.
Courses—Drawing, Framing, Matting, Photography

WAYNE

WAYNE ART CENTER, 413 Maplewood Ave, 19087. Tel 610-688-3553; *Pres* Mimi Green; *Exec Dir* Nancy Campell; *Instr* Lucy Edwards; *Instr* Edward Lis; *Instr* Carolyn Howard; *Instr* Constance Moore Simon; *Instr* Maevernon Varnum; *Instr* Paul Gorka; *Instr* Zhe-Zhou Jiang; *Instr* Diane Ippoldo; *Instr* Candace Stringer; *Instr* Nancy Barch; *Instr* Jill Rupinski; *Instr* Anna Park; *Instr* Vicki Koron; *Instr* Janice Strawder; *Instr* Richard M Moyer
Estab 1930; pvt; D & E; SC 25; enrl D 200, E 50, others 40
Ent Req: None; free program for senior citizens
Tuition: $140 for 12 wk session
Courses: Mixed Media, Painting, Sculpture, Pottery, Woodcarving
Children's Classes: Tuition $35 for 10 wk sem, yearly dues $6. Courses—Drawing, Painting, Sculpture
Summer School: Exec Dir, Meg Miller. Courses—same as above plus Landscape Painting

WAYNESBURG

WAYNESBURG COLLEGE, Dept of Fine Arts, 51 W College St, 15370. Tel 412-627-8191; FAX 412-627-6416; *Chmn* Daniel Morris, MA; *Asst Prof* Susan Howsare, MFA; *Instr* Robert Gay, BSJ
Estab 1849, dept estab 1971; pvt; D & E; scholarships; SC 25, LC 6; enrl D 131, E 3, maj 17
Ent Req: HS dipl
Degrees: BA(Visual Communication) 4 yrs, MBA
Tuition: res—$7030 per yr; nonres—$7220 per yr; campus res—room & board $10, 120 per yr
Courses: Art Education, Art History, Ceramics, Design, Drawing, Graphic Arts, Painting, Photography, Printmaking, Sculpture, Theatre Arts, Computer Applications for Visual Communication, Computer Graphics, Desk Top Publishing, Layout & Photography for Media, Photo-Journalism, Media Presentation, Television, Typography, †Visual Art, †Visual Communication, †Visual Communication-Print Media
Adult Hobby Classes: Courses—Art History, Graphic Design, Photography
Summer School: Dept Chmn, Daniel Morris. Tuition $270 for term of 5 wks beginning June 2 and July 7

WEST MIFFLIN

COMMUNITY COLLEGE OF ALLEGHENY COUNTY, Fine Arts Dept, South Campus, 1750 Clairton Rd, 15122. Tel 412-469-1100; FAX 412-469-6370; *Chmn* George Jaber
Degrees: AA, AS
Tuition: County res—$744 per yr, $62 per cr hr
Courses: Advertising Design, Art Appreciation, Calligraphy, Commercial Art, Ceramics, Design, Drawing, Handicrafts, Painting, Photography, Computer Graphics

WILKES-BARRE

WILKES UNIVERSITY, Dept of Art, Bedford Hall, 18766. Tel 717-831-4329; *Chmn & Prof* Richard A Fuller, MA; *Assoc Prof* William Sterling, PhD; *Assoc Prof* Sharon Bowar; *Adjunct Prof* Stanley Grand, PhD; *Adjunct Prof* Michael Thomas, BA; *Adjunct Prof* Michael Stanford, MFA; *Adjunct Prof* Jan Conway, MFA; *Adjunct Prof* Jean Adams, BA
Estab 1947; pvt; D & E; scholarships; SC 20, LC 7; enrl D 170, E 23, non-maj 120, maj 35
Ent Req: HS dipl, SAT
Degrees: BA 4 yr
Tuition: Undergrad $12,586 per yr, $6293 per sem, PT $350 per cr hr; campus res—room & board $3890 per yr
Courses: †Art Education, †Art History, †Ceramics, Drawing, Painting, †Photography, †Printmaking, †Sculpture, Teacher Training, Textile Design, †Communication Design, Surface Design
Adult Hobby Classes: Courses variable
Summer School: Dir, Henry Steuben. Tuition $350 per cr for 5 wk day, 8 wk evening or 3 wk presession. Courses—Art Studio, Ceramics, Photography, Surface Design

WILLIAMSPORT

LYCOMING COLLEGE, Art Dept, 17701. Tel 717-321-4000, 321-4002, 321-4240; *Chmn* Roger Douglas Shipley, MFA; *Prof* Jon Robert Bogle, MFA; *Assoc Prof* Amy Golahny; *Asst Prof* Lynn Estomin, MFA
Estab 1812; pvt; D & E; scholarships; SC 20, LC 7; enrl College 1500, Dept 500, maj 70
Ent Req: HS dipl, ACT or SAT
Degrees: BA 4 yr
Tuition: $14,700 per yr; campus res—room & board $4500 per yr
Courses: Advertising Design, †Art Education, †Art History, Ceramics, †Commercial Art, Costume Design & Construction, Design, Drawing, Graphic Arts, †History of Art & Archaeology, †Painting, †Photography, †Printmaking, †Sculpture, Stage Design, Teacher Training, Theatre Arts, Computer Graphics
Summer School: Dir, Roger Shipley. Enrl 25; May session. Courses—Art History, Drawing, Photography

PENNSYLVANIA COLLEGE OF TECHNOLOGY, Dept of Graphic Communications, 1 College Ave, 17701. Tel 717-326-3761; FAX 717-327-4503; *Dean Acad Studies* Veronica Muzic; *Prof* Ralph Horne, EdD; *Assoc Prof* Dale Metzker, AA; *Assoc Prof* Patrick Murphy, MSEd; *Asst Prof* William Ealer, BS; *Asst Prof* Steven Hirsch, MFA; *Instr* Kathy Y Walker, CET; *Instr* Tuna Saka, BArch; *Instr* Harold Newton
Estab 1965; pub; D & E; scholarships; enrl D 2903, E 2909
Ent Req: HS dipl, placement test
Degrees: AA 2 yr
Tuition: Res—$156.20 per hr; nonres—$238.60 per hr
Courses: †Advertising Design, Art History, Design, Drawing, Graphic Arts, Graphic Design, Lettering, Mixed Media, Painting, Photography, Technical Illustration

YORK

YORK COLLEGE OF PENNSYLVANIA, Dept of Music, Art & Speech Communications, Country Club Rd, 17405. Tel 717-846-7788; *Chmn Fine Arts* Dr Thomas Hall
Estab 1941; pvt; D & E; SC 17, LC 7
Ent Req: HS dipl, SAT or ACT
Degrees: BA 4 yrs & AA 2 yrs
Tuition: $2607.50 per yr; campus res available
Courses: Art Education, Art History, Commercial Art, Drawing, Painting, Photography, Sculpture
Adult Hobby Classes: Enrl 40; Courses—per regular session
Summer School: Dir, Thomas Michalski. Enrl 15; Term of 3 wks beginning May 19 & two 5 wk sessions beginning June & July

RHODE ISLAND

BRISTOL

ROGER WILLIAMS COLLEGE, Art Dept, One Old Ferry Rd, 02809-2921. Tel 401-253-1040; *Coordr* Ronald Wilczek; *Instr* Carol J Hathaway; *Instr* Thomas Russell, MFA; *Instr* Kathleen Hancock
Estab 1948, dept estab 1967; pvt; D & E; enrl D 1800, E 1500, maj 42
Ent Req: HS dipl
Degrees: AA 2 yr, BA 4 yr, apprenticeship and senior teaching
Tuition: Res—$16,290 per yr; nonres—$10,960 per yr; campus res—room & board $3130 per yr
Courses: Architecture, Art History, Drawing, Film, Graphic Design, Painting, Photography, Printmaking, Restoration & Conservation, Sculpture, Teacher Training, Theatre Arts, Weaving, Gallery Mgmt, 2-D & 3-D Design
Summer School: Dean, Bart Schiaro. Courses—Ceramics, Design, Drawing, Painting, Weaving

KINGSTON

UNIVERSITY OF RHODE ISLAND, Dept of Art, * Fine Arts Ctr, 02881-0820. Tel 401-874-2131, 874-5821; FAX 401-874-2729; *Chmn* Wendy B Holmes; *Prof* William Klenk, PhD; *Prof* William Leete, MFA; *Prof* Bart Parker, MFA; *Prof* Robert H Rohm, MFA; *Prof* Richard Calabro, MFA; *Prof* Marjorie Keller, PhD; *Prof* Wendy Roworth, PhD; *Prof* Gary Richman, MFA; *Asst Prof* Barbara Pagh, MFA; *Asst Prof* Mary Hollinshead. Instrs: Ft 12, PT 6
Estab 1892; pub; D & E; scholarships; SC 21, studio seminars 24, LC 23; enrl D 900, E 30, non-maj 725, maj 200, other 10 - 20
Ent Req: Same as required for Col of Arts & Sciences
Degrees: BA(Studio), BA(Art History) & BFA(Art Studio) 4 yrs
Tuition: Res—undergrad $3643 per yr, $2011 per sem, $1358 PT, $148 per cr hr; nonres—undergrad $9597 per yr, $4983 per sem, $4075 PT, $395 per cr hr; campus res—available
Courses: Aesthetics, Architecture, Art History, Conceptual Art, Drawing, Film, Graphic Arts, History of Art & Archaeology, Painting, Photography, Sculpture, Theatre Arts, Studio Art
Adult Hobby Classes: Art History, Drawing, Painting, Sculpture
Summer School: Chairperson Dept Art, Ronald Onorato, Enrl 45 - 50; tuition in-state—undergrad $121 per cr, out-of-state—undergrad $388 per cr for 5 wk terms beginning May 24 - June 25 & June 28 - July 30. Courses— Art History, Drawing, Photography

NEWPORT

NEWPORT ART MUSEUM SCHOOL, 76 Bellevue Ave, 02840. Tel 401-848-8200; FAX 401-848-8205; *Dir* Judith Sobol
Estab 1912; D & E; scholarships; SC 25, LC 3; enrl D 300 (total)
Ent Req: None
Degrees: None
Courses: Art History, Ceramics, Collages, Drawing, Jewelry, Painting, Photography, Printmaking, Sculpture, Etching, Multimedia, Pastels
Adult Hobby Classes: Enrl 200; tuition varies; 6, 8 or 10 wk courses
Children's Classes: Enrl 100 per term; tuition varies per 6, 8, or 10 wk session
Summer School: Enrl 160; tuition varies. Courses—Painting, Drawing, Workshops, Children's Multimedia

SALVE REGINA UNIVERSITY, Art Dept, Ochre Point Ave, 02840. Tel 401-847-6650; *Chmn* Jay Lacouture, MFA; *Assoc Prof* Barbara Shamblin, MFA; *Assoc Prof* Daniel Ludwig, MFA; *Assoc Prof* Gabrielle Bleek-Byrne, PhD; *Lectr* Bert Emerson, MAT
Estab 1947; den; D & E; scholarships; SC 28, LC 8; enrl D 270 per sem (dept), non-maj 95, maj 72
Ent Req: HS dipl, ent exam
Degrees: BA 4 yr
Tuition: Res—undergrad $7100 per sem, $330 per sem hr, grad $250 per cr
Courses: Art History, Ceramics, Commercial Art, Design, Drawing, Film, Graphic Arts, Graphic Design, History of Art & Archaeology, Illustration, Painting, Photography, Sculpture, Theatre Arts, Aesthetics, Anatomy, Environmental Design, 2 & 3-D Design
Summer School: Dir, Jay Lacouture

PROVIDENCE

BROWN UNIVERSITY
—**Dept History of Art & Architecture,** PO Box 1855, 02912. Tel 401-863-1174; FAX 401-863-7790; *Chmn* Jeffrey Muller
Pvt; D; scholarships; LC 13-15, GC 10-12; enrl maj 59, grad 47
Degrees: BA, MA, PhD
Tuition: $19,528 per yr
Courses: †Art History, History of Art & Archaeology, Chinese Art, 19th & 20th Century Architecture & Painting, Greek, Italian & Roman Art & Architecture, Introduction to Art
Summer School: Dean, Karen Sibley. Courses—limited
—**Dept of Visual Art,** PO Box 1861, 02912. Tel 401-863-2423; FAX 401-863-1680; *Chmn* Marlene Malik
Pvt; D; SC 19-21, LC 13-15, GC 10-12; enrl maj 140
Degrees: BA
Tuition: $19,528 per yr
Courses: Drawing, Painting, Printmaking, Sculpture, Art of the Book, Computer Art

PROVIDENCE COLLEGE, Art & Art History Dept, River Ave & Eaton St, 02918. Tel 401-865-2401, 865-2707; *Chmn* Dr Ann Wood Norton; *Assoc Prof* Adrian G Dabash, MFA; *Assoc Prof* Richard A McAlister, MFA; *Prof* James Baker, MFA; *Assoc Prof* Alice Beckwith, PhD; *Asst Prof* Suzanne H D'Avanzo; *Asst Prof* James Janecek, MFA; *Asst Prof* Dr David Gillerman, PhD; *Asst Prof* Deborah Johnson, PhD; *Slide Librn* Marie Woodard; *Slide Librn* John DiCicco
Estab 1917, dept estab 1969; pvt; D & E; SC 49, LC 8; enrl D 254, E 250, non-maj 209, maj 45
Ent Req: HS dipl, portfolio needed for transfer students
Degrees: BA 4 yr
Tuition: Res & nonres—undergrad $10,935 per yr; campus res—room & board $4700 per yr
Courses: †Art History, †Ceramics, †Drawing, †Painting, †Photography, †Printmaking, †Sculpture
Adult Hobby Classes: Dean, Dr O'Hara. Courses—History of Architecture, Art History, Calligraphy, Ceramics, Drafting, Drawing, Painting, Photography, Sculpture, Studio Art, Watercolor
Summer School: Dir, James M Murphy. Tuition $180 & $50 lab fee for three credit courses beginning mid-June through July. Courses—Art History, Calligraphy, Ceramics, Drawing, Painting, Photography, Printmaking, Soft and Hard Crafts. A summer program is offered at Pietrasanta, Italy: Dir, Richard A McAlister, MFA. Courses—Art History, Languages, Literature, Religious Studies, Studio Art, Drawing, Painting, Sculpture

RHODE ISLAND COLLEGE, Art Dept, * 600 Mt Pleasant, 02908. Tel 401-456-8054; *Prof* Ronald M Steinberg, PhD; *Prof* John DeMelim, MFA; *Prof* Curtis K LaFollette, MFA; *Prof* Donald C Smith, MA; *Prof* Krisjohn O Horvat, MFA; *Prof* Lawrence F Sykes, MS; *Prof* David M Hysell, PhD; *Chmn* Samuel B Ames, MFA; *Prof* Harriet Brissan, MFA; *Prof* Ronald M Steinberg, PhD; *Assoc Prof* Mary Ball Howkins, PhD; *Asst Prof* Heemong Kim, MFA; *Asst Prof* Stephen Fisher, MFA
Estab 1854, dept estab 1969; pub; D & E; SC 31, LC 10, GC 5; enrl D 443, E approx 50, non-maj approx 228, maj 357, grad 30
Ent Req: HS dipl, CEEB and SAT
Degrees: BA(Art History), BA & MA(Studio), BS(Art Educ) & BFA(Studio Art) 4 yr, MAT 1 yr
Tuition: Res—$910 plus fees $160, grad $60 per cr; nonres—$3174 plus fees $160, grad $125 per cr; campus res—room & board $1345 - $1396
Courses: †Art Education, †Art History, Ceramics, Drawing, Graphic Design, Painting, Photography, Printmaking, Sculpture, Teacher Training, Metals, Fibers
Adult Hobby Classes: Visual Arts in Society, Drawing, Design, Photography
Children's Classes: Enrl 165; tuition $175 per 20 wks. Courses—Ceramics, Drawing, Life Drawing, Painting, Printmaking
Summer School: Dir, W Swigert. Enrl 150; tuition $75 per cr, nonres—$135 per cr for term of 6 wks beginning June 26th. Courses—Ceramics, Drawing, Painting, Photography, Relief Printing

RHODE ISLAND SCHOOL OF DESIGN, Museum of Art, RISD, Two College St, 02903. Tel 401-454-6100; *Pres* Roger Mandle; *Communications* Frederick E Goff Jr
Estab 1877; pvt; endowed; scholarships, grants-in-aid to res, student loans, fels; enrl D 1960
Ent Req: HS grad, SAT, visual work
Degrees: BFA, BArch, BID, BLA, BIntArch, BGD, MFA, MID, MLA, MAE, MAT
Tuition: $14,036
Courses: †Architecture, †Ceramics, †Film, †Graphic Design, †Illustration, †Industrial Design, †Jewelry, †Landscape Architecture, †Painting, †Photography, †Printmaking, †Sculpture, †Teacher Training, †Textile Design, †Apparel Design, †Glass, †Interior Architecture, †Metalsmithing, †Television Studies, †Wood & Furniture Design
Adult Hobby Classes: Enrl 20; tuition $16,684 per yr. Courses—Apparel Design, Architecture, Art Education, Ceramics, Film/Video, Glass, Graphic Design, Illustrations, Industrial Design, Interior Architecture, Jewelry, Landscape Architecture, Liberal Arts, Lt Metals, Painting, Photography, Printmaking, Sculpture, Textiles

WARWICK

COMMUNITY COLLEGE OF RHODE ISLAND, Dept of Art, 400 East Ave, 02886. Tel 401-825-2220; FAX 401-825-2282; *Chmn* R Clark; *Prof* Frances Stanton; *Prof* Nancy Wyllie; *Instr* T Aitken; *Instr* R Judge; *Instr* F Robertson; *Instr* M Kelman; *Instr* C Smith; *Instr* S Hunnibell; *Instr* T Morrissey. Instrs: FT 10, PT 15
Estab 1964; pub; D & E; scholarships; SC 16, LC 3, seminar 1; enrl D 4600
Ent Req: HS dipl, ent exam, equivalency exam
Degrees: AA, AFA, AS & AAS 2 yr
Tuition: Res—$863 per sem, $73 per cr hr
Courses: Art Appreciation, Art Education, Art History, Ceramics, Commercial Art, Drawing, Graphic Arts, Graphic Design, Interior Design, Mixed Media, Painting, Photography, Sculpture, History of Modern Art, Life Drawing, Survey of Ancient Art
Summer School: Chmn, Rebecca Clark. Enrl 200; 7 wk term. Courses—Ceramics, Crafts History of Modern Art, Drawing

SOUTH CAROLINA

AIKEN

UNIVERSITY OF SOUTH CAROLINA AT AIKEN, Dept of Visual & Performing Arts, 171 University Pky, 29801. Tel 803-641-3305; *Chmn* Jack Benjamin
Estab 1961, dept estab 1985; pub; D & E; SC 31, LC 6; enrl D 180, E 60
Ent Req: HS dipl, GED, SAT
Tuition: $1060 per sem
Courses: Advertising Design, Art History, Ceramics, Commercial Art, Drawing, Graphic Design, Illustration, Painting, Photography, Printmaking, Sculpture, Theatre Arts
Adult Hobby Classes: Tuition $1060 per sem. Courses—Vary
Summer School: Dir, A Beyer. Tuition $91 per hr. Courses—Vary

CHARLESTON

CHARLESTON SOUTHERN UNIVERSITY, Dept of Language & Visual Art, PO Box 10087, 29411. Tel 803-863-7000; *Chmn* Dr Harold Overton
Estab 1960; den; D & E; scholarships; SC 14, LC 2; enrl D 80, E 71, maj 15
Ent Req: GED or HS dipl
Degrees: BA and BS 4 yrs
Tuition: $1975 per sem; campus res available
Courses: Art Education, Ceramics, Drawing, Graphic Arts, History of Art & Archaeology, Painting, Sculpture, Teacher Training
Summer School: Enrl 1500; tui $45 per sem hr; campus res—room and board $240 per sem; two 5 wk sessions beginning June. Courses—same as regular session

COLLEGE OF CHARLESTON, School of the Arts, 29424. Tel 803-953-5601; *Dean* Edward McQuire; *Chmn Music Dept* Steve Rosenberg; *Chmn Theatre Dept* Allen Lyndrup; *Chmn Studio Art* Michael Tyzack; *Chmn Art History* Diane Johnson
Estab 1966; pub; D & E; scholarships; SC 36, LC 24

Ent Req: HS dipl
Degrees: BA(Fine Arts) 4 yrs
Tuition: Res—$1470 per yr; nonres—$2670 per yr
Courses: Art History, Drawing, Painting, Printmaking, Sculpture, Theatre Arts, Music & Dance

GIBBES MUSEUM OF ART STUDIO, 76 Queen St, 29401. Tel 803-577-7275; *Studio Admin* Mary Jeffries. Instrs: PT 20
Estab 1969; pub; D & E; scholarships; SC 18; enrl D 150, E 150
Ent Req: None
Tuition: $35-$95 per course
Courses: Calligraphy, Drawing, Graphic Design, Handicrafts, Interior Design, Photography, Printmaking, Sculpture, Weaving, Air Brush, Book Binding, Pottery
Children's Classes: Enrl 15 per course; tuition $60 per course per sem.
Courses—Mixed Media (ages 4-7)
Summer School: Dir, Jean Smith. Courses—Same as regular session

CLEMSON

CLEMSON UNIVERSITY, College of Architecture, Lee Hall, 29634-0509. Tel 864-656-3881; *Head Dept* John Acorn
Estab 1967; pub; D; GC 24, SC 40, LC 29 (undergrad courses for service to pre-architecture and other Univ requirements); enrl approx 1500 annually, grad maj 10
Ent Req: Available on request
Degrees: MFA 60 hrs
Tuition: Res—$1500 per sem
Courses: Architecture, Art History, Ceramics, Drawing, Painting, Photography, Printmaking, Sculpture

CLINTON

PRESBYTERIAN COLLEGE, Fine Arts Dept, Harper Ctr, PO Box 975, 29325. Tel 864-833-2820, 833-8318; *Chmn* D O Raines; *Prof* C T Gaines; *Prof* Mark Anderson
Estab 1880, Dept estab 1966; den; D & E; scholarships; SC 8, LC 5; enrl D 200, non-maj 190, maj 10
Ent Req: HS dipl with C average, SAT
Degrees: BA & BS 4 yr
Tuition: $16,000 annual tuition; campus res available
Courses: Art Education, Art History, Drawing, Painting
Summer School: Dean, J W Moncrief. Enrl 150; tuition $120 per sem. Courses—Art Appreciation, Painting

COLUMBIA

BENEDICT COLLEGE, Fine Arts Dept, Harden & Blanding Sts, 29204. Tel 803-253-5290; FAX 803-253-5260; *Chmn* Scott Blanks
Estab 1870; pvt; D; scholarships; SC 11, LC 6
Ent Req: HS dipl
Degrees: BA(Teaching of Art), BA(Commercial Art)
Courses: Commercial Art, Teacher Training
Summer School: Term of two 5 wk sessions beginning June. Courses—Art Appreciation

COLUMBIA COLLEGE, Dept of Art, 1301 Columbia College Dr, 29203. Tel 803-786-3012; FAX 803-786-3893; *Chmn* Steve Nevitt
Scholarships
Degrees: BA, cert
Tuition: $10,425 per yr
Courses: Advertising Design, Art Appreciation, Art History, Ceramics, Design, Drawing, Painting, Photography, Printmaking, Crafts, 3-D Design
Adult Hobby Classes: Enrl 20 per class. Courses—Art Appreciation, Art History, Drawing, Photography
Summer School: Dir, Becky Hulion. Enrl 20 per class. Courses—Art Appreciation, Art History, Art Education, Drawing, Photography, Printmaking

UNIVERSITY OF SOUTH CAROLINA, Dept of Art, Sloan College, 29208. Tel 803-777-4236, 777-0535; *Chmn* Brad R Collins; *Chmn Studio* Roy Drasiten, MFA; *Chmn Art Educ* Cynthia Colbert, EdD; *Chmn Art History* Beverly Heisner, PhD; *Prof* Philip Mullen, PhD; *Prof* Howard Woody, MA
Estab 1801, dept estab 1924; pub; D & E; scholarships; SC 89, LC 57, GC 73; enrl D 1620, E 174, non-maj 1000, maj 620, grad 82
Ent Req: HS dipl
Degrees: BA, BFA & BS 4 yrs, MA & MAT 2 yr, MFA 3 yrs
Tuition: Res—undergrad $3810 pr yr; $1905 per sem, PT $127 per cr, grad $4230 per yr, $2115 per sem; nonres—undergrad $9240 per yr, $4620 per sem, PT undergrad $308 per cr, grad $282; Campus res—room $1800 per yr
Courses: †Advertising Design, †Art Education, †Art History, †Ceramics, †Commercial Art, †Drawing, †Graphic Arts, †Graphic Design, Illustration, Jewelry, Museum Staff Training, Painting, Photography, Printmaking, Restoration & Conservation
Adult Hobby Classes: Enrl 125; tuition $127 per hr for 16 wk term. Courses—Art for Elementary School, Basic Drawing, Ceramics, Fiber Arts, Fundamentals of Art, Interior Design, Intro to Art
Children's Classes: Enrl 100; tuition $30 for 9 wk term. Courses—Children's Art
Summer School: Dir, John O'Neil. Enrl 400; tuition undergrad $127 per hr, grad $141 per hr. Courses—Same as academic yr

FLORENCE

FRANCIS MARION UNIVERSITY, Fine Arts Dept, PO Box 100547, 29501-0547. Tel 803-661-1385; FAX 803-661-1219; *Chmn* Dennis C Sanderson
Scholarships
Degrees: BA
Tuition: Res—$1500 per yr; nonres—$3000 per yr
Courses: Art Appreciation, †Art Education, Art History, †Ceramics, Costume Design & Construction, Design, Drafting, Drawing, Film, †Painting, †Photography, Sculpture, †Stage Design, †Theatre Arts, Video, Graphic Design
Summer School: Dir, Dennis Sanderson. Enrl 50; 6 wk term. Courses—Art Appreciation, Art Education, Photography

GAFFNEY

LIMESTONE COLLEGE, Art Dept, 1115 College Dr, 29340. Tel 864-489-7151; *Chmn* Andy Cox
Estab 1845; pvt; D & E; scholarships; SC 19, LC 9; enrl D 112, maj 42, others 3
Ent Req: HS dipl, ent exam
Degrees: BS(Educ, Studio) 4 yrs
Tuition: $3800 full-time; campus res—$5600
Courses: Ceramics, Painting, Printmaking, 2-D & 3-D Design, Silk-Screen, Wood-Block

GREENVILLE

BOB JONES UNIVERSITY, School of Fine Arts, 29614. Tel 803-242-5100, Ext 2700; FAX 803-233-9829; *Dean* Dwight Gustafson, DMus; *Chmn Division of Art* David Appleman, MA; *Instr* Emery Bopp, MFA; *Instr* Kathy Bell, MA; *Instr* Carl Blair, MFA; *Instr* James Brooks, BA; *Instr* Karen Brinson, BA; *Instr* Darell Koons, MA; *Instr* Harrell Whittington, MA; *Instr* Michael Slattery, MA; *Instr* Mark Mulfinger, MA
Estab 1927, dept estab 1945; pvt; D; scholarships; SC 29, LC 12, GC 10; enrl M 59, W 57
Ent Req: HS dipl, letters of recommendation
Degrees: BA & BS 4 yrs, MA 1-2 yrs
Tuition: $4980 per yr, $2490 per sem; campus res—room & board $3900 per yr
Courses: Advertising Design, Aesthetics, Art Appreciation, †Art Education, Art History, Calligraphy, Ceramics, Costume Design & Construction, Drawing, †Film, Graphic Arts, †Graphic Design, Handicrafts, Illustration, Lettering, †Painting, Photography, Printmaking, Sculpture, Stage Design, Theatre Arts, Video

FURMAN UNIVERSITY, Dept of Art, 29613. Tel 864-294-2074; *Chmn* Jinger Simkins-Stuntz
Estab 1826; pvt den; D & E; scholarships; SC 21, LC 8; enrl D 245, non-maj 205, maj 40
Ent Req: HS dipl, SAT
Degrees: BA 4 yr
Courses: Advertising Design, Art Education, Art History, Ceramics, Drawing, Graphic Design, Handicrafts, History of Art & Archaeology, Lettering, Painting, Printmaking, Sculpture, Teacher Training, Art Criticism

GREENVILLE COUNTY MUSEUM OF ART, Museum School of Art, 420 College St, 29601. Tel 864-271-7570; FAX 803-271-7579; *Coordr* Robert A Strother. Instrs: PT 35
Estab 1960; pub; D & E; scholarships; SC 12, LC 2, GC 6; enrl D 250, E 170
Degrees: AAA and AFA 2-3 yr
Tuition: $50 regis fee, cost on per class basis
Courses: Art History, Drawing, Painting, Photography, †Printmaking, Sculpture, Philosophy of Art, †Pottery, Weaving
Adult Hobby Classes: Painting, Pottery, Watercolor
Children's Classes: Enrl 15 per course, ages 4 - 16. Courses—Clay, Drawing, Mixed Media, Painting
Summer School: Enrl approx 300 per sem; 6 or 7 wk term. Courses—same as regular sem

GREENWOOD

LANDER UNIVERSITY, Dept of Art, Stanley Ave, 29649. Tel 864-388-8323; *Chmn* Alan MacTaggart. Instrs: FT 5, PT 3
Estab 1872; pub; D & E; scholarships; SC 25, LC 5; enrl D 250, E 60, maj 91
Ent Req: HS dipl
Degrees: BA(Art) 4 yrs
Tuition: Res—$1700 per yr; nonres—$2513 per yr; campus res—$2800-$3350
Courses: Advertising Design, Art Appreciation, Art Education, Art History, Ceramics, Commercial Art, Costume Design & Construction, Display, Drawing, Film, Graphic Arts, Graphic Design, Painting, Photography, Printmaking, Sculpture, Stage Design, Theatre Arts, †Teacher Training, Mixed Media, Painting, Photography, Sculpture, Stage Design, Teacher Training, Video
Summer School: Enrl 300; tuition $136 per sem hr for 4 wks. Courses—Art Appreciation, Ceramics, Grad Art Education, Mass Media, Music Appreciation, Speech Fundamentals, Theatre & Film Appreciation, TV Production, Undergrad Art Education

GREER

GREENVILLE TECHNICAL COLLEGE, Visual Arts Dept, 2522 Locust Hill Rd, 29687. Tel 864-848-2024, 848-2023; *Acad Dean Educ* Dr Edward Opper
Degrees: AA
Tuition: $42 per cr hr; full-time $500 sem
Courses: Art Appreciation, Art History, Film
Adult Hobby Classes: Courses offered
Summer School: Dir, Dr David S Trask. Enrl 35. Courses—Art Appreciation

HARTSVILLE

COKER COLLEGE, Art Dept, 29550. Tel 803-383-8150; *Chmn* J Kim Chalmers. Instrs: FT 3
Estab 1908; pvt; D & E; scholarships; SC 26, LC 9; enrl 600, art maj 25
Ent Req: HS dipl, ent exam
Degrees: AB and BS 4 yrs
Tuition: $10,896 per yr; campus res—room & board $4516 per yr
Courses: Art Appreciation, Art Education, Art History, Ceramics, Design, Drawing, Graphic Design, Illustration, Painting, Photography, Printmaking, Sculpture
Summer School: Tuition $400 per sem hr for 8 wk term. Courses—Introduction Level Art

NEWBERRY

NEWBERRY COLLEGE, Dept of Art, 2100 College St, 29108. Tel 803-276-5010; FAX 803-321-5627; *Head Dept* Bruce Nell-Smith
Estab 1856, dept estab 1973; den; D & E; SC 35, LC 2; enrl D 114, non-maj 106, maj 15
Ent Req: HS dipl, SAT
Degrees: AB(Art) 4 yrs, BS(Arts Mgt), two courses in independent study, financial aid available
Tuition: $5097 per sem
Courses: Art History, Drawing, Mixed Media, Painting, Printmaking, Stage Design, Theatre Arts

ORANGEBURG

CLAFLIN COLLEGE, Dept of Art, * 400 College Ave, 29115. Tel 803-534-2710; *Chmn* Dr Kod Igwe; *Assoc Prof* Donna Bratcher; *Instr* Dan Smith
School estab 1869, dept estab 1888; pvt; D; scholarships; SC 10, LC 2; enrl D 20
Ent Req: HS dipl, SAT
Degrees: BA 4 years, BA Teacher Educ 4 years
Tuition: Res—undergrad $6510 including room & board; nonres—$4230
Courses: †Advertising Design, †Art Education, Art History, Ceramics, Drawing, Film, Graphic Arts, Lettering, Painting, Photography, Printmaking, Sculpture, Theatre Arts, Video, Afro-American Art History, Advanced Studio
Summer School: Dir, Karen Woodfaulk. Enrl 10-12, 6 wk term beginning June. Courses—Art Appreciation, Art-Elem School Crafts, Advertising Art, Textile Design

SOUTH CAROLINA STATE UNIVERSITY, Art Dept, 300 College St NE, 29117. Tel 803-536-7174, 8119; FAX 803-533-3824; *Chmn* Leo F Twiggs, EdD; *Cur Educ* Emily Scoville; *Assoc Prof* Terry K Hunter, PhD; *Cur Coll & Exhib* Frank Martin II, MA
Dept estab 1972; D & E; SC 15, LC 7; enrl D 73, nonmaj 8, maj 73
Ent Req: HS dipl
Degrees: BA & BS 4 yrs, MS approx 2 yrs
Tuition: Res—$1150 per sem, nonres—$1700 per sem; campus res available
Courses: †Art Education, Printmaking
Adult Hobby Classes: Ceramics, Sculpture
Summer School: Dir, Dr Leroy Davis. Tuition $90 per cr hr. Courses—Art Appreciation, Arts & Crafts for Children

ROCK HILL

WINTHROP UNIVERSITY, Dept of Art & Design, 29733. Tel 803-323-2126; *Chmn* Jerry Walden; *Asst Chmn* Curt Sherman; *Prof* E Wade Hobgood, MFA; *Prof* Mary Mintich, MFA; *Prof* John Olvera; *Prof* David Freeman; *Prof* Jean McFarland; *Assoc Prof* Alan Huston; *Assoc Prof* Paul Martyka, MFA; *Asst Prof* Jim Connell; *Asst Prof* Quentin Currie; *Asst Prof* Laura Dufresne; *Asst Prof* Jean Edwards; *Asst Prof* Charles Harmon; *Asst Prof* Carol Ivory; *Asst Prof* Margaret Johnson; *Asst Prof* Lynn Smith; *Asst Prof* David Stokes; *Asst Prof* Dr Eli Bentor; *Asst Prof* Dr Peg Delamater
Estab 1886; pub; D & E; SC 42, LC 10; enrl in college D 4983, non-maj 360, maj 147, grad 6
Ent Req: HS dipl, SAT, CEEB
Degrees: BA and BFA 4 yrs
Tuition: Res—undergrad $3600 per yr, $1800 per sem, grad $1800; nonres—undergrad $6380 per yr, $3190 per sem; campus res available
Courses: †Advertising Design, †Art Education, Art History, Calligraphy, †Ceramics, Collages, †Commercial Art, Conceptual Art, †Drawing, Fashion Arts, †Graphic Arts, †Graphic Design, Handicrafts, †Illustration, †Interior Design, †Jewelry, Lettering, Mixed Media, †Painting, †Photography, Art Appreciation, Design, Display, Drafting, History of Art & Archaeology, Industrial Design, Museum Staff Training, Printmaking, Sculpture, Silversmithing, Teacher Training, Textile Design, Weaving
Summer School: Dir, Wade Hobgood. Enrl 120. Courses—Art Appreciation, Art for Classroom Teacher, Creative Art for Children, Drawing, Painting, Photography

SPARTANBURG

CONVERSE COLLEGE, Art Dept, PO Box 29, 29302. Tel 803-569-9180, 596-9178, 596-9181; *Chmn Dept* Teresa Prater; *Prof* Mayo McBoggs, MFA; *Assoc Prof* Fraz Pajak, MA Arch; *Asst Prof* David Zacharias, MFA; *Asst Prof* Donn Britt Ping; *Asst Prof* Dr Suzanne Schuweiler-Daab; *Asst Prof* Douglas Whittle
Col estab 1889; pvt; D; scholarships; SC 40, LC 17; enrl D 290, non-maj 240, maj 90, others 12, double major available
Ent Req: HS dipl, SAT, CEEB, ACT, Advanced placement in Art & Art History
Degrees: BA & BFA 4 yrs
Tuition: $17,825 incl room & board
Courses: Advertising Design, Architecture, Art Appreciation, †Art Education, †Art History, Ceramics, Commercial Art, Design, Drafting, Drawing, †Interior Design, Jewelry, Mixed Media, Painting, Photography, Printmaking, Restoration & Conservation, Sculpture, Textile Design, Art Therapy, Studio Art
Adult Hobby Classes: Enrl 100; tuition $16,000 for 4 yrs. Courses—Art Education, Art History, Art Therapy, Interior Design, Studio Art
Summer School: Dir, Joe Dunn

SPARTANBURG COUNTY MUSEUM OF ART (Formerly Art Association School), Art School, 385 S Spring St, 29306. Tel 864-582-7616; FAX 803-948-5353; *Dir* Scott Cunningham
Estab 1970; D & E; SC 25; enrl 300-400
Ent Req: None
Tuition: $35-$90 for 4-8 wk classes & weekend workshops
Courses: Calligraphy, Drawing, Mixed Media, Painting, Sculpture, Cartooning, Figure Drawing, Portraiture, Pottery & Ceramic Design, Stained Glass
Children's Classes: $35-$90 for 4-8 wk classes & weekend workshops
Summer School: Dir, Jim Creal. Enrl 200. Art Camp, 3-1 wk sessions

SOUTH DAKOTA

ABERDEEN

NORTHERN STATE UNIVERSITY, Art Dept, 1200 S Jay St, 57401. Tel 605-626-2514; Elec Mail shekorem@wolf.northern.edu. *Chmn* Mark Shekore, MFA; *Prof* Mark McGinnis, MFA; *Asst Prof* Carlene Roters, PhD; *Assoc Prof* Bill Hoar, PhD; *Asst Prof* Lynn Carlsgaard, MA. Instrs: Estab 1901, dept estab 1920
Pub; D & E; scholarships; SC 40, LC 14, GC 6; enrl D 385, non-maj 300, maj 85
Ent Req: HS dipl
Degrees: AA 2 yrs, BA, BS, BSEd 4 yrs
Tuition: Res—undergrad $51.45 per cr, grad $78.25 per cr; nonres—undergrad $111.48 per cr, grad $151.13 per cr; campus res—room $568 per sem
Courses: Advertising Design, †Art Education, Art History, †Ceramics, †Commercial Art, †Drawing, Illustration, Mixed Media, Painting, Photography, Printmaking, Sculpture, Teacher Training, Video, Computer Graphics, Fiber Arts
Adult Hobby Classes: Enrl 30; tuition $45.78 per cr
Summer School: Dir, Mark Shekore

BROOKINGS

SOUTH DAKOTA STATE UNIVERSITY, Dept of Visual Arts, PO Box 2223, 57007. Tel 605-688-4103; FAX 605-688-6769; Elec Mail vanderd@ur.sdstate.edu. *Head Dept* Norman Gambill, PhD; *Prof* Helen Morgan; *Prof* Melvin Spinar, MFA; *Prof* Tim Steele, MFA; *Assoc Prof* Gerald Kruse, MFA; *Assoc Prof* Jeannie French; *Asst Prof* Rodney Nowosielski; *Asst Prof* Scott Wallace
Estab 1881; pub; D & E; scholarships; SC 26, LC 10
Ent Req: HS dipl, ent ACT
Degrees: BA & BS 128 sem cr
Tuition: Res—$80.45 per cr hr; nonres—$154.10 per cr hr; in- state tuition with Minnesota only
Courses: Advertising Design, Art Appreciation, †Art Education, Art History, †Ceramics, Design, Drawing, †Graphic Design, Intermedia, Mixed Media, †Painting, †Printmaking, †Sculpture, Museum Staff Training, Painting, Printmaking, Sculpture, General Art, History of Art & Design

HURON

HURON UNIVERSITY, Arts & Sciences Division, 333 Ninth St SW, 57350. Tel 605-352-8721; *Dean* Gretchen Rich
Pvt; scholarships; enrl 510
Ent Req: HS dipl or GED
Degrees: BA & BS 4 yrs
Tuition: $7260 per yr
Courses: Art Appreciation, Manual & Public School Art

MADISON

DAKOTA STATE UNIVERSITY, College of Liberal Arts, 57042. Tel 605-256-5270; *Dean* Eric Johnson. Instrs: FT 1, PT 1
Estab 1881; pub; D; scholarships; SC 16, LC 5; enrl D 120, maj 20
Ent Req: HS dipl, ACT
Degrees: BS 4 yrs
Tuition: Res—undergrad $1502 per yr
Courses: Art Education, Art History, Ceramics, Drawing, Jewelry, Painting, Sculpture, Teacher Training
Summer School: Term of 8 wks beginning June

SIOUX FALLS

AUGUSTANA COLLEGE, Art Dept, 2001 S Summit Ave, 57197. Tel 605-336-5428; WATS 800-727-2844. *Chmn* Carl A Grupp, MFA; *Prof* Robert Aldern, BFA; *Prof* Endre Gastony, PhD; *Assoc Prof* Steve Thomas, MFA; *Assoc Prof* Adrien Hannus, PhD; *Asst Prof* Tom Shields, MFA; *Instr* Gerry Punt, BA
Estab 1860; den; D & E; scholarships; SC 14, LC 3; enrl total 1861
Ent Req: HS dipl, ent exam
Degrees: BA & MAT
Tuition: $8640 annual tuition; campus res available
Courses: †Art Education, †Drawing, †Graphic Design, History of Art & Archaeology, Painting, Printmaking, Sculpture, Teacher Training, Etching, Lithography
Children's Classes: Enrl 15; tuition $600 fall & spring. Courses—Ceramics, Drawing
Summer School: Dir, Dr Gary D Olson. Term of 7 wks beginning June. Courses—Arts, Crafts, Drawing

SIOUX FALLS COLLEGE, Dept of Art, Division of Fine Arts/Music, 1501 S Prairie Ave, 57105-1699. Tel 605-331-6671; *Chmn* Nancy Olive
Estab 1883; pub; scholarships; SC, LC; enrl 1000
Degrees: BA with maj in Art or Art Educ 4 yrs
Tuition: $8990 per yr
Courses: Art Education, Art History, Ceramics, Drawing, Graphic Design, Handicrafts, Painting, Photography, Printmaking, Sculpture
Summer School: Terms one 3 wk session, two 4 wk sessions. Courses—Crafts, Design, Drawing, Education

SPEARFISH

BLACK HILLS STATE UNIVERSITY, Art Dept, 57799-9003. Tel 605-642-6011, 642-6420; *Chmn* Jim Cargill. Instrs: FT 13
Estab 1883; pub; D; scholarships; SC 15, LC 4; enrl maj 50
Ent Req: HS dipl, transcripts, ACT, physical exam
Degrees: BA 4 yrs
Tuition: Res—$76.70 per cr hr; nonres—$144 per cr hr
Courses: Art Education, Calligraphy, Ceramics, Commercial Art, Drafting, Drawing, Painting, Photography, Sculpture
Summer School: Art in our Lives, Ceramics, Drawing, Painting, School Arts & Crafts

VERMILLION

UNIVERSITY OF SOUTH DAKOTA, Department of Art, College of Fine Arts, 414 Clark St, 57069-2390. Tel 605-677-5636; *Dean* John A Day, MFA; *Chmn* Dennis Navrat, MFA; *Prof* Daniel Packard, MFA; *Prof* Kenneth Grizzell, MFA; *Prof* Lloyd Menard, MFA; *Prof* Jeff Freeman, MFA; *Prof* John Banasiak, MFA; *Assoc Prof* Lawrence Anderson, MFA; *Assoc Prof* Martin Wanserski, MFA; *Assoc Prof* Ann Balakier, PhD
Estab 1862, dept estab 1931; pub; D & E; scholarships; SC 32, LC 9, GC 9; enrl non-maj 300, maj 80, grad 17
Ent Req: HS dipl, ACT
Degrees: BFA, BFA with Teacher Cert, MFA
Tuition: Res—undergrad $53 per cr hr, grad $79.75 per cr hr; nonres—$168 per cr hr, grad $235.25 per cr hr; campus res—room & board $1392
Courses: Advertising Design, Aesthetics, Art Appreciation, †Art Education, Art History, †Ceramics, Commercial Art, Design, Drawing, Graphic Design, History of Art & Archaeology, Lettering, Mixed Media, Museum Staff Training, †Painting, †Photography, †Printmaking, †Sculpture, Teacher Training, Graphics
Summer School: Chmn, Dennis Navrat. Tuition per cr hr for terms of 4 wks to 15 wks. Courses—Variable offerings in summer-not disciplines are offered each summer

YANKTON

MOUNT MARTY COLLEGE, Art Dept, 1105 W Eighth St, 57078. Tel 605-668-1011, 668-1574; *Dept Head* David Kahle; *Lectr* Sr Kathleen Courtney, MA; *Lectr* Virgil Petrik
Estab 1936; den; D; SC 17, LC 5; enrl 9
Ent Req: HS dipl
Degrees: BA 4 yrs, MA(Anesthesia)
Tuition: $4950 two sem & interim; $195 per cr hr; campus res available
Courses: Art Appreciation, Calligraphy, Ceramics, Collages, Design, Drawing, Handicrafts, Mixed Media, Printmaking, Teacher Training, 2-D & 3-D Design
Adult Hobby Classes: Enrl 100-150; tuition $283 per 11 cr hrs, $3390 full time. Courses—Art Appreciation, Calligraphy, Ceramics, Crafts, Design, Painting & Drawing, Photography, Printmaking
Summer School: Dir, Sr Pierre Roberts. Tuition $100 per cr hr for term of wks beginning June & July

TENNESSEE

CHATTANOOGA

CHATTANOOGA STATE TECHNICAL COMMUNITY COLLEGE, Advertising Arts Dept, 4501 Amnicola Hwy, 37406. Tel 423-697-4400, 697-4441; *Dir Fine Arts* Denise Frank; *Asst Prof* Alan Wallace
Pub; D & E; scholarships; SC 30, LC 5; enrl D 3000, E 2000
Ent Req: HS dipl
Degrees: Certificate, AA(Advertising Art)
Tuition: Res—$505 per sem; nonres—$1898 per sem
Courses: Advertising Design, Art Education, Art History, Ceramics, Commercial Art, Drafting, Drawing, Graphic Arts, Graphic Design, Illustration, Painting, Photography, Teacher Training, Advertising Concepts, Air Brush, Internships, Production Art, Typography
Adult Hobby Classes: Tuition $45 per course. Courses—Painting, Photography
Children's Classes: Tuition $20 per course. Courses—Arts & Crafts, Ceramics & Sculpture
Summer School: Tuition $140 per term of 10 wks

UNIVERSITY OF TENNESSEE AT CHATTANOOGA, Dept of Art, 615 McCallie Ave, 37403. Tel 615-755-4178; *Head* E Alan White; *Prof* Anne Lindsey, PhD; *Prof* Maggie McMahon, MFA; *Assoc Prof* Bruce Wallace, MFA; *Assoc Prof* Gavin Townsend, PhD; *Assoc Prof* Stephen S LeWinter, MA
Estab 1928; pub; D & E; scholarships; SC 11, LC 13, GC 1; enrl D 420, E 80, non-maj 500, maj 130, grad 6, others 14
Ent Req: HS dipl, ACT or SAT, health exam
Degrees: BA and BFA 4 yrs
Tuition: Res—undergrad $746 per sem, grad $974 per sem; nonres—undergrad

$2428 per sem, grad $2656 per sem; campus res—room available
Courses: Art Education, Art History, Ceramics, Commercial Art, Drawing, Graphic Design, Painting, Printmaking, Sculpture
Summer School: Tuition $72 per sem hr

CLARKSVILLE

AUSTIN PEAY STATE UNIVERSITY, Dept of Art, * PO Box 4677, 37044. Tel 615-648-7333; *Acting Chair* Susan Bryant, MFA; *Prof* Max Hochstetler; *Prof* James T Diehr; *Assoc Prof* Bruce Childs, MFA; *Asst Prof* W Renkl; *Asst Prof* Bettye Holte; *Asst Prof* Gregg Schlanger, MFA; *Asst Prof* Dixie Webb, PhD; *Asst Prof* Kell Black
Estab 1927, dept estab 1930; pub; D & E; scholarships; GC 3; enrl D 740, E 75, non-maj 590, maj 150
Ent Req: HS dipl
Degrees: BFA, BA & BS 4 yrs
Tuition: Res—undergrad $761 per sem; nonres—$2363 per sem; campus residence available
Courses: †Art Education, Art History, †Ceramics, Drawing, †Graphic Design, Illustration, Lettering, †Painting, †Photography, †Printmaking, †Sculpture
Adult Hobby Classes: Enrl 15; tuition $332. Courses-Photography, Printmaking, Ceramics, Drawing, Painting
Summer School: Dir Max Hochstetler. Enrl 150; tuition $761 for 5 wks.
Courses—Art Appreciation, Art Education, Sculpture

CLEVELAND

CLEVELAND STATE COMMUNITY COLLEGE, Dept of Art, Adkisson Dr, PO Box 3570, 37320-3570. Tel 423-472-7141; FAX 423-478-6255; WATS 800-604-2722. *Assoc Prof* Jere Chumley, MA
Estab 1967; pub; D & E; scholarships; SC 6, LC 5; enrl D 95, E 20, non-maj 60, maj 35
Ent Req: HS dipl or GED
Degrees: AA and AS 2 yrs
Tuition: Res—$497 per sem; nonres—$1960 per sem
Courses: Architecture, Art Appreciation, Art Education, Art History, Calligraphy, Ceramics, Design, Drafting, Drawing, History of Art & Archaeology, Painting, Photography, Sculpture
Adult Hobby Classes: Drawing, Painting

LEE COLLEGE, Dept of Music & Fine Arts, 1120 N Ocoee St, 37311. Tel 423-614-8240; FAX 423-614-8242; *Chmn* Lonnie McCalister
Tuition: Res—$2616 per sem
Courses: Art Appreciation

COLLEGEDALE

SOUTHERN COLLEGE OF SEVENTH-DAY ADVENTISTS, Art Dept, PO Box 370, 37315. Tel 423-238-2732, 237-2111; *Chmn* Robert F Garren
Estab 1969; den; D & E; LC 4; enrl maj 12
Ent Req: HS dipl, ent exam
Degrees: BA(Art), BA(Art & Educ) & BA(Computer Graphic Design) 4 yr
Tuition: $8918 per yr, $12,414 with dorm
Courses: Art Education, Art, Computer Graphic Design

COLUMBIA

COLUMBIA STATE COMMUNITY COLLEGE, Dept of Art, 412 Hwy W, PO Box 1315, 38401. Tel 615-540-2722; *Head Dept* Fred Behrens, MFA
Estab 1966; pub; D & E; scholarships; SC 17, LC 4; enrl D 230, non-maj 215, maj 12-15
Ent Req: Open door institution
Degrees: AA & AS 2 yrs
Tuition: Res—$483 per sem; nonres—$1876 per sem
Courses: Art History, Design, Drawing, Film, Painting, Photography, Printmaking, †Art Studio, Visual Arts
Children's Classes: Enrl 18-20, tuition $30 per session

GATLINBURG

ARROWMONT GALLERY, Arrowmont School of Arts & Crafts, 556 Parkway, PO Box 567, 37738. Tel 423-436-5860; *Dir* Sandra J Blain; *Asst Dir* Bill Griffith
Estab 1945; pvt; D & E (operate mostly in spring & summer with special programs for fall & winter); scholarships; SC 44-50, GC 30; enrl D 1000
Degrees: None granted, though credit is offered for courses through the Univ of Tennessee, Knoxville
Tuition: $185 per wk, 1 & 2 wk sessions; campus res—room & board $135-$225 per wk
Courses: Ceramics, Drawing, Weaving, Jewelry, Painting, Photography, Textile Design, Basketry, Bookbinding, Enamel, Papermaking, Quilting Stained Glass, Woodturning

GOODLETTSVILLE

NOSSI COLLEGE OF ART, 907 Two Mile Pkwy, E-6, 37072. Tel 615-851-1088; *Exec Dir* Nossi Vatandoost, BA; *Instr* William H Nussle, BA; *Instr* Stephan LaSeurer; *Instr* Blake Long
Priv; D & E; SC 1, LC 4
Ent Req: HS dipl or GED
Degrees: Dipl in Fine Arts 2 yr; Dipl in Commercial Art 3 yr; degrees Dipl in Fashion Merchandising 2 yr
Tuition: $3000 per yr

Courses: Advertising Design, Architecture, Art Appreciation, Art Education, Art History, Conceptual Art, Design, Display, Drawing, Graphic Arts, Graphic Design, Illustration, Mixed Media, Lettering, Painting, Photography
Adult Hobby Classes: Enrl 120; tuition $3600 per yr. Courses—Commercial Art (3 yrs), Fashion Merchandising (2 yrs), Fine Arts (2 yrs)
Summer School: Dir, Nossi Vantandoost, BA. Enrol 40; $1200 tuition for 12 wks sem. Courses—Airbrush, Drawing, Painting, Photography, Watercolor

GREENEVILLE

TUSCULUM COLLEGE, Fine Arts Dept, Division of Arts & Humanities, 2299 Tusculum, PO Box 5084, 37743. Tel 423-636-7300; *Div Head* Clement Allison, MFA
Estab 1794; den; D; scholarships; SC 25, LC 3; enrl D 445, maj 18
Ent Req: HS dipl
Degrees: BA & BS 4 yrs
Tuition: $7700 per yr
Courses: Art Education, Ceramics, Drawing, History of Art & Archaeology, Painting, Printmaking, Sculpture
Adult Hobby Classes: Enrl 14. Courses—Painting

HARROGATE

LINCOLN MEMORIAL UNIVERSITY, Division of Humanities, Kimberland Gap Pky, PO Box 670, 37752. Tel 423-869-3611; *Chmn Humanities* Dr David McDonald; *Assoc Prof Art* Bebe DeBord; *Instr* Alex Buckland
Estab 1897, dept estab 1974; pvt; D & E; SC 30, LC 3; enrl D 120, E 75, non-maj 97, maj 98
Ent Req: HS dipl
Degrees: BA 4 yrs
Tuition: Res—$2975 per sem; campus res—room & board $1430
Courses: Aesthetics, Art Education, Art History, Ceramics, Commercial Art, Drawing, Film, Goldsmithing, †Graphic Arts, Jewelry, Lettering, Museum Staff Training, †Painting, †Photography, †Sculpture, Silversmithing, †Teacher Training, †Textile Design, †Theatre Arts, Weaving

JACKSON

LAMBUTH UNIVERSITY, Dept of Human Ecology & Visual Arts, 705 Lambuth Blvd, PO Box 431, 38301. Tel 901-425-3275, 425-2500; FAX 901-423-1990; *Chmn* Lawrence A Ray, PhD; *Assoc Prof* June Creasy, MS; *Asst Prof* Lendon H Noe, MS; *Lectr* Susan Haubold, MEd; *Lectr* Belinda A Patterson, BS; *Lectr* Glynn Weatherley, BS; *Lectr* Rosemary Carroway, BA
Estab 1843, dept estab 1950; den; D & E; scholarships; SC 21, LC 10
Ent Req: HS dipl
Degrees: BA, BS, B(Mus) & B(Bus Ad) 4 yrs
Tuition: $2317 per sem
Courses: Advertising Design, Aesthetics, †Art Education, †Art History, †Commercial Art, †Drawing, †Graphic Design, †Interior Design, †Painting, †Photography, †Printmaking, †Sculpture, Stage Design, Crafts, Fiber Crafts, Human Ecology, †Stained Glass, Visual Art
Adult Hobby Classes: Adult Evening Prog. $1800 per term
Children's Classes: Enrl 45-50; tuition $50 for 5 wk term. Courses—Elementary art classes
Summer School: Dir, William Shutowski. Courses—Art Appreciation, Art Education, Basic ID, Painting, Printmaking

UNION UNIVERSITY, Dept of Art, Hwy 45 Bypass, 38305. Tel 901-668-1818; FAX 901-664-7476; *Chmn* Michael Mallard
Estab 1824, dept estab 1958; den; D & E; scholarships; SC 20, LC 5; enrl D 200, E 40, maj 28
Ent Req: HS dipl, portfolio, ACT
Degrees: BA and BS 4 yrs
Tuition: $2125 per sem
Courses: Art Appreciation, Art Education, Art History, Ceramics, Drawing, Graphic Design, Painting, Photography, Printmaking, Sculpture, Teacher Training
Adult Hobby Classes: Enrl 20. Courses—Art History, Ceramics, Drawing, Metalsmithing, Painting, Sculpture

JEFFERSON CITY

CARSON-NEWMAN COLLEGE, Art Dept, PO Box 71911, 37760. Tel 423-471-3333; FAX 615-475-7956; *Chmn Dept* H T Niceley; *Prof* Derek Randle; *Prof* David Underwood; *Artist & Residence* William Houston. Instrs: FT 3
Col estab 1851; den; D & E; scholarships; SC 26, LC 7; enrl maj 36
Ent Req: HS dipl
Degrees: BA(Art & Photography) 4 yrs
Tuition: Res—$5980 per yr; nonres—$6080 per yr; campus res $1800
Courses: Aesthetics, Art Education, Art History, Drawing, Graphic Design, Painting, Photography, Printmaking, Computer Graphics, Senior Seminar, Support Systems
Summer School: Dir, H T Niceley. Enrl 25; tuition $80 per sem hr. Courses—Art Appreciation, Photography

JOHNSON CITY

EAST TENNESSEE STATE UNIVERSITY, Dept of Art & Design, PO Box 70708, 37614-0708. Tel 423-439-4247; *Chmn Dept* David G Logan; *Prof* Michael Smith, MFA; *Prof* James Mills, PhD; *Prof* Jean Miller, MFA; *Assoc Prof* David Dixon, MFA; *Assoc Prof* Vida Hull, PhD; *Assoc Prof* M Wayne Dyer, MFA; *Asst Prof* Anita DeAngelis; *Assoc Prof* Lynn Whitehead, MFA; *Assoc Prof* Peter Pawlowicz, PhD; *Assoc Prof* Ralph Slatton, MFA; *Asst Prof* Ann Clark, MFA; *Asst Prof* Catherine Murray, MFA

Estab 1909, dept estab 1949; pub; D & E; scholarships; SC 102, LC 30, GC 46; enrl D approx 1400
Ent Req: HS dipl, ACT or SAT
Degrees: BA, BS & BFA 4 yrs, MA, MFA
Tuition: Res—undergrad $77 per sem hr, $865 per sem, grad $113 per sem hr, $1128 per sem; nonres—undergrad $258 per sem hr, $2930 per sem
Courses: Advertising Design, †Art Education, †Art History, †Ceramics, Commercial Art, Conceptual Art, Design, Drawing, Goldsmithing, Graphic Arts, †Graphic Design, History of Art & Archaeology, Illustration, †Jewelry, Mixed Media, †Painting, †Photography, Printmaking, †Sculpture, Silversmithing, Teacher Training, Weaving, †Metalsmithing, †Weaving/Fibers
Adult Hobby Classes: Credit/no credit classes at night. Courses—Art History, Drawing, Photography, painting
Summer School: Dir, David G Logan. Enrl 300; tuition $77 per cr hr for May-Aug. Courses—Art Educ, Art History, Computer Art & Design, Drawing, Foreign Group-Travel, Graphic Design, Marketing, Painting, Photography

KNOXVILLE

UNIVERSITY OF TENNESSEE, KNOXVILLE, Dept of Art, 1715 Volunteer Blvd, 37996-2410. Tel 423-974-3408; FAX 423-974-3198; *Head Art Dept* Dr Norman Magden. Instrs: FT 25, PT 6
Estab 1794, dept estab 1951; pub; D & E; scholarships; SC 51, LC 23, GC 50; enrl D 1600, E 250, non-maj 300, maj 400, grad 40
Ent Req: HS dipl
Degrees: BA & BFA, MFA; both undergraduate & graduate credit may be earned through the affiliated program at Arrowmont School of Arts & Crafts, Gatlinburg, TN
Tuition: Res—undergrad $783 per sem. grad $975 per sem; nonres—undergrad $1682 per sem, grad $1682 per sem; campus res—room & board $3166 per yr
Courses: †Advertising Design, †Art History, †Ceramics, †Drawing, †Graphic Design, †Painting, †Photography, †Printmaking, †Sculpture, †Video, Computer Graphics
Adult Hobby Classes: Enrl 150. Courses - Ceramics, Drawing, Graphic Design, Photography
Summer School: Dir, Norman Magden. Enrl 400; term of 2 sessions beginning June & Aug. Courses—Art History, Design, Drawing

MARYVILLE

MARYVILLE COLLEGE, Dept of Fine Arts, 502 Lamar Alexander Pky, 37804. Tel 423-981-8000; *Chmn* Dan Taddie. Instrs: FT 2, PT 1
Estab 1937; den; scholarships; SC 10, LC 6
Degrees: 4 yr
Tuition: $1920 per term
Courses: Art Education, Art History, Ceramics, Drawing, Graphic Design, Painting, Photography, Printmaking, Weaving, Computer Graphics, Fabric Design, Visual Theory & Design
Adult Hobby Classes: Courses offered
Children's Classes: Art Education, Crafts

MEMPHIS

MEMPHIS COLLEGE OF ART, Overton Park, 1930 Poplar Ave, 38104-2764. Tel 901-726-4085; FAX 901-272-5830; *Pres* Jeffrey Nesin; *Exec VPres* Phillip S Morris, MFA; *Dean* Alonz Davis. Instrs: FT 18, PT 28
Estab 1936; pvt; D & E; scholarships; enrl D 200, E 300
Ent Req: HS dipl
Degrees: BFA 4 yrs, MFA 2 yrs
Tuition: $5125 per sem; women's campus res
Courses: †Advertising Design, Aesthetics, Architecture, Art Appreciation, Art History, Calligraphy, Ceramics, Collages, †Commercial Art, Conceptual Art, Constructions, †Design, Drawing, Goldsmithing, Graphic Arts, †Graphic Design, History of Art & Archaeology, †Illustration, Intermedia, †Jewelry, Lettering, Mixed Media, †Painting, Photography, †Printmaking, †Sculpture, †Silversmithing, Stage Design, †Textile Design, Weaving, Book Arts, Computer Arts, †Papermaking
Adult Hobby Classes: Enrl 200; tuition $95-$210 for 1 day to 7 wk term. Courses—Calligraphy, Collage, Computer, Drawing, Jewelry, Painting, Papermaking, Photography, Pottery, Printmaking, Sculpture
Children's Classes: Enrl 220; tuition $85-$135 for 10 wk term. Courses—Cartooning, Computer, Drawing, First Art, Painting, Photography, Pottery, Sculpture
Summer School: Dir, Jackie Ware. Enrl 400; tuition $85-$135 for 2 wk term. Courses—Same as above

RHODES COLLEGE, Dept of Art, 2000 N Pky, 38112. Tel 901-726-3833; FAX 901-726-3718; *Chmn* David McCarthy; *Asst Prof* Victor Coonin; *Instr* Carol Stewart, MFA; *Instr* Diane Hoffman, MFA; *Instr* James S Williamson; *Instr* Hallie Chalniz, MFA
Estab 1848, dept estab 1940; pvt; D & E; SC 17, LC 12; enrl D 250, non-maj 240, maj 10
Ent Req: SAT or ACT, 13 acad credits, 16 overall
Degrees: BA 4 yrs
Tuition: $16,392 per yr; campus res—room & board $5010 per yr
Courses: Aesthetics, Architecture, Art History, Drawing, History of Art & Archaeology, Museum Staff Training, Painting, Photography, Printmaking, Sculpture

UNIVERSITY OF MEMPHIS (Formerly Memphis State University), Art Dept, Campus Box 526715, 38152-6715. Tel 901-678-2216; FAX 901-678-2735; *Chmn Dept* Robert E Lewis; *Chmn Asst* Wayne Simpkins; *Chmn Asst* Brenda Landman
Estab 1912; pub; D & E; scholarships; SC 100, LC 40, GC 30; enrl D 2200, maj 467, grad 80
Ent Req: HS dipl, SAT
Degrees: BA & BFA 4 yrs, MA 1 yr, MFA 2 yrs
Tuition: Campus residence available
Courses: Art Education, Ceramics, Drawing, Graphic Design, History of Art &

Archaeology, Illustration, Interior Design, Museum Staff Training, Painting, Photography, Printmaking, Sculpture, Teacher Training
Adult Hobby Classes: Courses offered
Summer School: Dir, Robert E Lewis

MURFREESBORO

MIDDLE TENNESSEE STATE UNIVERSITY, Art Dept, * PO Box 25, 37132. Tel 615-898-2455; FAX 615-898-2254; *Chmn Art Dept* Carlyle Johnson
Estab 1911, dept estab 1952; pub; D & E; scholarships; SC 62, LC 10, GC 35; enrl non-maj 900, maj 200, grad 5
Ent Req: HS dipl
Degrees: BS(Art Educ), & BFA 4 yrs
Courses: †Art Education, †Ceramics, †Commercial Art, Drawing, Graphic Design, Goldsmithing, †Jewelry, †Painting, †Printmaking, †Sculpture, †Silversmithing, Textile Design
Adult Hobby Classes: Courses Offered
Children's Classes: Creative Art Clinic for Children; enrl 45; tuition $25 per term
Summer School: Courses Offered

NASHVILLE

CHEEKWOOD NASHVILLE'S HOME OF ART & GARDENS, Education Dept, 1200 Forrest Park Dr, 37205. Tel 615-353-2140; FAX 615-353-2162; *Pres* Jane Gerry; *Dir Educ* Donna Glasford; *Cur Coll* Christine Kreyling; *Cur Coll* Celia Walker; *Dir Botanical Gardens* Bob Brackman
Estab 1960; pvt; D & E; scholarships; SC 10-15, LC 5-10
Tuition: $60-$120 for 8 wk term
Courses: Art Appreciation, Art History, Ceramics, Drawing, Jewelry, Painting, Sculpture, Weaving, Landscape Design, Papermaking
Adult Hobby Classes: Calligraphy, Design, Life Drawing, Painting, Photography, Printmaking, Watercolor
Children's Classes: Art Start, Exploring Art

FISK UNIVERSITY, Art Dept, 1000 17th Ave N, 37208-3051. Tel 615-329-8674, 329-8500; *Chmn&Instr* Lifran Fort, MA
Estab 1867, dept estab 1937; pvt; D; scholarships; SC 10, LC 3; enrl 65, non-maj 40, maj 15
Ent Req: HS dipl, SAT
Degrees: BS & BA 4 yrs
Tuition: $6300 per sem; campus res & tuition $3910 per sem
Courses: Aesthetics, Art History, Drawing, Painting, Sculpture, African Art, Afro-American Art

VANDERBILT UNIVERSITY, Dept of Fine Arts, 23rd Ave S at West End Ave, PO Box 1801, Station B, 37235. Tel 615-322-0125; *Chmn* Robert L Mode, PhD; *Prof* F Hamilton Hazlehurst, PhD; *Assoc Prof* Robert A Baldwin, MFA; *Assoc Prof* Donald H Evans, MFA; *Assoc Prof* Leonard Folgarait, PhD; *Assoc Prof* Milan Mihal, PhD; *Assoc Prof* Robert L Mode, PhD; *Assoc Prof* Ljubica D Popovich, PhD; *Asst Prof* Barbara Tsakirgis, PhD; *Asst Prof* Marilyn Murphy, MFA; *Assoc Prof* Michael Aurbach, MFA; *Assoc Prof* Vivien G Fryd, PhD; *Asst Prof* Ellen Konowitz; *Sr Lectr* Amy Kirschke, PhD; *Lectr* Susan DeMay, MFA; *Lectr* Carlton Wilkinson, MFA
Estab 1873, dept estab 1944; pvt; D; scholarships; SC 19, LC 29, GC 2; enrl non-maj 367, maj 47, grad 10
Ent Req: HS dipl, ent exam
Degrees: BA 4 yrs, MA(Art Hist) 1-2 yrs
Tuition: $15,975 per yr; $7987.50 per sem; campus res—room & board $5764 per yr
Courses: Architecture, Art Appreciation, Ceramics, Design, Drawing, Film, Printmaking, Sculpture, Video, Painting, Photography, Multimedia Design
Summer School: Dean, John Venable. Tuition $666 per sem for two 4 wk terms beginning early June. Courses—Vary

WATKINS INSTITUTE, College of Art & Design, 601 Church St, 37219-2390. Tel 615-242-1851; *Dir Fine Arts* Madeline Reed. Instrs: 50
Estab 1885; pvt; D & E; SC 30, LC 5; enrl D 1000, E 1000
Ent Req: Noncredit adult educ program, must be 17 yrs of age or older
Degrees: AA in Art, approved by Tennessee Higher Education Commission, 2 yr
Tuition: $120 per cr hr
Courses: †Film, †Graphic Design, †Interior Design, †Photography, †Fine Art
Children's Classes: Enrl 500; tuition $150-$200 for 12 wks. Courses—Fine Arts
Summer School: Enrl 400; tuition $90 - $135 per course for 10 wks. Summer Art Camp for children, 2 wk sessions. Courses—Commercial Art, Fine Arts, Interior Design

SEWANEE

UNIVERSITY OF THE SOUTH, Dept of Fine Arts, Carnegie Hall, 37383. Tel 615-598-1537, 598-1000; Elec Mail pmalde@seraph1.sewaner.edu. *Chmn Dept* Pradip Malde. Instrs: FT 4
Pvt, den; D; SC 20, LC 20; enrl D 250, non-maj 225, maj 30
Degrees: BS & BA, MDivinity
Tuition: $9100 per yr
Courses: Art History, Drawing, History of Art & Archaeology, Painting, Photography, Printmaking, Sculpture, Video
Summer School: Dir, Dr John Reishman. Enrl 150 for term of 6 wks beginning June; tuition $400 per cr. Courses—History of Western Art II, Painting, Photography

TULLAHOMA

MOTLOW STATE COMMUNITY COLLEGE, Art Dept, PO Box 88100, 37388-8100. Tel 615-393-1700; WATS 800-654-4877. *Dean* Dr Mary McLemore; *Art Teacher* Jack Moore; *Art Teacher* Ann Smotherman
Scholarships
Tuition: Res—$387 per sem; nonres—$1602 sem
Courses: Art Appreciation, Ceramics, Commercial Art, Design, Drawing, Painting, Photography, Arts & Crafts
Adult Hobby Classes: Enrl 200
Children's Classes: Enrl 40

TEXAS

ABILENE

ABILENE CHRISTIAN UNIVERSITY, Dept of Art, ACU Sta, Box 7987, 79699. Tel 915-674-2085; FAX 915-674-2202; *Head Dept* Brent Green, PhD. Instrs: FT 6, PT 1
Estab 1906; den; D & E; SC 29, LC 8; enrl maj 79
Ent Req: Upper 3/4 HS grad class or at 19 standard score ACT composite
Degrees: BA, BA(Educ) & BFA 4 yrs
Tuition: $230 per sem hr
Courses: Art History, Drawing, Art Education, Ceramics, Graphic Design, Painting, Sculpture, Printmaking, Jewelry, Design, Pottery
Summer School: Dir, Dr Brent Green. Enrl 10; tuition $230 for 3 & 6 wk blocks. Courses— ceramics, Drawing, Introduction to Art History

HARDIN-SIMMONS UNIVERSITY, Art Dept, Hickory at Ambler St, PO Box 16085, 79698. Tel 915-670-1246, 670-1249; *Chmn* Linda D Fawcett, MFA; *Asst Prof* Don Stevenson, MFA; *Instr* Carrie Tucker, MFA; *Instr* Martha Kiel, MEd
Univ estab 1891; den; D & E; scholarships; SC 27, LC 5; enrl D 130, E 25, non-maj 65, maj 65
Ent Req: HS dipl, SAT, ACT
Degrees: BA & BBS 4 yrs
Tuition: $230 per cr hr; campus res—room & board $1195
Courses: Art Education, Art History, †Ceramics, †Drawing, †Graphic Design, †Painting, †Photography, †Printmaking, Sculpture, †Teacher Training, †Theatre Arts, †Teacher Training, †Theatre Arts
Children's Classes: Enrl summer only 110; tuition $160 per wk full day, $85 per wk half day. Courses—Art History, Ceramics, Drawing, Painting, Papermaking, Photography, Printmaking, Sculpture
Summer School: Dir, Linda D Fawcett. Enrl 30; tuition $230 per cr hr for term of 6 wks beginning June 2. Courses—Art Appreciation, Ceramics, Drawing, Photography

MCMURRY UNIVERSITY, Art Dept, McMurry Sta, PO Box 308, 79697. Tel 915-691-6200; *Head Dept* Kathy Walker-Millar; *Prof* Sherwood Suter, MFA; *Prof* J Robert Miller, BS; *Prof* Sara Beth Clevenger
Estab 1923; pvt; D & E; scholarships; SC 19, LC 1; enrl D 80, E 8, non-maj 18, maj 15
Ent Req: HS dipl
Degrees: BA, BFA & BS 4 yrs
Tuition: Res—undergrad $2772 per sem, $875 per sem (incl room), $231 per sem hr; nonres—same as res fees
Courses: Art Education, Art History, Ceramics, Drawing, Jewelry, Painting, Teacher Training, Assemblage Sculpture, Design
Adult Hobby Classes: Enrl 24; tuition $360 fall, spring & summer terms. Courses—Art Education I & II
Summer School: Dir, Bob Maniss. Two summer terms. Courses—Art Education I, Exploring the Visual Arts

ALPINE

SUL ROSS STATE UNIVERSITY, Dept of Fine Arts & Communications, * C-43, 79832. Tel 915-837-8130; FAX 915-837-8046; *Chmn* Dr George Bradley; *Prof* Charles R Hext; *Prof* Dr Roy Dodson
Estab 1920, dept estab 1922; pub; D & E; scholarships; SC 21, LC 3, GC 19; enrl D 183, E 32, non-maj 170, maj 25-30, GS 15
Ent Req: HS dipl, ACT or SAT
Degrees: BFA 4 yrs, MEd(Art) 1 1/2 yrs
Tuition: Res—12 hr $578 pr sem, nonres—12 hr $2210 per sem
Courses: Art History, Ceramics, Conceptual Art, Drawing, Jewelry, Mixed Media, Painting, Printmaking, Sculpture, Teacher Training, Advertising Art
Summer School: Tuition 6 hr $309 per term; nonres 6 hr $1125 per term

ALVIN

ALVIN COMMUNITY COLLEGE, Art Dept, 3110 Mustang Rd, 77511. Tel 281-388-6411, 331-6111, 388-4839; FAX 281-388-4903; *Chmn* Doris Burbank
Estab 1949; D & E
Ent Req: HS dipl
Degrees: AA 2 yrs
Tuition: In-district—$112; res—$240; nonres—$320
Courses: Art Appreciation, Art History, Ceramics, Drawing, Graphic Design, Painting, Sculpture, Design Communication, Graphic Media
Summer School: Dir, Bruce Turner. 6-12 wk term. Courses—Vary

AMARILLO

AMARILLO COLLEGE, Art Dept, PO Box 447, 79178. Tel 806-371-5000, Ext 5084; *Chmn* Denny Fraze, MFA; *Prof* William Burrell, MFA; *Instr* Dennis Olson; *Instr* Steven Cost; *Instr* Pedro Gonzalez
Estab 1926; pub; D & E; scholarships; SC 18, LC 2; enrl D 142, E 60
Ent Req: HS dipl, CEEB
Degrees: AA 2 yrs
Tuition: Res—undergrad $236.25 per sem, lab fee $8; nonres—undergrad $360 per sem; no campus res
Courses: Art History, Ceramics, Drawing, †Graphic Design, Illustration, Jewelry, †Painting, †Sculpture, †Fine Art, Layout, Typographics
Summer School: Chmn, Denny Fraze, MFA

ARLINGTON

UNIVERSITY OF TEXAS AT ARLINGTON, Dept of Art & Art History, 335 Fine Arts Bldg, PO Box 19089, 76019. Tel 817-272-2891; FAX 817-273-2805; *Chmn* Kenda North
Estab 1895, dept estab 1937; pub; D & E; scholarships; SC 46, LC 39, maj 400
Degrees: BFA 4 yrs
Tuition: Res—$497 for 15 cr hrs; nonres—$2057 for 15 cr hrs
Courses: Advertising Design, Art Appreciation, †Art History, †Ceramics, Commercial Art, Conceptual Art, Constructions, Design, Display, †Drawing, Film, Goldsmithing, Graphic Arts, †Graphic Design, History of Art & Archaeology, Illustration, Intermedia, †Jewelry, Mixed Media, Museum Staff Training, †Painting, †Photography, †Printmaking, †Sculpture, Silversmithing, Teacher Training, †Video, Glass Blowing, †Metalsmithing

AUSTIN

AUSTIN COMMUNITY COLLEGE, Dept of Commercial Art, North Ridge Campus, 11928 Stonehollow Dr, 78758. Tel 512-223-7000; *Head Dept* Daniel Traverso, MFA; *Head Dept South Campus* Steve Kramer. Instrs: FT 4, PT 20
Estab 1974; pub; D & E; enrl 386 per sem
Ent Req: HS dipl or GED
Degrees: AAS 2 yr
Tuition: Res—undergrad $21.50 per cr hr; nonres—undergrad $105.50 per cr hr
Courses: Art History, Calligraphy, Ceramics, Commercial Art, Drawing, Graphic Design, Illustration, Photography, Graphic Arts, Painting, †Photography, †Printmaking, †Sculpture, †Video, Advertising, Animation, Commercial Art History, Computer Layout & Design, Desktop Publishing, Environmental Graphics, Figure Drawing, Graphics Practicum, Illustrative Techniques, Metalsmithing, Production Art, Silkscreening, Typography Design

CONCORDIA UNIVERSITY, Dept of Fine Arts, 3400 I-35 N, 78705. Tel 512-452-7661; FAX 512-459-8517; *Chmn* Dr Milton Riemer. Instrs: FT 1
Estab 1925; den; D; scholarships; SC 1, LC 1; enrl D 350
Ent Req: HS dipl
Degrees: AA 2 yrs
Tuition: $175 per sem hr; campus res available
Courses: Ceramics, Design, Drawing, Art Fundamentals, Drawing Media, Relief Printing

UNIVERSITY OF TEXAS
—School of Architecture, Goldsmith Hall, 78712-1160. Tel 512-471-1922; FAX 512-471-0716; *Dean* Lawrence Speck. Instrs: FT 38, PT 9
Estab 1909; pub; scholarships; enrl undergrad 450, grad 210
Ent Req: Reasonable HS scholastic achievement, SAT, ACT
Degrees: BA, MA, PhD
Tuition: Res—$769 per sem; nonres—$2485 per sem
Courses: †Architecture, Community & Regional Planning
Adult Hobby Classes: Courses through Division of Continuing Education
Children's Classes: Six week summer program for high school
Summer School: Dir, Harold Box
—Dept of Art & Art History, 78712. Tel 512-471-3382; FAX 512-471-7801; *Acting Chair* Kenneth Hale. Instrs: FT & PT 80
Estab 1938; scholarships & fels; enrl grad 127, 900 undergrad maj
Degrees: BA 4yrs, BFA 4 yrs, MA 2 yrs, MFA 2 yrs, PhD
Tuition: Res—undergrad $584 per sem, grad $574 per sem; nonres—undergrad $2240 per sem, grad $1798 per sem
Courses: Art Education, Art History, Conceptual Art, Design, Drawing, Painting, Photography, Printmaking, Sculpture, Teacher Training, Video, †Criticism of Art, Installation Film Art, Metals, †Teacher Certificatoin, Trans Media, †Visual Communications
Summer School: Two 6 wk terms

BEAUMONT

LAMAR UNIVERSITY, Art Dept, PO Box 10027, LU Sta, 77710. Tel 409-880-8141; FAX 409-880-1799; *Head Dept* Donna M Meeks; *Prof* Jerry Newman, MFA; *Assoc Prof* Meredith M Jack MFA; *Assoc Prof* Philip Fitzpatrick, MFA; *Assoc Prof* Lynn Lokensgard, PhD; *Asst Prof* Stephen Hodges, MFA; *Assoc Prof* Keith Carter; *Asst Prof* James Nakagawa, MFA
Estab 1923, dept estab 1951; pub; D & E; scholarships; SC 60, LC 76; enrl D 604, E 40, non-maj 300, maj 150
Ent Req: HS dipl, SAT/ACT
Degrees: BFA, BS & MA, 4 yr
Tuition: Res—undergrad $120 for 3 sem hrs; nonres—undergrad $738 for 3 sem hrs; campus res available
Courses: Aesthetics, Art Appreciation, †Art Education, Art History, †Ceramics, †Commercial Art, Design, †Drawing, †Graphic Design, Illustration, Jewelry, Museum Staff Training, †Painting, †Photography, †Printmaking, †Sculpture, †Teacher Training, Weaving, Jewelry, Landscape Architecture, Lettering, Mixed

Media, Painting, Photography, Printmaking, Sculpture, Stage Design, Teacher Training, Computer Graphics
Summer School: Dir, Donna M Meeks. Enrl 125; tuition in state $96, out of state $738 per 3 sem hrs for two wk sessions. Courses—Art Appreciation, Art Education, Computers in Art, Drawing

BELTON

UNIVERSITY OF MARY HARDIN-BAYLOR, School of Fine Arts, PO Box 8012, 76513. Tel 817-939-4678, 939-8642; *Dean* George Stansbury; *Art Dept Head* Hershel Fields
Estab 1845; den; D & E; scholarships; SC 6, LC 1 and one independent learning course per sem
Ent Req: Upper half of HS grad class
Degrees: BA, BFA & BS 4 yrs
Tuition: $185 per sem hr
Courses: Art Education, Art History, Ceramics, Drawing, Graphic Arts, Jewelry, Painting, Design
Children's Classes: Summer Art Camp
Summer School: Sem of 5 wks, from 1 to 4 cr hrs. Courses—Crafts, Independent Learning

BIG SPRING

HOWARD COLLEGE, Art Dept, Division of Fine Arts, 1001 Birdwell Lane, 79720. Tel 915-264-5000; FAX 915-264-5082; *Chmn* Mary Dudley
Estab 1948, dept estab 1972; pub; D & E; scholarships; SC 5, LC 1; enrl D 70, E 20, non-maj 60, maj 10
Ent Req: HS dipl, ACT
Degrees: AA
Tuition: Res—$90 per sem cr hr; nonres—$276 per sem cr hr
Courses: Art Education, Art History, Ceramics, Drawing

BROWNSVILLE

UNIVERSITY OF TEXAS AT BROWNSVILLE & TEXAS SOUTHMOST COLLEGE, Fine Arts Dept, 80 Fort Brown, 78520. Tel 210-548-6525; *Chmn Fine Arts* Terry Tomlin
Estab 1973; pub; D & E; scholarships; SC 10, LC 10; enrl D 300, E 100
Ent Req: HS dipl
Degrees: AA (Fine Arts) 2-3 yrs, BA 4 yr
Tuition: Res—undergrad $386, grad $506 for 12 hrs or more; nonres—undergrad $1346, grad $2162 for 12 hrs or more
Courses: Art Education, Ceramics, Drawing, Graphic Design, History of Art & Archaeology, Painting, Photography, Sculpture, Design I and II
Adult Hobby Classes: Courses—Ceramics, Drawing
Summer School: Dir, Terry Tomlin. Courses—Art Appreciation, Art History

BROWNWOOD

HOWARD PAYNE UNIVERSITY, Dept of Art, School of Fine & Applied Arts, PO Box 839, HPU Sta, 76801. Tel 915-646-2502; *Dean* Donal Bird, PhD; *Chmn Dept Art* Ann Smith, MA. Instrs: FT 2, PT 2
Estab 1889; den; D & E; SC 18, LC 8; enrl D 120, E 25, maj 2
Ent Req: HS dipl, ent exam
Degrees: BA & BS 4 yrs
Tuition: $118 per sem hr
Courses: Advertising Design, Art Appreciation, Art Education, Art History, Ceramics, Commercial Art, Design, Drawing, Graphic Arts, Graphic Design, Handicrafts, Painting, Photography, Computer Graphics
Adult Hobby Classes: Enrl 30; tuition $50 per course. Courses—Crafts, Painting, Travel Seminars
Children's Classes: tuition $20-$50 per 2 wk course
Summer School: Enrl 75; tuition term of 6 wks beginning June. Courses—Crafts, Drawing, Painting, Photography

CANYON

WEST TEXAS A&M UNIVERSITY, Art, Communication & Theatre Dept, PO Box 747, WT Sta, 79016. Tel 806-656-2799; *Head Dept* Royal Brantley; *Prof* Robert Caruthers, MFA; *Prof* Darold Smith, MFA; *Assoc Prof* David Rindlisbacher, MFA; *Assoc Prof* Mary Ann Petry, PhD; *Asst Prof* Sven Anderson, MFA
Estab 1910; pub; D & E; scholarships; SC 70, LC 23, GC 50; enrl maj 120, grad 23
Ent Req: HS dipl
Degrees: BA, BS, BFA, MA & MFA
Tuition: Res—$192 per sem, $100 PT; non-res—$1440 per sem, $720 PT; foreign students $1140 per sem; campus res—$1154
Courses: †Advertising Design, Aesthetics, †Art Education, Art History, †Ceramics, Commercial Art, †Drawing, †Goldsmithing, Graphic Arts, †Graphic Design, Handicrafts, Illustration, †Jewelry, †Painting, †Printmaking, †Sculpture, †Silversmithing, Teacher Training
Children's Classes: Summer session offered by Gifted & Talented Dept
Summer School: Dir, Steven Mayes. Tuition res $108 per session, nonres $1080 per session; Session I from June 2 - July 8, Session II July 9 - Aug 20. All art courses offered

COLLEGE STATION

TEXAS A&M UNIVERSITY, College of Architecture, 77843-3137. Tel 409-845-1221; FAX 409-845-4491; *Dean* Walter V Wendler. Instrs: FT 92
Estab 1905; pub; D; scholarships; enrl maj Ed 800, total 1750
Ent Req: SAT; Achievement, HS rank
Degrees: BEenviron Design, BS(Building Construction), BLandscape Arch, MArch, MLandscape, MUrban Planning, PhD(Urban Science) 4 yr, MS(Construction Mgmt), MS(Land Development), MS(Architecture), PhD(Architecture), MS(Visualization) (Computer Animation)
Tuition: Res—$30 per sem cr hr; nonres—$162 per sem cr hr; fees $700
Courses: Architecture, Art History, Constructions, Design, Drafting, Drawing, History of Art & Archaeology, Illustration, Landscape Architecture, Photography, Restoration & Conservation, Video, Computer Animation
Adult Hobby Classes: Enrl 30; tuition $375 for one wk term. Courses—Career Horizons
Summer School: Dir, Rodney Hill. Enrl 1000; tuition same as above for two wk sessions. Courses—Arch Design, Arch History, Construction Science, Drawing, Planning

COMMERCE

EAST TEXAS STATE UNIVERSITY, Dept of Art, E Texas Sta, 75429. Tel 903-886-5208; FAX 214-886-5415; *Head* William Wadley; *Chmn Ceramics* Barbara Frey, MFA; *Chmn Printmaking* Lee Baxter Davis, MFA; *Chmn Sculpture* Jerry Dodd, MFA; *Chmn Art Ed* Dr James Allumbaugh; *Coordr Grad Programs* Gerard Huber, MFA; *Chmn Painting* Michael Miller; *Chmn Art History* Ivana Spalatin; *Prof* James Newberry; *Asst Prof* Stan Godwin; *Instr at Interim* Terry Falke
Pub; D & E; scholarships; SC 64, LC 29, GC 19; enrl maj 300, GS 30
Ent Req: HS dipl, ACT or SAT
Degrees: BA, BS & BFA 4 yr, MFA 2 yr, MA & MS 1 1/2 yr. There is a special prog called the Post Masters-MFA which is worked out on an individual basis
Courses: †Advertising Design, Aesthetics, †Art Education, Art History, †Ceramics, Collages, †Commercial Art, Constructions, Drafting, †Drawing, †Graphic Arts, †Graphic Design, History of Art & Archaeology, †Illustration, †Intermedia, Industrial Design, †Jewelry, Lettering, †Mixed Media, †Painting, †Photography, †Printmaking, †Sculpture, Silversmithing, †Teacher Training, Video, Lithography, Papermaking & Casting
Adult Hobby Classes: Enrl 15; tuition $77 per sem. Courses—Bonzai, Ceramics, Drawing, Painting, Watercolor
Summer School: Enrl 15; tuition res—$64.75-$393; nonres—$134.75-$2121, for 2 terms of 2 to 6 wks beginning June. Courses—Art Education, Ceramics, Design, Drawing, Painting, Printmaking

CORPUS CHRISTI

DEL MAR COLLEGE, Art Dept, 101 Baldwin, 78404-3897. Tel 512-886-1216; *Chmn* William E Lambert, MFA; *Prof* Jan R Ward, MFA; *Prof* Ronald Dee Sullivan, MA; *Prof* Randolph Flowers, MS; *Assoc Prof* Kitty Dudics MFA; *Assoc Prof* Ken Rosier, MFA
Estab 1941, dept estab 1965; pub; D & E; scholarships; SC 21, LC 3; enrl D 500, E 100, non-maj 400, maj 139
Ent Req: HS dipl, SAT score or any accepted test including GED
Degrees: AA 2 yr in studio, art educ
Tuition: Res—$16 per sem hr, $50 minimum; nonres—$40 per sem hr, $200 minimum; foreign students $40 per sem hr, $200 minimum; plus other fees; no campus res
Courses: Graphic Design, History of Art & Archaeology, Painting, Photography, Printmaking, Sculpture
Adult Hobby Classes: Tuition varies according to classes. Courses—same as above
Summer School: Chmn, W E Lambert, MFA. Enrl 60; tuition $16 per sem hr, $50 minimum, for 16 wks. Courses—Ceramics, Design, Drawing, Graphic Design, Painting, Principles of Art, Printmaking, Sculpture

CORSICANA

NAVARRO COLLEGE, Art Dept, 3200 W Seventh Ave, 75110. Tel 903-874-6501; FAX 903-874-4636; WATS: 800-NAVARRO. *Dir* Sandra Dowd. Instrs: FT2, PT2
Estab 1946; pub; D & E; scholarships; SC 11, LC 1; enrl D 300, maj 30
Ent Req: HS dipl, ent exam, special permission
Degrees: AA, AS, A Gen Educ & A Appl Sci 60 sem hr
Tuition: $450 per sem
Courses: Advertising Design, Art Appreciation, Calligraphy, Ceramics, Commercial Art, Design, Drafting, Drawing, Graphic Arts, Illustration, Painting, Photography, Sculpture, Video, 2-D & 3-D Design, †Computer Art, Multi-Media
Adult Hobby Classes: Enrl 200; tuition $30-$150 for sem of 6-12 wks. Courses—Art Appreciation, Crafts, Design, Drawing, Painting, Photography, Sculpture
Summer School: Dir, Evans David. Enrl 30; Courses—Art Appreciation

DALLAS

THE ART INSTITUTE OF DALLAS, 2 N Park East, 8080 Park Lane, 75231-9959. Tel 214-692-8080; FAX 214-692-6541; WATS 800-275-4243. *Registrar* Stuart Moore
Scholarships
Degrees: AA
Tuition: $2650 per qtr
Courses: Interior Design, Photography, Computer Animation Multimedia, Fashion Design, Fashion Marketing, Music & Video Business, Visual Communication
Adult Hobby Classes: Enrl 850; tuition $2050 per quarter. Courses—Commercial Art, Fashion Merchandising, Interior Design, Music Business, Photography, Video

DALLAS BAPTIST UNIVERSITY, Dept of Art, 3000 Mountain Creek Pky, 75211-9299. Tel 214-333-5316, 333-5300; FAX 214-333-5333; *Asst Prof* Dawna Hamm Walsh, PhD; *Asst Prof* Jim Colley, MFA; *Asst Prof* Rosalie Lemme; *Asst Prof* Morris Abernathy; *Asst Prof* Don Adair; *Artist in Residence* Jack Hamm
Estab 1965; pvt den; D & E; scholarships; enrl D 75, E 25, non-maj 75, maj 25
Ent Req: HS dipl
Degrees: BA & BS 4 yrs, Bachelor of Applied Studies 2-4 yrs, Grad Art Degree: MLA
Tuition: $200 per sem hr
Courses: Art Education, Art History, Ceramics, Commercial Art, Drawing, Graphic Design, Interior Design, Painting, Photography, Sculpture, Teacher Training, Theatre Arts, Crafts, Fine Arts
Adult Hobby Classes: Art Education, Art History, Ceramics, Commercial Art, Crafts, Drawing, Fine Arts, Graphic Design, Interior Design, Painting, Photography, Sculpture, Teacher Training
Children's Classes: Contact PBU Lab School
Summer School: Dir, Dr Dawna Walsh. Tuition $200 per cr hr. Courses—Ceramics, Drawing, Painting. Art Travel Program for cr available

SOUTHERN METHODIST UNIVERSITY, Division of Art, 75275-0356. Tel 214-768-2489; Elec Mail mvernon@sun.cis.smu.edu. *Chair* Jay Sullivan
Estab 1911, Meadows School of Arts estab 1964; pvt; D & E; scholarships; enrl maj 142, grad 41
Ent Req: Selective admis
Degrees: BFA(Art), BFA(Art Histroy), BA(Art History) 4 yr, MFA(Art) 2 yr, MA(Art History) 1 1/2 yr
Tuition: $400 per cr hr; campus res—room & board $4688
Courses: †Art History, †Ceramics, †Drawing, †Painting, †Photography, †Printmaking, †Sculpture
Summer School: Tuition $570 per course for term of 5 wks beginning June 4. Selected courses in art & art history at Taos, NM

DEER PARK

SAN JACINTO JUNIOR COLLEGE, Division of Fine Arts, * 8060 Spencer Hwy, PO Box 2007, 77536. Tel 713-476-1501; *Division Chmn Fine Arts* Jerry Callahan
Estab 1961; pub; D & E; SC 5, LC 1; enrl D 230, E 45, non-maj 120, maj 155
Ent Req: HS dipl, GED or individual approval
Degrees: AA and AS 2 yrs
Tuition: In district—$50 per 6 hr; out of district—$240 per 6 hr; out of state & non-citizens—$240 per 6 hr
Courses: Advertising Design, Art Appreciation, Art History, Ceramics, Commercial Art, Design, Drawing, Lettering, Painting, Photography, Sculpture, Advertising Art, Free Illustration
Summer School: Enrl 25; tuition $25 for term of 6 wks beginning June 5th. Courses—Design, Painting Workshop

DENISON

GRAYSON COUNTY COLLEGE, Art Dept, 6101 Grayson Dr, 75020. Tel 903-463-8662; FAX 903-463-5284; *Dept Head* Steve O Black; *Inst* Evette Moorman; *Instr* Terri Blair
Estab 1965; pub; D & E; scholarships; LC 3; enrl D 63, E 35
Ent Req: HS dipl
Degrees: AA 2 yrs
Courses: Art Appreciation, Art Education, Art History, Drawing, Painting, Color & Design, Foundations of Art, 3-D Design
Adult Hobby Classes: Ceramics, Drawing, Painting
Summer School: Dir, Steve O Black. Courses—Art Appreciation, Foundations of Art, Drawing, Painting

DENTON

TEXAS WOMAN'S UNIVERSITY, Dept of Visual Arts, PO Box 425469, 76204. Tel 817-898-2530; FAX 817-898-2496; *Chmn* Dr Betty D Copeland, EdD; *Prof* John B Miller; *Prof* Linda Stuckenbruck, MFA; *Prof* Dr John A Calabrese, PhD; *Prof* Susan Kae Grant, MFA; *Assoc Prof* Alfred E Green, MFA; *Assoc Prof* Jeanne Broussard; *Assoc Prof* Gary Washmon; *Adjunct Asst Prof* Don Radke; *Adjunct Asst Prof* Laurie Weller; *Adjunct Asst Prof* Millie Giles; *Adjunct Asst Prof* Cynthia Laughlin; *Adjunct Asst Prof* Cynthia Rodriquez; *Lectr* Tori Arpad
Estab 1901; pub; D & E; scholarships; SC 21, LC 34, GC 17; enrl non-maj 400, maj 110, undergrad 150, total 750
Ent Req: HS dipl, MA and MFA portfolio review required
Degrees: BA, BS and BFA 4 yrs, MA 1 yr, MFA 2 yrs
Tuition: Res—$16 per sem hr, $100 minimum; nonres—$120 per sem hr; campus res—$590 - $1180 for room only, meal plan available at extra charge
Courses: Art Education, Art History, Jewelry, Painting, Photography, Sculpture, Textile Design, Advertising Art, Bookmaking-Topography, Clay, Fibers, Fashion Illustration, Handmade Paper, Metalsmithing
Adult Hobby Classes: Art History, Children's Art, Studio Courses
Children's Classes: 10 wks. Courses—Clay, Drawing
Summer School: Dir, Dr Betty D Copeland. Enrl 150; tuition same as above for 2 5-wk sessions. Courses—Art Design, Art Education, Art History, Clay, Drawing, Fibers, Painting, Photography

UNIVERSITY OF NORTH TEXAS, School of Visual Arts, PO Box 5098, 76203. Tel 817-565-2855; FAX 817-565-4717; *Dean* D Jack Davis, PhD; *Interim Assoc Dean* Don R Schol, MFA; *Grad Studies Coordr* Dianne Taylor, PhD; *Undergrad Coordr* Mickey McCarter, MEd; *Interior Design Coordr* Bruce Nacke, MA; *Communications Design Coordr* Jack Sprague, MFA; *Printmaking Coordr* Judy Youngblood, MFA; *Photography Coordr* Brent Phelps, MFA; *Painting & Drawing Coordr* Rob Erdle, MFA; *Sculpture Coordr* Richard Davis, MA; *Art History Coordr* Larry Gleeson, PhD; *Fashion Design Coordr* Marian O'Rourke Kaplan, MBA; *Ceramics Coordr* Jerry Austin, MFA; *Jewelry & Metalsmithing Coordr* Harlan Butt, MFA; *Basic Drawing Coordr* Robert Jessup, MFA; *Fibers Coordr* Jennifer Sargent,

MFA; *Art Educ Coordr* Nancy Berry, MFA; *Basic Design Coordr* Don E Schel, MFA
Estab 1897, dept estab 1901; pub; D & E; scholarships; SC 92, LC 54, GC 83; enrl non-maj 500, maj 1500, grad 100, others 25
Ent Req: HS dipl, SAT, GRE, portfolio for MFA, letters of recommendation for PhD
Degrees: BFA 4 yrs, MFA, MA, PhD
Tuition: Res—undergrad & grad $24 per sem hr, minimum of $100 plus fees; nonres—undergrad, grad & foreign $162 per sem hr; campus res—room & board $1486.70 - $1984.70 per sem
Courses: Art Appreciation, †Art Education, †Art History, †Ceramics, Conceptual Art, Design, Drawing, †Fashion Arts, Graphic Design, Illustration, †Interior Design, †Jewelry, †Painting, †Photography, †Printmaking, †Sculpture, Silversmithing, Teacher Training, Textile Design, †Weaving, Communication Design
Adult Hobby Classes: Tuition determined by class. Courses—Mini-classes in arts and craft related areas
Children's Classes: Courses—Mini-classes in arts and crafts related areas; special prog for advanced students
Summer School: Dir, D Jack Davis. Enrl 700-900 per session; tuition $26 per sem hr for term of 6 wks; 2 summer sessions. Courses—Art Appreciation, Art Education, Art History, Design, Drawing, Fashion, Interior Design, Painting, Photography

EDINBURG

UNIVERSITY OF TEXAS PAN AMERICAN, Art Dept, 1201 W University Dr, 78539. Tel 210-381-3480, Main 381-2011; FAX 210-384-5072; Elec Mail nmoyer@panam.edu. *Chmn Dept* Nancy Moyer, PhD
Estab 1927, dept estab 1972; pub; D & E; scholarships; SC 43, LC 14; enrl D 1200, E 150, non-maj 650, maj 209
Ent Req: Open, immunization
Degrees: BA and BFA 4 yrs
Tuition: Res—$200.94 per 3 cr hr, $734.76 per 15 cr hr; nonres—$593.94 per 3 cr hr, $2879.76 per 15 cr hr
Courses: Advertising Design, Aesthetics, Art Appreciation, †Art Education, Art History, Calligraphy, †Ceramics, Collages, Design, Drawing, †Graphic Design, History of Art & Archaeology, Illustration, †Jewelry, Lettering, †Painting, Photography, †Printmaking, †Sculpture, Silversmithing, Computer Graphic
Summer School: Dir, Nancy Moyer. Enrl 20 per class; tuition $31-$78 for term of 5 wks beginning June 2 & July 9. Courses—Art Appreciation, Art Education, Basic Design, Beginning & Advanced Painting, Ceramics, Drawing, Elementary Art Educ, Printing

EL PASO

UNIVERSITY OF TEXAS AT EL PASO, Dept of Art, 79968. Tel 915-747-5181, 747-5000; *Head Dept* Albert Wong. Instrs: FT 12
Estab 1939; pub; D & E; scholarships; SC 24, GC 8; enrl 200
Degrees: BA & BFA 4 yrs, MA (Studio & Art Ed)
Tuition: $656.40 per sem
Courses: Art Education, Art History, Ceramics, Design, Drawing, Graphic Design, Painting, Printmaking, Sculpture, Metals
Adult Hobby Classes: Enrl 9; tuition varies from class to class. Courses—offered through Extension Division
Children's Classes: Enrl 25; tuition $25 for 6 week class. Courses—Kidzart
Summer School: Chmn, Charles Fensch. Enrl 150; tuition $80 for 3 hr course. Courses—Art Education, Intro to Art, Life Drawing, Painting, Printmaking

FORT WORTH

SAGER STUDIOS, 320 N Bailey Ave, 76107. Tel 817-626-3105; *Owner* Judy Sager
Estab 1964; pvt; D & E; enrl D 8, E 16
Ent Req: Entrance exam, portfolio preparation stressed
Degrees: BFA 4 yr
Courses: Ceramics, Collages, Design, Drawing, Lettering, Mixed Media, Painting, Photography, Printmaking, Sculpture, Teacher Training
Children's Classes: Special classes for gifted students ages 10-24

TEXAS CHRISTIAN UNIVERSITY, Art & Art History Dept, College of Fine Arts & Communication, PO Box 298000, 76129. Tel 817-921-7643; FAX 817-921-7703; *Dean of Fine Arts* Robert Garwell; *Chmn of Art & Art History* Ronald Watson; *Prof* Anne Helmreich, PhD; *Prof* David Conn, MFA; *Prof* Babette Bohn, PhD; *Prof* Thad Duhigg, MFA; *Prof* Linda Guy, MFA; *Prof* Lewis Glaser, MFA; *Prof* Susan Harrington, MFA; *Prof* Jim Woodson, MFA; *Prof* Mark Thistlethwaite, PhD; *Prof* Luther Smith, MFA; *Prof* Gail Gear, MFA. Instrs: FT 13, PT 9
Estab 1909; pvt; scholarships & grad fels; SC 35, LC 10, GC; enrl maj 150, others 450
Degrees: BA, BFA & BFA Art Ed, MFA 2 yrs
Tuition: $314 per sem hr
Courses: †Art Education, †Art History, Drawing, †Graphic Design, †Painting, †Photography, †Printmaking, †Sculpture
Summer School: Dir, Terri Cummings. Enrl 200; tuition $195 per sem hr. Courses—ARA Camp

TEXAS WESLEYAN UNIVERSITY, Dept of Art, 1201 Wesleyan St, 76105-1536. Tel 817-531-4444; FAX 817-531-4814; *Dean* Joe Brown; *Chmn Dept* Mary Apple McConnell
Den; D & E; scholarships; SC, LC
Ent Req: HS dipl
Degrees: BA 4 yrs
Tuition: $3950 per sem
Courses: Art Education, Ceramics, Drawing, History of Art & Archaeology, Painting, Printmaking, Teacher Training

GAINESVILLE

NORTH CENTRAL TEXAS COLLEGE, Division of Communications & Fine Arts, 1525 W California St, 76240. Tel 817-668-7731; FAX 817-668-6049; *Chmn* Mary Dell Heathington; *Prof* Mary Frances VanPelt
Estab 1924; pub; D & E; scholarships; SC 14, LC 1; enrl D 50
Ent Req: HS dipl, SAT or ACT, individual approval
Degrees: AA and AFA 2 yrs
Courses: Art Appreciation, Art History, Ceramics, Drawing, Jewelry, Painting, Sculpture, Figure Drawing
Adult Hobby Classes: Enrl 120; tuition $10 - $20. Courses—Basketry, Country Art, Drawing, Flower Arrangement, Painting, Weaving
Children's Classes: Enrl 20; tuition $15. Courses - Art

GEORGETOWN

SOUTHWESTERN UNIVERSITY, Art Dept, PO Box 770, 78627. Tel 512-863-6511; *Chmn* Thomas Howe, PhD; *Prof* Patrick Veerkamp; *Assoc Prof* Mary Visser, MFA; *Assoc Prof* Victoria Star Varner; *Instr* Judy Bullington
Estab 1840, dept estab 1940; pvt; D; scholarships; SC 28, LC 9; enrl D 160, maj 43
Ent Req: HS dipl, SAT, portfolio
Degrees: BA 4 yrs
Tuition: $13,400 per yr
Courses: Architecture, Art Education, Art History, Ceramics, Design, Drawing, Painting, Photography, Printmaking, Sculpture
Summer School: Courses—various

HILLSBORO

HILL COLLEGE, Fine Arts Dept, 112 Lamar Dr, PO Box 619, 76645. Tel 817-582-2555; FAX 817-582-5791; Elec Mail dotallen@hillcollege.hill-college.cc.tx.us. *Music Prog Coordr* Phillip Lowe; *Art Prog Coordr* Dottie Allen
Scholarships
Degrees: AA, cert
Tuition: In district—$30.50 per sem hr; res—$33 per sem hr; nonres—$76 per sem hr
Courses: †Advertising Design, Art History, Drafting, Drawing, †Graphic Design, Painting, Photography, Stage Design, Theatre Arts, Computer Graphics, Digital Imaging

HOUSTON

ART INSTITUTE OF HOUSTON, 1900 Yorktown, 77056. Tel 713-623-2040; WATS 800-275-4244. *Dir Educ* Kim Nugent; *School of Design* Kyle Rislow. Instrs: FT 25, PT 15
Estab 1964; pvt; D & E; scholarships; enrl D 800, E 145
Ent Req: Ent req HS transcripts & graduation or GED, interview
Tuition: $1990 per quarter
Courses: Graphic Design, Illustration, Interior Design, Photography, Fashion Merchandising
Adult Hobby Classes: Applied Photography, Interior Planning, Layout & Production

GLASSELL SCHOOL OF ART, The Museum of Fine Arts, 5101 Montrose Blvd, 77006. Tel 713-639-7500; *Dir* Joseph Havel; *Admin Dean* Valerie L Olsen; *Dean Jr School & Community Outreach Prog* Norma Jane Dolcater
Estab 1926. Under the auspices of the Museum of Fine Arts; pvt; D & E; fels; SC 34, LC 5; enrl studio 1552, Jr 2597
Ent Req: Ent req portfolio review, transfer students
Degrees: 4 yr cert
Tuition: FT $935, SC $275 each, Art History $210 each; no campus res
Courses: Art History, Ceramics, Design, Drawing, Jewelry, Painting, Photography, †Printmaking, †Sculpture, Visual Fundamentals
Children's Classes: 2597; tuition $85-$105 per class (4-17 yrs)

HOUSTON BAPTIST UNIVERSITY, Dept of Art, 7502 Fondren Rd, 77074. Tel 713-995-3309, 774-7661; FAX 713-995-3489; *Chmn* James Busby; *Instr* Erik Mandaville
Estab 1963; den; D & E; scholarships; SC 7, LC 9; enrl D 2500, maj 35
Ent Req: HS dipl, ent exam
Degrees: BA & BS
Tuition: $240 per sem hr
Courses: Art Appreciation, Art Education, Ceramics, Design, Drawing, History of Art & Archaeology, Painting, Printmaking, Sculpture, Elementary Art with Teacher Certification

RICE UNIVERSITY, Dept of Art & Art History, 6100 Main St, MS 21, 77005-1892. Tel 713-527-4815; FAX 713-527-4039; *Acting Chmn* K F Drew, PhD; *Dir Art Gallery* Kimberly Davenport; *Prof* William A Camfield, PhD; *Prof* Neil Havens, MA; *Prof* Basilios N Poulos; *Prof* Karin Broker, MFA; *Prof* George Smith, MFA; *Prof* Geoffrey Winningham; *Prof* Brian Huberman; *Assoc Prof* William A Camfield, PhD; *Assoc Prof* Rebecca Mersereau, PhD; *Assoc Prof* Hamid Naficy, PhD; *Asst Prof* John Sparagana; *Asst Prof* Darra Keeton; *Assoc* Linda Neagley, PhD; *Lectr* Bren DuBay; *Vis Lectr* Thomas McEvilley, PhD
Estab 1912, dept estab 1966-67; pvt; D; scholarships; SC 27, LC 31, GC (BFA) 7; enrl D 125, non-maj 75, maj 50, grad 2 (BFA)
Ent Req: HS dipl, CEEB, evaluations of HS counselors and teachers, interview
Degrees: BA 4 yrs, BFA 5 yrs, MA(Art History, Classical Archaeology)
Tuition: $12,800 per yr, $6400 per sem, grad $13,300 per yr, $6650 per sem; PT $740 per yr, $370 per sem; campus res—room & board $6000 per yr
Courses: †Art History, Design, Drawing, Film, History of Art & Archaeology, Painting, Photography, Printmaking, Sculpture, Theatre Arts, Video
Adult Hobby Classes: Classes offered for adults & children at university

SAN JACINTO COLLEGE-NORTH, Art Dept, 5800 Uvalde, 77049. Tel 713-458-4050; *Chmn* Dr Timothy Fleming; *Instr* Robert Hume; *Instr* Ken Luce
Estab 1972; pub; D & E; scholarships; SC 16, LC 3; enrl D 56, E 21, non-maj 50, maj 27
Ent Req: HS dipl
Degrees: AA 2 yrs
Tuition: Res—undergrad $318 per yr, $136 per 12 hrs, $80 for 6 hrs; nonres—undergrad $1286 per yr, $643 per sem, $270 per 6 hrs; no campus res
Courses: Art Appreciation, Art History, Drawing, Painting, Photography, Sculpture
Adult Hobby Classes: Enrl 50; tuition $15 - $40 per 6-18 hrs. Courses—Calligraphy, Ceramics, Origami, Pastel Art, Photography, Stained Glass
Children's Classes: Enrl 15, tuition $30 per 6 wks. Courses—Pastel Art
Summer School: Dir, Kenneth A Luce. Enrl 10 - 25; tuition $78 - $96. Courses—vary beginning May

TEXAS SOUTHERN UNIVERSITY, Dept of Fine Arts, 3100 Cleburne Ave, 77004. Tel 713-313-7337; FAX 713-313-7539; *Chmn* Dr Sarah Trotty; *Asst Prof* Mark Myers; *Asst Prof* Alvia Wardlaw; *Asst Prof* Harvey Johnson
Estab 1949; pub; D & E; scholarships; SC 31, LC 12, GC 4; enrl maj 85, other 100
Ent Req: HS dipl
Degrees: BFA & B(Art Educ) 5 yrs
Tuition: $412 annual tuition
Courses: Art Education, Ceramics, Design, Drawing, Weaving, Painting, Sculpture, Hot Print Making, Silk Screen Painting
Summer School: Dir, Joseph Jones, Jr. Enrl 100; for a term of 6 wks beginning June. Courses—Advanced Crafts for Teachers, Art Appreciation in Educational Program, Basic Art for Elementary Teachers, Exhibition; Mural Painting in School, Problems in Art Education, Problems in Secondary Art Education, Research Projects

UNIVERSITY OF HOUSTON, Dept of Art, 4800 Calhoun Rd, 77204-4893. Tel 713-743-3001; FAX 713-743-2823; *Chmn* Al Souza. Instrs: FT 29, PT 7
Estab 1927; pub; D & E; enrl D 600 maj
Ent Req: HS dipl, SAT
Degrees: BA, BFA, MFA
Tuition: Res—$4 per sem cr hr; nonres—$40 per sem cr hr; campus res available
Courses: Art History, Ceramics, Interior Design, Painting, Photography, Printmaking, †Sculpture, Silversmithing, Video, †Graphic Communications, Jewelry/Metals, †Paint/Drawing, †Photography/Video

UNIVERSITY OF SAINT THOMAS, Art Dept, 3800 Montrose Blvd, 77006. Tel 713-522-7911; *Chmn* Nancy L Jircik, MA
Den; D & E; scholarships; SC 15, LC 7; enrl E 30, maj 44
Ent Req: HS dipl
Degrees: BA(Liberal Arts), BA(Fine Arts-Drama & Music, Art History, BFA
Tuition: $285 per cr hr; campus res available
Courses: Art History

HUNTSVILLE

SAM HOUSTON STATE UNIVERSITY, Art Dept, 77341. Tel 409-294-1315; *Dept Head* Martin Amorous, MFA; *Prof* Gene M Eastman, MFA; *Prof* Darry Patrick, MFA; *Prof* William J Breitenbach, MFA; *Assoc Prof* Kenneth L Zonker, MA; *Asst Prof* Kate Borcherding; *Asst Prof* Elizabeth Akamatsu; *Asst Prof* Patric K Lawler; *Asst Prof* Leaha Hardy
Estab 1879, dept estab 1936; pub; D; SC 26, LC 7, GC 12; enrl D 844, non-maj 100, maj 170, grad 15
Ent Req: HS dipl, ACT or SAT
Degrees: BA, BFA 4 yrs, MFA 2 yrs, MA 1 1/2 yrs
Tuition: Res—$548 per 16 hrs; nonres—$2212 per 16 hrs; campus res—room $1040 per yr, board $1310 (7-day plan), $1210 (5-day plan)
Courses: Advertising Design, Art History, Ceramics, Drawing, Illustration, Jewelry, Painting, Printmaking, Sculpture, 2-D & 3-D Design, Life Drawing, Studio Art
Summer School: Chmn, Jimmy H Barker. Enrl 100; tuition 232 per term of 6 wks beginning June 5 & July 11. Courses—Art History, Crafts, Drawing, Watercolor, 2-D Design

HURST

TARRANT COUNTY JUNIOR COLLEGE, Art Dept, Northeast Campus, 76054. Tel 817-281-7860; *Chair* Martha Gordon, MA; *Asst Prof* Richard Hlad, MA; *Asst Prof* Arnold Leondar, MA; *Assoc Prof* Karmien Bowman, MA
Estab 1967, dept estab 1968; pub; D & E; SC 19, LC 3; enrl D 200, E 150, non-maj 150, maj 200
Ent Req: HS dipl, GED, admission by individual approval
Degrees: AA and AAS 2 yrs
Tuition: Res—$14 per hr, minimum $70 per sem; nonres—of county $8 per sem hr added to res fee, others $120 per sem hr with $200 minimum fee, aliens $120 per sem hr with $200 minimum fee; no campus res
Courses: Advertising Design, Art Appreciation, Art Education, Art History, Ceramics, Collages, Constructions, Drawing, Jewelry, Mixed Media, Painting, Photography, Printmaking, Sculpture
Adult Hobby Classes: Enrl 50; for 7 wks. Courses—Drawing, Oil-Acrylic, Tole Painting, Ceramics
Children's Classes: Enrl 100; 7 wks. Courses—Cartooning, Ceramics, College for Kids, Drawing, Painting
Summer School: Dir, Dr Jane Harper. Enrl 100; tuition as above for term of 6 wks beginning June. Courses—Art Appreciation

KILGORE

KILGORE COLLEGE, Visual Arts Dept, Fine Arts, 1100 Broadway, 75662-3299.
Tel 903-984-8531; FAX 903-983-8600; *Chmn* Frank Herbert; *Instr* John Hillier;
Instr Larry Kitchen; *Instr* O Rufus Lovett
Estab 1935; D & E; scholarships; SC 11, LC 3; enrl D 75, E 25, non-maj 25, maj 50
Ent Req: HS dipl
Degrees: AAAS & AA
Tuition: District res—$11 per sem hr; non-district res—$27 per sem hr; non-state
res—$39 per sem hr
Courses: †Art Education, †Art History, Commercial Art, †Drawing, Painting,
Photography, Printmaking, Sculpture

KINGSVILLE

TEXAS A&M UNIVERSITY-KINGSVILLE, Art Dept, 78363. Tel 512-593-2619;
Chmn Dr Richard Scherpereel
Estab 1925, dept estab 1930; pub; D & E; SC 21, LC 5, GC 2; enrl D 700, non-maj
300, maj 400, art maj 150, grad 20
Ent Req: HS dipl
Degrees: BFA & BA 4 yr
Tuition: Res $500; nonres $1400 per sem
Courses: Advertising Design, Art Education, Art History, Ceramics, Design,
Drawing, Graphic Arts, History of Art & Archaeology, Painting, Printmaking,
Sculpture, Teacher Training
Adult Hobby Classes: Courses offered
Summer School: Courses—full schedule

LAKE JACKSON

BRAZOSPORT COLLEGE, Art Dept, 500 College Dr, 77566. Tel 409-266-3000;
FAX 409-265-2944; *Fine Arts Dept Chmn* Richard Wilcher; *Asst Prof* Sandra Baker
Estab 1968; pub; D & E; scholarships; SC 10, LC 3; enrl D 50
Ent Req: HS dipl or GED
Degrees: AA 2 yrs
Tuition: In district—$60 per cr hr; out-of-district—$48 per cr hr; nonres—$233 per
3 cr hr
Courses: Art Appreciation, Art History, Ceramics, Design, Drawing, Mixed Media,
Painting, Sculpture, Theatre Arts
Adult Hobby Classes: Ceramics, China Painting, Painting, Weaving

LEVELLAND

SOUTH PLAINS COLLEGE, Fine Arts Dept, * 1401 College Ave, 79336. Tel
806-894-9611, Ext, 263; *Chmn* Jon Johnson. Instrs: FT 2, PT 1
Estab 1958; pub; D & E; SC 8, LC 5; enrl D 252, E 76, maj 52
Ent Req: HS dipl
Degrees: AA 2 yrs
Tuition: Res—$10 per sem hr; nonres—$14 per sem hr
Courses: Advertising Design, Art History, Ceramics, Commercial Art, Drafting,
Drawing, Graphic Arts, Graphic Design, Painting, Photography, Sculpture, Teacher
Training
Adult Hobby Classes: Enrl 62; tuition & duration vary. Courses—Drawing, Painting,
Photography, Sculpture
Children's Classes: Enrl 116; tuition & duration vary. Courses—Crafts, Drawing,
Painting
Summer School: Dir, Lynette Watkins. Ernl 66; tuition same as regular sem for 4
wk term. Courses—Art for Elementary Teachers, Art History, Photography

LUBBOCK

LUBBOCK CHRISTIAN UNIVERSITY, Dept of Communication & Fine Art,
5601 19th St, 79407-2099. Tel 806-796-8800; FAX 806-796-8917; *Prof* Karen
Randolph, MFA; *Assoc Prof* J Lee Roberts, MA; *Instr* Michelle Kraft, MA
Scholarships offered
Degrees: BA & BSID
Tuition: $2500 - $3000 annual tuition
Courses: Advertising Design, Art Appreciation, Art Education, Art History, Design,
Drawing, Graphic Arts, Graphic Design, Handicrafts, Painting, Printmaking,
Sculpture, Fine Arts
Summer School: Dir, K Randolph. Tuition $310 per course for 3-4 wk session.
Courses—Art, Art & Children, Art History, Desktop Publishing, 2-D Design

TEXAS TECH UNIVERSITY, Dept of Art, 79409. Tel 806-742-3825; *Chmn*
Melody Weiler, MFA; *Prof* Ken Dixon, MFA; *Prof* Frank Cheatham, MFA; *Prof*
Rick Dingus, MFA; *Prof* Verne Funk, MFA; *Prof* Hugh Gibbons, MA; *Prof* Terry
Morrow, MS; *Prof* Lynwood Kreneck, MFA; *Prof* Sara Waters, MFA; *Assoc Prof*
Bill Bagley, MFA; *Assoc Prof* Rob Glover, MFA; *Assoc Prof* Jane Cheatham, MFA;
Assoc Prof Tina Fuentes, MFA; *Assoc Prof* John Stinespring, PhD; *Asst Prof* Robin
Germany, MFA; *Asst Prof* Karen Keifer-Boyd, PhD; *Assoc Prof* Nancy Reed, PhD;
Asst Prof Juan Granados; *Assoc Prof* Brian Steele, PhD; *Assoc Prof* James Hanna,
MA; *Assoc Prof* Rick Dingus, MFA; *Asst Prof* Glen Brown, PhD; *Asst Prof* Nancy
Slagle, MFA; *Asst Prof* Carolyn Tate, PhD; *Asst Prof* Andrew Martin; *Asst Prof*
Phoebe Lloyd, PhD; *Instr* Charlotte Funk, MFA; *Asst Prof* Ed Check, PhD
Estab 1925, dept estab 1967; pub; D & E; scholarships; SC 60 undergrad, 20 grad,
LC 20 undergrad, 15 grad; enrl D 1400, non-maj 950, maj 400, grad 50
Ent Req: HS dipl, SAT or ACT test
Degrees: BFA & BA(Art History), MAE 36 hrs, MFA 60 hrs minimum, PhD 54 hrs
beyond MA minimum
Tuition: Variable for res and nonres; campus residence available
Courses: Aesthetics, Art Appreciation, †Art Education, †Art History, Ceramics,
Design, Drawing, Graphic Design, Illustration, Intermedia, Jewelry, Lettering,
Mixed Media, Painting, Photography, Printmaking, Sculpture, Silversmithing,
Teacher Training, Weaving, Computer-Aided Design, †Design Communication,

Digital Imaging, Installation, †Studio Art
Adult Hobby Classes: Computer-Aided Design, Photography, Studio Art
Children's Classes: Art Project for talented high school students, Artery; classes in
art for elementary & middle school students
Summer School: Dir, Betty Street. Courses—Art Education, Ceramics, Drawing,
Glassblowing, Jewelry & Metalsmithing, Painting, Papermaking, Photography,
Printmaking, Sculpture, Textile Design, Weaving

MARSHALL

WILEY COLLEGE, Dept of Fine Arts, 711 Wiley Ave, 75670. Tel 903-938-8341;
Head Dept Darrell Cason
Estab 1873, historically black college; den; D & E; scholarships; SC 16, LC 2; enrl D
56
Ent Req: HS dipl
Degrees: No art major
Tuition: $50 per hr, plus special fees; campus res—$500-$794 per yr
Courses: Advertising Design, Art Education, Art History, Ceramics, Commercial
Art, Drawing, Fashion Arts, Graphic Arts, Graphic Design, Painting, Theatre Arts,
Decoupage, Enameling
Summer School: Dir, Dr Joseph Capers. Tuition $1725 per sem

MESQUITE

EASTFIELD COLLEGE, Humanities Division, Art Dept, 3737 Motley Dr, 75150.
Tel 972-860-7100; *Dean* Enric Madriguera
Degrees: AA
Tuition: $36 per 3 cr hr
Courses: Art Appreciation, Art History, Ceramics, Design, Drawing, Jewelry,
Painting, Sculpture

MIDLAND

MIDLAND COLLEGE, Art Dept, 3600 N Garfield, 79705. Tel 915-685-4626;
FAX 915-685-4769; Elec Mail lgriffin@midland.cc.tx.us. *Chmn* Larry D Griffin,
PhD; *Instr* Warren Taylor, MFA; *Instr* Carol Bailey, MA; *Instr* Kent Moss, MFA
Estab 1972; pub; D & E; scholarships; SC 28, LC 4; enrl D 70, E 80, non-maj 125,
maj 25
Ent Req: HS dipl
Degrees: AA and AAA 2 yrs
Tuition: Res—undergrad $327 per 12 hrs plus $40 fee; nonres—undergrad $351 per
12 hrs plus $40 fee; no campus res
Courses: Art History, Collages, Drawing, Illustration, †Jewelry, Mixed Media,
†Painting, †Photography, †Sculpture, Teacher Training
Adult Hobby Classes: Ceramics, Painting, Photography
Children's Classes: Kid's College
Summer School: Dir, Larry D Griffin. Enrl 40. Courses—varied

NACOGDOCHES

STEPHEN F AUSTIN STATE UNIVERSITY, Art Dept, PO Box 13001, 75962.
Tel 409-568-4804; FAX 409-468-4041; *Chmn* Jon D Wink, MFA
Estab 1923; pub; D & E; scholarships; SC 28, LC 11, GC 11; enrl D 461, non-maj
150, maj 200, grad 20
Ent Req: HS dipl, ACT score 18
Degrees: BA & BFA 4 yrs, MFA 2 yrs, MA 1 yr
Tuition: Res—undergrad $360 per 15 hr, grad $288 per 12 hr; nonres—undergrad
$2430 per 15 hr, grad $1944 per 12 hr; campus res available
Courses: †Advertising Design, Art Appreciation, †Art Education, Art History,
†Ceramics, Design, †Drawing, Film, Illustration, †Interior Design, †Jewelry,
†Painting, †Photography, †Printmaking, †Sculpture, Silversmithing, Stage Design,
Teacher Training, Theatre Arts, Video, Cinematography
Summer School: Dir, Jon D Wink. Beginning & advanced art classes.
Courses—Varies summer to summer

ODESSA

UNIVERSITY OF TEXAS OF PERMIAN BASIN, Dept of Art, 4901 E
University Blvd, 79762. Tel 915-552-2286; *Chmn* Pam Price, MFA
Estab 1972; pub; D; scholarships; SC 45, LC 10; enrl non-maj 10, maj 30
Degrees: BA
Tuition: Campus residency available
Courses: Ceramics, Commercial Art, Painting, Printmaking, Sculpture
Summer School: Courses—varied

PARIS

PARIS JUNIOR COLLEGE, Art Dept, 2400 Clarksville St, 75460. Tel 913-785-
7661, Ext 460; FAX 913-784-9370; 800-441-1398 (TX), 800-232-5804 (US). *Coordr*
Cathie Tyler
Estab 1924; pub; D & E; scholarships; SC 11, LC 2; enrl D 30-60, E 50-70, non-maj
60-65, maj 15-20
Ent Req: None
Degrees: AA in Art 2 yrs
Tuition: $13-$20 per hr
Courses: Art Appreciation, Art History, Ceramics, Design, Painting, Photography,
Sculpture, Art Metals (General Art Preparatory Program), Foundation Graphic
Technologies
Adult Hobby Classes: Enrl 20. Courses—Art Appreciation, Art Metals, Ceramics,
Design, Drawing, Graphic Design, Painting, Photography
Children's Classes: 3 wk term in June. Courses—Arts, Computer, Math, Physical
Development, Science, Sports
Summer School: Dir, Cathie Tyler. 2-5 wk sessions June-Aug. Courses—Art
Appreciation, Ceramics, Painting, Photography

PLAINVIEW

WAYLAND BAPTIST UNIVERSITY, Dept of Art, Division of Communication Arts, Box 249, 79072. Tel 806-291-5050; *Assoc Prof* Candace Keller
Den; D & E; scholarships; SC 15, LC 2; enrl D 81, E 24, maj 10
Ent Req: HS dipl, ent exam
Degrees: BA and BS 4 yrs
Tuition: $98 per sem hr
Adult Hobby Classes: Enrl 90 - 100; 16 wk term. Courses—Art Appreciation, Ceramics, Design, Drawing, Painting, Sculpture, Watercolor
Children's Classes: Enrl 25-35; tuition $60 for 2 wk term. Courses offered through Llano Estacado Museum on Campus
Summer School: Art Cur, Candace Keller. Enrl 30-40; 3 wk term.
Courses—Ceramics, Crafts, Teacher Art Education, Watercolor

ROCKPORT

SIMON MICHAEL SCHOOL OF FINE ARTS, 510 E King St, PO Box 1283, 78382. Tel 512-729-6233; *Head Dept* Simon Michael. Instrs: FT 1
Estab 1947; pvt; enrl professionals & intermediates
Courses: Drawing, Landscape Architecture, Mixed Media, Painting, Sculpture
Summer School: Enrl varies; tuition varies for each 1 wk workshop. Courses—Travel Art Workshop in USA and Europe

SAN ANGELO

ANGELO STATE UNIVERSITY, Art & Music Dept, ASU Sta, PO Box 10906, 76909. Tel 915-942-2085, 942-2223; *Coordr* Dr Robert Prestiano; *Chmn Art & Music* Koste Belcheff
Estab 1963, dept estab 1976; pub; D & E; SC 15, LC 9; enrl D 400 (art), E 50, non-maj 320, maj 80
Ent Req: HS dipl
Degrees: BA(Art) & BA(Art) & Teaching Certification
Tuition: Res—$420 15 cr hr; nonres—$2565 15 cr hr; campus res—room & board $1027-$1866
Courses: Art Education, Art History, Ceramics, Drawing, Jewelry, Painting, †Printmaking, †Sculpture, Creative Design, Etchings, †Graphic Illustration, Greek & Roman Art, History of Contemporary Art, History of Italian Renaissance, Intaglio Processes, Introduction to Art, Primary Art Theory
Summer School: Tuition as above for term of 10 wks beginning June 1.
Courses—Art Education, Art History, Ceramics, Introduction to Art, Sculpture, Studio Courses incl Design & Drawing

SAN ANTONIO

INCARNATE WORD UNIVERSITY OF THE ARTS & SCIENCES, Art Dept, 4301 Broadway, 78209. Tel 210-829-6022; *Prof* William A Reily, MFA; *Prof* E Stoker, MA; *Prof* Sr Martha Ann Kirk, PhD; *Asst Prof* Taylor Mitchell, PhD; *Lectr* Nancy Pawel, MA; *Lectr* Don Ewers, MA
Estab 1881, dept estab 1948; den; D; scholarships; SC 14, LC 9; enrl D 195, non-maj 120, maj 30
Ent Req: HS dipl, ent exam
Degrees: BA 4 yrs
Courses: †Art Education, Art History, Ceramics, Design, History of Art & Archaeology, Museum Staff Training, Painting, Photography, Sculpture, Stage Design, Weaving

OUR LADY OF THE LAKE UNIVERSITY, Dept of Art, 411 SW 24 St, 78207-4689. Tel 210-434-6711; *Dean* Sr Isabel Ball, PhD; *Asst Prof* Jody Cariolano, MFA; *Asst Prof* Sr Jule Adele Espey, PhD. Instrs: FT 2, PT 1
Estab 1911, dept estab 1920; den; D & E; scholarships; SC 12, LC 3; enrl non-maj 62, maj 8
Ent Req: HS dipl, completion of GED tests, 35 on each test or average of 45 on tests
Degrees: BA(Art)
Tuition: Res—undergrad $2996 per sem; res—grad $201 per sem hr; campus res—room & board $1430-$1675 per yr
Courses: Art Appreciation, Art Education, Art History, Ceramics, Design, Drawing, Graphic Arts, Painting, Photography, Printmaking, Sculpture, Computer Design
Adult Hobby Classes: Courses offered

SAINT MARY'S UNIVERSITY, Dept of Fine Arts, One Camino Santa Maria, 78228. Tel 210-436-3797, 436-3011; *Chmn* Sharon McMahon. Instrs: FT 6, PT 8
Estab 1852; pvt; D & E; SC 10, LC 20; enrl D 60, maj 58
Ent Req: HS dipl or GED, ent exam
Degrees: BA 4-5 yrs
Tuition: $4339 per 12 cr hr, $284 per cr hr; campus res—room & board $1572-$2538 per sem
Courses: Art Education, Drawing, Graphic Design, History of Art & Archaeology, Painting, Photography, Printmaking, Sculpture, Teacher Training, Theatre Arts, 3-D Design
Adult Hobby Classes: Enrl 75-100; tuition $25. Courses—vary
Summer School: Courses—vary

SAN ANTONIO COLLEGE, Visual Arts & Technology, 1300 San Pedro Ave, 78212. Tel 210-733-2894, 733-2000; FAX 210-733-2338; *Prof* Thomas Willome. Instrs: FT 17, PT 20
Estab 1955; pub; D & E; SC 75, LC 4; enrl D 1000-1300, E 250-450
Ent Req: Ent req HS dipl, GED, TASP, ent exam
Degrees: AA & AS 2 yrs
Tuition: $298 per 12 sem hrs; no campus res
Courses: Advertising Design, Architecture, Art Appreciation, Art History, Ceramics, Design, Drafting, Drawing, Film, Goldsmithing, Graphic Arts, Graphic Design,

History of Art & Archaeology, Illustration, Intermedia, Interior Design, Jewelry, Landscape Architecture, Painting, Photography, Printmaking, Sculpture, Silversmithing, Stage Design, Theatre Arts, Video, Electronic Graphics, Jewelry Repair & Design, Production Pottery
Summer School: Dir, Thomas Willome. Enrl 400; tuition $150 per 6 sem hrs.
Courses—Same as for regular school yr

TRINITY UNIVERSITY, Dept of Art, 715 Stadium Dr, 78212-7200. Tel 210-736-7216, 736-7011; *Prof* Robert E Tiemann, MFA; *Prof* Kate Ritson, MFA; *Prof* William A Bristow, MFA
Estab 1869; pvt; D & E; SC 39, LC 20; enrl D 144, E 30, non-maj 50, maj 90
Ent Req: HS dipl, CEEB, SAT, 3 achievement tests
Degrees: BA 4 yrs
Tuition: $510 per sem hr; campus res available
Courses: Art Education, Drawing, Graphic Arts, Painting, Photography, Printmaking, Sculpture, †Studio Art
Adult Hobby Classes: Courses offered by Department of Continuing Educ
Summer School: Dir, Dept of Continuing Educ. Tuition $114 per hr. Courses vary

UNIVERSITY OF TEXAS AT SAN ANTONIO, Division of Visual Arts, 6900 N Loop 1604 W, 78249-0642. Tel 210-458-4352; FAX 210-458-4356; *Div Dir* James Broderick, MA; *Prof* Ronald Binks, MFA; *Prof* Charles Field, MFA; *Prof* Jacinto Quirarte, PhD; *Prof* Stephen Reynolds, MFA; *Prof* Judith Sobre, PhD; *Prof* Ken Little; *Assoc Prof* Kent Rush, MFA; *Assoc Prof* Dennis Olsen, MA; *Assoc Prof* Neil Maurer, MFA; *Assoc Prof* Frances Colpitt; *Asst Prof* Constance Lowe, MFA
Pub; D & E; scholarships; SC 31, LC 25, GC 17; enrl maj 200, grad 35
Ent Req: HS dipl, ACT, grad
Degrees: BFA 4 yrs, MFA 2 yrs
Tuition: $384 per sem (12 hrs or under)
Courses: Art History, †Ceramics, †Drawing, †Painting, †Photography, †Printmaking, †Sculpture
Summer School: Tuition $90 per sem. Courses—Art History, Ceramics, Drawing, Painting, Photography, Printmaking, Sculpture

SAN MARCOS

SOUTHWEST TEXAS STATE UNIVERSITY, Dept of Art, 601 University Dr, 78666. Tel 512-245-2611; *Dean* Richard Cheatham; *Chmn* Brian G Row, MFA; *Gallery Dir* Roger Colombik; *Prof* Mark Todd; *Prof* Jean Laman, MFA; *Prof* Marshall Wortham, MFA; *Prof* William Kolbe, MFA; *Prof* Erik Nielsen, PhD; *Prof* Eric Weller, MFA; *Prof* Neal Wilson, MFA; *Prof* Michel Conroy, MFA; *Assoc Prof* Carole Greer, MFA; *Assoc Prof* Diane Gregory, PhD; *Assoc Prof* Tom Williams, PhD; *Assoc Prof* Francine Carraro, PhD; *Assoc Prof* Roger Colombik, MFA; *Asst Prof* Beverly Penn, MFA; *Assoc Prof* Randall Reid, MFA; *Asst Prof* William Meek, MFA; *Asst Prof* Sandra McCollister, PhD; *Asst Prof* David Shields, MFA; *Instr* Chris Hill, BS; *Instr* Roger Christian; *Instr* Dana Holland; *Instr* Melissa Grimes; *Instr* Lewis Marquardtz; *Instr* Mary Mikel-Reid; *Instr* Pat Marince; *Instr* Robert Cordes, BA; *Instr* Marc English, BFA; *Instr* Joan Fabian, MFA; *Instr* Veronica Fernandez, MFA; *Instr* Thomas Fitzpatrick, MFA; *Instr* Jennifer Odem, MFA; *Instr* Alan Pizer, MA; *Instr* Caprice Taniguchi; *Lectr* Pat Taylor; *Lectr* Brad Lawton
Estab 1903, dept estab 1916; pub; D & E; scholarships; SC 31, LC 7, GC 6; enrl D 1600, E 150, non-maj 1350, maj 525
Ent Req: HS dipl, ACT, SAT
Degrees: BFA(Communication Design & Studio), BFA Art Ed all-level & secondary, BA secondary, BA 4 yr
Courses: Advertising Design, Art Appreciation, Art Education, Art History, Commercial Art, Design, Drawing, Graphic Arts, Graphic Design, Illustration, Photography, Painting, Printmaking, Teacher Training, Communication Design, Computer Graphics, Multi-Media
Summer School: Chmn, Brian Row. Two 6 week terms

SEGUIN

TEXAS LUTHERAN COLLEGE, Dept of Visual Arts, 1000 W Court St, 78155. Tel 210-372-8000, Ext 6017; *Chmn* T Paul Hernandez. Instrs: FT 2
Estab 1923; D; SC 18, LC 3; enrl 1000, maj 10
Ent Req: HS dipl
Degrees: BA(Art) 4 yrs
Tuition: $11,310 incl tuition room & board
Courses: Advertising Design, Art Appreciation, Art Education, Art History, Ceramics, Design, Drawing, Painting, Printmaking, Sculpture
Adult Hobby Classes: Enrl 12; tuition $72 for 6 wk term. Courses—Art Appreciation, Sketching
Summer School: Instr, John Nellermoe. Enrl 12; tuition $75 for 6 wk term.
Courses—Ceramics, Painting

SHERMAN

AUSTIN COLLEGE, Art Dept, 900 N Grande, Ste 61587, 75090-4440. Tel 903-813-2000; *Chmn* Tim Tracz; *Prof* Mark Smith; *Prof* Mark Monroe
Estab 1848; pvt; D; scholarships; SC 9, LC 5, GC 8; enrl D 350, maj 55, grad 2
Ent Req: Ent exam plus acceptance by admission committee
Degrees: BA 4 yrs, MA 5 yrs
Tuition: $7250 per yr, campus res—room & board $2260
Courses: Art History, Ceramics, Drawing, Photography, Printmaking, Sculpture

TEMPLE

TEMPLE COLLEGE, Art Dept, 2600 S First St, 76504. Tel 817-773-9961; *Chmn* Michael Donahue, MFA
Estab 1926; pub; D & E; scholarships; SC 4, LC 2; enrl D 100, E 15, non-maj 85, maj 15
Ent Req: HS dipl, ACT or SAT
Degrees: AA 2 yrs

Tuition: District res—$44 per sem hr; non-district res—$55 per sem hr; non-state res—$230 per sem hr; campus res available
Courses: Art Appreciation, Art History, Ceramics, Design, Drawing, Painting, Printmaking, Sculpture, Figure Drawing
Adult Hobby Classes: Enrl 15 per class; tuition $19 per 8 sessions. Courses—Arts & Crafts, Calligraphy, Drawing

TEXARKANA

TEXARKANA COLLEGE, Art Dept, 2500 N Robison Rd, 75599. Tel 903-838-4541; *Chmn* Dr Rolfe Wylie; *Prof* Mary Long
Estab 1927; D & E; scholarships
Ent Req: HS dipl
Tuition: District res—$280 for 15 cr hrs; out of district res—$300 for 15 cr hrs
Courses: Art Appreciation, Ceramics, Drawing, Painting, Sculpture, Weaving
Summer School: Dir, Rolfe Wylie. Enrl 20; tuition $200. Courses—Drawing & Ceramics

TYLER

TYLER JUNIOR COLLEGE, Art Program, PO Box 9020, 75711. Tel 903-510-2200, 510-2234; *Dept Dir* Chris Stewart
Scholarships
Degrees: AA
Tuition: Res—undergrad $578 per yr
Courses: Art Appreciation, Art Education, Art History, Ceramics, Design, Weaving, Drawing, Painting, Sculpture, Weaving
Adult Hobby Classes: Courses—Offered
Children's Classes: Courses—Offered for ages 5-8 & 9-12
Summer School: Courses—Offered

UNIVERSITY OF TEXAS AT TYLER, Dept of Art, * 3900 University Blvd, 75799. Tel 903-566-7250; *Chmn* James R Pace; *Prof* William B Stephens, EdD; *Assoc Prof* Gary Hatcher; *Asst Prof* Karen Roberson, MFA; *Instr* Rosalie Coggin, MA
Estab 1973; pub; D & E; scholarships; SC 28, LC 6, GC 11
Ent Req: AA degree or 60 hrs of college study
Degrees: BA and BFA
Tuition: Res—$173 per sem; nonres—$323 per sem
Courses: Aesthetics, †Art Education, †Art History, Ceramics, Drawing, Graphic Arts, Graphic Design, History of Art & Archaeology, Interior Design, Mixed Media, Painting, Photography, Printmaking, Sculpture, Teacher Training, †Studio Art
Summer School: Dir, Donald Van Horn. Tuition res $76, nonres $151. Courses—vary

VICTORIA

VICTORIA COLLEGE, Fine Arts Dept, 2200 E Red River, 77901. Tel 512-573-3291; FAX 512-572-3850; *Head Dept* Dr Marylynn Fletcher; *Prof* Nancy Bandy
Estab 1925; pub; D & E; SC 9, LC 3; enrl D 100, E 40, non-maj 40, maj 100
Ent Req: HS dipl
Tuition: Res—$100 per sem; nonres—$200 per sem; no campus res
Courses: Art Education, Art History, Commercial Art, Display, Drafting, Drawing, Graphic Design, Painting, Printmaking, Sculpture, Teacher Training, Art Fundamentals, Pottery
Summer School: Courses—as above

WACO

BAYLOR UNIVERSITY, Dept of Art, 76798-7263. Tel 817-755-1867; FAX 817-755-1765; *Chmn* John D McClanahan; *Prof* Karl Umlauf, MFA; *Prof* William M Jensen, PhD; *Prof* Berry J Klingman, MFA; *Assoc Prof* Terry M Roller, MFA; *Assoc Prof* Janice McCullagh, PhD; *Assoc Prof* Paul A McCoy, MFA; *Asst Prof* Heidi J Hornik, PhD; *Asst Prof* Michael Johnson; *Asst Prof* Mark W Moran, MFA; *Asst Prof* Mary Ruth Smith, PhD
Estab 1845, dept estab 1870; den; D & E; scholarships; SC 65, LC 24, GC 12; enrl D 1600, E60, non-maj 1300, maj 150
Ent Req: HS dipl, ent exam, SAT/ACT tests
Degrees: BA, BFA(Art Educ) & BFA(Studio) 4 yrs
Courses: †Art Education, †Art History, †Ceramics, Drawing, †Graphic Design, †Jewelry, †Painting, Photography, †Sculpture, Fibers, Metalsmithing, 2-D Design, 3-D Design
Summer School: Prof, John McClanahan

MCLENNAN COMMUNITY COLLEGE, Fine Arts Dept, 1400 College Dr, 76708. Tel 817-299-8000; *Chmn* Dr Don Balmos
Estab 1965; pub; D & E; SC 8, LC 3; enrl D 35, non-maj 20, maj 40
Ent Req: HS dipl
Degrees: AA 2 yrs
Tuition: Res—$17 per sem hr; nonres—$22 per sem hr; no campus res
Courses: Art History, Drawing, Painting, Photography, Sculpture, Art Appreciation, Color, Design, Problems in Contemporary Art
Adult Hobby Classes: Tuition depends on the class. Courses—Ceramics, Drawing, Jewelry, Painting, Sculpture, Stained Glass
Summer School: Tuition $42. Courses—Design, Drawing, Watercolor

WEATHERFORD

WEATHERFORD COLLEGE, Dept of Speech/Fine Arts, 308 E Park Ave, 76086. Tel 817-594-5471; *Head Dept of Art* Myrlan Coleman, MA & MFA
Estab 1856, dept estab 1959; pub; D & E; SC 10, LC 4; enrl D 58, non-maj 30, maj 16, others 12
Ent Req: HS dipl
Degrees: AA
Courses: Art History, Intermedia, Mixed Media, Painting
Summer School: Term May 24 & July 10

WHARTON

WHARTON COUNTY JUNIOR COLLEGE, Art Dept, * 911 Boling Hwy, 77488. Tel 409-532-4560, Ext 285; *Chmn* Morna Nation, MFA
Pub; D & E; SC 8, LC 2; enrl D 90, E 15
Ent Req: HS dipl, GED
Degrees: 2 yrs
Tuition: District res—$24 per sem hr; non-district—$43 per sem hr; non-state res—$69 per sem hr
Courses: Art Education, Art History, Ceramics, Drawing, History of Art & Archaeology, Painting, Sculpture, Teacher Training
Summer School: Dir Morna Nation. Enrl 10; 6 wk term. Courses—Ceramics

WICHITA FALLS

MIDWESTERN STATE UNIVERSITY, Div of Fine Arts, 3410 Taft Blvd, 76308. Tel 817-689-4264, Ext 4264; FAX 817-689-4511; *Art Coordr* Richard Ash
Estab 1926; pub; D & E; scholarships; SC 20-30, LC 406; enrl D 300 per sem, E 30-50 per sem, non-maj 60, maj 125, others 10
Ent Req: HS dipl, ACT, SAT
Degrees: BA, BFA and BSE 4 yrs
Tuition: In-state $131.50 per cr hr
Courses: †Advertising Design, Art Appreciation, Art Education, Art History, †Ceramics, †Commercial Art, Design, Drawing, †Graphic Design, †Jewelry, †Painting, †Photography, †Printmaking, †Sculpture, †Silversmithing, †Teacher Training
Summer School: Dir, Richard Ash. Enrl 15. Courses—Ceramics, Drama, Metalsmithing, Photography

UTAH

CEDAR CITY

SOUTHERN UTAH STATE UNIVERSITY, Dept of Art, 351 W Center, 84720. Tel 801-586-7962, 586-7700; *Chmn* Mark Talbert. Instrs: FT 4, PT 2
Estab 1897; pub; D & E; scholarships; SC 29, LC 6; enrl D 300, E 80, maj 60, minors 45
Ent Req: HS dipl ent exam
Degrees: BA and BS 4 yrs
Tuition: Res—$566 per qtr; nonres—$1876 per qtr
Courses: Ceramics, Commercial Art, Drawing, Graphic Arts, Graphic Design, History of Art & Archaeology, Illustration, Painting, Sculpture, Teacher Training
Summer School: Dir, Arlene Braithwaite. Tuition same as regular school. Courses—Drawing, Ceramics, Art Methods for Elementary School, Art Appreciation

EPHRAIM

SNOW COLLEGE, Art Dept, 150 E College Ave, 84627. Tel 801-283-4021, Ext 356; *Chmn* Osral Allred
Scholarships
Degrees: AA, AAS
Tuition: Res—$720 per yr; nonres— $1500 per yr
Courses: Art Appreciation, Ceramics, Design, Drawing, Interior Design, Jewelry, Painting, Photography, Printmaking, Sculpture

LOGAN

UTAH STATE UNIVERSITY
—Dept of Landscape Architecture Environmental Planning, 84322-4005. Tel 801-797-0500; *Head* Richard E Toth. Instrs: FT 6, PT 3
Degrees: BA, BLA & MLA 4 yr
Tuition: Res—$576 per qtr; nonres—$1706 per qtr
Courses: †Landscape Architecture, †Town & Regional Planning
—Dept of Art, UMC 4000, 84322. Tel 801-797-3460 3; FAX 801-797-3421; *Head* Craig J Law; *Prof* Glen Edwards; *Prof* Jon Anderson; *Prof* Adrian Van Suchtelen; *Assoc Prof* Christopher Terry; *Assoc Prof* Craig Law; *Assoc Prof* Susanne Warma; *Assoc Prof* John Neely; *Asst Prof* Thomas Toone; *Asst Prof* Alan Hashimoto; *Asst Prof* Sara Northerner; *Asst Prof* Greg Schulte; *Asst Prof* Janet Shapero
Estab 1890; D & E; scholarships; enrl D 300, maj 300, grad 35
Ent Req: HS dipl, HS transcript, ACT
Degrees: BA, BS & BSA 4 yr, MA 2 yr, MSA 3 yr
Tuition: Res—undergrad $573, grad $339; nonres—undergrad $1706, grad $1051
Courses: †Advertising Design, †Art Education, †Art History, †Ceramics, †Drawing, †Graphic Arts, †Illustration, †Painting, †Photography, †Printmaking, †Sculpture
Summer School: Head, Prof Marion R Hyde. 4 wk session. Courses—Ceramics, Ceramic Handbuilding, Ceramic Wheelthrow, Individual Projects, Photography

OGDEN

WEBER STATE UNIVERSITY, Dept of Visual Arts, 2001 University Circle, 84408-2001. Tel 801-626-6762; *Chmn* James C Jacobs; *Prof* Arthur R Adelmann, MFA; *Prof* Dale W Bryner, MFA; *Prof* David N Cox, MFA; *Prof* Richard J VanWagoner, MFA; *Prof* Mark Biddle, MFA; *Prof* Susan Makov, MFA; *Assoc Prof* Angelika Pagel, PhD; *Assoc Prof* Drex Brooks, MFA; *Asst Prof* Miguel Almanza, EdD; *Asst Prof* Naseem Banerji, PhD
Estab 1933, dept estab 1937; pub; D & E; scholarships; SC 66, LC 17; enrl D 2464, E 694, non-maj 700, maj 200
Ent Req: HS dipl, ACT

Degrees: BA, BS 4 yr
Tuition: Res—$1542 per yr; nonres— $4332 per yr; campus res available
Courses: Advertising Design, Art Appreciation, Art Education, Art History, Calligraphy, Ceramics, Commercial Art, Conceptual Art, Design, Drawing, Graphic Arts, Graphic Design, History of Art & Archaeology, Illustration, Jewelry, Lettering, Painting, Photography, Printmaking, Sculpture, Silversmithing, Textile Design, Weaving, Textile Design, †2-D, †3-D
Summer School: Dir, James R McBeth. Tuition $581 for term of 8 wks beginning June 19

PROVO

BRIGHAM YOUNG UNIVERSITY, Dept of Visual Arts, C-502 HFAC, 84602. Tel 801-378-4266; *Chmn* Michael Day. Instrs: FT 19, PT 5
Estab 1875, dept estab 1893; den; D & E; scholarships; SC 50; enrl E 1975, maj 352, grad 30
Ent Req: HS dipl or ACT
Degrees: BA and BFA 4 yrs, MFA 2 yrs and MA 1 1/2 yrs
Tuition: Undergrad $3550 per yr, $1775 per sem, PT $180 per cr hr; grad $2220 per yr, $1110 per sem, PT $123 per cr hr; non-church member—undergrad $2320 per yr, $1160 per sem, PT $120 per cr hr, grad $2700 per yr, $1350 per sem, PT $150 per cr hr; campus res—room & board $2420
Courses: †Art Education, †Art History, †Ceramics, †Drawing, †Painting, †Printmaking, †Sculpture, Teacher Training
Summer School: Courses same as regular session

SAINT GEORGE

DIXIE COLLEGE, Art Dept, 225 South & 700 East, 84770. Tel 801-652-7500, 652-7761; *Dean Div Fine & Performing Arts* C Paul Anderson; *Head Art Dept* Max Bunnell; *Prof* Glen Blakely; *Asst Prof* Del Parson
Estab 1911; pub; D & E; scholarships; SC 24, LC 7, GC 1; enrl D 400, maj 30
Ent Req: HS dipl, ACT
Degrees: AA and AS 2 yrs
Tuition: Res—$443.88 per qtr; nonres—$1593.48 per qtr
Courses: Advertising Design, Art Education, Art History, Ceramics, Commercial Art, Costume Design & Construction, Drafting, Drawing, Film, Illustration, Interior Design, Painting, Photography, Printmaking, Sculpture, Teacher Training, Textile Design, Theatre Arts, Video, Weaving, Life Drawing, Portrait Drawing, 3-D Design
Adult Hobby Classes: Enrl 14-16; tuition res —$355.43, nonres—$956.98; 10 wk term. Courses offered—Art Educ, Ceramics, Design, Drawing, Painting, Photography, Weaving
Children's Classes: Enrl 10-12; tuition res $103.96, nonres $257.87; 10 wk session
Summer School: Dir, Prof Glen Blakely. Enrl 100; tuition res $160.43, nonres $414.09; 8 wk session. Courses—Ceramics, Design, Drawing

SALT LAKE CITY

SALT LAKE COMMUNITY COLLEGE, Graphic Design Dept, * 4600 S Redwood Rd, PO Box 30808, 84130. Tel 801-957-4636; *Chmn* Don Merrill; *Dean* Elwood Zaugg; *Prof* Allen Reinhold, MA; *Prof* Grant Hulet, MA; *Asst Prof* Douglas Jordan, BA; *Asst Prof* Fred Van Dyke, BA; *Instr* Lana Hall; *Instr* Richard Graham; *Instr* Terry Martin. Instrs: FT 3, PT 3
Pub, D & E, scholarships, SC 44, LC 7, enrl D 123, E 10, non-maj 81, maj 42
Ent Req: HS dipl or equivalent, aptitude test
Degrees: Cert, Dipl, AAS(Design), AAS(Computer Graphics), AAS(Illustration)
Tuition: Res—$75 per cr hr, $380 per 12 cr hr; nonres—$194 per cr hr, $1040 per 12 cr hr;
Courses: Advertising Design, Drawing, Illustration, Photography, †Graphic Design, †Illustration, †Lettering, Photography, Art Principles, Computer Graphics
Summer School: Dean, James Schnirel. Enrl 30; tuition $145 for term of 10 wks beginning June. Courses—Aesthetics, Drawing, Lettering, Media & Techniques

UNIVERSITY OF UTAH, Art Dept, 200 S University St, 84112. Tel 801-581-7200; *Chmn* Nathan Winters, PhD; *Dean* Robert S Olpin, PhD; *Prof* Dorothy Bearnson, MA; *Prof* Paul H Davis MFA; *Prof* Frank Anthony Smith, MFA; *Prof* Lennox Tierney; *Prof* McRay Magleby, BA; *Prof* Robert W Kleinschmidt, MFA; *Assoc Prof* Sheila Muller, MA; *Assoc Prof* Brian Patrick, MFA; *Assoc Prof* David Pendell, MFA; *Assoc Prof* Raymond Morales, BA; *Asst Prof* Mary F Francey, PhD; *Asst Prof* Roger D (Sam) Wilson, MFA
Estab 1850, dept estab 1888; pub; D & E; scholarships; SC 79, LC 57, GC 27; enrl D 3624, E 465, non-maj 1347, maj 350, grad 10
Ent Req: HS dipl
Degrees: BA and BFA 4 yrs, MA and MFA 2 yrs
Tuition: Res—$831.90 for 16 hrs per qtr, $1023.90 for 21 hrs per qtr; nonres—$2555.90 for 16 hrs per qtr, $3195.40 for 21 hrs per qtr; campus res available
Courses: Art Education, †Art History, †Ceramics, †Film, †Graphic Design, †Illustration, †Painting, †Photography, †Printmaking, †Sculpture, Teacher Training

WESTMINSTER COLLEGE OF SALT LAKE CITY, Dept of Arts, 1840 S 13th East, 84105. Tel 801-484-7651, Ext 215; *Chmn Fine Arts Program* Catherine Kuzminski. Instrs: FT 1, PT 5
Estab 1875; pvt; D; scholarships; SC 25, LC 2; enrl D 900-1000, maj 25
Ent Req: HS dipl, ent exam acceptable, HS grade point average
Degrees: BA & BS 4 yrs
Tuition: $4410 12-16 cr hrs, $294 per cr hr after 16
Courses: Art Education, Art History, Ceramics, Drawing, Painting, Photography, Sculpture, Teacher Training, Weaving

VERMONT

BENNINGTON

BENNINGTON COLLEGE, Visual Arts Division, 05201. Tel 802-442-5401; FAX 802-442-5401, Ext 329; *Pres* Elizabeth Coleman. Instrs: FT E 70
Estab 1932; pvt; scholarships
Degrees: AB 4 yrs & MA 2 yrs
Tuition: $25,850 per yr; campus res
Courses: Architecture, Art History, Ceramics, Drawing, Painting, Photography, Printmaking, Sculpture, Animation Lithography, CAD, Cultural Studies, 3-D Modeling, Etching Studio, Graphics, Visual Arts

BURLINGTON

UNIVERSITY OF VERMONT, Dept of Art, 304 Williams Hall, 05405. Tel 802-656-2014; FAX 802-656-8429; *Chmn* Ted Lyman. Instrs: 24
Pub; D & E; enrl D 25
Degrees: BA 4 yrs
Tuition: Res—$176 per cr hr; nonres—$536 per cr hr
Courses: Art Education, Art History, Ceramics, Design, Drawing, Painting, Photography, Printmaking, Sculpture, Teacher Training, Video, Clay Silkscreen, Computer Art, Design, Fine Metals, Lithography, Visual Art
Adult Hobby Classes: College of Continuing Education
Summer School: Dir, Lynne Ballard. Two 9 wk sessions beginning in May

CASTLETON

CASTLETON STATE COLLEGE, Art Dept, 05735. Tel 802-468-5611; *Head Dept* Jonathon Scott; *Prof* William Ramage; *Assoc Prof* Rita Bernatowitz; *Coordr* Mariko Hancock
Estab 1787; Pub; D & E; scholarships; SC 31, LC 3, GC varies; enrl D 1900, E 1000, non-maj 300, maj 52, grad 5
Ent Req: HS dipl, ACT, SAT, CEEB
Degrees: BA(Art) & BA Art(2nd major Education) 4 yrs
Tuition: Res—undergrad & grad $3432 per yr, $1716 per sem, $97 per cr; nonres—undergrad & grad $7944 per yr, $3972 per sem, $224 per cr; campus res—room & board $2902
Courses: Advertising Design, Art History, Calligraphy, Drawing, Graphic Design, Lettering, Painting, Photography, Printmaking, Sculpture, Video, Computer Graphics, Education, Professional Studio Arts, Typography
Summer School: Enrl 24. Courses—Introduction to Art History, Introduction to Studio Art

COLCHESTER

ST MICHAEL'S COLLEGE, Fine Arts Dept, Winooski Park, 05439. Tel 802-654-2000; *Chmn* Donald A Rathgeb, MFA; *Assoc Prof* Lance Richbourg, MFA; *Asst Prof* Gregg Blasdel; *Asst Prof* Amy Werbel, MFA
Estab 1903, dept estab 1965; den; D & E; SC 8, LC 3
Ent Req: HS dipl
Degrees: BA 4 yrs
Tuition: Res—undergrad $11,800 per yr, campus res—available
Courses: Art Education, Art History, Calligraphy, Costume Design & Construction, Drawing, Graphic Arts, History of Art & Archaeology, Painting, Photography, Printmaking, Sculpture, Stage Design, Teacher Training, Theatre Arts, Art Theory
Summer School: Dir, Dr Art Hessler. Session 1, 5 wks beginning mid May, session 2, 6 wks beginning last wk in June. Courses—Calligraphy, Drawing, Painting

JOHNSON

JOHNSON STATE COLLEGE, Dept Fine & Performing Arts, Dibden Center for the Arts, 05656. Tel 802-635-2356; FAX 802-635-1248; *Chmn* Russ Longtin; *Gallery Dir* Roger Dell; *Photography Dept Head* Peter Moriarty; *Assoc Prof* Lisa Jablow; *Sculpture Instr* Susan Calza; *Painting Instr* Ken Lesley
Estab 1828; pub; D & E; SC 30, LC 6; enrl D 325, non-maj 200, maj 140
Ent Req: HS dipl
Degrees: BA & BFA 4 yrs
Tuition: Res—undergrad $1656 12-18 cr; nonres—undergrad $3828 12-18 cr; campus res—room & board $4690 per yr
Courses: Art Education, Art History, Ceramics, Design, Drawing, Painting, Photography, Printmaking, Sculpture, Studio Art
Children's Classes: Gifted & talented prog for high school students
Summer School: Enrl 40; tuition res—$75 per cr hr, nonres—$105 per cr hr for term of 6 wks beginning June. Courses—Mixed Media, Painting, Sculpture

MIDDLEBURY

MIDDLEBURY COLLEGE, Dept of Art, Johnson Memorial Bldg, 05753. Tel 802-443-5000; *Chmn* Kristen Powell; *Chmn* John Huddleston. Instrs: FT 9, PT 2
Estab 1800; pvt; D; SC 7, LC 30; enrl maj 77, others 500 per term
Ent Req: Exam and cert
Degrees: BA
Courses: Art History, Design, Drawing, Painting, Photography, Printmaking, Sculpture

NORTHFIELD

NORWICH UNIVERSITY, Dept of Philosophy, Religion & Fine Arts, S Main St, 05663. Tel 802-485-2000; FAX 802-485-2580; *Prof* Earl Fechter, MFA; *Assoc Prof* Dean Perkins, PhD; *Assoc Prof* Robert McKay, PhD; *Assoc Prof* James Bennett; *Assoc Prof* Sandra Vitzhum; *Assoc Prof* Robert Schmidt; *Assoc Prof* David Woolf; *Assoc Prof* Arnold Aho; *Assoc Prof* Elizabeth Church; *Assoc Prof* Mike Huffman; *Asst Prof* Benjamin Pfingstag
Pvt; D & E; enrl D 65 (studio art), E 8, non-maj 126
Ent Req: HS dipl
Degrees: AA
Tuition: Campus residency available
Courses: Architecture, Art Education, Art History, Drawing, Painting, Photography, Printmaking, Design
Adult Hobby Classes: Chmn, Harold Krauth, PhD

PLAINFIELD

GODDARD COLLEGE, Dept of Art, 05667. Tel 802-454-8311; *Instr* Jon Batdorff; *Instr* Cynthia Ross; *Instr* David Hale
Estab 1938; pvt; D & E
Degrees: BA 4 yr, MA 1-2 yr
Tuition: Res—undergrad $8750 (comprehensive) per sem, $6500 (tuition only) per sem; nonres—undergrad $3350 per sem, grad $3840 per sem; campus res available
Courses: Art Education, Art History, Ceramics, Drawing, Painting, Photography, Printmaking, Sculpture, Video, Weaving, Holography

POULTNEY

GREEN MOUNTAIN COLLEGE, Dept of Art, 05764. Tel 802-287-9313, Ext 251; FAX 802-287-9313, Ext 340; *Chmn* Susan Smith-Hunter; *Prof* Dick Weis; *Assoc Prof* Richard Weinstein
Estab 1834; enrl maj 60
Ent Req: Scholarships
Degrees: BFA 4 yrs
Tuition: Res—$13,120 per yr; nonres—$10,250 per yr
Courses: Art History, Ceramics, Design, Drawing, Graphic Design, Illustration, Painting, Photography, Printmaking, Sculpture, Graphic Design Studio, Fine Art Studio

VIRGINIA

ANNANDALE

NORTHERN VIRGINIA COMMUNITY COLLEGE, Art Dept, 8333 Little River Turnpike, 22003. Tel 703-323-3107; *Chmn* Dr Gladys Watkins
Pub; D & E; scholarships; enrl D 589, E 200
Ent Req: Open admis
Degrees: Degrees AA(Art Educ), AA(Art History) AAS(Commercial Art), AA(Fine Arts) & AA(Photography) 2 yrs
Tuition: Res—undergrad $33 per cr hr; nonres—undergrad $145 per cr hr; no campus res
Courses: Art History, Ceramics, Painting, Sculpture, Computer Graphics, †Fine Arts, Perpestive Drawing
Summer School: Chmn Humanities Div, Dr Jonathan Yoder. Tuition same as regular session; 2 five wk D sessions and 1 ten wk E session during Summer. Courses—varied, incl study abroad

ARLINGTON

MARYMOUNT UNIVERSITY OF VIRGINIA, School of Arts & Sciences Division, 2807 N Glebe Rd, 22207. Tel 703-522-5600; FAX 703-284-3859; *Dean* Robert Draghi, PhD; *Prof* Pamela Stoessell, MFA
Estab 1950; pvt; D & E; SC 14, LC 20
Ent Req: HS dipl, SAT results, letter of recommendation
Degrees: BA 4 yrs, AA 2 yrs
Tuition: Res—undergrad $6200 per sem, grad $430 per cr hr; campus res available
Courses: Advertising Design, Art History, Ceramics, Design, Drafting, Drawing, Fashion Arts, Graphic Design, Handicrafts, †Industrial Design, Painting, Sculpture, Textile Design, Clothing Design & Construction, †Studio Arts
Adult Hobby Classes: Courses—any course in fine arts
Summer School: Dir, Alice S Mandanis. Tuition $1600 per summer sem, for term of 5 wks beginning May

ASHLAND

RANDOLPH-MACON COLLEGE, Dept of the Arts, 23005-1698. Tel 804-798-8375, 798-8372; FAX 804-752-7231; *Chmn* E Raymond Berry; *Prof* R D Ward; *Assoc Prof* Joe Mattys; *Lectr* Evie Terrono
Estab 1830, dept estab 1953; pvt; D; SC 4, LC 4; enrl D 200, non-maj 200
Degrees: BA & BS 4 yrs
Tuition: Res—undergrad $9905 per yr; campus res available
Courses: †Art History, Drawing, Painting, †Art Management, †Drama, †Music, †Studio Art

BLACKSBURG

VIRGINIA POLYTECHNIC INSTITUTE & STATE UNIVERSITY, Dept of Art & Art History, 201 Draper Rd, 24061-0103. Tel 540-231-5547; FAX 703-231-5761; Elec Mail dmyers@vtum1.cc.vt.edu. *Head Dept* David Crane, MFA; *Prof* Jane Aiken, PhD; *Prof* Steve Bickley, MFA; *Prof* Derek Myers, MFA; *Prof* Thomas Carpenter, PhD; *Prof* Robert Fields, MFA; *Prof* Maryann Harman, MFA; *Prof* Robert Graham, MFA; *Prof* Ray Kass, MFA; *Prof* L Bailey Van Hook, PhD. Instrs: FT 13
Estab 1969; pub; scholarships; SC 25, LC 12
Degrees: BA 4 yrs, BFA 5 yrs
Tuition: In state $1699.50; out of state $4926
Courses: Advertising Design, Art Appreciation, Art History, Ceramics, Commercial Art, Design, Drawing, Graphic Arts, Graphic Design, Illustration, Mixed Media, Painting, Sculpture, Computer Art
Summer School: Dir, Derek Myers. Enrl 150; tuition proportional to acad yr for two 5 wk sessions. Courses—Advertising Design, Art History, Ceramics, Computer Art, Design, Drawing, Graphic Design, Illustration, Painting, Sculpture, Watercolor

BRIDGEWATER

BRIDGEWATER COLLEGE, Art Dept, 402 E College St, 22812. Tel 540-828-5396; FAX 703-828-2160; *Dept Head* Nan Covert, MFA; *Dept Head* Paul Kline, MFA
Scholarships
Degrees: BA 4 yr
Courses: Art History, Design, Drawing, Painting, Photography, Printmaking, Sculpture

BRISTOL

VIRGINIA INTERMONT COLLEGE, Fine Arts Division, Moore St, 24201. Tel 540-669-6101; FAX 540-669-5763; *Chmn* Dr Marvin Tadlock; *Instr* Tedd Blevins, MFA; *Instr* Chris Anderson
Estab 1884; den; D & E; scholarships; SC 15, LC 4; enrl D 35, non-maj 110
Ent Req: HS dipl, review of work
Degrees: BA(Art) & BA(Art Educ) 4 yrs, AA 2 yrs
Tuition: $3487.50 per sem (incl board)

BUENA VISTA

SOUTHERN VIRGINIA COLLEGE, One College Hill Dr, 24416. Tel 540-261-8400; FAX 540-261-8451; *Chmn* Dr Michael Platt
Estab 1867; pvt; D; SC 10, LC 5; enrl D 185, non-maj 175, maj 2
Ent Req: HS dipl, SAT or ACT
Degrees: AA & BA 2 yrs
Tuition: Res—undergrad $9500 per yr; nonres—undergrad $9500 per yr
Courses: Art Education, Art History, Design, Painting, Photography, Teacher Training, Italian Renaissance, Study Abroad
Summer School: Dir M Worth. Enrl 30; tuition $135 per cr hr for 4 wk term beginning May 17 - June 16. Courses—Art History, Photography

CHARLOTTESVILLE

UNIVERSITY OF VIRGINIA, McIntire Dept of Art, Fayerweather Hall, 22903. Tel 804-924-6123; FAX 804-924-3647; *Chmn* Lawrence Goedde. Instrs: FT 21
Estab 1819, dept estab 1951; pub; D; scholarships; SC 21, LC 21, GC 14; enrl D 1500, maj 150, grad 40 res, 18 nonres
Ent Req: HS dipl
Degrees: BA(Studio and Art History), MA(Art History) and PhD(Art History)
Courses: Art History, Drawing, Painting, Photography, Printmaking, Sculpture, Computer Graphics
Summer School: Enrl 15; tuition varies. Courses—Art History, Studio Art

DANVILLE

AVERETT COLLEGE, Art Dept, 420 W Main St, 24541. Tel 804-791-5600, 791-5797; FAX 804-791-5647; *Coordr* Diane Kendrick; *Prof* Robert Marsh, MFA; *Prof* Maud F Gatewood
Estab 1859, dept estab 1930; pvt; D & E; scholarships; SC 13, LC 5; enrl D 1000, non-maj 250, maj 25
Ent Req: HS dipl
Degrees: AB
Tuition: $9925 per yr; campus res available $4135 per yr
Courses: Advertising Design, Art Education, Art History, Ceramics, Commercial Art, Drawing, Fashion Arts, History of Art & Archaeology, Illustration, Jewelry, Lettering, Painting, Printmaking, Sculpture, Teacher Training, Textile Design
Summer School: Two 4 wk sessions

FAIRFAX

GEORGE MASON UNIVERSITY, Dept of Art & Art History, 4400 University Dr, 22030. Tel 703-993-1010; FAX 703-323-3849; *Chmn* Shelia Sfollite; *Prof* Carol C Mattusch, PhD. Instrs: FT 11, PT 4
Estab 1948, dept estab 1981; pub; D & E; SC 16, LC 15; enrl non-maj 200, maj 130
Ent Req: HS dipl, SAT or CEEB
Degrees: BA
Tuition: Res—$1400 per 12-17 sem hrs; nonres—$3280 per 12-17 sem hrs
Courses: †Art History, Drawing, Graphic Arts, Photography, Painting, Printmaking, Sculpture, Computer Graphics, †Studio Art
Summer School: Courses—Art Appreciation, Art Education, Studio Arts

FARMVILLE

LONGWOOD COLLEGE, Dept of Art, Pine St, 23901. Tel 804-395-2284; *Head Dept* Randall W Edmonson
Estab 1839, dept estab 1932; pub; D & E; scholarships; SC 59, LC 15; enrl non-maj 450 per sem maj 110 per sem
Ent Req: HS dipl
Degrees: BFA (Art Educ, Art History, Studio) 4 yr
Courses: Advertising Design, Art Education, Art History, Ceramics, Drawing, Illustration, Jewelry, Lettering, Museum Staff Training, Photography, †Printmaking, †Teacher Training, Basic Design, Crafts, Design, Fibers, Metalsmithing, Stained Glass, 3-D Design, Wood Design
Summer School: Dir, Randall W Edmonson. Tuition varies for one 3-wk & two 4-wk sessions. Courses—Varied

FREDERICKSBURG

MARY WASHINGTON COLLEGE, Art Dept, 22401. Tel 540-899-4357, 654-1937; *Prof* Steve Griffin, PhD; *Prof* Paul C Muick, PhD; *Prof* Cornelia Oliver, PhD; *Prof* Joseph Dreiss, PhD; *Assoc Prof* Lorene Nickel, MFA
Estab 1904; pub; D & E; scholarships; SC 18, LC 20; enrl maj 50
Ent Req: HS dipl, ent exam
Degrees: BA & BS 4 yrs
Tuition: Res—undergrad $95 per cr hr, grad $146 per cr hr; nonres—undergrad $220 per cr hr, grad $275 per cr hr; campus res available
Courses: †Art History, Ceramics, Drawing, Graphic Arts, Painting, Photography, Printmaking, Sculpture, †Studio Art

HAMPTON

HAMPTON UNIVERSITY, Dept of Fine & Performing Arts, 23668. Tel 804-727-5416; *Chmn* Dr Karen Ward. Instrs: FT 6, PT 1
Estab 1869; pvt; D; scholarships; SC 22, LC 7, GC 9; enrl maj 80, others 300, grad 7
Ent Req: HS grad
Degrees: BA, BS
Tuition: $8600 annual tuition; campus res available
Courses: Ceramics, Interior Design, Painting, Photography
Summer School: Dir, Sheila May. Courses—Advanced Workshop in Ceramics, Art Educ Methods, Art Methods for the Elementary School, Basic Design, Ceramics, Commercial Art, Design, Drawing & Composition, Graphics, Metalwork & Jewelry, Painting, Understanding the Arts

HARRISONBURG

JAMES MADISON UNIVERSITY, School of Art & Art History, 22807. Tel 540-568-6216; *Dir* Dr Cole H Welter; *Prof* Martha B Caldwell, PhD; *Prof* Jerry L Coulter, MFA; *Prof* Philip James; *Prof* Rebecca Humphrey, MFA; *Prof* James Crable, MFA; *Prof* Jay Kain, PhD; *Prof* Steve Zapton, MFA; *Prof* Barbara Lewis, MFA; *Prof* Ronald Wyancko, MFA; *Prof* Kathleen Arthur, PhD; *Prof* Gary Chatelain, MFA; *Prof* Jack McCaslin, MFA; *Prof* Robert Bersson, PhD; *Prof* Masako Miyata, MFA; *Assoc Prof* Alan Tschudi, MFA; *Prof* Kenneth Szmagaj, MFA; *Assoc Prof* Sang Yoon, MFA; *Assoc Prof* Trudy Cole-Zielanski, MFA; *Asst Prof* William Tate, MArch; *Asst Prof* Peter Ratner, MFA; *Asst Prof* Corinne Martin; *Instr* Stuart Downs, MA
Estab 1908; pub; D & E; scholarships; SC 31, LC 21, GC 22; enrl D & E 1254, maj 184, GS 12
Ent Req: HS dipl, grads must submit portfolio, undergrads selected on portfolio & acad merit
Degrees: BA(Art History), BS & BFA(Studio) 4 yrs, MA(Studio, Art History, Art Educ) 1 1/2 to 2 yrs, MFA 60 cr hrs
Tuition: Res—undergrad $1508 per sem, grad $94 per cr; nonres—undergrad $3002 per sem, grad $255 per cr; campus res—room & board $1954 per sem
Courses: Advertising Design, Aesthetics, †Art Education, †Art History, †Ceramics, Drafting, †Drawing, Goldsmithing, †Graphic Design, †Jewelry, Interior Design, Museum Staff Training, Painting, Photography, Printmaking, Sculpture, Silversmithing, Textile Design, Weaving, Art Therapy, Computer Graphics, Papermaking, Stained Glass, Typography
Adult Hobby Classes: Tuition res—$250, nonres—$658 for 1-3 cr hr.
Courses—Summer workshop, all beginning courses
Children's Classes: Enrl 260; tuition $40 for 8 sessions
Summer School: Prof, Philip James. Enrl 200; tuition res—undergrad $65 per cr hr, grad $109 per cr hr, nonres—undergrad $193 per cr hr, grad $322 per cr hr

LEXINGTON

WASHINGTON AND LEE UNIVERSITY, Division of Art, Dupont Hall, 24450. Tel 540-463-8857, 463-8861 (Art Dept); FAX 540-463-8104; Elec Mail psimpson@wlu.edu. *Head Art Div* Pamela H Simpson, PhD; *Prof* Larry M Stene, MFA; *Assoc Prof* Kathleen Olson-Janjic; *Assoc Dean* Joan O'Mara, PhD; *Asst Prof* George Bent
Estab 1742, dept 1949; pvt; D; scholarships; SC 14, LC 26; enrl D 1200 (in col) non-maj 200, maj 4-6
Ent Req: HS dipl, SAT, 3 CEEB, one English CEEB plus essay on skills in English, English composition test; entrance requirements most rigorous in English; required of all, including art majors
Degrees: BA 4 yrs
Tuition: Res—undergrad $10,850 per yr, grad $11,200 per yr; campus res—room & board available
Courses: Art History, Drawing, Graphic Arts, History of Art & Archaeology, Museum Staff Training, Painting, Printmaking, Sculpture, Stage Design, Theatre Arts, Study Art Abroad (Taiwan, Greece)

LYNCHBURG

LYNCHBURG COLLEGE, Art Dept, 1501 Lakeside Dr, 24501. Tel 804-522-8100; FAX 804-522-8499; *Chmn* Richard G Pumphrey, MFA; *Dir* Virginia Irby Davis, MEd; *Asst Prof* Pat Kiblinger; *Asst Prof* John Roark; *Asst Prof* Michelle Baldwin; *Asst Prof* Aubrey Wiley
Estab 1903, dept estab 1948; pvt; D & E; SC 26, LC 16, GC 2; enrl D 400, E 50, non-maj 410, maj 45
Ent Req: HS dipl
Degrees: BA & BS 4 yrs
Tuition: Res—undergrad $9000 per yr; nonres—undergrad $15,380; campus res available
Courses: Art Education, Art History, Ceramics, Design, Drawing, Graphic Arts, Graphic Design, Painting, Photography, Printmaking, Sculpture, Art for Therapy, Art for Communication, Crafts, Figure Drawing, History of Architecture
Summer School: Art Education, Art History & Studio

RANDOLPH-MACON WOMAN'S COLLEGE, Dept of Art, 2500 Rivermont Ave, 24503. Tel 804-947-8486; FAX 804-947-8138; *Chmn* Gina S Werfel. Instrs: FT 4
Estab 1891; pvt, W; D; scholarships; SC 18, LC 15; enrl maj 35, others 305
Degrees: BA 4 yrs
Tuition: $17,950 incl room & board
Courses: Art History, Ceramics, Drawing, Painting, Printmaking, Sculpture, American Art, Art Survey
Summer School: Dir, Dr John Justice. Enrl 30; 4 wk term. Courses—various

MCLEAN

MCLEAN ARTS CENTER, Art Dept, 1437 Emerson Ave, 22101. Tel 703-790-0861 (Art Dept); *Head Dept* John Bryans
Estab 1955; pvt; D & E; SC 1; enrl D 63, E 12
Tuition: Adults $140 for 10 lessons; children $110 for 10 lessons
Courses: Drawing, Painting
Adult Hobby Classes: 35; tuition $140 per 10 lessons. Courses—General Drawing & Painting
Children's Classes: 40; tuition $110 per 10 lessons. Courses—General Drawing & Painting
Summer School: Dir, John Bryans. Enrl 20; tuition $110 for 2 wk term.
Courses—General Drawing & Painting

NEWPORT NEWS

CHRISTOPHER NEWPORT UNIVERSITY, Arts & Communications, 50 Shoe Lane, 23606. Tel 757-594-7089, 594-7000; FAX 757-594-7389; *Head Dept* Rita Hubbard, PhD; *Prof* B Anglin, MA; *Faculty* David Alexick, PhD
Estab 1974; pub; D & E; SC 19, LC 4; enrl D 250, E 60, non-maj 200, maj 100
Ent Req: HS dipl, admis committee approval
Degrees: BA & BS 4 yrs
Tuition: Res—undergrad $3326 per yr, $139 per cr hr; nonres—undergrad $7946 per yr, $331 per cr hr; no campus res
Courses: Art Education, Art History, Ceramics, Collages, Costume Design & Construction, Drawing, Graphic Arts, Painting, Photography, Sculpture, Stage Design, Theatre Arts, †Art, †Music (BM)
Summer School: Dir, Dr Barry Woods. Enrl 25; tuition $300. Courses—Ceramics, Drawing, Painting

NORFOLK

NORFOLK STATE UNIVERSITY, Fine Arts Dept, 23504. Tel 804-683-8844; *Head Dept* Rod A Taylor, PhD
Estab 1935; pub; D & E; SC 50, LC 7; enrl D 355, E 18, non-maj 200, maj 155
Ent Req: HS dipl
Degrees: BA(Art Educ), BA(Fine Arts) and BA(Graphic Design) 4 yrs, MA and MFA in Visual Studies
Tuition: Res—undergrad $92 per sem hr, grad $147 per sem hr; nonres—students $193 per sem hr
Courses: History of Art & Archaeology, Jewelry, Lettering, Mixed Media, †Painting, Photography, Printmaking, Sculpture, Teacher Training
Adult Hobby Classes: Enrl 30. Courses—Ceramics, Crafts
Children's Classes: Enrl 45; tuition none. Courses—all areas

OLD DOMINION UNIVERSITY, Art Dept, 23529. Tel 757-683-4047; FAX 757-683-5923; *Chmn&Assoc Prof* Michael Fanizza; *Grad Prog Dir* Ron Snapp; *Gallery Dir* David Johnson; *Prof Emeriti* Ernest Mauer; *Prof* Victor Pickett; *Prof* Ken Daley; *Assoc Prof* Linda McGreevy; *Assoc Prof* Ronald Snapp; *Assoc Prof* William Wagner; *Assoc Prof* Carol Hines; *Assoc Prof* Robert Wotojwicz; *Assoc Prof* Elizabeth Lipsmeyer; *Asst Prof* Elliott Jones; *Adjunct Instr* Rita Marlier; *Asst Prof Art Educ* B Stephen Carpenter
Scholarships, fellowships & assistantships
Ent Req: HS, dipl, SAT
Degrees: BA(Art History, Art Education or Studio Art), BFA, MA & MFA
Tuition: Res—$1231 per sem; nonres—$2491 per sem
Courses: Aesthetics, Art Appreciation, †Art Education, †Art History, Ceramics, Design, †Drawing, †Goldsmithing, Graphic Arts, †Graphic Design, History of Art & Archaeology, Illustration, †Jewelry, Mixed Media, Museum Staff Training, †Painting, †Photography, †Printmaking, †Sculpture, †Silversmithing, Teacher Training, Textile Design, Weaving, Clay, Computer Imaging, Crafts, Metals, †Studio Art
Adult Hobby Classes: Enrl 75; tuition $60-$90 per 8 wk course. Courses—Clay, Drawing, Graphics, Mixed Media, Painting, Photography, Stained-Glass
Children's Classes: Enrl 25. Courses—2 semesters, Governor's Magnet School classes
Summer School: Dir, Carol Hines. Enrl 125; tuition res $126 per cr hr; nonres $313 per cr hr

VIRGINIA WESLEYAN COLLEGE, Art Dept of the Humanities Division, 1584 Wesleyan Dr, 23502. Tel 757-455-3200; FAX 757-461-5025; *Assoc Prof* Barclay Sheaks; *Prof* R E Neil Britton, MFA; *Assoc Prof* Joyce B Howell, PhD; *Adjunct Instr* Robert Karl, MA; *Adjunct Instr* Ken Bowen
Pvt, den; D & E; scholarships; SC 21, LC 8; enrl E 20
Ent Req: HS dipl, SAT
Degrees: BA(Liberal Arts) 4 yrs
Tuition: $12,700 per yr; campus res available
Courses: Aesthetics, Art Appreciation, Art Education, Art History, Ceramics, Drawing, Graphic Arts, Graphic Design, Handicrafts, History of Art & Archaeology, Jewelry, Mixed Media, Painting, Photography, Printmaking, Sculpture, Silversmithing, Stage Design, Teacher Training, Theatre Arts, Weaving, Computer Art, Fabric Enrichment
Adult Hobby Classes: Enrl 20

PETERSBURG

RICHARD BLAND COLLEGE, Art Dept, * 11301 Johnson Rd, 23805. Tel 804-862-6272, 862-6100; *Pres* Clarence Maze Jr, PhD; *Art Prof* Susan Brown
Estab 1960, dept estab 1963; pub; D & E; SC 3, LC 3; enrl D 73
Ent Req: HS dipl, SAT, recommendation of HS counselor
Degrees: AA(Fine Arts) 2 yrs
Tuition: Res—undergrad $860 per sem; nonres—$2475 per sem
Courses: Art History, Drawing, Painting, Sculpture, Art Appreciation, Basic Design
Adult Hobby Classes: Courses—Interior Design, Yoga

VIRGINIA STATE UNIVERSITY, Fine & Commercial Art, PO Box 9026, 23806. Tel 804-524-5000; *Chmn & Asst Prof* Eugene R Vango; *Prof* Valery Bates-Brown, PhD; *Inst* Charles Flynn, MA
Estab 1882, dept estab 1935; pub; D & E; SC 16, LC 6, GC 2; enrl D 400, E 60, non-maj 302, maj 98
Ent Req: HS dipl
Degrees: Degrees BFA(Art Educ) & BFA(Visual Commercial Art & Design) 4 yrs
Tuition: Res—undergrad $6160 per yr incl room & board; nonres—undergrad $6660 per yr
Courses: Advertising Design, Aesthetics, Art Appreciation, Art Education, Art History, Ceramics, Drawing, Lettering, Jewelry, Painting, Photography, Printmaking, Sculpture, Computer Graphics, Silkscreen, Typography
Adult Hobby Classes: Enrl 20; tuition $165 per course. Courses—Batik, Ceramics, Crafts, Jewelry, Macrame, Painting, Printmaking, Sculpture
Summer School: Dir, Dr M McCall. Enrl 20; tuition $55 per cr for term of 12 wks, beginning May 21. Courses—Basic Art, Ceramics, Crafts, Jewelry

PORTSMOUTH

TIDEWATER COMMUNITY COLLEGE, Art Dept, 340 High St, 23704. Tel 757-396-6999; FAX 757-396-6800; *Chmn* Harriette C F Laskin; *Dir* Anne Iott; *Prof* Ed Gibbs; *Prof* Rob Hawkes; *Prof* Craig Nilson; *Prof* George Tussing
Estab 1968; pub; D & E; SC 12, LC 3; enrl D 120, E 180, non-maj 190, maj 110
Ent Req: HS dipl
Degrees: AA(Fine Arts), AAS(Graphic Arts) 2 yrs
Tuition: Res—$52 per cr hr; nonres—$161 per cr hr; no campus res
Courses: †Advertising Design, Art Appreciation, Art History, Ceramics, Design, Drawing, Illustration, Lettering, Painting, Photography, Sculpture, Computer Graphics
Adult Hobby Classes: Offered through Continuing Educ Div
Summer School: Assoc Dir, H Laskin. Enrl 15 per course; tuition per course beginning May. Courses—Art History, Ceramics, Design, Drawing, Painting

RADFORD

RADFORD UNIVERSITY, Art Dept, PO Box 6965, 24142. Tel 540-831-5475; *Chmn* Arthur Jones; *Prof* Halide Salam; *Assoc Prof* Jerry Krebs, MFA; *Asst Prof* Pam F Lawson; *Asst Prof* Ed LeShock; *Asst Prof* Jennifer Spoon, MA; *Assoc Prof* Dr Dorothy Mercer; *Asst Prof* Charles Brouwer, MFA; *Assoc Prof* Stephen Arbury; *Asst Prof* Dr Eloise Philpot
Estab 1910, dept estab 1936; pub; D & E; scholarships; enrl D 1250, E 80, non-maj 1086, maj 164, grad 18
Ent Req: HS dipl, SAT
Degrees: BA, BFA, BS & BS (teaching) 4 yrs, MFA 2 yrs, MS 1 yr
Tuition: In-state undergrad $4250 per yr, out-of-state undergrad $7688 per yr; campus res—room & board $4248 per yr
Courses: Art Appreciation, Art Education, Art History, Ceramics, Drawing, Graphic Arts, Graphic Design, Handicrafts, Jewelry, Lettering, Painting, Photography, Printmaking, Sculpture, Teacher Training, Art Safety, Art Foundations, Baroque & Rococo Art, Contemporary Art, Fiber Design, Visual Arts
Summer School: Dir, James Knipe. Enrl 50; two 5 wk sessions each based on sem-hr charge. Courses—Art Appreciation, Studio Art

RICHMOND

J SARGEANT REYNOLDS COMMUNITY COLLEGE, Humanities & Social Science Division, PO Box 85622, 23285-5622. Tel 804-371-3263; *Chmn* Arthur L Dixon
Tuition: Res—$48.55 per sem hr; nonres—$157.90 per sem hr
Courses: Art Appreciation, Art History, Design, Drawing, Graphic Design, Handicrafts, Interior Design, Painting, Photography, Sculpture

UNIVERSITY OF RICHMOND, Dept of Art, 23173. Tel 804-289-8272, 289-8276; FAX 804-287-6006; *Chmn* Charles W Johnson Jr, PhD; *Prof* Stephen Addiss; *Assoc Prof* Ephraim Rubenstein; *Asst Prof* Margaret Denton; *Asst Prof* Mark Rhodes
Pvt; D & E; scholarships; SC 29, LC 15
Ent Req: HS dipl, CEEB

Degrees: BA and BS 4 yrs
Tuition: Res—&12,000 per yr
Courses: Art Appreciation, †Art History, Ceramics, Design, Drawing, History of Art & Archaeology, Museum Staff Training, Painting, Photography, Printmaking, Sculpture, Color & Design, Museum Studies, †Studio Art

VIRGINIA COMMONWEALTH UNIVERSITY
—Art History Dept, PO Box 3046, 23284-3046. Tel 804-828-2784; *Chmn* Bruce M Koplin; *Prof* Dr Baba Tunde Lawal; *Prof* Robert Hobbs; *Prof* Howard Risatti; *Assoc Prof* Dr Charles Brownell; *Assoc Prof* Fredrika H Jacobs; *Assoc Prof* Sharon Jones Hill; *Asst Prof* Dr Ann G Crowe; *Asst Prof* Dr James Farmer; *Asst Prof* Fredrika H Jacobs
Degrees: BA, MA, PhD
Tuition: Res—$1957 per sem; nonres—$5548 per sem
Courses: Motion Pictures Western Survey, Pre-Columbian Art & Architectures
—School of the Arts, 325 N Harrison St, 23284. Tel 804-828-2784; *Dean* Richard Toscan; *Dir Summer School* Sue F Murro. Instrs: FT 146, PT 24
Estab 1838; pub; D & E; scholarships, fels & grad assistantships; enrl 2699
Ent Req: Ent req portfoli
Degrees: BA, BFA, MFA
Tuition: Res—$1957 per sem; nonres—$5548
Courses: Art Education, Art History, Ceramics, Fashion Arts, Interior Design, Jewelry, Printmaking, Sculpture, Theatre Arts, Art Experience, 2-D Art, Exceptional Art, Fine Art, Print
Summer School: Dir, Sue F Murro. Courses 3 - 8 wks, most art disciplines; $105 per cr hr

ROANOKE

HOLLINS COLLEGE, Art Dept, 7916 Williamson Rd, 24020. Tel 540-362-6000; FAX 540-362-6642; *Chmn* Kathlee Nolen
Estab 1842; pvt; D; scholarships; SC 13; enrl D 380, maj 35
Ent Req: HS dipl
Degrees: BA 4 yrs
Tuition: $14,100
Courses: Architecture, Art Appreciation, Art Education, Art History, Drawing, Graphic Arts, History of Art & Archaeology, Painting, Photography, Printmaking, Sculpture, Teacher Training, Video, †Studio

VIRGINIA WESTERN COMMUNITY COLLEGE, Commercial Art, Fine Art & Photography, 3095 Colonial Ave SW, PO Box 14007, 24038. Tel 540-857-7385, 857-7255 (Dept Head); *Chmn Div Human* Dr Clarence C Mays Jr, EdD; *Dept Head* David Curtis, MFA; *Assoc Prof* Rudolph H Hotheinz, MAE; *Assoc Prof* Sherrye Lantz, MFA
Pub; D & E; SC 11, LC 2
Ent Req: HS dipl
Degrees: AA(Fine Art), AAS(Commercial Art)
Tuition: Res—$47.65 per cr hr; nonres—$157 per cr hr
Adult Hobby Classes: Oil Painting, Papermaking, Watercolor

SALEM

ROANOKE COLLEGE, Fine Arts Dept-Art, Olin Hall, High St, 24153. Tel 540-375-2354; *Chmn* Bruce Partin; *Prof* Scott Hardwig, MFA; *Assoc Prof* John Brust; *Asst Prof* Elizabeth Heil, MFA; *Asst Prof* Dr Jane Long
Estab 1842, dept estab 1930; den; D; scholarships; SC 16, LC 8; enrl D 130, non-maj 120, maj 40
Ent Req: HS dipl, SAT or ACT, 13 academic credits - 2 English, 2 Social Sciences, 5 Arts & Humanities, 2 Math, 2 Science
Degrees: BA 4 yrs
Tuition: Res—$17,850 per yr incl room & board; nonres—$13,425 per yr
Courses: Advertising Design, Art Education, †Art History, Ceramics, Drawing, Graphic Design, Painting, Photography, Printmaking, Sculpture, Stage Design, †Studio Arts
Children's Classes: Ceramics
Summer School: Dir, Dr Ed Whitson. Courses—Art History, Studio

STAUNTON

MARY BALDWIN COLLEGE, Dept of Art, Frederick and New Sts, 24401. Tel 540-887-7197; FAX 540-887-7139; *Sr Member* Marlena Hobson; *Prof* Paul Ryan; *Asst Prof* Kris Iden; *Asst Prof* Beth Young; *Asst Prof* Paula Rau
Estab 1842; pvt; D & E; scholarships; SC 16, LC 18; enrl D 173, E 32, non-maj 172, maj 33, others 4 non-credit
Ent Req: HS dipl
Degrees: BA & BS 4 yrs
Tuition: $12,000 annual tuition
Courses: Ceramics, Drawing, Film, Graphic Arts, Graphic Design, Interior Design, Museum Staff Training, Painting, Photography, Printmaking, Stage Design, Teacher Training, Theatre Arts, Video, Art for the Exceptional Child, Historical Preservation, Typography

SWEET BRIAR

SWEET BRIAR COLLEGE, Art History Dept, 24595. Tel 804-381-6125 (Art History Dept), 381-6100; *Chmn* Christopher Witcombe; *Prof* Aileen H Laing, PhD
Estab 1901, dept estab 1930; pvt; D; scholarships; SC 19, LC 19; enrl D 375 per term, maj 32
Ent Req: HS dipl, col boards
Degrees: BA 4 yrs
Tuition: $20,500 incl room & board
Courses: †Art History, Drawing, Graphic Arts, History of Art & Archaeology
Adult Hobby Classes: Fibre Art History, Graphic Design, Modern Art

WILLIAMSBURG

COLLEGE OF WILLIAM & MARY, Dept of Fine Arts, PO Box 8795, 23187. Tel 804-221-4000, 221-2537; *Chmn* Barbara Watkinson, PhD; *Prof* James D Kornwolf, PhD; *Prof* Miles Chappell, PhD; *Prof* Edwin Pease; *Prof* Dr Alan Wallach; *Prof* Henry Coleman; *Assoc Prof* Marlene Jack, MFA; *Assoc Prof* Paul Helfrich, MFA; *Assoc Prof* William Barnes, MFA; *Asst Prof* Lewis Choen, MFA; *Lectr* Muriel Christison; *Lectr* Mark Iwinski; *Lectr* Joseph Dye
Estab 1693, dept estab 1936; pub; D; SC 20, LC 22; enrl D 5000, non-maj 825, maj 64
Ent Req: HS dipl
Degrees: BA 4 yrs
Tuition: Res—$1483 per sem; nonres—$3906 per sem; campus res available
Courses: †Architecture, †Art History, †Ceramics, †Drawing, †Painting, †Printmaking, †Sculpture
Summer School: Dir, Nell Jones. Courses—Art History, Design, Painting, Drawing

WISE

CLINCH VALLEY COLLEGE OF THE UNIVERSITY OF VIRGINIA, Visual & Performing Arts Dept, One College Ave, 24293. Tel 540-328-0100; FAX 540-328-0115; *Dept Chmn* Suzanne Adams
Estab 1954, dept estab 1980; pub; D & E; scholarships; SC 9, LC 4
Ent Req: HS dipl, SAT or ACT
Degrees: BA & BS 4 yrs
Tuition: Res—$1546.50 per sem; nonres—$3584 per sem
Courses: Art Appreciation, Art History, Ceramics, Costume Design & Construction, Drawing, Film, History of Art & Archaeology, Painting, Sculpture, Stage Design, Teacher Training, Theatre Arts, Applied Music, Music History & Literature, Music Theory, Performance
Adult Hobby Classes: Dir, Dr Winston Ely
Summer School: Dir, Dr Winston Ely. Enrl 15 per course. Courses—Same as above

WASHINGTON

AUBURN

GREEN RIVER COMMUNITY COLLEGE, Art Dept, 12401 SE 320th St, 98092. Tel 206-833-9111; FAX 206-288-3465; *Chmn & Instr* Dr Bernie Bleha, EdD; *Instr* Ed Brannan, MFA; *Instr* Elayne Levensky-Vogel; *Instr* Patrick Navin
Estab 1965; pub; D & E; SC 31, LC 4; enrl D 330, E 120
Ent Req: HS dipl or 18 yrs old
Degrees: AA 2 yr
Tuition: Res—undergrad $43.20 per cr; nonres—undergrad $169.70 per cr
Courses: Art History, Ceramics, Drawing, Design, Painting, Photography, Weaving, Computer Enhanced Design, Craft, Papermaking
Summer School: Dir, Bruce Haulman. Tuition $193.66. Courses—Ceramics, Drawing, Painting, Photography

BELLEVUE

BELLEVUE COMMUNITY COLLEGE, Art Dept, 3000 Landerholme Circle SE, 98007. Tel 206-641-2341; FAX 206-453-3029; *Dept Chmn* Robert Purser
Estab 1966; pub; D & E; SC 15, LC 5; enrl 600, maj 50
Ent Req: No ent req
Degrees: AA 2 yrs
Tuition: Varies according to courses taken
Courses: Art History, Design, Drawing, Interior Design, Painting, Photography, Sculpture, Textile Design
Adult Hobby Classes: Enrl 600. Courses—Ceramics, Design, Drawing, Jewelry, Painting, Photography, Sculpture

BELLINGHAM

WESTERN WASHINGTON UNIVERSITY, Art Dept, Fine Arts Complex, Rm 116, 98225-9068. Tel 360-650-3660; FAX 360-647-6878; *Chmn Dept Art* Elisi Vassval Ellis. Instrs: FT 15, PT 6
Estab 1899; pub; D & E; scholarships; enrl D 1500, E 200
Ent Req: HS dipl, ent exam
Degrees: BA 4 yr, BA(Educ) 4 yr, BFA 5 yr, MEd 6 yr
Tuition: Res—undergrad $752 per quarter; nonres—undergrad $2658 per quarter
Courses: †Art History, †Ceramics, †Drawing, †Graphic Design, †Painting, †Sculpture, †Fibers, †Metals
Adult Hobby Classes: Enrl 200; tuition $43 per cr continuing educ; Courses—Ceramics, Drawing, Fibers, Paintings, Sculpture
Children's Classes: Enrl 100; tuition $125 one wk session; Courses—Adventures in Science/Arts
Summer School: Dir, Shirley Ennons. Tuition $404, six & nine week sessions; Courses—Art Education, Art History, Ceramics, Drawing, Fibers, Painting, Sculpture

BREMERTON

OLYMPIC COLLEGE, Social Sciences & Humanities Division, 1600 Chester Ave, 98337. Tel 360-478-4866; FAX 360-478-7161; *Dir* Lee Brock, MA; *Instr* Imy Klett, MA; *Instr* Mel R Wallis, MA
Estab 1946; pub; D & E; scholarships; LC 3; enrl D 125, E 75
Ent Req: HS dipl
Degrees: AA, AS & ATA 2 yrs, cert

Tuition: Res—undergrad $95.40 per cr hr; nonres—undergrad $369.40 per cr hr; no campus res
Courses: Art Appreciation, Art History, Ceramics, Drawing, Jewelry, Painting, Photography, Printmaking, Sculpture, Life Drawing, Native American Art History, Papermaking, Stained Glass
Adult Hobby Classes: Calligraphy, Painting

CHENEY

EASTERN WASHINGTON UNIVERSITY, Dept of Art, 99004. Tel 509-359-2493; FAX 509-359-7028; *Chmn* Richard L Twedt
Estab 1886; pub; D; scholarships; SC 58, LC 21, GC 18; enrl D 600, non-maj 200, maj 200, GS 20
Degrees: BA, BEd and BFA 4 yrs, MA and MEd 1 to 2 yrs
Tuition: Res—undergrad $81 per cr hr, grad $130 per cr hr; nonres—undergrad $287 per cr hr, grad $394 per cr hr
Courses: Aesthetics, Art Appreciation, Art Education, Art History, Ceramics, Design, Drawing, Graphic Design, Mixed Media, Painting, Photography, Printmaking, Sculpture, Teacher Training
Summer School: Dir, Richard L Twedt. Enrl 200; tuition $120 per cr undergrad, $190 per cr grad for 8 wk term. Courses—Art History, Art in Humanities, Drawing, Painting, Photography

ELLENSBURG

CENTRAL WASHINGTON UNIVERSITY, Dept of Art, 98926. Tel 509-963-2665; *Chmn* Michael Chinn. Instrs: 14
Estab 1891; pub; D; enrl maj 150, others 7134
Ent Req: GPA 2
Degrees: BA, MA and MFA 4-5 yrs
Tuition: Res—undergrad $810 per quarter, grad $1295 per quarter; nonres—undergrad $2872 per yr, grad $3939 per yr; campus res available
Courses: Art Appreciation, †Art Education, Art History, †Ceramics, Design, †Drawing, †Graphic Design, Illustration, †Jewelry, †Painting, †Photography, †Printmaking, †Sculpture, †Computer Art, Papermaking, †Wood Design
Adult Hobby Classes: Art in Elementary School, Art in Secondary School
Summer School: Dir, Michael Chinn. Tuition $75 per cr for 4, 6, 8 wk sessions. Courses—Art Appreciation, Ceramics, Computer Art, Drawing, Painting

EVERETT

EVERETT COMMUNITY COLLEGE, Art Dept, 801 Wetmore Ave, 98201. Tel 206-388-9378 (Art Dept), 388-9100; *Chmn* Lowell Hanson
Degrees: AA, AFA & ATA 2 yr
Tuition: $44.50 per cr hr
Courses: Graphic Arts, Photography, Media Production, Multimedia
Summer School: Dean of Instruction, Nicki Haynes.

LACEY

ST MARTINS COLLEGE, Humanities Dept, 5300 Pacific Ave SE, 98503-1297. Tel 360-491-4700; FAX 360-459-4124; *Dean* Dr David Suter
Courses: Art Appreciation, Art History, Ceramics, Design, Drawing, Painting, Printmaking

LONGVIEW

LOWER COLUMBIA COLLEGE, Art Dept, 1600 Maple, PO Box 3010, 98632. Tel 360-577-2300; *Art Instr* Rosemary Powelson, MFA; *Instr* Yvette O'Neill, MA
Estab 1934; pub; D & E; scholarships; SC 36, LC 8; enrl D 200, E 100
Ent Req: Open admis
Degrees: AAS 2 yrs
Tuition: Res—undergrad $1200 per yr, $67.80 per hr; nonres—undergrad $4000 per yr, $263.80 per hr; no campus res
Courses: Art History, Calligraphy, Ceramics, Drawing, Graphic Arts, Painting, Printmaking, Sculpture, Photography, Design
Adult Hobby Classes: Courses—Matting & Framing, Relief Woodcuts, Recreational Photography

MOSES LAKE

BIG BEND COMMUNITY COLLEGE, Art Dept, 98857. Tel 509-762-6269; *Dir* Christopher Garcia
Estab 1962; pub; D & E; SC 8, LC 1; enrl D 325, E 60, maj 10-15
Ent Req: HS dipl
Degrees: AA 2 yrs
Tuition: Res—undergrad $999 per yr; nonres—undergrad $3939 per yr; campus res available
Courses: Art Appreciation, Ceramics, Drawing, Lettering, Painting, Photography, Sculpture, Basic Design, Poster Art, Pottery
Adult Hobby Classes: Enrl 15. Courses—Drawing
Summer School: Dir, Joan Lucas. Enrl 180; tuition $31.50 per cr hr. Courses—Drawing, Painting, Pottery, Photography, Sculpture

MOUNT VERNON

SKAGIT VALLEY COLLEGE, Dept of Art, 2405 E College Way, 98273. Tel 360-416-7724 (Dept Art), 428-1261; FAX 360-416-7690; *Chmn* Ann Chadwick-Reid. Instrs: FT 2, PT 6
Estab 1926; pub; D & E; scholarships; SC 32, LC 1; enrl D 2500, E 3500
Ent Req: Open

Tuition: Res—$467 per quarter full-time; nonres—$1837 per quarter full-time
Courses: Art Appreciation, Art History, Ceramics, Design, Drawing, Jewelry, Painting, Photography, Printmaking, Sculpture, Figure Drawing
Adult Hobby Classes: Four nights a week
Summer School: Dir, Bert Williamson

PASCO

COLUMBIA BASIN COLLEGE, Esvelt Gallery, 2600 N 20th Ave, 99301. Tel 509-547-0511; FAX 509-546-0401; *Dean Arts & Humanities* Ted Neth; *Gallery Coordr* Susan Kimmel, MFA; *Art Dept Chmn* Morse Clary, MFA; *Instr* Janette Hopper
Scholarships
Degrees: AA & AS
Tuition: Res—$178.50; nonres—$684.50
Courses: Art Appreciation, Art History, Calligraphy, Ceramics, Design, Drawing, Graphic Design, Interior Design, Jewelry, Photography, Printmaking, Sculpture, Stage Design, Video, Metal Casting & Foundary
Adult Hobby Classes: Enrl 5000; tuition $400 per qtr. Courses—Art Appreciation, Fine Arts, Graphic Design
Summer School: Dir, Ted Neth. Enrl 1500; tuition $400 for 8 wks.
Courses—Ceramics, Drawing, Illustration, Introduction to Art

PULLMAN

WASHINGTON STATE UNIVERSITY, Fine Arts Dept, 99164-7450. Tel 509-335-8686; FAX 509-335-7742; *Chmn* Christopher Watts. Instrs: FT 11
Estab 1890, dept estab 1925; pub; D & E; scholarships; SC 29, LC 13, GC 25; enrl D 1593, E 131, maj 220, GS 25
Ent Req: HS dipl
Degrees: BA(Fine Arts) 4 yrs, BFA 4 yrs, MFA 2 yrs
Tuition: Res—$977; nonres— $2717
Courses: Ceramics, Drawing, Painting, Photography, Printmaking, Sculpture, Electronic Imaging

SEATTLE

THE ART INSTITUTES INTERNATIONAL, The Art Institute of Seattle, 2323 Elliot Ave, 98121-1622. Tel 206-448-0900; FAX 206-448-2501; *Pres* Les Pritchard; *VPres & Dir Educ* Daniel Lafferty, MS; *Instr* Fred Griffin, BFA; *Instr* William Cumming; *Instr* James Scott, BFA; *Instr* Nan Cooper; *Instr* Jim Richardson, BA; *Instr* John Hansen; *Instr* David Mercer; *Instr* Anita Griffin; *Instr* John Hildding; *Instr* David Danioth; *Instr* Sam Dimico
Estab 1946; pvt; D; scholarships; SC 2; enrl D 1300
Ent Req: HS dipl, portfolio approval recommended but not required
Degrees: Prof dipl, AAA 2 yr
Tuition: $2875 per qtr for 8 qtrs
Courses: Advertising Design, Commercial Art, Fashion Arts, Film, Graphic Arts, Graphic Design, Illustration, Lettering, Video, Interior Design, Photography, Fashion Merchandising, Layout & Production, Commercial Art Technician
Summer School: Enrl 975; tuition $2250 per term of 11 wks beginning July 7

CITY ART WORKS, Pratt Fine Arts Center, 1902 S Main St, 98144-2206. Tel 206-328-2200; FAX 206-328-1260; *Exec Dir* Gregory Robinson, MPA; *Educ Dir* Kristin Tollefson, MFA; *Development Dir* Patricia Warren, MA
Estab 1979; pvt; D & E; scholarships & fels; SC 300; enrl D 1000, E 1000
Ent Req: Open enrollment
Degrees: No degree prog
Tuition: $55 - $500 per class
Courses: Collages, Drawing, Goldsmithing, Illustration, Jewelry, Mixed Media, Painting, Printmaking, Sculpture, Silversmithing, Glass blowing & casting
Adult Hobby Classes: Enrl 2000; tuition $100-$500 for 8 wk class.
Classes—Drawing, Glass, Jewelry, Painting, Printmaking, Sculpture
Children's Classes: Drawing, Glass, Printmaking, Sculpture
Summer School: Educ Dir, Kristin Tollefson. Enrl 50; tuition $400-$650 per wk-long class. Classes—Glassblowing, Jewelry, Printmaking, Sculpture

CORNISH COLLEGE OF THE ARTS, Art Dept, 710 E Roy St, 98102. Tel 206-323-1400; *Pres* Sergei Eschernisch. Instrs: FT 32, PT 93
Estab 1914; pvt; D & E; scholarships; SC 57, LC 6; enrl non-maj 124 PT, maj 423 FT
Ent Req: HS dipl, portfolio review, fine arts, design, personal interview
Degrees: BAA, BFA
Tuition: $8650 per yr
Courses: Advertising Design, Art History, Calligraphy, Commercial Art, Conceptual Art, †Costume Design & Construction, Design, Display, Drafting, Drawing, Graphic Arts, Graphic Design, †Illustration, Industrial Design, Interior Design, Lettering, Mixed Media, Painting, Photography, Printmaking, Sculpture, Stage Design, Theatre Arts, Video, Furniture Design
Summer School: Dir, Greg Skinner. Enrl 50; tuition $329 per cr for 8 wk term.
Courses—Drawing, Painting, Photography, Print, Sculpture, Video

NORTH SEATTLE COMMUNITY COLLEGE, Art Dept, Humanities Division, 9600 College Way N, 98103. Tel 206-527-3709; FAX 206-527-3784; *Head Dept* Elroy Christenson, MFA; *Instr* Joan Ross Blaedel; *Instr* David J Harris, MFA
Estab 1970; pub; D & E; scholarships; SC 27, LC 7; enrl D 150, E 65
Ent Req: HS dipl
Degrees: AA 2 yr, AFA, CFA 2 yr
Tuition: Res—undergrad $459.50 per quarter, $42 per cr, nonres—$1829.50 per quarter; no campus res
Courses: Art History, Drawing, History of Art & Archaeology, Jewelry, Painting, Sculpture
Adult Hobby Classes: Enrl 6600; tuition $459.50 per quarter for res, $1829.50 per quarter for nonres. Courses—Art History, Basic Drawing, Ceramics, 2-D & 3-D Design, Intro to Art, Jewelry Design, Painting, Sculptures, Water Solvable Media

PILCHUCK GLASS SCHOOL, 315 Second Ave S, 98104-2618. Tel 206-621-8422; FAX 206-621-0713; *Exec Dir* Marjorie Levy. Instrs: FT 5, PT 30
Estab 1971; summer location: 1201 316th St NW, Stanwood, WA 98292-9600, Tel: 206-445-3111, Fax: 206-445-5515; pvt; D & E; scholarships; SC 25; enrl D & E 250
Ent Req: 18 years or older
Tuition: $1900-$2650 per class; campus res available
Courses: Constructions, Sculpture, Glass
Summer School: Exec Dir, Marjorie Levy. Enrl 250; tuition approx $2200 for 2 1/2 wk course. Courses—Casting, Cold Working, Flamework, Fusing, Glassblowing, Mosaic, Stained Glass

SEATTLE CENTRAL COMMUNITY COLLEGE, Humanities - Social Sciences Division, 1701 Broadway, 98122. Tel 206-587-3800; FAX 206-587-3878; *Chmn* Rosetta Hunter; *Prof* Ileana Leavens
Estab 1970; pub; D & E; scholarships; SC 15, LC 5; enrl D 70, E 50
Ent Req: HS dipl, ent exam
Degrees: AA 2 yrs
Tuition: Res—$426 per qtr; nonres—$1692 per qtr; no campus res
Courses: Art History, Painting
Summer School: Courses—Art History, Painting, Sculpture

SEATTLE PACIFIC UNIVERSITY, Art Dept, 3307 Third Ave W, 98119. Tel 206-281-2079; FAX 206-281-2500; *Chmn* Michael Caldwell
Scholarships & fellowships
Tuition: $4223 per qtr for 12-17 cr; campus res—$1620 room, board & meals
Courses: Art Appreciation, †Art Education, Ceramics, Design, Drawing, Fashion Arts, Handicrafts, Industrial Design, Interior Design, Jewelry, Painting, Printmaking, Sculpture, Textile Design, Weaving
Children's Classes: Tuition $23 for 8 wk session. Courses - General Art for Children
Summer School: Dir, Larry Metcalf. Two 4 wk sessions. Courses - Elementary Art Education Workshops, Fabrics, Monoprinting, Painting, Papermaking, Silkscreening

SEATTLE UNIVERSITY, Fine Arts Dept, Division of Art, Broadway & Madison, 98122-4460. Tel 206-296-5360 (Fine Arts Dept), 296-6000; FAX 206-296-5433; *Chmn* Carol Wolfe Clay; *Prof* William Dore; *Prof* Andrew Schoz; *Asst Prof Art* Ki Gottberg; *Asst Prof Art* Michael Holloman; *Asst Prof US Art* Joy Sherman; *Asst Prof US Art* Joseph Venker
D; scholarships
Ent Req: HS dipl and entrance exam
Degrees: BA prog offered
Tuition: $317 per cr hr
Courses: Art History, Design, Drawing, Painting, Printmaking, Sculpture, Drama, Studio Art
Summer School: Chmn, Kate Duncan. Courses—same as regular session

SHORELINE COMMUNITY COLLEGE, Humanities Division, 16101 Greenwood Ave N, 98133. Tel 206-546-4741; FAX 206-546-5869; *Interim Chmn* Sara Hart; *Acting Writing Dir* Chris Fisher; *Prof* Mike Larson, MA; *Prof* Chris Simons, MFA; *Prof* Willy Clark, PhD; *Prof* Bruce Armstutz; *Prof* Brian Edwards, MA; *Prof* K C Maxwell, MFA
Estab 1964; pub; D & E; scholarships; SC 9, LC Art History Survey; enrl D 5500
Ent Req: HS dipl, col ent exam
Degrees: AA & AFA
Tuition: Res—undergrad $436.35 per quarter, nonres—undergrad $1833.35 per quarter
Courses: †Advertising Design, Aesthetics, Art Appreciation, Art History, Ceramics, †Commercial Art, Conceptual Art, Constructions, †Costume Design & Construction, Design, †Drafting, Drawing, †Fashion Arts, Film, †Graphic Arts, †Graphic Design, History of Art & Archaeology, Mixed Media, Painting, †Photography, Sculpture, Stage Design, †Textile Design, †Video, Multimedia
Summer School: Dir, Marie Rosenwasser. Enrl 45 maximum; two 4 wk terms.
Courses—Ceramics, Design, Design Appreciation, Drawing, Electronic Design, Graphic Design, Painting, Photography, Sculpture

UNIVERSITY OF WASHINGTON, School of Art, PO Box 353440, 98195-3440. Tel 206-543-0970 (Admin), 543-0646 (Undergraduating Adv); FAX 206-685-1657; *Dir* Christopher Ozubko
Estab 1878; pub; D & E; scholarships; SC 113, LC 84, GC 30; enrl Maj 1100, grad 125
Ent Req: Must meet university admission req, must be matriculated to enroll in art classes in academic year
Degrees: BFA 5 yrs, BA 4 yrs, MA, PhD and MFA
Tuition: Res—undergrad $1046, grad $1644, nonres—undergrad $3251, grad $4121
Courses: †Art History, †Ceramics, Drawing, Goldsmithing, †Graphic Design, †Industrial Design, Jewelry, †Painting, †Photography, †Printmaking, †Sculpture, Silversmithing, Textile Design, Video, Weaving, Fibers, Interdisciplinery Visual Arts, Metals
Summer School: Dir, C Ozubko. Enrl 830; 2-month term. Various courses offered through UW Extension, open to community

SPOKANE

GONZAGA UNIVERSITY, Dept of Art, College of Arts & Sciences, 502 E Boone, 99258-0001. Tel 509-328-4220, Ext 3286; *Chmn* Terry Gieber; *Prof* J Scott Patnode; *Prof* R Gilmore; *Prof* Mary Farrell. Instrs: FT 3, PT 2
Estab 1962; pvt; D & E; SC 20, LC 5, GC 12; enrl D 250 incl maj 40, grad 1, others 80
Ent Req: HS dipl
Degrees: BA 4 yrs, grad cert in art
Tuition: $7450 per sem; campus res available
Courses: Art Education, Ceramics, Drawing, History of Art & Archaeology, Painting, Printmaking, Sculpture, Teacher Training, 2-D Design
Summer School: Dean, Richard Wolfe. Term of 8 wks beginning June.
Courses—Ceramics, Drawing, Painting, Printmaking

SPOKANE FALLS COMMUNITY COLLEGE, Fine Arts Dept, W 3410 Fort George Wright Dr, 99204. Tel 509-533-3500; 533-3710 (Art Dept); *Dean* Stan Lauderbaugh; *Dept Chmn* Jo Fyfe; *Asst Prof* Sharon Wilkin; *Asst Prof* Carolyn Stephens; *Asst Prof* Dick Ibach; *Asst Prof* Jeanette Kirishian; *Asst Prof* Patty Haag; *Asst Prof* Carl Richardson; *Asst Prof* Mardis Nenno; *Adjunct Asst Prof* Linda Kraus; *Adjunct Asst Prof* Gay Gardner; *Adjunct Asst Prof* Ann Lauderbaugh; *Adjunct Asst Prof* Lars Neises; *Adjunct Asst Prof* Bob Evans; *adjunct Asst Prof* Richard Schindler; *Adjunct Asst Prof* Karen Kaiser; *Adjunct Asst Prof* Harold Balazs; *Adjunct Asst Prof* Ken Speiring
Estab 1963; pub; D & E; scholarships; SC 41, LC 5; enrl D 600, E 200
Ent Req: HS dipl, GED
Degrees: AAA 3 yr, AA, AFA & CFA 2 yr
Tuition: Res—$467 per quarter; nonres—$1837 per quarter; no campus res
Courses: Art Education, Calligraphy, Ceramics, Drawing, Handicrafts, Illustration, Jewelry, Lettering, Mixed Media, Painting, Photography, Printmaking, Sculpture, Weaving, African, Native & Hispanic Arts, Computer Arts, Design 2D & 3D Advanced, Digital Paint, Exhibit, Fiber Arts, Health/Safety in Art, Intro to Art, Portfolio
Adult Hobby Classes: Enrl 10-20; tuition $25.60 for 6 week term. Courses—Art History, Calligraphy, Ceramics, Drawing, Watercolor, Weaving
Children's Classes: Enrl 20-22; tuition $30 for 4 wks. Art Experiences, Courses—Ceramics, Drawing
Summer School: Dir, Stan Lauderbaugh. Enrl 100; tuition $46.50 per cr or $467 per 10-18 cr; 6-8 wk term. Courses—Ceramics, Color & Design, Drawing, Figure Drawing, Intro to Art, Printmaking, Watercolor

WHITWORTH COLLEGE, Art Dept, 99251. Tel 509-466-1000, 466-3258 (Art Dept); *Chmn* Barbara Filo, MA; *Prof* Walter Grosvenor, MAT; *Assoc Prof* Gordon Wilson, MFA; *Asst Prof* Barbara Filo; *Instr* Jeff Harris; *Instr* John Blessant
Pvt; D & E; scholarships; SC 18, LC 6
Ent Req: HS dipl
Degrees: BA 4 yrs, MA, MAT & MEd 2 yrs
Courses: Art Education, Art History, Ceramics, Drawing, Graphic Design, Mixed Media, Painting, Printmaking, Art Administration, Leaded Glass

TACOMA

FORT STEILACOOM COMMUNITY COLLEGE, Fine Arts Dept, 9401 Farwest Dr SW, 98498. Tel 206-964-6500, 964-6717; *Dept Head* Bill Rades. Instrs: FT 2, PT 2
Estab 1966, dept estab 1972; pub; D & E; SC 20, LC 5; enrl D 3500
Ent Req: Ent exam
Degrees: AA 2yrs
Tuition: $343 per term; nonres—$1323 per term; no campus res
Courses: Drawing, Painting, Photography, Printmaking, Figure Drawing
Adult Hobby Classes: Courses vary
Summer School: Dir, Walt Boyden. Tuition $19 per cr hr. Courses—Ceramics, Drawing, Painting.

PACIFIC LUTHERAN UNIVERSITY, Dept of Art, School of the Arts, 98447. Tel 206-535-7573; FAX 206-536-5063; *Chmn* John Hallam, PhD; *Prof* David Keyes, Ma; *Assoc Prof* Dennis Cox, MFA; *Assoc Prof* Beatrice Geller, MFA; *Assoc Prof* Lawrence Gold, MFA; *Assoc Prof* Walt Tomsic, MFA
Estab 1890, dept estab 1960; den; D & E; scholarships; SC 29, LC 8; enrl D 800, E 75, maj 60
Ent Req: HS dipl, SAT
Degrees: BA, BAEd & BFA 4 yrs
Tuition: $14,560 per yr; PT students $455 per cr hr; campus res—room & board $4690 per yr
Courses: †Advertising Design, Aesthetics, Art Appreciation, Art Education, Art History, †Ceramics, †Commercial Art, †Constructions, †Design, †Drawing, †Graphic Arts, †Graphic Design, Illustration, †Mixed Media, †Painting, †Photography, †Printmaking, †Sculpture, †Teacher Training, Stained Glass
Summer School: Dean, Dr Richard Moe. Enrl 2000; tuition $190 per sem hr; $297 per grad cr, 3 - 4 wk sessions. Courses—Ceramics, Drawing, Jewelry, Photography

TACOMA COMMUNITY COLLEGE, Art Dept, 6501 S 19th St, 98466-6139. Tel 206-566-5000, 566-5300 (Art Dept); *Art Dept Chmn* Frank Dippolito, MFA; *Instr* Richard Mahaffey
Estab 1965; pub; D & E; scholarships; SC 35, LC 1; enrl D & E 1500
Degrees: AAS & Assoc in Liberal Arts 2 yrs
Tuition: Res—$467.30 per quarter, nonres—$1837.30 per quarter
Courses: Art History, Jewelry, Painting, Photography, Printmaking, Sculpture, 2-D & 3-D Design, Figure Drawing, Pottery

UNIVERSITY OF PUGET SOUND, Art Dept, 1500 N Warner St, 98416. Tel 206-756-3348; FAX 206-756-3500; *Chmn* Helen Nagy. Instrs: FT 7, PT 2
Estab 1935; den; D & E; scholarships; SC 41, LC 11; enrl maj 65, undergrad 455
Ent Req: HS grad
Degrees: BA 4 yrs
Tuition: $18,030 per yr; campus res—room & board $4800 per yr; student fee $140
Courses: Art History, Ceramics, Design, Drawing, Painting, Photography, Printmaking, Sculpture, Oriental Art, Studio Design
Summer School: Dir, Ron Fields. Enrl 15 per class; tuition $925 per unit for 4 wk course. Courses—Art Education, Art History, Ceramics, Drawing, Painting, Watercolor

VANCOUVER

CLARK COLLEGE, Art Dept, 1800 E McLoughlin Blvd, 98663. Tel 360-694-6521; *Coordr* Roger Baker; *Instr* Warren Dunn; *Instr* Carson Legree, MFA
Estab 1933, dept estab 1947; pub; D & E; scholarships; SC 87, LC 3; enrl D 300, E 400
Ent Req: Open door
Degrees: Assoc of Arts & Science, Assoc of Applied Science, & Assoc of General Studies 2 yr

Tuition: Res—$27.50 per cr hr, $247.50 (9 cr), $315 (10 cr); nonres—$104 per cr, $936 (9 cr), $1040 (10 cr)
Courses: Art History, Calligraphy, Ceramics, Drawing, Graphic Design, Handicrafts, Jewelry, Lettering, Painting, Photography, Sculpture
Adult Hobby Classes: Enrl 40 FTE; tuition $55 per 2 cr course. Courses—Air Brush, Art History, Calligraphy, Ceramics, Drawing, Photography
Summer School: Enrl 40 FTE; tuition $27.50 per cr. Courses—Art Appreciation, Art History, Calligraphy, Ceramics, Drawing, Photography, Watercolor

WALLA WALLA

WALLA WALLA COMMUNITY COLLEGE, Art Dept, 500 Tausick Way, 99362. Tel 509-527-4212, 527-4600; *Instr* Bill Piper; *Instr* Melissa Webster; *Instr* Jim Fritz
Scholarships
Degrees: AA 2 yr
Tuition: Res—$88.40 per cr hr; nonres—$341.60 per cr hr, minimum 2 cr
Courses: Art Appreciation, Ceramics, Design, Drawing, Handicrafts, Photography, Printmaking, Sculpture, Pottery
Summer School: Dir, Don Adams. Tuition same as regular quarter

WHITMAN COLLEGE, Art Dept, Olin Hall, 99362. Tel 509-527-5248, 527-5111; *Chmn* Ed Humphreys
Pvt; D; SC 15, LC 8; enrl D 250, maj 15
Ent Req: HS dipl, ent exam
Degrees: BA 4 yrs
Tuition: $1667 per yr
Courses: Aesthetics, Art History, Ceramics, Design, Drawing, History of Art & Archaeology, Painting, Photography, Printmaking, Sculpture, Book Arts

WENATCHEE

WENATCHEE VALLEY COLLEGE, Art Dept, 1300 Fifth St, 98801. Tel 509-662-1651; *Prof* Stephen Henderson; *Instr* Ruth Allan, MFA
Estab 1939; pub; D & E; scholarships; LC 6; enrl D 550, E 200, maj 45
Ent Req: HS dipl, open door policy
Degrees: AA 2 yrs
Tuition: Res—undergrad $780 per yr, $260 per quarter, $26 per cr hr; nonres—undergrad $3075 per yr, $1025 per quarter, $102.50 per cr; campus res available
Courses: Aesthetics, Art Appreciation, Art History, Ceramics, Design, Drawing, Painting, Printmaking, Color Theory
Summer School: Dir, Dr Joann Schoen

YAKIMA

YAKIMA VALLEY COMMUNITY COLLEGE, Art Dept, S 16th Ave & Nob Hill Blvd, PO Box 1647, 98907. Tel 509-574-4846 (Chair), 574-4844 (E Hayes), 574-4845 (Assoc faculty); *Dir* Robert A Fisher; *Faculty* Herb Blisard; *Faculty* Erin Hayes. Instrs: PT 5
Scholarships
Degrees: AA & AS offered
Tuition: Res—$477 per quarter, PT $42 per cr, nonres—$1847 per quarter
Courses: Art Appreciation, Art History, Calligraphy, Ceramics, Design, Drawing, Graphic Design, Jewelry, Mixed Media, Painting, Photography, Sculpture, Silversmithing
Summer School: Dir, Robert A Fisher. Tuition $477 per quarter, FT

WEST VIRGINIA

ATHENS

CONCORD COLLEGE, Fine Art Division, PO Box 50, 24712-1000. Tel 304-384-3115; FAX 304-384-9044; *Prof* Maynard R Coiner, MFA; *Prof* Gerald C Arrington, MFA; *Asst Prof* Sheila M Chipley, EdD; *Asst Prof* Steve Glazer
Estab 1872, dept estab 1925; pub; D & E; scholarships; SC 32, LC 3; enrl non-maj 200, maj 75, D 75
Ent Req: HS dipl
Degrees: BA & BS 4 yrs
Tuition: Res—$1109 per sem; nonres—$2399 per sem; campus res—room & board available
Courses: Advertising Design, Art Education, Art History, Ceramics, Collages, Commercial Art, Drawing, Graphic Arts, Graphic Design, Handicrafts, Illustration, Painting, Printmaking, Sculpture, Teacher Training, †Advertising
Adult Hobby Classes: Enrl varies; tuition based on part-time rates. Courses—Vary
Children's Classes: Enrl varies; tuition none for 4 wk sessions. Courses vary
Summer School: Tuition res—$420; nonres—$1150 for term of 5 wks beginning June. Courses—varied

BETHANY

BETHANY COLLEGE, Dept of Fine Arts, 26032. Tel 304-829-7000; FAX 304-829-7223, 829-7108; *Dean* William Whipple; *Head Dept* Herb Weaver; *Asst Prof* Wesley Wagner; *Asst Prof Studio Art* Kenneth Morgan
Estab 1840, dept estab 1958; den; D; scholarships; SC 27, LC 7; enrl D 136, non-maj 106, maj 30
Ent Req: HS dipl
Degrees: BA & BS 4 yrs
Tuition: $14,752 per yr; campus res available
Courses: Art History, Calligraphy, Ceramics, Drawing, Graphic Design, Illustration, Painting, Photography, Sculpture

BLUEFIELD

BLUEFIELD STATE COLLEGE, Art Dept, 24701. Tel 304-327-4171; *Prof* Joyce Shamro
Estab 1895; pub; D & E; scholarships & fels; SC 14, LC 4; enrl D 125, E 40, non-maj 150, minor 10, other 5
Ent Req: HS dipl, 18 yrs old
Degrees: BA, BA(Humanities), BS, BS(Educ) & BS(Engineering Technology) 4 yrs
Tuition: Res—$890 per term; nonres—$2023 per term
Courses: Art Education, Art History, Ceramics, Drawing, Painting, Photography, Printmaking, Sculpture, Computer Art
Adult Hobby Classes: Enrl 10-15. Courses—Art in Western World, Photography, Television, Woodcarving
Children's Classes: Enrl varies. Courses—Ceramics, Drawing
Summer School: Dir, Dwight Moore. Enrl 15-20; term of 5 wks beginning June/July. Courses—Art Educ & Appreciation (workshops on occasion)

BUCKHANNON

WEST VIRGINIA WESLEYAN COLLEGE, Dept of Fine Arts, 59 College Ave, 26201. Tel 304-473-8000, 473-8067; *Chmn* Dan Keegan; *Instr* William Oldaker; *Theatre Art Instr* John Urquhart
Estab 1890; den; D & E; SC 16, LC 6; enrl non-maj 120, maj 20, grad 2
Ent Req: HS dipl, ent exam
Degrees: BA
Tuition: $7488 per sem
Courses: Art Education, Art History, Ceramics, Design, Drawing, Graphic Design, Painting, Printmaking, Sculpture, Theatre Arts, Computer Graphics, Computer Illustration
Adult Hobby Classes: Tuition $50 per cr for 12-13 wks
Summer School: Dir, Dr Mark Defoe. Enrl 25; tuition $290 per cr hr for three 4 wk terms. Courses—Art History, Basic & Intermediate Stained Glass, Studio Arts

CHARLESTON

UNIVERSITY OF CHARLESTON, Carleton Varney Dept of Art & Design, 2300 MacCorkle Ave SE, 25304. Tel 304-357-4725; *Dir* Joellen Kerr; *Coordr* Steve Watts; *Instr* Holly Cline; *Instr* Linda Anderson. Instrs: FT 3, PT 3
Estab 1888; pvt; D & E; scholarships; enrl maj 55
Ent Req: Usual col req
Degrees: 4 yr
Tuition: $5495 per sem
Courses: †Art Education, Art History, Design, Drafting, Drawing, †Interior Design, Painting, Photography, Printmaking, Teacher Training, Advanced Studio, Art Administration, Art Appreciation, Color Theory
Children's Classes: Enrl 30; tuition by the wk. Courses—Summer Art Camp Program
Summer School: Dir, Joellen Kerr. Tuition $60 per wk. Courses—Summer Colors

ELKINS

DAVIS & ELKINS COLLEGE, Dept of Art, 100 Campus Dr, 26241. Tel 304-637-1254; FAX 304-637-1413; *Chmn* Jesse F Reed; *Lectr* Margo Blebin; *Lectr* Scottie Wiest; *Lectr* Donna Morgam. Instrs: FT 1, PT 3
Den; D; scholarships; SC 15, LC 5; enrl maj 3
Ent Req: HS dipl
Degrees: AA & AS 2 yrs, BA 2 yrs
Tuition: $5290 per sem; campus res available
Courses: Art Education, Art History, Drawing, Graphic Arts, Painting, Sculpture, Teacher Training, Weaving, †Computer Art, Pottery
Adult Hobby Classes: Enrl 90
Summer School: Augusta Heritage Arts Workshop. Courses—Appalachian Crafts, Basketry, Bushcraft, Calligraphy, Chairbottoming, Prospecting, Coopering, Dance, Folkcarving, Folklore Musical Instrument Construction & Repair, Papermaking, Pottery, Stained Glass, Treenware, Woodworking

FAIRMONT

FAIRMONT STATE COLLEGE, Division of Fine Arts, 26554. Tel 304-367-4000; *Chmn* Suzanne Snyder; *Prof* John Clovis, MFA; *Prof* Dr Stephen Smigocki, PhD; *Prof* Barry Snyder, MFA; *Asst Prof* Lynn Boggess
Pub; D & E; scholarships; enrl D maj 35, non-maj 15
Ent Req: HS dipl
Degrees: BA(Art Educ) and BS(Graphics, Fine Arts) 4 yrs
Tuition: $750 per sem
Courses: †Art Education, Art History, Ceramics, Design, Drawing, Graphic Arts, Painting, Photography, Printmaking, Sculpture, Commercial Design
Adult Hobby Classes: Two - three times a wk for 16 wks. Courses—same as above
Children's Classes: Enrl 20; tuition $25 per 6 wk term. Courses—Art for children ages 5 - 12, 2 - D & 3 - D Design
Summer School: Dir Dr S Snyder. Enrl 50; 4 wks per sessions. Courses—Art Education, Drawing, Design, Painting, Art Appreciation

GLENVILLE

GLENVILLE STATE COLLEGE, Dept of Fine Arts, 200 High St, 26351. Tel 304-462-7361, Ext 215; *Chmn* Gary Gillespie, PhD; *Prof* Charles C Scott, MFA; *Prof* James W Rogers, MFA; *Asst Prof* George D Harper, MFA
Estab 1872, dept estab 1952; pub; D & E; scholarships; SC 25, LC 3; enrl D 128, E 42, non-maj 14, maj 55
Ent Req: HS dipl
Degrees: AB 4 yrs
Tuition: Res—undergrad $840 per yr, $420 per sem; nonres—undergrad $2300 per

yr, $1150 per sem; campus residency available
Courses: †Art Education, Art History, †Ceramics, Drawing, Graphic Arts, Jewelry, Lettering, †Painting, Photography, Printmaking, Sculpture, Textile Design, Weaving
Summer School: Chmn, Gary Gillespie

HUNTINGTON

MARSHALL UNIVERSITY, Dept of Art, 400 Hal Greer Blvd, 25755. Tel 304-696-6760; FAX 304-696-6505, 696-6760; *Chmn* Michael Cornfeld; *Dean* Donald Van Horn; *Prof* Earlene Allen; *Prof* Mary Grassell; *Prof* Robert Hutton; *Prof* Susan Jackson; *Prof* Peter Massing; *Prof* Robert Rowe; *Prof* Stan Sporny; *Prof* Dr Beverly Marchant; *Prof* Dr Susan Power; *Office Mgr* Opal Turner. Instrs: FT 10
Estab 1903; pub; enrl maj incl grad 108
Ent Req: HS grad
Degrees: BFA & MA in art educ & studio 4 yrs
Tuition: Res—$1058 per sem; nonres—$2939 per sem; campus res available
Courses: Art Education, Ceramics, Graphic Design, Painting, Photography, Printmaking, Sculpture, Weaving
Children's Classes: Enrl 60; tuition $35 per student for 8 wks. Courses—Ceramics, Drawing, Mixed Media, Painting
Summer School: Tuition $427.10 for 6 sem hrs, nonres $1247.10 for 5 wk terms

INSTITUTE

WEST VIRGINIA STATE COLLEGE, Art Dept, Campus Box 4, 25112-1000. Tel 304-766-3196, 766-3198; FAX 304-768-9842; *Chair* Reidun Ovrebo, PhD; *Prof* Paul Nuchims, PhD; *Asst Prof* Molly Erlandson; *Asst Prof* Paula Clendenin
D & E; scholarships; SC 26, LC 11
Ent Req: HS dipl
Degrees: AB(Art) and BSEd(Art) 4 yrs
Tuition: Res—$1700 per sem; nonres—$1711 per sem
Courses: Art Education, Art History, Ceramics, Design, Drawing, Graphic Design, Painting, Photography, Printmaking, Sculpture, Teacher Training, Appalachian Art & Crafts, Computer Graphics, Figure Drawing
Summer School: Dir, R Ovrebo. Enrl 75.; 3 or 6 wk session. Courses—Art Appreciation, Basic Studio

KEYSER

POTOMAC STATE COLLEGE, Dept of Art, Mineral St at Fort Ave, 26726. Tel 304-788-6800; *Chmn* Edward M Wade, MA; *Div Chmn* Anthony Whitmore
College estab 1953, dept estab 1974; pub; D & E; SC 8, LC 2; enrl D 160, non-maj 150, others 10
Ent Req: HS dipl
Degrees: AA 2 yrs, AAS 2 yrs
Tuition: Res—undergrad $2311 per yr including room & board; nonres—$3714 per yr including room & board
Courses: Drawing, Painting, Sculpture, Visual Foundation
Summer School: Dir, Edward Wade. Enrl 10-20; tuition res—undergrad $77.25 per 3 hrs, nonres—undergrad $236.25 per 3 hrs for 5 wk term beginning June 1. Courses—Art Appreciation, Drawing, Painting

MONTGOMERY

WEST VIRGINIA INSTITUTE OF TECHNOLOGY, Creative Arts Dept, * 405 Fayette Pike, 25136. Tel 304-442-3192 (Dept), 442-3071; *Head Dept* Fred Meyer; *Assoc Prof* Robert Simile
Estab 1896; pub; scholarships; enrl 3500 (total)
Ent Req: HS grad
Degrees: AS, BA and BS 2-4 yrs
Tuition: Res—$765 per sem; nonres—$1800 per sem
Courses: Ceramics, Graphic Design, Painting, Art Appreciation, Design

MORGANTOWN

WEST VIRGINIA UNIVERSITY, College of Creative Arts, Division of Art, PO Box 6111, 26506-6111. Tel 304-293-3140; FAX 304-293-3550; *Chmn* Carmon Colangelo, MFA; *Prof* Robert Anderson, MFA; *Prof* Bernie Schultz, PhD; *Prof* Cara Jaye, MFA; *Prof* Victoria Fergus, PhD; *Prof* Iain Machell, MFA; *Prof* Kristina Olson, MA; *Prof* Clifford Harvey, BFA; *Prof* Alison Helm, MFA; *Prof* Marian Hollinger, PhD; *Prof* Ed Petrosky, MFA; *Prof* Eve Faulkes, MFA; *Prof* William Thomas, PhD; *Prof* Paul Krainak, MFA; *Prof* Christopher Hocking, MFA; *Prof* Sergio Soave, MFA
Estab 1867, div estab 1897; pub; D & E; scholarships; enrl D 250, maj 180, grad 28
Ent Req: HS dipl
Degrees: BA(Art Educ) and BFA 4 yrs, MA(Art) and MFA(Art) 2-4 yrs; grad degrees
Tuition: Res—undergrad $888.50 per sem, grad $935.50; nonres—undergrad $2322.50 per sem, grad $2432.50; campus residency available
Courses: †Art Education, Art History, †Ceramics, Drawing, †Graphic Design, †Painting, †Printmaking, †Sculpture, Basic Design
Children's Classes: Enrl 20; tuition $65 for 10 wks. Courses—Primary & Intermediate Studio
Summer School: Dir, Carmon Colangelo. Enrl 100; tuition $74 per cr hr res $251 per cr hr non res. Courses—Art History, Ceramics, Drawing, Painting, Printmaking

PARKERSBURG

WEST VIRGINIA UNIVERSITY AT PARKERSBURG, Art Dept, Rte 5, Box 167-A, 26101-9577. Tel 304-424-8000; *Chmn* Roger Allen; *Asst Prof* Henry Aglio, MFA
Estab 1961, dept estab 1973; pub; D & E; scholarships; SC 25, LC 5; enrl D 120, E 80, non-maj 125, maj 8
Ent Req: HS dipl plus diagnostic tests in Reading, Math & English
Degrees: AA 2 yrs
Tuition: Res—undergrad $49.50 per cr hr; nonres—$147 per cr hr
Courses: Art History, Ceramics, Drawing, Painting, Photography, Printmaking, Bronze Castings, Wood Carvings
Summer School: Dir, Roger Allen. Tuition $49.50 per cr hr

SHEPHERDSTOWN

SHEPHERD COLLEGE, Art Dept, A02 Frank Ctr, 25443. Tel 304-876-2511; FAX 304-876-3101; WATS 800-826-6807. *Chmn* Dow Benedict. Instrs: FT 9, PT 12
Estab 1872; pub; D; scholarships; SC 75, LC 15; enrl maj 200
Ent Req: HS dipl
Degrees: AA and BFA, BA(Educ) and BS 4 yrs
Tuition: $1020 per sem; campus res—$2610 per yr; nonres—$2335 per sem
Courses: Advertising Design, Aesthetics, Art Appreciation, †Art Education, Art History, Conceptual Art, Constructions, Design, Drawing, Film, †Graphic Design, History of Art & Archaeology, Intermedia, Interior Design, Mixed Media, †Painting, †Photography, †Printmaking, †Sculpture, Stage Design, Teacher Training, Theatre Arts, Video, Aesthetic Criticism, Art Therapy, Design
Summer School: Dir, Dow Benedict. Enrl 60; tuition $85 per cr hr, 2-5 wk sessions. Courses—Art Appreciation, Studio

WEST LIBERTY

WEST LIBERTY STATE COLLEGE, Art Dept, * 26074. Tel 304-336-8006; *Chmn* Charles Boggess, MusB; *Prof* Bernie K Peace, MFA; *Prof* Karen Rychlewski, MFA; *Assoc Prof* R Paul Padgett, MFA
Estab 1836; pub; D & E; scholarships; SC 40, LC 6; enrl D 855, E 140, non-maj 900, maj 90, others 12
Ent Req: HS dipl, score of 17 or higher on ACT test or cumulative HS GPA of at least 2.0 or a combined verbal/math score of 680 on the SAT
Degrees: BA and BS 4 yrs
Tuition: Res—undergrad $1590 per yr, $795 per sem, $101 per cr hr; nonres—undergrad $3630 per yr, $1830 per sem, $188 cr hr; campus res—available
Courses: Advertising Design, †Art Education, Art History, Ceramics, Drawing, Film, Graphic Arts, †Graphic Design, History of Art & Archaeology, Illustration, Jewelry, Lettering, Painting, Photography, Printmaking, Sculpture, Stage Design, Theatre Arts, Weaving, Computer Graphics, Studio Crafts
Summer School: Dir, David T Jauersak. Tuition res $100 per sem hr, nonres $190 per sem hr. Courses—Art Education, Special Education

WISCONSIN

APPLETON

LAWRENCE UNIVERSITY, Dept of Art, Wriston Art Ctr, 54912. Tel 414-832-6621; FAX 414-832-6606; *Chmn* Helen R Klebesadel. Instrs: FT 6
Estab 1847; scholarships; SC 8, LC 17
Ent Req: HS performance, CEEB scores, recommendation
Degrees: BA 4 yrs
Tuition: $23,000 includes room & board per 3 term yr
Courses: Art Education, Art History, Ceramics, Costume Design & Construction, Drawing, Jewelry, Mixed Media, Painting, Photography, Printmaking, Sculpture, Theatre Arts, Metalwork, †Studio Art, Studio Ceramics, 3-D Design

DE PERE

SAINT NORBERT COLLEGE, Division of Humanities & Fine Arts, 334 Boyle Hall, 100 Grant St, 54115. Tel 414-337-3181, 337-3105; *Chmn* Dr Lawrence McAndrews. Instrs: FT 4, PT 1
Estab 1898; pvt den; D; SC 19, LC 5; enrl D 60, maj 60
Ent Req: HS dipl, ent exam
Degrees: BA 4 yrs
Tuition: $13,900 per yr
Courses: Aesthetics, Art Education, Art History, Ceramics, Drawing, Graphic Arts, Graphic Design, Illustration, Jewelry, Painting, Photography, Sculpture, Teacher Training
Summer School: Dir, John Giovannini. Terms of 3 or 5 wks beginning June. Courses—Art Education, Ceramics, Drawing, History of Art, Painting, Sculpture

EAU CLAIRE

UNIVERSITY OF WISCONSIN-EAU CLAIRE, Dept of Art, Park & Garfield Ave, 54702-4004. Tel 715-836-3277; FAX 715-836-4882; *Chmn* Scott Robertson. Instrs: FT 15
Estab 1916; pub; D & E; scholarships; SC 31, LC 12; enrl maj 260
Ent Req: HS dipl, ent exam
Degrees: BA, BS & BFA 4 yrs
Tuition: Res—$1350 per sem, grad $1650; nonres—$4100 per sem, grad $5050
Courses: Advertising Design, Art Education, Art History, Ceramics, Drawing,

Illustration, Painting, Photography, Printmaking, Sculpture, Fibers, Metalsmithing
Adult Hobby Classes: Ceramics, Painting
Summer School: Chmn, Scott Roertson. Enrl 100; tuition res—$1165, nonres—$3550 for 8 wk, 8 cr term. Courses—Art Methods for Teachers, Drawing Painting

FOND DU LAC

MARIAN COLLEGE, Art Dept, 45 S National Ave, 54935. Tel 414-923-7602, Ext 7622; FAX 414-923-7154; *Coordr* Sr Mary Neff, MA; *Chmn Arts & Humanities* Dr Gary Boelhower; *Asst Prof* Frank Scotello; *Instr* Kris Krumenauer; *Adjunct Instr* Cal Jones
Estab 1936; pvt; E; scholarships; SC 20, LC 12; enrl D 107, E 35, maj 6
Ent Req: HS dipl, ACT or SAT
Degrees: BA and BA(Art Educ) 4 yrs
Tuition: $10,560 per yr, $230 per cr; campus res available
Courses: Aesthetics, Art Appreciation, Art Education, Art History, Calligraphy, Ceramics, Design, Drawing, Graphic Arts, Graphic Design, Handicrafts, Illustration, Jewelry, Lettering, Mixed Media, Painting, Photography, Printmaking, Restoration & Conservation, Sculpture, Teacher Training, Weaving, Fiber Arts, Puppetry
Adult Hobby Classes: Workshops, summer sessions, continuing education
Children's Classes: In Relationship with Art Education
Summer School: Workshops, credit art courses

GREEN BAY

UNIVERSITY OF WISCONSIN-GREEN BAY, Art-Communication & the Arts, 2420 Nicolet, 54311-7001. Tel 414-465-2348; FAX 414-465-2890; *Chmn* Curt Hever; *Concentration Chmn* Jeffrey Entwistle; *Instr* David Damkoehler. Instrs: FT 8, PT 2
Estab 1970; pub; D & E; SC 29, LC 3; enrl D 5500
Ent Req: HS dipl, ent exam
Degrees: BA and BS 4 yrs
Tuition: Res—$1142.75 per sem; nonres—$3536.75 per sem
Courses: Aesthetics, Art Education, Ceramics, Drawing, Graphic Design, Intermedia, Jewelry, Mixed Media, Painting, Photography, Printmaking, Sculpture, Stage Design, Textile Design, Theatre Arts, Acting & Directing, Costume & Makeup Design, Environmental Design, Graphic Communications, Styles
Children's Classes: Varies
Summer School: Courses—vary

KENOSHA

CARTHAGE COLLEGE, Art Dept, 2001 Alfred Dr, 53140-1994. Tel 414-551-5859; FAX 414-551-6208; *Chmn* Alane Bolton
Estab 1963; scholarships
Degrees: BA
Tuition: Res—$14,600 per term; campus res—room & board $4195
Courses: Advertising Design, Art Education, Art History, Ceramics, Design, Drawing, Graphic Design, Basic Photography

UNIVERSITY OF WISCONSIN-PARKSIDE, Art Dept, 900 Wood Rd, PO Box 2000, 53141. Tel 414-595-2581; FAX 414-595-2271; *Prof* David Holmes, MFA; *Prof* Douglas DeVinny, MFA; *Assoc Prof* Dennis Bayuzick, MFA; *Assoc Prof* John Satre Murphy; *Assoc Prof* Rollin Jansky, MS
Estab 1965; pub; D & E; scholarships; SC 25, LC 6
Ent Req: Ent req HS dipl, upper 50%
Degrees: BA and BS 4 yrs
Tuition: Res—undergrad $849 per sem; nonres—undergrad $2529.50 per sem; campus res—available
Courses: Aesthetics, Art Education, Art History, Ceramics, Drawing, †Jewelry, Painting, Printmaking, Sculpture, Teacher Training, Textile Design, Art Metals, Life Modeling
Summer School: Tuition $82.25 res hr for term of 8 wks beginning mid June. Courses—Vary from summer to summer

LA CROSSE

UNIVERSITY OF WISCONSIN-LA CROSSE, Center for the Arts, 1725 State St, 54601. Tel 608-785-8230; FAX 608-785-6719; *Chmn* D Tulla Lightfoot. Instrs: FT 8
Estab 1905; pub; D & E; scholarships; SC 25, LC 5; enrl (univ) 7600
Ent Req: HS dipl
Degrees: BA and BS 4 yrs
Tuition: Res—$112.15 per cr hr; nonres—$311.65 per cr hr
Courses: Art Education, Ceramics, Drawing, Graphic Arts, Painting, Printmaking, Sculpture, Ancient Art of the Western World, Computer Art, Holography, Medieval Art of the Western World, Renaissance Art of the Western World, Modern Art of the Western World, History of American Art, Aesthetics in Art Criticism in the Visual Arts, Art Metals, Blacksmithing, Figure Drawing, History of Animated Film, 2-D & 3-D Design
Adult Hobby Classes: Courses—Blacksmithing, Ceramics, Outreach Jewelry
Summer School: Courses—vary

VITERBO COLLEGE, Art Dept, 815 S Ninth, 54601. Tel 608-796-3000; FAX 608-791-0367; *Chmn* Peter Fletcher; *Assoc Prof* Edward Rushton; *Instr* Diane Crane
Estab 1890; pvt; D & E; scholarships; SC 10-12, LC 6; enrl D 55, maj 55
Degrees: BA, BAEd & BS 4 yrs
Tuition: $4500 per yr; campus res—room & board $3000 per yr
Courses: Advertising Design, Art Education, Art History, Ceramics, Commercial Art, Drawing, Graphic Arts, Illustration, Painting, Photography, Printmaking, Sculpture, Teacher Training, Weaving, Fibers

WESTERN WISCONSIN TECHNICAL COLLEGE, Graphics Division, 304 N Sixth St, PO Box 0908, 54602-0908. Tel 608-785-9200; FAX 608-785-9407; *Chmn* Richard Westpfahl
Estab 1911, dept estab 1964; pub; D & E; scholarships; SC & LC 16; enrl D 130, E 145, non-maj 132, maj 143
Ent Req: HS dipl or GED
Degrees: AAS 2 yrs
Courses: Advertising Design, †Commercial Art, Display, Film, †Graphic Arts, Graphic Design, Illustration, Lettering, Mixed Media, Painting, Photography, Stage Design, Video, Computer Graphics, Media, Printing & Publishing, Visual Communications
Adult Hobby Classes: Enrl 264. Courses—Color Photo Printing, Home Movie Making, Painting, Photography
Summer School: Dir, Richard Westpfahl. Courses—varied

MADISON

EDGEWOOD COLLEGE, Art Dept, 855 Woodrow St, 53711. Tel 608-257-4861, Ext 2307; *Chmn* Robert Tarrell; *Assoc Prof* David Smith; *Asst Prof* Melanie Herzog; *Asst Prof* Laurie Neustadt; *Instr* Mary Lybarger
Estab 1941; den; D & E; institutional grants based on financial needs; SC 20, LC 4; enrl D & E 500 (total), non-maj 70, maj 20
Ent Req: HS dipl, ACT
Degrees: BA or BS 4 yrs
Tuition: $5330 annual tuition; campus res available
Courses: †Art Education, Art History, Calligraphy, Ceramics, Drawing, Graphic Design, Painting, Photography, Sculpture, †Teacher Training, Video, Art Therapy
Summer School: Dir, Dr Joseph Schmiedicke. Tuition $110 per cr. Courses—vary

MADISON AREA TECHNICAL COLLEGE, Art Dept, 3550 Anderson St, 53704. Tel 608-246-6058, 246-6100, 246-6002; FAX 608-246-6880; *Chmn* Jerry E Butler, PhD
Estab 1911; pub; D & E; scholarships; SC 45, LC 12; enrl D 5300, E 23,000 (part-time)
Ent Req: HS dipl
Degrees: AA 2 yrs(Commercial Art, Interior Designing, Photography & Visual Communications)
Tuition: $57.35 per cr; other $46.10
Courses: Advertising Design, Art History, Calligraphy, Ceramics, †Commercial Art, Design, Display, Drawing, Handicrafts, Illustration, Jewelry, Lettering, Painting, †Photography, Printmaking, Visual Communications
Adult Hobby Classes: Enrl 1000. Courses—same as regular session

UNIVERSITY OF WISCONSIN, MADISON
—Dept of Art, 6241 Humanities Bldg, 455 N Park, 53706. Tel 608-262-1660; FAX 608-265-4593; *Chmn* Jim Escalante; *Prof* Leslie Nelson; *Prof* Jack Damer; *Prof* Fred Fenster; *Prof* Walter Hamady; *Prof* Philip Hamilton; *Prof* Cavaliere Ketchum; *Prof* Richard Lazzaro; *Prof* Richard Long; *Prof* Truman Lowe; *Prof* Patricia Fennell; *Prof* Edward Pope; *Prof* Eleanor Moty; *Prof* Ronald Neperud; *Prof* R Kenneth Ray; *Prof* Richard Reese; *Prof* Daniel Ramirez; *Prof* William Weege; *Prof* David Becker; *Assoc Prof* George Cramer; *Assoc Prof* Laurie Beth Clark; *Assoc Prof* Steve Feren; *Assoc Prof* Doug Marschlek; *Assoc Prof* Frances Meyers; *Assoc Prof* Carol Pylant; *Asst Prof* Elaine Scheer; *Asst Prof* John Rieben; *Asst Prof* Tom Loeser. Instrs: FT 32, PT 3
Estab 1911; pub; scholarships & fels; SC 68, LC 2, GC 19; enrl maj 500, grad 120
Degrees: MA, MFA
Tuition: Res—undergrad $1368 per sem, grad $1929 per sem; nonres—undergrad $4547 per sem, grad $5852 per sem
Courses: Ceramics, Drawing, Painting, Printmaking, Sculpture, Drawing, Goldsmithing, Graphic Arts, Graphic Design, Handicrafts, Illustration, Intermedia, Jewelry, Lettering, Mixed Media, Book Making, Glass, Papermaking, Wood, Serigraphy, Stage Design & Lighting, Typography, Woodworking
Summer School: Three wk intersession, 8 wk session
—Dept of Art History, Elvehjem Museum of Art, Rm 232, 800 University Ave, 53706. Tel 608-263-2340; *Art History Dept Chmn* Barbara C Buenger; *Prof* Henry J Drewal; *Prof* James M Dennis; *Prof* Frank R Horlbeck; *Prof* Narcisco G Menocal; *Assoc Prof* Barbara C Buenger; *Assoc Prof* Gail L Geiger; *Asst Prof* Nicholas D Mirzoeff; *Asst Prof* Julia K Murray; *Asst Prof* Quitman E Phillips
Estab 1848, dept estab 1925; pub; D; scholarships & fels; enrl 1500, maj 75, grad 69
Ent Req: HS dipl
Degrees: MA, PhD
Tuition: Res—$1929 per sem; nonres—$5852 per sem
Courses: †Art History, African Art, American Art, Asian Art, Dutch Painting, Greek Art & Society, Modern Art, 20th Century Photography, Venetian Painting, Western Architecture, Women's Art
—Graduate School of Business, Center for Arts Administration, 975 University Ave, 53706. Tel 608-263-4161; *Dir* E Arthur Prieve
Estab 1969
Tuition: Res—undergrad $1175 per sem, grad $1619 per sem; nonres—undergrad $3920 per sem, grad $4912 per sem; Minnesota res—undergrad $1625 per sem, grad $1825 per sem
Courses: Arts Administration Seminars, Colloquium in Arts Administration

MANITOWOC

SILVER LAKE COLLEGE, Art Dept, 2406 S Alverno Rd, 54220. Tel 414-684-6691, Ext 181; FAX 414-684-7082; *Chmn* Sr Mariella Erdmann, MA; *Instr* Donna Dart, MA; *Instr* Sr Andree DuCharme
Estab 1936, dept estab 1959; pvt; D & E; SC 21, LC 6; enrl D 50, E 10, non-maj 25, maj 25
Ent Req: HS dipl, ACT or SAT
Degrees: AA(Commercial Art) 2 yrs, BA(Studio Art) & BS or BA(Art Educ) 4 yrs
Tuition: Res & nonres—undergrad $8660 per yr
Courses: †Art Education, Art History, Calligraphy, Ceramics, †Commercial Art, Drawing, Graphic Arts, Graphic Design, Jewelry, Lettering, Mixed Media, Painting, Photography, Printmaking, Sculpture, Teacher Training, Textile Design, Computer

Graphics, †Studio Art
Children's Classes: Enrl 100; tuition $10-$25 per 6 wk term. Courses—Clay, Drawing, Fibers, Photography, Sculpture, Painting, Graphics
Summer School: Dir, Sr Lorita Gaffney. Enrl 350; tuition $155 per cr per 6 wk terms beginning June 18. Courses—vary

MARINETTE

UNIVERSITY OF WISCONSIN CENTER-MARINETTE COUNTY, Art Dept, Bay Shore, 54143. Tel 715-735-4301; FAX 715-735-4307; *Head Dept* James La Malfa, MFA
Estab 1850, dept estab 1946; pub; D & E; scholarships
Ent Req: HS dipl or GED
Degrees: AAS 2 yrs
Tuition: Res—undergrad $952.80 per sem; nonres—undergrad $3257.30 per sem
Courses: Art History, Drawing, Painting, Photography, Sculpture, Survey of Art, 2-D Design
Summer School: Dir, Sidney Bremer. Tuition $70 per cr. Courses—Art Appreciation, Art History

MENOMONIE

UNIVERSITY OF WISCONSIN-STOUT, Dept of Art & Design, 54751. Tel 715-232-1141; FAX 715-232-1669; *Head Dept* Ron Verdon, MFA; *Prof* Gene Bloedorn, MFA; *Prof* Todd Boppel, MFA; *Prof* Doug Cumming, MFA; *Prof* John Perri, MFA; *Prof* Eddie Wong, MFA; *Prof* Glen Bloedorn, MFA; *Prof* Dr Claudia Smith, PhD; *Prof* Susan Hunt, MFA; *Prof* Humphrey Gilbert, MFA; *Prof* Charles Wimmer; *Prof* Rob Price, MFA; *Prof* Paul De Long, MFA; *Assoc Prof* Sherri Klein; *Assoc Prof* Alan Gamache, MFA; *Asst Prof* Dion Manriquez, MFA; *Asst Prof* William De Hoff, MFA; *Asst Prof* Mark Kallsen; *Asst Prof* Kate Maury; *Asst Prof* Maureen Mitton; *Asst Prof* Timothy O'Keeffe; *Asst Prof* Benjamin Pratt; *Lectr* Tim Eaton, BFA
Estab 1893, dept estab 1965; pub; E; SC 60, LC 6; enrl D 24, non-maj 1200, maj 630
Ent Req: HS dipl
Degrees: BS(Art), BFA(Art) 4 yrs
Tuition: Res—undergrad $933 per sem, $78 per cr hr, grad $1115 per sem, $120 per cr hr; nonres—undergrad $2757 per sem, grad $3309 per sem; campus res—room & board $2158 per yr
Courses: †Art Education, Art History, Ceramics, Design, Drawing, †Graphic Design, †Industrial Design, †Interior Design, Painting, Printmaking, Sculpture, Silversmithing, Art Period Courses, Art Metals, Blacksmithing, Fashion Illustration
Children's Classes: Sat classes in Art Design, Art History, Fine Arts, Graphic Arts
Summer School: Dir, Gene Bloedorn. Enrl varies with class; tuition res—undergrad $452, grad $587; nonres—undergrad $1303, grad $1717 for term of 8 wks beginning June 1 - Aug 6. Courses—Advanced Graphic Design, Ceramics, Drawing, Design, Life Drawing, Painting, Printmaking

MEQUON

CONCORDIA UNIVERSITY, Division of Arts & Sciences, 12800 N Lake Shore Dr, 9 W, 53097. Tel 414-243-4208; FAX 414-243-4351; *Dean* Dr Gene Edward Veith
Estab 1881, dept estab 1971; den; D & E; SC 6, LC 1; enrl non-maj 100, maj 5
Ent Req: HS dipl
Degrees: AA 2 yrs, BA 2 yrs
Tuition: $5350 per sem; campus res—room & board $1800 per sem
Courses: Art History, Drawing, Graphic Design, Handicrafts, Painting, Sculpture, Design
Adult Hobby Classes: Art History, Ceramics, Design, Drawing, Introduction to Studio Art, Photography, Printmaking, Sculpture
Summer School: Terms of 5 wks. Courses—Drawing & Painting (outdoors)

MILWAUKEE

ALVERNO COLLEGE, Art Dept, 3401 S 39 St, PO Box 343922, 53234-3922. Tel 414-382-6000, 382-6148; FAX 414-382-6354; *Chmn* Nancy Lamers
Estab 1948; pvt, W only in degree program; D & E; scholarships; SC 20, LC 5; enrl D 2300, E 2300, maj 60
Ent Req: GPA, class rank and ACT or SAT
Degrees: BA 4 yrs (or 128 cr)
Tuition: $4644 per sem; campus res—room & board available
Courses: Art Education, Art History, Ceramics, Drawing, Painting, Printmaking, Sculpture, Teacher Training, Art Therapy, Computer Graphics, Enameling (Cloisonne), Fibers, General Crafts, Introduction to Visual Art, Metal Working
Summer School: Term June to August. Courses—Art Education, Studio Art

CARDINAL STRITCH COLLEGE, Art Dept, 6801 N Yates Rd, 53217-3985. Tel 414-352-5400, Ext 466; FAX 414-351-7516; *Asst Prof* Timothy Abler; *Asst Prof* William Carman; *Asst Prof* Peter Galante; *Asst Prof* Teri Wagner; *Adjunct Prof* Barbara Manger; *Lectr* Sr Jeanne Moynihan; *Lectr* Claire Pfleger
Estab 1937; den; D & E; scholarships; SC 29, LC 17; enrl maj 98
Ent Req: HS dipl, ent exam
Degrees: AA, BA, BFA, BA(Commercial Art), BA(Education)
Tuition: Undergrad $4480 per sem, $280 per cr hr; grad $290 per cr hr; campus—room & board $1910-$1985
Courses: †Art Education, †Art History, †Ceramics, †Drawing, †Film, †Graphic Design, Illustration, †Jewelry, Painting, †Photography, †Printmaking, †Sculpture, Textile Design, †Video, Computer Graphics, Fibers, Metalsmithing
Adult Hobby Classes: Enrl 200; tuition $40-$100 per 8-12 wk sessions. Courses—Basic, Ceramics, Drawing, Mixed Media, Painting, Watercolor
Children's Classes: Enrl 100; tuition $60 per child per 12 classes. Courses—traditional media plus various crafts

MILWAUKEE AREA TECHNICAL COLLEGE, Graphic Arts Division, 700 W State St, 53233. Tel 414-297-6433; FAX 414-271-2195; *Assoc Dean* James MacDonald; *Instr* Howard Austin, MS; *Instr* William Bonifay, BS; *Instr* Mary Anna Petrick, MFA; *Instr* Joseph D'Lugosz, BFA; *Instr* Geraldine Geischer, MFA; *Instr* John Strachota, MS; *Instr* Edward Adams, MFA; *Instr* Corrine Kraus, BFA; *Instr* Janice Mahlberg, BS; *Instr* Patrick Mitten, BS; *Instr* John Raymer, BS; *Instr* Mark Saxon, AAS; *Instr* Elliot Schnackenberg, BFA; *Instr* Robert Stocki; *Instr* James Surges, AAS; *Instr* Dewey Coerper, MS; *Instr* Sharman Hummel, BA; *Instr* Ted Joyce; *Instr* Thomas Kusz; *Instr* Leonard McGhee, MS; *Instr* Walter Royek, AAS; *Instr* Olga Schuster; *Instr* C Ryan Smith, MS; *Instr* Anne Steinberg, BA
Estab 1912, dept estab 1958; pub; D & E; financial aid; enrl D 240, E 150
Ent Req: HS dipl
Degrees: AA 2 yrs
Tuition: res—$35.25 per cr hr; $564 per sem; $1128 per yr; nonres—$235.80 per cr hr; no campus res
Courses: Advertising Design, Commercial Art, Design, Display, Drawing, Graphic Arts, Graphic Design, Illustration, Interior Design, Jewelry, Lettering, Mixed Media, Photography, Teacher Training, Video, Computer Graphics, Multimedia, Visual Communications, 3-D Modeling & Animation
Adult Hobby Classes: Tuition $46.10 per cr

MILWAUKEE INSTITUTE OF ART & DESIGN, 273 E Erie St, 53202. Tel 414-276-7889; FAX 414-291-8077; *Pres* Terrence J Coffman, BFA; *VPres Academic Affairs* John E Spurgin; *Dean Fine Arts* Deane Nesbitt; *Dean Design* Becky Balistreri; *Dean Liberal Studies* Steve Kapelke; *Assoc Dean Foundations* Jan Feldhausen. Instrs: FT 25, PT 50
Estab 1974; pvt; D; scholarships; enrl D 400, maj 472
Ent Req: HS dipl, portfolio
Degrees: BFA 4 yrs
Tuition: $7000 per yr
Courses: Advertising Design, Aesthetics, Art History, Conceptual Art, Constructions, Design, Display, Drafting, Drawing, Graphic Design, History of Art & Archaeology, Illustration, Industrial Design, Interior Design, Painting, Photography, Printmaking, Sculpture, Silversmithing
Summer School: Dir, John E Spurgin. Enrl, 25; tuition $256 per cr for 12 wk term. Courses—Art History, Basic Design, Drawing, English

MOUNT MARY COLLEGE, Art Dept, 2900 N Menomonee River Pky, 53222. Tel 414-258-4810; *Chmn* Sr Angelee Fuchs, MA; *Gallery Dir* Karen Olsen; *Prof* S Rosemarita Hubner, MFA; *Prof* Charles Kaiser, MFA; *Prof* Joseph Rozman, MFA; *Assoc Prof* Sandra Keiser; *Assoc Prof* Sr Aloyse Hessburg, MA; *Assoc Prof* Elaine Zarse, MA; *Assoc Prof* Pamela Steffen, MBS; *Assoc Prof* Lynn Kapitan, MPS; *Assoc Prof* Geraldine Wind; *Assoc Prof* Sr Carla Huebner, MS; *Asst Prof* Kay Hruska; *Asst Prof* Dennis Klopfer; *Instr* Melody Todd Ashby, MS; *Instr* Margie Zymbrzuski; *Instr* Mary Kuhnen, MA; *Instr* Greg Miller, MS; *Instr* Karen Olsen, MA; *Instr* Patty Rass, MA; *Instr* J Michael Tucci; *Instr* Martha Bolles, MA; *Instr* Lorrie Paepke, MA; *Instr* Sue Loesl, MA; *Instr* Luanne Alberts, MA; *Instr* Joanne Bowring; *Instr* Jackie Halverson, BA; *Instr* Karen McCormick, MA; *Instr* Laura Dralle; *Instr* Mary Elliott, BA; *Instr* Dawn Oertel; *Instr* Kathy Kubiak, BA
Estab 1913, dept estab 1929; den; D & E; scholarships for women only; SC 22, LC 12; enrl D 200, E 30, non-maj 50, maj 200
Ent Req: HS dipl
Degrees: BA 4 yrs
Tuition: $7300 per yr, $3650 per sem; campus res—available; board $750 - $1000 per sem
Courses: †Advertising Design, Aesthetics, Architecture, Art Appreciation, †Art Education, Art History, Calligraphy, Ceramics, Commercial Art, Constructions, Costume Design & Construction, Design, Display, Drawing, †Fashion Arts, Film, Graphic Arts, †Graphic Design, Handicrafts, †Occupational Therapy, Silversmithing, Stage Design, Teacher Training, Textile Design, Video, Weaving, Art Therapy
Adult Hobby Classes: Enrl 1300; tuition variable, on going year round. Courses—Varied, self-interest
Children's Classes: Enrl 125; tuition $55 for 2 wk term, summer only. Courses—Arts & Crafts
Summer School: Dir, Toni Wulff

UNIVERSITY OF WISCONSIN-MILWAUKEE, Dept of Art, School of Fine Arts, PO Box 413, 53201. Tel 414-229-4200; FAX 414-229-6154; *Dean* Catherine A Davy. Instrs: FT 30, PT 29
Scholarships; enrl maj 860
Degrees: BFA(Art), BFA with teachers cert, MA(Art), MS(Art Educ), MFA(Art), MFA with teachers cert
Tuition: Res—undergrad $1078.25 per sem
Courses: Art Education, Ceramics, Drawing, Painting, Photography, Printmaking, Sculpture, Graphic Design, Metals
Children's Classes: Enrl 100; tuition $20 for 1 month term. Courses—Clay, Drawing, Mixed Media, Painting
Summer School: Enrl 250. Courses—Vary

OSHKOSH

UNIVERSITY OF WISCONSIN-OSHKOSH, Dept of Art, 800 Algoma Blvd, 54901. Tel 414-424-2222; FAX 414-424-1738; *Chmn* David Hodge. Instrs: FT 24
Estab 1871; pub; D & E; scholarships for grad students; SC 56, LC 14, GC 31; enrl D 10,5000, E 2500, maj 350, minors 50
Ent Req: HS dipl
Degrees: BA, BAE and BS(Art) 4 yrs, BFA 82 cr
Courses: Advertising Design, Art Education, Art History, Ceramics, Commercial Art, Drawing, Graphic Arts, Jewelry, Lettering, Painting, Photography, Printmaking, Sculpture, Teacher Training, Textile Design, Woodcraft

PLATTEVILLE

UNIVERSITY OF WISCONSIN-PLATTEVILLE, Dept of Fine Art, * Art Bldg 212B, 53818. Tel 608-342-1781; *Chmn* Roger Gottschalk. Instrs: FT 8
Estab 1866; pub; D & E; SC 30, LC 5, GC 3; enrl maj 105
Ent Req: HS dipl, ent exam
Degrees: BA and BS 4 yrs
Tuition: Res—undergrad $1043, grad $1268; nonres—undergrad $3135, grad $3732
Courses: Ceramics, Drawing, Graphic Design, Illustration, Painting, Photography, Printmaking, Art Survey, Ethnic Art, Fiber & Fabrics, Lettering & Typographic, Art in Elementary Education
Summer School: Dir, Harold Hutchinson. Enrl 2200; term of 8 wks beginning June. Courses—same as regular session

RICE LAKE

UNIVERSITY OF WISCONSIN, Center-Barron County, Dept of Art, 1800 College Dr, 54868. Tel 715-234-8176, Ext 5408; FAX 715-234-1975; *Assoc Prof* Don Ruedy, MFA
Pub; D & E; scholarships; SC 8, LC 2; enrl D 63, E 10, non-maj 57, maj 16
Ent Req: HS dipl
Degrees: AA & AS 2 yrs
Tuition: Res—$843.75 per sem; nonres—$2693 per sem; no campus res
Courses: Art History, Calligraphy, Design, Drawing, Jewelry, Lettering, Painting, Printmaking, Theatre Arts
Children's Classes: Enrl 30; tuition $40 for 2 wks in summer. Courses—Art

RIPON

RIPON COLLEGE, Art Dept, PO Box 248, 54971. Tel 414-748-8110; *Chmn* Evelyn Kain. Instrs: FT 2, PT 1
Estab 1851; pvt; D; scholarships and financial aid; SC 13, LC 8; enrl maj 20
Ent Req: Grad from accredited secondary school, SAT or ACT is recommended, but not required
Degrees: AB 4 yrs
Tuition: $16,780 per yr
Courses: †Art History, Design, Drawing, Mixed Media, Painting

RIVER FALLS

UNIVERSITY OF WISCONSIN-RIVER FALLS, Art Dept, 54022. Tel 715-425-3266; FAX 715-425-0657; *Chmn* Michael Padgett
Estab 1874, major estab 1958; pub; D; scholarships; SC 26, LC 18; enrl non-maj 400, maj 170
Ent Req: HS dipl
Degrees: BA, BS(Educ), BFA and BS(Liberal Arts) 4 yrs
Courses: Aesthetics, †Art Education, Art History, Ceramics, Costume Design & Construction, Drawing, Film, Graphic Design, History of Art & Archaeology, Jewelry, Painting, Photography, Printmaking, Silversmithing, Textile Design, Glass Blowing, Fibers, Stained Glass
Summer School: Dir, Dr Roger Swanson. Enrl 1600; 4 wk sessions. Courses—Clay, Fibers, Glass, Painting, Printmaking, Sculpture

STEVENS POINT

UNIVERSITY OF WISCONSIN-STEVENS POINT, Dept of Art & Design, College of Fine Arts, 1801 Franklin St, 54481. Tel 715-346-2669, 346-4066; FAX 715-346-2718;
Internet Home Page Address http://www.uwsp.edu/acad/cofa/index.htm.
Chmn&Prof Gary Hagen, MFA; *Prof* Rex Dorethy; *Prof* Daniel Fabiano; *Assoc Prof* Patricia Kluetz; *Assoc Prof* Robert Stowers; *Assoc Prof* Diane Bywaters; *Assoc Prof* Anne-Bridget Gary; *Assoc Prof* Jeff Morin; *Asst Prof* Robert Erickson; *Asst Prof* Larry Ball; *Asst Prof* Rob Stolzer; *Asst Prof* Guillermo Penafiel; *Lectr* Jay Salinks; *Lectr* Mark Pohlkamp
Estab 1894; pub; D & E; enrl D 866, non-maj 666, maj 250
Ent Req: HS dipl
Degrees: BA(Fine Arts) & BFA(Art-Professional)
Tuition: Res $2680.15 per sem; non res $5074.15; campus res available
Courses: Ceramics, Drawing, Graphic Design, Painting, Photography, Printmaking, Sculpture, Computer Graphics, †Studio Art
Children's Classes: Art Workshop
Summer School: Chnm, Gary Hagen. Term of 8 wks beginning June 14. Courses—Art Education, Design, Drawing, Painting

SUPERIOR

UNIVERSITY OF WISCONSIN-SUPERIOR, Programs in the Visual Arts, 1800 Grand Ave, 54880. Tel 715-394-8391, 394-8101; *Chmn* James Grittner, MFA; *Prof* Mel Olsen, MFA; *Prof* William Morgan, MFA; *Prof* Linda Helender, MFA; *Assoc Prof* Laurel Scott, PhD; *Assoc Prof* Susan Loonsk, MFA; *Asst Prof* Joshua Doyle; *Lectr* Kim Borst, MFA; *Lectr* Pope Wright, MA
Estab 1896, dept estab 1930; pub; D & E; scholarships; enrl D 250, E 100-125, non-maj 250, maj 100, grad 30
Ent Req: HS dipl
Degrees: BS, BS(Photography), BS(Art Therapy), BFA & BFA(Photography) 4 yrs, BFA with cert 5 yrs, MA 5 - 6 yrs
Tuition: Res—undergrad $1300 per sem, grad $1600 per sem; nonres—undergrad $3000 per sem, grad $3600 per sem; campus res available
Courses: †Art Education, †Art History, †Ceramics, Collages, Design, Drawing, †Jewelry, †Painting, †Photography, †Printmaking, †Sculpture, †Silversmithing, †Teacher Training, †Weaving, †Art Therapy
Adult Hobby Classes: Ceramics, Crafts, Drawing, Fibers, Metalwork, Painting, Photography

Children's Classes: Summer session only
Summer School: Dir, James Grittner. Enrl 100; tuition varies for term of 3 & 4 wks beginning June 12th. Courses—Art History, Ceramics, Drawing, Painting, Photography

WAUKESHA

CARROLL COLLEGE, Art Dept, 100 N East Ave, 53186. Tel 414-547-1211, 524-7191; *Co-Chmn* Thomas Selle; *Assoc Prof* Philip Krejcarek, MFA
Estab 1846; pvt; D & E; scholarships; SC 21, LC 4; enrl D 1100, E 350
Ent Req: HS dipl, SAT or ACT
Degrees: BA
Tuition: $13,190 annual full-time tuition
Courses: Museum Staff Training, Sculpture, †Stage Design, †Teacher Training, Textile Design, †Theatre Arts, †Video, †Pre-Architecture; †Commercial Art; Weaving
Adult Hobby Classes: Enrl 20 per sess. Courses—Photographing Your Own Work
Children's Classes: New program
Summer School: Asst Prof, Thomas Selle. Enrl varies; tuition varies for term of 6 wks. Courses—Drawing, Graphics, Photography

WHITEWATER

UNIVERSITY OF WISCONSIN-WHITEWATER, Dept of Art, Ctr of the Arts 2073, 53190. Tel 414-472-1324; FAX 414-472-2808; *Chmn* William L Chandler. Instrs: FT 16, PT 1
Estab 1868; pub; D & E; SC 41, LC 18; enrl D 270, maj 200
Ent Req: HS dipl
Degrees: BA & BS(Art, Art Educ, Art History, Graphic Design), BFA 4 yrs
Tuition: Res—$825 per sem; nonres—$2366 per sem; campus res $994 per sem
Courses: Art Appreciation, †Art Education, †Art History, Ceramics, Design, Drawing, †Graphic Design, Illustration, Jewelry, Painting, Photography, Printmaking, Sculpture, Teacher Training
Adult Hobby Classes: Enrl 240; tuition non res—undergrad $296.40 per cr, res undergrad—$96.90 per cr
Summer School: Enrl 80; 3 & 6 wk terms, May- Aug. Courses—Art History, Ceramics, Drawing

WYOMING

CASPER

CASPER COLLEGE, Dept of Visual Arts, 125 College Dr, 82601. Tel 307-268-2110; FAX 307-268-2224; *Div Head* Lynn R Munns; *Instr* Richard Jacobi, MFA; *Instr* Linda Lee Ryan, MFA; *Instr* Nancy Madura, MFA; *Instr* James L Gaither, MED; *Instr* Michael Keogh, MFA
Pub; D & E; scholarships; LC 2; enrl D 3870
Ent Req: HS dipl
Degrees: AA 2 yrs
Tuition: Res—undergrad $26 per cr hr, $477 per sem nonres—undergrad $108 per cr hr, $1236 per sem; campus res—room & board $1075-$1275
Courses: Advertising Design, Art History, Ceramics, Collages, Commercial Art, Drafting, Drawing, Handicrafts, Illustration, Jewelry, Painting, Photography, Sculpture, Silversmithing, Textile Design, Theatre Arts
Adult Hobby Classes: Tuition $32 per cr hr. Courses—Air Brush, Ceramics, Drawing, Fiber Art, Jewelry, Painting, Photography, Watercolor
Summer School: Dir, Kathy Anderson. Enrl 100; tuition $126 for summer sem or $21 per hr. Courses—Air Brush, Ceramics, Drawing, Jewelry, Painting, Photography

CHEYENNE

LARAMIE COUNTY COMMUNITY COLLEGE, Division of Arts & Humanities, 1400 E College Dr, 82007. Tel 307-778-1158; *Asst Dean* Chuck Thompson, MA; *Instr* Matt West, MFA; *Instr* Joan Fullerton, MFA
Estab 1969; pub; D & E; scholarships; SC 19, LC 3; enrl D 125, E 100, non-maj 150, maj 20
Ent Req: HS dipl
Degrees: AA
Tuition: Res—$496 per sem; nonres—$1320 per sem
Courses: Ceramics, Drawing, Painting, Photography, Sculpture, Theatre Arts, Computer Graphics, Designs & Welded Sculpture, Metals
Summer School: Dir, Chuck Thompson. Enrl 40; tuition $34 per cr hr for 8 wk term. Courses—Ceramics, Computer Gaphics, Drawing, Metals

LARAMIE

UNIVERSITY OF WYOMING, Dept of Art, PO Box 3138, 82071-3138. Tel 307-766-3269; FAX 307-766-5468; Elec Mail bardin@uwyo.edu; mjclay@uwyo.edu. *Head Dept* Mary Jane Edwards. Instrs: FT 8
Estab 1886; dept estab 1946; pub; D; scholarships; SC 23, LC 6, GC 13; enrl D 80, non-maj 600, maj 120, grad 16
Ent Req: HS dipl
Degrees: BA, BS and BFA 4 yrs, MFA 2 yrs, MA and MAT 1 yr
Tuition: Res—$1072 per sem; nonres—$3436 per sem
Courses: Art Appreciation, †Art Education, Art History, †Ceramics, Design, Drawing, †Graphic Design, †Painting, †Printmaking, †Sculpture
Adult Hobby Classes: Courses offered through University of Wyoming Art Museum
Summer School: Dir, Mary Jane Edwards. Enrl 129; tuition res—undergrad $83.50 per cr hr 1-12, grad $102.50 per cr hr 1-12; non res—undergrad $231.50 per cr hr 1-12, grad $250.50 per cr hr 1-12, 4 & 8 wk sessions. Courses—Art Appreciation, Art History, Ceramics, Drawing, Graphic Design, Painting, Printmaking, Sculpture

POWELL

NORTHWEST COMMUNITY COLLEGE, Dept of Art, 231 W Sixth St, 82435. Tel 307-754-6111; *Chmn* Neil Hansen; *Instr* Lynn Thorpe; *Instr* John Giarrizzo; *Instr* DeBoer; *Instr* Micael Torre
Estab 1946, dept estab 1952; pub; D & E; scholarships; SC 12, LC 4; enrl D 130, E 222, non-maj 317, maj 35
Ent Req: HS dipl, nonres ACT
Degrees: AA 2 yrs
Tuition: Res—undergrad $472 per sem; nonres—undergrad $1172 per sem, WUE 1.50% res tuition
Courses: Advertising Design, Art Education, Ceramics, Commercial Art, Drawing, Graphic Arts, Graphic Design, Handicrafts, Lettering, Painting, Photography, Printmaking, History of Graphic Design
Adult Hobby Classes: Enrl 100. Courses—Vary each sem

RIVERTON

CENTRAL WYOMING COLLEGE, Art Center, 2660 Peck Ave, 82501. Tel 307-856-9291; *Div Head* Chet Rogalski; *Prof* Sallie Wesaw, MFA; *Prof* Willis R Patterson
Estab 1966; pub; D & E; scholarships; SC 20, LC 2; enrl D 1500, E 500, non-maj 100, maj 20, others 20
Ent Req: HS dipl, GED
Degrees: AA 2 yrs
Tuition: Res $312 per sem; nonres—$936 per sem; sr citizen free of charge; campus res—room & board $1138
Courses: Art Appreciation, Art Education, Art History, Ceramics, Drawing, Graphic Arts, Mixed Media, Painting, Photography, Printmaking, Sculpture, Stage Design, Teacher Training, Theatre Arts, Bronze Casting, Fiber Arts, Lapidary, Moldmaking, Stained Glass, Stone/Wood Carving, Weaving
Adult Hobby Classes: Enrl 12-20; tuition $15-$50. Courses—Varied Art & General Curriculum
Children's Classes: Enrl 200; classes for a day, wk or sem. Courses—varied
Summer School: Limited Art offerings

ROCK SPRINGS

WESTERN WYOMING COMMUNITY COLLEGE, Art Dept, PO Box 428, 82901. Tel 307-382-1600, Ext 723; *Head Dept* Dr Florence McEwin. Instrs: FT 3, PT 4
Estab 1959; pub; D & E; scholarships; SC 12, LC 1; enrl D 675, E 600, maj 20
Ent Req: HS dipl
Degrees: AA 2 yrs
Tuition: $431.50 full-time
Courses: Advertising Design, Art Appreciation, Art History, Ceramics, Collages, Design, Drafting, Drawing, Film, Graphic Design, History of Art & Archaeology, Mixed Media, Museum Staff Training, Painting, Photography, Printmaking, Sculpture, Stage Design, Theatre Arts, Video, Life Drawing
Adult Hobby Classes: Enrl 100. Courses—Crafts, Drawing, Painting, Pottery
Children's Classes: Dance
Summer School: Dir, Florence McEwin. Courses—Ceramics, Photography

SHERIDAN

SHERIDAN COLLEGE, Art Dept, 3059 Coffeen Ave, PO Box 1500, 82801-1500. Tel 307-674-6446, Ext 123; FAX 307-674-4293; *Head Dept* Jim Lawson; *Instr* Danna Hildebrand. Instrs: PT 3
Estab 1951; pub; D & E; scholarships; enrl maj 10
Ent Req: HS grad
Degrees: AA, AS & AAS 2 yrs
Tuition: In-state res—$440 per sem; out-of-state res—$1140 per sem; Western undergrads $615 per sem
Courses: Art Appreciation, Ceramics, Design, Drawing, Jewelry, Painting, Photography, Sculpture, Etching, Lithography, Pottery, Silk Screen
Adult Hobby Classes: Enrl 40-60; tuition varies. Courses—Drawing, Painting, Pottery, Stained Glass
Children's Classes: Enrl 10-15; tuition varies. Courses—Pottery
Summer School: Enrl 10-15; tuition varies. Courses—Painting, Pottery

TORRINGTON

EASTERN WYOMING COLLEGE, Art Dept, 3200 W C St, 82240. Tel 307-532-8291; FAX 307-532-8225; *Head Dept* Sue Milner. Instrs: FT 1, PT 2
Estab 1948; pub; D & E; scholarships; SC 9, LC 1; enrl D 60, 50, maj 6
Ent Req: Varied
Degrees: AA and AAS 2 yrs
Tuition: Res—$312 per sem; nonres—$936 per sem
Courses: Ceramics, Commercial Art, Drawing, Graphic Arts, History of Art & Archaeology, Painting, Sculpture, General Art, Design I
Adult Hobby Classes: Painting Workshops
Summer School: Dir, Sue Milner. Enrl 20; tuition $30 per cr hr for 6 wk term. Courses—Ceramics, Drawing

PUERTO RICO

MAYAGUEZ

UNIVERSITY OF PUERTO RICO, MAYAGUEZ, Dept of Humanities, College
of Arts & Sciences, PO Box 5000, 00681. Tel 787-832-4040, Ext 3160, 265-3846;
FAX 809-265-1225; *Dir* Carlos Casablanca; *Gallery Dir* Felix Zupata. Instrs: FT 40
Estab 1970; pub; D; SC 20, LC 15; enrl 402, maj 115
Ent Req: HS dipl
Degrees: BA(Art Theory) and BA(Plastic Arts) 4 yrs
Courses: Aesthetics, Art Appreciation, Art Education, Art History, Calligraphy,
Ceramics, Commercial Art, Design, Drawing, Graphic Arts, Illustration, Painting,
Photography, Printmaking, Restoration & Conservation, Sculpture, Stage Design,
Teacher Training, Theatre Arts
Adult Hobby Classes: Enrl 40

PONCE

CATHOLIC UNIVERSITY OF PUERTO RICO, Dept of Fine Arts, 2250 Las
Americas Ave, Ste 563, 00731-6382. Tel 809-841-2000, Ext 276; FAX 809-840-
9595; *Head Dept* Alfonso Santiago; *Prof* Ana Basso Bruno, MFA; *Prof* Mahir
Laracuente, MM; *Prof* Adrian N Ramirez, MA; *Prof* Julio Micheli, MFA
Estab 1948, dept estab 1964; den; D; scholarships; SC 22, LC 4; enrl D 50 maj
Ent Req: HS dipl
Degrees: BA 4 yrs
Tuition: Res—undergrad $95 per cr hr, grad $130 per cr hr
Courses: Advertising Design, Aesthetics, Art Appreciation, Art Education, Art
History, Ceramics, Conceptual Art, Constructions, Design, Drawing, Graphic
Design, Painting, Photography, Printmaking, Sculpture, History in Art in Puerto
Rico, Contemporary Form

RIO PIEDRAS

UNIVERSITY OF PUERTO RICO, Dept of Fine Arts, Ponce de Leon Ave
(Mailing add: UPR Sta, PO Box 21A49, San Juan, 00931). Tel 809-764-0000; *Dir*
Sylvia Velez; *Prof* Luis Hernandez-Cruz, MA; *Prof* Arturo Davila, PhD; *Prof* Rafael
Rivera-Garcia, MA; *Assoc Prof* Enrique Garcia-Gutierrez, MA; *Assoc Prof* Carola
Colom, MA; *Assoc Prof* Susana Herrero, MA; *Assoc Prof* Carmen A Rivera de
Figueroa; *Asst Prof* Maria L Moreno, MA; *Asst Prof* Carmen T Ruiz de Fischler,
MA; *Asst Prof* Pablo Rubio, MA; *Asst Prof* Jaime Romano, MA; *Asst Prof* Rene
Torres-Delgado, MA; *Instr* Nelson Millan, MFA; *Instr* Guy Paizy
Estab 1902, dept estab 1950; pub; D; scholarships; enrl D 200, maj 45
Ent Req: HS dipl
Degrees: BA 4 yrs
Tuition: Res—undergrad $15 per cr; grad $45 per cr; campus res available
Courses: Architecture, Art Appreciation, Art History, Commercial Art, Design,
Drawing, Graphic Arts, Painting, Photography, Sculpture, Video, Art in Puerto
Rico, Michelangelo: Artist & Poet, Color Theory, General Theory of Art, Pre-
Hispanic Art of Antilles
Adult Hobby Classes: Tuition $125-$375 per sem cr (Aug-Dec & Jan-May).
Courses—Art History, Design, Drawing, Painting, Printmaking
Summer School: Dir, Dr Juan Barragan. Tuition $15 per cr for 2 month session.
Courses—Art Appreciation, Art History, Design, Drawing

SAN GERMAN

INTER AMERICAN UNIVERSITY OF PUERTO RICO, Dept of Art, * Call Box
5100, 00753. Tel 809-763-1464; *Dir* Jaime Carrero, MS; *Auxiliary Prof* Fernando
Santiago, MA; *Auxiliary Prof* Maria Garcia Vera, MFA; *Assoc Prof* Paul Vivoni,
EdD; *Instr* Jose B Alvarez, BA
Estab 1912, dept estab 1947; pvt; D; SC 20, LC 12; enrl D 135, maj 135
Ent Req: HS dipl, college board, presentation of portfolio
Degrees: BA 4 yrs
Tuition: Res—undergrad $75 per cr, grad $110 per cr; campus res available
Courses: †Art Education, Art History, Calligraphy, †Ceramics, Drawing, †Graphic
Arts, Handicrafts, †Painting, †Photography, †Sculpture, Experimental Design in
Native Media, Leather, Macrame, Metals
Summer School: Dir, Jaime Carrero. Enrl 10; tuition $75 per cr hr for 5 wk term.
Courses—Art Appreciation

SAN JUAN

INSTITUTE OF PUERTO RICAN CULTURE, Escuela de Artes Plasticas, School
of Fine Arts, El Morro Grounds (Mailing add: Institute of Puerto Rican Culture, PO
Box 1112, PR 00905-1112). Tel 809-725-1522; FAX 809-725-8111; *Chancellor*
Maimar Benitez
Estab 1971; pub; D; scholarships; SC 38, LC 12, GC 10; enrl D 160
Ent Req: HS dipl, ent exam
Degrees: BA 4 yrs
Tuition: In-state or out-of-state $1543 per yr
Courses: †Sculpture, Teacher Training
Adult Hobby Classes: Enrl 150; tuition $40 per cr. Courses—Graphic, Painting,
Sculpture
Summer School: Basic Drawing, Painting, Sculpture

NEW BRUNSWICK

SUPERIOR

LOVEWELL STUDIOS (Formerly Plum Tree Fine Arts Program), RR 2, Box 48,
68978. Elec Mail lovewell2@americaonline.com. WATS 800-373-6028. *Dir* Rich
Thibodeau, BFA
Estab 1982; pvt; D; scholarships; SC 26; enrl D 140
Tuition: Campus res available
Courses: Painting, Photography, Woodblock Printing
Adult Hobby Classes: Enrl 120. Courses—same as above
Children's Classes: Enrl 120. Courses—same as above
Summer School: Dir, Rich Thibodeau. Tuition $250-$350 for 1 wk, $100-$150
weekend. Courses— same as above

Art Schools In Canada

ALBERTA

BANFF

BANFF CENTRE FOR THE ARTS, PO Box 1020, Sta 28, T0L 0C0. Tel 403-762-6180; FAX 403-762-6345; Elec Mail arts—info@banffcentre.ab.cacable. Cable ARTSBANFF. *VPres Educ* Carol Phillips; *Artistic Dir/Exec Producer* Sara Diamond
Estab 1933 for summer study, winter cycle prog began 1979; scholarships; enrl winter 78, summer 39
Ent Req: Resume, slides of work, post-secondary art training at a university or art school and/or professional experience in field
Courses: Ceramics, Photography, Art Studio, Media Arts
Adult Hobby Classes: Enrl 70; tuition $2730. Courses—Art Studio, Ceramics Studio, Photography Studio, Visual Community
Summer School: Enrl 140; tuition $2730. Courses—Art Studio, Ceramics Studio, Photography Studio, Visual Community

CALGARY

ALBERTA COLLEGE OF ART, 1407 14th Ave NW, T2N 4R3. Tel 403-284-7600; FAX 403-289-6682; *Acad Dean Fine Arts* Helen Sevelius; *Dean Design* Arwin Van Vorthuizen; *Dean Core & Humanities* Rob Milphorp
Estab 1926; pub; D & E; scholarships; SC approx 250, LC 14; enrl D 650, E 500, non-maj 200, maj 390, others 60
Ent Req: HS dipl, portfolio
Degrees: BFA
Tuition: $8633 per yr plus course costs
Courses: Ceramics, Drawing, Jewelry, Painting, Photography, Printmaking, Sculpture, Glass, Photographic Arts, Textiles, Visual Communications
Adult Hobby Classes: Enrl 1000; tuition varies per course. Courses—Ceramics, Art Fundamentals, Drawing, Jewelry, Painting, Printmaking, Sculpture, Glass, Textiles, Watercolor, Photography
Children's Classes: Enrl 560; tuition $95 per course; Pre-College Studio $110 for 18 hrs. Courses—Ceramics, Jewelry, Mixed Media, Painting, Painting for Teenagers, Puppetry, Sculpture

MOUNT ROYAL COLLEGE, Dept of Interior Design, 4825 Richard Rd SW, T3E 6K6. Tel 403-240-6100; FAX 403-240-6939; *Chmn* Jacqui McFarland. Instrs: FT 5, PT 10
Estab 1910; pub; D & E; scholarships; SC 12, LC 17
Ent Req: HS dipl
Degrees: 2 yr dipl
Tuition: $5000 per sem
Courses: Design, †Interior Design, Sculpture, Stage Design, Business Principles & Practices, Graphic Presentation, History of Art & Architecture, History of Furniture, Technical Design & Drafting
Adult Hobby Classes: Enrl 50. Courses—Interior Design Program

UNIVERSITY OF CALGARY, Dept of Art, 2500 University Dr NW, AB605, T2N 1N4. Tel 403-220-5252; FAX 403-289-7333; *Dean, Faculty Fine Arts* Dr Maurice Yacowar; *Dept Head* Eric Cameron. Instrs: FT 21, PT 6
Estab 1965; pub; D & E; SC 56, LC 19, GC 8; enrl D 263, E 31, all maj
Ent Req: HS dipl
Degrees: BA(Art History), BFA(School Art, Art), MFA(Studio)
Tuition: $1018.25 fall or winter sem
Courses: Art Education, Art History, Drawing, Painting, Photography, Sculpture, Printmaking, Art Fundamentals, Art Theory
Summer School: Two terms of 6 wks, May-July. Courses—Art History, Drawing, Printmaking, Painting, Art Fundamentals, Art Education, Sculpture

EDMONTON

UNIVERSITY OF ALBERTA, Dept of Art & Design, 398 Fine Arts Bldg, T6G 2C9. Tel 403-492-3261; FAX 403-492-7870; *Chmn* Dr Desmond Rochfort
Estab 1908, dept estab 1946; pub; D & E; scholarships; SC 51, LC 42, grad 23; enrl D 151, grad 15-20
Ent Req: HS dipl, portfolio
Degrees: BFA 4 yrs, MFA, MA 2 yrs
Tuition: Res—undergrad $2900 per yr, grad $3100 per yr; international—$6220; campus res available
Courses: †Art History, †Graphic Design, †Industrial Design, †Painting, †Printmaking, †Sculpture
Summer School: Dir, Rick Chenier. Enrl 150; tuition $420 per course. Courses—Art History, Drawing, Painting, Printmaking, Sculpture

LETHBRIDGE

UNIVERSITY OF LETHBRIDGE, Div of Art, 4401 University Dr, T1K 3M4. Tel 403-329-2691; FAX 403-382-7127; *Asst Dean* Open; *Asst Prof* Nichlos Wade; *Assoc Prof* Carl Granzow, MFA; *Asst Prof* Janet Cardiff, MFA; *Asst Prof* Leslie Dawn; *Asst Prof* Jennifer Gordon
Estab 1967; pub; D & E; scholarships; SC 26, LC 9
Ent Req: HS dipl
Degrees: BA and BFA 4 yrs
Tuition: Res—undergrad $238 for 3 cr hr; nonres—undergrad $476 for 3 cr hr
Courses: Aesthetics, Art Appreciation, Art Education, Art History, Conceptual Art, Costume Design & Construction, Design, Drawing, History of Art & Archaeology, Intermedia, Mixed Media, Museum Staff Training, Painting, Photography, Printmaking, Sculpture, Stage Design, Teacher Training, Theatre Arts, Video

RED DEER

RED DEER COLLEGE, Dept of Art & Design, 56th Ave & 32nd St, Box 5005, T4N 5H5. Tel 403-342-3300; FAX 403-347-0399; *Chmn* Ian Cook. Instrs: FT 6, PT 2
Estab 1973; pub; D & E; scholarships; enrl max 50 first yr students, 30 second yr
Ent Req: HS dipl, portfolio
Degrees: Dipl, BFA 2 yrs
Courses: Art History, Ceramics, Drawing, Painting, Printmaking, Sculpture, Fundamentals of Visual Communication
Adult Hobby Classes: Enrl 300; tuition $74 - $100 per course. Courses—Ceramics, Drawing, Glass Blowing
Children's Classes: Enrl 80; tuition $350 per wk. Courses—Drawing, Painting, Sculpture
Summer School: Dir, Ann Brodie. Enrl 500; tuition $200 per wk. Courses—Applied Arts, Drawing, Glass Blowing, Painting, Printmaking

BRITISH COLUMBIA

VANCOUVER

EMILY CARR INSTITUTE OF ART & DESIGN, 1399 Johnston St, V6H 3R9. Tel 604-844-3800; FAX 604-844-3801; *Pres* Dr Ronald Burnett; *Dir Student Services* Alan C McMillan; *Dean Studio* Renee Van Halm; *Dean Design* Tom Becher; *Dean Media* Jim Breukelman; *Dean First Yr* Monique Fouquet
Estab 1925; pub; D & E; scholarships; SC 20, LC 8; enrl 800
Ent Req: HS dipl plus presentation of folio of art work
Degrees: 4 yr dipl, 4 yr degree
Tuition: $2200; part-time courses $230 & up
Courses: Art History, Ceramics, Design, Drawing, Film, Graphic Design, Photography, Printmaking, Sculpture, Video, Animation, Intermedia Studies
Adult Hobby Classes: Enrl 2000; tuition $250 per course. Courses—Design, Fine Arts
Children's Classes: Enrl 70. Courses—Art Access
Summer School: Dir, Isabel Scott. Enrl 700; tuition $250. Courses—Design, Fine Arts

UNIVERSITY OF BRITISH COLUMBIA
—Dept of Fine Arts, 6333 Memorial Rd, V6T 1Z2. Tel 604-822-2757; FAX 604-822-9003; *Head* James O Caswell, PhD; *Prof* Serge Guilbaut, PhD; *Prof* Rhodri Windsor-Liscombe, PhD; *Prof* Jeff Wall, MA; *Assoc Prof* Richard Prince, BA; *Assoc Prof* Robert Young, BA; *Assoc Prof* Rose Marie San Juan, PhD; *Assoc Prof* Marvin Cohodas, PhD; *Assoc Prof* Moritaka Matsumoto, PhD; *Assoc Prof* Ken Lum, MFA; *Assoc Prof* John O Brian, PhD; *Assoc Prof* Barbara Z Sungur, MFA; *Asst Prof* Wendy Dobereiner, MA; *Asst Prof* Maureen Ryan, PhD; *Asst Prof* Judith Williams, BA; *Asst Prof* Katherine Hacker, PhD; *Asst Prof* Carol Knicely, PhD
Scholarships & fels
Courses: Art History, Graphic Arts, History of Art & Archaeology, Mixed Media, Painting, Photography, Printmaking, Sculpture, †Printmaking, †Sculpture, †Western, †Asian, †Indigenous Arts of the Americas
—School of Architecture, 6333 Memorial Rd, V6T 1Z2. Tel 604-822-2779; FAX 604-822-3808; *Dir* Sanford Hirshen. Instrs: FT 14
Estab 1946; pub; scholarships & fels
Degrees: MArchit & MPA
Tuition: $2400 per yr
Courses: Architecture, Architectural History, Computational Design, Design Studios, Environmental Design, Structures, Urban Design
Adult Hobby Classes: Enrl 170; tuition $2448 per yr for 3 yr program

VANCOUVER COMMUNITY COLLEGE, LANGARA CAMPUS, Dept of Fine Arts, 100 W 49th Ave, V5Y 2Z6. Tel 604-323-5511; FAX 604-323-5555; *Chmn Dept* Daryl Plater, BFA; *Div Chmn* Scott Plear, BFA; *Instr* Gordan Trick, MFA; *Instr* Gerald Formosa, Dipl Art; *Instr* Don Hutchinson, Dipl Art; *Instr* Barry Holmes, Nat Dipl; *Instr* Catherine Broderick-Lockhart, MFA; *Instr* Judith Brackman Sharp, MTA; *Instr* Lesley Finlayson, MFA
Estab 1970; pub; D & E; SC 7, LC 1; enrl D 160
Ent Req: HS dipl, portfolio
Degrees: 2 yr Fine Arts Dipl
Tuition: $700 per sem, $250 studio fees per sem
Courses: Ceramics, Design, Drawing, Painting, Printmaking, Sculpture
Adult Hobby Classes: Enrl 20 per class; tuition $100 per sem. Courses—Design, Drawing

VICTORIA

UNIVERSITY OF VICTORIA
—**Dept of Visual Arts,** MS 8011, V8W 2Y2. Tel 250-721-8011; FAX 250-721-6595; *Chmn* Robert Youds, MFA; *Prof* R Brener, Post Dipl, AD; *Assoc Prof* G Tiessen, MFA; *Assoc Prof* F Douglas; *Assoc Prof* Lynda Gammon, MFA; *Asst Prof* Vikky Alexander, BFA; *Asst Prof* S Meigs
Estab 1963; pub; D; enrl 50
Ent Req: HS dipl
Degrees: BFA, MFA
Tuition: Undergrad $2000 per yr
Courses: Drawing, Painting, Photography, Printmaking, Sculpture
Summer School: Drawing, Painting, Printmaking
—**Dept of History in Art,** V8W 2Y2. Tel 604-721-7942; FAX 604-721-7941; *Chair* Carol Gibson-Wood; *Dean* S Anthony Welch, PhD; *Prof* John L Osborne, PhD; *Assoc Prof* Nancy Micklewright, PhD; *Assoc Prof* Kathlyn Liscomb, PhD; *Assoc Prof* Elizabeth Tumasonis, PhD; *Assoc Prof* Victoria Wyatt, PhD; *Assoc Prof* Astri Wright, PhD; *Asst Prof* Lianne McLarty, PhD; *Asst Prof* Catherine Harding, PhD; *Asst Prof* Christopher Thomas, PhD
LC 52, grad 20
Degrees: BA, MA, PhD
Tuition: Undergrad $151 per unit, grad $966 per term
Courses: Art Therapy, Asian, Canadian, European & Native American Art, Chinese, Italian & Medieval Art, Islamic Architecture
Summer School: May-Aug

MANITOBA

WINNIPEG

UNIVERSITY OF MANITOBA
—**School of Art,** R3T 2N2. Tel 204-474-9303; FAX 204-275-3148; *Dir* Dale Amundson; *Chmn Drawing* Sharon Alward; *Co-Chmn Painting* Steven Higgins, MFA; *Co-Chmn Paintings* Diane Whitehouse, MFA; *Chmn Sculpture* Gordon Reeve, MFA; *Chmn Photography* David McMillan, MFA; *Chmn Graphic Design* Bruce Reimer; *Chmn Printmaking* William Pura, MFA; *Chmn Art History* Marilyn Baker, PhD; *Chmn Foundations* Charlotte Werner; *Chmn Ceramics* Robert Flynn
Estab 1950; pub; D; SC 35, LC 16; enrl D 420
Ent Req: HS dipl and portfolio
Degrees: BFA
Tuition: $1900 per yr
Courses: Art History, Drawing, Graphic Design, Painting, Photography, Printmaking, Sculpture, Foundations
Adult Hobby Classes: Courses offered
Summer School: Dir, Robert C Sakowski. Term of 6 wks. Courses—Studio & Art History
—**Faculty of Architecture,** R3T 2N2. Tel 204-474-6433; FAX 204-275-7198; *Dean* Michael Cox; *Assoc Dean* Mario Carvalho; *Head Environmental Design* Harlyn Thompson; *Head Landscape Archit* Charles Thomsen; *Head Dept Interior Design* Dana Stewart; *Acting Head Dept City Planning* Jeff Bargh; *Head Dept Archit* Herb Enns; *Prof* Thomas Hodne
Estab 1913; pub; scholarships; enrl Environmental Studies 218, Archit 110, Interior Design 284, City Planning 72, Landscape 60
Ent Req: Senior matriculation or Bachelor for particular subject
Degrees: BED, BID, MArchit, MCP, MID, M(Land Arch)
Tuition: $1900 per yr
Courses: Architecture, Interior Design, Landscape Architecture, Environmental Design, Landscape

NEW BRUNSWICK

EDMUNDSTON

UNIVERSITE DE MONCTON, CAMPUS D'EDMUNDSTON (Formerly Saint-Louis-Maillet), Dept of Visual Arts, 165 Blvd Hebert, E3V 2S8. Tel 506-737-5050; *Chief* Jacques Martin
Estab 1946, dept estab 1968; pub; D & E; scholarships; SC 12, LC 1; enrl D 20, E 11, non-maj 25, maj 6
Ent Req: HS dipl
Degrees: BA(Fine Arts) 4 yrs
Tuition: $2430; campus res—room & board $1545 per yr
Courses: Art History, Drawing, Painting, Sculpture

FREDERICTON

NEW BRUNSWICK COLLEGE OF CRAFT & DESIGN, PO Box 6000, E3B 5H1. Tel 506-453-2305; FAX 506-457-7352; *Dir Craft School* Janice Gillies
Estab 1946; pub; D; enrl 70 plus PT
Ent Req: HS dipl, transcript, questionnaire and interview
Degrees: 3 yr dipl
Tuition: $1600
Courses: Advertising Design, Art History, Ceramics, Design, Drawing, Fashion Arts, Graphic Arts, Illustration, Jewelry, Photography, Silversmithing, Textile Design, Weaving, †Clothing Design & Construction, Colour, †Creative Graphics, †Native Arts Studies
Adult Hobby Classes: Courses—Weekend workshops

UNIVERSITY OF NEW BRUNSWICK, Art Education Section, Faculty of Education, PO Box 4400, E3B 5A3. Tel 506-453-3500; FAX 506-453-3569; *Head Art Educ* Don Soucy
Tuition: Res—$1975 per yr
Courses: Art History, Art Education for Elementary Teachers, Art Media for Schools, Children's Art for Teachers, Art Seminar
Children's Classes: 70; tuition $15 for 6 weeks, one afternoon per wk

MONCTON

UNIVERSITE DE MONCTON, Dept of Visual Arts, E1A 3E9. Tel 506-858-4033; FAX 506-858-4166; *Chmn* Ghislain Clermont. Instrs: 6
Estab 1967; pub; D & E; SC 7, LC 3; enrl D 80, E 40, grad 10
Ent Req: HS dipl
Degrees: BA(Fine Arts) 4 yrs
Courses: Aesthetics, Art Education, †Ceramics, Drawing, †Painting, †Photography, †Printmaking, †Sculpture, †Teacher Training

SACKVILLE

MOUNT ALLISON UNIVERSITY, Fine Arts Dept, E0A 3C0. Tel 506-364-2490; FAX 506-364-2575; *Head* Virgil Hammock, MFA; *Prof* Thaddeus Holownia, BFA; *Prof* Rebecca Burke, MFA; *Assoc Prof* Thomas Henderson, MFA; *Assoc Prof* M J A Crooker, MA; *Asst Prof* Sylvat Aziz, MFA; *Asst Prof* Rita McKeough, MFA; *Lectr* Kelly Gemey, BFA
Estab 1854; pub; D & E; scholarships; SC 34, LC 19; enrl 85
Ent Req: HS dipl
Degrees: BFA 4 yrs
Tuition: $3665; campus res available
Courses: †Art History, †Drawing, †Painting, †Photography, †Printmaking, †Sculpture
Adult Hobby Classes: Enrl 20; 12 wk term. Courses—Drawing, Sculpture
Summer School: Dir, Virgil Hammock, MFA. Enrl 24; 5 day term. Courses—Accomodation Drawing, Printmaking

NEWFOUNDLAND

CORNER BROOK

MEMORIAL UNIVERSITY OF NEWFOUNDLAND, School of Fine Arts, Visual Arts Dept, University Dr, A2H 6P9. Tel 709-637-6333; FAX 709-637-6383; *Chmn* David Morrrish
Estab 1975, dept estab 1988; pub; D; scholarships; enrl D 50
Tuition: Res—undergrad $1344 yr; non-res—undergrad $1344 yr; campus res—room & board $2740 yr
Courses: Aesthetics, Art Appreciation, Art History, Design, Drawing, Mixed Media, Painting, Photography, Printmaking, Sculpture

NOVA SCOTIA

ANTIGONISH

ST FRANCIS XAVIER UNIVERSITY, Fine Arts Dept, B2G 2W5. Tel 902-867-2172; *Assoc Prof* T Roach. Instrs: PT 4
Scholarships
Courses: Art History, Design, Drawing, Painting, Printmaking, Stained Glass
Adult Hobby Classes: Courses - Drawing, General Studio, Painting
Children's Classes: Courses - Drawing, Painting, Printmaking
Summer School: Dir, Angus Braid. Enrl 15; 5 wk sem beginning July-Aug. Courses—General Studio

HALIFAX

NOVA SCOTIA COLLEGE OF ART & DESIGN, 5163 Duke St, B3J 3J6. Tel 902-422-7381; FAX 902-425-2420; *Pres* Alice Mansell; *Dean* Dr Jill Grant; *Assoc Dean* Dr Harold Pearse; *Dir Foundation Studies* Barbara Lowder; *Dir Grad Studies&Coordr MFA Prog* Susan McEachern
Estab 1887; pvt; D & E; SC 67, LC 31, GC 8 each sem; enrl 600, grad 17
Ent Req: HS dipl, portfolio or project
Degrees: BFA, BD(Environmental Planning or Graphic Design), BA, MFA & MA(Art Educ)

Tuition: $1670 per sem; visa students $2520 per sem; no campus res
Courses: Art Education, Art History, Ceramics, Design, Drawing, Graphic Arts, Graphic Design, Jewelry, Mixed Media, Painting, Photography, Printmaking, Sculpture, Textile Design, Video, Computer Art
Adult Hobby Classes: Enrl 300; tuition $80 - $175. Courses—Art History, Craft, Computer Art, Drawing, Graphic Technology, Painting, Photography, Sculpture
Children's Classes: Enrl 125; tuition, materials fee. Courses—Art
Summer School: Coordinator, Jerry Ferguson. Tuition $1670 ($2520 Visa students) for term of 14 wks beginning May 15. Half sessions offered

TECHNICAL UNIVERSITY OF NOVA SCOTIA, Faculty of Architecture, 5410 Spring Garden Rd, PO Box 1000, B3J 2X4. Tel 902-420-7692; FAX 902-423-6672; *Interim Dean* Grant Wanzel; *Prof* T Emodi; *Prof* Philip McAleer; *Prof* D Procos; *Prof* Michael Poulton; *Assoc Prof* S Parcell; *Assoc Prof* T Cavanagh; *Assoc Prof* B MacKay-Lyons; *Asst Prof* Susan Guppy; *Asst Prof* Richard Kroeker; *Asst Prof* Christine Macy; *Asst Prof* Christopher Quek
Estab 1911, faculty estab 1961; pvt; D; scholarships; enrl approx 200, maj 200, grad 2
Ent Req: Previous 2 yrs at univ
Degrees: MArchit 4 yrs, Post-professional MArchit 1 yr minimum
Tuition: $3000 per year; differential for foreign students
Courses: Architecture, Art History, Constructions, Drafting, Photography, Environmental Studies, Urban & Rural Planning
Summer School: Three terms per yr

WOLFVILLE

ACADIA UNIVERSITY, Art Dept, B0P 1X0. Tel 902-542-2201; FAX 902-542-4727; *Chmn & Prof* Wayne Staples
Scholarships
Tuition: $3850 per yr
Courses: Art History, Drawing, Painting
Summer School: Dir, Prof Wayne Stapler. Enrl 30

ONTARIO

BUCKHORN

BUCKHORN SCHOOL OF FINE ART, Hwy 36, Box 10, K0L 1J0. Tel 705-657-1107; FAX 705-657-8766; WATS 800-461-1787.
Estab 1976; pvt; D
Courses: Drawing, Painting
Adult Hobby Classes: Tuition $75 per 2 day workshop. Courses—Acrylic, Drawing, Oil, Pastel, Watercolor

DUNDAS

DUNDAS VALLEY SCHOOL OF ART, 21 Ogilvie St, L9H 2S1. Tel 905-628-6357; FAX 905-628-1087; *Dir* J Trevor Hodgson; *Coordr* J Wilkinson; *Registrar* Betty Abbey
Estab 1964; pvt; D & E; scholarships; SC 56, LC 2, GC 3; enrl D 500, E 2500, maj 20, grad 4
Ent Req: Part time no-req, full time interview with portfolio
Tuition: $1600 per yr
Courses: Art Appreciation, Art History, Ceramics, Collages, Commercial Art, Conceptual Art, Constructions, Design, Drawing, Graphic Arts, Graphic Design, Mixed Media, Painting, Photography, Printmaking, Sculpture
Adult Hobby Classes: Enrl 1500; tuition $115 for 10 wk term. Courses—Ceramics, Drawing, Painting, Photography, Printmaking, Sculpture
Children's Classes: Enrl 1500; tuition $85 for 10 wk term. Courses—Drawing, Painting, Pottery
Summer School: Enrl 300; tuition $95-$115 for 10 sessions

ETOBICOKE

HUMBER COLLEGE OF APPLIED ARTS & TECHNOLOGY, Applied Arts Div, 205 Humber College Blvd, M9W 5L7. Tel 416-675-3111, Ext 4470; *Chmn* Steven Bodsworth
Estab 1967; pub; D & E; SC 300, LC 75, GC 6; enrl grad 50, PT 25
Ent Req: HS dipl, mature student status, one yr of employment plus 19 yrs of age
Degrees: None, 2 & 3 yr dipl courses
Tuition: Canadian res—$1008 per yr
Courses: Art History, Drafting, Drawing, Film, Graphic Arts, †Graphic Design, †Industrial Design, †Interior Design, Photography, Furniture Design, †Landscape Technology, †Packaging Design, TV Production
Adult Hobby Classes: Enrl 4042; tuition & duration vary. Beginning classes in most regular courses
Children's Classes: Nature studies

GUELPH

UNIVERSITY OF GUELPH, Fine Art Dept, Zavitz Hall, N1G 2W1. Tel 519-824-4120, Ext 6106; *Acting Chmn Prof* Ron Shuebrook. Instrs: FT 11, PT 20
Estab 1966; pub; D; scholarships; SC 30, LC 30; enrl 959, maj 300
Ent Req: HS dipl
Degrees: BA 3 yrs, BA(Hons) 4 yrs
Tuition: Res—undergrad $1313.05 per sem; part-time $291.76 per course; campus res available
Courses: Aesthetics, †Art History, Collages, †Conceptual Art, †Drawing, History of Art & Archaeology, †Intermedia, †Painting, †Photography, †Printmaking, †Sculpture, Video, Alternative Media
Summer School: Chair, Thomas Tritschler. Courses—Vary

HAMILTON

MCMASTER UNIVERSITY, Dept of Art & Art History, 1280 Main St W, L8S 4M2. Tel 905-525-9140, Ext 27671; *Chmn* Dr H Hartwell. Instrs: FT 9
Estab 1934; SC 12, LC 29; enrl 85
Degrees: BA(Art History), Hons BA(Studio & Art History) 3-4 yrs
Tuition: $2572.79 per yr; campus res available
Courses: †Art History, Music Drama, †Studio Art Program

KINGSTON

QUEEN'S UNIVERSITY, Dept of Art, K7L 3N6. Tel 613-545-6166; *Dean* Robert Silverman. Instrs: FT 21, PT 1
Estab 1932; pub; D & E; SC 16, LC 25
Ent Req: Grade XIII
Degrees: BA 3 yrs, BA(hons) & BFA 4 yrs, MA(Conservation), MA(Art History), PhD(Art History)
Tuition: $445.60 per course, campus res available
Courses: Art History, Drawing, Painting, Printmaking, Restoration & Conservation, Sculpture, Art Conservation
Summer School: Drawing, Painting, Sculpture

ST LAWRENCE COLLEGE, Dept of Visual & Creative Arts, * King & Portsmouth, PO Box 6000, K7L 5A6. Tel 613-545-5400; FAX 613-545-3920; *Chmn* Don Niven; *Chmn* Michael Shumate; *Chmn* Charles Muli; *Chmn* Terry Pfliger
Estab 1967, dept estab 1969; pub; D & E
Ent Req: Hs dipl & portfolio
Degrees: Diploma (Visual & Creative Arts, Graphic Design) 3 yrs, Certificate (Basic Photography, Certificate Graphic Design)
Tuition: Res—grad $1074; international $8541
Courses: Art History, Commercial Art, Drawing, †Graphic Design, Illustration, Mixed Media, Painting, Photography, Printmaking, Marketing, Communications, Computer Graphics

LONDON

UNIVERSITY OF WESTERN ONTARIO, John Labatt Visual Arts Centre, N6A 5B7. Tel 519-661-3440; FAX 519-661-2020; *Chmn* Madeline Lennon. Instrs: FT 11, PT 10
Estab 1967; pub; D & E; SC 23, LC 31; enrl maj 235
Ent Req: HS dipl, portfolio and/or interview
Degrees: BA 3 yrs, BA(Hons) and BFA 4 yrs
Tuition: $2941
Courses: Drawing, †History of Art & Archaeology, Museum Staff Training, †Painting, †Photography, †Printmaking, †Sculpture
Summer School: Enrl limited; term of 6 wks beginning July. Courses—Visual Arts

NORTH YORK

KOFFLER CENTER SCHOOL OF VISUAL ART, 4588 Bathurst St, M2R 1W6. Tel 416-636-1880, Ext 270; FAX 416-636-5813; *Dir* Joan Tooke
Estab 1977; pub; D & E; enrl D 400, E 98; SC 35
Courses: Ceramics, Drawing, Mixed Media, Painting, Sculpture, Cartooning, Clay, Stone Sculpture
Adult Hobby Classes: Enrl 350-400. Courses—Design, Drawing, Painting, Sculpture

YORK UNIVERSITY, Dept of Visual Arts, Ctr for Fine Arts, 4700 Keele St, M3J 1P3. Tel 416-736-5187; FAX 416-736-5447; *Chmn Prof* Ken Carpenter. Instrs: FT 26, PT 13
Estab 1969; pub; D & E; scholarships; SC 53, LC 17; enrl D over 400, maj 400, others 120
Ent Req: HS dipl, interview and portfolio evaluation
Degrees: BA(Hons), BFA(Hons) 4 yrs, MA in Art History, MFA in Visual Arts
Tuition: Res—$554.02 per course; nonres—$1778.82 per course
Courses: Design, Drawing, Graphic Arts, Painting, Photography, Sculpture, Interdisciplinary Studio

OAKVILLE

SHERIDAN COLLEGE, School of Arts & Design, 1430 Trafalgar Rd, L6H 2L1. Tel 905-845-9430, Ext 2780; FAX 905-815-4041; *Exec Dir* Donald H Graves
Estab 1967; pub; D & E; enrl D 1250
Ent Req: HS dipl, ent exam
Degrees: Dip 3 yr
Courses: Advertising Design, Art Appreciation, Art Education, †Art History, †Ceramics, Conceptual Art, Costume Design & Construction, †Design, Display, Drafting, †Drawing, †Fashion Arts, †Film, Graphic Arts, †Graphic Design, Handicrafts, †Illustration, †Interior Design, †Mixed Media, †Painting, Photography, Printmaking, Sculpture, Stage Design, Textile Design, †Theatre Arts, †Video, Animation, Art Fundamentals, Computer Animation, Computer Graphics, Music Theatre
Adult Hobby Classes: Enrl 2600; tuition varies
Summer School: Enrl 600. Courses—various Visual & Performing Arts; International Summer School of Animation

OTTAWA

CARLETON UNIVERSITY, Dept of Art History, 1125 Colonel By Dr, K1S 5B6. Tel 613-520-2342; *Asst Dir* Roger Mesley. Instrs: FT 8, PT 2
Estab 1964; D & E; scholarships; SC 2, LC 25, GC 3; enrl D over 700, maj 135
Ent Req: HS dipl
Degrees: BA 6 Hons 3-4 yrs
Tuition: Res—$1353.19 per sem
Courses: Art History

SOUTHAMPTON

SOUTHAMPTON ART SCHOOL, * 20 Albert St S, N0H 2L0. Tel 519-797-5068; *Dir* Open ; *Instr* Gabor P Mezei; *Instr* Guttorm Otto; *Instr* Roly Fenivick
Estab 1958 as a summer school; pub; D, July and Aug
Tuition: Adults $125 per wk; students (14-18) $85 per wk; children (10-13) $35 per wk, half days only; no campus res
Courses: Art Education, Drawing, Mixed Media, Painting
Children's Classes: Tuition $30 per wk, summer only
Summer School: Tuition $75-$100 per wk. Courses—Acrylic, Drawing, Oil, Watercolor

THUNDER BAY

LAKEHEAD UNIVERSITY, Dept of Visual Arts, * 955 Oliver Rd, P7B 5E1. Tel 807-343-8787; FAX 807-345-2394; Telex 073-4594. *Dean Faculty of Arts & Sciences* Dr J Gellert, PhD; *Chmn* Patricia Vervoort, MA; *Prof* Mark Nisenholt, MFA; *Prof* Ann Clarke, MFA. Instrs: FT 4, PT 5
Div Estab 1976, dept estab 1988; pub; D & E; scholarships
Ent Req: HS dipl, portfolio
Degrees: HBFA, Dipl in Arts Administration
Tuition: Res—undergrad $1893 per yr, $390 per course, $195 per 1/2 cr; campus res—rooms & board $3109 - $4283
Courses: Art History, †Ceramics, Drawing, †Painting, †Printmaking, †Sculpture
Adult Hobby Classes: Studio and art history courses
Summer School: Dir, Dan Pakulak. Tuition $390 per course for 6 wks

TORONTO

GEORGE BROWN COLLEGE OF APPLIED ARTS & TECHNOLOGY, Dept of Visual Arts, * PO Box 1015, Sta B, M5T 2T9. Tel 416-867-2000, 867-2011; FAX 416-867-2600; *Chmn* Earl Walker. Instrs: FT 30, PT 60
Estab 1970; D & E; enrl D 900, E 2000
Ent Req: HS grade 12 dipl, entr exam
Degrees: 3 yr dipl
Courses: †Advertising Design, Calligraphy, †Commercial Art, Graphic Arts, Graphic Design, Illustration, †Lettering, Painting, Photography, Video, Air Brush Techniques, Cartooning, Computer Graphics, Marker Rendering Techniques

ONTARIO COLLEGE OF ART & DESIGN, 100 McCaul St, M5T 1W1. Tel 416-977-5311; FAX 416-977-0235; *Pres* Alan Barkley; *Dean of Acad Student Services* Arthur Wood; *VPres Finance/Admin* Peter Caldwell, MPA; *Financial Aid Officer* Josephine Polera; *Chair Foundation Studies* Catherine Wild; *Dean of Design* Lenore Richards; *Asst Dean* Heather Whitton; *Asst Dean* Steven Quinlan
Estab 1876; pub; D & E; scholarships; SC approx 450; enrl D 1300, E 2000, grad 25, summer 900
Ent Req: HS dipl, English requirement, interview
Degrees: Diploma AOCA 4 yrs
Tuition: $623 per cr, $311.50 per half-cr; international students $1987 per cr, $993.50 per half-cr; no campus res
Courses: †Advertising Design, Art History, †Ceramics, Collages, †Commercial Art, Conceptual Art, Display, †Drawing, Film, †Graphic Arts, †Graphic Design, History of Art & Archaeology, †Illustration, †Industrial Design, †Jewelry, Mixed Media, †Painting, †Photography, †Printmaking, Silversmithing, Stage Design, Video, †Weaving, Animation, Batik, Color, Composition, †Corporate Design, Design Management, †Editorial Design, †Environmental Arts, †Experimental Arts, †Fibre, Foundry, †Glass, Holography, Light, Materials & Processes, Metal Work, Moldmaking, †New Media, †Surface Design & Print
Adult Hobby Classes: Enro 2000; tuition $272 per course for 3 hrs per wk for 30 wks. Courses—Advertising Design, Art History, Ceramics, Color, Corporate Design, Drawing, Editorial Design, Fibre/Weaving, Glasss, Graphics, History of Ceramics & Glass History of Furniture, Illustration, Industrial Design, Painting, Photography, Printmaking, Sculpture, Surface Design/Print, Typography, Watercolor, Woodworking
Summer School: Registrar, Tom Kowall. Enrl 900; tuition $272 per course for term of 3 wks (5 days a wk) or 15 wks (2 evenings a wk) beginning May. Courses—Advertising Design, Art History, Ceramics, Color, Corporate Design, Drawing, Editorial Design, Environmental, Fibre/Weaving, Glass, Graphics, History of Ceramics & Glass, History of Furniture, Illustration, Industrial Design, Painting, Photography, Printmaking, Sculpture, Surface Design/Print, Typography, Watercolor, Woodworking

TORONTO ART THERAPY INSTITUTE, 216 St Clair Ave W, M4V 1R2. Tel 416-924-6221; *Dir Acad Prog & Internships* Gilda S Grossman, MSW; *Psychiatric Consultant to Training Prog* Dr Jodi Lofchy, MD; *Supervisor* Nell Bateman, MA; *Instr & Supervisor* Jacqueline Fehlner, BA; *Instr & Supervisor* Kathryn Hubner Kozman, BA; *Instr & Supervisor* Barbara Merkur, MA; *Instr* Ellen Bateman, BA; *Instr* Helen Burt, BA; *Instr* Mercedes Chacin De Fuchs, MEd; *Instr* Temmi Ungerman, MA; *Instr* Lyn Westwood, BA; *Instr* Val Zoulalian, BA; *Thesis Advisor* O Robert Bosso, PhD; *Thesis Advisor* Ruth Epstein, EdD; *Thesis Advisor* Vince Murphy, PhD; *Thesis Advisor* Ken Morrison, PhD
Estab 1968; D & E
Degrees: Dipl, BA and MA(Art Therapy) through affiliation with other US colleges; graduate level certificate program in art therapy
Tuition: $6750
Adult Hobby Classes: Enrl 6-12; fee $40 per session. Courses—workshops
Children's Classes: Enrl 6-12; fee $20 per session. Courses—workshops

TORONTO SCHOOL OF ART, 110 Spadina Ave, Ste 700, M5V 2K4. Tel 416-504-7910; *Prog Coordr* Gretchen Sankey; *Instr* Susan Beniston; *Instr* Brian Burnett; *Instr* Moira Clark; *Instr* Denis Cliff; *Instr* Andy Fabo; *Instr* Simon Glass; *Instr* Carl Skelton; *Instr* Megan Williams
Estab 1969; pvt; D & E; scholarships; enrl 959, maj 300
Ent Req: Portfolio
Tuition: $2079 full-time, $4158 foreign students; no campus res
Courses: Drawing, Mixed Media, Painting, Photography, Printmaking, Sculpture

UNIVERSITY OF TORONTO
—Dept of Fine Art, Sidney Smith Hall, 6th Flr, M5S 3G3. Tel 416-978-6272; FAX 416-978-1491; *Chmn* M Miller. Instrs: FT 14, PT 4
Estab 1934; pub; scholarships & fels; LC, GC
Degrees: BA 4 yrs, MA 2 yrs, PhD 5 yrs
Tuition: Nonres—undergrad $12,024; campus res available
Courses: Aesthetics, Architecture, Art History, Drawing, Graphic Arts, History of Art & Archaeology, Painting, Printmaking, Sculpture, Video, Art Studio
Adult Hobby Classes: Enrl 250
—School of Architecture & Landscape Architecture, 230 College St, M5T 1R2. Tel 416-978-5038; *Dean* Larry W Richars
Estab 1948; pub; D; scholarships; SC 5, LC 33, GC 11; enrl 299, non-maj 6, maj 293, grad 13
Ent Req: HS dipl, portfolio of work & interview
Degrees: BArchit
Tuition: Domestic students $2970 per sem; foreign students $14,250 per sem
Courses: Design, Construction Management, History & Theory Building Science, Professional Practice, Structural Design
—Programme in Landscape Architecture, 230 College St, M5T 1R2. Tel 416-978-6788; FAX 416-971-2094; *Chmn* Robert Wright; *Prof* Robert Allsopp, DipArch; *Assoc Prof* John Consolati, BSLA; *Assoc Prof* John Danahy, BLA
Estab 1827, dept estab 1965; pub; D; scholarships; enrl maj 100
Ent Req: Grad 13 dipl
Degrees: BA(Land Archit)
Tuition: Canadian Students $2970 per sem; foreign students $14,250 per sem
Courses: Design, Drawing, Computer Art, Computer Modeling, Environment, Research & Writing Studio
Summer School: Contact, Prof Gerald Englar. Enrl 20; tuition $1200 for 4 wks non-degree. Courses—Career initiation program for Architecture & Landscape Arthitecture

WATERLOO

UNIVERSITY OF WATERLOO, Fine Arts Dept, 200 University Ave W, N2L 3G1. Tel 519-885-1211, Ext 2442; FAX 519-888-4521; *Dean* B Hendley; *Chmn Dept* Don MacKay, MFA; *Prof* Virgil Burnett, MA; *Prof* Ann Roberts, MFA; *Prof* A M Urquhart, BFA; *Assoc Prof* Jan Uhde, PhD; *Assoc Prof* Art Green, BFA; *Assoc Prof* Eve Kliman, PhD; *Asst Prof* Jane Buyers, BA; *Asst Prof* Bruce Taylor, MFA
Estab 1958, dept estab 1968; pub; D & E; scholarships; SC 32, LC 27; enrl maj 100
Ent Req: HS dipl
Degrees: BA 3 yrs, BA(Hons) 4 yrs
Tuition: $2136 per yr; campus res available
Courses: †Art History, †Drawing, Illustration, †Painting, Photography, †Printmaking, †Sculpture, Ceramic Sculpture, †Film Theory & History, Computer Imaging, Applied Graphics
Summer School: Enrl 30. Courses—Drawing

WINDSOR

UNIVERSITY OF WINDSOR, School of Visual Arts, Huron Church Rd at College, N9B 3P4. Tel 519-253-4232, Ext 2828; FAX 519-971-3647; Instrs: FT 10, PT 4
Estab 1960; pub; D & E; scholarships & assistantships; SC 33, LC 21; enrl D 265, E approx 75, maj 340
Ent Req: Ontario Secondary School Graduation Dipl (OSSD) plus 6 Ontario Academic Courses (OAC) or equivalent
Degrees: BA 3 yrs, BA(Hons) and BFA 4 yrs, MFA 2 yrs
Tuition: Undergrad $1641.30 per sem, grad $1466.25 per sem
Courses: †Art History, †Drawing, †Painting, Photography, †Printmaking, †Sculpture, Multi Media

PRINCE EDWARD ISLAND

CHARLOTTETOWN

HOLLAND COLLEGE, Health, Science & Creative Arts, 140 Weymouth St, C1A 4Z1. Tel 902-566-9564; FAX 902-566-9505; *Prog Unit Coordr* Gaylene Smith
Estab 1977; scholarships; enrl D 100
Tuition: $1315 per yr
Courses: Photography, †Commercial Design, Woodworking
Adult Hobby Classes: Enrl 100; tuition $1315 per yr. Courses—Commercial Design, Photography, Wood
Children's Classes: Enrl 15; tuition $70 for 8 wks. Courses—Art Activities

QUEBEC

MONTREAL

CONCORDIA UNIVERSITY, Faculty of Fine Arts, 1395 Rene Levesque Blvd, H3G 2M5. Tel 514-848-4600; FAX 514-848-4599; *Dean* Christopher Jackson
D & E; scholarships
Ent Req: HS dipl, CEGEP dipl Prov of Quebec
Degrees: BFA, post-BFA Dipl in Art Educ & Art Therapy, full-time leading to teaching cert, MA(Art Educ), MA(Art History), MA(Art Therapy), PhD(Art Educ)
Courses: †Art Education, †Art History, †Ceramics, †Drawing, †Painting, †Photography, †Printmaking, †Sculpture, †Theatre Arts, †Art Therapy, Cinema, †Contemporary Dance, †Design Art, †Fibres, Interdisciplinary Studies, †Music, Women & the Fine Arts
Adult Hobby Classes: Courses offered
Children's Classes: Enrl 75; tuition $75 for 8 wk term, $125 for 2 terms
Summer School: Courses offered

MCGILL UNIVERSITY

—**Dept of Art History,** 853 Sherbrooke St W, H3A 2T6. Tel 514-398-6541; FAX 514-398-7247; *Chmn* John M Fossey; *Assoc Prof* T Glenn, Phd; *Faculty Lectr* R Meyer; *Asst Prof* C Solomon-Kiefer, PhD
Pvt; D; teaching assistantships; SC 2, LC 7, GC 12
Ent Req: HS dipl or CEGEP Dipl
Degrees: BA(Art History), 3 & 4 yr, MA(Art History) 2 yr, PhD(Art History)
Tuition: Res—$1500 per yr, nonres—$7000 per yr
Courses: †History of Art & Archaeology, Ancient Greek Art, Baroque Art, Medieval Art, Modern Art, Renaissance Art
—**School of Architecture,** 815 Sherbrooke St W, H3A 2K6. Tel 514-398-6704; FAX 514-398-7372; *Prof* David Covo; *Prof* Ricardo Castro. Instrs: FT 12, PT 21, FTE 9
Estab 1896; fels; SC 8, LC 32
Ent Req: Ent exam
Degrees: BArchit 4 yrs
Tuition: Res—$1500 per yr, nonres—$7000 per yr
Courses: Architecture, Architectural Design, History of Architecture

UNIVERSITE DE MONTREAL, Dept of Art History, PO Box 6128, Succursale Centre Ville, H3C 3J7. Tel 514-343-6184; FAX 514-343-2393; Elec Mail larouchm@ere.umontreal.ca. *Dir* Michel Larouche; *Instr* Yves Deschamps; *Instr* Nicole Dubreuil; *Instr* Francois Marc Gagnon; *Instr* Pierre Granche; *Instr* Chantal Hardy; *Instr* Alain Laframboise; *Instr* Lise Lamarche; *Instr* Johanne Lamoureux; *Instr* Luis de Moura Sobral; *Instr* Gilles Marsolais; *Instr* Constance Naubert-Riser; *Instr* Serge Tousignant; *Instr* Jean Trudel; *Instr* Peter Krausz; *Instr* David W Booth; *Instr* Andre Gaudreault; *Instr* Jean-Francois Lhote; *Instr* Sylvestra Mariniello
Dept estab 1961; pvt; D & E; SC 20, LC 70, GC 10; enrl D 270, non-maj 113, maj 106, grad 80, others 151
Ent Req: HS dipl
Degrees: BA & MA
Tuition: Campus res available
Courses: Art History, Film, Fine Arts

UNIVERSITE DU QUEBEC A MONTREAL, Famille des Arts, CP 8888, Succursale Center Ville, H3C 3P8. Tel 514-987-4545; *Dept Head* Louise Dusseault Letocha
Estab 1969
Ent Req: 2 yrs after HS
Degrees: Baccalaureat specialise 3 yrs; Master Degrees in Visual Arts; programs in Environmental Design, Graphic Design, History of Art, Visual Arts (engraving, sculpture, painting); MA(Musicology)
Tuition: $166.50 per cr
Courses: Drawing, Museum Staff Training, Painting, Teacher Training, Architectural Drafting, Ceramic Sculpture, Design, Etching and Engraving, Graphic Techniques, Modeling, Mural Painting, Scenography
Adult Hobby Classes: Certificate in visual arts available

QUEBEC

UNIVERSITE LAVAL CITE UNIVERSITAIRE, School of Visual Arts, Laval University, Edifice La Fabrique, G1K 7P4. Tel 418-656-7631; FAX 418-656-7678; Elec Mail arv@arv.ulaval.ca. *Dir Visual Arts* Andre Theberge; *Faculty Dean Arts, Architecture & Amenagement* Takashi Nakajima
Estab 1970; pub; D; enrl 550
Ent Req: 2 yrs col
Degrees: BA(Arts Plastiques, Communication Graphique, Enseignement des Arts Plastiques); cert(arts plastiques), MA(Visual Arts)
Tuition: Res—undergrad $1952 per yr, $558 per qtr
Courses: Drawing, Graphic Arts, Graphic Design, Illustration, Painting, Photography, Sculpture, Video, Computer Graphic, Engraving, Lithography, Silk Screen

TROIS RIVIERES

UNIVERSITY OF QUEBEC, TROIS RIVIERES, Fine Arts Section, * 3351 boul des Forges, PO Box 500, G9A 5H7. Tel 819-376-5136; FAX 819-376-5112; *Section Head* Graham Cantieni
Estab 1969; pub; D & E; SC 12, LC 8, GC 28; enrl D 150, E 100
Ent Req: Ent exam or DEC
Degrees: BA(Fine Arts) & BA(Art Education)
Tuition: $50 per course
Courses: Art Education, Art History, †Drawing, †Painting, †Printmaking, †Sculpture, †Glass, †Paper
Adult Hobby Classes: Enrl 100. Courses—Art History, Painting, Printmaking

SASKATCHEWAN

REGINA

UNIVERSITY OF REGINA

—**Visual Arts Dept,** S4S 0A2. Tel 306-585-5872; FAX 306-779-4744; *Head* Roger Lee. Instrs: FT 9
Pub; scholarships & fels; enrl 450
Ent Req: HS grad
Degrees: 2 yr cert, BA 3 yrs, BA 4 yrs, BFA 4 yrs, MFA 2 yrs
Tuition: $284 per class
Courses: Art Appreciation, Art History, Drawing, Intermedia, Mixed Media, Museum Staff Training, Painting, Printmaking, Sculpture
Summer School: Introductory courses offered
—**Art Education Program,** Faculty of Education, S4S 0A2. Tel 306-585-4519; *Dean Educ* Dr Michael Tymchak; *Dean Faculty Fine Arts* Dr Mary Blackstone. Instrs: FT 9
Estab 1965; pub; D & E; scholarships; LC 6; enrl D 160, E 20, maj 10
Ent Req: HS dipl, matriculation or degree for maj in art
Degrees: BA 3 & 4 yr, BEduc 3 yr
Tuition: Res—$2490 per sem, visa students $4110 per sem
Courses: Aesthetics, Art Education
Children's Classes: Sat
Summer School: Exten Courses, H Kindred; Dean Educ, Dr Toombs. Term of 3 to 6 wks beginning May

SASKATOON

UNIVERSITY OF SASKATCHEWAN, Dept of Art & Art History, 9 Campus Dr, S7N 5A5. Tel 306-966-4222; FAX 306-966-4266; *Head* Lynne Bell. Instrs: FT 13, PT 4
Estab 1936; pub; D; scholarships; SC, LC, GC; enrl approx 880, BFA prog 130, grad 9
Ent Req: HS grad
Degrees: BA 3 yrs, BAHons(Art History), BA(Advanced) 4 yrs, BFA 4 yrs, MFA(Studio Art), BEd(Art)
Tuition: $366 per class; 4 classes per acad yr
Courses: Art Education, Art History, Drawing, History of Art & Archaeology, Mixed Media, Painting, Photography, Printmaking, Sculpture
Summer School: Dir, Bob Cram, Extension Credit Studies. Enrl 200; tuition $366 per 6 wk term. Courses—Art Educ, Art History, Drawing, Painting, Photography, Printmaking, Sculpture

III ART INFORMATION

Major Museums Abroad

Major Art Schools Abroad

State Arts Councils

State Directors and Supervisors of Art Education

Art Magazines

Newspaper Art Editors and Critics

Scholarships and Fellowships

Open Exhibitions

Traveling Exhibition Booking Agencies

Major Museums Abroad

AFGHANISTAN

KABUL

M **KABUL MUSEUM,** Darul Aman. Tel 42656. *Dir* Ahamad Ali Motamedi
   Collections: Kushan art; archaeology of prehistoric, Greco-Roman, Islamic periods; ethnological collections

ALGERIA

ALGIERS

M **MUSEE NATIONAL DES ANTIQUITES,** Parc de la Liberte. Tel 74-66-86. *Dir* Drias Lakhdar; *Cur* Mohammed Temmam
   Collections: Algerian antiquities & Islamic art

M **MUSEE NATIONAL DES BEAUX ARTS D'ALGER,** National Museum of Algiers, Place Dar-el Salem, El Hamma. Tel 66-49-16. *Dir* Malika Bosabdellah
   Collections: Contemporary Algerian art; paintings; drawings; bronze reliefs

ARGENTINA

BUENOS AIRES

M **MUSEO DE ARTE MODERNO,** Museum of Modern Art, Teatro General San Martin, Corrientes 1530 y San Juan 350, 1042. Tel 49-4796. *Dir* Raul Santana
   Collections: Latin American paintings, especially Argentine, and contemporary schools

M **MUSEO DE BELLAS ARTES DE LA BOCA,** Fine Arts Museum, Pedro Mendoza 1835, 1169. Tel 21-1080. *Dir* Dr Guillermo C De La Canal
   Collections: Paintings, sculptures, engravings & maritime museum

M **MUSEO MUNICIPAL DE ARTE ESPANOL ENRIQUE LARRETA,** Municipal Museum of Spanish Art, Juramento 2291 y Obligado 2139, 1428. Tel 784-4040. *Dir* Mercedes di Paala de Picot
   Collections: 13th - 16th century wood carvings, gilt objects and painted panels, paintings of Spanish School of 16th and 17th centuries, tapestries, furniture

M **MUSEO NACIONAL DE ARTE DECORATIVO,** National Museum of Decorative Art, Avda del Libertador 1902, 1425. Tel 802-6606. *Dir* Alberto Guillermo Bellucci
   Collections: European and South American works; furniture, sculptures and tapestries

M **MUSEO NACIONAL DE BELLAS ARTES,** National Museum of Fine Arts, Avda del Libertador 1473, 1425. Tel 803-4062. *Dir* Alberto G Bellucci
   Collections: Argentine, American and European art, both modern and classical

CORDOBA

M **MUSEO PROVINCIAL DE BELLAS ARTES EMILIO A CARAFFA,** Provincial Museum of Fine Arts, Avenida Hipolito Irigoyen 651, 5000. Tel 69-0786. *Dir Lic* Graciela Elizabeth Palela
   Collections: Provincial art center, including art library and archives; Argentine and foreign paintings, sculptures, drawings and engravings

ROSARIO

M **MUSEO MUNICIPAL DE ARTE DECORATIVO FIRMA Y ODILO ESTEVEZ,** Municipal Decorative Arts Museum, Santa Fe 748, 2000. Tel 041-482544. *Cur* P A Sinopoli
   Collections: Antique glass; paintings by Van Utrecht, Antolinez, De Hondecoeter, Gerard, Lucas; 16th - 18th centuries furniture & silver; ceramics; antique glass; ivories; silver

M **MUSEO MUNICIPAL DE BELLAS ARTES JUAN B CASTAGNINO,** Municipal Museum of Fine Arts, Avda Pellegrini, 2202. Tel 041-21-73-10 /403948. *Dir* Horacio Quiroga
   Library with 3000 vols
   Collections: Works by Jose de Ribera, Goya, Valdes Leal & a complete collection of Argentine art from 19th century to present

SANTA FE

M **MUSEO DE BELLAS ARTES ROSA GALISTEO DE RODRIGUEZ,** Museum of Fine Arts, 4 de Enero 1510, 3000. Tel (042) 22142. *Dir* Nydia Pereyra Salva de Impini
   Library with 4000 vols
   Collections: Contemporary Argentine & modern art

TANDIL

M **MUSEO MUNICIPAL DE BELLAS ARTES DE TANDIL,** Municipal Museum of Fine Arts, Chacabuco 357, 7000. Tel 2000. *Dir* E Valor
   Collections: Paintings of classical, impressionist, cubist and modern schools

AUSTRALIA

ADELAIDE

M **ART GALLERY OF SOUTH AUSTRALIA,** North Terrace, 5000. Tel (08) 207-7000. *Dir* Ron Radford
   Collections: Representative selection of Australian, British and European paintings, prints, drawings and sculpture; large collection of ceramics, glass and silver; extensive South Australian Historical Collection; SE Asian ceramics; furniture

CANBERRA

M **AUSTRALIAN NATIONAL GALLERY,** PO Box 1150, ACT 2601. Telex 6-1500; Tel 062-71-2411. *Dir* Elizabeth Churcher
   Collections: Extensive Australian collection includes fine and decorative arts, folk art, commercial art, architecture and design; International collection contains arts from Asia, Southeast Asia, Oceania, Africa, Pre-Columbian America and Europe
L **Library,** ACT 2601. Tel 62-1111.
   Library Holdings: Monographs 70,000; Serials 3000; Other materials 200,000; Micro — Fiche 35,000; Other — Exhibition catalogs 12,000

HOBART

M **TASMANIAN MUSEUM AND ART GALLERY,** 40 Macquarie St, GPO Box 1164M, Tasmania 7001. Tel 02-350-777. *Dir* P Sabine
   Collections: Australian and Tasmanian art

LAUNCESTON

M **QUEEN VICTORIA MUSEUM AND ART GALLERY,** Wellington St, Tasmania 7250. Tel 03-31-6777. *Dir* C B Tassell
   Collections: Pure & applied art; Tasmanian history; Tasmanian & general anthropology; Tasmanian botany, geology, paleontology & zoology

MELBOURNE

M **NATIONAL GALLERY OF VICTORIA,** 180 St Kilda Rd, Victoria 3004. Tel 685-0222. *Dir* James Mollison
   Library with 20,000 vols
   Collections: Asian art; Australian art; pre-Columbian art; modern European art; antiquities, costumes, textiles, old master and modern drawings, paintings, photography, prints and sculpture

PERTH

M **ART GALLERY OF WESTERN AUSTRALIA,** 47 James St, Perth Cultural Centre, WA 6000. Tel (09) 328-7233. *Dir* Paula Latos-Valier
Library with 14,000 vols
Collections: †Australian aboriginal artifacts; †British, †European & †Australian paintings, prints, drawings, sculptures & crafts

SOUTH BRISBANE

M **QUEENSLAND ART GALLERY,** PO Box 3686, Queensland 4101. Tel (07) 840-7333. *Dir* Douglas Hall
Collections: Predominantly Australian art, ceramics, decorative arts, paintings and drawings; British and European paintings and sculpture

SYDNEY

M **ART GALLERY OF NEW SOUTH WALES,** Domain, New South Wales 2000. Tel (02) 225-1700. *Dir* Edmund Capon
Collections: Australian Aboriginal and Melanesian art; Australian art; collections of British and European painting and sculpture; Asian art, including Japanese ceramics and painting and Chinese ceramics

M **NICHOLSON MUSEUM OF ANTIQUITIES,** University of Sydney, New South Wales 2006. Tel 02-692-2812. *Cur* Prof A Cambitoglou
Collections: Antiquities of Egypt, Near East, Europe, Greece, Rome

M **POWERHOUSE MUSEUM OF APPLIED ARTS & SCIENCES,** 500 Harris St, Ultimo, New South Wales 2000. Tel 217-0111. *Dir* Terence Measham; *Dir* L G Sharp
Library with 20,000 vols
Collections: Scientific Instruments; Numismatics; Philately; Astronomy

AUSTRIA

INNSBRUCK

M **TIROLER LANDESMUSEUM FERDINANDEUM,** Tyrolese Provincial Museum, Museumst 15, 6020. Tel (0512) 59489. *Dir* Gert Ammann
Collections: Historical artifacts, sculptures, baroque & 19th century art

LINZ

M **NEUE GALERIE DER STADT LINZ-WOLFGANG GURLITT MUSEUM,** Lentia 2000, Blutenstrasse 15, 4040. Tel 0732-2393/3600. *Dir* Peter Baum
Collections: 19th & 20th century paintings, drawings, sculptures & prints

SALZBURG

M **RESIDENZGALERIE SALZBURG,** Residenzplatz 1, A-5010. Tel (0662) 84 04 51. *Dir* Dr Roswitha Juffinger
Collections: European paintings, 16th - 19th centuries

M **SALZBURGER MUSEUM CAROLINO-AUGUSTEUM,** Salzburg Museum, Museumsplatz 6, Postfach 525, A-5020. Tel 841134. *Dir* A Rohrmoser
Library with 100,000 vols
Collections: Art, coins, musical instruments, costumes, peasant art; Prehistoric & Roman archaeology

VIENNA

M **AKADEMIE DER BILDENDEN KUNSTE IN WIEN,** Gemaldegalerie der Akademie der bildenden Kunste in Wien, Schillerplatz 3, 1010. Tel 58816-225-231. *Dir* Dr Renate Trnek; *Asst* Dr Martina Fleischer
Collections: European Paintings of the 14th - 20th centuries - Hieronymus Bosch, Hans Baldung Grien; 17th century Dutch (Rembrandt, Ruisdael, van Goyen, Jan Both & others); Flemish, (Rubens, Jordaens, van Dyck), Guardi, Magnasco, Tiepolo, bequests by Count Lamberg, Prince Liechtenstein, Wolfgang von Wurzbach

M **GRAPHISCHE SAMMLUNG ALBERTINA,** Albertina Graphic Art Collection, Augustinerstrasse 1, 1010. Tel 0222-534-830. *Dir* Konrud Oberhuber
Estab 1796. Average Annual Attendance: 40,000
Collections: Drawings 44,000; sketchbooks, miniatures & posters. This is one of the largest (over one million) and best print collections in Europe

M **KUNSTHISTORISCHES MUSEUM,** Museum of Fine Arts, Burgring 5 & Neue Burg, 1010. Tel (0222) 52177. *Chief Dir* Dr Wilfried Seipel
Collections: Egyptian collection; antiquities, ceramics, historical carriages & costumes, jewelry, old musical instruments, paintings, tapestries, weapons; collection of secular & ecclesiastical treasures of Holy Roman Empire & Hapsburg dynasty

    MUSEUM MODERNER KUNST STIFUNG LUDWIG, Ludwig Foundation Museum of Art

M **Palais Liechtenstein,** Furstengasse 1, 1090. Tel 34-12-59. *Dir* Dieter Ronte
Collections: Modern classics & modern art

M **Museum des 20 Jahrhunderts,** Schweizergarten, 1030. Tel 78-25-50.
Collections: Works of the 20th century & a sculpture garden; artists represented include: Archipenko, Arp, Barlach, Beckman, Boeckl, Bonnard, Delaunay, Ernst, Gleizes, Hofer, Hoflehner, Jawlensky, Kandinsky, Kirchner, Klee, Kokoschka, Laurens, Leger, Marc, Matisse, Miro, Moore, Munch, Nolde, Picasso, Rodin, Rosso, Wotruba & others

M **OSTERREICHISCHE GALERIE,** Austrian Gallery, Oberes & Unteres Belvedere, Prinz Eugenstrasse 27, Postfach 134, A 1037. Tel 79557. *Dir* Dr Gerbert Frodl
Library with 210,000 vols
Collections: Austrian Gallery of 19th & 20th Century Art; Museum of Austrian Baroque Art; Museum of Austrian Medieval Art; Ambrosi Museum; Branch of the Austrian Gallery at Schloss Halbturn

M **Museum mittelalterlicher Kunst,** Orangerie des Belvedere, Rennweg 6A
Collections: Austrian medieval paintings & sculptures, especially 14th - 16th century

M **Osterreichisches Barockmuseum,** Unteres Belvedere, Rennweg 6A
Collections: Austrian Baroque art (paintings and sculptures)

M **Osterreichische Galerie und Internationale Kunst des XIX - Jahrhunderts,** Oberes Belvedere, Prinz Eugenstr 27
Collections: 19th - 20th century Austrian paintings & sculptures

M **Gustinus Ambrosi-Museum,** Scherzergasse 1A
Collections: Sculpture by G Ambrosi (1893-1975)

M **Expositur der Osterreichischen Galerie auf Schloss Halbturn,** Burgenland, Halbturn, A-7131. Tel (02172) 3307.
Collections: 20th century Austrian paintings & sculptures

M **Osterreichische Galerie und Internationale Kunst des XX - Jahrhunderts (International Art of the 19th & 20th Centuries),** Stallburg
Collections: International painting & sculpture

M **OSTERREICHISCHES MUSEUM FUR ANGEWANDTE KUNST,** Austrian Museum of Applied Art, Stubenring 5, 1010. Tel (0222) 71136-0. *Dir* Peter Noever
Library with 100,000 vols & 250,000 prints
Collections: Applied arts from Roman to modern age

BELGIUM

ANTWERP

M **CITY OF ANTWERP,** Kunsthistorische Musea, Museum Mayer van den Bergh, Lange Gasthuisstraat 19, 2000. Tel (03) 232-42-37. *Dir* Hans Nieuwdorp
Collections: Painting 13th-18th century; sculpture 14th-16th century; all decorative arts, mainly late medieval

M **Rubenshuis,** Wapper 9-11, 2000. Tel (03) 232-47-51. *Cur* Hans Nieuwdorp
Collections: Reconstruction of Rubens' house & studio; paintings by P P Rubens, his collaborators & pupils

L **Rubenianum,** Kolveniersstraat 20, 2000. Tel (03) 232-39-20. *Cur* Hans Nieuwdorp
Center for the study of 16th & 17th century Flemish art; library & photo archives
Publications: Corpus Rubenianum Ludwig Burchard

M **Openluchtmuseum voor Beeldhowwkunst Middleheim,** Middelheimlaan 61, 2020. Tel (03) 827-15-34. *Cur* M Meewis
Collections: Contemporary sculpture of Rodin, Maillol, Zadkine, Marini, Manzu, Gargallo, Moore, biennial exhibitions of modern sculpture

M **Museum Smidt van Gelder,** Belgielei 91, 2000. Tel (03) 239-06-52. *Asst Keeper* Clara Vanderhenst
Collections: Collections of Chinese & European porcelains, 17th century Dutch paintings, 18th century French furniture

M **Museum Mayer van den Bergh,** Lange Gasthuisstraat 19, 2000. Tel (03) 232-42-37. *Cur* Hans Nieuwdorp
Collections: Collection of paintings, including Breughel, Metsys, Aertsen, Mostaert, Bronzino, Heda, de Vos, & medieval sculpture

M **INTERNATIONAAL CULTUREEL CENTTRUM,** International Cultural Centre, Meir 50, 2000. Tel 03-226-03-06. *Dir* Willy Juwet

M **KONINKLIJK MUSEUM VOOR SCHONE KUNSTEN,** Royal Museum of Fine Arts, Leopold de Waelplein, 2000. Tel (03) 238-78-09. *Deputy Dir* L M A Schoonbaert
Library with 35,000 vols
Collections: Five Centuries of Flemish Painting: Flemish Primitifs, early foreign schools, 16th-17th century Antwerp School, 17th century Dutch School, 19th and 20th century Belgian artists; works of De Braekeleer, Ensor, Leys, Permeke, Smits and Wouters

M **MUSEUM PLANTIN-MORETUS,** Plantin-Moretus Museum, Vrijdagmarkt 22, 2000. Tel (03) 233-02-94. *Dir* Dr Francine de Nave
Library of 30,000 books of 15th - 18th centuries
Collections: Designs, copper and wood engravings, printing presses, typography

M **STEDELIJK PRENTENKABINET,** Municipal Gallery of Graphic Arts, Vrijdagmarkt 23, 2000. Tel 03-232-24-55. *Keeper* Dr Carl DePauw
Collections: Antwerp iconographic collection; modern drawings: J Ensor, F Jespers, H Leys, W Vaes, Rik Wouters; modern engravings: Cantre, Ensor, Masereel, J Minne, W Vaes; old drawings: Jordaens, E and A Quellin, Rubens, Schut, Van Dyck; old engravings: Galle, Goltzius, Hogenbergh, W Hollar, Jegher, Wiericx, etc

BRUGES

M **GROENINGEMUSEM,** Municipal Art Gallery, Dyver, 12, 8000. Tel (050) 44-87-11. *Chief Cur* Dr Valentin Vermeersch
Collections: Ancient & modern paintings, including works by Hieronymus Bosch, Gerard David, Hugo vanderGoes, Jan van Eyck, R van de Weyden & Hans Memling

M **STEDELIJK MUSEUM VOOR VOLKSKUNDE,** Municipal Museum of Folklore, Rolweg 40, 8000. Tel 050-33-00-44. *Cur* W P Dezutter
Collections: Collections including folklore, sculpture, applied arts, ancient and modern paintings, trades and crafts of 19th century, popular art

BRUSSELS

L **BIBLIOTHEQUE ROYALE ALBERT I,** The Belgian National Library, 4 blvd de l'Empereur, 1000. Tel (02) 519-53-11. *Dir* Pierre Cockshaw
Collections: Coins, medals, maps, manuscripts, prints, rare printed books housed in Belgian National Library

M **MUSEE HORTA,** 25 rue Americaine, 1050. Tel 537-16-92. *Dir* Francoise Dierkens-Aubry
Library with 2500 vols
Collections: Paintings & works of art by V Horta; architecture & furniture

M **MUSEES ROYAUX D'ART ET D'HISTOIRE,** Royal Museums of Art and History, 10 Parc du Cinquantenaire, 1040. Tel 02-741-72-11. *Dir* F Van Noten
Collections: Pre-Columbian art; Belgian, Egyptian, Japanese, Greek, Roman and classical art; Medieval, Renaissance and modern art - ceramics, furniture, glass, lace, silver, tapestries, textiles; ethnography; folklore

M **MUSEES ROYAUX DES BEAUX-ARTS DE BELGIQUE,** Royal Museums of Fine Arts of Belgium, 9 rue de Musee, 1000. Tel (02) 513-96-30, 508 32 11. *Dir* Eliane De Wilde
Collections: Medieval, Renaissance & modern paintings, drawings & sculptures
M **Musee d'Art Ancien,** 3 rue de la Regence, 1000. Tel 02-513-96-30. *Dept Head* Henri Pauwels
Collections: Paintings & drawings (15th - 19th centuries) & old & modern sculptures
M **Musee d'Art Moderne,** 1-2 Place Royale, Brussels, 1000. Tel 02-513-96-30. *Dept Head* Phil Mertens
Collections: Temporary exhibitions; 20th century paintings, drawings & sculptures
M **Musee Constantin Meunier,** 59 rue de l'Abbaye, 1000. Tel 02-648-44-49.
Collections: Paintings, drawings and sculptures by Constanin Meunier, the artist's house and studio
M **Musee Wiertz,** 62 rue Vautier, Brussels, 1000. Tel 02-648-17-18. *Head Cur* Philippe Roberts-Jones
Collections: Paintings by Antoine Wiertz

M **MUSEUM ERASMUS,** 31 Rue du Chapitre, 1070. Tel 521-13-83. *Cur* Alexandre Vanautgaerden
Library with 4000 vols
Collections: Documents, paintings, manuscripts relating to Erasmus & other humanists of the 16th century

LIEGE

M **MUSEES D'ARCHEOLOGIE ET DES ARTS DECORATIFS,** Musee d'Ansembourg, Feronstree 114, 4000. Tel 32-41-21.94.02. *Cur* Ann Chevalier
Collections: 18th century decorative arts of Liege, housed in a mansion of the same period
M **Musee Curtius,** 13 quai de Maastricht, 4000. Tel 32-41-21.94.04. *Cur* Ann Chevalier; *Cur* Marie-Claire Gueury
The museum is the headquarters of the Archaeological Institute of Liege
Collections: Prehistory, Romano-Belgian & Frankish; Liege coins, decorative arts from the Middle Ages to the 19th century; Annex: lapidary collection in Palais de Justice
M **Musee d'Ansembourg** 4000
Collections: 18th century decorative arts of Liege; reconstituted interiors
M **Musee du Verre,** 13 quai de Maastricht, 4000. Tel 32-41-21.94.04. *Cur* Ann Chevalier
Collections: Main centers of production, from the earliest times to the present, are represented

MARIEMONT

M **MUSEE ROYALE ET DOMAINE DE MARIEMONT,** Morlanwelz, 6510. Tel (064) 22-12-43. *Cur* Patrice Dartevelle
Maintains library with 70,000 volumes
Collections: Belgian archaeology; porcelain from Tournai; Egyptian, Grecian, Roman, Chinese & Japanese antiquities

VERVIERS

M **MUSEES COMMUNAUX DE VERVIERS: BEAUX-ARTS,** Community Museum of Fine Arts, Rue Renier 17, 4800. Tel 087-33-16-95. *Cur* V Bronowski
Collections: European & Asian painting and sculpture, ceramics, & folk arts

BOLIVIA

LA PAZ

M **MUSEO NACIONAL DE ARQUEOLOGIA,** National Museum, Calle Tihuanaco 93, Casilla oficial. Tel 29624. *Dir* Max Portugal Ortiz
Collections: Anthropology, archaeology, ethnology, folklore, Lake Titicaca district exhibitions, traditional native arts and crafts

M **MUSEO NACIONAL DE ARTE,** Calle Socabaya 485, Casilla 7038. Tel 371177. *Dir* Teresa Villegas de Aneiva
Collections: Colonial & local modern art

BOTSWANA

GABORONE

M **NATIONAL MUSEUM AND ART GALLERY,** Independence Ave, Private Bag 00114. Tel 374616. *Dir* T L Mpulubusi
Collections: Art of all races of Africa south of the Sahara; scientific collections relating to Botswana

BRAZIL

OURO PRETO

M **MUSEU DA INCONFIDENCIA,** History of Democratic Ideals and Culture, Praca Tiradentes, 139, 35400. Tel 031-551-1121. *Dir* Rui Mourao
Collections: Objects & documents related to the 1789 Revolutionaries of Minas Gerais (the Inconfidentes)

RIO DE JANEIRO

M **MUSEU DE ARTE MODERNA DO RIO DE JANIERO,** Museum of Modern Art, Av Infante Dom Henrique 85, CP 44, 20021. Tel 021-240-6351. *Pres* M F Nascimento Brito; *Exec Dir* Gustavo A Capanema
Collections: Collections representing different countries

M **MUSEU NACIONAL DE BELAS ARTES,** National Museum of Fine Arts, Ave Rio Branco 199, 20040. Tel 240-9869. *Dir* Prof Heloisa A Lustosa
Library with 12,000 vols
Collections: 19th & 20th century Brazilian art, works by outstanding painters; European paintings & sculptures - works by Dutch, English, French, German, Italian, Portuguese & Spanish masters; masterpieces of foreign collection: Dutch school - eight Brazilian landscapes by Frans Post; French school - 20 Paintings by Eugene Boudin; Ventania (Storm) by Alfred Sisley; Italian School Portrait of the Cardinal Amadei by Giovanni Battista Gaulli, Baciccia; Sao Caetano (circa 1730) by Giambattista Tiepolo. Graphic art department: Prints & drawings by Annibale Carracci, Chagall, Daumier, Durer, Toulouse Lautrec, Picasso, Guido Reni, Renoir, Tiepolo, etc

SALVADOR

M **MUSEO DE ARTE ANTIGA: INSTITUTO FEMENINO DA BAHIA,** Early Art Museum: Bahia Women's College, Rua Monsenhor Flaviano 2. *Dir* Henriqueta Martins Catharino
Collections: Religious art; Brazilian art; women's apparel, jewelry, gold, silver

SAO PAULO

M **MUSEU DE ARTE CONTEMPORANEA DA UNIVERSIDADE DE SAO PAULO,** Modern Art Museum of Sao Paulo University, CP22031, Parque Ibirapuera, Pavilhao da Bienal, 01499. Tel 211-0011. *Dir* Dr Lisbeth Rebollo Concalves
Collections: International & Brazilian plastic arts

M **MUSEU DE ARTE DE SAO PAULO,** Sao Paulo Art Museum, Ave Paulista 1578, 01310. Tel 251-5644. *Dir* Julio Neves
Collections: Representative works by Portinari & Lasar Segall; ancient & modern paintings & sculptures: American, 19th - 20th Centuries; Brazilian, 17th - 20th Centuries; British, 18th - 20th Centuries; Dutch, Flemish & German, 15th - 20th Centuries; French, 16th - 20th Centuries; Italian, 13th - 20th Centuries; Spanish & Portuguese, 16th - 19th Centuries

BULGARIA

PAZARDZIK

M **STANISLAV DOSPEVSKY MUSEUM,** Maria-Luisa 50, 4400. Tel 2-50-30. *Dir* N Dolchev
Collections: House where the painter lived & worked; exhibition of paintings, icons, personal effects & documents

PLOVDIV

M **REGIONAL MUSEUM OF ARCHAEOLOGY,** Pl Saedinenie 1, 4000. Tel 22-43-39, 23-17-60. *Dir* Dr Kostadin Kisyov
Library with 15,000 vols
Collections: Prehistory; classical & medieval archaeology; epigraphic monuments, jewelery, numismatics, toreutics & vessels

SOFIA

M **NATSIONALNA HUDOZHESTVENA GALERIJA,** National Art Gallery, Batemberg 6, 1000. Tel 044-88-35-59. *Dir* Svetlin Rusev
Collections: National & foreign art

CHILE

SANTIAGO

M **MUSEO DE ARTE COLONIAL DE SAN FRANCISCO,** Alameda Bernardo O'Higgins 834, PO Box 122D. Tel 398737. *Dir* Rosa Puga
Collections: 16th - 19th century art; important collection of 17th century paintings in Chile; the life of St Francis depicted in 53 pictures; other religious works of art, furniture

M **MUSEO DE ARTE POPULAR AMERICANO,** Museum of American Folk Art, Parque Forestal S/N, Casilla 2100, Univ of Chile. Tel 396-488. *Dir* Julio Tobar Urzua
Collections: Araucanian silver; American folk arts of pottery, basketware, metal & wood

M **MUSEO NACIONAL DE BELLAS ARTES,** National Museum of Fine Arts, Parque Forestal, Casilla 3209. Tel 330655. *Dir* Milan Ivelic
Collections: Baroque, Chilean & Spanish paintings; sculpture; engravings

CHINA, REPUBLIC OF

TAIPEI

M **NATIONAL PALACE MUSEUM,** Wai-Shuang-Hsi, Shih-Lin. Tel 02-882-1230. *Dir* Chin Hsiao-yi
Collections: Bronzes, calligraphy, carved lacquer, embroidery, enamelware, jades, miniature crafts, oracle bones, paintings, porcelain, pottery, rare and old books & documents from Shang Dynasty to Ch'ing Dynasty, tapestry, writing implements
L **Library**
Library Holdings: Vols 48,000; Per subs 683; Documents 395,000; Rare books 191,000

COLOMBIA

BOGOTA

M **MUSEO COLONIAL,** Museum of the Colonial Period, Carrera 6, No 9-77. Tel 2-41-60-17. *Dir* Teresa Morales de Gomez
Collections: Spanish colonial period art work: paintings, sculpture, furniture, gold and silver work, drawing

COSTA RICA

SAN JOSE

M **MUSEO DE ARTE COSTARRICENSE,** Apdo 378, Fe cosa, 1009. Tel 22-72-55. *Dir* Rocio Fernandez De Ulibarri
Collections: Representative Costa Rican art

M **MUSEO NACIONAL DE COSTA RICA,** Calle 17, Avda Central y 2, Apdo 749, 1000. Tel 57-14-33. *Dir* Melania Ortiz Volio
Collections: Pre-Columbian & colonial religious art; natural history

CROATIA

RIJEKA

M **MODERNA GALERIJA,** Museum of Modern Art, Dolac 1, 51000. Tel 334280. *Dir* Berislav Valusek
Library with 2000 vols
Collections: Paintings, sculptures & graphics

SPLIT

M **ARCHEOLOSKI MUZEJ U SPLITU,** Archaeological Museum, Zrinjsko-Frankopanska 25, 58000. Tel 05844574. *Dir* Emilio Marin
Library with 30,000 vols
Collections: Relics from the Greek colonies; prehistoric & numismatic collection; medieval monuments from the 9th to the 13th century

M **GALERIJA UMJETNINA,** Art Gallery, Lovretska 11, 58000. *Dir* Milan Ivanisevic
Library with 10,000 vols
Collections: Paintings & sculptures; ancient & modern art

ZAGREB

M **ARHEOLOSKI MUZEJ,** Archaelogical Museum, Zrinski trg 19, 41000. Tel 427600. *Dir* Ante Rendic-Miocevic
Collections: Neolithic 13th century

M **MODERNA GALERIJA,** Gallery of Modern Art, Brace Kavurica 1, 41000. Tel 433802. *Dir* Igor Zidic
Library with 2500 vols
Collections: Collection of sculptures, graphic arts & paintings

M **MUNZEJ SUVREMENE UMJETNOSTI,** Habdeliceva 2, 41000. Tel 041-431-343. *Dir* Davor Maticevi
Collections: Five galleries exhibiting contemporary art, antique & Renaissance works, primitive art, Ivan Mestrovic's sculpture & photography
M **Galerija Benko Horvat,** 41000. *Cur* Zelimir Koscevic
Collections: Antique & renaissance art
M **Galerija Primitivne Umjetnosti, Gallery of Naive Art,** Cirilometodska 3, 41000. Tel 041 423 669. *Cur* Nada Krizic
M **Galerija Suvremene Umjetnosti, Gallery of Contemporary Art,** Katarinin trg 2, 41000. Tel 041 425 227. *Cur* Marijan Susovski

M **MUZEJ ZA UMJETNOST I OBRT,** Museum of Applied Arts, Trg Marsala Tita 10, 41000. Tel 454-122. *Dir* Vladimir Malekovic
Library with 36,000 vols
Collections: Applied arts from the 14th to the 20th century; ceramics, glass, tapestries, textiles, paintings & sculptures

M **STROSSMAYEROVA GALERIJA STARIH MAJSTORA,** Strossmayer's Gallery of Old Masters, Trg Nikole Subica Zrinskog 11, 41000. Tel 041-433-504. *Dir* Prof Duro Vandura
Collections: Dutch 15th-18th century; French collection mostly 18th & 19th century; Italian collection, Fra Angelico - Piazzetta, six rooms, paintings & sculpture, 13th to 19th century

CUBA

HAVANA

M **MUSEO DE ARTES DECORATIVAS,** Calle 17, No 502 Vedado. Tel 320924. *Dir* Rebeca Gutierrez
Library with 2500 vols
Collections: Porcelain, bronzes, gold & silver work & tapestries

M **MUSEO NACIONAL DE BELLAS ARTES,** National Museum, Animas entre Zulueta y Monserate, CP 10200. Tel 621643. *Dir* Lucilla Villegas Oria
Collections: Renaissance and other European art; Cuban art from colonial times to the present

CYPRUS

NICOSIA

M **CYPRUS MUSEUM,** PO Box 2024. Tel (02) 30-2189. *Dir of Antiquities* Athanasios Papugeorghiou; *Cur* Open
Collections: Bronze cauldron from Salamis; middle and late Bronze-age Geometric, Archaic, Classical, Hellenistic and Graeco-Roman pottery; Mycenaean vases; Neolithic stone tools and vessels; sculpture from Archaic to Greco-Roman Age, including the Fine Arsos Head, the Aphrodite of Soli, and the bronze statue of Septimus Sevarus; silver trays from Lambousa

CZECH REPUBLIC

BRNO

M **MORAVSKA GALERIE V BRNE,** Moravian Gallery in Brno, Husova 14, 662 26. Tel 42-21-57-53. *Dir* Dr Jaroslav Kacer
Library with 120,000 vols
Collections: European Art Collection - ceramics, furniture, glass, graphic design, jewelry, photography, textiles; Fine Art Collection - graphic art, painting, sculpture, 14th century to present; Oriental Art Collection

JIRASKOVA

M **MUZEUM SKLA A BIZUTERIE,** Museum of Glass & Jewelry, Jablonec nad Nisou, 46600. Tel 22522. *Dir* Antonin Langhamer
Library with 11,500 vols
Collections: Bohemian glass making & jewelry; exhibitions

LITOMERICE

M **GALERIE VYTVARNEHO UMENI,** Gallery of Fine Arts, Michalska 7, 412-37. Tel 4127. *Dir* Jan Stibr
Collections: Art of the 19th century; Baroque Art of the 17th - 18th centuries; contemporary art; Gothic art of the 13th - 16th centuries; special collections of native paintings and sculpture; Renaissance paintings and sculptures of the 15th - 16th centuries

PRAGUE

M **GALERIE HLAVNIHO MESTA PRAHY,** Prague City Gallery, Mickiewiczova 3, 16000. Tel 341439. *Dir* Jaroslav Fatka
Collections: Pragensia work; 19th & 20th centuries Czech artists

M **NARODNI GALERIE V PRAZE,** National Gallery of Prague, Hradcanske Nam 15, 119 04. Tel 232-9331. *Dir* Dr Martin Zlatohlávek
Library with 75,000 vols
Collections: Architecture; Czech sculpture of the 19th and 20th century; French and European art of the 19th and 20th century; Old Czech art; Old European Art; graphic art, modern art; Oriental art

M **UMELECKOPRUMYSLOVE MUZEUM V PRAZE,** Ulice 17 listopadu 2, 110 01. Tel 2481 12 41. *Dir* Dr Helena Koenigsmarkova
Library with 150,000 vols
Collections: European applied art from 16th to 19th century; collections of glass, ceramics, china, furniture, textiles, tapestries, gold & silver work, iron, ivory, clocks, prints, posters, photography, contemporary design

M **ZIDOVSKE MUZEUM,** Jewish Museum, Jachymova 3, 110 01. Tel 24 81 00 99. *Dir* Jaroslav Stika
Library with 100,000 vols
Collections: Historical archival materials of Bohemian & Moravian Jewish religious communities; library of ancient books with a collection of Hebrew manuscripts; children's drawings & works of painters from the Terezin concentration camp; silver from Czech synagogues; textiles from synagogues of historic interest; Holocaust memorial

DENMARK

AALBORG

M **NORDJYLLANDS KUNSTMUSEUM,** Art Museum of Northern Jutland, Kong Christians Alle 50, 9000. Tel 98-13-80-88. *Dir* Nina Hobolth
Library with 7400 vols
Collections: Collection of graphics, painting & sculpture from 20th century, Danish & international

AARHUS

M **AARHUS KUNSTMUSEUM,** Aarhus Art Museum, Vennelystparken, 8000. Tel 86-13-52-55. *Dir* Jens Erik Sorensen
Library with 1000 vols
Collections: Danish & European art, Danish Golden ages, †Danish modernism-Asger Jorn, Richard Mortensen, †contemporay Danish & international, Jeff Koons, Gilbert & George

CHARLOTTENLUND

M **ORDRUPGAARDSAMLINGEN,** Vilvordevej 110, 2920. Tel 39-64-11-83. *Dir* Anne-Birgitte Fonsmark
Collections: Wilhelm Hansen Collection; paintings by Cezanne, Corot, Courbet, Degas, Delacroix, Gauguin, Manet, Pissarro, Renoir, Sisley & other French & Danish artists from the 19th century & the beginning of the century

COPENHAGEN

L **KUNSTAKADEMIETS BIBLIOTEK,** Royal Danish Academy of Fine Arts Library, 1 Kongens Nytoru, K 1050. Tel 33-12-86-59. *Dir* Hakon Lund
Library Holdings: Vols 115,000; Architectural Drawings 110,000; AV — Slides 100,000; Other — Photographs 300,000

M **KUNSTINDUSTRIMUSEET,** The Danish Museum of Decorative Art, Bredgade 68, 1260. Tel 33-14-94-52. *Pres* Olav Grue; *Dir* Kristian Jakobsen
Library with 60,000 vols
Collections: Chinese and Japanese art and handicrafts; European decorative and applied art from the Middle Ages to present - bookbindings, carpets and tapestries, furniture, jewelry, porcelain and pottery, silverware and textiles

M **NATIONALMUSEET,** National Museum, Prinsens Palae, Frederiksholms Kanal 12, 1220. Tel 33-13-44-11. *Dir* Dr Olaf Olsen
Collections: Museum has 5 divisions, including Danish historical collection, folk museum, ethnographic collection, classical antiquities collection, royal coin & medal collection

COPENHAGEN K

M **ROSENBORG SLOT,** Rosenborg Palace, Oster Voldgade 4A, 1350. Tel 33-15-76-19. *Dir* Mogens Bencard; *Dir Chamberlain* Niels Eilschou Holm
Collections: Crown Jewels; arms, apparel, jewelry & furniture from period 1470-1863

M **STATENS MUSEUM FOR KUNST,** Royal Museum of Fine Arts, Solvgade 48-50, DK 1307. Tel 33-91-21-26. *Dir* Allis Helleland
Collections: Danish paintings and sculpture; various other works by 19th and 20th century Scandinavian artists; old masters of Italian, Flemish, Dutch and German Schools; modern French art

M **THORVALDSENS MUSEUM,** Porthusgade 2, 1213. Tel 33-32-15-32. *Dir* Stig Miss; *Cur* Bjarne Jornas
Collections: 19th century European paintings & drawings; sculpture & drawings by Bertel Thorvaldsen (1770 - 1844) & his collections of contemporary paintings, drawings & prints

COPENHAGEN V

M **KOBENHAVNS BYMUSEUM,** Copenhagen City Museum, Absalonsgade 3, PO Box 3004, 1507. Tel 31-21-07-72. *Dir* Jørgen Selmer
Collections: Photographs 1850 to present; architecture; history of Copenhagen in pictures; The Soren Kierkegaard Collection; Kierkegaard relics; models

M **NY CARLSBERG GLYPTOTEK,** Carlsberg Gallery, Dantes Plads 7, 1556. Tel 33-41-81-41. *Dir* Flemming Johansen; *Pres* Hans Edvard Norregard-Nielsen
Collections: Danish & French paintings & sculptures from 19th & 20th centuries; Egyptian, Etruscan, Greek & Roman sculpture

HUMLEBAEK

M **LOUISIANA MUSEUM OF MODERN ART,** Gammel Strandvej 13, 3050. Tel 42-19-07-19. *Dir* Knud W Jensen
Collections: Danish, International & Modern art from 1950, including sculpture & paintings
Activities: Concerts; cinema; theatre

DOMINICAN REPUBLIC

SANTO DOMINGO

M **GALERIA NACIONAL DE BELLAS ARTES,** National Fine Arts Gallery, Avenida Independencia esq Maximo Gomez. Tel 687-3300. *Dir* Dr Jose de J Alvarez Valverde
Collections: Paintings and sculptures previously exhibited in the Museo Nacional

ECUADOR

QUITO

M **MUSEO DE ARTE COLONIAL,** Cuenca St & Mejia St, Apdo 2555. Tel 212-297. *Dir* Carlos A Rodriguez
Collections: Art from the Escuela Quitena of the Colonial epoch - 17th, 18th and 19th century art and some contemporary art

M **MUSEO MUNICIPAL DE ARTE E HISTORIA ALBERTO MENA CAAMANO,** Civic Museum of Arts and History, Calle Espejo 1147 y Benalcazar, Apdo 17-01-3346. Tel 214018. *Dir* Alfonso Ortiz Crespo
Collections: Sculptures; paintings; documents

EGYPT

ALEXANDRIA

M **GRECO-ROMAN MUSEUM,** Museum St. *Dir* Doreya Said
Library with 15,000 vols
Collections: Exhibits from the Byzantine, Greek and Roman eras

CAIRO

M **COPTIC MUSEUM,** Old Cairo. *Dir* Maher Sahib
Library with 6500 vols
Collections: Architecture, bone, ebony, frescos, glass, icons, ivory, manuscripts, metalwork, pottery, sculpture, textiles, woodcarvings

M **EGYPTIAN NATIONAL MUSEUM,** Midan-el-Tahrir Kasr El-Nil. Tel 754-310. *Dir* Mohammed Saleh
Library with 39,000 vols
Collections: Ancient Egyptian art from prehistoric times through 6th century AD (excluding Coptic & Islamic periods); houses the Department of Antiquities

M **MUSEUM OF ISLAMIC ART,** Ahmed Maher Sq, Bab al-Khalq, 11638. Tel 90-19-30. *Dir-Gen* Abd al-Rauf Ali Yousuf
Museum maintains library with 14,000 volumes
Collections: Works of art showing evolution of Islamic art up to 1879

ENGLAND

BATH

M **AMERICAN MUSEUM IN BRITAIN,** Claverton Manor, BA2 7BD. Tel (0225) 460503. *Dir* William McNaught
Collections: American decorative arts from 17th to 19th centuries

M **HOLBURNE MUSEUM & CRAFTS STUDY CENTRE,** Great Pulteney St, Avon BA2 4DB. Tel (0225) 466669. *Cur* Barley Roscoe
Collections: Paintings by 17th & 18th century masters, including Gainsborough, Turner, British & Continental; fine art, porcelain & silver, 20th century pottery, textiles & calligraphy

M **VICTORIA ART GALLERY,** Bridge St, BA2 4AT. Tel (0225) 461111, Ext 2772. *Cur* Stephen Bird; *Arts Officer* Victoria Barwell
Collections: British & European paintings from 17th to 20th century; English pottery, porcelain, antique glass

BIRMINGHAM

M **BIRMINGHAM MUSEUMS AND ART GALLERY,** Chamberlain Square, B3 3DH. Tel (021) 235-2834. *Dir* Michael Diamond
Collections: Fine and applied art, including English works since 17th century, foreign schools from Renaissance, Pre-Raphaelite works; silver, ceramics, coin, textile collections; Old and New World archeology, ethnography and local history collections; branch museums house furniture, machinery and applied arts

BRIGHTON

M **ROYAL PAVILION, ART GALLERY AND MUSEUMS,** Brighton Museum & Art Gallery, Church St, Sussex BN1 1UE. Tel (0273) 603005. *Dir* Jessica Rutherford
M **Brighton Art Gallery and Museum,** Tel (0273) 603005.
Collections: Early and modern paintings, watercolors, prints and drawings; English pottery and porcelain, including the Willett Collection; decorative art and furniture of Art Nouveau and Art Deco periods; ethnography and archaeology; musical instruments; Brighton history
M **Royal Pavilion,** Tel (0273) 603005.
Collections: Once the marine palace of King George IV (1787-1846); interior decorations restored and original furniture
M **Preston Manor,** Preston Park. Tel (0273) 603005.
Collections: Home of the Stanford family for nearly 200 years, this fully furnished Gregorian Era house illustrates the life of the wealthy preceeding the First World War; rebuilt 1738; remodelled 1905

BRISTOL

M **CITY OF BRISTOL MUSEUM AND ART GALLERY,** Queen's Rd, BS8 1RL. Tel (0117) 922 3571. *Divisional Dir, Museums & Heritage* Martyn Heighton
Collections: Fine and applied arts of Great Britain; archaeological and ethnological collection; Oriental Art

CAMBRIDGE

M **UNIVERSITY OF CAMBRIDGE,** Fitzwilliam Museum, Trumpington St, CB2 1RB. Tel (01223) 332900. *Dir* S S Jervis
Library with 200,000 vols
Collections: European ceramics; Greek, Roman, western Asiatic & Egyptian antiquities; arms & armor, coins, drawings, furniture, illuminated manuscripts, manuscripts, paintings, prints, sculpture, textiles

CARDIFF

M **NATIONAL MUSEUM OF WALES,** Amgueddfa Genedlaethol Cymru, Main Bldg, Cathays Park, CF1 3NP. Tel (0222) 397951. *Pres* C R T Edwards; *Dir* Colin Ford
Collections: Art, natural sciences, archaeology & industry of Wales

DONCASTER

M **DONCASTER MUSEUM AND ART GALLERY,** Chequer Rd, Yorks DN1 2AE. Tel 0302-734293. *Cur* T G Preece
Collections: European painting, ceramics and glass, silver and jewelry; The King's Own Yorkshire Light Infantry Regimental Collection

EAST MOLESEY

M **HAMPTON COURT PALACE,** Surrey KT8 9AU. Tel (081) 7819500. *Palace Adminr* Crawford McDonald; *Supt Royal Coll* J Cowell
Represents art, architecture & gardens from the Tudor Period to Georgian Period
Collections: Paintings & tapestries, including Andrea Mantegna's 9 paintings of The Triumph of Julius Caesar

KENDAL

M **ABBOT HALL ART GALLERY & MUSEUM OF LAKELAND LIFE & INDUSTRY,** Cumbria LA9 5AL. Tel (01539) 722464. *Dir* Edward King
Collections: Gallery provides changing exhibitions of local and international interest; houses permanent collections of 18th century furniture, paintings and objects d'art; modern paintings; sculpture; drawings; museum features working and social life of the area †18th century potraits, Esp Romney; watercolors & drawings, including Ruskin, Constable, Turner; †lake district landscapes; †modern British art

LEEDS

M **TEMPLE NEWSAM HOUSE,** LS15 0AE. Tel 247 7241. *Dir* Christopher Gilbert
Collections: Decorative arts; old master and Ingram family paintings
M **Leeds City Art Gallery,** Municipal Bldg, The Headrow, LS1 3AA. Tel (0532) 462-495.
Collections: Early English Watercolors; English & European paintings of 19th century; modern paintings & sculpture; Henry Moore Centre for the Study of Sculpture
M **Lotherton Hall,** Aberford. Tel (0532) 813259.
Collections: Gascoigne Collection of 17th to 19th century paintings, ceramics, silver, furniture; Oriental gallery; modern crafts

LEICESTER

M **LEICESTERSHIRE MUSEUMS, ARTS & RECORDS SERVICE,** 96 New Walk, LE2 0JJ. Tel (0533) 554100. *Dir* Dr R T Schalda-Hall
Collections: Major special collections include 18th, 19th and 20th century British Art, German Expressionists (largest public collection in Britain); European Art from Renaissance to present; contemporary art

LINCOLN

M **LINCOLNSHIRE MUSEUMS,** County Offices, Newland, LN1 1YL. Tel (0522) 552806. *Asst Dir Heritage Services* R E Taylor
Oversees 7 museums
M **Museum of Lincolnshire Life,** Burton Rd, LN1 1YL. Tel (0522) 528448. *Keeper of Social History* P R Cousins
Collections: Displays illustrating the social, agricultural & industrial history of Lincolnshire over the last three centuries
M **Usher Gallery,** Lindum Rd. Tel (0522) 527980. *Keeper* R H Wood
Collections: Exhibits the Usher collection of watches, miniatures, porcelain; special collection of works by Peter De Wint; a general collection of paintings, sculpture & decorative art; collection of coins & tokens from Lincolnshire
M **Lincoln City and County Museum,** Broadgate. Tel (0522) 530401. *Keeper of Archaeology* Antony Page
Collections: Natural history, archaeological & historical collections relating to Lincolnshire; large collection of Roman antiquities from Lincoln

LIVERPOOL

M WALKER ART GALLERY, William Brown St, L3 8EL. Tel 2070-001. *Cur* Edward Morris
Collections: English and European drawings, paintings, prints, sculpture, watercolors, including notable collections of Italian and Netherlandish primitives; pop art

LONDON

M BRITISH MUSEUM, Great Russell St, WC1B 3DG. Tel (071) 636-1555. *Dir* Dr Robert G W Anderson
Collections: Egyptian, Assyrian, Greek and Roman Prehistoric, Romano-British, Western Asiatic and other arts; coins and medals; prints and drawings

M DULWICH PICTURE GALLERY, College Rd, SE21 7AD. Tel (081) 693-5254. *Dir* G A Waterfield
Collections: Collections of Old Masters from 1626 onwards, including Claude, Cuyp, Gainsborough, Murillo, Poussin, Raphael, Rembrandt, Rubens, Teniers, Tiepolo, Van Dyck, Watteau & others

M NATIONAL GALLERY, Trafalgar Square, WC2N 5DN. Tel (071) 839-3321. *Chair* Jacob Rothschild; *Dir* Neil MacGregor
Collections: Principal schools, British, Dutch, Early Netherlandish, French, German, Italian; Western European painting up to early 20th century

M NATIONAL PORTRAIT GALLERY, 2 St Martin's Pl, WC2H 0HE. Tel (071) 306-0055. *Chmn Trustees* Henry Keswick; *Dir* Charles Sammarez Smith Phd
Collections: National Collection of portraits spanning last 500 years, including sculpture and photographs; caricatures, drawings, photographs; printings, watercolors

M QUEEN'S GALLERY, Buckingham Palace Rd, SW1A 1AA. Tel 799-2331.

M ROYAL ACADEMY OF ARTS, Burlington House, Piccadilly, W1V 0DS. Tel 734-9052. *Pres* Philip Dowson
Collections: Paintings, prints, architectural collection
L Library, W1V 0DS. Tel (071) 439-7438. *Libr* Mary Anne Stevens
Library Holdings: Vols 15,000; Engravings; Fine arts books 20,000; Manuscripts; Original drawings; Other — Manuscripts

M SOUTH LONDON GALLERY, 65 Peckham Rd, SE5 8UH. Tel (071) 703-6120. *Gallery Dir* David Thorp
Collections: Contemporary British art; 20th century original prints; paintings of the Victorian period; topographical paintings & drawings of local subjects permanent collection exhibited periodically
Exhibitions: Exhibitions from permanent collection

M TATE GALLERY, Millbank, SW1P 4RG. Tel (071) 887-8000. *Dir* Nicholas Serota
Collections: Works of Blake, Constable, Hogarth, Turner and the Pre-Raphaelites; British painting from the 16th century to present; modern foreign painting from Impressionism onward; modern sculpture; collection totals 12,000, including 5500 prints; Largest public collection of British Art of 20th Century

M UNIVERSITY OF LONDON, Courtauld Institute Galleries, Somerset House, Strand, WC2R 0RN. Tel (071) 873-2538. *Dir* Dr Dennis Farr
Collections: Samuel Courtauld Collection of French Impressionist and Post-Impressionist Paintings; other collections include old masters, early 20th century French and English paintings, modern British art, English landscape paintings and drawings

M VICTORIA & ALBERT MUSEUM, Cromwell Rd, South Kensington, SW7 2RL. Tel (071) 938-8500. *Dir* Alan Borg
Collections: Fine and applied arts of all countries, periods and styles, including Oriental art. European collections are mostly post-classical, architectural details, art of the book, bronzes, calligraphs, carpets, ceramics, clocks, costumes, cutlery, drawings, embroider, enamels, engravings, fabrics, furniture, glass, gold and silversmiths' work, ironwork, ivories, jewelry, lace, lithographs, manuscripts, metalwork, miniatures, musical instruments, oil paintings, posters, pottery and porcelain, prints, sculpture, stained glass, tapestries, theatre art, vestments, watches, watercolors, woodwork
M Apsley House (Wellington Museum), 149 Piccadilly Hyde Park Corner, W1V 9FA. Tel (071) 499-5676. *Cur* Jonathan Voak
Opened to the public 1952
Collections: Paintings, silver, porcelain, sculpture, orders and decorations, and personal relics of the first Duke of Wellington
M Bethnal Green Museum of Childhood, Cambridge Heath Rd, E2 9PA. Tel (081) 980-2415. *Cur* Anthony Burton
Collections: Dolls, ceramics, costumes, textiles, furniture & toys; articles related to childhood

M WALLACE COLLECTION, Hertford House, Manchester Square, W1M 6BN. Tel (071) 935-0687. *Dir* Rosalind Savill
Collections: Arms & Armour; French Furniture; Sevres Porcelain; paintings & works of art of all European schools; miniatures; sculpture

M WHITECHAPEL ART GALLERY, 80-82 Whitechapel High St, E1 7QX. Tel (171) 377-5015. *Dir* Catherine Lampert; *Press Officer* Mark Sladen
Collections: Changing exhibitions, primarily of modern & contemporary art

M WILLIAM MORRIS GALLERY, Lloyd Park, Forest Rd, E17 4PP. Tel (81) 527-3782. *Dir* Norah Gillow
Publications: Works of William Morris, pre-Raphaelites & the arts & crafts movement; sculpture by late 19th century artists; works by Frank Brangwyn

MANCHESTER

M MANCHESTER CITY ART GALLERIES, Corner of Mosley & Princess Sts, M2 3JL. Tel (061) 236-5244. *Dir* Richard Gray
Collections: British art; English costume, enamels, silver and decorative arts; Old Master and Dutch 17th century painting; pre-Raphaelite painting

M UNIVERSITY OF MANCHESTER, Whitworth Art Gallery, Oxford Rd, M15 6ER. Tel 0161-273-4865. *Dir* Alistair Smith
Collections: British drawings and watercolors; contemporary British paintings and sculpture; Old Master and modern prints; textiles, wallpapers

NEWCASTLE

M TYNE AND WEAR MUSEUMS, Newcastle Discovery, Blandford Square, NE1 4JA. Tel 091-232-6789. *Dir* David Fleming
Collections: British oil paintings since 1700 (with works by Burne-Jones, Gainsborough, Lansleer, Reynolds, Turner); British prints & watercolors; British (especially local) ceramics, costume, glass, pewter, silver of all periods; British textiles
M Sunderland Museum & Art Gallery, Borough Rd, NE1 4JA
Collections: Local history, pottery, paintings & glass
M Shipley Art Gallery, Prince Consort Rd
Collections: Contemporary craft & paintings from the old masters

NEWPORT

M BOROUGH OF NEWPORT MUSEUM AND ART GALLERY, John Frost Square, Gwent NP9 1PA. Tel (0633) 840064. *Cur* Robert Trett
Collections: Early English watercolors; oil paintings by British artists; local archeology (especially Roman); natural & social history

OXFORD

M MUSEUM OF MODERN ART OXFORD, 30 Pembroke St, 0X1 1BP. Telex 8-3147; Tel (0865) 722733. *Dir* David Elliott; *Cur* Chrissie Iles
Library with 15,000 vols
Exhibitions: Features changing international exhibitions of 20th century painting, photography, prints, sculpture, drawing, film & video

M OXFORD UNIVERSITY, Ashmolean Museum, Beaumont St, OX1 2PH. Tel (0865) 278000. *Dir* Dr C J White
Collections: British, European, Egyptian, Mediterranean & Near Eastern archaeology; Chinese Bronzes; Chinese & Japanese porcelain, painting & lacquer; Dutch, English, Flemish, French & Italian oil paintings; Indian sculpture & painting; Hope Collection of engraved portraits Tibetan, Indian and Islamic art objects; Extensive collection of coins from various countries and times; Old Master and modern drawings, prints and watercolors

PLYMOUTH

M PLYMOUTH CITY MUSEUM AND ART GALLERY, Drake Circus, Plymouth, Devon PL4 8AJ. Tel (0752) 264878. *Cur* Stephen Price
Estab to illustrate arts of the West Country
Collections: The Clarendon Collection of Portraits of 16th & 17th Century English worthies; Collection of Cookworthy's Plymouth & Bristol Porcelain; The Cottonian Collection of early printed & illuminated books

SHEFFIELD

M SHEFFIELD CITY MUSEUM, Weston Park, Yorks S10 2TP. Tel (0742) 768588. *Dir* Philip Broomhead
Estab 1875
Collections: Sheffield silver, Old Sheffield Plate, British and European cutlery, coins and medals, ceramics
M Abbeydale Hamlet, Abbeydale Rd S, S7 2QW. Tel (0742) 3677-31. *Dir* Philip Broomhead
Collections: An 18th century scytheworks with Huntsman type crucible steel furnace, tilt-hammers, grinding-shop and hand forges
M Bishop's House, Meersbrook Park, S8 9BE. Tel (0742) 557701. *Dir* Philip Broomhead
Collections: A late 15th century timber-framed domestic building with 16th - 17th century additions

SOUTHAMPTON

M SOUTHAMPTON CITY ART GALLERY, Civic Centre, Hants S09 4XF. Tel (0703) 632601. *Cur* Adrian B Rance; *Principal Officer Arts* Elizabeth Goodall
Collections: Continental Old Masters; French 19th & 20th centuries schools; British painting from the 18th century to present; contemporary sculpture & painting

SOUTHPORT

M ATKINSON ART GALLERY, Lord St, Merseyside PR8 No 1DH. Tel (0704) 533133, Ext 2110. *Keeper of Art Galleries & Museums* Anthony K Wray
Collections: British art - local, contemporary & historic; British 18th, 19th & 20th centuries oils; drawings, prints, sculptures & watercolors

STOKE ON TRENT

M **STOKE-ON-TRENT CITY MUSEUM AND ART GALLERY,** Hanley, Staffs ST1 3DW. Tel (0782) 202173. *Dir* P F Vigurs
Collections: One of the finest collections of English ceramics in the world, preeminent in Staffordshire ware; fine & decorative arts

WOLVERHAMPTON

M **WOLVERHAMPTON ART GALLERY AND MUSEUM,** Lichfield St, West Midlands WV1 1DU. Tel (0902) 312032. *Art Galleries & Museums Officer* Nicholas Dodd
Collections: Contemporary British art; 18th century British paintings; 19th & 20th centuries British painting & watercolors; branch museums have English enamels, japanning & porcelain

YORK

M **YORK CITY ART GALLERY,** Exhibition Square, Y01 2EW. Tel (0904) 551861. *Cur* Richard Green
Collections: British and European paintings, including the Lycett Green Collection of Old Masters; modern stoneware pottery; paintings and drawings by York artists, notably William Etty; watercolors, drawings and prints, mostly local topography

ETHIOPIA

ADDIS ABABA

M **MUSEUM OF THE INSTITUTE OF ETHIOPIAN STUDIES,** University of Addis Ababa, PO Box 1176. Tel 550844. *Cur* Ato Taye Taddese
Collections: Ethiopian cultural artifacts, ethnology collections, cultural history documents; religious art from 14th century to present

FINLAND

HELSINKI

M **SUOMEN KANSALLISMUSEO,** National Museum of Finland, Mannerheimintie 34, 00101. Tel 90-40251. *Dir* Ritva Ware
Numerous branch galleries throughout Finland
Collections: Ethnographical Department with Finnish, Finno-Ugrian & Comparative Ethnographical Collections; Finnish Historical Department with a collection of coins & medals; Prehistoric department with Finnish & Comparative Collections

M **SUOMEN RAKENNUSTAITEEN MUSEO,** Museum of Finnish Architecture, Kasarmikatu 24, 00130. Tel 66-19-18. *Dir* Marja-Riitta Norri
Library with 30,000 vols
Collections: Finnish architecture collection includes 70,000 photographs, 32,000 slides, 300,000 original drawings

TURKU

M **TURUN TAIDEMUSEO,** Turku Art Museum, Puolalanpuisto, 20100. Tel (921) 233-0954. *Dir* Erja Pusa
Collections: 19th & 20th centuries Finnish & Scandinavian art, drawings, paintings, prints & sculpture; 19th & 20th centuries international print collection

FRANCE

ALENCON

M **MUSEE DES BEAUX-ARTS ET DE LA DENTELLE,** Rue Charles Aveline, 61000. Tel 33-32-40-07. *Dir* Aude Pessey-Lux
Collections: 17th - 19th century French, Dutch & Flemish paintings; 16th - 19th century French, Italian & Dutch drawings; 16th - 20th century Alencon, Flemish, Italian & Eastern European lace

ANGERS

M **MUSEE DES BEAUX-ARTS,** Museum of Fine Arts, 10 rue du Musee, 49100. Tel 41-88-64-65. *Cur* Patrick Le Novene
Collections: Paintings of the 17th & 18th centuries; Dutch, Flemish & French schools; sculpture, including busts by Houdon

ANTIBES

M **MUSEE PICASSO,** Chateau Grimaldi, 06600. Tel 92-90-54-20. *Dir* Maurice Friehurst
Collections: Modern and contemporary art; 230 works by Picasso

AVIGNON

M **MUSEE DU PETIT PALAIS,** Place du Palais des Papes, 84000. Tel 90-86-44-58. *Dir* Esther Moench-Scherer
Collections: Italian paintings covering the period from 14th - 16th century; Medieval sculpture from Avignon from 12th - 15th century; paintings of the Avignon School of 14th - 15th centuries

CHANTILLY CEDEX

M **MUSEE ET CHATEAU DE CHANTILLY (MUSEE CONDE),** BP 243, 60631. Tel 44-57-08-00. *Cur* Amelie Lefebure; *Cur Libr* Fzederic Vezgne; *Cur Paintings* Nicole Gainier
Collections: Ceramics, manuscripts & paintings

DIJON

M **MUSEE DES BEAUX-ARTS DE DIJON,** Museum of Fine Arts, Palais des Etats Cour de Bour, 21000. Tel 80-74-52-70. *Chief Cur* Emmanuel Starcky
Collections: Furniture, objects of art, paintings of French & foreign schools, sculpture; Granville Collection

FONTAINEBLEAU

M **MUSEE NATIONAL DE FONTAINEBLEAU,** National Museum of Fontainebleau, Chateau de Fountainebleau, 77300. Tel 64-22-27-40. *Cur* Jean-Pierre Samoyault; *Cur* Colombe Samoyault-Yerlet; *Cur* Daniele Denise
Collections: Paintings, furniture and interiors of 1st Empire and 17th, 18th and 19th centuries

GRENOBLE

M **MUSEE DES BEAUX-ARTS,** Place de Verdun, 38000. Tel 76-54-09-82. *Chief Cur* Serge Lemoine
Collections: 16th, 17th and 18th century paintings; French, Italian, Spanish, Flemish schools; modern collection; Egyptology collection

LILLE

M **MUSEE DES BEAUX-ARTS DE LILLE,** Museum of Fine Arts, Place de la Republique, 59000. Tel 20-57-01-84. *Chief Cur* Arnauld Brejon de Lavergnee
Collections: Western European paintings from 15th - 20th centuries; collection of ceramics, objects of art and sculptures

LYON

M **MUSEE DES BEAUX-ARTS,** Museum of Fine Arts, Plais Saint Pierre, 20 Place des Terreaux, 69001. Tel 78-28-07-66. *Chief Cur* Philippe Durey
Collections: Ancient, Medieval & Modern sculpture; Egyptian, Greek & Roman antiquities; French art since the Middle Ages; French, Hispano-Moorish, Italian & Oriental ceramics; Gothic & Renaissance art; Islamic art; modern art & murals by Purvis de Chavannes; painting of the French, Flemish, Dutch, Italian & Spanish schools

M **MUSEE HISTORIQUE DES TISSUS, MUSEE LYONNAIS DES ARTS DECORATIFS,** 30-34 rue de la Charite, 69002. Tel 78-37-15-05. *Cur* Guy Balzy
Collections: Re-created French 18th century salons with furniture, objects d'art & decorative pieces; 15th & 16th centuries Italian majolicas; enamels, ivories & tapestries of Middle Ages & Renaissance; European drawings from 16th to 19th century

ORLEANS

M **MUSEE DES BEAUX-ARTS D'ORLEANS,** Museum of Fine Arts, Place Sainte-Croix, 45000. Tel 38-53-39-22. *Cur* E Moinet
Collections: Dutch, French, Flemish, German, Italian & Spanish paintings & drawings, primarily from 17th & 18th centuries; sculpture

PARIS

M **CENTRE NATIONAL D'ART ET DE CULTURE GEORGES POMPIDOU,** Musee National d'Art Moderne, 31 Rue Saint-Merri, Cedex 04, 75191. Telex 21-2726; Tel 44-78-12-33. *Pres* Francois Barre; *Dir* Germain Viatte
Collections: 20th century paintings, prints, drawings & sculpture; art films & photographs

L **ECOLE NATIONALE SUPERIEURE DES BEAUX-ARTS,** La Bibliotheque, 14 rue Bonaparte, 75272. Tel (1) 47-03-50-00. *Dir of School* Yves Michaud
120,000 vol library for school with 600 students & 75 instructors

M **MUSEE CARNAVALET,** 23 Rue de Sevigne, 75003. Tel (1) 42-72-21-13. *Chief Cur* Jean-Marc Leri
Collections: History and archaeology of Paris; prints and drawings

M **MUSEE COGNACQ-JAY**, Cognacq-Jay Museum, 8 rue Elzevir, 75003. Tel 40-27-07-21. *Cur* Pascal de la Vaissiere
Collections: 18th century works of art; English and French furniture, pastels, paintings, porcelain, sculpture

M **MUSEE D'ART MODERNE DE LA VILLE DE PARIS**, 11 ave du President Wilson, Post 9 Rue Gaston de St Paul, 75116. Tel 53-67-40-00. *Cur* Suzanne Page
Collections: Modern painting and sculpture

M **MUSEE DU LOUVRE**, Louvre Museum, Paris Cedex 01, 34-36 quai du Louvrel, 75058. Telex 21-4670; Tel 40-20-50-50. *Dir* Pierre Rosenberg
Collections: Islamic art; The Edmond de Rothschild Collection; Oriental, Greek, Roman and Egyptian antiquities; decorative arts, drawings, paintings; Medieval, Renaissance and modern sculpture
M **Musee du Jeu de Paume**, Place de la Concorde, 75001. Tel 47-03-12-36. *Chief Cur* Daniel Abadie

M **MUSEE DU PETIT PALAIS**, Municipal Museum, Ave Winston Churchill, 75008. Tel 42-65-12-73. *Cur* Therese Burollet
Collections: Egyptian, Etruscan and Greek antiquities; paintings, sculpture and other works of art to 19th century

M **MUSEE GUIMET**, 6 place d'Iena, 19 Ave d'Iena, 75116. Tel 47-23-61-65. *Chief Cur* Jean-Francois Jarrige
Maintains library with 100,000 vols
Collections: Art, archaeology, religions, history of India, Afghanistan, Central Asia, China, Korea, Japan, Khmer, Tibet, Thailand and Indonesia

M **MUSEE MARMOTTAN**, 2 rue Louis Boilly, 75016. Tel 42-24-07-02. *Cur* Arnaud D'Hauterives
Collections: Collection of Primitives, Renaissance, Empire and Impressionist works; medieval miniatures in Wildenstein collection

M **MUSEE NATIONAL DES MONUMENTS FRANCAIS**, Palais de Chaillot, Place du Trocadero, 75116. Tel 44-05-39-10. *Cur* Guy Cogeual
Library with 10,000 works on art history
Collections: Full scale casts of the principal French monuments and sculpture from the beginning of Christianity to the 19th century; full scale reproductions of Medieval murals

M **MUSEE NATIONAL DU MOYEN AGE THERMES DE CLUNY**, 6 Place Paul Painleve, 75005. Tel 43-25-62-00. *Dir* Viviane Huchard
Collections: Enamels, furniture, goldsmithery, ivories, paintings, sculptures & tapestries of the Middle Ages-from the 10th to the beginning of the 16th centuries

M **UNION DES ARTS DECORATIFS**, Central Union of Decorative Arts, 107 rue de Rivoli, 75001. Tel 44-55-57-50. *Pres* Antoine Riboud; *Conservateur Général* Pierre Arizzoli-Clémentel
Collections: Housed in four museums: Musées des Arts Decoratifs - decorative arts collection from Middle Ages to present; Western & Oriental Art; includes national arts information & documentation center; library with 100,000 vols; Musee Nissim de Camondo - unique 18th century objects bequeathed by Count Moise de Camondo; Musée de la Mode et du textile

RENNES

M **MUSEE DES BEAUX-ARTS ET D'ARCHEOLOGIE**, 20, quai Emile Zola, 35000. Tel 99-28-55-85. *Cur* Jean Aubert
Collections: Egyptian, Greek and Roman archeology; drawings, paintings and sculptures from 15th - 20th centuries

STRASBOURG

M **MUSEE DES BEAUX-ARTS**, Museum of Fine Arts, Chateau des Rohan, 2 Place du Chateau, 67000. Tel 88-52-50-00. *Cur* Jean-Louis Faure
Collections: Old Masters; 17th to 19th century French schools; Italian schools

TOULOUSE

M **MUSEE DES AUGUSTINS**, 21 rue de Metz, 31000. Tel 61-22-21-82. *Cur* Alain Daguerre de Hureaux
Collections: Medieval sculptures and paintings housed in former Augustine Convent

TOURS

M **MUSEE DES BEAUX-ARTS**, Museum of Fine Arts, 18 Place Francois Sicard, 37000. Tel 47-05-68-73. *Cur* Jacques Nicourt
Collections: Ancient and Modern Tapestries; Furniture; French School of 18th Century, including Boucher and Lancret; Italian Paintings of 13th to 16th Century, including Mantegna and primitives; 17th Century Paintings, including Rembrandt and Rubens; 19th Century Paintings, including Degas, Delacroix and Monet; Sculptures: Bourdelle, Houdon, Lemoyne

VERSAILLES

M **MUSEE NATIONAL DU CHATEAU DE VERSAILLES**, National Museum of the Chateau of Versailles, Chateau de Versailles, 78000. Tel 30-84-74-00. *Chief Cur* Jean-Pierre Babelon
Collections: Furniture from 17th to 19th centuries; painting and sculpture from 16th to 20th centuries

GERMANY

AACHEN

M **SUERMONDT-LUDWIG-MUSEUM**, Wilhelmstrasse 18, 5100. Telex 2-9166; Tel (0241) 47980-0. *Dir* Dr Ulrich Schneider
Collections: Paintings from the Middle Ages to the Baroque; portraits from Middle Ages to present; sculpture from the Middle Ages; graphic art (ceramics, textiles)

BERLIN

M **BRUCKE MUSEUM**, Bussardsteig 9, 14195. Tel 831-20-29. *Dir* Dr Magdalena Moeller
Collections: German expressionism, paintings, sculptures & graphic art of the Brucke group

M **STAATLICHE MUSEEN ZU BERLIN-PREUSSISCHER KULTURBESITZ**, State Museums, Foundation for Prussian Cultural Treasures, Stauffenbergstrasse 41, 10785. Tel 2662610. *Gen Dir* Prof Dr Wolf-Dieter Dube
Collections: Supervises 17 museums and departments, in addition to an art library and a museum library
—**Skulpturensammlung, Dept of Sculpture**, Tel 8301. *Dir* Dr Wolf-Dieter Dube
—**Kupferstichkabinett, Dept of Prints & Drawings**, 1000 Matthaikirchplatz 4, Berlin, 10785. Tel 2662002. *Dir* Dr Alexander Duckers
Library with 40,000 vols
Collections: Drawings, prints and illustrated books of all epochs of European art
—**Museum fur Volkerkunde, Ethnographical Museum**, Arminallee 27, 1000. Tel 8301-226. *Dir* Klaus Helfrich
Collections: Items of different cultures: Africa, East Asia (China, Tibet), Europe and North America
—**Museum fur Indische Kunst, Museum of Indian Art**, Takustrasse 40, Berlin, 14195. Tel 8301-392. *Dir* Prof Dr Marianne Yaldiz
Collections: Indian Art
—**Museum fur Ostasiatische Kunst, Museum of Far Eastern Art**, Takustrasse 40, 1000. Tel 8301-381. *Dir* Dr Willibald Veit
Collections: Paintings and ceramics of China and Japan
—**Museum fur Islamische Kunst, Museum of Islamic Art**, Bodestrasse 1-3, Berlin, 10178. Tel 20355 329. *Dir* Dr Michael Meinecke; *Dir* Volkman Enderlein
Library with 25,000 vols
—**Museum fur Volkskunde, Museum of German Ethnology**, Im Winkel 6/8, Berlin, D-14195. Tel 83901-01. *Dir* Dr Erika Karasek
Library with 25,000 vols
Collections: Folklore objects from German speaking population in Europe
—**Agyptisches Museum und Papyrussammlung, Egyptian Museum**, Schlosstrasse 70, 14059. Tel 32091-261. *Dir* Dr Dietrich Wildung
Library with 15,000 vols
Collections: Art & cultural history of ancient egypt
—**Antikensammlung, Greek & Roman Antiquities**, Bodestrasse 1-3, Berlin, D-10178. Tel 20355-401-504. *Dir* Prof Dr Wolf-Dieter Heilmeyer
Collections: Greek & Roman antiquities
—**Gemaldegalerie, Picture Gallery**, Arnimallee 23-27, 1000. Tel 8301-1. *Prof Dr* Henning Bock
—**Kunstgewerbemuseum, Museum of Arts & Crafts**, Tiergartenstrasse 6, 1000. Tel 266-29-02. *Dir* Dr Barbara Mundt
Collections: Arts & Crafts
—**Museum fur Vor- und Fruhgeschichte, Museum of Pre- & Proto-History**, Schloss Charlottenburg, 1000. Tel 32091-233. *Dir* Dr Wilfried Menghin
—**Nationalgalerie, National Gallery**, Potsdamerstrasse 50, 1000. Tel 266-26-62. *Dir* Peter-Klaus Schuster
Collections: 19th & 20th centuries works

BIELEFELD

M **KUNSTHALLE BIELEFELD**, Artur-Ladebeck-Strasse 5, 33602. Tel (0521) 51-24-80. *Dir* Dr Ulrich Weisner
Collections: 20th century art

BONN

M **KUNSTMUSEUM BONN**, Art Museum of Bonn, Friedrich-Ebert-Allee 2, 53113. Tel (0228) 776260. *Dir* Prof Dr Dieter Ronte
Collections: Art of the 20th century, especially August Macke & the Rhenish expressionists; German Art since 1945; contemporary international graphic arts

M **LANDSCHAFTS VERBAND RHEINLAND**, Rheinisches Landesmuseum Bonn, Colmantstrasse 14-16, 53115. Tel 72941. *Dir* Dr Hartwic Ludtke
Library with 105,000 vols
Collections: Rhenish sculpture, painting & applied arts from the Middle Ages up to the present; finds from the Stone Age, Roman times till the Middle Ages

BREMEN

M **KUNSTHALLE BREMEN**, Bremen Art Gallery, Am Wall 207, 28195. Tel 0421-32-90-80. *Dir* Dr Wulf Herzogenrath
Collections: Japanese drawings and prints; European paintings, Middle Ages to modern, especially French and German Art of the 19th century; 17th - 20th century sculpture; illustrated books

BRUNSWICK

M **HERZOG ANTON ULRICH-MUSEUM,** Museumstrasse 1, 38100. Tel 0531-484-2400. *Dir* Dr J Luckhardt
Library with 40,000 vols
Collections: European Paintings - Renaissance & Baroque; European Renaissance & Baroque decorative art, including bronzes, clocks, French 16th century enamels, furniture, glass, ivory & wood carvings, laces; Medieval art; prints & drawings from the 15th century to present

COLOGNE

M **MUSEEN DER STADT KOLN,** Cologne City Museums, Saint Apernstrasse 17-21, 5000. Tel 221-2301. *Dir* Prof Dr Hiltrud Kier
M **Wallraf-Richartz-Museum,** Bischofsgartenstrasse 1, 5000. Tel 221-23-72. *Dir* Dr Rainer Budde
Collections: Painting from 13th century to 1900; 19th century sculpture
M **Romisch-Germanisches Museum,** Roncalliplatz 4, 5000. Tel 221-44-38. *Dir* Prof Dr Hansgerd Hellenkemper
Collections: Early and pre-historic discoveries; gold ornaments; glass and industrial arts
L **Romisch-Germanisches Museum Bibliothek,** Roncalliplatz 4
Library Holdings: Vols 11,000
M **Rautenstrauch-Joest-Museum,** Ubierring 45, 50678. Tel 336940. *Dir* Dr Gisela Volger
Collections: Ethnological museum; folk culture
M **Kolnisches Stadtmuseum,** Zeughausstrasse 1-3, 5000. Tel 221-23-52. *Dir* Dr Werner Schafke
Collections: Graphic Arts of Cologne and the Rhineland; photograph collection of the Rhineland; industrial arts of Cologne; religious and rural art and culture
M **Museum fur Ostasiatische Kunst,** Universitatstrasse 100
Library with 18,000 vols
Collections: Art of China, Korea and Japan
M **Schnutgen-Museum,** Cacilienstrasse 29, 5000. Tel 0221-221-23-10. *Dir* Dr Hiltrud Westermann-Angerhausen
Collections: Art of the early Middle Ages to Baroque
M **Josef-Haubrich-Kunsthalle,** Josef-Haubrich-Hof, 5000. Tel 221-23-35.
M **Museum Ludwig,** Bischofsgartenstrass 1, 5000. Tel 221-2370. *Dir* Marc Scheps
Collections: Painting & sculpture from 1900 to present

DRESDEN

M **STAATLICHE KUNSTSAMMLUNGEN DRESDEN,** Postfach 450, Georg-Treu-Platz 1, Albertinum, 8012. Tel 4953056. *Gen Dir* Dr Werner Schmidt
Collections: Consists of 12 galleries & collections
M **Gemaldegalerie Alte Meister,** Sophienstrasse, 8010. *Dir* Dr Harald Marx
M **Gemaldegalerie Neue Meister,** Georg-Treu-Platz 1, Albertinum, 8010. Tel 4953056. *Dir* Dr Horst Zimmerman
M **Skulpturensammlung,** Georg-Treu-Platz 1, Albertinum, 8010. Tel 4953056. *Dir* Dr Heiner Protzmann
M **Historisches Museum,** Sophienstrasse, 8010. *Dir* Dr Dieter Schaal

DUSSELDORF

L **KUNSTAKADEMIE DUSSELDORF, HOCHSCHULE FUR BILDENDE KUNSTE - BIBLIOTHEK,** State Academy of Art - Library, Eiskellerstrasse 1, 40213. Tel (0211) 1396-0. *Librn* Helmut Kleinenbroich
Library with 90,000 vols

M **KUNSTMUSEUM DUSSELDORF,** Ehrenhof 5, 40479. Tel (0211) 899-2460. *Dir* Dr Hans Albert Peters
Collections: Collections of European & applied art from middle ages to 1800, prints & drawings, & contemporary art at 5 museum locations

M **STADTISCHE KUNSTHALLE DUSSELDORF,** Grabbeplatz 4, Postfach 1120, 40213. Tel (0211) 899-6241. *Dir* Jurgen Harten
Exhibitions: Contemporary art exhibitions

FRANKFURT

M **LIEBIEGHAUS, MUSEUM ALTER PLASTIK,** Museum of Sculpture, Schaumainkai 71, 6000. Tel 2123-38617. *Dir* Dr Herbert Beck
Collections: Sculpture of Egypt, Greece, Rome Medieval period, East Asia, Rococo style & Baroque period

M **MUSEUM FUR KUNSTHANDWERK,** Museum of Arts and Crafts, Schaumainkai 17, 60594. Tel (069) 2123-40-37. *Dir* Dr Arnulf Herbst
Collections: European applied art, from Gothic to art nouveau; Far Eastern & Islamic works of art

M **STADELSCHES KUNSTINSTITUT UND STADTISCHE GALERIE,** Durerstrasse 2, 60596. Tel (069) 605098-0. *Dir* Dr Herbert Beck
Library with 50,000 vols
Collections: Paintings, sculptures, prints, drawings

HAMBURG

M **HAMBURGER KUNSTHALLE,** Glockengiesserwall, 20095. Tel (040) 24862612. *Dir* Dr Uwe M Schneede
Library with 110,000 vols
Collections: Drawings, engravings & masterworks of painting from 14th century to present; sculpture from 19th and 20th centuries

M **MUSEUM FUR KUNST UND GEWERBE HAMBURG,** Steintorplatz 1, 2000. Tel (040) 2486-2732. *Dir* Dr Wilhelm Hornbostel
Collections: European art & sculpture from Middle Ages to present; Near & Far East art; European popular art

HANOVER

M **KESTNER-MUSEUM,** Trammplatz 3, 30159. Tel (0511) 1682120. *Dir* Dr Ulrich Gehrig; *Cur* Dr Helga Hilschenz-Mlynek
Collections: Ancient, medieval & modern coins & medals; Egyptian, Greek, Etruscan & Roman art objects & medieval art; handicrafts, illuminated manuscripts & incunabula of the 15th - 20th centuries

KARLSRUHE

M **BADISCHES LANDESMUSEUM,** Schlossplatz 1, 76131. Tel 926-6514. *Dir* Prof Dr Harald Siebenmorgen
Maintains library with 58,000 vols
Collections: Antiquities of Egypt, Greece & Rome; art from middle ages to present; medieval, Renaissance & baroque sculpture; coins, weapons & folklore

M **STAATLICHE KUNSTHALLE,** State Art Gallery, Hans-Thoma-Strasse 2-6, 76133. Tel 926-33-55. *Dir* Dr Horst Vey
Library with 110,000 vols
Collections: 15th - 20th century German painting & graphics; 16th - 20th century Dutch, Flemish & French paintings & graphics; 50,000 prints & drawings, sculptures, 19th - 20th century

KASSEL

M **STAATLICHE KASSEL MUSEEN,** State Museums of Kassel, Schloss Wilhelmshohe, 34131. Tel (0561) 9377-7. *Dir* Open
Library with 60,000 vols
Collections: Department of classical antiquities gallery of 15th - 18th century old master paintings, collection of drawings & engravings

MUNICH

M **BAYERISCHES NATIONALMUSEUM,** Bavarian National Museum, Prinzregentenstrasse 3, 80538. Tel (089) 21-12-41. *Gen Dir* Dr Reinhold Baumstark
Library with 70,000 vols
Collections: European fine arts: decorative arts, paintings, folk art, sculpture

A **BAYERISCHE STAATSGEMALDESAMMLUNGEN,** Bavarian State Art Galleries, Barerstrasse 29, 8000. Tel (089) 238050. *Dir* Bruno Heimberg
Consists of 5 galleries
Collections: Flemish, Spanish, Italian, German & other European paintings & sculpture; 20th century sculpture & art

M **STAATLICHE GRAPHISCHE SAMMLUNG,** National Graphic Collection, Meiserstrasse 10, D-80333. Tel (089) 5591490. *Dir* Dr Tilman Falk
Library with 38,000 vols
Collections: French, 15th to 20th century German, Italian & Dutch prints & drawings

M **STAATLICHE MUNZSAMMLUNG,** State Coin Collection, Residenzstrasse 1, 8000. Tel (089) 227221. *Dir* Dr Bernhard Overbeck
Library with 14,000 vols
Collections: Coins from different countries & centuries; medals; precious stones from antiquity, Middle Ages & Renaissance

M **STAATLICHE SAMMLUNG AEGYPTISCHER KUNST,** State Collection of Egyptian Art, Hofgartenstrasse 1, Meiserstrasse 10, 80333. Tel (089) 5591486. *Dir* Dr Sylvia Schoske

M **STADTISCHE GALERIE IM LENBACHHAUS,** Luisenstrasse 33, 8000. Tel (089) 521041 233 32000. *Dir* Dr Helmut Friedel
Collections: Art Nouveau; The Blue Rider and Kandinsky and Klee; paintings by Munich artists

NUREMBERG

M **GERMANISCHES NATIONAL MUSEUM,** Kartausergasse 1, Postf 11 95 80, D 90402. Tel (0911) 1331-0. *Chief Dir* Dr G Ulrich Grossmann
Library with 500,000 vols
Collections: Ancient historical objects, archives, books, folk art, furniture, manuscripts, musical instruments, paintings, sculpture, textiles, toys, weapons

RECKLINGHAUSEN

M **MUSEEN DER STADT RECKLINGHAUSEN,** Recklinghausen City Museums, Grosse Perdekamp Str 25-27, 45657. Tel (02361) 501931. *Dir* Dr Ferdinand Ullrich; *Dir* Dr Hans-Jurgen Schwalm
Collections: Paintings, sculpture, drawings & prints by contemporary artists

STUTTGART

M **STAATSGALERIE STUTTGART,** Konrad-Adenauer-Strasse 30-32, 70182. Tel (0711) 212-4050. *Dir* Christian Von Holst
Collections: European art, 14th - 20th centuries; international art of the 20th century; graphic art

WITTEN

M **MARKISCHES MUSEUM DER STADT WITTEN,** Husemannstrasse 12, 5810. Tel (02302) 1560/1569. *Dir* Dr Wolfgang Zemter
Collections: 20th century German paintings, drawings & graphics

GHANA

ACCRA

M **GHANA NATIONAL MUSEUM,** Barnes Rd, PO Box 3343. Tel 221633. *Actg Dir* I N Debrah
Collections: Art, archeological and ethnological collections for Ghana and West Africa

GREECE

ATHENS

M **BENAKI MUSEUM,** Odos Koumbari 1, 10674. Tel 361-16-17. *Dir* Dr Angelos Delivorrias
Library, historical archives and photographic archives are maintained
Collections: Ancient Greek art, chiefly jewelry; Byzantine and post-Byzantine art, icons and crafts; collections of Islamic art and Chinese porcelain; Greek popular art and historical relics; textiles from Far East and Western Europe

M **BYZANTINE MUSEUM,** 22 Vasilissis Sophias Ave, 10675. Tel 7211027, 7232178. *Dir* Myrtali Acheimastou-Potamianou
Library & photo archives are maintained
Collections: Byzantine & Post-Byzantine icons, ceramics, marbles, metalwork; Christian & Byzantine sculpture & pottery; liturgical items; Greek manuscripts

M **NATIONAL ARCHAEOLOGICAL MUSEUM,** Odos Patisson 44, 10682. Tel 8217724. *Dir* Olga Tzahou-Alexandri
Collections: Original Greek sculptures; Roman period sculptures; Bronze Age relics; Mycenaean treasures; Greek vases, terracottas; jewels; Egyptian antiquities

M **NATIONAL ART GALLERY & ALEXANDER SOUTZOS MUSEUM,** 50 Vassileos Konstantinou Ave, 11610. Tel 7211010. *Dir* Marina Lambraki-Plaka
Collections: Engravings; 14th - 20th century European painting; 17th - 20th century Greek engravings, paintings & sculpture; impressionist, post-impressionist & contemporary drawings

ATTICA

M **VORRES MUSEUM OF GREEK ART,** Paiania. Tel 6642520. *Dir* Ian Vorres
Collections: Contemporary Greek art

CORINTH

M **ARCHAEOLOGICAL MUSEUM OF CORINTH,** c/o Am Sch of Classical Studies, 54 Souideas, Athens. Tel 0741 31207. *Dir* Phani Pachiyanni

DELPHI

M **THE DELPHI MUSEUM,** I Ephorate of Prehistoric & Classical Antiquities, 33054. Tel (0265) 82 313. *Dir* Evangelos Pentazos; *Archaeologist* Rozina Kolonia
Library with 2392 vols

HERAKLION

M **ARCHAEOLOGICAL MUSEUM,** One Xanthoudidou St, 71202. Tel 081 226 092. *Dir* C H Kritzas
Collections: Development of Cretan & Minoan art

OLYMPIA

M **ARCHAEOLOGICAL MUSEUM OF OLYMPIA,** Tel 0624 22-529. *Dir* Xeni Arapoyanni
Collections: Greek & archaic bronzes

RHODES

M **ARCHAEOLOGICAL MUSEUM,** Tel 02 41 75674. *Dir* John Papachristodoulou
Library with 22,000 vols
Collections: Mycenean through to late Roman times

THESSALONIKI

M **ARCHAEOLOGICAL MUSEUM OF THESSALONIKI,** YMCA Sq, 54621. Tel 830538. *Dir* J Vokotopoulou
Collections: Macedonian archaeology, mainly from Thessaloniki, Chalkidiki and Kilkis

GUATEMALA

GUATEMALA CITY

M **MUSEO NACIONAL DE ARQUEOLOGIA Y ETNOLOGIA,** Archaeological & Ethnographical Museum, Edif No 5, La Aurora, Zona 13. *Dir* Licda Dora Guerra de Gonzalez
Collections: Mayan art

M **MUSEO NACIONAL DE ARTE MODERNO,** Edificio No 6, Finca La Aurora, Zona 13. Tel 310-403. *Dir* J Oscar Barrientos
Collections: Paintings, sculpture, engravings, drawings

HAITI

PORT AU PRINCE

M **CENTRE D'ART,** 58 rue Roy. Tel 2-2018. *Dir* Francine Murat
Collections: Haitian art

HONDURAS

COMAYAGUA

M **MUSEO ARQUEOLOGIA DE COMAYAGUA,** Ciudad de Comayagua. Tel 72-03-86. *Dir* Salvador Turcios
Collections: Archaeology dating back to 1000 BC; colonial collections

HONG KONG

KOWLOON

M **HONG KONG MUSEUM OF ART,** 10 Salisbury Rd, Tsim Sha Tsui. Tel 734-2167. *Cur* Gerard C C Tsang
Collections: Chinese antiquities; Chinese paintings & calligraphy with a specialization of Cantonese artists; historical collection of paintings, prints & drawings of Hong Kong, Macau & China; local & contemporary art

HUNGARY

BUDAPEST

M **MAGYAR NEMZETI GALERIA,** Hungarian National Gallery, Budavari Palota PF 31, 1250. Tel 1757-533. *Dir* Dr Lorand Bereczky
Collections: Ancient & modern Hungarian paintings & sculpture; medal cabinet; panel paintings

M **MUCSARNOK,** Palace of Exhibitions, PO Box 35, 1406. Tel 3437402. *Dir* Iren Pilaszanovich
Library with 15,000 vols
Collections: Hungarian & foreign art

M **SZEPMUVESZETI MUZEUM,** Museum of Fine Arts, Dozsa Gyorgy ut 41, 1146. Tel 1429-759. *Dir* Dr Miklos Mojzer
Library with 100,000 vols
Collections: Egyptian, Greek & Roman antiquities; paintings & sculpture †Old Masters, †Egyptian, †19th century art, †20th century art, sculpture collection

ESZTERGOM

M **KERESZTENY MUZEUM,** Christian Museum, Berenyi ZS U2, PF 25, 2501. Tel (36-33) 13-880. *Pres* Pal Csefalvay
Publications: Hungarian, Austrian, Dutch, French, German and Italian medieval panels, pictures, gold & silver artwork, miniatures, porcelain, statues, and tapestries

KECSKEMET

M **MAGYAR NAIV MUVESZEK MUZEUMA,** Museum of Hungarian Native Art, Gaspar A U 11, 6000. Tel 24767. *Dir* Dr Pal Banszky
Collections: Works of Hungarian primitive painters and sculptors

PECS

M **JANUS PANNONIUS MUZEUM,** Papnovelde U 5, 7601. Tel (72) 10-172. *Dir* Jeno Ujvari
Library with 20,000 vols
Collections: Modern Hungarian art; archaeology, ethnology, local history

SOPRON

M **SOPRONI MUZEUM,** Foter 8, 9400. Tel 99 311-327. *Dir* Dr Attila Kornyei
Library with 20,000 vols
Collections: Folk & local Baroque art

SZENTENDRE

M **FERENCZY MUZEUM,** Foter 6, PF 49, 2001. Tel (26) 10-244. *Dir* Sandor Soos
Library with 22,000 vols
Collections: Paintings, sculptures, drawings; archaeological, ethnographic & local history collections; Gobelin tapestries

ZALAEGERSZEG

M **GOCSEJI MUZEUM,** Batthyanyi U2, PO Box 176, 8900. Tel 9211-455. *Dir* Dr Laszlo Vandor
Library with 12,000 vols
Collections: Regional paintings & sculptures

ICELAND

REYKJAVIK

M **LISTASAFN EINARS JONSSONAR,** National Einar Jonsson Art Gallery, PO Box 1051. Tel 91-13797. *Dir* Dr Hrafnil Dur Schram
Collections: Sculpture and paintings by Einar Jonsson

M **THJODMINJASAFN,** National Museum Library, Sudurgata 41, PO Box 1489, 121. Tel 1-28888. *Dir* Thor Magnusson; *Head Librn* Groa Finnsdottir
Library with 9000 vols
Collections: Archaeological & ethnological artifacts, Icelandic antiquities, portraits, folk art

INDIA

BARODA

M **BARODA MUSEUM AND PICTURE GALLERY,** Sayaji Park, Gujarat 390005. Tel 64605. *Dir* S K Bhowmik
Library with 19,000 vols
Collections: Indian archeology & art, numismatic collections; Asiatic & Egyptian Collections; Greek, Roman, European civilizations & art; European paintings

BOMBAY

M **HERAS INSTITUTE OF INDIAN HISTORY AND CULTURE,** Heras institute Museum, St Xavier's College, 5, Mahapalika Marg, 400001. Tel 262-0662. *Dir* Desmond D'Monte
Library with 30,000 vols
Collections: Indian stone sculptures, woodwork, paintings; old rare maps, books, metal artifacts, coins, ivories, manuscripts, weapons, seals & amulets

M **PRINCE OF WALES MUSEUM OF WESTERN INDIA,** 159-61 Mahatma Gandhi Rd, Fort, 400023. Tel 244484. *Dir* S V Gorakshkar
Library with 11,000 vols
Collections: Paintings; archaeology; natural history

CALCUTTA

M **INDIAN MUSEUM,** 27 Jawaharlal Nehru Rd, 700016. Tel 29-5699. *Dir* R C Sharma
Collections: Bronzes and bronze figures, ceramic, coins, copper and stone implements of prehistoric and proto-historic origin; geology, botany and zoology collections

JUNAGADH

M **JUNAGADH MUSEUM,** Sakkar Bag, 362001. Tel 745. *Dir* P V Dholakia
Collections: Archaeology, miniature paintings, manuscripts, sculptures, decorative & applied arts

MADRAS

M **GOVERNMENT MUSEUM & NATIONAL ART GALLERY,** Pantheon Rd, Egmore, 600008. Tel 89638. *Dir* M Raman
Collections: Ancient & modern Indian art; Buddhist sculptures; bronzes; archaeology; natural sciences collection

NEW DELHI

M **CRAFTS MUSEUM,** All India Handicrafts Board, Bhairon Rd, Pragati Maidan, 110001. Tel 3317641. *Dir* Dr Jyotindra Jain
Collections: Indian traditional crafts, folk & tribal arts; folk crafts

M **NATIONAL GALLERY OF MODERN ART,** Jaipur House India Gate, Sher Shah Rd, 110003. Tel 382835. *Dir* Dr Anis Farooqi
Collections: Indian contemporary paintings, sculptures, graphics, drawings, architecture, industrial design, prints and minor arts

M **NATIONAL MUSEUM OF INDIA,** Janpath, 110011. Tel 3018159. *Dir-Gen* Dr R C Sharma
Library with 30,000 vols
Collections: Arabic, Indian, Persian, Sanskrit language manuscripts; Central Asian antiquities and murals; decorative arts

M **RABINDRA BHAVAN ART GALLERY,** Lalit Kala Akademi (National Academy of Art), 35 Ferozeshah Rd. Tel 38-72-41. *Chmn* Anand Dev
Collections: Permanent collection of graphics, paintings and sculpture

IRAN

ISFAHAN

M **ARMENIAN ALL SAVIOUR'S CATHEDRAL MUSEUM,** Julfa, PO Box 81735-115. Tel 243471. *Dir* Levon Minassian
Collections: 450 paintings, miniatures & tomb portraits; 700 ancient books

TEHERAN

M **TEHERAN MUSEUM OF MODERN ART,** Karegar Ave, Laleh Park, PO Box 41-3669. *Dir* Kamran Diba
Museum maintains library
Collections: Modern Western art works

IRAQ

BAGHDAD

M **DIRECTORATE - GENERAL OF ANTIQUITIES AND HERITAGE,** Risafa-Al-Qushla. *Dir Gen* Dr Muayad Said Basim Damerji
M **Babylon Museum**
Collections: Models, pictures & paintings of the remains at Babylon

M **IRAQI MUSEUM,** Salhiya Quarter. Tel 36121-5. *Dir* Sabah Jasim Alshakri
Collections: Antiquities from the Stone Age to the 17th century, including Islamic objects

IRELAND

DUBLIN

M **HUGH LANE MUNICIPAL GALLERY OF MODERN ART,** Charlemont House, Parnell Square N, 1. Tel 74-19-03. *Dir* Barbara Dawson
Collections: Works of Irish, English & European artists; sculptures; Sir Hugh Lane collection

M **NATIONAL GALLERY OF IRELAND,** Merrion Square W, 2. Tel (01) 6615133. *Dir* Raymond Keaveney
Library with 30,000 vols
Collections: British, Dutch, Flemish, French, German, Italian, Irish, Russian, & Spanish masters since 1250; drawings, prints, oil paintings, sculptures, watercolors

M **NATIONAL MUSEUM OF IRELAND,** Kildare St, 2. Tel 6618811. *Dir* Patrick F Wallace
Collections: Art and Industrial Division; Irish Antiquities Division; Irish Folklife Division; Natural History Division

ISRAEL

HAIFA

M **HAIFA MUSEUM OF MODERN ART,** 26 Shabbetai Levi St. Tel (04) 523255. *Cur* Meir Ahronson
Library with 10,000 vols
Collections: Israeli paintings, sculpture, drawings & prints; modern American, French, German & English paintings; art posters

M **MUSEUM OF ANCIENT ART,** 26 Shabbetai Levi St. Tel (972-4) 523255. *Cur* Zemer Avshalom
Collections: Ancient Haifa; ancient coins from Israel; antiquities from the excavations of Shikmona from the Bronze Age to Byzantine period; Biblical, Cypriot and Greek pottery and sculpture; Near Eastern figurines

M **TIKOTIN MUSEUM OF JAPANESE ART,** 89 Hanassi Ave, 34-642. Tel (04) 383554. *Dir* Eli Lancman
Collections: Ceramics, folk art, drawings, metalwork, netsuke, prints, paintings

JERUSALEM

M **ARCHAEOLOGICAL ROCKEFELLER MUSEUM,** Rockefeller Bldg, Suleiman, PO Box 586, 91004. Tel (2) 282251. *Cur* Ornit Ilan
Collections: Archaeology of Israel; Islamic period

M **BEIT HA'OMAMIM,** Jerusalem Artists' House, 12 Shmuel Hanagid St. Tel (972-2) 252-636.
Collections: Artwork of Jerusalem citizens

M **ISRAEL MUSEUM,** PO Box 71117, 91710. Tel (02) 708811. *Dir* Dr Martin Weyl
Collections: Consists of 6 collections
M **Bezalel National Art Museum,** *Chief Cur* Yigal Zalmona
Lending library of reproductions & slides
Collections: Jewish ceremonial art, ethnological objects, paintings, sculptures, drawings & prints
M **Billy Rose Art Garden,** *Cur* Dr Martin Weyl
Collections: Modern European, American & Israeli sculpture & Reuven Lipchitz collection of Jacques Lipchitz's bronze sketches
M **Bronfman Biblical and Archaeological Museum,** *Chief Cur* Ya'akov Meshorer
Collections: Collection of archaeology of Israel from earliest times to Islamic & Crusader periods; material found in excavations since 1948
L **Shrine of the Book,** *Cur* Magen Broshi
D Samuel & Jeanne H Gottesman Center for Biblical MSS
Collections: Houses the Dead Sea Scrolls (discovered in Qumran) & manuscripts from adjacent sites on western shore of the Dead Sea, Masada & Nahal Hever
L **Library,** *Librn* Elisheva Rechtman
Library Holdings: Vols 65,000; Other — Exhibition catalogs

POST KEFAR-MENAHEM

M **SHEPHELA MUSEUM,** Kibbutz Kefar-Menahem, 79875. Tel (9728) 501827. *Dir* M Israel
Collections: Collections of fine arts, children's art & antiquities

TEL AVIV

M **ERETZ-ISRAEL,** 2 Chaim Levanon St, PO Box 17068, 61 170. Tel (972-3) 415244. *General Mgr* Shild Sasson
Collections: Consists of 15 museums & collections; ancient glass; historical documents of Tel Aviv-Yafo; Jewish ritual & secular art objects; ceramics, coins, prehistoric finds, scientific & technical apparatus, traditional work tools & methods
M **Ceramics Museum,** Tel 03-41-52-44. *Cur* Mrs Yael Olenik
Collections: Pottery throughout history
M **Museum of Antiquities of Tel-Aviv-Jaffa,** 10 Mifratz Shlomo St, Jaffa, 680 38. *Dir* Dr Ivan Ordentlich
Collections: Archaeological findings from Tel Aviv-Yafo area, covering Neolithic to Byzantine periods

M **Museum of Ethnography and Folklore,** *Dir* D Davidowitz
Collections: Jewish popular art & costumes

M **TEL AVIV MUSEUM OF ART,** 27 Shaul Hamelech Blvd, POB 33288, 61332. Tel (972-3) 6957361. *Dir* Ronnie Dissentshik
Library with 50,000 vols
Collections: Works from 17th century to present; Israeli art

ITALY

BARI

M **PINACOTECA PROVINCIALE,** Via Spalato 19, 70121. Tel (080) 392-421. *Dir* Dr Clara Gelao
Collections: Apulian, Venetian and Neapolitan paintings and sculpture from 11th - 19th century

BERGAMO

M **GALLERIA DELL' ACCADEMIA CARRARA,** Piazza Giacomo Carrara 82/A, 24100. Tel (035) 399640. *Dir* Dr F Rossi
Collections: Paintings by: Bellini, Raffaello, Pisanello, Mantegna, Botticelli, Beato Angelico, Previtali, Tiepolo, Durer, Brueghel, Van Dyck

BOLOGNA

M **PINACOTECA NAZIONALE,** Via Belle Arti 56, 40100. Tel (051) 243222. *Dir* Prof Andrea Emiliani
Collections: 14th - 18th centuries Bolognese paintings; German & Italian engravings

FLORENCE

M **GALLERIA D'ARTE MODERNA DI PALAZZO PITTI,** Piazza Pitti 1, 50125. Tel 287096. *Dir* Ettore Spalletti
Collections: Paintings and sculptures of the 19th and 20th centuries

M **GALLERIA DEGLI UFFIZI,** Uffizi Gallery, Piazzale degli Uffizi, 50122. Tel (055) 2388651. *Dir* Annamaria Petrioli Tofani
Collections: Florentine Renaissance painting

M **GALLERIA DELL' ACCADEMIA,** Via Ricasoli 60, 50122. Tel (055) 2388609. *Dir* Franca Falletti
Collections: Michelangelo's statues in Florence & works of art of 13th - 19th centuries masters, mostly Tuscan

M **GALLERIA PALATINA,** Palazzo Pitti, Piazza Pitti, 50125. Tel (055) 2388611. *Dir* Dr Marco Chiarini
Collections: Paintings from 16th and 17th centuries

M **MUSEO DEGLI ARGENTI,** Palazzo Pitti, 50100. Tel 2125-57. *Dir* Dr Kirsten Piacenti
Collections: Summer state apartments of the Medici Grand Dukes; gold, silver, enamel, objets d'art, hardstones, ivory, amber, cameos and jewels, principally from the 15th to the 18th centuries; period costumes exhibited in Galleria del Costume on premises

M **MUSEO DELLA CASA BUONARROTI,** Via Ghibellina 70, 50100. Tel (055) 241-752. *Dir* Pina Ragionieri
Collections: Works by Michelangelo & others; items from the Buonarroti family collections

M **MUSEO DI SAN MARCO O DELL' ANGELICO,** Piazza San Marco, 50100. Tel (055) 210741. *Dir* Magnolia Scudieri
Collections: Fra Angelico frescoes, paintings & panels

GENOA

M **SERVIZIO BENI CULTURALI,** Via Garibaldi 18, 16124. Tel (010) 282641. *Dir* Laura Tagliaferro
M **Museo di Palazzo Rosso,** Via Garibaldi 18, 16124. Tel (010) 282641. *Cur* Piero Boccardo
Library with 35,000 vols
Collections: Ligurian ceramics
M **Galleria di Arte Moderna,** Villa Serra, Via Capolungo 3, Nervi, 16167. Tel (010) 3726025. *Cur* Maria Flora Giubilei
Collections: 19th & 20th centuries paintings
M **Museo Giannettino Luxoro,** Via Aurelia 29, Nervi, 16167. Tel (010) 322673.
Collections: Flemish & Genoese 17th & 18th centuries paintings, ceramics
M **Museo d'Arte Orientale Edoardo Chiossone,** Viletta di Negro, Piazzale Mazzini, 16122. Tel (010) 542285. *Cur* Donatella Failla
Collections: Chinese & Japanese works of art
M **Raccolte Frugone in Villa Grimaldi,** Villa Grimaldi, Via Capolungo 9, Nervi, 16167. Tel (010) 322 396. *Cur* Maria Flora Giubilei
Collections: 19th & 20th centuries Italian artists

LUCCA

M **MUSEO DI VILLA GUINIGI,** Villa Guinigi, Via della Quarquonia, 55100. Tel (0583) 46033. *Dir* Maria Teresa Filieri
Collections: Roman and late Roman sculptures and mosaics; Romanesque, Gothic, Renaissance and Neoclassical sculpture; paintings from 12th to 18th century

M **MUSEO E PINACOTECA NAZIONALE DI PALAZZO MANSI,** National Museum and Picture Gallery of the Palazzo Mansi, Via Galli Tassi 43, 55100. Tel (0583) 55570. *Dir* Dr Maria Teresa Filieri
Collections: Works of Tuscan, Venetian, French & Flemish Schools; paintings by such masters as Titian & Tintoretto

MANTUA

M **GALLERIA E MUSEO DI PALAZZO DUCALE,** Gallery and Museum of the Palazzo Ducale, Piazza Sordello 39, 46100. Tel (0376) 320586. *Dir* Dr Aldo Cicinelli
Collections: Classical Antiquities & Sculpture; picture gallery

MILAN

M **DIREZIONE CIVICHE RACCOLTE D'ARTE,** Castello Sforzesco, 20121. Tel 021-6236-3943. *Dir* Dr Mercedes Garberi
Governs several museums & collections
M **Civiche Raccolte di Arte Applicata,** Castello Sforzesco, 20121. Tel 869-30-71. *Dir* Dr Claudio Salsi
Collections: Armor, bronzes, ceramics, coins, ironworks, ivories, porcelains, sculpture, textiles
M **Raccolte delle Stampe Achille Bertarelli,** Castello Sforzesco, 20121. Tel 869-30-71. *Dir* Dr Claudio Salsi
M **Civiche Raccolte Archeologiche e Numismatiche,** Via B Luini 2, 20123. Tel 805-3972. *Dir* Dr Ermanno Arslan; *Cur* Dr Rina La Guardia
Collections: Ancient Egyptian, antique & modern coins; Etruscan, Greek & Roman Collections
M **Museo d'Arte Antica,** Castello Sforzesco, 20121. *Dir* Dr Teresa Fiorio
Maintains library
Collections: Paintings, including works by Bellini, Guardi, Lippi, Lotto, Mantegna, Tiepolo, Tintoretto & others; sculpture from early Middle Ages to 17th century, including masterpieces like Michelangelo's Pieta-Rondanini; furniture; silver, bronzes, tapestries
M **Galleria d'Arte Moderna,** Villa Reale, Via Palestro 16, 20121. Tel 76-00-28-19. *Dir* Dr Teresa Fiorio
Collections: Painting & sculpture from Neo-Classical period to present day; includes the Grassi Collection & Museo Marino Marini (approx 200 sculptures, portraits, paintings, drawings & etchings by Marini)

M **MUSEO POLDI PEZZOLI,** Via A Manzoni 12, 20121. Tel (02) 796-334. *Dir* Dr Alessandra Mottola Molfino
Collections: Paintings from 14th - 18th centuries; armor, tapestries, rugs, jewelry, porcelain, glass, textiles, furniture, clocks and watches

M **PINACOTECA AMBROSIANA,** Piazza Pio XI, 2, 20123. Tel (02) 86451436. *Dir* Dr Gianfranco Ravasi
Collections: Botticelli, Caravaggio, Luini, Raphael, Titian; drawings, miniatures, ceramics and enamels

M **PINACOTECA DI BRERA,** Via Brera 28, 20121. Tel 722631. *Dir* Pietro Petraroia
Collections: Pictures of all schools, especially Lombard and Venetian; paintings by Mantegna, Bellini, Crivelli, Lotto, Titian, Veronese, Tintoretto, Tiepolo, Foppa, Bergognone, Luini, Piero della Francesca, Bramante, Raphael, Caravaggio, Rembrandt, Van Dyck, Rubens; also Italian 20th century works

MODENA

M **GALLERIA, MUSEO E MEDAGLIERE ESTENSE,** Este Gallery, Museum and Coin Collection, Palazzo dei Musei, Piazza S Agostino 109, 41100. Tel 22-21-45. *Dir* Jadranka Bentini
Collections: Bronzes, coins, drawings, medals, minor arts, paintings, prints & sculptures, most from the Este family

NAPLES

M **MUSEO CIVICO GAETANO FILANGIERI,** Via Duomo 288, 80100. Tel (081) 203175. *Dir* Antonio Buccino Grimaldi
Collections: Paintings, furniture, archives, photographs

M **MUSEO E GALLERIE NAZIONALI DI CAPODIMONTE,** Palazzo di Capodimonte, 80100. Tel (081) 7410801. *Dir* Dr Nicola Spinosa
Library with 50,000 vols
Collections: Paintings from 13th to 18th centuries; paintings and sculptures of 19th century; arms and armor; medals and bronzes of the Renaissance; porcelain

M **MUSEO NAZIONALE DI SAN MARTINO,** National Museum of San Martino, Largo San Martino 5, 80129. Tel 5781769. *Dir* Dr T Fittipaldi
Collections: 16th - 18th century pictures & paintings; 13th - 19th century sculpture, majolicas & porcelains; section of modern prints, paintings & engravings; Neapolitan historical collection

PADUA

M **MUSEI CIVICI DI PADOVA,** Municipal Museum, Piazza Eremitani 8, 35121. Tel (049) 8750975. *Dir* Dr Gian Franco Martinoni
Collections: Archaeological Museum; Art Gallery - bronzes, ceramics, industrial arts, painting, sculpture; Bottacin Museum - Greco-Roman, Italian, Paduan, Venetian, Napoleonic coins and medals; Renaissance gallery

PARMA

M **GALLERIA NAZIONALE,** Palazzo Pilotta 15, 43100. Tel (0521) 233309. *Dir* Lucia Fornari Schianchi
Collections: Paintings from 13th to 19th centuries, including works by Correggio, Parmigianino, Cima, El Greco, Piazzetta, Tiepolo, Holbein, Van Dyck, Mor, Nattier & several painters of the school of Parma; modern art

PERUGIA

M **GALLERIA NAZIONALE DELL'UMBRIA,** Umbrian National Gallery, Corso Vannucci, Palazzo dei Priori, 06100. Tel (075) 20316. *Dir* Vittoria Garibaldi
Collections: Jewels; paintings from the Umbrian School from the 13th - 18th centuries; 13th, 14th and 15th century sculpture

PISA

M **MUSEO NAZIONALE DI SAN MATTEO,** Convento di San Matteo, Lungarno Mediceo, 56100. Tel (050) 23750. *Dir* Dr Mariagiulia Burresi
Collections: Sculptures by the Pisanos and their school; important collection of the Pisan school of the 13th and 14th centuries, and paintings of the 15th, 16th, and 17th centuries; ceramics; important collection of coins and medals

ROME

M **GALLERIA BORGHESE,** Borghese Gallery, Villa Borghese, 00197. Tel 06-85-85-77. *Dir* Claudio Strinati
Collections: Baroque & Classical; 580 paintings about XV-XVII-XVIII, 450 sculptures

M **GALLERIA DORIA PAMPHILJ,** Piazza del Collegio Romano 1/a, 00186. Tel (06) 679-43-65. *Dir* Dr Eduard A Safarik
Collections: Paintings by Caravaggio, Carracci, Correggio, Filippo Lippi, Lorrain, del Piombo, Titian, Velazquez

M **GALLERIA NAZIONALE DI ROMA,** National Gallery of Rome, Palazzo Barberini, Via Quattro Fontane 13, 00184. Tel (06) 4824184. *Dir* Dr Sivigliano Alloisi
Collections: Italian & European paintings from 12th - 18th century; Baroque architecture

M **ISTITUTO NAZIONALE PER LA GRAFICA,** National Institute for Graphic Arts, Farnesina, Via Della Lungara, 230, 00165. Tel (06) 699801. *Dir* Dr Serenita Papaldo
Collections: Italian & foreign prints & drawings from the 14th century to the present

M **MUSEI CAPITOLINI,** Piazza del Campidoglio 1471, 00186. Tel (06) 67109071. *Dir* M E Tittoni
Collections: Ancient sculptures, Art History

M **MUSEO NAZIONALE ROMANO,** National Museum of Rome, Piazza dei Cinquecento 79, 00185. Tel (06) 483617. *Dir* Prof Adriano La Regina
Collections: Archaeological collection; Roman bronzes and sculpture; numismatics

ROVIGO

M **PINACOTECA DELL'ACADEMIA DEI CONCORDI,** Piazza V Emanuele II 14, 45100. Tel (0425) 21654.
Collections: Venetian paintings from the 14th to the 18th century

SASSARI

M **MUSEO NAZIONALE G A SANNA,** G A Sanna National Museum, Via Roma 64, 07100. Tel 272-203. *Dir* Dr F Lo Schiavo
Collections: Archeological Collections; Picture Gallery with Medieval and Modern Art; Collection of Sardinian Ethnography

TURIN

M **ARMERIA REALE,** Royal Armory, Piazza Castello 191, 10122. Tel (011) 543889. *Dir* Paolo Venturoli
Collections: Archaeological Arms; Arms and Armours from 13th - 18th Century; Arms of the 19th and 20th Century; Oriental Arms; equestrian arms; engravings of Monaco de Baviera School

M **GALLERIA SABAUDA,** Via Accademia delle Scienze 6, 10123. Tel 54-74-40. *Dir* Paola Astrua
Library with 100 vols
Collections: Flemish Masters; French Masters; Italian Masters; Dutch & early Italian collections; Piedmontese Masters; furniture, sculpture, jewelry

M **MUSEI CIVICI DI TORINO,** Galleria d'Arte Moderna e Contemporanea, Via Magenta 31, 10128. Tel (011) 5629911. *Cur Ancient Art* Silvana Pettenati; *Cur Modern Art* Rosanna Maggio Serra
Library with 80,000 vols
Collections: Antique & modern art; coins, paintings; sculpture

VATICAN CITY

M **MONUMENTI, MUSEI E GALLERIE PONTIFICIE,** Vatican Museums and Galleries, 00120. Tel (06) 6983333.
Collections: Twelve museum sections with Byzantine, medieval & modern art; classical sculpture; liturgical art; minor arts
Publications: For all except Missionary Museum: Bollettino dei Monumenti, Musei, Gallerie Pontificie
M **Museo Pio Clementino,** *Cur* Paolo Liverani
Founded by Pope Clement XIV (1770-74) & enlarged by his successor, Pius VI; exhibits include the Apollo of Belvedere, the Apoxyomenos by Lysippus, the Laocoon Group, the Meleager of Skopas, the Apollo Sauroktonos by Praxiteles
M **Museo Sacro,** *Cur* Dr Giovanni Morello
Founded in 1756 by Pope Benedict XIV; administered by the Apostolic Vatican Library
Collections: Objects of liturgical art, historical relics & curios from the Lateran, objects of palaeolithic, medieval & Renaissance minor arts, paintings of the Roman era
M **Museo Profano,** *Cur* Dr Giovanni Morello
Founded in 1767 by Pope Clement XIII; administered by the Vatican Apostolic Library
Collections: Bronze sculpture & minor art of the classical era
M **Museo Chiaramonti e Braccio Nuovo,** *Cur* Paolo Liverani
Founded by Pope Pius VII at the beginning of the 19th century, to house the many new findings excavated in that period
Collections: Statues of the Nile, of Demosthenes & of the Augustus of Prima Porta
M **Museo Gregoriano Etrusco,** *Cur* Francesco Buranelli
Founded by Pope Gregory XVI in 1837
Collections: Objects from the Tomba Regolini Galassi of Cerveteri, the bronzes, terracottas & jewelry, & Greek vases from Etruscan tombs
M **Museo Gregoriano Egizio,** *Consultant* Prof Jean-Claude Grenier
Inaugurated by Pope Gregory XVI in 1839
Collections: Egyptian papyri, mummies, sarcophagi & statues, including statue of Queen Tuia (1300 BC)
M **Museo Gregoriano Profano,** *Cur* Paolo Liverani
Founded by Gregory XVI in 1844 & housed in the Lateran Palace, it was transferred to a new building in the Vatican & opened to the public in 1970
Collections: Roman sculptures from the Pontifical States; Portrait-statue of Sophocles, the Marsyas of the Myronian group of Athena & Marsyas, the Flavian reliefs from the Palace of the Apostolic Chancery
M **Museo Pio Cristiano,** *Cur* Giandomenico Spinola
Founded by Pius IX in 1854 & housed in the Lateran Palace; transferred to a new building in the Vatican & opened to the public in 1970
Collections: Sarcophagi; Latin & Greek inscriptions from Christian cemeteries & basilicas; the Good Shepherd
M **Museo Missionario Etnologico,** *Cur* Rev P J Penkowski
Founded by Pius XI in 1926 & housed in the Lateran Palace; transferred to a new building in the Vatican & opened to the public in 1973
Collections: Ethnographical collections from all over the world
Publications: Annali
M **Pinacoteca Vaticana,** *Cur* Dr Fabrizio Mancinelli
Inaugurated by Pope Pius XI in 1932
Collections: Paintings by Fra Angelico, Raphael, Leonardo da Vinci, Titian & Caravaggio, & the Raphael Tapestries
M **Collezione d'Arte Religiosa Moderna,** *Cur* Dr Mario Ferrazza
Founded in 1973 by Pope Paul VI; paintings, sculptures & drawings offered to the Pope by artists & donors
M **Vatican Palaces,** Tel 698-33-32. *Cur* Dr Arnold Nesserath
Chapel of Beato Angelico (or Niccolò V, 1448-1450); Sistine Chapel constructed for Sixtus IV (1471-1484); Borgia Apartment decorated by Pinturicchio; Chapel of Urbano VIII (1631-1635); rooms & loggias decorated by Raphael; Gallery of the Maps (1580-83)

VENICE

M **BIENNALE DI VENEZIA,** S Marco, Ca' Giustinian, 30124. Tel 5218711. *Pres* Gian Luigi Rondi
Collections: Visual arts, architecture, cinema, theatre, music. Owns historical archives of contemporary art

M **CIVICI MUSEI VENEZIANI D'ARTE E DI STORIA,** S Marco 52, 30100. Tel (041) 522625. *Dir* Prof Giandomenico Romanelli
M **Museo Correr,** Piazza San Marco, 30100
Collections: 13th - 16th centuries Venetian Art, Renaissance coins & ceramics
M **Ca'Rezzonico,** S Barnaba-Fondamenta Rezzonico, Canal Grande, 30100
Collections: 18th century Venetian art, sculpture, etc
M **Museo Vetario di Murano,** Fondamenta Giustiniani 8, Murano, 30121
Collections: Venetian glass from middle ages to the present
M **Palazzo Mocenigo** 30100
Collections: Palace of the Doges; collection of fabrics & costumes; library on history of fashion
M **Galleria Internazionale d'Arte Moderna di Ca'Pesaro,** Santa Croce, San Stae, Venice, 30100. Tel 041 721127.
Collections: 19th & 20th centuries works of art

M **GALLERIA DELL'ACCADEMIA,** Campo della Carita 1059A, 30100. Tel 22247. *Dir* Giovanna Scire Nepi
Collections: Venetian painting, 1310-1700

M **GALLERIA G FRANCHETTI,** Calle Ca d'Oro, Canal Grande, 30100. Tel 387-90. *Dir* Dr Adriana Augusti
Collections: Sculpture & paintings

M **GALLERIA QUERINI-STAMPALIA,** Palazzo Querini-Stampalia, Castello 4778, 30122. Tel (041) 5203433. *Dir* Dr Giorgio Busetto
Collections: 14th - 19th century Italian paintings

M **MUSEO ARCHEOLOGICO,** Piazza S Marco 17, 30122. Tel (041) 5225978. *Dir* Dr Giovanna Luisa Ravagnan
Collections: Greek & Roman sculpture, jewels, coins

M **MUSEO D'ARTE MODERNA,** Ca' Pesaro, Canal Grande, 30100. Tel (041) 24127. *Dir* Prof Giandomenico Romanelli
Collections: 19th & 20th century works of art

M **MUSEO D'ARTE ORIENTALE,** Ca' Pesaro, Canal Grande, 30100. Tel 27681. *Dir* Dr Adriana Ruggeri

M **PINACOTECA MANFREDINIANA,** Campo della Salute, 30123. Tel 041 525558. *Dir* Open
Collections: Paintings & sculptures of the Roman, Gothic, Renaissance & Neo-classical period

VERONA

M **MUSEI CIVICI D' ARTE DI VERONA,** Castelvecchio 2, 37121. Tel (045) 594734. *Dir* Sergio Marinelli
—**Galleria Comunale d' Arte Moderna e Contemporanea,** Vla Forti 1, 37121. Tel (045) 8001903. *Sr Dir Dotl* Grossi Cortenova
—**Museo Archeologico al Teatro Romano,** Regaste Redentore, 37129. Tel (045) 8000360. *S Dir Dssa* Margherita Bolla
—**Museo di Castelvecchio,** Corso Castelvecchio 3, 37121. Tel (045) 8005817. *S Dir Dssa* Paola Marini
—**Museo Lapidario Maffeiano,** Piazza Bra, 37121. Tel (045) 590087.
—**Museo degli Affreschi e Tomba di Giulietta,** Via del Pontiere, 37122. Tel (045) 8000361.

IVORY COAST

ABIDJAN

M **MUSEE DE LA COTE D'IVOIRE,** BP 1600. Tel 22-20-56. *Dir* Dr B Holas
Collections: Art, ethnographic, scientific & sociological exhibits

JAPAN

ATAMI

M **MOA BIJUTSUKAN,** MOA Museum of Art, 26-2 Momoyama-Cho, Shizuoka 413. Tel 84-2511. *Dir* Yoji Yoshioka
Library with 20,000 vols
Collections: Oriental fine arts; paintings, ceramics, lacquers and sculptures

HIROSHIMA

M **ITSUKUSHIMA JINJA HOMOTSUKAN,** Treasure Hall of the Isukushima Shinto Shrine, Miyajima-cho, Saeki-gun. *Cur & Chief Priest* Motoyoshi Nozaka
Collections: Paintings, calligraphy, sutras, swords, and other ancient weapons

KURASHIKI

M **OHARA BIJITSUKAN,** Ohara Museum of Art, 1-1-15 Chuo, 710. Tel 86-422-0005. *Cur* Shin-ichiro Foujita
Library with 30,000 vols
Collections: Ancient Egyptian, Persian & Turkish ceramics & sculpture; 19th & 20th century European paintings & sculpture; modern Japanese oil paintings, pottery, sculpture & textiles

KYOTO

M **KYOTO KOKURITSU HAKUBUTSUKAN,** Kyoto National Museum, 527 Chayamachi, Higashiyama-ku, 605. Tel (075) 541-1151. *Dir* Norio Fujisawa
Collections: Fine art; handicrafts & historical collections of Asia, chiefly Japan; over 65,000 research photographs

M **KYOTO KOKURITSU KINDAI BIJUTSUKAN,** National Museum of Modern Art, Enshoji-cho, Okazaki, Sakyo-ku, 606. Tel (075) 761-4111. *Dir* Tadao Ogura; *Chief Cur* Takeo Uchiyama
Collections: Contemporary print works in Japan & Japanese artists who are active abroad; contemporary sculpture, handicrafts works by contemporary artists, paintings by the artists who have been active in Kyoto mainly

M **KYOTO-SHI BIJUTSUKAN,** Kyoto City Art Museum, Okazaki Park, Sakyo-ku. Tel (075) 771-4107. *Dir* Mitsugu Uehira
Collections: Contemporary fine arts objects, including Japanese pictures, sculptures, decorative arts exhibits and prints

NAGOYA

M **TOKUGAWA REIMEIKAI FOUNDATION,** Tokugawa Art Museum, 27 Tokugawa-cho, 2-Chome, Higashi-ku, 461. Tel (052) 935-6262. *Dir* Yoshinoku Tokugawa
Collections: Tokugawa family collection of 12,000 treasures, including scrolls, swords, calligraphy & pottery

NARA

M **HORYUJI,** Horyuji Temple, Aza Horyuji, Ikaruga-cho, Ikoma-gun
Collections: Buddhist images and paintings; the buildings date from the Asuka, Nara, Heian, Kamakura, Ashikaga, Tokugawa periods

M **NARA KOKURITSU HAKUBUTSU-KAN,** Nara National Museum, 50 Nabori-oji-Cho, 630. Tel (0742) 22-7771. *Dir* Nobuyoshi Yamamoto
Collections: Art objects of Buddhist art, mainly of Japan, including applied arts and archaeological relics, calligraphy, paintings, sculptures

OSAKA

M **FUJITA BIJUTSUKAN,** Fujita Art Museum, 10-32 Amijima-cho, Miyakojima-ku. Tel (06) 351-0582. *Dir* Masako Fujita
Collections: Scroll paintings

M **OSAKA-SHIRITSU HAKUBUTSUKAN,** Osaka Municipal Museum of Art, 1-82 Chausuyama-Cho, Tennoji-ku, 543. Tel (06) 771-4874. *Dir* Kohyama Noboru
Collections: Art of China, Korea & Japan

TOKYO

M **BRIDGESTONE BIJUTSUKAN,** Bridgestone Museum of Art, 10-1, Kyobashi 1-chome, Chuo-ku, 104. Tel (03) 3563-0241. *Executive Dir* Yasuo Kamon
Collections: Foreign paintings, mainly Impressionism and after; western style paintings late 19th century to present

M **IDEMITSU MUSEUM OF ARTS,** 3-1-1 Marunouchi, Chiyoda-ku, 100. Tel 3213-9402. *Dir* Shosuke Idemitsu
Collections: Oriental art & ceramics; Japanese paintings; calligraphy; Chinese bronzes; lacquer wares & paintings by Georges Rouault, Sam Francis

M **KOKURITSU SEIYO BIJUTSUKAN,** National Museum of Western Art, Ueno-Koen 7-7, Taito-ku, 110. Tel 828-5131. *Dir* Tetsuo Misumi
Collections: Many works of European art from the 14th - 20th century; Matsukata Collection of 19th century French art, European paintings & sculpture; Old Master paintings

M **NEZU BIJUSUKAN,** Nezu Institute of Fine Arts, 6-5 Minami-aoyama, Minato-ku, 107. Tel 400-2536. *Dir* Hisao Sugahara
Collections: Kaichiro Nezu's private collection, including 7,195 paintings, calligraphy, sculpture, swords, ceramics, lacquer-ware, archeological exhibits; 184 items designated as national treasures

M **NIPPON MINGEI KAN,** Japanese Folk Crafts Museum, 4-3-33 Komaba, Meguro-ku, 153. Tel 467-4527. *Dir* Sori Yanagi
Collections: Folk-craft art objects from all parts of the world

M **TOKYO KOKURITSU HAKUBUTSUKAN,** Tokyo National Museum, 13-9 Ueno Koen, Taito-ku, 110. Tel (03) 3822-1111. *Dir Gen* Bunichiro Sano
Collections: Largest art museum in Japan; Eastern fine arts, including paintings, calligraphy, sculpture, metal work, ceramic art, textiles, lacquer ware, archaeological exhibits

M **TOKYO KOKURITSU KINDAI BUJUTSUKAN,** National Museum of Modern Art, Tokyo, 3 Kitanomaru Koen, Chiyoda-ku, 102. Tel (03) 3214-2561. *Dir* Hiroshi Veki
Collections: Calligraphy, drawings, paintings, prints, sculptures, watercolors
M **Crafts Gallery,** 1 Kitanomaru Koen, Chiyoda-ku. *Chief Cur* Mitsuhiki Hasebe
Collections: Ceramics, lacquer ware, metalworks

M **TOKYO NATIONAL UNIVERSITY OF FINE ARTS & MUSIC ART MUSEUM,** Ueno Park, Taito-ku. Tel (03) 3828-7745.
Collections: Paintings, sculptures & industrial art of Japan, China & Korea

M **TOKYO-TO BIJUTSUKAN,** Tokyo Metropolitan Art Museum, Ueno Park 8-36, Daito-ku, 110. Tel (03) 3823-6921. *Dir* Muneaki Murabayashi; *Deputy Dir* Yoshitake Mamuro
Collections: Sculptures

WAKAYAMA

M **KOYASAN REIHOKAN,** Museum of Buddhist Art on Mount Koya, Koyasan Koya-cho, Ito-gun. *Cur* Dr Chikyo Yamamoto
Collections: Buddhist paintings and images, sutras and old documents, some of them registered National Treasures and Important Cultural Properties

KOREA, REPUBLIC OF

SEOUL

M **NATIONAL MUSEUM OF KOREA,** 1 Sejong-ro, Chongno-ku, 110. Tel 720-2714. *Dir Gen* Yang-Mo Chung
Seven branch museums & library with 20,000 vols
Collections: Korean archaeology, culture & folklore

LEBANON

BEIRUT

M **ARCHAELOGICAL MUSEUM OF THE AMERICAN UNIVERSITY OF BEIRUT,** Bliss. Tel 350000, Ext 2523. *Dir* Dr Leila Badre
Collections: Bronze and Iron Age Near Eastern pottery collections; bronze figurines, weapons and implements of the Bronze Age Near East; Graeco-Roman imports of pottery from Near East sites; Palaeolithic-Neolithic flint collection; Phoenician glass collection; pottery collection of Islamic periods; substantial coin collection

M **DAHESHITE MUSEUM AND LIBRARY,** PO Box 202. *Dir* Dr A S M Dahesh
Library with 30,000 vols
Collections: Aquarelles, gouaches, original paintings, engravings, sculptures in marble, bronze, ivory and wood carvings

M **MUSEE NATIONAL,** National Museum of Lebanon, Rue de Damas. Tel 4-01-00/4-40. *Dir* Dr Camille Asmar
Collections: Anthropological sarcophagi of the Greco-Persian period; Byzantine mosaics; royal arms, jewels and statues of the Phoenician epoch; Dr C Ford Collection of 25 sarcophagi of the Greek and Helenistic epoch; goblets, mosaics, relief and sarcophagi of the Greco-Roman period; Arabic woods and ceramics

LIBERIA

MONROVIA

M **NATIONAL MUSEUM,** Broad & Buchanan Sts, PO Box 3223. *Dir* Burdie Urey-Weeks
Collections: Liberian history & art

LIBYA

TRIPOLI

M **ARCHAEOLOGICAL, NATURAL HISTORY, EPIGRAPHY, PREHISTORY AND ETHNOGRAPHY MUSEUMS,** Assarai al-Hamra. Tel 38116/7. *Pres* Dr Abdullah Shaiboub
Administered by Department of Antiquities
Collections: Archaeology from Libyan sites

LIECHTENSTEIN

VADUZ

M **LIECHTENSTEINISCHE STAATLICHE KUNSTSAMMLUNG,** Englander-Bau, Stadtle 37, 9490. Tel 232 23 41. *Dir* Dr George Malin

LITHUANIA

KAUNAS

M **M K CIURLIONIS STATE MUSEUM OF ART,** Vlado Putvinskio 55, LT-3000. Tel 22-97-38. *Dir* Osvaldas Daugelis
Collections: Lithuanian, European & Oriental art; 5 related galleries & museums in Kaunas & Druskininkai

VILNIUS

M **ART MUSEUM OF THE LITHUANIAN,** Ul Gorkio 55, 2024. Tel 62-80-30.
Dir Romualdas Budrys
Collections: Lithuanian art; English, Flemish, French, German & Italian art from
16th-19th centuries

MALAYSIA

KUALA LUMPUR

M **MUZIUM NEGARA,** National Museum of Malaysia, Jalan Damansara, 50566.
Tel (03) 2380255. *Dir-Gen* Haji Mohamed Zulkifli Bin Haji Abdul Aziz
Collections: Oriental & Islamic arts, ethnographical, archaeological & zoological
collections

MALTA

VALLETTA

M **MUSEUMS DEPARTMENT,** Auberge de Provence, Republic St. Tel 25293.
Dir T C Gouder
Collections: Fine arts; archaeology & natural history

MEXICO

GUADALAJARA

M **MUSEO DEL ESTADO DE JALISCO,** Liceo 60 S H, Jalisco 44100. Tel
145257. *Dir* C Sanchez Del Real
Collections: Archaeological discoveries; early Mexican objects; folk art &
costumes

M **MUSEO-TALLER JOSE CLEMENTE OROZCO,** Calle Aurelio Aceves 27,
Sector Juarez, Jalisco 44100. *Dir* Margarita V de Orozco
Collections: Paintings and sketches by the artist

MEXICO CITY

M **MUSEO DE ARTE MODERNO,** Museum of Modern Art, Bosque de
Chapultepec, Paseo de la Reforma y Gandhi, 11560. Tel 553-63-13. *Dir* Teresa
del Conde
Collections: International and Mexican collection of modern art

M **MUSEO DE SAN CARLOS,** Puente de Alvarado 50, 06030. Tel 592-37-21. *Dir*
Mtra Leonor Cortina
Collections: English, Flemish, French, German, Hungarian, Italian, Polish,
Netherlandish and Spanish paintings from 14th - 19th centuries
L **Library,** Puente de Alvarado No 50, 06030
Library Holdings: Vols 2000

M **MUSEO NACIONAL DE ANTROPOLOGIA,** National Museum of
Anthropology, Paseo de la Reforma y Gandhi, 11560. Tel 5-53-19-02. *Dir* Mari
Carmen Serra Puche
Collections: Anthropological, archaeological & ethnographical collections

M **MUSEO NACIONAL DE ARTES E INDUSTRIAS POPULARES DEL
INSTITUTO NACIONAL INDIGENISTA,** National Museum of Popular Arts
and Crafts, Avda Juarez 44, 06050. Tel 510-34-04. *Dir* Maria Teresa Pomar
Collections: Major permanent collections of Mexican popular arts and crafts

M **MUSEO NACIONAL DE HISTORIA,** National Historical Museum, Castillo
de Chapultepec, 5. Tel 553-62-02. *Dir* Lourdes Herrasti Macia
Collections: The history of Mexico from the Spanish Conquest to the 1917
Constitution, through collections of ceramics, costumes, documents, flags and
banners, furniture, jewelry & personal objects

M **PINACOTECA NACIONAL DE SAN DIEGO,** San Diego National Art
Gallery, Dr Mora 7, Alameda Central, 06050. Tel 5-10-27-93. *Dir* Mercedes
Meade de Angulo
Collections: Under auspices of Instituto Nacional de Bellas Artes; paintings of
the colonial era in Mexico

PUEBLA

M **MUSEO DE ARTE JOSE LUIS BELLO Y GONZALEZ,** Avenida 3 Poniente
302. Tel 32-94-75. *Dir* Alicia Torres de Araujo
Collections: Ivories; porcelain; wrought iron; furniture; clocks; watches; musical
instruments; Mexican, Chinese and European paintings, sculptures, pottery,
vestments, tapestries, ceramics, miniatures

TOLUCA

M **MUSEO DE LAS BELLAS ARTES,** Museum of Fine Arts, Calle de Santos
Degollado 102. *Dir* Prof Jose M Caballero-Barnard
Collections: Paintings; sculptures; Mexican colonial art

MYAHMAR (BURMA)

YANGON

M **NATIONAL MUSEUM OF ART AND ARCHAEOLOGY,** Jubilee Hall, 26/42
Pagoda Rd. Tel (01) 73706. *Dir* Dr Ye Tut
Collections: Antiquities; paintings; replica of King Mindon's Mandalay Palace

NEPAL

KATHMANDU

M **NATIONAL MUSEUM OF NEPAL,** Museum Rd, Chhauni. Tel 211504. *Chief*
Sanu Nani Kansakar
Collections: Art, history, culture, ethnology & natural history collections

NETHERLANDS

ALKMAAR

M **STEDELIJK MUSEUM ALKMAAR,** Alkmaar Municipal Museum, Nieuwe
Doelen, Doelenstraat 3-9, 1811 KX. Tel 11-07-37. *Dir* M E A de Vries
Collections: Collection from Alkmaar region, including archaeological items,
dolls and other toys, modern sculpture, paintings, silver tiles; works by
Honthorst, van Everdingen, van de Velde the Elder

AMSTERDAM

M **REMBRANDT-HUIS MUSEUM,** Rembrandthouse Museum, Jodenbreestraat
4-6, 1011 NK. Tel 020-624-9486. *Dir* E de Heer
Collections: Rembrandt's etchings and drawings; drawings and paintings by
Rembrandt's pupils

M **RIJKSMUSEUM,** State Museum, Stadhouderskade 42, PO Box 74888, 1070
DN. Tel 020-673-2121. *Dir Gen* Dr H W van Os
Library with 200,000 vols
Collections: Asiatic art; Dutch history & paintings; prints & drawings from all
parts of the world; sculpture & applied art

M **STEDLIJK MUSEUM,** Municipal Museum, Paulus Potterstraat 13, PO Box
5082, 1007 AB. Tel (020) 5732911. *Dir* R H Fuchs
Library with 20,000 vols & 90,000 catalogs
Collections: Applied art & design; European & American trends after 1960 in
paintings & sculptures

M **VAN GOGH MUSEUM** (Formerly Rijksmuseum Vincent Van Gogh), Paulus
Potterstraat 7, PO Box 75366, 1070 AJ. Tel (020) 570-5200. *Dir* Ronald de
Leeuw
Collections: 550 drawings & 200 paintings by Vincent Van Gogh; Van Gogh's
personal collection of English & French prints & Japanese woodcuts

ARNHEM

M **GEMEENTEMUSEUM ARNHEM,** Municipal Museum of Arnhem,
Utrechtseweg 87, Gelderland 6812 AA. Tel (085) 512431. *Dir* Dr L Brandt
Corstius
Library with 18,000 vols
Collections: Chinese porcelain; Delftware; Design; Dutch archaeological objects;
Dutch and international paintings, drawings and prints; Dutch contemporary
applied art; provincial archaeology and history; sculpture gardens; silverware;
topographical and historical maps of the Province of Gelderland

DELFT

M **STEDELIJK MUSEUM HET PRINSENHOF,** Het Prinsenhof State Museum,
St Agathaplein 1, 2611 HR. Tel (015) 602-357. *Dir* Dr D H A C Lokin
Library with 6000 vols
Collections: Delft silver, tapestries and ware; paintings of the Delft School;
modern art

DORDRECHT

M DORDRECHTS MUSEUM, Museumstraat 40, 3311 XP. Tel 13-41-00. *Dir* Dr S J M De Groot
Collections: Dutch paintings, prints, drawings & sculpture, 17th to 20th century drawings, paintings & prints

EINDHOVEN

M MUNICIPAL VAN ABBEMUSEUM INN EINDHOVEN, Eindhoven Municipal Museum, Bilderdijklaan 10, PO Box 235, 5600 AE. Tel (040) 389730. *Dir* J Debbaut
Library with 100,000 vols
Collections: Modern and contemporary art; Lissitzky Collection

ENSCHEDE

M RIJKSMUSEUM TWENTHE TE ENSCHEDE, Lasondersingel 129, 7514 BP. Tel (053) 358675. *Dir* Dr D A S Cannegieter
Library with 24,000 vols
Collections: Collection of paintings & sculptures from middle ages up until present

GRONINGEN

M GRONINGEN MUSEUM, Praediniussingel, 9711AG. Tel (050) 183343. *Dir* Dr F Haks
Library with 35,000 vols
Collections: Paintings & drawings from the 16th - 20th Century, mainly Dutch, including Averkamp, Cuyp, Fabritius, Jordaens, Rembrandt, Rubens, Teniers; Oriental ceramics; local archaeology & history

HAARLEM

M FRANS HALSMUSEUM, Groot Heiligland 62, 2011 ES. Tel 164200. *Dir* D P Snoep
Collections: Works by Frans Hals & Haarlem school; antique furniture; modern art collection

M TEYLERS MUSEUM, Spaarne 16, 2011 CH. Tel (023) 319010. *Dir* E Ebbinge
Library with 150,000 vols
Collections: Coins, drawings, fossils, historical physical instruments, medals, minerals & paintings

THE HAGUE

M HAAGS GEMEENTEMUSEUM, Municipal Museum of The Hague, Stadhouderslaan 41, 2517 HV. Telex 3-6990; Tel (070) 3381111. *Dir* Dr J L Locher
Collections: Decorative Arts Collection includes ceramics, furniture, glass, silver; modern art of 19th & 20th centuries; musical insturments; history of The Hague

M KONINKLIJK KABINET VAN SCHILDERIJEN MAURITSHUIS, Royal Picture Gallery, Korte Vijverberg 8, 2513 AB. Tel (070) 346-9244. *Dir* F J Duparc
Collections: Paintings of the Dutch and Flemish Masters of the 15th, 16th, 17th and 18th centuries, including G David, Holbein, Hals, Rembrandt, Van Dyck, Vermeer

HERTOGENBOSCH

M NOORDBRABANTS MUSEUM, Verwersstraat 41, PO Box 1004, 5200 BA. Tel 073-877 877. *Dir* M M A van Boven
Collections: All collections have an emphasis on local history: archaeology, arts & crafts, coins & medals, painting & sculpture

HOORN

M WESTFRIES MUSEUM, Rode Steen 1, Acherom 2, 1621 KV. Tel (02290) 15748. *Dir* R J Spruit
Collections: 17th & 18th century paintings, prints, oak panelling, glass, pottery, furniture, costumes, interiors; folk art; historical objects from Hoorn & West Friesland; West Friesland native painting; prehistoric finds

LEERDAM

M STICHTING NATIONAAL GLASMUSEUM, National Glass Museum, Lingedijk 28, 4142 LD. Tel (03451) 13662. *Cur* Dr T G Te Dhits
Collections: Antique, machine-made & packaging glass; art glass; unique pieces; contemporary Dutch collection & works from America & Europe

LEEUWARDEN

M FRIES MUSEUM, Turfmarkt 24, 8911 KT. Tel 058-123001 129085. *Dir* R Vos
Collections: Archaeology, ceramics, costumes, folk art, historical items, painting, prints and drawings, sculpture

LEIDEN

M STEDELIJK MUSEUM DE LAKENHAL, Leiden Municipal Museum, Oude Singel 28-32, PO Box 2044, 2301 CA. Tel 165360. *Dir* Dr H Bolten-Rempt
Collections: Altar pieces by Lucas van Leyden; paintings by Rembrandt, Steen, van Goyen; pictures of Leiden School & modern Leiden School; arms, ceramics, furniture, glass, period rooms, pewter, silver

MUIDEN

M MUIDERSLOT RIJKSMUSEUM, State Museum at Muiden, 1398 AA. Tel 02942-1325. *Dir* P W Mojet Loc
Collections: 13th century castle furnished in early 17th century style; paintings, tapestries, furniture & armory

NIJMEGEN

M NIJMEEGS MUSEUM COMMANDERIE VAN ST JAN, Franse Plaats 3, 6511 VS. Tel 080-22-91-93. *Dir* Dr G T M Lemmens
Collections: Art and history of Nijmegen and region: Middle Ages - 20th Century; modern international art

OTTERLO

M RIJKSMUSEUM KROLLER-MULLER, Foundation Kröller-Müller Museum, Nationale Park de Hoge Veluwe, Houtkampweg 6 (Mailing add: Box nr 1, 6730 AA). Tel 08382-1241. *Dir* Dr E J van Straaten; *Deputy Dir* Dr J B Bremmer; *Cur Sculpture* Dr M Brouwer; *Cur Paintings* Dr J van der Wolk; *Cur Works on Paper* Dr T van Kooten
Library with 35,000 vols
Collections: Van Gogh Collection; 19th and 20th century art - drawings, paintings, sculpture garden, ceramics, graphic arts, sculpture and sculpture drawings

ROTTERDAM

M MUSEUM BOYMANS-VAN BEUNINGEN, Museum Park 18-20, 3015 CK. Tel 010-441-9400.
Collections: Dutch school paintings including Bosch, Hals, Rembrandt, Van Eyck; 15th-20th centuries Dutch, Flemish, French, German, Italian & Spanish works; Baroque School; Impressionists; old, modern & contemporary sculpture; Dutch, Italian, Persian & Spanish pottery & tiles

NEW ZEALAND

AUCKLAND

M AUCKLAND CITY ART GALLERY, 5 Kitchener St, PO Box 5449, 1. Tel (09) 307-7700. *Dir* Christopher Johnstone
Library with 33,000 vols
Collections: American & Australian paintings; general collection of European paintings & sculpture from 12th century on; historical & contemporary New Zealand painting, sculpture & prints

L UNIVERSITY OF AUCKLAND, Elam School of Fine Arts Library, School of Fine Arts, Whitaker Pl. Tel 31 897. *Dean of Elam School of Fine Arts* Jolyon D Saunders
Library with 30,000 vols

DUNEDIN

M DUNEDIN PUBLIC ART GALLERY, Logan Park, PO Box 566. Tel (03) 4778-770. *Dir* John McCormack
Collections: 15th - 19th century European paintings; New Zealand paintings since 1876; Australian paintings 1900-60; British watercolors, portraits and landscapes; ancillary collections of furniture, ceramics, glass, silver, oriental rugs; De Beer collection of Old Masters, including Monet

INVERCARGILL

M ANDERSON PARK ART GALLERY, PO Box 755. *Pres* S Bradshaw
Collections: Contemporary New Zealand art

NAPIER

M HAWKES BAY ART GALLERY AND MUSEUM, 9 Herschell St, PO Box 248. Tel 8357781. *Deputy Dir* R B McGregor
Collections: Antiques; Maori & Pacific artifacts; New Zealand painting & sculpture

WANGANUI

M SARJEANT GALLERY, Queen's Park, PO Box 998. Tel 064-570-52.
Collections: European & English watercolors, 18th century to present; local works; New Zealand collection of paintings; First World War cartoons

WELLINGTON

M NATIONAL ART GALLERY OF NEW ZEALAND, Buckle St. Tel (04) 859-703. *Dir* Jenny Harper
Library with 20,000 vols
Collections: Australian, British, European & New Zealand art; Sir Harold Beauchamp Collection of early English drawings, illustrations & watercolors; Sir John Ilott Collection of prints; Nan Kivell Collection of British original prints; Monrad Collection of early European graphics; collection of Old Master drawings

NIGERIA

IFE

M MUSEUM OF THE IFE ANTIQUITIES, Enuwa Sq. Tel 21-50. *Dir* Frank Willett
Collections: Western Nigeria Archeology

NORWAY

BERGEN

M VESTLANDSKE KUNSTINDUSTRIMUSEUM, Western Norway Museum of Applied Art, Nordahl Brunsgate 9, 5014. Tel (05) 32-51-08. *Museum Dir* Widar Halen
Library with 20,000 vols
Collections: Contemporary Norwegian and European ceramics, furniture, textiles; The General Munthe Collection of Chinese Art; collections of old European arts and crafts; The Anna B and William H Singer Collection of art and antiquities

LILLEHAMMER

M LILLEHAMMER KUNSTNUSEUM (Formerly Lillehammer Bys Malerisamling), Lillehammer Municipal Art Gallery, Stortorget 2, PO Box 264, 2601. Tel 61269444. *Dir* Sucir Olaw Hoff
Collections: Norwegian paintings, sculpture and graphic art from 19th and 20th centuries

OSLO

M KUNSTINDUSTRIMUSEET I OSLO, Oslo Museum of Applied Art, St Olavs Gate 1, 0165. Tel 22 203578. *Dir* Anniken Thue
Library with 52,000 vols
Collections: Collection from the 600s to the present of applied arts, fashion & design with ceramics, furniture, glass, silver, textiles from Norway, Europe & Far East

M NASJONALGALLERIET, Universitetsgaten 13, PO Box 8157 Dep, 0033. Tel (22) 200404. *Dir* Knut Berg
Library with 30,000 vols
Collections: Norwegian paintings & sculpture; Old European paintings; icon collection; especially of modern French, Danish & Swedish art; a collection of prints & drawings; a small collection of Greek & Roman sculptures; the collections of paintings & sculpture up to 1945

M NORSK FOLKEMUSEUM, Norwegian Folk Museum, Bygdoy, Museum Veien 10, 2. Tel 22437020. *Dir* Erik Rudeng
Collections: The Lappish section provides an insight into the ancient culture of the Lapps. The Open Air Museum totals about 170 old buildings, all original. Among them are the 13th century Gol stave church; farmsteads from different districts of the country; single buildings of particular interest; The Old Town - 17th, 18th & 19th centuries town houses. Urban Collections; Henrik Ibsen's study; other collections include peasant art & church history

M NORSK SJOFARTSMUSEUM, Norwegian Maritime Museum, Bygdoynesveien 37, N-0286. Tel 22 438240. *Dir* Bard Kolltveit
Library with 28,000 vols
Collections: Amundsen's Gjoa; archives pertaining to maritime history; instruments, paintings, photographs of ships, ship models, tools & other items pertaining to maritime collections

M OSLO KOMMUNES KUNSTSAMLINGER, Munch museet, Toyengata 53, 0608. Tel (02) 673774. *Dir* Alf Boe; *Chief Cur* Arne Eggum
Collections: Paintings, sculptures, graphic works, prints and drawings of: Edvard Munch, Gustav Vigeland, Ludvig Ravensburg, Rolf E Stenersens

L STATENS KUNSTAKADEMI BIBLIOTEKET, National Academy of Fine Arts Library, St Olavs Gate 32, 0166. Tel 02-20-01-50. *Rector of Academy* Jan Ake Petterson
Library with 6000 volumes to support training by 14 teachers of 130 students

M UNIVERSITETETS SAMLING AV NORDISKE OLDSAKER, University Museum of National Antiquities, Frederiksgate 2, 0164. Tel 22 85 19 00. *Dir* Prof Erla B Hohler
Collections: Archaeological finds from Norwegian Stone, Bronze & Iron Ages, also Medieval age, including religious art, 70,000 exhibits from prehistoric & Viking times, including Middle Ages

PAKISTAN

KARACHI

M NATIONAL MUSEUM OF PAKISTAN, Burns Garden. Tel 211341. *Supt* Abdul Aziz Farooq
Collections: Antiquities dating from 2800 to 1500, large collection of coins and miniature paintings spreading from 6th century BC to present; ethnological material from the various regions of Pakistan; Buddhist and Hindu sculptures; paleolithic implements; handicrafts and manuscripts of the Muslim period

LAHORE

M LAHORE FORT MUSEUM, 54000. Tel 56747. *Dir Archaeology* Dr Muhammad Sharif
Collections: Mughal Gallery: Mughal paintings, coins, calligraphy, manuscripts, faience, carving, Sikh Gallery: arms and armor, paintings and art of Sikh period; Sikh Painting Gallery: oil paintings from the Princess Bamba Collection

M LAHORE MUSEUM, Sharah-i-Quaid-i-Azam. Tel 322835. *Dir* Dr F M Anjum Rehmani
Library with 35,000 vols
Collections: Greco-Buddhist sculpture; Indo-Pakistan coins; miniature paintings; local arts; armor; stamps; Oriental porcelain & manuscripts; Islamic calligraphy

PESHAWAR

M PESHAWAR MUSEUM, Tel 7-44-52. *Dir* Aurangzeb Khan
Collections: Architectural pieces and minor antiquities; mainly sculptures of the Gandhara School containing images of Buddha, Bodhisattvas, Buddhist deities, reliefs illustrating the life of the Buddha and Jataka stories; Koranic manuscripts

TAXILA

M ARCHAEOLOGICAL MUSEUM, Rawalpindi. *Custodian* Gulzar Mohammed Khan
Collections: Antiquities from Taxila Sites ranging from 6th Century BC to 5th Century AD; gold and silver ornaments; pottery; sculptures of stone and stucco of Gandhara School

PAPUA NEW GUINEA

BOROKO

M PAPUA NEW GUINEA NATIONAL MUSEUM & ART GALLERY, PO Box 5560. Tel 252405. *Dir* Soroi Marepo Eoe
Library with 4500 vols

PARAGUAY

ASUNCION

M MUSEO DE CERAMICA Y BELLAS ARTES JULIAN DE LA HERRERIA, Estados Unidos, 1120. *Dir* Josefina Pia
Library with 6000 vols
Collections: Modern works of Paraguayan artists; Paraguayan folk art

M MUSEO NACIONAL DE BELLAS ARTES, Mariscal Estigarribia y Iturbe. *Dir* Jose Laterza Parodi
Collections: Paintings from the work of Juan Silvano Godoy

PERU

LIMA

M **MUSEO DE ARTE DE LIMA,** Lima Museum of Art, Paseo Colon 125. Tel 23-4732. *Dir* Cecilia Alayza
Collections: Peruvian art throughout history; Colonial painting; carvings, ceramics, furniture, metals, modern paintings, religious art, sculpture, textiles; modern furniture & paintings

M **MUSEO NACIONAL DE LA CULTURA PERUANA,** National Museum of Peruvian Culture, Avenida Alfonso Ugarte 650, Apdo 3048, 100. Tel 235892. *Dir* Sara Acevedo Basurto
Collections: Ethnology, folklore, popular art

PHILIPPINES

MANILA

M **METROPOLITAN MUSEUM OF MANILA,** Central Bank Complex, Roxas Blvd. Tel 8323645. *Dir* Eric B Zerrudo
Collections: Fine arts museum; paintings, graphic arts, sculptures & decorative arts

M **NATIONAL MUSEUM OF THE PHILIPPINES,** POB 2659, Padre Burgos St, 1000. Tel 48-14-27. *Dir* Gabriel S Casal
Collections: Fine arts, cultural, archaeological, sciences collections

M **SANTO TOMAS MUSEUM,** Museum of Arts & Sciences, Main Bldg, University of Santo Tomas, Calle Espana, 1008. Tel 7313101. *Dir* Isidro Abano
Collections: Archaeology, cultural & historical items; Chinese trade pottery; ethnology of the Philippines; medals; Philippine art; popular Philippines religious art; stamps

POLAND

CRACOW

L **BIBLIOTEKA GLOWNA AKADEMII SZTUK PIEKNYCH,** Central Library of the Academy of Fine Arts, ul Smolensk 9, 31-108. Tel (0048-12) 22-15-46; 21-31-45. *Dir* Elzbieta Warchalowska
Collections: Over 71,000 vols, 30,000 other items in collection

M **MUZEUM NARODOWE W KRAKOWIE,** National Museum in Cracow, Ul J Pilsudskiego 12, 31-109. Tel 22-54-34. *Dir* Tadeusz Chruscicki
Collections: National Museum in Cracow consists of several departments with various collections: 3 galleries exhibit Polish painting and sculpture from 14th to 20th centuries; Emeryk Hutten-Czapski Dept has graphic, numismatic and old book collection; Jan Matejko's House exhibits relics and paintings of the eminent Polish painter; Czartoryski Collection contains national relics, armory, Polish and foreign crafts and paintings, archaeology; Czartoryski Library and Archives holds collections of documents, codices, books and incunabula; Stanislaw Wyspianski Museum exhibits works by the Polish Modernist artist, handicrafts, architecture and town planning; Karol Szymanowski Museum contains exhibits relating to the life of the eminent composer

M **PANSTWOWE ZBIORY SZTUKI NA WAWELU,** Wawel State Art Collections, Wawel 5, 31001. Tel 225155. *Dir* Jan Ostrowski
Collections: Collections of art in the royal castle; 16th century collection of Flemish tapestries; Italian & Dutch paintings; Oriental objects of art

M **ZAMEK KROLEWSKI NA WAWELU,** Wawel Royal Castle, Wawel 5, 31-001. Tel 22-51-55. *Dir* Jan Ostrowski; *Mgr* Stefan Zajac
Library with 11,500 vols
Collections: Italian Renaissance furniture; King Sigismund Augustus 16th Century Collection of Flemish Tapestries; Oriental art objects; Polish, Western-European Oriental weapons; Western-European & Oriental pottery; Western European painting; royal treasury of crown jewels, gold objects, historical relics; Western European furniture; Western European Oriental textiles

KIELCE

M **MUZEUM NARODOWE W KIELCACH,** National Museum in Kielce, Pl Zamkowy 1, 25-010. Tel 440-14. *Dir* Alojzy Oborny
Library with 31,500 vols
Collections: Polish paintings from 17th to 20th century; Polish baroque interiors; European-paintings, graphics, glass, pottery, gold, silver, furniture, arms & armour, coins, medals

LODZ

M **MUSEUM SZTUKI W LODZI,** Art Museum, Ul Wieckowskiego 36, 90-734. Tel (42) 33-97-90. *Dir* Jaromir Jedlinski
Collections: Gothic art; 15th to 19th century foreign paintings; 18th to 20th century Polish paintings; international modern art

POZNAN

M **MUZEUM NARODOWE,** National Museum, Al Marcinkowskiego 9, 61-745. Tel 52-80-11. *Dir* Dr Konstanty Kalinowski
Library has 85,000 vols; 8 branch museums
Collections: Polish paintings from 15th to 20th century; prints, drawings, sculpture; medieval art; European paintings from 14th to 19th century; modern art; numismatics

WARSAW

L **BIBLIOTEKA UNIWERSYTECKA W WARSZAWIE,** Library of the University of Warsaw, Ul Krakowskie Przedmiescie 32, 00-927. Tel 264-155. *Dir* Dr Henryk Hollender
Collections: Prints & drawings from 15th - 20th centuries; various memorial collections

M **MUZEUM NARODOWE,** National Museum, Al Jerozolimskie 3, 00495. Tel 211031. *Dir* Ferdynand Ruszczyc
Collections: Paintings, sculptures & drawings; Medieval & modern Polish 12th century art

M **PANSTWOWE MUZEUM ETNOGRAFICZNE W WARSZAWIE,** State Ethnographic Museum in Warsaw, Ul Kredytowa 1, 00-056. Tel 27-76-41. *Dir* Dr Jan Witold Suliga
Library has 23,000 vols
Collections: Polish & non-European ethnography collection

M **ZAMEK KROLEWSKI W WARSZAWIE POMNIK HISTORII I KULTRY NARODWEJ,** Royal Castle in Warsaw, National History & Culture Memorial, Zamkowy 4, 00-277. Tel 6350808. *Dir* Andrzej Rottermund
Library with 25,000 vols
Collections: Prints, paintings, sculptures & applied arts

WROCLAW

M **MUZEUM ARCHITEKTURY,** Museum of Architecture, Ul Bernardynska 5, 50-156. Tel 336-75. *Dir* Prof Olgierd Czerner
Collections: Polish & other architecture; modern art

M **MUZEUM NARODOWE WE WROCLAWIU,** National Museum in Wroclaw, Pl Powstancow Warszawy 5, 50-153. Tel 388-30. *Dir* Mariusz Hermansdorfer
Library with 77,000 vols
Collections: Medieval art; Polish paintings of the 17th, 18th, 19th & 20th centuries, European paintings; decorative arts, prints, ethnography & history relating to Silesia; numismatics

PORTUGAL

EVORA

M **MUSEU DE EVORA,** Largo do Conde de Vila Flor, 7000. Tel 22604. *Dir* Artur Goulart de Melo Borges
Collections: Paintings: 16th century Flemish & Portuguese works; local prehistoric tools & Roman art & archaelogy; sculpture from middle ages to the 19th century; 18th century Portuguese furniture & silver

LAMEGO

M **MUSEU DE LAMEGO,** 5100. Tel (054) 62008. *Dir* Dr Agostinlto Riberio
Collections: 16th century Brussels tapestries; Portuguese painting of 16th and 18th centuries; sculpture; religious ornaments

LISBON

M **MUSEU CALOUSTE GULBENKIAN,** Av de Berne 45 A, 1093. Tel 7935131. *Dir* Maria Teresa Gomes-Ferreira
Collections: Gulbenkian art collection covering the period 2800 BC to present; classical, Oriental, European art; manuscripts, furniture, gold and silver; medals; tapestries

M **MUSEU NACIONAL DE ARTE ANTIGA,** National Museum of Ancient Art, Rua das Janelas Verdes, 3703. Tel 397-2725. *Dir* Dra Ana Brandao
Library with 16,500 vols
Collections: Portuguese and foreign plastic and ornamental art from 12th to 19th centuries

M **MUSEU NACIONAL DE ARTE CONTEMPORANEA,** National Museum of Contemporary Art, Rua de Serpa Pinto 6. Tel (01) 36-8028. *Dir* Raquel Henriques
Collections: Contemporary painting and sculpture

PORTO

M MUSEU NACIONAL DE SOARES DOS REIS, National Museum of Soares Dos Reis, Palacio dos Carrancas, Rua de D Manuel II, 4000. Tel 20-81-956. *Dir* Dr Monica Baldaque
Collections: Furniture, glass, jewelry, old and modern paintings, porcelain, pottery, sculpture

VISEU

M MUSEU DE GRAO VASCO, Paco dos Tres Escaloes. Tel 422049. *Dir* Dr Alberto Correia
Collections: Flemish & Portuguese paintings; furniture, tapestries, ceramics & glassware

ROMANIA

BUCHAREST

L BIBLIOTECA ACADEMIEI ROMANE, Calea Victoriei 125, 71102. Tel 50-30-43. *Dir* Prof Victor Sahini
Library Holdings: Items over 9 million
Collections: National depository for Romanian & United Nations publications; Romania, Latin, Greek, Oriental & Slavonic manuscripts, engravings, documents, maps, medals & coins

M MUZEUL NATIONAL DE ARTA, National Museum of Art, Calea Victoriei 49-53, 70731. Tel 15-51-93. *Dir* Dr Theodor Enescu
Collections: Medieval Romanian art (9th - 18th centuries); National Gallery: national, old Romanian, modern & contemporary works of art; Universal Gallery: paintings, sculptures, European decorative arts & Oriental art; graphic art & prints
M Ansamblul Brincovenesc Mogosoaia, Str Donca Simo 18, 78911. Tel 667-02-40. *Dir* Alexandru Cebuc
Collections: Old Romanian art
M Muzeul Colectiilor de Arta, Calea Victoriei 111, 78911. Tel 659-66-93.
Collections: Romanian folk art; decorative arts; paintings, sculpture, graphic arts

CLUJ-NAPOCA

M MUZEUL ETNOGRAFIC AL TRANSILVANIEI, Transylvanian Museum of Ethnography, Str Memorandumului 21, 3400. Tel (95) 19-23-44. *Dir* Tiberiu Graur
Collections: Exhibits of Transylvanian traditional occupations; primitive people; Ethnographical Park, the first open-air museum in Romania

M MUZEUL NATIONAL DE ARTA CLUJ, National Museum of Art Cluj, Eroilor, 3400. Tel 40/064/116952. *Dir* Dr Livia Dragoi
Library with 80,475 vols
Collections: Decorative arts; European and Romanian art, including graphics, paintings and sculpture of the 16th - 20th centuries

CONSTANTA

M MUZEUL DE ARTA CONSTANTA, Bd Tomis 84, 8700. Tel (41) 61-80-19. *Dir* Simona Rusu
Collections: Modern & contemporary Romanian art

M MUZEUL DE ISTORIE NATIONALA SI ARHEOLOGIE DIN CONSTANTA, National History & Archaeology Museum, Piata Ovidiu 12, 8700. Tel (917) 61-39-25. *Dir* Dr A Radulesci
Library with 22,000 volumes
Collections: Prehistory, history & archaeology of the region; statues, coins, neolithic vessels

RUSSIA

KAZAN

M TATAR STATE MUSEUM OF FINE ARTS, Ul K Marska 64, 420015. Tel 366921.
Library with 10,000 exhibits
Collections: West European & Soviet paintings

MOSCOW

M KREMLIN MUSEUMS, Kremlin, 103073. Tel 928-44-56. *Dir* I A Rodimtseva
Collections: Collections housed in Armoury & various Kremlin cathedrals
M Kremlin Cathedrals, Cathedral Sq
Collections: Icons, tombs & applied arts found in Cathedral of the Assumption, Cathedral of the Annunciation, Archangel Cathedral, Rizpolozhensky Cathedral & Cathedral of the Twelve Apostles

M STATE MUSEUM OF CERAMICS, 111402. Tel 370-01-60. *Dir* E S Eritsan
Collections: Russian art; paintings, pottery, porcelain & tapestries

M STATE MUSEUM OF ORIENTAL ART, Suvorovskii bul 12A, 107120. Tel 291-03-9614. *Dir* V A Nabachikov
Collections: Art of the Republics of Soviet Central Asia; Chinese art; monuments of art of Japan, India, Vietnam, Korea, Mongolia, Iran and other countries of the Middle and Far East

M STATE PUSHKIN MUSEUM OF FINE ARTS, Volkhonka 12, 121019. Tel 203-69-74. *Dir* I A Antonova
Collections: Ancient Byzantine, Greek, Roman and European art; American art

M STATE TRETYAKOV GALLERY, Krymskii val 10-14, 117049. Tel 230-77-88. *Dir* P I Lebedev
Collections: 40,000 Russian icons; Russian & Soviet paintings, sculpture & graphic arts from 11th century to present

ROSTOV-ON-DON

M ROSTOV MUSEUM OF FINE ART, Ul Pushkinskaya 115, 344007. Tel 665907. *Dir* G S Alimurzaeva
Collections: Old Russian, Soviet art

SAINT PETERSBURG

M MUSEUM OF SCULPTURE, Pl A Nevskogo 1. *Dir* N H Belova
Collections: Collection of Russian sculpture; architectural drawings

M MUSEUM PALACES AND PARKS IN PAVLOVSK, Petrodvorets Ul Rasvodnaya 2, 188623. Tel 470-2155. *Dir* U V Murdrov
Collections: Russian garden architecture; 18th century sculptures & paintings by the Italian & French masters

M STATE HERMITAGE MUSEUM, M Dvortsovaya naberezhnaya 34. Tel 212-95-45. *Dir* Dr Mikhail Petrovsky
Collections: Collection of the arts of prehistoric, ancient Eastern, Graeco - Roman and medieval times; preserves over 2,600,000 objects d'art, including 40,000 drawings, 500,000 engravings; works by Leonardo da Vinci, Raphael, Titian, Rubens and Rembrandt; coins; weapons; applied art

M STATE RUSSIAN MUSEUM, Inzhenernaya 4. *Dir* V A Gusev
Collections: Collection of Russian icons; paintings, sculptures & drawings from the 11th to the 19th centuries

SARATOV

M SAROTOV A N RADISHCHEV ART MUSEUM, Ul Radishcheva 39, 410071. Tel 241918. *Dir* G M Kormakulina
Library with 34,000 vols & 20,000 exhibitions

ST PETERSBURG

M SUMMER GARDEN AND MUSEUM PALACE OF PETER THE GREAT, *Dir* K M Egorova
Collections: 18th century sculpture & architecture

TVER

M TVER ART GALLERY, Sovetskaya 3, 170640. Tel 32561. *Dir* Tatyana S Kuyukina
Library with 25,000 vols; 12,000 exhibits

VORONEZH

M VORONEZH ART MUSEUM, Pr Revolyutsii 18. Tel 552843. *Dir* Vladimir Y Ustinov
Library with 18,000 vols; 22,000 exhibits

YAKUTSK

M YAKUTSK MUSEUM OF FINE ARTS, Ul Khabarova 27, 677000. Tel 27798. *Dir* N M Vasileva
Collections: 17th to 20th century folk art

SCOTLAND

ABERDEEN

M ABERDEEN ART GALLERY & MUSEUMS, Schoolhill, AB9 1FQ. Telex 7-3366; Tel (0224) 646333. *Dir* Alexander Hidalgo
Collections: 20th century British art; fine & decorative arts; James McBey print room

DUNDEE

M DUNDEE ART GALLERIES & MUSEUMS, McManus Galleries, Albert Sq,
DD1 1DA. Tel 43-20-20. *Dir* A B Ritchie
Collections: 18th, 19th and 20th Century Scottish and English paintings; 17th
Century Venetian and Flemish works; varied selection of watercolors and prints
from the 18th - 20th Century; regional archaeology

EDINBURGH

M NATIONAL GALLERIES OF SCOTLAND, The Mound, EH2 2EL. Tel (031)
556-8921. *Dir* Timothy Clifford; *Keeper* Michael Clarke
Collections: European & Scottish drawings, paintings, prints & sculpture, 14th -
19th centuries
M Scottish National Gallery of Modern Art, Belford Rd, EH4 3DR. Tel 031 556
8921. *Dir* Timothy Clifford; *Keeper* Richard Calvocoressi

M NATIONAL MUSEUM OF SCOTLAND, Royal Museum of Scotland,
Chambers St, EH1 1JF. Tel 2257534. *Dir* M E P Jones
Collections: Collections of the Decorative Arts of the World; archaeology and
ethnography

GLASGOW

M GLASGOW MUSEUMS AND ART GALLERIES, Kelvingrove, G3 8AG. Tel
(041) 305-2600. *Dir* Julian Spalding
Library with 50,000 vols
Collections: Archaeology; British and Scottish art; Decorative Art Collection of
ceramics, glass, jewelry, silver (especially Scottish); ethnography; Fine Art
Collection representing the Dutch, Flemish, French and Italian schools; history;
natural history

M GLASGOW UNIVERSITY, Hunterian Museum, Main Bldg, G12 8QQ. Tel
(041) 330-4221. *Dir* Malcolm McLeod
Collections: Prehistoric, Roman, ethnographical & coin collections
M Hunterian Art Gallery, Hillhead St, G12 8QQ. Tel (041) 330-5431. *Dir*
Malcolm McLeod
Collections: J M Whistler & C R Mackintosh collections; Scottish painting from
the 18th century to the present; Old Master & modern prints

SENEGAL

DAKAR

M MUSEES DEL'INSTITUT FONDAMENTAL D'AFRIQUE NOIRE, Musee
D'art Africain de Dakar, BP 206. *Cur* Dr Massamba Ng Lame
Collections: African art; ethnography

SINGAPORE, REPUBLIC OF

SINGAPORE

M NATIONAL HERITAGE BOARD NATIONAL MUSEUM, Stamford Rd,
0617. Tel 3323656. *Chief Exec Officer* Lim Siam Kim
Houses the National Museum Art Gallery & the Children's Discovery Gallery;
Library with 15,000 vols
Collections: Paintings & sculpture by artists of Singapore & Southeast Asia
ethnology & history collections

SLOVAK, REPUBLIC OF

BRATISLAVA

M GALERIA MESTA BRATISLAVY, Municipal Gallery of Bratislava, Mirbachov
Palac, Frantiskanske Nam 11, 81535. Tel 33-51-02. *Dir* Fedor Kriska
Collections: Ancient European art; 18th-20th centuries art; Gothic painting &
sculpture; permanent Baroque art exhibition

M SLOVENSKA NARODNA GALERIA, Slovak National Gallery, Riecna 1, 815
13. Tel 3307-46. *Dir* Dr Juraj Zarv
Collections: Applied arts; European & Slovak paintings; Dutch, Flemish and
Italian works of art; graphics & drawings; sculpture

SLOVENIA

LJUBLJANA

M MODERNA GALERIJA, Museum of Modern Art, Tomsiceva 14, 61000. Tel
386-61-214-106. *Dir* Zdenka Badovinac
Library with 45,000 vols
Collections: Slovene art from Impressionists to present; international collection
containing works of major artists of contemporary world art

M NARODNA GALERIJA, National Art Gallery, Prezihova 1, 61000. Tel 061-
219-740. *Dir* Dr Andrej Smrekar
Library with 19,000 vols
Collections: Copies of medieval frescoes; Foreign Masters from the 14th Century
to the beginning of the 20th Century; Slovenian sculptures and paintings from
the 13th to the beginning of the 20th Century; Slovenian graphic arts

SOUTH AFRICA, REPUBLIC OF

CAPE TOWN

M MICHAELIS COLLECTION, Old Town House, Greenmarket Square. Tel
(021) 246367. *Dir* Dr H Fransen
Collections: Dutch and Flemish graphic art and paintings of the 16th - 18th
centuries

M SOUTH AFRICAN NATIONAL GALLERY, Government Ave, Gardens, PO
Box 2420, 8000. Tel (021) 45-1628. *Dir* M Martin
Collections: 19th and 20th century South African art; 15th - 20th century,
European art, including drawings, paintings, prints, sculptures and watercolors;
traditional African art; 20th century American Art

DURBAN

M DURBAN MUSEUMS, City Hall, Smith St, PO Box 4085, 4000. Tel (031)
3006911. *Dir* W J Oberholzer
Collections: Archaeology, paintings, graphic art, porcelain, sculptures, local
history

JOHANNESBURG

M JOHANNESBURG ART GALLERY, Joubert Park, PO Box 23561, 2044. Tel
(011) 725-3130. *Dir* R Keene
Collections: South African & international painting & sculpture; print collection;
small collection of ceramics & textiles

KIMBERLEY

M WILLIAM HUMPHREYS ART GALLERY, Civic Centre, PO Box 885, Cape
Province 8300. Tel (0531) 81-17-24. *Dir* Mrs R J Holloway
Collections: Representative collection of Old Masters; collection of South
African works of art

PIETERMARITZBURG

M TATHAM ART GALLERY, Opp City Hall, Commercial Rd. Tel (0331) 421804.
Dir Brendan Bell
Collections: 19th & 20th centuries English & French paintings & sculpture; 19th
& 20th centuries English graphics; modern European graphics; South African
painting & sculpture

PORT ELIZABETH

M KING GEORGE VI ART GALLERY, One Park Dr, 6001. Tel (041) 561030.
Dir Melanie Hillebrand
Collections: English painting; international graphics; Oriental ceramics and
miniatures; South African art

PRETORIA

M PRETORIA ART MUSEUM, Municipal Art Gallery, Arcadia Park, 0083. Tel
(012) 344-1807. *Dir* Dr L M De Waal
Collections: European graphics; 17th century Dutch art; 19th & 20th centuries
South African art

SPAIN

BARCELONA

M **MUSEO PICASSO,** Calle Montcada 15-19, 08003. Tel 3196310. *Dir* Maria
Teresa Ocana
Collections: Pablo Picasso, 1890-1972: paintings, sculpture, drawings and
engravings, including the series Las Meninas and the artist's donation, in 1970, of
940 works of art

M **MUSEU D'ART MODERN DE BARCELONA,** Museum of Modern Art, Parc
de la Ciutadella, 08003. Tel 93-319-5728. *Dir* Cristina Mendoza Garriga
Library with 50,000 vols
Collections: Modern art

M **MUSEU NACIONAL D'ART DE CATALUNYA,** National Art Museum, Parc
de Montjuic, Palau Nacional, 08038. Tel (93) 4237199. *Dir* Xavier Barral I Altet
Collections: Baroque & Renaissance paintings; Catalan Gothic & Romanesque
paintings & sculpture

BILBAO

M **MUSEO DE BELLAS ARTES,** Museum of Fine Arts, Plaza del Museo 2,
48009. Tel 441-95-36. *Dir* Jorge De Barandiaran
Collections: Paintings, sculpture; famous works by El Greco, Goya, Gauguin,
Velazquez; general contemporary art; early Spanish paintings

MADRID

M **MUSEO CERRALBO,** Ventura Rodriguez 17, 28008. Tel 547-36-46. *Dir* Pilar
De Navascues Benlloch
Library with 12,000 vols
Collections: Paintings; drawings; engravings; porcelain arms; carpets; coins;
furniture; includes paintings by: El Greco, Ribera, Titian, Van Dyck & Tintoretto

M **MUSEO LAZARO GALDIANO,** Calle Serrano 122, 28006. Tel 5616084. *Dir*
Don Enrique Pardo Canalis
Collections: Italian, Spanish and Flemish Renaissance paintings; primitives;
Golden Age 18th - 19th century Spanish paintings; 17th century Dutch
paintings; English 18th century collection ivories, enamels, furniture,
manuscripts, tapestries

M **MUSEO NACIONAL DEL PRADO,** National Museum of Paintings and
Sculpture, Paseo del Prado. Tel 420-28-36. *Dir* Jose M Luzon Nogue
Collections: Paintings by: Botticelli, Rembrandt, Velazquez, El Greco, Goya,
Murillo, Raphael, Bosch, Van der Weyden, Zurbaran, Van Dyck, Tiepolo,
Ribalta, Rubens, Titian, Veronese, Tintoretto, Moro, Juanes, Menendez, Poussin,
Ribera; classical and Renaissance sculpture; jewels and medals

M **MUSEO ROMANTICO,** Museum of the Romantic Period, Calle de San Mateo
13, 28004. Tel 448-10-45. *Dir* Maria Rosa Donoso Guerrero
Collections: Books, decorations, furniture and paintings of the Spanish Romantic
period

M **PATRIMONIO NACIONAL,** Calle de Bailen, 28071. Tel 248-74-04. *Dir* Julio
de la Guardi Garcia
Estab 1940 to administer former Crown property; it is responsible for all the
museums situated in Royal Palaces & properties & is governed by an
administrative council
Publications: Guides to all the Museums
M **Palacio Real de Madrid,** Calle Bailen s/n, 28071. Tel 248-74-04.
Also maintains armoury and coach museum. Library with 350,000 vols
Collections: Special room devoted to 16th-18th century tapestries, clocks,
paintings & porcelain from the Royal Palaces & Pharmacy
M **Palacio Real de Aranjuez,** Aranjuez, 28300. Tel 891-07-40.
Collections: Royal Palace of 18th century art
M **Monasterio de San Lorenzo de El Escorial,** San Lorenzo de El Escorial, El
Escorial, 28200. Tel 890-59-03.
Built by Juan B de Toledo & Juan de Herrera & contains many famous works by
international artists of the 16th & 18th centuries from royal residences
Collections: Royal Collection of famous international work by artists of 16th &
18th centuries; paintings, sculptures, tapestries, mobiliary, clocks, lamps,
porcelains, maps & prints
M **Museo-Monasterio de la Huelgas,** Burgos, 09001. Tel (947) 20-16-30.
Founded by Alfonso VIII in the ninth century
M **Museo-Monasterio de Santa Clara,** Tordesilla. Tel 7704-63.
Collections: 14th century art
M **Museo de la Encarnacion,** 28013. Tel 248-74-04, Ext 309.
Collections: Monastic life in the 16th & 17th centuries
M **Museo de las Descalzas Reales,** 28013. Tel 248-74-04, Ext 309.
Collections: Showing monastic life in the 16th & 17th centuries
M **Palacios de la Granja y Riofrio,** La Granja de San Ildefonso, Segovia, 40100. Tel
(911) 47-00-19.
Collections: Gardens & fountains in imitation of Versailles, tapestry museum
M **Museo de Ceramica,** Palacio de Pedralbes-Diagonal, Barcelona, 686-08034. Tel
(93) 2801621. *Dir* Trinidad Sanchez-Pacheco; *Cur* Dolors Giral; *Cur* Maria
Sanchez Pacheco
Library with 1920 vols
Collections: 19th century royal residence; tapestries, furniture
M **Palacio de la Almudaina,** Palma de Mallorca, Balearic Is, 07001. Tel (971) 72-
71-45.
Arab-Gothic palace

TOLEDO

M **CASA Y MUSEO DEL GRECO: FUNDACIONES VEGA INCLAN,** El
Greco's House, Calle Samuel Levi. Tel (925) 22-40-46. *Dir* Maria Elena Gomez-
Moreno
Collections: Artist's paintings and those of his followers; 16th century furniture
M **Museo del Greco**
Collections: El Greco's paintings, including portraits of Christ and the apostles
and other 16th and 17th century paintings

SRI LANKA

ANURADHAPURA

M **ARCHAEOLOGICAL MUSEUM,** Tel 411. *Keeper* J S A Uduwara
Collections: Stone sculptures, mural paintings & frescoes, coins, bronzes, pottery

COLOMBO

M **COLOMBO NATIONAL MUSEUM,** Sir Marcus Fernando Mawatha, PO Box
854, 7. Tel 94767. *Dir* W Thelma T P Gunawardane
Collections: Art, folk culture and antiquities of Sri Lanka

SWEDEN

GOTEBORG

M **ROHSSKA KONSTSLOJDMUSEET,** Rohss Museum of Arts and Crafts,
37-39 Vasagatan, PO Box 53178, 400 15. Tel 031-20-06-05. *Dir-Pro-Tem* B
Gyllenberg Pernevi
The arts and crafts section of the Goteborgs Museer (Museums of the City of
Gothenburg); Library with 33,000 vols

GOTHENBURG

M **GOTEBORGS KONSTMUSEUM,** Goteborg Art Gallery, Gotaplatsen, 41256.
Tel (031) 61-10-00. *Dir* Folke Edwards
Collections: French art from 1820 to present; Old Masters, especially Dutch and
Flemish; Scandinavian art

LANDSKRONA

M **LANDSKRONA MUSEUM,** Slottsgatan, 26131. Tel 0418-79000. *Dir* Christin
Nielsen
Collections: Swedish paintings since 1900; modern Swiss art; Nell Walden
collection of paintings & ethnology

LINKOPING

M **OSTERGOTLANDS LANS MUSEUM,** Raoul Wallerberg Pl, Vasaragen 16, PO
Box 232, 58102. Tel (013) 13-23-03-00. *Dir* M Ostergren
Collections: Dutch, Flemish & Swedish art; Swedish archaeology; furniture,
tapestries; Egyptian collection

STOCKHOLM

M **NATIONAL MUSEUM,** Sodra Blasieholmshamnen, PO Box 16176, 103 24. Tel
(08) 666-42-50. *Dir* Olle Granath
Collections: 6672 paintings, icons & miniatures; 4492 sculptures, including
antiquities; 202,000 drawings & prints; 29,000 items of applied art; collections of
several royal castles with 7440 works of art

M **NORDISKA MUSEET,** Scandinavian Museum, Djurgardsvagen 6-16, Box
27820, S-115 93. Tel (08) 666-46-00. *Dir* Benat Nystrom
Collections: Costumes, industrial art, handcrafts, period furnishings; over one
million exhibits

M **OSTASIATISKA MUSEET,** Museum of Far Eastern Antiquities,
Skeppsholmen, PO Box 163 81, S-103 27. Tel (08) 666-42-50. *Dir* Dr Jan Wirgin
Library with 30,000 vols
Collections: Chinese archaeology, Buddhist sculpture, bronzes, painting &
porcelain, Stone-age pottery; Indian, Japanese & Korean art

M **STOCKHOLMS STADSMUSEUM,** City Museum. Peter Myndes Backe 6. S-
11646. Tel (08) 70-00-500. *Dir* Nanna Hermansson
Collections: The Lohe Treasure. naive 19th century paintings of Josabeth Sjoberg
& armed 15th century vessel; photographs; paintings; drawings, sketches &
engravings

SWITZERLAND

AARAU

M **AARGAUER KUNSTHAUS,** Aargauer Platz, CH-5001. Tel (064) 21-21-30. *Dir* Beat Wismer
Collections: Swiss painting and sculpture from 1750 to the present day; Caspar Wolf paintings (1735-1783) - art of the first painter of the Alps; landscape painter Adolf Staebli and Auberjonois, Bruhlmann, Amiet, G Giacometti, Hodler, Meyer-Amden, Louis Soutter, Vallotton

BASEL

M **HISTORISCHES MUSEUM BASEL,** Verwaltung, Steinenberg 4, 4051. Tel (061) 271-05-05. *Dir* Dr Burkard von Roda
Collections: Collection of objects from prehistory to 19th century contained in 4 branches: Barfusserkirche, Haus zum Kirschgarten, Musikinstrum enten-Sammlung, Kutschen- und Schlittensammlung

M **MUSEUM FUR VOLKERKUNDE UND SCHWEIZERISCHES MUSEUM FUR VOLKSKUNDE BASEL,** Augustinergasse 2, PO Box 1048, 4001. Tel (061) 266-55-00. *Dir* Dr Gerhard Baer
Library with 58,000 vols
Collections: Ethnological collections from Indonesia, Europe, Oceania and South America

M **OEFFENTLICHE KUNSTSAMMLUNG BASEL KUNSTMUSEUM,** St Alben-Graben 16, 4010. Tel (061) 271-08-28. *Dir* Dr Katharina Schmidt
Library with 100,000 vols
Collections: Pictures from 15th century to present day, notably by Witz, Holbein & contemporary painters; collection includes Grunewald, Cranach the Elder, Rembrandt; 16th - 17th century Netherlandish painting, Cezanne, Gauguin & Van Gogh Impressionists; large collection of cubist art; sculptures by Rodin & 20th century artists; American art since 1945; German & Swiss masters, Klee, Matisse

BERN

M **KUNSTMUSEUM BERN,** Musee des Beaux-Arts de Berne, Hodlerstrasse 8-12, 3000. Tel 031-220944. *Dir* Dr Toni Stooss
Collections: Dutch & contemporary artists; French & other European Masters of the 19th & 20th centuries; Italian Masters; collection of Paul Klee works of 2600 items; Niklaus Manuel; Hermann & Margrit Rupf Foundation, Adolf Wolfli Foundation; Swiss Baroque Masters; Swiss 19th & 20th Century Masters, 38,000 drawings & engravings; illustrations; works by Sophie Taeuber-Arp

CHUR

M **BUNDNER KUNSTMUSEUM,** Postfach 107, 7002. Tel (081) 21-28-68. *Dir* Dr Beat Stutzer
Library with 3000 vols
Collections: Augusto, Alberto, Augusto & Giovanni Giacometti, Angelika Kauffmann, E L Kirchner; Swiss painting

GENEVA

M **MUSEE D'ART ET D'HISTOIRE,** 2 rue Charles Galland, Case Postale 516, 1211. Tel (022) 311-43-40. *Dir* C Menz
Collections: Swiss art works; primitive Italian, French, German & Flemish art; modern art; archaeology; European sculpture & decorative arts; six attached museums

LA CHAUX DE FONDS

M **MUSEE DES BEAUX-ARTS,** Museum of Fine Arts, 33 rue des Musees, 2300. Tel (039) 23-04-44. *Dir* Edmond Charriere
Collections: Works of local artists; Swiss works of the 19th & 20th centuries; modern European painting, sculpture & tapestries

LAUSANNE

M **MUSEE CANTONAL DES BEAUX-ARTS,** Palais de Rumine, 1014. Tel (021) 312-83-33. *Dir* Dr J Zutter
Collections: Works by Swiss artists & artists of other European countries; works of Vaudois artists from 15th century to present

LIGORNETTO

M **FEDERAL OFFICE OF CULTURE,** Museo Vela, 6853. Tel 091-47-32-68. *Cur* Dr Gianna A Mina Zeni
Collections: Works of art by Vela family; paintings from eighteenth & nineteenth centuries Italian schools; original monument plasters by Vinceno Vela (1820-1891); plasters by Lorenzo Vela (1812-1897); Pictures by Spartaco; Lombard & Piemontese paintings from the eighteenth & nineteenth centuries

LUCERNE

M **KUNSTMUSEUM LUZERN,** Robert - Zundstrasse 1, Postfach 3570, 6002. Tel (041) 23-10-24. *Dir* Martin Schwander
Collections: Swiss art from ancient times to 20th century; European expressionism and contemporary works

SAINT GALLEN

M **HISTORISCHES MUSEUM,** Historical Museum, Museumstrasse 50, CH-9000. Tel 071-25-22-44. *Cur* Dr Louis Specker
Collections: Furniture, glass & glass painting, graphics, period rooms, pewter, porcelain, stoves, weapons

SCHAFFHAUSEN

M **MUSEUM ZU ALLERHEILIGEN,** Klostergasse 1, CH-8200. Tel (053) 25-43-77. *Dir* Dr Gerard Seiterle
Collections: Prehistory, history and art of the region

SOLOTHURN

M **KUNSTMUSEUM SOLOTHURN,** Solothurn Art Museum, Werkhofstrasse 30, 4500. Tel (065) 22-23-07. *Cur* Andre Kamber
Collections: Swiss art from 1850 to 1980, including Amiet, Berger, Buscher, Frolicher, Hodler, Trachsel; small old master collection; private art section

WINTERTHUR

M **KUNSTMUSEUM WINTERTHUR,** Museumstrasse 52, PO Box 378, 8402. Tel (052) 84-51-62. *Pres* Urs Widmer; *Cur* Dr Dieter Schwarz
Collections: Swiss painting and sculpture from 18th century to present day; French, Italian and German painting and sculpture of 19th and 20th centuries, including Monet, Degas, Picasso, Gris, Leger, Klee, Schlemmer, Schwitters, Arp, Kandinsky, Renoir, Bonnard, Maillol, Van Gogh, Rodin, Brancusi, Morandi, Giacometti, de Stael; drawings and prints

M **MUSEUM STIFTUNG OSKAR REINHART,** Stadthausstrasse 6, 8400. Tel (052) 267-51-72. *Cur* Dr Peter Wegmann
Collections: Pictures & drawings by German, Swiss & Austrian Masters of the 18th & 19th century

ZURICH

M **KUNSTHAUS ZURICH,** Museum of Fine Arts, Heimplatz 1, 8024. Tel 01-251-67-65. *Dir* Dr Felix Baumann
Library with 55,000 vols
Collections: Alberto Giacometti works; medieval and modern sculptures; paintings; graphic arts, 16th - 20th centuries, mainly 19th and 20th

M **MUSEUM RIETBERG ZURICH,** Gablerstrasse 15, 8002. Tel (01) 202-45-28. *Dir* Dr Eberhard Fischer
Collections: Asiatic, Oceania and African art; Chinese bronzes; Baron von der Heydt Collection

M **SCHWEIZERISCHES LANDESMUSEUM-MUSEE NATIONAL SUISSSE,** Swiss National Museum, Museumstrasse 2, CH-8023. Tel 01-221-10-10. *Dir* Dr Andres Fuger
Library with 85,000 vols
Collections: History & cultural development of Switzerland since prehistoric times

SYRIA

DAMASCUS

M **MUSEE NATIONAL DE DAMAS,** National Museum, Syrian University St, 4. Tel 214-854. *General Dir* Dr Ali Abu Assaf
Collections: Ancient, Byzantine, Greek, Islamic, Modern, Oriental, Prehistoric and Roman art

TANZANIA

DAR ES SALAAM

M **NATIONAL MUSEUM OF TANZANIA,** PO Box 511. Tel 31365. *Dir* M L Mbago
Collections: Archaeology from Stone Age sites; ethnography & history collections

THAILAND

BANGKOK

M **NATIONAL MUSEUM,** Na Phra-dhart Rd, Amphoe Phda Nakhon, 10200. Tel 2241396. *Dir* Mrs Chira Chongkol
Collections: Bronze & stone sculptures, prehistoric artifacts, textiles, weapons, wood-carvings, royal regalia, theatrical masks, marionettes, shadow-play figures

TRINIDAD AND TOBAGO

PORT OF SPAIN

M **NATIONAL MUSEUM AND ART GALLERY,** 117 Frederick St. Tel 62-35941. *Dir* M P Alladin; *Cur* Claire Broadbridge
Collections: Fine art, archaeology, history & natural history collections

TUNISIA

TUNIS

M **MUSEE NATIONAL DU BARDO,** Bardo National Museum, 2000 Le Bardo. Tel 51-36-50. *Dir* Habib Ben Younes
Collections: Ancient & modern Islamic art; Greek & Roman antiquities; Roman mosaics

TURKEY

ISTANBUL

M **ISTANBUL ARKEOLOJI MUZELERI,** Archaeological Museums of Istanbul, Gulhane, 34400. Tel 5207740. *Dir* Alpay Pasinli
Library with 80,000 vols
Collections: Architectural pieces; Turkish tiles; Akkadian, Assyrian, Byzantine, Egyptian, Greek, Hittite, Roman, Sumerian and Urartu works of art

M **TOPKAPI PALACE MUSEUM,** Sultanahmed. Tel 28-35-47. *Dir* Ahmet Mentes
Library with 18,000 manuscripts and 23,000 archival documents
Collections: Chinese & Japanese porcelains; miniatures & portraits of Sultans; private collections of Kenan Ozbel; Sami Ozgiritli's collection of furniture; Islamic relics; Sultan's costumes; Turkish embroideries; armor; tiles; applied arts; paintings

M **TURK VE ISLAM ESERLERI MUZESI,** Museum of Turkish and Islamic Art, Ibrahim Pasa Sarayi, Sultanahmet. Tel 528-5158. *Dir* Nazan Tapan Olcer
Collections: Illuminated manuscripts; monuments of Islamic art; metalwork and ceramics; Turkish and Islamic carpets; sculpture in stone and stucco; wood carvings; traditional crafts gathered from Turkish mosques and tombs

UKRAINE

KIEV

M **KIEV STATE MUSEUM OF RUSSIAN ART,** Tereshchenkovska vul 9, Ukrainian 252 004. Tel 224-62-18. *Dir* M N Soldatova
Collections: 10,000 art objects

M **KIEV STATE MUSEUM OF UKRAINIAN ART,** Ul Kirova 6, Ukrainian 252004. *Dir* V F Yatsenko
Collections: Portraits, icons, wood carvings & paintings from the Middle Ages; exhibits covering 8 centuries

M **KIEV STATE MUSEUM OF WESTERN & ORIENTAL ART,** Ul Repina 15-17, Ukrainian. Tel 22-502-06. *Dir* V F Ovchinikov
Collections: 16,000 items of artistic interest

M **UKRAINIAN MUSEUM OF FOLK AND DECORATIVE ART,** Ul Yanvarskogo Vosstaniya 21, Ukrainian. *Dir* V G Nagai
Collections: Wood carvings, ceramics, weaving & applied arts from 16th century to present

ODESSA

M **ODESSA MUSEUM OF WESTERN AND EASTERN ART,** Ul Pushkinshaya 9, Ukrainian 270026. Tel 22-48-15. *Dir* N G Lutzkevich
Collections: Over 8000 art objects

URUGUAY

MONTEVIDEO

M **MUSEO MUNICIPAL DE BELLAS ARTES,** Avda Millan 4015. Tel 38-54-20. *Dir* Mario C Tempone
Collections: Paintings, sculptures, drawings, wood-carvings

M **MUSEO NACIONAL DE BELLAS ARTES,** National Museum of Fine Arts, Tomas Giribaldi 2283, Parque Rodo. Tel 438-00. *Dir* Angel Kalenberg
Collections: 4217 ceramics, drawings, engravings, paintings & sculptures

VENEZUELA

CARACAS

M **GALERIA DE ARTE NACIONAL,** Plaza Morelos-Los Caobos, Apartado 6729, 1010. Tel 571-3519. *Dir* Rafael Romero Diaz
Collections: Visual arts of Venezuela throughout history

M **MUSEO DE BELLAS ARTES,** Museum of Fine Arts, Plaza Morelos, Los Caobos, 105. Tel 571-01-69. *Dir* Maria Elena Ramos
Collections: Latin American & foreign paintings & sculpture

VIETNAM

HANOI

M **NATIONAL ART GALLERY,** 66 Nguyen Thai Hoc St. Tel 233084. *Dir* Nguyen Van Chung
Collections: Ancient & modern ceramics, fine arts & handicrafts; Vietnamese cultural heritage; specialized library of over 1100 volumes

YUGOSLAVIA

BELGRADE

M **MUSEUM OF CONTEMPORARY ART,** Usce Save bb, 11071. Tel 011-145-900. *Dir* Zoran Gavric
Collections: Yugoslav & foreign art

ZAIRE

KINSHASA

M **INSTITUT DES MUSEES NATIONAUX DU ZAIRE,** BP 4249, 2. Tel 59536. *Pres* Del-Gen Lema Gwete
Collections: Art, archaeology, traditional music & contemporary art

ZIMBABWE

CAUSEWAY HARARE

M **NATIONAL GALLERY OF ZIMBABWE,** 20 Julius Nyerere Way, PO Box CY 848. Tel 04666. *Dir* George P Kahari
Collections: African traditional & local contemporary sculpture & paintings; ancient & modern European paintings & sculpture, including works by Bellini, Caracciolo, Gainsborough, Murillo, Reynolds, Rodin

Major Art Schools Abroad

ARGENTINA

BUENOS AIRES

ESCUELA SUPERIOR DE BELLAS ARTES DE LA NACION ERNESTO DE LA CARCOVA, Tristan Aehaval Rodriguez 1701, 1107. Tel 31-5144. *Rector Prof* Eduardo A Audivert

AUSTRALIA

CANBERRA

ROYAL AUSTRALIAN INSTITUTE OF ARCHITECTS, 2A Mugga Way, ACT 2603. Telex 6-2428; Tel (062) 73-1548. *Dir* Chris Peters

DARLINGHURST

SCHOOL OF ART AND DESIGN (Formerly Sydney Institute of Technology), Forbes St, NSW 2010. Tel 339-0266. *Head* Ted Binder

GLEBE

SYDNEY COLLEGE OF THE ARTS, 266 Glebe Point Rd, PO Box 226, New South 2037. Tel (2) 9351-1000. *Dir* R Dunn

HOBART

UNIVERSITY OF TASMANIA, Tasmanian School of Art, GPO Box 252C, Tasmania 7001. Tel (002) 202101. *Dean* R H Ewins

MELBOURNE

VICTORIAN COLLEGE OF THE ARTS, School of Art, 234 St Kilda Rd, Victoria 3004. Tel (03) 616-9300. *Dir* Dr Alwynne Mackie

SYDNEY

UNIVERSITY OF SYDNEY, Dept of Archaeology, NSW 2006. Telex 20056; Tel 02-692-2222. *Chancellor* Dame Leonie Kramer

AUSTRIA

SALZBURG

INTERNATIONALE SOMMERAKADEMIE FUR BILDENDE KUNST, International Summer Academy of Fine Arts, PO Box 18, 5010. Tel 84-21-13, 84-37-27. *Pres* Dr Wieland Schmied

VIENNA

HOCHSCHULE FUR ANGEWANDTE KUNST IN WIEN, University of Applied Arts in Vienna, Oskar Kokoschkaplatz 2, 71010. Tel (01) 71133. *Rector* Oswald Oberhuber

BELGIUM

ANTWERP

NATIONAAL HOGER INSTITUUT EN KONINKLIJKE ACADEMIE VOOR SCHONE KUNSTEN, National Higher Institute and Royal Academy of Fine Arts, 31 Mutsaertstraat, 2000. Tel 03-232-41-61. *Dir* Garard Gaudaen

NATIONAAL HOGER INSTITUUT VAN HET RIJK, National Higher Institute of Architecture of the State, Mutsaertstraat 31, 2000. Tel 31-70-84. *Dir* W Toubhans

BRUSSELS

ACADEMIE ROYALE DES BEAUX-ARTS DE BRUXELLES, Brussels Royal Academy of Fine Arts, 144 rue du Midi, B-1000. Tel 02-511-04-91. *Dir* D Vienne

ECOLE NATIONALE SUPERIEURE DES ARTS VISUELS DE LA CAMBRE, 21 Abbaye de la Cambre, 1050. Tel 02-648-96-19. *Dir* France Borel

BRAZIL

RIO DE JANEIRO

ESCOLA DE ARTES VISUAIS, School of Visual Arts, 414 Rua Jardim Botanico, Parque Lage, 22461. *Dir* Joao Carlos Goldberg

BULGARIA

SOFIA

NIKOLAJ PAVLOVIC HIGHER INSTITUTE OF FINE ARTS, National Academy of Arts, Shipka 1, 1000. Tel 88-17-01. *Rector Prof* O Shoshev

CHINA, REPUBLIC OF

TAIPEI

NATIONAL TAIWAN ACADEMY OF ARTS, Pan-chiao Park, 22055. Tel 967-6414. *Pres* S L Ling

COLOMBIA

BOGOTA

PONTIFICIA UNIVERSIDAD JAVERIANA, Carrera 7, No 40-76, Apdo Aereo 56710. Tel 287-57-91. *Dean Faculty of Architecture* Rafael Uribe

CROATIA

ZAGREB

AKADEMIJA IIKOVNIJ UMJETNOSTI, Academy of Fine Arts, 85 Ilica, 41000. Tel (1) 177300. *Dir* Dubrkr Brbez

CZECH REPUBLIC

PRAGUE

AKADEMIE VYTVARNYCH UMENI, Academy of Fine Arts, U Akademie 4, Prague 7, 17022. Tel 37-36-41. *Rector* Milan Knizak

VYSOKA SKOLA UMELECKOPRUMYSLOVA, Academy of Applied Arts, Nam Jana Palacha 80, 116 93. Tel 2481-1172. *Rector* Dr Josef Hlavcek

DENMARK

AARHUS C

ARKITEKTSKOLEN I AARHUS, Aarhus School of Architecture, Norreport 20, 8000. Tel 89-36-00-00. *Rector* Gosta Knudsen

COPENHAGEN

KONGELIGE DANSKE KUNSTAKADEMI, The Royal Danish Academy of Fine Arts, Charlottenborg, Kongens Nytorv 1, 1050. Tel 33-12-68-60. *Rector School of Fine Arts* Else Marie Bukdahl

DOMINICAN REPUBLIC

SANTO DOMINGO

DIRECCION GENERAL DE BELLAS ARTES, Fine Arts Council, *Dir* Jose Delmonte Peguero

ENGLAND

BIRMINGHAM

BIRMINGHAM POLYTECHNIC, Faculty of Art & Design, Perry Barr, B42 7DX. Tel (021) 331-5886. *Dean Art & Design* J E C Price

BRIGHTON

BRIGHTON POLYTECHNIC, Faculty of Art & Design, Grand Parade, BN2 2JY. Tel (0273) 604-141. *Dean Art, Design & Humanities* D Brown

EXETER

EXETER COLLEGE OF ART & DESIGN, Earl Richards Rd N, EX2 6AS. Tel (392) 77977. *Head* Prof M Newby

FARNHAM

WEST SURREY COLLEGE OF ART & DESIGN, Falkner Rd, Surrey, GU9 7DS. Tel 0252-722441. *Dir* N J Taylor

GLOUCESTER

GLOUCESTERSHIRE COLLEGE OF ARTS & TECHNOLOGY, Brunswick Rd, GL1 1HS. 1452-42-66-50.

IPSWICH

SUFFOLK COLLEGE OF HIGHER & FURTHER EDUCATION, Department of Art & Design, Rope Walk, IP4 1LT. Tel 0473-255885. *Head* J Roger Lowe

LEICESTER

DEMONTSORT UNIVERSITY, Faculty of Art and Design, The Gateway, LE1 9BH. Tel (0533) 551551. *Dean Art & Design* N Witts

LIVERPOOL

LIVERPOOL JOHN MOORES UNIVERSITY, Aldham Robarts Learning Resource Centre, Mount Pleasant, L3 5UX. Tel (051) 231 21 21.

LONDON

CAMBERWELL COLLEGE OF ARTS, Peckham Rd, SE5 8UF. Tel (071) 514-6300. *Head Prof* Roger Breakwell

CHELSEA COLLEGE OF ART & DESIGN, Manresa Rd, SW3 6LS. Tel (0171) 514 7750. *Principal* Bridget Jackson

CITY AND GUILDS OF LONDON ART SCHOOL, 124 Kennington Park Rd, SE11 4DJ. Tel 071-735 2306, 5210. *Principal* Michael Kenny

LONDON INSTITUTE, Lethaby Gallery, Central Saint Martins College of Art & Design, London Institute Gallery, 65 Davies St, W1Y 2DA. Tel (071) 514 6000. *Rector* John McKenzie

ROYAL ACADEMY SCHOOLS, Burlington House, Piccadilly, W1V ODS. Tel 01-734-9052, Sch Ext 40. *Keeper Prof* Leonord McComd

ROYAL COLLEGE OF ART, Kensington Gore, SW7 2EU. Tel (071) 584-5020. *Rector Prof* Anthony Jones

SAINT MARTIN'S SCHOOL OF ART, 107 Charing Cross Rd, WC2H 0DU. Tel 437-0611; 7539090. *Principal* Ian Simpson

SLADE SCHOOL OF FINE ART, University College, Gower St, WC1. Tel (071) 387-7050. *Dir* Bernard Cohen

UNIVERSITY OF LONDON, Goldsmiths' College, Lewisham Way, New Cross, SE14 6NW. Tel 081-692-7171. *Warden* Prof Kenneth Gregory

WIMBLEDON SCHOOL OF ART, Merton Hall Rd, SW19 3QA. Tel 181-540-0231. *Prin* Colin Painter
—**Dept of Foundation Studies,** Palmerston Rd, SW19 1PB. Tel 181-540-0231; Student Tel 181-540-7504. *Dept Head* Yvonne Crossley
—**Dept of Theatre,** SW19 3QA. Tel 181-540-0231. *Dept Head* Malcolm Pride
—**Dept of Fine Arts,** SW19 3QA. Tel 181-540-0231. *Dept Head* Michael Ginsborg
—**Department of History of Art & Contextual Studies,** SW19 3QA. Tel 181-540-0231. *Dept Head* Dr Melissa McQuillan

MANCHESTER

MANCHESTER METROPOLITAN UNIVERSITY, Faculty of Art and Design, All Saints Bldg, Grosvenor Square, M15 6BH. Tel (061) 247-2000. *Dean Art & Design* R Wilson

NOTTINGHAM

NOTTINGHAM TRENT UNIVERSARY, School of Art and Design, Burton St, NG1 4BU. Telex 37-7534; Tel (0602) 941-8418. *Dean* J P Lesquereux

OXFORD

UNIVERSITY OF OXFORD, Ruskin School of Drawing and Fine Art, 74 High St, OX1 4BG. Tel 08-65-27-69-40. *Principal* Stephen Farthing

ESTONIA

TALLINN

TALLINN ART UNIVERSITY, Tartu Maantee 1, 0001. Tel 43-26-64. *Rector* J Kangilaski

FINLAND

HELSINKI

KUVATAIDEAKATEMIA, Academy of Fine Arts, Yrjonkatu 18, 00120. Tel 358-(9)0-680 3320. *Rector* Outi Heiskanen

FRANCE

PARIS

ECOLE DU LOUVRE, School of the Louvre, 34 quai du Louvre, 75001. Tel 40-20-56-14. *Principal* D Ponnau

ECOLE NATIONALE SUPERIEURE DES ARTS DECORATIFS, National College of Decorative Arts, 31 rue d'Ulm, 75005. Tel 43-29-86-79. *Dir* Richard Peduzzi

ECOLE NATIONALE SUPERIEURE DES BEAUX-ARTS, National College of Fine Arts, 14 rue Bonaparte, Cedex 06, 75272. Tel (1)47-03-50-00. *Dir* Y Michaud

ECOLE SPECIALE D'ARCHITECTURE, 254 blvd Raspail, 75014. Tel 40-47-40-47. *Dir* Michel Denes

UNIVERSITE DE PARIS I, PANTHEON-SORBONNE, UFR d'Art et d'Archeologie, 12 Place du Pantheon, 75231. Tel 1-46-34-97-00. *Actg Dir Art & Archaeology* L Pressouyre

VILLENEUVE D'ASCQ

ECOLE D'ARCHITECTURE DE LILLE ET DES REGIONS NORD, rue Verte, Quartier de l'Hotel de Ville, 59650. Tel 20 91 26 41. *Dir* Regis Lecterq

GERMANY

BERLIN

HOCHSCHULE DER KUNSTE BERLIN, 10 Ernst-Reuter-Platz 10, Postfac 126720, 1000. Tel 030-31-85-0. *Pres* Dr Olaf Schwencke

BRUNSWICK

HOCHSCHULE FUR BILDENDE KUNSTE, Johannes-Selenka-Platz 1, 38188. Tel 391-9122. *Rector* Dr Dieter Welzel

DRESDEN

HOCHSCHULE FUR BILDENE KUNSTE, Guntzstrasse 34, 01307. Tel (351) 4402-0. *Rector* Ingo Sandner

DUSSELDORF

STAATLICHE KUNSTAKADEMIE DUSSELDORF, Hochschule fur Bildende Kunste, State Academy of Art, Eiskellerstrasse 1, 4000. Tel (0211) 1396-0. *Dir* Markus Lupertz

FRANKFURT

STAEDELSCHULE, STAATLICHE HOCHSCHULE FUR BILDENE KUENSTE DUERERSTR, Schoene Aussicht 2, 60311. Tel 069-605-008-0. *Rector* *Prof* Kasper Koenig

HAMBURG

HOCHSCHULE FUR BILDENDE KUNSTE, College of Fine Arts, Lerchenfeld 2, 2000. Tel 040-29188. *Pres* Adrienne Goehler

KARLSRUHE

STAATLICHE AKADEMIE DER BILDENDEN KUNSTE, State Academy of Fine Arts, Reinhold-Frank-Strasse 81-83, 7500. Tel 0721-85018-0. *Rector* Dr Andreas Franzke

LEIPZIG

HOCHSCHULE FUR GRAFIK UND BUCHKUNST, State Academy of Graphic Arts and Book Production, Wachterstrasse 11, 04107. Tel 21 35 155. *Rector* Albrecht von Bodecker

MUNICH

AKADEMIE DER BILDENDEN KUNSTE, Academy of Fine Arts, Akademiestr 2, 80799. Tel 089-3852-0. *Pres* Dr Otto Steidle

NUREMBERG

AKADEMIE DER BILDENDEN KUNSTE IN NURNBERG, Academy of Fine Arts in Nuremberg, Bingstrasse 60, 90480. Tel 0911-94040. *Pres* Dr Rainer Beck

STUTTGART

STAATLICHE AKADEMIE DER BILDENDEN KUNSTE, State Academy of Fine Arts, Am Weissenhof 1, 7000. Tel 0711-2575-0. *Rector* Dr Paul Uwe Dreyer

GREECE

ATHENS

ECOLE FRANCAISE D'ATHENES, French Archeological School, 6 Ave Didotou, 16080. Tel 01-3612518. *Dir* R Etienne

HUNGARY

BUDAPEST

MAGYAR KEPZOMUVESZETI FOISKOLA, Hungarian Academy of Fine Arts, Andrassy vt 69-71, 1062. Tel 3421-738. *Rector* Szabados Arpad

INDIA

BARODA

MAHARAJA SAYAJIRAO UNIVERSITY OF BARODA, Faculty of Fine Arts, University Rd, Gujarat 390002. Tel 64721. *Dean Faculty Fine Arts* S G Kantawala

BOMBAY

ACADEMY OF ARCHITECTURE, Plot 278, Shankar Ghaneker Marg, Prabhadevi, 400025. *Principal* P P Amberkar

LUCKNOW

UNIVERSITY OF LUCKNOW, College of Arts and Crafts, Faculty of Fine Arts, Badshah Bagh, 226007. Tel 43138. *Dean* B N Arya

MYSORE

SRI VARALAKSHMI ACADEMIES OF FINE ARTS, Chamaraja Double Rd, Ramvilas, Kasphipathy Agarahar, 4. *Principal* C V Srivatsa

IRELAND

CO CLARE

BURREN COLLEGE OF ART, Newton Castle, Ballyvaughan. Tel 353-65-77200. *Pres* Eugene C Wicks; *Provost* Mary Hawkes-Greene

DUBLIN

COLAISTE NAISIUNTA EALAINE IS DEARTHA, National College of Art & Design, 100 Thomas St, 8. Tel 01-6711377. *Dir* Noel Sheridan

ISRAEL

JERUSALEM

BEZALEL ACADEMY OF ARTS & DESIGN, Mount Scopus, PO Box 24046, 91240. Tel 02-89-33-33. *Dir* Ran Sapoznik

ITALY

BOLOGNA

ACCADEMIA DI BELLE ARTI, Academy of Fine Arts, via Belle Arti 54, 40126. Tel 051-243 064. *Dir* A Baccilieri

FLORENCE

ACCADEMIA DI BELLE ARTI, Academy of Fine Arts, via Ricasoli 66, 50122. Tel 055-215-449. *Dir* D Viggiano

MILAN

ACCADEMIA DI BELLE ARTI, Academy of Fine Arts, Palazzo di Brera, via Brera 28, 20121. Tel 02-86-46-19-29. *Pres* Walter Fontana

NAPLES

ACCADEMIA DI BELLE ARTI E LICEO ARTISTICO, Academy of Fine Arts, via Bellini 36, 80135. *Dir* Constanza Lorenzetti

PERUGIA

ACCADEMIA DI BELLE ARTI, Academy of Fine Arts, Piazza San Francesco al Prato 5, 06123. Tel 075-5730631. *Dir* Edgardo Abbozzo

RAVENNA

ACCADEMIA DI BELLE ARTI, Academy of Fine Arts, Loggetta Lombardesca, Via di Roma 13, 48100. Tel 213641. *Dir* Vittorio D'Augusta

ROME

ACCADEMIA DI BELLE ARTI, Academy of Fine Arts, via di Ripetta 222, 00186. Tel 06-322-70-25. *Dir* Guido Strazza

AMERICAN ACADEMY IN ROME, Via Angelo Masina 5, 00153. Tel 06-58461. *Dir* Cardine Bruzelius

BRITISH SCHOOL AT ROME, Piazzale Winston Churchill 5, 00197. Tel 06-32-30-743. *Dir* R A Hodges

ISTITUTO CENTRALE DEL RESTAURO, Central Institute for the Restoration of Works of Art, Piazza San Francesco di Paola 9, 00184. Tel 48-27-142-5. *Dir* Dott M d'Elia

TURIN

ACCADEMIA ALBERTINA DI BELLE ARTI, via Accademia Albertina 6, 10123. Tel 011-889020. *Pres* P Delle Roncole

VENICE

ACCADEMIA DI BELLE ARTI, Academy of Fine Arts, Campo della Carita 1050, 30123. Tel 041-5225396. *Dir* Nedo Fiorentin

JAMAICA

KINGSTON

EDNA MANLEY COLLEGE OF VISUAL & PERFORMING ARTS (Formerly Edna Manley School for the Visual Arts), Cultural Training Center, One Arthur Wint Dr, Kingston 5. Tel 809-929-2352. *Libr Asst* Pamela James

JAPAN

KANAZAWA CITY

KANAZAWA COLLEGE OF ART, 5-11-1 Kodatsuno, Kanazawa-shi, Ishikawa 920, 920. Tel (0762) 62-3531. *Pres* Fujio Kitade

KYOTO

KYOTO CITY UNIVERSITY OF ARTS, 13-6 Kutsukake-Cho, Oheda, Nishikyo-Ku, 610-11. Tel 075-332-0701. *Pres* Shumpei Ueyama

TOKYO

TAMA BIJUTSU DAIGATU, Tama Art University, 3-15-34 Kaminoge, Setagaya-Ku, 158. Tel (03) 3702-1141. *Pres* K Goto

TOKYO GRIJUTSO DAIGAKU, Tokyo National University of Fine Arts & Music, 12-8 Ueno Park, Taito-Ku, 110. Tel 3828-7745. *Pres* Masao Yamamoto

KOREA, REPUBLIC OF

SEOUL

SEOUL NATIONAL UNIVERSITY, College of Fine Arts, Sinlim-dong, Kwanak-gu, 151. Tel 877-1601. *Dean* Se-ok Suh

LATVIA

RIGA

VALST MAKSLAS AKADEMIJA, Latvian Academy of Arts, Kalpaka blvd 13, 1867. Tel 33-22-02. *Rector* Indulis Zarins

LEBANON

BEIRUT

ACADEMIE LIBANAISE DES BEAUX-ARTS, PO Box 55251, Sin-El-Fil. Tel 480-056. *Chair* Georges Khodr

MEXICO

MEXICO CITY

ESCUELA NACIONAL DE ARTES PLASTICAS, National School of Plastic Arts, Ave Constitution 600, BO La Concha, Xochimilco, DF. Tel 52-5-06-30. *Dir* Jose De Santiago
Courses: Engraving

INSTITUTO NACIONAL DE BELLAS ARTES, Avda Juarez 1. Tel 585-4888. *Dir* Vicgor Sandoval de Leon

PUEBLA

UNIVERSIDAD DE LAS AMERICAS, Artes Graficas y Diseno, Apartado Postal 100, Santa Catarina Martir, 72820. Tel 29 20 00. *Rector* Dr Enrique Cardenas

MOROCCO

TETOUAN

ECOLE NATIONALE DES BEAUX ARTS, Ave Mohamed V, Cite Scolaire BP 89. *Dir* Mohammed M Serghini

NETHERLANDS

AMSTERDAM

ACADEMIE VAN BOUWKUNST, Academy of Architecture, Waterlooplein 211, 1011 PG. Tel 020-622-0188. *Dir* N Stam

RIJKSAKADEMIE VAN BEELDENDE KUNSTEN, State Academy of Fine Arts, Stadhouderskade 86, 1073 AT. Tel 020-679-7811. *Dir* J Schrofer

BREDA

ACADEMIE VOOR BEELDENDE KUNSTEN ST JOOST, St Joost Academy of Art and Design, 18 St Janstraat, 4811 ZM. Tel (31) 76250500. *Dir* M J M Regouin

GRONINGEN

AKADEMIE VOOR BEELDENDE KUNSTEN BOUWKUNST AKADEMIE MINERVA, School of Visual Arts and Architecture. Gedempte Zuiderdiep 158, 9711 HN. Tel 18-54-54. *Dir* A van Hijum

THE HAGUE

KONINKLIJKE ACADEMIE VAN BEELDENDE KUNSTEN, Royal Academy of Fine and Applied Arts, Prinsessegracht 4, 2514 AN. Tel 070-364-3835. *Dir* C M Rehorst

STICHTING DE VRIJE ACADEMIE VOOR BEELDENDE KUNSTEN, De Gheijnstraat 129, PO Box 61390, 2506 AJ. Tel 63-89-68. *Dir* Frans A M Zwartjes

HERTOGENBOSCH

AKADEMIE VOOR KUNST EN VORMGEVING, Academy of Art and Design, PO Box 91, 5201 AB. Tel 29-54-60. *Dir* L R Waale

ROTTERDAM

ACADEMIE VAN BEELDENDE KUNSTEN ROTTERDAM, Rotterdam Academy of Art, Blaak 10, 3011 TA. Tel 010-411-2853. *Pres* A C M Van Gemert

NEW ZEALAND

AUCKLAND

UNIVERSITY OF AUCKLAND, Elam School of Fine Arts, Whitaker Pl, Private Bag 92019, 1. Tel 737-999. *Dean* M R Dunn

NORWAY

OSLO

STATENS HANDVERKS-OG KUNSTINDUSTRISKOLE, National College of Art, Crafts and Design, Ullevalsveien 5, 0165. Tel 02-201-235. *Rector* Roar Hoyland

STATENS KUNSTAKADEMI, National Academy of Fine Art, St Olavs Gate 32, 0166. Tel 02-20-01-50. *Rector* Jan Ake Petterson

PERU

LIMA

ESCUELA NACIONAL SUPERIOR DE BELLAS ARTES, National School of Fine Arts, 681 Jiron Ancash. *Dir* Juan Manuel Ugarte Elespupu

POLAND

CRACOW

AKADEMIA SZTUK PIEKNYCH IM JANA MATEJKI W KRAKOWIE, Academy of Fine Arts in Cracow, Pl Matekji 13, 31-157. Tel 22-24-50. *Rector* Wlodzimierz Kunz

GDANSK

PANSTWOWA WYZSZA SZKOLA SZTUK PLASTYCZNYCH, Higher School of Fine Arts, Ul Targ Weglowy 6, 80-836. Tel 31-28-01. *Rector* Stanislaw Radwanski

LODZ

PANSTWOWA WYZSZA SZKOLA SZTUK PLASTYCZNYCH, Higher School of Applied Arts. Ul Wojska Polskiego 121, 91-726. Tel 56-97-56. *Rector* Jerzy Trelinski

WARSAW

AKADEMIA SZTUK PIEKNYCH, Academy of Fine Arts, Ul Krakowskie Przedmiescie 5, 00-068. Tel 26-19-72. *Rector* Adam Myjak

WROCLAW

PANSTWOWA WYZSZA SZKOLA SZTUK PLASTYCZYNCH, Higher School of Fine Arts, Pl Polski 3/4, 50-156. Tel 315-58. *Rector* Konrad Jarodzki

PORTUGAL

LISBON

ESCOLA SUPERIOR DE BELAS ARTES, School of Fine Arts, Largo da Academia Nacional de Belas-Artes, 1200. Tel 36-81-74. *Pres* Augusto Pereira Brandao

OPORTO

ESCOLA SUPERIOR DE BELAS ARTES, School of Fine Arts, Av Rodrigues de Freitas 265. Tel 228-77. *Dir* Carlos Ramos

RUSSIA

MOSCOW

MOSCOW V I SURIKOV STATE ART INSTITUTE (Formerly V I Surikov State Art Institute), 30 Tovarishcheskii Pereulok, 109004. Tel (095)912-39-32. *Dir* L V Shepelev

SAINT PETERSBURG

ST PETERSBURG REPIN INSTITUTE OF PAINTING, SCULPTURE AND ARCHITECTURE, Universitetskaya Nab 17, 199034. Tel 213-61-89. *Rector* O A Yeremeyev

SCOTLAND

DUNDEE

UNIVERSITY OF DUNDEE (Formerly Duncan of Jordanstone College of Art), Faculty of Duncan of Jordanstone College, 13 Perth Rd, DD1 4HN. Tel 1382-223181. *Principal* Dr Ian J Graham-Bryce

EDINBURGH

EDINBURGH COLLEGE OF ART, Lauriston Pl, EH3 9DF. Tel 031-221 6000. *Principal* Alistair Rowan

GLASGOW

GLASGOW SCHOOL OF ART, 167 Renfrew St, G3 6RQ. Tel 041-353-4500. *Dir* Dr J Whiteman

SLOVAK, REPUBLIC OF

BRATISLAVA

VYSOKA SKOLA VYTVARNYCH UMENI, Academy of Fine Arts, Hviezdoslavovo 18, 814 37. Tel 332-431. *Rector* Stefan Slachta

SOUTH AFRICA, REPUBLIC OF

CAPE TOWN

UNIVERSITY OF CAPE TOWN, Michaelis School of Fine Art, 31 Orange St, Private Bag, Rondebosch 7700. Tel 650911. *Dean* J W Rabie

JOHANNESBURG

TECHNIKON WITWATERSRAND, School of Art and Design, PO Box 3293, 2000. Tel 011-406-2381. *Chmn Art* P J Coetzee

SPAIN

BARCELONA

REAL ACADEMIA CATALANA DE BELLAS ARTES DE SAN JORGE, Royal Academy of Fine Arts, Casa Lonja, Paseo de Isabel II, 08003. Tel 319-24-32. *Pres* Joan Bassegoda Nonell

MADRID

CENTRO DE ESTUDIOS HISTORICOS, Departamento de Historia del Arte Diego Velazquez, CSIC, Duque de Medinaceli 4, 28014. Tel 429-20-17. *Chief of Dept* Enrique Arias Angles

SEVILLE

REAL ACADEMIA DE BELLAS ARTES DE SANTA ISABEL DE HUNGRIA DE SEVILLE, Abades 14, 41004. Tel 22-11-98. *Pres* Antona dela Banda y Vargas

VALENCIA

ESCUELA SUPERIOR DE BELLAS ARTES DE SAN CARLOS, Valencia School of Fine Arts, Calle del Museo 2. *Dir* Daniel de Nueda Llisiona

SWEDEN

STOCKHOLM

KONSTFACK, University College of Arts, Crafts and Design, Valhallavagan 191, PO Box 24115, 104 51. Tel 08-450-41-00. *Principal* Inez Svensson

KONSTHOGSKOLAN, College of Fine Arts, Fredsgatan 12, PO Box 16 315, 103 26. Tel 08-24-63-00. *Principal* Olle Kaks

SWITZERLAND

GENEVA

ECOLES D'ART DE GENEVE, Geneva Schools of Art, 9 blvd Helvetique, 1205. Tel 22-311-05-10. *Dir* Bernard Zumthor
—**Ecole Superieure D'Art Visuel,** Higher School of Visual Arts, 9 blvd Helvetique. Tel 22-311-05-10. *Dir* Bernard Zumthor
—**Ecole des Arts Decoratifs,** School of Decorative Arts, rue Jacques-Necker 2, Switzerland 1201. Tel 22-732-04-39. *Dir* Roger Fallet

LAUSANNE

ECOLE CANTONALE D'ART DE LAUSANNE, Lausanne College of Art, Ave de l'Elysee 4, 1006. Tel 021-617-75-23. *Dir* P Keller

VENEZUELA

CARACAS

ESCUELA DE ARTES VISUALES CRISTOBAL ROJAS, Cristobal Rojas School of Visual Arts, Avda Lecund-Este 10 bis, El Conde. *Dir* Carmen Julia Negron de Valery

State Arts Councils

NATIONAL ENDOWMENT FOR THE ARTS

Jane Alexander, Chmn
1100 Pennsylvania Ave NW
Washington, DC 20506-0001
Tel 202-682-5400

REGIONAL ORGANIZATIONS

Arts Midwest

David Fraher, Exec Dir
528 Hennepin Ave, Ste 310
Minneapolis, MN 55403-1899
Tel 612-341-0755; Fax 612-341-0902
TDD 612-341-0901
(IA, IL, IN, MI, MN, OH, ND, SD, WI)

Mid-America Arts Alliance/ExhibitsUSA

Henry Moran, Exec Dir
912 Baltimore Ave, Ste 700
Kansas City, MO 64105
Tel 816-421-1388; Fax 816-421-3918
(AR, KS, MO, NE, OK, TX)

Mid-Atlantic Arts Foundation

Alan Cooper, Exec Dir
11 E Chase St, Ste 2A
Baltimore, MD 21202
Tel 410-539-6656; Fax 410-837-5517
(DC, DE, MD, NJ, NY, PA, VA, VI, WV)

New England Foundation for the Arts

Sam Miller, Exec Dir
330 Congress St, 6th Flr
Boston, MA 02210
Tel 617-951-0010; Fax 617-951-0016
(CT, MA, ME, NH, RI, VT)

Southern Arts Federation

Jeffrey A Kesper, Exec Dir
181 14th St NE, Ste 400
Atlanta, GA 30309
Tel 404-874-7244; Fax 404-873-2148
(AL, FL, GA, KY, LA, MS, NC, SC, TN)

Western States Arts Federation

Donald A Mayer, Exec Dir
236 Montezuma Ave
Santa Fe, NM 87501-2641
Tel 505-988-1166
(AK, AZ, CA, CO, HI, ID, MT, NV, NM, OR, UT, WA, WY)

STATE ART AGENCIES

Alabama State Council on the Arts

Philip Sellers, Chmn
One Dexter Ave
Montgomery, AL 36130-1800
Tel 334-242-4076; Fax 334-240-3269

Albert B Head, Exec Dir
201 Monroe St
Montgomery, AL 36130-1800
Tel 334-242-4076; Fax 334-240-3269

Alaska State Council on the Arts

Bonnie Bernholz, Chmn
411 W Fourth Ave, Ste 1E
Anchorage, AK 99501-2343
Tel 907-269-6610; Fax 907-269-6601

Timothy Wilson, Exec Dir
411 W Fourth Ave, Ste 1E
Anchorage, AK 99501-2343
Tel 907-269-6610; Fax 907-269-6601

Arizona Commission on the Arts

Gerry Murphy, Chmn
417 W Roosevelt St
Phoenix, AZ 85003
Tel 602-255-5882; Fax 602-256-0282

Shelley M Cohn, Exec Dir
417 W Roosevelt Ave
Phoenix, AZ 85003
Tel 602-255-5882; Fax 602-256-0282

Arkansas Arts Council

Dr John Dahlquist
Lyon College
Batesville, AR 72501
Tel 501-698-4397; Fax 501-698-4622

Sally A Williams, Artist Servs Coordr
1500 Tower Bldg
323 Center St
Little Rock, AR 72201
Tel 501-324-9348; Fax 501-324-9154
WWW:http://www.heritage.state.ar.us

California Arts Council

Thomas R Hall, Chmn
1300 I St, Ste 930
Sacramento, CA 95814
Tel 916-322-6555; Fax 916-322-6575
E-mail: cac@cwo.com
WWW:http//www.cac.ca.gov

Gay Carroll, Pub Info Officer
1300 I St, Ste 930
Sacramento, CA 95814
Tel 916-322-6555; Fax 916-322-6575
E-mail cac@cwo.com
WWW: http://www.cac.ca.gov

Colorado Council on the Arts

Karen Reinertson, Chmn
1301 Pennsylvania St, Ste 900
Denver, CO 80203-3699
Tel 303-860-1616; Fax 303-860-0175

Fran Holden, Exec Dir
750 Pennsylvania St
Denver, CO 80203-3699
Tel 303-894-2617; Fax 303-894-2615

Connecticut Commission on the Arts

Michael Price, Chmn
One Financial Plaza,755 Main St
Hartford, CT 06103
Tel 860-566-4770; Fax 860-566-6462

John E Ostrout, Exec Dir
One Financial Plaza, 755 Main St
Hartford, CT 06103
Tel 860-566-4770; Fax 860-566-6462

Delaware Division of the Arts

Peggy Amsterdam, Dir
820 N French St
Wilmington, DE 19801
Tel 302-577-3540; Fax 302-577-6561

DC Commission on the Arts and Humanities

Anthony Gittens, Exec Dir
410 Eighth St NW, 5th Flr
Washington, DC 20004
Tel 202-724-5613; Fax 202-727-4135

Florida Arts Council

Paul Stavros, Chmn
Dept of State, Div of Cultural Affairs
Florida Arts Council , The Capitol
Tallahassee, FL 32399-0250
Tel 904-487-2980; Fax 904-922-5259

Peyton Fearington (Ms.), Dir
Div of Cultural Affairs,
Florida Dept of State, The Capitol
Tallahassee, FL 32399-0250
Tel 904-487-2980; Fax 904-922-5259

Georgia Council for the Arts

Caroline Ballard Leake, Exec Dir
530 Means St NW, Ste 115
Atlanta, GA 30318-5793
Tel 404-651-7920; Fax 404-651-7922

Cary Cleaver, Dir of Communications
530 Means St NW, Ste 115
Atlanta, GA 30318-5793
Tel 404-651-7920; Fax 404-651-7922

Hawaii State Foundation on Culture and the Arts

John M Hara, Chmn
44 Merchant St
Honolulu, HI 96813
Tel 808-586-0300; Fax 808-586-0308

Ronald K Yamakawa, Interim Exec Dir
44 Merchant St
Honolulu, HI 96813
Tel 808-586-0300; Fax 808-586-0308

Idaho Commission on the Arts

Delores Fery, Chmn
199 N Capital Blvd, Ste 1000
Boise, ID 83702-5921
Tel 208-343-5581

Margot H Knight, Dir
PO Box 83720
Boise, ID 83702-0008
Tel 208-334-2119; Fax 208-334-2488

Illinois Arts Council

Shirley R Madigan, Chmn
100 W Randolph, Ste 10-500
Chicago, IL 60601-3298
Tel 312-814-6750; Fax 312-814-1471

Lori S Montana, Exec Dir
100 W Randolph St, Ste 10-500
Chicago, IL 60601-3298
Tel 312-814-6750; Fax 312-814-1471

Indiana Arts Commission

Cliff Lambert, Chmn
402 W Washington St, Room 072
Indianapolis, IN 46204
Tel 317-232-1268; Fax 317-232-5595

Dorothy Ilgen, Dir
402 W Washington St, Room 072
Indianapolis, IN 46204
Tel 317-232-1268; Fax 317-232-5595

Iowa Arts Council

Phyllis Otto (Ms.), Chmn
Capitol Complex, 600 E Locust
Des Moines, IA 50319-0290
Tel 515-281-4451; Fax 515-242-6498

William Jackson, Exec Dir
Capitol Complex, 600 E Locust
Des Moines, IA 50319-0290
Tel 515-281-4013;
Fax 515-242-6498

Kansas Arts Commission

Clark Balderson, Pres
700 Jackson, Ste 1004
Topeka, KS 66603-3852
Tel 913-296-3335

Eric Hayashi, Exec Dir
700 Jackson, Ste 1004
Topeka, KS 66603-3852
Tel 913-296-3355

Kentucky Arts Council

Gerri Combs (Ms.), Exec Dir
31 Fountain Pl
Frankfort, KY 40601
Tel 502-564-3757

Louisiana State Arts Council

Chmn
PO Box 44247
Baton Rouge, LA 70804
Tel 504-342-8180; Fax 504-343-8173

James Borders, Dir
Louisiana Division of the Arts
PO Box 44247
Baton Rouge, LA 70804
Tel 504-342-8180; Fax 504-342-8173

Maine Arts Commission

Alden C Wilson, Dir
25 SHS, 55 Capitol St
Augusta, ME 04333-0025
Tel 207-287-2724; Fax 207-287-2335

Maryland State Arts Council

Shirley Giarritta, Past Pres
55 N Centre St
Cumberland, MD 21502
Tel 301-777-9234; Fax 301-777-7092

James Backas, Exec Dir
601 N Howard St
Baltimore, MD 21201
Tel 410-333-8232; Fax 410-333-1062

Massachusetts Cultural Council

Peter Nessen, Chmn
120 Boylston St, 2nd Flr
Boston, MA 02116
Tel 617-727-3668

Mary Kelley, Exec Dir
120 Boylston St, 2nd Flr
Boston, MA 02116
Tel 617-727-3668

Michigan Council for Arts and Cultural Affairs

Judith Ann Rapanos, Chmn
1012 W Sugnet
Midland, MI 48640
Tel 517-631-2544; Fax 517-631-4235

Betty Boone, Dir
1200 Sixth St, Ste 1180
Detroit, MI 48226
Tel 313-256-3735

Minnesota State Arts Board

Conrad Razidlo, Chmn
Park Square Ct,
400 Sibley St, Ste 200
Saint Paul, MN 55101-1928
Tel 612-297-2603; Fax 612-297-4304

Robert Booker, Actg Exec Dir
Park Square Ct, 400 Sibley St, Ste 200
Saint Paul, MN 55101-1928
Tel 612-297-2603; Fax 612-297-4304

Mississippi Arts Commission

George Thatcher, Chmn
239 N Lamar St, Ste 207
Jackson, MS 39201
Tel 601-359-6030; Fax 601-359-6008

Missouri Arts Council

Thomas Irwin, Chmn
111 N Seventh St, Ste 105
Saint Louis, MO 63101-2188
Tel 314-340-6845; Fax 314-340-7215

Flora Maria Garcia, Exec Dir
111 N Seventh St, Ste 105
Saint Louis, MO 63101
Tel 314-340-6845; Fax 314-340-7215

Montana Arts Council

Arlynn Fishbaugh, Exec Dir
316 N Park Ave, Room 252
Helena, MT 59620
Tel 406-444-6430; Fax 406-444-6548

Nebraska Arts Council

Gail Yanney, Chmn
3838 Davenport St
Omaha, NE 68131-2329
Tel 402-595-2122

Nevada State Council on the Arts

Roger Thomas, Chmn
602 N Curry St
Carson City, NV 89710
Tel 702-687-6680; Fax 702-687-6688

Susan Boskoff, Exec Dir
602 N Curry St
Carson City, NV 89710
Tel 702-687-6680; Fax 702-687-6688

New Hampshire State Council on the Arts

Chris Dwyer, Chmn
Phoenix Hall
40 N Main St
Concord, NH 03301
Tel 603-271-2789; Fax 603-271-3584

New Jersey State Council on the Arts

Lilian Levy, Chmn
20 W State St, 3rd Flr, CN 306
Trenton, NJ 08625
Tel 609-292-6130; Fax 609-989-1440

Barbara F Russo, Exec Dir
20 W State St, 3rd Flr, CN 306
Trenton, NJ 08625
Tel 609-292-6130; Fax 609-989-1440

New Mexico Arts

John Garcia, Officer of Cultural Affairs
228 E Palace Ave
Santa Fe, NM 87501
Tel 505-827-6490; Fax 505-827-6043

Louis Leroy, Dir
228 E Palace Ave
Santa Fe, NM 87501
Tel 505-827-6490; Fax 505-827-6043

New York State Council on the Arts

Earle I Mack, Chmn
915 Broadway, 8th Flr
New York, NY 10010
Tel 212-387-7003; Fax 212-387-7164

Nicolette Clarke, Exec Dir
915 Broadway, 8th Fl
New York, NY 10010
Tel 212-387-7000; Fax 212-387-7164

North Carolina Arts Council

Margaret S Newman, Chmn
221 E Lane St
Raleigh, NC 27601
Tel 919-733-2821; Fax 919-733-4834

Mary Regan, Exec Dir
Dept of Cultural Resources
Raleigh, NC 27601-2807
Tel 919-733-2821; Fax 919-733-4834

North Dakota Council on the Arts

Patsy Thompson, Exec Dir
418 E Broadway, Ste 70
Bismarck, ND 58501-4086
Tel 701-328-3954; Fax 701-328-3963

Ohio Arts Council

Barbara Robinson, Chmn
727 E Main St
Columbus, OH 43205-1796
Tel 614-466-2613; Fax 614-466-4496

Wayne Lawson, Exec Dir
727 E Main St
Columbus, OH 43205-1796
Tel 614-466-2613, Fax 614-466-4496

Oklahoma Arts Council

Linda S Frazier, Chmn
2101 N Lincoln, Rm 640
PO Box 52001-2001
Oklahoma City, OK 73152-2001
Tel 405-521-2931; Fax 405-521-6418

Betty Price, Exec Dir
2101 N Lincoln, Rm 640
PO Box 52001-2001
Oklahoma City, OK 73152-2001
Tel 405-521-2931; Fax 405-521-6418

Oregon Arts Commission

Christine T D'Arcy, Exec Dir
775 Summer St NE
Salem, OR 97310
Tel 503-986-0087; Fax 503-986-0260

Pennsylvania Council on the Arts

Dr Oscar E Remick, Chmn
Finance Bldg, Rm 216
Harrisburg, PA 17120
Tel 717-787-6883

Philip Horn, Exec Dir
Finance Bldg, Rm 216
Harrisburg, PA 17120
Tel 717-787-6883

Rhode Island State Council on the Arts

Thomas J Reilly, Chmn
95 Cedar St, Ste 103
Providence, RI 02903
Tel 401-277-3880

Randall Rosenbaum, Exec Dir
95 Cedar St, Ste 103
Providence, RI 02903
Tel 401-277-3880

South Carolina Arts Commission

Pat Wilson, Chmn
1800 Gervais St
Columbia, SC 29201
Tel 803-734-8696; Fax 803-734-8526

Suzette M Surkamer, Exec Dir
1800 Gervais St
Columbia, SC 29201
Tel 803-734-8696; Fax 803-734-8526

South Dakota Arts Council

Dennis Holub, Exec Dir
800 Governors Dr
Pierre, SD 57501
Tel 605-773-3131; Fax 605-773-6962
E-mail sdac@stlib.state.sd.us

Tennessee Arts Commission

Grace Spurell, Chmn
401 Charlotte Ave
Nashville, TN 37243-0780
Tel 615-741-1701; Fax 615-741-8559

Bennett Tarleton, Exec Dir
401 Charlotte Ave
Nashville, TN 37243-0780
Tel 615-741-1701; Fax 615-741-8559

Texas Commission on the Arts

Connie Ware, Chmn
PO Box 13406-3406
Austin, TX 78711
Tel 512-463-5535; Fax 512-475-2699
E-mail: front.desk@arts.state.tx.us

John Paul Batiste, Exec Dir
PO Box 13406-3406
Austin, TX 78711
Tel 512-463-5535; Fax 512-475-2699
E-mail: front.desk@arts.state.tx.us

Utah Arts Council

Robert S Olpin, Chmn
617 E South Temple
Salt Lake City, UT 84102-1177
Tel 801-533-5895; Fax 801-533-6196

Bonnie H Stephens, Exec Dir
617 E South Temple
Salt Lake City, UT 84102-1177
Tel 801-533-5895; Fax 801-533-6196

Vermont Arts Council

Margaret Kannenstin, Chmn
136 State St, Drawer 33
Montpelier, VT 05633-6001
Tel 802-828-3291; Fax 802-828-3363

Alexander L Aldri, Exec Dir
136 State St, Drawer 33
Montpelier, VT 05633-6001
Tel 802-828-3291; Fax 802-828-3363

Virginia Commission on the Arts

Janet Davis, Chmn
Lewis House, 2nd Flr
223 Governor St
Richmond, VA 23219-2010
Tel 540-225-3132; Fax 540-225-4327

Peggy Baggett, Exec Dir
Lewis House, 2nd Flr
223 Governor St
Richmond, VA 23219-2010
Tel 540-225-3132; Fax 540-225-4327

Washington State Arts Commission

Rosemary Selinger, Chmn
234 E Eighth Ave, PO Box 42675
Olympia, WA 98504-2675
Tel 360-753-3860; Fax 360-586-5351

Karen Kamara Gose, Exec Dir
234 E Eighth Ave, PO Box 42675
Olympia, WA 98504-2675
Tel 360-753-3860; Fax 360-586-5351

West Virginia Commission on the Arts

Bill Davis, Chmn
Arts & Humanities Section
West Virginia Div of Culture & History
1900 Kanawha Blvd E
Charleston, WV 25305-0300
Tel 304-558-0220; Fax 304-558-2779

Lakin Ray Cook, Exec Dir
Arts & Humanities Section
West Virginia Div of Culture & History
1900 Kanawha Blvd E
Charleston, WV 25305-0300
Tel 304-558-0220; Fax 304-558-2779

Wisconsin Arts Board

Kathryn M Burke, Chmn
101 E Wilson St, First Flr
Madison, WI 53702
Tel 608-266-0190; Fax 414-352-2686

George Tsougros, Exec Dir
101 E Wilson St, First Flr
Madison, WI 53702
Tel 608-266-0190; Fax 608-267-0380

Wyoming Arts Council

John G Coe, Dir
2320 Capitol Ave
Cheyenne, WY 82002
Tel 307-777-7742; Fax 307-777-5499

Nancy Curtis, Chmn
2320 Capitol Ave
Cheyenne, WY 82002
Tel 307-777-7742; Fax 307-777-5499

American Samoa Council on Art, Culture and Humanities

Fagafaga D Langkilde, Chmn
Territory of American Samoa
PO Box 1540
Pago Pago, AS 96799
Tel 684-633-4347; Fax 684-633-2059

Faailoilo Lauvao, Exec Dir
Territory of American Samoa
PO Box 1540
Pago Pago, AS 96799
Tel 684-633-4347; Fax 684-633-2059

Guam Council on the Arts and Humanities Agency

Deborah J Bordallo, Exec Dir
PO Box 2950
Agana, GU 96932
Tel 671-475-2242; Fax 671-472-2781

Commonwealth Council for Arts and Culture

Carmen Gaskins, Chmn
Dept of Community & Cultural Affairs
PO Box 553, CHRB
Saipan, MP 96950
Tel 670-322-9982

Genieve Cabrera, Exec Dir
Dept of Community & Cultural Affairs
PO Box 553, CHRB
Saipan, MP 96950
Tel 670-322-9982

Institute of Puerto Rican Culture

Chmn
Apartado Postal 4184
San Juan, PR 00902-4184
Tel 809-725-7570; Fax 809-724-8393

Dr. Luis Edgardo Diaz, Exec Dir
Apartado Postal 4184
San Juan, PR 00902-4184
Tel 809-725-7570; Fax 809-724-8393

Virgin Islands Council on the Arts

Harvey Henne, Chmn
41-42 Norre Gade
Saint Thomas, VI 00802
Tel 809-774-5984; Fax 809-774-6206

John M Jowers, Exec Dir
41-42 Norre Gade
Saint Thomas, VI 00802
Tel 809-774-5984; Fax 809-774-6206

State Directors and Supervisors of Art Education

ALABAMA

Bob G. Smith, Ed.D.
Arts in Education Specialist
State Department of Education
50 N. Ripley St, Rm 3339
PO Box 302101
Montgomery, AL 36130-2101
Tel 334-242-8059; Fax 334-242-0482
E-mail: bsmith@sdenet.alsde.edu

ALASKA

Judith Entwife
Arts Standards & Curriculum Framework Specialist
Alaska Department of Education
801 W Tenth, Ste 200
Juneau, AK 99801-1894
Tel 907-465-8721; Fax 907-465-3396
E-mail: jentwife@educ.state.ak.us

ARIZONA

Jeanne Belcheff
Arizona Department of Education
1535 W Jefferson St
Phoenix, AZ 85007
Tel 602-542-3710

ARKANSAS

Ms. Brenda Turner
Specialist, Art Education
State Department of Education
Education Bldg, Rm 107A
Little Rock, AR 72201
Tel 501-682-4397

CALIFORNIA

Diane L. Brooks, Ed. D.
Administrator
California Department of Education
Curriculum Frameworks & Instructional Resources Office
721 Capitol Mall, PO Box 944272
Sacramento, CA 94244-2720
Tel 916-657-3711

Patty Taylor, Consultant
California Department of Education
Middle Grades Academic Expectations
721 Capitol Mall, PO Box 944272
Sacramento, CA 94244-2720
Tel 916-654-5979

COLORADO

Jacquie Kitzelman
Fine Arts & Physical Education Consultant
Colorado Department of Education
201 E. Colfax Ave, Rm 400
Denver, CO 80203
Tel 303-866-6790

CONNECTICUT

Dr. Scott C. Shuler
Arts Education Consultant
Connecticut State Department of Education
PO Box 2219
Hartford, CT 06145
Tel 860-566-4565; Fax 860-566-5623

DELAWARE

Dr. Vicki S. Bodenhamer, Education Associate
Visual & Performing Arts
Department of Public Instruction
Townsend Bldg, POBox 1402
Dover, DE 19903
Tel 302-739-4670; Fax 302-739-4483

DISTRICT OF COLUMBIA

Rena Watson
Supervising Director of Art
Lingdon Elementary School
1900 Evart St NE
Washington, DC 20018
Tel 202-576-7813; Fax 202-576-7041

FLORIDA

June Hinckley, Fine Arts Specialist
Bureau of Curriculum, Instruction & Assessment
Florida Department of Education
444 Florida Education Center, 325 Gaines St
Tallahassee, FL 32399
Tel 904-488-6047

GEORGIA

Ruth Gassett
Coordinator, Arts Education
1958 Twin Towers East
Atlanta, GA 30334
Tel & Fax 404-651-7274

HAWAII

Kauanoelehua Chang
Educational Specialist
189 Lunalilo Home Road
Rm P-3
Honolulu, HI 96825
Tel 808-396-2526

IDAHO

Gale Maxey, Fine Arts Specialist
State Department of Education
PO Box 83720
Boise, ID 83720-0027
Tel 208-332-6941; Fax 208-334-4664

ILLINOIS

Pat Ryan
Policy Advisor
Quality Assurance & Accountability (Arts Consultant)
Illinois State Board of Education
100 N First St
Springfield, IL 62777
Tel 217-782-2948; Fax 217-524-8750

Ron Engstrom
Principal Consultant
Illinois State Board of Education
100 N First St
Springfield, IL 62777
Tel 217-782-8317; Fax 217-785-9210

INDIANA

Dr. N. Carlotta Parr
Fine Arts Consultant
Center for School Improvement
Indiana Department of Education
State House, Rm 229
Indianapolis, IN 46204-2798
Tel 317-232-9156; Fax 317-232-9121

IOWA

Mary Beth Schroeder Fracek
Consultant, Arts Education
Department of Education
Grimes State Office Building
Des Moines, IA 50319-0146
Tel 515-281-3160

KANSAS

Dr. Dee Hansen
Education Program Consultant
State Department of Education
120 E Tenth Ave
Topeka, KS 66612
Tel 913-296-4932; Fax 913-296-7933;
E-mail: dhansen@smtpgw.ksbe.state.ks.us

KENTUCKY

Arthur W. Patterson, Sr.
Arts & Humanities Consultant
Kentucky Department of Education
Capitol Plaza Tower 1808
500 Mero St
Frankfort, KY 40601
Tel 502-564-2106; Fax 502-564-9848

LOUISIANA

Martin Sotile
Acting Director
PO Box 94064
Baton Rouge, LA 70804
Tel 504-342-3393; 342-3395

MAINE

Sandra T. Long
Educational Consultant
Maine Department of Education
Station 23
Augusta, ME O4333
Tel 207-287-5884; Fax 207-287-5894

MARYLAND

James L. Tucker, Jr.
Chief, Arts and Humanities Section
Maryland State Department of Education
200 West Baltimore St.
Baltimore, MD 21201
Tel 410-767-0352

MASSACHUSETTS

Linda Beardsley, Executive Director
Instruction and Curriculum Services
Massachusetts Department of Education
350 Main St.
Malden, MA 02148
Tel 617-388-3300 ext. 203; Fax 617-388-3396

MICHIGAN

Michigan Department of Education
Curriculum Development Department
Box 30008
Lansing, MI 48909
Tel 517-373-3982; Fax 517-335-2473

MINNESOTA

Minnesota Center for Arts Education
6125 Olson Memorial Hwy
Golden Valley, MN 55422

MISSISSIPPI

K. Bitzi Moore
Fine & Performing Arts Specialist
Mississippi Department of Education
PO Box 771
Jackson, MS 39205-0771
Tel. 601-359-3778; Fax 601-359-3712

MISSOURI

Larry N. Peeno, Ed.D.
Coordinator, Fine Arts
Missouri State Department of Elementary & Secondary Education
PO Box 480
Jefferson City, MO 65102-0480
Tel 573-751-2625

MONTANA

Office of Public Instruction
State Capitol, Rm 106
PO Box 202501
Helena, MT 59620-2501
Tel 406-444-4442
Fax 406-444-3924

NEBRASKA

Sheila Brown
Director, Visual & Performing Arts Education
Department of Education
301 Centennial Mall South
Lincoln, NE 68509
Tel 402-471-4337; Fax 402-471-0117

NEVADA

Mary Peterson, Superintendent Public Instruction
Nevada Department of Education
700 E Fifth St
Carson City, NV 89701-5096
Tel 702-687-9200

NEW HAMPSHIRE

Pamela Murphy Flynn, Art Consultant
New Hampshire Department of Education
101 Pleasant St
Concord, NH 03301
Tel 603-271-2832

NEW JERSEY

Roberta Carol, Arts Education
New Jersey Department of Education, Office of Standards
100 Riverview, CN500
Trenton, NJ 08625
Tel 609-984-1805

NEW MEXICO

Vicki Breen, Director of the Arts
New Mexico State Department of Education
Education Building, 300 Don Gasper
Santa Fe, NM 87503
Tel 505-827-6559

NEW YORK

Roger E. Hyndman,
Associate in Art Education Curriculum & Assessment
New York State Department of Education, Rm 681EBA
Albany, NY 12234
Tel 518-474-5932; Fax 518-473-4884

NORTH CAROLINA

Dr. Roger Metcalf, Director
Western Regional Education
Service Alliance
118 Main St
Canton, NC 28716-4489
Tel 704-648-9424: Fax 704-648-9429

NORTH DAKOTA

Ann Clapper
Department of Public Instruction
600 E Boulevard Ave
Bismarck, ND 58505-0440
Tel 701-328-2260

OHIO

Susan Witten, Art Supervisor
Division of Professional Development
Ohio Department of Education
65 S Front St, Rm 1009
Columbus, OH 43215-4183
Tel 614-466-2761; Fax 614-728-3058

OKLAHOMA

Paulette Black, Director
Arts in Education Program
State Department of Education
2500 N Lincoln Blvd
Oklahoma City, OK 73105
Tel 405-521-3034

OREGON

Federal Programs Fine Arts
Oregon Department of Education
255 Capitol St NE
Salem, OR 97310-0203
Tel 503-378-8004; Fax 503-373-7968

PENNSYLVANIA

Dr. Gene Vandyke, Chief
Division of Arts & Sciences
Department of Education, 333 Market St
Harrisburg, PA 17126-0333
Tel 717-783-2642

Ms. Beth Cornell
Fine Arts Adviser
Division of Arts and Sciences
Department of Education, 333 Market St
Harrisburg, PA 17126-0333
Tel 717-787-5317

RHODE ISLAND

Richard Latham, Consultant
Rhode Island Department of Education
Shepard Bldg, 255 Westminster St
Providence, RI 02903
Tel 401-277-4600 ext 2371; Fax 401-277-4979

SOUTH CAROLINA

MacArthur Goodwin
Education Associate
Office of Education Design
State Department of Education
602-C Rutledge Bldg
Columbia, SC 29201
Tel 803-734-8382; Fax 803-734-5953

SOUTH DAKOTA

Colin Olsen
Arts Education Coordinator
Office of Arts
Department of Education & Cultural Affairs
800 Governors Drive
Pierre, SD 57501
Tel 605-773-3131
E-mail: sdac@stlib.state.sd.us.
World Wide Website: http//www.state.sd/state/executive/
    deca/sdarts/sdarts.htm

TENNESSEE

Joe Giles
Director, Arts Education
Tennessee Department of Education
Andrew Johnson Tower, 8th Flr
Nashville, TN 37243-0379
Tel 615-532-6273

Carolyn McDonald
Art Consultant
Tennessee Department of Education
Andrew Johnson Tower, 8th Flr
Nashville, TN 37243
Tel 615-532-6720

TEXAS

Jeanne Rollins
Director of Fine Arts Programs
Curriculum and Professional Development
Texas Education Agency
1701 N. Congress Avenue
Austin, TX 78701-1494
Tel 512-463-4341

UTAH

Carol Ann Goodson
State Specialist in Fine Arts Education
Utah State Office of Education
250 East Fifth South
Salt Lake City, UT 84111
Tel 801-538-7793; Fax 801-538-7769
E-mail: cgoodson@usoe.k12.ut.us

Tom Wood
State Visual Art Consultant
Utah State Office of Education
250 East Fifth South
Salt Lake City, UT 84111
Tel 801-572-7473; Fax 801-256-5270
E-mail: tdwood@sisna.com

VERMONT

Douglas Walker
Manager for School & Instructional Support Team
Department of Education, 120 State St
Montpelier, VT 05620
Tel 802-828-3111; Fax 802-828-3140

VIRGINIA

Cheryle C. Gardner
Principal Specialist of Fine Arts
Department of Education
P.O. Box 2120
Richmond, VA 23218-2120
Tel 804-225-2881
E-mail: cgardner@pen.k12.va.us

WASHINGTON

Gina May
Program Supervisor
Visual and Performing Arts
Office Superintendent of Public Information
Old Capitol Bldg
PO Box 47200
Olympia, WA 98504-7200
Tel 360-753-7389; Fax 360-586-2728

WEST VIRGINIA

Dr. Jeanne Moore
Coordinator of Fine Arts
West Virginia Department of Education
Capitol Complex, Bldg 6, Rm 330
1900 Kanawha Blvd E
Charleston, WV 25305
Tel 304-558-7805

WISCONSIN

Dr. Martin Rayala
Wisconsin Department of Public Instruction
PO Box 7841
Madison, WI 53707
Tel 608-267-7461

WYOMING

Judy Catchpole
Director, Public Instruction
Department of Education
Hathaway Bldg, 2300 Capitol, 2nd Flr
Cheyenne, WY 82002
Tel 307-777-6226

Art Magazines

A for Annuals; Bi-M for Bi-Monthlies; Bi-W for Bi-Weeklies;
M for Monthlies; Q for Quarterlies; Semi-A for Semi-Annually; W for Weeklies

African Arts (Q)—Don Consentino & Dawn Ross, Eds; James S. Coleman African Studies Center, University of California, 405 Hilgard Ave, Los Angeles, CA 90024. Tel 310-825-1218; Fax 310-206-2250. Yearly $42.00 (domestic)

Afterimage (6 Issues)—Michael Starenko, Ed; Visual Studies Workshop Inc, 31 Prince St, Rochester, NY 14607. Tel 716-442-8676. Yearly $30.00

Aha! Hispanic Arts News (9 Issues)—Sandra M Perez, Exec Dir; Association of Hispanic Arts, 173 E 116th St, 2nd Flr, New York, NY 10029. Tel 212-860-5445; Fax 212-427-2787. Yearly: $20.00 individuals; $40.00 institutions

American Art (Q)—Lisa Siequist, Ed; National Museum of American Art Smithsonian Institution, MRC-210, Washington, DC 20560. Tel 202-357-4836; Fax 202-357-2528. Yearly: $35.00 individuals; $70.00 to institutions

American Artist (M)—M Stephen Doherty, Ed; BPI Communications Inc, 1515 Broadway, New York, NY 10036. Tel 212-764-7300. Yearly $26.95

American Art Journal (Semi-A)—Jayne Kuchna, Ed; Kennedy Galleries, 730 Fifth Ave, 2nd Flr, New York, NY 10019. Tel 212-541-9600; Fax 212-977-3833. Yearly $35.00

American Craft (Bi-M)—Lois Moran, Ed; American Craft Council, 72 Spring St, New York, NY 10012. Tel 212-274-0630; Fax 212-274-0650. Yearly $40.00

American Folk Art (Q)—Rosemary Gabriel, Ed; Museum of American Folk Art, 61 W 62nd St, New York, NY 10023. Tel 212-977-7170; Fax 212-977-8134. Membership: $25.00 students and senior citizens; $35.00 individuals; $50.00 family

American Indian Art Magazine (Q)—Roanne Goldfein, Ed; American Indian Art Inc, 7314 E Osborn Dr, Scottsdale, AZ 85251. Tel 602-994-5445. Yearly $20.00

American Journal of Archaeology (Q)—Fred S Kleiner, Ed; 656 Beacon St, Boston, MA 02215. Tel 617-353-9364; Fax 617-353-6550; E-mail aja@bu.edu. Yearly: $60.00 individuals; $120.00 institutions

American Watercolor Society Newsletter (2 Issues)—Kent Coes, Ed; American Watercolor Society, 47 Fifth Ave, New York, NY 10003. Tel 212-206-8986. Membership

Antiquarian (A)—Allan Everest, Ed; Clinton County Historical Association, 48 Court St, Plattsburgh, NY 12901. Tel 518-561-0340. Membership fee $20.00

Aperture (Q)—Melissa Harris; Aperture Foundation, 20 E 23rd St, New York, NY 10010. Tel 212-505-5555; Fax 212-979-7759. Yearly: $40.00 domestic; $47.00 foreign

Archaeology (Bi-M)—Peter Young, Ed; Archaeological Institute of America, 135 William St, 8th Flr, New York, NY 10038. Tel 212-732-5154; Fax 212-732-5007. Yearly $20.00

Architectural Digest (M)—Paige Rense, Ed; Condi-Nast Publications, Inc, 6300 Wilshire Blvd, 11th Flr, Los Angeles, CA 90048. Tel 213-965-3700; Fax 213-937-1458. Yearly $40.00

Archives of American Art (Q)—Robert Brown, Ed; Smithsonian Institution, 1285 Avenue of the Americas, New York, NY 10019. Tel 212-399-5015; Fax 212-399-6890. Yearly $35.00

Art & Antiques (11 Issues)—Mark Mayfield, Ed; 3 E 54th St, 11th Flr, New York, NY 10022. Tel 212-752-5557

Art & Auction (11 Issues)—Bruce Wolmer, Ed; Auction Guild, 440 Park Ave S, 14th Flr, New York, NY 10016. Tel 212-447-9555; Fax 212-447-5221. Yearly $42.00

Art & Understanding (M)—David Waggoner, Ed; Art & Understanding, Inc., 25 Monroe St, Ste 205, Albany, NY 12743. Tel 518-426-9010. Yearly $24.95

Art Bulletin (Q)—John Paoletti, Ed; College Art Association of America Inc., 275 Seventh Ave, 5th Flr, New York, NY 10001-6708. Tel 212-691-1051; Fax 212-627-2381. Membership

Art Business News (M)—Avanstar Communications, 270 Madison Ave, New York, NY 10016. Tel 212-951-6600; Fax 212-481-6563. Yearly $43.00; Free to art dealers

Art Calendar (M)—Carolyn Blakeslee, Ed; Art Calendar, PO Box 199, Upper Fairmont, MD 21867-0199. Tel 410-651-9150; Fax 410-651-5313. Yearly $32.00

Art Com (Art Contemporary/la Mamelle) (Q)—Carl Loeffler, Ed; Contemporary Arts Press, PO Box 193123, Rincon Ctr, San Francisco, CA 94119. Tel 415-431-7524; Fax 415-431-7841; E-mail artcom.t.v.@well.com. Yearly $96.00. Electronically available

Art Documentation (Semi-A)—Judi Dyki, Ed; Art Libraries Society of North America, 4101 Lake Boone Trail, Ste 201, Raleigh, NC 27607. Tel 919-787-5181. Yearly: $65.00 individuals; $80.00 institutions

Art Education (Bi-M)—Mary Ann Stankiewicz, Ed; National Art Education Association, 1916 Association Dr, Reston, VA 20191-1590. Tel 703-860-8000; Fax 703-860-2960. Yearly $50.00 non-members

ArtFocus (Q)—Pat Fleisher, Ed; 15 McMurrich St, Ste 706, Toronto, ON M5R 3M6 Canada. Tel 416-925-5564; Fax 416-925-2972. Yearly $25.00 (US)

Artforum (10 Issues)—Jack Bankowsky, Ed; Artforum International Magazine Inc, 65 Bleecker St, New York, NY 10012. Tel 212-475-4000; Fax 212-529-1257. Yearly $46.00

Artibus Asiae (Q)—Thomas Lawton, Ed; Arthur M Sackler/Smithsonian Institution, 1050 Independence Ave SW, Washington, DC 20560. Tel 202-357-4880; Fax 202-357-4911. Yearly $75.00

Art in America (M)—Elizabeth C. Baker, Ed; Brant Publications, 575 Broadway, New York, NY 10012. Tel 212-941-2800. Yearly $39.95

Artist's Magazine (M)—Sandy Carpenter, Ed; F & W Publications Inc, 1507 Dana Ave, Cincinnati, OH 45207. Tel 513-531-2690, Ext 257. Yearly $24.00

Art Journal (Q)—Janet Kaplan, Ed; College Art Association of America Inc, 275 Seventh Ave, 5th Flr, New York, NY 10001-6708. Tel 212-691-1051. Yearly: $30.00 non-members; $36.00 foreign members; $45.00 local institutions; $51.00 foreign institutions

Art New England (6 Issues)—Carla Munsat, Ed; 425 Washington St, Brighton, MA 02135. Tel 617-782-3008. Yearly $24.00

Artnews (11 Issues)—Milton Esterow, Ed; Artnews Associates, 48 W 38th St, New York, NY 10018. Tel 212-398-1690. Yearly $39.95

Artnewsletter (Bi-W)—Barbara Pollack, Ed; Artnews Associates, 48 W 38th St, New York, NY 10018. Tel 212-398-1690. Yearly $249.00

Art of the West (Bi-M)—Vicki Stavig, Ed; Duerr and Tierney Ltd, 15612 Hwy 7, Ste 235, Minnetonka, MN 55345. Tel 612-935-5850; Fax 612-935-6546. Yearly $24.00

Art Papers (6 Issues)—Glenn Harper, Ed; Atlanta Art Papers, Inc, 1083 Austin Ave NE, Rm 206, PO Box H77348, Atlanta, GA 30357. Tel 404-588-1837. Fax: 404-588-1836. Yearly $25.00

Arts (M)—Amy Orchard, Ed; Minneapolis Institute of Arts, 2400 Third Ave S, Minneapolis, MN 55404. Tel 612-870-3046; Fax 612-870-3004. Yearly: $1.00 monthly (non-members); free (members)

Arts Quarterly (Q)—Wanda O'Shello, Ed; New Orleans Museum of Art, PO Box 19123, New Orleans, LA 70179. Tel 504-488-2631. Yearly $10.00

Art Students League News (Q)—Lawrence Campbell, Ed; 215 W 57th St, New York, NY 10019. Tel 212-247-4510. Membership

Art Therapy (3 Issues)—Cathy Malchiodi, Ed; American Art Therapy Association, Inc, 1202 Allanson Rd, Mundelein, IL 60060-2419. Tel 708-949-6064. Yearly: $40.00 individuals; $57.00 institutions

Artweek (Bi-M)—Bruce Nixon, Ed; 1249 Paragon Dr, Ste 100, San Jose, CA 95131. Tel 408-279-2293. Yearly: $30.00; $34.00 institutions

Art/World (10 Issues)—Bruce Duff Hooton, Ed; Arts Review Inc, 55 Wheatley Rd, Glen Head, NY 11545. Tel 516-626-1345. Yearly $20.00

Artworld Europe (Bi-M)—S R Howarth, Ed; Humanities Exchange Inc, PO Box 1608, Largo, FL 34649. Tel 813-581-7328. Yearly $69.00

Aviso (M)—Lauren Lantos, Ed; American Association of Museums, 1225 Eye St NW, Ste 200, Washington, DC 20005. Tel 202-289-1818. Yearly $30.00

Bomb (4 Issues)—Betsy Sussler, Ed; 594 Broadway, No 1002 A, New York, NY 10012-3233. Tel 212-431-3943. Yearly $18.00

Bulletin of the Cleveland Museum of Art (10 Issues)—Laurence Channing, Ed; Publications Dept, 11150 East Blvd, Cleveland, OH 44106. Tel 216-421-7340. Yearly $25.00 non-members

Bulletin of the Detroit Institute of Arts (2 Issues)—Judith A Ruskin, Ed; 5200 Woodward Ave, Detroit, MI 48202. Tel 313-833-7961. Yearly $16.00

Canadian Art (Q)—Sarah Milroy, Ed; Canadian Art Foundation, 6 Church St, 2nd Flr, Toronto, ON M5E 1M1, Canada. Tel 416-368-8854. Yearly $24.00 (CN)

Ceramics Monthly (M)—Ruth C Butler, Ed; American Ceramic Society, 735 Ceramic Place, Box 6102, Westerville, OH 43086. Tel 614-523-1660. Yearly $22.00

C Magazine (Q)—Joyce Mason, Ed; Box 5, Sta B, Toronto, ON M5T 2T2, Canada. Tel 416-539-9495. Yearly: $25.68 (CN) individuals; $36.38 (CN) institutions

Classical Realism Journal (Q)—Rebecca Anderson, Ed; American Society of Classical Realism, 1313 Fifth St SE, Minneapolis, MN 55414. Tel 612-379-3908. Yearly $15.00

Columbia-VLA Journal of Law & the Arts (Q)—Editorial Board - Columbia University School of Law, 435 W 116th St, PO Box D-28, New York, NY 10027. Tel 212-663-8719. Yearly: $35.00; $43.00 foreign

Communication Arts (8 Issues)—Patrick S Coyne, Ed; Coyne & Blanchard Inc, 410 Sherman Ave, PO Box 10300, Palo Alto, CA 94303. Tel 415-326-6040. Yearly $53.00

Connection's Monthly (M)—Jen Neiman, Ed; Americans for the Arts, 927 15th St NW, 12th Flr, Washington, DC 20005. Tel 202-371-2830

Dialogue (Columbus) (Bi-M)—Lorrie Dirkse, Ed; Dialogue Inc, Box 2572, Columbus, OH 43216-2572.Tel 614-621-3704. Yearly: $16.00 individuals; $20.00 institutions

Drawing (Bi-M)—Michael Flack, Ed; Drawing Society Inc., 15 Penn Plaza, Box 66, New York, NY 10001-2050. Tel 212-563-4822. Yearly $50.00

Evaluator (Q)—Elizabeth Carr, Ed; International Society of Fine Arts Appraisers, 7015 Euclid Ave, Oak Park, IL 60304. Tel 312-848-3340. Membership

Fiberarts (5 Issues)—Ann Batchelder, Ed; Altamont Press, 50 College St, Asheville, NC 28801. Tel 704-253-0468. Yearly $22.00

Frame/Work (Semi-A)—Leslie Ernst, Ed; Los Angeles Center for Photographic Studies, 6518 Hollywood Blvd, Los Angeles, CA 90028. Tel 213-466-6232. Individuals $18.00, institutions $28.00

Gesta (2 Issues)—Annemarie Weyl-Carr, Ed; International Center of Medieval Art, The Cloisters, Fort Tryon Park, New York, NY 10040. Tel 212-928-1146. Yearly: $15.00 students; $35.00 individuals; $50.00 institutions

Graphic Design: USA (M)—Gordon A Kaye, Ed; Kaye Publishing Corp, 1556 Third Ave, Ste 405, New York, NY 10128. Tel 212-534-5003. Yearly $60.00

Heresies (2 Issues)—Heresies Collective Inc, 280 Broadway, Ste 412, New York, NY 10007. Tel 212-227-2108. Four issues: $27.00 individuals; $38.00 institutions

ID: International Design (7 Issues)—Magazine Publication's LP, 440 Park Ave S, New York, NY 10016. Tel 212-447-1400. Yearly $60.00

IFAR Reports (10 Issues)—Constance Lowenthal, Ed; International Foundation for Art Research, 500 Fifth Ave, Ste 1234, New York, NY 10110. Tel 212-391-6234. Yearly $65.00

Illustrator (2 Issues)—Dr Don L Jardine, Ed; Art Instruction Schools, 3309 Broadway St NE, Minneapolis, MN 55413. Tel 612-788-1000. Two years $8.00

In Brief (formerly Graphiti) (Q)—R Biggs, Ed; Artists in Print Inc, 665 Third St, Ste 530, San Francisco, CA 94107. Tel 415-243-8244. Membership

Indianapolis Museum of Art Previews Magazine (Bi-M)—Rue Hostetler, Ed; 1200 W 38th St, Indianapolis, IN 46208. Tel 317-923-1331. Membership

Journal of Aesthetics & Art Criticism (Q)—Philip Alperson, Ed; American Society for Aesthetics, University of Wisconsin Press, Journal Division, 114 N Murray St, Madison, WI 53715. Tel 608-262-5839. Yearly: $36.00 non-members; $60.00 institutions

Journal of Canadian Art History (Semi-A)—Sandra Paikowsky, Ed; Concordia University, 1455 blvd de Maissoneuve Ouest, S-VA 432, Montreal, PQ H3G 1M8, Canada. Tel 514-848-4699. Yearly: $25.00 (CN); $30.00 (US)

Journal of Decorative and Propaganda Arts (A)—Cathy Leff, Ed; Wolfson Foundation of Decorative and Propaganda Arts, 2399 NE Second Ave, Miami, FL 33137. Tel 305-573-9170. Yearly: $19.00 individuals; $25.00 institutions

Journal of the American Institute for Conservation of Historic & Artistic Works (3 Issues)—Elisabeth West Fitzhugh, Ed; 1717 K St NW, Ste 301, Washington, DC 20006. Tel 202-452-9545. Yearly $63.00

Latin American Art (Q)—Juliana Murphy Campbell, Ed; PO Box 9888, Scottsdale, AZ 85252. Tel 602-947-8422. Yearly: $32.00 individuals; $48.00 institutions

Leonardo: Art, Science & Technology (5 Issues)—Roger Malina, Ed; MIT Press, 55 Hayward St, Cambridge, MA 02142. Tel 617-253-2889. Yearly $55.00 individuals

Letter Arts Review (Q)—Karyn L Gilman, Ed; Calligraphy Review, Inc, 1624 24th Ave SW, Norman, OK 73072-5709. Tel 405-364-8794. Yearly $42.00

Lightworks Magazine (Irregular)—Andrea D Martin, Ed; PO Box 1202, Birmingham, MI 48012-1203. Tel 810-626-8026. Yearly: $20.00 individuals; $25.00 institutions

Master Drawings (Q)—Anne-Marie Logan, Ed; Master Drawings Association Inc, 29 E 36th St, New York, NY 10016. Tel 212-685-0008. Yearly $60.00

Metropolitan Museum of Art Bulletin (Q)—Joan Holt, Ed; 1000 Fifth Ave, New York, NY 10028. Tel 212-535-7710. Yearly $25.00

Museum News (Bi-M)—John Strand, Ed; American Association of Museums, 1225 Eye St NW, Ste 200, Washington, DC 20005. Tel 202-289-9124. Yearly $38.00 non-members

Museum of Fine Arts Bulletin (2 Issues)—Diane Lovejoy, Ed; Museum of Fine Arts, Houston, 1001 Bissonnet, Houston, TX 77005. Tel 713-639-7512

Museum Studies (Semi-A)—Michael Sittenfeld, Ed; Art Institute of Chicago, Publications Dept, 111 S Michigan Ave, Chicago, IL 60603-6111. Tel 312-443-3540. Individuals $25.00, institutions $32.00

New Art Examiner (10 Issues)—Ann Wiens, Ed; 314 W Institute Pl, Chicago, IL 60610. Tel 312-649-9900. Yearly $35.00

New Observations (6 Issues)—Diane R Karp, Ed; New Observations Ltd, 611 Broadway, Ste 701, New York, NY 10012-2608. Tel 212-677-8561; E-mail newobs@inch.com. Yearly $22.00

North Country Notes—Jane E Rupp, Ed; 48 Court St, Plattsburgh, NY 12901. Tel 518-561-0340. Membership

October (Q)—Paul Dzus, Ed; MIT Press, 55 Hayward St, Cambridge, MA 02142. Tel 617-253-2889. Yearly: $35.00 individuals; $98.00 institutions

On Paper (Bi-M)—Gabriella Fanning, Ed; 39 E 78th St, New York, NY 10021. Tel 212-988-5959. Yearly $60.00

Ornament (Q)—Robert Liu, Ed; Ornament Inc, PO Box 2349, San Marcos, CA 92079-2349. Tel 619-599-0222. Yearly $23.00

Parachute (Q)—Chantal Pontbriand, Ed; Editions Parachute, 4060 Blvd St Laurent, Ste 501, Montreal, PQ H2W 1Y9, Canada. Tel 514-842-9805. Yearly: $44.00 (CN) individual; $60.00 (CN) institutions

Philadelphia Museum of Art Bulletin (4 Issues)—George H Marcus, Ed; PO Box 7646, Philadelphia, PA 19101. Tel 215-235-8700. Yearly: $20.00 domestic; $25.00 foreign

Print (Bi-M)—Martin Fox, Ed; RC Publications Inc, 104 Fifth Ave,19th Flr, New York, NY 10011. Tel 212-463-0600; Fax 212-989-9891. Yearly $55.00

Record of the Art Museum Princeton University (2 Issues)—Jill Guthrie, Ed; Princeton University Art Museum, Princeton, NJ 08544. Tel 609-258-4341; Fax 609-258-5949. Yearly $12.00

re: view (Q)—David Featherstone, Ed; Friends of Photography, 250 Fourth St, San Francisco, CA 94103. Tel 415-495-7000. Free membership

School Arts (9 Issues)—Eldon Katter, Ed; Davis Publications Inc, 50 Portland St, Worcester, MA 01608. Tel 508-754-7201; Fax 508-753-3834. Yearly $24.50 (domestic)

Sculpture (10 Issues)—International Sculpture Center, 1050 17th St NW, Ste 250, Washington, DC 20036. Tel 202-785-1144; Fax 202-785-0810. Yearly $45.00

Sculpture Review (Q)—David Finn, Ed; National Sculpture Society, 1177 Avenue of the Americas, New York, NY 10036. Tel 212-764-5645. Yearly $19.00

Society of Architectural Historians Journal (Q)—Nick Adams, Ed; 1232 Pine St, Philadelphia, PA 19107-5944. Tel 215-735-0224. Yearly $60.00

Source: Notes in the History of Art (Q)—Laurie Schneider, Ed; Ars Brevis Foundation, Inc, One E 87th St, Ste 8A, New York, NY 10128. Tel 212-397-5551; Fax 212-977-7032. Yearly $25.00

Southwest Art (M)—Susan Hallsten McGarry, Ed; 5444 Westheimer, Ste 1440, PO Box 460535, Houston, TX 77056-8535. Tel 713-850-0990. Monthly $32.00

Stained Glass (Q)—Richard Gross, Ed; Stained Glass Association of America, 6 SW Second St, No 7, Lees Summit, MO 64063. Tel 816-333-6690; Fax 816-524-9405. Yearly $30.00

Studies in Art Education (4 Issues)—Sally McRorie, Ed; National Art Education Association, 1916 Association Dr, Reston, VA 20191. Tel 703-860-8000; Fax 703-860-2960. Yearly $25.00 non-members

Studio Potter (Semi-A)—Gerry Williams, Ed; Box 70, Goffstown, NH 03045. Tel 603-774-3582; Fax 603-774-6313. Yearly $25.00

Sunshine Artists (M)—Amy Detwiler, Ed; Palmhouse Publications, 2600 Temple Dr, Winter Park, FL 32789. Tel 407-539-1399; Fax 407-539-1499. Yearly $29.95

Technology & Conservation (Q)—S E Schur, Ed; Technology Organization Inc., 76 Highland Ave, Somerville, MA 02143. Tel 617-623-4488. Yearly $28.00

Tole World (Bi-M)—Judy Swager, Ed; EGW Publishing Co, 1041 Shary Circle, Concord, CA 94518. Tel 510-671-9852. Yearly $23.70

Traveling Exhibition Information Service Newsletter (Bi-M)—S R Howarth, Ed; Humanities Exchange Inc, PO Box 1608, Largo, FL 33779. Tel 813-581-7328; Fax 813-585-6398. Yearly $35.00

Umbrella (4 Issues)—Judith A Hoffberg, Ed; Umbrella Associates, PO Box 40100, Pasadena, CA 91114. Tel 310-399-1146; Fax 310-399-5070; E-mail umbrella@ix.netcom.com. Yearly: $18.00 individuals; $25.00 institutions

Vie des Arts (Q)—Bernard Levy, Ed; 200 Saint Jacques St, Montreal, PQ H2Y 1M1, Canada. Tel 514-282-0205; Fax 514-282-0235. Yearly $39.00 (CN)

Views (3 Issues)—Darsie Alexander, Ed; Photographic Resource Center, Boston University, 602 Commonwealth Ave, Boston, MA 02215. Tel 617-353-0700; Fax 617-353-1662. Yearly $25.00

Walters Art Gallery Bulletin (10 Issues)—Nini Sarmiento, Ed; 600 N Charles St, Baltimore, MD 21201. Tel 410-547-9000; Fax 410-783-7969. Yearly $12.00

WestArt (24 Issues)—Martha Garcia, Ed; WestArt Publications, PO Box 6868, Auburn, CA 95604. Tel 916-885-0969. Yearly $16.00

White Walls (2 Issues)—Ann Torke, Ed; PO Box 8204, Chicago, IL 60680. Tel 773-862-5061. Yearly $15.00

Woman's Art Journal (2 Issues)—Elsa Honig Fine, Ed; 1711 Harris Rd, Laverock, PA 19038. Tel 215-233-0639. Yearly: $16.00 individuals; $25.00 institutions

Women Artists News Book Review (A)—Sylvia Moore, Ed; Midmarch Associates, 300 Riverside Dr, New York, NY 10025. Tel 212-666-6990. Yearly $6.00

Newspaper Art Editors and Critics

Cities for newspapers that do not start with city name
will have city name in parentheses as part of the listing

ALABAMA

Birmingham News—Fred Kaimann
Birmingham Post-Herald—Suzanne Dent
Florence Times—Terry Pace
Gadsden Times—Leigh Pritchett
Huntsville Times—Howard Miller
Lanett Valley Times-News—Cy Wood
Mobile Press Register—Gordon Tatum
Montgomery Advertiser—M.P. Wilkerson

ALASKA

Anchorage Daily News—Mike Dunham

ARIZONA

Bisbee Daily Review—Maureen McBride
(Flagstaff) Arizona Daily Sun—Becky Ramsdell
Mesa Tribune—Liz Belanger
(Phoenix) Arizona Republic—Richard Nilsen
Phoenix Gazette—Richard Nilsen
Scottsdale Daily Progress—Gary Rausch
(Tucson) Arizona Daily Star—Chuck Kramer
Tucson Citizen—Chuck Kramer

ARKANSAS

Batesville Guard—Jeff Porter
Fort Smith Southwest Times-Record—Nancy Steel
(Little Rock) Arkansas Democratic Gazette—Eric Harrison
Paragould Daily Press—Todd Nighswonger
(Rogers) Northwest Arkansas Morning News—Rachel Newton

CALIFORNIA

(Antioch) Daily Ledger-Post Dispatch—Curtis Corlew
(Bakersfield) Californian—Logan Molen
Beverly Hills Courier—March Schwartz
Chico News & Review—Gary Kupp
(Covina) San Gabriel Valley Tribune—Katherine Gaugh
Davis Enterprise—Debbie Davis
(El Centro) Imperial Valley Press—Peggy Dale
Fairfield Daily Republic—Matt Pelkin
Fresno Bee—David Hale
Hanford Sentinel—Joan Pegues
(Long Beach) Press-Telegram—Susan Jacobs
Los Angeles Daily News—Greg Miller
(Los Angeles) La Opinion—Hugo Quintana
Los Angeles Times—William Wilson

Madera Tribune—Robert Adams
Modesto Bee—Jim Lawrence
(Monterey) Herald—Fred Hernandez
Napa Valley Register—L. Pierce Carson
Oakland Tribune—Sharon Betz
(Palm Springs) Desert Sun—Bruce Fessier
Porterville Recorder—Darla Welles
(Riverside) Press-Enterprise—Cindy Friday
Sacramento Bee—Howard Shintaku or Scott Levar
San Bernardino Sun—Margo Wilson
San Diego Daily Transcript—Joley Cornett or Vera Fisher
San Diego Union Tribune—Robert Pincus
San Francisco Chronicle—Hilda Nelson
San Francisco Examiner—David Bonetti
(San Jose) Mercury News—Bruce Manuel
San Mateo Times—Debbie Morse
(Santa Ana) Orange County Register—David Whiting
Santa Barbara News-Press—Gary Robb
Santa Monica Daily Breeze—Terry Moore
Santa Rosa Press Democrat—Dan Taylor
Stockton Record—Erin Orr
Turlock Journal—Abbie Dutcher
Vallejo Times-Herald—Pat Poblete
Ventura County Star-Free Press—Rita Moran
(Walnut Creek) Contra Costa Times—Anita Amirrezvani
(Woodland Hills) Daily News—Mary Goetz

COLORADO

Boulder Daily Camera—Niki Hayden
Colorado Springs Gazette Telegraph—Trich Redman
Denver Post—Leavett Biles
(Denver) Rocky Mountain News—Mary Chandler
Fort Morgan Times—John LaPorte
Pueblo Chieftain—Margie Wood

CONNECTICUT

(Bridgeport) Connecticut Post—Patrick Quinn
Bristol Press—Maureen Hamel
Danbury News-Times—Jean Buoy
Greenwich Time—Dorothy Friedman
Hartford Courant—Frank Rizzo
New Britain Herald—Leslie Silverman
New Haven Register—Mary Colurso
Stamford Advocate—Linda O'Connell
Waterbury American & Republican—Claire LaFleniz

DELAWARE

Wilmington News-Journal—Gary Mullinay

DISTRICT OF COLUMBIA

Washington Post—Paul Richard
Washington Times—Cathy Donohoe

FLORIDA

Daytona Beach News Journal—Steve McLachlin
Fort Lauderdale Sun-Sentinel—Roger Hurlburt
Fort Myers News-Press—Randy Lovely
Fort Walton Northwest Florida Daily News—Brenda Shoffner
Gainesville Sun—Bill De Young
(Jacksonville) Florida Times-Union—Vasin Omer Douglas
Lakeland Ledger—Mark Williams
(Melbourne) Florida Today—Pam Harbough
Miami Herald—Elisa Turner
Ocala Star Banner—Rima Firrone
Orlando Sentinel—Barry Glenn
Palatka Daily News—Beth Hickenlooper
Palm Beach Daily News—Jan Sjostrom
Pensacola News-Journal—Donna Frackman
Saint Augustine Record—Jason Stott
Saint Petersburg Times—Maryanne Marger
Sarasota Herald Tribune—Joan Altabe
Tallahassee Democrat—Zilpha Underwood
Tampa Tribune—Joanne Milliani
West Palm Beach Post—Gary Schwan

GEORGIA

Albany Herald—Mandy Flynn
(Athens) Banner-Herald & Daily News—Jan Beckley
Atlanta Journal & Constitution—Cathy Fox
Augusta Herald & Chronicle—Elizabeth Adams
Cartersville Daily Tribune News—Priscilla Parkman
Columbus Enquirer—Don Coker
Macon Telegraph—Dan Maley
Savannah News—Marty Shuter
Waycross Journal Herald—Martha Davis

HAWAII

Honolulu Advertiser—Wayne Havada
(Honolulu) Star Bulletin—Cynthia Oi

IDAHO

(Boise) Idaho Statesman—Patrick Davis
Coeur d'Alene Press—Rita Hollinsworth
(Idaho Falls) Post-Register—John Jensen
Lewiston Morning Tribune—Todd Adams
(Pocatello) Idaho State Journal—Nick Dolby
(Twin Falls) Times-News—Steve Grump

ILLINOIS

Alton Telegraph—Mary Anne Mazenko
Arlington Heights Daily Herald—Jean Rudolph
Belleville News-Democrat—Patrick Kuhl
Bloomington Daily Pantagraph—Stephan Gleason
Centralia Sentinel—Luanne Droege
(Champaign) News-Gazette—Tom Kacich
Chicago Sun-Times—Char Searl, Toby Roberts
Chicago Tribune—Alan Artner
Decatur Herald-Review—Dave Burke, Fran Hall
DeKalb Daily Chronicle—Kurt Messler
Dixon Telegraph—Paula Sherman
(Galesburg) Register-Mail—Janet Saunders
Moline Daily Dispatch—Kathy Bush
Peoria Journal-Star—Gary Panetta
(Rockford) Register-Star—Doug Gass
(Springfield) State Journal-Register—Paul Povse
Watseka Times Republic—Sherry Waters

INDIANA

(Bedford) Times-Mail—Mark Hardman
Columbus Republic—Cheryl Fiscus
Connersville News-Examiner—Jodi Miller
Crawfordsville Journal-Review—Kevin Condon
Evansville Courier—Roger McBain
Evansville Press—Sandra Knipe
Fort Wayne News-Sentinel—Harriet Heithause
Gary Post-Tribune—Sharon Wilmore
Huntington Herald-Press—Cindy Klepper
Indianapolis News—Zach Dunkin
Indianapolis Star—Zach Dunkin
Muncie Star—Mitchelle Kinsey
Shelbyville News—Scarlet Syse
South Bend Tribune—Linda McManus
(Spencer) Evening World—Terry Schooling
Washington Times-Herald—Melody Maust

IOWA

(Burlington) Hawk Eye—Anne Riley
Cedar Rapids Gazette—Cindy Chapman
Centerville Iowegian—Amy Sinclair
Des Moines Register—Eliot Nusbaum
(Iowa City) Daily Iowan—Prasanti Kantamneni
Muscatine Journal—Jeff Tecklanburg
Newton Daily News—Michael Swanger
Oelwein Daily Register—Kaye Frazer
Sioux City Journal—Bruce Miller
Washington Evening Journal—Lisa Kruse
Waterloo Courier—Melody Parker

KANSAS

Concordia Blade-Empire—Robert Lowrey
Hutchinson News—Karen Martinez
(Independence) Daily Report—Donna Stockton
Lawrence Journal World—Jan Biles
(Liberal) Southwest Times—Lane Allison
Manhattan Mercury—Paul Bransom
Newton Kansan—Wendy Nugent
Norton Daily Telegram—Von Fowler
Pratt Tribune—Mitsi Welch
Russell Daily News—James Joule
Salina Journal—Sherida Warner
Topeka Capital-Journal—Mark Sommer
Wichita Eagle—Diana Lewis

KENTUCKY

(Ashland) Daily Independent—William E. Martin
(Covington) Kentucky Post—Michele Day
(Elizabethtown) News-Enterprise—David Greer
(Hopkinsville) Kentucky New Era—Cathy Kanadaugh
Lexington Herald-Leader—David Minton
Louisville Courier-Journal—Maureen McNerney
Murray Ledger & Times—Jim Mahanes
Paducah Sun—Landini Leigh
Winchester Sun—Betty Smith

LOUISIANA

Alexandria Daily Town Talk—Alice Storey
Bastrop Daily Enterprise—William Warner
Crowley Post-Signal—Janet Sarver
Hammond Daily Star—Joan Davis
Minden Press-Herald—Bryan Carlisle
(New Orleans) Times Picayune—Chris Waddington
Shreveport Times—Lane Crockett
Slidell Sentry-News—John Perkins

MAINE

Bangor Daily News—Alecia Armstead
(Lewiston) Sun-Journal—Heather McCarthy
Portland Press Herald—Jane Lord

MARYLAND

(Annapolis) Capital—Kathy Edwards
Baltimore Sun—John Dorsey
Columbia Flier—Geoffrey Himes & John Harding
(Hagerstown) Herald-Mail—Lisa Prejean
Salisbury Daily Times—Erick Sahler

MASSACHUSETTS

(Boston) Christian Science Monitor—Jennifer Wolcott
Boston Globe—Scott Powers
Boston Hellenic Chronicle—Nancy Agris-Savage
Boston Herald—Ed Barrett
Boston Phoenix—Jeffrey Gantz
(Brockton) Enterprise—David Laferriere
(East Boston) Post-Gazette—Hilda Morrill
(Framingham) Middlesex News—Carol Beggy
Haverhill Gazette—Molly Hartle
Lowell Sun—Otto Erbar
(North Andover) Eagle Tribune—Mary Fitzgerald
(Pittsfield) Berkshire Eagle—Jeffrey Borak
(Quincy) Patriot Ledger—Jon Lehman
Springfield Union News—Gloria Russell
Taunton Daily Gazette—Margo Moore
West Springfield Record—Marie A. Coburn
Worcester Telegram & Gazette—Frank Magiera

MICHIGAN

Alpena News—Richard Crofton
Ann Arbor News—Alan Bliss
Battle Creek Enquirer—Mark Schwerin
Bay City Times—Kathy Roberts
(Benton Harbor-St Joseph) Herald-Palladium—Steve Pepple
Big Rapids Pioneer—Judy Hale
Detroit Free Press—Marsha Miro
Detroit News—David Lyman
Flint Journal—Ed Bradley
Grand Rapids Press—Sylvia Krissoff
Jackson Citizen Patriot—Dave Hoger
Kalamazoo Gazette—Margaret DeRitter
Lansing State Journal—Kathleen Lavey
Ludington Daily News—Cheryl Higginson
(Mount Clemens) Macomb Daily—Debbie Komar
Muskegon Chronicle—Linda O'Dette
(Pontiac) Oakland Press—Mary Lynn Hewitt
Saginaw News—Janet Martineau

MINNESOTA

Austin Daily Herald—Rod Amland
Duluth News Tribune & Herald—Dominic Papatola
(Hibbing) Daily Tribune—Heather Barnick
Minneapolis Star & Tribune—Mary Abbe Martin
(Red Wing) Republican Eagle—Ruth Nerbaugen
(Rochester) Post-Bulletin—Janice McFarland
Saint Cloud Times—Becky Beyers
Saint Paul Pioneer Press—Jayne Blanchard
(Wilmar) West Central Tribune—Gary Miller & Sharon Bomstead
Worthington Daily Globe—Beth Rickers

MISSISSIPPI

(Biloxi) Sun Herald—Betty Attaway
(Greenville) Delta Democrat-Times—Lynne LaFoc
(Jackson) Clarion—Ledger—Nell Luter
(McComb) Enterprise-Journal—June Gilbert
Meridian Star—Dorothy Thompson
(Pascagoula) Mississippi Press—Charles Brooks
(Tupelo) Northeast Mississippi Daily Journal—Beth Clements

MISSOURI

Brookfield News-Bulletin—Gregory Orear
Farmington Press Leader—Kathy Emro
Independence Examiner—Jessicia Wagner
Jefferson City Capital News—Tim Dyke
Kansas City Star—Alice Thorson
Neosha Daily News—Chris Jackson
Saint Joseph News-Press—Vivian Letran
Saint Louis Post-Dispatch—Robert Duffy
Springfield News—Leader—Diane Robinson
West Plains Daily Quill—Vickie Taylor

MONTANA

Billings Gazette—Tim Jones
(Butte) Montana Standard—Carmen Winslow
(Missoula) Missoulian—Mike McInally

NEBRASKA

Kearney Hub—Steve Cahallan
Lincoln Journal—Linda Olig
McCook Daily Gazette—Connie Discoe
Omaha World-Herald—Kay MacMillian

NEVADA

(Carson City) Nevada Appeal—Rhonda C. Landers
Las Vegas Review-Journal—Frank Fertado
Las Vegas Sun—Phil Hagen
Reno Gazette-Journal—Peggy Santoro

NEW HAMPSHIRE

Manchester Union Leader—Barry Palmer

NEW JERSEY

Atlantic City Press—Gail Wilson
Bridgeton Evening News—Kay Budderow
The (Bridgewater) Courier News—Paul Grzella
(Cherry Hill) Courier-Post—Helene Driggs
(Hackensack) Record—John Zeaman
(Jersey City) Jersey Journal—Kay Kenney
(Morristown) Daily Record—Marion Filler
(Neptune) Asbury Park Press—A. R. Prendimano
Newark Star Ledger—Eileen Watkins
(New Brunswick) Home News—Mary Price
(Passaic) North Jersey Herald & News—Mary Noone
(Trenton) Trentonian—Andy McEwan
Woodbridge News Tribune—Mary Price
(Woodbury) Gloucester County Times—Jen Watson

NEW MEXICO

Albuquerque Journal—Dan Herrera
Albuquerque Tribune—Joline Glenn
Carlsbad Current-Argus—Valerie Cranston
Clovis News-Journal—Mike Wheeler
(Farmington) Daily Times—Michele Bruce
(Grants) Cibola County Grants Beacon—J. D. Miesner
Hobbs Daily News-Sun—Donita Evans
Roswell Daily Record—Jerry McCormack
(Santa Fe) New Mexican—Denise Kuzel

NEW YORK

Albany Times Union—Thomas Palmer
Batavia Daily News—Ben Beagle
(Binghamton) Press & Sun-Bulletin—Gene Gray

Buffalo News—Richard Huntington
Corning Leader—Jeremey Ehrenreich
(Herkimer) Evening Telegram—Donna Thompson
(Melville) Newsday—Barbara Schuler
Middletown Times Herald-Record—Dennis Sprick
New York Daily News—John Sullivan
New York Post—Matt Diebel
New York Times—Connie Rosenblum
(New York) Wall Street Journal—Terry Agins
(Nyack) Rockland Journal-News—John Cornell
Port Chester Daily Item—Tad Clark
Poughkeepsie Journal—Florence Schetzel
Rochester Democrat & Chronicle—Elizabeth Forbes
Rochester Times-Union—Elizabeth Forbes
(Saratoga Springs) Saratogian—Beverly McKim
Schenectady Gazette—Margaret Wright
(Southold) Long Island Traveler/Watchman—Dan McCarthy
Staten Island Advance—Michael Fressola
Syracuse Herald-Journal—Mary Fran Devendorf
Syracuse Post-Standard—Mary Fran Devendorf
(Troy) Record—Doug DeLisle & Steve Barnes
(Yorktown Heights) North County News—Lawrence Hutton

NORTH CAROLINA

Asheville Citizen-Times—Dale Neal
Charlotte Observer—Richard Maschel
Durham Herald-Sun—Blue Greenberg
Elizabeth City Daily Advance—Jim Roberts
Goldsboro News-Argus—Winkie Lee
Greensboro News & Record—Cathy Gant Hill
Greenville Daily Reflector—Lori Goodson
Hendersonville Times-News—Maryann Murdoch
(Lumberton) Robesonian—James Bass
(Raleigh) News & Observer—Suzanne Brown
Shelby Star—Chris Horeth
Washington Daily News—Mark Inabinett
Wilmington Star-News—Carole Collier
Wilson Daily Times—Lisa Battes
Winston-Salem Journal—Sara Fox

NORTH DAKOTA

Bismarck Tribune—Jeff Olson
Dickinson Press—Linda Sailer
Fargo Forum—Ross Raihala
Grand Forks Herald—Sally Thompson
Jamestown Sun—Gail Hogan
Minot Daily News—Shelley Beryantt

OHIO

Akron Beacon Journal—Dorothy Shinn
Athens Messenger—Meredeth Erlewine
Beavercreek News Current—Chris Mitsoff
Canton Repository—Gayle Beck
Cincinnati Enquirer—Owen Findsen
Cincinnati Post—Jerry Stein
Cleveland Plain Dealer—Robert Pinkus
Columbus Dispatch—Scott Minister
Dayton Daily News & Journal Herald—Lee Waigand
Galion Inquirer—Theresa Haferd
(Mansfield) News-Journal—Alisa Ness

Portsmouth Daily Times—Debbie Allard
Sandusky Register—John Bruno
Sidney Daily News—Jeffrey Billiel
Toledo Blade—Rick Nease
Troy Daily News—Kevin Tucker
Wapakoneta Daily News—Melanie Speicher
(Willoughby) News-Herald—Tricia Ambrose
(Youngstown) Vindicator—Robert McFerren

OKLAHOMA

Blackwell Journal-Tribune—Helene Seubert
Claremore Progress—Pat Reeder
Elk City Daily News—Jo Ann Medders
Lawton Constitution—Charles Clark
Muskogee Daily Phoenix & Times-Democrat—Lou Rohde
(Oklahoma City) Daily Oklahoman—Bill Sandlin
Pryor Daily Times—Betty Perkins
Seminole Producer—Karen Anson
Tulsa Tribune—Rusty Lang
Tulsa World—Cathy Logan

OREGON

(Coos Bay) World—Linda Meirjurgen
(Eugene) Register—Guard—Carl Davaz
(Grants Pass) Daily Courier—Edith Decker & Kathleen Alaks
(Medford) Mail Tribune—Al Reiss
(Ontario) Argus Observer—Larry Hurrie
(Portland) Oregonian—Randy Gragg
(Salem) Statesman-Journal—Kay Worthington

PENNSYLVANIA

Allentown Morning Call—Len Righi
Bradford Era—Natalie Montecaluo
(Doylestown) Intelligencer—Trilla Ramage
(DuBois) Courier-Express—Barbara Azzato
Greensburg Tribune-Review—Graham Shearing
(Harrisburg) Patriot-News—Sandy Cullen
(Huntingdon) Daily News—James D. Hunt
Johnstown Tribune Democrat—Clifford Kepple
(Lancaster) Sunday News—John Gates
(Levittown) Bucks County Courier Times—Jim Patrone
(Lewistown) Sentinel—John Tommasino
(Lock Haven) Express—Wendy Stiver
(New Kensington-Tarentum) Valley News-Dispatch—Sallie Webb
Philadelphia Daily News—Jill Williams
Philadelphia Inquirer—Ed Sozanski
Philadelphia New Observer—Hugo Warren
Pittsburgh Post-Gazette—Donald Miller
Pittsburgh Press—Donald Miller
(Reading) Times—George Hatza
Scranton Times—Daniel F. Cusick
(Towanda) Daily Review—Dave Colton
(Wilkes-Barre) Times Leader—Joe Butkewicz
York Dispatch—Dora Kluger

RHODE ISLAND

Providence Journal-Bulletin—Mick Cochran
(South Kingstown) Narragansett Times—Amy Dunne

SOUTH CAROLINA

Aiken Standard—Phillip Lord
Anderson Independent-Mail—Michelle Winter
Beaufort Gazette—Debbie Radford
Charleston News & Courier—Gill Guerry
Columbia Black News—Jeffrey Day
(Columbia) State—Bill Starr
Florence Morning News—Jeff Chatlosh
Greenville News—Staci Sturrock
Myrtle Beach Sun News—Mona Prufer
Orangeburg Times & Democrat—Joyce Milke
(Spartanburg) Herald-Journal—Jeff Zehr

SOUTH DAKOTA

(Mitchell) Republic—Nancy Correll
(Sioux Falls) Argus Leader—Michael Bennett

TENNESSEE

Chattanooga News-Free Press—Pete Hunter
Chattanooga Times—Steve Bonseld
(Clarksville) Leaf Chronicle—Leigh Anne Monitor
(Columbia) Daily Herald—Marvine Sugg
Elizabethton Starr—Bryan Stevens
Jackson Sun—Steve Manning
Johnson City Press—Lisa Paine-Brooks
Kingsport Times-News—Allison Mechem
Knoxville News-Sentinel—Barbara Asbury
Lebanon Democrat—Marcia Poley
(Memphis) Commercial Appeal—Jon Sparks
(Morristown) Citizen Tribune—Carolyn Walter
(Murfreesboro) Daily News Journal—Suzanne Ghianni
Nashville Banner—Tim Ghianni
Nashville Tennessean—D'Anna Sharon
(Oak Ridge) Oak Ridger—Bernadine Andrew

TEXAS

Abilene Reporter-News—Layne Smith
Amarillo Daily News—Jeff Rhoads
Austin American-Statesman—Larry Babb
Beaumont Enterprise—Sherri Fey
Big Spring Herald—Kelly Jones
(Clute) Brazosport Facts—Wayland Smart
(Corpus Christi) Caller-Times—Dollie Turpin
Dallas Morning News—Janet Kutner
El Paso Herald-Post—Nan E. Keck
El Paso Times—Jeff Carr
Fort Worth Star-Telegram—Janet Tyson
Houston Chronicle—Lindsay Heinsen
(Lubbock) Avalanche Journal—Bill Kerns
Midland Reporter-Telegram—Elizabeth Edwin
(Nacogdoches) Daily Sentinel—Judy Morgan

Odessa American—Janet Terry
Orange Leader—Ken Sury
Pecos Enterprise—Rosie Flores
Plainview Daily Herald—Nicki Logan
Port Arthur News—Darragh Castillo
San Angelo Standard Times—Diane Murray
San Antonio Express-News—Kristina Paledes
San Marcos Daily Record—Diana Finlay
(Tyler) Courier Times—Joyce Turner
Waco Tribune Herald—Jay Jeffers
Waxahachie Daily Light—Susan Roberts
Wichita Falls Times Record News—Bridget Knight

UTAH

Logan Herald Journal—Jared Thayne
Ogden Standard-Examiner—Larry Stephens
Provo Daily Herald—Tiffany Zweifel
(Salt Lake City) Deseret News—Dave Gagon
Salt Lake Tribune—Frank McEntire

VERMONT

Burlington Free Press—Casey Seiler
Saint Albans Messenger—Gary Rutkowski

VIRGINIA

(Arlington) USA Today—David Zimmerman
Bristol Herald Courier—Carla Twyman
(Charlottesville) Daily Progress—Mary Alice Blackwell
(Covington) Virginian Review—Horton P. Beirne
Fairfax Journal—Mary Ellen Webb
(Fredericksburg) Free Lance-Star—Anna Billingsley
Hopewell News—Kathy Slade
(Lynchburg) News & Advance—Donna Keesee
Newport News Daily Press—Michael Dabrowa
(Norfolk) Virginian-Pilot—Theresa Annas
Richmond Times-Dispatch—Robert Walsh
Roanoke Times & World News—Kevin Kittredge
(Waynesboro) News-Virginian—Theresa Reynolds

WASHINGTON

(Aberdeen) Daily World—Laura Chenoweth
Ellensburg Daily Record—Peggy Steward
(Everett) Herald—Ron Glowen
(Moses Lake) Columbia Basin Herald—Dan Black
Seattle Times—Robin Updike
Spokane Spokesman-Review—Susan English
Tacoma News Tribune—Don Ruiz
(Vancouver) Columbian—Stephanie Thomson
Wenatchee World—David Kraft

WEST VIRGINIA

Bluefield Daily Telegraph—Samantha Perry
Charleston Daily Mail—Julie Kemp
Charleston Gazette—Doug Imbrogno
Huntington Herald-Dispatch—Arlinda Broady
(Martinsburg) Journal—Peggy Swisher
(Wheeling) News-Register—Don Fise

WISCONSIN

(Appleton) Post-Crescent—Ed Berthiaume
(Chippewa Falls) Chippewa Herald-Telegram—Steve Massie
(Eau Claire) Leader-Telegram—Bill Foy
Green Bay Press-Gazette—Jeff Ash
Kenosha News—Elizabeth Snyder
(Madison) Capital Times—Jacob Stockinger
(Madison) Wisconsin State Journal—Brian Howell
Milwaukee Journal—James Auer
Milwaukee Sentinel—James Auer
(Racine) Journal Times—Barbara Schuetz
(Superior) Evening Telegram—Linda McGonigal
Wausau Daily Herald—Randy Riebe

WYOMING

(Casper) Star-Tribune—David Hipschman
(Cheyenne) Wyoming Eagle & State Tribune—C. J. Putname
Riverton Ranger—Steven Peck
Rock Springs Daily Rocket-Miner—Bruce Yoder

PUERTO RICO

(San Juan) El Nuevo Dia—Mario Aledre
(San Juan) El Vocero de Puerto Rico—Sonia L. Cordero

CANADA

ALBERTA

Calgary Herald—Nancy Tousley
Calgary Sun—David Veitch
Edmonton Journal—Bob Remington
Edmonton Sun—Tom Elsworthy

BRITISH COLUMBIA

Vancouver Province—Renee Doruxter
Vancouver Sun—Michael Scott
Victoria Times-Colonist—Adrian Chamberlin & Michael D. Reid

MANITOBA

Winnipeg Free Press—Gordon Preece

NOVA SCOTIA

Halifax Chronicle Herald—Grey Guy

ONTARIO

Hamilton Spectator—Jeff Mahoney
(Kitchener) Waterloo Record—Robert Reid
London Free Press—Bill McGrath
Ottawa Citizen—Don Butler
Toronto Globe & Mail—Katherine Ashenburg
Toronto Star—Christopher Hume
Toronto Sun—Linda Fox
Windsor Star—Ted Shaw

QUEBEC

Montreal Gazette—Lucinda Chodan
(Montreal) La Presse Ltée—Julien Chung
(Montreal) Le Journal de Montreal—Denis Trembley
(Quebec) Le Journal de Quebec—Jocelyn Bourque
(Quebec) Le Soleil—Jacques Samson

SASKATCHEWAN

Regina Leader-Post—Pat Carlson
(Saskatoon) Star Phoenix—Pat Macsymic

Scholarships and Fellowships

OFFERED BY	AMOUNT	OPEN TO	DURATION	WHEN OFFERED
ACA College of Design 2528 Kemper Lane Cincinnati, OH 45206	$6,780	First-year ACA student who has completed 11 months	One year	Annually
		Seven high school scholarships for senior students	Two years	
Adelphi University Garden City, NY 11530	$2000-$5000	All	Four years	Annually
Adrian College 110 S Madison Adrian, MI 49221	$1000-$2000	Transfer & freshmen; by portfolio review	Renewable up to four years	Annually to incoming Freshmen
	$1000-$2000	Upperclass	Renewable	Annually
	$1000-$2000	Upperclass art major	One year	Annually
	$2000	Incoming freshmen HS GPA 3.3; can be combined with any of the above	Renewable for four years	Annually
	Up to $11,000	Incoming freshmen HS GPA 3.5, can be combined with any of above	Renewable for four years	Annually
Allegheny College Art Department Meadville, PA 16335	Varies	All matriculated students	One year	Annually
The Alliance for Young Artists & Writers, the Scholastic Art & Writing Awards 555 Broadway New York, NY 10012	Varies: scholarship nominations to participating colleges and art institutions	Students graduating high school who submit outstanding portfolios of art and/or photography	Varies	Annually; write for details and entry info by Nov. 1
	Portfolio Awards; (5) $5000 each	Students graduating high school entering the scholarship nominations program (above)	One year	Annually; write for details and entry info by Nov. 1
Alma College, Dept of Art & Design 614 W Superior St Alma, MI 48877	$500-$1500	Entering students who submit portfolio and application	Renewable after first year, specific requirements for renewal	Annually
American Antiquarian Society 185 Salisbury St Worcester, MA 01609	Maximum available stipend $30,000 (AAS-NEH Fellowships)	Qualified scholars in American history and culture to 1877. Degree candidates are not eligible	Six months-one year at the Society's library (four or five month tenure may now be arranged)	Annually
	Peterson Fellowships $950 per month	Qualified scholars in American history and culture to 1877; open to graduate students at work on dissertations	One-three months at the Society's library	Annually
	AAS-ASECS Fellowships $950 per month	Qualified scholars in any area of American eighteenth-century studies. Degree candidates not eligible	One-three months at the Society's library	Annually
	AHPCS Fellowships $950 per month	Qualified scholars researching American prints of the 18th and 19th centuries		Annually

563

OFFERED BY	AMOUNT	OPEN TO	DURATION	WHEN OFFERED
American Film Institute, Center for Advanced Film & Television Study 2021 N Western Ave Los Angeles, CA 90027	$15,000	Incoming first year student; awarded in each discipline	One year	Annually
American Numismatic Society Broadway at 155th St New York, NY 10032	$2000 stipend in support of summer study	Students who have completed one year graduate study in classics, archeology, history, art history and related fields	Summer	
	$3500 dissertation fellowship	Individuals who have completed the ANS Graduate Seminar & general examinations for the doctorate	Academic year	
	$2000 Frances M Schwartz Fellowship	Individuals who have completed the BA	Academic year	
	Louise Wallace Hackney Fellowship for the Study Chinese Art- $7000	Post-Doctoral and Doctoral students who are US citizens	One year	July 1st to June 30th
American Scandinavian Foundation Exchange Division 725 Park Ave New York, NY 10021	$3000-$15000	Applicants with an undergraduate degree (unrestricted fields) for Denmark, Finland, Iceland, Norway and Sweden	Up to one year	Annually, deadline Nov 1
American University, Dept of Art 4400 Massachusetts Ave NW Washington, DC 20016	Varies	Graduate students	One year	Annually
American Watercolor Society 47 Fifth Ave New York, NY 10003	Varies	Art schools and museums with watercolor study. Society chooses schools; schools choose recipients	One year	Annually
Aquinas College 1607 Robinson Rd SE Grand Rapids, MI 49506	$3000-$7000	Incoming freshmen	Four years	Annually
Archaelogical Institute of America 656 Beacon St Boston, MA 02215-2010	$3000-$15,000	Graduate students or recent PhD recipients working in archaeology of Greece, Rome and Near East	One year	Annually
	$11,000	Graduate students or recent PhD recipients working in archaeology in Greece, Rome and Near East; must be accepted at the American School of Classical Studies, Athens	One year	Biennially
Arizona Commission on the Arts 417 W Roosevelt St Phoenix, AZ 85003	$500-$7500	Residents of Arizona, over 18; students are not eligible	One year	Annually
	Performing Arts Fellowship	Same as above	One year	Annually
	Writers Fellowship	Same as above	One year	Annually
	Visual Arts Fellowships			
Arizona State University, School of Art Tempe, AZ 85287-1505	Varies	Regularly admitted students	Varies	Annually
The Arkansas Art Center, Museum School PO Box 2137 Little Rock, AR 72203	From $75 and up	Children and adults	Per quarter	Quarterly
Arkansas State University, Dept of Art, PO Box 1920 State University, AR 72467	$100-$800 range, full or partial tuition, grants up to four each semester	Entering and current undergraduates	One semester-eight semesters	Reviewed each semester
Art Academy of Cincinnati 1125 St Gregory St Cincinnati, OH 45202	$500-$9000	All entering, degree-seeking students	Renewable	Annually

OFFERED BY	AMOUNT	OPEN TO	DURATION	WHEN OFFERED
Art Center College of Design 1700 Lida St, PO Box 7197 Pasadena, CA 91109	Variable	All students	One or two semesters at a time	Every semester
Art Guild of Burlington Arts for Living Center Seventh & Washington Sts PO Box 5 Burlington, IA 52601	$1000+	Students enrolled in School of Art at University of Iowa and live within 100 miles of Burlington	One year	Annually
Art Institute of Boston 700 Beacon St, Boston, MA 02215-2598	Ment Scholarships	Incoming students	Four years	Each semester
	DuPont Fellowship $15,000	Minority photographers	One semester	
The Art Institute of Dallas 2 N Park East 8080 Park Lane, Dallas, TX 75231	Full tuition only in each major	High school seniors	18-24 months	Annually
Art Institute of Philadelphia 1622 Chestnut St Philadelphia, PA 19103	Varied	Eligible students	One year	Annually
Art Institute of Pittsburgh 526 Penn Ave Pittsburgh, PA 15222	$1650	Current students	One quarter	Quarterly
	$500 and up	Based on need and minimum 2.5 GPA	One year to quarterly; based on length of program	Annual to quarterly
	$238,000	HS senior; 31 competitive scholarships; portfolio & application required	2 to 9 quarters	Annually
Arts Council of the Blue Ridge 20 E Church Ave Roanoke, VA 24011	$50-$250 - Laban Johnson Arts Scholarship	High school and college students to pursue visual, performing or literary arts experiences	One year	Annually
The Arts Partnership of Greater Spartanburg 385 S Spring St Spartanburg, SC 29306	Varies	Residents	Variable	Annually
	Mary Wheeler Scholarship $1000	Spartanburg county students pursuing studies toward career in the arts	One year	Annually
Artworks 19 Everett Alley Trenton, NJ 08611	$50 $200	Students enrolled in Artworks classes	One year	Bi-annually
Asbury College, Art Dept One Macklem Dr Wilmore, KY 40390	$500-$1000	Asbury College art students	One year	Annually
Ashland University Dept of Art, College Ave Ashland, OH 44805	$2500	Entering freshman and transfers	One year, renewable	Annually
Atlanta College of Art 1280 Peachtree St NE Atlanta, GA 30309	$500-$2500	Prospective students	One year	Annually
Auburn University at Montgomery Department of Fine Arts Montgomery, AL 36193	$2025	Incoming freshmen	One year	Annually
Augustana College Art & Art History Dept 639 38th St Rock Island, IL 61201	Up to $2000	Studio art majors and minors beginning in freshman year, based on talent and financial need	One year, renewable	Annually
Augustana College 29th & S Summit Sioux Falls, SD 57197	Varies; several thousand in scholarships available	Deserving sophomore and junior students		
Augusta State University Dept of Fine Arts 2500 Walton Way Augusta, GA 30904	Variable	Freshmen, sophomores, juniors	One year	Annually

OFFERED BY	AMOUNT	OPEN TO	DURATION	WHEN OFFERED
Austin College Art Dept PO Box 1177 Sherman, TX 75090	$500-$2000 Up to $1000	Incoming freshmen & transfer students Continuing students	Four years Reviewed annually	Annually
Austin Peay State University Dept of Art Clarksville, TN 37044	$500-$1000	Current full-time undergraduates	One year	Annually
Avila College, Art Division 11901 Wornall Rd Kansas City, MO 64145	$2000	Art majors	One year, renewable	Annually
Bakersfield Art Foundation PO Box 1911 Bakersfield, CA 933003	$500	All art students		Annually
Ball State University 2000 University Ave Muncie, IN 47306	$5000 graduate assistantship academic year (tuition waved)	Master's level art students	One year (assistantship)	Annually
Baltimore Watercolor Society c/o Marshall Kinsley 716 Hollen Rd Baltimore, MD 21212	$100	High school student in the Baltimore area	One year	Annually
Banff Centre for the Arts PO Box 1020 Banff, AB TOL OGO, Canada	Contact sponsor	Accepted applicants of applicable Banff Centre programs	Length of program (residency) accepted into	On acceptance
Barton College Art Department College Station Wilson, NC 27893	Varies $700 Bessie Massengill Scholarship $1000 Triangle East Advertising/Marketing	All art majors Juniors and seniors Juniors and seniors	Determined by Art Faculty One year One year	
Barton County Community College Fine Arts Department, RR3 Great Bend, KS 67530	$300-$400	All qualified, majoring in art	One year	Annually
Bassist College 2000 SW Fifth Ave Portland, OR 97201	$25,000 (The total represents the combined amounts for the first and second year students)	Bassist College students	One and two years	Annually
Battleship North Carolina Battleship Dr, Eagle Island PO Box 480 Wilmington, NC 28402	$1920	Graduate or undergraduate history major, with interest in the museum profession	Ten weeks, summer	Annually
Baylor University Department of Art Waco, TX 76798-7263	Varies		One year	Annually
F Lammot Belin Arts Scholarship Waverly Community House Waverly, PA 18471	$10,000	Exceptional ability in chosen field. Must be a US citizen. Must have been or presently be a resident of the Abingtons or Pocono Northeast of PA	One year	Annually, deadline Dec. 15
Bemidji State University 1500 Birchmont Dr Bemidji, MN 56601	Varies	Incoming freshmen		Annually
Bemis Center for Contemporary Arts 724 S 12th St Omaha, NE 68102-3202	$500-$1000 per month	Professional artists	Two-six months	Annually
Berkshire Artisans 28 Renne Ave Pittsfield, MA 01201	$3800	Massachusetts artists only	One year	Semi-annually

OFFERED BY	AMOUNT	OPEN TO	DURATION	WHEN OFFERED
Berry College Art Department Mt Berry, GA 30149	$3000-$5000	All art majors	One year	Annually
Bethany College 421 N First St Lindsborg, KS 67456	Up to $2500 Art Performance awards	Incoming freshmen & transfer students who qualify	One year, can continue for entire course if standards are maintained	Annually
Binghamton University, SUNY Department of Art History Binghamton, NY 13901	Variable	Art history graduate students only, with additional fellowships open to minorities	One year	Annually
Bloomsburg University, Dept of Art, Blakeless Center for the Humanities, Old Science Hall, Bloomsburg, PA 17815	$500 John Cook award	Freshmen	One year	Annually
Bob Jones University School of Fine Arts Wade Hampton Blvd Greenville, SC 29614	$125 to $325 per month	Undergraduate students with demonstrated financial need and satisfactory school record, campus work assignment required	One semester (renewable)	Semi-annually
Boise State University Art Department 1910 University Dr Boise, ID 83725	Varies	All art majors	One year	Annually
Bowling Green State University School of Art, Fine Arts Bldg Bowling Green, OH 43403-0211	Varies	BGSU art students	Per semester	Annually
Briar Cliff College 3303 Rebecca St Sioux City, IA 51104	$17,800	Freshmen and senior year	Four years (renewable each year)	Annually
Brigham Young University Harris Fine Arts Center 210 BRMB Provo, UT 84602-2500	Full and half tuition	Qualified freshmen applicants, transfer students and continuing students	One year	Annually
Brooklyn College, Art Dept Bedford Ave and Ave H Brooklyn, NY 11210	Varies	Painters	One year	Annually
Brooks Institute of Photography 801 Alston Rd Santa Barbara, CA 93108	Varies	Enrolled students	One year and two months	Varies
Cabrillo College, Visual & Performing Arts Division 6500 Soquel Dr Aptos, CA 95003	Varies	Art students	One year	Annually
John C Calhoun State Community College PO Box 2216 Decatur, AL 35609-2216	Varies	Art, graphic design and photography majors	Three quarters (nine-month period)	Annually
California College of Arts and Crafts 5212 Broadway Oakland, CA 94618	Variable. Scholarships, loans, grants; up to $2.5 million	Grants & loans, open to all CCAC students; based on need & merit	One year, renewable	Annually
California Institute of the Arts School of Art 24700 McBean Pkwy, Valencia, CA 91355	$500-$10,000	Registered students	One year	Annually
California State University, Art Dept 801 W Monte Vista Ave Turlock, CA 95382	Varies	Juniors and seniors; art majors only	One year	Annually

OFFERED BY	AMOUNT	OPEN TO	DURATION	WHEN OFFERED
California State University, Bakersfield Fine Arts Department 9001 Stockdale Hwy Bakersfield, CA 93311	$300	Art majors	One year	Annually
California State University, Chico Art Department First & Normal, Chico, CA 95929-0820	Varies	Art majors	One year	Annually
California State University, Los Angeles, Art Dept 5151 State Univ Dr Los Angeles, CA 90032	Varies	Undergraduates and graduates	One year	Annually
California State University, San Bernandino, Visual Arts Dept 5500 University Pkwy San Bernandino, CA 92407	$600	Art student with 3.0 GPA and above	One year	Annually
California State University, Sacramento, Art Department 6000 J Street Sacramento, CA 95819-6061	Varies	Art majors	One year	Annually
California Watercolor Association PO Box 4631 Walnut Creek, CA 94596	$1400	Local adult or high school students selected by their teachers at the request of the group	One time award	Annually
Canadian Scandinavian Foundation, McGill Univ 805 Sherbrook St W Montreal, PQ H3G 3G1 Canada	Brucebo scholarship, 5,000 SEK for travel, food stipend & cottage use	Talented, young Canadian artist-painter	Two months in Gotland	Annually
Canton Museum of Art 1001 Market Ave N Canton, OH 44702	$1000	High school seniors for college tuition	One	Annually
Cardinal Stritch College, Art Dept 6801 N. Yates Rd, Milwaukee, WI 53217-3985	$1000	BFA candidates	Four years	Annually
Carson-Newman College, Art Dept PO Box 71911 Jefferson City, TN 37760	Varies		By semester	Annually
Case Western Reserve University Dept of Art History & Art Mather House Cleveland, OH 44106-7110	Full tuition- $12,834 plus $6000 stipend	MA & PhD candidates	Two years	Annually
Century College, Humanities Dept 3401 Century Ave N White Bear Lake, MN 55110			One year	Annually
Chaffey College 5885 Haven Ave Alta Loma, CA 91701	Various	Qualified Chaffey students only; must have 24 units with a 2.75 cum GPA	Once a year	Annually
Chatham Historical Society 347 Stage Harbor Rd PO Box 381 Chatham, MA 02633	$1000	College juniors and seniors with history or related majors	One year	Annually
Chautauqua Institute/ The Art School Box 1098, Dept 6 Chautauqua, NY 14722	$27,000	Full term students	Eight weeks	Annually
Claremont Graduate School Art Dept 251 E Tenth St, Claremont, CA 91711	Varies	All	One year	Annually
	Matching	Minority student	One year	Annually
Clark College, Art Dept 1800 E McLoughlin Blvd Vancouver, WA 98663	Tuition waiver (up to $275/term)	All new or returning students who enroll for at least 6 credits	One year	Annually

OFFERED BY	AMOUNT	OPEN TO	DURATION	WHEN OFFERED
Clarke College 1550 Clarke Dr Dubuque, IA 52001	Up to $2000	High school graduates, based on portfolio review and 3.0 GPA in art classes	One year (renewable for four years)	Annually
The Clay Studio 139 N Second St Philadelphia, PA 19106	$500 stipend (free studio & materials)	Ceramic artists	One year	Annually
Cleveland State Community College Department of Art Adkisson Dr, PO Box 3570 Cleveland, TN 37320-3570	Varies	All qualified applicants	One year	Annually and semi-annually
Coe College, Art Dept 1221 First Ave NE Cedar Rapids, IA 52402	$3500 to full tuition	High school seniors and returning college students	Four years	Nov, Feb
Coffeyville Community College Art Dept, 400 W 11th St Coffeyville, KS 67337	$1238 (tuition, supplies, $500 for dorm)	Any applicant	Two years	Annually
Coker College, Art Dept College Ave Hartsville, SC 29550	$2000 $1900	Incoming freshman art majors All art majors	Four years Four years	Annually Annually
College of Eastern Utah, Gallery East 451 E Fourth St N Price, UT 84501	Full tuition ($395 per quarter)	Portfolio review	One year	Annually
College of Mt Saint Joseph Art Department 5701 Delhi Rd Cincinnati, OH 45233-1670	Full tuition Scholastic Art Scholarship	High school graduates	One year (renewable)	Annually
	$2000 Fine Arts Scholarship	High school graduates	One year (renewable)	Annually
	$2000 Selections Scholarship	High school graduates	One year (renewable)	Bi-annually
	$1000 Ohio Governor's Youth Art Scholarship	High school graduates	One year (renewable)	Annually
	$1000 S Augusta Zimmer Scholarship	High school graduates	One year	As available
	$1000 Moore-Eckel Scholarship	High school graduates	One year (renewable)	Annually
College of New Rochelle School of Arts & Sciences New Rochelle, NY 10805	Variable $500-$2000 Presidential and Academic scholarships	Incoming freshman with portfolio General student population	Four years (renewable) One year	Annually Annually
College of Notre Dame at Maryland, Art Department 4701 N Charles St Baltimore, MD 21210	$3200 $2500-$3000 $4000 $300	Art majors in continuing education programs Incoming freshmen Art majors Photography majors	One year One to four years One to two years One year	Annually Annually Annually Annually
College of St. Benedict, Admissions Office 37 S College Ave St Joseph, MN 56374-2099	$1000	Art majors and intended majors	One year	Annually
The College of Saint Rose 432 Western Ave Albany, NY 12203	$1500-$3000	Freshmen or transfer students (based on excellence of art portfolio)	Four years	Annually
The College of the Ozarks Department of Art Point Lookout, MO 65726	Full tuition Work/study grant	Preference to scholarships, financial need, geographic location	Four years	Each semester
Colley-Sawyer College, Dept of Fine & Performing Arts 100 Main St New London, NH 03257	$5000 (10-12) - Dean's Scholarship for Creativity $1200 (2) - Edith B Long Scholarship	Incoming freshmen	One year, renewable for four years One year, renewable for four years	Annually Annually
Colorado State University Dept of Art Fort Collins, CO 80523	Varies	All undergraduate art majors	One year	Annually

OFFERED BY	AMOUNT	OPEN TO	DURATION	WHEN OFFERED
Columbia Basin College, Esvelt Gallery 2600 N 20th Ave Pasco, WA 99301	$1500	Two for entering art majors (freshmen); Two for continuing art majors (sophomores)	One year	Annually
Columbia University School of the Arts 310 Dodge New York, NY 10027	Variable	All registered students in competition		Annually
Columbus College Department of Art 4225 University Ave Columbus, GA 31907-5645	$10,000 Varies	Art majors Art majors; transfer students and entering freshmen	One year	Spring quarter
Community Colleges of Spokane 2000 N Greene St Spokane, WA 99207-5499	Varies; $50 quarterly tuition	Art students		
Concordia College Art Department 901 S Eighth Moorhead, MN 56562	Variable	Freshmen, sophomores, juniors and upper classmen	One year	Annually
Concordia College Art Department 800 N Columbia Ave Seward, NE 68434	Variable	Entering freshmen and upper classmen	Four years	Annually
Converse College Dept of Art, PO Box 29 Spartanburg, SC 29302	Varies	Scholastic & athletic students	One-four years	Annually
Cooper-Hewitt, National Design Museum, Smithsonian Institution 2 E 91st St, New York, NY 10128	Peter Krueger-Christie's Fellowship -$17,000 per year $15,000 stipend; $2000 for research related travel	Pre-doctoral graduate students	One year	
The Cooper Union School of Art Cooper Sq New York, NY 10003	Full tuition	Entering freshmen accepted into a four-year undergraduate BFA program	Four years	Annually
Corcoran School of Art 500 17th St NW Washington, DC 20006-4808	Varies	BFA degree, full- time students only		
Cornell College 600 First St W Mt Vernon, IA 52314-1098	$7000 -George E Buzza Award $5000 -Cornell Award	Selected on recommendation of Art Dept	Four years if student remains art major in good academic standing	Annually to freshmen
The Corning Museum of Glass One Museum Way Corning, NY 14830-2253	$5000 Rakow Grant for Glass Research	Scholars and researchers - by competition	One year	Annually
Cornish College of the Arts 710 E Roy St Seattle, WA 98102	Kreielsheimer Scholarship: Full tuition plus books & supplies	Residents of WA, OR and AK; must be recent (within two years) high school graduate or earned GED	Four years	Annually
Cosanti Foundation, Arcosanti HCR 74, Box 4136, Mayer, AZ 86333	$700 (seminar/ workshop tuition)	Applicants over 18 years old - contact workshop coordinator for application	Five weeks	11 times a year - one per seminar/workshop
Cottey College Fine Arts Division Nevada, MO 64772	$750 $400 (Harry Chew Memorial Scholarship)	Students interested in art who are attending Cottey College Students interested in art who are attending Cottey College	One year (renewable) One year (renewable)	Annually Annually
Crazy Horse Memorial Avenue of the Chiefs Crazy Horse, SD 57730-9506	$15,000 - $18,000	College students from South Dakota Indian reservations		Annually
Crowder College 601 LacLede Neosho, MO 64850	Trustee Scholarship, full tuition up to 16 credit hours	All students	Two years	Semi-annually

OFFERED BY	AMOUNT	OPEN TO	DURATION	WHEN OFFERED
Culver-Stockton College One College Hill Canton, MO 63435	$750-$2500 - majors $400-$750 - minors	Incoming art majors & minors; continuing art majors	One year	Annually; renewable with faculty review and satisfactory progress
Cumberland College, Art Dept 7523 College Station Dr Williamsburg, KY 40769	$1200	All	One year (renewable)	Annually
Daemen College Art Department 4380 Main St Amherst, NY 14226	$500-$5000	Talented students with financial needs; two $5000 awards exclusive of need	One year; renewable based on academic average	Annually, with special emphasis on February portfolio review
Dallas Baptist University Department of Art 3000 Mountain Creek Pkwy Dallas, TX 75211-9299	$600-$1000	All art major students	One year	Annually
Dana College Blair, NE 68008	$500-$2000	Entering students	Four years with annual review	Annually
Davidson College, Art Dept 315 N Main St, PO Box 1720 Davidson, NC 28036	$10,000/year - Bearden Scholarship $4000/year - Pepper Scholarship	Students at Davidson College	One year (renewable after each year)	Annually
Delta State University Dept of Art, Box D-2 Cleveland, MS 38733	$800-$1500	Incoming freshmen	One year	Annually
Denison University, University Gallery PO Box M, Burke Hall Granville, OH 43023	Vail Scholarships in the Arts -$1000 McGaw Scholarship - $5000	Sophomores, juniors & seniors -competitive. Awarded on the basis of portfolio and general academic ability Sophomores, juniors & seniors	One year, renewable	Annually
DePaul University, Dept of Art 1150 W Fullerton Chicago, IL 60614	$1000 - $4000	Incoming freshmen	One for four years	Annually
The Detroit Institute of Arts 5200 Woodward Ave Detroit, MI 48202	Curatorial & Education Internships & Conservation Fellowships	Minority graduate students; all other students		
Dickinson State University, Department of Fine Arts & Humanities, Dickinson, ND 58601	$100-$750	All students	One year	Annually
Douglas County Historical Society 906 E Second St Superior, WI 54880	$500	University Wisconsin - Superior history students	One year	Annually
Drake University University Ave Des Moines, IA 50311	$500-$4000	All art students	One year- renewable for 4 years	Annually
Dundas Valley School of Art 21 Ogilvie St Dundas, ON L9H 2S1 Canada	$2000 - $16,000	Full and part-time students	One year or one term	Semi-annually
East Carolina University School of Art Greenville, NC 27858-4353	$1200	Incoming art majors	One year	Spring
	$200-$1300	All art majors	One semester- four years	Annually
	$475	All out-of-state entering freshmen art majors, based on a portfolio review during NASAD portfolio days or private review	One semester	Annually
	$500-$5200	Graduate students		Annually
East Central College PO Box 529 Union, MO 63084	$600	High school seniors or older who display artistic ability & discipline	One semester	Semi-annually
Eastern Illinois University Art Department Charleston, IL 61920	Tuition waiver	Undergraduate art majors and entering freshmen	One year	Annually

OFFERED BY	AMOUNT	OPEN TO	DURATION	WHEN OFFERED
Eastern Washington University Dept of Art, MS 102 526 Fifth St Cheney, WA 99004	Varies	Art majors only: scholarships to undergraduates; fellowships to graduates	One year	Annually
Eastern Wyoming College Art Department 3200 West C St Torrington, WY 82240	Value of tuition (in-state)	Art majors	Four semesters	Spring
East Tennessee State University Carroll Reece Museum Johnson City, TN 37614	Friends of the Reece Museum Scholarship $2000	Students in the Dept of Art and Design at ETSU	One year	Annually
Edgewood College, Art Dept 855 Woodrow St Madison, WI 53711	$500-$1500	Entering freshmen or transfer students	One year (renewable for 4 years)	Annually
Edinboro University of Pennsylvania Dept of Art Edinboro, PA 16444	Graduate Assistantships which include tuition waiver plus stipend	MFA students-Graduates, Undergraduates, BFA - Fine Arts, BA - Art History, Art Education	One year (renewable)	Annually
Emmanuel College 400 The Fenway Boston, MA 02115	$6250	Undergraduates	One year; renewable for four years	Annually
Emory University Art History Dept Atlanta, GA 30322	Competitive	PhD candidates	Four years	Annually
Fairbanks Arts Association PO Box 72786 Fairbanks, AK 99707	$400	Junior high students attending the University of Alaska summer fine arts camp	One year	Annually
Fashion Institute of Technology 227 W 27th St New York, NY 10001	Variable	All students who qualify	Renewable	Annually
First Street Gallery 560 Broadway New York, NY 10012	Up to $4000	All	One month	Semi-annually
Fitton Center for Creative Arts 101 S Monument Ave Hamilton, OH 45011-2833	Class fees	Those in need; accepting all ages and abilities	Six to eight weeks	Each session
Fort Hays State University Visual Arts Center 600 Park St Hays, KS 67601	$400	Freshmen	One year	Semi-annually
Franklin College, Art Dept 501 E Monroe Franklin, IN 46131	$500	Art minor	One year	Annually
Franklin and Marshall College Art Dept, PO Box 3003, Lancaster, PA 17604-3003	Variable $3000	Advanced students with experience A sophomore major	Summer Summer travel grant to study or research abroad	At request of professors Annually
Friends University Art Department 2100 University Ave Wichita, KS 67213	$600 and up	All art majors	One to four years if grades & work standards are maintained	Annually
Frostburg State University Dept of Visual Arts E College Ave Frostburg, MD 21532-1099	Tuition	Freshmen or transfer art students pursuing a BFA at FSU	Up to 8 semesters - freshmen Up to 4 semesters - transfer students	
Gallery Worth 90 N Country Rd Setauket, NY 11780	(10) $500	Students of SUNY at Stonybrook	Semester	By semester (short term emergency funds) through Chairman of Art Dept SUNY, Stony Brook

OFFERED BY	AMOUNT	OPEN TO	DURATION	WHEN OFFERED
Georgetown College, Art Dept Mulberry St, PO Box 201 Georgetown, KY 40324	$250-$4000	Art majors	Four years with 2.0 GPA for grants; four years with 3.1 GPA for scholarships	Annually
Georgian Court College 900 Lakewood Ave Lakewood, NJ 08701	$3200, $1000 and $750 per year	High school graduates who plan to major in art	Renewable for four years	Annually
The Glassell School of Art, The Museum of Fine Arts, Houston 5101 Montrose Blvd Houston, TX 77006	Tuition only	One studio class; portfolio review	One semester	Semi-annually
Grace College, Department of Art 200 Seminary Dr Winona Lake, IN 46590	Quarter of tuition	Incoming freshmen, art majors with portfolio	One year (renewable)	Annually
Graceland College, Fine Arts Dept 700 College Ave Lamoni, IA 50140	Varies	Art majors	Some one-time; others on-going (renewable)	Annually
Graduate School of Figurative Art of the New York Academy of Art 111 Franklin St New York, NY 10013	$500-$5000	MFA candidates	Two years	Annually
Grand Valley State University Art & Design Department Allendale, MI 49401	$15000 -approximately	New and continuing students	Renewable	Annually
Grants for Graduate Study Abroad Write: USIA Fulbright Student Programs Institute of International Education, 809 United Nations Plaza, New York, NY 10017		People in the arts may apply for any of these awards (Fulbright-Hays and Foreign Governments, Lusk Memorial Fellowships), but they must be affiliated with an educational institute abroad while pursuing their studies	One academic year	Annually
Grayson County College, Art Dept 6101 Grayson Dr Denison, TX 75020	Varies	Visual Arts full-time students	By semester	Semi-annually
Greater Lafayette Museum of Art 101 S Ninth St Lafayette, IN 47901	Full tuition	Citizens of Indiana	Per term	Semi-annually
Green Mountain College Dept of Art Poultney, VT 05764	$3000 $500-$1000	Art applicants; freshmen Art majors	Four years	Annually Once
Greensboro Artists League 200 N Davie St Greensboro, NC 27401	(4) $250	Guilford County high school seniors pursuing art as a career		Annually
Gulf Coast Community College PO Box 100 Gautier, MS 39553	Varies	All	One year	Annually
John Simon Guggenheim Memorial Foundation 90 Park Ave New York, NY 10016	Adjusted to needs of fellows; average award $28,000	Advanced professionals, citizens or permanent residents of US, Canada, Latin America and the Caribbean	Six months to one year	Annually
Gustavus Adolphus College Art Dept, Schaefer Fine Arts Center Saint Peter, MN 56082	$300-$850	40 studio and art history students	One year	Annually
Hallwalls Contemporary Arts Center 2495 Main St, Ste H25 Buffalo, NY 14214	$1500	Visual artists from Erie, Monroe, Wayne and Livingstone Counties in NY state	One month	Between July and Dec

OFFERED BY	AMOUNT	OPEN TO	DURATION	WHEN OFFERED
Hampton University, Dept of Fine and Performing Arts Hampton, VA 23668	Varies	Fine and performing arts majors	One year	Annually
Allan Hancock College, Fine Arts Dept 800 S College Dr Santa Maria, CA 93454	$100-$500	Enrolled students	One year	Annually
Hannibal-LaGrange College 2800 Palmyra Rd Hannibal, MO 63401	$2000, $250 per semester - divisional scholarship	Beginning freshmen	Per semester	Annually
	$2400, $300 per semester - performance scholarship	Art majors	Per semester	Annually
	$2000, $250 per semester - student assistantship	Art majors	Per semester	Annually
Harding University Department of Art Box 2253 Searcy, AR 72149-0001	$250-$1000	Art majors; selection by portfolio, high school transcript and reference letters from art teachers	One year; renewable	Annually
Hardin-Simmons University, Art Dept Hickory at Ambler St PO Box 16085, Univ Sta Abilene, TX 79698	Up to $500 per semester	Art majors, full-time students; based on financial need, then merit	One year	Annually
Hartford Art School University of Hartford 200 Bloomfield Ave West Hartford, CT 06117	Varies	Open to qualified applicants for full time study - undergraduate and graduate students	One year; renewable based upon performance	Annually
The Heritage Center, Inc PO Box 100 Pine Ridge, SD 57770	(5) $1000	Native American artists entering the "Red Cloud Indian Art Show"	One year	Annually
Hesston College, Art Dept Box 3000 Hesston, KS 67022	$3000 (varies by academic prowess)	Any student (not art specific)	Two years, contingent of maintaining standards	Annually
Hills College, Fine Arts Dept PO Box 619 Hillsboro, TX 76645	Variable	Anyone	Semester	Semi-annually
Hinds Community College Marie Hull Gallery Raymond, MS 39154	Tuition	Entering freshmen	One year	Annually
Historical Museum at Fort Missoula Bldg 322, Fort Missoula Missoula, MT 59801	$450	University students	Semester	
Historical Society of Kent County, Inc 101 Church Alley, PO Box 665 Chestertown, MD 21620	$500 book scholarship	Kent County High School seniors		Annually
Historic Deerfield, Inc The Street, PO 321 Deerfield, MA 01342	$1400 to Historic Deerfield Fellowship; financial aid available	College undergraduates	Nine weeks, from mid-June to mid-Aug.	Annually
History of Art & Architecture University of California Santa Barbara, CA 93106-7080	Variable	Graduate students approved by Art History Department Chairman. MA and PhD candidates are also eligible for consideration for departmental Vidda Foundation and Art Affiliate Awards	Academic year	
Hofstra University 1000 Fulton Ave Hempstead, NY 11550	$20,872	Undergrads	Variable	Annually
Hope College, Art Department De Pree Art Center 275 Columbia Ave Holland, MI 49423	$2500	Prospective Art Majors (and minors)	Four years (renewable)	Annually

OFFERED BY	AMOUNT	OPEN TO	DURATION	WHEN OFFERED
Houston Center for Photography 1441 W Alabama Houston, TX 77006	$1000 & exhibition	Photographers and artists who incorporate photographic media in their work	One year	Annually
Huguenot Historical Society PO Box 339 New Paltz, NY 12561	(5) $1200	Students in the museum field summer jobs	One year	Annually
Huntingdon College 1500 E Fairview Ave Montgomery, AL 36106	One full tuition and numerous partial tuitions	Any incoming art students	Four years	Annually
The Huntington Library and Art Gallery San Marino, CA 91108	$1800/month	Scholars doing research on British & American art	One to five months	Annually; applications received Oct 1 to Dec 15 for awards beginning the following June 1
Idaho State University Art Department Fifth & Dillon, PO Box 8004 Pocatello, ID 83209	Varies	Declared art undergraduates and graduate students		
Illinois State University Art Dept, CUA119 Normal, IL 61790-5620	Varies	All undergraduate and graduate students	One year; some are renewable	Annually
Illinois Wesleyan University School of Art Bloomington, IL 61702	$2000-$6800	Entering freshmen; based on portfolio review & academic background	Four years (renewable)	Annually
Indiana Purdue University Dept of Fine Arts 2101 Coliseum Blvd E Fort Wayne, IN 46805-1499	Varies	Full-time degree students	One year	Annually
Indiana State University, Department of Art, Terre Haute, IN 47809	$3500	MFA, MS, MA	One year	Annually
	$1100	BFA Freshmen Juniors/Seniors Painting	Four years One year	Annually
	$350-$1500	BS, BFA	One year	Annually
Indiana University of Pennsylvania Dept of Arts & Art Education 115 Sprowls Hall Indiana, PA 15705	$100-$4500	Graduate students	One year	Annually
Indiana Wesleyan University, Art Dept 4201 S Washington St Marion, IN 46953	$600	Any art major	One year	Annually
Indian Hills Community College Ottumwa Campus, Dept of Art 525 Grandview at Elm Ottumwa, IA 52501	$100-$400	Full-time students in art	One year	Annually
Industrial Designers Society of America, Ste E 1142 E Walker Rd, Great Falls, VA 22066	Varies	Graduate and undergraduate students	One year	Annually
Iowa State University Department of Art and Design 158 College of Design Bldg Ames, IA 50011-3092	Varies	Varies		Annually
Ithaca College, Art Dept 101 Ceracche Center Ithaca, NY 14850-7277	$600	Art majors with financial need	One year	Annually
Jackson State University Department of Art Lynch at Dalton St Jackson, MS 39217	Varies	All honor students; portfolios required		Annually
Jacksonville State University Department of Art 700 Pelham Rd N, Jacksonville, AL 36265	$970	Art majors	One year	Annually

OFFERED BY	AMOUNT	OPEN TO	DURATION	WHEN OFFERED
James Madison University School of Art and Art History Harrisonburg, VA 22807	$500-$4000	Undergraduate art and art history majors	One year (renewable)	Annually
Jersey City State College, Art Dept 2039 Kennedy Blvd Jersey City, NJ 07305	Varies	Applicants with appropriate SAT scores, recommendations	Varies	Annually
Johnson Atelier Technical Institute of Sculpture 60 Ward Ave Exten Mercerville, NJ 08619	$4800 (tuition grant)	Accepted students	Varies	Annually
Junior College of Albany Fine Arts Division 140 New Scotland Ave Albany, NY 12208	$3000	Freshmen and second year students	One and two years, over-all GPA	
Kalamazoo College 1200 Academy Kalamazoo, MI, 49006	$1500 - Art scholarship $3000-$10,000 - Honors scholarship	Accepted applicants Accepted applicants	One year (renewable) One year (renewable)	Annually Annually
Kansas City Art Institute 4415 Warwick Blvd KansasCity, MO 64111	Varies	All students accepted for admission	One year (renewable) with satisfactory GPA	Varies
Kansas State University Department of Art Manhattan, KS 66506	Variable scholarship awards	Freshmen-senior undergraduates & graduate students	One year	Annually
Kapioliani Community College Art Program 4303 Diamond Head Rd Honolulu, HI 96816	$500	Kapioliani Community College art majors	One year	Annually
Kappa Pi International Honorary Art Fraternity 9321 Paul Adrian Dr Crestwood, MO 63126	$200, $300 & $500-$1000	Active student members only	One year (renewable)	Annually
Kellogg Community College Visual & Performing Arts Dept 450 North Ave Battle Creek, MI 49017	$50-$150		Semester	Semi-annually
Kendall College of Art & Design 111 N Division Grand Rapids, MI 49503	Varies	All students	Renewable	Annually
Kent State University School of Art Kent, OH 44242	$500 per year; graduate fellowships, graduate teaching assistants (tuition waiver)	One year	Varies	Annually
Maude I Kerns, Art Center 1910 E 15th Ave Eugene, OR 97403	$1000 per year	Children through adults exhibiting motivation and/or financial need	One year for MKAC classes	Quarterly
Kresge Art Museum, Michigan State University East Lansing, MI 48824	$13,000 plus medical benefits	Interns with some graduate work in art history and some experience in museums	Ten months	Annually- apply between Jan-Mar each year
Lake Forest College 555 N Sheridan Rd Lake Forest, IL 60045	Varies	All students	One year to four full years	Annually
Lamar University, Dishman Art Gallery Box 10027 Beaumont, TX 77710	Varies	All students	One year, renewable	Semi-annually

OFFERED BY	AMOUNT	OPEN TO	DURATION	WHEN OFFERED
Lander University Greenwood, SC 29649	$15,000	Art majors	One year (renewable): based upon GPA up to graduation	Annually
Lane Community College 4000 E 30th Ave Eugene, OR 97405	$500	Graphic design students	One year	Annually
	$500-Wayne Shields Foundation	All art majors	One year	Annually
Laramie County Community College Div of Humanities 1400 E Colege Dr Cheyenne, WY 82007	Two at $496	All applicants	One year	Semi-annually
Lawrence University, Dept of Art Wriston Art Center Appleton, WI 54912	Varies	Students of academic merit and particular talent		Annually
Leo Baeck Institute 129 E 73rd St New York, NY 10021	Fritz Halbers Fellowship, up to $3000	Students enrolled in a PhD program in an accredited institution of higher education	One year	Annually; application deadline Nov 1
	David Baumgardt Memorial Fellowship	Academics affiliated with an accredited institution of higher education	One year; monthly installments	Annually; application deadline Nov 1
	LBI/DAAD Fellowship, stipend of $2000	Doctoral students or recent PhDs affiliated with an accredited American institute of higher education; must be US citizen and no older than 35-years-old	One year; paid in two installments	Annually; application deadline Nov 1
	LBI/DAAD Fellowship; stipend of DM 1600 monthly	Doctoral students or academics affiliated with an accredited institution of higher education that will do research in Federal Republic of Germany; must be US citizen and no older than 35-years-old	Six months; monthly installments	Annually; application deadline Nov 1
Lewis-Clark State College Art Department Lewiston, ID 83501	Varies	All students	Six months	Annually
Lewiston Art Center 801 W Broadway Lewiston, MT 59457	$500	College bound or college students majoring in performing or visual arts	One year	Annually
Library Company of Philadelphia 1314 Locust St Philadelphia, PA 19107	$1400	Those involved in both post-doctoral and dissertation research	One month	Annually
Limestone College 1115 College Dr Geffrey, SC 29340	$2500	Majors - studio & art education	One year (renewable)	Annually
Lindenwood College, Art Dept 209 S Kingshighway St. Charles, MO 63301	Variable	Basis of merit, talent & financial need	One year (renewable)	Annually & semi-annually
Lock Haven University Lock Haven, PA 17745	Varies	Variable	One year	
Long Island University Brooklyn Center, Art Dept University Plaza Brooklyn, NY 11201	One-half tuition	Art majors with 3.0 average	One year	Annually
Long Island University C.W. Post Campus, Art Dept Northern Blvd Brookville, NY 11548	$250-$500 O'-Malley Awards	Undergraduates and graduates attending LIU		By application, six times annually
	$1000 -O'Malley Research Travel Fellowship	Undergraduates and graduates attending LIU	One year	Annually
	$1500-$4000 - Portfolio award	Incoming freshmen and transfer students	Four years	Annually in Nov
	Posner Fund - $1000	Incoming freshmen	Four years	Annually
Longwood College Dept of Art, High St Farmville, VA 23909	$300-$500	Current students only	One year	Annually

OFFERED BY	AMOUNT	OPEN TO	DURATION	WHEN OFFERED
Louisiana College, Dept of Art 1140 College Dr Pineville, LA 71359		Studio art and graphic design majors (juniors & seniors)	One year	Annually
Lourdes College 6832 Convent Blvd Sylvania, OH 43560	$500	Any art major who has completed one semester at Lourdes College	One year	Annually
Lower East Side Printshop 59-61 E Fourth St, 6th Flr New York, NY 10003	50% workspace fee	Artists of color with a printmaking background	Six-month sessions; renewable	Continuous
Lubbock Christian University 5601 W 19th St Lubbock, TX 79407-2099	$500	All applicants; with portfolios	Semester	Annually
Lycoming College, Art Dept Williamsport, PA 17701	$1,500	Entering students	Renewable for four years	Semi-annually
Maine College of Art 97 Spring St Portland, ME 04101	Half or partial tuition	Qualified BFA degree students	Four years	Annually
Maine Line Art Center Old Buck Rd - Lancaster Ave Haverford, PA 19041	$100-$150	Students	Semester	Per semester
Malone College, Department of Art, Division of Fine Art, 515 25th St NW, Canton, OH 44709		Full-time students		
Manchester College, Art Dept 604 College Ave North Manchester, IN 46962	$1000 - $4000	Everyone	One year (renewable)	Annually
Manchester Institute of Arts & Sciences Gallery 148 Concord St Manchester, NH 03104	Tuition	All applicants		Each semester
Mankato State University, Art Dept PO Box 8400 Mankato, MN 56002-8400	Varies	Recommended by faculty	One year	Annually
Mansfield University Art Dept, Allen Hall Mansfield, PA 16933	Varies	Freshmen	One year	Annually
The Mariners' Museum 100 Museum Dr Newport News, VA 23606-3759	$750	All researchers interested in the holdings of the museum's collection, library and archives	Varies	Annually
Marion Art Center 80 Pleasant, Box 602 Marion, MA 02738	$500	High school seniors in southeastern Massachusetts	One year	Annually
Mars Hill College Art Department Mars Hill, NC 28754	Up to $1000	All students meeting the entrance criteria of Mars Hill College	One year	Annually
Marylhurst College Art Department Marylhurst, OR 97036	Varies	Continuing students	One year	Annually
Marymount College, Art Dept 100 Tarrytown Ave Tarrytown, NY 10591	Varies (up to $500)	Full-time students registered at the college	One year	Annually
Marywood College, Art Dept 2300 Adams Ave Scranton, PA 18509	Varies	All students; undergraduate and graduate	Undergraduate, four years; graduate, one year renewable	Annually
Massachusetts Historical Society, 1154 Boylston St Boston, MA 02215	$1500	Graduate students, faculty and independent scholars	Four to five weeks	Annually

OFFERED BY	AMOUNT	OPEN TO	DURATION	WHEN OFFERED
McMurry University Art Department PO Box 308, McMurry Sta Abilene, TX 79697	$2200	Art students who show special ability	One year	Annually
	$1000	Entering art students who show special ability	Four years	Annually
	$3000 with $1000 added each remaining year	Art scholarship (based on portfolio judging from local area high schools)	Four years	Annually
McNeese State University Department of Visual Arts Box 92295 Lake Charles, LA 70601	(15) $1000	Incoming freshmen	Two years	Annually
Memphis College of Art Overton Pk, 1930 Poplar Ave Memphis, TN 38104-2764	$1500-$5125	Entering freshmen and full-time students	Renewable	Annually
	Varies	Any applicant	Spring, summer and fall sessions	Spring, summer and fall sessions
Mendocino County Arts Council 400 E Commercial St Willits, CA 95490	$150 to $1800	Artists and arts organizations of Mendocino County only	Six months	Annually
Mercer University, Art Department College of Liberal Arts 1400 Coleman Ave Macon, GA 31207	$750-$1000	Two scholarships to rising seniors; five scholarships to continuing sophomores and juniors	One year	Annually
Mercyhurst College, Dept of Art Glenwood Hills Erie, PA 16546	$4000- 1st place $1500- 2nd place $1000- 3rd place	All freshmen art applicants, recent high school graduates, portfolio competition	One year (renewable)	Annually
Metropolitan Museum of Art Education Department 1000 Fifth Ave New York, NY 10028	Variable	Scholars researching art historical fields relating to Metropolitan Museum of Art Collections & Conservators	One year	Annually
Metropolitan State College of Denver Art Department PO Box 173362 Denver, CO 80217-3362	Full year tuition	All majors, after one year	One year	Annually
Miami-Dade Community College Visual Arts Dept 11011 SW 104th St Miami, FL 33176	$350-$500 per term; two at $1200 per year	New and continuing art majors	Varies	Annually; semi-annually
Michigan State University Department of Art 113 Kresge Art Center East Lansing, MI 48824-1119	$300-$10,000	Undergraduate and graduate students	One year	Annually
Midwestern State University Art Department 3410 Taft Blvd Wichita Falls, TX 76308	$100-$1500 per year	Full-time students; minimum 3.0 GPA	One year, must re-apply after each year	Semi-annually
Miles Community College Art Department 2715 Dickinson St Miles City, MT 59301	Based on need	Art students	One year	Annually
Millikin University Art Department 1184 W Main Decatur, IL 62522	$500 to one-half tuition	Qualified students	Four years	Annually
Milwaukee Institute of Art & Design 273 E Erie St Milwaukee, WI 53202	$2000 -full tuition	All applicants	One year, renewable for four years	Annually
Minnesota State Arts Board Park Square Court 400 Sibley St, Ste 200 Saint Paul, MN 55101-1928	$6000 (Fellowships only)	Professional artists in all disciplines who are residents of the state of Minnesota. Restriction: cannot be used for tuition, fees or work towards any degree	One year	Annually

OFFERED BY	AMOUNT	OPEN TO	DURATION	WHEN OFFERED
Minot State University Northwest Art Center 500 University Ave W Minot, ND 58707	Varies	All applicants	One year	Annually
Miracosta College One Barnard Dr Oceanside, CA 92056	$100-$800	All students	One year	Annually
Missouri Southern State College Art Department, 3950 E Newman Rd Joplin, MO 64801-1595	Henry Hornsby $1000; Thomas Hart Benton (4) $1150; Warten Fine Arts $1150; BL Parker $500; CL Hyde Specialty Scholarships - $500	Top quality students with art skills and financial needs	One year	Annually
Missouri Western State College Art Department 4525 Downs Dr St Joseph, MO 64507	Variable	Any qualifying student majoring in art	By semester	By semester
Montana State University School of Art Bozeman, MT 59717	(1) $5000 teaching assistantship	Graduate students	Ten months	Annually
	(2) $1000 presidential scholarship	Graduate students	Ten months	Annually
Montana State University - Billings Art Department 1500 N 30th St Billings, MT 59101-0298		Full time art majors	One semester to one year	Annually
Monterey Museum of Art 559 Pacific St Monterey, CA 93940	$100 monthly	All students	One year	Annually, deadline for application Nov 15
Montserrat College of Art 23 Essex St, Box 26 Beverly, MA 01915	Merit Awards starting at $1000	Incoming freshmen and transfer students	One year	
	Montserrat grants varying to $3000	Students eligible for financial aid	One year (renewable)	
	Dean's Scholarship starting at $1000	Incoming students, 3.0 GPA, SAT required for financial aid eligibility	One year (renewable)	
	(1) Presidential Scholarship	Incoming freshmen (minority applicant), 3.0 GPA, SAT required for financial aid eligibility	Four years (renewable)	
Moravian College, Dept of Art 1200 Main St, Church St Campus Bethlehem, PA 18018	$1000-$8000	Meritorious students in financial need	One year	Annually
Morningside College, Art Dept 1501 Morningside Ave Sioux City, IA 51106	$1000-$10,000	Incoming freshmen and transfer students	Four years	Semi-annually
Mount Allison University Dept of Fine Arts Sackville, NB E0A 3C0, Canada	$134-$1250	All students	One year	Annually
Mount Hood Community College Visual Arts Center 26000 SE Stark St Bresham, OR 97030	Varies	Varies	Quarterly; annually	Annually; semi-annually; quarterly
Mount Mary College 2900 N Menomonee River Pkwy Milwaukee, WI 53222	$3000	Entering freshmen (women)	One year (renewable)	Annually
Mount Mercy College, Art Dept 1330 Elmhurst Dr NE Cedar Rapids, IA 52402-4797	Up to $2500	Anyone interested in art participation	Yearly (renewable)	Annually
Mount Union College, Dept of Art 1972 Clark Dr Alliance, OH 44601	$6000 per year	Incoming freshmen		Annually

OFFERED BY	AMOUNT	OPEN TO	DURATION	WHEN OFFERED
Munson-Williams-Proctor Institute School of Art 310 Genesee St Utica, NY 13502		College credit students	One year	Semi-annually
Murray State University Dept of Art 15th St, PO Box 9 Murray, KY 42071-0009	Variable (Presidential University Scholars and Academic Scholarships)	Graduating high school seniors	One to four years	Annually
	$500 to $2000 departmental/ collegiate scholarships	Incoming freshman and students majoring in art at Murray State University (portfolio required)	One year	Annually
	Varies	All	Varies	Annually
Muscarelle Museum of Art College of William and Mary Williamsburg, VA 23187-8795		College of William and Mary students	One semester	Semi-annually
The Museum of Arts and Sciences Inc 1040 Museum Blvd Daytona Beach, FL 32114	Varies	Interns with college training	One year	Annually
Museum of Early Southern Decorative Arts Summer Institute PO Box 10310 Winston-Salem, NC 27108-0310	$150-$200 Fellowship for partial summer institute tuition	Graduate students in history, art history, preservation, museum studies; museum personnel	June-July (four weeks)	Annually
Muskoka Arts and Crafts Inc 15 King St, Box 376 Bracebridge, ON P1L 1S7 Canada	$1000	Graduating high school student from Muskoka pursuing a post-secondary education in the visual arts	One year	Annually
National Gallery of Canada 80 Sussex Dr Ottawa, ON K1N 9N4 Canada	$15,000 Claudia DeHueck Fellowship	Teachers, artists, scientists, art historians, curators, conservators and other scholars with at least an MA or equivalent	One year	Annually
	(4) Research Fellowships, up to $15,000 each	Canadian citizens and permanent residents of Canada; Liselte Model/Joseph G Blum Photography Fellowship is open to international applications	Three to nine months	
National League of American Pen Women 1300 17th St NW Washington, DC 20036	$1000 each in Letters, Music & Art	Non Pen Women Mature Women's Grant		Biennial on even-numbered years awarded
National Sculpture Society 1177 Avenue of the Americas New York, NY 10036	$1000	Figurative sculpture students	One year	Annually
Navarro College, Art Dept/ Computer Art Multimedia Technology, 3200 N Hwy 31 Corsicana, TX 75110	(20) $200-$600 each	Art majors or any art field, granted based on a portfolio review & interview	One year	Annually
Nazareth College of Rochester Art Dept, 4245 East Ave Rochester, NY 14618-3790	$2000	Qualified high school graduates	Four years	Annually
Nebraska Wesleyan University Art Department, 5000 St Paul Lincoln, NE 68504	$1000 per year	First year students	Four years	Annually
New Hampshire Institute of Art 148 Concord St Manchester, NH 03104	Up to $6000 per semester	Qualified applicants	Semester basis	Semester basis
New Haven Paint & Clay Club, Inc The John Slade Ely House 51 Trumbull St New Haven, CT 06510	$500	Local high school students who exhibit their artwork and submit a portfolio		Annually

OFFERED BY	AMOUNT	OPEN TO	DURATION	WHEN OFFERED
New Orleans School of Glassworks & Gallery 727 Magazine St New Orleans, LA 70130	Kotaro Hamada Scholarship	Glassworks faculty members		Annually
New World School of Arts 300 NE Second Ave Miami, FL 33132	$1000 to full tuition towards a BFA degree	All US and foreign students	One to four years	Semi-annually
New York Academy of Art 111 Franklin St New York, NY 10013	$500-$5000	MFA students	One year (renewable)	Annually
New York Institute of Technology Fine Arts Dept, Wheatley Rd Old Westbury, NY 11568	Varies			Semi-annually
North Central College Art Department 30 N Brainard Naperville, IL 60566	$4000	Incoming freshmen art majors; returning students; transfer students	One year	Annually
Northeast Louisiana University Dept of Art 700 University Ave, Stubbs 141 Monroe, LA 71209	$200	Top five full-time art students with portfolio	One year	Annually
Northeastern Illinois University Art Department 5500 N St Louis Chicago, IL 60625	Full tuition	Art majors	One semester; student re-applies each semester	Semi-annually
Northern Illinois University School of Art DeKalb, IL 60115-2883	Jack Arends Scholarship - approximately $800	Art majors with 3.0 overall GPA, one year residence at NIU, portfolio and three reco-mmendations (two from NIU School of Art)	One year	Annually
	James P Bates Memorial Scholarship - approximately $500	Rotated among NIU majors in the areas of School of Art	One year	Annually
	Richard Keefer Scholarship - approximately $300	Art majors-rotated among four areas-Art History and Art Education; Drawing, Painting & Printmaking; Crafts & Sculpture; Design & Photography	One year	Annually
	NIU Tuition Waiver- tuition fee for Illinois residents or out-of-state award equal to in-state amount	Incoming freshmen art majors; must maintain 2.5 overall GPA and 3.0 art GPA; awarded by Portfolio Competition	One year	Annually
	John X Koznarek Memorial Scholarship- approximately $900	Enrolled majors in studio art; portfolio and three recommendations	One year	Annually
	Cora B Miner Scholarship - approximately $300	Preferably to NIU student from DeKalb County with interest in realistic art	One year	Annually
	Frances E Gates Memorial Scholarship- approximately $400	Preferably a NIU graduate student specializing in watercolor	One year	Annually
	Peg Bond Scholarship- approximately $1000	Awarded to an undergraduate art education major; minimum 3.0 GPA overall, art portfolio and brief paper on subject of the teaching of art as a profession must be submitted	One year	Annually
Northern Michigan University Dept of Art & Design Marquette, MI 49855	$1000	Entering freshmen	One year	Annually
	$400	Continuing students	One year	Annually
	$200	Continuing students	One year	Annually
Northern Virginia Fine Arts Association at the Athenaeum, 20 Prince St Alexandria, VA 22314	Varies	Talented dancers for NVFAA's Alexandria Ballet	One year	Annually

OFFERED BY	AMOUNT	OPEN TO	DURATION	WHEN OFFERED
North Iowa Area Community College Department of Art 500 College Dr Mason City, IA 50401	$500-$1000	Art majors	One year	Annually
Northwest College Powell, WY 82435	Maximum $800 per person per year, plus three $1000 scholarships ships per year	All students, portfolio required	Two years	Annually
Northwest Missouri State University Department of Art Maryville, MO 64468	25-50% tuition	Freshmen & seniors	One year	Annually
Northwestern College Art Department Orange City, IA 51041	$500	Art majors competing as entering freshmen in portfolio reviews	One year (renewable)	Annually
Nova Scotia College of Art & Design 5163 Duke St Halifax, NS B3J 3J6 Canada	$500-$1500 (CN)	Students at NSCAD	One year	Annually
Ocean County College Humanities Department College Dr Toms River, NJ 08754-2001	Varies	Any Applicant	One year	Annually
Ohio State University Dept of History of Art 100 Hayes Hall Columbus, OH 43210	$7083 for first year students plus tuition waiver for teaching associateships	Students who demontrate accomplishment and evidence of potential excellence in teaching scholarship and/or research in History of Art		Annually
	University fellowship of $11,000 per year plus tuition waiver	First year students, graduate students; MA and PhD	One year	Annually
Ohio State University Graduate School Department of Art Education Columbus, OH 43210	(1) Graduate Associates; start at $6210, plus tuition waivers; (2) Fellowships; start at $10,260 plus tuition waivers	All MA and PhD candidates (special minority fellowships are also awarded)	9-12 months (renewable for three years)	Annually
Ohio University, School of Art College of Fine Arts Athens, OH 45701	Tuition scholarships, graduate teaching assistantships	Undergraduate students and graduates	One year (renewable)	Annually
Oklahoma Baptist University 500 W University Shawnee, OK 74801	$1500	Art majors	One year	Annually
Oklahoma Christian University of Science & Arts PO Box 11000 Oklahoma City, OK 73136-1100	$1000	Entering freshmen	Five years	Annually
Oklahoma City University 2501 N Blackwelder Oklahoma City, OK 73106	$1000-$1250	Freshmen, junior & senior art majors	One year	Annually
	(5) Regular Norick Art Scholarships $1000	Freshmen	One year	Annually
	(3) Native American Norick Art Scholarships $1000	Freshmen	One year	Annually
	Petree Scholarship in Art $1000	Freshmen	Four years	Annually
	Ruth Jeanette Brooks Scholarship in Fine Arts $3000	Sophomore and above	One year (renewable)	Annually
	Iva B Kelly Art Scholarship $2500	Juniors and seniors	One year (renewable)	Annually
	Roberta M Miller Art Scholarship $1500	Sophomore and above	One year (renewable)	Annually
	Fritz Ford Art Award $200	Sophomore and above	One year (renewable)	Annually

OFFERED BY	AMOUNT	OPEN TO	DURATION	WHEN OFFERED
Oklahoma State University Department of Art 108 Bartlett Center Stillwater, OK 74078-4085	$12,500	Incoming freshmen and continuing art majors	One year	Annually
Old Dominion University Art Dept Norfolk, VA 23529	Variable	Art majors, studio art history	One year	Annually
Oregon College of Art and Craft 8245 SW Barnes Rd Portland, OR 97225	$195-$2952	Full-time certificate programs; students and BFA students	One academic year	Annually - end of spring quarter, for the next academic year
Oregon Historical Society Library 1200 SW Park Ave Portland, OR 97205	$3000, plus tuition remission	Portland State University graduate history students	One year	Annually
Oregon State University, Dept of Art Corvallis, OR 97331-3702	$100-$1500	Anyone	One year (renewable)	Annually
Otis College of Art and Design 2401 Wilshire Blvd Los Angeles, CA 90057	Variable	Students enrolled at Otis in the BFA or MFA degree program	Academic year	Annually
Our Lady of the Lake University 411 SW 24th St San Antonio, TX 78207-4689	Varies	All undergraduate applicants based on ACT/SAT scores and high school GPA	Up to 8 semesters	Annually
Pacific Lutheran University Art Dept Tacoma, WA 98447	$500-$3000	All enrolled students	One year	Annually
Pacific Northwest College of Art 1219 SW Park St Portland, OR 97205	Variable Variable	Enrolled students Incoming freshmen	One school year One school year	Annually Annually
Pacific Union College Art Department Angwin, CA 94508	$1000	New students	One year	Annually
Pacific University on Oregon Arts Division, Dept of Art 2043 College Way Forest Grove, OR 97116	Varies	Anyone	One year, can be extended	Annually
Palm Beach Community College Division of Fine Arts 4200 Congress Ave, Central Campus Lake Worth, FL 33461	$5000 art scholarship	Entering freshmen; beginning sophomores; merit based on GPA	One year	Annually & semi-annually
Palomar College 1140 W Mission Rd San Marcos, CA 92069	$100 Lake San Marcos Art League Award	Returning sophomores majoring in art		
	$250 Fallbrook Art Association	Fallbrook resident, full time art student in the spring at a two year community college; must transfer to a 4-year course university in the fall		
	Ivie Frances Wickam Scholarships $500-$5000	Current women graduates of Palomar College who are evident of financial need, evidence of scholastic record; preference is given to art, music and education students		
	$200 John Barlow	Returning or transfer students		
Pasadena City College Art Department 1570 E Colorado Ave Pasadena, CA 91107	$18,000	Students with 3.5 GPA in art and have completed 12 units	One year	Annually
Pastel Society of the West Coast Roseville Arts Center 424 Oak Street Roseville, CA 95789	$300	Graduating high school seniors pursuing art		Annually; qualifying counties/school districts rotate
Peabody Essex Museum E India Sq Salem, MA 01970	Variable	Graduate students in American Studies at Boston University	One year	Annually

OFFERED BY	AMOUNT	OPEN TO	DURATION	WHEN OFFERED
The Pen and Brush, Inc 16 E Tenth St New York, NY 10003-5958	$1000	Chosen by governing board	One year	Annually
Pence Gallery 212 D St Davis, CA 95616	$200	Qualified university students seeking a career in museums	one semester; one quarter	Annually
Penland School of Crafts Penland, NC 28765	Varies	All students over 19 years old, all levels of experience		Annually
Pennsylvania Academy of the Fine Arts 1301 Cherry St Philadelphia, PA 19107	Varies	All full-time students who show need or merit	One year (renewable)	Annually
Pennsylvania School of Art & Design 704 N Prince St, PO Box 59 Lancaster, PA 17608-0059	$1950	Freshmen applicants	Three years if 3.0 GPA is maintained	Annually
Pensacola Junior College Visual Arts Department 1000 College Blvd Pensacola, FL 32504-8998	$1200	Incoming freshmen by portfolio review	One year	Annually
Peru State College Art Department PO Box 106, Peru, NE 68421	$300	All art majors, freshmen to seniors	One year (renewable); based on performance	Annually
Peters Valley Craftsmen, Inc 19 Kuhn Rd Layton, NJ 07851	Workshop fees	New Jersey art educators (K-12); Sussex County High School students (NJ)	Per workshop	Annually
Phillips Exeter Academy, Art Center & Lamont Gallery, Front St & Tan Line Exeter, NH 03833	Varies	Students with financial need		Annually
Pittsburg State University Art Department 1701 S Broadway St Pittsburg, KS 66762-7512	$1000	Art majors	Full semester	Annually
Plum Tree Fine Arts Program, PO Box 1-A Pilar, NM 97531	50% of tuition	Residents of New Mexico	Workshop session	Annually
Plymouth State College Plymouth, NH 03264	$1000-$2000	Various criteria, including high scholarship and achievement	Scholarships one year, fellowships one semester	Annually
Polk Community College Arts, Letters & Social Sciences 999 Ave H NE Winter Haven, FL 33881	Varies	Working students	One year	Semi-annually
Pomona College, Art Dept 333 College Way Claremont, CA 91711	Based on need	Enrolled students	Academic period	Annually
The Ponca City Art Association 819 E Central, Box 1394 Ponca City, OK 74602	$250	Local art student	One year	Annually
Portland Community College PO Box 19000 Portland, OR 97280-0990	Tuition grants	Art majors	One year	Annually
Portland State University Dept of Art PO Box 751 Portland, OR 97207	Varied	Art major currently enrolled at PSU with 20 hrs in art at time of application. Good accumulative GPA and portfolio also required	Academic year	Annually-Spring
Pratt Community College Art Department Hwy 61 Pratt, KS 67124	Varies; from $100 to full tuition and books	Qualified art majors	One year; renewable for two years	Annually; spring semester every year

OFFERED BY	AMOUNT	OPEN TO	DURATION	WHEN OFFERED
Pratt Manhattan 295 Lafayette St, 2nd Flr New York, NY 10012		All students	One year	Annually
Printmaking Workshop 55 W 17th St New York, NY 10011	Varies: scholarships, fellowships and guest residencies		Based on scholarship, fellowship and/or residency	Annually
Queen's Medical Auxiliary Queen Emma Gallery, PO Box 861 1301 Punchbowl St Honolulu, HI 96813	$500-$1000	Students in health services	One year	Annually
Randall Museum 199 Museum Way San Francisco, CA 94114	Up to half of class fee ($30 maximum)	Persons under 18 years of age	Per course	Annually
Harry Ransom Humanities Research Center PO Box 7219 Austin, TX 78713-7219	$1500-$2000 per month	Scholars pursuing post-doctoral research	One to four months	Annually
Rensselaer County Historical Society 59 Second St Troy, NY 12180		Juniors & seniors with art history and history of American studies majors	On-going	
Rhode Island School of Design Two College St Providence, RI 02903	Variable	Accepted degree candidates on undergraduate & graduate level based on financial need	One year	Annually
Rice University Dept of Art & Art History PO Box 1892 Houston, TX 77251	$1000-$9000 (plus tuition waiver)	Candidates of the Master of Arts degree in Art History	One year (renewable)	Annually
Richmond Art Museum McGuire Memorial Hall 350 Whitewater Blvd Richmond, IN 47374	$500 Anna Belle Henthorne Art Scholarship, $350	Richmond High School senior studying art Richmond High School senior studying art	One year One year	Annually Annually
Ricks College, Department of Art Rexburg, ID 83440	$200-$800	Art majors	One year	Fall
Ringling School of Art & Design 2700 N Tamiami Trail Sarasota, FL 34234	$500-$2500	All full-time Ringling students	One year, some semester grants, renewable	Annually
Roberts Wesleyan College Art Department 2301 W Side Dr Rochester, NY 14624	$500-$1500	Incoming new students, based on portfolio review		Annually; renewable
Rocky Mountain College of Art and Design 6875 E Evans Ave Denver, CO 80224	$750 $7500	Full-time students New full time students	One trimester (renewable) Program duration	Each trimester Each fall
Rutgers University, Newark Dept of Visual & Performing Arts University Heights, 110 Warren St Bradley Hall Newark, NJ 07102	$4000	Students in Visual Arts, Art History & Art Education	One year	Annually
Sacred Heart University Dept of Art 5151 Park Ave Fairfield, CT 06432-1000	$500-$2000	Full-time art majors	One year	Annually
Saginaw Valley State University 7400 Bay Rd University Center, MI 48710	Fine Arts Awards - full tuition and fees	HS seniors with 3.0 GPA; portfolio required	One year, renewable up to 3 years	Annually

OFFERED BY	AMOUNT	OPEN TO	DURATION	WHEN OFFERED
Saint Andrews Presbyterian College Art Program, 1700 Dogwood Mile, Laurinburg, NC 28352	Up to $2500	First year and transfer students	Renewable for four years total	Annually
Saint Anselm College 100 Anselm Dr Manchester, NH 03102	Varies	Full-time students		Annually
Saint Louis Community College Florissant Valley 3400 Pershall Rd Saint Louis, MO 63135-1499	Varies	High school graduates	Two years	Annually
Saint Louis University Fine and Performing Arts Department 221 N Grand Saint Louis, MO 63103	$500-$1000	Undergraduates	One year	Annually
Saint Mary College, Art Program 4100 S Fourth St Trafficway Leavenworth, KS 66048-5082	$300-$1000	Incoming freshmen	Four years (renewable) - participation required	Annually
Saint Mary's College, Dept of Art Notre Dame, IN 46556	$500; $1000; $2500	Freshmen; upperclassmen	One year	Annually
Saint Mary's University of Minnesota, Art & Design Dept 700 Terrace Heights Winona, MN 55987	$1000-$2000	Portfolio review	One year (renewable)	Annually
Saint Olaf College, Art Dept 1520 Saint Olaf Ave Northfield, MN 55057-1098	$1000 and up	Students based on need; competitive scholarship by portfolio	One year	Annually
Saint Xavier College, Dept of Art 3700 W 103rd St Chicago, IL 60655	Varies; covers course tuition	Smith Scholarship to School of Art Institute of Chicago open to Saint Xavier art majors for courses not offered at SXU	Per course	Each semester
Salem State College Art Department 352 Lafayette St Salem, MA 01970	Varies	Art majors with a 3.0 GPA and who exhibit creativity; minorities also	One year	Annually
Salisbury State University Art Dept College & Camden Ave Salisbury, MD 21801	BFA $300-$500 each	First-year students	One year (renewable)	Annually
Salve Regina University Art Department Ochre Point Ave Newport, RI 02840	Variable	Based on financial need	One to four years	Annually
San Bernardino Art Association 780 North E St San Bernardino, CA 92404	$500	2 High Schools (local) San Bernardino Valley College and California State College in San Bernardino	One year	Annually
San Diego State University College of Professional Studies & Fine Arts, School of Art Design & Art History San Diego, CA 92182-4805	Isabel Kraft Sculpture Scholarship, $3000	Sculpture students	Fall	Annually
	Patricia Clapp Scholarship, $500	Art majors	Fall	Annually
	Haystack Mountain School of Crafts Scholarship, summer fees paid for program in Deer Isle, ME	Crafts undergraduates & graduates	Spring	Annually
	Darryl Groover Memorial Scholarship ($500)	Painting students	Spring	Annually
	Paul Lingren Memorial Scholarship	Undergraduate studio students	Spring	Annually
	SDSU Art Council Scholarships	Art majors	Spring	Annually
	Ellamarie Wooley Art Student Assistance Scholarship ($2000)	Art majors	Fall	Annually

OFFERED BY	AMOUNT	OPEN TO	DURATION	WHEN OFFERED
San Joaquin Delta College 5151 Pacific Ave Stockton, CA 95207	Varies	Varies		Annually
San Jose State University School of Art & Design One Washington Square San Jose, CA 95192-0089	$200-$1000 scholarships; $1500-$3100 fellowships	Scholarships for graduate and undergraduate students; fellowships for graduate students	One year	Annually and semi-annually
School of American Research/ Indian Arts Research Center PO Box 2188 Santa Fe, NM 87504	$20,000-Harvey W Branigar, Jr, Native American Internship	Native Americans with a BA and an interest in museum studies	One year	Annually
The School of Fashion Design 136 Newbury St Boston, MA 02116	$1000	All currently enrolled full time students	One year	Annually (in May for Sept enrollment)
School of Fine Arts 38660 Mentor Ave Willoughby, OH 44094	Tuition	Talent plus need	One year	Annually
School of the Museum of Fine Arts 230 The Fenway Boston, MA 02115	Varies	Deserving students	One year	Annually
Seton Hall University College of Arts and Sciences 400 S Orange Ave South Orange, NJ 07079	$500-$1000	Art and art history majors	One year	Annually
Seton Hill College Greensburg, PA 15601	$1000 toward tuition	Incoming freshmen art majors	One year	Annually
Sharon Arts Center RR2 Box 361 Peterborough, NH 03458	$90 per quarter	All	Eight-week session	Quarterly
Shepherd College, Art Dept A02 Frank Center Shepherdstown, WV 25443	$1500	Residents of West Virginia	One year	Annually
Shoreline Community College Humanities Division 16101 Greenwood Ave N Seattle, WA 98133	$100-$1000	Art majors	One year	Semi-annually
Siena Heights College Studio Angelico-Art Dept 1247 E Siena Heights Dr Adrian, MI 49221	Varies	Undergraduates	One year	Annually
Simpson College 701 North C St Indianola, IA 50125	$1500		One year; renewable	Annually
Sinclair Community College Div of Performing & Fine Arts 444 W Third St Dayton, OH 45402	$300-$500	Fine arts majors enrolled in 12 or more hours of courses, must have taken 12 hours	Quarterly	Semi-annually
Sioux City Art Center 225 Nebraska St Sioux City, IA 51101	$800	Children and/or adults for art center art classes	Six-week art class	Quarterly
Skowhegan School of Painting and Sculpture 200 Park Ave S, Ste 1116 New York, NY 10003	(9) Full scholarships $5200	Artists 19 years of age and over (average age 27), slide review	Nine weeks June to Aug.	Annually
	(45) Partial scholarships	Artists 19 years of age and over (average age 27), slide review	Nine weeks June to Aug.	Annually

OFFERED BY	AMOUNT	OPEN TO	DURATION	WHEN OFFERED
Abigail Adams Smith Museum & Gardens 421 E 61st St New York, NY 10021	$2500	Undergraduate and graduate students in related courses of study - by open application	Eight weeks	Summer
Smithsonian Institute Office of Fellowships & Grants 955 L'Enfant Plaza, Ste 7000 Washington, DC 20560	$25,000	Post-doctoral scholars in American art history, Oriental art history and African art	3 - 12 months	Annual
	$14,000	Dissertation research for Doctoral candidates in American art history, Oriental art history and African art	3 - 12 months	Annual
	Freer Gallery Internship	Interns must have working knowledge of one or more of the pertinent Oriental languages & submit a proposal relevant to the Freer collections		
	Harold P Stern Memorial Fund at Freer Gallery	Selection of recipients is by invitation only & is based upon outstanding scholarly achievements in the field of Japanese art		
	Hirshhorn Museum & Sculpture Garden Internship	College juniors & seniors who have completed at least 12 semester hours in art history	Ten weeks	Annual
		Graduate student internships are available for students in accredited art history graduate programs	One Semester	Annual
	National Museum of African Art Internship	People enrolled in undergraduate & graduate programs of study & for people interested in exploring museum professions related to African art & museum work	Ten weeks minimum	Annual
	National Museum of American Art Internship	Museum training for college senior graduate students, in art history, studio art and American studies	Eight weeks, commence in June. Grad program during year	Annual
	National Portrait Gallery Internship		Three months	
	Sidney & Celia Siegel Fellowship Program at Cooper-Hewitt	Applicants with two years of college education, preference given to those without previous museum experience	Ten weeks	Annual
South Carolina Arts Commission 1800 Gervais St Columbia, SC 29201	(5) $7500	SC professional artists: visual arts, literary arts & composition, music performance, choreography and dance performance	One year	Annually on a rotating basis
South Dakota Art Museum Medary Ave at Harvey Dunn St Brookings, SD 57007	$500	Art students of South Dakota State Univ	One year	Annually
Southampton College Long Island University Arts & Media Division Southampton, NY 11968	$1000-$6000	Freshmen and transfer students who have applied for admission	Up to four years	Bi-annually
Southern Alberta Art Gallery 601 Third Ave S Lethbridge, AB T1J 0H4 Canada	Varies	Visual arts students at University of Lethbridge		Annually
Southern Arkansas University 100 E University Magnolia, AR 71753-5000	$7000-$8000	Beginning freshmen and returning students - performance based	One year, renewable	Semi-annually
Southern Illinois University, Carbondale School of Art and Design Carbondale, IL 62901-4301	$201,575	Graduating seniors, entering freshmen, transfer students, graduate students, some continuing undergraduates	One year	Annually
Southern Oregon State College Dept of Art 1250 Siskiyou Blvd, Ashland, OR 97520	$50-$1500	Enrolled art students		Annually

OFFERED BY	AMOUNT	OPEN TO	DURATION	WHEN OFFERED
Southern Utah State University Department of Art Cedar City, UT 84720	Part tuition	Residents of Utah and nonresidents	One year	Annually and quarterly
	$700 up	Freshmen, sophomores, juniors and seniors	One year	Annually
Southwest Baptist University, Art Dept 1601 S Springfield Bolivar, MO 65613	$600	Freshmen	One year	Annually
Southwestern Oklahoma State University Art Department 100 Campus Dr Weatherford, OK 73096	$5000 (approximately)	Art majors both lower and upper classmen	One year	Annually
Springfield College 263 Alden St Springfield, MA 01109	Varied	All students	One year	Annually
Springfield Museum of Art 107 Cliff Park Rd Springfield, OH 45501	$25-$100	Children, some adults	Nine weeks	Each quarter
State University of New York at Buffalo Art Department 202 Center for the Arts Buffalo, NY 14260	$1200	Junior level art majors	Summer	Annually
State University of New York, College at Geneseo, Dept of Art, Geneseo, NY 14454	(6) $500	Art studio & art history majors, minors, concentrates - juniors	One year	Annually
	$400-$500	Art studio & art history majors, minors, freshmen, sophomores, juniors	One year	Annually
	$500	Art studio majors, minors - any class year	One year	Annually
State University of New York at Plattsburgh, Art Dept Myers Fine Arts Bldg Plattsburgh, NY 12901	Varies	All art majors and one to two scholarships offered to art minors	One year	Spring
The State University of West Georgia Carrollton, GA 30118	$15,000	Enrolled art majors	One year	Annually
Stephen F Austin State University Art Dept, Box 13001 Nacogdoches, TX 75962	$5200	Graduates; portfolio review	Six semesters for MFA candidates, four semesters for MA candidates	Annually
The Strong Museum One Manhattan Sq Rochester, NY 14607	H J Swinney Museum Studies Internship Program	Graduate students who aspire to a career in the museum profession	Three months (summer)	Annually
Sul Ross State University Dept of Art, C-90 Alpine, TX 79832	$150 per semester (four scholarships)	All art majors, including graduate	One Year	Annually
Sullivan County Community College 1000 LeRoy Rod Loch Sheldrake, NY 12759-5151	Variable	Students in commercial art or photography	Varies	Annually
Sunbury Shores Arts and Nature Centre, Inc 139 Water St, PO Box 100 St Andrews, NB E0G 2X0 Canada	Approx $400 each; all costs covered	New Brunswick residents ages 12-21 inclusive	One to three weeks varying with art course	Annually, for July and Aug. Submit application by Mar. 31
Swarthmore College 500 College Ave Swarthmore, PA 19081	As much as student needs	All students in financial need	As long as student demonstrates financial need	Annually
Syracuse University School of Art & Design 203 Crouse College Syracuse, NY 13244-1010	$1000-$2000 art merit scholarships plus academic merit scholarship - amounts vary for undergraduates; partial & full tuition scholarships for graduate students	Freshmen	Four years	Annually
	$9,970 university fellowships (African-American) for graduates, half & full assistantships for graduate students	Graduates-30 credit hours of tuition per year	Up to 3 years	Annually

OFFERED BY	AMOUNT	OPEN TO	DURATION	WHEN OFFERED
Taylor University, Art Dept 500 W Read Ave Upland, IN 46989-1001	$600-$1000 for incoming students; $600-$1400 for continuing students	Incoming and continuing students	One year	Annually
Teikyo Westmar University, 1002 Third Ave SE Le Mars, IA 51031	$250	Outstanding art students; applicable to enrollment at Teikyo Westmar University only - not transferable	One year	Annually
Temple College, Art Dept 2600 S First St Temple, TX 76504	$100-$400	Art Majors	Per semester	Semi-annually
Tennessee Arts Commission 404 James Robertson Pkwy Nashville, TN 37243-0780	$2000	Fellowship for professional artists who are residents of Tennessee; students not eligible	One year	Annually
Texas Tech University Dept of Art, Box 42081 Lubbock, TX 79409-2081	$500-$11,000	BA, BFA, MAE, MFA, PhD applicants	One year (renewable)	Annually
Texas Woman's University Dept of Visual Arts PO Box 425469 Denton, TX 76204	Varies	All qualified students	One year	Annually
Truman State University Division of Fine Arts Kirksville, MO 63501	Varying amounts	High school seniors; other awards available to junior college graduates	One year (renewable)	Annually
Truro Center for the Arts at Castle Hill PO Box 756 Truro, MA 02666	$100	Local school children & provincetown AIDS Support Group; Also, work study opportunities	One class	Annually
Tucson Museum of Art Attn: Judith D'Agostino 140 N Main Tucson, AZ 85701	Varied Varies	Talented, needy and minority students for TMA school classes only All students	Each session Per semester	Quarterly All year
Tufts University Fine Arts Dept 11 Talbot Ave Medford, MA 02155	$5000-$10,000	First year graduate students	One year	Annually
UNC Pembroke Art Dept PO Box 1510 Pembroke, NC 28372-1510	Varies	Talented and/or academic gifted students	One year (renewable)	Annually
Union University Highway 45 Bypass Jackson, TN 38305	$100-$1000	Students/art majors	One year	Annually
United States Capitol Historical Society Architect of the Capitol U.S. Capitol Washington, DC 20515	$1500	Scholars and graduate students	One month to one year	Annually, starts Sept 1
Universal Technical Institute Commercial Art Div 4001 S 24th St Omaha, NE 68107	Varies	High school graduates	One year	Annually
The University of Akron School of Art, Folk Hall Akron, OH 44325-7801	Up to full tuition	All art students	One year (renewable)	Annually
The University of Alabama at Birmingham Department of Art, 113 Humanities Bldg University Sta Birmingham, AL 35294-1260	$2500 $500	Senior art majors Senior art history majors	One year One year	Annually Annually

OFFERED BY	AMOUNT	OPEN TO	DURATION	WHEN OFFERED
University of Alabama Dept of Art Huntsville, AL 35899	Varied	Art major with 2.5 GPA on 4.0 scale	One year	Annually
University of Alaska, Fairbanks Dept of Art, Fine Arts Complex Fairbanks, AK 99775-0200	Tuition $500-Painters Palette Artists Supply	Entering students Entering Alaskan students	One year One year	Annually Annually
University of Alberta Dept of Art & Design 3-98 Fine Arts Bldg Edmonton, AB T6G 2C9, Canada	$13,000	Incoming graduate students in MFA and M.Des program	One year	Annually
University of Arizona College of Fine Arts Department of Art Tucson, AZ 85721	Variable	Students enrolled in art program at UA	One year	Annually
University of Arkansas Art Department Fayetteville, AR 72701	Tuition & up to $5700 (GTA)	MFA Grad Students	One year	Annually
University of Arkansas at Little Rock 2801 S University Ave Little Rock, AR 72204	Up to $1000	Qualified applicants	Semester	Semi-annually
University of Arkansas at Monticello Fine Arts Dept PO Box 3607 Monticello, AR 71655	Tuition waiver	Talented art students; 3.0 GPA or better to continue	One year	Annually
The University of the Arts Broad & Pine Sts Philadelphia, PA 19102	Up to 50% tuition	All incoming students		Annually
University of Central Arkansas Dept of Art Conway, AR 72032	$500 per semester	Art majors	Continuation of eligibility	Semi-annually
University of Central Oklahoma Dept of Visual Arts & Design 100 N University Dr Edmond, OK 73034-0180	 Varies $500-Bob Aldridge Memorial	Undergraduate students Full-time students; in state students Full time students	One semester Semester One year	Semi-annually Semi-annually Annually
University of Charleston Dept of Art and Design 2300 MacCorkle Ave SE Charleston, WV 25304	Varies	Students with talent but of financial need	One year	Annually
University of Cincinnati School of Art 6431 Aronoff, ML 16 Cincinnati, OH 45221	Undergraduate, $500-$1000; Graduate, stipend & full tuition. $2500 Traveling Fellowships, graduates & undergraduates	Fine arts freshmen; SOA freshmen; University Graduate Scholarships and Minority Fellowships	One year	Annually
University of Connecticut Art Dept Storrs, CT 06269-1099	$150-$3000	Incoming freshmen and enrolled students	One year	Annually
University of Delaware Dept of History Newark, DE 19716	$9850 MA candidates; $10,700 PhD candidates	Students enrolled as MA and/or PhD candidates	Two to four year program	
University of Evansville Department of Art 1800 Lincoln Ave Evansville, IN 47722	Varies	Art majors; full-time undergraduate students	Four years	Annually
University of Georgia School of Art, Lamar Dodd Visual Arts Bldg Jackson St, Athens, GA 30602	$500-$1500	Undergraduate and graduate students	One year	Annually

OFFERED BY	AMOUNT	OPEN TO	DURATION	WHEN OFFERED
University of Hartford Hartford Art School 200 Bloomfield Ave West Hartford, CT 06117	Varies		Renewable to 4 years	Annually
University of Hawaii Kapiolani Community College 4303 Diamond Head Rd Honolulu, HI 96816	$500	Art majors	One year	Annually
University of Hawaii at Manoa Department of Art 2535 The Mall Honolulu, HI 96822	Varies $2500	All Museum students in the arts	One year, one semester One year	Annually, semi-annually Annually
University of Houston Dept of Art 4800 Calhoun Rd Houston, TX 77204-4893		Current students and incoming graduate students	One year	Annually
University of Idaho Department of Art & Architecture Moscow, ID 83843	Variable $400 (Commemorative Art Scholarship)	All majors in art, undergraduate and graduate; based on ability alone Upper division undergraduates in art; based on need and ability	One year	Annually Annually in the spring for fall semester
University of Illinois Urbana-Champaign College of Fine and Applied Arts 117 Architecture Bldg 608 Taft Dr Champaign, IL, 61820	Kate Neal Kinley Memorial Fellowship	Graduates of the College of Fine and Applied Arts of the University of Illinois, Urbana-Champaign and to graduates of similar institutions of equal educational standing. Preference is given to applicants under 25 years of age	One academic year	Annually
University of Indianapolis Art Dept 1400 E Hanna Ave Indianapolis, IN 46227	$15,000 Varies	Entering freshmen majors and returning majors Undergraduates	One year One year	Annually Annually
University of Iowa, School of Art and Art History E100 Art Bldg Iowa City, IA 52242	Varies	Undergraduates and graduate students	One year	Annually
University of Louisville Allen R Hite Art Institute Dept of Fine Arts Belkamp Campus Louisville, KY 40292	Varies- Hendershot Scholarship Varies-Hite Scholarship $5000- Don Payton Graduate Award	All Kentucky High School graduates Current and new students Graduate level degree student in art history	One year; four-year full scholarship for incoming freshmen One year One year	Annually Annually Annually, beginning 1998
University of Miami Dept of Art and Art History PO Box 248106 Coral Gables, FL 33124-4410	Partial tuition waiver - undergraduate art scholarships Tuition waiver stipend - graduate teaching assistantships	Qualified students Qualified students	One year (renewable) Two years	Annually Annually
University of Michigan, Ann Arbor History of Art Department Ann Arbor, MI 48109-1357	Charles L Freer Fellowships in Oriental Art, amounts vary Graduate Fellowships offered by Horace H Rackham School of Graduate Studies, amounts vary Rackham Predoctoral Fellowship; health insurance and $14,400 stipend for two and a half terms Regents Fellowships, minimum three years at $10,000 plus tuition, fees and health insurance Teaching Fellowships up to $8000 plus full tuition waiver Michigan Merit Fellowship for historically under-represented groups. Tuition, health insurance, $1000 per month offered by Horace H Rackham School of Graduate Studies, tuition plus up to $10000	Advanced graduate students in non-western art, residence at Freer Gallery, Washington, DC Graduate students Predoctoral students Beginning graduate students Graduate students of the second year & beyond Beginning graduate students, historically under-represented racial or ethnic groups	Half year One year One year Three years One year Up to five years	Annually Annually Annually Annually Annually Annually

OFFERED BY	AMOUNT	OPEN TO	DURATION	WHEN OFFERED
University of Minnesota, Duluth Department of Art 317 Humanities Bldg 10 University Dr Duluth, MN 55812	(4-6) $5000 Grad Teaching assistantships	Graduate students	One year	Annually
	(4) $250 scholarships (4)	Undergraduates, who are in at least their second quarter of study as an art major at UMD and who meet eligibility requirements	Summer session only	
	(6) $1000 awards	Undergrad/graduates, who are in at least their second quarter of study as an art major at UMD and who meet eligibility requirements	One year	Annually
	(5) $600 scholarships	Undergrad/graduates, who are in at least their second quarter of study as an art major at UMD and who meet eligibility requirements	One year	Annually
University of Minnesota Split Rock Arts Program 306 Wesbrook Hall 77 Pleasant St SE Minneapolis, MN 55455	$330-$450	Anyone; awards based on artistic merit & financial need	One workshop only	Annually
University of Minnesota, Minneapolis Department of Art Minneapolis, MN 55455	$200-$4000	Undergraduate and/or graduate	One year	Annually
University of Mississippi Art Dept University, MS 38677	$500-$1000 plus out-of-state tuition	Qualified students	Three years (renewable)	Annually
University of Missouri, Kansas City Art & Art History Department 5100 Rockhill Rd Kansas City, MO 64110		Incoming freshmen	One year	Annually
University of Missouri, Saint Louis Dept of Art & Art History 8001 Natural Bridge Saint Louis, MO 63121	Varies- William T Isbell II Art Scholarship	Art history students	One year	Annually
	Varies- Barbara St Cyr Scholarship	Art history or education majors	One year	Annually
University of Nebraska, Kearney Dept of Art & Art History Kearney, NE 68849	(8) $1000 tuition waiver in Art	Freshmen & upper classmen	One year	Annually
	$200-$300- other scholarships available	Any level	One year	Annually
University of Nebraska-Lincoln Department of Art & Art History Woods Hall Lincoln, NE 68588	Thomas Coleman Memorial Scholarship in Printmaking awards of $100 each	Outstanding graduate and undergraduate student in prints	One year	Annually
	Francis Vreeland Award in Art $1600	Outstanding graduate and undergraduate students in studio art	One year	Annually
	E Evelyn Peterson Memorial Fine Arts Scholarships $10,000	Outstanding students, sophomore and above, with high potential in art	One year	Annually
	Ruth Ann Sack Memorial Scholarship in Photography and Painting, five at $100	Outstanding upper division students in photography and painting	One year	Annually as income available
	Louise Esterday Munday Fine Arts Scholarship $600	Determined by financial need	One year	Annually
	Shelly Arnold Waggoner Memorial Scholarship Fund, four awards of $600 each	Based on exceptional talent	One year	Annually
	Art & Art History Dept Scholarships, three awards of $100 each	Demonstrated talent and need	One year	Annually
	Nellis Polly Hills & John Hills Scholarship $2400	Based on scholastic achievement, Willard professional potential and financial need	One year	Annually
	Henry Grabowski Memorial Award $100	Based on creativity in any medium		Annually
University of New Mexico Albuquerque, NM 87131	Varies	Undergraduates and graduates	Variable	Annually

OFFERED BY	AMOUNT	OPEN TO	DURATION	WHEN OFFERED
University of North Alabama Dept of Art, PO Box 5006 Florence, AL 35632-0001	$250-$3370	Entering freshmen, sophomores, juniors, seniors & transfers with art majors	One year (renewable)	Annually
University of North Carolina-Chapel Hill, Department of Art, CB# 3405, Hanes Art Center Chapel Hill, NC 27599-3405	Emily Pollard Fellowships, $2000-$3000	Graduate students only	One year	Annually
	UNC-CH Merit Assistantship $9000-$11,000	Graduate students only	One year	Annually
	Minority presence awards $9000-$11,000	Students	One year	First year
	Undergraduate Prize in Art History - $100	All students	One year	Annually
	The George Kachergis Memorial Scholarship - $300-$400	Junior & senior Studio Art majors	Two year eligibility	Annually
	The Jonathan E Sharpe Scholarship - $400-$500	Junior & senior Studio Art majors	Two year eligibility	Annually
	The Alexander Julian Prize - $300	Junior & senior Studio Art majors	Two year eligibility	Annually
University of North Carolina at Charlotte, Dept of Art Charlotte, NC 28223	$500-$1000	New freshmen & transfer students	One year	Annually
University of North Texas Art Dept, PO Box 5098, UNT Denton, TX 76201	Varies	Continuing students only	One year	Annually
University of Notre Dame, Graduate School, Art, Art History & Design Dept Notre Dame, IN 46556	Tuition $18,690; Stipend $8300	Teaching assistants chosen by faculty	Up to three years	Annually
University of Oklahoma, School of Art 520 Parrington Oval, Rm 202 Norman, OK 73019	$200-$8000	Varies: some open; some restricted	One year (renewable)	Annually
University of the Pacific Dept of Art & Art History 601 Pacific Ave Stockton, CA 95211	$18,000	Sophomore - Senior Art, Art History or Graphic Design major	One year	Annually
University of Pittsburgh Henry Clay Frick Dept of History of Art and Architecture Pittsburgh, PA 15260	$9,990-TA, $10,400-TF, $12,500-Mellon Tuition scholarships	Art History graduate students	One year (renewable)	Annually
University of Puget Sound 1500 N Warner St St, Tacoma, WA 98416	$1000-$1500	Freshmen, transfers and upper class	Renewable	Annually
University of Regina Department of Visual Arts Regina, SK S4S 0A2 Canada	$100-$2000	Visual Arts & Art History students	One year	Annually
	$3500-$4500	MFA students	One semester	Semi-annually
University of Rochester Dept of Art & Art History 424 Morey Hall Rochester, NY 14627	$7000	PhD candidates in Visual & Cultural Studies program	Three years, possibly four	Annually
University of San Diego Art History Area, Fine Arts Dept Alcala Park, San Diego, CA 92123	Variable		One year	Annually, semi-annually
University of Saskatchewan Dept of Art & Art History Saskatoon, SK S7N 0W0 Canada	$100-$1000	Second, third and fourth year students		Annually
University of Science and Arts of Oklahoma PO Box 82345 Chickasha, OK 73018-0001	$2100	Entering freshmen	One year	Annually

OFFERED BY	AMOUNT	OPEN TO	DURATION	WHEN OFFERED
University of South Carolina Dept of Art, Sloan College Columbia, SC 29208	$400 granted per semester ($800 per year)	Freshmen; continuing & transfer students	One year	June 1
University of South Dakota Dept of Art, CFA 179 414 E Clark St Vermillion, SD 57069	(5) Undergraduate Scholarships- $200		Academic year	Annually
	(5) Oscar Howe Scholarships- $400	Outstanding art students - Native American preference	Academic year	Annually
	(1) H J and A B Gunderson Scholarship-$750	Senior	Academic year	Annually
	(5) Graduate Assistantships- $4000		Academic year by contract	Annually
	(2) Louise Hansen Art Scholarships-$300	Outstanding art students	Academic year	Annually
	(1) Lance Hyde Memorial Scholarship-$200	Art Education major	Academic year	Annually
University of Southern California School of Fine Arts Watt Hall 103, University Park Los Angeles, CA 90089-0292	Variable	Fine arts undergraduate majors	One year	Annually
	Graduate teaching assistantships (tuition credit and stipend)- contact School of Fine Arts	Studio graduate students and Studio Art	One year	Annually
University of Southwestern Louisiana, College of the Arts USL Box 43850 Lafayette, LA 70504	$600	Juniors and seniors in visual arts	One year	Annually
University of Tampa, Dept of Art 401 W Kennedy Blvd Tampa, FL 33606	Varies	Entering freshmen and transfer students		Annually
University of Tennessee Dept of Art 1715 Volunteer Blvd Knoxville, TN 37996-2410	$5000 (total)	Currently enrolled art majors	One year	Annually
	$1000	Freshmen art majors	One year	Annually
University of Tennessee at Chattanooga Dept of Art 615 McCallie Ave Chattanooga, TN 37403	Tuition scholarships	Freshmen, sophomores, juniors	One - four years	Annually
University of Texas at Arlington Department of Art & Art History 335 Fine Arts Bldg, PO Box 19089 Arlington, TX 76019	Varies	Art majors		Annually
University of Texas at San Antonio Division of Visual Arts San Antonio, TX 78249-0642	$200 to $1000	Graduate MA and MFA applicants	One year	Fall
University of Texas of Permian Basin Department of Art Odessa, TX 79762	Varies	Currently enrolled art majors and minors	One year	Annually
University of Texas-Pan American Department of Art, Edinburg, TX 78539	$500	Entering, enrolled Art Majors	One year	Annually
University of Tulsa, School of Art 600 S College Ave Tulsa, OK 74104			One year	Annually
University of Utah Art Dept ART 161 Salt Lake City, UT 84112	Varied	MA, MFA, BA & BFA	One year	Annually
University of Virginia Bayly Art Museum Rugby Rd Charlottesville, VA 22903	$4000	Graduate students in the Department of Art	One year (10 hrs/week)	Annually
	$12,000	Advanced graduate students in the Dept of Art History, University of Virginia	One year (20 hrs/week)	Annually

OFFERED BY	AMOUNT	OPEN TO	DURATION	WHEN OFFERED
University of Washington School of Art Box 353440 Seattle, WA 98195-3440	Varies	Currently enrolled art and art history majors	One year	Annually
University of West Florida Dept of Art 11000 University Pkwy Pensacola, FL 32514	(8) $1,000 each	Incoming freshmen and junior transfers (Art Majors)	Freshmen (4 years); Junior (2 years); if GPA maintained	Annually
University of Windsor School of Visual Arts Windsor, ON, N9B 3P4 Canada	Variable	Visual arts students	One year	Annually
University of Wisconsin-Milwaukee Art History Dept, PO Box 413 Mitchell Hall 151 Milwaukee, WI 53201	$6500-$8300 for project and teaching assistants; also small cash grants to specific research projects	All graduate students	Academic year	Annually
University of Wyoming Art Dept, PO Box 3138 Laramie, WY 82071	$500-$3000	Freshmen, transfer and continuing art majors (studio)	One year	Annually
	Ten half assistantships, $3800 stipend plus half resident tuition reduction	Graduate students	One year	Annually
	$500-$3000	Undergraduate and graduate students; in state and out of state	One year; renewable	Annually
Utica College of Syracuse University Division of Humanities Burrstone Rd Utica, NY 13502	$100-$870	Full-time students	One year	Annually
Valdosta State University Dept of Art N Paterson St Valdosta, GA 31698	$425 per quarter	Art majors	Until graduation	As current recipients graduate
	Up to $500	Art majors	Freshmen year	Annually
Valley City State University Art Department, College St Valley City, ND 58072	Varies	All students, freshmen to seniors	Varies	Annually and semi-annually
Ventura College, Fine Arts Dept 4667 Telegraph Rd Ventura, CA 93003	Varies	Students	Varies	
Vermont State Craft Center at Frog Hollow, Mill St Middlebury, VT 05753	Open	Applicants who demonstrate a need	One class session	Quarterly
Vermont Studio Center PO Box 613 Johnson, VT 05656	Up to $2,700 per month	Painters, sculptors & writers	One month residency with access to visiting artists and writers	Ongoing
Vincennes University Junior College, Art Department Second & Harrison Sts Vincennes, IN 47591	Varies	Visual art students majoring in design, fine art and/or art education	One year	Semi-annually
Virginia Polytechnic Institute & State University, Department of Art & Art History, 201 Draper Rd, Mail Code 0103 Blacksburg, VA 24061-0103	$500-$1125	Entering freshmen and upper classmen	One year; renewable for four years	Annually
Wake Forest University, Dept of Art PO Box 7232 Reynolda Sta Winston Salem, NC 27109	$500 and up	Freshmen and junior art students	One year (renewable)	Annually
Warner House Association PO Box 895 Portsmouth, NH 03802-0895	$1500-$2000 (Summer fellowship)	Graduate students	Three months	Annually

OFFERED BY	AMOUNT	OPEN TO	DURATION	WHEN OFFERED
Wartburg College, Art Department 222 Ninth St NW, PO Box 1003 Waverly, IA 50677	$500	Those deemed artistically and academically qualified by the art department chairperson	One year	Annually
Washington and Lee University, Art Dept Lexington, VA 24450	Varies according to need	Art majors, coed	One year (renewable up to four years)	Annually
Washington University School of Art One Brookings Dr, CB 1031 Saint Louis, MO 63130	Full tuition	Entering freshmen and first year graduate students	Undergraduate - four years; graduate - two years	Annually
	Partial tuition	All students	Variable	Annually
Watercolor Society of Alabama PO Box 43011 Birmingham, AL 35243-0011	$200	Senior college student majoring in Fine Arts and attending Alabama College	One year	Annually
Wayne State College Wayne, NE	$500	Undergraduate	One year (renewable)	Semi-annually
Wayne State University Dept of Art & Art History 150 Community Arts Bldg Detroit, MI 48202	$1000	Entering undergraduate students in fine arts	Four years	Annually
	Variable amount	Graduate students in fine arts and fashion design	One year (renewable)	Annually
	Variable amount	Fine art undergraduate and graduate students	One year	Annually
	Variable amount	Fashion design students	One year	Annually
	$1000	Art History students	One year	Annually
Weber State University Dept of Visual Arts 2001 University Circle Ogden, UT 84408-2001	Tuition waiver	Art students	One year	Annually
Westchester Community College Art Workshop Westchester County Center White Plains, NY 10606	Varies	Based on merit; disabled and in need of financial assistance	Every semester	Semi-annually
Western Art Association PO Box 893 Ellensburg, WA 98926	$500	Kittitas County graduating high school seniors	One year	Annually
Western Carolina University Department of Art, Belk Bldg Cullowhee, NC 28723	$500-$6000	Undergraduate and graduate art majors	One year	Annually
Western Illinois University Art Department, Garwood 32 Macomb, IL 61455	$500	Students matriculating or new students with outstanding portfolios	Each semester	Semi-annually
	Tuition	Incoming freshmen with art portfolio	Semester	Semi-annually
	Bulkeley Scholarship - $800	Sophomores, juniors, seniors and transfers	One year	Annually
Western Michigan University Dept of Art Kalamazoo, MI 49008	Varies	Undergraduate and graduate	One year	Annually
Western Montana College, Art Dept 710 S Atlantic Dillon, MT 59725	$500	All art education students	One semester with a four-year maximum	Annually
Western New Mexico University Expressive Arts Dept 100 W College Ave, PO Box 680 Silver City, NM 88062	$400	HS seniors & undergraduates majoring in art	One year	Annually
Western Oregon State College Creative Arts Division 315 Monmouth Ave Monmouth, OR 97361	$300-$500	Returning art students	Term tuition	Annually

OFFERED BY	AMOUNT	OPEN TO	DURATION	WHEN OFFERED
Western Wyoming Community College, Art Dept, PO Box 428, Rock Springs, WY 82901	Partial and full tuition	Art majors with 3.5 and above GPA	One year (renewable) based on GPA	Annually
West Virginia University College of Creative Arts, PO Box 6111 Morgantown, WV 26506-6111	$2000-$6000	All art majors	One year, reviewed yearly	Annually
Whitney Museum of American Art Independent Study Program 384 Broadway, 4th Flr New York, NY 10013	$1800	Students of universities and art schools	Sept. to May	Annually
The Wichita Center for the Arts The Mary R Koch School of Visual Arts, 9112 E Central, Wichita, KS 67206	Tuition	Based on talent and need	Varies	Annually; classes offered Spring, Summer and Fall (three separate sessions)
Wiley College Department of Fine Arts 711 Wiley Ave Marshall, TX 75670	Varies	Financially qualifying students	One year	Annually
William Paterson College, Art Dept 300 Pompton Rd Wayne, NJ 07470	Varies	All WPC art students	One year	Annually
Winthrop University Rock Hill, SC 29733	$100-$1000	Freshmen	One year	Annually
Woodstock Art Gallery Volunteer Committee 447 Hunter St, Woodstock, ON N4S 4G7 Canada	$1000	Students of Oxford County high schools pursuing studies in visual arts	One year	Annually
Woodstock School of Art, PO Box 338AD, Woodstock, NY 12498	Variable	All who qualify by reason of merit and need	One month or longer	Annually
	Free studio space	Painters, sculptors, printmakers may apply	Three to five weeks	Spring & Fall
Wright State University Dept of Art & Art History Dayton, OH 45434	Variable, $1000 minimum	Art majors	Variable, one year minimum	Annually
Helene Wurlitzer Foundation of New Mexico Box 545 Taos, NM 87571	Free rent & utilities	Any artist in all media & allied fields, creative, not interpretive	Apr 1 to Sept 30	Annually
Xavier University Dept of Art 3800 Victory Pkwy Cincinnati, OH 45207-7311	$103,600	Incoming freshmen	Renewable - four years	Annually
Yale Center for British Art Yale University, Box 208280 New Haven, CT 06520-8280	Short-term resident visiting fellowships	Scholars in post-doctoral or equivalent research related to British art	One month	Monthly
	Andrew W Mellon Fellowship, $15,000 plus travel	Predoctoral candidate from British or other non-American University	One year	Annually
Yale University Beinecke Rare Book & Manuscript Library, Box 208240 New Haven, CT 06520-8240	(12-15) Fellowships each year: $2400, plus travel expenses	Post-doctoral researchers	One month	Annually
Yale University School of Art PO Box 208242 New Haven, CT 06520-8242	Variable	Eligible MFA students	Academic year	Annually
Young Harris College Department of Art Young Harris, GA 30582	(3) $1000	Art majors	One year	Annually

Open Exhibitions
National, Regional and State-Wide

ALABAMA

WATERCOLOR SOCIETY OF ALABAMA ANNUAL NATIONAL EXHIBITION. Held in April. Open to watercolor artists residing in the United States. $6000 in awards. For further information write Watercolor Society of Alabama, P.O. Box 43011, Birmingham, AL 35243. Tel 205-822-3721.

ARIZONA

MESA ARTS CENTER EXHIBITS, Mesa. Annual. Present up to seven national juried exhibits in all media. For further information, write Mesa Arts Center/Galeria Mesa, 155 N. Center St., P.O. Box 1466, Mesa, AZ 85211-1466. Tel 602-644-2056; Fax 602-644-2901.

SCOTTSDALE ARTS FESTIVAL, Scottsdale. Annual, mid-March. Any media. Juried. Entry Slides due Nov. 18 - prospectus mailed out in Sept. For further information write Scottsdale Center for the Arts, 7380 E. Second St., Scottsdale, AZ 85251. Tel 602-994-2787.

ARKANSAS

ARKANSAS ARTS CENTER REGIONAL CRAFT BIENNIAL, Little Rock. Biennial. Apr. 19-May 31, 1998. Objects made of craft media - clay, fiber, glass, metal, wood and mixed-media. Open to artists born or residing in Arkansas, Louisiana, Mississippi, Missouri, Oklahoma, Tennessee and Texas. Juried by slides. Juror's Award and up to $2000 in additional purchase awards. Fee $10 per entry, limit three. Deadline for slides late Dec. For further information write Decorative Arts Museum, The Arkansas Arts Center, MacArthur Park, Little Rock, AR 72203-2137.

CALIFORNIA

FEATS OF CLAY X, Lincoln. Annual national juried ceramic competition and exhibition. May 21 to June 14, 1997. Juror: Ken Ferguson. Purchase and cash merit awards. For prospectus: send legal sized SASE to Lincoln Arts, P.O. Box 1166, Lincoln, CA 95648. Tel 916-645-9713.

INK AND CLAY. Annual national juried ceramic competition and exhibition. MAy 21 to June 14, 1997. Juror: Ken Ferguson. Entry deadline March 19. Purchase and cash merit awards. For prospectus: Send legal-sized SASE to Lincoln Arts, PO Box 1166, Lincoln, CA 95648. Tel 916-645-9713.

MASKIBITION 12, Eureka. Oct. 1997. Handmade masks. Juried, prizes. For further information write The Ink People Center for the Arts, 411 12th St., Eureka, CA 95501. Tel 707-442-8413; Fax 707-444-8722.

OLIVE HYDE ART GALLERY ANNUAL TEXTILE COMPETITION, Annual. April 10-May18, 1997. Textiles. Open to any artist working in predominantly fiber media. Juried, awards. Fee $7 per item, limit three. Work must be hand delivered. Jury by Saturday, April 5. For further information write Olive Hyde Art Gallery, City of Fremont, Leisure Services Department, P.O. Box 5006, Fremont, CA 94537.

PALM SPRINGS DESERT MUSEUM ARTISTS COUNCIL 28th ANNUAL JURIED EXHIBITION, Palm Springs. Annual. Oil, watercolor, acrylic, drawings, mixed-media, graphics, photography and sculpture (not over 50 lbs.). No crafts or functional art. Open to all residents of the U.S., work previously exhibited by the Artists Council not eligible. Original art work must have been completed within past three years. For prospectus, write Palm Springs Desert Museum, P.O. Box 2288, Palm Springs, CA 92263. Tel 619-325-7186; Fax 619-327-5069.

SAN BERNARDINO ART ASSOCIATION INLAND EXHIBITION. Annual, May 21-June 28. Oil, acrylic, watercolor, mixed, collage, graphics (no sculpture or photography). Open to all artists. Cash awards and purchase awards. Fee $10 per slide entry, limit three, 30% commission. For further information write San Bernardino Art Association, PO Box 3574, San Bernardino, CA 92413.

WATERCOLOR WEST ANNUAL NATIONAL JURIED EXHIBITION XXIX, Riverside. Annual, Sept. 13-Nov.8, 1997, held at the Riverside Art Museum. Transparent water media. Open to all artists. Juror for selection and awards. Fee $25 for one or two slides. For further information write Watercolor West XXIX, PO Box 1181 Yucaipa, CA 92399.

WEST COAST WORKS ON/OF PAPER 1997, Eureka. Art made on and of paper. Juried for competition and prizes up to $1000. For further information write The Ink People Center for the Arts, 411 12th St., Eureka, CA 95501. Tel 707-442-8413; Fax 707-444-8722. E-mail: lmaynard@northcoast.com

COLORADO

COLORED PENCIL IN COLORADO, Craig. Oct. 6-25. Juried. For further information write to: Frances Williams-Reust, 615 Legion St., Craig, CO 81625. Tel 970-824-7643.

ANNUAL WATERMEDIA EXHIBIT, Denver. Annual, Apr. - May. Watermedia. Statewide, juried. For further information write Colorado Watercolor Society, 26406 Columbine Glen, Golden, CO 80401. Tel 970-526-0345.

CONNECTICUT

CELEBRATION OF AMERICAN CRAFTS, New Haven. Annual, Nov-Dec. Crafts. Open to U.S. artists. Juried. Deadline for slides June 15. For prospectus send SASE to: Creative Arts Workshop, 80 Audubon St, New Haven, CT 06510.

NEW HAVEN PAINT & CLAY CLUB. Annual, Mar. Oil, watercolor, acrylic, graphics and sculpture. Open to artists from the New England states & NY. Prizes and purchase awards. Fee $12 for first entry, $6 for second, 20% comm. Entry forms mailed out in Jan and Feb. For further information write NHP & C Club Secretary, 51 Trumbull St., New Haven, CT 06510.

DELAWARE

DELAWARE ART MUSEUM'S REGIONAL BIENNIAL, Wilmington, Spring 1998. All media (except video), must be original work executed by entrants. Open only to artists who reside in the following states and counties: New Castle, Kent and Sussex, Delaware; Chester, Delaware and Philadelphia, Pennsylvania; Cecil County, Maryland and Salem County, New Jersey. Juried by slides with cash prizes. Fee; limit of three works per person. For prospectus send SASE to: Nancy Miller Batty, Delaware Art Museum, 2301 Kentmere Pkwy., Wilmington, DE 19806. Tel 302-571-9590.

FLORIDA

ANNUAL SMALL WORKS SHOW, West Palm Beach. Annual. Subject: Human form. Juried by slides, artists may submit up to three entries. $5000 in prizes. Fee $25. Entry deadline March 10. Send SASE to: Small Works, Armory Art Center, 1703 S. Lake Ave., West Palm Beach, FL 33401. Tel 561-832-1776; Fax 561-832-0191.

COMBINED TALENTS: THE FLORIDA NATIONAL, Tallahassee. Annual, Sept. 2-Oct. 5. Open to artists over 18, students and faculty of FSU are ineligible. Juried by slides, entrants may submit up to two works. $1500 in monetary awards. Fee $15, deadline Oct. 31. For further information and/or prospectus write The Florida National, FSU Museum of Fine Arts, 250 FAB, corner of W Tennessee & Copeland, Tallahassee, FL 32306-2055. Tel 904-644-6836.

MIAMI BEACH OUTDOOR FESTIVAL OF THE ARTS, Miami Beach. Annual. All media $11,000 in awards. Entry slides due Dec 1. Fee $200. For further information write to: Miami Beach Fine Arts Board, Dept FL, PO Bin O, Miami Beach, FL 33119.

RIVERSIDE ARTS AND MUSIC FESTIVAL, Jacksonville. Sept 6-7. Over 150 artists and craftsmen. $6000 in awards. For application and further information write Riverside Avondale Preservation, Inc., 2623 Herschel St., Jacksonville, FL 32204. Tel 904-389-2449; Fax 904-389-0431.

THIRD ANNUAL ART OF PHOTOGRAPHY, Oct 16 - Nov 29. Traditional and non-traditional categories. Juried by slides, postmark deadline August 22, $2500 in awards. For prospectus send SASE to Armory Art Center, 1703 S Lake Avenue, West Palm Beach, FL 33401. Tel 561-832-1776.

GEORGIA

AFRICAN-AMERICAN ARTISTS ANNUAL, Saint Simons Island. Annual. Deadline: Jan. for Feb. exhibit. Work of African-American artists. Open to African-American artists from throughout the U.S. Juried exhibition. For further information write Coastal Center for the Arts, 2012 Demere Rd., Saint Simons Island, GA 31522. Tel & Fax 912-634-0404.

ARTIST NATIONAL, Saint Simons Island. Annual. Deadline: Jan. for Mar./Apr. exhibit. Various media. Open to artists throughout the U.S. National juror(s). For further information write Coastal Center for the Arts, 2012 Demere Rd., Saint Simons Island, GA 31522. Tel & Fax 912-634-0404.

NEW WORK OF THE NEW YEAR, Saint Simons Island. Annual. Open to established or emerging artists. For further information write Coastal Center for the Arts, 2012 Demere Rd., Saint Simons Island, GA 31522. Tel & Fax 912-634-0404.

SAINT SIMONS BY THE SEA: AN ARTS FEST, Saint Simons Island. Annual, first weekend in Oct. Juried exhibit, outdoors. For further information write Coastal Center for the Arts, 2012 Demere Rd., Saint Simons Island, GA 31522. Tel & Fax 912-634-0404.

UNDER THE OAKS, Saint Simons Island, Annual, quarterly, dates coincide with spring break, Memorial Day, Independence Day and Thanksgiving. For further information write Coastal Center for the Arts, 2012 Demere Rd., Saint Simons Island, GA 31522. Tel & Fax 912-634-0404.

HAWAII

PACIFIC STATES BIENNIAL NATIONAL PRINT EXHIBITION, Hilo. Biennial. All printmaking media including monoprints (no photographs). Open to all artists 18 years or older residing in the U.S. and territories. National juried print exhibition. Entry fee for all original work. For exhibition prospectus send SASE to: Art Dept, Attn: Professor W. Miyamoto, University of Hawaii at Hilo, 200 W. Kawli St., Hilo, HI 96720. Fax 808-933-3736.

IDAHO

ART ON THE GREEN, Coeur d'Alene. Annual, Aug. Arts and crafts, all media. Juried show, displayed and sold. $5000 cash prizes. For further information write Citizens' Council for the Arts, PO Box 901, Coeur d' Alene, ID 83816-0901. Tel 208-667-9346.

ILLINOIS

AMERICAN CENTER FOR DESIGN, THE 100 SHOW, Chicago. Annual. Books, brochures, announcements, invitations, stationery, annual reports, house organs, calendars, catalogs, posters, manuals, corporate graphics, packages, logos and trademarks. Juried exhibit. Fee $35 per entry for non-members, $25 per entry for members. Entry due mid-April. For further information write American Center for Design, 325 West Huron St, Suite 711, Chicago, IL 60610. Tel 800-257-8657.

ANNUAL FOUNTAIN SQUARE ARTS FESTIVAL, ART IN THE GARDEN, Evanston. Annual, June 28-29, 1997. Variety of media displayed and sold. Local and national artists. For further information write Evanston Chamber of Commerce, 1560 Sherman Ave., Ste. 860, Evanston, IL 60201. Tel 847-328-1500; 328-1510.

ANNUAL NATIONAL EXHIBITION OF TRANSPARENT WATERCOLORS, Annual, show will travel to different museums each year. Show for 1997 will be held at West Bend Art Museum in West Bend, WI. July 19 - September 7, 1997. Transparent watercolor. Open to all artists 18 years or older and living in the U.S. and Canada. Open juried. Fee $20 for non-members, free for members, one painting per entrant. $7800 and up in awards. For further information write Lori Fronczak, 924 David Drive, Bensenville, IL 60106-3414.

CHICAGO'S NEW EAST SIDE ARTWORKS, Chicago. Arts and Crafts. Open to all artists throughout the U.S. and Canada. Juried show, outdoor. For further information write to : Chicago's New Eastside Artworks, 200 N Michigan Ave, Ste 300, Chicago, IL 60601. Tel 312-551-9290; Fax 312-541-0253.

INDIANA

EVANSVILLE MUSEUM OF ARTS AND SCIENCE ANNUAL MID-STATES CRAFT EXHIBITION, Evansville. Biennial; Write or call for application in May-July. Ceramic, textile, metalwork, glass, wood, enamel and handcrafted materials. Open to residents of Indiana, Illinois, Kentucky, Missouri, Ohio, and Tennessee. Juried awards. Fee $15. For further information write Art Committee, Evansville Museum of Arts & Science, 411 SE Riverside Dr., Evansville, IN 47713. Tel 812-425-2406.

IOWA

35th ANNUAL 'ART IN THE PARK,' Riverview Park in Clinton. June 14-15. Fine arts and fine crafts only. Juried by 5 slides (1 of display). Application fee $5. Space fee $70 (12x12). No commission. Cash award ($2000). Application deadline Mar. 15. SASE to Art in the Park, Box 2164, Clinton, IA 52733 or call Carol Glahn, Tel 319-259-8308.

ANNUAL OCTAGON COMMUNITY OF ARTISTS EXHIBITION, Ames. Annual, Nov. 24 - Jan. 5. Open to artists in the Octagon Community. Juried exhibition. For further information write Octagon Center for the Arts, 427 Douglas Ave., Ames, IA 50010-6213. Tel 515-232-5331; Fax 515-232-5088.

IOWA CRAFTS ANNUAL, Mason City. Annual, Oct-Dec. Open to any and all craft media, such as clay, fiber, metals and others. Open to all artists, craftspersons residing within the State of Iowa. Juried by submission of the work, up to $2500 in cash awards. No fee. Entry deadline three weeks prior to opening of show. For further information write Richard Leet, Dir., Charles H MacNider Museum, 303 Second St. SE, Mason City, IA 50401.

OCTAGON'S CLAY, FIBER, PAPER, GLASS, METAL AND WOOD EXHIBITION, Ames. Annual, Mar. - April. Fine Arts. Open to established and emerging artists from around the U.S. Premier juried national exhibition. For further information write Octagon Center for the Arts, 427 Douglas Ave., Ames, IA 50010-6213. Tel 515-232-5331; Fax 515-232-5088.

KANSAS

SMOKY HILL RIVER FESTIVAL, Salina. Annual, June 13-15, 1997. Juried, art displayed and sold. $5300 in Merit awards; $1500 in Public Art Purchases. For further information write Salina Arts & Humanities Commission, P.O. Box 2181, Salina, KS 67402-2181. Tel 913-826-7410; Fax 913-826-7444.

LOUISIANA

NEW ORLEANS MUSEUM OF ART. Triennial. Focus on contemporary art in all media by professional artists from thirteen-state region of Southeastern U.S. single guest curator purchases. No fee. Next exhibition in series: 1998. For further information write New Orleans Triennial, New Orleans Museum of Art, P.O. Box 19123, One Collins Diboll Circle, City Park, New Orleans, LA 70179.

MAINE

MAINE OPEN JURIED ART SHOW, Waterville. Annual. Open to Maine artists only. Fee $15 for two entries. $1200 in cash prizes. For further information write Waterville Area Art Society, P.O. Box 41 China, Neck Rd., China, ME 04926. Tel 207-968-2871.

MARYLAND

MID-ATLANTIC REGIONAL WATERCOLOR EXHIBITION, Baltimore. Original aquamedia works on paper. Juried competition, over $4000 in prizes, juror: Judy Wagner, author of The Watercolor Fixit Book and Painting with the White of the Paper. For prospectus, send SASE to Liz Donovan, 4035 Roxmill Ct, Glenwood, MD 21738.

MICHIGAN

THE GREAT LAKES REGIONAL EXHIBITION (formerly Mid-Michigan Exhibition), Midland. Annual, spring. All media and mixed media (painting, drawing, print-making, sculpture, ceramics, fiber art, photography, jewelry and new forms). Open to artists 18 years or older residing in Michigan, Illinois, Indiana, Ohio and Wisconsin. Only original work completed within past three years. Juried, prizes and awards. Fee $15 per artist, maximum three entries, $10 fee for AC members. Preliminary jurying from slides. Final jurying from actual works. For further information and prospectus write Arts Midland: Galleries and School, Midland Center for the Arts, 1801 W. Saint Andrews, Midland, MI 48640.

MICHIGAN FINE ARTS COMPETITION, Birmingham. Annual. Juried, juror: James Walker. Thousands of dollars in awards. For further information write Birmingham Bloomfield Art Association, 1516 S. Cranbrook Rd., Birmingham, MI 48009. Tel 810-644-0866; Fax 810-644-7904.

MINNESOTA

SISTER KENNY 34th ANNUAL INTERNATIONAL ART SHOW BY ARTISTS WITH DISABILITIES, Minneapolis. Annual, deadline March 22nd. Fine art only. Open to all disabled artists worldwide. Two pieces per entrant; artwork sold at exhibit, profits returned to participating artists. For further information write Attn: Linda Frederickson, Abbott Northwestern Hospital, Sister Kenny Institute, 800 E. 28th St., Minneapolis, MN 55407-9923. Tel 612-863-4630; Fax 612-863-3299.

MISSOURI

GREATER MIDWEST INTERNATIONAL EXHIBITION, Warrensburg. No media restrictions. Open to artists 21 years or older. work must be original, completed within the last 3 years not and not previously exhibited at CMSU Art Center Gallery. Juried, $1600 in cash awards. Fee $20 for one to three slides, $25 for four or five slides. For further information and prospectus write Central Missouri State University, Art Center Gallery - GMI XII, c/o Dir. Morgan Gallatin, 217 Clark St., Warrensburg, MO 64093-5246.

NATIONAL OIL & ACRYLIC PAINTERS SOCIETY EXHIBIT, Osage Beach. Annual. Oil and acrylic paintings in all styles. Juried exhibit. Awards $4000. Slides deadline July 25, 1997. For entry forms send SASE to: NOAPS, Dept. R, P.O. Box 676, Osage Beach, MO 65065. Tel 573-346-3897.

PHOTOSPIVA, Joplin. Jan.-Feb., All photography processes. Open to U.S. artists. Juried. $1500 in cash awards. Fee $25, limit five. For further information write Spiva Center for the Arts, 222 W. Third St., Joplin, MO 64801.

NEBRASKA

PHI-THETA-KAPPA SIX-STATE COMPETITIVE, McCook. Annual, Feb. - Mar. All two-dimensional art except computer-generated and photography. Open to all artists 18 years and older living in Nebraska, Colorado, Iowa, Kansas, South Dakota and Wyoming. Juried by slides. $1200 and up in purchase and cash awards, 20% comm. in all art work sold. For prospectus write Don Dernovich, Art Dept., McCook Community College, 1205 E. Third, McCook, NE 69001. Tel 308-345-6303; Fax 308-345-3305.

NEW JERSEY

BOARDWALK INDIAN SUMMER CRAFT SHOW, Atlantic City. Annual, Sept. Craft. $3000 in awards. For further information write Florence Miller, Dir, 205 N. Montpelier Ave., Atlantic City, NJ 08401.

NEW MEXICO

PSNM NATIONAL ART EXHIBITION, Albuquerque. Oct. 27-Nov.15, 1997. Awards in excess of $3000. For prospectus write Pastel Society of New Mexico, 208 Cardenas NE, Albuquerque, NM 87108.

SOUTHWEST ARTS FESTIVAL, Albuquerque. Annual, Nov. Open to artists and craftspeople. Juried. Admission $4. For further information write Southwest Arts Festival, 1720 Louisiana Blvd NE, Suite 103, Albuquerque, NM 87110. Tel 505-262-2448.

NEW YORK

CERAMIC NATIONAL. Syracuse. Triennial, spring. Open to artists 21 years of age or older who reside in the U.S. Purchase prices. Fee. Artwork must be predominantly of fired clay. For further information write Everson Museum of Art, Public Info Dept., 401 Harrison St., Syracuse, NY 13202.

COOPERSTOWN ANNUAL NATIONAL SUMMER EXHIBITION, Cooperstown. Annual. All media. Prizes. Catalog. For further information write Janet Garber, Dir., Cooperstown Art Association, 22 Main St., Cooperstown, NY 13326.

EVERSON MUSEUM OF ART EVERSON BIENNIAL, Syracuse. Biennial, held during even years. Painting, prints, drawing, collage, photographs, sculpture, fiber. Open to artists over 18 years of age who reside in central NY. Fee for non-members. For further information write Everson Museum of Art, Public Info Dept., 401 Harrison St., Syracuse, NY 13202.

SALMAGUNDI CLUB ANNUAL OPEN NON-MEMBERS EXHIBITION, New York. June 2-20, 1997. All two dimensional media - no photography or sculpture. Juried, cash awards. Fee: $25 - 1 slide, $35 - 2 slides, $45 - 3 slides. For further information send SASE to Jo Ann Leiser, Open Show Chairman, Salmagundi Club, 47 Fifth Ave., New York, NY 10003. Tel 212-255-7740. Must send SASE for prospectus.

THE MINI PRINT INTERNATIONAL EXHIBITION, Binghamton. Print making, contemporary and traditional methods acceptable. Images submitted no larger then 4" x 4". For prospectus and further information write B. McLean, Studio School & Art Gallery, 3 Chestnut St., Binghamton, NY 13905. Tel 607-772-6867.

NORTH CAROLINA

NORTH CAROLINA ARTISTS EXHIBITION, Raleigh. Triennial, summer 1999. All media. Open to current North Carolina residents. For further information write Curatorial Dept. North Carolina Museum of Art, 2110 Blue Ridge Rd., Raleigh, NC 27607.

SHELBY ART LEAGUE, Shelby. Annual, Juried, $4000 in cash awards. For further information write before Aug, 1997, to Shelby Art League, P.O. Box 1708, Shelby, NC 28151.

OHIO

COLUMBUS ARTS FESTIVAL, COLUMBUS. Annual, June. Fine arts and crafts. Juried. For further information write Columbus Arts Festival, 55 E. State St., Columbus, OH 43215. Tel 614-224-2606.

SUMMERFAIR, Cincinnati, Annual, May 30-June 1, 1997. All fine arts and crafts. Juried Exhibition, sale. Processing fee $20. $8000 and up in cash awards. For further information write Summerfair, Dept. AAD, P.O. Box 8287, Cincinnati, OH 45208. Tel 513-531-0050.

OKLAHOMA

OKLAHOMA ART WORKSHOPS NATIONAL JURIED EXHIBITION, Tulsa. Sept. 7-30, 1997. Multi-media, open to all artists nationwide. Juror: Pat San Soucie $5000 in cash prizes. Entry deadline June 11, 1997. For further information send SASE Attn: Anne Nowak, Chmn, Oklahoma Art Workshops, 6953 S 66th E Ave, Tulsa, OK 74133-1747. Tel 918-492-8863.

PENNSYLVANIA

ANNUAL JURIED EXHIBITION OF THE ART ASSOCIATION OF HARRISBURG, Harrisburg. Annual, May 10 - June 13, 1997. Media categories include: oil and acrylic, sculpture and ceramics, photography, watercolor, prints and graphics, etc. Open to all artists in the U.S. and abroad. Juried by slides. Fee $12.50 per slide, two slides per entrant. Entry deadline Jan. 31, 1997. Send SASE to Art Association of Harrisburg, 21 N. Front St., Harrisburg, PA 17101. Tel 717-236-1432; Fax 717-236-6631.

CENTRAL PENNSYLVANIA FESTIVAL OF THE ARTS SIDEWALK SALE & EXHIBITION, State College. Annual, July 10 - 13, 1997. Media categories: ceramics, sculpture, glass, fiber, leather, jewelry, wood, painting, printmaking, watercolor, photography, drawing and graphics, mixed media, metal and paper. Juried, $15,000 in awards. $15 application fee, five slides submitted with fee. For entry and further information send SASE to: Visual Arts Director, Central Pennsylvania Festival of the Arts, P.O. Box 1023, State College, PA 16804-1023. Tel 814-237-3682; Fax 814-237-0708.

WASHINGTON & JEFFERSON COLLEGE NATIONAL PAINTING SHOW, Washington. Annual, Mar-Apr. All painting. Open to any U.S. artists, 18 years old. Prizes and purchase awards. Fee $10 for each slide entry. Entry cards and slides due Jan, work due Mar. For further information write Paul B. Edwards, Olin Art Center, Washington & Jefferson College, Washington, PA 15301.

RHODE ISLAND

PROVIDENCE ART CLUB. Annual. Three open, juried shows every year scheduled at various times. Limited to artists living in Southern New England. Shows are either media-specific (prints, sculpture, etc.) or theme-based. For further information write Sarah Farragher, Providence Art Club, 11 Thomas St., Providence, RI 02903. Tel 401-331-1114.

SOUTH CAROLINA

ANNUAL JUDGED SPRING ART SHOW, Myrtle Beach. Annual. Two- and three-dimensional fine art. $4000 total in awards. For prospectus write Waccamaw Arts & Crafts Guild, P.O. Box 1595, Myrtle Beach, SC 29578. Tel 803-497-3897.

ART-IN-THE-PARK, Myrtle Beach. Three shows annually: May 10-11; June 12-13; July 14-15. Handmade crafts and original fine art. Juried, outdoor. For application write Waccamaw Arts & Crafts Guild, Bruce Smith, Chmn., P.O. Box 3302, North Myrtle Beach, SC 29582. Tel 803-249-4937.

SOUTH DAKOTA

RED CLOUD INDIAN ART SHOW, Pine Ridge. June-Aug. Paintings, graphics, mixed media, 3-D work. Open to any tribal member of the native people of North America. Juried, $5500 in merit and purchase awards. Entries due May 22. For further information write Red Cloud Indian Art Show, Red Cloud Indian School, Pine Ridge, SD 57770.

TENNESSEE

CENTRAL SOUTH ART EXHIBITION, Nashville. Annual, summer. All media recognized for artists residing in Tennessee, each adjoining state within a 300-mile radius and/or a league member. Juried competition and exhibition. For entry and prospectus write Tennessee Art League, 3011 Poston Ave., Nashville, TN 37203. Tel 615-298-4072.

TEXAS

MUSEUMS OF ABILENE, Abilene. Annual. Exhibition and competition of conyemporary two- and three-dimensional art. Open to Texas artists. Juried. Cash prizes. Solo exhibition awarded. For information write to: MOA Annual Art Competition, Museums of Abilene, 102 Cypress, Abilene, TX 79601. Tel 915-673-4587.

UTAH

UTAH STATEWIDE ANNUAL COMPETITION AND EXHIBITION, Salt Lake City. This juried exhibit sponsored by the Utah Arts Council has a tradition spanning more than ninety years. Open to Utah artists only, at no charge, this exhibition is selected by at least one out-of-state juror. The annual format is hosted by Utah Museum with rotating disciplines. Up to $10,000 is allocated for cash awards and purchases. For further information write Utah Arts Council, 617 E. South Temple, Salt Lake City, UT 84102. Tel 801-533-4195.

VIRGINIA

NATIONAL JURIED SHOW, Richmond. Annual, June 7-29, 1997. All contemporary media will be considered except traditional craft. Open to all artists residing in the U.S. Juried. Entry fee, entry deadline April 1. For prospectus send SASE to: 1708 Gallery, Annual National Juried Exhibition, 103 E. Broad St., P.O. Box 12520, Richmond, VA 23241. Tel 804-643-7829.

STOCKLEY GARDENS ARTS FESTIVALS, Norfolk. Held twice a year, May 17-18 and Oct. 18-19, 1997. For further information write Hope House Foundation, 100 W. Plume St., No.244, Norfolk, VA 23510. Tel 757-625-6161; Fax 757-625-7775.

WASHINGTON

NORTHWEST PASTEL SOCIETY ANNUAL INTERNATIONAL EXHIBITION, For further information, send SASE to: Northwest Pastel; Society, 420 NW Gilman Blvd., No.2732, Issaquah, WA 98027-7001.

WISCONSIN

LAKEFRONT FESTIVAL OF ARTS, Milwaukee. Annual, June. Multi-media. Open to professional artists and fine craftsmen from across the country. Juried and $10,000 in prizes. Fee $25. For further information write Milwaukee Art Museum, 750 N. Lincoln Memorial Dr., Milwaukee, WI 53202. Tel 414-224-3850; Fax 414-271-7588.

Traveling Exhibition Booking Agencies

ADAMS COUNTY MUSEUM, 9601 Henderson Rd, Brighton, CO 80601-8100. *Exhibits*—Traveling suitcases, containing items from the early 1900s ranching and farming. Rental fees free to schools.

ALBERTA FOUNDATION FOR THE ARTS, 10158 103rd St, 5th Flr, Edmonton, AB T5J 0X6, Canada. *Arts Develop Officer* Ross Bradley.
Exhibits—Exhibitions are currently provided through a consortium of Alberta public art galleries. The programs vary from year to year and from region to region. Fees may vary and are subject to negotiation with participating galleries.

ALBRIGHT-KNOX ART GALLERY, 1285 Elmwood Ave, Buffalo, NY 14222. *Cur* Cheryl Brutvan & Marc Mayer; *Dir* Douglas G Schlutz.
Exhibits—Jenny Holzer: The Venice Installation; Abstract Expressionism: The Critical Developments. Susan Rothenberg: Paintings and Drawings; Clyfford Still: The Buffalo and San Francisco Collections; Jess: A Grand Collage, 1951-1993; The paintings of Sylvia Plimack Mangold. Arshile Gorky: The Breakthrough Years. Being & Time: The Emergence of Video Projection.

THE ALBUQUERQUE MUSEUM, 2000 Mountain Rd NW, Albuquerque, NM 87104. Tel 505-243-7255; Fax 505-764-6546. *Cur of Hist* John Grassham
Exhibits—Santiago-Saint of Two Worlds: Photographs by Joan Myers; Monuments of Adobe: Photographs by Kirk Gittings; Pueblo Deco: Photographs by Carla Breeze; Chaco Body: Photographs by Kirk Gittings, Poetry by V.B. Price; Chaco Past-Chaco Future: Photographs by Douglas Kent Hall. En Divina Luz; Photographs by Craig Varjabedian. Rental fees $350-$900. Insurance value $5000- $50,000.

AMERICAN JEWISH ART CLUB, 6301 N Sheridan Rd, Apt 8E, Chicago, IL 60660. *Pres* Mrs Irmgard Hess Rosenberger.
Exhibits—One and two group exhibitions per year-one is an annual exhibition at which awards are given to five artists. Membership is $35 annually.

AMERICAS SOCIETY INC, 680 Park Ave, New York, NY 10021. Tel 212-249-8950; Fax 212-249-5868. *Head Visual Arts* Elizabeth Ferrer; *Visual Arts and Education Programs Admin* Regina Smith.
Exhibits—Latin American, Caribbean and Canadian art from pre-Columbian to contemporary times. Details of programs available from Visual Arts Department. Rental fees are dependent on the nature of the exhibition.

ARC GALLERY, 1040 W Huron St, Chicago, IL 60622. Tel 312-733-2787. *Pres* Julia M Morrisroe; *VPres* Pamela Staker Matson.
Exhibits—Potentiality: Interactive Art Exhibition; Artists Invite Artists Group Exhibition; National Exposure Juried Photo Exhibition; ARC Regional IV . Major work by artists members. Exhibit costs-shipping only.

THE ARKANSAS ART CENTER, STATE SERVICES, PO Box 2137, Little Rock, AR 72203. *Dir State Svcs* Renee Bearfield; *Artmobile Educator* Virgil Lawrence.
Exhibits—Thematically organized exhibitions from the permanent collection which includes the 1996-98 Artmobile exhibition, Poetry in Drawing; as well as ten other traveling exhibitions including-Lithographs by Joseph Hirsch; Will Barnet: Drawings 1930-1990; African-American Artists; Old Master Prints and Prints by 20th Century Sculptors. Rental fees $1200 per month, outside AR. Shipping fees vary, but are the responsibility of the renter. Contact the Arts Center's State Services Dept for additional information on the availability of traveling programs.

ART CENTER OF BATTLE CREEK, 265 E Emmett St, Battle Creek, MI 49017. *Dir* A W Concannon; *Cur* Carol Snapp.
Exhibits—Affected Environments: Post-Industrial Visions by Michigan Artists. Rental fees $200-$400 for four weeks. Shipping fees are responsibility of renter.

ART GALLERY OF NEWFOUNDLAND AND LABRADOR, Arts & Culture Centre, PO Box 4200, St John's, NF A1C 5S7, Canada. *Dir* Patricia Grattan.
Exhibits—Contemporary art; folk art; traditional craft of Newfoundland & Labrador. Rental & shipping fees vary.

ART GALLERY OF YORK UNIVERSITY, Ross Bldg, 4700 Keele St, Rm N145, North York, ON M3J 1P3, Canada. *Dir & Cur* Loretta Yarlow; *Asst Cur* Jack Liang.
Exhibits—Robert Therrien; Roy Arden; Becky Singleton; Alison Wilding.

ART IN ARCHITECTURE, 7917 1/2 W Norton Ave, Los Angeles, CA 90046. Tel 213-654-0990. *Dir* Joseph Young; *Assoc* Millicent E Young.
Exhibits—Art in Architecture.

THE ASIA SOCIETY GALLERIES, 725 Park Ave, New York, NY 10021. *Dir* Vishakha Desai.
Exhibits—Asian art, usually on closely focused topics. Rental and shipping fees vary.

AUGUSTANA COLLEGE ART GALLERY, Art & Art History Dept, 3701 Seventh Ave, Rock Island, IL 61201. Tel 309-794-7231; Fax 309-794-7678; E-mail armaurer@augustana.edu. *Dir* Sherry C Maurer.
Exhibits—Swedish-American Artists. Rental fees $2000. Shipping fees $1500.

BALZEKAS MUSEUM OF LITHUANIAN CULTURE, 6500 S Pulaski Rd, Chicago, IL 60629. *Pres* Stanley Balzekas, Jr.
Exhibits—Six small portable cases which include history, maps and some memorabilia on Lithuania dating back 300 years. Rental fee is $150 plus transportation.

BATON ROUGE GALLERY, 1442 City Park Ave, Baton Rouge, LA 70808. Tel 504-383-1470. *Exec Dir* Kathleen Pheney; *Asst Dir* Nancy Stapleton; *Pub Dir* Larry Giacoletti.
Exhibits—Thirteen comtemporary art exhibitions each year featuring regionally- and nationally-recognized artists' works in all types of media; Frank Hayden Retrospective. Questions or comments, please call.

BINGHAMTON UNIVERSITY, Art Museum, PO Box 6000, Binghamton, NY 13902-6000. *Dir* Lynn Gamwell; *Cur* Lucie Nelson; *Secy* Norma Moses.
Exhibits—Josiah Wedgwood: Experimental Potter, tour schedule 1994-97. The Josiah Wedgwood exhibition is toured by Smith Kramer Fine Art Services of Kansas City, MO.

BLACKWOOD GALLERY, ERINDALE COLLEGE, UNIVERSITY OF TORONTO IN MISSISSAUGA, Mississauga Rd N, Mississauga, ON L5L 1C6 Canada. Tel 905-828-3789; Fax 905-828-5474. *Cur* Nancy Hazelgrove.
Exhibits—David Blackwood Travelling Survey Exhibition 1980-1990. Down North: A Coastal Journey. Prints and paintings by Anne Meredith Barry. Rental fees $750. Shipping fees paid by renting gallery.

B'NAI B'RITH KLUTZNICK NATIONAL JEWISH MUSEUM, 1640 Rhode Island Ave NW, Washington, DC 20036 *Dir* Ori Z Soltes.
Exhibits— Jews in Sports. Charles Stern: The Mysticism of Hebrew letters.

BUFFALO BILL HISTORICAL CENTER, 720 Sheridan Ave, Cody, WY 82414. *Interim Dir* Eugene W Reben.
Exhibits—"It Never Failed Me: The Arms and Art of the Remington Arms Company."

BURCHFIELD—PENNEY ART CENTER, Buffalo State College, 1300 Elmwood Ave, Buffalo, NY 14222-1095. *Actg Dir* Donald J Metz.
Exhibits—Life Cycles: The Charles E Burchfield Collection (presently being toured by the American Federation of Arts). Milton Rogovin: Buffalo's Lower West Side Revisited. Rental fees $2500 - $27,000.

BURLINGTON ART CENTER, 1333 Lakeshore Rd, Burlington, ON L7S 1A9 Canada. Tel 905-632-7796; Fax 905-632-7796. Internet Home Page Address: http://www.burlingtonartcenter.on.ca. *Exec Dir* Ian D Ross; *Dir of Programs* George Wale.
Exhibits—Earth and Fire: Contemporary Canadian Ceramic Art. Call for further information.

THE CASEMATE MUSEUM, PO Box 51341, Fort Monroe, VA 23651-0341. Tel 757-727-3935; Fax 757-727-3886. *Museum Dir* Dennis P Mroczkowski; *Museum Specialist* Kathy A Rothrock.
Exhibits—Postcard Images of Fort Monroe, exhibits restricted to local area, exceptions to be determined by Dir on a case-by-case basis.

CAZENOVIA COLLEGE, Cazenovia, NY 13035. *Dir, Art Gallery* John Aistars; *Dir, Cultural Center* Corky Goss.
Exhibits—Variety of media and stylistic approaches.

CENTER GALLERY OF BECKNELL UNIVERSITY, Elaine Langone Center, Lewisburg, PA 17837. Tel 717-524-3792; Fax 717-524-3480. *Asst Dir* Cynthia Peltier.
Exhibits—Varies. Rental & shipping fees vary.

CHAPEL ART CENTER, Saint Anselm College, 100 Saint Anselm Dr, Manchester, NH 03102. Tel 603-641-7470; Fax 603-641-7116. *Dir* Dr Donald Rosenthal; *Asst Dir* Adrienne LaVallée.
Exhibits—Guatemala: Holy Week (with catalogue). Colony Printmakers: MacDowell Colony Printmakers from 1925-1995 (co-sponsored & coordinated by Sharon Arts Center, Peterborough, NH, with catalogue).

CHATTAHOOCHEE VALLEY ART MUSEUM, 112 Hines St, La Grange, GA 30240. Tel 706-882-3267.
Exhibits—Bronislaw Bak: Graphic Works 1953-73. Rental fees $800, not including shipping.

CINCINNATI ART MUSEUM, Eden Park Dr, Cincinnati, OH 45202. *Head of Exhibitions & Registrations* Mary Ellen Goeke.
Exhibits—Pueblo Pottery; Avant-garde by the Yard Textiles; Women in Ancient Egypt.

THE COLLEGE OF SANTA FE, Art/Art History Dept, 1600 Saint Michaels Dr, Santa Fe, NM 87501. *Dir* Don Messec.
Exhibits—Monoprints. Rental fees $2 per monoprint, $50 minimum. Shipping fees cost only. They are shipped with foamcore backing and plastic glazing, unframed, ready for L-nails, screws or exhibitor's frames. 25% sales discount to exhibitors.

COLORADO SPRINGS FINE ARTS CENTER, 30 W Dale St, Colorado Springs, CO 80903. Tel 719-634-5581; Fax 719-634-0570. *Exec Dir* David J Wagner; *Dir of Collections* Cathy Wright; *Exhibition Coordr* Kathy Reynolds.
Exhibits—Walt Kuhn: An Imaginary History of the West; John James Audubon's The Birds of America: Double Elephant Folio; Posada: Major Works from the Taylor Museum Collection; Contemporary Native American Prints. Rental fees $1,000-$7,500, not including shipping.

CORNELL FINE ARTS MUSEUM, Rollins College, Winter Park, FL 32789. Tel 407-646-2526; Fax 407-646-2524. *Dir* Dr Arthur R Blumenthal.
Exhibits—Winslow Homer: American Illustrator. Rental fees $3500, shipping $2000 and up.

CORNING MUSEUM OF GLASS, One Museum Way, Corning, NY 14830-2253. Tel 607-937-5371. *Pub Rel* Lezli White.
Exhibits—Italian Glass 1930-1970:Masterpieces of Design from Murano and Milan.

CULVER-STOCKTON COLLEGE, One College Hill, Canton, MO 63435. Tel 217-231-6367; Fax 217-231-6611. *Gallery Dir* Catherine Royer.
Exhibits—Images of Faith; Eastern Christian Icons & Hispanic Catholic Saints. NCECA Connection: Teachers in Liberal Arts Programs. Missouri Fiber Artists 1998. Rental fees $100-200.

CUMMER GALLERY OF ART LIBRARY, The Cummer Museum of Art & Gardens, 829 Riverside Ave, Jacksonville, FL 32204. Tel 904-356-6857; Fax 904-353-4101. *Dir* Dr Kahren J Arbitman; *Cur* Dr Sally Metzle.
Exhibits—Russian Imperial Porcelain; California Impressionists; A Night at the Opera.

CUSTER COUNTY ART CENTER, Water Plant Rd, PO Box 1284, Miles City, MT 59301. Tel 406-232-0635. *Dir* Mark Browning; *Admin Asst* Brenda Kneeland
Exhibits—Blackfeet Tipis: Silkscreens by Jessie Wilbur; Photogravures - "Images of an Idyllic Past:" Edward S Curtis; "Why Killdeers Cry" and "The Prairie and I," watermedia paintings by Andrew L Hofmeister. Rental fees $350-$450 for four weeks. Exhibits are insured, crated and shipped one way pre-paid. For more information, please contact Mark Browning.

DENNOS MUSEUM CENTER, Northwestern Michigan College, 1701 E Front St, Traverse City, MI 49686. Tel 616-922-1055; Fax 616-922-1597. *Dir* Eugene A Jenneman; *Cur* Jacqueline Shinners.
Exhibits—Cultural Reflections: Inuit Art from the Dennos Museum Center Collection (consists of approximately 30 prints & 20 stone sculptures). Rental fees $2500, shipping is at cost.

DESERT CABALLEROS WESTERN MUSEUM, 21 N Frontier St, Wickenburg, AZ 85390. Tel 520-684-2272 *Cur* Sheila Kollasch.
Exhibits—Sole of the West: The Art and History of Cowboy Boots. Rental and shipping fees vary and are offered through the Arizona Commission on the Arts.

THE DETROIT INSTITUTE OF ARTS, 5200 Woodward Ave, Detroit, MI 48202. Tel 313-833-7976. *Exhibitor Coordr* Tara Robinson.
Exhibits—Images in Ivory. Splendors of Ancient Egypt.

DUKE UNIVERSITY, Museum of Art, PO Box 90732, Durham, NC 27708-0732. Tel 919-684-5135; Fax 919-681-8624. *Dir* Dr Michael P Mezzatesta.
Exhibits—Jerusalem & the Holy Land Rediscovered: The Prints of David Roberts; Lost Russia: Photographs by William Craft Brumfield; The Ancient Ones: Photographs by Hans Li. Rental fees $1500-$25,000.

EAST CAROLINA UNIVERSITY, School of Art, Gray Art Gallery, Greenville, NC 27858. Tel 919-328-6336; Fax 919-328-6441 *Gallery Dir* Gil Leebrick.
Exhibits—Baltic Ceramics: 96 (call for further information).

EASTERN ILLINOIS UNIVERSITY, Tarble Arts Center, 600 Lincoln Ave, Charleston, IL 61920-3099. *Dir* Michael Watts; *Reg* David Pooley.
Exhibits—Amish of Illinois (photo documentary). Rental and shipping fees are negotiable. This is a free-standing exhibit that includes didactic materials and some folk arts/artifacts.

EAST TENNESSEE STATE UNIVERSITY, Dept of Art & Design, Box 70708, Johnson City, TN 37614-0708. Tel 423-439-4247. *Dir* (Slocumb Gallery) Ann Ropp; *Chmn* (Art & Design Dept) David G Logan; *Cur* (Reece Museum) Blair H White.
Exhibits—Contemporary fine arts & crafts (Slocumb); contemporary & historical exhibits (Reece). Rental and shipping fees vary.

ELK RIVER AREA ARTS COUNCIL, 400 Jackson Ave, Ste 205, Elk River, MN 55330. Tel 612-441-4725. *Exec Dir* David Beauvais.
Exhibits—A Day in the Life of Elk River, consist of thirty-six 20"x 24" & 25"x 29" mounted photographs selected fom 1446 photographs taken by twenty-eight photographers on June 8, 1996. Rental fees $100, shipping $60 (return shipping paid by exhibitor).

EN FOCO, INC, 32 E Kingsbridge Rd, Bronx, NY 10468. Tel 718-584-7718. *Exec Dir* Charles Biasiny-Rivera; *Managing Dir* Miriam Romais.
Exhibits—Island Journey: Ten Puerto Rican Photographers (catalogue provided). En Foco Collection: Twenty Years. Saving the Light: New Works by Latino Photographers. Rental fees $1500 and up.

ERIE ART MUSEUM, 411 State St, Erie, PA 16501. *Dir* John Vanco.
Exhibits—The Tactile Vessel-New Basket forms; Daumier Lithographs; Art of the Comic Book; Edward Sheriff Curtis-People of the Pueblos; Nationals and Dobros—American Resophonic Instruments. Rental fees $1000-$5500. Shipping fees - borrower pays one way shipping to next site.

EVANSTON HISTORICAL SOCIETY, 225 Greenwood St, Evanston, IL 60201. *Dir* Joan M Costello.
Exhibits—The Sick Can't Wait: The story of Evanston Community Hospital, founded by African-Americans. Your Presence is Requested: The Story of African-American social activities in Evanston, including debutante balls, clubs and social organizations from the 1930s through 1970s. Evanston Tackles the Woman Question: Displays the role of Evanston women in the women's movement. Rental fees are to be determined. Shipping fees are as required.

FORUM FOR CONTEMPORARY ART, 3540 Washington, St Louis, MO 63103. Tel 314-535-4660; Fax 314-535-1226. E-mail forum@inlink.com. *Exec Dir* Elizabeth Wright Millard; *Cur* Mel Watkin.
Exhibits—Sabina Ott: Everywhere There is Somewhere #2. A survey of recent paintings & a new installation/incorporation of paintings, sculpture & video. Traveling 1998-99 (Catalogue available). Rental fees $12,000, shipping is prorated.

FUDAN MUSEUM FOUNDATION, 1522 Schoolhouse Rd, Ambler, PA 19002-1936. *Pres* Dr Alfonz Lengyel.
Exhibits—Chinese Humorous (Caricature), brush and ink paintings. Sizes 30"x 25" some smaller. Rental fees $500. Shipping fees UPS charges.

GALERIE RESTIGOUCHE GALLERY, 39 rue Andrew St, CP/PO Box 674, Campbellton, NB E3N 3H1, Canada. *Dir* Valerie Gilker.
Exhibits—Couleurs d'Acadie: Color photographs of brightly painted houses phenomena. 120 running feet. No rental fee. Borrower pays cost of transportation both ways. Catalogue available.

GETTYSBURG COLLEGE, Art Department, Box 2452, Gettysburg, PA 17325. *Gallery Dir* Norman Annis.
Exhibits—Steven H Warner, 1946-71: Words and Pictures from the Vietnam War; Seeing a New World: The Works of Carl Beam and Frederic Remington. No rental fees. Shipping fees-to cover shipping and insurance.

THE GREAT LAKES HISTORICAL SOCIETY, 480 Main St, PO Box 435, Vermilion, OH 44089. Tel 800-893-1485; Fax 216-967-1519. E-mail glhs1@aol.com *Exec Dir* William A O'Brien; *Bus Mgr* William Stark.
Exhibits—Great Lakes Ship Models; Steam and Out Board Engines; Fine Art. Rental and shipping fees vary with size and number of artifacts.

GREEN HILL CENTER FOR NORTH CAROLINA ART, 200 N Davie St, Greensboro, NC 27401. *Dir* Jennifer Moore.
Exhibits—Effective Sight: The Paintings of Juan Logan. Rental fees $500. Shipping fees are transportation one way.

THE SOLOMON R GUGGENHEIM MUSEUM, 1071 Fifth Ave, New York, NY 10128. *Cur* Lisa Dennison.
Exhibits—Concentrations of individual artists; European painting & sculpture; modern sculpture; European sources of American abstraction; American abstract painting and works on paper from the 1930s & 1940s; postwar American painting; postwar European painting; postwar art; Latin American art; works on paper. Borrowing institutions will remain responsible for shipping, insurance costs, packing & other charges. In addition, some loan exhibitions organized by the museum are available for travel tours.

HEARST ART GALLERY, Saint Mary's College of California, PO Box 5110, Moraga, CA 94575. Tel 510-631-4379. *Cur* Marvin Schenck.
Exhibits—William Keith: California's Poet-Printer. Stanley Truman: Fifty Years of Photography. Rental fees $1000-$5000.

THE HERITAGE CENTER, INC, PO Box 100, Pine Ridge, SD 57770. *Pres* Calvin Jumping Bull; *Dir* C M Simon.
Exhibits—Come Dance With Us: Selections from Permanent Collection Annual Art Show; Robert Freeman Retrospective; Ten Years of Winners; Northern Plains Tribal Arts. Contact center for shipping fees.

HIBEL MUSEUM OF ART, 150 Royal Poinciana Plaza, Palm Beach, FL 33480. Tel 561-833-6870; Fax 561-848-9640. E-mail hibel@worldnet.att.net. *Exec Trustee* Dr Andy Plotkin; *Dir* Mary Johnson; *Asst Dir & Ed Dir* Janet Tanis.
Exhibits—Paintings; Drawings; Sculptures; Graphics; Porcelain Art. Rental fees $200 - $500. Shipping fees are actual cost.

THE HIGH DESERT MUSEUM, 59800 S Hwy 97, Bend, OR 97702. *Exhibits Coordr* Barbara Reynolds. Tel 541-382-4754; Fax 541-382-5256.
Exhibits—Gum San: Land of the Golden Mountain; Amerikanuak! Basques in the High Desert. Call or write for information.

HISTORICAL MUSEUM AT FORT MISSOULA, Fort Missoula Bldg 322, Missoula, MT 59801. Tel 406-728-3476; Fax 406-728-5063. E-mail ftmslamuseum@marsweb.com. *Sen Cur* L Jane Richards.
Exhibits—"Victories" - World War II poster exhibit.

HUNT INSTITUTE FOR BOTANICAL DOCUMENTATION, Carnegie Mellon University, Pittsburgh, PA 15213. *Cur of Art* James J White.
Exhibits—International Exhibition; Marilena Pistoia: Botanical Watercolors; Poisonous Plants: Orchids from the Hunt Institute Collection; Iris from the Hunt Institute Collection. Rental fees $300-$750. Shipping fees vary.

HUNTSVILLE MUSEUM OF ART, 700 Monroe St SW, Huntsville, AL 35801. Tel 205-535-4350; Fax 205-532-1743. E-mail hma@traveller.com. Internet Home Page: NETSITE www.hsv.tis.net/hma.
Exhibits—Splendors of a Golden Age: Italian Paintings from Burghley House; White Mountain Painters. Encounters: Mark Marchlinski. Lost and Found: Sculpture by Jim Opasik and Mary Deacon Opasik. YAM: Exhibition for Youth Art Month. Frank Stella Prints. Golden Mouse Awards Computer Art Competition. Encounters: Will Berry. Embracing Beauty: Aesthetic Perfection in Contemporary Art. Intention/Invention: Advanced Photography in the 1990s.

INDEPENDENT CURATORS INCORPORATED, 799 Broadway, No 205, New York, NY 10003. *Assoc Dir* Judith Richards; *Exec Dir* Sandra Lang.
Exhibits—After Perestroika: Kitchenmaids or Stateswomen; Critiques of Pure Abstraction; Dark Decor; Departures: Photography 1923-1990; Drawn in the Nineties; Empty Dress: Clothing as Surrogate in Recent Art; The First Generation: Women and Video, 1970-75; From Media to Metaphor: Art about AIDS; Good Stories Well Told: Video Art for Young Audiences; Image and Memory: Latin American Photography, 1880-1992; Meret Oppenheim: Beyond the Teacup; Monumental Propaganda; Multiple Exposure: The Group Portrait in Photography; Content and Discontent in Today's Photography. At the Threshold of the Visible: Miniscule and Small-scale Art. David Smith: Medals for Dishonor. Do It. Embedded Metaphor. Liquiform: Visualizing Liquidity. Making It Real. Matters of Fact: New Art from Glasgow. Rental fees $500-$15,000, varying with exhibition.

INTERNATIONAL MUSEUM OF CARTOON ART, 5788 Notre Dame de Grace, Montreal, PQ H4A 1M4, Canada. Tel 514-489-0527. *VPres* Mark Scott.
Exhibits—Animation-Cartoon Film Exhibits:The Hollywood Cartoon; A History & Development of Animation; Homage to Walt Disney. Rental & shipping fees vary.

JAMES FORD BELL MUSEUM OF NATURAL HISTORY, University of Minnesota, 10 Church St, Minneapolis, MN 55455. Tel 612-624-2357; Fax 612-626-7704. *Touring Exhibits Coordr* Ian Dudley.
Exhibits—Exotic Aquatics, Return of the Peregrine Falcon, Saving Endangered Species-Saving ourselves, The Photography of Jim Brendenberg, The Net Result, Images of the North Country-Frances Lee Jacques. Rental fees from $500-$5000, shipping not included. The Museum has 18 touring exhibits ranging from Art, Natural History and AIDS.

KINGS COUNTY HISTORICAL SOCIETY AND MUSEUM, PO Box 5001, Hampton, NB E0G 1Z0, Canada. Tel 506-832-6009; Fax 506-832-6007. *Cur* A Faye Pearson.
Exhibits—Beulah Camp 1894-1994.

KITCHENER-WATERLOO ART GALLERY, 101 Queen St N, Kitchener, ON N2H 6P7, Canada. *Exten Cur & Educ Officer* Paul Blain.
Exhibits—Animal Images—Part II; Art: A Study of Realism; Canadian Landscape; Inuit Art; Face to Face; From Pen to Paper; Printmaking; Silkscreening; Watercolour and Waterloo County 1930-1960.

KRESGE ART MUSEUM, Michigan State University, East Lansing, MI 48824-1119. *Cur* Phylis Floyd.
Exhibits—Art and the Automobile; John Martin's Paradise Lost; The Prints of John Demartelley. Rental fees $850-$5000. Insurance coverage by borrowing institution.

THE KURDISH MUSEUM, 144 Underhill Ave, Brooklyn, NY 11238. Tel 718-783-7930; Fax 718-398-4365. *Dir* Vera Beaudin Saeedpour.
Exhibits—Jews of Kurdistan, largely textual with accompanying photos mounted on text boards which also includes a video. Rental fees $250, shipping $100.

MAITLAND ART CENTER TRAVELING EXHIBITION SERVICE (MACTES), 231 W Packwood Ave, Maitland, FL 32751-5596. Tel 407-539-2181; Fax 407-539-1198. *Cur* Leslie Tate Boles.
Exhibits—Currently twelve exhibitions of lithographs, watercolors, photography, textiles, sculpture, mixed-media, both foreign and American, range from 25-50 pieces per exhibit. Rental fees $650-$1200 for four-week booking period. The exhibitor is responsible for outgoing shipping. Annual and periodic catalogs available.

MERIDIAN INTERNATIONAL CENTER, 1624-30 Crescent Pl NW, Washington, DC 20009. Tel 202-939-5568; Fax 202-319-1306. E-mail meridian@dgs.dgsys.com. *VPres* (Arts) Nancy Matthews; *Dir* (Exhibitions) Curtis Sandburg; *Dir* (Educ) Susan Mordan.
Exhibits—Building Bridges: Israeli & Palestinian Artists Speak. Once Upon A Page: The Art of Children's Books. Panoramas of Passage: Changing Landscapes of South Africa. Wild Animals: Paintings by Sheila Isham. A Winding River: Contemporary Art From Vietnam (Nov 97). Imagining the World: Native Art from Latin America. Rental fees $5000-$20,000; shipping fees $800-$4000.

MESA ARTS CENTER, Galeria Mesa, 155 N Center, PO Box 1466, Mesa, AZ 85211-1466. *Visual Arts Supv* Robert Schultz; *Cur* Richard Wager; *Gallery Asst* Sandy Trant; *Gallery Aide* Tim Davidson.
Exhibits—Double Vision, Inside Story, From Every Angle, 19th Annual Vahki, Glass Act, Pulp Friction, Vaguely Familiar, Global Warning.

MEXIC-ARTE MUSEUM, 419 Congress Ave, PO Box 2632, Austin, TX 78768. *Exec Dir* Sylvia Orozco. *Exhibits*— Jean Charlot: Prints on Mexico; Masks from Guerrero: Rental fees $500, shipping $1000 - $1500 (for "masks" exhibition).

MIDWEST MUSEUM OF AMERICAN ART, 429 S Main, PO Box 1812, Elkhart, IN 46515. *Dir* Jane Burns; *Cur* Brian D Byrn. *Admin Asst* Martha Culp.
Exhibits—Viktoras Petravicius: Master of the Monoprint; John Doyle: The Great Human Race; William Gropper Lithographs. Rental fees $1200. Shipping fees one-way. Send for brochure.

MINNESOTA MUSEUM OF AMERICAN ART, Landmark Center, 75 W Fifth St, Saint Paul, MN 55102. *Dir* Ruth Appelhof.
Exhibits—Patrick DesJarlait and the Ojibwe Tradition. Rental fees $1500. Shipping fees pro-rated.

MONTANA HISTORICAL SOCIETY, 225 N Roberts, PO Box 201201, Helena, MT 59620-1201. Tel 406-444-4710. *Mus Registrar* Janet Sperry.
Exhibits—Lure of the Parks (National and State Parks of Montana); Photographing Montana 1894-1928: The World of Evelyn Cameron; Buildings in the Balance: Saving Montana's Historic Places; Butte in the Era of the Copper Kings; F Jay Haynes: Fifty Views; Children in Montana: 1864-1930; Montana Collage: Our History Through Photographs. Write or call for information.

MONTEREY MUSEUM OF ART, 559 Pacific St, Monterey, CA 93940. *Dir* Richard W Gadd.
Exhibits—The Monterey Photographic Tradition; The Weston Years; Colors and Impressions: The Early Work of E C Fortune: The Eye of the Child (International Folk Art); The Expressive Sculpture of Alvin Light; Photogravures: Edward Curtis; The Chicago Federal Act Project: WPA Prints; Joe Cole: A New Life's Work (Folk artist: oil pastels on paper); Wonderful Colors: The Paintings of August Gay; Jeannette Marfield Lewis: A Centennial Salute (prints and paintings).

MORAVIAN HISTORICAL SOCIETY, 214 E Center St, Nazareth, PA 18064. *Exec Dir* Susan M Dreydoppel.
Exhibits—Father of Modern Education: about Amos Comenius; Where in the World is the Moravian Church? Rental fees $20. Shipping fees as needed. For further information, contact MHS.

MUNICIPAL ART COMMISSION, City Hall, 17th Flr, 414 E 12th St, Kansas City, MO 64106. *Pub Art Adminr* Heidi Iverson Bilardo.
Exhibits—Winning entries of the annual Kansas City photography contest-shown at various public locations for one month at each site.

MUNSON-WILLIAMS-PROCTOR INSTITUTE MUSEUM OF ART, 310 Genesee St, Utica, NY 13502. *Dir & Chief Cur* Paul D Schweizer; *Cur* (20 Century) Mary Murray.
Exhibits—Shaker: The Art of Craftmanship.

THE MUSEUM OF ARTS AND SCIENCES INC, 1040 Museum Blvd, Daytona Beach, FL 32114. *Dir* Gary R Libby.
Exhibits—Indian and Persian Miniature Painting; Paul Jacoulet: Works on Paper; The New World in the Eyes of Explorers. Rental and shipping fees vary.

MUSEUM OF CONTEMPORARY ART, San Diego. Two locations: 700 Prospect St, LaJolla, CA 92037; and 1001 Kettner Blvd, San Diego, CA 92101. *Dir* Dr Hugh M Davies.
Exhibits—Bill Viola; Anish Kapoor; Edward and Nancy Reddin Kienholz; Kim MacConnel; Armando Rascon. For LaJolla location: Sebastiao Salgado, Nina Levy, Gabriel Orozco, and Joel Shapiro. Rental and shipping fees vary.

MUSEUM OF FINE ARTS, 255 Beach Dr NE, Saint Petersburg, FL 33701-3498. *Cur (Collections and Exhibitions)* Jennifer Hardin.
Exhibits—Later Chinese Jades from the Yangtze River Collection (catalogue); The Intriguing World of Glass: Two Prominent Florida Collections; Photographs from the MFA Collection; Large Contemporary Prints from the MFA Collection; Please Touch: Art from the MFA Collection. Rental and shipping fees depend upon exhibition and time. Call for further information.

MUSEUM OF MODERN ART, 11 W 53rd St, New York, NY 10019.
Exhibition Program: *Coordr of Exhibitions* Linda Thomas; *Assoc Coordr* Eleni Cocordas.
A number of exhibitions directed by members of the Museum's curatorial staff are offered to other qualified museums on a participating basis. These exhibitions are generally either full-scale projects or reduced versions of shows initially presented at The Museum of Modern Art. Although exhibitions are not necessarily available at all times in all media, the traveling program does cover the entire range of the Museum's New York program—painting, sculpture, drawings, prints, photography, architecture and design. Participating fees usually begin at $3500 for smaller exhibitions and range up to several thousand dollars for major exhibitions. Tour participants are also asked to cover pro-rated transport costs.

MUSEUM OF NORTHERN ARIZONA, 3101 N Fort Valley Rd, Flagstaff, AZ 86001. Tel 520-774-5211; Fax 520-779-1527. *Exhibit Coodr/Designer* Patrick Neary; *Exhibit Artist/Designer* Jodi Griffith.
Exhibits—Native American Anthropology and Art.

NATIONAL WATERCOLOR SOCIETY, 1149 McDonald Rd, Fallbrook, CA 92028. *Travel Show Dir* Joan Roche.
Exhibits—Travel shows are juried from the annual exhibitions and the all-membership Shows. Works are aquamedia on paper under plexi. The approximate number of works in each show is 30-100. NWS travel shows are available only to museums and galleries with adequate security and supervision. Commercial galleries are not eligible. National Watercolor Society requires that exhibiting galleries provide insurance during the exhibit and pay transportation and in-transit insurance one way. No other fee is charged. A limited number of annual exhibition catalogues are available for a nominal fee.

THE NEW YORK PUBLIC LIBRARY FOR THE PERFORMING ARTS, 40 Lincoln Center Plaza, New York, NY 10023. *Cur & Coordr of Exhibit* Barbara Stratyner.
Exhibits—New Performance in Found Space: Documentary Photographs by Tom Brazil & Dona Ann McAdams; Classic Black. Exhibitions travel with posters, audio/video components, brochures, bibliographics and more. Rental fees $1500-$5000

NEXUS CONTEMPORARY ART CENTER, 535 Means St, Atlanta, GA 30318. *Gallery Dir* Teresa Bramlette. *Exhibits*—Atlanta Biennial; ID Me; Poets Function.

NICOLAYSEN ART MUSEUM AND DISCOVERY CENTER, 400 E Collins Dr, Casper, WY 82601. Tel 307-235-5247; Fax 307-235-0923. *Dir* Karen R Mobley.
Exhibits—Call for information.

NORTH CENTRAL COLLEGE, Art Department, 30 N Brainard, Naperville, IL 60566. *Chmn Art Dept* Barry Skurkis; *Asst Gallery Dir* Maria Morelli.
Exhibits—Block Print Exhibit; Printmaking Exhibit. Rental fees $100. Shipping fees $65.

NORTHWEST FILM CENTER, 1219 SW Park, Portland, OR 97205.
Exhibits—Best of the Northwest: New work by film and video artists in Oregon, Alaska, Idaho, Montana, Washington and British Columbia.

OCTAGON CENTER FOR THE ARTS, 427 Douglas Ave, Ames, IA 50010-6281. Tel 515-232-5331; Fax 515-232-5088.
Exhibits—Watercolor Society. The Two Bill Zimmermans: Portraits, Landscapes and Wildlife Art. Ohio Star Quilts: New Quilts fron an Old Favorite. Community of Arts.

OREGON HISTORICAL SOCIETY, Education and Outreach, 1200 Park Ave, Portland, OR 97205. Tel 503-306-5280; Fax 503-221-2035. *Contact* Patti Larkin.
Exhibits—Trails to Oregon: A History of Migration to the Oregon Country; Northwest Black Heritage: The Pioneers; All For Organization: Inventing Government in Oregon 1843-1848; Something to Consider: The Editorial Cartoons of Art Bimrose; Adventure and Encounter: Captain Gray on the Columbia; The Columbia: America's Great Highway, Past, Present and Future; The Art Perfected; Differences & Discriminations: The Oregon Perspective. Oregon Main Street: A Rephotographic Survey. Celebrating Traditions, Strenghtening Community: Hermiston's Hispanic Heritage. Shipping fees vary, please call for more informationn

OWATONNA ARTS CENTER, 435 Dunnell Dr, PO Box 134, Owatonna, MN 55060. *Dir* Silvan Durben.
Exhibits—The Marianne Young Costume Collection. This collection includes 98 garments from twenty-five countries and is complete with accessories such as hats, jewelry, gloves and boots.

PALO ALTO CULTURAL CENTER, 1313 Newell Rd, Palo Alto, CA 94303. *Dir* Linda Craighead; *Cur* Signe Mayfield; *Registrar* Mark Ellen Daly.
Exhibits—Dominic Di Mare: A Retrospective. Rental fees $4000, shipping fees pro-rated among venues.

PARIS GIBSON SQUARE, MUSEUM OF ART, 1400 First Ave N, Great Falls, MT 59401. *Cur of Art* Jessica Hunter.
Exhibits—Two in Montana: Deborah Butterfield and John Buck, Sculpture and Woodblock Prints. Rental fees $7000, includes shipping. Must be insured for $400,000. Available November and December 1997.

PASTEL SOCIETY OF AMERICA, 15 Gramercy Park S, New York, NY 10003. *Chmn* Flora B Giffuni. *Pres* Sidney Hermel
Exhibits—National Arts Club at Roundabout Theater- 45th St and Broadway, New York, NY.

PENSACOLA JUNIOR COLLEGE, Visual Arts Department, 1000 College Blvd, Pensacola, FL 32504-8998. *Dir* Allan Peterson.
Exhibits—Regional exhibits loaned to museums and sister institutions. No rental fees. Borrower pays shipping fees and insurance.

THE PHOTOGRAPHERS GALLERY, 12 23rd St E, 2nd Flr, Saskatoon, SK S7K 0H5, Canada, Tel 306-244-8018; Fax 306-665-6568. *Dir* Monte Greenshields; *Admin Asst* Jeff Gee; *Prog Coordr/Exhib Officer* Brenda Barry Byrne.
Exhibits—Contemporary photographic art. Rental and shipping fees are available upon request.

PRAIRIE ART GALLERY, 10209 99th St, Grande Prairie, AB T8V 2H3, Canada. Tel 403-532-8111; Fax 403-539-1991. *Dir & Cur* Laura Van Haven.
Exhibits—Barbara Roe Hicklin, Terry Greguroschon, Katie One, Bill Morton: Between 4; Janet Mitchell, Marcia Perkins, Wendy Toogood, Don Mabie, Robert Char Michael, The Artists Guild, Franklin Heisler and William McDonnell. Some forty exhibitions are produced by the Prairie Art Gallery.

PRATT COMMUNITY COLLEGE, Art Department, 348 NE SR 61, Pratt, KS 67124. *Art Instructor* Gene Wineland.
Exhibits—Evolutions: Lithographs by Gene Wineland. Rental fees $500 plus shipping.

THE PRINT CENTER, 1614 Latimer St, Philadelphia, PA 19103. *Dir* Kathleen Edwards. Tel 215-735-6090; Fax 215-735-5511
Exhibits—Contemporary Latvian and Bulgarian prints; 71st Annual International Competition: Prints. Rental fees $500

THE PRINT CONSORTIUM, 6121 NW 77th St, Kansas City, MO 64151. *Exec Dir* Dr William S Eickhorst.
Exhibits—Museum quality exhibits of works by established American & European printmakers. Rental fees $300-$500, shipping paid by exhibitor. Catalogue available.

QCC ART GALLERY, 222-05 56th Ave, Bayside, NY 11364-1497. *Dir* Faustino Quintanilla; *Admin Asst* Deanne DeNyse; *Conservator* Oscar Sossa.
Exhibits—Hats & Hats Not: Photographs by Jules Allen. Rental fees $1500. Borrowing institutions must provide shipping and insurance.

RAMAPO COLLEGE GALLERY, 505 Ramapo Valley Rd, Mahwah, NJ 07430. Tel 201-529-7587. *Dir* Shalom Gorewitz.
Exhibits—Passing the Torch: Paintings on the Holocaust by David Boscovitch. Shipping fees assumed by borrower.

RED ROCK STATE PARK MUSEUM, PO Box 328, Church Rock, NM 87311. Tel 505-863-1337.
Exhibits—Anasazi artifacts; Pueblo and Navajo culture; Southwestern Native American fine art and crafts (jewelry, baskets, pottery, rugs and Kachina carvings). Call for information on further traveling exhibits.

THE ROCKWELL MUSEUM, 111 Cedar St, Corning, NY 14830. Tel 607-937-5386; Fax 607-974-4536. *Cur* (Collections) Robyn G. Peterson.
Exhibits—Fabric of Life: The Photographs of John Smart; Edward Borein; Warp and Weft: Cross-cultural Exchange in Navajo Weavings from the Rockwell Museum. Rental fees $2500-$7500. Shipping fees vary.

ROSENBERG GALLERY, Goucher College, 1021 Dulaney Valley Rd, Baltimore, MD 21204. *Exhib Dir* Helen Glazer.
Exhibits—Handkerchief Quilts by Pat Long Gardner. Rental and shipping fees upon request.

C M RUSSELL MUSEUM, 400 13th St N, Great Falls, MT 59401. *Dir* Lorne E Render; *Cur* Elizabeth Dear; *Registrar* Nancy Wheeler.
Exhibits—The West of Julius Seyler - 50 pieces; Winold Reiss - 25 pieces; American Indian Trade Blankets - 62 pieces. Rental fees $2500-$3500.

SALEM ART ASOCIATION, 600 Mission St SE, Salem, OR 97302. Tel 503-581-2228. *Exhibitions Dir* Salaryn Hilde.
Exhibits—Paintings & Parfleches: Native American Abstract Design.

SCHWEINFURTH ART CENTER, 205 Genesee St, Auburn, NY 13021. Tel 315-255-1553. E-mail smac@relex.com. *Dir* David Kwasigroh; *Educ Coordr* Jude Valentine; *Admin Asst* Mary Ellen Kliss.
Exhibits—Quilts=Art=Quilts; Upstate Invitational; Both Ends of the Rainbow; The Gardens of Ellen Shippman; Women's Installations; and Made in New York (juried).

SIOUX CITY ART CENTER, 225 Nebraska St, Sioux City, IA 51101. *Interim Dir* Janet A Brown; *Educ Cur* Sandi Beaubien; *Reg/Preparator* Chuck Jenkins.
Exhibits—Exhibitions focus on Upper Midwest contemporary artists.

SLATER HILL HISTORIC SITES, PO Box 696, Pawtucket, RI 02862. *Cur* Karin Conopask and Louis Hutchins.
Exhibits—Vanishing Rhode Island (rental fees $100 monthly). Nature to Profit: The Transformation of RI Waterways (rental fees $200 for 6 weeks period). Shipping fees paid by borrowing agency.

SOUTH CAROLINA ARTS COMMISSION MEDIA ARTS CENTER, 1800 Gervais St, Columbia, SC 29201. *Dir* Susan Leonard.
Exhibits—Southern Circuit (film/video artist tour).

SOUTHERN ALBERTA ART GALLERY, 601 Third Ave S, Lethbridge, AB T1J 0H4, Canada. *Dir & Cur* Joan Stebbins.
Exhibits—Ian Carr-Harris; Janet Werner.

SOUTHERN ILLINOIS UNIVERSITY MUSEUM, Faner Hall 2469, Carbondale, IL 62901-4508. *Dir* John J Whitlock; *Educ Coordr* Robert De Hoet; *Cur of Coll* Lorilee Hoffman.
Exhibits—Visions of the unseen. Contact Curator for rental and shipping fees information.

TEXAS FINE ARTS ASSOCIATION, 3809-B W 35th St, Austin, TX 78703. Tel 512-453-5312; Fax 512-459-4830. *Exec Dir* Sandra Gregor; *Art-on-Tour Coordr* Kelly Tankersley.
Exhibits—New American Talent, Texas Abstract and Pulp Fictions. Rental fees $800-$2000. Shipping fees $120. Currently touring in Texas only.

TUCSON MUSEUM OF ART, 140 N Main Ave, Tucson, AZ 85701. *Cur of Exhib* Joanne Stuhr.
Exhibits—Louise Serpa Photographs: Thirty years in the Arena. Icalido! Contemporary Warm Glass. Symbols of Life: Ritual Art of the Amazon people.

TWEED MUSEUM OF ART, 10 University Dr, Duluth, MN 55812. *Dir* Martin DeWitt; *Cur/Registrar* Peter Spooner. Tel 218-725-7056; Fax 218-762-8503. E-mail pspooner@d.umn.edu
Exhibits—Three Regionalists: Lithographs by Benton, Curry and Wood. American Art from the Tweed Museum. The Barbizon School: Painting and Prints by Millet Rousseau, Daubigney, Jacque, et al. The Potlatch Collection of RCMP Paintings. George Morrison: Minnesota Ojibwe Artist/World Artists.

THE UKRAINIAN MUSEUM, 203 Second Ave, New York, NY 10003. *Dir* Maria Shust.
Exhibits—Masterpieces in Wood: Houses of Worship in Ukraine; Ukraine Folk Art; To Preserve a Heritage: The Story of the Ukrainian Immigration in the USA. Rental fees $450-$1000. Packets of information on particular traveling exhibitions are available.

UNIVERSITY ART MUSEUM, California State University, Long Beach, 1250 Bellflower Blvd, Long Beach, CA 90840. Tel 562-985-5761; Fax 562-985-7602. E-mail uam@csulb.edu. *Dir* Constance W Glenn; *Cur* Gwen Hill.
Exhibits—Contemporary art, including photography. The Great American Pop: Multiples of the Sixties (offered at present). Rental fee $15,000; one tour vacancy.

UNIVERSITY GALLERY, University of Delaware, 114 Old College, Newark, DE 19716. Dir Belena S Chapp.
Exhibits—PH Polk: American Photographer, available Fall 1998. Rental fees $3500. Borrowing institution pays shipping fees. Send for further information, available upon request.

UNIVERSITY MUSEUMS, The University of Mississippi, University, MS 38677. *Dir* Bonnie J Krause; *Coordr* Susan V Hannah.
Exhibits—Olynthus 348 BC: The Destruction and Resurrection of a Greek City (photographic). Rental fees $100, shipping one way.

UNIVERSITY OF HAWAII ART GALLERY, Dept of Art, 2535 The Mall, Honolulu, HI 96822. *Dir* Tom Klobe.
Exhibits—The International Shoebox Sculpture Exhibitions (triennial) and others. Rental fees $1400. Shipping fees-outgoing ($800 average).

UNIVERSITY OF HOUSTON, Sarah Campbell Blaffer Gallery, Entrance 16 off Cullen Blvd, Houston, TX 77204-4891. *Dir and Chief Cur* Don Bacigalupi; *Asst Dir* Nancy Hixon; *Coordr of Develop* Ellen Efsic
Exhibits—Michael Ray Charles, 1989-97. Rental fees $10,000. Shipping fees are pro-rated.

UNIVERSITY OF MARYLAND AT COLLEGE PARK, The Art Gallery, Art-Sociology Bldg, College Park, MD 20742. *Dir* Terry Gips; *Exhib Designer* Karen Werth; *Asst to the Dir & Reg* Rob Blitz. *Exhib Asst* Kimberly Gladfelter.
Exhibits—The Helen D Ling Collection of Chinese Ceramics. Russian Constructionist Roots: Present Concerns. David C. Briskell: Collections of the African Diaspora. Rental fees $3000-$6000.

UNIVERSITY OF MIAMI, Department of Art & Art History, PO Box 248106, Coral Gables, FL 33124. Tel 305-284-2542; Fax 305-284-2115. *Dir* (New Gallery) Lise Drost.
Exhibits—Florida Craftsmen Annual Exhibition; 3 Generations of Swedish Photography; Art by the Mentally Ill; Denis Defibaugh. Rental and shipping fees vary.

UNIVERSITY OF SOUTH DAKOTA, 414 E Clark St, Vermillion, SD 57069. *Dir* John A Day.
Exhibits—Jim D Butler: Twenty-five Years of Printmaking. Robert Aldern Retrospective. Robert Freeman Retrospective. Northern Plains Tribal Arts: 10th Anniversary Invitational Exhibition. Rental fees $800, shipping $200.

UTAH ARTS COUNCIL, 617 E South Temple, Salt Lake City, UT 84102. Tel 801-533-5757.
Exhibits—The exhibition program is designed to provide traveling exhibitions to a statewide audience. Approximately twenty exhibitions are available which vary in size and subject matter. They include works from the permanent collections of the Utah Arts Council, Utah Museums and from special collections contributed by organizations and individuals. Exhibitions are scheduled for one month at $100 per exhibit. They may be booked by museums, college and public galleries, community groups or institutions such as libraries, schools, or other non-profit organizations. The Visual Arts staff transports the exhibitions and supervises installation.

VALDOSTA STATE UNIVERSITY, Art Dept, Valdosta, GA 31698. *Actg Head* J Stephen Lahn; *Gallery Dir* Karin Murray.
Exhibits—Nine exhibits annually. Rental & shipping fees vary.

VANDERBILT UNIVERSITY, Fine Arts Gallery, Box 1801, Sta B, Nashville, TN 37235. Tel 615-322-0605; Fax 615-343-1382. *Cur* Joseph Mella.
Exhibits—Witness to Our Century: An Artistic Biography of Fritz Eichenberg. Rental fees $3500, shipping fees $1500.

VESTERHEIM NORWEGIAN-AMERICAN MUSEUM, 502 W Water St, Decorah, IA 52101. *Dir* Darrell Henning; *Reg* Carol Hasvold; *Textile Cur* Laurann Figg; *Farm Cur* Steven Johnson.
Exhibits—Norwegian-American Woodcarvings. Leaving Norway, The Voyage to Amerika: Content of an Immigrant's Trunk. Photographs by Andreas Dahl: 43 photos of Norwegian immigrant life in southern Wisconsin, 1870-1880 (general frontier interest).

WASHINGTON COUNTY MUSEUM OF FINE ARTS, PO Box 423, Hagerstown, MD 21741. Tel 301-739-5727; Fax 301-745-3741. *Dir* Jean Woods; *Admin Asst* Christine Shives.
Exhibits—Prints of Salvador Dali: Watercolors by Edmund Darch Lewis; Paperweights from the Bryden Collection; Art of the 60s and 70s; The Photographs of Mathew Brady (Civil War); Korean Watercolors; WPA Collection. Rental fees $200-$500 monthly, plus shipping charges.

WASHINGTON SCULPTORS GROUP, 2735 McKinley St NW, Washington, DC 20015. Tel 202-362-7707. *Co-Dirs* (Exhibition Installations) Tom Rooney and Lee Aks; (Exhibition Sites) Sam Noto .
Exhibits—Sculpture 97-members annual juried exhibition survey. Landscapes: An Exhibition of Sculpture (available 1998), in collaboration with Art Museum of the Americas (AOS), WOC. Rental and shipping fees vary, call for information.

WHARTON ESHERICK MUSEUM, Horseshoe Trail, PO Box 595, Paoli, PA 19301-0595. Tel 610-644-5822. *Dir* Robert Leonard; *Cur* Mansfield Bascom.
Exhibits—Half a Century in Wood: 1920-1970—a photographic exhibition of furniture created by Wharton Esherick, including a catalogue. Rental fees $250. Shipping fees $50-$100. Contact Museum Director.

WHITNEY MUSEUM OF AMERICAN ART, 945 Madison Ave, New York, NY 10021. *Dir* (Collections Mgmt) Nancy McGary.
Exhibits—Vary; primarily 20th century American art.

WICHITA FALLS MUSEUM & ART CENTER, 2 Eureka Circle, Wichita Falls, TX 76308. *Dir* Carole Borgman; *Exhibits Cur* Janelle Redlaczyk; *Laser Dir* Jeff Desborough.
Exhibits—Art & Science; Children's Gallery; Discovery Center; Laser light show; Planetarium. Rental fees vary.

THE WINNIPEG ART GALLERY, 300 Memorial Blvd, Winnipeg, MB R3C 1V1, Canada. Tel 204-786-6641. Fax 204-788-4998. *Exten Serv Coordr* Robert Epp.
Exhibits—Several exhibitions of contemporary Canadian and international art organized each year by The Winnipeg Art Gallery are offered to other qualified galleries and museums in Canada, the United States and abroad, on a participating basis. Borrowing fees and loan terms vary.

WOMEN IN THE ARTS FOUNDATION, INC, 1175 York Ave, No 2G, New York, NY 10021. *Pres* Roberta Crown.
Exhibits—Work of the members with various themes. Rental fees are open. Shipping fees depend upon exhibit.

LEIGH YAWKEY WOODSON ART MUSEUM, 700 N 12th St, Wausau, WI 54403-5007. Tel 715-845-7010; Fax 715-845-7103. *Dir* Robert A Kret; *Assoc Dir* Marcia M Theel; *Cur of Exhib* Andrew J McGivern; *Cur of Coll* Jane M Weinke; *Cur of Educ* Michael Baechler.
Exhibits—Beyond the Lens: Compositions by Art Wolfe. Rental fees $2000 plus pro-rated shipping. Birds in Art: Rental fees $8000 plus pro-rated shipping, 100 catalogues included in rental fees. Natural Wonders: The John and Alice Woodson Forester Miniature Collection. Rental fees $2500 plus pro-rated shipping, 50 catalogues included in rental fees. Naturally Drawn. Rental fees $2000 plus pro-rated shipping, 50 catalogues included in rental fees. Only Owls. Rental fees $750 plus incoming and outgoing shipping. Wildlife: The Artist's View. Rental fees $7000 plus pro-rated shipping, 100 catalogues included in rental fees.

YESHIVA UNIVERSITY MUSEUM, 2520 Amsterdam Ave at W 185th St, New York, NY 10033. Tel 212-960-5390; Fax 212-960-5406. *Dir* Sylvia Herskowitz.
Exhibits—Aishet Hagil: Woman of Valor. Sir Moses Montefiore. Letters Dipped in Honey: Children's Literature. Rental and shipping fees vary.

IV INDEXES

Subject

Personnel

Organizational

Subject Index

Major subjects are listed first, followed by named collections.

AFRICAN ART

Albany Museum of Art, Albany GA
Albion College, Bobbitt Visual Arts Center, Albion MI
Anchorage Museum of History & Art, Anchorage AK
The Art Institute of Chicago, Chicago IL
Art Museum of Missoula, Missoula MT
Arts Council of Fayetteville-Cumberland County, The Arts Center, Fayetteville NC
Baltimore Museum of Art, Baltimore MD
Barnes Foundation, Merion PA
Baylor University, Martin Museum of Art, Waco TX
Berea College, Doris Ulmann Galleries, Berea KY
Blanden Memorial Art Museum, Fort Dodge IA
Bower's Museum, Santa Ana CA
Brandeis University, Rose Art Museum, Waltham MA
Brevard Museum of Art & Science, Melbourne FL
The Buffalo Fine Arts Academy, Albright-Knox Art Gallery, Buffalo NY
California College of Arts & Crafts, Steven Oliver Art Center, Oakland CA
California State University, Hayward, C E Smith Museum of Anthropology, Hayward CA
California State University Stanislaus, University Art Gallery, Turlock CA
Capital University, Schumacher Gallery, Columbus OH
Center for Puppetry Arts, Atlanta GA
Center for the Arts at Yerba Buena Gardens, San Francisco CA
Chicago Department of Cultural Affairs, Chicago Cultural Center, Chicago IL
Cincinnati Museum Association, Cincinnati Art Museum, Cincinnati OH
Cleveland State University, Art Gallery, Cleveland OH
College of William & Mary, Joseph & Margaret Muscarelle Museum of Art, Williamsburg VA
The College of Wooster, Art Museum, Wooster OH
Concordia Historical Institute, Saint Louis MO
C W Post Campus of Long Island University, Hillwood Art Museum, Brookville NY
Dallas Museum of Art, Dallas TX
Danforth Museum of Art, Framingham MA
Dartmouth College, Hood Museum of Art, Hanover NH
Denison University, Art Gallery, Granville OH
Denver Art Museum, Denver CO
Detroit Institute of Arts, Detroit MI
Dickinson College, Trout Gallery, Carlisle PA
Duke University Museum of Art, Durham NC
East Carolina University, Wellington B Gray Gallery, Greenville NC
East Los Angeles College, Vincent Price Gallery, Monterey Park CA
Edmundson Art Foundation, Inc, Des Moines Art Center, Des Moines IA
Emory University, Michael C Carlos Museum, Atlanta GA
Evansville Museum of Arts & Science, Evansville IN

Everhart Museum, Scranton PA
Everson Museum of Art, Syracuse NY
Fayette Art Museum, Fayette AL
Fine Arts Museums of San Francisco, M H de Young Memorial Museum & California Palace of the Legion of Honor, San Francisco CA
The First National Bank of Chicago, Art Collection, Chicago IL
Fisk University, University Galleries, Nashville TN
Fitton Center For Creative Arts, Hamilton OH
Flint Institute of Arts, Flint MI
Florence Museum of Art, Science & History, Florence SC
Florida State University Foundation - Central Florida Community College Foundation, The Appleton Museum of Art, Ocala FL
Fort Worth Art Association, Modern Art Museum of Fort Worth, Fort Worth TX
Freeport Arts Center, Freeport IL
Fuller Museum of Art, Brockton MA
Grand Rapids Art Museum, Grand Rapids MI
Greenwood Museum, Greenwood SC
Hampton University, University Museum, Hampton VA
Heard Museum, Phoenix AZ
Hofstra University, Hofstra Museum, Hempstead NY
Hollywood Art Museum, Hollywood FL
Honolulu Academy of Arts, Honolulu HI
Howard University, Gallery of Art, Washington DC
Indiana University, Art Museum, Bloomington IN
The Interchurch Center, Galleries at the Interchurch Center, New York NY
Jacksonville University, Alexander Brest Museum & Gallery, Jacksonville FL
Martin & Osa Johnson Safari Museum, Inc, Chanute KS
Joslyn Art Museum, Omaha NE
Kansas City Art Institute, Kemper Museum of Contemporary Art & Design, Kansas City MO
Kelowna Museum, Kelowna BC
Kimbell Art Foundation, Kimbell Art Museum, Fort Worth TX
Lafayette Natural History Museum, Planetarium & Nature Station, Lafayette LA
Louisiana Arts & Science Center, Baton Rouge LA
McPherson Museum, McPherson KS
Marietta College, Grover M Hermann Fine Arts Center, Marietta OH
Menil Collection, Houston TX
Minneapolis Institute of Arts, Minneapolis MN
Minnesota Museum of American Art, Saint Paul MN
Mint Museum of Art, Charlotte NC
Mobile Museum of Art, Mobile AL
Montreal Museum of Fine Arts, Montreal PQ
Morris Museum, Morristown NJ
Musee des Augustines de l'Hotel Dieu de Quebec, Quebec PQ
Museum of African American Art, Tampa FL
The Museum of Arts & Sciences Inc, Daytona Beach FL
Museum of Contemporary Art, North Miami FL

Museum of Fine Arts, Saint Petersburg, Florida, Inc, Saint Petersburg FL
Museum of York County, Rock Hill SC
National Conference of Artists, Michigan Chapter Gallery, Detroit MI
National Museum of African Art, Washington DC
Nelson-Atkins Museum of Art, Kansas City MO
Newark Museum Association, The Newark Museum, Newark NJ
New Brunswick Museum, Saint John NB
New Orleans Museum of Art, New Orleans LA
New Visions Gallery, Inc, Marshfield WI
North Carolina Central University, NCCU Art Museum, Durham NC
North Carolina Museum of Art, Raleigh NC
North Country Museum of Arts, Park Rapids MN
Oakland University, Meadow Brook Art Gallery, Rochester MI
Ohio University, Kennedy Museum of American Art, Athens OH
Oklahoma Center for Science & Art, Kirkpatrick Center, Oklahoma City OK
Orlando Museum of Art, Orlando FL
Page-Walker Arts & History Center, Cary NC
Pennsylvania State University, Palmer Museum of Art, University Park PA
Pensacola Museum of Art, Pensacola FL
Philbrook Museum of Art, Tulsa OK
Plains Art Museum, Fargo ND
Port Authority of New York & New Jersey, Art Collection, New York NY
Portland Art Museum, Portland OR
Purdue University Galleries, West Lafayette IN
Royal Ontario Museum, Toronto ON
St Lawrence University, Richard F Brush Art Gallery, Canton NY
Santa Barbara Museum of Art, Santa Barbara CA
Santa Clara University, de Saisset Museum, Santa Clara CA
Schenectady Museum Planetarium & Visitors Center, Schenectady NY
Slater-Norton Corporation, Slater Memorial Museum & Converse Art Gallery, Norwich CT
Southern Connecticut State University, Art Gallery, New Haven CT
Southern Illinois University, University Museum, Carbondale IL
Springfield Library & Museums Association, Springfield Science Museum, Springfield MA
Stanford University, Museum of Art, Stanford CA
State University of New York at New Paltz, College Art Gallery, New Paltz NY
State University of New York at Purchase, Neuberger Museum of Art, Purchase NY
Syracuse University, Art Collection, Syracuse NY
Topeka & Shawnee County Public Library, Gallery of Fine Arts, Topeka KS
Tubman African American Museum, Macon GA
University of Alabama at Birmingham, Visual Arts Gallery, Birmingham AL
University of California, Berkeley Art Museum & Pacific Film Archive, Berkeley CA
University of California, Los Angeles, Fowler Museum of Cultural History, Los Angeles CA

University of California, Santa Barbara, University Art Museum, Santa Barbara CA
University of Delaware, University Gallery, Newark DE
University of Florida, Samuel P Harn Museum of Art, Gainesville FL
University of Iowa, Museum of Art, Iowa City IA
University of Kentucky, Art Museum, Lexington KY
University of Maryland, College Park, Art Gallery, College Park MD
University of Memphis, Art Museum, Memphis TN
University of Miami, Lowe Art Museum, Coral Gables FL
University of Michigan, Museum of Art, Ann Arbor MI
University of Mississippi, University Museums, Oxford MS
University of Notre Dame, Snite Museum of Art, Notre Dame IN
University of Oklahoma, Fred Jones Jr Museum of Art, Norman OK
University of Pennsylvania, Arthur Ross Gallery, Philadelphia PA
University of Rochester, Memorial Art Gallery, Rochester NY
University of South Florida, Contemporary Art Museum, Tampa FL
University of Virginia, Bayly Art Museum, Charlottesville VA
University of Wisconsin-Stout, J Furlong Gallery, Menomonie WI
Valdosta State University, Art Gallery, Valdosta GA
Vancouver Museum Commission, Vancouver Museum, Vancouver BC
Wayne Center for the Arts, Wooster OH
Williams College, Museum of Art, Williamstown MA
Winston-Salem State University, Diggs Gallery, Winston Salem NC
Wiregrass Museum of Art, Dothan AL
Wustum Museum Art Association, Racine WI

AFRO-AMERICAN ART

Afro-American Historical & Cultural Museum, Philadelphia PA
Albany Museum of Art, Albany GA
Anacostia Museum, Washington DC
Arkansas Territorial Restoration, Little Rock AR
The Art Institute of Chicago, Chicago IL
Art Museum of Missoula, Missoula MT
Arts Council of Fayetteville-Cumberland County, The Arts Center, Fayetteville NC
ArtSpace-Lima, Lima OH
Asheville Art Museum, Asheville NC
Brandywine Workshop, Philadelphia PA
Bronx River Art Center, Gallery, Bronx NY
California College of Arts & Crafts, Steven Oliver Art Center, Oakland CA
Cartoon Art Museum, San Francisco CA
Center for Puppetry Arts, Atlanta GA
Center for the Arts at Yerba Buena Gardens, San Francisco CA
Central United Methodist Church, Swords Info Plowshares Peace Center & Gallery, Detroit MI
Charleston Museum, Joseph Manigault House, Charleston SC
Chattahoochee Valley Art Museum, LaGrange GA
Chicago Department of Cultural Affairs, Chicago Cultural Center, Chicago IL
CIGNA Corporation, CIGNA Museum & Art Collection, Philadelphia PA
Cincinnati Institute of Fine Arts, Taft Museum, Cincinnati OH
Cleveland State University, Art Gallery, Cleveland OH
Columbus Museum, Columbus GA
Cooper-Hewitt, National Design Museum, New York NY
County of Henrico, Meadow Farm Museum, Glen Allen VA
Danforth Museum of Art, Framingham MA
Davidson College Visual Arts Center, William H Van Every Jr & Edward M Smith Galleries, Davidson NC
Detroit Institute of Arts, Detroit MI

Detroit Repertory Theatre Gallery, Detroit MI
DuSable Museum of African American History, Chicago IL
East Baton Rouge Parks & Recreation Commission, Baton Rouge Gallery Inc, Baton Rouge LA
East Carolina University, Wellington B Gray Gallery, Greenville NC
Elmhurst Art Museum, Elmhurst IL
El Paso Museum of Art, El Paso TX
Fairfield University, Thomas J Walsh Art Gallery, Fairfield CT
Fayette Art Museum, Fayette AL
The First National Bank of Chicago, Art Collection, Chicago IL
Fisk University, University Galleries, Nashville TN
Fitton Center For Creative Arts, Hamilton OH
Florence Museum of Art, Science & History, Florence SC
Fort Worth Art Association, Modern Art Museum of Fort Worth, Fort Worth TX
Gonzaga University, Jundt Art Museum, Ad Art Gallery, Spokane WA
Grand Rapids Art Museum, Grand Rapids MI
Greater Lafayette Museum of Art, Lafayette IN
Hampton University, University Museum, Hampton VA
Hirshhorn Museum & Sculpture Garden, Washington DC
Howard University, Gallery of Art, Washington DC
Huntington Museum of Art, Huntington WV
Intar Latin American Gallery, New York NY
The Interchurch Center, Galleries at the Interchurch Center, New York NY
Kansas City Art Institute, Kemper Museum of Contemporary Art & Design, Kansas City MO
Knoxville Museum of Art, Knoxville TN
Lafayette Natural History Museum, Planetarium & Nature Station, Lafayette LA
Longview Art Museum, Longview TX
Maryland Art Place, Baltimore MD
Maryland Hall for the Creative Arts, Cardinal Gallery, Annapolis MD
Metropolitan State College of Denver, Center for the Visual Arts, Denver CO
Mint Museum of Art, Charlotte NC
Mississippi Department of Archives & History, Old Capitol Museum, Jackson MS
Mississippi River Museum at Mud-Island, Memphis TN
Mobile Museum of Art, Mobile AL
Museum of African American Art, Tampa FL
The Museum of Arts & Sciences Inc, Daytona Beach FL
Museum of Contemporary Art, North Miami FL
Museum of Fine Arts, Saint Petersburg, Florida, Inc, Saint Petersburg FL
Museum of the National Center of Afro-American Artists, Boston MA
National Conference of Artists, Michigan Chapter Gallery, Detroit MI
National Infantry Museum, Fort Benning GA
National Museum of American Art, Washington DC
National Museum of Women in the Arts, Washington DC
Nelson-Atkins Museum of Art, Kansas City MO
Newark Museum Association, The Newark Museum, Newark NJ
Niagara University, Castellani Art Museum, Niagara NY
Ohio Historical Society, National Afro American Museum & Cultural Center, Wilberforce OH
Orlando Museum of Art, Orlando FL
Page-Walker Arts & History Center, Cary NC
Palm Springs Desert Museum, Palm Springs CA
Pennsylvania Academy of the Fine Arts, Museum of American Art, Philadelphia PA
Port Authority of New York & New Jersey, Art Collection, New York NY
Purdue University Galleries, West Lafayette IN
Rollins College, George D & Harriet W Cornell Fine Arts Museum, Winter Park FL
Saint Louis Artists' Guild, Saint Louis MO
School of Visual Arts, Visual Arts Museum, New York NY
Scripps College, Clark Humanities Museum, Claremont CA
South Carolina State Museum, Columbia SC

Southeastern Center for Contemporary Art, Winston-Salem NC
Southern Alleghenies Museum of Art, Southern Alleghenies Museum of Art at Johnstown, Loretto PA
The Studio Museum in Harlem, New York NY
Tubman African American Museum, Macon GA
University of Alabama at Birmingham, Visual Arts Gallery, Birmingham AL
University of California, Berkeley Art Museum & Pacific Film Archive, Berkeley CA
University of Colorado at Colorado Springs, Gallery of Contemporary Art, Colorado Springs CO
University of Memphis, Art Museum, Memphis TN
University of Mississippi, University Museums, Oxford MS
University of Pennsylvania, Arthur Ross Gallery, Philadelphia PA
University of Rhode Island, Fine Arts Center Galleries, Kingston RI
University of Rochester, Memorial Art Gallery, Rochester NY
The University of Texas, Institute of Texan Cultures, San Antonio TX
University of Texas at Austin, Archer M Huntington Art Gallery, Austin TX
Viridian Artists Inc, New York NY
Waterworks Visual Arts Center, Salisbury NC
Williams College, Museum of Art, Williamstown MA
Winston-Salem State University, Diggs Gallery, Winston Salem NC
Wiregrass Museum of Art, Dothan AL

AMERICAN INDIAN ART

Academy of the New Church, Glencairn Museum, Bryn Athyn PA
Alabama Department of Archives & History, Museum Galleries, Montgomery AL
Alaska Department of Education, Division of Libraries, Archives & Museums, Sheldon Jackson Museum, Sitka AK
The Albrecht-Kemper Museum of Art, Saint Joseph MO
Albuquerque Museum of Art & History, Albuquerque NM
Anchorage Museum of History & Art, Anchorage AK
Archaeological Society of Ohio, Indian Museum of Lake County, Ohio, Painesville OH
Arkansas Territorial Restoration, Little Rock AR
The Art Institute of Chicago, Chicago IL
Art Museum of Missoula, Missoula MT
Arts Council of Fayetteville-Cumberland County, The Arts Center, Fayetteville NC
ArtSpace-Lima, Lima OH
Ataloa Lodge Museum, Muskogee OK
Atlanta Museum, Atlanta GA
Aurora University, Schingoethe Center for Native American Cultures, Aurora IL
Bay County Historical Society, Historical Museum of Bay County, Bay City MI
Bent Museum & Gallery, Taos NM
Berea College, Doris Ulmann Galleries, Berea KY
Berkshire Museum, Pittsfield MA
Jesse Besser Museum, Alpena MI
Bowdoin College, Peary-MacMillan Arctic Museum, Brunswick ME
Bower's Museum, Santa Ana CA
Brandeis University, Rose Art Museum, Waltham MA
Brandywine Workshop, Philadelphia PA
The Bruce Museum, Greenwich CT
Butler Institute of American Art, Art Museum, Youngstown OH
Capital University, Schumacher Gallery, Columbus OH
Carmel Mission & Gift Shop, Carmel CA
Carson County Square House Museum, Panhandle TX
Cayuga Museum of History & Art, Auburn NY
Center for the Arts at Yerba Buena Gardens, San Francisco CA
Central United Methodist Church, Swords Info Plowshares Peace Center & Gallery, Detroit MI
Chattahoochee Valley Art Museum, LaGrange GA

Chelan County Public Utility District, Rocky Reach Dam, Wenatchee WA

Chicago Department of Cultural Affairs, Chicago Cultural Center, Chicago IL

Chief Plenty Coups Museum, Pryor MT

Chilkat Valley Historical Society, Sheldon Museum & Cultural Center, Haines AK

Church of Jesus Christ of Latter-Day Saints, Museum of Church History & Art, Salt Lake City UT

Cincinnati Museum Association, Cincinnati Art Museum, Cincinnati OH

Cleveland State University, Art Gallery, Cleveland OH

Colby College, Museum of Art, Waterville ME

College of Southern Idaho, Herrett Center for Arts & Science, Twin Falls ID

College of William & Mary, Joseph & Margaret Muscarelle Museum of Art, Williamsburg VA

The College of Wooster, Art Museum, Wooster OH

Colorado Historical Society, Colorado History Museum, Denver CO

Colorado Springs Fine Arts Center, Colorado Springs CO

Columbus Museum, Columbus GA

Community Fine Arts Center, Halseth Gallery, Rock Springs WY

The Currier Gallery of Art, Manchester NH

Dacotah Prairie Museum, Lamont Gallery, Aberdeen SD

Dartmouth College, Hood Museum of Art, Hanover NH

Deming-Luna Mimbres Museum, Deming NM

Denison University, Art Gallery, Granville OH

Denver Art Museum, Denver CO

Detroit Institute of Arts, Detroit MI

DeWitt Historical Society of Tompkins County, Ithaca NY

Dickinson College, Trout Gallery, Carlisle PA

Douglas County Historical Society, Fairlawn Mansion & Museum, Superior WI

Duke University Museum of Art, Durham NC

East Carolina University, Wellington B Gray Gallery, Greenville NC

Eastern Washington State Historical Society, Cheney Cowles Museum, Spokane WA

East Los Angeles College, Vincent Price Gallery, Monterey Park CA

Eiteljorg Museum of American Indians & Western Art, Indianapolis IN

El Paso Museum of Art, Wilderness Park Museum, El Paso TX

Enook Galleries, Waterloo ON

Erie Art Museum, Erie PA

Evanston Historical Society, Charles Gates Dawes House, Evanston IL

Everhart Museum, Scranton PA

Favell Museum of Western Art & Indian Artifacts, Klamath Falls OR

Fine Arts Museums of San Francisco, M H de Young Memorial Museum & California Palace of the Legion of Honor, San Francisco CA

Five Civilized Tribes Museum, Muskogee OK

Florence Museum of Art, Science & History, Florence SC

Freeport Arts Center, Freeport IL

Fruitlands Museum, Inc, Harvard MA

Galleries of the Claremont Colleges, Claremont CA

Gilcrease Museum Institute of American History & Art, Tulsa OK

Goshen Historical Society, Goshen CT

Grand Rapids Art Museum, Grand Rapids MI

Greater Lafayette Museum of Art, Lafayette IN

Hamilton College, Fred L Emerson Gallery, Clinton NY

Hampton University, University Museum, Hampton VA

Hartwick College, Museum at Hartwick, Oneonta NY

Heard Museum, Phoenix AZ

Heritage Center, Inc, Pine Ridge SD

Heritage Plantation of Sandwich, Sandwich MA

Honolulu Academy of Arts, Honolulu HI

Huronia Museum, Midland ON

Idaho Historical Museum, Boise ID

Illinois State Museum, Illinois Art Gallery, Chicago IL

Imperial Calcasieu Museum, Gibson-Barham Gallery, Lake Charles LA

Indian Arts & Crafts Board, Sioux Indian Museum, Rapid City SD

Indian Pueblo Cultural Center, Albuquerque NM

Institute of American Indian Arts Museum, Santa Fe NM

Institute of the Great Plains, Museum of the Great Plains, Lawton OK

Intar Latin American Gallery, New York NY

The Interchurch Center, Galleries at the Interchurch Center, New York NY

Iowa State University, Brunnier Art Museum, Ames IA

Jefferson County Open Space, Hiwan Homestead Museum, Evergreen CO

Johnson-Humrickhouse Museum, Coshocton OH

Joslyn Art Museum, Omaha NE

Kansas City Art Institute, Kemper Museum of Contemporary Art & Design, Kansas City MO

Kelly-Griggs House Museum, Red Bluff CA

Kelowna Museum, Kelowna BC

Kiah Museum, Savannah GA

Koshare Indian Museum, Inc, La Junta CO

Lac du Flambeau Band of Lake Superior Chippewa Indians, George W Brown Jr Ojibwe Museum & Cultural Center, Lac du Flambeau WI

Leanin' Tree Museum of Western Art, Boulder CO

Leelanau Historical Museum, Leland MI

Lehigh County Historical Society, Allentown PA

Lightner Museum, Saint Augustine FL

Maryhill Museum of Art, Goldendale WA

Metropolitan State College of Denver, Center for the Visual Arts, Denver CO

Mid-America All-Indian Center, Indian Center Museum, Wichita KS

Midwest Museum of American Art, Elkhart IN

Minneapolis Institute of Arts, Minneapolis MN

Minnesota Museum of American Art, Saint Paul MN

Mint Museum of Art, Charlotte NC

Mission San Luis Rey de Francia, Mission San Luis Rey Museum, San Luis Rey CA

Mississippi Department of Archives & History, Old Capitol Museum, Jackson MS

Mississippi River Museum at Mud-Island, Memphis TN

Arthur Roy Mitchell Memorial Inc, Museum of Western Art, Trinidad CO

Mobile Museum of Art, Mobile AL

Mohave Museum of History & Arts, Kingman AZ

Montana State University, Museum of the Rockies, Bozeman MT

Montclair Art Museum, Montclair NJ

Moose Jaw Art Museum & National Exhibition Centre, Art & History Museum, Moose Jaw SK

Morris Museum, Morristown NJ

Musee d'Art de Saint-Laurent, Saint-Laurent PQ

Musee des Augustines de l'Hotel Dieu de Quebec, Quebec PQ

Museum of Arts & History, Port Huron MI

The Museum of Arts & Sciences Inc, Daytona Beach FL

Museum of Fine Arts, Houston, Houston TX

Museum of Fine Arts, Saint Petersburg, Florida, Inc, Saint Petersburg FL

Museum of New Mexico, Museum of Fine Arts, Santa Fe NM

Museum of Northern Arizona, Flagstaff AZ

Museum of Northern British Columbia, Ruth Harvey Art Gallery, Prince Rupert BC

Museum of the Plains Indian & Crafts Center, Browning MT

Museum of the Southwest, Midland TX

National Cowboy Hall of Fame & Western Heritage Center Museum, Oklahoma City OK

National Hall of Fame for Famous American Indians, Anadarko OK

National Infantry Museum, Fort Benning GA

National Museum of American Art, Washington DC

National Museum of the American Indian, George Gustav Heye Center, New York NY

National Museum of Women in the Arts, Washington DC

National Native American Co-Operative, North American Indian Information & Trade Center, Tucson AZ

Navajo Nation Museum, Window Rock AZ

Nelson-Atkins Museum of Art, Kansas City MO

Nevada Museum of Art, Reno NV

Newark Museum Association, The Newark Museum, Newark NJ

New Brunswick Museum, Saint John NB

New Visions Gallery, Inc, Marshfield WI

No Man's Land Historical Society Museum, Goodwell OK

North Carolina Museum of Art, Raleigh NC

Northern Illinois University, NIU Art Museum, De Kalb IL

The Ohio Historical Society, Inc, Campus Martius Museum & Ohio River Museum, Marietta OH

Ohio University, Kennedy Museum of American Art, Athens OH

Oklahoma Historical Society, State Museum of History, Oklahoma City OK

Oysterponds Historical Society, Museum, Orient NY

Page-Walker Arts & History Center, Cary NC

Palm Springs Desert Museum, Palm Springs CA

Panhandle-Plains Historical Society Museum, Canyon TX

Paris Gibson Square, Museum of Art, Great Falls MT

Philbrook Museum of Art, Tulsa OK

Frank Phillips Foundation Inc, Woolaroc Museum, Bartlesville OK

George Phippen Memorial Foundation, Phippen Museum of Western Art, Prescott AZ

Piatt Castles, West Liberty OH

Plains Art Museum, Fargo ND

Plains Indians & Pioneers Historical Foundation, Museum & Art Center, Woodward OK

Plumas County Museum, Quincy CA

Ponca City Cultural Center & Museum, Ponca City OK

Pope County Historical Society, Pope County Museum, Glenwood MN

Port Authority of New York & New Jersey, Art Collection, New York NY

Portland Art Museum, Portland OR

Marjorie Merriweather Post Foundation of DC, Hillwood Museum, Washington DC

Principia College, School of Nations Museum, Elsah IL

Purdue University Galleries, West Lafayette IN

Rahr-West Art Museum, Manitowoc WI

Randall Museum Junior Museum, San Francisco CA

Redding Museum of Art & History, Redding CA

Red River Valley Museum, Vernon TX

Red Rock State Park, Red Rock Museum, Church Rock NM

Riverside Municipal Museum, Riverside CA

Roberts County Museum, Miami TX

The Rockwell Museum, Corning NY

Millicent Rogers Museum of Northern New Mexico, Taos NM

Rollins College, George D & Harriet W Cornell Fine Arts Museum, Winter Park FL

Roswell Museum & Art Center, Roswell NM

C M Russell Museum, Great Falls MT

Safety Harbor Museum of Regional History, Safety Harbor FL

Saint Bonaventure University, Regina A Quick Fine Art Center, Saint Bonaventure NY

Saint Joseph Museum, Saint Joseph MO

The Saint Louis Art Museum, Saint Louis MO

Saint Louis County Historical Society, Duluth MN

Schenectady Museum Planetarium & Visitors Center, Schenectady NY

School of American Research, Indian Arts Research Center, Santa Fe NM

School of Visual Arts, Visual Arts Museum, New York NY

Seneca-Iroquois National Museum, Salamanca NY

Slater-Norton Corporation, Slater Memorial Museum & Converse Art Gallery, Norwich CT

Sooke Region Museum & Art Gallery, Sooke BC

South Dakota State University, South Dakota Art Museum, Brookings SD

Southern Illinois University, University Museum, Carbondale IL

Southern Plains Indian Museum, Anadarko OK

Southwest Museum, Los Angeles CA

Springfield Library & Museums Association, Springfield Science Museum, Springfield MA
Stamford Museum & Nature Center, Stamford CT
Stanford University, Museum of Art, Stanford CA
Nelda C & H J Lutcher Stark Foundation, Stark Museum of Art, Orange TX
State Capitol Museum, Olympia WA
State Historical Society of Wisconsin, State Historical Museum, Madison WI
Strasburg Museum, Strasburg VA
Stratford Historical Society, Katherine Mitchel Museum, Stratford CT
US Coast Guard Museum, New London CT
United States Military Academy, West Point Museum, West Point NY
University of Alabama at Birmingham, Visual Arts Gallery, Birmingham AL
University of British Columbia, Museum of Anthropology, Vancouver BC
University of California, Los Angeles, Fowler Museum of Cultural History, Los Angeles CA
University of California, Santa Barbara, University Art Museum, Santa Barbara CA
University of Colorado at Colorado Springs, Gallery of Contemporary Art, Colorado Springs CO
University of Iowa, Museum of Art, Iowa City IA
University of Miami, Lowe Art Museum, Coral Gables FL
University of Notre Dame, Snite Museum of Art, Notre Dame IN
University of Rhode Island, Fine Arts Center Galleries, Kingston RI
University of Rochester, Memorial Art Gallery, Rochester NY
University of Southern Colorado, College of Liberal & Fine Arts, Pueblo CO
University of Victoria, Maltwood Art Museum and Gallery, Victoria BC
University of Virginia, Bayly Art Museum, Charlottesville VA
University of Washington, Thomas Burke Memorial Washington State Museum, Seattle WA
Vancouver Museum Commission, Vancouver Museum, Vancouver BC
Vermilion County Museum Society, Danville IL
Wayne County Historical Society, Museum, Honesdale PA
T T Wentworth Jr Museum, Florida State Museum, Pensacola FL
Whatcom Museum of History and Art, Bellingham WA
Wheelwright Museum of the American Indian, Santa Fe NM
Witte Museum, San Antonio TX
Wyoming State Museum, State Art Gallery, Cheyenne WY
Yosemite Museum, Yosemite National Park CA

AMERICAN WESTERN ART

Alaska Department of Education, Division of Libraries, Archives & Museums, Sheldon Jackson Museum, Sitka AK
The Albrecht-Kemper Museum of Art, Saint Joseph MO
Albuquerque Museum of Art & History, Albuquerque NM
Artesia Historical Museum & Art Center, Artesia NM
Art Gallery of Hamilton, Hamilton ON
Art Museum of Missoula, Missoula MT
ArtSpace-Lima, Lima OH
Berkshire Museum, Pittsfield MA
Birmingham Museum of Art, Birmingham AL
Brigham Young University, B F Larsen Gallery, Provo UT
Brigham Young University, Museum of Art, Provo UT
Brookgreen Gardens, Murrells Inlet SC
California College of Arts & Crafts, Steven Oliver Art Center, Oakland CA
Canajoharie Library & Art Gallery, Canajoharie NY
Kit Carson Historic Museums, Ernest Blumenschein Home & Studio, Taos NM
Kit Carson Historic Museums, Home & Museum, Taos NM
Amon Carter Museum, Fort Worth TX

Cartoon Art Museum, San Francisco CA
Cedar Rapids Museum of Art, Cedar Rapids IA
Cheekwood-Tennessee Botanical Gardens & Museum of Art, Nashville TN
Church of Jesus Christ of Latter-Day Saints, Museum of Church History & Art, Salt Lake City UT
Cincinnati Institute of Fine Arts, Taft Museum, Cincinnati OH
Colorado Historical Society, Colorado History Museum, Denver CO
Community Fine Arts Center, Halseth Gallery, Rock Springs WY
Coutts Memorial Museum of Art, Inc, El Dorado KS
Crook County Museum & Art Gallery, Sundance WY
Denver Art Museum, Denver CO
Detroit Institute of Arts, Detroit MI
East Carolina University, Wellington B Gray Gallery, Greenville NC
Eiteljorg Museum of American Indians & Western Art, Indianapolis IN
Ellen Noel Art Museum of the Permian Basin, Odessa TX
Elmhurst Art Museum, Elmhurst IL
El Paso Museum of Art, El Paso TX
Favell Museum of Western Art & Indian Artifacts, Klamath Falls OR
Frontier Times Museum, Bandera TX
Genesee Country Museum, John L Wehle Gallery of Sporting Art, Mumford NY
Gonzaga University, Jundt Art Museum, Ad Art Gallery, Spokane WA
Grand Rapids Art Museum, Grand Rapids MI
Nora Eccles Harrison Museum of Art, Logan UT
Headquarters Fort Monroe, Dept of Army, Casemate Museum, Fort Monroe VA
Heard Museum, Phoenix AZ
Honolulu Academy of Arts, Honolulu HI
Huntington Museum of Art, Huntington WV
Idaho Historical Museum, Boise ID
Indiana University, Art Museum, Bloomington IN
Institute of the Great Plains, Museum of the Great Plains, Lawton OK
Joslyn Art Museum, Omaha NE
Koshare Indian Museum, Inc, La Junta CO
Leanin' Tree Museum of Western Art, Boulder CO
Maricopa County Historical Society, Desert Caballeros Western Museum, Wickenburg AZ
Marietta College, Grover M Hermann Fine Arts Center, Marietta OH
Maryhill Museum of Art, Goldendale WA
Mexican Museum, San Francisco CA
Midwest Museum of American Art, Elkhart IN
Mississippi Museum of Art, Jackson MS
Arthur Roy Mitchell Memorial Inc, Museum of Western Art, Trinidad CO
Mobile Museum of Art, Mobile AL
MonDak Heritage Center, Sidney MT
Montana State University, Museum of the Rockies, Bozeman MT
Monterey Museum of Art Association, Monterey CA
The Museum of Arts & Sciences Inc, Daytona Beach FL
Museum of Fine Arts, Saint Petersburg, Florida, Inc, Saint Petersburg FL
Museum of New Mexico, Museum of Fine Arts, Santa Fe NM
Museum of Northern Arizona, Flagstaff AZ
Museum of Western Art, Denver CO
The Museums at Stony Brook, Stony Brook NY
National Cowboy Hall of Fame & Western Heritage Center Museum, Oklahoma City OK
National Infantry Museum, Fort Benning GA
National Museum of American Art, Washington DC
National Museum of Wildlife Art, Jackson WY
National Museum of Women in the Arts, Washington DC
National Park Service, Hubbell Trading Post National Historic Site, Ganado AZ
Natural History Museum of Los Angeles County, Los Angeles CA
Nelson-Atkins Museum of Art, Kansas City MO
Nevada Museum of Art, Reno NV

No Man's Land Historical Society Museum, Goodwell OK
Oklahoma Historical Society, State Museum of History, Oklahoma City OK
Orlando Museum of Art, Orlando FL
Page-Walker Arts & History Center, Cary NC
Panhandle-Plains Historical Society Museum, Canyon TX
George Phippen Memorial Foundation, Phippen Museum of Western Art, Prescott AZ
Pioneer Town, Pioneer Museum of Western Art, Wimberley TX
Redding Museum of Art & History, Redding CA
Red Rock State Park, Red Rock Museum, Church Rock NM
Frederic Remington Art Museum, Ogdensburg NY
Sid W Richardson Foundation, Collection of Western Art, Fort Worth TX
The Rockwell Museum, Corning NY
Millicent Rogers Museum of Northern New Mexico, Taos NM
Ross Memorial Museum, Saint Andrews NB
Roswell Museum & Art Center, Roswell NM
C M Russell Museum, Great Falls MT
R W Norton Art Gallery, Shreveport LA
Saint Johnsbury Athenaeum, Saint Johnsbury VT
South Dakota State University, South Dakota Art Museum, Brookings SD
Southwest Museum, Los Angeles CA
Nelda C & H J Lutcher Stark Foundation, Stark Museum of Art, Orange TX
State Historical Society of Wisconsin, State Historical Museum, Madison WI
Texas Tech University, Museum, Lubbock TX
The Turner Museum, Denver CO
United States Military Academy, West Point Museum, West Point NY
University of British Columbia, Museum of Anthropology, Vancouver BC
University of Colorado at Colorado Springs, Gallery of Contemporary Art, Colorado Springs CO
University of Florida, Samuel P Harn Museum of Art, Gainesville FL
University of Rhode Island, Fine Arts Center Galleries, Kingston RI
University of Texas at Austin, Archer M Huntington Art Gallery, Austin TX
University of Victoria, Maltwood Art Museum and Gallery, Victoria BC
University of Virginia, Bayly Art Museum, Charlottesville VA
USS Constitution Museum, Boston MA
Wells Fargo Bank, Wells Fargo History Museum, San Francisco CA
Wyoming State Museum, State Art Gallery, Cheyenne WY

ANTHROPOLOGY

Alaska Department of Education, Division of Libraries, Archives & Museums, Sheldon Jackson Museum, Sitka AK
Anchorage Museum of History & Art, Anchorage AK
ArtSpace-Lima, Lima OH
Bay County Historical Society, Historical Museum of Bay County, Bay City MI
Beloit College, Wright Museum of Art, Beloit WI
Berkshire Museum, Pittsfield MA
Bowdoin College, Peary-MacMillan Arctic Museum, Brunswick ME
California State University, Hayward, C E Smith Museum of Anthropology, Hayward CA
Carson County Square House Museum, Panhandle TX
Chelan County Public Utility District, Rocky Reach Dam, Wenatchee WA
College of Southern Idaho, Herrett Center for Arts & Science, Twin Falls ID
Colorado Historical Society, Colorado History Museum, Denver CO
Dartmouth College, Hood Museum of Art, Hanover NH
Deming-Luna Mimbres Museum, Deming NM
Department of Natural Resources of Missouri, Missouri State Museum, Jefferson City MO
Detroit Institute of Arts, Detroit MI

DeWitt Historical Society of Tompkins County, Ithaca NY

Douglas County Historical Society, Fairlawn Mansion & Museum, Superior WI

East Carolina University, Wellington B Gray Gallery, Greenville NC

Evansville Museum of Arts & Science, Evansville IN

The First National Bank of Chicago, Art Collection, Chicago IL

Hampton University, University Museum, Hampton VA

Heritage Hjemkomst Interpretive Center, Moorhead MN

Indiana University, William Hammond Mathers Museum, Bloomington IN

Institute of the Great Plains, Museum of the Great Plains, Lawton OK

Lafayette Natural History Museum, Planetarium & Nature Station, Lafayette LA

Loveland Museum Gallery, Loveland CO

McAllen International Museum, McAllen TX

The Mariners' Museum, Newport News VA

Maryhill Museum of Art, Goldendale WA

Milwaukee Public Museum, Milwaukee WI

Mississippi Department of Archives & History, Old Capitol Museum, Jackson MS

Mississippi River Museum at Mud-Island, Memphis TN

Mohave Museum of History & Arts, Kingman AZ

Montana State University, Museum of the Rockies, Bozeman MT

Morris Museum, Morristown NJ

Museo De Las Americas, Denver CO

Museum of Arts & History, Port Huron MI

The Museum of Arts & Sciences Inc, Daytona Beach FL

Museum of Northern Arizona, Flagstaff AZ

Museum of Northern British Columbia, Ruth Harvey Art Gallery, Prince Rupert BC

Museum of the City of New York, New York NY

Museum of York County, Rock Hill SC

National Museum of the American Indian, George Gustav Heye Center, New York NY

Natural History Museum of Los Angeles County, Los Angeles CA

Navajo Nation Museum, Window Rock AZ

No Man's Land Historical Society Museum, Goodwell OK

Oklahoma Historical Society, State Museum of History, Oklahoma City OK

Palm Beach County Parks & Recreation Department, Morikami Museum & Japanese Gardens, Delray Beach FL

Panhandle-Plains Historical Society Museum, Canyon TX

Pennsylvania Historical & Museum Commission, State Museum of Pennsylvania, Harrisburg PA

Phelps County Historical Society, Phelps County Museum, Holdrege NE

Plumas County Museum, Quincy CA

Red Rock State Park, Red Rock Museum, Church Rock NM

Riverside Municipal Museum, Riverside CA

Roberts County Museum, Miami TX

Rollins College, George D & Harriet W Cornell Fine Arts Museum, Winter Park FL

Royal Ontario Museum, Toronto ON

C M Russell Museum, Great Falls MT

Saint Joseph Museum, Saint Joseph MO

Abigail Adams Smith Museum, New York NY

Southern Illinois University, University Museum, Carbondale IL

Springfield Library & Museums Association, Springfield Science Museum, Springfield MA

State Historical Society of Wisconsin, State Historical Museum, Madison WI

University of British Columbia, Museum of Anthropology, Vancouver BC

University of California, Los Angeles, Fowler Museum of Cultural History, Los Angeles CA

University of Memphis, Art Museum, Memphis TN

University of Mississippi, University Museums, Oxford MS

University of Pennsylvania, Museum of Archaeology & Anthropology, Philadelphia PA

The University of Texas, Institute of Texan Cultures, San Antonio TX

University of Victoria, Maltwood Art Museum and Gallery, Victoria BC

University of Washington, Thomas Burke Memorial Washington State Museum, Seattle WA

Wheelwright Museum of the American Indian, Santa Fe NM

Witte Museum, San Antonio TX

Xavier University, Xavier Art Gallery, Cincinnati OH

ANTIQUITIES - ASSYRIAN

Academy of the New Church, Glencairn Museum, Bryn Athyn PA

Bowdoin College, Museum of Art, Brunswick ME

Cincinnati Museum Association, Cincinnati Art Museum, Cincinnati OH

Dartmouth College, Hood Museum of Art, Hanover NH

Harvard University, Semitic Museum, Cambridge MA

Huntington Museum of Art, Huntington WV

Indiana University, Art Museum, Bloomington IN

Kimbell Art Foundation, Kimbell Art Museum, Fort Worth TX

Maryland Hall for the Creative Arts, Cardinal Gallery, Annapolis MD

The Metropolitan Museum of Art, New York NY

Mint Museum of Art, Charlotte NC

Nelson-Atkins Museum of Art, Kansas City MO

Polk Museum of Art, Lakeland FL

Rosicrucian Egyptian Museum & Art Gallery, San Jose CA

Southern Baptist Theological Seminary, Joseph A Callaway Archaeological Museum, Louisville KY

Toledo Museum of Art, Toledo OH

University of Chicago, Oriental Institute Museum, Chicago IL

University of Missouri, Museum of Art & Archaeology, Columbia MO

University of Rochester, Memorial Art Gallery, Rochester NY

Walters Art Gallery, Baltimore MD

ANTIQUITIES - BYZANTINE

The Buffalo Fine Arts Academy, Albright-Knox Art Gallery, Buffalo NY

Cincinnati Museum Association, Cincinnati Art Museum, Cincinnati OH

Duke University Museum of Art, Durham NC

The First National Bank of Chicago, Art Collection, Chicago IL

Florence Museum of Art, Science & History, Florence SC

Harvard University, Dumbarton Oaks Research Library & Collections, Washington DC

Harvard University, Semitic Museum, Cambridge MA

Huntington Museum of Art, Huntington WV

Indiana University, Art Museum, Bloomington IN

Maryland Hall for the Creative Arts, Cardinal Gallery, Annapolis MD

Menil Collection, Houston TX

The Metropolitan Museum of Art, New York NY

Michigan State University, Kresge Art Museum, East Lansing MI

Mint Museum of Art, Charlotte NC

Newark Museum Association, The Newark Museum, Newark NJ

Princeton University, The Art Museum, Princeton NJ

Royal Arts Foundation, Belcourt Castle, Newport RI

Southern Baptist Theological Seminary, Joseph A Callaway Archaeological Museum, Louisville KY

State University of New York at New Paltz, College Art Gallery, New Paltz NY

University of Delaware, University Gallery, Newark DE

University of Illinois, World Heritage Museum, Champaign IL

University of Missouri, Museum of Art & Archaeology, Columbia MO

University of Virginia, Bayly Art Museum, Charlottesville VA

Walters Art Gallery, Baltimore MD

ANTIQUITIES - EGYPTIAN

Academy of the New Church, Glencairn Museum, Bryn Athyn PA

Albany Museum of Art, Albany GA

Lyman Allyn Art Museum, New London CT

Arnot Art Museum, Elmira NY

The Art Institute of Chicago, Chicago IL

Barnes Foundation, Merion PA

Beloit College, Wright Museum of Art, Beloit WI

Berkshire Museum, Pittsfield MA

Brevard Museum of Art & Science, Melbourne FL

The Buffalo Fine Arts Academy, Albright-Knox Art Gallery, Buffalo NY

Cincinnati Museum Association, Cincinnati Art Museum, Cincinnati OH

Cleveland Museum of Art, Cleveland OH

The College of Wooster, Art Museum, Wooster OH

C W Post Campus of Long Island University, Hillwood Art Museum, Brookville NY

Dickinson College, Trout Gallery, Carlisle PA

Duke University Museum of Art, Durham NC

Emory University, Michael C Carlos Museum, Atlanta GA

Evansville Museum of Arts & Science, Evansville IN

Fine Arts Museums of San Francisco, M H de Young Memorial Museum & California Palace of the Legion of Honor, San Francisco CA

Florence Museum of Art, Science & History, Florence SC

Florida State University Foundation - Central Florida Community College Foundation, The Appleton Museum of Art, Ocala FL

Freeport Arts Center, Freeport IL

Grand Rapids Art Museum, Grand Rapids MI

Hamilton College, Fred L Emerson Gallery, Clinton NY

Harvard University, William Hayes Fogg Art Museum, Cambridge MA

Harvard University, Arthur M Sackler Museum, Cambridge MA

Harvard University, Semitic Museum, Cambridge MA

Indiana University, Art Museum, Bloomington IN

Johns Hopkins University, Archaeological Collection, Baltimore MD

Joslyn Art Museum, Omaha NE

Kelowna Museum, Kelowna BC

Kimbell Art Foundation, Kimbell Art Museum, Fort Worth TX

Louisiana Arts & Science Center, Baton Rouge LA

Maryland Hall for the Creative Arts, Cardinal Gallery, Annapolis MD

The Metropolitan Museum of Art, New York NY

Michigan State University, Kresge Art Museum, East Lansing MI

Milwaukee Art Museum, Milwaukee WI

Mount Holyoke College, Art Museum, South Hadley MA

Museum of Fine Arts, Boston MA

Newark Museum Association, The Newark Museum, Newark NJ

Panhandle-Plains Historical Society Museum, Canyon TX

Princeton University, The Art Museum, Princeton NJ

Purdue University Galleries, West Lafayette IN

Putnam Museum of History & Natural Science, Davenport IA

Queens College, City University of New York, Godwin-Ternbach Museum, Flushing NY

Rollins College, George D & Harriet W Cornell Fine Arts Museum, Winter Park FL

Rosicrucian Egyptian Museum & Art Gallery, San Jose CA

Royal Arts Foundation, Belcourt Castle, Newport RI

Saint Gregory's Abbey & College, Mabee-Gerrer Museum of Art, Shawnee OK

The Saint Louis Art Museum, Saint Louis MO

San Antonio Museum of Art, San Antonio TX

Southern Baptist Theological Seminary, Joseph A Callaway Archaeological Museum, Louisville KY

Stanford University, Museum of Art, Stanford CA

State University of New York at New Paltz,
College Art Gallery, New Paltz NY
Toledo Museum of Art, Toledo OH
Tufts University, Art Gallery, Medford MA
University of Chicago, Oriental Institute Museum,
Chicago IL
University of Delaware, University Gallery, Newark
DE
University of Illinois, World Heritage Museum,
Champaign IL
University of Memphis, Art Museum, Memphis TN
University of Michigan, Kelsey Museum of
Archaeology, Ann Arbor MI
University of Missouri, Museum of Art &
Archaeology, Columbia MO
University of Puerto Rico, Museum of
Anthropology, History & Art, San Juan PR
University of Rochester, Memorial Art Gallery,
Rochester NY
University of Utah, Utah Museum of Fine Arts, Salt
Lake City UT
University of Wisconsin-Madison, Elvehjem
Museum of Art, Madison WI
Wadsworth Atheneum, Hartford CT
Walters Art Gallery, Baltimore MD
Worcester Art Museum, Worcester MA

ANTIQUITIES - ETRUSCAN

Arnot Art Museum, Elmira NY
Berkshire Museum, Pittsfield MA
Bowdoin College, Museum of Art, Brunswick ME
The Buffalo Fine Arts Academy, Albright-Knox Art
Gallery, Buffalo NY
Dartmouth College, Hood Museum of Art, Hanover
NH
Duke University Museum of Art, Durham NC
Emory University, Michael C Carlos Museum,
Atlanta GA
Fine Arts Museums of San Francisco, M H de
Young Memorial Museum & California Palace
of the Legion of Honor, San Francisco CA
The First National Bank of Chicago, Art Collection,
Chicago IL
Florence Museum of Art, Science & History,
Florence SC
Florida State University Foundation - Central
Florida Community College Foundation, The
Appleton Museum of Art, Ocala FL
Freeport Arts Center, Freeport IL
Indiana University, Art Museum, Bloomington IN
The Metropolitan Museum of Art, New York NY
Putnam Museum of History & Natural Science,
Davenport IA
Rollins College, George D & Harriet W Cornell
Fine Arts Museum, Winter Park FL
Tampa Museum of Art, Tampa FL
University of British Columbia, Museum of
Anthropology, Vancouver BC
University of Iowa, Museum of Art, Iowa City IA
University of Missouri, Museum of Art &
Archaeology, Columbia MO
University of Virginia, Bayly Art Museum,
Charlottesville VA
Vassar College, The Frances Lehman Loeb Art
Center, Poughkeepsie NY
Walters Art Gallery, Baltimore MD

ANTIQUITIES - GREEK

Academy of the New Church, Glencairn Museum,
Bryn Athyn PA
Albany Museum of Art, Albany GA
Lyman Allyn Art Museum, New London CT
Baltimore Museum of Art, Baltimore MD
Beloit College, Wright Museum of Art, Beloit WI
Berea College, Doris Ulmann Galleries, Berea KY
Berkshire Museum, Pittsfield MA
Bowdoin College, Museum of Art, Brunswick ME
The Buffalo Fine Arts Academy, Albright-Knox Art
Gallery, Buffalo NY
Chrysler Museum of Art, Norfolk VA
Cleveland Museum of Art, Cleveland OH
The College of Wooster, Art Museum, Wooster OH
Corcoran Gallery of Art, Washington DC
Dartmouth College, Hood Museum of Art, Hanover
NH
Duke University Museum of Art, Durham NC

Emory University, Michael C Carlos Museum,
Atlanta GA
Fine Arts Museums of San Francisco, M H de
Young Memorial Museum & California Palace
of the Legion of Honor, San Francisco CA
Florida State University Foundation - Central
Florida Community College Foundation, The
Appleton Museum of Art, Ocala FL
Freeport Arts Center, Freeport IL
Isabella Stewart Gardner Museum, Boston MA
Getty Center for the History of Art & the
Humanities Trust Museum, The J Paul Getty
Museum, Santa Monica CA
Hamilton College, Fred L Emerson Gallery, Clinton
NY
Harvard University, William Hayes Fogg Art
Museum, Cambridge MA
Harvard University, Semitic Museum, Cambridge
MA
Hispanic Society of America, Museum, New York
NY
Indiana University, Art Museum, Bloomington IN
James Madison University, Sawhill Gallery,
Harrisonburg VA
Kelowna Museum, Kelowna BC
Kimbell Art Foundation, Kimbell Art Museum,
Fort Worth TX
Louisiana Arts & Science Center, Baton Rouge LA
Maryhill Museum of Art, Goldendale WA
The Metropolitan Museum of Art, New York NY
Michigan State University, Kresge Art Museum,
East Lansing MI
Milwaukee Art Museum, Milwaukee WI
Minneapolis Institute of Arts, Minneapolis MN
Mobile Museum of Art, Mobile AL
Mount Holyoke College, Art Museum, South
Hadley MA
The Museum of Arts & Sciences Inc, Daytona
Beach FL
Museum of Fine Arts, Boston MA
Museum of Fine Arts, Houston, Houston TX
New Brunswick Museum, Saint John NB
Portland Art Museum, Portland OR
Princeton University, The Art Museum, Princeton
NJ
Putnam Museum of History & Natural Science,
Davenport IA
Queens College, City University of New York,
Godwin-Ternbach Museum, Flushing NY
Queen's University, Agnes Etherington Art Centre,
Kingston ON
Rhode Island School of Design, Museum of Art,
Providence RI
Saint Gregory's Abbey & College, Mabee-Gerrer
Museum of Art, Shawnee OK
San Antonio Museum of Art, San Antonio TX
Santa Barbara Museum of Art, Santa Barbara CA
Seattle Art Museum, Seattle WA
Stanford University, Museum of Art, Stanford CA
Staten Island Institute of Arts & Sciences, Staten
Island NY
Tampa Museum of Art, Tampa FL
Toledo Museum of Art, Toledo OH
Tufts University, Art Gallery, Medford MA
University of British Columbia, Museum of
Anthropology, Vancouver BC
University of Chicago, David & Alfred Smart
Museum of Art, Chicago IL
University of Cincinnati, DAAP Galleries-College
of Design Architecture, Art & Planning,
Cincinnati OH
University of Delaware, University Gallery, Newark
DE
University of Illinois, World Heritage Museum,
Champaign IL
University of Manitoba, Faculty of Architecture
Exhibition Centre, Winnipeg MB
University of Michigan, Kelsey Museum of
Archaeology, Ann Arbor MI
University of Mississippi, University Museums,
Oxford MS
University of Missouri, Museum of Art &
Archaeology, Columbia MO
University of Texas at Austin, Archer M
Huntington Art Gallery, Austin TX
University of Vermont, Robert Hull Fleming
Museum, Burlington VT

University of Virginia, Bayly Art Museum,
Charlottesville VA
University of Wisconsin-Madison, Elvehjem
Museum of Art, Madison WI
Vassar College, The Frances Lehman Loeb Art
Center, Poughkeepsie NY
Virginia Museum of Fine Arts, Richmond VA
Wadsworth Atheneum, Hartford CT
Walters Art Gallery, Baltimore MD
Yale University, Art Gallery, New Haven CT

ANTIQUITIES - ORIENTAL

Academy of the New Church, Glencairn Museum,
Bryn Athyn PA
Arnot Art Museum, Elmira NY
Asian Art Museum of San Francisco, Avery
Brundage Collection, San Francisco CA
Atlanta Museum, Atlanta GA
Barnes Foundation, Merion PA
Bass Museum of Art, Miami Beach FL
Beloit College, Wright Museum of Art, Beloit WI
The Buffalo Fine Arts Academy, Albright-Knox Art
Gallery, Buffalo NY
Billie Trimble Chandler Arts Foundation, Asian
Cultures Museum & Educational Center, Corpus
Christi TX
Cincinnati Institute of Fine Arts, Taft Museum,
Cincinnati OH
The College of Wooster, Art Museum, Wooster OH
Denver Art Museum, Denver CO
Erie Art Museum, Erie PA
The First National Bank of Chicago, Art Collection,
Chicago IL
Harvard University, William Hayes Fogg Art
Museum, Cambridge MA
Indiana University, Art Museum, Bloomington IN
McPherson Museum, McPherson KS
Maryland Hall for the Creative Arts, Cardinal
Gallery, Annapolis MD
Michigan State University, Kresge Art Museum,
East Lansing MI
Mint Museum of Art, Charlotte NC
Mobile Museum of Art, Mobile AL
The Museum of Arts & Sciences Inc, Daytona
Beach FL
National Infantry Museum, Fort Benning GA
Newark Museum Association, The Newark
Museum, Newark NJ
New Brunswick Museum, Saint John NB
Old Jail Art Center, Albany TX
Pacific - Asia Museum, Pasadena CA
Panhandle-Plains Historical Society Museum,
Canyon TX
Peabody Essex Museum, Salem MA
Portland Art Museum, Portland OR
Putnam Museum of History & Natural Science,
Davenport IA
Rosicrucian Egyptian Museum & Art Gallery, San
Jose CA
Royal Arts Foundation, Belcourt Castle, Newport
RI
San Antonio Museum of Art, San Antonio TX
Staten Island Institute of Arts & Sciences, Staten
Island NY
State University of New York at New Paltz,
College Art Gallery, New Paltz NY
Toledo Museum of Art, Toledo OH
University of British Columbia, Museum of
Anthropology, Vancouver BC
University of Florida, Samuel P Harn Museum of
Art, Gainesville FL
University of Illinois, World Heritage Museum,
Champaign IL
University of Virginia, Bayly Art Museum,
Charlottesville VA
Vizcaya Museum & Gardens, Miami FL
Woodmere Art Museum, Philadelphia PA
Worcester Art Museum, Worcester MA

ANTIQUITIES - PERSIAN

Asian Art Museum of San Francisco, Avery
Brundage Collection, San Francisco CA
The Buffalo Fine Arts Academy, Albright-Knox Art
Gallery, Buffalo NY
C W Post Campus of Long Island University,
Hillwood Art Museum, Brookville NY

Detroit Institute of Arts, Detroit MI
Florida State University Foundation - Central
    Florida Community College Foundation, The
    Appleton Museum of Art, Ocala FL
Edsel & Eleanor Ford House, Grosse Pointe Shores
    MI
Harvard University, Semitic Museum, Cambridge
    MA
Huntington Museum of Art, Huntington WV
Indiana University, Art Museum, Bloomington IN
Jacksonville University, Alexander Brest Museum &
    Gallery, Jacksonville FL
The Metropolitan Museum of Art, New York NY
Mint Museum of Art, Charlotte NC
Mobile Museum of Art, Mobile AL
The Museum of Arts & Sciences Inc, Daytona
    Beach FL
Newark Museum Association, The Newark
    Museum, Newark NJ
Panhandle-Plains Historical Society Museum,
    Canyon TX
Putnam Museum of History & Natural Science,
    Davenport IA
Royal Arts Foundation, Belcourt Castle, Newport
    RI
University of Missouri, Museum of Art &
    Archaeology, Columbia MO
Walters Art Gallery, Baltimore MD
Woodmere Art Museum, Philadelphia PA

ANTIQUITIES - ROMAN

Academy of the New Church, Glencairn Museum,
    Bryn Athyn PA
Albany Museum of Art, Albany GA
Lyman Allyn Art Museum, New London CT
Baltimore Museum of Art, Baltimore MD
Beloit College, Wright Museum of Art, Beloit WI
Bowdoin College, Museum of Art, Brunswick ME
The Buffalo Fine Arts Academy, Albright-Knox Art
    Gallery, Buffalo NY
Chrysler Museum Of Art, Norfolk VA
Cincinnati Museum Association, Cincinnati Art
    Museum, Cincinnati OH
Cleveland Museum of Art, Cleveland OH
C W Post Campus of Long Island University,
    Hillwood Art Museum, Brookville NY
Detroit Institute of Arts, Detroit MI
Dickinson College, Trout Gallery, Carlisle PA
Duke University Museum of Art, Durham NC
Emory University, Michael C Carlos Museum,
    Atlanta GA
The First National Bank of Chicago, Art Collection,
    Chicago IL
Florida State University Foundation - Central
    Florida Community College Foundation, The
    Appleton Museum of Art, Ocala FL
Freeport Arts Center, Freeport IL
Isabella Stewart Gardner Museum, Boston MA
Getty Center for the History of Art & the
    Humanities Trust Museum, The J Paul Getty
    Museum, Santa Monica CA
Harvard University, William Hayes Fogg Art
    Museum, Cambridge MA
Harvard University, Semitic Museum, Cambridge
    MA
Hebrew Union College - Jewish Institute of
    Religion, Skirball Museum-Cincinnati Branch,
    Cincinnati OH
Indiana University, Art Museum, Bloomington IN
James Madison University, Sawhill Gallery,
    Harrisonburg VA
Johns Hopkins University, Archaeological
    Collection, Baltimore MD
Kelowna Museum, Kelowna BC
Kimbell Art Foundation, Kimbell Art Museum,
    Fort Worth TX
Louisiana Arts & Science Center, Baton Rouge LA
The Metropolitan Museum of Art, New York NY
Michigan State University, Kresge Art Museum,
    East Lansing MI
Milwaukee Art Museum, Milwaukee WI
Minneapolis Institute of Arts, Minneapolis MN
Mint Museum of Art, Charlotte NC
Mobile Museum of Art, Mobile AL
Mount Holyoke College, Art Museum, South
    Hadley MA
Museum of Fine Arts, Boston MA

Museum of Fine Arts, Houston, Houston TX
Newark Museum Association, The Newark
    Museum, Newark NJ
New Brunswick Museum, Saint John NB
Princeton University, The Art Museum, Princeton
    NJ
Putnam Museum of History & Natural Science,
    Davenport IA
Queen's University, Agnes Etherington Art Centre,
    Kingston ON
Rhode Island School of Design, Museum of Art,
    Providence RI
Rollins College, George D & Harriet W Cornell
    Fine Arts Museum, Winter Park FL
Saginaw Art Museum, Saginaw MI
Saint Gregory's Abbey & College, Mabee-Gerrer
    Museum of Art, Shawnee OK
San Antonio Museum of Art, San Antonio TX
Santa Barbara Museum of Art, Santa Barbara CA
Seattle Art Museum, Seattle WA
Stanford University, Museum of Art, Stanford CA
Staten Island Institute of Arts & Sciences, Staten
    Island NY
Tampa Museum of Art, Tampa FL
Toledo Museum of Art, Toledo OH
Tufts University, Art Gallery, Medford MA
University of Chicago, David & Alfred Smart
    Museum of Art, Chicago IL
University of Delaware, University Gallery, Newark
    DE
University of Illinois, World Heritage Museum,
    Champaign IL
University of Manitoba, Faculty of Architecture
    Exhibition Centre, Winnipeg MB
University of Michigan, Kelsey Museum of
    Archaeology, Ann Arbor MI
University of Mississippi, University Museums,
    Oxford MS
University of Missouri, Museum of Art &
    Archaeology, Columbia MO
University of Texas at Austin, Archer M
    Huntington Art Gallery, Austin TX
University of Vermont, Robert Hull Fleming
    Museum, Burlington VT
University of Virginia, Bayly Art Museum,
    Charlottesville VA
Vassar College, The Frances Lehman Loeb Art
    Center, Poughkeepsie NY
Vizcaya Museum & Gardens, Miami FL
Wadsworth Atheneum, Hartford CT
Walters Art Gallery, Baltimore MD
Yale University, Art Gallery, New Haven CT

ARCHAEOLOGY

Academy of the New Church, Glencairn Museum,
    Bryn Athyn PA
African Art Museum of Maryland, Columbia MD
Alabama Department of Archives & History,
    Museum Galleries, Montgomery AL
Alaska State Museum, Juneau AK
American Architectural Foundation, The Octagon
    Museum, Washington DC
Anchorage Museum of History & Art, Anchorage
    AK
Archaeological Society of Ohio, Indian Museum of
    Lake County, Ohio, Painesville OH
Arkansas Territorial Restoration, Little Rock AR
ArtSpace-Lima, Lima OH
Association for the Preservation of Virginia
    Antiquities, John Marshall House, Richmond
    VA
Augusta Richmond County Museum, Augusta GA
Aurora University, Schingoethe Center for Native
    American Cultures, Aurora IL
Balzekas Museum of Lithuanian Culture, Chicago
    IL
Bay County Historical Society, Historical Museum
    of Bay County, Bay City MI
Beloit College, Wright Museum of Art, Beloit WI
Jesse Besser Museum, Alpena MI
California State University, Hayward, C E Smith
    Museum of Anthropology, Hayward CA
Calvert Marine Museum, Solomons MD
Canadian Museum of Civilization, Hull PQ
Carson County Square House Museum, Panhandle
    TX

Kit Carson Historic Museums, Home & Museum,
    Taos NM
Charleston Museum, Joseph Manigault House,
    Charleston SC
Chelan County Public Utility District, Rocky Reach
    Dam, Wenatchee WA
Cherokee National Historical Society, Inc,
    Tahlequah OK
Clinton County Historical Association, Clinton
    County Historical Museum, Plattsburgh NY
College of Southern Idaho, Herrett Center for Arts
    & Science, Twin Falls ID
Colorado Historical Society, Colorado History
    Museum, Denver CO
Columbus Museum, Columbus GA
County of Henrico, Meadow Farm Museum, Glen
    Allen VA
Crow Wing County Historical Society, Brainerd
    MN
Department of Community Development,
    Provincial Museum of Alberta, Edmonton AB
Detroit Institute of Arts, Detroit MI
DeWitt Historical Society of Tompkins County,
    Ithaca NY
Douglas County Historical Society, Fairlawn
    Mansion & Museum, Superior WI
Dundurn Castle, Hamilton ON
Edgecombe County Cultural Arts Council, Inc,
    Blount-Bridgers House, Hobson Pittman
    Memorial Gallery, Tarboro NC
El Paso Museum of Art, Wilderness Park Museum,
    El Paso TX
Emory University, Michael C Carlos Museum,
    Atlanta GA
Eskimo Museum, Churchill MB
Fairfield University, Thomas J Walsh Art Gallery,
    Fairfield CT
Farmington Village Green & Library Association,
    Stanley-Whitman House, Farmington CT
The First National Bank of Chicago, Art Collection,
    Chicago IL
Forges du Saint-Maurice National Historic Site,
    Trois Rivieres PQ
Fort Ticonderoga Association, Ticonderoga NY
Freer Gallery of Art Gallery, Arthur M Sackler
    Gallery, Washington DC
Gunston Hall Plantation, Mason Neck VA
Hampton University, University Museum, Hampton
    VA
Harvard University, Semitic Museum, Cambridge
    MA
Heard Museum, Phoenix AZ
Hebrew Union College, Skirball Cultural Center,
    Los Angeles CA
Hebrew Union College - Jewish Institute of
    Religion, Skirball Museum-Cincinnati Branch,
    Cincinnati OH
Hebrew Union College-Jewish Institute of Religion,
    New York NY
Hispanic Society of America, Museum, New York
    NY
Historical & Cultural Affairs, Delaware State
    Museums, Dover DE
Historical Society of Rockland County, New City
    NY
Huguenot Historical Society of New Paltz Galleries,
    New Paltz NY
Huronia Museum, Midland ON
Illinois Historic Preservation Agency, Bishop Hill
    State Historic Site, Bishop Hill IL
Institute of the Great Plains, Museum of the Great
    Plains, Lawton OK
The Jewish Museum, New York NY
Johns Hopkins University, Homewood House
    Museum, Baltimore MD
Kelowna Museum, Kelowna BC
Kern County Museum, Bakersfield CA
Koshare Indian Museum, Inc, La Junta CO
Lac du Flambeau Band of Lake Superior Chippewa
    Indians, George W Brown Jr Ojibwe Museum &
    Cultural Center, Lac du Flambeau WI
Lafayette Natural History Museum, Planetarium &
    Nature Station, Lafayette LA
Lakeview Museum of Arts & Sciences, Peoria IL
Louisiana State Exhibit Museum, Shreveport LA
Loveland Museum Gallery, Loveland CO
McPherson Museum, McPherson KS

Maine Historical Society, Maine History Gallery, Portland ME

Maryhill Museum of Art, Goldendale WA

Mississippi Department of Archives & History, Old Capitol Museum, Jackson MS

Mississippi River Museum at Mud-Island, Memphis TN

Mohave Museum of History & Arts, Kingman AZ

Moncur Gallery, Boissevain MB

Montana State University, Museum of the Rockies, Bozeman MT

Morris Museum, Morristown NJ

Musee Regional de la Cote-Nord, Sept-Iles PQ

Museo De Las Americas, Denver CO

Museum of Arts & History, Port Huron MI

The Museum of Arts & Sciences Inc, Daytona Beach FL

Museum of Mobile, Mobile AL

Museum of Northern Arizona, Flagstaff AZ

Museum of Northern British Columbia, Ruth Harvey Art Gallery, Prince Rupert BC

Museum of the City of New York, New York NY

Museum of York County, Rock Hill SC

National Museum of the American Indian, George Gustav Heye Center, New York NY

Natural History Museum of Los Angeles County, Los Angeles CA

Naval Historical Center, The Navy Museum, Washington DC

Newark Museum Association, The Newark Museum, Newark NJ

No Man's Land Historical Society Museum, Goodwell OK

The Ohio Historical Society, Inc, Campus Martius Museum & Ohio River Museum, Marietta OH

Oklahoma Historical Society, State Museum of History, Oklahoma City OK

Oshkosh Public Museum, Oshkosh WI

Palm Springs Desert Museum, Palm Springs CA

Panhandle-Plains Historical Society Museum, Canyon TX

Peabody Essex Museum, Salem MA

Pennsylvania Historical & Museum Commission, State Museum of Pennsylvania, Harrisburg PA

Frank Phillips Foundation Inc, Woolaroc Museum, Bartlesville OK

Ponca City Cultural Center & Museum, Ponca City OK

Putnam Museum of History & Natural Science, Davenport IA

Redding Museum of Art & History, Redding CA

Red Rock State Park, Red Rock Museum, Church Rock NM

Riverside Municipal Museum, Riverside CA

Roberts County Museum, Miami TX

Rollins College, George D & Harriet W Cornell Fine Arts Museum, Winter Park FL

Rome Historical Society Museum, Rome NY

Royal Ontario Museum, Toronto ON

C M Russell Museum, Great Falls MT

Saint Augustine Historical Society, Oldest House & Museums, Saint Augustine FL

Saint Joseph Museum, Saint Joseph MO

Seneca-Iroquois National Museum, Salamanca NY

Shaker Village of Pleasant Hill, Harrodsburg KY

Abigail Adams Smith Museum, New York NY

Sooke Region Museum & Art Gallery, Sooke BC

Southern Baptist Theological Seminary, Joseph A Callaway Archaeological Museum, Louisville KY

Southern Illinois University, University Museum, Carbondale IL

Southern Oregon Historical Society, Jacksonville Museum of Southern Oregon History, Medford OR

South Street Seaport Museum, New York NY

Spertus Institute of Jewish Studies, Spertus Museum, Chicago IL

Springfield Art & Historical Society, Miller Art Center, Springfield VT

Springfield Library & Museums Association, Springfield Science Museum, Springfield MA

State Art Museum of Florida, John & Mable Ringling Museum of Art, Sarasota FL

State Historical Society of Wisconsin, State Historical Museum, Madison WI

Tallahassee Museum of History & Natural Science, Tallahassee FL

The Temple-Tifereth Israel, The Temple Museum of Religious Art, Beachwood OH

Texas A&M University, J Wayne Stark University Center Galleries, College Station TX

Tryon Palace Historic Sites & Gardens, New Bern NC

Turtle Mountain Chippewa Historical Society, Turtle Mountain Heritage Center, Belcourt ND

University of British Columbia, Museum of Anthropology, Vancouver BC

University of California, Los Angeles, Fowler Museum of Cultural History, Los Angeles CA

University of Chicago, Oriental Institute Museum, Chicago IL

University of Illinois, World Heritage Museum, Champaign IL

University of Manitoba, Faculty of Architecture Exhibition Centre, Winnipeg MB

University of Memphis, Art Museum, Memphis TN

University of Pennsylvania, Museum of Archaeology & Anthropology, Philadelphia PA

University of Puerto Rico, Museum of Anthropology, History & Art, San Juan PR

University of Tennessee, Frank H McClung Museum, Knoxville TN

University of Victoria, Maltwood Art Museum and Gallery, Victoria BC

University of Washington, Thomas Burke Memorial Washington State Museum, Seattle WA

Vancouver Museum Commission, Vancouver Museum, Vancouver BC

Vassar College, The Frances Lehman Loeb Art Center, Poughkeepsie NY

Wade House & Wesley W Jung Carriage Museum, Historic House & Carriage Museum, Greenbush WI

Wayne County Historical Society, Museum, Honesdale PA

Western Kentucky University, Kentucky Museum, Bowling Green KY

Wethersfield Historical Society Inc, Museum, Wethersfield CT

Woodlawn Plantation, Mount Vernon VA

York Institute Museum, Saco ME

ARCHITECTURE

Academy of the New Church, Glencairn Museum, Bryn Athyn PA

African Art Museum of Maryland, Columbia MD

Agecroft Association, Museum, Richmond VA

Allentown Art Museum, Allentown PA

Arkansas Territorial Restoration, Little Rock AR

Artesia Historical Museum & Art Center, Artesia NM

The Art Institute of Chicago, Chicago IL

Art Museum of Missoula, Missoula MT

Arts Council of Fayetteville-Cumberland County, The Arts Center, Fayetteville NC

ArtSpace-Lima, Lima OH

Association for the Preservation of Virginia Antiquities, John Marshall House, Richmond VA

Athenaeum of Philadelphia, Philadelphia PA

Atlanta Historical Society Inc, Atlanta History Center, Atlanta GA

Leo Baeck Institute, New York NY

Baltimore Museum of Art, Baltimore MD

The Bartlett Museum, Amesbury MA

Beloit College, Wright Museum of Art, Beloit WI

Boston Public Library, Albert H Wiggin Gallery & Print Department, Boston MA

Burchfield-Penney Art Center, Buffalo NY

California College of Arts & Crafts, Steven Oliver Art Center, Oakland CA

Kit Carson Historic Museums, Ernest Blumenschein Home & Studio, Taos NM

Kit Carson Historic Museums, Home & Museum, Taos NM

Cedar Rapids Museum of Art, Cedar Rapids IA

Central United Methodist Church, Swords Info Plowshares Peace Center & Gallery, Detroit MI

Charleston Museum, Joseph Manigault House, Charleston SC

Chatillon-DeMenil House Foundation, DeMenil Mansion, Saint Louis MO

Chicago Architecture Foundation, Chicago IL

Chicago Athenaeum, Museum of Architecture & Design, Chicago IL

Chicago Department of Cultural Affairs, Chicago Cultural Center, Chicago IL

Chinati Foundation, Marfa TX

Church of Jesus Christ of Latter-Day Saints, Museum of Church History & Art, Salt Lake City UT

CIGNA Corporation, CIGNA Museum & Art Collection, Philadelphia PA

Cincinnati Institute of Fine Arts, Taft Museum, Cincinnati OH

City of Atlanta, City Gallery at Chastain, Atlanta GA

The City of Petersburg Museums, Petersburg VA

City of Springdale, Shiloh Museum, Springdale AR

Clemson University, Rudolph E Lee Gallery, Clemson SC

Cohasset Historical Society, Cohasset Maritime Museum, Cohasset MA

Columbus Museum, Columbus GA

Cooper-Hewitt, National Design Museum, New York NY

Cosanti Foundation, Arcosanti, Scottsdale AZ

County of Henrico, Meadow Farm Museum, Glen Allen VA

Craigdarroch Castle Historical Museum Society, Victoria BC

Cranbrook Art Museum, Bloomfield Hills MI

Crow Wing County Historical Society, Brainerd MN

The Currier Gallery of Art, Manchester NH

Davidson College Visual Arts Center, William H Van Every Jr & Edward M Smith Galleries, Davidson NC

Denver Art Museum, Denver CO

DeWitt Historical Society of Tompkins County, Ithaca NY

Douglas County Historical Society, Fairlawn Mansion & Museum, Superior WI

Dundurn Castle, Hamilton ON

Eastern Washington State Historical Society, Cheney Cowles Museum, Spokane WA

Edgecombe County Cultural Arts Council, Inc, Blount-Bridgers House, Hobson Pittman Memorial Gallery, Tarboro NC

Elmhurst Art Museum, Elmhurst IL

Ephraim McDowell-Cambus-Kenneth Foundation, McDowell House & Apothecary Shop, Danville KY

Wharton Esherick Museum, Paoli PA

Evanston Historical Society, Charles Gates Dawes House, Evanston IL

Farmington Village Green & Library Association, Stanley-Whitman House, Farmington CT

Federal Reserve Board, Art Gallery, Washington DC

The First National Bank of Chicago, Art Collection, Chicago IL

Florida Gulf Coast Art Center, Inc, Belleair FL

Edsel & Eleanor Ford House, Grosse Pointe Shores MI

Fort Worth Art Association, Modern Art Museum of Fort Worth, Fort Worth TX

Glanmore, Hastings County Museum, Belleville ON

Gunston Hall Plantation, Mason Neck VA

Hebrew Union College, Skirball Cultural Center, Los Angeles CA

Hebrew Union College-Jewish Institute of Religion, New York NY

Hillel Foundation, Hillel Jewish Student Center Gallery, Cincinnati OH

Historical & Cultural Affairs, Delaware State Museums, Dover DE

Historical Society of Old Newbury, Cushing House Museum, Newburyport MA

Historical Society of Pennsylvania, Philadelphia PA

Historical Society of Washington DC, Heurich House Museum, Washington DC

Historic Landmarks Foundation of Indiana, Morris-Butler House, Indianapolis IN

House of Roses, Senator Wilson Home, Deadwood SD

The Hudson River Museum of Westchester, Yonkers NY

Huguenot Historical Society of New Paltz Galleries, New Paltz NY

The Huntington Library, Art Collections & Botanical Gardens, San Marino CA
Illinois Historic Preservation Agency, Bishop Hill State Historic Site, Bishop Hill IL
Institute for Contemporary Art, Project Studio One (P S 1), Long Island City NY
Institute of the Great Plains, Museum of the Great Plains, Lawton OK
Jefferson County Open Space, Hiwan Homestead Museum, Evergreen CO
Jersey City Museum, Jersey City NJ
The Jewish Museum, New York NY
Johns Hopkins University, Homewood House Museum, Baltimore MD
Kansas City Art Institute, Kemper Museum of Contemporary Art & Design, Kansas City MO
Kemerer Museum of Decorative Arts, Bethlehem PA
Kern County Museum, Bakersfield CA
Landmark Society of Western New York, Inc, Rochester NY
LeSueur County Historical Museum, Chapter One, Elysian MN
Lockwood-Mathews Mansion Museum, Norwalk CT
Longfellow-Evangeline State Commemorative Area, Saint Martinville LA
Louisa May Alcott Memorial Association, Orchard House, Concord MA
Louisiana State University, School of Art Gallery, Baton Rouge LA
Maine Historical Society, Wadsworth-Longfellow House, Portland ME
Maryland Hall for the Creative Arts, Cardinal Gallery, Annapolis MD
Maryland Historical Society, Museum of Maryland History, Baltimore MD
Massachusetts Institute of Technology, MIT Museum, Cambridge MA
Mattatuck Historical Society, Mattatuck Museum, Waterbury CT
Milwaukee Art Museum, Milwaukee WI
Mint Museum of Art, Charlotte NC
Mission San Luis Rey de Francia, Mission San Luis Rey Museum, San Luis Rey CA
Mississippi Department of Archives & History, Old Capitol Museum, Jackson MS
Mississippi River Museum at Mud-Island, Memphis TN
Arthur Roy Mitchell Memorial Inc, Museum of Western Art, Trinidad CO
Mobile Museum of Art, Mobile AL
Moore College of Art & Design, Goldie Paley Gallery, Philadelphia PA
Morris-Jumel Mansion, Inc, New York NY
Museo De Las Americas, Denver CO
The Museum of Arts & Sciences Inc, Daytona Beach FL
Museum of Contemporary Art, North Miami FL
Museum of Contemporary Art, San Diego-Downtown, San Diego CA
Museum of Modern Art, New York NY
Museum of the City of New York, New York NY
The Museums at Stony Brook, Stony Brook NY
Muttart Public Art Gallery, Calgary AB
National Park Service, Weir Farm National Historic Site, Wilton CT
The National Park Service, United States Department of the Interior, The Statue of Liberty National Monument, New York NY
National Society of the Colonial Dames, Wilton House Museum, Richmond VA
Naval Historical Center, The Navy Museum, Washington DC
Nebraska State Capitol, Lincoln NE
Norfolk Historical Society Inc, Museum, Norfolk CT
Old Jail Art Center, Albany TX
Old York Historical Society, Old Gaol Museum, York ME
Page-Walker Arts & History Center, Cary NC
Palm Springs Desert Museum, Palm Springs CA
Panhandle-Plains Historical Society Museum, Canyon TX
Peabody Essex Museum, Salem MA
Pennsylvania Academy of the Fine Arts, Museum of American Art, Philadelphia PA

Pennsylvania Historical & Museum Commission, Railroad Musuem of Pennsylvania, Harrisburg PA
Phelps County Historical Society, Phelps County Museum, Holdrege NE
Philadelphia Museum of Art, Philadelphia PA
Pioneer Town, Pioneer Museum of Western Art, Wimberley TX
Plumas County Museum, Quincy CA
Pope County Historical Society, Pope County Museum, Glenwood MN
Purdue University Galleries, West Lafayette IN
Riley County Historical Society, Riley County Historical Museum, Manhattan KS
Riverside Municipal Museum, Riverside CA
Millicent Rogers Museum of Northern New Mexico, Taos NM
Ross Memorial Museum, Saint Andrews NB
Royal Arts Foundation, Belcourt Castle, Newport RI
Royal Ontario Museum, Toronto ON
San Francisco Museum of Modern Art, San Francisco CA
Santarella, Tyringham's Gingerbread House, Tyringham MA
Shaker Village of Pleasant Hill, Harrodsburg KY
Abigail Adams Smith Museum, New York NY
Southern Alleghenies Museum of Art, Southern Alleghenies Museum of Art at Johnstown, Loretto PA
South Street Seaport Museum, New York NY
Springfield Art & Historical Society, Miller Art Center, Springfield VT
State Historical Society of Wisconsin, State Historical Museum, Madison WI
State University of New York College at Fredonia, M C Rockefeller Arts Center Gallery, Fredonia NY
Stratford Historical Society, Katherine Mitchel Museum, Stratford CT
Tallahassee Museum of History & Natural Science, Tallahassee FL
The Temple-Tifereth Israel, The Temple Museum of Religious Art, Beachwood OH
Tryon Palace Historic Sites & Gardens, New Bern NC
Tulane University, University Art Collection, New Orleans LA
Tulane University, Dept Art Newcomb Col Art Galleries, New Orleans LA
Turtle Mountain Chippewa Historical Society, Turtle Mountain Heritage Center, Belcourt ND
United States Capitol, Architect of the Capitol, Washington DC
University of Alabama at Birmingham, Visual Arts Gallery, Birmingham AL
University of British Columbia, Museum of Anthropology, Vancouver BC
University of California, Berkeley Art Museum & Pacific Film Archive, Berkeley CA
University of California, Santa Barbara, University Art Museum, Santa Barbara CA
University of Chicago, Oriental Institute Museum, Chicago IL
University of Manitoba, Faculty of Architecture Exhibition Centre, Winnipeg MB
University of Memphis, Art Museum, Memphis TN
University of Rhode Island, Fine Arts Center Galleries, Kingston RI
University of Victoria, Maltwood Art Museum and Gallery, Victoria BC
Vassar College, The Frances Lehman Loeb Art Center, Poughkeepsie NY
Vesterheim Norwegian-American Museum, Decorah IA
Wade House & Wesley W Jung Carriage Museum, Historic House & Carriage Museum, Greenbush WI
West Baton Rouge Historical Association, Museum, Port Allen LA
Westover, Charles City VA
White House, Washington DC
Willard House & Clock Museum, Inc, North Grafton MA
Kemper & Leila Williams Foundation, New Orleans LA
Woodrow Wilson House, Washington DC
Wistariahurst Museum, Holyoke MA

Woodlawn Plantation, Mount Vernon VA
Woodmere Art Museum, Philadelphia PA
Frank Lloyd Wright Pope-Leighey House, Mount Vernon VA
Yale University, Yale Center for British Art, New Haven CT
York Institute Museum, Saco ME

ASIAN ART

Academy of the New Church, Glencairn Museum, Bryn Athyn PA
Arnot Art Museum, Elmira NY
Art Complex Museum, Duxbury MA
Art Gallery of Greater Victoria, Victoria BC
The Art Institute of Chicago, Chicago IL
ArtSpace-Lima, Lima OH
Asian Art Museum of San Francisco, Avery Brundage Collection, San Francisco CA
The Asia Society Galleries, New York NY
Barnes Foundation, Merion PA
Beloit College, Wright Museum of Art, Beloit WI
Berea College, Doris Ulmann Galleries, Berea KY
Birmingham Museum of Art, Birmingham AL
Bowdoin College, Museum of Art, Brunswick ME
Bower's Museum, Santa Ana CA
Brevard Museum of Art & Science, Melbourne FL
Brigham Young University, Museum of Art, Provo UT
The Buffalo Fine Arts Academy, Albright-Knox Art Gallery, Buffalo NY
California College of Arts & Crafts, Steven Oliver Art Center, Oakland CA
California State University Stanislaus, University Art Gallery, Turlock CA
Capital University, Schumacher Gallery, Columbus OH
Center for Puppetry Arts, Atlanta GA
Billie Trimble Chandler Arts Foundation, Asian Cultures Museum & Educational Center, Corpus Christi TX
Chicago Department of Cultural Affairs, Chicago Cultural Center, Chicago IL
China Institute in America, China Institute Gallery, New York NY
Cincinnati Institute of Fine Arts, Taft Museum, Cincinnati OH
Cincinnati Museum Association, Cincinnati Art Museum, Cincinnati OH
College of William & Mary, Joseph & Margaret Muscarelle Museum of Art, Williamsburg VA
Columbus Museum, Columbus GA
Concordia Historical Institute, Saint Louis MO
Cornell University, Herbert F Johnson Museum of Art, Ithaca NY
Craft & Folk Art Museum, Los Angeles CA
The Currier Gallery of Art, Manchester NH
C W Post Campus of Long Island University, Hillwood Art Museum, Brookville NY
Davidson College Visual Arts Center, William H Van Every Jr & Edward M Smith Galleries, Davidson NC
Denison University, Art Gallery, Granville OH
Detroit Institute of Arts, Detroit MI
Dickinson College, Trout Gallery, Carlisle PA
Duke University Museum of Art, Durham NC
Elmhurst Art Museum, Elmhurst IL
Emory University, Michael C Carlos Museum, Atlanta GA
Erie Art Museum, Erie PA
The First National Bank of Chicago, Art Collection, Chicago IL
Fitton Center For Creative Arts, Hamilton OH
Florida State University Foundation - Central Florida Community College Foundation, The Appleton Museum of Art, Ocala FL
Edsel & Eleanor Ford House, Grosse Pointe Shores MI
Freeport Arts Center, Freeport IL
Freer Gallery of Art Gallery, Arthur M Sackler Gallery, Washington DC
Galleries of the Claremont Colleges, Claremont CA
Hammond Museum & Japanese Stroll Garden, Cross-Cultural Center, North Salem NY
Hampton University, University Museum, Hampton VA
Harvard University, Arthur M Sackler Museum, Cambridge MA

Headley-Whitney Museum, Lexington KY
Honolulu Academy of Arts, Honolulu HI
Indiana University, Art Museum, Bloomington IN
The Interchurch Center, Galleries at the
    Interchurch Center, New York NY
Jacksonville University, Alexander Brest Museum &
    Gallery, Jacksonville FL
James Madison University, Sawhill Gallery,
    Harrisonburg VA
Kelowna Museum, Kelowna BC
Kimbell Art Foundation, Kimbell Art Museum,
    Fort Worth TX
Lizzardo Museum of Lapidary Art, Elmhurst IL
Los Angeles County Museum of Art, Los Angeles
    CA
McMaster University, Museum of Art, Hamilton
    ON
Mary Washington College, Ridderhof Martin
    Gallery, Fredericksburg VA
Memphis Brooks Museum of Art, Memphis TN
Michigan State University, Kresge Art Museum,
    East Lansing MI
Minnesota Museum of American Art, Saint Paul
    MN
Mint Museum of Art, Charlotte NC
Mobile Museum of Art, Mobile AL
Monterey Museum of Art Association, Monterey
    CA
Morris Museum, Morristown NJ
Mount Holyoke College, Art Museum, South
    Hadley MA
The Museum at Drexel University, Philadelphia PA
National Gallery of Canada, Ottawa ON
National Infantry Museum, Fort Benning GA
National Museum of Women in the Arts,
    Washington DC
Naval Historical Center, The Navy Museum,
    Washington DC
Nelson-Atkins Museum of Art, Kansas City MO
Newark Museum Association, The Newark
    Museum, Newark NJ
New York University, Grey Art Gallery & Study
    Center, New York NY
Northern Illinois University, NIU Art Museum, De
    Kalb IL
Oklahoma City Art Museum, Oklahoma City OK
Pacific - Asia Museum, Pasadena CA
Palm Beach County Parks & Recreation
    Department, Morikami Museum & Japanese
    Gardens, Delray Beach FL
Peabody Essex Museum, Salem MA
Pennsylvania State University, Palmer Museum of
    Art, University Park PA
Philadelphia Museum of Art, Philadelphia PA
Philbrook Museum of Art, Tulsa OK
Phoenix Art Museum, Phoenix AZ
Polk Museum of Art, Lakeland FL
Port Authority of New York & New Jersey, Art
    Collection, New York NY
Portland Art Museum, Portland OR
Principia College, School of Nations Museum,
    Elsah IL
Purdue University Galleries, West Lafayette IN
Putnam Museum of History & Natural Science,
    Davenport IA
Rollins College, George D & Harriet W Cornell
    Fine Arts Museum, Winter Park FL
Royal Arts Foundation, Belcourt Castle, Newport
    RI
Royal Ontario Museum, Toronto ON
San Antonio Museum of Art, San Antonio TX
Santa Barbara Museum of Art, Santa Barbara CA
Seattle Art Museum, Seattle WA
Slater-Norton Corporation, Slater Memorial
    Museum & Converse Art Gallery, Norwich CT
Society of the Cincinnati, Museum & Library at
    Anderson House, Washington DC
Southern Alleghenies Museum of Art, Southern
    Alleghenies Museum of Art at Johnstown,
    Loretto PA
Springfield Art Museum, Springfield MO
State University of New York at New Paltz,
    College Art Gallery, New Paltz NY
Sheldon Swope Art Museum, Terre Haute IN
Tacoma Art Museum, Tacoma WA
Towson State University, Asian Arts Center,
    Towson MD

University of Akron, University Galleries, Akron
    OH
University of Alabama at Birmingham, Visual Arts
    Gallery, Birmingham AL
University of British Columbia, Museum of
    Anthropology, Vancouver BC
University of California, Richard L Nelson Gallery
    & Fine Arts Collection, Davis CA
University of California, Berkeley Art Museum &
    Pacific Film Archive, Berkeley CA
University of California, Los Angeles, Fowler
    Museum of Cultural History, Los Angeles CA
University of Cincinnati, DAAP Galleries-College
    of Design Architecture, Art & Planning,
    Cincinnati OH
University of Colorado at Colorado Springs, Gallery
    of Contemporary Art, Colorado Springs CO
University of Florida, Samuel P Harn Museum of
    Art, Gainesville FL
University of Iowa, Museum of Art, Iowa City IA
University of Kansas, Spencer Museum of Art,
    Lawrence KS
University of Michigan, Museum of Art, Ann Arbor
    MI
University of Mississippi, University Museums,
    Oxford MS
University of Missouri, Museum of Art &
    Archaeology, Columbia MO
University of North Carolina at Greensboro,
    Weatherspoon Art Gallery, Greensboro NC
University of Oregon, Museum of Art, Eugene OR
University of San Diego, Founders' Gallery, San
    Diego CA
University of Victoria, Maltwood Art Museum and
    Gallery, Victoria BC
University of Virginia, Bayly Art Museum,
    Charlottesville VA
Vancouver Museum Commission, Vancouver
    Museum, Vancouver BC
Virginia Museum of Fine Arts, Richmond VA
Washburn University, Mulvane Art Museum,
    Topeka KS
Williams College, Museum of Art, Williamstown
    MA
Wing Luke Asian Museum, Seattle WA
Woodmere Art Museum, Philadelphia PA

BAROQUE ART

Allentown Art Museum, Allentown PA
Art Gallery of Hamilton, Hamilton ON
The Art Institute of Chicago, Chicago IL
Bass Museum of Art, Miami Beach FL
Beloit College, Wright Museum of Art, Beloit WI
The Buffalo Fine Arts Academy, Albright-Knox Art
    Gallery, Buffalo NY
College of William & Mary, Joseph & Margaret
    Muscarelle Museum of Art, Williamsburg VA
Columbia Museum of Art, Columbia Art
    Association, Columbia SC
The Currier Gallery of Art, Manchester NH
Denison University, Art Gallery, Granville OH
Detroit Institute of Arts, Detroit MI
Dickinson College, Trout Gallery, Carlisle PA
El Paso Museum of Art, El Paso TX
Fairfield University, Thomas J Walsh Art Gallery,
    Fairfield CT
Fine Arts Museums of San Francisco, M H de
    Young Memorial Museum & California Palace
    of the Legion of Honor, San Francisco CA
Guilford College, Art Gallery, Greensboro NC
Hartwick College, Foreman Gallery, Oneonta NY
Hispanic Society of America, Museum, New York
    NY
The Huntington Library, Art Collections &
    Botanical Gardens, San Marino CA
Indiana University, Art Museum, Bloomington IN
Knights of Columbus Supreme Council,
    Headquarters Museum, New Haven CT
Michigan State University, Kresge Art Museum,
    East Lansing MI
Mint Museum of Art, Charlotte NC
Mobile Museum of Art, Mobile AL
Museo De Las Americas, Denver CO
The Museum of Arts & Sciences Inc, Daytona
    Beach FL
National Gallery of Canada, Ottawa ON
Nelson-Atkins Museum of Art, Kansas City MO

Phoenix Art Museum, Phoenix AZ
Purdue University Galleries, West Lafayette IN
Rollins College, George D & Harriet W Cornell
    Fine Arts Museum, Winter Park FL
San Diego Museum of Art, San Diego CA
Society of the Cincinnati, Museum & Library at
    Anderson House, Washington DC
Southern Methodist University, Meadows Museum,
    Dallas TX
Stanford University, Museum of Art, Stanford CA
State Art Museum of Florida, John & Mable
    Ringling Museum of Art, Sarasota FL
University of Kansas, Spencer Museum of Art,
    Lawrence KS
University of Miami, Lowe Art Museum, Coral
    Gables FL
University of Notre Dame, Snite Museum of Art,
    Notre Dame IN
University of Texas at Austin, Archer M
    Huntington Art Gallery, Austin TX
University of Virginia, Bayly Art Museum,
    Charlottesville VA
Wadsworth Atheneum, Hartford CT
Williams College, Museum of Art, Williamstown
    MA

BOOKPLATES & BINDINGS

Agecroft Association, Museum, Richmond VA
Beloit College, Wright Museum of Art, Beloit WI
Center for Book Arts, New York NY
Cooper-Hewitt, National Design Museum, New
    York NY
The Currier Gallery of Art, Manchester NH
C W Post Campus of Long Island University,
    Hillwood Art Museum, Brookville NY
Farmington Village Green & Library Association,
    Stanley-Whitman House, Farmington CT
The First National Bank of Chicago, Art Collection,
    Chicago IL
Fort Ticonderoga Association, Ticonderoga NY
Hebrew Union College-Jewish Institute of Religion,
    New York NY
Hispanic Society of America, Museum, New York
    NY
Huronia Museum, Midland ON
The Interchurch Center, Galleries at the
    Interchurch Center, New York NY
Johns Hopkins University, Evergreen House,
    Baltimore MD
La Casa del Libro Museum, San Juan PR
Lafayette Natural History Museum, Planetarium &
    Nature Station, Lafayette LA
Judah L Magnes Museum, Berkeley CA
Mankato State University, Conkling Gallery Art
    Dept, Mankato MN
The Mariners' Museum, Newport News VA
Maryland Hall for the Creative Arts, Cardinal
    Gallery, Annapolis MD
National Gallery of Canada, Ottawa ON
Natural History Museum of Los Angeles County,
    Los Angeles CA
Panhandle-Plains Historical Society Museum,
    Canyon TX
Lauren Rogers Museum of Art, Laurel MS
South Carolina Artisans Center, Walterboro SC
Yale University, Yale Center for British Art, New
    Haven CT

BRONZES

African Art Museum of Maryland, Columbia MD
Albuquerque Museum of Art & History,
    Albuquerque NM
Allentown Art Museum, Allentown PA
Appaloosa Museum, Inc, Moscow ID
Arnot Art Museum, Elmira NY
The Art Institute of Chicago, Chicago IL
Art Museum of Missoula, Missoula MT
ArtSpace-Lima, Lima OH
Asian Art Museum of San Francisco, Avery
    Brundage Collection, San Francisco CA
Atlanta Museum, Atlanta GA
Baltimore Museum of Art, Baltimore MD
Blanden Memorial Art Museum, Fort Dodge IA
Roy Boyd Gallery, Chicago IL
Brigham Young University, Museum of Art, Provo
    UT

Brookgreen Gardens, Murrells Inlet SC
Canajoharie Library & Art Gallery, Canajoharie NY
Carson County Square House Museum, Panhandle TX
Billie Trimble Chandler Arts Foundation, Asian Cultures Museum & Educational Center, Corpus Christi TX
Cincinnati Museum Association, Cincinnati Art Museum, Cincinnati OH
College of William & Mary, Joseph & Margaret Muscarelle Museum of Art, Williamsburg VA
The College of Wooster, Art Museum, Wooster OH
Concordia University Wisconsin, Fine Art Gallery, Mequon WI
Corcoran Gallery of Art, Washington DC
Coutts Memorial Museum of Art, Inc, El Dorado KS
C W Post Campus of Long Island University, Hillwood Art Museum, Brookville NY
Dahesh Museum, New York NY
Danville Museum of Fine Arts & History, Danville VA
Dartmouth College, Hood Museum of Art, Hanover NH
Eiteljorg Museum of American Indians & Western Art, Indianapolis IN
Ellen Noel Art Museum of the Permian Basin, Odessa TX
Erie Art Museum, Erie PA
Fine Arts Museums of San Francisco, M H de Young Memorial Museum & California Palace of the Legion of Honor, San Francisco CA
The First National Bank of Chicago, Art Collection, Chicago IL
Five Civilized Tribes Museum, Muskogee OK
Florida State University Foundation - Central Florida Community College Foundation, The Appleton Museum of Art, Ocala FL
Franklin Mint Museum, Franklin Center PA
Freer Gallery of Art Gallery, Arthur M Sackler Gallery, Washington DC
The Frick Art & Historical Center, Frick Art Museum, Pittsburgh PA
Frick Collection, New York NY
Gallery 53, Cooperstown NY
Gallery One, Ellensburg WA
Gonzaga University, Jundt Art Museum, Ad Art Gallery, Spokane WA
Harness Racing & Hall of Fame, Goshen NY
Harvard University, William Hayes Fogg Art Museum, Cambridge MA
Harvard University, Arthur M Sackler Museum, Cambridge MA
Headquarters Fort Monroe, Dept of Army, Casemate Museum, Fort Monroe VA
Heard Museum, Phoenix AZ
Hebrew Union College-Jewish Institute of Religion, New York NY
Hermitage Foundation Museum, Norfolk VA
Honolulu Academy of Arts, Honolulu HI
The Huntington Library, Art Collections & Botanical Gardens, San Marino CA
Indianapolis Museum of Art, Indianapolis IN
Indiana University, Art Museum, Bloomington IN
Jacksonville University, Alexander Brest Museum & Gallery, Jacksonville FL
Kelowna Museum, Kelowna BC
Kentucky Derby Museum, Louisville KY
Knoxville Museum of Art, Knoxville TN
Koshare Indian Museum, Inc, La Junta CO
Leanin' Tree Museum of Western Art, Boulder CO
Lighthouse Gallery & School of Art, Tequesta FL
Los Angeles County Museum of Natural History, William S Hart Museum, Newhall CA
Louisiana Arts & Science Center, Baton Rouge LA
Loyola University of Chicago, Martin D'Arcy Gallery of Art, Chicago IL
Judah L Magnes Museum, Berkeley CA
Maricopa County Historical Society, Desert Caballeros Western Museum, Wickenburg AZ
Maryhill Museum of Art, Goldendale WA
Maryland Art Place, Baltimore MD
Michigan State University, Kresge Art Museum, East Lansing MI
Montana State University, Museum of the Rockies, Bozeman MT
Morris Museum, Morristown NJ

Musee du Quebec, Quebec PQ
Museo De Las Americas, Denver CO
The Museum of Arts & Sciences Inc, Daytona Beach FL
National Art Museum of Sport, Indianapolis IN
National Gallery of Canada, Ottawa ON
National Hall of Fame for Famous American Indians, Anadarko OK
National Museum of Racing, National Museum of Racing & Hall of Fame, Saratoga Springs NY
National Museum of Wildlife Art, Jackson WY
National Portrait Gallery, Washington DC
National Trust for Historic Preservation, Chesterwood Museum, Glendale MA
Naval Historical Center, The Navy Museum, Washington DC
Nevada Museum Of Art, Reno NV
Norton Gallery & School of Art, Inc, Norton Museum of Art, West Palm Beach FL
Old Jail Art Center, Albany TX
Order Sons of Italy in America, Garibaldi & Meucci Museum, Staten Island NY
Owensboro Museum of Fine Art, Owensboro KY
Pacific - Asia Museum, Pasadena CA
Pennsylvania Academy of the Fine Arts, Museum of American Art, Philadelphia PA
Phelps County Historical Society, Phelps County Museum, Holdrege NE
George Phippen Memorial Foundation, Phippen Museum of Western Art, Prescott AZ
Pioneer Town, Pioneer Museum of Western Art, Wimberley TX
Princeton University, The Art Museum, Princeton NJ
Purdue University Galleries, West Lafayette IN
Queens College, City University of New York, Godwin-Ternbach Museum, Flushing NY
Frederic Remington Art Museum, Ogdensburg NY
Sid W Richardson Foundation, Collection of Western Art, Fort Worth TX
The Rockwell Museum, Corning NY
Rollins College, George D & Harriet W Cornell Fine Arts Museum, Winter Park FL
Ross Memorial Museum, Saint Andrews NB
C M Russell Museum, Great Falls MT
Saint Louis Artists' Guild, Saint Louis MO
The Saint Louis Art Museum, Saint Louis MO
Santa Barbara Museum of Art, Santa Barbara CA
Santarella, Tyringham's Gingerbread House, Tyringham MA
Society of the Cincinnati, Museum & Library at Anderson House, Washington DC
Southern Alleghenies Museum of Art, Southern Alleghenies Museum of Art at Johnstown, Loretto PA
Springville Museum of Art, Springville UT
Stanford University, Museum of Art, Stanford CA
Nelda C & H J Lutcher Stark Foundation, Stark Museum of Art, Orange TX
Syracuse University, Art Collection, Syracuse NY
Topeka & Shawnee County Public Library, Gallery of Fine Arts, Topeka KS
UMLAUF Sculpture Garden & Museum, Austin TX
United States Capitol, Architect of the Capitol, Washington DC
United States Figure Skating Association, World Figure Skating Museum & Hall of Fame, Colorado Springs CO
United States Military Academy, West Point Museum, West Point NY
University of Chicago, Oriental Institute Museum, Chicago IL
University of Cincinnati, DAAP Galleries-College of Design Architecture, Art & Planning, Cincinnati OH
University of Florida, Samuel P Harn Museum of Art, Gainesville FL
University of Kansas, Spencer Museum of Art, Lawrence KS
University of Michigan, Kelsey Museum of Archaeology, Ann Arbor MI
University of Nebraska, Lincoln, Sheldon Memorial Art Gallery & Sculpture Garden, Lincoln NE
Virginia Museum of Fine Arts, Richmond VA
Vizcaya Museum & Gardens, Miami FL
Wadsworth Atheneum, Hartford CT
Wayne Center for the Arts, Wooster OH

Westmoreland Museum of American Art, Greensburg PA

CALLIGRAPHY

Art Museum of Missoula, Missoula MT
ArtSpace-Lima, Lima OH
Asian Art Museum of San Francisco, Avery Brundage Collection, San Francisco CA
Beloit College, Wright Museum of Art, Beloit WI
Central United Methodist Church, Swords Info Plowshares Peace Center & Gallery, Detroit MI
Billie Trimble Chandler Arts Foundation, Asian Cultures Museum & Educational Center, Corpus Christi TX
Cincinnati Museum Association, Cincinnati Art Museum, Cincinnati OH
Cooper-Hewitt, National Design Museum, New York NY
Dickinson College, Trout Gallery, Carlisle PA
Dundurn Castle, Hamilton ON
Freer Gallery of Art Gallery, Arthur M Sackler Gallery, Washington DC
Guilford College, Art Gallery, Greensboro NC
Hebrew Union College-Jewish Institute of Religion, New York NY
Heritage Center of Lancaster County Museum, Lancaster PA
Hispanic Society of America, Museum, New York NY
Indiana University, Art Museum, Bloomington IN
The Interchurch Center, Galleries at the Interchurch Center, New York NY
Lighthouse Gallery & School of Art, Tequesta FL
Judah L Magnes Museum, Berkeley CA
Mint Museum of Art, Charlotte NC
Musee des Augustines de l'Hotel Dieu de Quebec, Quebec PQ
The Museum of Arts & Sciences Inc, Daytona Beach FL
National Museum of Women in the Arts, Washington DC
Naval Historical Center, The Navy Museum, Washington DC
Nelson-Atkins Museum of Art, Kansas City MO
Pacific - Asia Museum, Pasadena CA
Phoenix Art Museum, Phoenix AZ
Portland Art Museum, Portland OR
Saint John's University, Chung-Cheng Art Gallery, Jamaica NY
George Walter Vincent Smith Art Museum, Springfield MA
Southern Alleghenies Museum of Art, Southern Alleghenies Museum of Art at Johnstown, Loretto PA
State University of New York at New Paltz, College Art Gallery, New Paltz NY
The Temple-Tifereth Israel, The Temple Museum of Religious Art, Beachwood OH
University of Kansas, Spencer Museum of Art, Lawrence KS
Willard House & Clock Museum, Inc, North Grafton MA

CARPETS & RUGS

Academy of the New Church, Glencairn Museum, Bryn Athyn PA
Agecroft Association, Museum, Richmond VA
Amherst Museum, Amherst NY
Anchorage Museum of History & Art, Anchorage AK
Arkansas Territorial Restoration, Little Rock AR
Asian Art Museum of San Francisco, Avery Brundage Collection, San Francisco CA
Barnes Foundation, Merion PA
Brigham Young University, Museum of Art, Provo UT
Carson County Square House Museum, Panhandle TX
Kit Carson Historic Museums, Ernest Blumenschein Home & Studio, Taos NM
Chattahoochee Valley Art Museum, LaGrange GA
Chicago Department of Cultural Affairs, Chicago Cultural Center, Chicago IL
Clinton County Historical Association, Clinton County Historical Museum, Plattsburgh NY
The College of Wooster, Art Museum, Wooster OH

Colorado Historical Society, Colorado History Museum, Denver CO

Cooper-Hewitt, National Design Museum, New York NY

County of Henrico, Meadow Farm Museum, Glen Allen VA

Coutts Memorial Museum of Art, Inc, El Dorado KS

Craigdarroch Castle Historical Museum Society, Victoria BC

Crow Wing County Historical Society, Brainerd MN

DAR Museum, National Society Daughters of the American Revolution, Washington DC

Dundurn Castle, Hamilton ON

Ephraim McDowell-Cambus-Kenneth Foundation, McDowell House & Apothecary Shop, Danville KY

Evanston Historical Society, Charles Gates Dawes House, Evanston IL

Fetherston Foundation, Packwood House Museum, Lewisburg PA

Fine Arts Museums of San Francisco, M H de Young Memorial Museum & California Palace of the Legion of Honor, San Francisco CA

The First National Bank of Chicago, Art Collection, Chicago IL

Florida State University Foundation - Central Florida Community College Foundation, The Appleton Museum of Art, Ocala FL

Edsel & Eleanor Ford House, Grosse Pointe Shores MI

General Board of Discipleship, The United Methodist Church, The Upper Room Chapel & Museum, Nashville TN

Hermitage Foundation Museum, Norfolk VA

Hispanic Society of America, Museum, New York NY

Historic Landmarks Foundation of Indiana, Morris-Butler House, Indianapolis IN

Huguenot Historical Society of New Paltz Galleries, New Paltz NY

The Huntington Library, Art Collections & Botanical Gardens, San Marino CA

Huntington Museum of Art, Huntington WV

Imperial Calcasieu Museum, Gibson-Barham Gallery, Lake Charles LA

Indiana University, Art Museum, Bloomington IN

Institute of American Indian Arts Museum, Santa Fe NM

Iowa State Education Association, Salisbury House, Des Moines IA

Jacksonville University, Alexander Brest Museum & Gallery, Jacksonville FL

The Jewish Museum, New York NY

Johns Hopkins University, Evergreen House, Baltimore MD

Kemerer Museum of Decorative Arts, Bethlehem PA

Koshare Indian Museum, Inc, La Junta CO

Lac du Flambeau Band of Lake Superior Chippewa Indians, George W Brown Jr Ojibwe Museum & Cultural Center, Lac du Flambeau WI

Leroy Historical Society, LeRoy NY

LeSueur County Historical Museum, Chapter One, Elysian MN

Los Angeles County Museum of Natural History, William S Hart Museum, Newhall CA

Judah L Magnes Museum, Berkeley CA

Marquette University, Haggerty Museum of Art, Milwaukee WI

Mississippi River Museum at Mud-Island, Memphis TN

Arthur Roy Mitchell Memorial Inc, Museum of Western Art, Trinidad CO

Montana State University, Museum of the Rockies, Bozeman MT

Morris Museum, Morristown NJ

Munson-Williams-Proctor Institute, Museum of Art, Utica NY

Museum of Arts & History, Port Huron MI

Muttart Public Art Gallery, Calgary AB

National Infantry Museum, Fort Benning GA

Nelson-Atkins Museum of Art, Kansas City MO

New Visions Gallery, Inc, Marshfield WI

North Carolina State University, Visual Arts Center, Raleigh NC

The Ohio Historical Society, Inc, Campus Martius Museum & Ohio River Museum, Marietta OH

Old Jail Art Center, Albany TX

Panhandle-Plains Historical Society Museum, Canyon TX

Pasadena Historical Museum, Pasadena CA

Phelps County Historical Society, Phelps County Museum, Holdrege NE

Plumas County Museum, Quincy CA

Polk Museum of Art, Lakeland FL

Portland Art Museum, Portland OR

Marjorie Merriweather Post Foundation of DC, Hillwood Museum, Washington DC

Putnam Museum of History & Natural Science, Davenport IA

Rensselaer County Historical Society, Hart-Cluett Mansion, 1827, Troy NY

Rhode Island Historical Society, John Brown House, Providence RI

Riverside Municipal Museum, Riverside CA

The Rosenbach Museum & Library, Philadelphia PA

Ross Memorial Museum, Saint Andrews NB

Abigail Adams Smith Museum, New York NY

George Walter Vincent Smith Art Museum, Springfield MA

Society of the Cincinnati, Museum & Library at Anderson House, Washington DC

South Carolina Artisans Center, Walterboro SC

South Dakota State University, South Dakota Art Museum, Brookings SD

Southern Alleghenies Museum of Art, Southern Alleghenies Museum of Art at Johnstown, Loretto PA

Southern Illinois University, University Museum, Carbondale IL

Nelda C & H J Lutcher Stark Foundation, Stark Museum of Art, Orange TX

State Historical Society of Wisconsin, State Historical Museum, Madison WI

Swedish American Museum Association of Chicago, Chicago IL

Textile Museum, Washington DC

Topeka & Shawnee County Public Library, Gallery of Fine Arts, Topeka KS

Tryon Palace Historic Sites & Gardens, New Bern NC

US Department of State, Diplomatic Reception Rooms, Washington DC

University of Kansas, Spencer Museum of Art, Lawrence KS

University of Pennsylvania, Arthur Ross Gallery, Philadelphia PA

Vesterheim Norwegian-American Museum, Decorah IA

Vizcaya Museum & Gardens, Miami FL

Westmoreland Museum of American Art, Greensburg PA

Wheelwright Museum of the American Indian, Santa Fe NM

Willard House & Clock Museum, Inc, North Grafton MA

Woodlawn Plantation, Mount Vernon VA

Woodmere Art Museum, Philadelphia PA

CARTOONS

American Kennel Club, Museum of the Dog, Saint Louis MO

American Museum of the Moving Image, Astoria NY

ArtSpace-Lima, Lima OH

Leo Baeck Institute, New York NY

Brigham Young University, Museum of Art, Provo UT

Cartoon Art Museum, San Francisco CA

Central United Methodist Church, Swords Info Plowshares Peace Center & Gallery, Detroit MI

Cooper-Hewitt, National Design Museum, New York NY

Denison University, Art Gallery, Granville OH

Erie Art Museum, Erie PA

The First National Bank of Chicago, Art Collection, Chicago IL

Fort George G Meade Museum, Fort Meade MD

Hartwick College, Foreman Gallery, Oneonta NY

Historical Society of Pennsylvania, Philadelphia PA

International Museum of Cartoon Art, Boca Raton FL

International Museum of Cartoon Art, Montreal PQ

The Jewish Museum, New York NY

Kansas State Historical Society, Kansas Museum of History, Topeka KS

Marylhurst College, The Art Gym, Marylhurst OR

Montana State University, Museum of the Rockies, Bozeman MT

Museum of Arts & History, Port Huron MI

Museum of the City of New York, New York NY

National Art Museum of Sport, Indianapolis IN

National Portrait Gallery, Washington DC

Naval Historical Center, The Navy Museum, Washington DC

Panhandle-Plains Historical Society Museum, Canyon TX

George Phippen Memorial Foundation, Phippen Museum of Western Art, Prescott AZ

Prairie Art Gallery, Grande Prairie AB

Rollins College, George D & Harriet W Cornell Fine Arts Museum, Winter Park FL

C M Russell Museum, Great Falls MT

Saint Louis Artists' Guild, Saint Louis MO

School of Visual Arts, Visual Arts Museum, New York NY

State Historical Society of Missouri, Columbia MO

State Historical Society of Wisconsin, State Historical Museum, Madison WI

Syracuse University, Art Collection, Syracuse NY

United States Military Academy, West Point Museum, West Point NY

CERAMICS

Agecroft Association, Museum, Richmond VA

Alabama Department of Archives & History, Museum Galleries, Montgomery AL

Albany Institute of History & Art, Albany NY

Albion College, Bobbitt Visual Arts Center, Albion MI

Allentown Art Museum, Allentown PA

Charles Allis Art Museum, Milwaukee WI

The American Ceramic Society, Ross C Purdy Museum of Ceramics, Westerville OH

American Kennel Club, Museum of the Dog, Saint Louis MO

American Swedish Institute, Minneapolis MN

Walter Anderson Museum of Art, Ocean Springs MS

Arizona State University, ASU Art Museum, Tempe AZ

Arkansas Territorial Restoration, Little Rock AR

Arnot Art Museum, Elmira NY

Art Gallery of Nova Scotia, Halifax NS

The Art Institute of Chicago, Chicago IL

Art Museum of Missoula, Missoula MT

ArtSpace-Lima, Lima OH

Asbury College, Student Center Gallery, Wilmore KY

Asian Art Museum of San Francisco, Avery Brundage Collection, San Francisco CA

Association for the Preservation of Virginia Antiquities, John Marshall House, Richmond VA

Baldwin Historical Society Museum, Baldwin NY

Baltimore Museum of Art, Baltimore MD

Barnes Foundation, Merion PA

Bass Museum of Art, Miami Beach FL

Bennington Museum, Bennington Museum, Bennington VT

Berea College, Doris Ulmann Galleries, Berea KY

Berkshire Museum, Pittsfield MA

Jesse Besser Museum, Alpena MI

Bethany College, Mingenback Art Center, Lindsborg KS

Blanden Memorial Art Museum, Fort Dodge IA

The Bostonian Society, Old State House Museum, Boston MA

Bowdoin College, Museum of Art, Brunswick ME

Brandeis University, Rose Art Museum, Waltham MA

Brigham City Museum-Gallery, Brigham City UT

Brigham Young University, Museum of Art, Provo UT

Bradford Brinton Memorial Museum & Historic Ranch, Big Horn WY

Butler Institute of American Art, Art Museum, Youngstown OH

California College of Arts & Crafts, Steven Oliver Art Center, Oakland CA

Calvin College, Center Art Gallery, Grand Rapids MI

The Canadian Craft Museum, Vancouver BC

Canadian Museum of Nature, Musee Canadien de la Nature, Ottawa ON

Kit Carson Historic Museums, Ernest Blumenschein Home & Studio, Taos NM

Central United Methodist Church, Swords Info Plowshares Peace Center & Gallery, Detroit MI

Charleston Museum, Charleston SC

Chattahoochee Valley Art Museum, LaGrange GA

Chicago Department of Cultural Affairs, Chicago Cultural Center, Chicago IL

CIGNA Corporation, CIGNA Museum & Art Collection, Philadelphia PA

Cincinnati Museum Association, Cincinnati Art Museum, Cincinnati OH

City of Atlanta, Southeast Arts Center, Atlanta GA

City of Austin Parks & Recreation, O Henry Museum, Austin TX

Clay Studio, Philadelphia PA

Cleveland Museum of Art, Cleveland OH

Cleveland State University, Art Gallery, Cleveland OH

Clinton County Historical Association, Clinton County Historical Museum, Plattsburgh NY

College of Saint Benedict, Art Gallery, Saint Joseph MN

College of William & Mary, Joseph & Margaret Muscarelle Museum of Art, Williamsburg VA

The College of Wooster, Art Museum, Wooster OH

Colorado Historical Society, Colorado History Museum, Denver CO

Columbus Museum of Art, Columbus OH

Community Fine Arts Center, Halseth Gallery, Rock Springs WY

Concordia College, Marx Hausen Art Gallery, Seward NE

Cooper-Hewitt, National Design Museum, New York NY

Cornwall Gallery Society, Regional Art Gallery, Cornwall ON

County of Henrico, Meadow Farm Museum, Glen Allen VA

Coutts Memorial Museum of Art, Inc, El Dorado KS

Craigdarroch Castle Historical Museum Society, Victoria BC

Cranbrook Art Museum, Bloomfield Hills MI

Creighton University, Fine Arts Gallery, Omaha NE

C W Post Campus of Long Island University, Hillwood Art Museum, Brookville NY

DAR Museum, National Society Daughters of the American Revolution, Washington DC

Dartmouth Heritage Museum, Dartmouth NS

Davidson College Visual Arts Center, William H Van Every Jr & Edward M Smith Galleries, Davidson NC

Denison University, Art Gallery, Granville OH

Dickinson College, Trout Gallery, Carlisle PA

East Baton Rouge Parks & Recreation Commission, Baton Rouge Gallery Inc, Baton Rouge LA

Edgecombe County Cultural Arts Council, Inc, Blount-Bridgers House, Hobson Pittman Memorial Gallery, Tarboro NC

Ellen Noel Art Museum of the Permian Basin, Odessa TX

Elmhurst Art Museum, Elmhurst IL

Emory University, Michael C Carlos Museum, Atlanta GA

Erie Art Museum, Erie PA

Wharton Esherick Museum, Paoli PA

Evanston Historical Society, Charles Gates Dawes House, Evanston IL

Everson Museum of Art, Syracuse NY

Farmington Village Green & Library Association, Stanley-Whitman House, Farmington CT

Fine Arts Museums of San Francisco, M H de Young Memorial Museum & California Palace of the Legion of Honor, San Francisco CA

The First National Bank of Chicago, Art Collection, Chicago IL

Florence Museum of Art, Science & History, Florence SC

Florida Gulf Coast Art Center, Inc, Belleair FL

Fondo del Sol, Visual Art & Media Center, Washington DC

Fort Worth Art Association, Modern Art Museum of Fort Worth, Fort Worth TX

Freer Gallery of Art Gallery, Arthur M Sackler Gallery, Washington DC

Fuller Museum of Art, Brockton MA

Galleries of the Claremont Colleges, Claremont CA

Gallery One, Ellensburg WA

George R Gardiner Museum of Ceramic Art, Toronto ON

Glanmore, Hastings County Museum, Belleville ON

Gonzaga University, Jundt Art Museum, Ad Art Gallery, Spokane WA

Goucher College, Rosenberg Gallery, Baltimore MD

Grand Rapids Art Museum, Grand Rapids MI

Greater Lafayette Museum of Art, Lafayette IN

Greenwood Museum, Greenwood SC

Gunston Hall Plantation, Mason Neck VA

Harrison County Historical Museum, Marshall TX

Nora Eccles Harrison Museum of Art, Logan UT

Harvard University, William Hayes Fogg Art Museum, Cambridge MA

Harvard University, Arthur M Sackler Museum, Cambridge MA

Haystack Mountain School of Crafts, Gallery, Deer Isle ME

Headley-Whitney Museum, Lexington KY

Heard Museum, Phoenix AZ

Hebrew Union College-Jewish Institute of Religion, New York NY

Hispanic Society of America, Museum, New York NY

Historical Society of Bloomfield, Bloomfield NJ

Historic Cherry Hill, Albany NY

Historic Deerfield, Inc, Deerfield MA

Historic Landmarks Foundation of Indiana, Morris-Butler House, Indianapolis IN

Honolulu Academy of Arts, Honolulu HI

House of Roses, Senator Wilson Home, Deadwood SD

Huguenot Historical Society of New Paltz Galleries, New Paltz NY

The Huntington Library, Art Collections & Botanical Gardens, San Marino CA

Huntington Museum of Art, Huntington WV

Huronia Museum, Midland ON

Hutchinson Art Association, Hutchinson Art Center, Hutchinson KS

Hyde Park Art Center, Chicago IL

Idaho Historical Museum, Boise ID

Imperial Calcasieu Museum, Gibson-Barham Gallery, Lake Charles LA

Indianapolis Museum of Art, Indianapolis IN

Indiana University, Art Museum, Bloomington IN

Institute of American Indian Arts Museum, Santa Fe NM

The Interchurch Center, Galleries at the Interchurch Center, New York NY

Iowa State University, Brunnier Art Museum, Ames IA

Jersey City Museum, Jersey City NJ

The Jewish Museum, New York NY

Johns Hopkins University, Evergreen House, Baltimore MD

Johns Hopkins University, Homewood House Museum, Baltimore MD

Joslyn Art Museum, Omaha NE

Kansas City Art Institute, Kemper Museum of Contemporary Art & Design, Kansas City MO

Kelowna Museum, Kelowna BC

Kemerer Museum of Decorative Arts, Bethlehem PA

Maude I Kerns Art Center Galleries, Eugene OR

Kings County Historical Society and Museum, Hampton NB

Kohler Co, Art Collection, Kohler WI

Lemoyne Art Foundation, Inc, Tallahassee FL

Leroy Historical Society, LeRoy NY

LeSueur County Historical Museum, Chapter One, Elysian MN

Lighthouse Gallery & School of Art, Tequesta FL

Lightner Museum, Saint Augustine FL

Longfellow-Evangeline State Commemorative Area, Saint Martinville LA

Longue Vue House & Gardens, New Orleans LA

Longview Art Museum, Longview TX

Louisiana Arts & Science Center, Baton Rouge LA

Louisiana State University, School of Art Gallery, Baton Rouge LA

Loyola Marymount University, Laband Art Gallery, Los Angeles CA

Luther College, Fine Arts Collection, Decorah IA

Charles H MacNider Museum, Mason City IA

Judah L Magnes Museum, Berkeley CA

Maine Historical Society, Wadsworth-Longfellow House, Portland ME

The Mariners' Museum, Newport News VA

Maryland Art Place, Baltimore MD

Marylhurst College, The Art Gym, Marylhurst OR

Mattatuck Historical Society, Mattatuck Museum, Waterbury CT

Mercer County Community College, The Gallery, Trenton NJ

Mexican Museum, San Francisco CA

Michigan State University, Kresge Art Museum, East Lansing MI

Midwest Museum of American Art, Elkhart IN

Mint Museum of Art, Charlotte NC

Mississippi Department of Archives & History, Old Capitol Museum, Jackson MS

Arthur Roy Mitchell Memorial Inc, Museum of Western Art, Trinidad CO

Mobile Museum of Art, Mobile AL

James Monroe Museum, Fredericksburg VA

Montana State University, Museum of the Rockies, Bozeman MT

Moore College of Art & Design, Goldie Paley Gallery, Philadelphia PA

Morris-Jumel Mansion, Inc, New York NY

Morris Museum, Morristown NJ

Mount Saint Vincent University, Art Gallery, Halifax NS

Musee d'Art de Saint-Laurent, Saint-Laurent PQ

Musee des Augustines de l'Hotel Dieu de Quebec, Quebec PQ

Musee Regional de la Cote-Nord, Sept-Iles PQ

The Museum at Drexel University, Philadelphia PA

Museum of Art, Fort Lauderdale, Fort Lauderdale FL

The Museum of Arts & Sciences Inc, Daytona Beach FL

Museum of Contemporary Art, North Miami FL

Museum of Mobile, Mobile AL

Museum of New Mexico, Museum of Fine Arts, Santa Fe NM

Museum of Northern Arizona, Flagstaff AZ

Museum of Northern British Columbia, Ruth Harvey Art Gallery, Prince Rupert BC

Museum of the City of New York, New York NY

Museum of York County, Rock Hill SC

The Museums at Stony Brook, Stony Brook NY

Muttart Public Art Gallery, Calgary AB

National Museum of American History, Washington DC

National Museum of the American Indian, George Gustav Heye Center, New York NY

National Museum of Women in the Arts, Washington DC

National Society of the Colonial Dames, Wilton House Museum, Richmond VA

Naval Historical Center, The Navy Museum, Washington DC

Nelson-Atkins Museum of Art, Kansas City MO

Nevada Museum Of Art, Reno NV

New Mexico State University, University Art Gallery, Las Cruces NM

North Carolina State University, Visual Arts Center, Raleigh NC

North Central Washington Museum, Gallery, Wenatchee WA

Oglebay Institute, Mansion Museum, Wheeling WV

Old Jail Art Center, Albany TX

Old Salem Inc, Museum of Early Southern Decorative Arts, Winston-Salem NC

One West Art Center, Fort Collins CO

Owensboro Museum of Fine Art, Owensboro KY

Pacific - Asia Museum, Pasadena CA

Palm Beach Community College Foundation, Museum of Art, Lake Worth FL

Panhandle-Plains Historical Society Museum, Canyon TX
Paris Gibson Square, Museum of Art, Great Falls MT
Pasadena Historical Museum, Pasadena CA
Peabody Essex Museum, Salem MA
Pennsylvania State University, Palmer Museum of Art, University Park PA
Pewabic Society Inc, Pewabic Pottery, Detroit MI
Phelps County Historical Society, Phelps County Museum, Holdrege NE
Philbrook Museum of Art, Tulsa OK
Phillips County Museum, Helena AR
George Phippen Memorial Foundation, Phippen Museum of Western Art, Prescott AZ
Plumas County Museum, Quincy CA
Portland Art Museum, Portland OR
Portsmouth Historical Society, John Paul Jones House, Portsmouth NH
Marjorie Merriweather Post Foundation of DC, Hillwood Museum, Washington DC
Principia College, School of Nations Museum, Elsah IL
Purdue University Galleries, West Lafayette IN
Putnam Museum of History & Natural Science, Davenport IA
Randall Museum Junior Museum, San Francisco CA
Randolph-Macon Woman's College, Maier Museum of Art, Lynchburg VA
Redding Museum of Art & History, Redding CA
Rensselaer County Historical Society, Hart-Cluett Mansion, 1827, Troy NY
Rhode Island Historical Society, John Brown House, Providence RI
Millicent Rogers Museum of Northern New Mexico, Taos NM
Rollins College, George D & Harriet W Cornell Fine Arts Museum, Winter Park FL
Ross Memorial Museum, Saint Andrews NB
Royal Arts Foundation, Belcourt Castle, Newport RI
Saint Louis Artists' Guild, Saint Louis MO
The Sandwich Historical Society, Inc, Sandwich Glass Museum, Sandwich MA
Santa Clara University, de Saisset Museum, Santa Clara CA
The Seagram Museum, Waterloo ON
Seneca-Iroquois National Museum, Salamanca NY
Ella Sharp Museum, Jackson MI
Shelburne Museum, Shelburne VT
Sioux City Art Center, Sioux City IA
Abigail Adams Smith Museum, New York NY
George Walter Vincent Smith Art Museum, Springfield MA
Society of the Cincinnati, Museum & Library at Anderson House, Washington DC
South Carolina Artisans Center, Walterboro SC
South Dakota State University, South Dakota Art Museum, Brookings SD
Southeastern Center for Contemporary Art, Winston-Salem NC
Southern Alleghenies Museum of Art, Loretto PA
Southern Alleghenies Museum of Art, Southern Alleghenies Museum of Art at Johnstown, Loretto PA
Southern Illinois University, University Museum, Carbondale IL
Southern Oregon State College, Schneider Museum of Art, Ashland OR
Spartanburg County Museum of Art, Spartanburg SC
Springfield Art & Historical Society, Miller Art Center, Springfield VT
Springfield Art Museum, Springfield MO
State Historical Society of Wisconsin, State Historical Museum, Madison WI
State University of New York at Geneseo, Bertha V B Lederer Gallery, Geneseo NY
State University of New York at New Paltz, College Art Gallery, New Paltz NY
Stetson University, Duncan Gallery of Art, De Land FL
Stratford Historical Society, Katherine Mitchel Museum, Stratford CT
Swedish American Museum Association of Chicago, Chicago IL
Syracuse University, Art Collection, Syracuse NY

Tacoma Arts Commission, Commencement Art Gallery, Tacoma WA
Tampa Museum of Art, Tampa FL
Thomas More College, TM Gallery, Crestview KY
Toledo Museum of Art, Toledo OH
Topeka & Shawnee County Public Library, Gallery of Fine Arts, Topeka KS
Touchstone Center for Crafts, Farmington PA
Towson State University, Asian Arts Center, Towson MD
Trenton City Museum, Trenton NJ
Triton Museum of Art, Santa Clara CA
Tryon Palace Historic Sites & Gardens, New Bern NC
Mark Twain Memorial, Hartford CT
The Ukrainian Museum, New York NY
UMLAUF Sculpture Garden & Museum, Austin TX
US Coast Guard Museum, New London CT
United States Figure Skating Association, World Figure Skating Museum & Hall of Fame, Colorado Springs CO
United States Naval Academy Museum, Annapolis MD
University of Akron, University Galleries, Akron OH
University of Alabama at Birmingham, Visual Arts Gallery, Birmingham AL
University of British Columbia, Museum of Anthropology, Vancouver BC
University of California, Richard L Nelson Gallery & Fine Arts Collection, Davis CA
University of California, Los Angeles, Fowler Museum of Cultural History, Los Angeles CA
University of Chicago, Oriental Institute Museum, Chicago IL
University of Colorado, Art Galleries, Boulder CO
University of Florida, Samuel P Harn Museum of Art, Gainesville FL
University of Iowa, Museum of Art, Iowa City IA
University of Manitoba, Faculty of Architecture Exhibition Centre, Winnipeg MB
University of Michigan, Museum of Art, Ann Arbor MI
University of Montana, Paxson Gallery, Missoula MT
University of Nebraska, Lincoln, Sheldon Memorial Art Gallery & Sculpture Garden, Lincoln NE
University of Rochester, Memorial Art Gallery, Rochester NY
University of Victoria, Maltwood Art Museum and Gallery, Victoria BC
University of Virginia, Bayly Art Museum, Charlottesville VA
University of Washington, Henry Art Gallery, Seattle WA
USS Constitution Museum, Boston MA
Vassar College, The Frances Lehman Loeb Art Center, Poughkeepsie NY
Vizcaya Museum & Gardens, Miami FL
Volcano Art Center, Hawaii National Park HI
Wade House & Wesley W Jung Carriage Museum, Historic House & Carriage Museum, Greenbush WI
Wadsworth Atheneum, Hartford CT
Washburn University, Mulvane Art Museum, Topeka KS
Waterworks Visual Arts Center, Salisbury NC
Wayne Center for the Arts, Wooster OH
Western Illinois University, Art Gallery-Museum, Macomb IL
Westmoreland Museum of American Art, Greensburg PA
Wheelwright Museum of the American Indian, Santa Fe NM
Wiregrass Museum of Art, Dothan AL
Woodlawn Plantation, Mount Vernon VA
Woodmere Art Museum, Philadelphia PA
Xavier University, Xavier Art Gallery, Cincinnati OH
York Institute Museum, Saco ME

COINS & MEDALS

Academy of the New Church, Glencairn Museum, Bryn Athyn PA
Alaska State Museum, Juneau AK
Albuquerque Museum of Art & History, Albuquerque NM
ArtSpace-Lima, Lima OH
Balzekas Museum of Lithuanian Culture, Chicago IL
Bennington Museum, Bennington Museum, Bennington VT
Berea College, Doris Ulmann Galleries, Berea KY
Berkshire Museum, Pittsfield MA
The Bostonian Society, Old State House Museum, Boston MA
Bowdoin College, Museum of Art, Brunswick ME
Brookgreen Gardens, Murrells Inlet SC
Cape Ann Historical Museum, Gloucester MA
Kit Carson Historic Museums, Home & Museum, Taos NM
Church of Jesus Christ of Latter-day Saints, Museum of Church History & Art, Salt Lake City UT
Clinton County Historical Association, Clinton County Historical Museum, Plattsburgh NY
College of William & Mary, Joseph & Margaret Muscarelle Museum of Art, Williamsburg VA
The College of Wooster, Art Museum, Wooster OH
Colorado Historical Society, Colorado History Museum, Denver CO
Concordia Historical Institute, Saint Louis MO
DAR Museum, National Society Daughters of the American Revolution, Washington DC
Dartmouth Heritage Museum, Dartmouth NS
Dawson City Museum & Historical Society, Dawson City YT
Department of Community Development, Provincial Museum of Alberta, Edmonton AB
Duke University Museum of Art, Durham NC
Dundurn Castle, Hamilton ON
Ephraim McDowell-Cambus-Kenneth Foundation, McDowell House & Apothecary Shop, Danville KY
Farmington Village Green & Library Association, Stanley-Whitman House, Farmington CT
Franklin Mint Museum, Franklin Center PA
General Board of Discipleship, The United Methodist Church, The Upper Room Chapel & Museum, Nashville TN
Glanmore, Hastings County Museum, Belleville ON
Grand Rapids Art Museum, Grand Rapids MI
Guilford College, Art Gallery, Greensboro NC
Hastings Museum, Hastings NE
Headquarters Fort Monroe, Dept of Army, Casemate Museum, Fort Monroe VA
Hebrew Union College, Skirball Cultural Center, Los Angeles CA
Hispanic Society of America, Museum, New York NY
House of Roses, Senator Wilson Home, Deadwood SD
Huguenot Historical Society of New Paltz Galleries, New Paltz NY
Huntington Museum of Art, Huntington WV
Huronia Museum, Midland ON
Idaho Historical Museum, Boise ID
Imperial Calcasieu Museum, Gibson-Barham Gallery, Lake Charles LA
Indiana University, Art Museum, Bloomington IN
Jacksonville University, Alexander Brest Museum & Gallery, Jacksonville FL
Jersey City Museum, Jersey City NJ
The Jewish Museum, New York NY
Kings County Historical Society and Museum, Hampton NB
Knights of Columbus Supreme Council, Headquarters Museum, New Haven CT
Koochiching County Historical Society Museum, International Falls MN
Liberty Memorial Museum & Archives, Kansas City MO
Longfellow-Evangeline State Commemorative Area, Saint Martinville LA
McPherson Museum, McPherson KS
Judah L Magnes Museum, Berkeley CA
The Mariners' Museum, Newport News VA
Maryhill Museum of Art, Goldendale WA

Mattatuck Historical Society, Mattatuck Museum, Waterbury CT
Michigan State University, Kresge Art Museum, East Lansing MI
Mississippi Department of Archives & History, Old Capitol Museum, Jackson MS
Mississippi River Museum at Mud-Island, Memphis TN
Musee des Augustines de l'Hotel Dieu de Quebec, Quebec PQ
The Museum of Arts & Sciences Inc, Daytona Beach FL
Museum of Mobile, Mobile AL
Museum of Northern British Columbia, Ruth Harvey Art Gallery, Prince Rupert BC
Museum of the City of New York, New York NY
The Museums at Stony Brook, Stony Brook NY
National Infantry Museum, Fort Benning GA
National Museum of the American Indian, George Gustav Heye Center, New York NY
Naval Historical Center, The Navy Museum, Washington DC
Northern Arizona University, Art Museum & Galleries, Flagstaff AZ
Ohio Historical Society, National Afro American Museum & Cultural Center, Wilberforce OH
Order Sons of Italy in America, Garibaldi & Meucci Museum, Staten Island NY
Pacific - Asia Museum, Pasadena CA
Peabody Essex Museum, Salem MA
Pennsylvania Academy of the Fine Arts, Museum of American Art, Philadelphia PA
Phelps County Historical Society, Phelps County Museum, Holdrege NE
Plainsman Museum, Aurora NE
Plumas County Museum, Quincy CA
Polish Museum of America, Chicago IL
Portland Art Museum, Portland OR
Marjorie Merriweather Post Foundation of DC, Hillwood Museum, Washington DC
Putnam Museum of History & Natural Science, Davenport IA
Rhode Island Historical Society, John Brown House, Providence RI
Rollins College, George D & Harriet W Cornell Fine Arts Museum, Winter Park FL
Royal Ontario Museum, Dept of Western Art & Culture, Toronto ON
Society of the Cincinnati, Museum & Library at Anderson House, Washington DC
State Art Museum of Florida, John & Mable Ringling Museum of Art, Sarasota FL
State Historical Society of Wisconsin, State Historical Museum, Madison WI
Swedish American Museum Association of Chicago, Chicago IL
Tampa Museum of Art, Tampa FL
Temple Beth Israel, Sylvia Plotkin Judaica, Phoenix AZ
The Temple-Tifereth Israel, The Temple Museum of Religious Art, Beachwood OH
The Ukrainian Museum, New York NY
US Coast Guard Museum, New London CT
United States Figure Skating Association, World Figure Skating Museum & Hall of Fame, Colorado Springs CO
United States Military Academy, West Point Museum, West Point NY
University of British Columbia, Museum of Anthropology, Vancouver BC
University of Calgary, The Nickle Arts Museum, Calgary AB
University of California, Santa Barbara, University Art Museum, Santa Barbara CA
University of Virginia, Bayly Art Museum, Charlottesville VA
USS Constitution Museum, Boston MA
Wells Fargo Bank, Wells Fargo History Museum, San Francisco CA
T T Wentworth Jr Museum, Florida State Museum, Pensacola FL
Wheaton College, Watson Gallery, Norton MA
Willard House & Clock Museum, Inc, North Grafton MA
Woodlawn Plantation, Mount Vernon VA
Yarmouth County Historical Society, Yarmouth County Museum, Yarmouth NS
York Institute Museum, Saco ME

COLLAGES

Alaska State Museum, Juneau AK
Albany Institute of History & Art, Albany NY
Albuquerque Museum of Art & History, Albuquerque NM
The Art Institute of Chicago, Chicago IL
Art Museum of Missoula, Missoula MT
Arts Council of Fayetteville-Cumberland County, The Arts Center, Fayetteville NC
ArtSpace-Lima, Lima OH
Bank One Gallery, Louisville KY
Beaumont Art League, Beaumont TX
Bowdoin College, Museum of Art, Brunswick ME
Roy Boyd Gallery, Chicago IL
Chicago Department of Cultural Affairs, Chicago Cultural Center, Chicago IL
CIGNA Corporation, CIGNA Museum & Art Collection, Philadelphia PA
College of William & Mary, Joseph & Margaret Muscarelle Museum of Art, Williamsburg VA
The College of Wooster, Art Museum, Wooster OH
Community Fine Arts Center, Halseth Gallery, Rock Springs WY
Coutts Memorial Museum of Art, Inc, El Dorado KS
C W Post Campus of Long Island University, Hillwood Art Museum, Brookville NY
Davidson College Visual Arts Center, William H Van Every Jr & Edward M Smith Galleries, Davidson NC
Detroit Institute of Arts, Detroit MI
Detroit Repertory Theatre Gallery, Detroit MI
Ellen Noel Art Museum of the Permian Basin, Odessa TX
Erie Art Museum, Erie PA
Federal Reserve Board, Art Gallery, Washington DC
Florence Museum of Art, Science & History, Florence SC
Fort Worth Art Association, Modern Art Museum of Fort Worth, Fort Worth TX
Gallery One, Ellensburg WA
Grand Rapids Art Museum, Grand Rapids MI
Hebrew Union College, Skirball Cultural Center, Los Angeles CA
Hebrew Union College-Jewish Institute of Religion, New York NY
Hirshhorn Museum & Sculpture Garden, Washington DC
Huntington Museum of Art, Huntington WV
Institute for Contemporary Art, Project Studio One (P S 1), Long Island City NY
Institute of American Indian Arts Museum, Santa Fe NM
The Interchurch Center, Galleries at the Interchurch Center, New York NY
Kansas City Art Institute, Kemper Museum of Contemporary Art & Design, Kansas City MO
Knoxville Museum of Art, Knoxville TN
Lighthouse Gallery & School of Art, Tequesta FL
Longview Museum of Art, Longview TX
Judah L Magnes Museum, Berkeley CA
Maitland Art Center, Maitland FL
Maryhill Museum of Art, Goldendale WA
Maryland Art Place, Baltimore MD
Marylhurst College, The Art Gym, Marylhurst OR
Mint Museum of Art, Charlotte NC
Mobile Museum of Art, Mobile AL
Monroe County Historical Association, Elizabeth D Walters Library, Stroudsburg PA
Montana State University, Museum of the Rockies, Bozeman MT
Morris Museum, Morristown NJ
Museum of Contemporary Art, North Miami FL
The Museums at Stony Brook, Stony Brook NY
Muttart Public Art Gallery, Calgary AB
Nassau County Museum of Fine Art, Roslyn Harbor NY
National Gallery of Canada, Ottawa ON
New Brunswick Museum, Saint John NB
Niagara University, Castellani Art Museum, Niagara NY
Owensboro Museum of Fine Art, Owensboro KY
Pennsylvania Academy of the Fine Arts, Museum of American Art, Philadelphia PA
Provincetown Art Association & Museum, Provincetown MA
Purdue University Galleries, West Lafayette IN

Randolph-Macon Woman's College, Maier Museum of Art, Lynchburg VA
Rollins College, George D & Harriet W Cornell Fine Arts Museum, Winter Park FL
Roswell Museum & Art Center, Roswell NM
School of Visual Arts, Visual Arts Museum, New York NY
South Carolina Artisans Center, Walterboro SC
Southeastern Center for Contemporary Art, Winston-Salem NC
Southern Alleghenies Museum of Art, Southern Alleghenies Museum of Art at Johnstown, Loretto PA
Springfield Art Museum, Springfield MO
University of Alabama at Birmingham, Visual Arts Gallery, Birmingham AL
University of Rhode Island, Fine Arts Center Galleries, Kingston RI
Viridian Artists Inc, New York NY

COSTUMES

Academy of the New Church, Glencairn Museum, Bryn Athyn PA
Adams County Historical Society, Museum & Cultural Center, Brighton CO
African Art Museum of Maryland, Columbia MD
Agecroft Association, Museum, Richmond VA
Albany Institute of History & Art, Albany NY
American Museum of the Moving Image, Astoria NY
Amherst Museum, Amherst NY
Anchorage Museum of History & Art, Anchorage AK
Arapahoe Community College, Colorado Gallery of the Arts, Littleton CO
Arkansas Territorial Restoration, Little Rock AR
Arts & Science Center, Statesville NC
ArtSpace-Lima, Lima OH
Association for the Preservation of Virginia Antiquities, John Marshall House, Richmond VA
Atlanta Historical Society Inc, Atlanta History Center, Atlanta GA
Leo Baeck Institute, New York NY
Baldwin Historical Society Museum, Baldwin NY
The Bartlett Museum, Amesbury MA
Bennington Museum, Bennington Museum, Bennington VT
Berea College, Doris Ulmann Galleries, Berea KY
Berkshire Museum, Pittsfield MA
Jesse Besser Museum, Alpena MI
Canton Museum of Art, Canton OH
Carson County Square House Museum, Panhandle TX
Kit Carson Historic Museums, Home & Museum, Taos NM
Center for Puppetry Arts, Atlanta GA
Billie Trimble Chandler Arts Foundation, Asian Cultures Museum & Educational Center, Corpus Christi TX
Chicago Department of Cultural Affairs, Chicago Cultural Center, Chicago IL
Church of Jesus Christ of Latter-day Saints, Museum of Church History & Art, Salt Lake City UT
City of Atlanta, Atlanta Cyclorama, Atlanta GA
Clark County Historical Society, Pioneer - Krier Museum, Ashland KS
Clinton County Historical Association, Clinton County Historical Museum, Plattsburgh NY
Cohasset Historical Society, Cohasset Maritime Museum, Cohasset MA
Colorado Historical Society, Colorado History Museum, Denver CO
Concordia Historical Institute, Saint Louis MO
Craft & Folk Art Museum, Los Angeles CA
Crow Wing County Historical Society, Brainerd MN
DAR Museum, National Society Daughters of the American Revolution, Washington DC
Dartmouth Heritage Museum, Dartmouth NS
Department of Natural Resources of Missouri, Missouri State Museum, Jefferson City MO
Detroit Institute of Arts, Detroit MI
DeWitt Historical Society of Tompkins County, Ithaca NY

CRAFTS

Burchfield-Penney Art Center, Buffalo NY
California College of Arts & Crafts, Steven Oliver Art Center, Oakland CA
The Canadian Craft Museum, Vancouver BC
Carson County Square House Museum, Panhandle TX
Center for Book Arts, New York NY
Chicago Department of Cultural Affairs, Chicago Cultural Center, Chicago IL
Chinese Culture Foundation, Chinese Culture Center Gallery, San Francisco CA
CIGNA Corporation, CIGNA Museum & Art Collection, Philadelphia PA
City of Pittsfield, Berkshire Artisans, Pittsfield MA
City of Springdale, Shiloh Museum, Springdale AR
Clark County Historical Society, Pioneer - Krier Museum, Ashland KS
Cleveland State University, Art Gallery, Cleveland OH
College of Saint Benedict, Art Gallery, Saint Joseph MN
Concordia Historical Institute, Saint Louis MO
Confederation Centre Art Gallery and Museum, Charlottetown PE
Contemporary Crafts Association & Gallery, Portland OR
Cooper-Hewitt, National Design Museum, New York NY
Cornwall Gallery Society, Regional Art Gallery, Cornwall ON
County of Henrico, Meadow Farm Museum, Glen Allen VA
Craft & Folk Art Museum, Los Angeles CA
Cranbrook Art Museum, Bloomfield Hills MI
DeWitt Historical Society of Tompkins County, Ithaca NY
Douglas County Historical Society, Fairlawn Mansion & Museum, Superior WI
Durham Art Guild Inc, Durham NC
East Tennessee State University, Carroll Reece Museum, Johnson City TN
Enook Galleries, Waterloo ON
Erie Art Museum, Erie PA
Wharton Esherick Museum, Paoli PA
Essex Historical Society, Essex Shipbuilding Museum, Essex MA
Evanston Historical Society, Charles Gates Dawes House, Evanston IL
Farmington Village Green & Library Association, Stanley-Whitman House, Farmington CT
Favell Museum of Western Art & Indian Artifacts, Klamath Falls OR
Florida Gulf Coast Art Center, Inc, Belleair FL
Gallery 53, Cooperstown NY
Gallery One, Ellensburg WA
G B Gate & Sons, Asheville NC
Georgetown College Gallery, Georgetown KY
Grand Rapids Art Museum, Grand Rapids MI
Greater Lafayette Museum of Art, Lafayette IN
Hebrew Union College, Skirball Cultural Center, Los Angeles CA
Hebrew Union College-Jewish Institute of Religion, New York NY
Hershey Museum, Hershey PA
Hispanic Society of America, Museum, New York NY
Huntington Museum of Art, Huntington WV
Huronia Museum, Midland ON
Hyde Park Art Center, Chicago IL
Imperial Calcasieu Museum, Gibson-Barham Gallery, Lake Charles LA
Indian Arts & Crafts Board, Sioux Indian Museum, Rapid City SD
Institute of the Great Plains, Museum of the Great Plains, Lawton OK
The Interchurch Center, Galleries at the Interchurch Center, New York NY
Jersey City Museum, Jersey City NJ
Kansas City Art Institute, Kemper Museum of Contemporary Art & Design, Kansas City MO
Kelowna Museum, Kelowna BC
Maude I Kerns Art Center Galleries, Eugene OR
Koochiching County Historical Society Museum, International Falls MN
Koshare Indian Museum, Inc, La Junta CO
Lac du Flambeau Band of Lake Superior Chippewa Indians, George W Brown Jr Ojibwe Museum & Cultural Center, Lac du Flambeau WI

Lafayette Natural History Museum, Planetarium & Nature Station, Lafayette LA
Leelanau Historical Museum, Leland MI
Long Beach Museum of Art, Long Beach CA
Longfellow-Evangeline State Commemorative Area, Saint Martinville LA
McAllen International Museum, McAllen TX
Carrie McLain Museum, Nome AK
Judah L Magnes Museum, Berkeley CA
Maison Saint-Gabriel Museum, Montreal PQ
Maitland Art Center, Maitland FL
Mankato State University, Conkling Gallery Art Dept, Mankato MN
Marietta College, Grover M Hermann Fine Arts Center, Marietta OH
The Mariners' Museum, Newport News VA
Maryland Art Place, Baltimore MD
Massillon Museum, Massillon OH
Mexican Museum, San Francisco CA
Minnesota Museum of American Art, Saint Paul MN
Mint Museum of Art, Charlotte NC
Mississippi Department of Archives & History, Old Capitol Museum, Jackson MS
Mobile Museum of Art, Mobile AL
Moore College of Art & Design, Goldie Paley Gallery, Philadelphia PA
Morris Museum, Morristown NJ
Museum of Northern Arizona, Flagstaff AZ
Museum of Northern British Columbia, Ruth Harvey Art Gallery, Prince Rupert BC
Museum of the American Quilter's Society, Paducah KY
Museum of the City of New York, New York NY
Museum of the Plains Indian & Crafts Center, Browning MT
The Museums at Stony Brook, Stony Brook NY
National Museum of American Art, Renwick Gallery, Washington DC
National Museum of Women in the Arts, Washington DC
Newark Museum Association, The Newark Museum, Newark NJ
New Brunswick Museum, Saint John NB
New Mexico State University, University Art Gallery, Las Cruces NM
New Visions Gallery, Inc, Marshfield WI
New York State Historical Association, Farmers' Museum, Inc, Cooperstown NY
Nippon Club Gallery, New York NY
North Carolina State University, Visual Arts Center, Raleigh NC
Nova Scotia Museum, Maritime Museum of the Atlantic, Halifax NS
Noyes Museum, Oceanville NJ
Oakland Museum of California, Art Dept, Oakland CA
Ohio Historical Society, National Afro American Museum & Cultural Center, Wilberforce OH
The Ohio Historical Society, Inc, Campus Martius Museum & Ohio River Museum, Marietta OH
Okefenokee Heritage Center, Inc, Waycross GA
Old Dartmouth Historical Society, New Bedford Whaling Museum, New Bedford MA
One West Art Center, Fort Collins CO
Oshkosh Public Museum, Oshkosh WI
Owensboro Museum of Fine Art, Owensboro KY
Palm Beach County Parks & Recreation Department, Morikami Museum & Japanese Gardens, Delray Beach FL
Panhandle-Plains Historical Society Museum, Canyon TX
Pasadena Historical Museum, Pasadena CA
Phelps County Historical Society, Phelps County Museum, Holdrege NE
George Phippen Memorial Foundation, Phippen Museum of Western Art, Prescott AZ
Pioneer Town, Pioneer Museum of Western Art, Wimberley TX
Plumas County Museum, Quincy CA
Pope County Historical Society, Pope County Museum, Glenwood MN
Principia College, School of Nations Museum, Elsah IL
Randall Museum Junior Museum, San Francisco CA
Red Rock State Park, Red Rock Museum, Church Rock NM

Rensselaer County Historical Society, Hart-Cluett Mansion, 1827, Troy NY
Rhode Island Historical Society, John Brown House, Providence RI
Millicent Rogers Museum of Northern New Mexico, Taos NM
Rollins College, George D & Harriet W Cornell Fine Arts Museum, Winter Park FL
Rome Historical Society Museum, Rome NY
Roswell Museum & Art Center, Roswell NM
Saint Louis Artists' Guild, Saint Louis MO
San Diego State University, University Gallery, San Diego CA
San Francisco Maritime National Historical Park, National Maritime Museum, San Francisco CA
Seneca-Iroquois National Museum, Salamanca NY
Shaker Village of Pleasant Hill, Harrodsburg KY
Sooke Region Museum & Art Gallery, Sooke BC
South Carolina Artisans Center, Walterboro SC
South Carolina State Museum, Columbia SC
Southeastern Center for Contemporary Art, Winston-Salem NC
Southern Illinois University, University Museum, Carbondale IL
Southern Plains Indian Museum, Anadarko OK
Southwest Museum, Los Angeles CA
Springfield Art & Historical Society, Miller Art Center, Springfield VT
Stamford Museum & Nature Center, Stamford CT
State Historical Society of Wisconsin, State Historical Museum, Madison WI
Swedish American Museum Association of Chicago, Chicago IL
Tallahassee Museum of History & Natural Science, Tallahassee FL
The Temple-Tifereth Israel, The Temple Museum of Religious Art, Beachwood OH
Tubman African American Museum, Macon GA
Ukrainian Canadian Archives & Museum of Alberta, Edmonton AB
The Ukrainian Museum, New York NY
United Society of Shakers, Shaker Museum, New Glocester ME
University of British Columbia, Museum of Anthropology, Vancouver BC
University of Colorado at Colorado Springs, Gallery of Contemporary Art, Colorado Springs CO
University of Rochester, Memorial Art Gallery, Rochester NY
University of Victoria, Maltwood Art Museum and Gallery, Victoria BC
Utah Arts Council, Chase Home Museum of Utah Folk Art, Salt Lake City UT
Vermont State Craft Center at Frog Hollow, Middlebury VT
Vesterheim Norwegian-American Museum, Decorah IA
Volcano Art Center, Hawaii National Park HI
Wade House & Wesley W Jung Carriage Museum, Historic House & Carriage Museum, Greenbush WI
West Baton Rouge Historical Association, Museum, Port Allen LA
Whatcom Museum of History and Art, Bellingham WA
Wheelwright Museum of the American Indian, Santa Fe NM
Wiregrass Museum of Art, Dothan AL
Worcester Center for Crafts, Worcester MA
Xavier University, Xavier Art Gallery, Cincinnati OH
Yarmouth County Historical Society, Yarmouth County Museum, Yarmouth NS

DECORATIVE ARTS

Alabama Department of Archives & History, Museum Galleries, Montgomery AL
Alaska State Museum, Juneau AK
Albany Institute of History & Art, Albany NY
Albuquerque Museum of Art & History, Albuquerque NM
Allentown Art Museum, Allentown PA
Lyman Allyn Art Museum, New London CT
American Architectural Foundation, The Octagon Museum, Washington DC
Americas Society Art Gallery, New York NY
Amherst Museum, Amherst NY

Maine Historical Society, Wadsworth-Longfellow House, Portland ME

Maine Historical Society, Maine History Gallery, Portland ME

Mamie McFaddin Ward Heritage Historic Foundation Inc, Beaumont TX

Maricopa County Historical Society, Desert Caballeros Western Museum, Wickenburg AZ

The Mariners' Museum, Newport News VA

Marquette University, Haggerty Museum of Art, Milwaukee WI

Maryhill Museum of Art, Goldendale WA

Mattatuck Historical Society, Mattatuck Museum, Waterbury CT

Meridian Museum of Art, Meridian MS

The Metropolitan Museum of Art, New York NY

Miami University, Art Museum, Oxford OH

Midwest Museum of American Art, Elkhart IN

Milwaukee Public Museum, Milwaukee WI

Minneapolis Institute of Arts, Minneapolis MN

Mint Museum of Art, Charlotte NC

Mission San Luis Rey de Francia, Mission San Luis Rey Museum, San Luis Rey CA

Mississippi Department of Archives & History, Old Capitol Museum, Jackson MS

Arthur Roy Mitchell Memorial Inc, Museum of Western Art, Trinidad CO

Mobile Museum of Art, Mobile AL

Monroe County Historical Association, Elizabeth D Walters Library, Stroudsburg PA

Montana State University, Museum of the Rockies, Bozeman MT

Monterey Museum of Art Association, Monterey CA

Montreal Museum of Fine Arts, Montreal PQ

Moravian Historical Society, Whitefield House Museum, Nazareth PA

Morris-Jumel Mansion, Inc, New York NY

Morris Museum, Morristown NJ

Munson-Williams-Proctor Institute, Museum of Art, Utica NY

Muscatine Art Center, Muscatine IA

Musee du Quebec, Quebec PQ

The Museum at Drexel University, Philadelphia PA

Museum of Arts & History, Port Huron MI

The Museum of Arts & Sciences Inc, Daytona Beach FL

Museum of Fine Arts, Boston MA

Museum of Fine Arts, Houston, Houston TX

Museum of Fine Arts, Saint Petersburg, Florida, Inc, Saint Petersburg FL

Museum of Mobile, Mobile AL

Museum of Our National Heritage, Lexington MA

Museum of the American Quilter's Society, Paducah KY

Museum of the City of New York, New York NY

Museum of York County, Rock Hill SC

The Museums at Stony Brook, Stony Brook NY

National Gallery of Canada, Ottawa ON

National Museum of American Art, Washington DC

National Museum of the American Indian, George Gustav Heye Center, New York NY

National Museum of Women in the Arts, Washington DC

National Park Service, Weir Farm National Historic Site, Wilton CT

The National Park Service, United States Department of the Interior, The Statue of Liberty National Monument, New York NY

National Society of Colonial Dames of America in the State of Maryland, Mount Clare Mansion, Baltimore MD

National Society of the Colonial Dames, Wilton House Museum, Richmond VA

National Society of Tole & Decorative Painters, Inc, Wichita KS

National Trust for Historic Preservation, Chesterwood Museum, Glendale MA

National Trust for Historic Preservation, Washington DC

Naval Historical Center, The Navy Museum, Washington DC

Nebraska State Capitol, Lincoln NE

Nelson-Atkins Museum of Art, Kansas City MO

Newark Museum Association, The Newark Museum, Newark NJ

New Brunswick Museum, Saint John NB

Newburyport Maritime Society, Custom House Maritime Museum, Newburyport MA

New Jersey Historical Society, Newark NJ

New Jersey State Museum, Trenton NJ

New Orleans School of GlassWorks, Gallery & Printmaking Studio, New Orleans LA

New Visions Gallery, Inc, Marshfield WI

New York State Historical Association, Fenimore House Museum, Cooperstown NY

New York State Museum, Albany NY

Nichols House Museum, Inc, Boston MA

North Carolina Museum of Art, Raleigh NC

North Carolina State University, Visual Arts Center, Raleigh NC

The Ohio Historical Society, Inc, Campus Martius Museum & Ohio River Museum, Marietta OH

Oklahoma Historical Society, State Museum of History, Oklahoma City OK

Old Barracks Museum, Trenton NJ

Old Dartmouth Historical Society, New Bedford Whaling Museum, New Bedford MA

Old Salem Inc, Museum of Early Southern Decorative Arts, Winston-Salem NC

Old York Historical Society, Old Gaol Museum, York ME

Order Sons of Italy in America, Garibaldi & Meucci Museum, Staten Island NY

Oshkosh Public Museum, Oshkosh WI

Owensboro Museum of Fine Art, Owensboro KY

Oysterponds Historical Society, Museum, Orient NY

Pacific - Asia Museum, Pasadena CA

Palisades Interstate Park Commission, Senate House State Historic Site, Kingston NY

Palm Beach County Parks & Recreation Department, Morikami Museum & Japanese Gardens, Delray Beach FL

Panhandle-Plains Historical Society Museum, Canyon TX

Pasadena Historical Museum, Pasadena CA

Passaic County Historical Society, Paterson NJ

Peabody Essex Museum, Salem MA

Pennsylvania Historical & Museum Commission, State Museum of Pennsylvania, Harrisburg PA

Pensacola Museum of Art, Pensacola FL

Phoenix Art Museum, Phoenix AZ

Pilgrim Society, Pilgrim Hall Museum, Plymouth MA

Pioneer Town, Pioneer Museum of Western Art, Wimberley TX

Plumas County Museum, Quincy CA

Polish Museum of America, Chicago IL

Polk Museum of Art, Lakeland FL

Pope County Historical Society, Pope County Museum, Glenwood MN

Porter-Phelps-Huntington Foundation, Inc, Historic House Museum, Hadley MA

Portland Art Museum, Portland OR

Portland Museum of Art, Portland ME

Marjorie Merriweather Post Foundation of DC, Hillwood Museum, Washington DC

Prairie Art Gallery, Grande Prairie AB

Principia College, School of Nations Museum, Elsah IL

Putnam Museum of History & Natural Science, Davenport IA

Quapaw Quarter Association, Inc, Villa Marre, Little Rock AR

Rensselaer County Historical Society, Hart-Cluett Mansion, 1827, Troy NY

Rhode Island Historical Society, John Brown House, Providence RI

Rhode Island School of Design, Museum of Art, Providence RI

Riley County Historical Society, Riley County Historical Museum, Manhattan KS

Ringwood Manor House Museum, Ringwood NJ

Riverside County Museum, Edward-Dean Museum, Cherry Valley CA

Roberson Museum & Science Center, Binghamton NY

Rock Ford Foundation, Inc, Historic Rock Ford & Kauffman Museum, Lancaster PA

Millicent Rogers Museum of Northern New Mexico, Taos NM

Rollins College, George D & Harriet W Cornell Fine Arts Museum, Winter Park FL

Rome Historical Society Museum, Rome NY

Roosevelt-Vanderbilt National Historic Sites, Hyde Park NY

Ross Memorial Museum, Saint Andrews NB

Royal Ontario Museum, Dept of Western Art & Culture, Toronto ON

C M Russell Museum, Great Falls MT

Saginaw Art Museum, Saginaw MI

Saint Anselm College, Chapel Art Center, Manchester NH

The Saint Louis Art Museum, Saint Louis MO

San Diego Museum of Art, San Diego CA

The Sandwich Historical Society, Inc, Sandwich Glass Museum, Sandwich MA

San Joaquin Pioneer & Historical Society, The Haggin Museum, Stockton CA

Schuyler-Hamilton House, Morristown NJ

The Seagram Museum, Waterloo ON

Seneca Falls Historical Society Museum, Seneca Falls NY

Seneca-Iroquois National Museum, Salamanca NY

Shaker Museum & Library, Old Chatham NY

Shaker Village of Pleasant Hill, Harrodsburg KY

Shelburne Museum, Shelburne VT

Siena Heights College, Klemm Gallery, Studio Angelico, Adrian MI

Smith College, Museum of Art, Northampton MA

South Carolina Artisans Center, Walterboro SC

South Carolina State Museum, Columbia SC

Southern Illinois University, University Museum, Carbondale IL

Southern Oregon Historical Society, Jacksonville Museum of Southern Oregon History, Medford OR

Springfield Art & Historical Society, Miller Art Center, Springfield VT

Springfield Art Museum, Springfield MO

Springfield Library & Museums Association, Connecticut Valley Historical Museum, Springfield MA

Stanford University, Museum of Art, Stanford CA

Nelda C & H J Lutcher Stark Foundation, Stark Museum of Art, Orange TX

Sunrise Museum, Inc, Sunrise Art Museum & Sunrise Science Museum, Charleston WV

Susquehanna University, Lore Degenstein Gallery, Selinsgrove PA

Swedish American Museum Association of Chicago, Chicago IL

Sheldon Swope Art Museum, Terre Haute IN

Syracuse University, Art Collection, Syracuse NY

Telfair Museum of Art, Savannah GA

The Temple-Tifereth Israel, The Temple Museum of Religious Art, Beachwood OH

Toledo Museum of Art, Toledo OH

Topeka & Shawnee County Public Library, Gallery of Fine Arts, Topeka KS

Tulane University, University Art Collection, New Orleans LA

Tulane University, Dept Art Newcomb Col Art Galleries, New Orleans LA

Mark Twain Memorial, Hartford CT

The Ukrainian Museum, New York NY

United Methodist Historical Society, Lovely Lane Museum, Baltimore MD

United States Capitol, Architect of the Capitol, Washington DC

US Coast Guard Museum, New London CT

United States Figure Skating Association, World Figure Skating Museum & Hall of Fame, Colorado Springs CO

University of Alabama at Birmingham, Visual Arts Gallery, Birmingham AL

University of British Columbia, Museum of Anthropology, Vancouver BC

University of Chicago, David & Alfred Smart Museum of Art, Chicago IL

University of Illinois, Krannert Art Museum, Champaign IL

University of Illinois, World Heritage Museum, Champaign IL

University of Iowa, Museum of Art, Iowa City IA

University of Manitoba, Faculty of Architecture Exhibition Centre, Winnipeg MB

University of Miami, Lowe Art Museum, Coral Gables FL

University of Michigan, Museum of Art, Ann Arbor MI

DIORAMAS

DOLLS

Presidential Museum, Odessa TX
Principia College, School of Nations Museum, Elsah IL
Putnam Museum of History & Natural Science, Davenport IA
Rensselaer County Historical Society, Hart-Cluett Mansion, 1827, Troy NY
Rhode Island Historical Society, John Brown House, Providence RI
Riley County Historical Society, Riley County Historical Museum, Manhattan KS
Riverside Municipal Museum, Riverside CA
Millicent Rogers Museum of Northern New Mexico, Taos NM
Saint Joseph Museum, Saint Joseph MO
Santa Barbara Museum of Art, Santa Barbara CA
Seneca-Iroquois National Museum, Salamanca NY
Shaker Museum & Library, Old Chatham NY
Shelburne Museum, Shelburne VT
Sooke Region Museum & Art Gallery, Sooke BC
South Carolina Artisans Center, Walterboro SC
Southern Illinois University, University Museum, Carbondale IL
Southern Oregon Historical Society, Jacksonville Museum of Southern Oregon History, Medford OR
Springfield Art & Historical Society, Miller Art Center, Springfield VT
Stratford Historical Society, Katherine Mitchel Museum, Stratford CT
University of Chicago, Oriental Institute Museum, Chicago IL
University of Mississippi, University Museums, Oxford MS
Wellfleet Historical Society Museum, Wellfleet MA
Westmoreland Museum of American Art, Greensburg PA
Whatcom Museum of History and Art, Bellingham WA
Wheelwright Museum of the American Indian, Santa Fe NM
Willard House & Clock Museum, Inc, North Grafton MA
Witte Museum, San Antonio TX
Yarmouth County Historical Society, Yarmouth County Museum, Yarmouth NS
York Institute Museum, Saco ME

DRAWINGS

Academy of the New Church, Glencairn Museum, Bryn Athyn PA
Alaska State Museum, Juneau AK
Albany Institute of History & Art, Albany NY
The Albrecht-Kemper Museum of Art, Saint Joseph MO
Albuquerque Museum of Art & History, Albuquerque NM
Allentown Art Museum, Allentown PA
American Kennel Club, Museum of the Dog, Saint Louis MO
American University, Watkins Collection, Washington DC
Anchorage Museum of History & Art, Anchorage AK
Walter Anderson Museum of Art, Ocean Springs MS
Arkansas Arts Center, Little Rock AR
Arkansas Territorial Restoration, Little Rock AR
Artesia Historical Museum & Art Center, Artesia NM
Art Gallery of Nova Scotia, Halifax NS
Art Museum of the Americas, Washington DC
Arts & Science Center, Statesville NC
Arts Council of Fayetteville-Cumberland County, The Arts Center, Fayetteville NC
ArtSpace-Lima, Lima OH
Asbury College, Student Center Gallery, Wilmore KY
Austin Peay State University, Margaret Fort Trahern Gallery, Clarksville TN
Leo Baeck Institute, New York NY
Baldwin-Wallace College, Fawick Art Gallery, Berea OH
Ball State University, Museum of Art, Muncie IN
Baltimore Museum of Art, Baltimore MD
Bank One Gallery, Louisville KY
Barnes Foundation, Merion PA

Baruch College of the City University of New York, Sidney Mishkin Gallery, New York NY
Baylor University, Martin Museum of Art, Waco TX
Beaverbrook Art Gallery, Fredericton NB
Bennington Museum, Bennington Museum, Bennington VT
Berea College, Doris Ulmann Galleries, Berea KY
Berkshire Museum, Pittsfield MA
Jesse Besser Museum, Alpena MI
The Bostonian Society, Old State House Museum, Boston MA
Bowdoin College, Museum of Art, Brunswick ME
Roy Boyd Gallery, Chicago IL
Brandywine River Museum, Chadds Ford PA
Brigham Young University, B F Larsen Gallery, Provo UT
Brigham Young University, Museum of Art, Provo UT
Butler Institute of American Art, Art Museum, Youngstown OH
California Historical Society, El Molino Viejo, San Marino CA
California State University Stanislaus, University Art Gallery, Turlock CA
Calvin College, Center Art Gallery, Grand Rapids MI
Canadian Museum of Nature, Musee Canadien de la Nature, Ottawa ON
Carnegie Institute, Carnegie Museum of Art, Pittsburgh PA
Carson County Square House Museum, Panhandle TX
Kit Carson Historic Museums, Ernest Blumenschein Home & Studio, Taos NM
Cartoon Art Museum, San Francisco CA
Cedar Rapids Museum of Art, Cedar Rapids IA
Chattahoochee Valley Art Museum, LaGrange GA
Chicago Department of Cultural Affairs, Chicago Cultural Center, Chicago IL
CIGNA Corporation, CIGNA Museum & Art Collection, Philadelphia PA
City of Atlanta, Chastain Arts Center, Atlanta GA
City of Cedar Falls, Iowa, James & Meryl Hearst Center for the Arts, Cedar Falls IA
City of Pittsfield, Berkshire Artisans, Pittsfield MA
Sterling & Francine Clark Art Institute, Williamstown MA
Cleveland State University, Art Gallery, Cleveland OH
Clinton County Historical Association, Clinton County Historical Museum, Plattsburgh NY
College of New Jersey, Art Gallery, Trenton NJ
College of Saint Benedict, Art Gallery, Saint Joseph MN
College of William & Mary, Joseph & Margaret Muscarelle Museum of Art, Williamsburg VA
Colorado Springs Fine Arts Center, Colorado Springs CO
Columbus Museum, Columbus GA
Columbus Museum of Art, Columbus OH
Community Fine Arts Center, Halseth Gallery, Rock Springs WY
Concordia University, Leonard & Bina Ellen Art Gallery, Montreal PQ
Cooper-Hewitt, National Design Museum, New York NY
Corcoran Gallery of Art, Washington DC
Cornell University, Herbert F Johnson Museum of Art, Ithaca NY
Cornish College of the Arts, Fisher Gallery, Seattle WA
Cornwall Gallery Society, Regional Art Gallery, Cornwall ON
Cranbrook Art Museum, Bloomfield Hills MI
Creighton University, Fine Arts Gallery, Omaha NE
Crow Wing County Historical Society, Brainerd MN
The Currier Gallery of Art, Manchester NH
C W Post Campus of Long Island University, Hillwood Art Museum, Brookville NY
Dahesh Museum, New York NY
Danforth Museum of Art, Framingham MA
Dartmouth College, Hood Museum of Art, Hanover NH
Dartmouth Heritage Museum, Dartmouth NS

Davidson College Visual Arts Center, William H Van Every Jr & Edward M Smith Galleries, Davidson NC
Del Mar College, Joseph A Cain Memorial Art Gallery, Corpus Christi TX
Detroit Institute of Arts, Detroit MI
Detroit Repertory Theatre Gallery, Detroit MI
Dickinson College, Trout Gallery, Carlisle PA
Duke University Museum of Art, Durham NC
Eiteljorg Museum of American Indians & Western Art, Indianapolis IN
Ellen Noel Art Museum of the Permian Basin, Odessa TX
Elmhurst Art Museum, Elmhurst IL
Farmington Village Green & Library Association, Stanley-Whitman House, Farmington CT
Fayette Art Museum, Fayette AL
Federal Reserve Board, Art Gallery, Washington DC
Fine Arts Museums of San Francisco, M H de Young Memorial Museum & California Palace of the Legion of Honor, San Francisco CA
The First National Bank of Chicago, Art Collection, Chicago IL
Fitchburg Art Museum, Fitchburg MA
Florence Museum of Art, Science & History, Florence SC
Edsel & Eleanor Ford House, Grosse Pointe Shores MI
Fort Hays State University, Moss-Thorns Gallery of Arts, Hays KS
Fort Smith Art Center, Fort Smith AR
Frick Collection, New York NY
Fuller Museum of Art, Brockton MA
Gallery 53, Cooperstown NY
Gallery One, Ellensburg WA
Getty Center for the History of Art & the Humanities Trust Museum, The J Paul Getty Museum, Santa Monica CA
Glanmore, Hastings County Museum, Belleville ON
Gonzaga University, Jundt Art Museum, Ad Art Gallery, Spokane WA
Goucher College, Rosenberg Gallery, Baltimore MD
Greater Lafayette Museum of Art, Lafayette IN
Great Lakes Historical Society, Island Seas Maritime Museum, Vermilion OH
Greenville College, Richard W Bock Sculpture Collection, Greenville IL
Grinnell College, Print & Drawing Study Room/ Gallery, Grinnell IA
Guggenheim Museum Soho, New York NY
Solomon R Guggenheim Museum, New York NY
Guilford College, Art Gallery, Greensboro NC
Hamilton College, Fred L Emerson Gallery, Clinton NY
Hampton University, University Museum, Hampton VA
Hartwick College, Foreman Gallery, Oneonta NY
Harvard University, William Hayes Fogg Art Museum, Cambridge MA
Headquarters Fort Monroe, Dept of Army, Casemate Museum, Fort Monroe VA
Heard Museum, Phoenix AZ
Hebrew Union College, Skirball Cultural Center, Los Angeles CA
Heckscher Museum of Art, Huntington NY
Henry Gallery Association, Henry Art Gallery, Seattle WA
Hirshhorn Museum & Sculpture Garden, Washington DC
Hispanic Society of America, Museum, New York NY
Historical Society of Pennsylvania, Philadelphia PA
Housatonic Community-Technical College, Housatonic Museum of Art, Bridgeport CT
Huguenot Historical Society of New Paltz Galleries, New Paltz NY
The Huntington Library, Art Collections & Botanical Gardens, San Marino CA
Huronia Museum, Midland ON
Hyde Park Art Center, Chicago IL
Illinois Wesleyan University, Merwin & Wakeley Galleries, Bloomington IL
Imperial Calcasieu Museum, Gibson-Barham Gallery, Lake Charles LA
Indianapolis Museum of Art, Indianapolis IN
Indiana University, Art Museum, Bloomington IN

University of California, Richard L Nelson Gallery & Fine Arts Collection, Davis CA
University of California, Berkeley Art Museum & Pacific Film Archive, Berkeley CA
University of California, Santa Barbara, University Art Museum, Santa Barbara CA
University of Chicago, David & Alfred Smart Museum of Art, Chicago IL
University of Cincinnati, DAAP Galleries-College of Design Architecture, Art & Planning, Cincinnati OH
University of Colorado, Art Galleries, Boulder CO
University of Colorado at Colorado Springs, Gallery of Contemporary Art, Colorado Springs CO
University of Delaware, University Gallery, Newark DE
University of Florida, Samuel P Harn Museum of Art, Gainesville FL
University of Georgia, Georgia Museum of Art, Athens GA
University of Illinois, Krannert Art Museum, Champaign IL
University of Iowa, Museum of Art, Iowa City IA
University of Kansas, Spencer Museum of Art, Lawrence KS
University of Louisville, Allen R Hite Art Institute Gallery, Louisville KY
University of Manitoba, Faculty of Architecture Exhibition Centre, Winnipeg MB
University of Massachusetts, Amherst, University Gallery, Amherst MA
University of Memphis, Art Museum, Memphis TN
University of Minnesota, Weisman Art Museum, Minneapolis MN
University of Mississippi, University Museums, Oxford MS
University of Missouri, Museum of Art & Archaeology, Columbia MO
University of Nebraska, Lincoln, Sheldon Memorial Art Gallery & Sculpture Garden, Lincoln NE
University of New Hampshire, The Art Gallery, Durham NH
University of New Mexico, University Art Museum, Albuquerque NM
University of North Carolina at Greensboro, Weatherspoon Art Gallery, Greensboro NC
University of Notre Dame, Snite Museum of Art, Notre Dame IN
University of Pennsylvania, Arthur Ross Gallery, Philadelphia PA
University of Pittsburgh, University Art Gallery, Pittsburgh PA
University of Rhode Island, Fine Arts Center Galleries, Kingston RI
University of Rochester, Memorial Art Gallery, Rochester NY
University of Southern Colorado, College of Liberal & Fine Arts, Pueblo CO
University of South Florida, Contemporary Art Museum, Tampa FL
University of Texas at Austin, Archer M Huntington Art Gallery, Austin TX
University of Vermont, Robert Hull Fleming Museum, Burlington VT
University of Victoria, Maltwood Art Museum and Gallery, Victoria BC
University of Washington, Henry Art Gallery, Seattle WA
University of Wisconsin Oshkosh, Allen R Priebe Gallery, Oshkosh WI
University of Wisconsin-Stout, J Furlong Gallery, Menomonie WI
Upstairs Gallery, Winnipeg MB
Ursinus College, Philip & Muriel Berman Museum of Art, Collegeville PA
Valparaiso University, Brauer Museum of Art, Valparaiso IN
Vassar College, The Frances Lehman Loeb Art Center, Poughkeepsie NY
Virginia Museum of Fine Arts, Richmond VA
Viridian Artists Inc, New York NY
Wadsworth Atheneum, Hartford CT
Walker Art Center, Minneapolis MN
Washington County Museum of Fine Arts, Hagerstown MD
Waterworks Visual Arts Center, Salisbury NC
Wesleyan University, Davison Art Center, Middletown CT

West Bend Art Museum, West Bend WI
Western Illinois University, Art Gallery-Museum, Macomb IL
Westminster College, Art Gallery, New Wilmington PA
Westmoreland Museum of American Art, Greensburg PA
Whatcom Museum of History and Art, Bellingham WA
Wheaton College, Watson Gallery, Norton MA
Wheelwright Museum of the American Indian, Santa Fe NM
Whitney Museum of American Art, New York NY
Wichita Art Museum, Wichita KS
Wilfrid Laurier University, Robert Langen Gallery, Waterloo ON
Kemper & Leila Williams Foundation, New Orleans LA
Woodlawn Plantation, Mount Vernon VA
Woodmere Art Museum, Philadelphia PA
Xavier University, Xavier Art Gallery, Cincinnati OH
Yale University, Yale Center for British Art, New Haven CT
Yarmouth County Historical Society, Yarmouth County Museum, Yarmouth NS

EMBROIDERY

Academy of the New Church, Glencairn Museum, Bryn Athyn PA
Albany Institute of History & Art, Albany NY
Allentown Art Museum, Allentown PA
Amherst Museum, Amherst NY
Arkansas Territorial Restoration, Little Rock AR
Artesia Historical Museum & Art Center, Artesia NM
Art Museum of Missoula, Missoula MT
Asian Art Museum of San Francisco, Avery Brundage Collection, San Francisco CA
Association for the Preservation of Virginia Antiquities, John Marshall House, Richmond VA
Leo Baeck Institute, New York NY
Baltimore Museum of Art, Baltimore MD
Bank One Gallery, Louisville KY
Bennington Museum, Bennington Museum, Bennington VT
Cape Ann Historical Museum, Gloucester MA
Kit Carson Historic Museums, Hacienda Martinez, Taos NM
Central United Methodist Church, Swords Info Plowshares Peace Center & Gallery, Detroit MI
Chicago Department of Cultural Affairs, Chicago Cultural Center, Chicago IL
Clinton County Historical Association, Clinton County Historical Museum, Plattsburgh NY
Cooper-Hewitt, National Design Museum, New York NY
Cornwall Gallery Society, Regional Art Gallery, Cornwall ON
County of Henrico, Meadow Farm Museum, Glen Allen VA
Craft & Folk Art Museum, Los Angeles CA
Craigdarroch Castle Historical Museum Society, Victoria BC
Crow Wing County Historical Society, Brainerd MN
The Currier Gallery of Art, Manchester NH
DAR Museum, National Society Daughters of the American Revolution, Washington DC
Dartmouth Heritage Museum, Dartmouth NS
Davidson College Visual Arts Center, William H Van Every Jr & Edward M Smith Galleries, Davidson NC
Douglas County Historical Society, Fairlawn Mansion & Museum, Superior WI
Ellen Noel Art Museum of the Permian Basin, Odessa TX
Ephraim McDowell-Cambus-Kenneth Foundation, McDowell House & Apothecary Shop, Danville KY
Erie Art Museum, Erie PA
Farmington Village Green & Library Association, Stanley-Whitman House, Farmington CT
Fine Arts Museums of San Francisco, M H de Young Memorial Museum & California Palace of the Legion of Honor, San Francisco CA

Glanmore, Hastings County Museum, Belleville ON
Hebrew Union College, Skirball Cultural Center, Los Angeles CA
Historical Society of Old Newbury, Cushing House Museum, Newburyport MA
Historic Deerfield, Inc, Deerfield MA
House of Roses, Senator Wilson Home, Deadwood SD
Huguenot Historical Society of New Paltz Galleries, New Paltz NY
Imperial Calcasieu Museum, Gibson-Barham Gallery, Lake Charles LA
The Interchurch Center, Galleries at the Interchurch Center, New York NY
The Jewish Museum, New York NY
Kemerer Museum of Decorative Arts, Bethlehem PA
Kings County Historical Society and Museum, Hampton NB
Koochiching County Historical Society Museum, International Falls MN
Lac du Flambeau Band of Lake Superior Chippewa Indians, George W Brown Jr Ojibwe Museum & Cultural Center, Lac du Flambeau WI
Lafayette Natural History Museum, Planetarium & Nature Station, Lafayette LA
Leroy Historical Society, LeRoy NY
Litchfield Historical Society, Litchfield CT
Longfellow-Evangeline State Commemorative Area, Saint Martinville LA
Judah L Magnes Museum, Berkeley CA
Maine Historical Society, Wadsworth-Longfellow House, Portland ME
Maison Saint-Gabriel Museum, Montreal PQ
Mexican Museum, San Francisco CA
Mississippi Department of Archives & History, Old Capitol Museum, Jackson MS
Monroe County Historical Association, Elizabeth D Walters Library, Stroudsburg PA
Montana State University, Museum of the Rockies, Bozeman MT
Moravian College, Payne Gallery, Bethlehem PA
Musee des Augustines de l'Hotel Dieu de Quebec, Quebec PQ
Museum of Arts & History, Port Huron MI
Museum of the American Quilter's Society, Paducah KY
Museum of the City of New York, New York NY
The Museums at Stony Brook, Stony Brook NY
National Infantry Museum, Fort Benning GA
Naval Historical Center, The Navy Museum, Washington DC
Neville Public Museum, Green Bay WI
No Man's Land Historical Society Museum, Goodwell OK
North Carolina State University, Visual Arts Center, Raleigh NC
Old Dartmouth Historical Society, New Bedford Whaling Museum, New Bedford MA
Old York Historical Society, Old Gaol Museum, York ME
Oshkosh Public Museum, Oshkosh WI
Panhandle-Plains Historical Society Museum, Canyon TX
Pasadena Historical Museum, Pasadena CA
Peabody Essex Museum, Salem MA
Phelps County Historical Society, Phelps County Museum, Holdrege NE
Plainsman Museum, Aurora NE
Plumas County Museum, Quincy CA
Pope County Historical Society, Pope County Museum, Glenwood MN
Portsmouth Historical Society, John Paul Jones House, Portsmouth NH
Marjorie Merriweather Post Foundation of DC, Hillwood Museum, Washington DC
Putnam Museum of History & Natural Science, Davenport IA
Rensselaer County Historical Society, Hart-Cluett Mansion, 1827, Troy NY
Rhode Island Historical Society, John Brown House, Providence RI
Millicent Rogers Museum of Northern New Mexico, Taos NM
Royal Arts Foundation, Belcourt Castle, Newport RI
The Sandwich Historical Society, Inc, Sandwich Glass Museum, Sandwich MA

Shaker Museum & Library, Old Chatham NY
Southern Oregon Historical Society, Jacksonville Museum of Southern Oregon History, Medford OR
Stratford Historical Society, Katherine Mitchel Museum, Stratford CT
Swedish American Museum Association of Chicago, Chicago IL
The Temple-Tifereth Israel, The Temple Museum of Religious Art, Beachwood OH
The Ukrainian Museum, New York NY
Ukrainian National Museum & Library, Chicago IL
University of Kansas, Spencer Museum of Art, Lawrence KS
Wheelwright Museum of the American Indian, Santa Fe NM
Willard House & Clock Museum, Inc, North Grafton MA
Witte Museum, San Antonio TX
Woodlawn Plantation, Mount Vernon VA
Woodmere Art Museum, Philadelphia PA
Xavier University, Xavier Art Gallery, Cincinnati OH
Yarmouth County Historical Society, Yarmouth County Museum, Yarmouth NS

ENAMELS

Academy of the New Church, Glencairn Museum, Bryn Athyn PA
The Art Institute of Chicago, Chicago IL
ArtSpace-Lima, Lima OH
Bank One Gallery, Louisville KY
The Currier Gallery of Art, Manchester NH
The First National Bank of Chicago, Art Collection, Chicago IL
Gallery One, Ellensburg WA
Glanmore, Hastings County Museum, Belleville ON
Hispanic Society of America, Museum, New York NY
House of Roses, Senator Wilson Home, Deadwood SD
The Interchurch Center, Galleries at the Interchurch Center, New York NY
Iowa State University, Brunnier Art Museum, Ames IA
Johns Hopkins University, Evergreen House, Baltimore MD
LeSueur County Historical Museum, Chapter One, Elysian MN
Loyola University of Chicago, Martin D'Arcy Gallery of Art, Chicago IL
Mint Museum of Art, Charlotte NC
The Museum of Arts & Sciences Inc, Daytona Beach FL
New Orleans School of GlassWorks, Gallery & Printmaking Studio, New Orleans LA
Marjorie Merriweather Post Foundation of DC, Hillwood Museum, Washington DC
Southern Illinois University, University Museum, Carbondale IL
Topeka & Shawnee County Public Library, Gallery of Fine Arts, Topeka KS
Virginia Museum of Fine Arts, Richmond VA

ESKIMO ART

Alaska State Museum, Juneau AK
Anchorage Museum of History & Art, Anchorage AK
Archaeological Society of Ohio, Indian Museum of Lake County, Ohio, Painesville OH
Art Gallery of Hamilton, Hamilton ON
Art Gallery of Nova Scotia, Halifax NS
Art Museum of Missoula, Missoula MT
Aurora University, Schingoethe Center for Native American Cultures, Aurora IL
Bowdoin College, Peary-MacMillan Arctic Museum, Brunswick ME
Brevard Museum of Art & Science, Melbourne FL
Capital University, Schumacher Gallery, Columbus OH
Chilkat Valley Historical Society, Sheldon Museum & Cultural Center, Haines AK
CIGNA Corporation, CIGNA Museum & Art Collection, Philadelphia PA
College of Southern Idaho, Herrett Center for Arts & Science, Twin Falls ID

College of William & Mary, Joseph & Margaret Muscarelle Museum of Art, Williamsburg VA
Columbus Museum of Art, Columbus OH
C W Post Campus of Long Island University, Hillwood Art Museum, Brookville NY
Deming-Luna Mimbres Museum, Deming NM
Denver Art Museum, Denver CO
Discovery Place Inc, Charlotte NC
Eiteljorg Museum of American Indians & Western Art, Indianapolis IN
Eskimo Museum, Churchill MB
The First National Bank of Chicago, Art Collection, Chicago IL
Genesee Country Museum, John L Wehle Gallery of Sporting Art, Mumford NY
Heritage Center, Inc, Pine Ridge SD
Huronia Museum, Midland ON
Institute of American Indian Arts Museum, Santa Fe NM
The Interchurch Center, Galleries at the Interchurch Center, New York NY
Johnson-Humrickhouse Museum, Coshocton OH
Kelowna Museum, Kelowna BC
Kendall Whaling Museum, Sharon MA
Koshare Indian Museum, Inc, La Junta CO
Louisiana Arts & Science Center, Baton Rouge LA
Luther College, Fine Arts Collection, Decorah IA
MacDonald Stewart Art Centre, Guelph ON
Carrie McLain Museum, Nome AK
Maitland Art Center, Maitland FL
Maryhill Museum of Art, Goldendale WA
Moravian Historical Society, Whitefield House Museum, Nazareth PA
Musee Regional de la Cote-Nord, Sept-Iles PQ
Museum of Northern British Columbia, Ruth Harvey Art Gallery, Prince Rupert BC
National Art Museum of Sport, Indianapolis IN
National Museum of the American Indian, George Gustav Heye Center, New York NY
Northwestern Michigan College, Dennos Museum Center, Traverse City MI
Panhandle-Plains Historical Society Museum, Canyon TX
Peabody Essex Museum, Salem MA
Pope County Historical Society, Pope County Museum, Glenwood MN
Port Authority of New York & New Jersey, Art Collection, New York NY
Portland Art Museum, Portland OR
Riverside Municipal Museum, Riverside CA
Saint Joseph Museum, Saint Joseph MO
South Dakota State University, South Dakota Art Museum, Brookings SD
Topeka & Shawnee County Public Library, Gallery of Fine Arts, Topeka KS
US Coast Guard Museum, New London CT
United States Department of the Interior Museum, Washington DC
University of Alabama at Birmingham, Visual Arts Gallery, Birmingham AL
University of Delaware, University Gallery, Newark DE
University of Michigan, Museum of Art, Ann Arbor MI
University of Washington, Thomas Burke Memorial Washington State Museum, Seattle WA
Upstairs Gallery, Winnipeg MB
Vancouver Museum Commission, Vancouver Museum, Vancouver BC
Peter & Catharine Whyte Foundation, Whyte Museum of the Canadian Rockies, Banff AB
Wilfrid Laurier University, Robert Langen Gallery, Waterloo ON
Winnipeg Art Gallery, Winnipeg MB
Wistariahurst Museum, Holyoke MA
Wustum Museum Art Association, Racine WI
York University, Art Gallery of York University, North York ON
Yugtarvik Regional Museum & Bethel Visitors Center, Bethel AK

ETCHINGS & ENGRAVINGS

Alaska State Museum, Juneau AK
Albany Institute of History & Art, Albany NY
The Albrecht-Kemper Museum of Art, Saint Joseph MO
Albuquerque Museum of Art & History, Albuquerque NM
Allentown Art Museum, Allentown PA
American Kennel Club, Museum of the Dog, Saint Louis MO
American University, Watkins Collection, Washington DC
Anchorage Museum of History & Art, Anchorage AK
Arkansas Territorial Restoration, Little Rock AR
Arnot Art Museum, Elmira NY
Art Gallery of Hamilton, Hamilton ON
The Art Institute of Chicago, Chicago IL
Art Museum of Missoula, Missoula MT
ArtSpace-Lima, Lima OH
Asbury College, Student Center Gallery, Wilmore KY
Leo Baeck Institute, New York NY
Baldwin Historical Society Museum, Baldwin NY
Baruch College of the City University of New York, Sidney Mishkin Gallery, New York NY
Berea College, Doris Ulmann Galleries, Berea KY
Berkshire Museum, Pittsfield MA
Jesse Besser Museum, Alpena MI
Blanden Memorial Art Museum, Fort Dodge IA
Brandywine River Museum, Chadds Ford PA
Brigham Young University, Museum of Art, Provo UT
Brown University, David Winton Bell Gallery, Providence RI
The Buffalo Fine Arts Academy, Albright-Knox Art Gallery, Buffalo NY
California State University, Chico, Janet Turner Print Gallery & Collection, Chico CA
Cape Ann Historical Museum, Gloucester MA
Carson County Square House Museum, Panhandle TX
Cartoon Art Museum, San Francisco CA
Cedar Rapids Museum of Art, Cedar Rapids IA
Center for Book Arts, New York NY
Central United Methodist Church, Swords Info Plowshares Peace Center & Gallery, Detroit MI
Chattahoochee Valley Art Museum, LaGrange GA
CIGNA Corporation, CIGNA Museum & Art Collection, Philadelphia PA
Cincinnati Institute of Fine Arts, Taft Museum, Cincinnati OH
Cleveland State University, Art Gallery, Cleveland OH
Clinton Art Association Gallery, Clinton IA
Clinton County Historical Association, Clinton County Historical Museum, Plattsburgh NY
College of William & Mary, Joseph & Margaret Muscarelle Museum of Art, Williamsburg VA
Columbus Museum, Columbus GA
Columbus Museum of Art, Columbus OH
Community Fine Arts Center, Halseth Gallery, Rock Springs WY
Concordia Historical Institute, Saint Louis MO
Concordia University, Leonard & Bina Ellen Art Gallery, Montreal PQ
Cooper-Hewitt, National Design Museum, New York NY
Cranbrook Art Museum, Bloomfield Hills MI
Crow Wing County Historical Society, Brainerd MN
The Currier Gallery of Art, Manchester NH
Dahesh Museum, New York NY
Danforth Museum of Art, Framingham MA
Dartmouth Heritage Museum, Dartmouth NS
Davidson College Visual Arts Center, William H Van Every Jr & Edward M Smith Galleries, Davidson NC
DeCordova Museum & Sculpture Park, Lincoln MA
Delaware Art Museum, Wilmington DE
Denison University, Art Gallery, Granville OH
Detroit Institute of Arts, Detroit MI
Detroit Repertory Theatre Gallery, Detroit MI
Dickinson College, Trout Gallery, Carlisle PA
Duke University Museum of Art, Durham NC
Dundurn Castle, Hamilton ON
Durham Art Guild Inc, Durham NC

East Baton Rouge Parks & Recreation Commission, Baton Rouge Gallery Inc, Baton Rouge LA

Eastern Illinois University, Tarble Arts Center, Charleston IL

Eiteljorg Museum of American Indians & Western Art, Indianapolis IN

Ellen Noel Art Museum of the Permian Basin, Odessa TX

Elmhurst Art Museum, Elmhurst IL

Emory University, Michael C Carlos Museum, Atlanta GA

Erie Art Museum, Erie PA

Evansville Museum of Arts & Science, Evansville IN

Farmington Village Green & Library Association, Stanley-Whitman House, Farmington CT

Federal Reserve Board, Art Gallery, Washington DC

Fine Arts Museums of San Francisco, M H de Young Memorial Museum & California Palace of the Legion of Honor, San Francisco CA

The First National Bank of Chicago, Art Collection, Chicago IL

First Tennessee National Corp, First Tennessee Heritage Collection, Memphis TN

Florence Museum of Art, Science & History, Florence SC

Florida Gulf Coast Art Center, Inc, Belleair FL

Freeport Arts Center, Freeport IL

Fuller Museum of Art, Brockton MA

Galleries of the Claremont Colleges, Claremont CA

Gallery 53, Cooperstown NY

Gallery One, Ellensburg WA

Gonzaga University, Jundt Art Museum, Ad Art Gallery, Spokane WA

Grand Rapids Art Museum, Grand Rapids MI

Greater Lafayette Museum of Art, Lafayette IN

Grinnell College, Print & Drawing Study Room/Gallery, Grinnell IA

Guilford College, Art Gallery, Greensboro NC

Hamilton College, Fred L Emerson Gallery, Clinton NY

Hebrew Union College, Skirball Cultural Center, Los Angeles CA

Hebrew Union College-Jewish Institute of Religion, New York NY

Henry Gallery Association, Henry Art Gallery, Seattle WA

Hispanic Society of America, Museum, New York NY

Historical Society of Pennsylvania, Philadelphia PA

Historical Society of the Town of Greenwich, Inc, Bush-Holley House Museum, Cos Cob CT

Honolulu Academy of Arts, Honolulu HI

The Huntington Library, Art Collections & Botanical Gardens, San Marino CA

Huronia Museum, Midland ON

Hyde Park Art Center, Chicago IL

Imperial Calcasieu Museum, Gibson-Barham Gallery, Lake Charles LA

Indiana University, Art Museum, Bloomington IN

The Interchurch Center, Galleries at the Interchurch Center, New York NY

Jersey City Museum, Jersey City NJ

The Jewish Museum, New York NY

Joslyn Art Museum, Omaha NE

Kamloops Art Gallery, Kamloops BC

Kansas City Art Institute, Kemper Museum of Contemporary Art & Design, Kansas City MO

Maude I Kerns Art Center Galleries, Eugene OR

Knights of Columbus Supreme Council, Headquarters Museum, New Haven CT

Knoxville Museum of Art, Knoxville TN

Lafayette Natural History Museum, Planetarium & Nature Station, Lafayette LA

Leroy Historical Society, LeRoy NY

LeSueur County Historical Museum, Chapter One, Elysian MN

Lockwood-Mathews Mansion Museum, Norwalk CT

Longview Art Museum, Longview TX

Luther College, Fine Arts Collection, Decorah IA

Charles H MacNider Museum, Mason City IA

Judah L Magnes Museum, Berkeley CA

Maitland Art Center, Maitland FL

The Mariners' Museum, Newport News VA

Maryhill Museum of Art, Goldendale WA

Marylhurst College, The Art Gym, Marylhurst OR

Mary Washington College, Belmont, The Gari Melchers, Fredericksburg VA

Mexican Museum, San Francisco CA

Michigan State University, Kresge Art Museum, East Lansing MI

Midwest Museum of American Art, Elkhart IN

Mint Museum of Art, Charlotte NC

Mobile Museum of Art, Mobile AL

Mohawk Valley Heritage Association, Inc, Walter Elwood Museum, Amsterdam NY

Montana State University, Museum of the Rockies, Bozeman MT

Montgomery Museum of Fine Arts, Montgomery AL

Morris-Jumel Mansion, Inc, New York NY

Morris Museum, Morristown NJ

Murray State University, Eagle Gallery, Murray KY

Museo De Las Americas, Denver CO

The Museum of Arts & Sciences Inc, Daytona Beach FL

Museum of Contemporary Art, North Miami FL

Museum of the Americas, Brookfield VT

Museum of the City of New York, New York NY

Muttart Public Art Gallery, Calgary AB

National Art Museum of Sport, Indianapolis IN

National Gallery of Canada, Ottawa ON

National Infantry Museum, Fort Benning GA

National Museum of American Art, Washington DC

National Museum of Wildlife Art, Jackson WY

National Museum of Women in the Arts, Washington DC

National Park Service, Weir Farm National Historic Site, Wilton CT

Naval Historical Center, The Navy Museum, Washington DC

Nelson-Atkins Museum of Art, Kansas City MO

Nevada Museum Of Art, Reno NV

Neville Public Museum, Green Bay WI

New Mexico State University, University Art Gallery, Las Cruces NM

New Orleans School of GlassWorks, Gallery & Printmaking Studio, New Orleans LA

Newport Art Museum, Newport RI

New Visions Gallery, Inc, Marshfield WI

New York Studio School of Drawing, Painting & Sculpture, Gallery, New York NY

Northern Illinois University, NIU Art Museum, De Kalb IL

Northwestern College, Te Paske Gallery, Orange City IA

Oklahoma City Art Museum, Oklahoma City OK

Old Dartmouth Historical Society, New Bedford Whaling Museum, New Bedford MA

Owensboro Museum of Fine Art, Owensboro KY

Page-Walker Arts & History Center, Cary NC

Palm Springs Desert Museum, Palm Springs CA

Panhandle-Plains Historical Society Museum, Canyon TX

The Parrish Art Museum, Southampton NY

Peabody Essex Museum, Salem MA

Pennsylvania Academy of the Fine Arts, Museum of American Art, Philadelphia PA

Pensacola Museum of Art, Pensacola FL

George Phippen Memorial Foundation, Phippen Museum of Western Art, Prescott AZ

Port Authority of New York & New Jersey, Art Collection, New York NY

Portland Art Museum, Portland OR

Provincetown Art Association & Museum, Provincetown MA

Randolph-Macon Woman's College, Maier Museum of Art, Lynchburg VA

Rensselaer County Historical Society, Hart-Cluett Mansion, 1827, Troy NY

Rhode Island Historical Society, John Brown House, Providence RI

The Rockwell Museum, Corning NY

Roswell Museum & Art Center, Roswell NM

C M Russell Museum, Great Falls MT

Rutgers University, Stedman Art Gallery, Camden NJ

Saint Gregory's Abbey & College, Mabee-Gerrer Museum of Art, Shawnee OK

Santa Barbara Museum of Art, Santa Barbara CA

School of Visual Arts, Visual Arts Museum, New York NY

The Seagram Museum, Waterloo ON

1708 Gallery, Richmond VA

Sioux City Art Center, Sioux City IA

Southern Alleghenies Museum of Art, Southern Alleghenies Museum of Art at Johnstown, Loretto PA

Southern Illinois University, University Museum, Carbondale IL

Southern Methodist University, Meadows Museum, Dallas TX

Springfield Art & Historical Society, Miller Art Center, Springfield VT

Springfield Art Museum, Springfield MO

Stanford University, Museum of Art, Stanford CA

Nelda C & H J Lutcher Stark Foundation, Stark Museum of Art, Orange TX

State Capitol Museum, Olympia WA

State Historical Society of Wisconsin, State Historical Museum, Madison WI

State University of New York at New Paltz, College Art Gallery, New Paltz NY

Susquehanna University, Lore Degenstein Gallery, Selinsgrove PA

Swedish American Museum Association of Chicago, Chicago IL

Syracuse University, Art Collection, Syracuse NY

The Temple-Tifereth Israel, The Temple Museum of Religious Art, Beachwood OH

Topeka & Shawnee County Public Library, Gallery of Fine Arts, Topeka KS

The Turner Museum, Denver CO

The Ukrainian Museum, New York NY

United States Capitol, Architect of the Capitol, Washington DC

US Coast Guard Museum, New London CT

United States Figure Skating Association, World Figure Skating Museum & Hall of Fame, Colorado Springs CO

United States Military Academy, West Point Museum, West Point NY

University of Alabama at Birmingham, Visual Arts Gallery, Birmingham AL

University of California, Richard L Nelson Gallery & Fine Arts Collection, Davis CA

University of California, Santa Barbara, University Art Museum, Santa Barbara CA

University of Cincinnati, DAAP Galleries-College of Design Architecture, Art & Planning, Cincinnati OH

University of Colorado at Colorado Springs, Gallery of Contemporary Art, Colorado Springs CO

University of Delaware, University Gallery, Newark DE

University of Florida, Samuel P Harn Museum of Art, Gainesville FL

University of Iowa, Museum of Art, Iowa City IA

University of Kansas, Spencer Museum of Art, Lawrence KS

University of Manitoba, Faculty of Architecture Exhibition Centre, Winnipeg MB

University of Memphis, Art Museum, Memphis TN

University of Mississippi, University Museums, Oxford MS

University of New Hampshire, The Art Gallery, Durham NH

University of Pennsylvania, Arthur Ross Gallery, Philadelphia PA

University of Texas at Austin, Archer M Huntington Art Gallery, Austin TX

University of Victoria, Maltwood Art Museum and Gallery, Victoria BC

University of Virginia, Bayly Art Museum, Charlottesville VA

Upstairs Gallery, Winnipeg MB

Ursinus College, Philip & Muriel Berman Museum of Art, Collegeville PA

Vassar College, The Frances Lehman Loeb Art Center, Poughkeepsie NY

Virginia Museum of Fine Arts, Richmond VA

Washburn University, Mulvane Art Museum, Topeka KS

Wesleyan University, Davison Art Center, Middletown CT

Westmoreland Museum of American Art, Greensburg PA

Peter & Catharine Whyte Foundation, Whyte Museum of the Canadian Rockies, Banff AB

Wichita State University, Edwin A Ulrich Museum of Art, Wichita KS

Grand Rapids Art Museum, Grand Rapids MI
Greater Lafayette Museum of Art, Lafayette IN
Halifax Historical Society, Inc, Halifax Historical Museum, Daytona Beach FL
Hambidge Center Gallery, Rabun Gap GA
Hebrew Union College, Skirball Cultural Center, Los Angeles CA
Hebrew Union College - Jewish Institute of Religion, Skirball Museum-Cincinnati Branch, Cincinnati OH
Hebrew Union College-Jewish Institute of Religion, New York NY
Heritage Center, Inc, Pine Ridge SD
Heritage Center of Lancaster County Museum, Lancaster PA
Heritage Hjemkomst Interpretive Center, Moorhead MN
Heritage Plantation of Sandwich, Sandwich MA
High Point Historical Society Inc, Museum, High Point NC
Hinckley Foundation Museum, Ithaca NY
Hispanic Society of America, Museum, New York NY
Huguenot Historical Society of New Paltz Galleries, New Paltz NY
Huntington Museum of Art, Huntington WV
Huronia Museum, Midland ON
Hyde Park Art Center, Chicago IL
Illinois Historic Preservation Agency, Bishop Hill State Historic Site, Bishop Hill IL
Illinois State Museum, Illinois Art Gallery & Lockport Gallery, Springfield IL
Illinois State Museum, Illinois Art Gallery, Chicago IL
Imperial Calcasieu Museum, Gibson-Barham Gallery, Lake Charles LA
Indiana University, William Hammond Mathers Museum, Bloomington IN
Jamestown-Yorktown Foundation, Williamsburg VA
Jefferson County Open Space, Hiwan Homestead Museum, Evergreen CO
Jersey City Museum, Jersey City NJ
Kelowna Museum, Kelowna BC
Kemerer Museum of Decorative Arts, Bethlehem PA
Key West Art & Historical Society, East Martello Museum & Gallery, Key West FL
Kiah Museum, Savannah GA
Knoxville Museum of Art, Knoxville TN
Koshare Indian Museum, Inc, La Junta CO
Lafayette Natural History Museum, Planetarium & Nature Station, Lafayette LA
Lakeview Museum of Arts & Sciences, Peoria IL
Leelanau Historical Museum, Leland MI
LeSueur County Historical Museum, Chapter One, Elysian MN
Litchfield Historical Society, Litchfield CT
Louisiana Arts & Science Center, Baton Rouge LA
Loyola Marymount University, Laband Art Gallery, Los Angeles CA
McAllen International Museum, McAllen TX
McCord Museum of Canadian History, Montreal PQ
Judah L Magnes Museum, Berkeley CA
Maine Historical Society, Maine History Gallery, Portland ME
Manhattan Psychiatric Center, East River Gallery, New York NY
Maricopa County Historical Society, Desert Caballeros Western Museum, Wickenburg AZ
The Mariners' Museum, Newport News VA
Marylhurst College, The Art Gym, Marylhurst OR
Mendocino County Arts Council, Westport CA
Mercer County Community College, The Gallery, Trenton NJ
Mexican Fine Arts Center Museum, Chicago IL
Mexican Museum, San Francisco CA
Miami University, Art Museum, Oxford OH
Midwest Museum of American Art, Elkhart IN
Milwaukee Public Museum, Milwaukee WI
Mingei International, Inc, Mingei International Museum Satellite of World Folk Art, San Diego CA
Mississippi Department of Archives & History, Old Capitol Museum, Jackson MS
Mississippi River Museum at Mud-Island, Memphis TN

Arthur Roy Mitchell Memorial Inc, Museum of Western Art, Trinidad CO
Mobile Museum of Art, Mobile AL
Montana State University, Museum of the Rockies, Bozeman MT
Monterey Museum of Art Association, Monterey CA
Montgomery Museum of Fine Arts, Montgomery AL
Moore College of Art & Design, Goldie Paley Gallery, Philadelphia PA
Moose Jaw Art Museum & National Exhibition Centre, Art & History Museum, Moose Jaw SK
Moravian Historical Society, Whitefield House Museum, Nazareth PA
Morris Museum of Art, Augusta GA
Musee d'Art de Saint-Laurent, Saint-Laurent PQ
Museo De Las Americas, Denver CO
Museum of American Folk Art, New York NY
Museum of Arts & History, Port Huron MI
Museum of New Mexico, Museum of International Folk Art, Santa Fe NM
Museum of Northern Arizona, Flagstaff AZ
Museum of the American Quilter's Society, Paducah KY
Museum of the Americas, Brookfield VT
Museum of the City of New York, New York NY
The Museums at Stony Brook, Stony Brook NY
Muttart Public Art Gallery, Calgary AB
National Museum of American Art, Washington DC
The National Park Service, United States Department of the Interior, The Statue of Liberty National Monument, New York NY
Naval Historical Center, The Navy Museum, Washington DC
Neville Public Museum, Green Bay WI
Newark Museum Association, The Newark Museum, Newark NJ
New Brunswick Museum, Saint John NB
New Mexico State University, University Art Gallery, Las Cruces NM
New York State Historical Association, Fenimore House Museum, Cooperstown NY
No Man's Land Historical Society Museum, Goodwell OK
North Carolina State University, Visual Arts Center, Raleigh NC
Northern Kentucky University Gallery, Highland Heights KY
Noyes Museum, Oceanville NJ
Ohio Historical Society, National Afro American Museum & Cultural Center, Wilberforce OH
The Ohio Historical Society, Inc, Campus Martius Museum & Ohio River Museum, Marietta OH
Old Dartmouth Historical Society, New Bedford Whaling Museum, New Bedford MA
Old Salem Inc, Museum of Early Southern Decorative Arts, Winston-Salem NC
Oshkosh Public Museum, Oshkosh WI
Owensboro Museum of Fine Art, Owensboro KY
Pacific - Asia Museum, Pasadena CA
Page-Walker Arts & History Center, Cary NC
Palm Beach County Parks & Recreation Department, Morikami Museum & Japanese Gardens, Delray Beach FL
Panhandle-Plains Historical Society Museum, Canyon TX
Paris Gibson Square, Museum of Art, Great Falls MT
Pasadena Historical Museum, Pasadena CA
Passaic County Historical Society, Paterson NJ
Peabody Essex Museum, Salem MA
Pensacola Museum of Art, Pensacola FL
Philadelphia Museum of Art, Philadelphia PA
Plainsman Museum, Aurora NE
Polish Museum of America, Chicago IL
Port Authority of New York & New Jersey, Art Collection, New York NY
Prairie Art Gallery, Grande Prairie AB
Promote Art Works Inc (PAWI), Laziza Videodance Lumia Project, Brooklyn NY
Randolph-Macon Woman's College, Maier Museum of Art, Lynchburg VA
Reading Public Museum, Reading PA
Rensselaer County Historical Society, Hart-Cluett Mansion, 1827, Troy NY
Riverside Municipal Museum, Riverside CA

Rock Ford Foundation, Inc, Historic Rock Ford & Kauffman Museum, Lancaster PA
Millicent Rogers Museum of Northern New Mexico, Taos NM
Rollins College, George D & Harriet W Cornell Fine Arts Museum, Winter Park FL
Roswell Museum & Art Center, Roswell NM
C M Russell Museum, Great Falls MT
Saint Mary's Romanian Orthodox Church, Romanian Ethnic Museum, Cleveland OH
San Antonio Museum of Art, San Antonio TX
Shaker Village of Pleasant Hill, Harrodsburg KY
Shelburne Museum, Shelburne VT
South Carolina Artisans Center, Walterboro SC
South Carolina State Museum, Columbia SC
Southeastern Center for Contemporary Art, Winston-Salem NC
Southern Alleghenies Museum of Art, Southern Alleghenies Museum of Art at Johnstown, Loretto PA
Southern Illinois University, University Museum, Carbondale IL
Southern Oregon Historical Society, Jacksonville Museum of Southern Oregon History, Medford OR
South Street Seaport Museum, New York NY
Spartanburg County Museum of Art, Spartanburg SC
Springfield Art Museum, Springfield MO
State Historical Society of Wisconsin, State Historical Museum, Madison WI
Stratford Historical Society, Katherine Mitchel Museum, Stratford CT
Swedish American Museum Association of Chicago, Chicago IL
Tallahassee Museum of History & Natural Science, Tallahassee FL
The Temple-Tifereth Israel, The Temple Museum of Religious Art, Beachwood OH
Towson State University, Asian Arts Center, Towson MD
Tubman African American Museum, Macon GA
The Ukrainian Museum, New York NY
Ukrainian National Museum & Library, Chicago IL
United States Military Academy, West Point Museum, West Point NY
University of British Columbia, Museum of Anthropology, Vancouver BC
University of California, Berkeley Art Museum & Pacific Film Archive, Berkeley CA
University of California, Los Angeles, Fowler Museum of Cultural History, Los Angeles CA
University of Colorado at Colorado Springs, Gallery of Contemporary Art, Colorado Springs CO
University of Florida, University Gallery, Gainesville FL
University of Florida, Samuel P Harn Museum of Art, Gainesville FL
University of Memphis, Art Museum, Memphis TN
University of Mississippi, University Museums, Oxford MS
University of Nebraska, Lincoln, Sheldon Memorial Art Gallery & Sculpture Garden, Lincoln NE
University of Rochester, Memorial Art Gallery, Rochester NY
The University of Texas, Institute of Texan Cultures, San Antonio TX
University of Victoria, Maltwood Art Museum and Gallery, Victoria BC
Upstairs Gallery, Winnipeg MB
Ursinus College, Philip & Muriel Berman Museum of Art, Collegeville PA
Utah Arts Council, Chase Home Museum of Utah Folk Art, Salt Lake City UT
Vancouver Museum Commission, Vancouver Museum, Vancouver BC
Wadsworth Atheneum, Hartford CT
Waterworks Visual Arts Center, Salisbury NC
Western Kentucky University, Kentucky Museum, Bowling Green KY
Westmoreland Museum of American Art, Greensburg PA
Wethersfield Historical Society Inc, Museum, Wethersfield CT
Whatcom Museum of History and Art, Bellingham WA
Wheelwright Museum of the American Indian, Santa Fe NM

Willard House & Clock Museum, Inc, North Grafton MA

Williams College, Museum of Art, Williamstown MA

Witte Museum, San Antonio TX

Woodmere Art Museum, Philadelphia PA

Yarmouth County Historical Society, Yarmouth County Museum, Yarmouth NS

York Institute Museum, Saco ME

FURNITURE

Academy of the New Church, Glencairn Museum, Bryn Athyn PA

Alaska State Museum, Juneau AK

Albany Institute of History & Art, Albany NY

Allentown Art Museum, Allentown PA

Lyman Allyn Art Museum, New London CT

Americas Society Art Gallery, New York NY

Amherst Museum, Amherst NY

Anna Maria College, Saint Luke's Gallery, Paxton MA

Anson County Historical Society, Inc, Wadesboro NC

Arizona Historical Society-Yuma, Century House Museum & Garden, Yuma AZ

Arkansas Territorial Restoration, Little Rock AR

Artesia Historical Museum & Art Center, Artesia NM

Arts & Science Center, Statesville NC

ArtSpace-Lima, Lima OH

Association for the Preservation of Virginia Antiquities, John Marshall House, Richmond VA

Atlanta Museum, Atlanta GA

Baldwin Historical Society Museum, Baldwin NY

Ball State University, Museum of Art, Muncie IN

Baltimore Museum of Art, Baltimore MD

Barnes Foundation, Merion PA

The Bartlett Museum, Amesbury MA

Bass Museum of Art, Miami Beach FL

Bennington Museum, Bennington Museum, Bennington VT

Berkshire Museum, Pittsfield MA

Jesse Besser Museum, Alpena MI

Bradford Brinton Memorial Museum & Historic Ranch, Big Horn WY

Brooklyn Historical Society, Brooklyn OH

California College of Arts & Crafts, Steven Oliver Art Center, Oakland CA

California Historical Society, El Molino Viejo, San Marino CA

Cambria Historical Society, New Providence NJ

The Canadian Craft Museum, Vancouver BC

Cape Ann Historical Museum, Gloucester MA

Carnegie Institute, Carnegie Museum of Art, Pittsburgh PA

Carson County Square House Museum, Panhandle TX

Kit Carson Historic Museums, Taos NM

Kit Carson Historic Museums, Ernest Blumenschein Home & Studio, Taos NM

Kit Carson Historic Museums, Home & Museum, Taos NM

Kit Carson Historic Museums, Hacienda Martinez, Taos NM

Charleston Museum, Charleston SC

Charleston Museum, Joseph Manigault House, Charleston SC

Chatillon-DeMenil House Foundation, DeMenil Mansion, Saint Louis MO

Chicago Athenaeum, Museum of Architecture & Design, Chicago IL

Chicago Department of Cultural Affairs, Chicago Cultural Center, Chicago IL

Church of Jesus Christ of Latter-day Saints, Museum of Church History & Art, Salt Lake City UT

Cincinnati Institute of Fine Arts, Taft Museum, Cincinnati OH

City of Austin Parks & Recreation, O Henry Museum, Austin TX

City of Gainesville, Thomas Center Galleries - Cultural Affairs, Gainesville FL

The City of Petersburg Museums, Petersburg VA

Clinton County Historical Association, Clinton County Historical Museum, Plattsburgh NY

Cohasset Historical Society, Caleb Lothrop House, Cohasset MA

The College of Wooster, Art Museum, Wooster OH

Colorado Historical Society, Colorado History Museum, Denver CO

Columbia County Historical Society, Columbia County Museum, Kinderhook NY

Columbia Museum of Art, Columbia SC

Columbia Museum of Art, Columbia Art Association, Columbia SC

Columbus Chapel & Boal Mansion Museum, Boalsburg PA

Concordia Historical Institute, Saint Louis MO

Cooper-Hewitt, National Design Museum, New York NY

Corcoran Gallery of Art, Washington DC

Cortland County Historical Society, Suggett House Museum, Cortland NY

County of Henrico, Meadow Farm Museum, Glen Allen VA

Coutts Memorial Museum of Art, Inc, El Dorado KS

Craft & Folk Art Museum, Los Angeles CA

Craigdarroch Castle Historical Museum Society, Victoria BC

Cranbrook Art Museum, Bloomfield Hills MI

Crow Wing County Historical Society, Brainerd MN

DAR Museum, National Society Daughters of the American Revolution, Washington DC

Dartmouth Heritage Museum, Dartmouth NS

Dawson City Museum & Historical Society, Dawson City YT

Dawson County Historical Society, Museum, Lexington NE

Deming-Luna Mimbres Museum, Deming NM

Denison University, Art Gallery, Granville OH

Denver Art Museum, Denver CO

DeWitt Historical Society of Tompkins County, Ithaca NY

Discovery Museum, Bridgeport CT

Douglas County Historical Society, Fairlawn Mansion & Museum, Superior WI

Dundurn Castle, Hamilton ON

Durham Art Guild Inc, Durham NC

Ellis County Museum Inc, Waxahachie TX

Ephraim McDowell-Cambus-Kenneth Foundation, McDowell House & Apothecary Shop, Danville KY

Wharton Esherick Museum, Paoli PA

Evanston Historical Society, Charles Gates Dawes House, Evanston IL

Evansville Museum of Arts & Science, Evansville IN

Farmington Village Green & Library Association, Stanley-Whitman House, Farmington CT

Fetherston Foundation, Packwood House Museum, Lewisburg PA

Fine Arts Museums of San Francisco, M H de Young Memorial Museum & California Palace of the Legion of Honor, San Francisco CA

Flint Institute of Arts, Flint MI

Florence Museum of Art, Science & History, Florence SC

Florida Department of Environmental Protection, Stephen Foster State Folk Culture Center, White Springs FL

Florida Gulf Coast Art Center, Inc, Belleair FL

Florida State University Foundation - Central Florida Community College Foundation, The Appleton Museum of Art, Ocala FL

Edsel & Eleanor Ford House, Grosse Pointe Shores MI

Fort Worth Art Association, Modern Art Museum of Fort Worth, Fort Worth TX

The Frick Art & Historical Center, Frick Art Museum, Pittsburgh PA

Frick Collection, New York NY

Fuller Museum of Art, Brockton MA

General Board of Discipleship, The United Methodist Church, The Upper Room Chapel & Museum, Nashville TN

Girard College, Stephen Girard Collection, Philadelphia PA

Glanmore, Hastings County Museum, Belleville ON

Grand Rapids Art Museum, Grand Rapids MI

Greenville College, Richard W Bock Sculpture Collection, Greenville IL

Gunston Hall Plantation, Mason Neck VA

Halifax Historical Society, Inc, Halifax Historical Museum, Daytona Beach FL

Hammond-Harwood House Association, Inc, Annapolis MD

Headquarters Fort Monroe, Dept of Army, Casemate Museum, Fort Monroe VA

Hebrew Union College, Skirball Cultural Center, Los Angeles CA

Heritage Center of Lancaster County Museum, Lancaster PA

Hermitage Foundation Museum, Norfolk VA

Hershey Museum, Hershey PA

Edna Hibel Art Foundation, Hibel Museum of Art, Palm Beach FL

High Point Historical Society Inc, Museum, High Point NC

Historical & Cultural Affairs, Delaware State Museums, Dover DE

Historical Society of Bloomfield, Bloomfield NJ

Historical Society of Old Newbury, Cushing House Museum, Newburyport MA

Historical Society of the Town of Greenwich, Inc, Bush-Holley House Museum, Cos Cob CT

Historical Society of Washington DC, Heurich House Museum, Washington DC

Historic Cherry Hill, Albany NY

Historic Deerfield, Inc, Deerfield MA

Historic Landmarks Foundation of Indiana, Morris-Butler House, Indianapolis IN

Historic Northampton Museum, Northampton MA

Honolulu Academy of Arts, Honolulu HI

House of Roses, Senator Wilson Home, Deadwood SD

Houston Baptist University, Museum of American Architecture and Decorative Arts, Houston TX

Houston Museum of Decorative Arts, Chattanooga TN

Huguenot Historical Society of New Paltz Galleries, New Paltz NY

The Huntington Library, Art Collections & Botanical Gardens, San Marino CA

Huntington Museum of Art, Huntington WV

Hyde Collection Trust, Glens Falls NY

Idaho Historical Museum, Boise ID

Illinois Historic Preservation Agency, Bishop Hill State Historic Site, Bishop Hill IL

Imperial Calcasieu Museum, Gibson-Barham Gallery, Lake Charles LA

Indianapolis Museum of Art, Indianapolis IN

Iowa State University, Brunnier Art Museum, Ames IA

Jacksonville University, Alexander Brest Museum & Gallery, Jacksonville FL

Jefferson County Historical Society, Watertown NY

Jefferson County Open Space, Hiwan Homestead Museum, Evergreen CO

Jekyll Island Museum, Jekyll Island GA

Kansas City Art Institute, Kemper Museum of Contemporary Art & Design, Kansas City MO

Kelly-Griggs House Museum, Red Bluff CA

Kelowna Museum, Kelowna BC

Kemerer Museum of Decorative Arts, Bethlehem PA

Maude I Kerns Art Center Galleries, Eugene OR

Kiah Museum, Savannah GA

Kings County Historical Society and Museum, Hampton NB

Koochiching County Historical Society Museum, International Falls MN

Lafayette Natural History Museum, Planetarium & Nature Station, Lafayette LA

Landmark Society of Western New York, Inc, Rochester NY

Leroy Historical Society, LeRoy NY

LeSueur County Historical Museum, Chapter One, Elysian MN

Lightner Museum, Saint Augustine FL

Litchfield Historical Society, Litchfield CT

Livingston County Historical Society, Cobblestone Museum, Geneseo NY

Lockwood-Mathews Mansion Museum, Norwalk CT

Longfellow-Evangeline State Commemorative Area, Saint Martinville LA

Longfellow's Wayside Inn Museum, South Sudbury MA

Longue Vue House & Gardens, New Orleans LA

Los Angeles County Museum of Natural History, William S Hart Museum, Newhall CA
Louisa May Alcott Memorial Association, Orchard House, Concord MA
Loveland Museum Gallery, Loveland CO
Lyndhurst, Tarrytown NY
McCord Museum of Canadian History, Montreal PQ
McPherson Museum, McPherson KS
Judah L Magnes Museum, Berkeley CA
Maine Historical Society, Wadsworth-Longfellow House, Portland ME
Maison Saint-Gabriel Museum, Montreal PQ
Maricopa County Historical Society, Desert Caballeros Western Museum, Wickenburg AZ
Mark Twain Birthplace State Historic Site Birthplace Museum, Stoutsville MO
Maryhill Museum of Art, Goldendale WA
Marylhurst College, The Art Gym, Marylhurst OR
Mattatuck Historical Society, Mattatuck Museum, Waterbury CT
Midwest Museum of American Art, Elkhart IN
Minnesota Museum of American Art, Saint Paul MN
Mississippi Department of Archives & History, Old Capitol Museum, Jackson MS
Mississippi River Museum at Mud-Island, Memphis TN
Mobile Museum of Art, Mobile AL
Monroe County Historical Association, Elizabeth D Walters Library, Stroudsburg PA
James Monroe Museum, Fredericksburg VA
Montana State University, Museum of the Rockies, Bozeman MT
Moravian Historical Society, Whitefield House Museum, Nazareth PA
Morris-Jumel Mansion, Inc, New York NY
Mount Mary College, Tower Gallery, Milwaukee WI
Mount Vernon Ladies' Association of the Union, Mount Vernon VA
Munson-Williams-Proctor Institute, Museum of Art, Utica NY
Murray State University, Eagle Gallery, Murray KY
Musee d'Art de Saint-Laurent, Saint-Laurent PQ
Musee des Augustines de l'Hotel Dieu de Quebec, Quebec PQ
Musee Regional de la Cote-Nord, Sept-Iles PQ
Musee Regional de Vaudreuil-Soulanges, Vaudreuil PQ
Museo De Las Americas, Denver CO
Museum of American Folk Art, New York NY
Museum of Arts & History, Port Huron MI
The Museum of Arts & Sciences Inc, Daytona Beach FL
Museum of Contemporary Art, North Miami FL
Museum of the City of New York, New York NY
Museum of Western Art, Denver CO
The Museums at Stony Brook, Stony Brook NY
Muttart Public Art Gallery, Calgary AB
National Gallery of Canada, Ottawa ON
National Infantry Museum, Fort Benning GA
National Museum of American Art, Washington DC
National Park Service, Weir Farm National Historic Site, Wilton CT
National Society of Colonial Dames of America in the State of Maryland, Mount Clare Mansion, Baltimore MD
National Society of the Colonial Dames, Wilton House Museum, Richmond VA
National Trust for Historic Preservation, Washington DC
National Trust for Historic Preservation, Decatur House, Washington DC
Naval Historical Center, The Navy Museum, Washington DC
Nebraska State Capitol, Lincoln NE
Nemours Mansion & Gardens, Wilmington DE
Neville Public Museum, Green Bay WI
Newark Museum Association, The Newark Museum, Newark NJ
New Brunswick Museum, Saint John NB
New Hampshire Antiquarian Society, Hopkinton NH
New Orleans School of GlassWorks, Gallery & Printmaking Studio, New Orleans LA

New York State Office of Parks Recreation & Historic Preservation, John Jay Homestead State Historic Site, Katonah NY
Norfolk Historical Society Inc, Museum, Norfolk CT
North Carolina State University, Visual Arts Center, Raleigh NC
North Carolina State University, Chinqua-Penn Plantation House, Garden & Greenhouses, Reidsville NC
Oatlands, Inc, Leesburg VA
The Ohio Historical Society, Inc, Campus Martius Museum & Ohio River Museum, Marietta OH
Olana State Historic Site, Hudson NY
Old Colony Historical Society, Museum, Taunton MA
Old Dartmouth Historical Society, New Bedford Whaling Museum, New Bedford MA
Old Jail Art Center, Albany TX
Old Salem Inc, Museum of Early Southern Decorative Arts, Winston-Salem NC
Old York Historical Society, Old Gaol Museum, York ME
Owensboro Museum of Fine Art, Owensboro KY
Oysterponds Historical Society, Museum, Orient NY
Pacific - Asia Museum, Pasadena CA
Page-Walker Arts & History Center, Cary NC
Palm Springs Desert Museum, Palm Springs CA
Panhandle-Plains Historical Society Museum, Canyon TX
Pasadena Historical Museum, Pasadena CA
Passaic County Historical Society, Paterson NJ
Patterson Homestead, Dayton OH
Peabody Essex Museum, Salem MA
Pennsylvania Historical & Museum Commission, Railroad Museum of Pennsylvania, Harrisburg PA
Philadelphia Museum of Art, Philadelphia PA
Philbrook Museum of Art, Tulsa OK
Pilgrim Society, Pilgrim Hall Museum, Plymouth MA
Plainsman Museum, Aurora NE
Plumas County Museum, Quincy CA
Pope County Historical Society, Pope County Museum, Glenwood MN
Portsmouth Historical Society, John Paul Jones House, Portsmouth NH
Marjorie Merriweather Post Foundation of DC, Hillwood Museum, Washington DC
Putnam County Historical Society, Foundry School Museum, Cold Spring NY
Putnam Museum of History & Natural Science, Davenport IA
Quapaw Quarter Association, Inc, Villa Marre, Little Rock AR
Rahr-West Art Museum, Manitowoc WI
Frederic Remington Art Museum, Ogdensburg NY
Rensselaer County Historical Society, Hart-Cluett Mansion, 1827, Troy NY
Rhode Island Historical Society, John Brown House, Providence RI
Rhode Island School of Design, Museum of Art, Providence RI
Riley County Historical Society, Riley County Historical Museum, Manhattan KS
Riverside Municipal Museum, Riverside CA
Roberson Museum & Science Center, Binghamton NY
Roberts County Museum, Miami TX
Rowland Evans Robinson Memorial Association, Rokeby Museum, Ferrisburgh VT
Rock Ford Foundation, Inc, Historic Rock Ford & Kauffman Museum, Lancaster PA
Millicent Rogers Museum of Northern New Mexico, Taos NM
Rome Historical Society Museum, Rome NY
Ross Memorial Museum, Saint Andrews NB
Royal Arts Foundation, Belcourt Castle, Newport RI
Saint Joseph Museum, Saint Joseph MO
Saint Louis Artists' Guild, Saint Louis MO
Saint Louis County Historical Society, Duluth MN
Salem Art Association, Bush House, Salem OR
San Diego Museum of Art, San Diego CA
The Sandwich Historical Society, Inc, Sandwich Glass Museum, Sandwich MA

Santa Clara University, de Saisset Museum, Santa Clara CA
The Seagram Museum, Waterloo ON
Seneca-Iroquois National Museum, Salamanca NY
Shaker Museum & Library, Old Chatham NY
Shaker Village of Pleasant Hill, Harrodsburg KY
Ella Sharp Museum, Jackson MI
Shirley Plantation, Charles City VA
Slater-Norton Corporation, Slater Memorial Museum & Converse Art Gallery, Norwich CT
Society of the Cincinnati, Museum & Library at Anderson House, Washington DC
South Carolina Artisans Center, Walterboro SC
Southern Illinois University, University Museum, Carbondale IL
Southern Lorain County Historical Society, Spirit of '76 Museum, Wellington OH
Southern Oregon Historical Society, Jacksonville Museum of Southern Oregon History, Medford OR
Springfield Art & Historical Society, Miller Art Center, Springfield VT
Springfield Art Museum, Springfield MO
Springfield Library & Museums Association, Connecticut Valley Historical Museum, Springfield MA
Stanford University, Museum of Art, Stanford CA
Nelda C & H J Lutcher Stark Foundation, Stark Museum of Art, Orange TX
State Historical Society of Wisconsin, State Historical Museum, Madison WI
T C Steele State Historic Site, Nashville IN
Stratford Historical Society, Katherine Mitchel Museum, Stratford CT
Summit County Historical Society, Akron OH
Susquehanna University, Lore Degenstein Gallery, Selinsgrove PA
Swedish American Museum Association of Chicago, Chicago IL
Towson State University, Asian Arts Center, Towson MD
Tryon Palace Historic Sites & Gardens, New Bern NC
Mark Twain Memorial, Hartford CT
United Society of Shakers, Shaker Museum, New Glocester ME
US Department of State, Diplomatic Reception Rooms, Washington DC
University of Alabama at Birmingham, Visual Arts Gallery, Birmingham AL
University of Chicago, Oriental Institute Museum, Chicago IL
University of Manitoba, Faculty of Architecture Exhibition Centre, Winnipeg MB
University of Mississippi, University Museums, Oxford MS
University of Montana, Paxson Gallery, Missoula MT
University of Rochester, Memorial Art Gallery, Rochester NY
University of San Diego, Founders' Gallery, San Diego CA
University of Tampa, Henry B Plant Museum, Tampa FL
University of Tennessee, Frank H McClung Museum, Knoxville TN
University of Tennessee, Eleanor Dean Audigier Art Collection, Knoxville TN
University of Utah, Utah Museum of Fine Arts, Salt Lake City UT
University of Wisconsin-Madison, Elvehjem Museum of Art, Madison WI
Ursinus College, Philip & Muriel Berman Museum of Art, Collegeville PA
USS Constitution Museum, Boston MA
Van Cortlandt House Museum, Bronx NY
Vermilion County Museum Society, Danville IL
Virginia Museum of Fine Arts, Richmond VA
Vizcaya Museum & Gardens, Miami FL
Wade House & Wesley W Jung Carriage Museum, Historic House & Carriage Museum, Greenbush WI
Wadsworth Atheneum, Hartford CT
Warner House Association, MacPheadris-Warner House, Portsmouth NH
Wayne County Historical Society, Museum, Honesdale PA

GLASS

Palm Beach Community College Foundation, Museum of Art, Lake Worth FL
Palm Springs Desert Museum, Palm Springs CA
Panhandle-Plains Historical Society Museum, Canyon TX
Pasadena Historical Museum, Pasadena CA
Pensacola Museum of Art, Pensacola FL
Philadelphia Museum of Art, Philadelphia PA
Philbrook Museum of Art, Tulsa OK
Phillips County Museum, Helena AR
Plainsman Museum, Aurora NE
Plumas County Museum, Quincy CA
Pope County Historical Society, Pope County Museum, Glenwood MN
Portland Museum of Art, Portland ME
Portsmouth Historical Society, John Paul Jones House, Portsmouth NH
Marjorie Merriweather Post Foundation of DC, Hillwood Museum, Washington DC
Potsdam Public Museum, Potsdam NY
Principia College, School of Nations Museum, Elsah IL
Promote Art Works Inc (PAWI), Laziza Videodance Lumia Project, Brooklyn NY
Putnam Museum of History & Natural Science, Davenport IA
Queens College, City University of New York, Godwin-Ternbach Museum, Flushing NY
Queen's Medical Center Auxiliary, Queen Emma Gallery, Honolulu HI
Rahr-West Art Museum, Manitowoc WI
Walter Cecil Rawls Museum, Courtland VA
Frederic Remington Art Museum, Ogdensburg NY
Rensselaer County Historical Society, Hart-Cluett Mansion, 1827, Troy NY
Rhode Island Historical Society, John Brown House, Providence RI
Riley County Historical Society, Riley County Historical Museum, Manhattan KS
Rome Historical Society Museum, Rome NY
Saint Joseph Museum, Saint Joseph MO
Saint Louis Artists' Guild, Saint Louis MO
The Sandwich Historical Society, Inc, Sandwich Glass Museum, Sandwich MA
San Jose Museum of Art, San Jose CA
The Seagram Museum, Waterloo ON
Shaker Museum & Library, Old Chatham NY
Abigail Adams Smith Museum, New York NY
Society of the Cincinnati, Museum & Library at Anderson House, Washington DC
South Carolina Artisans Center, Walterboro SC
Southeastern Center for Contemporary Art, Winston-Salem NC
Southern Illinois University, University Museum, Carbondale IL
Southern Oregon Historical Society, Jacksonville Museum of Southern Oregon History, Medford OR
Southern Oregon State College, Schneider Museum of Art, Ashland OR
Springfield Art Museum, Springfield MO
Nelda C & H J Lutcher Stark Foundation, Stark Museum of Art, Orange TX
State University of New York at Geneseo, Bertha V B Lederer Gallery, Geneseo NY
Stratford Historical Society, Katherine Mitchel Museum, Stratford CT
Summit County Historical Society, Akron OH
Susquehanna University, Lore Degenstein Gallery, Selinsgrove PA
Swedish American Museum Association of Chicago, Chicago IL
Syracuse University, Art Collection, Syracuse NY
Tacoma Art Museum, Tacoma WA
Toledo Museum of Art, Toledo OH
Topeka & Shawnee County Public Library, Gallery of Fine Arts, Topeka KS
Triton Museum of Art, Santa Clara CA
Tryon Palace Historic Sites & Gardens, New Bern NC
Tulane University, Dept Art Newcomb Col Art Galleries, New Orleans LA
Mark Twain Memorial, Hartford CT
University of Chicago, Oriental Institute Museum, Chicago IL
University of Colorado at Colorado Springs, Gallery of Contemporary Art, Colorado Springs CO

University of Kansas, Spencer Museum of Art, Lawrence KS
University of Mississippi, University Museums, Oxford MS
Valentine Museum, Richmond VA
Vesterheim Norwegian-American Museum, Decorah IA
Virginia Museum of Fine Arts, Richmond VA
Volcano Art Center, Hawaii National Park HI
Washburn University, Mulvane Art Museum, Topeka KS
Washington County Museum of Fine Arts, Hagerstown MD
Wayne County Historical Society, Museum, Honesdale PA
Westmoreland Museum of American Art, Greensburg PA
Wheaton College, Watson Gallery, Norton MA
White House, Washington DC
Willard House & Clock Museum, Inc, North Grafton MA
Wiregrass Museum of Art, Dothan AL
Wistariahurst Museum, Holyoke MA
Woodlawn Plantation, Mount Vernon VA
Wustum Museum Art Association, Racine WI
Yarmouth County Historical Society, Yarmouth County Museum, Yarmouth NS
York Institute Museum, Saco ME

GOLD

Alaska State Museum, Juneau AK
Albany Institute of History & Art, Albany NY
The Art Institute of Chicago, Chicago IL
Beloit College, Wright Museum of Art, Beloit WI
Cincinnati Institute of Fine Arts, Taft Museum, Cincinnati OH
Cooper-Hewitt, National Design Museum, New York NY
Denver Art Museum, Denver CO
Franklin Mint Museum, Franklin Center PA
Freer Gallery of Art Gallery, Arthur M Sackler Gallery, Washington DC
Glanmore, Hastings County Museum, Belleville ON
Jacksonville University, Alexander Brest Museum & Gallery, Jacksonville FL
Loyola University of Chicago, Martin D'Arcy Gallery of Art, Chicago IL
Judah L Magnes Museum, Berkeley CA
Museo De Las Americas, Denver CO
The Museum of Arts & Sciences Inc, Daytona Beach FL
Museum of Fine Arts, Houston, Houston TX
Museum of Northern British Columbia, Ruth Harvey Art Gallery, Prince Rupert BC
Muttart Public Art Gallery, Calgary AB
National Museum of American Art, Washington DC
New Brunswick Museum, Saint John NB
Old Salem Inc, Museum of Early Southern Decorative Arts, Winston-Salem NC
Plumas County Museum, Quincy CA
Polk Museum of Art, Lakeland FL
Marjorie Merriweather Post Foundation of DC, Hillwood Museum, Washington DC
Royal Arts Foundation, Belcourt Castle, Newport RI
United States Figure Skating Association, World Figure Skating Museum & Hall of Fame, Colorado Springs CO
University of Chicago, Oriental Institute Museum, Chicago IL
Virginia Museum of Fine Arts, Richmond VA
Wells Fargo Bank, Wells Fargo History Museum, San Francisco CA
Willard House & Clock Museum, Inc, North Grafton MA

GRAPHICS

Alaska State Museum, Juneau AK
Alberta College of Art & Design, Illingworth Kerr Gallery, Calgary AB
Albuquerque Museum of Art & History, Albuquerque NM
Art Gallery of Hamilton, Hamilton ON
Art Museum of Southeast Texas, Beaumont TX
Augusta Richmond County Museum, Augusta GA

Leo Baeck Institute, New York NY
Baltimore City Community College, Art Gallery, Baltimore MD
Baltimore Museum of Art, Baltimore MD
Balzekas Museum of Lithuanian Culture, Chicago IL
Baylor University, Martin Museum of Art, Waco TX
Beloit College, Wright Museum of Art, Beloit WI
Jesse Besser Museum, Alpena MI
Brown University, David Winton Bell Gallery, Providence RI
The Buffalo Fine Arts Academy, Albright-Knox Art Gallery, Buffalo NY
John C Calhoun State Community College, Art Gallery, Decatur AL
California College of Arts & Crafts, Steven Oliver Art Center, Oakland CA
Canton Museum of Art, Canton OH
Capital University, Schumacher Gallery, Columbus OH
Central United Methodist Church, Swords Info Plowshares Peace Center & Gallery, Detroit MI
Chattahoochee Valley Art Museum, LaGrange GA
Cheekwood-Tennessee Botanical Gardens & Museum of Art, Nashville TN
Chelan County Public Utility District, Rocky Reach Dam, Wenatchee WA
Chicago Athenaeum, Museum of Architecture & Design, Chicago IL
Chicago Department of Cultural Affairs, Chicago Cultural Center, Chicago IL
Cincinnati Institute of Fine Arts, Taft Museum, Cincinnati OH
City of Gainesville, Thomas Center Galleries - Cultural Affairs, Gainesville FL
Clemson University, Rudolph E Lee Gallery, Clemson SC
Cleveland State University, Art Gallery, Cleveland OH
College of William & Mary, Joseph & Margaret Muscarelle Museum of Art, Williamsburg VA
The College of Wooster, Art Museum, Wooster OH
Colorado Springs Fine Arts Center, Colorado Springs CO
Columbia Museum of Art, Columbia SC
Columbus Museum, Columbus GA
Concordia University Wisconsin, Fine Art Gallery, Mequon WI
Cornell University, Herbert F Johnson Museum of Art, Ithaca NY
Cranbrook Art Museum, Bloomfield Hills MI
Creighton University, Fine Arts Gallery, Omaha NE
Cummer Museum of Art & Gardens, DeEtte Holden Cummer Museum Foundation, Jacksonville FL
C W Post Campus of Long Island University, Hillwood Art Museum, Brookville NY
Dahesh Museum, New York NY
Danforth Museum of Art, Framingham MA
DeCordova Museum & Sculpture Park, Lincoln MA
Delaware Art Museum, Wilmington DE
Dickinson College, Trout Gallery, Carlisle PA
Dickinson State University, Mind's Eye Gallery, Dickinson ND
Edmundson Art Foundation, Inc, Des Moines Art Center, Des Moines IA
El Paso Museum of Art, El Paso TX
Erie Art Museum, Erie PA
Fine Arts Museums of San Francisco, M H de Young Memorial Museum & California Palace of the Legion of Honor, San Francisco CA
Fitton Center For Creative Arts, Hamilton OH
Florence Museum of Art, Science & History, Florence SC
Fort George G Meade Museum, Fort Meade MD
Fuller Museum of Art, Brockton MA
Galleries of the Claremont Colleges, Claremont CA
Gallery One, Ellensburg WA
Georgetown College Gallery, Georgetown KY
Georgetown University, Art & History Museum, Washington DC
George Washington University, The Dimock Gallery, Washington DC
Grand Rapids Art Museum, Grand Rapids MI
Greater Lafayette Museum of Art, Lafayette IN

HISPANIC ART

Millicent Rogers Museum of Northern New Mexico, Taos NM
Roswell Museum & Art Center, Roswell NM
Royal Ontario Museum, Toronto ON
San Antonio Museum of Art, San Antonio TX
San Jose Museum of Art, San Jose CA
Santa Barbara Museum of Art, Santa Barbara CA
South Carolina State Museum, Columbia SC
Southeastern Center for Contemporary Art, Winston-Salem NC
Southern Alleghenies Museum of Art, Southern Alleghenies Museum of Art at Johnstown, Loretto PA
University of Puerto Rico, Museum of Anthropology, History & Art, San Juan PR
University of Rochester, Memorial Art Gallery, Rochester NY
University of Texas at Austin, Archer M Huntington Art Gallery, Austin TX

HISTORICAL MATERIAL

Adams County Historical Society, Museum & Cultural Center, Brighton CO
Agecroft Association, Museum, Richmond VA
Alabama Department of Archives & History, Museum Galleries, Montgomery AL
Alaska State Museum, Juneau AK
Albuquerque Museum of Art & History, Albuquerque NM
Allentown Art Museum, Allentown PA
American Kennel Club, Museum of the Dog, Saint Louis MO
Americas Society Art Gallery, New York NY
Amherst Museum, Amherst NY
Anchorage Museum of History & Art, Anchorage AK
Appaloosa Museum, Inc, Moscow ID
Archives & History Center of the United Methodist Church, Madison NJ
Arizona Historical Society-Yuma, Century House Museum & Garden, Yuma AZ
Arkansas Territorial Restoration, Little Rock AR
Artesia Historical Museum & Art Center, Artesia NM
Art Gallery of Nova Scotia, Halifax NS
Arts & Science Center, Statesville NC
Ashland Historical Society, Ashland MA
Association for the Preservation of Virginia Antiquities, John Marshall House, Richmond VA
Ateneo Puertorriqueno, San Juan PR
Atlanta Historical Society Inc, Atlanta History Center, Atlanta GA
Leo Baeck Institute, New York NY
Baker University, Old Castle Museum, Baldwin City KS
The Bartlett Museum, Amesbury MA
Battleship North Carolina, Wilmington NC
Bay County Historical Society, Historical Museum of Bay County, Bay City MI
Beverly Historical Society, Cabot, Hale & Balch House Museums, Beverly MA
Bowdoin College, Peary-MacMillan Arctic Museum, Brunswick ME
Brant Historical Society, Brant County Museum, Brantford ON
Brooklyn Historical Society, Brooklyn OH
California State University Stanislaus, University Art Gallery, Turlock CA
Calvert Marine Museum, Solomons MD
Canadian Museum of Civilization, Hull PQ
Canajoharie Library & Art Gallery, Canajoharie NY
Carson County Square House Museum, Panhandle TX
Kit Carson Historic Museums, Ernest Blumenschein Home & Studio, Taos NM
Kit Carson Historic Museums, Home & Museum, Taos NM
Kit Carson Historic Museums, Hacienda Martinez, Taos NM
Cartoon Art Museum, San Francisco CA
Casa Amesti, Monterey CA
Center for Puppetry Arts, Atlanta GA
Chatham Historical Society, Old Atwood House Museum, Chatham MA

Chatillon-DeMenil House Foundation, DeMenil Mansion, Saint Louis MO
Chelan County Public Utility District, Rocky Reach Dam, Wenatchee WA
Cherokee National Historical Society, Inc, Tahlequah OK
Chesapeake Bay Maritime Museum, Saint Michaels MD
Chief Plenty Coups Museum, Pryor MT
Chinese Culture Foundation, Chinese Culture Center Gallery, San Francisco CA
Church of Jesus Christ of Latter-day Saints, Museum of Church History & Art, Salt Lake City UT
City of Atlanta, Atlanta Cyclorama, Atlanta GA
City of Gainesville, Thomas Center Galleries - Cultural Affairs, Gainesville FL
The City of Petersburg Museums, Petersburg VA
City of Springdale, Shiloh Museum, Springdale AR
Clark County Historical Society, Springfield OH
Clark County Historical Society, Pioneer - Krier Museum, Ashland KS
Cleveland State University, Art Gallery, Cleveland OH
Cliveden, Philadelphia PA
Cohasset Historical Society, Cohasset Maritime Museum, Cohasset MA
Cohasset Historical Society, Captain John Wilson Historical House, Cohasset MA
The College of Wooster, Art Museum, Wooster OH
Colorado Historical Society, Colorado History Museum, Denver CO
Columbus & Lowndes County Historical Society, Blewett-Lee Museum, Columbus MS
Columbus Museum, Columbus GA
Connecticut Historical Commission, Sloane-Stanley Museum, Kent CT
Cooper-Hewitt, National Design Museum, New York NY
Craigdarroch Castle Historical Museum Society, Victoria BC
C W Post Campus of Long Island University, Hillwood Art Museum, Brookville NY
Dacotah Prairie Museum, Lamont Gallery, Aberdeen SD
Davidson College Visual Arts Center, William H Van Every Jr & Edward M Smith Galleries, Davidson NC
Deming-Luna Mimbres Museum, Deming NM
Department of Natural Resources of Missouri, Missouri State Museum, Jefferson City MO
Dickinson College, Trout Gallery, Carlisle PA
Eva Brook Donly Museum, Simcoe ON
Douglas County Historical Society, Fairlawn Mansion & Museum, Superior WI
Drew County Historical Society, Museum, Monticello AR
East Bay Asian Local Development Corp, Asian Resource Gallery, Oakland CA
Eastern Washington State Historical Society, Cheney Cowles Museum, Spokane WA
East Tennessee State University, Carroll Reece Museum, Johnson City TN
Eberdt Museum of Communications, Heritage Sutton, Sutton PQ
Elmhurst Art Museum, Elmhurst IL
Ephraim McDowell-Cambus-Kenneth Foundation, McDowell House & Apothecary Shop, Danville KY
Eskimo Museum, Churchill MB
Evanston Historical Society, Charles Gates Dawes House, Evanston IL
Fetherston Foundation, Packwood House Museum, Lewisburg PA
Fitton Center For Creative Arts, Hamilton OH
Florence Museum of Art, Science & History, Florence SC
Floyd County Museum, New Albany IN
Fort George G Meade Museum, Fort Meade MD
Fort Morgan Heritage Foundation, Fort Morgan CO
Fort Ticonderoga Association, Ticonderoga NY
Gadsden Museum, Mesilla NM
Gananoque Historical Museum, Gananoque ON
General Board of Discipleship, The United Methodist Church, The Upper Room Chapel & Museum, Nashville TN

Gilcrease Museum Institute of American History & Art, Tulsa OK
Glanmore, Hastings County Museum, Belleville ON
Glenbow Museum, Calgary AB
Goshen Historical Society, Goshen CT
Great Lakes Historical Society, Island Seas Maritime Museum, Vermilion OH
Gunston Hall Plantation, Mason Neck VA
Hampton University, University Museum, Hampton VA
Harrison County Historical Museum, Marshall TX
Headquarters Fort Monroe, Dept of Army, Casemate Museum, Fort Monroe VA
Heard Museum, Phoenix AZ
Hebrew Union College, Skirball Cultural Center, Los Angeles CA
Hebrew Union College-Jewish Institute of Religion, New York NY
Hispanic Society of America, Museum, New York NY
Historical Society of Cheshire County, Archive Center of the Society, Keene NH
Historical Society of Old Newbury, Cushing House Museum, Newburyport MA
Historical Society of Pennsylvania, Philadelphia PA
Historical Society of Rockland County, New City NY
Historical Society of Washington DC, Heurich House Museum, Washington DC
Historical Society of York County, York PA
House of Roses, Senator Wilson Home, Deadwood SD
Huguenot Historical Society of New Paltz Galleries, New Paltz NY
Hunterdon Historical Museum, Clinton NJ
Idaho Historical Museum, Boise ID
Illinois State Museum, Illinois Art Gallery, Chicago IL
Imperial Calcasieu Museum, Gibson-Barham Gallery, Lake Charles LA
Independence Seaport Museum, Philadelphia PA
Indiana University, William Hammond Mathers Museum, Bloomington IN
Institute of the Great Plains, Museum of the Great Plains, Lawton OK
Jackson County Historical Society, The 1859 Jail, Marshal's Home & Museum, Independence MO
Jamestown-Yorktown Foundation, Williamsburg VA
Jefferson County Historical Museum, Pine Bluff AR
Jefferson County Historical Society, Watertown NY
Jefferson County Open Space, Hiwan Homestead Museum, Evergreen CO
Jordan Historical Museum of The Twenty, Jordan ON
Joslyn Art Museum, Omaha NE
Kansas State Historical Society, Kansas Museum of History, Topeka KS
Kentucky Historical Society, Old State Capitol & Annex, Frankfort KY
Kern County Museum, Bakersfield CA
Kings County Historical Society and Museum, Hampton NB
Klamath County Museum, Klamath Falls OR
Lac du Flambeau Band of Lake Superior Chippewa Indians, George W Brown Jr Ojibwe Museum & Cultural Center, Lac du Flambeau WI
Lafayette Museum Association, Lafayette Museum-Alexandre Mouton House, Lafayette LA
Lafayette Natural History Museum, Planetarium & Nature Station, Lafayette LA
Landmark Society of Western New York, Inc, Rochester NY
Leroy Historical Society, LeRoy NY
LeSueur County Historical Museum, Chapter One, Elysian MN
Lightner Museum, Saint Augustine FL
Long Branch Historical Museum, Long Branch NJ
Longfellow-Evangeline State Commemorative Area, Saint Martinville LA
Los Angeles County Museum of Natural History, William S Hart Museum, Newhall CA
Louisiana State Exhibit Museum, Shreveport LA
Loveland Museum Gallery, Loveland CO
Lyme Historical Society, Florence Griswold Museum, Old Lyme CT
McCord Museum of Canadian History, Montreal PQ

Woodrow Wilson Birthplace & Museum, Staunton VA

Woodrow Wilson House, Washington DC

Witte Museum, San Antonio TX

Woodlawn Plantation, Mount Vernon VA

Yarmouth County Historical Society, Yarmouth County Museum, Yarmouth NS

ISLAMIC ART

Academy of the New Church, Glencairn Museum, Bryn Athyn PA

African Art Museum of Maryland, Columbia MD

The Art Institute of Chicago, Chicago IL

Asian Art Museum of San Francisco, Avery Brundage Collection, San Francisco CA

Cincinnati Institute of Fine Arts, Taft Museum, Cincinnati OH

Cincinnati Museum Association, Cincinnati Art Museum, Cincinnati OH

College of William & Mary, Joseph & Margaret Muscarelle Museum of Art, Williamsburg VA

Detroit Institute of Arts, Detroit MI

Dickinson College, Trout Gallery, Carlisle PA

Florida State University Foundation - Central Florida Community College Foundation, The Appleton Museum of Art, Ocala FL

Freer Gallery of Art Gallery, Arthur M Sackler Gallery, Washington DC

Harvard University, Arthur M Sackler Museum, Cambridge MA

Harvard University, Semitic Museum, Cambridge MA

Los Angeles County Museum of Art, Los Angeles CA

Michigan State University, Kresge Art Museum, East Lansing MI

State University of New York at New Paltz, College Art Gallery, New Paltz NY

University of Chicago, Oriental Institute Museum, Chicago IL

University of Florida, Samuel P Harn Museum of Art, Gainesville FL

University of Iowa, Museum of Art, Iowa City IA

University of Victoria, Maltwood Art Museum and Gallery, Victoria BC

Virginia Museum of Fine Arts, Richmond VA

Williams College, Museum of Art, Williamstown MA

IVORY

Academy of the New Church, Glencairn Museum, Bryn Athyn PA

African Art Museum of Maryland, Columbia MD

Alaska Department of Education, Division of Libraries, Archives & Museums, Sheldon Jackson Museum, Sitka AK

Alaska State Museum, Juneau AK

Anchorage Museum of History & Art, Anchorage AK

Asian Art Museum of San Francisco, Avery Brundage Collection, San Francisco CA

Beloit College, Wright Museum of Art, Beloit WI

Bowdoin College, Peary-MacMillan Arctic Museum, Brunswick ME

Brigham Young University, Museum of Art, Provo UT

The Bruce Museum, Greenwich CT

Billie Trimble Chandler Arts Foundation, Asian Cultures Museum & Educational Center, Corpus Christi TX

Chilkat Valley Historical Society, Sheldon Museum & Cultural Center, Haines AK

C W Post Campus of Long Island University, Hillwood Art Museum, Brookville NY

Detroit Institute of Arts, Detroit MI

Elmhurst Art Museum, Elmhurst IL

Fine Arts Museums of San Francisco, M H de Young Memorial Museum & California Palace of the Legion of Honor, San Francisco CA

Florida State University Foundation - Central Florida Community College Foundation, The Appleton Museum of Art, Ocala FL

Freer Gallery of Art Gallery, Arthur M Sackler Gallery, Washington DC

Glanmore, Hastings County Museum, Belleville ON

Greenwood Museum, Greenwood SC

Harvard University, Dumbarton Oaks Research Library & Collections, Washington DC

Jacksonville University, Alexander Brest Museum & Gallery, Jacksonville FL

Koshare Indian Museum, Inc, La Junta CO

Lizzardo Museum of Lapidary Art, Elmhurst IL

Loyola University of Chicago, Martin D'Arcy Gallery of Art, Chicago IL

The Mariners' Museum, Newport News VA

Mitchell Museum, Mount Vernon IL

Naval Historical Center, The Navy Museum, Washington DC

Nelson-Atkins Museum of Art, Kansas City MO

Oklahoma Center for Science & Art, Kirkpatrick Center, Oklahoma City OK

Oklahoma City Art Museum, Oklahoma City OK

Old Dartmouth Historical Society, New Bedford Whaling Museum, New Bedford MA

Pacific - Asia Museum, Pasadena CA

Panhandle-Plains Historical Society Museum, Canyon TX

Peabody Essex Museum, Salem MA

Marjorie Merriweather Post Foundation of DC, Hillwood Museum, Washington DC

Rahr-West Art Museum, Manitowoc WI

Rensselaer County Historical Society, Hart-Cluett Mansion, 1827, Troy NY

Robert W Ryerss Library & Museum, Philadelphia PA

Saint John's University, Chung-Cheng Art Gallery, Jamaica NY

Santa Clara University, de Saisset Museum, Santa Clara CA

Society of the Cincinnati, Museum & Library at Anderson House, Washington DC

University of Chicago, Oriental Institute Museum, Chicago IL

University of Michigan, Kelsey Museum of Archaeology, Ann Arbor MI

University of Victoria, Maltwood Art Museum and Gallery, Victoria BC

Warther Museum Inc, Dover OH

Yarmouth County Historical Society, Yarmouth County Museum, Yarmouth NS

Yugtarvik Regional Museum & Bethel Visitors Center, Bethel AK

JADE

Alaska Department of Education, Division of Libraries, Archives & Museums, Sheldon Jackson Museum, Sitka AK

Alaska State Museum, Juneau AK

Allentown Art Museum, Allentown PA

Asian Art Museum of San Francisco, Avery Brundage Collection, San Francisco CA

Beloit College, Wright Museum of Art, Beloit WI

Brigham Young University, Museum of Art, Provo UT

Cape Ann Historical Museum, Gloucester MA

Billie Trimble Chandler Arts Foundation, Asian Cultures Museum & Educational Center, Corpus Christi TX

Denver Art Museum, Denver CO

Detroit Institute of Arts, Detroit MI

Emory University, Michael C Carlos Museum, Atlanta GA

Florida State University Foundation - Central Florida Community College Foundation, The Appleton Museum of Art, Ocala FL

Freeport Arts Center, Freeport IL

Harvard University, William Hayes Fogg Art Museum, Cambridge MA

Harvard University, Arthur M Sackler Museum, Cambridge MA

Hermitage Foundation Museum, Norfolk VA

Honolulu Academy of Arts, Honolulu HI

Indianapolis Museum of Art, Indianapolis IN

Iowa State University, Brunnier Art Museum, Ames IA

Jacksonville University, Alexander Brest Museum & Gallery, Jacksonville FL

Johns Hopkins University, Evergreen House, Baltimore MD

Lizzadro Museum of Lapidary Art, Elmhurst IL

Mitchell Museum, Mount Vernon IL

Museo De Las Americas, Denver CO

Norton Gallery & School of Art, Inc, Norton Museum of Art, West Palm Beach FL

Pacific - Asia Museum, Pasadena CA

Panhandle-Plains Historical Society Museum, Canyon TX

Peabody Essex Museum, Salem MA

Pennsylvania State University, Palmer Museum of Art, University Park PA

Marjorie Merriweather Post Foundation of DC, Hillwood Museum, Washington DC

Saint John's University, Chung-Cheng Art Gallery, Jamaica NY

Santa Barbara Museum of Art, Santa Barbara CA

Seattle Art Museum, Seattle WA

Society of the Cincinnati, Museum & Library at Anderson House, Washington DC

University of Alabama at Birmingham, Visual Arts Gallery, Birmingham AL

University of Florida, Samuel P Harn Museum of Art, Gainesville FL

University of Iowa, Museum of Art, Iowa City IA

Virginia Museum of Fine Arts, Richmond VA

Washington County Museum of Fine Arts, Hagerstown MD

JEWELRY

Academy of the New Church, Glencairn Museum, Bryn Athyn PA

African Art Museum of Maryland, Columbia MD

Alaska State Museum, Juneau AK

Allentown Art Museum, Allentown PA

Art Museum of Missoula, Missoula MT

Asian Art Museum of San Francisco, Avery Brundage Collection, San Francisco CA

Baldwin Historical Society Museum, Baldwin NY

Baltimore Museum of Art, Baltimore MD

Beloit College, Wright Museum of Art, Beloit WI

Berea College, Doris Ulmann Galleries, Berea KY

Berkshire Museum, Pittsfield MA

Bradford Brinton Memorial Museum & Historic Ranch, Big Horn WY

California College of Arts & Crafts, Steven Oliver Art Center, Oakland CA

The Canadian Craft Museum, Vancouver BC

Billie Trimble Chandler Arts Foundation, Asian Cultures Museum & Educational Center, Corpus Christi TX

Chicago Department of Cultural Affairs, Chicago Cultural Center, Chicago IL

City of Atlanta, Chastain Arts Center, Atlanta GA

City of Atlanta, Southeast Arts Center, Atlanta GA

Clinton County Historical Association, Clinton County Historical Museum, Plattsburgh NY

Cooper-Hewitt, National Design Museum, New York NY

Crow Wing County Historical Society, Brainerd MN

C W Post Campus of Long Island University, Hillwood Art Museum, Brookville NY

DAR Museum, National Society Daughters of the American Revolution, Washington DC

Dartmouth Heritage Museum, Dartmouth NS

Denver Art Museum, Denver CO

Eiteljorg Museum of American Indians & Western Art, Indianapolis IN

Ellen Noel Art Museum of the Permian Basin, Odessa TX

Emory University, Michael C Carlos Museum, Atlanta GA

Ephraim McDowell-Cambus-Kenneth Foundation, McDowell House & Apothecary Shop, Danville KY

Evanston Historical Society, Charles Gates Dawes House, Evanston IL

Fine Arts Museums of San Francisco, M H de Young Memorial Museum & California Palace of the Legion of Honor, San Francisco CA

Fitton Center For Creative Arts, Hamilton OH

Florida Gulf Coast Art Center, Inc, Belleair FL

Freer Gallery of Art Gallery, Arthur M Sackler Gallery, Washington DC

Fuller Museum of Art, Brockton MA

Gallery 53, Cooperstown NY

Gallery One, Ellensburg WA

G B Gate & Sons, Asheville NC

Glanmore, Hastings County Museum, Belleville ON

Gunston Hall Plantation, Mason Neck VA

Walter Anderson Museum of Art, Ocean Springs MS

Artesia Historical Museum & Art Center, Artesia NM

Art Museum of Missoula, Missoula MT

Arts & Science Center, Statesville NC

Arts Council of Fayetteville-Cumberland County, The Arts Center, Fayetteville NC

Asbury College, Student Center Gallery, Wilmore KY

Leo Baeck Institute, New York NY

Bay County Historical Society, Historical Museum of Bay County, Bay City MI

Berkshire Museum, Pittsfield MA

Jesse Besser Museum, Alpena MI

Brandywine River Museum, Chadds Ford PA

Brigham Young University, Museum of Art, Provo UT

Brown University, David Winton Bell Gallery, Providence RI

California Center for the Arts Museum, Escondido CA

California College of Arts & Crafts, Steven Oliver Art Center, Oakland CA

Canadian Museum of Contemporary Photography, Ottawa ON

Cape Ann Historical Museum, Gloucester MA

Cedar Rapids Museum of Art, Cedar Rapids IA

Central United Methodist Church, Swords Info Plowshares Peace Center & Gallery, Detroit MI

Chicago Department of Cultural Affairs, Chicago Cultural Center, Chicago IL

Church of Jesus Christ of Latter-day Saints, Museum of Church History & Art, Salt Lake City UT

Cincinnati Museum Association, Cincinnati Art Museum, Cincinnati OH

City of Gainesville, Thomas Center Galleries - Cultural Affairs, Gainesville FL

City of Pittsfield, Berkshire Artisans, Pittsfield MA

College of William & Mary, Joseph & Margaret Muscarelle Museum of Art, Williamsburg VA

Columbus Museum, Columbus GA

Columbus Museum of Art, Columbus OH

Community Fine Arts Center, Halseth Gallery, Rock Springs WY

Concordia University, Leonard & Bina Ellen Art Gallery, Montreal PQ

Connecticut Historical Commission, Sloane-Stanley Museum, Kent CT

Coutts Memorial Museum of Art, Inc, El Dorado KS

C W Post Campus of Long Island University, Hillwood Art Museum, Brookville NY

Dahesh Museum, New York NY

Danforth Museum of Art, Framingham MA

Dartmouth College, Hood Museum of Art, Hanover NH

Dartmouth Heritage Museum, Dartmouth NS

DeCordova Museum & Sculpture Park, Lincoln MA

Denver Art Museum, Denver CO

Detroit Institute of Arts, Detroit MI

DeWitt Historical Society of Tompkins County, Ithaca NY

Dickinson College, Trout Gallery, Carlisle PA

Durham Art Guild Inc, Durham NC

East Baton Rouge Parks & Recreation Commission, Baton Rouge Gallery Inc, Baton Rouge LA

Eiteljorg Museum of American Indians & Western Art, Indianapolis IN

Ellen Noel Art Museum of the Permian Basin, Odessa TX

Erie Art Museum, Erie PA

Essex Historical Society, Essex Shipbuilding Museum, Essex MA

Evanston Historical Society, Charles Gates Dawes House, Evanston IL

Fayette Art Museum, Fayette AL

Federal Reserve Board, Art Gallery, Washington DC

Fine Arts Museums of San Francisco, M H de Young Memorial Museum & California Palace of the Legion of Honor, San Francisco CA

Fitton Center For Creative Arts, Hamilton OH

Florence Museum of Art, Science & History, Florence SC

Florida State University Foundation - Central Florida Community College Foundation, The Appleton Museum of Art, Ocala FL

Fort Ticonderoga Association, Ticonderoga NY

Fort Worth Art Association, Modern Art Museum of Fort Worth, Fort Worth TX

Gallery 53, Cooperstown NY

Gallery One, Ellensburg WA

Glanmore, Hastings County Museum, Belleville ON

Headquarters Fort Monroe, Dept of Army, Casemate Museum, Fort Monroe VA

Hebrew Union College, Skirball Cultural Center, Los Angeles CA

Henry Gallery Association, Henry Art Gallery, Seattle WA

Hispanic Society of America, Museum, New York NY

Historic Cherry Hill, Albany NY

Historic Landmarks Foundation of Indiana, Morris-Butler House, Indianapolis IN

Honolulu Academy of Arts, Honolulu HI

House of Roses, Senator Wilson Home, Deadwood SD

The Interchurch Center, Galleries at the Interchurch Center, New York NY

Joslyn Art Museum, Omaha NE

Kansas City Art Institute, Kemper Museum of Contemporary Art & Design, Kansas City MO

Knoxville Museum of Art, Knoxville TN

Koochiching County Historical Society Museum, International Falls MN

Lafayette Natural History Museum, Planetarium & Nature Station, Lafayette LA

Landmark Society of Western New York, Inc, Rochester NY

LeSueur County Historical Museum, Chapter One, Elysian MN

LeSueur Museum, LeSueur MN

Longview Art Museum, Longview TX

Louisiana Arts & Science Center, Baton Rouge LA

Charles H MacNider Museum, Mason City IA

Maine Historical Society, Wadsworth-Longfellow House, Portland ME

Maitland Art Center, Maitland FL

Maricopa County Historical Society, Desert Caballeros Western Museum, Wickenburg AZ

The Market Gallery of the City of Toronto Archives, Toronto ON

Maryhill Museum of Art, Goldendale WA

Maryland Art Place, Baltimore MD

Marylhurst College, The Art Gym, Marylhurst OR

Mattatuck Historical Society, Mattatuck Museum, Waterbury CT

Maui Historical Society, Bailey House, Wailuku HI

Michigan State University, Kresge Art Museum, East Lansing MI

Midwest Museum of American Art, Elkhart IN

Arthur Roy Mitchell Memorial Inc, Museum of Western Art, Trinidad CO

Morris Museum of Art, Augusta GA

Munson-Williams-Proctor Institute, Museum of Art, Utica NY

Musee Regional de la Cote-Nord, Sept-Iles PQ

Museum of Arts & History, Port Huron MI

Museum of Contemporary Art, North Miami FL

Museum of the City of New York, New York NY

Museum of Western Art, Denver CO

Muttart Public Art Gallery, Calgary AB

National Cowboy Hall of Fame & Western Heritage Center Museum, Oklahoma City OK

National Gallery of Canada, Ottawa ON

National Museum of American Art, Washington DC

National Museum of Wildlife Art, Jackson WY

National Museum of Women in the Arts, Washington DC

National Park Service, Weir Farm National Historic Site, Wilton CT

Nelson-Atkins Museum of Art, Kansas City MO

Nevada Museum Of Art, Reno NV

New Brunswick Museum, Saint John NB

New Mexico State University, University Art Gallery, Las Cruces NM

The Ohio Historical Society, Inc, Campus Martius Museum & Ohio River Museum, Marietta OH

Oklahoma City Art Museum, Oklahoma City OK

Old Salem Inc, Museum of Early Southern Decorative Arts, Winston-Salem NC

One West Art Center, Fort Collins CO

Oshkosh Public Museum, Oshkosh WI

Owensboro Museum of Fine Art, Owensboro KY

Palm Springs Desert Museum, Palm Springs CA

Panhandle-Plains Historical Society Museum, Canyon TX

Passaic County Historical Society, Paterson NJ

Pennsylvania Academy of the Fine Arts, Museum of American Art, Philadelphia PA

George Phippen Memorial Foundation, Phippen Museum of Western Art, Prescott AZ

Pope County Historical Society, Pope County Museum, Glenwood MN

Rensselaer County Historical Society, Hart-Cluett Mansion, 1827, Troy NY

Rhode Island Historical Society, John Brown House, Providence RI

Ross Memorial Museum, Saint Andrews NB

Abigail Adams Smith Museum, New York NY

South Dakota State University, South Dakota Art Museum, Brookings SD

Southeastern Center for Contemporary Art, Winston-Salem NC

Southern Alleghenies Museum of Art, Southern Alleghenies Museum of Art at Johnstown, Loretto PA

Southern Methodist University, Meadows Museum, Dallas TX

Spartanburg County Museum of Art, Spartanburg SC

Springfield Art Museum, Springfield MO

State University of New York at New Paltz, College Art Gallery, New Paltz NY

Susquehanna University, Lore Degenstein Gallery, Selinsgrove PA

Syracuse University, Art Collection, Syracuse NY

Tampa Museum of Art, Tampa FL

Texas A&M University, J Wayne Stark University Center Galleries, College Station TX

Topeka & Shawnee County Public Library, Gallery of Fine Arts, Topeka KS

The Ukrainian Museum, New York NY

United Society of Shakers, Shaker Museum, New Glocester ME

United States Capitol, Architect of the Capitol, Washington DC

University of Alabama at Birmingham, Visual Arts Gallery, Birmingham AL

University of Cincinnati, DAAP Galleries-College of Design Architecture, Art & Planning, Cincinnati OH

University of Colorado at Colorado Springs, Gallery of Contemporary Art, Colorado Springs CO

University of Delaware, University Gallery, Newark DE

University of New Hampshire, The Art Gallery, Durham NH

University of Rochester, Memorial Art Gallery, Rochester NY

University of Virginia, Bayly Art Museum, Charlottesville VA

Upstairs Gallery, Winnipeg MB

Ursinus College, Philip & Muriel Berman Museum of Art, Collegeville PA

Vesterheim Norwegian-American Museum, Decorah IA

Viridian Artists inc, New York NY

Wadsworth Atheneum, Hartford CT

Waterworks Visual Arts Center, Salisbury NC

Wells Fargo Bank, Wells Fargo History Museum, San Francisco CA

Whatcom Museum of History and Art, Bellingham WA

Peter & Catharine Whyte Foundation, Whyte Museum of the Canadian Rockies, Banff AB

Wilfrid Laurier University, Robert Langen Gallery, Waterloo ON

Woodmere Art Museum, Philadelphia PA

Yale University, Yale Center for British Art, New Haven CT

Yarmouth County Historical Society, Yarmouth County Museum, Yarmouth NS

York Institute Museum, Saco ME

Mattatuck Historical Society, Mattatuck Museum, Waterbury CT

Mexican Museum, San Francisco CA

Mississippi Department of Archives & History, Old Capitol Museum, Jackson MS

Mississippi River Museum at Mud-Island, Memphis TN

Mohave Museum of History & Arts, Kingman AZ

Musee des Augustines de l'Hotel Dieu de Quebec, Quebec PQ

Museum of Mobile, Mobile AL

Museum of the City of New York, New York NY

National Museum of the American Indian, George Gustav Heye Center, New York NY

Naval Historical Center, The Navy Museum, Washington DC

Naval War College Museum, Newport RI

Nevada Museum Of Art, Reno NV

New Brunswick Museum, Saint John NB

New York State Office of Parks Recreation & Historic Preservation, John Jay Homestead State Historic Site, Katonah NY

The John A Noble Collection, Staten Island NY

Ohio Historical Society, National Afro American Museum & Cultural Center, Wilberforce OH

Old Dartmouth Historical Society, New Bedford Whaling Museum, New Bedford MA

Old Jail Art Center, Albany TX

Old Slater Mill Association, Slater Mill Historic Site, Pawtucket RI

Old York Historical Society, Old Gaol Museum, York ME

Oshkosh Public Museum, Oshkosh WI

Page-Walker Arts & History Center, Cary NC

Passaic County Historical Society, Paterson NJ

Pope County Historical Society, Pope County Museum, Glenwood MN

Putnam Museum of History & Natural Science, Davenport IA

Redding Museum of Art & History, Redding CA

Rensselaer County Historical Society, Hart-Cluett Mansion, 1827, Troy NY

Riley County Historical Society, Riley County Historical Museum, Manhattan KS

Rowland Evans Robinson Memorial Association, Rokeby Museum, Ferrisburgh VT

The Rosenbach Museum & Library, Philadelphia PA

C M Russell Museum, Great Falls MT

Saint Joseph Museum, Saint Joseph MO

The Seagram Museum, Waterloo ON

Shaker Village of Pleasant Hill, Harrodsburg KY

Abigail Adams Smith Museum, New York NY

Society of the Cincinnati, Museum & Library at Anderson House, Washington DC

South Street Seaport Museum, New York NY

Springfield Art & Historical Society, Miller Art Center, Springfield VT

Nelda C & H J Lutcher Stark Foundation, Stark Museum of Art, Orange TX

Stratford Historical Society, Katherine Mitchel Museum, Stratford CT

Susquehanna University, Lore Degenstein Gallery, Selinsgrove PA

Swedish American Museum Association of Chicago, Chicago IL

The Temple-Tifereth Israel, The Temple Museum of Religious Art, Beachwood OH

Tryon Palace Historic Sites & Gardens, New Bern NC

Tulane University, University Art Collection, New Orleans LA

Turtle Mountain Chippewa Historical Society, Turtle Mountain Heritage Center, Belcourt ND

United States Capitol, Architect of the Capitol, Washington DC

US Coast Guard Museum, New London CT

United States Figure Skating Association, World Figure Skating Museum & Hall of Fame, Colorado Springs CO

United States Naval Academy Museum, Annapolis MD

University of Chicago, Oriental Institute Museum, Chicago IL

University of Manitoba, Faculty of Architecture Exhibition Centre, Winnipeg MB

USS Constitution Museum, Boston MA

Vermilion County Museum Society, Danville IL

Wadsworth Atheneum, Hartford CT

Washington County Museum of Fine Arts, Hagerstown MD

Washington State History Museum, Tacoma WA

Wayne County Historical Society, Museum, Honesdale PA

Wells Fargo Bank, Wells Fargo History Museum, San Francisco CA

West Baton Rouge Historical Association, Museum, Port Allen LA

Wheelwright Museum of the American Indian, Santa Fe NM

White House, Washington DC

Peter & Catharine Whyte Foundation, Whyte Museum of the Canadian Rockies, Banff AB

Winterthur Museum, Winterthur DE

Yale University, Yale Center for British Art, New Haven CT

Yarmouth County Historical Society, Yarmouth County Museum, Yarmouth NS

York Institute Museum, Saco ME

MAPS

African Art Museum of Maryland, Columbia MD

Agecroft Association, Museum, Richmond VA

Alabama Department of Archives & History, Museum Galleries, Montgomery AL

Albuquerque Museum of Art & History, Albuquerque NM

Amherst Museum, Amherst NY

Anchorage Museum of History & Art, Anchorage AK

Arizona Historical Society-Yuma, Century House Museum & Garden, Yuma AZ

Arkansas Territorial Restoration, Little Rock AR

Artesia Historical Museum & Art Center, Artesia NM

Atlanta Historical Society Inc, Atlanta History Center, Atlanta GA

Baldwin Historical Society Museum, Baldwin NY

Balzekas Museum of Lithuanian Culture, Chicago IL

The Bartlett Museum, Amesbury MA

Jesse Besser Museum, Alpena MI

Bowdoin College, Peary-MacMillan Arctic Museum, Brunswick ME

Brooklyn Historical Society, Brooklyn OH

Calvert Marine Museum, Solomons MD

Carson County Square House Museum, Panhandle TX

Central United Methodist Church, Swords Info Plowshares Peace Center & Gallery, Detroit MI

Chicago Department of Cultural Affairs, Chicago Cultural Center, Chicago IL

City of Springdale, Shiloh Museum, Springdale AR

Clinton County Historical Association, Clinton County Historical Museum, Plattsburgh NY

Colorado Historical Society, Colorado History Museum, Denver CO

Crow Wing County Historical Society, Brainerd MN

Dartmouth Heritage Museum, Dartmouth NS

Douglas County Historical Society, Fairlawn Mansion & Museum, Superior WI

Eastern Washington State Historical Society, Cheney Cowles Museum, Spokane WA

Ephraim McDowell-Cambus-Kenneth Foundation, McDowell House & Apothecary Shop, Danville KY

Evanston Historical Society, Charles Gates Dawes House, Evanston IL

Evansville Museum of Arts & Science, Evansville IN

Five Civilized Tribes Museum, Muskogee OK

Florida State University Foundation - Central Florida Community College Foundation, The Appleton Museum of Art, Ocala FL

Fort George G Meade Museum, Fort Meade MD

Fort Ticonderoga Association, Ticonderoga NY

Great Lakes Historical Society, Island Seas Maritime Museum, Vermilion OH

Hebrew Union College-Jewish Institute of Religion, New York NY

Hispanic Society of America, Museum, New York NY

Historical Society of Pennsylvania, Philadelphia PA

Huguenot Historical Society of New Paltz Galleries, New Paltz NY

Imperial Calcasieu Museum, Gibson-Barham Gallery, Lake Charles LA

Institute of the Great Plains, Museum of the Great Plains, Lawton OK

Kern County Museum, Bakersfield CA

Kings County Historical Society and Museum, Hampton NB

Koochiching County Historical Society Museum, International Falls MN

La Casa del Libro Museum, San Juan PR

Lafayette Natural History Museum, Planetarium & Nature Station, Lafayette LA

Lehigh County Historical Society, Allentown PA

Leroy Historical Society, LeRoy NY

LeSueur County Historical Museum, Chapter One, Elysian MN

Liberty Memorial Museum & Archives, Kansas City MO

McPherson Museum, McPherson KS

Judah L Magnes Museum, Berkeley CA

The Mariners' Museum, Newport News VA

The Market Gallery of the City of Toronto Archives, Toronto ON

Mason County Museum, Maysville KY

Massachusetts Institute of Technology, MIT Museum, Cambridge MA

Massachusetts Institute of Technology, Hart Nautical Galleries & Collections, Cambridge MA

Mattatuck Historical Society, Mattatuck Museum, Waterbury CT

Mississippi Department of Archives & History, Old Capitol Museum, Jackson MS

Mississippi River Museum at Mud-Island, Memphis TN

Moravian Historical Society, Whitefield House Museum, Nazareth PA

Museum of Arts & History, Port Huron MI

Museum of Mobile, Mobile AL

Museum of Northern British Columbia, Ruth Harvey Art Gallery, Prince Rupert BC

Museum of the Americas, Brookfield VT

Museum of the City of New York, New York NY

National Infantry Museum, Fort Benning GA

National Society of the Colonial Dames, Wilton House Museum, Richmond VA

Naval Historical Center, The Navy Museum, Washington DC

Naval War College Museum, Newport RI

New Brunswick Museum, Saint John NB

New York State Office of Parks Recreation & Historic Preservation, John Jay Homestead State Historic Site, Katonah NY

Norfolk Historical Society Inc, Museum, Norfolk CT

Oklahoma City Art Museum, Oklahoma City OK

Old Dartmouth Historical Society, New Bedford Whaling Museum, New Bedford MA

Old Jail Art Center, Albany TX

Old Salem Inc, Museum of Early Southern Decorative Arts, Winston-Salem NC

Oshkosh Public Museum, Oshkosh WI

Oysterponds Historical Society, Museum, Orient NY

Page-Walker Arts & History Center, Cary NC

Panhandle-Plains Historical Society Museum, Canyon TX

Passaic County Historical Society, Paterson NJ

Pennsylvania Historical & Museum Commission, Railroad Museum of Pennsylvania, Harrisburg PA

Plainsman Museum, Aurora NE

Polish Museum of America, Chicago IL

Port Authority of New York & New Jersey, Art Collection, New York NY

Portsmouth Historical Society, John Paul Jones House, Portsmouth NH

Putnam Museum of History & Natural Science, Davenport IA

Queens Historical Society, Flushing NY

Redding Museum of Art & History, Redding CA

Rensselaer County Historical Society, Hart-Cluett Mansion, 1827, Troy NY

Rhode Island Historical Society, John Brown House, Providence RI

Riley County Historical Society, Riley County
Historical Museum, Manhattan KS
San Francisco Maritime National Historical Park,
National Maritime Museum, San Francisco CA
Seneca-Iroquois National Museum, Salamanca NY
Abigail Adams Smith Museum, New York NY
South Street Seaport Museum, New York NY
Springfield Art & Historical Society, Miller Art
Center, Springfield VT
David M Stewart Museum, Montreal PQ
Stratford Historical Society, Katherine Mitchel
Museum, Stratford CT
Towson State University, The Holtzman Art
Gallery, Towson MD
Tryon Palace Historic Sites & Gardens, New Bern
NC
Tulane University, University Art Collection, New
Orleans LA
Turtle Mountain Chippewa Historical Society,
Turtle Mountain Heritage Center, Belcourt ND
Vermilion County Museum Society, Danville IL
Washington State History Museum, Tacoma WA
Wayne County Historical Society, Museum,
Honesdale PA
Wells Fargo Bank, Wells Fargo History Museum,
San Francisco CA
West Baton Rouge Historical Association, Museum,
Port Allen LA
Westminster College, Winston Churchill Memorial
& Library in the United States, Fulton MO
Wethersfield Historical Society Inc, Museum,
Wethersfield CT
Peter & Catharine Whyte Foundation, Whyte
Museum of the Canadian Rockies, Banff AB
Woodlawn Plantation, Mount Vernon VA
Yale University, Yale Center for British Art, New
Haven CT
York Institute Museum, Saco ME

MARINE PAINTING

Alaska State Museum, Juneau AK
Albany Institute of History & Art, Albany NY
The Albrecht-Kemper Museum of Art, Saint Joseph
MO
Battleship North Carolina, Wilmington NC
Jesse Besser Museum, Alpena MI
The Bostonian Society, Old State House Museum,
Boston MA
Brigham Young University, Museum of Art, Provo
UT
Butler Institute of American Art, Art Museum,
Youngstown OH
Calvert Marine Museum, Solomons MD
Cape Ann Historical Museum, Gloucester MA
Chatham Historical Society, Old Atwood House
Museum, Chatham MA
Chattahoochee Valley Art Museum, LaGrange GA
Chesapeake Bay Maritime Museum, Saint Michaels
MD
Columbia River Maritime Museum, Astoria OR
Douglas County Historical Society, Fairlawn
Mansion & Museum, Superior WI
Federal Reserve Board, Art Gallery, Washington
DC
Florida State University Foundation - Central
Florida Community College Foundation, The
Appleton Museum of Art, Ocala FL
Gallery One, Ellensburg WA
Great Lakes Historical Society, Island Seas
Maritime Museum, Vermilion OH
Headquarters Fort Monroe, Dept of Army,
Casemate Museum, Fort Monroe VA
Heckscher Museum of Art, Huntington NY
Independence Seaport Museum, Philadelphia PA
The Interchurch Center, Galleries at the
Interchurch Center, New York NY
International Society of Marine Painters, Oneco FL
Kendall Whaling Museum, Sharon MA
Knoxville Museum of Art, Knoxville TN
Maine Maritime Museum, Bath ME
The Mariners' Museum, Newport News VA
The Market Gallery of the City of Toronto
Archives, Toronto ON
Massachusetts Institute of Technology, MIT
Museum, Cambridge MA

Massachusetts Institute of Technology, Hart
Nautical Galleries & Collections, Cambridge
MA
Monterey History & Art Association, Maritime
Museum of Monterey, Monterey CA
Munson-Williams-Proctor Institute, Museum of Art,
Utica NY
Museum of Arts & History, Port Huron MI
Museum of the City of New York, New York NY
National Museum of American Art, Washington
DC
Naval Historical Center, The Navy Museum,
Washington DC
Naval War College Museum, Newport RI
Nevada Museum Of Art, Reno NV
Newburyport Maritime Society, Custom House
Maritime Museum, Newburyport MA
The John A Noble Collection, Staten Island NY
Nova Scotia Museum, Maritime Museum of the
Atlantic, Halifax NS
The Ohio Historical Society, Inc, Campus Martius
Museum & Ohio River Museum, Marietta OH
Old Dartmouth Historical Society, New Bedford
Whaling Museum, New Bedford MA
Oysterponds Historical Society, Museum, Orient
NY
Pennsylvania Academy of the Fine Arts, Museum
of American Art, Philadelphia PA
Provincetown Art Association & Museum,
Provincetown MA
Rhode Island Historical Society, John Brown
House, Providence RI
San Diego Maritime Museum, San Diego CA
San Francisco Maritime National Historical Park,
National Maritime Museum, San Francisco CA
South Street Seaport Museum, New York NY
Stratford Historical Society, Katherine Mitchel
Museum, Stratford CT
Towson State University, The Holtzman Art
Gallery, Towson MD
University of Rochester, Memorial Art Gallery,
Rochester NY
Upstairs Gallery, Winnipeg MB
Ursinus College, Philip & Muriel Berman Museum
of Art, Collegeville PA
USS Constitution Museum, Boston MA
Wilfrid Laurier University, Robert Langen Gallery,
Waterloo ON
Yarmouth County Historical Society, Yarmouth
County Museum, Yarmouth NS

MEDIEVAL ART

Academy of the New Church, Glencairn Museum,
Bryn Athyn PA
Lyman Allyn Art Museum, New London CT
The Art Institute of Chicago, Chicago IL
Beloit College, Wright Museum of Art, Beloit WI
Cincinnati Institute of Fine Arts, Taft Museum,
Cincinnati OH
Cincinnati Museum Association, Cincinnati Art
Museum, Cincinnati OH
College of William & Mary, Joseph & Margaret
Muscarelle Museum of Art, Williamsburg VA
Florida State University Foundation - Central
Florida Community College Foundation, The
Appleton Museum of Art, Ocala FL
General Board of Discipleship, The United
Methodist Church, The Upper Room Chapel &
Museum, Nashville TN
Hebrew Union College, Skirball Cultural Center,
Los Angeles CA
Hebrew Union College-Jewish Institute of Religion,
New York NY
Honolulu Academy of Arts, Honolulu HI
Joslyn Art Museum, Omaha NE
Marion Koogler McNay Art Museum, San Antonio
TX
The Metropolitan Museum of Art, New York NY
Michigan State University, Kresge Art Museum,
East Lansing MI
Museum of Fine Arts, Houston, Houston TX
National Gallery of Canada, Ottawa ON
Nelson-Atkins Museum of Art, Kansas City MO
Rensselaer Newman Foundation Chapel & Cultural
Center, The Gallery, Troy NY
Royal Ontario Museum, Toronto ON

Saint Mary's College of California, Hearst Art
Gallery, Moraga CA
Santa Barbara Museum of Art, Santa Barbara CA
Southern Methodist University, Meadows Museum,
Dallas TX
Stanford University, Museum of Art, Stanford CA
Toledo Museum of Art, Toledo OH
University of Chicago, Oriental Institute Museum,
Chicago IL
University of Illinois, Krannert Art Museum,
Champaign IL
University of Kansas, Spencer Museum of Art,
Lawrence KS
University of Rochester, Memorial Art Gallery,
Rochester NY
University of Vermont, Robert Hull Fleming
Museum, Burlington VT
University of Victoria, Maltwood Art Museum and
Gallery, Victoria BC
University of Wisconsin-Madison, Elvehjem
Museum of Art, Madison WI
Vassar College, The Frances Lehman Loeb Art
Center, Poughkeepsie NY
Williams College, Museum of Art, Williamstown
MA
Worcester Art Museum, Worcester MA

METALWORK

Agecroft Association, Museum, Richmond VA
Alaska State Museum, Juneau AK
Arkansas Territorial Restoration, Little Rock AR
Art Museum of Missoula, Missoula MT
Asian Art Museum of San Francisco, Avery
Brundage Collection, San Francisco CA
Leo Baeck Institute, New York NY
Beloit College, Wright Museum of Art, Beloit WI
California College of Arts & Crafts, Steven Oliver
Art Center, Oakland CA
The Canadian Craft Museum, Vancouver BC
Kit Carson Historic Museums, Home & Museum,
Taos NM
Kit Carson Historic Museums, Hacienda Martinez,
Taos NM
Chilkat Valley Historical Society, Sheldon Museum
& Cultural Center, Haines AK
Cincinnati Institute of Fine Arts, Taft Museum,
Cincinnati OH
College of William & Mary, Joseph & Margaret
Muscarelle Museum of Art, Williamsburg VA
Cooper-Hewitt, National Design Museum, New
York NY
Cranbrook Art Museum, Bloomfield Hills MI
Durham Art Guild Inc, Durham NC
Evanston Historical Society, Charles Gates Dawes
House, Evanston IL
Florida Gulf Coast Art Center, Inc, Belleair FL
Florida State University Foundation - Central
Florida Community College Foundation, The
Appleton Museum of Art, Ocala FL
Edsel & Eleanor Ford House, Grosse Pointe Shores
MI
Forges du Saint-Maurice National Historic Site,
Trois Rivieres PQ
Fort Worth Art Association, Modern Art Museum
of Fort Worth, Fort Worth TX
Gallery One, Ellensburg WA
Grand Rapids Art Museum, Grand Rapids MI
Hambidge Center Gallery, Rabun Gap GA
Harvard University, Dumbarton Oaks Research
Library & Collections, Washington DC
Harvard University, Arthur M Sackler Museum,
Cambridge MA
Hebrew Union College, Skirball Cultural Center,
Los Angeles CA
Heritage Center of Lancaster County Museum,
Lancaster PA
Hutchinson Art Association, Hutchinson Art
Center, Hutchinson KS
Institute of American Indian Arts Museum, Santa
Fe NM
Kelowna Museum, Kelowna BC
Knoxville Museum of Art, Knoxville TN
Leroy Historical Society, LeRoy NY
LeSueur County Historical Museum, Chapter One,
Elysian MN
McCord Museum of Canadian History, Montreal
PQ

Judah L Magnes Museum, Berkeley CA
Maryland Historical Society, Museum of Maryland History, Baltimore MD
Mattatuck Historical Society, Mattatuck Museum, Waterbury CT
Musee d'Art de Saint-Laurent, Saint-Laurent PQ
Musee Regional de la Cote-Nord, Sept-Iles PQ
Museum of the City of New York, New York NY
Muttart Public Art Gallery, Calgary AB
Naval Historical Center, The Navy Museum, Washington DC
New Orleans School of GlassWorks, Gallery & Printmaking Studio, New Orleans LA
Old Salem Inc, Museum of Early Southern Decorative Arts, Winston-Salem NC
One West Art Center, Fort Collins CO
Pioneer Town, Pioneer Museum of Western Art, Wimberley TX
Plumas County Museum, Quincy CA
Pope County Historical Society, Pope County Museum, Glenwood MN
Principia College, School of Nations Museum, Elsah IL
Millicent Rogers Museum of Northern New Mexico, Taos NM
Saint Clair County Community College, Jack R Hennesey Art Galleries, Port Huron MI
Seneca-Iroquois National Museum, Salamanca NY
Southeastern Center for Contemporary Art, Winston-Salem NC
Tacoma Arts Commission, Commencement Art Gallery, Tacoma WA
Topeka & Shawnee County Public Library, Gallery of Fine Arts, Topeka KS
Towson State University, Asian Arts Center, Towson MD
The Ukrainian Museum, New York NY
United States Naval Academy Museum, Annapolis MD
Wheelwright Museum of the American Indian, Santa Fe NM
White House, Washington DC
Wilfrid Laurier University, Robert Langen Gallery, Waterloo ON
York Institute Museum, Saco ME

MEXICAN ART

Americas Society Art Gallery, New York NY
Arts Council of Fayetteville-Cumberland County, The Arts Center, Fayetteville NC
Aurora University, Schingoethe Center for Native American Cultures, Aurora IL
Bard College, Center for Curatorial Studies Museum, Annandale on Hudson NY
Brown University, David Winton Bell Gallery, Providence RI
The Buffalo Fine Arts Academy, Albright-Knox Art Gallery, Buffalo NY
Kit Carson Historic Museums, Hacienda Martinez, Taos NM
Chicago Department of Cultural Affairs, Chicago Cultural Center, Chicago IL
Cleveland State University, Art Gallery, Cleveland OH
Coutts Memorial Museum of Art, Inc, El Dorado KS
Craft & Folk Art Museum, Los Angeles CA
Davenport Museum of Art, Davenport IA
Davidson College Visual Arts Center, William H Van Every Jr & Edward M Smith Galleries, Davidson NC
East Carolina University, Wellington B Gray Gallery, Greenville NC
Ellen Noel Art Museum of the Permian Basin, Odessa TX
El Paso Museum of Art, El Paso TX
Emory University, Michael C Carlos Museum, Atlanta GA
Edsel & Eleanor Ford House, Grosse Pointe Shores MI
Fort Worth Art Association, Modern Art Museum of Fort Worth, Fort Worth TX
Fresno Arts Center & Museum, Fresno CA
Gonzaga University, Jundt Art Museum, Ad Art Gallery, Spokane WA
Guadalupe Historic Foundation, Santuario de Guadalupe, Santa Fe NM

Heard Museum, Phoenix AZ
Intar Latin American Gallery, New York NY
The Interchurch Center, Galleries at the Interchurch Center, New York NY
Jefferson County Open Space, Hiwan Homestead Museum, Evergreen CO
Kansas City Art Institute, Kemper Museum of Contemporary Art & Design, Kansas City MO
Knoxville Museum of Art, Knoxville TN
Koshare Indian Museum, Inc, La Junta CO
McAllen International Museum, McAllen TX
Mercer County Community College, The Gallery, Trenton NJ
Mexican Fine Arts Center Museum, Chicago IL
Mexican Museum, San Francisco CA
MEXIC-ARTE Museum, Austin TX
Museum of New Mexico, Museum of Fine Arts, Santa Fe NM
Museum of the Americas, Brookfield VT
Panhandle-Plains Historical Society Museum, Canyon TX
Phoenix Art Museum, Phoenix AZ
Roswell Museum & Art Center, Roswell NM
C M Russell Museum, Great Falls MT
San Antonio Museum of Art, San Antonio TX
Santa Barbara Museum of Art, Santa Barbara CA
University of Colorado at Colorado Springs, Gallery of Contemporary Art, Colorado Springs CO
University of Illinois, World Heritage Museum, Champaign IL
University of Texas at Austin, Archer M Huntington Art Gallery, Austin TX
Wichita Art Museum, Wichita KS

MILITARY ART

Alabama Department of Archives & History, Museum Galleries, Montgomery AL
Arts Council of Fayetteville-Cumberland County, The Arts Center, Fayetteville NC
Battleship North Carolina, Wilmington NC
Kit Carson Historic Museums, Home & Museum, Taos NM
Clark County Historical Society, Pioneer - Krier Museum, Ashland KS
Evanston Historical Society, Charles Gates Dawes House, Evanston IL
Fort George G Meade Museum, Fort Meade MD
Fort Ticonderoga Association, Ticonderoga NY
Headquarters Fort Monroe, Dept of Army, Casemate Museum, Fort Monroe VA
Huntington Museum of Art, Huntington WV
Liberty Memorial Museum & Archives, Kansas City MO
The Mariners' Museum, Newport News VA
National Infantry Museum, Fort Benning GA
Naval Historical Center, The Navy Museum, Washington DC
Naval War College Museum, Newport RI
Oklahoma Historical Society, State Museum of History, Oklahoma City OK
Polish Museum of America, Chicago IL
Marjorie Merriweather Post Foundation of DC, Hillwood Museum, Washington DC
Society of the Cincinnati, Museum & Library at Anderson House, Washington DC
State Historical Society of Wisconsin, State Historical Museum, Madison WI
David M Stewart Museum, Montreal PQ
US Navy Supply Corps School, US Navy Supply Corps Museum, Athens GA
USS Constitution Museum, Boston MA

MINIATURES

Arts & Science Center, Statesville NC
Carolina Art Association, Gibbes Museum of Art, Charleston SC
Cincinnati Institute of Fine Arts, Taft Museum, Cincinnati OH
Cincinnati Museum Association, Cincinnati Art Museum, Cincinnati OH
DAR Museum, National Society Daughters of the American Revolution, Washington DC
Ephraim McDowell-Cambus-Kenneth Foundation, McDowell House & Apothecary Shop, Danville KY

Favell Museum of Western Art & Indian Artifacts, Klamath Falls OR
Fayette Art Museum, Fayette AL
Glanmore, Hastings County Museum, Belleville ON
Grand Rapids Art Museum, Grand Rapids MI
Hebrew Union College-Jewish Institute of Religion, New York NY
Houston Baptist University, Museum of American Architecture and Decorative Arts, Houston TX
Kelowna Museum, Kelowna BC
Knoxville Museum of Art, Knoxville TN
LeSueur County Historical Museum, Chapter One, Elysian MN
Maine Historical Society, Wadsworth-Longfellow House, Portland ME
Maryhill Museum of Art, Goldendale WA
Munson-Williams-Proctor Institute, Museum of Art, Utica NY
Napoleonic Society of America, Museum & Library, Clearwater FL
National Portrait Gallery, Washington DC
Navajo Nation Museum, Window Rock AZ
Naval Historical Center, The Navy Museum, Washington DC
Naval War College Museum, Newport RI
New Jersey Historical Society, Newark NJ
New Orleans Museum of Art, New Orleans LA
Old Dartmouth Historical Society, New Bedford Whaling Museum, New Bedford MA
Pacific - Asia Museum, Pasadena CA
Phoenix Art Museum, Phoenix AZ
Rhode Island Historical Society, John Brown House, Providence RI
R W Norton Art Gallery, Shreveport LA
Society of the Cincinnati, Museum & Library at Anderson House, Washington DC
South Carolina State Museum, Columbia SC
Wheelwright Museum of the American Indian, Santa Fe NM
Woodlawn Plantation, Mount Vernon VA
Yale University, Yale Center for British Art, New Haven CT
York Institute Museum, Saco ME

MOSAICS

Academy of the New Church, Glencairn Museum, Bryn Athyn PA
Leo Baeck Institute, New York NY
Baltimore Museum of Art, Baltimore MD
Chicago Department of Cultural Affairs, Chicago Cultural Center, Chicago IL
Community Fine Arts Center, Halseth Gallery, Rock Springs WY
Harvard University, Dumbarton Oaks Research Library & Collections, Washington DC
The Interchurch Center, Galleries at the Interchurch Center, New York NY
Lizzadro Museum of Lapidary Art, Elmhurst IL
Plainsman Museum, Aurora NE
Stanford University, Museum of Art, Stanford CA
University of Manitoba, Faculty of Architecture Exhibition Centre, Winnipeg MB
Worcester Art Museum, Worcester MA

ORIENTAL ART

Allentown Art Museum, Allentown PA
Lyman Allyn Art Museum, New London CT
Amherst College, Mead Art Museum, Amherst MA
Art Gallery of Greater Victoria, Victoria BC
The Art Institute of Chicago, Chicago IL
Art Museum of Western Virginia, Roanoke VA
Arts Council of Fayetteville-Cumberland County, The Arts Center, Fayetteville NC
Asian Art Museum of San Francisco, Avery Brundage Collection, San Francisco CA
Baltimore Museum of Art, Baltimore MD
Bates College, Museum of Art, Lewiston ME
Beloit College, Wright Museum of Art, Beloit WI
Blanden Memorial Art Museum, Fort Dodge IA
Boise Art Museum, Boise ID
Brigham Young University, Museum of Art, Provo UT
The Buffalo Fine Arts Academy, Albright-Knox Art Gallery, Buffalo NY
California State University Stanislaus, University Art Gallery, Turlock CA

PAINTING - AMERICAN

Bates College, Museum of Art, Lewiston ME
Battleship North Carolina, Wilmington NC
Baylor University, Martin Museum of Art, Waco TX
Beaumont Art League, Beaumont TX
Beloit College, Wright Museum of Art, Beloit WI
Bergstrom Mahler Museum, Neenah WI
Berkshire Museum, Pittsfield MA
Jesse Besser Museum, Alpena MI
Birmingham Museum of Art, Birmingham AL
Blanden Memorial Art Museum, Fort Dodge IA
Board of Parks & Recreation, The Parthenon, Nashville TN
Boise Art Museum, Boise ID
The Bostonian Society, Old State House Museum, Boston MA
Bowdoin College, Peary-MacMillan Arctic Museum, Brunswick ME
Bowdoin College, Museum of Art, Brunswick ME
Roy Boyd Gallery, Chicago IL
Brandeis University, Rose Art Museum, Waltham MA
Brandywine River Museum, Chadds Ford PA
Brigham Young University, B F Larsen Gallery, Provo UT
Brigham Young University, Museum of Art, Provo UT
Bradford Brinton Memorial Museum & Historic Ranch, Big Horn WY
Brown County Art Gallery Association Inc, Brown County Art Gallery & Museum, Nashville IN
Brown University, David Winton Bell Gallery, Providence RI
The Bruce Museum, Greenwich CT
The Buffalo Fine Arts Academy, Albright-Knox Art Gallery, Buffalo NY
Burchfield-Penney Art Center, Buffalo NY
Butler Institute of American Art, Art Museum, Youngstown OH
California Center for the Arts Museum, Escondido CA
California College of Arts & Crafts, Steven Oliver Art Center, Oakland CA
California State University Stanislaus, University Art Gallery, Turlock CA
Canadian Wildlife & Wilderness Art Museum, Ottawa ON
Canajoharie Library & Art Gallery, Canajoharie NY
Canton Museum of Art, Canton OH
Cape Ann Historical Museum, Gloucester MA
Capital University, Schumacher Gallery, Columbus OH
Cardinal Stritch College, Layton Honor Gallery, Milwaukee WI
Carnegie Institute, Carnegie Museum of Art, Pittsburgh PA
Carolina Art Association, Gibbes Museum of Art, Charleston SC
Carson County Square House Museum, Panhandle TX
Kit Carson Historic Museums, Ernest Blumenschein Home & Studio, Taos NM
Kit Carson Historic Museums, Home & Museum, Taos NM
Amon Carter Museum, Fort Worth TX
Cartoon Art Museum, San Francisco CA
Radio-Canada SRC CBC, Galerie Georges Goguen, Moncton NB
Cedar Rapids Museum of Art, Cedar Rapids IA
Central United Methodist Church, Swords Info Plowshares Peace Center & Gallery, Detroit MI
Chatillon-DeMenil House Foundation, DeMenil Mansion, Saint Louis MO
Chattahoochee Valley Art Museum, LaGrange GA
Cheekwood-Tennessee Botanical Gardens & Museum of Art, Nashville TN
Chicago Department of Cultural Affairs, Chicago Cultural Center, Chicago IL
Chrysler Museum Of Art, Norfolk VA
Church of Jesus Christ of Latter-day Saints, Museum of Church History & Art, Salt Lake City UT
Cincinnati Institute of Fine Arts, Taft Museum, Cincinnati OH
City of Atlanta, Atlanta Cyclorama, Atlanta GA

City of Cedar Falls, Iowa, James & Meryl Hearst Center for the Arts, Cedar Falls IA
City of Gainesville, Thomas Center Galleries - Cultural Affairs, Gainesville FL
The City of Petersburg Museums, Petersburg VA
City of Pittsfield, Berkshire Artisans, Pittsfield MA
Clark County Historical Society, Pioneer - Krier Museum, Ashland KS
Clemson University, Rudolph E Lee Gallery, Clemson SC
Cleveland Museum of Art, Cleveland OH
Cleveland State University, Art Gallery, Cleveland OH
Clinton Art Association Gallery, Clinton IA
Clinton County Historical Association, Clinton County Historical Museum, Plattsburgh NY
Colby College, Museum of Art, Waterville ME
College of Saint Benedict, Art Gallery, Saint Joseph MN
College of Saint Rose, Picotte Hall Art Gallery, Albany NY
College of William & Mary, Joseph & Margaret Muscarelle Museum of Art, Williamsburg VA
The College of Wooster, Art Museum, Wooster OH
Colorado Historical Society, Colorado History Museum, Denver CO
Colorado Springs Fine Arts Center, Colorado Springs CO
Columbia County Historical Society, Columbia County Museum, Kinderhook NY
Columbia Museum of Art, Columbia SC
Columbus Chapel & Boal Mansion Museum, Boalsburg PA
Columbus Museum, Columbus GA
Columbus Museum of Art, Columbus OH
Community Fine Arts Center, Halseth Gallery, Rock Springs WY
Concordia Historical Institute, Saint Louis MO
Confederation Centre Art Gallery and Museum, Charlottetown PE
Connecticut Historical Commission, Sloane-Stanley Museum, Kent CT
Coos Art Museum, Coos Bay OR
Corcoran Gallery of Art, Washington DC
Cornell University, Herbert F Johnson Museum of Art, Ithaca NY
Coutts Memorial Museum of Art, Inc, El Dorado KS
Craigdarroch Castle Historical Museum Society, Victoria BC
Cranbrook Art Museum, Bloomfield Hills MI
Crane Collection Gallery, Boston MA
Crawford County Historical Society, Baldwin-Reynolds House Museum, Meadville PA
Crazy Horse Memorial, Indian Museum of North America & Native American Educational & Cultural Center, Crazy Horse SD
Creighton University, Fine Arts Gallery, Omaha NE
Cripple Creek District Museum, Cripple Creek CO
Crocker Art Museum, Sacramento CA
Crow Wing County Historical Society, Brainerd MN
Cummer Museum of Art & Gardens, DeEtte Holden Cummer Museum Foundation, Jacksonville FL
The Currier Gallery of Art, Manchester NH
Custer County Art Center, Miles City MT
C W Post Campus of Long Island University, Hillwood Art Museum, Brookville NY
Dallas Museum of Art, Dallas TX
Danforth Museum of Art, Framingham MA
DAR Museum, National Society Daughters of the American Revolution, Washington DC
Dartmouth College, Hood Museum of Art, Hanover NH
Davenport Museum of Art, Davenport IA
Davidson College Visual Arts Center, William H Van Every Jr & Edward M Smith Galleries, Davidson NC
Dayton Art Institute, Dayton OH
DeCordova Museum & Sculpture Park, Lincoln MA
Delaware Art Museum, Wilmington DE
Denison University, Art Gallery, Granville OH
Department of Natural Resources of Missouri, Missouri State Museum, Jefferson City MO
Detroit Institute of Arts, Detroit MI

DeWitt Historical Society of Tompkins County, Ithaca NY
Dezign House, Jefferson OH
Dickinson College, Trout Gallery, Carlisle PA
Dickinson State University, Mind's Eye Gallery, Dickinson ND
Discovery Museum, Bridgeport CT
Dixie College, Southwestern Utah Art Gallery, Saint George UT
The Dixon Gallery & Gardens, Memphis TN
Douglas County Historical Society, Fairlawn Mansion & Museum, Superior WI
East Baton Rouge Parks & Recreation Commission, Baton Rouge Gallery Inc, Baton Rouge LA
East Carolina University, Wellington B Gray Gallery, Greenville NC
Eastern Washington State Historical Society, Cheney Cowles Museum, Spokane WA
East Tennessee State University, Carroll Reece Museum, Johnson City TN
Edmonton Art Gallery, Edmonton AB
Edmundson Art Foundation, Inc, Des Moines Art Center, Des Moines IA
Eiteljorg Museum of American Indians & Western Art, Indianapolis IN
Elmhurst Art Museum, Elmhurst IL
El Paso Museum of Art, El Paso TX
Enook Galleries, Waterloo ON
Ephraim McDowell-Cambus-Kenneth Foundation, McDowell House & Apothecary Shop, Danville KY
Erie Art Museum, Erie PA
Wharton Esherick Museum, Paoli PA
Evanston Historical Society, Charles Gates Dawes House, Evanston IL
Evansville Museum of Arts & Science, Evansville IN
Everhart Museum, Scranton PA
Everson Museum of Art, Syracuse NY
Fairbanks Museum & Planetarium, Saint Johnsbury VT
Fairfield University, Thomas J Walsh Art Gallery, Fairfield CT
Fall River Historical Society, Fall River MA
William A Farnsworth Library & Art Museum, Rockland ME
Fayette Art Museum, Fayette AL
Federal Reserve Board, Art Gallery, Washington DC
Fetherston Foundation, Packwood House Museum, Lewisburg PA
Fine Arts Center for the New River Valley, Pulaski VA
Fine Arts Museums of San Francisco, M H de Young Memorial Museum & California Palace of the Legion of Honor, San Francisco CA
First Tennessee National Corp, First Tennessee Heritage Collection, Memphis TN
Fitchburg Art Museum, Fitchburg MA
Fitton Center For Creative Arts, Hamilton OH
Henry Morrison Flagler Museum, Whitehall Mansion, Palm Beach FL
Flint Institute of Arts, Flint MI
Florence Museum of Art, Science & History, Florence SC
Florida Gulf Coast Art Center, Inc, Belleair FL
Florida State University, Museum of Fine Arts, Tallahassee FL
Florida State University Foundation - Central Florida Community College Foundation, The Appleton Museum of Art, Ocala FL
Edsel & Eleanor Ford House, Grosse Pointe Shores MI
Fort Hays State University, Moss-Thorns Gallery of Arts, Hays KS
Fort Smith Art Center, Fort Smith AR
Fort Ticonderoga Association, Ticonderoga NY
Fort Wayne Museum of Art, Inc, Fort Wayne IN
Fort Worth Art Association, Modern Art Museum of Fort Worth, Fort Worth TX
Freeport Arts Center, Freeport IL
Frye Art Museum, Seattle WA
Fuller Museum of Art, Brockton MA
Galeria Mesa, Mesa Arts Center, Mesa AZ
Galleries of the Claremont Colleges, Claremont CA
Gallery 53, Cooperstown NY
Gallery One, Ellensburg WA
Isabella Stewart Gardner Museum, Boston MA

Museum of Modern Art, New York NY
Museum of Northern Arizona, Flagstaff AZ
Museum of Our National Heritage, Lexington MA
Museum of the Americas, Brookfield VT
Museum of Western Art, Denver CO
Museum of York County, Rock Hill SC
The Museums at Stony Brook, Stony Brook NY
Museums of Abilene, Inc, Abilene TX
Muskegon Museum of Art, Muskegon MI
Nantucket Historical Association, Historic
    Nantucket, Nantucket MA
Nassau County Museum of Fine Art, Roslyn
    Harbor NY
National Air and Space Museum, Washington DC
National Art Museum of Sport, Indianapolis IN
National Gallery of Canada, Ottawa ON
National Museum of American Art, Washington
    DC
National Museum of the American Indian, George
    Gustav Heye Center, New York NY
National Museum of Wildlife Art, Jackson WY
National Museum of Women in the Arts,
    Washington DC
National Park Service, Weir Farm National Historic
    Site, Wilton CT
National Portrait Gallery, Washington DC
National Society of Colonial Dames of America in
    the State of Maryland, Mount Clare Mansion,
    Baltimore MD
National Society of the Colonial Dames, Wilton
    House Museum, Richmond VA
National Society of Tole & Decorative Painters,
    Inc, Wichita KS
Naval Historical Center, The Navy Museum,
    Washington DC
Nebraska State Capitol, Lincoln NE
Nebraska Wesleyan University, Elder Gallery,
    Lincoln NE
Nevada Museum Of Art, Reno NV
Neville Public Museum, Green Bay WI
New Britain Museum of American Art, New
    Britain CT
New Brunswick Museum, Saint John NB
New England Maple Museum, Rutland VT
New Jersey State Museum, Trenton NJ
New Mexico State University, University Art
    Gallery, Las Cruces NM
New Orleans Museum of Art, New Orleans LA
Newport Art Museum, Newport RI
New York State Historical Association, Fenimore
    House Museum, Cooperstown NY
New York State Office of Parks Recreation &
    Historic Preservation, John Jay Homestead State
    Historic Site, Katonah NY
New York Studio School of Drawing, Painting &
    Sculpture, Gallery, New York NY
New York University, Grey Art Gallery & Study
    Center, New York NY
Niagara University, Castellani Art Museum,
    Niagara NY
No Man's Land Historical Society Museum,
    Goodwell OK
North Carolina Central University, NCCU Art
    Museum, Durham NC
North Carolina Museum of Art, Raleigh NC
North Dakota State University, Memorial Union
    Art Gallery, Fargo ND
Northern Illinois University, NIU Art Museum, De
    Kalb IL
Norton Gallery & School of Art, Inc, Norton
    Museum of Art, West Palm Beach FL
Noyes Museum, Oceanville NJ
Oakland Museum of California, Art Dept, Oakland
    CA
Oberlin College, Allen Memorial Art Museum,
    Oberlin OH
Ogunquit Museum of American Art, Ogunquit ME
Ohio Historical Society, National Afro American
    Museum & Cultural Center, Wilberforce OH
The Ohio Historical Society, Inc, Campus Martius
    Museum & Ohio River Museum, Marietta OH
Ohio State University, Wexner Center for the Arts,
    Columbus OH
Ohio University, Kennedy Museum of American
    Art, Athens OH
Okefenokee Heritage Center, Inc, Waycross GA
Oklahoma Center for Science & Art, Kirkpatrick
    Center, Oklahoma City OK

Oklahoma City Art Museum, Oklahoma City OK
Oklahoma Historical Society, State Museum of
    History, Oklahoma City OK
Olana State Historic Site, Hudson NY
Old Dartmouth Historical Society, New Bedford
    Whaling Museum, New Bedford MA
Old Jail Art Center, Albany TX
Old York Historical Society, Old Gaol Museum,
    York ME
One West Art Center, Fort Collins CO
Orange County Museum of Art, Newport Harbor
    Art Museum, Newport Beach CA
Orlando Museum of Art, Orlando FL
Oshkosh Public Museum, Oshkosh WI
Owensboro Museum of Fine Art, Owensboro KY
Page-Walker Arts & History Center, Cary NC
Palm Springs Desert Museum, Palm Springs CA
Panhandle-Plains Historical Society Museum,
    Canyon TX
Paris Gibson Square, Museum of Art, Great Falls
    MT
The Parrish Art Museum, Southampton NY
Passaic County Historical Society, Paterson NJ
Pennsylvania Academy of the Fine Arts, Museum
    of American Art, Philadelphia PA
Pennsylvania Historical & Museum Commission,
    Railroad Museum of Pennsylvania, Harrisburg
    PA
Pennsylvania State University, Palmer Museum of
    Art, University Park PA
Pensacola Museum of Art, Pensacola FL
Philadelphia Museum of Art, Philadelphia PA
Philbrook Museum of Art, Tulsa OK
Phillips Academy, Addison Gallery of American
    Art, Andover MA
The Phillips Collection, Washington DC
Phillips County Museum, Helena AR
George Phippen Memorial Foundation, Phippen
    Museum of Western Art, Prescott AZ
Phoenix Art Museum, Phoenix AZ
Plainsman Museum, Aurora NE
Plumas County Museum, Quincy CA
Polk Museum of Art, Lakeland FL
Pope County Historical Society, Pope County
    Museum, Glenwood MN
Port Authority of New York & New Jersey, Art
    Collection, New York NY
Portland Art Museum, Portland OR
Portland Museum of Art, Portland ME
Portsmouth Athenaeum, Portsmouth NH
Portsmouth Historical Society, John Paul Jones
    House, Portsmouth NH
Portsmouth Museums, Art Center, Portsmouth VA
Potsdam College of the State University of New
    York, Roland Gibson Gallery, Potsdam NY
Prairie Art Gallery, Grande Prairie AB
Princeton University, The Art Museum, Princeton
    NJ
Provincetown Art Association & Museum,
    Provincetown MA
Putnam County Historical Society, Foundry School
    Museum, Cold Spring NY
Queensborough Community College, Art Gallery,
    Bayside NY
Rahr-West Art Museum, Manitowoc WI
Rapid City Arts Council, Dahl Fine Arts Center,
    Rapid City SD
Reading Public Museum, Reading PA
Red Rock State Park, Red Rock Museum, Church
    Rock NM
Frederic Remington Art Museum, Ogdensburg NY
Reynolda House Museum of American Art,
    Winston-Salem NC
Rhode Island Historical Society, John Brown
    House, Providence RI
Rhode Island School of Design, Museum of Art,
    Providence RI
Sid W Richardson Foundation, Collection of
    Western Art, Fort Worth TX
Roberson Museum & Science Center, Binghamton
    NY
The Rockwell Museum, Corning NY
Lauren Rogers Museum of Art, Laurel MS
Rogue Community College, Wiseman Gallery -
    Firehouse Gallery, Grants Pass OR
Rollins College, George D & Harriet W Cornell
    Fine Arts Museum, Winter Park FL
Ross Memorial Museum, Saint Andrews NB

Roswell Museum & Art Center, Roswell NM
Round Top Center for the Arts Inc, Arts Gallery,
    Damariscotta ME
Royal Arts Foundation, Belcourt Castle, Newport
    RI
C M Russell Museum, Great Falls MT
Rutgers University, Stedman Art Gallery, Camden
    NJ
R W Norton Art Gallery, Shreveport LA
Robert W Ryerss Library & Museum, Philadelphia
    PA
Saginaw Art Museum, Saginaw MI
Saint Anselm College, Chapel Art Center,
    Manchester NH
Saint Clair County Community College, Jack R
    Hennesey Art Galleries, Port Huron MI
Saint Gregory's Abbey & College, Mabee-Gerrer
    Museum of Art, Shawnee OK
Saint Johnsbury Athenaeum, Saint Johnsbury VT
St Lawrence University, Richard F Brush Art
    Gallery, Canton NY
Saint Louis Artists' Guild, Saint Louis MO
The Saint Louis Art Museum, Saint Louis MO
Saint Mary's College of California, Hearst Art
    Gallery, Moraga CA
San Antonio Museum of Art, San Antonio TX
San Diego Museum of Art, San Diego CA
San Diego State University, University Gallery, San
    Diego CA
The Sandwich Historical Society, Inc, Sandwich
    Glass Museum, Sandwich MA
San Francisco Museum of Modern Art, San
    Francisco CA
San Joaquin Pioneer & Historical Society, The
    Haggin Museum, Stockton CA
San Jose Museum of Art, San Jose CA
Santa Barbara Museum of Art, Santa Barbara CA
Santa Clara University, de Saisset Museum, Santa
    Clara CA
Schenectady Museum Planetarium & Visitors
    Center, Schenectady NY
School of Visual Arts, Visual Arts Museum, New
    York NY
Seattle Art Museum, Seattle WA
Seneca-Iroquois National Museum, Salamanca NY
1708 Gallery, Richmond VA
Ella Sharp Museum, Jackson MI
Shelburne Museum, Shelburne VT
Silverado Museum, Saint Helena CA
Sioux City Art Center, Sioux City IA
Slater-Norton Corporation, Slater Memorial
    Museum & Converse Art Gallery, Norwich CT
Smith College, Museum of Art, Northampton MA
George Walter Vincent Smith Art Museum,
    Springfield MA
Society of the Cincinnati, Museum & Library at
    Anderson House, Washington DC
South Carolina State Museum, Columbia SC
South Dakota State University, South Dakota Art
    Museum, Brookings SD
Southeastern Center for Contemporary Art,
    Winston-Salem NC
Southern Alleghenies Museum of Art, Loretto PA
Southern Alleghenies Museum of Art, Southern
    Alleghenies Museum of Art at Johnstown,
    Loretto PA
Southern Lorain County Historical Society, Spirit of
    '76 Museum, Wellington OH
Southern Oregon Historical Society, Jacksonville
    Museum of Southern Oregon History, Medford
    OR
Southern Oregon State College, Schneider Museum
    of Art, Ashland OR
Southern Utah University, Braithwaite Fine Arts
    Gallery, Cedar City UT
Spark Gallery, Denver CO
Spartanburg County Museum of Art, Spartanburg
    SC
Springfield Art & Historical Society, Miller Art
    Center, Springfield VT
Springfield Art Museum, Springfield MO
Springfield Library & Museums Association,
    Connecticut Valley Historical Museum,
    Springfield MA
Springville Museum of Art, Springville UT
Stamford Museum & Nature Center, Stamford CT
Stanford University, Museum of Art, Stanford CA

PAINTING - AUSTRALIAN

PAINTING - BRITISH

Bradford Brinton Memorial Museum & Historic
Ranch, Big Horn WY
The Buffalo Fine Arts Academy, Albright-Knox Art
Gallery, Buffalo NY
Capital University, Schumacher Gallery, Columbus
OH
College of William & Mary, Joseph & Margaret
Muscarelle Museum of Art, Williamsburg VA
Columbus Museum, Columbus GA
Columbus Museum of Art, Columbus OH
Corcoran Gallery of Art, Washington DC
Coutts Memorial Museum of Art, Inc, El Dorado
KS
The Currier Gallery of Art, Manchester NH
Dahesh Museum, New York NY
Davenport Museum of Art, Davenport IA
Delaware Art Museum, Wilmington DE
Denver Art Museum, Denver CO
Detroit Institute of Arts, Detroit MI
Evansville Museum of Arts & Science, Evansville
IN
Fine Arts Museums of San Francisco, M H de
Young Memorial Museum & California Palace
of the Legion of Honor, San Francisco CA
Fort Worth Art Association, Modern Art Museum
of Fort Worth, Fort Worth TX
Glanmore, Hastings County Museum, Belleville ON
Heckscher Museum of Art, Huntington NY
Huntington Museum of Art, Huntington WV
Joslyn Art Museum, Omaha NE
Kendall Whaling Museum, Sharon MA
Louisiana State University, Museum of Arts, Baton
Rouge LA
McMaster University, Museum of Art, Hamilton
ON
Maryhill Museum of Art, Goldendale WA
Montreal Museum of Fine Arts, Montreal PQ
Museum of Fine Arts, Springfield MA
Museum of the Americas, Brookfield VT
National Gallery of Canada, Ottawa ON
New Brunswick Museum, Saint John NB
New Orleans Museum of Art, New Orleans LA
New York Studio School of Drawing, Painting &
Sculpture, Gallery, New York NY
Niagara University, Castellani Art Museum,
Niagara NY
Panhandle-Plains Historical Society Museum,
Canyon TX
Pennsylvania State University, Palmer Museum of
Art, University Park PA
Phoenix Art Museum, Phoenix AZ
Princeton University, The Art Museum, Princeton
NJ
The Rosenbach Museum & Library, Philadelphia
PA
Royal Arts Foundation, Belcourt Castle, Newport
RI
San Diego Museum of Art, San Diego CA
Santa Barbara Museum of Art, Santa Barbara CA
Society of the Cincinnati, Museum & Library at
Anderson House, Washington DC
Stanford University, Museum of Art, Stanford CA
State University of New York at Oswego, Tyler Art
Gallery, Oswego NY
The Turner Museum, Denver CO
University of California, Berkeley Art Museum &
Pacific Film Archive, Berkeley CA
University of California, Los Angeles, UCLA at the
Armand Hammer Museum of Art & Cultural
Center, Los Angeles CA
University of Florida, University Gallery,
Gainesville FL
University of Kansas, Spencer Museum of Art,
Lawrence KS
University of Notre Dame, Snite Museum of Art,
Notre Dame IN
University of Southern California, Fisher Gallery,
Los Angeles CA
University of Utah, Utah Museum of Fine Arts, Salt
Lake City UT
Ursinus College, Philip & Muriel Berman Museum
of Art, Collegeville PA
Wadsworth Atheneum, Hartford CT
Walters Art Gallery, Baltimore MD
Wilfrid Laurier University, Robert Langen Gallery,
Waterloo ON
Woodlawn Plantation, Mount Vernon VA
Worcester Art Museum, Worcester MA

Yale University, Yale Center for British Art, New
Haven CT

PAINTING - CANADIAN

Algonquin Arts Council, Art Gallery of Bancroft,
Bancroft ON
Art Gallery of Nova Scotia, Halifax NS
Bowdoin College, Peary-MacMillan Arctic
Museum, Brunswick ME
Canadian Museum of Nature, Musee Canadien de
la Nature, Ottawa ON
Cartoon Art Museum, San Francisco CA
Radio-Canada SRC CBC, Galerie Georges Goguen,
Moncton NB
Central United Methodist Church, Swords Info
Plowshares Peace Center & Gallery, Detroit MI
Concordia University, Leonard & Bina Ellen Art
Gallery, Montreal PQ
Cornwall Gallery Society, Regional Art Gallery,
Cornwall ON
Craigdarroch Castle Historical Museum Society,
Victoria BC
Dartmouth Heritage Museum, Dartmouth NS
Dundurn Castle, Hamilton ON
Edmonton Art Gallery, Edmonton AB
Enook Galleries, Waterloo ON
Estevan National Exhibition Centre Inc, Estevan
SK
Fayette Art Museum, Fayette AL
Fort Worth Art Association, Modern Art Museum
of Fort Worth, Fort Worth TX
Glanmore, Hastings County Museum, Belleville ON
Heritage Center, Inc, Pine Ridge SD
Huntington Museum of Art, Huntington WV
Institute for Contemporary Art, Project Studio One
(P S 1), Long Island City NY
Kamloops Art Gallery, Kamloops BC
Kansas City Art Institute, Kemper Museum of
Contemporary Art & Design, Kansas City MO
Kings County Historical Society and Museum,
Hampton NB
Kitchener-Waterloo Art Gallery, Kitchener ON
Laurentian University, Museum & Art Centre,
Sudbury ON
L'Universite Laval, Ecole des Arts Visuels, Quebec
PQ
McCord Museum of Canadian History, Montreal
PQ
McMaster University, Museum of Art, Hamilton
ON
The Market Gallery of the City of Toronto
Archives, Toronto ON
Mendel Art Gallery & Civic Conservatory,
Saskatoon SK
Montreal Museum of Fine Arts, Montreal PQ
Moose Jaw Art Museum & National Exhibition
Centre, Art & History Museum, Moose Jaw SK
Musee du Quebec, Quebec PQ
Musee Regional de la Cote-Nord, Sept-Iles PQ
Museum of Arts & History, Port Huron MI
Museum of Northern British Columbia, Ruth
Harvey Art Gallery, Prince Rupert BC
National Gallery of Canada, Ottawa ON
National Society of Tole & Decorative Painters,
Inc, Wichita KS
New Brunswick Museum, Saint John NB
Niagara University, Castellani Art Museum,
Niagara NY
Prairie Art Gallery, Grande Prairie AB
Prince George Art Gallery, Prince George BC
Red Deer & District Museum & Archives, Red
Deer AB
Ross Memorial Museum, Saint Andrews NB
University of Calgary, The Nickle Arts Museum,
Calgary AB
University of Manitoba, Faculty of Architecture
Exhibition Centre, Winnipeg MB
Upstairs Gallery, Winnipeg MB
Vancouver Art Gallery, Vancouver BC
Peter & Catharine Whyte Foundation, Whyte
Museum of the Canadian Rockies, Banff AB
Wilfrid Laurier University, Robert Langen Gallery,
Waterloo ON
Winnipeg Art Gallery, Winnipeg MB
Yarmouth County Historical Society, Yarmouth
County Museum, Yarmouth NS

York University, Art Gallery of York University,
North York ON

PAINTING - DUTCH

Allentown Art Museum, Allentown PA
Arnot Art Museum, Elmira NY
Barnes Foundation, Merion PA
Bass Museum of Art, Miami Beach FL
Berkshire Museum, Pittsfield MA
Bowdoin College, Museum of Art, Brunswick ME
Chicago Department of Cultural Affairs, Chicago
Cultural Center, Chicago IL
Chrysler Museum Of Art, Norfolk VA
Sterling & Francine Clark Art Institute,
Williamstown MA
College of William & Mary, Joseph & Margaret
Muscarelle Museum of Art, Williamsburg VA
Columbus Museum of Art, Columbus OH
Corcoran Gallery of Art, Washington DC
Coutts Memorial Museum of Art, Inc, El Dorado
KS
The Currier Gallery of Art, Manchester NH
Detroit Institute of Arts, Detroit MI
Elmhurst Art Museum, Elmhurst IL
Evansville Museum of Arts & Science, Evansville
IN
Fine Arts Museums of San Francisco, M H de
Young Memorial Museum & California Palace
of the Legion of Honor, San Francisco CA
Fort Worth Art Association, Modern Art Museum
of Fort Worth, Fort Worth TX
Isabella Stewart Gardner Museum, Boston MA
Grand Rapids Art Museum, Grand Rapids MI
Heckscher Museum of Art, Huntington NY
Huguenot Historical Society of New Paltz Galleries,
New Paltz NY
Huntington Museum of Art, Huntington WV
Institute for Contemporary Art, Project Studio One
(P S 1), Long Island City NY
Kansas City Art Institute, Kemper Museum of
Contemporary Art & Design, Kansas City MO
Kendall Whaling Museum, Sharon MA
McMaster University, Museum of Art, Hamilton
ON
The Mariners' Museum, Newport News VA
Memphis Brooks Museum of Art, Memphis TN
Michigan State University, Kresge Art Museum,
East Lansing MI
Montreal Museum of Fine Arts, Montreal PQ
Museum of Fine Arts, Springfield MA
National Gallery of Canada, Ottawa ON
National Society of Tole & Decorative Painters,
Inc, Wichita KS
Oberlin College, Allen Memorial Art Museum,
Oberlin OH
Panhandle-Plains Historical Society Museum,
Canyon TX
Phoenix Art Museum, Phoenix AZ
Prairie Art Gallery, Grande Prairie AB
San Diego Museum of Art, San Diego CA
Timken Museum of Art, San Diego CA
University of California, Santa Barbara, University
Art Museum, Santa Barbara CA
University of Kansas, Spencer Museum of Art,
Lawrence KS
University of Southern California, Fisher Gallery,
Los Angeles CA
Ursinus College, Philip & Muriel Berman Museum
of Art, Collegeville PA
Wadsworth Atheneum, Hartford CT
Western Kentucky University, Kentucky Museum,
Bowling Green KY
Worcester Art Museum, Worcester MA

PAINTING - EUROPEAN

Agecroft Association, Museum, Richmond VA
Allentown Art Museum, Allentown PA
American Kennel Club, Museum of the Dog, Saint
Louis MO
American University, Watkins Collection,
Washington DC
Art Complex Museum, Duxbury MA
Art Gallery of Greater Victoria, Victoria BC
Art Gallery of Hamilton, Hamilton ON
Art Gallery of Ontario, Toronto ON
Ball State University, Museum of Art, Muncie IN

Barnes Foundation, Merion PA
Bass Museum of Art, Miami Beach FL
Blanden Memorial Art Museum, Fort Dodge IA
Bob Jones University, Museum & Art Gallery, Greenville SC
Boise Art Museum, Boise ID
The Buffalo Fine Arts Academy, Albright-Knox Art Gallery, Buffalo NY
Capital University, Schumacher Gallery, Columbus OH
Carnegie Institute, Carnegie Museum of Art, Pittsburgh PA
Cartoon Art Museum, San Francisco CA
Radio-Canada SRC CBC, Galerie Georges Goguen, Moncton NB
Cleveland Museum of Art, Cleveland OH
College of William & Mary, Joseph & Margaret Muscarelle Museum of Art, Williamsburg VA
Columbia Museum of Art, Columbia SC
Columbus Museum of Art, Columbus OH
Corcoran Gallery of Art, Washington DC
Cornell University, Herbert F Johnson Museum of Art, Ithaca NY
Crocker Art Museum, Sacramento CA
Cummer Museum of Art & Gardens, DeEtte Holden Cummer Museum Foundation, Jacksonville FL
Dahesh Museum, New York NY
Dallas Museum of Art, Dallas TX
Davenport Museum of Art, Davenport IA
Dayton Art Institute, Dayton OH
Denison University, Art Gallery, Granville OH
Denver Art Museum, Denver CO
Detroit Institute of Arts, Detroit MI
Dezign House, Jefferson OH
Edmonton Art Gallery, Edmonton AB
El Paso Museum of Art, El Paso TX
Evansville Museum of Arts & Science, Evansville IN
Everhart Museum, Scranton PA
Fairbanks Museum & Planetarium, Saint Johnsbury VT
Fairfield University, Thomas J Walsh Art Gallery, Fairfield CT
William A Farnsworth Library & Art Museum, Rockland ME
Flint Institute of Arts, Flint MI
Florida State University Foundation - Central Florida Community College Foundation, The Appleton Museum of Art, Ocala FL
Fort Worth Art Association, Modern Art Museum of Fort Worth, Fort Worth TX
Freeport Arts Center, Freeport IL
Frick Collection, New York NY
Harvard University, Busch-Reisinger Museum, Cambridge MA
Harvard University, William Hayes Fogg Art Museum, Cambridge MA
Heckscher Museum of Art, Huntington NY
Gertrude Herbert Institute of Art, Augusta GA
Hirshhorn Museum & Sculpture Garden, Washington DC
Hofstra University, Hofstra Museum, Hempstead NY
Honolulu Academy of Arts, Honolulu HI
Hyde Collection Trust, Glens Falls NY
Indianapolis Museum of Art, Indianapolis IN
Kendall Whaling Museum, Sharon MA
Kimbell Art Foundation, Kimbell Art Museum, Fort Worth TX
Knights of Columbus Supreme Council, Headquarters Museum, New Haven CT
Knoxville Museum of Art, Knoxville TN
La Salle University, Art Museum, Philadelphia PA
Los Angeles County Museum of Art, Los Angeles CA
Louisiana Arts & Science Center, Baton Rouge LA
Loyola University of Chicago, Martin D'Arcy Gallery of Art, Chicago IL
McAllen International Museum, McAllen TX
McMaster University, Museum of Art, Hamilton ON
Marion Koogler McNay Art Museum, San Antonio TX
Merrick Art Gallery, New Brighton PA
The Metropolitan Museum of Art, New York NY
Michigan State University, Kresge Art Museum, East Lansing MI

Milwaukee Art Museum, Milwaukee WI
Minneapolis Institute of Arts, Minneapolis MN
Mount Holyoke College, Art Museum, South Hadley MA
Musee d'Art de Joliette, Joliette PQ
Musee des Augustines de l'Hotel Dieu de Quebec, Quebec PQ
Museum of Arts & History, Port Huron MI
Museum of Arts & Sciences, Inc, Macon GA
Museum of Fine Arts, Springfield MA
Museum of Fine Arts, Houston, Houston TX
Muskegon Museum of Art, Muskegon MI
Nassau County Museum of Fine Art, Roslyn Harbor NY
National Gallery of Canada, Ottawa ON
Nevada Museum Of Art, Reno NV
New Orleans Museum of Art, New Orleans LA
New York Studio School of Drawing, Painting & Sculpture, Gallery, New York NY
New York University, Grey Art Gallery & Study Center, New York NY
North Carolina Museum of Art, Raleigh NC
North Country Museum of Arts, Park Rapids MN
Oklahoma City Art Museum, Oklahoma City OK
Philadelphia Museum of Art, Philadelphia PA
Philbrook Museum of Art, Tulsa OK
The Phillips Collection, Washington DC
Phoenix Art Museum, Phoenix AZ
Portland Art Museum, Portland OR
Portland Museum of Art, Portland ME
Prairie Art Gallery, Grande Prairie AB
Princeton University, The Art Museum, Princeton NJ
Queens College, City University of New York, Godwin-Ternbach Museum, Flushing NY
Reading Public Museum, Reading PA
Frederic Remington Art Museum, Ogdensburg NY
Lauren Rogers Museum of Art, Laurel MS
Royal Arts Foundation, Belcourt Castle, Newport RI
R W Norton Art Gallery, Shreveport LA
Saginaw Art Museum, Saginaw MI
Saint Gregory's Abbey & College, Mabee-Gerrer Museum of Art, Shawnee OK
St Lawrence University, Richard F Brush Art Gallery, Canton NY
The Saint Louis Art Museum, Saint Louis MO
San Antonio Museum of Art, San Antonio TX
San Diego Museum of Art, San Diego CA
San Joaquin Pioneer & Historical Society, The Haggin Museum, Stockton CA
Santa Barbara Museum of Art, Santa Barbara CA
Seattle Art Museum, Seattle WA
Shelburne Museum, Shelburne VT
Smith College, Museum of Art, Northampton MA
George Walter Vincent Smith Art Museum, Springfield MA
Society of the Cincinnati, Museum & Library at Anderson House, Washington DC
Springfield Art Museum, Springfield MO
Stanford University, Museum of Art, Stanford CA
State Art Museum of Florida, John & Mable Ringling Museum of Art, Sarasota FL
State University of New York at Purchase, Neuberger Museum of Art, Purchase NY
Swiss Institute, New York NY
Toledo Museum of Art, Toledo OH
Tucson Museum of Art & Historic Block, Tucson AZ
The Turner Museum, Denver CO
Twin City Art Foundation, Masur Museum of Art, Monroe LA
University of California, Berkeley Art Museum & Pacific Film Archive, Berkeley CA
University of California, Los Angeles, UCLA at the Armand Hammer Museum of Art & Cultural Center, Los Angeles CA
University of California, Santa Barbara, University Art Museum, Santa Barbara CA
University of Chicago, David & Alfred Smart Museum of Art, Chicago IL
University of Connecticut, William Benton Museum of Art, Storrs CT
University of Illinois, Krannert Art Museum, Champaign IL
University of Kansas, Spencer Museum of Art, Lawrence KS

University of Kentucky, Art Museum, Lexington KY
University of Missouri, Museum of Art & Archaeology, Columbia MO
University of North Carolina at Greensboro, Weatherspoon Art Gallery, Greensboro NC
University of Northern Iowa, Gallery of Art, Cedar Falls IA
University of Notre Dame, Snite Museum of Art, Notre Dame IN
University of Oklahoma, Fred Jones Jr Museum of Art, Norman OK
University of Wisconsin-Madison, Elvehjem Museum of Art, Madison WI
University of Wyoming, University of Wyoming Art Museum, Laramie WY
Ursinus College, Philip & Muriel Berman Museum of Art, Collegeville PA
Vanderbilt University, Fine Arts Gallery, Nashville TN
Vassar College, The Frances Lehman Loeb Art Center, Poughkeepsie NY
Virginia Museum of Fine Arts, Richmond VA
Wadsworth Atheneum, Hartford CT
Walters Art Gallery, Baltimore MD
Widener University, Art Museum, Chester PA
Wilfrid Laurier University, Robert Langen Gallery, Waterloo ON
Wilkes University, Sordoni Art Gallery, Wilkes-Barre PA
Woodmere Art Museum, Philadelphia PA
Yale University, Art Gallery, New Haven CT
Zigler Museum, Jennings LA

PAINTING - FLEMISH

Agecroft Association, Museum, Richmond VA
Allentown Art Museum, Allentown PA
Arnot Art Museum, Elmira NY
Barnes Foundation, Merion PA
Bass Museum of Art, Miami Beach FL
Berkshire Museum, Pittsfield MA
Bowdoin College, Museum of Art, Brunswick ME
Chrysler Museum Of Art, Norfolk VA
Cincinnati Museum Association, Cincinnati Art Museum, Cincinnati OH
Sterling & Francine Clark Art Institute, Williamstown MA
Clemson University, Fort Hill Plantation, Clemson SC
College of William & Mary, Joseph & Margaret Muscarelle Museum of Art, Williamsburg VA
Columbus Chapel & Boal Mansion Museum, Boalsburg PA
Columbus Museum of Art, Columbus OH
Corcoran Gallery of Art, Washington DC
Detroit Institute of Arts, Detroit MI
El Paso Museum of Art, El Paso TX
Evansville Museum of Arts & Science, Evansville IN
Fort Worth Art Association, Modern Art Museum of Fort Worth, Fort Worth TX
Freeport Arts Center, Freeport IL
The Frick Art & Historical Center, Frick Art Museum, Pittsburgh PA
Isabella Stewart Gardner Museum, Boston MA
Heckscher Museum of Art, Huntington NY
Honolulu Academy of Arts, Honolulu HI
Memphis Brooks Museum of Art, Memphis TN
Musee des Augustines de l'Hotel Dieu de Quebec, Quebec PQ
National Gallery of Canada, Ottawa ON
Oberlin College, Allen Memorial Art Museum, Oberlin OH
Phoenix Art Museum, Phoenix AZ
Prairie Art Gallery, Grande Prairie AB
San Diego Museum of Art, San Diego CA
University of Southern California, Fisher Gallery, Los Angeles CA
University of Virginia, Bayly Art Museum, Charlottesville VA
Ursinus College, Philip & Muriel Berman Museum of Art, Collegeville PA
Virginia Museum of Fine Arts, Richmond VA
Wadsworth Atheneum, Hartford CT
Worcester Art Museum, Worcester MA

PAINTING - FRENCH

Charles Allis Art Museum, Milwaukee WI
Arnot Art Museum, Elmira NY
Baltimore Museum of Art, Baltimore MD
Barnes Foundation, Merion PA
Bates College, Museum of Art, Lewiston ME
Bowdoin College, Museum of Art, Brunswick ME
Brigham Young University, Museum of Art, Provo UT
The Buffalo Fine Arts Academy, Albright-Knox Art Gallery, Buffalo NY
Cartoon Art Museum, San Francisco CA
Radio-Canada SRC CBC, Galerie Georges Goguen, Moncton NB
Centenary College of Louisiana, Meadows Museum of Art, Shreveport LA
Central United Methodist Church, Swords Info Plowshares Peace Center & Gallery, Detroit MI
Chrysler Museum Of Art, Norfolk VA
Cincinnati Museum Association, Cincinnati Art Museum, Cincinnati OH
Sterling & Francine Clark Art Institute, Williamstown MA
College of William & Mary, Joseph & Margaret Muscarelle Museum of Art, Williamsburg VA
The College of Wooster, Art Museum, Wooster OH
Columbus Museum of Art, Columbus OH
Corcoran Gallery of Art, Washington DC
Coutts Memorial Museum of Art, Inc, El Dorado KS
Dahesh Museum, New York NY
Davenport Museum of Art, Davenport IA
Denver Art Museum, Denver CO
Dickinson College, Trout Gallery, Carlisle PA
The Dixon Gallery & Gardens, Memphis TN
Elmhurst Art Museum, Elmhurst IL
El Paso Museum of Art, El Paso TX
Florida State University Foundation - Central Florida Community College Foundation, The Appleton Museum of Art, Ocala FL
Edsel & Eleanor Ford House, Grosse Pointe Shores MI
Fort Worth Art Association, Modern Art Museum of Fort Worth, Fort Worth TX
The Frick Art & Historical Center, Frick Art Museum, Pittsburgh PA
Frye Art Museum, Seattle WA
Isabella Stewart Gardner Museum, Boston MA
Glanmore, Hastings County Museum, Belleville ON
Guggenheim Museum Soho, New York NY
Solomon R Guggenheim Museum, New York NY
Heckscher Museum of Art, Huntington NY
Henry Gallery Association, Henry Art Gallery, Seattle WA
Hill-Stead Museum, Farmington CT
Honolulu Academy of Arts, Honolulu HI
Institute for Contemporary Art, Project Studio One (P S 1), Long Island City NY
Johns Hopkins University, Evergreen House, Baltimore MD
Kansas City Art Institute, Kemper Museum of Contemporary Art & Design, Kansas City MO
Knoxville Museum of Art, Knoxville TN
Lockwood-Mathews Mansion Museum, Norwalk CT
McMaster University, Museum of Art, Hamilton ON
The Mariners' Museum, Newport News VA
Michelson Museum of Art, Marshall TX
Michigan State University, Kresge Art Museum, East Lansing MI
Mint Museum of Art, Charlotte NC
Montreal Museum of Fine Arts, Montreal PQ
Musee des Augustines de l'Hotel Dieu de Quebec, Quebec PQ
The Museum at Drexel University, Philadelphia PA
Museum of Fine Arts, Springfield MA
Napoleonic Society of America, Museum & Library, Clearwater FL
Nassau County Museum of Fine Art, Roslyn Harbor NY
National Gallery of Canada, Ottawa ON
New York Studio School of Drawing, Painting & Sculpture, Gallery, New York NY
Niagara University, Castellani Art Museum, Niagara NY
Norton Gallery & School of Art, Inc, Norton Museum of Art, West Palm Beach FL

Oklahoma City Art Museum, Oklahoma City OK
Old Jail Art Center, Albany TX
Panhandle-Plains Historical Society Museum, Canyon TX
Marjorie Merriweather Post Foundation of DC, Hillwood Museum, Washington DC
Prairie Art Gallery, Grande Prairie AB
The Saint Louis Art Museum, Saint Louis MO
San Joaquin Pioneer & Historical Society, The Haggin Museum, Stockton CA
Santa Barbara Museum of Art, Santa Barbara CA
Springfield Art Museum, Springfield MO
Syracuse University, Art Collection, Syracuse NY
Tacoma Art Museum, Tacoma WA
Telfair Museum of Art, Savannah GA
Timken Museum of Art, San Diego CA
Tufts University, Art Gallery, Medford MA
University of California, Los Angeles, UCLA at the Armand Hammer Museum of Art & Cultural Center, Los Angeles CA
University of Manitoba, Faculty of Architecture Exhibition Centre, Winnipeg MB
University of Notre Dame, Snite Museum of Art, Notre Dame IN
University of Pennsylvania, Arthur Ross Gallery, Philadelphia PA
University of Rochester, Memorial Art Gallery, Rochester NY
University of Southern California, Fisher Gallery, Los Angeles CA
University of Virginia, Bayly Art Museum, Charlottesville VA
Ursinus College, Philip & Muriel Berman Museum of Art, Collegeville PA
Wadsworth Atheneum, Hartford CT
Worcester Art Museum, Worcester MA

PAINTING - GERMAN

Allentown Art Museum, Allentown PA
Arnot Art Museum, Elmira NY
Leo Baeck Institute, New York NY
Bard College, Center for Curatorial Studies Museum, Annandale on Hudson NY
Barnes Foundation, Merion PA
Bowdoin College, Museum of Art, Brunswick ME
The Buffalo Fine Arts Academy, Albright-Knox Art Gallery, Buffalo NY
Central United Methodist Church, Swords Info Plowshares Peace Center & Gallery, Detroit MI
Chicago Department of Cultural Affairs, Chicago Cultural Center, Chicago IL
Cincinnati Institute of Fine Arts, Taft Museum, Cincinnati OH
Cincinnati Museum Association, Cincinnati Art Museum, Cincinnati OH
College of William & Mary, Joseph & Margaret Muscarelle Museum of Art, Williamsburg VA
Columbus Chapel & Boal Mansion Museum, Boalsburg PA
Columbus Museum of Art, Columbus OH
Coutts Memorial Museum of Art, Inc, El Dorado KS
Davenport Museum of Art, Davenport IA
Florida State University Foundation - Central Florida Community College Foundation, The Appleton Museum of Art, Ocala FL
Fort Worth Art Association, Modern Art Museum of Fort Worth, Fort Worth TX
Frye Art Museum, Seattle WA
Guggenheim Museum Soho, New York NY
Solomon R Guggenheim Museum, New York NY
Heckscher Museum of Art, Huntington NY
Institute for Contemporary Art, Project Studio One (P S 1), Long Island City NY
Kansas City Art Institute, Kemper Museum of Contemporary Art & Design, Kansas City MO
McMaster University, Museum of Art, Hamilton ON
The Metropolitan Museum of Art, New York NY
Michigan State University, Kresge Art Museum, East Lansing MI
Milwaukee Art Museum, Milwaukee WI
Mint Museum of Art, Charlotte NC
The Museum at Drexel University, Philadelphia PA
Nassau County Museum of Fine Art, Roslyn Harbor NY
National Gallery of Canada, Ottawa ON

National Museum of Wildlife Art, Jackson WY
Niagara University, Castellani Art Museum, Niagara NY
Old Jail Art Center, Albany TX
Panhandle-Plains Historical Society Museum, Canyon TX
Prairie Art Gallery, Grande Prairie AB
The Saint Louis Art Museum, Saint Louis MO
State University of New York at New Paltz, College Art Gallery, New Paltz NY
Syracuse University, Art Collection, Syracuse NY
Telfair Museum of Art, Savannah GA
Tufts University, Art Gallery, Medford MA
University of Cincinnati, DAAP Galleries-College of Design Architecture, Art & Planning, Cincinnati OH
University of Manitoba, Faculty of Architecture Exhibition Centre, Winnipeg MB
University of Virginia, Bayly Art Museum, Charlottesville VA
Ursinus College, Philip & Muriel Berman Museum of Art, Collegeville PA
Wadsworth Atheneum, Hartford CT

PAINTING - ISRAELI

Leo Baeck Institute, New York NY
The Buffalo Fine Arts Academy, Albright-Knox Art Gallery, Buffalo NY
Central United Methodist Church, Swords Info Plowshares Peace Center & Gallery, Detroit MI
Fort Worth Art Association, Modern Art Museum of Fort Worth, Fort Worth TX
Hebrew Union College - Jewish Institute of Religion, Skirball Museum-Cincinnati Branch, Cincinnati OH
Hebrew Union College-Jewish Institute of Religion, New York NY
Institute for Contemporary Art, Project Studio One (P S 1), Long Island City NY
Kansas City Art Institute, Kemper Museum of Contemporary Art & Design, Kansas City MO
Temple Beth Israel, Sylvia Plotkin Judaica, Phoenix AZ
The Temple-Tifereth Israel, The Temple Museum of Religious Art, Beachwood OH
Ursinus College, Philip & Muriel Berman Museum of Art, Collegeville PA

PAINTING - ITALIAN

Allentown Art Museum, Allentown PA
Arnot Art Museum, Elmira NY
Ball State University, Museum of Art, Muncie IN
Bard College, Center for Curatorial Studies Museum, Annandale on Hudson NY
Bates College, Museum of Art, Lewiston ME
Berea College, Doris Ulmann Galleries, Berea KY
Berkshire Museum, Pittsfield MA
The Buffalo Fine Arts Academy, Albright-Knox Art Gallery, Buffalo NY
Canton Museum of Art, Canton OH
Chicago Department of Cultural Affairs, Chicago Cultural Center, Chicago IL
Chrysler Museum Of Art, Norfolk VA
Cincinnati Institute of Fine Arts, Taft Museum, Cincinnati OH
Cincinnati Museum Association, Cincinnati Art Museum, Cincinnati OH
Sterling & Francine Clark Art Institute, Williamstown MA
College of William & Mary, Joseph & Margaret Muscarelle Museum of Art, Williamsburg VA
Columbia Museum of Art, Columbia SC
Columbus Chapel & Boal Mansion Museum, Boalsburg PA
Columbus Museum of Art, Columbus OH
Cuneo Foundation, Museum & Gardens, Vernon Hills IL
C W Post Campus of Long Island University, Hillwood Art Museum, Brookville NY
Denver Art Museum, Denver CO
El Paso Museum of Art, El Paso TX
Fort Worth Art Association, Modern Art Museum of Fort Worth, Fort Worth TX
Freeport Arts Center, Freeport IL
The Frick Art & Historical Center, Frick Art Museum, Pittsburgh PA

PERIOD ROOMS

Academy of the New Church, Glencairn Museum, Bryn Athyn PA
Adams National Historic Site, Quincy MA
Agecroft Association, Museum, Richmond VA
Alabama Department of Archives & History, Museum Galleries, Montgomery AL
Albany Institute of History & Art, Albany NY
Allentown Art Museum, Allentown PA
American Kennel Club, Museum of the Dog, Saint Louis MO
Amherst Museum, Amherst NY
Arizona Historical Society-Yuma, Century House Museum & Garden, Yuma AZ
Arkansas Territorial Restoration, Little Rock AR
Artesia Historical Museum & Art Center, Artesia NM
Ashland Historical Society, Ashland MA
Association for the Preservation of Virginia Antiquities, John Marshall House, Richmond VA
Atlanta Historical Society Inc, Atlanta History Center, Atlanta GA
Audubon Wildlife Sanctuary, Audubon PA
The Bartlett Museum, Amesbury MA
Bartow-Pell Mansion Museum & Gardens, Bronx NY
Bay County Historical Society, Historical Museum of Bay County, Bay City MI
Bradford Brinton Memorial Museum & Historic Ranch, Big Horn WY
Brooklyn Historical Society, Brooklyn OH
Canadian Heritage - Parks Canada, Laurier House, Ottawa ON
Cape Ann Historical Museum, Gloucester MA
Carson County Square House Museum, Panhandle TX
Kit Carson Historic Museums, Taos NM
Kit Carson Historic Museums, Ernest Blumenschein Home & Studio, Taos NM
Kit Carson Historic Museums, Home & Museum, Taos NM
Kit Carson Historic Museums, Hacienda Martinez, Taos NM
Chateau Ramezay Museum, Montreal PQ
Chatillon-DeMenil House Foundation, DeMenil Mansion, Saint Louis MO
City of Austin Parks & Recreation, O Henry Museum, Austin TX
City of Gainesville, Thomas Center Galleries - Cultural Affairs, Gainesville FL
The City of Petersburg Museums, Petersburg VA
City of Springdale, Shiloh Museum, Springdale AR
Clark County Historical Society, Pioneer - Krier Museum, Ashland KS
Clemson University, Fort Hill Plantation, Clemson SC
Cliveden, Philadelphia PA
Colonel Black Mansion, Ellsworth ME
Concord Museum, Concord MA
Craigdarroch Castle Historical Museum Society, Victoria BC
Crane Collection Gallery, Boston MA
Crawford County Historical Society, Baldwin-Reynolds House Museum, Meadville PA
Creek Council House Museum, Okmulgee OK
Cuneo Foundation, Museum & Gardens, Vernon Hills IL
DAR Museum, National Society Daughters of the American Revolution, Washington DC
Dartmouth Heritage Museum, Dartmouth NS
Douglas County Historical Society, Fairlawn Mansion & Museum, Superior WI
Dundurn Castle, Hamilton ON
East Tennessee State University, Carroll Reece Museum, Johnson City TN
Ephraim McDowell-Cambus-Kenneth Foundation, McDowell House & Apothecary Shop, Danville KY
Evanston Historical Society, Charles Gates Dawes House, Evanston IL
Evansville Museum of Arts & Science, Evansville IN
Fetherston Foundation, Packwood House Museum, Lewisburg PA
Henry Morrison Flagler Museum, Whitehall Mansion, Palm Beach FL
Captain Robert Bennet Forbes House, Milton MA

Edsel & Eleanor Ford House, Grosse Pointe Shores MI
The Frick Art & Historical Center, Frick Art Museum, Pittsburgh PA
Gananoque Historical Museum, Gananoque ON
Gibson Society, Inc, Gibson House Museum, Boston MA
Girard College, Stephen Girard Collection, Philadelphia PA
Glanmore, Hastings County Museum, Belleville ON
Gunston Hall Plantation, Mason Neck VA
Hancock Shaker Village, Inc, Pittsfield MA
Headquarters Fort Monroe, Dept of Army, Casemate Museum, Fort Monroe VA
Historical & Cultural Affairs, Delaware State Museums, Dover DE
Historical Society of Old Newbury, Cushing House Museum, Newburyport MA
Historical Society of the Town of Greenwich, Inc, Bush-Holley House Museum, Cos Cob CT
Historical Society of Washington DC, Heurich House Museum, Washington DC
Historic Cherry Hill, Albany NY
Historic Landmarks Foundation of Indiana, Morris-Butler House, Indianapolis IN
Hopewell Museum, Hopewell NJ
House of Roses, Senator Wilson Home, Deadwood SD
Huguenot Historical Society of New Paltz Galleries, New Paltz NY
Huntington Museum of Art, Huntington WV
Stan Hywet Hall & Gardens, Inc, Akron OH
Idaho Historical Museum, Boise ID
Imperial Calcasieu Museum, Lake Charles LA
Imperial Calcasieu Museum, Gibson-Barham Gallery, Lake Charles LA
Independence Museum, Independence KS
Independence National Historical Park, Philadelphia PA
Indianapolis Museum of Art, Indianapolis IN
Institute of the Great Plains, Museum of the Great Plains, Lawton OK
Jackson County Historical Society, The 1859 Jail, Marshal's Home & Museum, Independence MO
Jefferson County Open Space, Hiwan Homestead Museum, Evergreen CO
Thomas Jefferson Memorial Foundation, Monticello, Charlottesville VA
Johns Hopkins University, Evergreen House, Baltimore MD
Johns Hopkins University, Homewood House Museum, Baltimore MD
Jordan Historical Museum of The Twenty, Jordan ON
Kentucky Historical Society, Old State Capitol & Annex, Frankfort KY
Kern County Museum, Bakersfield CA
Knoxville Museum of Art, Knoxville TN
Koochiching County Historical Society Museum, International Falls MN
Landmark Society of Western New York, Inc, Rochester NY
Lehigh County Historical Society, Allentown PA
Leroy Historical Society, LeRoy NY
LeSueur County Historical Museum, Chapter One, Elysian MN
LeSueur Museum, LeSueur MN
Liberty Hall Historic Site, Liberty Hall Museum, Frankfort KY
Lockwood-Mathews Mansion Museum, Norwalk CT
Longfellow-Evangeline State Commemorative Area, Saint Martinville LA
Longfellow National Historic Site, Cambridge MA
Longfellow's Wayside Inn Museum, South Sudbury MA
Los Angeles County Museum of Natural History, William S Hart Museum, Newhall CA
Louisa May Alcott Memorial Association, Orchard House, Concord MA
Loveland Museum Gallery, Loveland CO
McPherson Museum, McPherson KS
Maine Historical Society, Wadsworth-Longfellow House, Portland ME
Mamie McFaddin Ward Heritage Historic Foundation Inc, Beaumont TX
Manitoba Historical Society, Dalnavert Museum, Winnipeg MB

Maricopa County Historical Society, Desert Caballeros Western Museum, Wickenburg AZ
Marquette University, Haggerty Museum of Art, Milwaukee WI
Mattatuck Historical Society, Mattatuck Museum, Waterbury CT
Minneapolis Institute of Arts, Minneapolis MN
Mint Museum of Art, Charlotte NC
Mississippi River Museum at Mud-Island, Memphis TN
MonDak Heritage Center, Sidney MT
Monroe County Historical Association, Elizabeth D Walters Library, Stroudsburg PA
Morris-Jumel Mansion, Inc, New York NY
Morris Museum, Morristown NJ
Mount Vernon Ladies' Association of the Union, Mount Vernon VA
Muchnic Foundation & Atchison Art Association, Muchnic Gallery, Atchison KS
Munson-Williams-Proctor Institute, Museum of Art, Utica NY
Musee des Augustines de l'Hotel Dieu de Quebec, Quebec PQ
Museum of Fine Arts, Boston MA
Museum of Fine Arts, Saint Petersburg, Florida, Inc, Saint Petersburg FL
National Cowboy Hall of Fame & Western Heritage Center Museum, Oklahoma City OK
National Infantry Museum, Fort Benning GA
National Museum of American Art, Renwick Gallery, Washington DC
National Society of the Colonial Dames, Wilton House Museum, Richmond VA
National Trust for Historic Preservation, Decatur House, Washington DC
Nelson-Atkins Museum of Art, Kansas City MO
Newark Museum Association, The Newark Museum, Newark NJ
New Brunswick Museum, Saint John NB
Newport Art Museum, Newport RI
New York State Office of Parks Recreation & Historic Preservation, John Jay Homestead State Historic Site, Katonah NY
New York State Office of Parks, Recreation & Historical Preservation, Mills Mansion State Historical Site, Staatsburg NY
Nichols House Museum, Inc, Boston MA
North Country Museum of Arts, Park Rapids MN
Oatlands, Inc, Leesburg VA
Oglebay Institute, Mansion Museum, Wheeling WV
The Ohio Historical Society, Inc, Campus Martius Museum & Ohio River Museum, Marietta OH
Oklahoma Historical Society, State Museum of History, Oklahoma City OK
Old Barracks Museum, Trenton NJ
Old Fort Harrod State Park Mansion Museum, Harrodsburg KY
Old York Historical Society, Elizabeth Perkins House, York ME
Old York Historical Society, Old Gaol Museum, York ME
Palm Springs Desert Museum, Palm Springs CA
Panhandle-Plains Historical Society Museum, Canyon TX
Passaic County Historical Society, Paterson NJ
Peabody Essex Museum, Salem MA
Pennsylvania Historical & Museum Commission, Railroad Museum of Pennsylvania, Harrisburg PA
Penobscot Marine Museum, Searsport ME
Peoria Historical Society, Peoria IL
Phelps County Historical Society, Phelps County Museum, Holdrege NE
Philadelphia Museum of Art, Philadelphia PA
Piatt Castles, West Liberty OH
Plainsman Museum, Aurora NE
Pope County Historical Society, Pope County Museum, Glenwood MN
Portsmouth Historical Society, John Paul Jones House, Portsmouth NH
Putnam County Historical Society, Foundry School Museum, Cold Spring NY
Queens Historical Society, Flushing NY
Rahr-West Art Museum, Manitowoc WI
Red Deer & District Museum & Archives, Red Deer AB
Rhode Island Historical Society, John Brown House, Providence RI

PEWTER

PHOTOGRAPHY

Clark County Historical Society, Pioneer - Krier Museum, Ashland KS

Clinton Art Association Gallery, Clinton IA

Clinton County Historical Association, Clinton County Historical Museum, Plattsburgh NY

College of William & Mary, Joseph & Margaret Muscarelle Museum of Art, Williamsburg VA

Colorado Photographic Arts Center, Denver CO

Columbia College, The Museum of Contemporary Photography, Chicago IL

Columbus Museum, Columbus GA

Columbus Museum of Art, Columbus OH

Community Fine Arts Center, Halseth Gallery, Rock Springs WY

Corcoran Gallery of Art, Washington DC

Cornell University, Herbert F Johnson Museum of Art, Ithaca NY

Cornish College of the Arts, Fisher Gallery, Seattle WA

Cornwall Gallery Society, Regional Art Gallery, Cornwall ON

Cranbrook Art Museum, Bloomfield Hills MI

Creighton University, Fine Arts Gallery, Omaha NE

Crocker Art Museum, Sacramento CA

Crow Wing County Historical Society, Brainerd MN

The Currier Gallery of Art, Manchester NH

Custer County Art Center, Miles City MT

C W Post Campus of Long Island University, Hillwood Art Museum, Brookville NY

Danforth Museum of Art, Framingham MA

Dartmouth Heritage Museum, Dartmouth NS

Daytona Beach Community College, Southeast Museum of Photography, Daytona Beach FL

DeCordova Museum & Sculpture Park, Lincoln MA

Delaware Art Museum, Wilmington DE

Denison University, Art Gallery, Granville OH

Detroit Repertory Theatre Gallery, Detroit MI

DeWitt Historical Society of Tompkins County, Ithaca NY

Dickinson College, Trout Gallery, Carlisle PA

Dundurn Castle, Hamilton ON

Durham Art Guild Inc, Durham NC

DuSable Museum of African American History, Chicago IL

East Baton Rouge Parks & Recreation Commission, Baton Rouge Gallery Inc, Baton Rouge LA

East Bay Asian Local Development Corp, Asian Resource Gallery, Oakland CA

Eastern Washington State Historical Society, Cheney Cowles Museum, Spokane WA

George Eastman House-International Museum of Photography & Film, Rochester NY

Edmonton Art Gallery, Edmonton AB

Eiteljorg Museum of American Indians & Western Art, Indianapolis IN

Elk River Area Arts Council, Elk River MN

Ellen Noel Art Museum of the Permian Basin, Odessa TX

El Paso Museum of Art, El Paso TX

Emory University, Michael C Carlos Museum, Atlanta GA

Erie Art Museum, Erie PA

Essex Historical Society, Essex Shipbuilding Museum, Essex MA

Evanston Historical Society, Charles Gates Dawes House, Evanston IL

Fayette Art Museum, Fayette AL

Federal Reserve Board, Art Gallery, Washington DC

Fetherston Foundation, Packwood House Museum, Lewisburg PA

Fitton Center For Creative Arts, Hamilton OH

Five Civilized Tribes Museum, Muskogee OK

Focal Point Gallery, Bronx NY

Fort George G Meade Museum, Fort Meade MD

Fort Smith Art Center, Fort Smith AR

Fort Ticonderoga Association, Ticonderoga NY

Fuller Museum of Art, Brockton MA

Galeria Mesa, Mesa Arts Center, Mesa AZ

Galleries of the Claremont Colleges, Claremont CA

Gallery 53, Cooperstown NY

Gallery One, Ellensburg WA

George Washington University, The Dimock Gallery, Washington DC

Getty Center for the History of Art & the Humanities Trust Museum, The J Paul Getty Museum, Santa Monica CA

Glanmore, Hastings County Museum, Belleville ON

Goshen Historical Society, Goshen CT

Goucher College, Rosenberg Gallery, Baltimore MD

Greater Lafayette Museum of Art, Lafayette IN

Great Lakes Historical Society, Island Seas Maritime Museum, Vermilion OH

Greenwood Museum, Greenwood SC

Arthur Griffin Center for Photographic Art, Winchester MA

Grinnell College, Print & Drawing Study Room/Gallery, Grinnell IA

Grossmont Community College, Hyde Gallery, El Cajon CA

Guggenheim Museum Soho, New York NY

Solomon R Guggenheim Museum, New York NY

Guild Hall of East Hampton, Inc, Guild Hall Museum, East Hampton NY

Guilford College, Art Gallery, Greensboro NC

Hammond Museum & Japanese Stroll Garden, Cross-Cultural Center, North Salem NY

Harvard University, William Hayes Fogg Art Museum, Cambridge MA

Headquarters Fort Monroe, Dept of Army, Casemate Museum, Fort Monroe VA

Heard Museum, Phoenix AZ

Hebrew Union College-Jewish Institute of Religion, New York NY

Heckscher Museum of Art, Huntington NY

Henry Gallery Association, Henry Art Gallery, Seattle WA

Hispanic Society of America, Museum, New York NY

Historical Society of Pennsylvania, Philadelphia PA

Historic Northampton Museum, Northampton MA

Hofstra University, Hofstra Museum, Hempstead NY

Honolulu Academy of Arts, Honolulu HI

House of Roses, Senator Wilson Home, Deadwood SD

The Hudson River Museum of Westchester, Yonkers NY

Huguenot Historical Society of New Paltz Galleries, New Paltz NY

Hunter Museum of American Art, Chattanooga TN

Huntington Museum of Art, Huntington WV

Huntsville Museum of Art, Huntsville AL

Hyde Park Art Center, Chicago IL

Illinois State Museum, Illinois Art Gallery & Lockport Gallery, Springfield IL

Illinois State Museum, Illinois Art Gallery, Chicago IL

Imperial Calcasieu Museum, Gibson-Barham Gallery, Lake Charles LA

Institute for Contemporary Art, Project Studio One (P S 1), Long Island City NY

Institute of American Indian Arts Museum, Santa Fe NM

Institute of the Great Plains, Museum of the Great Plains, Lawton OK

Intar Latin American Gallery, New York NY

International Center of Photography, New York NY

International Museum of Cartoon Art, Montreal PQ

Irving Arts Center, Main Gallery & New Talent Gallery, Irving TX

Joslyn Art Museum, Omaha NE

Kalamazoo Institute of Arts, Kalamazoo MI

Kamloops Art Gallery, Kamloops BC

Kansas City Art Institute, Kemper Museum of Contemporary Art & Design, Kansas City MO

Kentucky Derby Museum, Louisville KY

Kern County Museum, Bakersfield CA

Kings County Historical Society and Museum, Hampton NB

Knoxville Museum of Art, Knoxville TN

Koochiching County Historical Society Museum, International Falls MN

Lac du Flambeau Band of Lake Superior Chippewa Indians, George W Brown Jr Ojibwe Museum & Cultural Center, Lac du Flambeau WI

Lafayette College, Morris R Williams Center for the Arts, Art Gallery, Easton PA

Lafayette Natural History Museum, Planetarium & Nature Station, Lafayette LA

Lehigh University Art Galleries, Bethlehem PA

Leroy Historical Society, LeRoy NY

LeSueur County Historical Museum, Chapter One, Elysian MN

LeSueur Museum, LeSueur MN

Lewistown Art Center, Lewistown MT

Liberty Memorial Museum & Archives, Kansas City MO

Lighthouse Gallery & School of Art, Tequesta FL

Light Work, Syracuse NY

Longview Art Museum, Longview TX

Louisa May Alcott Memorial Association, Orchard House, Concord MA

Louisiana Department of Culture, Recreation & Tourism, Louisiana State Museum, New Orleans LA

Loyola Marymount University, Laband Art Gallery, Los Angeles CA

McCord Museum of Canadian History, Montreal PQ

McLean County Historical Society, Bloomington IL

Charles H MacNider Museum, Mason City IA

Maitland Art Center, Maitland FL

Maricopa County Historical Society, Desert Caballeros Western Museum, Wickenburg AZ

The Mariners' Museum, Newport News VA

Mark Twain Birthplace State Historic Site Birthplace Museum, Stoutsville MO

Marquette University, Haggerty Museum of Art, Milwaukee WI

Maryland Hall for the Creative Arts, Cardinal Gallery, Annapolis MD

Marylhurst College, The Art Gym, Marylhurst OR

Massachusetts Institute of Technology, List Visual Arts Center, Cambridge MA

Massachusetts Institute of Technology, MIT Museum, Cambridge MA

Mattatuck Historical Society, Mattatuck Museum, Waterbury CT

Mendel Art Gallery & Civic Conservatory, Saskatoon SK

Meridian Museum of Art, Meridian MS

The Metropolitan Museum of Art, New York NY

Mexican Fine Arts Center Museum, Chicago IL

Mexican Museum, San Francisco CA

Miami-Dade Community College, Kendal Campus, Art Gallery, Miami FL

Miami University, Art Museum, Oxford OH

James A Michener Art Museum, Doylestown PA

Michigan State University, Kresge Art Museum, East Lansing MI

Middle Tennessee State University, Baldwin Photographic Gallery, Murfreesboro TN

Midwest Museum of American Art, Elkhart IN

Mills College, Art Gallery, Oakland CA

Milwaukee Public Museum, Milwaukee WI

Minneapolis Institute of Arts, Minneapolis MN

Mint Museum of Art, Charlotte NC

Arthur Roy Mitchell Memorial Inc, Museum of Western Art, Trinidad CO

Monterey Museum of Art Association, Monterey CA

Moore College of Art & Design, Goldie Paley Gallery, Philadelphia PA

Moravian College, Payne Gallery, Bethlehem PA

Munson-Williams-Proctor Institute, Museum of Art, Utica NY

Murray State University, Eagle Gallery, Murray KY

Musee des Augustines de l'Hotel Dieu de Quebec, Quebec PQ

Musee du Quebec, Quebec PQ

Musee Regional de la Cote-Nord, Sept-Iles PQ

Museo De Las Americas, Denver CO

Museum of Arts & History, Port Huron MI

Museum of Contemporary Art, San Diego-Downtown, San Diego CA

Museum of Fine Arts, Houston, Houston TX

Museum of Holography - Chicago, Chicago IL

Museum of Modern Art, New York NY

Museum of New Mexico, Museum of Fine Arts, Santa Fe NM

Museum of Northern Arizona, Flagstaff AZ

National Gallery of Canada, Ottawa ON

National Museum of American Art, Washington DC

National Museum of the American Indian, George Gustav Heye Center, New York NY

National Museum of Wildlife Art, Jackson WY

Wiregrass Museum of Art, Dothan AL
Woodmere Art Museum, Philadelphia PA
Yarmouth County Historical Society, Yarmouth
County Museum, Yarmouth NS
Peter Yegen Jr Yellowstone County Museum,
Billings MT
York Institute Museum, Saco ME
Yosemite Museum, Yosemite National Park CA

PORCELAIN

Agecroft Association, Museum, Richmond VA
American Kennel Club, Museum of the Dog, Saint
Louis MO
American Swedish Institute, Minneapolis MN
Arizona Historical Society-Yuma, Century House
Museum & Garden, Yuma AZ
Arkansas Territorial Restoration, Little Rock AR
Asian Art Museum of San Francisco, Avery
Brundage Collection, San Francisco CA
Association for the Preservation of Virginia
Antiquities, John Marshall House, Richmond
VA
Atlanta Museum, Atlanta GA
Leo Baeck Institute, New York NY
Baltimore Museum of Art, Baltimore MD
Beaverbrook Art Gallery, Fredericton NB
Bellingrath Gardens & Home, Theodore AL
Beloit College, Wright Museum of Art, Beloit WI
Jesse Besser Museum, Alpena MI
The Bradford Museum of Collector's Plates, Niles
IL
The Bruce Museum, Greenwich CT
Cape Ann Historical Museum, Gloucester MA
Chatillon-DeMenil House Foundation, DeMenil
Mansion, Saint Louis MO
Cheekwood-Tennessee Botanical Gardens &
Museum of Art, Nashville TN
Cincinnati Institute of Fine Arts, Taft Museum,
Cincinnati OH
Sterling & Francine Clark Art Institute,
Williamstown MA
College of William & Mary, Joseph & Margaret
Muscarelle Museum of Art, Williamsburg VA
The College of Wooster, Art Museum, Wooster OH
Columbus Museum, Columbus GA
Columbus Museum of Art, Columbus OH
Cooper-Hewitt, National Design Museum, New
York NY
Cornwall Gallery Society, Regional Art Gallery,
Cornwall ON
Cranbrook Art Museum, Bloomfield Hills MI
Cummer Museum of Art & Gardens, DeEtte
Holden Cummer Museum Foundation,
Jacksonville FL
The Currier Gallery of Art, Manchester NH
C W Post Campus of Long Island University,
Hillwood Art Museum, Brookville NY
Danville Museum of Fine Arts & History, Danville
VA
DAR Museum, National Society Daughters of the
American Revolution, Washington DC
Dartmouth Heritage Museum, Dartmouth NS
The Dixon Gallery & Gardens, Memphis TN
Dundurn Castle, Hamilton ON
Ellen Noel Art Museum of the Permian Basin,
Odessa TX
Erie Art Museum, Erie PA
Evanston Historical Society, Charles Gates Dawes
House, Evanston IL
Everson Museum of Art, Syracuse NY
Fetherston Foundation, Packwood House Museum,
Lewisburg PA
Florida State University Foundation - Central
Florida Community College Foundation, The
Appleton Museum of Art, Ocala FL
Captain Robert Bennet Forbes House, Milton MA
Edsel & Eleanor Ford House, Grosse Pointe Shores
MI
Fort Smith Art Center, Fort Smith AR
Franklin Mint Museum, Franklin Center PA
The Frick Art & Historical Center, Frick Art
Museum, Pittsburgh PA
Frick Collection, New York NY
Gallery 53, Cooperstown NY
Gallery One, Ellensburg WA

General Board of Discipleship, The United
Methodist Church, The Upper Room Chapel &
Museum, Nashville TN
Girard College, Stephen Girard Collection,
Philadelphia PA
Greater Lafayette Museum of Art, Lafayette IN
Gunston Hall Plantation, Mason Neck VA
Hammond-Harwood House Association, Inc,
Annapolis MD
Headquarters Fort Monroe, Dept of Army,
Casemate Museum, Fort Monroe VA
Hershey Museum, Hershey PA
Hill-Stead Museum, Farmington CT
Historical & Cultural Affairs, Delaware State
Museums, Dover DE
Historic Cherry Hill, Albany NY
Historic Landmarks Foundation of Indiana, Morris-
Butler House, Indianapolis IN
Honolulu Academy of Arts, Honolulu HI
House of Roses, Senator Wilson Home, Deadwood
SD
Huguenot Historical Society of New Paltz Galleries,
New Paltz NY
Indianapolis Museum of Art, Indianapolis IN
Iowa State University, Brunnier Art Museum, Ames
IA
Jacksonville University, Alexander Brest Museum &
Gallery, Jacksonville FL
Johns Hopkins University, Evergreen House,
Baltimore MD
Johns Hopkins University, Homewood House
Museum, Baltimore MD
Knoxville Museum of Art, Knoxville TN
Koochiching County Historical Society Museum,
International Falls MN
Lehigh University Art Galleries, Bethlehem PA
Lewistown Art Center, Lewistown MT
Longfellow-Evangeline State Commemorative Area,
Saint Martinville LA
Louisa May Alcott Memorial Association, Orchard
House, Concord MA
Maitland Art Center, Maitland FL
Maryland Historical Society, Museum of Maryland
History, Baltimore MD
Memphis Brooks Museum of Art, Memphis TN
Michigan State University, Kresge Art Museum,
East Lansing MI
Midwest Museum of American Art, Elkhart IN
Mint Museum of Art, Charlotte NC
Montgomery Museum of Fine Arts, Montgomery
AL
Montreal Museum of Fine Arts, Montreal PQ
Musee des Augustines de l'Hotel Dieu de Quebec,
Quebec PQ
Musee Regional de la Cote-Nord, Sept-Iles PQ
Museo De Las Americas, Denver CO
Museum of Fine Arts, Boston MA
Museum of Northern British Columbia, Ruth
Harvey Art Gallery, Prince Rupert BC
National Society of Colonial Dames of America in
the State of Maryland, Mount Clare Mansion,
Baltimore MD
National Society of Tole & Decorative Painters,
Inc, Wichita KS
Naval Historical Center, The Navy Museum,
Washington DC
Neville Public Museum, Green Bay WI
Newark Museum Association, The Newark
Museum, Newark NJ
North Carolina State University, Visual Arts
Center, Raleigh NC
The Ohio Historical Society, Inc, Campus Martius
Museum & Ohio River Museum, Marietta OH
Old York Historical Society, Old Gaol Museum,
York ME
Pacific - Asia Museum, Pasadena CA
Panhandle-Plains Historical Society Museum,
Canyon TX
Pennsylvania State University, Palmer Museum of
Art, University Park PA
Penobscot Marine Museum, Searsport ME
Philadelphia Museum of Art, Philadelphia PA
Marjorie Merriweather Post Foundation of DC,
Hillwood Museum, Washington DC
Red Deer & District Museum & Archives, Red
Deer AB
Frederic Remington Art Museum, Ogdensburg NY

Rhode Island Historical Society, John Brown
House, Providence RI
Rhode Island School of Design, Museum of Art,
Providence RI
The Rosenbach Museum & Library, Philadelphia
PA
Royal Arts Foundation, Belcourt Castle, Newport
RI
Robert W Ryerss Library & Museum, Philadelphia
PA
Saint John's University, Chung-Cheng Art Gallery,
Jamaica NY
The Saint Louis Art Museum, Saint Louis MO
The Seagram Museum, Waterloo ON
Seattle Art Museum, Seattle WA
Ella Sharp Museum, Jackson MI
Ships of The Sea Maritime Museum, Savannah GA
Society of the Cincinnati, Museum & Library at
Anderson House, Washington DC
Springfield Art Museum, Springfield MO
Nelda C & H J Lutcher Stark Foundation, Stark
Museum of Art, Orange TX
Stratford Historical Society, Katherine Mitchel
Museum, Stratford CT
Swedish American Museum Association of Chicago,
Chicago IL
Towson State University, Asian Arts Center,
Towson MD
Trenton City Museum, Trenton NJ
Tryon Palace Historic Sites & Gardens, New Bern
NC
US Department of State, Diplomatic Reception
Rooms, Washington DC
United States Figure Skating Association, World
Figure Skating Museum & Hall of Fame,
Colorado Springs CO
University of Mississippi, University Museums,
Oxford MS
University of Notre Dame, Snite Museum of Art,
Notre Dame IN
University of Rochester, Memorial Art Gallery,
Rochester NY
University of Tampa, Henry B Plant Museum,
Tampa FL
University of Tennessee, Eleanor Dean Audigier
Art Collection, Knoxville TN
University of Victoria, Maltwood Art Museum and
Gallery, Victoria BC
University of Virginia, Bayly Art Museum,
Charlottesville VA
Vesterheim Norwegian-American Museum,
Decorah IA
Virginia Museum of Fine Arts, Richmond VA
Wadsworth Atheneum, Hartford CT
Wayne Center for the Arts, Wooster OH
Wells Fargo Bank, Wells Fargo History Museum,
San Francisco CA
T T Wentworth Jr Museum, Florida State Museum,
Pensacola FL
White House, Washington DC
Wichita Art Museum, Wichita KS
Winterthur Museum, Winterthur DE
Woodlawn Plantation, Mount Vernon VA
Woodmere Art Museum, Philadelphia PA
Yarmouth County Historical Society, Yarmouth
County Museum, Yarmouth NS
York Institute Museum, Saco ME

PORTRAITS

Agecroft Association, Museum, Richmond VA
Albany Institute of History & Art, Albany NY
Albuquerque Museum of Art & History,
Albuquerque NM
American Kennel Club, Museum of the Dog, Saint
Louis MO
Walter Anderson Museum of Art, Ocean Springs
MS
Arizona Historical Society-Yuma, Century House
Museum & Garden, Yuma AZ
Arkansas Territorial Restoration, Little Rock AR
Arts Council of Fayetteville-Cumberland County,
The Arts Center, Fayetteville NC
Asbury College, Student Center Gallery, Wilmore
KY
Ashland Historical Society, Ashland MA
Asian Art Museum of San Francisco, Avery
Brundage Collection, San Francisco CA

University of Mississippi, University Museums, Oxford MS
University of Nebraska, Lincoln, Sheldon Memorial Art Gallery & Sculpture Garden, Lincoln NE
University of Rochester, Memorial Art Gallery, Rochester NY
University of Southern California, Fisher Gallery, Los Angeles CA
University of Victoria, Maltwood Art Museum and Gallery, Victoria BC
University of Virginia, Bayly Art Museum, Charlottesville VA
Ursinus College, Philip & Muriel Berman Museum of Art, Collegeville PA
USS Constitution Museum, Boston MA
Vesterheim Norwegian-American Museum, Decorah IA
Viridian Artists Inc, New York NY
Warner House Association, MacPheadris-Warner House, Portsmouth NH
Wayne County Historical Society, Museum, Honesdale PA
Westmoreland Museum of American Art, Greensburg PA
Whatcom Museum of History and Art, Bellingham WA
White House, Washington DC
Wilfrid Laurier University, Robert Langen Gallery, Waterloo ON
Willard House & Clock Museum, Inc, North Grafton MA
Winterthur Museum, Winterthur DE
Woodlawn Plantation, Mount Vernon VA
Woodmere Art Museum, Philadelphia PA
Yale University, Yale Center for British Art, New Haven CT
Yarmouth County Historical Society, Yarmouth County Museum, Yarmouth NS
York Institute Museum, Saco ME

POSTERS

Algonquin Arts Council, Art Gallery of Bancroft, Bancroft ON
American Kennel Club, Museum of the Dog, Saint Louis MO
American University, Watkins Collection, Washington DC
Arts Council of Fayetteville-Cumberland County, The Arts Center, Fayetteville NC
Leo Baeck Institute, New York NY
Jesse Besser Museum, Alpena MI
Brigham Young University, Museum of Art, Provo UT
Brown University, David Winton Bell Gallery, Providence RI
The Buffalo Fine Arts Academy, Albright-Knox Art Gallery, Buffalo NY
Canadian Museum of Nature, Musee Canadien de la Nature, Ottawa ON
Cartoon Art Museum, San Francisco CA
Radio-Canada SRC CBC, Galerie Georges Goguen, Moncton NB
Cedar Rapids Museum of Art, Cedar Rapids IA
Center for Puppetry Arts, Atlanta GA
Central United Methodist Church, Swords Info Plowshares Peace Center & Gallery, Detroit MI
Chicago Athenaeum, Museum of Architecture & Design, Chicago IL
City of Cedar Falls, Iowa, James & Meryl Hearst Center for the Arts, Cedar Falls IA
Clinton County Historical Association, Clinton County Historical Museum, Plattsburgh NY
Columbus Museum, Columbus GA
Cooper-Hewitt, National Design Museum, New York NY
Dartmouth Heritage Museum, Dartmouth NS
Delaware Art Museum, Wilmington DE
DeWitt Historical Society of Tompkins County, Ithaca NY
Dickinson College, Trout Gallery, Carlisle PA
Ellen Noel Art Museum of the Permian Basin, Odessa TX
Evanston Historical Society, Charles Gates Dawes House, Evanston IL
Fairfield University, Thomas J Walsh Art Gallery, Fairfield CT
Fitton Center For Creative Arts, Hamilton OH

Fort George G Meade Museum, Fort Meade MD
Greenville College, Richard W Bock Sculpture Collection, Greenville IL
Historical Society of Pennsylvania, Philadelphia PA
International Museum of Cartoon Art, Montreal PQ
Iowa State University, Brunnier Art Museum, Ames IA
Kansas City Art Institute, Kemper Museum of Contemporary Art & Design, Kansas City MO
Knights of Columbus Supreme Council, Headquarters Museum, New Haven CT
Kurdish Museum, Brooklyn NY
La Casa del Libro Museum, San Juan PR
Lac du Flambeau Band of Lake Superior Chippewa Indians, George W Brown Jr Ojibwe Museum & Cultural Center, Lac du Flambeau WI
Lafayette Natural History Museum, Planetarium & Nature Station, Lafayette LA
Leroy Historical Society, LeRoy NY
LeSueur County Historical Museum, Chapter One, Elysian MN
LeSueur Museum, LeSueur MN
Lewistown Art Center, Lewistown MT
Liberty Memorial Museum & Archives, Kansas City MO
Livingston County Historical Society, Cobblestone Museum, Geneseo NY
Longview Art Museum, Longview TX
Luther College, Fine Arts Collection, Decorah IA
Maitland Art Center, Maitland FL
The Mariners' Museum, Newport News VA
Mattatuck Historical Society, Mattatuck Museum, Waterbury CT
Michigan State University, Kresge Art Museum, East Lansing MI
Musee Regional de la Cote-Nord, Sept-Iles PQ
Museum of Modern Art, New York NY
Museum of Movie Art, Calgary AB
Museum of York County, Rock Hill SC
National Portrait Gallery, Washington DC
Naval Historical Center, The Navy Museum, Washington DC
Nebraska State Capitol, Lincoln NE
New Jersey Historical Society, Newark NJ
New Visions Gallery, Inc, Marshfield WI
One West Art Center, Fort Collins CO
Oshkosh Public Museum, Oshkosh WI
Panhandle-Plains Historical Society Museum, Canyon TX
Pennsylvania Academy of the Fine Arts, Museum of American Art, Philadelphia PA
Pennsylvania Historical & Museum Commission, Railroad Museum of Pennsylvania, Harrisburg PA
School of Visual Arts, Visual Arts Museum, New York NY
The Seagram Museum, Waterloo ON
Southern Alleghenies Museum of Art, Southern Alleghenies Museum of Art at Johnstown, Loretto PA
South Street Seaport Museum, New York NY
State University of New York at New Paltz, College Art Gallery, New Paltz NY
State University of New York at Oswego, Tyler Art Gallery, Oswego NY
Stratford Historical Society, Katherine Mitchel Museum, Stratford CT
Temple Beth Israel, Sylvia Plotkin Judaica, Phoenix AZ
United States Figure Skating Association, World Figure Skating Museum & Hall of Fame, Colorado Springs CO
University of California, Richard L Nelson Gallery & Fine Arts Collection, Davis CA
University of California, Berkeley Art Museum & Pacific Film Archive, Berkeley CA
University of California, Santa Barbara, University Art Museum, Santa Barbara CA
University of Cincinnati, DAAP Galleries-College of Design Architecture, Art & Planning, Cincinnati OH
University of South Florida, Contemporary Art Museum, Tampa FL
University of Virginia, Bayly Art Museum, Charlottesville VA
Ursinus College, Philip & Muriel Berman Museum of Art, Collegeville PA
Viridian Artists inc, New York NY

Washington State History Museum, Tacoma WA
Wells Fargo Bank, Wells Fargo History Museum, San Francisco CA

POTTERY

Agecroft Association, Museum, Richmond VA
Alabama Department of Archives & History, Museum Galleries, Montgomery AL
Albany Institute of History & Art, Albany NY
Algonquin Arts Council, Art Gallery of Bancroft, Bancroft ON
Allegheny College, Bowman, Megahan & Penelec Galleries, Meadville PA
American Kennel Club, Museum of the Dog, Saint Louis MO
Art Association of Jacksonville, David Strawn Art Gallery, Jacksonville IL
Artesia Historical Museum & Art Center, Artesia NM
Art Gallery of Nova Scotia, Halifax NS
Arts Council of Fayetteville-Cumberland County, The Arts Center, Fayetteville NC
Asbury College, Student Center Gallery, Wilmore KY
Asian Art Museum of San Francisco, Avery Brundage Collection, San Francisco CA
Baker University, Old Castle Museum, Baldwin City KS
Barnes Foundation, Merion PA
Jesse Besser Museum, Alpena MI
Brevard College, Sims Art Center, Brevard NC
Brigham Young University, Museum of Art, Provo UT
The Canadian Craft Museum, Vancouver BC
Cape Ann Historical Museum, Gloucester MA
Kit Carson Historic Museums, Ernest Blumenschein Home & Studio, Taos NM
Central United Methodist Church, Swords Info Plowshares Peace Center & Gallery, Detroit MI
Billie Trimble Chandler Arts Foundation, Asian Cultures Museum & Educational Center, Corpus Christi TX
Chattahoochee Valley Art Museum, LaGrange GA
Cherokee National Historical Society, Inc, Tahlequah OK
Church of Jesus Christ of Latter-Day Saints, Museum of Church History & Art, Salt Lake City UT
City of Atlanta, Chastain Arts Center, Atlanta GA
City of Atlanta, Southeast Arts Center, Atlanta GA
City of Gainesville, Thomas Center Galleries - Cultural Affairs, Gainesville FL
City of Pittsfield, Berkshire Artisans, Pittsfield MA
Clinton Art Association Gallery, Clinton IA
Clinton County Historical Association, Clinton County Historical Museum, Plattsburgh NY
Columbus Museum, Columbus GA
Columbus Museum of Art, Columbus OH
Community Fine Arts Center, Halseth Gallery, Rock Springs WY
Cooper-Hewitt, National Design Museum, New York NY
Cornwall Gallery Society, Regional Art Gallery, Cornwall ON
Craft & Folk Art Museum, Los Angeles CA
Cranbrook Art Museum, Bloomfield Hills MI
Creighton University, Fine Arts Gallery, Omaha NE
Custer County Art Center, Miles City MT
C W Post Campus of Long Island University, Hillwood Art Museum, Brookville NY
DAR Museum, National Society Daughters of the American Revolution, Washington DC
Dartmouth Heritage Museum, Dartmouth NS
Deming-Luna Mimbres Museum, Deming NM
Dickinson College, Trout Gallery, Carlisle PA
Dundurn Castle, Hamilton ON
Eiteljorg Museum of American Indians & Western Art, Indianapolis IN
Emory University, Michael C Carlos Museum, Atlanta GA
Enook Galleries, Waterloo ON
Ephraim McDowell-Cambus-Kenneth Foundation, McDowell House & Apothecary Shop, Danville KY
Erie Art Museum, Erie PA

Favell Museum of Western Art & Indian Artifacts, Klamath Falls OR

Fetherston Foundation, Packwood House Museum, Lewisburg PA

Fitton Center For Creative Arts, Hamilton OH

Five Civilized Tribes Museum, Muskogee OK

Fuller Museum of Art, Brockton MA

Gadsden Museum, Mesilla NM

Galeria Mesa, Mesa Arts Center, Mesa AZ

Gallery 53, Cooperstown NY

Gallery One, Ellensburg WA

Gonzaga University, Jundt Art Museum, Ad Art Gallery, Spokane WA

Greater Lafayette Museum of Art, Lafayette IN

Grossmont Community College, Hyde Gallery, El Cajon CA

Halifax Historical Society, Inc, Halifax Historical Museum, Daytona Beach FL

Hambidge Center Gallery, Rabun Gap GA

Harvard University, Dumbarton Oaks Research Library & Collections, Washington DC

Headquarters Fort Monroe, Dept of Army, Casemate Museum, Fort Monroe VA

Heard Museum, Phoenix AZ

Hershey Museum, Hershey PA

High Point Historical Society Inc, Museum, High Point NC

Hispanic Society of America, Museum, New York NY

Historical Society of Cheshire County, Archive Center of the Society, Keene NH

Historical Society of the Town of Greenwich, Inc, Bush-Holley House Museum, Cos Cob CT

Historic Cherry Hill, Albany NY

Huguenot Historical Society of New Paltz Galleries, New Paltz NY

Imperial Calcasieu Museum, Gibson-Barham Gallery, Lake Charles LA

Institute of American Indian Arts Museum, Santa Fe NM

Iowa State University, Brunnier Art Museum, Ames IA

Irving Arts Center, Main Gallery & New Talent Gallery, Irving TX

Johnson-Humrickhouse Museum, Coshocton OH

Joslyn Art Museum, Omaha NE

Kenosha Public Museum, Kenosha WI

Koochiching County Historical Society Museum, International Falls MN

Koshare Indian Museum, Inc, La Junta CO

Leroy Historical Society, LeRoy NY

LeSueur County Historical Museum, Chapter One, Elysian MN

Lewistown Art Center, Lewistown MT

Livingston County Historical Society, Cobblestone Museum, Geneseo NY

Louisiana Arts & Science Center, Baton Rouge LA

Luther College, Fine Arts Collection, Decorah IA

McCord Museum of Canadian History, Montreal PQ

Charles H MacNider Museum, Mason City IA

Maitland Art Center, Maitland FL

The Mariners' Museum, Newport News VA

Maryland Historical Society, Museum of Maryland History, Baltimore MD

Meridian Museum of Art, Meridian MS

Mexican Museum, San Francisco CA

Michigan State University, Kresge Art Museum, East Lansing MI

Midwest Museum of American Art, Elkhart IN

Mills College, Art Gallery, Oakland CA

Mississippi River Museum at Mud-Island, Memphis TN

Arthur Roy Mitchell Memorial Inc, Museum of Western Art, Trinidad CO

Morris Museum, Morristown NJ

Mount Saint Vincent University, Art Gallery, Halifax NS

Munson-Williams-Proctor Institute, Museum of Art, Utica NY

Musee des Augustines de l'Hotel Dieu de Quebec, Quebec PQ

Musee Regional de la Cote-Nord, Sept-Iles PQ

Musee Regional de Vaudreuil-Soulanges, Vaudreuil PQ

Museum of Northern Arizona, Flagstaff AZ

National Museum of the American Indian, George Gustav Heye Center, New York NY

Navajo Nation Museum, Window Rock AZ

Newark Museum Association, The Newark Museum, Newark NJ

New Visions Gallery, Inc, Marshfield WI

North Carolina State University, Visual Arts Center, Raleigh NC

The Ohio Historical Society, Inc, Campus Martius Museum & Ohio River Museum, Marietta OH

One West Art Center, Fort Collins CO

Oshkosh Public Museum, Oshkosh WI

Pacific - Asia Museum, Pasadena CA

Palm Beach County Parks & Recreation Department, Morikami Museum & Japanese Gardens, Delray Beach FL

Paris Gibson Square, Museum of Art, Great Falls MT

Peabody Essex Museum, Salem MA

Peoria Historical Society, Peoria IL

Phelps County Historical Society, Phelps County Museum, Holdrege NE

George Phippen Memorial Foundation, Phippen Museum of Western Art, Prescott AZ

Potsdam Public Museum, Potsdam NY

Rensselaer County Historical Society, Hart-Cluett Mansion, 1827, Troy NY

Millicent Rogers Museum of Northern New Mexico, Taos NM

Roswell Museum & Art Center, Roswell NM

C M Russell Museum, Great Falls MT

R W Norton Art Gallery, Shreveport LA

Saint Louis Artists' Guild, Saint Louis MO

The Seagram Museum, Waterloo ON

Seneca-Iroquois National Museum, Salamanca NY

Abigail Adams Smith Museum, New York NY

South Dakota State University, South Dakota Art Museum, Brookings SD

Southern Baptist Theological Seminary, Joseph A Callaway Archaeological Museum, Louisville KY

Spartanburg County Museum of Art, Spartanburg SC

Springfield Art & Historical Society, Miller Art Center, Springfield VT

Springfield Art Museum, Springfield MO

Stanford University, Museum of Art, Stanford CA

State University of New York at New Paltz, College Art Gallery, New Paltz NY

State University of New York at Oswego, Tyler Art Gallery, Oswego NY

Summit County Historical Society, Akron OH

Swedish American Museum Association of Chicago, Chicago IL

Tallahassee Museum of History & Natural Science, Tallahassee FL

Tampa Museum of Art, Tampa FL

Topeka & Shawnee County Public Library, Gallery of Fine Arts, Topeka KS

Towson State University, Asian Arts Center, Towson MD

Tulane University, University Art Collection, New Orleans LA

Tulane University, Dept Art Newcomb Col Art Galleries, New Orleans LA

The Ukrainian Museum, New York NY

University of Chicago, Oriental Institute Museum, Chicago IL

University of Delaware, University Gallery, Newark DE

University of Iowa, Museum of Art, Iowa City IA

University of Manitoba, Faculty of Architecture Exhibition Centre, Winnipeg MB

University of Michigan, Kelsey Museum of Archaeology, Ann Arbor MI

University of Rochester, Memorial Art Gallery, Rochester NY

University of Virginia, Bayly Art Museum, Charlottesville VA

University of Washington, Henry Art Gallery, Seattle WA

Ursinus College, Philip & Muriel Berman Museum of Art, Collegeville PA

Vesterheim Norwegian-American Museum, Decorah IA

Virginia Museum of Fine Arts, Richmond VA

Westmoreland Museum of American Art, Greensburg PA

Wheelwright Museum of the American Indian, Santa Fe NM

Winston-Salem State University, Diggs Gallery, Winston Salem NC

PRE-COLUMBIAN ART

Americas Society Art Gallery, New York NY

Anchorage Museum of History & Art, Anchorage AK

Art Association of Jacksonville, David Strawn Art Gallery, Jacksonville IL

Aurora University, Schingoethe Center for Native American Cultures, Aurora IL

Birmingham Museum of Art, Birmingham AL

Bowdoin College, Museum of Art, Brunswick ME

Bower's Museum, Santa Ana CA

Brandeis University, Rose Art Museum, Waltham MA

Brevard Museum of Art & Science, Melbourne FL

California State University, Hayward, C E Smith Museum of Anthropology, Hayward CA

California State University Stanislaus, University Art Gallery, Turlock CA

Capital University, Schumacher Gallery, Columbus OH

Center for Puppetry Arts, Atlanta GA

Cincinnati Museum Association, Cincinnati Art Museum, Cincinnati OH

Colgate University, Picker Art Gallery, Hamilton NY

College of Southern Idaho, Herrett Center for Arts & Science, Twin Falls ID

The College of Wooster, Art Museum, Wooster OH

Columbus Museum, Columbus GA

Columbus Museum of Art, Columbus OH

Concordia University, Leonard & Bina Ellen Art Gallery, Montreal PQ

C W Post Campus of Long Island University, Hillwood Art Museum, Brookville NY

Dallas Museum of Art, Dallas TX

Denver Art Museum, Denver CO

Dickinson College, Trout Gallery, Carlisle PA

Discovery Place Inc, Charlotte NC

East Tennessee State University, Carroll Reece Museum, Johnson City TN

El Paso Museum of Art, El Paso TX

Emory University, Michael C Carlos Museum, Atlanta GA

Erie Art Museum, Erie PA

Fitton Center For Creative Arts, Hamilton OH

Florida State University Foundation - Central Florida Community College Foundation, The Appleton Museum of Art, Ocala FL

Freeport Arts Center, Freeport IL

Fuller Museum of Art, Brockton MA

Hampton University, University Museum, Hampton VA

Harvard University, Dumbarton Oaks Research Library & Collections, Washington DC

Hofstra University, Hofstra Museum, Hempstead NY

Honolulu Academy of Arts, Honolulu HI

Jacksonville Museum of Contemporary Art, Jacksonville FL

Jacksonville University, Alexander Brest Museum & Gallery, Jacksonville FL

Joslyn Art Museum, Omaha NE

Kimbell Art Foundation, Kimbell Art Museum, Fort Worth TX

Luther College, Fine Arts Collection, Decorah IA

The Mariners' Museum, Newport News VA

Mexican Museum, San Francisco CA

Michigan State University, Kresge Art Museum, East Lansing MI

Minneapolis Institute of Arts, Minneapolis MN

Mount Holyoke College, Art Museum, South Hadley MA

Musee d'Art de Joliette, Joliette PQ

Museum of Fine Arts, Houston, Houston TX

Museum of Fine Arts, Saint Petersburg, Florida, Inc, Saint Petersburg FL

Museum of the Americas, Brookfield VT

National Museum of the American Indian, George Gustav Heye Center, New York NY

Newark Museum Association, The Newark Museum, Newark NJ

New Mexico State University, University Art Gallery, Las Cruces NM

New Orleans Museum of Art, New Orleans LA

Niagara University, Castellani Art Museum, Niagara NY
North Carolina Museum of Art, Raleigh NC
North Carolina State University, Visual Arts Center, Raleigh NC
Oakland University, Meadow Brook Art Gallery, Rochester MI
Oklahoma Center for Science & Art, Kirkpatrick Center, Oklahoma City OK
Old Jail Art Center, Albany TX
Orlando Museum of Art, Orlando FL
Palm Springs Desert Museum, Palm Springs CA
Polk Museum of Art, Lakeland FL
Portland Art Museum, Portland OR
Princeton University, The Art Museum, Princeton NJ
Rhode Island School of Design, Museum of Art, Providence RI
Rice University, Art Gallery, Houston TX
Riverside Municipal Museum, Riverside CA
Millicent Rogers Museum of Northern New Mexico, Taos NM
Royal Ontario Museum, Toronto ON
C M Russell Museum, Great Falls MT
Saint Gregory's Abbey & College, Mabee-Gerrer Museum of Art, Shawnee OK
The Saint Louis Art Museum, Saint Louis MO
San Antonio Museum of Art, San Antonio TX
Santa Barbara Museum of Art, Santa Barbara CA
Southern Connecticut State University, Art Gallery, New Haven CT
Southwest Museum, Los Angeles CA
Stanford University, Museum of Art, Stanford CA
State University of New York at New Paltz, College Art Gallery, New Paltz NY
Tucson Museum of Art & Historic Block, Tucson AZ
Tulane University, Dept Art Newcomb Col Art Galleries, New Orleans LA
University of California, Los Angeles, Fowler Museum of Cultural History, Los Angeles CA
University of Cincinnati, DAAP Galleries-College of Design Architecture, Art & Planning, Cincinnati OH
University of Florida, University Gallery, Gainesville FL
University of Florida, Samuel P Harn Museum of Art, Gainesville FL
University of Illinois, Krannert Art Museum, Champaign IL
University of Iowa, Museum of Art, Iowa City IA
University of Kentucky, Art Museum, Lexington KY
University of Miami, Lowe Art Museum, Coral Gables FL
University of Missouri, Museum of Art & Archaeology, Columbia MO
University of Notre Dame, Snite Museum of Art, Notre Dame IN
University of South Florida, Contemporary Art Museum, Tampa FL
University of Virginia, Bayly Art Museum, Charlottesville VA
Vancouver Museum Commission, Vancouver Museum, Vancouver BC
Wichita Art Museum, Wichita KS
Williams College, Museum of Art, Williamstown MA
Worcester Art Museum, Worcester MA

PRIMITIVE ART

Lyman Allyn Art Museum, New London CT
American Kennel Club, Museum of the Dog, Saint Louis MO
Artesia Historical Museum & Art Center, Artesia NM
Art Gallery of Greater Victoria, Victoria BC
Boise Art Museum, Boise ID
Bowdoin College, Peary-MacMillan Arctic Museum, Brunswick ME
Capital University, Schumacher Gallery, Columbus OH
Carson County Square House Museum, Panhandle TX
Church of Jesus Christ of Latter-day Saints, Museum of Church History & Art, Salt Lake City UT

City of Springdale, Shiloh Museum, Springdale AR
Columbus Museum, Columbus GA
Davidson College Visual Arts Center, William H Van Every Jr & Edward M Smith Galleries, Davidson NC
Dickinson College, Trout Gallery, Carlisle PA
Discovery Place Inc, Charlotte NC
Enook Galleries, Waterloo ON
Fayette Art Museum, Fayette AL
Field Museum, Chicago IL
Fitton Center For Creative Arts, Hamilton OH
Freeport Arts Center, Freeport IL
Gallery of Prehistoric Paintings, New York NY
Heard Museum, Phoenix AZ
Heritage Plantation of Sandwich, Sandwich MA
Historic Landmarks Foundation of Indiana, Morris-Butler House, Indianapolis IN
Illinois Historic Preservation Agency, Bishop Hill State Historic Site, Bishop Hill IL
Indiana University, Art Museum, Bloomington IN
Knoxville Museum of Art, Knoxville TN
Lafayette Natural History Museum, Planetarium & Nature Station, Lafayette LA
Lightner Museum, Saint Augustine FL
Luther College, Fine Arts Collection, Decorah IA
The Mariners' Museum, Newport News VA
The Metropolitan Museum of Art, New York NY
Michigan State University, Kresge Art Museum, East Lansing MI
Morris Museum, Morristown NJ
Morris Museum of Art, Augusta GA
Museum of Fine Arts, Springfield MA
Museum of Fine Arts, Houston, Houston TX
Museum of Northern British Columbia, Ruth Harvey Art Gallery, Prince Rupert BC
National Museum of American Art, Washington DC
Olivet College, Armstrong Museum of Art & Archaeology, Olivet MI
Paris Gibson Square, Museum of Art, Great Falls MT
Red Deer & District Museum & Archives, Red Deer AB
Riverside Municipal Museum, Riverside CA
Rollins College, George D & Harriet W Cornell Fine Arts Museum, Winter Park FL
Royal Ontario Museum, Toronto ON
Seattle Art Museum, Seattle WA
Southern Alleghenies Museum of Art, Southern Alleghenies Museum of Art at Johnstown, Loretto PA
Southwest Museum, Los Angeles CA
Stanford University, Museum of Art, Stanford CA
Staten Island Institute of Arts & Sciences, Staten Island NY
State University of New York at New Paltz, College Art Gallery, New Paltz NY
Stephens College, Lewis James & Nellie Stratton Davis Art Gallery, Columbia MO
Stratford Historical Society, Katherine Mitchel Museum, Stratford CT
Tattoo Art Museum, San Francisco CA
The Ukrainian Museum, New York NY
University of California, Richard L Nelson Gallery & Fine Arts Collection, Davis CA
University of California, Los Angeles, Fowler Museum of Cultural History, Los Angeles CA
University of Rochester, Memorial Art Gallery, Rochester NY
University of Victoria, Maltwood Art Museum and Gallery, Victoria BC
Wheelwright Museum of the American Indian, Santa Fe NM
Winston-Salem State University, Diggs Gallery, Winston Salem NC

PRINTS

Adirondack Historical Association, Adirondack Museum, Blue Mountain Lake NY
Albany Institute of History & Art, Albany NY
Albertson College of Idaho, Rosenthal Art Gallery, Caldwell ID
Albion College, Bobbitt Visual Arts Center, Albion MI
The Albrecht-Kemper Museum of Art, Saint Joseph MO
Albright College, Freedman Gallery, Reading PA

Albuquerque Museum of Art & History, Albuquerque NM
Aldrich Museum of Contemporary Art, Ridgefield CT
American Kennel Club, Museum of the Dog, Saint Louis MO
American Textile History Museum, Lowell MA
American University, Watkins Collection, Washington DC
Anchorage Museum of History & Art, Anchorage AK
Arizona State University, ASU Art Museum, Tempe AZ
Arkansas Arts Center, Little Rock AR
The Art Galleries of Ramapo College, Mahwah NJ
Art Gallery of Nova Scotia, Halifax NS
The Art Institute of Chicago, Chicago IL
Art Museum of South Texas, Corpus Christi TX
Art Museum of the Americas, Washington DC
Art Museum of Western Virginia, Roanoke VA
Art Resources International, Washington DC
Asbury College, Student Center Gallery, Wilmore KY
Asheville Art Museum, Asheville NC
Attleboro Museum, Center for the Arts, Attleboro MA
Augustana College, Art Gallery, Rock Island IL
Austin College, Ida Green Gallery, Sherman TX
Austin Peay State University, Margaret Fort Trahern Gallery, Clarksville TN
Leo Baeck Institute, New York NY
Baldwin-Wallace College, Fawick Art Gallery, Berea OH
Ball State University, Museum of Art, Muncie IN
Baltimore City Life Museums, Baltimore MD
Baltimore Museum of Art, Baltimore MD
Bates College, Museum of Art, Lewiston ME
Baylor University, Martin Museum of Art, Waco TX
Beaverbrook Art Gallery, Fredericton NB
Jesse Besser Museum, Alpena MI
The Bostonian Society, Old State House Museum, Boston MA
Boston Public Library, Albert H Wiggin Gallery & Print Department, Boston MA
Bowdoin College, Museum of Art, Brunswick ME
Roy Boyd Gallery, Chicago IL
Brandeis University, Rose Art Museum, Waltham MA
Brandywine River Museum, Chadds Ford PA
Brandywine Workshop, Philadelphia PA
Brevard College, Sims Art Center, Brevard NC
Brigham City Museum-Gallery, Brigham City UT
Brigham Young University, B F Larsen Gallery, Provo UT
Brigham Young University, Museum of Art, Provo UT
Bradford Brinton Memorial Museum & Historic Ranch, Big Horn WY
Brown County Art Gallery Association Inc, Brown County Art Gallery & Museum, Nashville IN
Brown University, David Winton Bell Gallery, Providence RI
Burnaby Art Gallery, Burnaby BC
Butler Institute of American Art, Art Museum, Youngstown OH
California College of Arts & Crafts, Steven Oliver Art Center, Oakland CA
California State University, Chico, Janet Turner Print Gallery & Collection, Chico CA
Calvin College, Center Art Gallery, Grand Rapids MI
Canadian Museum of Contemporary Photography, Ottawa ON
Canadian Museum of Nature, Musee Canadien de la Nature, Ottawa ON
Carnegie Institute, Carnegie Museum of Art, Pittsburgh PA
Carolina Art Association, Gibbes Museum of Art, Charleston SC
Carson County Square House Museum, Panhandle TX
Amon Carter Museum, Fort Worth TX
Cartoon Art Museum, San Francisco CA
Radio-Canada SRC CBC, Galerie Georges Goguen, Moncton NB
Cedar Rapids Museum of Art, Cedar Rapids IA

Museum of Fine Arts, Boston MA
Museum of Modern Art, New York NY
Museum of Movie Art, Calgary AB
Museum of the Americas, Brookfield VT
The Museums at Stony Brook, Stony Brook NY
Museums of Abilene, Inc, Abilene TX
Nassau Community College, Firehouse Art Gallery, Garden City NY
National Air and Space Museum, Washington DC
National Museum of Racing, National Museum of Racing & Hall of Fame, Saratoga Springs NY
National Museum of Wildlife Art, Jackson WY
National Portrait Gallery, Washington DC
Naval Historical Center, The Navy Museum, Washington DC
Nebraska Wesleyan University, Elder Gallery, Lincoln NE
Nelson-Atkins Museum of Art, Kansas City MO
Nevada Museum Of Art, Reno NV
Neville Public Museum, Green Bay WI
New Mexico State University, University Art Gallery, Las Cruces NM
New Orleans School of GlassWorks, Gallery & Printmaking Studio, New Orleans LA
Newport Art Museum, Newport RI
New Visions Gallery, Inc, Marshfield WI
New York University, Grey Art Gallery & Study Center, New York NY
Niagara University, Castellani Art Museum, Niagara NY
The John A Noble Collection, Staten Island NY
North Central Washington Museum, Gallery, Wenatchee WA
Northern Kentucky University Gallery, Highland Heights KY
Noyes Museum, Oceanville NJ
Oakland Museum of California, Art Dept, Oakland CA
Ohio University, Kennedy Museum of American Art, Athens OH
Okefenokee Heritage Center, Inc, Waycross GA
Oklahoma Center for Science & Art, Kirkpatrick Center, Oklahoma City OK
Oklahoma City Art Museum, Oklahoma City OK
Old Dartmouth Historical Society, New Bedford Whaling Museum, New Bedford MA
Old Jail Art Center, Albany TX
Olivet College, Armstrong Museum of Art & Archaeology, Olivet MI
One West Art Center, Fort Collins CO
Order Sons of Italy in America, Garibaldi & Meucci Museum, Staten Island NY
Owensboro Museum of Fine Art, Owensboro KY
Pacific - Asia Museum, Pasadena CA
Palm Springs Desert Museum, Palm Springs CA
Paris Gibson Square, Museum of Art, Great Falls MT
Passaic County Historical Society, Paterson NJ
Pennsylvania Academy of the Fine Arts, Museum of American Art, Philadelphia PA
Pennsylvania Historical & Museum Commission, Railroad Museum of Pennsylvania, Harrisburg PA
Pennsylvania State University, Palmer Museum of Art, University Park PA
Pensacola Museum of Art, Pensacola FL
Philbrook Museum of Art, Tulsa OK
Phillips Academy, Addison Gallery of American Art, Andover MA
Phoenix Art Museum, Phoenix AZ
Plains Art Museum, Fargo ND
Polk Museum of Art, Lakeland FL
Port Authority of New York & New Jersey, Art Collection, New York NY
Portland Art Museum, Portland OR
Portland Museum of Art, Portland ME
Portsmouth Museums, Art Center, Portsmouth VA
Potsdam College of the State University of New York, Roland Gibson Gallery, Potsdam NY
Provincetown Art Association & Museum, Provincetown MA
Putnam Museum of History & Natural Science, Davenport IA
Queensborough Community College, Art Gallery, Bayside NY
Queen's Medical Center Auxiliary, Queen Emma Gallery, Honolulu HI

Queen's University, Agnes Etherington Art Centre, Kingston ON
Quincy University, The Gray Gallery, Quincy IL
Rahr-West Art Museum, Manitowoc WI
Rapid City Arts Council, Dahl Fine Arts Center, Rapid City SD
Reed College, Douglas F Cooley Memorial Art Gallery, Portland OR
Rensselaer County Historical Society, Hart-Cluett Mansion, 1827, Troy NY
Reynolda House Museum of American Art, Winston-Salem NC
Rhode Island School of Design, Museum of Art, Providence RI
Rice University, Art Gallery, Houston TX
Roberson Museum & Science Center, Binghamton NY
The Rockwell Museum, Corning NY
Lauren Rogers Museum of Art, Laurel MS
Rogue Community College, Wiseman Gallery - Firehouse Gallery, Grants Pass OR
The Rosenbach Museum & Library, Philadelphia PA
Roswell Museum & Art Center, Roswell NM
C M Russell Museum, Great Falls MT
Rutgers University, Stedman Art Gallery, Camden NJ
Robert W Ryerss Library & Museum, Philadelphia PA
Saint Anselm College, Chapel Art Center, Manchester NH
Saint Clair County Community College, Jack R Hennesey Art Galleries, Port Huron MI
Saint Gregory's Abbey & College, Mabee-Gerrer Museum of Art, Shawnee OK
St Lawrence University, Richard F Brush Art Gallery, Canton NY
Saint Louis Artists' Guild, Saint Louis MO
The Saint Louis Art Museum, Saint Louis MO
Saint Mary's College, Moreau Galleries, Notre Dame IN
Salisbury State University, University Gallery, Salisbury MD
San Diego Museum of Art, San Diego CA
San Diego State University, University Gallery, San Diego CA
San Jose Museum of Art, San Jose CA
Santa Barbara Museum of Art, Santa Barbara CA
School of Visual Arts, Visual Arts Museum, New York NY
Scottsdale Center for the Arts, Scottsdale AZ
The Seagram Museum, Waterloo ON
Seattle Art Museum, Seattle WA
1708 Gallery, Richmond VA
Ella Sharp Museum, Jackson MI
Silvermine Guild Arts Center, Silvermine Galleries, New Canaan CT
Sioux City Art Center, Sioux City IA
Skidmore College, Schick Art Gallery, Saratoga Springs NY
Smith College, Museum of Art, Northampton MA
Sonoma State University, Art Gallery, Rohnert Park CA
Southeastern Center for Contemporary Art, Winston-Salem NC
Southern Alleghenies Museum of Art, Loretto PA
Southern Alleghenies Museum of Art, Southern Alleghenies Museum of Art at Johnstown, Loretto PA
Southern Arkansas University, Art Dept Gallery & Magale Art Gallery, Magnolia AR
Southern Oregon State College, Schneider Museum of Art, Ashland OR
South Street Seaport Museum, New York NY
Spark Gallery, Denver CO
Spartanburg County Museum of Art, Spartanburg SC
Springfield Art Museum, Springfield MO
Stamford Museum & Nature Center, Stamford CT
Nelda C & H J Lutcher Stark Foundation, Stark Museum of Art, Orange TX
State Art Museum of Florida, John & Mable Ringling Museum of Art, Sarasota FL
State Historical Society of Missouri, Columbia MO
State Historical Society of Wisconsin, State Historical Museum, Madison WI
Staten Island Institute of Arts & Sciences, Staten Island NY

State University of New York at New Paltz, College Art Gallery, New Paltz NY
State University of New York at Oswego, Tyler Art Gallery, Oswego NY
State University of New York at Purchase, Neuberger Museum of Art, Purchase NY
State University of New York College at Fredonia, M C Rockefeller Arts Center Gallery, Fredonia NY
Stetson University, Duncan Gallery of Art, De Land FL
Stratford Historical Society, Katherine Mitchel Museum, Stratford CT
Swedish American Museum Association of Chicago, Chicago IL
Tacoma Art Museum, Tacoma WA
Tampa Museum of Art, Tampa FL
Toledo Museum of Art, Toledo OH
Topeka & Shawnee County Public Library, Gallery of Fine Arts, Topeka KS
Towson State University, The Holtzman Art Gallery, Towson MD
Tryon Palace Historic Sites & Gardens, New Bern NC
Tufts University, Art Gallery, Medford MA
Tulane University, University Art Collection, New Orleans LA
Twin City Art Foundation, Masur Museum of Art, Monroe LA
Ulster County Community College, Muroff-Kotler Visual Arts Gallery, Stone Ridge NY
United States Capitol, Architect of the Capitol, Washington DC
United States Figure Skating Association, World Figure Skating Museum & Hall of Fame, Colorado Springs CO
United States Naval Academy Museum, Annapolis MD
University at Albany, State University of New York, University Art Museum, Albany NY
University of Alabama at Birmingham, Visual Arts Gallery, Birmingham AL
University of Alabama at Huntsville, Gallery of Art, Huntsville AL
University of Calgary, The Nickle Arts Museum, Calgary AB
University of California, Richard L Nelson Gallery & Fine Arts Collection, Davis CA
University of California, Berkeley Art Museum & Pacific Film Archive, Berkeley CA
University of Chicago, David & Alfred Smart Museum of Art, Chicago IL
University of Cincinnati, DAAP Galleries-College of Design Architecture, Art & Planning, Cincinnati OH
University of Colorado, Art Galleries, Boulder CO
University of Colorado at Colorado Springs, Gallery of Contemporary Art, Colorado Springs CO
University of Delaware, University Gallery, Newark DE
University of Findlay, Egner Fine Arts Center, Findlay OH
University of Florida, University Gallery, Gainesville FL
University of Florida, Samuel P Harn Museum of Art, Gainesville FL
University of Illinois, Krannert Art Museum, Champaign IL
University of Iowa, Museum of Art, Iowa City IA
University of Kansas, Spencer Museum of Art, Lawrence KS
University of Louisville, Allen R Hite Art Institute Gallery, Louisville KY
University of Manitoba, Faculty of Architecture Exhibition Centre, Winnipeg MB
University of Maryland, College Park, Art Gallery, College Park MD
University of Massachusetts, Amherst, University Gallery, Amherst MA
University of Memphis, Art Museum, Memphis TN
University of Minnesota, Weisman Art Museum, Minneapolis MN
University of Minnesota, Duluth, Tweed Museum of Art, Duluth MN
University of Missouri, Museum of Art & Archaeology, Columbia MO
University of Nebraska at Omaha, Art Gallery, Omaha NE

RELIGIOUS ART

University of Wisconsin-Madison, Elvehjem Museum of Art, Madison WI
Ursinus College, Philip & Muriel Berman Museum of Art, Collegeville PA
Valparaiso University, Brauer Museum of Art, Valparaiso IN
Waterworks Visual Arts Center, Salisbury NC
Wheelwright Museum of the American Indian, Santa Fe NM
Williams College, Museum of Art, Williamstown MA
Winston-Salem State University, Diggs Gallery, Winston Salem NC
Yeshiva University Museum, New York NY

RENAISSANCE ART

Agecroft Association, Museum, Richmond VA
Charles Allis Art Museum, Milwaukee WI
Art Gallery of Nova Scotia, Halifax NS
Ball State University, Museum of Art, Muncie IN
Baltimore Museum of Art, Baltimore MD
Berea College, Doris Ulmann Galleries, Berea KY
Brigham Young University, Museum of Art, Provo UT
Cincinnati Museum Association, Cincinnati Art Museum, Cincinnati OH
College of William & Mary, Joseph & Margaret Muscarelle Museum of Art, Williamsburg VA
Columbia Museum of Art, Columbia SC
Columbia Museum of Art, Columbia Art Association, Columbia SC
Columbus Museum of Art, Columbus OH
Denver Art Museum, Denver CO
Dickinson College, Trout Gallery, Carlisle PA
East Los Angeles College, Vincent Price Gallery, Monterey Park CA
Ellen Noel Art Museum of the Permian Basin, Odessa TX
El Paso Museum of Art, El Paso TX
Fairfield University, Thomas J Walsh Art Gallery, Fairfield CT
Flint Institute of Arts, Flint MI
Frick Collection, New York NY
Guadalupe Historic Foundation, Santuario de Guadalupe, Santa Fe NM
Guilford College, Art Gallery, Greensboro NC
Hartwick College, Foreman Gallery, Oneonta NY
Harvard University, Busch-Reisinger Museum, Cambridge MA
Gertrude Herbert Institute of Art, Augusta GA
Honolulu Academy of Arts, Honolulu HI
Howard University, Gallery of Art, Washington DC
Indianapolis Museum of Art, Clowes Fund Collection, Indianapolis IN
Joslyn Art Museum, Omaha NE
Memphis Brooks Museum of Art, Memphis TN
Michigan State University, Kresge Art Museum, East Lansing MI
Montclair State University, Art Galleries, Upper Montclair NJ
Nassau County Museum of Fine Art, Roslyn Harbor NY
New Orleans Museum of Art, New Orleans LA
The Parrish Art Museum, Southampton NY
Phoenix Art Museum, Phoenix AZ
Portland Art Museum, Portland OR
Rhode Island School of Design, Museum of Art, Providence RI
Royal Arts Foundation, Belcourt Castle, Newport RI
San Diego Museum of Art, San Diego CA
Santa Barbara Museum of Art, Santa Barbara CA
Society of the Cincinnati, Museum & Library at Anderson House, Washington DC
Stanford University, Museum of Art, Stanford CA
University of Arizona, Museum of Art, Tucson AZ
University of California, Santa Barbara, University Art Museum, Santa Barbara CA
University of Illinois, World Heritage Museum, Champaign IL
University of Kansas, Spencer Museum of Art, Lawrence KS
University of Rochester, Memorial Art Gallery, Rochester NY
University of Texas at Austin, Archer M Huntington Art Gallery, Austin TX

University of Utah, Utah Museum of Fine Arts, Salt Lake City UT
University of Victoria, Maltwood Art Museum and Gallery, Victoria BC
University of Wisconsin-Madison, Elvehjem Museum of Art, Madison WI
Vanderbilt University, Fine Arts Gallery, Nashville TN
Virginia Museum of Fine Arts, Richmond VA
Vizcaya Museum & Gardens, Miami FL
Williams College, Museum of Art, Williamstown MA
Woodmere Art Museum, Philadelphia PA

REPRODUCTIONS

American Kennel Club, Museum of the Dog, Saint Louis MO
Appaloosa Museum, Inc, Moscow ID
Art Gallery of Nova Scotia, Halifax NS
Leo Baeck Institute, New York NY
Canadian Museum of Contemporary Photography, Ottawa ON
Cartoon Art Museum, San Francisco CA
Central United Methodist Church, Swords Info Plowshares Peace Center & Gallery, Detroit MI
Cincinnati Institute of Fine Arts, Taft Museum, Cincinnati OH
City of Cedar Falls, Iowa, James & Meryl Hearst Center for the Arts, Cedar Falls IA
Clark County Historical Society, Pioneer - Krier Museum, Ashland KS
Detroit Repertory Theatre Gallery, Detroit MI
Douglas County Historical Society, Fairlawn Mansion & Museum, Superior WI
Dundurn Castle, Hamilton ON
Fitton Center For Creative Arts, Hamilton OH
General Board of Discipleship, The United Methodist Church, The Upper Room Chapel & Museum, Nashville TN
Great Lakes Historical Society, Island Seas Maritime Museum, Vermilion OH
Historical Society of Pennsylvania, Philadelphia PA
House of Roses, Senator Wilson Home, Deadwood SD
Lewistown Art Center, Lewistown MT
Mexican Museum, San Francisco CA
Museum of Movie Art, Calgary AB
New York State Office of Parks Recreation & Historic Preservation, John Jay Homestead State Historic Site, Katonah NY
C M Russell Museum, Great Falls MT
The Sandwich Historical Society, Inc, Sandwich Glass Museum, Sandwich MA
Seneca-Iroquois National Museum, Salamanca NY
Abigail Adams Smith Museum, New York NY
Tallahassee Museum of History & Natural Science, Tallahassee FL
The Temple-Tifereth Israel, The Temple Museum of Religious Art, Beachwood OH
University of Manitoba, Faculty of Architecture Exhibition Centre, Winnipeg MB
University of Texas at Austin, Archer M Huntington Art Gallery, Austin TX
Wells Fargo Bank, Wells Fargo History Museum, San Francisco CA
Western Kentucky University, Kentucky Museum, Bowling Green KY

RESTORATIONS

Agecroft Association, Museum, Richmond VA
Association for the Preservation of Virginia Antiquities, John Marshall House, Richmond VA
Brookgreen Gardens, Murrells Inlet SC
Center for Puppetry Arts, Atlanta GA
Cincinnati Institute of Fine Arts, Taft Museum, Cincinnati OH
City of San Rafael, Falkirk Cultural Center, San Rafael CA
Craigdarroch Castle Historical Museum Society, Victoria BC
Denver Art Museum, Denver CO
Douglas County Historical Society, Fairlawn Mansion & Museum, Superior WI
Dundurn Castle, Hamilton ON
Gunston Hall Plantation, Mason Neck VA

Heard Museum, Phoenix AZ
Historic Landmarks Foundation of Indiana, Morris-Butler House, Indianapolis IN
House of Roses, Senator Wilson Home, Deadwood SD
Huguenot Historical Society of New Paltz Galleries, New Paltz NY
Illinois Historic Preservation Agency, Bishop Hill State Historic Site, Bishop Hill IL
Institute of the Great Plains, Museum of the Great Plains, Lawton OK
International Museum of Cartoon Art, Montreal PQ
Johns Hopkins University, Homewood House Museum, Baltimore MD
Lafayette Natural History Museum, Planetarium & Nature Station, Lafayette LA
Landmark Society of Western New York, Inc, Rochester NY
Lockwood-Mathews Mansion Museum, Norwalk CT
Mission San Luis Rey de Francia, Mission San Luis Rey Museum, San Luis Rey CA
Mohave Museum of History & Arts, Kingman AZ
The National Park Service, United States Department of the Interior, The Statue of Liberty National Monument, New York NY
Nebraska State Capitol, Lincoln NE
Nelson-Atkins Museum of Art, Kansas City MO
New York State Office of Parks Recreation & Historic Preservation, John Jay Homestead State Historic Site, Katonah NY
The Ohio Historical Society, Inc, Campus Martius Museum & Ohio River Museum, Marietta OH
Old Dartmouth Historical Society, New Bedford Whaling Museum, New Bedford MA
Page-Walker Arts & History Center, Cary NC
Pennsylvania Historical & Museum Commission, Railroad Musuem of Pennsylvania, Harrisburg PA
Port Authority of New York & New Jersey, Art Collection, New York NY
Queens Historical Society, Flushing NY
Red Deer & District Museum & Archives, Red Deer AB
Ringwood Manor House Museum, Ringwood NJ
Santarella, Tyringham's Gingerbread House, Tyringham MA
The Seagram Museum, Waterloo ON
Abigail Adams Smith Museum, New York NY
Springfield Art & Historical Society, Miller Art Center, Springfield VT
Nelda C & H J Lutcher Stark Foundation, Stark Museum of Art, Orange TX
United States Capitol, Architect of the Capitol, Washington DC
Vermilion County Museum Society, Danville IL
West Baton Rouge Historical Association, Museum, Port Allen LA
Wilfrid Laurier University, Robert Langen Gallery, Waterloo ON
Willard House & Clock Museum, Inc, North Grafton MA
Woodlawn Plantation, Mount Vernon VA

SCRIMSHAW

Alaska Department of Education, Division of Libraries, Archives & Museums, Sheldon Jackson Museum, Sitka AK
The Bostonian Society, Old State House Museum, Boston MA
Chilkat Valley Historical Society, Sheldon Museum & Cultural Center, Haines AK
Community Fine Arts Center, Halseth Gallery, Rock Springs WY
Dartmouth Heritage Museum, Dartmouth NS
Dawson City Museum & Historical Society, Dawson City YT
Denver Art Museum, Denver CO
Eiteljorg Museum of American Indians & Western Art, Indianapolis IN
Enook Galleries, Waterloo ON
Gallery One, Ellensburg WA
Heritage Plantation of Sandwich, Sandwich MA
Independence Seaport Museum, Philadelphia PA
Institute of American Indian Arts Museum, Santa Fe NM
Kendall Whaling Museum, Sharon MA

SCULPTURE

Hartwick College, Foreman Gallery, Oneonta NY
Harvard University, Dumbarton Oaks Research Library & Collections, Washington DC
Harvard University, William Hayes Fogg Art Museum, Cambridge MA
Harvard University, Arthur M Sackler Museum, Cambridge MA
Headquarters Fort Monroe, Dept of Army, Casemate Museum, Fort Monroe VA
Heard Museum, Phoenix AZ
Hebrew Union College-Jewish Institute of Religion, New York NY
Henry Gallery Association, Henry Art Gallery, Seattle WA
Gertrude Herbert Institute of Art, Augusta GA
Heritage Center of Lancaster County Museum, Lancaster PA
Hirshhorn Museum & Sculpture Garden, Washington DC
Hispanic Society of America, Museum, New York NY
Historic Landmarks Foundation of Indiana, Morris-Butler House, Indianapolis IN
Housatonic Community-Technical College, Housatonic Museum of Art, Bridgeport CT
House of Roses, Senator Wilson Home, Deadwood SD
Howard University, Gallery of Art, Washington DC
The Hudson River Museum of Westchester, Yonkers NY
Hunter Museum of American Art, Chattanooga TN
Huntsville Museum of Art, Huntsville AL
Hyde Collection Trust, Glens Falls NY
Hyde Park Art Center, Chicago IL
Illinois State Museum, Illinois Art Gallery & Lockport Gallery, Springfield IL
Illinois State Museum, Illinois Art Gallery, Chicago IL
Institute for Contemporary Art, Project Studio One (P S 1), Long Island City NY
Institute of American Indian Arts Museum, Santa Fe NM
Intar Latin American Gallery, New York NY
Iowa State Education Association, Salisbury House, Des Moines IA
Irving Arts Center, Main Gallery & New Talent Gallery, Irving TX
Jacksonville University, Alexander Brest Museum & Gallery, Jacksonville FL
Japan Society, Inc, Japan Society Gallery, New York NY
Joslyn Art Museum, Omaha NE
Kalamazoo Institute of Arts, Kalamazoo MI
Kamloops Art Gallery, Kamloops BC
Kansas City Art Institute, Kemper Museum of Contemporary Art & Design, Kansas City MO
Kent State University, School of Art Gallery, Kent OH
Kimbell Art Foundation, Kimbell Art Museum, Fort Worth TX
Knights of Columbus Supreme Council, Headquarters Museum, New Haven CT
Lafayette Natural History Museum, Planetarium & Nature Station, Lafayette LA
Laumeier Sculpture Park & Museum, Saint Louis MO
Leanin' Tree Museum of Western Art, Boulder CO
Lehigh University Art Galleries, Bethlehem PA
Lewistown Art Center, Lewistown MT
Lighthouse Gallery & School of Art, Tequesta FL
Lightner Museum, Saint Augustine FL
Long Beach Museum of Art, Long Beach CA
Longview Art Museum, Longview TX
Los Angeles County Museum of Art, Los Angeles CA
Louisa May Alcott Memorial Association, Orchard House, Concord MA
Louisiana Arts & Science Center, Baton Rouge LA
Loveland Museum Gallery, Loveland CO
Loyola University of Chicago, Martin D'Arcy Gallery of Art, Chicago IL
L'Universite Laval, Ecole des Arts Visuels, Quebec PQ
Luther College, Fine Arts Collection, Decorah IA
The Robert McLaughlin Gallery, Oshawa ON
Marion Koogler McNay Art Museum, San Antonio TX
Charles H MacNider Museum, Mason City IA

Maison Saint-Gabriel Museum, Montreal PQ
Maitland Art Center, Maitland FL
Manhattan Psychiatric Center, Sculpture Garden, New York NY
Maricopa County Historical Society, Desert Caballeros Western Museum, Wickenburg AZ
Marietta College, Grover M Hermann Fine Arts Center, Marietta OH
The Mariners' Museum, Newport News VA
Marquette University, Haggerty Museum of Art, Milwaukee WI
Maryland Hall for the Creative Arts, Cardinal Gallery, Annapolis MD
Marylhurst College, The Art Gym, Marylhurst OR
Massachusetts Institute of Technology, List Visual Arts Center, Cambridge MA
Mattatuck Historical Society, Mattatuck Museum, Waterbury CT
Memphis Brooks Museum of Art, Memphis TN
Meridian Museum of Art, Meridian MS
The Metropolitan Museum of Art, New York NY
Mexican Museum, San Francisco CA
Miami-Dade Community College, Kendal Campus, Art Gallery, Miami FL
Miami University, Art Museum, Oxford OH
James A Michener Art Museum, Doylestown PA
Michigan State University, Kresge Art Museum, East Lansing MI
Middlebury College, Museum of Art, Middlebury VT
Midwest Museum of American Art, Elkhart IN
Millikin University, Perkinson Gallery, Decatur IL
Minneapolis Institute of Arts, Minneapolis MN
Minnesota Museum of American Art, Saint Paul MN
Mississippi Valley Conservation Authority, Mill of Kintail Museum, Almonte ON
Arthur Roy Mitchell Memorial Inc, Museum of Western Art, Trinidad CO
Mitchell Museum, Mount Vernon IL
James Monroe Museum, Fredericksburg VA
Moore College of Art & Design, Goldie Paley Gallery, Philadelphia PA
Morris Museum, Morristown NJ
Mount Allison University, Owens Art Gallery, Sackville NB
Mount Holyoke College, Art Museum, South Hadley MA
Munson-Williams-Proctor Institute, Museum of Art, Utica NY
Murray State University, Eagle Gallery, Murray KY
Musee du Quebec, Quebec PQ
Musee Regional de la Cote-Nord, Sept-Iles PQ
Musee Regional de Vaudreuil-Soulanges, Vaudreuil PQ
Museo De Las Americas, Denver CO
The Museum at Drexel University, Philadelphia PA
Museum of Art & History, Santa Cruz CA
Museum of Art, Fort Lauderdale, Fort Lauderdale FL
Museum of Arts & Sciences, Inc, Macon GA
Museum of Contemporary Art, San Diego, La Jolla CA
Museum of Contemporary Art, San Diego-Downtown, San Diego CA
Museum of Contemporary Impressionism, New Milford CT
Museum of Fine Arts, Springfield MA
Museum of Fine Arts, Boston MA
Museum of Fine Arts, Houston, Houston TX
Museum of Modern Art, New York NY
Museum of New Mexico, Museum of Fine Arts, Santa Fe NM
Museum of Western Art, Denver CO
Museum of York County, Rock Hill SC
Nassau Community College, Firehouse Art Gallery, Garden City NY
Nassau County Museum of Fine Art, Roslyn Harbor NY
National Air and Space Museum, Washington DC
National Cowboy Hall of Fame & Western Heritage Center Museum, Oklahoma City OK
National Museum of the American Indian, George Gustav Heye Center, New York NY
National Museum of Wildlife Art, Jackson WY
National Portrait Gallery, Washington DC
National Trust for Historic Preservation, Chesterwood Museum, Glendale MA

Navajo Nation Museum, Window Rock AZ
Naval Historical Center, The Navy Museum, Washington DC
Nebraska State Capitol, Lincoln NE
Nebraska Wesleyan University, Elder Gallery, Lincoln NE
Nevada Museum of Art, Reno NV
Neville Public Museum, Green Bay WI
New Canaan Historical Society, New Canaan CT
New Orleans Museum of Art, New Orleans LA
New Orleans School of GlassWorks, Gallery & Printmaking Studio, New Orleans LA
Newport Art Museum, Newport RI
New York Studio School of Drawing, Painting & Sculpture, Gallery, New York NY
Elisabet Ney Museum, Austin TX
Niagara University, Castellani Art Museum, Niagara NY
Isamu Noguchi Foundation, Isamu Noguchi Garden Museum, Long Island City NY
North Carolina Central University, NCCU Art Museum, Durham NC
North Carolina Museum of Art, Raleigh NC
Northern Kentucky University Gallery, Highland Heights KY
Norton Gallery & School of Art, Inc, Norton Museum of Art, West Palm Beach FL
Noyes Museum, Oceanville NJ
Oakland Museum of California, Art Dept, Oakland CA
Oberlin College, Allen Memorial Art Museum, Oberlin OH
Ogunquit Museum of American Art, Ogunquit ME
Ohio Historical Society, National Afro American Museum & Cultural Center, Wilberforce OH
Ohio University, Kennedy Museum of American Art, Athens OH
Oklahoma City Art Museum, Oklahoma City OK
Old Dartmouth Historical Society, New Bedford Whaling Museum, New Bedford MA
Old Jail Art Center, Albany TX
Olivet College, Armstrong Museum of Art & Archaeology, Olivet MI
One West Art Center, Fort Collins CO
Oshkosh Public Museum, Oshkosh WI
Otis College of Art & Design, Los Angeles CA
Owensboro Museum of Fine Art, Owensboro KY
Pacific - Asia Museum, Pasadena CA
Page-Walker Arts & History Center, Cary NC
Palm Beach Community College Foundation, Museum of Art, Lake Worth FL
Palm Springs Desert Museum, Palm Springs CA
Paris Gibson Square, Museum of Art, Great Falls MT
Pennsylvania Academy of the Fine Arts, Museum of American Art, Philadelphia PA
Pennsylvania State University, Palmer Museum of Art, University Park PA
Phelps County Historical Society, Phelps County Museum, Holdrege NE
Philbrook Museum of Art, Tulsa OK
Phillips Academy, Addison Gallery of American Art, Andover MA
George Phippen Memorial Foundation, Phippen Museum of Western Art, Prescott AZ
Phoenix Art Museum, Phoenix AZ
Pioneer Town, Pioneer Museum of Western Art, Wimberley TX
Plains Art Museum, Fargo ND
Ponca City Cultural Center & Museum, Ponca City OK
Port Authority of New York & New Jersey, Art Collection, New York NY
Portland Art Museum, Portland OR
Portland Museum of Art, Portland ME
Potsdam College of the State University of New York, Roland Gibson Gallery, Potsdam NY
Prince George Art Gallery, Prince George BC
Provincetown Art Association & Museum, Provincetown MA
Queen's Medical Center Auxiliary, Queen Emma Gallery, Honolulu HI
Queen's University, Agnes Etherington Art Centre, Kingston ON
Redding Museum of Art & History, Redding CA
Red River Valley Museum, Vernon TX
Frederic Remington Art Museum, Ogdensburg NY

York Institute Museum, Saco ME
York University, Art Gallery of York University, North York ON
Zigler Museum, Jennings LA

SILVER

Agecroft Association, Museum, Richmond VA
Lyman Allyn Art Museum, New London CT
American Kennel Club, Museum of the Dog, Saint Louis MO
Leo Baeck Institute, New York NY
Baltimore Museum of Art, Baltimore MD
The Bartlett Museum, Amesbury MA
Battleship North Carolina, Wilmington NC
Birmingham Museum of Art, Birmingham AL
Bowdoin College, Museum of Art, Brunswick ME
Cape Ann Historical Museum, Gloucester MA
Cincinnati Institute of Fine Arts, Taft Museum, Cincinnati OH
The City of Petersburg Museums, Petersburg VA
Sterling & Francine Clark Art Institute, Williamstown MA
College of William & Mary, Joseph & Margaret Muscarelle Museum of Art, Williamsburg VA
Colorado Historical Society, Colorado History Museum, Denver CO
Cranbrook Art Museum, Bloomfield Hills MI
The Currier Gallery of Art, Manchester NH
DAR Museum, National Society Daughters of the American Revolution, Washington DC
Dartmouth Heritage Museum, Dartmouth NS
Dundurn Castle, Hamilton ON
Ellen Noel Art Museum of the Permian Basin, Odessa TX
Ephraim McDowell-Cambus-Kenneth Foundation, McDowell House & Apothecary Shop, Danville KY
Erie Art Museum, Erie PA
Evanston Historical Society, Charles Gates Dawes House, Evanston IL
Fetherston Foundation, Packwood House Museum, Lewisburg PA
Fitton Center for Creative Arts, Hamilton OH
The Frick Art & Historical Center, Frick Art Museum, Pittsburgh PA
Fuller Museum of Art, Brockton MA
Gallery One, Ellensburg WA
Girard College, Stephen Girard Collection, Philadelphia PA
Gunston Hall Plantation, Mason Neck VA
Hammond-Harwood House Association, Inc, Annapolis MD
Harvard University, William Hayes Fogg Art Museum, Cambridge MA
Heard Museum, Phoenix AZ
Heritage Center of Lancaster County Museum, Lancaster PA
Hill-Stead Museum, Farmington CT
Historical & Cultural Affairs, Delaware State Museums, Dover DE
Historical Society of Cheshire County, Archive Center of the Society, Keene NH
Historic Cherry Hill, Albany NY
Historic Deerfield, Inc, Deerfield MA
Historic Landmarks Foundation of Indiana, Morris-Butler House, Indianapolis IN
House of Roses, Senator Wilson Home, Deadwood SD
Institute of American Indian Arts Museum, Santa Fe NM
Johns Hopkins University, Homewood House Museum, Baltimore MD
Kelowna Museum, Kelowna BC
Kings County Historical Society and Museum, Hampton NB
Leroy Historical Society, LeRoy NY
Lewistown Art Center, Lewistown MT
Livingston County Historical Society, Cobblestone Museum, Geneseo NY
Los Angeles County Museum of Natural History, William S Hart Museum, Newhall CA
Louisa May Alcott Memorial Association, Orchard House, Concord MA
Louisiana State University, Museum of Arts, Baton Rouge LA
Loyola University of Chicago, Martin D'Arcy Gallery of Art, Chicago IL

Maryland Historical Society, Museum of Maryland History, Baltimore MD
Mattatuck Historical Society, Mattatuck Museum, Waterbury CT
Mitchell Museum, Mount Vernon IL
James Monroe Museum, Fredericksburg VA
Montclair Art Museum, Montclair NJ
Munson-Williams-Proctor Institute, Museum of Art, Utica NY
Musee d'Art de Saint-Laurent, Saint-Laurent PQ
Museo De Las Americas, Denver CO
Museum of Arts & History, Port Huron MI
Museum of Fine Arts, Boston MA
Museum of Mobile, Mobile AL
Museum of Northern Arizona, Flagstaff AZ
National Society of Colonial Dames of America in the State of Maryland, Mount Clare Mansion, Baltimore MD
National Society of the Colonial Dames, Wilton House Museum, Richmond VA
Navajo Nation Museum, Window Rock AZ
Naval Historical Center, The Navy Museum, Washington DC
Newark Museum Association, The Newark Museum, Newark NJ
New York State Office of Parks Recreation & Historic Preservation, John Jay Homestead State Historic Site, Katonah NY
The Ohio Historical Society, Inc, Campus Martius Museum & Ohio River Museum, Marietta OH
Old Colony Historical Society, Museum, Taunton MA
Phoenix Art Museum, Phoenix AZ
Plumas County Museum, Quincy CA
Portland Art Museum, Portland OR
Putnam Museum of History & Natural Science, Davenport IA
Walter Cecil Rawls Museum, Courtland VA
Frederic Remington Art Museum, Ogdensburg NY
Rensselaer County Historical Society, Hart-Cluett Mansion, 1827, Troy NY
Rhode Island Historical Society, John Brown House, Providence RI
Lauren Rogers Museum of Art, Laurel MS
Millicent Rogers Museum of Northern New Mexico, Taos NM
The Rosenbach Museum & Library, Philadelphia PA
Royal Arts Foundation, Belcourt Castle, Newport RI
R W Norton Art Gallery, Shreveport LA
Saint Louis Artists' Guild, Saint Louis MO
San Antonio Museum of Art, San Antonio TX
San Diego Museum of Art, San Diego CA
Santa Clara University, de Saisset Museum, Santa Clara CA
The Seagram Museum, Waterloo ON
Seneca-Iroquois National Museum, Salamanca NY
Shirley Plantation, Charles City VA
Abigail Adams Smith Museum, New York NY
Spertus Institute of Jewish Studies, Spertus Museum, Chicago IL
Springfield Art Museum, Springfield MO
State Historical Society of Wisconsin, State Historical Museum, Madison WI
State University of New York at New Paltz, College Art Gallery, New Paltz NY
Stratford Historical Society, Katherine Mitchel Museum, Stratford CT
Summit County Historical Society, Akron OH
Temple Beth Israel, Sylvia Plotkin Judaica, Phoenix AZ
The Temple-Tifereth Israel, The Temple Museum of Religious Art, Beachwood OH
Mark Twain Memorial, Hartford CT
US Department of State, Diplomatic Reception Rooms, Washington DC
United States Naval Academy Museum, Annapolis MD
University of Alabama at Birmingham, Visual Arts Gallery, Birmingham AL
University of Iowa, Museum of Art, Iowa City IA
University of Kansas, Spencer Museum of Art, Lawrence KS
University of Mississippi, University Museums, Oxford MS
University of South Carolina, McKissick Museum, Columbia SC

University of Tennessee, Eleanor Dean Audigier Art Collection, Knoxville TN
University of Utah, Utah Museum of Fine Arts, Salt Lake City UT
Valentine Museum, Richmond VA
Virginia Museum of Fine Arts, Richmond VA
Westmoreland Museum of American Art, Greensburg PA
Wheelwright Museum of the American Indian, Santa Fe NM
Willard House & Clock Museum, Inc, North Grafton MA
Witte Museum, San Antonio TX
Woodlawn Plantation, Mount Vernon VA
Yale University, Art Gallery, New Haven CT
York Institute Museum, Saco ME

SOUTHWESTERN ART

Albuquerque Museum of Art & History, Albuquerque NM
Artesia Historical Museum & Art Center, Artesia NM
Aurora University, Schingoethe Center for Native American Cultures, Aurora IL
Barnes Foundation, Merion PA
Bradford Brinton Memorial Museum & Historic Ranch, Big Horn WY
California State University, Hayward, C E Smith Museum of Anthropology, Hayward CA
Kit Carson Historic Museums, Ernest Blumenschein Home & Studio, Taos NM
Church of Jesus Christ of Latter-Day Saints, Museum of Church History & Art, Salt Lake City UT
Colorado Historical Society, Colorado History Museum, Denver CO
Colorado Springs Fine Arts Center, Colorado Springs CO
Craft & Folk Art Museum, Los Angeles CA
Custer County Art Center, Miles City MT
Dickinson College, Trout Gallery, Carlisle PA
Douglas Art Association, Little Gallery, Douglas AZ
Eiteljorg Museum of American Indians & Western Art, Indianapolis IN
Ellen Noel Art Museum of the Permian Basin, Odessa TX
El Paso Museum of Art, El Paso TX
Enook Galleries, Waterloo ON
Erie Art Museum, Erie PA
Galeria Mesa, Mesa Arts Center, Mesa AZ
Genesee Country Museum, John L Wehle Gallery of Sporting Art, Mumford NY
Greater Lafayette Museum of Art, Lafayette IN
Heard Museum, Phoenix AZ
Heritage Center, Inc, Pine Ridge SD
Institute of American Indian Arts Museum, Santa Fe NM
Institute of the Great Plains, Museum of the Great Plains, Lawton OK
Intar Latin American Gallery, New York NY
Jefferson County Open Space, Hiwan Homestead Museum, Evergreen CO
Joslyn Art Museum, Omaha NE
Luther College, Fine Arts Collection, Decorah IA
Maricopa County Historical Society, Desert Caballeros Western Museum, Wickenburg AZ
Metropolitan State College of Denver, Center for the Visual Arts, Denver CO
Mexican Museum, San Francisco CA
Midwest Museum of American Art, Elkhart IN
Mills College, Art Gallery, Oakland CA
Mission San Luis Rey de Francia, Mission San Luis Rey Museum, San Luis Rey CA
Arthur Roy Mitchell Memorial Inc, Museum of Western Art, Trinidad CO
Museo De Las Americas, Denver CO
Museum of Fine Arts, Saint Petersburg, Florida, Inc, Saint Petersburg FL
Museum of Northern Arizona, Flagstaff AZ
National Cowboy Hall of Fame & Western Heritage Center Museum, Oklahoma City OK
Newark Museum Association, The Newark Museum, Newark NJ
New Mexico State University, University Art Gallery, Las Cruces NM

No Man's Land Historical Society Museum,
Goodwell OK
Northern Arizona University, Art Museum &
Galleries, Flagstaff AZ
Ohio University, Kennedy Museum of American
Art, Athens OH
Palm Springs Desert Museum, Palm Springs CA
George Phippen Memorial Foundation, Phippen
Museum of Western Art, Prescott AZ
Red Rock State Park, Red Rock Museum, Church
Rock NM
Riverside Municipal Museum, Riverside CA
Millicent Rogers Museum of Northern New
Mexico, Taos NM
Roswell Museum & Art Center, Roswell NM
Royal Ontario Museum, Toronto ON
C M Russell Museum, Great Falls MT
South Dakota State University, South Dakota Art
Museum, Brookings SD
Springfield Art Museum, Springfield MO
Nelda C & H J Lutcher Stark Foundation, Stark
Museum of Art, Orange TX
Texas A&M University, J Wayne Stark University
Center Galleries, College Station TX
Towson State University, Asian Arts Center,
Towson MD
University of Colorado at Colorado Springs, Gallery
of Contemporary Art, Colorado Springs CO
University of New Mexico, The Harwood
Foundation, Taos NM
University of Texas at Austin, Archer M
Huntington Art Gallery, Austin TX
Washburn University, Mulvane Art Museum,
Topeka KS
Wichita Art Museum, Wichita KS
Yuma Fine Arts Association, Art Center, Yuma AZ

STAINED GLASS

Agecroft Association, Museum, Richmond VA
Albany Institute of History & Art, Albany NY
Algonquin Arts Council, Art Gallery of Bancroft,
Bancroft ON
Asbury College, Student Center Gallery, Wilmore
KY
Chattahoochee Valley Art Museum, LaGrange GA
Chicago Department of Cultural Affairs, Chicago
Cultural Center, Chicago IL
Church of Jesus Christ of Latter-Day Saints,
Museum of Church History & Art, Salt Lake
City UT
City of Atlanta, Chastain Arts Center, Atlanta GA
The City of Petersburg Museums, Petersburg VA
Corcoran Gallery of Art, Washington DC
Craigdarroch Castle Historical Museum Society,
Victoria BC
Custer County Art Center, Miles City MT
DeWitt Historical Society of Tompkins County,
Ithaca NY
Dundurn Castle, Hamilton ON
Evanston Historical Society, Charles Gates Dawes
House, Evanston IL
Gallery One, Ellensburg WA
General Board of Discipleship, The United
Methodist Church, The Upper Room Chapel &
Museum, Nashville TN
Headquarters Fort Monroe, Dept of Army,
Casemate Museum, Fort Monroe VA
Higgins Armory Museum, Worcester MA
Jekyll Island Museum, Jekyll Island GA
Johns Hopkins University, Evergreen House,
Baltimore MD
Lewistown Art Center, Lewistown MT
The Mariners' Museum, Newport News VA
National Infantry Museum, Fort Benning GA
National Museum of American Art, Washington
DC
Newark Museum Association, The Newark
Museum, Newark NJ
Owensboro Museum of Fine Art, Owensboro KY
Royal Arts Foundation, Belcourt Castle, Newport
RI
Swedish American Museum Association of Chicago,
Chicago IL
The Temple-Tifereth Israel, The Temple Museum of
Religious Art, Beachwood OH
Tulane University, Dept Art Newcomb Col Art
Galleries, New Orleans LA

Mark Twain Memorial, Hartford CT
United States Capitol, Architect of the Capitol,
Washington DC
University of Pennsylvania, Arthur Ross Gallery,
Philadelphia PA
Workman & Temple Family Homestead Museum,
City of Industry CA

TAPESTRIES

Agecroft Association, Museum, Richmond VA
American Swedish Institute, Minneapolis MN
Barnes Foundation, Merion PA
The Canadian Craft Museum, Vancouver BC
Kit Carson Historic Museums, Ernest Blumenschein
Home & Studio, Taos NM
Chicago Department of Cultural Affairs, Chicago
Cultural Center, Chicago IL
Cincinnati Institute of Fine Arts, Taft Museum,
Cincinnati OH
City of Pittsfield, Berkshire Artisans, Pittsfield MA
The College of Wooster, Art Museum, Wooster OH
Corcoran Gallery of Art, Washington DC
Cranbrook Art Museum, Bloomfield Hills MI
Cummer Museum of Art & Gardens, DeEtte
Holden Cummer Museum Foundation,
Jacksonville FL
Cuneo Foundation, Museum & Gardens, Vernon
Hills IL
The Currier Gallery of Art, Manchester NH
Dundurn Castle, Hamilton ON
Evansville Museum of Arts & Science, Evansville
IN
The Frick Art & Historical Center, Frick Art
Museum, Pittsburgh PA
General Board of Discipleship, The United
Methodist Church, The Upper Room Chapel &
Museum, Nashville TN
Gonzaga University, Jundt Art Museum, Ad Art
Gallery, Spokane WA
Heard Museum, Phoenix AZ
Higgins Armory Museum, Worcester MA
Hyde Collection Trust, Glens Falls NY
Iowa State Education Association, Salisbury House,
Des Moines IA
Lafayette Natural History Museum, Planetarium &
Nature Station, Lafayette LA
Michigan State University, Kresge Art Museum,
East Lansing MI
National Infantry Museum, Fort Benning GA
Nebraska State Capitol, Lincoln NE
Nemours Mansion & Gardens, Wilmington DE
Newark Museum Association, The Newark
Museum, Newark NJ
North Carolina State University, Visual Arts
Center, Raleigh NC
Pacific - Asia Museum, Pasadena CA
Pennsylvania Academy of the Fine Arts, Museum
of American Art, Philadelphia PA
Port Authority of New York & New Jersey, Art
Collection, New York NY
Marjorie Merriweather Post Foundation of DC,
Hillwood Museum, Washington DC
Royal Arts Foundation, Belcourt Castle, Newport
RI
R W Norton Art Gallery, Shreveport LA
Santa Barbara Museum of Art, Santa Barbara CA
Santa Clara University, de Saisset Museum, Santa
Clara CA
Norton Simon Museum, Pasadena CA
Temple Beth Israel, Sylvia Plotkin Judaica, Phoenix
AZ
University of Manitoba, Faculty of Architecture
Exhibition Centre, Winnipeg MB
University of San Diego, Founders' Gallery, San
Diego CA
University of Utah, Utah Museum of Fine Arts, Salt
Lake City UT
Ursinus College, Philip & Muriel Berman Museum
of Art, Collegeville PA
Virginia Museum of Fine Arts, Richmond VA
Vizcaya Museum & Gardens, Miami FL
Wayne Center for the Arts, Wooster OH
Wilfrid Laurier University, Robert Langen Gallery,
Waterloo ON

TEXTILES

Agecroft Association, Museum, Richmond VA
Alabama Department of Archives & History,
Museum Galleries, Montgomery AL
Albany Institute of History & Art, Albany NY
Albuquerque Museum of Art & History,
Albuquerque NM
Algonquin Arts Council, Art Gallery of Bancroft,
Bancroft ON
American Swedish Institute, Minneapolis MN
American Textile History Museum, Lowell MA
Anchorage Museum of History & Art, Anchorage
AK
Artesia Historical Museum & Art Center, Artesia
NM
Asian Art Museum of San Francisco, Avery
Brundage Collection, San Francisco CA
Association for the Preservation of Virginia
Antiquities, John Marshall House, Richmond
VA
Atlanta Historical Society Inc, Atlanta History
Center, Atlanta GA
Aurora University, Schingoethe Center for Native
American Cultures, Aurora IL
Leo Baeck Institute, New York NY
Balzekas Museum of Lithuanian Culture, Chicago
IL
Barnes Foundation, Merion PA
Battleship North Carolina, Wilmington NC
Bay County Historical Society, Historical Museum
of Bay County, Bay City MI
Berea College, Doris Ulmann Galleries, Berea KY
Bowdoin College, Museum of Art, Brunswick ME
Bower's Museum, Santa Ana CA
Brooklyn Historical Society, Brooklyn OH
California College of Arts & Crafts, Steven Oliver
Art Center, Oakland CA
California State University, Hayward, C E Smith
Museum of Anthropology, Hayward CA
Calvin College, Center Art Gallery, Grand Rapids
MI
The Canadian Craft Museum, Vancouver BC
Kit Carson Historic Museums, Ernest Blumenschein
Home & Studio, Taos NM
Kit Carson Historic Museums, Home & Museum,
Taos NM
Kit Carson Historic Museums, Hacienda Martinez,
Taos NM
Cedar Rapids Museum of Art, Cedar Rapids IA
Charleston Museum, Charleston SC
Chattahoochee Valley Art Museum, LaGrange GA
Cherokee National Historical Society, Inc,
Tahlequah OK
Chicago Athenaeum, Museum of Architecture &
Design, Chicago IL
Chicago Department of Cultural Affairs, Chicago
Cultural Center, Chicago IL
Church of Jesus Christ of Latter-Day Saints,
Museum of Church History & Art, Salt Lake
City UT
City of Gainesville, Thomas Center Galleries -
Cultural Affairs, Gainesville FL
City of Pittsfield, Berkshire Artisans, Pittsfield MA
Clark County Historical Society, Pioneer - Krier
Museum, Ashland KS
Cleveland Museum of Art, Cleveland OH
Clinton County Historical Association, Clinton
County Historical Museum, Plattsburgh NY
The College of Wooster, Art Museum, Wooster OH
Colorado Historical Society, Colorado History
Museum, Denver CO
Columbia Museum of Art, Columbia SC
Columbia Museum of Art, Columbia Art
Association, Columbia SC
Columbus Museum, Columbus GA
Craft & Folk Art Museum, Los Angeles CA
Craigdarroch Castle Historical Museum Society,
Victoria BC
Cranbrook Art Museum, Bloomfield Hills MI
The Currier Gallery of Art, Manchester NH
C W Post Campus of Long Island University,
Hillwood Art Museum, Brookville NY
DAR Museum, National Society Daughters of the
American Revolution, Washington DC
Dartmouth Heritage Museum, Dartmouth NS
Davidson College Visual Arts Center, William H
Van Every Jr & Edward M Smith Galleries,
Davidson NC

Dawson County Historical Society, Museum, Lexington NE
Denison University, Art Gallery, Granville OH
Detroit Repertory Theatre Gallery, Detroit MI
DeWitt Historical Society of Tompkins County, Ithaca NY
Douglas County Historical Society, Fairlawn Mansion & Museum, Superior WI
Dundurn Castle, Hamilton ON
Durham Art Guild Inc, Durham NC
Eiteljorg Museum of American Indians & Western Art, Indianapolis IN
Evanston Historical Society, Charles Gates Dawes House, Evanston IL
Evansville Museum of Arts & Science, Evansville IN
Fetherston Foundation, Packwood House Museum, Lewisburg PA
The First National Bank of Chicago, Art Collection, Chicago IL
Fitton Center for Creative Arts, Hamilton OH
Flint Institute of Arts, Flint MI
Florida State University Foundation - Central Florida Community College Foundation, The Appleton Museum of Art, Ocala FL
Fort George G Meade Museum, Fort Meade MD
Freeport Arts Center, Freeport IL
Galeria Mesa, Mesa Arts Center, Mesa AZ
Gaston County Museum of Art & History, Dallas NC
Greater Lafayette Museum of Art, Lafayette IN
Gunston Hall Plantation, Mason Neck VA
Harvard University, Dumbarton Oaks Research Library & Collections, Washington DC
Harvard University, Arthur M Sackler Museum, Cambridge MA
Headley-Whitney Museum, Lexington KY
Headquarters Fort Monroe, Dept of Army, Casemate Museum, Fort Monroe VA
Heard Museum, Phoenix AZ
Hebrew Union College - Jewish Institute of Religion, Skirball Museum-Cincinnati Branch, Cincinnati OH
Henry Gallery Association, Henry Art Gallery, Seattle WA
Hershey Museum, Hershey PA
High Point Historical Society Inc, Museum, High Point NC
Historical Society of Old Newbury, Cushing House Museum, Newburyport MA
Historic Cherry Hill, Albany NY
Historic Deerfield, Inc, Deerfield MA
Historic Landmarks Foundation of Indiana, Morris-Butler House, Indianapolis IN
Historic Northampton Museum, Northampton MA
Honolulu Academy of Arts, Honolulu HI
House of Roses, Senator Wilson Home, Deadwood SD
Houston Baptist University, Museum of American Architecture and Decorative Arts, Houston TX
Hyde Park Art Center, Chicago IL
Idaho Historical Museum, Boise ID
Illinois Historic Preservation Agency, Bishop Hill State Historic Site, Bishop Hill IL
Indianapolis Museum of Art, Indianapolis IN
Institute of American Indian Arts Museum, Santa Fe NM
Japan Society, Inc, Japan Society Gallery, New York NY
Jefferson County Historical Society, Watertown NY
Johns Hopkins University, Homewood House Museum, Baltimore MD
Kansas City Art Institute, Kemper Museum of Contemporary Art & Design, Kansas City MO
Kelowna Museum, Kelowna BC
Kings County Historical Society and Museum, Hampton NB
Knights of Columbus Supreme Council, Headquarters Museum, New Haven CT
Koochiching County Historical Society Museum, International Falls MN
Koshare Indian Museum, Inc, La Junta CO
Kurdish Museum, Brooklyn NY
Leroy Historical Society, LeRoy NY
Lewistown Art Center, Lewistown MT
Lightner Museum, Saint Augustine FL
Livingston County Historical Society, Cobblestone Museum, Geneseo NY

Longfellow-Evangeline State Commemorative Area, Saint Martinville LA
Longue Vue House & Gardens, New Orleans LA
Los Angeles County Museum of Art, Los Angeles CA
Los Angeles County Museum of Natural History, William S Hart Museum, Newhall CA
Louisa May Alcott Memorial Association, Orchard House, Concord MA
Louisiana Arts & Science Center, Baton Rouge LA
Loveland Museum Gallery, Loveland CO
Loyola University of Chicago, Martin D'Arcy Gallery of Art, Chicago IL
McAllen International Museum, McAllen TX
McCord Museum of Canadian History, Montreal PQ
Maricopa County Historical Society, Desert Caballeros Western Museum, Wickenburg AZ
Maryland Historical Society, Museum of Maryland History, Baltimore MD
Memphis Brooks Museum of Art, Memphis TN
Miami University, Art Museum, Oxford OH
Mills College, Art Gallery, Oakland CA
Minnesota Museum of American Art, Saint Paul MN
Mission San Luis Rey de Francia, Mission San Luis Rey Museum, San Luis Rey CA
Monroe County Historical Association, Elizabeth D Walters Library, Stroudsburg PA
Moore College of Art & Design, Goldie Paley Gallery, Philadelphia PA
Morris-Jumel Mansion, Inc, New York NY
Morris Museum of Art, Augusta GA
Murray State University, Eagle Gallery, Murray KY
Musee d'Art de Saint-Laurent, Saint-Laurent PQ
Musee Regional de la Cote-Nord, Sept-Iles PQ
Museo De Las Americas, Denver CO
The Museum at Drexel University, Philadelphia PA
Museum of Arts & History, Port Huron MI
Museum of New Mexico, Museum of International Folk Art, Santa Fe NM
Museum of Northern Arizona, Flagstaff AZ
Museum of Northern British Columbia, Ruth Harvey Art Gallery, Prince Rupert BC
Museum of the American Quilter's Society, Paducah KY
Museum of York County, Rock Hill SC
National Infantry Museum, Fort Benning GA
National Museum of American Art, Washington DC
National Museum of American History, Washington DC
National Museum of the American Indian, George Gustav Heye Center, New York NY
National Society of the Colonial Dames, Wilton House Museum, Richmond VA
Navajo Nation Museum, Window Rock AZ
Nevada Museum of Art, Reno NV
Newark Museum Association, The Newark Museum, Newark NJ
New York State Office of Parks Recreation & Historic Preservation, John Jay Homestead State Historic Site, Katonah NY
No Man's Land Historical Society Museum, Goodwell OK
North Carolina State University, Visual Arts Center, Raleigh NC
The Ohio Historical Society, Inc, Campus Martius Museum & Ohio River Museum, Marietta OH
Ohio University, Kennedy Museum of American Art, Athens OH
Olana State Historic Site, Hudson NY
Old Colony Historical Society, Museum, Taunton MA
Old Slater Mill Association, Slater Mill Historic Site, Pawtucket RI
Old York Historical Society, Old Gaol Museum, York ME
Owensboro Museum of Fine Art, Owensboro KY
Pacific - Asia Museum, Pasadena CA
Page-Walker Arts & History Center, Cary NC
Peabody Essex Museum, Salem MA
Philadelphia College of Textiles & Science, Paley Design Center, Philadelphia PA
Phoenix Art Museum, Phoenix AZ
Plainsman Museum, Aurora NE
Port Authority of New York & New Jersey, Art Collection, New York NY

Marjorie Merriweather Post Foundation of DC, Hillwood Museum, Washington DC
Principia College, School of Nations Museum, Elsah IL
Putnam Museum of History & Natural Science, Davenport IA
Quapaw Quarter Association, Inc, Villa Marre, Little Rock AR
Red Deer & District Museum & Archives, Red Deer AB
Rensselaer County Historical Society, Hart-Cluett Mansion, 1827, Troy NY
Rhode Island Historical Society, John Brown House, Providence RI
Rhodes College, Jessie L Clough Art Memorial for Teaching, Memphis TN
Riley County Historical Society, Riley County Historical Museum, Manhattan KS
Riverside Municipal Museum, Riverside CA
Rowland Evans Robinson Memorial Association, Rokeby Museum, Ferrisburgh VT
Millicent Rogers Museum of Northern New Mexico, Taos NM
Rollins College, George D & Harriet W Cornell Fine Arts Museum, Winter Park FL
Roswell Museum & Art Center, Roswell NM
Royal Arts Foundation, Belcourt Castle, Newport RI
Saginaw Art Museum, Saginaw MI
Scalamandre Museum of Textiles, New York NY
Schenectady Museum Planetarium & Visitors Center, Schenectady NY
Scripps College, Clark Humanities Museum, Claremont CA
The Seagram Museum, Waterloo ON
Shaker Museum & Library, Old Chatham NY
Shaker Village of Pleasant Hill, Harrodsburg KY
Shelburne Museum, Shelburne VT
Slater-Norton Corporation, Slater Memorial Museum & Converse Art Gallery, Norwich CT
South Carolina State Museum, Columbia SC
South Dakota State University, South Dakota Art Museum, Brookings SD
Southern Alleghenies Museum of Art, Southern Alleghenies Museum of Art at Johnstown, Loretto PA
Southern Baptist Theological Seminary, Joseph A Callaway Archaeological Museum, Louisville KY
Southern Oregon Historical Society, Jacksonville Museum of Southern Oregon History, Medford OR
Spartanburg County Museum of Art, Spartanburg SC
Spertus Institute of Jewish Studies, Spertus Museum, Chicago IL
Springfield Art & Historical Society, Miller Art Center, Springfield VT
T C Steele State Historic Site, Nashville IN
Stratford Historical Society, Katherine Mitchel Museum, Stratford CT
Swedish American Museum Association of Chicago, Chicago IL
Temple Beth Israel, Sylvia Plotkin Judaica, Phoenix AZ
The Temple-Tifereth Israel, The Temple Museum of Religious Art, Beachwood OH
Textile Arts Centre, Chicago IL
Textile Museum, Washington DC
Towson State University, Asian Arts Center, Towson MD
Mark Twain Memorial, Hartford CT
Ucross Foundation, Big Red Barn Gallery, Clearmont WY
The Ukrainian Museum, New York NY
United Society of Shakers, Shaker Museum, New Glocester ME
University of British Columbia, Museum of Anthropology, Vancouver BC
University of California, Los Angeles, Fowler Museum of Cultural History, Los Angeles CA
University of California, Santa Barbara, University Art Museum, Santa Barbara CA
University of Chicago, Oriental Institute Museum, Chicago IL
University of Colorado at Colorado Springs, Gallery of Contemporary Art, Colorado Springs CO

University of Delaware, University Gallery, Newark DE
University of Iowa, Museum of Art, Iowa City IA
University of Kansas, Spencer Museum of Art, Lawrence KS
University of Manitoba, Faculty of Architecture Exhibition Centre, Winnipeg MB
University of Miami, Lowe Art Museum, Coral Gables FL
University of Michigan, Kelsey Museum of Archaeology, Ann Arbor MI
University of Minnesota, Goldstein Gallery, Saint Paul MN
University of Mississippi, University Museums, Oxford MS
University of Oregon, Museum of Art, Eugene OR
University of San Diego, Founders' Gallery, San Diego CA
University of Texas at Austin, Archer M Huntington Art Gallery, Austin TX
University of Washington, Henry Art Gallery, Seattle WA
Ursinus College, Philip & Muriel Berman Museum of Art, Collegeville PA
Vizcaya Museum & Gardens, Miami FL
Westmoreland Museum of American Art, Greensburg PA
Wethersfield Historical Society Inc, Museum, Wethersfield CT
Whatcom Museum of History and Art, Bellingham WA
Wheaton College, Watson Gallery, Norton MA
Wichita Art Museum, Wichita KS
Wilfrid Laurier University, Robert Langen Gallery, Waterloo ON
Willard House & Clock Museum, Inc, North Grafton MA
Winston-Salem State University, Diggs Gallery, Winston Salem NC
Winterthur Museum, Winterthur DE
Witte Museum, San Antonio TX
Woodlawn Plantation, Mount Vernon VA
York Institute Museum, Saco ME

WATERCOLORS

The Albrecht-Kemper Museum of Art, Saint Joseph MO
Albuquerque Museum of Art & History, Albuquerque NM
Algonquin Arts Council, Art Gallery of Bancroft, Bancroft ON
American Kennel Club, Museum of the Dog, Saint Louis MO
American University, Watkins Collection, Washington DC
Anchorage Museum of History & Art, Anchorage AK
Walter Anderson Museum of Art, Ocean Springs MS
Artesia Historical Museum & Art Center, Artesia NM
Art Gallery of Nova Scotia, Halifax NS
Asbury College, Student Center Gallery, Wilmore KY
Asheville Art Museum, Asheville NC
Leo Baeck Institute, New York NY
Barnes Foundation, Merion PA
Baylor University, Martin Museum of Art, Waco TX
Bethany College, Mingenback Art Center, Lindsborg KS
The Bostonian Society, Old State House Museum, Boston MA
Bowdoin College, Museum of Art, Brunswick ME
Roy Boyd Gallery, Chicago IL
Brandywine River Museum, Chadds Ford PA
Brevard College, Sims Art Center, Brevard NC
Brigham Young University, Museum of Art, Provo UT
Brown County Art Gallery Association Inc, Brown County Art Gallery & Museum, Nashville IN
Brown University, David Winton Bell Gallery, Providence RI
Butler Institute of American Art, Art Museum, Youngstown OH
California Historical Society, El Molino Viejo, San Marino CA

Calvert Marine Museum, Solomons MD
Canadian Museum of Nature, Musee Canadien de la Nature, Ottawa ON
Cape Ann Historical Museum, Gloucester MA
Capital University, Schumacher Gallery, Columbus OH
Cartoon Art Museum, San Francisco CA
Radio-Canada SRC CBC, Galerie Georges Goguen, Moncton NB
Chattahoochee Valley Art Museum, LaGrange GA
Church of Jesus Christ of Latter-Day Saints, Museum of Church History & Art, Salt Lake City UT
CIAO, Gallery & Art Center, Bronx NY
City of Gainesville, Thomas Center Galleries - Cultural Affairs, Gainesville FL
The City of Petersburg Museums, Petersburg VA
City of Pittsfield, Berkshire Artisans, Pittsfield MA
Clinton County Historical Association, Clinton County Historical Museum, Plattsburgh NY
Columbus Museum, Columbus GA
Community Fine Arts Center, Halseth Gallery, Rock Springs WY
Corcoran Gallery of Art, Washington DC
Cornwall Gallery Society, Regional Art Gallery, Cornwall ON
The Currier Gallery of Art, Manchester NH
Custer County Art Center, Miles City MT
Dahesh Museum, New York NY
Danforth Museum of Art, Framingham MA
Davidson College Visual Arts Center, William H Van Every Jr & Edward M Smith Galleries, Davidson NC
Detroit Repertory Theatre Gallery, Detroit MI
DeWitt Historical Society of Tompkins County, Ithaca NY
The Dixon Gallery & Gardens, Memphis TN
Dundurn Castle, Hamilton ON
East Baton Rouge Parks & Recreation Commission, Baton Rouge Gallery Inc, Baton Rouge LA
Eastern Illinois University, Tarble Arts Center, Charleston IL
Edmonton Art Gallery, Edmonton AB
Eiteljorg Museum of American Indians & Western Art, Indianapolis IN
Ellen Noel Art Museum of the Permian Basin, Odessa TX
Elmhurst Art Museum, Elmhurst IL
El Paso Museum of Art, El Paso TX
Emory University, Michael C Carlos Museum, Atlanta GA
Evansville Museum of Arts & Science, Evansville IN
Fayette Art Museum, Fayette AL
The First National Bank of Chicago, Art Collection, Chicago IL
First Tennessee National Corp, First Tennessee Heritage Collection, Memphis TN
Florida State University Foundation - Central Florida Community College Foundation, The Appleton Museum of Art, Ocala FL
Fort Smith Art Center, Fort Smith AR
Fuller Museum of Art, Brockton MA
Galeria Mesa, Mesa Arts Center, Mesa AZ
Girard College, Stephen Girard Collection, Philadelphia PA
Greater Lafayette Museum of Art, Lafayette IN
Grinnell College, Print & Drawing Study Room/ Gallery, Grinnell IA
Guggenheim Museum Soho, New York NY
Solomon R Guggenheim Museum, New York NY
Guilford College, Art Gallery, Greensboro NC
Hamilton College, Fred L Emerson Gallery, Clinton NY
Headquarters Fort Monroe, Dept of Army, Casemate Museum, Fort Monroe VA
Heard Museum, Phoenix AZ
Heckscher Museum of Art, Huntington NY
Henry Gallery Association, Henry Art Gallery, Seattle WA
Historical Society of Pennsylvania, Philadelphia PA
Historic Landmarks Foundation of Indiana, Morris-Butler House, Indianapolis IN
Howard University, Gallery of Art, Washington DC
Huntsville Museum of Art, Huntsville AL
Hutchinson Art Association, Hutchinson Art Center, Hutchinson KS
Hyde Park Art Center, Chicago IL

Indianapolis Museum of Art, Indianapolis IN
Institute of American Indian Arts Museum, Santa Fe NM
Irving Arts Center, Main Gallery & New Talent Gallery, Irving TX
Jacksonville University, Alexander Brest Museum & Gallery, Jacksonville FL
Johns Hopkins University, Evergreen House, Baltimore MD
Joslyn Art Museum, Omaha NE
Kalamazoo Institute of Arts, Kalamazoo MI
Kamloops Art Gallery, Kamloops BC
Kansas City Art Institute, Kemper Museum of Contemporary Art & Design, Kansas City MO
Koshare Indian Museum, Inc, La Junta CO
La Salle University, Art Museum, Philadelphia PA
Leroy Historical Society, LeRoy NY
Lewistown Art Center, Lewistown MT
Lighthouse Gallery & School of Art, Tequesta FL
Longview Art Museum, Longview TX
Los Angeles County Museum of Natural History, William S Hart Museum, Newhall CA
Louisa May Alcott Memorial Association, Orchard House, Concord MA
Louisiana State University, Museum of Arts, Baton Rouge LA
Luther College, Fine Arts Collection, Decorah IA
Charles H MacNider Museum, Mason City IA
McPherson College Gallery, McPherson KS
Maitland Art Center, Maitland FL
Maricopa County Historical Society, Desert Caballeros Western Museum, Wickenburg AZ
The Mariners' Museum, Newport News VA
The Market Gallery of the City of Toronto Archives, Toronto ON
Marquette University, Haggerty Museum of Art, Milwaukee WI
Maryland Hall for the Creative Arts, Cardinal Gallery, Annapolis MD
Massachusetts Institute of Technology, MIT Museum, Cambridge MA
Mattatuck Historical Society, Mattatuck Museum, Waterbury CT
Michelson Museum of Art, Marshall TX
James A Michener Art Museum, Doylestown PA
Midwest Museum of American Art, Elkhart IN
Millikin University, Perkinson Gallery, Decatur IL
Arthur Roy Mitchell Memorial Inc, Museum of Western Art, Trinidad CO
Moore College of Art & Design, Goldie Paley Gallery, Philadelphia PA
Moravian College, Payne Gallery, Bethlehem PA
Moravian Historical Society, Whitefield House Museum, Nazareth PA
Morris Museum, Morristown NJ
Mount Mary College, Tower Gallery, Milwaukee WI
Munson-Williams-Proctor Institute, Museum of Art, Utica NY
Musee Regional de la Cote-Nord, Sept-Iles PQ
Museo De Las Americas, Denver CO
Museum of Arts & History, Port Huron MI
Museum of Contemporary Art, San Diego-Downtown, San Diego CA
Museum of Contemporary Impressionism, New Milford CT
Museum of Western Art, Denver CO
Nassau County Museum of Fine Art, Roslyn Harbor NY
National Infantry Museum, Fort Benning GA
National Museum of American Art, Washington DC
National Park Service, Weir Farm National Historic Site, Wilton CT
National Portrait Gallery, Washington DC
National Society of Tole & Decorative Painters, Inc, Wichita KS
Navajo Nation Museum, Window Rock AZ
Naval Historical Center, The Navy Museum, Washington DC
Nevada Museum of Art, Reno NV
Neville Public Museum, Green Bay WI
Newport Art Museum, Newport RI
New York Studio School of Drawing, Painting & Sculpture, Gallery, New York NY
New York University, Grey Art Gallery & Study Center, New York NY

Niagara University, Castellani Art Museum, Niagara NY

No Man's Land Historical Society Museum, Goodwell OK

Northern Illinois University, NIU Art Museum, De Kalb IL

Noyes Museum, Oceanville NJ

Oklahoma City Art Museum, Oklahoma City OK

Old Jail Art Center, Albany TX

One West Art Center, Fort Collins CO

Owensboro Museum of Fine Art, Owensboro KY

Paris Gibson Square, Museum of Art, Great Falls MT

Passaic County Historical Society, Paterson NJ

Peabody Essex Museum, Salem MA

Pensacola Museum of Art, Pensacola FL

Philbrook Museum of Art, Tulsa OK

George Phippen Memorial Foundation, Phippen Museum of Western Art, Prescott AZ

Phoenix Art Museum, Phoenix AZ

Port Authority of New York & New Jersey, Art Collection, New York NY

Provincetown Art Association & Museum, Provincetown MA

Putnam Museum of History & Natural Science, Davenport IA

Rahr-West Art Museum, Manitowoc WI

Rapid City Arts Council, Dahl Fine Arts Center, Rapid City SD

Frederic Remington Art Museum, Ogdensburg NY

Rhode Island Historical Society, John Brown House, Providence RI

Sid W Richardson Foundation, Collection of Western Art, Fort Worth TX

Rowland Evans Robinson Memorial Association, Rokeby Museum, Ferrisburgh VT

Millicent Rogers Museum of Northern New Mexico, Taos NM

Ross Memorial Museum, Saint Andrews NB

Roswell Museum & Art Center, Roswell NM

Rutgers University, Stedman Art Gallery, Camden NJ

Saint Louis Artists' Guild, Saint Louis MO

School of Visual Arts, Visual Arts Museum, New York NY

The Seagram Museum, Waterloo ON

Seneca-Iroquois National Museum, Salamanca NY

Shaker Museum & Library, Old Chatham NY

Society of the Cincinnati, Museum & Library at Anderson House, Washington DC

South Dakota State University, South Dakota Art Museum, Brookings SD

Southern Alleghenies Museum of Art, Southern Alleghenies Museum of Art at Johnstown, Loretto PA

Southern Oregon Historical Society, Jacksonville Museum of Southern Oregon History, Medford OR

Spartanburg County Museum of Art, Spartanburg SC

Springfield Art & Historical Society, Miller Art Center, Springfield VT

Springfield Art Museum, Springfield MO

Stanford University, Museum of Art, Stanford CA

State Historical Society of Missouri, Columbia MO

Stetson University, Duncan Gallery of Art, De Land FL

Stratford Historical Society, Katherine Mitchel Museum, Stratford CT

Swedish American Museum Association of Chicago, Chicago IL

Tampa Museum of Art, Tampa FL

Topeka & Shawnee County Public Library, Gallery of Fine Arts, Topeka KS

Tulane University, University Art Collection, New Orleans LA

The Turner Museum, Denver CO

Twin City Art Foundation, Masur Museum of Art, Monroe LA

Ucross Foundation, Big Red Barn Gallery, Clearmont WY

The Ukrainian Museum, New York NY

UMLAUF Sculpture Garden & Museum, Austin TX

United States Capitol, Architect of the Capitol, Washington DC

United States Department of the Interior Museum, Washington DC

United States Figure Skating Association, World Figure Skating Museum & Hall of Fame, Colorado Springs CO

University of Calgary, The Nickle Arts Museum, Calgary AB

University of California, Richard L Nelson Gallery & Fine Arts Collection, Davis CA

University of California, Santa Barbara, University Art Museum, Santa Barbara CA

University of Chicago, Oriental Institute Museum, Chicago IL

University of Cincinnati, DAAP Galleries-College of Design Architecture, Art & Planning, Cincinnati OH

University of Colorado, Art Galleries, Boulder CO

University of Colorado at Colorado Springs, Gallery of Contemporary Art, Colorado Springs CO

University of Florida, Samuel P Harn Museum of Art, Gainesville FL

University of Iowa, Museum of Art, Iowa City IA

University of Kansas, Spencer Museum of Art, Lawrence KS

University of Manitoba, Faculty of Architecture Exhibition Centre, Winnipeg MB

University of Mississippi, University Museums, Oxford MS

University of Nebraska, Lincoln, Sheldon Memorial Art Gallery & Sculpture Garden, Lincoln NE

University of Rochester, Memorial Art Gallery, Rochester NY

University of Texas at Austin, Archer M Huntington Art Gallery, Austin TX

University of Wisconsin-Madison, Wisconsin Union Galleries, Madison WI

Ursinus College, Philip & Muriel Berman Museum of Art, Collegeville PA

Valentine Museum, Richmond VA

Vassar College, The Frances Lehman Loeb Art Center, Poughkeepsie NY

Vesterheim Norwegian-American Museum, Decorah IA

Washburn University, Mulvane Art Museum, Topeka KS

Waterworks Visual Arts Center, Salisbury NC

Westmoreland Museum of American Art, Greensburg PA

Whatcom Museum of History and Art, Bellingham WA

Peter & Catharine Whyte Foundation, Whyte Museum of the Canadian Rockies, Banff AB

Wichita Art Museum, Wichita KS

Wilfrid Laurier University, Robert Langen Gallery, Waterloo ON

Winston-Salem State University, Diggs Gallery, Winston Salem NC

Woodlawn Plantation, Mount Vernon VA

Wustum Museum Art Association, Charles A Wustum Museum of Fine Arts, Racine WI

Yale University, Yale Center for British Art, New Haven CT

York Institute Museum, Saco ME

WOODCARVINGS

Agecroft Association, Museum, Richmond VA

A I R Gallery, New York NY

Alaska Department of Education, Division of Libraries, Archives & Museums, Sheldon Jackson Museum, Sitka AK

Albuquerque Museum of Art & History, Albuquerque NM

American Kennel Club, Museum of the Dog, Saint Louis MO

Walter Anderson Museum of Art, Ocean Springs MS

Arnold Mikelson Mind & Matter Gallery, White Rock BC

Art Gallery of Hamilton, Hamilton ON

Art Gallery of Nova Scotia, Halifax NS

Asian Art Museum of San Francisco, Avery Brundage Collection, San Francisco CA

Beaumont Art League, Beaumont TX

Bowdoin College, Museum of Art, Brunswick ME

Brigham Young University, Museum of Art, Provo UT

Brown University, David Winton Bell Gallery, Providence RI

Calvert Marine Museum, Solomons MD

The Canadian Craft Museum, Vancouver BC

Canadian Museum of Nature, Musee Canadien de la Nature, Ottawa ON

Kit Carson Historic Museums, Hacienda Martinez, Taos NM

Radio-Canada SRC CBC, Galerie Georges Goguen, Moncton NB

Center for Puppetry Arts, Atlanta GA

Central United Methodist Church, Swords Info Plowshares Peace Center & Gallery, Detroit MI

Chattahoochee Valley Art Museum, LaGrange GA

Chicago Department of Cultural Affairs, Chicago Cultural Center, Chicago IL

Chilkat Valley Historical Society, Sheldon Museum & Cultural Center, Haines AK

Church of Jesus Christ of Latter-Day Saints, Museum of Church History & Art, Salt Lake City UT

City of Gainesville, Thomas Center Galleries - Cultural Affairs, Gainesville FL

Clark County Historical Society, Pioneer - Krier Museum, Ashland KS

Clinton Art Association Gallery, Clinton IA

Columbus Museum, Columbus GA

Community Fine Arts Center, Halseth Gallery, Rock Springs WY

The Currier Gallery of Art, Manchester NH

Custer County Art Center, Miles City MT

Davidson College Visual Arts Center, William H Van Every Jr & Edward M Smith Galleries, Davidson NC

Denison University, Art Gallery, Granville OH

Detroit Repertory Theatre Gallery, Detroit MI

Dundurn Castle, Hamilton ON

Eastern Washington State Historical Society, Cheney Cowles Museum, Spokane WA

Ellen Noel Art Museum of the Permian Basin, Odessa TX

Elmhurst Art Museum, Elmhurst IL

Emory University, Michael C Carlos Museum, Atlanta GA

Enook Galleries, Waterloo ON

Wharton Esherick Museum, Paoli PA

Essex Historical Society, Essex Shipbuilding Museum, Essex MA

Fayette Art Museum, Fayette AL

The First National Bank of Chicago, Art Collection, Chicago IL

Five Civilized Tribes Museum, Muskogee OK

Gallery 53, Cooperstown NY

General Board of Discipleship, The United Methodist Church, The Upper Room Chapel & Museum, Nashville TN

Wendell Gilley Museum, Southwest Harbor ME

Gloridale Partnership, National Museum of Woodcarving, Custer SD

Greater Lafayette Museum of Art, Lafayette IN

Greenwood Museum, Greenwood SC

Harness Racing & Hall of Fame, Goshen NY

Headquarters Fort Monroe, Dept of Army, Casemate Museum, Fort Monroe VA

Heard Museum, Phoenix AZ

Hermitage Foundation Museum, Norfolk VA

Hershey Museum, Hershey PA

Higgins Armory Museum, Worcester MA

Historical Society of Washington DC, Heurich House Museum, Washington DC

Jacksonville University, Alexander Brest Museum & Gallery, Jacksonville FL

Kiah Museum, Savannah GA

Koshare Indian Museum, Inc, La Junta CO

Lac du Flambeau Band of Lake Superior Chippewa Indians, George W Brown Jr Ojibwe Museum & Cultural Center, Lac du Flambeau WI

Los Angeles County Museum of Natural History, William S Hart Museum, Newhall CA

Luther College, Fine Arts Collection, Decorah IA

Maitland Art Center, Maitland FL

The Mariners' Museum, Newport News VA

Maryland Hall for the Creative Arts, Cardinal Gallery, Annapolis MD

Michigan State University, Kresge Art Museum, East Lansing MI

Midwest Museum of American Art, Elkhart IN

Mills College, Art Gallery, Oakland CA

Mitchell Museum, Mount Vernon IL

Musee d'Art de Saint-Laurent, Saint-Laurent PQ

Musee du Quebec, Quebec PQ

WOODCUTS

Winston-Salem State University, Diggs Gallery,
Winston Salem NC

Collections

Aboriginal Artifacts

Moncur Gallery, Boissevain MB

Acadian Artifacts

Lafayette Natural History Museum, Planetarium &
Nature Station, Lafayette LA

Adler Collection

Lehigh University Art Galleries, Bethlehem PA

Blanche Adler Graphic Arts Collection

Baltimore Museum of Art, Baltimore MD

Adolf Austrian Academic Painting Collection

Pennsylvania State University, Palmer Museum of
Art, University Park PA

African-American Art Collection

Winston-Salem State University, Diggs Gallery,
Winston Salem NC

African Art

College of William & Mary, Joseph & Margaret
Muscarelle Museum of Art, Williamsburg VA
Slater-Norton Corporation, Slater Memorial
Museum & Converse Art Gallery, Norwich CT

African Artifacts

University of Illinois, World Heritage Museum,
Champaign IL

African Collection

Albany Museum of Art, Albany GA

Agricultural Equipment

Dawson County Historical Society, Museum,
Lexington NE

Agriculture

Adams County Historical Society, Museum &
Cultural Center, Brighton CO
New York State Historical Association, Farmers'
Museum, Inc, Cooperstown NY

Ala Story Print Collection

University of California, Santa Barbara, University
Art Museum, Santa Barbara CA

**Lucy Truman Aldrich Collection of
Porcelains & Textiles**

Rhode Island School of Design, Museum of Art,
Providence RI

Washington Allston Trust Collection

University of Miami, Lowe Art Museum, Coral
Gables FL

American Art

Saint Mary's College of California, Hearst Art
Gallery, Moraga CA

American Art Collection

James A Michener Art Museum, Doylestown PA

**American Art; Conceptual Art;
Contemporary Art**

University of California, Berkeley Art Museum &
Pacific Film Archive, Berkeley CA

**American Art & Furniture from the
Seventeenth - Twentieth Centuries**

Slater-Norton Corporation, Slater Memorial
Museum & Converse Art Gallery, Norwich CT

American Coverlet

Columbus Museum of Art, Columbus OH

American Craft Collection

San Angelo Museum of Fine Arts, San Angelo TX

**American Decorative Arts, 19th-20th
Centuries**

Birmingham Museum of Art, Birmingham AL

American Fine Arts

Fetherston Foundation, Packwood House Museum,
Lewisburg PA

American Folk Art Collection

University Of Wisconsin-Whitewater, Crossman
Gallery, Whitewater WI

American Furniture

US Department of State, Diplomatic Reception
Rooms, Washington DC

American Historical Artifacts

The Museums at Stony Brook, Stony Brook NY

American Illustration

Brandywine River Museum, Chadds Ford PA

American Impressionism

Historical Society of the Town of Greenwich, Inc,
Bush-Holley House Museum, Cos Cob CT
National Museum of American Art, Washington
DC

**American Impressionism & Realism
Collection**

Sterling Portfolio Inc, New York NY

American Impressionist Paintings

National Park Service, Weir Farm National Historic
Site, Wilton CT

American Jewish Ethnographic Collection

Hebrew Union College, Skirball Cultural Center,
Los Angeles CA

American Painting & Sculpture Collection

San Angelo Museum of Fine Arts, San Angelo TX

American Portraits & Paintings

US Department of State, Diplomatic Reception
Rooms, Washington DC

American Revolutionary War

Society of the Cincinnati, Museum & Library at
Anderson House, Washington DC

American Silver

US Department of State, Diplomatic Reception
Rooms, Washington DC

Ancient Art

Albany Museum of Art, Albany GA

Carl Andre Collection

Chinati Foundation, Marfa TX

Animation

International Museum of Cartoon Art, Montreal PQ

Antique Electrical Signs

Museum of Neon Art, Los Angeles CA

Antiquities - Cycladic

Kimbell Art Foundation, Kimbell Art Museum,
Fort Worth TX

Karel Appel Graphics Collection

Art Gallery of Hamilton, Hamilton ON

Archdiocese Santa Fe Collection

Guadalupe Historic Foundation, Santuario de
Guadalupe, Santa Fe NM

Archeological Collection

Clark County Historical Society, Pioneer - Krier
Museum, Ashland KS

**Archives; Photos & Maps; Trade & Business
Items**

Arizona Historical Society-Yuma, Century House
Museum & Garden, Yuma AZ

Arensberg Collection

Philadelphia Museum of Art, Philadelphia PA

J Chester Armstrong Collection

Zigler Museum, Jennings LA

Grant Arnold Fine Print Collection

State University of New York at Oswego, Tyler Art
Gallery, Oswego NY

Matthias H Arnot Collection

Arnot Art Museum, Elmira NY

Art Education

Brookgreen Gardens, Murrells Inlet SC
The Turner Museum, Denver CO

Art History

Adams County Historical Society, Museum &
  Cultural Center, Brighton CO
Brookgreen Gardens, Murrells Inlet SC
The Turner Museum, Denver CO

**Art Mouveau Glass-Nineteenth Century
Chinese Decorative Arts**

Topeka & Shawnee County Public Library, Gallery
  of Fine Arts, Topeka KS

Art Preservation

The Bartlett Museum, Amesbury MA

Asian Art

College of William & Mary, Joseph & Margaret
  Muscarelle Museum of Art, Williamsburg VA

Asian & Guatemalan Collection

Mills College, Art Gallery, Oakland CA

Asnis Collection

Sonoma State University, Art Gallery, Rohnert
  Park CA

**Lady Nancy Astor Collection of English
China**

Virginia Museum of Fine Arts, Richmond VA

Eleanor Deane Audigier Art Collection

University of Tennessee, Frank H McClung
  Museum, Knoxville TN

Audubon Prints

Lafayette Natural History Museum, Planetarium &
  Nature Station, Lafayette LA

Aultman Collection

Arthur Roy Mitchell Memorial Inc, Museum of
  Western Art, Trinidad CO

Australian Aboriginal Art Collection

New Visions Gallery, Inc, Marshfield WI

Autio Ceramics Collection

University of Montana, Paxson Gallery, Missoula
  MT

Alice Baber Midwest Collection

Greater Lafayette Museum of Art, Lafayette IN

Manson F Backus Print Collection

Seattle Art Museum, Seattle WA

Hetty Gray Baker Bookplate Collection

Wadsworth Atheneum, Hartford CT

Baker Collection of Porcelain

Lehigh University Art Galleries, Bethlehem PA

Bryant Baker Sculpture Collection

Ponca City Cultural Center & Museum, Ponca City
  OK

Cyrus Baldridge Drawings

Fisk University, University Galleries, Nashville TN

**Ball-Kraft Collection of Roman & Syrian
Glass**

Ball State University, Museum of Art, Muncie IN

Bancroft Collection

Delaware Art Museum, Wilmington DE

**John Chandler Bancroft Collection of
Japanese Prints**

Worcester Art Museum, Worcester MA

Barbed Wire Collection

Clark County Historical Society, Pioneer - Krier
  Museum, Ashland KS

Barberini-Kress Foundation Collection

Philadelphia Museum of Art, Philadelphia PA

Virgil Barker Collection

University of Miami, Lowe Art Museum, Coral
  Gables FL

David Barry Photography Collection

Douglas County Historical Society, Fairlawn
  Mansion & Museum, Superior WI

Alfred I Barton Collection

University of Miami, Lowe Art Museum, Coral
  Gables FL

Bernard Baruch Silver Collection

University of South Carolina, McKissick Museum,
  Columbia SC

Antoine Louis Barye Collection of Bronzes

Corcoran Gallery of Art, Washington DC

Baseball-Related Contemporary Art

Gallery 53, Cooperstown NY

Ellen H Bayard Painting Collection

Baltimore Museum of Art, Baltimore MD

Zoe Beiler Paintings Collection

Dickinson State University, Mind's Eye Gallery,
  Dickinson ND

David Belasco Collection

Neville Public Museum, Green Bay WI

Bell Collection

Deming-Luna Mimbres Museum, Deming NM

**Thomas E Benesch Memorial Drawing
Collection**

Baltimore Museum of Art, Baltimore MD

Bennington Pottery Collection

Bennington Museum, Bennington VT

Berman Collection

Lehigh University Art Galleries, Bethlehem PA
Ursinus College, Philip & Muriel Berman Museum
  of Art, Collegeville PA

Bernat Oriental Collection

Colby College, Museum of Art, Waterville ME

**Harry A Bernstein Memorial Painting
Collection**

Baltimore Museum of Art, Baltimore MD

Joseph Beuys Collection

Walker Art Center, Minneapolis MN

Biblical Archaeology

Hebrew Union College, Skirball Cultural Center,
  Los Angeles CA

Biblical Archaeology Collection

Hebrew Union College-Jewish Institute of Religion,
  New York NY

Biggs Sculpture Collection

Red River Valley Museum, Vernon TX

Birds of America

Audubon Wildlife Sanctuary, Audubon PA

Joseph Blackburn Collection

Warner House Association, MacPheadris-Warner
  House, Portsmouth NH

Black Diaspora Exhibits & Artifacts

Anacostia Museum, Washington DC

Vyvyan Blackford Collection

Fort Hays State University, Moss-Thorns Gallery of
  Arts, Hays KS

Wendel Black Print Collection

Oregon State University, Fairbanks Gallery,
  Corvallis OR

Blacksmithing

Kit Carson Historic Museums, Hacienda Martinez,
  Taos NM

Edwin M Blake Memorial Collection

Trinity College, Austin Arts Center, Hartford CT

Ernest L Blumenschein & Family Collection

Kit Carson Historic Museums, Ernest Blumenschein Home & Studio, Taos NM

Aubrey Bodine Collection

Calvert Marine Museum, Solomons MD

Bodmer Collection

Joslyn Art Museum, Omaha NE

Boehm Collection

Bellingrath Gardens & Home, Theodore AL

J S Bohannon Folk Art Steamboat Collection

Calvert Marine Museum, Solomons MD

Bone & Ivory

Agecroft Association, Museum, Richmond VA

Frederick T Bonham Collection

University of Tennessee, Frank H McClung Museum, Knoxville TN

Book Arts

Art Resources International, Washington DC

Bower Collection

Red Deer & District Museum & Archives, Red Deer AB

Bradley Collection

Milwaukee Art Museum, Milwaukee WI

Branch Collection of Renaissance Art

Virginia Museum of Fine Arts, Richmond VA

Constantin Brancusi Sculpture Collection

Guggenheim Museum Soho, New York NY
Solomon R Guggenheim Museum, New York NY

Brass Measures (1854)

Kings County Historical Society and Museum, Hampton NB

British Contemporary Paintings

Old Jail Art Center, Albany TX

Saidye & Samuel Bronfman Collection of Canadian Art

Montreal Museum of Fine Arts, Montreal PQ

Ailsa Mellon Bruce Collection of Decorative Arts

Virginia Museum of Fine Arts, Richmond VA

Buchanan Collection of City of Lethbridge

Southern Alberta Art Gallery, Lethbridge AB

Buddhist Art Collection

Jacques Marchais Museum of Tibetan Art Center of Tibetan Art, Tibetan Museum, Staten Island NY

Ottilia Buerger Collection of Ancient Coins

Lawrence University, Wriston Art Center Galleries, Appleton WI

George Burchett Collection

Tattoo Art Museum, San Francisco CA

Charles E Burchfield

Burchfield-Penney Art Center, Buffalo NY

Burnap Collection

Nelson-Atkins Museum of Art, Kansas City MO

Burnap English Pottery Collection

Potsdam Public Museum, Potsdam NY

Burrison Folklife Collection

Atlanta Historical Society Inc, Atlanta History Center, Atlanta GA

James F Byrnes Collection

University of South Carolina, McKissick Museum, Columbia SC

Caballeria Collection of Oils

Southwest Museum, Los Angeles CA

Canadian Historical & Contemporary Art Collection

Moose Jaw Art Museum & National Exhibition Centre, Art & History Museum, Moose Jaw SK

Canadian & International Photography Collection

Stephen Bulger Gallery, Toronto ON

B G Canton Gallery

Stanford University, Museum of Art, Stanford CA

Caplan Collection

Children's Museum, Rauh Memorial Library, Indianapolis IN

Carl VanVechten Photographs

Hammond Museum & Japanese Stroll Garden, Cross-Cultural Center, North Salem NY

Carl von Marr Collection

West Bend Art Museum, West Bend WI

Carnegie Collection of Prints

Dickinson College, Trout Gallery, Carlisle PA

Carrington Collection

Rhode Island Historical Society, John Brown House, Providence RI

Kit Carson Collection

Kit Carson Historic Museums, Home & Museum, Taos NM

Carter Collection of Peruvian Art

Florida State University, Museum of Fine Arts, Tallahassee FL

Clarence Carter Paintings

Southern Ohio Museum Corporation, Southern Ohio Museum & Cultural Center, Portsmouth OH

George Washington Carver Artifacts

Tuskegee Institute National Historic Site, George Washington Carver & The Oaks, Tuskegee Institute AL

Mary Cassatt Collection

Saint John's Museum of Art, Wilmington NC

John H Cassell Collection of Political Cartoons

Hartwick College, Foreman Gallery, Oneonta NY

Cass Wedgewood Collection

Wheaton College, Watson Gallery, Norton MA

Central Pennsylvania Artifacts

Fetherston Foundation, Packwood House Museum, Lewisburg PA

Cesnola Collection

Stanford University, Museum of Art, Stanford CA

Lynn Chadwick Sculpture Collection

Ursinus College, Philip & Muriel Berman Museum of Art, Collegeville PA

John Chamberlain Collection

Chinati Foundation, Marfa TX

Clara Champlain Griswold Toy Collection

Lyme Historical Society, Florence Griswold Museum, Old Lyme CT

Conrad Wise Chapman Oils Collection

Valentine Museum, Richmond VA

Charles Umlauf Collection

UMLAUF Sculpture Garden & Museum, Austin TX

Benjamin Chee Chee Collection

Enook Galleries, Waterloo ON

Contemporary Print Collection

Wake Forest University, Fine Arts Gallery, Winston Salem NC

Contemporary Realism Collection

Sterling Portfolio Inc, New York NY

Contemporary Visual Art

A Space, Toronto ON

Contemporary Western Art

Favell Museum of Western Art & Indian Artifacts, Klamath Falls OR

Contemporary Western Artists

Pioneer Town, Pioneer Museum of Western Art, Wimberley TX

Coons Collection

Carrie McLain Museum, Nome AK

J C Coovert Collection

Arts & Science Center for Southeast Arkansas, Pine Bluff AR

Copeland Collection

Delaware Art Museum, Wilmington DE

Cosla Collection

Saint Mary's Romanian Orthodox Church, Romanian Ethnic Museum, Cleveland OH

Cosla Collection of Renaissance Art

Montclair State University, Art Galleries, Upper Montclair NJ

Cotter Collection

Saint Mary's College, Moreau Galleries, Notre Dame IN

Couldery European Art Collection

Glanmore, Hastings County Museum, Belleville ON

Coverlet Collection

Houston Museum of Decorative Arts, Chattanooga TN

Cowan Collection

Board of Parks & Recreation, The Parthenon, Nashville TN

Craft Art

Burchfield-Penney Art Center, Buffalo NY

Craig Collection of Edna Hibel

Edna Hibel Art Foundation, Hibel Museum of Art, Palm Beach FL

Alexander M Craighead Collection of European & American Military Art

United States Military Academy, West Point Museum, West Point NY

Charles Cristadoro Sculptures

Los Angeles County Museum of Natural History, William S Hart Museum, Newhall CA

Crozier Collection of Chinese Art

Philadelphia Museum of Art, Philadelphia PA

Cuban Collection

The Museum of Arts & Sciences Inc, Daytona Beach FL

Cummings Collection

Colby College, Museum of Art, Waterville ME

Edward S Curtis Photographic Collection

Custer County Art Center, Miles City MT

Custis-Washington-Lee Art Collection

Washington & Lee University, Lee Chapel & Museum, Lexington VA

Charles Cutts Collection

Nevada Museum Of Art, Reno NV

Cybis Collection

Mercer County Community College, The Gallery, Trenton NJ

Elise Agnus Daingerfield 18th Century Collection

Baltimore Museum of Art, Baltimore MD

Chester Dale Collection

National Gallery of Art, Washington DC

Cyrus Dallin Bronze Collection

Springville Museum of Art, Springville UT

Dana Collection

University of Montana, Paxson Gallery, Missoula MT

Joseph E Davies Collection of Russian Icons & Paintings

University of Wisconsin-Madison, Elvehjem Museum of Art, Madison WI

Jacqueline Davis China Collection

Ross Memorial Museum, Saint Andrews NB

Cecil Clark Davis Collection

Marion Art Center, Marion MA

Norman Davis Collection of Classical Art

Seattle Art Museum, Seattle WA

D'Berger Collection

Santa Clara University, de Saisset Museum, Santa Clara CA

Decorative Arts

National Park Service, Weir Farm National Historic Site, Wilton CT

Decorative Arts Collection

National Society of Tole & Decorative Painters, Inc, Wichita KS

Agness Delano Watercolor & Print Collection

Howard University, Gallery of Art, Washington DC

Joe DeYong Paintings

Los Angeles County Museum of Natural History, William S Hart Museum, Newhall CA

Thomas S Dickey Civil War Ordiance Collection

Atlanta Historical Society Inc, Atlanta History Center, Atlanta GA

John G Diefenbaker Memorabilia & Archives

University of Saskatchewan, Diefenbaker Canada Centre, Saskatoon SK

Frank & Mary Alice Diener Collection of Ancient Snuff Bottles

Fresno Metropolitan Museum, Fresno CA

Harvey Dienn Collection

Arthur Roy Mitchell Memorial Inc, Museum of Western Art, Trinidad CO

Digget Collection of Wooden Models

Halifax Historical Society, Inc, Halifax Historical Museum, Daytona Beach FL

Maynard Dixon Collection

Brigham Young University, B F Larsen Gallery, Provo UT

F B Doane Collection of Western American Art

Frontier Times Museum, Bandera TX

Domestic Arts

Hinckley Foundation Museum, Ithaca NY

Dorflinger Glass Collection

Everhart Museum, Scranton PA

Dorsky & Tannenbaum Collection

Fort Wayne Museum of Art, Inc, Fort Wayne IN

Peter Carl Faberge Collection of Czarist Jewels

Virginia Museum of Fine Arts, Richmond VA

Faberge objects d'art

Marjorie Merriweather Post Foundation of DC, Hillwood Museum, Washington DC

Fairbanks Collection

Fort Wayne Museum of Art, Inc, Fort Wayne IN

Farm Machinery

Jefferson County Open Space, Hiwan Homestead Museum, Evergreen CO

Edith H K Featherston Collection

Fetherston Foundation, Packwood House Museum, Lewisburg PA

Brigadier General Bonner F Fellers Collection

MacArthur Memorial, Library & Archives, Norfolk VA

Dexter M Ferry Collection

Vassar College, The Frances Lehman Loeb Art Center, Poughkeepsie NY

Louis Feuchter Collection

Calvert Marine Museum, Solomons MD

Clark Field Collection of American Indian Crafts

Philbrook Museum of Art, Tulsa OK

Fifteenth-Nineteenth Century European Ceramic Collection

Polk Museum of Art, Lakeland FL

Fine Art Permanent Collection of Northwestern College (Iowa)

Northwestern College, Te Paske Gallery, Orange City IA

Fine Arts

Knights of Columbus Supreme Council, Headquarters Museum, New Haven CT

Fire Fighting

CIGNA Corporation, CIGNA Museum & Art Collection, Philadelphia PA

Elizabeth Parke Firestone Collection of French Silver

Detroit Institute of Arts, Detroit MI

Elizabeth Holmes Fisher Collection

University of Southern California, Fisher Gallery, Los Angeles CA

Fisher Memorial Collection

Beloit College, Wright Museum of Art, Beloit WI

Fitzgerald Study Collection

University of Manitoba, Gallery III, Winnipeg MB

Fitz Hugh Lane Collection

Cape Ann Historical Museum, Gloucester MA

Flagg Collection

Milwaukee Art Museum, Milwaukee WI

James M Flagg Paintings

Los Angeles County Museum of Natural History, William S Hart Museum, Newhall CA

Julius Fleischman Collection

University of Cincinnati, DAAP Galleries-College of Design Architecture, Art & Planning, Cincinnati OH

Florida Contemporary Collection

The Museum of Arts & Sciences Inc, Daytona Beach FL

Focus Gallery Collection

Santa Clara University, de Saisset Museum, Santa Clara CA

Fowler Collection

Gadsden Museum of Fine Arts, Inc, Gadsden AL

Charles L Franck Photograph Collection

Kemper & Leila Williams Foundation, New Orleans LA

Robert Frank Photography Collection

Stanford University, Museum of Art, Stanford CA

Simon Fraser Collection

Simon Fraser University, Simon Fraser Gallery, Burnaby BC

Laura G Fraser Studio Collection of Western Art

National Cowboy Hall of Fame & Western Heritage Center Museum, Oklahoma City OK

Grace & Abigail French Collection

Rapid City Arts Council, Dahl Fine Arts Center, Rapid City SD

Samuel Friedenberg Collection of Plaques & Medals

The Jewish Museum, New York NY

Harry G Friedman Collection of Ceremonial Objects

The Jewish Museum, New York NY

Patricia & Phillip Frost Collection

National Museum of American Art, Washington DC

Laura Anne Fry American Art Pottery & Art Glass

Greater Lafayette Museum of Art, Lafayette IN

Eugene Fuller Memorial Collection of Chinese Jades

Seattle Art Museum, Seattle WA

Fulton-Meyer Collection of African Art

University of Mississippi, University Museums, Oxford MS

Edward J Gallagher Jr Collection

University of Arizona, Museum of Art, Tucson AZ

Gallatin Collection

Philadelphia Museum of Art, Philadelphia PA

Gallier Architectural Drawings Collection

Kemper & Leila Williams Foundation, New Orleans LA

Gardens & Gardening

The Dixon Gallery & Gardens, Memphis TN

Garfield Collection

Sonoma State University, Art Gallery, Rohnert Park CA

T Harrison Garrett Graphic Arts Collection

Baltimore Museum of Art, Baltimore MD

Garvan Collection of American Decorative Art

Yale University, Art Gallery, New Haven CT

Gebauer Collection of Cameroon Art

Portland Art Museum, Portland OR

Geesey Collection of Pennsylvania Dutch Folk Art

Philadelphia Museum of Art, Philadelphia PA

John Gellatly Collection

National Museum of American Art, Washington DC

Genealogy

Artesia Historical Museum & Art Center, Artesia NM
The Bartlett Museum, Amesbury MA

Genealogy of Northeastern US & Eastern Canada

Springfield Library & Museums Association, Connecticut Valley Historical Museum, Springfield MA

Hawaiian Art

Volcano Art Center, Hawaii National Park HI

William Randolph Hearst Collection of Arms & Armour

Detroit Institute of Arts, Detroit MI

Heeramaneck Collection of Asian Art

Virginia Museum of Fine Arts, Richmond VA

Heeramaneck Collection of Primitive Art

Seattle Art Museum, Seattle WA

Herbert Waide Hemphill Jr Collection

National Museum of American Art, Washington DC

Heritage Buildings

Peter & Catharine Whyte Foundation, Whyte Museum of the Canadian Rockies, Banff AB

Abby Williams Hill Collection

University of Puget Sound, Kittredge Art Gallery, Tacoma WA

Lida Hilton Print Collection

Montclair State University, Art Galleries, Upper Montclair NJ

Hinkhouse Contemporary Art Collection

Coe College, Gordon Fennell Gallery & Marvin Cone Gallery, Cedar Rapids IA

Hirschberg West African Arts Collection

Topeka & Shawnee County Public Library, Gallery of Fine Arts, Topeka KS

Hirsch Collection of Oriental Rugs

Portland Art Museum, Portland OR

Hispanic Collection

Hispanic Society of America, Museum, New York NY

Historical Louisiana Maps

Lafayette Natural History Museum, Planetarium & Nature Station, Lafayette LA

Historic Naval Uniforms

USS Constitution Museum, Boston MA

Historic Southern Plains Indian Arts

Southern Plains Indian Museum, Anadarko OK

History of Holyoke 1850-1930

Wistariahurst Museum, Holyoke MA

HMS Debraak, 18th century British Warship

Historical & Cultural Affairs, Delaware State Museums, Dover DE

Gene Hoback woodcarvings

Los Angeles County Museum of Natural History, William S Hart Museum, Newhall CA

Morris Henry Hobbs Print Collection

Kemper & Leila Williams Foundation, New Orleans LA

Hogarth & Caroline Durieux Graphics Collection

Louisiana State University, Museum of Arts, Baton Rouge LA

Albert Gallatin Hoit Paintings

Sandwich Historical Society, Center Sandwich NH

Alfred H & Eva Underhill Holbrook Collection of American Art

University of Georgia, Georgia Museum of Art, Athens GA

Willitts J Hole Collection

University of California, Los Angeles, UCLA at the Armand Hammer Museum of Art & Cultural Center, Los Angeles CA

Mary Hollen Collection

Huronia Museum, Midland ON

Holliday Collection of Neo-Impressionist Paintings

Indianapolis Museum of Art, Indianapolis IN

Oliver Wendell Holmes Stereographic Collection

Canton Museum of Art, Canton OH

Winslow Homer Collection

Colby College, Museum of Art, Waterville ME

Winslow Homer Woodcut Collection

State Capitol Museum, Olympia WA

Samuel Houghton Great Basin Collection

Nevada Museum Of Art, Reno NV

F B Housser Memorial Collection

London Regional Art & Historical Museums, London ON

John M Howard Collection

Arts & Science Center for Southeast Arkansas, Pine Bluff AR

J Harry Howard Gemstone Collection

University of South Carolina, McKissick Museum, Columbia SC

Oscar Howe Collection

University of South Dakota Art Galleries, Vermillion SD

Joe and Lucy Howorth Collection

Delta State University, Fielding L Wright Art Center, Cleveland MS

Anna C Hoyt Collection of Old Masters

Vanderbilt University, Fine Arts Gallery, Nashville TN

Winifred Kimball Hudnut Collection

University of Utah, Utah Museum of Fine Arts, Salt Lake City UT

Hudson River Paintings

Putnam County Historical Society, Foundry School Museum, Cold Spring NY

Marie Hull Collection

Delta State University, Fielding L Wright Art Center, Cleveland MS

Human History Artifacts Collection

Moose Jaw Art Museum & National Exhibition Centre, Art & History Museum, Moose Jaw SK

J Marvin Hunter Western Americana Collection

Frontier Times Museum, Bandera TX

Charles & Elsa Hutzler Memorial Collection of Contemporary Sculpture

Baltimore Museum of Art, Baltimore MD

Illinois Art, Historical & Contemporary

Illinois State Museum, Illinois Art Gallery, Chicago IL

Illustrations

International Museum of Cartoon Art, Montreal PQ

Incunabula

La Casa del Libro Museum, San Juan PR

Indian Baskets

Deming-Luna Mimbres Museum, Deming NM

Industrial Artifacts

The Seagram Museum, Waterloo ON

Industrial Design

Chicago Athenaeum, Museum of Architecture & Design, Chicago IL
Cooper-Hewitt, National Design Museum, New York NY
Craft & Folk Art Museum, Los Angeles CA

Industrial & Domestic Artifacts

Dawson City Museum & Historical Society, Dawson City YT

William Inge Memorabilia Collection

Independence Museum, Independence KS

Korean Pottery Collection

Allegheny College, Bowman, Megahan & Penelec
Galleries, Meadville PA

Krannert Memorial Collection

University of Indianapolis, Christel DeHaan Fine
Arts Gallery, Indianapolis IN

Samuel H Kress Collection

Allentown Art Museum, Allentown PA
Columbia Museum of Art, Columbia SC
El Paso Museum of Art, El Paso TX
Howard University, Gallery of Art, Washington DC
Memphis Brooks Museum of Art, Memphis TN
National Gallery of Art, Washington DC
North Carolina Museum of Art, Raleigh NC
Philbrook Museum of Art, Tulsa OK
Portland Art Museum, Portland OR
Trinity College, Austin Arts Center, Hartford CT
University of Arizona, Museum of Art, Tucson AZ
University of Miami, Lowe Art Museum, Coral
Gables FL
Vanderbilt University, Fine Arts Gallery, Nashville
TN

**Samuel H Kress Collection of Renaissance
Art**

Berea College, Doris Ulmann Galleries, Berea KY
Honolulu Academy of Arts, Honolulu HI
New Orleans Museum of Art, New Orleans LA

Samuel H Kress Study Collection

University of Georgia, Georgia Museum of Art,
Athens GA
University of Notre Dame, Snite Museum of Art,
Notre Dame IN

Irma Kruse Collection

Hastings Museum, Hastings NE

Kurdian Collection of Mexican Art

Wichita Art Museum, Wichita KS

**Mary Andresw Ladd Collection of Japanese
Prints**

Portland Art Museum, Portland OR

**William S Ladd Collection of Pre-Columbian
Art**

Portland Art Museum, Portland OR

B Lafon Drawing Collection

Kemper & Leila Williams Foundation, New Orleans
LA

Fannie Lager Collection

Museum of Contemporary Impressionism, New
Milford CT

Lake Superior Ojibwes Collection

Lac du Flambeau Band of Lake Superior Chippewa
Indians, George W Brown Jr Ojibwe Museum &
Cultural Center, Lac du Flambeau WI

Norman LaLiberte Collection

Saint Mary's College, Moreau Galleries, Notre
Dame IN

Robert L Lambdin Paintings

Los Angeles County Museum of Natural History,
William S Hart Museum, Newhall CA

Dr Paul Lamp Collection

Glanmore, Hastings County Museum, Belleville ON

Landscape Architecture

Brookgreen Gardens, Murrells Inlet SC

**John D Lankenau Collection of 19th
Century Paintings & Sculptures**

The Museum at Drexel University, Philadelphia PA

Larson Drawing Collection

Austin Peay State University, Margaret Fort
Trahern Gallery, Clarksville TN

Mauricio Lasansky Print Collection

University of Iowa, Museum of Art, Iowa City IA

**Late Medival, Renaissance & Baroque
Sculpture Collection**

Harvard University, Busch-Reisinger Museum,
Cambridge MA

Samuel K Lathrop Collection

University of Miami, Lowe Art Museum, Coral
Gables FL

Latter-Schlesinger Miniature Collection

New Orleans Museum of Art, New Orleans LA

Clarence Laughlin Photograph Collection

Kemper & Leila Williams Foundation, New Orleans
LA

**Roberta Campbell Lawson Collection of
Indian Artifacts; Tabor Collection of
Oriental Art**

Philbrook Museum of Art, Tulsa OK

Lawther Collection of Ethiopian Crosses

Portland Art Museum, Portland OR

Layton Collection

Milwaukee Art Museum, Milwaukee WI

Robert Lehman Collection

The Metropolitan Museum of Art, New York NY

Bernard Lennon Collection

Museum of Contemporary Impressionism, New
Milford CT

Roy C Leventritt Collection

Asian Art Museum of San Francisco, Avery
Brundage Collection, San Francisco CA

Levy Collection

McMaster University, Museum of Art, Hamilton
ON

Dr Louis Levy Collection of American Prints

Memphis Brooks Museum of Art, Memphis TN

**Robert H & Ryda Levy Collection of
Contemporary Sculpture**

Baltimore Museum of Art, Baltimore MD

**Julius Levy Memorial Collection of Oriental
Art**

Baltimore Museum of Art, Baltimore MD

Lewis Collection of Classical Antiquities

Portland Art Museum, Portland OR

Lewis-Kneberg Collection

University of Tennessee, Frank H McClung
Museum, Knoxville TN

Lewisohn Collection of Caribbean Art

University of Mississippi, University Museums,
Oxford MS

Dan Leyrer Photograph Collection

Kemper & Leila Williams Foundation, New Orleans
LA

Joans Lie Collection of Panama Canal Oils

United States Military Academy, West Point
Museum, West Point NY

Liedesdorf Collection of European Armor

United States Military Academy, West Point
Museum, West Point NY

Linoleum Blocks & Prints

Walter Anderson Museum of Art, Ocean Springs
MS

Jacques Lipchitz Sculpture Collection

University of Arizona, Museum of Art, Tucson AZ

Liquor Bottle Collection

Deming-Luna Mimbres Museum, Deming NM

Local & State History

Palm Springs Desert Museum, Palm Springs CA

Locke Collection

Roberts County Museum, Miami TX

Michener Collection of Prints & Paintings

Kent State University, School of Art Gallery, Kent OH

Midwestern Art

Nobles County Art Center Gallery, Worthington MN

Mielke Collection

Carrie McLain Museum, Nome AK

Arnold Mikelson Wood Sculpture

Arnold Mikelson Mind & Matter Gallery, White Rock BC

Military Art Collection

Fort George G Meade Museum, Fort Meade MD
National Infantry Museum, Fort Benning GA

Military Artifacts

United States Military Academy, West Point Museum, West Point NY

Military Equipment Relating to Mech Cavalry & Armor

Cavalry - Armor Foundation, Patton Museum of Cavalry & Armor, Fort Knox KY

Samuel & Tobie Miller Collection

Baltimore Museum of Art, Baltimore MD

Anna L Miller Paintings

Viterbo College Art Gallery, La Crosse WI

John Miller Photography Collection

Delta State University, Fielding L Wright Art Center, Cleveland MS

Millington-Barnard Collection

University of Mississippi, University Museums, Oxford MS

Rose & Benjamin Mintz Collection of Eastern European Art

The Jewish Museum, New York NY

A R Mitchell Collection

Arthur Roy Mitchell Memorial Inc, Museum of Western Art, Trinidad CO

Albert K Mitchell Russell-Remington Collection

National Cowboy Hall of Fame & Western Heritage Center Museum, Oklahoma City OK

Model Airplanes

US Coast Guard Museum, New London CT

Model Ships

US Coast Guard Museum, New London CT

Andrew Molles Collection

Riverside Art Museum, Riverside CA

James Montgomery Ward Permanent Collection

Palette & Chisel Academy of Fine Arts, Chicago IL

Marianne Moore Archive Collection

The Rosenbach Museum & Library, Philadelphia PA

Moore Collection

London Regional Art & Historical Museums, London ON
University of Illinois, Krannert Art Museum, Champaign IL
University of Tennessee, Frank H McClung Museum, Knoxville TN

Henry Moore Sculpture Collection

Art Gallery of Ontario, Toronto ON

Thomas Moran & J M W/Turner Original Prints, Watercolor & Oil Collections

The Turner Museum, Denver CO

Morgenroth Renaissance Medals & Plaquettes Collection

University of California, Santa Barbara, University Art Museum, Santa Barbara CA

Mormon Collection

Church of Jesus Christ of Latter-Day Saints, Museum of Church History & Art, Salt Lake City UT

Howard J Morrison Jr Osteological Collection

Kiah Museum, Savannah GA

Morse Collection

Beloit College, Wright Museum of Art, Beloit WI

Pfeffer Moser Glass Collection

University of the Ozarks, Stephens Gallery, Clarksville AR

Mountain Sculpture-Carving

Crazy Horse Memorial, Indian Museum of North America & Native American Educational & Cultural Center, Crazy Horse SD

William Sidney Mount Collection

The Museums at Stony Brook, Stony Brook NY

Arnold Mountfort Collection

Santa Clara University, de Saisset Museum, Santa Clara CA

Mourot Collection of Meissen Porcelain

Virginia Museum of Fine Arts, Richmond VA

Mowat Loyalist Collection

Ross Memorial Museum, Saint Andrews NB

Munich School Paintings

Frye Art Museum, Seattle WA

Roland P Murdock Collection of American Art

Wichita Art Museum, Wichita KS

Musical Instruments

The Metropolitan Museum of Art, New York NY

Eadwaerd Muybridge Photography Collection

Stanford University, Museum of Art, Stanford CA

Mystic Art Colony Collection

Mystic Art Association, Inc, Mystic CT

Gwen Houston Naftzger Collection of Porcelain Birds

Wichita Art Museum, Wichita KS

L S and Ida L Naftzger Collection of Prints and Drawings

Wichita Art Museum, Wichita KS

M C Naftzger Collection of Russell Paintings

Wichita Art Museum, Wichita KS

Nagel Collection of Chinese & Tibetan Sculpture & Textiles

Scripps College, Clark Humanities Museum, Claremont CA

Thomas Nast Collection

Cornell College, Armstrong Gallery, Mount Vernon IA

Native American Art

Carson County Square House Museum, Panhandle TX
College of William & Mary, Joseph & Margaret Muscarelle Museum of Art, Williamsburg VA
Florence Museum of Art, Science & History, Florence SC
Newark Museum Association, The Newark Museum, Newark NJ

Native American Artifacts

Artesia Historical Museum & Art Center, Artesia NM
Coos County Historical Society Museum, North Bend OR
Piatt Castles, West Liberty OH

Native American Artifacts Collection

Willard House & Clock Museum, Inc, North Grafton MA

Paintings

National Museum of Women in the Arts, Washington DC

Paintings-Hungarian

The Turner Museum, Denver CO

Painting - Spanish Colonial

San Antonio Museum of Art, San Antonio TX

Paintings - Susan Eakins, Gustavus Gronewald, Antonio Martino, Elmer Schofield

Moravian College, Payne Gallery, Bethlehem PA

Papua New Guinea Artifacts

Enook Galleries, Waterloo ON

Parish Collection of Furniture

Frederic Remington Art Museum, Ogdensburg NY

Parker Lace Collection

Montreal Museum of Fine Arts, Montreal PQ

Samuel Parrish Collection of Renaissance Art

The Parrish Art Museum, Southampton NY

J G D'Arcy Paul Collection

Baltimore Museum of Art, Baltimore MD

The Paulson Collection of Ancient Near Eastern Coins

University of Georgia, Georgia Museum of Art, Athens GA

John Barton Payne Collection

Virginia Museum of Fine Arts, Richmond VA

Peabody Institute Collection

Baltimore Museum of Art, Baltimore MD

Adelaide Pearson Collection

Colby College, Museum of Art, Waterville ME

Samuel Pees Contemporary Painting Collection

Allegheny College, Bowman, Megahan & Penelec Galleries, Meadville PA

Pendleton Collection

Kelly-Griggs House Museum, Red Bluff CA

Pendleton House Decorative Arts Collection

Rhode Island School of Design, Museum of Art, Providence RI

Joseph Pennell Collection

George Washington University, The Dimock Gallery, Washington DC

E Wood Perry Paintings

Sandwich Historical Society, Center Sandwich NH

Leonard Pfeiffer Collection

University of Arizona, Museum of Art, Tucson AZ

Phelps Collection

Delaware Art Museum, Wilmington DE

Phillips-Burrows-Faulkner Collection

Glanmore, Hastings County Museum, Belleville ON

Walter J Phillips Collection

Banff Centre, Walter Phillips Gallery, Banff AB

George Phippen Memorial Western Bronze Collection

Maricopa County Historical Society, Desert Caballeros Western Museum, Wickenburg AZ

Duncan Phyfe Furniture Collection

Cincinnati Institute of Fine Arts, Taft Museum, Cincinnati OH

Albert Pilavin Collection of 20th Century American Arts

Rhode Island School of Design, Museum of Art, Providence RI

Lucile Pillow Porcelain Collection

Montreal Museum of Fine Arts, Montreal PQ

Pioneer Memorabilia

Crazy Horse Memorial, Indian Museum of North America & Native American Educational & Cultural Center, Crazy Horse SD

Pitkin Asian Art Collection

Beloit College, Wright Museum of Art, Beloit WI

Pohl Collection - German Expressionism

Lawrence University, Wriston Art Center Galleries, Appleton WI

Sigmar Polke Collection

Walker Art Center, Minneapolis MN

William J Pollock Collection of American Indian Art

Colby College, Museum of Art, Waterville ME

H V Poor

Birger Sandzen Memorial Gallery, Lindsborg KS

Porter-Phelps-Huntington Family Collection

Porter-Phelps-Huntington Foundation, Inc, Historic House Museum, Hadley MA

Portsmouth Furniture Collection

Warner House Association, MacPheadris-Warner House, Portsmouth NH

Potamkin Collection of 19th & 20th Century Work

Dickinson College, Trout Gallery, Carlisle PA

Potlatch Collection of Royal Canadian Mounted Police Illustrations

University of Minnesota, Duluth, Tweed Museum of Art, Duluth MN

Charles Pratt Collection of Chinese Jades

Vassar College, The Frances Lehman Loeb Art Center, Poughkeepsie NY

Lillian Thomas Pratt Collection of Czarist Jewels

Virginia Museum of Fine Arts, Richmond VA

Pre-Columbian Art

Blanden Memorial Art Museum, Fort Dodge IA

Pre-Columbian Collection

Polk Museum of Art, Lakeland FL

Pre-Columbian Pottery

George R Gardiner Museum of Ceramic Art, Toronto ON
Luther College, Fine Arts Collection, Decorah IA

William Henry Price Memorial Collection of Oil Paintings

Oregon State University, Memorial Union Art Gallery, Corvallis OR

Public Art

Capp Street Project, San Francisco CA

Public Sculpture

Art Resources International, Washington DC

Puerto Rican Art

University of Puerto Rico, Museum of Anthropology, History & Art, San Juan PR

Puppetry

Center for Puppetry Arts, Atlanta GA

Putnam Collection

Timken Museum of Art, San Diego CA

Quadrupeds of North America Collection

Audubon Wildlife Sanctuary, Audubon PA

Natacha Rambova Egyptian Collection

University of Utah, Utah Museum of Fine Arts, Salt Lake City UT

Rand Collection of American Indian Art

Montclair Art Museum, Montclair NJ

Rasmussen Collection of Eskimo Arts

Portland Art Museum, Portland OR

Ray American Indian Collection

Red River Valley Museum, Vernon TX

Lester Raymer

Birger Sandzen Memorial Gallery, Lindsborg KS

Regional Folk Art

Columbus Museum of Art, Columbus OH

Remington Bronze Collection

Pioneer Town, Pioneer Museum of Western Art,
Wimberley TX

Frederic Remington Collection

Bradford Brinton Memorial Museum & Historic
Ranch, Big Horn WY
R W Norton Art Gallery, Shreveport LA
St Lawrence University, Richard F Brush Art
Gallery, Canton NY

Remington Drawings

Headquarters Fort Monroe, Dept of Army,
Casemate Museum, Fort Monroe VA

Frederic Remington Paintings

Los Angeles County Museum of Natural History,
William S Hart Museum, Newhall CA

Fredrick Remington Sculpture Collection

Coutts Memorial Museum of Art, Inc, El Dorado
KS

Frederic Remington Western Art Paintings

Sid W Richardson Foundation, Collection of
Western Art, Fort Worth TX

Renaissance & Baroque Period Collection

Guilford College, Art Gallery, Greensboro NC

Richards Coin Collection

Hastings Museum, Hastings NE

General Lawrason Riggs Collection

Baltimore Museum of Art, Baltimore MD

Rindisbacher Watercolors

United States Military Academy, West Point
Museum, West Point NY

William Ritschel Collection

Monterey Museum of Art Association, Monterey
CA

David Roberts Collection

Riverside County Museum, Edward-Dean Museum,
Cherry Valley CA

Roberts Sculpture Collection

Portland Art Museum, Portland OR

Marion Sharp Robinson Collection

University of Utah, Utah Museum of Fine Arts, Salt
Lake City UT

David Robinson Collection of Antiquities

University of Mississippi, University Museums,
Oxford MS

Sara Roby Foundation Collection

National Museum of American Art, Washington
DC

**Abby Aldrich Rockefeller Collection of
Japanese Art**

Rhode Island School of Design, Museum of Art,
Providence RI

Rockefeller Third Collection of Asian Art

The Asia Society Galleries, New York NY

Norman Rockwell Collection

Norman Rockwell Museum at Stockbridge,
Stockbridge MA

Robert F Rockwell Foundation Collection

The Rockwell Museum, Corning NY

Rodeo Portrait Collection

National Cowboy Hall of Fame & Western Heritage
Center Museum, Oklahoma City OK

Auguste Rodin Collection

Stanford University, Museum of Art, Stanford CA

Rodin Sculpture Collection

Gonzaga University, Jundt Art Museum, Ad Art
Gallery, Spokane WA

Rodman Collection of Popular Art

The Art Galleries of Ramapo College, Mahwah NJ

Nicholas Roerich Collection

Nicholas Roerich Museum, New York NY

John Rogers Sculpture Collection

Saginaw Art Museum, Saginaw MI

August H O Rolle Collection

Calvert Marine Museum, Solomons MD

Edward Rose Collection of Ceramics

Brandeis University, Rose Art Museum, Waltham
MA

Ross Decorative Art Collection

Ross Memorial Museum, Saint Andrews NB

Guy Rowe Wax Drawings Collection

Angelo State University, Houston Harte University
Center, San Angelo TX

Roycroft Objects

Burchfield-Penney Art Center, Buffalo NY

Edmond R Ruben Film Study Collection

Walker Art Center, Minneapolis MN

Peter Paul Rubens Collection

State Art Museum of Florida, John & Mable
Ringling Museum of Art, Sarasota FL

Rugs

Deming-Luna Mimbres Museum, Deming NM

Charles M Russell Collection

Bradford Brinton Memorial Museum & Historic
Ranch, Big Horn WY
C M Russell Museum, Great Falls MT
R W Norton Art Gallery, Shreveport LA

Charles M Russell Paintings

Los Angeles County Museum of Natural History,
William S Hart Museum, Newhall CA
Wichita Art Museum, Wichita KS

Charles M Russell Western Art Paintings

Sid W Richardson Foundation, Collection of
Western Art, Fort Worth TX

Russian & Baltic Photography

Roy Boyd Gallery, Chicago IL

Sackler Collection

The Metropolitan Museum of Art, New York NY

**Oscar & Maria Salzer Collection of Still
Life & Trompe L'oeil Paintings**

Fresno Metropolitan Museum, Fresno CA

**Oscar & Maria Salzer Collection of 16th &
17th Century Dutch & Flemish Paintings**

Fresno Metropolitan Museum, Fresno CA

Wilbur Sandison Photography Collection

Whatcom Museum of History and Art, Bellingham
WA

Sandwich Glass Collection

Fuller Museum of Art, Brockton MA

Birger Sandzen

Birger Sandzen Memorial Gallery, Lindsborg KS

Sargent Collection of American Indian Art

Montclair Art Museum, Montclair NJ

Sawhill Artifact Collection

James Madison University, Sawhill Gallery, Harrisonburg VA

Jonathan Sax Print Collection

University of Minnesota, Duluth, Tweed Museum of Art, Duluth MN

Scandinavian Immigrant Painting

Luther College, Fine Arts Collection, Decorah IA

Eugene Schaefer Collection

Newark Museum Association, The Newark Museum, Newark NJ

Richard Schmid Permanent Collection

Palette & Chisel Academy of Fine Arts, Chicago IL

Alice F Schott Doll Collection

Santa Barbara Museum of Art, Santa Barbara CA

Schreyvogel Collection

National Cowboy Hall of Fame & Western Heritage Center Museum, Oklahoma City OK

Charles Schreyvogel Paintings

Los Angeles County Museum of Natural History, William S Hart Museum, Newhall CA

Schuette Woodland Indian Collection

Rahr-West Art Museum, Manitowoc WI

Schwartz Collection of Chinese Ivories

Rahr-West Art Museum, Manitowoc WI

Hazel Schwentker Collection

Rapid City Arts Council, Dahl Fine Arts Center, Rapid City SD

Scotese Collection of Graphics

Columbia Museum of Art, Columbia SC

Philip Sears Sculpture Collection

Fruitlands Museum, Inc, Harvard MA

Seibels Collection of Renaissance Art

Columbia Museum of Art, Columbia SC

Shaker Collection

Hancock Shaker Village, Inc, Pittsfield MA

Shaker Culture

Shaker Village of Pleasant Hill, Harrodsburg KY

Shaker History & Culture Collection

Shaker Museum & Library, Old Chatham NY

Sharp Collection of Glass

Frederic Remington Art Museum, Ogdensburg NY

Sheet Music Covers

Liberty Memorial Museum & Archives, Kansas City MO

Inglis Sheldon-Williams Collection

Regina Public Library, Dunlop Art Gallery, Regina SK

William Ludwell Sheppard Watercolor Collection

Valentine Museum, Richmond VA

Shipbuilding

Essex Historical Society, Essex Shipbuilding Museum, Essex MA

Henrietta Shore Collection

Santa Clara University, de Saisset Museum, Santa Clara CA

David M Shoup Collection of Korean Pottery

Allegheny College, Bowman, Megahan & Penelec Galleries, Meadville PA

Philip Trammell Shutze Collection

Atlanta Historical Society Inc, Atlanta History Center, Atlanta GA

B Simon Lithography Collection

Kemper & Leila Williams Foundation, New Orleans LA

John Singer Sargent Collection

Isabella Stewart Gardner Museum, Boston MA

Sixteenth Century Porcelain Collection

Harvard University, Busch-Reisinger Museum, Cambridge MA

Sixteenth-Twentieth Century American & European Works

College of William & Mary, Joseph & Margaret Muscarelle Museum of Art, Williamsburg VA

Sixteenth-Twentieth Century Books

La Casa del Libro Museum, San Juan PR

Dorothy D Skewis Print Collection

Witter Gallery, Storm Lake IA

SLA Corporate Collection

SLA Arch-Couture Inc, Art Collection, Denver CO

Sloan Collection

Valparaiso University, Brauer Museum of Art, Valparaiso IN

Eric Sloane Collection

Connecticut Historical Commission, Sloane-Stanley Museum, Kent CT

Helen S Slosberg Collection of Oceanic Art

Brandeis University, Rose Art Museum, Waltham MA

C R Smith Collection of Western American Art

University of Texas at Austin, Archer M Huntington Art Gallery, Austin TX

Smith Painting Collection

Woodmere Art Museum, Philadelphia PA

Smith-Patterson Memorial Collection

Delta State University, Fielding L Wright Art Center, Cleveland MS

Smith Watch Key Collection

Rollins College, George D & Harriet W Cornell Fine Arts Museum, Winter Park FL

Snelgrove Historical Collection

Gadsden Museum of Fine Arts, Inc, Gadsden AL

Steamer W P Snyder Jr

The Ohio Historical Society, Inc, Campus Martius Museum & Ohio River Museum, Marietta OH

Society of Cincinnati

Society of the Cincinnati, Museum & Library at Anderson House, Washington DC

Soldiers' Art & Crafts

Liberty Memorial Museum & Archives, Kansas City MO

Sonnenschein Collection

Cornell College, Armstrong Gallery, Mount Vernon IA

Southern Mississippi Delta Art

Arts & Science Center for Southeast Arkansas, Pine Bluff AR

Leon Spilliaert Collection

The Metropolitan Museum of Art, New York NY

Sporting Art

Genesee Country Museum, John L Wehle Gallery of Sporting Art, Mumford NY

Springfield & Connecticut Valley History

Springfield Library & Museums Association, Connecticut Valley Historical Museum, Springfield MA

Tufnell Watercolor Collection

Calvert Marine Museum, Solomons MD

J M W Turner Watercolor Collection

Indianapolis Museum of Art, Indianapolis IN

Lyle Tuttle Collection

Tattoo Art Museum, San Francisco CA

George P Tweed Memorial Collection of American & European Paintings

University of Minnesota, Duluth, Tweed Museum of Art, Duluth MN

Twentieth Century American Art

Albany Museum of Art, Albany GA
Guilford College, Art Gallery, Greensboro NC

Twentieth Century American Sculpture Collection

James A Michener Art Museum, Doylestown PA

Twentieth Century Art

San Jose Museum of Art, San Jose CA
State University of New York at Stony Brook, University Art Gallery, Stony Brook NY

Twentieth Century Artists

University of Wisconsin-Eau Claire, Foster Gallery, Eau Claire WI

Twentieth Century German Works Collection

Harvard University, Busch-Reisinger Museum, Cambridge MA

Twentieth Century Paintings

Moravian College, Payne Gallery, Bethlehem PA

Twentieth Century Realism & Abstraction

National Museum of American Art, Washington DC

Two & Three-Dimensional Designs

Coutts Memorial Museum of Art, Inc, El Dorado KS

Tyson Collection

Philadelphia Museum of Art, Philadelphia PA

Ukrainian Paintings; Archives

The Ukrainian Museum, New York NY

Doris Ulmann Photography Collection

Berea College, Doris Ulmann Galleries, Berea KY

United States & Foreign Military Equipment

National Infantry Museum, Fort Benning GA

United States Military History

Roswell P Flower Memorial Library, Watertown NY

Nora S Unwin Collection of Wood Engravings, Drawings, Watercolors

Sharon Arts Center, Peterborough NH

USS Constitution Models

USS Constitution Museum, Boston MA

Edward Virginius Valentine Sculpture Collection

Valentine Museum, Richmond VA

Vanderpoel Oriental Art Collection

Slater-Norton Corporation, Slater Memorial Museum & Converse Art Gallery, Norwich CT

Van Ess Collection of Renaissance & Baroque Art

Hartwick College, Foreman Gallery, Oneonta NY

Carl Van Vechten Photographs

Fisk University, University Galleries, Nashville TN

Edward Burr Van Vleck Collection of Japanese Prints

University of Wisconsin-Madison, Elvehjem Museum of Art, Madison WI

Matthew Vassar Collection

Vassar College, The Frances Lehman Loeb Art Center, Poughkeepsie NY

James Ven Der Zee Photography Collection

The Studio Museum in Harlem, New York NY

Ellis Verink Photograph Collection

Polk Museum of Art, Lakeland FL

David T Vernon Indian Arts Collection

Grand Teton National Park Service, Colter Bay Indian Arts Museum, Moose WY

Victor Talking Machine Company Phonographs & Records

Historical & Cultural Affairs, Delaware State Museums, Dover DE

Voertman Collection

University of North Texas, Art Gallery, Denton TX

Von Schleinitz Collection

Milwaukee Art Museum, Milwaukee WI

Wachovia Permanent Collection

Burke Arts Council, Jailhouse Galleries, Morganton NC

Wagner Collection of African Sculpture

Scripps College, Clark Humanities Museum, Claremont CA

Waldo Peirce Collection

Southern Oregon State College, Schneider Museum of Art, Ashland OR

Walker Collection of French Impressionists

Corcoran Gallery of Art, Washington DC

C G Wallace Collection

Heard Museum, Phoenix AZ

Wallcoverings

Cooper-Hewitt, National Design Museum, New York NY

Cloud Wampler Collection of Oriental Art

Everson Museum of Art, Syracuse NY

Felix M Warburg Collection of Medieval Sculpture

Vassar College, The Frances Lehman Loeb Art Center, Poughkeepsie NY

Austen D Warburton Native American Art & Artifacts Collection

Triton Museum of Art, Santa Clara CA

Andy Warhol Collection

University of Maryland, College Park, Art Gallery, College Park MD

Booker T Washington Collection

Tuskegee Institute National Historic Site, George Washington Carver & The Oaks, Tuskegee Institute AL

George Washington Memorabilia

Mount Vernon Ladies' Association of the Union, Mount Vernon VA

Wassenberg Collection

Wassenberg Art Center, Van Wert OH

Watkins Collection of American and European Paintings

American University, Watkins Collection, Washington DC

Homer Watson Collection

Kitchener-Waterloo Art Gallery, Kitchener ON

William Watson Collection of Ceramics

Lemoyne Art Foundation, Inc, Tallahassee FL

Ernest C & Jane Werner Watson Collection of Indian Miniatures

University of Wisconsin-Madison, Elvehjem Museum of Art, Madison WI

Watson Family Artifacts

Homer Watson House & Gallery, Kitchener ON

Homer Watson Paintings Collection

Homer Watson House & Gallery, Kitchener ON

Frederick J Waugh Paintings (Ulrich Collection)

Wichita State University, Edwin A Ulrich Museum of Art, Wichita KS

John Wayne Collection

National Cowboy Hall of Fame & Western Heritage Center Museum, Oklahoma City OK

Weatherhead Collection

Fort Wayne Museum of Art, Inc, Fort Wayne IN

Weaving

Kit Carson Historic Museums, Hacienda Martinez, Taos NM

Esther Webster Art Collection

Port Angeles Fine Arts Center, Port Angeles WA

Wedgewood Collection

Birmingham Museum of Art, Birmingham AL

Wedgwood Collection

R W Norton Art Gallery, Shreveport LA

Teresa Jackson Weill Collection

Brandeis University, Rose Art Museum, Waltham MA

J Alden Weir Archive & Manuscript Collection

National Park Service, Weir Farm National Historic Site, Wilton CT

J Alden Weir Collection

Brigham Young University, B F Larsen Gallery, Provo UT

Wellington Collection of Wood Engravings

Mobile Museum of Art, Mobile AL

Maurice Wertheim Collection

Harvard University, William Hayes Fogg Art Museum, Cambridge MA

West African Art Collection

New Visions Gallery, Inc, Marshfield WI

Benjamin West Collection

Bob Jones University, Museum & Art Gallery, Greenville SC

Western & Contemporary Western

Coutts Memorial Museum of Art, Inc, El Dorado KS

Western Indian Artifacts

Favell Museum of Western Art & Indian Artifacts, Klamath Falls OR

Western New York Regional Art

Burchfield-Penney Art Center, Buffalo NY

Candace Wheeler Collection

Mark Twain Memorial, Hartford CT

Peter Whitebird Collection of WPA Project Paintings

Viterbo College Art Gallery, La Crosse WI

White Collection

Baltimore Museum of Art, Baltimore MD
Philadelphia Museum of Art, Philadelphia PA
Sumter Gallery of Art, Sumter SC

Major General Courtney Whitney Collection

MacArthur Memorial, Library & Archives, Norfolk VA

Whitney Silver Collection

Montclair Art Museum, Montclair NJ

Whittington Memorial Collection

Delta State University, Fielding L Wright Art Center, Cleveland MS

Wiant Collection of Chinese Art

Ohio State University, Wexner Center for the Arts, Columbus OH

Bartlett Wicks Collection

University of Utah, Utah Museum of Fine Arts, Salt Lake City UT

Widener Collection

National Gallery of Art, Washington DC

Albert H Wiggin Collection

Boston Public Library, Albert H Wiggin Gallery & Print Department, Boston MA

Margurite Wildenhain Collection

Luther College, Fine Arts Collection, Decorah IA

Wilder Art Glass & Pottery Collection

Topeka & Shawnee County Public Library, Gallery of Fine Arts, Topeka KS

Wildlife Art (North American & European)

Genesee Country Museum, John L Wehle Gallery of Sporting Art, Mumford NY

John Wiley Collection

Concordia University Wisconsin, Fine Art Gallery, Mequon WI

Willard Clockmaking Collection

Willard House & Clock Museum, Inc, North Grafton MA

Archibald M Willard Paintings Collection

Southern Lorain County Historical Society, Spirit of '76 Museum, Wellington OH

Will Collection of Paintings & Drawings

Jersey City Museum, Jersey City NJ

William Rufus King Collection

Alabama Department of Archives & History, Museum Galleries, Montgomery AL

Adolph D & Wilkins C Williams Collection

Virginia Museum of Fine Arts, Richmond VA

Lois Wilson Collection

Fayette Art Museum, Fayette AL
Huntington College, Robert E Wilson Art Gallery, Huntington IN
Lehigh University Art Galleries, Bethlehem PA

Wilstach Collection of Old Masters

Philadelphia Museum of Art, Philadelphia PA

Wingert Collection of African & Oceanic Art

Montclair State University, Art Galleries, Upper Montclair NJ

Wisconsin Art History Collection

West Bend Art Museum, West Bend WI

Ella Witter Collection

Witter Gallery, Storm Lake IA

Women Artists

La Centrale Powerhouse Gallery, Montreal PQ

Woodblock (Ukiyo-e) Prints

Lauren Rogers Museum of Art, Laurel MS

Grant Wood Collection

Davenport Museum of Art, Davenport IA
Huronia Museum, Midland ON

Jack Woods Collection

Pioneer Town, Pioneer Museum of Western Art, Wimberley TX

William Woodward Collection

Baltimore Museum of Art, Baltimore MD

Theodore Wores Collection

Triton Museum of Art, Santa Clara CA

World War I Covers

Liberty Memorial Museum & Archives, Kansas City MO

Frank Lloyd Wright Collection

Allentown Art Museum, Allentown PA
George Washington University, The Dimock Gallery, Washington DC

Wutzburger Collection

Baltimore Museum of Art, Baltimore MD

Wyeth Family Collection

Brandywine River Museum, Chadds Ford PA

Yena Collection

Witte Museum, San Antonio TX

Mahonri Young Collection of Manuscripts

Brigham Young University, B F Larsen Gallery, Provo UT

Karl Zerbe Collection of Serigraphs

Lemoyne Art Foundation, Inc, Tallahassee FL

Zogbaum Drawings

Headquarters Fort Monroe, Dept of Army, Casemate Museum, Fort Monroe VA

Adams, Marlin, *Instr,* Gordon College, Dept of Fine Arts, Barnesville GA (S)

Adams, Meg, *Educ,* Blanden Memorial Art Museum, Fort Dodge IA

Adams, Nicholas, *Chmn,* Vassar College, Art Dept, Poughkeepsie NY (S)

Adams, Roger J, *Assoc Prof,* Nazareth College of Rochester, Art Dept, Rochester NY (S)

Adams, Rosemary, *Ed,* Chicago Historical Society, Chicago IL

Adams, Sally, *Business Mgr,* Western Reserve Historical Society, Cleveland OH

Adams, Sharon, *Specialist Ceramic Educ,* Duke University Union, Durham NC

Adams, Stan, *Instr,* Illinois Central College, Dept of Fine Arts, East Peoria IL (S)

Adams, Suzanne, *Dept Chmn,* Clinch Valley College of the University of Virginia, Visual & Performing Arts Dept, Wise VA (S)

Adams-O'Brien, Frances, *Technical Servs Librn,* Ringling School of Art & Design, Verman Kimbrough Memorial Library, Sarasota FL

Adamson, Jim, *Instr,* Sierra Community College, Art Dept, Rocklin CA (S)

Adamy, George E, *Dir,* Adamy's Concrete & Cast Paper Workshops, Ossining NY (S)

Adato, Linda, *Treas,* Society of American Graphic Artists, New York NY

Addington, Aldon, *Assoc Prof,* Southern Illinois University, School of Art & Design, Carbondale IL (S)

Addison, Elizabeth, *Librn,* Morris Museum, Library, Morristown NJ

Addison, E W, *Dir,* Brewton-Parker College, Visual Arts, Mount Vernon GA (S)

Addison, Les, *Instr,* Maryville University of Saint Louis, Art Division, Saint Louis MO (S)

Addiss, Stephen, *Prof,* University of Richmond, Dept of Art, Richmond VA (S)

Addleman, Roger, *Dir Communications,* Ohio State University, Wexner Center for the Arts, Columbus OH

Ade, Shirley, *Museum Dir,* McPherson Museum, McPherson KS

Adelman, Charles, *Assoc Prof,* University of Northern Iowa, Dept of Art, Cedar Falls IA (S)

Adelman, Everett Mayo, *Instr,* North Carolina Wesleyan College, Dept of Visual & Performing Arts, Rocky Mount NC (S)

Adelman, Meri, *Cur Educ,* Woodmere Art Museum, Library, Philadelphia PA

Adelmann, Arthur R, *Prof,* Weber State University, Dept of Visual Arts, Ogden UT (S)

Adkins, William, *Dir & Cur Art Gallery,* Indiana University - Purdue University at Indianapolis, Indianapolis Center for Contemporary Art-Herron Gallery, Indianapolis IN

Adkins, William, *Dir Visual Arts,* Jay County Arts Council, Hugh N Ronald Memorial Gallery, Portland IN

Adleburg, Frances S, *Chmn,* North Florida Community College, Dept Humanities & Art, Madison FL (S)

Adney, Carol, *Dir,* City of San Rafael, Falkirk Cultural Center, San Rafael CA

Adrean, Louis V, *Asst Librn Public Serv,* Cleveland Museum of Art, Ingalls Library, Cleveland OH

Affleck, John, *VPres,* Woodmere Art Museum, Philadelphia PA

Aframe, Debby, *Slide Librn,* Worcester Art Museum, Library, Worcester MA

Agard, James, *Assoc Prof,* Gettysburg College, Dept of Visual Arts, Gettysburg PA (S)

Agdanowski, Debbie, *Exhib Coordr,* Creative Arts Center, Pontiac MI

Agee, Nelle, *Asst Prof,* Oklahoma Baptist University, Art Dept, Shawnee OK (S)

Agel, Lillian, *Pres,* Arts Council of Greater Kingsport, Renaissance Center Main Gallery, Kingsport TN

Ageloff, Scott, *Assoc Prof,* Marymount College, Art Dept, Tarrytown NY (S)

Aglio, Henry, *Asst Prof,* West Virginia University at Parkersburg, Art Dept, Parkersburg WV (S)

Agnew, Ellen Schall, *Dir Colls & Progs,* Randolph-Macon Woman's College, Maier Museum of Art, Lynchburg VA

Agnew, L Jack, *Prof,* Sullivan County Community College, Division of Commercial Art & Photography, Loch Sheldrake NY (S)

Aguado, William, *Council Dir,* Bronx Council on the Arts, Longwood Arts Gallery, Bronx NY

Aguayo, Jose, *Exec Dir,* Museo De Las Americas, Denver CO

Aguero, Clara, *Asst Prof,* Savannah State University, Dept of Fine Arts, Savannah GA (S)

Aguilo, Sister, *Instr,* University of North Carolina at Charlotte, Dept of Visual Arts, Charlotte NC (S)

Ahearn, Maureen, *Dir,* Keene State College, Thorne-Sagendorph Art Gallery, Keene NH

Ahern, Vincent, *Coordr Pub Art,* University of South Florida, Contemporary Art Museum, Tampa FL

Ahlstrom, Romaine, *Dept Mgr,* Los Angeles Public Library, Arts & Recreation Dept, Los Angeles CA

Ahmad, Sufi, *Assoc Prof,* Saint Francis College, Art Dept, Fort Wayne IN (S)

Aho, Arnold, *Assoc Prof,* Norwich University, Dept of Philosophy, Religion & Fine Arts, Northfield VT (S)

Aho, Charles, *Adjunct Instr,* Le Moyne College, Fine Arts Dept, Syracuse NY (S)

Ahrens, Kent, *Dir,* Civic Fine Arts Center, Sioux Falls SD

Ahrens, Kent, *Dir,* Civic Fine Arts Center, Library, Sioux Falls SD

Ahwesh, Peggy, *Instr,* Bard College, Milton Avery Graduate School of the Arts, Annandale-on-Hudson NY (S)

Aichele, K Porter, *Head,* University of North Carolina at Greensboro, Art Dept, Greensboro NC (S)

Aidinoff, M Bernard, *Treas,* Guild Hall of East Hampton, Inc, Guild Hall Museum, East Hampton NY

Aiello, Eugene, *Treas,* Arthur Roy Mitchell Memorial Inc, Museum of Western Art, Trinidad CO

Aiken, Edward A, *Dir,* Syracuse University, Joe & Emily Lowe Art Gallery, Syracuse NY

Aiken, Jane, *Prof,* Virginia Polytechnic Institute & State University, Dept of Art & Art History, Blacksburg VA (S)

Aiken, Suzanne, *Instr,* University of Evansville, Art Dept, Evansville IN (S)

Aikens, Martha, *Supt,* Independence National Historical Park, Philadelphia PA

Aikin, Roger, *Chmn Fine & Performing Arts Dept,* Creighton University, Fine Arts Gallery, Omaha NE

Aikin, Roger, *Chmn&prof,* Creighton University, Fine & Performing Arts Dept, Omaha NE (S)

Aikman, John, *Instr,* Linn Benton Community College, Fine & Applied Art Dept, Albany OR (S)

Aimesto, Laura, *Dean,* Barry University, Dept of Fine Arts, Miami Shores FL (S)

Ainslie, Patricia, *VPres Coll,* Glenbow Museum, Calgary AB

Aistars, John, *Dir,* Cazenovia College, Chapman Art Center Gallery, Cazenovia NY

Aistars, Kohn, *Prof,* Cazenovia College, Center for Art & Design Studies, Cazenovia NY (S)

Aitken, T, *Instr,* Community College of Rhode Island, Dept of Art, Warwick RI (S)

Ajootian, Aileen, *Asst Prof,* University of Mississippi, Dept of Art, University MS (S)

Akamatsu, Elizabeth, *Asst Prof,* Sam Houston State University, Art Dept, Huntsville TX (S)

Akgulian, Mark, *Dir Design,* Spertus Institute of Jewish Studies, Spertus Museum, Chicago IL

Akuna-Hanson, Chris, *Gallery Dir,* Rio Hondo College Art Gallery, Whittier CA

Alaggia, Dominick, *VPres,* Bowne House Historical Society, Flushing NY

Alaniz, Anet, *Admin Asst,* Contemporary Art for San Antonio Blue Star Art Space, San Antonio TX

Alartoski, Richard, *Head Art Dept,* School of Fashion Design, Boston MA (S)

Albacete, Manuel J, *Exec Dir,* Canton Museum of Art, Canton OH

Albacete, Manuel J, *Exec Dir,* Canton Museum of Art, Art Library, Canton OH

Albacete, Manuel J, *Dir,* Canton Museum of Art, Canton OH (S)

Albert, Karen, *Exhibit Designer & Preparation,* Hofstra University, Hofstra Museum, Hempstead NY

Alberti, Janet, *Controller,* Museum of Contemporary Art, Chicago IL

Alberts, Luanne, *Instr,* Mount Mary College, Art Dept, Milwaukee WI (S)

Albrecht, Carl, *Head Natural History,* Ohio Historical Society, Columbus OH

Albrecht, Sterling, *Dir Libraries,* Brigham Young University, Harold B Lee Library, Provo UT

Albritton, Leigh, *Registrar,* Milwaukee Art Museum, Milwaukee WI

Alderette, Bob, *Assoc Prof,* University of Southern California, School of Fine Arts, Los Angeles CA (S)

Aldern, Robert, *Prof,* Augustana College, Art Dept, Sioux Falls SD (S)

Alderson, Marge, *Treas,* Art League, Alexandria VA

Aldred, Chris, *Coordr Pub Progs,* London Regional Art & Historical Museums, London ON

Aldrich, Jonathan, *Instr,* Maine College of Art, Portland ME (S)

Aldridge, Alexander Q, *VPres Development,* Philadelphia Museum of Art, Philadelphia PA

Alegria, Ricardo E, *Dir,* Museo de la Americas, Old San Juan PR

Alexander, Andrew, *Dir,* Mason City Public Library, Mason City IA

Alexander, Anita Harris, *Artist Serv Dir,* Arts Council of Fayetteville-Cumberland County, The Arts Center, Fayetteville NC

Alexander, Barbara, *Assoc Prof,* University of Alaska-Fairbanks, Dept of Art, Fairbanks AK (S)

Alexander, Brian, *Dir,* Shelburne Museum, Shelburne VT

Alexander, Brian, *Dir,* Shelburne Museum, Library, Shelburne VT

Alexander, Brooke, *Cur,* Fried, Frank, Harris, Shriver & Jacobson, Art Collection, New York NY

Alexander, Carolyn, *VPres,* Artists Space, New York NY

Alexander, Franklin, *Instr,* Woodstock School of Art, Inc, Woodstock NY (S)

Alexander, Irene, *Cur,* Stephens College, Lewis James & Nellie Stratton Davis Art Gallery, Columbia MO

Alexander, James, *Assoc Prof,* University of Alabama at Birmingham, Dept of Art, Birmingham AL (S)

Alexander, Jane, *Chmn,* National Endowment for the Arts, Washington DC

Alexander, Kathie, *Communication Specialist,* First Tennessee National Corp, First Tennessee Heritage Collection, Memphis TN

Alexander, Lo, *Pres,* Arts on the Park, Lakeland FL

Alexander, Mark, *Dir,* University of Texas at El Paso, Glass Gallery, El Paso TX

Alexander, Mary Veitch, *Owner,* Gadsden Museum, Mesilla NM

Alexander, Melissa, *Vol Coordr,* Bellevue Art Museum, Bellevue WA

Alexander, Robert, *Interim Asst Dean,* North Hennepin Community College, Art Dept, Brooklyn Park MN (S)

Alexander, Ronald J, *Head Dept,* Northeast Louisiana University, Dept of Art, Monroe LA (S)

Alexander, Ron J, *Head,* Northeast Louisiana University, Bry Gallery, Monroe LA

Alexander, Vikky, *Asst Prof,* University of Victoria, Dept of Visual Arts, Victoria BC (S)

Alexander-Grohman, Martha, *Asst Dir,* Columbia College, The Museum of Contemporary Photography, Chicago IL

Alexenberg, Mel, *Dean Visual Arts,* New World School of the Arts, Gallery, Miami FL

Alexenberg, Mel, *Dean Visual Arts,* New World School of the Arts, Miami FL (S)

Alexick, David, *Faculty,* Christopher Newport University, Arts & Communications, Newport News VA (S)

Alfano, Domenic, *Asst Prof*, New York Institute of Technology, Fine Arts Dept, Old Westbury NY (S)

Alfied, Ted, *VPres*, Intermuseum Conservation Association, Oberlin OH

Alford, John, *Asst Prof*, Mississippi University for Women, Division of Fine & Performing Arts, Columbus MS (S)

Algermissen, Elizabeth, *Asst Dir Exhib*, Los Angeles County Museum of Art, Los Angeles CA

Ali, Ronald, *Instr*, Indiana University of Pennsylvania, Dept of Art & Art Education, Indiana PA (S)

Alkema, Chester, *Prof*, Grand Valley State University, Art & Design Dept, Allendale MI (S)

Allaben, Craig, *Gallery Mgr*, University of Massachusetts, Amherst, University Gallery, Amherst MA

Allan, Ruth, *Instr*, Wenatchee Valley College, Art Dept, Wenatchee WA (S)

Allard, L, *Chief Librn*, Musee du Quebec, Bibliotheque des Arts, Quebec PQ

Allen, Bruce, *Chmn Dept & Prof*, Centenary College of Louisiana, Dept of Art, Shreveport LA (S)

Allen, Chas, *Pres*, San Diego Maritime Museum, San Diego CA

Allen, Dottie, *Art Prog Coordr*, Hill College, Fine Arts Dept, Hillsboro TX (S)

Allen, Earlene, *Prof*, Marshall University, Dept of Art, Huntington WV (S)

Allen, Eleanor, *Prof*, Florida Community College at Jacksonville, South Campus, Art Dept, Jacksonville FL (S)

Allen, Elizabeth, *Pres*, Alberta Society of Artists, Calgary AB

Allen, Francie, *Bookstore Mgr*, Fort Worth Art Association, Modern Art Museum of Fort Worth, Fort Worth TX

Allen, Frederick E, *Dean Instruction*, Butte College, Dept of Fine Arts, Oroville CA (S)

Allen, F Robert, *Instr*, Saint Louis Community College at Meramec, Art Dept, Saint Louis MO (S)

Allen, Gwen, *Dir*, Plainsman Museum, Aurora NE

Allen, Heidi, *Asst Prof*, Concordia College, Art Dept, Moorhead MN (S)

Allen, Jacqueline, *Art Reference Librn*, Museum of Fine Arts, Houston, Hirsch Library, Houston TX

Allen, James, *Dir*, Daemen College, Fanette Goldman & Carolyn Greenfield Gallery, Amherst NY

Allen, James, *Chmn Dept*, Daemen College, Art Dept, Amherst NY (S)

Allen, Jan, *Cur Contemporary Art*, Queen's University, Agnes Etherington Art Centre, Kingston ON

Allen, Jere H, *Prof*, University of Mississippi, Dept of Art, University MS (S)

Allen, Jim, *Instr*, Springfield College in Illinois, Dept of Art, Springfield IL (S)

Allen, Jules, *Asst Prof*, Queensborough Community College, Dept of Art & Photography, Bayside NY (S)

Allen, Kay, *Assoc to Dir*, University of Southern California, Fisher Gallery, Los Angeles CA

Allen, Lucy, *Progs Coordr*, Mississippi Department of Archives & History, Old Capitol Museum, Jackson MS

Allen, Lynne, *Asst Prof*, Rutgers, the State University of New Jersey, Mason Gross School of the Arts, New Brunswick NJ (S)

Allen, Margaret, *Fine Arts Reference Librn*, Grace A Dow Memorial Library, Fine Arts Dept, Midland MI

Allen, Nancy S, *Chief Librn*, Museum of Fine Arts, William Morris Hunt Memorial Library, Boston MA

Allen, Pamela, *Asst Prof*, Troy State University, Dept of Art & Classics, Troy AL (S)

Allen, Rachel, *Research & Scholars Center Chief*, National Museum of American Art, Washington DC

Allen, Richard, *Cur*, The Southland Corporation, Art Collection, Dallas TX

Allen, Roger, *Chmn*, West Virginia University at Parkersburg, Art Dept, Parkersburg WV (S)

Allen, Skip, *Instr*, Millsaps College, Dept of Art, Jackson MS (S)

Allen, Stan, *Chmn Div Urban Design*, Columbia University, Graduate School of Architecture, Planning & Preservation, New York NY (S)

Allen, Virginia, *Chmn Critical Studies*, Massachusetts College of Art, Boston MA (S)

Allen, Virginia, *VPres*, Almond Historical Society, Inc, Hagadorn House, The 1800-37 Museum, Almond NY

Allen, Walter, *Div Chmn of Art*, James H Faulkner Community College, Art Dept, Bay Minette AL (S)

Allen, William, *Prof*, Arkansas State University, Dept of Art, State University AR (S)

Alley, Jon, *Instr*, Bucks County Community College, Fine Arts Dept, Newtown PA (S)

Alley, Mark, *Exec Dir*, Davidson County Museum of Art, Lexington NC

Alley, Perry, *Treas*, Hudson Valley Art Association, Hastings On Hudson NY

Alley, William, *Archivist & Historian*, Southern Oregon Historical Society, Library, Medford OR

Allison, Andrea, *Librn*, Quetico Park, John B Ridley Research Library, Atikokan ON

Allison, Angie, *VPres*, Peninsula Fine Arts Center, Newport News VA

Allison, Brooke, *Instr*, Dunedin Fine Arts & Cultural Center, Dunedin FL (S)

Allison, Clement, *Div Head*, Tusculum College, Fine Arts Dept, Greeneville TN (S)

Allison, Glenn, *Dir*, The Art Gallery of Southwestern Manitoba, Brandon MB

Allison, Wayne, *Assoc Prof*, Graceland College, Fine Arts Dept, Lamoni IA (S)

Allman, Anne, *Prof*, College of the Ozarks, Dept of Art, Point Lookout MO (S)

Allman, Marion, *Pres*, ACA College of Design, Cincinnati OH (S)

Allo, Anthony, *Instr*, Indian River Community College, Fine Arts Dept, Fort Pierce FL (S)

Allred, Osral, *Chmn*, Snow College, Art Dept, Ephraim UT (S)

Allsopp, Robert, *Prof*, University of Toronto, Programme in Landscape Architecture, Toronto ON (S)

Allumbaugh, James, *Chmn Art Ed*, East Texas State University, Dept of Art, Commerce TX (S)

Allwenss, Sissy, *Second VPres*, North Shore Art League, Winnetka IL

Alm, Rebecca, *Acting Visual Studies*, Minneapolis College of Art & Design, Minneapolis MN (S)

Almanza, Miguel, *Asst Prof*, Weber State University, Dept of Visual Arts, Ogden UT (S)

Almquist, Karl, *Bus Mgr*, Heard Museum, Phoenix AZ

Alperson, Philip, *Journal Ed*, American Society for Aesthetics, Edmonton AB

Alpert, L, *Assoc Prof*, University of Oregon, Dept of Fine & Applied Arts, Eugene OR (S)

Alsip, James, *Dir*, Grace A Dow Memorial Library, Fine Arts Dept, Midland MI

Alston, Littleton, *Artist-in-Res*, Creighton University, Fine & Performing Arts Dept, Omaha NE (S)

Alswang, Hope, *Exec Dir*, New Jersey Historical Society, Library, Newark NJ

Altamura, Mauro, *Asst Prof*, Jersey City State College, Art Dept, Jersey City NJ (S)

Altemus, Anne R, *Lectr*, Johns Hopkins University, School of Medicine, Dept of Art as Applied to Medicine, Baltimore MD (S)

Alter-Muri, Simone, *Asst Prof*, Springfield College, Dept of Visual & Performing Arts, Springfield MA (S)

Altieri, Charles, *Chmn*, University of California, Berkeley, College of Letters & Sciences-Art Dept, Berkeley CA (S)

Altshuler, Bruce, *Dir*, Isamu Noguchi Foundation, Isamu Noguchi Garden Museum, Long Island City NY

Alvarez, Jose B, *Instr*, Inter American University of Puerto Rico, Dept of Art, San German PR (S)

Alvarez, Suzanne E, *Educ Dir*, McAllen International Museum, McAllen TX

Alves, C Douglass, *Dir*, Calvert Marine Museum, Solomons MD

Alward, Sharon, *Chmn Drawing*, University of Manitoba, School of Art, Winnipeg MB (S)

Amadei, Daniel, *Asst Dir Exhib & Installations*, National Gallery of Canada, Ottawa ON

Amandson, Garth, *Asst Prof*, College of Wooster, Dept of Art, Wooster OH (S)

Amason, Alvin, *Asst Prof*, University of Alaska-Fairbanks, Dept of Art, Fairbanks AK (S)

Amato, Carol, *Deputy Dir*, Virginia Museum of Fine Arts, Richmond VA

Amatore, Edward, *Registrar*, State Art Museum of Florida, John & Mable Ringling Museum of Art, Sarasota FL

Amatore, Edward, *Registrar*, Dayton Art Institute, Dayton OH

Ambroge, Patti, *Assoc Prof*, Rochester Institute of Technology, School of Photographic Arts & Sciences, Rochester NY (S)

Ambrogio, Lucy Sant, *Cur*, Historical Society of Bloomfield, Bloomfield NJ

Ambrose, Andrea, *Prog Dir*, Sunrise Museum, Inc, Sunrise Art Museum & Sunrise Science Museum, Charleston WV

Ambrose, Gail, *Recording Secy*, South County Art Association, Kingston RI

Ambrose, Richard, *Chief Cur*, Sunrise Museum, Inc, Sunrise Art Museum & Sunrise Science Museum, Charleston WV

Ambrose, Robin, *Prog Coordr*, Maitland Art Center, Maitland FL

Ambrosino, Thomas, *Prof*, Sullivan County Community College, Division of Commercial Art & Photography, Loch Sheldrake NY (S)

Ambrosio, Katherine, *Shop Mgr*, Carmel Mission & Gift Shop, Carmel CA

Ambroson, Rodd, *Instr*, Marylhurst College, Art Dept, Marylhurst OR (S)

Amenoff, Gregory, *Instr*, Columbia University, School of the Arts, Division of Visual Arts, New York NY (S)

Amerson, L Price, *Dir*, University of California, Richard L Nelson Gallery & Fine Arts Collection, Davis CA

Ames, Madge, *Treas*, Kennebec Valley Art Association, Harlow Gallery, Hallowell ME

Ames, Michael M, *Dir & Prof*, University of British Columbia, Museum of Anthropology, Vancouver BC

Ames, Robert, *Pres*, Timken Museum of Art, San Diego CA

Ames, Samuel B, *Chmn*, Rhode Island College, Art Dept, Providence RI (S)

Ames-Bell, Linda, *Prof*, University of Toledo, Dept of Art, Toledo OH (S)

Amez, Martha, *Asst Prof*, Wesleyan University, Art Dept, Middletown CT (S)

Amico, David, *Vis Instr*, Claremont Graduate School, Dept of Fine Arts, Claremont CA (S)

Ammons, Betty, *Asst Librn*, United Methodist Historical Society, Library, Baltimore MD

Amorous, Martin, *Dept Head*, Sam Houston State University, Art Dept, Huntsville TX (S)

Amory, Claudia, *Dir*, School 33 Art Center, Baltimore MD

Amory, Dita, *Cur Drawings, Prints & Paintings*, National Academy of Design, New York NY

Amos, Emma, *Dir Undergrad Prog*, Rutgers, the State University of New Jersey, Mason Gross School of the Arts, New Brunswick NJ (S)

Amos, Emma, *Prof*, Rutgers, the State University of New Jersey, Mason Gross School of the Arts, New Brunswick NJ (S)

Amos, Maria, *Admin Asst*, Oklahoma City University, Hulsey Gallery-Norick Art Center, Oklahoma City OK

Amrhein, John, *Dean Library Serv*, California State University Stanislaus, Vasche Library, Turlock CA

Ams, Charles M, *Pres*, Southern Vermont Art Center, Manchester VT

Amsler, Cory, *Cur Coll*, Bucks County Historical Society, Mercer Museum, Doylestown PA

Amt, Richard, *Chief Photographic Services*, National Gallery of Art, Washington DC

Amundson, Dale, *Dir*, University of Manitoba, Gallery III, Winnipeg MB

Amundson, Dale, *Dir*, University of Manitoba, School of Art, Winnipeg MB (S)

Amyx, Guyla Call, *Instr,* Cuesta College, Art Dept, San Luis Obispo CA (S)

Anacker, John, *Gallery Dir,* Montana State University, Helen E Copeland Gallery, Bozeman MT

Ananian, Elissa, *Prof,* Salem State College, Art Dept, Salem MA (S)

Anawalt, Patricia, *Consulting Cur Costumes & Textiles,* University of California, Los Angeles, Fowler Museum of Cultural History, Los Angeles CA

Anders, Maribeth, *Instr,* The Arkansas Arts Center, Museum School, Little Rock AR (S)

Andersen, Jay, *Adminr,* Grand Marais Art Colony, Grand Marais MN (S)

Andersen, Jeffrey W, *Dir,* Lyme Historical Society, Florence Griswold Museum, Old Lyme CT

Andersen, Paul, *Registrar,* Fine Arts Museum of Long Island, Hempstead NY

Andersen, Stephen, *Gallery Dir,* Valdosta State University, Art Gallery, Valdosta GA

Anderson, Arthur, *Assoc Prof,* York College of the City University of New York, Fine & Performing Arts, Jamaica NY (S)

Anderson, Barbara, *Instr,* Concordia College, Art Dept, Moorhead MN (S)

Anderson, Barbara, *Assoc Dean,* Carnegie Mellon University, College of Fine Arts, Pittsburgh PA (S)

Anderson, Betsy, *Lectr,* Saint Joseph's University, Dept of Fine & Performing Arts, Philadelphia PA (S)

Anderson, Brooke Davis, *Dir,* Winston-Salem State University, Diggs Gallery, Winston Salem NC

Anderson, Camille, *Adminr,* The Metal Arts Guild, Toronto ON

Anderson, Chris, *Instr,* Virginia Intermont College, Fine Arts Division, Bristol VA (S)

Anderson, Ciel, *Cur Horticulture,* Paine Art Center & Arboretum, Oshkosh WI

Anderson, C Paul, *Dean Div Fine & Performing Arts,* Dixie College, Art Dept, Saint George UT (S)

Anderson, Craig, *Assoc Dir,* NAB Gallery, Chicago IL

Anderson, Daniel J, *Head Ceramic,* Southern Illinois University at Edwardsville, Dept of Art & Design, Edwardsville IL (S)

Anderson, Diana, *Exhibits Coordr,* Red Deer & District Museum & Archives, Red Deer AB

Anderson, Dorothy, *Prog Dir,* Lizzadro Museum of Lapidary Art, Elmhurst IL

Anderson, Douglas, *Asst Prof,* University of Hartford, Hartford Art School, West Hartford CT (S)

Anderson, Duane, *VPres,* School of American Research, Indian Arts Research Center, Santa Fe NM

Anderson, Ellen, *Chmn Dept,* Saint Mary's College, Art Dept, Raleigh NC (S)

Anderson, Eric, *Prof,* University of North Carolina at Charlotte, Dept of Visual Arts, Charlotte NC (S)

Anderson, Gail, *Mgr Arts & Recreation,* Calgary Public Library, Arts & Recreation Dept, Calgary AB

Anderson, Gail Kana, *Asst Dir & Acting Registrar,* University of Oklahoma, Fred Jones Jr Museum of Art, Norman OK

Anderson, Hugh B, *Dir,* Polk Community College, Art, Letters & Social Sciences, Winter Haven FL (S)

Anderson, J, *Gallery Cur,* Real Art Ways (RAW), Hartford CT

Anderson, James C, *Cur,* University of Louisville, Photographic Archives, Louisville KY

Anderson, Janice, *Asst Prof,* University of Minnesota, Duluth, Art Dept, Duluth MN (S)

Anderson, Jeannine, *Assoc Prof,* Berea College, Art Dept, Berea KY (S)

Anderson, Jeffrey C, *Assoc Prof,* George Washington University, Dept of Art, Washington DC (S)

Anderson, Jess, *Pres,* Rutland Area Art Association, Inc, Chaffee Art Center, Rutland VT

Anderson, Jim, *Chmn,* Armstrong Atlantic State University, Art & Music Dept, Savannah GA (S)

Anderson, Joan, *Music Librn & Cataloger,* California Institute of the Arts Library, Santa Clarita CA

Anderson, Joe, *Achaeologist,* Institute of the Great Plains, Museum of the Great Plains, Lawton OK

Anderson, John, *Business Mgr,* Brandywine River Museum, Chadds Ford PA

Anderson, John, *Assoc Prof,* Framingham State College, Art Dept, Framingham MA (S)

Anderson, Jon, *Prof,* Utah State University, Dept of Art, Logan UT (S)

Anderson, Judi, *Head Technical Servs,* Ponca City Library, Art Dept, Ponca City OK

Anderson, Julia, *Art Cur,* Safeco Insurance Company, Art Collection, Seattle WA

Anderson, Ken, *Assoc Prof,* University of Missouri, Saint Louis, Dept of Art & Art History, Saint Louis MO (S)

Anderson, Kenneth, *Prof,* Peru State College, Art Dept, Peru NE (S)

Anderson, Kristin, *Chmn,* Augsburg College, Art Dept, Minneapolis MN (S)

Anderson, Larry, *Drawing Chmn,* Atlanta College of Art, Atlanta GA (S)

Anderson, Lawrence, *Assoc Prof,* University of South Dakota, Department of Art, College of Fine Arts, Vermillion SD (S)

Anderson, Linda, *Instr,* University of Charleston, Carleton Varney Dept of Art & Design, Charleston WV (S)

Anderson, Mark, *Prof,* Presbyterian College, Fine Arts Dept, Clinton SC (S)

Anderson, Martin, *Chmn,* Henry Ford Community College, Art Dept, Dearborn MI (S)

Anderson, Maxwell, *Dir,* Art Gallery of Ontario, Toronto ON

Anderson, Maxwell L, *Dir,* Emory University, Michael C Carlos Museum, Atlanta GA

Anderson, Nancy, *Cur Asst,* Manitoba Historical Society, Dalnavert Museum, Winnipeg MB

Anderson, Nancy B, *Exec Dir,* Museum of Arts & Sciences, Inc, Macon GA

Anderson, Neil, *Prof,* Bucknell University, Dept of Art, Lewisburg PA (S)

Anderson, Patricia, *Dir,* New Rochelle Public Library, Art Section, New Rochelle NY

Anderson, Paul, *Head Exhib Develop,* Brigham Young University, Museum of Art, Provo UT

Anderson, Richita, *Librn,* Aesthetic Realism Foundation, Eli Siegel Collection, New York NY

Anderson, Richita, *Librn,* Aesthetic Realism Foundation, Aesthetic Realism Foundation Library, New York NY

Anderson, Robert, *Prof,* West Virginia University, College of Creative Arts, Morgantown WV (S)

Anderson, Stanford, *Head Dept,* Massachusetts Institute of Technology, School of Architecture and Planning, Cambridge MA (S)

Anderson, Susan, *Develop Officer,* Bellevue Art Museum, Bellevue WA

Anderson, Susan, *Acting Dir & Cur Exhib,* Laguna Art Museum of the Orange County Museum of Art, Laguna Beach CA

Anderson, Susan, *Dir,* Bloomington Art Center, Bloomington MN

Anderson, Susan B, *Treas,* Madison & Main Gallery, Greeley CO

Anderson, Sven, *Asst Prof,* West Texas A&M University, Art, Communication & Theatre Dept, Canyon TX (S)

Anderson, Ted, *Designer,* Gallery Association of New York State, Hamilton NY

Anderson, Terrance A, *Dir,* Savannah State University, Dept of Fine Arts, Savannah GA (S)

Anderson, Terry, *Instr,* Northeast Mississippi Junior College, Art Dept, Booneville MS (S)

Anderson, Tobey, *Artistic Dir,* Niagara Artists' Centre, Saint Catharines ON

Anderson, Tom, *Prof,* Florida State University, Art Education Dept, Tallahassee FL (S)

Anderson, W, *Instr,* Humboldt State University, College of Arts & Humanities, Arcata CA (S)

Anderson, Wayne, *Prof,* Wayne State College, Art Dept, Wayne NE (S)

Anderson, Wm, *VPres,* Hunterdon Art Center, Clinton NJ

Anderson, Wyatt, *Dean,* University of Georgia, Franklin College of Arts & Sciences, Lamar Dodd School of Art, Athens GA (S)

Anderson Lawrence, Jennifer, *Cur,* Abigail Adams Smith Museum, New York NY

Andersson, Christiane, *Prof,* Bucknell University, Dept of Art, Lewisburg PA (S)

Anderton, Jaye, *Coordr,* Rice University, Art Gallery, Houston TX

Andes, Charles L, *Chmn Board,* Pennsylvania Academy of the Fine Arts, Museum of American Art, Philadelphia PA

Andrad, Tina, *Dir Develop,* The Currier Gallery of Art, Manchester NH

Andraka, Judith, *Chmn,* Prince George's Community College, Art Dept, Largo MD (S)

Andrea, Martha, *Prof,* Colby-Sawyer College, Dept of Fine & Performing Arts, New London NH (S)

Andress, Thomas, *Print Selection Committee Chmn,* Print Club of Albany, Albany NY

Andrew, David, *Prof,* University of New Hampshire, Dept of Arts & Art History, Durham NH (S)

Andrews, Edwin, *Asst Prof,* Northeastern University, Dept of Art & Architecture, Boston MA (S)

Andrews, Luann, *Cur Educ,* University of Missouri, Museum of Art & Archaeology, Columbia MO

Andrews, Mel, *Exhib Adminr,* Muckenthaler Cultural Center, Fullerton CA

Andrews, Nancy, *Librn,* Mingei International, Inc, Reference Library, San Diego CA

Andrews, Richard, *Dir,* University of Washington, Henry Art Gallery, Seattle WA

Andrews, Richard, *Dir,* Henry Gallery Association, Henry Art Gallery, Seattle WA

Andrews, Terry, *Registrar,* Contemporary Arts Museum, Houston TX

Andrews, Tex, *Prog Dir,* Maryland Art Place, Baltimore MD

Andrus, Beryl, *Branch Adminr,* Las Vegas-Clark County Library District, Las Vegas NV

Andrus, David, *Asst Prof,* John Brown University, Art Dept, Siloam Springs AR (S)

Andrus, Lisa, *Assoc Prof,* Portland State University, Dept of Art, Portland OR (S)

Andrus-Walck, Kathryn, *Asst Prof,* University of Colorado-Colorado Springs, Fine Arts Dept, Colorado Springs CO (S)

Angeline, M, *Prof,* Madonna University, Art Dept, Livonia MI (S)

Angeloch, Eric, *Instr,* Woodstock School of Art, Inc, Woodstock NY (S)

Angeloch, Robert, *Instr,* Woodstock School of Art, Inc, Woodstock NY (S)

Angert, Joe C, *Instr,* Saint Louis Community College at Forest Park, Art Dept, Saint Louis MO (S)

Angie, Joanna, *Founder & Dir,* Art Studios of Western New York, Buffalo NY

Anglin, B, *Prof,* Christopher Newport University, Arts & Communications, Newport News VA (S)

Anglin, Barbara, *Technical Services Librn,* Lee County Library, Tupelo MS

Annau, Ernest, *Pres,* Royal Canadian Academy of Arts, Toronto ON

Annis, Norman, *Prof,* Gettysburg College, Dept of Visual Arts, Gettysburg PA (S)

Anreus, Alejandro, *Cur,* Jersey City Museum, Jersey City NJ

Antaki, Karen, *Dir & Cur,* Concordia University, Leonard & Bina Ellen Art Gallery, Montreal PQ

Antal, Bev, *Clerical Asst,* Regina Public Library, Dunlop Art Gallery, Regina SK

Antel, Barbara, *Corporate Art Cur,* Westinghouse Electric Corporation, Art Collection, Pittsburgh PA

Anthony, Carolyn, *Dir,* Skokie Public Library, Skokie IL

Anthony, David, *Dean,* Golden West College, Visual Art Dept, Huntington Beach CA (S)

Anthony, Stuart, *Asst Dir,* Exit Art-The First World, Inc, New York NY

Anthony, Vincent, *Exec Dir,* Center for Puppetry Arts, Atlanta GA

Anthony, Vincent, *Exec Dir,* Center for Puppetry Arts, Library, Atlanta GA

Anthrop, Mary, *Archivist*, Tippecanoe County Historical Museum, Alameda McCollough Library, Lafayette IN

Antoime, Janeen, *Exec Dir*, American Indian Contemporary Arts, San Francisco CA

Anton, D, *Instr*, Humboldt State University, College of Arts & Humanities, Arcata CA (S)

Anton, Waldo, *Treas*, Guadalupe Historic Foundation, Santuario de Guadalupe, Santa Fe NM

Antonetti, Martin, *Librn*, Grolier Club Library, New York NY

Antonovics, Lilian, *Admin & Personnel Mgr*, Duke University Museum of Art, Durham NC

Antonsen, Lasse, *Coordr Gallery*, University of Massachusetts Dartmouth, College of Visual & Performing Arts, North Dartmouth MA (S)

Antrim, Elizabeth, *Slide Cur*, San Jose State University, Robert D Clark Library, San Jose CA

Aona, Gretchen, *Treas*, Queen's Medical Center Auxiliary, Queen Emma Gallery, Honolulu HI

Apesos, Anthony, *Chmn Fine Arts Dept*, Art Institute of Boston, Boston MA (S)

Apfelstadt, Eric, *Asst Prof*, Santa Clara University, Art Dept, Santa Clara CA (S)

Apgar, Peter, *Dir*, Morris-Jumel Mansion, Inc, New York NY

Apostolos, Margaret, *Reference Librn*, Kutztown University, Rohrbach Library, Kutztown PA

Appelhof, Ruth Stevens, *Dir*, Minnesota Museum of American Art, Saint Paul MN

Applebaun, Ronald, *Pres*, Kean College of New Jersey, Union NJ

Appleman, David, *Chmn Division of Art*, Bob Jones University, School of Fine Arts, Greenville SC (S)

Apraxine, Pierre, *Cur*, The Gilman Paper Company, New York NY

Aquilino, Marie, *Asst Prof*, University of Kansas, Kress Foundation Dept of Art History, Lawrence KS (S)

Aquirre, Carlos, *Assoc Prof*, University of Miami, Dept of Art & Art History, Coral Gables FL (S)

Arat, Serdar, *Dir Art Dept*, Concordia College, Bronxville NY (S)

Arbitmam, Kahren, *Dir*, Cummer Museum of Art & Gardens, DeEtte Holden Cummer Museum Foundation, Jacksonville FL

Arbury, Stephen, *Assoc Prof*, Radford University, Art Dept, Radford VA (S)

Arceneaux, Pamela D, *Reference Librn*, Kemper & Leila Williams Foundation, Historic New Orleans Collection, New Orleans LA

Arceo, Rene, *Visual Arts Coord*, Mexican Fine Arts Center Museum, Chicago IL

Archabal, Nina M, *Dir*, Minnesota Historical Society, Saint Paul MN

Arche, Harvey, *Asst Prof*, Murray State University, Dept of Art, Murray KY (S)

Archer, Richard, *Asst Prof*, Southern Illinois University, School of Art & Design, Carbondale IL (S)

Archibald, Robert, *Pres*, Missouri Historical Society, Saint Louis MO

Archibald, Robert R, *Pres*, Missouri Historical Society, Library & Research Center, Saint Louis MO

Archibald, Tamara, *Admin Asst*, Rogue Valley Art Association, Rogue Gallery & Art Center, Medford OR

Archuleta, Margaret, *Cur of Fine Art*, Heard Museum, Phoenix AZ

Arellanes, Audrey Spencer, *Dir & Ed*, American Society of Bookplate Collectors & Designers, Alhambra CA

Arentz, Donald, *Asst Prof Philosophy*, LeMoyne College, Wilson Art Gallery, Syracuse NY

Argabrite, Diana, *Asst*, De Anza College, Euphrat Museum of Art, Cupertino CA

Arimitsu, Joe, *Chmn Art 3-D Media*, California State University, Northridge, Dept of Art-Two Dimensional Media, Northridge CA (S)

Armantrout, Les, *Prof*, Maryville University of Saint Louis, Art Division, Saint Louis MO (S)

Armas-Garcia, Daisy, *Treas*, Miami Watercolor Society, Inc, Miami FL

Arminio, Roberta Y, *Dir*, Museum of Ossining Historical Society, Ossining NY

Armstead, Keneth, *Asst Cur*, Alternative Museum, New York NY

Armstrong, Carmen, *Grad Coordr*, Northern Illinois University, School of Art, De Kalb IL (S)

Armstrong, Carol, *Assoc Prof*, City University of New York, PhD Program in Art History, New York NY (S)

Armstrong, James A, *Asst Cur*, Harvard University, Semitic Museum, Cambridge MA

Armstrong, Lilian, *Prof*, Wellesley College, Art Dept, Wellesley MA (S)

Armstrong, Linda, *Lectr*, Emory University, Art History Dept, Atlanta GA (S)

Armstrong, Martha, *Assoc Prof*, Smith College, Art Dept, Northampton MA (S)

Armstrong, Matthew, *Cur*, Paine Webber Inc, New York NY

Armstrong, Rachel, *VPres*, Lyme Art Association, Inc, Old Lyme CT

Armstrong, Richard, *Dir & Cur Contemporary Arts*, Carnegie Institute, Carnegie Museum of Art, Pittsburgh PA

Armstrong, Robert, *Chmn*, Treasure Valley Community College, Art Dept, Ontario OR (S)

Armstrong, Susan, *Assoc Prof*, Malone College, Dept of Art, Canton OH (S)

Armstrong-Friedmann, Janee, *Chmn Trustee Committee*, George Walter Vincent Smith Art Museum, Springfield MA

Armstrong Morgan, Debra, *Registrar*, University of Texas at Austin, Harry Ransom Humanities Research Center, Austin TX

Armstutz, Bruce, *Prof*, Shoreline Community College, Humanities Division, Seattle WA (S)

Arndorter, Tom, *Cur Arts. Humanities Educ*, Omaha Childrens Museum, Inc, Omaha NE

Arndt, Susan, *Art Instr*, Red Rocks Community College, Arts & Humanities Dept, Lakewood CO (S)

Arneill, Porter, *Cur*, Laumeier Sculpture Park & Museum, Saint Louis MO

Arneson, Wendell, *Chmn*, Saint Olaf College, Art Dept, Northfield MN (S)

Arnette, Laura, *Visual Resources Library Asst*, Colonial Williamsburg Foundation, John D Rockefeller, Jr Library, Williamsburg VA

Arnold, Craig, *Librn*, San Diego Maritime Museum, San Diego CA

Arnold, Dorothea, *Cur Egyptian Art*, The Metropolitan Museum of Art, New York NY

Arnold, Mary Koniz, *Assoc Dir*, Dutchess County Arts Council, Poughkeepsie NY

Arnold, Patrick, *Instr*, Main Line Art Center, Haverford PA (S)

Arnold, Ralph, *Prof*, Loyola University of Chicago, Fine Arts Dept, Chicago IL (S)

Arnold, Willard B, *Pres Historical Society*, Waterville Historical Society, Redington Museum, Waterville ME

Arnts, Otis, *Pres*, Guild of Creative Art, Shrewsbury NJ (S)

Aronson, Carol, *Prof*, University of New Hampshire, Dept of Arts & Art History, Durham NH (S)

Aronson, Julie, *Asst Cur American Art*, Nelson-Atkins Museum of Art, Kansas City MO

Arp, Kimberly, *Prof*, Louisiana State University, School of Art, Baton Rouge LA (S)

Arpad, Tori, *Lectr*, Texas Woman's University, Dept of Visual Arts, Denton TX (S)

Arpadi, Allen, *Instr*, Saint Louis Community College at Forest Park, Art Dept, Saint Louis MO (S)

Arpin, Pierre, *Dir & Cur*, Laurentian University, Museum & Art Centre, Sudbury ON

Arpin, Pierre, *Dir*, Laurentian University, Art Centre Library, Sudbury ON

Arraras, Maria Teresa, *Dir*, La Casa del Libro Museum, San Juan PR

Arrasmith, Lynnda, *Cur Exhibits & Registrar*, Canton Museum of Art, Canton OH (S)

Arrington, Gerald C, *Prof*, Concord College, Fine Art Division, Athens WV (S)

Arrison, John, *Librn*, Penobscot Marine Museum, Searsport ME

Arrison, John, *Librn*, Penobscot Marine Museum, Stephen Phillips Memorial Library, Searsport ME

Arrowo, Imna, *Chmn*, Eastern Connecticut State University, Fine Arts Dept, Willimantic CT (S)

Arrowwood, Rick, *Chief Exec Officer & Pres*, Art & Culture Center of Hollywood, Hollywood FL

Arsem, Marilyn, *Co-Dir*, Mobius Inc, Boston MA

Arseneault, Celine, *Botanist & Librn*, Jardin Botanique de Montreal, Bibliotheque, Montreal PQ

Arthur, Kathleen, *Prof*, James Madison University, School of Art & Art History, Harrisonburg VA (S)

Artzberger, John A, *Dir*, Oglebay Institute, Mansion Museum, Wheeling WV

Artzberger, John A, *Dir*, Oglebay Institute, Library, Wheeling WV

Asano, Hisako, *Adjunct Asst Prof*, University of Southern California, School of Fine Arts, Los Angeles CA (S)

Asaro, Meg, *Asst Dir*, School of Visual Arts, Visual Arts School, New York NY

Asaro, Meg, *Asst Dir*, School of Visual Arts, New York NY (S)

Asch, Howard, *Dir Public Prog*, Jamaica Arts Center, Jamaica NY

Aschkenes, Anna M, *Exec Dir*, Middlesex County Cultural & Heritage Commission, North Brunswick NJ

Ash, Carla Caccamise, *Cur*, Joseph E Seagram & Sons, Inc, Gallery, New York NY

Ash, Richard, *Art Coordr*, Midwestern State University, Div of Fine Arts, Wichita Falls TX (S)

Ashbaugh, Sue, *Educ Coordr*, Jefferson County Open Space, Hiwan Homestead Museum, Evergreen CO

Ashby, Andrea, *Librn Technician*, Independence National Historical Park, Library, Philadelphia PA

Ashby, Anna Lou, *Assoc Cur Printed Books*, Pierpont Morgan Library, New York NY

Ashby, Lisa Baylis, *Lectr*, Oakland University, Dept of Art & Art History, Rochester MI (S)

Ashby, Marty, *Dir Performing Arts*, Manchester Craftsmen's Guild, Pittsburgh PA

Ashby, Melody Todd, *Instr*, Mount Mary College, Art Dept, Milwaukee WI (S)

Asher, Catherine, *Assoc Prof*, University of Minnesota, Minneapolis, Art History, Minneapolis MN (S)

Asher, Frederick, *Chmn*, University of Minnesota, Minneapolis, Art History, Minneapolis MN (S)

Asher, Martha, *Registrar*, Sterling & Francine Clark Art Institute, Williamstown MA

Asherman, Edward G, *Pres*, Victoria Mansion, Inc, Victoria Mansion - Morse Libby House, Portland ME

Ashley, Peter, *Chmn*, Baltimore City Community College, Dept of Fine Arts, Baltimore MD (S)

Ashlstrom, Ed, *Chmn*, Montgomery College, Dept of Art, Rockville MD (S)

Ashman, Stuart, *Dir*, Museum of New Mexico, Museum of Fine Arts, Santa Fe NM

Ashton, Lynn, *Dir Marketing & Develop*, Kentucky Derby Museum, Louisville KY

Ashton, Rick J, *Librn*, Denver Public Library, General Reference, Denver CO

Ashworth, Judie, *Cur*, Franklin Mint Museum, Franklin Center PA

Asmus, Collin, *Asst Prof*, Millsaps College, Dept of Art, Jackson MS (S)

Asper, Lynn, *Chmn*, Grand Rapids Community College, Art Dept, Grand Rapids MI (S)

Aspin, Toni, *Exec Dir*, Centrum Foundation, Port Townsend WA

Asti, Martha, *Chmn Div*, Wingate University, Division of Fine Arts, Wingate NC (S)

Aszling, Jill, *Registrar*, Massachusetts Institute of Technology, List Visual Arts Center, Cambridge MA

Aten, Duane, *Dir*, College of Marin, Art Gallery, Kentfield CA

Athan, Jean, *Art Consultant*, Wilmington Trust Company, Wilmington DE

Atherly, Mary, *Collections Mgr*, Iowa State University, Brunnier Art Museum, Ames IA

Atherton, Charles H, *Secy*, United States Commission of Fine Arts, Washington DC

Atherton, Tom, *Treas.* Revelstoke Art Group, Revelstoke BC

Atkinson, Alan, *Instr.* University of Alabama at Birmingham, Dept of Art, Birmingham AL (S)

Atkinson, Daniel, *Prog Dir.* Library Association of La Jolla, Athenaeum Music & Arts Library, La Jolla CA

Atkinson, D Scott, *Cur.* Terra Museum of American Art, Chicago IL

Atkinson, Jennifer, *Cur.* Fuller Museum of Art, Brockton MA

Attenborough, Debra, *Cur Educ.* Rodman Hall Arts Centre, Saint Catharines ON

Attenborough, Debra, *Librn.* Rodman Hall Arts Centre, Library, Saint Catharines ON

Attie, Diana, *Prof.* University of Toledo, Dept of Art, Toledo OH (S)

Attwood, Maryon, *Exec Dir.* Worcester Center for Crafts, Worcester MA

Attwood, Maryon M, *Exec Dir.* Worcester Center for Crafts, Worcester MA (S)

Atwater, H Brewster, *Chmn Board,* Walker Art Center, Minneapolis MN

Atwateraws, John, *Pres.* Connecticut Watercolor Society, Farmington CT

Atwell, Michael, *Asst Dir.* Purdue University Galleries, West Lafayette IN

Au, Jeri, *Asst Prof.* Webster University, Art Dept, Webster Groves MO (S)

Aubourg, Vickie, *Asst,* California Polytechnic State University, College of Architecture & Environmental Design-Art Collection, San Luis Obispo CA

Aucella, Frank J, *Asst Dir,* Woodrow Wilson House, Washington DC

Audet, M, *Asst Librn.* Musee du Quebec, Bibliotheque des Arts, Quebec PQ

Audrey, Laura, *Instr.* University of Southern Colorado, Belmont Campus, Dept of Art, Pueblo CO (S)

Auerbach, James, *Exec Dir.* Pasadena Historical Museum, Pasadena CA

Auerbach, Seymour, *Prof.* Catholic University of America, School of Architecture & Planning, Washington DC (S)

Aufderheide, Larry, *Chmn & Dir of Humanities Div,* Lakeland Community College, Visual Arts Dept, Mentor OH (S)

Augaitis, Diana, *Chief Cur.* Vancouver Art Gallery, Vancouver BC

Auger, Jane, *Cur & Caretaker,* South County Art Association, Kingston RI

Augusztiny, Roxana, *Asst Dir.* University of Washington, Thomas Burke Memorial Washington State Museum, Seattle WA

Aul, Billie, *Sr Librn,* New York State Library, Manuscripts & Special Collections, Albany NY

Aumann, Karen, *Asst Prof.* Philadelphia Community College, Dept of Art, Philadelphia PA (S)

Aumont, Jean-Pierre, *Dir.* Saint Joseph's Oratory, Museum, Montreal PQ

Aunspaugh, Richard, *Chmn.* Young Harris College, Dept of Art, Young Harris GA (S)

Auping, Michael, *Chief Cur.* Fort Worth Art Association, Modern Art Museum of Fort Worth, Fort Worth TX

Aurandt, David, *Dir.* Rodman Hall Arts Centre, Saint Catharines ON

Aurbach, Michael, *Assoc Prof.* Vanderbilt University, Dept of Fine Arts, Nashville TN (S)

Ausfeld, Margaret, *Cur, Paintings & Sculpture,* Montgomery Museum of Fine Arts, Montgomery AL

Austin, Beverly, *Lectr,* Harding University, Dept of Art, Searcy AR (S)

Austin, Carole, *Cur,* San Francisco Craft & Folk Art Museum, San Francisco CA

Austin, Helen C, *Instr.* John C Calhoun State Community College, Department of Fine Arts, Decatur AL (S)

Austin, Helen C, *Dir.* John C Calhoun State Community College, Art Gallery, Decatur AL

Austin, Howard, *Instr.* Milwaukee Area Technical College, Graphic Arts Division, Milwaukee WI (S)

Austin, Jerry, *Ceramics Coordr.* University of North Texas, School of Visual Arts, Denton TX (S)

Austin, Jon, *Dir.* Rome Historical Society Museum, Rome NY

Austin, Linda, *Dir.* Michelson Museum of Art, Marshall TX

Austin-Mckillop, Mardonna, *Pres.* Legacy Ltd, Seattle WA

Auth, Susan H, *Cur Classical Coll.* Newark Museum Association, The Newark Museum, Newark NJ

Autry, Carolyn, *Assoc Prof.* University of Toledo, Dept of Art, Toledo OH (S)

Avens, Irene, *Reference Librn,* Frick Art Reference Library, New York NY

Averilo, Barbara, *Media Relations Mgr.* Minnesota Historical Society, Saint Paul MN

Avitabile, Gunhild, *Dir.* Japan Society, Inc, Japan Society Gallery, New York NY

Avril, Ellen, *Assoc Cur Far Eastern Art.* Cincinnati Museum Association, Cincinnati Art Museum, Cincinnati OH

Ayer, Elizabeth, *Asst Prof.* Hartwick College, Art Dept, Oneonta NY (S)

Ayers, Lucie, *Exhibit Coordr.* Tennessee Valley Art Association & Center, Tuscumbia AL

Aylmer, Annabelle, *Instr.* Glendale Community College, Visual & Performing Arts Division, Glendale CA (S)

Ayres, Anne, *Dir.* Otis College of Art & Design, Los Angeles CA

Ayscue, Beverly, *Coordr.* City Of Raleigh Arts Commission, Municipal Building Art Exhibitions, Raleigh NC

Ayson, Maud V, *Asst Dir Prog & Educ.* Norman Rockwell Museum at Stockbridge, Stockbridge MA

Aziz, Sylvat, *Asst Prof.* Mount Allison University, Fine Arts Dept, Sackville NB (S)

B, Aline, *Asst Cur Contemporary Art.* Museum of New Mexico, Museum of Fine Arts, Santa Fe NM

Baas, Jacquelynn, *Dir.* University of California, Berkeley Art Museum & Pacific Film Archive, Berkeley CA

Babb, Julia, *Pres.* Pemaquid Group of Artists, Pemaquid Art Gallery, Pemaquid Point ME

Babcock, Catherine M, *Dir Communications.* The Huntington Library, Art Collections & Botanical Gardens, San Marino CA

Babcock, Herb, *Chmn Crafts,* Center for Creative Studies, College of Art & Design, Detroit MI (S)

Babel, Deborah, *Branch Head,* Clemson University, Emery A Gunnin Architectural Library, Clemson SC

Baca, Judith F, *Artistic Dir.* Social & Public Art Resource Center, (SPARC), Venice CA

Bacarella, Flavia, *Dir.* Prince Street Gallery, New York NY

Bach, Beverly, *Registrar.* Miami University, Art Museum, Oxford OH

Bach, Claudia, *Public Information Dir.* University of Washington, Henry Art Gallery, Seattle WA

Bach, Claudia, *Deputy Dir.* Henry Gallery Association, Henry Art Gallery, Seattle WA

Bach, Penny Balkin, *Exec Dir.* Fairmount Park Art Association, Philadelphia PA

Bachsbaum, Betty, *Sr VPres,* Massachusetts College of Art, Boston MA (S)

Bachtell, Barbara, *Assoc Dir,* New Organization for the Visual Arts, (NOVA), Cleveland OH

Bacigalupi, Don, *Dir.* University of Houston, Sarah Campbell Blaffer Gallery, Houston TX

Bacon, Mardges, *Prof.* Northeastern University, Dept of Art & Architecture, Boston MA (S)

Bacon, Nancy M, *Pres.* San Antonio Art League, San Antonio TX

Bacon, Nancy M, *Pres.* San Antonio Art League, Library, San Antonio TX

Bacot, H Parrott, *Dir & Cur.* Louisiana State University, Museum of Arts, Baton Rouge LA

Bacot, H Perrott, *Dir.* Louisiana State University, Library, Baton Rouge LA

Baden, Linda, *Assoc Dir Editorial Servs.* Indiana University, Art Museum, Bloomington IN

Bader, Emily, *Dir.* Springfield Library & Museums Association, Art & Music Dept, Springfield MA

Bader, James, *Pres.* Wayne County Historical Society, Museum, Honesdale PA

Badger, Linda, *Coll Mgr.* Indiana State Museum, Indianapolis IN

Badt, Pat, *Asst Prof.* Cedar Crest College, Art Dept, Allentown PA (S)

Baer, Mark, *Adminr.* The Trustees of Reservations, The Mission House, Stockbridge MA

Bagley, Bill, *Assoc Prof.* Texas Tech University, Dept of Art, Lubbock TX (S)

Bagley, Robert, *Prof.* Princeton University, Dept of Art & Archaeology, Princeton NJ (S)

Bagnall, Bill, *Pres.* Santa Cruz Art League, Inc, Center for the Arts, Santa Cruz CA

Bagnatori, Paola, *VPres.* Museo Italo Americano, San Francisco CA

Bagnuolo, Peter, *Coordr Commercial Art.* College of DuPage, Humanities Division, Glen Ellyn IL (S)

Bahm, Linda, *Assoc Dir.* University of New Mexico, University Art Museum, Albuquerque NM

Bahr, David, *Assoc Prof.* Baltimore City Community College, Dept of Fine Arts, Baltimore MD (S)

Bahrani, Zaihab, *Asst Prof.* State University of New York at Stony Brook, Art Dept, Stony Brook NY (S)

Baigell, Matthew, *Prof.* Rutgers, the State University of New Jersey, Graduate Program in Art History, New Brunswick NJ (S)

Baigell, Naomi, *Mgr.* Prudential Art Program, Newark NJ

Baile, Beth, *Adjunct Instr.* Maryville University of Saint Louis, Art Division, Saint Louis MO (S)

Bailey, Barry, *Asst Prof.* Tulane University, Sophie H Newcomb Memorial College, New Orleans LA (S)

Bailey, Carol, *Instr.* Midland College, Art Dept, Midland TX (S)

Bailey, Colin, *Chief Cur.* National Gallery of Canada, Ottawa ON

Bailey, Daniel, *Assoc Prof.* University of Maryland, Baltimore County, Visual Arts Dept, Baltimore MD (S)

Bailey, Debra J, *Registrar,* Pacific - Asia Museum, Pasadena CA

Bailey, Deirdre Windsor, *Textile Conservator.* American Textile History Museum, Lowell MA

Bailey, Erin, *Dir.* City of Atlanta, Gilbert House, Atlanta GA

Bailey, Forrest, *Chief Conservator.* Nelson-Atkins Museum of Art, Kansas City MO

Bailey, Jann L M, *Dir & Cur.* Kamloops Art Gallery, Kamloops BC

Bailey, Ken, *Controller,* Polk Museum of Art, Lakeland FL

Bailey, Lebe, *Asst Prof.* Wesleyan College, Art Dept, Macon GA (S)

Bailey, Nolan, *Asst Prof.* Northwestern State University of Louisiana, Dept of Art, Natchitoches LA (S)

Bailey, Pamela, *Dir.* University of California at Santa Cruz, Mary Porter Sesnon Art Gallery, Santa Cruz CA

Bailey, Rebecca, *Chmn.* Meredith College, Art Dept, Raleigh NC (S)

Bailey, Regina C, *Asst Dir.* Florida International University, The Art Museum at FIU, Miami FL

Bailey, Roger, *Prof.* St Lawrence University, Dept of Fine Arts, Canton NY (S)

Bailey, Walter J, *Chmn.* Baker University, Dept of Art, Baldwin City KS (S)

Bailey, William, *Prof.* Yale University, School of Art, New Haven CT (S)

Bailey, Willis, *Cur Oriental Art.* Zanesville Art Center, Zanesville OH

Bains, Sneh, *Library Dir.* Bayonne Free Public Library, Art Dept, Bayonne NJ

Bair, Miles, *Dir.* Illinois Wesleyan University, School of Art, Bloomington IL (S)

Baird, Ellen, *Dean.* University of Illinois at Chicago, College of Architecture, Chicago IL (S)

Baird, Marjorie Gee, *Secy.* Acadia University Art Gallery, Wolfville NS

Baird, M M, *Instr.* Peace College, Art Dept, Raleigh NC (S)

Bairnsfather, Ragnhild, *Real Estate Librn.* Massachusetts Institute of Technology, Rotch Library of Architecture & Planning, Cambridge MA

Baizerman, Suzanne, *Dir.* University of Minnesota, Goldstein Gallery, Saint Paul MN

Bajko, Daria, *Admin Dir.* The Ukrainian Museum, New York NY

Baken, James, *Chmn.* Rocky Mountain College, Art Dept, Billings MT (S)

Baker, Alden, *First VPres.* Art Centre of New Jersey, Livingston NJ (S)

Baker, Carl, *Fine Arts Librn.* Beverly Hills Public Library, Fine Arts Library, Beverly Hills CA

Baker, Cassandra, *Exec Dir.* Morgan County Foundation, Inc, Madison-Morgan Cultural Center, Madison GA

Baker, David R, *Instr.* Southwestern Michigan College, Fine & Performing Arts Dept, Dowagiac MI (S)

Baker, Edward R, *Division Dean.* Orange Coast College, Division of Fine Arts, Costa Mesa CA (S)

Baker, Elizabeth B, *Acting Dir.* Halifax Historical Society, Inc, Halifax Historical Museum, Daytona Beach FL

Baker, Gary, *Prof.* Polk Community College, Art, Letters & Social Sciences, Winter Haven FL (S)

Baker, Hollis M, *VPres.* The Society of the Four Arts, Palm Beach FL

Baker, James, *Prof.* Providence College, Art & Art History Dept, Providence RI (S)

Baker, Janet, *Chief Cur of Educ.* Bower's Museum, Santa Ana CA

Baker, Jerry E, *Pres.* Gadsden Museum of Fine Arts, Inc, Gadsden AL

Baker, Jim, *Pres.* St Genevieve Museum, Sainte Genevieve MO

Baker, Laura, *Colors Dir.* Spartanburg County Museum of Art, Spartanburg SC

Baker, Loren, *Dir.* Roberts Wesleyan College, Art Dept, Rochester NY (S)

Baker, Marilyn, *Chmn Art History.* University of Manitoba, School of Art, Winnipeg MB (S)

Baker, Michael, *Asst Cur Mus.* London Regional Art & Historical Museums, London ON

Baker, Patsy Collins, *Gallery Dir & Admnr.* New Orleans Academy of Fine Arts, Academy Gallery, New Orleans LA

Baker, Peggy M, *Dir & Librn.* Pilgrim Society, Pilgrim Hall Museum, Plymouth MA

Baker, Peggy M, *Dir & Librn.* Pilgrim Society, Library, Plymouth MA

Baker, Robert, *Cur Natural Science Research Lab.* Texas Tech University, Museum, Lubbock TX

Baker, Roger, *Coordr.* Clark College, Art Dept, Vancouver WA (S)

Baker, Sandra, *Asst Prof.* Brazosport College, Art Dept, Lake Jackson TX (S)

Baker, Scott, *Asst Dir.* Howard University, Gallery of Art, Washington DC

Baker, Victoria, *Asst Cur Early Canadian Art.* National Gallery of Canada, Ottawa ON

Baker, Wes, *Pres.* Museum of Northern British Columbia, Ruth Harvey Art Gallery, Prince Rupert BC

Baker, W Lowell, *Chmn Dept,* University of Alabama, Art Dept, Tuscaloosa AL (S)

Bakke, Julia Addison, *Registrar,* Menil Collection, Houston TX

Bakken, Jim, *Instr.* Charles Stewart Mott Community College, Art Area, School of Arts & Humanities, Flint MI (S)

Bakker, Dirk, *Photographer,* Detroit Institute of Arts, Detroit MI

Bakos, Stephanie, *Dir.* Berkeley Heights Free Public Library, Berkeley Heights NJ

Bakovych, A, *Asst Prof.* Northern Arizona University, School of Art & Design, Flagstaff AZ (S)

Balakier, Ann, *Assoc Prof.* University of South Dakota, Department of Art, College of Fine Arts, Vermillion SD (S)

Balas, Andrea, *Educ Exten Coordr.* Ukrainian Cultural & Educational Centre, Winnipeg MB

Balas, Shawna, *Cur.* Ukrainian Cultural & Educational Centre, Winnipeg MB

Balas, Shawna, *Gallery Cur.* Ukrainian Cultural & Educational Centre, Gallery, Winnipeg MB

Balazs, Harold, *Adjunct Asst Prof.* Spokane Falls Community College, Fine Arts Dept, Spokane WA (S)

Balbach, Charles E, *Pres.* The Buffalo Fine Arts Academy, Albright-Knox Art Gallery, Buffalo NY

Balch, Inge, *Assoc Prof.* Baker University, Dept of Art, Baldwin City KS (S)

Baldaia, Peter, *Chief Cur.* Huntsville Museum of Art, Huntsville AL

Baldaia, Peter J, *Chief Cur.* Huntsville Museum of Art, Reference Library, Huntsville AL

Baldwin, Dana, *Educ Dir.* Portland Museum of Art, Portland ME

Baldwin, Guy, *Assoc Prof.* University of Minnesota, Minneapolis, Dept of Art, Minneapolis MN (S)

Baldwin, Michelle, *Asst Prof.* Lynchburg College, Art Dept, Lynchburg VA (S)

Baldwin, Robert, *Assoc Prof.* Connecticut College, Dept of Art History, New London CT (S)

Baldwin, Robert A, *Assoc Prof.* Vanderbilt University, Dept of Fine Arts, Nashville TN (S)

Balentine, Susan, *Theatre Dir.* Hill Country Arts Foundation, Duncan-McAshan Visual Arts Center, Ingram TX

Balester, John, *Dir.* American Academy of Art, Chicago IL (S)

Balfour, Alan, *Dean.* Rensselaer Polytechnic Institute, School of Architecture, Troy NY (S)

Balistreri, Becky, *Dean Design.* Milwaukee Institute of Art & Design, Milwaukee WI (S)

Ball, Dan, *VPres.* Southern Arkansas University, Art Dept Gallery & Magale Art Gallery, Magnolia AR

Ball, Isabel, *Dean.* Our Lady of the Lake University, Dept of Art, San Antonio TX (S)

Ball, Jeff, *Instr.* William Woods-Westminster Colleges, Art Dept, Fulton MO (S)

Ball, Kathy, *Registrar.* Lafayette Natural History Museum, Planetarium & Nature Station, Lafayette LA

Ball, Larry, *Asst Prof.* University of Wisconsin-Stevens Point, Dept of Art & Design, Stevens Point WI (S)

Ball, Martin, *Asst Prof.* Rutgers, the State University of New Jersey, Mason Gross School of the Arts, New Brunswick NJ (S)

Ball, Rex, *Exec Dir.* The University of Texas, Institute of Texan Cultures, San Antonio TX

Ball, Susan L, *Exec Dir.* College Art Association, New York NY

Balla, Wes, *Cur History.* Albany Institute of History & Art, Albany NY

Ballance, Stephen, *Chmn Dept.* Northwestern Michigan College, Art Dept, Traverse City MI (S)

Ballantine, Robert, *Graphic Designer.* London Regional Art & Historical Museums, London ON

Ballard, Helen, *Chief Visitors Services.* Lightner Museum, Saint Augustine FL

Ballard, Maria, *Bus Mgr.* University of South Carolina, McKissick Museum, Columbia SC

Ballard Leake, Caroline, *Exec Dir.* Georgia Council for the Arts, Atlanta GA

Balleau, Pat, *Pres.* Allied Arts Gallery of the Yakima Valley, Yakima WA

Balliet, Nancy, *Dir.* Atlantic Gallery, New York NY

Ballinger, James K, *Dir.* Phoenix Art Museum, Phoenix AZ

Ballweg, Janet, *Assoc Dir.* Bowling Green State University, School of Art, Bowling Green OH (S)

Balmos, Don, *Chmn.* McLennan Community College, Fine Arts Dept, Waco TX (S)

Balmuth, Miriam, *Prof.* Tufts University, Dept of Art & Art History, Medford MA (S)

Balogh, Anthony, *Instr.* Madonna University, Art Dept, Livonia MI (S)

Baltosser, Virginia, *Instr.* The Arkansas Arts Center, Museum School, Little Rock AR (S)

Baltrushunas, John, *Asst Prof.* Maryville University of Saint Louis, Art Division, Saint Louis MO (S)

Balzekas, Stanley, *Pres.* Balzekas Museum of Lithuanian Culture, Chicago IL

Balzekas, Stanley, *Pres.* Balzekas Museum of Lithuanian Culture, Research Library, Chicago IL

Bambrick, Barbara, *Exec Dir.* Saint Bernard Foundation & Monastery, North Miami Beach FL

Banaian, Nancy, *Admin Asst.* Manchester Institute of Arts & Sciences Gallery, Manchester NH

Banas, Lillian, *Treas.* Jesse Besser Museum, Alpena MI

Banasiak, John, *Prof.* University of South Dakota, Department of Art, College of Fine Arts, Vermillion SD (S)

Banchs, William, *Pres.* National Foundation for Advancement in the Arts, Miami FL

Bancou, Marielle, *Exec Dir.* Color Association of The US, New York NY

Bandes, Susan, *Dir.* Michigan State University, Kresge Art Museum, East Lansing MI

Bandy, Mary Lee, *Chief Cur, Dept Film & Video.* Museum of Modern Art, New York NY

Bandy, Nancy, *Prof.* Victoria College, Fine Arts Dept, Victoria TX (S)

Banerji, Naseem, *Asst Prof.* Weber State University, Dept of Visual Arts, Ogden UT (S)

Bang, Peggy L, *Instr.* North Iowa Area Community College, Dept of Art, Mason City IA (S)

Banks, Barbara, *Membership & Program Liaison.* Madison Art Center, Madison WI

Banks, Charles, *Dir.* Butera School of Art, Boston MA (S)

Bannard, Darby, *Chmn.* University of Miami, Dept of Art & Art History, Coral Gables FL (S)

Bannigan, Patrick G, *Pres.* New Jersey Water-Color Society, Chester NJ

Bannon, Anthony, *Dir.* George Eastman House-International Museum of Photography & Film, Rochester NY

Bantens, Robert, *Art Historian.* University of South Alabama, Dept of Art & Art History, Mobile AL (S)

Bantle, Thomas, *Cur Exhib.* Public Museum of Grand Rapids, Grand Rapids MI

Baptie, Sue M, *Dir.* Vancouver City Archives, Vancouver BC

Barabe, Bryon, *Secy.* Xicanindio, Inc, Mesa AZ

Baraetucci, Mauricio, *Gallery Chmn.* Santa Monica College Art Gallery, Santa Monica CA

Barasch, Shirley, *Chmn.* Point Park College, Performing Arts Dept, Pittsburgh PA (S)

Barbash, Steven, *Prof.* State University of New York, College at Cortland, Art Dept, Cortland NY (S)

Barber, Christy, *Campaign-Marketing Mgr.* Allied Arts Council of St Joseph, Saint Joseph MO

Barber, Judith, *Exec Dir.* Hambidge Center Gallery, Rabun Gap GA

Barberia, Julia, *Museum Shop Mgr.* Philbrook Museum of Art, Tulsa OK

Barbieri, Frances, *Educ Coordr.* Seneca Falls Historical Society Museum, Seneca Falls NY

Barboni, Gwen, *Exec Dir.* Meadville Council on the Arts, Meadville PA

Barch, Nancy, *Instr.* Wayne Art Center, Wayne PA (S)

Barcheck, Rick, *Cur.* Mark Twain Bancshares, Saint Louis MO

Barde, Alex, *Prof.* Pittsburg State University, Art Dept, Pittsburg KS (S)

Barden, John, *Librn.* Tryon Palace Historic Sites & Gardens, Library, New Bern NC

Barden, John R, *Historian.* Tryon Palace Historic Sites & Gardens, New Bern NC

Bardenheuer, Lee, *Treas.* Kent Art Association, Inc, Gallery, Kent CT

Bardieri, Frances, *Acting Exec Dir.* Seneca Falls Historical Society Museum, Seneca Falls NY

Bardon, Donna, *Friends of Lovejoy Librn.* Southern Illinois University, Lovejoy Library, Edwardsville IL

Barello, Julia, *Asst Prof.* New Mexico State University, Art Dept, Las Cruces NM (S)

Barger, Judy, *Dir Develop.* Polk Museum of Art, Lakeland FL

Bargh, Jeff, *Acting Head Dept City Planning.* University of Manitoba, Faculty of Architecture, Winnipeg MB (S)

Barhaug, Shirley, *Pres.* Cody Country Art League, Cody WY

Barilleaux, Renee, *Asst Cur & Registrar.* Mississippi Museum of Art, Jackson MS

Barker, Marie, *Cur.* Sturdivant Hall, Selma AL

Barker, Norman, *Instr.* Johns Hopkins University, School of Medicine, Dept of Art as Applied to Medicine, Baltimore MD (S)

Barker, Stephen, *Dean.* University of California, Irvine, Studio Art Dept, Irvine CA (S)

Barkley, Alan, *Pres.* Ontario College of Art & Design, Toronto ON (S)

Barksdale, Jody, *Exec Dir.* Saint Louis Artists' Guild, Saint Louis MO

Barksdale, Kit, *Exec Dir.* Craftsmen's Guild of Mississippi, Inc, Agriculture & Forestry Museum, Jackson MS

Barletta, Barbara, *Assoc Prof.* University of Florida, Dept of Art, Gainesville FL (S)

Barletta, Guido, *Adminr.* Institute of Puerto Rican Culture, Museo de Arte Religioso Porta Coeli, San Juan PR

Barley, Gerlinde, *Coll Develop.* State University of New York at New Paltz, Sojourner Truth Library, New Paltz NY

Barlow, Barbara, *Membership Chmn.* Blacksburg Regional Art Association, Christiansburg VA

Barlow, Deborah, *Librn.* Los Angeles County Museum of Art, Allan C Balch Art Research Library, Los Angeles CA

Barlow, Deborah, *Head Librn.* Corcoran Gallery of Art, Corcoran Museum & School of Art Library, Washington DC

Barmann, Floyd, *Exec Dir & Cur Museum,* Clark County Historical Society, Springfield OH

Barmann, Floyd, *Dir.* Clark County Historical Society, Library, Springfield OH

Barnes, Bernadine, *Assoc Prof.* Wake Forest University, Dept of Art, Winston-Salem NC (S)

Barnes, Bridget, *Asst Dir,* University of California at Santa Cruz, Mary Porter Sesnon Art Gallery, Santa Cruz CA

Barnes, Carl F, *Prof.* Oakland University, Dept of Art & Art History, Rochester MI (S)

Barnes, Gary, *Assoc Prof.* Arkansas Tech University, Dept of Art, Russellville AR (S)

Barnes, Laurie, *Cur of Asian Art.* Detroit Institute of Arts, Detroit MI

Barnes, Lisa Tremper, *Dir.* Ursinus College, Philip & Muriel Berman Museum of Art, Collegeville PA

Barnes, Marilyn, *Office Mgr.* Oakville Galleries, Centennial Gallery and Gairloch Gallery, Oakville ON

Barnes, Raymond S, *Asst Prof.* Muhlenberg College, Dept of Art, Allentown PA (S)

Barnes, Reinaldo, *Mgr.* Longfellow-Evangeline State Commemorative Area, Saint Martinville LA

Barnes, Rick, *Adjunct Prof.* Oklahoma Christian University of Science & Arts, Dept of Art & Design, Oklahoma City OK (S)

Barnes, Robert, *Prof.* Indiana University, Bloomington, Henry Radford Hope School of Fine Arts, Bloomington IN (S)

Barnes, Sharron, *Assoc Prof.* Gulf Coast Community College, Division of Visual & Performing Arts, Panama City FL (S)

Barnes, Susan, *Bus Mgr.* American Society for Aesthetics, Edmonton AB

Barnes, Ted, *Chair.* Louisiana College, Dept of Art, Pineville LA (S)

Barnes, William, *Assoc Prof.* College of William & Mary, Dept of Fine Arts, Williamsburg VA (S)

Barnett, James F, *Dir Historic Properties,* Mississippi Department of Archives & History, Library, Jackson MS

Barnett, John, *Chmn Dept,* California State University, Art Dept, Turlock CA (S)

Barnett, Loretta, *Assoc Prof.* Colby-Sawyer College, Dept of Fine & Performing Arts, New London NH (S)

Barnett, Patricia, *Andrew W Mellon Librn.* Frick Art Reference Library, New York NY

Barnett, Patricia J, *Systems Librn,* The Metropolitan Museum of Art, Thomas J Watson Library, New York NY

Barnett, Richard, *Prof.* College of Mount Saint Vincent, Fine Arts Dept, Riverdale NY (S)

Barnett, Robert, *Secy Board of Trustees,* Royal Ontario Museum, Toronto ON

Barnette, Joan, *Museum Cur,* Red Rock State Park, Library, Church Rock NM

Barnhard, Sherry, *Pres.* Lahaina Arts Society, Art Organization, Lahaina HI

Barnhill, Georgia, *Pres.* Fitchburg Art Museum, Fitchburg MA

Barnhill, Georgia B, *Cur Graphic Arts.* American Antiquarian Society, Worcester MA

Barnitz, Downing, *Dir.* Florida Southern College, Melvin Art Gallery, Lakeland FL

Barnitz, Downing, *Chmn Dept,* Florida Southern College, Art Dept, Lakeland FL (S)

Barnitz, Gwenda, *Vol Coordr.* Salvador Dali Museum, Saint Petersburg FL

Barnum, Amy, *Dir.* New York State Historical Association, Library, Cooperstown NY

Baroff, Debby, *Cur Spec Coll.* Institute of the Great Plains, Museum of the Great Plains, Lawton OK

Baroff, Deborah, *Cur Spec Coll.* Institute of the Great Plains, Research Library, Lawton OK

Baron, Donna, *Registrar.* Alaska State Museum, Juneau AK

Baron, Richard, *Exec Dir.* Bridge Center for Contemporary Art, El Paso TX

Barone, Deborah, *Cur.* Connecticut State Library, Museum of Connecticut History, Hartford CT

Barone, Isabella, *Co-Dir.* McGroarty Cultural Art Center, Tujunga CA (S)

Barr, David, *Prof.* Macomb Community College, Art Dept, Warren MI (S)

Barr, Donald, *Assoc Prof.* College of the Ozarks, Dept of Art, Point Lookout MO (S)

Barraclough, Dennis, *Assoc Prof.* Daemen College, Art Dept, Amherst NY (S)

Barret, Dale, *Information Officer,* Ontario Crafts Council, Craft Resource Centre, Toronto ON

Barrett, Dale, *Cur.* Ontario Crafts Council, The Craft Gallery, Toronto ON

Barrett, Evelyn, *Chmn.* Warner House Association, MacPheadris-Warner House, Portsmouth NH

Barrett, Joann, *Mgr Pub Information,* Institute of Contemporary Art, Boston MA

Barrett, Nancy, *Cur Photog.* New Orleans Museum of Art, New Orleans LA

Barrett, Ned, *Humanities Chmn.* Idyllwild Arts Academy, Idyllwild CA (S)

Barrett, Robert, *Dir & Chief Cur.* Fresno Arts Center & Museum, Fresno CA

Barrett, Terry, *Assoc Prof.* Ohio State University, Dept of Art Education, Columbus OH (S)

Barrett, Wayne, *Dir Colonial Williamsburg Journal.* Colonial Williamsburg Foundation, Williamsburg VA

Barrett, William O, *Exec Dir.* Association of Independent Colleges of Art & Design, San Francisco CA

Barrie, Shirley, *Adminr.* Canadian Society of Painters In Watercolour, Toronto ON

Barrineau, Annette W, *VPres Student Servs.* Florida School of the Arts, Visual Arts, Palatka FL (S)

Barringer, George M, *Special Collections Librn.* Georgetown University, Lauinger Library-Special Collections Division, Washington DC

Barrington, Susan T, *Supt.* Old Fort Harrod State Park Mansion Museum, Harrodsburg KY

Barron, Stephanie, *Cur 20th Century Art.* Los Angeles County Museum of Art, Los Angeles CA

Barrow, Jane, *Head Painting.* Southern Illinois University at Edwardsville, Dept of Art & Design, Edwardsville IL (S)

Barry, Claire, *Chief Conservator.* Kimbell Art Foundation, Kimbell Art Museum, Fort Worth TX

Barry, Maureen, *Pub Relations Dir.* Embarcadero Center Ltd, San Francisco CA

Barry, William D, *Reference Asst.* Maine Historical Society, Library, Portland ME

Barryte, Bernard, *Assoc Dir & Chief Cur.* Stanford University, Museum of Art, Stanford CA

Barsotti, Frank, *Prof.* School of the Art Institute of Chicago, Chicago IL (S)

Bart, Sharon, *Supv Branches,* Miami-Dade Public Library, Miami FL

Bartel, Katherine, *Asst Prof.* Eastern Illinois University, Art Dept, Charleston IL (S)

Bartel, Marvin, *Chmn.* Goshen College, Art Dept, Goshen IN (S)

Bartell, Lorinda B, *Pres.* Springfield Museum of Art, Springfield OH

Bartelo, Jose, *Dir.* Institute of Puerto Rican Culture, Museo y Parque Historico de Caparra, San Juan PR

Bartels, Kathleen, *Dir Admin.* The Museum of Contemporary Art, Los Angeles CA

Barter, Judith, *Cur American Arts.* The Art Institute of Chicago, Chicago IL

Bartfield, Ira, *Coordr of Photography.* National Gallery of Art, Washington DC

Barth, Charles, *Prof.* Mount Mercy College, Art Dept, Cedar Rapids IA (S)

Barth, Cynthia, *Librn.* Munson-Williams-Proctor Institute, Museum of Art, Utica NY

Barth, Cynthia M, *Head Librn.* Munson-Williams-Proctor Institute, Art Reference Library, Utica NY

Barth, Miles, *Cur of Coll.* International Center of Photography, New York NY

Barth, Uta, *Asst Prof.* University of California, Riverside, Dept of Art, Riverside CA (S)

Bartholomew, Terese Tse, *Cur Indian Art.* Asian Art Museum of San Francisco, Avery Brundage Collection, San Francisco CA

Bartlett, Christopher, *Dir & Prof.* Towson State University, The Holtzman Art Gallery, Towson MD

Bartlett, Jack, *Assoc Prof.* Mississippi State University, Art Dept, Mississippi State MS (S)

Bartner, Howard C, *Asst Prof.* Johns Hopkins University, School of Medicine, Dept of Art as Applied to Medicine, Baltimore MD (S)

Barton, James, *Pres.* Johnson Atelier Technical Institute of Sculpture, Mercerville NJ (S)

Barton, William, *Dir.* Historical Society of Old Newbury, Cushing House Museum, Newburyport MA

Barton, William, *Dir & Cur.* Newburyport Maritime Society, Custom House Maritime Museum, Newburyport MA

Bartos, Armand, *Pres.* Sculpture Center School & Studios, New York NY

Bartz, Marilyn, *Pres.* Safety Harbor Museum of Regional History, Safety Harbor FL

Barwick, Kent, *Pres.* New York State Historical Association, Fenimore House Museum, Cooperstown NY

Barwick, Kent, *Pres.* New York State Historical Association, Farmers' Museum, Inc, Cooperstown NY

Barzman, Karen-edis, *Asst Prof.* Cornell University, Dept of the History of Art, Ithaca NY (S)

Bascom, Mansfield, *Cur.* Wharton Esherick Museum, Paoli PA

Bascom, Ruth E, *Pres.* Wharton Esherick Museum, Paoli PA

Bash, Lee, *Chair.* Illinois Benedictine University, Fine Arts Dept, Lisle IL (S)

Basha, Regine, *Cur.* Saidye Bronfman Centre for the Arts Centre, Montreal PQ

Basham, Kathleen, *Deputy Dir Admin.* Baltimore Museum of Art, Baltimore MD

Basile, Kenneth, *Gallery Dir.* Salisbury State University, University Gallery, Salisbury MD

Basinger, Jeanine, *Prof.* Wesleyan University, Art Dept, Middletown CT (S)

Basista, Paul, *Exec Dir.* Graphic Artists Guild, New York NY

Bass, Clayton, *Exec Dir.* Walter Anderson Museum of Art, Ocean Springs MS

Bass, Deborah, *Registrar.* The Dixon Gallery & Gardens, Memphis TN

Bass, Deborah, *Registrar.* The Dixon Gallery & Gardens, Library, Memphis TN

Bass, Linda, *Dir Marketing.* Stan Hywet Hall & Gardens, Inc, Akron OH

Bass, W Clayton, *Exhib Design Supv.* Emory University, Michael C Carlos Museum, Atlanta GA

Bassett, Lynne, *Cur Colls.* Historic Northampton Museum, Northampton MA

Bassett, Ruth, *Librn.* Brandywine River Museum, Chadds Ford PA

Bassett, Ruth, *Librn.* Brandywine River Museum, Library, Chadds Ford PA

Bassi, George, *Dir.* Lauren Rogers Museum of Art, Laurel MS

Bassin, Joan, *Exec Dir.* National Institute for Architectural Education, New York NY

Bassinger, Marilyn, *Dir.* Ellen Noel Art Museum of the Permian Basin, Odessa TX

Bassis, Michael, *Pres.* Olivet College, Armstrong Museum of Art & Archaeology, Olivet MI

Bassolos, Arturo, *Art Dept Chmn.* Delaware State College, Dept of Art & Art Education, Dover DE (S)

Basson, David, *Reference,* New York University, Institute of Fine Arts Visual Resources Collection, New York NY

Baster, Victoria V, *Asst Cur.* University of Lethbridge, Art Gallery, Lethbridge AB

Bastian, Duane, *Prof.* University of Toledo, Dept of Art, Toledo OH (S)

Batchelor, Anthony, *Chmn.* Art Academy of Cincinnati, Cincinnati OH (S)

Batchelor, Betsey, *Assoc Prof.* Beaver College, Dept of Fine Arts, Glenside PA (S)

Batdorff, Jon, *Instr.* Goddard College, Dept of Art, Plainfield VT (S)

Bateman, Ellen, *Instr.* Toronto Art Therapy Institute, Toronto ON (S)

Bateman, Nell, *Supervisor,* Toronto Art Therapy Institute, Toronto ON (S)

Bater, Richard, *Dir Libr Servs,* Presbyterian Historical Society, Library, Philadelphia PA

Bates, Craig D, *Cur Ethnography,* Yosemite Museum, Yosemite National Park CA

Bates, Geoff, *Asst Prof.* Salem College, Art Dept, Winston-Salem NC (S)

Bates, Lenny, *Asst Cur.* Sloss Furnaces National Historic Landmark, Birmingham AL

Bates, Tom, *Prof.* La Roche College, Division of Graphics, Design & Communication, Pittsburgh PA (S)

Bates-Brown, Valery, *Prof.* Virginia State University, Fine & Commercial Art, Petersburg VA (S)

Batkin, Jonathan, *Dir.* Wheelwright Museum of the American Indian, Santa Fe NM

Batkin, Jonathan, *Dir.* Wheelwright Museum of the American Indian, Mary Cabot Wheelwright Research Library, Santa Fe NM

Batkin, Norton, *Dir.* Bard College, Center for Curatorial Studies Graduate Program, Annandale-on-Hudson NY (S)

Batson, Darrell, *Dir.* Las Vegas-Clark County Library District, Las Vegas NV

Batson, Darrell, *Branch Adminr,* Las Vegas-Clark County Library District, Las Vegas NV

Batson, Gayle, *Instr.* The Arkansas Arts Center, Museum School, Little Rock AR (S)

Batter, John, *Area Head,* Kentucky State University, Jackson Hall Gallery, Frankfort KY

Battis, Nicholas, *Registrar,* Pratt Institute Library, Rubelle & Norman Schafler Gallery, Brooklyn NY

Batty, Ellen, *Circulation Librn,* Athenaeum of Philadelphia, Philadelphia PA

Batty, Ellen, *Circulation Librn,* Athenaeum of Philadelphia, Library, Philadelphia PA

Batty, Nancy Miller, *Assoc Dir & Chief Cur,* Delaware Art Museum, Wilmington DE

Batzka, Stephen, *Prof.* Manchester College, Art Dept, North Manchester IN (S)

Bauche, Dean, *Cur.* Allen Sapp Gallery, North Battleford SK

Baucom, Ronda, *Vol Spec Events,* Chrysler Museum Of Art, Norfolk VA

Baucus, Joan, *Interim Dir,* Hockaday Center for the Arts, Kalispell MT

Bauer, Brent A, *Asst Prof.* Johns Hopkins University, School of Medicine, Dept of Art as Applied to Medicine, Baltimore MD (S)

Bauer, Douglas, *Pres.* Bowne House Historical Society, Flushing NY

Bauer, Florence, *Librn & Treas,* Pennsylvania Dutch Folk Culture Society Inc, Baver Genealogical Library, Lenhartsville PA

Bauer, Susie, *Asst to Dir.* Oklahoma City Art Museum, Oklahoma City OK

Bauknight, Alice R, *Cur of Exhib,* University of South Carolina, McKissick Museum, Columbia SC

Bauman, Patricia, *Pres,* G G Drayton Club, Salem OH

Bauman, Thomas, *VPres,* G G Drayton Club, Salem OH

Baumann, Richard, *Instr.* Columbia College, Art Dept, Columbia MO (S)

Baure, Thomson B, *VPres,* New Mexico Art League, Gallery, Albuquerque NM

Baxa, Kathryn, *Asst Prof.* North Central College, Dept of Art, Naperville IL (S)

Baxter, Joan, *Exec Secy,* Greene County Historical Society, Xenia OH

Baxter, Paula A, *Cur Art & Arch Coll,* The New York Public Library, Art, Prints & Photographs Division, New York NY

Baxter, Violet, *Treas,* New York Artists Equity Association, Inc, New York NY

Bayles, Jennifer, *Cur Educ,* The Buffalo Fine Arts Academy, Albright-Knox Art Gallery, Buffalo NY

Bayless, Frederick, *Treas.* Almond Historical Society, Inc, Hagadorn House, The 1800-37 Museum, Almond NY

Baynes, Gloretta, *Asst to Dir.* Museum of the National Center of Afro-American Artists, Boston MA

Bayrus, Kristin, *Catalog Librn,* Moore College of Art & Design, Library, Philadelphia PA

Bayuzick, Dennis, *Assoc Prof.* University of Wisconsin-Parkside, Art Dept, Kenosha WI (S)

Baza, Larry, *Board Exec Dir,* Centro Cultural De La Raza, San Diego CA

Beach, Milo, *Adjunct Prof.* University of Michigan, Ann Arbor, Dept of History of Art, Ann Arbor MI (S)

Beach, Milo C, *Dir.* Freer Gallery of Art Gallery, Arthur M Sackler Gallery, Washington DC

Beagle, Charles, *Dir Facility Servs & Security,* Memphis Brooks Museum of Art, Memphis TN

Beaird, Elisabeth, *Admin Dir.* The Lab, San Francisco CA

Beal, Bruce, *Commissioner,* Boston Art Commission of the City of Boston, Boston MA

Beal, Graham W J, *Dir.* Los Angeles County Museum of Art, Los Angeles CA

Beale, Arthur, *Dir Research,* Museum of Fine Arts, Boston MA

Beals, Stuart, *Instr.* Johnson County Community College, Visual Arts Program, Overland Park KS (S)

Beam, Patrice K, *Exec Dir.* Octagon Center for the Arts, Ames IA

Beam, Philip C, *Emeritus Prof.* Bowdoin College, Art Dept, Brunswick ME (S)

Beamer, Karl, *Assoc Prof.* Bloomsburg University, Dept of Art, Bloomsburg PA (S)

Beane, Frances A, *Deputy Dir.* Harvard University, Harvard University Art Museums, Cambridge MA

Beane, Frances A, *Deputy Dir.* Harvard University, William Hayes Fogg Art Museum, Cambridge MA

Beane, Frances A, *Deputy Dir.* Harvard University, Arthur M Sackler Museum, Cambridge MA

Beard, Kimberly, *Registrar,* Port Authority of New York & New Jersey, Art Collection, New York NY

Beard, Rick, *Exec Dir.* Atlanta Historical Society Inc, Atlanta History Center, Atlanta GA

Beardsley, Kelcey, *Instr.* Marylhurst College, Art Dept, Marylhurst OR (S)

Beardsley, Theodore S, *Pres.* Hispanic Society of America, Museum, New York NY

Bearnson, Dorothy, *Prof.* University of Utah, Art Dept, Salt Lake City UT (S)

Bearor, Karen, *Assoc Prof.* Florida State University, Art History Dept (R133B), Tallahassee FL (S)

Beasterfeld, Lila, *Cur.* Wabaunsee County Historical Museum, Alma KS

Beattie, Bruce, *Pres.* National Cartoonists Society, New York NY

Beauchamp, Darrell, *Dir.* Navarro College, Gaston T Gooch Library & Learning Resource Center, Corsicana TX

Beaudoin-Ross, Jacqueline, *Cur Costume,* McCord Museum of Canadian History, Montreal PQ

Beauvais, David, *Exec Dir.* Elk River Area Arts Council, Elk River MN

Becher, Tom, *Dean Design,* Emily Carr Institute of Art & Design, Vancouver BC (S)

Bechet, Ron, *Acting Chmn.* Southern University in New Orleans, Fine Arts & Philosophy Dept, New Orleans LA (S)

Becht, Mary A, *Dir.* Broward County Board of Commissioners Cultural Affairs Divison, Fort Lauderdale FL

Bechwith, Wendy, *Instr.* La Roche College, Division of Graphics, Design & Communication, Pittsburgh PA (S)

Beck, Albert, *Prof.* Culver-Stockton College, Art Dept, Canton MO (S)

Beck, Kimberly, *Bus Mgr.* Columbus Museum, Columbus GA

Beck, Martin, *Registrar,* Dahesh Museum, New York NY

Beck, Sachiko, *Asst Prof.* Framingham State College, Art Dept, Framingham MA (S)

Beckelman, John, *Chmn Art Dept,* Coe College, Gordon Fennell Gallery & Marvin Cone Gallery, Cedar Rapids IA

Beckelman, John, *Chmn.* Coe College, Dept of Art, Cedar Rapids IA (S)

Becken, Bradford A, *Pres.* Newport Historical Society, Newport RI

Becker, Beverly, *Public Prog Cur.* Redding Museum of Art & History, Redding CA

Becker, David, *Prof.* University of Wisconsin, Madison, Dept of Art, Madison WI (S)

Becker, Heather, *Exec Dir.* Rock Ford Foundation, Inc, Historic Rock Ford & Kauffman Museum, Lancaster PA

Becker, Jack, *Cur & Librn.* Lyme Historical Society, Florence Griswold Museum, Old Lyme CT

Becker, Jack, *Cur.* Lyme Historical Society, Archives, Old Lyme CT

Becker, James, *Cur.* First Bank System, Art Collection, Minneapolis MN

Becker, Randy, *Gallery Dir.* Teikyo Westmar University, Westmar Art Gallery, LeMars IA

Becker, Randy, *Dir.* Teikyo Westmar University, Mock Library Art Dept, LeMars IA

Beckerman, Lilyan, *Treas.* Hollywood Art Museum, Hollywood FL

Beckman, Thomas, *Registrar,* Historical Society of Delaware, Delaware History Museum, Wilmington DE

Beckstrom, Robert, *Chmn.* Lorain County Community College, Elyria OH (S)

Beckwith, Alice, *Assoc Prof.* Providence College, Art & Art History Dept, Providence RI (S)

Beckwith, Claudia, *Head Collections Management & Security,* Greenville County Museum of Art, Greenville SC

Beckwith, Herbert, *Technical Services,* San Francisco Maritime National Historical Park, J Porter Shaw Library, San Francisco CA

Becky, Tawney, *Cur Asst.* Harvard University, Busch-Reisinger Museum, Cambridge MA

Beda, Gaye Elise, *Chmn Scholarship Members,* Salmagundi Club, New York NY

Bedard, Robert J, *Treas.* Art PAC, Washington DC

Bedell, Cindy, *Asst Cur Educ,* Tippecanoe County Historical Museum, Lafayette IN

Bedford, Scott, *Public Relations Dir,* Arts & Science Council, Charlotte VA

Bedno, Jane, *Graduate Prog.* University of the Arts, Philadelphia College of Art & Design, Philadelphia PA (S)

Bedoya, Roberto, *Exec Dir.* National Association of Artists' Organizations (NAAO), Washington DC

Beebe, Mary Livingstone, *Dir.* University of California, San Diego, Stuart Collection, La Jolla CA

Beecher, Raymond, *Librn.* Greene County Historical Society, Bronck Museum, Coxsackie NY

Beeching, Lynne, *Develop.* Hidalgo County Historical Museum, Edinburg TX

Beelick, Susan, *Humanities Reference & Slide Librn.* California State University at Sacramento, Library - Humanities Reference Dept, Sacramento CA

Beesch, Ruth K, *Dir.* University of North Carolina at Greensboro, Weatherspoon Art Gallery, Greensboro NC

Begland, Mary Anne, *Chmn Graphic Design & Prof.* Rochester Institute of Technology, School of Art & Design, Rochester NY (S)

Begley, John P, *Exec Dir,* Louisville Visual Art Association, Louisville KY

Behler, Mark, *Cur,* North Central Washington Museum, Gallery, Wenatchee WA

Behnk, Elisa, *Media Relations Mgr,* Carnegie Institute, Carnegie Museum of Art, Pittsburgh PA

Behnk, Elisa, *Media Relations Mgr,* Carnegie Institute, Carnegie Museum of Art, Pittsburgh PA

Behrends, Carey, *Exec Dir,* Presidential Museum, Odessa TX

Behrends, Carey, *Exec Dir,* Presidential Museum, Library of the Presidents, Odessa TX

Behrens, Fred, *Head Dept,* Columbia State Community College, Dept of Art, Columbia TN (S)

Behrens, Roy, *Prof,* University of Northern Iowa, Dept of Art, Cedar Falls IA (S)

Beiersdorfer, Ann, *Prof,* Xavier University, Dept of Art, Cincinnati OH (S)

Beil, Eloise, *Dir Coll,* Shelburne Museum, Shelburne VT

Beil, Eloise, *Dir Coll,* Shelburne Museum, Library, Shelburne VT

Beiman, Frances, *Supv Art & Music Div,* Newark Public Library, Art & Music Div, Newark NJ

Belan, Kyra, *Gallery Dir,* Broward Community College - South Campus, Art Gallery, Pembroke Pines FL

Beland, Mario, *Conservator Early Art,* Musee du Quebec, Quebec PQ

Belanger, Alain, *Coordr,* Vu Centre D'Animation Et de Diffusion De La Photographie, Quebec PQ

Belcheff, Koste, *Chmn Art & Music,* Angelo State University, Art & Music Dept, San Angelo TX (S)

Beldin-Reed, Elaine, *Exec Dir,* Mendocino Art Center, Gallery, Mendocino CA

Beldin-Reed, Elaine, *Exec Dir,* Mendocino Art Center, Library, Mendocino CA

Beldin-Reed, Elaine, *Exec Dir,* Mendocino Art Center, Mendocino CA (S)

Belesco, Ruth, *Asst Prof,* Spring Hill College, Fine Arts Dept, Mobile AL (S)

Belfort-Chalat, Jacqueline, *Chmn & Prof,* Le Moyne College, Fine Arts Dept, Syracuse NY (S)

Belknap, Beth, *Assoc,* College of Mount Saint Joseph, Art Dept, Cincinnati OH (S)

Bell, Christine, *Lectr,* Lake Forest College, Dept of Art, Lake Forest IL (S)

Bell, Eugene, *Instr,* Cuyahoga Valley Art Center, Cuyahoga Falls OH (S)

Bell, Eunice, *Exec Dir,* Ocean City Art Center, Ocean City NJ (S)

Bell, Eunice, *Exec Dir,* Ocean City Art Center, Ocean City NJ

Bell, Eunice, *Exec Dir,* Ocean City Art Center, Art Library, Ocean City NJ

Bell, Greg, *Dir,* University of Puget Sound, Kittredge Art Gallery, Tacoma WA

Bell, Janis, *Assoc Prof,* Kenyon College, Art Dept, Gambier OH (S)

Bell, Judith, *Instr,* San Jose City College, School of Fine Arts, San Jose CA (S)

Bell, Kathy, *Instr,* Bob Jones University, School of Fine Arts, Greenville SC (S)

Bell, Lesley, *Mgr,* Metropolitan Toronto Library Board, Main Reference, Toronto ON

Bell, Lynne, *Head,* University of Saskatchewan, Dept of Art & Art History, Saskatoon SK (S)

Bell, Roberley, *Instr,* Villa Maria College of Buffalo, Art Dept, Buffalo NY (S)

Bell, Robert, *Instr,* Umpqua Community College, Fine & Performing Arts Dept, Roseburg OR (S)

Bell, Trevor, *Prof,* Florida State University, Art Dept, Tallahassee FL (S)

Bellah, Mary S, *Cur,* Carnegie Art Museum, Oxnard CA

Bellais, Leslie, *Cur Costumes & Textiles,* State Historical Society of Wisconsin, State Historical Museum, Madison WI

Bellas, Gerald, *Dir,* College of Mount Saint Joseph, Studio San Giuseppe, Cincinnati OH

Bellas, Gerry, *Asst Prof,* College of Mount Saint Joseph, Art Dept, Cincinnati OH (S)

Belle, Randolph, *Board Pres,* Pro Arts, Oakland CA

Bellerby, Greg, *Cur,* Emily Carr Institute of Art & Design, The Charles H Scott Gallery, Vancouver BC

Belleville, Patricia, *Asst Prof,* Eastern Illinois University, Art Dept, Charleston IL (S)

Bell-Garvin, Donna, *Cur,* New Hampshire Historical Society, Concord NH

Bellingham, Susan, *Spec Coll Librn,* University of Waterloo, Dana Porter Library, Waterloo ON

Bellov, Anthony, *Prog & Public Information,* Abigail Adams Smith Museum, New York NY

Belmonte, Maria Luisa, *Exec Dir,* Detroit Artists Market, Detroit MI

Belluscio, Lynne, *Dir,* Leroy Historical Society, LeRoy NY

Belnap, Gillian, *Head Publ,* Carnegie Institute, Carnegie Museum of Art, Pittsburgh PA

Belovitch, Carol, *Human Resources Specialist,* National Museum of the American Indian, George Gustav Heye Center, New York NY

Belson, Anne M, *Cultural Affairs Coordr,* Federal Reserve Bank of Boston, Boston MA

Beltemacchi, Peter, *Assoc Dean,* Illinois Institute of Technology, College of Architecture, Chicago IL (S)

Belvo, Hazel, *Faculty,* Grand Marais Art Colony, Grand Marais MN (S)

Belvo, Hazel, *Chmn Fine Arts,* Minneapolis College of Art & Design, Minneapolis MN (S)

Belz, Carl I, *Dir,* Brandeis University, Rose Art Museum, Waltham MA

Belz, Scott, *Instr,* Mississippi State University, Art Dept, Mississippi State MS (S)

Beman, Lynn S, *Exec Dir,* Amherst Museum, Amherst NY

Benckenstein, Eunice R, *VChmn,* Nelda C & H J Lutcher Stark Foundation, Stark Museum of Art, Orange TX

Bendel, D, *Prof,* Northern Arizona University, School of Art & Design, Flagstaff AZ (S)

Bender, David R, *Exec Dir,* Special Libraries Association, Museum, Arts & Humanities Division, Washington DC

Bender, Jennifer, *Asst Dir,* Art Com-La Mamelle, Inc, San Francisco CA

Bender, Phil, *Dir,* Pirate-A Contemporary Art Oasis, Denver CO

Bendit, Jo-Anne, *Gallery Asst,* City of Woodstock, Woodstock Art Gallery, Woodstock ON

Benedetti, Joan, *Librn,* Craft & Folk Art Museum, Los Angeles CA

Benedetti, Joan M, *Museum Librn,* Craft & Folk Art Museum, Edith R Wyle Research Library, Los Angeles CA

Benedetti, Susan, *Librn & Archivist,* San Joaquin Pioneer & Historical Society, The Haggin Museum, Stockton CA

Benedict, Dow, *Chmn,* Shepherd College, Art Dept, Shepherdstown WV (S)

Benedict, Mary Jane, *Librn,* J B Speed Art Museum, Art Reference Library, Louisville KY

Benefield, Richard, *Adminr,* Brown University, David Winton Bell Gallery, Providence RI

Benezra, Neal, *Dir Public Programs & Chief Cur,* Hirshhorn Museum & Sculpture Garden, Washington DC

Bengston, Charlotte, *Treas,* Essex Historical Society, Essex Shipbuilding Museum, Essex MA

Bengston, Rod, *Gallery Dir,* University of Akron, University Galleries, Akron OH

Benini, Lorraine, *Chmn,* The Art Foundation, Hot Springs National Park AR

Benio, Pauleve, *Chmn Art Dept,* Adrian College, Art & Design Dept, Adrian MI (S)

Beniston, Susan, *Instr,* Toronto School of Art, Toronto ON (S)

Benites, Marimar, *Dir,* Institute of Puerto Rican Culture, Escuela de Artes Plasticas Galleria, San Juan PR

Benitez, Maimar, *Chancellor,* Institute of Puerto Rican Culture, Escuela de Artes Plasticas, San Juan PR (S)

Benjamin, Brent, *Deputy Dir Curatorial Affairs,* Museum of Fine Arts, Boston MA

Benjamin, Jack, *Chmn,* University of South Carolina at Aiken, Dept of Visual & Performing Arts, Aiken SC (S)

Benjamin, Karl, *Prof,* Claremont Graduate School, Dept of Fine Arts, Claremont CA (S)

Benjamin, Tritobia, *Chmn,* Howard University, Gallery of Art, Washington DC

Benn, Carl, *Cur,* Toronto Historical Board, Historic Fort York, Toronto ON

Bennett, Anne, *Registrar,* University of California, Los Angeles, Grunwald Center for the Graphic Arts, Los Angeles CA

Bennett, Archie, *Instr,* Surry Community College, Art Dept, Dobson NC (S)

Bennett, Bill, *Pres,* Summit County Historical Society, Akron OH

Bennett, Claude, *Pres,* University of Alabama at Birmingham, Visual Arts Gallery, Birmingham AL

Bennett, Fernanda, *Registrar,* Nassau County Museum of Fine Art, Roslyn Harbor NY

Bennett, James, *Assoc Prof,* Norwich University, Dept of Philosophy, Religion & Fine Arts, Northfield VT (S)

Bennett, Kate, *Cur Edu,* Birmingham Museum of Art, Birmingham AL

Bennett, Kelly, *Budget Analyst,* National Museum of the American Indian, George Gustav Heye Center, New York NY

Bennett, K Sharon, *Archivist,* Charleston Museum, Charleston SC

Bennett, K Sharon, *Librn,* Charleston Museum, Library, Charleston SC

Bennett, Laura, *Museum Educ Specialist,* Frederic Remington Art Museum, Ogdensburg NY

Bennett, Mary, *VPres,* Miami Watercolor Society, Inc, Miami FL

Bennett, Michael J, *Chief Cur,* Tampa Museum of Art, Tampa FL

Bennett, Michael J, *Sr Cur,* Tampa Museum of Art, Library, Tampa FL

Bennett, Shelley, *Cur British & Continental Art,* The Huntington Library, Art Collections & Botanical Gardens, San Marino CA

Bennett, Shelley, *Adjunct Asst Prof,* University of Southern California, School of Fine Arts, Los Angeles CA (S)

Bennett, Steven, *Public Relations,* Marion Koogler McNay Art Museum, San Antonio TX

Bennett, Swannee, *Cur,* Arkansas Territorial Restoration, Little Rock AR

Bennett, Swannee, *Cur,* Arkansas Territorial Restoration, Library, Little Rock AR

Bennett, Valerie, *Cur,* City of Austin Parks & Recreation, O Henry Museum, Austin TX

Benoit, Claude, *Exec Dir,* McCord Museum of Canadian History, Montreal PQ

Benoit, George N, *Chmn Board,* Bronx Museum of the Arts, Bronx NY

Benoy, Cecilia, *Cur Educ,* Gaston County Museum of Art & History, Dallas NC

Benson, Anita, *Instr,* Monterey Peninsula College, Art Dept, Monterey CA (S)

Benson, Barbara E, *Exec Dir,* Historical Society of Delaware, Delaware History Museum, Wilmington DE

Benson, Barbara E, *Exec Dir,* Historical Society of Delaware, Library, Wilmington DE

Benson, David, *Mus Cur,* Chatham Cultural Centre, Thames Art Gallery, Chatham ON

Benson, Eugenia, *Fine Arts,* Silas Bronson Library, Art, Theatre & Music Services, Waterbury CT

Benson, Jack, *Emeritus Prof,* University of Massachusetts, Amherst, Art History Program, Amherst MA (S)

Benson, Kerry J, *Dir,* Santa Fe Arts Institute, Santa Fe NM (S)

Benson, Mark, *Assoc Prof,* Auburn University at Montgomery, Dept of Fine Arts, Montgomery AL (S)

Benson, M D, *Instr,* Humboldt State University, College of Arts & Humanities, Arcata CA (S)

Benson, Richard, *Dean,* Yale University, School of Art, New Haven CT (S)

Benson, Sarah, *Publicity/Publications Coordr,* Cornell University, Herbert F Johnson Museum of Art, Ithaca NY

Benson, Timothy, *Assoc Cur*. Los Angeles County Museum of Art, Robert Gore Rifkind Center for German Expressionist Studies, Los Angeles CA

Bent, George, *Asst Prof*. Washington and Lee University, Division of Art, Lexington VA (S)

Bentley, Eden R, *Librn*. Johnson Atelier Technical Institute of Sculpture, Johnson Atelier Library, Mercerville NJ

Benton, Janetta, *Prof*. Pace University, Dyson College of Arts & Sciences, Pleasantville NY (S)

Benton, Steve, *Dir*. Massachusetts Institute of Technology, Center for Advanced Visual Studies, Cambridge MA (S)

Bentor, Eli, *Asst Prof*. Winthrop University, Dept of Art & Design, Rock Hill SC (S)

Benvenuti, Noella, *Registrar*. San Bernardino County Museum, Fine Arts Institute, Redlands CA

Benz, Blair, *Dir*. University of Northern Iowa, Gallery of Art, Cedar Falls IA

Ben'zvi, Paul, *Instr*. Indiana University of Pennsylvania, Dept of Art & Art Education, Indiana PA (S)

Berard, Guy, *Prof*. St Lawrence University, Dept of Fine Arts, Canton NY (S)

Berens, Stephen, *Prof*. Chapman University, Art Dept, Orange CA (S)

Berg, Kathy L, *Librn*. Worcester Art Museum, Library, Worcester MA

Berg, Mona, *Gallery Dir*. Purdue University Galleries, West Lafayette IN

Berg, Niels, *VPres*. Ages of Man Fellowship, Amenia NY

Berg, Susan, *Dir*. Colonial Williamsburg Foundation, John D Rockefeller, Jr Library, Williamsburg VA

Bergan, Elizabeth, *VPres*. Mingei International, Inc, Mingei International Museum Satellite of World Folk Art, San Diego CA

Bergeman, Rich, *Instr*. Linn Benton Community College, Fine & Applied Art Dept, Albany OR (S)

Berger, Jerry A, *Dir*. Springfield Art Museum, Springfield MO

Berger, M, *Librn*. McGill University, Blackader-Lauterman Library of Architecture and Art, Montreal PQ

Bergeron, Father Andre, *Artistic Cur*. Saint Joseph's Oratory, Museum, Montreal PQ

Bergeron, Jack, *Assoc Prof*. Lansing Community College, Art Program, Lansing MI (S)

Bergeron, Suzanne K, *Asst Dir*. Bowdoin College, Museum of Art, Brunswick ME

Bergeron, Yves, *Cur*. Musee du Seminaire de Quebec, Quebec PQ

Bergfeld, Mary Ann, *Assoc Prof*. Saint Xavier University, Dept of Art, Chicago IL (S)

Berg-Johnson, Karen, *Asst Prof*. Bethel College, Dept of Art, Saint Paul MN (S)

Bergles, Frances, *Librn*. Mendel Art Gallery & Civic Conservatory, Reference Library, Saskatoon SK

Bergman, Joseph, *Assoc Prof*. Siena Heights College, Studio Angelico-Art Dept, Adrian MI (S)

Bergman, Robert, *Chair*. American Association of Museums, US National Committee of the International Council of Museums (AAM-ICOM), Washington DC

Bergman, Robert P, *Dir*. Cleveland Museum of Art, Cleveland OH

Bergman, Sky, *Prof*. California Polytechnic State University at San Luis Obispo, Dept of Art & Design, San Luis Obispo CA (S)

Bergmann, Frank, *Assoc Dean Humanities*. Utica College of Syracuse University, Division of Humanities, Utica NY (S)

Bergmann, Merrie, *Chmn*. Town of Cummington Historical Commission, Kingman Tavern Historical Museum, Cummington MA

Bergs, Lilita, *Public Relations & Marketing Mgr*. The Rockwell Museum, Corning NY

Bergsieker, David, *Instr*. Illinois Valley Community College, Division of Humanities & Fine Arts, Oglesby IL (S)

Berguson, Robert, *Interim Dir*. Louisiana Tech, School of Art, Ruston LA (S)

Berk, Penny, *Exec Dir*. Glass Art Society, Seattle WA

Berke, Debra, *Museum Cur*. United States Department of the Interior Museum, Washington DC

Berko, Linda, *Technician Mus Coll & Exhib*. London Regional Art & Historical Museums, London ON

Berkow, Ita, *Art Cur*. The Museums at Stony Brook, Kate Strong Historical Library, Stony Brook NY

Berkowitz, Lynn, *Cur Educ*. Allentown Art Museum, Allentown PA

Berkowitz, Rita, *Asst Prof*. Bradford College, Creative Arts Division, Bradford MA (S)

Berkowitz, Roger M, *Deputy Dir*. Toledo Museum of Art, Toledo OH

Berliant, Jenny Rosenthal, *VPres*. Contemporary Arts Center, Cincinnati OH

Berlo, Janet, *Prof*. University of Missouri, Saint Louis, Dept of Art & Art History, Saint Louis MO (S)

Berlyn, Judith, *Librn*. Chateau Ramezay Museum, Library, Montreal PQ

Berman, Brad, *Develop & Traveling Exhib*. Judah L Magnes Museum, Berkeley CA

Berman, Mary Jane, *Dir*. Wake Forest University, Museum of Anthropology, Winston Salem NC

Berman, Nancy, *Dir*. Hebrew Union College, Skirball Cultural Center, Los Angeles CA

Berman, Patricia, *Exec Dir*. East End Arts & Humanities Council, Riverhead NY

Berman, Patricia, *Asst Prof*. Wellesley College, Art Dept, Wellesley MA (S)

Berman, Philip, *Chmn Board*. Philadelphia Museum of Art, Philadelphia PA

Berman, Tosh, *Dir*. Beyond Baroque Foundation, Beyond Baroque Literary/Arts Center, Venice CA

Berman-Enn, Beate, *Chmn*. San Diego Mesa College, Fine Arts Dept, San Diego CA (S)

Bermingham, Peter, *Dir & Chief Cur*. University of Arizona, Museum of Art, Tucson AZ

Bernal, Rudy, *Preparator*. University of Chicago, David & Alfred Smart Museum of Art, Chicago IL

Bernard, Catherine, *Asst Prof*. Southampton College of Long Island University, Arts & Media Division, Southampton NY (S)

Bernardi, Rosemarie, *Assoc Prof Painting, Drawing & Printmaking*. University of Arizona, Dept of Art, Tucson AZ (S)

Bernatowitz, Rita, *Assoc Prof*. Castleton State College, Art Dept, Castleton VT (S)

Berner, Andrew, *Dir*. University Club Library, New York NY

Berns, Marla, *Dir*. University of California, Santa Barbara, University Art Museum, Santa Barbara CA

Bernstein, Ed, *Assoc Prof*. Indiana University, Bloomington, Henry Radford Hope School of Fine Arts, Bloomington IN (S)

Bernstein, Jill, *Presenting, Touring & Literature Dir*. Arizona Commission on the Arts, Phoenix AZ

Bernstein, Joanne, *Chmn*. Mills College, Art Dept, Oakland CA (S)

Bernstein, Michael, *Dir Finanical Affairs*. The Phillips Collection, Washington DC

Bernstein, Roberta, *Art Historian*. University at Albany, State University of New York, Art Dept Slide Library, Albany NY

Bernstein, Roberta, *Chair Dept*. State University of New York at Albany, Art Dept, Albany NY (S)

Bernstein, Roberta, *Assoc Prof*. State University of New York at Albany, Art Dept, Albany NY (S)

Bernstock, Judith E, *Assoc Prof*. Cornell University, Dept of the History of Art, Ithaca NY (S)

Beroza, Barbara, *Coll Mgr*. Yosemite Museum, Yosemite National Park CA

Berreth, David, *Dir*. Mary Washington College, Belmont, The Gari Melchers, Fredericksburg VA

Berrin, Kathleen, *Cur African, Oceania & the Americas*. Fine Arts Museums of San Francisco, M H de Young Memorial Museum & California Palace of the Legion of Honor, San Francisco CA

Berrones-Molina, Patricia, *Acting Dir*. Pimeria Alta Historical Society, Nogales AZ

Berrones-Molina, Patricia, *Acting Dir*. Pimeria Alta Historical Society, Library, Nogales AZ

Berry, Christine, *Assoc Registrar & Asst Cur*. Fort Worth Art Association, Modern Art Museum of Fort Worth, Fort Worth TX

Berry, E Raymond, *Chmn*. Randolph-Macon College, Dept of the Arts, Ashland VA (S)

Berry, Ethan, *Printmaking*. Monserrat College of Art, Beverly MA (S)

Berry, Janet, *VPres*. Shelby Art League, Inc, Shelby NC

Berry, Jim, *Dir*. City of Atlanta, Chastain Arts Center, Atlanta GA

Berry, Lloyd, *Pres*. North Central Washington Museum, Gallery, Wenatchee WA

Berry, Margaret, *Exec Dir*. Lincoln Arts Council, Lincoln NE

Berry, Nancy, *Art Educ Coordr*. University of North Texas, School of Visual Arts, Denton TX (S)

Berry, Paul, *Librn*. Calvert Marine Museum, Library, Solomons MD

Berry, Paula, *Assoc Dir*. University of California, Los Angeles, UCLA at the Armand Hammer Museum of Art & Cultural Center, Los Angeles CA

Berry, William, *Chmn*. University of Missouri, Art Dept, Columbia MO (S)

Bershad, Deborah, *Exec Dir*. Art Commission of the City of New York, New York NY

Berson, Ruth, *Assoc Dir*. Rutgers, The State University of New Jersey, Jane Voorhees Zimmerli Art Museum, New Brunswick NJ

Bersson, Robert, *Prof*. James Madison University, School of Art & Art History, Harrisonburg VA (S)

Berthol, Jake, *Instr*. New York Studio School of Drawing, Painting & Sculpture, New York NY (S)

Bertin, Maggie, *Asst Dir NMAI National Campaign*. National Museum of the American Indian, George Gustav Heye Center, New York NY

Bertoia, Roberto, *Assoc Prof*. Cornell University, Dept of Art, Ithaca NY (S)

Berube, Georgette, *VPres*. Musee d'Art de Saint-Laurent, Saint-Laurent PQ

Beslanovits, Denise, *Asst to Dir*. Lehigh University Art Galleries, Bethlehem PA

Besom, Bob, *Dir*. City of Springdale, Shiloh Museum, Springdale AR

Besore, Arlene, *Instr*. Grand Canyon University, Art Dept, Phoenix AZ (S)

Bessey, Richard B, *Dir*. The Rockwell Museum, Corning NY

Bessey, Richard B, *Dir*. The Rockwell Museum, Library, Corning NY

Best, Don, *Pres*. Kelowna Museum, Kelowna BC

Best, Doug, *Instr*. ACA College of Design, Cincinnati OH (S)

Best, Jonathan, *Chmn*. Wesleyan University, Art Dept, Middletown CT (S)

Best, Jonathan, *Prof*. Wesleyan University, Art Dept, Middletown CT (S)

Betancourt, Philip, *Chmn Art History*. Temple University, Tyler School of Art, Philadelphia PA (S)

Beth, Dana, *Art & Architecture Librn*. Washington University, Art & Architecture Library, Saint Louis MO

Bethany, Adeline, *Chmn Dept*. Cabrini College, Dept of Fine Arts, Radnor PA (S)

Bethke, Karl, *Prof*. University of Minnesota, Minneapolis, Dept of Art, Minneapolis MN (S)

Betsch, William, *Asst Prof*. University of Miami, Dept of Art & Art History, Coral Gables FL (S)

Betts, Katheleen, *Museum Dir*. Society of the Cincinnati, Museum & Library at Anderson House, Washington DC

Betty, Michelle, *Reference Librn*. Art Center College of Design, James Lemont Fogg Memorial Library, Pasadena CA

Beveridge, Nancy, *Librn*. Litchfield Historical Society, Ingraham Memorial Research Library, Litchfield CT

Bey, Amir, *Gallery Coordr*. Bronx River Art Center, Gallery, Bronx NY

Bezaire, Bruce, *Chmn*, Belhaven College, Art Dept, Jackson MS (S)

Bezner, Lili, *Prof*, University of North Carolina at Charlotte, Dept of Visual Arts, Charlotte NC (S)

Bhargava, Sudeep, *Bus Mgr*, University of Regina, MacKenzie Art Gallery, Regina SK

Bherer, Carole, *Gallery Coordr*, Bishop University, Artists' Centre, Lennoxville PQ

Bialy, Mark G, *Prof*, Passaic County Community College, Division of Humanities, Paterson NJ (S)

Bianco, Joseph P, *Exec VPres*, Detroit Institute of Arts, Founders Society, Detroit MI

Bianco, Juliette, *Exhib Coordr*, Dartmouth College, Hood Museum of Art, Hanover NH

Biasiny-Rivera, Charles, *Exec Dir*, En Foco, Inc, Bronx NY

Biblarz, Dora, *Assoc Dean Coll Develop*, Arizona State University, Hayden Library, Tempe AZ

Bible, Ann Vollmann, *Asst Museum Librn*, The Metropolitan Museum of Art, Photograph & Slide Library, New York NY

Bibler, Helen Ann, *Dir*, Ravalli County Museum, Hamilton MT

Bibler, Robert, *Instr*, Chemeketa Community College, Dept of Humanities & Communications, Salem OR (S)

Bickley, Steve, *Prof*, Virginia Polytechnic Institute & State University, Dept of Art & Art History, Blacksburg VA (S)

Bickley, Thomas, *Branch Librn*, Anacostia Museum, Branch Library, Washington DC

Biddle, Mark, *Prof*, Weber State University, Dept of Visual Arts, Ogden UT (S)

Bidler, A, *Dept Chmn*, University of California, Los Angeles, Dept Art History, Los Angeles CA (S)

Bidstrup, Wendy, *Dir*, Marion Art Center, Marion MA

Biegon, Glenn, *Assoc Prof*, College of Visual Arts, Saint Paul MN (S)

Bienvenu, Yvonne D, *Pres*, Lafayette Museum Association, Lafayette Museum-Alexandre Mouton House, Lafayette LA

Bier, Carol, *Cur Eastern Hemisphere*, Textile Museum, Washington DC

Bier, Martha, *Chmn & Librn*, Polk Museum of Art, Penfield Library, Lakeland FL

Biers, Jane C, *Cur Ancient Art*, University of Missouri, Museum of Art & Archaeology, Columbia MO

Biers, William R, *Prof*, University of Missouri, Art History & Archaeology Dept, Columbia MO (S)

Biferie, Dan, *Prof*, Daytona Beach Community College, Dept of Fine Arts & Visual Arts, Daytona Beach FL (S)

Bigazzi, Anna, *Library Coordr*, University of Hartford, Anne Bunce Cheney Library, West Hartford CT

Bigazzi, Anna, *Art Coordr*, University of Hartford, Mortensen Library, West Hartford CT

Biggs, George, *Instr*, New Mexico Junior College, Arts & Sciences, Hobbs NM (S)

Bigler, Steve, *Prof*, University of Northern Iowa, Dept of Art, Cedar Falls IA (S)

Bilardo, Heidi Iverson, *Public Art Adminr*, Kansas City Municipal Art Commission, Kansas City MO

Bilbo, Rebecca, *Chmn*, Thomas More College, Art Dept, Crestview Hills KY (S)

Bilder, Dorothea, *Dir Coordr*, Northern Illinois University, School of Art, De Kalb IL (S)

Bilger, Betsy, *Instr*, University of North Carolina at Charlotte, Dept of Visual Arts, Charlotte NC (S)

Bilger, Betsy, *Dir Educ*, Light Factory, Charlotte NC

Bilich, Sheila, *Pres*, San Mateo County Arts Council, Belmont CA

Billeit, Monica, *Asst Cur*, Hebrew Union College, Skirball Cultural Center, Los Angeles CA

Billings, Loren, *Dir*, Museum of Holography - Chicago, Chicago IL

Billings, Loren, *Exec Dir*, Museum of Holography - Chicago, David Wender Library, Chicago IL

Billings, Robert H, *Chmn Humanities & Fine Arts*, Los Angeles Harbor College, Art Dept, Wilmington CA (S)

Billingsley, Robert, *Technology Prog Coordr*, National Museum of the American Indian, George Gustav Heye Center, New York NY

Billington, James H, *Librn*, Library of Congress, Prints & Photographs Division, Washington DC

Bilsky, Thelma, *Registrar*, Temple Beth Israel, Sylvia Plotkin Judaica, Phoenix AZ

Bilyeu, Elizabeth, *Librn*, Oregon College of Art Craft, Library, Portland OR

Binder, Donald J, *Dir & Cur*, Yankton County Historical Society, Dakota Territorial Museum, Yankton SD

Bingham, Drake, *Dir*, New Mexico Highlands University, Dept of Communications & Fine Arts, Las Vegas NM (S)

Bingham, Georganne, *Dir External Affairs*, North Carolina Museum of Art, Raleigh NC

Binkley, David A, *Cur, Arts of Africa, Oceania & the Americas*, Nelson-Atkins Museum of Art, Kansas City MO

Binks, Ronald, *Prof*, University of Texas at San Antonio, Division of Visual Arts, San Antonio TX (S)

Biondi, Priscilla, *Archival Librn*, Wentworth Institute of Technology Library, Boston MA

Bippes, Bill, *Division Dir Music Arts*, Spring Arbor College, Art Dept, Spring Arbor MI (S)

Birch, James A, *Cur Education*, Cleveland Museum of Art, Cleveland OH

Bird, Donal, *Dean*, Howard Payne University, Dept of Art, Brownwood TX (S)

Bird, Mary Alice, *Develop Dir*, William A Farnsworth Library & Art Museum, Rockland ME

Bird, Richard, *Coordr*, Chadron State College, Arts Gallery, Chadron NE

Bird, Richard, *Chmn*, Ricks College, Dept of Art, Rexburg ID (S)

Bird, Richard, *Chmn*, Chadron State College, Dept of Art, Speech & Theatre, Chadron NE (S)

Birkett, Barbara, *Prof*, Rochester Institute of Technology, School of Printing, Rochester NY (S)

Birkett, William H, *Assoc Prof*, Rochester Institute of Technology, School of Printing, Rochester NY (S)

Birmingham, Doris A, *Prof*, New England College, Art & Art History, Henniker NH (S)

Biro, Matthew, *Asst Prof*, University of Michigan, Ann Arbor, Dept of History of Art, Ann Arbor MI (S)

Bisaillon, Blaise, *Dir*, Forbes Library, Northampton MA

Bisbee, John, *Vis Instr*, Bowdoin College, Art Dept, Brunswick ME (S)

Bischoff, Roger, *Instr*, Woodstock School of Art, Inc, Woodstock NY (S)

Bischoff, William L, *Cur Coin Coll*, Newark Museum Association, The Newark Museum, Newark NJ

Bishop, Budd Harris, *Dir*, University of Florida, Samuel P Harn Museum of Art, Gainesville FL

Bishop, Christine, *Dir*, Carnegie Art Center, Walla Walla WA

Bishop, Henry, *Cur*, Society for the Protection & Preservation of Black Culture in Nova Scotia, Black Cultural Center for Nova Scotia, Dartmouth NS

Bishop, Jerold, *Assoc Prof Graphic Illustration*, University of Arizona, Dept of Art, Tucson AZ (S)

Bishop, Michael, *Graduate Advisor, Instr & Prof*, California State University, Chico, Art Dept, Chico CA (S)

Bishop, Samuel, *Assoc Prof*, Northeastern University, Dept of Art & Architecture, Boston MA (S)

Bishop, Steve, *Assoc Prof*, Murray State University, Dept of Art, Murray KY (S)

Bissaccia, Giusseppe, *Cur Manuscripts*, Boston Public Library, Rare Book & Manuscripts Dept, Boston MA

Bissell, R Ward, *Prof*, University of Michigan, Ann Arbor, Dept of History of Art, Ann Arbor MI (S)

Bissell, Tina, *Assoc Cur*, University of Michigan, Slide & Photograph Collection, Ann Arbor MI

Bissonnette, Daniel, *Dir*, Musee Regional de Vaudreuil-Soulanges, Vaudreuil PQ

Bissonnette, Daniel, *Dir*, Musee Regional de Vaudreuil-Soulanges, Library, Vaudreuil PQ

Bitz, Gwen, *Registrar*, Walker Art Center, Minneapolis MN

Bitzan, Robert, *Public Affairs*, University of Minnesota, Weisman Art Museum, Minneapolis MN

Bizzarro, Tina Walduier, *Chmn Div*, Rosemont College, Division of the Arts, Rosemont PA (S)

Bjelajac, David, *Asst Prof*, George Washington University, Dept of Art, Washington DC (S)

Bjurlin, Marvin, *Gallery Dir*, State University of New York College at Fredonia, M C Rockefeller Arts Center Gallery, Fredonia NY

Black, Bettie, *Cur*, Langston University, Melvin B Tolson Black Heritage Center, Langston OK

Black, Bonnie, *Chmn*, Clinton Community College, Art Dept, Plattsburgh NY (S)

Black, Jack, *Board Chmn & Cur*, Fayette Art Museum, Fayette AL

Black, Kell, *Asst Prof*, Austin Peay State University, Dept of Art, Clarksville TN (S)

Black, Larry, *Exec Dir*, Columbus Metropolitan Library, Humanities, Fine Art & Recreation Division, Columbus OH

Black, Randolph, *Registrar*, Montclair Art Museum, Art School, Montclair NJ (S)

Black, Randy, *Curatorial Registrar*, Montclair Art Museum, Montclair NJ

Black, Steve, *Assoc Prof*, Vincennes University Junior College, Art Dept, Vincennes IN (S)

Black, Steve O, *Dept Head*, Grayson County College, Art Dept, Denison TX (S)

Black, Vonnel, *Gift Shop Mgr*, African American Historical & Cultural Society, San Francisco CA

Blackaby, Anita D, *Dir*, Pennsylvania Historical & Museum Commission, Harrisburg PA

Blackaby, Anita D, *Dir*, Pennsylvania Historical & Museum Commission, State Museum of Pennsylvania, Harrisburg PA

Blackadar, Lisa, *Cur*, Headley-Whitney Museum, Library, Lexington KY

Blackadar, Lisa K, *Cur*, Headley-Whitney Museum, Lexington KY

Blackbeard, Bill, *Dir*, San Francisco Academy of Comic Art, Library, San Francisco CA

Blackburn, Robert, *Exec Dir*, Printmaking Workshop, New York NY

Blackburn, Selma, *Instr*, The Arkansas Arts Center, Museum School, Little Rock AR (S)

Blackley, Terrence, *Chmn Division Fine Arts*, Fullerton College, Division of Fine Arts, Fullerton CA (S)

Blackmon, Mary Collins, *Dir*, Elisabet Ney Museum, Austin TX

Blackmon, Mary Collins, *Dir*, Elisabet Ney Museum, Library, Austin TX

Blackmun, Barbara, *Instr*, San Diego Mesa College, Fine Arts Dept, San Diego CA (S)

Blackstein, Mike, *Dir*, Southern Exposure Gallery, San Francisco CA

Blackstone, Julie, *Instr*, Oklahoma Baptist University, Art Dept, Shawnee OK (S)

Blackstone, Mary, *Dean Faculty Fine Arts*, University of Regina, Art Education Program, Regina SK (S)

Blackwood, C Roy, *Chmn*, Southeastern Louisiana University, Dept of Visual Arts, Hammond LA (S)

Blades, John, *Dir*, Henry Morrison Flagler Museum, Whitehall Mansion, Palm Beach FL

Blades, Margaret Bleecker, *Mus Cur*, Chester County Historical Society, West Chester PA

Blaedel, Joan Ross, *Instr*, North Seattle Community College, Art Dept, Seattle WA (S)

Blain, Brad, *Dir*, Kitchener-Waterloo Art Gallery, Kitchener ON

Blain, Brad, *Dir*, Kitchener-Waterloo Art Gallery, Eleanor Calvert Memorial Library, Kitchener ON

Blain, Sandra J, *Dir*, Arrowmont Gallery, Arrowmont School of Arts & Crafts, Gatlinburg TN (S)

Blaine, Johnnie L, *General Mgr*, International Institute of Pigeons & Doves, Oklahoma City OK

Blair, Brent, *Instr*, Gettysburg College, Dept of Visual Arts, Gettysburg PA (S)

Blair, Carl, *Instr*, Bob Jones University, School of Fine Arts, Greenville SC (S)

Blair, Edward, *Pres.* The Art Institute of Chicago, Print & Drawing Dept, Chicago IL

Blair, Jean duP, *Pres.* New Orleans School of GlassWorks, Gallery & Printmaking Studio, New Orleans LA

Blair, Terri, *Instr.* Grayson County College, Art Dept, Denison TX (S)

Blais, Louise, *Cultural Counsellor,* Canadian Embassy, Art Gallery, Washington DC

Blaisdell, Phillip, *Instr.* Joe Kubert School of Cartoon & Graphic Art, Inc, Dover NJ (S)

Blake, Beth, *Asst Prof.* State University of New York College at Brockport, Dept of Art, Brockport NY (S)

Blake, Elizabeth, *Chmn,* The American Federation of Arts, New York NY

Blake, Hortense, *Dir,* Clinton Art Association Gallery, Clinton IA

Blake, Jeff, *Lectr,* Saint Joseph's University, Dept of Fine & Performing Arts, Philadelphia PA (S)

Blake, Jody, *Prof.* Bucknell University, Dept of Art, Lewisburg PA (S)

Blake, Michael, *Cur Archaeology,* University of British Columbia, Museum of Anthropology, Vancouver BC

Blake, Nathan, *Prog Coordr,* Franklin Furnace Archive, Inc, New York NY

Blakely, George C, *Prof.* Florida State University, Art Dept, Tallahassee FL (S)

Blakely, Glen, *Prof.* Dixie College, Art Dept, Saint George UT (S)

Blandford, Robert, *Assoc Dir,* Children's Museum of Manhattan, New York NY

Blandon-Lawrence, Patty, *Cur Educ,* Memphis Brooks Museum of Art, Memphis TN

Blank, Peter, *Asst Librn,* Stanford University, Art & Architecture Library, Stanford CA

Blankenship, Tiska, *Assoc Cur,* University of New Mexico, Jonson Library, Albuquerque NM

Blankenshop, Tiska, *Assoc Cur,* University of New Mexico, Jonson Gallery, Albuquerque NM

Blankinship, Sue, *Museum Store Mgr,* University of Tampa, Henry B Plant Museum, Tampa FL

Blanks, Scott, *Chmn,* Benedict College, Fine Arts Dept, Columbia SC

Blaschke, Shirley, *Dir,* Individual Artists of Oklahoma, Oklahoma City OK

Blasdel, Gregg, *Asst Prof.* St Michael's College, Fine Arts Dept, Colchester VT (S)

Blather, Mary, *Pres,* Sunbury Shores Arts & Nature Centre, Inc, Gallery, Saint Andrews NB

Blatti, Jo, *Dir,* Harriet Beecher Stowe Center, Hartford CT

Blatti, Jo, *Dir,* Harriet Beecher Stowe Center, Stowe-Day Library, Hartford CT

Blaugher, Kurt E, *Prof.* Mount Saint Mary's College, Visual & Performing Arts Dept, Emmitsburg MD (S)

Blebin, Margo, *Lectr,* Davis & Elkins College, Dept of Art, Elkins WV (S)

Bleck, Carol, *Bus Mgr,* Tucson Museum of Art & Historic Block, Tucson AZ

Bleek-Byrne, Gabrielle, *Assoc Prof.* Salve Regina University, Art Dept, Newport RI (S)

Bleha, Bernie, *Chmn & Instr,* Green River Community College, Art Dept, Auburn WA (S)

Bleick, Chuck, *Actg Dir,* Virginia Commonwealth University, Anderson Gallery, Richmond VA

Blessant, John, *Instr,* Whitworth College, Art Dept, Spokane WA (S)

Blessin, Sylvia, *Prog Coordr,* Contemporary Art Gallery Society of British Columbia, Vancouver BC

Blessin, Sylvia, *Prog Coordr,* Contemporary Art Gallery Society of British Columbia, Art Library Service, Vancouver BC

Bletter, Rosemarie Haag, *Prof.* City University of New York, PhD Program in Art History, New York NY (S)

Blevins, Anne, *Dir Admis,* The New England School of Art & Design at Suffolk University, Boston MA (S)

Blevins, Tedd, *Instr.* Virginia Intermont College, Fine Arts Division, Bristol VA (S)

Bliese, Nina, *Chair Board,* Textile Arts Centre, Chicago IL

Blinderman, Barry, *Dir.* Illinois State University, University Galleries, Normal IL

Blinn, Jean, *Sr Librn in Charge.* Oakland Public Library, Art, Music & Recreation Section, Oakland CA

Blisard, Herb, *Faculty,* Yakima Valley Community College, Art Dept, Yakima WA (S)

Bliss, Harry, *Gallery Dir.* Palomar Community College, Boehm Gallery, San Marcos CA

Bliss, Harry E, *Assoc Prof.* Palomar Community College, Art Dept, San Marcos CA (S)

Bliss, Jerry, *Asst Prof.* Colby-Sawyer College, Dept of Fine & Performing Arts, New London NH (S)

Blitz, Robert, *Asst to Dir & Registrar,* University of Maryland, College Park, Art Gallery, College Park MD

Blixt, Rose, *Accounts Supvr.* University of Minnesota, Weisman Art Museum, Minneapolis MN

Blizard, Bill, *Chmn.* Springfield College, Hasting Gallery, Springfield MA

Blizard, William, *Chmn Dept.* Springfield College, Dept of Visual & Performing Arts, Springfield MA (S)

Bloch, Kathleen, *Assoc Dir.* Spertus Institute of Jewish Studies, Asher Library, Chicago IL

Blochowiak, Mary, *Publ.* Oklahoma Historical Society, State Museum of History, Oklahoma City OK

Block, Carol M, *Dir.* Academy of Art, College Library, San Francisco CA

Block, Diana, *Gallery Dir.* University of North Texas, Art Gallery, Denton TX

Block, Holly, *Exec Dir.* Art in General, New York NY

Block, Jane, *Librn.* University of Illinois, Ricker Library of Architecture & Art, Champaign IL

Block, Jay, *Museum Mgr.* State University of New York at Purchase, Neuberger Museum of Art, Purchase NY

Block, Laura, *Pres.* Pastel Society of Oregon, Roseburg OR

Block, Philip, *Dir Educ.* International Center of Photography, New York NY

Blocker, Julia, *Shop Mgr.* Green Hill Center for North Carolina Art, Greensboro NC

Blocton, Lula, *Asst Prof.* Eastern Connecticut State University, Fine Arts Dept, Willimantic CT (S)

Bloedhorn, Gene, *Cur.* University of Wisconsin-Stout, J Furlong Gallery, Menomonie WI

Bloedorn, Ellena, *Dir Admis & Records,* John F Kennedy University, Graduate School for Holistic Studies, Orinda CA (S)

Bloedorn, Gene, *Prof.* University of Wisconsin-Stout, Dept of Art & Design, Menomonie WI (S)

Bloff, Wally, *Exec Dir.* Allied Arts Council of St Joseph, Saint Joseph MO

Blondin, Bruce, *Instr.* Solano Community College, Division of Fine & Applied Art, Suisun City CA (S)

Bloom, Arthur W, *Dean,* Kutztown University, College of Visual & Performing Arts, Kutztown PA (S)

Bloom, Beth, *Art Librn.* Seton Hall University, Library, South Orange NJ

Bloom, Billie, *Adminr,* Art Museum of Missoula, Missoula MT

Bloom, Leslye, *Pres.* Blacksburg Regional Art Association, Christiansburg VA

Bloom, Sharon, *Chmn.* West Shore Community College, Division of Humanities & Fine Arts, Scottville MI (S)

Bloom, Stephen, *Library Dir.* University of the Arts, Albert M Greenfield Library, Philadelphia PA

Bloom, Sue, *Dept Head,* Western Maryland College, Dept of Art & Art History, Westminster MD (S)

Bloomberg, Louise, *Cur Visual Coll.* University of Massachusetts, Amherst, Dorothy W Perkins Slide Library, Amherst MA

Bloomberg, Sally, *Shop Mgr.* Farmington Valley Arts Center, Avon CT

Bloomer, Jerry M, *Secy Board,* R W Norton Art Gallery, Shreveport LA

Bloomer, Jerry M, *Librn,* R W Norton Art Gallery, Library, Shreveport LA

Bloomfield, Debra, *Instr.* Solano Community College, Division of Fine & Applied Art, Suisun City CA (S)

Blore, Bill, *Vol Coordr.* Craigdarroch Castle Historical Museum Society, Victoria BC

Blosser, John, *Head Dept.* Hesston College, Art Dept, Hesston KS (S)

Blouin, Joy, *Cur.* University of Michigan, Slide & Photograph Collection, Ann Arbor MI

Blum, Harlo, *Chmn Dept.* Monmouth College, Dept of Art, Monmouth IL (S)

Blum, Zevi, *Assoc Prof.* Cornell University, Dept of Art, Ithaca NY (S)

Blumberg, Linda, *Exec Dir.* Capp Street Project, San Francisco CA

Blume, Peter F, *Dir.* Allentown Art Museum, Allentown PA

Blumenfeld, Erica, *Cur Exhib,* Museum of African Art, New York NY

Blumenthal, Arthur R, *Dir.* Rollins College, George D & Harriet W Cornell Fine Arts Museum, Winter Park FL

Blumenthal, Elizabeth, *Asst Prof.* Johns Hopkins University, School of Medicine, Dept of Art as Applied to Medicine, Baltimore MD (S)

Blundell, Harry, *Dir of Theatre.* Arts Center of the Ozarks Gallery, Springdale AR

Blundell, Kathi, *Dir.* Arts Center of the Ozarks Gallery, Springdale AR

Bluthardt, Valerie C, *Asst Dir & Registrar.* San Angelo Museum of Fine Arts, San Angelo TX

Board, Michael, *Instr.* Columbia University, School of the Arts, Division of Visual Arts, New York NY (S)

Bob, Murray L, *Dir.* James Prendergast Library Association, Jamestown NY

Bober, Jonathan, *Cur Prints & Drawings,* University of Texas at Austin, Archer M Huntington Art Gallery, Austin TX

Bober, Phyllis B, *Prof.* Bryn Mawr College, Dept of the History of Art, Bryn Mawr PA (S)

Bobick, Bruce, *Chmn,* State University of West Georgia, Art Dept, Carrollton GA (S)

Bobulsky, Kathy, *Pres.* Ashtabula Arts Center, Ashtabula OH

Boch, Suzanne, *Librn.* Alaska Watercolor Society, Anchorage AK

Bochicchio, Nicholas, *Dir Admin Servs.* Ferguson Library, Stamford CT

Bock, Catherine, *Prof.* School of the Art Institute of Chicago, Chicago IL (S)

Bock, Julia, *Librn.* Leo Baeck Institute, New York NY

Bockelman, Jim, *Prof.* Concordia College, Art Dept, Seward NE (S)

Bockrath, Mark F, *Paintings Conservator.* Pennsylvania Academy of the Fine Arts, Museum of American Art, Philadelphia PA

Bockwoldt, Michael, *VPres,* House of Roses, Senator Wilson Home, Deadwood SD

Bocz, George, *Assoc Prof.* Florida State University, Art Dept, Tallahassee FL (S)

Bodem, Dennis R, *Dir.* Jesse Besser Museum, Alpena MI

Bodem, Dennis R, *Dir.* Jesse Besser Museum, Philip M Park Library, Alpena MI

Bodily, Vince, *Instr.* Ricks College, Dept of Art, Rexburg ID (S)

Bodine, Paul, *Assoc Prof.* Eastern Illinois University, Art Dept, Charleston IL (S)

Bodine, William, *Cur Coll.* Columbia Museum of Art, Columbia SC

Bodnar, Alice Wernimont, *Asst Librn.* Minneapolis Institute of Arts, Library, Minneapolis MN

Bodogaard, Grete, *Cur.* Rapid City Arts Council, Dahl Fine Arts Center, Rapid City SD

Bodsworth, Steven, *Chmn.* Humber College of Applied Arts & Technology, Applied Arts Div, Etobicoke ON (S)

Bodwitch, Lucy, *Asst Prof.* College of Saint Rose, Dept of Art, Albany NY (S)

Boe, Michael, *Assoc Librn.* Minneapolis Institute of Arts, Library, Minneapolis MN

Boehm, Louise Kirtland, *Assoc Prof.* Palomar Community College, Art Dept, San Marcos CA (S)

Bourcier, Claudette, *Gift Shop Mgr*, Cascade County Historical Society, Cascade County Historical Museum & Archives, Great Falls MT

Bourcier, Paul, *Chief Cur*, State Historical Society of Wisconsin, State Historical Museum, Madison WI

Bourdon, Donald, *Archives*, Peter & Catharine Whyte Foundation, Whyte Museum of the Canadian Rockies, Banff AB

Bourque, Paul, *Technician*, Galerie d'art de l'Universite de Moncton, Moncton NB

Bous, Klaus, *Managing Dir*, SIAS International Art Society, Sherwood Park AB

Bousard-Hui, Eva, *Lectr*, Georgian Court College, Dept of Art, Lakewood NJ (S)

Bouyack, Kay, *Admin Dir*, Southern Ohio Museum Corporation, Southern Ohio Museum & Cultural Center, Portsmouth OH

Bova, Joe, *Dir*, Ohio University, Seigfred Gallery, Athens OH

Bovey, John A, *Provincial Archivist*, British Columbia Information Management Services, Victoria BC

Bovey, Patricia A, *Dir*, Art Gallery of Greater Victoria, Victoria BC

Bowar, Sharon, *Assoc Prof*, Wilkes University, Dept of Art, Wilkes-Barre PA (S)

Bowen, Ken, *Adjunct Instr*, Virginia Wesleyan College, Art Dept of the Humanities Division, Norfolk VA (S)

Bowen, Linnell R, *Exec Dir*, Maryland Hall for the Creative Arts, Cardinal Gallery, Annapolis MD

Bowen, Nancy, *Instr*, Sarah Lawrence College, Dept of Art History, Bronxville NY (S)

Bowen, Nancy, *Instr*, Columbia University, School of the Arts, Division of Visual Arts, New York NY (S)

Bowen, Paul, *Instr*, Truro Center for the Arts at Castle Hill, Inc, Truro MA (S)

Bowen, Robert, *Asst to Dir External Affairs*, Fort Worth Art Association, Modern Art Museum of Fort Worth, Fort Worth TX

Bowen, Susan, *Admin Asst*, City of Atlanta, Bureau of Cultural Affairs, Atlanta GA

Bower, Bob, *Div Dir*, Southwestern Oregon Community College, Visual Arts Dept, Coos Bay OR (S)

Bower, Gerald, *Prof*, Louisiana State University, School of Art, Baton Rouge LA (S)

Bower, Peter, *Provincial Archivist*, Provincial Archives of Manitoba, Winnipeg MB

Bowers, John, *Asst Prof*, Oregon State University, Dept of Art, Corvallis OR (S)

Bowers, Sally, *Chief Adminr*, The Robert McLaughlin Gallery, Oshawa ON

Bowie, Barbara, *Museum Store Mgr*, Marion Koogler McNay Art Museum, San Antonio TX

Bowie, Eleanor, *Div Chmn Humanities*, Penn Valley Community College, Art Dept, Kansas City MO (S)

Bowie, Kim, *Dean*, Art Association of Harrisburg, School & Galleries, Harrisburg PA

Bowie, Lucille, *Librn*, Southern University, Art & Architecture Library, Baton Rouge LA

Bowie, Mary Ann, *Registrar*, Rollins College, George D & Harriet W Cornell Fine Arts Museum, Winter Park FL

Bowitz, John, *Chmn*, Morningside College, Art Dept, Sioux City IA (S)

Bowler, Laura, *Rights & Reproductions Coordr*, Nelda C & H J Lutcher Stark Foundation, Stark Museum of Art, Orange TX

Bowles, Bryan, *Dir*, Polynesian Cultural Center, Laie HI

Bowles, K Johnson, *Gallery Dir*, Saint Mary's College, Moreau Galleries, Notre Dame IN

Bowles, Sandra, *Exec Dir & Ed*, Handweavers Guild of America, Duluth GA

Bowley, Michael, *Instr*, Marylhurst College, Art Dept, Marylhurst OR (S)

Bowling, Marilyn, *Design Coordr*, Ritz-Carlton Hotel Company, Art Collection, Atlanta GA

Bowlt, John, *Adjunct Prof*, University of Southern California, School of Fine Arts, Los Angeles CA (S)

Bowman, Brice, *Instr*, Solano Community College, Division of Fine & Applied Art, Suisun City CA (S)

Bowman, David, *Chmn Basic Arts*, Moore College of Art & Design, Philadelphia PA (S)

Bowman, Debbie, *Dir Operations*, Cincinnati Museum Association, Cincinnati Art Museum, Cincinnati OH

Bowman, Karmien, *Assoc Prof*, Tarrant County Junior College, Art Dept, Hurst TX (S)

Bowman, Leah, *Prof*, School of the Art Institute of Chicago, Chicago IL (S)

Bowman, Leslie, *Adjunct Asst Prof*, University of Southern California, School of Fine Arts, Los Angeles CA (S)

Bowman, Marty, *Dir*, Central Iowa Art Association, Inc, Marshalltown IA

Bowman, Marty, *Dir*, Central Iowa Art Association, Inc, Art Reference Library, Marshalltown IA

Bowman, Roger, *Assoc Prof*, University of Central Arkansas, Art Dept, Conway AR (S)

Bowman, Russell, *Dir*, Milwaukee Art Museum, Milwaukee WI

Bowman, Stanley J, *Assoc Prof*, Cornell University, Dept of Art, Ithaca NY (S)

Bowring, Joanne, *Instr*, Mount Mary College, Art Dept, Milwaukee WI (S)

Bowring, Sally, *Dir*, 1708 Gallery, Richmond VA

Bowser, Barbara, *Dir*, City of Atlanta, Bureau of Cultural Affairs, Atlanta GA

Box, Bobby, *Producer*, Center for Puppetry Arts, Atlanta GA

Boyce, John, *Lectr*, University of Pennsylvania, Graduate School of Fine Arts, Philadelphia PA (S)

Boyce, Margaret, *Treas*, Shoreline Historical Museum, Seattle WA

Boyce, Robert, *Dir*, Berea College, Doris Ulmann Galleries, Berea KY

Boyce, Robert, *Chmn*, Berea College, Art Dept, Berea KY (S)

Boyd, Ann, *Co-Dir*, Roy Boyd Gallery, Chicago IL

Boyd, Karen W, *Prof*, Murray State University, Dept of Art, Murray KY (S)

Boyd, Lorraine, *Dir*, Brooklyn Arts Council, Brooklyn NY

Boyd, Norree, *VPres*, Palm Beach County Cultural Council, West Palm Beach FL

Boyd, Roy, *Co-Dir*, Roy Boyd Gallery, Chicago IL

Boyd, Teresa, *Business Mgr*, Ward Foundation, Ward Museum of Wildfowl Art, Salisbury MD

Boyd, Willard L, *Pres Emeritus*, Field Museum, Chicago IL

Boyd, William L, *Head Dept*, Alabama A & M University, Art & Art Education Dept, Normal AL (S)

Boydston, Linda, *Exec Dir*, South Arkansas Arts Center, Library, El Dorado AR

Boyer, Irene, *Cur Asst Decorative Art*, Illinois State Museum, Illinois Art Gallery & Lockport Gallery, Springfield IL

Boyer, John, *Exec Dir*, Mark Twain Memorial, Hartford CT

Boyer, John, *Exec Dir*, Mark Twain Memorial, Mark Twain House Research Library, Hartford CT

Boyer, Lise, *Pub Relations*, Musee du Quebec, Quebec PQ

Boyer, Mindy, *Pres*, West Hills Unitarian Fellowship, Portland OR

Boyer, Yvonne, *Librn*, Vanderbilt University, Arts Library, Nashville TN

Boyle, Kevin, *Exhib Cur*, University of California, California Museum of Photography, Riverside CA

Boysen, Bill H, *Crafts Area Head*, Southern Illinois University, School of Art & Design, Carbondale IL (S)

Boyston, Linda, *Exec Dir*, South Arkansas Arts Center, El Dorado AR

Bracalente, Anita, *Asst Registrar*, Indiana University, Art Museum, Bloomington IN

Bracco, Sal, *Treas*, New York Society of Architects, New York NY

Bracewell, Ruth, *Chmn Board*, Morgan County Foundation, Inc, Madison-Morgan Cultural Center, Madison GA

Brack, Lillie, *Central Reference Coordr*, Kansas City Public Library, Kansas City MO

Brackbill, Eleanor, *Head Museum Educ*, State University of New York at Purchase, Neuberger Museum of Art, Purchase NY

Brackman, Bob, *Dir Botanical Gardens*, Cheekwood Nashville's Home of Art & Gardens, Education Dept, Nashville TN (S)

Brackman Sharp, Judith, *Instr*, Vancouver Community College, Langara Campus, Dept of Fine Arts, Vancouver BC (S)

Brackney, Kathryn S, *Librn*, Georgia Institute of Technology, College of Architecture Library, Atlanta GA

Bradd, Cheryl, *Asst Dir*, Anniston Museum of Natural History, Anniston AL

Braddock, Jane, *VPres*, Visual Arts Alliance of Nashville, Nashville TN

Bradford, Barry, *Head of Dept*, Chattanooga-Hamilton County Bicentennial Library, Fine Arts Dept, Chattanooga TN

Bradford, Colleen H, *Chmn*, Brigham City Museum-Gallery, Brigham City UT

Bradford, David, *Chmn*, Laney College, Art Dept, Oakland CA (S)

Bradford, Hugh, *Exec Dir*, Gallery Association of New York State, Hamilton NY

Bradford, John, *Instr*, Woodstock School of Art, Inc, Woodstock NY (S)

Bradley, David, *Develop Dir*, Virginia Museum of Fine Arts, Richmond VA

Bradley, Douglas, *Cur*, University of Notre Dame, Snite Museum of Art, Notre Dame IN

Bradley, George, *Chmn*, Sul Ross State University, Dept of Fine Arts & Communications, Alpine TX (S)

Bradley, James A, *Exec Dir Jekyll Island*, Jekyll Island Museum, Jekyll Island GA

Bradley, Laura, *Archivist*, Yarmouth County Historical Society, Yarmouth County Museum, Yarmouth NS

Bradley, Loris, *Performing Arts Dir*, Diverse Works, Houston TX

Bradley, Mark, *Instr*, Campbellsville College, Fine Arts Division, Campbellsville KY (S)

Bradley, Norman, *Assoc Prof*, Indiana-Purdue University, Dept of Fine Arts, Fort Wayne IN (S)

Bradley, Ross, *Arts Develop Officer*, Alberta Foundation for the Arts, Edmonton AB

Bradley, Ross, *VPres*, Canadian Crafts Council, Conseil Canadien de l'Artisanat, Ottawa ON

Bradley, Tim, *Photography Dept Chmn*, Art Center College of Design, Pasadena CA (S)

Bradley, Tom, *Asst Dean*, University of Hartford, Hartford Art School, West Hartford CT (S)

Bradley, Virginia, *Dir*, Saint Cloud State University, Kiehle Gallery, Saint Cloud MN

Bradley, Virginia, *Assoc Prof*, Saint Cloud State University, Dept of Art, Saint Cloud MN (S)

Bradley, Wm Steven, *Dir*, Davenport Museum of Art, Davenport IA

Bradley-Johnson, Gayle V, *Prof*, North Park College, Art Dept, Chicago IL (S)

Bradt, Rochelle, *Cur Educ*, Yeshiva University Museum, New York NY

Brady, Patricia, *Dir Public & Academic Affairs*, Kemper & Leila Williams Foundation, New Orleans LA

Brady, Robert J, *Mgr Bldgs & Secy*, Frick Collection, New York NY

Braeutigam, Peggy, *Pres*, Northwest Pastel Society (NPS), Issaquah WA

Bragg, Nicholas B, *Exec Dir*, Reynolda House Museum of American Art, Winston-Salem NC

Braig, Kathryn B, *Asst to Librn*, The Mariners' Museum, Library, Newport News VA

Brako, Jeanne, *Coll Mgr*, Colorado Historical Society, Colorado History Museum, Denver CO

Bramhall, Mary A, *Pres*, Concord Art Association, Concord MA

Bramlette, Teresa, *Dir Nexus Gallery*, Nexus Contemporary Art Center, Atlanta GA

Brancaccio, Jim, *Cur*, Living Arts & Science Center, Inc, Lexington KY

Branch, Harrison, *Prof*, Oregon State University, Dept of Art, Corvallis OR (S)

Branch, Susan, *Mgr*, Scalamandre Museum of Textiles, New York NY

Brand, Myra, *Chmn Creative Arts,* Western Oregon State College, Creative Arts Division, Visual Arts, Monmouth OR (S)

Branden, Mack, *Chmn,* California Baptist College, Art Dept, Riverside CA (S)

Branden, Shirley, *Head Reference Dept,* University of Delaware, Morris Library, Newark DE

Brander, Susan, *Admin Dir,* Museum of the Hudson Highlands, Cornwall on Hudson NY

Brandoli, Susan, *Dir,* Vernon Art Gallery, Vernon BC

Brandon, Reiko, *Cur Textile Coll,* Honolulu Academy of Arts, Honolulu HI

Brandrup, Jessica, *Sales Assoc,* Fort Worth Art Association, Modern Art Museum of Fort Worth, Fort Worth TX

Brandson, Lorraine, *Cur,* Eskimo Museum, Churchill MB

Brandson, Lorraine, *Cur,* Eskimo Museum, Library, Churchill MB

Brandyberg, Tyrone, *Museum Technician,* Tuskegee Institute National Historic Site, George Washington Carver & The Oaks, Tuskegee Institute AL

Branham, Erin, *Dir Science & Educ,* Arts & Science Center for Southeast Arkansas, Pine Bluff AR

Branham, Mary, *Asst Dir,* Wheelwright Museum of the American Indian, Santa Fe NM

Brannah, Beverly W, *Photographs,* Library of Congress, Prints & Photographs Division, Washington DC

Brannan, Ed, *Instr,* Green River Community College, Art Dept, Auburn WA (S)

Brannan, John, *Cultural Travel,* Texas A&M University, Visual Arts Committee, College Station TX

Branning, Katherine, *Librn,* French Institute-Alliance Francaise, Library, New York NY

Bransford, Pamela, *Registrar,* Montgomery Museum of Fine Arts, Montgomery AL

Branson, Edward V, *Instr,* Yavapai College, Visual & Performing Arts Division, Prescott AZ (S)

Branston, Stu, *Chmn,* Oral Roberts University, Fine Arts Dept, Tulsa OK (S)

Brant, Patricia, *Acting Dir,* Widener University, Art Museum, Chester PA

Brantley, Royal, *Head Dept,* West Texas A&M University, Art, Communication & Theatre Dept, Canyon TX (S)

Bratcher, Donna, *Assoc Prof,* Claflin College, Dept of Art, Orangeburg SC (S)

Brauer, Daniel R, *Publications Dir,* University of California, Los Angeles, Fowler Museum of Cultural History, Los Angeles CA

Brauer, Deborah, *Exhib Coordr,* Menil Collection, Houston TX

Braufman, Sheila, *Cur,* Judah L Magnes Museum, Berkeley CA

Braun, Bettina, *Adjunct Instr,* Maryville University of Saint Louis, Art Division, Saint Louis MO (S)

Braun, Suzan, *Prof,* Eastern Illinois University, Art Dept, Charleston IL (S)

Bravender, Suzanne, *Acting Area Head Art,* Pasadena City College, Art Dept, Pasadena CA (S)

Bravo, M, *Instr,* Humboldt State University, College of Arts & Humanities, Arcata CA (S)

Braxton, Anne, *Art Librn,* Ohio University, Fine Arts Library, Athens OH

Bray, Ann, *Vis Instr,* Claremont Graduate School, Dept of Fine Arts, Claremont CA (S)

Bray, Jim, *Dept Head,* Missouri Southern State College, Dept of Art, Joplin MO (S)

Bray, Marsha, *VPres,* Missouri Historical Society, Saint Louis MO

Brayham, Angela, *Exec Dir,* One West Art Center, Fort Collins CO

Braysmith, Eric, *Instr,* University of Southern Indiana, Art Dept, Evansville IN (S)

Braysmith, Hilary, *Prof,* University of Southern Indiana, Art Dept, Evansville IN (S)

Brayton, Diane, *Business Mgr,* Birmingham-Bloomfield Art Association, Birmingham MI

Brazile, Orella R, *Dir,* Southern University Library, Shreveport LA

Bredendick, Joan, *Adjunct Prof,* North Central College, Dept of Art, Naperville IL (S)

Brehm, Georgia L, *Dir,* Black River Historical Society, Black River Academy Museum, Ludlow VT

Breiling, Roy, *Instr,* Yavapai College, Visual & Performing Arts Division, Prescott AZ (S)

Breimayer, Mary Phyllis, *Prof,* Georgian Court College, Dept of Art, Lakewood NJ (S)

Breitenbach, Eric, *Prof,* Daytona Beach Community College, Dept of Fine Arts & Visual Arts, Daytona Beach FL (S)

Breitenbach, William J, *Prof,* Sam Houston State University, Art Dept, Huntsville TX (S)

Brekke, Michael, *Assoc Prof,* Atlanta College of Art, Atlanta GA (S)

Brendel-PanDich, Susanne, *Dir,* Lyndhurst, Tarrytown NY

Brener, R, *Prof,* University of Victoria, Dept of Visual Arts, Victoria BC (S)

Brengle, Anne, *Dir,* Old Dartmouth Historical Society, New Bedford Whaling Museum, New Bedford MA

Brennan, Anne, *Cur & Registrar Colls,* Saint John's Museum of Art, Wilmington NC

Brennan, Beth, *Librn,* Mitchell Museum, Cedar Hurst Library, Mount Vernon IL

Brennan, Ruth, *Exec Dir,* Rapid City Arts Council, Dahl Fine Arts Center, Rapid City SD

Brenneman, David, *Cur European Art,* High Museum of Art, Atlanta GA

Brenneman, Jan, *Dir,* Sid W Richardson Foundation, Collection of Western Art, Fort Worth TX

Brenner, Ed, *VPres Finance & Admin,* American Association of Museums, US National Committee of the International Council of Museums (AAM-ICOM), Washington DC

Brenner, M Diane, *Archivist,* Anchorage Museum of History & Art, Anchorage AK

Brenner, M Diane, *Museum Archivist,* Anchorage Museum of History & Art, Archives, Anchorage AK

Brenner, Stephen, *VPres,* Sitka Historical Society, Isabel Miller Museum, Sitka AK

Brenner, Susan, *Prof,* University of North Carolina at Charlotte, Dept of Visual Arts, Charlotte NC (S)

Bresnahan, Edith, *Chmn,* Dominican College of San Rafael, Art Dept, San Rafael CA (S)

Bresnan, Susan M, *Assoc Museum Librn,* The Metropolitan Museum of Art, Photograph & Slide Library, New York NY

Bressett, Ken, *Pres,* American Numismatic Association, Museum, Colorado Springs CO

Brett-Smith, Sarah, *Assoc Prof,* Rutgers, the State University of New Jersey, Graduate Program in Art History, New Brunswick NJ (S)

Breukelman, Jim, *Dean Media,* Emily Carr Institute of Art & Design, Vancouver BC (S)

Brew, Michael G, *Asst Dir,* Broward County Board of Commissioners Cultural Affairs Divison, Fort Lauderdale FL

Brewer, Barbara, *Cur Colls,* Cascade County Historical Society, Cascade County Historical Museum & Archives, Great Falls MT

Brewer, Douglas, *Dir,* University of Illinois, Museum of Natural History, Champaign IL

Brewer, Esther Vivian, *Asst Proj Dir,* National Conference of Artists, Michigan Chapter Gallery, Detroit MI

Brewer, Tom, *Coordr Art Educ,* University of Southern Mississippi, Dept of Art, Hattiesburg MS (S)

Brewster, Michael, *Prof,* Claremont Graduate School, Dept of Fine Arts, Claremont CA (S)

Brewster, Riley, *Instr,* New York Studio School of Drawing, Painting & Sculpture, New York NY (S)

Brezzo, Steven L, *Dir,* San Diego Museum of Art, San Diego CA

Bridenstine, James A, *Exec Dir,* Kalamazoo Institute of Arts, Kalamazoo MI

Bridges, Edwin C, *Dir,* Alabama Department of Archives & History, Museum Galleries, Montgomery AL

Bridges, Kimberly B, *Librn,* Honolulu Academy of Arts, Robert Allerton Library, Honolulu HI

Bridges, Robert, *Cur Asst,* The First National Bank of Chicago, Art Collection, Chicago IL

Bridson, Gavin D R, *Bibliographer,* Carnegie Mellon University, Hunt Institute for Botanical Documentation, Pittsburgh PA

Bridwell, Nancy, *Adjunct Instr,* Maryville University of Saint Louis, Art Division, Saint Louis MO (S)

Brienza, Barney, *Chmn Dept,* Western Montana College, Art Dept, Dillon MT (S)

Brierley, David, *Cur,* San Diego Maritime Museum, San Diego CA

Briese, Judge Shawn, *Second VPres,* Halifax Historical Society, Inc, Halifax Historical Museum, Daytona Beach FL

Briggs, Larry S, *Design Area Head,* Southern Illinois University, School of Art & Design, Carbondale IL (S)

Briggs, Larry S, *Assoc Prof,* Southern Illinois University, School of Art & Design, Carbondale IL (S)

Briggs, Peter, *Cur Coll,* University of Arizona, Museum of Art, Tucson AZ

Bright, Jane, *Cur,* Roberts County Museum, Miami TX

Bright, Randall, *First VPres,* Rome Historical Society Museum, Rome NY

Brigmann, Birgitte, *Prof,* New Mexico Highlands University, Dept of Communications & Fine Arts, Las Vegas NM (S)

Briley, John B, *Mgr,* The Ohio Historical Society, Inc, Campus Martius Museum & Ohio River Museum, Marietta OH

Brill, Margaret, *Prof,* Corning Community College, Division of Humanities, Corning NY (S)

Brill, Peter S, *Head Exhib NY,* National Museum of the American Indian, George Gustav Heye Center, New York NY

Brill, Robert H, *Research Scientist,* Corning Museum of Glass, Corning NY

Brill, Wayne, *Instr,* Interlochen Arts Academy, Dept of Visual Art, Interlochen MI (S)

Brilla, Maureen, *Prof,* Nazareth College of Rochester, Art Dept, Rochester NY (S)

Bringle, Edwina, *Prof,* University of North Carolina at Charlotte, Dept of Visual Arts, Charlotte NC (S)

Bringle, Mel, *Chmn Dept Humanities & Fine Arts,* Saint Andrews Presbyterian College, Art Program, Laurinburg NC (S)

Brinkerhoff, Derioksen M, *Prof Emeriti,* University of California, Riverside, Dept of the History of Art, Riverside CA (S)

Brinson, Karen, *Instr,* Bob Jones University, School of Fine Arts, Greenville SC (S)

Brisebois, Marcel, *Dir,* Musee d'art Contemporain de Montreal, Montreal PQ

Brissan, Harriet, *Prof,* Rhode Island College, Art Dept, Providence RI (S)

Bristah, James W, *Exec Dir,* Central United Methodist Church, Swords Info Plowshares Peace Center & Gallery, Detroit MI

Bristol, Joanna, *Dir Information Serv,* Cleveland Botanical Garden, Eleanor Squire Library, Cleveland OH

Bristow, William A, *Prof,* Trinity University, Dept of Art, San Antonio TX (S)

Britt, Sam Glenn, *Prof,* Delta State University, Dept of Art, Cleveland MS (S)

Brittain, Patsy, *Admin Asst,* Art Museum of Southeast Texas, Beaumont TX

Britton, Benjamin, *Prof Fine Arts,* University of Cincinnati, School of Art, Cincinnati OH (S)

Britton, Bonnie, *Instr,* Monterey Peninsula College, Art Dept, Monterey CA (S)

Britton, R E Neil, *Prof,* Virginia Wesleyan College, Art Dept of the Humanities Division, Norfolk VA (S)

Britton, Virginia, *Ballet Headmistress,* Northern Virginia Fine Arts Association, The Athenaeum, Alexandria VA

Britz, Kevin, *Exhibits Dir,* High Desert Museum, Bend OR

Bro, Lu, *Coordr Drawing & Painting,* Iowa State University, Dept of Art & Design, Ames IA (S)

Broad, Deborah, *Prof.* Moorhead State University, Dept of Art, Moorhead MN (S)

Broadfoot, Claire, *Asst Dir Exhibitions & Events.* School of the Art Institute of Chicago, Gallery 2, Chicago IL

Brock, Jill, *Sr Recreation Therapist.* Manhattan Psychiatric Center, East River Gallery, New York NY

Brock, Lee, *Dir.* Olympic College, Social Sciences & Humanities Division, Bremerton WA (S)

Brock, Sally, *Dir.* Sun Valley Center for the Arts & Humanities, Dept of Fine Art, Sun Valley ID (S)

Brocker, Pam, *Pres.* Art Guild of Burlington, Arts for Living Center, Burlington IA

Brockman, Cathy, *Registrar.* New Mexico State University, University Art Gallery, Las Cruces NM

Broda, Alysan, *Dir Visual & Performing Arts.* Aims Community College, Visual & Performing Arts, Greeley CO (S)

Brode, Carol, *Dir Gallery & Instr.* Seton Hill College, Dept of Art, Greensburg PA (S)

Broderick, Herbert R, *Chmn.* Herbert H Lehman College, Art Dept, Bronx NY (S)

Broderick, James, *Div Dir.* University of Texas at San Antonio, Division of Visual Arts, San Antonio TX (S)

Broderick-Lockhart, Catherine, *Instr.* Vancouver Community College, Langara Campus, Dept of Fine Arts, Vancouver BC (S)

Brodeur, Danyelle, *Coordr.* Dorval Cultural Centre, Dorval PQ

Brodhead, Heather, *Staff Librn.* Carnegie Library of Pittsburgh, Pittsburgh PA

Brodie, Lee, *Educ Liaison.* University of Saskatchewan, Diefenbaker Canada Centre, Saskatoon SK

Brodie, Scott, *Asst Prof.* College of Saint Rose, Dept of Art, Albany NY (S)

Brodnax, Vicki, *Admin Asst.* Rollins College, George D & Harriet W Cornell Fine Arts Museum, Winter Park FL

Brodsky, Joyce, *Chmn.* University of California, Santa Cruz, Board of Studies in Art, Santa Cruz CA (S)

Brodsky, Judith, *Prof.* Rutgers, the State University of New Jersey, Mason Gross School of the Arts, New Brunswick NJ (S)

Brodsky, Michael, *Prof.* Loyola Marymount University, Art & Art History Dept, Los Angeles CA (S)

Brody, Arthur W, *Prof.* University of Alaska-Fairbanks, Dept of Art, Fairbanks AK (S)

Brody, Lauren, *Secy & Treas.* Art Dealers Association of America, Inc, New York NY

Brody, Myron, *Prof.* University of Arkansas, Art Dept, Fayetteville AR (S)

Brofman, Lucy, *Dir Educ.* Newark Museum Association, The Newark Museum, Newark NJ

Brohel, Edward R, *Dir.* State University of New York, SUNY Plattsburgh Art Museum, Plattsburgh NY

Broker, Karin, *Prof.* Rice University, Dept of Art & Art History, Houston TX (S)

Bromberg, Anne R, *Assoc Cur Ancient Art.* Dallas Museum of Art, Dallas TX

Bromberg, Nicolette, *Cur Visual Materials.* State Historical Society of Wisconsin, State Historical Museum, Madison WI

Bromley, Diana, *Asst Dir.* Arts & Science Center, Statesville NC

Bromley, Kimble, *Asst Prof.* North Dakota State University, Division of Fine Arts, Fargo ND (S)

Broner, Megan, *VPres.* Canadian Crafts Council, Conseil Canadien de l'Artisanat, Ottawa ON

Bronson, A A, *Dir.* Art Metropole, Toronto ON

Broodwell, Caroyln, *Prof.* Napa Valley College, Art Dept, Napa CA (S)

Brooke, Anna, *Librn.* Hirshhorn Museum & Sculpture Garden, Library, Washington DC

Brookhouse, Jon, *Chmn Dept.* Suomi International College of Art & Design, Fine Arts Dept, Hancock MI (S)

Brookner, Jacalyn, *Lectr.* University of Pennsylvania, Graduate School of Fine Arts, Philadelphia PA (S)

Brooks, Angela, *Operations Coordr.* Tubman African American Museum, Macon GA

Brooks, Bradley C, *Dir.* Mamie McFaddin Ward Heritage Historic Foundation Inc, Beaumont TX

Brooks, Bradley C, *Dir.* Mamie McFaddin Ward Heritage Historic Foundation Inc, McFaddin-Ward House, Beaumont TX

Brooks, Carol, *Cur.* Arizona Historical Society-Yuma, Century House Museum & Garden, Yuma AZ

Brooks, Drex, *Assoc Prof.* Weber State University, Dept of Visual Arts, Ogden UT (S)

Brooks, Gordon, *Dean.* University of Southwestern Louisiana, College of the Arts, Lafayette LA (S)

Brooks, Helen M, *Dir.* Arts & Science Center for Southeast Arkansas, Pine Bluff AR

Brooks, James, *Instr.* Bob Jones University, School of Fine Arts, Greenville SC (S)

Brooks, Jamie, *VPres.* Art League, Alexandria VA

Brooks, Jeffrey, *Archives.* University of Arizona, College of Architecture Library, Tucson AZ

Brooks, John H, *Assoc Dir.* Sterling & Francine Clark Art Institute, Williamstown MA

Brooks, Leonard, *Dir.* United Society of Shakers, The Shaker Library, New Glocester ME

Brooks, Leonard L, *Dir.* United Society of Shakers, Shaker Museum, New Glocester ME

Brooks, Ruth, *Assoc Educ.* Old Salem Inc, Museum of Early Southern Decorative Arts, Winston-Salem NC

Brooks, Steven, *Photographer.* University of California, Architecture Slide Library, Berkeley CA

Brooks, Wendell, *Assoc Prof.* College of New Jersey, Art Dept, Trenton NJ (S)

Broome, Skooker, *Designer & Technician.* University of British Columbia, Museum of Anthropology, Vancouver BC

Brophy, Kathleen L, *Dept Head.* Hartford Public Library, Art Dept, Hartford CT

Broske, Jan, *Asst Cur.* University of Delaware, University Gallery, Newark DE

Bross, John, *Instr.* Greenfield Community College, Art, Graphic Design & Media Communication Dept, Greenfield MA (S)

Brothers, Leslie, *Registrar.* Virginia Commonwealth University, Anderson Gallery, Richmond VA

Brothers, Stacy, *Publicity.* Iowa State University, Brunnier Art Museum, Ames IA

Broude, Norma, *Prof.* American University, Dept of Art, Washington DC (S)

Broudo, J David, *Head Dept.* Endicott College, Art Dept, Beverly MA (S)

Brougher, Dale, *Dir.* University of Findlay, Egner Fine Arts Center, Findlay OH

Brougher, Dale, *Dean College & Liberal Arts.* University of Findlay, Art Dept, Findlay OH (S)

Brouillard, William, *Assoc Prof.* Cleveland Institute of Art, Cleveland OH (S)

Brouillet, Johanne, *Dir.* University of Sherbrooke, Art Gallery, Sherbrooke PQ

Broun, Elizabeth, *Dir.* National Museum of American Art, Washington DC

Brous, Ellen, *Treas.* Long Island Graphic Eye Gallery, Port Washington NY

Broussard, Jeanne, *Assoc Prof.* Texas Woman's University, Dept of Visual Arts, Denton TX (S)

Brouwer, Charles, *Asst Prof.* Radford University, Art Dept, Radford VA (S)

Brouwer, Norman, *Historian & Librn.* South Street Seaport Museum, New York NY

Brouwer, Norman, *Historian & Librn.* South Street Seaport Museum, Library, New York NY

Browdo, Bar, *Cur.* Wenham Museum, Wenham MA

Brower, Paul, *Cur.* Western Washington University, Viking Union Gallery, Bellingham WA

Brown, Ann Barton, *Dir.* American Swedish Historical Foundation & Museum, Philadelphia PA

Brown, Ann Barton, *Exec Dir.* American Swedish Historical Foundation & Museum, Library, Philadelphia PA

Brown, Barbara J, *Head Librn.* Washington & Lee University, Leyburn Library, Lexington VA

Brown, Bernadette, *Cur Educational Serv.* University of Utah, Utah Museum of Fine Arts, Salt Lake City UT

Brown, Brad, *Display Artist.* City of Lethbridge, Sir Alexander Galt Museum, Lethbridge AB

Brown, Bruce, *Cur.* Maine Coast Artists, Art Gallery, Rockport ME

Brown, Bruce R, *Assoc Prof.* Monroe Community College, Art Dept, Rochester NY (S)

Brown, Charlotte V, *Dir.* North Carolina State University, Visual Arts Center, Raleigh NC

Brown, Christopher, *Communications Mgr.* Winnipeg Art Gallery, Winnipeg MB

Brown, Claire H, *Marketing & Public Relations Dir.* Louisiana Department of Culture, Recreation & Tourism, Louisiana State Museum, New Orleans LA

Brown, Clinton, *Prof.* Oregon State University, Dept of Art, Corvallis OR (S)

Brown, Clyde, *Chmn.* Texas A&M University, Visual Arts Committee, College Station TX

Brown, C Reynolds, *Dir.* Saint John's Museum of Art, Wilmington NC

Brown, Dan, *Dept Chmn.* Towson State University, Dept of Art, Towson MD (S)

Brown, Darlene, *Dir.* George Spiva Center for the Arts, Joplin MO

Brown, David, *Cur Renaissance Painting.* National Gallery of Art, Washington DC

Brown, David, *Cur.* Contemporary Arts Center, Library, Cincinnati OH

Brown, David H, *Asst Prof.* Emory University, Art History Dept, Atlanta GA (S)

Brown, David R, *Pres.* Art Center College of Design, Pasadena CA (S)

Brown, D Gregg, *Pres.* Riverside Art Museum, Riverside CA

Brown, Dorothy D, *Chmn.* Georgia College, Art Dept, Milledgeville GA (S)

Brown, Dottie, *Instr.* Sierra Community College, Art Dept, Rocklin CA (S)

Brown, Eden, *Gallery Dir.* Mississippi State University, Art Dept, Mississippi State MS (S)

Brown, Edward, *Prof.* Barton College, Art Dept, Wilson NC (S)

Brown, Elizabeth, *Cur.* University of California, Santa Barbara, University Art Museum, Santa Barbara CA

Brown, Elly Sparks, *Admin Dir.* Wesley Theological Seminary Center for the Arts & Religion, Dadian Gallery, Washington DC

Brown, Geoffrey, *Conservator.* University of Michigan, Kelsey Museum of Archaeology, Ann Arbor MI

Brown, Gerard, *Exec Dir.* Cheltenham Center for the Arts, Cheltenham PA (S)

Brown, Glen, *Asst Prof.* Texas Tech University, Dept of Art, Lubbock TX (S)

Brown, Jackie, *Coordr.* Frostburg State University, The Stephanie Ann Roper Gallery, Frostburg MD

Brown, Jack Perry, *Dir of Libraries.* The Art Institute of Chicago, Ryerson & Burnham Libraries, Chicago IL

Brown, Jane, *Chmn.* University of Arkansas at Little Rock, Fine Arts Galleries, Little Rock AR (S)

Brown, Janet, *Interim Dir.* Sioux City Art Center, Sioux City IA

Brown, Janet, *Interim Dir.* Sioux City Art Center, Sioux City IA (S)

Brown, J Carter, *Chmn.* United States Commission of Fine Arts, Washington DC

Brown, Jeff, *Chmn Fine Arts.* Jones County Junior College, Art Dept, Ellisville MS (S)

Brown, Jess, *Pres.* Monterey Museum of Art Association, Monterey CA

Brown, Jesse, *Curatorial Asst.* California State University, Chico, Janet Turner Print Gallery & Collection, Chico CA

Brown, Joe, *Dean.* Texas Wesleyan University, Dept of Art, Fort Worth TX (S)

Brown, Judith, *Controller.* New Brunswick Museum, Saint John NB

Brown, Laura, *Preparator.* Art Complex Museum, Duxbury MA

Brown, Laurie, *Educ Coordr.* Abigail Adams Smith Museum, New York NY

Brown, Lindie K, *Develop Officer,* Anniston Museum of Natural History, Anniston AL

Brown, Louise Freshman, *Prof,* University of North Florida, Dept of Communications & Visual Arts, Jacksonville FL (S)

Brown, Lyn, *Secy,* Mississippi Art Colony, Pascagoula MS

Brown, Maren, *Asst Cur Educ,* George Walter Vincent Smith Art Museum, Springfield MA

Brown, Marilyn R, *Assoc Prof,* Tulane University, Sophie H Newcomb Memorial College, New Orleans LA (S)

Brown, Mary, *Dir Admin,* The Queens Museum of Art, Flushing NY

Brown, Mary, *Dir,* Mount Vernon Public Library, Fine Art Dept, Mount Vernon NY

Brown, Michael, *Cur Bayou Bend,* Museum of Fine Arts, Houston, Houston TX

Brown, Milton, *Prof Emeritus,* City University of New York, PhD Program in Art History, New York NY (S)

Brown, N, *Exec Dir,* Center for History of American Needlework, Butler PA

Brown, Nancy, *Asst Exec Dir,* Manchester Craftsmen's Guild, Pittsburgh PA

Brown, Nell, *Business Mgr,* Arts & Science Center for Southeast Arkansas, Pine Bluff AR

Brown, Osa, *Dir Publications,* Museum of Modern Art, New York NY

Brown, Pam, *Cur & Ethnology/Media,* University of British Columbia, Museum of Anthropology, Vancouver BC

Brown, Pat, *Prof,* Princeton University, Dept of Art & Archaeology, Princeton NJ (S)

Brown, Patricia, *Exhib Chmn,* Delta State University, Fielding L Wright Art Center, Cleveland MS

Brown, Patricia L, *Asst Prof,* Delta State University, Dept of Art, Cleveland MS (S)

Brown, Regina, *Exec Secy,* National Council on Education for the Ceramic Arts (NCECA), Bandon OR

Brown, R Kelley, *Trustee,* Hill-Stead Museum, Farmington CT

Brown, Robert, *Dir,* Historical Museum at Fort Missoula, Missoula MT

Brown, Robert F, *Dir & Journal Ed,* Archives of American Art, New England Regional Center, Washington DC

Brown, Robin, *Chmn Dept,* Southern Illinois University at Edwardsville, Dept of Art & Design, Edwardsville IL (S)

Brown, Robin, *Photography & Graphic Design,* Southern Illinois University at Edwardsville, Dept of Art & Design, Edwardsville IL (S)

Brown, Ruth, *Dir,* Deming-Luna Mimbres Museum, Deming NM

Brown, Ruth A, *Gallery Mgr,* North Shore Arts Association, Inc, Art Gallery, Gloucester MA

Brown, Scott M, *Exec Dir,* Spartanburg County Museum of Art, Spartanburg SC

Brown, Shary, *Art Fair Dir,* Michigan Guild of Artists & Artisans, Michigan Guild Gallery, Ann Arbor MI

Brown, Shoko, *Cur Exhib,* Palm Beach County Parks & Recreation Department, Morikami Museum & Japanese Gardens, Delray Beach FL

Brown, Shoko, *Coll Cur,* Palm Beach County Parks & Recreation Department, Donald B Gordon Memorial Library, Delray Beach FL

Brown, Stephen, *Assoc Prof,* University of Hartford, Hartford Art School, West Hartford CT (S)

Brown, Susan, *Art Prof,* Richard Bland College, Art Dept, Petersburg VA (S)

Brown, Susan, *Cur,* Laumeier Sculpture Park & Museum, Saint Louis MO

Brown, Terrence, *Dir,* Society of Illustrators, New York NY

Brown, Terrence, *Dir,* Society of Illustrators, Museum of American Illustration, New York NY

Brown, Timothy P, *Pres,* Lancaster Museum of Art, Lancaster PA

Brown, Tonja, *Asst Dir,* Stephen Bulger Gallery, Toronto ON

Brown, William, *Cur Glass,* Zanesville Art Center, Zanesville OH

Brown, William, *Asst Prof,* University of Evansville, Art Dept, Evansville IN (S)

Brown, William A, *Lectr,* Emory University, Art History Dept, Atlanta GA (S)

Brown, Yvonne S, *Head Art Information Center,* Chicago Public Library, Harold Washington Library Center, Chicago IL

Brownawell, Christopher, *Dir & Cur,* Academy of the Arts, Easton MD

Browne, Charles C, *Dir,* Fairbanks Museum & Planetarium, Saint Johnsbury VT

Brownell, Charles, *Assoc Prof,* Virginia Commonwealth University, Art History Dept, Richmond VA (S)

Brownfield, John, *Chmn,* University of Redlands, Dept of Art, Redlands CA (S)

Browning, Louis N, *Adminr,* Mason County Museum, Maysville KY

Browning, Mark, *Exec Dir,* Custer County Art Center, Miles City MT

Browning, Rob, *Preparator,* University of Virginia, Bayly Art Museum, Charlottesville VA

Brown-Lee, Barbara, *Dir Educ,* Milwaukee Art Museum, Milwaukee WI

Brownrigg, Elizabeth, *Dir,* Omaha Childrens Museum, Inc, Omaha NE

Brownscombe, Martha, *Dir,* Lansing Art Gallery, Lansing MI

Brozovich, Tom J, *Instr,* American River College, Dept of Art, Sacramento CA (S)

Brozynski, Dennis, *Coordr Fashion Design,* Columbia College, Art Dept, Chicago IL (S)

Brubaker, Ann, *Dir Educ,* Nelson-Atkins Museum of Art, Kansas City MO

Brubaker, Diane, *Adminr,* Philadelphia Art Alliance, Philadelphia PA

Bruce, Bonnie, *Instr,* Marylhurst College, Art Dept, Marylhurst OR (S)

Bruce, Chris, *Sr Cur,* University of Washington, Henry Art Gallery, Seattle WA

Bruce, Dan, *Asst Cur,* Kelowna Museum, Kelowna BC

Bruce, Donald, *Cur,* Cambria Historical Society, New Providence NJ

Brucker, Jane, *Asst Prof,* Loyola Marymount University, Art & Art History Dept, Los Angeles CA (S)

Brudsky, Judith, *Pres,* College Art Association, New York NY

Bruggen, Willard, *Dir Budget & Finance,* Indiana State Museum, Indianapolis IN

Bruhl, Win, *Prof,* Concordia College, Art Dept, Saint Paul MN (S)

Bruhn, Jutta-Annette, *Cur European Glass,* Corning Museum of Glass, Corning NY

Bruhn, Thomas P, *Acting Dir,* University of Connecticut, William Benton Museum of Art, Storrs CT

Bruker, David, *Exhibits Mgr,* Indiana University, William Hammond Mathers Museum, Bloomington IN

Brumback, Charlie, *VChmn,* Chicago Historical Society, Chicago IL

Brumbaugh, Mary, *Exec Dir,* Lynchburg Fine Arts Center Inc, Lynchburg VA

Brumgardt, John R, *Dir,* Charleston Museum, Charleston SC

Brun, Laura, *Artistic Dir,* The Lab, San Francisco CA

Brunchwyler, Greta, *Cur Exhib,* Southern Oregon Historical Society, Jacksonville Museum of Southern Oregon History, Medford OR

Brundage, Harvey, *Facilities Dept,* R J R Nabisco, Inc, New York NY

Brunez, Fred, *Asst Prof,* College of DuPage, Humanities Division, Glen Ellyn IL (S)

Bruni, Stephen T, *Dir,* Delaware Art Museum, Wilmington DE

Brunken, Glen, *Chmn Dept,* Slippery Rock University of Pennsylvania, Dept of Art, Slippery Rock PA (S)

Brunner, Christal, *Reference Librn,* Mexico-Audrain County Library, Mexico MO

Brunner, Helen M, *Dir Spec Projects,* Art Resources International, Washington DC

Brunning, Margaret, *Prog Coordr,* Tempe Arts Center, Tempe AZ

Bruno, Ana Basso, *Prof,* Catholic University of Puerto Rico, Dept of Fine Arts, Ponce PR (S)

Brusati, Celeste, *Assoc Prof,* University of Michigan, Ann Arbor, Dept of History of Art, Ann Arbor MI (S)

Brusca, Maureen, *VPres Finance Admin,* Pennsylvania Academy of the Fine Arts, Museum of American Art, Philadelphia PA

Brush, Gloria D, *Head Dept,* University of Minnesota, Duluth, Art Dept, Duluth MN (S)

Brush, Leif, *Prof,* University of Minnesota, Duluth, Art Dept, Duluth MN (S)

Brust, John, *Assoc Prof,* Roanoke College, Fine Arts Dept-Art, Salem VA (S)

Brutger, James H, *Assoc Prof,* University of Minnesota, Duluth, Art Dept, Duluth MN (S)

Brutuan, Cheryl A, *Cur,* The Buffalo Fine Arts Academy, Albright-Knox Art Gallery, Buffalo NY

Bruya, Marilyn, *Prof,* University of Montana, Dept of Art, Missoula MT (S)

Bruzelius, Caroline, *Prof,* Duke University, Dept of Art & Art History, Durham NC (S)

Bryan, Betsy, *Cur Near Eastern & Egyptian Art,* Johns Hopkins University, Archaeological Collection, Baltimore MD

Bryan, Charles F, *Dir,* Virginia Historical Society, Richmond VA

Bryan, Charles F, *Dir,* Virginia Historical Society, Library, Richmond VA

Bryan, Jack, *Chmn,* Cameron University, Art Dept, Lawton OK (S)

Bryan, James B, *Dean of Faculty,* Manhattanville College, Brownson Art Gallery, Purchase NY

Bryan, Jerry, *Chmn,* Western Oklahoma State College, Art Dept, Altus OK (S)

Bryan, Joseph, *VPres,* Key West Art & Historical Society, East Martello Museum & Gallery, Key West FL

Bryan Hood, Mary, *Dir,* Owensboro Museum of Fine Art, Art Library, Owensboro KY

Bryans, John, *Head Dept,* McLean Arts Center, Art Dept, McLean VA (S)

Bryant, Anne L, *Exec Dir,* American Association of University Women, Washington DC

Bryant, Bill, *Pres,* Cuyahoga Valley Art Center, Cuyahoga Falls OH (S)

Bryant, David, *Dir,* New Canaan Library, New Canaan CT

Bryant, Hal, *Pres,* Shelby Art League, Inc, Shelby NC

Bryant, Susan, *Acting Chair,* Austin Peay State University, Dept of Art, Clarksville TN (S)

Brydon, Irene Ward, *Exec Dir,* Creative Growth Art Center, Oakland CA

Bryner, Dale W, *Prof,* Weber State University, Dept of Visual Arts, Ogden UT (S)

Brynolf, Anita, *Instr,* San Diego Mesa College, Fine Arts Dept, San Diego CA (S)

Brynteson, Susan, *Dir Libraries,* University of Delaware, Morris Library, Newark DE

Bucanek, James, *Chmn,* Movimiento Artistico del Rio Salado, Inc (MARS) Artspace, Phoenix AZ

Buchanan, Bryan, *Pres,* Mohawk Valley Heritage Association, Inc, Walter Elwood Museum, Amsterdam NY

Buchanan, David, *Dir Develop,* Atlanta Historical Society Inc, Atlanta History Center, Atlanta GA

Buchanan, John, *Exec Dir,* Portland Art Museum, Portland OR

Buchanan, John, *Instr,* Alcorn State University, Dept of Fine Arts, Lorman MS (S)

Buchanan, Lucy, *Develop,* Portland Art Museum, Portland OR

Buchanan, Richard, *Head,* Carnegie Mellon University, Dept of Design, Pittsburgh PA (S)

Buchanan, Sidney, *Prof,* University of Nebraska at Omaha, Dept of Art & Art History, Omaha NE (S)

Bucher, Francois, *Prof,* Florida State University, Art History Dept (R133B), Tallahassee FL (S)

Buchloh, Benjamin, *Chmn,* Columbia University, Barnard College, New York NY (S)

Buchman, Lorne, *Pres,* California College of Arts & Crafts, Oakland CA (S)

Buchter, Thomas, *Head of Gardens,* Winterthur Museum, Winterthur DE

Buck, Dana, *Exhibit Preparator,* University of Michigan, Kelsey Museum of Archaeology, Ann Arbor MI

Burton, Ann Betts, *Lectr*, Trinity College, Art Program, Washington DC (S)

Burton, Carol, *Pres*, Minneapolis Institute of Arts, Friends of the Institute, Minneapolis MN

Burton, Douglas, *Asst Prof*, Lenoir Rhyne College, Dept of Art, Hickory NC (S)

Burton, Judith, *Dir*, Columbia University, Teachers Col Program in Art & Art Educ, New York NY (S)

Burton, Margaret, *Mgr*, Forest Lawn Museum, Glendale CA

Burton, Margaret, *Cur*, Forest Lawn Museum, Library, Glendale CA

Burwell, Sandra, *Instr*, Indiana University of Pennsylvania, Dept of Art & Art Education, Indiana PA (S)

Burwell, Sandra, *Instr*, Indiana University of Pennsylvania, Dept of Art & Art Education, Indiana PA (S)

Busby, James, *Chmn*, Houston Baptist University, Dept of Art, Houston TX (S)

Busby, Ken, *Asst to Dir & Dir Public Relations*, Gilcrease Museum Institute of American History & Art, Tulsa OK

Busceme, Greg, *Dir*, The Art Studio Inc, Beaumont TX

Busch, Cindy, *Dir Public Relations*, Indiana State Museum, Indianapolis IN

Busch, W Larry, *Assoc Prof*, Southern Illinois University, School of Art & Design, Carbondale IL (S)

Buscho, Qwen, *VPres*, Owatonna Arts Center, Community Arts Center, Owatonna MN

Bush, Kimberly, *Registrar*, Dallas Museum of Art, Dallas TX

Bush, Teresia, *Sr Educator*, Hirshhorn Museum & Sculpture Garden, Washington DC

Busse, Carol, *Librn*, Southern Alberta Art Gallery, Library, Lethbridge AB

Bustamante, Cody, *Chmn Dept Art*, Southern Oregon State College, Central Art Gallery, Ashland OR

Bustamante, Cody, *Chmn Dept Art*, Southern Oregon State College, Dept of Art, Ashland OR (S)

Butcher, Larry, *Assoc Prof*, Delta College, Art Dept, University Center MI (S)

Butchovitz, Dean, *Prof*, University of North Carolina at Charlotte, Dept of Visual Arts, Charlotte NC (S)

Butckovitz, Jane, *Instr*, University of North Carolina at Charlotte, Dept of Visual Arts, Charlotte NC (S)

Butera, Joseph L, *Pres*, Butera School of Art, Boston MA (S)

Buth-Furness, Christine, *VPres-Nominations*, Coalition of Women's Art Organizations, Port Washington WI

Butler, Charles T, *Dir*, Columbus Museum, Columbus GA

Butler, David, *Dir*, Sheldon Swope Art Museum, Terre Haute IN

Butler, David, *Dir*, Sheldon Swope Art Museum, Research Library, Terre Haute IN

Butler, Erin, *Newsletter Ed*, Women in the Arts Foundation, Inc, New York NY

Butler, Janine, *Registrar*, Art Gallery of Windsor, Windsor ON

Butler, Janine, *Librn*, Art Gallery of Windsor, Reference Library, Windsor ON

Butler, Jerry E, *Chmn*, Madison Area Technical College, Art Dept, Madison WI (S)

Butler, Joyce, *Manuscrips Cur*, Brick Store Museum & Library, Kennebunk ME

Butler, Kenneth, *Treas*, Contemporary Arts Center, Cincinnati OH

Butler, Mike, *Nature Park Mgr*, Iroquois Indian Museum, Howes Cave NY

Butler, Monte, *Bookstore Mgr*, Laguna Art Museum of the Orange County Museum of Art, Laguna Beach CA

Butler, Owen, *Assoc Prof*, Rochester Institute of Technology, School of Photographic Arts & Sciences, Rochester NY (S)

Butler, Pamela, *Shop Mgr*, Iowa State University, Brunnier Art Museum, Ames IA

Butler, Ruth, *Emeritus Prof*, University of Massachusetts - Boston, Art Dept, Boston MA (S)

Butler-Ludwig, John L, *Cur*, University of Chicago, Art Slide Collection, Chicago IL

Butridge, Julie, *Gallery Preparator*, City of Austin Parks & Recreation Department, Dougherty Arts Center Gallery, Austin TX

Butt, Harlan, *Jewelry & Metalsmithing Coordr*, University of North Texas, School of Visual Arts, Denton TX (S)

Butterfield, Michelle, *Registrar*, Portland Museum of Art, Portland ME

Butterfield, Thomas F, *Art Dir*, Virginia Polytechnic Institute & State University, Perspective Gallery, Blacksburg VA

Butterworth, James M, *Dean College Fine Arts*, Western Illinois University, Art Dept, Macomb IL (S)

Butts, H Daniel, *Dir*, Mansfield Fine Arts Guild, Mansfield Art Center, Mansfield OH

Butts, H Daniel, *Art Dir*, Mansfield Fine Arts Guild, Library, Mansfield OH

Butts, Patricia, *Asst to the Dir*, Columbus Museum, Columbus GA

Buttwinick, Edward, *Dir*, Brentwood Art Center, Los Angeles CA (S)

Buyers, Jane, *Asst Prof*, University of Waterloo, Fine Arts Dept, Waterloo ON (S)

Byard, Anne, *Asst Cur*, Brant Historical Society, Brant County Museum, Brantford ON

Byers, Julia, *Prog Dir*, Lesley College, Arts Institute, Cambridge MA (S)

Byers, Laura, *Cur Rare Books*, Norfolk Historical Society Inc, Museum, Norfolk CT

Bykonen, P Lisa, *Visitor Servs*, Alaska Department of Education, Division of Libraries, Archives & Museums, Sheldon Jackson Museum, Sitka AK

Byrd, Dejay, *Gallery Assoc*, Nexus Contemporary Art Center, Atlanta GA

Byrd, Jeff, *Assoc Prof*, University of Northern Iowa, Dept of Art, Cedar Falls IA (S)

Byrd, Joan, *Prof*, Western Carolina University, Dept of Art, Cullowhee NC (S)

Byrd, Kathleen, *Staff Performing Artist*, Jay County Arts Council, Hugh N Ronald Memorial Gallery, Portland IN

Byrd, Mora, *Dir Spec Projects*, Caribbean Cultural Center, Cultural Arts Organization & Resource Center, New York NY

Byrn, Brian D, *Cur Exhib & Educ*, Midwest Museum of American Art, Elkhart IN

Byrne, Brenda Barry, *Prog Coordr*, Photographers Gallery, Saskatoon SK

Byrne, Elizabeth, *Head*, University of California, Environmental Design Library, Berkeley CA

Byrne, Jeri, *Fine Art Librn*, Beverly Hills Public Library, Fine Arts Library, Beverly Hills CA

Byrne, Richard, *Pres & Dir*, Norfolk Historical Society Inc, Museum, Norfolk CT

Byrum, Donald, *Chmn*, Wichita State University, School of Art & Design, Wichita KS (S)

Bytnerowicz, Dasia, *Exhib Designer*, Riverside Municipal Museum, Riverside CA

Bywater, Roger, *Asst Cur*, Art Metropole, Toronto ON

Bywaters, Diane, *Assoc Prof*, University of Wisconsin-Stevens Point, Dept of Art & Design, Stevens Point WI (S)

Bzdak, Michael J, *Art Cur*, Johnson & Johnson, Art Program, New Brunswick NJ

Cabarga, Paul, *Bookstore Mgr*, University of Washington, Henry Art Gallery, Seattle WA

Caddell, Foster, *Head Dept*, Foster Caddell's Art School, Voluntown CT (S)

Cadigan, Edward, *Supv of Operations*, Memorial University of Newfoundland, Art Gallery of Newfoundland & Labrador, Saint John's NF

Cadogan, Jean, *Assoc Prof*, Trinity College, Dept of Fine Arts, Hartford CT (S)

Caesar, Pauline, *Project Coordr*, Public Relations & Fund Develop, City of Atlanta, Bureau of Cultural Affairs, Atlanta GA

Caglioti, Victory, *Assoc Prof*, University of Minnesota, Minneapolis, Dept of Art, Minneapolis MN (S)

Cahalan, Joseph M, *VPres Xerox Foundation*, Xerox Corporation, Art Collection, Stamford CT

Cahill, Stephen, *Photography*, Pitzer College, Dept of Art, Claremont CA (S)

Cahoon, John, *Col Mgr*, Los Angeles County Museum of Natural History, William S Hart Museum, Newhall CA

Cain, Mark, *Dir*, College of Mount Saint Joseph, Archbishop Alter Library, Cincinnati OH

Caine, Joan, *Asst Dir*, University of Washington, Henry Art Gallery, Seattle WA

Cairns, R Christopher, *Prof*, Haverford College, Fine Arts Dept, Haverford PA (S)

Cairns, Roger, *Assoc Prof*, Montgomery County Community College, Art Dept, Blue Bell PA (S)

Caivano, Felice, *Cur*, Trinity College, Austin Arts Center, Hartford CT

Caivano, Nicholas, *Lectr*, Georgian Court College, Dept of Art, Lakewood NJ (S)

Cajori, Charles, *Instr*, New York Studio School of Drawing, Painting & Sculpture, New York NY (S)

Calabrese, John A, *Prof*, Texas Woman's University, Dept of Visual Arts, Denton TX (S)

Calabro, Richard, *Prof*, University of Rhode Island, Dept of Art, Kingston RI (S)

Caldarelli, Janet, *Gallery Assoc*, International Images, Ltd, Sewickley PA

Calden, Lisa, *Coll & Exhib Admin*, University of California, Berkeley Art Museum & Pacific Film Archive, Berkeley CA

Calder, Jacqueline, *Cur*, Vermont Historical Society, Museum, Montpelier VT

Calder-Lacroix, Jenny, *Admin Asst*, Concordia University, Leonard & Bina Ellen Art Gallery, Montreal PQ

Calderwood, Kathy, *Prof*, Nazareth College of Rochester, Art Dept, Rochester NY (S)

Caldwell, Blaine, *Prof*, University of the Ozarks, Dept of Art, Clarksville AR (S)

Caldwell, Cathy, *Assoc Prof*, University of Central Arkansas, Art Dept, Conway AR (S)

Caldwell, Danette, *Exec Dir*, Northfield Arts Guild, Northfield MN

Caldwell, Desiree, *Exec Dir*, Concord Museum, Concord MA

Caldwell, Jody, *Reference Librn*, Drew University, Art Dept Library, Madison NJ

Caldwell, Lantz, *Dir*, Dubuque Art Association, Dubuque Museum of Art, Dubuque IA

Caldwell, Martha B, *Prof*, James Madison University, School of Art & Art History, Harrisonburg VA (S)

Caldwell, Michael, *Chmn*, Seattle Pacific University, Art Dept, Seattle WA (S)

Caldwell, Peter, *VPres Finance/Admin*, Ontario College of Art & Design, Toronto ON (S)

Caldwell, Robert, *Gallery Asst*, Fund for the Borough of Brooklyn, Rotunda Gallery, Brooklyn NY

Calhoun, Larry, *Chmn Art Dept*, MacMurray College, Art Dept, Jacksonville IL (S)

Calhoun, Paul S, *Instr*, Johns Hopkins University, School of Medicine, Dept of Art as Applied to Medicine, Baltimore MD (S)

Calinescu, Adriana, *Cur Ancient Art*, Indiana University, Art Museum, Bloomington IN

Calkins, Robert G, *Prof*, Cornell University, Dept of the History of Art, Ithaca NY (S)

Callahan, Diane, *Adjunct Prof*, Southwest Baptist University, Art Dept, Bolivar MO (S)

Callahan, Jerry, *Division Chmn Fine Arts*, San Jacinto Junior College, Division of Fine Arts, Deer Park TX (S)

Callahan, Nancy, *Instr*, State University of New York College at Oneonta, Dept of Art, Oneonta NY (S)

Callahan-Dolcater, Katrina, *Prof*, Dickinson State University, Dept of Art, Dickinson ND (S)

Callahon, Christine, *Dir Admin*, Newport Art Museum, Newport RI

Callan, Josi I, *Dir*, San Jose Museum of Art, San Jose CA

Calleri, Daniel V, *Instr*, Villa Maria College of Buffalo, Art Dept, Buffalo NY (S)

Callery, Bernadette, *VPres*, Guild of Book Workers, New York NY

Callis, Dan, *Assoc Prof*, Biola University, Art Dept, La Mirada CA (S)

Callis, Marion M, *Dir*, Twin City Art Foundation, Masur Museum of Art, Monroe LA

Callow, Bette Ray, *Slide Cur*, Memphis College of Art, Library, Memphis TN

Callus, Tom, *Registrar*, Orange County Museum of Art, Newport Harbor Art Museum, Newport Beach CA

Calman, Wendy, *Assoc Prof*, Indiana University, Bloomington, Henry Radford Hope School of Fine Arts, Bloomington IN (S)

Calo, Mary Ann, *Asst Prof*, Colgate University, Dept of Art & Art History, Hamilton NY (S)

Calvert, Jean W, *Dir*, Mason County Museum, Maysville KY

Calvert, Sheena, *Asst Prof*, Rutgers, the State University of New Jersey, Mason Gross School of the Arts, New Brunswick NJ (S)

Calvi, Elise, *Head Librn*, Walters Art Gallery, Library, Baltimore MD

Calza, Susan, *Sculpture Instr*, Johnson State College, Dept Fine & Performing Arts, Dibden Center for the Arts, Johnson VT (S)

Calzonetti, Jo Ann, *Head Librn*, West Virginia University, Evansdale Library, Morgantown WV

Camarigg, Elizabeth, *Art Librn*, Mason City Public Library, Mason City IA

Camber, Diane W, *Dir*, Bass Museum of Art, Miami Beach FL

Cameron, Ben, *Instr*, Columbia College, Art Dept, Columbia MO (S)

Cameron, Eric, *Dept Head*, University of Calgary, Dept of Art, Calgary AB (S)

Cameron, Gregory, *Dir Foundations & Corporate Relations*, The Art Institute of Chicago, Chicago IL

Cameron, Jan, *Pres*, Redding Museum of Art & History, Redding CA

Cameron, John B, *Prof*, Oakland University, Dept of Art & Art History, Rochester MI (S)

Camfield, William A, *Prof*, Rice University, Dept of Art & Art History, Houston TX (S)

Camfield, William A, *Assoc Prof*, Rice University, Dept of Art & Art History, Houston TX (S)

Camilli, Adrienne, *Co-Pres*, Greenwich Art Society Inc, Greenwich CT

Camp, Carl, *Cur*, Utah Department of Natural Resources, Division of Parks & Recreation, Territorial Statehouse, Fillmore UT

Camp, Edward, *Prof*, Manatee Community College, Dept of Art & Humanities, Bradenton FL (S)

Camp, Michelle M, *Exec Dir*, Florida Pastel Association, Hollywood FL

Camp, Orton P, *Chmn*, Mattatuck Historical Society, Mattatuck Museum, Waterbury CT

Camp, Roger, *Chmn & Instr*, Golden West College, Visual Art Dept, Huntington Beach CA (S)

Campagna, Roxane, *Dir Library*, Bronxville Public Library, Bronxville NY

Campbell, Ann, *Marketing Dir*, Arts of the Southern Finger Lakes, Corning NY

Campbell, Bob, *Deputy Dir*, California Museum of Science and Industry, Los Angeles CA

Campbell, Clayton, *Exec Dir*, 18th Street Arts Complex, Santa Monica CA

Campbell, Cyndie, *Head Archives*, National Gallery of Canada, Library, Ottawa ON

Campbell, Francis D, *Librn*, American Numismatic Society, New York NY

Campbell, Francis D, *Librn*, American Numismatic Society, Library, New York NY

Campbell, James, *Librn*, New Haven Colony Historical Society, Whitney Library, New Haven CT

Campbell, Kay, *Treas*, Surface Design Association, Inc, Oakland CA

Campbell, Laura, *Dir Develop & Marketing*, Please Touch Museum, Philadelphia PA

Campbell, Lynne, *Registrar*, Michigan State University, Kresge Art Museum, East Lansing MI

Campbell, Mary, *Assoc Prof*, Jersey City State College, Art Dept, Jersey City NJ (S)

Campbell, Mei Wan, *Cur Clothing & Textile*, Texas Tech University, Museum, Lubbock TX

Campbell, Michael, *Asst Prof*, Shippensburg University, Art Dept, Shippensburg PA (S)

Campbell, Nancy, *Dir*, Wayne Art Center, Wayne PA

Campbell, Nancy, *Asst Chmn*, Mount Holyoke College, Art Dept, South Hadley MA (S)

Campbell, Nancy, *Cur*, MacDonald Stewart Art Centre, Guelph ON

Campbell, Phil, *Dir*, Southern Oregon State College, Stevenson Union Gallery, Ashland OR

Campbell, Phyllis, *Prog Assoc & On-Site Dir*, University of Minnesota, Minneapolis, Split Rock Arts Program, Minneapolis MN (S)

Campbell, Richard, *Dir*, LA Art Association, Los Angeles CA

Campbell, Richard, *Cur Prints & Drawings*, Minneapolis Institute of Arts, Minneapolis MN

Campbell, Rochelle, *Instr*, Keystone Junior College, Fine Arts Dept, Factoryville PA (S)

Campbell, Rusty, *Adminr*, University of Houston, Sarah Campbell Blaffer Gallery, Houston TX

Campbell, Sara, *Dir Art*, Norton Simon Museum, Pasadena CA

Campbell, Stephen, *Asst Prof*, Spring Hill College, Fine Arts Dept, Mobile AL (S)

Campbell-Smith, Douglas, *Prof*, Central Oregon Community College, Dept of Art, Bend OR (S)

Campell, Nancy, *Exec Dir*, Wayne Art Center, Wayne PA (S)

Campion, William, *Pres*, Central Florida Community College Art Collection, Ocala FL

Campolo, Sandie, *Artists in Educ Dir*, Arizona Commission on the Arts, Phoenix AZ

Campulli, Eleanor, *Prof*, Jersey City State College, Art Dept, Jersey City NJ (S)

Campus, Peter, *Assoc Prof*, New York University, Dept of Art & Art Professions, New York NY (S)

Camurati, Al, *VPres*, National Art League Inc, Douglaston NY

Canada, Gayle, *Adjunct Prof*, Oklahoma Christian University of Science & Arts, Dept of Art & Design, Oklahoma City OK (S)

Canaves, Marie, *Prof*, Cape Cod Community College, Art Dept, West Barnstable MA (S)

Candau, Eugenie, *Librn*, San Francisco Museum of Modern Art, Library, San Francisco CA

Candel, Sol, *General Mgr*, Museum of Movie Art, Calgary AB

Candelari, Patti, *Dir*, Hera Education Foundation, Hera Gallery, Wakefield RI

Canedy, Norman, *Prof*, University of Minnesota, Minneapolis, Art History, Minneapolis MN (S)

Cannahan, Paul, *Librn*, Vermont Historical Society, Museum, Montpelier VT

Cannell, Susan, *Asst Prof*, Florida State University, Art Dept, Tallahassee FL (S)

Canning, Shirley, *Pres*, Emerald Empire Art Gallery Association, Springfield OR

Canning, Susan, *Chmn*, College of New Rochelle School of Arts & Sciences, Art Dept, New Rochelle NY (S)

Cannon, Robert, *Dir*, Public Library of Charlotte & Mecklenburg County, Charlotte NC

Cannuli, Richard, *Chmn*, Villanova University, Dept of Art & Art History, Villanova PA (S)

Cannup, John, *VPres Facilities Management*, The Mariners' Museum, Newport News VA

Cano, Rose, *Exec Dir*, Plaza de la Raza Cultural Center, Los Angeles CA

Cantieni, Graham, *Section Head*, University of Quebec, Trois Rivieres, Fine Arts Section, Trois Rivieres PQ (S)

Cantley, John, *Dir*, County of Los Angeles, Century Gallery, Sylmar CA

Cantor, Dorothy, *Cur Educ Servs*, Mattatuck Historical Society, Mattatuck Museum, Waterbury CT

Cantor, Mira, *Asst Prof*, Northeastern University, Dept of Art & Architecture, Boston MA (S)

Cantrell, Carol S, *Admin Human Resources*, The Metropolitan Museum of Art, New York NY

Cantrell, Gary, *Performing Arts Librn*, Adelphi University, Fine & Performing Arts Library, Garden City NY

Cantrell, Jimmy, *Instr*, John C Calhoun State Community College, Department of Fine Arts, Decatur AL (S)

Cantu, Anthony, *Dean*, Fresno City College, Art Dept, Fresno CA (S)

Capawana, Sarah, *Chmn Art Dept*, Mesa Community College, Dept of Art & Art History, Mesa AZ (S)

Capone, John, *Bookkeeper*, Lahaina Arts Society, Art Organization, Lahaina HI

Capote, Melody, *Dir*, Caribbean Cultural Center, Cultural Arts Organization & Resource Center, New York NY

Cappellazzo, Amy, *Gallery Dir*, Miami-Dade Community College, Frances Wolfson Art Gallery, Miami FL

Cappellazzo, Amy, *Gallery Dir*, Miami-Dade Community College, InterAmerican Art Gallery, Miami FL

Cappellazzo, Amy, *Gallery Dir*, Miami-Dade Community College, Wolfson Galleries, Miami FL

Capps, Patricia, *Admin Mgr*, University of California, Los Angeles, UCLA at the Armand Hammer Museum of Art & Cultural Center, Los Angeles CA

Cappuccio, Thomas, *Prof*, Northern Michigan University, Dept of Art & Design, Marquette MI (S)

Capture, George Horse, *Deputy Asst Dir Cultural Resources*, National Museum of the American Indian, George Gustav Heye Center, New York NY

Carbonaro, Richard, *Treas*, Woodmere Art Museum, Philadelphia PA

Carbone, David, *Assoc Prof*, State University of New York at Albany, Art Dept, Albany NY (S)

Carboni, Tamra, *Dir Progs*, Louisiana Department of Culture, Recreation & Tourism, Louisiana State Museum, New Orleans LA

Carden, Marianne, *Visual Resources Librn*, Colonial Williamsburg Foundation, John D Rockefeller, Jr Library, Williamsburg VA

Cardiff, Janet, *Asst Prof*, University of Lethbridge, Div of Art, Lethbridge AB (S)

Cardoni, Edmund, *Dir*, Hallwalls Contemporary Arts Center, Buffalo NY

Carey, Brian, *Dir & Custodian Holdings*, National Archives of Canada, Visual & Sound Archives, Ottawa ON

Carey, Ellen, *Assoc Prof*, University of Hartford, Hartford Art School, West Hartford CT (S)

Carey, Frank, *Technical Servs Librn*, Daemen College, Marian Library, Amherst NY

Carey, John, *Acting Acad Dean*, Tunxis Community College, Graphic Design Dept, Farmington CT (S)

Carey Lester, William, *Prof*, Delta State University, Dept of Art, Cleveland MS (S)

Cargill, Jim, *Chmn*, Black Hills State University, Art Dept, Spearfish SD (S)

Cariolano, Jody, *Asst Prof*, Our Lady of the Lake University, Dept of Art, San Antonio TX (S)

Carl, Joan, *Pres*, LA Art Association, Los Angeles CA

Carlberg, Norman, *Dir*, Maryland Institute, Rinehart School of Sculpture, Baltimore MD (S)

Carlean, E A, *Dir*, Memphis Brooks Museum of Art, Memphis TN

Carlile, Margie, *Office Mgr*, Toledo Artists' Club, Toledo OH

Carlin, Jane, *DAAP Librn*, University of Cincinnati, Design, Architecture, Art & Planning Library, Cincinnati OH

Carline, Gina, *Gift Shop Mgr*, Nelda C & H J Lutcher Stark Foundation, Stark Museum of Art, Orange TX

Carlisle, Elizabeth, *VPres*, Porter-Phelps-Huntington Foundation, Inc, Historic House Museum, Hadley MA

Carlisle, Macleah, *Dir*, Hinckley Foundation Museum, Ithaca NY

Carlisle, Roger, *Assoc Prof*, Arkansas State University, Dept of Art, State University AR (S)

Carlone, Christine, *Cur Architecture*, Library of Congress, Prints & Photographs Division, Washington DC

Carlsgaard, Lynn, *Asst Prof*, Northern State University, Art Dept, Aberdeen SD (S)

Carlson, Denise, *Head Reference Serv*, Minnesota Historical Society, Library, Saint Paul MN

Carlson, Donna, *Dir Admin*, Art Dealers Association of America, Inc, New York NY

Carlson, Eleanor, *Chmn Music Dept*, University of Massachusetts Dartmouth, College of Visual & Performing Arts, North Dartmouth MA (S)

Carlson, Karen, *Exec Dir*, Textile Arts Centre, Chicago IL

Carlson, Kristi, *Chair*, Waldorf College, Art Dept, Forest City IA (S)

Carlson, Lance, *Dean*, Rio Hondo College, Visual Arts Dept, Whittier CA (S)

Carlson, Shala, *Operations Mgr*, Shadows-on-the-Teche, New Iberia LA

Carlson, Victor, *Sr Cur Prints & Drawings*, Los Angeles County Museum of Art, Los Angeles CA

Carlson, William, *In Charge Glass & Sculpture*, University of Illinois, Urbana-Champaign, School of Art & Design, Champaign IL (S)

Carlstrom, Jon, *Building Consultant*, Mankato Area Arts Council, Carnegie Art Center, Mankato MN

Carlton, Caroline, *Librn*, North Carolina State University, Harrye Lyons Design Library, Raleigh NC

Carlton, Lance, *Div Dean*, Rio Hondo College Art Gallery, Whittier CA

Carlton, Rosemary, *Interpretation Specialist*, Alaska Department of Education, Division of Libraries, Archives & Museums, Sheldon Jackson Museum, Sitka AK

Carman, William, *Asst Prof*, Cardinal Stritch College, Art Dept, Milwaukee WI (S)

Carmichael, Lisa, *Office Mgr & Asst to Dir*, Ball State University, Museum of Art, Muncie IN

Carmoney, Pat, *Div Chmn*, Thomas College, Humanities Division, Thomasville GA (S)

Carnes, Sandra, *Chmn Fine Arts*, Malone College, Dept of Art, Canton OH (S)

Carney, Gay, *Dir Educ*, Columbus Museum, Columbus GA

Carns, Janet, *Asst to Dir External Affairs*, Westmoreland Museum of American Art, Greensburg PA

Carol, Jane, *Instr*, Lincoln University, Dept Fine Arts, Jefferson City MO (S)

Carolyn-Gluckman, Dale, *Cur Costumes & Textiles*, Los Angeles County Museum of Art, Los Angeles CA

Caron, Jacqueline, *Dir*, Institut des Arts au Saguenay, Centre National D'Exposition a Jonquiere, Jonquiere PQ

Caron, Linda, *Chmn*, Wright State University, Dept of Art & Art History, Dayton OH (S)

Carothers, Martha, *Chmn*, University of Delaware, Dept of Art, Newark DE (S)

Carothers, Peggy, *Adjunct Instr*, Maryville University of Saint Louis, Art Division, Saint Louis MO (S)

Carp, Richard M, *Chmn, School of Art*, Northern Illinois University, School of Art, De Kalb IL (S)

Carpenter, B Stephen, *Asst Prof Art Educ*, Old Dominion University, Art Dept, Norfolk VA (S)

Carpenter, Cheslie, *Treas*, South County Art Association, Kingston RI

Carpenter, Clair E, *Asst Dir Admin & Information*, Ohio University, Kennedy Museum of American Art, Athens OH

Carpenter, Janice, *Travel Publications Specialist*, Utah Travel Council, Salt Lake City UT

Carpenter, Ken, *Chmn Prof*, York University, Dept of Visual Arts, North York ON (S)

Carpenter, Margot, *Exec Dir*, Aesthetic Realism Foundation, New York NY

Carpenter, Margot, *Exec Dir*, Aesthetic Realism Foundation, New York NY (S)

Carpenter, Mary Jo, *Asst Dir Publications & Spec Projects*, Sterling & Francine Clark Art Institute, Williamstown MA

Carpenter, Richard, *Pres*, John C Calhoun State Community College, Art Gallery, Decatur AL

Carpenter, Syd, *Asst Prof*, Swarthmore College, Dept of Art, Swarthmore PA (S)

Carpenter, Thomas, *Prof*, Virginia Polytechnic Institute & State University, Dept of Art & Art History, Blacksburg VA (S)

Carr, Carol, *Mgr Library Serv*, Hallmark Cards, Inc, Creative Library, Kansas City MO

Carr, Carolyn, *Deputy Dir*, National Portrait Gallery, Washington DC

Carr, Jeffrey, *Assoc Prof*, Saint Mary's College of Maryland, Art Dept, Saint Mary's City MD (S)

Carr, Ken, *Pres*, Owen Sound Historical Society, Marine & Rail Heritage Museum, Owen Sound ON

Carr, Margaret S, *Museum Registrar*, East Tennessee State University, Carroll Reece Museum, Johnson City TN

Carr, Melissa, *Dir*, Daniel Boone Regional Library, Columbia MO

Carracio, Kahleen, *Lectr*, Coe College, Dept of Art, Cedar Rapids IA (S)

Carrageorge, Adrianne, *Asst Prof*, Rochester Institute of Technology, School of Photographic Arts & Sciences, Rochester NY (S)

Carrard, Mary, *Prof*, American University, Dept of Art, Washington DC (S)

Carraro, Francine, *Assoc Prof*, Southwest Texas State University, Dept of Art, San Marcos TX (S)

Carrell, Dan, *Chmn*, Benedictine College, Art Dept, Atchison KS (S)

Carrera, Magali M, *Chmn Art History*, University of Massachusetts Dartmouth, College of Visual & Performing Arts, North Dartmouth MA (S)

Carrero, Jaime, *Dir*, Inter American University of Puerto Rico, Dept of Art, San German PR (S)

Carrico, Anita, *Head*, University of Maryland, College Park, Architecture Library, College Park MD

Carrier, Rock, *Dir*, The Canada Council, Conseil des Arts du Canada, Ottawa ON

Carrington, Mark, *Dir Music*, The Phillips Collection, Washington DC

Carrol, Charles, *Registrar*, Museum of Fine Arts, Houston, Houston TX

Carroll, Ann, *Dir Public Affairs*, Adirondack Historical Association, Adirondack Museum, Blue Mountain Lake NY

Carroll, Charlie, *Dir*, Lake City Community College, Art Dept, Lake City FL (S)

Carroll, David, *Registrar*, University of Utah, Utah Museum of Fine Arts, Salt Lake City UT

Carroll, E A, *Prof*, Vassar College, Art Dept, Poughkeepsie NY (S)

Carroll, James F L, *Dir*, New Arts Program, Inc, Kutztown PA

Carroll, Karen, *Dir*, Maryland Institute, Art Education Graduate Studies, Baltimore MD (S)

Carroll, Lori, *Pub Relations & Exec Asst to Pres*, Cosanti Foundation, Arcosanti, Scottsdale AZ

Carroll, Margaret, *Chmn*, Wellesley College, Art Dept, Wellesley MA (S)

Carroll, Roger, *Div Head*, J Erie Johnson Library, Fine Arts Division, Dallas TX

Carroll, Susan, *Educ Dir*, Adirondack Historical Association, Adirondack Museum, Blue Mountain Lake NY

Carron, Christian, *Cur Coll*, Public Museum of Grand Rapids, Grand Rapids MI

Carroway, Rosemary, *Lectr*, Lambuth University, Dept of Human Ecology & Visual Arts, Jackson TN (S)

Carson, Denise, *Librn*, Bethany College, Library, Lindsborg KS

Carson, JoAnne, *Assoc Prof*, State University of New York at Albany, Art Dept, Albany NY (S)

Carson, Lew, *Prof*, California State University, Hayward, University Art Gallery, Hayward CA

Carson, Nan, *Performing Arts Coordr*, Organization of Saskatchewan Arts Councils (OSAC), Regina SK

Cart, Doran L, *Dir*, Liberty Memorial Museum & Archives, Kansas City MO

Carter, Alice T, *Librn*, Montgomery Museum of Fine Arts, Library, Montgomery AL

Carter, Charles Hill, *Owner*, Shirley Plantation, Charles City VA

Carter, Cooper, *Cur Asst*, Portsmouth Museums, Art Center, Portsmouth VA

Carter, Curtis L, *Dir*, Marquette University, Haggerty Museum of Art, Milwaukee WI

Carter, Curtis L, *Secy-Treas*, American Society for Aesthetics, Edmonton AB

Carter, Greg, *Temporary Asst Prof*, Georgia Southern University, Dept of Art, Statesboro GA (S)

Carter, Harold, *Chmn Dept*, Mansfield University, Art Dept, Mansfield PA (S)

Carter, John S, *Pres*, Independence Seaport Museum, Philadelphia PA

Carter, Joseph, *Dir*, Will Rogers Memorial & Museum, Claremore OK

Carter, Joseph, *Dir*, Will Rogers Memorial & Museum, Media Center Library, Claremore OK

Carter, Keith, *Assoc Prof*, Lamar University, Art Dept, Beaumont TX (S)

Carter, Linda Haag, *Exec Dir*, Art League of Houston, Houston TX

Carter, Lynn, *Dir*, American-Scandinavian Foundation, New York NY

Carter, Mary, *Dir*, Museum of Neon Art, Los Angeles CA

Carter, Nathan, *Dept Chmn*, Morgan State University, Dept of Art, Baltimore MD (S)

Carter, Panchita, *Instr*, Dowling College, Dept of Visual Arts, Oakdale NY (S)

Carter, Patricia, *Temporary Asst Prof*, Georgia Southern University, Dept of Art, Statesboro GA (S)

Carter, Rand, *Instr*, Hamilton College, Art Dept, Clinton NY (S)

Carter, Robert, *Prof*, Nassau Community College, Art Dept, Garden City NY (S)

Carter, Susan, *Cur & Registrar*, University of Tampa, Henry B Plant Museum, Tampa FL

Carter, Thelma, *Pres*, Sitka Historical Society, Isabel Miller Museum, Sitka AK

Carter, Yvonne, *Prof*, University of the District of Columbia, Dept of Mass Media, Visual & Performing Arts, Washington DC (S)

Carter-Carter, Susan, *VPres*, Society of American Graphic Artists, New York NY

Carter Southard, Edna, *Cur Coll*, Miami University, Art Museum, Oxford OH

Carter Stevenson, Ruth, *Chmn Board Trustees*, National Gallery of Art, Washington DC

Cartiere, Cameron, *Cur*, City of San Rafael, Falkirk Cultural Center, San Rafael CA

Cartland, John D, *First VPres*, The Arts Club of Chicago, Chicago IL

Cartmell, Robert, *Assoc Prof*, State University of New York at Albany, Art Dept, Albany NY (S)

Cartmell, Timothy, *Museum Store Mgr*, Board of Parks & Recreation, The Parthenon, Nashville TN

Cartwright, Derrick, *Dir*, University of San Diego, Founders' Gallery, San Diego CA

Cartwright, Guenther, *Assoc Prof*, Rochester Institute of Technology, School of Photographic Arts & Sciences, Rochester NY (S)

Cartwright, Rick, *Assoc Prof*, Saint Francis College, Art Dept, Fort Wayne IN (S)

Cartwright, Roy, *Prof Fine Arts*, University of Cincinnati, School of Art, Cincinnati OH (S)

Caruthers, Robert, *Prof*, West Texas A&M University, Art, Communication & Theatre Dept, Canyon TX (S)

Caruthers, Russell, *Pres*, Waterloo Art Association, Waterloo IA

Carvalho, Mario, *Assoc Dean*, University of Manitoba, Faculty of Architecture, Winnipeg MB (S)

Carver, Dan, *Exec Dir*, Yeiser Art Center Inc, Paducah KY

Carver, Melvin, *Chmn*, North Carolina Central University, Art Dept, Durham NC (S)

Cary, Richard, *Chmn*, Mars Hill College, Art Dept, Mars Hill NC (S)

Casablanca, Carlos, *Dir*, University of Puerto Rico, Mayaguez, Dept of Humanities, College of Arts & Sciences, Mayaguez PR (S)

Casares, Eduardo, *Dir*, Intar Latin American Gallery, New York NY

Cascieri, Arcangelo, *Dean*, Boston Architectural Center, Boston MA

Case, Harold, *Head*, Allan Hancock College, Fine Arts Dept, Santa Maria CA (S)

Case, Rebecca, *Library Asst*, Mount Vernon Ladies' Association of the Union, Library, Mount Vernon VA

Case, Rita, *Marketing Coordr*, Lafayette Natural History Museum, Planetarium & Nature Station, Lafayette LA

Case, Sue G, *Cur*. Mason County Museum, Maysville KY

Cash, G Gerald, *Chmn Fine Arts Div*. Florida Keys Community College, Fine Arts Div, Key West FL (S)

Cash, Sarah, *Exec Dir*. Randolph-Macon Woman's College, Maier Museum of Art, Lynchburg VA

Cashman, Carol, *Instr*. Bismarck State College, Fine Arts Dept, Bismarck ND (S)

Casillas, Marlene Hernandez, *Registrar*. Museo de la Americas, Old San Juan PR

Caskey, Christin, *Asst Prof*. McPherson College, Art Dept, McPherson KS (S)

Caslin, Jean, *Exec Dir*. Houston Center For Photography, Houston TX

Cason, Darrell, *Head Dept*. Wiley College, Dept of Fine Arts, Marshall TX (S)

Casper, Joseph, *Pres*. Caspers, Inc, Art Collection, Tampa FL

Cass, Doug, *Archivist*. Glenbow Museum, Library, Calgary AB

Cassara, Tina, *Prof*. Cleveland Institute of Art, Cleveland OH (S)

Cassel, Valerie, *Asst Dir Exhibitions & Events*. School of the Art Institute of Chicago, Gallery 2, Chicago IL

Cassell, Linda, *Mgr*. Arts Club of Washington, James Monroe House, Washington DC

Casselman, Carol-Ann, *Information Officer*, Ontario Crafts Council, Craft Resource Centre, Toronto ON

Cassidy, Brendan, *Dir*, Princeton University, Index of Christian Art, Princeton NJ

Cassidy, Tim, *Adjunct Asst Prof*, Drew University, Art Dept, Madison NJ (S)

Cassino, Michael, *Prof*, Adrian College, Art & Design Dept, Adrian MI (S)

Cassone, John, *Assoc Prof*. Los Angeles Harbor College, Art Dept, Wilmington CA (S)

Cast, David, *Chmn Dept*, Bryn Mawr College, Dept of the History of Art, Bryn Mawr PA (S)

Castellani, Carla, *Museum Shop*, Niagara University, Castellani Art Museum, Niagara NY

Castelluzzo, Julie, *Electronic Serv*, Cooper Union for the Advancement of Science & Art, Library, New York NY

Castelnuovo, Sheri, *Cur Educ & Public Programming*, Madison Art Center, Madison WI

Casteras, Nancy, *Prog Coordr*, Woodbridge Township Cultural Arts Commission, Barron Arts Center, Woodbridge NJ

Casteras, Susan, *Cur Paintings*, Yale University, Yale Center for British Art, New Haven CT

Castle, Charles, *Assoc Dir*, Museum of Contemporary Art, San Diego, La Jolla CA

Castle, Charles, *Assoc Dir*, Museum of Contemporary Art, San Diego-Downtown, San Diego CA

Castle, Delphine, *Registrar & Technician*, Craigdarroch Castle Historical Museum Society, Victoria BC

Castle, Wendell, *Prof*. Rochester Institute of Technology, School of Art & Design, Rochester NY (S)

Castleberry, May, *Librn & Assoc Cur Spec Coll*, Whitney Museum of American Art, New York NY

Castleberry, May, *Librn*, Whitney Museum of American Art, Library, New York NY

Castleman, Riva, *Chief Cur, Prints & Illustrated Books*, Museum of Modern Art, New York NY

Castonguay, Gerald, *Chmn*, Clark University, Dept of Visual & Performing Arts, Worcester MA (S)

Castriota, David, *Instr*. Sarah Lawrence College, Dept of Art History, Bronxville NY (S)

Castro, Ricardo, *Prof*. McGill University, School of Architecture, Montreal PQ (S)

Caswell, James O, *Head*, University of British Columbia, Dept of Fine Arts, Vancouver BC (S)

Caswell, Lucy Shelton, *Cur*, Ohio State University, Cartoon, Graphic & Photographic Arts Research Library, Columbus OH

Catalano, Laura, *Registrar*, The Buffalo Fine Arts Academy, Albright-Knox Art Gallery, Buffalo NY

Catalina, Lynn, *Dir Marketing*, The University of Texas, Institute of Texan Cultures, San Antonio TX

Cate, Barbara, *Assoc Prof*. Seton Hall University, College of Arts & Sciences, South Orange NJ (S)

Cate, Phillip Dennis, *Dir*. Rutgers, The State University of New Jersey, Jane Voorhees Zimmerli Art Museum, New Brunswick NJ

Cateforts, David, *Asst Prof*. University of Kansas, Kress Foundation Dept of Art History, Lawrence KS (S)

Catherall, Virginia, *Assoc Cur Educ*. University of Utah, Utah Museum of Fine Arts, Salt Lake City UT

Catling, William, *Asst Prof*. Azusa Pacific University, College of Liberal Arts, Art Dept, Azusa CA (S)

Caton, Mary Anne, *Cur*. Agecroft Association, Agecroft Hall, Richmond VA

Caton, Mary Anne, *Cur Coll*. Agecroft Association, Museum, Richmond VA

Catron, Joanna D, *Cur*. Mary Washington College, Belmont, The Gari Melchers, Fredericksburg VA

Catterall, John E, *Chmn*. University of Florida, Dept of Art, Gainesville FL (S)

Caugant, John, *Asst Dir Admin*. Walters Art Gallery, Baltimore MD

Caulkins, Beth, *Co-owner & Creative Dir*. Frank Lloyd Wright Museum, AD German Warehouse, Richland Center WI

Caulkins, Deborah, *Coordr*. Lycoming College Gallery, Williamsport PA

Cauthen, Gene, *Dir Fine Arts Gallery*. Mount Wachusett Community College, Art Galleries, Gardner MA

Cavalier, Joseph, *Prof*. School of the Art Institute of Chicago, Chicago IL (S)

Cavanagh, T, *Assoc Prof*. Technical University of Nova Scotia, Faculty of Architecture, Halifax NS (S)

Cavanaugh, Marianne L, *Assoc Librn*. The Saint Louis Art Museum, Richardson Memorial Library, Saint Louis MO

Cavanaugh, Theresa A, *Pres*. New Rochelle Public Library, New Rochelle Art Association, New Rochelle NY

Caviness, Madeline H, *Prof*. Tufts University, Dept of Art & Art History, Medford MA (S)

Caylor, Lawrence M, *Dir*. Fort Hays State University, Forsyth Library, Hays KS

Cazort, Mimi, *Cur Prints & Drawings*. National Gallery of Canada, Ottawa ON

Cecil, Sarah, *Asst Dir Develop*. Worcester Art Museum, Worcester MA

Cederna, Ann, *Vis Asst Prof*. Catholic University of America, School of Architecture & Planning, Washington DC (S)

Celaya, Enrique Martinez, *Prof*. Pomona College, Dept of Art & Art History, Claremont CA (S)

Celdran, Carlos, *Asst Ad*. Socrates Sculpture Park, Long Island City NY

Celenko, Theodore, *Cur African, S Pacific, Pre-Columbian*, Indianapolis Museum of Art, Indianapolis IN

Celi, Maria, *Adminr*, Dahesh Museum, New York NY

Cembrola, Robert, *Sr Cur*. Naval War College Museum, Newport RI

Cendrowski, Harry, *VPres*. Birmingham-Bloomfield Art Association, Birmingham MI

Cent, Judy, *Head Dept*. Atlanta Area Technical School, Visual Communications Class, Atlanta GA (S)

Center, Williams, *Asst Dir*. Lafayette College, Morris R Williams Center for the Arts, Art Gallery, Easton PA

Centini, Gail, *Exec Dir*. Georgia Volunteer Lawyers for the Arts, Inc, Atlanta GA

Cerny, Charlene, *Dir*. Museum of New Mexico, Museum of International Folk Art, Santa Fe NM

Ceruti, Mary, *Prog Dir*. Capp Street Project, San Francisco CA

Cervantes, James, *Cur Military History*. Heritage Plantation of Sandwich, Sandwich MA

Cetlin, Cynthia, *Assoc Prof*. Ohio Wesleyan University, Fine Arts Dept, Delaware OH (S)

Chabolla, Luis, *Exec Dir*. La Raza-Galeria Posada, Sacramento CA

Chabot, Aurore, *Assoc Prof Ceramics*. University of Arizona, Dept of Art, Tucson AZ (S)

Chacon, Rafael, *Asst Prof*. University of Montana, Dept of Art, Missoula MT (S)

Chadbourne, Janice, *Cur of Fine Arts*. Boston Public Library, Fine Arts Dept, Boston MA

Chadwick-Reid, Ann, *Chmn*. Skagit Valley College, Dept of Art, Mount Vernon WA (S)

Chafe, Anne, *Cur*. The Seagram Museum, Waterloo ON

Chaffee, Tom, *Prof*. Arkansas State University, Dept of Art, State University AR (S)

Chaiken, Paula, *Asst Cur Educ*. Spertus Institute of Jewish Studies, Spertus Museum, Chicago IL

Chait, Andrew, *Secy*. National Antique & Art Dealers Association of America, Inc, New York NY

Chait, Andrew, *Treas*. National Antique & Art Dealers Association of America, Inc, New York NY

Challener, Elizbeth, *Exec Dir*. Montalvo Center for the Arts, Saratoga CA

Chalmers, J Kim, *Chmn*. Coker College, Art Dept, Hartsville SC (S)

Chalniz, Hallie, *Instr*. Rhodes College, Dept of Art, Memphis TN (S)

Chamberland, Alan, *Supt*. Sterling & Francine Clark Art Institute, Williamstown MA

Chamberlin, Emila, *Prog Dir*. Southern Oregon Historical Society, Jacksonville Museum of Southern Oregon History, Medford OR

Chamberlin, Marsha, *Exec Dir*. Ann Arbor Art Association, Art Center, Ann Arbor MI

Chamberlin-Hellman, Maria, *Assoc Prof*. Marymount College, Art Dept, Tarrytown NY (S)

Chambers, Kelly, *Dir Archives*. Jackson County Historical Society, Research Library & Archives, Independence MO

Chambliss, Charles, *Pres*. Arts Council of Richmond, Inc, Richmond VA

Chametzky, Peter, *Asst Prof*. Adelphi University, Dept of Art & Art History, Garden City NY (S)

Champ, Joan, *Archivist*. University of Saskatchewan, Diefenbaker Canada Centre, Saskatoon SK

Champagne, Anne, *Head Technical Servs*. The Art Institute of Chicago, Ryerson & Burnham Libraries, Chicago IL

Champeau, Sylvie, *Dir*. La Societe des Decorateurs-Ensembliers du Quebec, Interior Designers Society of Quebec, Montreal PQ

Chan, Elise, *Cur Coll*. Jefferson County Historical Society, Watertown NY

Chandler, John, *Dir*. Maine Coast Artists, Art Gallery, Rockport ME

Chandler, William L, *Chmn*. University of Wisconsin-Whitewater, Dept of Art, Whitewater WI (S)

Chang, John K, *Records Mgr*. Vancouver City Archives, Vancouver BC

Chanlatte, Luis A, *Archaeologist*, University of Puerto Rico, Museum of Anthropology, History & Art, San Juan PR

Channing, Laurence, *Head Publications*, Cleveland Museum of Art, Cleveland OH

Channing, Susan R, *Dir*. SPACES, Cleveland OH

Chao, Anita, *Admin Coordr*. Franklin Furnace Archive, Inc, New York NY

Chao, Paul, *Assoc Dean*. Seton Hall University, Library, South Orange NJ

Chapin, Mona L, *Head Librn*. Cincinnati Museum Association, Mary R Schiff Library, Cincinnati OH

Chaplock, Sharon Kayne, *Dir Audio-Visual*. Milwaukee Public Museum, Milwaukee WI

Chapman, Gary, *Asst Prof*. University of Alabama at Birmingham, Dept of Art, Birmingham AL (S)

Chapman, Gretel, *Assoc Prof*. Southern Illinois University, School of Art & Design, Carbondale IL (S)

Chapman, Jefferson, *Dir*. University of Tennessee, Frank H McClung Museum, Knoxville TN

Chapman, Jefferson, *Dir*. University of Tennessee, Eleanor Dean Audigier Art Collection, Knoxville TN

Chapman, Joanna, *Pres Board*. Pacific Grove Art Center, Pacific Grove CA

Chapman, Susan, *Instr*. Truett-McConnell College, Fine Arts Dept & Arts Dept, Cleveland GA (S)

Chapman, William, *Treas.* Second Street Gallery, Charlottesville VA

Chapp, Belena S, *Dir.* University of Delaware, University Gallery, Newark DE

Chappell, Berkley, *Prof.* Oregon State University, Dept of Art, Corvallis OR (S)

Chappell, Bonnie, *Pres.* Prince George Art Gallery, Prince George BC

Chappell, Miles, *Prof.* College of William & Mary, Dept of Fine Arts, Williamsburg VA (S)

Charette, Luc, *Dir.* Galerie d'art de l'Universite de Moncton, Moncton NB

Charlap, Peter, *Assoc Prof.* Vassar College, Art Dept, Poughkeepsie NY (S)

Charles, Charles, *Assoc Prof.* University of North Florida, Dept of Communications & Visual Arts, Jacksonville FL (S)

Charles, Ellen MacNeile, *Pres.* Marjorie Merriweather Post Foundation of DC, Hillwood Museum, Washington DC

Charles, Peter, *Assoc Prof.* Georgetown University, Dept of Art, Music & Theatre, Washington DC (S)

Charles, Sophie, *Museum Shop Mgr & Arts & Crafts Dir.* Yugtarvik Regional Museum & Bethel Visitors Center, Bethel AK

Charney, Edward, *Asst Prof.* Wartburg College, Dept of Art, Waverly IA (S)

Charnow, Elliott, *Chmn.* Chabot College, Humanities Division, Hayward CA (S)

Chase, Guy M, *Dir & Cur.* Greenville College, Richard W Bock Sculpture Collection, Greenville IL

Chase, Guy M, *Librn.* Greenville College, The Richard W Bock Sculpture Collection & Art Library, Greenville IL

Chase, Guy M, *Dept Head.* Greenville College, Division of Language, Literature & Fine Arts, Greenville IL (S)

Chase, Linda, *Asst University Librn.* American University, Jack I Dorothy G Bender Library, Washington DC

Chatelain, Gary, *Prof.* James Madison University, School of Art & Art History, Harrisonburg VA (S)

Chatfield Taylor, Adele, *Pres.* American Academy in Rome, New York NY (S)

Chatham, Walter F, *Pres.* Architectural League of New York, New York NY

Chatland, Gordon, *Park Mgr.* Utah Department of Natural Resources, Division of Parks & Recreation, Territorial Statehouse, Fillmore UT

Chatman, Sue, *Ref Librn.* Indianapolis Marion County Public Library, Arts Division, Indianapolis IN

Chatterjee, Sankar, *Cur Vertebrate Paleontology.* Texas Tech University, Museum, Lubbock TX

Chauteau, Suzanne, *Prof.* Xavier University, Dept of Art, Cincinnati OH (S)

Chave, Anna, *Prof.* City University of New York, PhD Program in Art History, New York NY (S)

Chavez, Thomas, *Assoc Dir.* Museum of New Mexico, Palace of Governors, Santa Fe NM

Cheatham, Frank, *Prof.* Texas Tech University, Dept of Art, Lubbock TX (S)

Cheatham, Jane, *Assoc Prof.* Texas Tech University, Dept of Art, Lubbock TX (S)

Cheatham, Richard, *Dean.* Southwest Texas State University, Dept of Art, San Marcos TX (S)

Checefsky, Bruce, *Gallery Dir.* Cleveland Institute of Art, Reinberger Galleries, Cleveland OH

Check, Ed, *Asst Prof.* Texas Tech University, Dept of Art, Lubbock TX (S)

Cheek, Belinda, *Technician.* North Central College, Oesterle Library, Naperville IL

Cheevers, James W, *Sr Cur.* United States Naval Academy Museum, Annapolis MD

Cheff, Michel V, *Dir.* Winnipeg Art Gallery, Winnipeg MB

Chehab, Hafez, *Asst Prof.* State University of New York College at Brockport, Dept of Art, Brockport NY (S)

Chellstrop, Marjorie, *Instr.* Madonna University, Art Dept, Livonia MI (S)

Chen, Abre, *Prog Dir.* Westchester Community College, Westchester Art Workshop, White Plains NY (S)

Chen, Chiong-Yiao, *Asst Prof.* University of North Alabama, Dept of Art, Florence AL (S)

Chen, Lynn, *Librn.* American Numismatic Association, Library, Colorado Springs CO

Chen, Michael, *Instr.* Joe Kubert School of Cartoon & Graphic Art, Inc, Dover NJ (S)

Chen, Suzy, *Fine Arts Librn.* Beverly Hills Public Library, Fine Arts Library, Beverly Hills CA

Chen-Courtin, Dorothy, *Dir Marketing.* Peabody Essex Museum, Salem MA

Cheng, Albert, *Pres.* Chinese Culture Foundation, Chinese Culture Center Gallery, San Francisco CA

Cheng, Jane, *Sr Oriental Cataloger.* Nelson-Atkins Museum of Art, Spencer Art Reference Library, Kansas City MO

Chenoweth, Marjorie, *Library Dir.* Maryland Institute, Decker Library, Baltimore MD

Chepp, Mark, *Dir.* Springfield Museum of Art, Library, Springfield OH

Chepp, Mark, *Dir.* Springfield Museum of Art, Springfield OH (S)

Chepp, Mark J, *Dir.* Springfield Museum of Art, Springfield OH

Chermayeff, Ivan, *Art Consultant.* Mobil Corporation, Art Collection, Fairfax VA

Chervenie, Paul B, *Dir Library.* College of Saint Elizabeth, Mahoney Library, Morristown NJ

Chervrier, Herbert, *Chmn.* United Westurne Inc, Art Collection, Montreal PQ

Chesbrough, David, *Dir.* Roberson Museum & Science Center, Binghamton NY

Cheshire, Craig, *Prof.* Portland State University, Dept of Art, Portland OR (S)

Chesser, Bruce, *Chmn.* Ohio Northern University, Dept of Art, Ada OH (S)

Chester, Kay, *Treas.* Lyme Art Association, Inc, Old Lyme CT

Chester, Timothy J, *Dir.* Public Museum of Grand Rapids, Grand Rapids MI

Chevian, Margaret, *Specialist.* Providence Public Library, Art & Music Services, Providence RI

Chew, Ron, *Dir.* Wing Luke Asian Museum, Seattle WA

Cheyno, Susan, *Co-Dir.* McGroarty Cultural Art Center, Tujunga CA (S)

Chibnik, Kitty, *Assoc Dir.* Columbia University, Avery Architectural & Fine Arts Library, New York NY

Chiburis, Nick J, *Prof Art.* Iowa Western Community College, Art Dept, Council Bluffs IA (S)

Chickanzeff, Sharon, *Dir.* New York University, Stephen Chan Library of Fine Arts, New York NY

Chickering, F William, *Dean.* Pratt Institute Library, Art & Architecture Dept, Brooklyn NY

Chieffo, Beverly, *Instr.* Albertus Magnus College, Art Dept, New Haven CT (S)

Chieffo, Clifford T, *Cur.* Georgetown University, Art & History Museum, Washington DC

Chieffo, Patricia H, *Assoc Cur.* Georgetown University, Art & History Museum, Washington DC

Chiego, William J, *Dir.* Marion Koogler McNay Art Museum, San Antonio TX

Chiesa, Wilfredo, *Assoc Prof.* University of Massachusetts - Boston, Art Dept, Boston MA (S)

Chiger, Eleanor, *Office Mgr.* Yeshiva University Museum, New York NY

Chijioke, Mary Ellen, *Cur.* Swarthmore College, Friends Historical Library of Swarthmore College, Swarthmore PA

Child, Abigail, *Instr.* Sarah Lawrence College, Dept of Art History, Bronxville NY (S)

Child, Kent, *Gallery Advisor & Humanities Div Dir.* Gavilan College, Art Gallery, Gilroy CA

Childers, Ann, *Southern Illinois Representative.* American Society of Artists, Inc, Chicago IL

Childers, Martha P, *Assoc Librn Technical Servs.* Nelson-Atkins Museum of Art, Spencer Art Reference Library, Kansas City MO

Childs, Bruce, *Assoc Prof.* Austin Peay State University, Dept of Art, Clarksville TN (S)

Childs, William A P, *Chmn Prog in Classical Archaeology.* Princeton University, Dept of Art & Archaeology, Princeton NJ (S)

Chilla, Benigna, *Instr.* Berkshire Community College, Dept of Fine Arts, Pittsfield MA (S)

Chillman, Helen, *Slide & Photograph.* Yale University, Art & Architecture Library, New Haven CT

Chilton, Meredith, *Cur.* George R Gardiner Museum of Ceramic Art, Toronto ON

Chin, Cecilia, *Chief Librn.* National Museum of American Art, Library of the National Museum of American Art & the National Portrait Gallery, Washington DC

Chin, Cecilia H, *Chief Librn.* National Portrait Gallery, Library, Washington DC

Chin, Wanda W, *Coordr Exhib & Exhib Designer.* University of Alaska, Museum, Fairbanks AK

Chinn, Cassie, *Exhibit Coordr.* Wing Luke Asian Museum, Seattle WA

Chinn, Michael, *Chmn.* Central Washington University, Dept of Art, Ellensburg WA (S)

Chipley, Sheila M, *Asst Prof.* Concord College, Fine Art Division, Athens WV (S)

Chiss, Judy, *Assoc Exec Dir.* Chicago Children's Museum, Chicago IL

Chiu, Fabiana, *Deputy Dir.* Museum of Chinese in the Americas, New York NY

Chmel, Patrick, *Chmn.* Rider College, Dept of Fine Arts, Lawrenceville NJ (S)

Chmielewski, Wendy, *Cur Peace Collection.* Swarthmore College, Friends Historical Library of Swathmore College, Swarthmore PA

Choate, Jerry, *Instr.* Northwestern State university, Tahlequah OK (S)

Chodkowski, Henry J, *Prof.* University of Louisville, Allen R Hite Art Institute, Louisville KY (S)

Choen, Lewis, *Asst Prof.* College of William & Mary, Dept of Fine Arts, Williamsburg VA (S)

Chojecki, Randolph, *Ref Librn.* Daemen College, Marian Library, Amherst NY

Choo, Chunghi, *Prof Metalsmithing & Jewelry.* University of Iowa, School of Art & Art History, Iowa City IA (S)

Chouinard, Denis, *Pres.* La Societe des Decorateurs-Ensembliers du Quebec, Interior Designers Society of Quebec, Montreal PQ

Chouinard, Gaetan, *Dir Admin.* Musee du Quebec, Quebec PQ

Chouinard, Terry, *Resident Letter Press.* Pyramid Atlantic, Riverdale MD

Chow, Alan, *Exec Dir.* Chinese-American Arts Council, New York NY

Chow, David, *Instr.* Columbia University, School of the Arts, Division of Visual Arts, New York NY (S)

Chrisman, Diane J, *Deputy Dir Public Services.* Buffalo & Erie County Public Library, Buffalo NY

Chrisman, George, *Dir.* Avila College, Thornhill Art Gallery, Kansas City MO

Christ, Ronald, *Graduate Coordr.* Wichita State University, School of Art & Design, Wichita KS (S)

Christensen, George C, *Pres.* Octagon Center for the Arts, Ames IA

Christensen, V A, *Prof.* Missouri Southern State College, Dept of Art, Joplin MO (S)

Christenson, Edwin, *Asst Prof.* Elmira College, Art Dept, Elmira NY (S)

Christenson, Elroy, *Head Dept.* North Seattle Community College, Art Dept, Seattle WA (S)

Christian, Roger, *Instr.* Southwest Texas State University, Dept of Art, San Marcos TX (S)

Christiana, David, *Assoc Prof Graphic Design-Illustration.* University of Arizona, Dept of Art, Tucson AZ (S)

Christison, Muriel, *Lectr.* College of William & Mary, Dept of Fine Arts, Williamsburg VA (S)

Christman, David C, *Dir.* Hofstra University, Hofstra Museum, Hempstead NY

Christman, George, *Instr.* Avila College, Art Division, Dept of Humanities, Kansas City MO (S)

Christoforidis, Sandra, *Dir.* Wistariahurst Museum, Holyoke MA

Christopher, Theresa, *Registrar.* DuSable Museum of African American History, Chicago IL

Christovich, Mary Louise, *Pres of Board.* Kemper & Leila Williams Foundation, New Orleans LA

Chu, Petra, *Chmn*, Seton Hall University, College of Arts & Sciences, South Orange NJ (S)

Chu, Petrateu Doesschate, *Dir*, Seton Hall University, South Orange NJ

Chudzik, Theresa, *Instr*, Hibbing Community College, Art Dept, Hibbing MN (S)

Chumley, Jere, *Assoc Prof*, Cleveland State Community College, Dept of Art, Cleveland TN (S)

Chung, Robert Y, *Asst Prof*, Rochester Institute of Technology, School of Printing, Rochester NY (S)

Chupa, Anna, *Asst Prof*, Mississippi State University, Art Dept, Mississippi State MS (S)

Church, Elizabeth, *Assoc Prof*, Norwich University, Dept of Philosophy, Religion & Fine Arts, Northfield VT (S)

Church, John, *Instr*, Interlochen Arts Academy, Dept of Visual Art, Interlochen MI (S)

Church, Sara, *Exec Asst*, SLA Arch-Couture Inc, Art Collection, Denver CO

Churches, Roger, *Prof*, La Sierra University, Art Dept, Riverside CA (S)

Churchill, Angiola, *Co-Dir*, International Center for Advanced Studies in Art, New York NY

Churchill, Angiola R, *Prof*, New York University, Dept of Art & Art Professions, New York NY (S)

Churchuan, Michael, *Dir Capital Campaign*, Nelson-Atkins Museum of Art, Kansas City MO

Churdar, Janice, *Staff Supvr*, Bob Jones University, Museum & Art Gallery, Greenville SC

Chytilo, Lynne, *Asst Prof*, Albion College, Dept of Visual Arts, Albion MI (S)

Ciampa, John, *Chmn American Video Institute*, Rochester Institute of Technology, School of Photographic Arts & Sciences, Rochester NY (S)

Cianfoni, Emilio, *Chief Conservator*, Vizcaya Museum & Gardens, Miami FL

Ciatto, Deana, *Dir Membership*, The Phillips Collection, Washington DC

Ciccone, Amy Navratil, *Head Librn*, University of Southern California, Helen Topping Architecture & Fine Arts Library, Los Angeles CA

Cichy, Barbara, *Instr*, Bismarck State College, Fine Arts Dept, Bismarck ND (S)

Cicierski, Eernie, *Exec Dir*, Ukrainian Cultural & Educational Centre, Winnipeg MB

Cicotello, Louis, *Chmn*, University of Colorado-Colorado Springs, Fine Arts Dept, Colorado Springs CO (S)

Cigliano, Flavia, *Exec Dir*, Whistler House Museum of Art, Lowell MA

Cikovsky, Nicholai, *Cur American Art*, National Gallery of Art, Washington DC

Cilella, Salvatore G, *Dir*, Columbia Museum of Art, Columbia SC

Cilella, Salvatore G, *Dir*, Columbia Museum of Art, Columbia Art Association, Columbia SC

Cimerman, Sue, *Admin Asst*, Florida Gulf Coast Art Center, Inc, Belleair FL

Cinelli, Michael J, *Head Dept*, Northern Michigan University, Dept of Art & Design, Marquette MI (S)

Cino, John, *Chmn Board Dir*, Cultural Council Foundation, Fourteen Sculptors Gallery, New York NY

Ciofalo, John, *Asst Prof*, Indiana University, Bloomington, Henry Radford Hope School of Fine Arts, Bloomington IN (S)

Cipriano, M, *Chmn Dept*, Central Connecticut State University, Dept of Art, New Britain CT (S)

Cirone, Christie, *Instr*, Illinois Central College, Dept of Fine Arts, East Peoria IL (S)

Citron, Harvey, *Instr*, New York Academy of Art, Graduate School of Figurative Art, New York NY (S)

Citty, Betty, *Admin Sec*, North Carolina State University, Chinqua-Penn Plantation House, Garden & Greenhouses, Reidsville NC

Clabaugh, John, *Assoc Prof*, Nebraska Wesleyan University, Art Dept, Lincoln NE (S)

Clahassey, Patricia, *Prof*, College of Saint Rose, Dept of Art, Albany NY (S)

Clair, Mike, *Dir*, Newfoundland Museum, Saint John's NF

Clampitt, Susan, *Deputy Chmn Prog*, National Endowment for the Arts, Washington DC

Clancy, Patrick, *Chmn Photo*, Kansas City Art Institute, Kansas City MO (S)

Clapp, Anne, *Prof*, Wellesley College, Art Dept, Wellesley MA (S)

Clapper, Peter, *Instr*, Woodstock School of Art, Inc, Woodstock NY (S)

Clarien, Gary, *Workshop Supv*, Palo Alto Cultural Center, Palo Alto CA

Clark, Andrea, *Registrar*, Norton Simon Museum, Pasadena CA

Clark, Ann, *Asst Prof*, East Tennessee State University, Dept of Art & Design, Johnson City TN (S)

Clark, Bob, *Head Librn & Archivist*, Montana Historical Society, Library, Helena MT

Clark, Bob, *Head Dept*, Southwestern Community College, Commercial Art & Advertising Design Dept, Sylva NC (S)

Clark, Bruce, *VPres for Mgt*, Meridian International Center, Cafritz Galleries, Washington DC

Clark, Elizabeth, *Curatorial Asst (Art)*, University of Calgary, The Nickle Arts Museum, Calgary AB

Clark, Erica, *Dir Develop*, The Museum of Contemporary Art, Los Angeles CA

Clark, Gary F, *Asst Prof*, Bloomsburg University, Dept of Art, Bloomsburg PA (S)

Clark, Gregor, *Project Mgr*, Public Art Fund, Inc, New York NY

Clark, James, *Exec Dir*, Clay Studio, Philadelphia PA

Clark, James M, *Chmn*, Blackburn College, Dept of Art, Carlinville IL (S)

Clark, Jennifer, *Public Serv Intern*, Broward County Board of Commissioners Cultural Affairs Divison, Fort Lauderdale FL

Clark, Joan, *Head Main Library*, Cleveland Public Library, Fine Arts & Special Collections Dept, Cleveland OH

Clark, John B, *Dir*, The Bruce Museum, Greenwich CT

Clark, John B, *Dir*, Lakeview Museum of Arts & Sciences, Peoria IL

Clark, Jon, *Chmn Crafts*, Temple University, Tyler School of Art, Philadelphia PA (S)

Clark, Joyce, *Cur Asst*, Regina Public Library, Dunlop Art Gallery, Regina SK

Clark, Joyce, *Instr*, Monterey Peninsula College, Art Dept, Monterey CA (S)

Clark, Kim, *Pres*, Owatonna Arts Center, Community Arts Center, Owatonna MN

Clark, Kimball, *Cataloger*, National Portrait Gallery, Library, Washington DC

Clark, Laurie Beth, *Assoc Prof*, University of Wisconsin, Madison, Dept of Art, Madison WI (S)

Clark, Lynda K, *Dir*, South Dakota State University, South Dakota Art Museum, Brookings SD

Clark, Michael, *Chmn*, Elmira College, Art Dept, Elmira NY (S)

Clark, Michelle, *Asst Cur*, Longfellow National Historic Site, Cambridge MA

Clark, Moira, *Instr*, Toronto School of Art, Toronto ON (S)

Clark, Nick, *Cur American Art*, Chrysler Museum Of Art, Norfolk VA

Clark, Pam, *Gift Adminr*, University of Lethbridge, Art Gallery, Lethbridge AB

Clark, Peter P, *Registrar*, National Baseball Hall of Fame & Museum, Inc, Art Collection, Cooperstown NY

Clark, R, *Chmn*, Community College of Rhode Island, Dept of Art, Warwick RI (S)

Clark, Raymond R, *Chmn Cincinnati Inst Fine Arts & Mus Comt*, Cincinnati Institute of Fine Arts, Taft Museum, Cincinnati OH

Clark, Raymond R, *Chmn Board & Pres*, Cincinnati Institute of Fine Arts, Cincinnati OH

Clark, Rebecca, *Chairwoman*, Community College of Rhode Island, Art Department Gallery, Warwick RI

Clark, Richard, *Cur Design*, United States Military Academy, West Point Museum, West Point NY

Clark, R J, *Prof*, Princeton University, Dept of Art & Archaeology, Princeton NJ (S)

Clark, Ron, *Independent Study Prog Dir*, Whitney Museum of American Art, New York NY

Clark, Sara B, *Adjunct Instr*, Saginaw Valley State University, Dept of Art & Design, University Center MI (S)

Clark, Tommy, *Asst Prof*, Campbellsville College, Fine Arts Division, Campbellsville KY (S)

Clark, William, *Asst Prof*, Cedar Crest College, Art Dept, Allentown PA (S)

Clark, Willy, *Prof*, Shoreline Community College, Humanities Division, Seattle WA (S)

Clarke, Allan, *Exhib Officer*, Newfoundland Museum, Saint John's NF

Clarke, Ann, *Prof*, Lakehead University, Dept of Visual Arts, Thunder Bay ON (S)

Clarke, Cecilia C, *Exec Dir Develop & Admin*, Skowhegan School of Painting & Sculpture, New York NY (S)

Clarke, Eugenia, *Archivist*, Planting Fields Foundation, Coe Hall at Planting Fields Arboretum, Oyster Bay NY

Clarke, Jude, *Art Educ*, Vernon Art Gallery, Vernon BC

Clarke, Mary V, *Asst Cur*, Mason County Museum, Maysville KY

Clarke, Robert, *Asst Prof*, Mohawk Valley Community College, Advertising Design & Production, Utica NY (S)

Clarkin, William, *Librn & Archivist*, Print Club of Albany, Albany NY

Clark-Langager, Sarah, *Dir*, Western Washington University, Western Gallery, Bellingham WA

Clark-Stone, Lynn, *Museum Shop Mgr*, Frederic Remington Art Museum, Ogdensburg NY

Clary, Morse, *Art Dept Chmn*, Columbia Basin College, Esvelt Gallery, Pasco WA (S)

Clausen, Charles, *Coll Mgr*, Hartwick College, Foreman Gallery, Oneonta NY

Claussen, Louise Keith, *Dir*, Morris Museum of Art, Augusta GA

Clavir, Miriam, *Conservator*, University of British Columbia, Museum of Anthropology, Vancouver BC

Claxton-Oldfield, Patricia, *Librn*, The Robert McLaughlin Gallery, Library, Oshawa ON

Clay, Carol Wolfe, *Chmn*, Seattle University, Fine Arts Dept, Division of Art, Seattle WA (S)

Clay, Joe, *Exec Dir*, Koshare Indian Museum, Inc, La Junta CO

Clay, Joe, *Exec Dir*, Koshare Indian Museum, Inc, Library, La Junta CO

Clay, Vaughn, *Gallery Dir*, Indiana University of Pennsylvania, Kipp Gallery, Indiana PA

Clay, Vaughn, *Instr*, Indiana University of Pennsylvania, Dept of Art & Art Education, Indiana PA (S)

Clayden, Stephen, *Natural Sciences-Botany*, New Brunswick Museum, Saint John NB

Clayson, Hollis, *Assoc Prof*, Northwestern University, Evanston, Dept of Art History, Evanston IL (S)

Claytor, Pat, *Admin Dir*, National Institute of Art & Disabilities (NIAD), Richmond CA

Cleary, John R, *Assoc Prof*, Salisbury State University, Art Dept, Salisbury MD (S)

Cleary, Manon, *Coordr*, University of the District of Columbia, Dept of Mass Media, Visual & Performing Arts, Washington DC (S)

Cleaver, J D, *Cur of Coll*, Oregon Historical Society, Portland OR

Cleland, Camille, *Asst Dir for Technical Servs*, Skokie Public Library, Skokie IL

Clem, Debra, *Assoc Prof*, Indiana University-Southeast, Fine Arts Dept, New Albany IN (S)

Clemans, Chuck, *Chmn*, Regional Arts & Culture Council, Metropolitan Center for Public Arts, Portland OR

Clemans, H, *Instr*, Golden West College, Visual Art Dept, Huntington Beach CA (S)

Clemenson, Gay, *Dir*, Jackson County Historical Society, The 1859 Jail, Marshal's Home & Museum, Independence MO

Clement, Constance, *Asst Dir*, Yale University, Yale Center for British Art, New Haven CT

Clement, Louise, *Instr*, Samuel S Fleisher Art Memorial, Philadelphia PA (S)

Clement, Nathan, *Instr*, Indiana Wesleyan University, Art Dept, Marion IN (S)

Clement, Rika, *Assoc Dir Develop & Membership*, Danforth Museum of Art, Framingham MA

Clement, Winifred, *Registrar*, Springfield Art Museum, Springfield MO

Clementi, Bobbie, *Prof*, Daytona Beach Community College, Dept of Fine Arts & Visual Arts, Daytona Beach FL (S)

Clements, Brian, *Instructional Aide*, Victor Valley College, Art Dept, Victorville CA (S)

Clements, Kitty, *VPres*, Key West Art & Historical Society, East Martello Museum & Gallery, Key West FL

Clements, Martin, *Instr*, New York Institute of Technology, Fine Arts Dept, Old Westbury NY (S)

Cleminshaw, Doug, *Asst Prof*, Rochester Institute of Technology, School of Art & Design, Rochester NY (S)

Clemmer, Joel, *Library Dir*, MacAlester College, DeWitt Wallace Library, Saint Paul MN

Clemmons, Sarah, *Dean Fine Arts Div*, Chipola Junior College, Dept of Fine & Performing Arts, Marianna FL (S)

Clendenin, Paula, *Asst Prof*, West Virginia State College, Art Dept, Institute WV (S)

Clerk, Bryon, *Prof*, University of Idaho, College of Art & Architecture, Moscow ID (S)

Clermont, Ghislain, *Chmn*, Universite de Moncton, Dept of Visual Arts, Moncton NB (S)

Clervi, Paul, *Chmn*, William Woods-Westminster Colleges, Art Dept, Fulton MO (S)

Clevand, Hiliary P, *Pres*, New Hampshire Historical Society, Concord NH

Clevenger, Sara Beth, *Prof*, McMurry University, Art Dept, Abilene TX (S)

Cleverdon, John H, *Acting Chmn*, University of South Alabama, Ethnic American Slide Library, Mobile AL

Cleverdon, John H, *Chmn & Printmaker*, University of South Alabama, Dept of Art & Art History, Mobile AL (S)

Clevett, Don, *Asst Dir Exhibits & Visitor Servs*, Department of Community Development, Provincial Museum of Alberta, Edmonton AB

Clews, Christopher S, *Pres*, La Napoule Art Foundation, Portsmouth NH

Cleyne, Patricia, *Instr*, Pacific University in Oregon, Arts Div, Dept of Art, Forest Grove OR (S)

Clich, Carol, *Exec Secy & Operations Mgr*, Mingei International, Inc, Mingei International Museum Satellite of World Folk Art, San Diego CA

Cliff, Denis, *Instr*, Toronto School of Art, Toronto ON (S)

Clifford, Christina, *Librn*, San Diego Public Library, Art & Music Section, San Diego CA

Cline, Holly, *Instr*, University of Charleston, Carleton Varney Dept of Art & Design, Charleston WV (S)

Cline-Cordonier, Susan, *Pres*, North Carolina State University, Chinqua-Penn Plantation House, Garden & Greenhouses, Reidsville NC

Clinger, Catherine, *Prof*, New Mexico Highlands University, Dept of Communications & Fine Arts, Las Vegas NM (S)

Clinger, Melinda, *Admin Asst*, Fulton County Historical Society Inc, Fulton County Museum, Rochester IN

Clinkingbeard, Brian, *Cur*, Kentucky Art & Craft Gallery, Louisville KY

Close, John, *Instr*, Harriet FeBland Art Workshop, New York NY (S)

Close, Tim, *Exec Dir*, Albany Museum of Art, Albany GA

Cloudman, Ruth, *Cur*, J B Speed Art Museum, Louisville KY

Clough, J, *Instr*, Western Illinois University, Art Dept, Macomb IL (S)

Clouten, Neville, *Dean*, Lawrence Technological University, College of Architecture, Southfield MI (S)

Cloutier, Nadine, *Pres*, Hartland Art Council, Hartland MI

Cloutier, Nicole, *Dir*, Artexte Information & Documentation Centre, Montreal PQ

Cloutier, Therese, *Dir*, Maison Saint-Gabriel Museum, Montreal PQ

Clovis, John, *Prof*, Fairmont State College, Division of Fine Arts, Fairmont WV (S)

Clubb, Barbara, *Dir*, Ottawa Public Library, Fine Arts Dept, Ottawa ON

Cluse, Nancy, *Instr*, Grand Rapids Community College, Art Dept, Grand Rapids MI (S)

Clymer, Frances, *Librn*, Buffalo Bill Memorial Association, Buffalo Bill Historical Center, Cody WY

Clymer, Frances, *Acting Librn*, Buffalo Bill Memorial Association, Harold McCracken Research Library, Cody WY

Clymer, Steve, *Pres*, Lincoln Arts Council, Lincoln NE

Coady, Wanda, *VPres*, International Society of Marine Painters, Oneco FL

Coaston, Shirley, *Art Librn*, Laney College Library, Art Section, Oakland CA

Coates, Ann S, *Cur Slides*, University of Louisville, Slide Collection, Louisville KY

Coates, Darcy, *Registrar*, University of Vermont, Robert Hull Fleming Museum, Burlington VT

Coates, James, *Assoc Prof*, University of Massachusetts Lowell, Dept of Art, Lowell MA (S)

Coates, Sue S, *Head Dept*, Mississippi University for Women, Division of Fine & Performing Arts, Columbus MS (S)

Coats, Bruce, *Chmn Dept*, Scripps College, Millard Sheets Art Center, Claremont CA (S)

Cobb, Beth, *Receptionist & Tour Coordr*, University of Missouri, Museum of Art & Archaeology, Columbia MO

Cobb, Henry Ives, *VChmn Emeritus*, Museum of Modern Art, New York NY

Cobb, June, *Gen Servs*, Museum of Our National Heritage, Lexington MA

Cobb, Stanley, *Art Instr*, Phillips County Community College, Dept of English & Fine Arts, Helena AR (S)

Cobbs, David, *Chmn*, Compton Community College, Art Dept, Compton CA (S)

Coburn, Oakley H, *Dir*, Wofford College, Sandor Teszler Library Gallery, Spartanburg SC

Cocaougher, Robert L, *Assoc Prof*, University of North Florida, Dept of Communications & Visual Arts, Jacksonville FL (S)

Cocchiarelli, Maria, *Cur Educ*, University of Wyoming, University of Wyoming Art Museum, Laramie WY

Cochran, Dorothy, *Cur*, The Interchurch Center, Galleries at the Interchurch Center, New York NY

Cochran, Dorothy, *Dir & Cur Galleries*, The Interchurch Center, The Interchurch Center, New York NY

Cochran, Marie, *Asst Prof*, Georgia Southern University, Dept of Art, Statesboro GA (S)

Cochran, Michael, *Dir*, Sculpture Center Gallery & School, New York NY (S)

Cochran, Michael, *School Dir*, Sculpture Center School & Studios, New York NY

Cochran, Michael, *School Dir*, Sculpture Center School & Studios, Gallery, New York NY

Cochran, Patricia, *Comptroller*, Museum of African Art, New York NY

Cochran, Virginia, *Public Relations*, Santa Barbara Museum of Art, Santa Barbara CA

Cochrane, Virginia, *Pres*, Santa Cruz Valley Art Association, Tubac Center of the Arts, Tubac AZ

Cockhill, Brian, *Dir*, Montana Historical Society, Helena MT

Cockhill, Brian, *Dir*, Montana Historical Society, Library, Helena MT

Cockrell, Lila, *Dir Development*, San Antonio Museum of Art, San Antonio TX

Codding, Mitchell A, *Dir*, Hispanic Society of America, Museum, New York NY

Codell, Julie, *Dir*, Arizona State University, School of Art, Tempe AZ (S)

Codo, Norman, *Pres*, Boca Raton Museum of Art, Boca Raton FL

Cody, Donna, *Pres*, Art Association of Jacksonville, David Strawn Art Gallery, Jacksonville IL

Coe, Henry H R, *Chmn*, Buffalo Bill Memorial Association, Buffalo Bill Historical Center, Cody WY

Coerper, Dewey, *Instr*, Milwaukee Area Technical College, Graphic Arts Division, Milwaukee WI (S)

Coffey, John, *Acting Chief Cur*, North Carolina Museum of Art, Raleigh NC

Coffin, David, *Pres*, Old State House, Hartford CT

Coffman, Rebecca L, *Asst Prof*, Huntington College, Art Dept, Huntington IN (S)

Coffman, Terrence J, *Pres*, Milwaukee Institute of Art & Design, Milwaukee WI (S)

Cogan, Nelly Bly, *Exhib*, Fitton Center For Creative Arts, Hamilton OH

Cogan, Nelly Bly, *Exhibitions*, Fitton Center for Creative Arts, Hamilton OH (S)

Cogar, William B, *Dir*, United States Naval Academy Museum, Annapolis MD

Cogar, William B, *Dir*, United States Naval Academy Museum, Library, Annapolis MD

Coggin, Rosalie, *Instr*, University of Texas at Tyler, Dept of Art, Tyler TX (S)

Cogswell, Arnold, *Exec Dir*, Hickory Museum of Art, Inc, Hickory NC

Cohalan, Mary Lou, *Exec Dir*, Islip Art Museum, East Islip NY

Cohan, Allan L, *Chmn*, Ulster County Community College, Muroff-Kotler Visual Arts Gallery, Stone Ridge NY

Cohen, Allan, *Head Dept*, Ulster County Community College, Dept of Visual Arts, Stone Ridge NY (S)

Cohen, Andrew, *Assoc Prof*, University of Central Arkansas, Art Dept, Conway AR (S)

Cohen, Corey, *Gallery Bookstore Mgr*, San Francisco Camerawork Inc, San Francisco CA

Cohen, David, *Exec Dir*, Salem Art Association, Salem OR

Cohen, David, *Exec Dir*, Salem Art Association, Bush Barn Art Center, Salem OR

Cohen, Janie, *Cur*, University of Vermont, Robert Hull Fleming Museum, Burlington VT

Cohen, Madeline, *Assoc Prof*, Philadelphia Community College, Dept of Art, Philadelphia PA (S)

Cohen, Marcia R, *Prof*, Atlanta College of Art, Atlanta GA (S)

Cohen, Marvin, *Pres*, National Assembly of State Arts Agencies, Washington DC

Cohen, Meryl, *Registrar*, Drawing Center, New York NY

Cohen, Mildred Thaler, *Dir*, The Marbella Gallery Inc, New York NY

Cohen, Rosalie, *Dir of Sales*, Cleveland Center for Contemporary Art, Cleveland OH

Cohen, Sarah, *Art Historian*, University at Albany, State University of New York, Art Dept Slide Library, Albany NY

Cohen, Sarah, *Asst Prof*, State University of New York at Albany, Art Dept, Albany NY (S)

Cohen, Ted, *Pres*, American Society for Aesthetics, Edmonton AB

Cohn, Anna, *Dir Traveling Exhib Serv*, Smithsonian Institution, Washington DC

Cohn, Marjorie B, *Cur Prints*, Harvard University, William Hayes Fogg Art Museum, Cambridge MA

Cohn, Shelley, *Exec Dir*, Arizona Commission on the Arts, Phoenix AZ

Cohodas, Marvin, *Assoc Prof*, University of British Columbia, Dept of Fine Arts, Vancouver BC (S)

Cohon, Robert, *Cur Ancient Art*, Nelson-Atkins Museum of Art, Kansas City MO

Coiner, Maynard R, *Prof*, Concord College, Fine Art Division, Athens WV (S)

Coish, Terry, *Dir*, New Bedford Free Public Library, Art Dept, New Bedford MA

Colaguori, Louis, *VPres*, Burlington County Historical Society, Burlington NJ

Colangelo, Carmon, *Chmn*, West Virginia University, College of Creative Arts, Morgantown WV (S)

Colanoelo, Nicole, *Public Relations Officer*, Fraunces Tavern Museum, New York NY

Colaricci, Susan P, *Registrar*, Evansville Museum of Arts & Science, Evansville IN

Colarusso, Corrine, *Assoc Prof*, Atlanta College of Art, Atlanta GA (S)

Colbert, Cynthia, *Chmn Art Educ*, University of South Carolina, Dept of Art, Columbia SC (S)

Colburn, Bolton, *Cur Colls*, Laguna Art Museum of the Orange County Museum of Art, Laguna Beach CA

Colburn, Richard, *Assoc Prof,* University of Northern Iowa, Dept of Art, Cedar Falls IA (S)

Colby, Gary, *Photography,* University of La Verne, Dept of Art, La Verne CA (S)

Cole, Bruce, *Prof,* Indiana University, Bloomington, Henry Radford Hope School of Fine Arts, Bloomington IN (S)

Cole, Carol, *Instr,* Main Line Art Center, Haverford PA (S)

Cole, Charlene, *Dir Library Services,* Tougaloo College, Coleman Library, Tougaloo MS

Cole, Charles T, *Exec VPres,* Wachovia Bank of South Carolina, Columbia SC

Cole, Charlie, *VPres,* Columbia Museum of Art, Columbia SC

Cole, Dorothy Orr, *Pres,* The National Society of The Colonial Dames of America in the State of New Hampshire, Moffatt-Ladd House, Portsmouth NH

Cole, Harold D, *Chmn Div,* Baldwin-Wallace College, Dept of Art, Berea OH (S)

Cole, Herbert M, *Adjunct Cur Ethnic Art,* University of California, Santa Barbara, University Art Museum, Santa Barbara CA

Cole, Michael, *Instr,* De Anza College, Creative Arts Division, Cupertino CA (S)

Cole, Paul, *Supt,* Roosevelt-Vanderbilt National Historic Sites, Hyde Park NY

Cole, Robert A, *Prof,* Rochester Institute of Technology, School of Art & Design, Rochester NY (S)

Cole, Steve, *Assoc Prof,* Birmingham-Southern College, Art Dept, Birmingham AL (S)

Cole, Theresa, *Prof,* Tulane University, Sophie H Newcomb Memorial College, New Orleans LA (S)

Colebeck, Donna, *Dir,* Marietta-Cobb Museum of Art, Marietta GA

Colegrove, Jim, *Computer Systems Mgr,* Fort Worth Art Association, Modern Art Museum of Fort Worth, Fort Worth TX

Colegrove, Susan, *Admin Asst to Cur,* Fort Worth Art Association, Modern Art Museum of Fort Worth, Fort Worth TX

Coleman, Dorothy J, *Pres,* New Orleans Academy of Fine Arts, Academy Gallery, New Orleans LA

Coleman, Elizabeth, *Pres,* Bennington College, Visual Arts Division, Bennington VT (S)

Coleman, Henry, *Prof,* College of William & Mary, Dept of Fine Arts, Williamsburg VA (S)

Coleman, Johnny, *Asst Prof,* Oberlin College, Dept of Art, Oberlin OH (S)

Coleman, Marybeth, *Instr,* East Central University, Art Dept, Ada OK (S)

Coleman, Myrlan, *Head Dept of Art,* Weatherford College, Dept of Speech/Fine Arts, Weatherford TX (S)

Coleman, Thomas, *Prof,* Indiana University, Bloomington, Henry Radford Hope School of Fine Arts, Bloomington IN (S)

Colescott, Robert, *Regents Prof,* University of Arizona, Dept of Art, Tucson AZ (S)

Colet, Thora, *Dir Retail Operations,* The Phillips Collection, Washington DC

Coley, Philip, *Prof,* Auburn University at Montgomery, Dept of Fine Arts, Montgomery AL (S)

Cole-Zielanski, Trudy, *Assoc Prof,* James Madison University, School of Art & Art History, Harrisonburg VA (S)

Colglazier, Gail, *Dir,* Museum of Fine Arts, Springfield MA

Colglazier, Gail N, *Dir,* Springfield Library & Museums Association, Connecticut Valley Historical Museum, Springfield MA

Colglazier, Galil Nessel, *Dir,* Springfield Library & Museums Association, Springfield Science Museum, Springfield MA

Collazo, Evelyn, *Asst Dir,* Fotografica, New York NY

Collens, David R, *Dir,* Storm King Art Center, Mountainville NY

Collet, Lee, *Chmn,* Muskegon Community College, Dept of Creative & Performing Arts, Muskegon MI (S)

Collette, Alfred T, *Dir,* Syracuse University, Art Collection, Syracuse NY

Colley, Jim, *Asst Prof,* Dallas Baptist University, Dept of Art, Dallas TX (S)

Colliar, Ric, *Dir,* Salt Lake Art Center, Salt Lake City UT

Collier, James, *Chmn Photo,* Fashion Institute of Technology, Art & Design Division, New York NY (S)

Collier, Jean, *Registrar,* University of Virginia, Bayly Art Museum, Charlottesville VA

Collier, Will, *Instr,* Santa Rosa Junior College, Art Dept, Santa Rosa CA (S)

Collin, Margot, *Reference Librn,* Santa Barbara Public Library, Faulkner Memorial Art Wing, Santa Barbara CA

Collings, Ed, *Chmn,* Columbia College, Art Dept, Columbia MO (S)

Collingwood, Halimah, *Prog Dir,* Humboldt Arts Council, Eureka CA

Collins, Brad R, *Chmn,* University of South Carolina, Dept of Art, Columbia SC (S)

Collins, Dana, *Instr,* Illinois Valley Community College, Division of Humanities & Fine Arts, Oglesby IL (S)

Collins, D Cheryl, *Dir,* Riley County Historical Society, Riley County Historical Museum, Manhattan KS

Collins, Jeanne, *VPres Communications,* American Museum of Natural History, New York NY

Collins, Joel, *Chmn,* Mount Union College, Dept of Art, Alliance OH (S)

Collins, John, *Exec Dir,* Museums of Abilene, Inc, Abilene TX

Collins, John, *Dean,* Surry Community College, Art Dept, Dobson NC (S)

Collins, Julie, *Educ & Tours,* Northwestern University, Mary & Leigh Block Gallery, Evanston IL

Collins, Kathleen, *Pres,* Kansas City Art Institute, Kansas City MO (S)

Collins, Kelly, *Pub Servs Librn,* North Central College, Oesterle Library, Naperville IL

Collins, Kim, *Librn,* High Museum of Art, Library, Atlanta GA

Collins, Midge, *Asst Cur,* Gonzaga University, Jundt Art Museum, Ad Art Gallery, Spokane WA

Collins, Patrick, *Chmn,* John Jay College of Criminal Justice, Dept of Art, Music & Philosophy, New York NY (S)

Collins, Susan, *State Archaeologist,* Colorado Historical Society, Colorado History Museum, Denver CO

Collins, Toni, *Adminr,* Pennsylvania Historical & Museum Commission, Brandywine Battlefield Park, Harrisburg PA

Collinson, Howard, *Dept Head,* Royal Ontario Museum, Dept of Western Art & Culture, Toronto ON

Collischan, Judy, *Admin Dir,* Printmaking Workshop, New York NY

Colo, Papo, *Co-Founder-Official Poet,* Exit Art-The First World, Inc, New York NY

Colodny, Lou Anne, *Dir,* Museum of Contemporary Art, North Miami FL

Colom, Carola, *Assoc Prof,* University of Puerto Rico, Dept of Fine Arts, Rio Piedras PR (S)

Colombik, Roger, *Gallery Dir,* Southwest Texas State University, Dept of Art, San Marcos TX (S)

Colombik, Roger, *Assoc Prof,* Southwest Texas State University, Dept of Art, San Marcos TX (S)

Colonghi, John, *Dir NMAI National Campaign,* National Museum of the American Indian, George Gustav Heye Center, New York NY

Colpitt, Frances, *Assoc Prof,* University of Texas at San Antonio, Division of Visual Arts, San Antonio TX (S)

Colton, Stan, *Library Develop,* Las Vegas-Clark County Library District, Las Vegas NV

Colvin, Richard D, *Exhibit Designer,* Rollins College, George D & Harriet W Cornell Fine Arts Museum, Winter Park FL

Colvin, William, *Act Dept Chmn,* Alabama State University, Art Dept, Montgomery AL (S)

Comba, Steve, *Registrar,* Galleries of the Claremont Colleges, Claremont CA

Comella, Frank, *Mgr Marketing,* Art Gallery of Ontario, Toronto ON

Comer, Eugenia, *Asst Prof,* Augusta College, Dept of Fine Arts, Augusta GA

Comer, Fred, *Exec Dir,* Iowa State Education Association, Salisbury House, Des Moines IA

Cominotto, Gary, *Instr,* Mount San Jacinto College, Art Dept, San Jacinto CA (S)

Comport, Jean, *Mgr Art & Literature Dept,* Detroit Public Library, Art & Literature Dept, Detroit MI

Compton, Douglas, *Instr,* Joe Kubert School of Cartoon & Graphic Art, Inc, Dover NJ (S)

Comstock, Joy, *Dir Educ,* Buffalo Bill Memorial Association, Buffalo Bill Historical Center, Cody WY

Conacchione, Matthew, *Controller,* Indianapolis Museum of Art, Indianapolis IN

Conant, Rita, *Cur,* Portsmouth Athenaeum, Library, Portsmouth NH

Conarroe, Joel, *Pres,* John Simon Guggenheim Memorial Foundation, New York NY

Conaty, Gerald, *Cur Ethnology,* Glenbow Museum, Calgary AB

Conaty, Siobhan, *Instr,* Dowling College, Dept of Visual Arts, Oakdale NY (S)

Concannon, Ann, *Dir,* Art Center of Battle Creek, Michigan Art & Artist Archives, Battle Creek MI

Concannon, Ann Worth, *Dir,* Art Center of Battle Creek, Battle Creek MI

Concannon, L O, *Pres,* First State Bank, Norton KS

Concholar, Dan, *Pres & Dir,* Art Information Center, Inc, New York NY

Condon, Lorna, *Cur Archives,* Society for the Preservation of New England Antiquities, Archives, Boston MA

Cone, John, *Asst Prof of Art,* Thomas College, Humanities Division, Thomasville GA (S)

Conforti, Michael, *Dir,* Sterling & Francine Clark Art Institute, Williamstown MA

Conger, William, *Chmn Art Dept,* Northwestern University, Evanston, Dept of Art Theory & Practice, Evanston IL (S)

Conisbee, Philip, *Cur European Paintings & Sculpture,* Los Angeles County Museum of Art, Los Angeles CA

Conkelton, Sheryl, *Sr Cur,* Henry Gallery Association, Henry Art Gallery, Seattle WA

Conklin, Jo-Ann, *Dir,* Brown University, David Winton Bell Gallery, Providence RI

Conklin, Michelle, *Dir,* Crooked Tree Arts Council, Virginia M McCune Community Arts Center, Petoskey MI

Conlee, Julie, *Cataloger,* Colonial Williamsburg Foundation, John D Rockefeller, Jr Library, Williamsburg VA

Conley, Alston, *Cur,* Boston College, Museum of Art, Chestnut Hill MA

Conley, James D, *VPres,* Historic Landmarks Foundation of Indiana, Information Center Library, Indianapolis IN

Conlin, Kathleen F, *Dean,* University of Illinois, Urbana-Champaign, College of Fine & Applied Arts, Champaign IL (S)

Conlin, Pete, *Cur,* Heritage Hjemkomst Interpretive Center, Moorhead MN

Conlon, James, *Sculptor,* University of South Alabama, Dept of Art & Art History, Mobile AL (S)

Conlon, William, *Div Chmn,* Fordham University, Art Dept, New York NY (S)

Conn, David, *Prof,* Texas Christian University, Art & Art History Dept, Fort Worth TX (S)

Connell, Ann, *School Dir,* Silvermine Guild Arts Center, Silvermine Galleries, New Canaan CT

Connell, Ann, *Asst Dir,* Silvermine Guild Arts Center, New Canaan CT

Connell, Anne, *School Dir,* Guild Art Center, New Canaan CT (S)

Connell, Jim, *Asst Prof,* Winthrop University, Dept of Art & Design, Rock Hill SC (S)

Connell, Steven, *Chmn,* University of Montana, Dept of Art, Missoula MT (S)

Connelly, Christy, *Co-Dir,* Antonelli Institute of Art & Photography, Cincinnati OH (S)

Connelly, Frances, *Chmn,* University of Missouri-Kansas City, Dept of Art & Art History, Kansas City MO (S)

Conner, Ann Louise, *Prof,* University of North Carolina at Wilmington, Dept of Fine Arts - Division of Art, Wilmington NC (S)

Conner, Jill, *Asst Mgr & Gallery Dir,* Brand Library & Art Galleries, Glendale CA

Conner, Neppie, *Prof Emeritus,* University of Arkansas, Art Dept, Fayetteville AR (S)

Connett, Dee, *Prof,* Hutchinson Community Junior College, Visual Arts Dept, Hutchinson KS (S)

Connolly, Bruce E, *Access Serv Librn,* New York State College of Ceramics at Alfred University, Scholes Library of Ceramics, Alfred NY

Connolly, Edith, *Asst Dir,* Gallery One, Ellensburg WA

Connolly, Felicia, *Office Admin,* Wenham Museum, Wenham MA

Connor, Cynthia, *Registrar,* Columbia Museum of Art, Columbia SC

Connors, Becky, *Dir,* Freeport Arts Center, Freeport IL

Connors, Becky, *Dir,* Freeport Arts Center, Library, Freeport IL

Connors, Hope, *Prog Coordr,* Museum of New Mexico, Museum of International Folk Art, Santa Fe NM

Connors, Jeanne Moffatt, *Prof,* Community College of Allegheny County, Boyce Campus, Art Dept, Monroeville PA (S)

Connor-Talasek, Catherine, *Chmn Dept,* Fontbonne College, Art Dept, Saint Louis MO (S)

Connorton, Judy, *Librn,* City College of the City University of New York, Architecture Library, New York NY

Conolly, H Neal, *Pres,* Columbia County Historical Society, Columbia County Museum, Kinderhook NY

Conopash, Karin, *Cur,* Old Slater Mill Association, Slater Mill Historic Site, Pawtucket RI

Conrad, Dennis, *Ed,* Nathanael Green Papers, Rhode Island Historical Society, Providence RI

Conrad, Geoffrey W, *Dir,* Indiana University, William Hammond Mathers Museum, Bloomington IN

Conrad, John, *Instr,* San Diego Mesa College, Fine Arts Dept, San Diego CA (S)

Conrads, Margaret, *Samuel Sosland Cur American Art,* Nelson-Atkins Museum of Art, Kansas City MO

Conrey, Joseph, *Coordr,* Ocean County College, Humanities Dept, Toms River NJ (S)

Conroy, Michel, *Prof,* Southwest Texas State University, Dept of Art, San Marcos TX (S)

Consagra, Francesca, *Cur,* Vassar College, The Frances Lehman Loeb Art Center, Poughkeepsie NY

Consey, Kevin, *Dir,* Museum of Contemporary Art, Chicago IL

Considine, Raymond, *Asst Dean of Arts & Sciences,* Indian River Community College, Fine Arts Dept, Fort Pierce FL (S)

Consolati, John, *Assoc Prof,* University of Toronto, Programme in Landscape Architecture, Toronto ON (S)

Consragra, Pier, *Instr,* Columbia University, School of the Arts, Division of Visual Arts, New York NY (S)

Constans, Mary, *Dept Chmn&Prof,* Portland State University, Dept of Art, Portland OR (S)

Constantine, Gregory, *Prof,* Andrews University, Dept of Art, Art History & Design, Berrien Springs MI (S)

Constantine, Jay, *Chmn Foundation & Fine Arts,* Kendall College of Art & Design, Frank & Lyn Van Steenberg Library, Grand Rapids MI

Contes, Anna, *Instr,* Woodstock School of Art, Inc, Woodstock NY (S)

Contiguglia, Georgianna, *Cur Decorative & Fine Arts,* Colorado Historical Society, Colorado History Museum, Denver CO

Convertino, Karen, *Asst Dir,* College of New Rochelle, Castle Gallery, New Rochelle NY

Conway, Jan, *Adjunct Prof,* Wilkes University, Dept of Art, Wilkes-Barre PA (S)

Conway, Patricia, *Prof,* University of Pennsylvania, Graduate School of Fine Arts, Philadelphia PA (S)

Conwill, Kinshasha Holman, *Dir,* The Studio Museum in Harlem, New York NY

Conyers, Wayne, *Dir,* McPherson College Gallery, McPherson KS

Conyers, Wayne, *Chmn,* McPherson College, Art Dept, McPherson KS (S)

Cook, Debbie, *Mem,* Yale University, Art Gallery, New Haven CT

Cook, Hope, *Gallery Coordr,* Mankato Area Arts Council, Carnegie Art Center, Mankato MN

Cook, Ian, *Chmn,* Red Deer College, Dept of Art & Design, Red Deer AB (S)

Cook, James, *Prof,* Elmira College, Art Dept, Elmira NY (S)

Cook, Jennifer, *Visual Art Cur,* Sangre de Cristo Arts & Conference Center, Pueblo CO

Cook, Joyce A, *Exec Asst,* Queens Historical Society, Flushing NY

Cook, Kim, *Operations Mgr,* Women And Their Work, Austin TX

Cook, Lia, *Textiles,* California College of Arts & Crafts, Oakland CA (S)

Cook, Peter J, *Pres,* Belle Grove Plantation, Middletown VA

Cooke, Adrian G, *Chief Preparator,* University of Lethbridge, Art Gallery, Lethbridge AB

Cooke, Constance B, *Pres,* The Queens Museum of Art, Flushing NY

Cooke, Judith M, *Acting Dir Develop,* Nelson-Atkins Museum of Art, Kansas City MO

Cooke, Judith M, *Asst Dir of Develop & Mem,* Nelson-Atkins Museum of Art, Friends of Art, Kansas City MO

Cooke, Judy, *Instr,* Pacific Northwest College of Art, Portland OR (S)

Cooke, Lynne, *Cur,* Dia Center for the Arts, New York NY

Cooke, Robert T, *Assoc Prof,* Rutgers, the State University of New Jersey, Mason Gross School of the Arts, New Brunswick NJ (S)

Cooke, S Tucker, *Chmn,* University of North Carolina at Asheville, Dept of Art, Asheville NC (S)

Coolidge, Christina, *Asst Librn,* Mount Wachusett Community College, Library, Gardner MA

Coombe, JoAnne, *Dir,* Saint Louis County Historical Society, Duluth MN

Coon, A W, *VPres Board,* R W Norton Art Gallery, Shreveport LA

Coon, Cheryl, *Asst Dir,* San Francisco Art Commission, Gallery & Slide Registry, San Francisco CA

Coones, R C, *Instr,* Northwestern State university, Tahlequah OK (S)

Cooney, Roberta, *Exec Dir,* Audrain County Historical Society, Graceland Museum & American Saddlehorse Museum, Mexico MO

Cooney, Ross, *Pres,* Boulder Museum of Contemporary Art, Boulder CO

Coonin, Victor, *Asst Prof,* Rhodes College, Dept of Art, Memphis TN (S)

Cooper, Adrienne, *Prog Dir,* Museum of Chinese in the Americas, New York NY

Cooper, Charisse, *Facility Coordr,* Philbrook Museum of Art, Tulsa OK

Cooper, David, *Chmn,* Butte College, Dept of Fine Arts, Oroville CA (S)

Cooper, Diana, *Cur,* Potsdam College of the State University of New York, Roland Gibson Gallery, Potsdam NY

Cooper, Diana, *Reference Librn,* University of British Columbia, Fine Arts Library, Vancouver BC

Cooper, Ginnie, *Dir,* Multnomah County Library, Henry Failing Art & Music Dept, Portland OR

Cooper, Helen, *Cur American Painting,* Yale University, Art Gallery, New Haven CT

Cooper, Jack, *Communications Dir,* High Desert Museum, Bend OR

Cooper, Ken, *Community Services Dir,* Gavilan College, Art Gallery, Gilroy CA

Cooper, Linda G, *Asst VPres,* Wachovia Bank of North Carolina, Winston-Salem NC

Cooper, Michael, *Instr,* De Anza College, Creative Arts Division, Cupertino CA (S)

Cooper, Nan, *Instr,* The Art Institutes International, The Art Institute of Seattle, Seattle WA (S)

Cooper, Patty, *Exec VPres,* South Carolina State Museum, Columbia SC

Cooper, Paula, *Cur,* Fried, Frank, Harris, Shriver & Jacobson, Art Collection, New York NY

Cooper, Rhonda, *Dir,* State University of New York at Stony Brook, University Art Gallery, Stony Brook NY

Cooper, Wendy, *Coordr Public Relations,* University of Georgia, Georgia Museum of Art, Athens GA

Cootner, Cathryn, *Cur Rugs,* Fine Arts Museums of San Francisco, M H de Young Memorial Museum & California Palace of the Legion of Honor, San Francisco CA

Copeland, Betty D, *Chmn,* Texas Woman's University, Dept of Visual Arts, Denton TX (S)

Copeley, William, *Librn,* New Hampshire Historical Society, Library, Concord NH

Coppage, Carol B, *Exec Dir,* Northwood University, Alden B Dow Creativity Center, Midland MI (S)

Coppin, Kerry, *Assoc Prof,* Rochester Institute of Technology, School of Photographic Arts & Sciences, Rochester NY (S)

Copping, Lisette, *Chmn Fine Arts,* Delgado College, Dept of Fine Arts, New Orleans LA (S)

Coppola, Regina, *Cur,* University of Massachusetts, Amherst, University Gallery, Amherst MA

Coraor, John E, *Dir,* Heckscher Museum of Art, Huntington NY

Corbett, Frank, *VPres,* Peninsula Fine Arts Center, Newport News VA

Corbin, George, *Prof,* City University of New York, PhD Program in Art History, New York NY (S)

Corbin, Tarrence, *Prof Fine Arts,* University of Cincinnati, School of Art, Cincinnati OH (S)

Corcoran, Kathryn, *Art Librn,* Joslyn Art Museum, Omaha NE

Corder, Ronald, *Sr Exhibit Specialist,* United States Naval Academy Museum, Annapolis MD

Cordes, Robert, *Instr,* Southwest Texas State University, Dept of Art, San Marcos TX (S)

Cordi, Jill, *Prog Dir,* Sierra Arts Foundation, Reno NV

Cordova, Ralph, *Pres,* Movimiento Artistico del Rio Salado, Inc (MARS) Artspace, Phoenix AZ

Cores, Ellen, *Dir,* South Peace Art Society, Dawson Creek Art Gallery, Dawson Creek BC

Corey, Liz, *Vol Coordr,* Pacific - Asia Museum, Pasadena CA

Corey, Peter, *Cur Coll,* Alaska Department of Education, Division of Libraries, Archives & Museums, Sheldon Jackson Museum, Sitka AK

Corey, Sharon, *Prof,* Chapman University, Art Dept, Orange CA (S)

Corey, Shirley Trusty, *Exec Dir,* Arts Council Of New Orleans, New Orleans LA

Corley, Elke G, *Supv Corporate Admin Serv,* Times Mirror Company, Los Angeles CA

Cormack, Sarah, *Asst Prof,* Duke University, Dept of Art & Art History, Durham NC (S)

Cormier, Cynthia, *Cur Educ,* Wadsworth Atheneum, Hartford CT

Cormier, Robert, *Chmn,* Boston Art Commission of the City of Boston, Boston MA

Cornelius, Phil, *Acting Area Head Ceramics,* Pasadena City College, Art Dept, Pasadena CA (S)

Cornell, Beth, *Sr Adviser,* Pennsylvania Department of Education, Arts in Education Program, Harrisburg PA

Cornell, Roger C, *Pres,* Mingei International, Inc, Mingei International Museum Satellite of World Folk Art, San Diego CA

Cornell, Sylvia, *Acting Dir,* Jacksonville Public Library, Fine Arts & Recreation Dept, Jacksonville FL

Cornell, Thomas B, *Prof,* Bowdoin College, Art Dept, Brunswick ME (S)

Cornett, J, *Assoc Prof,* Northern Arizona University, School of Art & Design, Flagstaff AZ (S)

Cornett, James W, *Cur Natural Science,* Palm Springs Desert Museum, Palm Springs CA

Cornett, James W, *Natural Sciences,* Palm Springs Desert Museum, Library, Palm Springs CA

Cornfeld, Michael, *Chmn,* Marshall University, Dept of Art, Huntington WV (S)

Cornier, Caroline, *Secy,* Musee Regional de la Cote-Nord, Sept-Iles PQ

Corning, Marilyn, *Librn*, Wenham Museum, Timothy Pickering Library, Wenham MA

Cornish, Glenn, *Music Instr*, Edison Community College, Dept of Fine & Performing Arts, Fort Myers FL (S)

Cornish, Jack, *Chmn*, Kean College of New Jersey, Fine Arts Dept, Union NJ (S)

Cornrich, Bill, *Dir*, Rose Center & Council for the Arts, Morristown TN

Corral, Laurie, *Dir Educ*, Hickory Museum of Art, Inc, Hickory NC

Correa, Laura, *Dir*, Van Cortlandt House Museum, Bronx NY

Correia, Peter, *Prof*, Ulster County Community College, Dept of Visual Arts, Stone Ridge NY (S)

Correro, Guido, *Prof*, Herkimer County Community College, Liberal Arts & Public Service Division, Herkimer NY (S)

Corrie, Rebecca, *Chmn*, Bates College, Art Dept, Lewiston ME (S)

Corrigan, Carol, *Gallery Dir*, Southern Oregon State College, Central Art Gallery, Ashland OR

Corrigan, David J, *Cur*, Connecticut State Library, Museum of Connecticut History, Hartford CT

Corrigan, Kathleen, *Chmn*, Dartmouth College, Dept of Art History, Hanover NH (S)

Corrin, Lisa, *Cur & Educator*, The Contemporary, Museum for Contemporary Arts, Baltimore MD

Corsaro, James, *Assoc Librn*, New York State Library, Manuscripts & Special Collections, Albany NY

Corser, James B, *Bus Mgr*, Fort Worth Art Association, Modern Art Museum of Fort Worth, Fort Worth TX

Cost, Steven, *Instr*, Amarillo College, Art Dept, Amarillo TX (S)

Costanzo, Nancy, *Chmn Dept*, Our Lady of Elms College, Dept of Fine Arts, Chicopee MA (S)

Costello, Joan M, *Dir*, Evanston Historical Society, Charles Gates Dawes House, Evanston IL

Costigan, Constance C, *Prof*, George Washington University, Dept of Art, Washington DC (S)

Cote, Alan, *Instr*, Bard College, Milton Avery Graduate School of the Arts, Annandale-on-Hudson NY (S)

Cote, Claire, *Dir Cultural Serv*, Pointe Claire Cultural Centre, Stewart Hall Art Gallery, Pointe Claire PQ

Cote, Marc, *Asst Prof*, Framingham State College, Art Dept, Framingham MA (S)

Cotter, Ann, *Ed*, Cincinnati Museum Association, Cincinnati Art Museum, Cincinnati OH

Cotter, James H, *Treas*, Old Jail Art Center, Albany TX

Cottong, Kathy, *Dir*, The Arts Club of Chicago, Reference Library, Chicago IL

Cottong, Kathy S, *Dir*, The Arts Club of Chicago, Chicago IL

Cottrill, Thomas, *Dean Arts & Letters*, Northwestern State university, Tahlequah OK (S)

Cotugno, H Arthur P, *Supt Greater Amsterdam School Dist*, Mohawk Valley Heritage Association, Inc, Walter Elwood Museum, Amsterdam NY

Couch, Jennie, *Asst Prof*, Concordia College, Art Dept, Moorhead MN (S)

Couch, N C Christopher, *Asst Prof*, Smith College, Art Dept, Northampton MA (S)

Couchon, Marie-Paule, *Archivist*, Musee des Augustines de l'Hotel Dieu de Quebec, Archive, Quebec PQ

Coughin, Marge, *Dir Special Events*, American Society of Artists, Inc, Chicago IL

Coughlin, Joan Hopkins, *Cur*, Wellfleet Historical Society Museum, Wellfleet MA

Coulet du Gard, Dominique, *Cur Exhib*, Historical & Cultural Affairs, Delaware State Museums, Dover DE

Coulter, Gary, *Chmn*, Fort Hays State University, Moss-Thorns Gallery of Arts, Hays KS

Coulter, Gary, *Chmn*, Fort Hays State University, Dept of Art, Hays KS (S)

Coulter, Jerry L, *Prof*, James Madison University, School of Art & Art History, Harrisonburg VA (S)

Coumbe, Robert E, *Dir*, Free Public Library, Art & Music Dept, Trenton NJ

Couper, James M, *Prof*, Florida International University, Visual Arts Dept, Miami FL (S)

Courson, Bruce, *Dir*, The Sandwich Historical Society, Inc, Sandwich Glass Museum, Sandwich MA

Courson, Bruce, *Dir*, The Sandwich Historical Society, Inc, Library, Sandwich MA

Court, Elizabeth, *Chief Paintings Conservator*, Balboa Art Conservation Center, San Diego CA

Courtemanche, Susan, *Dir Develop & Mem*, Worcester Art Museum, Worcester MA

Courtmanche, Susan, *Dir Develop & External Affairs*, Whitney Museum of American Art, New York NY

Courtney, Kathleen, *Lectr*, Mount Marty College, Art Dept, Yankton SD (S)

Courtney, Vernon, *Asst Dir*, Ohio Historical Society, National Afro American Museum & Cultural Center, Wilberforce OH

Coutant, Tricia, *Dept Head*, Jacksonville Public Library, Fine Arts & Recreation Dept, Jacksonville FL

Couture, Marie, *Co-Chmn*, Rivier College, Art Dept, Nashua NH (S)

Couture, Theresa, *Co-Chmn*, Rivier College, Art Dept, Nashua NH (S)

Covert, Nan, *Dept Head*, Bridgewater College, Art Dept, Bridgewater VA (S)

Covington, Betsy, *Dir Develop*, Columbus Museum, Columbus GA

Covington, Joseph F, *Dir Educ*, North Carolina Museum of Art, Raleigh NC

Covington-Vogl, Laurel, *Assoc Prof*, Fort Lewis College, Art Dept, Durango CO (S)

Covo, David, *Prof*, McGill University, School of Architecture, Montreal PQ (S)

Cowart, Jack, *Deputy Dir & Chief Cur*, Corcoran Gallery of Art, Washington DC

Cowden, Chris, *Dir*, Women And Their Work, Austin TX

Cowden, Dorothy, *Dir*, University of Tampa, Lee Scarfone Gallery, Tampa FL

Cowdery, Sue, *Registrar*, Mid-America All-Indian Center, Library, Wichita KS

Cowette, Thomas, *Assoc Prof*, University of Minnesota, Minneapolis, Dept of Art, Minneapolis MN (S)

Cowish, Doug, *Prof*, Wabash College, Art Dept, Crawfordsville IN (S)

Cowles, Virginia, *Pres*, Artists Space, New York NY

Cox, Abbe Rose, *Instr*, Surry Community College, Art Dept, Dobson NC (S)

Cox, Andy, *Chmn*, Limestone College, Art Dept, Gaffney SC (S)

Cox, Anne, *Dir*, Atlanta College of Art, Georgia Artists Registry, Atlanta GA

Cox, Beverly, *Cur Exhib*, National Portrait Gallery, Washington DC

Cox, David N, *Prof*, Weber State University, Dept of Visual Arts, Ogden UT (S)

Cox, Dennis, *Assoc Prof*, Pacific Lutheran University, Dept of Art, Tacoma WA (S)

Cox, Jean, *Assoc Prof*, Oakland City College, Division of Fine Arts, Oakland City IN (S)

Cox, Jonathan, *VPres Coll*, Historical Society of Pennsylvania, Philadelphia PA

Cox, Leslie, *Office Mgr*, Texas Fine Arts Association, Austin TX

Cox, Michael, *Dean*, University of Manitoba, Faculty of Architecture, Winnipeg MB (S)

Cox, Nicole, *Coordr*, C W Post Campus of Long Island University, Hillwood Art Museum, Brookville NY

Cox, Peggy, *Chmn*, Westminster College, Art Dept, New Wilmington PA (S)

Cox, Richard, *Prof*, Louisiana State University, School of Art, Baton Rouge LA (S)

Cox, Sharon, *Chmn*, Jamestown College, Art Dept, Jamestown ND (S)

Cox, Thomas, *VChmn*, Detroit Artists Market, Detroit MI

Cox, William, *Gallery Dir*, Edinboro University of Pennsylvania, Art Dept, Edinboro PA (S)

Cox-Rearick, Janet, *Distinguished Prof*, City University of New York, PhD Program in Art History, New York NY (S)

Cox-Smith, Susan, *Membership Coordr*, Southern Oregon Historical Society, Jacksonville Museum of Southern Oregon History, Medford OR

Coyle, Jack, *Registrar*, Independent Curators Inc, New York NY

Crabb, Christine, *Public Relations Coordr*, Dartmouth College, Hood Museum of Art, Hanover NH

Crabb, Patrick, *Instr*, Rancho Santiago College, Art Dept, Santa Ana CA (S)

Crabb, Ted, *Dir*, University of Wisconsin-Madison, Wisconsin Union Galleries, Madison WI

Crable, James, *Prof*, James Madison University, School of Art & Art History, Harrisonburg VA (S)

Craddock, Robert, *Visual Arts Dir*, Jamaica Arts Center, Jamaica NY

Craig, Andrew B, *Pres & Chmn*, The Boatmen's National Bank of St Louis, Art Collection, Saint Louis MO

Craig, Christina, *Assoc Prof*, College of New Jersey, Art Dept, Trenton NJ (S)

Craig, Susan V, *Librn*, University of Kansas, Murphy Library of Art & Architecture, Lawrence KS

Craighead, Linda, *Dir*, Palo Alto Cultural Center, Palo Alto CA

Craighead, Tim, *Instr*, Monterey Peninsula College, Art Dept, Monterey CA (S)

Cramer, Carole, *Supv*, Brown University, Annmary Brown Memorial, Providence RI

Cramer, George, *Assoc Prof*, University of Wisconsin, Madison, Dept of Art, Madison WI (S)

Cramer, Patricia T, *Dir*, Westfield Athenaeum, Jasper Rand Art Museum, Westfield MA

Cramer, Sam, *Instr*, Luzerne County Community College, Commercial Art Dept, Nanticoke PA (S)

Cramer, Wendy, *Pres*, Mankato Area Arts Council, Carnegie Art Center, Mankato MN

Crane, Barbara, *Prof*, School of the Art Institute of Chicago, Chicago IL (S)

Crane, Bonnie L, *Pres*, Crane Collection Gallery, Boston MA

Crane, David, *Head Art Chair*, Virginia Polytechnic Institute & State University, Armory Art Gallery, Blacksburg VA

Crane, David, *Head Dept*, Virginia Polytechnic Institute & State University, Dept of Art & Art History, Blacksburg VA (S)

Crane, Diane, *Instr*, Viterbo College, Art Dept, La Crosse WI (S)

Crane, Elizabeth, *Cur Asst*, Aurora University, Schingoethe Center for Native American Cultures, Aurora IL

Crane, James, *Prof*, Eckerd College, Art Dept, Saint Petersburg FL (S)

Crane, Lois F, *Librn*, Wichita Art Museum, Library, Wichita KS

Crane, Michael, *Assoc Cur*, Bellevue Art Museum, Bellevue WA

Crane, Tim, *Dir*, Viterbo College Art Gallery, La Crosse WI

Crank, Frank, *Prof*, University of Idaho, College of Art & Architecture, Moscow ID (S)

Crasco, Gael, *Asst to Pres*, Crane Collection Gallery, Boston MA

Crawford, Cameron, *Instr*, California State University, Chico, Art Dept, Chico CA (S)

Crawford, Henry, *Registrar*, Texas Tech University, Museum, Lubbock TX

Crawford, J, *Instr*, Humboldt State University, College of Arts & Humanities, Arcata CA (S)

Crawford, James, *Cur & Historical Cur*, Canajoharie Library & Art Gallery, Canajoharie NY

Crawford, James, *Cur*, Canajoharie Library & Art Gallery, Library, Canajoharie NY

Crawford, James, *Chmn*, Humboldt State University, College of Arts & Humanities, Arcata CA (S)

Crawford, Margaret, *Second VPres*, New Jersey Water-Color Society, Chester NJ

Crawford, Nina, *Adminr*, Dauphin & District Allied Arts Council, Dauphin MB

Crawford, Randal, *Instr*, Delta College, Art Dept, University Center MI (S)

Crawford, Rebecca H, *Pres*, Florence Museum of Art, Science & History, Florence SC

Crawford, Stan, *Pres*, Taos Art Association Inc, Stables Art Center, Taos NM

Creal, Jim, *Dir*, Converse College, Milliken Art Gallery, Spartanburg SC

Creamer, George, *Foundation Dept*, Monserrat College of Art, Beverly MA (S)

Creasy, June, *Assoc Prof*, Lambuth University, Dept of Human Ecology & Visual Arts, Jackson TN (S)

Creedon, Denise, *Asst Dir*, Perkins Center for the Arts, Moorestown NJ

Creemers, Harry, *VPres Develop & Marketing*, Mint Museum of Art, Charlotte NC

Creighton, Sandra, *Visitor Services*, National Gallery of Art, Washington DC

Creighton, Valerie, *Exec Dir*, Saskatchewan Arts Board, Regina SK

Crespo, Michael, *Dir*, Louisiana State University, School of Art Gallery, Baton Rouge LA

Cress, George, *Gallery Coordr*, University of Tennessee at Chattanooga, George Ayers Cress Gallery of Art, Chattanooga TN

Cress, Robert, *Pres Board Trustees*, Roswell Museum & Art Center, Roswell NM

Cresson, Pat, *Prof*, Monmouth University, Dept of Art & Design, West Long Branch NJ (S)

Crew, Roger T, *Archivist*, The Mariners' Museum, Library, Newport News VA

Crew, Spencer, *Dir*, National Museum of American History, Washington DC

Cribelli, Susan, *Chmn Div Communications & Humanities*, Aims Community College, Visual & Performing Arts, Greeley CO (S)

Crimson, Linda, *Adjunct Asst Prof*, Indiana University South Bend, Fine Arts Dept, South Bend IN (S)

Cripps, Andrew, *Coordr Art Placement*, Visual Arts Ontario, Toronto ON

Cripps, Stephen, *Pres*, Kings County Historical Society and Museum, Hampton NB

Crise, Robert, *Gallery Mgr*, Detroit Focus, Detroit MI

Crismon, David, *Asst Prof*, Oklahoma Christian University of Science & Arts, Dept of Art & Design, Oklahoma City OK (S)

Crisp, Lynn, *Librn Asst*, North Carolina State University, Harrye Lyons Design Library, Raleigh NC

Critchfield, Ann, *Head Visual Communications & Graphic Arts*, Art Institute of Atlanta, Atlanta GA (S)

Croce, Judith, *Dir*, Caldwell College, Art Gallery, Caldwell NJ

Croce, Judith, *Chmn*, Caldwell College, Art Dept, Caldwell NJ (S)

Crocker, Kyle, *Prof*, Bemidji State University, Visual Arts Dept, Bemidji MN (S)

Croft, Michael, *Prof Jewelry & Metalsmithing*, University of Arizona, Dept of Art, Tucson AZ (S)

Croggon, Asha, *Exec Adminr*, Professional Art Dealers Association of Canada, Toronto ON

Cromley, Elizabeth, *Chmn*, Northeastern University, Dept of Art & Architecture, Boston MA (S)

Croneberger, Robert B, *Dir*, Carnegie Institute, Library, Pittsburgh PA

Cronin, Allison, *Asst Coll Mgr*, University of British Columbia, Museum of Anthropology, Vancouver BC

Cronin, Mary, *Supv Educ*, Brandywine River Museum, Chadds Ford PA

Cronin, Patricia, *Prog Educ Coordr*, Arts Council of the Blue Ridge, Roanoke VA

Crooker, M J A, *Assoc Prof*, Mount Allison University, Fine Arts Dept, Sackville NB (S)

Crooks, William C, *Pres*, Historical Society of the Town of Greenwich, Inc, Bush-Holley House Museum, Cos Cob CT

Crosby, Bobbie, *VPres*, Norman Rockwell Museum at Stockbridge, Stockbridge MA

Crosby, Rancie W, *Dir Emerita*, Johns Hopkins University, School of Medicine, Dept of Art as Applied to Medicine, Baltimore MD (S)

Crosby, Suzanne, *Assoc Prof*, Hillsborough Community College, Fine Arts Dept, Tampa FL (S)

Croskrey, Wendy, *Asst Prof*, University of Alaska-Fairbanks, Dept of Art, Fairbanks AK (S)

Crosman, Christopher B, *Dir*, William A Farnsworth Library & Art Museum, Rockland ME

Crosman, Christopher B, *Dir*, William A Farnsworth Library & Art Museum, Library, Rockland ME

Cross, Berri, *Prog Advisor*, University of Tennessee, Visual Arts Committee, Knoxville TN

Cross, Sharon, *Spec Appointment*, Moravian College, Dept of Art, Bethlehem PA (S)

Cross, Tony, *Instr*, Cuyahoga Valley Art Center, Cuyahoga Falls OH (S)

Crossan, Melanie, *Admin Asst*, Ursinus College, Philip & Muriel Berman Museum of Art, Collegeville PA

Crossett, Arlene, *Asst Librn*, Manchester Historic Association, Library, Manchester NH

Crossley, Connie, *Dept Head Fashion Merchandise*, Antonelli Institute of Art & Photography, Cincinnati OH (S)

Crossman, Rodney, *Instr*, Indiana Wesleyan University, Art Dept, Marion IN (S)

Crosson, David, *Exec Dir*, Praire Avenue House Museums, Glesser House, Chicago IL

Crosson, David, *Exec Dir*, Praire Avenue House Museums, Henry B Clarke House Museum, Chicago IL

Croston, Robert B, *Assoc Prof*, Southern Illinois University, School of Art & Design, Carbondale IL (S)

Croton, Lynn, *Dean Visual & Performing Arts*, C W Post Center of Long Island University, School of Visual & Performing Arts, Brookville NY (S)

Crouch, D E, *Instr*, Western Illinois University, Art Dept, Macomb IL (S)

Crouse, Michael, *Chmn Art & Art History Dept*, University of Alabama in Huntsville, Dept of Art & Art History, Huntsville AL (S)

Crouther, Betty, *Assoc Prof*, University of Mississippi, Dept of Art, University MS (S)

Crowe, Ann G, *Asst Prof*, Virginia Commonwealth University, Art History Dept, Richmond VA (S)

Crowe, Edith, *Art Reference Librn*, San Jose State University, Robert D Clark Library, San Jose CA

Crowe, M, *Lectr*, Mount Ida College, Chamberlayne School of Design & Merchandising, Boston MA (S)

Crowley, J Anthony, *Chmn Dept & Instr*, Grinnell College, Dept of Art, Grinnell IA (S)

Crowley, William, *Museum Adminr*, State Historical Society of Wisconsin, State Historical Museum, Madison WI

Crown, Patricia, *Prof*, University of Missouri, Art History & Archaeology Dept, Columbia MO (S)

Crown, Roberta, *Exec Coordr*, Women in the Arts Foundation, Inc, New York NY

Crowston, Catherine, *Dir & Cur*, Banff Centre, Walter Phillips Gallery, Banff AB

Crozier, Richard F, *Deputy Dir Finance & Adminr*, Winterthur Museum, Winterthur DE

Cruickshank, Marilyn W, *Dir Educ*, USS Constitution Museum, Boston MA

Crum, Katherine B, *Dir*, Mills College, Art Gallery, Oakland CA

Crum, Roger, *Asst Prof*, University of Dayton, Visual Arts Dept, Dayton OH (S)

Crumbley, Amelia, *VPres*, Mississippi Art Colony, Pascagoula MS

Crusan, Ronald L, *Chief Exec Officer & Exec Dir*, Waterworks Visual Arts Center, Salisbury NC

Cruz, Maria de Lourdes Morales, *Public Relations*, Museo de las Americas, Old San Juan PR

Cruz, Michele A, *Instr*, North Carolina Wesleyan College, Dept of Visual & Performing Arts, Rocky Mount NC (S)

Cruz, Patricia, *Deputy Dir Progs*, The Studio Museum in Harlem, New York NY

Cruz, Ruben, *Instr*, New York Institute of Technology, Fine Arts Dept, Old Westbury NY (S)

Cubbs, Joanne, *Cur Folk Art*, High Museum of Art, Atlanta GA

Cucchi, Paolo, *Dean*, Drew University, Elizabeth P Korn Gallery, Madison NJ

Culbertson, Ben, *Coordr*, Hagerstown Junior College, Art Dept, Hagerstown MD (S)

Culbertson, Margaret, *Librn*, University of Houston, William R Jenkins Architecture & Art Library, Houston TX

Cull, John, *Head Librn*, Vancouver Public Library, Fine Arts & Music Div, Vancouver BC

Cullen, Charles T, *Pres & Librn*, Newberry Library, Chicago IL

Cullen, Debbie, *Cur & Registrar*, Printmaking Workshop, New York NY

Culley, Lou Ann, *Assoc Prof*, Kansas State University, Art Dept, Manhattan KS (S)

Culley, Paul T, *Technical Serv Librn & Engineering Bibliographer*, New York State College of Ceramics at Alfred University, Scholes Library of Ceramics, Alfred NY

Culp, Martha, *Admin Asst*, Midwest Museum of American Art, Elkhart IN

Culver, Michael, *Assoc Dir & Cur*, Ogunquit Museum of American Art, Ogunquit ME

Cumine, Lynn, *Pres*, Lyceum Club and Women's Art Association of Canada, Toronto ON

Cummin, Joyce, *Supv Security*, University of Oklahoma, Fred Jones Jr Museum of Art, Norman OK

Cumming, Doug, *Prof*, University of Wisconsin-Stout, Dept of Art & Design, Menomonie WI (S)

Cumming, Nan, *Asst Dir*, Maine Historical Society, Portland ME

Cumming, Nan, *Asst Dir*, Maine Historical Society, Wadsworth-Longfellow House, Portland ME

Cumming, William, *Instr*, The Art Institutes International, The Art Institute of Seattle, Seattle WA (S)

Cummings, Angela, *Instr*, The Arkansas Arts Center, Museum School, Little Rock AR (S)

Cummings, Mary Lou, *Cur & Registrar*, Knights of Columbus Supreme Council, Headquarters Museum, New Haven CT

Cummins, Karen, *Cur Education*, New Jersey State Museum, Trenton NJ

Cunard, Gail, *Dir*, Harness Racing & Hall of Fame, Goshen NY

Cunard, Tim, *Chmn Dept*, Wheaton College, Art Dept, Norton MA (S)

Cundiff, Linda, *Asst Prof*, Campbellsville College, Fine Arts Division, Campbellsville KY (S)

Cuneo, Pia, *Asst Prof Art History*, University of Arizona, Dept of Art, Tucson AZ (S)

Cunning, John, *Dir*, Department of Natural Resources of Missouri, Missouri State Museum, Jefferson City MO

Cunning, John, *Dir*, Department of Natural Resources of Missouri, Elizabeth Rozier Gallery, Jefferson City MO

Cunningham, David, *Designer/Exhib*, University of British Columbia, Museum of Anthropology, Vancouver BC

Cunningham, Dennis, *Instr*, Marylhurst College, Art Dept, Marylhurst OR (S)

Cunningham, Denyse M, *Asst Cur*, Aurora University, Schingoethe Center for Native American Cultures, Aurora IL

Cunningham, Elizabeth, *Registrar*, Cheekwood-Tennessee Botanical Gardens & Museum of Art, Nashville TN

Cunningham, Linda, *Instr*, Franklin & Marshall College, Art Dept, Lancaster PA (S)

Cunningham, Lynn, *Visual Resources Coll Cur*, University of Memphis, Visual Resource Collection, Memphis TN

Cunningham, Michael R, *Chief Cur Asian Art*, Cleveland Museum of Art, Cleveland OH

Cunningham, Sam, *Div Dir*, Tallahassee Community College, Art Dept, Tallahassee FL (S)

Cunningham, Scott, *Dir*, Spartanburg County Museum of Art, Art School, Spartanburg SC (S)

Cunningham, Scott, *Art School Dir*, Spartanburg County Museum of Art, Spartanburg SC

Cunningham, William, *Treas*, Pennsylvania Academy of the Fine Arts, Fellowship of the Pennsylvania Academy of the Fine Arts, Philadelphia PA

Cuno, James, *Dir*, Harvard University, Harvard University Art Museums, Cambridge MA

Cuno, James, *Dir*, Harvard University, William Hayes Fogg Art Museum, Cambridge MA

Cuno, James, *Dir*, Harvard University, Arthur M Sackler Museum, Cambridge MA

Curcic, Slobodan, *Prof*, Princeton University, Dept of Art & Archaeology, Princeton NJ (S)

Curcio, Robert, *Dir*, Ward-Nasse Gallery, New York NY

Curfman, Robert, *Asst Prof*, Indiana Wesleyan University, Art Dept, Marion IN (S)

Curl, Alan, *Admin Cur*, Riverside Municipal Museum, Riverside CA

Curl, David, *Prof*, Kalamazoo College, Art Dept, Kalamazoo MI (S)

Curl, Sheila, *Librn*, University of Notre Dame, Architecture Library, Notre Dame IN

Curler, Dawna, *VIP Coordr*, Southern Oregon Historical Society, Jacksonville Museum of Southern Oregon History, Medford OR

Curley, Arthur, *Dir*, Boston Public Library, Central Library, Boston MA

Curling, Marianne, *Cur*, Mark Twain Memorial, Hartford CT

Curling, Marianne, *Cur*, Mark Twain Memorial, Mark Twain House Research Library, Hartford CT

Curran, Darryl J, *Chmn Dept*, California State University, Fullerton, Art Dept, Fullerton CA (S)

Curran, John, *VPres Merchandising Activities*, The Metropolitan Museum of Art, New York NY

Curren, Kathleen, *Asst Prof*, Trinity College, Dept of Fine Arts, Hartford CT (S)

Curreri, Dyana, *Dir*, California College of Arts & Crafts, Steven Oliver Art Center, Oakland CA

Currie, Quentin, *Asst Prof*, Winthrop University, Dept of Art & Design, Rock Hill SC (S)

Curry, Colleen, *Coll Mgr*, Lehigh County Historical Society, Allentown PA

Curry, Heidi, *Pres*, San Angelo Museum of Fine Arts, San Angelo TX

Curry, Larrie, *Dir Museum*, Shaker Village of Pleasant Hill, Harrodsburg KY

Curry, Michael P, *Dir*, City of Hampton, Hampton Arts Commission, Hampton VA

Curtin, Nancy, *Dir*, Port Washington Public Library, Port Washington NY

Curtin-Stevenson, Mary, *Librn*, Massachusetts College of Art, Morton R Godine Library, Boston MA

Curtis, Brian, *Assoc Prof*, University of Miami, Dept of Art & Art History, Coral Gables FL (S)

Curtis, David, *Dept Head*, Virginia Western Community College, Commercial Art, Fine Art & Photography, Roanoke VA (S)

Curtis, George H, *Asst Dir*, National Archives & Records Administration, Harry S Truman Library, Independence MO

Curtis, Marilyn D, *Acting Dir*, Redwood Library & Athenaeum, Newport RI

Curtis, Steven, *Cur Historic Bldgs*, Historical & Cultural Affairs, Delaware State Museums, Dover DE

Curtis, Verna, *Photographs*, Library of Congress, Prints & Photographs Division, Washington DC

Curtis, Walter D, *Asst Prof*, University of Arkansas, Art Dept, Fayetteville AR (S)

Cushing, John D, *Pres*, Essex Historical Society, Essex Shipbuilding Museum, Essex MA

Cushman, Brad, *Chmn*, Southeastern Oklahoma State University, Art Dept, Durant OK (S)

Cushman, Dennis, *Marketing Dir*, San Diego Museum of Art, San Diego CA

Cutler, Jerry, *Assoc Prof*, University of Florida, Dept of Art, Gainesville FL (S)

Cutler, Phyllis L, *Librn*, Williams College, Sawyer Library, Williamstown MA

Cutler, Walter L, *Pres, Ambassador*, Meridian International Center, Cafritz Galleries, Washington DC

Cutting, Richard W, *Treas*, The Buffalo Fine Arts Academy, Albright-Knox Art Gallery, Buffalo NY

Cyr, Ann, *Art Cur*, State Street Corporation, Concourse Gallery, Boston MA

Cyr, Louis, *Dir*, Kateri Tekakwitha Shrine, Kahnawake PQ

Cyr, Paul, *Dept Head Genealogy & Whaling Coll*, New Bedford Free Public Library, Art Dept, New Bedford MA

Czarnecki, James, *Assoc Prof*, University of Nebraska at Omaha, Dept of Art & Art History, Omaha NE (S)

Czerniejewski, Marilyn, *Asst Librn (Technical)*, Toledo Museum of Art, Library, Toledo OH

Czestochowski, Joseph S, *Dir*, The Dixon Gallery & Gardens, Memphis TN

Czestochowski, Joseph S, *Dir*, The Dixon Gallery & Gardens, Library, Memphis TN

Czichos, Raymond L, *Dir*, Pioneer Town, Pioneer Museum of Western Art, Wimberley TX

Czuma, Stanislaw, *Cur Indian & SE Asian Art*, Cleveland Museum of Art, Cleveland OH

Dabakis, Melissa, *Assoc Prof*, Kenyon College, Art Dept, Gambier OH (S)

Dabash, Adrian G, *Assoc Prof*, Providence College, Art & Art History Dept, Providence RI (S)

D'Abate, Richard, *Exec Dir*, Maine Historical Society, Portland ME

Dabrowski, Gina, *Prof*, Indiana University, Bloomington, Henry Radford Hope School of Fine Arts, Bloomington IN (S)

Dacey, Jill, *Dept Chmn*, University of Idaho, College of Art & Architecture, Moscow ID (S)

Da Costa Nunes, Jadviga, *Chmn*, Muhlenberg College, Dept of Art, Allentown PA (S)

Dadess, Margret, *Sr VPres Corp Communications*, Burroughs Wellcome Company, Art Collection, Research Triangle Park NC

Daggett, Patsy, *Instr*, The Arkansas Arts Center, Museum School, Little Rock AR (S)

D'Agostino, Fernanda, *Instr*, Marylhurst College, Art Dept, Marylhurst OR (S)

D'Agostino, Judith, *School Mgr*, Tucson Museum of Art & Historic Block, Tucson AZ

D'Agostino, Judith, *Dir Educ*, Tucson Museum of Art School, Tucson AZ (S)

Dahill, Barbara A, *Gallery Mgr*, Guild of Boston Artists, Boston MA

Dahlstrom, Harry, *Pres*, Phelps County Historical Society, Phelps County Museum, Holdrege NE

Dahlstrom, Harry D, *Pres*, Phelps County Historical Society, Library, Holdrege NE

Daignault, Janet, *Bus Mgr*, University of Vermont, Robert Hull Fleming Museum, Burlington VT

Dajani, Virginia, *Exec Dir*, American Academy of Arts & Letters, New York NY

Dake, Dennis, *Coordr Art Educ*, Iowa State University, Dept of Art & Design, Ames IA (S)

Dale, Alison, *Asst Prof*, Seton Hall University, College of Arts & Sciences, South Orange NJ (S)

Dale, Cindi, *Dir Educ & Community Develop*, University of California, Los Angeles, Grunwald Center for the Graphic Arts, Los Angeles CA

Dale, Cindi, *Dir Educ & Community Develop*, University of California, Los Angeles, UCLA at the Armand Hammer Museum of Art & Cultural Center, Los Angeles CA

Dale, Ron, *Prof*, University of Mississippi, Dept of Art, University MS (S)

Daley, Judy, *Asst Cur*, Art Gallery of Peel, Library, Brampton ON

Daley, Ken, *Prof*, Old Dominion University, Art Dept, Norfolk VA (S)

Daley, William, *Instr*, Chautauqua Institution, School of Art, Chautauqua NY (S)

Dalkey, F, *Instr*, Sacramento City College, Art Dept, Sacramento CA (S)

Dallas, Sally, *Second VPres*, Arizona Watercolor Association, Phoenix AZ

Dalling, Harvey, *Genealogist*, Kings County Historical Society and Museum, Hampton NB

Dalton, Rick, *Equipment Coordr*, South Carolina Arts Commission, Columbia SC

Dalton, Tessa, *Office & Sales Mgr (Oct-Apr)*, Bradford Brinton Memorial Museum & Historic Ranch, Big Horn WY

Damaska, Maureen, *Admin Officer*, National Museum of American Art, Washington DC

D'Ambra, Eve, *Asst Prof*, Vassar College, Art Dept, Poughkeepsie NY (S)

D'Ambrosio, Anna T, *Decorative Arts Cur*, Munson-Williams-Proctor Institute, Museum of Art, Utica NY

D'Ambrosio, Vinni Marie, *Pres*, Pen & Brush, Inc, New York NY

D'Ambrosio, Vinni Marie, *Pres*, Pen & Brush, Inc, Library, New York NY

Damer, Jack, *Prof*, University of Wisconsin, Madison, Dept of Art, Madison WI (S)

Damiam, Carol, *Instr & Art Historian*, Florida International University, Visual Arts Dept, Miami FL (S)

Damiels, Brian, *Union Dir*, Duke University Union, Durham NC

Damkoehler, David, *Instr*, University of Wisconsin-Green Bay, Art-Communication & the Arts, Green Bay WI (S)

Danahy, John, *Assoc Prof*, University of Toronto, Programme in Landscape Architecture, Toronto ON (S)

Danciger, Alain, *Exec Dir*, Saidye Bronfman Centre for the Arts Centre, Montreal PQ

Danciger, Alain, *Asst Dir*, Saidye Bronfman Centre for the Arts Centre, Montreal PQ

Dandois, Leslie, *ARTLINKS Coordr*, Nevada Museum Of Art, Reno NV

Danford, Gerald, *VPres*, Fort Morgan Heritage Foundation, Fort Morgan CO

D'Angelo, Joseph, *Pres*, International Museum of Cartoon Art, Boca Raton FL

Daniel, Betty, *Circulation & Reserve Supv*, Washington University, Art & Architecture Library, Saint Louis MO

Daniel, Mike, *Instr*, Long Beach City College, Dept of Art, Long Beach CA (S)

Daniels, Christopher, *Preparator*, Greenville Museum of Art, Inc, Greenville NC

Daniels, Eve, *Registar*, Roberson Museum & Science Center, Binghamton NY

Daniels, John P, *Dir*, Historic Pensacola Preservation Board, Historic Pensacola Village, Pensacola FL

Daniels, Kevin, *Asst Prof*, University of Florida, Dept of Art, Gainesville FL (S)

Daniels, Maygene, *Gallery Archivist*, National Gallery of Art, Washington DC

Daniels, Robert, *Dir*, Nashua Center for Arts, Nashua NH (S)

Danielson, Deborah, *Assoc Prof*, Siena Heights College, Studio Angelico-Art Dept, Adrian MI (S)

Danioth, David, *Instr*, The Art Institutes International, The Art Institute of Seattle, Seattle WA (S)

Danly, Susan, *Cur American Art*, Amherst College, Mead Art Museum, Amherst MA

Dannenbaum, Claire, *Library Asst*, University of California, Architecture Slide Library, Berkeley CA

Danoff, I Michael, *Dir*, Edmundson Art Foundation, Inc, Des Moines Art Center, Des Moines IA

Danuser, Lois, *Circulation Library Asst*, Colonial Williamsburg Foundation, John D Rockefeller, Jr Library, Williamsburg VA

D'Aponte, Mimi, *Chmn*, Bernard M Baruch College of the City University of New York, Art Dept, New York NY (S)

Daraska, Jessie, *Librn*, Balzekas Museum of Lithuanian Culture, Research Library, Chicago IL

Darby, Laurie, *Spec Events Coordr*, Museum of Fine Arts, Springfield MA

Daringer, David, *Cur*, National Academy of Design, New York NY

Daringer, David, *Cur*, National Academy of Design, Archives, New York NY

Darish, Patricia, *Asst Prof*, University of Kansas, Kress Foundation Dept of Art History, Lawrence KS (S)

Darling, Barry, *Adjunct Asst Prof*, Le Moyne College, Fine Arts Dept, Syracuse NY (S)

Daro, Hazel E, *Asst to Dir*, University of Alaska, Museum, Fairbanks AK

Da Rold, Joseph H, *Dir*, Plainfield Public Library, Plainfield NJ

Darr, Alan, *Cur European Sculpture & Decorative Arts*, Detroit Institute of Arts, Detroit MI

Darst, Lise, *Museum Cur*, Rosenberg Library, Galveston TX

Dart, Donna, *Instr*, Silver Lake College, Art Dept, Manitowoc WI (S)

Daschle, Thomas A, *VChmn*, United States Senate Commission on Art, Washington DC

DaSilva, Marilyn, *Jewelry & Metal Arts*, California College of Arts & Crafts, Oakland CA (S)

D'Astolfo, Frank, *Deputy Chair*, Rutgers University, Newark, Dept of Visual & Performing Arts, Newark NJ (S)

Daubert, Debra, *Cur*, Oshkosh Public Museum, Oshkosh WI

Daugherty, Michael, *Dir*, Louisiana State University, School of Art, Baton Rouge LA (S)

Daughhetee, Mark, *Cur Exhib*, Alaska State Museum, Juneau AK

Daulton, Christine, *Conservator*, Westmoreland Museum of American Art, Greensburg PA

D'Avanzo, Suzanne H, *Asst Prof*, Providence College, Art & Art History Dept, Providence RI (S)

Davenny, Ward, *Assoc Prof*, Dickinson College, Fine Arts Dept, Carlisle PA (S)

Davenport, Ellen, *VPres*, Plastic Club, Art Club, Philadelphia PA

Davenport, Kimberly, *Dir*, Rice University, Art Gallery, Houston TX

Davenport, Kimberly, *Dir Art Gallery*, Rice University, Dept of Art & Art History, Houston TX (S)

Davey, Tara P, *Deputy Dir*, Dahesh Museum, New York NY

Davezac, Bertrand, *Cur*, Menil Collection, Houston TX

Davezac, Shehira, *Assoc Prof*, Indiana University, Bloomington, Henry Radford Hope School of Fine Arts, Bloomington IN (S)

Davi, Susan A, *Subject Librn (Art & Art History)*, University of Delaware, Morris Library, Newark DE

David, Christiane, *Pres*, Berks Art Alliance, Reading PA

David, Michelle, *Admin Asst*, Fort Morgan Heritage Foundation, Fort Morgan CO

Davidhazy, Andrew, *Chmn Imaging & Photographic Technology*, Rochester Institute of Technology, School of Photographic Arts & Sciences, Rochester NY (S)

Davidson, David, *Assoc Dean*, New York Academy of Art, Graduate School of Figurative Art, New York NY (S)

Davidson, Richard, *Chmn Trustees*, Longfellow's Wayside Inn Museum, South Sudbury MA

Davidson, Susan, *Assoc Cur*, Menil Collection, Houston TX

Davidson, Todd, *Mgr*, City of Scarborough, Cedar Ridge Creative Centre, Scarborough ON

Davies, Bruce W, *Exec Dir*, Craigdarroch Castle Historical Museum Society, Victoria BC

Davies, Hanlyn, *Chmn Dept*, University of Massachusetts, Amherst, College of Arts & Sciences, Amherst MA (S)

Davies, Harry, *Chmn*, Adelphi University, Dept of Art & Art History, Garden City NY (S)

Davies, Hugh M, *Dir*, Museum of Contemporary Art, San Diego, La Jolla CA

Davies, Hugh M, *Dir*, Museum of Contemporary Art, San Diego-Downtown, San Diego CA

Davila, Arturo, *Prof*, University of Puerto Rico, Dept of Fine Arts, Rio Piedras PR (S)

Davis, Allen, *Asst Prof*, Alabama A & M University, Art & Art Education Dept, Normal AL (S)

Davis, Alonzo, *Dean*, Memphis College of Art, Memphis TN (S)

Davis, Alonzo, *Dean*, Memphis College of Art, G Pillow Lewis Memorial Library, Memphis TN

Davis, Ann, *Dir*, University of Calgary, The Nickle Arts Museum, Calgary AB

Davis, Ann, *Dir*, University of Calgary, Faculty of Environmental Design, Calgary AB

Davis, Arcenia, *Interim Chmn*, Winston-Salem State University, Art Dept, Winston-Salem NC (S)

Davis, Art, *Head Dept*, Grace College, Dept of Art, Winona Lake IN (S)

Davis, Beth, *Cur*, United States Figure Skating Association, World Figure Skating Museum & Hall of Fame, Colorado Springs CO

Davis, Beth, *Cur*, United States Figure Skating Association, Library, Colorado Springs CO

Davis, Bill, *Asst Prof*, Shippensburg University, Art Dept, Shippensburg PA (S)

Davis, Bruce, *Dir*, Arts Council of Santa Clara County, Santa Clara CA

Davis, Caecilia W, *Prof*, Tulane University, Sophie H Newcomb Memorial College, New Orleans LA (S)

Davis, Clifford, *Prof*, Asbury College, Student Center Gallery, Wilmore KY

Davis, Clifford, *Instr*, Asbury College, Art Dept, Wilmore KY (S)

Davis, Colonel W J, *Deputy Dir*, Marine Corps Museum, Art Collection, Washington DC

Davis, Craig, *Library Dir*, Harrington Institute of Interior Design, Design Library, Chicago IL

Davis, David, *Co Chair Interior Design*, Academy of Art College, Fine Arts Dept, San Francisco CA (S)

Davis, Deb, *Asst Prof*, University of West Florida, Dept of Art, Pensacola FL (S)

Davis, D Jack, *Dean*, University of North Texas, School of Visual Arts, Denton TX (S)

Davis, Don, *Prof*, Northwest Nazarene College, Art Dept, Nampa ID (S)

Davis, Dorothy, *Librn*, Southern University, Art & Architecture Library, Baton Rouge LA

Davis, Dustin P, *Head Dept*, Frostburg State University, Dept of Visual Arts, Frostburg MD (S)

Davis, Dustin P, *Head*, Frostburg State University, The Stephanie Ann Roper Gallery, Frostburg MD

Davis, Enid, *Asst to Dir*, Museum of the Southwest, Midland TX

Davis, Eric, *Curatorial Consultant*, Wright State University, Dayton Art Institute, Dayton OH

Davis, Gainor B, *Dir*, Vermont Historical Society, Museum, Montpelier VT

Davis, Gainor, *Dir*, Longue Vue House & Gardens, New Orleans LA

Davis, Gainor B, *Dir*, Vermont Historical Society, Library, Montpelier VT

Davis, Jack R, *Chmn*, Oklahoma City University, Norick Art Center, Oklahoma City OK (S)

Davis, Jan Friend, *VPres*, Chautauqua Center for the Visual Arts, Chautauqua NY

Davis, Jim, *Facilities Mgr*, International Institute of Pigeons & Doves, Oklahoma City OK

Davis, Joan C, *Dir*, Bob Jones University, Museum & Art Gallery, Greenville SC

Davis, John, *Cur Exhibits*, Schenectady Museum Planetarium & Visitors Center, Schenectady NY

Davis, J R Leighton, *Dir & Cur*, St Mary's University, Art Gallery, Halifax NS

Davis, Katherine, *Exhibit Designer*, Pratt Institute Library, Rubelle & Norman Schafler Gallery, Brooklyn NY

Davis, Keith E, *Supt of Grounds*, North Carolina State University, Chinqua-Penn Plantation House, Garden & Greenhouses, Reidsville NC

Davis, Keith F, *Dir Fine Art Prog*, Hallmark Cards, Inc, Fine Art Programs, Kansas City MO

Davis, Larry, *Faculty Coordr Fine Arts*, Florida Community College at Jacksonville, South Campus, Art Dept, Jacksonville FL (S)

Davis, Leah, *Library Asst*, National Museum of Women in the Arts, Library & Research Center, Washington DC

Davis, Lee Baxter, *Chmn Printmaking*, East Texas State University, Dept of Art, Commerce TX (S)

Davis, Lydia, *Instr*, Bard College, Milton Avery Graduate School of the Arts, Annandale-on-Hudson NY (S)

Davis, Lynn, *Store Mgr*, Museum of Contemporary Art, Chicago IL

Davis, Marsh, *Dir Community Servs*, Historic Landmarks Foundation of Indiana, Information Center Library, Indianapolis IN

Davis, Mary, *Exec Dir*, American Center for Design, Chicago IL

Davis, Meredith, *Head Graphic Design Dept*, North Carolina State University at Raleigh, School of Design, Raleigh NC (S)

Davis, Meredith, *Pres*, American Center for Design, Chicago IL

Davis, Myrna, *Exec Dir*, Art Directors Club, Inc, New York NY

Davis, Nancy, *Cur & Coll*, Maryland Historical Society, Museum of Maryland History, Baltimore MD

Davis, Nancy, *Cur & Coll*, Maryland Historical Society, Library, Baltimore MD

Davis, Nathalie, *Second VPres*, Toledo Museum of Art, Toledo OH

Davis, Paul, *Dir*, University of Utah, Owen Library, Salt Lake City UT

Davis, Richard, *Sculpture Coordr*, University of North Texas, School of Visual Arts, Denton TX (S)

Davis, Ronald O, *Dir*, Florida A & M University, Dept of Visual Arts, Humanities & Theatre, Tallahassee FL (S)

Davis, Ruth C, *Exec VPres*, Pennsylvania Academy of the Fine Arts, Fellowship of the Pennsylvania Academy of the Fine Arts, Philadelphia PA

Davis, Scott M, *Asst to the Pres*, Cosanti Foundation, Scottsdale AZ

Davis, Shawn, *Dir*, Yuma Fine Arts Association, Art Center, Yuma AZ

Davis, Susan, *Bus Mgr for the Arts*, University of Wisconsin - Platteville, Harry Nohr Art Gallery, Platteville WI

Davis, Susan S, *Dir*, Stanley Museum, Inc, Kingfield ME

Davis, Thelma, *VPres*, Pastel of the West Coast, Sacramento Fine Arts Center, Carmichael CA

Davis, Virginia Irby, *Dir*, Lynchburg College, Art Dept, Lynchburg VA (S)

Davis, Walter R, *Dir*, Panhandle-Plains Historical Society Museum, Canyon TX

Davis, Whitney, *Assoc Prof*, Northwestern University, Evanston, Dept of Art History, Evanston IL (S)

Davis, William, *Pres*, The New England School of Art & Design at Suffolk University, Boston MA (S)

Davis, William J, *Dir*, MacArthur Memorial, Norfolk VA

Davis, Willis, *Chmn*, Central State University, Dept of Art, Wilberforce OH (S)

Davis, Zina, *Dir*, University of Hartford, Joseloff Gallery, West Hartford CT

Davish, Peggy, *Adminr*, Middletown Fine Arts Center, Middletown OH

Davis MFA, Paul H, *Prof*, University of Utah, Art Dept, Salt Lake City UT (S)

Davison, Liane, *Cur*, Surrey Art Gallery, Surrey BC

Davison, Liane, *Cur Exhib & Coll*, Surrey Art Gallery, Library, Surrey BC

Davis-Rosenbaum, Kate, *Instr*, Midway College, Art Dept, Midway KY (S)

Davis-Rosenbaum, Steve, *Instr*, Midway College, Art Dept, Midway KY (S)

Davson, Victor, *Exec Dir*, Aljira Center for Contemporary Art, Newark NJ

Davy, Catherine A, *Dean*, University of Wisconsin-Milwaukee, Dept of Art, Milwaukee WI (S)

Davy, Edgar W, *Librn*, Ghost Ranch Living Museum, Conference Center Library, Abiquiu NM

Davy, Susan, *Dir Admin & Finance*, Peabody Essex Museum, Salem MA

Dawkins, Jimmie, *Assoc Prof*, Alabama A & M University, Art & Art Education Dept, Normal AL (S)

Dawn, Leslie, *Asst Prof*, University of Lethbridge, Div of Art, Lethbridge AB (S)

Daws, Russell S, *Dir*, Tallahassee Museum of History & Natural Science, Tallahassee FL

Daws, Russell S, *Chief Exec Officer & Exec Dir*, Tallahassee Museum of History & Natural Science, Library, Tallahassee FL

Dawson, Amy, *Dir*, Randall Museum Junior Museum, San Francisco CA

Day, Brenda, *Dir*, Baker University, Old Castle Museum, Baldwin City KS

Day, C, *VPres*, Rodman Hall Arts Centre, Saint Catharines ON

Day, Gary, *Assoc Prof*, University of Nebraska at Omaha, Dept of Art & Art History, Omaha NE (S)

Day, Holliday T, *Cur Contemporary Art*, Indianapolis Museum of Art, Indianapolis IN

Day, Jacqueline, *Dir.* Adirondack Historical Association, Adirondack Museum, Blue Mountain Lake NY

Day, John, *Board Dirs Pres*, Sioux City Art Center, Sioux City IA

Day, John A, *Dir.* University of South Dakota Art Galleries, Vermillion SD

Day, John A, *Dean,* University of South Dakota, Department of Art, College of Fine Arts, Vermillion SD (S)

Day, Michael, *Pres-Elect,* National Art Education Association, Reston VA

Day, Michael, *Chmn.* Brigham Young University, Dept of Visual Arts, Provo UT (S)

Day, Paul, *City Mgr.* Carrie McLain Museum, Nome AK

Day, Pip, *Cur.* Artists Space, Unaffiliated Artists File, New York NY

Day, Ross, *Head Librn.* The Metropolitan Museum of Art, Robert Goldwater Library, New York NY

Day, Sharon, *Office Mgr.* Beaumont Art League, Beaumont TX

Days, Russell, *Facilities Dir.* Florida State University Foundation - Central Florida Community College Foundation, The Appleton Museum of Art, Ocala FL

Dayton, Diana, *Library Asst,* East Hampton Library, Pennypacker Long Island Collection, East Hampton NY

Deahl, Beth, *Reference Librn.* Library Association of La Jolla, Athenaeum Music & Arts Library, La Jolla CA

Deal, Cliff, *Cur Exhibits,* Lafayette Natural History Museum, Planetarium & Nature Station, Lafayette LA

Deal, Georgia, *Chmn Printmaking,* Corcoran School of Art, Washington DC (S)

Deal, Joe, *Dean School,* Washington University, School of Art, Saint Louis MO (S)

Deal, Michelle, *Registrar/Cur.* Octagon Center for the Arts, Ames IA

Dean, Ann, *Distribution Coordr,* Art Metropole, Toronto ON

Dean, David, *Dir.* Printed Matter, Inc, New York NY

Dean, David K, *Assoc Dir Operations,* Texas Tech University, Museum, Lubbock TX

Dean, Jim, *Dean Admis,* Ringling School of Art & Design, Sarasota FL (S)

Dean, Joseph, *Dir General Serv,* Colorado Historical Society, Colorado History Museum, Denver CO

Dean, Paul, *Asst Prof,* Louisiana State University, School of Art, Baton Rouge LA (S)

Deane, Dennis, *Assoc Prof,* Ohio University-Chillicothe Campus, Fine Arts & Humanities Division, Chillicothe OH (S)

DeAngelis, Anita, *Asst Prof,* East Tennessee State University, Dept of Art & Design, Johnson City TN (S)

DeAngelo, Michael, *Librn.* Independence Seaport Museum, Philadelphia PA

DeAngelo, Michael, *Librn.* Independence Seaport Museum, Library, Philadelphia PA

Deans, John, *Pres,* Jefferson Community College, Art Dept, Watertown NY (S)

Deans, Thomas A, *Pres,* Lemoyne Art Foundation, Inc, Tallahassee FL

Dear, Elizabeth, *Cur,* C M Russell Museum, Great Falls MT

Deaton, Linda, *Cur Coll & Exhib,* Tallahassee Museum of History & Natural Science, Tallahassee FL

De Biaso, Thomas, *Chmn Media Arts,* Minneapolis College of Art & Design, Minneapolis MN (S)

Debla, Acha, *Prof,* North Carolina Central University, Art Dept, Durham NC (S)

DeBoer, Brett, *Instr.* Northwest Community College, Dept of Art, Powell WY (S)

DeBolt, Dean, *Dir Spec Coll,* University of West Florida, Library, Pensacola FL

DeBord, Bebe, *Assoc Prof Art,* Lincoln Memorial University, Division of Humanities, Harrogate TN (S)

de Bretteville, Sheila, *Prof,* Yale University, School of Art, New Haven CT (S)

Decker, David, *Assoc Prof,* University of Maine, Dept of Art, Orono ME (S)

Decker, Linda, *Pres,* Maui Historical Society, Bailey House, Wailuku HI

Decker, Tim, *Registrar,* Berkshire Museum, Pittsfield MA

Decorso, Debra, *Interim Dir.* Manhattanville College, Library, Purchase NY

DeCosmo, Jan, *Chair,* Florida A & M University, Dept of Visual Arts, Humanities & Theatre, Tallahassee FL (S)

Decoteau, Pamela, *Head Art History,* Southern Illinois University at Edwardsville, Dept of Art & Design, Edwardsville IL (S)

DeDonato, Louis, *Chmn Jr Members,* Salmagundi Club, New York NY

Deegan, Denis, *Prof,* Daytona Beach Community College, Dept of Fine Arts & Visual Arts, Daytona Beach FL (S)

Deely, Philip S, *Assoc Dir External Relations,* Norman Rockwell Museum at Stockbridge, Stockbridge MA

Deeming, George, *Cur.* Pennsylvania Historical & Museum Commission, Railroad Musuem of Pennsylvania, Harrisburg PA

DeFalla, Josie E, *Dir.* Maryhill Museum of Art, Goldendale WA

de Fato, Elizabeth, *Librn.* Seattle Art Museum, Library, Seattle WA

DeFazio, Raymond, *Assoc Prof,* Seton Hill College, Dept of Art, Greensburg PA (S)

Defenbaugh, Deni, *Asst Prof,* Rochester Institute of Technology, School of Photographic Arts & Sciences, Rochester NY (S)

Defoor, T, *Music Instr.* Edison Community College, Dept of Fine & Performing Arts, Fort Myers FL (S)

De Fuchs, Mercedes Chacin, *Instr.* Toronto Art Therapy Institute, Toronto ON (S)

DeFurio, A G, *Chmn,* Indiana University of Pennsylvania, Dept of Art & Art Education, Indiana PA (S)

de gennaro, Cristina, *Asst Prof,* College of New Rochelle School of Arts & Sciences, Art Dept, New Rochelle NY (S)

DeGennaro, Mark, *Preparator,* Miami University, Art Museum, Oxford OH

Degler, Suzanne, *Acting Dir.* Minneapolis College of Art & Design, Library, Minneapolis MN

De Graff, Lee, *Pres,* Canton Museum of Art, Canton OH

DeGrange, Elmore, *Humanities,* Southern University in New Orleans, Fine Arts & Philosophy Dept, New Orleans LA (S)

DeGrazia, Diane, *Cur Southern Baroque Painting,* National Gallery of Art, Washington DC

de Guzman, Rene, *Asst Artistic Dir Visual Arts,* Center for the Arts at Yerba Buena Gardens, San Francisco CA

De Hoet, Robert, *Prog Educational-Community Servs Coordr,* Southern Illinois University, University Museum, Carbondale IL

De Hoff, William, *Asst Prof,* University of Wisconsin-Stout, Dept of Art & Design, Menomonie WI (S)

Deicher, Cate, *Fine Arts Mgr.* Alverno College Gallery, Milwaukee WI

Deihl, Nancy, *Asst Cur & Registrar.* Equitable Life Assurance Society, The Equitable Gallery, New York NY

Deitrick, Pam, *Head Librn,* Public Library of Des Moines, Central Library Information Services, Des Moines IA

Dejardin, Fiona, *Assoc Prof,* Hartwick College, Art Dept, Oneonta NY (S)

DeJong, J D, *Asst Prof,* Central University of Iowa, Art Dept, Pella IA (S)

Delacote, Goery, *Dir.* Exploratorium, San Francisco CA

Delago, Gary, *Deputy Dir,* Arizona Commission on the Arts, Phoenix AZ

Delahoyd, Mary, *Instr.* Sarah Lawrence College, Dept of Art History, Bronxville NY (S)

del Alamo, Constancio, *Cur Archaeology & Sculpture,* Hispanic Society of America, Museum, New York NY

Delamater, Peg, *Asst Prof,* Winthrop University, Dept of Art & Design, Rock Hill SC (S)

DeLaney, Charles, *Dean,* New York Institute of Photography, New York NY (S)

Delaney, Esmeralda, *Res Artist,* Grand Canyon University, Art Dept, Phoenix AZ (S)

Delaney, Marina, *Instr.* Dowling College, Dept of Visual Arts, Oakdale NY (S)

Delaney, Susan, *Instr.* Miracosta College, Art Dept, Oceanside CA (S)

de la Noval, Rossana, *Graduate Cur,* University of Illinois, Museum of Natural History, Champaign IL

DeLap, Amy, *Prof,* Vincennes University Junior College, Art Dept, Vincennes IN (S)

DeLape, Christine, *Registrar,* State University of New York at New Paltz, College Art Gallery, New Paltz NY

De La Sota, Raoul, *Prof,* Los Angeles City College, Dept of Art, Los Angeles CA (S)

de la Torre, David, *Assoc Dir.* Honolulu Academy of Arts, Honolulu HI

deLaubenfels, Pat, *Library Technical Asst II,* University of Maryland, College Park, Art Library, College Park MD

Delbo, Jose, *Instr.* Joe Kubert School of Cartoon & Graphic Art, Inc, Dover NJ (S)

DeLelys, Mark, *Museum Shop Mgr.* Pennsylvania Academy of the Fine Arts, Museum of American Art, Philadelphia PA

Delemare, Theresa, *Bus Asst,* Dartmouth College, Hood Museum of Art, Hanover NH

de Leon, Perla, *Exec Dir,* Fotografica, New York NY

Delgado, Jane, *Exec Dir,* Bronx Museum of the Arts, Bronx NY

Delgado, Sally, *Asst Dir Exhib & Prog,* Ohio University, Kennedy Museum of American Art, Athens OH

DeLillo, John, *Div Coordr,* Northern Illinois University, School of Art, De Kalb IL (S)

Delin, Nancy, *Art Librn.* Hewlett-Woodmere Public Library, Hewlett NY

Delisle, Andre, *Dir.* Chateau Ramezay Museum, Montreal PQ

Dell, Irve, *Asst Prof,* Saint Olaf College, Art Dept, Northfield MN (S)

Dell, Roger, *Gallery Dir.* Johnson State College, Dept Fine & Performing Arts, Dibden Center for the Arts, Johnson VT (S)

Della-Piana, Elissa, *Illustration,* Monserrat College of Art, Beverly MA (S)

Dellavalle, Jacques A, *Prof,* Daytona Beach Community College, Dept of Fine Arts & Visual Arts, Daytona Beach FL (S)

Deller, Harris, *Asst Dir.* Southern Illinois University, School of Art & Design, Carbondale IL (S)

Delli Quadri, Lyn, *Exec Dir Graphics & Communications,* The Art Institute of Chicago, Chicago IL

Dellis, Arlene, *Registrar,* Metro-Dade, Miami Art Museum of Dade County, Miami FL

Dellisanti, Laura, *Office Mgr.* Firelands Association for the Visual Arts, Oberlin OH

Dell'Olio, L, *Prof,* Camden County College, Dept of Art, Blackwood NJ (S)

DelMonico, Mary, *Head Publ,* Whitney Museum of American Art, New York NY

DeLong, Marilyn, *Costume Cur,* University of Minnesota, Goldstein Gallery, Saint Paul MN

De Long, Paul, *Prof,* University of Wisconsin-Stout, Dept of Art & Design, Menomonie WI (S)

DeLorme, Harry H, *Cur Educ,* Telfair Museum of Art, Savannah GA

Delos, Kate, *Instr.* Solano Community College, Division of Fine & Applied Art, Suisun City CA (S)

Deluca, Carolyn, *Dir.* Rockford Art Museum, Rockford IL

DeLuca, Carolyn, *Exec Dir.* Rockford Art Museum, Library, Rockford IL

DeLuca, E P, *Chmn Div Fine Arts, Language, Literature,* Peace College, Art Dept, Raleigh NC (S)

de Luise, Alexandra, *Cur.* Queens College, City University of New York, Queens College Art Center, Flushing NY

de Luise, Alexandra, *Art Librn.* Queens College, City University of New York, Art Library, Flushing NY del Valle, Ed, *Assoc Prof*, Florida International University, Visual Arts Dept, Miami FL (S)

DelValle, Helen, *VPres*, American Society of Artists, Inc, Chicago IL

Delvin, Robert C, *Fine Arts Librn*, Illinois Wesleyan University, Slide Library, Bloomington IL

De Marcos, Sally, *Asst Prof*, Baltimore City Community College, Dept of Fine Arts, Baltimore MD (S)

Demaree, Robert W, *Chmn*, Indiana University South Bend, Fine Arts Dept, South Bend IN (S)

Dematera, Gretchen, *Co-Dir*, Carnegie Mellon University, Forbes Gallery, Pittsburgh PA

DeMay, Susan, *Lectr*, Vanderbilt University, Dept of Fine Arts, Nashville TN (S)

Dembrowsky, Louise, *Registrar*, Kendall Whaling Museum, Sharon MA

DeMedeiros, Melissa, *Librn*, M Knoedler & Co, Inc, Library, New York NY

DeMelim, John, *Prof*, Rhode Island College, Art Dept, Providence RI (S)

De Menil, Dominique, *Pres*, Menil Collection, Houston TX

Demerling, Rod, *Installations & Registrar*, Oakville Galleries, Centennial Gallery and Gairloch Gallery, Oakville ON

Demerling, Rod, *Dir*, Lynnwood Arts Centre, Simcoe ON

Demers, Sheryl, *Bus Mgr*, Fitchburg Art Museum, Fitchburg MA

Demerson, Bamidele, *Cur Exhib*, National Conference of Artists, Michigan Chapter Gallery, Detroit MI

Demetrion, James, *Dir*, Hirshhorn Museum & Sculpture Garden, Washington DC

DeMichiel, Helen, *National Coordr*, National Alliance for Media Arts & Culture, San Francisco CA

D'Emilio, Sandra, *Cur Painting*, Museum of New Mexico, Museum of Fine Arts, Santa Fe NM

de Montebello, Philippe, *Dir*, The Metropolitan Museum of Art, New York NY

DeMoss, Max, *Instr*, Mount San Jacinto College, Art Dept, San Jacinto CA (S)

DeMots, Lois, *Instr*, Siena Heights College, Studio Angelico-Art Dept, Adrian MI (S)

Demott, Judith, *Dir Develop*, Penobscot Marine Museum, Searsport ME

DeMoulpied, Deborah, *Prof*, University of Maine, Dept of Art, Orono ME (S)

Dempsey, Anne, *Reference Librn*, Germantown Historical Society, Library, Philadelphia PA

Dempsey, Bruce, *Dean*, The Illinois Institute of Art, Chicago IL (S)

Dempsey, Connie, *Dir Educ Serv*, ICS Learning Systems, School of Interior Design, Scranton PA (S)

Dempsey, Connie, *Dir Educ Serv*, ICS Learning Systems, School of Art, Scranton PA (S)

Dempsey, Harlon, *Pres*, San Angelo Art Club, Helen King Kendall Memorial Art Gallery, San Angelo TX

Dempsey, Mary A, *Commissioner*, Chicago Public Library, Harold Washington Library Center, Chicago IL

Dempster, Dora, *Asst Dir Reference Div*, Metropolitan Toronto Library Board, Main Reference, Toronto ON

Demulder, Kum, *Instr*, Joe Kubert School of Cartoon & Graphic Art, Inc, Dover NJ (S)

DeMurias, Elaena, *Pres*, Discovery Museum, Bridgeport CT

DeNatale, Carol, *Registrar*, Cornell University, Herbert F Johnson Museum of Art, Ithaca NY

Denby, Greg, *Head Preparator*, University of Notre Dame, Snite Museum of Art, Notre Dame IN

Dengate, James, *Cur Numismatics*, University of Illinois, World Heritage Museum, Champaign IL

Denham, Karen, *Gallery Coordr*, Bank One Gallery, Louisville KY

Denison, Cara D, *Cur Drawings & Prints*, Pierpont Morgan Library, New York NY

Denison, Dirk, *Assoc Dean*, Illinois Institute of Technology, College of Architecture, Chicago IL (S)

Deniston, Grace, *Asst Prof*, University of Northern Iowa, Dept of Art, Cedar Falls IA (S)

Denker, Bert, *Librn in Charge Visual Resources Coll*, Winterthur Museum, Library, Winterthur DE

Denning, Elizabeth, *Pres*, Fall River Historical Society, Fall River MA

Dennis, David, *Technical Dir*, University of Iowa, Museum of Art, Iowa City IA

Dennis, James M, *Prof*, University of Wisconsin, Madison, Dept of Art History, Madison WI (S)

Dennis, Terry, *Instr*, Rochester Community & Technical College, Art Dept, Rochester MN (S)

Dennis, Tom, *Assoc Prof*, University of Nebraska, Kearney, Dept of Art & Art History, Kearney NE (S)

Dennison, Lisa, *Cur Col & Exhib*, Solomon R Guggenheim Museum, New York NY

Dennison, Lisa, *Cur Coll & Exhib*, Guggenheim Museum Soho, New York NY

Dennison, Sandra, *Instr*, Cuyahoga Valley Art Center, Cuyahoga Falls OH (S)

Denny, Paul C, *Chmn*, University of Arkansas at Monticello, Fine Arts Dept, Monticello AR (S)

Denny, Walter B, *Prof*, University of Massachusetts, Amherst, Art History Program, Amherst MA (S)

Densham, Robert, *Prof*, California Polytechnic State University at San Luis Obispo, Dept of Art & Design, San Luis Obispo CA (S)

Denslow, Orriene First, *Adminr*, Sitka Historical Society, Isabel Miller Museum, Sitka AK

Dentelinger, Jolene, *Pres*, Witter Gallery, Storm Lake IA

Denton, Margaret, *Asst Prof*, University of Richmond, Dept of Art, Richmond VA (S)

De Nunzio, Annette, *Pres*, Museo Italo Americano, San Francisco CA

De Nunzio, John, *Chmn*, Lackawanna Junior College, Fine Arts Dept, Scranton PA (S)

Denyes, Kaaren, *Dept Head*, Ferris State University, Visual Communication Dept, Big Rapids MI (S)

DePalma-Sadzkoski, Elaine, *Museum Educator*, Munson-Williams-Proctor Institute, Museum of Art, Utica NY

DePass, Penney, *Exec Dir*, Art Libraries Society of North America, Raleigh NC

DePietro, Anne Cohen, *Cur*, Heckscher Museum of Art, Huntington NY

DePopolo, Margaret, *Librn*, Massachusetts Institute of Technology, Rotch Library of Architecture & Planning, Cambridge MA

DeProspero, Al, *Prof*, Delaware County Community College, Communications & Humanities House, Media PA (S)

Deranian, Janet, *Cur Coll*, Historical Society of York County, York PA

Derbes, Anne, *Chmn*, Hood College, Dept of Art, Frederick MD (S)

Derby, Midge, *Dir*, Johnson-Humrickhouse Museum, Coshocton OH

Derman, Asher, *Coordr Interior Design*, Kean College of New Jersey, Fine Arts Dept, Union NJ (S)

Der Manuelian, Lucy, *Adjunct Prof*, Tufts University, Dept of Art & Art History, Medford MA (S)

Dermody, Bill, *Visual Arts Dir*, Community Council for the Arts, Kinston NC

de Roquebrune, Sylviane, *Dir & Cur*, York University, Glendon Gallery, North York ON

DeRosa, Elizabeth, *Cur Coll*, New Jersey Historical Society, Newark NJ

DeRosa, Libby, *Cur Coll*, New Jersey Historical Society, Library, Newark NJ

DeRosa, Michael, *Head Dept*, Coffeyville Community College, Art Dept, Coffeyville KS (S)

DeRoux, Ken, *Cur Museum Serv*, Alaska State Museum, Juneau AK

Derrevere, William, *Instr*, Tulsa Junior College, Art Dept, Tulsa OK (S)

DeRuiter, Garret, *Prof*, Eastern Illinois University, Art Dept, Charleston IL (S)

Dery, Joanne, *Librn*, Montreal Museum of Fine Arts, Library, Montreal PQ

Desabritas, Elizabeth, *Instr*, Centenary College, Humanities Dept, Hackettstown NJ (S)

Desai, Vishakha, *Dir Galleries*, The Asia Society Galleries, New York NY

de Sales Dinneen, Marie, *Chmn*, Regis College, Dept of Art, Weston MA (S)

DeSaussure, Charlton, *Pres Board*, Carolina Art Association, Gibbes Museum of Art, Charleston SC

DeSaussure, Charlton, *Pres Board*, Carolina Art Association, Library, Charleston SC

Desch, Philip, *Instr*, ACA College of Design, Cincinnati OH (S)

DeSchamps, Francois, *Chmn Art Studio & Art Educ*, State University of New York College at New Paltz, Art Studio Dept, New Paltz NY (S)

Deschamps, Yves, *Instr*, Universite de Montreal, Dept of Art History, Montreal PQ (S)

De Seve, Karen, *Archivist*, Eastern Washington State Historical Society, Cheney Cowles Museum, Spokane WA

De Seve, Karen, *Archivists*, Eastern Washington State Historical Society, Library, Spokane WA

des Grange, Jane, *Dir*, Hartwick College, Museum at Hartwick, Oneonta NY

Deshauteurs, Aurora, *Librn*, Pennsylvania Academy of the Fine Arts, Library, Philadelphia PA

DeShaw, Katie, *Dir Develop*, Walker Art Center, Minneapolis MN

DeSiano, Michael, *Coordr Art Educ*, Kean College of New Jersey, Fine Arts Dept, Union NJ (S)

Desiderio, Vincent, *Instr*, New York Academy of Art, Graduate School of Figurative Art, New York NY (S)

De Silvo, Verneal, *Prof*, Compton Community College, Art Dept, Compton CA (S)

Desjardins, Robert Y, *Dir*, Shawinigan Art Center, Shawinigan PQ

DeSloover, Rose, *Prof*, Marygrove College, Visual & Performing Arts Div, Detroit MI (S)

Desmarais, Charles, *Dir*, Contemporary Arts Center, Cincinnati OH

Desmarais, Charles, *Dir*, Contemporary Arts Center, Library, Cincinnati OH

de Smet, Louis, *Treas*, Art Centre of New Jersey, Livingston NJ (S)

DeSmett, Don, *Dir Exhib*, Temple University, Tyler School of Art-Galleries, Tyler Gallery, Elkins PA

Desmond, Kathleen, *Prof*, Central Missouri State University, Art Dept, Warrensburg MO (S)

DeSoto, Lewis, *Graduate Studies*, California College of Arts & Crafts, Oakland CA (S)

Despres, Rene, *VPres*, Musee d'Art de Joliette, Joliette PQ

Dessornes, Maria, *Pres*, Conejo Valley Art Museum, Thousand Oaks CA

Dessureault, Pierre, *Assoc Cur*, Canadian Museum of Contemporary Photography, Ottawa ON

Detweiler, Robert K, *Chmn*, Santa Clara University, Art Dept, Santa Clara CA (S)

Deutsch, Sanna, *Registrar*, Honolulu Academy of Arts, Honolulu HI

deVallet, Christine, *Asst Librn*, Yale University, Art & Architecture Library, New Haven CT

Devereaux, Donna, *Dir Visual Arts*, Spirit Square Center for Arts & Education, Charlotte NC

de Ville, Roy V, *Gallery Dir*, Louisiana State University at Alexandria, University Gallery, Alexandria LA

deVille, Roy V, *Prof Art*, Louisiana State University at Alexandria, Dept of Fine Arts & Design, Alexandria LA (S)

Devine, Denise, *Coll Mgr*, California State University, Chico, Janet Turner Print Gallery & Collection, Chico CA

Devine, Jack, *Board Pres*, Ocean City Art Center, Ocean City NJ

Devine, Maureen, *Head Cur & Registrar*, Edsel & Eleanor Ford House, Grosse Pointe Shores MI

Devine, Rose, *Anti-Drug APPLE Corps Dir*, Arizona Commission on the Arts, Phoenix AZ

Devine-Reed, Pat, *Exec Dir*, Boulevard Arts Center, Chicago IL

DeVinny, Douglas, *Prof*, University of Wisconsin-Parkside, Art Dept, Kenosha WI (S)

Devlin, Dan, *Instr*, ACA College of Design, Cincinnati OH (S)

Devlin, Joseph T, *Head*, Girard College, Stephen Girard Collection, Philadelphia PA

Devlin, Margaret, *Dir Library Serv*. Kutztown University, Rohrbach Library, Kutztown PA

Devlin, Richard, *Chmn Dept*. Carlow College, Art Dept, Pittsburgh PA (S)

DeVoll, Michael G, *Assoc Dir*. Houston Center For Photography, Houston TX

Devon, Marjorie, *Dir*. University of New Mexico, Tamarind Institute, Albuquerque NM (S)

Dew, Patsy, *Theater Mgr*. Northfield Arts Guild, Northfield MN

Dew, **Roderick**, *Librn*, Colorado Springs Fine Arts Center, Colorado Springs CO

Dew, Roderick, *Librn*, Colorado Springs Fine Arts Center, Library, Colorado Springs CO

Dewald, Ann, *Asst Dir*, Archaeological Society of Ohio, Indian Museum of Lake County, Ohio, Painesville OH

Dewar, Les, *Pres*. Manitoba Society of Artists, Winnipeg MB

Dewey, Pamela, *Head Photo Archives*, National Museum of the American Indian, George Gustav Heye Center, New York NY

Dewey, Toby, *Dir*, Charles River School, Creative Arts Program, Dover MA (S)

Dewey, Tom, *Assoc Prof*. University of Mississippi, Dept of Art, University MS (S)

Dewhitt, Karen, *Office Mgr*, Huntsville Art League, Huntsville AL

DeWitt, Martin, *Dir*. University of Minnesota, Duluth, Tweed Museum of Art, Duluth MN

DeWitt, Rick, *Treas*, CIAO, Gallery & Art Center, Bronx NY

DeWoody, James, *Instr*. New York Institute of Technology, Fine Arts Dept, Old Westbury NY (S)

DeYoung Kohler, Ruth, *Dir*, Sheboygan Arts Foundation, Inc, John Michael Kohler Arts Center, Sheboygan WI

d'Harnoncourt, Anne, *The George D Widener Dir*. Philadelphia Museum of Art, Philadelphia PA

Dial, Gail, *Dir*, Idaho State University, John B Davis Gallery of Fine Art, Pocatello ID

Dial, Gail, *Chmn*. Idaho State University, Dept of Art, Pocatello ID (S)

Diament, Elizabeth, *Asst Cur Educ*, Yeshiva University Museum, New York NY

Diamond, Sara, *Artistic Dir & Exec Producer*, Banff Centre for the Arts, Banff AB (S)

Diamond, Stuart, *Instr*. Columbia University, School of the Arts, Division of Visual Arts, New York NY (S)

Diamond-Nigh, John, *Asst*, Elmira College, Art Dept, Elmira NY (S)

Diaz, Carlos, *Chmn Photography*, Center for Creative Studies, College of Art & Design, Detroit MI (S)

Dibert, Rita, *Prof*, University of North Carolina at Charlotte, Dept of Visual Arts, Charlotte NC (S)

Dicey, Mark, *Technician*, Alberta College of Art & Design, Illingworth Kerr Gallery, Calgary AB

Dichtl, William, *Exhib Dir*, Tippecanoe County Historical Museum, Lafayette IN

DiCicco, John, *Slide Librn*, Providence College, Art & Art History Dept, Providence RI (S)

Dickens, Denise, *Exec Dir*, City Gallery of Contemporary Art, Raleigh NC

Dickerson, Amy Vigilante, *Gallery Coordr*, City of Gainesville, Thomas Center Galleries - Cultural Affairs, Gainesville FL

Dickerson, Lydia, *Asst to Dir*, Angels Gate Cultural Center, The Gate Gallery, San Pedro CA

Dickerson, Roger, *Music*, Southern University in New Orleans, Fine Arts & Philosophy Dept, New Orleans LA (S)

Dickert, Carol, *Exec Dir*, Institute for Arts & Humanities Education, New Jersey Summer Arts Institute, New Brunswick NJ (S)

Dickey, Elizabeth, *Dean*, New School for Social Research, Adult Education Division, New York NY (S)

Dickey, Mike, *Admin*, Arrow Rock State Historic Site, Arrow Rock MO

Dickey, Terry P, *Coordr Public Servs & Educ*, University of Alaska, Museum, Fairbanks AK

Dickinson, Carol, *Exec Dir*, Foothills Art Center, Inc, Golden CO

Dickinson, Carol V, *Exec Dir*. Foothills Art Center, Inc, Golden CO

Dickinson, Carolyn, *Head Fine Arts & Audiovisual Dept*, Salt Lake City Public Library, Fine Arts, Audiovisual Dept and Atrium Gallery, Salt Lake City UT

Dickinson, Pat, *Coordr*, Baycrest Centre for Geriatric Care, Irving E & Ray Kanner Heritage Museum, Toronto ON

Dickinson, Sarah, *Asst Librn*. Boston Architectural Center, Memorial Library, Boston MA

Dickson, Anita, *Asst Prof*. College of DuPage, Humanities Division, Glen Ellyn IL (S)

Dickson, Janet S, *Cur Educ*. Yale University, Art Gallery, New Haven CT

Dickson, Jean, *Office Mgr*. Palo Alto Cultural Center, Palo Alto CA

Dickson, Kathy, *Mus Div*. Oklahoma Historical Society, State Museum of History, Oklahoma City OK

DiCostanza, C, *Instr*. Humboldt State University, College of Arts & Humanities, Arcata CA (S)

Diduk, Barbara, *Chmn*. Dickinson College, Fine Arts Dept, Carlisle PA (S)

Diebold, William J, *Chmn Art History & Humanities*, Reed College, Dept of Art, Portland OR (S)

Diebold, William J, *Assoc Prof Art History*, Reed College, Dept of Art, Portland OR (S)

Diehl, Anna Grace, *VChmn*, Moncur Gallery, Boissevain MB

Diehl, Steve, *Assoc Prof*, Rochester Institute of Technology, School of Photographic Arts & Sciences, Rochester NY (S)

Diehr, James T, *Prof*. Austin Peay State University, Dept of Art, Clarksville TN (S)

Diercks, Robert, *Co-Chmn*, Franklin Pierce College, Dept of Fine Arts & Graphic Communications, Rindge NH (S)

Dierdorff, Jo, *Chmn*. Riverside Community College, Dept of Art & Mass Media, Riverside CA (S)

Dierfeldt, Jerry, *Dir*. Hastings Museum, Hastings NE

Dieter, Joseph, *Lectr*. Johns Hopkins University, School of Medicine, Dept of Art as Applied to Medicine, Baltimore MD (S)

Diethorn, Karie, *Chief Museum Branch*, Independence National Historical Park, Philadelphia PA

Dietrich, Dorothea, *Prof*. Princeton University, Dept of Art & Archaeology, Princeton NJ (S)

Dietz, Judy, *Mgr Coll & Gallery Services*, Art Gallery of Nova Scotia, Halifax NS

Dietz, Ulysses G, *Cur Decorative Arts*. Newark Museum Association, The Newark Museum, Newark NJ

DiFate, Vincent, *Pres*. Society of Illustrators, New York NY

Differding, Paula, *Coordr Visual Communications*, Indiana University-Purdue University, Indianapolis, Herron School of Art, Indianapolis IN (S)

Dige, Becky, *Admin Asst*. MonDak Heritage Center, Sidney MT

Digesare, John, *Registrar*. Mingei International, Inc, Mingei International Museum Satellite of World Folk Art, San Diego CA

Digrys, Mary, *Admin Asst*. Beaufort County Arts Council, Washington NC

Dill, William, *Interim Pres*. Boston Architectural Center, Boston MA

Dillihay, Ernest, *Performing Arts Dir*. City of Los Angeles, Cultural Affairs Dept, Los Angeles CA

Dillon, Eve, *Secy*. Oakland Community College, Art Dept, Farmington Hills MI (S)

Dillon, John, *Cur Natural Sciences*. Randall Museum Junior Museum, San Francisco CA

Dillon, John W, *Prof*. University of Alabama at Birmingham, Dept of Art, Birmingham AL (S)

Dillon, Ruth, *Pres*. Hutchinson Art Association, Hutchinson Art Center, Hutchinson KS

Dills, Keith, *Prof*. California Polytechnic State University at San Luis Obispo, Dept of Art & Design, San Luis Obispo CA (S)

Dilts, Susan, *Public Relations*. Library Association of La Jolla, Athenaeum Music & Arts Library, La Jolla CA

Dilworth, Kirby, *Asst Head*. Carnegie Library of Pittsburgh, Pittsburgh PA

DiMattia, Ernest A, *Pres*. Ferguson Library, Stamford CT

Dimattio, Vincent, *Chmn*. Monmouth University, Dept of Art & Design, West Long Branch NJ (S)

Dimico, Sam, *Instr*. The Art Institutes International, The Art Institute of Seattle, Seattle WA (S)

Dimon, Heather, *Assoc Cur & Registrar*, Guild Hall of East Hampton, Inc, Guild Hall Museum, East Hampton NY

Dimond, Thomas, *Asst Prof Art*. Eastern Oregon State College, Arts & Humanities Dept, La Grande OR (S)

Dingman, Kevin, *Lectr*, Culver-Stockton College, Art Dept, Canton MO (S)

Dingus, Rick, *Prof. & Assoc Prof*, Texas Tech University, Dept of Art, Lubbock TX (S)

Dingwall, Kenneth, *Prof*. Cleveland Institute of Art, Cleveland OH (S)

Dinkelspiel, Edgar N, *Pres*. Long Branch Historical Museum, Long Branch NJ

Dinsmore, John, *Chmn*, University of Nebraska, Kearney, Dept of Art & Art History, Kearney NE (S)

Dion, Ray, *Develop Dir*. Conejo Valley Art Museum, Thousand Oaks CA

DiPilla, Michela, *Adminr*, Museo Italo Americano, San Francisco CA

Dippolito, Frank, *Art Dept Chmn*. Tacoma Community College, Art Dept, Tacoma WA (S)

Diracles, Naomi, *Pres*, Long Beach Art League, Island Park NY

Dirks, John, *Dir*. Ogunquit Museum of American Art, Ogunquit ME

Dirks, John, *Dir*. Ogunquit Museum of American Art, Reference Library, Ogunquit ME

Dirkse, Lorrie, *Exec Ed*, Dialogue Inc, Columbus OH

Disbro, Bill, *Div Chmn*, Jamestown Community College, Arts & Humanities Division, Jamestown NY (S)

Dismore, Grant, *Instr*. La Roche College, Division of Graphics, Design & Communication, Pittsburgh PA (S)

Disney, Betty, *Dir*. Cypress College, Fine Arts Gallery, Cypress CA

DiTeresa, Neil, *Prof*. Berea College, Art Dept, Berea KY (S)

Ditler, Joe, *Develop Dir*. San Diego Maritime Museum, San Diego CA

Di Tommaso, Francis, *Dir*. School of Visual Arts, Visual Arts Museum, New York NY

Di Tommaso, Francis, *Dir*. School of Visual Arts, New York NY (S)

Divelbiss, Maggie, *Dir*, Sangre de Cristo Arts & Conference Center, Pueblo CO

Divola, John, *Chmn*, University of California, Riverside, Dept of Art, Riverside CA (S)

Dixon, Annette, *Cur Western Art*. University of Michigan, Museum of Art, Ann Arbor MI

Dixon, Arthur L, *Chmn*. J Sargeant Reynolds Community College, Humanities & Social Science Division, Richmond VA (S)

Dixon, Bob, *Assoc Prof*. University of Illinois at Springfield, Visual Arts Program, Springfield IL (S)

Dixon, Claudine, *Office Mgr*, University of California, Los Angeles, Grunwald Center for the Graphic Arts, Los Angeles CA

Dixon, David, *Assoc Prof*, East Tennessee State University, Dept of Art & Design, Johnson City TN (S)

Dixon, F Eugene, *Pres*, The Society of the Four Arts, Palm Beach FL

Dixon, Gerald, *VPres*, No Man's Land Historical Society Museum, Goodwell OK

Dixon, Jeannette, *Librn*. Museum of Fine Arts, Houston, Hirsch Library, Houston TX

Dixon, Ken, *Prof*. Texas Tech University, Dept of Art, Lubbock TX (S)

Dixon, Laurinda, *Prof*. Syracuse University, Dept of Fine Arts (Art History), Syracuse NY (S)

Dixon, Susan, *Asst Prof*. Murray State University, Dept of Art, Murray KY (S)

Dixon, Yvonne, *Head Dept*. Trinity College, Art Program, Washington DC (S)

Douke, Daniel, *Dir.* California State University, Los Angeles, Fine Arts Gallery, Los Angeles CA

Doumato, Lamia, *Reader Services Librn.* National Gallery of Art, Library, Washington DC

Dove, Judy, *Pres.* Gallery XII, Wichita KS

Dove, Ronald, *Pres.* Hussian School of Art, Commercial Art Dept, Philadelphia PA (S)

Dovman, Claudia, *Asst Librn.* Historic Hudson Valley, Library, Tarrytown NY

Dowd, Sandra, *Dir.* Navarro College, Art Dept, Corsicana TX (S)

Dowdy, William, *Chmn Dept,* Blue Mountain College, Art Dept, Blue Mountain MS (S)

Dowell, Cheryl, *Asst Site Mgr,* Illinois Historic Preservation Agency, Bishop Hill State Historic Site, Bishop Hill IL

Dowell, Michael B, *Exec Dir,* Fine Arts Center for the New River Valley, Pulaski VA

Dowell-Dennis, Terri, *Educ Coordr,* Southeastern Center for Contemporary Art, Winston-Salem NC

Dowhie, Leonard, *Asst Prof,* University of Southern Indiana, Art Dept, Evansville IN (S)

Dowis, William S, *VPres,* Florence Museum of Art, Science & History, Florence SC

Dowlin, Kenneth E, *Dir,* San Francisco Public Library, Art & Music Center, San Francisco CA

Dowling, Russell, *Chmn Board,* High Plains Museum, McCook NE

Downey, Christina, *Prof,* Blackburn College, Dept of Art, Carlinville IL (S)

Downey, Judith, *Librn,* Old Dartmouth Historical Society, Whaling Museum Library, New Bedford MA

Downey, Kay, *Serials Librn,* Cleveland Museum of Art, Ingalls Library, Cleveland OH

Downey, Laura, *Paper Conservator,* Balboa Art Conservation Center, San Diego CA

Downey, Martha J, *Site Mgr,* Illinois Historic Preservation Agency, Bishop Hill State Historic Site, Bishop Hill IL

Downs, Linda, *Cur Educ,* National Gallery of Art, Washington DC

Downs, Stuart, *Instr,* James Madison University, School of Art & Art History, Harrisonburg VA (S)

Downs, Stuart C, *Gallery Dir,* James Madison University, Sawhill Gallery, Harrisonburg VA

Doyle, Cheri, *Cur Coll,* Southwest Museum, Los Angeles CA

Doyle, Christopher, *Facilities Mgr,* Headlands Center for the Arts, Sausalito CA

Doyle, Erin T, *Asst Chief Librn,* Medicine Hat Public Library, Medicine Hat AB

Doyle, Glenn, *Exec Dir,* Arthur Griffin Center for Photographic Art, Winchester MA

Doyle, Joshua, *Asst Prof,* University of Wisconsin-Superior, Programs in the Visual Arts, Superior WI (S)

Doyle, Leo, *Instr,* California State University, San Bernardino, Visual Arts, San Bernardino CA (S)

Doyle, Marilyn, *Visitor Serv,* Alaska State Museum, Juneau AK

Doyle, Richard, *Dir Library Services & Academic Computing,* Coe College, Stewart Memorial Library & Gallery, Cedar Rapids IA

Doyon, Lena, *Asst Librn,* Musee du Quebec, Bibliotheque des Arts, Quebec PQ

Doyon-Bernard, Suzette J, *Asst Prof,* University of West Florida, Dept of Art, Pensacola FL (S)

Drachler, Carole, *Instr,* Mesa Community College, Dept of Art & Art History, Mesa AZ (S)

Drafen, Jennifer, *Cur Coll,* Schenectady Museum Planetarium & Visitors Center, Schenectady NY

Draghi, Robert, *Dean,* Marymount University of Virginia, School of Arts & Sciences Division, Arlington VA (S)

Drahos, Dean, *Dir,* Baldwin-Wallace College, Fawick Art Gallery, Berea OH

Drahos, Dean, *Head Dept,* Baldwin-Wallace College, Dept of Art, Berea OH (S)

Drake, Tommi, *Dir,* Rogue Community College, Wiseman Gallery - Firehouse Gallery, Grants Pass OR

Dralle, Laura, *Instr,* Mount Mary College, Art Dept, Milwaukee WI (S)

Dransfield, Charles, *Second VPres,* Kent Art Association, Inc, Gallery, Kent CT

Draper, Jerry L, *Dean School Visual Arts,* Florida State University, Art History Dept (R133B), Tallahassee FL (S)

Draper, Stacy F Pomeroy, *Cur,* Rensselaer County Historical Society, Hart-Cluett Mansion, 1827, Troy NY

Drasiten, Roy, *Chmn Studio,* University of South Carolina, Dept of Art, Columbia SC (S)

Dreeszen, Craig, *Dir,* Arts Extension Service, Amherst MA

Dreiling, Janet, *Registrar,* University of Kansas, Spencer Museum of Art, Lawrence KS

Dreishpoon, Douglas, *Cur Coll,* University of North Carolina at Greensboro, Weatherspoon Art Gallery, Greensboro NC

Dreiss, Joseph, *Prof,* Mary Washington College, Art Dept, Fredericksburg VA (S)

Drennen, Barbara, *Asst Prof,* Malone College, Dept of Art, Canton OH (S)

Drescher, Judith, *Dir,* Memphis-Shelby County Public Library & Information Center, Dept of Art, Music & Films, Memphis TN

Dressler, Rachel, *Asst Prof,* State University of New York at Albany, Art Dept, Albany NY (S)

Drew, K F, *Acting Chmn,* Rice University, Dept of Art & Art History, Houston TX (S)

Drewal, Henry J, *Prof,* University of Wisconsin, Madison, Dept of Art History, Madison WI (S)

Drexler, Nancy, *Marketing Mgr,* State University of New York at Purchase, Neuberger Museum of Art, Purchase NY

Dreydoppel, Susan, *Exec Dir,* Moravian Historical Society, Whitefield House Museum, Nazareth PA

Dreyer, Donna Jean, *Develop Dir,* Penland School of Crafts, Penland NC (S)

Dreyfus, Renee, *Cur Interpretation,* Fine Arts Museums of San Francisco, M H de Young Memorial Museum & California Palace of the Legion of Honor, San Francisco CA

Drieband, Laurence, *Fine Arts Dept Chmn,* Art Center College of Design, Pasadena CA (S)

Driesbach, Janice T, *Cur,* Crocker Art Museum, Sacramento CA

Drinkard, Joel F, *Cur,* Southern Baptist Theological Seminary, Joseph A Callaway Archaeological Museum, Louisville KY

Driscoll, James, *Research Analyst,* Queens Historical Society, Flushing NY

Drittler, John, *Librn,* Museum of Ossining Historical Society, Library, Ossining NY

Droega, Anthony, *Adjunct Asst Prof,* Indiana University South Bend, Fine Arts Dept, South Bend IN (S)

Droege, John, *Prof,* Bridgewater State College, Art Dept, Bridgewater MA (S)

Drosny, Mary, *Prog Dir,* Palos Verdes Art Center, Rancho Palos Verdes CA

Drost, Lise, *Asst Prof,* University of Miami, Dept of Art & Art History, Coral Gables FL (S)

Drost, Romola, *Pres,* Cumberland Art Society Inc, Cookeville Art Gallery, Cookeville TN

Druback, Diana, *Asst,* Ohio State University, Fine Arts Library, Columbus OH

Drubner, Sharon, *Pres,* Mattatuck Historical Society, Mattatuck Museum, Waterbury CT

Druckenbrod, Mark, *Asst Dir,* Cleveland Botanical Garden, Eleanor Squire Library, Cleveland OH

Drucker, Virginia, *Librn,* The Parrish Art Museum, Aline B Saarinen Library, Southampton NY

Druick, Douglas W, *Cur European Painting,* The Art Institute of Chicago, Chicago IL

Druick, Douglas W, *Cur Prints & Drawings,* The Art Institute of Chicago, Chicago IL

Druick, Douglas W, *Prince Trust Cur Prints & Drawings & Searle Cur European Drawings,* The Art Institute of Chicago, Print & Drawing Dept, Chicago IL

Drum, Karen, *Pub Relations,* Laguna Art Museum of the Orange County Museum of Art, Laguna Beach CA

Drumheller, Grant, *Assoc Prof,* University of New Hampshire, Dept of Arts & Art History, Durham NH (S)

Drummey, Peter, *Librn,* Massachusetts Historical Society, Library, Boston MA

Drury, Doug, *Gallery Coordr,* ArtSpace-Lima, Lima OH

Dryfhout, John H, *Supt & Cur,* Saint-Gaudens National Historic Site, Cornish NH

Dryfhout, John H, *Cur,* Saint-Gaudens National Historic Site, Library, Cornish NH

Drysdale, Andrew, *Dir,* Hunterdon Historical Museum, Clinton NJ

D'Spain, Pat, *Pres,* Frontier Times Museum, Bandera TX

Duarte, Gema, *Pres,* Xicanindio, Inc, Mesa AZ

Dubansky, Mindell, *Conservation Librn,* The Metropolitan Museum of Art, Thomas J Watson Library, New York NY

DuBay, Bren, *Lectr,* Rice University, Dept of Art & Art History, Houston TX (S)

Dubberly, Ronald A, *Dir,* Altanta-Fulton Public Library, Art-Humanities Dept, Atlanta GA

Dubler, Linda, *Cur Media Art,* High Museum of Art, Atlanta GA

DuBois, Alan, *Cur Decorative Arts,* Arkansas Arts Center, Little Rock AR

DuBois, Doug, *Asst Prof,* New Mexico State University, Art Dept, Las Cruces NM (S)

DuBois, Henry J, *Art Bibliographer,* California State University, Long Beach, University Library, Long Beach CA

DuBois, Jeanne, *Dir,* Housatonic Community-Technical College, Housatonic Museum of Art, Bridgeport CT

Dubose, Frank, *Grad Div Chair,* School of the Art Institute of Chicago, Chicago IL (S)

Dubreuil, Nicole, *Instr,* Universite de Montreal, Dept of Art History, Montreal PQ (S)

Dubsky, Selagh, *Dance Coordr,* Ashtabula Arts Center, Ashtabula OH

DuCharme, Andree, *Instr,* Silver Lake College, Art Dept, Manitowoc WI (S)

Duckett, Sarah, *Museum Asst,* Fort Worth Art Association, Modern Art Museum of Fort Worth, Fort Worth TX

Duckwall, J Robert, *Instr,* Johns Hopkins University, School of Medicine, Dept of Art as Applied to Medicine, Baltimore MD (S)

Duckworth, W Donald, *Dir,* Bernice Pauahi Bishop Museum, Honolulu HI

Dudek, Steve, *Instr,* Barton County Community College, Fine Arts Dept, Great Bend KS (S)

Dudics MFA, Kitty, *Assoc Prof,* Del Mar College, Art Dept, Corpus Christi TX (S)

Dudley, Ian, *Touring Exhib Coordr,* University of Minnesota, James Ford Bell Museum of Natural History, Minneapolis MN

Dudley, Janice Stafford, *Admin Asst,* MacArthur Memorial, Norfolk VA

Dudley, Mary, *Chmn,* Howard College, Art Dept, Big Spring TX (S)

Dudley, Russell, *Gallery Dir,* Sierra Nevada College, Visual & Performing Arts Dept, Incline Village NV (S)

Duensing, Sally, *Museum Liaison,* Exploratorium, San Francisco CA

Duerr, Mark, *Dir,* Steep & Brew Gallery, Madison WI

Duesing, James, *Prof Fine Arts,* University of Cincinnati, School of Art, Cincinnati OH (S)

Duff, Charles, *Act Dept Head,* Ancilla College, Art Dept, Donaldson IN (S)

Duff, James H, *Dir,* Brandywine River Museum, Chadds Ford PA

Duffek, Robert, *Asst Prof,* Mohawk Valley Community College, Advertising Design & Production, Utica NY (S)

Duffy, Alan, *Gallery Mgr,* Calgary Contemporary Arts Society, Triangle Gallery of Visual Arts, Calgary AB

Duffy, Anne Marie, *Office Mgr,* Cliveden, Philadelphia PA

Duffy, Brian R, *Chmn,* Villa Maria College of Buffalo, Art Dept, Buffalo NY (S)

Duffy, Joe, *Info Contact,* National Cartoonists Society, New York NY

Duffy, Michael, *Pres,* Rensselaer Newman Foundation Chapel & Cultural Center, The Gallery, Troy NY

Dufilho, Diane, *Assoc Dir Educ,* Asheville Art Museum, Asheville NC

Dufort, Robert, *Chmn Dept of Art & Design,* Schoolcraft College, Dept of Art & Design, Livonia MI (S)

Dufour, Lydia, *Reference Letters*, Frick Art Reference Library, New York NY

Dufresne, Daphne, *Dir*, Universite du Quebec, Bibliotheque des Arts, Montreal PQ

Dufresne, Laura, *Asst Prof*, Winthrop University, Dept of Art & Design, Rock Hill SC (S)

Dugan, Alan, *Instr*, Truro Center for the Arts at Castle Hill, Inc, Truro MA (S)

Dugan, Charles H, *Asst Prof*, Clarion University of Pennsylvania, Dept of Art, Clarion PA (S)

Dugan, Ellen, *Cur Photography*, High Museum of Art, Atlanta GA

Dugan, George, *Prof*, State University of New York, College at Cortland, Art Dept, Cortland NY (S)

Dugdale, James, *Instr*, Joliet Junior College, Fine Arts Dept, Joliet IL (S)

Duggan, Jane E, *Librn*, Boston Public Library, Albert H Wiggin Gallery & Print Department, Boston MA

Duggan, Lynn, *Prof*, Nazareth College of Rochester, Art Dept, Rochester NY (S)

Duggan, Mona, *Assoc Dir External Affairs*, Stanford University, Museum of Art, Stanford CA

Duhigg, Thad, *Prof*, Texas Christian University, Art & History Dept, Fort Worth TX (S)

Duillo, John, *Pres*, Society of American Historical Artists, Osysterbay NY

Duke, Linda, *Dir Educ*, University of Illinois, Krannert Art Museum, Champaign IL

DuLong, Bridget, *Mem Coordr*, Los Angeles Contemporary Exhibitions, Hollywood CA

Dunbeck, Helen, *Adminr*, Museum of Contemporary Art, Chicago IL

Duncan, Carol, *Prof Art History*, Ramapo College of New Jersey, School of Contemporary Arts, Mahwah NJ (S)

Duncan, Gloria, *Instr*, Oklahoma Baptist University, Art Dept, Shawnee OK (S)

Duncan, Karen, *Registrar*, University of Minnesota, Weisman Art Museum, Minneapolis MN

Duncan, Norine, *Cur*, Brown University, Art Slide Library, Providence RI

Duncan, Richard, *Assoc Prof*, Florida International University, Visual Arts Dept, Miami FL (S)

Duncan, Sam, *Asst Librn*, Amon Carter Museum, Library, Fort Worth TX

Duncan, Shelby, *In Charge*, Nations Bank, Art Collection, Richmond VA

Dundon, Margo, *Exec Dir*, Museum Science & History, Jacksonville FL

Dundore, Mary Margaret, *Co-Dir*, University of Portland, Buckley Center Gallery, Portland OR

Dunifon, Don, *Prof*, Wittenberg University, Art Dept, Springfield OH (S)

Dunkley, Diane, *Dir & Chief Cur*, DAR Museum, National Society Daughters of the American Revolution, Washington DC

Dunlap, Ellen S, *Pres*, American Antiquarian Society, Worcester MA

Dunn, Alberta S, *Pres*, Livingston County Historical Society, Cobblestone Museum, Geneseo NY

Dunn, Carol, *Exec Dir*, San Luis Obispo Art Center, San Luis Obispo CA

Dunn, Josephine, *Cur Art*, Everhart Museum, Scranton PA

Dunn, Mary Maples, *VPres*, Historic Deerfield, Inc, Deerfield MA

Dunn, Nancy, *Dir*, Artesia Historical Museum & Art Center, Artesia NM

Dunn, Robert, *VPres*, National Society of Painters in Casein & Acrylic, Inc, Whitehall PA

Dunn, Roger, *Prof*, Bridgewater State College, Art Dept, Bridgewater MA (S)

Dunn, Warren, *Instr*, Clark College, Art Dept, Vancouver WA (S)

Dunne, Jane, *Deputy Dir Adminr*, The Jewish Museum, New York NY

Dunning, Clara, *VPres*, Arthur Roy Mitchell Memorial Inc, Museum of Western Art, Trinidad CO

Dunning, Gail, *Instr*, Creighton University, Fine & Performing Arts Dept, Omaha NE (S)

Dunwoodie, Jane, *Librn*, Dayton Art Institute, Library, Dayton OH

duPont, Diana, *Cur 20th Century Art*, Santa Barbara Museum of Art, Santa Barbara CA

Dupont, Inge, *Head Reader Serv*, Pierpont Morgan Library, New York NY

DuPuy, David, *Head Librn*, Maryland College of Art & Design Library, Silver Spring MD

Durand, Mark, *Librn*, Playboy Enterprises, Inc, Library, Chicago IL

Durben, Silvan A, *Dir & Cur*, Owatonna Arts Center, Community Arts Center, Owatonna MN

Durbin, Mary L, *Asst Dir*, Southern Alleghenies Museum of Art, Loretto PA

Durden, Robert, *Cur*, Yellowstone Art Center, Billings MT

Durham, David, *Chmn Dept*, Saint Louis Community College at Meramec, Art Dept, Saint Louis MO (S)

Durham, Suzanne, *Archivist*, Virginia Dept Historic Resources, Research Library, Richmond VA

Durrant, G D, *Assoc Prof*, Palomar Community College, Art Dept, San Marcos CA (S)

durRussell, Kent, *Dir*, Higgins Armory Museum, Worcester MA

Dursi, Pat A, *Registrar*, United States Military Academy, West Point Museum, West Point NY

Dursum, Brian, *Dir*, University of Miami, Lowe Art Museum, Coral Gables FL

Dusanek, Joyce, *Pres*, Paint 'N Palette Club, Grant Wood Memorial Park & Gallery, Anamosa IA

Dusenbury, Carolyn, *Art Librn*, California State University, Chico, Meriam Library, Chico CA

Dustin, Robin, *Dir & Cur*, Sandwich Historical Society, Center Sandwich NH

Dutka, Marie, *Dir*, Illinois Wesleyan University, Merwin & Wakeley Galleries, Bloomington IL

Dutka, Marie, *Instr*, Illinois Wesleyan University, School of Art, Bloomington IL (S)

Dutton, Richard H, *Dept Head*, Indian Hills Community College, Ottumwa Campus, Dept of Art, Ottumwa IA (S)

Dutton, Richard H, *Head Dept*, Indian Hills Community College, Dept of Art, Centerville IA (S)

Duvigneaud, Diane, *Prof Emeritus*, North Central College, Dept of Art, Naperville IL (S)

Dvorak, Anna, *Librn*, North Carolina Museum of Art, Raleigh NC

Dvorak, Anna, *Librn*, North Carolina Museum of Art, Reference Library, Raleigh NC

Dwyer, Eugene J, *Prof*, Kenyon College, Art Dept, Gambier OH (S)

Dwyer, Penny, *Asst Cur*, George Washington University, The Dimock Gallery, Washington DC

Dwyer, Rob, *Dir*, Quincy Society of Fine Arts, Quincy IL

Dyckes, Martha, *Dir Educ*, Colorado Historical Society, Colorado History Museum, Denver CO

Dye, David, *Assoc Prof*, Hillsborough Community College, Fine Arts Dept, Tampa FL (S)

Dye, Donna, *Dir*, Mississippi Department of Archives & History, Old Capitol Museum, Jackson MS

Dye, Donna, *Dir State Historical Museum*, Mississippi Department of Archives & History, Library, Jackson MS

Dye, Emma, *Exec Dir*, Hendersonville Arts Council, Hendersonville TN

Dye, Joseph, *Lectr*, College of William & Mary, Dept of Fine Arts, Williamsburg VA (S)

Dyer, Don, *Develop Mgr*, Missouri State Council on the Arts, Saint Louis MO

Dyer, J T, *Cur Art*, Marine Corps Museum, Art Collection, Washington DC

Dyer, Michael P, *Cur*, Kendall Whaling Museum, Sharon MA

Dyer, Michael P, *Librn*, Kendall Whaling Museum, Library, Sharon MA

Dyer, M Wayne, *Assoc Prof*, East Tennessee State University, Dept of Art & Design, Johnson City TN (S)

Dykes, Stephen E, *Deputy Dir Admin*, Fine Arts Museums of San Francisco, M H de Young Memorial Museum & California Palace of the Legion of Honor, San Francisco CA

Dyki, Judy, *Head Librn*, Cranbrook Art Museum, Library, Bloomfield Hills MI

Dynak, Sharon, *Exec Dir*, Ucross Foundation, Big Red Barn Gallery, Clearmont WY

Dynneson, Donald, *Prof*, Concordia College, Art Dept, Seward NE (S)

Dytri, Sheelagh, *Asst Dir*, University of Denver, School of Art & Art History, Denver CO (S)

Dzwonchyk, Joseph, *Adminr*, Fetherston Foundation, Packwood House Museum, Lewisburg PA

Eagar, Jorge, *VPres*, Xicanindio, Inc, Mesa AZ

Eagen, Kip, *Dir*, Palm Beach Community College Foundation, Museum of Art, Lake Worth FL

Eagerton, Robert, *Coordr Fine Arts*, Indiana University-Purdue University, Indianapolis, Herron School of Art, Indianapolis IN (S)

Ealer, William, *Asst Prof*, Pennsylvania College of Technology, Dept of Graphic Communications, Williamsport PA (S)

Earhart, Jeanne, *Exec Dir*, Worthington Arts Council, Worthington OH

Earle, Edward W, *Assoc Dir New Media & Colls*, University of California, California Museum of Photography, Riverside CA

Earle, Susan, *Cur European & American Art*, University of Kansas, Spencer Museum of Art, Lawrence KS

Earls-Solari, Bonnie, *Cur*, Bank of America Galleries, San Francisco CA

Early, James, *Asst Secy Educ & Pub Serv*, Smithsonian Institution, Washington DC

Earnest, Greta, *Art & Architecture Librn*, Pratt Institute Library, Art & Architecture Dept, Brooklyn NY

Earnest, Nancy, *Slide Cur*, East Tennessee State University, Carroll Reece Museum, Johnson City TN

Easby, Rebecca, *Assoc Prof*, Trinity College, Art Program, Washington DC (S)

Eastep, Jim, *Cur*, Oklahoma Center for Science & Art, Kirkpatrick Center, Oklahoma City OK

Eastman, Gene M, *Prof*, Sam Houston State University, Art Dept, Huntsville TX (S)

Eaton, Charlotte B, *Cur*, Putnam County Historical Society, Foundry School Museum, Cold Spring NY

Eaton, Tim, *Lectr*, University of Wisconsin-Stout, Dept of Art & Design, Menomonie WI (S)

Ebben, James, *Pres*, Edgewood College, DeRicci Gallery, Madison WI

Eberdt, Edmund, *Cur*, Eberdt Museum of Communications, Heritage Sutton, Sutton PQ

Eberly, John, *Instr*, Hutchinson Community Junior College, Visual Arts Dept, Hutchinson KS (S)

Ebert, D, *Instr*, Golden West College, Visual Art Dept, Huntington Beach CA (S)

Ebert, Mary Beth, *Museum Store Mgr*, Fort Worth Art Association, Modern Art Museum of Fort Worth, Fort Worth TX

Ebie, Theresa, *Cur Painting/Registrar*, Roswell Museum & Art Center, Roswell NM

Ebie, William D, *Dir*, Roswell Museum & Art Center, Roswell NM

Ebitz, David, *Dir*, State Art Museum of Florida, John & Mable Ringling Museum of Art, Sarasota FL

Eby, Jeff, *Asst Dir Finance & Admin*, Seattle Art Museum, Seattle WA

Eccles, Tom, *Dir*, Public Art Fund, Inc, New York NY

Echeverria, Durand, *Co-Cur*, Wellfleet Historical Society Museum, Wellfleet MA

Echeverria, Felipe, *Prof*, University of Northern Iowa, Dept of Art, Cedar Falls IA (S)

Ecker, David W, *Prof*, New York University, Dept of Art & Art Professions, New York NY (S)

Ecker, Gary, *Restoration Specialist*, Riverside Municipal Museum, Riverside CA

Eckert, Charles, *Head of Dept*, Middlesex Community Technical College, Fine Arts Division, Middletown CT (S)

Eckhart, Susan, *Educ Dir*, Art Center of Battle Creek, Battle Creek MI

Eckhart, Karen, *Communications Coordr*, Mendel Art Gallery & Civic Conservatory, Saskatoon SK

Eckley, Thomas, *Pres*, Cincinnati Art Club, Cincinnati OH

Edborg, Judy A, *American Artisans Dir*, American Society of Artists, Inc, Chicago IL

Eddey, Roy R, *Acting Pres*, Brooklyn Museum, Brooklyn NY

Eddins, Emily, *Asst Dir*, Leedy Voulko's Art Center Gallery, Kansas City MO

Eddy, Becky, *Asst Dir Admin.* Rochester Institute of Technology, College of Imaging Arts & Sciences, Rochester NY (S)

Eddy, Warren S, *Dir.* Cortland Free Library, Cortland NY

Edelson, Gilbert S, *Admin VPres & Counsel.* Art Dealers Association of America, Inc, New York NY

Edelson, Michael, *Assoc Prof.* State University of New York at Stony Brook, Art Dept, Stony Brook NY (S)

Edelstein, Teri J, *Deputy Dir.* The Art Institute of Chicago, Chicago IL

Edens, Marjorie, *Oral Historian.* Southern Oregon Historical Society, Jacksonville Museum of Southern Oregon History, Medford OR

Eder, Elizabeth, *Asst Dir.* Sculpture Center School & Studios, New York NY

Edgecombe, Wallace I, *Dir.* Hostos Center for the Arts & Culture, Bronx NY

Edidin, Stephen, *Cur.* Dahesh Museum, New York NY

Edinberg, Lucinda, *Outreach Coordr.* Saint John's College, Elizabeth Myers Mitchell Art Gallery, Annapolis MD

Edison, Carol, *Folk Arts Coordr.* Utah Arts Council, Chase Home Museum of Utah Folk Art, Salt Lake City UT

Edmonds, Carolyn, *Pres.* Shoreline Historical Museum, Seattle WA

Edmonds, Nicolas, *Assoc Prof,* Boston University, School of Visual Arts, Boston MA (S)

Edmonson, Randall W, *Head Dept,* Longwood College, Dept of Art, Farmville VA (S)

Edmunds, Allan L, *Pres & Exec Dir.* Brandywine Workshop, Philadelphia PA

Edmunds, Anne, *Exec Dir.* Afro-American Historical & Cultural Museum, Philadelphia PA

Edson, Gary, *Exec Dir,* Texas Tech University, Museum, Lubbock TX

Edward, Deborah, *Dir.* Austin Children's Museum, Austin TX

Edwards, Beth, *Assoc Prof,* University of Dayton, Visual Arts Dept, Dayton OH (S)

Edwards, Brian, *Prof,* Shoreline Community College, Humanities Division, Seattle WA (S)

Edwards, C William, *Chief Finance Officer,* Bellevue Art Museum, Bellevue WA

Edwards, Ethel, *Instr.* Truro Center for the Arts at Castle Hill, Inc, Truro MA (S)

Edwards, Frederick C, *Pres.* Redlands Art Association, Redlands CA

Edwards, Glen, *Prof,* Utah State University, Dept of Art, Logan UT (S)

Edwards, Heather, *Assoc Dir.* Contemporary Art for San Antonio Blue Star Art Space, San Antonio TX

Edwards, Jean, *Asst Prof.* Winthrop University, Dept of Art & Design, Rock Hill SC (S)

Edwards, Jim, *Dir,* Texas A&M University-Corpus Christi, Weil Art Gallery, Corpus Christi TX

Edwards, Joel, *Chmn,* California Lutheran University, Art Dept, Thousand Oaks CA (S)

Edwards, Kathleen, *Dir,* The Print Center, Philadelphia PA

Edwards, Lucy, *Instr.* Wayne Art Center, Wayne PA (S)

Edwards, Mary Jane, *Head Dept,* University of Wyoming, Dept of Art, Laramie WY (S)

Edwards, Melvin, *Prof,* Rutgers, the State University of New Jersey, Mason Gross School of the Arts, New Brunswick NJ (S)

Edwards, Nancy, *Asst Dir Academic Affairs.* Kimbell Art Foundation, Kimbell Art Museum, Fort Worth TX

Edwards, Page, *Dir.* Saint Augustine Historical Society, Oldest House & Museums, Saint Augustine FL

Edwards, Paul B, *Gallery Dir.* Washington & Jefferson College, Olin Art Gallery, Washington PA

Edwards, Paul B, *Chmn Art Dept,* Washington & Jefferson College, Art Dept, Washington PA (S)

Edwards, Richard, *Prof Emeritus.* University of Michigan, Ann Arbor, Dept of History of Art, Ann Arbor MI (S)

Edwards, Susan C S, *Dir.* Brick Store Museum & Library, Kennebunk ME

Edwards, William, *Chmn Board of Trustees.* Visual Studies Workshop, Rochester NY

Edwins, Steve, *Asst Prof.* Saint Olaf College, Art Dept, Northfield MN (S)

Efland, Arthur, *Prof.* Ohio State University, Dept of Art Education, Columbus OH (S)

Efsic, Ellen, *Coordr Develop.* University of Houston, Sarah Campbell Blaffer Gallery, Houston TX

Eggebrecht, David, *Academic Dean.* Concordia University Wisconsin, Fine Art Gallery, Mequon WI

Egleston, Robert, *Dir.* New Haven Colony Historical Society, New Haven CT

Egli, Herbert, *Treas.* Greenwich Art Society Inc, Greenwich CT

Eglinski, Edmund, *Assoc Prof.* University of Kansas, Kress Foundation Dept of Art History, Lawrence KS (S)

Egolof, Jacklyn, *Pub Servs Librn.* North Central College, Oesterle Library, Naperville IL

Eguargie, Frank, *Educ Dir.* Ohio Historical Society, National Afro American Museum & Cultural Center, Wilberforce OH

Ehlers, Carol, *Dir Develop.* Davenport Museum of Art, Davenport IA

Ehrhardt, Ursula M, *Asst Prof.* Salisbury State University, Art Dept, Salisbury MD (S)

Ehringer, Martha, *Dir Public Relations.* Mingei International, Inc, Mingei International Museum Satellite of World Folk Art, San Diego CA

Ehrlich, Richard, *Exec Dir.* Western Reserve Historical Society, Cleveland OH

Eicher, Diana J, *Coordr.* University of Minnesota, Coffman Union Third Floor Gallery, Minneapolis MN

Eichner, Steven A, *Head Librn.* Chrysler Museum Of Art, Norfolk VA

Eichner, Steven A, *Library Asst.* Chrysler Museum Of Art, Jean Outland Chrysler Library, Norfolk VA

Eickhorst, William, *Chmn Dept.* Missouri Western State College, Art Dept, Saint Joseph MO (S)

Eickhorst, William, *Chmn Dept of Art.* Missouri Western State College, Fine Arts Gallery, Saint Joseph MO

Eickhorst, William S, *Exec Dir.* Print Consortium, Kansas City MO

Eickmeier, Valerie, *Assoc Dean.* Indiana University-Purdue University, Indianapolis, Herron School of Art, Indianapolis IN (S)

Eickoff, Harold, *Pres.* College of New Jersey, Art Gallery, Trenton NJ

Eide, Joel S, *Dir.* Northern Arizona University, School of Art & Design, Flagstaff AZ (S)

Eide, Joel S, *Dir.* Northern Arizona University, Art Museum & Galleries, Flagstaff AZ

Eide, John, *Instr.* Maine College of Art, Portland ME (S)

Eidelberg, Martin, *Prof.* Rutgers, the State University of New Jersey, Graduate Program in Art History, New Brunswick NJ (S)

Eige, G Eason, *Sr Cur.* Huntington Museum of Art, Huntington WV

Eike, Claire, *Dir.* School of the Art Institute of Chicago, John M Flaxman Library, Chicago IL

Eiland, William, *Acting Museum Adminr.* University of Georgia, Georgia Museum of Art, Athens GA

Einecke, Claudia, *Assoc Cur European Art.* Joslyn Art Museum, Omaha NE

Einfalt, Linda, *Chmn Fine Arts & Prof.* University of Cincinnati, School of Art, Cincinnati OH (S)

Einreinhofer, Nancy, *Dir.* William Paterson College of New Jersey, Ben Shahn Galleries, Wayne NJ

Einthoven, Wink, *Gallery Dir.* Printmaking Council of New Jersey, North Branch NJ

Eis, Andrea, *Lectr.* Oakland University, Dept of Art & Art History, Rochester MI (S)

Eis, Ruth, *Cur Emertius.* Judah L Magnes Museum, Berkeley CA

Eischen, Patricia, *Registrar.* Louisiana Department of Culture, Recreation & Tourism, Louisiana State Museum, New Orleans LA

Eisenberg, Marvin, *Prof Emeritus.* University of Michigan, Ann Arbor, Dept of History of Art, Ann Arbor MI (S)

Eisenhardt, Roy, *Treas.* The Friends of Photography, Ansel Adams Center for Photography, San Francisco CA

Eisenmenger, Michael, *Asst Prof.* Rutgers, the State University of New Jersey, Mason Gross School of the Arts, New Brunswick NJ (S)

Eisman, Hy, *Instr.* Joe Kubert School of Cartoon & Graphic Art, Inc, Dover NJ (S)

Eiswerth, Barbara, *Instr.* Marylhurst College, Art Dept, Marylhurst OR (S)

Eiteljorg, Harrison, *Chmn.* Eiteljorg Museum of American Indians & Western Art, Indianapolis IN

Ekdahl, Janis, *Chief Librn Adminr.* Museum of Modern Art, Library, New York NY

Ekdahl, Janis, *Pres.* Art Libraries Society of North America, Raleigh NC

Ekins, Roger, *Assoc Dean,* Butte College, Dept of Performing Arts, Oroville CA (S)

Ekiss, Joan, *Librn.* Springfield Art Association of Edwards Place, Michael Victor II Art Library, Springfield IL

Eklund, Lori, *Programs.* University of Kansas, Spencer Museum of Art, Lawrence KS

Elam, Leslie A, *Dir.* American Numismatic Society, New York NY

El-A-Min, Kathann, *Controller,* Marion Koogler McNay Art Museum, San Antonio TX

Elder, Bev, *Reference,* Mason City Public Library, Mason City IA

Elder, Patti, *Instr.* University of North Carolina at Charlotte, Dept of Visual Arts, Charlotte NC (S)

Elder, Sarah M, *Cur Hist & Librn.* Saint Joseph Museum, Saint Joseph MO

Elder, Sarah M, *Co-Dir Alaska Native Heritage Film Center.* University of Alaska, Museum, Fairbanks AK

Elder, William Voss, *Consultant Cur Decorative Arts.* Baltimore Museum of Art, Baltimore MD

Eldredge, Charles, *Prof.* University of Kansas, Kress Foundation Dept of Art History, Lawrence KS (S)

Eldridge, Jan, *Instr.* Solano Community College, Division of Fine & Applied Art, Suisun City CA (S)

Elfers, John, *Music Librn.* J Erie Johnson Library, Fine Arts Division, Dallas TX

Elfvin, John T, *VPres.* The Buffalo Fine Arts Academy, Albright-Knox Art Gallery, Buffalo NY

Elgstrand, Gregory, *Dir.* Struts Gallery, Sackville NB

Elias, Margery M, *Assoc,* Dezign House, Jefferson OH

Elias, Ramon J, *Dir.* Dezign House, Jefferson OH

Elias, Ramon J, *Dir.* Dezign House, Library, Jefferson OH

Eliasoph, Philip, *Dir Walsh Art Gallery.* Fairfield University, Thomas J Walsh Art Gallery, Fairfield CT

Elkins, Stanley, *Trustee.* Historic Northampton Museum, Northampton MA

Eller, Matt, *Design Dir.* Walker Art Center, Minneapolis MN

Ellingson, JoAnn, *Dir.* Saint Xavier University, Byrne Memorial Library, Chicago IL

Ellington, Carol, *Board Dir.* Artists' Cooperative Gallery, Omaha NE

Ellingwood, Sue A, *Supv Art, Music & Video.* Saint Paul Public Library, Art, Music & Video Dept, Saint Paul MN

Elliot, Barbara, *Dir of Admis.* University of the Arts, Philadelphia College of Art & Design, Philadelphia PA (S)

Elliot, Gillian, *Dir.* Place des Arts, Coquitlam BC

Elliot, Gregory, *Asst Prof.* Louisiana State University, School of Art, Baton Rouge LA (S)

Elliot, Mary Gene, *Cur.* Atlanta Museum, Atlanta GA

Elliot, Thomas, *Dir.* Iroquois Indian Museum, Howes Cave NY

Elliott, Bob, *Instr.* William Woods-Westminster Colleges, Art Dept, Fulton MO (S)

Elliott, Deann, *Chmn Humanities Div.* Quincy College, Fine Arts Dept, Quincy MA (S)

Elliott, Elizabeth, *Shows.* Society of Canadian Artists, Toronto ON

Elliott, J H, *Dir.* Atlanta Museum, Atlanta GA

Elliott, John T, *Pres*, Oil Pastel Association, Nyack NY

Elliott, Joseph, *Asst Prof*, Muhlenberg College, Dept of Art, Allentown PA (S)

Elliott, Mary, *Instr*, Mount Mary College, Art Dept, Milwaukee WI (S)

Elliott, Sheila, *Executive Dir*, Oil Pastel Association, Nyack NY

Elliott, Susan, *River Museum Mgr*, Mississippi River Museum at Mud-Island, Memphis TN

Ellis, Anita, *Chief Cur & Cur Decorative Arts*, Cincinnati Museum Association, Cincinnati Art Museum, Cincinnati OH

Ellis, Cathryn, *Performing Arts Coordr*, St Mary's University, Art Gallery, Halifax NS

Ellis, David M, *1st VPres*, Crawford County Historical Society, Baldwin-Reynolds House Museum, Meadville PA

Ellis, Elisi Vassval, *Chmn Dept Art*, Western Washington University, Art Dept, Bellingham WA (S)

Ellis, George R, *Dir*, Honolulu Academy of Arts, Honolulu HI

Ellis, Kay, *Asst Dir*, Texas A&M University - Commerce, University Gallery, Commerce TX

Ellis, Mary Ann, *Dir of Educ*, Museum of Arts & Sciences, Inc, Macon GA

Ellis, Mel, *Business Mgr*, New Britain Museum of American Art, New Britain CT

Ellis, Robert M, *Dir*, University of New Mexico, The Harwood Foundation, Taos NM

Ellis, Steve, *Exhibit Designer*, Columbus Museum, Columbus GA

Ellis, Steven, *Electronic Text Librn*, Pennsylvania State University, Arts Library, University Park PA

Ellison, Rosemary, *Chief Cur*, Southern Plains Indian Museum, Anadarko OK

Ellison, Scott, *VPres Exec Committee*, Bank of Oklahoma NA, Art Collection, Tulsa OK

Elloian, Peter, *Prof*, University of Toledo, Dept of Art, Toledo OH (S)

Ellsworth, Linda V, *Dir*, Conservation Center for Art & Historic Artifacts, Philadelphia PA

Elman, Erin, *Dir Pre-College Prog*, University of the Arts, Philadelphia College of Art & Design, Philadelphia PA (S)

Elmendorf, Diane, *Exec Dir*, New York Society of Architects, New York NY

Elmore, Dennis, *Prof*, Los Angeles City College, Dept of Art, Los Angeles CA (S)

El-Omami, Anne, *Chmn Museum Educ*, University of the Arts, Philadelphia College of Art & Design, Philadelphia PA (S)

Elsmo, Nancy, *Librn*, Wustum Museum Art Association, Wustum Art Library, Racine WI

Elson, James M, *Exec Dir*, Patrick Henry Memorial Foundation, Red Hill National Memorial, Brookneal VA

Elstein, Rochelle S, *Bibliographer*, Northwestern University, Art Library, Evanston IL

Elston, Sandra, *Dean Art*, Eastern Oregon State College, Arts & Humanities Dept, La Grande OR (S)

Efy, Ervin, *Chmn*, Bismarck State College, Fine Arts Dept, Bismarck ND (S)

Emack-Cambra, Jane, *Cur*, Old Colony Historical Society, Museum, Taunton MA

Emack-Cambra, Jane, *Cur*, Old Colony Historical Society, Library, Taunton MA

Emanuel, Martin, *Prof*, Atlanta College of Art, Atlanta GA (S)

Emeeita, Mary Risley, *Adjunct Assoc Prof*, Wesleyan University, Art Dept, Middletown CT (S)

Emerick, David, *Dir*, St Mary's College of Maryland, The Dwight Frederick Boyden Gallery, Saint Mary City MD

Emerick, Judson, *Chmn Art & Art History Dept & Assoc Prof*, Pomona College, Dept of Art & Art History, Claremont CA (S)

Emerick, Peter, *Photo Archives*, New York University, Institute of Fine Arts Visual Resources Collection, New York NY

Emerson, Bert, *Lectr*, Salve Regina University, Art Dept, Newport RI (S)

Emerson, Nancy, *Library Mgr*, San Diego Museum of Art, Art Reference Library, San Diego CA

Emerson, Robert L, *Dir*, Pennsylvania Historical & Museum Commission, Railroad Museum of Pennsylvania, Harrisburg PA

Emil, Carla, *Pres*, The Friends of Photography, Ansel Adams Center for Photography, San Francisco CA

Eminent, Morris, *Scholar in Art*, Augusta College, Dept of Fine Arts, Augusta GA (S)

Emmerich, Carl, *Prof*, Eastern Illinois University, Art Dept, Charleston IL (S)

Emmons, Tonya, *Registrar*, Cincinnati Academy of Design, Cincinnati OH (S)

Emodi, T, *Prof*, Technical University of Nova Scotia, Faculty of Architecture, Halifax NS (S)

Emory, Sue, *Cur*, Appaloosa Museum, Inc, Moscow ID

Enck, Edward, *Treas*, Art Information Center, Inc, New York NY

Endacott, Pamela, *Treas*, Sculptors Guild, Inc, New York NY

Endress, Lawrence, *Instr*, Saint Francis College, Art Dept, Fort Wayne IN (S)

Endsley, William, *Provost*, Bassist College Library, Portland OR

Endslow, Ellen, *Cur*, Fairfield Historical Society, Fairfield CT

Engelbrecht, Lloyd, *Chmn Art History & Prof*, University of Cincinnati, School of Art, Cincinnati OH (S)

Engell, Bettianne, *Office Mgr*, Lynnwood Arts Centre, Simcoe ON

Engelmann, Lothar K, *Prof*, Rochester Institute of Technology, School of Photographic Arts & Sciences, Rochester NY (S)

Engelson, Robert, *Head Dept*, Mount Saint Clare College, Art Dept, Clinton IA (S)

Engeman, Richard, *Photog & Graphics Librn*, University of Washington, Libraries, Seattle WA

Engen, Donald D, *Dir*, National Air and Space Museum, Washington DC

Engglezos, Yvonne, *Dir*, Bowne House Historical Society, Flushing NY

England, Ann, *Cur*, Georgia State University, School of Art & Design, Visual Resource Center, Atlanta GA

English, Chuck, *Science Educator*, Sunrise Museum, Inc, Sunrise Art Museum & Sunrise Science Museum, Charleston WV

English, Marc, *Instr*, Southwest Texas State University, Dept of Art, San Marcos TX (S)

Engman, Margaret, *VPres*, Pennsylvania Academy of the Fine Arts, Fellowship of the Pennsylvania Academy of the Fine Arts, Philadelphia PA

Enns, Herb, *Co-Dir & Prof*, University of Manitoba, Faculty of Architecture Exhibition Centre, Winnipeg MB

Enns, Herb, *Head Dept Archit*, University of Manitoba, Faculty of Architecture, Winnipeg MB (S)

Enos, Chris, *Assoc Prof*, University of New Hampshire, Dept of Arts & Art History, Durham NH (S)

Enright, Robyn, *Public Events Dir*, The Albrecht-Kemper Museum of Art, Saint Joseph MO

Enriquez, Carola R, *Dir*, Kern County Museum, Bakersfield CA

Ensign, William L, *Acting Architect of the Capitol*, United States Capitol, Architect of the Capitol, Washington DC

Enstice, Wayne, *Chmn Art Dept*, Indiana State University, Turman Art Gallery, Terre Haute IN

Enstice, Wayne, *Dir*, University of Cincinnati, School of Art, Cincinnati OH (S)

Entin, Daniel, *Exec Dir*, Nicholas Roerich Museum, New York NY

Entwistle, Jeanette, *Cur Educ*, University of New Mexico, University Art Museum, Albuquerque NM

Entwistle, Jeffrey, *Concentration Chmn*, University of Wisconsin-Green Bay, Art-Communication & the Arts, Green Bay WI (S)

Enz Finken, Kathleen, *Asst Prof*, Moorhead State University, Dept of Art, Moorhead MN (S)

Enzweiler, Joan, *Asst Dir*, Thomas More College, TM Gallery, Crestview KY

Epp, Ron, *Treas*, Prince George Art Gallery, Prince George BC

Eppich, Linda, *Museum Cur*, Rhode Island Historical Society, Providence RI

Eppich, Linda, *Cur*, Rhode Island Historical Society, John Brown House, Providence RI

Epstein, Beatrice, *Assoc Museum Librn*, The Metropolitan Museum of Art, Photograph & Slide Library, New York NY

Epstein, Robert, *Chmn Ceramics*, Corcoran School of Art, Washington DC (S)

Epstein, Ruth, *Thesis Advisor*, Toronto Art Therapy Institute, Toronto ON (S)

Epstein, Stephan, *Assoc Dir*, University of Pennsylvania, Museum of Archaeology & Anthropology, Philadelphia PA

Epting, Marion, *Instr*, California State University, Chico, Art Dept, Chico CA (S)

Erbacher, Ann E, *Registrar*, Nelson-Atkins Museum of Art, Kansas City MO

Erbe, Gary, *Pres*, The Allied Artists of America, Inc, New York NY

Erbe, Gary, *VPres Oils*, Audubon Artists, Inc, New York NY

Erbolato-Ramsey, Christiane, *Fine Arts Librn*, Brigham Young University, Harold B Lee Library, Provo UT

Erdle, Rob, *Painting & Drawing Coordr*, University of North Texas, School of Visual Arts, Denton TX (S)

Erdmann, Mariella, *Chmn*, Silver Lake College, Art Dept, Manitowoc WI (S)

Erf, Greg, *Dir*, Eastern New Mexico University, Dept of Art, Portales NM

Erf, Greg, *Dir Art Dept*, Eastern New Mexico University, Golden Library, Portales NM

Erf, Greg, *Chmn*, Eastern New Mexico University, Dept of Art, Portales NM (S)

Erf, Lisa K, *Cur*, The First National Bank of Chicago, Art Collection, Chicago IL

Erger, Patricia, *Adminr*, Adams County Historical Society, Museum & Cultural Center, Brighton CO

Erhard, Peter, *Asst Prof*, Andrews University, Dept of Art, Art History & Design, Berrien Springs MI (S)

Ericksen, Mary, *Prog-Shop Mgr*, Northfield Arts Guild, Northfield MN

Erickson, Crista, *Prof*, Indiana University, Bloomington, Henry Radford Hope School of Fine Arts, Bloomington IN (S)

Erickson, Edmunbd, *Library Dir*, Black Hills State University, Library, Spearfish SD

Erickson, Elizabeth, *Faculty*, Grand Marais Art Colony, Grand Marais MN (S)

Erickson, Jeff, *Dir*, Southern Oregon State College, Stevenson Union Gallery, Ashland OR

Erickson, Robert, *Asst Prof*, University of Wisconsin-Stevens Point, Dept of Art & Design, Stevens Point WI (S)

Ericsson, Dwight, *Dir*, Huntington College, Robert E Wilson Art Gallery, Huntington IN

Erie, Mary, *Bus Mgr*, Lehigh County Historical Society, Allentown PA

Erikson, Christine, *Chmn*, University of Alaska Anchorage, Dept of Art, Anchorage AK (S)

Erlandson, Molly, *Asst Prof*, West Virginia State College, Art Dept, Institute WV (S)

Erlebacher, Martha Mayer, *Chmn*, New York Academy of Art, Graduate School of Figurative Art, New York NY (S)

Ermenc, Christine, *Dir Educ*, Connecticut Historical Society, Hartford CT

Erwin, Sarah, *Cur Archival Colls*, Gilcrease Museum Institute of American History & Art, Library, Tulsa OK

Esau, Kaia Stavig, *Reference Librn*, University of Oregon, Architecture & Allied Arts Library, Eugene OR

Escalante, Jim, *Chmn*, University of Wisconsin, Madison, Dept of Art, Madison WI (S)

Escallon, Ana Maria, *Dir*, Art Museum of the Americas, Washington DC

Escandor, Betsy, *Admin Asst*, University of California, Los Angeles, Fowler Museum of Cultural History, Los Angeles CA

Esch, Pam, *Dir Educ*, Cleveland Center for Contemporary Art, Cleveland OH

Eschernisch, Sergei, *Pres*, Cornish College of the Arts, Art Dept, Seattle WA (S)

Escobar, Gloria, *Asst Prof,* Hartwick College, Art Dept, Oneonta NY (S)

Esh, Sharise, *Bulletin Educ,* Special Libraries Association, Museum, Arts & Humanities Division, Washington DC

Eshoo, Virginia H, *Mgr Museum Progs,* The Currier Gallery of Art, Manchester NH

Eskind, Andrew, *Mgr Information Technologies,* George Eastman House-International Museum of Photography & Film, Rochester NY

Esler, Jennifer, *Exec Dir,* Cliveden, Philadelphia PA

Eslick, Amber, *Finance & Mem,* University of Illinois, World Heritage Museum, Champaign IL

Esparsen, Ray P, *Prof,* Lewis-Clark State College, Art Dept, Lewiston ID (S)

Esparza, Richard, *Historic Resources International Dir,* Riverside Municipal Museum, Riverside CA

Espey, Jule Adele, *Asst Prof,* Our Lady of the Lake University, Dept of Art, San Antonio TX (S)

Esping-Swanson, Gretchen, *Inter-Library Loan Librn,* Bethany College, Library, Lindsborg KS

Esposito, Tara, *Office Mgr,* Elmhurst Art Museum, Elmhurst IL

Esquibel, George A, *Instr,* Sacramento City College, Art Dept, Sacramento CA (S)

Esser, Cary, *Chmn Ceramics,* Kansas City Art Institute, Kansas City MO (S)

Esser, John, *Asst Dean,* State University of New York College at Purchase, Division of Visual Arts, Purchase NY (S)

Esslinger, Claudia, *Assoc Prof,* Kenyon College, Art Dept, Gambier OH (S)

Esterly, Diane, *VPres,* Boothbay Region Art Foundation, Boothbay Harbor ME

Estes, Curtis, *Chmn Interior Design,* Moore College of Art & Design, Philadelphia PA (S)

Estes, Jim, *Prof,* Missouri Western State College, Art Dept, Saint Joseph MO (S)

Estes, Judy, *Coll Mgr,* The Museums at Stony Brook, Kate Strong Historical Library, Stony Brook NY

Estomin, Lynn, *Asst Prof,* Lycoming College, Art Dept, Williamsport PA (S)

Etier, Marc, *Instr,* East Central University, Art Dept, Ada OK (S)

Eubanks, Paula, *Asst Prof,* University of Northern Iowa, Dept of Art, Cedar Falls IA (S)

Eugene, Robert, *Adminr,* Princeton Antiques Bookservice, Art Marketing Reference Library, Atlantic City NJ

Evangelista, Mary, *Cur,* New England Center for Contemporary Art, Brooklyn CT

Evans, Bob, *Adjunct Asst Prof,* Spokane Falls Community College, Fine Arts Dept, Spokane WA (S)

Evans, Bruce, *Chief Librn,* Medicine Hat Public Library, Medicine Hat AB

Evans, Bruce, *Chief Exec Officer & Pres,* Mint Museum of Art, Charlotte NC

Evans, Constance, *Exec Dir,* Weir Farm Heritage Trust, National Park Service, Weir Farm National Historic Site, Wilton CT

Evans, Dan, *Assoc Prof,* Philadelphia Community College, Dept of Art, Philadelphia PA (S)

Evans, David, *Fine Arts Chmn,* Queens College, Fine Arts Dept, Charlotte NC (S)

Evans, Donald H, *Assoc Prof,* Vanderbilt University, Dept of Fine Arts, Nashville TN (S)

Evans, Dorinda, *Assoc Prof,* Emory University, Art History Dept, Atlanta GA (S)

Evans, Douglas W, *Registrar,* Westmoreland Museum of American Art, Greensburg PA

Evans, Elaine A, *Cur Coll,* University of Tennessee, Frank H McClung Museum, Knoxville TN

Evans, Elaine A, *Cur,* University of Tennessee, Eleanor Dean Audigier Art Collection, Knoxville TN

Evans, Garth, *Instr,* New York Studio School of Drawing, Painting & Sculpture, New York NY (S)

Evans, Gregory, *Exec Dir,* British Columbia Museums Association, Victoria BC

Evans, Jon, *Library Asst,* Museum of Fine Arts, Houston, Hirsch Library, Houston TX

Evans, Lee, *Chmn,* University, Theatre & Fine Arts Dept, New York NY (S)

Evans, Margaret, *Artistic Dir,* Acme Art Co, Columbus OH

Evans, Micki, *Mem Coordr,* Rollins College, George D & Harriet W Cornell Fine Arts Museum, Winter Park FL

Evans, Oliver, *Pres,* Kendall College of Art & Design, Grand Rapids MI (S)

Evans, Oliver, *Pres,* Kendall College of Art & Design, Frank & Lyn Van Steenberg Library, Grand Rapids MI

Evans, Peggy, *Treasurer,* French Art Colony, Gallipolis OH

Evans, Scott, *Faculty,* Idaho State University, Dept of Art, Pocatello ID (S)

Evans, Tom, *Librn,* East Carolina University, Art Library, Greenville NC

Evans-Tibbs, Thurlow, *Dir,* Evans-Tibbs Collection, Washington DC

Evans-Tibbs, Thurlow, *Dir,* Evans-Tibbs Collection, Archives, Washington DC

Evarts, Wilbur, *VPres,* Paint 'N Palette Club, Grant Wood Memorial Park & Gallery, Anamosa IA

Evelyn, Douglas E, *Deputy Dir,* National Museum of the American Indian, George Gustav Heye Center, New York NY

Even, Yael, *Assoc Prof,* University of Missouri, Saint Louis, Dept of Art & Art History, Saint Louis MO (S)

Evenhouse, Raymon, *Assoc Prof,* University of Illinois, Chicago, Health Science Center, Biomedical Visualizations, Chicago IL (S)

Everett, Kristie, *Registrar,* Flint Institute of Arts, Flint MI

Everett, Kristie, *Registrar,* Flint Institute of Arts, Library, Flint MI

Everidge, Janice, *Registrar,* University of Florida, University Gallery, Gainesville FL

Evers, Fred, *Asst Prof,* Bradford College, Creative Arts Division, Bradford MA (S)

Everson, Dave, *Instr,* Cuyahoga Valley Art Center, Cuyahoga Falls OH (S)

Ewart, Tom, *Exhib Designer,* Calvert Marine Museum, Solomons MD

Ewers, Don, *Lectr,* Incarnate Word University of the Arts & Sciences, Art Dept, San Antonio TX (S)

Ewick, Cynthia, *Dept Educ,* Indiana State Museum, Indianapolis IN

Ewing, Dan, *Chmn,* Hobart & William Smith Colleges, Art Dept, Geneva NY (S)

Ewing, Lauren, *Prof,* Rutgers, the State University of New Jersey, Mason Gross School of the Arts, New Brunswick NJ (S)

Ewing, Warren, *Dir Visual Arts,* Rutgers, the State University of New Jersey, Mason Gross School of the Arts, New Brunswick NJ (S)

Exxon, Randall L, *Chmn Dept Art & Assoc Prof,* Swarthmore College, Dept of Art, Swarthmore PA (S)

Eyerdam, Pamela, *Supvr Art Serv,* Cleveland State University, Library & Art Services, Cleveland OH

Eyestone, June, *Asst Prof,* Florida State University, Art Education Dept, Tallahassee FL (S)

Eyraud, Cole H, *Pres,* Cabot's Old Indian Pueblo Museum, Pueblo Art Gallery, Desert Hot Springs CA

Eyrich, Ruth, *VPres,* LA Art Association, Los Angeles CA

Fabbri, Anne R, *Dir,* Philadelphia College of Textiles & Science, Paley Design Center, Philadelphia PA

Faber, Carol, *Instr,* North Iowa Area Community College, Dept of Art, Mason City IA (S)

Faber, David, *Assoc Prof,* Wake Forest University, Dept of Art, Winston-Salem NC (S)

Faber, Mindy, *Assoc Dir,* School of Art Institute of Chicago, Video Data Bank, Chicago IL

Faberman, Hilarie, *Cur of Modern & Contemporary,* Stanford University, Museum of Art, Stanford CA

Fabian, Joan, *Instr,* Southwest Texas State University, Dept of Art, San Marcos TX (S)

Fabiano, Daniel, *Prof,* University of Wisconsin-Stevens Point, Dept of Art & Design, Stevens Point WI (S)

Fabiano, Michele, *Instr,* University of North Alabama, Dept of Art, Florence AL (S)

Fabing, Suzannah J, *Dir & Chief Cur,* Smith College, Museum of Art, Northampton MA

Faccinto, Victor, *Gallery Dir,* Wake Forest University, Dept of Art, Winston-Salem NC (S)

Faccinto, Victor, *Dir,* Wake Forest University, Fine Arts Gallery, Winston Salem NC

Face, Jo, *Prof Art History,* University of Cincinnati, School of Art, Cincinnati OH (S)

Facos, Michelle, *Asst Prof,* Indiana University, Bloomington, Henry Radford Hope School of Fine Arts, Bloomington IN (S)

Fagaly, William A, *Asst Dir Art,* New Orleans Museum of Art, New Orleans LA

Fagan, Charlin Chang, *Librn,* Sarah Lawrence College Library, Esther Raushenbush Library, Bronxville NY

Fagan-Affleck, Diane, *Cur,* American Textile History Museum, Lowell MA

Faggioli, Renzo, *Ceramist-in-Residence,* Moravian College, Dept of Art, Bethlehem PA (S)

Fago, Margaret, *Treas,* California Watercolor Association, Walnut Creek CA

Fago, Nancy E, *Colls Mgr,* Ursinus College, Philip & Muriel Berman Museum of Art, Collegeville PA

Fahey, Patrick, *Asst Prof,* Moorhead State University, Dept of Art, Moorhead MN (S)

Fahlen, Charles, *Chmn 3-D Fine Arts,* Moore College of Art & Design, Philadelphia PA (S)

Fahlund, Michael J, *Asst Dir,* Carnegie Institute, Carnegie Museum of Art, Pittsburgh PA

Fahy, Everett, *Chmn European Paintings,* The Metropolitan Museum of Art, New York NY

Fairbanks, Jonathan, *Cur American Decorative Arts,* Museum of Fine Arts, Boston MA

Fairbrother, Trevor, *Cur Contemporary Art,* Museum of Fine Arts, Boston MA

Fairchild MFA, Martha, *Prof,* La Roche College, Division of Graphics, Design & Communication, Pittsburgh PA (S)

Fairchild-Shepler, Martha, *Chmn,* La Roche College, Division of Graphics, Design & Communication, Pittsburgh PA (S)

Faircloth, Norman D, *Head,* Guilford Technical Community College, Commercial Art Dept, Jamestown NC (S)

Falana, Kenneth, *Prof,* Florida A & M University, Dept of Visual Arts, Humanities & Theatre, Tallahassee FL (S)

Falcone, Paul, *Asst Prof,* Northwest Missouri State University, Dept of Art, Maryville MO (S)

Falk, Karen, *Gallery Dir,* Jewish Community Center of Greater Washington, Jane L & Robert H Weiner Judaic Museum, Rockville MD

Falke, Herman, *Treas,* Sculptor's Society of Canada, Toronto ON

Falke, Terry, *Instr at Interim,* East Texas State University, Dept of Art, Commerce TX (S)

Falkner, Avery, *Instr,* Pepperdine University, Seaver College, Dept of Art, Malibu CA (S)

Falkner, Lorett, *Asst Prof,* Rochester Institute of Technology, School of Photographic Arts & Sciences, Rochester NY (S)

Falls, David, *Installations Officer & Registrar,* University of Western Ontario, McIntosh Gallery, London ON

Fane, Diana, *Chmn Arts of Africa, Pacific & Americas,* Brooklyn Museum, Brooklyn NY

Fanivza, Michael, *Art Chmn,* Old Dominion University, Gallery, Norfolk VA

Fanizza, Michael, *Chmn&Assoc Prof,* Old Dominion University, Art Dept, Norfolk VA (S)

Fannin, Bill, *Cur Exhib,* Department of Natural Resources of Missouri, Missouri State Museum, Jefferson City MO

Fantaski, Dennis, *Pres,* Art Institute of Pittsburgh, Pittsburgh PA (S)

Faoro, Victoria, *Exec Dir,* Museum of the American Quilter's Society, Paducah KY

Faquin, Jane, *Vol Coordr,* The Dixon Gallery & Gardens, Memphis TN

Farah, Priscilla, *Chief Librn,* The Metropolitan Museum of Art, Photograph & Slide Library, New York NY

Farber, Alan, *Chmn,* State University of New York College at Oneonta, Dept of Art, Oneonta NY (S)

Farber, Allen, *Chmn Art Dept,* State University of New York College at Oneonta, Art Gallery & Sculpture Court, Oneonta NY

Farber, Janet, *Assoc Cur 20th Century Art*, Joslyn Art Museum, Omaha NE

Farbo, Karen, *Art Educ Cur*, Louisiana Arts & Science Center, Baton Rouge LA

Faries, Molly, *Prof*, Indiana University, Bloomington, Henry Radford Hope School of Fine Arts, Bloomington IN

Faries, Molly, *Asst Prof*, Indiana University, Bloomington, Henry Radford Hope School of Fine Arts, Bloomington IN (S)

Faris, Brunel, *Dir*, Oklahoma City University, Hulsey Gallery-Norick Art Center, Oklahoma City OK

Farlowe, Horace, *Sculpture*, University of Georgia, Franklin College of Arts & Sciences, Lamar Dodd School of Art, Athens GA (S)

Farmer, Ann, *Educ Coordr*, Fort Worth Art Association, Modern Art Museum of Fort Worth, Fort Worth TX

Farmer, James, *Asst Prof*, Virginia Commonwealth University, Art History Dept, Richmond VA (S)

Farmer, J David, *Dir*, Dahesh Museum, New York NY

Farr, Carol, *Asst Prof*, University of Alabama in Huntsville, Dept of Art & Art History, Huntsville AL (S)

Farr, Dorothy, *Assoc Dir & Cur*, Queen's University, Agnes Etherington Art Centre, Kingston ON

Farr, Dorothy, *Pres*, Ontario Association of Art Galleries, Toronto ON

Farrah, James, *Pres*, Arizona Watercolor Association, Phoenix AZ

Farrel, Damien, *Pres*, Ann Arbor Art Association, Art Center, Ann Arbor MI

Farrell, Anne, *Develop Dir*, Museum of Contemporary Art, San Diego, La Jolla CA

Farrell, Anne, *Develop Dir*, Museum of Contemporary Art, San Diego-Downtown, San Diego CA

Farrell, Bill, *Prof*, School of the Art Institute of Chicago, Chicago IL (S)

Farrell, C F, *Chmn*, University of Minnesota, Morris, Humanities Division, Morris MN (S)

Farrell, Mary, *Prof*, Gonzaga University, Dept of Art, Spokane WA (S)

Farrell, M Mildred, *Dir*, Boston Art Commission of the City of Boston, Boston MA

Farrell, Nancy, *Gallery Dir*, University of the Ozarks, Stephens Gallery, Clarksville AR

Farrell, Nancy, *Asst Prof*, University of the Ozarks, Dept of Art, Clarksville AR (S)

Farrington, Rusty, *Instr*, Iowa Central Community College, Dept of Art, Fort Dodge IA (S)

Farris, Carolyn P, *Pres Bd Trustees*, Museum of Contemporary Art, San Diego, La Jolla CA

Farris, Carolyn P, *Pres Board Trustees*, Museum of Contemporary Art, San Diego-Downtown, San Diego CA

Farrow, Susan, *Exec Dir*, Vermont State Craft Center at Frog Hollow, Middlebury VT

Farver, Jane, *Dir Exhib*, The Queens Museum of Art, Flushing NY

Farver, Suzanne, *Dir*, The Aspen Art Museum, Aspen CO

Farwell, Richard, *Dir*, Vizcaya Museum & Gardens, Miami FL

Farwell, Robert D, *Dir*, Fruitlands Museum, Inc, Harvard MA

Farwell, Robert D, *Dir*, Fruitlands Museum, Inc, Library, Harvard MA

Fasanella, R Marc, *Div Dir*, Southampton College of Long Island University, Arts & Media Division, Southampton NY (S)

Fasoldt, Statts, *Instr*, Woodstock School of Art, Inc, Woodstock NY (S)

Fasolino, William, *Dean*, Pratt Institute, School of Art & Design, Brooklyn NY (S)

Fass, Philip, *Asst Prof*, University of Northern Iowa, Dept of Art, Cedar Falls IA (S)

Fassett, Brian, *Instr*, Northeast Louisiana University, Dept of Art, Monroe LA (S)

Fast, Susan, *Coll Gallery Mgr*, Mingei International, Inc, Mingei International Museum Satellite of World Folk Art, San Diego CA

Fastuca, Carol, *Asst Prof*, University of Maryland, Baltimore County, Visual Arts Dept, Baltimore MD (S)

Faude, Wilson H, *Exec Dir*, Old State House, Hartford CT

Faudie, Fred, *Chmn Dept*, University of Massachusetts Lowell, Dept of Art, Lowell MA (S)

Faul, Karene, *Chmn*, College of Saint Rose, Dept of Art, Albany NY (S)

Faulkes, Eve, *Prof*, West Virginia University, College of Creative Arts, Morgantown WV (S)

Faunce, Sarah, *Cur European Paintings & Sculpture*, Brooklyn Museum, Brooklyn NY

Faunt, Peggy, *Secy*, Monroe County Community College, Humanities Division, Monroe MI (S)

Faust, Charles B, *Asst Cur*, Bradford Brinton Memorial Museum & Historic Ranch, Big Horn WY

Faust, Jennifer, *Pres-Elect*, Watercolor Society of Alabama, Birmingham AL

Favell, Gene H, *Pres & Cur*, Favell Museum of Western Art & Indian Artifacts, Klamath Falls OR

Favell, Winifred L, *VPres & Treas*, Favell Museum of Western Art & Indian Artifacts, Klamath Falls OR

Faver, Jack, *Chmn*, Kansas Wesleyan University, Art Dept, Salina KS (S)

Favis, Roberta, *Head Dept*, Stetson University, Art Dept, De Land FL (S)

Fawcett, Linda D, *Chmn*, Hardin-Simmons University, Art Dept, Abilene TX (S)

Fawkes, Tom, *Instr*, Pacific Northwest College of Art, Portland OR (S)

Faxon, Susan, *Asst Dir & Cur Paintings, Sculpture, Prints & Drawings*, Phillips Academy, Addison Gallery of American Art, Andover MA

Fayerman, Faye, *Prof*, New York Institute of Technology, Fine Arts Dept, Old Westbury NY (S)

Fazzini, Richard, *Cur Egyptian & Classical Art*, Brooklyn Museum, Brooklyn NY

Fearington, Peyton T, *Dir*, Florida Department of State, Division of Cultural Affairs, Florida Arts Council, Tallahassee FL

Fearon, Chris, *Museum Educator*, University of Vermont, Robert Hull Fleming Museum, Burlington VT

Fears, Eileen, *Prof*, California State Polytechnic University, Pomona, Art Dept, Pomona CA (S)

FeBland, Harriet, *Dir*, Harriet FeBland Art Workshop, New York NY (S)

Fechter, Claudia Z, *Museum Dir*, The Temple-Tifereth Israel, The Temple Museum of Religious Art, Beachwood OH

Fechter, Claudia Z, *Dir*, The Temple-Tifereth Israel, Library, Beachwood OH

Fechter, Earl, *Prof*, Norwich University, Dept of Philosophy, Religion & Fine Arts, Northfield VT (S)

Federhen, Deborah Anne, *Cur Coll*, Bennington Museum, Bennington Museum, Bennington VT

Federighi, Christine, *Prof*, University of Miami, Dept of Art & Art History, Coral Gables FL (S)

Feeley, Noel, *Blair Art Extension Coordr*, Southern Alleghenies Museum of Art, Loretto PA

Feeney, Larry, *Dir Gallery, Cur Museum & Permanent Coll*, Mississippi University for Women, Fine Arts Gallery, Columbus MS

Feeny, Lawrence, *Prof*, Mississippi University for Women, Division of Fine & Performing Arts, Columbus MS (S)

Fees, Paul, *Cur Buffalo Bill Museum*, Buffalo Bill Memorial Association, Buffalo Bill Historical Center, Cody WY

Fehlner, Jacqueline, *Instr & Supervisor*, Toronto Art Therapy Institute, Toronto ON (S)

Fehr, Shirley, *Graphics Supv*, SaskPower, Gallery on the Roof, Regina SK

Fehrenbach, Julie, *Assoc Dir*, SPACES, Cleveland OH

Fehrenbacher, Margaret, *Registrar*, Art Museum of Southeast Texas, Beaumont TX

Feinberg, David, *Assoc Prof*, University of Minnesota, Minneapolis, Dept of Art, Minneapolis MN (S)

Feinberg, Elen, *Chmn*, University of New Mexico, Dept of Art & Art History, Albuquerque NM (S)

Feinberg, Jean, *Instr*, Bard College, Milton Avery Graduate School of the Arts, Annandale-on-Hudson NY (S)

Feinberg, Jean E, *Cur Contemporary Art*, Cincinnati Museum Association, Cincinnati Art Museum, Cincinnati OH

Feinstein, Rochelle, *Prof*, Yale University, School of Art, New Haven CT (S)

Fekner, John, *Asst Prof*, C W Post Center of Long Island University, School of Visual & Performing Arts, Brookville NY (S)

Felberbaum, Carol A, *Adjunct Instr*, Maryville University of Saint Louis, Art Division, Saint Louis MO (S)

Feldberg, Michael, *Dir*, American Jewish Historical Society, Waltham MA

Feldhausen, Jan, *Assoc Dean Foundations*, Milwaukee Institute of Art & Design, Milwaukee WI (S)

Feldman, Bob, *Pres*, Key West Art & Historical Society, East Martello Museum & Gallery, Key West FL

Feldman, Devin, *Music & Art Librn*, Queensborough Community College Library, Bayside NY

Feldman, Joan, *Admin*, National Society of Colonial Dames of America in the State of Maryland, Mount Clare Mansion, Baltimore MD

Feldman, Joel B, *Assoc Prof*, Southern Illinois University, School of Art & Design, Carbondale IL (S)

Feldman, Kaywin, *Dir Exhib*, Fresno Metropolitan Museum, Fresno CA

Feldman, Roger, *Assoc Prof*, Biola University, Art Dept, La Mirada CA (S)

Feldman, Ronald, *VPres*, Art Dealers Association of America, Inc, New York NY

Feldman, Sally, *Branch Adminr*, Las Vegas-Clark County Library District, Las Vegas NV

Feldstein, Barbara, *Dir Pub Information*, Worcester Art Museum, Worcester MA

Feliciano, Awilda, *Instr*, Guilford Technical Community College, Commercial Art Dept, Jamestown NC (S)

Fell, Carolyn, *Dir Asst*, Gallery North, Setauket NY

Feller-Kuppman, Michele, *Librn*, American Jewish Historical Society, Lee M Friedman Memorial Library, Waltham MA

Felling, Wendy, *Cur Educ & Assoc Dir*, Nevada Museum of Art, Art Library, Reno NV

Felling, Wendy Thomas, *Cur Educ*, Nevada Museum Of Art, Reno NV

Felos, Charlene, *Chairperson*, Cypress College, Cypress CA (S)

Felshin, Nina, *Cur Exhib*, Wesleyan University, Ezra & Cecile Zilkha Gallery, Middletown CT

Felter, Susan, *Assoc Prof*, Santa Clara University, Art Dept, Santa Clara CA (S)

Felton, Craig, *Assoc Prof*, Smith College, Art Dept, Northampton MA (S)

Fenety, Lois, *Dir*, Sunbury Shores Arts & Nature Centre, Inc, Gallery, Saint Andrews NB

Fenety, Lois, *Dir*, Sunbury Shores Arts & Nature Centre, Inc, Library, Saint Andrews NB

Fenger, Anne-Marie, *Mgr Admin*, University of British Columbia, Museum of Anthropology, Vancouver BC

Fenivick, Roly, *Instr*, Southampton Art School, Southampton ON (S)

Fennell, Nancy, *Pres*, Nevada Museum Of Art, Reno NV

Fennell, Patricia, *Prof*, University of Wisconsin, Madison, Dept of Art, Madison WI (S)

Fenoglio, Andy, *Visitor Services Mgr*, Omaha Childrens Museum, Inc, Omaha NE

Fenster, Fred, *Prof*, University of Wisconsin, Madison, Dept of Art, Madison WI (S)

Fenton, Terry, *Dir*, Mendel Art Gallery & Civic Conservatory, Saskatoon SK

Ferber, Linda, *Cur American Paintings & Sculpture*, Brooklyn Museum, Brooklyn NY

Ferber, Linda S, *Acting Dir & Chief Cur*, Brooklyn Museum, Brooklyn NY

Feren, Steve, *Assoc Prof*, University of Wisconsin, Madison, Dept of Art, Madison WI (S)

Ferger, Jane, *Slide Coordr*, Indianapolis Museum of Art, Slide Collection, Indianapolis IN

Fergueson, Janene, *Educ Dir*, Palos Verdes Art Center, Rancho Palos Verdes CA

Fergus, Victoria, *Prof*, West Virginia University, College of Creative Arts, Morgantown WV (S)

Ferguson, Nancy, *Exec Dir*, Marblehead Arts Association, Inc, Marblehead MA

Ferguson, Bruce W, *Pres*, New York Academy of Art, Graduate School of Figurative Art, New York NY (S)

Ferguson, Carra, *Assoc Prof*, Georgetown University, Dept of Art, Music & Theatre, Washington DC (S)

Ferguson, Jay R, *Dir Cur Services*, Kentucky Derby Museum, Louisville KY

Ferguson, Joan, *VChmn*, Detroit Artists Market, Detroit MI

Ferguson, John, *Instr*, Saint Louis Community College at Meramec, Art Dept, Saint Louis MO (S)

Ferguson, Judy, *Educ Coordr*, Witter Gallery, Storm Lake IA

Ferguson, Ken, *Bus Mgr*, Art Gallery of Windsor, Windsor ON

Ferguson, Sandra, *Chief Financial Officer*, San Antonio Museum of Art, San Antonio TX

Fergusson, Mary E D'Aquin, *Asst Dir*, Longue Vue House & Gardens, New Orleans LA

Fergusson, Peter J, *Prof*, Wellesley College, Art Dept, Wellesley MA (S)

Fern, Alan, *Dir*, National Portrait Gallery, Washington DC

Fernandez, Diana, *Chmn & Dean*, Hillsborough Community College, Fine Arts Dept, Tampa FL (S)

Fernandez, Leo, *Dir*, Western Kentucky University, University Gallery, Bowling Green KY

Fernandez, Leo, *Chmn*, Western Kentucky University, Art Dept, Bowling Green KY (S)

Fernandez, Veronica, *Instr*, Southwest Texas State University, Dept of Art, San Marcos TX (S)

Ferrell, John, *Co-Dir*, 1078 Gallery, Chico CA

Ferrell, Mike, *Exhib Design*, San Joaquin Pioneer & Historical Society, The Haggin Museum, Stockton CA

Ferrer, Elizabeth, *Head Visual Arts Dept*, Americas Society Art Gallery, New York NY

Ferrin, Richard I, *Dir*, Knoxville Museum of Art, Knoxville TN

Ferris, Alison, *Cur*, Bowdoin College, Museum of Art, Brunswick ME

Ferris, Alison, *Cur*, Sheboygan Arts Foundation, Inc, John Michael Kohler Arts Center, Sheboygan WI

Ferris, Robert, *Treas*, Cortland County Historical Society, Suggett House Museum, Cortland NY

Ferstrom, Katharine, *Assoc Cur Art Of Africa, Americas, Oceania*, Baltimore Museum of Art, Baltimore MD

Feser, Ken, *Systems Librn*, Cleveland Museum of Art, Ingalls Library, Cleveland OH

Festa, Gioranni, *Admin Dir*, The Canadian Craft Museum, Vancouver BC

Fetchko, Peter, *Dir Curatorial Operations*, Peabody Essex Museum, Salem MA

Fett, Richard, *Preparator*, Florida State University, Museum of Fine Arts, Tallahassee FL

Fetterolf, Susan, *Pres*, Organization of Independent Artists, New York NY

Fetters, Mike, *Public Relations*, National Air and Space Museum, Washington DC

Fetzer, Rachel, *Treas*, Wayne County Historical Society, Wooster OH

Fewkes, Nancy, *Curatorial Asst Preparator*, Columbia College, The Museum of Contemporary Photography, Chicago IL

Fey, Mike, *Dir Exhibits*, South Carolina State Museum, Columbia SC

Ffrench, Robert, *Prog Coordr*, Society for the Protection & Preservation of Black Culture in Nova Scotia, Black Cultural Center for Nova Scotia, Dartmouth NS

Fiacco, Lori, *Cur Educ*, University of California, California Museum of Photography, Riverside CA

Fichner-Rathus, Lois, *Assoc Prof*, College of New Jersey, Art Dept, Trenton NJ (S)

Fichter, Robert, *Prof*, Florida State University, Art Dept, Tallahassee FL (S)

Fidler, Spencer, *Prof*, New Mexico State University, Art Dept, Las Cruces NM (S)

Field, Charles, *Prof*, University of Texas at San Antonio, Division of Visual Arts, San Antonio TX (S)

Field, John, *Chmn*, Holyoke Community College, Dept of Art, Holyoke MA (S)

Field, Katheryn, *Lectr*, Lake Forest College, Dept of Art, Lake Forest IL (S)

Field, Richard, *Pres*, Print Council of America, New Haven CT

Field, Richard Henning, *Dir*, Dartmouth Heritage Museum, Dartmouth NS

Field, Richard S, *Cur Prints, Drawings & Photographs*, Yale University, Art Gallery, New Haven CT

Field, Virginia, *Admin Asst*, University of California, University Art Gallery, Riverside CA

Fields, Catherine Keene, *Dir*, Litchfield Historical Society, Litchfield CT

Fields, Catherine Keene, *Dir*, Litchfield Historical Society, Ingraham Memorial Research Library, Litchfield CT

Fields, Hershel, *Art Dept Head*, University of Mary Hardin-Baylor, School of Fine Arts, Belton TX (S)

Fields, Laura Kemper, *Dir Art Coll*, Commerce Bancshares, Inc, Art Collection, Kansas City MO

Fields, Robert, *Prof*, Virginia Polytechnic Institute & State University, Dept of Art & Art History, Blacksburg VA (S)

Fieno, Rosina, *Assoc Dean*, Delaware County Community College, Communications & Humanities House, Media PA (S)

Fife, Laurie G, *Cur*, North Canton Public Library, Little Art Gallery, North Canton OH

Fife, Lin, *Prof*, University of Colorado-Colorado Springs, Fine Arts Dept, Colorado Springs CO (S)

Figg, Laurann, *Textiles Cur & Conservator*, Vesterheim Norwegian-American Museum, Decorah IA

Figgins-Fuchs, Kim, *Marketing Coordr*, Heard Museum, Phoenix AZ

Figueroa, Paul C, *Dir*, Carolina Art Association, Gibbes Museum of Art, Charleston SC

Figueroa, Paul C, *Dir*, Carolina Art Association, Library, Charleston SC

Fike, Charles, *Technical Coordr*, Ashtabula Arts Center, Ashtabula OH

Filipczak, Zirka, *Chmn Art History*, Williams College, Dept of Art, Williamstown MA (S)

Filkosky, Josefa, *Prof*, Seton Hill College, Dept of Art, Greensburg PA (S)

Fillin-Yeh, Susan, *Dir & Cur*, Reed College, Douglas F Cooley Memorial Art Gallery, Portland OR

Fillos, Debra, *Cur*, Harriet Beecher Stowe Center, Hartford CT

Filo, Barbara, *Chmn*, Whitworth College, Art Dept, Spokane WA (S)

Filo, Barbara, *Asst Prof*, Whitworth College, Art Dept, Spokane WA (S)

Finch, Don, *Dir Air Space Museum*, Oklahoma Center for Science & Art, Kirkpatrick Center, Oklahoma City OK

Finch, Robert, *Instr*, Main Line Art Center, Haverford PA (S)

Findlay, James, *Head Librn*, Wolfsonian Foundation, Miami Beach FL

Findley, David, *Chief Conservator*, North Carolina Museum of Art, Raleigh NC

Fine, Jud, *Prof*, University of Southern California, School of Fine Arts, Los Angeles CA (S)

Fine, Milton, *Chmn Mus Art Board*, Carnegie Institute, Carnegie Museum of Art, Pittsburgh PA

Fineman, Richard, *Prof*, Northwestern Connecticut Community College, Fine Arts Dept, Winsted CT (S)

Fineman, Yale, *Staff Librn*, Carnegie Library of Pittsburgh, Pittsburgh PA

Finger, H Ellis, *Center Dir*, Lafayette College, Morris R Williams Center for the Arts, Art Gallery, Easton PA

Fink, John, *Prof*, Nassau Community College, Art Dept, Garden City NY (S)

Finkel, Susan, *Cur Cultural History*, New Jersey State Museum, Trenton NJ

Finkelpearl, Tom, *Exec Dir Prog*, Skowhegan School of Painting & Sculpture, New York NY (S)

Finkler, Robert, *Chmn*, Mankato State University, Art Dept, Mankato MN (S)

Finlayson, Lesley, *Instr*, Vancouver Community College, Langara Campus, Dept of Fine Arts, Vancouver BC (S)

Finley, Linda, *Dir*, Rome Art & Community Center, Rome NY

Finn, David, *Vis Asst Prof*, Wake Forest University, Dept of Art, Winston-Salem NC (S)

Finnemore, Donnice, *Resident Cur*, Waterville Historical Society, Redington Museum, Waterville ME

Finnemore, Harry, *Resident Cur*, Waterville Historical Society, Redington Museum, Waterville ME

Finneran, Mary, *Asst Prof*, Eastern New Mexico University, Dept of Art, Portales NM (S)

Finney, Barbara, *Office Mgr*, Crawford County Historical Society, Baldwin-Reynolds House Museum, Meadville PA

Finney, John, *Adjunct Prof*, Oklahoma Christian University of Science & Arts, Dept of Art & Design, Oklahoma City OK (S)

Fiorentino, Francis, *Instr*, Munson-Williams-Proctor Institute, School of Art, Utica NY (S)

Fiorese, Lisa, *Bookkeeper*, Dutchess County Arts Council, Poughkeepsie NY

Fiori, Dennis, *Dir*, Maryland Historical Society, Museum of Maryland History, Baltimore MD

Fiori, Dennis, *Dir*, Maryland Historical Society, Library, Baltimore MD

Firestone, Evan R, *Dir*, University of Georgia, Dept of Art Lamar Dodd School of Art, Athens GA

Firestone, Evan R, *Dir*, University of Georgia, Franklin College of Arts & Sciences, Lamar Dodd School of Art, Athens GA (S)

Firmani, Domenico, *Chmn & Assoc Prof*, College of Notre Dame of Maryland, Art Dept, Baltimore MD (S)

Fisch, Arline, *Chmn Board*, Haystack Mountain School of Crafts, Gallery, Deer Isle ME

Fisch, Robert W, *Cur Weapons*, United States Military Academy, West Point Museum, West Point NY

Fischer, Adam D, *Treas*, The Florida Museum of Hispanic & Latin American Art, Miami FL

Fischer, Billie, *Chmn Dept*, Kalamazoo College, Art Dept, Kalamazoo MI (S)

Fischer, Carl, *Pres*, Art Directors Club, Inc, New York NY

Fischer, Ellen E, *Cur*, Greater Lafayette Museum of Art, Lafayette IN

Fischer, Linda, *Pres*, Grand Prairie Arts Council, Inc, Arts Center of the Grand Prairie, Stuttgart AR

Fischl, Eric, *Instr*, New York Academy of Art, Graduate School of Figurative Art, New York NY (S)

Fischler, Carmen, *Exec Dir*, Museo de Arte de Ponce, Ponce Art Museum, Ponce PR

Fischler, Carmen, *Exec Dir*, Museo de Arte de Ponce, Library, Ponce PR

Fish, Alida, *Chmn Photography, Media Arts, Film & Animation*, University of the Arts, Philadelphia College of Art & Design, Philadelphia PA (S)

Fish, Jozina, *Asst Librn*, Atlanta College of Art Library, Atlanta GA

Fish, Vinnie, *Pres*, Gallery North, Setauket NY

Fisher, Anne F, *Pres*, Lancaster County Art Association, Inc, Lancaster PA

Fisher, B C, *Owner*, Westover, Charles City VA

Fisher, Bruce, *Coordr Sanamu African Gallery*, Oklahoma Center for Science & Art, Kirkpatrick Center, Oklahoma City OK

Fisher, Carol, *Educ Coordr*, Michigan State University, Kresge Art Museum, East Lansing MI

Fisher, Chris, *Acting Writing Dir*, Shoreline Community College, Humanities Division, Seattle WA (S)

Fontana, Lilia M, *Asst Dir*, Miami-Dade Community College, Kendal Campus, Art Gallery, Miami FL

Fontenot, Bill, *Cur Natural Science*, Lafayette Natural History Museum, Planetarium & Nature Station, Lafayette LA

Fonvielle, Betsy, *Treas*, Shelby Art League, Inc, Shelby NC

Forbes, Donna M, *Dir*, Yellowstone Art Center, Billings MT

Forbes, Jim, *Dir Develop*, Peabody Essex Museum, Salem MA

Forbes, Krina, *Communications & Pub Prog*, Kamloops Art Gallery, Kamloops BC

Forbes, Pamela, *Ed Dir Media Relations*, Fine Arts Museums of San Francisco, M H de Young Memorial Museum & California Palace of the Legion of Honor, San Francisco CA

Forbes, Susan, *Chmn Interior Design*, Fashion Institute of Technology, Art & Design Division, New York NY (S)

Forbes, Wayne, *Instr*, Illinois Central College, Dept of Fine Arts, East Peoria IL (S)

Forbes, William, *Pres*, Rome Historical Society Museum, Rome NY

Forcinito, Anne, *Asst Cur Coll*, Mint Museum of Art, Charlotte NC

Ford, Beth M, *Asst Prof*, Florida Southern College, Art Dept, Lakeland FL (S)

Ford, Derna, *Chmn Fine Arts Dept*, Barry University, Dept of Fine Arts, Miami Shores FL (S)

Ford, Janice, *Gallery Dir*, Pikeville College, Humanities Division, Pikeville KY (S)

Ford, Sharon, *Instr*, Rancho Santiago College, Art Dept, Santa Ana CA (S)

Forehand, Darin, *Studio Mgr*, Printmaking Workshop, New York NY

Forell, Jean, *Cur of Educ*, Flint Institute of Arts, Flint MI

Forest Wilson, Ernest, *Prof*, Catholic University of America, School of Architecture & Planning, Washington DC (S)

Forgang, David M, *Chief Cur*, Yosemite Museum, Yosemite National Park CA

Formigoni, Mauri, *Asst Prof*, University of Illinois at Springfield, Visual Arts Program, Springfield IL (S)

Formo, Peter L, *VPres*, Amerind Foundation, Inc, Amerind Museum, Fulton-Hayden Memorial Art Gallery, Dragoon AZ

Formo, Peter L, *VPres*, Amerind Foundation, Inc, Fulton-Hayden Memorial Library, Dragoon AZ

Formosa, Gerald, *Instr*, Vancouver Community College, Langara Campus, Dept of Fine Arts, Vancouver BC (S)

Forney, Darrell, *Instr*, Sacramento City College, Art Dept, Sacramento CA (S)

Forrest, Anne Mane, *Head Children's Prog*, Kalamazoo Institute of Arts, KIA School, Kalamazoo MI (S)

Forrester, Vivian, *House Mgr*, North Carolina State University, Chinqua-Penn Plantation House, Garden & Greenhouses, Reidsville NC

Forst, Ed, *Chmn*, Waubonsee Community College, Art Dept, Sugar Grove IL (S)

Forst, George William, *Chmn*, Sterling College, Art Dept, Sterling KS (S)

Forster-Hahn, Francoise, *Prof*, University of California, Riverside, Dept of the History of Art, Riverside CA (S)

Forsyth, Ilene H, *Prof*, University of Michigan, Ann Arbor, Dept of History of Art, Ann Arbor MI (S)

Fort, Karen, *Exhib Prog Mgr*, National Museum of the American Indian, George Gustav Heye Center, New York NY

Fort, Lifran, *Chmn&Instr*, Fisk University, Art Dept, Nashville TN (S)

Fort, Tom, *Asst Dir & Cur Exhibits*, Hidalgo County Historical Museum, Edinburg TX

Forte, Joseph C, *Instr*, Sarah Lawrence College, Dept of Art History, Bronxville NY (S)

Fortescue, Donald, *Wood & Furniture Design*, California College of Arts & Crafts, Oakland CA (S)

Fortier, Rollin, *Preparator*, University of California, Santa Barbara, University Art Museum, Santa Barbara CA

Fortreide, Steven, *Assoc Dir*, Allen County Public Library, Art, Music & Audiovisual Services, Fort Wayne IN

Fortson, Kay, *Pres*, Kimbell Art Foundation, Kimbell Art Museum, Fort Worth TX

Fortunas-Whatley, Angela, *Cur Museum Educ*, Florida State University Foundation - Central Florida Community College Foundation, The Appleton Museum of Art, Ocala FL

Foshay, Susan, *Exhib Cur*, Art Gallery of Nova Scotia, Halifax NS

Foss, Maggie, *Cur of Educ*, San Bernardino County Museum, Fine Arts Institute, Redlands CA

Fossey, John M, *Chmn*, McGill University, Dept of Art History, Montreal PQ (S)

Foster, April, *Instr*, Art Academy of Cincinnati, Cincinnati OH (S)

Foster, Bill, *Dir*, Portland Art Museum, Northwest Film Center, Portland OR

Foster, David, *Chmn Art Dept*, Lake Tahoe Community College, Art Dept, South Lake Tahoe CA (S)

Foster, Elaine, *Prof*, Jersey City State College, Art Dept, Jersey City NJ (S)

Foster, Hal, *Assoc Prof*, Cornell University, Dept of the History of Art, Ithaca NY (S)

Foster, John, *Chmn*, Victor Valley College, Art Dept, Victorville CA (S)

Foster, Kathleen, *Cur 19th & 20th Century Art*, Indiana University, Art Museum, Bloomington IN

Foster, Laura, *Cur*, Frederic Remington Art Museum, Ogdensburg NY

Foster, Laura, *Cur*, Frederic Remington Art Museum, Library, Ogdensburg NY

Foster, Suzanne, *Assoc Chmn*, University of Colorado, Boulder, Dept of Fine Arts, Boulder CO (S)

Foti-Soublet, Silvana, *Chmn*, Methodist College, Art Dept, Fayetteville NC (S)

Fought, Rick, *Librn*, Art Institute of Fort Lauderdale, Technical Library, Fort Lauderdale FL

Founds, George, *Assoc Prof*, La Roche College, Division of Graphics, Design & Communication, Pittsburgh PA (S)

Fouquet, Monique, *Dean First Yr*, Emily Carr Institute of Art & Design, Vancouver BC (S)

Fournet, Annette E, *Assoc Prof*, University of New Orleans-Lake Front, Dept of Fine Arts, New Orleans LA (S)

Fournier, Arthur, *Public Relations Coordr*, Hyde Park Art Center, Chicago IL

Fournier, Marthe, *Serials Librn*, Universite du Quebec, Bibliotheque des Arts, Montreal PQ

Fowler, Harriet, *Dir*, University of Kentucky, Art Museum, Lexington KY

Fowler, Jon H, *Prof*, Missouri Southern State College, Dept of Art, Joplin MO (S)

Fowler, Larry, *Chmn Human & Fine Arts*, Garden City Community College, Art Dept, Garden City KS (S)

Fowler, Sherry, *Asst Prof*, Lewis & Clark College, Dept of Art, Portland OR (S)

Fox, Anne, *House Adminr*, Charleston Museum, Joseph Manigault House, Charleston SC

Fox, Carson, *Instr*, Main Line Art Center, Haverford PA (S)

Fox, Chris, *Instr*, Main Line Art Center, Haverford PA (S)

Fox, Christopher D, *Cur*, Fort Ticonderoga Association, Ticonderoga NY

Fox, Christopher D, *Cur*, Fort Ticonderoga Association, Thompson-Pell Research Center, Ticonderoga NY

Fox, Edward, *Prof*, Nassau Community College, Art Dept, Garden City NY (S)

Fox, Elizabeth P, *Cur*, Connecticut Historical Society, Hartford CT

Fox, Gail, *Instr*, Delaware County Community College, Communications & Humanities House, Media PA (S)

Fox, Howard, *Cur Contemporary Art*, Los Angeles County Museum of Art, Los Angeles CA

Fox, Hugh R, *Asst Prof*, Rochester Institute of Technology, School of Printing, Rochester NY (S)

Fox, John, *Asst Prof*, Finger Lakes Community College, Visual & Performing Arts Dept, Canandaigua NY (S)

Fox, Judith Hoos, *Cur*, Wellesley College, Davis Museum & Cultural Center, Wellesley MA

Fox, Larnie, *Children's Prog*, Palo Alto Cultural Center, Palo Alto CA

Fox, Linda, *Reference Head*, Berkeley Heights Free Public Library, Berkeley Heights NJ

Fox, Michael J, *Dir*, Museum of Northern Arizona, Flagstaff AZ

Fox, Paulette, *Public Relations Mgr*, Tennessee State Museum, Nashville TN

Fox, Randall, *Supt*, Game and Parks Commission, Arbor Lodge State Historical Park, Nebraska City NE

Fox, Robert, *Chmn*, National Institute for Architectural Education, New York NY

Fox, Ross, *Instr*, Springfield College, Dept of Visual & Performing Arts, Springfield MA (S)

Fox, Terri, *Asst Dir*, The Art Studio Inc, Beaumont TX

Foxley, William C, *Pres*, Museum of Western Art, Denver CO

Foy, Donna, *Area Coordr*, Saint Mary-of-the-Woods College, Art Dept, Saint Mary-of-the-Woods IN (S)

Foy, Jessica, *Cur of Coll*, Mamie McFaddin Ward Heritage Historic Foundation Inc, Beaumont TX

Fraas, Kathleen, *Registrar*, Niagara University, Castellani Art Museum, Niagara NY

Fragua Hevey, Janet, *Cur*, Wheelwright Museum of the American Indian, Santa Fe NM

Fragua Hevey, Janet, *Cur*, Wheelwright Museum of the American Indian, Mary Cabot Wheelwright Research Library, Santa Fe NM

Fraher, David J, *Exec Dir*, Arts Midwest, Minneapolis MN

Fraizer, Steve, *Preparator*, Southern Oregon State College, Schneider Museum of Art, Ashland OR

Frajzyngier, Anna, *Library Asst*, University of Colorado, Art & Architecture Library, Boulder CO

Fraker, Harrison, *Dean Environmental Design*, University of California, Berkeley, College of Environmental Design, Berkeley CA (S)

Frampton, Doris, *Dir Annual Giving*, Philbrook Museum of Art, Tulsa OK

Frances, Carole, *Studio Dir*, Huntington Beach Art Center, Huntington Beach CA

Francey, Mary F, *Asst Prof*, University of Utah, Art Dept, Salt Lake City UT (S)

Francis, Frances, *Registrar*, High Museum of Art, Atlanta GA

Francis, Irma Talabi, *Asst Dir Spec Projects*, Fondo del Sol, Visual Art & Media Center, Washington DC

Francis, Richard, *Chief Cur*, Museum of Contemporary Art, Chicago IL

Francis, Tom, *Painting Chmn*, Atlanta College of Art, Atlanta GA (S)

Francis, Wayne, *Gallery Dir*, Northern Michigan University Art Museum, Marquette MI

Francisco, Alan, *Coll Mgr*, Hartwick College, Museum at Hartwick, Oneonta NY

Francisco, Rae Lynn, *Museum Clerk*, Red Rock State Park, Library, Church Rock NM

Franco, Barbara, *Exec Dir*, Historical Society of Washington DC, Heurich House Museum, Washington DC

Franco, Barbara, *Exec Dir*, Historical Society of Washington DC, Research Collections, Washington DC

Francuz, Liliane, *Visual Arts Prog Mgr*, Department of Commerce, Wyoming Arts Council Gallery, Cheyenne WY

Frandrup, Dennis, *Assoc Prof*, College of Saint Benedict, Art Dept, Saint Joseph MN (S)

Frandrup, Dennis, *Asst Prof*, Saint John's University, Art Dept, Collegeville MN (S)

Franeasis, Evelyn, *Treas*, San Bernardino Art Association, Inc, San Bernardino CA

Franits, Wayne, *Prof*, Syracuse University, Dept of Fine Arts (Art History), Syracuse NY (S)

Frank, Barbara, *Asst Prof*, State University of New York at Stony Brook, Art Dept, Stony Brook NY (S)

Frank, Brian, *Dir*, Mankato State University, Conkling Gallery Art Dept, Mankato MN

Frank, Charles, *Executive Dir*, Fine Arts Association, School of Fine Arts, Willoughby OH

Frank, Charles M, *Dir*, School of Fine Arts, Visual Arts Dept, Willoughby OH (S)

Frank, David, *Prof*, Mississippi University for Women, Division of Fine & Performing Arts, Columbus MS (S)

Frank, Denise, *Dir Fine Arts*, Chattanooga State Technical Community College, Advertising Arts Dept, Chattanooga TN (S)

Frank, Eric, *Chmn*, Occidental College, Dept of Art History & Visual Arts, Los Angeles CA (S)

Frank, Henry B, *VPres*, Detroit Institute of Arts, Founders Society, Detroit MI

Frank, Irene, *Art Reference Librn*, University of South Florida, Library, Tampa FL

Frank, Jacqueline, *Assoc Prof*, C W Post Center of Long Island University, School of Visual & Performing Arts, Brookville NY (S)

Frank, Micheline, *Co-Chmn*, Studio Gallery, Washington DC

Frank, Stuart M, *Dir*, Kendall Whaling Museum, Sharon MA

Frank, Stuart M, *Dir*, Kendall Whaling Museum, Library, Sharon MA

Frankel, Robert, *Acting Dir*, Santa Barbara Museum of Art, Santa Barbara CA

Frankel, Robert H, *Dir*, Santa Barbara Museum of Art, Library, Santa Barbara CA

Frankenbach, Susan, *Registrar*, Yale University, Art Gallery, New Haven CT

Franklin, Carolyn, *Catalog Librn*, San Francisco Art Institute, Anne Bremer Memorial Library, San Francisco CA

Franklin, Dwayne, *Registrar & Exhib Preparator*, Dickinson College, Trout Gallery, Carlisle PA

Franklin, Hardy R, *Dir Library*, Public Library of the District of Columbia, Art Division, Washington DC

Franklin, Oliver, *Educ*, Hidalgo County Historical Museum, Edinburg TX

Franklin, Ralph W, *Dir*, Yale University, Beinecke Rare Book & Manuscript Library, New Haven CT

Franklin, Ruth, *Cur of African & Oceanic Art*, Stanford University, Museum of Art, Stanford CA

Franks, Mary, *Asst Cur Educ*, George Walter Vincent Smith Art Museum, Springfield MA

Franks, Steffi, *Instr*, Chautauqua Institution, School of Art, Chautauqua NY (S)

Franson, Scott, *Instr*, Ricks College, Dept of Art, Rexburg ID (S)

Frantz, James H, *Conservator Objects*, The Metropolitan Museum of Art, New York NY

Frantz, Susanne, *Cur 20th Century Glass*, Corning Museum of Glass, Corning NY

Franzini, Robert, *Chmn*, Morehead State University, Art Dept, Morehead KY (S)

Franzini, Robert, *Dir*, Morehead State University, Claypool-Young Art Gallery, Morehead KY

Frasczak, Mary Beth, *Librn*, College of Visual Arts, Library, Saint Paul MN

Fraser, A Ian, *Research Cur*, Indianapolis Museum of Art, Indianapolis IN

Fraser, A Ian, *Cur*, Indianapolis Museum of Art, Clowes Fund Collection, Indianapolis IN

Fraser, Bill, *Chmn Management Comt*, Manitoba Historical Society, Dalnavert Museum, Winnipeg MB

Fraser, David, *Pres & Board Trustees*, Textile Museum, Washington DC

Fraser, James, *Librn Dir*, Fairleigh Dickinson University, Florham Madison Campus Library - Art Dept, Madison NJ

Fraser, Ted, *Exec Dir*, London Regional Art & Historical Museums, London ON

Frauenglass, M, *Chmn Fine Arts*, Fashion Institute of Technology, Art & Design Division, New York NY (S)

Fraze, Denny, *Chmn*, Amarillo College, Art Dept, Amarillo TX (S)

Frazer, John, *Prof*, Wesleyan University, Art Dept, Middletown CT (S)

Frazier, Clifton T, *Assoc Prof*, Rochester Institute of Technology, School of Printing, Rochester NY (S)

Frazier, Diane, *Finance Officer*, Chattahoochee Valley Art Museum, LaGrange GA

Frazier, James, *Pres*, Headley-Whitney Museum, Lexington KY

Frazier, James, *Chmn Board*, Headley-Whitney Museum, Library, Lexington KY

Frazier, Steve, *Prof*, Shorter College, Art Dept, Rome GA (S)

Freaney, Linda, *Head Archivist*, Woodstock Artists Association, WAA Archives, Woodstock NY

Frechette, Suzy Enns, *Mgr Fine Arts Dept*, Saint Louis Public Library, Saint Louis MO

Frederick, Frances A, *Exec Dir*, Associated Artists of Pittsburgh, Pittsburgh PA

Frederick, Helen C, *Artistic Dir*, Pyramid Atlantic, Riverdale MD

Frederick, Jennie, *Head Dept*, Maple Woods Community College, Dept of Art & Art History, Kansas City MO (S)

Fredrick, Charles, *Prof*, California State Polytechnic University, Pomona, Art Dept, Pomona CA (S)

Free, Abigail, *Exec Dir*, Hammond Museum & Japanese Stroll Garden, Cross-Cultural Center, North Salem NY

Freed, Rita, *Cur Egyptian & Ancient Near Eastern*, Museum of Fine Arts, Boston MA

Freedman, Susan K, *Pres*, Public Art Fund, Inc, New York NY

Freehling, Stanley M, *Pres*, The Arts Club of Chicago, Chicago IL

Freel, Mirle E, *Prof*, College of Great Falls, Humanities Division, Great Falls MT (S)

Freeman, Carla C, *Dir*, New York State College of Ceramics at Alfred University, Scholes Library of Ceramics, Alfred NY

Freeman, Carolyn, *Interior Design*, La Roche College, Division of Graphics, Design & Communication, Pittsburgh PA (S)

Freeman, Craig, *Asst Prof*, University of Florida, Dept of Art, Gainesville FL (S)

Freeman, Dana, *Asst Prof*, Aquinas College, Art Dept, Grand Rapids MI (S)

Freeman, David, *Prof*, Winthrop University, Dept of Art & Design, Rock Hill SC (S)

Freeman, Gary, *Dept Chmn*, Gaston College, Art Dept, Dallas NC (S)

Freeman, Jeff, *Prof*, University of South Dakota, Department of Art, College of Fine Arts, Vermillion SD (S)

Freeman, Kirk, *Assoc Prof*, Bethel College, Dept of Art, Saint Paul MN (S)

Freeman, Marina, *Registrar*, California State University, Long Beach, University Art Museum, Long Beach CA

Freeman, Mary Ann C, *Develop*, Discovery Museum, Bridgeport CT

Freeman, Nancy, *Pres*, Round Top Center for the Arts Inc, Arts Gallery, Damariscotta ME

Freeman, Nancy, *Pres*, Round Top Center for the Arts Inc, Round Top Library, Damariscotta ME

Freeman, Robert, *Dir*, Stratford Art Association, The Gallery Stratford, Stratford ON

Freeman, Scott, *Dir Public Prog*, University of Washington, Thomas Burke Memorial Washington State Museum, Seattle WA

Freeman, Susanne, *Librn*, Virginia Museum of Fine Arts, Library, Richmond VA

Freer, Elene J, *Cur*, Muskoka Arts & Crafts Inc, Chapel Gallery, Bracebridge ON

Fregin, Nancy J, *Pres*, American Society of Artists, Inc, Chicago IL

Freiberg, Jack, *Asst Prof*, Florida State University, Art History Dept (R133B), Tallahassee FL (S)

Freilach, David, *Chief Admin*, Alternative Museum, New York NY

Freitag, Amy, *Supv*, Robert W Ryerss Library & Museum, Philadelphia PA

Freitag, Amy, *Supv*, Robert W Ryerss Library & Museum, Library, Philadelphia PA

Freitag, Sally, *Registrar*, National Gallery of Art, Washington DC

French, Jeannie, *Assoc Prof*, South Dakota State University, Dept of Visual Arts, Brookings SD (S)

French, Kate Pearson, *Pres*, Wave Hill, Bronx NY

French, La Wanda, *Dir*, Ponca City Cultural Center & Museum, Ponca City OK

French, La Wanda, *Dir*, Ponca City Cultural Center & Museum, Library, Ponca City OK

French, Stephanie, *VPres*, The American Federation of Arts, New York NY

French, Stephanie, *VPres Corporate Contributions & Cultural Programs*, Philip Morris Companies Inc, New York NY

Frenzel, Peter M, *Pres*, Wesleyan University, Friends of the Davison Art Center, Middletown CT

Freudenheim, Tom, *Asst Secy Arts & Humanities*, Smithsonian Institution, Washington DC

Freudenheim, Tom L, *VPres*, The American Federation of Arts, New York NY

Freund, David, *Assoc Prof Photo*, Ramapo College of New Jersey, School of Contemporary Arts, Mahwah NJ (S)

Freund, Debbie, *Asst Cur*, Hebrew Union College, Skirball Cultural Center, Los Angeles CA

Freund, Louise, *Publicity*, Gallery 9, Los Altos CA

Frew, Rachel, *Librn Asst*, University of North Carolina at Chapel Hill, Joseph Curtis Sloane Art Library, Chapel Hill NC

Frey, Barbara, *Dir*, Texas A&M University - Commerce, University Gallery, Commerce TX

Frey, Barbara, *Chmn Ceramics*, East Texas State University, Dept of Art, Commerce TX (S)

Frey, Jay, *VPres Develop & External Affairs*, Chicago Historical Society, Chicago IL

Frey, Mary, *Assoc Prof*, University of Hartford, Hartford Art School, West Hartford CT (S)

Frey, Viola, *Ceramics*, California College of Arts & Crafts, Oakland CA (S)

Freye, Melissa, *Public Relations Coordr*, Muskegon Museum of Art, Muskegon MI

Freyer, Jon, *Darkroom Mgr*, Light Work, Syracuse NY

Friars, Ernest, *Co-Genealogist*, Kings County Historical Society and Museum, Hampton NB

Friary, Donald R, *Exec Dir & Secy*, Historic Deerfield, Inc, Deerfield MA

Frick, Aida, *Asst Prof*, Wartburg College, Dept of Art, Waverly IA (S)

Frick, Arthur C, *Prof Emeritus*, Wartburg College, Dept of Art, Waverly IA (S)

Frick, Henry Clay, *Pres*, Frick Collection, New York NY

Fricker, Geoff, *Prof*, Butte College, Dept of Fine Arts, Oroville CA (S)

Fridge, Jennifer, *Sales Assoc*, Fort Worth Art Association, Modern Art Museum of Fort Worth, Fort Worth TX

Fridrich, Debbie, *Fiscal Officer*, University of Missouri, Museum of Art & Archaeology, Columbia MO

Fried, Geoffry, *Chmn Design Dept*, Art Institute of Boston, Boston MA (S)

Frieden, Bernard, *Assoc Dean*, Massachusetts Institute of Technology, School of Architecture and Planning, Cambridge MA (S)

Friedlander, Michal, *Cur Judaica*, Judah L Magnes Museum, Berkeley CA

Friedly, Milt, *Pres*, Doshi Center for Contemporary Art, Harrisburg PA

Friedman, Alice T, *Assoc Prof*, Wellesley College, Art Dept, Wellesley MA (S)

Friedman, Barbara, *Prof*, Pace University, Dyson College of Arts & Sciences, Pleasantville NY (S)

Friedman, Betty, *Exec Dir*, Farmington Valley Arts Center, Avon CT

Friedman, Donna, *Coordr Visual Studies*, Iowa State University, Dept of Art & Design, Ames IA (S)

Friedman, Paula, *Public Relations*, Judah L Magnes Museum, Berkeley CA

Friedman, Robert, *Instr*, Stephens College, Art & Fashion Dept, Columbia MO (S)

Friedrich, Richard, *Chmn*, Herkimer County Community College, Liberal Arts & Public Service Division, Herkimer NY (S)

Friend, Grover J, *Chairperson*, Bucks County Historical Society, Mercer Museum, Doylestown PA

Friend, Miles E, *Faculty*, Idaho State University, Dept of Art, Pocatello ID (S)

Frierson, Amy, *Dir*, Houston Museum of Decorative Arts, Chattanooga TN

Frigon, Elaine, *Coordr*, La Centrale Powerhouse Gallery, Montreal PQ

Friis-Hansen, Dana, *Sr Cur*, Contemporary Arts Museum, Houston TX

Frisbee, John, *Dir*, New Hampshire Historical Society, Concord NH

Frisch, Jefferey, *Dir*, Orange County Center for Contemporary Art, Santa Ana CA

Frisch, Marianne Brunson, *Cur*, The Reader's Digest Association Inc, Pleasantville NY

Fritz, Berry, *Public Relations*, McAllen International Museum, McAllen TX

Fritz, Don, *Instr*, Monterey Peninsula College, Art Dept, Monterey CA (S)

Fritz, Jim, *Instr*, Walla Walla Community College, Art Dept, Walla Walla WA (S)

Fritz, Martin, *Managing Dir*, Institute for Contemporary Art, Project Studio One (P S 1), Long Island City NY

Frizzle, Donald, *Secy*, Pocumtuck Valley Memorial Association, Memorial Hall, Deerfield MA

Froehlich, Conrad G, *Dir*, Martin & Osa Johnson Safari Museum, Inc, Chanute KS

Froehlich, Conrad G, *Dir*, Martin & Osa Johnson Safari Museum, Inc, Imperato Collection of West African Artifacts, Chanute KS

Froehlich, Conrad G, *Dir*, Martin & Osa Johnson Safari Museum, Inc, Johnson Collection of Photographs, Movies & Memorabilia, Chanute KS

Froehlich, Conrad G, *Dir*, Martin & Osa Johnson Safari Museum, Inc, Selsor Gallery of Art, Chanute KS

Froehlich, Conrad G, *Dir*, Martin & Osa Johnson Safari Museum, Inc, Scott Explorers Library, Chanute KS

Froem, Rosemary, *Grantsperson-Historian*, Mankato Area Arts Council, Carnegie Art Center, Mankato MN

Fromer, Seymour, *Dir*, Judah L Magnes Museum, Berkeley CA

Fromm, Martin, *Asst Prof*, University of Montana, Dept of Art, Missoula MT (S)

Froncek, Joyce, *First VPres*, Arizona Artist Guild, Phoenix AZ

Frontz, Stephanie J, *Librn*, University of Rochester, Art Library, Rochester NY

Frost, J William, *Dir*, Swarthmore College, Friends Historical Library of Swathmore College, Swarthmore PA

Frudakis, Tony, *Asst Prof*, Hillsdale College, Art Dept, Hillsdale MI (S)

Fruhan, Catherine, *Chmn*, DePauw University, Art Dept, Greencastle IN (S)

Frushour, Steve, *Assoc Coordr Exhib*, Toledo Museum of Art, Toledo OH

Fry, Eileen, *Slide Librn*, Indiana University, Fine Arts Library, Bloomington IN

Fry, Joseph, *Asst Dir*, Kent State University, School of Art, Kent OH (S)

Fryberger, Betsy G, *Cur of Prints & Drawings*, Stanford University, Museum of Art, Stanford CA

Fryd, Vivien G, *Assoc Prof*, Vanderbilt University, Dept of Fine Arts, Nashville TN (S)

Frye, Nancy, *Dir*, Bainbridge Island Arts Council, Bainbridge Isle WA

Frye, Todd, *Actg Dir*, Brigham Young University, B F Larsen Gallery, Provo UT

Fuchs, Angelee, *Chmn*, Mount Mary College, Tower Gallery, Milwaukee WI

Fuchs, Angelee, *Chmn*, Mount Mary College, Art Dept, Milwaukee WI (S)

Fuchs, Joseph, *Library Mgr*, Brand Library & Art Galleries, Glendale CA

Fuentes, Tina, *Assoc Prof*, Texas Tech University, Dept of Art, Lubbock TX (S)

Fugate-Wilcox, Perry, *Treas*, Actual Art Foundation, New York NY

Fuglie, Gordon, *Dir*, Loyola Marymount University, Laband Art Gallery, Los Angeles CA

Fuhro, Laura, *Asst Dir*, Berkeley Heights Free Public Library, Berkeley Heights NJ

Fukawa, Hirokazu, *Asst Prof*, University of Hartford, Hartford Art School, West Hartford CT (S)

Fuller, George, *Co-Dir*, University of Manitoba, Faculty of Architecture Exhibition Centre, Winnipeg MB

Fuller, Richard A, *Chmn & Prof*, Wilkes University, Dept of Art, Wilkes-Barre PA (S)

Fullerton, Jane, *Assoc Dir*, New Brunswick Museum, Saint John NB

Fullerton, Joan, *Instr*, Laramie County Community College, Division of Arts & Humanities, Cheyenne WY (S)

Fullerton, Mark, *Chmn Dept*, Ohio State University, Dept of the History of Art, Columbus OH (S)

Fullerton-Ferrigno, Deborah, *Educator*, Art Museum of South Texas, Corpus Christi TX

Fullerton-Ferrigno, Deborah, *Cur Educ*, Art Museum of South Texas, Library, Corpus Christi TX

Fullford, Gladys, *Business Mgr*, Whatcom Museum of History and Art, Bellingham WA

Fulton, Carol, *Exhibition Designer*, Craft & Folk Art Museum, Los Angeles CA

Fulton, Duncan, *Pres*, Amerind Foundation, Inc, Fulton-Hayden Memorial Library, Dragoon AZ

Fulton, Jeff, *Exec Dir*, Ships of The Sea Maritime Museum, Savannah GA

Fulton, Marianne, *Chief Cur*, George Eastman House-International Museum of Photography & Film, Rochester NY

Fulton, William Duncan, *Pres*, Amerind Foundation, Inc, Amerind Museum, Fulton-Hayden Memorial Art Gallery, Dragoon AZ

Fundenburke, Amy, *Exhib Cur*, Arts Council of Winston-Salem & Forsyth County, Winston-Salem NC

Funderburk, Brent, *Head*, Mississippi State University, Art Dept, Mississippi State MS (S)

Funderburk, Danielle, *Registrar*, Columbus Museum, Columbus GA

Funk, Charlotte, *Instr*, Texas Tech University, Dept of Art, Lubbock TX (S)

Funk, Verne, *Prof*, Texas Tech University, Dept of Art, Lubbock TX (S)

Funtleroy, Carma, *Exec Dir*, The Queens Museum of Art, Flushing NY

Furgol, Edward, *Cur*, Naval Historical Center, The Navy Museum, Washington DC

Furlong, James, *Gallery Dir*, Hudson Guild, Joe & Emily Lowe Art Gallery, New York NY

Furman, David, *Prof Ceramics*, Pitzer College, Dept of Art, Claremont CA (S)

Furman, Evelyn E, *Cur*, Tabor Opera House Museum, Leadville CO

Furman, Serena, *Designer*, Museum of Our National Heritage, Lexington MA

Furst, Donald, *Prof*, University of North Carolina at Wilmington, Dept of Fine Arts - Division of Art, Wilmington NC (S)

Furst, Jill, *Chmn Liberal Arts*, Moore College of Art & Design, Philadelphia PA (S)

Furtak, Rosemary, *Librn*, Walker Art Center, Staff Reference Library, Minneapolis MN

Fusco, Peter, *Cur of European Sculpture & Works of Art*, Getty Center for the History of Art & the Humanities Trust Museum, Santa Monica CA

Fusco, Peter, *Cur European Sculpture & Works of Art*, Getty Center for the History of Art & the Humanities Trust Museum, The J Paul Getty Museum, Santa Monica CA

Fustukian, Sam, *Dir*, University of South Florida, Library, Tampa FL

Futernick, Robert, *Conservator Paper*, Fine Arts Museums of San Francisco, M H de Young Memorial Museum & California Palace of the Legion of Honor, San Francisco CA

Futter, Ellen V, *Pres*, American Museum of Natural History, New York NY

Fyfe, Jo, *Dept Chmn*, Spokane Falls Community College, Fine Arts Dept, Spokane WA (S)

Fzalay, Marilyn, *Instr*, Cuyahoga Community College, Dept of Art, Cleveland OH (S)

Gabarra, Ed, *Adminr*, Mission San Luis Rey de Francia, Mission San Luis Rey Museum, San Luis Rey CA

Gabarro, Marilyn, *Co-Chmn Design*, Massachusetts College of Art, Boston MA (S)

Gabel, Marlene, *Exec Dir*, Contemporary Crafts Association & Gallery, Portland OR

Gabin, George, *Painting*, Monserrat College of Art, Beverly MA (S)

Gable, Jane, *Public Relations & Mem Coordr*, Southern Alleghenies Museum of Art, Loretto PA

Gabriel, Laurie, *Admin Asst*, Children's Art Foundation, Museum of International Children's Art, Santa Cruz CA

Gadd, Richard W, *Dir*, Monterey Museum of Art Association, Monterey CA

Gaddis, Robert, *Div Head*, Campbellsville College, Fine Arts Division, Campbellsville KY (S)

Gadson, James, *Assoc Prof*, University of North Carolina at Chapel Hill, Art Dept, Chapel Hill NC (S)

Gadson, Lynn, *Pres*, Philadelphia Museum of Art, Women's Committee, Philadelphia PA

Gaffin, Harold, *Dir*, Rochester Institute of Technology, School of Printing, Rochester NY (S)

Gaffney, Gary, *Chmn*, Art Academy of Cincinnati, Cincinnati OH (S)

Gaffney, Richard W, *Chmn*, Wagner College, Performing & Visual Arts Dept, Staten Island NY (S)

Gage, Mary M, *Dir*, Mohawk Valley Heritage Association, Inc, Walter Elwood Museum, Amsterdam NY

Gagnier, Bruce, *Instr*, New York Studio School of Drawing, Painting & Sculpture, New York NY (S)

Gagnon, Francois Marc, *Instr*, Universite de Montreal, Dept of Art History, Montreal PQ (S)

Gagnon, Jean, *Assoc Cur Film & Video*, National Gallery of Canada, Ottawa ON

Gagnon, Paulette, *Cur-in-Chief*, Musee d'art Contemporain de Montreal, Montreal PQ

Gagnon, Sylvie, *Dir*, Societe des Musees Quebecois, Montreal PQ

Gagnon, Sylvie, *Exec Dir*, Societe des Musees Quebecois, Association of Museums, Montreal PQ

Gaiber, Maxine, *Dir Educ*, Orange County Museum of Art, Newport Harbor Art Museum, Newport Beach CA

Gaillard, K, *Admin Serv*, Heublein, Inc, Hartford CT

Gaines, C T, *Prof*, Presbyterian College, Fine Arts Dept, Clinton SC (S)

Gaither, Edmund B, *Dir & Cur*, Museum of the National Center of Afro-American Artists, Boston MA

Gaither, James L, *Instr*, Casper College, Dept of Visual Arts, Casper WY (S)

Galante, Peter, *Asst Prof*, Cardinal Stritch College, Art Dept, Milwaukee WI (S)

Galassi, Peter, *Chief Cur, Dept Photography*, Museum of Modern Art, New York NY

Galassi, Susan Grace, *Assoc Cur*, Frick Collection, New York NY

Galban, Victoria, *Art Reference Librn*, The Society of the Four Arts, Library, Palm Beach FL

Galbraith, Lynn, *Assoc Prof Art Educ*, University of Arizona, Dept of Art, Tucson AZ (S)

Galczenski, Marian, *Instr*, Cuesta College, Art Dept, San Luis Obispo CA (S)

Gale, Gayle, *Sunday Coordr*, Cultural Affairs Department City of Los Angeles, Junior Arts Center, Los Angeles CA

Galehouse, Ida, *Librn*, Cheekwood-Tennessee Botanical Gardens & Museum of Art, Botanic Hall Library, Nashville TN

Galembo, Phyllis, *Assoc Prof*, State University of New York at Albany, Art Dept, Albany NY (S)

Galichia, Kathy, *Treas*, Wichita Center for the Arts, Wichita KS

Galizia, Ed, *Dir Music & Video Bus*, Art Institute of Fort Lauderdale, Fort Lauderdale FL (S)

Gall, Dolores, *Pres*, New Haven Paint & Clay Club, Inc, New Haven CT

Gallagher, Edward, *Pres.* American-Scandinavian Foundation, New York NY

Gallagher, James, *Pres.* Philadelphia College of Textiles & Science, School of Textiles, Philadelphia PA (S)

Gallagher, Jean, *Instr.* California State University, Chico, Art Dept, Chico CA (S)

Gallagher, Joanne, *Pres.* Jesse Besser Museum, Alpena MI

Gallagher, Marsha V, *Chief Cur, Cur Material Culture,* Joslyn Art Museum, Omaha NE

Gallant, Michele, *Registrar & Preparator.* Dalhousie University, Art Gallery, Halifax NS

Gallas, Ron, *Asst Prof.* Saint Olaf College, Art Dept, Northfield MN (S)

Gallatin, Gaile, *Prof.* Muskingum College, Art Department, New Concord OH (S)

Gallatin, Morgan Dean, *Gallery Dir.* Central Missouri State University, Art Center Gallery, Warrensburg MO

Gallaty, Tomas, *Dir.* University of Wisconsin, Green Bay, Lawton & Weidner, Green Bay WI

Galligan, David, *Admin Dir.* Walker Art Center, Minneapolis MN

Galloway, Bart, *Lect.* Mississippi State University, Art Dept, Mississippi State MS (S)

Galloway, Elizabeth, *VPres & Dir.* Art Center College of Design, James Lemont Fogg Memorial Library, Pasadena CA

Galloway, Gail, *Cur.* Supreme Court of the United States, Washington DC

Galloway, Mary Lou, *Mgr IL Artisans Shop.* Illinois State Museum, Illinois Artisans & Visitors Centers, Chicago IL

Galloway, Patricia, *Dir Spec Projects.* Mississippi Department of Archives & History, Library, Jackson MS

Galloway, Robert, *Instr.* Mesa Community College, Dept of Art & Art History, Mesa AZ (S)

Galloway, Thomas D, *Dean.* Georgia Institute of Technology, College of Architecture, Atlanta GA (S)

Galow, Carl, *Exhibits Preparator.* Valparaiso University, Brauer Museum of Art, Valparaiso IN

Galperin, Mischa, *Dir.* Education Alliance, Art School, New York NY (S)

Galvin, Mary D, *Intern.* Detroit Institute of Arts, Research Library, Detroit MI

Gamache, Alan, *Assoc Prof.* University of Wisconsin-Stout, Dept of Art & Design, Menomonie WI (S)

Gambil, Jim, *Pres.* Eastern Shore Art Association, Inc, Eastern Shore Art Center, Fairhope AL

Gambill, Norman, *Head Dept.* South Dakota State University, Dept of Visual Arts, Brookings SD (S)

Gamble, Steven G, *Pres.* Southern Arkansas University, Art Dept Gallery & Magale Art Gallery, Magnolia AR

Gambone, Robert L, *Dir.* Valparaiso University, Brauer Museum of Art, Valparaiso IN

Games, Ruth, *Art Librn.* J Erie Johnson Library, Fine Arts Division, Dallas TX

Gammon, Lynda, *Assoc Prof.* University of Victoria, Dept of Visual Arts, Victoria BC (S)

Gamwell, Lyn, *Dir.* State University of New York at Binghamton, University Art Gallery, Vestal NY

Gandara, Nancy, *Asst Dir.* Central Library, Dept of Fine Arts, San Antonio TX

Gandee, Cynthia, *Dir.* University of Tampa, Henry B Plant Museum, Tampa FL

Gandell, Suzanne, *Assoc Dir.* Dartmouth College, Hood Museum of Art, Hanover NH

Gander, Chris, *Instr.* Pacific Northwest College of Art, Portland OR (S)

Gandy, Janice, *Art Historian.* University of South Alabama, Dept of Art & Art History, Mobile AL (S)

Ganem, Cynthia, *Pres.* Arizona Artist Guild, Library, Phoenix AZ

Gangitano, Lia, *Asst Cur Registrar.* Institute of Contemporary Art, Boston MA

Gann, Dan, *Div Head.* Indianapolis Marion County Public Library, Arts Division, Indianapolis IN

Gann, Pat, *Exec Dir.* Arts Festival of Atlanta, Atlanta GA

Ganong, Overton G, *Exec Dir.* South Carolina State Museum, Columbia SC

Gans, Lucy, *Prof.* Lehigh University, Dept of Art & Architecture, Bethlehem PA (S)

Ganstrom, Linda, *Asst Prof.* Fort Hays State University, Dept of Art, Hays KS (S)

Gant, Laurie, *Instr.* Hamilton College, Art Dept, Clinton NY (S)

Gant, Sally, *Educ Coordr.* Old Salem Inc, Museum of Early Southern Decorative Arts, Winston-Salem NC

Gantner, Ellen, *Dir ILL Artisans Prog.* Illinois State Museum, Illinois Artisans Shop, Chicago IL

Gantner, Ellen, *Dir ILL Artisans Prog.* Illinois State Museum, Illinois Artisans & Visitors Centers, Chicago IL

Gantner, Ellen, *IL Artisans Prog.* Illinois State Museum, Museum Shop, Chicago IL

Gantz, Richard A, *Exec Dir.* Indiana State Museum, Indianapolis IN

Garanoes, Darren, *Prog Asst.* Civic Fine Arts Center, Sioux Falls SD

Garay, Olga, *Dir Cultural Affairs.* Miami-Dade Community College, Frances Wolfson Art Gallery, Miami FL

Garay, Olga, *Dir Cultural Affairs.* Miami-Dade Community College, InterAmerican Art Gallery, Miami FL

Garay, Olga, *Dir Cultural Affairs.* Miami-Dade Community College, Wolfson Galleries, Miami FL

Garballey, Jim, *Head Sign Painting.* Butera School of Art, Boston MA (S)

Garber, Elizabeth, *Assoc Prof Art Educ.* University of Arizona, Dept of Art, Tucson AZ (S)

Garber, Janet, *Dir.* Cooperstown Art Association, Cooperstown NY

Garcia, Carole J, *International Representative.* National Native American Co-Operative, North American Indian Information & Trade Center, Tucson AZ

Garcia, Christopher, *Dir.* Big Bend Community College, Art Dept, Moses Lake WA (S)

Garcia, Debbie, *Unit Registrar.* Museum of New Mexico, Museum of International Folk Art, Santa Fe NM

Garcia, E Meren, *Traveling Exhib Officer.* Musee d'art Contemporain de Montreal, Montreal PQ

Garcia, Flora Maria, *Exec Dir.* Missouri State Council on the Arts, Saint Louis MO

Garcia, Hector, *Assoc Prof.* Indiana-Purdue University, Dept of Fine Arts, Fort Wayne IN (S)

Garcia, June, *Dir.* Central Library, Dept of Fine Arts, San Antonio TX

Garcia, Maria Teresa, *Cur Educ.* Southern Methodist University, Meadows Museum, Dallas TX

Garcia, Tony, *Dir Design & Graphics.* Indiana State Museum, Indianapolis IN

Garcia-Gutierrez, Enrique, *Assoc Prof.* University of Puerto Rico, Dept of Fine Arts, Rio Piedras PR (S)

Gardiner, Allen R, *Instr.* Maine College of Art, Portland ME (S)

Gardiner, George, *Pres.* Gilbert Stuart Memorial, Inc Memorial Association, Inc, Museum, Saunderstown RI

Gardiner, Mary, *Vol & Progs Coordr.* Southern Oregon State College, Schneider Museum of Art, Ashland OR

Gardiner, Rita, *Develop Mgr.* Memorial University of Newfoundland, Art Gallery of Newfoundland & Labrador, Saint John's NF

Gardinier, Paul, *Temporary Exhibits.* Alaska State Museum, Juneau AK

Gardner, Doll, *Office Admin.* West Hills Unitarian Fellowship, Portland OR

Gardner, Donald, *Admin Dir.* Marblehead Historical Society, Marblehead MA

Gardner, Frederick, *Dean.* California Institute of the Arts Library, Santa Clarita CA

Gardner, Gay, *Adjunct Asst Prof.* Spokane Falls Community College, Fine Arts Dept, Spokane WA (S)

Gardner, William, *Chmn Div Communications & Humanities.* Lewis & Clark Community College, Art Dept, Godfrey IL (S)

Gardner, William F, *Instr.* North Florida Community College, Dept Humanities & Art, Madison FL (S)

Garfield, Alan, *Chmn.* Teikyo Marycrest University, Art & Computer Graphics Dept, Davenport IA (S)

Garhart, Martin, *Prof.* Kenyon College, Art Dept, Gambier OH (S)

Garland, Jeff, *Head Dept.* Springfield College in Illinois, Dept of Art, Springfield IL (S)

Garland, Kathleen, *Conservator of Objects.* Nelson-Atkins Museum of Art, Kansas City MO

Garland, Robin K, *Pub Relations Dir.* Cheltenham Center for the Arts, Cheltenham PA (S)

Garner, Gretchen, *Dean.* Moore College of Art & Design, Philadelphia PA (S)

Garoza, Valdis, *Chmn.* Marietta College, Grover M Hermann Fine Arts Center, Marietta OH

Garoza, Valdis, *Chmn.* Marietta College, Art Dept, Marietta OH (S)

Garreck, Dennis, *Exec Dir.* Organization of Saskatchewan Arts Councils (OSAC), Regina SK

Garrels, Gary, *Chief Cur.* San Francisco Museum of Modern Art, San Francisco CA

Garren, Robert F, *Chmn.* Southern College of Seventh-Day Adventists, Art Dept, Collegedale TN (S)

Garrett, Barbara, *Mgr Visual Arts & Crafts.* Idaho Commission on the Arts, Boise ID

Garrett, Cheri S, *Office Mgr.* Pennsylvania Historical & Museum Commission, Railroad Museum of Pennsylvania, Harrisburg PA

Garriot-Stejskal, Richard, *Exhib Coordr.* Very Special Arts New Mexico, Enabled Arts Center, Albuquerque NM (S)

Garriott-Stejskal, Richard, *Exhib Coordr.* Very Special Arts New Mexico, Very Special Arts Gallery, Albuquerque NM

Garrison, Helene, *Chmn Liberal Arts.* Art Institute of Southern California, Ruth Salyer Library, Laguna Beach CA

Garrison, Jim, *Instr.* Mesa Community College, Dept of Art & Art History, Mesa AZ (S)

Garrison, Mary, *Pres.* Glynn Art Association, Saint Simons Island GA

Garrison, William, *Colls Mgr.* Saratoga County Historical Society, Brookside Museum, Ballston Spa NY

Garrity, Noreen Scott, *Cur Educ.* Rutgers University, Stedman Art Gallery, Camden NJ

Garrott, Martha, *Dir.* Craftsmen's Guild of Mississippi Crafts Center Mississippi, Inc, Ridgeland MS

Garten, Clifford, *Prof.* Hamline University, Dept of Art & Art History, Saint Paul MN (S)

Gartenmann, Donna, *City of Boulder Arts Commission.* Boulder Public Library & Gallery, Dept of Fine Arts Gallery, Boulder CO

Garthwaite, Ernest, *Assoc Prof.* York College of the City University of New York, Fine & Performing Arts, Jamaica NY (S)

Gartner, Mary, *Cur.* LeSueur Museum, LeSueur MN

Gartrell, Ellen, *Dir.* Duke University Library, Hartman Center for Sales, Advertising & Marketing History, Durham NC

Gartrell, Roberta, *Asst.* Ponca City Cultural Center & Museum, Library, Ponca City OK

Garvey, Susan Gibson, *Adjunct Cur.* Dalhousie University, Art Gallery, Halifax NS

Garvey, Timothy, *Instr.* Illinois Wesleyan University, School of Art, Bloomington IL (S)

Garwell, Robert, *Dean of Fine Arts.* Texas Christian University, Art & Art History Dept, Fort Worth TX (S)

Gary, Anne-Bridget, *Assoc Prof.* University of Wisconsin-Stevens Point, Dept of Art & Design, Stevens Point WI (S)

Gascon, France, *Dir.* Musee d'Art de Joliette, Library, Joliette PQ

Gascon, France, *Dir.* Musee d'Art de Joliette, Joliette PQ

Gaskell, Ivan, *Cur Painting.* Harvard University, William Hayes Fogg Art Museum, Cambridge MA

Gasparro, Frank, *Instr.* Samuel S Fleisher Art Memorial, Philadelphia PA (S)

Gass, Katherine, *Registrar*, The Chase Manhattan Bank, NA, Art Collection, New York NY

Gastonguay, N, *Asst Librn*, Musee du Quebec, Bibliotheque des Arts, Quebec PQ

Gastony, Endre, *Prof*, Augustana College, Art Dept, Sioux Falls SD (S)

Gates, Carole C, *Instr*, Villa Maria College of Buffalo, Art Dept, Buffalo NY (S)

Gates, Elaine, *Assoc Prof*, Hood College, Dept of Art, Frederick MD (S)

Gates, H I, *Assoc Prof*, George Washington University, Dept of Art, Washington DC (S)

Gates, James L, *Librn*, National Baseball Hall of Fame & Museum, Inc, Art Collection, Cooperstown NY

Gates, Jay, *Dir*, Dallas Museum of Art, Dallas TX

Gates, Leigh, *Head Slide Librn*, The Art Institute of Chicago, Ryerson & Burnham Libraries, Chicago IL

Gates, Mimi, *Dir*, Seattle Art Museum, Seattle WA

Gates, Sue, *Dir*, Dacotah Prairie Museum, Lamont Gallery, Aberdeen SD

Gates, Sue, *Dir*, Dacotah Prairie Museum, Ruth Bunker Memorial Library, Aberdeen SD

Gates, William, *Cur*, The American Ceramic Society, Ross C Purdy Museum of Ceramics, Westerville OH

Gatewood, Maud F, *Prof*, Averett College, Art Dept, Danville VA (S)

Gatlin, Sally, *Gallery Mgr*, Coppini Academy of Fine Arts, San Antonio TX

Gattis, Tom, *Instr*, Suomi International College of Art & Design, Fine Arts Dept, Hancock MI (S)

Gatzke, Donald, *Dean*, Tulane University, School of Architecture, New Orleans LA (S)

Gauchier, Michelle, *Librn*, Musee d'art Contemporain de Montreal, Mediatheque, Montreal PQ

Gaudet, Art, *Dir*, Peter Yegen Jr Yellowstone County Museum, Billings MT

Gaudieri, Millicent Hall, *Exec Dir*, Association of Art Museum Directors, New York NY

Gaudreault, Andre, *Instr*, Universite de Montreal, Dept of Art History, Montreal PQ (S)

Gaughan, Tom, *Instr*, Samuel S Fleisher Art Memorial, Philadelphia PA (S)

Gaugler, William, *Assoc Chair, Art History*, San Jose State University, School of Art & Design, San Jose CA (S)

Gaul, Elaine, *Designer*, Indiana University, William Hammond Mathers Museum, Bloomington IN

Gaul, Mitchell, *Head Design & Installation*, San Diego Museum of Art, San Diego CA

Gauron, Carole, *Pres*, Conseil des Arts Textiles du Quebec (CATQ), Centre de Documentation, Montreal PQ

Gauvreau, Robert, *Division Dean*, Modesto Junior College, Arts Humanities & Communications Division, Modesto CA (S)

Gauza, Kenneth, *Asst Prof*, Colby College, Art Dept, Waterville ME (S)

Gavin, John, *Cur Coll*, Museum of Mobile, Mobile AL

Gavin, Robin Farwell, *Cur Spanish Colonial Coll*, Museum of New Mexico, Museum of International Folk Art, Santa Fe NM

Gawron, Carol, *Supv Branches*, Miami-Dade Public Library, Miami FL

Gay, Robert, *Instr*, Waynesburg College, Dept of Fine Arts, Waynesburg PA (S)

Gayer, Don, *Vol Librn*, Vizcaya Museum & Gardens, Library, Miami FL

Gaylor, Gregory, *Dir*, Community Fine Arts Center, Halseth Gallery, Rock Springs WY

Gazda, Elaine K, *Dir*, University of Michigan, Kelsey Museum of Archaeology, Ann Arbor MI

Gazda, Elaine K, *Dir Kelsey Museum*, University of Michigan, Ann Arbor MI, Dept of History of Art, Ann Arbor MI (S)

Gazit, Tova, *Librn*, Judah L Magnes Museum, Berkeley CA

Gazit, Tova, *Librn*, Judah L Magnes Museum, Blumenthal Rare Book & Manuscript Library, Berkeley CA

Gealt, Adelheid, *Dir*, Indiana University, Art Museum, Bloomington IN

Gealt, Barry, *Prof*, Indiana University, Bloomington, Henry Radford Hope School of Fine Arts, Bloomington IN (S)

Gear, Gail, *Prof*, Texas Christian University, Art & Art History Dept, Fort Worth TX (S)

Geare, J Scott, *VPres*, Allegany County Historical Society, History House, Cumberland MD

Gearey, Dave, *Instr*, Sarah Lawrence College, Dept of Art History, Bronxville NY (S)

Gebb, Wayne, *Instr*, Midway College, Art Dept, Midway KY (S)

Gebbie, Robert, *Deputy Dir Finance & Adminr*, Solomon R Guggenheim Museum, New York NY

Gebbie, Robert, *Deputy Dir Finance & Admin*, Guggenheim Museum Soho, New York NY

Gebhard, David, *Cur Architectural Drawings*, University of California, Santa Barbara, University Art Museum, Santa Barbara CA

Geddes, Mathew, *Instr*, Ricks College, Dept of Art, Rexburg ID (S)

Gedeon, Lucinda H, *Dir*, State University of New York at Purchase, Neuberger Museum of Art, Purchase NY

Gedraicis, Nancy, *Asst to Dir*, Plymouth Antiquarian Society, Plymouth MA

Gee, Jeff, *Admin Asst*, Photographers Gallery, Saskatoon SK

Geers, Robert, *Dir Performing Arts*, Colorado Springs Fine Arts Center, Colorado Springs CO

Gehret, L Alan, *Asst Adminr*, Audubon Wildlife Sanctuary, Audubon PA

Gehrm, Barbara, *Archives*, Ward Foundation, Ward Museum of Wildfowl Art, Salisbury MD

Geibert, Ron, *Prof*, Wright State University, Dept of Art & Art History, Dayton OH (S)

Geier, Bob, *Exec Dir*, Ogden Union Station, Myra Powell Art Gallery, Ogden UT

Geier, Bob, *Exec Dir*, Ogden Union Station, Union Station Museums, Ogden UT

Geiger, Gail L, *Assoc Prof*, University of Wisconsin, Madison, Dept of Art History, Madison WI (S)

Geiger, Mary Ann, *Exec Dir*, Center for History of American Needlework, Butler PA

Geimzer, Eugene, *Chmn Fine Arts Dept*, Loyola University of Chicago, Fine Arts Dept, Chicago IL (S)

Geis, Mary Christina, *Dir*, Georgian Court College Gallery, M Christina Geis Gallery, Lakewood NJ

Geis, Mary Christina, *Head Dept*, Georgian Court College, Dept of Art, Lakewood NJ (S)

Geischer, Geraldine, *Instr*, Milwaukee Area Technical College, Graphic Arts Division, Milwaukee WI (S)

Geisinger, William, *Instr*, De Anza College, Creative Arts Division, Cupertino CA (S)

Geist, Ronnie, *Dir Programming*, Women's Interart Center, Inc, Interart Gallery, New York NY

Gelarden, Martha, *Gallery Dir*, Eastern Michigan University, Ford Gallery, Ypsilanti MI

Geldin, Sherri, *Dir*, Ohio State University, Wexner Center for the Arts, Columbus OH

Gelinas, Andre, *VPres*, Fitchburg Art Museum, Fitchburg MA

Geller, Beatrice, *Assoc Prof*, Pacific Lutheran University, Dept of Art, Tacoma WA (S)

Gellert, J, *Dean Faculty of Arts & Sciences*, Lakehead University, Dept of Visual Arts, Thunder Bay ON (S)

Gellert, Michael E, *Chmn Board of Trustees*, Caramoor Center for Music & the Arts, Inc, Caramoor House Museum, Katonah NY

Gelles, Ann, *Comptroller*, Nassau County Museum of Fine Art, Roslyn Harbor NY

Gellman, Lola B, *Chmn*, Queensborough Community College, Dept of Art & Photography, Bayside NY (S)

Geltner, Frank, *Asst Dir*, University of Oregon, Aperture Photo Gallery - EMU Art Gallery, Eugene OR

Gemey, Kelly, *Lectr*, Mount Allison University, Fine Arts Dept, Sackville NB (S)

General, John, *Dir Electronics & Kinetics*, Museum of Holography - Chicago, Chicago IL

Genevro, Rosalie, *Exec Dir*, Architectural League of New York, New York NY

Genshaft, Carole, *Dir Educ*, Columbus Museum of Art, Columbus OH

Genshaft, Carole, *Dir Educ*, Columbus Museum of Art, Resource Center, Columbus OH

Genszler, Leslie, *Gallery Shop Mgr*, Madison Art Center, Madison WI

Gentile, Anthony M, *Dir Finance*, Cleveland Museum of Art, Cleveland OH

Gentis, Thierry, *Assoc Cur & Coll Mgr*, Brown University, Haffenreffer Museum, Providence RI

Gentry, James, *Instr*, Eastern Arizona College, Art Dept, Thatcher AZ (S)

Gentry, Sandra, *Admin Asst*, Pensacola Museum of Art, Pensacola FL

Genzlinger, Grant, *VPres*, Wayne County Historical Society, Museum, Honesdale PA

Geoffrion, Moira, *Prof Sculpture*, University of Arizona, Dept of Art, Tucson AZ (S)

Geoghan, Kevin, *Exec Dir*, Arts of the Southern Finger Lakes, Corning NY

George, Candace, *Treas*, Ravalli County Museum, Hamilton MT

George, David N, *Prof*, Truett-McConnell College, Fine Arts Dept & Arts Dept, Cleveland GA (S)

George, Mary Z, *Pres Cultural Heritage Commission*, City of Los Angeles, Cultural Affairs Dept, Los Angeles CA

Georgia, Olivia, *Dir Visual Arts*, Snug Harbor Cultural Center, Newhouse Center for Contemporary Art, Staten Island NY

Georgias, Andrew, *Prof*, Glendale Community College, Visual & Performing Arts Division, Glendale CA (S)

Georgilas, Elaine, *Cur Educ*, Florida Gulf Coast Art Center, Inc, Belleair FL

Georgilas, Elaine, *Cur Educ*, Florida Gulf Coast Art Center, Inc, Art Reference Library, Belleair FL

Georgilas, Elaine, *Cur Educ*, Florida Gulf Coast Art Center, Inc, Belleair FL (S)

Gephart, Geoff, *Pres*, Arts United of Greater Fort Wayne, Fort Wayne IN

Gerber, Daryl, *Pres*, The Art Institute of Chicago, Society for Contemporary Arts, Chicago IL

Gerber, John H, *Cur Native American Coll*, Ohio University, Kennedy Museum of American Art, Athens OH

Gerdts, William H, *Prof*, City University of New York, PhD Program in Art History, New York NY (S)

Gerharz, Ellen, *Dir*, Lewistown Art Center, Lewistown MT

Geritz, Kathy, *Cur Film*, University of California, Berkeley Art Museum & Pacific Film Archive, Berkeley CA

Geritz, Kathy, *Assoc Film Cur*, University of California, Pacific Film Archive, Berkeley CA

Gerlach, Michael, *Chmn*, Mesa College, Art Dept, Grand Junction CO (S)

Gerlach, Monte, *Assoc Prof*, Saint Xavier University, Dept of Art, Chicago IL (S)

Gerlough, Kate, *Mgr Sales & Info*, Frick Collection, New York NY

Germany, Robin, *Asst Prof*, Texas Tech University, Dept of Art, Lubbock TX (S)

Germer, Mark, *Music Librn*, University of the Arts, Albert M Greenfield Library, Philadelphia PA

Germin, Pierre, *Librn*, Saint Joseph's Oratory, Library, Montreal PQ

Gerratt, Bradley, *Dir*, National Archives & Records Administration, John F Kennedy Library & Museum, Boston MA

Gerry, Jane, *Pres*, Cheekwood Nashville's Home of Art & Gardens, Education Dept, Nashville TN (S)

Gersan, Denise, *Cur Exhib*, University of Miami, Lowe Art Museum, Coral Gables FL

Gersan, Denise, *Assoc Dir*, University of Miami, Lowe Art Museum Reference Library, Coral Gables FL

Gershen, Linda M, *Pres*, Florida Pastel Association, Hollywood FL

Gershon, Stacy, *Asst Cur*, The Chase Manhattan Bank, NA, Art Collection, New York NY

Gerson, Paula, *Treas*, International Center of Medieval Art, Inc, New York NY

Gilmore, Mark, *Dir Develop*, Arts United of Greater Fort Wayne, Fort Wayne IN

Gilmore, Peter, *Dir Operations*, Drawing Center, New York NY

Gilmore, R, *Prof*, Gonzaga University, Dept of Art, Spokane WA (S)

Gilmore, Roger, *Pres*, Maine College of Art, Portland ME (S)

Gilmore-House, Gloria, *Dir*, Fuller Lodge Art Center & Gallery, Los Alamos NM

Gilpin, Darcy, *Vice Dir Develop*, Brooklyn Museum, Brooklyn NY

Gilpin, Risa, *Head Adult Services*, Providence Athenaeum, Library, Providence RI

Gilrain, Kathleen, *Dir*, Socrates Sculpture Park, Long Island City NY

Gilson, Barry, *Pres Board Trustees*, Burnaby Art Gallery, Burnaby BC

Gimse, Malcolm, *Prof*, Saint Olaf College, Art Dept, Northfield MN (S)

Gioffre, Dolores, *Chmn*, Woodbridge Township Cultural Arts Commission, Barron Arts Center, Woodbridge NJ

Giordana, Enrico, *Prof*, College of Mount Saint Vincent, Fine Arts Dept, Riverdale NY (S)

Gipe, Thomas D, *Head Sculpture*, Southern Illinois University at Edwardsville, Dept of Art & Design, Edwardsville IL (S)

Gips, Terry, *Dir*, University of Maryland, College Park, Art Gallery, College Park MD

Giral, Angela, *Dir*, Columbia University, Avery Architectural & Fine Arts Library, New York NY

Girard, Jack, *Prof*, Transylvania University, Studio Arts Dept, Lexington KY (S)

Girardi, Guido, *Instr*, Glendale Community College, Visual & Performing Arts Division, Glendale CA (S)

Girshman, Beth, *Adult Service Librn*, Jones Library, Inc, Amherst MA

Giuliano, Marie, *Business Office Supv*, Ferguson Library, Stamford CT

Giuntini, Gilles, *Assoc Prof*, University of Hartford, Hartford Art School, West Hartford CT (S)

Givnish, Gerry, *Exec Dir*, Painted Bride Art Center, The Gallery at the Painted Bride, Philadelphia PA

Gladfelter, Kimberly, *Exhib Asst*, University of Maryland, College Park, Art Gallery, College Park MD

Gladstone, Caroline T, *Mgr Vol Services*, Philadelphia Museum of Art, Mount Pleasant, Philadelphia PA

Gladstone, Patricia, *Asst to Dir*, Hartwick College, Museum at Hartwick, Oneonta NY

Glanton, Richard H, *Pres Board of Trustees*, Barnes Foundation, Merion PA

Glantz, Johnnie Sue, *Chmn*, Art & Culture Center of Hollywood, Hollywood FL

Glanzer, Harvey W, *Co-owner Mgr*, Frank Lloyd Wright Museum, AD German Warehouse, Richland Center WI

Glaser, Lewis, *Prof*, Texas Christian University, Art & Art History Dept, Fort Worth TX (S)

Glaser, Miles R, *Financial Dir*, Menil Collection, Houston TX

Glasford, Donna, *Dir Educ*, Cheekwood Nashville's Home of Art & Gardens, Education Dept, Nashville TN (S)

Glasgow, Andrew, *Educ Dir*, Southern Highland Craft Guild, Folk Art Center, Asheville NC

Glasgow, Joanne, *Museum Shop Mgr*, The Dixon Gallery & Gardens, Memphis TN

Glasgow, Vaughn L, *Dir Spec Projects*, Louisiana Department of Culture, Recreation & Tourism, Louisiana State Museum, New Orleans LA

Glasper, Mark, *Dir Communications*, The American Ceramic Society, Ross C Purdy Museum of Ceramics, Westerville OH

Glass, Christopher, *Vis Instr*, Bowdoin College, Art Dept, Brunswick ME (S)

Glass, Dorothy F, *VPres*, International Center of Medieval Art, Inc, New York NY

Glass, Simon, *Instr*, Toronto School of Art, Toronto ON (S)

Glassell, Alfred C, *Chmn Board*, Museum of Fine Arts, Houston, Houston TX

Glasser, Dale, *Dir*, Union of American Hebrew Congregations, Synagogue Art & Architectural Library, New York NY

Glassford, C, *Instr*, Golden West College, Visual Art Dept, Huntington Beach CA (S)

Glassford, Donna, *Dir Educ*, Cheekwood-Tennessee Botanical Gardens & Museum of Art, Nashville TN

Glassheim, Elliot, *Asst to Dir*, North Dakota Museum of Art, Grand Forks ND

Glassman, Paul, *Art & Architecture Librn*, Pratt Institute Library, Art & Architecture Dept, Brooklyn NY

Glasson, Lloyd, *Prof*, University of Hartford, Hartford Art School, West Hartford CT (S)

Glatt, Robert, *Chmn Art Dept*, Sullivan County Community College, Division of Commercial Art & Photography, Loch Sheldrake NY (S)

Glavin, Ellen M, *Chmn Art Dept*, Emmanuel College, Art Dept, Boston MA (S)

Glaze, Ruth, *Heat Art Dept*, Mississippi College, Art Dept, Clinton MS (S)

Glazer, Helen, *Exhib Dir & Coll Coordr*, Goucher College, Rosenberg Gallery, Baltimore MD

Glazer, Steve, *Asst Prof*, Concord College, Fine Art Division, Athens WV (S)

Gleason, Mary Joan, *Ref Librn*, Daemen College, Marian Library, Amherst NY

Gleaves, Charles T, *Dir Horticulture*, Indianapolis Museum of Art, Indianapolis IN

Gleeman, E L, *Instr*, Normandale Community College, Bloomington MN (S)

Gleeson, Larry, *Art History Coordr*, University of North Texas, School of Visual Arts, Denton TX (S)

Glenn, Constance W, *Dir & Chief Cur*, California State University, Long Beach, University Art Museum, Long Beach CA

Glenn, Dennis, *Dept Head*, The Illinois Institute of Art, Chicago IL (S)

Glenn, Ralph F, *Chmn Art Dept*, Madonna University, Art Dept, Livonia MI (S)

Glenn, T, *Assoc Prof*, McGill University, Dept of Art History, Montreal PQ (S)

Glennon, Rose M, *Cur Educ*, Marion Koogler McNay Art Museum, San Antonio TX

Gleysteen, William H, *Pres Japan Society*, Japan Society, Inc, Japan Society Gallery, New York NY

Glibbery, Sheilagh, *Treas*, South Peace Art Society, Dawson Creek Art Gallery, Dawson Creek BC

Glickberg, Randi, *Deputy Dir*, Yeshiva University Museum, New York NY

Glidden, Linda, *Mgr*, Oatlands, Inc, Leesburg VA

Gliniecki, Anita, *Dean*, Saint Clair County Community College, Jack R Hennesey Gallery, Art Dept, Port Huron MI (S)

Globensky, Bridiged, *Dir Educ*, Baltimore Museum of Art, Baltimore MD

Globus, Dorothy Twining, *Dir*, Fashion Institute of Technology, Museum at FIT, New York NY

Gloeckler, Terry, *Asst Prof*, Eastern Oregon State College, Arts & Humanities Dept, La Grande OR (S)

Glonski, Dan, *Cur Astronomy*, Hastings Museum, Hastings NE

Glousky, Alan, *Chmn*, Promote Art Works Inc (PAWI), Laziza Videodance Lumia Project, Brooklyn NY

Glover, Rob, *Assoc Prof*, Texas Tech University, Dept of Art, Lubbock TX (S)

Glowski, Janice, *Assoc Cur*, Ohio State University, Slide & Photograph Library, Columbus OH

Glueckert, Stephen, *Educ Cur*, Art Museum of Missoula, Missoula MT

Glusberg, Jorge, *Co-Dir*, International Center for Advanced Studies in Art, New York NY

Glusman, Gayle, *Challenger Center Sr Flight Dir*, Louisiana Arts & Science Center, Baton Rouge LA

Glynn, Edward, *Dean*, Maryland College of Art & Design, Silver Spring MD (S)

Goad, Albert, *Chmn*, Ashland College Arts & Humanities Gallery, Ashland OH

Goad, Albert W, *Chmn*, Ashland University, Art Dept, Ashland OH (S)

Gochman, Stanley I, *Prog Coordr*, International Council for Cultural Exchange (ICCE), Bellport NY (S)

Goddard, Stephen, *Cur Prints & Drawings*, University of Kansas, Spencer Museum of Art, Lawrence KS

Godel, Larry, *Chmn Dept*, Northeast Community College, Dept of Liberal Arts, Norfolk NE (S)

Godfrey, Judy, *Lectr*, Centenary College of Louisiana, Dept of Art, Shreveport LA (S)

Godfrey, Judy, *Dir*, Centenary College of Louisiana, Meadows Museum of Art, Shreveport LA

Godfrey, Robert, *Head Dept*, Western Carolina University, Dept of Art, Cullowhee NC (S)

Godfrey, William, *Pres*, The Art Guild, Farmington CT

Godin, Nathalie, *Chmn*, Galerie Restigouche Gallery, Campbellton NB

Godlewski, Henry, *Assoc Prof*, Mohawk Valley Community College, Advertising Design & Production, Utica NY (S)

Godsey, William, *Instr*, John C Calhoun State Community College, Department of Fine Arts, Decatur AL (S)

Godwin, Stan, *Asst Prof*, East Texas State University, Dept of Art, Commerce TX (S)

Goebel, C C, *Chmn Dept*, Augustana College, Art & Art History Dept, Rock Island IL (S)

Goedde, Lawrence, *Chmn*, University of Virginia, McIntire Dept of Art, Charlottesville VA (S)

Goeke, Mary Ellen, *Head Exhibits & Registration*, Cincinnati Museum Association, Cincinnati Art Museum, Cincinnati OH

Goering, Doug, *Chmn*, Albion College, Bobbitt Visual Arts Center, Albion MI

Goering, Douglas, *Chmn Dept Visual Arts & Assoc Prof*, Albion College, Dept of Visual Arts, Albion MI (S)

Goering, Douglas, *Prof*, Albion College, Dept of Visual Arts, Albion MI (S)

Goering, Karen M, *Exec VPres*, Missouri Historical Society, Saint Louis MO

Goerler, Nancy N, *Dir Develop*, Palm Beach County Parks & Recreation Department, Morikami Museum & Japanese Gardens, Delray Beach FL

Goetemann, Gordon, *Chmn*, College of Saint Benedict, Art Dept, Saint Joseph MN (S)

Goetemann, Gordon, *Chmn*, Saint John's University, Art Dept, Collegeville MN (S)

Goethals, Marion, *Asst Dir*, Williams College, Museum of Art, Williamstown MA

Goettemann, Gordon, *Chmn Art Dept*, College of Saint Benedict, Art Gallery, Saint Joseph MN

Goetz, Linda, *Librn*, West Bend Art Museum, West Bend WI

Goetz, Mary Anna, *Instr*, Woodstock School of Art, Inc, Woodstock NY (S)

Goff, Frederick E, *Communications*, Rhode Island School of Design, Museum of Art, RISD, Providence RI (S)

Goff, Lila J, *Asst to Dir for Libraries & Museum Coll*, Minnesota Historical Society, Saint Paul MN

Goffe, Gwen, *Assoc Dir Finance & Admin*, Museum of Fine Arts, Houston, Houston TX

Goffen, Rona, *Prof*, Rutgers, the State University of New Jersey, Graduate Program in Art History, New Brunswick NJ (S)

Goffredo, Sam, *Chmn*, Los Angeles Valley College, Art Dept, Van Nuys CA (S)

Golahny, Amy, *Assoc Prof*, Lycoming College, Art Dept, Williamsport PA (S)

Gold, Arnold, *Pres*, New York Artists Equity Association, Inc, New York NY

Gold, Lawrence, *Assoc Prof*, Pacific Lutheran University, Dept of Art, Tacoma WA (S)

Goldberg, Alan, *Chmn*, Albany Institute of History & Art, Albany NY

Goldberg, Beth, *Assoc Dir*, San Francisco Camerawork Inc, San Francisco CA

Goldberg, Glenn, *Instr*, New York Studio School of Drawing, Painting & Sculpture, New York NY (S)

Goldberg, Ira, *Admin Mgr*, Art Students League of New York, New York NY

Goldberg, Ira, *Admin Mgr*, Art Students League of New York, Library, New York NY

Goldberg, Ira, *Admin Mgr*, American Fine Arts Society, New York NY

Goldberg, Joshua, *Cur Educ*, University of Arizona, Museum of Art, Tucson AZ

Goldberg, Kenneth, *Information Specialist*, Northeast Ohio Areawide Coordinating Agency (NOACA), Information Resource Center, Cleveland OH

Goldberg, Steven, *Art & AV Librn*, Portland Public Library, Art - Audiovisual Dept, Portland ME

Goldblat, Aaron, *Dir Exhibits*, Please Touch Museum, Philadelphia PA

Golden, Jacqueline, *Asst Prof*, University of Arkansas, Art Dept, Fayetteville AR (S)

Golden, Jennifer, *Educ Dir*, Tallahassee Museum of History & Natural Science, Tallahassee FL

Golden, Joe, *Pres*, Spirit Square Center for Arts & Education, Charlotte NC

Golden, Judith, *Prof Emerita*, University of Arizona, Dept of Art, Tucson AZ (S)

Golden, Thelma, *Branch Dir, Philip Morris & Assoc Cur*, Whitney Museum of American Art, New York NY

Golden, Thelma, *Branch Dir*, Whitney Museum of American Art, Whitney Museum at Philip Morris, New York NY

Golden, Vivian, *Trustee*, Foundation for Today's Art, Nexus Gallery, Philadelphia PA

Goldenstein, Sonny, *Div Chmn*, Governors State University, College of Arts & Science, Art Dept, University Park IL (S)

Goldfarb, Barbara, *Second VPres*, Monmouth Museum & Cultural Center, Lincroft NJ

Goldfarb, Hilliard T, *Cur*, Isabella Stewart Gardner Museum, Boston MA

Goldfarb, Joan, *Chmn Bd Trustees*, McMichael Canadian Art Collection, Kleinburg ON

Goldich, Louis, *Registrar*, San Diego Museum of Art, San Diego CA

Goldin, Ellen, *Instr*, Dowling College, Dept of Visual Arts, Oakdale NY (S)

Goldman, Beverly, *Shop Mgr*, B'nai B'rith International, B'nai B'rith Klutznick National Jewish Museum, Washington DC

Goldman, Debra, *Asst Prof*, University of Colorado at Denver, Dept of Fine Arts, Denver CO (S)

Goldman, Harvey, *Chmn Design*, University of Massachusetts Dartmouth, College of Visual & Performing Arts, North Dartmouth MA (S)

Goldman, Nancy, *Library Head*, University of California, Pacific Film Archive, Berkeley CA

Goldman, Stewart, *Chmn*, Art Academy of Cincinnati, Cincinnati OH (S)

Goldman, Susan, *Resident Printer*, Pyramid Atlantic, Riverdale MD

Goldner, George R, *Cur in Charge*, The Metropolitan Museum of Art, Dept of Drawings & Prints, New York NY

Goldsleger, Cheryl, *Dept Head*, Piedmont College, Art Dept, Demorest GA (S)

Goldsmith, Christopher, *Admin Dir*, Milwaukee Art Museum, Milwaukee WI

Goldsmith, Robert B, *Deputy Dir Admin*, Frick Collection, New York NY

Goldsmith, Shelly, *Admin Asst*, Marquette University, Haggerty Museum of Art, Milwaukee WI

Goldstein, Alan, *Instr*, Bucks County Community College, Fine Arts Dept, Newtown PA (S)

Goldstein, Andrea, *Librn*, Temple University, Tyler School of Art Library, Elkins PA

Goldstein, Audrey, *Chmn Fine Arts*, The New England School of Art & Design at Suffolk University, Boston MA (S)

Goldstein, Gabriel, *Cur*, Yeshiva University Museum, New York NY

Goldstein, Karen, *Cur Exhib*, Pilgrim Society, Pilgrim Hall Museum, Plymouth MA

Goldstein, Leslie, *Librn*, New York Institute of Technology, Art & Architectural Library, Old Westbury NY

Goldstein, Marilyn, *Prof*, C W Post Center of Long Island University, School of Visual & Performing Arts, Brookville NY (S)

Goldstein, Mark, *Library Technician*, San Francisco Maritime National Historical Park, J Porter Shaw Library, San Francisco CA

Goldstein, Nathan, *Chmn Found Dept*, Art Institute of Boston, Boston MA (S)

Goldstone, Adrienne, *Pres*, Los Angeles Center for Photographic Studies, Hollywood CA

Goley, Mary Anne, *Dir*, Federal Reserve Board, Art Gallery, Washington DC

Golik, Jay, *Prof*, Napa Valley College, Art Dept, Napa CA (S)

Golisek, Lisa, *Visitor Serv*, Alaska State Museum, Juneau AK

Golly, Laura, *Chmn Dept Graphic Design*, The New England School of Art & Design at Suffolk University, Boston MA (S)

Golomb, Katherine, *Dir Pub Servs*, Ferguson Library, Stamford CT

Gomberg, Betsy, *Assoc Dir*, Spertus Institute of Jewish Studies, Spertus Museum, Chicago IL

Gomez, Ariela, *School Arts Coordr*, Museum of New Mexico, Museum of International Folk Art, Santa Fe NM

Gomez, Martin, *Dir Library Servs*, Oakland Public Library, Art, Music & Recreation Section, Oakland CA

Gomez, Mirta, *Assoc Prof*, Florida International University, Visual Arts Dept, Miami FL (S)

Goncher, Dennis D, *Dir*, The Creative Solutions, Villa Park IL (S)

Gong, Stephen, *Assoc Dir*, University of California, Berkeley Art Museum & Pacific Film Archive, Berkeley CA

Gonzales, Chinyere, *Public Relations Coordr*, Nexus Contemporary Art Center, Atlanta GA

Gonzales, Paul, *Dir*, Institute of American Indian Arts Museum, Santa Fe NM

Gonzalez, Jorge, *Asst Dir*, Metro-Dade, Miami Art Museum of Dade County, Miami FL

Gonzalez, Manuel, *Exec Dir & VPres*, The Chase Manhattan Bank, NA, Art Collection, New York NY

Gonzalez, Mia, *Asst Dir*, Galeria de la Raza, Studio 24, San Francisco CA

Gonzalez, Pedro, *Instr*, Amarillo College, Art Dept, Amarillo TX (S)

Gonzalez, Ruben, *Artist-in-Residence*, Western New Mexico University, Dept of Expressive Arts, Silver City NM (S)

Gonzalez-Cid, Malena, *Exec Dir*, Centro Cultural Aztlan, San Antonio TX

Gooch, Peter, *Assoc Prof*, University of Dayton, Visual Arts Dept, Dayton OH (S)

Good, Joan, *Exec Dir*, New Jersey Center for Visual Arts, Summit NJ

Goodale, Jennifer, *Mgr Cultural Affairs*, Philip Morris Companies Inc, New York NY

Goode, Carm, *Assoc Prof*, Loyola Marymount University, Art & Art History Dept, Los Angeles CA (S)

Goodenough, Daniel W, *Pres*, Academy of the New Church, Glencairn Museum, Bryn Athyn PA

Goodheart, John, *Prof*, Indiana University, Bloomington, Henry Radford Hope School of Fine Arts, Bloomington IN (S)

Goodhue, Timothy, *Registrar*, Yale University, Yale Center for British Art, New Haven CT

Goodison, Michael, *Prog Coordr & Archivist*, Smith College, Museum of Art, Northampton MA

Goodkind, Joan, *Librn*, Simon's Rock College of Bard, Library, Great Barrington MA

Goodman, Bill, *Instr*, Hibbing Community College, Art Dept, Hibbing MN (S)

Goodman, Carl, *Cur Digital Media*, American Museum of the Moving Image, Astoria NY

Goodman, Herb, *Asst Prof*, Louisiana State University, School of Art, Baton Rouge LA (S)

Goodman, James, *Pres*, Art Dealers Association of America, Inc, New York NY

Goodman, Laine, *Dir Develop*, National Museum of Wildlife Art, Jackson WY

Goodman, Marcie, *Dir Develop*, Cleveland Center for Contemporary Art, Cleveland OH

Goodman, Sherry, *Cur Educ*, University of California, Berkeley Art Museum & Pacific Film Archive, Berkeley CA

Goodman, Susan T, *Chief Cur*, The Jewish Museum, New York NY

Goodman, Ted, *Ed*, Columbia University, Avery Architectural & Fine Arts Library, New York NY

Goodrich, James W, *Exec Dir*, State Historical Society of Missouri, Columbia MO

Goodrich, James W, *Dir & Librn*, State Historical Society of Missouri, Library, Columbia MO

Goodrich, Margaret, *Reference Librn*, Denver Art Museum, Library, Denver CO

Goodridge, James, *Instr*, University of Evansville, Art Dept, Evansville IN (S)

Goodridge, Lawrence W, *Instr*, Art Academy of Cincinnati, Cincinnati OH (S)

Goodson, Lucy, *Asst Prof*, Coe College, Dept of Art, Cedar Rapids IA (S)

Goodspeed, Rupert, *Pres*, Ojai Valley Art Center, Ojai CA

Goodstein, Barbara, *Instr*, Chautauqua Institution, School of Art, Chautauqua NY (S)

Goodwin, David, *Assoc Prof*, Coe College, Dept of Art, Cedar Rapids IA (S)

Goodwin, Mary, *Instr*, California State University, San Bernardino, Visual Arts, San Bernardino CA (S)

Goody, Stephen, *Lectr*, Oakland University, Dept of Art & Art History, Rochester MI (S)

Goodyear, John, *Prof*, Rutgers, the State University of New Jersey, Mason Gross School of the Arts, New Brunswick NJ (S)

Gootee, Marita, *Assoc Prof*, Mississippi State University, Art Dept, Mississippi State MS (S)

Gordening, Genice, *Asst Dir*, Dawson County Historical Society, Museum, Lexington NE

Gordon, Alden R, *Prof*, Trinity College, Dept of Fine Arts, Hartford CT (S)

Gordon, Ann, *Secy*, Stanley Museum, Inc, Kingfield ME

Gordon, David, *Gallery Dir*, St Lawrence College, Art Gallery, Kingston ON

Gordon, Deborah, *Exec Ed*, Number Inc, Memphis TN

Gordon, Derek, *Head Educ Dept*, The John F Kennedy Center for the Performing Arts, Education Resources Center, Washington DC

Gordon, Edward, *Dir*, Gibson Society, Inc, Gibson House Museum, Boston MA

Gordon, Elliott, *Chmn*, Pratt Institute, Pratt Manhattan, New York NY (S)

Gordon, Geri, *School Dir*, Art League, Alexandria VA

Gordon, Irene, *Lectr*, John Jay College of Criminal Justice, Dept of Art, Music & Philosophy, New York NY (S)

Gordon, Jayne, *Coordr of Educ*, Concord Museum, Concord MA

Gordon, Jennifer, *Asst Prof*, University of Lethbridge, Div of Art, Lethbridge AB (S)

Gordon, Josephine, *Reference Librn*, Nelson-Atkins Museum of Art, Spencer Art Reference Library, Kansas City MO

Gordon, Kathy, *Dir*, Colby Community College, Visual Arts Dept, Colby KS (S)

Gordon, Leslie, *Artistic Dir*, Arts Festival of Atlanta, Atlanta GA

Gordon, Lewis, *Assoc Head Music*, Saint Joseph's University, Dept of Fine & Performing Arts, Philadelphia PA (S)

Gordon, Lori, *Development Officer*, Heckscher Museum of Art, Huntington NY

Gordon, Martha, *Chair*, Tarrant County Junior College, Art Dept, Hurst TX (S)

Gordon, Peter, *Cur*, San Jose Museum of Art, San Jose CA

Gordon, Richard, *Asst Cur*, Alberta College of Art & Design, Illingworth Kerr Gallery, Calgary AB

Gordon, Wendy, *Assoc Dir*, Boulder Historical Society Inc, Museum of History, Boulder CO

Gore, Eugenia, *VPres for North Jersey*, Federated Art Associations of New Jersey, Inc, Maplewood NJ

Goree, Joan, *Instr*, John C Calhoun State Community College, Department of Fine Arts, Decatur AL (S)

Gorewitz, Shalom, *Dir*, Ramapo College of New Jersey, School of Contemporary Arts, Mahwah NJ (S)

Gorewitz, Shalom, *Dir*, The Art Galleries of Ramapo College, Mahwah NJ

Goring, Rich, *Historic Site Mgr,* Palisades Interstate Park Commission, Senate House State Historic Site, Kingston NY

Goring, Rich, *Historic Site Mgr,* Palisades Interstate Park Commission, Reference Library, Kingston NY

Gorka, Paul, *Instr,* Wayne Art Center, Wayne PA (S)

Gorman, Donna, *Exec Dir,* The Art Guild, Farmington CT

Gormley, Jim, *Chmn Div,* Saint Louis Community College at Florissant Valley, Liberal Arts Division, Ferguson MO (S)

Gormley, Kate, *Dir Marketing,* Edsel & Eleanor Ford House, Grosse Pointe Shores MI

Gormley, Nina Z, *Exec Dir,* Wendell Gilley Museum, Southwest Harbor ME

Gormley, Tom, *Assoc Prof,* University of Miami, Dept of Art & Art History, Coral Gables FL (S)

Gorove, Margaret, *Dir,* University of Mississippi, University Gallery, Oxford MS

Gorove, Margaret, *Chmn,* University of Mississippi, Dept of Art, University MS (S)

Gorse, George, *Prof,* Pomona College, Dept of Art & Art History, Claremont CA (S)

Gorsengner, Ronald H, *Dir,* Carnegie Public Library, Delta Blues Museum, Clarksdale MS

Gort, Gene, *Asst Prof,* University of Hartford, Hartford Art School, West Hartford CT (S)

Goslin, Anne, *Asst Dir,* University of New Hampshire, The Art Gallery, Durham NH

Goss, Charles, *Assoc Prof,* Cazenovia College, Center for Art & Design Studies, Cazenovia NY (S)

Goss, David K, *Dir & Cur,* Beverly Historical Society, Cabot, Hale & Balch House Museums, Beverly MA

Goss, David K, *Dir,* Beverly Historical Society, Library, Beverly MA

Goss, Hanna, *Public Information,* Carolina Art Association, Gibbes Museum of Art, Charleston SC

Gossel, Deborah S, *Asst to Dir,* Flint Institute of Arts, Flint MI

Gosselin, Gaetan, *Dir,* Vu Centre D'Animation Et de Diffusion de La Photographie, Quebec PQ

Gostin, Arlene, *Lectr,* University of Pennsylvania, Graduate School of Fine Arts, Philadelphia PA (S)

Gotbaum, Betsy, *Exec Dir,* New York Historical Society, New York NY

Gothard, Paul, *Prof,* Lake Erie College, Fine Arts Dept, Painesville OH (S)

Gotlieb, Marc J, *Assoc Prof,* Emory University, Art History Dept, Atlanta GA (S)

Gotlob, Mark, *Deputy Dir,* The American Federation of Arts, New York NY

Gott, Wesley A, *Chmn,* Southwest Baptist University, Art Dept, Bolivar MO (S)

Gottberg, Ki, *Asst Prof Art,* Seattle University, Fine Arts Dept, Division of Art, Seattle WA (S)

Gottesfeld, Linda, *Prof,* Pace University, Dyson College of Arts & Sciences, Pleasantville NY (S)

Gottfried, Michael D, *Cur Paleontology,* Calvert Marine Museum, Solomons MD

Gottlieb, Peter, *Archivist,* State Historical Society of Wisconsin, Archives, Madison WI

Gottlieb, Wendy, *Public Affairs Asst Dir,* Kimbell Art Foundation, Kimbell Art Museum, Fort Worth TX

Gottschalk, Roger, *Chmn,* University of Wisconsin-Platteville, Dept of Fine Art, Platteville WI (S)

Gough-DiJulio, Betsy, *Dir Educ,* Virginia Beach Center for the Arts, Virginia Beach VA

Goughnour, David, *Instr,* Iowa Lakes Community College, Dept of Art, Estherville IA (S)

Gould, Anne, *Asst Cur,* Eskimo Museum, Churchill MB

Gould, Claudia, *Dir,* Artists Space, New York NY

Gould, Claudia, *Dir,* Artists Space, Artists Space Gallery, New York NY

Gould, Jim, *Instr,* Charles Stewart Mott Community College, Art Area, School of Arts & Humanities, Flint MI (S)

Gould, Rosemary F, *Graphic Design,* La Roche College, Division of Graphics, Design & Communication, Pittsburgh PA (S)

Gouma-Peterson, Thalia, *Prof,* College of Wooster, Dept of Art, Wooster OH (S)

Gouma-Peterson, Thalia, *Dir,* The College of Wooster, Art Museum, Wooster OH

Gourley, Hugh J, *Dir,* Colby College, Museum of Art, Waterville ME

Gourley, Richard, *Dir & Pres,* Triton Museum of Art, Santa Clara CA

Govan, Michael, *Exec Dir,* Dia Center for the Arts, New York NY

Govin, Marilyn, *Gallery Coordr,* Michigan Guild of Artists & Artisans, Michigan Guild Gallery, Ann Arbor MI

Gowen, John R, *Prof,* Ocean County College, Humanities Dept, Toms River NJ (S)

Grabania, Nadine, *Asst Cur & Registrar,* The Frick Art & Historical Center, Frick Art Museum, Pittsburgh PA

Grabbe, Kaye, *Admin Librn,* Lake Forest Library, Fine Arts Dept, Lake Forest IL

Grabill, Vin, *Assoc Prof,* University of Maryland, Baltimore County, Visual Arts Dept, Baltimore MD (S)

Grabowski, Beth, *Asst Chmn Studio Art,* University of North Carolina at Chapel Hill, Art Dept, Chapel Hill NC (S)

Grabowski, Beth, *Prof,* University of North Carolina at Chapel Hill, Art Dept, Chapel Hill NC (S)

Graboys, Caroline, *Dir,* Fuller Museum of Art, Brockton MA

Grace, Debbie, *Library Technician,* San Francisco Maritime National Historical Park, J Porter Shaw Library, San Francisco CA

Grace, Laura, *Slide Cur,* University of Arkansas, Art Slide Library, Little Rock AR

Grace, Robert M, *VPres,* The Society of the Four Arts, Palm Beach FL

Grachos, Louis, *Cur,* Museum of Contemporary Art, San Diego, La Jolla CA

Grachos, Louis, *Cur,* Museum of Contemporary Art, San Diego-Downtown, San Diego CA

Grady, Edward, *Asst Cur,* Langston University, Melvin B Tolson Black Heritage Center, Langston OK

Grady, John, *Instr,* Elgin Community College, Fine Arts Dept, Elgin IL (S)

Graef, Dorothy, *Regent,* Schuyler-Hamilton House, Morristown NJ

Graff, Terry, *Dir,* Confederation Centre Art Gallery and Museum, Charlottetown PE

Graham, Ann, *Visual Resources Cur,* University of North Texas, Visual Resources Collection, Denton TX

Graham, Anne, *Coordr Jewelry,* University of Delaware, Dept of Art, Newark DE (S)

Graham, Carann, *Instr,* Salem College, Art Dept, Winston-Salem NC (S)

Graham, Conrad, *Cur Decorative Arts,* McCord Museum of Canadian History, Montreal PQ

Graham, Cynthia, *Vis Prof,* Atlanta College of Art, Atlanta GA (S)

Graham, Douglas, *Founder & Treas,* The Turner Museum, Denver CO

Graham, Greg, *Dir,* Canadian Artists' Representation-Le Front Des Artistes Canadiens, Aylmer PQ

Graham, Heather, *Exhibit Gallery Dir,* Ann Arbor Art Association, Art Center, Ann Arbor MI

Graham, John R, *Cur Exhib,* Western Illinois University, Art Gallery-Museum, Macomb IL

Graham, Linda, *Dir & VPres,* The Turner Museum, Denver CO

Graham, Lonnie, *Dir Photography,* Manchester Craftsmen's Guild, Pittsburgh PA

Graham, Mayo, *Chief Conservator,* Montreal Museum of Fine Arts, Montreal PQ

Graham, Michael, *Cur,* United Society of Shakers, Shaker Museum, New Glocester ME

Graham, Michael, *Cur,* United Society of Shakers, The Shaker Library, New Glocester ME

Graham, Michael, *Assoc Prof,* American University, Dept of Art, Washington DC (S)

Graham, Richard, *Instr,* Salt Lake Community College, Graphic Design Dept, Salt Lake City UT (S)

Graham, Robert, *Prof,* Virginia Polytechnic Institute & State University, Dept of Art & Art History, Blacksburg VA (S)

Grainger, Nessa, *VPres Aqua Media,* Audubon Artists, Inc, New York NY

Grais, Stephanie, *Admin Servs Mgr,* Terra Museum of American Art, Chicago IL

Gralapp, Marcelee, *Library Dir,* Boulder Public Library & Gallery, Dept of Fine Arts Gallery, Boulder CO

Grams, Diane, *Dir,* Peace Museum, Chicago IL

Granados, Juan, *Asst Prof,* Texas Tech University, Dept of Art, Lubbock TX (S)

Granche, Pierre, *Instr,* Universite de Montreal, Dept of Art History, Montreal PQ (S)

Grand, Stanley, *Adjunct Prof,* Wilkes University, Dept of Art, Wilkes-Barre PA (S)

Grand, Stanley I, *Dir,* Wilkes University, Sordoni Art Gallery, Wilkes-Barre PA

Grandbois, Michele, *Prints & Drawings,* Musee du Quebec, Quebec PQ

Granderson, Eddie, *Dir,* City of Atlanta, City Gallery East, Atlanta GA

Grandmaitre, Robert, *Chief Coll Consultation,* National Archives of Canada, Visual & Sound Archives, Ottawa ON

Grandy, Stuart, *Pres,* Arts & Crafts Association of Meriden Inc, Gallery 53, Meriden CT

Granelina, Michelle, *Assoc Prof,* Assumption College, Dept of Art & Music, Worcester MA (S)

Graney, Carol Homan, *Assoc Dir,* University of the Arts, Albert M Greenfield Library, Philadelphia PA

Granger, Robert, *Faculty,* Idaho State University, Dept of Art, Pocatello ID (S)

Granger, Steven T, *Archivist,* Archives of the Archdiocese of St Paul & Minneapolis, Saint Paul MN

Granne, Regina, *Instr,* Bard College, Milton Avery Graduate School of the Arts, Annandale-on-Hudson NY (S)

Grant, Alicia D, *Bibliographic Instruction & Branch Librn,* Sweet Briar College, Martin C Shallenberger Art Library, Sweet Briar VA

Grant, Jill, *Dean,* Nova Scotia College of Art & Design, Halifax NS (S)

Grant, Marion, *Dir Art Educ,* Berkshire Museum, Pittsfield MA

Grant, Michele, *Exec Dir,* Prints In Progress, Philadelphia PA

Grant, Scott, *Building Engineer,* Fort Worth Art Association, Modern Art Museum of Fort Worth, Fort Worth TX

Grant, Susan, *Librn,* University Club Library, New York NY

Grant, Susan Kae, *Prof,* Texas Woman's University, Dept of Visual Arts, Denton TX (S)

Granzow, Carl, *Assoc Prof,* University of Lethbridge, Div of Art, Lethbridge AB (S)

Grass, Kevin, *Instr,* Gordon College, Dept of Fine Arts, Barnesville GA (S)

Grassell, Mary, *Prof,* Marshall University, Dept of Art, Huntington WV (S)

Grassham, John, *Cur History,* Albuquerque Museum of Art & History, Albuquerque NM

Grattan, Patricia, *Dir,* Memorial University of Newfoundland, Art Gallery of Newfoundland & Labrador, Saint John's NF

Gratzer, Peggy, *Pres,* Klamath Falls Art Association, Klamath Art Gallery, Klamath Falls OR

Grauer, Michael R, *Cur Art,* Panhandle-Plains Historical Society Museum, Canyon TX

Grauer, Rita, *Dir Asst,* Rogue Community College, Wiseman Gallery - Firehouse Gallery, Grants Pass OR

Gravef, Donna, *Prog Dir,* Headlands Center for the Arts, Sausalito CA

Graveline, Michelle, *Chmn,* Assumption College, Dept of Art & Music, Worcester MA (S)

Graves, Charles E, *Chmn,* Xavier University of Louisiana, Dept of Fine Arts, New Orleans LA (S)

Graves, Donald H, *Exec Dir,* Sheridan College, School of Arts & Design, Oakville ON (S)

Graves, Jane, *Fine & Performing Arts Librn,* Skidmore College, Lucy Scribner Library, Saratoga Springs NY

Graves, Kreta, *Educ Asst*, Green Hill Center for North Carolina Art, Greensboro NC

Graves, Lawanda, *Bookkeeper*, Printmaking Workshop, New York NY

Gray, Beth, *Dir*, East Hampton Library, Pennypacker Long Island Collection, East Hampton NY

Gray, Brian, *Dir Design & Facility*, Orange County Museum of Art, Newport Harbor Art Museum, Newport Beach CA

Gray, Kenneth, *Prof*, Glendale Community College, Visual & Performing Arts Division, Glendale CA (S)

Gray, Lynn, *Assoc Prof*, University of Minnesota, Minneapolis, Dept of Art, Minneapolis MN (S)

Gray, Noel, *Prof*, Chadron State College, Dept of Art, Speech & Theatre, Chadron NE (S)

Gray, Sharon L, *Sr Cur*, Amherst Museum, Amherst NY

Gray, Sharon R, *Asst Dir*, Springville Museum of Art, Springville UT

Gray, Sonia, *Dir Neighborhood Art Prog*, San Francisco City & County Art Commission, San Francisco CA

Graybill, Maribeth, *Assoc Prof*, Swarthmore College, Dept of Art, Swarthmore PA (S)

Grazzini, Patricia, *Assoc Dir*, Minneapolis Institute of Arts, Minneapolis MN

Greco, Anthony, *Prof*, Atlanta College of Art, Atlanta GA (S)

Green, Alfred E, *Assoc Prof*, Texas Woman's University, Dept of Visual Arts, Denton TX (S)

Green, Art, *Assoc Prof*, University of Waterloo, Fine Arts Dept, Waterloo ON (S)

Green, Brent, *Head Dept*, Abilene Christian University, Dept of Art, Abilene TX (S)

Green, Doris, *Office Mgr*, Freeport Arts Center, Freeport IL

Green, Ellen, *Cur Oppertshauser House*, Multicultural Heritage Centre, Stony Plain AB

Green, Eveleth, *Dir*, Gallery One, Ellensburg WA

Green, Harriett, *Visual Arts Dir*, South Carolina Arts Commission, Columbia SC

Green, James, *Asst Librn*, Library Company of Philadelphia, Philadelphia PA

Green, Jerold, *Dir & Cur*, Queens College, City University of New York, Godwin-Ternbach Museum, Flushing NY

Green, John, *Asst Dir*, Plainsman Museum, Aurora NE

Green, Jonathan W, *Prof*, University of California, Riverside, Dept of the History of Art, Riverside CA (S)

Green, Jonathan W, *Dir*, University of California, California Museum of Photography, Riverside CA

Green, Joshua, *Dir Ceramic Arts*, Manchester Craftsmen's Guild, Pittsburgh PA

Green, Kelli, *Educ Coordr*, Litchfield Historical Society, Litchfield CT

Green, Louise, *Acting Asst Librn*, University of Maryland, College Park, Art Library, College Park MD

Green, Marua, *Treas*, Key West Art & Historical Society, East Martello Museum & Gallery, Key West FL

Green, Mary, *VPres*, Monterey Museum of Art Association, Monterey CA

Green, Michael, *Assoc Prof*, College of Southern Idaho, Art Dept, Twin Falls ID (S)

Green, Mike, *Art Gallery Mgr*, College of Southern Idaho, Herrett Center for Arts & Science, Twin Falls ID

Green, Mimi, *Pres*, Wayne Art Center, Wayne PA (S)

Green, Nancy E, *Asst Dir Coll & Progs & Cur Prints, Drawings & Photographs*, Cornell University, Herbert F Johnson Museum of Art, Ithaca NY

Green, Richard, *Instr*, Eastern Arizona College, Art Dept, Thatcher AZ (S)

Green, Stephen, *Librn*, The University of Texas, Institute of Texan Cultures, San Antonio TX

Green, William, *Asst Prof*, New Mexico State University, Art Dept, Las Cruces NM (S)

Greenberg, Douglas, *Pres*, Chicago Historical Society, Chicago IL

Greenberg, Gary, *Asst Prof*, Clarion University of Pennsylvania, Dept of Art, Clarion PA (S)

Greenberg, Judi, *VPres*, California Watercolor Association, Walnut Creek CA

Greenberg, Lisa, *Cur Exhib*, Art Complex Museum, Duxbury MA

Greenberg, Marice R, *Chmn Society Board Trustees*, The Asia Society Galleries, New York NY

Greenberg, Ted, *Registrar*, Fine Arts Museums of San Francisco, M H de Young Memorial Museum & California Palace of the Legion of Honor, San Francisco CA

Greene, Allison, *Assoc Cur 20th Century Art*, Museum of Fine Arts, Houston, Houston TX

Greene, Canon James J, *Pres*, Burlington County Historical Society, Burlington NJ

Greene, Casey, *Head Spec Coll*, Rosenberg Library, Galveston TX

Greene, Eric A, *Educ*, Edgecombe County Cultural Arts Council, Inc, Blount-Bridgers House, Hobson Pittman Memorial Gallery, Tarboro NC

Greene, Janice, *Instr*, University of Evansville, Art Dept, Evansville IN (S)

Greene, Joseph A, *Asst Dir*, Harvard University, Semitic Museum, Cambridge MA

Greene, Judith, *Museum Dir*, Seneca-Iroquois National Museum, Salamanca NY

Greene, Ken, *Instr*, William Woods-Westminster Colleges, Art Dept, Fulton MO (S)

Greene, Rhonda, *Co-Site Supv*, Fort Totten State Historic Site, Pioneer Daughters Museum, Fort Totten ND

Greene, Ryland W, *Prof*, Cedar Crest College, Art Dept, Allentown PA (S)

Greene, Theodore, *VPres Develop*, Pennsylvania Academy of the Fine Arts, Museum of American Art, Philadelphia PA

Greene, Tom, *Instr*, ACA College of Design, Cincinnati OH (S)

Greene, William, *Public Relations*, Rhode Island Historical Society, Providence RI

Greenfield, Dorothy, *Treas*, Historical Society of Bloomfield, Bloomfield NJ

Greenhill, Patricia, *Coordr Public Information*, State University of New York at Purchase, Neuberger Museum of Art, Purchase NY

Greenland, Dorothy, *Sr Libr Specialist*, Fine Arts Dept, University of Utah, Marriott Library, Salt Lake City UT

Greenlee, Bob, *Instr*, Hannibal La Grange College, Art Dept, Hannibal MO (S)

Greenlee, Hugh, *Prof*, Cleveland Institute of Art, Cleveland OH (S)

Greenquist, Steve, *Asst Prof*, Graceland College, Fine Arts Dept, Lamoni IA (S)

Greenshields, Monte, *Dir*, Photographers Gallery, Saskatoon SK

Greenshields, Monte, *Dir*, Photographers Gallery, Library, Saskatoon SK

Greenspan, Jack, *Chmn*, Feather River Community College, Art Dept, Quincy CA (S)

Greenwall, Steven R, *Dept Head*, Allen County Community College, Art Dept, Iola KS (S)

Greenwold, Mark, *Assoc Prof*, State University of New York at Albany, Art Dept, Albany NY (S)

Greenwood, Scott, *Dir*, Willamette University, George Putnam University Center, Salem OR

Greenwood, William, *VPres*, Pennsylvania Academy of the Fine Arts, Fellowship of the Pennsylvania Academy of the Fine Arts, Philadelphia PA

Greer, Carole, *Assoc Prof*, Southwest Texas State University, Dept of Art, San Marcos TX (S)

Greer, Dwaine, *Prof Art Educ*, University of Arizona, Dept of Art, Tucson AZ (S)

Greer, Nelson, *Chmn Illustration*, Center for Creative Studies, College of Art & Design, Detroit MI (S)

Greer, Rina, *Dir*, Toronto Sculpture Garden, Toronto ON

Gregersen, Thomas, *Cur*, Palm Beach County Parks & Recreation Department, Morikami Museum & Japanese Gardens, Delray Beach FL

Gregg-Wightman, Lisa, *Instr*, Munson-Williams-Proctor Institute, School of Art, Utica NY (S)

Gregoire, Collene Z, *Assoc Prof*, Baker University, Dept of Art, Baldwin City KS (S)

Gregoire, Mathieu, *Project Mgr*, University of California, San Diego, Stuart Collection, La Jolla CA

Gregor, Sandra, *Dir*, Texas Fine Arts Association, Austin TX

Gregory, Diane, *Assoc Prof*, Southwest Texas State University, Dept of Art, San Marcos TX (S)

Gregory, Fred, *Assoc Prof*, Atlanta College of Art, Atlanta GA (S)

Gregory, J, *Instr*, Western Illinois University, Art Dept, Macomb IL (S)

Gregory, Peg, *VPres*, South County Art Association, Kingston RI

Gregory, Shirley, *Dir*, Barton College, Library, Wilson NC

Greig, Rick E, *Program Dir*, Angelo State University, Houston Harte University Center, San Angelo TX

Greiner, William, *Prof*, Olivet Nazarene University, Dept of Art, Kankakee IL (S)

Grenda, C, *Prof*, City Colleges of Chicago, Daley College, Chicago IL (S)

Greone Bowman, Leslie, *Cur Decorative Arts*, Los Angeles County Museum of Art, Los Angeles CA

Gresham, Jesse, *Chief Financial Officer*, Memphis Brooks Museum of Art, Memphis TN

Gresham, Paul A, *Instr*, Oklahoma State University, Graphic Arts Dept, Okmulgee OK (S)

Gressom, Harriette, *Asst Prof*, Atlanta College of Art, Atlanta GA (S)

Greve, Gail, *Spec Coll Librn & Assoc Cur Rare Books & Manuscripts*, Colonial Williamsburg Foundation, John D Rockefeller, Jr Library, Williamsburg VA

Grew, Douglas, *Dir*, School of the Art Institute of Chicago, Gallery 2, Chicago IL

Grey, Campbell, *Dir*, Brigham Young University, Museum of Art, Provo UT

Grey, Campbell, *Dir*, Brigham Young University, Fritz B Burns Library, Provo UT

Gribbon, Debra, *Assoc Dir*, Getty Center for the History of Art & the Humanities Trust Museum, Santa Monica CA

Grider, George, *Cur*, Ephraim McDowell-Cambus-Kenneth Foundation, McDowell House & Apothecary Shop, Danville KY

Griep, Mary, *Asst Prof*, Saint Olaf College, Art Dept, Northfield MN (S)

Grier, Ted, *Chmn*, College of Marin, Dept of Art, Kentfield CA (S)

Griesell, Mary, *Coordr*, Lewis & Clark Community College, Art Dept, Godfrey IL (S)

Griesemer, Allan, *Dir*, San Bernardino County Museum, Fine Arts Institute, Redlands CA

Griesinger, Pamela, *Prof*, Daytona Beach Community College, Dept of Fine Arts & Visual Arts, Daytona Beach FL (S)

Grieve, Suzanne, *VPres*, Revelstoke Art Group, Revelstoke BC

Griffel, Lois, *Dir*, Cape Cod School of Art, Provincetown MA (S)

Griffen, Richard, *Instr*, Hannibal La Grange College, Art Dept, Hannibal MO (S)

Griffin, Anita, *Instr*, The Art Institutes International, The Art Institute of Seattle, Seattle WA (S)

Griffin, Cathryn, *Assoc Prof*, Western Carolina University, Dept of Art, Cullowhee NC (S)

Griffin, Christine, *Chmn*, State University of New York College at Old Westbury, Visual Arts Dept, Old Westbury NY (S)

Griffin, Christine, *Dir*, State University of New York College at Old Westbury, Amelie A Wallace Gallery, Old Westbury NY

Griffin, David, *Asst Prof*, Eastern Illinois University, Art Dept, Charleston IL (S)

Griffin, Fred, *Instr*, The Art Institutes International, The Art Institute of Seattle, Seattle WA (S)

Griffin, Gary, *Head Metalsmithing Dept*, Cranbrook Academy of Art, Bloomfield Hills MI (S)

Griffin, Gerald, *Instr*, Ricks College, Dept of Art, Rexburg ID (S)

Griffin, Janice, *Cur*, Praire Avenue House Museums, Glesser House, Chicago IL

Griffin, Jerri, *Ceramics & Sculpture Instr*, Hutchinson Community Junior College, Visual Arts Dept, Hutchinson KS (S)

Griffin, Justice, *Cur*, Praire Avenue House Museums, Henry B Clarke House Museum, Chicago IL

Griffin, Kathleen, *Sr Librn*, San Diego Public Library, Art & Music Section, San Diego CA

Griffin, Larry D, *Chmn*, Midland College, Art Dept, Midland TX (S)

Griffin, Penny, *Asst Prof*, Salem College, Art Dept, Winston-Salem NC (S)

Griffin, Steve, *Chmn*, Mary Washington College, Art Dept, Fredericksburg VA (S)

Griffis, Larry, *Chief Exec Officer*, Ashford Hollow Foundation for Visual & Performing Arts, Griffis Sculpture Park, East Otto NY

Griffis, Larry L, *Dir*, Birger Sandzen Memorial Gallery, Lindsborg KS

Griffis, Mark B, *Dir*, Ashford Hollow Foundation for Visual & Performing Arts, Griffis Sculpture Park, East Otto NY

Griffis, Simon, *Exec Dir*, Ashford Hollow Foundation for Visual & Performing Arts, Griffis Sculpture Park, East Otto NY

Griffith, Bill, *Asst Dir*, Arrowmont Gallery, Arrowmont School of Arts & Crafts, Gatlinburg TN (S)

Griffith, Daniel, *Div Dir*, Historical & Cultural Affairs, Delaware State Museums, Dover DE

Griffith, Denny, *Deputy Dir*, Columbus Museum of Art, Columbus OH

Griffith, June B, *Librn*, Lehigh County Historical Society, Allentown PA

Griffith, Laura S, *Asst Dir*, Fairmount Park Art Association, Philadelphia PA

Griffith, Marion, *Gallery Dir*, Sculpture Center Gallery & School, New York NY (S)

Griffith, Roberta, *Prof*, Hartwick College, Art Dept, Oneonta NY (S)

Griffith, William, *Coll Mgr*, University of Mississippi, University Museums, Oxford MS

Griffiths, June B, *Librn & Archivist*, Lehigh County Historical Society, Scott Andrew Trexler II Library, Allentown PA

Griffiths, Sharon, *Librn*, Canadian Conference of the Arts, Ottawa ON

Grilli, Stephanie, *Asst Prof*, University of Colorado at Denver, Dept of Fine Arts, Denver CO (S)

Grillo, Michael, *Asst Prof*, University of Maine, Dept of Art, Orono ME (S)

Grimaldi, Anthony, *Instr*, Dowling College, Dept of Visual Arts, Oakdale NY (S)

Grimaldi, Anthony, *Architecture Coordr*, New Jersey Institute of Technology, Architecture Library, Newark NJ

Grimaldi, Mary Ellen, *Historic Site Asst*, Schuyler Mansion State Historic Site, Albany NY

Grimes, Carroll, *Chmn*, University of Pittsburgh at Johnstown, Dept of Fine Arts, Johnstown PA (S)

Grimes, Melissa, *Instr*, Southwest Texas State University, Dept of Art, San Marcos TX (S)

Grinnell, Nancy Whipple, *Cur Colls*, Art Complex Museum, Duxbury MA

Grissano, Joan, *Reference Coordr*, New York City Technical College, Namm Hall Library and Learning Resource Center, Brooklyn NY

Griswold, James R, *Treas*, The Currier Gallery of Art, Manchester NH

Griswold, Justin, *Preparator*, University of Massachusetts, Amherst, University Gallery, Amherst MA

Griswold, Mac, *Instr*, Sarah Lawrence College, Dept of Art History, Bronxville NY (S)

Grittner, James, *Chmn*, University of Wisconsin-Superior, Programs in the Visual Arts, Superior WI (S)

Grivetti, Albert, *Asst Prof*, Eastern Illinois University, Art Dept, Charleston IL (S)

Grizzell, Kenneth, *Prof*, University of South Dakota, Department of Art, College of Fine Arts, Vermillion SD (S)

Groce, Susan, *Prof*, University of Maine, Dept of Art, Orono ME (S)

Grochowski, Paul, *Head Librn*, University of Michigan, Art Media Union Library, Ann Arbor MI

Groefe, Richard, *Assoc Dir*, American Institute of Graphic Arts, New York NY

Groeneveld, Paul, *Asst to Dir*, Civic Fine Arts Center, Sioux Falls SD

Groft, Tammis, *Chief Cur*, Albany Institute of History & Art, Albany NY

Grogan, John, *VPres*, Children's Museum, Rauh Memorial Library, Indianapolis IN

Grogan, Kevin, *Dir*, Fisk University, University Galleries, Nashville TN

Grogan, Kevin, *Dir*, Fisk University, Florine Stettheimer Library, Nashville TN

Gron, Jack, *Chmn*, University of Kentucky, Dept of Art, Lexington KY (S)

Grootkerk, Paul, *Prof*, Mississippi State University, Art Dept, Mississippi State MS (S)

Groover, Charles, *Head*, Jacksonville State University, Art Dept, Jacksonville AL (S)

Grose, Donald, *Dir*, University of North Texas, Willis Library, Denton TX

Grosfils, Cathy, *Visual Resources Editorial Librn*, Colonial Williamsburg Foundation, John D Rockefeller, Jr Library, Williamsburg VA

Grosowsky, Vern, *Instr*, Solano Community College, Division of Fine & Applied Art, Suisun City CA (S)

Gross, Chaim, *Dir*, The Chaim Gross Studio Museum, New York NY

Gross, Charles M, *Prof*, University of Mississippi, Dept of Art, University MS (S)

Gross, Jennifer, *Communications Coordr*, Arts & Education Council of Greater Saint Louis, Saint Louis MO

Gross, Jennifer, *Dir*, Maine College of Art, The Institute of Contemporary Art, Portland ME

Gross, Kelly M, *Dir*, Art Association of Jacksonville, David Strawn Art Gallery, Jacksonville IL

Gross, Margarete K, *Picture Coll Librn*, Chicago Public Library, Harold Washington Library Center, Chicago IL

Gross, Meir, *Dept Head*, University of Massachusetts, Amherst, Dept of Landscape Architecture & Regional Planning, Amherst MA (S)

Grossman, Barbara, *Instr*, Chautauqua Institution, School of Art, Chautauqua NY (S)

Grossman, Barbara, *Lectr*, University of Pennsylvania, Graduate School of Fine Arts, Philadelphia PA (S)

Grossman, Cissy, *Cur*, Congregation Emanu-El, New York NY

Grossman, Gilda S, *Dir Acad Prog & Internships*, Toronto Art Therapy Institute, Toronto ON (S)

Grossman, Grace Cohen, *Cur*, Hebrew Union College, Skirball Cultural Center, Los Angeles CA

Grossman, Orin, *Dean*, Fairfield University, Visual & Performing Arts, Fairfield CT (S)

Grosvenor, Walter, *Prof*, Whitworth College, Art Dept, Spokane WA (S)

Grote, Bob, *Exec Dir*, Pittsburgh Center for the Arts, Pittsburgh PA

Grote, William M, *Chmn*, Loyola University of New Orleans, Dept of Visual Arts, New Orleans LA (S)

Grove, Dana, *Dir of Arts & Sciences*, Indian Hills Community College, Ottumwa Campus, Dept of Art, Ottumwa IA (S)

Groves, Will E, *Admin Asst*, Broward County Board of Commissioners Cultural Affairs Divison, Fort Lauderdale FL

Growborg, Erik, *Instr*, Miracosta College, Art Dept, Oceanside CA (S)

Grubb, Tom, *Dir*, Fayetteville Museum of Art, Inc, Fayetteville NC

Gruber, Doris, *Periodicals*, Trinity College Library, Washington DC

Gruber, J Richard, *Deputy Dir*, Morris Museum of Art, Augusta GA

Gruber, Sharon White, *Dir*, Gertrude Herbert Institute of Art, Augusta GA

Grubola, James, *Chmn*, University of Louisville, Allen R Hite Art Institute Gallery, Louisville KY

Grubola, James T, *Chmn*, University of Louisville, Allen R Hite Art Institute, Louisville KY (S)

Gruenwald, Helen, *Asst Prof*, Kirkwood Community College, Dept of Fine Arts, Cedar Rapids IA (S)

Gruenwald, Larry, *Technician*, University of Minnesota, Duluth, Tweed Museum of Art, Duluth MN

Grundberg, Andy, *Exec Dir*, The Friends of Photography, Ansel Adams Center for Photography, San Francisco CA

Grundset, Eric, *Librn*, DAR Museum, Library, Washington DC

Grunenberg, Christoph, *Cur*, Institute of Contemporary Art, Boston MA

Gruner, Charles J, *Dir Lecture & Demonstration Serv*, American Society of Artists, Inc, Chicago IL

Gruninger, Sandi, *Pres*, Wood Tobe-Coburn School, New York NY (S)

Grunwald, Fela, *Pres*, Professional Art Dealers Association of Canada, Toronto ON

Grupp, Carl A, *Chmn*, Augustana College, Art Dept, Sioux Falls SD (S)

Gualtieri, Joseph P, *Dir*, Slater-Norton Corporation, Slater Memorial Museum & Converse Art Gallery, Norwich CT

Guarll, Kris, *Secy*, Concord Art Association, Concord MA

Guava, Sig, *Chmn Div Urban Planning*, Columbia University, Graduate School of Architecture, Planning & Preservation, New York NY (S)

Gudmundson, Jane, *Dir Educ*, Plains Art Museum, Fargo ND

Guenther, Bruce, *Chief Cur*, Orange County Museum of Art, Newport Harbor Art Museum, Newport Beach CA

Guenthler, John R, *Assoc Prof*, Indiana University-Southeast, Fine Arts Dept, New Albany IN (S)

Guerin, Charles, *Dir*, University of Wyoming, University of Wyoming Art Museum, Laramie WY

Guerin, Joan, *Dir Educ*, Westmoreland Museum of American Art, Greensburg PA

Guernsey, David T, *Exec Dir*, Ships of the Sea Maritime Museum, Library, Savannah GA

Guffey, Elizabeth, *Asst Prof*, State University of New York College at Purchase, Art History Board of Study, Purchase NY (S)

Guffin, R L, *Prof*, Stillman College, Stillman Art Gallery & Art Dept, Tuscaloosa AL (S)

Guggenheimer, Doni, *Museum Educator*, Randolph-Macon Woman's College, Maier Museum of Art, Lynchburg VA

Guglielmo, Rudy, *Expansion Arts Dir*, Arizona Commission on the Arts, Phoenix AZ

Guiby, Marillyn, *Cur Educ*, San Joaquin Pioneer & Historical Society, The Haggin Museum, Stockton CA

Guichet, Melody, *Prof*, Louisiana State University, School of Art, Baton Rouge LA (S)

Guido, Anthony, *Chmn Industrial Design*, University of the Arts, Philadelphia College of Art & Design, Philadelphia PA (S)

Guig, Karen, *Dir*, University of Maine at Augusta, Jewett Hall Gallery, Augusta ME

Guilbaut, Serge, *Prof*, University of British Columbia, Dept of Fine Arts, Vancouver BC (S)

Guilfoile, William J, *VPres*, National Baseball Hall of Fame & Museum, Inc, Art Collection, Cooperstown NY

Guilfoyle, Marvin, *Acquistions Librn*, University of Evansville, University Library, Evansville IN

Guilmain, Jacques, *Prof*, State University of New York at Stony Brook, Art Dept, Stony Brook NY (S)

Guip, David, *Prof*, University of Toledo, Dept of Art, Toledo OH (S)

Guiwits, Bruce, *Chmn*, Blue Mountain Community College, Fine Arts Dept, Pendleton OR (S)

Gulacsy, Elizabeth, *Art Reference Librn & Archivist*, New York State College of Ceramics at Alfred University, Scholes Library of Ceramics, Alfred NY

Gumina, Peter, *VPres*, Museo Italo Americano, San Francisco CA

Gump, Betse, *Pres*, New Jersey Center for Visual Arts, Summit NJ

Gumpert, Lynn, *Dir*, New York University, Grey Art Gallery & Study Center, New York NY

Gund, Agnes, *Pres & Chmn Board*, Museum of Modern Art, New York NY

Gundermann, Donald E, *Chmn Board Trustees*, Heckscher Museum of Art, Huntington NY

Gundersheimer, Werner, *Dir*, Folger Shakespeare Library, Washington DC

Gunderson, Barry, *Prof*, Kenyon College, Art Dept, Gambier OH (S)

Gunderson, Jeff, *Librn*, San Francisco Art Institute, Anne Bremer Memorial Library, San Francisco CA

Gunn, Nancy, *Asst Dir Museum Develop*, Wellesley College, Davis Museum & Cultural Center, Wellesley MA

Gunsalus, Heather, *Educator*, Cayuga Museum of History & Art, Auburn NY

Gunyon, Randi, *Instr*, Indiana Wesleyan University, Art Dept, Marion IN (S)

Guppy, Susan, *Asst Prof*, Technical University of Nova Scotia, Faculty of Architecture, Halifax NS (S)

Guraedy, J Bruce, *Head Dept*, East Central Community College, Art Dept, Decatur MS (S)

Gursoy, Ahmet, *Pres*, Federation of Modern Painters & Sculptors, New York NY

Gurth, Barbara, *Exec Dir*, Arts Council of the Mid-Columbia Region, Kennewick WA

Gustafson, Dwight, *Dean*, Bob Jones University, School of Fine Arts, Greenville SC (S)

Gustafson, Maureen, *Dir*, Rockford College Art Gallery, Rockford IL

Gustafson, Roger, *Instr*, Elgin Community College, Fine Arts Dept, Elgin IL (S)

Gustavson, Carrie, *Cur Archival Coll*, Bisbee Arts & Humanities Council, Lemuel Shattuck Memorial Library, Bisbee AZ

Gustavson, Todd, *Cur Technology Coll*, George Eastman House-International Museum of Photography & Film, Rochester NY

Gutekunst, B, *Head Humanities Div*, Catholic University of America, Humanities Div, Mullen Library, Washington DC

Guthrie, Carole, *Instr*, Bay Path College, Dept of Art, Longmeadow MA (S)

Guthrie, Gregg, *Acting Dir*, Lac du Flambeau Band of Lake Superior Chippewa Indians, George W Brown Jr Ojibwe Museum & Cultural Center, Lac du Flambeau WI

Guthrie, Jill, *Managing Ed*, Princeton University, The Art Museum, Princeton NJ

Guthrie, Lisa, *Mailing Coordr*, Marin County Watercolor Society, Greenbrae CA

Guthrie, Marcus, *Archivist & Cur*, Lac du Flambeau Band of Lake Superior Chippewa Indians, George W Brown Jr Ojibwe Museum & Cultural Center, Lac du Flambeau WI

Gutierrez, Rafael, *Dir*, Indian Pueblo Cultural Center, Albuquerque NM

Gutride, Doug, *Pres*, Greater Lafayette Museum of Art, Library, Lafayette IN

Gutridge, Doug, *Pres*, Greater Lafayette Museum of Art, Lafayette IN

Guttenberg, Rick, *Dir Educ*, Peabody Essex Museum, Salem MA

Gutterman, Scott, *Dir Cmmunications*, Solomon R Guggenheim Museum, New York NY

Gutterman, Scott, *Dir Public Affairs*, Guggenheim Museum Soho, New York NY

Guv, Michael, *Instr*, Dickinson College, Fine Arts Dept, Carlisle PA (S)

Guy, Jody, *Exec Dir*, Silver Eye Center for Photography, Pittsburgh PA

Guy, Linda, *Prof*, Texas Christian University, Art & Art History Dept, Fort Worth TX (S)

Guyer, Rod, *Instr*, Solano Community College, Division of Fine & Applied Art, Suisun City CA (S)

Guynes, Jason, *Chmn*, University of West Alabama, Division of Fine Arts, Livingston AL (S)

Guynn, William, *Art Chmn*, Sonoma State University, Art Dept, Rohnert Park CA (S)

Guzman, Diane, *Librn*, Brooklyn Museum, Wilbour Library of Egyptology, Brooklyn NY

Guzman, Marcy, *Rights & Reproductions*, Norton Simon Museum, Pasadena CA

Guzman, Ruben, *Asst Cur & Gallery Coordr*, Galeria de la Raza, Studio 24, San Francisco CA

Gyorgy, Suzanne, *Dir Exhib & Coll*, Morris Museum, Morristown NJ

Ha, Paul, *Exec Dir*, White Columns, New York NY

Haag, Patty, *Asst Prof*, Spokane Falls Community College, Fine Arts Dept, Spokane WA (S)

Haagenson, Lynne, *Prof*, University of Idaho, College of Art & Architecture, Moscow ID (S)

Haak, Kellen, *Registrar*, Dartmouth College, Hood Museum of Art, Hanover NH

Haarer, Ann, *Chmn Dept*, College of Saint Elizabeth, Art Dept, Morristown NJ (S)

Haas, Charles W, *Asst Prof*, Monroe Community College, Art Dept, Rochester NY (S)

Haazen, Vince, *Prof*, Chadron State College, Dept of Art, Speech & Theatre, Chadron NE (S)

Haberman, David, *Prof*, Cuyahoga Community College, Dept of Art, Cleveland OH (S)

Haberman, Patty, *Exhib Coordr*, Tempe Arts Center, Tempe AZ

Hack, Gary, *Dean*, University of Pennsylvania, Graduate School of Fine Arts, Philadelphia PA (S)

Hack, Rosalinda I, *Head Visual & Performing Arts Div*, Chicago Public Library, Harold Washington Library Center, Chicago IL

Hacker, Katherine, *Asst Prof*, University of British Columbia, Dept of Fine Arts, Vancouver BC (S)

Hacker, Robert G, *Paul & Louise Miller Prof*, Rochester Institute of Technology, School of Printing, Rochester NY (S)

Hacklin, Alan, *Chmn*, Columbia University, School of the Arts, Division of Visual Arts, New York NY (S)

Hackman, Larry J, *Dir*, National Archives & Records Administration, Harry S Truman Library, Independence MO

Hadaway, Sandra S, *Admin*, Telfair Museum of Art, Savannah GA

Haddad, Farid A, *Prof*, New England College, Art & Art History, Henniker NH (S)

Haddad, Rosemary, *Assoc Librn*, Canadian Centre for Architecture, Library, Montreal PQ

Hadden, Helen, *Librn*, Art Gallery of Hamilton, Muriel Isabel Bostwick Library, Hamilton ON

Haddock, Brent, *Chmn*, College of Eastern Utah, Gallery East, Price UT

Hadler, Mona, *Prof*, City University of New York, PhD Program in Art History, New York NY (S)

Hadley, Valorie, *Admis Counselor*, Oregon School of Arts & Crafts, Portland OR (S)

Hafer, Linda, *Asst Dir*, Art League, Alexandria VA

Hafertepe, Kenneth, *Dir Acad Progs*, Historic Deerfield, Inc, Deerfield MA

Hagan, Kay, *Instr*, Saint Louis Community College at Meramec, Art Dept, Saint Louis MO (S)

Hagedorn, Bernard, *Assoc Prof*, Vincennes University Junior College, Art Dept, Vincennes IN (S)

Hagedorn, Deborah, *Assoc Prof*, Vincennes University Junior College, Art Dept, Vincennes IN (S)

Hagel, Scott, *Dir Public Relations*, Buffalo Bill Memorial Association, Buffalo Bill Historical Center, Cody WY

Hagel, Scott, *Dir Communications*, Buffalo Bill Memorial Association, Buffalo Bill Historical Center, Cody WY

Hageman, Lee, *Chmn Dept Art*, Northwest Missouri State University, DeLuce Art Gallery, Maryville MO

Hageman, Lee, *Chmn*, Northwest Missouri State University, Dept of Art, Maryville MO (S)

Hagen, Gary, *Chmn & Prof*, University of Wisconsin-Stevens Point, Dept of Art & Design, Stevens Point WI (S)

Hagerstrand, Martin A, *Pres*, Five Civilized Tribes Museum, Muskogee OK

Haggard, Amy, *Treas*, Lubbock Art Association, Inc, Lubbock TX

Haglich, Bianca, *Prof*, Marymount College, Art Dept, Tarrytown NY (S)

Hagloch, Jennifer, *Bush House Cur*, Salem Art Association, Bush House, Salem OR

Hagloch, Jennifer, *Cur*, Salem Art Association, Archives, Salem OR

Hagstrom, Fred, *Chmn*, Carleton College, Dept of Art & Art History, Northfield MN (S)

Hahn, Cynthia J, *Assoc Prof*, Florida State University, Art History Dept (R133B), Tallahassee FL (S)

Hahn, Dorothy, *Instr*, Hannibal La Grange College, Art Dept, Hannibal MO (S)

Hahne, Freddie, *Pres*, Eyes & Ears Foundation, San Francisco CA

Haight, Bonnie, *Gallery Mgr*, Creative Growth Art Center, Oakland CA

Hail, Barbara A, *Deputy Dir & Cur*, Brown University, Haffenreffer Museum, Providence RI

Haile, Priscilla, *Exec Dir*, Sumter Gallery of Art, Sumter SC

Haines, Annette, *Library Asst*, Michigan State University, Fine Arts Library, East Lansing MI

Haines, Carol, *Public Relations Officer*, Concord Museum, Concord MA

Haines, Melissa J, *Site Coordr*, Association for the Preservation of Virginia Antiquities, John Marshall House, Richmond VA

Hajduczok, Lydia, *Public Relations*, The Ukrainian Museum, New York NY

Hajic, Maria, *Cur*, National Museum of Wildlife Art, Jackson WY

Hajic, Maria, *Cur*, National Museum of Wildlife Art, Library, Jackson WY

Hake, Carol, *Exhibits Chmn*, Gallery 9, Los Altos CA

Halaby, Raouf, *Chmn*, Ouachita Baptist University, Dept of Art, Arkadelphia AR (S)

Halbreich, Kathy, *Dir*, Walker Art Center, Minneapolis MN

Hale, David, *Instr*, Goddard College, Dept of Art, Plainfield VT (S)

Hale, Kenneth, *Acting Chair*, University of Texas, Dept of Art & Art History, Austin TX (S)

Hale, Nathan Cabot, *Pres*, Ages of Man Fellowship, Amenia NY

Hales, David, *Head Alaska & Polar Regions Colls*, University of Alaska, Elmer E Rasmuson Library, Fairbanks AK

Haley, Brian, *Chmn*, Heidelberg College, Dept of Art, Tiffin OH (S)

Halford-MacLeoud, Johanna, *Exec Asst to Dir*, The Phillips Collection, Washington DC

Halinan, Joy, *Dir Corporate & Foundation Relations*, The Phillips Collection, Washington DC

Halkin, Theodore, *Prof*, School of the Art Institute of Chicago, Chicago IL (S)

Halkovic, Marilyn, *Art Librn*, University of Georgia, University of Georgia Libraries, Athens GA

Hall, Allen, *Pres*, Rhode Island Watercolor Society, Pawtucket RI

Hall, Andrew, *Instr*, Cedar Crest College, Art Dept, Allentown PA (S)

Hall, Ann, *Office Asst*, Art League of Manatee County, Bradenton FL

Hall, Ann Medlin, *Office Asst*, Art League of Manatee County, Library, Bradenton FL

Hall, Bonnie, *Pres*, Artist's Alliance of California, Nevada City CA

Hall, Danelle, *Dir*, Oklahoma City University, Reference, Oklahoma City OK

Hall, Doug, *Prof*, Kirkwood Community College, Dept of Fine Arts, Cedar Rapids IA (S)

Hall, James, *Dir Finance*, Please Touch Museum, Philadelphia PA

Hall, Janice, *Asst Dir Mus Servs*, Putnam Museum of History & Natural Science, Davenport IA

Hall, Lana, *Instr*, Salt Lake Community College, Graphic Design Dept, Salt Lake City UT (S)

Hall, Lane, *Asst Prof*, Teikyo Marycrest University, Art & Computer Graphics Dept, Davenport IA (S)

Hall, Mark, *Chmn & Instr*, Marian College, Art Dept, Indianapolis IN (S)

Hall, Martha, *Access Servs & Visual Resources Librn*, University of the Arts, Albert M Greenfield Library, Philadelphia PA

Hall, Mary-Anne, *Cur Educ*, Slater-Norton Corporation, Slater Memorial Museum & Converse Art Gallery, Norwich CT

Hall, N Terry, *Pres*, Goshen Historical Society, Goshen CT

Hall, Richard, *Assoc Prof*, Cleveland Institute of Art, Cleveland OH (S)

Hall, Rick, *Instr*, The Arkansas Arts Center, Museum School, Little Rock AR (S)

Hall, Robert, *Chmn*, Flagler College, Visual Arts Dept, Saint Augustine FL (S)

Hall, Robert, *Acting Dir Educ & Outreach*, Anacostia Museum, Washington DC

Hall, Thom, *Registrar*, Arkansas Arts Center, Little Rock AR

Hall, Thomas, *Chmn Fine Arts*, York College of Pennsylvania, Dept of Music, Art & Speech Communications, York PA (S)

Hall, Tod, *Cur Educ*, Ward Foundation, Ward Museum of Wildfowl Art, Salisbury MD

Hall, Walter, *Assoc Prof*, University of Hartford, Hartford Art School, West Hartford CT (S)

Hall, Wendy, *Fine Arts Librn*, Columbia College, Library, Chicago IL

Hallam, John, *Chmn*, Pacific Lutheran University, Dept of Art, Tacoma WA (S)

Hallatt, Kim, *Asst Dir Admin*, University of Rochester, Memorial Art Gallery, Rochester NY

Hall-Duncan, Nancy, *Cur Art*, The Bruce Museum, Greenwich CT

Halle, Fiti, *VPres*, National Antique & Art Dealers Association of America, Inc, New York NY

Hallenbeck, Bob, *Asst Dir*, George Phippen Memorial Foundation, Phippen Museum of Western Art, Prescott AZ

Haller, Linda, *Public Relations Dir*, National Cowboy Hall of Fame & Western Heritage Center Museum, Oklahoma City OK

Hallman, Gary, *Assoc Prof*, University of Minnesota, Minneapolis, Dept of Art, Minneapolis MN (S)

Hall-Smith, Arthur, *Prof*, George Washington University, Dept of Art, Washington DC (S)

Hallum, John, *Colls Mgr*, Sitka Historical Society, Isabel Miller Museum, Sitka AK

Halpin, Marjorie, *Cur Ethnology*, University of British Columbia, Museum of Anthropology, Vancouver BC

Halsey, Louise, *Educ Dir*, Owensboro Museum of Fine Art, Owensboro KY

Halter, Ellen F, *Asst Prof*, Concordia College, Bronxville NY (S)

Halverson, Aniko, *Reference & Instruction Librn*, University of Southern California, Helen Topping Architecture & Fine Arts Library, Los Angeles CA

Halverson, Jackie, *Instr*, Mount Mary College, Art Dept, Milwaukee WI (S)

Hamady, Walter, *Prof*, University of Wisconsin, Madison, Dept of Art, Madison WI (S)

Hambleton, Judy, *Art School Dir*, Newport Art Museum, Newport RI

Hamblin, Diane, *Doll Cur*, Wenham Museum, Wenham MA

Hambourg, Maria, *Cur Photographs*, The Metropolitan Museum of Art, New York NY

Hamburger, Jeffrey, *Assoc Prof*, Oberlin College, Dept of Art, Oberlin OH (S)

Hamel, Regina, *Board Pres*, Pence Gallery, Davis CA

Hamic, Steve, *Treas*, Arts on the Park, Lakeland FL

Hamil, Sherrie, *Dir*, Gadsden Museum of Fine Arts, Inc, Gadsden AL

Hamilton, David Verner, *Pres*, Tradd Street Press, Elizabeth O'Neill Verner Studio Museum, Charleston SC

Hamilton, Esley, *Adjunct Instr*, Maryville University of Saint Louis, Art Division, Saint Louis MO (S)

Hamilton, J Hank, *Chmn*, Cheyney University of Pennsylvania, Dept of Art, Cheyney PA (S)

Hamilton, John, *Cur Colls*, Museum of Our National Heritage, Lexington MA

Hamilton, Laurie, *Fine Arts Conservator*, Art Gallery of Nova Scotia, Halifax NS

Hamilton, Mort, *Dir*, Charles B Goddard Center for the Visual & Performing Arts, Ardmore OK

Hamilton, Paula, *Head Librn*, Mount Angel Abbey Library, Saint Benedict OR

Hamilton, Philip, *Prof*, University of Wisconsin, Madison, Dept of Art, Madison WI (S)

Hamilton, Robert, *Instr*, Indiana University of Pennsylvania, Dept of Art & Art Education, Indiana PA (S)

Hamm, Jack, *Artist in Residence*, Dallas Baptist University, Dept of Art, Dallas TX (S)

Hamma, Kenneth, *Adjunct Asst Prof*, University of Southern California, School of Fine Arts, Los Angeles CA (S)

Hammell, Peter, *Dir*, National Museum of Racing, National Museum of Racing & Hall of Fame, Saratoga Springs NY

Hammell, Peter H, *Dir*, National Museum of Racing, Reference Library, Saratoga Springs NY

Hammett, Beverly, *Asst Librn*, Webster Parish Library, Minden LA

Hammock, Virgil, *Head*, Mount Allison University, Fine Arts Dept, Sackville NB (S)

Hammond, Christie, *Assoc Archivist*, Lincoln Memorial Shrine, Redlands CA

Hammond, Harmony, *Prof Painting & Drawing*, University of Arizona, Dept of Art, Tucson AZ (S)

Hammond, Theresa, *Dir & Cur*, Guilford College, Art Gallery, Greensboro NC

Hammond, Tom, *Printmaking*, University of Georgia, Franklin College of Arts & Sciences, Lamar Dodd School of Art, Athens GA (S)

Hammond, Wayne G, *Asst Librn*, Williams College, Chapin Library, Williamstown MA

Hammonter, Eddie, *Librn*, Webster Parish Library, Minden LA

Hamm Walsh, Dawna, *Asst Prof*, Dallas Baptist University, Dept of Art, Dallas TX (S)

Hamshaw, Rallou, *Acting Dir*, First Street Gallery, New York NY

Hanchrow, Grace M, *Deputy Dir*, Montgomery Museum of Fine Arts, Montgomery AL

Hancock, Beverlye, *Cur*, Wake Forest University, Museum of Anthropology, Winston Salem NC

Hancock, Blair, *Dir*, Wilkes Community College, Arts & Science Division, Wilkesboro NC (S)

Hancock, Elliott, *Music Dir*, Ozark Folk Center, Ozark Cultural Resource Center, Mountain View AR

Hancock, Jason, *Gallery Cur*, University of Minnesota, Paul Whitney Larson Gallery, Saint Paul MN

Hancock, John, *Asst Prof*, Barton College, Art Dept, Wilson NC (S)

Hancock, Kathleen, *Instr*, Roger Williams College, Art Dept, Bristol RI (S)

Hancock, Lisa, *Registrar*, Virginia Museum of Fine Arts, Richmond VA

Hancock, Mariko, *Coordr*, Castleton State College, Art Dept, Castleton VT (S)

Hand, Donald, *Horticulture*, National Gallery of Art, Washington DC

Hand, Ronald, *Exhib Designer*, Pennsylvania State University, Palmer Museum of Art, University Park PA

Handler, Linda, *Dir*, Phoenix Gallery, New York NY

Handy, Riley, *Dept Head*, Western Kentucky University, Kentucky Museum, Bowling Green KY

Handy, Riley, *Dept Head*, Western Kentucky University, Kentucky Library, Bowling Green KY

Haney, Kristine, *Assoc Prof*, University of Massachusetts, Amherst, Art History Program, Amherst MA (S)

Hanft, Margie, *Film & Reference Librn*, California Institute of the Arts Library, Santa Clarita CA

Hankins, Roger, *Dir*, University of California, Memorial Union Art Gallery, Davis CA

Hanks, Ken, *Pres*, Burke Arts Council, Jailhouse Galleries, Morganton NC

Hanley, Lynn, *Instr*, Gettysburg College, Dept of Visual Arts, Gettysburg PA (S)

Hanna, Annette Adrian, *Dir*, Blackwell Street Center for the Arts, Denville NJ

Hanna, Carole, *Clerical Hostess*, Red River Valley Museum, Vernon TX

Hanna, James, *Assoc Prof*, Texas Tech University, Dept of Art, Lubbock TX (S)

Hanna, Martha, *Acting Dir*, Canadian Museum of Contemporary Photography, Ottawa ON

Hanna, Susan, *Cur Coll*, Landis Valley Museum, Lancaster PA

Hanna, Tony, *Dir*, Kemerer Museum of Decorative Arts, Bethlehem PA

Hanna, William J, *Dir Records Management*, Mississippi Department of Archives & History, Library, Jackson MS

Hannah, Susan, *Prog Coordr*, University of Mississippi, University Museums, Oxford MS

Hannan, William, *Assoc Prof*, Black Hawk College, Art Dept, Moline IL (S)

Hannen, Kathryn M, *Asst Art Cur*, Vanderbilt University, Fine Arts Gallery, Nashville TN

Hanner, Frank, *Dir & Cur*, National Infantry Museum, Fort Benning GA

Hanner, Frank, *Dir*, National Infantry Museum, Library, Fort Benning GA

Hannibal, Joe, *Prof*, California State Polytechnic University, Pomona, Art Dept, Pomona CA (S)

Hanning, Christine, *Cur Educ*, Museum of East Texas, Lufkin TX

Hannon, Brian, *Dir*, Center for Book Arts, New York NY

Hannus, Adrien, *Assoc Prof*, Augustana College, Art Dept, Sioux Falls SD (S)

Hanrahan, Thomas, *Dean*, Pratt Institute, School of Architecture, Brooklyn NY (S)

Hansen, Alissa, *Shop Mgr*, Octagon Center for the Arts, Ames IA

Hansen, Elisa, *Dir Adult Educ*, State Art Museum of Florida, John & Mable Ringling Museum of Art, Sarasota FL

Hansen, John, *Instr*, The Art Institutes International, The Art Institute of Seattle, Seattle WA (S)

Hansen, Neil, *Chmn*, Northwest Community College, Dept of Art, Powell WY (S)

Hansen, Pearl, *Prof*, Wayne State College, Art Dept, Wayne NE (S)

Hansen, Rena, *VPres*, CIAO, Gallery & Art Center, Bronx NY

Hansen, Roland, *Head Readers Services*, School of the Art Institute of Chicago, John M Flaxman Library, Chicago IL

Hansen, Steve, *Prof*, Andrews University, Dept of Art, Art History & Design, Berrien Springs MI (S)

Hansen, Trudy, *Cur Prints & Drawings*, Rutgers, The State University of New Jersey, Jane Voorhees Zimmerli Art Museum, New Brunswick NJ

Hanson, David A, *Prof*, Fairleigh Dickinson University, Fine Arts Dept, Teaneck NJ (S)

Hanson, Debbie, *Registrar & Public Relations Coordr*, Eastern Shore Art Association, Inc, Library, Fairhope AL

Hanson, Emma, *Cur Plains Indian Museum*, Buffalo Bill Memorial Association, Buffalo Bill Historical Center, Cody WY

Hanson, Lowell, *Chmn*, Everett Community College, Art Dept, Everett WA (S)

Hanson, Robert, *Instr*, Pacific Northwest College of Art, Portland OR (S)

Hanson, Steven, *Circulations Supv*, Art Center College of Design, James Lemont Fogg Memorial Library, Pasadena CA

Hanson, Susan, *Historic Preservation Supv*, County of Henrico, Meadow Farm Museum, Glen Allen VA

Hanzal, Carla M, *Deputy Dir*, International Sculpture Center, Washington DC

Happe, Renetta, *Mem Asst*, Library Association of La Jolla, Athenaeum Music & Arts Library, La Jolla CA

Harakal, Eileen E, *Exec Dir Pub Affairs*, The Art Institute of Chicago, Chicago IL

Harasimowicz, Alan, *Exhibits Designer*, Southern Illinois University, University Museum, Carbondale IL

Harber, Margaret Neiman, *Pres*, Society of Scribes, Ltd, New York NY

Harbison, Craig, *Prof*, University of Massachusetts, Amherst, Art History Program, Amherst MA (S)

Harbison-Samuelson, Carol, *Library Mgr*, Southern Oregon Historical Society, Library, Medford OR

Harcada, Gwen, *Keeper*, *Lending Center*, Honolulu Academy of Arts, Honolulu HI

Hard, Michael W, *Treas*, Amerind Foundation, Inc, Amerind Museum, Fulton-Hayden Memorial Art Gallery, Dragoon AZ

Hard, Michael W, *Treas.* Amerind Foundation, Inc, Fulton-Hayden Memorial Library, Dragoon AZ

Hardberger, Linda, *Cur Tobin Theatre Coll & Library.* Marion Koogler McNay Art Museum, San Antonio TX

Harden, Jeanette, *Librn Asst.* Johns Hopkins University, George Peabody Library, Baltimore MD

Harders, Faith, *Librn.* University of Kentucky, Hunter M Adams Architecture Library, Lexington KY

Hardesty, David, *Chmn.* Oregon State University, Dept of Art, Corvallis OR (S)

Hardesty, Ron, *Registrar,* Owensboro Museum of Fine Art, Owensboro KY

Hardginski, Jean, *Mgr Bldg Servs,* The Pillsbury Company, Art Collection, Minneapolis MN

Hardiman, Thomas, *Cur.* York Institute Museum, Saco ME

Hardin, Jennifer, *Cur Coll & Exhib.* Museum of Fine Arts, Saint Petersburg, Florida, Inc, Saint Petersburg FL

Hardine, Shirley, *Cur.* National Park Service, Hubbell Trading Post National Historic Site, Ganado AZ

Harding, Catherine, *Asst Prof.* University of Victoria, Dept of History in Art, Victoria BC (S)

Harding, Taylce, *Dir,* North Dakota State University, Division of Fine Arts, Fargo ND (S)

Hardwig, Scott, *Prof.* Roanoke College, Fine Arts Dept-Art, Salem VA (S)

Hardy, Chantal, *Instr.* Universite de Montreal, Dept of Art History, Montreal PQ (S)

Hardy, David, *Gallery Supt & Preparator,* University of Utah, Utah Museum of Fine Arts, Salt Lake City UT

Hardy, Dominick, *Prog Asst.* Art Gallery of Peterborough, Peterborough ON

Hardy, Leaha, *Asst Prof.* Sam Houston State University, Art Dept, Huntsville TX (S)

Hardy, Myra, *Librn.* Mason County Museum, Maysville KY

Hardy, Neil, *Asst Prof.* Johns Hopkins University, School of Medicine, Dept of Art as Applied to Medicine, Baltimore MD (S)

Hardy, Saralyn Reece, *Dir.* Salina Art Center, Salina KS

Hare, John, *Chief Preparator,* Hunter Museum of American Art, Chattanooga TN

Harger, Elaine, *Head Librn,* New Jersey Historical Society, Newark NJ

Harger, Elaine, *Head Librn,* New Jersey Historical Society, Library, Newark NJ

Hargraves, Martine, *Dept Head Reference,* New Bedford Free Public Library, Art Dept, New Bedford MA

Harington, Donald, *Assoc Prof,* University of Arkansas, Art Dept, Fayetteville AR (S)

Harkavy, Donna, *Cur Contemporary Art,* Worcester Art Museum, Worcester MA

Harleman, Kathleen, *Assoc Dir,* Wellesley College, Davis Museum & Cultural Center, Wellesley MA

Harley, Timothy F, *Dir,* Huguenot Historical Society of New Paltz Galleries, New Paltz NY

Harlow, Ann, *Dir,* Saint Mary's College of California, Hearst Art Gallery, Moraga CA

Harman, Maryann, *Prof,* Virginia Polytechnic Institute & State University, Dept of Art & Art History, Blacksburg VA (S)

Harmon, Charles, *Asst Prof,* Winthrop University, Dept of Art & Design, Rock Hill SC (S)

Harmon, Jean, *Assoc Prof,* Missouri Western State College, Art Dept, Saint Joseph MO (S)

Harmon, Rick, *Quarterly Ed,* Oregon Historical Society, Library, Portland OR

Harmsen, Jeri, *Educ Officer,* Queen's University, Agnes Etherington Art Centre, Kingston ON

Harmsen, Phyllis, *Secy,* Augustana College, Center for Western Studies, Sioux Falls SD

Harowitz, Lisa, *Dir,* University of Pennsylvania, Museum Library, Philadelphia PA

Harper, George D, *Asst Prof,* Glenville State College, Dept of Fine Arts, Glenville WV (S)

Harper, Katherine, *Assoc Prof,* Loyola Marymount University, Art & Art History Dept, Los Angeles CA (S)

Harper, Lucy Bjorklund, *Librn.* University of Rochester, Charlotte W Allen Library-Memorial Art Gallery, Rochester NY

Harper, Margaret, *Div Chair Arts & Science.* Oakland City College, Division of Fine Arts, Oakland City IN (S)

Harper, Paula, *Assoc Prof.* University of Miami, Dept of Art & Art History, Coral Gables FL (S)

Harper, Prudence O, *Chmn Ancient Near Eastern Art.* The Metropolitan Museum of Art, New York NY

Harper, Robert W, *Exec Dir.* Lightner Museum, Saint Augustine FL

Harper, Robert W, *Exec Dir.* Lightner Museum, Library, Saint Augustine FL

Harper, Suzanne, *Dir of Fine Arts.* Museum of Arts & Sciences, Inc, Macon GA

Harreld Love, Josephine, *Dir.* Your Heritage House, Detroit MI

Harreld Love, Josephine, *Dir.* Your Heritage House, Library, Detroit MI

Harrington, Kelly, *Educ Prog Coordr.* Glenhyrst Art Gallery of Brant, Library, Brantford ON

Harrington, Susan, *Prof.* Texas Christian University, Art & Art History Dept, Fort Worth TX (S)

Harris, Albert, *Museum Coordr.* Portsmouth Museums, Art Center, Portsmouth VA

Harris, Anne, *Prof.* Bowdoin College, Art Dept, Brunswick ME (S)

Harris, Caroline, *Dir Develop.* Drawing Center, New York NY

Harris, Christie, *Librn.* Watkins Institute College of Art & Design, Library, Nashville TN

Harris, David J, *Instr.* North Seattle Community College, Art Dept, Seattle WA (S)

Harris, Donald, *Dean Col.* Ohio State University, College of the Arts, Columbus OH (S)

Harris, Ellen, *Dir.* Montclair Art Museum, Montclair NJ

Harris, Ellen, *Dir.* Montclair Art Museum, Art School, Montclair NJ (S)

Harris, Gene E, *Cur Coll.* Brandywine River Museum, Chadds Ford PA

Harris, George, *Dir & Cur.* Prince George Art Gallery, Prince George BC

Harris, Jane, *Dir.* Amos Eno Gallery, New York NY

Harris, Jeff, *Instr.* Whitworth College, Art Dept, Spokane WA (S)

Harris, Joe, *Assoc Prof.* Culver-Stockton College, Art Dept, Canton MO (S)

Harris, Karen, *Dir.* Marymount Manhattan College Gallery, New York NY

Harris, Mac, *Admin.* Cherokee National Historical Society, Inc, Tahlequah OK

Harris, Marie Joan, *Acadmic Dean.* Avila College, Thornhill Art Gallery, Kansas City MO

Harris, Michael, *Asst Prof.* University of North Carolina at Chapel Hill, Art Dept, Chapel Hill NC (S)

Harris, Michael, *Coordr Photography Hall Fame.* Oklahoma Center for Science & Art, Kirkpatrick Center, Oklahoma City OK

Harris, Michele, *Dir Admin.* Mississippi Museum of Art, Jackson MS

Harris, Miriam B, *Dir.* Colorado State University, Curfman Gallery, Fort Collins CO

Harris, Mona, *Gallery Dir.* Lahaina Arts Society, Art Organization, Lahaina HI

Harris, Robert A, *Dir.* Helen M Plum Memorial Library, Lombard IL

Harris, Ronna, *Asst Prof.* Tulane University, Sophie H Newcomb Memorial College, New Orleans LA (S)

Harrison, Allen, *Dir.* Pasadena City College, Art Gallery, Pasadena CA

Harrison, Cheryl, *Chmn.* High Point College, Fine Arts Dept, High Point NC (S)

Harrison, Davina, *Technical Servs Asst.* The Saint Louis Art Museum, Richardson Memorial Library, Saint Louis MO

Harrison, Eugene, *Asst Prof.* Eastern Illinois University, Art Dept, Charleston IL (S)

Harrison, Jeff, *Chief Cur.* Chrysler Museum of Art, Norfolk VA

Harrison, Katie, *Ed-Asst.* Artist's Alliance of California, Nevada City CA

Harrison, Nancy, *Pres.* Creative Arts Guild, Dalton GA

Harrison, Susan, *Chief Art-in-Architecture Prog.* General Services Administration, Washington DC

Harrist, Robert, *Asst Prof.* Oberlin College, Dept of Art, Oberlin OH (S)

Harrold, Marty, *Museum Coordr.* Hastings Museum, Hastings NE

Hart, Arnold, *Instr.* Okaloosa-Walton Community College, Dept of Fine & Performing Arts, Niceville FL (S)

Hart, Barbara A, *Assoc Dir Admin.* National Portrait Gallery, Washington DC

Hart, E J, *Dir.* Peter & Catharine Whyte Foundation, Whyte Museum of the Canadian Rockies, Banff AB

Hart, Katherine, *Cur Academic Progs,* Dartmouth College, Hood Museum of Art, Hanover NH

Hart, Sara, *Interim Chmn.* Shoreline Community College, Humanities Division, Seattle WA (S)

Hart, Tom, *Head Fine Arts.* Colorado Mountain College, Fine Arts Gallery, Breckenridge CO

Hart, Vincent, *Asst Prof.* Georgian Court College, Dept of Art, Lakewood NJ (S)

Hart-Agee, Diane, *Registrar.* Williams College, Museum of Art, Williamstown MA

Hartcourt, Glenn, *Asst Prof.* University of Southern California, School of Fine Arts, Los Angeles CA (S)

Hartfield, Ronne, *Exec Dir Museum Educ.* The Art Institute of Chicago, Chicago IL

Harth, Marjorie L, *Dir.* Galleries of the Claremont Colleges, Claremont CA

Harthorn, Sandy, *Cur Exhib.* Boise Art Museum, Boise ID

Hartigan, Grace, *Dir.* Maryland Institute, Hoffberger School of Painting, Baltimore MD (S)

Hartke, Mary, *VPres.* Iroquois County Historical Society Museum, Old Courthouse Museum, Watseka IL

Hartline, Angelia, *Public Information.* Cheekwood-Tennessee Botanical Gardens & Museum of Art, Nashville TN

Hartman, Bruce, *Dir Art Gallery,* Johnson County Community College, Visual Arts Program, Overland Park KS (S)

Hartman, Eleanor, *Librn.* Los Angeles County Museum of Art, Los Angeles CA

Hartman, Hedy, *Pres & Chief Exec Officer.* Staten Island Institute of Arts & Sciences, Staten Island NY

Hartman, Terry L, *Instr.* Modesto Junior College, Arts Humanities & Communications Division, Modesto CA (S)

Hartshorn, Willis, *Dir.* International Center of Photography, New York NY

Hartshorn, Willis, *Dir.* International Center of Photography, Midtown, New York NY

Hartswick, Kim, *Assoc Prof.* George Washington University, Dept of Art, Washington DC (S)

Hartung, Angela, *Operations Dir.* Art Center of Battle Creek, Michigan Art & Artist Archives, Battle Creek MI

Hartwell, Carroll T, *Cur Photo.* Minneapolis Institute of Arts, Minneapolis MN

Hartwell, H, *Chmn.* McMaster University, Dept of Art & Art History, Hamilton ON (S)

Hartwell, Janice E, *Assoc Prof.* Florida State University, Art Dept, Tallahassee FL (S)

Hartzold, Susan, *Cur.* McLean County Historical Society, Bloomington IL

Harvath, John, *Mgr. Fine Arts & Recreation.* Houston Public Library, Houston TX

Harvey, Alan, *Dean.* Foothill College, Fine Arts & Communications Div, Los Altos Hills CA (S)

Harvey, Archer, *Assoc Prof.* Rutgers, the State University of New Jersey, Graduate Program in Art History, New Brunswick NJ (S)

Harvey, Bruce, *Dir.* Housatonic Community-Technical College, Library, Bridgeport CT

Harvey, Bunny, *Assoc Prof.* Wellesley College, Art Dept, Wellesley MA (S)

Harvey, Clifford, *Prof.* West Virginia University, College of Creative Arts, Morgantown WV (S)

Harvey, Emily, *Discipline Coordr.* Rockland Community College, Graphic Arts & Advertising Tech Dept, Suffern NY (S)

Heffner, Jinger, *Gallery Coordr*, Otis College of Art & Design, Los Angeles CA

Heffner, Terry, *Assoc Dir*, Meredith Gallery, Baltimore MD

Heflin, Patricia, *Fine Arts Support Specialist*, US Department of State, Diplomatic Reception Rooms, Washington DC

Hegarty, Melinda, *Prof*, Eastern Illinois University, Art Dept, Charleston IL (S)

Hegeman, William, *Media Relations Supv*, Minnesota Museum of American Art, Saint Paul MN

Heger, Carol, *Educ Coordr*, Anderson Fine Arts Center, Anderson IN

Hehman, Jennifer, *Assoc Librn*, Indiana University - Purdue University at Indianapolis, Herron School of Art Library, Indianapolis IN

Heidorf, Christine, *Cur*, Historic Cherry Hill, Albany NY

Heil, Elizabeth, *Asst Prof*, Roanoke College, Fine Arts Dept-Art, Salem VA (S)

Heil, Harry, *Gallery Dir*, Western State College of Colorado, Quigley Hall Art Gallery, Gunnison CO

Heil, Mary Colleen, *Pres*, Pennsylvania School of Art & Design, Lancaster PA (S)

Heilbrun, Margaret, *Library Dir*, New York Historical Society, Library, New York NY

Heimann, Nora, *Instr & Art Historian*, Florida International University, Visual Arts Dept, Miami FL (S)

Heimdal, Georg, *Chmn*, Ohio State University, Dept of Art, Columbus OH (S)

Heineman, Stephanie, *Dir*, Northport-East Northport Public Library, Northport NY

Heinicke, Janet, *Chmn Dept*, Simpson College, Art Dept, Indianola IA (S)

Heinicke, Janet, *Head Art Dept*, Simpson College, Farnham Gallery, Indianola IA

Heinrich, Milton, *Chmn*, Dana College, Art Dept, Blair NE (S)

Heinson, Lillian, *Slide Librn*, York University, Fine Arts Phase II Slide Library, North York ON

Heintz, David, *Film-Video*, California College of Arts & Crafts, Oakland CA

Heintzman, John, *Dir Art & Cur Gallery*, Bradley University, Heuser Art Center, Peoria IL

Heipp, Richard, *Assoc Prof*, University of Florida, Dept of Art, Gainesville FL (S)

Heisch, Melvena, *Preservation Dir*, Oklahoma Historical Society, State Museum of History, Oklahoma City OK

Heischman, Robert, *Prof*, Rochester Institute of Technology, School of Art & Design, Rochester NY (S)

Heise, Lane, *Instr*, Harcum Junior College, Illustrations & Graphic Design Dept, Bryn Mawr PA (S)

Heisner, Beverly, *Chmn Art History*, University of South Carolina, Dept of Art, Columbia SC (S)

Heiss, Alanna, *Exec Dir*, Institute for Contemporary Art, Project Studio One (P S 1), Long Island City NY

Heit, Dorothea, *Adjunct Prof*, Oral Roberts University, Fine Arts Dept, Tulsa OK (S)

Heitner, Devorah, *Educ Coordr*, Spertus Institute of Jewish Studies, Spertus Museum, Chicago IL

Held, Nancy L, *Lectr*, Johns Hopkins University, School of Medicine, Dept of Art as Applied to Medicine, Baltimore MD (S)

Helender, Linda, *Prof*, University of Wisconsin-Superior, Programs in the Visual Arts, Superior WI (S)

Helfrich, Paul, *Assoc Prof*, College of William & Mary, Dept of Fine Arts, Williamsburg VA (S)

Helland, Karen, *Museum Dir*, Saint Olaf College, Art Dept, Northfield MN (S)

Heller, Barbara, *Head Conservator*, Detroit Institute of Arts, Detroit MI

Heller, John, *Chmn*, Bridgewater State College, Art Dept, Bridgewater MA (S)

Heller, Kevin, *Asst Supv*, Newark Museum Association, Junior Museum, Newark NJ

Heller, Susanna, *Instr*, Sarah Lawrence College, Dept of Art History, Bronxville NY (S)

Hellier, Bob, *Preparator*, Tampa Museum of Art, Tampa FL

Helm, Alison, *Prof*, West Virginia University, College of Creative Arts, Morgantown WV (S)

Helm, Charles R, *Dir Performing Arts*, Ohio State University, Wexner Center for the Arts, Columbus OH

Helm, Richard, *Dir*, Western Colorado Center for the Arts, Inc, Grand Junction CO

Helmick, Robert, *Pres Board Trustees*, Edmundson Art Foundation, Inc, Des Moines Art Center, Des Moines IA

Helmreich, Anne, *Prof*, Texas Christian University, Art & Art History Dept, Fort Worth TX (S)

Helsell, Charles, *Cur Art Coll*, 3M, Art Collection, Saint Paul MN

Helzel, Florence, *Cur*, Judah L Magnes Museum, Berkeley CA

Helzer, Richard, *Interim Dir Art*, Montana State University, Bozeman MT (S)

Hench, Robert, *Assoc Prof*, University of Southern Colorado, Belmont Campus, Dept of Art, Pueblo CO (S)

Hendershot, James, *Assoc Prof*, College of Saint Benedict, Art Dept, Saint Joseph MN (S)

Hendershot, James, *Assoc Prof*, Saint John's University, Art Dept, Collegeville MN (S)

Henderson, Amy, *Librn*, Terra Museum of American Art, Chicago IL

Henderson, Amy, *Librn*, Terra Museum of American Art, Chicago IL

Henderson, Barry, *Librn*, Beaverbrook Art Gallery, Library, Fredericton NB

Henderson, Debra, *Dir Educ & Training*, The American Film Institute, Center for Advanced Film & Television, Los Angeles CA (S)

Henderson, Jamesina, *Dir*, California African-American Museum, Los Angeles CA

Henderson, Janet, *Office Mgr*, Maryland-National Capital Park & Planning Commission, Montpelier Cultural Arts Center, Laurel MD

Henderson, Lana, *Prof*, North Carolina Central University, Art Dept, Durham NC (S)

Henderson, Maren, *Chair*, California State Polytechnic University, Pomona, Art Dept, Pomona CA (S)

Henderson, Robbin, *Exec Dir*, Berkeley Art Center, Berkeley CA

Henderson, Stephen, *Prof*, Wenatchee Valley College, Art Dept, Wenatchee WA (S)

Henderson, Thomas, *Assoc Prof*, Mount Allison University, Fine Arts Dept, Sackville NB (S)

Hendig, Cathy, *Instr*, Monterey Peninsula College, Art Dept, Monterey CA (S)

Hendley, B, *Dean*, University of Waterloo, Fine Arts Dept, Waterloo ON (S)

Hendrick, Joe, *Assoc Prof*, Monroe Community College, Art Dept, Rochester NY (S)

Hendricks, Barkley L, *Prof*, Connecticut College, Dept of Art, New London CT (S)

Hendricks, Geoffrey, *Prof*, Rutgers, the State University of New Jersey, Mason Gross School of the Arts, New Brunswick NJ (S)

Hendricks, Joan, *Registrar*, State University of New York at Purchase, Neuberger Museum of Art, Purchase NY

Hendricks, Larry, *Dir Humanities & Fine Arts*, Sacramento City College, Art Dept, Sacramento CA (S)

Hendricks, Leta, *Librn*, Ohio State University, Human Ecology Library, Columbus OH

Hendricks, Patricia, *Cur Exhib*, University of Texas at Austin, Archer M Huntington Art Gallery, Austin TX

Hendricks, Susan, *Public Relations Officer*, Lyman Allyn Art Museum, New London CT

Hendrickson, Bill, *Pres*, Mason County Museum, Maysville KY

Hendrickson, Ted, *Asst Prof*, Connecticut College, Dept of Art, New London CT (S)

Hendrickx, Jim, *Chmn*, Mount Vernon Nazarene College, Art Dept, Mount Vernon OH (S)

Hendrix, Randy P, *Asst to the Dir*, Westminster College, Winston Churchill Memorial & Library in the United States, Fulton MO

Hendry, Leigh, *Dir Spec Projects*, Tennessee State Museum, Nashville TN

Henke, Dellas, *Assoc Prof*, Grand Valley State University, Art & Design Dept, Allendale MI (S)

Henke, Jerry D, *Exec Dir*, Fillmore County Historical Society, Fountain MN

Henkel, James, *Assoc Prof*, University of Minnesota, Minneapolis, Dept of Art, Minneapolis MN (S)

Henley, David, *Assoc Prof*, C W Post Center of Long Island University, School of Visual & Performing Arts, Brookville NY (S)

Hennessey, Colleen, *Archivist*, Freer Gallery of Art Gallery, Library, Washington DC

Hennessey, Maureen Hart, *Cur*, Norman Rockwell Museum at Stockbridge, Stockbridge MA

Hennessey, Maureen Hart, *Cur*, Norman Rockwell Museum at Stockbridge, Library, Stockbridge MA

Hennessey, William, *Dir*, University of Michigan, Museum of Art, Ann Arbor MI

Hennessey, William, *Dir Museum Art*, University of Michigan, Ann Arbor, Dept of History of Art, Ann Arbor MI (S)

Hennessey, William J, *Dir*, Chrysler Museum Of Art, Norfolk VA

Hennigar, Robert, *Computer Graphics Chmn*, Art Center College of Design, Pasadena CA (S)

Henning, Darrell D, *Dir*, Vesterheim Norwegian-American Museum, Decorah IA

Henning, Darrell D, *Dir*, Vesterheim Norwegian-American Museum, Reference Library, Decorah IA

Henning, Jean, *Coordr Young People's Prog*, Nassau County Museum of Fine Art, Roslyn Harbor NY

Henning, Robert, *Asst Dir Curatorial Servs*, Santa Barbara Museum of Art, Santa Barbara CA

Henning, William T, *Exec Dir*, Rosemount Museum, Inc, Pueblo CO

Hennings, Pat, *Chmn*, California State University, Fresno, Art & Design, Fresno CA (S)

Hennum, Paulette, *Registrar*, Crocker Art Museum, Sacramento CA

Henrey, Michael, *Dept Chmn*, Prairie State College, Art Dept, Chicago Heights IL (S)

Henri, Janine, *Head Librn*, University of Texas at Austin, Architecture & Planning Library, Austin TX

Henrich, Biff, *Pres*, Center for Exploratory & Perceptual Art, CEPA Gallery, Buffalo NY

Henrich, Gary, *Chair*, Historical Society of Washington DC, Heurich House Museum, Washington DC

Henrich, Sarah E, *Exec Dir*, Historical Society of Rockland County, New City NY

Henrickson, Steve, *Cur Coll*, Alaska State Museum, Juneau AK

Henry, Ed, *Deputy Dir Admin & Finance*, Museum of the City of New York, New York NY

Henry, Eileen, *Prog Coordr*, Hunter Museum of American Art, Chattanooga TN

Henry, John, *Exec Secy & Mgr*, Brown County Art Gallery Association Inc, Brown County Art Gallery & Museum, Nashville IN

Henry, John, *Coordr of Galleries*, Saint Clair County Community College, Jack R Hennesey Art Galleries, Port Huron MI

Henry, John B, *Dir*, Flint Institute of Arts, Flint MI

Henry, Karen, *Dir & Cur*, Burnaby Art Gallery, Burnaby BC

Henry, Kevin, *Coordr Pkg Designs*, Columbia College, Art Dept, Chicago IL (S)

Henry, Lawrence, *Pres*, Brookgreen Gardens, Murrells Inlet SC

Henry, Michelle, *Dir*, Jamestown Community College, The Forum Gallery, Jamestown NY

Henry, Michelle, *Asst to Dir*, Jamestown Community College, The Forum Gallery, Jamestown NY

Henry, Sara, *Chmn Dept*, Drew University, Art Dept, Madison NJ (S)

Henry, Sue, *VPres*, Biloxi Art Association Inc & Gallery, Biloxi MS

Henry, Wayne, *Dir*, Arapahoe Community College, Colorado Gallery of the Arts, Littleton CO

Henshall, Barbara E, *Cur*, Martin & Osa Johnson Safari Museum, Inc, Chanute KS

Hensler, Ruth, *Instr*, Saint Louis Community College at Meramec, Art Dept, Saint Louis MO (S)

Hensley, Fred Owen, *Prof.* University of North Alabama, Dept of Art, Florence AL (S)

Henson, Harvey, *Adjunct Cur Geology,* Southern Illinois University, University Museum, Carbondale IL

Hentchel, Fred, *Instr.* Illinois Central College, Dept of Fine Arts, East Peoria IL (S)

Henthorne, Michael, *Dir.* Oregon State University, Memorial Union Art Gallery, Corvallis OR

Henton, Marty, *Dir.* Living Arts & Science Center, Inc, Lexington KY

Hentz, Christopher, *Prof.* Louisiana State University, School of Art, Baton Rouge LA (S)

Henzy, John, *Head,* Gloucester County College, Liberal Arts Dept, Sewell NJ

Hepburn, Tony, *Head Ceramics Dept,* Cranbrook Academy of Art, Bloomfield Hills MI (S)

Hepner, Edward, *Chief Preparator,* Marion Koogler McNay Art Museum, San Antonio TX

Heppner, Richard, *Chmn Dept,* Orange County Community College, Art Dept, Middletown NY (S)

Hepworth, Russell, *Assoc Prof.* College of Southern Idaho, Art Dept, Twin Falls ID (S)

Herbeck, Edward, *Adjunct Prof.* North Central College, Dept of Art, Naperville IL (S)

Herberg, Mayde, *Instr.* Rancho Santiago College, Art Dept, Santa Ana CA (S)

Herbert, Ann, *Vol Coordr,* UMLAUF Sculpture Garden & Museum, Austin TX

Herbert, Frank, *Chmn,* Kilgore College, Visual Arts Dept, Kilgore TX (S)

Herbert, Kimberly, *Children's Art Museum Adminr,* San Angelo Museum of Fine Arts, San Angelo TX

Herbert, Linda M, *Pub Information Officer,* Everson Museum of Art, Syracuse NY

Herbert, Lynn, *Assoc Cur,* Contemporary Arts Museum, Houston TX

Herbert, Mark E, *Asst Librn,* Natural History Museum of Los Angeles County, Research Library, Los Angeles CA

Herbig, Matt, *Cur Coll,* Rockford Art Museum, Rockford IL

Herden, Irene, *Dir Humanities,* Bay Path College, Dept of Art, Longmeadow MA (S)

Herdrich, Donald, *Treas,* Katonah Museum of Art, Katonah NY

Herdy, Sarah, *Dir,* Center for Critical Architecture, AAES (Art & Architecture Exhibition Space), San Francisco CA

Heredia, Ruben, *Vis Prof.* Butte College, Dept of Fine Arts, Oroville CA (S)

Hereth, Jennifer, *Asst Prof.* College of DuPage, Humanities Division, Glen Ellyn IL (S)

Heriard, Robert T, *Chair Reference Servs,* University of New Orleans, Earl K Long Library, New Orleans LA

Heric, John, *Assoc Prof Sculpture,* University of Arizona, Dept of Art, Tucson AZ (S)

Hering, Michael J, *Dir,* School of American Research, Indian Arts Research Center, Santa Fe NM

Herman, Judy, *Exec Dir,* Main Line Art Center, Haverford PA

Herman, Judy S, *Admin Exec Dir,* Main Line Art Center, Haverford PA (S)

Herman, Ladell, *Technical Advisor,* Hickory Museum of Art, Inc, Hickory NC

Herman, Ralph, *Pres,* San Fernando Valley Historical Society, Andres Pico Adobe Library, Mission Hills CA

Hern, Mary Ellen, *Dir,* Shaker Museum & Library, Emma B King Library, Old Chatham NY

Hern, Mary Ellen W, *Dir.* Shaker Museum & Library, Old Chatham NY

Hernandez, Alberto, *Librn,* University of Northern Iowa, Art & Music Section Rod Library, Cedar Falls IA

Hernandez, Carlos, *Chmn,* Jersey City Museum, Jersey City NJ

Hernandez, Connie, *Board VPres,* Centro Cultural De La Raza, San Diego CA

Hernandez, Daniel, *Board Pres,* Centro Cultural De La Raza, San Diego CA

Hernandez, Dora, *Visual Arts Dir,* Arizona Commission on the Arts, Phoenix AZ

Hernandez, John, *Cur Exhib,* Institute of the Great Plains, Museum of the Great Plains, Lawton OK

Hernandez, Lorna, *Asst Chmn Advertising Design,* Art Institute of Fort Lauderdale, Fort Lauderdale FL (S)

Hernandez, Luis A Diaz, *Dir,* Institute of Puerto Rican Culture, Instituto de Cultura Puertorriquena, San Juan PR

Hernandez, Luis Cruz, *Dir,* University of Puerto Rico, Museum of Anthropology, History & Art, San Juan PR

Hernandez, Sam, *Assoc Prof.* Santa Clara University, Art Dept, Santa Clara CA (S)

Hernandez, T Paul, *Chmn,* Texas Lutheran College, Dept of Visual Arts, Seguin TX (S)

Hernandez-Cruz, Luis, *Prof.* University of Puerto Rico, Dept of Fine Arts, Rio Piedras PR (S)

Herr, Marcianne, *Dir Educ,* Akron Art Museum, Akron OH

Herr, Marcianne, *Educ Dir,* Akron Art Museum, Martha Stecher Reed Art Library, Akron OH

Herrera, Luis, *Dir,* Pasadena Public Library, Fine Arts Dept, Pasadena CA

Herrero, Susana, *Assoc Prof.* University of Puerto Rico, Dept of Fine Arts, Rio Piedras PR (S)

Herrick, Cindee, *Cur,* US Coast Guard Museum, New London CT

Herrick, Kristine, *Assoc Prof.* College of Saint Rose, Dept of Art, Albany NY (S)

Herring, Howard, *Exec Dir,* Caramoor Center for Music & the Arts, Inc, Caramoor House Museum, Katonah NY

Herrington, Thomas E, *Chief Preparator,* New Orleans Museum of Art, New Orleans LA

Herrity, Carol M, *Asst Librn,* Lehigh County Historical Society, Scott Andrew Trexler II Library, Allentown PA

Herrmann, Frank, *Prof Fine Arts,* University of Cincinnati, School of Art, Cincinnati OH (S)

Herrmann, John, *Cur Classical Art,* Museum of Fine Arts, Boston MA

Herrold, David, *Prof.* DePauw University, Art Dept, Greencastle IN (S)

Herron, Cliff, *Chmn,* Okaloosa-Walton Community College, Dept of Fine & Performing Arts, Niceville FL (S)

Hersey, Irwin, *Pres,* The Chaim Gross Studio Museum, New York NY

Hersh, Lela, *Registrar,* Museum of Contemporary Art, Chicago IL

Hershberger, Abner, *Prof.* Goshen College, Art Dept, Goshen IN (S)

Herskowitz, Sylvia A, *Dir,* Yeshiva University Museum, New York NY

Hertel, Christiane, *Asst Prof.* Bryn Mawr College, Dept of the History of Art, Bryn Mawr PA (S)

Hertz, Betti-Sue, *Longwood Dir,* Bronx Council on the Arts, Longwood Arts Gallery, Bronx NY

Hertz, Richard, *Liberal Arts, Sciences & Graduate Studies Chmn,* Art Center College of Design, Pasadena CA (S)

Hertzson, Joyce, *Chmn Foundation Studies & Assoc Prof.* Rochester Institute of Technology, School of Art & Design, Rochester NY (S)

Herzog, Melanie, *Asst Prof.* Edgewood College, Art Dept, Madison WI (S)

Hess, Anthony P, *Librn,* Colby College, Bixler Art & Music Library, Waterville ME

Hess, Garry J, *Prof.* Missouri Southern State College, Dept of Art, Joplin MO (S)

Hess, Honee A, *Dir Educ,* Worcester Art Museum, Worcester MA

Hess, Ralph, *VPres,* Prescott Fine Arts Association, Gallery, Prescott AZ

Hess, Richard, *First VPres,* Brown County Art Gallery Association Inc, Brown County Art Gallery & Museum, Nashville IN

Hessburg, Aloyse, *Assoc Prof.* Mount Mary College, Art Dept, Milwaukee WI (S)

Hesse, Gary, *Assoc Dir,* Light Work, Syracuse NY

Hessel, Jan, *Facilities Tech,* Washington University, Gallery of Art, Saint Louis MO

Hessemer, Peter, *Assoc Prof.* Oakton Community College, Art & Architecture Dept, Des Plaines IL (S)

Heth, Charlotte, *Asst Dir Public Progs,* National Museum of the American Indian, George Gustav Heye Center, New York NY

Hetherington, Lillian, *AV Coordr,* Academy of Art, College Library, San Francisco CA

Heuler, Henry J, *Assoc Prof.* University of West Florida, Dept of Art, Pensacola FL (S)

Heuser, Frederick J, *Dir.* Presbyterian Historical Society, Philadelphia PA

Hever, Curt, *Chmn,* University of Wisconsin-Green Bay, Art-Communication & the Arts, Green Bay WI (S)

Hewitt, Clarissa, *Prof.* California Polytechnic State University at San Luis Obispo, Dept of Art & Design, San Luis Obispo CA (S)

Hewitt, Marsha, *Assoc Prof.* University of Nebraska, Kearney, Dept of Art & Art History, Kearney NE (S)

Hewitt, Timothy, *Cur,* Presidential Museum, Odessa TX

Hext, Charles R, *Prof.* Sul Ross State University, Dept of Fine Arts & Communications, Alpine TX (S)

Heyler, Joanne, *Acting Cur,* SunAmerica, Inc, The SunAmerica-Kaufman & Broad Home Corporation Collection, Los Angeles CA

Heyman, Ira Michael, *Secy,* Smithsonian Institution, Washington DC

Heyrmon, Joy, *Dir Develop,* Walters Art Gallery, Baltimore MD

Hibbard, James, *Prof.* Portland State University, Dept of Art, Portland OR (S)

Hickey, Carol, *Instr.* Franklin & Marshall College, Art Dept, Lancaster PA (S)

Hickey, Christopher, *Chmn Dept.* Clark-Atlanta University, School of Arts & Sciences, Atlanta GA (S)

Hickey, Joe, *Pres.* Crooked Tree Arts Council, Virginia M McCune Community Arts Center, Petoskey MI

Hickey, Margaret, *Chmn Design.* Massachusetts College of Art, Boston MA (S)

Hickman, Paul, *Asst Prof.* Arkansas State University, Dept of Art, State University AR (S)

Hicks, Amy, *Develop Assoc,* New Langton Arts, San Francisco CA

Hicks, Hilarie M, *Cur Interpretation,* Tryon Palace Historic Sites & Gardens, New Bern NC

Hicks, Jim, *Instr.* Pacific Northwest College of Art, Portland OR (S)

Hicks, Katie, *Gallery Dir,* University of South Carolina at Spartanburg, Art Gallery, Spartanburg SC

Hicks, Laurie E, *Chair,* University of Maine, Dept of Art, Orono ME (S)

Hicks, Leon, *Assoc Prof.* Webster University, Art Dept, Webster Groves MO (S)

Hicks, Leslie, *Cur of Educ.* Jekyll Island Museum, Jekyll Island GA

Hicks, Linda, *Admin.* University of Pittsburgh, University Art Gallery, Pittsburgh PA

Hicks, Pam, *Pres.* Hoosier Salon Patrons Association, Hoosier Salon Art Gallery, Indianapolis IN

Hicks, Ron, *Instr.* Johnson County Community College, Visual Arts Program, Overland Park KS (S)

Hicks, Steve, *Chmn,* Oklahoma Baptist University, Art Dept, Shawnee OK (S)

Hicks, Timothy O, *Chmn.* North Carolina Agricultural & Technical State University, Art Dept, Greensboro NC (S)

Hidley, Charles, *Cur,* Art Association of Harrisburg, School & Galleries, Harrisburg PA

Hiebert, Helen, *Prog Dir,* Dieu Donne Papermill, Inc, New York NY

Hieblinger, Faith, *Mgr,* Homer Watson House & Gallery, Kitchener ON

Hiester, Jan, *Registrar,* Charleston Museum, Charleston SC

Higa, Yosh, *Prof.* Southampton College of Long Island University, Arts & Media Division, Southampton NY (S)

Higgins, Isabelle, *Librn,* Brooks Institute Photography Library, Santa Barbara CA

Higgins, Larkin, *Prof.* California Lutheran University, Art Dept, Thousand Oaks CA (S)

Higgins, Steven, *Co-Chmn Painting,* University of Manitoba, School of Art, Winnipeg MB (S)

Higgins-Jacob, Coleen, *Treas,* John Simon Guggenheim Memorial Foundation, New York NY

Higginson, Genevra, *Special Events Officer,* National Gallery of Art, Washington DC

High, Steven S, *Exec Dir,* Nevada Museum of Art, Reno NV

High, Steven S, *Exec Dir,* Nevada Museum of Art, Art Library, Reno NV

Hightower, John B, *Pres,* The Mariners' Museum, Newport News VA

Hightower, Nancy, *Finance Officer,* Laguna Art Museum of the Orange County Museum of Art, Laguna Beach CA

Hightower, Samantha, *School & Community Outreach Asst.* Dartmouth College, Hood Museum of Art, Hanover NH

Hignite, Daniel, *Prof,* Antioch College, Visual Arts Dept, Yellow Springs OH (S)

Higonnet, Anne, *Asst Prof,* Wellesley College, Art Dept, Wellesley MA (S)

Hilde, Saralyn, *Exhib Dir,* Salem Art Association, Bush Barn Art Center, Salem OR

Hildebrand, Danna, *Instr,* Sheridan College, Art Dept, Sheridan WY (S)

Hile, Jeanette, *Assoc Prof,* Seton Hall University, College of Arts & Sciences, South Orange NJ (S)

Hileman, Jayne, *Chmn,* Saint Xavier University, Dept of Art, Chicago IL (S)

Hileman, Nancy, *Dir Develop,* Lyman Allyn Art Museum, New London CT

Hilger, Charles, *Exec Dir,* Museum of Art & History, Santa Cruz CA

Hilkin, Jim, *VPres,* Art Guild of Burlington, Arts for Living Center, Burlington IA

Hill, Barbara, *Prog Dir,* Hand Workshop Art Center, Richmond VA

Hill, Barbara A, *Prog Coordr,* City of Tampa, Art in Public Places, Tampa FL

Hill, Carolyn, *Dir & Chief Cur,* Oklahoma City Art Museum, Oklahoma City OK

Hill, Carolyn, *Dir & Cur,* Oklahoma City Art Museum, Library, Oklahoma City OK

Hill, Carolyn, *Dean,* Notre Dame College, Art Dept, Manchester NH (S)

Hill, Charles, *Cur Canadian Art,* National Gallery of Canada, Ottawa ON

Hill, Chris, *Instr,* Southwest Texas State University, Dept of Art, San Marcos TX (S)

Hill, Dennis, *Music Instr,* Edison Community College, Dept of Fine & Performing Arts, Fort Myers FL (S)

Hill, Elen, *Resident Printer,* Pyramid Atlantic, Riverdale MD

Hill, Gwen, *Cur,* California State University, Long Beach, University Art Museum, Long Beach CA

Hill, Heidi, *Site Asst,* Olana State Historic Site, Hudson NY

Hill, James K, *Head Dept,* Southwest Missouri State University, Dept of Art & Design, Springfield MO (S)

Hill, Jan, *Pres Museum Board Trustees,* Chilkat Valley Historical Society, Sheldon Museum & Cultural Center, Haines AK

Hill, Jo, *Conservator,* University of California, Los Angeles, Fowler Museum of Cultural History, Los Angeles CA

Hill, Joyce, *Pres,* Buffalo Society of Artists, Williamsville NY

Hill, Liz, *Dir Public Affairs,* National Museum of the American Indian, George Gustav Heye Center, New York NY

Hill, Lynn, *Asst Prof,* Elmhurst College, Art Dept, Elmhurst IL (S)

Hill, Pamela, *Cur Educ,* University of North Carolina at Greensboro, Weatherspoon Art Gallery, Greensboro NC

Hill, Peter, *Prof,* University of Nebraska at Omaha, Dept of Art & Art History, Omaha NE (S)

Hill, Ron, *Transportation Design Chmn,* Art Center College of Design, Pasadena CA (S)

Hill, Sherri, *Prof,* Manatee Community College, Dept of Art & Humanities, Bradenton FL (S)

Hill, Thom, *Dean of Fine & Performing Arts,* Rancho Santiago College, Art Dept, Santa Ana CA (S)

Hill, Thomas, *Librn,* Vassar College, Art Library, Poughkeepsie NY

Hillbruner, Fred, *Head Technical Services,* School of the Art Institute of Chicago, John M Flaxman Library, Chicago IL

Hillding, John, *Instr,* The Art Institutes International, The Art Institute of Seattle, Seattle WA (S)

Hilliard, Elbert R, *Dir,* Mississippi Department of Archives & History, Library, Jackson MS

Hillier, John, *Instr,* Kilgore College, Visual Arts Dept, Kilgore TX (S)

Hillman, Arthur, *Instr,* Simon's Rock College of Bard, Visual Arts Dept, Great Barrington MA (S)

Hillman, Eric, *VPres,* Southern Alberta Art Gallery, Lethbridge AB

Hillman, Ernest, *Assoc Pres,* Marcella Sembrich Memorial Association Inc, Opera Museum, Bolton Landing NY

Hillman, Judy, *Instr,* Hope College, Art Dept, Holland MI (S)

Hills, Helen, *Asst Prof,* University of North Carolina at Chapel Hill, Art Dept, Chapel Hill NC (S)

Hillsberg, Meryl, *Prog Coordr,* Montclair Art Museum, Art School, Montclair NJ (S)

Hills-Nova, Clare, *Reference Librn,* New York University, Stephen Chan Library of Fine Arts, New York NY

Hillstrom, Richard L, *Consultant & Cur,* Lutheran Brotherhood Gallery, Gallery of Religious Art, Minneapolis MN

Hillyer, Debbie, *Instructor Arts & Crafts,* Palo Alto Junior Museum & Zoo, Palo Alto CA

Hilmer, Dick, *Performing Arts,* Sun Valley Center for the Arts & Humanities, Dept of Fine Art, Sun Valley ID (S)

Hilton, Alison, *Assoc Prof,* Georgetown University, Dept of Art, Music & Theatre, Washington DC (S)

Hime, Gary D, *Asst Librn,* Wichita Public Library, Wichita KS

Himer, Rachelle, *Admin Asst,* Prairie Art Gallery, Grande Prairie AB

Hinckley, Robert L, *VPres,* Wendell Gilley Museum, Southwest Harbor ME

Hindman, Sandra, *Chmn Dept,* Northwestern University, Evanston, Dept of Art History, Evanston IL (S)

Hinds, B G, *Mgr,* Eastern Shore Art Association, Inc, Eastern Shore Art Center, Fairhope AL

Hinds, Jill, *Instr,* Northwestern Michigan College, Art Dept, Traverse City MI (S)

Hinds, Pat, *Prof,* Antelope Valley College, Art Dept, Division of Fine Arts, Lancaster CA (S)

Hindson, Bradley T, *Assoc Prof,* Rochester Institute of Technology, School of Photographic Arts & Sciences, Rochester NY (S)

Hines, Carol, *Assoc Prof,* Old Dominion University, Art Dept, Norfolk VA (S)

Hines, Jean, *Librn,* New York School of Interior Design Library, New York NY

Hines, Jessica, *Assoc Prof,* Georgia Southern University, Dept of Art, Statesboro GA (S)

Hines, Norman, *Prof,* Pomona College, Dept of Art & Art History, Claremont CA (S)

Hing, Allan, *Interior Design Chmn,* Atlanta College of Art, Atlanta GA (S)

Hinken, Susan, *Technical Services Librn,* University of Portland, Wilson W Clark Memorial Library, Portland OR

Hinkhouse, Jim, *Prof,* Fort Hays State University, Dept of Art, Hays KS (S)

Hinkley, James, *Dir Educ,* Carson County Square House Museum, Panhandle TX

Hinson, Mary Joan, *Dir,* Florida Community College at Jacksonville, South Gallery, Jacksonville FL

Hinson, Monica R, *Exec Dir,* Fremont Center for the Arts, Canon City CO

Hinson, Tom E, *Cur Contemporary Art,* Cleveland Museum of Art, Cleveland OH

Hinton, David, *Dean Academic Affairs,* Watkins Institute College of Art & Design, Nashville TN

Hinton, Don, *Dir,* Dixie College, Southwestern Utah Art Gallery, Saint George UT

Hinton, William, *Dir & Cur,* Louisburg College, Art Gallery, Louisburg NC

Hintz, Glen, *Asst Prof,* Rochester Institute of Technology, School of Art & Design, Rochester NY (S)

Hintze, Rick, *Prof,* Kirkwood Community College, Dept of Fine Arts, Cedar Rapids IA (S)

Hios, Theo, *VPres,* Federation of Modern Painters & Sculptors, New York NY

Hiott, Will, *Dir Historic Houses & Cur,* Clemson University, Fort Hill Plantation, Clemson SC

Hipp, Francis M, *Chmn,* Liberty Life Insurance Company, Greenville SC

Hipsley, Vicky, *Artist,* San Bernardino County Museum, Fine Arts Institute, Redlands CA

Hirano, M, *Assoc Prof,* American University, Dept of Art, Washington DC (S)

Hiratsuka, Yuji, *Asst Prof,* Oregon State University, Dept of Art, Corvallis OR (S)

Hirsch, Barron, *Prof,* Saginaw Valley State University, Dept of Art & Design, University Center MI (S)

Hirsch, Karen, *Dir,* 911 Arts Media Center, Seattle WA

Hirsch, Richard, *Prof,* Rochester Institute of Technology, School of Art & Design, Rochester NY (S)

Hirsch, Robert, *Exec Dir,* Center for Exploratory & Perceptual Art, CEPA Gallery, Buffalo NY

Hirsch, Steven, *Asst Prof,* Pennsylvania College of Technology, Dept of Graphic Communications, Williamsport PA (S)

Hirschel, Anthony, *Dir,* University of Virginia, Bayly Art Museum, Charlottesville VA

Hirschfeld, Barbara, *Dir,* Cuneo Foundation, Museum & Gardens, Vernon Hills IL

Hirschfield, Jim, *Assoc Prof,* University of North Carolina at Chapel Hill, Art Dept, Chapel Hill NC (S)

Hirschorn, Paul, *Head Dept Architecture,* Drexel University, Nesbitt College of Design Arts, Philadelphia PA (S)

Hirshen, Sanford, *Dir,* University of British Columbia, School of Architecture, Vancouver BC (S)

Hisaw, Ruth, *Admin Asst,* Columbia Museum of Art, Columbia SC

Hiscox, Ingeborg, *Art Gallery Dir,* Pointe Claire Cultural Centre, Stewart Hall Art Gallery, Pointe Claire PQ

Hislop, David, *First VPres,* Rochester Historical Society, Rochester NY

Hitch, Henry C, *Pres,* No Man's Land Historical Society Museum, Goodwell OK

Hitchcock, Alix, *Instr,* Wake Forest University, Dept of Art, Winston-Salem NC (S)

Hitchcock, D Michael, *Assoc Prof,* George Washington University, Dept of Art, Washington DC (S)

Hitchings, Sinclair H, *Keeper of Prints,* Boston Public Library, Albert H Wiggin Gallery & Print Department, Boston MA

Hite, Ms Jessie O, *Dir,* University of Texas at Austin, Archer M Huntington Art Gallery, Austin TX

Hitner, Chuck, *Prof Painting & Drawing,* University of Arizona, Dept of Art, Tucson AZ (S)

Hitt, Terri, *Assoc Prof,* University of Dayton, Visual Arts Dept, Dayton OH (S)

Hixon, Nancy, *Asst Dir,* University of Houston, Sarah Campbell Blaffer Gallery, Houston TX

Hlad, Richard, *Asst Prof,* Tarrant County Junior College, Art Dept, Hurst TX (S)

Hluszok, Zenon, *Archivist,* Ukrainian Cultural & Educational Centre, Winnipeg MB

Ho, Abraham P, *Cur,* Saint John's University, Chung-Cheng Art Gallery, Jamaica NY

Ho, Rosa, *Cur Art & Pub Programmes,* University of British Columbia, Museum of Anthropology, Vancouver BC

Hoadley, Mary, *Admin,* Cosanti Foundation, Scottsdale AZ

Hoadley, Mary, *Admin,* Cosanti Foundation, Arcosanti, Scottsdale AZ

Hoar, Bill, *Assoc Prof,* Northern State University, Art Dept, Aberdeen SD (S)

Hoard, Curtis, *Prof,* University of Minnesota, Minneapolis, Dept of Art, Minneapolis MN (S)

Hoback, Mary, *Instr,* Bay De Noc Community College, Art Dept, Escanaba MI (S)

Hobbs, Patricia, *Dir Coll.* Woodrow Wilson Birthplace & Museum, Staunton VA

Hobbs, Robert, *Prof.* Virginia Commonwealth University, Art History Dept, Richmond VA (S)

Hobgood, E Wade, *Prof.* Winthrop University, Dept of Art & Design, Rock Hill SC (S)

Hobgood, Wade, *Dean.* California State University, Long Beach, Art Dept, Long Beach CA (S)

Hobgood, Wade, *Dean.* California State University, Long Beach, Design Dept, Long Beach CA (S)

Hobson, Marlena, *Sr Member.* Mary Baldwin College, Dept of Art, Staunton VA (S)

Hochhausen, Bill, *Co-Pres.* 55 Mercer, New York NY

Hochstetler, Max, *Prof.* Austin Peay State University, Dept of Art, Clarksville TN (S)

Hock, Louis, *Dept Chmn.* University of California, San Diego, Visual Arts Dept, La Jolla CA (S)

Hockett, Roland L, *Assoc Prof.* Gulf Coast Community College, Division of Visual & Performing Arts, Panama City FL (S)

Hocking, Christopher, *Prof.* West Virginia University, College of Creative Arts, Morgantown WV (S)

Hodecker, Paula, *Instr.* Springfield College, Dept of Visual & Performing Arts, Springfield MA (S)

Hodge, David, *Chmn.* University of Wisconsin-Oshkosh, Dept of Art, Oshkosh WI (S)

Hodgens, Mary Lee, *Admin Asst.* Light Work, Syracuse NY

Hodges, Rhoda, *Chmn Board.* Coutts Memorial Museum of Art, Inc, El Dorado KS

Hodges, Stephen, *Asst Prof.* Lamar University, Art Dept, Beaumont TX (S)

Hodgson, J Trevor, *Dir.* Dundas Valley School of Art, Dundas ON (S)

Hodik, Barbara, *Prof.* Rochester Institute of Technology, School of Art & Design, Rochester NY (S)

Hodne, Thomas, *Prof.* University of Manitoba, Faculty of Architecture, Winnipeg MB (S)

Hodnicki, Jill, *Chmn Holyoke Historical Commission.* Wistariahurst Museum, Holyoke MA

Hodosy, Kenneth, *Dir.* Roswell P Flower Memorial Library, Watertown NY

Hodson, Carol, *Asst Prof.* Webster University, Art Dept, Webster Groves MO (S)

Hoel, Randall, *Cur.* Sharon Arts Center, Peterborough NH

Hoell, Peter, *Instr.* Saint Louis Community College at Meramec, Art Dept, Saint Louis MO (S)

Hoeltzel, Susan, *Dir.* Lehman College Art Gallery, Bronx NY

Hoey, Kimberlee, *VPres.* Hunterdon Art Center, Clinton NJ

Hofacket, Katy, *Coordr.* Deming-Luna Mimbres Museum, Deming NM

Hoff, Ken, *Instr.* Century College, Humanities Dept, White Bear Lake MN (S)

Hoff, Leslie, *Head Children's Prog.* Kalamazoo Institute of Arts, KIA School, Kalamazoo MI (S)

Hoff, Roger, *VPres.* Wustum Museum Art Association, Racine WI

Hoffman, Barbara, *Bus Mgr & Art Cur.* Playboy Enterprises, Inc, Chicago IL

Hoffman, Diane, *Instr.* Rhodes College, Dept of Art, Memphis TN (S)

Hoffman, Eva, *Asst Prof.* Tufts University, Dept of Art & Art History, Medford MA (S)

Hoffman, John, *Chmn.* Loras College, Dept of Art, Dubuque IA (S)

Hoffman, Katherine, *Chmn.* Saint Anselm College, Dept of Fine Arts, Manchester NH (S)

Hoffman, Kim, *Assoc Prof.* Western Oregon State College, Creative Arts Division, Visual Arts, Monmouth OR (S)

Hoffman, Lawrence, *Chief Conservator.* Hirshhorn Museum & Sculpture Garden, Washington DC

Hoffman, Lee, *Painting & Drawing.* University of South Alabama, Dept of Art & Art History, Mobile AL (S)

Hoffman, Lorre, *Asst Prof.* University of Colorado at Denver, Dept of Fine Arts, Denver CO (S)

Hoffman, Lothar, *Chmn Graphic Design.* Center for Creative Studies, College of Art & Design, Detroit MI (S)

Hoffman, Neil, *Pres.* Otis School of Art & Design, Fine Arts, Los Angeles CA (S)

Hoffman, Susan, *Exec Dir.* California Confederation of the Arts, Sacramento CA

Hoffman, Tom, *Prof.* University of Maine at Augusta, Division of Fine & Performing Arts, Augusta ME (S)

Hoffmann, John, *Dir Research.* Museum of Holography - Chicago, Chicago IL

Hoffmann, Robert, *Asst Secy for the Sciences.* Smithsonian Institution, Washington DC

Hofmann, Irene, *Asst Cur.* Cranbrook Art Museum, Bloomfield Hills MI

Hogan, James, *Dir & Col Librn.* College of the Holy Cross, Dinand Library, Worcester MA

Hogan, Jean, *Pres.* Concord Museum, Concord MA

Hogarth, Brian, *Cur Educ.* Asian Art Museum of San Francisco, Avery Brundage Collection, San Francisco CA

Hogarth, Brian, *Interim Dir Educ.* Indianapolis Museum of Art, Indianapolis IN

Hoge, Robert W, *Museum Cur.* American Numismatic Association, Museum, Colorado Springs CO

Hogge, David, *Asst Cur.* University of Michigan, Slide & Photograph Collection, Ann Arbor MI

Hogu, Barbara J, *Asst Prof.* City Colleges of Chicago, Malcolm X College, Chicago IL (S)

Hogue, James, *VPres.* Washington Art Association, Washington Depot CT

Hogue, Phillip, *Asst Gen Mgr.* Ozark Folk Center, Ozark Cultural Resource Center, Mountain View AR

Hoi, Samuel, *Dean.* Corcoran School of Art, Washington DC (S)

Holabind, Robin, *VPres.* Sierra Arts Foundation, Reno NV

Holahan, Elizabeth G, *Pres.* Rochester Historical Society, Rochester NY

Holahan, Mary, *Registrar.* Delaware Art Museum, Wilmington DE

Holbach, Joseph, *Registrar.* The Phillips Collection, Washington DC

Holbert, Raymond, *Chairperson.* City College of San Francisco, Art Dept, San Francisco CA (S)

Holbrook, W Paul, *Exec Dir.* American Ceramic Society, Westerville OH

Holcomb, Anna, *Head Dept.* Kansas State University, Art Dept, Manhattan KS (S)

Holcomb, Grant, *Dir.* University of Rochester, Memorial Art Gallery, Rochester NY

Holden, John, *Asst Prof.* Bemidji State University, Visual Arts Dept, Bemidji MN (S)

Holden, Rebecca, *Pres.* Seneca Falls Historical Society Museum, Seneca Falls NY

Holden, Wendy, *Sr Assoc Cur.* University of Michigan, Asian Art Archives, Ann Arbor MI

Holden, Wendy, *Sr Assoc Cur & Asian Art Archives.* University of Michigan, Slide & Photograph Collection, Ann Arbor MI

Holder, Thomas J, *Instr.* University of Nevada, Las Vegas, Dept of Art, Las Vegas NV (S)

Holihan, Michael, *Prof.* Cleveland Institute of Art, Cleveland OH (S)

Holland, Dana, *Instr.* Southwest Texas State University, Dept of Art, San Marcos TX (S)

Holland, Matthew, *VChmn.* Detroit Artists Market, Detroit MI

Holleran, Owen, *Admin Officer.* Chattahoochee Valley Art Museum, LaGrange GA

Holley, Brian, *Dir.* Cleveland Botanical Garden, Eleanor Squire Library, Cleveland OH

Holley, Tara, *Dir Development.* Austin Museum of Art at Laguna Gloria, Austin TX

Holliday, Judith, *Librn.* Cornell University, Fine Arts Library, Ithaca NY

Holliday, Peter, *Instr.* California State University, San Bernardino, Visual Arts, San Bernardino CA (S)

Holliman, Lilly, *Treas.* Biloxi Art Association Inc & Gallery, Biloxi MS

Hollinger, Marian, *Prof.* West Virginia University, College of Creative Arts, Morgantown WV (S)

Hollingsworth, Teresa, *Folklife Adminr.* Florida Folklife Programs, Tallahassee FL

Hollingworth, Keith, *Art Historian.* Greenfield Community College, Art, Graphic Design & Media Communication Dept, Greenfield MA (S)

Hollinshead, Mary, *Asst Prof.* University of Rhode Island, Dept of Art, Kingston RI (S)

Hollis, Sara, *Prof.* Southern University in New Orleans, Fine Arts & Philosophy Dept, New Orleans LA (S)

Hollis, Violet Angeles, *Dir Dance.* Jacksonville University, Dept of Art, Jacksonville FL (S)

Hollis, Wayne, *Instr.* Iowa Lakes Community College, Dept of Art, Estherville IA (S)

Holloman, Michael, *Asst Prof Art.* Seattle University, Fine Arts Dept, Division of Art, Seattle WA (S)

Hollomon, Jim, *Adminr.* National Society of the Colonial Dames, Wilton House Museum, Richmond VA

Hollosy, E Gyuri, *Acad Asst.* Johnson Atelier Technical Institute of Sculpture, Mercerville NJ (S)

Hollow, Michele, *Dir Public Relations.* Jamaica Arts Center, Jamaica NY

Holloway, Amy, *Librn.* African American Historical & Cultural Society, Library, San Francisco CA

Holloway, Ray, *Instr.* Millsaps College, Dept of Art, Jackson MS (S)

Hollrah, Warren, *Archivist.* Westminster College, Winston Churchill Memorial & Library in the United States, Fulton MO

Holly, Michael Ann, *Chmn.* University of Rochester, Dept of Art & Art History, Rochester NY (S)

Holm, Jack, *Asst Prof.* Rochester Institute of Technology, School of Photographic Arts & Sciences, Rochester NY (S)

Holm, Steve, *Prof.* Hillsborough Community College, Fine Arts Dept, Tampa FL (S)

Holma, Viviana, *Deputy.* Howard County Arts Council, Ellicott City MD

Holman, L Bruce, *Instr.* Cottey College, Art Dept, Nevada MO (S)

Holmes, Anne, *Librn.* Maine Photographic Workshops, Carter-Haas Library, Rockport ME

Holmes, Barry, *Instr.* Vancouver Community College, Langara Campus, Dept of Fine Arts, Vancouver BC (S)

Holmes, Carry, *Grad Coordr.* University of Delaware, Dept of Art, Newark DE (S)

Holmes, David, *Prof.* University of Wisconsin-Parkside, Art Dept, Kenosha WI (S)

Holmes, Elizabeth, *Technical Servs.* Wentworth Institute of Technology Library, Boston MA

Holmes, H T, *Dir Archives & Library.* Mississippi Department of Archives & History, Library, Jackson MS

Holmes, Ira, *Dean.* Central Florida Community College, Humanities Dept, Ocala FL (S)

Holmes, Karen, *Cur.* City of Ukiah, Grace Hudson Museum & The Sun House, Ukiah CA

Holmes, Martha, *Asst Prof.* Fort Hays State University, Dept of Art, Hays KS (S)

Holmes, Wendy B, *Chmn.* University of Rhode Island, Dept of Art, Kingston RI (S)

Holmes, Willard, *Deputy Dir.* Whitney Museum of American Art, New York NY

Holmguist, Russell, *Treas.* Swedish American Museum Association of Chicago, Chicago IL

Holo, Selma, *Adjunct Assoc Prof.* University of Southern California, School of Fine Arts, Los Angeles CA (S)

Holo, Selma, *Dir.* University of Southern California, Fisher Gallery, Los Angeles CA

Holoday, Carol, *Instr.* Monterey Peninsula College, Art Dept, Monterey CA (S)

Holownia, Thaddeus, *Prof.* Mount Allison University, Fine Arts Dept, Sackville NB (S)

Holsing, Marilyn, *Chmn Univ Art & Art Educ.* Temple University, Tyler School of Art, Philadelphia PA (S)

Holst, Lise, *Dir.* Hamilton College, Fred L Emerson Gallery, Clinton NY

Holt, Alison, *Catalog Librn.* Art Center College of Design, James Lemont Fogg Memorial Library, Pasadena CA

Holt, Bonnie, *Book Librn.* University of California, Art Dept Library, Davis CA

Holt, Daniel, *Dir.* Dwight D Eisenhower Presidential Library, Abilene KS

Holt, David, *Chmn.* Marymount College, Art Dept, Tarrytown NY (S)

Holt, Jack, *Pres*. Monterey History & Art Association, Monterey CA

Holt, Laura, *Librn*. Museum of New Mexico, Laboratory of Anthropology, Santa Fe NM

Holte, Bettye, *Dir*. Austin Peay State University, Margaret Fort Trahern Gallery, Clarksville TN

Holte, Bettye, *Gallery Cur*. Austin Peay State University, Art Dept Library, Clarksville TN

Holte, Bettye, *Asst Prof*. Austin Peay State University, Dept of Art, Clarksville TN (S)

Holte, Bettye S, *Dir*. Austin Peay State University, Harned Gallery, Clarksville TN

Holtgrewe, Doug, *Prof*. Elmira College, Art Dept, Elmira NY (S)

Holubar, Michael, *Museum Preparator*. Oberlin College, Allen Memorial Art Museum, Oberlin OH

Holubec, Marie, *Slide Librn*. York University, Fine Arts Phase II Slide Library, North York ON

Holubizky, Ihor, *Sr Cur*. Art Gallery of Hamilton, Hamilton ON

Holubizky, Ihor, *Sr Cur*. Art Gallery of Hamilton, Muriel Isabel Bostwick Library, Hamilton ON

Holz, Ronald W, *Div Head Music & Art*. Asbury College, Art Dept, Wilmore KY (S)

Holzer, Harold, *Dir Communications*. The Metropolitan Museum of Art, New York NY

Hom, Meiling, *Asst Prof*. Philadelphia Community College, Dept of Art, Philadelphia PA (S)

Homan, Geoff, *Exec Dir*. Association of Artist-Run Galleries, New York NY

Homan, Geoffrey, *VPres*. New York Artists Equity Association, Inc, New York NY

Homan, Ralph, *Instr*. College of the Sequoias, Art Dept, Visalia CA (S)

Homburg, Connie, *Cur*. Washington University, Gallery of Art, Saint Louis MO

Hommel, William L, *Chmn*. University of Central Oklahoma, Dept of Visual Arts & Design, Edmond OK (S)

Hong, Lynda, *Slide Librn Cur*. Montclair State University, Calcia Fine Arts Slide Library, Upper Montclair NJ

Honig, Ethelyn, *Co-Pres*. 55 Mercer, New York NY

Hood, Craig, *Assoc Prof*. University of New Hampshire, Dept of Arts & Art History, Durham NH (S)

Hood, Gail, *Assoc Prof*. Southeastern Louisiana University, Dept of Visual Arts, Hammond LA (S)

Hood, Gina, *Office Mgr*. Ellen Noel Art Museum of the Permian Basin, Odessa TX

Hood, Graham S, *VPres Coll & Museums*. Colonial Williamsburg Foundation, Williamsburg VA

Hood, Kristine, *Dir Mem & Museum Servs*. Newark Museum Association, The Newark Museum, Newark NJ

Hood, Mary Bryan, *Dir*. Owensboro Museum of Fine Art, Owensboro KY

Hood, Susan, *Assoc Prof*. Auburn University at Montgomery, Dept of Fine Arts, Montgomery AL (S)

Hood, William, *Chmn*. Oberlin College, Dept of Art, Oberlin OH (S)

Hoogstoel, Jewel, *Membership Mgr*. State University of New York at Purchase, Neuberger Museum of Art, Purchase NY

Hook, Charles E, *Assoc Prof*. Florida State University, Art Dept, Tallahassee FL (S)

Hooker, Tony, *Pres*. The Friends of Photography, Ansel Adams Center for Photography, San Francisco CA

Hooks, Judith, *Pres*. Walker's Point Artists Assoc, Gallery 218, Milwaukee WI

Hoone, Jeffrey, *Dir*. Light Work, Syracuse NY

Hooper, Letha, *Asst Cur*. Ellen Noel Art Museum of the Permian Basin, Odessa TX

Hooper, Percy, *Head Design & Technology Dept*. North Carolina State University at Raleigh, School of Design, Raleigh NC (S)

Hoopingarner, Tim, *Dir*. Colorado Mountain College, Fine Arts Gallery, Breckenridge CO

Hoort, Rebecca, *Sr Assoc Cur*. University of Michigan, Slide & Photograph Collection, Ann Arbor MI

Hooten, Joseph, *Instr*. Long Beach City College, Dept of Art, Long Beach CA (S)

Hoover, Heather, *Instr*. University of North Carolina at Charlotte, Dept of Visual Arts, Charlotte NC (S)

Hoover, Jeff, *Chmn*. Illinois Central College, Dept of Fine Arts, East Peoria IL (S)

Hope, Samuel, *Executive Dir*. National Association of Schools of Art & Design, Reston VA

Hopela, Charlene, *Exec Dir*. Saint Cloud Community Arts Council, Saint Cloud MN

Hopkins, Bryan, *Gallery Co-Cur*. Art Studios of Western New York, Buffalo NY

Hopkins, Debra, *Asst Dir Visual Arts*. Scottsdale Center for the Arts, Scottsdale AZ

Hopkins, Henry T, *Dir*. University of California, Los Angeles, UCLA at the Armand Hammer Museum of Art & Cultural Center, Los Angeles CA

Hopkins, Terri, *Instr*. Marylhurst College, Art Dept, Marylhurst OR (S)

Hopkins, Terri M, *Dir*. Marylhurst College, The Art Gym, Marylhurst OR

Hoppa, Doug, *Assoc Dean*. Charles Stewart Mott Community College, Art Area, School of Arts & Humanities, Flint MI (S)

Hoppe, David, *Instr*. California State University, Chico, Art Dept, Chico CA (S)

Hopper, India, *Registrar*. Carolina Art Association, Gibbes Museum of Art, Charleston SC

Hopper, Janette, *Instr*. Columbia Basin College, Esvelt Gallery, Pasco WA (S)

Hopper, W Kenneth, *Asst Prof*. Huntington College, Art Dept, Huntington IN (S)

Hopps, Walter, *Consulting Cur*. Menil Collection, Houston TX

Horan, Pam, *Reference Librn*. University of Portland, Wilson W Clark Memorial Library, Portland OR

Horewitz, Deborah, *Instr*. College of the Canyons, Art Dept, Valencia CA (S)

Hori, Robert, *Gallery Dir*. Japanese American Cultural & Community Center, George J Doizaki Gallery, Los Angeles CA

Horigan, Carol, *Asst Dir*. Pensacola Junior College, Visual Arts Gallery, Pensacola FL

Horigan, Evelyn, *Art & Slide Librn*. California Institute of the Arts Library, Santa Clarita CA

Horlbeck, Frank R, *Prof*. University of Wisconsin, Madison, Dept of Art History, Madison WI (S)

Horn, B, *Assoc Prof*. Northern Arizona University, School of Art & Design, Flagstaff AZ (S)

Horn, Larry, *Dir Educ*. Colorado Institute of Art, Denver CO (S)

Horn, Ralph, *Chmn*. First Tennessee National Corp, First Tennessee Heritage Collection, Memphis TN

Horn, Robert, *Assoc Dir*. NAB Gallery, Chicago IL

Horn, Susan, *Vis Prof*. Nebraska Wesleyan University, Art Dept, Lincoln NE (S)

Hornbuckle, Heather, *Coll Mgr*. Marion Koogler McNay Art Museum, San Antonio TX

Horne, Adele, *Membership Asst*. Houston Center For Photography, Houston TX

Horne, Field, *Cur*. National Museum of Racing, National Museum of Racing & Hall of Fame, Saratoga Springs NY

Horne, Meade B, *Dir*. Edgecombe County Cultural Arts Council, Inc, Blount-Bridgers House, Hobson Pittman Memorial Gallery, Tarboro NC

Horne, Ralph, *Prof*. Pennsylvania College of Technology, Dept of Graphic Communications, Williamsport PA (S)

Horne-Leshinsky, Jody, *Marketing Adminr*. Broward County Board of Commissioners Cultural Affairs Divison, Fort Lauderdale FL

Horner, Dick, *Dir Performing Arts*. Palm Springs Desert Museum, Palm Springs CA

Horner, Edward W, *Exec VPres Develop & Public Affairs*. The Art Institute of Chicago, Chicago IL

Hornik, Heidi, *Dir*. Baylor University, Martin Museum of Art, Waco TX

Hornik, Heidi J, *Asst Prof*. Baylor University, Dept of Art, Waco TX (S)

Horning, Lisa, *Prof*. Ocean County College, Humanities Dept, Toms River NJ (S)

Hornor, Elizabeth S, *Coordr Educ Progs*. Emory University, Michael C Carlos Museum, Atlanta GA

Horowicz, Kari E, *Librn*. The Buffalo Fine Arts Academy, G Robert Strauss Jr Memorial Library, Buffalo NY

Horowitz, Corinne Gillet, *Cur Educ*. University of California, Santa Barbara, University Art Museum, Santa Barbara CA

Horrell, Jeffrey L, *Librn*. Harvard University, Fine Arts Library, Cambridge MA

Horrocks, Sandra, *Public Relations Mgr*. Philadelphia Museum of Art, Philadelphia PA

Horsey, Ann, *Cur Coll*. Historical & Cultural Affairs, Delaware State Museums, Dover DE

Horsfield, Kate, *Dir*. School of Art Institute of Chicago, Video Data Bank, Chicago IL

Horst, Randy, *Dir*. Western Montana College, Art Gallery/Museum, Dillon MT

Horsting, Archana, *Exec Dir*. Kala Institute, Berkeley CA

Hortas, Carlos, *Dean*. Hunter College, Art Dept, New York NY (S)

Horth, Monique, *Temporary Exhib*. Canadian Museum of Nature, Musee Canadien de la Nature, Ottawa ON

Horton, Anna, *Head Art & Music Dept*. Public Library of Cincinnati & Hamilton County, Art & Music Dept, Cincinnati OH

Horton, Christopher, *Assoc Prof*. University of Hartford, Hartford Art School, West Hartford CT (S)

Horton, Constance, *Pres*. Kent Art Association, Inc, Gallery, Kent CT

Horton, Lon, *Pres*. Wisconsin Fine Arts Association, Inc, Ozaukee Art Center, Cedarburg WI

Horton, Lynne M, *Cur Hist*. The Sandwich Historical Society, Inc, Sandwich Glass Museum, Sandwich MA

Horton, Nell, *Librn*. Nelda C & H J Lutcher Stark Foundation, Stark Museum of Art, Orange TX

Horton-Trippe, Shelley, *Adjunct Assoc*. College of Santa Fe, Art Dept, Santa Fe NM (S)

Horvat, Krisjohn O, *Prof*. Rhode Island College, Art Dept, Providence RI (S)

Horvitz, Suzanne, *Foundation Dir & Trustee*. Foundation for Today's Art, Nexus Gallery, Philadelphia PA

Horwitz, Michael J, *Pres*. Cleveland Museum of Art, Cleveland OH

Hose, Henry, *Gallery Dir*. Mercer County Community College, The Gallery, Trenton NJ

Hose, Henry, *Cur*. Mercer County Community College, Arts & Communication/Engineering Technology, Trenton NJ (S)

Hosey, Terrie, *VPres*. Art Association of Harrisburg, School & Galleries, Harrisburg PA

Hoshine, Marvin, *Chmn*. Queens College, Art Dept, Flushing NY (S)

Hoskin, Denise, *Office Mgr*. Dalhousie University, Art Gallery, Halifax NS

Hosley, William, *Cur Decorative Arts*. Wadsworth Atheneum, Hartford CT

Hostetter, David, *Cur Planetarium*. Lafayette Natural History Museum, Planetarium & Nature Station, Lafayette LA

Hotchkiss, Holly, *Treas*. Arts Iowa City, Art Center & Gallery, Iowa City IA

Hotchkiss, Rollin, *Librn*. Berkshire Museum, Pittsfield MA

Hotchner, Holly, *Dir*. American Craft Council, American Craft Museum, New York NY

Hotheinz, Rudolph H, *Assoc Prof*. Virginia Western Community College, Commercial Art, Fine Art & Photography, Roanoke VA (S)

Hough, Katherine, *Cur*. Palm Springs Desert Museum, Library, Palm Springs CA

Hough, Katherine Plake, *Dir Coll & Exhib*. Palm Springs Desert Museum, Palm Springs CA

Hough, Melissa, *Dir*. CIGNA Corporation, CIGNA Museum & Art Collection, Philadelphia PA

Houghtaling, Kim, *Dir & Cur*. Swift Current National Exhibition Centre, Swift Current SK

Houghton, Barbara, *Chmn*. Northern Kentucky University, Art Dept, Highland Heights KY (S)

Houlihan, Genni, *Librn*. Phoenix Art Museum, Art Research Library, Phoenix AZ

House, Pat, *Dir Develop & Marketing*. Bower's Museum, Santa Ana CA

Houseman, John, *Dir.* Portland Children's Museum, Portland OR

Houser, Caroline, *Assoc Prof.* Smith College, Art Dept, Northampton MA (S)

Housman, Russell, *Prof.* Nassau Community College, Art Dept, Garden City NY (S)

Houston, David, *Dir.* Clemson University, Rudolph E Lee Gallery, Clemson SC

Houston, William, *Artist & Residence.* Carson-Newman College, Art Dept, Jefferson City TN (S)

Hoveman, Alice, *Dir.* Redding Museum of Art & History, Redding CA

Howard, Angela, *Assoc Prof.* Rutgers, the State University of New Jersey, Graduate Program in Art History, New Brunswick NJ (S)

Howard, Carolyn, *Instr.* Wayne Art Center, Wayne PA (S)

Howard, Cordelia, *Dir Libr Servs.* Long Beach Public Library, Long Beach CA

Howard, Deborah, *Museum Shop Mgr.* Danville Museum of Fine Arts & History, Danville VA

Howard, Jan, *Assoc Cur Prints Drawings & Photographs,* Baltimore Museum of Art, Baltimore MD

Howard, Joey, *Admin Asst & Preparator,* City Gallery of Contemporary Art, Raleigh NC

Howard, Peter, *Chmn.* Troy State University, Dept of Art & Classics, Troy AL (S)

Howat, John K, *Chmn American Art Dept,* The Metropolitan Museum of Art, New York NY

Howe, Eunice, *Assoc Prof.* University of Southern California, School of Fine Arts, Los Angeles CA (S)

Howe, Katherine, *Cur Decorative Arts.* Museum of Fine Arts, Houston TX

Howe, Kathleen, *Cur Prints/Photos.* University of New Mexico, University Art Museum, Albuquerque NM

Howe, Thomas, *Chmn.* Southwestern University, Art Dept, Georgetown TX (S)

Howell, Anthony, *Prof,* Western New Mexico University, Dept of Expressive Arts, Silver City NM (S)

Howell, Bob, *Prof,* Louisiana College, Dept of Art, Pineville LA (S)

Howell, Joyce B, *Assoc Prof.* Virginia Wesleyan College, Art Dept of the Humanities Division, Norfolk VA (S)

Howell, Robert D, *Prof.* California Polytechnic State University at San Luis Obispo, Dept of Art & Design, San Luis Obispo CA (S)

Howell, Susan, *Adminr,* University of Virginia, Bayly Art Museum, Charlottesville VA

Howell, Tom, *Chmn.* Porterville College, Dept of Fine Arts, Porterville CA (S)

Howes, Stephen, *VChmn,* Town of Cummington Historical Commission, Kingman Tavern Historical Museum, Cummington MA

Howk, Cynthia, *Res Coordr,* Landmark Society of Western New York, Inc, Wenrich Memorial Library, Rochester NY

Howkins, Mary Ball, *Assoc Prof.* Rhode Island College, Art Dept, Providence RI (S)

Howland, Margaret, *Visitor Servs.* Harvard University, Harvard University Art Museums, Cambridge MA

Hownion, Morris, *Chief Cataloguer,* New York City Technical College, Namm Hall Library and Learning Resource Center, Brooklyn NY

Howorth, Patricia, *Projects Mgr.* Queen's University, Agnes Etherington Art Centre, Kingston ON

Howsare, Susan, *Asst Prof.* Waynesburg College, Dept of Fine Arts, Waynesburg PA (S)

Hoxie, Fredrick E, *VPres Research & Educ.* Newberry Library, Chicago IL

Hoy, Harold, *Dir.* Lane Community College, Art Dept Gallery, Eugene OR

Hoydysh, Daria, *Cur.* Ukrainian Institute of America, Inc, New York NY

Hoyt, Edward, *Pres.* Museum of the Hudson Highlands, Cornwall on Hudson NY

Hranka, T, *Cur & Mgr.* Wilfrid Laurier University, Robert Langen Gallery, Waterloo ON

Hrehov, John, *Asst Prof.* Indiana-Purdue University, Dept of Fine Arts, Fort Wayne IN (S)

Hruska, Kay, *Asst Prof.* Mount Mary College, Art Dept, Milwaukee WI (S)

Hrycelak, George, *Dir & Pres.* Ukrainian National Museum & Library, Chicago IL

Hsu, Ginger C, *Asst Prof.* University of California, Riverside, Dept of the History of Art, Riverside CA (S)

Hu, Zheng, *Exhib Designer.* University at Albany, State University of New York, University Art Museum, Albany NY

Hua, Alina, *Special Events Coordr.* Wing Luke Asian Museum, Seattle WA

Hubbard, John D, *Prof.* Northern Michigan University, Dept of Art & Design, Marquette MI (S)

Hubbard, Martin, *Art Instr.* Kellogg Community College, Visual & Performing Arts Dept, Battle Creek MI (S)

Hubbard, Peggy, *Dir Develop.* University of Rochester, Memorial Art Gallery, Rochester NY

Hubbard, Rita, *Head Dept.* Christopher Newport University, Arts & Communications, Newport News VA (S)

Huber, Fran, *Registrar.* Indiana University, Art Museum, Bloomington IN

Huber, Gerard, *Coordr Grad Programs.* East Texas State University, Dept of Art, Commerce TX (S)

Huber, Mary, *Dir.* City of Cedar Falls, Iowa, James & Meryl Hearst Center for the Arts, Cedar Falls IA

Huberman, Brian, *Prof.* Rice University, Dept of Art & Art History, Houston TX (S)

Hubert, Thomas, *Dept Chmn.* Mercyhurst College, Dept of Art, Erie PA (S)

Hubner, S Rosemarita, *Prof.* Mount Mary College, Art Dept, Milwaukee WI (S)

Hubschmitt, William, *Dept Chmn.* Eastern Illinois University, Art Dept, Charleston IL (S)

Huculak, Father Larry, *Dir.* Basilian Fathers, Mundare AB

Huculak, Father Larry, *Dir.* Basilian Fathers, Library, Mundare AB

Hudak, Jane R, *Assoc Prof.* Georgia Southern University, Dept of Art, Statesboro GA (S)

Huddleston, John, *Chmn.* Middlebury College, Dept of Art, Middlebury VT (S)

Hudnut, David, *Pres.* California Historical Society, El Molino Viejo, San Marino CA

Hudson, Bradiey, *Registrar & Preparator.* Syracuse University, Joe & Emily Lowe Art Gallery, Syracuse NY

Hudson, Carol J, *Public Information.* Schenectady Museum Planetarium & Visitors Center, Schenectady NY

Hudson, David C, *Pres & Exec Dir.* Arts Council of Winston-Salem & Forsyth County, Winston-Salem NC

Hudson, Eldered, *Prof.* University of North Carolina at Charlotte, Dept of Visual Arts, Charlotte NC (S)

Hudson, Jennifer, *Cur Coll.* Dacotah Prairie Museum, Ruth Bunker Memorial Library, Aberdeen SD

Hudson, Joseph, *Pres.* Detroit Institute of Arts, Founders Society, Detroit MI

Hudson, Kimberly, *Cur Educ.* Visual Arts Center of Northwest Florida, Panama City FL

Hudson, Myrna, *Adult Serv Div Coordr.* Wichita Public Library, Wichita KS

Hudson, Raiph M, *VPres.* Kappa Pi International Honorary Art Fraternity, Crestwood MO

Hudson, Rod, *General Mgr.* Chilliwack Community Arts Council, Chilliwack BC

Hudson, Susan M, *Registrar.* Cincinnati Institute of Fine Arts, Taft Museum, Cincinnati OH

Huebler, Douglas, *Instr.* Truro Center for the Arts at Castle Hill, Inc, Truro MA (S)

Huebner, Carla, *Assoc Prof.* Mount Mary College, Art Dept, Milwaukee WI (S)

Huebner, Gregory, *Chmn.* Wabash College, Art Dept, Crawfordsville IN (S)

Huebner, Roger, *Prof.* East Central University, Art Dept, Ada OK (S)

Huebner-Venezia, Carol, *Asst Prof.* C W Post Center of Long Island University, School of Visual & Performing Arts, Brookville NY (S)

Huebsch, Randolph, *VPres.* Manhattan Graphics Center, New York NY (S)

Huenink, Peter, *Assoc Prof.* Vassar College, Art Dept, Poughkeepsie NY (S)

Huether, Mary, *Asst Instr.* Dickinson State University, Dept of Art, Dickinson ND (S)

Huff, David, *Educ.* Tom Thomson Memorial Art Gallery, Owen Sound ON

Huff, David, *Educ.* Tom Thomson Memorial Art Gallery, Library, Owen Sound ON

Huff, John, *Interior Design.* University of Georgia, Franklin College of Arts & Sciences, Lamar Dodd School of Art, Athens GA (S)

Huff, Richard E, *Exec Dir.* Irving Arts Center, Main Gallery & New Talent Gallery, Irving TX

Huff, Robert, *Chmn.* Miami-Dade Community College, Visual Arts Dept, Miami FL (S)

Huffman, Bill, *Admin Dir.* A Space, Toronto ON

Huffman, Lorilee, *Cur Colls.* Southern Illinois University, University Museum, Carbondale IL

Huffman, Mike, *Assoc Prof.* Norwich University, Dept of Philosophy, Religion & Fine Arts, Northfield VT (S)

Hufford, Gary, *Instr.* The Arkansas Arts Center, Museum School, Little Rock AR (S)

Hughen, Dan, *Dir Admin.* Tallahassee Museum of History & Natural Science, Tallahassee FL

Hughen, Lawrence, *Pres.* Sturdivant Hall, Selma AL

Hughes, Danny R, *Arts Educ Dir.* Arts Partnership of Greater Spartanburg, Inc, Spartanburg Arts Center, Spartanburg SC

Hughes, Gary, *Chief Cur.* New Brunswick Museum, Saint John NB

Hughes, Gary, *Head.* New Brunswick Museum, Library, Saint John NB

Hughes, Jeffrey, *Asst Prof.* Webster University, Art Dept, Webster Groves MO (S)

Hughes, John, *Assoc Prof.* Missouri Western State College, Art Dept, Saint Joseph MO (S)

Hughes, Julie, *Treas.* Kings County Historical Society and Museum, Hampton NB

Hughes, Kathleen R, *Educ Coordr.* Washburn University, Mulvane Art Museum, Topeka KS

Hughes, Kevin, *Asst Prof.* Vincennes University Junior College, Art Dept, Vincennes IN (S)

Hughes, Susan, *Educ Specialist.* Shaker Village of Pleasant Hill, Harrodsburg KY

Hughes, Woody, *Instr.* Dowling College, Dept of Visual Arts, Oakdale NY (S)

Hughley, John, *Prof.* North Carolina Central University, Art Dept, Durham NC (S)

Hughston, Milan R, *Librn.* Amon Carter Museum, Library, Fort Worth TX

Huisman, Carl J, *Prof.* Calvin College, Art Dept, Grand Rapids MI (S)

Hulet, Grant, *Prof.* Salt Lake Community College, Graphic Design Dept, Salt Lake City UT (S)

Hull, David, *Librn.* San Francisco Maritime National Historical Park, National Maritime Museum, San Francisco CA

Hull, David, *Principal Librn.* San Francisco Maritime National Historical Park, J Porter Shaw Library, San Francisco CA

Hull, Joan C, *Exec Dir.* The Bostonian Society, Old State House Museum, Boston MA

Hull, John, *Asst Prof.* University of Mississippi, Dept of Art, University MS (S)

Hull, Orris, *Acting Cur.* Owen Sound Historical Society, Marine & Rail Heritage Museum, Owen Sound ON

Hull, Susan, *Exec Dir.* Community Arts Council of Vancouver, Vancouver BC

Hull, Vida, *Assoc Prof.* East Tennessee State University, Dept of Art & Design, Johnson City TN (S)

Huls, Chris, *Asst Building Engineer.* Fort Worth Art Association, Modern Art Museum of Fort Worth, Fort Worth TX

Hulten, Kim, *Bookkeeper,* Cascade County Historical Society, Cascade County Historical Museum & Archives, Great Falls MT

Hultman, John, *VPres.* Roswell Museum & Art Center, Roswell NM

Hults, Linda, *Chmn.* College of Wooster, Dept of Art, Wooster OH (S)

Humberston, Margaret, *Head Library & Archive Coll.* Springfield Library & Museums Association, Connecticut Valley Historical Museum, Springfield MA

Humble, Douglas, *Galleries Asst.* Galleries of the Claremont Colleges, Claremont CA

Hume, Robert, *Instr.* San Jacinto College-North, Art Dept, Houston TX (S)

Hummel, Sharman, *Instr.* Milwaukee Area Technical College, Graphic Arts Division, Milwaukee WI (S)

Hummer, Philip, *Chmn.* Chicago Historical Society, Chicago IL

Humphery, Meeghan, *Admin Asst & Visual Arts & Exhibit Coordr.* Ashtabula Arts Center, Ashtabula OH

Humphrey, John, *Assoc Prof.* University of Michigan, Ann Arbor, Dept of History of Art, Ann Arbor MI (S)

Humphrey, Karen, *Pres.* Minnesota Historical Society, Saint Paul MN

Humphrey, Rebecca, *Prof.* James Madison University, School of Art & Art History, Harrisonburg VA (S)

Humphrey, Rita S, *Cur Manuscripts.* Baylor University, Armstrong Browning Library, Waco TX

Humphreys, Ed, *Chmn.* Whitman College, Art Dept, Walla Walla WA (S)

Humphries, Kim, *Preparator.* Contemporary Arts Center, Cincinnati OH

Hungerford, Constance Cain, *Prof.* Swarthmore College, Dept of Art, Swarthmore PA (S)

Hunnibell, S, *Instr.* Community College of Rhode Island, Dept of Art, Warwick RI (S)

Hunt, David, *Dir.* Nelda C & H J Lutcher Stark Foundation, Stark Museum of Art, Orange TX

Hunt, David, *Assoc Prof.* Fort Lewis College, Art Dept, Durango CO (S)

Hunt, Dot, *Librn Asst.* North Carolina State University, Harrye Lyons Design Library, Raleigh NC

Hunt, Garrett, *Visual Arts Dir.* Arts Center of the Ozarks Gallery, Springdale AR

Hunt, Gregory K, *Dean.* Catholic University of America, School of Architecture & Planning, Washington DC (S)

Hunt, John Dixon, *Chmn.* University of Pennsylvania, Dept of Landscape Architecture & Regional Planning, Philadelphia PA (S)

Hunt, Mary, *Exec Dir.* South Carolina Artisans Center, Walterboro SC

Hunt, Susan, *Prof.* University of Wisconsin-Stout, Dept of Art & Design, Menomonie WI (S)

Hunter, Carolyn, *Art Librn.* Public Library of Charlotte & Mecklenburg County, Charlotte NC

Hunter, James, *Dir.* Huronia Museum, Midland ON

Hunter, Jessica, *Cur.* Paris Gibson Square, Museum of Art, Great Falls MT

Hunter, John, *Art & Theatre Arts Chmn.* Washburn University of Topeka, Dept of Art & Theatre Arts, Topeka KS (S)

Hunter, John, *Chmn & Prof.* Cleveland State University, Art Dept, Cleveland OH (S)

Hunter, John K, *VPres Admin.* Philadelphia Art Alliance, Philadelphia PA

Hunter, Lance, *Gallery Dir.* Brescia College, Anna Eaton Stout Memorial Art Gallery, Owensboro KY

Hunter, Rosetta, *Chmn.* Seattle Central Community College, Humanities - Social Sciences Division, Seattle WA (S)

Hunter, Sharon, *Acad Dean.* Lyme Academy of Fine Arts, Old Lyme CT (S)

Hunter, Sharon, *Acad Dean.* Lyme Academy of Fine Arts, Old Lyme CT

Hunter, Sue, *Western Representative.* Arizona Watercolor Association, Phoenix AZ

Hunter, Terry K, *Assoc Prof.* South Carolina State University, Art Dept, Orangeburg SC (S)

Hurbet, Tom, *Second VPres Exhib.* Arizona Artist Guild, Phoenix AZ

Hurlbert, Susan, *Clerk.* Burbank Public Library, Warner Research Collection, Burbank CA

Hurrigan, William, *Cur Media Arts.* Ohio State University, Wexner Center for the Arts, Columbus OH

Hurry, Robert J, *Registrar.* Calvert Marine Museum, Solomons MD

Hursh, Robert D, *Pres Board of Mgrs.* University of Rochester, Memorial Art Gallery, Rochester NY

Hurst, Andrew W, *Exhib Coordr.* University of Tennessee, Frank H McClung Museum, Knoxville TN

Hurst, Andrew W, *Exhibits Coodr.* University of Tennessee, Eleanor Dean Audigier Art Collection, Knoxville TN

Hurst, Louann, *Dir.* Lee County Library, Tupelo MS

Hurst, William, *Dir Dept Arts & Science.* Dominican College of Blauvelt, Art Dept, Orangeburg NY (S)

Hurt, Laquita, *Office Mgr.* Carson County Square House Museum, Panhandle TX

Hurt, Susanne, *Recording Secy.* American Artists Professional League, Inc, New York NY

Hurwitz, Jeffrey, *Photographer in Residence.* Moravian College, Dept of Art, Bethlehem PA (S)

Husband, Timothy, *Cur.* The Metropolitan Museum of Art, The Cloisters, New York NY

Huseboe, Arthur R, *Dir.* Augustana College, Center for Western Studies, Sioux Falls SD

Huskey, Susan, *Instr.* Dunedin Fine Arts & Cultural Center, Dunedin FL (S)

Huskinson, Ann G, *Exec Dir.* Red River Valley Museum, Vernon TX

Huss, Kathryn, *Admin.* University of Michigan, Museum of Art, Ann Arbor MI

Hussey, Christopher, *Pres.* Pilgrim Society, Pilgrim Hall Museum, Plymouth MA

Hussey, Kathryn, *Registrar.* Brick Store Museum & Library, Kennebunk ME

Hustboe, Arthur R, *Exec Dir.* Augustana College, Center for Western Studies, Sioux Falls SD

Huston, Alan, *Assoc Prof.* Winthrop University, Dept of Art & Design, Rock Hill SC (S)

Huston, Kathleen, *City Librn.* Milwaukee Public Library, Art, Music & Recreation Dept, Milwaukee WI

Hutchens, James, *Chmn Dept.* Ohio State University, Dept of Art Education, Columbus OH (S)

Hutchins, Lee, *Exec Dir.* Society for Photographic Education, Dallas TX

Hutchins, Louis, *Cur.* Old Slater Mill Association, Slater Mill Historic Site, Pawtucket RI

Hutchinson, Don, *Instr.* Vancouver Community College, Langara Campus, Dept of Fine Arts, Vancouver BC (S)

Hutchinson, Max, *Pres.* Max Hutchinson's Sculpture Fields, Kenoza Lake NY

Hutchinson, William, *Acting Chmn.* University of California, Los Angeles, Dept of Design, Los Angeles CA (S)

Hutflies, Ann, *Educ & Outreach.* University of Illinois, Museum of Natural History, Champaign IL

Huth, Nancy, *Asst Dir & Cur Educ.* Ball State University, Museum of Art, Muncie IN

Huts, Linda C, *Pres.* Midwest Art History Society, Wooster OH

Hutsell, Barbara, *Dir.* Atlanta College of Art Library, Atlanta GA

Hutson, Bill, *Instr.* Creighton University, Fine & Performing Arts Dept, Omaha NE (S)

Hutson, Victoria, *Instr.* Vermilion Community College, Art Dept, Ely MN (S)

Hutterer, Karl, *Dir.* University of Washington, Thomas Burke Memorial Washington State Museum, Seattle WA

Hutto, Samuel L, *Assoc Prof.* Mercer University, Art Dept, Macon GA (S)

Hutton, John, *Instr.* Salem College, Art Dept, Winston-Salem NC (S)

Hutton, Kathleen F B, *Coordr Educ.* Reynolda House Museum of American Art, Winston-Salem NC

Hutton, Peter, *Instr.* Bard College, Milton Avery Graduate School of the Arts, Annandale-on-Hudson NY (S)

Hutton, Robert, *Prof.* Marshall University, Dept of Art, Huntington WV (S)

Hutton, Tom, *Asst Prof.* Salem College, Art Dept, Winston-Salem NC (S)

Hyden, John, *Registrar.* Nicolaysen Art Museum & Discovery Center, Childrens Discovery Center, Casper WY

Hyden, John, *Registrar.* Nicolaysen Art Museum & Discovery Center, Museum, Casper WY

Hyland, Douglas, *Dir.* San Antonio Museum of Art, San Antonio TX

Hyleck, Walter, *Dept Chair.* Berea College, Art Dept Library, Berea KY

Hyleck, Walter, *Prof.* Berea College, Art Dept, Berea KY (S)

Hylle, John, *Treas.* Owatonna Arts Center, Community Arts Center, Owatonna MN

Hyman, Debra, *Coll Mgr.* International Museum of Cartoon Art, Library, Boca Raton FL

Hyman, Lewis B, *VPres.* Wilmington Trust Company, Wilmington DE

Hynes, William, *Chmn Art Dept.* Shippensburg University, Art Dept, Shippensburg PA (S)

Hynes, William Q, *Dir.* Shippensburg University, Kauffman Gallery, Shippensburg PA

Hysell, David M, *Prof.* Rhode Island College, Art Dept, Providence RI (S)

Iacono, Domenic J, *Assoc Dir.* Syracuse University, Art Collection, Syracuse NY

Iannone, Mary, *Textile Cur.* Amherst Museum, Amherst NY

Ibach, Dick, *Asst Prof.* Spokane Falls Community College, Fine Arts Dept, Spokane WA (S)

Ibbitson, R, *Fine Arts Technician.* Mount Allison University, Owens Art Gallery, Sackville NB

Iberti, Elissa, *Instr.* Dowling College, Dept of Visual Arts, Oakdale NY (S)

Ice, Joyce, *Asst Dir.* Museum of New Mexico, Museum of International Folk Art, Santa Fe NM

Ichelson, Myrna, *Coordr Coll.* Shell Canada Ltd, Calgary AB

Ichiyama, D Y, *Head Dept.* Purdue University, West Lafayette, Dept of Visual & Performing Arts, Div of Art & Design, West Lafayette IN (S)

Ida, Richard, *Div Dean.* Solano Community College, Division of Fine & Applied Art, Suisun City CA (S)

Ide, Harriett, *Pres.* Almond Historical Society, Inc, Hagadorn House, The 1800-37 Museum, Almond NY

Iden, Kris, *Asst Prof.* Mary Baldwin College, Dept of Art, Staunton VA (S)

Igler, Aaron, *Public Relations Dir.* Fabric Workshop & Museum, Philadelphia PA

Igwe, Kod, *Chmn.* Claflin College, Dept of Art, Orangeburg SC (S)

Ikedo, Yoshiro, *Prof.* Kansas State University, Art Dept, Manhattan KS (S)

Iler, Henry, *Assoc Prof.* Georgia Southern University, Dept of Art, Statesboro GA (S)

Iles, Bill R, *Chmn.* McNeese State University, Dept of Visual Arts, Lake Charles LA (S)

Imami-Paydar, Niloofar, *Assoc Cur Textiles & Costumes.* Indianapolis Museum of Art, Indianapolis IN

Imm-Stroukoff, Eumie, *Assoc Librn Reference.* Museum of Modern Art, Library, New York NY

Indeck, Karen, *Dir.* University of Illinois At Chicago, Gallery 400, Chicago IL

Indick, Janet, *Pres.* National Association of Women Artists, Inc, New York NY

Infantino, Cynthia, *Adult Servs Coordr.* Lake Forest Library, Fine Arts Dept, Lake Forest IL

Ingalls, Chris, *Cur Educ.* Florida International University, The Art Museum at FIU, Miami FL

Ingber, Rabbi Abie, *Exec Dir.* Hillel Foundation, Hillel Jewish Student Center Gallery, Cincinnati OH

Ingberman, Jeannette, *Dir.* Exit Art-The First World, Inc, New York NY

Inglat, Amy, *Gift Shop Mgr.* Muskegon Museum of Art, Muskegon MI

Inks, Ed, *Chmn.* Santa Barbara City College, Fine Arts Dept, Santa Barbara CA (S)

Inlow, Terry, *Prof.* Wilmington College, Art Dept, Wilmington OH (S)

Inman, Jan, *Instr.* La Sierra University, Art Dept, Riverside CA (S)

Inman, Marcie J, *Cur.* Irving Arts Center, Main Gallery & New Talent Gallery, Irving TX

Inness, Carrie J, *Dir.* Galesburg Civic Art Center, Galesburg IL

Insalaco, Thomas F, *Prof*, Finger Lakes Community College, Visual & Performing Arts Dept, Canandaigua NY (S)

Inserra, Margaret, *Acting Dir*, Lighthouse Gallery & School of Art, Tequesta FL

Inserra, Margaret, *Acting Dir*, Lighthouse Gallery & School of Art, Library, Tequesta FL

Insield, Warren, *Chmn*, Hofstra University, Department of Fine Arts, Hempstead NY (S)

Inwood, Judy, *First Asst*, Public Library of Cincinnati & Hamilton County, Art & Music Dept, Cincinnati OH

Iott, Anne, *Dir*, Tidewater Community College, Art Dept, Portsmouth VA (S)

Ippoldo, Diane, *Instr*, Wayne Art Center, Wayne PA (S)

Ipson, Daniel A, *Dean Fine Arts*, Hartnell College, Art & Photography Dept, Salinas CA (S)

Iraheta, Oscar, *Human Resources*, The Phillips Collection, Washington DC

Irby, Frank, *Instr*, Pacific Northwest College of Art, Portland OR (S)

Ireland, Lynda, *Cur*, Autozone, Autozone Corporation Collection, Memphis TN

Ireland, Martha, *Cur*, Princeton Antiques Bookservice, Art Marketing Reference Library, Atlantic City NJ

Irestone, Sally, *Business Adminr*, Fresno Metropolitan Museum, Fresno CA

Irvan, Alice M, *Dir Marketing & Communications*, Indianapolis Museum of Art, Indianapolis IN

Irvin, Stan, *Dir*, Saint Edward's University, Fine Arts Exhibit Program, Austin TX

Irvine, Betty Jo, *Head Librn*, Indiana University, Fine Arts Library, Bloomington IN

Irvine, Brenda, *Educ Officer*, City of Woodstock, Woodstock Art Gallery, Woodstock ON

Irvine, Doug, *Asst Artifact Center Cur*, Spertus Institute of Jewish Studies, Spertus Museum, Chicago IL

Irvine, Mary, *Visitor Serv*, Alaska State Museum, Juneau AK

Isaacson, Gene, *Art Instr*, Rancho Santiago College, Art Dept, Santa Ana CA (S)

Isaacson, Gene, *Advisor to Board*, Orange County Center for Contemporary Art, Santa Ana CA

Isaacson, Joel, *Prof*, University of Michigan, Ann Arbor, Dept of History of Art, Ann Arbor MI (S)

Isaacson, M, *Instr*, Humboldt State University, College of Arts & Humanities, Arcata CA (S)

Isaacson, Marcia, *Prof*, University of Florida, Dept of Art, Gainesville FL (S)

Isabelle, Margot, *Librn*, Massachusetts College of Art, Morton R Godine Library, Boston MA

Isaksen, Mark, *Acting Cur*, Independence Seaport Museum, Philadelphia PA

Isenberg, E Duane, *Asst Prof*, Mohawk Valley Community College, Advertising Design & Production, Utica NY (S)

Ishikawa, Joseph, *Dir Emeritus*, Michigan State University, Kresge Art Museum, East Lansing MI

Isman, Bonnie, *Dir*, Jones Library, Inc, Amherst MA

Ison, Mary M, *Head Reference Section*, Library of Congress, Prints & Photographs Division, Washington DC

Ison, Susan, *Dir*, Loveland Museum Gallery, Loveland CO

Isto, Ted, *Instr*, Umpqua Community College, Fine & Performing Arts Dept, Roseburg OR (S)

Istrabadi, Juliet, *Asst Cur*, Valparaiso University, Brauer Museum of Art, Valparaiso IN

Itami, Michi, *Dir Grad Studies*, City College of New York, Art Dept, New York NY (S)

Itter, William, *Prof*, Indiana University, Bloomington, Henry Radford Hope School of Fine Arts, Bloomington IN (S)

Iuorno-Shirley, Mary Rose, *Public Relations Coordr*, Lehigh County Historical Society, Allentown PA

Ivers, Bob, *Pres*, Chautauqua Center for the Visual Arts, Chautauqua NY

Ivers, Louise, *Chmn*, California State University, Dominguez Hills, Art Dept, Carson CA (S)

Ives, Colta, *Cur-in-Charge Prints & Illustrated Books*, The Metropolitan Museum of Art, New York NY

Ives, Jack, *Asst Dir Archaeology & Ethnology*, Department of Community Development, Provincial Museum of Alberta, Edmonton AB

Ivey, Paul, *Asst Prof Art History*, University of Arizona, Dept of Art, Tucson AZ (S)

Ivins, Millie, *Chmn Illustration*, Moore College of Art & Design, Philadelphia PA (S)

Ivory, Carol, *Asst Prof*, Winthrop University, Dept of Art & Design, Rock Hill SC (S)

Ivory, Paul W, *Dir*, National Trust for Historic Preservation, Chesterwood Museum, Glendale MA

Iwinski, Mark, *Lectr*, College of William & Mary, Dept of Fine Arts, Williamsburg VA (S)

Jaber, George, *Chmn*, Community College of Allegheny County, Fine Arts Dept, West Mifflin PA (S)

Jablon, Linda, *Audio & Visual Dir*, Fine Arts Museums of San Francisco, M H de Young Memorial Museum & California Palace of the Legion of Honor, San Francisco CA

Jablow, Lisa, *Assoc Prof*, Johnson State College, Dept Fine & Performing Arts, Dibden Center for the Arts, Johnson VT (S)

Jack, Marlene, *Assoc Prof*, College of William & Mary, Dept of Fine Arts, Williamsburg VA (S)

Jacka, Doris M, *Pres*, San Bernardino Art Association, Inc, San Bernardino CA

Jack MFA, Meredith M, *Assoc Prof*, Lamar University, Art Dept, Beaumont TX (S)

Jackovich, Sheila, *Gallery Hostess*, Pemaquid Group of Artists, Pemaquid Art Gallery, Pemaquid Point ME

Jackson, A, *Instr*, Golden West College, Visual Art Dept, Huntington Beach CA (S)

Jackson, Absalon, *Assoc Prof*, Xavier University of Louisiana, Dept of Fine Arts, New Orleans LA (S)

Jackson, Amy, *Admin*, Illinois State Museum, Illinois Art Gallery & Lockport Gallery, Springfield IL

Jackson, Anke, *Assoc Dir*, The Parrish Art Museum, Southampton NY

Jackson, Arnold, *Dir Promotional Servs*, American Society of Artists, Inc, Chicago IL

Jackson, B, *Secy-Registrar*, University of Victoria, Maltwood Art Museum and Gallery, Victoria BC

Jackson, Bev, *Adminr*, Favell Museum of Western Art & Indian Artifacts, Klamath Falls OR

Jackson, Bill, *Chmn Art Dept*, Simon's Rock College of Bard, Great Barrington MA

Jackson, Chris, *Admin Asst*, University of Arizona, Museum of Art, Tucson AZ

Jackson, Christopher, *Dean*, Concordia University, Faculty of Fine Arts, Montreal PQ (S)

Jackson, Craig, *Reference Librn*, Mechanics' Institute Library, San Francisco CA

Jackson, Dale, *Dir Art Dept*, Southwestern Community College, Art Dept, Creston IA (S)

Jackson, Doug, *Dir*, Chatham Cultural Centre, Thames Art Gallery, Chatham ON

Jackson, Duke, *Chmn Fine Arts*, Georgia Southwestern State University, Art Gallery, Americus GA

Jackson, Duke, *Chmn*, Georgia Southwestern State University, Dept of Fine Arts, Americus GA (S)

Jackson, Greg, *Staff Librn*, Children's Museum, Rauh Memorial Library, Indianapolis IN

Jackson, Herb, *Chmn*, Davidson College, Art Dept, Davidson NC (S)

Jackson, Ilene, *Adminr*, Portage and District Arts Council, Portage Arts Centre, Portage la Prairie MB

Jackson, Jan, *Dir & Chmn Exhib Committee*, State University of New York at Geneseo, Bertha V B Lederer Gallery, Geneseo NY

Jackson, Jed, *Asst Prof*, Southern Illinois University, School of Art & Design, Carbondale IL (S)

Jackson, Kathryn A, *Art Librn*, Southern Methodist University, Hamon Arts Library, Dallas TX

Jackson, Marian, *Chmn*, Wayne State University, Dept of Art & Art History, Detroit MI (S)

Jackson, Marsha, *Deputy Dir*, Museum of New Mexico, Santa Fe NM

Jackson, Mary Gaissert, *Dir*, Northern Virginia Fine Arts Association, The Athenaeum, Alexandria VA

Jackson, Mavis, *Mgr*, Atlanta-Fulton Public Library, Art-Humanities Dept, Atlanta GA

Jackson, Milton, *Div Chmn of Music*, James H Faulkner Community College, Art Dept, Bay Minette AL (S)

Jackson, Steve, *Cur Art & Photo*, Montana State University, Museum of the Rockies, Bozeman MT

Jackson, Susan, *Prof*, Marshall University, Dept of Art, Huntington WV (S)

Jackson, Walter C, *Exec Dir*, Bronx River Art Center, Gallery, Bronx NY

Jackson, William, *Chmn Studio Arts Dept*, Simon's Rock College of Bard, Visual Arts Dept, Great Barrington MA (S)

Jackson-Beck, Lauren, *Assoc Museum Librn*, The Metropolitan Museum of Art, The Cloisters Library, New York NY

Jackson-Reese, Carla, *Instr*, Tuskegee University, Liberal Arts & Education, Tuskegee AL (S)

Jacob, Johanna, *Asst Prof*, College of New Jersey, Art Dept, Trenton NJ (S)

Jacob, John P, *Dir*, Photographic Resource Center, Boston MA

Jacobi, Richard, *Instr*, Casper College, Dept of Visual Arts, Casper WY (S)

Jacobs, Bill, *Pres*, Rogue Valley Art Association, Rogue Gallery & Art Center, Medford OR

Jacobs, Carl, *Pres*, Rock Valley College, Dept of Art, Rockford IL (S)

Jacobs, Ellen, *Prof*, Florida International University, Visual Arts Dept, Miami FL (S)

Jacobs, Fredrika H, *Assoc Prof*, Virginia Commonwealth University, Art History Dept, Richmond VA (S)

Jacobs, Fredrika H, *Asst Prof*, Virginia Commonwealth University, Art History Dept, Richmond VA (S)

Jacobs, Jack, *Production Mgr*, Hostos Center for the Arts & Culture, Bronx NY

Jacobs, James C, *Chmn*, Weber State University, Dept of Visual Arts, Ogden UT (S)

Jacobs, Jennifer, *Cur*, Litchfield Historical Society, Litchfield CT

Jacobs, Joseph, *Cur Painting & Sculpture*, Newark Museum Association, The Newark Museum, Newark NJ

Jacobs, Joyce, *Asst Prof*, Georgian Court College, Dept of Art, Lakewood NJ (S)

Jacobs, Les, *Prof*, Oakton Community College, Art & Architecture Dept, Des Plaines IL (S)

Jacobs, Lynn, *Asst Prof*, University of Arkansas, Art Dept, Fayetteville AR (S)

Jacobs, Nina S, *Dir*, Jersey City Museum, Jersey City NJ

Jacobs, P J, *Adminr*, University of Nebraska, Lincoln, Sheldon Memorial Art Gallery & Sculpture Garden, Lincoln NE

Jacobs, Robin, *Co-Educ Dir*, Center for Puppetry Arts, Atlanta GA

Jacobsen, Don, *Dir Library*, Englewood Library, Fine Arts Dept, Englewood NJ

Jacobsen, Robert, *Cur Oriental Arts*, Minneapolis Institute of Arts, Minneapolis MN

Jacobsen, Terry D, *Asst Dir*, Carnegie Mellon University, Hunt Institute for Botanical Documentation, Pittsburgh PA

Jacobson, Betty Jean, *VPres*, Toledo Artists' Club, Toledo OH

Jacobson, Frank, *Dir*, Scottsdale Center for the Arts, Scottsdale AZ

Jacobson, Jake, *Assoc Prof*, University of Nebraska, Kearney, Dept of Art & Art History, Kearney NE (S)

Jacobson, Lee, *Instr*, Chemeketa Community College, Dept of Humanities & Communications, Salem OR (S)

Jacobson, Leslie, *VPres*, Katonah Museum of Art, Katonah NY

Jacobson, Paul, *Chmn Div Language*, Western Nebraska Community College, Division of Language & Arts, Scottsbluff NE (S)

Jacobson, Thora, *Pres*, Philadelphia Art Commission, Philadelphia PA

Jacobson, Thora E, *Dir*, Philadelphia Museum of Art, Samuel S Fleisher Art Memorial, Philadelphia PA

Jacobson, Thora E, *Dir*, Samuel S Fleisher Art Memorial, Philadelphia PA (S)

Jacoby, Patricia, *Deputy Dir Marketing & Develop*, Museum of Fine Arts, Boston MA

Jacoby, Thomas J, *Head*, University of Connecticut, Art & Design Library, Storrs CT

Jacomini, Ronald, *Chmn Design Studies*, Bowling Green State University, School of Art, Bowling Green OH (S)

Jacquard, Jerry, *Prof*, Indiana University, Bloomington, Henry Radford Hope School of Fine Arts, Bloomington IN (S)

Jaeger, Al, *Lectr*, Notre Dame College, Art Dept, Manchester NH (S)

Jaffe, Amanda, *Assoc Prof*, New Mexico State University, Art Dept, Las Cruces NM (S)

Jaffe, David, *Cur Paintings & Drawings*, Getty Center for the History of Art & the Humanities Trust Museum, Santa Monica CA

Jaffe, David, *Cur Paintings & Drawings*, Getty Center for the History of Art & the Humanities Trust Museum, The J Paul Getty Museum, Santa Monica CA

Jaffe, Jeanne, *Chmn Crafts*, University of the Arts, Philadelphia College of Art & Design, Philadelphia PA (S)

Jaffe, John G, *Dir*, Sweet Briar College, Martin C Shallenberger Art Library, Sweet Briar VA

Jaffe, R, *Prof*, Maryville University of Saint Louis, Art Division, Saint Louis MO (S)

Jaffee, Richard, *VChmn*, Chicago Historical Society, Chicago IL

Jahn, Deborah, *Develop Dir*, Ann Arbor Art Association, Art Center, Ann Arbor MI

Jahnke, Karen, *Registrar*, San Joaquin Pioneer & Historical Society, The Haggin Museum, Stockton CA

Jahns, Tim, *Educ Coordr*, City of Irvine, Irvine Fine Arts Center, Irvine CA

Jahns, Tim, *Educ Coordr*, City of Irvine, Fine Arts Center, Irvine CA (S)

Jahos, Catherine, *Prog Adminr*, Monmouth Museum & Cultural Center, Lincroft NJ

Jalenak, Mala, *Museum Cur*, Louisiana Arts & Science Center, Baton Rouge LA

James, Anne, *Museum Specialist*, United States Department of the Interior Museum, Washington DC

James, Christopher, *Chmn Photography Dept*, Art Institute of Boston, Boston MA (S)

James, David, *Prof*, University of Montana, Dept of Art, Missoula MT (S)

James, John W, *Chmn*, Manatee Community College, Dept of Art & Humanities, Bradenton FL (S)

James, Louise, *Dir & Cur*, Plains Indians & Pioneers Historical Foundation, Museum & Art Center, Woodward OK

James, Nancy, *Dir*, Santa Cruz Valley Art Association, Tubac Center of the Arts, Tubac AZ

James, Nancy, *Dir*, Santa Cruz Valley Art Association, Library, Tubac AZ

James, Peggy, *Treas*, Coquille Valley Art Association, Coquille OR

James, Philip, *Prof*, James Madison University, School of Art & Art History, Harrisonburg VA (S)

James, Portia P, *Historian*, Anacostia Museum, Washington DC

James, Theodore, *Coll & Exhib Mgr*, Joslyn Art Museum, Omaha NE

James, Thomas A, *Pres*, Salvador Dali Museum, Saint Petersburg FL

Jameson, Nancy O, *Dir*, Old Island Restoration Foundation Inc, Wrecker's Museum - Oldest House, Key West FL

Janecek, James, *Asst Prof*, Providence College, Art & Art History Dept, Providence RI (S)

Janes, R, *Pres*, Glenbow Museum, Calgary AB

Janick, Richard, *Instr*, Monterey Peninsula College, Art Dept, Monterey CA (S)

Janis, Richard, *Chmn Dept*, Central Michigan University, Dept of Art, Mount Pleasant MI (S)

Jankowski, Edward, *Asst Prof*, Monmouth University, Dept of Art & Design, West Long Branch NJ (S)

Janovy, Karen, *Cur Educ*, University of Nebraska, Lincoln, Sheldon Memorial Art Gallery & Sculpture Garden, Lincoln NE

Janpol, Matthew, *Dir Musical Prog*, Art & Culture Center of Hollywood, Hollywood FL

Jansen, Catherine, *Instr*, Bucks County Community College, Fine Arts Dept, Newtown PA (S)

Jansky, Rollin, *Assoc Prof*, University of Wisconsin-Parkside, Art Dept, Kenosha WI (S)

Janson, Anthony F, *Chmn*, University of North Carolina at Wilmington, Dept of Fine Arts - Division of Art, Wilmington NC (S)

Jantzen, Franz, *Photograph Coll Coordr*, Supreme Court of the United States, Washington DC

Janzen, Joan, *Educ Coordr*, Hastings Museum, Hastings NE

Jareckie, Stephen B, *Cur Photography*, Worcester Art Museum, Worcester MA

Jaremba, Tom, *Prof*, School of the Art Institute of Chicago, Chicago IL (S)

Jarvinen, Lisa, *Educ Coordr*, Colgate University, Picker Art Gallery, Hamilton NY

Jaskot, Paul, *Asst Prof*, DePaul University, Dept of Art, Chicago IL (S)

Jaskowiak, Jennifer, *Exhib Coordr*, University of Southern California, Fisher Gallery, Los Angeles CA

Javan, Marjorie, *Pres*, Boston Printmakers, Boston MA

Javorski, Susanne, *Art Librn*, Wesleyan University, Art Library, Middletown CT

Jaworski, Lee, *Information Serv Supv*, Ferguson Library, Stamford CT

Jay, Robert, *Chmn*, University of Hawaii at Manoa, Dept of Art, Honolulu HI (S)

Jay, Stephen, *Dean, College of Performing Arts*, University of the Arts, Philadelphia College of Art & Design, Philadelphia PA (S)

Jaye, Cara, *Prof*, West Virginia University, College of Creative Arts, Morgantown WV (S)

Jebsen, Mary, *Librn*, Museum of New Mexico, Museum of Fine Arts, Santa Fe NM

Jebsen, Mary, *Librn*, Museum of New Mexico, Museum of Fine Arts Library, Santa Fe NM

Jedda, Barbara, *Cur & Mgr*, American Kennel Club, Museum of the Dog, Saint Louis MO

Jedlicka, Judith A, *Pres*, Business Committee for the Arts, Inc, New York NY

Jeffers, Susan, *Instr Asst*, Ulster County Community College, Dept of Visual Arts, Stone Ridge NY (S)

Jefferson, Lori, *Publicity Dir*, East Baton Rouge Parks & Recreation Commission, Baton Rouge Gallery Inc, Baton Rouge LA

Jefferson, Marion, *Assoc Chmn*, University of Miami, Dept of Art & Art History, Coral Gables FL (S)

Jeffreys, Jennifer, *Museum Shop Mgr*, University of Connecticut, William Benton Museum of Art, Storrs CT

Jeffries, Mary, *Studio Admin*, Gibbes Museum of Art Studio, Charleston SC (S)

Jelenfy, Karen, *Asst Prof*, Maryland College of Art & Design, Silver Spring MD (S)

Jellinghaus, Fritz, *Dir Develop*, International Museum of Cartoon Art, Boca Raton FL

Jelsing, Terry, *Dir*, Plains Art Museum, Fargo ND

Jendrzejewski, Andrew, *Chmn*, Vincennes University Junior College, Art Dept, Vincennes IN (S)

Jendyk, Khrystyna, *Pres*, Ukrainian Canadian Archives & Museum of Alberta, Edmonton AB

Jenkins, Bruce, *Dir Film & Video*, Walker Art Center, Minneapolis MN

Jenkins, Donald, *Cur Asian Art*, Portland Art Museum, Portland OR

Jenkins, Jon, *Pres*, Art League of Houston, Houston TX

Jenkins, Lawrence, *Asst*, University of New Orleans-Lake Front, Dept of Fine Arts, New Orleans LA (S)

Jenkins, Rupert, *Dir*, San Francisco Art Commission, Gallery & Slide Registry, San Francisco CA

Jenkins, Suzanne, *Registrar*, National Portrait Gallery, Washington DC

Jenkinson, Pamela, *Public Information Progs*, Los Angeles County Museum of Art, Los Angeles CA

Jenkner, Ingrid, *Dir Art Gallery*, Mount Saint Vincent University, Art Gallery, Halifax NS

Jenneman, Eugene A, *Museum Dir*, Northwestern Michigan College, Dennos Museum Center, Traverse City MI

Jennette, Judy, *Dir*, Beaufort County Arts Council, Washington NC

Jennings, Ann, *Chmn*, College of Saint Catherine, Art & Art History Dept, Saint Paul MN (S)

Jennings, Corrine, *Dir*, Kenkeleba House, Inc, Kenkeleba Gallery, New York NY

Jennings, C W, *Prof*, California Polytechnic State University at San Luis Obispo, Dept of Art & Design, San Luis Obispo CA (S)

Jennings, DeAnn, *Instr*, Los Angeles Harbor College, Art Dept, Wilmington CA (S)

Jennings, Jack, *Pres*, Greenwood Museum, Greenwood SC

Jennings, Susan, *Exec Dir*, Arts Council of the Blue Ridge, Roanoke VA

Jenny, Barbara R, *Interim Dir*, Phillips Exeter Academy, Frederic R Mayer Art Center & Lamont Gallery, Exeter NH

Jensen, Carl, *Art Dept Chmn*, University of Southern Colorado, College of Liberal & Fine Arts, Pueblo CO

Jensen, Carl, *Chmn*, University of Southern Colorado, Belmont Campus, Dept of Art, Pueblo CO (S)

Jensen, Carl, *Asst Prof*, University of Southern Colorado, Belmont Campus, Dept of Art, Pueblo CO (S)

Jensen, James, *Assoc Dir*, The Contemporary Museum, Honolulu HI

Jensen, James, *Assoc Prof*, Loyola University of Chicago, Fine Arts Dept, Chicago IL (S)

Jensen, Joan, *Cur Educ*, Hunterdon Historical Museum, Clinton NJ

Jensen, Kari, *Asst to Dir*, Community Fine Arts Center, Halseth Gallery, Rock Springs WY

Jensen, Ken, *Chief Librn*, Regina Public Library, Art Dept, Regina SK

Jensen, Mark, *Interior Architecture Design*, California College of Arts & Crafts, Oakland CA (S)

Jensen, Michelle, *Discovery Room Mgr*, University of Illinois, Museum of Natural History, Champaign IL

Jensen, Sue, *Asst Prof*, Auburn University at Montgomery, Dept of Fine Arts, Montgomery AL (S)

Jensen, William M, *Prof*, Baylor University, Dept of Art, Waco TX (S)

Jenson, Carie, *Develop*, Texas A&M University, Visual Arts Committee, College Station TX

Jentis, William R, *Pres*, The Art Institute of Chicago, Woman's Board, Chicago IL

Jercich, George, *Prof*, California Polytechnic State University at San Luis Obispo, Dept of Art & Design, San Luis Obispo CA (S)

Jeremias, Trudy, *VPres*, Artist-Craftsmen of New York, New York NY

Jernegan, Jeremy, *Asst Prof*, Tulane University, Sophie H Newcomb Memorial College, New Orleans LA (S)

Jernigan, Bonnie, *Communications Coordr*, Art Complex Museum, Duxbury MA

Jerry, Jane, *Pres*, Cheekwood-Tennessee Botanical Gardens & Museum of Art, Nashville TN

Jesburg, Bob, *Treas*, LA Art Association, Los Angeles CA

Jesse, Bernd, *Asst Cur Japanese Art*, The Art Institute of Chicago, Department of Asian Art, Chicago IL

Jessiman, John, *Prof*, State University of New York, College at Cortland, Art Dept, Cortland NY (S)

Jessop, Brad, *Instr*, East Central University, Art Dept, Ada OK (S)

Jessup, Philip C, *Secy & Gen Counsel*, National Gallery of Art, Washington DC

Jessup, Robert, *Basic Drawing Coordr*, University of North Texas, School of Visual Arts, Denton TX (S)

Jetter, Charyl, *Assoc Prof*, Andrews University, Dept of Art, Art History & Design, Berrien Springs MI (S)

Ji, Hongyu, *Asst Prof*, Eastern Illinois University, Art Dept, Charleston IL (S)

Jiang, Zhe-Zhou, *Instr*, Wayne Art Center, Wayne PA (S)

Jicha, Jon, *Prof*, Western Carolina University, Dept of Art, Cullowhee NC (S)

Jilg, Michael, *Prof*, Fort Hays State University, Dept of Art, Hays KS (S)

Jimenez-Torres, Maria, *School Coordr*, Plaza de la Raza Cultural Center, Los Angeles CA

Jimison, Tom, *Cur*, Middle Tennessee State University, Baldwin Photographic Gallery, Murfreesboro TN

Jipson, Jim, *Chmn*, University of West Florida, Dept of Art, Pensacola FL (S)

Jircik, Nancy L, *Chmn*, University of Saint Thomas, Art Dept, Houston TX (S)

Joanis, Marc, *Chef de Bibliotheque*, Universite de Montreal, Bibliotheque d'Amenagement, Montreal PQ

Jobe, Barbara, *Coordr Indian Gallery*, Oklahoma Center for Science & Art, Kirkpatrick Center, Oklahoma City OK

Jobe, Brock, *Deputy Dir Coll*, Winterthur Museum, Winterthur DE

Jobin, Pamela A, *Asst Dir*, Saint John's Museum of Art, Wilmington NC

Jodderell, Lynne, *Asst*, Louisiana State University, School of Art, Baton Rouge LA (S)

Joelson, Suzanne, *Instr*, Columbia University, School of the Arts, Division of Visual Arts, New York NY (S)

Johansen, Bill, *Drawing & Painting*, University of Georgia, Franklin College of Arts & Sciences, Lamar Dodd School of Art, Athens GA (S)

Johanson, Richard, *Pres & Board Trustees*, Fresno Metropolitan Museum, Fresno CA

Johns, Barbara, *Sr Cur & Cur Exhib*, Tacoma Art Museum, Tacoma WA

Johns, Dana, *Mus Admin*, The Contemporary, Museum for Contemporary Arts, Baltimore MD

Johnson, Anne, *Instr*, Pacific Northwest College of Art, Portland OR (S)

Johnson, Arthur, *Arts Instr*, Kalani Honua Institute for Cultural Studies, Pahoa HI (S)

Johnson, Betsy, *Dir*, Jackson County Historical Society, John Wornall House Museum, Independence MO

Johnson, Brooks, *Cur Photo*, Chrysler Museum of Art, Norfolk VA

Johnson, Buck, *Chair*, Koochiching County Historical Society Museum, International Falls MN

Johnson, Byron, *Dir & Supt*, Texas Ranger Hall of Fame & Museum, Waco TX

Johnson, Carl, *Conservatrice en Art Contemporain*, Le Musee Regional de Rimouski, Centre National d'Exposition, Rimouski PQ

Johnson, Carl, *Asst Prof*, Ithaca College, Fine Art Dept, Ithaca NY (S)

Johnson, Carla, *Asst Prof*, Marymount College, Art Dept, Tarrytown NY (S)

Johnson, Carlyle, *Chmn Art Dept*, Middle Tennessee State University, Art Dept, Murfreesboro TN (S)

Johnson, Celeste, *Admin Asst*, Newburyport Maritime Society, Custom House Maritime Museum, Newburyport MA

Johnson, Charles, *Res Librn*, Ventura County Historical Society, Museum of History & Art, Ventura CA

Johnson, Charles W, *Chmn*, University of Richmond, Dept of Art, Richmond VA (S)

Johnson, Dale, *Pres*, Moody County Historical Society, Flandreau SD

Johnson, Dale R, *Prof*, Bethel College, Dept of Art, Saint Paul MN (S)

Johnson, David, *Dir*, Old Dominion University, Gallery, Norfolk VA

Johnson, David, *Gallery Dir*, Old Dominion University, Art Dept, Norfolk VA (S)

Johnson, David B, *Chmn*, William Jewell College, Art Dept, Liberty MO (S)

Johnson, David J, *Archivist*, Headquarters Fort Monroe, Dept of Army, Casemate Museum, Fort Monroe VA

Johnson, David T, *Asst Dir Curatorial Affairs*, Cincinnati Institute of Fine Arts, Taft Museum, Cincinnati OH

Johnson, Deborah, *Asst Prof*, Providence College, Art & Art History Dept, Providence RI (S)

Johnson, Deborah, *Library Dir*, Ringling School of Art & Design, Verman Kimbrough Memorial Library, Sarasota FL

Johnson, Deborah J, *Pres*, The Museums at Stony Brook, Stony Brook NY

Johnson, Delton, *Personnel Mgr*, Kalani Honua Institute for Cultural Studies, Pahoa HI (S)

Johnson, Denise, *Registrar*, Phillips Academy, Addison Gallery of American Art, Andover MA

Johnson, Diana, *Project Coordr*, University of Illinois, World Heritage Museum, Champaign IL

Johnson, Diane, *Chmn Art History*, College of Charleston, School of the Arts, Charleston SC (S)

Johnson, Diane, *Librn*, Waterville Historical Society, Redington Museum, Waterville ME

Johnson, Donald, *Asst Dir*, Oregon State University, Memorial Union Art Gallery, Corvallis OR

Johnson, Dorothy, *Dir*, University of Iowa, School of Art & Art History, Iowa City IA (S)

Johnson, Eileen, *Cur Anthropology*, Texas Tech University, Museum, Lubbock TX

Johnson, E J, *Supt*, Davenport Museum of Art, Davenport IA

Johnson, Elizabeth, *Cur & Educ*, Landis Valley Museum, Lancaster PA

Johnson, Eric, *Dean*, Dakota State University, College of Liberal Arts, Madison SD (S)

Johnson, Eric B, *Prof*, California Polytechnic State University at San Luis Obispo, Dept of Art & Design, San Luis Obispo CA (S)

Johnson, Gary, *Sr Mgr Humanities*, Memphis-Shelby County Public Library & Information Center, Dept of Art, Music & Films, Memphis TN

Johnson, Gay, *Assoc Prof*, Los Angeles City College, Dept of Art, Los Angeles CA (S)

Johnson, Harvey, *Asst Prof*, Texas Southern University, Dept of Fine Arts, Houston TX (S)

Johnson, Herbert H, *Assoc Prof*, Rochester Institute of Technology, School of Printing, Rochester NY (S)

Johnson, James A, *Chmn*, The John F Kennedy Center for the Performing Arts, Washington DC

Johnson, Jeanne, *Exec Dir*, Thornton W Burgess Society, Inc, Museum, Sandwich MA

Johnson, Jennifer, *Dir*, Columbus Cultural Arts Center, Columbus OH

Johnson, Jerry, *Acting Co-Chair*, University of Colorado at Denver, Dept of Fine Arts, Denver CO (S)

Johnson, Jerry, *Chmn*, Southern Arkansas University, Dept of Art, Magnolia AR (S)

Johnson, Jerry, *Chmn Art Dept*, Southern Arkansas University, Art Dept Gallery & Magale Art Gallery, Magnolia AR

Johnson, Jon, *Chmn*, South Plains College, Fine Arts Dept, Levelland TX (S)

Johnson, Joyce, *Curatorial Asst Archaeology*, University of British Columbia, Museum of Anthropology, Vancouver BC

Johnson, Kate, *Librn*, Historic Hudson Valley, Library, Tarrytown NY

Johnson, Kathleen E, *Cur*, Historic Hudson Valley, Tarrytown NY

Johnson, Kathryn C, *Chmn Educ*, Minneapolis Institute of Arts, Minneapolis MN

Johnson, Kitty, *Instr*, Dunedin Fine Arts & Cultural Center, Dunedin FL (S)

Johnson, Laura, *Educ Dir*, Rockford Art Museum, Library, Rockford IL

Johnson, Lee, *Art Area Coordr*, Western State College of Colorado, Quigley Hall Art Gallery, Gunnison CO

Johnson, Linda K, *Pres & Exec Dir*, Witte Museum, San Antonio TX

Johnson, Lois, *Chmn Fine Arts Dept*, University of the Arts, Philadelphia College of Art & Design, Philadelphia PA (S)

Johnson, Lydia, *Dir*, Southern Utah University, Braithwaite Fine Arts Gallery, Cedar City UT

Johnson, Margaret, *Asst Prof*, Winthrop University, Dept of Art & Design, Rock Hill SC (S)

Johnson, Marge, *Office & Sales Mgr (May-Sept)*, Bradford Brinton Memorial Museum & Historic Ranch, Big Horn WY

Johnson, Mark, *Instr*, Maine College of Art, Portland ME (S)

Johnson, Mark M, *Dir*, Montgomery Museum of Fine Arts, Montgomery AL

Johnson, Mary, *Dir*, Edna Hibel Art Foundation, Hibel Museum of Art, Palm Beach FL

Johnson, Mary, *Dir*, Edna Hibel Art Foundation, Gallery, Palm Beach FL

Johnson, Michael, *Assoc Prof*, Murray State University, Dept of Art, Murray KY (S)

Johnson, Michael, *Asst Prof*, Baylor University, Dept of Art, Waco TX (S)

Johnson, Neil, *Lectr*, Centenary College of Louisiana, Dept of Art, Shreveport LA (S)

Johnson, Norma, *Librn*, University of Arkansas, Fine Arts Library, Fayetteville AR

Johnson, Osie, *Asst Prof*, University of Northern Iowa, Dept of Art, Cedar Falls IA (S)

Johnson, Pam, *Instr*, Sierra Community College, Art Dept, Rocklin CA (S)

Johnson, Pat, *Coordr*, Spectrum Gallery, Toledo OH

Johnson, Patricia, *VPres for Develop*, Meridian International Center, Cafritz Galleries, Washington DC

Johnson, Patty, *Office*, McPherson Museum, McPherson KS

Johnson, Paul, *Cur of Exhibit*, Bower's Museum, Santa Ana CA

Johnson, Peter, *Instr*, Butler County Community College, Art Dept, El Dorado KS (S)

Johnson, Philip H, *Chmn Dept*, Black Hawk College, Art Dept, Moline IL (S)

Johnson, R, *Instr*, Humboldt State University, College of Arts & Humanities, Arcata CA (S)

Johnson, Rhonda, *Strings Dir*, Elk River Area Arts Council, Elk River MN

Johnson, Richard, *Gallery Dir*, University of New Orleans, Fine Arts Gallery, New Orleans LA

Johnson, Richard A, *Prof*, University of New Orleans-Lake Front, Dept of Fine Arts, New Orleans LA (S)

Johnson, Robert S, *Cur*, Fort George G Meade Museum, Fort Meade MD

Johnson, Roy, *Dept Head*, Eastern Michigan University, Ford Gallery, Ypsilanti MI

Johnson, Sallie, *Deputy Dir*, Memphis-Shelby County Public Library & Information Center, Dept of Art, Music & Films, Memphis TN

Johnson, Sally, *Admin Asst*, Cornish College of the Arts, Fisher Gallery, Seattle WA

Johnson, Sara, *Dir Planning*, Southern Ohio Museum Corporation, Southern Ohio Museum & Cultural Center, Portsmouth OH

Johnson, Sherry, *Librn Asst*, North Carolina State University, Harrye Lyons Design Library, Raleigh NC

Johnson, Shirley G, *Pres*, Kansas Watercolor Society, Wichita Art Museum, Wichita KS

Johnson, Stephen, *Installationist*, Arizona State University, ASU Art Museum, Tempe AZ

Johnson, Steven, *Asst Cur & Site Mgr*, Vesterheim Norwegian-American Museum, Decorah IA

Johnson, Steven, *Asst Cur & Site Mgr*, Vesterheim Norwegian-American Museum, Reference Library, Decorah IA

Johnson, Sue, *Asst Prof*, Saint Mary's College of Maryland, Art Dept, Saint Mary's City MD (S)

Johnson, Thomas B, *Acting Dir & Cur*, Old York Historical Society, York ME

Johnson, Thomas B, *Acting Dir & Cur*, Old York Historical Society, Old Gaol Museum, York ME

Johnson, Twig, *Cur Educ*, Montclair Art Museum, Montclair NJ

Johnson, Twig, *Cur Educ*, Montclair Art Museum, Art School, Montclair NJ (S)

Johnson, Wanda, *Gallery & Public Relations*, Beaufort County Arts Council, Washington NC

Johnson, William, *Coordr*, Visual Studies Workshop, Research Center, Rochester NY

Johnson, William B, *Chmn*, Ritz-Carlton Hotel Company, Art Collection, Atlanta GA

Johnston, Amanda, *Mgr*, Wilkes Art Gallery, North Wilkesboro NC

Johnston, Catherine, *Cur European Art*, National Gallery of Canada, Ottawa ON

Johnston, D M, *Librn*, Lyceum Club and Women's Art Association of Canada, Library, Toronto ON

Johnston, Eileen, *Registrar*, Howard University, Gallery of Art, Washington DC

Johnston, Francis E, *Physical Anthropology Cur*, University of Pennsylvania, Museum of Archaeology & Anthropology, Philadelphia PA

Johnston, Jeff, *Assoc Prof*, College of the Ozarks, Dept of Art, Point Lookout MO (S)

Johnston, Lisa N, *Public Serv*, Sweet Briar College, Martin C Shallenberger Art Library, Sweet Briar VA

Johnston, Marshall, *Library Asst*, Bryn Mawr College, Art & Archaeology Library, Bryn Mawr PA

Johnston, Patricia, *Prof*, Salem State College, Art Dept, Salem MA (S)

Johnston, Richard, *Chmn Art Dept & Gallery Dir*, California State University, San Bernardino, University Art Galleries, San Bernardino CA

Johnston, Richard M, *Gallery Dir*, California State University, San Bernardino, Visual Arts, San Bernardino CA (S)

Johnston, Robert, *External Affairs Chief*, National Museum of American Art, Washington DC

Johnston, Roy E, *Head Dept*, Eastern Michigan University, Dept of Art, Ypsilanti MI (S)

Johnston, Sally S, *Dir*, Star-Spangled Banner Flag House Association, Museum, Baltimore MD

Johnston, Sona, *Cur Painting & Sculpture Before 1900*, Baltimore Museum of Art, Baltimore MD

Johnston, William R, *Assoc Dir*, Walters Art Gallery, Baltimore MD

Joiner, J Brooks, *Dir*, Gilcrease Museum Institute of American History & Art, Tulsa OK

Jokay, Alex, *Chmn*, Arts United of Greater Fort Wayne, Fort Wayne IN

Jokinen, David, *Assoc Prof*, Denison University, Dept of Art, Granville OH (S)

Jolicoeur, Anne, *Nat & International Prog Mgr*, Canadian Museum of Contemporary Photography, Ottawa ON

Jolliff, Joyce, *Undergrad Admissions*, Southern Illinois University, School of Art & Design, Carbondale IL (S)

Jonaitis, Aldona, *Dir*, University of Alaska, Museum, Fairbanks AK

Jonas, Joe, *Instr*, North Idaho College, Art Dept, Coeur D'Alene ID (S)

Jones, Amelia G, *Asst Prof*, University of California, Riverside, Dept of the History of Art, Riverside CA (S)

Jones, Anita, *Assoc Cur Textiles*, Baltimore Museum of Art, Baltimore MD

Jones, Ann, *Librn*, Marion Koogler McNay Art Museum, San Antonio TX

Jones, Ann, *Librn*, Marion Koogler McNay Art Museum, Reference Library, San Antonio TX

Jones, Ann, *Serials Librn*, The Art Institute of Chicago, Ryerson & Burnham Libraries, Chicago IL

Jones, Anthony, *School Pres*, The Art Institute of Chicago, Chicago IL

Jones, Arthur, *Chmn*, Radford University, Art Dept, Radford VA (S)

Jones, Barbara, *Cur*, Westmoreland Museum of American Art, Greensburg PA

Jones, Becky, *Admin Asst*, Charles B Goddard Center for the Visual & Performing Arts, Ardmore OK

Jones, Ben, *Prof*, Jersey City State College, Art Dept, Jersey City NJ (S)

Jones, Betty, *Bus Mgr*, Danville Museum of Fine Arts & History, Danville VA

Jones, Betty Ann, *Office Mgr*, Lancaster County Art Association, Inc, Lancaster PA

Jones, Bob, *Chmn of the Board*, Bob Jones University, Museum & Art Gallery, Greenville SC

Jones, Brian H, *Coordr & Assoc Prof*, Indiana University-Southeast, Fine Arts Dept, New Albany IN (S)

Jones, Cal, *Adjunct Instr*, Marian College, Art Dept, Fond Du Lac WI (S)

Jones, Charles E, *Librn*, University of Chicago, Oriental Institute Research Archives, Chicago IL

Jones, Chris, *Dir Sales Shop*, Colorado Springs Fine Arts Center, Colorado Springs CO

Jones, Christine, *Comptroller*, Arts United of Greater Fort Wayne, Fort Wayne IN

Jones, Cynthia L, *Dir & Cur Sheldon Museum*, Chilkat Valley Historical Society, Sheldon Museum & Cultural Center, Haines AK

Jones, Diane E, *Cur*, Genesee Country Museum, John L Wehle Gallery of Sporting Art, Mumford NY

Jones, Dina, *Admin Asst*, International Institute of Pigeons & Doves, Oklahoma City OK

Jones, Don R, *Chmn*, Iowa Wesleyan College, Art Dept, Mount Pleasant IA (S)

Jones, Doris, *Public Affairs Mgr*, Danville Museum of Fine Arts & History, Danville VA

Jones, Eileen, *VPres*, Lahaina Arts Society, Art Organization, Lahaina HI

Jones, Eleanor, *Assoc Cur American Art*, Dallas Museum of Art, Dallas TX

Jones, Elliott, *Asst Prof*, Old Dominion University, Art Dept, Norfolk VA (S)

Jones, F G, *Instr*, Western Illinois University, Art Dept, Macomb IL (S)

Jones, Frank, *Preparator*, University of Kentucky, Art Museum, Lexington KY

Jones, Frank, *Assoc Prof*, Palomar Community College, Art Dept, San Marcos CA (S)

Jones, Frederick N, *Instr*, Guilford Technical Community College, Commercial Art Dept, Jamestown NC (S)

Jones, George, *Assoc Prof*, Saint Thomas Aquinas College, Art Dept, Sparkhill NY (S)

Jones, Gerard, *Secy*, Louis Comfort Tiffany Foundation, New York NY

Jones, Harold, *Prof Photography*, University of Arizona, Dept of Art, Tucson AZ (S)

Jones, Harvey L, *Sr Cur Art*, Oakland Museum of California, Art Dept, Oakland CA

Jones, Janet, *Co-Pres*, Greenwich Art Society Inc, Greenwich CT

Jones, Jo Ann, *Gift Shop Mgr*, Koshare Indian Museum, Inc, La Junta CO

Jones, Joseph Howard, *Prof*, University of New Orleans-Lake Front, Dept of Fine Arts, New Orleans LA (S)

Jones, Julie, *Cur Arts of Africa, Oceania & the Americas*, The Metropolitan Museum of Art, New York NY

Jones, Justin, *Conservator*, Saint Gregory's Abbey & College, Mabee-Gerrer Museum of Art, Shawnee OK

Jones, Kathleen, *Registrar*, University of Illinois, Krannert Art Museum, Champaign IL

Jones, Kenneth, *Exec Dir*, Peters Valley Craft Center, Layton NJ

Jones, Kimberly Koller, *Exec Dir*, Hoyt Institute of Fine Arts, New Castle PA

Jones, Kirsten, *Public Art Coordr*, City of Eugene, Hult Center, Jacobs Gallery, Eugene OR

Jones, Lewis L, *VPres Academic Affairs*, Tougaloo College, Art Collection, Tougaloo MS

Jones, Lial, *Dir Educ*, Delaware Art Museum, Wilmington DE

Jones, Lynn, *Asst Prof*, Brenau University, Art Dept, Gainesville GA (S)

Jones, Malde, *Instr*, Ouachita Baptist University, Dept of Art, Arkadelphia AR (S)

Jones, Margaret, *Children's Librn*, Mexico-Audrain County Library, Mexico MO

Jones, Marvin H, *Prog*, Cleveland State University, Art Dept, Cleveland OH (S)

Jones, Maureen, *Asst to Dir*, Skidmore College, Schick Art Gallery, Saratoga Springs NY

Jones, Mike, *Animal Cur*, Tallahassee Museum of History & Natural Science, Tallahassee FL

Jones, Nancy, *Cur Educ*, Detroit Institute of Arts, Detroit MI

Jones, Nanette L, *Pres*, Watercolor Society of Alabama, Birmingham AL

Jones, Pat, *VChair*, Old Jail Art Center, Albany TX

Jones, Patrick, *Gallery Coordr*, Texas A&M University, Visual Arts Committee, College Station TX

Jones, Patty Sue, *International Child Art Coordr*, Cultural Affairs Department City of Los Angeles, Junior Arts Center, Los Angeles CA

Jones, Peggy, *Prof*, Peru State College, Art Dept, Peru NE (S)

Jones, Reba, *Coll Mgr*, Amarillo Art Association, Amarillo Art Center, Amarillo TX

Jones, Richard, *Chmn*, Russell Sage College, Visual & Performing Arts Dept, Troy NY (S)

Jones, Rick H, *Exec Dir*, Fitton Center for Creative Arts, Hamilton OH

Jones, Rick H, *Exec Dir*, Fitton Center for Creative Arts, Hamilton OH (S)

Jones, Robert L, *Head Div Fine Arts*, Truman State University, Art Dept, Kirksville MO (S)

Jones, Steve, *Pres*, South Arkansas Arts Center, El Dorado AR

Jones, Susan, *Gallery Dir*, Firelands Association for the Visual Arts, Oberlin OH

Jones, Thomas W, *Dir*, Museum of the Southwest, Midland TX

Jones, Tony, *Pres*, School of the Art Institute of Chicago, Chicago IL (S)

Jones, Virginia, *Prof*, Marygrove College, Visual & Performing Arts Div, Detroit MI (S)

Jones Hill, Sharon, *Assoc Prof*, Virginia Commonwealth University, Art History Dept, Richmond VA (S)

Jones MLS, Dolores A, *Cur*, University of Southern Mississippi, McCain Library & Archives, Hattiesburg MS

Jones-Rothwell, Pamela, *Assoc Prof*, University of Massachusetts - Boston, Art Dept, Boston MA (S)

Jonson AACR, Laurence, *Coll Conservator*, Deere & Company, Moline IL

Jordan, Daniel P, *Pres*, Thomas Jefferson Memorial Foundation, Monticello, Charlottesville VA

Jordan, Douglas, *Asst Prof*, Salt Lake Community College, Graphic Design Dept, Salt Lake City UT (S)

Jordan, Eddie J, *Prof*, Southern University in New Orleans, Fine Arts & Philosophy Dept, New Orleans LA (S)

Jordan, Sandra, *Chmn*, University of Montevallo, College of Fine Arts, Montevallo AL (S)

Jordon, Amy, *Pres Board*, Fort Smith Art Center, Fort Smith AR

Jordon, Barbara, *Chief Cur*, Craft Alliance Gallery & Education Center for the Visual Arts, Saint Louis MO

Jordon, Martha, *Instr*, The Arkansas Arts Center, Museum School, Little Rock AR (S)

Jordon, Shelley, *Assoc Prof*, Oregon State University, Dept of Art, Corvallis OR (S)

Jorgensen, Joseph, *Assoc Prof*, Culver-Stockton College, Art Dept, Canton MO (S)

Jorgensen, Susan, *VPres*, Santa Barbara Contemporary Arts Forum, Santa Barbara CA

Joseph, Phil, *Art Coordr*, Miami University, Dept Fine Arts, Hamilton OH (S)

Josepher, Susan, *Chmn*, Metropolitan State College of Denver, Art Dept, Denver CO (S)

Josephson, Ken, *Prof*, School of the Art Institute of Chicago, Chicago IL (S)

Josephy, Mariah, *Pres*, Washington Sculptors Group, Washington DC

Josey, Alley, *Dir*, Art Community Center, Art Center of Corpus Christi, Corpus Christi TX

Joslin, Richard, *Lecturer*, Smith College, Art Dept, Northampton MA (S)

Jossredo, Samuel, *Dir*, Los Angeles Valley College, Art Gallery, Van Nuys CA

Joyaux, Alain, *Dir*, Ball State University, Museum of Art, Muncie IN

Joyce, Daniel, *Cur Exhib & Coll*, Kenosha Public Museum, Kenosha WI

Joyce, Rosemary, *Dir*, University of California, Phoebe Apperson Hearst Museum of Anthropology, Berkeley CA

Joyce, Ted, *Instr*, Milwaukee Area Technical College, Graphic Arts Division, Milwaukee WI (S)

Joyce, Walker, *Artistic Dir The Bickford Theatre*, Morris Museum, Morristown NJ

Joye, Tyson, *Dir.* Peoria Art Guild, Peoria IL

Joyner, Eloise, *Dir Asst.* City of Atlanta, Bureau of Cultural Affairs, Atlanta GA

Juchniewich, Dan, *Asst Dir.* Rahr-West Art Museum, Library, Manitowoc WI

Juchniewich, Daniel, *Asst Dir.* Rahr-West Art Museum, Manitowoc WI

Judge, R, *Instr.* Community College of Rhode Island, Dept of Art, Warwick RI (S)

Judson, William D, *Cur Film & Video.* Carnegie Institute, Carnegie Museum of Art, Pittsburgh PA

Julian, Joanne, *Head Dept.* College of the Canyons, Art Dept, Valencia CA (S)

Juliano, Annette, *Chair.* Rutgers University, Newark, Dept of Visual & Performing Arts, Newark NJ (S)

Juliusburger, Thomas, *Art Dept Chmn.* University of Bridgeport Gallery, Bridgeport CT

Jumonville, Florence, *Head Librn.* Kemper & Leila Williams Foundation, New Orleans LA

Jumonville, Florence M, *Head Librn.* Kemper & Leila Williams Foundation, Historic New Orleans Collection, New Orleans LA

Juneau, Andre, *Dir.* Musee du Seminaire de Quebec, Quebec PQ

Junes, Tony, *Pres.* DuPage Art League School & Gallery, Wheaton IL

Jung, Michael, *Prof.* Denison University, Dept of Art, Granville OH (S)

Junker, Patti, *Assoc Cur American Painting.* Fine Arts Museums of San Francisco, M H de Young Memorial Museum & California Palace of the Legion of Honor, San Francisco CA

Jurey, Mark, *Chmn General Studies.* California State University, Northridge, Dept of Art-Two Dimensional Media, Northridge CA (S)

Jurgemeyer, Marne, *Dir.* Fort Morgan Heritage Foundation, Fort Morgan CO

Jurist, Susan, *Visual Arts Librn.* University of California, San Diego, Art & Architecture Library, La Jolla CA

Just, William, *Exec Dir.* Association of Medical Illustrators, Atlanta GA

Kabella, Chris R, *Pres.* College of Visual Arts, Gallery, Saint Paul MN

Kabella, Chris R, *Pres.* College of Visual Arts, Saint Paul MN (S)

Kabriel, J Ronald, *Asst Prof.* Catholic University of America, School of Architecture & Planning, Washington DC (S)

Kach, Claire, *Division Mgr.* Queens Borough Public Library, Fine Arts & Recreation Division, Jamaica NY

Kaczmarek, Pat, *Exhibits Coordr.* Oregon Historical Society, Library, Portland OR

Kaczorowski, Dr, *Academic Dean.* Camden County College, Dept of Art, Blackwood NJ (S)

Kadis, Averil, *Chief Pub Relations Div.* Enoch Pratt Free Library of Baltimore City, Baltimore MD

Kadish, Skip, *Instr.* Monterey Peninsula College, Art Dept, Monterey CA (S)

Kadoche, Salomon, *Second VPres.* Art Centre of New Jersey, Livingston NJ (S)

Kaericher, John, *Exhib Coordr.* Northwestern College, Te Paske Gallery, Orange City IA

Kaericher, John, *Chmn.* Northwestern College, Art Dept, Orange City IA (S)

Kagan, Judy, *Asst Dir.* Wooster Community Art Center, Danbury CT

Kager, Stephen J, *Dir.* Woodbridge Township Cultural Arts Commission, Barron Arts Center, Woodbridge NJ

Kagle, Joseph L, *Dir.* The Art Center of Waco, Library, Waco TX

Kagle, Joseph L, *Dir.* The Art Center of Waco, Waco TX

Kahan, Mitchell, *Dir.* Akron Art Museum, Akron OH

Kahle, David, *Dept Head.* Mount Marty College, Art Dept, Yankton SD (S)

Kahler, Bruce, *Assoc Prof.* Bethany College, Mingenback Art Center, Lindsborg KS

Kahler, Caroline, *Chmn Dept.* Bethany College, Mingenback Art Center, Lindsborg KS

Kahler, Caroline, *Head Art Dept.* Bethany College, Art Dept, Lindsborg KS (S)

Kahn, David, *Pres.* American Jewish Congress, New York NY

Kahn, David, *Exec Dir.* Connecticut Historical Society, Hartford CT

Kahn, Deborah, *Assoc Prof.* American University, Dept of Art, Washington DC (S)

Kahn, Deborah, *Prof.* Princeton University, Dept of Art & Archaeology, Princeton NJ (S)

Kahn, Elizabeth, *Assoc Prof.* St Lawrence University, Dept of Fine Arts, Canton NY (S)

Kahn, Herbert, *Cur.* Exchange National Bank of Chicago, Chicago IL

Kahn, James S, *Pres & Chief Exec Officer.* Museum of Science & Industry, Chicago IL

Kahn, Miriam, *Cur Asian & Pacific Ethnology.* University of Washington, Thomas Burke Memorial Washington State Museum, Seattle WA

Kahute, Robert M, *Assoc Prof.* Rochester Institute of Technology, School of Art & Design, Rochester NY (S)

Kailey, Dennis, *Architectural Admin.* Glendale Federal Bank, Glendale CA

Kaimal, Padma, *Asst Prof.* Colgate University, Dept of Art & Art History, Hamilton NY (S)

Kain, Evelyn, *Chmn.* Ripon College Art Gallery, Ripon WI

Kain, Evelyn, *Chmn.* Ripon College, Art Dept, Ripon WI (S)

Kain, Jay, *Prof.* James Madison University, School of Art & Art History, Harrisonburg VA (S)

Kainer, Michael, *Preparator.* Pacific Grove Art Center, Pacific Grove CA

Kaiser, Amanda M, *Librn.* Museum of Contemporary Art, Library, Chicago IL

Kaiser, Charles, *Prof.* Mount Mary College, Art Dept, Milwaukee WI (S)

Kaiser, Gina, *Assoc Librn.* Philadelphia Museum of Art, Library, Philadelphia PA

Kaiser, Karen, *Adjunct Asst Prof.* Spokane Falls Community College, Fine Arts Dept, Spokane WA (S)

Kaiser, Kurt, *Sr Lectr.* Aquinas College, Art Dept, Grand Rapids MI (S)

Kaiser, Michel, *Instr Commercial Art.* Honolulu Community College, Commercial Art Dept, Honolulu HI (S)

Kaiser-Kaplan, Nancy, *Cur.* Muchnic Foundation & Atchison Art Association, Muchnic Gallery, Atchison KS

Kajitani, Nobuko, *Conservator Textiles.* The Metropolitan Museum of Art, New York NY

Kalavrezou, I, *Chmn Dept.* Harvard University, Dept of Fine Arts, Sackler Museum, Cambridge MA (S)

Kalb, Marty J, *Prof.* Ohio Wesleyan University, Fine Arts Dept, Delaware OH (S)

Kalemkerian, Nairy, *Managing Dir.* Guilde Canadienne des Metiers d'Art Quebec, Canadian Guild of Crafts Quebec, Montreal PQ

Kalin, Louise, *Dir.* Gallery North, Setauket NY

Kalinovska, Milena, *Dir.* Institute of Contemporary Art, Boston MA

Kallenberger, Christine, *Dir Exhib & Coll.* Philbrook Museum of Art, Tulsa OK

Kallsen, Mark, *Asst Prof.* University of Wisconsin-Stout, Dept of Art & Design, Menomonie WI (S)

Kalmbach, Ann, *Exec Dir.* Women's Studio Workshop, Inc, Rosendale NY

Kalogeropoulos, Astero, *Prog Coordr.* Homer Watson House & Gallery, Kitchener ON

Kaloyanides, Michael G, *Chmn.* University of New Haven, Dept of Visual & Performing Arts & Philosophy, West Haven CT (S)

Kalvee, Debbie, *Head Bibliographic Access Management.* University of Alaska, Elmer E Rasmuson Library, Fairbanks AK

Kam, Betty Lou, *Archivist.* Bernice Pauahi Bishop Museum, Archives, Honolulu HI

Kamansky, David, *Exec Dir.* Pacific - Asia Museum, Pasadena CA

Kamerling, Leonard J, *Co-Dir Alaska Native Heritage Film Center.* University of Alaska, Museum, Fairbanks AK

Kamin, Benjamin Alon, *Sr Rabbi.* The Temple-Tifereth Israel, The Temple Museum of Religious Art, Beachwood OH

Kaminishi, Ikumi, *Asst Prof.* Tufts University, Dept of Art & Art History, Medford MA (S)

Kaminitz, Marian, *Head Conservation.* National Museum of the American Indian, George Gustav Heye Center, New York NY

Kaminsky, Lauren, *Dir.* Fraunces Tavern Museum, New York NY

Kaminsky, Vera, *Coordr Fibers.* University of Delaware, Dept of Art, Newark DE (S)

Kamm, David, *Gallery Coordr.* Luther College, Fine Arts Collection, Decorah IA

Kamm, James J, *Assoc Dir.* Wolfsonian Foundation, Miami Beach FL

Kammer, Linda, *Slide Cur.* College of Wooster, Dept of Art, Wooster OH (S)

Kamoche, Niambi, *Dir Library.* Langston University, Melvin B Tolson Black Heritage Center, Langston OK

Kampen, Michael, *Prof.* University of North Carolina at Charlotte, Dept of Visual Arts, Charlotte NC (S)

Kamps, Toby, *Cur Exhib.* Madison Art Center, Madison WI

Kan, Joseph, *Interim Dir.* University of Alaska, Elmer E Rasmuson Library, Fairbanks AK

Kan, Michael, *Cur African, Oceanic & New World Cultures Art.* Detroit Institute of Arts, Detroit MI

Kanatsiz, Suzanne, *Dir & Cur.* University of Nevada, Sheppard Fine Art Gallery, Reno NV

Kane, Katherine, *Dir Coll Servs.* Colorado Historical Society, Colorado History Museum, Denver CO

Kane, Mary Ann, *Dir.* Cortland County Historical Society, Suggett House Museum, Cortland NY

Kane, Mary Ann, *Exec Dir.* Cortland County Historical Society, Kellogg Memorial Research Library, Cortland NY

Kane, Patricia, *Cur American Decorative Arts.* Yale University, Art Gallery, New Haven CT

Kane, Susan, *Assoc Prof.* Oberlin College, Dept of Art, Oberlin OH (S)

Kane, Virginia C, *Assoc Prof.* University of Michigan, Ann Arbor, Dept of History of Art, Ann Arbor MI (S)

Kaneko, James, *Instr.* American River College, Dept of Art, Sacramento CA (S)

Kaneshiro, Carolyn, *Instr.* Mount San Jacinto College, Art Dept, San Jacinto CA (S)

Kangas, Gene, *Prof.* Cleveland State University, Art Dept, Cleveland OH (S)

Kanter, Laurence, *Cur Robert Lehman Collection.* The Metropolitan Museum of Art, New York NY

Kanz, Debbie, *Coordr Educ.* Walter Anderson Museum of Art, Ocean Springs MS

Kapan, Hillary, *Asst Prof.* University of Maryland, Baltimore County, Visual Arts Dept, Baltimore MD (S)

Kapelke, Steve, *Dean Liberal Studies.* Milwaukee Institute of Art & Design, Milwaukee WI (S)

Kapinan, Catherine, *Artistic Dir.* Wesley Theological Seminary Center for the Arts & Religion, Dadian Gallery, Washington DC

Kapitan, Lynn, *Assoc Prof.* Mount Mary College, Art Dept, Milwaukee WI (S)

Kaplan, Ilee, *Assoc Dir.* California State University, Long Beach, University Art Museum, Long Beach CA

Kaplan, Janice, *Pub Affairs Dir.* National Museum of African Art, Washington DC

Kaplan, Julius, *Instr.* California State University, San Bernardino, Visual Arts, San Bernardino CA (S)

Kaplan, Marian O'Rourke, *Fashion Design Coordr.* University of North Texas, School of Visual Arts, Denton TX (S)

Kaplan, Paul, *Assoc Prof.* State University of New York College at Purchase, Art History Board of Study, Purchase NY (S)

Kaplan, Ruth, *Public Information Officer.* National Gallery of Art, Washington DC

Kaplan, Stanley, *Chmn.* Contemporary Arts Center, Cincinnati OH

Kaplan, Stanley, *Prof.* Nassau Community College, Art Dept, Garden City NY (S)

Kaplan, Susan A, *Dir.* Bowdoin College, Peary-MacMillan Arctic Museum, Brunswick ME

Kaplowitz, Kenneth, *Assoc Prof,* College of New Jersey, Art Dept, Trenton NJ (S)

Kapplinger, Kent, *Lectr,* North Dakota State University, Division of Fine Arts, Fargo ND (S)

Karagheus-Murphy, Marsha, *Prof,* Xavier University, Dept of Art, Cincinnati OH (S)

Karalias, Ioannis, *Dir Exhib,* Chicago Athenaeum, Museum of Architecture & Design, Chicago IL

Karcheski, Walter J, *Cur & Librn,* Higgins Armory Museum, Library, Worcester MA

Kardon, Carol, *Instr,* Main Line Art Center, Haverford PA (S)

Kardon, Peter, *Dir Planning & Latin America Prog,* John Simon Guggenheim Memorial Foundation, New York NY

Kares, Jean, *Pres,* Canadian Crafts Council, Conseil Canadien de l'Artisanat, Ottawa ON

Karetzky, Patricia, *Instr,* Sarah Lawrence College, Dept of Art History, Bronxville NY (S)

Karg, Anita L, *Archivist,* Carnegie Mellon University, Hunt Institute for Botanical Documentation, Pittsburgh PA

Karibo, Lou, *Cur,* Kentucky New State Capitol, Division of Historic Properties, Frankfort KY

Karl, Brian, *Exec Dir,* Los Angeles Contemporary Exhibitions, Hollywood CA

Karl, Robert, *Adjunct Instr,* Virginia Wesleyan College, Art Dept of the Humanities Division, Norfolk VA (S)

Karlen, Mark, *Dean,* Fashion Institute of Technology, Art & Design Division, New York NY (S)

Karlins, Mary Lee, *Assoc Prof,* Bradford College, Creative Arts Division, Bradford MA (S)

Karlstrom, Ann, *Publs Mgr,* Fine Arts Museums of San Francisco, M H de Young Memorial Museum & California Palace of the Legion of Honor, San Francisco CA

Karlstrom, Paul J, *Regional Dir,* Archives of American Art, Archives of American Art, Washington DC

Karmal, Kathleen, *Asst Prof,* College of DuPage, Humanities Division, Glen Ellyn IL (S)

Karnes, Andrea, *Registrar,* Fort Worth Art Association, Modern Art Museum of Fort Worth, Fort Worth TX

Karp, Essie, *Exec Dir,* Women's Caucus For Art, Philadelphia PA

Karp, Marilynn, *Faculty Dir,* New York University, Washington Square East Galleries, New York NY

Karp, Marilynn G P, *Prof,* New York University, Dept of Art & Art Professions, New York NY (S)

Karpen, John E, *Prof,* Rochester Institute of Technology, School of Photographic Arts & Sciences, Rochester NY (S)

Karpiscak, Adeline, *Asst Dir,* University of Arizona, Museum of Art, Tucson AZ

Karraker, Jack, *Prof,* University of Nebraska, Kearney, Dept of Art & Art History, Kearney NE (S)

Karsina, James S, *Prof,* Aquinas College, Art Dept, Grand Rapids MI (S)

Karstadt, Bruce, *Dir,* American Swedish Institute, Minneapolis MN

Kartzinel, Wayne, *Dir,* Westchester Community College, Westchester Art Workshop, White Plains NY (S)

Kasfir, Sidney L, *Assoc Prof,* Emory University, Art History Dept, Atlanta GA (S)

Kaskell, Robert, *Cur,* Art Gallery of Windsor, Windsor ON

Kasl, Ronda J, *Cur Painting & Sculpture,* Indianapolis Museum of Art, Indianapolis IN

Kaspar, Ruth, *Exec Dir,* Scottsdale Artists' School, Scottsdale AZ (S)

Kaspar, Thomas L, *Preservation,* Nebraska State Capitol, Lincoln NE

Kasper, Michael, *Reference & Fine Arts Librn,* Amherst College, Frost Library, Amherst MA

Kasprzak, Constance, *Dir Display & Design,* Museum of Holography - Chicago, Chicago IL

Kass, Emily S, *Dir,* Tampa Museum of Art, Tampa FL

Kass, Emily S, *Dir,* Tampa Museum of Art, Library, Tampa FL

Kass, Ray, *Gallery Dir,* Virginia Polytechnic Institute & State University, Armory Art Gallery, Blacksburg VA

Kass, Ray, *Prof,* Virginia Polytechnic Institute & State University, Dept of Art & Art History, Blacksburg VA (S)

Kasser, Lucinda, *Chmn,* University of the Pacific, College of the Pacific, Dept of Art & Art History, Stockton CA (S)

Kassoy, Bernard, *Instr,* Harriet FeBland Art Workshop, New York NY (S)

Kastin, Judith B, *Treas,* Society of Scribes, Ltd, New York NY

Kaszarski, Richard, *Sr Historian,* American Museum of the Moving Image, Astoria NY

Katauskas, Joseph, *VPres,* Balzekas Museum of Lithuanian Culture, Chicago IL

Kates, Sam W, *Dir,* Wiregrass Museum of Art, Dothan AL

Kather, Jan, *Asst,* Elmira College, Art Dept, Elmira NY (S)

Kato, Bruce, *Chief Cur,* Alaska State Museum, Juneau AK

Katsiaficas, Mary Diane, *Prof,* University of Minnesota, Minneapolis, Dept of Art, Minneapolis MN (S)

Katsiff, Bruce, *Dir,* James A Michener Art Museum, Doylestown PA

Katsimpalis, Tom, *Cur Interpretation,* Loveland Museum Gallery, Loveland CO

Katsourides, Andrew, *Assoc Prof,* Central Missouri State University, Art Dept, Warrensburg MO (S)

Katz, Harry, *Popular & Applied Graphic Arts,* Library of Congress, Prints & Photographs Division, Washington DC

Katz, Jonathan, *Exec Dir,* National Assembly of State Arts Agencies, Washington DC

Katz, Lynda, *Instr,* Southeastern Louisiana University, Dept of Visual Arts, Hammond LA (S)

Katz, Melvin, *Prof,* Portland State University, Dept of Art, Portland OR (S)

Katz, Milton, *Chmn Liberal Arts,* Kansas City Art Institute, Kansas City MO (S)

Katz, Paul, *Exec Dir,* Carson County Square House Museum, Panhandle TX

Katz, Robert, *Prof,* University of Maine at Augusta, Division of Fine & Performing Arts, Augusta ME (S)

Katzenberg, Dena, *Consultant Cur Textiles,* Baltimore Museum of Art, Baltimore MD

Kaucher, Jackie, *Instr,* The Arkansas Arts Center, Museum School, Little Rock AR (S)

Kauders, Audrey, *Deputy Dir,* Joslyn Art Museum, Omaha NE

Kauffmann-Hay, Margaret, *Dir Develop,* Indiana State Museum, Indianapolis IN

Kaufman, Glen, *Fabric Design,* University of Georgia, Franklin College of Arts & Sciences, Lamar Dodd School of Art, Athens GA (S)

Kaufman, Jim, *Chmn,* Ohio State University, Dept of Industrial Interior & Visual Communication Design, Columbus OH (S)

Kaufman, Jolene, *Business Mgr,* Oregon Trail Museum Association, Scotts Bluff National Monument, Gering NE

Kaufman, Joshua, *Exec Dir,* Lawyers Committee for the Arts, Volunteer Lawyers for the Arts, Washington DC

Kaufmann, Faith, *Arts & Music Librn,* Forbes Library, Northampton MA

Kaufmann, Lon, *Chmn,* Taylor University, Chronicle-Tribune Art Gallery, Upland IN

Kaufmann, Lon D, *Chmn,* Taylor University, Art Dept, Upland IN (S)

Kaufmann, Thomas, *Prof,* Princeton University, Dept of Art & Archaeology, Princeton NJ (S)

Kaul, Marley, *Chmn,* Bemidji State University, Visual Arts Dept, Bemidji MN (S)

Kaumeyer, Kenneth, *Cur Estuarine Biology,* Calvert Marine Museum, Solomons MD

Kavanagh, Thomas, *Cur Coll,* Indiana University, William Hammond Mathers Museum, Bloomington IN

Kavanagli, Brian, *Registrar,* Hirshhorn Museum & Sculpture Garden, Washington DC

Kaven, Dennis, *Dept Head,* Grand View College, Art Dept, Des Moines IA (S)

Kavr, Amrita, *Library Asst,* University of Maryland, College Park, Art Library, College Park MD

Kawamoto, Wayne, *Design Asst,* University of Hawaii at Manoa, Art Gallery, Honolulu HI

Kay, Helen, *Co-Pres,* Wing Luke Asian Museum, Seattle WA

Kay, Mary, *Asst Prof,* Bethany College, Mingenback Art Center, Lindsborg KS

Kay, Mary, *Prof,* Bethany College, Art Dept, Lindsborg KS (S)

Kay, Terry, *Dir System Develop,* Museum of Holography - Chicago, Chicago IL

Kaya, Kathy, *Librn,* Montana State University, Creative Arts Library, Bozeman MT

Kaye, Garry, *Pres,* Southern Alberta Art Gallery, Lethbridge AB

Kaye, Jennifer, *Head Learning Servs,* Art Gallery of Hamilton, Hamilton ON

Kaye, Sheldon, *Dir,* Portland Public Library, Art - Audiovisual Dept, Portland ME

Kaylor, Scot, *Lectr,* University of Pennsylvania, Graduate School of Fine Arts, Philadelphia PA (S)

Kays, Elena, *Asst Prof Interior Design,* Centenary College, Humanities Dept, Hackettstown NJ (S)

Kayser, Peggy, *Adminr,* Hebrew Union College, Skirball Cultural Center, Los Angeles CA

Kayser, Robert, *Assoc Prof,* Rochester Institute of Technology, School of Photographic Arts & Sciences, Rochester NY (S)

Keane, Richard, *Prof,* School of the Art Institute of Chicago, Chicago IL (S)

Kear, Teline, *Pres Manitoba Historical Society,* Manitoba Historical Society, Dalnavert Museum, Winnipeg MB

Kearney, John, *Pres,* Contemporary Art Workshop, Chicago IL

Kearney, Lynn, *Dir,* Contemporary Art Workshop, Chicago IL

Kearney, Lynn, *Dir,* Contemporary Art Workshop, Chicago IL (S)

Kearns, Lola, *Dir Arts in Special Education Project,* Pennsylvania Department of Education, Arts in Education Program, Harrisburg PA

Kearns, Stapleton, *Pres,* Rockport Art Association, Rockport MA

Keating, John, *Librn,* Massachusetts College of Art, Morton R Godine Library, Boston MA

Keator, Carol, *Dir,* Santa Barbara Public Library, Faulkner Memorial Art Wing, Santa Barbara CA

Keber, Eloise Quinones, *Prof,* City University of New York, PhD Program in Art History, New York NY (S)

Keckeisen, Robert, *Museum Dir,* Kansas State Historical Society, Kansas Museum of History, Topeka KS

Kecskes, Lily C J, *Head Librn,* Freer Gallery of Art Gallery, Library, Washington DC

Kee, Cynthia, *Instr,* Northeast Louisiana University, Dept of Art, Monroe LA (S)

Keech, John, *Prof,* Arkansas State University, Dept of Art, State University AR (S)

Keefe, Jill, *Librn,* Museum of American Folk Art, Library, New York NY

Keefe, John W, *Cur Decorative Arts,* New Orleans Museum of Art, New Orleans LA

Keefe, Maureen, *Prog Dir,* San Francisco Artspace & Artspace Annex, San Francisco CA

Keegan, Dan, *Chmn,* West Virginia Wesleyan College, Dept of Fine Arts, Buckhannon WV (S)

Keegan, Kim, *Program & Educ Coordr,* Manchester Institute of Arts & Sciences Gallery, Manchester NH

Keegan, Trish, *Registrar,* Kamloops Art Gallery, Kamloops BC

Keenan, Jon, *Asst Prof,* Colby-Sawyer College, Dept of Fine & Performing Arts, New London NH (S)

Keenan, Joseph, *Dir,* Free Public Library of Elizabeth, Fine Arts Dept, Elizabeth NJ

Keene, Charles, *Dir,* Museum of the Hudson Highlands, Cornwall on Hudson NY

Keener, Alberta, *Educ Coordr,* Wiregrass Museum of Art, Dothan AL

Keeney, Bill, *Chmn Graphic Design,* Woodbury University, Dept of Graphic Design, Burbank CA (S)

Keesee, Tom, *Instr*, Saint Francis College, Art Dept, Fort Wayne IN (S)

Keeton, Darra, *Asst Prof*, Rice University, Dept of Art & Art History, Houston TX (S)

Kehoe, Tim, *Chief Admin Officer*, Royal Architectural Institute of Canada, Ottawa ON

Keifer-Boyd, Karen, *Asst Prof*, Texas Tech University, Dept of Art, Lubbock TX (S)

Keil, Bob, *Dir Opera*, Arts Festival of Atlanta, Atlanta GA

Keim, Barbara, *Chmn*, Westfield State College, Art Dept, Westfield MA (S)

Keiser, Sandra, *Assoc Prof*, Mount Mary College, Art Dept, Milwaukee WI (S)

Keith, Gary, *Galleries Mgr*, Galleries of the Claremont Colleges, Claremont CA

Keith, Marie C, *Assoc Librn*, Frick Art Reference Library, New York NY

Keith, Morrison, *Dean*, San Francisco State University, Art Dept, San Francisco CA (S)

Kekke, Rhonda, *Head Dept*, Kirkwood Community College, Dept of Fine Arts, Cedar Rapids IA (S)

Keland, Bill, *Treas*, Monterey Museum of Art Association, Monterey CA

Kelder, Diane, *Prof*, City University of New York, PhD Program in Art History, New York NY (S)

Keller, Candace, *Assoc Prof*, Wayland Baptist University, Dept of Art, Plainview TX (S)

Keller, Carol, *Dir*, Auraria Higher Education Center, Emmanuel Gallery, Denver CO

Keller, Deane, *Instr*, Woodstock School of Art, Inc, Woodstock NY (S)

Keller, Diane, *Lectr*, University of Pennsylvania, Graduate School of Fine Arts, Philadelphia PA (S)

Keller, Dorothy Bosch, *Chmn Dept*, Saint Joseph College, Dept of Fine Arts, West Hartford CT (S)

Keller, Emily, *Cultural Arts Mgr*, Brea Civic & Cultural Center Gallery, Brea CA

Keller, John, *Assoc Prof*, Harding University, Dept of Art, Searcy AR (S)

Keller, Kara, *Dir Finance & Operations*, Institute of Contemporary Art, Boston MA

Keller, Marjorie, *Prof*, University of Rhode Island, Dept of Art, Kingston RI (S)

Keller, Peter, *Exec Dir*, Bower's Museum, Santa Ana CA

Keller, Stephen, *Assoc Dean*, University of Hartford, Hartford Art School, West Hartford CT (S)

Keller, Tobin, *Instr*, Monterey Peninsula College, Art Dept, Monterey CA (S)

Keller, Ulrich, *Adjunct Cur Photo*, University of California, Santa Barbara, University Art Museum, Santa Barbara CA

Kelley, Daisy, *Prog Coordr*, Adirondack Lakes Center for the Arts, Blue Mountain Lake NY

Kelley, Don, *Prof Fine Arts*, University of Cincinnati, School of Art, Cincinnati OH (S)

Kelley, Regina, *Instr*, Maine College of Art, Portland ME (S)

Kellner, Sara, *Visual Arts Dir*, Hallwalls Contemporary Arts Center, Buffalo NY

Kellner, Tana, *Artistic Dir*, Women's Studio Workshop, Inc, Rosendale NY

Kellum, Barbara, *Asst Prof*, Smith College, Art Dept, Northampton MA (S)

Kelly, Amy Frushour, *Bus Mgr*, National Sculpture Society, Library, New York NY

Kelly, Cathie, *Asst Prof*, University of Nevada, Las Vegas, Dept of Art, Las Vegas NV (S)

Kelly, Clovis, *Pres*, Biloxi Art Association Inc & Gallery, Biloxi MS

Kelly, David C, *Head Dept*, University of Connecticut, Dept of Art & Art History, Storrs CT (S)

Kelly, D J, *Instr*, Western Illinois University, Art Dept, Macomb IL (S)

Kelly, Gemey, *Dir*, Mount Allison University, Owens Art Gallery, Sackville NB

Kelly, James, *Asst Dir*, Virginia Historical Society, Richmond VA

Kelly, Jennifer, *Registrar*, Ohio University, Kennedy Museum of American Art, Athens OH

Kelly, Jessie, *Pres*, Brooklyn Historical Society, Brooklyn NY

Kelly, Jim, *Exec Dir*, King County Arts Commission, Seattle WA

Kelly, Keith, *National Dir*, Canadian Conference of the Arts, Ottawa ON

Kelly, Madeline, *Supv Reference*, Berkshire Athenaeum Library, Reference Dept, Pittsfield MA

Kelly, Maggie, *Cur Architecture*, Chicago Historical Society, Chicago IL

Kelly, Margaret, *Dir*, Forbes Magazine, Inc, New York NY

Kelly, Mary, *Chmn*, University of California, Los Angeles, Dept of Art, Los Angeles CA (S)

Kelly, Nancy, *Dir*, University of Nebraska at Omaha, Art Gallery, Omaha NE

Kelly, Nannette, *Asst Prof Art*, Imperial Valley College, Art Dept, Imperial CA (S)

Kelly, Vincent, *Instr*, Yavapai College, Visual & Performing Arts Division, Prescott AZ (S)

Kelly-Zimmers, Claire, *Assoc Prof*, Portland State University, Dept of Art, Portland OR (S)

Kelm, Bonnie G, *Dir*, College of William & Mary, Joseph & Margaret Muscarelle Museum of Art, Williamsburg VA

Kelman, M, *Instr*, Community College of Rhode Island, Dept of Art, Warwick RI (S)

Keltner, K Kelly, *Exec Dir*, Visual Arts Center of Northwest Florida, Panama City FL

Keltner, K Kelly, *Exec Dir*, Visual Arts Center of Northwest Florida, Visual Arts Center Library, Panama City FL

Keltner, Stephen, *Pres*, Sculptors Guild, Inc, New York NY

Kemmerer, Allison, *Asst Cur*, Phillips Academy, Addison Gallery of American Art, Andover MA

Kemp, Jane, *Supv*, Luther College, Fine Arts Collection, Decorah IA

Kemp, Weston D, *Prof*, Rochester Institute of Technology, School of Photographic Arts & Sciences, Rochester NY (S)

Kemper, David W, *Chief Exec Officer & Pres*, Commerce Bancshares, Inc, Art Collection, Kansas City MO

Kemper, Mark, *Asst Supt*, Game and Parks Commission, Arbor Lodge State Historical Park, Nebraska City NE

Kemper, R Crosby, *Chmn of Board*, Kansas City Art Institute, Kemper Museum of Contemporary Art & Design, Kansas City MO

Kemper, R Crosby, *Chmn*, UMB Financial Corporation, Kansas City MO

Kempton, Peggy, *Admin Dir*, Morgan County Foundation, Inc, Madison-Morgan Cultural Center, Madison GA

Kenagy, G James, *Cur Mammalogy*, University of Washington, Thomas Burke Memorial Washington State Museum, Seattle WA

Kendall, Donald M, *Former Chmn & Chief Exec Officer*, PepsiCo Inc, Donald M Kendall Sculpture Garden, Purchase NY

Kendall, Douglas, *Cur Art Coll*, State Historical Society of Wisconsin, State Historical Museum, Madison WI

Kendall, Ginny, *Instr*, Main Line Art Center, Haverford PA (S)

Kendall, Thomas, *Dir*, Hand Workshop Art Center, Richmond VA

Kendall, William, *Prof*, Bridgewater State College, Art Dept, Bridgewater MA (S)

Kendrick, Diane, *Coordr*, Averett College, Art Dept, Danville VA (S)

Keneally, Michael, *Cur Exhib*, Dacotah Prairie Museum, Lamont Gallery, Aberdeen SD

Kenfield, John F, *Assoc Prof*, Rutgers, the State University of New Jersey, Graduate Program in Art History, New Brunswick NJ (S)

Kennedy, Arlene, *Dir*, University of Western Ontario, McIntosh Gallery, London ON

Kennedy, Caroline, *Dir*, West Baton Rouge Historical Association, Museum, Port Allen LA

Kennedy, Greg, *Visual Arts Chmn*, Idyllwild Arts Academy, Idyllwild CA (S)

Kennedy, Janet, *Assoc Prof*, Indiana University, Bloomington, Henry Radford Hope School of Fine Arts, Bloomington IN (S)

Kennedy, Nella, *Prof*, Northwestern College, Art Dept, Orange City IA (S)

Kennedy, Patricia, *Prof*, Ocean County College, Humanities Dept, Toms River NJ (S)

Kennedy, Paul, *Cur Educ*, El Paso Museum of Art, Library, El Paso TX

Kennedy, Philip, *Exhibits Designer Art*, Illinois State Museum, Illinois Art Gallery & Lockport Gallery, Springfield IL

Kennedy, Ronald, *Prof*, Southeastern Louisiana University, Dept of Visual Arts, Hammond LA (S)

Kennedy, Susan, *Dir Development*, Creative Time, New York NY

Kennedy, Terrence, *Cur*, Maharishi University of Management, Department of Fine Arts, Fairfield IA

Kennedy, Thomas, *VPres*, Everson Museum of Art, Syracuse NY

Kennell, Elizabeth, *Head Exhib*, McCord Museum of Canadian History, Montreal PQ

Kennington, Sarah J, *Registrar*, University of California, Los Angeles, Fowler Museum of Cultural History, Los Angeles CA

Kennon, Arthur B, *Pres*, Kappa Pi International Honorary Art Fraternity, Crestwood MO

Kenny, Peter, *VPres*, High Wire Gallery, Philadelphia PA

Kent, Diane, *Pres*, Arizona Artist Guild, Phoenix AZ

Kent, Renee, *Slide Librn*, Sarah Lawrence College Library, Esther Raushenbush Library, Bronxville NY

Kenyon, Colleen, *Exec Dir*, Center for Photography at Woodstock Inc, Woodstock NY

Keogh, Michael, *Instr*, Casper College, Dept of Visual Arts, Casper WY (S)

Keown, Gary, *Asst Prof*, Southeastern Louisiana University, Dept of Visual Arts, Hammond LA (S)

Kerber, Gwen, *Instr*, Bucks County Community College, Fine Arts Dept, Newtown PA (S)

Kerl, John, *Educator*, Prairie Art Gallery, Grande Prairie AB

Kern, Arthur E, *Prof*, Tulane University, Sophie H Newcomb Memorial College, New Orleans LA (S)

Kern, Dennis D, *Dir*, University of Montana, Gallery of Visual Arts, Missoula MT

Kern, Dennis D, *Dir*, University of Montana, Paxson Gallery, Missoula MT

Kern, Steven, *Cur of Paintings*, Sterling & Francine Clark Art Institute, Williamstown MA

Kernan, Thomas, *Exec Dir*, Madison County Historical Society, Cottage Lawn, Oneida NY

Kerns, Ed, *Dept Head*, Lafayette College, Dept of Art, Easton PA (S)

Kerns, Ginger, *Head Dept*, Eastern Community College, Dept of Art, Venice Beach CA (S)

Kerr, Donald, *Prof*, Grand Valley State University, Art & Design Dept, Allendale MI (S)

Kerr, Gloria, *Exec Asst*, London Regional Art & Historical Museums, London ON

Kerr, Joellen, *Dir*, University of Charleston, Carleton Varney Dept of Art & Design, Charleston WV (S)

Kerr, Nancy, *Div Chmn*, Dean College, Visual Art Dept, Franklin MA (S)

Kerr, Norwood, *Archival Librn*, Alabama Department of Archives & History, Library, Montgomery AL

Kerrigan, Thomas, *Prof*, University of Minnesota, Duluth, Art Dept, Duluth MN (S)

Kerrin, Jessica, *Dir*, Nova Scotia College of Art and Design, Anna Leonowens Gallery, Halifax NS

Kerslake, Kenneth A, *Distinctive Serv Prof*, University of Florida, Dept of Art, Gainesville FL (S)

Keser, Kerry, *Outreach Coordr*, Captain Robert Bennet Forbes House, Milton MA

Kessel, Suzan, *Librn*, Fairfield Art Association, Fairfield IA

Kessler, Herbert L, *Chmn*, Johns Hopkins University, Dept of the History of Art, Baltimore MD (S)

Kessler, Jonathan, *Instr*, Columbia University, School of the Arts, Division of Visual Arts, New York NY (S)

Kestenbaum, Stuart J, *Dir*, Haystack Mountain School of Crafts, Gallery, Deer Isle ME

Kestenbaum, Stuart J, *Dir*, Haystack Mountain School of Crafts, Library, Deer Isle ME

Kestenbaum, Stuart J, *Dir*, Haystack Mountain School of Crafts, Deer Isle ME (S)

Kester, Susanne, *Media Resources Coordr*, Hebrew Union College, Skirball Cultural Center, Los Angeles CA

Kester, William, *Interim Pres*, San Jose City College, School of Fine Arts, San Jose CA (S)

Kesterson, Sharon, *Prof*, College of Mount Saint Joseph, Art Dept, Cincinnati OH (S)

Ketchum, Cavaliere, *Prof*, University of Wisconsin, Madison, Dept of Art, Madison WI (S)

Ketner, Joseph D, *Dir*, Washington University, Gallery of Art, Saint Louis MO

Kettells, Margaret, *Office Supv*, Pope County Historical Society, Pope County Museum, Glenwood MN

Kettering, Karen, *Asst Prof*, University of Dayton, Visual Arts Dept, Dayton OH (S)

Ketwin, Barbara, *Instr*, College of the Canyons, Art Dept, Valencia CA (S)

Kew, Michael, *Cur Ethnography*, University of British Columbia, Museum of Anthropology, Vancouver BC

Key, Kathleen, *Art Reference Librn*, West Virginia University, Evansdale Library, Morgantown WV

Keyes, David, *Prof*, Pacific Lutheran University, Dept of Art, Tacoma WA (S)

Keyes, Donald, *Cur Paintings*, University of Georgia, Georgia Museum of Art, Athens GA

Keyes, George, *Cur European Painting*, Detroit Institute of Arts, Detroit MI

Keyes, Shira, *Assoc Dir*, Studio Gallery, Washington DC

Keyser, William, *Prof*, Rochester Institute of Technology, School of Art & Design, Rochester NY (S)

Khalidi, Omar, *Librn Aga Khan Program for Islamic Architecture*, Massachusetts Institute of Technology, Rotch Library of Architecture & Planning, Cambridge MA

Khalsa, Sant, *Instr*, California State University, San Bernardino, Visual Arts, San Bernardino CA (S)

Khera, Susheila, *Exec Dir*, Institute of Alaska Native Arts, Inc, Fairbanks AK

Khewhok, Carol, *Cur Art Center*, Honolulu Academy of Arts, Honolulu HI

Khewhok, Carol, *Cur*, Honolulu Academy of Arts, The Art Center at Linekona, Honolulu HI (S)

Khewhok, Sanit, *Gallery Dir*, Hawaii Pacific University, Gallery, Kaneohe HI

Khouri, Virginia, *Librn*, Cheekwood-Tennessee Botanical Gardens & Museum of Art, Museum of Art Library, Nashville TN

Kiah, Virginia J, *Dir & Founder*, Kiah Museum, Savannah GA

Kibler, Robert, *Assoc Prof*, Glendale Community College, Visual & Performing Arts Division, Glendale CA (S)

Kiblinger, Pat, *Asst Prof*, Lynchburg College, Art Dept, Lynchburg VA (S)

Kichingbird, Robin, *Librn*, Cherokee National Historical Society, Inc, Library, Tahlequah OK

Kickingbird, Lynn, *Develop Officer*, Oklahoma City Art Museum, Oklahoma City OK

Kidd, Betty, *Dir*, National Archives of Canada, Visual & Sound Archives, Ottawa ON

Kiddie, David, *Prof*, Chapman University, Art Dept, Orange CA (S)

Kiebvesadel, Helen, *Pres*, Women's Caucus For Art, Philadelphia PA

Kiel, Dennis, *Assoc Cur Photography & Design*, Cincinnati Museum Association, Cincinnati Art Museum, Cincinnati OH

Kiel, Martha, *Instr*, Hardin-Simmons University, Art Dept, Abilene TX (S)

Kierstead, Anne, *Office Mgr*, Noah Webster House, Inc, Noah Webster House, West Hartford CT

Kietzman, K M, *Dept Head*, College of Saint Francis, Fine Arts Dept, Joliet IL (S)

Kietzman, William, *Slide & Ill Librn*, Plymouth State College, Herbert H Lamson Library, Plymouth NH

Kiger, Robert W, *Dir*, Carnegie Mellon University, Hunt Institute for Botanical Documentation, Pittsburgh PA

Kihata, Hideki, *Assoc Prof*, Saginaw Valley State University, Dept of Art & Design, University Center MI (S)

Kiker, Evelyn, *Instr*, Mississippi Delta Community College, Dept of Fine Arts, Moorhead MS (S)

Kilfoyle, Sharon, *Instr*, William Woods-Westminster Colleges, Art Dept, Fulton MO (S)

Kilgore, Ron, *Studio Mgr*, Creative Growth Art Center, Oakland CA

Killoren, Michael, *Arts Coordr*, King County Arts Commission, Seattle WA

Kim, Carole, *Admin Dir*, Fellows of Contemporary Art, Los Angeles CA

Kim, Heemong, *Asst Prof*, Rhode Island College, Art Dept, Providence RI (S)

Kim, Kumja, *Cur Korean Art*, Asian Art Museum of San Francisco, Avery Brundage Collection, San Francisco CA

Kim, Kyu Hugh, *Chief Librn*, Queensborough Community College Library, Bayside NY

Kim, Ron, *Instr*, Greenfield Community College, Art, Graphic Design & Media Communication Dept, Greenfield MA (S)

Kimball, Athena, *Pres*, Katonah Museum of Art, Katonah NY

Kimball, Kathryn, *Upper Room Cur*, General Board of Discipleship, The United Methodist Church, The Upper Room Chapel & Museum, Nashville TN

Kimball-Moulton, Rosalind, *Dir*, Stephens College, Lewis James & Nellie Stratton Davis Art Gallery, Columbia MO

Kimball-Moulton, Rosalind, *Instr*, Stephens College, Art & Fashion Dept, Columbia MO (S)

Kimbrell, Leonard B, *Prof*, Portland State University, Dept of Art, Portland OR (S)

Kimes, Don, *Dir Art School*, Chautauqua Institution, School of Art, Chautauqua NY (S)

Kimes, Don, *Chmn Dept*, American University, Dept of Art, Washington DC (S)

Kimmel, Kent N, *Chmn*, Salisbury State University, Art Dept, Salisbury MD (S)

Kimmel, Susan, *Gallery Coordr*, Columbia Basin College, Esvelt Gallery, Pasco WA (S)

Kimmerle, Constance, *Cur Art Coll*, The Rosenbach Museum & Library, Philadelphia PA

Kimmerman, Tim, *Art Dept Chair*, Grand Canyon University, Art Dept, Phoenix AZ (S)

Kimura, Alma, *VPres*, Wing Luke Asian Museum, Seattle WA

Kinard, Spence, *Asst Dir*, Utah Travel Council, Salt Lake City UT

Kincaid, Carol, *Treas*, DuPage Art League School & Gallery, Wheaton IL

Kindy, Julia F, *Prog Representative*, University of California, San Diego, Stuart Collection, La Jolla CA

King, Anthony G, *Deputy Dir*, Worcester Art Museum, Worcester MA

King, Betty L, *Asst Dir*, State of Hawaii, Dept of Land & Natural Resources, Wailoa Visitor Center, Hilo HI

King, Clive, *Chmn*, Florida International University, Visual Arts Dept, Miami FL (S)

King, Cornelia, *Asst Head*, Free Library of Philadelphia, Rare Book Dept, Philadelphia PA

King, Dorothy, *Librn*, East Hampton Library, Pennypacker Long Island Collection, East Hampton NY

King, Duane, *Exec Dir*, Southwest Museum, Los Angeles CA

King, George G, *Exec Dir*, Katonah Museum of Art, Katonah NY

King, Gwen, *Dir*, Archaeological Society of Ohio, Indian Museum Library, Painesville OH

King, Gwen G, *Dir*, Archaeological Society of Ohio, Indian Museum of Lake County, Ohio, Painesville OH

King, Jack, *Dir & Cur*, Hamline University Learning Center Gallery, Library, Saint Paul MN

King, Jack, *Dept Chmn*, University of Tampa, Dept of Art, Tampa FL (S)

King, Jeanne, *Assoc Prof*, Cazenovia College, Center for Art & Design Studies, Cazenovia NY (S)

King, Jennifer, *Coordr*, Diverse Works, Houston TX

King, Karen, *Cur Historic Houses*, Charleston Museum, Charleston SC

King, Linda, *Instr*, Long Beach City College, Dept of Art, Long Beach CA (S)

King, Luci, *Library Chmn*, Grand Rapids Art Museum, McBride Art Reference Library, Grand Rapids MI

King, Lyndel, *Dir*, University of Minnesota, Weisman Art Museum, Minneapolis MN

King, Mary, *Librn*, Madison County Historical Society, Library, Oneida NY

King, Maureen, *Dir Public Relations*, Museum of Contemporary Art, Chicago IL

King, Maureen, *Secy*, Cypress College, Fine Arts Gallery, Cypress CA

King, Pam, *Pres*, Artists' Cooperative Gallery, Omaha NE

King, Samuel O, *Pres*, Southwest Missouri Museum Associates Inc, Springfield MO

King, Sharon, *Dir*, Las Vegas Art Museum, Las Vegas NV

King, Valeria, *Music*, Southern University in New Orleans, Fine Arts & Philosophy Dept, New Orleans LA (S)

Kingery, Trudy, *Pres*, Marion Art Center, Marion MA

Kingery, Victor, *Dir*, Quincy University, Brenner Library, Quincy IL

King-Hammond, Leslie, *VPres*, College Art Association, New York NY

Kingsley, Susan, *Instr*, Monterey Peninsula College, Art Dept, Monterey CA (S)

Kingsolver, Joy, *Serials & Archivist*, Spertus Institute of Jewish Studies, Asher Library, Chicago IL

Kinnaird, R, *Prof*, University of North Carolina at Chapel Hill, Art Dept, Chapel Hill NC (S)

Kinne, Carol, *Asst Prof*, Colgate University, Dept of Art & Art History, Hamilton NY (S)

Kinney, Gilbert H, *VPres*, The American Federation of Arts, New York NY

Kinnison, William, *Pres*, Clark County Historical Society, Springfield OH

Kintzler, David, *Faculty*, Housatonic Community & Technical College, Art Dept, Bridgeport CT (S)

Kinyon, Mary Lou, *Librn*, Amherst Museum, Amherst NY

Kiphart, Jan, *Registrar*, St Mary's College of Maryland, The Dwight Frederick Boyden Gallery, Saint Mary City MD

Kiphuth, Rebecca, *Registrar*, Florida Gulf Coast Art Center, Inc, Belleair FL

Kirby, John, *Pres*, Manhattan Graphics Center, New York NY (S)

Kirby, Patricia, *Asst to Dir*, Hermitage Foundation Museum, Norfolk VA

Kirby-Smith, Matilda, *Instr*, Guilford Technical Community College, Commercial Art Dept, Jamestown NC (S)

Kirishian, Jeanette, *Asst Prof*, Spokane Falls Community College, Fine Arts Dept, Spokane WA (S)

Kirjakovic, Dusica, *Exec Dir*, Lower East Side Printshop, Inc, New York NY

Kirjakovic, Dusica, *Exec Dir*, Lower East Side Printshop, New York NY (S)

Kirk, Jonathan, *Studio Mgr*, Sculpture Space, Inc, Utica NY

Kirk, Judith, *Asst Dir*, Indiana University, William Hammond Mathers Museum, Bloomington IN

Kirk, Martha Ann, *Prof*, Incarnate Word University of the Arts & Sciences, Art Dept, San Antonio TX (S)

Kirk, Muriel S, *Library Vol*, Museum of Fine Arts, Saint Petersburg, Florida, Inc, Art Reference Library, Saint Petersburg FL

Kirking, Clayton C, *Libr Dir*, Parsons School of Design, Adam & Sophie Gimbel Design Library, New York NY

Kirkpatrick, Andrea, *Cur Canada & International Art*, New Brunswick Museum, Saint John NB

Kirkpatrick, Diane, *Prof*, University of Michigan, Ann Arbor, Dept of History of Art, Ann Arbor MI (S)

Kirkpatrick, Nancy, *Head Mus Servs*, Vancouver Art Gallery, Vancouver BC

Kirsch, Edith, *Assoc Prof*, Colorado College, Dept of Art, Colorado Springs CO (S)

Kirschbaum, Robert, *Assoc Prof of Fine Arts & Dir of Studio Arts*, Trinity College, Dept of Fine Arts, Hartford CT (S)

Kirschberg, Reva G, *Dir*, Congregation Emanu-El, New York NY

Kirschenbaum, Jules, *Chmn Dept*, Drake University, Art Dept, Des Moines IA (S)

Kirscher, Don, *Treas*, Arizona Artist Guild, Phoenix AZ

Kirschke, Amy, *Sr Lectr*, Vanderbilt University, Dept of Fine Arts, Nashville TN (S)

Kirshner, Judith, *Dir School Art & Design*, University of Illinois at Chicago, College of Architecture, Chicago IL (S)

Kirstner, Diane L, *Dir Interpretive Serv*, Rock Ford Foundation, Inc, Historic Rock Ford & Kauffman Museum, Lancaster PA

Kirt, Julia, *Develop*, Oklahoma City Art Museum, Oklahoma City OK

Kisluk, Anna J, *Dir*, International Foundation for Art Research, Inc, Art Loss Register, New York NY

Kismaric, Carole, *Publications Dir*, Institute for Contemporary Art, Project Studio One (P S 1), Long Island City NY

Kissinger, Lori, *Dir*, Arts Council of Southwestern Indiana, Evansville IN

Kistler, Helen Kisthardt, *Pres*, Pennsylvania Dutch Folk Culture Society Inc, Baver Genealogical Library, Lenhartsville PA

Kistler, Kathleen, *Dir Division Fine Arts*, Shasta College, Art Dept, Fine Arts Division, Redding CA (S)

Kitao, T Kaori, *Prof*, Swarthmore College, Dept of Art, Swarthmore PA (S)

Kitchen, Larry, *Instr*, Kilgore College, Visual Arts Dept, Kilgore TX (S)

Kitchen, Tiffany, *Cur Educ*, Saint John's Museum of Art, Wilmington NC

Kittle, Barbara, *Librn*, University of Arizona, Museum of Art Library, Tucson AZ

Kittner, Craig, *Membership Dir*, National Artists Equity Association Inc, Washington DC

Kittredge, Cindy, *Dir & Cur*, Cascade County Historical Society, Cascade County Historical Museum & Archives, Great Falls MT

Kizik, Roger, *Preparator*, Brandeis University, Rose Art Museum, Waltham MA

Kjelgaard, Julia, *Lectr*, Emory University, Art History Dept, Atlanta GA (S)

Klapmeyer, Brian, *Instr*, Avila College, Art Division, Dept of Humanities, Kansas City MO (S)

Klassen, Heather, *Admin Coordr*, Banff Centre, Walter Phillips Gallery, Banff AB

Klassen, John, *Dir*, Massillon Museum, Massillon OH

Klassen, Marlene, *Develop Officer*, Oakville Galleries, Centennial Gallery and Gairloch Gallery, Oakville ON

Klausmeyer, David L, *Pres*, Norman Rockwell Museum at Stockbridge, Stockbridge MA

Klazek, Nancy, *Educ Officer*, Art Gallery of Greater Victoria, Victoria BC

Klebesadel, Helen R, *Chmn*, Lawrence University, Dept of Art, Appleton WI (S)

Kleckler, Curtis, *Financial Officer*, Rockford Art Museum, Rockford IL

Kleeblatt, Norman, *Cur Fine Arts*, The Jewish Museum, New York NY

Klein, Emanuel, *Pres*, Brown County Art Gallery Association Inc, Brown County Art Gallery & Museum, Nashville IN

Klein, Jeanette, *Asst Prof*, Berea College, Art Dept, Berea KY (S)

Klein, John, *Asst Prof*, University of Missouri, Art History & Archaeology Dept, Columbia MO (S)

Klein, Richard, *Asst Dir*, Aldrich Museum of Contemporary Art, Ridgefield CT

Klein, Sherri, *Assoc Prof*, University of Wisconsin-Stout, Dept of Art & Design, Menomonie WI (S)

Klein, Shirley, *Second VPres*, New York Society of Architects, New York NY

Kleinbauer, Eugene, *Prof*, Indiana University, Bloomington, Henry Radford Hope School of Fine Arts, Bloomington IN (S)

Kleinerman, Lori, *Dir Marketing*, Museum of Contemporary Art, Chicago IL

Kleinfelder, Arthur, *Dept Head*, Suffolk County Community College, Art Dept, Selden NY (S)

Kleinschmidt, Kelly A, *Dir Public Relations*, Stan Hywet Hall & Gardens, Inc, Akron OH

Kleinschmidt, Robert W, *Prof*, University of Utah, Art Dept, Salt Lake City UT (S)

Kleinsmith, Louise, *Instr*, Adrian College, Art & Design Dept, Adrian MI (S)

Klem, Alan, *Instr*, Creighton University, Fine & Performing Arts Dept, Omaha NE (S)

Klema, Stephen A, *Graphic Design Coordr*, Tunxis Community College, Graphic Design Dept, Farmington CT (S)

Klenk, William, *Prof*, University of Rhode Island, Dept of Art, Kingston RI (S)

Klett, Jim, *Instr*, Olympic College, Social Sciences & Humanities Division, Bremerton WA (S)

Kley, Gwen, *Pres*, Washington Art Association, Washington Depot CT

Klima, Stefan, *Supv Fine Arts Servs*, Beverly Hills Public Library, Fine Arts Library, Beverly Hills CA

Kliman, Eve, *Assoc Prof*, University of Waterloo, Fine Arts Dept, Waterloo ON (S)

Klimaszewski, Cathy, *Ames Cur Educ*, Cornell University, Herbert F Johnson Museum of Art, Ithaca NY

Klimiades, Mario Nick, *Librn*, Heard Museum, Phoenix AZ

Klimiades, Mario Nick, *Library Archives Mgr*, Heard Museum, Library & Archives, Phoenix AZ

Klindt, Steven, *Exec Dir*, Morris Museum, Morristown NJ

Kline, Katy, *Dir*, Massachusetts Institute of Technology, List Visual Arts Center, Cambridge MA

Kline, Paul, *Dept Head*, Bridgewater College, Art Dept, Bridgewater VA (S)

Klinedinst, Mary, *Dir Governor's School for the Arts*, Pennsylvania Department of Education, Arts in Education Program, Harrisburg PA

Klingensmith, Ann, *Assoc Prof*, Iowa Wesleyan College, Art Dept, Mount Pleasant IA (S)

Klingman, Berry J, *Prof*, Baylor University, Dept of Art, Waco TX (S)

Klinkon, Heinz, *Asst Prof*, Rochester Institute of Technology, School of Art & Design, Rochester NY (S)

Kliss, Mary Ellen, *Admin Asst*, Schweinfurth Art Center, Auburn NY

Kliwinski, Leonard M, *Deputy Cur*, Chicago Athenaeum, Museum of Architecture & Design, Chicago IL

Klobe, Delmarie, *Chmn*, University of Hawaii, Kapiolani Community College, Honolulu HI (S)

Klobe, Tom, *Dir*, University of Hawaii at Manoa, Art Gallery, Honolulu HI

Klonarides, Carole Ann, *Media Arts Cur*, Long Beach Museum of Art, Long Beach CA

Kloongian, Harold, *VPres*, North Shore Arts Association, Inc, Art Gallery, Gloucester MA

Klopfer, Dennis, *Asst Prof*, Mount Mary College, Art Dept, Milwaukee WI (S)

Kloppe, Linda, *IL Artisans Shop*, Illinois State Museum, Museum Shop, Chicago IL

Klos, Sheila M, *Head Librn*, University of Oregon, Architecture & Allied Arts Library, Eugene OR

Klosky, Peter, *Chief Designer*, Roberson Museum & Science Center, Binghamton NY

Klotter, James, *Dir*, Kentucky Historical Society, Old State Capitol & Annex, Frankfort KY

Kluba, William, *Instr*, Tunxis Community College, Graphic Design Dept, Farmington CT (S)

Klueg, James, *Assoc Prof*, University of Minnesota, Duluth, Art Dept, Duluth MN (S)

Kluetz, Patricia, *Assoc Prof*, University of Wisconsin-Stevens Point, Dept of Art & Design, Stevens Point WI (S)

Kluge, Janice, *Assoc Prof*, University of Alabama at Birmingham, Dept of Art, Birmingham AL (S)

Klukas, Carrie, *Technician*, Prairie Art Gallery, Grande Prairie AB

Kluttz, Ann, *Instr*, University of North Carolina at Charlotte, Dept of Visual Arts, Charlotte NC (S)

Klyberg, Albert T, *Dir*, Rhode Island Historical Society, Providence RI

Knab, Bernie, *Dir*, Chemeketa Community College, Dept of Humanities & Communications, Salem OR (S)

Knapp, M Jason, *Chmn*, Anderson University, Art Dept, Anderson IN (S)

Knapp, Tim, *Asst Dir*, Cleveland State University, Art Gallery, Cleveland OH

Knash, Bob, *Treas*, Wayne County Historical Society, Museum, Honesdale PA

Knaub, Donald E, *Dir*, Wichita State University, Edwin A Ulrich Museum of Art, Wichita KS

Knauer, Del, *Dir & VPres*, Hutchinson Art Association, Hutchinson Art Center, Hutchinson KS

Knauer, Scott, *Acting Dir*, New Harmony Gallery of Contemporary Art, New Harmony IN

Knauth, Sharon, *Dir*, Butte Silver Bow Arts Chateau, Butte MT

Knebel, Mary, *Reference Librn*, Hallmark Cards, Inc, Creative Library, Kansas City MO

Knecht, Elizabeth, *Graphic Designer*, Alaska State Museum, Juneau AK

Knecht, John, *Chmn*, Colgate University, Dept of Art & Art History, Hamilton NY (S)

Knecht, Samuel, *Dir*, Hillsdale College, Art Dept, Hillsdale MI (S)

Kneeland, Brenda, *Admin Asst*, Custer County Art Center, Miles City MT

Kneeland, Donna, *Develop Dir*, Monterey Museum of Art Association, Monterey CA

Kneppelt, Sue, *Exec Dir*, Associated Artists of Winston-Salem, Winston-Salem NC

Knepper, Alice, *Adjunct Prof*, Missouri Southern State College, Dept of Art, Joplin MO (S)

Knicely, Carol, *Asst Prof*, University of British Columbia, Dept of Fine Arts, Vancouver BC (S)

Knight, Clarence, *Chmn*, Bowie State University, Fine Arts Dept, Bowie MD (S)

Knight, David, *Dir*, Northern Kentucky University Gallery, Highland Heights KY

Knight, Gregory G, *Dir Visual Arts*, Chicago Department of Cultural Affairs, Chicago Cultural Center, Chicago IL

Knight, Margot H, *Exec Dir*, Idaho Commission on the Arts, Boise ID

Knight, Mary Ann, *Music & Arts Librn*, Berkshire Athenaeum Library, Reference Dept, Pittsfield MA

Knight, Michael, *Cur Chinese Art*, Asian Art Museum of San Francisco, Avery Brundage Collection, San Francisco CA

Knight, Robert, *VPres Visual Arts*, Scottsdale Center for the Arts, Scottsdale AZ

Knodel, Gerhardt, *Dir*, Cranbrook Academy of Art, Bloomfield Hills MI (S)

Knoke, Elisabeth, *Pres*, Association of Hawaii Artists, Honolulu HI

Knoll, Ann, *Dir*, Saginaw Art Museum, Couse Memorial Library, Saginaw MI

Knoll, Ann M, *Dir*, Saginaw Art Museum, Saginaw MI

Knopf, David, *Business Mgr*, J B Speed Art Museum, Louisville KY

Knott, Mike, *Pres*, Muscatine Art Center, Muscatine IA

Knott, Patricia, *Bus Mgr*, Oklahoma City Art Museum, Library, Oklahoma City OK

Knott, Robert, *Chmn*, Wake Forest University, Dept of Art, Winston-Salem NC (S)

Knott, Trish, *Adminr*, Oklahoma City Art Museum, Oklahoma City OK

Knowles, Karen, *Asst to Cur*, University of Louisville, Slide Collection, Louisville KY

Knowles, Millard B, *Pres*, United Methodist Historical Society, Lovely Lane Museum, Baltimore MD

Knowlton, Kenn, *Instr*, Art Academy of Cincinnati, Cincinnati OH (S)

Knox, Northrup R, *VPres*, The Buffalo Fine Arts Academy, Albright-Knox Art Gallery, Buffalo NY

Knox, Tyra, *Admin Asst*, Springfield Art Museum, Springfield MO

Knudsen, Dean, *Historian*, Oregon Trail Museum Association, Scotts Bluff National Monument, Gering NE

Knutsen, Jim, *Dir*, Black Hills State University, Ruddell Gallery, Spearfish SD

Knutson, Michael, *Prof Art*, Reed College, Dept of Art, Portland OR (S)

Knutson, Norman, *Prof*, Adrian College, Art & Design Dept, Adrian MI (S)

Kobrynich, Bill, *Dir Interior Design*, Art Institute of Fort Lauderdale, Fort Lauderdale FL (S)

Koby, Saundra, *Cur*, French Art Colony, Gallipolis OH

Koch, George C, *Pres*, National Artists Equity Association Inc, Washington DC

Koch, Loretta, *Humanities Librn*, Southern Illinois University, Morris Library, Carbondale IL

Koch, Paula, *Dir*, Wilkes Art Gallery, North Wilkesboro NC

Kochan, Roman V, *Acting Dir*, California State University, Long Beach, University Library, Long Beach CA

Kocher, Robert, *Prof*, Coe College, Dept of Art, Cedar Rapids IA (S)

Kocot, Marion, *Traveling Exhibits Coordr*, International Center of Photography, New York NY

Koehler, Ron, *Prof*, Delta State University, Dept of Art, Cleveland MS (S)

Koehn, Judd R, *Assoc Prof Art*, Eastern Oregon State College, Arts & Humanities Dept, La Grande OR (S)

Koenig, Jennifer, *Dir Educ*, New Jersey Center for Visual Arts, Summit NJ

Koerlin, Ernest, *Assoc Prof*, Wright State University, Dept of Art & Art History, Dayton OH (S)

Koetter, Fred, *Dean*, Yale University, School of Architecture, New Haven CT (S)

Koetting, Delores, *Treas*, St Genevieve Museum, Sainte Genevieve MO

Kohl, Allan, *Slide Librn*, Minneapolis College of Art & Design, Library, Minneapolis MN

Kohloff, R Skip, *Pres*, Colorado Photographic Arts Center, Denver CO

Kohn, Hannah, *House Chmn*, Plastic Club, Art Club, Philadelphia PA

Kohn, Mary Ann, *Treas*, Watercolor Society of Alabama, Birmingham AL

Kolb, Nancy D, *Exec Dir*, Please Touch Museum, Philadelphia PA

Kolbe, William, *Prof*, Southwest Texas State University, Dept of Art, San Marcos TX (S)

Koletar, Martha, *Dir Human Resources*, Whitney Museum of American Art, New York NY

Kolinski, Laura, *Cur Educ*, Canton Museum of Art, Canton OH (S)

Kolisnyk, Anne, *Exec Dir*, Ontario Association of Art Galleries, Toronto ON

Kollasch, Sheila, *Cur*, Maricopa County Historical Society, Desert Caballeros Western Museum, Wickenburg AZ

Kolmstetter, Ursual, *Reference Librn*, Indianapolis Museum of Art, Stout Reference Library, Indianapolis IN

Kolok, William, *Chmn*, Kentucky Wesleyan College, Dept Art, Owensboro KY (S)

Kolt, Ingrid, *Cur Programs*, Surrey Art Gallery, Surrey BC

Kolt, Ingrid, *Cur Prog*, Surrey Art Gallery, Library, Surrey BC

Koltun, Nancy, *First VPres*, North Shore Art League, Winnetka IL

Komor, Valerie, *Supv & Archivist*, Archives of American Art, New York Regional Center, Washington DC

Kong, Ron, *Cur*, The Canadian Craft Museum, Vancouver BC

Konkus, Helene, *Lending Dept Supv*, Newark Museum Association, The Newark Museum, Newark NJ

Konowitz, Ellen, *Asst Prof*, Vanderbilt University, Dept of Fine Arts, Nashville TN (S)

Konyer, Valerie, *Pres*, The Lindsay Gallery, Lindsay ON

Koob, Richard, *Exec Dir*, Kalani Honua Institute for Cultural Studies, Pahoa HI (S)

Koolman, Bill, *Library Technician*, San Francisco Maritime National Historical Park, J Porter Shaw Library, San Francisco CA

Koons, Darell, *Instr*, Bob Jones University, School of Fine Arts, Greenville SC (S)

Koonts, Russell, *Reference Archivist*, Duke University Library, Hartman Center for Sales, Advertising & Marketing History, Durham NC

Koop, Kathy, *Dir*, Westminster College, Art Gallery, New Wilmington PA

Koop, Rebecca, *Instr*, William Jewell College, Art Dept, Liberty MO (S)

Koos, Greg, *Exec Dir*, McLean County Historical Society, Bloomington IL

Kopatz, Kim, *Slide Cur*, University of Rochester, Art Library, Rochester NY

Kopf, Vicki, *Asst Dir*, Southeastern Center for Contemporary Art, Winston-Salem NC

Koplin, Bruce M, *Chmn*, Virginia Commonwealth University, Art History Dept, Richmond VA (S)

Koplinka-Loehr, Michael, *Dir*, DeWitt Historical Society of Tompkins County, Ithaca NY

Kopp, James J, *Dir*, University of Portland, Wilson W Clark Memorial Library, Portland OR

Koppy, Ann, *Dir*, Coos County Historical Society Museum, North Bend OR

Kopran, Eileen, *Public Servs Dir*, Dickinson State University, Stoxen Library, Dickinson ND

Kordich, Diane D, *Prof*, Northern Michigan University, Dept of Art & Design, Marquette MI (S)

Korenic, Lynette, *Head Arts Library*, University of California, Santa Barbara, Arts Library, Santa Barbara CA

Korman, Joseph, *Coll Mgr*, Douglas County Historical Society, Fairlawn Mansion & Museum, Superior WI

Korman, Joseph, *Coll Mgr*, Douglas County Historical Society, Archives, Superior WI

Korn, Henry, *Exec Dir*, Guild Hall of East Hampton, Inc, Guild Hall Museum, East Hampton NY

Kornacki, Frances E, *Asst to Dir*, Slater-Norton Corporation, Slater Memorial Museum & Converse Art Gallery, Norwich CT

Kornetchuk, Elena, *Pres*, International Images, Ltd, Sewickley PA

Kornfeld, Fran, *Asst to Dir*, Viridian Artists inc, New York NY

Kornhauser, Stephen, *Head Conservator*, Wadsworth Atheneum, Hartford CT

Kornwolf, James D, *Prof*, College of William & Mary, Dept of Fine Arts, Williamsburg VA (S)

Korol, Korene, *Arts Specialist*, Patterson Library & Art Gallery, Westfield NY

Korom, Frank, *Cur Middle Eastern-Asian Coll*, Museum of New Mexico, Museum of International Folk Art, Santa Fe NM

Koron, Vicki, *Instr*, Wayne Art Center, Wayne PA (S)

Koropp, Robert G, *Pres*, Gilpin County Arts Association, Central City CO

Koroscik, Judith, *Assoc Prof*, Ohio State University, Dept of Art Education, Columbus OH (S)

Korshak, Yvonne, *Prof*, Adelphi University, Dept of Art & Art History, Garden City NY (S)

Korte, Gerald, *Faculty*, Grand Marais Art Colony, Grand Marais MN (S)

Korten, Noel, *Prog Dir*, Los Angeles Municipal Art Gallery, Los Angeles CA

Kortun, Vasif, *Dir*, Bard College, Center for Curatorial Studies Museum, Annandale on Hudson NY

Korzun, Jonathan, *Instr*, Southwestern Michigan College, Fine & Performing Arts Dept, Dowagiac MI (S)

Koschmann, Edward, *VPres*, Brooklyn Historical Society, Brooklyn OH

Koshalek, Richard, *Dir*, The Museum of Contemporary Art, Los Angeles CA

Koshel, Terry, *Instr*, Sarah Lawrence College, Dept of Art History, Bronxville NY (S)

Kosinski, Joanna, *Pres*, Polish Museum of America, Chicago IL

Koski, Ann L, *Dir*, Neville Public Museum, Green Bay WI

Koski, Beth, *Exec Dir*, Ashtabula Arts Center, Ashtabula OH

Koslosky, Robert, *Prof*, Bloomsburg University, Dept of Art, Bloomsburg PA (S)

Koslow, Susan, *Prof*, City University of New York, PhD Program in Art History, New York NY (S)

Kosmere, Ellen, *Chmn*, Worcester State College, Visual & Performing Arts Dept, Worcester MA (S)

Koss, Allen, *Chmn Graphic Arts & Design*, Temple University, Tyler School of Art, Philadelphia PA (S)

Koss, Elaine, *Vice Dir Publications*, Brooklyn Museum, Brooklyn NY

Koss, Gene H, *Assoc Prof*, Tulane University, Sophie H Newcomb Memorial College, New Orleans LA (S)

Kossan, Carolyn, *Educ Cur*, Art & Culture Center of Hollywood, Hollywood FL

Kostel, Karen, *Educ Dir*, Arts Council of Fayetteville-Cumberland County, The Arts Center, Fayetteville NC

Kostelny, Elizabeth, *Cur*, Association for the Preservation of Virginia Antiquities, Library, Richmond VA

Koster, Anna, *Coll Mgr & Public Relations Officer*, Santa Clara University, de Saisset Museum, Santa Clara CA

Kostuch, Dorothy, *Chmn Academic Studies*, Center for Creative Studies, College of Art & Design, Detroit MI (S)

Kosuge, Michihiro, *Prof*, Portland State University, Dept of Art, Portland OR (S)

Kot, Malgorzata, *Librn*, Polish Museum of America, Research Library, Chicago IL

Kotik, Charlotta, *Cur Contemporary Art*, Brooklyn Museum, Brooklyn NY

Kotter, Paulette, *Dir*, Lewis County Historical Museum, Chehalis WA

Kotter, Paulette, *Dir*, Lewis County Historical Museum, Library, Chehalis WA

Koutecky, Judy, *Admin Asst*, Mendel Art Gallery & Civic Conservatory, Saskatoon SK

Koutroulis, Aris, *Chmn Fine Arts*, Center for Creative Studies, College of Art & Design, Detroit MI (S)

Kovach, Sally, *Chmn*, University of North Carolina at Charlotte, Dept of Visual Arts, Charlotte NC (S)

Kovacs, Rudy, *Faculty*, Idaho State University, Dept of Art, Pocatello ID (S)

Kovacs, Thomas, *In Charge Graphic Design*, University of Illinois, Urbana-Champaign, School of Art & Design, Champaign IL (S)

Kovatch, Ron, *In Charge Ceramics*, University of Illinois, Urbana-Champaign, School of Art & Design, Champaign IL (S)

Kowal, Calvin, *Instr*, Art Academy of Cincinnati, Cincinnati OH (S)

Kowalchek, Elizabeth, *Asst Prof*, University of Kansas, Dept of Art & Music Education & Music Therapy, Lawrence KS (S)

Kowalski, Jeff, *Div Coordr*, Northern Illinois University, School of Art, De Kalb IL (S)

Kowalski, Libby, *Instr*, Chautauqua Institution, School of Art, Chautauqua NY (S)

Kowalski, Libby, *Assoc Prof*, State University of New York, College at Cortland, Art Dept, Cortland NY (S)

Kowaski, Paul, *Adjunct Instr*, Saginaw Valley State University, Dept of Art & Design, University Center MI (S)

Kownacki, William, *Librn*, Bassist College Library, Portland OR

Kowski, Robert, *Prof*, Greensboro College, Dept of Art, Division of Fine Arts, Greensboro NC (S)

Kowski, Robert, *Assoc Prof*, Greensboro College, Irene Cullis Gallery, Greensboro NC

Kozak, Nancy, *Coordr*, Cumberland County College, Humanities Div, Vineland NJ (S)

Kozbial, Ardys, *Librn*, Payette Associates Architects Planners, Library, Boston MA

Kozik, Patricia, *Dir*, University of Wisconsin, Union Art Gallery, Milwaukee WI

Kozloff, Arielle P, *Cur Ancient Art*, Cleveland Museum of Art, Cleveland OH

Kozlowski, Barbara, *Assoc Dir Public Servs*, Skokie Public Library, Skokie IL

Kozman, Kathryn Hubner, *Instr & Supervisor*, Toronto Art Therapy Institute, Toronto ON (S)

Kraball, Merrill, *Chmn*, Bethel College, Dept of Art, North Newton KS (S)

Kraemer, Pat, *Instr*, Rochester Community & Technical College, Art Dept, Rochester MN (S)

Kraft, Ann, *Asst to Dir*, Solomon R Guggenheim Museum, New York NY

Kraft, Ann, *Asst to Dir*, Guggenheim Museum Soho, New York NY

Kraft, Michelle, *Instr*, Lubbock Christian University, Dept of Communication & Fine Art, Lubbock TX (S)

Kraft, Richard, *Instr*, Pacific Northwest College of Art, Portland OR (S)

Kraichnan, Lajla, *Registrar*, Sharon Arts Center, Peterborough NH

Krainak, Paul, *Prof*, West Virginia University, College of Creative Arts, Morgantown WV (S)

Kram, Barbara, *Acting Dir*, The Barnum Museum, Bridgeport CT

Kramer, Carol, *Preparator*, Mary Washington College, Ridderhof Martin Gallery, Fredericksburg VA

Kramer, Edith, *Cur Film*, University of California, Berkeley Art Museum & Pacific Film Archive, Berkeley CA

Kramer, Edith, *Cur Film*, University of California, Pacific Film Archive, Berkeley CA

Kramer, Gerald, *Prof*, Cuyahoga Community College, Dept of Art, Cleveland OH (S)

Kramer, Jim, *Gallery Operations Mgr*, Madison Art Center, Madison WI

Kramer, Larry, *Pres*, Avila College, Thornhill Art Gallery, Kansas City MO

Kramer, Leslie, *Dir*, Elmira College, George Waters Gallery, Elmira NY

Kramer, Leslie, *Asst Prof*, Elmira College, Art Dept, Elmira NY (S)

Kramer, Sandra, *VPres*, San Bernardino County Museum, Fine Arts Institute, Redlands CA

Kramer, Steve, *Head Dept South Campus*, Austin Community College, Dept of Commercial Art, North Ridge Campus, Austin TX (S)

Kramer, Trudy, *Dir*, The Parrish Art Museum, Southampton NY

Kramer, Vallery, *Dir Marketing*, Kentucky Art & Craft Gallery, Louisville KY

Krammes, Barry A, *Chmn Dept*, Biola University, Art Dept, La Mirada CA (S)

Krane, Susan, *Dir*, University of Colorado, Art Galleries, Boulder CO

Kraning, Al, *Prof*, University of Nebraska, Kearney, Dept of Art & Art History, Kearney NE (S)

Kraskin, Sandra, *Dir*, Baruch College of the City University of New York, Sidney Mishkin Gallery, New York NY

Krathwohl, Kristin, *Dir Public Relations*, The Phillips Collection, Washington DC

Kraus, Corrine, *Instr*, Milwaukee Area Technical College, Graphic Arts Division, Milwaukee WI (S)

Kraus, Linda, *Adjunct Asst Prof*, Spokane Falls Community College, Fine Arts Dept, Spokane WA (S)

Kraus, Russell C, *Prof*, Rochester Institute of Technology, School of Photographic Arts & Sciences, Rochester NY (S)

Krause, Bonnie J, *Dir*, University of Mississippi, University Museums, Oxford MS

Krause, Bonnie J, *Dir*, University of Mississippi, University Museums Library, Oxford MS

Krause, Carolyn, *Communications*, Contemporary Arts Center, Cincinnati OH

Krause, Darrell R, *Park Mgr*, Florida Department of Environmental Protection, Stephen Foster State Folk Culture Center, White Springs FL

Krause, Lawrence, *Prof*, Cleveland Institute of Art, Cleveland OH (S)

Krause, Martin F, *Cur Prints & Drawings*, Indianapolis Museum of Art, Indianapolis IN

Krauss, James A, *Chmn & Prof*, Oakton Community College, Art & Architecture Dept, Des Plaines IL (S)

Krauss, Rosalind, *Prof*, City University of New York, PhD Program in Art History, New York NY (S)

Krausz, Peter, *Instr*, Universite de Montreal, Dept of Art History, Montreal PQ (S)

Kraut, Adrienne, *Art Educ Coordn*, San Jose State University, School of Art & Design, San Jose CA (S)

Kraut, Barbara, *VPres*, Washington Art Association, Washington Depot CT

Krawczyk, Joan, *Dir*, Viridian Artists inc, New York NY

Kray, Gordon, *Adjunct Prof*, Trinity College, Art Program, Washington DC (S)

Kray, Hazele, *Cur*, The Bartlett Museum, Amesbury MA

Krebs, Jerry, *Assoc Prof*, Radford University, Art Dept, Radford VA (S)

Krech, Shepard, *Dir*, Brown University, Haffenreffer Museum, Providence RI

Kreft, Barbara, *Prof*, Hamline University, Dept of Art & Art History, Saint Paul MN (S)

Kreger, Philip, *Dir Exhib*, Tennessee State Museum, Nashville TN

Krehbiel, James, *Assoc Prof*, Ohio Wesleyan University, Fine Arts Dept, Delaware OH (S)

Krehe, Lynette, *Co-Dir*, 1078 Gallery, Chico CA

Krehmeier, Bill, *Instr*, Hannibal La Grange College, Art Dept, Hannibal MO (S)

Kreilick, Cynthia, *Educ Prog Specialist*, Please Touch Museum, Philadelphia PA

Kreipe de Montano, Marty, *Resource Center Mgr*, National Museum of the American Indian, George Gustav Heye Center, New York NY

Kreischer, Patricia, *Graphic Artist*, Lake Forest Library, Fine Arts Dept, Lake Forest IL

Kreisher, Katharine, *Chmn*, Hartwick College, Art Dept, Oneonta NY (S)

Krejcarek, Philip, *Assoc Prof*, Carroll College, Art Dept, Waukesha WI (S)

Kremer, William, *Chmn*, University of Notre Dame, Dept of Art, Art History & Design, Notre Dame IN (S)

Kremgold, David, *Assoc Prof*, University of Florida, Dept of Art, Gainesville FL (S)

Kren, Margo, *Assoc Prof*, Kansas State University, Art Dept, Manhattan KS (S)

Kren, Thom, *Cur Manuscripts*, Getty Center for the History of Art & the Humanities Trust Museum, Santa Monica CA

Kren, Thomas, *Cur Manuscripts*, Getty Center for the History of Art & the Humanities Trust Museum, The J Paul Getty Museum, Santa Monica CA

Kreneck, Lynwood, *Prof*, Texas Tech University, Dept of Art, Lubbock TX (S)

Krens, Thomas, *Dir*, Solomon R Guggenheim Museum, New York NY

Krens, Thomas, *Dir*, Guggenheim Museum Soho, New York NY

Kreplin, Bill, *Lectr*, Webster University, Art Dept, Webster Groves MO (S)

Krepp, Sarah, *In Charge Painting*, University of Illinois, Urbana-Champaign, School of Art & Design, Champaign IL (S)

Krepps, Jerald, *Assoc Prof*, University of Minnesota, Minneapolis, Dept of Art, Minneapolis MN (S)

Kresse, Kevin, *Instr*, The Arkansas Arts Center, Museum School, Little Rock AR (S)

Kret, Robert A, *Dir*, Leigh Yawkey Woodson Art Museum, Inc, Wausau WI

Kretz, Kate, *Instr & Art Historian*, Florida International University, Visual Arts Dept, Miami FL (S)

Krevenas, Michel, *Exec Dir*, Springfield Art Association of Edwards Place, Springfield IL

Kreyling, Christine, *Cur Coll*, Cheekwood Nashville's Home of Art & Gardens, Education Dept, Nashville TN (S)

Kreyling, Christine, *Cur Coll & Exhib*, Cheekwood-Tennessee Botanical Gardens & Museum of Art, Nashville TN

Krichman, Michael, *Exec Dir*, Installation Gallery, San Diego CA

Kridel, Craig, *Cur Education Museum*, University of South Carolina, McKissick Museum, Columbia SC

Kriebel, Marjorie, *Head Dept Interiors & Graphic Studies*, Drexel University, Nesbitt College of Design Arts, Philadelphia PA (S)

Krieger, Brad, *Vis Prof*, Nebraska Wesleyan University, Art Dept, Lincoln NE (S)

Kriegsman, Bethany, *Dir*, University of Denver, School of Art & Art History, Denver CO (S)

Kriekle, Donna, *Visual Arts Coordr*, Organization of Saskatchewan Arts Councils (OSAC), Regina SK

Kriele, Shelby, *Cur*, Greene County Historical Society, Bronck Museum, Coxsackie NY

Kriley, James D, *Dean*, University of Montana, Paxson Gallery, Missoula MT

Krist, Dennis, *Asst Prof*, Indiana-Purdue University, Dept of Fine Arts, Fort Wayne IN (S)

Kristof, Jane, *Assoc Prof*, Portland State University, Dept of Art, Portland OR (S)

Krivitz, James, *Deputy Operations Dir*, Milwaukee Public Museum, Milwaukee WI

Kroeber, Jean T, *Pres*, Catharine Lorillard Wolfe Art Club, Inc, New York NY

Kroeker, Marvin E, *Pres Board Trustees*, Oklahoma Historical Society, State Museum of History, Oklahoma City OK

Kroeker, Melanie, *Marketing & Develop Officer*, Prince George Art Gallery, Prince George BC

Kroeker, Richard, *Asst Prof*, Technical University of Nova Scotia, Faculty of Architecture, Halifax NS (S)

Kroff, Linda, *Prof*, University of North Carolina at Charlotte, Dept of Visual Arts, Charlotte NC (S)

Krol, Penne, *Instr*, Greenfield Community College, Art, Graphic Design & Media Communication Dept, Greenfield MA (S)

Kroll, James, *Head Dept*, Denver Public Library, General Reference, Denver CO

Kroll, Zoey, *Asst Develop Dir*, The Lab, San Francisco CA

Kromm, Jane, *Coordr*, State University of New York College at Purchase, Art History Board of Study, Purchase NY (S)

Krone, Ted, *Chmn*, Friends University, Art Dept, Wichita KS (S)

Kronewetter, Justin, *Chmn*, Ohio Wesleyan University, Fine Arts Dept, Delaware OH (S)

Kroning, Melissa, *Registrar*, National Museum of American Art, Washington DC

Kroop, Bernie, *Instructional Asst*, Sullivan County Community College, Division of Commercial Art & Photography, Loch Sheldrake NY (S)

Kropf, Joan R, *Librn*, Salvador Dali Museum, Library, Saint Petersburg FL

Krueger, Donald W, *Dir Studio Art Prog*, Clark University, Dept of Visual & Performing Arts, Worcester MA (S)

Krueger, J, *VPres*, American Institute for Conservation of Historic & Artistic Works (AIC), Washington DC

Krueger, Lou, *Dir*, Bowling Green State University, School of Art, Bowling Green OH (S)

Krueger, Nancy L, *Asst Dir*, Wilkes University, Sordoni Art Gallery, Wilkes-Barre PA

Krug, Kersti, *Dir Communications*, University of British Columbia, Museum of Anthropology, Vancouver BC

Kruger, Laura, *Chair, Exhib Advisory Committee*, Hebrew Union College-Jewish Institute of Religion, New York NY

Krule, Bernard K, *Assoc Prof*, Oakton Community College, Art & Architecture Dept, Des Plaines IL (S)

Krulik, Barbara S, *Dir*, New York Academy of Art, Graduate School of Figurative Art, New York NY (S)

Krull, Jeffrey R, *Dir*, Allen County Public Library, Art, Music & Audiovisual Services, Fort Wayne IN

Krumenauer, Kris, *Instr*, Marian College, Art Dept, Fond Du Lac WI (S)

Kruse, Donald, *Assoc Prof*, Indiana-Purdue University, Dept of Fine Arts, Fort Wayne IN (S)

Kruse, Gerald, *Assoc Prof*, South Dakota State University, Dept of Visual Arts, Brookings SD (S)

Krushenisky, Laurie, *Educ Coordr*, Michelson Museum of Art, Marshall TX

Krute, Carol, *Cur Costume & Textiles*, Wadsworth Atheneum, Hartford CT

Kryszko, Karen, *Assoc Prof*, Saint Mary's University of Minnesota, Art & Design Dept, Winona MN (S)

Kuan, Baulu, *Assoc Prof*, College of Saint Benedict, Art Dept, Saint Joseph MN (S)

Kuan, Baulu, *Assoc Prof*, Saint John's University, Art Dept, Collegeville MN (S)

Kubert, Joe, *Pres*, Joe Kubert School of Cartoon & Graphic Art, Inc, Dover NJ (S)

Kubiak, Kathy, *Instr*, Mount Mary College, Art Dept, Milwaukee WI (S)

Kuchar, Kathleen, *Prof*, Fort Hays State University, Dept of Art, Hays KS (S)

Kucharski, Malcolm E, *Assoc Prof*, Pittsburg State University, Art Dept, Pittsburg KS (S)

Kuchta, Ronald A, *Dir*, Everson Museum of Art, Syracuse NY

Kuczek, Lorraine, *Slide Cur*, School of Visual Arts Library, New York NY

Kuczynski, John D, *Art Dept Chmn*, Pierce College, Art Dept, Woodland Hills CA (S)

Kudder-Sullivan, P, *Assoc Prof*, Southampton College of Long Island University, Arts & Media Division, Southampton NY (S)

Kuehn, Gary, *Prof*, Rutgers, the State University of New Jersey, Mason Gross School of the Arts, New Brunswick NJ (S)

Kuehne, Kleda, *Office Mgr*, 2nd Crossing Arts Center, Valley City ND

Kueppers, Brigitte, *Arts Special Coll Librn*, University of California, Los Angeles, Arts Library, Los Angeles CA

Kugler, Sharon, *Asst Mgr*, Queens Borough Public Library, Fine Arts & Recreation Division, Jamaica NY

Kuhl, Nora, *Exec Dir*, Dinnerware Artist's Cooperative, Tucson AZ

Kuhnen, Mary, *Instr*, Mount Mary College, Art Dept, Milwaukee WI (S)

Kuhta, Richard J, *Librn*, Folger Shakespeare Library, Washington DC

Kuiper, James, *Instr*, California State University, Chico, Art Dept, Chico CA (S)

Kuipers, Margorie, *Exec Dir*, Urban Institute for Contemporary Arts, Grand Rapids MI

Kukla, Jon, *Dir*, Kemper & Leila Williams Foundation, New Orleans LA

Kulik, Gary, *Dir*, Winterthur Museum, Library, Winterthur DE

Kulpas, Dennis, *Financial Mgr*, Contemporary Art Gallery Society of British Columbia, Vancouver BC

Kumnick, Charles, *Assoc Prof*, College of New Jersey, Art Dept, Trenton NJ (S)

Kuncevich, Michael, *Pres*, American Color Print Society, Philadelphia PA

Kundar, Cynthia A, *Dir & Educ Dir*, Merrick Art Gallery, New Brighton PA

Kuniholm, Peter I, *Assoc Prof*, Cornell University, Dept of the History of Art, Ithaca NY (S)

Kuntz, Karen, *Coll Develop*, Chicago Public Library, Harold Washington Library Center, Chicago IL

Kuoni, Carin, *Dir*, Swiss Institute, New York NY

Kuper, Nora, *Registrar*, University of North Carolina at Greensboro, Weatherspoon Art Gallery, Greensboro NC

Kupper, Ketti, *Asst Prof*, University of Bridgeport, School of Arts, Humanities & Social Sciences, Bridgeport CT (S)

Kupris, Valdis, *Prof*, New York Institute of Technology, Fine Arts Dept, Old Westbury NY (S)

Kurany, Jain, *Gallery Adminr*, Latitude 53 Society of Artists, Edmonton AB

Kurcz, A, *Pres*, Rodman Hall Arts Centre, Saint Catharines ON

Kuretsky, Susan D, *Prof*, Vassar College, Art Dept, Poughkeepsie NY (S)

Kurlander, Amy, *Cur Modern Art*, Oberlin College, Allen Memorial Art Museum, Oberlin OH

Kurti, Esther, *Instr*, University of North Carolina at Charlotte, Dept of Visual Arts, Charlotte NC (S)

Kurtich, John, *Prof*, School of the Art Institute of Chicago, Chicago IL (S)

Kurutz, K D, *Cur Educ*, Crocker Art Museum, Sacramento CA

Kurytnik, Kevin, *Pres*, Quickdraw Animation Society, Calgary AB

Kurzbauer, Ruth, *Asst Dir*, Utah Travel Council, Salt Lake City UT

Kusaba, Yoshio, *Instr*, California State University, Chico, Art Dept, Chico CA (S)

Kuspit, Donald B, *Prof*, State University of New York at Stony Brook, Art Dept, Stony Brook NY (S)

Kusz, Thomas, *Instr*, Milwaukee Area Technical College, Graphic Arts Division, Milwaukee WI (S)

Kutbay, Bonnie, *Asst Prof*, Mansfield University, Art Dept, Mansfield PA (S)

Kutchins, Alex, *Chmn*, Park College, Dept of Art, Parkville MO (S)

Kuwayama, George, *Cur Far Eastern Art*, Los Angeles County Museum of Art, Los Angeles CA

Kuykendall, Alan, *Pres*, Rosemount Museum, Inc, Pueblo CO

Kuzminski, Catherine, *Chmn Fine Arts Program*, Westminster College of Salt Lake City, Dept of Arts, Salt Lake City UT (S)

Kwasigroh, David, *Dir*, Schweinfurth Art Center, Auburn NY

Kwiatkowski, Phillip C, *Exec Dir*, Tippecanoe County Historical Museum, Lafayette IN

Kyle, Jane, *Chief Academic Officer*, Oregon College of Art Craft, Hoffman Gallery, Portland OR

Kzapil, Jay, *Chmn*, California State University, Long Beach, Art Dept, Long Beach CA (S)

LaBarbera, Anne, *Museum Shop*, Niagara University, Castellani Art Museum, Niagara NY

LaBat, Karen, *Textile Cur*, University of Minnesota, Goldstein Gallery, Saint Paul MN

Labbe, Armand J, *Chief Cur*, Bower's Museum, Santa Ana CA

Labe, Paul, *Prof*, Harford Community College, Fine & Applied Arts Division, Bel Air MD (S)

LaBelle, Marguarite, *Assoc Prof*, Jersey City State College, Art Dept, Jersey City NJ (S)

Laber, Philip, *Olive DeLuce Art Gallery Coll Cur*, Northwest Missouri State University, DeLuce Art Gallery, Maryville MO

Laber, Philip, *Assoc Prof*, Northwest Missouri State University, Dept of Art, Maryville MO (S)

LaBey, Armand, *Treas*, Mingei International, Inc, Mingei International Museum Satellite of World Folk Art, San Diego CA

LaBlanc, Necol, *Secy*, Galerie d'art de l'Universite de Moncton, Moncton NB

LaBonte, Linelle, *Prof*, College of Notre Dame of Maryland, Art Dept, Baltimore MD (S)

LaBossiere, Holly, *Prof*, Ponca City Library, Art Dept, Ponca City OK

Labranche, John, *Cur*, Old York Historical Society, Old Gaol Museum, York ME

Labuz, Ronald, *Head Dept*, Mohawk Valley Community College, Advertising Design & Production, Utica NY (S)

Lacey, Thomas, *Instr*, Indiana University of Pennsylvania, Dept of Art & Art Education, Indiana PA (S)

Lachapelle, Francois, *Dir Mus*, Le Musee Regional de Rimouski, Centre National d'Exposition, Rimouski PQ

Lachman, Diane, *Lectr*, University of Pennsylvania, Graduate School of Fine Arts, Philadelphia PA (S)

Lachowicz, Keith, *Asst Dir*, Mills College, Art Gallery, Oakland CA

Lackey, Jane, *Chmn Fiber*, Kansas City Art Institute, Kansas City MO (S)

LaCour, Beth, *Instr*, Yavapai College, Visual & Performing Arts Division, Prescott AZ (S)

LaCouture, Jay, *Chmn*, Salve Regina University, Art Dept, Newport RI (S)

LaCroix, Catherine, *Educ Dir*, Billie Trimble Chandler Arts Foundation, Asian Cultures Museum & Educational Center, Corpus Christi TX

Laczko, Gina, *Educ Servs Mgr*, Heard Museum, Phoenix AZ

Ladd, Vivian, *School & Community Outreach Coordr*, Dartmouth College, Hood Museum of Art, Hanover NH

Ladd-Simmons, Marilyn, *Gallery Mgr*, SPACES, Cleveland OH

Ladin, Stephen, *Grants Coordr*, Dutchess County Arts Council, Poughkeepsie NY

Ladis, Andrew, *Art History*, University of Georgia, Franklin College of Arts & Sciences, Lamar Dodd School of Art, Athens GA (S)

Ladkin, Nicola, *Coll Mgr (Anthropology)*, Texas Tech University, Museum, Lubbock TX

Ladnier, Paul, *Assoc Prof*, University of North Florida, Dept of Communications & Visual Arts, Jacksonville FL (S)

LaDouceur, Philip, *Dir*, Zanesville Art Center, Zanesville OH

Lafargue, Philippe, *Conservator*, Tryon Palace Historic Sites & Gardens, New Bern NC

Lafaye, Bryan F, *Cur*, Alexandria Museum of Art, Alexandria LA

Lafferty, Daniel, *VPres & Dir Educ*, The Art Institutes International, The Art Institute of Seattle, Seattle WA (S)

Laffitte, Polly, *Chief Cur Art*, South Carolina State Museum, Columbia SC

Lafkas, Marion, *Site Selector*, Marin County Watercolor Society, Greenbrae CA

Lafo, Rachel, *Cur*, DeCordova Museum & Sculpture Park, Lincoln MA

LaFollette, Curtis K, *Prof*, Rhode Island College, Art Dept, Providence RI (S)

La Follette, Laetitia, *Assoc Prof*, University of Massachusetts, Amherst, Art History Program, Amherst MA (S)

LaFontaine, Charles, *Cur*, Wells Fargo Bank, Wells Fargo History Museum, San Francisco CA

Laframboise, Alain, *Instr*, Universite de Montreal, Dept of Art History, Montreal PQ (S)

La France, Liselle, *Dir*, Historic Cherry Hill, Albany NY

LaFrance, Michael, *VPres*, LeSueur County Historical Museum, Chapter One, Elysian MN

Lagerkvist, Irmfriede, *Chmn Art Dept*, Barat College, Dept of Art, Lake Forest IL (S)

Lagimodiere, Claudette, *Educ Mgr*, Winnipeg Art Gallery, Winnipeg MB

Lagoria, Georgianna M, *Dir*, The Contemporary Museum, Honolulu HI

Lagos, Marta, *Co-Dir*, Casa de Unidad Unity House, Detroit MI

LaGreca, Mary, *Pres*, Hudson Valley Art Association, Hastings On Hudson NY

LaGue, Mary, *Registrar*, Art Museum of Western Virginia, Roanoke VA

Lahaye, Francois, *Dir*, Centre Culturel de Trois Rivieres, Trois Rivieres PQ

Lahikainen, Dean, *Cur*, Peabody Essex Museum, John Ward House, Salem MA

Lahikainen, Dean, *Cur*, Peabody Essex Museum, Andrew-Safford House, Salem MA

Lahr, Dr J Stephen, *Head Dept*, Valdosta State University, Dept of Art, Valdosta GA (S)

Lai, Charlie, *Co-Founder*, Museum of Chinese in the Americas, New York NY

Lai, Waihang, *Faculty*, Kauai Community College, Dept of Art, Lihue HI (S)

Laing, Aileen H, *Prof*, Sweet Briar College, Art History Dept, Sweet Briar VA (S)

Laing-Malcolmson, Bonnie, *Dir*, Paris Gibson Square, Museum of Art, Great Falls MT

Lainhoff, Thomas, *Dir*, Gunston Hall Plantation, Library, Mason Neck VA

Lainhoff, Thomas A, *Dir*, Gunston Hall Plantation, Mason Neck VA

Laiou, Angeliki, *Dir*, Harvard University, Dumbarton Oaks Research Library & Collections, Washington DC

Laird, Diane, *Instr*, College of New Jersey, Art Dept, Trenton NJ (S)

Laird, Lucinda, *Dir Public Relations*, Brandywine River Museum, Chadds Ford PA

Lake, Bob, *Dir*, Hot Springs Art Center, Fine Arts Center, Hot Springs AR

Lake, Ellen, *Head Dept*, Central Community College - Platte Campus, Business & Arts Cluster, Columbus NE (S)

Lake, Jerry L, *Prof*, George Washington University, Dept of Art, Washington DC (S)

Lakin, Debbie, *Public Relations Dir*, Laumeier Sculpture Park & Museum, Saint Louis MO

Lakin-Hayes, Mollie, *Public Information & Locals Dir*, Arizona Commission on the Arts, Phoenix AZ

Lakin-Hayes, Mollie, *Public Information & Locals Dir*, Arizona Commission on the Arts, Reference Library, Phoenix AZ

Laleian, Aida, *Chmn Studio Art*, Williams College, Dept of Art, Williamstown MA (S)

Lalima, Maria, *Ed Publications*, Walters Art Gallery, Baltimore MD

L'Allier, Pierre, *Conservator Modern Art*, Musee du Quebec, Quebec PQ

Lally, Ann, *Librn*, University of Arizona, College of Architecture Library, Tucson AZ

Lalonde, Jerome, *Asst Prof*, Mohawk Valley Community College, Advertising Design & Production, Utica NY (S)

Lalumiere, Marilyn, *Develop Dir*, Portland Museum of Art, Portland ME

Lamagna, Carlo, *Assoc Prof*, New York University, Dept of Art & Art Professions, New York NY (S)

La Malfa, James, *Head Dept*, University of Wisconsin Center-Marinette County, Art Dept, Marinette WI (S)

Laman, Jean, *Prof*, Southwest Texas State University, Dept of Art, San Marcos TX (S)

Lamar, Kent, *Prof*, University of Science & Arts of Oklahoma, Arts Dept, Chickasha OK (S)

Lamarche, Lise, *Instr*, Universite de Montreal, Dept of Art History, Montreal PQ (S)

LaMarcz, Howard, *Prof*, C W Post Center of Long Island University, School of Visual & Performing Arts, Brookville NY (S)

Lamb, Donna, *Transit Coordr*, Gallery Association of New York State, Hamilton NY

Lamb, Keith, *Instr*, Saint Louis Community College at Meramec, Art Dept, Saint Louis MO (S)

Lamb, Kurt H, *Dir*, Mexico-Audrain County Library, Mexico MO

Lambard, Richard, *Owner*, Art Questers, Cottonwood AZ

Lambert, Alice, *Chmn Art Dept*, Anna Maria College, Saint Luke's Gallery, Paxton MA

Lambert, Alice, *Chmn Dept*, Anna Maria College, Dept of Art, Paxton MA (S)

Lambert, Anne, *Cur Educ*, University of Wisconsin-Madison, Elvehjem Museum of Art, Madison WI

Lambert, Frederick A, *Exec Dir*, Oglebay Institute, Mansion Museum, Wheeling WV

Lambert, Kirby, *Cur Coll*, Montana Historical Society, Library, Helena MT

Lambert, Lisa Shippee, *Archivist & Librn*, Panhandle-Plains Historical Society Museum, Research Center, Canyon TX

Lambert, Phyllis, *Dir*, Canadian Centre for Architecture, Library, Montreal PQ

Lambert, William E, *Dir*, Del Mar College, Joseph A Cain Memorial Art Gallery, Corpus Christi TX

Lambert, William E, *Chmn*, Del Mar College, Art Dept, Corpus Christi TX (S)

Lambl, Christopher, *Asst Prof*, Clarion University of Pennsylvania, Dept of Art, Clarion PA (S)

Lambrechts, Lillian, *Dir & Cur*, Bank Boston, Gallery, Boston MA

Lamers, Clara, *Acting Head Librn*, Brooklyn Historical Society, Library, Brooklyn NY

Lamers, Nancy, *Chmn*, Alverno College, Art Dept, Milwaukee WI (S)

Lamia, Stephen, *Div Coordr*, Dowling College, Dept of Visual Arts, Oakdale NY (S)

Lamm, Gary, *Dept Dir Finance & Admin*, State Art Museum of Florida, John & Mable Ringling Museum of Art, Sarasota FL

Lamothe, Dona, *Prof*, Assumption College, Dept of Art & Music, Worcester MA (S)

Lamoureux, Johanne, *Instr*, Universite de Montreal, Dept of Art History, Montreal PQ (S)

La Moy, William T, *Librn*, Peabody Essex Museum, Phillips Library, Salem MA

Lamp, Frederick, *Cur Art of Africa, Americas, Oceania*, Baltimore Museum of Art, Baltimore MD

Lampe, William, *Technical Dir*, University of Minnesota, Weisman Art Museum, Minneapolis MN

Lampela, Laurel, *Assoc Prof*, Cleveland State University, Art Dept, Cleveland OH (S)

Lancaster, Ann, *Operations Mgr*, Houston Center For Photography, Houston TX

Lance, Janie, *Chmn*, Crowder College, Art & Design, Neosho MO (S)

Lancefield, Robert C, *Registrar*, Wesleyan University, Davison Art Center, Middletown CT

Lancet, Marc, *Instr*, Solano Community College, Division of Fine & Applied Art, Suisun City CA (S)

Land, Chris, *Art Handler*, Columbus Museum, Columbus GA

Land, Norman, *Prof*, University of Missouri, Art History & Archaeology Dept, Columbia MO (S)

Landau, Ellen G, *Prof*, Case Western Reserve University, Dept of Art History & Art, Cleveland OH (S)

Landau, Laureen, *Instr*, Sacramento City College, Art Dept, Sacramento CA (S)

Landay, Janet, *Assoc Dir Spec Projects*, Museum of Fine Arts, Houston, Houston TX

Landess, Sara, *Second VPres*, Springfield Museum of Art, Springfield OH

Landis, Dick, *Pres*, Southern Lorain County Historical Society, Spirit of '76 Museum, Wellington OH

Landis, Ellen J, *Cur Art*, Albuquerque Museum of Art & History, Albuquerque NM

Landman, Brenda, *Chmn Asst*, University of Memphis, Art Dept, Memphis TN (S)

Landon, Ellen, *VPres*, Octagon Center for the Arts, Ames IA

Landry, Jean, *Assoc Prof*, Notre Dame College, Art Dept, Manchester NH (S)

Landry, Pierre, *Asst Cur Later Canadian Art*, National Gallery of Canada, Ottawa ON

Landry, Yves, *Animatic*, Le Musee Regional de Rimouski, Centre National d'Exposition, Rimouski PQ

Landus, Matt, *Publicity Officer*, University of Louisville, Allen R Hite Art Institute Gallery, Louisville KY

Land-Weber, E, *Instr*, Humboldt State University, College of Arts & Humanities, Arcata CA (S)

Lane, Betty, *Librn*, Arkansas Arts Center, Elizabeth Prewitt Taylor Memorial Library, Little Rock AR

Lane, Bruce, *Asst Prof*, Rochester Institute of Technology, School of Photographic Arts & Sciences, Rochester NY (S)

Lane, Diane, *Admin Asst*, Art Gallery of Windsor, Windsor ON

Lane, Georgia, *Registrar*, Carson County Square House Museum, Panhandle TX

Lane, Hugh C, *Pres*, Charleston Museum, Charleston SC

Lane, John R, *Dir*, San Francisco Museum of Modern Art, San Francisco CA

Lane, Kerstin B, *Exec Dir*, Swedish American Museum Association of Chicago, Chicago IL

Lane, Linn, *Contact*, WomanKraft, Tucson AZ

Lane, Richard, *Treas-Secy*, The American Federation of Arts, New York NY

Lane, Rosemary, *Coordr Printmaking*, University of Delaware, Dept of Art, Newark DE (S)

Lane, Thomas, *Assoc Prof*, University of Minnesota, Minneapolis, Dept of Art, Minneapolis MN (S)

Lang, Brian, *Cur*, Jefferson County Open Space, Hiwan Homestead Museum, Evergreen CO

Lang, Brian J, *Art Dir*, Mellon Bank Corporation, Pittsburgh PA

Lang, Gary, *Vis Instr*, Claremont Graduate School, Dept of Fine Arts, Claremont CA (S)

Lang, James, *Prof*, La Salle University, Dept of Art, Philadelphia PA (S)

Lang, R Park, *Chmn*, Southwestern Oklahoma State University, Art Dept, Weatherford OK (S)

Lang, Sandra, *Exec Dir*, Independent Curators Inc, New York NY

Lang, Tom, *Adminr*, Webster University, Cecille R Hunt Gallery, Saint Louis MO

Lang, Tom, *Chmn*, Webster University, Art Dept, Webster Groves MO (S)

Lang, William, *Head Librn, Art Dept*, Free Library of Philadelphia, Art Dept, Philadelphia PA

Langa, Helen, *Asst Prof*, American University, Dept of Art, Washington DC (S)

Langevin, Ann, *Extension Serv*, Las Vegas-Clark County Library District, Las Vegas NV

Langkilde, Fagafaga D, *Chmn Board Trustees*, Jean P Haydon Museum, Pago Pago, American Samoa PI

Langley, James LeRoy, *Master Woodcarver*, Calvert Marine Museum, Solomons MD

Langmann, Saren, *Trustee*, Hill-Stead Museum, Farmington CT

Langston-Harrison, Lee, *Cur*, James Monroe Museum, Fredericksburg VA

Langston-Harrison, Lee, *Cur*, James Monroe Museum, James Monroe Memorial Library, Fredericksburg VA

Lanier, David, *Prof*, University of the District of Columbia, Dept of Mass Media, Visual & Performing Arts, Washington DC (S)

Lankford, Louis, *Assoc Prof*, Ohio State University, Dept of Art Education, Columbus OH (S)

Lanmon, Dwight P, *Dir*, Winterthur Museum, Winterthur DE

Lannon, John, *Assoc Dir*, Boston Athenaeum, Boston MA

Lansbury, Edgar, *Pres*, Nicholas Roerich Museum, New York NY

Lansdown, Robert R, *Dir*, Frank Phillips Foundation Inc, Library, Bartlesville OK

Lantz, David, *Publicist*, Madison Art Center, Madison WI

Lantz, Elizabeth A, *Asst Librn Technical Serv*, Cleveland Museum of Art, Ingalls Library, Cleveland OH

Lantz, Sherrye, *Assoc Prof*, Virginia Western Community College, Commercial Art, Fine Art & Photography, Roanoke VA (S)

Lantzy, Donald M, *Dean*, Syracuse University, College of Visual & Performing Arts, Syracuse NY (S)

Lao, Lincoln, *Prof*, Schoolcraft College, Dept of Art & Design, Livonia MI (S)

Lapalombara, David, *Prof*, Antioch College, Visual Arts Dept, Yellow Springs OH (S)

Lapelle, Rodger, *Pres*, Pennsylvania Academy of the Fine Arts, Fellowship of the Pennsylvania Academy of the Fine Arts, Philadelphia PA

LaPierre, Barbara, *Treas*, Rhode Island Watercolor Society, Pawtucket RI

Lapilio, Lani, *Dir*, Judiciary History Center, Honolulu HI

Lapkus, Danas, *Cur*, Balzekas Museum of Lithuanian Culture, Research Library, Chicago IL

LaPlantz, D M, *Instr*, Humboldt State University, College of Arts & Humanities, Arcata CA (S)

La Porte, Mary, *Prof*, California Polytechnic State University at San Luis Obispo, Dept of Art & Design, San Luis Obispo CA (S)

Lapp, Jennifer, *Dir Educ*, Old York Historical Society, York ME

Lapp, Jennifer, *Educator*, Old York Historical Society, Old Gaol Museum, York ME

Lapsansky, Philip, *Chief Reference*, Library Company of Philadelphia, Philadelphia PA

Laracuente, Mahir, *Prof*, Catholic University of Puerto Rico, Dept of Fine Arts, Ponce PR (S)

Laris, Georgia, *Instr*, San Diego Mesa College, Fine Arts Dept, San Diego CA (S)

Lark, Tom, *Cur Coll*, Albuquerque Museum of Art & History, Albuquerque NM

Larken, Dan, *Lectr*, Rochester Institute of Technology, School of Photographic Arts & Sciences, Rochester NY (S)

Larkin, Alan, *Prof*, Indiana University South Bend, Fine Arts Dept, South Bend IN (S)

Larkin, Frank Y, *VChmn*, Museum of Modern Art, New York NY

Larkin, Linda, *Dir Mem*, San Jose Museum of Art, San Jose CA

Larmann, Ralph, *Instr*, Southern Arkansas University, Dept of Art, Magnolia AR (S)

Larmann, Ralph, *Instructor*, Southern Arkansas University, Art Dept Gallery & Magale Art Gallery, Magnolia AR

Larmer, Oscar V, *Emeritus Prof*, Kansas State University, Art Dept, Manhattan KS (S)

LaRoche, Christian S, *Dir*, Heritage Museum Association, Inc, Valparaiso FL

Larochelle, Steven, *Librn*, Thomas College Art Gallery, Library, Waterville ME

Larocque, Peter, *Cur New Brunswick Art*, New Brunswick Museum, Saint John NB

Larose, Tom, *Cur Exhib & Programs*, Florida State University Foundation - Central Florida Community College Foundation, The Appleton Museum of Art, Ocala FL

LaRou, George, *Instr*, Maine College of Art, Portland ME (S)

Larouche, Michel, *Dir*, Universite de Montreal, Dept of Art History, Montreal PQ (S)

Larris, Jeffrey, *Deputy Dir*, College Art Association, New York NY

Larry, Charles, *Arts Librn*, Northern Illinois University, Library, De Kalb IL

Larsen, Anna-Marie, *Cur*, City of Woodstock, Woodstock Art Gallery, Woodstock ON

Larsen, Devon, *Registrar*, Florida Gulf Coast Art Center, Inc, Belleair FL (S)

Larsen, Donna, *Dir*, Santa Rosa Junior College, Art Gallery, Santa Rosa CA

Larsen, Ken, *Assoc Dir*, California Confederation of the Arts, Sacramento CA

Larsen, Patrick, *Prof*, University of Central Arkansas, Art Dept, Conway AR (S)

Larsen-Martin, Susan, *Prof*, University of Southern California, School of Fine Arts, Los Angeles CA (S)

Larson, Bradley, *Dir*, Oshkosh Public Museum, Oshkosh WI

Larson, Daniel, *Chmn*, Avila College, Art Division, Dept of Humanities, Kansas City MO (S)

Larson, Daniel, *Chmn Humanities*, Avila College, Thornhill Art Gallery, Kansas City MO

Larson, John, *Archivist*, University of Chicago, Oriental Institute Museum, Chicago IL

Larson, Judy L, *Cur American Art*, High Museum of Art, Atlanta GA

Larson, Karen, *Asst Dir Educ*, Putnam Museum of History & Natural Science, Davenport IA

Larson, Mary, *Library Technician*, University of Colorado, Art & Architecture Library, Boulder CO

Larson, Mike, *Prof*, Shoreline Community College, Humanities Division, Seattle WA (S)

Larson, Preston K, *Chmn*, Brigham Young University, Hawaii Campus, Division of Fine Arts, Laie HI (S)

Larson, Sidney, *Cur*, State Historical Society of Missouri, Columbia MO

Larson, Sidney, *Instr*, Columbia College, Art Dept, Columbia MO (S)

Larson, Stephen, *Asst Prof*, University of Mississippi, Dept of Art, University MS (S)

Larson, Susan, *Cur*, William A Farnsworth Library & Art Museum, Rockland ME

Larson, Susan, *Cur*, William A Farnsworth Library & Art Museum, Library, Rockland ME

Larson, Will, *Dir*, Maryland Institute, Graduate Photography, Baltimore MD (S)

La Rue, Lisa, *Dir*, Thousand Islands Craft School & Textile Museum, Clayton NY (S)

Lasansky, Leonardo, *Chmn*, Hamline University Learning Center Gallery, Library, Saint Paul MN

Lasansky, Leonardo, *Head Dept*, Hamline University, Dept of Art & Art History, Saint Paul MN (S)

Lasansky, William, *Head Dept*, Bucknell University, Dept of Art, Lewisburg PA (S)

LaSeurer, Stephan, *Instr*, Nossi College of Art, Goodlettsville TN (S)

Laske, Lyle, *Prof*, Moorhead State University, Dept of Art, Moorhead MN (S)

Laskin, Harriette C F, *Chmn*, Tidewater Community College, Art Dept, Portsmouth VA (S)

Lasko, Katrinal, *Adjunct Assoc*, College of Santa Fe, Art Dept, Santa Fe NM (S)

Lasko, Maureen, *Head Reader Servs*, The Art Institute of Chicago, Ryerson & Burnham Libraries, Chicago IL

Lasky, Carole, *Adjunct Instr*, Maryville University of Saint Louis, Art Division, Saint Louis MO (S)

Lasry, James, *Pres*, Balboa Art Conservation Center, San Diego CA

Lassiter, Christine M, *Adminr*, Port Authority of New York & New Jersey, Art Collection, New York NY

Lassiter, Christine Moss, *Cur*, Port Authority of New York & New Jersey, Art Collection, New York NY

Lassiter, Kathleen, *Dir*, State of Hawaii, Dept of Land & Natural Resources, Wailoa Visitor Center, Hilo HI

Laszlo, Elaine, *Visitor Services Coordr*, London Regional Art & Historical Museums, London ON

Latham, Ron, *Dir*, Berkshire Athenaeum Library, Reference Dept, Pittsfield MA

Lathan, Marty, *Admin Officer NY*, National Museum of the American Indian, George Gustav Heye Center, New York NY

Lathrop, Randi, *Gallery Mgr*, The Society of Arts & Crafts, Boston MA

Latka, Nick, *Asst Prof*, University of Southern Colorado, Belmont Campus, Dept of Art, Pueblo CO (S)

LaTrespo, Brigitte, *Chmn*, Pikeville College, Humanities Division, Pikeville KY (S)

Latta, Douglas, *Assoc Prof*, Oral Roberts University, Fine Arts Dept, Tulsa OK (S)

Lattie, Martha, *Museum Shop Mgr*, Joslyn Art Museum, Omaha NE

Lattimore, Walter, *Asst Prof*, University of the District of Columbia, Dept of Mass Media, Visual & Performing Arts, Washington DC (S)

LaTurner, Gary, *Cur Educ*, Tacoma Art Museum, Tacoma WA

Latzki, Eric, *Publicity Dir*, The Kitchen Center, New York NY

Laubach, Gale C, *Coordr Exhib*, Museum of Fine Arts, Saint Petersburg, Florida, Inc, Saint Petersburg FL

Lauder, Ronald S, *VChmn*, Museum of Modern Art, New York NY

Lauderbaugh, Ann, *Adjunct Asst Prof*, Spokane Falls Community College, Fine Arts Dept, Spokane WA (S)

Lauderbaugh, Stan, *Dean*, Spokane Falls Community College, Fine Arts Dept, Spokane WA (S)

Lauderdale, M, *Dir*, Jacksonville University, Alexander Brest Museum & Gallery, Jacksonville FL

Laughlin, Cynthia, *Adjunct Asst Prof*, Texas Woman's University, Dept of Visual Arts, Denton TX (S)

Laughlin, Margarita, *Registrar*, Museum of Fine Arts, Saint Petersburg, Florida, Inc, Saint Petersburg FL

Laughlin, Page, *Assoc Prof*, Wake Forest University, Dept of Art, Winston-Salem NC (S)

Laurent, Elizabeth, *Cur Coll*, Cliveden, Philadelphia PA

Laurette, Sandy, *Treas*, Beaumont Art League, Beaumont TX

Lauria, Deborah, *Exec Dir*, Maude I Kerns Art Center School, Eugene OR (S)

Lauria, Deborah K, *Exec Dir*, Maude I Kerns Art Center Galleries, Eugene OR

Laurin, Gordon, *Asst Dir & Cur*, St Mary's University, Art Gallery, Halifax NS

Lautanen-Raleigh, Marcia, *Cur*, Aurora University, Schingoethe Center for Native American Cultures, Aurora IL

Lauterbach, Ann, *Instr*, Bard College, Milton Avery Graduate School of the Arts, Annandale-on-Hudson NY (S)

Lauvao, Foailoilo, *Exec Dir & Cur*, Jean P Haydon Museum, Pago Pago, American Samoa PI

LaVallee, Adrian, *Asst Dir*, Saint Anselm College, Chapel Art Center, Manchester NH

Lavallee, Paul, *Dir Admin*, Montreal Museum of Fine Arts, Montreal PQ

Lavenstein, Hollie, *Asst Prof*, University of Maryland, Baltimore County, Visual Arts Dept, Baltimore MD (S)

Laventhol, David, *Chmn*, The Museum of Contemporary Art, Los Angeles CA

Laverty, Bruce, *Architectural Archivist*, Athenaeum of Philadelphia, Philadelphia PA

Laville, Margo, *Registrar*, Louisiana Arts & Science Center, Baton Rouge LA

Lavin, Marguerite, *Rights & Reproductions*, Museum of the City of New York, Library, New York NY

Lavine, Steven D, *Pres*, California Institute of the Arts, School of Art, Valencia CA (S)

Lavioette, Suzanna, *Site & Museum Cur*, Longfellow-Evangeline State Commemorative Area, Saint Martinville LA

Law, Craig, *Assoc Prof*, Utah State University, Dept of Art, Logan UT (S)

Law, Craig J, *Head*, Utah State University, Dept of Art, Logan UT (S)

Law, Dennis, *Dean*, Kansas State University, College of Architecture & Design, Manhattan KS (S)

Law, Jane, *Librn*, Queen's University, Art Library, Kingston ON

Lawal, Baba Tunde, *Prof*, Virginia Commonwealth University, Art History Dept, Richmond VA (S)

Lawler, Patric K, *Asst Prof*, Sam Houston State University, Art Dept, Huntsville TX (S)

Lawless, Patrick, *Managing Librn*, Banff Centre, Centre for the Arts Library, Banff AB

Lawlor, Susan, *Coordr*, Avila College, Art Division, Dept of Humanities, Kansas City MO (S)

Lawn, Robert, *Prof*, Nassau Community College, Art Dept, Garden City NY (S)

Lawrason, Helena, *Cur*, Shorncliffe Park Improvement Assoc, Prairie Panorama Museum, Czar AB

Lawrence, Brenda, *Lectr*, Oakland University, Dept of Art & Art History, Rochester MI (S)

Lawrence, David, *Head Dept*, San Bernardino Valley College, Art Dept, San Bernardino CA (S)

Lawrence, Deirdre, *Librn*, Brooklyn Museum, Brooklyn NY

Lawrence, Deirdre E, *Principal Librn Libraries & Archives*, Brooklyn Museum, Libraries/Archives, Brooklyn NY

Lawrence, Ellen, *Gallery Dir*, College of the Holy Cross, Dept of Visual Arts, Worcester MA (S)

Lawrence, Ellen, *Lectr*, College of the Holy Cross, Dept of Visual Arts, Worcester MA (S)

Lawrence, Jacob, *Board Dir Member*, Art Information Center, Inc, New York NY

Lawrence, John, *Board Trustees*, Sioux City Art Center, Sioux City IA

Lawrence, John, *Dir Museum Prog*, Kemper & Leila Williams Foundation, New Orleans LA

Lawrence, John D, *Dept Head*, La Grange College, Lamar Dodd Art Center Museum, La Grange GA (S)

Lawrence, John D, *Dir*, La Grange College, Lamar Dodd Art Center Museum, La Grange GA

Lawrence, Katherine, *Asst Dir*, The Dixon Gallery & Gardens, Library, Memphis TN

Lawrence, Molly, *Marketing Mgr*, Caspers, Inc, Art Collection, Tampa FL

Lawrence, Pat, *Dir & Exhib Coordr*, Parkersburg Art Center, Parkersburg WV

Lawrence, Pat, *Exec Dir*, Parkersburg Art Center, Art Center, Parkersburg WV

Lawrence, Patricia, *Prof*, Louisiana State University, School of Art, Baton Rouge LA (S)

Lawrence, Priscilla, *Coll Mgr*, Kemper & Leila Williams Foundation, New Orleans LA

Lawrence, Sallee, *Cur*, Saint Johnsbury Athenaeum, Saint Johnsbury VT

Lawrence, Sally, *Pres*, Pacific Northwest College of Art, Portland OR (S)

Lawrence, Sidney, *Head Public Affairs*, Hirshhorn Museum & Sculpture Garden, Washington DC

Lawrie, Irene L, *Registrar*, Lightner Museum, Saint Augustine FL

Lawson, Jeannette, *Dir Educ*, Philbrook Museum of Art, Tulsa OK

Lawson, Jim, *Head Dept*, Sheridan College, Art Dept, Sheridan WY (S)

Lawson, John, *Bemis Art School Dir*, Colorado Springs Fine Arts Center, Colorado Springs CO

Lawson, Pam F, *Asst Prof*, Radford University, Art Dept, Radford VA (S)

Lawson, Roger, *Catalogue Librn*, National Gallery of Art, Library, Washington DC

Lawson, Scott, *Dir*, Plumas County Museum, Quincy CA

Lawson, Scott, *Dir*, Plumas County Museum, Museum Archives, Quincy CA

Lawson, Thomas, *Dean*, California Institute of the Arts, School of Art, Valencia CA (S)

Lawton, A Marshall, *Dir*, Sharon Arts Center, Peterborough NH (S)

Lawton, Brad, *Lectr.* Southwest Texas State University, Dept of Art, San Marcos TX (S)

Lawton, Marshall, *Dir.* Sharon Arts Center, Peterborough NH

Lawton, Mary, *Lectr.* Lake Forest College, Dept of Art, Lake Forest IL (S)

Layer, Julie, *Exec Dir.* Taos Art Association Inc, Stables Art Center, Taos NM

Lazar, Burton, *Pres.* Tucson Museum of Art & Historic Block, Tucson AZ

Lazar, Howard, *Dir Street Artist Prog.* San Francisco City & County Art Commission, San Francisco CA

Lazarus, Eleanor, *Assoc Dir Educ.* DeCordova Museum & Sculpture Park, Lincoln MA

Lazarus, Fred, *Pres.* Maryland Institute, College of Art Exhibitions, Baltimore MD

Lazarus, Fred, *Pres.* Maryland Institute, College of Art, Baltimore MD (S)

Laziza, Kathleen, *Artistic Dir.* Promote Art Works Inc (PAWI), Laziza Videodance Lumia Project, Brooklyn NY

Laziza, William, *Technical Dir.* Promote Art Works Inc (PAWI), Laziza Videodance Lumia Project, Brooklyn NY

Lazzari, Margaret, *Assoc Prof.* University of Southern California, School of Fine Arts, Los Angeles CA (S)

Lazzaro, Claudia, *Assoc Prof.* Cornell University, Dept of the History of Art, Ithaca NY (S)

Lazzaro, Richard, *Prof.* University of Wisconsin, Madison, Dept of Art, Madison WI (S)

Lea, Kathy, *Mgr Library Servs.* Lethbridge Community College, Buchanan Library, Lethbridge AB

Leach, David, *Assoc Prof.* Wright State University, Dept of Art & Art History, Dayton OH (S)

Leach, Sally, *Assoc Dir.* University of Texas at Austin, Harry Ransom Humanities Research Center, Austin TX

Leaf, Bill, *Instr.* University of Nevada, Las Vegas, Dept of Art, Las Vegas NV (S)

Leahy, Jean Louise, *Assoc Prof.* Marygrove College, Visual & Performing Arts Div, Detroit MI (S)

Leake, Caroline Paget, *VPres.* Society of Scribes, Ltd, New York NY

Leamon, David L, *Dir.* Topeka & Shawnee County Public Library, Gallery of Fine Arts, Topeka KS

Lean, Larry, *Chmn.* Mount Olive College, Dept of Art, Mount Olive NC (S)

Learned, Elizabeth Peck, *Architecture Librn.* Roger Williams University, Architecture Library, Bristol RI

Learner, Lisa, *Instr.* Main Line Art Center, Haverford PA (S)

Leary, Edward, *Assoc Prof.* Boston University, School of Visual Arts, Boston MA (S)

Leary, Judy, *Comptroller.* Museum of Northern Arizona, Flagstaff AZ

Leary, Nadine, *Exec Secy.* Captain Robert Bennet Forbes House, Milton MA

Leathem, Karen, *Dir Interpretive Servs.* Louisiana Department of Culture, Recreation & Tourism, Louisiana State Museum, New Orleans LA

Leatherbarrow, David, *Chmn.* University of Pennsylvania, Dept of Architecture, Philadelphia PA (S)

Leavens, Ileana, *Prof.* Seattle Central Community College, Humanities - Social Sciences Division, Seattle WA (S)

Leavitt, Ruth, *Assoc Prof.* University of Maryland, Baltimore County, Visual Arts Dept, Baltimore MD (S)

Lebergoh, Karen, *Prof Emeritus.* Lake Forest College, Dept of Art, Lake Forest IL (S)

LeBlanc, Anne-Marie, *Assoc Prof.* Indiana-Purdue University, Dept of Fine Arts, Fort Wayne IN (S)

LeBlanc, Suzanne, *Cur Ed.* Cincinnati Museum Association, Cincinnati Art Museum, Cincinnati OH

LeBlanc, Suzanne, *Dean Communications.* Musee du Quebec, Quebec PQ

Lechoco, Carole, *Grants Financial Analyst.* Broward County Board of Commissioners Cultural Affairs Division, Fort Lauderdale FL

Lecky, James, *VPres.* Gallery North, Setauket NY

LeClaire, Michael, *Principal.* Nutana Collegiate Institute, Memorial Library and Art Gallery, Saskatoon SK

LeClerc, Denise, *Asst Cur Later Canadian Art.* National Gallery of Canada, Ottawa ON

LeClerc, Paul, *Pres.* The New York Public Library, New York NY

Lecuna, Enrique, *Electronic Arts Head.* Atlanta College of Art, Atlanta GA (S)

Lederer, Carrie, *Cur.* Dean Lesher Regional Center for the Arts, Bedford Gallery, Walnut Creek CA

LeDoux, Dexter, *Museum & Planetarium Tech.* Lafayette Natural History Museum, Planetarium & Nature Station, Lafayette LA

Lee, Chui-Chun, *Dir.* State University of New York at New Paltz, Sojourner Truth Library, New Paltz NY

Lee, Colin, *Instr.* Dowling College, Dept of Visual Arts, Oakdale NY (S)

Lee, Ellen, *Chief Cur.* Indianapolis Museum of Art, Indianapolis IN

Lee, Henry, *Commissioner.* Boston Art Commission of the City of Boston, Boston MA

Lee, Hyosoo, *Technical Servs Librn.* Cleveland Institute of Art, Jessica Gund Memorial Library, Cleveland OH

Lee, Jim, *Assoc Prof.* University of Hartford, Hartford Art School, West Hartford CT (S)

Lee, Joe A, *Pres.* Tougaloo College, Art Collection, Tougaloo MS

Lee, Katharine C, *Dir.* Virginia Museum of Fine Arts, Richmond VA

Lee, Leslie, *Tours.* First Tennessee National Corp, First Tennessee Heritage Collection, Memphis TN

Lee, Martha J, *Registrar.* Yosemite Museum, Yosemite National Park CA

Lee, Mary Wood, *Dir.* Campbell Center for Historic Preservation Studies, Mount Carroll IL (S)

Lee, Molly, *Cur Ethnology.* University of Alaska, Museum, Fairbanks AK

Lee, Ok Hi, *Registrar.* Pennsylvania State University, Palmer Museum of Art, University Park PA

Lee, Robert, *Dir.* Asian-American Arts Centre, New York NY

Lee, Robert E, *Regent.* Mount Vernon Ladies' Association of the Union, Mount Vernon VA

Lee, Roger, *Head.* University of Regina, Visual Arts Dept, Regina SK (S)

Lee, Seung, *Instr.* Dowling College, Dept of Visual Arts, Oakdale NY (S)

Lee, Vicky, *Admin Asst.* Santa Clara University, de Saisset Museum, Santa Clara CA

Leebrick, Gilbert, *Dir.* East Carolina University, Wellington B Gray Gallery, Greenville NC

Leeder, Alex, *Dir.* Mendocino County Arts Council, Westport CA

Leedy, Sherry, *Dir.* Leedy Voulko's Art Center Gallery, Kansas City MO

Leedy, Walter, *Prof.* Cleveland State University, Art Dept, Cleveland OH (S)

Leen, Mary, *Acting Dir.* Massachusetts Institute of Technology, MIT Museum, Cambridge MA

Leeper, John P, *Dir Emeritus.* Marion Koogler McNay Art Museum, San Antonio TX

Lees, Gary P, *Dir Dept.* Johns Hopkins University, School of Medicine, Dept of Art as Applied to Medicine, Baltimore MD (S)

Lees, William, *Historical Sites.* Oklahoma Historical Society, State Museum of History, Oklahoma City OK

Leese, Craig, *Lectr.* California Lutheran University, Art Dept, Thousand Oaks CA (S)

Leese, David, *Dir Educ.* Hunterdon Art Center, Clinton NJ

Leese, Marianne, *Publications.* Historical Society of Rockland County, New City NY

Leese, Stephanie, *Dir Develop & Membership.* Terra Museum of American Art, Chicago IL

Leet, Clinton, *VPres.* Wayne County Historical Society, Museum, Honesdale PA

Leet, Richard E, *Dir.* Charles H MacNider Museum, Mason City IA

Leete, William, *Prof.* University of Rhode Island, Dept of Art, Kingston RI (S)

Leete, William C, *Prof.* Northern Michigan University, Dept of Art & Design, Marquette MI (S)

Lefevre, Susan, *Cur Educ.* Tyler Museum of Art, Reference Library, Tyler TX

Leffel, Larry, *Chmn.* Bay De Noc Community College, Art Dept, Escanaba MI (S)

Leftwich, Robin, *Gallery Asst.* Winston-Salem State University, Diggs Gallery, Winston Salem NC

LeFure, Susan, *Cur Educ.* Tyler Museum of Art, Tyler TX

Legassie, Norman, *Pres.* Lyme Art Association, Inc, Old Lyme CT

Leger, Danielle, *Librn.* Artexte Information & Documentation Centre, Montreal PQ

Legere, Diane, *Exec Dir.* Western Art Association, Ellensburg WA

Legree, Carson, *Instr.* Clark College, Art Dept, Vancouver WA (S)

Legree, Carson, *Instr.* Treasure Valley Community College, Art Dept, Ontario OR (S)

Lehane, Debra, *Mgr Civic Art Coll.* San Francisco City & County Art Commission, San Francisco CA

Lehman, Arnold L, *Dir.* Baltimore Museum of Art, Baltimore MD

Lehman, Harry, *Pres.* House of Roses, Senator Wilson Home, Deadwood SD

Lehman, Mark, *Asst Prof.* College of New Jersey, Art Dept, Trenton NJ (S)

Lehr, Lydia, *Instr.* Main Line Art Center, Haverford PA (S)

Lehrer, Leonard, *Chmn.* New York University, Dept of Art & Art Professions, New York NY (S)

Lehrer, Leonard, *Chmn.* International Center for Advanced Studies in Art, New York NY

Lehrman, Samuel, *Pres.* Jewish Community Center of Greater Washington, Jane L & Robert H Weiner Judaic Museum, Rockville MD

Leibert, Peter, *Prof.* Connecticut College, Dept of Art, New London CT (S)

Leibold, Cheryl, *Archivist.* Pennsylvania Academy of the Fine Arts, Archives, Philadelphia PA

Leibsohn, Dana, *Asst Prof.* Smith College, Art Dept, Northampton MA (S)

Leichty, Erle, *Babylonian Section Cur.* University of Pennsylvania, Museum of Archaeology & Anthropology, Philadelphia PA

Leider, Karen, *Dir.* Trinity College Library, Washington DC

Leidich, David, *Asst to Dir.* Moravian College, Payne Gallery, Bethlehem PA

Leidy, Susan, *Deputy Dir.* The Currier Gallery of Art, Manchester NH

Leifer, Elizabeth, *Instr.* Suomi International College of Art & Design, Fine Arts Dept, Hancock MI (S)

Leighton, Jennifer, *Asst to Dir.* Greater Lafayette Museum of Art, Lafayette IN

Leighton, Walter, *Instr.* New York Institute of Technology, Fine Arts Dept, Old Westbury NY (S)

Leinbach, Charles, *Chmn.* California State University, Long Beach, Design Dept, Long Beach CA (S)

Leininger, Michael, *Architecture Librn.* Massachusetts Institute of Technology, Rotch Library of Architecture & Planning, Cambridge MA

Leininger-Miller, Theresa, *Prof Art History.* University of Cincinnati, School of Art, Cincinnati OH (S)

Leinroth, Martha, *Asst Prof.* Rochester Institute of Technology, School of Photographic Arts & Sciences, Rochester NY (S)

Leipzig, Mel, *Prof.* Mercer County Community College, Arts & Communication/Engineering Technology, Trenton NJ (S)

Leiter, Franziska Kruschen, *Dir.* Acadia University Art Gallery, Wolfville NS

Leith, Christine, *Div Chmn.* Emma Willard School, Arts Division, Troy NY (S)

Leivick, Joe, *Cur of Photography.* Stanford University, Museum of Art, Stanford CA

Leja, Ilga, *Dir.* Nova Scotia College of Art and Design, Library, Halifax NS

Leja, Michael, *Asst Prof*, Northwestern University, Evanston, Dept of Art History, Evanston IL (S)

Lekberg, Barbara, *VPres Annual Exhib*, Sculptors Guild, Inc, New York NY

Lemakis, Suzy, *Cur*, Citibank, NA, Long Island City NY

Lemecha, Vera, *Cur*, Regina Public Library, Dunlop Art Gallery, Regina SK

LeMelle, Veronique, *Exec Dir*, Jamaica Arts Center, Jamaica NY

Lemire, Liz, *Gallery Dir*, Ann Arbor Art Association, Art Center, Ann Arbor MI

Lemme, Rosalie, *Asst Prof*, Dallas Baptist University, Dept of Art, Dallas TX (S)

Lemmerman, Harold, *Dir*, Jersey City State College, Courtney Art Gallery, Jersey City NJ

Lemmerman, Harold, *Dir*, Jersey City State College, Art Space, Jersey City NJ

Lemmerman, Harold, *Prof*, Jersey City State College, Art Dept, Jersey City NJ (S)

Lemmon, Alfred, *Cur Manuscripts*, Kemper & Leila Williams Foundation, New Orleans LA

Lemmon, Colette, *Dir Children's Museum*, Iroquois Indian Museum, Howes Cave NY

LeMoine, Genevieve, *Cur*, Bowdoin College, Peary-MacMillan Arctic Museum, Brunswick ME

Lemon, Robert, *Chmn*, Rollins College, Dept of Art, Main Campus, Winter Park FL (S)

Lemons, Charles R, *Cur*, Cavalry - Armor Foundation, Patton Museum of Cavalry & Armor, Fort Knox KY

Lemp, Frank J, *Chmn*, Ottawa University, Dept of Art, Ottawa KS (S)

Lemstrom-Sheedy, Kaarin, *Head, Mus Sales*, Whitney Museum of American Art, New York NY

Lenaghan, Patrick, *Cur Iconography*, Hispanic Society of America, Museum, New York NY

Lenderman, Max, *Prof*, Rochester Institute of Technology, School of Art & Design, Rochester NY (S)

Lenfestey, Harriett, *Cur Educ*, University of Tampa, Henry B Plant Museum, Tampa FL

Lengel, Kemper, *Admin Asst*, Art Community Center, Art Center of Corpus Christi, Corpus Christi TX

L'Engle, Madeleine, *Vol Librn*, Cathedral of Saint John the Divine, Library, New York NY

Lennig, Arthur, *Assoc Prof*, State University of New York at Albany, Art Dept, Albany NY (S)

Lennon, Madeline, *Chmn*, University of Western Ontario, John Labatt Visual Arts Centre, London ON (S)

Lennox, Judith L, *Asst to Dir*, Washburn University, Mulvane Art Museum, Topeka KS

Lent, Anthony, *Chmn Jewelry Design*, Fashion Institute of Technology, Art & Design Division, New York NY (S)

Lenz, Mary Jane, *Acting Head Curatorial*, National Museum of the American Indian, George Gustav Heye Center, New York NY

Leon, Edgardo, *Controller*, Florida Gulf Coast Art Center, Inc, Belleair FL

Leonard, David, *Provincial Archivist*, Department of Community Development, Provincial Archives of Alberta, Edmonton AB

Leonard, Douglas, *Assoc Dir*, Peter & Catharine Whyte Foundation, Whyte Museum of the Canadian Rockies, Banff AB

Leonard, Glen, *Dir*, Church of Jesus Christ of Latter-day Saints, Museum of Church History & Art, Salt Lake City UT

Leonard, Mike, *Head Art & Media*, Southern Oregon Historical Society, Jacksonville Museum of Southern Oregon History, Medford OR

Leonard, Robert, *Dir*, Wharton Esherick Museum, Paoli PA

Leonard, Susan, *Head Media*, South Carolina Arts Commission, Columbia SC

Leonard, Susan, *Dir*, South Carolina Arts Commission, Media Center, Columbia SC

Leonard, Susan, *Librn*, Bard College, Library, Annandale on Hudson NY

Leonard-Cravens, Mary, *Assoc Prof*, Eastern Illinois University, Art Dept, Charleston IL (S)

Leonardi, Joe, *Mgr Media Arts Center*, Long Beach Museum of Art, Long Beach CA

Leondar, Arnold, *Asst Prof*, Tarrant County Junior College, Art Dept, Hurst TX (S)

Leonhard, Aimee, *Asst Conservator*, University of Missouri, Museum of Art & Archaeology, Columbia MO

Le Page, Carmen D, *Supt*, Forges du Saint-Maurice National Historic Site, Trois Rivieres PQ

Lepine, Micheline, *Business Operations Mgr*, Burchfield-Penney Art Center, Buffalo NY

Lepka, Victoria, *Cur Educ*, University of Georgia, Georgia Museum of Art, Athens GA

Lequire, Stephen, *Assoc Prof*, University of North Carolina at Wilmington, Dept of Fine Arts - Division of Art, Wilmington NC (S)

Lerch, Dawn, *Public Relations*, M Grumbacher Inc, Bloomsbury NJ

Lerdahl, Alan, *Dir*, Oscar Howe Art Center, Mitchell SD

Lerma, Liz, *Exec Dir*, Galeria de la Raza, Studio 24, San Francisco CA

Lerner, A, *Prof*, City Colleges of Chicago, Daley College, Chicago IL (S)

Lerner, Alexandra, *Trustee*, Foundation for Today's Art, Nexus Gallery, Philadelphia PA

Lerner, Lynne, *Asst Dir*, Greenwich House Pottery, New York NY (S)

Lerner, Lynne, *Asst Dir*, Greenwich House, Pottery Library, New York NY

Lerner, Martin, *Cur Asian Art*, The Metropolitan Museum of Art, New York NY

Lerner, Ralph, *Dean*, Princeton University, School of Architecture, Princeton NJ (S)

Lernia, Jose R, *Gallery Docent*, Galeria de la Raza, Studio 24, San Francisco CA

Lesher, Pete, *Cur*, Chesapeake Bay Maritime Museum, Saint Michaels MD

Lesher, Pete, *Cur*, Chesapeake Bay Maritime Museum, Howard I Chapelle Memorial Library, Saint Michaels MD

LeShock, Ed, *Asst Prof*, Radford University, Art Dept, Radford VA (S)

Lesko, Diane, *Dir*, Telfair Museum of Art, Telfair Academy of Arts & Sciences Library, Savannah GA

Lesko, Jim, *Assoc Prof*, University of Bridgeport, School of Arts, Humanities & Social Sciences, Bridgeport CT (S)

Lesley, Ken, *Painting Instr*, Johnson State College, Dept Fine & Performing Arts, Dibden Center for the Arts, Johnson VT (S)

Leslie, Nancy, *Lectr*, State University of New York College at Brockport, Dept of Art, Brockport NY (S)

Lessard, Elizabeth, *Librn*, Manchester Historic Association, Library, Manchester NH

Lesser, Ann, *Pres & Chief Exec Officer*, Crary Art Gallery Inc, Warren PA

Lessley, Merrill, *Chmn*, University of Colorado, Boulder, Dept of Fine Arts, Boulder CO (S)

Lester, Harry T, *Pres Board of Trustees*, Chrysler Museum Of Art, Norfolk VA

Lester, Howard, *Chmn Film/Video*, Rochester Institute of Technology, School of Photographic Arts & Sciences, Rochester NY (S)

Lester, Howard, *Assoc Prof*, Rochester Institute of Technology, School of Photographic Arts & Sciences, Rochester NY (S)

LeSueur, Bill, *Design & Installation*, Fort Worth Art Association, Modern Art Museum of Fort Worth, Fort Worth TX

LeSueur, Marc, *Art History*, California College of Arts & Crafts, Oakland CA (S)

Letocha, Louise Dusseault, *Dept Head*, Universite du Quebec a Montreal, Famille des Arts, Montreal PQ (S)

Lettenstrom, Dean R, *Prof*, University of Minnesota, Duluth, Art Dept, Duluth MN (S)

Lettieri, Robin, *Dir*, Port Chester Public Library, Fine Arts Dept, Port Chester NY

Leval, Susana Torruella, *Exec Dir*, El Museo del Barrio, New York NY

LeVant, Howard, *Assoc Prof*, Rochester Institute of Technology, School of Photographic Arts & Sciences, Rochester NY (S)

Leven, Ann, *Treas*, National Gallery of Art, Washington DC

Levensky-Vogel, Elayne, *Instr*, Green River Community College, Art Dept, Auburn WA (S)

Leventhal, Micki, *Prog Dir*, Praire Avenue House Museums, Henry B Clarke House Museum, Chicago IL

Leventhal, Nathan, *Pres*, Lincoln Center for the Performing Arts, Cork Gallery, New York NY

Leventon, Melissa, *Cur Textiles*, Fine Arts Museums of San Francisco, M H de Young Memorial Museum & California Palace of the Legion of Honor, San Francisco CA

Leverette, Carlton, *Coordr Arts*, Baltimore City Community College, Art Gallery, Baltimore MD

Leveson, Meg, *Treas*, Blue Mountain Gallery, New York NY

Levesque, Francine, *Animator & Educ*, Musee Regional de la Cote-Nord, Sept-Iles PQ

Levesque, Kristen, *Pub Relations Dir*, Portland Museum of Art, Portland ME

Levesque, Sophie, *Technician*, Musee Regional de la Cote-Nord, Sept-Iles PQ

Levi, Toby, *Admin Officer*, Massachusetts Institute of Technology, List Visual Arts Center, Cambridge MA

Levin, David S, *Dean*, Mercer County Community College, Arts & Communication/Engineering Technology, Trenton NJ (S)

Levin, Gail, *Prof*, City University of New York, PhD Program in Art History, New York NY (S)

Levin, Pamela, *Assoc Dir*, Temple Beth Israel, Sylvia Plotkin Judaica, Phoenix AZ

Levin, Ruth, *Registrar*, Bennington Museum, Bennington Museum, Bennington VT

Levine, Julius S, *Assoc Prof*, Catholic University of America, School of Architecture & Planning, Washington DC (S)

Levine, Kathy, *Instr*, Dowling College, Dept of Visual Arts, Oakdale NY (S)

Levine, Louis D, *Dir & Asst Commissioner*, New York State Museum, Albany NY

Levine, Martin, *Pres*, Society of American Graphic Artists, New York NY

Levine, Martin, *Asst Prof*, State University of New York at Stony Brook, Art Dept, Stony Brook NY (S)

Levine, May, *Dir*, The American Foundation for the Arts, Miami FL

LeVine, Newton, *Assoc Prof Architecture*, Ramapo College of New Jersey, School of Contemporary Arts, Mahwah NJ (S)

Levine, Phyllis, *Public Information Dir*, International Center of Photography, New York NY

Levine, Phyllis, *Public Information Dir*, International Center of Photography, Library, New York NY

Levine, Richard, *Pres*, The American Foundation for the Arts, Miami FL

Levine, Steven, *Prof*, Bryn Mawr College, Dept of the History of Art, Bryn Mawr PA (S)

Levinson, Jude, *Chmn Theater*, Idyllwild Arts Academy, Idyllwild CA (S)

Levinthal, Beth, *Coordr Educ*, Heckscher Museum of Art, Huntington NY

Levitt, Isabell, *Prof*, North Carolina Central University, Art Dept, Durham NC (S)

Levitz, Dale R, *Asst Prof*, Johns Hopkins University, School of Medicine, Dept of Art as Applied to Medicine, Baltimore MD (S)

Levy, David C, *Pres & Dir*, Corcoran Gallery of Art, Washington DC

Levy, Elissa, *Presentations Coordr*, Los Angeles Contemporary Exhibitions, Hollywood CA

Levy, Marjorie, *Exec Dir*, Pilchuck Glass School, Seattle WA (S)

Levy, Maryse, *Dean*, International Fine Arts College, Miami FL (S)

Levy, Sue, *Cur*, CIGNA Corporation, CIGNA Museum & Art Collection, Philadelphia PA

Lew, William W, *Head Dept*, University of Northern Iowa, Dept of Art, Cedar Falls IA (S)

Lewanbowski, Rachel, *Registrar*, San Antonio Museum of Art, San Antonio TX

LeWinter, Stephen S, *Assoc Prof*, University of Tennessee at Chattanooga, Dept of Art, Chattanooga TN (S)

Lewis, Barbara, *Prof*, James Madison University, School of Art & Art History, Harrisonburg VA (S)

Lewis, C Douglas, *Cur Sculpture*, National Gallery of Art, Washington DC

Lewis, C Stanley, *Prof*, American University, Dept of Art, Washington DC (S)

Lewis, Elma, *Artistic Dir*, Museum of the National Center of Afro-American Artists, Boston MA

Lewis, Jack R, *Art Coordr*, Georgia Southwestern State University, Art Gallery, Americus GA

Lewis, Janice, *Chmn Fashion Design*, Moore College of Art & Design, Philadelphia PA (S)

Lewis, Jerry, *Chmn Dept*, Joliet Junior College, Fine Arts Dept, Joliet IL (S)

Lewis, Joe, *Dept Chmn*, California State University, Northridge, Dept of Art-Two Dimensional Media, Northridge CA (S)

Lewis, Keevin, *Community Serv Coordr*, National Museum of the American Indian, George Gustav Heye Center, New York NY

Lewis, Linda, *Asst Cur Educ*, Davenport Museum of Art, Davenport IA

Lewis, Louise, *Dir*, California State University, Northridge, Art Galleries, Northridge CA

Lewis, Marcia, *Instr*, Long Beach City College, Dept of Art, Long Beach CA (S)

Lewis, Mary, *Visiting Asst Prof*, Trinity College, Dept of Fine Arts, Hartford CT (S)

Lewis, Michael H, *Prof*, University of Maine, Dept of Art, Orono ME (S)

Lewis, Midge, *Head Weaving Dept*, Kalamazoo Institute of Arts, KIA School, Kalamazoo MI (S)

Lewis, Monty, *Dir*, Coronado School of Fine Arts, Coronado CA (S)

Lewis, Richard, *Prof*, Salem State College, Art Dept, Salem MA (S)

Lewis, Robert E, *Chmn Dept*, University of Memphis, Art Dept, Memphis TN (S)

Lewis, Russell, *Deputy Dir Research*, Chicago Historical Society, Chicago IL

Lewis, Samella, *Founder*, Museum of African American Art, Tampa FL

Lewis, Stanley, *Instr*, Chautauqua Institution, School of Art, Chautauqua NY (S)

Lewis, Susan, *Chief Librn*, Boston Architectural Center, Memorial Library, Boston MA

Lewis, Tom, *Controller*, Art Gallery of Ontario, Toronto ON

Lewis, Wallace, *Dir Educ*, Art Institute of Fort Lauderdale, Fort Lauderdale FL (S)

Lewitin, Margot, *Artistic Dir*, Women's Interart Center, Inc, Interart Gallery, New York NY

Ley, Jennifer, *Exec Dir*, Saratoga County Historical Society, Brookside Museum, Ballston Spa NY

Leys, Dale, *Prof*, Murray State University, Dept of Art, Murray KY (S)

Leyva, Maria, *Cur Reference Center*, Art Museum of the Americas, Washington DC

Leyva, Maria, *Cur*, Art Museum of the Americas, Archive of Contemporary Latin American Art, Washington DC

Lhote, Jean-Francois, *Instr*, Universite de Montreal, Dept of Art History, Montreal PQ (S)

L'Hote, Williard, *Prof*, University of Idaho, College of Art & Architecture, Moscow ID (S)

Li, Chu-tsing, *Res Cur Far Eastern Art*, Nelson-Atkins Museum of Art, Kansas City MO

Li, Chu-tsing, *Prof Emeritus*, University of Kansas, Kress Foundation Dept of Art History, Lawrence KS (S)

Liang, Jack, *Asst Cur*, York University, Art Gallery of York University, North York ON

Libbey, Lizabeth, *Prof*, University of Maine at Augusta, Division of Fine & Performing Arts, Augusta ME (S)

Libby, Gary R, *Pres & Dir Museum Arts*, Florida Art Museum Directors Association, Vero Beach FL

Libby, Gary Russell, *Dir*, The Museum of Arts & Sciences Inc, Daytona Beach FL

Libby, Robert E, *Board Chmn*, American Craft Council, New York NY

Libin, Laurence, *Cur Musical Instruments*, The Metropolitan Museum of Art, New York NY

Lichtenstein, Laura, *Lectr*, University of Pennsylvania, Graduate School of Fine Arts, Philadelphia PA (S)

Lichtman, Susan, *Chmn*, Brandeis University, Dept of Fine Arts, Waltham MA (S)

Lichty, Kay Grever, *Treas*, American Color Print Society, Philadelphia PA

Liddle, Matt, *Asst Prof*, Western Carolina University, Dept of Art, Cullowhee NC (S)

Lidtke, Thomas D, *Exec Dir*, West Bend Art Museum, West Bend WI

Lidtke, Thomas D, *Exec Dir*, West Bend Art Museum, Library, West Bend WI

Lie, Henry, *Dir Straus Center Conservation*, Harvard University, Harvard University Art Museums, Cambridge MA

Lieberman, Claire, *Sculpture*, Monserrat College of Art, Beverly MA (S)

Lieberman, Jack, *Instr*, Cuyahoga Valley Art Center, Cuyahoga Falls OH (S)

Lieberman, Laura, *Dir*, City of Atlanta, Arts Clearinghouse, Atlanta GA

Lieberman, William S, *Chmn Twentieth Century Art*, The Metropolitan Museum of Art, New York NY

Liell, Lilli, *Museum Shop Mgr*, National Museum of the American Indian, George Gustav Heye Center, New York NY

Lierheimer, Violet, *Acquisitions Librn*, Mexico-Audrain County Library, Mexico MO

Lightfoot, D Tulla, *Chmn*, University of Wisconsin-La Crosse, Center for the Arts, La Crosse WI (S)

Lightfoot, Thomas, *Asst Prof*, Rochester Institute of Technology, School of Art & Design, Rochester NY (S)

Lightner, Karen, *Ref Librn*, Free Library of Philadelphia, Rare Book Dept, Philadelphia PA

Ligo, Larry L, *Prof*, Davidson College, Art Dept, Davidson NC (S)

Ligon, Doris Hillian, *Dir*, African Art Museum of Maryland, Columbia MD

Liks, Melissa, *Registrar*, College of William & Mary, Joseph & Margaret Muscarelle Museum of Art, Williamsburg VA

Likvan, Kate, *Museum Shop Mgr*, Art Museum of Missoula, Missoula MT

Lillehoj, Elizabeth, *Assoc Prof*, DePaul University, Dept of Art, Chicago IL (S)

Lillich, Meredith, *Prof*, Syracuse University, Dept of Fine Arts (Art History), Syracuse NY (S)

Lillie, Lloyd, *Prof*, Boston University, School of Visual Arts, Boston MA (S)

Lilly, Robert C, *Dir*, Adirondack Lakes Center for the Arts, Blue Mountain Lake NY

Lilyquist, Christine, *Lila Acheson Wallace Research Cur Egyptology*, The Metropolitan Museum of Art, New York NY

Limondjian, Hilde, *Program Mgr Concerts & Lectures*, The Metropolitan Museum of Art, New York NY

LiMouze, Dorothy, *Assoc Prof*, St Lawrence University, Dept of Fine Arts, Canton NY (S)

Lincer, Catherin, *Libr Dir*, Cochise College, Charles Di Peso Library, Douglas AZ

Lincoln, Louise, *Cur Ethnographic Arts*, Minneapolis Institute of Arts, Minneapolis MN

Lind, Jennifer, *Registrar*, University of Massachusetts, Amherst, University Gallery, Amherst MA

Lind, Julie A, *Dir*, Fort Smith Art Center, Fort Smith AR

Linda, Mary F, *Asst Dir*, Pennsylvania State University, Palmer Museum of Art, University Park PA

Lindblom, Michelle, *Instr*, Bismarck State College, Fine Arts Dept, Bismarck ND (S)

Lindbloom, Terri, *Assoc Prof*, Florida State University, Art Dept, Tallahassee FL (S)

Lindenberger, Beth, *Instr*, Cuyahoga Valley Art Center, Cuyahoga Falls OH (S)

Lindenheim, Diane, *Instr*, Bucks County Community College, Fine Arts Dept, Newtown PA (S)

Linder, Brad, *Exec Dir*, Southern Oregon Historical Society, Jacksonville Museum of Southern Oregon History, Medford OR

Lindland, Pauline, *Art Cur*, Petro-Canada, Corporate Art Programme, Calgary AB

Lindner, Harry, *Instr*, Northeast Community College, Dept of Liberal Arts, Norfolk NE (S)

Lindquist, Evan, *Prof*, Arkansas State University, Dept of Art, State University AR (S)

Lindquist, Fred, *Chmn Board Dir*, Atwater Kent Museum, Philadelphia PA

Lindsay, Betsy, *Instr*, Pacific Northwest College of Art, Portland OR (S)

Lindsey, Anne, *Prof*, University of Tennessee at Chattanooga, Dept of Art, Chattanooga TN (S)

Lindsey, Jack, *Cur American Decorative Arts*, Philadelphia Museum of Art, Mount Pleasant, Philadelphia PA

Lindstrom, Janet, *Exec Dir*, New Canaan Historical Society, New Canaan CT

Lineberry, Heather, *Cur*, Arizona State University, ASU Art Museum, Tempe AZ

Linehan, James, *Prof*, University of Maine, Dept of Art, Orono ME (S)

Linehan, Thomas E, *Pres*, Ringling School of Art & Design, Sarasota FL (S)

Lineker, Bruce, *Exec Dir*, Light Factory, Charlotte NC

Lingeman, Thomas, *Chmn University Educ*, Toledo Museum of Art, Toledo OH

Lingeman, Tom, *Chmn*, University of Toledo, Dept of Art, Toledo OH (S)

Linhares, Philip, *Chief Cur Art*, Oakland Museum of California, Art Dept, Oakland CA

Linhart, Lucie E, *Registrar*, University of Lethbridge, Art Gallery, Lethbridge AB

Linick, Barbara, *Dir Public Affairs*, State Art Museum of Florida, John & Mable Ringling Museum of Art, Sarasota FL

Link, Henry, *Cur*, Green Hill Center for North Carolina Art, Greensboro NC

Linker, Wayne, *Exec VPres*, American Academy in Rome, New York NY (S)

Linowitz, June, *Dir*, Studio Gallery, Washington DC

Linsky, Carol, *Exec Dir*, Rockport Art Association, Rockport MA

Lintault, M Joan, *Prof*, Southern Illinois University, School of Art & Design, Carbondale IL (S)

Lintault, Roger, *Instr*, California State University, San Bernardino, Visual Arts, San Bernardino CA (S)

Linton, Henri, *Dept Chmn*, University of Arkansas at Pine Bluff, Art Dept, Pine Bluff AR (S)

Linton, Laura, *Develop Officer*, Barnes Foundation, Merion PA

Linton, Liz, *Serials Librn*, Sweet Briar College, Martin C Shallenberger Art Library, Sweet Briar VA

Linton, Margot, *VPres*, The American Federation of Arts, New York NY

Linton, Susan, *Finance Mgr*, Shaker Museum & Library, Old Chatham NY

Lintz, Rebecca, *Librn*, Colorado Historical Society, Stephen H Hart Library, Denver CO

Lionette, Gina, *Dir Pub Affairs*, Worcester Art Museum, Worcester MA

Lipfert, Nathan, *Library Dir*, Maine Maritime Museum, Bath ME

Lipfert, Nathan, *Library Dir*, Maine Maritime Museum, Archives Library, Bath ME

Lipinski, Marlene, *Coordr Graphics*, Columbia College, Art Dept, Chicago IL (S)

Lipp, Frederick, *Prof*, Rochester Institute of Technology, School of Art & Design, Rochester NY (S)

Lippincott, Bertram, *Librn*, Newport Historical Society, Library, Newport RI

Lippincott, Louise W, *Cur Fine Art*, Carnegie Institute, Carnegie Museum of Art, Pittsburgh PA

Lippman, Barbara, *Dir Continuing Studies*, University of the Arts, Philadelphia College of Art & Design, Philadelphia PA (S)

Lippman, Irvin, *Dir*, Columbus Museum of Art, Columbus OH

Lippman, Judith, *Dir*, Meredith Gallery, Baltimore MD

Lipschutz, Jeff, *Dir*, University of Wisconsin Oshkosh, Allen R Priebe Gallery, Oshkosh WI

Lipscomb, Bill, *Pres*, Intermuseum Conservation Association, Oberlin OH

Lipsett, Katherine, *Art Cur*, Peter & Catharine Whyte Foundation, Whyte Museum of the Canadian Rockies, Banff AB

Lipsett, Kathryn, *Pres*, Western Canada Art Association Inc, Vance AB

Long, Robert, *Asst Prof*, Mississippi State University, Art Dept, Mississippi State MS (S)

Longen, Neal, *VPres*, San Fernando Valley Historical Society, Andres Pico Adobe Library, Mission Hills CA

Longhauser, Elsa, *Gallery Dir*, Moore College of Art & Design, Goldie Paley Gallery, Philadelphia PA

Longmire, Sam, *Cur Educ*, Evansville Museum of Arts & Science, Evansville IN

Longobardi, Zita, *Mgr Marketing & Develop*, New Brunswick Museum, Saint John NB

Longstreth, Richard, *First VPres*, Society of Architectural Historians, Chicago IL

Longstreth-Brown, Kitty, *Registrar*, University of New Mexico, University Art Museum, Albuquerque NM

Longtin, Barbara C, *Dir*, Muscatine Art Center, Muscatine IA

Longtin, Russ, *Chmn*, Johnson State College, Dept Fine & Performing Arts, Dibden Center for the Arts, Johnson VT (S)

Lonnberg, Thomas R, *Asst Cur*, Evansville Museum of Arts & Science, Evansville IN

Loomis, Tom, *Assoc Prof*, Mansfield University, Art Dept, Mansfield PA (S)

Looney, Elizabeth Olson, *Develop Dir*, Fresno Metropolitan Museum, Fresno CA

Looney, Roberta, *Exec Dir*, Wayne Center for the Arts, Wooster OH

Loonsk, Susan, *Assoc Prof*, University of Wisconsin-Superior, Programs in the Visual Arts, Superior WI (S)

Loord, Leon, *Pres*, American Society of Portrait Artists (ASOPA), Montgomery AL

Loord McRae, Joy, *Treas*, American Society of Portrait Artists (ASOPA), Montgomery AL

Loosle, Richard, *Asst Prof*, Catholic University of America, School of Architecture & Planning, Washington DC (S)

Lopez, Barbara, *Bus Mgr*, Tulane University, Gallier House Museum, New Orleans LA

Lopez, Diana, *Cur Archaeology*, University of Puerto Rico, Museum of Anthropology, History & Art, San Juan PR

Lopez, Gildardo, *Museum Aide*, Spanish Governor's Palace, San Antonio TX

Lopez, J Tomas, *Assoc Prof*, University of Miami, Dept of Art & Art History, Coral Gables FL (S)

Lopez, Tom, *Asst Prof*, Rochester Institute of Technology, School of Photographic Arts & Sciences, Rochester NY (S)

Lopez-Isnardi, C Sandy, *Asst Prof*, Alma College, Clack Art Center, Alma MI (S)

Lopez-Woodward, Dina, *Exec Dir*, Xicanindio, Inc, Mesa AZ

Lorance, Jane, *Branch Adminr*, Las Vegas-Clark County Library District, Las Vegas NV

Loranth, Alice N, *Head Fine Arts & Special Colls Dept*, Cleveland Public Library, Fine Arts & Special Collections Dept, Cleveland OH

Lord, Catharine, *Dir*, University of California, Irvine, Fine Art Gallery, Irvine CA

Lordi, Michael, *Librn*, California College of Arts & Crafts Library, Oakland CA

Loriaux, Maurice, *Dir*, Southwest Art League Seminars, Santa Fe NM (S)

Lorigan, Martin, *Equipment Technician*, California State University, Fullerton, Art Gallery, Visual Arts Center, Fullerton CA

Loring, Richard, *Pres*, Huntsville Museum of Art, Huntsville AL

Lorinskas, Robert, *Museology*, Southern Illinois University, University Museum, Carbondale IL

Lorys, Jan M, *Dir*, Polish Museum of America, Chicago IL

Lorys, Jan M, *Cur*, Polish Museum of America, Research Library, Chicago IL

Losavio, Sam, *Asst Dir*, Louisiana Arts & Science Center, Baton Rouge LA

Losch, Michael, *Dir*, Western Maryland College, Esther Prangley Rice Gallery, Westminster MD

Losch, Michael, *Assoc Prof*, Western Maryland College, Dept of Art & Art History, Westminster MD (S)

Lotstein, Norman, *Pres*, Stamford Museum & Nature Center, Stamford CT

Lott, Trent, *Chmn*, United States Senate Commission on Art, Washington DC

Lottes, John W, *Pres*, Art Institute of Southern California, Ruth Salyer Library, Laguna Beach CA

Lott-Gerlach, Linda, *Librn*, Harvard University, Studies in Landscape Architecture & Garden Library, Washington DC

Lottis, Lynnea, *Outreach Coordr*, Ella Sharp Museum, Jackson MI

Lou, Richard, *Instr*, San Diego Mesa College, Fine Arts Dept, San Diego CA (S)

Loucks, Carlton, *Pres*, New Haven Colony Historical Society, New Haven CT

Loucks, John, *Chmn Humanities*, Seward County Community College, Art Dept, Liberal KS (S)

Loudenback, Brad, *Asst Prof*, Webster University, Art Dept, Webster Groves MO (S)

Loudon, George, *Organization Servs & Outreach Dir*, Arts Partnership of Greater Spartanburg, Inc, Spartanburg Arts Center, Spartanburg SC

Louie, Debbie, *Communications Mgr*, Wing Luke Asian Museum, Seattle WA

Louis, Elizabeth Souder, *Pres*, The Art Institute of Chicago, Auxiliary Board, Chicago IL

Lovano-Kerr, Jessie, *Prof*, Florida State University, Art Education Dept, Tallahassee FL (S)

Lovato, Manuelita, *Cur Coll*, Institute of American Indian Arts Museum, Santa Fe NM (S)

Love, Ed, *Prof*, Florida State University, Art Dept, Tallahassee FL (S)

Loveday, Amos, *Chief Educ Division*, Ohio Historical Society, Columbus OH

Loveday, Amos, *Head Historic Preservation*, Ohio Historical Society, Columbus OH

Lovejoy, Barbara, *Registrar*, University of Kentucky, Art Museum, Lexington KY

Lovejoy, Claudine, *Admin Asst*, Museum of East Texas, Lufkin TX

Lovejoy, Thomas, *Asst Secy External Affairs*, Smithsonian Institution, Washington DC

Loveless, Jim, *Prof*, Colgate University, Dept of Art & Art History, Hamilton NY (S)

Lovell, Carol, *Dir*, Kauai Museum, Lihue HI

Lovell, Charles, *Gallery Dir*, New Mexico State University, University Art Gallery, Las Cruces NM

Loven, Del Rey, *Chmn*, Judson College, Division of Fine Arts, Elgin IL (S)

Lovett, Margaret, *Cur*, Kauai Museum, Lihue HI

Lovett, O Rufus, *Instr*, Kilgore College, Visual Arts Dept, Kilgore TX (S)

Lovett, Thomas, *Dir*, Museum of Our National Heritage, Lexington MA

Loveys, Geraldine, *Registrar*, McMaster University, Museum of Art, Hamilton ON

Loving, Richard, *Prof*, School of the Art Institute of Chicago, Chicago IL (S)

Lovins, Mona, *Dir*, Hollywood Art Center School, Hollywood CA (S)

Low, Bill, *Asst Cur*, Bates College, Museum of Art, Lewiston ME

Lowder, Barbara, *Dir Foundation Studies*, Nova Scotia College of Art & Design, Halifax NS (S)

Lowe, Arline, *Asst Prof*, Seton Hall University, College of Arts & Sciences, South Orange NJ (S)

Lowe, Constance, *Asst Prof*, University of Texas at San Antonio, Division of Visual Arts, San Antonio TX (S)

Lowe, Darrell, *Theatre Coordr & Public Relations Coordr*, Ashtabula Arts Center, Ashtabula OH

Lowe, J Michael, *Prof*, St Lawrence University, Dept of Fine Arts, Canton NY (S)

Lowe, Patricia, *Librn*, Will Rogers Memorial & Museum, Media Center Library, Claremore OK

Lowe, Phillip, *Music Prog Coordr*, Hill College, Fine Arts Dept, Hillsboro TX (S)

Lowe, Truman, *Prof*, University of Wisconsin, Madison, Dept of Art, Madison WI (S)

Lowenberg, Susan, *Info Resources & Dance & Theater Librn*, California Institute of the Arts Library, Santa Clarita CA

Lowenstein, J, *Reference Librn*, McGill University, Blackader-Lauterman Library of Architecture and Art, Montreal PQ

Lowenthal, Constance, *Exec Dir*, International Foundation for Art Research, Inc, New York NY

Lowenthal, Constance, *Dir*, International Foundation for Art Research, Inc, Authentication Service, New York NY

Lowenthal, Elaine, *Asst Librn Cataloging*, Harrington Institute of Interior Design, Design Library, Chicago IL

Lowery, Stephen, *Prof*, Aurora University, Art Dept, Aurora IL (S)

Lowly, Tim, *Gallery Dir*, North Park College, Carlson Tower Gallery, Chicago IL

Lowman, Joyce, *Instr*, John C Calhoun State Community College, Department of Fine Arts, Decatur AL (S)

Lowrey, Annie, *Cur*, Friends University, Whittier Fine Arts Gallery, Wichita KS

Lowrey, Charles B, *University Librn*, Carnegie Mellon University, Hunt Library, Pittsburgh PA

Lowry, Glenn D, *Dir Museum*, Museum of Modern Art, New York NY

Lowry, Keith, *Prof*, University of Nebraska, Kearney, Dept of Art & Art History, Kearney NE (S)

Lowry, Michael, *Chmn Landscape Architecture*, University of California, Berkeley, College of Environmental Design, Berkeley CA (S)

Lowry, Sara Jane, *Dir External Affairs & Chief Financial Officer*, Westmoreland Museum of American Art, Greensburg PA

Loy, Jessica, *Asst Prof*, College of Saint Rose, Dept of Art, Albany NY (S)

Luallen, Sally, *Exec Dir*, Wichita Center for the Arts, Wichita KS

Luallen, Sally, *Exec Dir*, Wichita Center for the Arts, Wichita KS (S)

Lubben, Anne, *Instr*, Teikyo Westmar University, Art Dept, LeMars IA (S)

Lubell, Ruth, *VPres*, Art Directors Club, Inc, New York NY

Luber, Katherine Crawford, *Asst Cur*, Philadelphia Museum of Art, John G Johnson Collection, Philadelphia PA

Lubin, David, *Prof*, Colby College, Art Dept, Waterville ME (S)

Lubove, Rebecca, *Chief Develop Officer, Individual Giving*, The American Federation of Arts, New York NY

Lubrano, Joseph V, *Pres*, American Society of Contemporary Artists (ASCA), New York NY

Lucas, Dan, *Library Dir*, Portland Art Museum, Rex Arragon Library, Portland OR

Lucas, John, *Chief Exec Officer*, Lovelace Medical Foundation, Art Collection, Albuquerque NM

Lucas, Judith S, *Cur*, Hebrew Union College - Jewish Institute of Religion, Skirball Museum-Cincinnati Branch, Cincinnati OH

Lucas, Margaret, *Dean Col*, Rochester Institute of Technology, College of Imaging Arts & Sciences, Rochester NY (S)

Lucas, Margaret, *Dean*, Rochester Institute of Technology, School of Art & Design & School for American Craft, Rochester NY (S)

Luce, Charles, *Chmn & Prof*, County College of Morris, Art Dept, Randolph Township NJ (S)

Luce, Donald T, *Cur Exhib*, University of Minnesota, James Ford Bell Museum of Natural History, Minneapolis MN

Luce, Ken, *Instr*, San Jacinto College-North, Art Dept, Houston TX (S)

Lucero, Henry, *Treas*, Roswell Museum & Art Center, Roswell NM

Lucero, Keith, *Retail Marketing Mgr*, Indian Pueblo Cultural Center, Albuquerque NM

Lucero, Manuel, *Instr*, California State University, Chico, Art Dept, Chico CA (S)

Lucey, Susan, *Assoc Prof*, University of Minnesota, Minneapolis, Dept of Art, Minneapolis MN (S)

Luchinsky, Ellen, *Dept Head*, Enoch Pratt Free Library of Baltimore City, Baltimore MD

Lucic, Karen, *Assoc Prof*, Vassar College, Art Dept, Poughkeepsie NY (S)

Luck, Mickey, *Instr*, Mississippi State University, Art Dept, Mississippi State MS (S)

Lucke, Susan, *Registrar*, University of Miami, Lowe Art Museum, Coral Gables FL

Luckman, Stewart, *Prof*, Bethel College, Dept of Art, Saint Paul MN (S)

Luckner, Kurt T, *Cur Ancient Art*, Toledo Museum of Art, Toledo OH

Luderowski, Barbara, *Exec Dir*, Mattress Factory, Pittsburgh PA

Ludwig, Daniel, *Assoc Prof*, Salve Regina University, Art Dept, Newport RI (S)

Ludwig, James, *Dir Div of Art*, Bradley University, Heuser Art Center, Peoria IL

Ludwig, James, *Chair*, Bradley University, Dept of Art, Peoria IL (S)

Ludwig, Marjorie, *VPres Board Dir*, Plains Art Museum, Fargo ND

Ludwig, Petra, *School Dir*, Rockland Center for the Arts, West Nyack NY (S)

Lue, Joanne, *Admin Asst*, University at Albany, State University of New York, University Art Museum, Albany NY

Luebbers, Leslie L, *Dir*, University of Memphis, Art Museum, Memphis TN

Luecking, Stephen, *Chmn Dept*, DePaul University, Dept of Art, Chicago IL (S)

Luers, William H, *Pres*, The Metropolitan Museum of Art, New York NY

Luft, Margaret, *Cur*, Uptown Center Hull House Association, Chicago IL

Lugo, Anthony J, *Assoc Prof*, Palomar Community College, Art Dept, San Marcos CA (S)

Luhr, Zenaide, *Board Dir*, Artists' Cooperative Gallery, Omaha NE

Lukacher, Brian, *Assoc Prof*, Vassar College, Art Dept, Poughkeepsie NY (S)

Lukas, Vicki A, *Dept Head Technical Service*, New Bedford Free Public Library, Art Dept, New Bedford MA

Lukehart, Peter, *Asst Prof*, Dickinson College, Fine Arts Dept, Carlisle PA (S)

Lukehart, Peter M, *Dir*, Dickinson College, Trout Gallery, Carlisle PA

Lukkas, Lynn, *Asst Prof*, Oberlin College, Dept of Art, Oberlin OH (S)

Lum, Harry, *Chmn Art Dept*, Grossmont Community College, Hyde Gallery, El Cajon CA

Lum, Ken, *Assoc Prof*, University of British Columbia, Dept of Fine Arts, Vancouver BC (S)

Luman, Mitch, *Science Planetarium Dir*, Evansville Museum of Arts & Science, Evansville IN

Lumpkin, Farnese, *Asst Prof*, Savannah State University, Dept of Fine Arts, Savannah GA (S)

Lumsden, Ian G, *Dir*, Beaverbrook Art Gallery, Fredericton NB

Lund, Cheri, *Admin Asst*, Bemis Center for Contemporary Arts, New Gallery, Omaha NE

Lund, David, *Instr*, Chautauqua Institution, School of Art, Chautauqua NY (S)

Lund, Judith N, *Cur*, Old Dartmouth Historical Society, New Bedford Whaling Museum, New Bedford MA

Lund, Raymond, *Asst Prof*, Johns Hopkins University, School of Medicine, Dept of Art as Applied to Medicine, Baltimore MD (S)

Lund, Richard, *Prof*, College of DuPage, Humanities Division, Glen Ellyn IL (S)

Lunde, Mary Lee, *Chmn*, State University College at Fredonia, Dept of Art, Fredonia NY (S)

Lundgren, Nancy, *Dir Library Services*, Milwaukee Institute of Art Design, Library, Milwaukee WI

Lundstrom, Mike, *Instr*, Treasure Valley Community College, Art Dept, Ontario OR (S)

Lunn, Gerry, *Cur*, Nova Scotia Museum, Maritime Museum of the Atlantic, Halifax NS

Lunning, Elizabeth, *Paper Conservator*, Menil Collection, Houston TX

Lunsford, John L, *Dir*, Southern Methodist University, Meadows Museum, Dallas TX

Lunsford, W Hal, *Chmn*, Middle Georgia College, Dept of Art, Cochran GA (S)

Lupin, E Ralph, *Chmn*, Louisiana Department of Culture, Recreation & Tourism, Louisiana State Museum, New Orleans LA

Lupmanis, Sarah, *Exec Dir*, Ontario Crafts Council, The Craft Gallery, Toronto ON

Lupton, Ellen, *Cur Contemporary Design*, Cooper-Hewitt, National Design Museum, New York NY

Lurie, Janice, *Asst Librn*, The Buffalo Fine Arts Academy, G Robert Strauss Jr Memorial Library, Buffalo NY

Lutchmansingh, Larry D, *Prof*, Bowdoin College, Art Dept, Brunswick ME (S)

Luther, Lacinda, *Cur*, Wells Fargo & Co, History Museum, Los Angeles CA

Lutomski, James, *Assoc Prof*, Marygrove College, Visual & Performing Arts Div, Detroit MI (S)

Luton, Barbara, *Deputy Dir & Asst Dir Admin*, Santa Barbara Museum of Art, Santa Barbara CA

Lutsch, Gail, *Assoc Prof*, Bethel College, Dept of Art, North Newton KS (S)

Luttropp, John, *Dir Art Dept*, Montclair State University, Art Galleries, Upper Montclair NJ

Lutz, Cullen, *Cur Educ*, Art Museum of Southeast Texas, Beaumont TX

Lutz, Cullen, *Educ Cur*, Art Museum of Southeast Texas, Library, Beaumont TX

Lutz, Dianne, *Asst*, Artist's Alliance of California, Nevada City CA

Lutzker, Mary-Ann, *Prof Hist*, Mills College, Art Dept, Oakland CA (S)

Ly, Vi, *Instr*, Monterey Peninsula College, Art Dept, Monterey CA (S)

Lybarger, Mary, *Instr*, Edgewood College, Art Dept, Madison WI (S)

Lydecker, Kent, *Assoc Dir Educ*, The Metropolitan Museum of Art, New York NY

Lydon, Catherine, *Instr*, Springfield College, Dept of Visual & Performing Arts, Springfield MA (S)

Lykins, Anne, *Staff Site Interpreter*, Patterson Homestead, Dayton OH

Lykins, Beth, *Dir Permanent Coll*, Earlham College, Leeds Gallery, Richmond IN

Lykins, Jere, *Asst Prof*, Berry College, Art Dept, Mount Berry GA (S)

Lyle, Janice, *Dir*, Palm Springs Desert Museum, Palm Springs CA

Lyle, Janice, *Dir*, Palm Springs Desert Museum, Library, Palm Springs CA

Lyman, David H, *Founder & Dir*, Maine Photographic Workshops, Rockport ME

Lyman, David H, *Founder & Dir*, Maine Photographic Workshops, Rockport ME (S)

Lyman, Merlene, *Prof*, Fort Hays State University, Dept of Art, Hays KS (S)

Lyman, Sophia, *Project Coordr, Contracts for Art Servs*, City of Atlanta, Bureau of Cultural Affairs, Atlanta GA

Lyman, Ted, *Chmn*, University of Vermont, Dept of Art, Burlington VT (S)

Lymon, Keith, *Asst Bookstore Mgr*, Fort Worth Art Association, Modern Art Museum of Fort Worth, Fort Worth TX

Lynagh, Pat, *Asst Librn*, National Portrait Gallery, Library, Washington DC

Lynagh, Patricia, *Asst Librn*, National Museum of American Art, Library of the National Museum of American Art & the National Portrait Gallery, Washington DC

Lynch, Harry, *Exec Dir*, Stan Hywet Hall & Gardens, Inc, Akron OH

Lynch, Jerri, *Head AV Services*, Westport Public Library, Westport CT

Lynch, John W, *Assoc Prof*, Central Missouri State University, Art Dept, Warrensburg MO (S)

Lynch, Matt, *Preparator*, New Mexico State University, University Art Gallery, Las Cruces NM

Lynch, Peter, *Head Archit Dept*, Cranbrook Academy of Art, Bloomfield Hills MI (S)

Lynch, Robert L, *Pres & Chief Exec Officer*, Americans for the Arts, Washington DC

Lynde, Richard, *VPres*, Montclair State University, Art Galleries, Upper Montclair NJ

Lyndrup, Allen, *Chmn Theatre Dept*, College of Charleston, School of the Arts, Charleston SC (S)

Lynes, Lisa, *Instr*, North Idaho College, Art Dept, Coeur D'Alene ID (S)

Lynlyndon, Don, *Chmn Architecture*, University of California, Berkeley, College of Environmental Design, Berkeley CA (S)

Lynn, Judy, *Dir*, Coupeville Arts Center, Coupeville WA

Lynne, Michael, *VChmn*, Guild Hall of East Hampton, Inc, Guild Hall Museum, East Hampton NY

Lyon, Dorothy, *Cataloger*, Saint Augustine Historical Society, Library, Saint Augustine FL

Lyon, Jean, *Shop*, New England Maple Museum, Rutland VT

Lyon, Joyce, *Faculty*, Grand Marais Art Colony, Grand Marais MN (S)

Lyon, Joyce, *Assoc Prof*, University of Minnesota, Minneapolis, Dept of Art, Minneapolis MN (S)

Lyon, Robert F, *Head*, Auburn University, Dept of Art, Auburn AL (S)

Lyons, Anne, *Asst Librn*, Wadsworth Atheneum, Auerbach Art Library, Hartford CT

Lyons, Bob, *Financial Aid*, Rocky Mountain College of Art & Design, Denver CO (S)

Lyons, Nathan, *Dir*, Visual Studies Workshop, Rochester NY

Lyons, Thomas F, *Pres Board Trustees*, Anderson Fine Arts Center, Anderson IN

Lysniak, Wolodymyr, *Admin Dir*, Ukrainian Institute of America, Inc, New York NY

Lyss, Michael, *Adjunct Instr*, Maryville University of Saint Louis, Art Division, Saint Louis MO (S)

Lytle, Hubert, *Pres*, Iroquois County Historical Society Museum, Old Courthouse Museum, Watseka IL

Lytle, Richard, *Prof*, Yale University, School of Art, New Haven CT (S)

Maag, Albert, *Dir*, Capital University, Art Library, Columbus OH

Maas, Bernard, *Chmn Crafts*, Edinboro University of Pennsylvania, Art Dept, Edinboro PA (S)

Maas, Jim Stipe, *Acting Preparator*, University of Georgia, Georgia Museum of Art, Athens GA

Maass, R Andrew, *Exec Dir*, Mississippi Museum of Art, Jackson MS

Mabe, John, *Chmn*, City Of Raleigh Arts Commission, Municipal Building Art Exhibitions, Raleigh NC

Maberry, Sue, *Dir*, Otis College of Art & Design, Library, Los Angeles CA

MacAdam, Barbara, *Cur American Art*, Dartmouth College, Hood Museum of Art, Hanover NH

Macaulay, Scott, *Prog Dir*, The Kitchen Center, New York NY

Macaulay, Thomas, *Prof*, Wright State University, Dept of Art & Art History, Dayton OH (S)

Macaw, Lee, *Curatorial Asst*, Artesia Historical Museum & Art Center, Artesia NM

MacCollum, Lisa, *Exhibit Coordr*, Heard Museum, Phoenix AZ

MacDonald, Anne, *Dir*, San Francisco Artspace & Artspace Annex, San Francisco CA

MacDonald, Bernadette, *Pres*, Peter & Catharine Whyte Foundation, Whyte Museum of the Canadian Rockies, Banff AB

MacDonald, George, *Exec Dir*, Canadian Museum of Civilization, Hull PQ

MacDonald, Gerald J, *Cur*, Hispanic Society of America, Library, New York NY

MacDonald, J, *Pres Board*, Oakville Galleries, Centennial Gallery and Gairloch Gallery, Oakville ON

MacDonald, James, *Assoc Dean*, Milwaukee Area Technical College, Graphic Arts Division, Milwaukee WI (S)

MacDonald, John, *Dir Corp Affairs*, Rothmans, Benson & Hedges, Art Collection, Don Mills ON

MacDonald, Linda, *Asst Dir*, Connecticut Institute of Art, Greenwich CT (S)

Macdonald, Robert R, *Dir*, Museum of the City of New York, New York NY

MacDonald, Sara, *Reference Librn*, University of the Arts, Albert M Greenfield Library, Philadelphia PA

MacDonald, Scott, *Instr*, Hamilton College, Art Dept, Clinton NY (S)

MacEachern, David F, *Prof*, New England College, Art & Art History, Henniker NH (S)

Macecchak, Jeffrey, *Chief Historical Interpreter*, Old Barracks Museum, Trenton NJ

MacFarland, Brian, *Cur Educ*, Norton Gallery & School of Art, Inc, Norton Museum of Art, West Palm Beach FL

Macfee, Laurie, *Prog Cur*, Nevada Museum Of Art, Reno NV

Machell, Iain, *Prof*, West Virginia University, College of Creative Arts, Morgantown WV (S)

Machlin, Daniel, *Exec Dir*, Segue Foundation, Reading Room-Archive, New York NY

Macias, Nanette Yannuzzi, *Asst Prof*, Oberlin College, Dept of Art, Oberlin OH (S)

Maciejunes, Nanette, *Sr Cur*. Columbus Museum of Art, Columbus OH

MacInnis, Karen, *Research*. Marblehead Historical Society, Library, Marblehead MA

Macintyre, Bob, *Preparator*. Burnaby Art Gallery, Burnaby BC

Mack, Angela, *Cur Coll*. Carolina Art Association, Gibbes Museum of Art, Charleston SC

Mack, James, *Chmn Humanities*. City Colleges of Chicago, Harold Washington College, Chicago IL (S)

Mack, James, *Chmn*. City Colleges of Chicago, Wright College, Chicago IL (S)

MacKay, Don, *Chmn Dept*. University of Waterloo, Fine Arts Dept, Waterloo ON (S)

MacKay, Robert, *Dir Educ*. Museum of Our National Heritage, Lexington MA

MacKay-Lyons, B, *Assoc Prof*. Technical University of Nova Scotia, Faculty of Architecture, Halifax NS (S)

Mackenzie, Colin, *Asian*. Yale University, Art Gallery, New Haven CT

Mackenzie, Lynn, *Asst Prof*. College of DuPage, Humanities Division, Glen Ellyn IL (S)

MacKenzie, Warren, *Prof Emeritus*. University of Minnesota, Minneapolis, Dept of Art, Minneapolis MN (S)

Mackey, David, *Pres*. Hopewell Museum, Hopewell NJ

Mackie, Elizabeth, *Assoc Prof*. College of New Jersey, Art Dept, Trenton NJ (S)

MacKillop, Rod, *Prof*. University of North Carolina at Charlotte, Dept of Visual Arts, Charlotte NC (S)

Mackin, Myrna, *Admin Secy*. Wake Forest University, Museum of Anthropology, Winston Salem NC

Macklin, A D, *Chmn*. Jackson State University, Dept of Art, Jackson MS (S)

Maclean, Donald, *Operations Mgr*. Whitney Museum of American Art, New York NY

Macleish, A Bruce, *Dir Coll*. New York State Historical Association, Farmers' Museum, Inc, Cooperstown NY

MacLennan, Toby, *Dir Graduate Prog*. Rutgers, the State University of New Jersey, Mason Gross School of the Arts, New Brunswick NJ (S)

MacLennan, Toby, *Assoc Prof*. Rutgers, the State University of New Jersey, Mason Gross School of the Arts, New Brunswick NJ (S)

Macleod, Melissa, *Dir*. Artists Association of Nantucket, Nantucket MA

MacNabb, Vicki, *Admin Dir*. Women's Art Registry of Minnesota Gallery, Saint Paul MN

MacNulty, Jay F, *Pres*. Rensselaer County Historical Society, Hart-Cluett Mansion, 1827, Troy NY

MacNulty, Thomas, *Assoc Prof*. Adelphi University, Dept of Art & Art History, Garden City NY (S)

MacTaggart, Alan, *Chmn*. Lander University, Dept of Art, Greenwood SC (S)

Macy, Christine, *Asst Prof*. Technical University of Nova Scotia, Faculty of Architecture, Halifax NS (S)

Macy, Jean, *Pres Board*. Coos Art Museum, Coos Bay OR

Madaus, Howard M, *Cur Cody Firearms Museum*. Buffalo Bill Memorial Association, Buffalo Bill Historical Center, Cody WY

Madd, Vikki, *Museum Shop Mgr*. Taos Art Association Inc, Stables Art Center, Taos NM

Maddaus, Elsie, *Archivist Librn*. Schenectady County Historical Society, Library, Schenectady NY

Madden, Dennis, *Archivist*. Arizona State University, Architecture & Environmental Design Library, Tempe AZ

Madden, Peter, *Assoc Circulation Mgr*. Massachusetts College of Art, Morton R Godine Library, Boston MA

Maddock, Pam, *Instr*. American River College, Dept of Art, Sacramento CA (S)

Maddox, Gene, *Instr*. College of the Sequoias, Art Dept, Visalia CA (S)

Madeja, Stanley, *Div Coordr*. Northern Illinois University, School of Art, De Kalb IL (S)

Mader, Daniel, *Chmn*. College of Mount Saint Joseph, Art Dept, Cincinnati OH (S)

Madigan, Kathleen, *Adjunct Prof*. Washington & Jefferson College, Art Dept, Washington PA (S)

Madison, Willie C, *Park Supt*. Tuskegee Institute National Historic Site, George Washington Carver & The Oaks, Tuskegee Institute AL

Madkour, Christopher, *Dir*. Southern Vermont Art Center, Manchester VT

Madonia, Ann, *Cur*. College of William & Mary, Joseph & Margaret Muscarelle Museum of Art, Williamsburg VA

Madrigal, Carlos, *Admin Dir*. El Paso Museum of Art, Wilderness Park Museum, El Paso TX

Madriguera, Enric, *Dean*. Eastfield College, Humanities Division, Art Dept, Mesquite TX (S)

Madura, Nancy, *Instr*. Casper College, Dept of Visual Arts, Casper WY (S)

Maeckelbergh, Kenneth, *Instr*. Century College, Humanities Dept, White Bear Lake MN (S)

Maeder, Edward, *Adjunct Asst Prof*. University of Southern California, School of Fine Arts, Los Angeles CA (S)

Magavern, William J, *VPres*. The Buffalo Fine Arts Academy, Albright-Knox Art Gallery, Buffalo NY

Magden, Norman, *Head Art Dept*. University of Tennessee, Knoxville, Dept of Art, Knoxville TN (S)

Magee, Catherine, *Dir*. Henry Francis DuPont Winter Thur, Camden NJ

Magee, Eileen, *Program Coordr*. Athenaeum of Philadelphia, Philadelphia PA

Maggio, Bill, *Second VPres*. Buffalo Society of Artists, Williamsville NY

Maggio, Ron, *Assoc Prof*. Springfield College, Dept of Visual & Performing Arts, Springfield MA (S)

Maggio, Ronald, *Coordr*. Springfield College, Hasting Gallery, Springfield MA

Magistro, Charles J, *Chmn*. William Paterson College, Art Dept, Wayne NJ (S)

Magleby, McRay, *Prof*. University of Utah, Art Dept, Salt Lake City UT (S)

Magnan, Oscar, *Dir*. Saint Peter's College, Art Gallery, Jersey City NJ

Magness, Jodi, *Asst Prof*. Tufts University, Dept of Art & Art History, Medford MA (S)

Magnoni, Corinne, *Assoc Dir*. University of Wisconsin-Madison, Elvehjem Museum of Art, Madison WI

Magnuson, Gabriela, *Asst Cur Coll Management*. Wichita State University, Edwin A Ulrich Museum of Art, Wichita KS

Magnusson, Paul, *Pres*. Oregon School of Arts & Crafts, Portland OR (S)

Magowan, Robert A, *VPres*. The Society of the Four Arts, Palm Beach FL

Magri, Ken, *Instr*. American River College, Dept of Art, Sacramento CA (S)

Maguire, Eunice, *Cur*. University of Illinois, Krannert Art Museum, Champaign IL

Maguire, Nancy, *Asst Dir & Assoc Cur*. Rutgers University, Stedman Art Gallery, Camden NJ

Maguire, William, *Prof*. Florida International University, Visual Arts Dept, Miami FL (S)

Mahaffey, Richard, *Instr*. Tacoma Community College, Art Dept, Tacoma WA (S)

Mahar, William J, *Head Humanities*. Penn State Harrisburg, Humanities Division, Middletown PA (S)

Maher, Kathleen, *Asst Dir*. Lockwood-Mathews Mansion Museum, Norwalk CT

Maher, Kim L, *Exec Dir*. Museum of Discovery & Science, Fort Lauderdale FL

Mahlberg, Janice, *Instr*. Milwaukee Area Technical College, Graphic Arts Division, Milwaukee WI (S)

Mahmoudi, Hoda, *Library Dir*. Olivet College, Library, Olivet MI

Mahnke, Helen, *Museum Educator*. Pennsylvania Historical & Museum Commission, Brandywine Battlefield Park, Harrisburg PA

Mahones, Robert, *Public Information Officer*. The Queens Museum of Art, Flushing NY

Mahoney, M, *Instr*. Western Illinois University, Art Dept, Macomb IL (S)

Mahoney, Olivia, *Cur Decorative Arts*. Chicago Historical Society, Chicago IL

Mahoney, Toella-Jean, *Painting*. University of La Verne, Dept of Art, La Verne CA (S)

Mahsun, Carol Anne, *Assoc Prof*. Hope College, Art Dept, Holland MI (S)

Mai, James, *Dept Coordr*. Graceland College, Fine Arts Dept, Lamoni IA (S)

Main, Sally, *Asst Dir*. Tulane University, Dept Art Newcomb Col Art Galleries, New Orleans LA

Mainardi, Patricia, *Prof*. City University of New York, PhD Program in Art History, New York NY (S)

Maines, Clark, *Prof*. Wesleyan University, Art Dept, Middletown CT (S)

Mainiero, Elizabeth, *Dir*. Greenwich Library, Greenwich CT

Maiolo, Mimmo, *Preparator*. Banff Centre, Walter Phillips Gallery, Banff AB

Maize, Shirley, *Dir Visual Arts*. Tennessee Valley Art Association & Center, Tuscumbia AL

Majaras, Eileen, *Librn*. Solomon R Guggenheim Museum, Library, New York NY

Majeske, Robert, *Instr*. Illinois Central College, Dept of Fine Arts, East Peoria IL (S)

Majeski, Thomas, *Asst Prof*. University of Nebraska at Omaha, Dept of Art & Art History, Omaha NE (S)

Majewski, Shirley, *Library Aide*. Historic Deerfield, Inc, Henry N Flynt Library, Deerfield MA

Major, Sharon, *Pub Relations Coordr*. University of California, Santa Barbara, University Art Museum, Santa Barbara CA

Majors, Elaine, *Instr*. Creighton University, Fine & Performing Arts Dept, Omaha NE (S)

Majusiak, Anne, *Gallery Dir*. Vermont State Craft Center at Frog Hollow, Middlebury VT

Makar, Alexandra, *Spec Project Dir*. Ukrainian Canadian Archives & Museum of Alberta, Edmonton AB

Makela, Laurie, *Co-Head 2-D Design Dept*. Cranbrook Academy of Art, Bloomfield Hills MI (S)

Makela, P Scott, *Co-Head 2-D Design Dept*. Cranbrook Academy of Art, Bloomfield Hills MI (S)

Makinson, Randel, *Dir*. University of Southern California, Greene & Greene Library of the Arts & Crafts Movement, San Marino CA

Makov, Susan, *Prof*. Weber State University, Dept of Visual Arts, Ogden UT (S)

Makow, Yoram, *Prof*. California State Polytechnic University, Pomona, Art Dept, Pomona CA (S)

Malak, Greg, *Cur*. Will Rogers Memorial & Museum, Media Center Library, Claremore OK

Malak, Gregory, *Cur*. Will Rogers Memorial & Museum, Claremore OK

Malarcher, Patricia, *Ed Surface Design Journal*. Surface Design Association, Inc, Oakland CA

Malarney, Marge, *Pres*. Lansing Art Gallery, Lansing MI

Malavet, Juanita, *Museum Shop Mgr*. The Rockwell Museum, Corning NY

Malcolm-Arnold, Gloria, *VPres*. Kent Art Association, Inc, Gallery, Kent CT

Malde, Pradip, *Chmn Dept*. University of the South, Dept of Fine Arts, Sewanee TN (S)

Maldonado, Edward, *Assoc Cur*. Chicago Department of Cultural Affairs, Chicago Cultural Center, Chicago IL

Malecha, Marvin J, *Dean*. North Carolina State University at Raleigh, School of Design, Raleigh NC (S)

Malesky, Barney J, *Cur Educ*. San Diego Museum of Art, San Diego CA

Malgeri, Dina G, *Librn*. Malden Public Library, Art Dept & Gallery, Malden MA

Malik, Marlene, *Chmn*. Brown University, Dept of Visual Art, Providence RI (S)

Malinski, Richard M, *Chief Librn*. Ryerson Polytechnical Institute, Library, Toronto ON

Malkoff-Moon, Susan, *Head Librn*. Nelson-Atkins Museum of Art, Kansas City MO

Malkoff Moon, Susan, *Head Librn*. Nelson-Atkins Museum of Art, Spencer Art Reference Library, Kansas City MO

Mallard, Michael, *Chmn*. Union University, Dept of Art, Jackson TN (S)

Malley, Diane, *Dir*. Clarion University, Hazel Sandford Gallery, Clarion PA

Malley, Richard C, *Registrar.* Connecticut Historical Society, Hartford CT

Mallin, Joel, *Chmn.* Aldrich Museum of Contemporary Art, Ridgefield CT

Mallory, Jane, *Information Officer.* Ontario Crafts Council, Craft Resource Centre, Toronto ON

Mallory, Michael, *Prof.* City University of New York, PhD Program in Art History, New York NY (S)

Mallory, Michael, *Chmn.* Brooklyn College, Art Dept, Brooklyn NY (S)

Mallory, Nina, *Prof.* State University of New York at Stony Brook, Art Dept, Stony Brook NY (S)

Mallory, Sidney, *Chief Exec Officer.* Austin Museum of Art at Laguna Gloria, Austin TX

Malm, Linda, *Div Dean.* Pasadena City College, Art Dept, Pasadena CA (S)

Malmstrom, Susan, *Member Serv Liaison.* Public Corporation for the Arts, Visual & Performing Arts Registry, Long Beach CA

Malone, Carolyn, *Assoc Prof.* University of Southern California, School of Fine Arts, Los Angeles CA (S)

Malone, Leslie, *Instr.* University of North Carolina at Charlotte, Dept of Visual Arts, Charlotte NC (S)

Malone, Peter, *Gallery Asst.* Kingsborough Community College, City University of New York, Art Gallery, Brooklyn NY

Malone, Robert, *Pres.* Skaneateles Library Association, Skaneateles NY

Malone, Robert R, *Head Printmaking.* Southern Illinois University at Edwardsville, Dept of Art & Design, Edwardsville IL (S)

Malone, Terry, *Exec Dir.* Sooke Region Museum & Art Gallery, Sooke BC

Maloney, Kathleen, *Managing Dir.* Intermedia Arts Minnesota, Minneapolis MN

Maloney, Leslie, *Curatorial Asst Preparator.* Phillips Academy, Addison Gallery of American Art, Andover MA

Maloney, Patricia, *Asst Prof.* Washington & Jefferson College, Art Dept, Washington PA (S)

Maloney, Sarah, *Coordr.* Organization for the Development of Artists, Gallery Connexion, Fredericton NB

Maltais, Marie, *Dir.* University of New Brunswick, UNB Art Centre, Fredericton NB

Malus, Mary June, *Dir.* Imperial Calcasieu Museum, Lake Charles LA

Malus, Mary June, *Coordr.* Imperial Calcasieu Museum, Gibson-Barham Gallery, Lake Charles LA

Malus, Mary June, *Coordr.* Imperial Calcasieu Museum, Gibson Library, Lake Charles LA

Mamer, Helen, *Cur.* Weyburn Arts Council, Allie Griffin Art Gallery, Weyburn SK

Manbooh, Komar, *Asst Finance.* Institute of Contemporary Art, Boston MA

Manca, Maggi, *Special Events Coordr.* Marin County Watercolor Society, Greenbrae CA

Mancusi-Ungaro, Carol, *Chief Conservator.* Menil Collection, Houston TX

Mancuso, Bill, *Dir of Permanent Coll.* Thiel College, Sampson Art Gallery, Greenville PA

Mandaville, Erik, *Instr.* Houston Baptist University, Dept of Art, Houston TX (S)

Mandel, Gerry, *VPres.* Children's Art Foundation, Museum of International Children's Art, Santa Cruz CA

Manderen, Elizabeth, *Exec Dir.* Firelands Association for the Visual Arts, Oberlin OH

Mandle, Roger, *Pres.* Rhode Island School of Design, Museum of Art, RISD, Providence RI (S)

Maneen, Thomas, *Instr.* Mohawk Valley Community College, Advertising Design & Production, Utica NY (S)

Mangel, Deborah T, *Museum Shop Dir.* Philadelphia College of Textiles & Science, Paley Design Center, Philadelphia PA

Mangelli, Jennifer L, *Asst to Dir.* Philadelphia College of Textiles & Science, Paley Design Center, Philadelphia PA

Manger, Barbara, *Dir.* Cardinal Stritch College, Layton Honor Gallery, Milwaukee WI

Manger, Barbara, *Adjunct Prof.* Cardinal Stritch College, Art Dept, Milwaukee WI (S)

Mangers, Marvin, *Gen Mgr.* Harold Warp Pioneer Village Foundation, Minden NE

Mangus, Kirk, *Div Coordr Crafts.* Kent State University, School of Art, Kent OH (S)

Manhart, Marcia, *Dir.* Philbrook Museum of Art, Tulsa OK

Manifold, Gregory, *Interim Dir.* Fort Wayne Museum of Art, Inc, Fort Wayne IN

Maniscalco, Nelson R, *Chmn.* Cedar Crest College, Art Dept, Allentown PA (S)

Manjon, Sonia, *Arts Specialist.* Berkeley Civic Arts Program, Berkeley CA

Manley, Beverley, *Pres.* Arthur Manley Society, Tampa FL

Mann, Jack, *Assoc Prof.* Wittenberg University, Art Dept, Springfield OH (S)

Mann, James, *Cur.* Las Vegas Art Museum, Las Vegas NV

Mann, Janice, *Prof.* Bucknell University, Dept of Art, Lewisburg PA (S)

Mann, Judith, *Asst Prof.* University of Missouri, Saint Louis, Dept of Art & Art History, Saint Louis MO (S)

Mann, Katinka, *Treas.* American Abstract Artists, New York NY

Mann, Linda, *Dean.* Grossmont College, Art Dept, El Cajon CA (S)

Mann, Theresa, *Exhibits Coordr.* Spartanburg County Museum of Art, Spartanburg SC

Mann, Tina, *Instr.* William Woods-Westminster Colleges, Art Dept, Fulton MO (S)

Mann, Vivian B, *Cur of Judaica.* The Jewish Museum, New York NY

Mann, Vivian B, *Cur of Judaica.* The Jewish Museum, Library, New York NY

Mannheimer, Marc, *Prof.* Bradford College, Creative Arts Division, Bradford MA (S)

Mannikka, Eleanor, *Instr.* University of Michigan, Ann Arbor, Dept of History of Art, Ann Arbor MI (S)

Manning, Anne Marie, *Museum Educator.* Dartmouth College, Hood Museum of Art, Hanover NH

Manning, Larry, *Instructor.* Jefferson Davis Community College, Art Dept, Brewton AL (S)

Manning, Mary, *Dir Libraries.* California College of Arts & Crafts Library, Oakland CA

Mano, Charlene, *Educ Coordr.* Wing Luke Asian Museum, Seattle WA

Manos, George, *Asst to Dir of Music.* National Gallery of Art, Washington DC

Manring, Yvonne, *Asst Cur.* The American Ceramic Society, Ross C Purdy Museum of Ceramics, Westerville OH

Manriquez, Dion, *Asst Prof.* University of Wisconsin-Stout, Dept of Art & Design, Menomonie WI (S)

Mansdorf, Eve, *Asst Prof.* Indiana University, Bloomington, Henry Radford Hope School of Fine Arts, Bloomington IN (S)

Manseau, Marlene, *Marketing.* Ford Motor Company, Henry Ford Museum & Greenfield Village, Dearborn MI

Mansell, Alice, *Pres.* Nova Scotia College of Art & Design, Halifax NS (S)

Mansell, Alice, *Pres.* Nova Scotia College of Art and Design, Anna Leonowens Gallery, Halifax NS

Manthorne, Katherine, *In Charge History.* University of Illinois, Urbana-Champaign, School of Art & Design, Champaign IL (S)

Mantin, Regina, *Mgr Temporary Exhibits.* New Brunswick Museum, Saint John NB

Manton, Jill, *Dir Pub Art Prog.* San Francisco City & County Art Commission, San Francisco CA

Manuele, Lisa, *Instr.* Springfield College in Illinois, Dept of Art, Springfield IL (S)

Manzo, Helene, *Co-Dir.* Blue Mountain Gallery, New York NY

Maple, Amanda, *Music Librn.* Pennsylvania State University, Arts Library, University Park PA

Maples, Sharon, *Admin Asst.* Carson County Square House Museum, Panhandle TX

Mapp, Thomas, *Dir.* University of Chicago, Lorado Taft Midway Studios, Chicago IL

Marak, L B, *Instr.* Humboldt State University, College of Arts & Humanities, Arcata CA (S)

Marcel, Francine, *Exhib Cur.* South Dakota State University, South Dakota Art Museum, Brookings SD

March, Paula, *Deputy Dir.* Fine Arts Museums of San Francisco, San Francisco CA

March, Sally Cooper, *Pres.* Council of Delaware Artists, Elkton MD

Marchant, Beverly, *Asst Prof.* La Salle University, Dept of Art, Philadelphia PA (S)

Marchant, Beverly, *Prof.* Marshall University, Dept of Art, Huntington WV (S)

Marchlinski, Mark, *Asst Prof.* University of Alabama in Huntsville, Dept of Art & Art History, Huntsville AL (S)

Marcia, Graff, *Dir.* Chatillon-DeMenil House Foundation, DeMenil Mansion, Saint Louis MO

Marcinowski, Gary, *Asst Prof.* University of Dayton, Visual Arts Dept, Dayton OH (S)

Marconi, Nello, *Chief Design & Production.* National Portrait Gallery, Washington DC

Marcou, George T, *Prof.* Catholic University of America, School of Architecture & Planning, Washington DC (S)

Marcum-Estes, Leah, *Dir.* Oak Ridge Art Center, Oak Ridge TN

Marcum-Estes, Leah, *Dir.* Oak Ridge Art Center, Library, Oak Ridge TN

Marcus, Evelyn, *Cur Exhib.* Dartmouth College, Hood Museum of Art, Hanover NH

Marcus, Linda, *Dir Educ.* Fuller Museum of Art, Brockton MA

Marcus, Susan Bass, *Artifact Center Cur.* Spertus Institute of Jewish Studies, Spertus Museum, Chicago IL

Marcusen, Richard, *Chmn.* Yavapai College, Visual & Performing Arts Division, Prescott AZ (S)

Marder, Tod, *Prof.* Rutgers, the State University of New Jersey, Graduate Program in Art History, New Brunswick NJ (S)

Margalit, Nathan, *Visiting Assoc Prof.* Trinity College, Dept of Fine Arts, Hartford CT (S)

Margol, Deborah, *Deputy Dir.* South Florida Cultural Consortium, Metropolitan Dade County Cultural Affairs Council, Miami FL

Margulies, Stephen, *Cur Works on Paper.* University of Virginia, Bayly Art Museum, Charlottesville VA

Marichal, Flavia, *Cur Art.* University of Puerto Rico, Museum of Anthropology, History & Art, San Juan PR

Marien, Mary, *Prof.* Syracuse University, Dept of Fine Arts (Art History), Syracuse NY (S)

Marince, Pat, *Instr.* Southwest Texas State University, Dept of Art, San Marcos TX (S)

Marincola, Paula, *Gallery Dir.* Beaver College Art Gallery, Glenside PA

Maring, Joel, *Adjunct Cur Anthropology.* Southern Illinois University, University Museum, Carbondale IL

Mariniello, Sylvestra, *Instr.* Universite de Montreal, Dept of Art History, Montreal PQ (S)

Marino, Charles, *Assoc Prof.* University of Southern Colorado, Belmont Campus, Dept of Art, Pueblo CO (S)

Marino, Vicki L, *Asst Cur.* Wells Fargo & Co, History Museum, Los Angeles CA

Marinsky, Jane, *Instr.* Daemen College, Art Dept, Amherst NY (S)

Marioni, Tom, *Dir.* Archives of MOCA (Museum of Conceptual Art), San Francisco CA

Marioni, Tom, *Dir.* Archives of MOCA (Museum of Conceptual Art), Library, San Francisco CA

Mariott, W B, *VPres.* Ventura County Historical Society, Museum of History & Art, Ventura CA

Mark, Peter, *Assoc Prof.* Wesleyan University, Art Dept, Middletown CT (S)

Mark, Phyllis, *VPres Publications.* Sculptors Guild, Inc, New York NY

Markey, Mary, *Supv.* Baltimore City Life Museums, Library, Baltimore MD

Markham, Sandra, *Chief Librn.* Albany Institute of History & Art, Albany NY

Markham, Sandra, *Chief Librn.* Albany Institute of History & Art, McKinney Library, Albany NY

Markle, Greer, *Dir.* Southern Oregon State College, Schneider Museum of Art, Ashland OR

Markness, Toni M, *VPres Develop.* Newberry Library, Chicago IL

Marvel, Marcia, *Pres Board*, Rehoboth Art League, Inc, Rehoboth Beach DE

Marvin, Anne, *Cur Fine Art*, Kansas State Historical Society, Kansas Museum of History, Topeka KS

Marvin, Miranda, *Prof*, Wellesley College, Art Dept, Wellesley MA (S)

Marx, Robert, *Exec Dir*, The New York Public Library, Shelby Cullom Davis Museum, New York NY

Marxhausen, Reinhold P, *Prof*, Concordia College, Art Dept, Seward NE (S)

Marzio, Peter C, *Dir*, Museum of Fine Arts, Houston, Houston TX

Marzo, Janet, *Dir*, Nassau Community College, Firehouse Art Gallery, Garden City NY

Marzolf, Helen, *Dir & Cur*, Regina Public Library, Dunlop Art Gallery, Regina SK

Maschino, David, *Exhib Coordr*, Bowdoin College, Peary-MacMillan Arctic Museum, Brunswick ME

Mashibini, Deborah, *Dir Enabled Arts Center*, Very Special Arts New Mexico, Very Special Arts Gallery, Albuquerque NM

Mashke, Kathy, *Dir Develop*, Nexus Contemporary Art Center, Atlanta GA

Masich, Andrew E, *VPres*, Colorado Historical Society, Colorado History Museum, Denver CO

Maslansky, Pamela, *Art Cur*, Mobil Corporation, Art Collection, Fairfax VA

Masley, Mary, *Circulation Asst*, Roger Williams University, Architecture Library, Bristol RI

Mason, Bonnie C, *Cur Educ*, Miami University, Art Museum, Oxford OH

Mason, Charles, *Cur Asian Art*, Oberlin College, Allen Memorial Art Museum, Oberlin OH

Mason, Gary, *Exec Dir*, Providence Athenaeum, Providence RI

Mason, Gary, *Dir*, Providence Athenaeum, Library, Providence RI

Mason, George, *Chmn*, Saint Meinrad College, Humanities Dept, Saint Meinrad IN (S)

Mason, Glen, *Dir*, Eastern Washington State Historical Society, Library, Spokane WA

Mason, Glenn, *Dir*, Eastern Washington State Historical Society, Cheney Cowles Museum, Spokane WA

Mason, Henri, *Dir*, Drew County Historical Society, Museum, Monticello AR

Mason, Jeffrey, *Chmn*, California State University, Bakersfield, Fine Arts Dept, Bakersfield CA (S)

Mason, Joel, *Chmn*, New York City Technical College of the City University of New York, Dept of Art & Advertising Design, Brooklyn NY (S)

Mason, Julienne T, *Fiscal Officer & Designer*, *Museum Press*, Florida State University, Museum of Fine Arts, Tallahassee FL

Mason, Karen, *Pres*, California Watercolor Association, Walnut Creek CA

Mason, Marilyn Gell, *Dir*, Cleveland Public Library, Fine Arts & Special Collections Dept, Cleveland OH

Mason, Mary Ellen, *Membership & Public Relations Coordr*, Bennington Museum, Bennington Museum, Bennington VT

Mason, Terry, *Pres*, Douglas Art Association, Little Gallery, Douglas AZ

Massar, Phyllis, *Adult Servs Supv*, Ferguson Library, Stamford CT

Massaroni, Dino, *Instr*, Cuyahoga Valley Art Center, Cuyahoga Falls OH (S)

Massey, Bryan, *Assoc Prof*, University of Central Arkansas, Art Dept, Conway AR (S)

Massey, Lew, *Property Mgr*, Bank One Fort Worth, Fort Worth TX

Massie-Lane, Rebecca, *Dir*, Sweet Briar College, Art Gallery, Sweet Briar VA

Massier, John, *Asst Cur*, Jewish Community Centre of Toronto, The Koffler Gallery, North York ON

Massing, Peter, *Prof*, Marshall University, Dept of Art, Huntington WV (S)

Master-Karnik, Paul, *Dir*, DeCordova Museum & Sculpture Park, Lincoln MA

Masters, Cherryl, *Museum Shop Mgr*, The Canadian Craft Museum, Vancouver BC

Masterson, Judith P, *Gallery Coordr*, College of New Jersey, Art Gallery, Trenton NJ

Masterson, Nancy, *Color & Graphic Instr*, Hutchinson Community Junior College, Visual Arts Dept, Hutchinson KS (S)

Mastin, Cathy, *Cur Art*, Glenbow Museum, Calgary AB

Masuoka, Susan, *Interim Dir*, Tufts University, Art Gallery, Medford MA

Mates, Judy, *Instr*, Joe Kubert School of Cartoon & Graphic Art, Inc, Dover NJ (S)

Mathe, Barbara, *Librn*, The Metropolitan Museum of Art, Robert Goldwater Library, New York NY

Mather, Charles E, *Pres*, Fairmount Park Art Association, Philadelphia PA

Mather, Tim, *Asst Prof*, Indiana University, Bloomington, Henry Radford Hope School of Fine Arts, Bloomington IN (S)

Matherly, John, *Tech*, The Hudson River Museum of Westchester, Yonkers NY

Matheson, Pat, *Cur*, University of Regina, Slide Library, Regina SK

Matheson, Susan, *Assoc Cur Ancient Art*, Yale University, Art Gallery, New Haven CT

Mathews, John, *Instr*, Bucks County Community College, Fine Arts Dept, Newtown PA (S)

Mathews, Karen, *Asst Prof*, University of Colorado at Denver, Dept of Fine Arts, Denver CO (S)

Mathews, Nancy, *Cur Educ*, Kenosha Public Museum, Kenosha WI

Mathews, Nancy Mowll, *Prendergast Cur*, Williams College, Museum of Art, Williamstown MA

Mathews, Patricia, *Assoc Prof*, Oberlin College, Dept of Art, Oberlin OH (S)

Mathews, Wyhomme, *Chmn*, Kellogg Community College, Visual & Performing Arts Dept, Battle Creek MI (S)

Mathey, Carole, *Coll Mgr*, St Lawrence University, Richard F Brush Art Gallery, Canton NY

Mathis, Doyle, *VPres*, Berry College, Moon Gallery, Mount Berry GA

Matilsky, Barbara, *Exhib Cur*, University of North Carolina at Chapel Hill, Ackland Art Museum, Chapel Hill NC

Matisoo, Antionette, *Financial Dir*, Danforth Museum of Art, Framingham MA

Matlock, Jayne, *Asst Prof*, University of Dayton, Visual Arts Dept, Dayton OH (S)

Matlock-Hinkle, Maryann, *Instr*, Main Line Art Center, Haverford PA (S)

Mato, Nancy, *Deputy Dir*, The Society of the Four Arts, Palm Beach FL

Matson, Bob, *Coordr Art Gallery*, Willmar Community College, Art Dept, Willmar MN (S)

Matson, Isabel, *Asst to Dir*, Wayne Center for the Arts, Wooster OH

Matson, Karen, *Coordr Technical Communications*, Kalamazoo Valley Community College, Humanities Dept, Kalamazoo MI (S)

Matsumoto, Moritaka, *Assoc Prof*, University of British Columbia, Dept of Fine Arts, Vancouver BC (S)

Matta, Eugene, *Dir*, College of Staten Island, Performing & Creative Arts Dept, Staten Island NY (S)

Matter, Mercedes, *Instr*, New York Studio School of Drawing, Painting & Sculpture, New York NY (S)

Matteson, Charles C, *Chmn Art Dept*, State University of New York, Agricultural & Technical College, Art Dept, Cobleskill NY (S)

Matteson, Lynn, *Dean*, University of Southern California, School of Fine Arts, Los Angeles CA (S)

Matthews, Harriett, *Prof*, Colby College, Art Dept, Waterville ME (S)

Matthews, Henry, *Dir*, Muskegon Museum of Art, Muskegon MI

Matthews, Julia, *Head Librn*, Royal Ontario Museum, Library & Archives, Toronto ON

Matthews, Nancy, *VPres for Arts*, Meridian International Center, Cafritz Galleries, Washington DC

Matthias, Diana, *Coordr Community Prog*, University of Notre Dame, Snite Museum of Art, Notre Dame IN

Mattice, Matt, *Educ Specialist*, Judiciary History Center, Honolulu HI

Mattson, John, *Co-Site Supv*, Fort Totten State Historic Site, Pioneer Daughters Museum, Fort Totten ND

Mattusch, Carol C, *Prof*, George Mason University, Dept of Art & Art History, Fairfax VA (S)

Mattys, Joe, *Assoc Prof*, Randolph-Macon College, Dept of the Arts, Ashland VA (S)

Mauck, Marchita, *Prof*, Louisiana State University, School of Art, Baton Rouge LA (S)

Maudlin-Jeronimo, John, *Exec Dir*, National Architectural Accrediting Board, Inc, Washington DC

Mauer, Ernest, *Prof Emeriti*, Old Dominion University, Art Dept, Norfolk VA (S)

Mauersberger, George, *Assoc Prof*, Cleveland State University, Art Dept, Cleveland OH (S)

Maughan, William, *Co Chair Fine Art*, Academy of Art College, Fine Arts Dept, San Francisco CA (S)

Maul, John, *Asst Prof*, Oregon State University, Dept of Art, Corvallis OR (S)

Mauldin, Barbara, *Cur Latin American Folk Art*, Museum of New Mexico, Museum of International Folk Art, Santa Fe NM

Mauner, George L, *Prof*, Pennsylvania State University, University Park, Dept of Art History, University Park PA (S)

Mauren, Paul, *Assoc Prof*, College of Saint Rose, Dept of Art, Albany NY (S)

Maurer, Evan, *Dir*, Minneapolis Institute of Arts, Minneapolis MN

Maurer, Neil, *Assoc Prof*, University of Texas at San Antonio, Division of Visual Arts, San Antonio TX (S)

Maurer, Sherry C, *Gallery Dir*, Augustana College, Art Gallery, Rock Island IL

Mauro, Robert, *Chmn*, Beaver College, Dept of Fine Arts, Glenside PA (S)

Maury, Kate, *Asst Prof*, University of Wisconsin-Stout, Dept of Art & Design, Menomonie WI (S)

Maveety, Patrick, *Cur of Oriental Art*, Stanford University, Museum of Art, Stanford CA

Mavigliano, George, *Assoc Prof*, Southern Illinois University, School of Art & Design, Carbondale IL (S)

Mavor, Carol, *Assoc Prof*, University of North Carolina at Chapel Hill, Art Dept, Chapel Hill NC (S)

Mavrogenes, Sylvia, *Youth Serv Adminr*, Miami-Dade Public Library, Miami FL

Maw, Nicholas, *Instr*, Bard College, Milton Avery Graduate School of the Arts, Annandale-on-Hudson NY (S)

Mawani, Salma, *Admin Asst*, University of British Columbia, Museum of Anthropology, Vancouver BC

Mawdsley, Richard, *Prof*, Southern Illinois University, School of Art & Design, Carbondale IL (S)

Maxedon, Ed, *Cur Educ*, Indiana University, Art Museum, Bloomington IN

Maxwell, Belle, *Pres Board*, Seattle Art Museum, Seattle WA

Maxwell, Diane, *Dir Public Relations*, San Jose Museum of Art, San Jose CA

Maxwell, Kathleen, *Lectr*, Santa Clara University, Art Dept, Santa Clara CA (S)

Maxwell, K C, *Prof*, Shoreline Community College, Humanities Division, Seattle WA (S)

Maxwell, Margaret, *VPres*, Children's Museum, Rauh Memorial Library, Indianapolis IN

Maxwell, Stephanie, *Asst Prof*, Rochester Institute of Technology, School of Photographic Arts & Sciences, Rochester NY (S)

Maxwell, William C, *Prof*, College of New Rochelle School of Arts & Sciences, Art Dept, New Rochelle NY (S)

May, D L, *Assoc Prof*, Andrews University, Dept of Art, Art History & Design, Berrien Springs MI (S)

May, Gerald, *Secy Treas*, Moncur Gallery, Boissevain MB

May, Hayden B, *Dean School Fine Arts*, Miami University, Art Dept, Oxford OH (S)

May, James M, *Asst Prof*, University of Nebraska, Kearney, Dept of Art & Art History, Kearney NE (S)

May, Larry, *Instr.* Art Academy of Cincinnati, Cincinnati OH (S)

Maya, Gloria, *Prof.* Western New Mexico University, Dept of Expressive Arts, Silver City NM (S)

Mayberry, Martha, *Registrar,* Mint Museum of Art, Charlotte NC

Maycock, Susan, *Survey Dir.* City of Cambridge Historical Commission, Cambridge MA

Mayer, Carol, *Cur Ethnology & Ceramics,* University of British Columbia, Museum of Anthropology, Vancouver BC

Mayer, Edward, *Prof.* State University of New York at Albany, Art Dept, Albany NY (S)

Mayer, Jan, *VPres.* The American Federation of Arts, New York NY

Mayer, Jesse, *Treas,* Essex Art Association, Inc, Essex CT

Mayer, John, *Dir.* Manchester Historic Association, Manchester NH

Mayer, Lance, *Conservator,* Lyman Allyn Art Museum, New London CT

Mayer, Marc, *Cur.* The Buffalo Fine Arts Academy, Albright-Knox Art Gallery, Buffalo NY

Mayer, Robert A, *Pres.* Cleveland Institute of Art, Reinberger Galleries, Cleveland OH

Mayer, Robert A, *Pres.* Cleveland Institute of Art, Cleveland OH (S)

Mayer, William, *Chmn.* Hope College, Art Dept, Holland MI (S)

Mayes, Steven, *Dir.* Arkansas State University-Art Department, Jonesboro, Fine Arts Center Gallery, Jonesboro AR

Mayes, Steven L, *Prof.* Arkansas State University, Dept of Art, State University AR (S)

Mayfield, Signe, *Cur.* Palo Alto Cultural Center, Palo Alto CA

Mayhall, Dorothy, *Dir of Art,* Stamford Museum & Nature Center, Stamford CT

Maylone, R Russell, *Head Spec Art Library,* Northwestern University, Art Library, Evanston IL

Mayo, David, *Exhib Designer,* University of California, Los Angeles, Fowler Museum of Cultural History, Los Angeles CA

Mayo, Marti, *Dir.* Contemporary Arts Museum, Houston TX

Mayor, Babette, *Assoc Prof.* California State Polytechnic University, Pomona, Art Dept, Pomona CA (S)

Mayrhofer, Ingrid, *Prog Dir.* A Space, Toronto ON

Mays, Clarence C, *Chmn Div Human,* Virginia Western Community College, Commercial Art, Fine Art & Photography, Roanoke VA (S)

Mazanowski V, Ron, *Div Coordr,* Northern Illinois University, School of Art, De Kalb IL (S)

Maze, Clarence, *Pres,* Richard Bland College, Art Dept, Petersburg VA (S)

Mazeau, Mary, *Vol Librn.* Heckscher Museum of Art, Library, Huntington NY

Mazeika, George, *Registrar,* University of Connecticut, William Benton Museum of Art, Storrs CT

Mazellen, Ron, *Instr.* Indiana Wesleyan University, Art Dept, Marion IN (S)

Mazonowicz, Douglas, *Dir.* Gallery of Prehistoric Paintings, New York NY

Mazonowicz, Douglas, *Dir.* Gallery of Prehistoric Paintings, Library, New York NY

Mazur, Robert, *Chmn 2-D Studies,* Bowling Green State University, School of Art, Bowling Green OH (S)

McAdams, Margaret, *Assoc Prof.* Ohio University-Chillicothe Campus, Fine Arts & Humanities Division, Chillicothe OH (S)

McAfee, Michael J, *Cur History.* United States Military Academy, West Point Museum, West Point NY

McAleer, Philip, *Prof.* Technical University of Nova Scotia, Faculty of Architecture, Halifax NS (S)

McAlister, Richard A, *Assoc Prof.* Providence College, Art & Art History Dept, Providence RI (S)

McAlister-Curtis, Judith, *Cur.* Adams National Historic Site, Quincy MA

McAllister, Lowell, *Exec Dir.* Frederic Remington Art Museum, Ogdensburg NY

McAllister, Lowell, *Exec Dir.* Frederic Remington Art Museum, Library, Ogdensburg NY

McAllister, Michael, *Chmn Dept.* North Carolina Wesleyan College, Dept of Visual & Performing Arts, Rocky Mount NC (S)

McAlpine, Donald, *Natural Sciences-Zoology.* New Brunswick Museum, Saint John NB

McAndrews, Lawrence, *Chmn.* Saint Norbert College, Division of Humanities & Fine Arts, De Pere WI (S)

McArt, Craig, *Prof.* Rochester Institute of Technology, School of Art & Design, Rochester NY (S)

McArthur, Seonaid, *Educ Cur.* Museum of Contemporary Art, San Diego, La Jolla CA

McArthur, Seonaid, *Educ Cur.* Museum of Contemporary Art, San Diego-Downtown, San Diego CA

McAvity, John G, *Exec Dir.* Canadian Museums Association, Association des Musees Canadiens, Ottawa ON

McBeth, James, *Cur.* Lightner Museum, Saint Augustine FL

McBoggs, Mayo, *Prof.* Converse College, Art Dept, Spartanburg SC (S)

McBratney-Stapleton, Deborah, *Exec Dir.* Anderson Fine Arts Center, Anderson IN

McBrearty, Mary Jo, *Mgr Community Develop.* Sheboygan Arts Foundation, Inc, John Michael Kohler Arts Center, Sheboygan WI

McBride, Carolyn N, *Secy.* National Hall of Fame for Famous American Indians, Anadarko OK

McBride, Joe, *Dir & Exec VPres.* National Hall of Fame for Famous American Indians, Anadarko OK

McBride, Peggy, *Reference Librn.* University of British Columbia, Fine Arts Library, Vancouver BC

McBride, Peggy, *Gallery Coordr.* Hambidge Center Gallery, Rabun Gap GA

McCabe, Mary Kennedy, *Dir.* Mid America Arts Alliance & Exhibits USA, Kansas City MO

McCabe, Maureen, *Prof.* Connecticut College, Dept of Art, New London CT (S)

McCabe, Michael M, *Library Dir.* Brevard College, James A Jones Library, Brevard NC

McCabe, Nancy, *Development Officer,* John Simon Guggenheim Memorial Foundation, New York NY

McCabe, Sharon, *Business Mgr.* Montana Historical Society, Helena MT

McCafferty, Jay, *Instr.* Los Angeles Harbor College, Art Dept, Wilmington CA (S)

McCaffrey, Morra, *Cur Ethnology.* McCord Museum of Canadian History, Montreal PQ

McCain, Diana, *Public Information Officer,* Connecticut Historical Society, Hartford CT

McCain, Keith, *Pres.* Charles Morse Museum of American Art, Winter Park FL

McCalister, Lonnie, *Chmn.* Lee College, Dept of Music & Fine Arts, Cleveland TN (S)

McCall, Sara, *Secy & Registrar.* Zanesville Art Center, Zanesville OH

McCall, Sara, *Registrar & Librn.* Zanesville Art Center, Library, Zanesville OH

McCallig, Patrick, *VPres.* Museum of Holography - Chicago, Chicago IL

McCallum, Tracy, *Librn.* Taos Public Library, Taos NM

McCampbell, Jerry, *Chmn Math & Science.* Idyllwild Arts Academy, Idyllwild CA (S)

McCandless, Barbara, *Cur Paintings & Sculpture.* Amon Carter Museum, Fort Worth TX

McCandless, Harry, *Treas.* Lancaster County Art Association, Inc, Lancaster PA

McCann, James, *Business Mgr.* Historical Society of Pennsylvania, Philadelphia PA

McCann, Michael, *Exec Dir.* Center for Safety in the Arts, New York NY

McCarter, John W, *Pres.* Field Museum, Chicago IL

McCarter, Mickey, *Undergrad Coordr.* University of North Texas, School of Visual Arts, Denton TX (S)

McCarthy, Christine, *Asst to Dir.* Institute of Contemporary Art, Boston MA

McCarthy, David, *Chmn.* Rhodes College, Dept of Art, Memphis TN (S)

McCarthy, Frank, *Exec VPres.* North Central Life Insurance Company, Art Collection, Saint Paul MN

McCarthy, John, *Chmn Board.* Salmagundi Club, New York NY

McCarthy, John R, *Treas.* Artists' Fellowship, Inc, New York NY

McCarthy, Kevin, *Dir Human Resources.* Ferguson Library, Stamford CT

McCarthy, Rita E, *Acting Dir.* Loyola University of Chicago, Martin D'Arcy Gallery of Art, Chicago IL

McCartney, Henry, *Dir.* Landmark Society of Western New York, Inc, Rochester NY

McCarty, Gayle, *Dir.* Hinds Community College District, Marie Hull Gallery, Raymond MS

McCaslin, Jack, *Prof.* James Madison University, School of Art & Art History, Harrisonburg VA (S)

McCaulay, Janet, *Mgr Facility.* Arts United of Greater Fort Wayne, Fort Wayne IN

McCauley, Anne, *Chmn.* University of Massachusetts - Boston, Art Dept, Boston MA (S)

McCauley, Robert N, *Chmn Dept Fine Arts.* Rockford College, Dept of Fine Arts, Rockford IL (S)

McCean, David, *Board Pres.* Jamaica Arts Center, Jamaica NY

McClanahan, John D, *Chmn.* Baylor University, Dept of Art, Waco TX (S)

McCleary, M Cecile, *Mus Supv.* City of Lethbridge, Sir Alexander Galt Museum, Lethbridge AB

McCleery, Steve, *Dean.* New Mexico Junior College, Arts & Sciences, Hobbs NM (S)

McClellan, Andrew, *Chmn Art & Art History.* Tufts University, Dept of Art & Art History, Medford MA (S)

McClellan, Lynette, *Cur.* Gananoque Historical Museum, Gananoque ON

McClellan, Nancy, *Exec Dir.* Firehouse Art Center, Norman OK

McClemey-Brooker, Cheryl, *VPres External Affairs,* Philadelphia Museum of Art, Philadelphia PA

McClendon, Robert, *Cur Exhibits.* Museum of Mobile, Mobile AL

McClish, Jerry, *Pres.* International Society of Marine Painters, Oneco FL

McCloat, Elizabeth, *Dir.* Bryant Library, Roslyn NY

McCloskey, William, *Chmn.* Monroe County Community College, Fine Arts Council, Monroe MI

McClung, Elizabeth, *Exec Dir.* Belle Grove Plantation, Middletown VA

McCluskey, Holly, *Cur Colls & Educ,* Oglebay Institute, Mansion Museum, Wheeling WV

McCollister, Ellen, *Asst Dir Public Affairs.* Cornell University, Herbert F Johnson Museum of Art, Ithaca NY

McCollister, Sandra, *Asst Prof.* Southwest Texas State University, Dept of Art, San Marcos TX (S)

McComb, Ronald G, *Librn.* Cornish College of the Arts, Cornish Library, Seattle WA

McCombs, Bruce, *Prof.* Hope College, Art Dept, Holland MI (S)

McComell, Sharon, *Asst Prof.* College of the Holy Cross, Dept of Visual Arts, Worcester MA (S)

McCone, John, *Pres.* The Bartlett Museum, Amesbury MA

McCone, Michael, *Dir.* California Historical Society, Schubert Hall Library, San Marino CA

McConnell, Angela, *Dir Develop.* San Jose Museum of Art, San Jose CA

McConnell, Gordon, *Asst Dir & Sr Cur.* Yellowstone Art Center, Billings MT

McConnell, Jeanne, *Librn.* National Endowment for the Arts, Library, Washington DC

McConnell, Linda, *Gift Shop Coordr,* Vernon Art Gallery, Vernon BC

McConnell, Mary Apple, *Chmn Dept.* Texas Wesleyan University, Dept of Art, Fort Worth TX (S)

McConnell, Michael, *Prof.* University of New Hampshire, Dept of Arts & Art History, Durham NH (S)

McCool, Gary, *Coordr Public Servs*, Plymouth State College, Herbert H Lamson Library, Plymouth NH

McCormick, Charles James, *Chmn*, Georgetown College, Art Dept, Georgetown KY (S)

McCormick, Daniel Y, *Operations & Finance*, George Eastman House-International Museum of Photography & Film, Rochester NY

McCormick, David, *Instr*, Southeastern Community College, Dept of Art, Whiteville NC (S)

McCormick, Donald, *Recordings Cur*, The New York Public Library, Shelby Cullom Davis Museum, New York NY

McCormick, James, *Chmn*, Georgetown College Gallery, Georgetown KY

McCormick, John, *Assoc Prof*, Delta College, Art Dept, University Center MI (S)

McCormick, Karen, *Instr*, Mount Mary College, Art Dept, Milwaukee WI (S)

McCormick, Maureen, *Registrar*, Princeton University, The Art Museum, Princeton NJ

McCormick, Pauline, *Cataloger*, Worcester Art Museum, Library, Worcester MA

McCosker, Jane, *First VPres*, Monmouth Museum & Cultural Center, Lincroft NJ

McCoy, Beth, *Sales Mgr*, Vermont State Craft Center at Frog Hollow, Middlebury VT

McCoy, Carolyn, *Asst Dir Admin & Develop*, Cincinnati Institute of Fine Arts, Taft Museum, Cincinnati OH

McCoy, Karen, *Chmn Sculpture*, Kansas City Art Institute, Kansas City MO (S)

McCoy, L Frank, *Dean*, University of Montevallo, College of Fine Arts, Montevallo AL (S)

McCoy, Paul A, *Assoc Prof*, Baylor University, Dept of Art, Waco TX (S)

McCracken, Patrick, *Dir & Cur*, Amarillo Art Association, Amarillo Art Center, Amarillo TX

McCracken, Peter, *Dir Prog*, Centrum Foundation, Port Townsend WA

McCracken, Ursula E, *Dir*, Textile Museum, Washington DC

McCrea, Ann, *Dir Pub*, Worcester Art Museum, Worcester MA

McCrea, Judith, *Chmn*, University of Kansas, Dept of Art, Lawrence KS (S)

McCredie, James R, *Dir*, New York University, Institute of Fine Arts, New York NY (S)

McCreight, Tim, *Instr*, Maine College of Art, Portland ME (S)

McCroskey, Nancy, *Asst Prof*, Indiana-Purdue University, Dept of Fine Arts, Fort Wayne IN (S)

McCue, Donald, *Cur*, Lincoln Memorial Shrine, Redlands CA

McCue, Harry, *Chmn*, Ithaca College, Fine Art Dept, Ithaca NY (S)

McCue, Kaz, *Operations Mgr*, University of Bridgeport Gallery, Bridgeport CT

McCulla, George Ann, *Pres*, Mississippi Art Colony, Pascagoula MS

McCullagh, Janice, *Assoc Prof*, Baylor University, Dept of Art, Waco TX (S)

McCullagh, Suzanne, *Cur Prints & Drawings*, The Art Institute of Chicago, Chicago IL

McCulley, Clyde E, *Dir*, Munson-Williams-Proctor Institute, School of Art, Utica NY (S)

McCulloch, Gretchen, *Cur/Admnr*, Homer Watson House & Gallery, Kitchener ON

McCulloch, Judith, *Dir*, Cape Ann Historical Museum, Gloucester MA

McCulloch, Judith, *Dir*, Cape Ann Historical Museum, Library, Gloucester MA

McCullough-Hudson, Mary, *Exec Dir*, Cincinnati Institute of Fine Arts, Cincinnati OH

McCusker, Patrick, *Assoc Dir Public Affairs*, Ohio State University, Wexner Center for the Arts, Columbus OH

McCutcheon, Paul, *Reference Librn*, National Air and Space Museum, Library MRC 314, Washington DC

McDade, Elizabeth, *Dir*, Pyramid Arts Center, Rochester NY

McDade, George C, *Prof*, Monroe Community College, Art Dept, Rochester NY (S)

McDaniel, Jerry, *Chmn Advertising Design*, Fashion Institute of Technology, Art & Design Division, New York NY (S)

McDaniel, Nancy, *Assoc Dir*, Boise Art Museum, Boise ID

McDaniel, Richard, *Instr*, Woodstock School of Art, Inc, Woodstock NY (S)

McDaniel, Todd, *Preparator*, Cheekwood-Tennessee Botanical Gardens & Museum of Art, Nashville TN

McDavid, Stephanie, *Chmn Art Dept&Instr*, Saint Andrews Presbyterian College, Art Program, Laurinburg NC (S)

McDermid, James, *Instr*, Munson-Williams-Proctor Institute, School of Art, Utica NY (S)

McDermoth, Terrence M, *Exec VPres*, American Institute of Architects, Washington DC

McDermott, LeRoy, *Assoc Prof*, Central Missouri State University, Art Dept, Warrensburg MO (S)

McDevitt, Chuck, *Public Information Officer*, Pennsylvania Academy of the Fine Arts, Museum of American Art, Philadelphia PA

McDonald, Betty, *Pres*, Philadelphia Sketch Club, Inc, Philadelphia PA

McDonald, David, *Chmn Humanities*, Lincoln Memorial University, Division of Humanities, Harrogate TN (S)

McDonald, Douglass W, *Chief Exec Officer & Pres*, Genesee Country Museum, John L Wehle Gallery of Sporting Art, Mumford NY

McDonald, Evelyn, *Admin Asst*, City of Hampton, Hampton Arts Commission, Hampton VA

McDonald, J P, *Exec Dir*, Museum of East Texas, Lufkin TX

McDonald, Michele A, *Cur*, Vizcaya Museum & Gardens, Miami FL

McDonald, Robert, *Coordr Art*, Cape Cod Community College, Art Dept, West Barnstable MA (S)

McDonald, Susan, *Dir*, North Hennepin Community College, Art Gallery, Brooklyn Park MN

McDonell, Sally, *Treas*, Huntsville Art League, Huntsville AL

McDonnell, Anne, *Head Librn*, Kentucky Historical Society, Library, Frankfort KY

McDonnell, Patricia, *Cur*, University of Minnesota, Weisman Art Museum, Minneapolis MN

McDougal, O J, *Pres Board of Trustees*, Hastings Museum, Hastings NE

McDowell, Jerry, *Prof*, Wright State University, Dept of Art & Art History, Dayton OH (S)

McDowell, Sandy, *Instr*, Ouachita Baptist University, Dept of Art, Arkadelphia AR (S)

McDowell, Tim, *Chmn*, Connecticut College, Dept of Art, New London CT (S)

McEachern, Susan, *Dir Grad Studies&Coordr MFA Prog*, Nova Scotia College of Art & Design, Halifax NS (S)

McElroy, Keith, *Assoc Prof Art History*, University of Arizona, Dept of Art, Tucson AZ (S)

McElroy, Richard, *Librn*, Wellesley College, Art Library, Wellesley MA

McElroy, Sherri, *Instr*, Illinois Wesleyan University, School of Art, Bloomington IL (S)

McElroy-Edwards, J, *Chmn*, University of North Dakota, Visual Arts Dept, Grand Forks ND (S)

McEnroe, John, *Instr*, Hamilton College, Art Dept, Clinton NY (S)

McEntire, Ann, *In Charge of Art Coll*, First Tennessee Bank, Maryville TN

McEvilley, Thomas, *Vis Lectr*, Rice University, Dept of Art & Art History, Houston TX (S)

McEvoy, Maureen, *Prog Mgr*, Canadian Museum of Contemporary Photography, Ottawa ON

McEwen, Virginia, *Librn*, Shaker Museum & Library, Emma B King Library, Old Chatham NY

McEwin, Florence, *Head Dept*, Western Wyoming Community College, Art Dept, Rock Springs WY (S)

McFadden, David R, *Exec Dir*, Millicent Rogers Museum of Northern New Mexico, Taos NM

McFadden, David R, *Exec Dir*, Millicent Rogers Museum of Northern New Mexico, Library, Taos NM

McFadden, Robert, *Prog Coordr*, Pennsylvania Historical & Museum Commission, Railroad Museum of Pennsylvania, Harrisburg PA

McFall, Jena, *Admin Asst*, Amarillo Art Association, Amarillo Art Center, Amarillo TX

McFarland, Jacqui, *Chmn*, Mount Royal College, Dept of Interior Design, Calgary AB (S)

McFarland, Jean, *Prof*, Winthrop University, Dept of Art & Design, Rock Hill SC (S)

McFarland, Will Ellyn, *Pres*, National Watercolor Society, Downey CA

McFarlane, Leesa, *Sales Dir*, Battleship North Carolina, Wilmington NC

McFee, Doris, *Asst Librn*, Chappell Memorial Library and Art Gallery, Chappell NE

McGaffey, Beth, *Cur Educ Public Prog*, Marquette University, Haggerty Museum of Art, Milwaukee WI

McGary, Nancy, *Dir, Coll Management*, Whitney Museum of American Art, New York NY

McGee, Jack, *Pres*, Portsmouth Athenaeum, Portsmouth NH

McGee, J David, *Chmn*, Grand Valley State University, Art & Design Dept, Allendale MI (S)

McGee, Jerry, *Exec Dir*, Lexington Art League, Inc, Lexington KY

McGee, Joe, *Cur Exhib*, Kentucky Derby Museum, Louisville KY

McGee, Mike, *Dir*, California State University, Fullerton, Art Gallery, Visual Arts Center, Fullerton CA

McGee, Monicah, *Dir Develop & Marketing*, Light Factory, Charlotte NC

McGeehan, John, *General Mgr*, Harvestworks, Inc, New York NY

McGehee, Terry, *Chmn Art Dept*, Agnes Scott College, Dalton Gallery, Decatur GA

McGehee, Thomas C, *Museum Dir*, Bellingrath Gardens & Home, Theodore AL

McGhee, Leonard, *Instr*, Milwaukee Area Technical College, Graphic Arts Division, Milwaukee WI (S)

McGill, Dave, *Asst Prof*, Azusa Pacific University, College of Liberal Arts, Art Dept, Azusa CA (S)

McGill, Forrest, *Dir*, Mary Washington College, Ridderhof Martin Gallery, Fredericksburg VA

McGill, Heather, *Head Sculpture Dept*, Cranbrook Academy of Art, Bloomfield Hills MI (S)

McGillivray, Bruce, *Asst Dir Natural History & Coll Admin*, Department of Community Development, Provincial Museum of Alberta, Edmonton AB

McGinness, Karin, *Instr*, Century College, Humanities Dept, White Bear Lake MN (S)

McGinnis, George, *Instr*, California State University, San Bernardino, Visual Arts, San Bernardino CA (S)

McGinnis, Helen F, *Slide Cur*, Moore College of Art & Design, Library, Philadelphia PA

McGinnis, Mark, *Prof*, Northern State University, Art Dept, Aberdeen SD (S)

McGire, Ross, *Dir*, Sunrise Museum, Inc, Sunrise Art Museum & Sunrise Science Museum, Charleston WV

McGivern, Andrew J, *Cur of Exhib*, Leigh Yawkey Woodson Art Museum, Inc, Wausau WI

Mcgloughlin, Kate, *Instr*, Woodstock School of Art, Inc, Woodstock NY (S)

McGough, Stephen C, *Dir*, Crocker Art Museum, Sacramento CA

McGovern, Robert, *Co-Chmn Foundation Prog*, University of the Arts, Philadelphia College of Art & Design, Philadelphia PA (S)

McGrady, Patrick J, *Cur Ed*, Pennsylvania State University, Palmer Museum of Art, University Park PA

McGranahan, Doris, *Cur Educ*, Oklahoma City Art Museum, Oklahoma City OK

McGranahan, Doris, *Cur Educ*, Oklahoma City Art Museum, Library, Oklahoma City OK

McGrann, Michael, *Public Relations & Marketing Coordr*, Bellevue Art Museum, Bellevue WA

McGrath, Bryan, *Instr*, Munson-Williams-Proctor Institute, School of Art, Utica NY (S)

McGreevy, Linda, *Assoc Prof*, Old Dominion University, Art Dept, Norfolk VA (S)

McGrew, Bruce, *Prof Painting & Drawing*, University of Arizona, Dept of Art, Tucson AZ (S)

McGrew, Kim, *Asst Mgr*, The Ohio Historical Society, Inc, Campus Martius Museum & Ohio River Museum, Marietta OH

McGuire, Frank, *Adjunct Instr*, Maryville University of Saint Louis, Art Division, Saint Louis MO (S)

McGuire, Julie, *Temporary Instr*, Georgia Southern University, Dept of Art, Statesboro GA (S)

McGuire, Kay, *Museum Shop Mgr*, University of Minnesota, Weisman Art Museum, Minneapolis MN

McGuire, Michael C, *Dean Educ*, Cincinnati Academy of Design, Cincinnati OH (S)

McGuire, Susan, *Exec Dir*, Indian Arts & Crafts Association, Albuquerque NM

McHale, Ellen, *Folklorist*, Schoharie County Arts Council, Cobleskill NY

McHam, Sarah, *Prof*, Rutgers, the State University of New Jersey, Graduate Program in Art History, New Brunswick NJ (S)

McIlrath, Timothy J, *Assoc Chair*, Iowa State University, Dept of Art & Design, Ames IA (S)

McInerney, Gay, *Dir*, Bay County Historical Society, Historical Museum of Bay County, Bay City MI

McIntee, Terrence, *Exhib Design & Preparator*, Ball State University, Museum of Art, Muncie IN

McIntire, Nancy, *Dir*, Dunedin Fine Arts & Cultural Center, Dunedin FL (S)

McIntosh, Carl, *VPres*, North Carolina Museums Council, Raleigh NC

McIntosh, Henry P, *Treas*, The Society of the Four Arts, Palm Beach FL

McIntosh, Jenny C, *Chmn*, Elizabeth City State University, Dept of Art, Elizabeth City NC (S)

McIntyre, Donald, *Assoc Prof*, University of Bridgeport, School of Arts, Humanities & Social Sciences, Bridgeport CT (S)

McIntyre, Phyllis, *Instr*, Suomi International College of Art & Design, Fine Arts Dept, Hancock MI (S)

McKay, Gayle H, *Bus Mgr*, Mason County Museum, Maysville KY

McKay, Robert, *Assoc Prof*, Norwich University, Dept of Philosophy, Religion & Fine Arts, Northfield VT (S)

McKay, Terrence, *Adjunct Assoc*, College of Santa Fe, Art Dept, Santa Fe NM (S)

McKay, Yolanda, *Asst Prof*, Indiana University, Bloomington, Henry Radford Hope School of Fine Arts, Bloomington IN (S)

McKeand, Barbara, *Cur*, Barr Colony Heritage Cultural Centre, Lloydminster SK

McKeand, Barbara, *Cur*, Imhoff Art Gallery, Alberta SK

McKee, David, *Chmn*, New York Studio School of Drawing, Painting & Sculpture, Gallery, New York NY

McKee, Donna, *Educ Dir*, The Phillips Collection, Washington DC

McKee, Fred, *Instr*, Miles Community College, Dept of Fine Arts & Humanities, Miles City MT (S)

McKee, John, *Lectr*, Bowdoin College, Art Dept, Brunswick ME (S)

McKee, Linda, *Librn*, State Art Museum of Florida, John & Mable Ringling Museum of Art, Sarasota FL

McKee, Linda R, *Librn*, State Art Museum of Florida, Ringling Museum Library, Sarasota FL

McKemie, William, *Third VPres*, Halifax Historical Society, Inc, Halifax Historical Museum, Daytona Beach FL

McKenna, George L, *Cur Prints, Drawings & Photography*, Nelson-Atkins Museum of Art, Kansas City MO

McKenna, Jan B, *Slide Librn*, Nelson-Atkins Museum of Art, Spencer Art Reference Library, Kansas City MO

McKenna, Mary, *Admin Asst to Dir*, Dartmouth College, Hood Museum of Art, Hanover NH

McKenna, Paul, *Chmn*, University at Buffalo, State University of New York, Fine Arts Dept, Buffalo NY (S)

McKenzie, Catherine, *Cur Old Governor's Mansion*, Louisiana Arts & Science Center, Baton Rouge LA

McKenzie, Karen, *Chief Librn*, Art Gallery of Ontario, Edward P Taylor Research Library & Archives, Toronto ON

McKenzie, Stephen, *Arts Workshop Supv*, Newark Museum Association, The Newark Museum, Newark NJ

McKeough, Rita, *Asst Prof*, Mount Allison University, Fine Arts Dept, Sackville NB (S)

McKernan, Robert, *Cur Natural History*, San Bernardino County Museum, Fine Arts Institute, Redlands CA

McKiernan, Susan, *Asst Dir*, University of Akron, University Galleries, Akron OH

McKillop, Debra, *Gallery Dir*, Ventura College, Art Galleries, Ventura CA

McKim, Hazel, *Librn*, Redding Museum of Art & History, Shasta Historical Society Research Library, Redding CA

McKim-Smith, Gridley, *Prof*, Bryn Mawr College, Dept of the History of Art, Bryn Mawr PA (S)

McKinley, Paula, *Admin*, Greenwood Museum, Greenwood SC

McKinley-Martin, George, *Chief Art Division*, Public Library of the District of Columbia, Art Division, Washington DC

McKinney, Art, *Assoc Dir*, Art Institute of Fort Lauderdale, Technical Library, Fort Lauderdale FL

McKinney, Hal, *Assoc Dir Admin*, North Carolina Museum of Art, Raleigh NC

McKinney, Nancy, *Deputy Dir & Assoc Ed Publs*, California African-American Museum, Los Angeles CA

McKinney, Thomas R, *Dir*, Ataloa Lodge Museum, Muskogee OK

McKinney, Venora, *Supvr Central Servs*, Milwaukee Public Library, Art, Music & Recreation Dept, Milwaukee WI

McKinsey, Kristan, *Cur*, Lakeview Museum of Arts & Sciences, Peoria IL

McKinstry, Richard, *Librn in Charge Joseph Downs Coll of Manuscripts & Printed Ephemera*, Winterthur Museum, Library, Winterthur DE

McKinstry, Skip, *Adjunct Prof*, Oklahoma Christian University of Science & Arts, Dept of Art & Design, Oklahoma City OK (S)

McKinzie, Mack, *Treas*, Hoosier Salon Patrons Association, Hoosier Salon Art Gallery, Indianapolis IN

McKinzie, Mack P, *Dir Institutional Advancement*, Indianapolis Museum of Art, Indianapolis IN

McLachlan, Elizabeth, *Assoc Prof*, Rutgers, the State University of New Jersey, Graduate Program in Art History, New Brunswick NJ (S)

McLain, Nancy, *Financial Mgr*, Dartmouth College, Hood Museum of Art, Hanover NH

McLallen, Helen, *Cur*, Columbia County Historical Society, Columbia County Museum, Kinderhook NY

McLallen, Helen M, *Cur*, Columbia County Historical Society, Library, Kinderhook NY

McLane, Michael, *Dir*, State University of New York at Oswego, Penfield Library, Oswego NY

McLaren, Margot, *Cataloger*, Maine Historical Society, Library, Portland ME

McLarty, Lianne, *Asst Prof*, University of Victoria, Dept of History in Art, Victoria BC (S)

McLary, Kathleen, *Cur Costumes & Flat Textiles*, Indiana State Museum, Indianapolis IN

McLaughlin, Kevin, *Instr*, South Central Technical College, Commercial & Technical Art Dept, North Mankato MN (S)

McLaughlin, Cheryl, *Dir*, Crook County Museum & Art Gallery, Sundance WY

McLaughlin, Claudia, *Education Dir*, Saratoga County Historical Society, Brookside Museum, Ballston Spa NY

McLaughlin, Robert, *Dir*, Springfield Art & Historical Society, Springfield VT

McLean, Genetta, *Dir*, Bates College, Museum of Art, Lewiston ME

McLean, Linda E, *Historic Site Mgr III*, New York State Office of Parks Recreation & Historic Preservation, John Jay Homestead State Historic Site, Katonah NY

McLean, Peter, *Prof*, University of Hartford, Hartford Art School, West Hartford CT (S)

McLeish, A Bruce, *Dir Coll*, New York State Historical Association, Fenimore House Museum, Cooperstown NY

McLemore, Mary, *Dean*, Motlow State Community College, Art Dept, Tullahoma TN (S)

McLennan, Bill, *Designer Graphics*, University of British Columbia, Museum of Anthropology, Vancouver BC

McLeod, Kaye, *Second VPres*, Brown County Art Gallery Association Inc, Brown County Art Gallery & Museum, Nashville IN

McLoone, Patricia, *Instr*, Cottey College, Art Dept, Nevada MO (S)

McLoughlin, Rosemary, *Museum Educator*, New Mexico State University, University Art Gallery, Las Cruces NM

McMahan, Evadine, *Dir Admin*, Tennessee State Museum, Nashville TN

McMahan, Robert, *Prof*, Antelope Valley College, Art Dept, Division of Fine Arts, Lancaster CA (S)

McMahon, Ellen, *Asst Prof Graphic Design-Illustration*, University of Arizona, Dept of Art, Tucson AZ (S)

McMahon, Maggie, *Prof*, University of Tennessee at Chattanooga, Dept of Art, Chattanooga TN (S)

McMahon, Sharon, *Chmn*, Saint Mary's University, Dept of Fine Arts, San Antonio TX (S)

McManus, James, *Instr*, California State University, Chico, Art Dept, Chico CA (S)

McManus-Zurko, Kathleen, *Cur*, The College of Wooster, Art Museum, Wooster OH

McMillan, Alan C, *Dir Student Services*, Emily Carr Institute of Art & Design, Vancouver BC (S)

McMillan, Barbara, *Librn*, Mount Vernon Ladies' Association of the Union, Mount Vernon VA

McMillan, Barbara, *Librn*, Mount Vernon Ladies' Association of the Union, Library, Mount Vernon VA

McMillan, David, *Chmn Photography*, University of Manitoba, School of Art, Winnipeg MB (S)

McMillan, Dorothea, *Pres Board Dir*, Associates for Community Development, Boarman Arts Center, Martinsburg WV

McMillan, Melanie, *Dir Pub Relations*, Ferguson Library, Stamford CT

McMillan, Patsy, *Dir*, Klamath County Museum, Klamath Falls OR

McMillan, Patsy, *Dir*, Klamath County Museum, Research Library, Klamath Falls OR

McMillan, Patsy, *Dir*, Klamath County Museum, Baldwin Hotel Museum Annex, Klamath Falls OR

McMillan, R Bruce J, *Dir*, Illinois State Museum, Illinois Art Gallery & Lockport Gallery, Springfield IL

McMillan, Richard, *Instr*, La Sierra University, Art Dept, Riverside CA (S)

McMillian, Bruce, *Dir*, Illinois State Museum, Museum Shop, Chicago IL

McMorris, Penny, *Cur*, Owens-Corning Corporation, Art Collection, Toledo OH

McNabb, Michele, *Librn & Archivist*, McLean County Historical Society, Bloomington IL

McNair, Lee, *Chmn*, Des Moines Area Community College, Art Dept, Boone IA (S)

McNamara, Carole A, *Registrar*, University of Michigan, Museum of Art, Ann Arbor MI

McNamara, Marnie, *Dir*, Visual Arts Alliance of Nashville, Nashville TN

McNamara, Mary, *Pres Exec Dir of Interchurch Center*, The Interchurch Center, The Interchurch Center, New York NY

McNamee, Donald W, *Chief Librn*, Natural History Museum of Los Angeles County, Research Library, Los Angeles CA

McNaughton, Mary, *Cur Exhib*, Galleries of the Claremont Colleges, Claremont CA

McNaughton, Patrick, *Assoc Prof*, Indiana University, Bloomington, Henry Radford Hope School of Fine Arts, Bloomington IN (S)

McNeal, Brenda, *Registrar*, Florida State University Foundation - Central Florida Community College Foundation, The Appleton Museum of Art, Ocala FL

McNeal, Meridith, *Dir Educ*, Fund for the Borough of Brooklyn, Rotunda Gallery, Brooklyn NY

McNeal Few, Sarah, *Chmn Board of Governors*, J B Speed Art Museum, Louisville KY

McNeese, Kay, *Educ Cur*, Heritage Museum Association, Inc, Valparaiso FL

McNeil, W K, *Folklorist & Archivist*, Ozark Folk Center, Ozark Cultural Resource Center, Mountain View AR

McNeill, Janice, *Librn*, Chicago Historical Society, Chicago IL

McNeill, John, *Dir*, Royal Ontario Museum, Toronto ON

McNeill, Lloyd, *Assoc Prof*, Rutgers, the State University of New Jersey, Mason Gross School of the Arts, New Brunswick NJ (S)

McNeill, Winifred, *Asst Prof*, Jersey City State College, Art Dept, Jersey City NJ (S)

McNeman, Don, *Pres*, Guilford College, Art Gallery, Greensboro NC

McNichol, Theresa, *Dir*, Trenton City Museum, Trenton NJ

McNicholas, Mary Ann, *Adminr*, San Francisco Craft & Folk Art Museum, San Francisco CA

McNulty, John, *Shop Mgr*, Tucson Museum of Art & Historic Block, Tucson AZ

McNutt, James, *Adjunct Prof*, Washington & Jefferson College, Art Dept, Washington PA (S)

McOmber, Christina, *Dir Gallery*, Cornell College, Armstrong Gallery, Mount Vernon IA

McPhee, Sarah, *Asst Prof*, Emory University, Art History Dept, Atlanta GA (S)

McPherron, Sharon, *Exec Dir*, Craft Alliance Gallery & Education Center for the Visual Arts, Saint Louis MO

McPherson, Heather, *Assoc Prof*, University of Alabama at Birmingham, Dept of Art, Birmingham AL (S)

McQuade, Jayne, *Head*, Arlington County Department of Public Libraries, Fine Arts Section, Arlington VA

McQuire, Edward, *Dean*, College of Charleston, School of the Arts, Charleston SC (S)

McQuiston, William, *Dir*, Rensselaer Newman Foundation Chapel & Cultural Center, The Gallery, Troy NY

McRaven, Donald B, *Prof*, Moorhead State University, Dept of Art, Moorhead MN (S)

McRoberts, Jerry, *Prof*, Eastern Illinois University, Art Dept, Charleston IL (S)

McRorie, Sally, *Chmn*, Florida State University, Art Education Dept, Tallahassee FL (S)

McShea, Kate, *Pub Relations*, Harvard University, Harvard University Art Museums, Cambridge MA

McTavish, David, *Dir*, Queen's University, Agnes Etherington Art Centre, Kingston ON

McThail, Donald, *Treas*, The Print Center, Philadelphia PA

McTique, Mary, *Exec Dir*, Boston Center for Adult Education, Boston MA (S)

McVaugh, Robert, *Assoc Prof*, Colgate University, Dept of Art & Art History, Hamilton NY (S)

McVey, John, *Graphic Design*, Monserrat College of Art, Beverly MA (S)

McVicker, Charles, *Asst Prof*, College of New Jersey, Art Dept, Trenton NJ (S)

McVity, Patsy B, *Cur*, Concord Art Association, Concord MA

McWayne, Barry J, *Coordr Fine Arts*, University of Alaska, Museum, Fairbanks AK

McWeeney, Jim, *Instr*, Joe Kubert School of Cartoon & Graphic Art, Inc, Dover NJ (S)

McWhorter, Jack, *Coordr*, Kent State University, Stark Campus, School of Art, Canton OH (S)

McWhorter, Mark, *Instructor*, Indian Hills Community College, Dept of Art, Centerville IA (S)

McWhorter, Mark, *Instr*, Indian Hills Community College, Ottumwa Campus, Dept of Art, Ottumwa IA (S)

McWilliam, Deb, *Main Library Dir*, Columbus Metropolitan Library, Humanities, Fine Art & Recreation Division, Columbus OH

McWilliams, John, *Dir School*, Georgia State University, School of Art & Design, Atlanta GA (S)

McWilliams, Maria E, *Registrar*, The Rockwell Museum, Corning NY

Mead, Gerald, *Exhib Cur*, Burchfield-Penney Art Center, Buffalo NY

Mead, Margaret, *Spec Coordr*, Saint Bonaventure University, Regina A Quick Fine Art Center, Saint Bonaventure NY

Mead-Donaldson, Susan, *Technical Serv Adminr*, Miami-Dade Public Library, Miami FL

Meade, JoAnn, *Cur*, Alcan Aluminium Ltd, Montreal PQ

Meader, Abbott, *Prof*, Colby College, Art Dept, Waterville ME (S)

Meador-Woodruff, Robin, *Assoc Cur Photo & Slides*, University of Michigan, Kelsey Museum of Archaeology, Ann Arbor MI

Meadows, Christine, *Cur*, Mount Vernon Ladies' Association of the Union, Mount Vernon VA

Meadows-Rogers, Robert, *Asst Prof*, Concordia College, Art Dept, Moorhead MN (S)

Meager, Timothy J, *Dir Admin*, Ohio State University, Wexner Center for the Arts, Columbus OH

Means, Juli, *Mem Coordr*, Columbus Museum, Columbus GA

Mear, Margaret, *Assoc Prof*, Saint Mary's University of Minnesota, Art & Design Dept, Winona MN (S)

Meares, Maria, *VPres*, Artists' Cooperative Gallery, Omaha NE

Mears, Graham, *Lectr*, Centenary College of Louisiana, Dept of Art, Shreveport LA (S)

Mears, Peter, *Cur*, Austin Museum of Art at Laguna Gloria, Austin TX

Meckel, David, *Architecture*, California College of Arts & Crafts, Oakland CA (S)

Mecklenburg, Frank, *Chief Archivist*, Leo Baeck Institute, New York NY

Mecklenburg, Frank, *Archivist*, Leo Baeck Institute, Library, New York NY

Mecky, Debra Walker, *Exec Dir*, Historical Society of the Town of Greenwich, Inc, Bush-Holley House Museum, Cos Cob CT

Medd, Ken, *Dir Develop*, Fuller Museum of Art, Brockton MA

Medina, Dennis, *Museum Cur*, Dwight D Eisenhower Presidential Library, Abilene KS

Medina, Jacqueline, *Slide Librn*, Hamilton College, Art Dept, Clinton NY (S)

Medley, Chris, *Asst Prof*, Maryland College of Art & Design, Silver Spring MD (S)

Medlock, Rudy, *Head Art Dept*, Asbury College, Student Center Gallery, Wilmore KY

Medlock, Rudy, *Art Dept Head*, Asbury College, Art Dept, Wilmore KY (S)

Medway, F Michael, *Pres*, The Print Center, Philadelphia PA

Meehan, Brian, *Dir*, Tom Thomson Memorial Art Gallery, Owen Sound ON

Meehan, Brian, *Dir*, Tom Thomson Memorial Art Gallery, Library, Owen Sound ON

Meehan, Tracy, *Registrar*, Adirondack Historical Association, Adirondack Museum, Blue Mountain Lake NY

Meek, A J, *Prof*, Louisiana State University, School of Art, Baton Rouge LA (S)

Meek, Ken, *Cur Coll*, Frank Phillips Foundation Inc, Woolaroc Museum, Bartlesville OK

Meek, William, *Asst Prof*, Southwest Texas State University, Dept of Art, San Marcos TX (S)

Meeker, Benjamin, *Gallery Coordr*, Tacoma Arts Commission, Commencement Art Gallery, Tacoma WA

Meeks, Donna M, *Head Dept*, Lamar University, Art Dept, Beaumont TX (S)

Meeks, James, *Preparator*, University of Oklahoma, Fred Jones Jr Museum of Art, Norman OK

Meeks, Maryann, *Exec Dir*, Words & Pictures Museum, Northampton MA

Meier, Jan, *Mgr*, Maritz, Inc, Library, Fenton MO

Meier, Lucille, *Librn*, Muskegon Museum of Art, Library, Muskegon MI

Meier, Tom, *Dir*, Boulder Historical Society Inc, Museum of History, Boulder CO

Meiers, Susanna, *Dir*, El Camino College Art Gallery, Torrance CA

Meigs, S, *Asst Prof*, University of Victoria, Dept of Visual Arts, Victoria BC (S)

Meillon, Eileen, *Librn*, David M Stewart Museum, Library, Montreal PQ

Meir, Katia, *Asst Dir*, Saidye Bronfman Centre for the Arts Centre, Montreal PQ

Meisamy, Hoda, *Chmn Fashion Design*, Woodbury University, Dept of Graphic Design, Burbank CA (S)

Meister, Mark J, *Exec Dir*, Archaeological Institute of America, Boston MA

Meiver, Katherine, *Asst Prof*, University of Alabama at Birmingham, Dept of Art, Birmingham AL (S)

Meixner, Laura L, *Assoc Prof*, Cornell University, Dept of the History of Art, Ithaca NY (S)

Mejer, Robert Lee, *Gallery Dir*, Quincy University, The Gray Gallery, Quincy IL

Mejer, Robert Lee, *Prof Art*, Quincy University, Dept of Art, Quincy IL (S)

Mekal, Christopher, *Bus*, Isabella Stewart Gardner Museum, Boston MA

Melcher-Brethorst, Barbara, *Cur Educ*, Lakeview Museum of Arts & Sciences, Peoria IL

Melenbrink, Michael, *Bus Mgr*, Flint Institute of Arts, Flint MI

Meley, Tricia, *Cur Education*, Heritage Center of Lancaster County Museum, Lancaster PA

Melick, Randolph, *Instr*, New York Academy of Art, Graduate School of Figurative Art, New York NY (S)

Melis, Alan, *Assoc Prof*, University of Toledo, Dept of Art, Toledo OH (S)

Mella, Joseph, *Pres*, Visual Arts Alliance of Nashville, Nashville TN

Mella, Joseph S, *Dir*, Vanderbilt University, Fine Arts Gallery, Nashville TN

Mellon, Marc Richard, *Pres*, Artists' Fellowship, Inc, New York NY

Mello-nee, Mary, *Coordr Educ*, Charles H MacNider Museum, Mason City IA

Melson, Claudia F, *Cur Registration*, Historical & Cultural Affairs, Delaware State Museums, Dover DE

Melton, Laura, *Chmn Music*, Idyllwild Arts Academy, Idyllwild CA (S)

Melton, Terri, *Bus Mgr*, Owensboro Museum of Fine Art, Owensboro KY

Melton, Terry R, *Exec Dir*, McAllen International Museum, McAllen TX

Meltzer, Robert M, *Pres*, The American Federation of Arts, New York NY

Melvin, Douglas, *Chmn*, North Central Michigan College, Art Dept, Petoskey MI (S)

Memeger, Harriet B, *Head Librn*, Delaware Art Museum, Helen Farr Sloan Library, Wilmington DE

Menard, Lloyd, *Prof*, University of South Dakota, Department of Art, College of Fine Arts, Vermillion SD (S)

Menchaca, Belinda, *Dance Prog Dir*, Guadalupe Cultural Arts Center, San Antonio TX

Mendell, Cyndi, *Instr*, ACA College of Design, Cincinnati OH (S)

Mendelsohn, Loren, *Chief Reference Division*, City College of the City University of New York, Morris Raphael Cohen Library, New York NY

Mendelson, Haim, *Pres*, Federation of Modern Painters & Sculptors, New York NY

Mendelson, Shari, *Instr*, Chautauqua Institution, School of Art, Chautauqua NY (S)

Mendenhall, John, *Prof*, California Polytechnic State University at San Luis Obispo, Dept of Art & Design, San Luis Obispo CA (S)

Meneray, Bill, *Chmn Memorial Hall Committee*, Louisiana Historical Association, Confederate Museum, New Orleans LA

Mengel, Claudia, *VPres & Cur*, Chase Manhattan, New York NY

Menger, Linda, *Assoc Prof*, Delta College, Art Dept, University Center MI (S)

Menger, Mary Ann, *Prog Coordr*, Fitchburg Art Museum, Fitchburg MA

Menges, Gary, *Librn*, University of Washington, Libraries, Seattle WA

Menken, Ingrid, *Treas*, Haystack Mountain School of Crafts, Gallery, Deer Isle ME

Menn, Richard J, *Cur*, Carmel Mission & Gift Shop, Carmel CA

Menn, Richard J, *Cur*, Carmel Mission & Gift Shop, Archive of Old Spanish Missions, Diocese of Monterey, Carmel CA

Menna, Sari, *Recording Coordr*, Women in the Arts Foundation, Inc, New York NY

Menning, Daleene, *Prof.* Grand Valley State University, Art & Design Dept, Allendale MI (S)

Menocal, Narciso G, *Prof.* University of Wisconsin, Madison, Dept of Art History, Madison WI (S)

Mensing, Iris, *Auditorium Mgr & Book Store Mgr.* University of Notre Dame, Snite Museum of Art, Notre Dame IN

Mensing, Margo, *Interim Head Fiber Dept.* Cranbrook Academy of Art, Bloomfield Hills MI (S)

Menzies, Janet, *Registrar.* Simon Fraser University, Simon Fraser Gallery, Burnaby BC

Mercer, Bill, *Asst Cur Africa & Americas.* Cincinnati Museum Association, Cincinnati Art Museum, Cincinnati OH

Mercer, David, *Instr.* The Art Institutes International, The Art Institute of Seattle, Seattle WA (S)

Mercer, Dorothy, *Assoc Prof.* Radford University, Art Dept, Radford VA (S)

Mercer, John, *Coordr, Photograph Dept.* Phoenix College, Dept of Art & Photography, Phoenix AZ (S)

Mercer, Valerie J, *Cur.* The Studio Museum in Harlem, New York NY

Merchant, John, *Instr.* Lakeland Community College, Visual Arts Dept, Mentor OH (S)

Merdzinski, Marilyn, *Colls Mgr.* Public Museum of Grand Rapids, Grand Rapids MI

Meredith, Janet, *Head Marketing Develop.* Vancouver Art Gallery, Vancouver BC

Merendino, Janice, *Lectr,* Rosemont College, Division of the Arts, Rosemont PA (S)

Meretta, Anne, *Museum Shop Mgr.* Rhode Island School of Design, Museum of Art, Providence RI

Meride, Sally, *Instr.* College of Notre Dame of Maryland, Art Dept, Baltimore MD (S)

Merkens, Dionne, *Earned Income Dir.* Plains Art Museum, Fargo ND

Merkur, Barbara, *Instr & Supervisor,* Toronto Art Therapy Institute, Toronto ON (S)

Merling, Mitchell, *Cur Old Masters,* Montreal Museum of Fine Arts, Montreal PQ

Merrick, Robert S, *Trustee,* Merrick Art Gallery, New Brighton PA

Merrill, Don, *Chmn.* Salt Lake Community College, Graphic Design Dept, Salt Lake City UT (S)

Merrill, Joyce, *VPres.* Indian Pueblo Cultural Center, Albuquerque NM

Merrill, Kathleen, *Dir, Art Prog.* Lannan Foundation, Los Angeles CA

Merrill, Ross, *Chief Conservation.* National Gallery of Art, Washington DC

Merrill, Scotti, *Corresp Secy,* Key West Art & Historical Society, East Martello Museum & Gallery, Key West FL

Merriman, Larry, *Dir,* Cecelia Coker Bell Gallery, Hartsville SC

Merritt, Scott, *Head Coll,* National Museum of the American Indian, George Gustav Heye Center, New York NY

Mersereau, Rebecca, *Assoc Prof.* Rice University, Dept of Art & Art History, Houston TX (S)

Merson, Jeanne, *Adjunct Instr,* Maryville University of Saint Louis, Art Division, Saint Louis MO (S)

Mertens, Joan R, *Cur Greek & Roman Art,* The Metropolitan Museum of Art, New York NY

Merwin, Laura, *Item Dir,* McLean County Art Association, Arts Center, Bloomington IL

Meschutt, David, *Cur Art,* United States Military Academy, West Point Museum, West Point NY

Mesley, Roger, *Asst Dir,* Carleton University, Dept of Art History, Ottawa ON (S)

Messec, Don, *Adjunct Assoc,* College of Santa Fe, Art Dept, Santa Fe NM (S)

Messer, David, *Dir,* Bergen Museum of Art & Science, Paramus NJ

Messersmith, Mark, *Assoc Prof,* Florida State University, Art Dept, Tallahassee FL (S)

Messersmith, Mary, *Museum Store Mgr.* Terra Museum of American Art, Chicago IL

Messier, Arthur, *Head Adult Information Serv.* Springfield Library & Museums Association, Art & Music Dept, Springfield MA

Messina, Mitchell, *Asst Prof.* Nazareth College of Rochester, Art Dept, Rochester NY (S)

Messinger, Faye, *Librn.* Monterey History & Art Association, Library, Monterey CA

Metcalf, Elizabeth, *Develop Assoc.* Artists Space, New York NY

Metcalf, Lisa, *Developmental Assoc,* Artists Space, Artists Space Gallery, New York NY

Metcalf, Michael, *Prof.* Western New Mexico University, Dept of Expressive Arts, Silver City NM (S)

Metcalf, Preston, *Dir.* San Jose Institute of Contemporary Art, San Jose CA

Metcalf, William E, *Chief Cur.* American Numismatic Society, New York NY

Metcalfe, Elizabeth, *Adjunct Instr.* Maryville University of Saint Louis, Art Division, Saint Louis MO (S)

Metcoff, Donald, *Chicago Representative.* American Society of Artists, Inc, Chicago IL

Metcoff, Donald, *Librn.* American Society of Artists, Inc, Library Organization, Chicago IL

Metheny, Jacqueline, *Visiting Asst Prof.* Trinity College, Dept of Fine Arts, Hartford CT (S)

Metraux, M, *Cur.* York University, Fine Arts Phase II Slide Library, North York ON

Mettala, Teri, *Mgr.* Ojai Valley Art Center, Ojai CA

Mettler, Bonnie, *Instr.* Main Line Art Center, Haverford PA

Metz, Janice, *Instr.* College of the Canyons, Art Dept, Valencia CA (S)

Metz, Martha A, *Community Outreach.* Dickinson College, Trout Gallery, Carlisle PA

Metz, Rinda, *Assoc Prof.* Ohio Wesleyan University, Fine Arts Dept, Delaware OH (S)

Metzger, Lynn, *VPres.* Summit County Historical Society, Akron OH

Metzger, Michael, *Coordr Studio Prog.* Kean College of New Jersey, Fine Arts Dept, Union NJ (S)

Metzger, Robert, *Dir & Cur Fine Arts.* Reading Public Museum, Reading PA

Metzger, Robert, *Dir.* Reading Public Museum, Library, Reading PA

Metzker, Dale, *Assoc Prof.* Pennsylvania College of Technology, Dept of Graphic Communications, Williamsport PA (S)

Metzler, B G, *VPres Marketing.* Discovery Place Inc, Charlotte NC

Metzon, Greg, *Chmn.* Ellsworth Community College, Dept of Fine Arts, Iowa Falls IA (S)

Meunier, Brian A, *Assoc Prof.* Swarthmore College, Dept of Art, Swarthmore PA (S)

Meunier, John, *Dean.* Arizona State University, College of Architecture & Environmental Design, Tempe AZ (S)

Mew, T J, *Chmn.* Berry College, Art Dept, Mount Berry GA (S)

Mew, T J, *Prof of Art.* Berry College, Memorial Library, Mount Berry GA

Mey, Andree, *Cur Coll.* Lehigh County Historical Society, Allentown PA

Meyer, Elisabeth, *Assoc Prof.* Cornell University, Dept of Art, Ithaca NY (S)

Meyer, Elizabeth, *Instr.* Main Line Art Center, Haverford PA

Meyer, Ellen, *Pres.* Atlanta College of Art, Atlanta GA (S)

Meyer, Fred, *Head Dept.* West Virginia Institute of Technology, Creative Arts Dept, Montgomery WV (S)

Meyer, Helen, *Pres.* LeSueur Museum, LeSueur MN

Meyer, Hugo, *Prof.* Princeton University, Dept of Art & Archaeology, Princeton NJ (S)

Meyer, James S, *Asst Prof.* Emory University, Art History Dept, Atlanta GA (S)

Meyer, Jerry D, *Asst Chmn.* Northern Illinois University, School of Art, De Kalb IL (S)

Meyer, Joan L, *Head Technical Servs.* Springfield Free Public Library, Donald B Palmer Museum, Springfield NJ

Meyer, R, *Faculty Lectr.* McGill University, Dept of Art History, Montreal PQ (S)

Meyer, Robert, *Exec Dir.* Silvermine Guild Arts Center, Silvermine Galleries, New Canaan CT

Meyer, Ursula, *Prof Emeritus.* Herbert H Lehman College, Art Dept, Bronx NY (S)

Meyer, Wayne, *Librn.* Ball State University, Architecture Library, Muncie IN

Meyers, Amanda, *Develop Assoc.* The Museums at Stony Brook, Stony Brook NY

Meyers, Amy, *Cur American Art.* The Huntington Library, Art Collections & Botanical Gardens, San Marino CA

Meyers, Dale, *Pres.* American Watercolor Society, New York NY

Meyers, Frances, *Assoc Prof.* University of Wisconsin, Madison, Dept of Art, Madison WI (S)

Meyers, Pieter, *Head Conservation.* Los Angeles County Museum of Art, Los Angeles CA

Meyers, Tom, *Dir,* Highland Community College, Freeport IL (S)

Meyrick, Charles, *Pres.* Sarasota Visual Art Center, Sarasota FL

Meza, John, *Prof.* Maryland College of Art & Design, Silver Spring MD (S)

Mezei, Gabor P, *Instr.* Southampton Art School, Southampton ON (S)

Mezzatesta, Michael, *Adjunct Prof.* Duke University, Dept of Art & Art History, Durham NC (S)

Mezzatesta, Michael P, *Dir.* Duke University Museum of Art, Durham NC

Mhiripiri, Julie, *Co-Owner.* Mhiripiri Gallery, Minneapolis MN

Mhiripiri, Rex, *Co-Owner.* Mhiripiri Gallery, Minneapolis MN

Micas, Nieves, *Assoc Prof.* New York Institute of Technology, Fine Arts Dept, Old Westbury NY (S)

Micas, Stephanie, *Exec Dir.* Arts Council of Richmond, Inc, Richmond VA

Micchelli, Tom, *Slide & Picture.* Cooper Union for the Advancement of Science & Art, Library, New York NY

Miceli, Maryanne, *Mgr ILL Artisans Shop,* Illinois State Museum, Illinois Artisans Shop, Chicago IL

Michael, Shirley, *Head Art & Music Dept.* Free Public Library, Art & Music Dept, Trenton NJ

Michael, Simon, *Head Dept.* Simon Michael School of Fine Arts, Rockport TX (S)

Michaels, Bonni-Dara, *Cur & Registrar.* Yeshiva University Museum, New York NY

Michaels, Glorianne, *Third VPres.* Arizona Watercolor Association, Phoenix AZ

Michalczyk, John, *Chmn.* Boston College, Fine Arts Dept, Chestnut Hill MA (S)

Micheals, Beth, *Head Div.* Chowan College, Division of Art, Murfreesboro NC (S)

Michel, Delbert, *Prof.* Hope College, Art Dept, Holland MI (S)

Micheli, Julio, *Prof.* Catholic University of Puerto Rico, Dept of Fine Arts, Ponce PR (S)

Michels, Dana, *Registrar & Cur Asst.* Charles H MacNider Museum, Mason City IA

Mick, Cheryl, *Asst Dir.* Dallas Visual Art Center, Dallas TX

Mickelson, Duane, *Chmn.* Concordia College, Art Dept, Moorhead MN (S)

Mickenberg, David, *Dir.* Northwestern University, Mary & Leigh Block Gallery, Evanston IL

Micklewright, Nancy, *Assoc Prof.* University of Victoria, Dept of History in Art, Victoria BC (S)

Micots, Cory, *Cur.* Albany Museum of Art, Albany GA

Middlebrook, David, *Assoc Chair, Studio.* San Jose State University, School of Art & Design, San Jose CA (S)

Midkiff, David, *Asst Prof Art.* Williams Baptist College, Dept of Art, Walnut Ridge AR (S)

Mieczinkowski, Richard, *Dept Chmn.* California University of Pennsylvania, Dept of Art, California PA (S)

Mielnick, Matthew, *Dir.* Kirkland Art Center, Clinton NY

Miera, Lucille M, *Pres.* New Mexico Art League, Gallery, Albuquerque NM

Mieras, Marta, *Cur & Dir.* Edison Community College, Gallery of Fine Art, Fort Myers FL

Miers, Shep, *Instr.* The Arkansas Arts Center, Museum School, Little Rock AR (S)

Miesel, Victor H, *Prof.* University of Michigan, Ann Arbor, Dept of History of Art, Ann Arbor MI (S)

Migliori, Larry, *Asst Prof,* Mohawk Valley Community College, Advertising Design & Production, Utica NY (S)

Mihal, Milan, *Assoc Prof,* Vanderbilt University, Dept of Fine Arts, Nashville TN (S)

Miho, James, *Communication Design Chmn,* Art Center College of Design, Pasadena CA (S)

Mikel-Reid, Mary, *Instr,* Southwest Texas State University, Dept of Art, San Marcos TX (S)

Mikelson, Arnold, *Mgr,* Arnold Mikelson Mind & Matter Gallery, White Rock BC

Mikelson, Mary, *Dir,* Arnold Mikelson Mind & Matter Gallery, White Rock BC

Mikelson, Myra, *Asst Dir,* Arnold Mikelson Mind & Matter Gallery, White Rock BC

Mikelson, Sapphire, *Asst Mgr,* Arnold Mikelson Mind & Matter Gallery, White Rock BC

Mikesell, A David, *Board Chmn,* Detroit Artists Market, Detroit MI

Mikkelson, Rick, *Chmn,* State University of New York at Plattsburgh, Art Dept, Plattsburgh NY (S)

Milakovich, Jeannie, *Chmn,* Gogebic Community College, Fine Arts Dept, Ironwood MI (S)

Milbauer, Donna, *Instr,* Siena Heights College, Studio Angelico-Art Dept, Adrian MI (S)

Milbrandt, Lanny, *Head Art Dept,* Valdosta State University, Art Gallery, Valdosta GA

Miles, Carolyn, *Dir,* Atrium Gallery, Saint Louis MO

Miles, Carolyn, *Dir,* Aiken County Historical Museum, Aiken SC

Miles, Christine M, *Dir,* Albany Institute of History & Art, Albany NY

Miles, David, *Prof,* Ohio University-Eastern Campus, Dept Comparitive Arts, Saint Clairsville OH (S)

Miles, Ellen G, *Cur Paintings & Sculpture,* National Portrait Gallery, Washington DC

Miles, Steven, *Chmn Humanities Div,* New College of the University of South Florida, Fine Arts Dept, Humanities Division, Sarasota FL (S)

Miley, E J, *Assoc Prof,* Lincoln College, Art Dept, Lincoln IL (S)

Miley, Les, *Chmn Art Dept,* University of Evansville, Krannert Gallery, Evansville IN

Miley, Les, *Dept Head & Prof,* University of Evansville, Art Dept, Evansville IN (S)

Miley, Randy, *Instr,* Northeast Louisiana University, Dept of Art, Monroe LA (S)

Milkie, Jane, *Asst Prof,* Northern Michigan University, Dept of Art & Design, Marquette MI (S)

Milkofsky, Brenda, *Dir,* Wethersfield Historical Society Inc, Museum, Wethersfield CT

Milkofsky, Brenda, *Dir,* Wethersfield Historical Society Inc, Old Academy Library, Wethersfield CT

Milkovich, Michael, *Dir,* Museum of Fine Arts, Saint Petersburg, Florida, Inc, Saint Petersburg FL

Millan, Nelson, *Instr,* University of Puerto Rico, Dept of Fine Arts, Rio Piedras PR (S)

Millard, Elizabeth Wright, *Exec Dir,* Forum for Contemporary Art, Saint Louis MO

Millei, John, *Vis Instr,* Claremont Graduate School, Dept of Fine Arts, Claremont CA (S)

Millen, Brian, *Dir,* Gallery 53, Cooperstown NY

Miller, Amelia, *Pres,* Pocumtuck Valley Memorial Association, Memorial Hall, Deerfield MA

Miller, Christine, *Instr,* Mohawk Valley Community College, Advertising Design & Production, Utica NY (S)

Miller, Christopher A, *Dir,* Berea College, Appalachian Museum, Berea KY

Miller, Dale, *VPres,* Beaumont Art League, Beaumont TX

Miller, Darby, *Museum Relations,* University of Tampa, Henry B Plant Museum, Tampa FL

Miller, David, *Dir,* Skidmore College, Schick Art Gallery, Saratoga Springs NY

Miller, Dick, *Dir,* Frank Phillips Foundation Inc, Woolaroc Museum, Bartlesville OK

Miller, Don, *Treas,* Arizona Watercolor Association, Phoenix AZ

Miller, Doretta M, *Chmn,* Skidmore College, Dept of Art & Art History, Saratoga Springs NY (S)

Miller, Edward C, *Assoc Prof,* Rochester Institute of Technology, School of Art & Design, Rochester NY (S)

Miller, Elaine, *Asst Cur Photo,* Washington State History Museum, Special Collections Div, Tacoma WA

Miller, Elizabeth, *Exec Dir,* Allied Arts Gallery of the Yakima Valley, Yakima WA

Miller, Elizabeth, *Exec Dir,* Allied Arts Gallery of the Yakima Valley, Library, Yakima WA

Miller, George, *Dir,* California State University, Hayward, C E Smith Museum of Anthropology, Hayward CA

Miller, Glen, *Asst Prof,* Rochester Institute of Technology, School of Photographic Arts & Sciences, Rochester NY (S)

Miller, Glen, *Dir Information Serv,* Palm Beach County Cultural Council, West Palm Beach FL

Miller, Greg, *Instr,* Mount Mary College, Art Dept, Milwaukee WI (S)

Miller, Harriet S, *Dir,* Cultural Affairs Department City of Los Angeles, Junior Arts Center, Los Angeles CA

Miller, Harriet S, *Dir,* Cultural Affairs Department City of Los Angeles, Library, Los Angeles CA

Miller, Jane, *Instr,* Monterey Peninsula College, Art Dept, Monterey CA (S)

Miller, Jean, *Prof,* East Tennessee State University, Dept of Art & Design, Johnson City TN (S)

Miller, Jerry, *Chair Dept,* Central Missouri State University, Art Dept, Warrensburg MO (S)

Miller, John B, *Prof,* Texas Woman's University, Dept of Visual Arts, Denton TX (S)

Miller, Joseph, *Head International Design,* Antonelli Institute of Art & Photography, Cincinnati OH (S)

Miller, Joseph, *Dir Grad Studies,* Catholic University of America, School of Architecture & Planning, Washington DC (S)

Miller, J Robert, *Prof,* McMurry University, Art Dept, Abilene TX (S)

Miller, Karen, *Secy,* Lafayette Natural History Museum, Planetarium & Nature Station, Lafayette LA

Miller, Kate, *Dir Educ,* The Art Center of Waco, Waco TX

Miller, Kate, *Admin Asst,* Emily Carr Institute of Art & Design, The Charles H Scott Gallery, Vancouver BC

Miller, Kathryn, *Drawing,* Pitzer College, Dept of Art, Claremont CA (S)

Miller, Lenore D, *Dir,* George Washington University, The Dimock Gallery, Washington DC

Miller, Leslie, *Asst to Dir,* Oberlin College, Allen Memorial Art Museum, Oberlin OH

Miller, Lillian B, *Ed Charles Willson Peale Papers,* National Portrait Gallery, Washington DC

Miller, Lisa, *Bus Mgr,* Allentown Art Museum, Allentown PA

Miller, Lynn, *Dir,* Houston Baptist University, Museum of American Architecture and Decorative Arts, Houston TX

Miller, M, *Chmn,* University of Toronto, Dept of Fine Art, Toronto ON (S)

Miller, Margaret A, *Dir & Chief Cur,* University of South Florida, Contemporary Art Museum, Tampa FL

Miller, Marie Celeste, *Assoc Prof,* Aquinas College, Art Dept, Grand Rapids MI (S)

Miller, Marlene, *Instr,* Bucks County Community College, Fine Arts Dept, Newtown PA (S)

Miller, Marlene, *Instr,* Illinois Central College, Dept of Fine Arts, East Peoria IL (S)

Miller, Marlin, *Pres,* Haystack Mountain School of Crafts, Gallery, Deer Isle ME

Miller, Mary, *Chmn,* Yale University, Dept of the History of Art, New Haven CT (S)

Miller, Michael, *Prof,* School of the Art Institute of Chicago, Chicago IL (S)

Miller, Michael, *Chmn Painting,* East Texas State University, Dept of Art, Commerce TX (S)

Miller, Michael, *Co-Dir,* University of Portland, Buckley Center Gallery, Portland OR

Miller, Pamela, *Archivist,* McCord Museum of Canadian History, Montreal PQ

Miller, Penelope, *Instr,* Arkansas State University, Dept of Art, State University AR (S)

Miller, Randy, *Educ Officer Natural Science,* New Brunswick Museum, Saint John NB

Miller, Richard McDermott, *Pres,* National Sculpture Society, New York NY

Miller, Robert B, *Visiting Lect,* Lewis & Clark College, Dept of Art, Portland OR (S)

Miller, Roger, *Asst Dir,* Battleship North Carolina, Wilmington NC

Miller, Ron, *Dir,* World Archaeological Society, Information Center & Library, Hollister MO

Miller, Ruane, *Chmn Dept,* College of New Jersey, Art Dept, Trenton NJ (S)

Miller, Ruane, *Chmn & Prof,* College of New Jersey, Art Gallery, Trenton NJ

Miller, Ruth, *Instr,* New York Studio School of Drawing, Painting & Sculpture, New York NY (S)

Miller, Samantha, *Develop Coordr,* San Angelo Museum of Fine Arts, San Angelo TX

Miller, Skip, *Co-Dir,* Kit Carson Historic Museums, Taos NM

Miller, Skip, *Co-Dir,* Kit Carson Historic Museums, Archives, Taos NM

Miller, Skip, *Co-Dir,* Kit Carson Historic Museums, Ernest Blumenschein Home & Studio, Taos NM

Miller, Skip, *Co-Dir,* Kit Carson Historic Museums, Home & Museum, Taos NM

Miller, Skip, *Co-Dir,* Kit Carson Historic Museums, Hacienda Martinez, Taos NM

Miller, Stephanie, *Chief Designer,* North Carolina Museum of Art, Raleigh NC

Miller, Stephen, *Marketing Support,* Arts of the Southern Finger Lakes, Corning NY

Miller, Steve, *Assoc Prof,* Palomar Community College, Art Dept, San Marcos CA (S)

Miller, Steven, *Exec Dir,* Bennington Museum, Bennington Museum, Bennington VT

Miller, Susan, *Slide Coll Supv,* Syracuse University, Library, Syracuse NY

Miller, Susan, *Exec Dir,* New Langton Arts, San Francisco CA

Miller Clark, Denise, *Dir,* Columbia College, The Museum of Contemporary Photography, Chicago IL

Miller-Keller, Andrea, *Cur Contemporary Art,* Wadsworth Atheneum, Hartford CT

Millie, Elena G, *Posters,* Library of Congress, Prints & Photographs Division, Washington DC

Milligan, Bryce, *Literature Prog Dir,* Guadalupe Cultural Arts Center, San Antonio TX

Milligan, Frank, *Dir,* New Brunswick Museum, Saint John NB

Milligan, Shirley, *Exec Asst to Chmn,* Blount Inc, Blount Corporate Collection, Montgomery AL

Milligan Ryan, Barbara J, *Dir & Cur,* Plymouth Antiquarian Society, Plymouth MA

Millin, Laura J, *Dir,* Art Museum of Missoula, Missoula MT

Millis, Louise, *Library Chmn,* University of Southern California, Greene & Greene Library of the Arts & Crafts Movement, San Marino CA

Milloff, Mark, *Chmn Dept,* Berkshire Community College, Dept of Fine Arts, Pittsfield MA (S)

Millon, Henry A, *Dean, Center for Advanced Study in Visual Arts,* National Gallery of Art, Washington DC

Mills, Anne, *Exec Secy,* University of Notre Dame, Snite Museum of Art, Notre Dame IN

Mills, Cynthia, *Asst Dir,* Birmingham-Bloomfield Art Association, Birmingham MI

Mills, Dan, *Dir,* Potsdam College of the State University of New York, Roland Gibson Gallery, Potsdam NY

Mills, Don, *Chief Librn,* Mississauga Library System, Mississauga ON

Mills, Gene, *Pres College,* Earlham College, Leeds Gallery, Richmond IN

Mills, James, *Pres,* Montclair Art Museum, Montclair NJ

Mills, James, *Prof,* East Tennessee State University, Dept of Art & Design, Johnson City TN (S)

Mills, Jeanette C, *Dir Visual Servs,* University of Washington, Art Slide Library, Seattle WA

Mills, Kelly, *Instr,* Avila College, Art Division, Dept of Humanities, Kansas City MO (S)

Mills, Lea, *Dean,* College of the Redwoods, Arts & Languages Dept Division, Eureka CA (S)

Mills, Richard, *Prof.* Auburn University at Montgomery, Dept of Fine Arts, Montgomery AL (S)

Mills, Richard, *Asst Prof.* C W Post Center of Long Island University, School of Visual & Performing Arts, Brookville NY (S)

Millsaps, Lucy, *Assoc Prof.* Millsaps College, Dept of Art, Jackson MS (S)

Mills-Varnell, Ruth B, *Dir.* Art Association of Richmond, Richmond Art Museum, Richmond IN

Mills-Varnell, Ruth B, *Dir.* Art Association of Richmond, Library, Richmond IN

Milne, Norman F, *Clerk,* The Currier Gallery of Art, Manchester NH

Milner, Sue, *Head Dept.* Eastern Wyoming College, Art Dept, Torrington WY (S)

Milnes, Robert, *Dir.* San Jose State University, School of Art & Design, San Jose CA (S)

Milosevich, Joe, *Instr.* Joliet Junior College, Fine Arts Dept, Joliet IL (S)

Milosevich, Joe B, *Gallery Dir.* Joliet Junior College, Laura A Sprague Art Gallery, Joliet IL (S)

Milot, Barbara, *Asst Prof.* Framingham State College, Art Dept, Framingham MA (S)

Milovich, Rose M, *Assoc Cur.* Nora Eccles Harrison Museum of Art, Logan UT

Milphorp, Rob, *Dean Core & Humanities.* Alberta College of Art, Calgary AB (S)

Milroy, Elizabeth, *Assoc Prof.* Wesleyan University, Art Dept, Middletown CT (S)

Milroy, John, *First VPres.* Jesse Besser Museum, Alpena MI

Milsoch, Jane, *Asst Cur Coll.* Davenport Museum of Art, Davenport IA

Mimeault, Sonia, *Registrar.* Musee du Seminaire de Quebec, Quebec PQ

Mims, Michael, *Acting Area Head Photography.* Pasadena City College, Art Dept, Pasadena CA (S)

Minet, Cynthia, *Asst Prof.* Antelope Valley College, Art Dept, Division of Fine Arts, Lancaster CA (S)

Mingalone, Mimi, *Asst Dir.* Socrates Sculpture Park, Long Island City NY

Mingledorff, Susan, *Instr.* Northeast Louisiana University, Dept of Art, Monroe LA (S)

Minkkinen, Arno, *Prof.* University of Massachusetts Lowell, Dept of Art, Lowell MA (S)

Minkler, Christine, *Develop & Membership,* Columbia Museum of Art, Columbia SC

Minnelli, Peter, *Area Mgr.* Canadian Heritage - Parks Canada, Laurier House, Ottawa ON

Minogue, Eileen, *Asst Dir.* Northport-East Northport Public Library, Northport NY

Mintich, Mary, *Prof.* Winthrop University, Dept of Art & Design, Rock Hill SC (S)

Mints, Carolyn, *Dir Community Relations.* Mint Museum of Art, Charlotte NC

Mintz, Deborah, *VPres,* Arts Council of Fayetteville-Cumberland County, The Arts Center, Fayetteville NC

Mintz, Mary, *Head Reference,* American University, Jack I Dorothy G Bender Library, Washington DC

Mintz, Ward, *Deputy Dir Prog & Coll.* Newark Museum Association, The Newark Museum, Newark NJ

Minvielle, Shereen H, *Dir.* Shadows-on-the-Teche, New Iberia LA

Miot, Sandra, *VPres.* Miami Watercolor Society, Inc, Miami FL

Miraglia, Anthony J, *Chmn Fine Art.* University of Massachusetts Dartmouth, College of Visual & Performing Arts, North Dartmouth MA (S)

Mirandette, Marle Claude, *Cur Prints & Drawings.* Montreal Museum of Fine Arts, Montreal PQ

Mirzoeff, Nicholas D, *Asst Prof.* University of Wisconsin, Madison, Dept of Art History, Madison WI (S)

Misfeldt, Willard, *Chmn Art History.* Bowling Green State University, School of Art, Bowling Green OH (S)

Mishkin, Janet, *Dir.* Monroe County Historical Association, Elizabeth D Walters Library, Stroudsburg PA

Mishler, John, *Asst Prof.* Goshen College, Art Dept, Goshen IN (S)

Misite, Phyllis, *School Dir.* Mount Ida College, Chamberlayne School of Design & Merchandising, Boston MA (S)

Miskuly, Mary Helen, *Registrar.* Burchfield-Penney Art Center, Buffalo NY

Miskuly, Mary Helen, *Registrar.* Burchfield-Penney Art Center, Archives, Buffalo NY

Misner, Mary, *Coordr Cultural Servs.* Cambridge Public Library and Gallery, Cambridge ON

Misraje, Jenee A, *Prog Asst.* Art Prog, Lannan Foundation, Los Angeles CA

Missal, Paul, *Instr.* Pacific Northwest College of Art, Portland OR (S)

Mitchell, Brenda, *Instr.* Indiana University of Pennsylvania, Dept of Art & Art Education, Indiana PA (S)

Mitchell, David, *Dir.* Ella Sharp Museum, Jackson MI

Mitchell, Deborah, *Cur.* Art Museum of Missoula, Missoula MT

Mitchell, Dolores, *Instr.* California State University, Chico, Art Dept, Chico CA (S)

Mitchell, Jo, *Registrar.* Old Jail Art Center, Green Research Library, Albany TX

Mitchell, Katherine, *Lectr.* Emory University, Art History Dept, Atlanta GA (S)

Mitchell, Leah, *Pres.* Licking County Art Association, Art Gallery, Newark OH

Mitchell, Liz, *Community Relations,* Art Gallery of Hamilton, Hamilton ON

Mitchell, Pauline, *Registrar.* Shelburne Museum, Shelburne VT

Mitchell, Robert, *Bus Mgr.* Society of North American Goldsmiths, Tampa FL

Mitchell, Ron, *Instr.* West Hills Community College, Fine Arts Dept, Coalinga CA (S)

Mitchell, Sandy, *Librn.* Jesse Besser Museum, Philip M Park Library, Alpena MI

Mitchell, Stanley A, *Prof.* Chowan College, Division of Art, Murfreesboro NC (S)

Mitchell, Starr, *Educ Coordr.* Arkansas Territorial Restoration, Little Rock AR

Mitchell, Starr, *Educ Coordr.* Arkansas Territorial Restoration, Library, Little Rock AR

Mitchell, Taylor, *Asst Prof.* Incarnate Word University of the Arts & Sciences, Art Dept, San Antonio TX (S)

Mitchell, William J, *Dean.* Massachusetts Institute of Technology, School of Architecture and Planning, Cambridge MA (S)

Mitchell, Wilma Jo, *Registrar.* Old Jail Art Center, Albany TX

Mithen, Jeanne C, *Archivist.* Riley County Historical Society, Riley County Historical Museum, Manhattan KS

Mithen, Jeanne C, *Archivist.* Riley County Historical Society, Seaton Library, Manhattan KS

Mitsanas, D, *Instr.* Humboldt State University, College of Arts & Humanities, Arcata CA (S)

Mitten, David Gordon, *Cur Ancient Art,* Harvard University, Arthur M Sackler Museum, Cambridge MA

Mitten, Patrick, *Instr.* Milwaukee Area Technical College, Graphic Arts Division, Milwaukee WI (S)

Mittlestadt, Linda, *Archivist.* Oshkosh Public Museum, Library, Oshkosh WI

Mitton, Maureen, *Asst Prof.* University of Wisconsin-Stout, Dept of Art & Design, Menomonie WI (S)

Miura, Carol, *Instr.* Rancho Santiago College, Art Dept, Santa Ana CA (S)

Mixon, Jamie, *Asst Prof.* Mississippi State University, Art Dept, Mississippi State MS (S)

Miyata, Masako, *Prof.* James Madison University, School of Art & Art History, Harrisonburg VA (S)

Miyata, Wayne A, *Faculty,* Kauai Community College, Dept of Art, Lihue HI (S)

Miyazaki, Hiroshi, *Instr.* San Diego Mesa College, Fine Arts Dept, San Diego CA (S)

Mo, Charles, *Dir Coll & Exhib.* Mint Museum of Art, Charlotte NC

Moats, Tamara, *Cur Educ.* University of Washington, Henry Art Gallery, Seattle WA

Moats, Tamara, *Educ Dir.* Henry Gallery Association, Henry Art Gallery, Seattle WA

Moberg, David, *Chmn Fine Arts,* Indian River Community College, Fine Arts Dept, Fort Pierce FL (S)

Mobley, Karen, *Dir.* Nicolaysen Art Museum & Discovery Center, Childrens Discovery Center, Casper WY

Mobley, Karen, *Dir.* Nicolaysen Art Museum & Discovery Center, Museum, Casper WY

Mobley, Russell, *Instr.* Campbellsville College, Fine Arts Division, Campbellsville KY (S)

Modder, Susan, *Acting Admin Dir.* Charles Allis Art Museum, Milwaukee WI

Mode, Robert L, *Chmn.* Vanderbilt University, Dept of Fine Arts, Nashville TN (S)

Modica, Andrea, *Instr.* State University of New York College at Oneonta, Dept of Art, Oneonta NY (S)

Modica, Lee, *Arts Adminr.* Florida Department of State, Division of Cultural Affairs, Florida Arts Council, Tallahassee FL

Moe, Richard, *Pres.* National Trust for Historic Preservation, Washington DC

Moeller, Gary E, *Dir.* Rogers State College, Art Dept, Claremore OK (S)

Moeller, G Martin, *Exec Dir.* Association of Collegiate Schools of Architecture, Washington DC

Moezena, Darryl, *Pres.* Dubuque Art Association, Dubuque Museum of Art, Dubuque IA

Moffatt, Constance, *Assoc Prof.* Pierce College, Art Dept, Woodland Hills CA (S)

Moffatt, Laurie Norton, *Dir.* Norman Rockwell Museum at Stockbridge, Stockbridge MA

Moffet, David, *Pres.* Contemporary Arts Center, Cincinnati OH

Moffett, Charles S, *Dir.* The Phillips Collection, Washington DC

Moffett, Kenworth W, *Exec Dir.* Museum of Art, Fort Lauderdale, Fort Lauderdale FL

Moffett, Susan M, *Assoc Prof.* Indiana University-Southeast, Fine Arts Dept, New Albany IN (S)

Moffett, William, *Instr.* Wilkes Community College, Arts & Science Division, Wilkesboro NC (S)

Moffitt, Ann, *Store Mgr.* Penobscot Marine Museum, Searsport ME

Moffitt, John, *Prof.* New Mexico State University, Art Dept, Las Cruces NM (S)

Mohabali, Mohammed, *Bus Mgr.* Paine Art Center & Arboretum, Oshkosh WI

Mohr, Jani, *VPres.* Surface Design Association, Inc, Oakland CA

Mohr, John, *Cur Exhibits.* New Jersey State Museum, Trenton NJ

Mohr, Ken, *Adjunct Instr.* Maryville University of Saint Louis, Art Division, Saint Louis MO (S)

Moir, Alfred, *Adjunct Cur Drawings.* University of California, Santa Barbara, University Art Museum, Santa Barbara CA

Moir, Lindsay, *Librn.* Glenbow Museum, Library, Calgary AB

Moldenhauer, Richard, *Bus Mgr.* Mendel Art Gallery & Civic Conservatory, Saskatoon SK

Moldenhauer, Susan, *Cur Museum & Progs,* University of Wyoming, University of Wyoming Art Museum, Laramie WY

Moldwin, Jennifer L S, *Library Consultant.* Detroit Institute of Arts, Research Library, Detroit MI

Molen, Jan, *Dir.* Napa Valley College, Art Dept, Napa CA (S)

Molina, Samuel B, *Assoc Prof.* George Washington University, Dept of Art, Washington DC (S)

Molnar, Mike, *Instr.* Luzerne County Community College, Commercial Art Dept, Nanticoke PA (S)

Molner, Frank, *Instr.* Rancho Santiago College, Art Dept, Santa Ana CA (S)

Monaco, Theresa, *Prof.* Emmanuel College, Art Dept, Boston MA (S)

Monaghan, Kathleen, *Dir.* Hyde Collection Trust, Glens Falls NY

Monaghan, Kathleen, *Dir.* Hyde Collection Trust, Library, Glens Falls NY

Monaghan, Susan, *Dir of Operations.* Ann Arbor Art Association, Art Center, Ann Arbor MI

Monahan, Bob, *Co-Chmn*, Studio Gallery, Washington DC

Moncur, Shannon, *Chmn*, Moncur Gallery, Boissevain MB

Mondor, Karen, *Performing Arts Coordr*, Organization of Saskatchewan Arts Councils (OSAC), Regina SK

Monge-Rasuls, Pedro, *Exec Dir*, Ollantay Center for the Arts, Jackson Heights NY

Monk, Dan, *Asst Prof*, State University of New York at Stony Brook, Art Dept, Stony Brook NY (S)

Monkhouse, Christopher, *Chief Cur & Cur Decorative Arts*, Minneapolis Institute of Arts, Minneapolis MN

Monkhouse, Christopher, *Cur Architecture*, Carnegie Institute, Carnegie Museum of Art, Pittsburgh PA

Monkman, Betty C, *Assoc Cur*, White House, Washington DC

Monroe, Alden, *Asst Dir Spec Coll*, Alabama Department of Archives & History, Museum Galleries, Montgomery AL

Monroe, Arthur, *Registrar*, Oakland Museum of California, Art Dept, Oakland CA

Monroe, Dan L, *Exec Dir*, Peabody Essex Museum, Salem MA

Monroe, Gary, *Prof*, Daytona Beach Community College, Dept of Fine Arts & Visual Arts, Daytona Beach FL (S)

Monroe, Joan, *Tour Coordr*, Dartmouth College, Hood Museum of Art, Hanover NH

Monroe, Mark, *Prof*, Austin College, Art Dept, Sherman TX (S)

Monroe, Michael W, *Exec Dir Council*, American Craft Council, New York NY

Monroe, P Jensen, *Supv Public Programs*, The Rockwell Museum, Corning NY

Monson, Richard D, *Prof*, Central Missouri State University, Art Dept, Warrensburg MO (S)

Montague, Angela, *Fel Coordr*, College Art Association, New York NY

Monteolive, Leonardo, *Technician*, Promote Art Works Inc (PAWI), Laziza Videodance Lumia Project, Brooklyn NY

Montgomery, Edward, *Prof*, Miami University, Dept Fine Arts, Hamilton OH (S)

Montgomery, Florence, *Pres*, Bromfield Art Gallery, Boston MA

Montgomery, Jane, *Registrar*, Harvard University, Harvard University Art Museums, Cambridge MA

Montgomery, Katherine, *Instr*, Davidson County Community College, Humanities Div, Lexington NC (S)

Montgomery, Marilyn, *Dir External Affairs*, The Phillips Collection, Washington DC

Montgomery, Pat, *Admin Asst*, Alaska State Museum, Juneau AK

Montgomery, Renee, *Registrar*, Los Angeles County Museum of Art, Los Angeles CA

Montgomery, Wanda, *Instr*, Cuyahoga Valley Art Center, Cuyahoga Falls OH (S)

Montileaux, Paulette, *Cur*, Indian Arts & Crafts Board, Sioux Indian Museum, Rapid City SD

Moody, Barbara, *Dean*, Monserrat College of Art, Beverly MA (S)

Moody, Larrie J, *Chairperson*, Pittsburg State University, Art Dept, Pittsburg KS (S)

Moone, Charles, *Acting Co-Chair*, University of Colorado at Denver, Dept of Fine Arts, Denver CO (S)

Mooney, Allen, *Asst Prof*, State University of New York, College at Cortland, Art Dept, Cortland NY (S)

Mooney, Sandra, *Librn*, Louisiana State University, Design Resource Center, Baton Rouge LA

Mooney, Wanda, *Admin Staff Specialist*, Memorial University of Newfoundland, Art Gallery of Newfoundland & Labrador, Saint John's NF

Moore, Allison, *Develop Coordr*, Dallas Visual Art Center, Dallas TX

Moore, Ann, *Asst Cur Educ*, New Orleans Museum of Art, New Orleans LA

Moore, Anne F, *Dir*, Oberlin College, Allen Memorial Art Museum, Oberlin OH

Moore, Carol, *Dir Graduate Prog*, University of the Arts, Philadelphia College of Art & Design, Philadelphia PA (S)

Moore, Christine, *Admin Asst*, Southern Methodist University, Meadows Museum, Dallas TX

Moore, Dana, *Asst Dir*, Penland School of Crafts, Penland NC (S)

Moore, Debbie, *Registrar*, Touchstone Center for Crafts, Farmington PA

Moore, Del, *Reference Librn*, Colonial Williamsburg Foundation, John D Rockefeller, Jr Library, Williamsburg VA

Moore, Donald Everett, *Chmn*, Mitchell Community College, Visual Art Dept, Statesville NC (S)

Moore, Fay, *VPres*, The Allied Artists of America, Inc, New York NY

Moore, Jack, *Art Teacher*, Motlow State Community College, Art Dept, Tullahoma TN (S)

Moore, James C, *Dir*, Albuquerque Museum of Art & History, Albuquerque NM

Moore, Jane, *Mgr Resource Centre*, Ontario Crafts Council, The Craft Gallery, Toronto ON

Moore, Jeffrey, *Dir*, Contemporary Art for San Antonio Blue Star Art Space, San Antonio TX

Moore, Jennifer W, *Exec Dir & Cur*, Green Hill Center for North Carolina Art, Greensboro NC

Moore, Jerry, *VPres Operations*, High Desert Museum, Bend OR

Moore, Jim, *Instr*, Campbellsville College, Fine Arts Division, Campbellsville KY (S)

Moore, John, *Prof*, Boston University, School of Visual Arts, Boston MA (S)

Moore, John, *Asst Prof*, Smith College, Art Dept, Northampton MA (S)

Moore, Juanita, *Pres*, African American Museums Association, Wilberforce OH

Moore, Julia Muney, *Exhib Cur*, Indianapolis Art Center, Churchman-Fehsenfeld Gallery, Indianapolis IN

Moore, Kathleen A, *Asst Librn*, University of Louisville, Margaret M Bridwell Art Library, Louisville KY

Moore, Kemille, *Assoc Prof*, University of North Carolina at Wilmington, Dept of Fine Arts - Division of Art, Wilmington NC (S)

Moore, Lester, *Pres & Gen Mgr*, Polynesian Cultural Center, Laie HI

Moore, Marilyn, *Asst to Dir*, California State University, Fullerton, Art Gallery, Visual Arts Center, Fullerton CA

Moore, Melodye, *Historic Site Mgr*, New York State Office of Parks, Recreation & Historical Preservation, Mills Mansion State Historical Site, Staatsburg NY

Moore, Monica L, *Bus Mgr*, Rosemount Museum, Inc, Pueblo CO

Moore, Nevalyn, *Instr*, Campbellsville College, Fine Arts Division, Campbellsville KY (S)

Moore, Owen, *Colls Mgr*, University of California, Los Angeles, Fowler Museum of Cultural History, Los Angeles CA

Moore, Ray, *Admin Dir*, Appalshop Inc, Appalshop Films Media Center, Whitesburg KY

Moore, Richard, *Supt*, Yale University, Art Gallery, New Haven CT

Moore, Sarah, *Asst Prof Art History*, University of Arizona, Dept of Art, Tucson AZ (S)

Moore, Sherrod, *Chmn Board*, Glenbow Museum, Calgary AB

Moore, Stuart, *Registrar*, The Art Institute of Dallas, Dallas TX (S)

Moore, Susan, *Chmn Painting, Drawing, & Sculpture*, Temple University, Tyler School of Art, Philadelphia PA (S)

Moore, Sylvia, *Ed*, Midmarch Associates, Women Artists News Archive, New York NY

Moore, Tiffany, *Admin Asst*, York University, Glendon Gallery, North York ON

Moore, William, *Instr*, Pacific Northwest College of Art, Portland OR (S)

Moore Simon, Constance, *Instr*, Wayne Art Center, Wayne PA (S)

Moorman, Evette, *Inst*, Grayson County College, Art Dept, Denison TX (S)

Moppett, George, *Asst Cur*, Mendel Art Gallery & Civic Conservatory, Saskatoon SK

Moppett, Ron, *Dir & Cur*, Alberta College of Art & Design, Illingworth Kerr Gallery, Calgary AB

Morais, Lee, *Asst Dir Educ*, New Orleans Museum of Art, New Orleans LA

Morales, Michael, *Assoc Cur Geology*, Museum of Northern Arizona, Flagstaff AZ

Morales, Raymond, *Assoc Prof*, University of Utah, Art Dept, Salt Lake City UT (S)

Morales-Coll, Eduardo, *Pres*, Ateneo Puertorriqueno, San Juan PR

Morales-Coll, Eduardo, *Pres*, Ateneo Puertorriqueno, Library, San Juan PR

Moran, George F, *Treas*, National Hall of Fame for Famous American Indians, Anadarko OK

Moran, Joe, *Instr*, California State University, San Bernardino, Visual Arts, San Bernardino CA (S)

Moran, Lois, *Ed-in-Chief American Craft Magazine*, American Craft Council, New York NY

Moran, Mark W, *Asst Prof*, Baylor University, Dept of Art, Waco TX (S)

Moran, Susan, *Resource Center Dir*, John P Barclay Memorial Gallery, Pittsburgh PA

Moran, Susan, *Resource Center Dir*, John P Barclay Memorial Gallery, Resource Center, Pittsburgh PA

Moran, Susan, *Assoc Dean of Students*, Corcoran School of Art, Washington DC (S)

Morandi, Thomas, *Prof*, Oregon State University, Dept of Art, Corvallis OR (S)

Mordecai, Jo, *Coordr Exhib*, Schenectady County Historical Society, Schenectady NY

Mordus, Diane, *VPres*, Madison County Historical Society, Cottage Lawn, Oneida NY

More, Mary Thomas, *Libr Dir*, Lourdes College, Duns Scotus Library, Sylvania OH

Morec, Marti, *Librn*, Berkeley Public Library, Berkeley CA

Morehouse, Dorothy V, *Pres*, Monmouth Museum & Cultural Center, Lincroft NJ

Morel, Sylvie, *Dir Exhib*, Canadian Museum of Civilization, Hull PQ

Moreland, Paige, *Marketing Mgr*, Anniston Museum of Natural History, Anniston AL

Morell, Abelardo, *Chmn Media*, Massachusetts College of Art, Boston MA (S)

Morello, Samuel E, *Instr*, Charles Stewart Mott Community College, Art Area, School of Arts & Humanities, Flint MI (S)

Morello, S E, *Pres*, Buckham Fine Arts Project, Gallery, Flint MI

Moreno, Barry, *Libr Technician*, The National Park Service, United States Department of the Interior, The Statue of Liberty National Monument, New York NY

Moreno, Laura, *Deputy Dir*, Caribbean Cultural Center, Cultural Arts Organization & Resource Center, New York NY

Moreno, Maria L, *Asst Prof*, University of Puerto Rico, Dept of Fine Arts, Rio Piedras PR (S)

Moretta, Eleanor, *Dir Exhib*, Pratt Institute Library, Rubelle & Norman Schafler Gallery, Brooklyn NY

Morey, Mark, *Cur Educ*, Amarillo Art Association, Amarillo Art Center, Amarillo TX

Morgam, Donna, *Lectr*, Davis & Elkins College, Dept of Art, Elkins WV (S)

Morgan, Barbara, *Coordr Pub*, State University of New York at Purchase, Neuberger Museum of Art, Purchase NY

Morgan, Barbara, *Instr*, University of Alabama at Birmingham, Dept of Art, Birmingham AL (S)

Morgan, Clarence, *Prof*, University of Minnesota, Minneapolis, Dept of Art, Minneapolis MN (S)

Morgan, Dahlia, *Gallery Dir & Lecturer*, Florida International University, Visual Arts Dept, Miami FL (S)

Morgan, Dahlia, *Dir*, Florida International University, The Art Museum at FIU, Miami FL

Morgan, Elizabeth L, *Assoc Dir Planning & Develop*, Reynolda House Museum of American Art, Winston-Salem NC

Morgan, Ellen, *Exec Dir*, Association of Community Arts Agencies of Kansas, Salina KS

Morgan, George, *Dir*, Massachusetts College of Art, Morton R Godine Library, Boston MA

Morgan, Helen, *Prof.* South Dakota State University, Dept of Visual Arts, Brookings SD (S)

Morgan, Joann, *Instr.* Cottey College, Art Dept, Nevada MO (S)

Morgan, Kenneth, *Asst Prof Studio Art.* Bethany College, Dept of Fine Arts, Bethany WV (S)

Morgan, Laura, *Serials.* Chicago Public Library, Harold Washington Library Center, Chicago IL

Morgan, Linda D, *Instructional Media Specialist.* University of South Carolina, Art Library, Columbia SC

Morgan, M, *Instr.* Humboldt State University, College of Arts & Humanities, Arcata CA (S)

Morgan, Robert C, *Prof.* Rochester Institute of Technology, School of Art & Design, Rochester NY (S)

Morgan, Susan, *Cur & Registrar.* Museum of the American Quilter's Society, Paducah KY

Morgan, William, *Prof.* University of Wisconsin-Superior, Programs in the Visual Arts, Superior WI (S)

Morgenstern, Joan, *Pres.* Houston Center For Photography, Houston TX

Mori, John, *Asst Prof.* Arkansas Tech University, Dept of Art, Russellville AR (S)

Mori, Lynne, *Admin Asst.* Angels Gate Cultural Center, The Gate Gallery, San Pedro CA

Moriarty, Ellen, *Acting Adminr.* Chinati Foundation, Marfa TX

Moriarty, John, *Instr.* Springfield College, Dept of Visual & Performing Arts, Springfield MA (S)

Moriarty, Laura, *Prog Dir.* Women's Studio Workshop, Inc, Rosendale NY

Moriarty, Peter, *Photography Dept Head.* Johnson State College, Dept Fine & Performing Arts, Dibden Center for the Arts, Johnson VT (S)

Morice, Kit, *Cur Educ.* Eastern Illinois University, Tarble Arts Center, Charleston IL

Morin, Jeff, *Assoc Prof.* University of Wisconsin-Stevens Point, Dept of Art & Design, Stevens Point WI (S)

Morin, Mark, *Treas.* Westfield Athenaeum, Jasper Rand Art Museum, Westfield MA

Morin, Shawn, *Chmn 3-D Studies.* Bowling Green State University, School of Art, Bowling Green OH (S)

Morin, Thomas, *Dir.* Rochester Institute of Technology, School of Art & Design & School for American Craft, Rochester NY (S)

Morin, Tom, *Dir.* Rochester Institute of Technology, College of Imaging Arts & Sciences, Rochester NY (S)

Morin, Virginia E, *Dir.* Portsmouth Historical Society, John Paul Jones House, Portsmouth NH

Moriority, Kaleen, *Asst Prof.* Rochester Institute of Technology, School of Photographic Arts & Sciences, Rochester NY (S)

Morita, Linda, *Librn & Archivist,* McMichael Canadian Art Collection, Library & Archives, Kleinburg ON

Moritz, Evelyn, *Museum Coordr.* Ogden Union Station, Union Station Museums, Ogden UT

Morlan, Jenny, *Asst Prof.* DePaul University, Dept of Art, Chicago IL (S)

Morley, Anne, *Dir Admis.* School of the Art Institute of Chicago, Chicago IL (S)

Morley, Ruth, *Assoc Dir.* Boston Athenaeum, Boston MA

Morley, Stephen H, *Dir.* Academy of the New Church, Glencairn Museum, Bryn Athyn PA

Morman-Graham, Mary, *Librn.* Edmundson Art Foundation, Inc, Des Moines Art Center Library, Des Moines IA

Mornes, Joon, *Library Head.* University of Minnesota, Architecture & Landscape Library, Minneapolis MN

Morningstar, William, *Assoc Prof.* Berea College, Art Dept, Berea KY (S)

Morphis, Thomas, *Chmn.* Pacific Union College, Art Dept, Angwin CA (S)

Morrell, John, *Gallery Dir.* Georgetown University, Dept of Art, Music & Theatre, Washington DC (S)

Morrill, Allen, *Library Dir.* Kansas City Art Institute, Library, Kansas City MO

Morrill, Michael, *Chmn.* University of Pittsburgh, Dept of Studio Arts, Pittsburgh PA (S)

Morrin, Peter, *Dir.* J B Speed Art Museum, Louisville KY

Morris, Angie, *Facility Mgr.* Artspace Inc, Raleigh NC

Morris, Anne, *Exhib Dir.* Palos Verdes Art Center, Rancho Palos Verdes CA

Morris, Anne O, *Librn.* Toledo Museum of Art, Library, Toledo OH

Morris, Daniel, *Chmn.* Waynesburg College, Dept of Fine Arts, Waynesburg PA (S)

Morris, Daphne, *Archivist.* Town of Cummington Historical Commission, Kingman Tavern Historical Museum, Cummington MA

Morris, Jerry W, *Chmn.* Miami University, Art Dept, Oxford OH (S)

Morris, John, *Chmn.* East Central College, Art Dept, Union MO (S)

Morris, Kathleen, *Information Officer.* Ontario Crafts Council, Craft Resource Centre, Toronto ON

Morris, Kay T, *Registrar.* Tampa Museum of Art, Tampa FL

Morris, Kay T, *Registrar.* Tampa Museum of Art, Library, Tampa FL

Morris, Lois, *Gallery Educator.* Pence Gallery, Davis CA

Morris, Phillip S, *Exec VPres.* Memphis College of Art, Memphis TN (S)

Morris, Robert C, *Visiting Prof.* Trinity College, Dept of Fine Arts, Hartford CT (S)

Morris, Stephen, *Treas.* Maricopa County Historical Society, Desert Caballeros Western Museum, Wickenburg AZ

Morris, Susan, *Archivist.* Judah L Magnes Museum, Berkeley CA

Morris, Thomas, *Pres.* Morris-Jumel Mansion, Inc, New York NY

Morris, W S, *Chmn & Chief Exec Officer.* Morris Communications Corporation, Corporate Collection, Augusta GA

Morris, W S, *Chmn Board.* Morris Museum of Art, Augusta GA

Morrisey, Bob, *Prof.* Polk Community College, Art, Letters & Social Sciences, Winter Haven FL (S)

Morrisey, Marena Grant, *Dir.* Orlando Museum of Art, Orlando FL

Morrisey, Marena Grant, *Exec Dir.* Orlando Museum of Art, Orlando Sentinel Library, Orlando FL

Morrison, Alan E, *Librn.* University of Pennsylvania, Fisher Fine Arts Library, Philadelphia PA

Morrison, Anise, *Asst Cur.* Chattahoochee Valley Art Museum, LaGrange GA

Morrison, Bill, *Exec Dir.* Public Art Works, San Rafael CA

Morrison, Darrin, *Research Assoc Conservation.* University of British Columbia, Museum of Anthropology, Vancouver BC

Morrison, Ken, *Thesis Advisor.* Toronto Art Therapy Institute, Toronto ON (S)

Morrison, Philip, *Instr.* College of the Canyons, Art Dept, Valencia CA (S)

Morrison, Philip R, *Dir.* Hermitage Foundation Museum, Norfolk VA

Morrison, Philip R, *Dir.* Hermitage Foundation Museum, Library, Norfolk VA

Morrisroe, Julia, *Pres.* ARC Gallery, Chicago IL

Morrissey, T, *Instr.* Community College of Rhode Island, Dept of Art, Warwick RI (S)

Morrissey, Tom, *Dir & Librn.* Community College of Rhode Island, Flanagan Valley Campus Art Gallery, Warwick RI

Morro, Mary, *Interior Design Dept Head.* The Illinois Institute of Art, Chicago IL (S)

Morrow, Delores, *Photograph Cur.* Montana Historical Society, Library, Helena MT

Morrow, Terry, *Prof.* Texas Tech University, Dept of Art, Lubbock TX (S)

Morrish, David, *Chmn.* Memorial University of Newfoundland, School of Fine Arts, Visual Arts Dept, Corner Brook NF (S)

Morsberger, Philip, *Scholar in Art.* Augusta College, Dept of Fine Arts, Augusta GA (S)

Morsches, Richard, *VPres Operations.* The Metropolitan Museum of Art, New York NY

Morse, A Reynolds, *Chmn.* Salvador Dali Museum, Saint Petersburg FL

Morse, Bart, *Assoc Prof.* University of Arizona, Dept of Art, Tucson AZ (S)

Mortenson, K Hauser, *Instr.* Golden West College, Visual Art Dept, Huntington Beach CA (S)

Mortimer, Ruth, *Lectr.* Smith College, Art Dept, Northampton MA (S)

Morton, Gregory, *Cur Educ.* Chattahoochee Valley Art Museum, LaGrange GA

Morton, Jean Pell, *Staff.* Gallery 9, Los Altos CA

Morton, Patricia M, *Asst Prof.* University of California, Riverside, Dept of the History of Art, Riverside CA (S)

Morton, Robert, *Head Dept.* Plymouth State College, Art Dept, Plymouth NH (S)

Mortonson, Sheila, *Librn.* Tucson Museum of Art & Historic Block, Tucson AZ

Mortonson, Sheila, *Librn.* Tucson Museum of Art & Historic Block, Library, Tucson AZ

Mosby, Dewey F, *Dir.* Colgate University, Picker Art Gallery, Hamilton NY

Moseley, Bill, *Prof.* University of Maine at Augusta, Division of Fine & Performing Arts, Augusta ME (S)

Moser, Christopher L, *Cur Anthropology.* Riverside Municipal Museum, Riverside CA

Moser, Jan, *Pres.* Merced College, Arts Division, Merced CA (S)

Moser, Ken, *Vice Dir Coll & Chief Conservator.* Brooklyn Museum, Brooklyn NY

Moses, H Vincent, *Cur History.* Riverside Municipal Museum, Riverside CA

Moses, Jennifer, *Asst Prof.* University of New Hampshire, Dept of Arts & Art History, Durham NH (S)

Moses, Nancy, *Dir.* Atwater Kent Museum, Philadelphia PA

Mosgrove, Michelle Z, *Operations Mgr.* Contemporary Crafts Association & Gallery, Portland OR

Moskowitz, Anita, *Prof.* State University of New York at Stony Brook, Art Dept, Stony Brook NY (S)

Moskowitz, Bob, *Adjunct Instr.* Maryville University of Saint Louis, Art Division, Saint Louis MO (S)

Moss, Frances, *Dept Chair.* John C Calhoun State Community College, Department of Fine Arts, Decatur AL (S)

Moss, Joe, *Coordr Sculpture.* University of Delaware, Dept of Art, Newark DE (S)

Moss, Kent, *Instr.* Midland College, Art Dept, Midland TX (S)

Moss, Michael E, *Dir Museum.* United States Military Academy, West Point Museum, West Point NY

Moss, Rick, *Cur History.* California African-American Museum, Los Angeles CA

Moss, Roger W, *Dir.* Athenaeum of Philadelphia, Philadelphia PA

Most, Gregory P J, *Chief Slide Librn.* National Gallery of Art, Slide Library, Washington DC

Motes, J Barry, *Asst Prof.* Jefferson Community College, Fine Arts, Louisville KY (S)

Motley, A J, *Cur Manuscripts Coll.* Chicago Historical Society, Chicago IL

Motley, Anne, *Librn.* Colonial Williamsburg Foundation, Abby Aldrich Rockefeller Folk Art Center Library, Williamsburg VA

Mott, Eileen, *Statewide Exhib Coordr.* Virginia Museum of Fine Arts, Richmond VA

Mott, Rebecca, *Assoc Prof.* West Shore Community College, Division of Humanities & Fine Arts, Scottville MI (S)

Mott, Sarah, *Pres Board Trustees.* Attleboro Museum, Center for the Arts, Attleboro MA

Mottram, Ron, *Chmn.* Illinois State University, Art Dept, Normal IL (S)

Moty, Eleanor, *Prof.* University of Wisconsin, Madison, Dept of Art, Madison WI (S)

Motz, Leslie P, *Chmn.* Indiana-Purdue University, Dept of Fine Arts, Fort Wayne IN (S)

Moudry, Mary Lou, *Exec Dir.* Crow Wing County Historical Society, Brainerd MN

Mount, Pamela, *Co-Chmn Board Trustees.* Artworks, The Visual Art School of Princeton & Trenton, Trenton NJ

Mounty, Pamela, *Co-Chmn Board Trustees.* Artworks, Library, Trenton NJ

Nazionale, Nina, *Reference*, School of Visual Arts Library, New York NY

Neaderland, Louise, *Dir*, International Society of Copier Artists (ISCA), Brooklyn NY

Neagley, Linda, *Assoc*, Rice University, Dept of Art & Art History, Houston TX (S)

Neal, Berna, *Architecture Librn*, Arizona State University, Hayden Library, Tempe AZ

Neal, Berna E, *Dept Head*, Arizona State University, Architecture & Environmental Design Library, Tempe AZ

Neal, Christine Crafts, *Cur European & American Art*, University of Missouri, Museum of Art & Archaeology, Columbia MO

Neal, Gilbert L, *Chmn Dept*, Hastings College, Art Dept, Hastings NE (S)

Neal, Kenneth, *Art Librn*, Mayfield Regional Library, Mayfield Village OH

Nealis, Sharon, *Dir*, Allegany County Historical Society, History House, Cumberland MD

Near, Sue, *Cur*, Montana Historical Society, Helena MT

Neault, Carolyn, *Cur*, Columbus & Lowndes County Historical Society, Blewett-Lee Museum, Columbus MS

Nedelka, Helen, *Treas*, Brooklyn Historical Society, Brooklyn OH

Needle, Annette, *Treas*, Pen & Brush, Inc, New York NY

Neely, John, *Assoc Prof*, Utah State University, Dept of Art, Logan UT (S)

Neff, George, *Chmn Dept*, Rowan College of New Jersey, Dept of Art, Glassboro NJ (S)

Neff, Jean W, *Educ Cur*, Amherst Museum, Amherst NY

Neff, John Hallmark, *Dir Art Prog*, The First National Bank of Chicago, Art Collection, Chicago IL

Neff, Mary, *Coordr*, Marian College, Art Dept, Fond Du Lac WI (S)

Neidhardt, Jane, *Admin*, Washington University, Gallery of Art, Saint Louis MO

Neill, Peter, *Pres*, South Street Seaport Museum, New York NY

Neils, Jenifer, *Chmn*, Case Western Reserve University, Dept of Art History & Art, Cleveland OH (S)

Neiman, Jennifer, *Communications Dir*, Americans for the Arts, New York NY

Neimanas, Joyce, *Prof*, School of the Art Institute of Chicago, Chicago IL (S)

Neises, Lars, *Adjunct Asst Prof*, Spokane Falls Community College, Fine Arts Dept, Spokane WA (S)

Nell-Smith, Bruce, *Head Dept*, Newberry College, Dept of Art, Newberry SC (S)

Nelsen, Betty, *Instr*, American River College, Dept of Art, Sacramento CA (S)

Nelsen, Kenneth, *Assoc Prof*, Northwest Missouri State University, Dept of Art, Maryville MO (S)

Nelson, Arlyn, *Dept Head*, North Dakota State College of Science, Dept of Graphic Arts, Wahpeton ND (S)

Nelson, Bob, *Garden Cur*, Palm Beach County Parks & Recreation Department, Morikami Museum & Japanese Gardens, Delray Beach FL

Nelson, Burton R, *Cur Exhib*, Hastings Museum, Hastings NE

Nelson, Christina H, *Cur Decorative Arts*, Nelson-Atkins Museum of Art, Kansas City MO

Nelson, Craig, *Co Chair Fine Art*, Academy of Art College, Fine Arts Dept, San Francisco CA (S)

Nelson, David, *Pres*, Strasburg Museum, Strasburg VA

Nelson, Dean, *Museum Adminr*, Connecticut State Library, Museum of Connecticut History, Hartford CT

Nelson, Diane, *Pres*, Association of Medical Illustrators, Atlanta GA

Nelson, Ellen, *Exec Dir*, ArtSpace-Lima, Lima OH

Nelson, Fred, *Coordr Illustration*, Columbia College, Art Dept, Chicago IL (S)

Nelson, Gene, *Asst Dir*, Las Vegas-Clark County Library District, Las Vegas NV

Nelson, Harold, *Dir*, Long Beach Museum of Art, Long Beach CA

Nelson, Harold, *Cur*, Long Beach Museum of Art, Long Beach CA

Nelson, Irving, *Librn*, Navajo Nation Library System, Window Rock AZ

Nelson, James, *Preparator*, Westmoreland Museum of American Art, Greensburg PA

Nelson, John, *Lectr*, Culver-Stockton College, Art Dept, Canton MO (S)

Nelson, Julie D, *Exec Dir*, Quincy Art Center, Quincy IL

Nelson, Kierstie, *Admin Mgr*, Washington State University, Museum of Art, Pullman WA

Nelson, Kirk J, *Cur Glass*, The Sandwich Historical Society, Inc, Sandwich Glass Museum, Sandwich MA

Nelson, Kristi, *Prof Art History*, University of Cincinnati, School of Art, Cincinnati OH (S)

Nelson, Leslie, *Prof*, University of Wisconsin, Madison, Dept of Art, Madison WI (S)

Nelson, Lucie, *Cur*, State University of New York at Binghamton, University Art Gallery, Vestal NY

Nelson, Marilyn, *Asst Prof*, University of Arkansas, Art Dept, Fayetteville AR (S)

Nelson, Mary Carroll, *Founder*, Society of Layerists in Multi Media (SLMM), Albuquerque NM

Nelson, Michael, *Cur Educ*, Leigh Yawkey Woodson Art Museum, Inc, Wausau WI

Nelson, Michael, *Cur Educ*, Leigh Yawkey Woodson Art Museum, Inc, Art Library, Wausau WI

Nelson, Naomi, *Exec Dir*, The Community Education Center, Philadelphia PA

Nelson, Paula, *Dir*, Woodstock School of Art, Inc, Woodstock NY (S)

Nelson, Sarah, *Educ Cur*, Lehigh County Historical Society, Allentown PA

Nelson, Steve, *Asst Prof*, Hope College, Art Dept, Holland MI (S)

Nelson, Steven, *Lectr*, Tufts University, Dept of Art & Art History, Medford MA (S)

Nelson, Susan, *Prog Dir*, Saint Mary College, Art Program, Leavenworth KS (S)

Nelson, Susan, *Assoc Prof*, Indiana University, Bloomington, Henry Radford Hope School of Fine Arts, Bloomington IN (S)

Nelson, Warren C, *VPres & Treas*, Naples Art Gallery, Naples FL

Nelson Hoyle, Karen, *Cur*, University of Minnesota, Children's Literature Research Collections, Minneapolis MN

Nelson-Mayson, Lin, *Assoc Cur*, Minnesota Museum of American Art, Saint Paul MN

Nemec, Vernita, *Exec Dir & Pres*, Artists Talk on Art, New York NY

Nemiroff, Diane, *Cur Contemporary Art*, National Gallery of Canada, Ottawa ON

Nemour, Leslie, *Instr*, Miracosta College, Art Dept, Oceanside CA (S)

Nenno, Mardis, *Asst Prof*, Spokane Falls Community College, Fine Arts Dept, Spokane WA (S)

Neperud, Ronald, *Prof*, University of Wisconsin, Madison, Dept of Art, Madison WI (S)

Nervig, Denis J, *Photographer*, University of California, Los Angeles, Fowler Museum of Cultural History, Los Angeles CA

Nesbit, Molly, *Assoc Prof*, Vassar College, Art Dept, Poughkeepsie NY (S)

Nesbitt, Bill, *Cur*, Dundurn Castle, Hamilton ON

Nesbitt, Deane, *Dean Fine Arts*, Milwaukee Institute of Art & Design, Milwaukee WI (S)

Nesbitt, Perry L, *Dir*, Davidson College Visual Arts Center, William H Van Every Jr & Edward M Smith Galleries, Davidson NC

Neshat, Shirin, *Dir*, Storefront for Art & Architecture, New York NY

Nesin, Jeffrey, *Pres*, Memphis College of Art, Memphis TN (S)

Nesin, Jeffrey D, *Pres*, Memphis College of Art, G Pillow Lewis Memorial Library, Memphis TN

Ness, Gary, *Dir*, Ohio Historical Society, Columbus OH

Ness, Karla, *Prof*, Concordia College, Art Dept, Saint Paul MN (S)

Ness, Kim G, *Dir & Cur*, McMaster University, Museum of Art, Hamilton ON

Ness, Sharon, *Meeting Room Hostess*, Patterson Homestead, Dayton OH

Nesteruk, Janet, *Prof*, Northwestern Connecticut Community College, Fine Arts Dept, Winsted CT (S)

Nestor, James, *Instr*, Indiana University of Pennsylvania, Dept of Art & Art Education, Indiana PA (S)

Neth, Ted, *Dean Arts & Humanities*, Columbia Basin College, Esvelt Gallery, Pasco WA (S)

Netsky, Ron, *Head Dept*, Nazareth College of Rochester, Art Dept, Rochester NY (S)

Netsky, Ron, *Instr*, Woodstock School of Art, Inc, Woodstock NY (S)

Nettles, Bea, *In Charge Photography*, University of Illinois, Urbana-Champaign, School of Art & Design, Champaign IL (S)

Netzer, Nancy, *Dir*, Boston College, Museum of Art, Chestnut Hill MA

Netzer, Sylvia, *Deputy Chair*, City College of New York, Art Dept, New York NY (S)

Neu, Noreen, *Pub Relations*, Mendel Art Gallery & Civic Conservatory, Saskatoon SK

Neubert, George W, *Dir*, University of Nebraska, Lincoln, Sheldon Memorial Art Gallery & Sculpture Garden, Lincoln NE

Neumaiere, Diane, *Assoc Prof*, Rutgers, the State University of New Jersey, Mason Gross School of the Arts, New Brunswick NJ (S)

Neuman, Robert M, *Prof*, Florida State University, Art History Dept (R133B), Tallahassee FL (S)

Neuman de Vegvar, Carol, *Prof*, Ohio Wesleyan University, Fine Arts Dept, Delaware OH (S)

Neumann, J E, *Instr*, Western Illinois University, Art Dept, Macomb IL (S)

Neumann, Timothy C, *Dir*, Pocumtuck Valley Memorial Association, Memorial Hall, Deerfield MA

Neuroth, Karl O, *Chmn Fine Arts*, Keystone Junior College, Fine Arts Dept, Factoryville PA (S)

Neustadt, Laurie, *Asst Prof*, Edgewood College, Art Dept, Madison WI (S)

Nevadomi, Kenneth, *Prof*, Cleveland State University, Art Dept, Cleveland OH (S)

Nevens, Yvonne, *Dir Marketing*, San Jose Museum of Art, San Jose CA

Nevin, James, *Pres*, Danville Museum of Fine Arts & History, Danville VA

Nevins, Jerry, *Dir*, Albertus Magnus College, Art Dept, New Haven CT (S)

Nevitt, Steve, *Chmn*, Columbia College, Dept of Art, Columbia SC (S)

Newberry, James, *Prof*, East Texas State University, Dept of Art, Commerce TX (S)

Newbold, Theodore T, *Treas*, Fairmount Park Art Association, Philadelphia PA

Newhouse, Kathy, *VPres Board*, Coos Art Museum, Coos Bay OR

Newirth, Richard, *Asst Dir*, San Francisco City & County Art Commission, San Francisco CA

Newkirk, Dale, *Asst Prof*, Indiana University, Bloomington, Henry Radford Hope School of Fine Arts, Bloomington IN (S)

Newkirk, Sally, *Coordr*, Floyd County Museum, New Albany IN

Newland, Elaine, *Librn*, Museum of Art, Fort Lauderdale, Library, Fort Lauderdale FL

Newman, Alan B, *Exec Dir Imaging & Technical Serv*, The Art Institute of Chicago, Chicago IL

Newman, Constance Berry, *Under Secy*, Smithsonian Institution, Washington DC

Newman, Geoffrey, *Dean*, Montclair State University, Fine Arts Dept, Upper Montclair NJ (S)

Newman, Geoffrey, *Dean*, Montclair State University, Art Galleries, Upper Montclair NJ

Newman, Jerry, *Prof*, Lamar University, Art Dept, Beaumont TX (S)

Newman, Joanne K, *Exec Dir*, Mystic Art Association, Inc, Mystic CT

Newman, John, *Asst Prof*, University of Arkansas, Art Dept, Fayetteville AR (S)

Newman, Richard, *Prof*, Bradford College, Creative Arts Division, Bradford MA (S)

Newman, Ruth D, *Dir*, New York University, Washington Square East Galleries, New York NY

Newran, Sasha, *European & Contemporary*, Yale University, Art Gallery, New Haven CT

Newsome, Steven, *Dir,* Anacostia Museum, Washington DC

Newton, Earle W, *Dir,* Museum of the Americas, Brookfield VT

Newton, Earle W, *Dir,* Museum of the Americas, Library, Brookfield VT

Newton, Earle W, *Exec Dir,* Historic Saint Augustine Preservation Board, Saint Augustine FL

Newton, Harold, *Instr,* Pennsylvania College of Technology, Dept of Graphic Communications, Williamsport PA (S)

Newton, Verne W, *Dir,* National Archives & Records Administration, Franklin D Roosevelt Museum, Hyde Park NY

Newton, Verne W, *Dir,* National Archives & Records Administration, Franklin D Roosevelt Library, Hyde Park NY

Ney, Susan, *Chmn Dept,* Azusa Pacific University, College of Liberal Arts, Art Dept, Azusa CA (S)

Ng, Anthony, *Pub Relations & Develpment Dir,* Afro-American Historical & Cultural Museum, Philadelphia PA

Ngote, Lisa, *Lectr,* Oakland University, Dept of Art & Art History, Rochester MI (S)

Nian, Zhang Hong, *Instr,* Woodstock School of Art, Inc, Woodstock NY (S)

Nicandri, David, *Dir,* Washington State History Museum, Tacoma WA

Niceley, H T, *Chmn Dept,* Carson-Newman College, Art Dept, Jefferson City TN (S)

Nichelson, Jack C, *Prof,* University of Florida, Dept of Art, Gainesville FL (S)

Nicholas, Grace, *Admin Asst,* 1890 House-Museum & Center for The Arts, Cortland NY

Nicholas, Grace, *Admin Asst,* 1890 House-Museum & Center for The Arts, Kellogg Library & Reading Room, Cortland NY

Nicholls, Dave, *Cur Exhibits,* Anchorage Museum of History & Art, Anchorage AK

Nichols, Adele, *Gallery Dir,* Kennebec Valley Art Association, Harlow Gallery, Hallowell ME

Nichols, Charlotte, *Asst Prof,* Seton Hall University, College of Arts & Sciences, South Orange NJ (S)

Nichols, Charlotte, *Head Dept,* Adams State College, Dept of Visual Arts, Alamosa CO (S)

Nichols, Cheryl G, *Exec Dir,* Quapaw Quarter Association, Inc, Villa Marre, Little Rock AR

Nichols, Cheryl G, *Exec Dir,* Quapaw Quarter Association, Inc, Preservation Resource Center, Little Rock AR

Nichols, Frank, *Prof,* Fort Hays State University, Dept of Art, Hays KS (S)

Nichols, John D, *Chmn Board Trustees,* The Art Institute of Chicago, Chicago IL

Nichols, Judy, *Youth Serv Div Coordr,* Wichita Public Library, Wichita KS

Nichols, Lawrence, *Cur European Painting & Sculpture Before 1900,* Toledo Museum of Art, Toledo OH

Nichols, Madeleine, *Dance Cur,* The New York Public Library, Shelby Cullom Davis Museum, New York NY

Nichols, Ray, *Coordr Visual Communication,* University of Delaware, Dept of Art, Newark DE (S)

Nichols, Sarah C, *Cur Decorative Arts,* Carnegie Institute, Carnegie Museum of Art, Pittsburgh PA

Nichols, Walter, *Prof,* Mount Saint Mary's College, Visual & Performing Arts Dept, Emmitsburg MD (S)

Nicholson, Freda, *Chief Exec Officer,* Discovery Place Inc, Charlotte NC

Nicholson, Gail, *Assoc Dir,* Center for Exploratory & Perceptual Art, CEPA Gallery, Buffalo NY

Nicholson, Jane, *Cur Educ,* Paine Art Center & Arboretum, Oshkosh WI

Nicholson, Marilyn L, *Exec Dir,* Volcano Art Center, Hawaii National Park HI

Nicholson, Roy, *Assoc Prof,* Southampton College of Long Island University, Arts & Media Division, Southampton NY (S)

Nick, George, *VPres,* Concord Art Association, Concord MA

Nickel, Lorene, *Assoc Prof,* Mary Washington College, Art Dept, Fredericksburg VA (S)

Nickell, Jeff, *Cur,* Kern County Museum, Bakersfield CA

Nickell, Jeff, *Cur,* Kern County Museum, Library, Bakersfield CA

Nickels, Sara, *Grants Adminr,* Broward County Board of Commissioners Cultural Affairs Divison, Fort Lauderdale FL

Nickerson, Joseph, *Cur,* Chatham Historical Society, Old Atwood House Museum, Chatham MA

Nicklaus, Mike, *District Naturalist,* Grand Teton National Park Service, Colter Bay Indian Arts Museum, Moose WY

Nickson, Graham, *Dean,* New York Studio School of Drawing, Painting & Sculpture, New York NY (S)

Nickson, Graham, *Dean,* New York Studio School of Drawing, Painting & Sculpture, Gallery, New York NY

Nickson, Graham, *Dean,* New York Studio School of Drawing, Painting & Sculpture, Library, New York NY

Nickson, Guy, *Asst Dir,* Randolph Street Gallery, Chicago IL

Nicolescu, Alec, *Gallery Dir,* Kean College of New Jersey, Union NJ

Nicolescu, Alec, *Gallery Dir,* Kean College of New Jersey, Fine Arts Dept, Union NJ (S)

Nicoll, Jessica, *Cur Coll,* Portland Museum of Art, Portland ME

Nicolosi, Anthony S, *Dir,* Naval War College Museum, Newport RI

Nielsen, Christine, *Registrar,* Vancouver Art Gallery, Vancouver BC

Nielsen, Erik, *Prof,* Southwest Texas State University, Dept of Art, San Marcos TX (S)

Nielson, Nancy, *Team Leader Coll & Facilities,* State University of New York at New Paltz, Sojourner Truth Library, New Paltz NY

Nieman, John, *Dir Vol Servs,* Paine Art Center & Arboretum, Oshkosh WI

Niemiec, Ted, *Dir Educ,* Museum of Holography - Chicago, Chicago IL

Nierengarten-Smith, Beej, *Dir,* Laumeier Sculpture Park & Museum, Saint Louis MO

Nietcr, Gary, *Assoc Prof,* Grace College, Dept of Art, Winona Lake IN (S)

Niki, Kenji, *Librn,* Saint John's University, Asian Collection, Jamaica NY

Niles, Fred, *Assoc Prof,* University of Dayton, Visual Arts Dept, Dayton OH (S)

Niles, Katherine F, *Dir Art Prog,* PepsiCo Inc, Donald M Kendall Sculpture Garden, Purchase NY

Nill, Annegreth, *Assoc Cur Contemporary Art,* Dallas Museum of Art, Dallas TX

Nilsen, Norman, *Museum School Dir,* Philbrook Museum of Art, Tulsa OK

Nilson, Craig, *Prof,* Tidewater Community College, Art Dept, Portsmouth VA (S)

Nimmer, Dean, *Chmn Fine Arts, 2D,* Massachusetts College of Art, Boston MA (S)

Nirenberg, Jackie, *Public Relations,* Hidalgo County Historical Museum, Edinburg TX

Nisbet, Peter, *Cur,* Harvard University, Busch-Reisinger Museum, Cambridge MA

Nisenholt, Mark, *Prof,* Lakehead University, Dept of Visual Arts, Thunder Bay ON (S)

Nishimura, Tadaye, *Asst,* Phillips Exeter Academy, Frederic R Mayer Art Center & Lamont Gallery, Exeter NH

Nishioka, Reiko, *Educ Dir,* Palm Beach County Parks & Recreation Department, Morikami Museum & Japanese Gardens, Delray Beach FL

Niswonger, Gary, *Asst Prof,* Smith College, Art Dept, Northampton MA (S)

Niven, Don, *Chmn,* St Lawrence College, Dept of Visual & Creative Arts, Kingston ON (S)

Nivens, Charles, *Prof,* Eastern Illinois University, Art Dept, Charleston IL (S)

Nixon, Rick, *Exec Dir,* St Thomas Elgin Art Gallery, Saint Thomas ON

Nixon, Sean, *Assoc Prof,* University of Bridgeport, School of Arts, Humanities & Social Sciences, Bridgeport CT (S)

Nobili, Nicolas, *Chief Preparator,* Dartmouth College, Hood Museum of Art, Hanover NH

Noble, Cynthia, *Asst Prof,* Springfield College, Dept of Visual & Performing Arts, Springfield MA (S)

Noble, Joni, *Instr,* Northeast Louisiana University, Dept of Art, Monroe LA (S)

Noblett, David, *Prof,* Missouri Southern State College, Dept of Art, Joplin MO (S)

Noblett, Duane, *Assoc Prof,* Kansas State University, Art Dept, Manhattan KS (S)

Nochberg, Edwin, *VPres,* Sculpture Center School & Studios, New York NY

Nochin, Gail J, *Library Dir,* Paier College of Art, Inc, Library, Hamden CT

Nock, Walter J, *Museum Specialist,* United States Military Academy, West Point Museum, West Point NY

Noda, Takayo, *VPres Graphics,* Audubon Artists, Inc, New York NY

Nodal, Adolfo V, *General Mgr,* City of Los Angeles, Cultural Affairs Dept, Los Angeles CA

Noe, Cynthia, *Publicity & Gallery Dir,* Women And Their Work, Austin TX

Noe, Jerry, *Prof,* University of North Carolina at Chapel Hill, Art Dept, Chapel Hill NC (S)

Noe, Lendon H, *Asst Prof,* Lambuth University, Dept of Human Ecology & Visual Arts, Jackson TN (S)

Noe, Rita, *Treas,* Keokuk Art Center, Keokuk IA

Noeding, Faye S, *Owner,* Bent Museum & Gallery, Taos NM

Noeding, Otto T, *Owner,* Bent Museum & Gallery, Taos NM

Noffke, Gary, *Jewelry & Metalwork,* University of Georgia, Franklin College of Arts & Sciences, Lamar Dodd School of Art, Athens GA (S)

Nofziger, Lori, *Circulation Supvr,* Cleveland Institute of Art, Jessica Gund Memorial Library, Cleveland OH

Noga, Joseph L, *Coordr Grad Prog,* Rochester Institute of Technology, School of Printing, Rochester NY (S)

Nokes, Jack, *Dir Admin,* Austin Museum of Art at Laguna Gloria, Austin TX

Nolan, Ed, *Cur Spec Coll,* Washington State History Museum, Special Collections Div, Tacoma WA

Nolan, John, *Asst Dir,* Bob Jones University, Museum & Art Gallery, Greenville SC

Nolan, Liesel, *Head Art & Architecture Library,* University of Colorado, Art & Architecture Library, Boulder CO

Nolan, Mary, *Asst Dir & Ed,* C G Jung Institute of Chicago, Evanston IL

Nolan, Patricia E, *Special Arts Servs Dir,* American Society of Artists, Inc, Chicago IL

Nolan, Sandra, *Admin Support,* Arts of the Southern Finger Lakes, Corning NY

Nolan, William, *Visual Studies Chmn,* Atlanta College of Art, Atlanta GA (S)

Noland, Laura, *Lectr,* Centenary College of Louisiana, Dept of Art, Shreveport LA (S)

Noland, William, *Asst Prof Practice,* Duke University, Dept of Art & Art History, Durham NC (S)

Nolen, Kathlee, *Chmn,* Hollins College, Art Dept, Roanoke VA (S)

Nolf, Richard A, *Dir,* Saint Joseph Museum, Saint Joseph MO

Nolf, Richard A, *Dir,* Saint Joseph Museum, Library, Saint Joseph MO

Nolin, Anne-Marie, *Dir Communications,* Montclair Art Museum, Montclair NJ

Nonack, Steve, *Research Librn,* Boston Athenaeum, Boston MA

Nonn, Thomas I, *Chmn,* Kingsborough Community College, Dept of Art, Brooklyn NY (S)

Noon, Patrick, *Cur Prints Drawings & Rare Books,* Yale University, Yale Center for British Art, New Haven CT

Noon, Rosemary, *Dir,* Regis College, Fine Arts Center, Weston MA

Noone, Fran, *Info Servs Librn,* Lethbridge Community College, Buchanan Library, Lethbridge AB

Norberg, Deborah, *Deputy Dir,* San Jose Museum of Art, San Jose CA

Norbut, Tess, *Photo Research Cur*, Art Center College of Design, James Lemont Fogg Memorial Library, Pasadena CA

Nordan, Antoinette, *Cur*, University of Alabama at Birmingham, Visual Arts Gallery, Birmingham AL

Nordberg, Paul C, *Instr*, Pierce College, Art Dept, Woodland Hills CA (S)

Nordimann, Marie, *Registrar*, Washington University, Gallery of Art, Saint Louis MO

Nordstrom, Alison, *Dir*, Daytona Beach Community College, Southeast Museum of Photography, Daytona Beach FL

Nordtorp-Madson, Michelle, *Adjunct Asst Prof*, Hamline University, Dept of Art & Art History, Saint Paul MN

Nore, Nano, *Instr*, William Jewell College, Art Dept, Liberty MO (S)

Norman, Guy, *Asst Prof*, College of New Jersey, Art Dept, Trenton NJ (S)

Norman, Janis, *Chmn Educ Art*, University of the Arts, Philadelphia College of Art & Design, Philadelphia PA (S)

Norman, John, *Chmn*, College of the Desert, Art Dept, Palm Desert CA (S)

Norris, Andrea, *Dir*, University of Kansas, Spencer Museum of Art, Lawrence KS

Norris, Andrea, *Museum Dir*, University of Kansas, Kress Foundation Dept of Art History, Lawrence KS (S)

Norris, Debbie Hess, *Pres*, American Institute for Conservation of Historic & Artistic Works (AIC), Washington DC

Norris, E George, *Asst Dir*, University of West Florida, Art Gallery, Pensacola FL

Norris, Emilie, *Asst Cur*, Harvard University, Busch-Reisinger Museum, Cambridge MA

Norris, Julie, *Office Mgr*, Mississippi Museum of Art, Jackson MS

Norris, Trevor, *Exhib Designer*, University of Southern California, Fisher Gallery, Los Angeles CA

North, Kenda, *Chmn*, University of Texas at Arlington, Dept of Art & Art History, Arlington TX (S)

Northam, Cal, *Pres Board*, Yellowstone Art Center, Billings MT

Northern, Tamara, *Sr Cur Ethnographic Art*, Dartmouth College, Hood Museum of Art, Hanover NH

Northerner, Sara, *Asst Prof*, Utah State University, Dept of Art, Logan UT (S)

Northrop, Eileen, *Dir Admis*, Art Institute of Fort Lauderdale, Fort Lauderdale FL

Northrup, Jo Anne Severns, *Cur Exhibits & Coll*, Santa Clara University, de Saisset Museum, Santa Clara CA

Northup, Marjorie J, *Asst Dir Prog*, Reynolda House Museum of American Art, Winston-Salem NC

Norton, Ann Wood, *Chmn*, Providence College, Art & Art History Dept, Providence RI (S)

Norton, Elaine, *Exec Secy*, Jefferson County Historical Society, Watertown NY

Norton, James, *Instr*, Northeast Louisiana University, Dept of Art, Monroe LA (S)

Norton, Paul, *Prof*, University of Massachusetts, Amherst, Art History Program, Amherst MA (S)

Norton, Richard W, *Pres Board*, R W Norton Art Gallery, Shreveport LA

Noto, Sam, *VPres*, Washington Sculptors Group, Washington DC

Notz, John K, *Pres*, The Art Institute of Chicago, Textile Society, Chicago IL

Novacek, Vera, *Secy*, Art Gallery of Peterborough, Peterborough ON

Novak, Allen, *AV Librn*, Ringling School of Art & Design, Verman Kimbrough Memorial Library, Sarasota FL

Novak, Constance, *Supervising Librn*, The New York Public Library, Mid-Manhattan Library, Picture Collection, New York NY

Novak, Janos, *Frames Technician*, Balboa Art Conservation Center, San Diego CA

Novak, Philip, *Asst Dir*, Stamford Museum & Nature Center, Stamford CT

Novelli, Martin, *Dean Humanities*, Ocean County College, Humanities Dept, Toms River NJ (S)

Novetsky, Jason, *Instr*, Interlochen Arts Academy, Dept of Visual Art, Interlochen MI (S)

Nowosielski, Rodney, *Asst Prof*, South Dakota State University, Dept of Visual Arts, Brookings SD (S)

Noyes, Alex, *Studio Mgr*, Harvestworks, Inc, New York NY

Noyes, Julia, *Dir*, Noyes Art Gallery, Lincoln NE

Noyes, Julie, *Instr*, Northeast Community College, Dept of Liberal Arts, Norfolk NE (S)

Noyes, Nicholas, *Dir Library Servs*, Maine Historical Society, Library, Portland ME

Nozynski, John H, *Dir*, 1890 House-Museum & Center for The Arts, Cortland NY

Nuchims, Paul, *Prof*, West Virginia State College, Art Dept, Institute WV (S)

Nuetzel, Ron, *Adjunct Instr*, Maryville University of Saint Louis, Art Division, Saint Louis MO (S)

Nugent, Kim, *Dir Educ*, Art Institute of Houston, Houston TX (S)

Nugent, Kristina, *Dir*, Miracosta College, Art Dept, Oceanside CA (S)

Nugent, Patricia, *Assoc Prof*, Rosemont College, Division of the Arts, Rosemont PA (S)

Null, Charleen A, *Instr*, Pearl River Community College, Art Dept, Division of Fine Arts, Poplarville MS (S)

Nunez, Carla, *Coordr Community Servs*, Arts United of Greater Fort Wayne, Fort Wayne IN

Nunez, Mercedes, *Assoc Prof*, Bridgewater State College, Art Dept, Bridgewater MA (S)

Nunn, Nancy, *Exec Dir*, Historical Society of Kent County, Chestertown MD

Nunn, Natalee, *Dir*, Cowboy Artists of America Museum, Kerrville TX

Nunoo-Quarcoo, Franc, *Asst Prof*, University of Maryland, Baltimore County, Visual Arts Dept, Baltimore MD (S)

Nurse, Margaret, *Treas*, Society of Canadian Artists, Toronto ON

Nusbaum, Daniel C, *Chmn*, Mount Saint Mary's College, Visual & Performing Arts Dept, Emmitsburg MD (S)

Nussbaum, Donna Moog, *Pres*, Forum for Contemporary Art, Saint Louis MO

Nussle, William H, *Instr*, Nossi College of Art, Goodlettsville TN (S)

Nutting, David, *Pres*, Everson Museum of Art, Syracuse NY

Nuvayestewa, Grace, *Asst Librn*, Institute of American Indian Arts Museum, Alaska Native Culture & Arts Development, Santa Fe NM

Nuzum, Thomas, *Instr*, Charles Stewart Mott Community College, Art Area, School of Arts & Humanities, Flint MI (S)

Nybak, Arne, *Cur*, San Luis Obispo Art Center, San Luis Obispo CA

Nydorf, Roy, *Chmn*, Guilford College, Art Dept, Greensboro NC (S)

Nye, Timothy, *Dir Visual Arts Prog*, Thread Waxing Space, New York NY

Nyerges, Alex, *Dir*, Dayton Art Institute, Dayton OH

Nygren, Edward J, *Dir Art Division*, The Huntington Library, Art Collections & Botanical Gardens, San Marino CA

Nyhammer, Jayne, *VPres*, Pope County Historical Society, Pope County Museum, Glenwood MN

Nylander, Jane, *Dir*, Society for the Preservation of New England Antiquities, Boston MA

Nyman, William, *Asst Prof*, College of New Jersey, Art Dept, Trenton NJ (S)

Nyquist, John, *Chmn*, Association of Medical Illustrators, Atlanta GA

Oakley, Ron, *Chmn*, Davidson County Community College, Humanities Div, Lexington NC (S)

Oaks, Dallin H, *Chmn Board*, Polynesian Cultural Center, Laie HI

Oaks, Gary, *Asst Prof*, Southern University in New Orleans, Fine Arts & Philosophy Dept, New Orleans LA (S)

Oates, Robert, *Mgr Personnel*, Toledo Museum of Art, Toledo OH

Oatess, Jennifer, *Gallery Asst*, Loyola University of Chicago, Martin D'Arcy Gallery of Art, Chicago IL

Oats, Joclyn, *Architectural Studies & Graduate Studies*, Columbia College, Art Dept, Chicago IL (S)

Obata, Sue, *Pres*, Ontario Crafts Council, Artists in Stained Glass, Toronto ON

Obed, Martin, *Dept Chair Humanities*, Kalamazoo Valley Community College, Humanities Dept, Kalamazoo MI (S)

Oberndorf, Caroline, *Pres*, Cleveland Museum of Art, Print Club of Cleveland, Cleveland OH

Oberndorf, Caroline, *Pres*, Cleveland Institute of Art, Cleveland Art Association, Cleveland OH

Obershan, Micheal, *Temporary Asst Prof*, Georgia Southern University, Dept of Art, Statesboro GA (S)

Oberweiser, Don, *Staff Artist*, Oshkosh Public Museum, Oshkosh WI

Obetz, Tim, *Exhib Mgr*, Institute of Contemporary Art, Boston MA

O'Bourke, Rosemarie, *Dir*, Gulf Coast Community College, Division of Visual & Performing Arts, Panama City FL (S)

O'Brian, John, *Assoc Prof*, University of British Columbia, Dept of Fine Arts, Vancouver BC (S)

O'Brien, Barbara, *Gallery Dir*, Monserrat College of Art, Beverly MA (S)

O'Brien, Carole, *Dir Educ*, Butler Institute of American Art, Art Museum, Youngstown OH

O'Brien, Cookie, *Info Officer*, Historic Saint Augustine Preservation Board, Saint Augustine FL

O'Brien, Jerry, *Photo Acquisition*, National Archives of Canada, Visual & Sound Archives, Ottawa ON

O'Brien, Kevin, *Exec Dir*, Key West Art & Historical Society, East Martello Museum & Gallery, Key West FL

O'Brien, Mern, *Dir*, Dalhousie University, Art Gallery, Halifax NS

O'Brien, Nancy, *Dir*, Rehoboth Art League, Inc, Rehoboth Beach DE (S)

O'Brien, Walt, *Instr*, Umpqua Community College, Fine & Performing Arts Dept, Roseburg OR (S)

O'Brien, William, *Sales Mgr*, Walters Art Gallery, Baltimore MD

O'Brien, William A, *Exec Dir*, Great Lakes Historical Society, Island Seas Maritime Museum, Vermilion OH

Occhiuto, Joseph, *Rector*, San Carlos Cathedral, Monterey CA

Ocepek, Louis, *Prof*, New Mexico State University, Art Dept, Las Cruces NM (S)

Ochele, Claudia, *Cur Educ*, New Jersey Historical Society, Library, Newark NJ

Ochoa, Cristina, *Cur*, Self Help Graphics, Los Angeles CA

Ochoa, Jody, *Registrar*, Idaho Historical Museum, Boise ID

Ochoa, Maria, *Dir*, Hayward Area Forum of the Arts, Sun Gallery, Hayward CA

Ochs, Steven, *Asst Prof*, Southern Arkansas University, Dept of Art, Magnolia AR (S)

Ochs, Steven, *Asst Prof*, Southern Arkansas University, Art Dept Gallery & Magale Art Gallery, Magnolia AR

Ocken, Bob, *Instr*, The Arkansas Arts Center, Museum School, Little Rock AR (S)

Ockershausen, Cindylou, *Conservator*, National Portrait Gallery, Washington DC

O'Connell, Bonnie, *Asst Prof*, University of Nebraska at Omaha, Dept of Art & Art History, Omaha NE (S)

O'Connell, Clare, *Assoc Dir Develop*, Worcester Art Museum, Worcester MA

O'Connell, Daniel M, *Commissioner of Cultural Affairs & Artistic Dir*, City of Pittsfield, Berkshire Artisans, Pittsfield MA

O'Conner, David, *VPres*, Thornton W Burgess Society, Inc, Museum, Sandwich MA

O'Conner, Jim, *Finance Mgr*, Omaha Childrens Museum, Inc, Omaha NE

O'Connor, Charles, *Dir*, National Academy School of Fine Arts, New York NY (S)

O'Connor, Elizabeth, *Chair*, City College of New York, Art Dept, New York NY (S)

O'Connor, Harold, *Head*, Dunconor Workshops, Salida CO (S)

O'Connor, John A, *Prof*, University of Florida, Dept of Art, Gainesville FL (S)

O'Connor, Linda, *Asst*, Arts Council of Southwestern Indiana, Evansville IN

O'Connor, Martha Wilcox, *Cur Educ*, Morris Museum, Morristown NJ

O'Connor, Stanley J, *Prof*, Cornell University, Dept of the History of Art, Ithaca NY (S)

O'Connor, Thom, *Prof*, State University of New York at Albany, Art Dept, Albany NY (S)

O'Day, Kathy, *Pres*, Art League, Alexandria VA

Odden, Jan, *Shop Coordr*, Mankato Area Arts Council, Carnegie Art Center, Mankato MN

Oddo, Lynn, *Chmn*, New York Institute of Technology, Gallery, Old Westbury NY

Odel, Bill, *Chmn*, University of Massachusetts, Amherst, Art History Program, Amherst MA (S)

Odell, John B, *Coll Mgr*, United States Senate Commission on Art, Washington DC

Odem, Jennifer, *Instr*, Southwest Texas State University, Dept of Art, San Marcos TX (S)

Odevseff, Barbara, *Registrar*, Wichita Art Museum, Wichita KS

Odom, Anne, *Cur*, Marjorie Merriweather Post Foundation of DC, Hillwood Museum, Washington DC

Odom, Patt, *Head Visual Arts*, Mississippi Gulf Coast Community College-Jackson County Campus, Art Dept, Gautier MS (S)

Odoms, Carol, *Mgr*, Snake River Heritage Center, Weiser ID

O'Donnell, Hugh, *Dir*, Boston University, School of Visual Arts, Boston MA (S)

O'Donnell, Hugh, *Instr*, New York Studio School of Drawing, Painting & Sculpture, New York NY (S)

O'Donnell, Kendra, *Principal*, Phillips Exeter Academy, Frederic R Mayer Art Center & Lamont Gallery, Exeter NH

O'Donnell, Mark Stansbury, *Chmn*, University of Saint Thomas, Dept of Art History, Saint Paul MN (S)

O'Donnell, Pamela, *Gallery & Coll Asst*, Lawrence University, Wriston Art Center Galleries, Appleton WI

O'Donnell, Patricia, *Office Mgr*, Art Complex Museum, Duxbury MA

Oehler, Bonnie, *Adminr*, Door County, Miller Art Center, Sturgeon Bay WI

Oehlschlaeger, Frank, *Asst Prof*, Notre Dame College, Art Dept, Manchester NH (S)

Oertel, Dawn, *Instr*, Mount Mary College, Art Dept, Milwaukee WI (S)

Oertling, Sewall, *Chmn*, State University of New York College at Oswego, Art Dept, Oswego NY (S)

Oestreicher, Alene D, *Asst*, Baltimore Museum of Art, E Kirkbride Miller Art Library, Baltimore MD

Oettinger, Marion, *Sr Cur*, San Antonio Museum of Art, San Antonio TX

Offner, Elliot, *VPres*, National Sculpture Society, New York NY

Offner, Elliot, *Prof*, Smith College, Art Dept, Northampton MA (S)

Ogden, Dale, *Cur History*, Indiana State Museum, Indianapolis IN

Ogle, Philip, *Prof*, College of Visual Arts, Saint Paul MN (S)

O'Gorman, James F, *Prof*, Wellesley College, Art Dept, Wellesley MA (S)

O'Hara, Bruce, *Assoc Prof*, Tougaloo College, Art Dept, Tougaloo MS (S)

O'Hara, Cate, *Pub Affairs Mgr*, Cincinnati Institute of Fine Arts, Taft Museum, Cincinnati OH

O'Hara, J, *Assoc Prof*, Northern Arizona University, School of Art & Design, Flagstaff AZ (S)

O'Hara, Laura, *Photo Archivist*, Judah L Magnes Museum, Berkeley CA

O'Hara, Virginia, *Assoc Cur*, Brandywine River Museum, Chadds Ford PA

Ohashi, Ross, *Treas*, Wing Luke Asian Museum, Seattle WA

O'Hear, James, *Assoc Dean*, Catholic University of America, School of Architecture & Planning, Washington DC (S)

O'Hern, John D, *Dir*, Arnot Art Museum, Elmira NY

Ohr, Christine, *Services Dir*, Sierra Arts Foundation, Reno NV

Oja, Vivien, *Prog Assoc*, University of Minnesota, Minneapolis, Split Rock Arts Program, Minneapolis MN (S)

Ojala, Meg, *Asst Prof*, Saint Olaf College, Art Dept, Northfield MN (S)

Okada, Connie, *Librn*, University of Washington, Art Library, Seattle WA

Okada, Merle, *Asst Librn*, Japan Society, Inc, Library, New York NY

Okaya, Michiko, *Gallery Dir*, Lafayette College, Morris R Williams Center for the Arts, Art Gallery, Easton PA

Okazaki, Arthur, *Prof*, Tulane University, Sophie H Newcomb Memorial College, New Orleans LA (S)

O'Keefe, Michael J, *Chmn*, Oklahoma Christian University of Science & Arts, Dept of Art & Design, Oklahoma City OK (S)

O'Keefe, Paul, *Div Coordr Fine Art*, Kent State University, School of Art, Kent OH (S)

O'Keefe, Ruth, *Chmn Art History & Liberal Arts*, Kendall College of Art & Design, Frank & Lyn Van Steenberg Library, Grand Rapids MI

O'Keefe, Tom, *Pres*, North Shore Arts Association, Inc, Art Gallery, Gloucester MA

O'Keeffe, Timothy, *Asst Prof*, University of Wisconsin-Stout, Dept of Art & Design, Menomonie WI (S)

Okosh, Hanan, *Grants Asst*, Broward County Board of Commissioners Cultural Affairs Divison, Fort Lauderdale FL

Okoye, Ikem, *Lectr*, Northwestern University, Evanston, Dept of Art History, Evanston IL (S)

O'Laughlin, Thomas C, *Admin Mgr*, Albuquerque Museum of Art & History, Albuquerque NM

Olbrantz, John, *Deputy Dir*, Whatcom Museum of History and Art, Bellingham WA

Oldach, Linda R, *Dir*, Mount Wachusett Community College, Library, Gardner MA

Oldaker, William, *Instr*, West Virginia Wesleyan College, Dept of Fine Arts, Buckhannon WV (S)

Olds, Clifton C, *Dir Art History*, Bowdoin College, Art Dept, Brunswick ME (S)

Olds, Susan, *Gallery & Events Coordr*, Cornish College of the Arts, Fisher Gallery, Seattle WA

O'Leary, Daniel, *Dir*, Portland Museum of Art, Portland ME

O'Leary, Dennis, *Dir*, Boise Art Museum, Boise ID

O'Leary, Jay, *Division Chmn of Fine Arts*, Wayne State College, Nordstrand Visual Arts Gallery, Wayne NE

O'Leary, Jay, *Div Chmn*, Wayne State College, Art Dept, Wayne NE (S)

Olijnyk, Michael, *Cur*, Mattress Factory, Pittsburgh PA

Olin, Ferris, *Cur*, Rutgers, The State University of New Jersey, Mary H Dana Women Artists Series, New Brunswick NJ

Oliner, Stan, *Cur Books & Manuscripts*, Colorado Historical Society, Colorado History Museum, Denver CO

Olitski, Eve, *Asst Prof*, University of Hartford, Hartford Art School, West Hartford CT (S)

Olivant, David, *Prof*, California State University, Art Dept, Turlock CA (S)

Olive, Nancy, *Chmn*, Sioux Falls College, Dept of Art, Sioux Falls SD (S)

Oliver, Cornelia, *Prof*, Mary Washington College, Art Dept, Fredericksburg VA (S)

Oliver, Donna, *Dir Tours*, Edsel & Eleanor Ford House, Grosse Pointe MI

Oliver, Judith, *Assoc Prof*, Colgate University, Dept of Art & Art History, Hamilton NY (S)

Oliver, Patricia, *Environmental Design Chmn*, Art Center College of Design, Pasadena CA (S)

Oliver-Smith, Kerry, *Cur Educ*, University of Florida, Samuel P Harn Museum of Art, Gainesville FL

Ollman, Arthur, *Dir*, Museum of Photographic Arts, San Diego CA

O'Looney, James, *Assoc Prof*, Mohawk Valley Community College, Advertising Design & Production, Utica NY (S)

O'Loughlin, Deborah, *Educ Coordr*, Noah Webster House, Inc, Noah Webster House, West Hartford CT

Olpin, Robert, *Chmn*, Utah Arts Council, Chase Home Museum of Utah Folk Art, Salt Lake City UT

Olpin, Robert S, *Dean*, University of Utah, Art Dept, Salt Lake City UT (S)

Olsberg, Nicholas, *Chief Cur*, Canadian Centre for Architecture, Library, Montreal PQ

Olsen, Caren, *Cur*, Honeywell Inc, Art Collection, Minneapolis MN

Olsen, Charles, *Chmn*, St Francis College, Fine Arts Dept, Loretto PA (S)

Olsen, Dennis, *Assoc Prof*, University of Texas at San Antonio, Division of Visual Arts, San Antonio TX (S)

Olsen, Jim, *Prof*, Dana College, Art Dept, Blair NE (S)

Olsen, Karen, *Gallery Dir*, Mount Mary College, Art Dept, Milwaukee WI (S)

Olsen, Kathleen, *Dir*, Washington & Lee University, Gallery of DuPont Hall, Lexington VA

Olsen, Kathy, *Pres*, Coppini Academy of Fine Arts, San Antonio TX

Olsen, Kathy, *Pres*, Coppini Academy of Fine Arts, Library, San Antonio TX

Olsen, Mel, *Prof*, University of Wisconsin-Superior, Programs in the Visual Arts, Superior WI (S)

Olsen, Sandra H, *Dir*, Niagara University, Castellani Art Museum, Niagara NY

Olsen, Steven, *Operation Mgr*, Church of Jesus Christ of Latter-day Saints, Museum of Church History & Art, Salt Lake City UT

Olsen, Susan, *Dir*, Frank Lloyd Wright Pope-Leighey House, Mount Vernon VA

Olsen, Susan, *Dir*, Woodlawn Plantation, Mount Vernon VA

Olsen, Valerie L, *Admin Dean*, Glassell School of Art, Houston TX (S)

Olshan, Bernard, *VPres*, New York Artists Equity Association, Inc, New York NY

Olson, Dennis, *Instr*, Amarillo College, Art Dept, Amarillo TX (S)

Olson, Dona, *Cur & Mgr*, New England Maple Museum, Rutland VT

Olson, Eva M, *Exec Dir*, Hyde Park Art Center, Chicago IL

Olson, George, *Prof*, College of Wooster, Dept of Art, Wooster OH (S)

Olson, James, *Chief Exhib*, Natural History Museum of Los Angeles County, Los Angeles CA

Olson, Janis, *Cur Coll*, Whatcom Museum of History and Art, Bellingham WA

Olson, Jim, *Dir*, Colorado Mountain College, Visual & Performing Arts, Vale CO (S)

Olson, Joann, *Librn*, Miami University, Wertz Art & Architecture Library, Oxford OH

Olson, Kristina, *Cur*, West Virginia University, Laura & Paul Mesaros Galleries, Morgantown WV

Olson, Kristina, *Prof*, West Virginia University, College of Creative Arts, Morgantown WV (S)

Olson, Linda, *Dir*, Minot State University, Northwest Art Center, Minot ND

Olson, Marilyn, *Treas*, Muttart Public Art Gallery, Calgary AB

Olson, Maude, *Treas*, Pemaquid Group of Artists, Pemaquid Art Gallery, Pemaquid Point ME

Olson, Patricia, *Instr*, Saint Olaf College, Art Dept, Northfield MN (S)

Olson, Sarah, *Supt*, National Park Service, Weir Farm National Historic Site, Wilton CT

Olson, Thomas H, *Pres*, New England Maple Museum, Rutland VT

Olson-Janjic, Kathleen, *Assoc Prof*, Washington and Lee University, Division of Art, Lexington VA (S)

Olson-Rudenko, Jennifer, *Registrar*, Colgate University, Picker Art Gallery, Hamilton NY

Olsson, Kathy, *Chmn*, Lynnwood Arts Centre, Simcoe ON

Olszewski, Edward J, *Prof*, Case Western Reserve University, Dept of Art History & Art, Cleveland OH (S)

Olt, Frank, *Assoc Prof*, C W Post Center of Long Island University, School of Visual & Performing Arts, Brookville NY (S)

Olton, Charles S, *Dean*, Parsons School of Design, New York NY (S)

Oltvedt, Carl, *Prof*, Moorhead State University, Dept of Art, Moorhead MN (S)

Olvera, John, *Prof*, Winthrop University, Dept of Art & Design, Rock Hill SC (S)

O'Malley, Dennis M, *Dir*, Rhode Island College, Edward M Bannister Gallery, Providence RI

O'Malley, Jeannette, *Asst Dir*, Southwest Museum, Los Angeles CA

O'Malley, Karen, *Instr*, Marylhurst College, Art Dept, Marylhurst OR (S)

O'Malley, Kathleen, *Assoc Registrar*, Dartmouth College, Hood Museum of Art, Hanover NH

O'Malley, William, *Rare Books Cur*, Columbia University, Avery Architectural & Fine Arts Library, New York NY

O'Malley, William, *Instr*, Charles Stewart Mott Community College, Art Area, School of Arts & Humanities, Flint MI (S)

Omar, Margit, *Assoc Prof*, University of Southern California, School of Fine Arts, Los Angeles CA (S)

O'Mara, Joan, *Assoc Dean*, Washington and Lee University, Division of Art, Lexington VA (S)

Omari, Mikelle, *Assoc Prof Art History*, University of Arizona, Dept of Art, Tucson AZ (S)

O'Meara, Nancy G, *Exec Dir*, Philadelphia Museum of Art, Women's Committee, Philadelphia PA

Omelia, John F, *Chmn Fine Arts Dept*, Manhattan College, School of Arts, Bronx NY (S)

Omogbai, Meme, *Deputy Dir Finance*, Newark Museum Association, The Newark Museum, Newark NJ

Ondrizek, Geraldine, *Asst Prof Art*, Reed College, Dept of Art, Portland OR (S)

O'Neal, Mary, *Prof*, University of California, Berkeley, College of Letters & Sciences-Art Dept, Berkeley CA (S)

O'Neil, Elaine, *Dir*, Rochester Institute of Technology, School of Photographic Arts & Sciences, Rochester NY (S)

O'Neil, Julie, *Secy*, Wing Luke Asian Museum, Seattle WA

O'Neil, Karen, *Instr*, Woodstock School of Art, Inc, Woodstock NY (S)

O'Neil, William, *Pres*, Massachusetts College of Art, Boston MA (S)

O'Neill, Colleen, *Dir & Cur*, Memorial University of Newfoundland, Sir Wilfred Grenfell College Art Gallery, Corner Brook NF

O'Neill, John, *Cur Manuscripts & Rare Books*, Hispanic Society of America, Library, New York NY

O'Neill, Yvette, *Instr*, Lower Columbia College, Art Dept, Longview WA (S)

Onken, Michael O, *Grad Studies*, Southern Illinois University, School of Art & Design, Carbondale IL (S)

Onyile, Onyile B, *Assoc Prof*, Georgia Southern University, Dept of Art, Statesboro GA (S)

Opar, Barbara A, *Architecture Librn & Dept Head*, Syracuse University, Library, Syracuse NY

Opodocer, Paul, *Cur Native American Art*, Bower's Museum, Santa Ana CA

Oppenheim, Phyllis, *Colls Mgr*, College of Southern Idaho, Herrett Center for Arts & Science, Twin Falls ID

Opper, Edward, *Acad Dean Educ*, Greenville Technical College, Visual Arts Dept, Greer SC (S)

Oppio, Amy, *Public Relations Officer*, Nevada Museum Of Art, Reno NV

Orcutt, William, *Pres*, Ventura County Historical Society, Museum of History & Art, Ventura CA

Ore, Joyce, *Dir Pub Relations*, Hastings College, Art Dept, Hastings NE (S)

Orenstein, Cindy, *Assoc Dir*, Allentown Art Museum, Allentown PA

Orenstein, Phil, *Assoc Prof*, Rutgers, the State University of New Jersey, Mason Gross School of the Arts, New Brunswick NJ (S)

Oresky, Melissa, *Conservator*, Spertus Institute of Jewish Studies, Asher Library, Chicago IL

Oritsky, Mimi, *Instr*, Main Line Art Center, Haverford PA (S)

Orkiszewski, Paul, *Music Librn*, Rice University, Alice Pratt Brown Library of Art, Architecture & Music, Houston TX

Orlando, Fran, *Dir Exhib*, Bucks County Community College, Hicks Art Center, Newtown PA

Orloff, Chet, *Exec Dir*, Oregon Historical Society, Portland OR

Ornelas, La Verne, *Chmn*, Northeastern Illinois University, Art Dept, Chicago IL (S)

O'Rourke, Marilyn, *Librn*, New Canaan Historical Society, New Canaan CT

Orozco, Sylvia, *Exec Dir*, MEXIC-ARTE Museum, Austin TX

Orr, Amy, *Asst Prof*, Rosemont College, Division of the Arts, Rosemont PA (S)

Orr, Clint, *Graphic Design*, University of South Alabama, Dept of Art & Art History, Mobile AL (S)

Orr, Estelle, *Instr*, Rancho Santiago College, Art Dept, Santa Ana CA (S)

Orr-Cahall, Christina, *Dir*, Norton Gallery & School of Art, Inc, Norton Museum of Art, West Palm Beach FL

Orr-Cahall, Christina, *Dir*, Norton Gallery & School of Art, Inc, Library, West Palm Beach FL

Orr-Cahall, Christina, *Exec Dir Norton Museum*, Florida Art Museum Directors Association, Vero Beach FL

Orsine, Gary, *Chmn*, Boise State University, Art Dept, Boise ID (S)

Orta, Wilda, *Dean*, Hostos Center for the Arts & Culture, Bronx NY

Orth, Fredrick, *Dir*, San Diego State University, University Gallery, San Diego CA

Orth, Fredrick, *Dir*, San Diego State University, School of Art, Design & Art History, San Diego CA (S)

Ortiz, Benjamin, *Cur Art*, Discovery Museum, Bridgeport CT

Ortiz, Donald J, *VPres*, Guadalupe Historic Foundation, Santuario de Guadalupe, Santa Fe NM

Ortiz, Emilio I, *Dir*, Guadalupe Historic Foundation, Santuario de Guadalupe, Santa Fe NM

Ortiz, John, *Exec Dir*, Mid-America All-Indian Center, Indian Center Museum, Wichita KS

Ortiz, Jose, *Asst mgr*, The Metropolitan Museum of Art, The Cloisters, New York NY

Ortiz, Raphael, *Prof*, Rutgers, the State University of New Jersey, Mason Gross School of the Arts, New Brunswick NJ (S)

Ortner, Frederick, *Chmn*, Knox College, Dept of Art, Galesburg IL (S)

Orwig, Rosemarie, *Arts Outreach Coordr*, Redding Museum of Art & History, Redding CA

Osborne, Frederick S, *Dir*, Pennsylvania Academy of the Fine Arts, Philadelphia PA (S)

Osborne, John L, *Prof*, University of Victoria, Dept of History in Art, Victoria BC (S)

Osbun, Jack, *Chmn*, Wittenberg University, Art Dept, Springfield OH (S)

Oser, Marilyn, *Public Relations Dir*, Wave Hill, Bronx NY

O'Shello, Wanda, *Ed Arts Quarterly*, New Orleans Museum of Art, New Orleans LA

Osler, John C, *Chmn*, Alberta Foundation for the Arts, Edmonton AB

Osline, Naida, *Dir*, Huntington Beach Art Center, Huntington Beach CA

Osmond, Lynn J, *Pres*, Chicago Architecture Foundation, Chicago IL

Ostby, Lloyd, *Librn*, Memphis College of Art, G Pillow Lewis Memorial Library, Memphis TN

Ostby, Lloyd, *Librn*, Memphis College of Art, Library, Memphis TN

Oste-Alexander, Pia, *Instr*, Woodstock School of Art, Inc, Woodstock NY (S)

Osterhus, Cynthia B, *Dir*, Horizons Unlimited Supplementary Educational Center, Art Gallery, Salisbury NC

Osterman, Greg, *Instr*, Grand Canyon University, Art Dept, Phoenix AZ (S)

Osterman, William, *Asst Prof*, Rochester Institute of Technology, School of Photographic Arts & Sciences, Rochester NY (S)

Ostermiller, Jerry, *Exec Dir*, Columbia River Maritime Museum, Astoria OR

Ostheimer, Andy, *Dir*, San Jose State University, Art Gallery, San Jose CA

Ostman, Jessica, *Prog Dir*, Saint Cloud State University, Atwood Center Gallery Lounge, Saint Cloud MN

Ostrow, Mindy, *Asst Dir*, State University of New York at Oswego, Tyler Art Gallery, Oswego NY

Ostrow, Stephen E, *Chief*, Library of Congress, Prints & Photographs Division, Washington DC

Ostrow, Steven F, *Chmn & Assoc Prof*, University of California, Riverside, Dept of the History of Art, Riverside CA (S)

Ostrzewski, Donna, *Exhibits Coordr*, Gallery Association of New York State, Hamilton NY

O'Sullivan, Thomas, *Cur Art*, Minnesota Historical Society, Library, Saint Paul MN

Oszuscik, Philippe, *Art Historian*, University of South Alabama, Dept of Art & Art History, Mobile AL (S)

Otis, Helen K, *Conservator-in-Charge Paper*, The Metropolitan Museum of Art, New York NY

Otis, James, *Facilities Chmn*, Print Club of Albany, Albany NY

O'Toole, Judith H, *Chief Exec Officer & Dir*, Westmoreland Museum of American Art, Greensburg PA

O'Toole, Judith H, *Dir*, Westmoreland Museum of American Art, Art Reference Library, Greensburg PA

Ott, Greg, *Headmaster*, Delphian School, Sheridan OR (S)

Ott, Lili, *Dir*, Johns Hopkins University, Evergreen House, Baltimore MD

Ott, Lili, *Dir*, Johns Hopkins University, Homewood House Museum, Baltimore MD

Ott, Wendell, *Dir*, Tyler Museum of Art, Tyler TX

Ott, Wendell, *Dir*, Tyler Museum of Art, Reference Library, Tyler TX

Ottaviano, Scott, *Prof*, Cazenovia College, Center for Art & Design Studies, Cazenovia NY (S)

Otto, Guttorn, *Instr*, Southampton Art School, Southampton ON (S)

Otto, Jeffrey, *Asst Prof*, College of New Jersey, Art Dept, Trenton NJ (S)

Otto, Martha, *Head Archaeology*, Ohio Historical Society, Columbus OH

Otton, William, *Dir*, Art Museum of South Texas, Corpus Christi TX

Oubre, Jean, *Coordr*, Crowley Art Association, The Gallery, Crowley LA

Ouellette, David, *Dir Galleries*, Florida School of the Arts, Visual Arts, Palatka FL (S)

Ourecky, Irma, *Pres*, Wilber Czech Museum, Wilber NE

Overby, Osmund, *Prof*, University of Missouri, Art History & Archaeology Dept, Columbia MO (S)

Overson, Kristin, *Asst to Dir*, The One Club for Art & Copy, New York NY

Overstreet, Joe, *Art Dir*, Kenkeleba House, Inc, Kenkeleba Gallery, New York NY

Overton, Harold, *Chmn*, Charleston Southern University, Dept of Language & Visual Art, Charleston SC (S)

Overvoorde, Chris Stoffel, *Prof*, Calvin College, Art Dept, Grand Rapids MI (S)

Ovrebo, Reidun, *Chair*, West Virginia State College, Art Dept, Institute WV (S)

Owczarek, Robert, *Div Chmn*, Pine Manor College, Visual Arts Dept, Chestnut Hill MA (S)

Owczarski, Marian, *Dir*, St Mary's Galeria, Orchard Lake MI

Owen, Paula, *Dir*, Southwest Craft Center, Emily Edwards & Ursuline Sales Gallery, San Antonio TX

Owen, Robert, *Public Relations & Marketing*, Tyler Museum of Art, Reference Library, Tyler TX

Owens, Arthur, *Asst Dir Operations*, Los Angeles County Museum of Art, Los Angeles CA

Owens, Carlotta, *Asst Cur*, National Gallery of Art, Index of American Design, Washington DC

Owens, Chris, *Coll Mgr*, Saint Gregory's Abbey & College, Mabee-Gerrer Museum of Art, Shawnee OK

Owens, David, *Instr*, Okaloosa-Walton Community College, Dept of Fine & Performing Arts, Niceville FL (S)

Owens, Helen McKenzie, *Pres*, Kelly-Griggs House Museum, Red Bluff CA

Owens, John, *Asst Prof*, Central Missouri State University, Art Dept, Warrensburg MO (S)

Owens, Melissa, *Dir*, Saint Gregory's Abbey & College, Mabee-Gerrer Museum of Art, Shawnee OK

Owens, Nancy, *Admin Asst*, Kamloops Art Gallery, Kamloops BC

Owens, Robert G, *Head Div Fine Arts & Humanities*, Fayetteville State University, Fine Arts & Humanities, Fayetteville NC (S)

Owens, Robert L, *Chmn*, North Georgia College, Fine Arts Dept, Dahlonega GA (S)

Owens, Wendy, *Asst Dir Museum Serv*, Canadian Centre for Architecture, Library, Montreal PQ

Ownbey, Ronald B, *Chmn*, Mount San Antonio College, Art Dept, Walnut CA (S)

Oxman, M, *Prof*, American University, Dept of Art, Washington DC (S)

Oyuela, Raul, *Dir*, The Florida Museum of Hispanic & Latin American Art, Miami FL

Ozdogan, Turker, *Prof*, George Washington University, Dept of Art, Washington DC (S)

Ozolis, Auseklis, *Academy Dir*, New Orleans Academy of Fine Arts, Academy Gallery, New Orleans LA

Ozubko, Christopher, *Dir*, University of Washington, School of Art, Seattle WA (S)

Pabst, K T, *Dir*, Mechanics' Institute Library, San Francisco CA

Pace, Gary, *Asst Dir*, Board of Parks & Recreation, The Parthenon, Nashville TN

Pace, James R, *Chmn*, University of Texas at Tyler, Dept of Art, Tyler TX (S)

Pace, Lorenzo, *Dir*, Montclair State University, Art Galleries, Upper Montclair NJ

Pacheco, Diana, *Acting Dir*, Brockton Public Library System, Joseph A Driscoll Art Gallery, Brockton MA

Pacini, Marina, *Cur*, Rhodes College, Jessie L Clough Art Memorial for Teaching, Memphis TN

Packard, Daniel, *Prof*, University of South Dakota, Department of Art, College of Fine Arts, Vermillion SD (S)

Packard, Leo, *Dir SIACM*, Illinois State Museum, Illinois Artisans & Visitors Centers, Chicago IL

Paddock, Eric, *Cur Photog*, Colorado Historical Society, Colorado History Museum, Denver CO

Padfield, Clive, *Exec Dir*, Alberta Foundation for the Arts, Edmonton AB

Padgett, James, *Advisor*, Wilberforce University, Art Dept, Wilberforce OH (S)

Padgett, Michael, *Assoc Cur*, Princeton University, The Art Museum, Princeton NJ

Padgett, Michael, *Gallery Dir*, University of Wisconsin, Gallery 101, River Falls WI

Padgett, Michael, *Chmn*, University of Wisconsin-River Falls, Art Dept, River Falls WI (S)

Padgett, R Paul, *Assoc Prof*, West Liberty State College, Art Dept, West Liberty WV (S)

Padilla, Debra, *Assoc Dir*, Social & Public Art Resource Center, (SPARC), Venice CA

Paepke, Lorrie, *Instr*, Mount Mary College, Art Dept, Milwaukee WI (S)

Paganco, Don, *Pres*, Pastel of the West Coast, Sacramento Fine Arts Center, Carmichael CA

Page, Amanda, *Cur*, Springfield Art & Historical Society, Miller Art Center, Springfield VT

Page, Casey, *Gallery Asst*, St Mary's College of Maryland, The Dwight Frederick Boyden Gallery, Saint Mary City MD

Page, Colin, *Dir Admis*, Pacific Northwest College of Art, Portland OR (S)

Page, Debra, *Grad Res Asst*, University of Missouri, Museum of Art & Archaeology, Columbia MO

Page, Donna, *Adjunct Asst Prof*, Drew University, Art Dept, Madison NJ (S)

Page, Greg, *Assoc Prof*, Cornell University, Dept of Art, Ithaca NY (S)

Page, Kathryn, *Cur Maps & Documents*, Louisiana Department of Culture, Recreation & Tourism, Louisiana Historical Center Library, New Orleans LA

Page, Marcia, *Project Dir*, Craft & Folk Art Museum, Los Angeles CA

Pageau, Yvan, *Coordr*, Les Editions Intervention, Inter-Le Lieu, Documentation Center, Quebec PQ

Pagel, Angelika, *Assoc Prof*, Weber State University, Dept of Visual Arts, Ogden UT (S)

Paggie, Michael, *Bus Mgr*, Madison Art Center, Madison WI

Pagh, Barbara, *Asst Prof*, University of Rhode Island, Dept of Art, Kingston RI (S)

Paglia, Lenora, *Asst Museum Librn*, The Metropolitan Museum of Art, Photograph & Slide Library, New York NY

Pai, John, *Videographer*, Wing Luke Asian Museum, Seattle WA

Pai, Yun-feng, *Dir*, Taipei Economic & Cultural Office, Chinese Information & Culture Center Library, New York NY

Paier, Daniel, *VPres*, Paier College of Art, Inc, Library, Hamden CT

Paier, Jonathan E, *Pres*, Paier College of Art, Inc, Hamden CT (S)

Paier, Jonathan E, *Pres*, Paier College of Art, Inc, Library, Hamden CT

Paige, J M, *Librn*, Art Gallery of Greater Victoria, Library, Victoria BC

Paige, Robert, *Prof*, Philadelphia Community College, Dept of Art, Philadelphia PA (S)

Paine, Rosalie, *Pres*, Pence Gallery, Davis CA

Paine, Wesley M, *Dir*, Board of Parks & Recreation, The Parthenon, Nashville TN

Painter, Wendy, *Pres*, Visual Art Exchange, Raleigh NC

Paizy, Guy, *Instr*, University of Puerto Rico, Dept of Fine Arts, Rio Piedras PR (S)

Pajak, Fraz, *Assoc Prof*, Converse College, Art Dept, Spartanburg SC (S)

Pakasaar, Helga, *Cur*, Art Gallery of Windsor, Windsor ON

Pakhlazhgan, Tanya, *Librn*, The Metropolitan Museum of Art, Robert Lehman Collection Library, New York NY

Pal, Pratapaditya, *Cur Indian & Southeast Asian Art*, Los Angeles County Museum of Art, Los Angeles CA

Palazzolo, T, *Prof*, City Colleges of Chicago, Daley College, Chicago IL (S)

Palchick, Bernard, *Prof*, Kalamazoo College, Art Dept, Kalamazoo MI (S)

Palermo, James, *Dir Admis*, Art Institute of Philadelphia, Philadelphia PA (S)

Palermo, Joseph, *Dir*, Las Vegas Art Museum, Las Vegas NV

Paley, Albert, *Prof*, Rochester Institute of Technology, School of Art & Design, Rochester NY (S)

Palijczuk, Wasyl, *Prof*, Western Maryland College, Dept of Art & Art History, Westminster MD (S)

Palisin, B, *Instr*, Sacramento City College, Art Dept, Sacramento CA (S)

Palladino-Craig, Allys, *Dir*, Florida State University, Museum of Fine Arts, Tallahassee FL

Pallas, James, *Prof*, Macomb Community College, Art Dept, Warren MI (S)

Palma, Madelon, *Book & Gift Shop Mgr*, San Jose Museum of Art, San Jose CA

Palmer, Charles, *Dir*, Rehoboth Art League, Inc, Rehoboth Beach DE

Palmer, Cheryl, *Dir Educ*, Mint Museum of Art, Charlotte NC

Palmer, David, *Dir Exhib*, Newark Museum Association, The Newark Museum, Newark NJ

Palmer, Nancy, *Chmn Fine Arts*, Corcoran School of Art, Washington DC (S)

Palmer, Richard, *Coordr Exhib*, Museum of Modern Art, New York NY

Palmer, Robert, *Assoc Prof*, Cleveland Institute of Art, Cleveland OH (S)

Palmer, Sharon S, *Exec Dir*, Columbia County Historical Society, Columbia County Museum, Kinderhook NY

Palmer, Sharon S, *Dir*, Columbia County Historical Society, Library, Kinderhook NY

Palmer Adisa, Opal, *Ethnic Art Studies*, California College of Arts & Crafts, Oakland CA (S)

Palumbo, Nancy, *Deputy Commissioner Admin & Fiscal Prog Affairs*, New York Office of Parks, Recreation & Historic Preservation, Natural Heritage Trust, Albany NY

Palusky, Robert, *Instr*, Hamilton College, Art Dept, Clinton NY (S)

Paluzzi, Karen A, *Asst Dir*, Sculpture Chicago, Inc, Chicago IL

Pamer, Laurence, *Cur Exhib*, Museum of Art, Fort Lauderdale, Fort Lauderdale FL

Panczenko, Russell, *Dir*, University of Wisconsin-Madison, Elvehjem Museum of Art, Madison WI

Panepinto, Tressa, *Marketing Coordr*, Sangre de Cristo Arts & Conference Center, Pueblo CO

Pang, Toni, *Supv*, City of Irvine, Fine Arts Center, Irvine CA (S)

Pang, Tony, *Dir*, City of Irvine, Irvine Fine Arts Center, Irvine CA

Panko, Walter, *Head*, University of Illinois, Chicago, Health Science Center, Biomedical Visualizations, Chicago IL (S)

Pankow, David P, *Asst Prof*, Rochester Institute of Technology, School of Printing, Rochester NY (S)

Pantazzi, Michael, *Assoc Cur European Art*, National Gallery of Canada, Ottawa ON

Panyard, Gerry, *Instr*, Madonna University, Art Dept, Livonia MI (S)

Panzer, Mary, *Cur Photographs*, National Portrait Gallery, Washington DC

Panzer, Nora, *Educ Prog Chief*, National Museum of American Art, Washington DC

Panzer, Robert, *Exec Dir*, Visual Artists & Galleries Association (VAGA), New York NY

Paoletta, Donald, *Dir*, Nebraska Wesleyan University, Elder Gallery, Lincoln NE

Paoletta, Donald, *Chmn*, Nebraska Wesleyan University, Art Dept, Lincoln NE (S)

Paoletti, John T, *Prof*, Wesleyan University, Art Dept, Middletown CT (S)

Papadopoulos, Joan, *Pres*, Swedish American Museum Association of Chicago, Chicago IL

Papageorge, Tod, *Prof*, Yale University, School of Art, New Haven CT (S)

Papanek-Miller, Mary-Ann, *Assoc Prof*, Bemidji State University, Visual Arts Dept, Bemidji MN (S)

Papas, Diana, *Pres*, Springfield Art League, Springfield MA

Pape, David, *Pres*, Thornton W Burgess Society, Inc, Museum, Sandwich MA

Pape, Eva, *Cur*, New England Center for Contemporary Art, Brooklyn CT

Papich, Paul, *Deputy Dir External Affairs*, Baltimore Museum of Art, Baltimore MD

Papier, Maurice A, *Head Dept*, Saint Francis College, Art Dept, Fort Wayne IN (S)

Papineau, Karen, *Registrar*, George Walter Vincent Smith Art Museum, Springfield MA

Pappas, David, *Dir*, Friends University, Edmund Stanley Library, Wichita KS

Pappas, Marilyn, *Chmn Fine Arts, 3-D*, Massachusetts College of Art, Boston MA (S)

Paratore, Philip, *Prof*, University of Maine at Augusta, Division of Fine & Performing Arts, Augusta ME (S)

Parcell, S, *Assoc Prof*, Technical University of Nova Scotia, Faculty of Architecture, Halifax NS (S)

Pardington, Ralph, *Instr*, College of Santa Fe, Art Dept, Santa Fe NM (S)

Pardo, Jorge, *Public Arts Mgr*, Public Corporation for the Arts, Visual & Performing Arts Registry, Long Beach CA

Pardue, Diana, *Cur Colls*, Heard Museum, Phoenix AZ

Pardue, Diana, *Chief Cur*, The National Park Service, United States Department of the Interior, The Statue of Liberty National Monument, New York NY

Pare, Jean-Pierre, *Asst to Cur*, Musee du Seminaire de Quebec, Quebec PQ

Paredes, Gusteavo, *Exec Dir*, Randolph Street Gallery, Chicago IL

Paret, John J, *Dir*, Kateri Galleries, The National Shrine of the North American Martyrs, Auriesville NY

Parfitt, Chris, *Pres*, Birmingham-Bloomfield Art Association, Birmingham MI

Parfitt, Tina, *VPres*, Birmingham-Bloomfield Art Association, Birmingham MI

Parham, Annette, *Acquisitions Librn*, Colonial Williamsburg Foundation, John D Rockefeller, Jr Library, Williamsburg VA

Parham, Shannon, *General Mgr*, Association of American Editorial Cartoonists, Raleigh NC

Parisi, Beulah, *Acting Librn*, Contemporary Crafts Association & Gallery, Library, Portland OR

Parisi, Salvador, *Pastor*, Mission San Miguel Museum, San Miguel CA

Parisien, Diane, *Comptroller*, Montclair Art Museum, Montclair NJ

Parisien, Louise, *Coordr Expositions*, La Galerie Montcalm la galerie d'art de la Villede Hull, Hull PQ

Park, Anna, *Instr*, Wayne Art Center, Wayne PA (S)

Park, Christy, *Chmn Art*, Massachusetts College of Art, Boston MA (S)

Park, Kyong, *Founder*, Storefront for Art & Architecture, New York NY

Park, Leland, *Librn*, Davidson College Visual Arts Center, Library, Davidson NC

Park, Marlene, *Prof*, John Jay College of Criminal Justice, Dept of Art, Music & Philosophy, New York NY (S)

Park, Marlene, *Prof*, City University of New York, PhD Program in Art History, New York NY (S)

Park, Seho, *Assoc Prof*, Winona State University, Dept of Art, Winona MN (S)

Parke, David L, *Dir*, Hershey Museum, Hershey PA

Parke-Harrison, Robert, *Asst Prof*, College of the Holy Cross, Dept of Visual Arts, Worcester MA (S)

Parker, Bart, *Prof*, University of Rhode Island, Dept of Art, Kingston RI (S)

Parker, Carolyn, *Head Dept*, Peace College, Art Dept, Raleigh NC (S)

Parker, Cheryl Ann, *Asst Dir*, West Bend Art Museum, West Bend WI

Parker, Collier B, *Chmn Dept*, Delta State University, Fielding L Wright Art Center, Cleveland MS

Parker, Collier B, *Chmn*, Delta State University, Dept of Art, Cleveland MS (S)

Parker, Cynthia, *Office Mgr*, Ella Sharp Museum, Jackson MI

Parker, Dana, *Dir*, Florence Museum of Art, Science & History, Florence SC

Parker, Donna, *Cur Exhib*, Western Kentucky University, Kentucky Museum, Bowling Green KY

Parker, Elizabeth, *Asst Chief*, Library of Congress, Prints & Photographs Division, Washington DC

Parker, Ethel, *Treas*, Wayne County Historical Society, Wooster OH

Parker, Harry S, *Dir*, Fine Arts Museums of San Francisco, M H de Young Memorial Museum & California Palace of the Legion of Honor, San Francisco CA

Parker, Phil, *Coordr Graphic Design*, Florida School of the Arts, Visual Arts, Palatka FL (S)

Parker, Robert, *Treas*, Octagon Center for the Arts, Ames IA

Parker, Robert, *Dir*, Church of Jesus Christ of Latter Day Saints, Mormon Visitors' Center, Independence MO

Parker, S M, *Instr*, Western Illinois University, Art Dept, Macomb IL (S)

Parker, Sue T, *Assoc Librn*, Ohio Historical Society, National Afro American Museum & Cultural Center, Wilberforce OH

Parker, Teresa J, *Cur*, Elmhurst Art Museum, Elmhurst IL

Parker, Thomas, *Chmn Dept*, Drury College, Art & Art History Dept, Springfield MO (S)

Parker-Bell, Barbara, *Asst Prof*, Pittsburg State University, Art Dept, Pittsburg KS (S)

Parkerson, Jane, *Cur Educ*, Polk Museum of Art, Lakeland FL

Parkhurst, Charles, *Trustee*, Hill-Stead Museum, Farmington CT

Parkinson, Carol, *Dir*, Harvestworks, Inc, New York NY

Parkinson, George, *Division Chief & State Archivist*, Ohio Historical Society, Archives-Library Division, Columbus OH

Parkinson, John, *Treas*, Museum of Modern Art, New York NY

Parks, Ann B, *Asst Dir*, Landmark Society of Western New York, Inc, Wenrich Memorial Library, Rochester NY

Parks, Ann Laura, *Dir Visual Arts*, Morgan County Foundation, Inc, Madison-Morgan Cultural Center, Madison GA

Parks, Janet, *Cur Drawings & Archives*, Columbia University, Avery Architectural & Fine Arts Library, New York NY

Parks, Leroy B, *Pres Board Trustees*, Beck Center for the Cultural Arts, Lakewood OH

Parks, Maggie, *Gallery Co-Cur*, Art Studios of Western New York, Buffalo NY

Parks, Robert, *Cur Autograph Manuscripts*, Pierpont Morgan Library, New York NY

Parks-Kirby, Carie, *Chmn*, Alma College, Clack Art Center, Alma MI (S)

Parmenter, Marian Wintersteen, *Dir*, San Francisco Museum of Modern Art, Rental Gallery, San Francisco CA

Parmet, Joe, *Exec Dir*, Long Beach Jewish Community Center, Center Gallery, Long Beach CA

Parris, David, *Cur Science*, New Jersey State Museum, Trenton NJ

Parrish, Maurice, *Deputy Dir*, Detroit Institute of Arts, Detroit MI

Parrott, Frances, *Chmn*, Iowa Western Community College, Art Dept, Council Bluffs IA (S)

Parry, Lee, *Prof Art History*, University of Arizona, Dept of Art, Tucson AZ (S)

Parry, Pamela, *Registrar*, Norton Gallery & School of Art, Inc, Norton Museum of Art, West Palm Beach FL

Parshall, Peter W, *Prof Art History & Humanities*, Reed College, Dept of Art, Portland OR (S)

Parsley, Jacque, *Dir*, Bank One Gallery, Louisville KY

Parson, Del, *Asst Prof*, Dixie College, Art Dept, Saint George UT (S)

Parson, Leon, *Instr*, Ricks College, Dept of Art, Rexburg ID (S)

Parsons, Bernard, *Pres*, Arthur Roy Mitchell Memorial Inc, Museum of Western Art, Trinidad CO

Parsons, Jean, *Acad Visual Arts Chmn*, Interlochen Arts Academy, Dept of Visual Art, Interlochen MI (S)

Parsons, Jeanette, *VPres*, West Hills Unitarian Fellowship, Portland OR

Parsons, Marcia M, *Head Librn*, University of Texas at Austin, Fine Arts Library, Austin TX

Parsons, Oz, *Pres*, Ontario Crafts Council, The Craft Gallery, Toronto ON

Parsons, Richard, *Prof*, Lakeland Community College, Visual Arts Dept, Mentor OH (S)

Parsons, Susan, *Registrar*, Dawson City Museum & Historical Society, Dawson City YT

Partin, Bruce, *Chmn*, Roanoke College, Fine Arts Dept-Art, Salem VA (S)

Partington, Judith, *Librn*, The Filson Club, Reference & Research Library, Louisville KY

Partridge, Kathleen, *Instr*, Mohawk Valley Community College, Advertising Design & Production, Utica NY (S)

Parvis, Paul B, *Asst Dir*, Connecticut Historical Society, Hartford CT

Paschall, Jo Anne, *Dir Nexus Press*, Nexus Contemporary Art Center, Atlanta GA

Paschen, Stephen H, *Dir*, Summit County Historical Society, Akron OH

Pask, Kelly, *Asst Cur*, Dartmouth College, Hood Museum of Art, Hanover NH

Pasquine, Ruth, *Cur*, Arkansas Arts Center, Little Rock AR

Pass, Dwayne, *Instr*, Tulsa Junior College, Art Dept, Tulsa OK (S)

Passanise, Gary, *Artist-in-Residence*, Webster University, Art Dept, Webster Groves MO (S)

Pastan, Elizabeth Carson, *Assoc Prof*, Emory University, Art History Dept, Atlanta GA (S)

Paster, Carol, *Exec Dir*, Creative Art Center, Pontiac MI (S)

Paster, Carol, *Exec Dir*, Creative Arts Center, Pontiac MI

Pasternak, Anne, *Exec Dir*, Creative Time, New York NY

Pastore, Shiela, *Vol Coordr*, Palo Alto Cultural Center, Palo Alto CA

Pasztorri, Esther, *Dir Grad Studies*, Columbia University, Dept of Art History & Archaeology, New York NY (S)

Patano, Tony, *Coordr Interior Design*, Columbia College, Art Dept, Chicago IL (S)

Patch, Charles, *Systems Dir*, Kemper & Leila Williams Foundation, New Orleans LA

Pate, Annette, *Med Adjunct Prof*, Oklahoma Christian University of Science & Arts, Dept of Art & Design, Oklahoma City OK (S)

Paterakis, Angela, *Prof*, School of the Art Institute of Chicago, Chicago IL (S)

Paterniti, John, *Chief Financial Officer*, San Diego Museum of Art, San Diego CA

Patierno, Mary, *Instr*, Sarah Lawrence College, Dept of Art History, Bronxville NY (S)

Patnode, J Scott, *Prof*, Gonzaga University, Dept of Art, Spokane WA (S)

Patnode, J Scott, *Dir & Cur*, Gonzaga University, Jundt Art Museum, Ad Art Gallery, Spokane WA

Patrick, Brian, *Assoc Prof*, University of Utah, Art Dept, Salt Lake City UT (S)

Patrick, Darry, *Prof*, Sam Houston State University, Art Dept, Huntsville TX (S)

Patrick, Jill, *Dir*, Ontario College of Art & Design, Dorothy H Hoover Library, Toronto ON

Patrick, Rick, *Chmn Dept*, Holy Names College, Art Dept, Oakland CA (S)

Patrick, Vernon, *Chmn*, California State University, Chico, University Art Gallery, Chico CA

Patrick, Vernon, *Chmn*, California State University, Chico, Art Dept, Chico CA (S)

Patrick, Vernon, *Instr*, California State University, Chico, Art Dept, Chico CA (S)

Patridge, Margaret, *Pub Information*, Walker Art Center, Minneapolis MN

Patt, Susan, *Prof*, La Sierra University, Art Dept, Riverside CA (S)

Patten, James, *Cur Contemporary Art*, London Regional Art & Historical Museums, London ON

Pattern, Lloyd, *Ceramisist*, University of South Alabama, Dept of Art & Art History, Mobile AL (S)

Patterson, Aubrey B, *Pres*, Bank of Mississippi, Art Collection, Tupelo MS

Patterson, Belinda A, *Lectr*, Lambuth University, Dept of Human Ecology & Visual Arts, Jackson TN (S)

Patterson, Burns, *Public Affairs*, Historic Hudson Valley, Tarrytown NY

Patterson, Curtis, *Assoc Prof*, Atlanta College of Art, Atlanta GA (S)

Patterson, Don, *Cur Asst*, Dundurn Castle, Hamilton ON

Patterson, Joanne, *Registrar*, Buffalo Bill Memorial Association, Buffalo Bill Historical Center, Cody WY

Patterson, L Dale, *Archivist*, Archives & History Center of the United Methodist Church, Madison NJ

Patterson, Michelle, *Prof*, North Carolina Central University, Art Dept, Durham NC (S)

Patterson, Myron, *Fine Arts Librn*, University of Utah, Marriott Library, Salt Lake City UT

Patterson, Richard, *Instr*, Marian College, Art Dept, Indianapolis IN (S)

Patterson, Richard, *Dir*, Old Barracks Museum, Trenton NJ

Patterson, Vivian, *Assoc Cur Coll*, Williams College, Museum of Art, Williamstown MA

Patterson, Willis R, *Prof*, Central Wyoming College, Art Center, Riverton WY (S)

Patton, Larry, *Dean*, Butler County Community College, Art Dept, El Dorado KS (S)

Patton, Oscar, *Chmn*, Abraham Baldwin Agricultural College, Art & Humanities Dept, Tifton GA (S)

Patton, Sharon, *Assoc Prof,* University of Michigan, Ann Arbor, Dept of History of Art, Ann Arbor MI (S)

Patton, Thomas, *Prof,* University of Missouri, Saint Louis, Dept of Art & Art History, Saint Louis MO (S)

Paukert, Karel, *Chief Cur Musical Arts,* Cleveland Museum of Art, Cleveland OH

Paul, Alison, *Exec Dir,* Pelham Art Center, Pelham NY

Paul, April, *Coll Cur,* The Chaim Gross Studio Museum, New York NY

Paul, Gayle, *Cur Art,* Portsmouth Museums, Art Center, Portsmouth VA

Paul, John, *VPres,* Heritage Center, Inc, Pine Ridge SD

Paul, Kathy, *Dir Develop & Community Relations,* Madison Art Center, Madison WI

Pauley, Ed, *Dir Education,* Huntington Museum of Art, Huntington WV

Paulnisano, Susan, *Instr,* Indiana University of Pennsylvania, Dept of Art & Art Education, Indiana PA (S)

Paulsen, Richard, *Chmn,* Elmhurst College, Art Dept, Elmhurst IL (S)

Paulson, Alan, *Prof,* Gettysburg College, Dept of Visual Arts, Gettysburg PA (S)

Paulson, Robert, *Dir,* Southern Illinois University, School of Art & Design, Carbondale IL (S)

Paulson, Sheryl, *Coordr Art Gallery,* Willmar Community College, Art Dept, Willmar MN (S)

Paulson, Wesley E, *Pres,* Maryland College of Art & Design, Silver Spring MD (S)

Pavlik, John, *Dir,* Fisher Scientific Company, Fisher Collection of Alchemical & Historical Pictures, Pittsburgh PA

Pavovic, Miutin, *Designer,* Telfair Museum of Art, Savannah GA

Pawel, Nancy, *Lectr,* Incarnate Word University of the Arts & Sciences, Art Dept, San Antonio TX (S)

Pawlicki, Patti, *Instr,* Suomi International College of Art & Design, Fine Arts Dept, Hancock MI (S)

Pawloski, Carole, *Librn,* Eastern Michigan University, Art Dept Slide Collection, Ypsilanti MI

Pawlowicz, Peter, *Assoc Prof,* East Tennessee State University, Dept of Art & Design, Johnson City TN (S)

Pawlowski, Andrew, *Pres,* Sculptor's Society of Canada, Toronto ON

Payne, Christopher, *Chmn,* Huntingdon College, Dept of Art, Montgomery AL (S)

Payne, Chuck, *Exhibit Specialist,* Headquarters Fort Monroe, Dept of Army, Casemate Museum, Fort Monroe VA

Payne, Couric, *Gen Mgr Museum Stores,* Fine Arts Museums of San Francisco, M H de Young Memorial Museum & California Palace of the Legion of Honor, San Francisco CA

Payne, Jennifer Cover, *Exec Dir,* Cultural Alliance of Greater Washington, Washington DC

Payne, Marlene, *Dir,* Rocky Mount Arts Center, Rocky Mount NC

Payne, Thomas, *Dept Head,* Wartburg College, Dept of Art, Waverly IA (S)

Payton, Cydney, *Dir,* Boulder Museum of Contemporary Art, Boulder CO

Payton, Neal, *Vis Asst Prof,* Catholic University of America, School of Architecture & Planning, Washington DC (S)

Peace, Bernie K, *Prof,* West Liberty State College, Art Dept, West Liberty WV (S)

Peak, Elizabeth, *Assoc Prof,* Georgia Southern University, Dept of Art, Statesboro GA (S)

Peak, Marianne, *Supt,* Adams National Historic Site, Quincy MA

Peak, Sarah, *Acting Dir,* Northern Illinois University, Art Gallery in Chicago, Chicago IL

Peaney, Diane, *Dir Literature,* Idaho Commission on the Arts, Boise ID

Pear, William H, *Cur,* Nichols House Museum, Inc, Boston MA

Pearce, John N, *Dir Planning & Prog,* James Monroe Museum, James Monroe Memorial Library, Fredericksburg VA

Pearce-Moses, Richard, *Documenting Coll Archivist & Automation Coordr,* Heard Museum, Library & Archives, Phoenix AZ

Peard Lawson, Karol Anne, *Chief Cur,* Columbus Museum, Columbus GA

Pearlstein, Connie, *Office Mgr,* Pacific Grove Art Center, Pacific Grove CA

Pearlstein, Elinor, *Assoc Cur Chinese Art,* The Art Institute of Chicago, Department of Asian Art, Chicago IL

Pearman, Sara Jane, *Slide Librn,* Cleveland Museum of Art, Ingalls Library, Cleveland OH

Pearse, Harold, *Assoc Dean,* Nova Scotia College of Art & Design, Halifax NS (S)

Pearson, A Faye, *Cur,* Kings County Historical Society and Museum, Hampton NB

Pearson, Gary, *Instr,* Ricks College, Dept of Art, Rexburg ID (S)

Pearson, Jim, *Prof,* Vincennes University Junior College, Art Dept, Vincennes IN (S)

Pearson, John, *Prof,* Oberlin College, Dept of Art, Oberlin OH (S)

Pearson, J Robert, *Exec Dir,* Bellingrath Gardens & Home, Theodore AL

Pearson, Mary, *Pub Relations,* Green Hill Center for North Carolina Art, Greensboro NC

Pearson, Stacey, *Art, Music & Audiovisual Mgr,* Allen County Public Library, Art, Music & Audiovisual Services, Fort Wayne IN

Pease, Edwin, *Prof,* College of William & Mary, Dept of Fine Arts, Williamsburg VA (S)

Peatross, C Ford, *Cur Architecture,* Library of Congress, Prints & Photographs Division, Washington DC

Peck, Judith, *Prof,* Ramapo College of New Jersey, School of Contemporary Arts, Mahwah NJ (S)

Peck, Susan, *Grants Coordr,* Arts of the Southern Finger Lakes, Corning NY

Peck, William H, *Cur Ancient Art,* Detroit Institute of Arts, Detroit MI

Peckam, Cynthia A, *Cur,* Sandy Bay Historical Society & Museums, Sewall Scripture House-Old Castle, Rockport MA

Pecoravo, Patricia, *Asst Registrar & Cur Traveling Exhib,* New Orleans Museum of Art, New Orleans LA

Pederson, Ron, *Chmn Dept,* Aquinas College, Art Dept, Grand Rapids MI (S)

Pedley, John G, *Prof,* University of Michigan, Ann Arbor, Dept of History of Art, Ann Arbor MI (S)

Peebler, Anna, *Rare Books Librn,* Rosenberg Library, Galveston TX

Peebles, Billy, *Instr,* The Arkansas Arts Center, Museum School, Little Rock AR (S)

Peer, Charles, *Head Dept,* John Brown University, Art Dept, Siloam Springs AR (S)

Pefferman, Curt, *Instr,* Eastern Iowa Community College, Art Dept, Clinton IA (S)

Peglau, Michael, *Asst Prof,* Drew University, Art Dept, Madison NJ (S)

Pehrson, Clint, *Pres,* Allied Arts of Seattle, Inc, Seattle WA

Peirce, Donald, *Cur Decorative Art,* High Museum of Art, Atlanta GA

Peiser, Judy, *Exec Dir,* Center for Southern Folklore, Memphis TN

Pelfrey, Bob, *Chmn Fine Arts Div & Instr,* Cuesta College, Art Dept, San Luis Obispo CA (S)

Pelfrey, Don, *Pres,* Middletown Fine Arts Center, Middletown OH

Pelham, Jennifer, *Publicity,* Marin County Watercolor Society, Greenbrae CA

Pell, Anthony D, *Pres,* Fort Ticonderoga Association, Ticonderoga NY

Pellerito, Marlene, *Adjunct Instr,* Saginaw Valley State University, Dept of Art & Design, University Center MI (S)

Pelrine, Diane, *Assoc Dir Curatorial Services & Cur African & Oceanic Pre-Columbian Art,* Indiana University, Art Museum, Bloomington IN

Pels, Marsha, *Instr,* Sarah Lawrence College, Dept of Art History, Bronxville NY (S)

Peltier, Cynthia, *Asst Dir,* Bucknell University, Center Gallery, Lewisburg PA

Pelton, Robert, *Cur,* The Barnum Museum, Bridgeport CT

Peluso, Marta, *Dir,* Cuesta College, Cuesta College Art Gallery, San Luis Obispo CA

Pelzel, Thomas O, *Prof Emeriti,* University of California, Riverside, Dept of the History of Art, Riverside CA (S)

Penafiel, Guillermo, *Asst Prof,* University of Wisconsin-Stevens Point, Dept of Art & Design, Stevens Point WI (S)

Pence, Marc, *Registrar,* Portland Art Museum, Portland OR

Pendell, David, *Assoc Prof,* University of Utah, Art Dept, Salt Lake City UT (S)

Pendergraft, Norman, *Prof,* North Carolina Central University, Art Dept, Durham NC (S)

Pendlebury, Theresa, *Slide Cur,* Art Center College of Design, James Lemont Fogg Memorial Library, Pasadena CA

Pendleton, Debbie, *Asst Dir Public Services,* Alabama Department of Archives & History, Museum Galleries, Montgomery AL

Pendleton, Edith, *Head Dept Fine & Performing Arts,* Edison Community College, Dept of Fine & Performing Arts, Fort Myers FL (S)

Peniston, Robert C, *Dir,* Washington & Lee University, Lee Chapel & Museum, Lexington VA

Peniston, William A, *Librn,* Newark Museum Association, Newark Museum Library, Newark NJ

Penka, Ruth, *Exec Dir,* Fitchburg Historical Society, Fitchburg MA

Penn, Barbara, *Assoc Prof Painting & Drawing,* University of Arizona, Dept of Art, Tucson AZ (S)

Penn, Beverly, *Asst Prof,* Southwest Texas State University, Dept of Art, San Marcos TX (S)

Penn, Doris Brown, *Public Art & Design Asst,* Broward County Board of Commissioners Cultural Affairs Divison, Fort Lauderdale FL

Pennell, Allison, *Librn,* Fine Arts Museums of San Francisco, Library, San Francisco CA

Pennington, Claudia L, *Assoc Dir,* Naval Historical Center, The Navy Museum, Washington DC

Pennington, Estill Curtis, *Cur,* Morris Museum of Art, Augusta GA

Pennington, Mary Anne, *Dir,* Huntington Museum of Art, Huntington WV

Penny, Carl O, *Librn,* New Orleans Museum of Art, New Orleans LA

Penny, Carl O, *Librn,* New Orleans Museum of Art, Felix J Dreyfous Library, New Orleans LA

Penny, David, *VChmn,* Detroit Artists Market, Detroit MI

Pennypacker, Mona, *Prog Coordr,* Bridge Center for Contemporary Art, El Paso TX

Penuel, Jaime, *Lectr,* North Dakota State University, Division of Fine Arts, Fargo ND (S)

Penwell, Donna, *Dir,* Monterey History & Art Association, Maritime Museum of Monterey, Monterey CA

Pepall, Rosalina, *Cur Early Canadian Art,* Montreal Museum of Fine Arts, Montreal PQ

Pepich, Bruce W, *Dir,* Wustum Museum Art Association, Racine WI

Pepich, Bruce W, *Dir,* Wustum Museum Art Association, Charles A Wustum Museum of Fine Arts, Racine WI

Pepich, Bruce W, *Dir,* Wustum Museum Art Association, Wustum Art Library, Racine WI

Pepin, Suzanne, *Visual Arts Coordr,* City of Eugene, Hult Center, Jacobs Gallery, Eugene OR

Pepion, Loretta F, *Cur,* Museum of the Plains Indian & Crafts Center, Browning MT

Pepp, Lara, *Asst Dir,* Cartoon Art Museum, San Francisco CA

Pepper, Jerold, *Librn,* Adirondack Historical Association, Adirondack Museum, Blue Mountain Lake NY

Pepper, Jerold L, *Librn,* Adirondack Historical Association, Library, Blue Mountain Lake NY

Perchinske, Marlene, *Dir,* University of Missouri, Museum of Art & Archaeology, Columbia MO

Percy, Ann, *Cur Drawings,* Philadelphia Museum of Art, Philadelphia PA

Perdue, Lynne, *Registrar*, University of Georgia, Georgia Museum of Art, Athens GA

Peres, Michael, *Chmn Biomedical Photo Communications*, Rochester Institute of Technology, School of Photographic Arts & Sciences, Rochester NY (S)

Perez, Angel, *Dir*, Institute of Puerto Rican Culture, Centro Ceremonial de Caguana, San Juan PR

Perez, Sandra M, *Exec Dir*, Association of Hispanic Arts, New York NY

Perez, Vince, *Drawing*, California College of Arts & Crafts, Oakland CA (S)

Perih, Catrin, *Dir Educ*, South Street Seaport Museum, New York NY

Perinet, Francine, *Dir*, Oakville Galleries, Centennial Gallery and Gairloch Gallery, Oakville ON

Perisho, Sally L, *Dir*, Metropolitan State College of Denver, Center for the Visual Arts, Denver CO

Perkins, Dean, *Assoc Prof*, Norwich University, Dept of Philosophy, Religion & Fine Arts, Northfield VT (S)

Perkins, Jane, *Chair Art Committee (Exhibits)*, New Canaan Library, New Canaan CT

Perkins, Judy, *Librn*, Akron Art Museum, Martha Stecher Reed Art Library, Akron OH

Perkins, Larry David, *Cur Coll*, University of Florida, Samuel P Harn Museum of Art, Gainesville FL

Perkins, Phyllis, *VPres*, Southern Lorain County Historical Society, Spirit of '76 Museum, Wellington OH

Perks, Anne-Marie, *Pres*, San Bernardino County Museum, Fine Arts Institute, Redlands CA

Perlin, Ruth, *Head Educ Resources Progs*, National Gallery of Art, Washington DC

Perlman, Bill, *VPres*, Women's Interart Center, Inc, Interart Gallery, New York NY

Perlus, Barry, *Assoc Prof*, Cornell University, Dept of Art, Ithaca NY (S)

Pernish, Paul, *Dept Head*, Contra Costa Community College, Dept of Art, San Pablo CA (S)

Pernot, M M, *Dir*, Burlington County Historical Society, Burlington NJ

Perreault, John, *Dir*, Urban Glass, Brooklyn NY

Perri, John, *Prof*, University of Wisconsin-Stout, Dept of Art & Design, Menomonie WI (S)

Perrizo, James, *Prof*, California State University, Hayward, University Art Gallery, Hayward CA

Perrizo, James, *Chmn*, California State University, Hayward, Art Dept, Hayward CA (S)

Perron, Nicole, *Dir Mus*, Musee des Augustines de l'Hotel Dieu de Quebec, Quebec PQ

Perron, Nicole, *Dir Mus*, Musee des Augustines de l'Hotel Dieu de Quebec, Archive, Quebec PQ

Perry, Andy, *Exec Dir*, Artswatch, Louisville KY

Perry, Barbara A, *Dir*, State University of New York at Oswego, Tyler Art Gallery, Oswego NY

Perry, Birthe, *Pres*, Allied Arts Council of Lethbridge, Bowman Arts Center, Lethbridge AB

Perry, Candace, *Cur Coll*, Kentucky Derby Museum, Louisville KY

Perry, Daniel K, *Dir*, Everhart Museum, Scranton PA

Perry, Donald, *Chmn*, Emporia State University, Division of Art, Emporia KS (S)

Perry, Donald, *Dir*, Emporia State University, Norman R Eppink Art Gallery, Emporia KS

Perry, Donna, *Registrar*, Kalani Honua Institute for Cultural Studies, Pahoa HI

Perry, Elizabeth, *Corporate Relations Officer*, National Gallery of Art, Washington DC

Perry, Jennifer, *Registrar*, The Museum of Arts & Sciences Inc, Daytona Beach FL

Perry, Nancy, *Dir*, Danville Museum of Fine Arts & History, Danville VA

Perry, Patricia, *Business Mgr*, Maryhill Museum of Art, Goldendale WA

Perry, Sheryl, *Spec Events Dir*, Art Museum of Western Virginia, Roanoke VA

Perry, Susan L, *Dir*, Mount Holyoke College, Art Library, South Hadley MA

Perryman, Thomas, *Asst Dir*, Hickory Museum of Art, Inc, Hickory NC

Perryman, Thomas, *Asst Dir*, Hickory Museum of Art, Inc, Library, Hickory NC

Person, Ann I, *Educ Coordr*, Danforth Museum of Art, Framingham MA

Person, Deanna, *Public Relations Dir*, Denver Art Museum, Denver CO

Pertl, Susan, *Cur*, McDonald's Corporation, Art Collection, Oakbrook IL

Pesqueira, Randy, *Dir Operations*, Huntington Beach Art Center, Huntington Beach CA

Pestel, Michael, *Dir*, Chatham College, Art Gallery, Pittsburgh PA

Pestel, Michael, *Asst Prof*, Chatham College, Fine & Performing Arts, Pittsburgh PA (S)

Peterlin, Michelle, *Exhibits Preparator*, New Harmony Gallery of Contemporary Art, New Harmony IN

Peters, Judy, *Instr*, West Shore Community College, Division of Humanities & Fine Arts, Scottville MI (S)

Peters, Larry D, *Gallery Dir*, Topeka & Shawnee County Public Library, Gallery of Fine Arts, Topeka KS

Peters, Martha, *Visual Arts Mgr*, City of Austin Parks & Recreation Department, Dougherty Arts Center Gallery, Austin TX

Peters, Nevin, *Library Technical Asst*, Harrington Institute of Interior Design, Design Library, Chicago IL

Peters, Susan Dodge, *Asst Dir Educ*, University of Rochester, Memorial Art Gallery, Rochester NY

Peters, Thomas, *Prof*, Lehigh University, Dept of Art & Architecture, Bethlehem PA (S)

Peters-Campbell, John, *Asst Prof*, University of Colorado-Colorado Springs, Fine Arts Dept, Colorado Springs CO (S)

Petersen, Alessandra, *Board Dir*, Artists' Cooperative Gallery, Omaha NE

Petersen, Cheryl, *Controller*, Southwest Museum, Los Angeles CA

Petersen, Daniel W, *Instr*, Modesto Junior College, Arts Humanities & Communications Division, Modesto CA (S)

Peterson, Allan, *Head Dept*, Pensacola Junior College, Dept of Visual Arts, Pensacola FL (S)

Peterson, Allan, *Dir*, Pensacola Junior College, Visual Arts Gallery, Pensacola FL

Peterson, Brian, *Cur Exhib*, James A Michener Art Museum, Doylestown PA

Peterson, Carole, *Registrar Art*, Illinois State Museum, Illinois Art Gallery & Lockport Gallery, Springfield IL

Peterson, Chuck, *VPres*, Caspers, Inc, Art Collection, Tampa FL

Peterson, Constance, *Instr*, Lansing Community College, Art Program, Lansing MI (S)

Peterson, Dean A, *Asst Prof*, Salisbury State University, Art Dept, Salisbury MD (S)

Peterson, D R, *Instr*, Normandale Community College, Bloomington MN (S)

Peterson, Eric, *Acting Area Head Design*, Pasadena City College, Art Dept, Pasadena CA (S)

Peterson, Frederick, *Coordr*, University of Minnesota, Morris, Humanities Division, Morris MN (S)

Peterson, Gaylen, *Head Dept*, Lutheran Brethren Schools, Art Dept, Fergus Falls MN (S)

Peterson, Glen L, *Instr*, Yavapai College, Visual & Performing Arts Division, Prescott AZ (S)

Peterson, Harold, *Librn*, Minneapolis Institute of Arts, Library, Minneapolis MN

Peterson, James, *Chmn Dept*, Franklin & Marshall College, Art Dept, Lancaster PA (S)

Peterson, John, *Dir*, Timken Museum of Art, San Diego CA

Peterson, John E, *Cur Archives*, Lutheran Theological Seminary, Krauth Memorial Library, Philadelphia PA

Peterson, Kathy, *Bookkeeper*, Northfield Arts Guild, Northfield MN

Peterson, Kip, *Registrar*, Memphis Brooks Museum of Art, Memphis TN

Peterson, Larry D, *Prof*, University of Nebraska, Kearney, Dept of Art & Art History, Kearney NE (S)

Peterson, Margaret, *Prof*, Central Missouri State University, Art Dept, Warrensburg MO (S)

Peterson, Marge, *Treas*, High Wire Gallery, Philadelphia PA

Peterson, Merlin, *Pres*, Pope County Historical Society, Pope County Museum, Glenwood MN

Peterson, Nick, *Display Technician*, College of Southern Idaho, Herrett Center for Arts & Science, Twin Falls ID

Peterson, Pauline M, *Reference Librn*, Jones Library, Inc, Amherst MA

Peterson, Penny, *First VPres*, Arizona Watercolor Association, Phoenix AZ

Peterson, Robert, *Film Dept Chmn*, Art Center College of Design, Pasadena CA (S)

Peterson, Robyn G, *Cur*, The Rockwell Museum, Corning NY

Peterson, Russell O, *VPres Curriculum & Educ Affairs*, College of Lake County, Art Dept, Grayslake IL (S)

Peterson, Sue, *Instr*, Elgin Community College, Fine Arts Dept, Elgin IL (S)

Peterson, Willard, *Prof*, Roberts Wesleyan College, Art Dept, Rochester NY (S)

Petheo, Bela, *Prof*, College of Saint Benedict, Art Dept, Saint Joseph MN (S)

Petheo, Bela, *Prof*, Saint John's University, Art Dept, Collegeville MN (S)

Petore, Rebecca, *Mus Shop Mgr*, Hancock Shaker Village, Inc, Pittsfield MA

Petrick, Mary Anna, *Instr*, Milwaukee Area Technical College, Graphic Arts Division, Milwaukee WI (S)

Petrik, Virgil, *Lectr*, Mount Marty College, Art Dept, Yankton SD (S)

Petrillo, Jane, *Asst Prof*, Colby-Sawyer College, Dept of Fine & Performing Arts, New London NH (S)

Petrosky, Ed, *Prof*, West Virginia University, College of Creative Arts, Morgantown WV (S)

Petrovich-Mwaniki, Lois, *Asst Prof*, Western Carolina University, Dept of Art, Cullowhee NC (S)

Petrulis, Allen, *Asst Mgr*, First Street Gallery, New York NY

Petrulis, Elizabeth, *Registrar*, Sheldon Swope Art Museum, Terre Haute IN

Petruso, John D, *Pres*, Crawford County Historical Society, Baldwin-Reynolds House Museum, Meadville PA

Petry, Mary Ann, *Assoc Prof*, West Texas A&M University, Art, Communication & Theatre Dept, Canyon TX (S)

Petteplace, Jennifer, *Preparator*, McMaster University, Museum of Art, Hamilton ON

Pettibone, John W, *Exec Dir & Cur*, Hammond Castle Museum, Gloucester MA

Pettijohn, JuDee, *Asst Dir*, Florida Department of State, Division of Cultural Affairs, Florida Arts Council, Tallahassee FL

Pettus, Mary, *Dir*, Whatcom Museum of History and Art, Bellingham WA

Pettus, Theodore, *Treas*, Art Directors Club, Inc, New York NY

Peven, Michael, *Dept Chairperson*, University of Arkansas, Art Dept, Fayetteville AR (S)

Pevny, Chrystyna, *Archivist*, The Ukrainian Museum, New York NY

Peyrat, Jean, *Librn*, Center for Creative Studies, College of Art & Design Library, Detroit MI

Peyton, Judy, *Adminr*, Associates for Community Development, Boarman Arts Center, Martinsburg WV

Pfaff, Larry, *Deputy Librn*, Art Gallery of Ontario, Edward P Taylor Research Library & Archives, Toronto ON

Pfanschmidt, Martha, *Instr*, Marylhurst College, Art Dept, Marylhurst OR (S)

Pfefferman, Arthur, *Pres Cultural Affairs Commission*, City of Los Angeles, Cultural Affairs Dept, Los Angeles CA

Pfeifer, Natalie, *Gallery Mgr*, Volcano Art Center, Hawaii National Park HI

Pfeifer, William, *Dir*, Colonial Williamsburg Foundation, Visitor Center, Williamsburg VA

Pfingstag, Benjamin, *Asst Prof*, Norwich University, Dept of Philosophy, Religion & Fine Arts, Northfield VT (S)

Pfleger, Claire, *Lectr*, Cardinal Stritch College, Art Dept, Milwaukee WI (S)

Pfliger, Terry, *Chmn*, St Lawrence College, Dept of Visual & Creative Arts, Kingston ON (S)

Pfliger, Terry, *Dept Coordr*, St Lawrence College, Art Gallery, Kingston ON

Pfotenhauer, Louise, *Recorder*, Neville Public Museum, Library, Green Bay WI

Pfrehm, Paul, *Asst Prof*, Southeastern Oklahoma State University, Art Dept, Durant OK (S)

Phagan, Patricia, *Cur Prints & Drawings*, University of Georgia, Georgia Museum of Art, Athens GA

Pharp, Brent, *Cur*, Jamestown-Yorktown Foundation, Williamsburg VA

Phegley, John, *Exhib Designer*, University of Notre Dame, Snite Museum of Art, Notre Dame IN

Phelan, Andrew, *Dir*, University of Oklahoma, School of Art, Norman OK (S)

Phelan, Mary, *Graduate Prog*, University of the Arts, Philadelphia College of Art & Design, Philadelphia PA (S)

Phelan, Thomas, *Treas*, Rensselaer Newman Foundation Chapel & Cultural Center, The Gallery, Troy NY

Phelps, Bob, *VPres*, Shoreline Historical Museum, Seattle WA

Phelps, Brent, *Photography Coordr*, University of North Texas, School of Visual Arts, Denton TX (S)

Phelps, David, *Museum Preparator*, Loveland Museum Gallery, Loveland CO

Phelps, Timothy H, *Assoc Prof*, Johns Hopkins University, School of Medicine, Dept of Art as Applied to Medicine, Baltimore MD (S)

Pheney, Kathleen, *Dir*, East Baton Rouge Parks & Recreation Commission, Baton Rouge Gallery Inc, Baton Rouge LA

Philabaum, Bill, *Admin Coordr*, Licking County Art Association, Art Gallery, Newark OH

Philbin, Ann, *Dir*, Drawing Center, New York NY

Philbrick, Ruth, *Cur Photo Archives*, National Gallery of Art, Washington DC

Philbrick, Ruth, *Cur*, National Gallery of Art, Photographic Archives, Washington DC

Philipps, Alice, *Financial Coordr*, Women in the Arts Foundation, Inc, New York NY

Phillbrick, Stephanie, *Reference Asst*, Maine Historical Society, Library, Portland ME

Phillips, Anthony, *Prof*, School of the Art Institute of Chicago, Chicago IL (S)

Phillips, Carol, *VPres Educ*, Banff Centre for the Arts, Banff AB (S)

Phillips, Duane L, *Asst Prof*, University of North Alabama, Dept of Art, Florence AL (S)

Phillips, Francis, *Dir*, Intersection for the Arts, San Francisco CA

Phillips, Helen, *Prof*, University of Central Arkansas, Art Dept, Conway AR (S)

Phillips, James Duncan, *Librn*, Peabody Essex Museum, Phillips Library, Salem MA

Phillips, Joan, *Registrar-Archivist*, Kit Carson Historic Museums, Archives, Taos NM

Phillips, Kathryn D, *Librn*, Freer Gallery of Art Gallery, Library, Washington DC

Phillips, Kris, *Instr*, Sarah Lawrence College, Dept of Art History, Bronxville NY (S)

Phillips, Lisa, *Cur*, Whitney Museum of American Art, New York NY

Phillips, Mary, *Cur Dir*, Phillips University, Grace Phillips Johnson Art Gallery, Enid OK

Phillips, Mary, *Chmn*, Phillips University, Dept of Art, Enid OK (S)

Phillips, Patsy, *Prog Coordr*, Atlatl, Phoenix AZ

Phillips, Quitman E, *Asst Prof*, University of Wisconsin, Madison, Dept of Art History, Madison WI (S)

Phillips, Robert F, *Cur Contemporary Art*, Toledo Museum of Art, Toledo OH

Phillips, Romy, *Dir*, Alternative Museum, New York NY

Phillips, Stephen, *Asst Cur*, The Phillips Collection, Washington DC

Phillips, Stephen, *Librn*, Peabody Essex Museum, Phillips Library, Salem MA

Phillips-Abbott, Rebecca, *Admin Dir*, National Museum of Women in the Arts, Washington DC

Philpot, Eloise, *Asst Prof*, Radford University, Art Dept, Radford VA (S)

Phinney, Gail, *Educ Coordr*, Muskegon Museum of Art, Muskegon MI

Piasecki, Jane, *Assoc Dir*, Institute of American Indian Arts Museum, Santa Fe NM

Piatt, Margaret, *Dir*, Piatt Castles, West Liberty OH

Piazza, Paul J, *Controller*, George Eastman House-International Museum of Photography & Film, Rochester NY

Picco, Ronald, *Prof*, College of Santa Fe, Art Dept, Santa Fe NM (S)

Piche, Thomas, *Cur*, Everson Museum of Art, Syracuse NY

Pickard, Carey, *Exec Dir*, Tubman African American Museum, Macon GA

Pickett, Patricia, *Instr*, Dowling College, Dept of Visual Arts, Oakdale NY (S)

Pickett, Scott, *Pres*, Salt Lake Art Center, Salt Lake City UT

Pickett, Victor, *Prof*, Old Dominion University, Art Dept, Norfolk VA (S)

Picon, Carlos A, *Cur-in-Charge Greek & Roman Art*, The Metropolitan Museum of Art, New York NY

Picquet, Glenn, *Chair*, Old Jail Art Center, Albany TX

Piehl, Walter, *Chmn Div Humanities*, Minot State University, Dept of Art, Division of Humanities, Minot ND (S)

Piejko, Alex, *Instr*, Mohawk Valley Community College, Advertising Design & Production, Utica NY (S)

Pier, Gwen M, *Exec Dir*, National Sculpture Society, Library, New York NY

Pier, Gwen M, *Exec Dir*, National Sculpture Society, New York NY

Pierce, Beverly, *Adminr*, Hirshhorn Museum & Sculpture Garden, Washington DC

Pierce, Charles E, *Dir*, Pierpont Morgan Library, New York NY

Pierce, Christopher, *Asst Prof*, Berea College, Art Dept, Berea KY (S)

Pierce, Donald, *VPres*, New York Artists Equity Association, Inc, New York NY

Pierce, Sally, *Print Dept Cur*, Boston Athenaeum, Boston MA

Piersol, Daniel, *Chief Cur Exhib*, New Orleans Museum of Art, New Orleans LA

Pierson, Frank, *Dir CAFTS*, The American Film Institute, Center for Advanced Film & Television, Los Angeles CA (S)

Pierson, Richard, *Dean Admissions*, Clark University, Dept of Visual & Performing Arts, Worcester MA (S)

Pierson, Sallie, *Dir*, Estevan National Exhibition Centre Inc, Estevan SK

Pierson Ellingson, Susan, *Asst Prof*, Concordia College, Art Dept, Moorhead MN (S)

Piesentin, Joe, *Prof*, Pepperdine University, Seaver College, Dept of Art, Malibu CA (S)

Pietrzak, Ted, *Dir*, Art Gallery of Hamilton, Hamilton ON

Pietsch, Theodore, *Cur Fishes*, University of Washington, Thomas Burke Memorial Washington State Museum, Seattle WA

Piggott, Sylvia E A, *Pres*, Special Libraries Association, Museum, Arts & Humanities Division, Washington DC

Piispanen, Ruth, *Dir Arts Educ*, Idaho Commission on the Arts, Boise ID

Pike, Jeffrey C, *Assoc Dean School*, Washington University, School of Art, Saint Louis MO (S)

Pike, Jo, *Dir Visitor Servs*, Museum of Modern Art, New York NY

Pike, Kermit J, *Dir*, Western Reserve Historical Society, Cleveland OH

Pike, Kermit J, *Dir*, Western Reserve Historical Society, Library, Cleveland OH

Pike, Lorraine, *Librn*, Ascension Lutheran Church Library, Milwaukee WI

Pilgram, Suzanne, *Asst Prof*, Georgian Court College, Dept of Art, Lakewood NJ (S)

Pilgrim, Dianne, *Dir*, Cooper-Hewitt, National Design Museum, New York NY

Pilliod, Elizabeth, *Prof*, Oregon State University, Dept of Art, Corvallis OR (S)

Pillsbury, Edmund P, *Dir*, Kimbell Art Foundation, Kimbell Art Museum, Fort Worth TX

Pina, Bob, *Gallery Dir*, Florida Community College at Jacksonville, South Campus, Art Dept, Jacksonville FL (S)

Pina, Jorge, *Theater Arts Prog Dir*, Guadalupe Cultural Arts Center, San Antonio TX

Pinardi, Brenda, *Prof*, University of Massachusetts Lowell, Dept of Art, Lowell MA (S)

Pincus-Witten, Robert, *Prof Emeritus*, City University of New York, PhD Program in Art History, New York NY (S)

Pindell, Howardena, *Prof*, State University of New York at Stony Brook, Art Dept, Stony Brook NY (S)

Pinedo, Maria, *Dir*, Galeria de la Raza, Studio 24, San Francisco CA

Pines, Doralynn S, *Assoc Dir*, The Metropolitan Museum of Art, New York NY

Pines, Doralynn S, *Chief Librn*, The Metropolitan Museum of Art, Thomas J Watson Library, New York NY

Ping, Donn Britt, *Asst Prof*, Converse College, Art Dept, Spartanburg SC (S)

Pink, Jim, *Instr*, University of Nevada, Las Vegas, Dept of Art, Las Vegas NV (S)

Pinkel, Sheila, *Assoc Prof*, Pomona College, Dept of Art & Art History, Claremont CA (S)

Pinkert, Marvin, *VPres Prog*, Museum of Science & Industry, Chicago IL

Pinkston, H C, *Prof*, Pierce College, Art Dept, Woodland Hills CA (S)

Pinson, Penelope, *VPres*, Arts on the Park, Lakeland FL

Pinto, John, *Prof*, Princeton University, Dept of Art & Archaeology, Princeton NJ (S)

Pionk, Richard, *Pres*, Salmagundi Club, New York NY

Piotrowski, C, *Assoc Prof*, Northern Arizona University, School of Art & Design, Flagstaff AZ (S)

Piotrowski, Ronald, *Prof*, Northern Arizona University, School of Art & Design, Flagstaff AZ (S)

Piper, Bill, *Instr*, Walla Walla Community College, Art Dept, Walla Walla WA (S)

Piranio, Michelle, *Publication & Design Mgr*, Walker Art Center, Minneapolis MN

Pires, George, *Pres*, Museum of Ossining Historical Society, Ossining NY

Pirie, Marjorie L, *Treas-Membership*, Marin County Watercolor Society, Greenbrae CA

Pisciotta, Henry, *Fine Arts Librn*, Carnegie Mellon University, Hunt Library, Pittsburgh PA

Piskoti, James, *Prof*, California State University, Art Dept, Turlock CA (S)

Pison, Edna, *Librn*, Arts & Crafts Association of Meriden Inc, Library, Meriden CT

Pissarro, Joachim, *Chief Cur*, Kimbell Art Foundation, Kimbell Art Museum, Fort Worth TX

Pitman, Dianne, *Asst Prof*, Northeastern University, Dept of Art & Architecture, Boston MA (S)

Pitman, Ursula, *Dir of Docents*, Fitchburg Art Museum, Fitchburg MA

Pitt, Paul, *Prof*, Harding University, Dept of Art, Searcy AR (S)

Pitt, Sheila, *Asst Prof Gallery Management*, University of Arizona, Dept of Art, Tucson AZ (S)

Pittenger, Charles, *Registrar*, J B Speed Art Museum, Louisville KY

Pittini, Michelle, *Educ Coordr*, Jewish Community Centre of Toronto, The Koffler Gallery, North York ON

Pittman, David, *Fellowship Coordr*, Virginia Museum of Fine Arts, Richmond VA

Pitts, Barbara, *Treas*, Northwest Watercolor Society, Bellevue WA

Pitts, Bill, *State Mus Dir*, Oklahoma Historical Society, State Museum of History, Oklahoma City OK

Pitts, Laura, *Ursuline Gallery Mgr*, Southwest Craft Center, Emily Edwards & Ursuline Sales Gallery, San Antonio TX

Pitts, Terence, *Dir*, University of Arizona, Center for Creative Photography, Tucson AZ

Pittsley, Rich, *Dir*, Chief Plenty Coups Museum, Pryor MT

Pitynski, Andrew, *VPres Sculpture*, Audubon Artists, Inc, New York NY

Pivorun, Phyllis, *Media Resources Cur*, Clemson University, Emery A Gunnin Architectural Library, Clemson SC

Pivovar, Ronald A, *Dir*, Thiel College, Sampson Art Gallery, Greenville PA

Pivovar, Ronald A, *Chmn Dept*, Thiel College, Dept of Art, Greenville PA (S)

Pizer, Alan, *Instr*, Southwest Texas State University, Dept of Art, San Marcos TX (S)

Pizzollo, Sissy, *Dir*, Muse Art Gallery, Philadelphia PA

Plant, Anthony, *Chmn Dept Art*, Cornell College, Armstrong Gallery, Mount Vernon IA

Plante, Mary Gene, *Asst Treas*, Rhode Island Watercolor Society, Pawtucket RI

Plater, Daryl, *Chmn Dept*, Vancouver Community College, Langara Campus, Dept of Fine Arts, Vancouver BC (S)

Plato, Geraldine, *Asst Dir*, Penland School of Crafts, Penland NC (S)

Platou, Dode, *Dir Emerita*, Kemper & Leila Williams Foundation, New Orleans LA

Platt, Michael, *Chmn*, Southern Virginia College, Buena Vista VA (S)

Platt, Nicholas, *Pres*, The Asia Society Galleries, New York NY

Platt, Susan, *Reference Technician*, Sheridan College of Applied Arts and Technology, Trafalgar Campus Library, Oakville ON

Platzer, Eryl J, *Dir*, American Architectural Foundation, Washington DC

Platzer, Eryl J, *Dir*, American Architectural Foundation, The Octagon Museum, Washington DC

Plaut, T, *Head Dept*, Cornell College, Art Dept, Mount Vernon IA (S)

Plax, Julie, *Asst Prof Art History*, University of Arizona, Dept of Art, Tucson AZ (S)

Plear, Scott, *Div Chmn*, Vancouver Community College, Langara Campus, Dept of Fine Arts, Vancouver BC (S)

Pleasants, Craig, *Acting Dir*, Virginia Center for the Creative Arts, Camp Gallery, Sweet Briar VA

Pleasants, Sheila Gully, *Admissions Coordr*, Virginia Center for the Creative Arts, Camp Gallery, Sweet Briar VA

Plehaty, Phyllis, *Cur Costumes*, Boulder Historical Society Inc, Museum of History, Boulder CO

Plosky, Charles, *Assoc Prof*, Jersey City State College, Art Dept, Jersey City NJ (S)

Plotkin, Andy, *Exec Trustee*, Edna Hibel Art Foundation, Hibel Museum of Art, Palm Beach FL

Plotkin, Andy, *Exec Trustee*, Edna Hibel Art Foundation, Gallery, Palm Beach FL

Plotkin, Theodore, *Pres*, Edna Hibel Art Foundation, Hibel Museum of Art, Palm Beach FL

Plourde, Nelie, *Exec Dir*, UMLAUF Sculpture Garden & Museum, Austin TX

Plumb, Susan, *Assoc Cur Educ*, James A Michener Art Museum, Doylestown PA

Plummer, Ann, *Asst Prof*, Winona State University, Dept of Art, Winona MN (S)

Plummer, Bill, *Pres Board Trustees*, Zanesville Art Center, Zanesville OH

Plummer, John H, *Cur Medieval & Renaissance Manuscripts*, Pierpont Morgan Library, New York NY

Plyler, Anne, *Gallery Coordr*, James Prendergast Library Association, Jamestown NY

Poeschl, Paul, *Prog Coordr*, Oshkosh Public Museum, Oshkosh WI

Pogue, Dwight, *Chmn Art Dept*, Smith College, Art Dept, Northampton MA (S)

Pogue, Stephanie, *Chmn*, University of Maryland, Department of Art, College Park MD (S)

Pohl, Brian, *Adjunct Prof*, Oral Roberts University, Fine Arts Dept, Tulsa OK (S)

Pohl, Frances, *Assoc Prof*, Pomona College, Dept of Art & Art History, Claremont CA (S)

Pohlad, Mark, *Asst Prof*, DePaul University, Dept of Art, Chicago IL (S)

Pohli, Richard, *2nd VPres*, Historical Society of Bloomfield, Bloomfield NJ

Pohlkamp, Mark, *Lectr*, University of Wisconsin-Stevens Point, Dept of Art & Design, Stevens Point WI (S)

Pohlman, Ken, *Preparator Designer*, Middlebury College, Museum of Art, Middlebury VT

Pohlman, Lynette, *Dir*, Iowa State University, Brunnier Art Museum, Ames IA

Poirier, Ivanhoe, *Pastor & Dir*, Musee de la Basilique Notre-Dame, Montreal PQ

Pokinski, Deborah, *Chmn*, Hamilton College, Art Dept, Clinton NY (S)

Polan, Louise, *Chief Cur*, Huntington Museum of Art, Huntington WV

Poland, Barbara, *Research Librn*, Warner Bros Research Library, North Hollywood CA

Polatti, Gaylon, *Librn*, Dallas Historical Society, Research Center Library, Dallas TX

Polcari, Stephen, *Dir*, Archives of American Art, New York Regional Center, Washington DC

Polenberg, Marcia, *Instr*, Barton County Community College, Fine Arts Dept, Great Bend KS (S)

Polera, Josephine, *Financial Aid Officer*, Ontario College of Art & Design, Toronto ON (S)

Poleskie, Steve, *Prof*, Cornell University, Dept of Art, Ithaca NY (S)

Poley, Darren, *Head Public Serv*, Lutheran Theological Seminary, Krauth Memorial Library, Philadelphia PA

Poliakov, Lev, *Asst Prof*, New York Institute of Technology, Fine Arts Dept, Old Westbury NY (S)

Polich, Debra, *Exec Dir*, Artrain, Inc, Ann Arbor MI

Poling, Clark V, *Prof*, Emory University, Art History Dept, Atlanta GA (S)

Polishook, Mark, *Prof*, University of Maine at Augusta, Division of Fine & Performing Arts, Augusta ME (S)

Poliszczuk, Orest S, *Prof*, Montgomery College, Dept of Art, Rockville MD (S)

Polito, Ronald, *Assoc Prof*, University of Massachusetts - Boston, Art Dept, Boston MA (S)

Politsky, Rosalie, *Chmn Art Educ*, Bowling Green State University, School of Art, Bowling Green OH (S)

Polk, Andrew, *Assoc Prof Printmaking*, University of Arizona, Dept of Art, Tucson AZ (S)

Polk, Andrew W, *Foundations, Dept Head*, University of Arizona, Dept of Art, Tucson AZ (S)

Polk, Tom, *Undergrad Coordr*, University of Georgia, Franklin College of Arts & Sciences, Lamar Dodd School of Art, Athens GA (S)

Poll, Irene, *Publicity Dir*, American Jewish Art Club, Chicago IL

Pollack, Rhoda-Gale, *Dean*, University of Kentucky, Dept of Art, Lexington KY (S)

Pollari, Linda, *Chmn Interior Design*, Woodbury University, Dept of Graphic Design, Burbank CA (S)

Pollen, Jason, *Pres*, Surface Design Association, Inc, Oakland CA

Poller, Lisa, *Assoc Dir Develop*, Danforth Museum of Art, Framingham MA

Pollera, Anthony, *Dir*, Fine Arts Museum of Long Island, Hempstead NY

Pollifren, Sally, *Librn*, Center for History of American Needlework, Butler PA

Pollini, John, *Prof*, University of Southern California, School of Fine Arts, Los Angeles CA (S)

Pollock, John, *Head*, Montana State University-Billings, Art Dept, Billings MT (S)

Polowy, Barbara, *Librn*, Smith College, Hillyer Art Library, Northampton MA

Polskin, Philippa, *Pres*, Ruder Finn Inc, New York NY

Polster, Nancy, *Chmn Dept*, Iowa State University, Dept of Art & Design, Ames IA (S)

Pomeroy, Dan, *Dir Coll*, Tennessee State Museum, Nashville TN

Pomeroy, Dan, *Dir Coll*, Tennessee State Museum, Library, Nashville TN

Pomeroy, Lily, *Asst Prof*, Dickinson State University, Dept of Art, Dickinson ND (S)

Pomeroy Draper, Stacy, *Cur*, Rensselaer County Historical Society, Library, Troy NY

Pompelia, Mark, *Asst Cur*, Ohio State University, Slide & Photograph Library, Columbus OH

Pond, Ann, *Educ Cur*, Mobile Museum of Art, Library, Mobile AL

Ponder, Anita, *Asst Dir*, Tubman African American Museum, Macon GA

Pondone, Marc, *Instr*, Solano Community College, Division of Fine & Applied Art, Suisun City CA (S)

Ponte, Jamey, *Pres*, Cincinnati Artists' Group Effort, Cincinnati OH

Poole, Jeanne, *Head Resource Center*, The Art Institute of Chicago, Teacher Resource Center, Chicago IL

Poole, Katherine K, *Visual Coll Librn*, Massachusetts Institute of Technology, Rotch Library of Architecture & Planning, Cambridge MA

Pooley, David, *Registrar*, Eastern Illinois University, Tarble Arts Center, Charleston IL

Poor, Anna, *Instr*, Truro Center for the Arts at Castle Hill, Inc, Truro MA (S)

Poor, Robert, *Prof*, University of Minnesota, Minneapolis, Art History, Minneapolis MN (S)

Pope, Edward, *Prof*, University of Wisconsin, Madison, Dept of Art, Madison WI (S)

Pope, John C, *Trustee*, Hill-Stead Museum, Farmington CT

Pope, Linda, *Dir*, University of California at Santa Cruz, Eloisa Pickard Smith Gallery, Santa Cruz CA

Popovich, Ljubica D, *Assoc Prof*, Vanderbilt University, Dept of Fine Arts, Nashville TN (S)

Popowcer, Stuart, *Dir & Chief Financial Officer*, Terra Museum of American Art, Chicago IL

Popp, Jan, *Asst Dir*, Capital University, Schumacher Gallery, Columbus OH

Porada, Edith, *Honorary Cur Seals & Tablets*, Pierpont Morgan Library, New York NY

Poras, E Linda, *Exec Dir*, The Brush Art Gallery & Studios, Lowell MA

Porcari, George, *Acquisitions Librn*, Art Center College of Design, James Lemont Fogg Memorial Library, Pasadena CA

Porps, Ernest O, *Prof*, University of Colorado at Denver, Dept of Fine Arts, Denver CO (S)

Portell, Cristina, *Asst Cur*, Dahesh Museum, New York NY

Porter, Ann, *Dir*, University of Vermont, Robert Hull Fleming Museum, Burlington VT

Porter, Carol, *VPres*, Everson Museum of Art, Syracuse NY

Porter, Dave, *Media Dir*, Utah Travel Council, Salt Lake City UT

Porter, David S, *Assoc Prof*, University of North Florida, Dept of Communications & Visual Arts, Jacksonville FL (S)

Porter, Dean A, *Dir*, University of Notre Dame, Snite Museum of Art, Notre Dame IN

Porter, Edward, *Pres College*, International Fine Arts College, Miami FL (S)

Porter, Elwin, *Dir*, South Florida Art Institute of Hollywood, Dania FL (S)

Porter, James M, *Chmn Board*, New Jersey Historical Society, Newark NJ

Porter, Jane, *Keeper*, Portsmouth Athenaeum, Library, Portsmouth NH

Porter, Jane M, *Keeper*, Portsmouth Athenaeum, Portsmouth NH

Porter, Jeanne Chenault, *Assoc Prof*, Pennsylvania State University, University Park, Dept of Art History, University Park PA (S)

Porter, John, *Prof*, Gavilan College, Art Dept, Gilroy CA (S)

Porter, John R, *Dir*, Musee du Quebec, Quebec PQ

Porter, Tom, *Instr*, Bismarck State College, Fine Arts Dept, Bismarck ND (S)

Porterfield, Todd, *Prof*, Princeton University, Dept of Art & Archaeology, Princeton NJ (S)

Posner, Helaine, *Cur*, Massachusetts Institute of Technology, List Visual Arts Center, Cambridge MA

Post, Wendy, *Art Prog Cur*, Louisiana Arts & Science Center, Baton Rouge LA

Post, William, *Cur Ornithology*, Charleston Museum, Charleston SC

Poster, Amy, *Cur Asian Art*, Brooklyn Museum, Brooklyn NY

Potoft, Reeva, *Instr.* Columbia University, School of the Arts, Division of Visual Arts, New York NY (S)

Potratz, Wayne, *Chmn Dept.* University of Minnesota, Minneapolis, Dept of Art, Minneapolis MN (S)

Pottenger, David, *Pres.* Cohasset Historical Society, Caleb Lothrop House, Cohasset MA

Pottenget, David, *Pres.* Cohasset Historical Society, Captain John Wilson Historical House, Cohasset MA

Potter, G W, *Instr.* Western Illinois University, Art Dept, Macomb IL (S)

Potter, Joann, *Registrar.* Vassar College, The Frances Lehman Loeb Art Center, Poughkeepsie NY

Potter, Leslie, *Exhib Coordr.* Saskatchewan Craft Gallery, Saskatoon SK

Potter, Ted, *Exec Dir.* Contemporary Arts Center, New Orleans LA

Potters, Stephen, *VChmn.* National Institute for Architectural Education, New York NY

Potterson, Jim, *Interim Dean Humanities & Social Science.* San Jose City College, School of Fine Arts, San Jose CA (S)

Potts, Lesley, *Co-Educ Dir.* Center for Puppetry Arts, Atlanta GA

Poulet, Anne, *Cur European Decorative Arts & Sculpture.* Museum of Fine Arts, Boston MA

Poulos, Basilios N, *Prof.* Rice University, Dept of Art & Art History, Houston TX (S)

Poulos, Helen, *Pres.* Federated Art Associations of New Jersey, Inc, Maplewood NJ

Poulton, Michael, *Prof.* Technical University of Nova Scotia, Faculty of Architecture, Halifax NS (S)

Poundstone, Sally H, *Dir.* Westport Public Library, Westport CT

Pouse, Matt, *Chmn.* Marywood College, Art Dept, Scranton PA (S)

Pover, Bonnie L, *Dir.* Noyes Museum, Oceanville NJ

Pover, Bonnie L, *Dir.* Noyes Museum, Library, Oceanville NJ

Poveymrov, Frank, *Gallery Mgr & Assoc Dir.* New York University, Grey Art Gallery & Study Center, New York NY

Powell, Bobbie, *Dir.* Riverside Art Museum, Riverside CA

Powell, Bobbie, *Dir.* Riverside Art Museum, Library, Riverside CA

Powell, Dianne Garrett, *Develop Dir.* Marion Koogler McNay Art Museum, San Antonio TX

Powell, Earl A, *Dir.* National Gallery of Art, Washington DC

Powell, James, *Dir.* Natural History Museum of Los Angeles County, Los Angeles CA

Powell, Janice J, *Librn.* Princeton University, Marquand Library of Art & Archaeology, Princeton NJ

Powell, Kristen, *Chmn.* Middlebury College, Dept of Art, Middlebury VT (S)

Powell, Linda, *Cur Educ.* Kimbell Art Foundation, Kimbell Art Museum, Fort Worth TX

Powell, Mary Eleen, *Registrar.* Frederick R Weisman Art Foundation, Los Angeles CA

Powell, Nancy, *Registrar.* CIGNA Corporation, CIGNA Museum & Art Collection, Philadelphia PA

Powell, Patricia, *Ed.* University of Wisconsin-Madison, Elvehjem Museum of Art, Madison WI

Powell, Richard, *Assoc Prof.* Duke University, Dept of Art & Art History, Durham NC (S)

Powelson, Rosemary, *Art Instr.* Lower Columbia College, Art Dept, Longview WA (S)

Power, Christine T, *Cur.* Federal Reserve Bank of Minneapolis, Minneapolis MN

Power, Susan, *Prof.* Marshall University, Dept of Art, Huntington WV (S)

Power, Tracy, *Conservator.* Asian Art Museum of San Francisco, Avery Brundage Collection, San Francisco CA

Powers, Everett G, *Pres & Chief Operating Officer.* Arts Partnership of Greater Spartanburg, Inc, Spartanburg Arts Center, Spartanburg SC

Powers, Jack, *Asst to Dir.* Southern Methodist University, Meadows Museum, Dallas TX

Powers, Joan, *Assoc Prof.* C W Post Center of Long Island University, School of Visual & Performing Arts, Brookville NY (S)

Powers, Leland, *Asst Prof.* Fort Hays State University, Dept of Art, Hays KS (S)

Powers, Linda, *Develop Dir.* Koshare Indian Museum, Inc, La Junta CO

Powers, Martin, *Assoc Prof.* University of Michigan, Ann Arbor, Dept of History of Art, Ann Arbor MI (S)

Powers, Mary Ann, *Asst Prof.* Assumption College, Dept of Art & Music, Worcester MA (S)

Powers, Ramon, *Exec Dir.* Kansas State Historical Society, Kansas Museum of History, Topeka KS

Powers, Sandra L, *Library Dir.* Society of the Cincinnati, Museum & Library at Anderson House, Washington DC

Powlowski, Eugene, *Prof.* Cleveland Institute of Art, Cleveland OH (S)

Poynor, Robin, *Assoc Prof.* University of Florida, Dept of Art, Gainesville FL (S)

Poznansky, Jonathan, *Chmn Board.* Staten Island Institute of Arts & Sciences, Staten Island NY

P'Pool, Kenneth M, *Dir Historic Preservation.* Mississippi Department of Archives & History, Library, Jackson MS

Pramuk, Ed, *Prof.* Louisiana State University, School of Art, Baton Rouge LA (S)

Prater, Teresa, *Chmn Dept.* Converse College, Art Dept, Spartanburg SC (S)

Pratt, Benjamin, *Asst Prof.* University of Wisconsin-Stout, Dept of Art & Design, Menomonie WI (S)

Pratt, Vernon, *Assoc Prof.* Duke University, Dept of Art & Art History, Durham NC (S)

Pratzon, Jill, *Painting Restorer.* Illustration House Inc, Gallery Auction House, New York NY

Pratzon, Jim, *Gallery Mgr.* Illustration House Inc, Gallery Auction House, New York NY

Preble, Michael, *Dir Museum School.* The Arkansas Arts Center, Museum School, Little Rock AR (S)

Prekop, Martin, *Dean.* Carnegie Mellon University, College of Fine Arts, Pittsburgh PA (S)

Prelinger, Elizabeth, *Chmn.* Georgetown University, Dept of Art, Music & Theatre, Washington DC (S)

Premer, Nancy, *Instr.* Avila College, Art Division, Dept of Humanities, Kansas City MO (S)

Prendeville, Jet M, *Art Librn.* Rice University, Alice Pratt Brown Library of Art, Architecture & Music, Houston TX

Prenezost, William, *Mgr Marketing & Commission.* Cleveland Museum of Art, Cleveland OH

Prente, Jeffrey, *Asst Prog.* University of New Orleans-Lake Front, Dept of Fine Arts, New Orleans LA (S)

Press, Elizabeth, *Dir.* Historical Society of Martin County, Elliott Museum, Stuart FL

Pressly, William L, *Chmn.* University of Maryland, Dept of Art History, College Park MD (S)

Prestiano, Robert, *Coordr.* Angelo State University, Art & Music Dept, San Angelo TX (S)

Preston, Carol, *Cur Natural Sciences.* Randall Museum Junior Museum, San Francisco CA

Preston, Teresa, *Art History Instr.* Hutchinson Community Junior College, Visual Arts Dept, Hutchinson KS (S)

Pretola, John, *Cur Anthropology.* Springfield Library & Museums Association, Springfield Science Museum, Springfield MA

Preudergast, David, *VPres Coll & Research.* Royal Ontario Museum, Toronto ON

Prevec, Rose Anne, *Head Information.* McMaster University, Library, Hamilton ON

Price, Barbara Gillette, *Pres.* Moore College of Art & Design, Philadelphia PA (S)

Price, B Byron, *Acting Dir.* Buffalo Bill Memorial Association, Buffalo Bill Historical Center, Cody WY

Price, Boyce, *Pres.* Essex Art Association, Inc, Essex CT

Price, Jerry, *Develop Dir.* Southern Oregon Historical Society, Jacksonville Museum of Southern Oregon History, Medford OR

Price, Joan, *Supervisor Art Education.* City College of New York, Art Dept, New York NY (S)

Price, L, *Instr.* Humboldt State University, College of Arts & Humanities, Arcata CA (S)

Price, Lois, *Assoc Conservator Librn Coll.* Winterthur Museum, Library, Winterthur DE

Price, Marla, *Dir.* Fort Worth Art Association, Modern Art Museum of Fort Worth, Fort Worth TX

Price, Mary Jo, *Exhib Librn.* Frostburg State University, Lewis J Ort Library, Frostburg MD

Price, Mary Sue Sweeney, *Dir.* Newark Museum Association, The Newark Museum, Newark NJ

Price, Michael, *Prof.* Hamline University, Dept of Art & Art History, Saint Paul MN (S)

Price, Pam, *Library Dir.* Mercer County Community College, Library, Trenton NJ

Price, Pam, *Chmn.* University of Texas of Permian Basin, Dept of Art, Odessa TX (S)

Price, Priscilla B, *Registrar.* Corning Museum of Glass, Corning NY

Price, Ramon, *Chief Cur.* DuSable Museum of African American History, Chicago IL

Price, Richard W, *Managing Editor.* Corning Museum of Glass, Corning NY

Price, Rita, *Pres.* North Shore Art League, Winnetka IL

Price, Rita, *Pres.* North Shore Art League, Winnetka IL (S)

Price, Rob, *Prof.* University of Wisconsin-Stout, Dept of Art & Design, Menomonie WI (S)

Price, Sally Irwin, *Dir.* Baycrafters, Inc, Bay Village OH

Priede, Zigmunds, *Instr.* Johnson County Community College, Visual Arts Program, Overland Park KS (S)

Priegel, Mike, *Bus Mgr.* Nexus Contemporary Art Center, Atlanta GA

Priester, Anne, *Adjunct Prof.* Lehigh University, Dept of Art & Architecture, Bethlehem PA (S)

Prieve, E Arthur, *Dir.* University of Wisconsin, Madison, Graduate School of Business, Center for Arts Administration, Madison WI (S)

Priggee, Milt, *Pres.* Association of American Editorial Cartoonists, Raleigh NC

Prince, David, *Cur.* Syracuse University, Art Collection, Syracuse NY

Prince, Paul, *Designer Exhib.* University of California, Santa Barbara, University Art Museum, Santa Barbara CA

Prince, Richard, *Assoc Prof.* University of British Columbia, Dept of Fine Arts, Vancouver BC (S)

Prior, Barbara, *Asst Librn.* Cornell University, Fine Arts Library, Ithaca NY

Prioul, Didier, *Head Educative Serv & Cur.* Musee du Quebec, Quebec PQ

Prisco, Mario, *Interim Dean.* New York State College of Ceramics at Alfred University, School of Art & Design, Alfred NY (S)

Pritchard, C William, *Assoc Exec Dir.* Iowa State Education Association, Salisbury House, Des Moines IA

Pritchard, Les, *Pres.* The Art Institutes International, The Art Institute of Seattle, Seattle WA (S)

Pritikin, Renny, *Artistic Dir Visual Arts.* Center for the Arts at Yerba Buena Gardens, San Francisco CA

Privatsky, Benni, *Assoc Dir.* Dickinson State University, Mind's Eye Gallery, Dickinson ND

Privitt, Bob, *Prof.* Pepperdine University, Seaver College, Dept of Art, Malibu CA (S)

Probes, Anna Greidanus, *Assoc Prof.* Calvin College, Art Dept, Grand Rapids MI (S)

Procos, D, *Prof.* Technical University of Nova Scotia, Faculty of Architecture, Halifax NS (S)

Prohaska, Albert, *Assoc Prof.* New York Institute of Technology, Fine Arts Dept, Old Westbury NY (S)

Prohaska, Edward, *Dir Admin.* Pacific - Asia Museum, Pasadena CA

Prokof, Carol, *Asst Cur.* Surrey Art Gallery, Surrey BC

Prokop, Clifton A, *Assoc Prof.* Keystone Junior College, Fine Arts Dept, Factoryville PA (S)

Prokopoff, Stephen S, *Dir.* University of Iowa, Museum of Art, Iowa City IA

Prol, Elbertus, *Cur.* Ringwood Manor House Museum, Ringwood NJ

Ragsdale, Jana, *Admin Asst,* Columbia University, School of the Arts, Division of Visual Arts, New York NY (S)

Raguin, Virginia C, *Prof,* College of the Holy Cross, Dept of Visual Arts, Worcester MA (S)

Rahmi, Stanley, *Exhib Dir,* Royal Ontario Museum, Toronto ON

Raimo, John, *Pres,* Monserrat College of Art, Beverly MA (S)

Raine, Clifford, *Glass,* California College of Arts & Crafts, Oakland CA (S)

Raines, D O, *Chmn,* Presbyterian College, Fine Arts Dept, Clinton SC (S)

Raines, Kevin, *Prof,* College of Notre Dame of Maryland, Art Dept, Baltimore MD (S)

Rains, Jerry, *Chmn,* Northeast Mississippi Junior College, Art Dept, Booneville MS (S)

Rainwater, Robert, *Asst Dir for Art, Prints & Photographs & Cur Spencer Coll,* The New York Public Library, Spencer Collection, New York NY

Rait, Elearnor, *Cur Coll,* Hofstra University, Hofstra Museum, Hempstead NY

Raithel, Jan, *Dept Chmn,* Chaffey Community College, Art Dept, Rancho Cucamonga CA (S)

Raizman, David, *Head Dept Fashion & Visual Studies,* Drexel University, Nesbitt College of Design Arts, Philadelphia PA (S)

Rakoncay, Arlene, *Exec Dir,* Chicago Artists' Coalition, Chicago IL

Ralya, Kelyn, *Head Librn,* Birmingham Public Library, Arts, Music & Recreation Department, Birmingham AL

Ramage, Andrew, *Prof,* Cornell University, Dept of the History of Art, Ithaca NY (S)

Ramage, William, *Prof,* Castleton State College, Art Dept, Castleton VT (S)

Raman, Anne, *Gallery Dir,* Foundation for Today's Art, Nexus Gallery, Philadelphia PA

Ramberg, W Dodd, *Prof,* Catholic University of America, School of Architecture & Planning, Washington DC (S)

Ramers, Del, *Asst Cur,* Temple University, Slide Library, Elkins PA

Ramirez, Adrian N, *Prof,* Catholic University of Puerto Rico, Dept of Fine Arts, Ponce PR (S)

Ramirez, Daniel, *Prof,* University of Wisconsin, Madison, Dept of Art, Madison WI (S)

Ramirez, Jan, *Assoc Dir Coll,* Museum of the City of New York, New York NY

Ramirez, Jan S, *Assoc Dir Coll,* Museum of the City of New York, Library, New York NY

Ramirez, Luis, *Chmn & Prof,* La Sierra University, Art Dept, Riverside CA (S)

Ramirez, Mari Carmen, *Cur Latin American Art,* University of Texas at Austin, Archer M Huntington Art Gallery, Austin TX

Ramirez, Michael, *Pres-Elect,* Association of American Editorial Cartoonists, Raleigh NC

Ramos, Jim, *Instr,* Gettysburg College, Dept of Visual Arts, Gettysburg PA (S)

Ramos , Julianne, *Exec Dir,* Rockland Center for the Arts, West Nyack NY

Ramos, Julianne, *Exec Dir,* Rockland Center for the Arts, West Nyack NY (S)

Ramsaran, Helen, *Assoc Prof,* John Jay College of Criminal Justice, Dept of Art, Music & Philosophy, New York NY (S)

Ramsay, George, *Prof,* Wittenberg University, Art Dept, Springfield OH (S)

Ramsey, Bonnie, *Dir Publications,* University of Georgia, Georgia Museum of Art, Athens GA

Ramsey, Peter, *Dir,* Evergreen State College, Evergreen Galleries, Olympia WA

Rance, Donald, *Information Systems Librn,* Art Gallery of Ontario, Edward P Taylor Research Library & Archives, Toronto ON

Rand, Anne Gimes, *Cur,* USS Constitution Museum, Boston MA

Rand, Archie, *Instr,* Columbia University, School of the Arts, Division of Visual Arts, New York NY (S)

Rand, Duncan, *Librn,* Lethbridge Public Library, Art Gallery, Lethbridge AB

Rand, Richard, *Cur European Art,* Dartmouth College, Hood Museum of Art, Hanover NH

Randall, Lawrence E, *Dir,* State University of New York at Purchase, Library, Purchase NY

Randall, Lilian M C, *Research Cur Manuscripts & Rare Books,* Walters Art Gallery, Baltimore MD

Randall, Ross G, *Asst Dir,* Gunston Hall Plantation, Mason Neck VA

Randel, Patricia, *Exec Dir,* Palette & Chisel Academy of Fine Arts, Chicago IL

Randle, Derek, *Prof,* Carson-Newman College, Art Dept, Jefferson City TN (S)

Randolph, Karen, *Prof,* Lubbock Christian University, Dept of Communication & Fine Art, Lubbock TX (S)

Rands, Robert L, *Adjunct Cur Archaeology,* Southern Illinois University, University Museum, Carbondale IL

Raneses, Tom, *Asst Dir,* American University, Watkins Collection, Washington DC

Rankin, Shan, *Exec Dir,* Hidalgo County Historical Museum, Edinburg TX

Rankin, Tom, *Assoc Prof,* University of Mississippi, Dept of Art, University MS (S)

Ranmey, Brooks, *Pres,* Yankton County Historical Society, Dakota Territorial Museum, Yankton SD

Ranspach, Ernest, *Prof,* Lynn University, Art & Design Dept, Boca Raton FL (S)

Rantoul, T Neal, *Assoc Prof,* Northeastern University, Dept of Art & Architecture, Boston MA (S)

Raphoon, Michele, *Communications Specialist,* Tryon Palace Historic Sites & Gardens, New Bern NC

Rapkievian, Carolyn, *Public Prog Coordr,* National Museum of the American Indian, George Gustav Heye Center, New York NY

Rappaport, Wendy, *Educ Dir,* Farmington Valley Arts Center, Avon CT

Rasbury, Patricia, *Dir Educ,* Tennessee State Museum, Nashville TN

Rash, Brennan, *Public Affairs Officer,* National Portrait Gallery, Washington DC

Rash, Nancy, *Prof,* Connecticut College, Dept of Art History, New London CT (S)

Rasmussen, Gerald E, *Dir,* Stamford Museum & Nature Center, Stamford CT

Rasmussen, Jack, *Exec Dir,* Maryland Art Place, Baltimore MD

Rasmussen, Keith, *Exec Dir,* Chattahoochee Valley Art Museum, LaGrange GA

Rasmussen, Marie, *Chmn Fine & Performing Arts,* Umpqua Community College, Fine & Performing Arts Dept, Roseburg OR (S)

Rasmussen, Mary, *Assoc Prof,* University of Illinois, Chicago, Health Science Center, Biomedical Visualizations, Chicago IL (S)

Rass, Patty, *Instr,* Mount Mary College, Art Dept, Milwaukee WI (S)

Rassweiler, Janet, *Asst Dir Museum,* New Jersey Historical Society, Library, Newark NJ

Ratcliff, Gary, *Instr,* Northeast Louisiana University, Dept of Art, Monroe LA (S)

Rathbone, Eliza, *Chief Cur,* The Phillips Collection, Washington DC

Rathbone, Eliza, *Chief Cur,* The Phillips Collection, Library, Washington DC

Ratheum, Charlie, *Arts Coordr,* King County Arts Commission, Seattle WA

Rathgeb, Donald A, *Chmn,* St Michael's College, Fine Arts Dept, Colchester VT (S)

Rathwell, George, *VPrincipal,* Nutana Collegiate Institute, Memorial Library and Art Gallery, Saskatoon SK

Ratner, Peter, *Asst Prof,* James Madison University, School of Art & Art History, Harrisonburg VA (S)

Ratner, Rhoda, *Librn,* National Museum of American History, Branch Library, Washington DC

Rattazzi, Serena, *Dir,* The American Federation of Arts, New York NY

Rattner, Carl, *Prof,* Saint Thomas Aquinas College, Art Dept, Sparkhill NY (S)

Rau, David D J, *Cur Educ,* Cranbrook Art Museum, Bloomfield Hills MI

Rau, Paula, *Asst Prof,* Mary Baldwin College, Dept of Art, Staunton VA (S)

Rauch, Emily, *Dir,* Schoharie County Arts Council, Cobleskill NY

Rauch, Kristin, *Dir,* State University of New York College at New Paltz, Art Education Program, New Paltz NY (S)

Raudzens, Ingrida, *Chmn Dept,* Salem State College, Art Dept, Salem MA (S)

Raudzens, Mark, *Prof,* Salem State College, Art Dept, Salem MA (S)

Rauf, Barb, *Dir,* Thomas More College, TM Gallery, Crestview KY

Rauf, Barbara, *Assoc Prof,* Thomas More College, Art Dept, Crestview Hills KY (S)

Rauner, Michael, *Prog & Educ Coordr,* San Francisco Camerawork Inc, San Francisco CA

Rauschenberg, Brad, *Dir Research,* Old Salem Inc, Museum of Early Southern Decorative Arts, Winston-Salem NC

Rauschenberg, Bradford L, *Dir Research,* Old Salem Inc, Library, Winston-Salem NC

Rauschenberg, Chris, *Dir,* Blue Sky, Oregon Center for the Photographic Arts, Portland OR

Rauschenberg, Christopher, *Instr,* Marylhurst College, Art Dept, Marylhurst OR (S)

Rausmussen, Neil, *Coordr Tennessee State Museum Foundation,* Tennessee State Museum, Nashville TN

Rautman, Marcus, *Assoc Prof,* University of Missouri, Art History & Archaeology Dept, Columbia MO (S)

Ravenal, C, *Assoc Prof,* American University, Dept of Art, Washington DC (S)

Ravenel, Gaillard, *Chief of Design & Installation,* National Gallery of Art, Washington DC

Ravenhill, Philip, *Chief Cur,* National Museum of African Art, Washington DC

Raverty, Dennis, *Asst Prof,* Pittsburg State University, Art Dept, Pittsburg KS (S)

Rawlins, Dori, *Cur,* City of Irvine, Fine Arts Center, Irvine CA (S)

Rawlins, Kathleen, *Asst Dir,* City of Cambridge Historical Commission, Cambridge MA

Rawlins, Scott, *Asst Prof,* Beaver College, Dept of Fine Arts, Glenside PA (S)

Rawls, James A, *Chmn,* Pearl River Community College, Art Dept, Division of Fine Arts, Poplarville MS (S)

Rawson, Gale, *Museum Registrar,* Pennsylvania Academy of the Fine Arts, Museum of American Art, Philadelphia PA

Rawstern, Sherri, *Cur Educ,* Dacotah Prairie Museum, Lamont Gallery, Aberdeen SD

Ray, David, *Campus Dir,* The Illinois Institute of Art, Chicago IL (S)

Ray, Jeffrey, *Cur Coll,* Atwater Kent Museum, Philadelphia PA

Ray, Lawrence A, *Chmn,* Lambuth University, Dept of Human Ecology & Visual Arts, Jackson TN (S)

Ray, R Kenneth, *Prof,* University of Wisconsin, Madison, Dept of Art, Madison WI (S)

Ray, Timothy, *Prof,* Moorhead State University, Dept of Art, Moorhead MN (S)

Ray, Will, *Dir,* Palm Beach County Cultural Council, West Palm Beach FL

Rayen, James W, *Prof,* Wellesley College, Art Dept, Wellesley MA (S)

Raymer, John, *Instr,* Milwaukee Area Technical College, Graphic Arts Division, Milwaukee WI (S)

Rayse, Lisa, *Acting Cur,* United States Navy, Art Gallery, Washington DC

Raz, Robert, *Dir Library,* Grand Rapids Public Library, Music & Art Dept, Grand Rapids MI

Rea, Douglas F, *Assoc Prof,* Rochester Institute of Technology, School of Photographic Arts & Sciences, Rochester NY (S)

Read, Bob, *Art Dir,* New Mexico Highlands University, Arrott Art Gallery, Las Vegas NM

Read, Charles, *Prof,* Ocean County College, Humanities Dept, Toms River NJ (S)

Reagan, Robert, *Pres,* Gaston County Museum of Art & History, Dallas NC

Real, William A, *Chief Conservator,* Carnegie Institute, Carnegie Museum of Art, Pittsburgh PA

Reasoner, Kathryn, *Exec Dir,* Headlands Center for the Arts, Sausalito CA

Reaves, Wendy W, *Cur Prints & Drawings,* National Portrait Gallery, Washington DC

Renick, Patricia, *Prof Fine Arts*, University of Cincinnati, School of Art, Cincinnati OH (S)

Renkl, W, *Asst Prof*, Austin Peay State University, Dept of Art, Clarksville TN (S)

Renner, Linda, *Coordr Marketing & Development*, Houston Center For Photography, Houston TX

Rennie, Heather, *Dir*, Algonquin Arts Council, Art Gallery of Bancroft, Bancroft ON

Rennie, Mairi C, *Dir*, Baylor University, Armstrong Browning Library, Waco TX

Rennie, Mark, *Exec Dir*, Eyes & Ears Foundation, San Francisco CA

Rensink, Mark, *Public Relations Coordr*, Whatcom Museum of History and Art, Library, Bellingham WA

Rensberger, John, *Cur Vertebrate Paleontology*, University of Washington, Thomas Burke Memorial Washington State Museum, Seattle WA

Rensink, Mark, *Public Relations*, Whatcom Museum of History and Art, Bellingham WA

Rentof, Beryl, *Reference Head*, Fashion Institute of Technology, Gladys Marcus Library, New York NY

Reo, Danielle, *Assoc Dir*, Installation Gallery, San Diego CA

Repinski, Robert, *Asst Prof*, University of Minnesota, Duluth, Art Dept, Duluth MN (S)

Replogle, Ray, *Prof*, Wayne State College, Art Dept, Wayne NE (S)

Replogle, Rex, *Assoc Prof*, Kansas State University, Art Dept, Manhattan KS (S)

Repman, Martha, *Head*, Free Library of Philadelphia, Rare Book Dept, Philadelphia PA

Resch, Tyler, *Librn*, Bennington Museum, Library, Bennington VT

Resnik, Kim, *Dir Communications*, Atlanta Historical Society Inc, Atlanta History Center, Atlanta GA

Retallack, John, *Assoc Prof*, Rochester Institute of Technology, School of Photographic Arts & Sciences, Rochester NY (S)

Retfalvi, A, *Librn*, University of Toronto, Fine Art Library, Toronto ON

Rettew, Robert H, *Librn*, Saint Paul's School, Ohrstrom Library, Concord NH

Reubain, Patricia, *Dir*, University of Northern Colorado, John Mariani Art Gallery, Greeley CO

Reusch, Johann J K, *Dir*, Bucknell University, Center Gallery, Lewisburg PA

Reuter, Laurel J, *Dir & Head Cur*, North Dakota Museum of Art, Grand Forks ND

Reveley, W Taylor, *Pres*, Virginia Museum of Fine Arts, Richmond VA

ReVille, Grayson, *Pres*, Portraits South, Raleigh NC

ReVille, Jac F, *Pres*, Portraits South, Raleigh NC

Revoal, Marvin, *Pres*, Maude I Kerns Art Center Galleries, Eugene OR

Rexine, John, *Registrar*, Brandeis University, Rose Art Museum, Waltham MA

Rey, Alberto, *Dir*, Chautauqua Center for the Visual Arts, Chautauqua NY

Reydburd, Pola, *Dir*, Bakehouse Art Complex, Inc, Miami FL

Reyes, David, *Registrar*, Huntsville Museum of Art, Huntsville AL

Reyes, Marisa, *Dean*, Elgin Community College, Fine Arts Dept, Elgin IL (S)

Reynolds, Ed, *Interim Cur*, Silverado Museum, Reference Library, Saint Helena CA

Reynolds, Edmond, *Dir*, Silverado Museum, Saint Helena CA

Reynolds, Harold M, *Assoc Prof*, Central Missouri State University, Art Dept, Warrensburg MO (S)

Reynolds, Jim, *Assoc Archivist*, Heard Museum, Library & Archives, Phoenix AZ

Reynolds, Jock, *Dir & Cur Photo*, Phillips Academy, Addison Gallery of American Art, Andover MA

Reynolds, John R, *Chief Preparator & Exhib Designer*, Worcester Art Museum, Worcester MA

Reynolds, Jonathan, *Asst Prof*, University of Michigan, Ann Arbor, Dept of History of Art, Ann Arbor MI (S)

Reynolds, Liz, *Registrar*, Brooklyn Museum, Brooklyn NY

Reynolds, Robert, *Prof*, California Polytechnic State University at San Luis Obispo, Dept of Art & Design, San Luis Obispo CA (S)

Reynolds, Ron, *Head Dept*, Arkansas Tech University, Dept of Art, Russellville AR (S)

Reynolds, Sandy, *VPres*, Davidson County Museum of Art, Lexington NC

Reynolds, Stephen, *Prof*, University of Texas at San Antonio, Division of Visual Arts, San Antonio TX (S)

Reynolds, Valrae, *Cur Asian Coll*, Newark Museum Association, The Newark Museum, Newark NJ

Reynolds, Vic, *Prof*, Wayne State College, Art Dept, Wayne NE (S)

Reynolds, Wiley R, *VPres*, The Society of the Four Arts, Palm Beach FL

Rezelman, Betsy, *Chmn*, St Lawrence University, Dept of Fine Arts, Canton NY (S)

Rhei, Marylin, *Prof*, Smith College, Art Dept, Northampton MA (S)

Rhodes, Brian, *Head Librn*, Willard Library, Dept of Fine Arts, Evansville IN

Rhodes, David, *Pres*, School of Visual Arts, New York NY (S)

Rhodes, Kimberly, *Educ Dir*, The Parrish Art Museum, Southampton NY

Rhodes, Lisa, *Admin Dir*, Center for Puppetry Arts, Atlanta GA

Rhodes, Marcus A, *Pres*, Old Colony Historical Society, Museum, Taunton MA

Rhodes, Mark, *Asst Prof*, University of Richmond, Dept of Art, Richmond VA (S)

Rhodes, Richard, *Adjunct Cur*, Oakville Galleries, Centennial Gallery and Gairloch Gallery, Oakville ON

Rhodes, Rita, *Exec Dir*, Arts & Science Center, Statesville NC

Rhodes, Silas H, *Chmn*, School of Visual Arts, New York NY (S)

Rian, Kirsten, *Gallery Coordr*, Blue Sky, Oregon Center for the Photographic Arts, Portland OR

Riberin, Helene, *Dir Develop*, Musee du Quebec, Quebec PQ

Ribkoff, Natalie, *Cur Art*, Toronto Dominion Bank, Toronto ON

Riccardi, Elsebeth, *Dir Human Resources*, Royal Ontario Museum, Toronto ON

Ricci, Pat, *Cur*, Louisiana Historical Association, Confederate Museum, New Orleans LA

Ricciardelli, Catherine, *Registrar*, Minneapolis Institute of Arts, Minneapolis MN

Ricciardi, Dana D, *Dir*, Captain Robert Bennet Forbes House, Milton MA

Ricciotti, Dominic, *Chmn*, Winona State University, Dept of Art, Winona MN (S)

Rice, Arthur, *Head Landscape Architecture Dept*, North Carolina State University at Raleigh, School of Design, Raleigh NC (S)

Rice, Danielle, *Cur Educ*, Philadelphia Museum of Art, Philadelphia PA

Rice, James, *Chmn Photographic Processing & Finishing Management*, Rochester Institute of Technology, School of Photographic Arts & Sciences, Rochester NY (S)

Rice, Jane G, *Dep Dir*, San Diego Museum of Art, San Diego CA

Rice, Joey, *Art Specialist & Cur*, Walter Anderson Museum of Art, Ocean Springs MS

Rice, Kevin, *Registrar*, Confederation Centre Art Gallery and Museum, Charlottetown PE

Rice, Kevin, *Registrar*, Confederation Centre Art Gallery and Museum, Library, Charlottetown PE

Rice, Nancy, *Prof*, Maryville University of Saint Louis, Art Division, Saint Louis MO (S)

Rice, Nancy N, *Gallery Dir*, Maryville University Saint Louis, Morton J May Foundation Gallery, Saint Louis MO

Rice, Parker, *Treas*, Fitchburg Art Museum, Fitchburg MA

Rice, Tom, *Prof*, Kalamazoo College, Art Dept, Kalamazoo MI (S)

Ricetti, Angela, *Cataloger*, Spertus Institute of Jewish Studies, Asher Library, Chicago IL

Rich, Adelle, *Instr*, Fort Hays State University, Dept of Art, Hays KS (S)

Rich, Andrea L, *Pres & Chief Exec Officer*, Los Angeles County Museum of Art, Los Angeles CA

Rich, Danny C, *Secy*, Inter-Society Color Council, Lawrenceville NJ

Rich, Elizabeth, *Librn*, Columbia Museum of Art, Library, Columbia SC

Rich, Fred, *Preparator*, College of William & Mary, Joseph & Margaret Muscarelle Museum of Art, Williamsburg VA

Rich, Gretchen, *Dean*, Huron University, Arts & Sciences Division, Huron SD (S)

Rich, Merle, *Registrar*, Artesia Historical Museum & Art Center, Artesia NM

Rich, Nancy, *Cur Educ*, Smith College, Museum of Art, Northampton MA

Rich, Patricia, *Pres*, Arts & Education Council of Greater Saint Louis, Saint Louis MO

Richard, Charles, *Chmn*, Riverside Community College, Dept of Art & Mass Media, Riverside CA (S)

Richard, Harold James, *Prof*, University of New Orleans-Lake Front, Dept of Fine Arts, New Orleans LA (S)

Richard, Jack, *Dir*, Richard Gallery & Almond Tea Gallery, Divisions of Studios of Jack Richard, Cuyahoga Falls OH

Richard, Jack, *Dir*, Studios of Jack Richard Creative School of Design, Cuyahoga Falls OH (S)

Richard, Paul, *VPres*, Children's Museum, Rauh Memorial Library, Indianapolis IN

Richards, Anita, *Admin Dir*, Marcella Sembrich Memorial Association Inc, Opera Museum, Bolton Landing NY

Richards, David, *Librn*, University of Southern Mississippi, McCain Library & Archives, Hattiesburg MS

Richards, Evann, *Asst Prof*, Saint Louis Community College at Forest Park, Art Dept, Saint Louis MO (S)

Richards, Evann, *Adjunct Instr*, Maryville University of Saint Louis, Art Division, Saint Louis MO (S)

Richards, Janet, *Vis Cur*, University of Michigan, Kelsey Museum of Archaeology, Ann Arbor MI

Richards, Judith Olch, *Assoc Dir*, Independent Curators Inc, New York NY

Richards, Lenore, *Dean of Design*, Ontario College of Art & Design, Toronto ON (S)

Richards, L Jane, *Sr Cur*, Historical Museum at Fort Missoula, Missoula MT

Richards, Peter, *Artist Coordr*, Exploratorium, San Francisco CA

Richards, Ronald, *Cur in Charge*, Indiana State Museum, Indianapolis IN

Richardson, Brenda, *Deputy Dir & Cur Modern Paintings & Sculpture*, Baltimore Museum of Art, Baltimore MD

Richardson, Carl, *Dir*, League of New Hampshire Craftsmen, League Gallery, Concord NH

Richardson, Carl, *Dir*, League of New Hampshire Craftsmen, Library, Concord NH

Richardson, Carl, *Asst Prof*, Spokane Falls Community College, Fine Arts Dept, Spokane WA (S)

Richardson, Charlotte, *Events Coordr*, Dallas Visual Art Center, Dallas TX

Richardson, Dennis, *Dir Human Resources*, M Grumbacher Inc, Bloomsbury NJ

Richardson, Francoise, *Pres Board*, New Orleans Museum of Art, New Orleans LA

Richardson, Frederick, *Pres*, Springfield Art & Historical Society, Springfield VT

Richardson, Frederick, *Pres*, Springfield Art & Historical Society, Miller Art Center, Springfield VT

Richardson, Jim, *Instr*, The Art Institutes International, The Art Institute of Seattle, Seattle WA (S)

Richardson, Lynn, *Comm Dir*, Public Art Fund, Inc, Library, New York NY

Richardson, Martha, *Chmn Fine Arts Dept*, Mississippi Gulf Coast Community College-Jackson County Campus, Art Dept, Gautier MS (S)

Richardson, Peggy, *Librn*, Eastern Shore Art Association, Inc, Library, Fairhope AL

Richardson, Sue, *Registrar*, California State University, Chico, Janet Turner Print Gallery & Collection, Chico CA

Richardson, Susan, *Librn*, Birmingham Public Library, Arts, Music & Recreation Department, Birmingham AL

Richardson, Trevor, *Cur*, MacAlester College, Galleries, Saint Paul MN

Richardson, Wallace, *Chmn*, Mid America Arts Alliance & Exhibits USA, Kansas City MO

Richars, Larry W, *Dean*, University of Toronto, School of Architecture & Landscape Architecture, Toronto ON (S)

Richbourg, Lance, *Assoc Prof*, St Michael's College, Fine Arts Dept, Colchester VT (S)

Richell, Michael, *Asst to Dir*, Cummer Museum of Art & Gardens, DeEtte Holden Cummer Museum Foundation, Jacksonville FL

Richendrfer, Dolly, *Mgr Community Relations*, Spokane Public Library Gallery, Spokane WA

Richert, Phyllis, *Cur*, Chalet of the Golden Fleece, New Glarus WI

Richman, Gary, *Prof*, University of Rhode Island, Dept of Art, Kingston RI (S)

Richman, Irwin, *Prof*, Penn State Harrisburg, Humanities Division, Middletown PA (S)

Richman, Roger, *Prof*, University of Maine at Augusta, Division of Fine & Performing Arts, Augusta ME (S)

Richmond, William, *Asst Prof*, University of Evansville, Art Dept, Evansville IN (S)

Richter, Susan, *Cur*, Vermilion County Museum Society, Danville IL

Richter, Susan E, *Prog Dir*, Vermilion County Museum Society, Library, Danville IL

Richwagen, Pat, *Pres*, Marblehead Arts Association, Inc, Marblehead MA

Rickard, Marcia R, *Chmn*, Saint Mary's College, Dept of Art, Notre Dame IN (S)

Rideout, Janice, *Historian*, Marblehead Historical Society, Library, Marblehead MA

Rider, Diane, *Library-LRC Dir*, Art Institute of Fort Lauderdale, Technical Library, Fort Lauderdale FL

Ridewood, Donna M, *Dir*, Victoria Mansion, Inc, Victoria Mansion - Morse Libby House, Portland ME

Ridgeway, Teresa M, *Registrar*, Bower's Museum, Santa Ana CA

Riebel, Danielle, *Cur*, Old Barracks Museum, Trenton NJ

Rieben, John, *Asst Prof*, University of Wisconsin, Madison, Dept of Art, Madison WI (S)

Riedinger, Robert J, *Correspondence Secy*, Artists' Fellowship, Inc, New York NY

Riegel, James, *Head Photography Dept*, Kalamazoo Institute of Arts, KIA School, Kalamazoo MI (S)

Rieger, Sonja, *Chmn Dept*, University of Alabama at Birmingham, Dept of Art, Birmingham AL (S)

Rieke, Gail, *Adjunct Assoc*, College of Santa Fe, Art Dept, Santa Fe NM (S)

Riemer, Milton, *Chmn*, Concordia University, Dept of Fine Arts, Austin TX (S)

Riese, Beatrice, *Pres*, American Abstract Artists, New York NY

Riess, Jonathan, *Prof Art History*, University of Cincinnati, School of Art, Cincinnati OH (S)

Rietveld, Rickard, *Chmn*, Valencia Community College - East Campus, Art Dept, Orlando FL (S)

Riffle, Brenda, *Librn*, Hampshire County Public Library, Romney WV

Rifkin, Ned, *Dir*, High Museum of Art, Atlanta GA

Rigby, Bruce, *Prof*, College of New Jersey, Art Dept, Trenton NJ (S)

Rigby, Ida K, *Art History Graduate Coordr*, San Diego State University, School of Art, Design & Art History, San Diego CA (S)

Rigdon, Lois, *Dir*, Art Guild of Burlington, Arts for Living Center, Burlington IA

Rigg, Frank, *Cur*, National Archives & Records Administration, John F Kennedy Library & Museum, Boston MA

Rigg, Margaret, *Assoc Prof*, Eckerd College, Art Dept, Saint Petersburg FL (S)

Riggins-Ezzell, Lois, *Exec Dir*, Tennessee State Museum, Nashville TN

Riggs, Gerry, *Dir & Cur*, University of Colorado at Colorado Springs, Gallery of Contemporary Art, Colorado Springs CO

Rights, Edith A, *Librn*, Montclair Art Museum, LeBrun Library, Montclair NJ

Riker, Janet, *Dir*, Fund for the Borough of Brooklyn, Rotunda Gallery, Brooklyn NY

Riley, Amy, *Admin Asst to Dir*, Fort Worth Art Association, Modern Art Museum of Fort Worth, Fort Worth TX

Riley, Cathy F, *Adminr*, Maui Historical Society, Bailey House, Wailuku HI

Riley, Dixie, *Head Librn*, Chappell Memorial Library and Art Gallery, Chappell NE

Riley, Gary, *Visual Arts Dir*, Sun Valley Center for the Arts & Humanities, Dept of Fine Art, Sun Valley ID (S)

Riley, Gresham, *Pres*, Pennsylvania Academy of the Fine Arts, Museum of American Art, Philadelphia PA

Riley, Gresham, *Pres*, Pennsylvania Academy of the Fine Arts, Philadelphia PA (S)

Riley, Sarah, *Chmn*, Southeast Missouri State University, Dept of Art, Cape Girardeau MO (S)

Riley, Terence, *Chief Cur, Dept Architecture & Design*, Museum of Modern Art, New York NY

Rimington, Paul, *First VPres*, Swedish American Museum Association of Chicago, Chicago IL

Rimpela, Cindy, *Business Mgr*, Ashtabula Arts Center, Ashtabula OH

Rinder, Lawrence, *Cur*, University of California, Berkeley Art Museum & Pacific Film Archive, Berkeley CA

Rindfleisch, Jan, *Dir*, De Anza College, Euphrat Museum of Art, Cupertino CA

Rindler, Robert, *Dean*, Cooper Union, School of Art, New York NY (S)

Rindlisbacher, David, *Assoc Prof*, West Texas A&M University, Art, Communication & Theatre Dept, Canyon TX (S)

Riner, Camille, *Instr*, Southwestern Michigan College, Fine & Performing Arts Dept, Dowagiac MI (S)

Ring, Dan, *Asst Cur*, Mendel Art Gallery & Civic Conservatory, Saskatoon SK

Ring, Dan, *Extension Coordr*, Mendel Art Gallery & Civic Conservatory, Saskatoon SK

Ring, John, *Chief Protection Serv*, Cincinnati Institute of Fine Arts, Taft Museum, Cincinnati OH

Ringering, Dennis L, *Head Drawing*, Southern Illinois University at Edwardsville, Dept of Art & Design, Edwardsville IL (S)

Ringle, Stephen, *Exhibits Preparator*, University of Maine, Museum of Art, Orono ME

Ringler, Sara, *Prof*, Cape Cod Community College, Art Dept, West Barnstable MA (S)

Rini, David, *Instr*, Johns Hopkins University, School of Medicine, Dept of Art as Applied to Medicine, Baltimore MD (S)

Rinne, Nicola, *Marketing Coordr*, Institute of Contemporary Art, Boston MA

Riof-Metcalf, Silva, *Prof*, Gavilan College, Art Dept, Gilroy CA (S)

Riopelle, Christopher, *Assoc Cur*, Philadelphia Museum of Art, Rodin Museum of Philadelphia, Philadelphia PA

Riordan, John, *Prof*, State University of New York College at Potsdam, Dept of Fine Arts, Potsdam NY (S)

Riordon, Bernard, *Dir*, Art Gallery of Nova Scotia, Halifax NS

Rios, Sylvia, *Gallery Dir*, Gavilan College, Art Gallery, Gilroy CA

Rios-Samaniego, Milita, *Dir Coll*, Louisiana Department of Culture, Recreation & Tourism, Louisiana State Museum, New Orleans LA

Ripley, Karen, *Exhib Coordr*, Boulder Public Library & Gallery, Dept of Fine Arts Gallery, Boulder CO

Ripley, Robert C, *Mgr Capitol Restoration & Promotion*, Nebraska State Capitol, Lincoln NE

Rippee, Marilyn, *Pres*, Oklahoma Center for Science & Art, Kirkpatrick Center, Oklahoma City OK

Risatti, Howard, *Prof*, Virginia Commonwealth University, Art History Dept, Richmond VA (S)

Risbeck, Phil, *Chmn*, Colorado State University, Dept of Art, Fort Collins CO (S)

Risberg, Debra, *Cur*, Illinois State University, Museum Library, Normal IL

Risberg, Debra, *Cur*, Illinois State University, University Galleries, Normal IL

Riseman, Henry, *Dir*, New England Center for Contemporary Art, Brooklyn CT

Riser, Harry, *First VPres*, Hoosier Salon Patrons Association, Hoosier Salon Art Gallery, Indianapolis IN

Rishel, Joseph, *Cur of Pre-1900 European Painting & Sculpture*, Philadelphia Museum of Art, Rodin Museum of Philadelphia, Philadelphia PA

Rishel, Joseph, *Cur*, Philadelphia Museum of Art, John G Johnson Collection, Philadelphia PA

Rislow, Kyle, *School of Design*, Art Institute of Houston, Houston TX (S)

Rison, Carolyn, *Admin Asst*, Cincinnati Institute of Fine Arts, Taft Museum, Cincinnati OH

Ritchie, Charles, *Asst Cur*, National Gallery of Art, Index of American Design, Washington DC

Ritchie, Robert, *Dir Research*, The Huntington Library, Art Collections & Botanical Gardens, San Marino CA

Ritchie, Sherri, *Coordr*, Edmonton Public Library, Foyer Gallery, Edmonton AB

Ritsch, Joan, *Chmn*, Phoenix College, Dept of Art & Photography, Phoenix AZ (S)

Ritson, Kate, *Prof*, Trinity University, Dept of Art, San Antonio TX (S)

Rittenhouse, Cheri, *Prof*, Rock Valley College, Dept of Art, Rockford IL (S)

Ritter, Hannah, *Pres*, Long Island Graphic Eye Gallery, Port Washington NY

Ritter, Josef, *Prof*, Cazenovia College, Center for Art & Design Studies, Cazenovia NY (S)

Ritter, Katharine L, *Librn*, The Currier Gallery of Art, Library, Manchester NH

Rivard, Paul, *Dir*, American Textile History Museum, Lowell MA

Rivard-Shaw, Nancy, *Cur American Art*, Detroit Institute of Arts, Detroit MI

Rivera, Frank, *Prof*, Mercer County Community College, Arts & Communication/Engineering Technology, Trenton NJ (S)

Rivera, George, *Asst Dir & Chief Cur*, Triton Museum of Art, Santa Clara CA

Rivera, George, *Acting Dir*, Triton Museum of Art, Library, Santa Clara CA

Rivera de Figueroa, Carmen A, *Assoc Prof*, University of Puerto Rico, Dept of Fine Arts, Rio Piedras PR (S)

Rivera-Garcia, Rafael, *Prof*, University of Puerto Rico, Dept of Fine Arts, Rio Piedras PR (S)

Rivres, Helen, *Dir*, Danforth Gallery, the Maine Artists' Space, Portland ME

Rizk, Ron, *Prof*, University of Southern California, School of Fine Arts, Los Angeles CA (S)

Riznyk, Myroslaw, *Facilities Mgr NY*, National Museum of the American Indian, George Gustav Heye Center, New York NY

Rizzo, Tania, *Archivist*, Pasadena Historical Museum, Pasadena CA

Roach, T, *Assoc Prof*, St Francis Xavier University, Fine Arts Dept, Antigonish NS (S)

Roach, Wendy, *Community Relations*, University of North Carolina at Greensboro, Weatherspoon Art Gallery, Greensboro NC

Roane, Teresa, *Librn*, Valentine Museum, Library, Richmond VA

Roark, John, *Asst Prof*, Lynchburg College, Art Dept, Lynchburg VA (S)

Robb, Carole, *Instr*, New York Studio School of Drawing, Painting & Sculpture, New York NY (S)

Robb, Martha, *Pres*, Harrison County Historical Museum, Marshall TX

Robbin, C Roxanne, *Prof*, California State University, Art Dept, Turlock CA (S)

Robbins, Carol, *Cur Textiles*, Dallas Museum of Art, Dallas TX

Robbins, Mark, *Cur Architecture*, Ohio State University, Wexner Center for the Arts, Columbus OH

Roberga, Celesk, *Asst Prof*, University of Florida, Dept of Art, Gainesville FL (S)

Roberson, Karen, *Asst Prof*, University of Texas at Tyler, Dept of Art, Tyler TX (S)

Roberson, Sam, *Coordr Art History*, Indiana University-Purdue University, Indianapolis, Herron School of Art, Indianapolis IN (S)

Roberston, Anne, *Assoc Dir*, College of New Rochelle, Castle Gallery, New Rochelle NY

Robert, Brenda, *Dean*, Anoka Ramsey Community College, Art Dept, Coon Rapids MN (S)

Robert, Henry Flood, *Dir*, Jacksonville Museum of Contemporary Art, Jacksonville FL

Roberts, Ann, *Lectr*, Centenary College of Louisiana, Dept of Art, Shreveport LA (S)

Roberts, Ann, *Prof*, University of Waterloo, Fine Arts Dept, Waterloo ON (S)

Roberts, Anne, *Chmn*, Lake Forest College, Dept of Art, Lake Forest IL (S)

Roberts, Betty, *Dir Educ & Exhib*, Wichita Center for the Arts, Wichita KS (S)

Roberts, Bill, *Div Chmn*, Wells College, Dept of Art, Aurora NY (S)

Roberts, Brady, *Cur Coll & Exhib*, Davenport Museum of Art, Davenport IA

Roberts, Carla A, *Exec Dir*, Atlatl, Phoenix AZ

Roberts, Eileen, *Assoc Prof*, Northern Michigan University, Dept of Art & Design, Marquette MI (S)

Roberts, J Lee, *Assoc Prof*, Lubbock Christian University, Dept of Communication & Fine Art, Lubbock TX (S)

Roberts, Karen, *Admin Secy*, Arizona Historical Society-Yuma, Century House Museum & Garden, Yuma AZ

Roberts, Kim, *Educ Dir*, Ann Arbor Art Association, Art Center, Ann Arbor MI

Roberts, Marie, *Assoc Prof*, Fairleigh Dickinson University, Fine Arts Dept, Teaneck NJ (S)

Roberts, Mary, *Public Prog Mgr*, Workman & Temple Family Homestead Museum, City of Industry CA

Roberts, Nita, *Photographer*, New York University, Institute of Fine Arts Visual Resources Collection, New York NY

Roberts, Paul, *Pres Board of Dir*, Santa Barbara Contemporary Arts Forum, Santa Barbara CA

Roberts, Perri Lee, *Assoc Prof*, University of Miami, Dept of Art & Art History, Coral Gables FL (S)

Roberts, Prudence, *Sr Cur American, Contemporary & European Art*, Portland Art Museum, Portland OR

Roberts, Suzanne O, *Visual Resource Cur*, New York State College of Ceramics at Alfred University, Scholes Library of Ceramics, Alfred NY

Roberts, Wesley, *Instr*, Campbellsville College, Fine Arts Division, Campbellsville KY (S)

Robertshaw, Mary Jane, *Assoc Prof*, College of New Rochelle School of Arts & Sciences, Art Dept, New Rochelle NY (S)

Roberts-Manganelli, Susan, *Head Registration-Conservation*, Stanford University, Museum of Art, Stanford CA

Robertson, Barbara, *Dir Educ*, Williams College, Museum of Art, Williamstown MA

Robertson, Charles, *Deputy Dir*, National Museum of American Art, Washington DC

Robertson, David, *Dir*, University of Oregon, Museum of Art, Eugene OR

Robertson, David J, *Prof*, Rochester Institute of Technology, School of Photographic Arts & Sciences, Rochester NY (S)

Robertson, Dennis, *Pres*, Dillman's Bay Properties, Dillman's Creative Arts Foundation, Lac Du Flambeau WI

Robertson, Dennis, *Pres*, Dillman's Bay Properties, Tom Lynch Resource Center, Lac Du Flambeau WI

Robertson, Donna, *Dean*, Illinois Institute of Technology, College of Architecture, Chicago IL (S)

Robertson, F, *Instr*, Community College of Rhode Island, Dept of Art, Warwick RI (S)

Robertson, Jack, *Librn*, University of Virginia, Fiske Kimball Fine Arts Library, Charlottesville VA

Robertson, James, *Instr Pottery*, Red Rocks Community College, Arts & Humanities Dept, Lakewood CO (S)

Robertson, Jim, *Architecture Librn*, New Jersey Institute of Technology, Architecture Library, Newark NJ

Robertson, Karen, *Dir*, Morgan State University, Library, Baltimore MD

Robertson, Kimberly, *Museum Educ*, Wake Forest University, Museum of Anthropology, Winston Salem NC

Robertson, Lynn, *Dir*, University of South Carolina, McKissick Museum, Columbia SC

Robertson, Prudence, *Pres*, Hill-Stead Museum, Farmington CT

Robertson, Roderick, *Head Dept*, Saint Mary's University of Minnesota, Art & Design Dept, Winona MN (S)

Robertson, Scott, *Chmn*, University of Wisconsin-Eau Claire, Dept of Art, Eau Claire WI (S)

Robertson, Sherry, *Mgr Develop & Marketing*, Muttart Public Art Gallery, Calgary AB

Robertson, Sue, *VPres*, Dillman's Bay Properties, Dillman's Creative Arts Foundation, Lac Du Flambeau WI

Robeson, James, *Acting Dir*, Miami University, Art Museum, Oxford OH

Robicheau, Dick, *Pres*, Yarmouth County Historical Society, Yarmouth County Museum, Yarmouth NS

Robin, Madeleine, *Dir Art*, L'Universite Laval, Library, Quebec PQ

Robings, Edward, *Exec Dir*, Ventura County Historical Society, Museum of History & Art, Ventura CA

Robinow, Pat, *Slide Cur*, Wright State University, Dept of Art & Art History Resource Center & Slide Library, Dayton OH

Robins, Henriann, *Ref Dept*, Springfield Free Public Library, Donald B Palmer Museum, Springfield NJ

Robins, Rosemary Gay, *Assoc Prof*, Emory University, Art History Dept, Atlanta GA (S)

Robinson, Barbara, *Chmn*, National Assembly of State Arts Agencies, Washington DC

Robinson, Bonnell, *Dir Gallery & Exhib*, The Art Institute of Boston, Main Gallery, Boston MA

Robinson, Darlene, *Acting ExecDir*, Portage and District Arts Council, Portage Arts Centre, Portage la Prairie MB

Robinson, Deborah, *Corporate Press Officer*, Public Corporation for the Arts, Visual & Performing Arts Registry, Long Beach CA

Robinson, Don D, *Chmn Dept*, Harding University, Dept of Art, Searcy AR (S)

Robinson, Duncan, *Dir*, Yale University, Yale Center for British Art, New Haven CT

Robinson, Fern, *Young Adult*, Mason City Public Library, Mason City IA

Robinson, Franklin W, *Co-Dir*, Cornell University, Herbert F Johnson Museum of Art, Ithaca NY

Robinson, Franklin W, *Dir*, Cornell University, Museum Library, Ithaca NY

Robinson, George, *Prof*, Bethel College, Dept of Art, Saint Paul MN (S)

Robinson, Gregory, *Exec Dir*, City Art Works, Pratt Fine Arts Center, Seattle WA (S)

Robinson, Gregory, *Exec Dir*, Pratt Fine Arts Center, Gallery, Seattle WA

Robinson, Imogene, *Dir*, Willard House & Clock Museum, Inc, North Grafton MA

Robinson, James, *Cur Asian Art*, Indianapolis Museum of Art, Indianapolis IN

Robinson, Kim, *Museum Specialist*, United States Department of the Interior Museum, Washington DC

Robinson, Lilien, *Chmn*, George Washington University, Dept of Art, Washington DC (S)

Robinson, Mark, *Mem Coordr*, Terra Museum of American Art, Chicago IL

Robinson, Patricia, *Dir Development*, Painted Bride Art Center, The Gallery at the Painted Bride, Philadelphia PA

Robinson, Pearl, *Educ Dir*, Afro-American Historical & Cultural Museum, Philadelphia PA

Robinson, Regan, *Dir*, Westerly Public Library, Hoxie Gallery, Westerly RI

Robinson, Roger W, *Pres*, Willard House & Clock Museum, Inc, North Grafton MA

Robinson, Sally, *Exhib Coordr*, Dawson City Museum & Historical Society, Dawson City YT

Robinson, Sandra, *Instr*, Mount San Jacinto College, Art Dept, San Jacinto CA (S)

Robinson, Stephen, *Dir*, Glenhyrst Art Gallery of Brant, Brantford ON

Robinson, Steve, *Prog Coordr*, MacDonald Stewart Art Centre, Guelph ON

Robinson, Sue Ann, *Educator*, Long Beach Museum of Art, Long Beach CA

Robinson, Susan, *Prof*, Loyola Marymount University, Art & Art History Dept, Los Angeles CA (S)

Robinson, William, *Head*, Purdue University Calumet, Dept of Communication & Creative Arts, Hammond IN (S)

Robinson, William W, *Cur Drawings*, Harvard University, William Hayes Fogg Art Museum, Cambridge MA

Robison, Andrew, *Sr Cur Print, Drawing & Sculpture*, National Gallery of Art, Washington DC

Robison, Tim, *Dir Admissions*, San Francisco Art Institute, San Francisco CA (S)

Roby, Thomas, *Chmn*, City Colleges of Chicago, Kennedy-King College, Chicago IL (S)

Roche, James, *Prof*, Florida State University, Art Dept, Tallahassee FL (S)

Roche, Joanne, *Librn*, Yonkers Public Library, Fine Arts Dept, Yonkers NY

Roche, Joanne, *Librn*, Yonkers Public Library, Will Library, Yonkers NY

Roche, Roger, *Pres*, Boothbay Region Art Foundation, Boothbay Harbor ME

Roche, Valerie, *Instr*, Creighton University, Fine & Performing Arts Dept, Omaha NE (S)

Rochfort, Desmond, *Chmn*, University of Alberta, Dept of Art & Design, Edmonton AB (S)

Rock, Rodney, *Dir*, University of Connecticut, Jorgensen Gallery, Storrs CT

Rockefeller, David, *Chmn Emeritus*, Museum of Modern Art, New York NY

Rockefeller, Steven C, *Pres*, Wendell Gilley Museum, Southwest Harbor ME

Rockhill, King, *Pres*, Appaloosa Museum, Inc, Moscow ID

Rockwell, Dan, *Registrar*, Southern Methodist University, Meadows Museum, Dallas TX

Rodda, Jenni, *Cur*, New York University, Institute of Fine Arts Visual Resources Collection, New York NY

Rode, Meredith, *Prof*, University of the District of Columbia, Dept of Mass Media, Visual & Performing Arts, Washington DC (S)

Rodciro, Jose, *Assoc Prof*, Jersey City State College, Art Dept, Jersey City NJ (S)

Rodes, David S, *Dir*, University of California, Los Angeles, Grunwald Center for the Graphic Arts, Los Angeles CA

Rodgers, Dick, *Chmn Dept*, Earlham College, Art Dept, Richmond IN (S)

Rodgers, Jeanne, *Dir*, Minot Art Association, Minot Art Gallery, Minot ND

Rodgers, Kenneth G, *Dir*, North Carolina Central University, NCCU Art Museum, Durham NC

Rodgers, Richard, *Art Dept Convener*, Earlham College, Leeds Gallery, Richmond IN

Rodgers, Richelle, *Registrar*, Pennsylvania Historical & Museum Commission, State Museum of Pennsylvania, Harrisburg PA

Rodgers, Tommie, *Registrar*, Lauren Rogers Museum of Art, Laurel MS

Rodman, Cathie, *Develop Officer*, Civic Fine Arts Center, Sioux Falls SD

Rodman, Judith, *Museum Shop Mgr*, Bennington Museum, Bennington Museum, Bennington VT

Rodrigues-Boette, Taryn, *Library Dir*, Saint Augustine Historical Society, Library, Saint Augustine FL

Rodriguez, Anita, *Instr*, Mount San Jacinto College, Art Dept, San Jacinto CA (S)

Rodriguez, Geno, *Dir Advertising*, Alternative Museum, New York NY

Rodriguez, Maria del Carmen, *Staff Supv*, Museo de la Americas, Old San Juan PR

Rodriguez, Pedro A, *Exec Dir*, Guadalupe Cultural Arts Center, San Antonio TX

Rodriguez, Ruth, *Admin Asst*, University of Puerto Rico, Museum of Anthropology, History & Art, San Juan PR

Rodriguez, Vivian, *Interim Dir*, Metro-Dade, Miami Art Museum of Dade County, Miami FL

Rodriguez, Yolanda, *Asst,* University of Houston, William R Jenkins Architecture & Art Library, Houston TX

Rodriguiz, Sandria, *Dean,* College of Lake County, Art Dept, Grayslake IL (S)

Rodriquez, Cynthia, *Adjunct Asst Prof,* Texas Woman's University, Dept of Visual Arts, Denton TX (S)

Roe, Ruth, *Librn,* Orange County Museum of Art, Library, Newport Beach CA

Roehl, Paul, *Instr,* Monterey Peninsula College, Art Dept, Monterey CA (S)

Roelfsema-Hummel, Chris, *Dir,* Moody County Historical Society, Flandreau SD

Roemer, Carol, *Instr,* Long Beach City College, Dept of Art, Long Beach CA (S)

Roese, Ronnie L, *Dir,* Miracle at Pentecost Foundation, Biblical Arts Center, Dallas TX

Roever, James, *VPres,* Missouri Western State College, Fine Arts Gallery, Saint Joseph MO

Roeyer, Mark, *Exhib Designer,* University of Kansas, Spencer Museum of Art, Lawrence KS

Rogal, Samuel J, *Chmn,* Illinois Valley Community College, Division of Humanities & Fine Arts, Oglesby IL (S)

Rogalski, Chet, *Div Head,* Central Wyoming College, Art Center, Riverton WY (S)

Roger, Leon, *Mgr,* Virginia Commonwealth University, Anderson Gallery, Richmond VA

Rogers, Barbara, *Prof Painting & Drawing,* University of Arizona, Dept of Art, Tucson AZ (S)

Rogers, Byran, *Head,* Carnegie Mellon University, Dept of Art, Pittsburgh PA (S)

Rogers, Dan, *Instr,* Bismarck State College, Fine Arts Dept, Bismarck ND (S)

Rogers, Elizabeth, *Membership Coordr,* Organization of Independent Artists, New York NY

Rogers, Elizabeth, *Asst Dir,* Japan Society, Inc, Japan Society Gallery, New York NY

Rogers, Eric, *Exec Dir,* Jay County Arts Council, Hugh N Ronald Memorial Gallery, Portland IN

Rogers, Floretta, *Cur,* Clark County Historical Society, Pioneer - Krier Museum, Ashland KS

Rogers, James, *Pres,* Westfield Athenaeum, Jasper Rand Art Museum, Westfield MA

Rogers, James W, *Prof,* Glenville State College, Dept of Fine Arts, Glenville WV (S)

Rogers, John F W, *Chmn Fine Arts Committee,* US Department of State, Diplomatic Reception Rooms, Washington DC

Rogers, Judith, *Instr,* Linn Benton Community College, Fine & Applied Art Dept, Albany OR (S)

Rogers, Malcolm, *Dir,* Museum of Fine Arts, Boston MA

Rogers, Nancy M, *Exec Dir,* Wooster Community Art Center, Danbury CT

Rogers, Nancy M, *Exec Dir,* Wooster Community Art Center, Library, Danbury CT

Rogers, Patricia J, *Librn,* Corning Museum of Glass, Rakow Library, Corning NY

Rogers, Richard L, *Pres,* Center for Creative Studies, College of Art & Design, Detroit MI (S)

Rogers, Robert, *Cur Antique Auto Mus,* Heritage Plantation of Sandwich, Sandwich MA

Rogers, Robert, *Assoc Prof,* Queensborough Community College, Dept of Art & Photography, Bayside NY (S)

Rogerson, Lynn K, *Dir,* Art Services International, Alexandria VA

Rohlf, Jason, *Preparator Asst,* Marquette University, Haggerty Museum of Art, Milwaukee WI

Rohlfing, John, *Assoc Prof,* University of Hartford, Hartford Art School, West Hartford CT (S)

Rohm, Robert H, *Prof,* University of Rhode Island, Dept of Art, Kingston RI (S)

Rohn, Mathew, *Asst Prof,* Saint Olaf College, Art Dept, Northfield MN (S)

Rohr, Tom, *Vis Asst Prof,* University of Alaska-Fairbanks, Dept of Art, Fairbanks AK (S)

Rohrer, Judith, *Chmn,* Emory University, Art History Dept, Atlanta GA (S)

Rohwer, Sievert, *Cur Birds,* University of Washington, Thomas Burke Memorial Washington State Museum, Seattle WA

Roison, Morrie, *Prof,* Gavilan College, Art Dept, Gilroy CA (S)

Roizen, Morry, *Chmn,* West Valley College, Art Dept, Saratoga CA (S)

Rojers, June, *Exec Dir,* Fairbanks Arts Association, Fairbanks AK

Rokfalusi, J Mark, *Asst Prof,* Atlanta College of Art, Atlanta GA (S)

Roland, Craig, *Asst Prof,* University of Florida, Dept of Art, Gainesville FL (S)

Roland, George, *Chair Art Dept,* Allegheny College, Art Dept, Meadville PA (S)

Roland, Marya, *Asst Prof,* Western Carolina University, Dept of Art, Cullowhee NC (S)

Roll, Jon, *Gallery Mgr,* Massachusetts Institute of Technology, List Visual Arts Center, Cambridge MA

Roller, Marion, *Pres,* Audubon Artists, Inc, New York NY

Roller, Terry M, *Assoc Prof,* Baylor University, Dept of Art, Waco TX (S)

Rolling, Hubert, *Dir Performing Arts,* Arts & Science Center for Southeast Arkansas, Pine Bluff AR

Rollins, Fred H, *Dir,* Jefferson County Historical Society, Watertown NY

Rollins, Fred H, *Dir,* Jefferson County Historical Society, Library, Watertown NY

Rollins, Jane, *Events Coordr,* Ward Foundation, Ward Museum of Wildfowl Art, Salisbury MD

Rollins, Ken, *Exec Dir,* Florida Gulf Coast Art Center, Inc, Belleair FL

Rollins, Ken, *Exec Dir,* Florida Gulf Coast Art Center, Inc, Belleair FL (S)

Rollins, Rich, *Instr,* Marylhurst College, Art Dept, Marylhurst OR (S)

Rolnick, Neil, *Chmn,* Rensselaer Polytechnic Institute, Dept of Art, Troy NY (S)

Rolstad Triek, May, *VPres,* Pen & Brush, Inc, New York NY

Rom, Cristine, *Library Dir,* Cleveland Institute of Art, Jessica Gund Memorial Library, Cleveland OH

Rom, Cynthia, *Registrar,* Corcoran Gallery of Art, Washington DC

Romais, Miriam, *Prog Dir,* Organization of Independent Artists, New York NY

Romais, Miriam, *Managing Dir,* En Foco, Inc, Bronx NY

Romani, Daniel, *Dir Educ,* Rhode Island Historical Society, Providence RI

Romano, Enola R, *Art Asst,* Newark Museum Association, Junior Museum, Newark NJ

Romano, Filomena, *Instr,* Dowling College, Dept of Visual Arts, Oakdale NY (S)

Romano, Jaime, *Asst Prof,* University of Puerto Rico, Dept of Fine Arts, Rio Piedras PR (S)

Romano, Pia, *Reference,* Wentworth Institute of Technology Library, Boston MA

Romano, Salvatore, *Asst Prof,* Herbert H Lehman College, Art Dept, Bronx NY (S)

Romeo, Louise, *Asst Dean,* New World School of the Arts, Gallery, Miami FL

Romeo, Louise, *Asst Dean,* New World School of the Arts, Miami FL (S)

Romero, Brenda, *Dir,* Douglas Art Association, Little Gallery, Douglas AZ

Romero, Orlando, *Librn,* Museum of New Mexico, Fray Angelico Chavez History Library, Santa Fe NM

Romine, June, *Pub Relations Dir,* Palos Verdes Art Center, Rancho Palos Verdes CA

Romley, Janice, *Educ Coordr,* Whitney Museum of American Art at Champion, Stamford CT

Romo, Tere, *Cur,* Mexican Museum, San Francisco CA

Ronalds, William, *Chmn,* Saint John's University, Dept of Fine Arts, Jamaica NY (S)

Ronolich, Jean F, *Admnr,* CIGNA Corporation, CIGNA Museum & Art Collection, Philadelphia PA

Roode, William, *Assoc Prof,* University of Minnesota, Minneapolis, Dept of Art, Minneapolis MN (S)

Roof, Joan, *Treas,* Connecticut Watercolor Society, Farmington CT

Rooney, Denise, *Mgr Develop & Pub Relations,* Art Gallery of Nova Scotia, Halifax NS

Rooney, Jan, *Asst Dir,* Alternative Museum, New York NY

Rooney, Steve, *Deputy Dir for Adminr,* International Center of Photography, New York NY

Rooney, Thomas, *Assoc Prof,* Catholic University of America, Dept of Art, Washington DC (S)

Rooney, Tom, *VPres,* Washington Sculptors Group, Washington DC

Roop, Ophelia, *Head Librn,* Indiana University - Purdue University at Indianapolis, Herron School of Art Library, Indianapolis IN

Roos, Jane, *Assoc Prof,* City University of New York, PhD Program in Art History, New York NY (S)

Roosa, Wayne L, *Prof,* Bethel College, Dept of Art, Saint Paul MN (S)

Roosevelt, Janice, *Dir Public Relations,* Winterthur Museum, Winterthur DE

Root, Linda, *Office Mgr,* Koshare Indian Museum, Inc, La Junta CO

Root, Margaret, *Chmn,* University of Michigan, Ann Arbor, Dept of History of Art, Ann Arbor MI (S)

Root, Margaret, *Prof,* University of Michigan, Ann Arbor, Dept of History of Art, Ann Arbor MI (S)

Root, Maryann, *Dir,* Danbury Scott-Fanton Museum & Historical Society, Inc, Danbury CT

Root, Maryann, *Dir,* Danbury Scott-Fanton Museum & Historical Society, Inc, Library, Danbury CT

Root, Nina J, *Dir Library Servs,* American Museum of Natural History, Library, New York NY

Roover, Sarah, *Educ Dir,* Vermont Historical Society, Museum, Montpelier VT

Roozen, Kenneth, *Exec VPres,* University of Alabama at Birmingham, Visual Arts Gallery, Birmingham AL

Roper, Matthew, *Acting Dir,* University of Pittsburgh, University Art Gallery, Pittsburgh PA

Ropp, Ann, *Dir Exhib,* East Tennessee State University, Elizabeth Slocumb Galleries, Johnson City TN

Roraback, Dorothy, *Asst Cur,* Pacific - Asia Museum, Pasadena CA

Rorschach, Kimerly, *Dir,* University of Chicago, David & Alfred Smart Museum of Art, Chicago IL

Ros, Karen, *Asst Prof,* Indiana University, Bloomington, Henry Radford Hope School of Fine Arts, Bloomington IN (S)

Rosa, Rose, *Chmn Fashion Design,* Fashion Institute of Technology, Art & Design Division, New York NY (S)

Rosasco, Betsy, *Assoc Cur,* Princeton University, The Art Museum, Princeton NJ

Rose, Frank, *VPres,* San Angelo Museum of Fine Arts, San Angelo TX

Rose, George, *Instr,* Chautauqua Institution, School of Art, Chautauqua NY (S)

Rose, George, *Assoc Prof,* Northwest Missouri State University, Dept of Art, Maryville MO (S)

Rose, J, *Instr,* Western Illinois University, Art Dept, Macomb IL (S)

Rose, Joshua, *Dept Head,* New Mexico State University, Art Dept, Las Cruces NM (S)

Rose, Robert, *Asst Dir,* University of Northern Iowa, Art & Music Section Rod Library, Cedar Falls IA

Rose, Steve, *VPres,* Passaic County Community College, Division of Humanities, Paterson NJ (S)

Rose, Thomas, *Prof,* University of Minnesota, Minneapolis, Dept of Art, Minneapolis MN (S)

Rosell, Karen, *Chmn Dept,* Juniata College, Dept of Art, Huntingdon PA (S)

Roselli, Bart A, *Dir,* Schenectady Museum Planetarium & Visitors Center, Hall of Electrical History, Schenectady NY

Roselli, David, *Registrar,* Duke University Museum of Art, Durham NC

Roselli, Laura, *Gallery Dir,* Durham Art Guild Inc, Durham NC

Rosen, James, *Asst Prof,* Augusta College, Dept of Fine Arts, Augusta GA (S)

Rosen, Leila, *Librn,* Aesthetic Realism Foundation, Eli Siegel Collection, New York NY

Rosen, M, *Prof,* City Colleges of Chicago, Daley College, Chicago IL (S)

Rosen, Robert, *Dir,* University of Southern California, Cinema-Television Library & Archives of Performing Arts, Los Angeles CA

Rosen, Seymour, *Dir,* Saving & Preserving Arts & Cultural Environments, Los Angeles CA

Rosen, Seymour, *Dir,* Saving & Preserving Arts & Cultural Environments, Spaces Library & Archive, Los Angeles CA

Rosen, Steven W, *Dir & Chief Cur,* Nora Eccles Harrison Museum of Art, Logan UT

Rosenbaum, Allen, *Dir,* Princeton University, The Art Museum, Princeton NJ

Rosenbaum, Arthur, *Drawing & Painting,* University of Georgia, Franklin College of Arts & Sciences, Lamar Dodd School of Art, Athens GA (S)

Rosenbaum, Joan H, *Dir,* The Jewish Museum, New York NY

Rosenberg, Eric, *Assoc Prof,* Tufts University, Dept of Art & Art History, Medford MA (S)

Rosenberg, Herbert, *Assoc Prof,* Jersey City State College, Art Dept, Jersey City NJ (S)

Rosenberg, Lisa, *Advisor,* Western Washington University, Viking Union Gallery, Bellingham WA

Rosenberg, Martin, *Chmn Dept,* University of Nebraska at Omaha, Dept of Art & Art History, Omaha NE (S)

Rosenberg, Sarah Z, *Exec Dir,* American Institute for Conservation of Historic & Artistic Works (AIC), Washington DC

Rosenberg, Steve, *Chmn Music Dept,* College of Charleston, School of the Arts, Charleston SC (S)

Rosenberger, Irmgard Hess, *Pres,* American Jewish Art Club, Chicago IL

Rosenberger, Pat, *Exec Dir,* Valley Art Center Inc, Clarkston WA

Rosenberger, Stephen, *Reference & ILL,* Fashion Institute of Technology, Gladys Marcus Library, New York NY

Rosenblatt, Lisa, *Asst Dir,* B'nai B'rith International, B'nai B'rith Klutznick National Jewish Museum, Washington DC

Rosenblum, Paul, *Gen Mgr,* Caramoor Center for Music & the Arts, Inc, Caramoor House Museum, Katonah NY

Rosenblum, Peter, *Assoc Prof,* Seton Hall University, College of Arts & Sciences, South Orange NJ (S)

Rosenfeld, Alla, *Cur of Russian & Soviet Art,* Rutgers, The State University of New Jersey, Jane Voorhees Zimmerli Art Museum, New Brunswick NJ

Rosenfeld, Susan, *Asst Cur,* University of California, Los Angeles, Visual Resource Collection, Los Angeles CA

Rosenfield, Allan, *Pres,* Albuquerque United Artists, Albuquerque NM

Rosenholtz, Ellen M, *Dir,* Lancaster Museum of Art, Lancaster PA

Rosensaft, Jean Bloch, *Exhib Dir,* Hebrew Union College-Jewish Institute of Religion, New York NY

Rosenstein, Lynne, *Asst Dir,* Long Beach Jewish Community Center, Center Gallery, Long Beach CA

Rosensweig, Larry, *Dir,* Palm Beach County Parks & Recreation Department, Morikami Museum & Japanese Gardens, Delray Beach FL

Rosenthal, Deborah, *Cur,* Door County, Miller Art Center, Sturgeon Bay WI

Rosenthal, Donald, *Dir,* Saint Anselm College, Chapel Art Center, Manchester NH

Rosenthal, Ted, *Facilities Mgr,* Angels Gate Cultural Center, The Gate Gallery, San Pedro CA

Rosenwald, Jean, *Admin Asst,* Putnam County Historical Society, Foundry School Museum, Cold Spring NY

Rosier, Ken, *Assoc Prof,* Del Mar College, Art Dept, Corpus Christi TX (S)

Roskill, Mark, *Prof,* University of Massachusetts, Amherst, Art History Program, Amherst MA (S)

Roslak, Robyn, *Assoc Prof,* University of Minnesota, Duluth, Art Dept, Duluth MN (S)

Ross, Alex, *Head Librn,* Stanford University, Art & Architecture Library, Stanford CA

Ross, Barbara, *Assoc Cur,* Princeton University, The Art Museum, Princeton NJ

Ross, Carole, *Assoc Dean Grad Studies,* University of Kansas, School of Fine Arts, Lawrence KS (S)

Ross, Colleen, *Accounts Receivable & Donations Clerk,* London Regional Art & Historical Museums, London ON

Ross, Cynthia, *Instr,* Goddard College, Dept of Art, Plainfield VT (S)

Ross, David, *Alice Pratt Brown Dir,* Whitney Museum of American Art, New York NY

Ross, Doran H, *Asst Dir & Cur Africa, Oceania & Indonesia,* University of California, Los Angeles, Fowler Museum of Cultural History, Los Angeles CA

Ross, Gail, *Exec Dir,* Burke Arts Council, Jailhouse Galleries, Morganton NC

Ross, Gary, *Chmn,* Capital University, Fine Arts Dept, Columbus OH (S)

Ross, Gayle, *Instr,* Arkansas State University, Dept of Art, State University AR (S)

Ross, Hal, *Chmn Board,* Wichita Center for the Arts, Wichita KS

Ross, Harold, *Dean,* Cottey College, Art Dept, Nevada MO (S)

Ross, Ian D, *Exec Dir,* Burlington Art Centre, Burlington ON

Ross, Johnnie, *Instr,* Maine College of Art, Portland ME (S)

Ross, Judith, *Dir Marketing & Public Relations,* Westmoreland Museum of American Art, Greensburg PA

Ross, Margaret, *Dir,* Chatham College, Fine & Performing Arts, Pittsburgh PA (S)

Ross, Mary Anne, *Assoc Prof,* Delta State University, Dept of Art, Cleveland MS (S)

Ross, Novelene, *Chief Cur,* Wichita Art Museum, Wichita KS

Ross, Richard, *Chmn Dept,* University of California, Santa Barbara, Dept of Art Studio, Santa Barbara CA (S)

Ross, Robert, *Assoc Prof,* University of Arkansas, Art Dept, Fayetteville AR (S)

Ross, Robert, *Asst Prof,* Catholic University of America, Dept of Art, Washington DC (S)

Ross, S, *Instr,* Humboldt State University, College of Arts & Humanities, Arcata CA (S)

Ross, Wendy, *Cur Educ,* Parkersburg Art Center, Parkersburg WV

Ross, Wendy, *Educ Coordr,* Parkersburg Art Center, Art Center, Parkersburg WV

Rosselli, Bart A, *Dir,* Schenectady Museum Planetarium & Visitors Center, Schenectady NY

Rossen, Arlene, *Dir Development,* Akron Art Museum, Akron OH

Rossen, Susan F, *Exec Dir Publications,* The Art Institute of Chicago, Chicago IL

Rosser, Warren, *Chmn Painting & Printmaking,* Kansas City Art Institute, Kansas City MO (S)

Rosset, Carol, *Coll Mgr & Registrar,* University of California, Richard L Nelson Gallery & Fine Arts Collection, Davis CA

Rossi, Dianna, *Memberships,* Pastel of the West Coast, Sacramento Fine Arts Center, Carmichael CA

Rossley, Bruce R, *Commissioner,* Boston Art Commission of the City of Boston, Boston MA

Rossman, Michael, *Co-Chmn Foundation Prog,* University of the Arts, Philadelphia College of Art & Design, Philadelphia PA (S)

Rossman, Val, *Instr,* Main Line Art Center, Haverford PA (S)

Rossol, Monona, *Pres,* Artist-Craftsmen of New York, New York NY

Roston-Warren, Netra, *Dir & Pres,* African-American Historical & Cultural Society, San Francisco CA

Roters, Carlene, *Asst Prof,* Northern State University, Art Dept, Aberdeen SD (S)

Roth, Dan, *Cur,* US Navy Supply Corps School, US Navy Supply Corps Museum, Athens GA

Roth, Darlene, *Dir Exhib & Coll,* Atlanta Historical Society Inc, Atlanta History Center, Atlanta GA

Roth, Moira, *Prof Art Hist,* Mills College, Art Dept, Oakland CA (S)

Rothermel, Joan Ashley, *Treas,* American Watercolor Society, New York NY

Rothkopf, Katherine, *Asst Cur,* The Phillips Collection, Washington DC

Rothman, Deborah, *Public Relations Mgr,* University of Rochester, Memorial Art Gallery, Rochester NY

Rothman, Louise, *Asst Art Prof,* University of Florida, Dept of Art, Gainesville FL (S)

Rothrock, Kathy, *History Specialist,* Headquarters Fort Monroe, Dept of Army, Casemate Museum, Fort Monroe VA

Rothschild, Deborah Menaker, *Assoc Cur Exhib,* Williams College, Museum of Art, Williamstown MA

Rothwell, Elaine B, *Treas,* Gallery 9, Los Altos CA

Rotondi, Michael, *Dir,* Southern California Institute of Architecture, Los Angeles CA (S)

Rouleau, Bishop Reynald, *Dir,* Eskimo Museum, Churchill MB

Rouse, Father Warren, *Local Minister,* Mission San Luis Rey de Francia, Mission San Luis Rey Museum, San Luis Rey CA

Rousseas, Ermioni, *Librn,* Robert W Ryerss Library & Museum, Library, Philadelphia PA

Rousseau, Stacey, *Cur,* Key West Art & Historical Society, East Martello Museum & Gallery, Key West FL

Rousseau, T Marshall, *Exec Dir,* Salvador Dali Museum, Saint Petersburg FL

Routledge, Marie, *Asst Cur Inuit Art,* National Gallery of Canada, Ottawa ON

Routon, David, *Chmn Graduate Committee,* University of Nebraska-Lincoln, Dept of Art & Art History, Lincoln NE (S)

Rovine, Victoria, *Cur,* University of Iowa, Museum of Art, Iowa City IA

Row, Brian G, *Chmn,* Southwest Texas State University, Dept of Art, San Marcos TX (S)

Rowan, Dennis, *In Charge Printmaking,* University of Illinois, Urbana-Champaign, School of Art & Design, Champaign IL (S)

Rowan, Gerald, *Prog Coordr,* Northampton Community College, Art Dept, Bethlehem PA (S)

Rowan, Herman, *Prof,* University of Minnesota, Minneapolis, Dept of Art, Minneapolis MN (S)

Rowars, Lorelei, *Merchandise Mgr,* Newark Museum Association, The Newark Museum, Newark NJ

Rowe, Ann P, *Cur Western Hemisphere,* Textile Museum, Washington DC

Rowe, A W, *Pres,* Colorado City Historical Museum, Colorado City TX

Rowe, Charles, *Coordr Illustration,* University of Delaware, Dept of Art, Newark DE (S)

Rowe, Donald, *Dir,* Olivet College, Armstrong Museum of Art & Archaeology, Olivet MI

Rowe, Donald, *Prof,* Olivet College, Art Dept, Olivet MI (S)

Rowe, Duane, *Dir Marketing,* First National Bank, Fort Collins CO

Rowe, Ken, *Chmn & Dir Summer Arts Prog,* Sierra Nevada College, Visual & Performing Arts Dept, Incline Village NV (S)

Rowe, Kenneth, *Head Librn,* Archives & History Center of the United Methodist Church, Library, Madison NJ

Rowe, Kenneth E, *Librn,* Archives & History Center of the United Methodist Church, Madison NJ

Rowe, Martha, *Research Assoc,* Old Salem Inc, Museum of Early Southern Decorative Arts, Winston-Salem NC

Rowe, Martha, *Research Assoc,* Old Salem Inc, Library, Winston-Salem NC

Rowe, Robert, *Prof,* Marshall University, Dept of Art, Huntington WV (S)

Rowe, Sandra, *Assoc Prof,* California State Polytechnic University, Pomona, Art Dept, Pomona CA (S)

Rowe, Susan, *Instr,* Olivet College, Art Dept, Olivet MI (S)

Rowe, William, *Prof,* Arkansas State University, Dept of Art, State University AR (S)

Rowell, Margot, *Chief Cur. Drawings,* Museum of Modern Art, New York NY

Rowe-Scheel, Michelle, *Dir School,* Evanston Art Center, Evanston IL

Rowland, Cynthia, *Exec Dir,* Washington Center For Photography, Washington DC

Rowlands, J, *Prof,* Camden County College, Dept of Art, Blackwood NJ (S)

Rowlands, Thomas, *Asst Prof,* North Central College, Dept of Art, Naperville IL (S)

Rowlatt, Don, *VPres,* University of Victoria, Maltwood Art Museum and Gallery, Victoria BC

Rowley, Roger, *Dir.* State University of New York, College at Brockport, Tower Fine Arts Gallery, Brockport NY

Roworth, Wendy, *Prof,* University of Rhode Island, Dept of Art, Kingston RI (S)

Roy, Constance, *Assoc Prof,* Cazenovia College, Center for Art & Design Studies, Cazenovia NY (S)

Roy, Denise, *Instr,* Marylhurst College, Art Dept, Marylhurst OR (S)

Roy, Raona, *Pres,* Rensselaer County Council for the Arts, RCCA: The Arts Center, Troy NY

Royal, West, *Dir Public Relations,* Colorado Springs Fine Arts Center, Colorado Springs CO

Royce, Diana, *Librn,* Harriet Beecher Stowe Center, Stowe-Day Library, Hartford CT

Royce, Jodi, *Personnel Supv,* Minnesota Museum of American Art, Saint Paul MN

Royek, Walter, *Instr,* Milwaukee Area Technical College, Graphic Arts Division, Milwaukee WI (S)

Royer, Catherine M, *Gallery Dir,* Culver-Stockton College, Art Dept, Canton MO (S)

Royer, Jean, *Pres,* Musee d'Art de Saint-Laurent, Saint-Laurent PQ

Rozene, Janette, *Catalog Head,* Fashion Institute of Technology, Gladys Marcus Library, New York NY

Rozman, Joseph, *Prof,* Mount Mary College, Art Dept, Milwaukee WI (S)

Roznoy, Cynthia, *Mgr,* Whitney Museum of American Art at Champion, Stamford CT

Ruana, Maria, *Asst Dir,* Spanish Institute, Inc, Center for American-Spanish Affairs, New York NY

Rub, Timothy, *Dir,* Dartmouth College, Hood Museum of Art, Hanover NH

Rubel, William, *Pres,* Children's Art Foundation, Museum of International Children's Art, Santa Cruz CA

Rubenstein, Elliott, *Assoc Prof,* Rochester Institute of Technology, School of Photographic Arts & Sciences, Rochester NY (S)

Rubenstein, Ephraim, *Assoc Prof,* University of Richmond, Dept of Art, Richmond VA (S)

Rubin, James, *Chmn,* State University of New York at Stony Brook, Art Dept, Stony Brook NY (S)

Rubin, Robert S, *Chmn Board of Trustees,* Brooklyn Museum, Brooklyn NY

Rubio, Pablo, *Asst Prof,* University of Puerto Rico, Dept of Fine Arts, Rio Piedras PR (S)

Ruble, Jacqueline, *Admin Dir,* Institute for Arts & Humanities Education, New Jersey Summer Arts Institute, New Brunswick NJ (S)

Ruby, Julianne, *Archives,* Cascade County Historical Society, Cascade County Historical Museum & Archives, Great Falls MT

Rucker, Jack, *Chmn,* Northeastern Oklahoma A & M College, Art Dept, Miami OK (S)

Ruda, Jeffrey, *Dir Art History,* University of California, Davis, Art Dept, Davis CA (S)

Rudey, Liz, *Chmn,* Long Island University, Brooklyn Campus, Art Dept, Brooklyn NY (S)

Rudolph, Beth, *Exec Dir,* Very Special Arts New Mexico, Enabled Arts Center, Albuquerque NM (S)

Rudolph, Beth, *Exec Dir,* Very Special Arts New Mexico, Very Special Arts Gallery, Albuquerque NM

Rudolph, Conrad, *Assoc Prof,* University of California, Riverside, Dept of the History of Art, Riverside CA (S)

Rudolph, Jeffrey, *Dir,* California Museum of Science and Industry, Los Angeles CA

Rudolph, Wolf, *Assoc Prof,* Indiana University, Bloomington, Henry Radford Hope School of Fine Arts, Bloomington IN (S)

Rudy, Jenny, *Development Officer,* Nevada Museum Of Art, Reno NV

Ruedi, Katerina, *Dir School Archit,* University of Illinois at Chicago, College of Architecture, Chicago IL (S)

Ruedy, Don, *Assoc Prof,* University of Wisconsin, Center-Barron County, Dept of Art, Rice Lake WI (S)

Ruege, Ruth, *Coordr Fine Arts,* Milwaukee Public Library, Art, Music & Recreation Dept, Milwaukee WI

Ruess, Diane, *Acting Head Instructional Media Serv,* University of Alaska, Elmer E Rasmuson Library, Fairbanks AK

Rufe, Laurie J, *Asst Dir,* Roswell Museum & Art Center, Roswell NM

Ruff, Eric, *Cur,* Yarmouth County Historical Society, Yarmouth County Museum, Yarmouth NS

Ruff, Gloria, *Registrar,* Valparaiso University, Brauer Museum of Art, Valparaiso IN

Ruffo, Joseph M, *Chmn & Dir,* University of Nebraska, Lincoln, The Gallery of the Department of Art & Art History, Lincoln NE

Ruffo, Joseph M, *Chmn Dept,* University of Nebraska-Lincoln, Dept of Art & Art History, Lincoln NE (S)

Ruffolo, Robert E, *Pres,* Princeton Antiques Bookservice, Art Marketing Reference Library, Atlantic City NJ

Rugg, Ruth Ann, *Public Affairs,* Amon Carter Museum, Fort Worth TX

Ruggiero, Laurence, *Dir,* Charles Morse Museum of American Art, Winter Park FL

Ruggie Saunders, Cathie, *Assoc Prof,* Saint Xavier University, Dept of Art, Chicago IL (S)

Ruggles, Janet, *General Mgr & Chief Paper Conservator,* Balboa Art Conservation Center, San Diego CA

Ruggles, Janet, *General Mgr,* Balboa Art Conservation Center, Richard D Buck Memorial Library, San Diego CA

Ruggles, Joanne, *Prof,* California Polytechnic State University at San Luis Obispo, Dept of Art & Design, San Luis Obispo CA (S)

Ruhstaller, Tod, *Dir & Cur of History,* San Joaquin Pioneer & Historical Society, The Haggin Museum, Stockton CA

Ruhstaller, Tod, *Dir,* San Joaquin Pioneer & Historical Society, Petzinger Memorial Library, Stockton CA

Ruiz, Tony, *Chmn,* Gavilan College, Art Dept, Gilroy CA (S)

Ruiz de Fischler, Carmen T, *Asst Prof,* University of Puerto Rico, Dept of Fine Arts, Rio Piedras PR (S)

Rule, Amy, *Archivist,* University of Arizona, Center for Creative Photography, Tucson AZ

Rumrill, Alan, *Dir,* Historical Society of Cheshire County, Archive Center of the Society, Keene NH

Runcevich, Michael, *Pres,* Plastic Club, Art Club, Philadelphia PA

Rundels, Donna, *Slide Librn,* Center for Creative Studies, College of Art & Design Library, Detroit MI

Rundquist, Leisa, *Cur,* South Bend Regional Museum of Art, South Bend IN

Runyan, Sue, *Head Public Information,* Getty Center for the History of Art & the Humanities Trust Museum, Santa Monica CA

Runyard, Sue, *Head Public Information,* Getty Center for the History of Art & the Humanities Trust Museum, The J Paul Getty Museum, Santa Monica CA

Runyon, Dianne, *Registrar,* Art Institute of Philadelphia, Philadelphia PA (S)

Runyon, John M, *Prof,* Corning Community College, Division of Humanities, Corning NY (S)

Rupinski, Jill, *Instr,* Wayne Art Center, Wayne PA (S)

Rupp, Cora, *Exec Dir,* Art League, Alexandria VA

Rupp, Jane E, *Dir & Cur,* Clinton County Historical Association, Clinton County Historical Museum, Plattsburgh NY

Ruprecht, Carl, *Supt of Grounds,* Stan Hywet Hall & Gardens, Inc, Akron OH

Rusak, Halina, *Art Librn,* Rutgers, The State University of New Jersey, Art Library, New Brunswick NJ

Rusfvold, Georgia, *Prog Coordr,* SVACA - Sheyenne Valley Arts & Crafts Association, Bjarne Ness Gallery at Bear Creek Hall, Fort Ransom ND

Rush, Kent, *Assoc Prof,* University of Texas at San Antonio, Division of Visual Arts, San Antonio TX (S)

Rush, Laurie, *Cur,* DeWitt Historical Society of Tompkins County, Ithaca NY

Rush, Rob, *Cur,* University of Chicago, Max Epstein Archive, Chicago IL

Rush, Sallee, *Instr,* Main Line Art Center, Haverford PA (S)

Rushing, Kim, *Asst Prof,* Delta State University, Dept of Art, Cleveland MS (S)

Rushing, Molly, *Instr,* Delta State University, Dept of Art, Cleveland MS (S)

Rushing, Sandra, *Registrar,* University of California, Santa Barbara, University Art Museum, Santa Barbara CA

Rushing, W Jackson, *Assoc Prof,* University of Missouri, Saint Louis, Dept of Art & Art History, Saint Louis MO (S)

Rushton, Edward, *Assoc Prof,* Viterbo College, Art Dept, La Crosse WI (S)

Rusitzky, Harris H, *Chmn,* George Eastman House-International Museum of Photography & Film, Rochester NY

Ruskey, John, *Cur,* Carnegie Public Library, Delta Blues Museum, Clarksdale MS

Rusnell, Wesley A, *Cur Coll,* Roswell Museum & Art Center, Roswell NM

Russell, Barbara, *Fine Arts Mgr,* Cypress College, Cypress CA (S)

Russell, Bryan, *Treas,* Redding Museum of Art & History, Redding CA

Russell, Donald H, *Exec Dir,* Art Resources International, Washington DC

Russell, Douglas, *Gallery Dir,* Oregon State University, Fairbanks Gallery, Corvallis OR

Russell, Douglas, *Gallery Dir,* Oregon State University, Giustina Gallery, Corvallis OR

Russell, Douglas, *Sr Research Assoc,* Oregon State University, Dept of Art, Corvallis OR (S)

Russell, Fiona, *Cur,* Words & Pictures Museum, Northampton MA

Russell, Geraldine, *Curatorial Asst (Numismatics),* University of Calgary, The Nickle Arts Museum, Calgary AB

Russell, Graham, *Dir Membership,* Norton Gallery & School of Art, Inc, Norton Museum of Art, West Palm Beach FL

Russell, James, *Dir,* Attleboro Museum, Center for the Arts, Attleboro MA

Russell, Janet, *Asst to Dir,* Jackson County Historical Society, John Wornall House Museum, Independence MO

Russell, John I, *Exec Dir,* Brookfield Craft Center, Inc, Gallery, Brookfield CT

Russell, Lisa, *Asst. Cultural & Community Relations,* Bristol-Myers Squibb Pharmaceutical Group, Gallery at Bristol-Myers Squibb, Princeton NJ

Russell, Marilyn M, *Cur Educ,* Carnegie Institute, Carnegie Museum of Art, Pittsburgh PA

Russell, Nadine, *Pres,* Louisiana State University, Museum of Arts, Baton Rouge LA

Russell, Rebecca, *Cur Educ,* Museum of Fine Arts, Saint Petersburg, Florida, Inc, Saint Petersburg FL

Russell, Robert P, *Prof,* Pittsburg State University, Art Dept, Pittsburg KS (S)

Russell, Thomas, *Instr,* Roger Williams College, Art Dept, Bristol RI (S)

Russo, Edward G, *Registrar,* Florida International University, The Art Museum at FIU, Miami FL

Russo, Howard, *Instr,* Elgin Community College, Fine Arts Dept, Elgin IL (S)

Russo, Kathleen, *Chmn,* Florida Atlantic University, Art Dept, Boca Raton FL (S)

Russo, Susan, *Chmn,* Youngstown State University, Art Dept, Youngstown OH (S)

Rust, Brian, *Instr,* Augusta College, Dept of Fine Arts, Augusta GA (S)

Rustige, Rona, *Cur,* Glanmore, Hastings County Museum, Belleville ON

Rutberg, Alan, *Asst Prof,* University of Maryland, Baltimore County, Visual Arts Dept, Baltimore MD (S)

Rutberg, Carl, *Cur Exhibits,* The National Park Service, United States Department of the Interior, The Statue of Liberty National Monument, New York NY

Ruthenberg, Donald, *Pres,* National Oil & Acrylic Painters Society, Osage Beach MO

Rutherford, Mary Jane, *Community Relations Officer,* University of Oklahoma, Fred Jones Jr Museum of Art, Norman OK

Rutkovsky, Paul, *Assoc Prof,* Florida State University, Art Dept, Tallahassee FL (S)

Rutland, Jack, *Sr Cur,* New York Historical Society, New York NY

Rutledge, Margaret, *Asst Prof,* Delta State University, Dept of Art, Cleveland MS (S)

Ruttinger, Jacquelyn, *Exhib Dir,* Western Michigan University-Art Dept, Dept of Art Galleries, Kalamazoo MI

Ruttner, Nancy, *Dir,* John P Barclay Memorial Gallery, Pittsburgh PA

Ryan, David, *Cur Coll,* Norwest Corporation, Minneapolis, Arts Program, Minneapolis MN

Ryan, James, *Historic Site Mgr,* Olana State Historic Site, Hudson NY

Ryan, James, *Historic Site Mgr,* Olana State Historic Site, David Huntington Archive, Hudson NY

Ryan, Linda Lee, *Instr,* Casper College, Dept of Visual Arts, Casper WY (S)

Ryan, Martin, *Assoc Prof,* Monmouth University, Dept of Art & Design, West Long Branch NJ (S)

Ryan, Maureen, *Asst Prof,* University of British Columbia, Dept of Fine Arts, Vancouver BC (S)

Ryan, Patricia, *Asst Cur,* Honeywell Inc, Art Collection, Minneapolis MN

Ryan, Paul, *Prof,* Mary Baldwin College, Dept of Art, Staunton VA (S)

Ryan, Susan, *Asst,* Louisiana State University, School of Art, Baton Rouge LA (S)

Rychlak, Bonnie, *Dir Coll,* Isamu Noguchi Foundation, Isamu Noguchi Garden Museum, Long Island City NY

Rychlewski, Karen, *Prof,* West Liberty State College, Art Dept, West Liberty WV (S)

Ryckbosch, Bart, *Archivist,* The Art Institute of Chicago, Ryerson & Burnham Libraries, Chicago IL

Ryckman, Pat, *Dir,* Union County Public Library Union Room, Monroe NC

Rydell, Christine, *Instr,* Solano Community College, Division of Fine & Applied Art, Suisun City CA (S)

Ryer, Laurie, *Dir Administration,* Mattatuck Historical Society, Mattatuck Museum, Waterbury CT

Rykwert, Joseph, *Chmn Grad Group,* University of Pennsylvania, Dept of Architecture, Philadelphia PA (S)

Rylance, Keli, *Prof,* Hamline University, Dept of Art & Art History, Saint Paul MN (S)

Rynd, Chase W, *Exec Dir,* Tacoma Art Museum, Tacoma WA

Ryuto, Setsuko, *Controller,* San Joaquin Pioneer & Historical Society, The Haggin Museum, Stockton CA

Saab, Nina, *Librn,* California College of Arts & Crafts Library, Oakland CA

Saarnio, Robert, *Cur,* Peabody Essex Museum, Gardner-Pingree House, Salem MA

Saarnio, Robert, *Cur,* Peabody Essex Museum, Crowninshield-Bentley House, Salem MA

Sabatella, Joseph, *Prof,* University of Florida, Dept of Art, Gainesville FL (S)

Sabin, Kevin, *In Charge Art Coll & Prog,* First Commercial Bank in Little Rock, Little Rock AR

Sabloff, Jeremy A, *Dir,* University of Pennsylvania, Museum of Archaeology & Anthropology, Philadelphia PA

Sacchetti, Gina, *Cur Coll,* Wade House & Wesley W Jung Carriage Museum, Historic House & Carriage Museum, Greenbush WI

Saccopoulos, Christos, *Head Architecture Dept,* North Carolina State University at Raleigh, School of Design, Raleigh NC (S)

Sacher, Pamela, *Instr,* Greenfield Community College, Art, Graphic Design & Media Communication Dept, Greenfield MA (S)

Sachs, Samuel, *Dir,* Detroit Institute of Arts, Detroit MI

Sack, Carol, *Assoc Dean Col,* Rochester Institute of Technology, College of Imaging Arts & Sciences, Rochester NY (S)

Sackett, Margot Magee, *Dir,* Ross Memorial Museum, Saint Andrews NB

Sackman, Elmer, *Librn,* Fort Worth Public Library, Fine Arts Section, Fort Worth TX

Sacoman, Mariah, *Cur Southwestern Hispanic,* Museum of New Mexico, Museum of International Folk Art, Santa Fe NM

Sadinsky, Rachel, *Cur,* University of Kentucky, Art Museum, Lexington KY

Sadler, Cody, *Asst to Dir,* Canadian Wildlife & Wilderness Art Museum, Ottawa ON

Sadler, Cody, *Co-Dir,* Canadian Wildlife & Wilderness Art Museum, Library, Ottawa ON

Sadler, Donna, *Chmn,* Agnes Scott College, Dept of Art, Decatur GA (S)

Sadongei, Alyce, *Training Coordr,* National Museum of the American Indian, George Gustav Heye Center, New York NY

Saeedpour, Vera Beaudin, *Dir,* Kurdish Museum, Brooklyn NY

Safford, Herbert D, *Dir,* University of Northern Iowa, Art & Music Section Rod Library, Cedar Falls IA

Safrin, Robert W, *Dir,* The Society of the Four Arts, Palm Beach FL

Saganic, Livio, *Chmn Art Dept,* Drew University, Elizabeth P Korn Gallery, Madison NJ

Saganic, Livio, *Prof,* Drew University, Art Dept, Madison NJ (S)

Sage, Deby, *Arts in Common Dir,* Fitton Center For Creative Arts, Hamilton OH

Sage, Deby, *Arts in Common Dir,* Fitton Center for Creative Arts, Hamilton OH (S)

Sage, Priscilla, *Coordr Crafts,* Iowa State University, Dept of Art & Design, Ames IA (S)

Sager, Judy, *Owner,* Sager Studios, Fort Worth TX (S)

Sager, Judy, *Art Show Coordr,* University of North Texas Health Science Center Forth Worth, Atrium Gallery, Fort Worth TX

Sager, Robert, *Pres,* Schenectady County Historical Society, Schenectady NY

Sager, Rochelle, *Dir,* Fashion Institute of Technology, Gladys Marcus Library, New York NY

Sahlstrand, James, *Dir Art Gallery,* Central Washington University, Sarah Spurgeon Gallery, Ellensburg WA

Saidel, Alice, *Ref Librn,* Dayton Art Institute, Library, Dayton OH

Saiget, Jan, *Dir Develop,* Pacific - Asia Museum, Pasadena CA

Sainte-Marie, G, *Dir,* National Museum of Science & Technology, Ottawa ON

Saka, Tuna, *Instr,* Pennsylvania College of Technology, Dept of Graphic Communications, Williamsport PA (S)

Sakamoto, Kerri, *Writer,* Art in General, New York NY

Sakoulas, Thomas, *Gallery Mgr,* Maryland Institute, College of Art Exhibitions, Baltimore MD

Salam, Halide, *Prof,* Radford University, Art Dept, Radford VA (S)

Salerni, Luigi, *Performing Arts Interim Chair,* University of Illinois at Chicago, College of Architecture, Chicago IL (S)

Saliga, Pauline, *Exec Dir,* Society of Architectural Historians, Chicago IL

Salinks, Jay, *Lectr,* University of Wisconsin-Stevens Point, Dept of Art & Design, Stevens Point WI (S)

Salisbury, Ann, *Instr,* College of Saint Benedict, Art Dept, Saint Joseph MN (S)

Sall, Lauretta, *Dir Admis,* Cheltenham Center for the Arts, Cheltenham PA (S)

Sallee, Tiffany C, *Adminr,* Historic Landmarks Foundation of Indiana, Morris-Butler House, Indianapolis IN

Salmon, Mark, *Acad Dean,* Atlanta College of Art, Atlanta GA (S)

Salmon, Ray, *Instr,* Solano Community College, Division of Fine & Applied Art, Suisun City CA (S)

Salmon, Robin, *VPres Academic Affairs & Cur,* Brookgreen Gardens, Murrells Inlet SC

Salmon, Robin, *VPres & Cur,* Brookgreen Gardens, Library, Murrells Inlet SC

Salmond, Wendy, *Chmn,* Chapman University, Art Dept, Orange CA (S)

Salomon, Carol, *Engineering & Science,* Cooper Union for the Advancement of Science & Art, Library, New York NY

Salpeter, Ellen, *Exec Dir,* Thread Waxing Space, New York NY

Saltalamacchia, Karen, *Adjunct Instr,* Emmanuel College, Art Dept, Boston MA (S)

Salter, Richard, *Dir,* Museum of Contemporary Impressionism, New Milford CT

Saltzman, Marvin, *Prof,* University of North Carolina at Chapel Hill, Art Dept, Chapel Hill NC (S)

Saluato, Michael, *Asst Prof,* Philadelphia Community College, Dept of Art, Philadelphia PA (S)

Salvage, Barbara, *Art Librn,* Jacksonville Museum of Contemporary Art, Jacksonville FL

Salvage, Barbara, *Registrar,* Jacksonville Museum of Contemporary Art, Library, Jacksonville FL

Salvest, John J, *Assoc Prof,* Arkansas State University, Dept of Art, State University AR (S)

Salzberg, Rick, *Public Relations Mgr,* Chrysler Museum Of Art, Norfolk VA

Salzillo, Marjorie, *Instr,* Munson-Williams-Proctor Institute, School of Art, Utica NY (S)

Salzillo, William, *Instr,* Hamilton College, Art Dept, Clinton NY (S)

Samek, Susan, *Cur Costumes,* Chicago Historical Society, Chicago IL

Sammon, Christine E, *Library Dir,* Alberta College of Art & Design, Luke Lindoe Library, Calgary AB

Sammons, JoAnn, *Dir,* Dane G Hansen Memorial Museum, Logan KS

Sammons, Richard, *Instr,* Bismarck State College, Fine Arts Dept, Bismarck ND (S)

Samms, Mary Mallia, *Librn,* Textile Museum, Arthur D Jenkins Library, Washington DC

Samonides, William, *Asst Prof,* University of Kansas, Kress Foundation Dept of Art History, Lawrence KS (S)

Sample, George, *Asst Prof,* Central Missouri State University, Art Dept, Warrensburg MO (S)

Sampson, Cheryl E, *Staff Asst,* Nora Eccles Harrison Museum of Art, Logan UT

Sampson, Gary, *Asst Prof,* Grand Valley State University, Art & Design Dept, Allendale MI (S)

Samson, Allen L, *Pres Bd Trustees,* Milwaukee Art Museum, Milwaukee WI

Samuel, Elizabeth, *Chmn Board of Trustees,* Royal Ontario Museum, Toronto ON

Samuels, Allen, *Dean,* University of Michigan, Slusser Gallery, Ann Arbor MI

Samuels, Allen, *Dean,* University of Michigan, Ann Arbor, School of Art & Design, Ann Arbor MI (S)

Samuels, Clifford, *Dir,* Trova Foundation, Philip Samuels Fine Art, St Louis MO

Samuels, Philip, *Pres,* Trova Foundation, Philip Samuels Fine Art, St Louis MO

Samuelson, Jerry, *Dean School of Arts,* California State University, Fullerton, Art Dept, Fullerton CA (S)

Sanchez, Ramon Vasquez Y, *Arts Prog Dir,* Centro Cultural Aztlan, San Antonio TX

Sanchez, Richard, *Technical Asst,* Galeria de la Raza, Studio 24, San Francisco CA

Sanchez, Rosa, *Asst,* Louisiana State University, School of Art, Baton Rouge LA (S)

Sanchez-Walsh, Arlene, *Circulation Supv,* Art Center College of Design, James Lemont Fogg Memorial Library, Pasadena CA

Schachter, Ruth, *Librn.* Art Institute of Philadelphia Library, Philadelphia PA

Schaefer, Charles, *Pres.* Greene County Historical Society, Bronck Museum, Coxsackie NY

Schaeffer, Carl, *Pres Board of Dir.* Lake County Civic Center Association, Inc, Heritage Museum & Gallery, Leadville CO

Schafer, Barbara, *Cur Coll.* Rome Historical Society Museum, William E Scripture Memorial Library, Rome NY

Schafer, Carl, *Registrar,* Allentown Art Museum, Allentown PA

Schafer, Carrie, *Pres.* South Peace Art Society, Dawson Creek Art Gallery, Dawson Creek BC

Schafer, Michael L, *Pres.* Mohawk Valley Community College, Advertising Design & Production, Utica NY (S)

Schafer, Sheldon, *Science Planetarium Dir.* Lakeview Museum of Arts & Sciences, Peoria IL

Schaffer, Anne Louise, *Asst Cur Africa, Oceania & the Americas,* Museum of Fine Arts, Houston, Houston TX

Schaffer, Bonnie, *Coordr Communications,* University of Regina, MacKenzie Art Gallery, Regina SK

Schaffer, Dale E, *Co-owner,* Gloridale Partnership, National Museum of Woodcarving, Custer SD

Schaffer, D D, *Cur,* State University of New York, College at Cortland, Art Dept, Cortland NY (S)

Schaffer, Gloria, *Co-owner,* Gloridale Partnership, National Museum of Woodcarving, Custer SD

Schaffer, Jo, *Cur,* State University of New York College at Cortland, Art Slide Library, Cortland NY

Schaffer, Richard, *Registrar,* University of Arizona, Museum of Art, Tucson AZ

Schafroth, Colleen, *Cur Education,* Maryhill Museum of Art, Goldendale WA

Schall, Jan, *Asst Cur 20th Century Art,* Nelson-Atkins Museum of Art, Kansas City MO

Schall, Jan, *Asst Prof,* University of Florida, Dept of Art, Gainesville FL (S)

Schaller, Hydee, *Dir,* Saint John's College, Elizabeth Myers Mitchell Art Gallery, Annapolis MD

Schantz, Michael W, *Dir,* Woodmere Art Museum, Philadelphia PA

Schapp, Rebecca M, *Dir,* Santa Clara University, de Saisset Museum, Santa Clara CA

Schar, Stuart, *Dean,* University of Hartford, Hartford Art School, West Hartford CT (S)

Schatz, Charlotte, *Instr,* Bucks County Community College, Fine Arts Dept, Newtown PA (S)

Scheer, Elaine, *Asst Prof,* University of Wisconsin, Madison, Dept of Art, Madison WI (S)

Scheer, Lisa, *Dept Chmn & Assoc Prof,* Saint Mary's College of Maryland, Art Dept, Saint Mary's City MD (S)

Scheer, Stephen, *Photography,* University of Georgia, Franklin College of Arts & Sciences, Lamar Dodd School of Art, Athens GA (S)

Schefcik, Jerry, *Dir,* University of Nevada, Las Vegas, Donna Beam Fine Art Gallery, Las Vegas NV

Scheibraur, Kim, *Office Mgr,* Santa Cruz Art League, Inc, Center for the Arts, Santa Cruz CA

Scheifele, Eleanor, *Assoc Prof,* Indiana University, Bloomington, Henry Radford Hope School of Fine Arts, Bloomington IN (S)

Schel, Don E, *Basic Design Coordr,* University of North Texas, School of Visual Arts, Denton TX (S)

Schell, Edwin, *Librn.* United Methodist Historical Society, Library, Baltimore MD

Schell, William H, *Dir,* Martin Memorial Library, York PA

Scheller, Bonnie, *Instr,* Villa Maria College of Buffalo, Art Dept, Buffalo NY (S)

Schellhorn, Mary, *Dir,* Columbia College, Library, Chicago IL

Schelling, George, *Instr,* Luzerne County Community College, Commercial Art Dept, Nanticoke PA (S)

Schelsser, Edward, *Chief Exhib.* Hirshhorn Museum & Sculpture Garden, Washington DC

Schenck, Marvin, *Cur,* Saint Mary's College of California, Hearst Art Gallery, Moraga CA

Schendel, Jan, *Events Coordr.* Loveland Museum Gallery, Loveland CO

Schenk, Joseph B, *Dir,* Mobile Museum of Art, Mobile AL

Scher, Anne J, *Dir Public Relations,* The Jewish Museum, New York NY

Scherer, Herbert G, *Librn.* University of Minnesota, Art Book Collection, Minneapolis MN

Scherpereel, Richard, *Dir,* Texas A&M University, Art Gallery, Kingsville TX

Scherpereel, Richard, *Chmn.* Texas A&M University-Kingsville, Art Dept, Kingsville TX (S)

Scheu, David R, *Dir,* Battleship North Carolina, Wilmington NC

Schick, Marjorie K, *Prof,* Pittsburg State University, Art Dept, Pittsburg KS (S)

Schieferdecker, Marilyn, *Dir,* Arts Council of Greater Kingsport, Renaissance Center Main Gallery, Kingsport TN

Schieffed, Janelle, *Lirn.* Memphis Brooks Museum of Art, Library, Memphis TN

Schieffer, Janelle, *Librn.* Memphis Brooks Museum of Art, Memphis TN

Schienbaum, David, *Asst Prof.* College of Santa Fe, Art Dept, Santa Fe NM (S)

Schietinger, James, *Dir,* Millikin University, Perkinson Gallery, Decatur IL

Schietinger, James, *Chmn Art Dept,* Millikin University, Art Dept, Decatur IL (S)

Schieve, Catherine, *Asst Prof,* Southeastern Louisiana University, Dept of Visual Arts, Hammond LA (S)

Schiff, Jeffrey, *Assoc Prof,* Wesleyan University, Art Dept, Middletown CT (S)

Schiffer, Tim, *Cur,* Ventura County Historical Society, Museum of History & Art, Ventura CA

Schiffers, Richard, *Assoc Dir,* California State University at Sacramento, University Union Exhibit Lounge, Sacramento CA

Schimelfenig, Rachel Kay, *Educ Mgr,* Aurora University, Schingoethe Center for Native American Cultures, Aurora IL

Schimenti, Margie, *Board Dir,* Artists' Cooperative Gallery, Omaha NE

Schimmelman, Janice C, *Chmn Dept,* Oakland University, Dept of Art & Art History, Rochester MI (S)

Schindle, A, *Instr,* Western Illinois University, Art Dept, Macomb IL (S)

Schindler, Richard, *Adjunct Asst Prof.* Spokane Falls Community College, Fine Arts Dept, Spokane WA (S)

Schira, Peter, *Chmn.* Bronx Community College, Music & Art Dept, Bronx NY (S)

Schlanger, Gregg, *Asst Prof.* Austin Peay State University, Dept of Art, Clarksville TN (S)

Schlauder, Diana, *Pres.* Allied Arts Association, Allied Arts Center & Gallery, Richland WA

Schlawin, Judy, *Prof.* Winona State University, Dept of Art, Winona MN (S)

Schlechter, Jack W, *Exhib Coordr.* Carnegie Institute, Carnegie Museum of Art, Pittsburgh PA

Schleupner, Lynn, *Bookkeeper,* Arts Council of the Blue Ridge, Roanoke VA

Schlitt, Melinda, *Asst Prof.* Dickinson College, Fine Arts Dept, Carlisle PA (S)

Schloder, John, *Dir,* Joslyn Art Museum, Omaha NE

Schlossberg, Leon, *Assoc Prof.* Johns Hopkins University, School of Medicine, Dept of Art as Applied to Medicine, Baltimore MD (S)

Schlosser, Anne G, *Dir.* Warner Bros Research Library, North Hollywood CA

Schlosser, David, *Instr.* Cincinnati Academy of Design, Cincinnati OH (S)

Schlosser, Tom, *Chmn Dept,* College of Saint Mary, Art Dept, Omaha NE (S)

Schmaeling, Susan, *Public Relations Dir.* Contemporary Arts Museum, Houston TX

Schmaljohn, Russell, *Asst Prof.* Northwest Missouri State University, Dept of Art, Maryville MO (S)

Schmalz, Lydia H, *Cur.* Longue Vue House & Gardens, New Orleans LA

Schmandt, Marianne, *FAU Marketing Intern.* Broward County Board of Commissioners Cultural Affairs Divison, Fort Lauderdale FL

Schmidlapp, Don, *Assoc Prof.* Winona State University, Dept of Art, Winona MN (S)

Schmidt, Aaron, *Photographs,* Boston Public Library, Albert H Wiggin Gallery & Print Department, Boston MA

Schmidt, Bernard L, *Dir.* Xavier University, Xavier Art Gallery, Cincinnati OH

Schmidt, Bernard L, *Chmn.* Xavier University, Dept of Art, Cincinnati OH (S)

Schmidt, Edward, *Instr.* New York Academy of Art, Graduate School of Figurative Art, New York NY (S)

Schmidt, Eleanore, *Assoc Dir Adult Servs.* Long Beach Public Library, Long Beach CA

Schmidt, Kathleen, *Instr.* Northwestern State university, Tahlequah OK (S)

Schmidt, Kirsten, *Dir Pub Relations & Publ.* California State University, Long Beach, University Art Museum, Long Beach CA

Schmidt, Lawrence, *Cur Educ & Military Historian.* Old Barracks Museum, Trenton NJ

Schmidt, Mary, *Assoc Dept Head Admin Affair.* Carnegie Mellon University, Dept of Art, Pittsburgh PA (S)

Schmidt, Robert, *Assoc Prof.* Norwich University, Dept of Philosophy, Religion & Fine Arts, Northfield VT (S)

Schmidt, Sherri, *Dean University Libraries,* Arizona State University, Hayden Library, Tempe AZ

Schmidt, Steve, *Planetarium Dir,* Museum of the Southwest, Midland TX

Schmidt, Steve, *Planetarium Dir,* Museum of the Southwest, Library, Midland TX

Schmidt, Susan S, *Assoc Prof.* College of the Holy Cross, Dept of Visual Arts, Worcester MA (S)

Schmidt, Wendy, *Dir Educ,* American Academy of Art, Chicago IL (S)

Schmidt, Wilma, *Team Leader Information Resources & Delivery,* State University of New York at New Paltz, Sojourner Truth Library, New Paltz NY

Schmitt, Helmut, *Dir,* Merritt College, Art Dept, Oakland CA (S)

Schmitz, Robert, *Prof.* Rochester Institute of Technology, School of Art & Design, Rochester NY (S)

Schnabel, JoAnn, *Assoc Prof.* University of Northern Iowa, Dept of Art, Cedar Falls IA (S)

Schnackenberg, Elliot, *Instr.* Milwaukee Area Technical College, Graphic Arts Division, Milwaukee WI (S)

Schnee, Alix Sandra, *Historic Site Mgr.* Philipse Manor Hall State Historic Site, Yonkers NY

Schneider, Beth, *Eduction Dir.* Museum of Fine Arts, Houston, Houston TX

Schneider, Cynthia, *Assoc Prof.* Georgetown University, Dept of Art, Music & Theatre, Washington DC (S)

Schneider, Elsa, *Public Relations Dir.* Kemper & Leila Williams Foundation, New Orleans LA

Schneider, Emery E, *Chmn Design Composition Division.* Rochester Institute of Technology, School of Printing, Rochester NY (S)

Schneider, Karen, *Librn.* The Phillips Collection, Washington DC

Schneider, Karen, *Librn.* The Phillips Collection, Library, Washington DC

Schneider, Laurie, *Prof.* John Jay College of Criminal Justice, Dept of Art, Music & Philosophy, New York NY (S)

Schneider, Mimi, *Dir Asst.* Bemis Center for Contemporary Arts, New Gallery, Omaha NE

Schneider, Russell, *Chmn.* Hinds Community College District, Marie Hull Gallery, Raymond MS

Schneider, Russell, *Chmn.* Hinds Community College, Dept of Art, Raymond MS (S)

Schneider, U, *Instr.* Sarah Lawrence College, Dept of Art History, Bronxville NY (S)

Schneiderman, Kara, *Coll & Information Mgr.* Massachusetts Institute of Technology, MIT Museum, Cambridge MA

Schneiderman, Nancy, *Cur.* Rochester Historical Society, Rochester NY

Schnell, Frank T, *Cur Archaeology.* Columbus Museum, Columbus GA

Schnell, Ron, *Dir.* Tougaloo College, Art Collection, Tougaloo MS

Schnellman, Lew, *Instr.* Century College,
Humanities Dept, White Bear Lake MN (S)

Schnepf, Scott, *Assoc Prof.* University of New
Hampshire, Dept of Arts & Art History, Durham
NH (S)

Schnepper, Mary, *Cur of Coll.* Evansville Museum
of Arts & Science, Evansville IN

Schnepper, Mary, *Cur.* Evansville Museum of Arts
& Science, Henry R Walker Jr Memorial Art
Library, Evansville IN

Schnider, Richard, *Assoc Prof.* Cleveland State
University, Art Dept, Cleveland OH (S)

Schnitmann, Sylvia, *Publicity Dir.* American Jewish
Art Club, Chicago IL

Schnorr, Emil G, *Conservator,* George Walter
Vincent Smith Art Museum, Springfield MA

Schnorrenberg, John, *Prof.* University of Alabama
at Birmingham, Dept of Art, Birmingham AL (S)

Schnur, Barbara, *Mgr Cataloging Servs,*
Presbyterian Historical Society, Philadelphia PA

Schoenborn, Amy, *Acting Dir Develop,* Mexican
Museum, San Francisco CA

Schoenbrun, Jodi, *Community Outreach Dir,* Arts
Council of Fayetteville-Cumberland County, The
Arts Center, Fayetteville NC

Schoenfeld, Alissa, *Dir.* A I R Gallery, New York
NY

Schoenherr, Douglas, *Assoc Cur European &
American Prints & Drawings,* National Gallery of
Canada, Ottawa ON

Schoenthaler, Jean, *Dir.* Drew University, Art Dept
Library, Madison NJ

Schoenwetter, Hilda, *Treas,* Plastic Club, Art Club,
Philadelphia PA

Schoer, Alan, *Asst Prof.* Fort Hays State
University, Dept of Art, Hays KS (S)

Schofield, Peg, *Lectr,* Saint Joseph's University,
Dept of Fine & Performing Arts, Philadelphia PA
(S)

Schol, Don R, *Interim Assoc Dean,* University of
North Texas, School of Visual Arts, Denton TX
(S)

Schonlau, Ree, *Dir.* Bemis Center for
Contemporary Arts, New Gallery, Omaha NE

Schoonover, Larry, *Deputy Dir,* Eastern
Washington State Historical Society, Cheney
Cowles Museum, Spokane WA

Schoonover, Larry, *Deputy Dir.* Eastern
Washington State Historical Society, Library,
Spokane WA

Schor, Mira, *Instr,* Sarah Lawrence College, Dept of
Art History, Bronxville NY (S)

Schorr, David, *Prof,* Wesleyan University, Art
Dept, Middletown CT (S)

Schorsch, Ismar, *Pres.* Leo Baeck Institute, New
York NY

Schott, Gene A, *Dir,* Heritage Plantation of
Sandwich, Sandwich MA

Schousen, Steve, *Assoc Prof.* Aquinas College, Art
Dept, Grand Rapids MI (S)

Schoz, Andrew, *Prof,* Seattle University, Fine Arts
Dept, Division of Art, Seattle WA (S)

Schrock, Eileen, *VPres,* Phelps County Historical
Society, Phelps County Museum, Holdrege NE

Schrock, Peggy, *Asst Prof,* Murray State University,
Dept of Art, Murray KY (S)

Schroeder, Marsy, *Events Coordr,* North Dakota
Museum of Art, Grand Forks ND

Schroeder, Patrick, *Admin Asst,* Patrick Henry
Memorial Foundation, Red Hill National
Memorial, Brookneal VA

Schroeter, Annette, *Exhibition Technician,* Prince
George Art Gallery, Prince George BC

Schroth, Sarah, *Cur Coll,* Duke University Museum
of Art, Durham NC

Schuartz, Jessica, *Dir Public Information,* Museum
of Modern Art, New York NY

Schueckler, Valerie, *Asst Comptroller,* Sterling &
Francine Clark Art Institute, Williamstown MA

Schueler, Dean A, *Development Dir,* Augustana
College, Center for Western Studies, Sioux Falls
SD

Schueler, Dean A, *Development Dir,* Augustana
College, Center for Western Studies, Sioux Falls
SD

Schuessler, Richard, *Asst Prof,* University of
Nebraska, Kearney, Dept of Art & Art History,
Kearney NE (S)

Schuette, Lynn, *Dir.* Sushi-Performance & Visual
Art Gallery, San Diego CA

Schuetze, Frederick, *Assoc Prof.* Bradford College,
Creative Arts Division, Bradford MA (S)

Schukai, Charles, *Chmn,* Arts & Education Council
of Greater Saint Louis, Saint Louis MO

Schuler, Hans C, *Dir.* Schuler School of Fine Arts,
Baltimore MD (S)

Schuler, Jane, *Prof.* York College of the City
University of New York, Fine & Performing
Arts, Jamaica NY (S)

Schulhof, Hannelore, *VPres.* The American
Federation of Arts, New York NY

Schulte, Greg, *Asst Prof.* Utah State University,
Dept of Art, Logan UT (S)

Schultz, Bernie, *Prof.* West Virginia University,
College of Creative Arts, Morgantown WV (S)

Schultz, Douglas G, *Dir.* The Buffalo Fine Arts
Academy, Albright-Knox Art Gallery, Buffalo
NY

Schultz, Jeffrey, *Dir.* Wade House & Wesley W
Jung Carriage Museum, Historic House &
Carriage Museum, Greenbush WI

Schultz, Judy, *Acting Cur Educ,* Portland Art
Museum, Portland OR

Schultz, Rebecca, *Librn.* Milwaukee Art Museum,
Library, Milwaukee WI

Schultz, Robert, *Supv.* Galeria Mesa, Mesa Arts
Center, Mesa AZ

Schultze, Raymond W, *Prof.* University of
Nebraska, Kearney, Dept of Art & Art History,
Kearney NE (S)

Schulze, Paula, *Curatorial Asst.* Marquette
University, Haggerty Museum of Art, Milwaukee
WI

Schuman, Vincent B, *Pres.* Baldwin Historical
Society Museum, Baldwin NY

Schumann, Elka, *Mgr.* Bread & Puppet Theater
Museum, Glover VT

Schumann, Peter, *Artist.* Bread & Puppet Theater
Museum, Glover VT

Schupp, Catherine, *Educ Coordr,* Tulane
University, Gallier House Museum, New Orleans
LA

Schuster, David, *Chmn Illustration Dept,* Art
Institute of Boston, Boston MA (S)

Schuster, Jerry, *Pres.* Prescott Fine Arts
Association, Gallery, Prescott AZ

Schuster, Kenneth L, *Dir & Chief Cur.* Bradford
Brinton Memorial Museum & Historic Ranch,
Big Horn WY

Schuster, Olga, *Instr.* Milwaukee Area Technical
College, Graphic Arts Division, Milwaukee WI
(S)

Schuster, Sarah, *Asst Prof.* Oberlin College, Dept of
Art, Oberlin OH (S)

Schuster, Willa T, *VPres.* Mystic Art Association,
Inc, Mystic CT

Schutte, Richard, *Treas.* Valley Art Center Inc,
Clarkston WA

Schuweiler-Daab, Suzanne, *Asst Prof.* Converse
College, Art Dept, Spartanburg SC (S)

Schuyler, Michael, *Asst Librn,*
Munson-Williams-Proctor Institute, Art
Reference Library, Utica NY

Schuyler, Robert L, *American History Arch Assoc
Cur,* University of Pennsylvania, Museum of
Archaeology & Anthropology, Philadelphia PA

Schwab, Catherine, *Chmn.* Fairfield University,
Visual & Performing Arts, Fairfield CT (S)

Schwab, Debbie, *Dir Museum Shop.* The Jewish
Museum, New York NY

Schwab, Norman, *Chmn & Prof.* Mount Saint
Mary's College, Art Dept, Los Angeles CA (S)

Schwabach, James Bruce, *Instr.* Herkimer County
Community College, Liberal Arts & Public
Service Division, Herkimer NY (S)

Schwager, Michael, *Dir.* Sonoma State University,
Art Gallery, Rohnert Park CA

Schwager, Michael, *Interim Chair.* Sonoma State
University, Art Dept, Rohnert Park CA (S)

Schwager, Sue, *Assoc Secy.* John Simon
Guggenheim Memorial Foundation, New York
NY

Schwalm, Terry, *Dir.* Saskatchewan Craft Gallery,
Saskatoon SK

Schwanke, Harriet, *Asst Dir.* Miami-Dade Public
Library, Miami FL

Schwartz, Abby S, *Cur Educ,* Cincinnati Institute of
Fine Arts, Taft Museum, Cincinnati OH

Schwartz, Constance, *Dir & Chief Cur.* Nassau
County Museum of Fine Art, Roslyn Harbor NY

Schwartz, David, *Chief Cur Film & Video,*
American Museum of the Moving Image, Astoria
NY

Schwartz, Deborah, *Vice Dir Educ Div.* Brooklyn
Museum, Brooklyn NY

Schwartz, Douglas W, *Pres,* School of American
Research, Indian Arts Research Center, Santa Fe
NM

Schwartz, Judith, *Dir.* University of Toronto,
Justina M Barnicke Gallery, Toronto ON

Schwartz, Judith S, *Dir Undergraduate Studies,*
New York University, Dept of Art & Art
Professions, New York NY (S)

Schwartz, Laura, *Art Librn,* University of Texas at
Austin, Fine Arts Library, Austin TX

Schwartz, L C, *Instr,* Western Illinois University,
Art Dept, Macomb IL (S)

Schwartz, Melanie, *Prof,* Southwestern Oregon
Community College, Visual Arts Dept, Coos Bay
OR (S)

Schwartz, Michael, *Asst Prof,* Augusta College,
Dept of Fine Arts, Augusta GA (S)

Schwartz, Mike, *VChmn,* Detroit Artists Market,
Detroit MI

Schwartz, Richard J, *Co-Dir,* Cornell University,
Herbert F Johnson Museum of Art, Ithaca NY

Schwartz, Robert T, *Exec Dir,* Industrial Designers
Society of America, Great Falls VA

Schwartz, Samuel, *Chmn,* Winterthur Museum,
Winterthur DE

Schwartzbaum, Paul, *Conservator,* Solomon R
Guggenheim Museum, New York NY

Schwartzbaum, Paul, *Conservator,* Guggenheim
Museum Soho, New York NY

Schwartzman, Marci, *Fiscal Mgr,* Gallery 53,
Cooperstown NY

Schwarz, Joseph, *Head Dept,* Auburn University at
Montgomery, Dept of Fine Arts, Montgomery
AL (S)

Schwarzbek, Ellen, *Registrar,* Hickory Museum of
Art, Inc, Hickory NC

Schwarzer, Lynn, *Assoc Prof,* Colgate University,
Dept of Art & Art History, Hamilton NY (S)

Schwebel, Renata Manasse, *VPres Admissions,*
Sculptors Guild, Inc, New York NY

Schweitzer, Julie, *Art Dir,* Floyd County Museum,
New Albany IN

Schweizer, Paul D, *Dir,* Munson-Williams-Proctor
Institute, Museum of Art, Utica NY

Schwenger, Frances, *Libr Bd Dir,* Metropolitan
Toronto Library Board, Main Reference, Toronto
ON

Schwenkmeyer, Karen, *Treas,* Foundation for Art
Resources, Los Angeles CA

Schwerdtfeger, Toshiko, *Asst Dir,* Saint Cloud State
University, Atwood Center Gallery Lounge, Saint
Cloud MN

Schwertfeger, Ronald, *Serials Librn,* Harvard
University, Byzantine Library, Washington DC

Schwertley, Mark, *Chmn Humanities,* City Colleges
of Chicago, Malcolm X College, Chicago IL (S)

Schwieger, Robert, *Prof,* Missouri Southern State
College, Dept of Art, Joplin MO (S)

Schwoeffermann, Catherine, *Cur Folklife,* Roberson
Museum & Science Center, Binghamton NY

Scillia, Charles, *Chmn,* John Carroll University,
Dept of Art History & Humanities, Cleveland
OH (S)

Scoles, Diane, *Asst Librn (Reference),* Toledo
Museum of Art, Library, Toledo OH

Scotello, Frank, *Asst Prof,* Marian College, Art
Dept, Fond Du Lac WI (S)

Scott, A M, *Instr,* Humboldt State University,
College of Arts & Humanities, Arcata CA (S)

Scott, Ann, *Ref Librn,* Kansas State University,
Paul Weigel Library of Architecture Planning &
Design, Manhattan KS

Scott, Brigette D, *Assoc Dir,* University of Illinois,
Krannert Art Museum, Champaign IL

Scott, Carson, *Dept Chmn,* East Los Angeles
College, Art Dept, Monterey Park CA (S)

Scott, Charles C, *Prof*, Glenville State College, Dept of Fine Arts, Glenville WV (S)

Scott, Deborah Emont, *Sanders Sosland Cur 20th Century Art*, Nelson-Atkins Museum of Art, Kansas City MO

Scott, Don, *Dir*, Confederation Centre Art Gallery and Museum, Library, Charlottetown PE

Scott, Donna A, *Asst Dir Administration*, National Museum of the American Indian, George Gustav Heye Center, New York NY

Scott, Donna M, *Chmn*, The Canada Council, Conseil des Arts du Canada, Ottawa ON

Scott, Gerry, *Cur Western Antiquities*, San Antonio Museum of Art, San Antonio TX

Scott, James, *Instr*, The Art Institutes International, The Art Institute of Seattle, Seattle WA (S)

Scott, Jim, *Exhib Designer*, Ohio State University, Wexner Center for the Arts, Columbus OH

Scott, John, *Assoc Prof*, University of Florida, Dept of Art, Gainesville FL (S)

Scott, John T, *Prof*, Xavier University of Louisiana, Dept of Fine Arts, New Orleans LA (S)

Scott, Jonathon, *Head Dept*, Castleton State College, Art Dept, Castleton VT (S)

Scott, Julie, *Dir*, Rosicrucian Egyptian Museum & Art Gallery, San Jose CA

Scott, Laurel, *Assoc Prof*, University of Wisconsin-Superior, Programs in the Visual Arts, Superior WI (S)

Scott, Mark, *VPres*, International Museum of Cartoon Art, Montreal PQ

Scott, Polly, *Dir Communications*, Milwaukee Art Museum, Milwaukee WI

Scott, Robert Montgomery, *Pres*, Philadelphia Museum of Art, Philadelphia PA

Scott, Sandra, *Head*, Mississippi Valley State University, Fine Arts Dept, Itta Bena MS (S)

Scott, William, *Coll Mgr*, Indiana University, William Hammond Mathers Museum, Bloomington IN

Scott-Stewart, Diane, *Exec Dir*, Nova Scotia Association of Architects, Halifax NS

Scouten, Rex W, *Cur*, White House, Washington DC

Scoville, Emily, *Cur Educ*, South Carolina State University, Art Dept, Orangeburg SC (S)

Scully, Cammie V, *Dir*, Waterloo Museum of Art, Waterloo IA

Scully, Helen G, *Dir*, Coos Art Museum, Coos Bay OR (S)

Scully, Helen G, *Admin*, Coos Art Museum, Coos Bay OR

Scully, S, *Chmn of Board*, University of Victoria, Maltwood Art Museum and Gallery, Victoria BC

Scuvvia, Thomas, *VPres*, The Print Center, Philadelphia PA

Seabold, Tom, *Dir*, Keokuk Art Center, Keokuk IA

Seabury, Linda, *Public Relations & Membership Coordr*, Manchester Institute of Arts & Sciences Gallery, Manchester NH

Seage, Robin, *Exec Dir*, Cottonlandia Museum, Greenwood MS

Seale, Laurie, *Dir Public Information*, Austin Museum of Art at Laguna Gloria, Austin TX

Seamonds, Maureen, *Assoc Prof*, Iowa Central Community College, Dept of Art, Fort Dodge IA (S)

Searing, Helen, *Prof*, Smith College, Art Dept, Northampton MA (S)

Searles, Judith, *Head Circulation Dept*, Springfield Free Public Library, Donald B Palmer Museum, Springfield NJ

Searls-McConnel, Maryse, *Assoc Prof*, University of New Hampshire, Dept of Arts & Art History, Durham NH (S)

Sears, Elizabeth, *Asst Prof*, University of Michigan, Ann Arbor, Dept of History of Art, Ann Arbor MI (S)

Sears, Stanton, *Head Dept*, Macalester College, Dept of Art, Saint Paul MN (S)

Sebrell, Alice, *Asst Dir*, Light Factory, Charlotte NC

Seckelson, Linda, *Reader Servs Librn*, The Metropolitan Museum of Art, Thomas J Watson Library, New York NY

Seckinger, Linda, *Assoc Prof*, Mississippi State University, Art Dept, Mississippi State MS (S)

Secrest, Donna, *Office Mgr*, Ponca City Art Association, Ponca City OK

Sedlock, Marilen, *Public Affairs*, San Diego Museum of Art, San Diego CA

Seed, John, *Dept Chair*, Mount San Jacinto College, Art Dept, San Jacinto CA (S)

Seeley, J, *Prof*, Wesleyan University, Art Dept, Middletown CT (S)

Seely, Ella, *Head Art & Music Dept*, Multnomah County Library, Henry Failing Art & Music Dept, Portland OR

Seem, Olga, *Gallery Dir*, Mount Saint Mary's College, Jose Drudis-Biada Art Gallery, Los Angeles CA

Seeman, Helene Zucker, *Dir Art Program*, Prudential Art Program, Newark NJ

Seeman, Rebecca, *Instr*, Art Academy of Cincinnati, Cincinnati OH (S)

Sefcik, James F, *Museum Dir*, Louisiana Department of Culture, Recreation & Tourism, Louisiana State Museum, New Orleans LA

Sefcik, James F, *Dir*, Louisiana Department of Culture, Recreation & Tourism, Louisiana Historical Center Library, New Orleans LA

Sefton, Susan, *Exec Dir*, Huntsville Art League, Huntsville AL

Segall, Andrea, *Librn*, Berkeley Public Library, Berkeley CA

Segalman, Richard, *Instr*, Woodstock School of Art, Inc, Woodstock NY (S)

Segger, Martin, *Dir & Cur*, University of Victoria, Maltwood Art Museum and Gallery, Victoria BC

Sehlier, Debbie, *Cur Coll*, Springfield Art Museum, Springfield MO

Seibert, Peter S, *Exec Dir*, Heritage Center of Lancaster County Museum, Lancaster PA

Seid, Carrie, *Co-Pres*, Artemisia Gallery, Chicago IL

Seid, Steve, *Asst Cur Video*, University of California, Berkeley Art Museum & Pacific Film Archive, Berkeley CA

Seiden, Don, *Prof*, School of the Art Institute of Chicago, Chicago IL (S)

Seif, Denise, *Gallery Dir*, Parkland College, Art Gallery, Champaign IL

Seifert, Jan E, *Fine Arts Librn*, University of Oklahoma, Fine Arts Library, Norman OK

Seigal, Debra, *Cur Permanent Colls & Exhib Dir*, Hamline University Learning Center Gallery, Saint Paul MN

Seigel, Judy, *Ed*, Midmarch Associates, Women Artists News Archive, New York NY

Seitz, Amy, *Develop Dir*, McAllen International Museum, McAllen TX

Seitz, Becca, *Pub Relations & Marketing*, Baltimore Museum of Art, Baltimore MD

Seitz, Carole, *Instr*, Creighton University, Fine & Performing Arts Dept, Omaha NE (S)

Seivert, Lisa A, *Research Librn*, Buffalo Museum of Science, Research Library, Buffalo NY

Seiz, Janet, *Faculty*, Saint Ambrose University, Art Dept, Davenport IA (S)

Seiz, John, *Instr*, Springfield College in Illinois, Dept of Art, Springfield IL (S)

Seland, Paul, *Chmn*, Niagara County Community College, Fine Arts Division, Sanborn NY (S)

Selander, Lisa, *Cur Educ*, Rome Historical Society Museum, William E Scripture Memorial Library, Rome NY

Seley, Beverly, *Assoc Prof*, Grand Valley State University, Art & Design Dept, Allendale MI (S)

Self, Dana, *Cur Exhib*, Wichita State University, Edwin A Ulrich Museum of Art, Wichita KS

Self, Dana, *Cur*, Kansas City Art Institute, Kemper Museum of Contemporary Art & Design, Kansas City MO

Seligman, Rachel, *Asst Dir*, Lake George Arts Project, Courthouse Gallery, Lake George NY

Seligman, Thomas K, *Dir*, Stanford University, Museum of Art, Stanford CA

Seligsohn, Valerie, *Assoc Prof*, Philadelphia Community College, Dept of Art, Philadelphia PA (S)

Seline, Janice, *Asst Cur Contemporary Art*, National Gallery of Canada, Ottawa ON

Sellars, Judith, *Librn*, Museum of New Mexico, Museum of International Folk Art, Santa Fe NM

Sellars, Judith, *Librn*, Museum of New Mexico, Library, Santa Fe NM

Selle, Thomas, *Co-Chmn*, Carroll College, Art Dept, Waukesha WI (S)

Sellers, Kate M, *Dir Development*, Cleveland Museum of Art, Cleveland OH

Selter, Dan S, *Prog Dir*, Transylvania University, Studio Arts Dept, Lexington KY (S)

Semergieff, Chris, *Instr*, Chautauqua Institution, School of Art, Chautauqua NY (S)

Semiven, Douglas, *Instr*, Madonna University, Art Dept, Livonia MI (S)

Semmel, Joan, *Prof*, Rutgers, the State University of New Jersey, Mason Gross School of the Arts, New Brunswick NJ (S)

Semmens, Beverly, *Prof Fine Arts*, University of Cincinnati, School of Art, Cincinnati OH (S)

Semmes, Tom, *Pres*, Marion Koogler McNay Art Museum, San Antonio TX

Semowich, Charles, *Pres*, Print Club of Albany, Albany NY

Sengel, Jill, *VPres Educ*, DuPage Art League School & Gallery, Wheaton IL

Senie, Harriet F, *Dir Museum Studies*, City College of New York, Art Dept, New York NY (S)

Seniuk, Jake, *Dir*, Port Angeles Fine Arts Center, Port Angeles WA

Senn, Barbara, *Admin Asst*, Galleries of the Claremont Colleges, Claremont CA

Senn, Carol Johnson, *Dir*, Ephraim McDowell-Cambus-Kenneth Foundation, McDowell House & Apothecary Shop, Danville KY

Senn, Greg, *Asst Prof*, Eastern New Mexico University, Dept of Art, Portales NM (S)

Sennett, Arthur, *Prof*, State University of New York College at Potsdam, Dept of Fine Arts, Potsdam NY (S)

Sensemann, Susan, *Co-Pres*, Artemisia Gallery, Chicago IL

Senter, Renee, *Educ Coordr*, Iowa State University, Brunnier Art Museum, Ames IA

Senti, Manuel, *Exhibits*, Hutchinson Art Association, Hutchinson Art Center, Hutchinson KS

Senton, Luis, *Pres*, Casa Amesti, Monterey CA

Serebrennikov, Nina, *Asst Prof*, Davidson College, Art Dept, Davidson NC (S)

Seremet, Peter M, *Corporate VPres*, Heublein, Inc, Hartford CT

Serenco, Henry, *Assoc Prof*, University of Nebraska at Omaha, Dept of Art & Art History, Omaha NE (S)

Serfaty, Gail F, *Dir*, US Department of State, Diplomatic Reception Rooms, Washington DC

Sergovic, John, *VPres Finance*, Philadelphia Museum of Art, Philadelphia PA

Serio, Faye, *Assoc Prof*, St Lawrence University, Dept of Fine Arts, Canton NY (S)

Serlin-Cobb, Fran, *Dir Marketing*, Milwaukee Art Museum, Milwaukee WI

Serra, Lauriann, *Mem & Develop*, Photographic Resource Center, Boston MA

Serroes, Richard, *Instr*, Modesto Junior College, Arts Humanities & Communications Division, Modesto CA (S)

Servetas, John, *Treas*, Federation of Modern Painters & Sculptors, New York NY

Servis, Nancy M, *Dir*, Pence Gallery, Davis CA

Serwer, Jacquelyn, *Chief Cur*, National Museum of American Art, Washington DC

Sessions, Billie, *Instr*, California State University, San Bernardino, Visual Arts, San Bernardino CA (S)

Setford, David F, *Cur*, Norton Gallery & School of Art, Inc, Norton Museum of Art, West Palm Beach FL

Setford, David F, *Cur*, Norton Gallery & School of Art, Inc, Library, West Palm Beach FL

Seto, John H, *Exec Dir*, Chinese Culture Foundation, Chinese Culture Center Gallery, San Francisco CA

Settle, Gerda, *Dir*, Brownsville Art League Museum, Brownsville TX

Settle-Cooney, Mary, *Exec Dir*, Tennessee Valley Art Association & Center, Tuscumbia AL

Settler, Faye, *Dir & Owner*, Upstairs Gallery, Winnipeg MB

Setzer, Barbara, *Asst Dir*, Waterworks Visual Arts Center, Salisbury NC

Sevelius, Helen, *Acad Dean Fine Arts*, Alberta College of Art, Calgary AB (S)

Sever, Ziya, *Chmn Art*, Western Nebraska Community College, Division of Language & Arts, Scottsbluff NE (S)

Severtson, Johan, *Chmn Graphic Design*, Corcoran School of Art, Washington DC (S)

Sewell, Darrel, *McNeil Cur American Art*, Philadelphia Museum of Art, Philadelphia PA

Sexton, Brendan, *Pres*, Municipal Art Society of New York, New York NY

Seydel, Robert E, *Cur*, Photographic Resource Center, Boston MA

Seyl, Susan, *Dir Image Coll*, Oregon Historical Society, Library, Portland OR

Seyller, Anna, *Bus Mgr*, University of Vermont, Robert Hull Fleming Museum, Burlington VT

Seymour, Dottie, *Board Dir*, Artists' Cooperative Gallery, Omaha NE

Seymour, Gayle, *Assoc Prof*, University of Central Arkansas, Art Dept, Conway AR (S)

Seymour, Libby, *Pres*, Arts Council of Fayetteville-Cumberland County, The Arts Center, Fayetteville NC

Seymour, Lisa, *Dir*, Northeastern Nevada Historical Society Museum, Elko NV

Seymour, Lisa, *Dir*, Northeastern Nevada Historical Society Museum, Library, Elko NV

Sfirri, Mark, *Instr*, Bucks County Community College, Fine Arts Dept, Newtown PA (S)

Sfollite, Shelia, *Chmn*, George Mason University, Dept of Art & Art History, Fairfax VA (S)

Sha, Marjorie, *Head of Reference*, New Rochelle Public Library, Art Section, New Rochelle NY

Shackelford, George, *Cur European Art*, Museum of Fine Arts, Houston, Houston TX

Shackelford, George, *Cur European Paintings*, Museum of Fine Arts, Boston MA

Shacter, Joe, *Dir Exhibits*, Museum of Science & Industry, Chicago IL

Shade, Nancy, *Admin Asst*, Allied Arts Association, Allied Arts Center & Gallery, Richland WA

Shadrach, Jean, *Librn*, Alaska Watercolor Society, Anchorage AK

Shady, Ronald, *Asst Prof*, University of North Alabama, Dept of Art, Florence AL (S)

Shafer, Carolyn, *Cur*, Wiregrass Museum of Art, Dothan AL

Shafer, Phyllis, *Painting Instr*, Lake Tahoe Community College, Art Dept, South Lake Tahoe CA (S)

Shaffer, Mary, *Art Head*, Northwest Nazarene College, Art Dept, Nampa ID (S)

Shaffstall, James W, *Chmn Dept*, Hanover College, Dept of Art, Hanover IN (S)

Shaker, Andrea, *Asst Prof*, College of Saint Benedict, Art Dept, Saint Joseph MN (S)

Shakespeare, Valerie, *Pres*, Actual Art Foundation, New York NY

Shale, Frederick, *Treas*, Beverly Historical Society, Cabot, Hale & Balch House Museums, Beverly MA

Shamblin, Barbara, *Assoc Prof*, Salve Regina University, Art Dept, Newport RI (S)

Shames, Susan, *Decorative Arts Librn*, Colonial Williamsburg Foundation, John D Rockefeller, Jr Library, Williamsburg VA

Shamro, Joyce, *Prof*, Bluefield State College, Art Dept, Bluefield WV (S)

Shamy, Pat, *Treas*, New Jersey Water-Color Society, Chester NJ

Shanahan, Carl, *Chmn*, State University of New York College at Geneseo, Dept of Art, Geneseo NY (S)

Shanchuk, Victor, *Treas*, Buffalo Society of Artists, Williamsville NY

Shanck, Gregory S, *Theater Mgr*, Hostos Center for the Arts & Culture, Bronx NY

Shandor, Mary, *Art*, Nabisco, Inc, East Hanover NJ

Shaner, Carol, *Exhibits Librn*, Sarah Lawrence College Library, Esther Raushenbush Library, Bronxville NY

Shaner, Susan, *Cur*, Judiciary History Center, Honolulu HI

Shanis, Carole Price, *Pres*, Philadelphia Art Alliance, Philadelphia PA

Shankle, Charity, *Mem*, Ward Foundation, Ward Museum of Wildfowl Art, Salisbury MD

Shanley, Kevin, *Pres & Chmn Board of Trustees*, Newark Museum Association, The Newark Museum, Newark NJ

Shannahan, John W, *Dir*, Connecticut Historical Commission, Sloane-Stanley Museum, Kent CT

Shannon, Connie, *Exec Dir*, Friends of the Arts & Sciences, Hilton Leech Studio Workshops, Sarasota FL (S)

Shannon, Dolly, *Archives*, Deming-Luna Mimbres Museum, Deming NM

Shannon, George Ward, *Dir*, Louisiana State Exhibit Museum, Shreveport LA

Shannon, Joseph, *Prof*, College of New Jersey, Art Dept, Trenton NJ (S)

Shannon, Judith V, *Community Affairs Dir*, Heard Museum, Phoenix AZ

Shannon, Martha, *Exec Dir*, City Of Raleigh Arts Commission, Municipal Building Art Exhibitions, Raleigh NC

Shao, John, *Pres*, Community Council for the Arts, Kinston NC

Shapero, Janet, *Asst Prof*, Utah State University, Dept of Art, Logan UT (S)

Shapiro, Babe, *Faculty*, Maryland Institute, Mount Royal School of Art, Baltimore MD (S)

Shapiro, Cara, *Asst Dir*, Louisa May Alcott Memorial Association, Orchard House, Concord MA

Shapiro, Denise, *District Gallery Mgr*, Las Vegas-Clark County Library District, Flamingo Gallery, Las Vegas NV

Shapiro, Laura, *Volunteer Coordr*, Wing Luke Asian Museum, Seattle WA

Shapiro, Martin, *Head Coll Develop*, American University, Jack I Dorothy G Bender Library, Washington DC

Shapiro, Michael E, *Deputy Dir & Chief Cur*, High Museum of Art, Atlanta GA

Sharer, Robert, *American Sections Cur*, University of Pennsylvania, Museum of Archaeology & Anthropology, Philadelphia PA

Sharkey, Cindy, *Asst to Dir*, College of William & Mary, Joseph & Margaret Muscarelle Museum of Art, Williamsburg VA

Sharma, Martha, *Registrar*, University of Chicago, David & Alfred Smart Museum of Art, Chicago, IL

Sharma, Sue, *Division Chief*, Brooklyn Public Library, Art & Music Division, Brooklyn NY

Sharon, Dan, *Reference Librn*, Spertus Institute of Jewish Studies, Asher Library, Chicago IL

Sharp, Elbert L, *Chief Preparator*, Memphis Brooks Museum of Art, Memphis TN

Sharp, Ellen, *Graphic Arts*, Detroit Institute of Arts, Detroit MI

Sharp, Lewis, *Dir*, Denver Art Museum, Denver CO

Sharp, Pamela, *Art Educ Coordr*, San Jose State University, School of Art & Design, San Jose CA (S)

Sharp, Steven, *First VPres*, Springfield Museum of Art, Springfield OH

Sharpe, Yolanda, *Instr*, State University of New York College at Oneonta, Dept of Art, Oneonta NY (S)

Shaskan, I, *Instr*, Sacramento City College, Art Dept, Sacramento CA (S)

Shatto, Gloria, *Pres*, Berry College, Moon Gallery, Mount Berry GA

Shattum, Gerald, *Prof*, California Lutheran University, Art Dept, Thousand Oaks CA (S)

Shatzman, Merrill, *Asst Prof Practice*, Duke University, Dept of Art & Art History, Durham NC (S)

Shaver, Page, *Dir*, China Institute in America, China Institute Gallery, New York NY

Shaw, Catherine Elliot, *Cur*, University of Western Ontario, McIntosh Gallery, London ON

Shaw, Catherine Elliot, *VPres*, Ontario Association of Art Galleries, Toronto ON

Shaw, Frank, *Asst Prof*, Bethany College, Mingenback Art Center, Lindsborg KS

Shaw, Frank, *Asst Prof*, Bethany College, Art Dept, Lindsborg KS (S)

Shaw, Karen, *Cur*, Islip Art Museum, East Islip NY

Shaw, Louise E, *Exec Dir*, Nexus Contemporary Art Center, Atlanta GA

Shaw, Meg, *Librn*, University of Kentucky, Edward Warder Rannells Art Library, Lexington KY

Shaw, Reesey, *Dir*, California Center for the Arts Museum, Escondido CA

Shaw, Richard, *Prof*, University of California, Berkeley, College of Letters & Sciences-Art Dept, Berkeley CA (S)

Shaw, Wayne, *Dept Head*, Belleville Area College, Art Dept, Belleville IL (S)

Shay, Ed, *Two-Dimensional Area Head*, Southern Illinois University, School of Art & Design, Carbondale IL (S)

Shay, Robert, *Dean*, Indiana University-Purdue University, Indianapolis, Herron School of Art, Indianapolis IN (S)

Shea, John, *Cur*, Longfellow National Historic Site, Cambridge MA

Shea, Michael, *Installation Officer*, City of Woodstock, Woodstock Art Gallery, Woodstock ON

Shea, Stephen C, *Pres*, Colonel Black Mansion, Ellsworth ME

Sheaks, Barclay, *Assoc Prof*, Virginia Wesleyan College, Art Dept of the Humanities Division, Norfolk VA (S)

Shear, T Leslie, *Prof*, Princeton University, Dept of Art & Archaeology, Princeton NJ (S)

Sheardy, Robert, *Chmn Art History & Liberal Arts*, Kendall College of Art & Design, Grand Rapids MI (S)

Shearer, Linda, *Dir*, Williams College, Museum of Art, Williamstown MA

Shebairo, Richard, *Treas*, Artists Space, New York NY

Shechter, Jack, *Dir*, University of Judaism, Dept of Continuing Education, Los Angeles CA (S)

Sheckler, Allyson, *Asst Prof*, Florida Southern College, Art Dept, Lakeland FL (S)

Shedaker, Rachel, *Gallery Asst*, Salisbury State University, University Gallery, Salisbury MD

Shedd, Isabel McIlvain, *Assoc Prof*, Boston University, School of Visual Arts, Boston MA (S)

Shedd, Peggy, *Museum Shop Mgr*, Flint Institute of Arts, Flint MI

Sheedy, Madelon, *Johnstown Art Extension Coordr*, Southern Alleghenies Museum of Art, Loretto PA

Sheedy, Madelon, *Cur*, Southern Alleghenies Museum of Art, Southern Alleghenies Museum of Art at Johnstown, Loretto PA

Sheehan, Aurele, *Prog Coordr*, Ucross Foundation, Big Red Barn Gallery, Clearmont WY

Sheehan, Michael T, *Dir*, Woodrow Wilson House, Washington DC

Sheehy, Carolyn A, *Dir*, North Central College, Oesterle Library, Naperville IL

Sheehy, Colleen, *Educ Dir*, University of Minnesota, Weisman Art Museum, Minneapolis MN

Sheer, Doug, *Board of Dir*, Artists Talk on Art, New York NY

Sheets, Allen, *Chmn*, Moorhead State University, Dept of Art, Moorhead MN (S)

Sheets, Mary Bea, *Dir*, French Art Colony, Gallipolis OH

Sheets, Mary Bea, *Dir*, French Art Colony, Library, Gallipolis OH

Sheff, Donald, *Dir*, New York Institute of Photography, New York NY (S)

Sheffield, Ellen, *Gallery Dir*, Kenyon College, Art Dept, Gambier OH (S)

Sheffield, Ellen, *Coordr*, Kenyon College, Art Gallery, Gambier OH

Shekore, Mark, *Chmn*, Northern State University, Art Dept, Aberdeen SD (S)

Shelby, Jim, *Treas*, Knoxville Museum of Art, Knoxville TN

Sheldon, Janine, *Develop Dir*, University of California, Berkeley Art Museum & Pacific Film Archive, Berkeley CA

Sheldon, Sara, *Assoc Museum Dir*, Leanin' Tree Museum of Western Art, Boulder CO

Sheley, David, *Dir & Cur*, Turner House Museum, Hattiesburg MS

Shelkrot, Elliot, *Library Pres & Dir*, Free Library of Philadelphia, Art Dept, Philadelphia PA

Shell, Martin, *Asst Prof*, Springfield College, Dept of Visual & Performing Arts, Springfield MA (S)

Shelton, Bob, *Prof*, Birmingham-Southern College, Art Dept, Birmingham AL (S)

Shelton, Carol, *Gallery Asst*, Saint Paul's School, Art Center in Hargate, Concord NH

Shelton, Kay, *Head Librn*, Alaska State Library, Alaska Historical Collections, Juneau AK

Shelton, L T, *Cur Coll*, Department of Natural Resources of Missouri, Missouri State Museum, Jefferson City MO

Shelton, Robert, *Dir*, Birmingham Southern College, Doris Wainwright Kennedy Art Center, Birmingham AL

Shelton, Tom, *Photo Archivist*, The University of Texas, Institute of Texan Cultures, San Antonio TX

Shepard, Bruce, *Dir*, University of Saskatchewan, Diefenbaker Canada Centre, Saskatoon SK

Shepard, Charles A, *Dir*, Lyman Allyn Art Museum, New London CT

Shepard, Fred, *Preparator*, Santa Clara University, de Saisset Museum, Santa Clara CA

Shepard, Fred, *Prof*, Murray State University, Dept of Art, Murray KY (S)

Shepard, Piper, *Instr*, Chautauqua Institution, School of Art, Chautauqua NY (S)

Shepherd, Elizabeth, *Cur Exhibit*, University of California, Los Angeles, UCLA at the Armand Hammer Museum of Art & Cultural Center, Los Angeles CA

Shepherd, Lori, *Art Consultant*, Mobil Corporation, Art Collection, Fairfax VA

Shepherd, Murray, *Univ Librn*, University of Waterloo, Dana Porter Library, Waterloo ON

Shepp, James G, *Exec Dir*, Maitland Art Center, Maitland FL

Shepp, James G, *Dir*, Maitland Art Center, Library, Maitland FL

Sheppard, Carroll Anne, *Dir Develop*, Historical Society of Pennsylvania, Philadelphia PA

Sheppart, Luvon, *Chmn Fine Arts & Prof*, Rochester Institute of Technology, School of Art & Design, Rochester NY (S)

Sheret, Mary Ames, *Cur Coll*, Southern Oregon Historical Society, Jacksonville Museum of Southern Oregon History, Medford OR

Sheridan, Clare, *Librn*, American Textile History Museum, Library, Lowell MA

Sheridan, Georgine, *Pres*, CIAO, Gallery & Art Center, Bronx NY

Sheriff, Alice D, *Adminr*, New London County Historical Society, New London CT

Sheriff, Mary, *Prof*, University of North Carolina at Chapel Hill, Art Dept, Chapel Hill NC (S)

Sherin, Pamela V, *Cur, Cultural & Community Relations*, Bristol-Myers Squibb Pharmaceutical Group, Gallery at Bristol-Myers Squibb, Princeton NJ

Sherk, Jeffrey L, *Librn*, Maritz, Inc, Library, Fenton MO

Sherk, Scott, *Assoc Prof*, Muhlenberg College, Dept of Art, Allentown PA (S)

Sherman, Curt, *Asst Chmn*, Winthrop University, Dept of Art & Design, Rock Hill SC (S)

Sherman, Joy, *Asst Prof US Art*, Seattle University, Fine Arts Dept, Division of Art, Seattle WA (S)

Sherman, Paul T, *Admin Services Librn*, New York City Technical College, Namm Hall Library and Learning Resource Center, Brooklyn NY

Sherman, Tisa Rodriquez, *Admin Asst*, Tucson Museum of Art & Historic Block, Tucson AZ

Sherman, Todd, *Asst Prof*, University of Alaska-Fairbanks, Dept of Art, Fairbanks AK (S)

Sherman, Tom, *Dir*, Syracuse University, College of Visual & Performing Arts, Syracuse NY (S)

Sherrell, Steve, *Instr*, Joliet Junior College, Fine Arts Dept, Joliet IL (S)

Sherrill, Martine, *Cur Slides & Prints*, Wake Forest University, A Lewis Aycock Art Slide Library & Print Collection, Winston Salem NC

Sherry, James, *Pres*, Segue Foundation, Reading Room-Archive, New York NY

Sherwood, Katherine, *Prof*, University of California, Berkeley, College of Letters & Sciences-Art Dept, Berkeley CA (S)

Shestack, Alan, *Deputy Dir*, National Gallery of Art, Washington DC

Shetabi, Mark, *Asst Gallery Dir*, Western Washington University, Viking Union Gallery, Bellingham WA

Shetka, Stanley, *Chmn*, Gustavus Adolphus College, Art & Art History Dept, Saint Peter MN (S)

Shevburn, Earl, *Community Arts Dir*, City of Los Angeles, Cultural Affairs Dept, Los Angeles CA

Shiba, Hiromi, *Registrar*, Museo de Arte de Ponce, Ponce Art Museum, Ponce PR

Shick, Andrew, *Acting Dir*, Passaic County Historical Society, Paterson NJ

Shick, Andrew, *Acting Dir*, Passaic County Historical Society, Library, Paterson NJ

Shickman, Allan, *Assoc Prof*, University of Northern Iowa, Dept of Art, Cedar Falls IA (S)

Shieh, Suewhei T, *Cur*, Towson State University, Asian Arts Center, Towson MD

Shield, Jan, *Prof*, Pacific University in Oregon, Arts Div, Dept of Art, Forest Grove OR (S)

Shields, Ann, *Dir*, Pennsylvania State University, HUB Galleries, University Park PA

Shields, Catherine, *Librn*, Winnipeg Art Gallery, Clara Lander Library, Winnipeg MB

Shields, David, *Asst Prof*, Southwest Texas State University, Dept of Art, San Marcos TX (S)

Shields, D H, *Asst Librn*, University of Michigan, Art Media Union Library, Ann Arbor MI

Shields, Paul M, *Asst Prof*, York College, Art Dept, York NE (S)

Shields, Shannon, *Chmn Art Committee*, Angelo State University, Houston Harte University Center, San Angelo TX

Shields, Tom, *Asst Prof*, Augustana College, Art Dept, Sioux Falls SD (S)

Shields, Van W, *Exec Dir*, Museum of York County, Rock Hill SC

Shifman, Barry, *Cur Decorative Arts*, Indianapolis Museum of Art, Indianapolis IN

Shiga-Gattullo, Kathy, *Dir Educ*, The Hudson River Museum of Westchester, Yonkers NY

Shigaki, B J, *Dir*, Rochester Art Center, Rochester MN

Shih, Chia-Chun, *Librn*, Kimbell Art Foundation, Kimbell Art Museum, Fort Worth TX

Shih, Chia-Chun, *Librn*, Kimbell Art Foundation, Library, Fort Worth TX

Shill, Nancy, *Dir*, Harcum Junior College, Illustrations & Graphic Design Dept, Bryn Mawr PA (S)

Shillabeer, S L, *Asst Prof*, Troy State University, Dept of Art & Classics, Troy AL (S)

Shilland, Kimberly, *Cur Architecture*, Massachusetts Institute of Technology, MIT Museum, Cambridge MA

Shimizu, Yoshiaki, *Prof*, Princeton University, Dept of Art & Archaeology, Princeton NJ (S)

Shine, Pablo, *Instr*, Woodstock School of Art, Inc, Woodstock NY (S)

Shinn, Deborah, *Cur Applied Arts*, Cooper-Hewitt, National Design Museum, New York NY

Shinners, Jackie, *Art Historian*, Northwestern Michigan College, Art Dept, Traverse City MI (S)

Shinners, Jacqueline, *Cur*, Northwestern Michigan College, Dennos Museum Center, Traverse City MI

Shipley, Roger, *Co-Dir*, Lycoming College Gallery, Williamsport PA

Shipley, Roger Douglas, *Chmn*, Lycoming College, Art Dept, Williamsport PA (S)

Shipley, Walter B, *Instr*, Okaloosa-Walton Community College, Dept of Fine & Performing Arts, Niceville FL (S)

Shipman, Alan, *Coordr Exhib & Coll*, Washington State University, Museum of Art, Pullman WA

Shireman, Candace, *Cur*, Historical Society of Washington DC, Heurich House Museum, Washington DC

Shirley, Karen, *Prof Art*, Antioch College, Noyes & Read Galleries, Yellow Springs OH

Shirley, Karen, *Prof*, Antioch College, Visual Arts Dept, Yellow Springs OH (S)

Shirley, Margaret, *Instr*, Marylhurst College, Art Dept, Marylhurst OR (S)

Shives, Christine, *Admin Asst*, Washington County Museum of Fine Arts, Hagerstown MD

Shives, Rebecca, *Adult Servs*, Martin Memorial Library, York PA

Shockley, Evelyn, *Prog Mgr*, Xerox Corporation, Art Collection, Stamford CT

Shoemaker, Ed, *Library Resources*, Oklahoma Historical Society, State Museum of History, Oklahoma City OK

Shoemaker, Edward C, *Dir Library Resources Div*, Oklahoma Historical Society, Library Resources Division, Oklahoma City OK

Shoemaker, Innis, *Sr Cur Prints, Drawings & Photographs*, Philadelphia Museum of Art, Philadelphia PA

Shoger, Jan, *Assoc Prof*, Saint Olaf College, Art Dept, Northfield MN (S)

Shogren, Samuel W, *Cur*, Penobscot Marine Museum, Searsport ME

Shomstien, Cathy, *Chief Develop Officer, Corporate Foundation & Government Giving*, The American Federation of Arts, New York NY

Shook, Melissa, *Assoc Prof*, University of Massachusetts - Boston, Art Dept, Boston MA (S)

Shore, Francine, *Instr*, Main Line Art Center, Haverford PA (S)

Shore, Mark, *Prom Dir*, Battleship North Carolina, Wilmington NC

Shore, Stephen, *Instr*, Bard College, Milton Avery Graduate School of the Arts, Annandale-on-Hudson NY (S)

Shoreman, Mike, *VPres Bus Affairs & Operations*, Royal Ontario Museum, Toronto ON

Shorr, Ken, *Assoc Prof Photography*, University of Arizona, Dept of Art, Tucson AZ (S)

Short, Dale, *Instr*, New Mexico Junior College, Arts & Sciences, Hobbs NM (S)

Short, Frank, *Coordr*, Montgomery County Community College, Art Dept, Blue Bell PA (S)

Shortt, A J (Fred), *Cur*, National Museum of Science & Technology Corporation, National Aviation Museum, Ottawa ON

Shostak, Anthony, *Educ Coordr*, Bates College, Museum of Art, Lewiston ME

Shotwell, Clayton, *Chmn*, Augusta College, Dept of Fine Arts, Augusta GA (S)

Shoughnessy, Michael, *Chmn*, University of Southern Maine, Art Dept, Gorham ME (S)

Shoulders, Patrick, *Pres Board Dir*, Evansville Museum of Arts & Science, Evansville IN

Shoulet, Susan, *Exec Dir*, College of New Rochelle, Castle Gallery, New Rochelle NY

Showalter, Melissa, *Pres*, Scottsdale Artists' League, Scottsdale AZ

Shreve, Larry, *Prof*, Lenoir Community College, Dept of Visual Art, Kinston NC (S)

Shu, Beth, *Prog Dir*, Chinese-American Arts Council, New York NY

Shuck, Ann, *Archives Technician*, The Saint Louis Art Museum, Richardson Memorial Library, Saint Louis MO

Shuck, Patrick, *Instr*, Saint Louis Community College at Meramec, Art Dept, Saint Louis MO (S)

Shuckerow, Tim, *Asst Prof*, Case Western Reserve University, Dept of Art History & Art, Cleveland OH (S)

Shuebrook, Ron, *Acting Chmn Prof*, University of Guelph, Fine Art Dept, Guelph ON (S)

Shultes, Stephanie, *Cur*, Iroquois Indian Museum, Howes Cave NY

Shultz, Jay, *Assoc Prof*, Palomar Community College, Art Dept, San Marcos CA (S)

Shultz, Mike, *Head Librn*, Western Montana College, Lucy Carson Memorial Library, Dillon MT

Shumate, Michael, *Chmn*, St Lawrence College, Dept of Visual & Creative Arts, Kingston ON (S)

Shunk, Hal, *Asst Prof*, Wilmington College, Art Dept, Wilmington OH (S)

Shupe, Kevin, *Head Librn*, Manchester Historic Association, Library, Manchester NH

Shurkus, Marie, *Communications Coordr*, Randolph Street Gallery, Chicago IL

Shurtleff, Carol B, *Membership & Staff Coordr*, Maitland Art Center, Maitland FL

Shurtleff, Carol B, *Membership & Staff Coordr*, Maitland Art Center, Library, Maitland FL

Shust, Maria, *Dir*, The Ukrainian Museum, New York NY

Shust, Maria, *Dir*, The Ukrainian Museum, Library, New York NY

Shuttleworth, Roseanne, *Pres*, Allegany County Historical Society, History House, Cumberland MD

Siano, Mary Ann, *Assoc Dir*, Lehman College Art Gallery, Bronx NY

Sias, James H, *Prof*, Rochester Institute of Technology, School of Art & Design, Rochester NY (S)

Siboroski, Paul, *Cur Exhibits*, Anniston Museum of Natural History, Anniston AL

Sichel, Kim, *Dir*, Boston University, Art Gallery, Boston MA

Sicola, Kimberly, *Coll Mgr*, County of Henrico, Meadow Farm Museum, Glen Allen VA

Siddens, Vera Jo, *Prof*, University of Northern Iowa, Dept of Art, Cedar Falls IA (S)

Sider, Sandra, *Instr*, Sarah Lawrence College, Dept of Art History, Bronxville NY (S)

Sides, Wayne, *Asst Prof*, University of North Alabama, Dept of Art, Florence AL (S)

Sidner, Rob, *Asst Dir*, Mingei International, Inc, Mingei International Museum Satellite of World Folk Art, San Diego CA

Sido, Lee, *Chmn*, University of Nevada, Las Vegas, Dept of Art, Las Vegas NV (S)

Sieber, Matthew, *Designer*, Indiana University, William Hammond Mathers Museum, Bloomington IN

Sieber, Roy, *Prof*, Indiana University, Bloomington, Henry Radford Hope School of Fine Arts, Bloomington IN (S)

Siedell, Daniel, *Cur*, University of Nebraska, Lincoln, Sheldon Memorial Art Gallery & Sculpture Garden, Lincoln NE

Siefert, Chris, *Asst*, Louisiana State University, School of Art, Baton Rouge LA (S)

Sieg, Robert, *Chmn*, East Central University, Art Dept, Ada OK (S)

Siegel, Cheryl A, *Librn*, Vancouver Art Gallery, Library, Vancouver BC

Siegel, Judith, *Dir Educ*, The Jewish Museum, New York NY

Siegfried, Jay, *Chmn*, Middlesex County College, Visual Arts Dept, Edison NJ (S)

Siegmann, William, *Cur Arts of Africa & Pacific*, Brooklyn Museum, Brooklyn NY

Siers, Pamela, *Exec Dir*, Angels Gate Cultural Center, The Gate Gallery, San Pedro CA

Siersma, Betsy, *Dir*, University of Massachusetts, Amherst, University Gallery, Amherst MA

Sievers, Ann H, *Assoc Cur Prints*, Smith College, Museum of Art, Northampton MA

Sigaca, Patricia, *Dir Educ*, Museo De Las Americas, Denver CO

Sigala, Stephanie C, *Librn*, The Saint Louis Art Museum, Richardson Memorial Library, Saint Louis MO

Sigel, Deborah, *Vis Prof*, Hamline University, Dept of Art & Art History, Saint Paul MN (S)

Sigel, Milt, *Instr*, Bucks County Community College, Fine Arts Dept, Newtown PA (S)

Sigerson, Marge, *Librn*, The Museum of Arts & Sciences Inc, Library, Daytona Beach FL

Sigler, Doug, *Prof*, Rochester Institute of Technology, School of Art & Design, Rochester NY (S)

Sigman, D L, *Chmn Div*, Purdue University, West Lafayette, Dept of Visual & Performing Arts, Div of Art & Design, West Lafayette IN (S)

Sihota, Raj, *Admin Asst*, Community Arts Council of Vancouver, Vancouver BC

Sikkema, Scott, *Mgr School & Teacher Progs*, Terra Museum of American Art, Chicago IL

Silagyi, Lisa, *Dir*, Nelson-Atkins Museum of Art, Creative Arts Center, Kansas City MO

Silas, Anna, *Dir*, Hopi Cultural Center Museum, Second Mesa AZ

Silberman, Barbara, *Exec Dir*, Germantown Historical Society, Philadelphia PA

Silberman, Robert, *Assoc Prof*, University of Minnesota, Minneapolis, Art History, Minneapolis MN (S)

Silcox, Tinsley, *Dir*, Southern Methodist University, Hamon Arts Library, Dallas TX

Silhan, William A, *Prof*, University of West Florida, Dept of Art, Pensacola FL (S)

Sill, Diane, *Gallery Mgr*, Gilpin County Arts Association, Central City CO

Sill, Robert, *Cur Art*, Illinois State Museum, Illinois Art Gallery & Lockport Gallery, Springfield IL

Silliman, Mark, *Dean*, Leeward Community College, Arts & Humanities Division, Pearl City HI (S)

Silliman, Thomas, *Dir*, East Los Angeles College, Vincent Price Gallery, Monterey Park CA

Silosky, Daniel, *Registrar*, Huntington Museum of Art, Huntington WV

Silva, Laverne, *Mgr Museum Shop*, Kauai Museum, Lihue HI

Silva, Robin, *Cataloger*, Portsmouth Athenaeum, Portsmouth NH

Silva, Robin, *Cataloger*, Portsmouth Athenaeum, Library, Portsmouth NH

Silver, Beverly, *Educ Coordr*, Bellevue Art Museum, Bellevue WA

Silver, Florence, *Assoc VPres Exhibits & Marketing*, Royal Ontario Museum, Toronto ON

Silver, Larry, *Prof*, Northwestern University, Evanston, Dept of Art History, Evanston IL (S)

Silverman, David, *Egyptian Section Cur*, University of Pennsylvania, Museum of Archaeology & Anthropology, Philadelphia PA

Silverman, Gilbert B, *Treas*, Detroit Institute of Arts, Founders Society, Detroit MI

Silverman, Lanny, *Assoc Cur*, Chicago Department of Cultural Affairs, Chicago Cultural Center, Chicago IL

Silverman, Richard T, *Pres*, Saint Louis Artists' Guild, Saint Louis MO

Silverman, Robert, *Dean*, Queen's University, Dept of Art, Kingston ON (S)

Silverstein Scott, Susan, *Pub Prog*, Naval Historical Center, The Navy Museum, Washington DC

SilverThorne, Jeanette, *Admin Asst*, York University, Art Gallery of York University, North York ON

Sim, Richard, *Prof*, Antelope Valley College, Art Dept, Division of Fine Arts, Lancaster CA (S)

Simak, Ellen, *Cur Coll*, Hunter Museum of American Art, Chattanooga TN

Simile, Robert, *Assoc Prof*, West Virginia Institute of Technology, Creative Arts Dept, Montgomery WV (S)

Simio, Frank, *VPres*, National Baseball Hall of Fame & Museum, Inc, Art Collection, Cooperstown NY

Simkin, Phillips, *Assoc Prof*, York College of the City University of New York, Fine & Performing Arts, Jamaica NY (S)

Simkins-Stuntz, Jinger, *Chmn*, Furman University, Dept of Art, Greenville SC (S)

Simmons, Catherine T, *Community Relations Coordr*, Maitland Art Center, Library, Maitland FL

Simmons, Dominique, *Instr*, The Arkansas Arts Center, Museum School, Little Rock AR (S)

Simmons, E H, *Dir*, Marine Corps Museum, Art Collection, Washington DC

Simmons, Michael, *Instr*, California State University, Chico, Art Dept, Chico CA (S)

Simon, Ann, *Instr*, Main Line Art Center, Haverford PA (S)

Simon, Carla, *Cur Coll*, Oregon Historical Society, Portland OR

Simon, C M, *Dir*, Heritage Center, Inc, Pine Ridge SD

Simon, David, *Prof*, Colby College, Art Dept, Waterville ME (S)

Simon, Dorothy, *Asst Cur*, New York University, Institute of Fine Arts Visual Resources Collection, New York NY

Simon, Marilyn, *Asst Dir*, The Queens Museum of Art, Flushing NY

Simon, Meryl, *Librn*, Aesthetic Realism Foundation, Eli Siegel Collection, New York NY

Simon, Nancy, *Dir*, Denver Art Museum, Library, Denver CO

Simon, Sherri, *Exec Dir*, High Point Historical Society Inc, Museum, High Point NC

Simon, Sidney, *Instr*, Truro Center for the Arts at Castle Hill, Inc, Truro MA (S)

Simon, Sonia, *Assoc Prof*, Colby College, Art Dept, Waterville ME (S)

Simoneau, Christiane, *Dir*, Galerie d'Art du Parc-Manoir de Tonnancour, Manoir de Tonnancour, Trois Rivieres PQ

Simonian, Vahe, *Deputy Dir*, California Museum of Science and Industry, Los Angeles CA

Simonis, James J, *Library Dir*, LeMoyne College, Wilson Art Gallery, Syracuse NY

Simonitsch, Jake, *Operating Committee Chmn*, Jackson County Historical Society, The 1859 Jail, Marshal's Home & Museum, Independence MO

Simons, Anneke Prins, *Prof*, Jersey City State College, Art Dept, Jersey City NJ (S)

Simons, Chris, *Prof*, Shoreline Community College, Humanities Division, Seattle WA (S)

Simons, Patricia, *Assoc Prof*, University of Michigan, Ann Arbor, Dept of History of Art, Ann Arbor MI (S)

Simons, Sheri, *Instr*, California State University, Chico, Art Dept, Chico CA (S)

Simonsen, Oliver, *Pres of Board*, Canajoharie Library & Art Gallery, Canajoharie NY

Simonsen, Oliver, *Pres of Board*, Canajoharie Library & Art Gallery, Library, Canajoharie NY

Simonsson, Maria, *Asst Executive Dir*, Art League, Alexandria VA

Simonton, David, *Photo*, City Gallery of Contemporary Art, Raleigh NC

Simor, Suzanna, *Dir*, Queens College, City University of New York, Queens College Art Center, Flushing NY

Simor, Suzanna, *Head*, Queens College, City University of New York, Art Library, Flushing NY

Simpkins, Wayne, *Chmn Asst*, University of Memphis, Art Dept, Memphis TN (S)

Simple, Heather, *Art Dir*, PNC Bank, Art Collection, Pittsburgh PA

Simpson, Barbara, *Librn*, Kean College of New Jersey, Nancy Thompson Library, Union NJ

Simpson, Ellen, *Library Dir*, Valley Cottage Library, Gallery, Valley Cottage NY

Simpson, Gayle, *VPres*, Conejo Valley Art Museum, Thousand Oaks CA

Simpson, Glen C, *Prof*, University of Alaska-Fairbanks, Dept of Art, Fairbanks AK (S)

Simpson, Janet F, *Exec Dir*, Kansas City Artists Coalition, Kansas City MO

Simpson, Kay, *Public Prog*, Springfield Library & Museums Association, Springfield Science Museum, Springfield MA

Simpson, Kay, *Dir Public Progs*, Museum of Fine Arts, Springfield MA

Simpson, Kay, *Dir Educ*, George Walter Vincent Smith Art Museum, Springfield MA

Simpson, Larry, *Graphic Design*, University of South Alabama, Dept of Art & Art History, Mobile AL (S)

Simpson, Leslie T, *Dir*, Winfred L & Elizabeth C Post Foundation, Post Memorial Art Reference Library, Joplin MO

Simpson, Pamela H, *Head Art Div*, Washington and Lee University, Division of Art, Lexington VA (S)

Simpson, Paula, *Dir*, Monterey Public Library, Art & Architecture Dept, Monterey CA

Simpson, Shannon, *Cur*, Ellis County Museum Inc, Waxahachie TX

Simpson, Shrebe, *Asst Dir Curatorial Affairs & Cur Medieval Art*, Walters Art Gallery, Baltimore MD

Sims, Judith, *Dir Prog*, Austin Museum of Art at Laguna Gloria, Austin TX

Sims, Richard S, *Dir*, Museum of Western Colorado, Grand Junction CO

Sims, William R, *Chmn Dept*, Cornell University, New York State College of Human Ecology, Ithaca NY (S)

Sincavage, Marie, *Dir Develop*, Kemerer Museum of Decorative Arts, Bethlehem PA

Sinclair, Jane, *Prof*, Chapman University, Art Dept, Orange CA (S)

Sinclair, Susan, *Librn & Archivist*, Isabella Stewart Gardner Museum, Rare Book Collection & Archives, Boston MA

Sincox, Kim Robinson, *Cur*, Battleship North Carolina, Wilmington NC

Sindelar, Norma, *Archivist*, The Saint Louis Art Museum, Richardson Memorial Library, Saint Louis MO

Sindelir, Robert J, *Dir*, Miami-Dade Community College, Kendal Campus, Art Gallery, Miami FL

Sing, Susan, *Instr*, Glendale Community College, Visual & Performing Arts Division, Glendale CA (S)

Singer, Clyde, *Assoc Dir*, Butler Institute of American Art, Art Museum, Youngstown OH

Singer, Shirlee, *Coordr Interior Design*, Iowa State University, Dept of Art & Design, Ames IA (S)

Singleton, David, *Deputy Dir*, Philbrook Museum of Art, Tulsa OK

Singleton, Sheila, *Museum Shop Mgr*, The Studio Museum in Harlem, New York NY

Sinsheimer, Karen, *Cur Photo*, Santa Barbara Museum of Art, Santa Barbara CA

Sipiorski, Dennis, *Art Dept Head*, Nicholls State University, Dept of Art, Thibodaux LA (S)

Sippel, Jeffrey, *Educ Dir*, University of New Mexico, Tamarind Institute, Albuquerque NM (S)

Sirna, Jessie, *Instr*, Charles Stewart Mott Community College, Art Area, School of Arts & Humanities, Flint MI (S)

Siroti, Alice, *Interim Dir*, Turtle Mountain Chippewa Historical Society, Turtle Mountain Heritage Center, Belcourt ND

Sirotti, Kaye, *Exec Dir*, Michigan Guild of Artists & Artisans, Michigan Guild Gallery, Ann Arbor MI

Siry, Joseph, *Prof*, Wesleyan University, Art Dept, Middletown CT (S)

Siska, Patricia D, *Cataloguer*, Frick Art Reference Library, New York NY

Sislen, Dayne, *Adjunct Instr*, Maryville University of Saint Louis, Art Division, Saint Louis MO (S)

Sissen, Melissa M, *Public Servs Librn*, Siena Heights College, Art Library, Adrian MI

Sisto, Elena, *Instr*, New York Studio School of Drawing, Painting & Sculpture, New York NY (S)

Sistro, Elena, *Instr*, Columbia University, School of the Arts, Division of Visual Arts, New York NY (S)

Sitterly, Glenn F, *Cur*, Baldwin Historical Society Museum, Baldwin NY

Sivers, Cora, *Cur Marghab Coll*, South Dakota State University, South Dakota Art Museum, Brookings SD

Skaggs, Dale, *Asst Cur*, Fairfield University, Thomas J Walsh Art Gallery, Fairfield CT

Skaggs, Robert, *Prof*, School of the Art Institute of Chicago, Chicago IL (S)

Skari, Trudy, *Dir*, Liberty Village Arts Center & Gallery, Chester MT

Skelley, Robert C, *Prof*, University of Florida, Dept of Art, Gainesville FL (S)

Skelton, Carl, *Instr*, Toronto School of Art, Toronto ON (S)

Skelton, Scott, *Asst Mgr*, Houston Public Library, Houston TX

Skidmore, Gail, *Exec Dir*, Arts Council of Tuscaloosa County, Inc, Tuscaloosa AL

Skidmore, Margaret, *Assoc Dir Develop*, Museum of Fine Arts, Houston, Houston TX

Skidmore, Mercedes C, *Asst Dir Admin*, The Rockwell Museum, Corning NY

Skinezelewski, Kelly, *Gallery Coordr*, Banc One Wisconsin Corp, Milwaukee WI

Skinner, Arthur, *Asst Prof*, Eckerd College, Art Dept, Saint Petersburg FL (S)

Skinner, Bill, *Chmn Div of Communications & Arts*, North Arkansas Community-Technical College, Art Dept, Harrison AR (S)

Skinner, Carise, *Coordr Book Distribution*, Visual Studies Workshop, Rochester NY

Skinner, Greg, *Dept Chair*, Cornish College of the Arts, Fisher Gallery, Seattle WA

Skinner, Jaineth, *Asst Prof*, Bemidji State University, Visual Arts Dept, Bemidji MN (S)

Sklar, Hinda F, *Librn*, Harvard University, Frances Loeb Library, Cambridge MA

Sklarski, Bonnie, *Prof*, Indiana University, Bloomington, Henry Radford Hope School of Fine Arts, Bloomington IN (S)

Sklarva, Diane, *Cur*, United States Senate Commission on Art, Reference Library, Washington DC

Skoglond, Margaret, *Chmn*, University of Southern Indiana, Art Dept, Evansville IN (S)

Skoog, William, *Chmn*, Southwestern Michigan College, Fine & Performing Arts Dept, Dowagiac MI (S)

Skory, Gary, *Dir*, Midland County Historical Society, Midland MI

Skotheim, Robert Allen, *Pres*, The Huntington Library, Art Collections & Botanical Gardens, San Marino CA

Skove, Margaret, *Dir*, Blanden Memorial Art Museum, Fort Dodge IA

Skove, Margaret, *Dir*, Blanden Memorial Art Museum, Museum Library, Fort Dodge IA

Skurkis, Barry, *Chmn*, North Central College, Dept of Art, Naperville IL (S)

Skvarla, Diane, *Cur*, United States Senate Commission on Art, Washington DC

Skwerski, Tom, *Registrar*, Beloit College, Wright Museum of Art, Beloit WI

Sky, Carol, *VPres*, National Artists Equity Association Inc, Washington DC

Slade, Rona, *Assoc Dean of Faculty*, Corcoran School of Art, Washington DC (S)

Slade, Terry, *Asst Prof*, Hartwick College, Art Dept, Oneonta NY (S)

Slagle, Nancy, *Asst Prof*, Texas Tech University, Dept of Art, Lubbock TX (S)

Slamm, Susan, *Public Relations Dir*, Museum of American Folk Art, New York NY

Slaney, Debra, *Registrar*, Heard Museum, Phoenix AZ

Slater, Robert, *Treas*, Phelps County Historical Society, Phelps County Museum, Holdrege NE

Slater, Sandra, *Librn*, Phelps County Historical Society, Library, Holdrege NE

Slatery, W Patrick, *Art Prog Leader*, Palm Beach Community College, Dept of Art, Lake Worth FL (S)

Slattery, Michael, *Instr*, Bob Jones University, School of Fine Arts, Greenville SC (S)

Slatton, Ralph, *Assoc Prof*, East Tennessee State University, Dept of Art & Design, Johnson City TN (S)

Slaughter, Louise, *Acting Chmn*, Congressional Arts Caucus, Washington DC

Slaughter, Neill, *Assoc Prof*, Southampton College of Long Island University, Arts & Media Division, Southampton NY (S)

Slaughter, Thomas, *Dir*, Soho 20 Gallery, New York NY

Slavick, Sarah, *Asst Prof*, College of the Holy Cross, Dept of Visual Arts, Worcester MA (S)

Slavik, Barbara, *Asst Dir*, Port Angeles Fine Arts Center, Port Angeles WA

Slawson, Brian, *Asst Prof*, University of Florida, Dept of Art, Gainesville FL (S)

Slayton, John A, *Pres*, Leigh Yawkey Woodson Art Museum, Inc, Wausau WI

Slayton, Linda, *Cur Educ*, Visual Arts Center of Northwest Florida, Visual Arts Center Library, Panama City FL

Sledd, Michael, *Instr*, Columbia College, Art Dept, Columbia MO (S)

Slegtenhorst, Hendrik, *Interim Dir*, Vancouver Museum Commission, Vancouver Museum, Vancouver BC

Slenker, Elizabeth, *Instr*, Saint Thomas Aquinas College, Art Dept, Sparkhill NY (S)

Slenker, Jean, *Instr*, Indiana University of Pennsylvania, Dept of Art & Art Education, Indiana PA (S)

Slenker, Robert, *Instr*, Indiana University of Pennsylvania, Dept of Art & Art Education, Indiana PA (S)

Slichter, Jennifer, *Cur Coll*, Loveland Museum Gallery, Loveland CO

Slimon, Gary, *Dir*, Canadian Wildlife & Wilderness Art Museum, Ottawa ON

Slimon, Gary, *Dir*, Canadian Wildlife & Wilderness Art Museum, Library, Ottawa ON

Sloan, Charles, *Preparator*, Museum of New Mexico, Museum of Fine Arts, Santa Fe NM

Sloan, David, *Chmn*, Whittier College, Dept of Art, Whittier CA (S)

Sloan, Margaret, *Asst to Dir*, Greenville Museum of Art, Inc, Greenville NC

Sloane, Robert, *Dance Librn*, Chicago Public Library, Harold Washington Library Center, Chicago IL

Slocumb, Franklyn, *Supt*, Norton Gallery & School of Art, Inc, Norton Museum of Art, West Palm Beach FL

Slone, Lloyd, *Prof*, Birmingham-Southern College, Art Dept, Birmingham AL (S)

Slonim, Jillian, *Dir Pub Relations*, The American Federation of Arts, New York NY

Slorp, John S, *Pres*, Minneapolis College of Art & Design, Minneapolis MN (S)

Sloshberg, Leah P, *Dir*, New Jersey State Museum, Trenton NJ

Slouffman, James, *Dept Head Commercial Arts*, Antonelli Institute of Art & Photography, Cincinnati OH (S)

Slovin, Rochelle, *Dir*, American Museum of the Moving Image, Astoria NY

Slusarenko, Kay, *Chmn*, Marylhurst College, Art Dept, Marylhurst OR (S)

Slusher, Chris, *Asst Dir*, National Trust for Historic Preservation, Decatur House, Washington DC

Sluterbeck, Kay R, *Office Mgr*, Wassenberg Art Center, Van Wert OH

Slutsky, Madeleine, *Dept Head*, The Illinois Institute of Art, Chicago IL (S)

Slutzky, Robert, *Prof*, University of Pennsylvania, Graduate School of Fine Arts, Philadelphia PA (S)

Sly, Melissa, *Dir Annual Giving & Mem*, Pennsylvania Academy of the Fine Arts, Museum of American Art, Philadelphia PA

Slyfield, Donna, *Readers' Services*, Helen M Plum Memorial Library, Lombard IL

Small, Carol, *Asst Prof*, Gettysburg College, Dept of Visual Arts, Gettysburg PA (S)

Small, James, *Asst Prof*, Rutgers, the State University of New Jersey, Graduate Program in Art History, New Brunswick NJ (S)

Small, Janus, *Exec Dir*, New Organization for the Visual Arts, (NOVA), Cleveland OH

Small, Jocelyn, *Prof*, Rutgers, the State University of New Jersey, Graduate Program in Art History, New Brunswick NJ (S)

Small, John, *First Deputy Commissioner*, Chicago Department of Cultural Affairs, Chicago Cultural Center, Chicago IL

Small, Marcella, *Asst Prof*, Delta State University, Dept of Art, Cleveland MS (S)

Small, Martha, *Registrar*, Wadsworth Atheneum, Hartford CT

Smalley, David, *Prof*, Connecticut College, Dept of Art, New London CT (S)

Smalley, Stephen, *Prof*, Bridgewater State College, Art Dept, Bridgewater MA (S)

Smar, Joyce, *Mgr Performing Arts*, Toledo Museum of Art, Toledo OH

Smart, Sonny, *Chief Exec Officer & General Mgr*, Chelan County Public Utility District, Rocky Reach Dam, Wenatchee WA

Smart, Tom, *Assoc Dir, Curatorial Servs*, Winnipeg Art Gallery, Winnipeg MB

Smart, Tom, *Cur*, Beaverbrook Art Gallery, Fredericton NB

Smart, Tom, *Cur*, Beaverbrook Art Gallery, Fredericton NB

Smids, Nora, *Store Mgr*, Bellevue Art Museum, Bellevue WA

Smigocki, Stephen, *Prof*, Fairmont State College, Division of Fine Arts, Fairmont WV (S)

Smigrod, Claudia, *Chmn Photography*, Corcoran School of Art, Washington DC (S)

Smila, Carolyn, *Librn*, Johns Hopkins University, George Peabody Library, Baltimore MD

Smiley, Mary Ellen, *Asst Dir*, Beverly Historical Society, Cabot, Hale & Balch House Museums, Beverly MA

Smith, Alice, *Cur Educ*, Springfield Library & Museums Association, Connecticut Valley Historical Museum, Springfield MA

Smith, Allison, *Registrar*, Marquette University, Haggerty Museum of Art, Milwaukee WI

Smith, Allyson, *Dir Design & Production*, Colorado Historical Society, Colorado History Museum, Denver CO

Smith, Andrea, *Cur*, T C Steele State Historic Site, Nashville IN

Smith, Ann, *Cur*, Mattatuck Historical Society, Mattatuck Museum, Waterbury CT

Smith, Ann, *Chmn Dept Art*, Howard Payne University, Dept of Art, Brownwood TX (S)

Smith, Barbara, *Bus Mgr*, Carolina Art Association, Gibbes Museum of Art, Charleston SC

Smith, Barbara A, *Gallery Mgr*, Guild of Boston Artists, Boston MA

Smith, Beryl K, *Asst Librn*, Rutgers, The State University of New Jersey, Art Library, New Brunswick NJ

Smith, Betsy, *Librn*, Bucks County Historical Society, Spruance Library, Doylestown PA

Smith, Bill, *Photographer & Cur*, Huronia Museum, Midland ON

Smith, Brian, *Photo Lab Technician*, Institute of the Great Plains, Museum of the Great Plains, Lawton OK

Smith, Brydon, *Cur 20th Century Art*, National Gallery of Canada, Ottawa ON

Smith, C, *Instr*, Community College of Rhode Island, Dept of Art, Warwick RI (S)

Smith, Carion, *Cur Galleries*, The Asia Society Galleries, New York NY

Smith, Carrie, *Pres*, Columbia Museum of Art, Columbia Art Association, Columbia SC

Smith, Cary K, *Pres*, Columbia Museum of Art, Columbia SC

Smith, Catherine, *Instr*, Charles Stewart Mott Community College, Art Area, School of Arts & Humanities, Flint MI (S)

Smith, Catherine Howett, *Asst Dir*, Emory University, Michael C Carlos Museum, Atlanta GA

Smith, C J, *VPres*, Buckham Fine Arts Project, Gallery, Flint MI

Smith, Claude, *Prof*, Western New Mexico University, Dept of Expressive Arts, Silver City NM (S)

Smith, Claudia, *Prof*, University of Wisconsin-Stout, Dept of Art & Design, Menomonie WI (S)

Smith, C Martin, *Product Design Chmn*, Art Center College of Design, Pasadena CA (S)

Smith, Connie, *Mgr Mus Shop*, Glenbow Museum, Calgary AB

Smith, Constance, *Dir*, ArtNetwork, Penn Valley CA

Smith, Courtenay, *Asst Cur*, University of Chicago, David & Alfred Smart Museum of Art, Chicago IL

Smith, C Ryan, *Instr*, Milwaukee Area Technical College, Graphic Arts Division, Milwaukee WI (S)

Smith, Dan, *Instr*, Claflin College, Dept of Art, Orangeburg SC (S)

Smith, Darold, *Prof*, West Texas A&M University, Art, Communication & Theatre Dept, Canyon TX (S)

Smith, David, *Assoc Prof*, Edgewood College, Art Dept, Madison WI (S)

Smith, David, *Assoc Prof*, University of New Hampshire, Dept of Arts & Art History, Durham NH (S)

Smith, David, *Art Dept Chmn*, Edgewood College, DeRicci Gallery, Madison WI

Smith, Delta, *Dir & Cur*, University of Oregon, Aperture Photo Gallery - EMU Art Gallery, Eugene OR

Smith, Diane, *Dir Marketing*, Cincinnati Museum Association, Cincinnati Art Museum, Cincinnati OH

Smith, Donald C, *Prof*, Rhode Island College, Art Dept, Providence RI (S)

Smith, Donna, *Head Librn*, Lauren Rogers Museum of Art, Laurel MS

Smith, Donna, *Head Librn*, Lauren Rogers Museum of Art, Library, Laurel MS

Smith, Dorothy V, *Publicity*, Leatherstocking Brush & Palette Club Inc, Cooperstown NY

Smith, Doug, *Instr*, Modesto Junior College, Arts Humanities & Communications Division, Modesto CA (S)

Smith, Ed, *Instr*, Chautauqua Institution, School of Art, Chautauqua NY (S)

Smith, Elise, *Chmn*, Millsaps College, Dept of Art, Jackson MS (S)

Smith, Elizabeth B, *Assoc Prof*, Pennsylvania State University, University Park, Dept of Art History, University Park PA (S)

Smith, Frank Anthony, *Prof*, University of Utah, Art Dept, Salt Lake City UT (S)

Smith, Fred T, *Dir*, Kent State University, School of Art Gallery, Kent OH

Smith, Fred T, *Div Coordr Art History*, Kent State University, School of Art, Kent OH (S)

Smith, Gary, *Pres*, Bassist College Library, Portland OR

Smith, Gary T, *Dir*, Hartnell College Gallery, Salinas CA

Smith, Gaylene, *Prog Unit Coordr*, Holland College, Health, Science & Creative Arts, Charlottetown PE (S)

Smith, George, *VPres Admin*, Museum of Science & Industry, Chicago IL

Smith, George, *Dean*, Maine College of Art, Portland ME (S)

Smith, George, *Prof*, Rice University, Dept of Art & Art History, Houston TX (S)

Smith, George, *Asst Prof*, University of the District of Columbia, Dept of Mass Media, Visual & Performing Arts, Washington DC (S)

Smith, Gerald D, *Dean*, Huntington College, Art Dept, Huntington IN (S)

Smith, Gil R, *Chmn*, Eastern Kentucky University, Art Dept, Richmond KY (S)

Smith, Gregory A, *Dir*, Art Academy of Cincinnati, Cincinnati OH (S)

Smith, Gregory H, *VPres*, Ventura County Historical Society, Museum of History & Art, Ventura CA

Smith, Greta, *Library Asst*, Old Colony Historical Society, Library, Taunton MA

Smith, Harriet, *First VPres*, Huntsville Art League, Huntsville AL

Smith, Heather, *Cur*, Moose Jaw Art Museum & National Exhibition Centre, Art & History Museum, Moose Jaw SK

Smith, Heather, *Dir Operations & Member Services*, Arts Council of the Blue Ridge, Roanoke VA

Smith, Howard, *Slide Cur*, University of Southern California, Helen Topping Architecture & Fine Arts Library, Los Angeles CA

Smith, Jackie R, *Admin Asst*, Amarillo Art Association, Amarillo Art Center, Amarillo TX

Smith, Jan, *Cur*, Bergstrom Mahler Museum, Neenah WI

Smith, Jan, *Cur*, Bergstrom Mahler Museum, Library, Neenah WI

Smith, Jana Hallmark, *Cur Exhib & Coll*, Museums of Abilene, Inc, Abilene TX

Smith, Jean, *Librn*, Woodrow Wilson Birthplace & Museum, Library, Staunton VA

Smith, Jim, *Chmn*, Knoxville Museum of Art, Knoxville TN

Smith, Jo, *Office Mgr*, Marin Society of Artists Inc, Ross CA

Smith, Jonathan, *Cur Coll*, Burlington Art Centre, Burlington ON

Smith, Joseph E, *Assoc Prof*, Oakland City College, Division of Fine Arts, Oakland City IN (S)

Smith, Judith, *Coordr Marketing & Pub Relations*, Reynolda House Museum of American Art, Winston-Salem NC

Smith, Judith Chiba, *Cur European & American Coll*, Museum of New Mexico, Museum of International Folk Art, Santa Fe NM

Smith, J Weldon, *Dir*, San Francisco Craft & Folk Art Museum, San Francisco CA

Smith, Karen Burgess, *Dir Art Center*, Saint Paul's School, Art Center in Hargate, Concord NH

Smith, Kathy, *Admin Asst*, Plains Indians & Pioneers Historical Foundation, Museum & Art Center, Woodward OK

Smith, Kent J, *Dir Art*, Illinois State Museum, Illinois Art Gallery & Lockport Gallery, Springfield IL

Smith, Kris Runberg, *Dir Educ*, Missouri Historical Society, Saint Louis MO

Smith, Laura, *Sr VPres Admin*, Arts & Science Council, Charlotte VA

Smith, Lawry, *Dir & Cur*, Lamama La Galleria, New York NY

Smith, Luther, *Prof*, Texas Christian University, Art & Art History Dept, Fort Worth TX (S)

Smith, Lynn, *Asst Prof*, Winthrop University, Dept of Art & Design, Rock Hill SC (S)

Smith, Margaret Supplee, *Prof*, Wake Forest University, Dept of Art, Winston-Salem NC (S)

Smith, Marilyn, *Adminr*, Art Museum of South Texas, Corpus Christi TX

Smith, Mark, *Prof*, Austin College, Art Dept, Sherman TX (S)

Smith, Mark A, *Information Systems Librn*, New York State College of Ceramics at Alfred University, Scholes Library of Ceramics, Alfred NY

Smith, Martha C, *Reference-Visual Arts Specialist*, State University of New York at Purchase, Library, Purchase NY

Smith, Mary, *Dir Develop*, Arts Partnership of Greater Spartanburg, Inc, Spartanburg Arts Center, Spartanburg SC

Smith, Mary Elizabeth, *Cur*, Liberty Hall Historic Site, Liberty Hall Museum, Frankfort KY

Smith, Mary Jane, *Acting Dir*, Wayne State University, Community Arts Gallery, Detroit MI

Smith, Mary Jane, *Exhib Coordr*, Detroit Artists Market, Detroit MI

Smith, Mary Ruth, *Asst Prof*, Baylor University, Dept of Art, Waco TX (S)

Smith, Maureen, *Finance Dir*, Southern Oregon Historical Society, Jacksonville Museum of Southern Oregon History, Medford OR

Smith, McKelden, *Marketing*, Historic Hudson Valley, Tarrytown NY

Smith, Megan, *Dir & Cur*, T W Wood Gallery & Arts Center, Montpelier VT

Smith, Melinda K, *Registrar*, United States Senate Commission on Art, Washington DC

Smith, Merrill W, *Assoc Librn & Col Mgr*, Massachusetts Institute of Technology, Rotch Library of Architecture & Planning, Cambridge MA

Smith, Michael, *Prof*, East Tennessee State University, Dept of Art & Design, Johnson City TN (S)

Smith, Michele L, *Dir*, Wassenberg Art Center, Van Wert OH

Smith, Mike, *Dir Admins*, Mint Museum of Art, Charlotte NC

Smith, Monica, *Conservator*, Vancouver Art Gallery, Vancouver BC

Smith, Nan, *Assoc Prof*, University of Florida, Dept of Art, Gainesville FL (S)

Smith, Nancy M, *Exec Dir*, Rosenberg Library, Galveston TX

Smith, Owen, *Asst Prof*, University of Maine, Dept of Art, Orono ME (S)

Smith, Patricia, *Exec Dir*, Sierra Arts Foundation, Reno NV

Smith, Patricia, *Head Technical Serv*, Columbia College, Library, Chicago IL

Smith, Patti, *Cur Exhib*, Atwater Kent Museum, Philadelphia PA

Smith, Paul, *VPres*, Louis Comfort Tiffany Foundation, New York NY

Smith, Pauline, *Dir*, City of Atlanta, Atlanta Cyclorama, Atlanta GA

Smith, Randy, *Asst Library Dir*, Boulder Public Library & Gallery, Dept of Fine Arts Gallery, Boulder CO

Smith, Rob, *Dir*, Lachenmeyer Arts Center, Art Resource Library, Cushing OK

Smith, Robert H, *Pres*, National Gallery of Art, Washington DC

Smith, Sam, *Instr*, Marian College, Art Dept, Indianapolis IN (S)

Smith, Sara, *Dir Develop*, Norton Gallery & School of Art, Inc, Norton Museum of Art, West Palm Beach FL

Smith, Scott, *Treas*, Attleboro Museum, Center for the Arts, Attleboro MA

Smith, Sharon, *Instr*, California State University, Chico, Art Dept, Chico CA (S)

Smith, Shaw, *Assoc Prof*, Davidson College, Art Dept, Davidson NC (S)

Smith, Stacy, *Cur Coll & Exhib*, Noyes Museum, Oceanville NJ

Smith, Sue, *Exec Dir*, Greensboro Artists' League, Greensboro NC

Smith, Terri, *House Committee Chmn.* Colonel Black Mansion, Ellsworth ME

Smith, Thomas G, *Aquarium Dir.* Berkshire Museum, Pittsfield MA

Smith, Thomas O, *Chmn.* Grambling State University, Art Dept, Grambling LA (S)

Smith, Virginia, *Ed.* Ontario Crafts Council, Artists in Stained Glass, Toronto ON

Smith-Abbott, Katherine, *Asst Prof.* Saint Olaf College, Art Dept, Northfield MN (S)

Smith-Ferri, Sherrie, *Cur.* City of Ukiah, Grace Hudson Museum & The Sun House, Ukiah CA

Smith-Fisher, Laura, *Develop Officer.* National Gallery of Art, Washington DC

Smith-Hunter, Susan, *Chmn.* Green Mountain College, Dept of Art, Poultney VT (S)

Smith-Hurd, Diane, *Instr.* Art Academy of Cincinnati, Cincinnati OH (S)

Smith Shafts, Karen, *Asst Keeper of Prints.* Boston Public Library, Albert H Wiggin Gallery & Print Department, Boston MA

Smith-Willow, Neal, *Asst Prof.* Brenau University, Art Dept, Gainesville GA (S)

Smogor, Robert, *Registrar.* University of Notre Dame, Snite Museum of Art, Notre Dame IN

Smoke, Joe, *Dir.* Los Angeles Center For Photographic Studies, Hollywood CA

Smolkis, Georgia, *Cur Educ.* Schenectady Museum Planetarium & Visitors Center, Schenectady NY

Smotherman, Ann, *Art Teacher.* Motlow State Community College, Art Dept, Tullahoma TN (S)

Smutko, Paul, *Collections.* Museum of New Mexico, Museum of International Folk Art, Santa Fe NM

Smyrnios, Arleigh, *Instr.* Kalamazoo Valley Community College, Humanities Dept, Kalamazoo MI (S)

Smyser, Michael, *Assoc Prof.* Montgomery County Community College, Art Dept, Blue Bell PA (S)

Smyth, Carolyn, *Asst Prof.* Pennsylvania State University, University Park, Dept of Art History, University Park PA (S)

Smyth, Frances, *Ed.* National Gallery of Art, Washington DC

Smyth, Tim, *Treas.* Erie Art Museum, Erie PA

Smythe, James E, *Prof.* Western Carolina University, Dept of Art, Cullowhee NC (S)

Snapp, Caral, *Cur.* Art Center of Battle Creek, Battle Creek MI

Snapp, Ron, *Grad Prog Dir.* Old Dominion University, Art Dept, Norfolk VA (S)

Snapp, Ronald, *Assoc Prof.* Old Dominion University, Art Dept, Norfolk VA (S)

Snavely, Loanne, *Arts & Architecture Librn.* Pennsylvania State University, Arts Library, University Park PA

Snavely, Loanne, *Arts & Architecture Librn.* Pennsylvania State University, Architecture Library, University Park PA

Sneddeker, Duane, *Cur Photographs.* Missouri Historical Society, Saint Louis MO

Snellenberger, Earl, *Prof.* University of Indianapolis, Art Dept, Indianapolis IN (S)

Snibbe, Robert M, *Pres.* Napoleonic Society of America, Museum & Library, Clearwater FL

Snoddy, Donald, *Museum Dir.* Union Pacific Railroad, Historical Museum, Omaha NE

Snodgrass, John, *Treas.* Charles B Goddard Center for the Visual & Performing Arts, Ardmore OK

Snooks, A Nancy, *Asst Prof.* Pierce College, Art Dept, Woodland Hills CA (S)

Snow, Beverly, *Mus School Dir.* Danforth Museum of Art, Framingham MA

Snow, Beverly, *Dir.* Danforth Museum of Art School, Framingham MA (S)

Snow, Maryly, *Librn.* University of California, Architecture Slide Library, Berkeley CA

Snowden, Gilda, *Gallery Dir.* Detroit Repertory Theatre Gallery, Detroit MI

Snowden, Mary, *Painting.* California College of Arts & Crafts, Oakland CA (S)

Snowman, Tracy, *Instr.* Spoon River College, Art Dept, Canton IL (S)

Snydacker, Daniel, *Exec Dir.* Newport Historical Society, Newport RI

Snyder, Barry, *Prof.* Fairmont State College, Division of Fine Arts, Fairmont WV (S)

Snyder, Craig, *Dir.* Gallery West Ltd, Alexandria VA

Snyder, Dan, *Dir Develop & Center Operations.* Jay County Arts Council, Hugh N Ronald Memorial Gallery, Portland IN

Snyder, James, *Deputy Dir. Planning & Prog Support.* Museum of Modern Art, New York NY

Snyder, Jill, *Dir.* Aldrich Museum of Contemporary Art, Ridgefield CT

Snyder, Jill, *Dir.* Cleveland Center for Contemporary Art, Cleveland OH

Snyder, Jill, *Dir.* Cleveland Center for Contemporary Art, Library, Cleveland OH

Snyder, Joel, *Chmn.* University of Chicago, Dept of Art History & Committee on Art & Design, Chicago IL (S)

Snyder, Mark, *Asst Prof.* University of Hartford, Hartford Art School, West Hartford CT (S)

Snyder, Mary, *Dir of Non-Print Coll.* Nova Scotia College of Art and Design, Library, Halifax NS

Snyder, Mary Catherine, *Asst Head.* Girard College, Stephen Girard Collection, Philadelphia PA

Snyder, R B, *Pres.* Norton Gallery & School of Art, Inc, Norton Museum of Art, West Palm Beach FL

Snyder, Robert, *Prof.* School of the Art Institute of Chicago, Chicago IL (S)

Snyder, Scott, *Cur Exhib.* Rockford Art Museum, Rockford IL

Snyder, Scott, *Cur.* Rockford Art Museum, Library, Rockford IL

Snyder, Suzanne, *Chmn.* Fairmont State College, Division of Fine Arts, Fairmont WV (S)

Soave, Sergio, *Prof.* West Virginia University, College of Creative Arts, Morgantown WV (S)

Sobel, Judith, *Dir.* Newport Art Museum, Newport RI

Sobey, Edwin J C, *Exec Dir.* Fresno Metropolitan Museum, Fresno CA

Sobieszek, Robert A, *Cur Photo.* Los Angeles County Museum of Art, Los Angeles CA

Sobol, Judith, *Dir.* Newport Art Museum School, Newport RI (S)

Sobral, Luis de Moura, *Instr.* Universite de Montreal, Dept of Art History, Montreal PQ (S)

Sobre, Judith, *Prof.* University of Texas at San Antonio, Division of Visual Arts, San Antonio TX (S)

Socha, H Norman, *Dir.* Enook Galleries, Waterloo ON

Sockol, Michael, *Pub Relations Dir.* DeCordova Museum & Sculpture Park, Lincoln MA

Soderberg, Vicki, *Adminr.* William Bonifas Fine Art Center Gallery, Alice Powers Art Gallery, Escanaba MI

Sodervick, Bruce, *Assoc Prof.* Rochester Institute of Technology, School of Art & Design, Rochester NY (S)

Soehner, Kenneth, *Acquisitions Librn & Bibliographer.* The Metropolitan Museum of Art, Thomas J Watson Library, New York NY

Soganic, Barbara, *Sr Interpreter.* New Jersey State Museum, Historical Morven, Trenton NJ

Sohi, Marilyn, *Registrar.* Madison Art Center, Madison WI

Soklove, Deborah, *Cur.* Wesley Theological Seminary Center for the Arts & Religion, Dadian Gallery, Washington DC

Soldate, Joe, *Chmn.* California State University, Los Angeles, Art Dept, Los Angeles CA (S)

Soleri, Paolo, *Pres.* Cosanti Foundation, Scottsdale AZ

Soleri, Paolo, *Pres.* Cosanti Foundation, Arcosanti, Scottsdale AZ

Soles, Kathleen A, *Assoc Prof.* Emmanuel College, Art Dept, Boston MA (S)

Soles, Teresa, *Instr.* West Shore Community College, Division of Humanities & Fine Arts, Scottville MI (S)

Solheim, David, *Chmn.* Dickinson State University, Dept of Art, Dickinson ND (S)

Solmssen, Peter, *Pres.* University of the Arts, Philadelphia PA

Solmssen, Peter, *Pres.* University of the Arts, Philadelphia College of Art & Design, Philadelphia PA (S)

Solomon, Melanie, *Cur.* Historical Society of Rockland County, New City NY

Solomon, Richard E, *VChmn.* Museum of Modern Art, New York NY

Solomon-Kiefer, C, *Asst Prof.* McGill University, Dept of Art History, Montreal PQ (S)

Soloway, Lynn, *Dir.* Concordia College, Marx Hausen Art Gallery, Seward NE

Soloway, Lynn, *Prof.* Concordia College, Art Dept, Seward NE (S)

Solt, Mary, *Exec Dir of Museum Registration.* The Art Institute of Chicago, Chicago IL

Soltes, Ori Z, *Dir.* B'nai B'rith International, B'nai B'rith Klutznick National Jewish Museum, Washington DC

Somaio, Theresa, *Visual Resource Assoc.* Skidmore College, Lucy Scribner Library, Saratoga Springs NY

Sombille, Marilyn, *Dean.* Rutgers, the State University of New Jersey, Mason Gross School of the Arts, New Brunswick NJ (S)

Somers, David, *Cur.* Art Gallery of Peel, Peel Heritage Complex, Brampton ON

Somers, David, *Cur.* Art Gallery of Peel, Library, Brampton ON

Somers, Eric, *Dir.* Dutchess Community College, Dept of Visual Arts, Poughkeepsie NY (S)

Somerville, Barbara, *Admin Asst.* Museum of Fine Arts, Saint Petersburg, Florida, Inc, Saint Petersburg FL

Somerville, Mary R, *Dir.* Miami-Dade Public Library, Miami FL

Sommer, Susan, *Chief Librn Circulations Coll Mgr.* The New York Public Library, Shelby Cullom Davis Museum, New York NY

Sommers, Joyce, *Exec Dir.* Indianapolis Art Center, Churchman-Fehsenfeld Gallery, Indianapolis IN

Sonday, Milton, *Cur Textiles.* Cooper-Hewitt, National Design Museum, New York NY

Sonkevitch, Anatole, *Assoc Prof.* University of Michigan, Ann Arbor, Dept of History of Art, Ann Arbor MI (S)

Sonneborn, Sydney R, *Head Dept.* Miles Community College, Dept of Fine Arts & Humanities, Miles City MT (S)

Sonnema, Roy B, *Assoc Prof.* Georgia Southern University, Dept of Art, Statesboro GA (S)

Sonner, Grace, *Dir Fine Arts.* College of San Mateo, Creative Arts Dept, San Mateo CA (S)

Sons, Ruth, *Controller.* Tucson Museum of Art & Historic Block, Tucson AZ

Sopher, Sonja, *Conservator.* Portland Art Museum, Portland OR

Sopka, Elaine C, *Dir.* Newark School of Fine & Industrial Art, Newark NJ (S)

Soppelsa, Robert T, *Dir.* Washburn University, Mulvane Art Museum, Topeka KS

Sorell, Carole, *VPres Prog.* Americans for the Arts, New York NY

Sorensen, Lee, *Librn & Art Bibliographer.* Duke University Museum of Art, Lilly Art Library, Durham NC

Sorento, Bruno, *Prof.* Community College of Allegheny County, Boyce Campus, Art Dept, Monroeville PA (S)

Sorge, Walter, *Prof.* Eastern Illinois University, Art Dept, Charleston IL (S)

Sorkow, Janice, *Dir.* Museum of Fine Arts, Dept of Photographic Services, Boston MA

Sormson, Lillian, *Cataloging Dir.* Dickinson State University, Stoxen Library, Dickinson ND

Sorrell, Robert, *Asst Prof.* College of Santa Fe, Art Dept, Santa Fe NM (S)

Sorrell, Sonya, *Instr.* Pepperdine University, Seaver College, Dept of Art, Malibu CA (S)

Sossa, Oscar, *Gallery Conservator.* Queensborough Community College, Art Gallery, Bayside NY

Soucy, Don, *Head Art Educ.* University of New Brunswick, Art Education Section, Fredericton NB (S)

Sourakli, Judy, *Cur Coll.* University of Washington, Henry Art Gallery, Seattle WA

Sourakli, Judy, *Cur Coll.* Henry Gallery Association, Henry Art Gallery, Seattle WA

Sousa, Jean, *Assoc Dir of Museum Educ.* The Art Institute of Chicago, Kraft Education Center, Chicago IL

South, Allison, *Asst Dir*, University of Utah, Utah Museum of Fine Arts, Salt Lake City UT

South, Carissa, *Asst Cur Colls & Exhibit*, Art Museum of Western Virginia, Roanoke VA

Southall, Tom, *Cur Photographic Coll*, Amon Carter Museum, Fort Worth TX

Southard, Doug, *Librn*, The Bostonian Society, Library, Boston MA

Southworth, Michael, *Chmn City & Regional Planning*, University of California, Berkeley, College of Environmental Design, Berkeley CA (S)

Southworth, Miles F, *Prof*, Rochester Institute of Technology, School of Printing, Rochester NY (S)

Souza, Al, *Chmn*, University of Houston, Dept of Art, Houston TX (S)

Sova, Jessie, *Asst to Dir*, Fayetteville Museum of Art, Inc, Fayetteville NC

Sovern, Michael I, *Chmn*, American Academy in Rome, New York NY (S)

Sowden, Alison, *VPres Financial Affairs*, The Huntington Library, Art Collections & Botanical Gardens, San Marino CA

Sowell, Juliette, *Cur*, Berea College, Appalachian Museum, Berea KY

Sowiak, Christine, *Curatorial Asst (Art)*, University of Calgary, The Nickle Arts Museum, Calgary AB

Sowiski, Peter, *Chmn*, State University College at Buffalo, Fine Arts Dept, Buffalo NY (S)

Spack, Carol, *Dir*, Boston Visual Artists Union, Newton MA

Spahr, P Andrew, *Cur*, The Currier Gallery of Art, Manchester NH

Spain, Susan M, *Asst to Dir*, Edgecombe County Cultural Arts Council, Inc, Blount-Bridgers House, Hobson Pittman Memorial Gallery, Tarboro NC

Spalatin, Ivana, *Chmn Art History*, East Texas State University, Dept of Art, Commerce TX (S)

Spald, Gregory P, *Prof*, Kenyon College, Art Dept, Gambier OH (S)

Spalding, Ann E, *Educ Coordr*, Maitland Art Center, Maitland FL

Spalding, Jeffrey, *Gallery Dir & Cur*, University of Lethbridge, Art Gallery, Lethbridge AB

Spangenberg, Kristin L, *Cur Prints & Drawings*, Cincinnati Museum Association, Cincinnati Art Museum, Cincinnati OH

Spangler, Cindy, *Registrar*, University of Tennessee, Ewing Gallery of Art and Architecture, Knoxville TN

Sparagana, John, *Asst Prof*, Rice University, Dept of Art & Art History, Houston TX (S)

Sparkes, Kristina, *Spec Projects Officer*, Oakville Galleries, Centennial Gallery and Gairloch Gallery, Oakville ON

Sparks, Kevin, *Prof*, Asbury College, Student Center Gallery, Wilmore KY

Sparks, Sherry, *Chmn Design*, Kansas City Art Institute, Kansas City MO (S)

Sparr, Michael, *Assoc*, Brigham Young University, Museum of Art, Provo UT

Sparrow, Diane, *Office Coordr*, Boston Architectural Center, Boston MA

Sparrow, Marcheta, *Public Relations Dir*, Shaker Village of Pleasant Hill, Harrodsburg KY

Spartz, India, *Photographs Librn*, Alaska State Library, Alaska Historical Collections, Juneau AK

Spaziani, Carol, *Pres*, Arts Iowa City, Art Center & Gallery, Iowa City IA

Speach, Bernadette, *Exec Dir*, The Kitchen Center, New York NY

Spear, Richard, *Prof*, Oberlin College, Dept of Art, Oberlin OH (S)

Speare, Jed, *Co-Dir*, Mobius Inc, Boston MA

Spearing, Laurie, *Educ Coordr*, Swift Current National Exhibition Centre, Swift Current SK

Spears, Dolores, *Cur*, Zigler Museum, Jennings LA

Spears, Kimberly, *Exec Dir*, Anderson County Arts Council, Anderson SC

Speck, Lawrence, *Dean*, University of Texas, School of Architecture, Austin TX (S)

Spector, Jack J, *Prof*, Rutgers, the State University of New Jersey, Graduate Program in Art History, New Brunswick NJ (S)

Spector, Nancy, *Assoc Cur*, Solomon R Guggenheim Museum, New York NY

Spector, Nancy, *Assoc Cur*, Guggenheim Museum Soho, New York NY

Speed, Bonnie, *Cur*, Mitchell Museum, Mount Vernon IL

Speed, John S, *Pres Board Governor*, J B Speed Art Museum, Louisville KY

Speer, Jean, *Museum Dir*, East Tennessee State University, Carroll Reece Museum, Johnson City TN

Speight, Jerry, *Prof*, Murray State University, Dept of Art, Murray KY (S)

Speight, Pamela, *Cur*, Malaspina College, Nanaimo Art Gallery & Exhibition Centre, Nanaimo BC

Speiring, Ken, *Adjunct Asst Prof*, Spokane Falls Community College, Fine Arts Dept, Spokane WA (S)

Speller, Virginia, *Librn*, Old York Historical Society, Administration Building & Library, York ME

Spellman, Bryan D, *Admin Officer*, University of Montana, Gallery of Visual Arts, Missoula MT

Spellman, Bryan D, *Admin Officer*, University of Montana, Paxson Gallery, Missoula MT

Spence, Cable, *Pres*, Palette & Chisel Academy of Fine Arts, Chicago IL

Spence, Muheeva, *Assoc Prof*, University of Florida, Dept of Art, Gainesville FL (S)

Spencer, Anne M, *Cur Africa, Americas & Pacific*, Newark Museum Association, The Newark Museum, Newark NJ

Spencer, Deirdre, *Head Fine Arts Library*, University of Michigan, Fine Arts Library, Ann Arbor MI

Spencer, Donald, *Pres*, Western Illinois University, Art Gallery-Museum, Macomb IL

Spencer, Howard DaLee, *Cur*, Nevada Museum Of Art, Reno NV

Spencer, Marilyn, *Membership & Spec Events*, Southern Methodist University, Meadows Museum, Dallas TX

Spencer, Mark J, *Dir*, The Albrecht-Kemper Museum of Art, Saint Joseph MO

Spencer, Sue, *Dir*, Spoon River College, Art Dept, Canton IL (S)

Spencer, Sue, *Pres Heritage Foundation*, Fort Morgan Heritage Foundation, Fort Morgan CO

Spencer, T W, *Admin VPres*, Transco Energy Company Inc, Transco Gallery, Houston TX

Spencer, William T, *Cur Exhibits*, National Baseball Hall of Fame & Museum, Inc, Art Collection, Cooperstown NY

Speranza, Linda, *Instr*, Mesa Community College, Dept of Art & Art History, Mesa AZ (S)

Sperath, Albert, *Gallery Dir*, Murray State University, Eagle Gallery, Murray KY

Sperath, Albert, *Gallery Dir*, Murray State University, Dept of Art, Murray KY (S)

Sperling, Christine, *Chmn*, Bloomsburg University, Dept of Art, Bloomsburg PA (S)

Sperling, L Joy, *Assoc Prof*, Denison University, Dept of Art, Granville OH (S)

Sperow, Donna Wilt, *Adminr*, Bakehouse Art Complex, Inc, Miami FL

Spevers, Franklin, *Assoc Prof*, Calvin College, Art Dept, Grand Rapids MI (S)

Spicher, Valerie, *Graphic Designer*, University of Kansas, Spencer Museum of Art, Lawrence KS

Spiekler, Robert, *Assoc Dir*, Canadian Centre for Architecture, Library, Montreal PQ

Spikes, Tracy, *Cur*, Historic Saint Augustine Preservation Board, Saint Augustine FL

Spillman, Jane, *Cur American Glass*, Corning Museum of Glass, Corning NY

Spinar, Melvin, *Prof*, South Dakota State University, Dept of Visual Arts, Brookings SD (S)

Spindler, Virginia, *Cur Educ*, Terra Museum of American Art, Chicago IL

Spink, Walter M, *Prof*, University of Michigan, Ann Arbor, Dept of History of Art, Ann Arbor MI (S)

Spink, William B, *Pres*, Naples Art Gallery, Naples FL

Spinka, William, *Sr VPres*, Audubon Artists, Inc, New York NY

Spinski, Victor, *Coordr Ceramics*, University of Delaware, Dept of Art, Newark DE (S)

Spiro, Edmund, *Treas*, Middlesex County Cultural & Heritage Commission, North Brunswick NJ

Spiro, Stephen B, *Cur*, University of Notre Dame, Snite Museum of Art, Notre Dame IN

Spitler, Carol, *Assoc Prof*, Oakland City College, Division of Fine Arts, Oakland City IN (S)

Spitzmueller, Pamela, *Librn*, Guild of Book Workers, Library, New York NY

Spitzner, Joanna, *Gallery Coordr*, Art in General, New York NY

Splendore, Patricia, *Prog Dir*, American-Scandinavian Foundation, New York NY

Spnung, Loa, *Dir Communications*, National Watercolor Society, Downey CA

Spoerner, Thomas, *Chmn*, Ball State University, Dept of Art, Muncie IN (S)

Spohn, Jennifer, *Chief Conservator*, Worcester Art Museum, Worcester MA

Sponenberg, Susan, *Coordr*, Luzerne County Community College, Commercial Art Dept, Nanticoke PA (S)

Spoo, Corinne H, *Librn*, Paine Art Center & Arboretum, George P Nevitt Library, Oshkosh WI

Spoon, Jennifer, *Asst Prof*, Radford University, Art Dept, Radford VA (S)

Spooner, Peter, *Asst Cur*, University of Minnesota, Duluth, Tweed Museum of Art, Duluth MN

Sporny, Stan, *Prof*, Marshall University, Dept of Art, Huntington WV (S)

Spradling, Kim, *Asst Prof*, Northwest Missouri State University, Dept of Art, Maryville MO (S)

Sprague, Jack, *Communications Design Coordr*, University of North Texas, School of Visual Arts, Denton TX (S)

Sprigg, June, *Cur Coll*, Hancock Shaker Village, Inc, Pittsfield MA

Spring, Kathy, *Dir Pub Relations*, Ella Sharp Museum, Jackson MI

Spring, Michael, *Exec Dir*, South Florida Cultural Consortium, Metropolitan Dade County Cultural Affairs Council, Miami FL

Sproule, Sue, *Corporate Consultant*, San Francisco Museum of Modern Art, Rental Gallery, San Francisco CA

Sprout, Sally, *Art Cur*, Transco Energy Company Inc, Transco Gallery, Houston TX

Spruance, Jim, *Interim Dir*, Virginia Beach Center for the Arts, Virginia Beach VA

Spruce, Duane Blue, *Facilities Planning Mgr*, National Museum of the American Indian, George Gustav Heye Center, New York NY

Sprules, Nancy, *Head Systems & Cataloging*, National Gallery of Canada, Library, Ottawa ON

Spurgin, John E, *VPres Academic Affairs*, Milwaukee Institute of Art & Design, Milwaukee WI (S)

Spurling, Norine, *First VPres*, Buffalo Society of Artists, Williamsville NY

Squier, Jack L, *Prof*, Cornell University, Dept of Art, Ithaca NY (S)

Squire, Margaret, *Pres*, Canadian Society of Painters In Watercolour, Toronto ON

Squires, William, *Grad Coordr & Chmn Art Educ*, University of Georgia, Franklin College of Arts & Sciences, Lamar Dodd School of Art, Athens GA (S)

Srinivasan, Doris, *Assoc Cur Southeast Asian & Indian Art*, Nelson-Atkins Museum of Art, Kansas City MO

Sroka, Steven, *Cur*, University of Illinois, Museum of Natural History, Champaign IL

Srsen, Judy, *Dir Educ*, Owatonna Arts Center, Community Arts Center, Owatonna MN

Stacey, Robert, *Supvr*, New York University, Stephen Chan Library of Fine Arts, New York NY

Stachura, Irene, *Reference*, San Francisco Maritime National Historical Park, J Porter Shaw Library, San Francisco CA

Stack, Lotus, *Cur Textiles*, Minneapolis Institute of Arts, Minneapolis MN

Stack, Trudy Wilner, *Cur*, University of Arizona, Center for Creative Photography, Tucson AZ

Stackhouse, Mary, *Dir*, Truro Center for the Arts at Castle Hill, Inc, Truro MA (S)

Stackpole, Renny A, *Dir*, Penobscot Marine Museum, Searsport ME

Staebell, Sandra, *Cur Coll & Registrar*, Western Kentucky University, Kentucky Museum, Bowling Green KY

Staebler, Tom, *VPres & Art Dir*, Playboy Enterprises, Inc, Chicago IL

Staffne, Dennis, *Prof*, Northern Michigan University, Dept of Art & Design, Marquette MI (S)

Stafford, F Eugene, *Instr*, Guilford Technical Community College, Commercial Art Dept, Jamestown NC (S)

Stafford, Jennifer, *Registrar*, Nelda C & H J Lutcher Stark Foundation, Stark Museum of Art, Orange TX

Stager, Lawrence, *Dir*, Harvard University, Semitic Museum, Cambridge MA

Staggs, Jo, *Library Technician*, University of Kentucky, Hunter M Adams Architecture Library, Lexington KY

Stahl, Judith R, *Art Dir*, Louisiana State University, Union Art Gallery, Baton Rouge LA

Stahl, Stef, *Chmn Museum Educ*, Toledo Museum of Art, Toledo OH

Stahler, Hank, *Building Dir*, Institute for Contemporary Art, Project Studio One (P S 1), Long Island City NY

Staiger, Marsha, *Gallery Dir*, Art League, Alexandria VA

Staiger, Paul, *Graduate Prog Coordr*, San Jose State University, School of Art & Design, San Jose CA (S)

Staler, W, *Treas*, Springfield Museum of Art, Springfield OH

Staley, Allen, *Chmn*, Columbia University, Dept of Art History & Archaeology, New York NY (S)

Staley, Thomas F, *Dir*, University of Texas at Austin, Harry Ransom Humanities Research Center, Austin TX

Stallings, Tyler, *Dir Programming*, Huntington Beach Art Center, Huntington Beach CA

Stalnaker, Budd, *Prof*, Indiana University, Bloomington, Henry Radford Hope School of Fine Arts, Bloomington IN (S)

Stalsworth, Lee, *Chief Photography*, Hirshhorn Museum & Sculpture Garden, Washington DC

Stalvey, Dorrance, *Dir Music Progs*, Los Angeles County Museum of Art, Los Angeles CA

Stamm, Geoffrey E, *Dir*, United States Department of the Interior, Indian Arts & Crafts Board, Washington DC

Stammler, Ursula, *Dir*, University of Kansas, Architectural Resource Center, Lawrence KS

Stampfle, Felice, *Emeritus Cur Drawings & Prints*, Pierpont Morgan Library, New York NY

Stamps, Ray, *VPres*, Lake County Civic Center Association, Inc, Heritage Museum & Gallery, Leadville CO

Stancliffe, Thomas, *Assoc Prof*, University of Northern Iowa, Dept of Art, Cedar Falls IA (S)

Stand, Luis, *Cur*, Centro Cultural De La Raza, San Diego CA

Standridge, Christine, *Admin Asst*, Nassau County Museum of Fine Art, Roslyn Harbor NY

Stanfield, Alyson, *Mus Educator*, University of Oklahoma, Fred Jones Jr Museum of Art, Norman OK

Stanford, Linda O, *Chmn*, Michigan State University, Dept of Art, East Lansing MI (S)

Stanford, Michael, *Adjunct Prof*, Wilkes University, Dept of Art, Wilkes-Barre PA

Stangland-Cameron, Lyn, *Asst Prof*, Dean College, Visual-Art Dept, Franklin MA (S)

Stanislaus, Grace, *Exec Dir*, Museum of African Art, New York NY

Stanitz, Mark, *Prof*, Rochester Institute of Technology, School of Art & Design, Rochester NY (S)

Stanley, David, *Assoc Prof*, University of Florida, Dept of Art, Gainesville FL (S)

Stanley, Diane, *Cur*, Southern Lorain County Historical Society, Spirit of '76 Museum, Wellington OH

Stanley, Janet L, *Librn*, National Museum of African Art, Branch Library, Washington DC

Stanley, John, *Deputy Dir Operations*, Museum of Fine Arts, Boston MA

Stanley, John S, *Asst to Dir*, Toledo Museum of Art, Toledo OH

Stanley, Robert A, *Prof*, Oakton Community College, Art & Architecture Dept, Des Plaines IL (S)

Stanley, T, *Instr*, Humboldt State University, College of Arts & Humanities, Arcata CA (S)

Stanley, Tom, *Dir*, Winthrop University Galleries, Rock Hill SC

Stansbury, George, *Dean*, University of Mary Hardin-Baylor, School of Fine Arts, Belton TX (S)

Stanton, Anne Rudloff, *Asst Prof*, University of Missouri, Art History & Archaeology Dept, Columbia MO (S)

Stanton, Donna, *Asst Prof*, Daemen College, Art Dept, Amherst NY (S)

Stanton, Frances, *Prof*, Community College of Rhode Island, Dept of Art, Warwick RI (S)

Staples, Thornton, *Info Technology Chief*, National Museum of American Art, Washington DC

Staples, Wayne, *Chmn & Prof*, Acadia University, Art Dept, Wolfville NS (S)

Stapleton, Nancy, *Asst Dir*, East Baton Rouge Parks & Recreation Commission, Baton Rouge Gallery Inc, Baton Rouge LA

Starbuck, Robin, *Asst Prof*, Wesleyan College, Art Dept, Macon GA (S)

Stark, Nelda C, *Chmn*, Nelda C & H J Lutcher Stark Foundation, Stark Museum of Art, Orange TX

Stark, Robert, *Dir*, Art Exchange, Union Dale PA

St-Arnaud, Jacques, *Guide*, Musee des Augustines de l'Hotel Dieu de Quebec, Quebec PQ

Starr, Barbara, *Chmn*, Spring Hill College, Fine Arts Dept, Mobile AL (S)

Starr, Daniel, *Chief Librn Technical Servs & Planning*, Museum of Modern Art, Library, New York NY

Starr, Sydney, *Chmn*, Pratt Institute Library, Art & Architecture Dept, Brooklyn NY

Stathis, Peter, *Head 3-D Design Dept*, Cranbrook Academy of Art, Bloomfield Hills MI (S)

Statlander, Raymond, *Assoc Prof*, Jersey City State College, Art Dept, Jersey City NJ (S)

Stauage, Willis, *VPres*, Yankton County Historical Society, Dakota Territorial Museum, Yankton SD

Staubo, Judy, *VPres*, Mattatuck Historical Society, Mattatuck Museum, Waterbury CT

Staudt, Christina, *Instr*, Dowling College, Dept of Visual Arts, Oakdale NY (S)

Stave, Pari, *Cur*, Equitable Life Assurance Society, The Equitable Gallery, New York NY

Stavitsky, Gail, *Cur Coll*, Montclair Art Museum, Montclair NJ

Stavitsky, Gail, *Cur Coll*, Montclair Art Museum, Art School, Montclair NJ (S)

Stayman, Wendy, *Coll Mgr*, Museum of Fine Arts, Springfield MA

Stayton, Kevin, *Cur Decorative Arts*, Brooklyn Museum, Brooklyn NY

St Denis, Paul, *Prof*, Cleveland Institute of Art, Cleveland OH (S)

Steadman, Clinton, *Treas*, Rochester Historical Society, Rochester NY

Steadman, David, *Dir*, Toledo Museum of Art, Toledo OH

Steadman, David W, *Dir*, Toledo Museum of Art, Toledo OH

Steadman, Thomas, *Prof*, Georgia Southern University, Dept of Art, Statesboro GA (S)

Steans, Joan, *Asst Prof*, Jersey City State College, Art Dept, Jersey City NJ (S)

Stearns, Daniel, *Instr*, Glendale Community College, Visual & Performing Arts Division, Glendale CA (S)

Stebbins, Joan, *Dir & Cur*, Southern Alberta Art Gallery, Lethbridge AB

Stebbins, Theodore E, *Cur American Painting*, Museum of Fine Arts, Boston MA

Stebinger, Patricia, *Instr*, Marylhurst College, Art Dept, Marylhurst OR (S)

Steck, Janet, *Gallery Dir*, State University of New York, College at Cortland, Art Dept, Cortland NY (S)

Stecker, Barbara, *Librn*, DeCordova Museum & Sculpture Park, DeCordova Museum Library, Lincoln MA

Steedle, William J, *Dept Chmn*, State University of New York at Farmingdale, Advertising Art Design Dept, Farmingdale NY (S)

Steehler, Kirk, *Pres*, Erie Art Museum, Erie PA

Steel, LaVar, *Chmn*, College of Southern Idaho, Art Dept, Twin Falls ID (S)

Steel, Rebecca D, *Head Librn*, Kalamazoo Institute of Arts, Library, Kalamazoo MI

Steel, Virginia Oberlin, *Dir & Cur*, Rutgers University, Stedman Art Gallery, Camden NJ

Steele, Ana, *Sr Deputy Chmn*, National Endowment for the Arts, Washington DC

Steele, Brian, *Assoc Prof*, Texas Tech University, Dept of Art, Lubbock TX (S)

Steele, Chris, *Photo*, Massachusetts Historical Society, Library, Boston MA

Steele, Curtis, *Chair Art Dept*, Arkansas State University-Art Department, Jonesboro, Fine Arts Center Gallery, Jonesboro AR

Steele, Curtis, *Chmn*, Arkansas State University, Dept of Art, State University AR (S)

Steele, Curtis, *Assoc Prof*, Arkansas State University, Dept of Art, State University AR (S)

Steele, Jonathan, *Acting Dir*, Saint Petersburg Junior College, Humanities Dept, Saint Petersburg FL (S)

Steele, Lisa, *Academic Dean*, Rocky Mountain College of Art & Design, Denver CO (S)

Steele, Pamela, *Visual Resources Coordr*, The Phillips Collection, Washington DC

Steele, Steven M, *Dir*, Rocky Mountain College of Art & Design, Denver CO (S)

Steele, Tim, *Prof*, South Dakota State University, Dept of Visual Arts, Brookings SD (S)

Steen, Karen, *Asst Prof*, Cazenovia College, Center for Art & Design Studies, Cazenovia NY (S)

Stefaniak, Regina, *Asst Prof*, University of California, Riverside, Dept of the History of Art, Riverside CA (S)

Steffen, Pamela, *Assoc Prof*, Mount Mary College, Art Dept, Milwaukee WI (S)

Steffenson, Sally, *Cur Art*, Plains Art Museum, Fargo ND

Stefl, Bob, *Assoc Prof*, Lincoln College, Art Dept, Lincoln IL (S)

Stegeman, Charles, *Prof*, Haverford College, Fine Arts Dept, Haverford PA (S)

Stegleder, Linda, *Dir*, Danforth Museum of Art, Framingham MA

Stegleder, Linda, *Dir*, Danforth Museum of Art, Library, Framingham MA

Steier, Paul, *Treas*, Ukiyo-e Society of America, Inc, New York NY

Steiff, Charles, *Pres*, Star-Spangled Banner Flag House Association, Flag House & 1812 Museum, Baltimore MD

Stein, Anna R, *Exec Dir*, Pennsylvania Dutch Folk Culture Society Inc, Baver Genealogical Library, Lenhartsville PA

Stein, Donna, *Cur*, Guild Hall of East Hampton, Inc, Guild Hall Museum, East Hampton NY

Stein, Ed, *Chmn*, Brookdale Community College, Art Dept, Lincroft NJ (S)

Stein, Emily, *Asst Prof*, College of New Rochelle School of Arts & Sciences, Art Dept, New Rochelle NY (S)

Stein, Harvey, *Adjunct Asst Prof*, Drew University, Art Dept, Madison NJ (S)

Stein, Jane, *Prog Coordr*, Newark Museum Association, The Newark Museum, Newark NJ

Stein, Julie, *Cur Archaeology*, University of Washington, Thomas Burke Memorial Washington State Museum, Seattle WA

Stein, Marty, *Image Librn*, Museum of Fine Arts, Houston, Hirsch Library, Houston TX

Stein, Michael, *Faculty*, Housatonic Community & Technical College, Art Dept, Bridgeport CT (S)

Stein, Renata, *Art Cur*, Leo Baeck Institute, New York NY

Stein, Renata, *Cur*, Leo Baeck Institute, Library, New York NY

Steinberg, Anne, *Instr*, Milwaukee Area Technical College, Graphic Arts Division, Milwaukee WI (S)

Sticha, Denise, *Reference & Public Servs Librn,* Seton Hill College, Reeves Memorial Library, Greensburg PA

Stickhweh, Jo Anne, *Chmn,* Otterbein College, Art Dept, Westerville OH (S)

Stickney, Laura, *Teacher Outreach Coordr,* Cultural Affairs Department City of Los Angeles, Junior Arts Center, Los Angeles CA

Stidsen, Donald, *Mgr Exhibits,* Massachusetts Institute of Technology, MIT Museum, Cambridge MA

Stieber, Nancy, *Assoc Prof,* University of Massachusetts - Boston, Art Dept, Boston MA (S)

Stier, David, *Cur Natural Science,* Springfield Library & Museums Association, Springfield Science Museum, Springfield MA

Stiger, Lucille, *Registrar,* Oberlin College, Allen Memorial Art Museum, Oberlin OH

Stiger, Lucille, *Registrar,* University of Wisconsin-Madison, Elvehjem Museum of Art, Madison WI

Stiles, Kristine, *Assoc Prof,* Duke University, Dept of Art & Art History, Durham NC (S)

Stiles, Terry W, *Trustee Pres,* Museum of Discovery & Science, Fort Lauderdale FL

Stiles, Vicki, *Dir,* Shoreline Historical Museum, Seattle WA

Still, Chris, *Instr,* Dunedin Fine Arts & Cultural Center, Dunedin FL (S)

Still, Sandra, *Dir Educ,* Monterey Museum of Art Association, Monterey CA

Stillman, Diane Brandt, *Dir Educ,* Walters Art Gallery, Baltimore MD

Stillman, Wadell, *Dir Admin & Finance,* Historic Hudson Valley, Tarrytown NY

Stinchcomb, Donna, *Dir Educ,* Sangre de Cristo Arts & Conference Center, Pueblo CO

Stinespring, John, *Assoc Prof,* Texas Tech University, Dept of Art, Lubbock TX (S)

Stinson, Lisa, *Asst Prof,* University of Hartford, Hartford Art School, West Hartford CT (S)

Stitt, Susan, *Pres,* Historical Society of Pennsylvania, Philadelphia PA

Stiver, Greg, *Instr,* Oral Roberts University, Fine Arts Dept, Tulsa OK (S)

Stivers, David, *Archivist,* Nabisco, Inc, East Hanover NJ

St John, Terry, *Head Dept,* College of Notre Dame, Dept of Art, Belmont CA (S)

St Michael, Sean, *Head Develop,* Art Gallery of Ontario, Toronto ON

Stockebrand, Marianne, *Dir,* Chinati Foundation, Marfa TX

Stockholder, Jessica, *Instr,* Bard College, Milton Avery Graduate School of the Arts, Annandale-on-Hudson NY (S)

Stocki, Robert, *Instr,* Milwaukee Area Technical College, Graphic Arts Division, Milwaukee WI (S)

Stockwell, Ross, *Instr,* San Diego Mesa College, Fine Arts Dept, San Diego CA (S)

Stoddard, Barbara R, *Secy Art Committee,* Purdue University Calumet, Bicentennial Library Gallery, Hammond IN

Stoddard, Brooks, *Assoc Prof,* University of Maine at Augusta, Division of Fine & Performing Arts, Augusta ME (S)

Stoe, Jennifer, *Dir Public Relations,* Special Libraries Association, Museum, Arts & Humanities Division, Washington DC

Stoessell, Pamela, *Prof,* Marymount University of Virginia, School of Arts & Sciences Division, Arlington VA (S)

Stoker, E, *Prof,* Incarnate Word University of the Arts & Sciences, Art Dept, San Antonio TX (S)

Stokes, David, *Asst Prof,* Winthrop University, Dept of Art & Design, Rock Hill SC (S)

Stokes, Sally Sims, *Librn,* University of Maryland, College Park, National Trust for Historic Preservation Library Collection, College Park MD

Stokley, Susan, *Prog Dir,* Pointe Claire Cultural Centre, Stewart Hall Art Gallery, Pointe Claire PQ

Stokstad, Marilyn, *Consult Cur Medieval Art,* Nelson-Atkins Museum of Art, Kansas City MO

Stokstad, Marilyn, *Prof,* University of Kansas, Kress Foundation Dept of Art History, Lawrence KS (S)

Stolin, Alexander, *Instr,* Southeastern Louisiana University, Dept of Visual Arts, Hammond LA (S)

Stollhans, Cindy, *Chmn,* Saint Louis University, Fine & Performing Arts Dept, Saint Louis MO (S)

Stolper, Carolyn, *Dir Develop,* Museum of Contemporary Art, Chicago IL

Stolzer, Rob, *Asst Prof,* University of Wisconsin-Stevens Point, Dept of Art & Design, Stevens Point WI (S)

Stomberg, John R, *Asst Dir,* Boston University, Art Gallery, Boston MA

Stone, Caroline, *Educ & Exhib Cur,* Memorial University of Newfoundland, Art Gallery of Newfoundland & Labrador, Saint John's NF

Stone, Carolyn, *Chmn Art Educ,* Delta State University, Fielding L Wright Art Center, Cleveland MS

Stone, Carolyn Rea, *Prof,* Delta State University, Dept of Art, Cleveland MS (S)

Stone, Denise, *Asst Prof,* University of Kansas, Dept of Art & Music Education & Music Therapy, Lawrence KS (S)

Stone, Elizabeth, *Pres,* Wenham Museum, Wenham MA

Stone, Evalyn, *Serials Librn,* The Metropolitan Museum of Art, Thomas J Watson Library, New York NY

Stone, Gaylund, *Gallery Dir,* Concordia University Wisconsin, Fine Art Gallery, Mequon WI

Stone, George, *Sculpture,* University of La Verne, Dept of Art, La Verne CA (S)

Stone, Gerald, *Descriptive Servs Section,* National Archives of Canada, Visual & Sound Archives, Ottawa ON

Stone, Hazel, *Mem-at-Large,* Arizona Watercolor Association, Phoenix AZ

Stone, James, *Chmn,* Hannibal La Grange College, Art Dept, Hannibal MO (S)

Stone, Karen E, *Cur Educ,* Calvert Marine Museum, Solomons MD

Stone, Kenneth H, *Deputy Dir Finance,* Buffalo & Erie County Public Library, Buffalo NY

Stone, Lawre, *Admin Dir,* Isamu Noguchi Foundation, Isamu Noguchi Garden Museum, Long Island City NY

Stone, Paul, *Pres,* Brattleboro Museum & Art Center, Brattleboro VT

Stone, Robbie, *Supv,* Page-Walker Arts & History Center, Cary NC

Stone, Thelma, *Arts Unit Mgr,* Fort Worth Public Library, Fine Arts Section, Fort Worth TX

Stone-Ferrier, Linda, *Prof,* University of Kansas, Kress Foundation Dept of Art History, Lawrence KS (S)

Stone-Miller, Rebecca, *Assoc Prof,* Emory University, Art History Dept, Atlanta GA (S)

Stonestreet, Robert, *Dir & Treas,* Public Library of Cincinnati & Hamilton County, Art & Music Dept, Cincinnati OH

Stoops, Susan, *Cur,* Brandeis University, Rose Art Museum, Waltham MA

Stopka, Christina, *Librn & Archivist,* Texas Ranger Hall of Fame & Museum, Moody Texas Ranger Memorial Library, Waco TX

Stoppert, Mary, *Dir,* Northeastern Illinois University, Gallery, Chicago IL

Storke, Ed, *Assoc Dean Liberal Arts,* College of DuPage, Humanities Division, Glen Ellyn IL (S)

Storm, Harriet, *Pres,* Peninsula Fine Arts Center, Newport News VA

Storwick, Michael, *Spec Serv Librn,* University of Portland, Wilson W Clark Memorial Library, Portland OR

Story, Charlotte, *Assoc Prof,* American University, Dept of Art, Washington DC (S)

Story, Dana A, *Historian,* Essex Historical Society, Essex Shipbuilding Museum, Essex MA

Stouffer, Vicki, *Exec Dir,* Tempe Arts Center, Tempe AZ

Stoughton, Kathleen, *Dir,* University of California-San Diego, University Art Gallery, La Jolla CA

Stoughton, Michael, *Assoc Prof,* University of Minnesota, Minneapolis, Art History, Minneapolis MN (S)

Stout, Ken, *Prof,* University of Arkansas, Art Dept, Fayetteville AR (S)

Stout, Sarah, *Lectr,* Trinity College, Art Program, Washington DC (S)

Stout, Sarah, *Lectr,* Trinity College, Art Program, Washington DC (S)

Stout, William G, *Registrar,* Frick Collection, New York NY

Stover, Nan, *Librn,* Cowboy Artists of America Museum, Library, Kerrville TX

Stowell, Carol, *Dir Science,* Roberson Museum & Science Center, Binghamton NY

Stowers, John Walter, *Pres,* Montgomery Museum of Fine Arts, Montgomery AL

Stowers, Robert, *Assoc Prof,* University of Wisconsin-Stevens Point, Dept of Art & Design, Stevens Point WI (S)

Strachota, John, *Instr,* Milwaukee Area Technical College, Graphic Arts Division, Milwaukee WI (S)

Straight, Robert, *Coordr Foundations,* University of Delaware, Dept of Art, Newark DE (S)

Strand, Laura, *Head Fiber & Fabric,* Southern Illinois University at Edwardsville, Dept of Art & Design, Edwardsville IL (S)

Strandberg, Kevin, *Instr,* Illinois Wesleyan University, School of Art, Bloomington IL (S)

Strange, Georgia, *Assoc Prof,* Indiana University, Bloomington, Henry Radford Hope School of Fine Arts, Bloomington IN (S)

Strathman-Becker, Randy, *Art Prog Dir,* Teikyo Westmar University, Art Dept, LeMars IA (S)

Stratton, Donald, *Prof,* University of Maine at Augusta, Division of Fine & Performing Arts, Augusta ME (S)

Stratton, Gerald, *Prof Fine Arts,* University of Cincinnati, School of Art, Cincinnati OH (S)

Stratton, John, *Dir,* Bethany College, Library, Lindsborg KS

Stratton, Priscilla, *Operations Mgr,* University of Chicago, David & Alfred Smart Museum of Art, Chicago IL

Stratyner, Barbara, *Cur Exhib,* The New York Public Library, Shelby Cullom Davis Museum, New York NY

Straub, Louise, *Pres of Board,* Potsdam Public Museum, Potsdam NY

Strauss, Carol Kahn, *Exec Dir,* Leo Baeck Institute, New York NY

Strauss, Carol Kahn, *Dir,* Leo Baeck Institute, Library, New York NY

Strauss, Linda, *Cur Visual Resources Coll,* Columbia University, Dept of Art History & Archeology, New York NY

Strauss, Melville, *Chmn,* Guild Hall of East Hampton, Inc, Guild Hall Museum, East Hampton NY

Strawder, Janice, *Instr,* Wayne Art Center, Wayne PA (S)

Strawn, Martha, *Prof,* University of North Carolina at Charlotte, Dept of Visual Arts, Charlotte NC (S)

Strawn, Rachel, *Educator,* College of William & Mary, Joseph & Margaret Muscarelle Museum of Art, Williamsburg VA

Strean, Jeffrey, *Chief Designer,* Cleveland Museum of Art, Cleveland OH

Streed, Crit, *Assoc Prof,* University of Northern Iowa, Dept of Art, Cedar Falls IA (S)

Streetman, Evon, *Prof,* University of Florida, Dept of Art, Gainesville FL (S)

Streetman, John W, *Dir,* Evansville Museum of Arts & Science, Evansville IN

Strehlke, Carl B, *Adjunct Cur,* Philadelphia Museum of Art, John G Johnson Collection, Philadelphia PA

Streibert, Elizabeth, *Acting Dir International Prog,* Museum of Modern Art, New York NY

Streitz, Ronald, *Exec Dir,* Pewabic Society Inc, Pewabic Pottery, Detroit MI

Stremsterfer, Marianne, *Instr,* Springfield College in Illinois, Dept of Art, Springfield IL (S)

Stricevic, George, *Prof Art History,* University of Cincinnati, School of Art, Cincinnati OH (S)

Strick, Jeremy, *Cur 20th Century Painting & Sculpture*, The Art Institute of Chicago, Chicago IL

Strickland, Alice, *Exec Dir*, Goldsboro Art Center, Goldsboro NC (S)

Strickland, Barbour, *Exec Dir*, Greenville Museum of Art, Inc, Greenville NC

Strickland, Barbour, *Exec Dir*, Greenville Museum of Art, Inc, Reference Library, Greenville NC

Strickland, Eycke, *Lectr*, Emory University, Art History Dept, Atlanta GA (S)

Strickland, Ken, *Dean*, State University of New York College at Purchase, Division of Visual Arts, Purchase NY (S)

Strickland, Mary, *Cur*, Tulane University, Gallier House Museum, New Orleans LA

Strickland, William, *Exec Dir*, Manchester Craftsmen's Guild, Pittsburgh PA

Strickler, Ivy, *Dir*, The Museum at Drexel University, Philadelphia PA

Strickler, Susan E, *Dir Curatorial Affairs*, Worcester Art Museum, Worcester MA

Stringer, Candace, *Instr*, Wayne Art Center, Wayne PA (S)

Strohm, Robert, *Assoc Dir*, Virginia Historical Society, Richmond VA

Strohman, Barbara J, *Assoc Prof*, Bloomsburg University, Dept of Art, Bloomsburg PA (S)

Stromberg, Linda, *Admin Asst*, Northern Arizona University, Art Museum & Galleries, Flagstaff AZ

Strombotne, James S, *Prof*, University of California, Riverside, Dept of Art, Riverside CA (S)

Strong, Barbara, *Chmn Art Dept*, College of the Sequoias, Art Dept, Visalia CA (S)

Strong, David F, *Pres*, University of Victoria, Maltwood Art Museum and Gallery, Victoria BC

Strong, Donald, *Chmn Art History*, California State University, Northridge, Dept of Art-Two Dimensional Media, Northridge CA (S)

Strong, Gary, *Dir*, Queens Borough Public Library, Fine Arts & Recreation Division, Jamaica NY

Strong, John, *Dir*, Lake George Arts Project, Courthouse Gallery, Lake George NY

Strong, Scott M, *Adminr*, United States Senate Commission on Art, Washington DC

Strong, Susan, *Financial Mgr*, Millicent Rogers Museum of Northern New Mexico, Taos NM

Stroot, Scott, *Assoc Prof*, Bradford College, Creative Arts Division, Bradford MA (S)

Strother, Robert A, *Coordr*, Greenville County Museum of Art, Museum School of Art, Greenville SC (S)

Stroud, Betty, *Dept Head*, Union College, Art Dept, Barbourville KY (S)

Stroud, Jane, *Partner*, Stroud Wright Associates, Winnetka IL

Stroud, Marion Boulton, *Dir*, Fabric Workshop & Museum, Philadelphia PA

Stroud, Wilfred, *Prog Coordr*, Tubman African American Museum, Macon GA

Stroup, Rodger, *Dir Coll & Interpretation*, South Carolina State Museum, Columbia SC

Strueber, Michael M, *Dir*, Southern Alleghenies Museum of Art, Loretto PA

Struthers, Sally A, *Chmn Fine Arts*, Sinclair Community College, Division of Fine & Performing Arts, Dayton OH (S)

Struthers, Sharon, *Instr*, The Arkansas Arts Center, Museum School, Little Rock AR (S)

Stryklin, Susan, *Dir*, The Currier Gallery of Art, Manchester NH

Stuart, Lorraine, *Archivist*, Museum of Fine Arts, Houston, Hirsch Library, Houston TX

Stuart, Lynne, *Dir Performing Arts*, Palm Springs Desert Museum, Palm Springs CA

Stuart, Nancy, *Assoc Dir*, Rochester Institute of Technology, School of Photographic Arts & Sciences, Rochester NY (S)

Stuart, Nancy, *Assoc Prof*, Rochester Institute of Technology, School of Photographic Arts & Sciences, Rochester NY (S)

Stuart, Peter F, *Treas*, Mystic Art Association, Inc, Mystic CT

Stuckenbruck, Linda, *Prof*, Texas Woman's University, Dept of Visual Arts, Denton TX (S)

Stuckert, Caroline, *Dir*, Landis Valley Museum, Lancaster PA

Stuckert, Caroline M, *Dir*, Landis Valley Museum, Library, Lancaster PA

Stuckey, Charles, *Cur Paintings*, Minneapolis Institute of Arts, Minneapolis MN

Stucky, John, *Librn*, Asian Art Museum of San Francisco, Avery Brundage Collection, San Francisco CA

Stucky, John Carl, *Librn*, Asian Art Museum of San Francisco, Library, San Francisco CA

Studenroth, Zachary, *Dir*, Lockwood-Mathews Mansion Museum, Norwalk CT

Stuff, Paola Muggia, *Dir*, Cartoon Art Museum, San Francisco CA

Stuhlman, Rachel, *Librn*, George Eastman House-International Museum of Photography & Film, Library, Rochester NY

Stuhr, Joanne, *Cur Exhib*, Tucson Museum of Art & Historic Block, Tucson AZ

Stuhr, Pat, *Asst Prof*, Ohio State University, Dept of Art Education, Columbus OH (S)

Stule, Will, *Prof*, Butte College, Dept of Fine Arts, Oroville CA (S)

Stull, Staci, *Slide Cur*, Massachusetts College of Art, Morton R Godine Library, Boston MA

Stuntz, Susan M, *Dir Marketing Communications*, Colonial Williamsburg Foundation, Williamsburg VA

Stupler, Harvey, *Instr*, Long Beach City College, Dept of Art, Long Beach CA (S)

Stupp-Greer, Mary, *Div Dean*, Portland Community College, Visual & Performing Arts Division, Portland OR (S)

Sturgeon, Catherine Sullivan, *Cur*, California State University, Chico, Janet Turner Print Gallery & Collection, Chico CA

Sturgeon, John, *Assoc Dept Head Acad Affairs*, Carnegie Mellon University, Dept of Art, Pittsburgh PA (S)

Sturgeon, Mary C, *Chmn*, University of North Carolina at Chapel Hill, Art Dept, Chapel Hill NC (S)

Sturgeon, Thelma M, *Exec Coordr*, Bicentennial Art Center & Museum, Paris IL

Sturges, Hollister, *Dir*, George Walter Vincent Smith Art Museum, Springfield MA

Sturgess, Louise, *Exec Dir*, Pittsburgh History & Landmarks Foundation, James D Van Trump Library, Pittsburgh PA

Stutts, Lora, *Instr*, Barton College, Art Dept, Wilson NC (S)

Stutz, Sallie, *VDir Marketing*, Brooklyn Museum, Brooklyn NY

Styka, Wanda Magdeleine, *Archivist*, National Trust for Historic Preservation, Chesterwood Museum Archives, Glendale MA

Styron, Thomas W, *Exec Dir*, Greenville County Museum of Art, Greenville SC

Subler, Craig, *Dir*, University of Missouri-Kansas City, Gallery of Art, Kansas City MO

Sudbrink, Todd, *Museum Technician*, US Department of State, Diplomatic Reception Rooms, Washington DC

Sudeburg, Erika, *Assoc Prof*, University of California, Riverside, Dept of Art, Riverside CA (S)

Suelflow, August R, *Dir*, Concordia Historical Institute, Saint Louis MO

Sugarman, Matthew, *Assoc Prof*, University of Northern Iowa, Dept of Art, Cedar Falls IA (S)

Sugimoto, Lisa, *Instr*, Avila College, Art Division, Dept of Humanities, Kansas City MO (S)

Suhrcke, Patricia, *Dir Research & Educ*, Atlanta Historical Society Inc, Atlanta History Center, Atlanta GA

Suhre, Terry, *Asst Prof*, University of Missouri, Saint Louis, Dept of Art & Art History, Saint Louis MO (S)

Suhre, Terry, *Dir*, University of Missouri, Saint Louis, Gallery 210, Saint Louis MO

Sulkin, Howard, *Dir*, Spertus Institute of Jewish Studies, Spertus Museum, Chicago IL

Sullivan, Anne, *Registrar*, University of Arizona, Center for Creative Photography, Tucson AZ

Sullivan, Carol, *Dir*, Arlington Arts Center, Arlington VA

Sullivan, Charles M, *Exec Dir*, City of Cambridge Historical Commission, Cambridge MA

Sullivan, Eugene, *Chmn*, Framingham State College, Art Dept, Framingham MA (S)

Sullivan, Gerald P, *Sr Lect*, Santa Clara University, Art Dept, Santa Clara CA (S)

Sullivan, Jacqueline, *Asst Dir Admin*, New Orleans Museum of Art, New Orleans LA

Sullivan, James E, *Assoc Prof*, Southern Illinois University, School of Art & Design, Carbondale IL (S)

Sullivan, Jay, *Chair*, Southern Methodist University, Division of Art, Dallas TX (S)

Sullivan, John, *Assoc Prof*, Arkansas Tech University, Dept of Art, Russellville AR (S)

Sullivan, Kristina, *Asst Librn*, Dayton Art Institute, Library, Dayton OH

Sullivan, Kyra, *VPres-Programs*, Coalition of Women's Art Organizations, Port Washington WI

Sullivan, Mark, *Asst Prof*, Villanova University, Dept of Art & Art History, Villanova PA (S)

Sullivan, Martin, *Dir*, Heard Museum, Phoenix AZ

Sullivan, Pauline, *Pres*, Coquille Valley Art Association, Coquille OR

Sullivan, Pauline, *Pres*, Coquille Valley Art Association, Library, Coquille OR

Sullivan, Ronald Dee, *Prof*, Del Mar College, Art Dept, Corpus Christi TX (S)

Sultan, Larry, *Photography*, California College of Arts & Crafts, Oakland CA (S)

Sultan, Mara, *Cur Asst*, Montclair Art Museum, Art School, Montclair NJ (S)

Sultan, Terrie, *Cur*, Corcoran Gallery of Art, Washington DC

Sulyok, Laszlo, *Exec Dir*, NAME Gallery, Documents, Chicago IL

Sulyok, Laszlo, *Exec Dir*, NAME Gallery, Chicago IL

Sulzberger, Arthur Ochs, *Chmn Board Trustees*, The Metropolitan Museum of Art, New York NY

Sulzner, Nathalie, *Slide Librn*, University of Massachusetts, Amherst, Dorothy W Perkins Slide Library, Amherst MA

Summers, Cherie, *Registrar*, Santa Barbara Museum of Art, Santa Barbara CA

Summers, Elaine, *Co-Gallery Dir*, Sarasota Visual Art Center, Sarasota FL

Summers, Nancy, *Instr*, Woodstock School of Art, Inc, Woodstock NY (S)

Summers, Ruth, *Dir*, Southern Highland Craft Guild, Folk Art Center, Asheville NC

Sumner, Stephen, *Dir*, University of Tulsa, School of Art, Tulsa OK (S)

Sumner, Steven, *Dir*, University of Tulsa, Alexandre Hogue Gallery, Tulsa OK

Sumrall, Robert F, *Cur Ship Models*, United States Naval Academy Museum, Annapolis MD

Sundahl, Steve, *Asst Prof*, Bemidji State University, Visual Arts Dept, Bemidji MN (S)

Sundby, Mel, *Instr*, Century College, Humanities Dept, White Bear Lake MN (S)

Sundet, E S, *Instr*, Humboldt State University, College of Arts & Humanities, Arcata CA (S)

Sundstrand, Jacquelyn, *Library Archives Coordr*, Southern Oregon Historical Society, Library, Medford OR

Sundt, Christine L, *Visual Resources Cur*, University of Oregon, Architecture & Allied Arts Library, Eugene OR

Sung, Yunah, *Asian Bibliographer*, Cleveland Museum of Art, Ingalls Library, Cleveland OH

Sungur, Barbara Z, *Assoc Prof*, University of British Columbia, Dept of Fine Arts, Vancouver BC (S)

Sunkel, Robert, *Percival DeLuce Art Gallery Coll Cur*, Northwest Missouri State University, DeLuce Art Gallery, Maryville MO

Sunkel, Robert, *Assoc Prof*, Northwest Missouri State University, Dept of Art, Maryville MO (S)

Supino, David, *VPres*, The American Federation of Arts, New York NY

Sur, Sue, *Admin Mgr*, Green Hill Center for North Carolina Art, Greensboro NC

Surdo, Bruno, *Illustration Dept Head*, The Illinois Institute of Art, Chicago IL (S)

Surges, James, *Instr*, Milwaukee Area Technical College, Graphic Arts Division, Milwaukee WI (S)

Surkmer, Suzette, *Exec Dir*, South Carolina Arts Commission, Columbia SC

Surratt, Monte, *Instr Dept Head,* Cochise College, Art Dept, Douglas AZ (S)

Surtees, Ursula, *Dir & Cur,* Kelowna Museum, Kelowna BC

Susi, Frank, *Grad Coordr,* Kent State University, School of Art, Kent OH (S)

Sussman, Elisabeth, *Cur,* Whitney Museum of American Art, New York NY

Sussman, Wendy, *Prof,* University of California, Berkeley, College of Letters & Sciences-Art Dept, Berkeley CA (S)

Susstrink, Sabrine, *Asst Prof,* Rochester Institute of Technology, School of Photographic Arts & Sciences, Rochester NY (S)

Sutcliffe, Nina, *Asst Prof,* University of Maine, Dept of Art, Orono ME (S)

Suter, Catherine, *Dean,* St Martins College, Humanities Dept, Lacey WA (S)

Suter, Sherwood, *Prof,* McMurry University, Art Dept, Abilene TX (S)

Sutherin, Judy, *Dir Communications,* Arts Council of Winston-Salem & Forsyth County, Winston-Salem NC

Sutherland, Barbara, *Librn,* Yonkers Public Library, Fine Arts Dept, Yonkers NY

Sutherland, Barbara, *Librn,* Yonkers Public Library, Will Library, Yonkers NY

Sutherland, Cara, *Cur of Exhibits,* Museum of Our National Heritage, Lexington MA

Suthren, V J H, *Dir,* Canadian War Museum, Ottawa ON

Sutinen, Paul, *Asst Chmn,* Marylhurst College, Art Dept, Marylhurst OR (S)

Suttenfield, Nancy, *Asst Secy Finance & Admin,* Smithsonian Institution, Washington DC

Sutter, James, *Chmn & Prof,* State University of New York College at Potsdam, Dept of Fine Arts, Potsdam NY (S)

Sutton, Judith, *Assoc Dir,* Public Library of Charlotte & Mecklenburg County, Charlotte NC

Sutton, Patricia, *Assoc Prof,* University of Hartford, Hartford Art School, West Hartford CT (S)

Sutton, Peter C, *Dir,* Wadsworth Atheneum, Hartford CT

Suzor, Mary, *Registrar,* Cleveland Museum of Art, Cleveland OH

Svedlow, Andrew, *Pres,* New Hampshire Institute of Art, Manchester NH (S)

Svedlow, Jay, *Pres,* Manchester Institute of Arts & Sciences Gallery, Manchester NH

Swackhammer, Mac, *Dir,* Dawson City Museum & Historical Society, Dawson City YT

Swackhammer, Mac, *Dir & Cur,* Dawson City Museum & Historical Society, Resource Room Library, Dawson City YT

Swain, Darlene, *Instr,* Mesa Community College, Dept of Art & Art History, Mesa AZ (S)

Swain, Judy, *Admin Dir,* Anderson County Arts Council, Anderson SC

Swain, Tim, *Gallery Asst,* Anderson Fine Arts Center, Anderson IN

Swaminadhan, Anand, *Pres,* Musee d'Art de Joliette, Joliette PQ

Swan, Susan, *Treas,* National Institute for Architectural Education, New York NY

Swanson, Erik, *Dir,* Cripple Creek District Museum, Cripple Creek CO

Swanson, Gunnar, *Asst Prof,* University of Minnesota, Duluth, Art Dept, Duluth MN (S)

Swanson, Jean, *Admin Coordr,* Farmington Valley Arts Center, Avon CT

Swanson, Judy, *Pres,* Galesburg Civic Art Center, Galesburg IL

Swanson, Kenneth J, *Museum Adminr,* Idaho Historical Museum, Boise ID

Swanson, Laurie, *Dir Public Relations & Marketing,* Tucson Museum of Art & Historic Block, Tucson AZ

Swanson, Linda, *Adjunct Assoc,* College of Santa Fe, Art Dept, Santa Fe NM (S)

Swanson, Mark, *Librn & AV Production Mgr,* C G Jung Institute of Chicago, Evanston IL

Swanson, Mary T, *Prof,* University of Saint Thomas, Dept of Art History, Saint Paul MN (S)

Swanson, Michael, *Chmn Dept,* Franklin College, Art Dept, Franklin IN (S)

Swanson, Roy, *Prof,* Hutchinson Community Junior College, Visual Arts Dept, Hutchinson KS (S)

Swanson, Vern G, *Dir,* Springville Museum of Art, Springville UT

Swarez, Bibiana, *Assoc Prof,* DePaul University, Dept of Art, Chicago IL (S)

Swartz, Helen, *Adminr,* Boston College, Museum of Art, Chestnut Hill MA

Sweatt, Lilla, *Slide Cur,* San Diego State University, Art Department Slide Library, San Diego CA

Sweeney, Megan, *Instr,* Cuyahoga Community College, Dept of Art, Cleveland OH (S)

Sweeney, Patrick, *Curatorial Registrar,* Davenport Museum of Art, Davenport IA

Sweeney, Vince, *Cur History,* Staten Island Institute of Arts & Sciences, Staten Island NY

Sweeney, Vince, *Cur Archives & Library,* Staten Island Institute of Arts & Sciences, Archives Library, Staten Island NY

Sweet, Marvin, *Asst Prof,* Bradford College, Creative Arts Division, Bradford MA (S)

Swenson, Christine, *Cur Graphic Arts,* Toledo Museum of Art, Toledo OH

Swenson, David, *Lectr,* North Dakota State University, Division of Fine Arts, Fargo ND (S)

Swenson, Lisa, *Exec Dir,* Peninsula Fine Arts Center, Newport News VA

Swenson-Wolsey, Sonja, *Chmn,* Taft College, Art Department, Taft CA (S)

Swid, Steve, *Chmn,* Municipal Art Society of New York, New York NY

Swider, Bougdon, *Prof,* Colorado College, Dept of Art, Colorado Springs CO (S)

Swider, Tony, *Instr,* University of North Carolina at Charlotte, Dept of Visual Arts, Charlotte NC (S)

Swiderski, Christine, *Cur,* Ontario College of Art & Design, OCAD Gallery, Toronto ON

Swinton, Elizabeth de Sabato, *Cur Asian Art,* Worcester Art Museum, Worcester MA

Swisher, Michael, *Chmn Humanities,* City Colleges of Chicago, Truman College, Chicago IL (S)

Swithenbanik, Gail, *VPres,* Art Information Center, Inc, New York NY

Swope, John, *VPres,* The Currier Gallery of Art, Manchester NH

Swoyer, David, *Cur,* The Museum of Arts & Sciences Inc, Daytona Beach FL

Swyrydenko, Walter, *Prof,* Lakeland Community College, Visual Arts Dept, Mentor OH (S)

Sykes, Lawrence F, *Prof,* Rhode Island College, Art Dept, Providence RI (S)

Sykes, Mary, *Dir Research & Child Develop,* Please Touch Museum, Philadelphia PA

Sylvester, Judith, *Conservator,* Indiana University, William Hammond Mathers Museum, Bloomington IN

Sylvester, Steve, *Art Dept Chmn,* Montana State University-Northern, Humanities & Social Sciences, Havre MT (S)

Symmes, Edwin C, *Pres,* Symmes Systems, Photographic Investments Gallery, Atlanta GA

Symmes, Marilyn, *Cur Drawings & Prints,* Cooper-Hewitt, National Design Museum, New York NY

Synder, Fred, *Dir & Consultant,* National Native American Co-Operative, North American Indian Information & Trade Center, Tucson AZ

Sypoelt, Terrie, *Reference Librn,* Arkansas State University-Art Department, Jonesboro, Library, Jonesboro AR

Syvertson, Alma, *Asst Dir,* Fillmore County Historical Society, Fountain MN

Szabla, Joanne, *Prof,* Rochester Institute of Technology, School of Art & Design, Rochester NY (S)

Szeitz, P R, *Prof,* Moorhead State University, Dept of Art, Moorhead MN (S)

Szekely, Linda, *Asst Cur,* Norman Rockwell Museum at Stockbridge, Library, Stockbridge MA

Szmagaj, Kenneth, *Prof,* James Madison University, School of Art & Art History, Harrisonburg VA (S)

Szoke, Andrew, *Asst Prof,* Northampton Community College, Art Dept, Bethlehem PA (S)

Szott, Brian, *Dir Continuing Studies,* Minneapolis College of Art & Design, Minneapolis MN (S)

Szpila, Kathleen, *Slide Cur,* Temple University, Slide Library, Elkins PA

Szuszitzky, Blanche, *Treas,* North Country Museum of Arts, Park Rapids MN

Tabakoff, Sheila K, *Cur Coll,* The Dixon Gallery & Gardens, Memphis TN

Tabakoff, Sheila K, *Cur Coll,* The Dixon Gallery & Gardens, Library, Memphis TN

Tabbaa, Yasser, *Asst Prof,* University of Michigan, Ann Arbor, Dept of History of Art, Ann Arbor MI (S)

Tabor, Marlene, *Chmn Fine Arts Div,* College of the Sequoias, Art Dept, Visalia CA (S)

Tacang, Lee, *Instr,* De Anza College, Creative Arts Division, Cupertino CA (S)

Tacha, Athena, *Prof,* Oberlin College, Dept of Art, Oberlin OH (S)

Tack, Catherine, *Staff Librn,* Carnegie Library of Pittsburgh, Pittsburgh PA

Taddie, Dan, *Chmn,* Maryville College, Dept of Fine Arts, Maryville TN (S)

Taddie, Daniel, *Chmn,* Maryville College, Fine Arts Center Gallery, Maryville TN

Tadlock, Marvin, *Chmn,* Virginia Intermont College, Fine Arts Division, Bristol VA (S)

Taff, Cavett, *Cur Exhib,* Mississippi Department of Archives & History, Old Capitol Museum, Jackson MS

Tafler, David, *Lectr,* Rosemont College, Division of the Arts, Rosemont PA (S)

Tafoya, Guadalupe, *Coll Mgr,* Millicent Rogers Museum of Northern New Mexico, Taos NM

Tafoya, Joan, *Registrar,* Museum of New Mexico, Museum of Fine Arts, Santa Fe NM

Taft, Dudley S, *VChmn,* Cincinnati Institute of Fine Arts, Cincinnati OH

Taft, W Stanley, *Asst Prof,* Cornell University, Dept of Art, Ithaca NY (S)

Tai, Susan Shin-Tsu, *Cur Asian Art,* Santa Barbara Museum of Art, Santa Barbara CA

Taira, Masa Morioka, *Dir,* Queen's Medical Center Auxiliary, Queen Emma Gallery, Honolulu HI

Tait, Jen, *Distribution,* Art Com-La Mamelle, Inc, San Francisco CA

Takacs, Sharon, *System Librn,* North Central College, Oesterle Library, Naperville IL

Takahashi, Mina, *Exec Dir,* Dieu Donne Papermill, Inc, New York NY

Tako-Girard, Katherine, *Cur Educ,* Rutgers, The State University of New Jersey, Jane Voorhees Zimmerli Art Museum, New Brunswick NJ

Talalay, Lauren E, *Assoc Dir & Assoc Cur Educ,* University of Michigan, Kelsey Museum of Archaeology, Ann Arbor MI

Talar, Anita, *Acting Dean,* Seton Hall University, Library, South Orange NJ

Talarico, Sandra, *Dir,* Florida State University Foundation - Central Florida Community College Foundation, The Appleton Museum of Art, Ocala FL

Talbert, Hope C, *Dir,* Santarella, Tyringham's Gingerbread House, Tyringham MA

Talbert, Mark, *Chmn,* Southern Utah State University, Dept of Art, Cedar City UT (S)

Talbot, Annette, *Pres,* Plymouth Antiquarian Society, Plymouth MA

Talbot, Tonya, *Retail Dir,* Words & Pictures Museum, Northampton MA

Talbott, Linda, *Dir,* Copper Village Museum & Arts Center, Anaconda MT

Talbott, Linda, *Dir,* Copper Village Museum & Arts Center, Library, Anaconda MT

Talbott, Ronald, *Instr,* Harrisburg Area Community College, Division of Communication & the Arts, Harrisburg PA (S)

Talbott, Susan L, *Dir,* Southeastern Center for Contemporary Art, Winston-Salem NC

Talerman, Margaretha, *Cur Exhib,* American Swedish Historical Foundation & Museum, Library, Philadelphia PA

Talley, Dan R, *Gallery Dir,* Kutztown University, Sharadin Art Gallery, Kutztown PA

Talley, Shaunach, *Co-Dir,* Carnegie Mellon University, Forbes Gallery, Pittsburgh PA

Tallman, Carol W, *Librn,* Pennsylvania Historical & Museum Commission, Library, Harrisburg PA

Tambucci, Sarah, *Pres,* National Art Education Association, Reston VA

Tamisiea, Jeanne, *Asst Prof,* Black Hawk College, Art Dept, Moline IL (S)

Tamplin, Illi-Maria, *Dir.* Art Gallery of Peterborough, Peterborough ON

Tamrong, Nicky, *Presenting Progs Mgr.* Intermedia Arts Minnesota, Minneapolis MN

Tamura, Tomiaki, *Dir of Design*, Cosanti Foundation, Scottsdale AZ

Tamura, Tomiaki, *Planning & Exhib Coordr.* Cosanti Foundation, Arcosanti, Scottsdale AZ

Tan, Gustin, *VPres.* Ukiyo-e Society of America, Inc, New York NY

Tancin, Charlotte, *Librn.* Carnegie Mellon University, Hunt Institute for Botanical Documentation, Pittsburgh PA

Tandy, Jean C, *Chmn Dept Art,* Mount Wachusett Community College, Art Galleries, Gardner MA

Taniguchi, Caprice, *Instr.* Southwest Texas State University, Dept of Art, San Marcos TX (S)

Taniguchi, Dennis, *Exec Dir.* Japantown Art & Media Workshop, San Francisco CA

Tanis, Janet E, *Asst Dir.* Edna Hibel Art Foundation, Hibel Museum of Art, Palm Beach FL

Tanis, Janet E, *Asst Dir & Dir Educ.* Edna Hibel Art Foundation, Gallery, Palm Beach FL

Tanis, Steven, *Coordr Drawing & Painting,* University of Delaware, Dept of Art, Newark DE (S)

Tankersley, Kelly, *Art on Tour Coordr,* Texas Fine Arts Association, Austin TX

Tannebaum, Marilyn, *Instr.* Solano Community College, Division of Fine & Applied Art, Suisun City CA (S)

Tannen, Jason, *Art Commission Gallery,* San Francisco City & County Art Commission, San Francisco CA

Tannenbaum, Barbara, *Chief Cur.* Akron Art Museum, Akron OH

Tannenbaum, Judith, *Asst Dir.* Institute of Contemporary Art, Philadelphia PA

Tanner, Richard, *Prof.* Rochester Institute of Technology, School of Art & Design, Rochester NY (S)

Tanselle, G Thomas, *VPres & Secy,* John Simon Guggenheim Memorial Foundation, New York NY

Taormina, John J, *Cur.* Ohio State University, Slide & Photograph Library, Columbus OH

Taraba, Fred, *Asst Dir.* Illustration House Inc, Gallery Auction House, New York NY

Taragin, Davira, *Cur 19th & 20th Century Glass,* Toledo Museum of Art, Toledo OH

Tarango, Christina, *Admin Asst.* La Raza-Galeria Posada, Sacramento CA

Tarantal, Stephen, *Dean, College of Art & Design,* University of the Arts, Philadelphia College of Art & Design, Philadelphia PA (S)

Tarapor, Mahrukh, *Assoc Dir Exhibits.* The Metropolitan Museum of Art, New York NY

Tarbell, Mike, *Museum Educator,* Iroquois Indian Museum, Howes Cave NY

Tarchi, Claudio, *Treas,* Museo Italo Americano, San Francisco CA

Tardif, Jacqueline, *Dir Serv Arts Culture,* La Galerie Montcalm la galerie d'art de la Villede Hull, Hull PQ

Tardif, Jacqueline, *Dir.* La Galerie Montcalm la galerie d'art de la Villede Hull, Hull PQ

Tardo, Barbara, *Assoc Prof.* Southeastern Louisiana University, Dept of Visual Arts, Hammond LA (S)

Tarnowski, Thomas, *Instr.* Johnson County Community College, Visual Arts Program, Overland Park KS (S)

Tarpey, Sean, *Registrar & Preparator.* Mount Holyoke College, Art Museum, South Hadley MA

Tarr, Blair, *Cur of Decorative Art.* Kansas State Historical Society, Kansas Museum of History, Topeka KS

Tarrell, Robert, *Chmn,* Edgewood College, Art Dept, Madison WI (S)

Tartakov, Gary, *Coordr Art History,* Iowa State University, Dept of Art & Design, Ames IA (S)

Tarter, Diane, *Head Art Dept.* Western Oregon State College, Campbell Hall Gallery, Monmouth OR

Tarver, Paul, *Registrar.* New Orleans Museum of Art, New Orleans LA

Tasaka, Sharon, *Assoc Dir.* University of Hawaii at Manoa, Art Gallery, Honolulu HI

Tate, Barbara, *Dir.* Henry Street Settlement Arts for Living Center, New York NY (S)

Tate, Carolyn, *Asst Prof.* Texas Tech University, Dept of Art, Lubbock TX (S)

Tate, Gayle B, *Pres.* G B Gate & Sons, Asheville NC

Tate, George, *Cur.* Sturdivant Hall, Selma AL

Tate, Hephziah M, *Chmn.* G B Gate & Sons, Asheville NC

Tate, Jamie, *Dir.* Mississippi Art Colony, Pascagoula MS

Tate, Linda, *Accounting Mgr.* Hunter Museum of American Art, Chattanooga TN

Tate, Pat, *Cur.* Sturdivant Hall, Selma AL

Tate, Theresa, *Coordr.* Portland State University, Littman Gallery, Portland OR

Tate, Theresa, *Coordr.* Portland State University, White Gallery, Portland OR

Tate, William, *Asst Prof.* James Madison University, School of Art & Art History, Harrisonburg VA (S)

Tatham, David, *Prof.* Syracuse University, Dept of Fine Arts (Art History), Syracuse NY (S)

Tatum, James, *Chmn,* Lincoln University, Dept Fine Arts, Jefferson City MO (S)

Taubner, Joan, *Pres.* Bartow-Pell Mansion Museum & Gardens, Bronx NY

Taurins, Irene, *Registrar,* Philadelphia Museum of Art, Philadelphia PA

Tavani, Robert, *Gallery Dir.* DePaul University, Dept of Art, Chicago IL (S)

Taylor, Barbara E, *Dir.* Museum of Mobile, Mobile AL

Taylor, Barbara E, *Dir.* Museum of Mobile, Reference Library, Mobile AL

Taylor, Barbara E, *Dir.* Museum of Mobile, Carlen House, Mobile AL

Taylor, Barry, *Pres.* Wheaton Cultural Alliance Inc, Millville NJ

Taylor, Beverly A, *Pres.* Northwest Watercolor Society, Bellevue WA

Taylor, Brian, *Prof.* Shorter College, Art Dept, Rome GA (S)

Taylor, Brie, *Pres.* South County Art Association, Kingston RI

Taylor, Bruce, *Asst Prof.* University of Waterloo, Fine Arts Dept, Waterloo ON (S)

Taylor, Carole, *Library Dir.* Fort Valley State College, H A Hunt Memorial Library, Fort Valley GA

Taylor, Charles, *Preparator.* Philbrook Museum of Art, Tulsa OK

Taylor, Cheryl, *Dir.* Maricopa County Historical Society, Desert Caballeros Western Museum, Wickenburg AZ

Taylor, Cheryl, *Dir.* Maricopa County Historical Society, Eleanor Blossom Memorial Library, Wickenburg AZ

Taylor, David, *Cur.* Gallery Lambton, Sarnia ON

Taylor, David, *Dir.* L'Universite Laval, Ecole des Arts Visuels, Quebec PQ

Taylor, Deborah, *Educ Dir.* Huntsville Museum of Art, Huntsville AL

Taylor, Deborah, *Educ Dir.* Huntsville Museum of Art, Reference Library, Huntsville AL

Taylor, Dianne, *Grad Studies Coordr.* University of North Texas, School of Visual Arts, Denton TX (S)

Taylor, Frazine, *Readi Reference Librn.* Alabama Department of Archives & History, Library, Montgomery AL

Taylor, Howard J, *Dir.* San Angelo Museum of Fine Arts, San Angelo TX

Taylor, Hugh H, *Prof.* Washington & Jefferson College, Art Dept, Washington PA (S)

Taylor, Joan, *Assoc Prof.* Fairleigh Dickinson University, Fine Arts Dept, Teaneck NJ (S)

Taylor, Judith, *Asst Prof.* Beaver College, Dept of Fine Arts, Glenside PA (S)

Taylor, Marcia, *Assoc Prof.* College of New Jersey, Art Dept, Trenton NJ (S)

Taylor, Marilyn S, *Cur Ethnology,* Saint Joseph Museum, Saint Joseph MO

Taylor, Mary Diane, *Chmn Dept Art,* Brescia College, Anna Eaton Stout Memorial Art Gallery, Owensboro KY

Taylor, Mary Diane, *Chmn,* Brescia College, Dept of Art, Owensboro KY (S)

Taylor, Mary Jane, *Dir.* Brenau University, Art Dept, Gainesville GA (S)

Taylor, Michael, *Assoc Prof.* Lewis & Clark College, Dept of Art, Portland OR (S)

Taylor, Michael, *Prof.* Rochester Institute of Technology, School of Art & Design, Rochester NY (S)

Taylor, Michael D, *Dean Col.* University of Massachusetts Dartmouth, College of Visual & Performing Arts, North Dartmouth MA (S)

Taylor, Morgan, *Dir.* Blue Mountain Gallery, New York NY

Taylor, Odelle, *Bookkeeper,* Community Council for the Arts, Kinston NC

Taylor, Pat, *Lectr.* Southwest Texas State University, Dept of Art, San Marcos TX (S)

Taylor, Peter, *Cur.* Greensboro Artists' League, Greensboro NC

Taylor, Rene, *Emeritus Dir.* Museo de Arte de Ponce, Ponce Art Museum, Ponce PR

Taylor, Robert, *Theatre Cur.* The New York Public Library, Shelby Cullom Davis Museum, New York NY

Taylor, Rod A, *Head Dept.* Norfolk State University, Fine Arts Dept, Norfolk VA (S)

Taylor, Romalis, *Asst Dir Facilities.* Los Angeles County Museum of Art, Los Angeles CA

Taylor, Ron, *Prof.* University of North Carolina at Charlotte, Dept of Visual Arts, Charlotte NC (S)

Taylor, Ruth, *Grants & Membership.* Newport Art Museum, Newport RI

Taylor, Susan, *Dir.* Wellesley College, Davis Museum & Cultural Center, Wellesley MA

Taylor, Tom, *Coordr Fine Arts,* Columbia College, Art Dept, Chicago IL (S)

Taylor, Walter, *VPres Operations.* Philadelphia Museum of Art, Philadelphia PA

Taylor, Warren, *Instr.* Midland College, Art Dept, Midland TX (S)

Tchen, John K W, *Co-Founder,* Museum of Chinese in the Americas, New York NY

Teague, Edward H, *Architecture Fine Arts Bibliographer & Head Librn,* University of Florida, Architecture & Fine Arts Library, Gainesville FL

Teahan, John W, *Librn.* Wadsworth Atheneum, Auerbach Art Library, Hartford CT

Teats, Gloria, *Co-Chmn.* Valley Art Center Inc, Clarkston WA

Teczar, Steven, *Art Division Chmn.* Maryville University of Saint Louis, Art Division, Saint Louis MO (S)

Tedesco, Robin, *Instr.* Main Line Art Center, Haverford PA (S)

Tedford, Catherine, *Dir.* St Lawrence University, Richard F Brush Art Gallery, Canton NY

Teel, Gina, *Dir Public Relations.* Arts & Science Center for Southeast Arkansas, Pine Bluff AR

Teeter, Emily, *Assoc Cur.* University of Chicago, Oriental Institute Museum, Chicago IL

Tefft, Tom, *Art Dept Chmn.* Citrus College, Art Dept, Glendora CA (S)

Teilhet-Fisk, Jehnne, *Prof.* Florida State University, Art History Dept (R133B), Tallahassee FL (S)

Teitelbaum, Matthew, *Chief Cur.* Art Gallery of Ontario, Toronto ON

Teixido, Mercedes, *Asst Prof.* Pomona College, Dept of Art & Art History, Claremont CA (S)

Tejeda, Juan, *Xicano Music Prog Dir.* Guadalupe Cultural Arts Center, San Antonio TX

Telfair, Tula, *Assoc Prof.* Wesleyan University, Art Dept, Middletown CT (S)

Tellander, Bob, *Chmn,* San Joaquin Delta College, Art Dept, Stockton CA (S)

Teller, Douglas H, *Prof.* George Washington University, Dept of Art, Washington DC (S)

Tellier, Cassandra Lee, *Dir.* Capital University, Schumacher Gallery, Columbus OH

Telseyan, Madeleine, *Dir.* Rhode Island Historical Society, Library, Providence RI

Temple, Jimmy, *Pres.* Huntsville Art League, Huntsville AL

Temple, Leslie Alcott, *Pres.* SLA Arch-Couture Inc, Art Collection, Denver CO

Temple, Murray C, *Pres.* Art Gallery of Windsor, Windsor ON

Temple, Paula, *Assoc Prof*, University of Mississippi, Dept of Art, University MS (S)

Temple-Sullivan, Laura, *Dir Educ*, Museum of New Mexico, Museum of International Folk Art, Santa Fe NM

Templeton, Rijn, *Librn*, University of Iowa, Art Library, Iowa City IA

Templin, Pat, *Exec Dir*, Hoosier Salon Patrons Association, Hoosier Salon Art Gallery, Indianapolis IN

Tenabe, Gabriel S, *Dir & Cur*, Morgan State University, James E Lewis Museum of Art, Baltimore MD

Tennant, Phil, *Coordr Foundation*, Indiana University-Purdue University, Indianapolis, Herron School of Art, Indianapolis IN (S)

Tennent, Elaine, *Dir*, Tennent Art Foundation Gallery, Honolulu HI

Tennessen, Margaret, *Art Coordr*, University of Wisconsin-Madison, Wisconsin Union Galleries, Madison WI

Tenuth, Jeffrey, *Registrar*, Indiana State Museum, Indianapolis IN

Teodorowych, Oksana, *Cur*, Ukrainian National Museum & Library, Chicago IL

Teramoto, John, *Asst Prof*, University of Kansas, Kress Foundation Dept of Art History, Lawrence KS (S)

Terentieff, Robert, *Prof*, Mount Saint Mary's College, Visual & Performing Arts Dept, Emmitsburg MD (S)

Terenzio, Marion, *Dir Creative Arts*, Russell Sage College, Visual & Performing Arts Dept, Troy NY (S)

Terlinden, Rene, *Pres & Dir*, Revelstoke Art Group, Revelstoke BC

Terner, Ron, *Dir*, Focal Point Gallery, Bronx NY

Ternes, William, *Treas*, Guild of Boston Artists, Boston MA

Terra, Daniel J, *Founder*, Terra Museum of American Art, Chicago IL

Terrassa, Jacqueline, *Educ Dir*, Hyde Park Art Center, Chicago IL

Terrell, Janie, *VPres*, Gadsden Museum of Fine Arts, Inc, Gadsden AL

Terrell, Richard, *Head Dept*, Doane College, Dept of Art, Crete NE (S)

Terris, Andrew, *Exec Dir*, Visual Arts Nova Scotia, Halifax NS

Terrono, Evie, *Lectr*, Randolph-Macon College, Dept of the Arts, Ashland VA (S)

Terry, Ann, *Assoc Prof*, Wittenberg University, Art Dept, Springfield OH (S)

Terry, C, *Dir*, National Museum of Science & Technology Corporation, National Aviation Museum, Ottawa ON

Terry, Carol, *Dir*, Rhode Island School of Design, Library, Providence RI

Terry, Christopher, *Assoc Prof*, Utah State University, Dept of Art, Logan UT (S)

Terry, Michael, *Dir*, Spertus Institute of Jewish Studies, Asher Library, Chicago IL

Tersteeg, William, *Prof*, Keystone Junior College, Fine Arts Dept, Factoryville PA (S)

Tesman, Betty, *Center Adminr*, Muckenthaler Cultural Center, Fullerton CA

Tessman, Nancy, *Dir*, Salt Lake City Public Library, Fine Arts/Audiovisual Dept and Atrium Gallery, Salt Lake City UT

Tesso, Jane B, *Art Admin Consultant*, B P America, Cleveland OH

Testa, Adena, *Pres Board Trustees*, Walters Art Gallery, Baltimore MD

Tetzlaff, Julie Dodd, *Art Instr*, Randall Museum Junior Museum, San Francisco CA

Teverow, Lee, *Asst Dir*, Providence Athenaeum, Providence RI

Teverow, Lee, *Asst Dir*, Providence Athenaeum, Library, Providence RI

Thacher, Anne, *Librn*, Harvard University, Studies in Landscape Architecture & Garden Library, Washington DC

Thaler, Janice M, *Cur*, French Art Colony, Gallipolis OH

Thatcher, Becky, *Treas*, Society of North American Goldsmiths, Tampa FL

Thatcher, C Gregory, *Dir*, Maharishi University of Management, Department of Fine Arts, Fairfield IA

Thayer, Russel, *Chmn Dept*, Delta College, Art Dept, University Center MI (S)

Theberge, Andre, *Dir Visual Arts*, Universite Laval Cite Universitaire, School of Visual Arts, Quebec PQ (S)

Theberge, Pierre, *Dir*, Montreal Museum of Fine Arts, Montreal PQ

Theberge, Pierre, *Cur Contemporary Art*, Montreal Museum of Fine Arts, Montreal PQ

Theel, Marcia M, *Assoc Dir*, Leigh Yawkey Woodson Art Museum, Inc, Wausau WI

Theide, Billie, *In Charge Metals*, University of Illinois, Urbana-Champaign, School of Art & Design, Champaign IL (S)

Theide, Billie Jean, *Pres*, Society of North American Goldsmiths, Tampa FL

Thein, John, *Instr*, Creighton University, Fine & Performing Arts Dept, Omaha NE (S)

Theis, Leah, *Slide Librn*, University of California, Art Dept Library, Davis CA

Thesing, Claudia I, *Develop Coordr*, New Britain Museum of American Art, New Britain CT

Thibault, Barbara, *Dir*, Andover Historical Society, Andover MA

Thibault, Manon B, *Coordr*, La Centrale Powerhouse Gallery, Montreal PQ

Thibodeau, Rich, *Dir*, Lovewell Studios, Superior NB (S)

Thiele, John, *VPres*, Timken Museum of Art, San Diego CA

Thieme, Marilyn, *Art & Music*, San Francisco Public Library, Art & Music Center, San Francisco CA

Thiesen, John D, *Archivist*, Bethel College, Mennonite Library & Archives, North Newton KS

Thine, Anthony, *Dir*, Mayville State University Gallery, Mayville ND

Thistlethwaite, Mark, *Prof*, Texas Christian University, Art & Art History Dept, Fort Worth TX (S)

Thom, Ian, *Sr Cur*, Vancouver Art Gallery, Vancouver BC

Thomas, Ann, *Acting Cur Photo Coll*, National Gallery of Canada, Ottawa ON

Thomas, Arthur D, *Dir*, United Methodist Historical Society, Lovely Lane Museum, Baltimore MD

Thomas, Bruce, *Asst Prof*, Lehigh University, Dept of Art & Architecture, Bethlehem PA (S)

Thomas, C David, *Prof*, Emmanuel College, Art Dept, Boston MA (S)

Thomas, Christopher, *Asst Prof*, University of Victoria, Dept of History in Art, Victoria BC (S)

Thomas, David, *Assoc Dir*, Indianapolis Art Center, Churchman-Fehsenfeld Gallery, Indianapolis IN

Thomas, Donald, *Mgr*, Colonial Williamsburg Foundation, DeWitt Wallace Decorative Arts Gallery, Williamsburg VA

Thomas, Floyd, *Cur*, Ohio Historical Society, National Afro American Museum & Cultural Center, Wilberforce OH

Thomas, James C, *Pres & Chief Exec Officer*, Shaker Village of Pleasant Hill, Harrodsburg KY

Thomas, James E, *Prof*, Rochester Institute of Technology, School of Art & Design, Rochester NY (S)

Thomas, JoAnn, *Instr*, Marylhurst College, Art Dept, Marylhurst OR (S)

Thomas, Joe, *Chmn*, Clarion University of Pennsylvania, Dept of Art, Clarion PA (S)

Thomas, Joe, *Chmn*, Clarion University, Hazel Sandford Gallery, Clarion PA

Thomas, John Larry, *Instr*, Johnson County Community College, Visual Arts Program, Overland Park KS (S)

Thomas, Kay, *Crafts Dir*, Ozark Folk Center, Ozark Cultural Resource Center, Mountain View AR

Thomas, Lorelle, *Asst Prof*, Grand Valley State University, Art & Design Dept, Allendale MI (S)

Thomas, Madeline, *Cur Educ*, Historical & Cultural Affairs, Delaware State Museums, Dover DE

Thomas, Mark, *Prof*, Art Academy of Cincinnati, Cincinnati OH (S)

Thomas, Michael, *Adjunct Prof*, Wilkes University, Dept of Art, Wilkes-Barre PA (S)

Thomas, Ronald, *Instr*, Saint Louis Community College at Meramec, Art Dept, Saint Louis MO (S)

Thomas, Sam, *Assoc Prof*, Mansfield University, Art Dept, Mansfield PA (S)

Thomas, Sean, *Registrar & Researcher*, The Seagram Museum, Library, Waterloo ON

Thomas, Steve, *Assoc Prof*, Augustana College, Art Dept, Sioux Falls SD (S)

Thomas, Thelma, *Assoc Cur*, University of Michigan, Kelsey Museum of Archaeology, Ann Arbor MI

Thomas, Thelma, *Assoc Prof*, University of Michigan, Ann Arbor, Dept of History of Art, Ann Arbor MI (S)

Thomas, Troy, *Assoc Prof*, Penn State Harrisburg, Humanities Division, Middletown PA (S)

Thomas, William, *Prof*, West Virginia University, College of Creative Arts, Morgantown WV (S)

Thomas, William G, *Supt*, San Francisco Maritime National Historical Park, National Maritime Museum, San Francisco CA

Thomas, Wilma, *Treas*, Fulton County Historical Society Inc, Fulton County Museum, Rochester IN

Thomasgard, Robert, *Assoc Dir*, State Historical Society of Wisconsin, State Historical Museum, Madison WI

Thomason, Barbara, *Gallery Dir*, University of Redlands, Peppers Gallery, Redlands CA

Thomas-Williams, Helen, *Project Coordr*, Manhattan Psychiatric Center, Sculpture Garden, New York NY

Thommen, Lynn, *Deputy Dir External Affairs*, The Jewish Museum, New York NY

Thompson, Angelle, *Vol Dir*, Longue Vue House & Gardens, New Orleans LA

Thompson, Bradley, *Asst Dir*, Center on Contemporary Art, Seattle WA

Thompson, Bryan, *Exec Dir*, Golden Isles Arts & Humanities Association, Brunswick GA

Thompson, Carol, *Assoc Cur*, Museum of African Art, New York NY

Thompson, Christine M, *In Charge Art Educ*, University of Illinois, Urbana-Champaign, School of Art & Design, Champaign IL (S)

Thompson, Chuck, *Asst Dean*, Laramie County Community College, Division of Arts & Humanities, Cheyenne WY (S)

Thompson, Claire Holman, *Dir Develop*, University of Virginia, Bayly Art Museum, Charlottesville VA

Thompson, Deborah, *Cur*, Gilbert Stuart Memorial, Inc Memorial Association, Inc, Museum, Saunderstown RI

Thompson, Eleanor E, *Dir*, Wenham Museum, Wenham MA

Thompson, George, *Dir*, Johnson County Community College, Visual Arts Program, Overland Park KS (S)

Thompson, Gia, *Library Serv Supv*, Miami Dade Public Library, Miami Beach Branch, Miami Beach FL

Thompson, Greig, *Preparator*, University of Missouri, Museum of Art & Archaeology, Columbia MO

Thompson, Harlyn, *Head Environmental Design*, University of Manitoba, Faculty of Architecture, Winnipeg MB (S)

Thompson, Harry F, *Cur & Managing Ed*, Augustana College, Center for Western Studies, Sioux Falls SD

Thompson, Harry F, *Cur & Managing Ed*, Augustana College, Center for Western Studies, Sioux Falls SD

Thompson, James, *Assoc Prof*, Western Carolina University, Dept of Art, Cullowhee NC (S)

Thompson, James, *Assoc Prof*, Azusa Pacific University, College of Liberal Arts, Art Dept, Azusa CA (S)

Thompson, James C, *University Librn*, University of California, Tomas Rivera Library, Riverside CA

Thompson, Jim, *Account Mgr*, Memphis Brooks Museum of Art, Memphis TN

Tolnick, Judith, *Galleries Dir*, University of Rhode Island, Fine Arts Center Galleries, Kingston RI

Tolpa, Jennifer, *Reference Librn*, Massachusetts Historical Society, Library, Boston MA

Tolstedt, Lowell, *Dean*, Columbus College of Art & Design, Fine Arts Dept, Columbus OH (S)

Toluse, Joe, *Cur*, Idaho Historical Museum, Boise ID

Tom, Robert, *Prof*, Moorhead State University, Dept of Art, Moorhead MN (S)

Tomlin, Terry, *Chmn Fine Arts*, University of Texas at Brownsville & Texas Southmost College, Fine Arts Dept, Brownsville TX (S)

Tomlinson, Bill, *Assoc Cur*, Algonquin Arts Council, Art Gallery of Bancroft, Bancroft ON

Tomor, Michael, *Cur*, Southern Alleghenies Museum of Art, Loretto PA

Tomsen, Mary, *Dir Public Relations*, North Central Washington Museum, Gallery, Wenatchee WA

Tomsic, Walt, *Assoc Prof*, Pacific Lutheran University, Dept of Art, Tacoma WA (S)

Toner, Rochelle, *Dean*, Temple University, Tyler School of Art-Galleries, Tyler Gallery, Elkins PA

Toner, Rochelle, *Dean*, Temple University, Tyler School of Art, Philadelphia PA (S)

Tong, Darlene, *Art Librn*, San Francisco State University, J Paul Leonard Library, San Francisco CA

Toogood, James, *Instr*, Main Line Art Center, Haverford PA (S)

Tooke, Joan, *Dir*, Koffler Center School of Visual Art, North York ON (S)

Toomey, Tina, *Cur*, York Institute Museum, Saco ME

Toone, Thomas, *Asst Prof*, Utah State University, Dept of Art, Logan UT (S)

Tootle, Ann, *Registrar*, The Albrecht-Kemper Museum of Art, Saint Joseph MO

Toperzer, Thomas R, *Dir*, University of Oklahoma, Fred Jones Jr Museum of Art, Norman OK

Toplovich, Ann, *Exec Dir*, Tennessee Historical Society, Nashville TN

Topping, Margaret, *Exec Dir*, Saskatchewan Association of Architects, Saskatoon SK

Torcoletti, Enzo, *Prof*, Flagler College, Visual Arts Dept, Saint Augustine FL (S)

Tornell, Arnold, *VPres*, Fairbanks Arts Association, Fairbanks AK

Tornheim, N, *Instr*, Golden West College, Visual Art Dept, Huntington Beach CA (S)

Torno, Janet E, *Exec Dir*, Birmingham-Bloomfield Art Association, Birmingham MI

Torno, Janet E, *Exec Dir*, Birmingham-Bloomfield Art Association, Birmingham MI (S)

Torntore, Susan, *Cur Exhib*, State Capitol Museum, Olympia WA

Torre, Micael, *Instr*, Northwest Community College, Dept of Art, Powell WY (S)

Torre, Rosemary, *Pres*, Ukiyo-e Society of America, Inc, New York NY

Torreano, John, *Assoc Prof*, New York University, Dept of Art & Art Professions, New York NY (S)

Torres, Harold, *Tourism Mgr*, Pueblo of San Ildefonso, Maria Martinez Museum, Santa Fe NM

Torres, Jennifer, *Asst Prof*, Bethany College, Mingenback Art Center, Lindsborg KS

Torres, Jennifer, *Asst Prof*, Bethany College, Art Dept, Lindsborg KS (S)

Torres, Manuel, *Assoc Prof*, Florida International University, Visual Arts Dept, Miami FL (S)

Torres-Delgado, Rene, *Asst Prof*, University of Puerto Rico, Dept of Fine Arts, Rio Piedras PR (S)

Torrey, Charles, *Researcher*, Museum of Mobile, Mobile AL

Torri, Erika, *Exec Dir & Librn*, Library Association of La Jolla, Athenaeum Music & Arts Library, La Jolla CA

Tortolero, Carlos, *Exec Dir*, Mexican Fine Arts Center Museum, Chicago IL

Toscan, Richard, *Dean*, Virginia Commonwealth University, School of the Arts, Richmond VA (S)

Toth, Carl, *Head Photo Dept*, Cranbrook Academy of Art, Bloomfield Hills MI (S)

Toth, George, *Commercial Art*, Madonna University, Art Dept, Livonia MI (S)

Toth, Julie, *Cur Educ*, Paine Art Center & Arboretum, Oshkosh WI

Toth, Mary, *Exec Dir*, Howard County Arts Council, Ellicott City MD

Toth, Myra, *Chmn*, Ventura College, Fine Arts Dept, Ventura CA (S)

Toth, Richard E, *Head*, Utah State University, Dept of Landscape Architecture Environmental Planning, Logan UT (S)

Toth, Robert, *Dir*, Rhinelander District Library, Rhinelander WI

Touchette, Lori-Ann, *Cur*, Johns Hopkins University, Archaeological Collection, Baltimore MD

Touchine, Maxine A, *Museum Clerk*, Red Rock State Park, Red Rock Museum, Church Rock NM

Touhey, Paula, *Dir*, Kenosha Public Museum, Kenosha WI

Tousignant, Serge, *Instr*, Universite de Montreal, Dept of Art History, Montreal PQ (S)

Tovell, Rosemarie, *Assoc Cur Canadian Prints & Drawings*, National Gallery of Canada, Ottawa ON

Tow, Kelly, *Instr*, Antonelli Institute of Art & Photography, Cincinnati OH (S)

Towers, Debbie, *Admin Assoc*, Palm Beach County Parks & Recreation Department, Morikami Museum & Japanese Gardens, Delray Beach FL

Townsend, Allen, *Librn*, Philadelphia Museum of Art, Library, Philadelphia PA

Townsend, Allen, *Head*, Dallas Museum of Art, Mildred R & Frederick M Mayer Library, Dallas TX

Townsend, Andrew, *Art Asst*, University Club Library, New York NY

Townsend, Carol, *Part-time Assoc Prof*, Daemen College, Art Dept, Amherst NY (S)

Townsend, Gavin, *Assoc Prof*, University of Tennessee at Chattanooga, Dept of Art, Chattanooga TN (S)

Townsend, Ken, *Exec Dir*, National Cowboy Hall of Fame & Western Heritage Center Museum, Oklahoma City OK

Townsend, Richard, *Hardman Cur*, Philbrook Museum of Art, Tulsa OK

Townsend, Richard F, *Cur Africa, Oceania & the Americas*, The Art Institute of Chicago, Chicago IL

Townson, Lowell, *Pres*, Cherokee National Historical Society, Inc, Tahlequah OK

Toyce, Peter, *VPres*, Monterey Museum of Art Association, Monterey CA

Trachtenberg-Patent, Amy, *Coordr Educ*, University of Houston, Sarah Campbell Blaffer Gallery, Houston TX

Tracy, Paul, *Asst Preparator*, Memphis Brooks Museum of Art, Memphis TN

Tracz, Tim, *Chmn*, Austin College, Art Dept, Sherman TX (S)

Tracz, Timothy, *Chair*, Austin College, Ida Green Gallery, Sherman TX

Trafford, Hal, *Head Commercial Art*, Butera School of Art, Boston MA (S)

Trafton, Robin, *Cur Art Coll*, Commerce Bancshares, Inc, Art Collection, Kansas City MO

Trager, Neil C, *Dir*, State University of New York at New Paltz, College Art Gallery, New Paltz NY

Trahan, Eric, *Dir*, Canajoharie Library & Art Gallery, Canajoharie NY

Trahan, Eric, *Dir Library*, Canajoharie Library & Art Gallery, Library, Canajoharie NY

Traiger, Bernadette, *Bookshop*, University of Kansas, Spencer Museum of Art, Lawrence KS

Trama, Ellen G, *Spec Events*, Newark Museum Association, The Newark Museum, Newark NJ

Tran, Thuy, *Coordr Public Information & Membership*, University of Houston, Sarah Campbell Blaffer Gallery, Houston TX

Tran, Thuy M, *Prog Coordr*, Houston Center For Photography, Houston TX

Tranbarger, Ossie E, *Coordr*, Independence Museum, Independence KS

Tranter, Adele, *VPres*, Crary Art Gallery Inc, Warren PA

Trapani, Denise, *Assoc Dir Develop*, DeCordova Museum & Sculpture Park, Lincoln MA

Trapp, Catherine, *Cur Art*, Bank One Arizona, Phoenix AZ

Trapp, Ken, *Renwick Gallery Cur-in-Charge*, National Museum of American Art, Washington DC

Trapp, Kenneth, *Cur-in-Charge*, National Museum of American Art, Renwick Gallery, Washington DC

Trask, Benjamin, *Librn*, The Mariners' Museum, Library, Newport News VA

Trauger, Susan, *Librn*, Los Angeles County Museum of Art, Robert Gore Rifkind Center for German Expressionist Studies, Los Angeles CA

Traugott, Joseph, *Cur*, University of New Mexico, Jonson Gallery, Albuquerque NM

Traugott, Joseph, *Cur 20th Century Painting*, Museum of New Mexico, Museum of Fine Arts, Santa Fe NM

Traverso, Daniel, *Head Dept*, Austin Community College, Dept of Commercial Art, North Ridge Campus, Austin TX (S)

Travis, Betsy, *Dir*, Potsdam Public Museum, Potsdam NY

Travis, David, *Cur Photography*, The Art Institute of Chicago, Chicago IL

Travis, Jane, *Library Technician*, University of Oklahoma, Architecture Library, Norman OK

Travis, Jessica, *Reference Librn*, Kemper & Leila Williams Foundation, Historic New Orleans Collection, New Orleans LA

Travis, Susan, *Asst Slide Cur*, Roger Williams University, Architecture Library, Bristol RI

Treacy, Thomas D, *Dir*, Antonelli Institute, Professional Photography, Commercial Art & Interior Design, Erdenheim PA (S)

Treadway, Beth A, *Gallery Dir*, Pace University Gallery, Pleasantville NY

Treadwell, Ann, *Dir*, Creative Arts Guild, Dalton GA

Treanor, Dennis, *Art Instr*, Randall Museum Junior Museum, San Francisco CA

Trechsel, Gail, *Dir*, Birmingham Museum of Art, Birmingham AL

Trecker, Stan, *Pres*, The Art Institute of Boston, Main Gallery, Boston MA

Trecker, Stan, *Pres*, Art Institute of Boston, Boston MA (S)

Tredway, Cherry, *Assoc Prof*, Oklahoma Christian University of Science & Arts, Dept of Art & Design, Oklahoma City OK (S)

Trelstad, Barbara, *Registrar*, Rutgers, The State University of New Jersey, Jane Voorhees Zimmerli Art Museum, New Brunswick NJ

Tremblay, Guy, *Dir & Cur*, Musee Regional de la Cote-Nord, Sept-Iles PQ

Trend, David, *Dean Creative Arts*, De Anza College, Creative Arts Division, Cupertino CA (S)

Trent, Andrienne, *Reprography Coordr*, Visual Arts Ontario, Toronto ON

Trentham, Rod, *Interpretive Prog Coordr*, Red Deer & District Museum & Archives, Red Deer AB

Trepanier, Peter, *Head Reader Serv*, National Gallery of Canada, Library, Ottawa ON

Trepp, George, *Dir*, Long Beach Public Library, Long Beach NY

Trevelyan, Amelia M, *Chmn*, Gettysburg College, Dept of Visual Arts, Gettysburg PA (S)

Trevorrow, Todd, *Dir Library Services*, Plymouth State College, Herbert H Lamson Library, Plymouth NH

Triano, Anthony, *Asst Prof*, Seton Hall University, College of Arts & Sciences, South Orange NJ (S)

Tribush, Brenda, *VPres*, New York Artists Equity Association, Inc, New York NY

Trick, Gordan, *Instr*, Vancouver Community College, Langara Campus, Dept of Fine Arts, Vancouver BC (S)

Trickey, Karen, *Asst Prof*, Nazareth College of Rochester, Art Dept, Rochester NY (S)

Trien, Susan, *Pub Relations*, Strong Museum, Rochester NY

Trimpe, Pamela White, *Cur*, University of Iowa, Museum of Art, Iowa City IA

Trippett, Lorraine, *Controller*, Craft & Folk Art Museum, Los Angeles CA

Tyzack, Michael, *Chmn Studio Art*, College of Charleston, School of the Arts, Charleston SC (S)

Udein, Mohommed, *Interim Dean*, Southern University A & M College, School of Architecture, Baton Rouge LA (S)

Ugent, Donald, *Adjunct Cur Botany*, Southern Illinois University, University Museum, Carbondale IL

Uglow, Sadie, *Librn*, Tacoma Art Museum, Reference Library, Tacoma WA

Uhde, Jan, *Assoc Prof*, University of Waterloo, Fine Arts Dept, Waterloo ON (S)

Ulloa, Derby, *Prof*, Florida Community College at Jacksonville, South Campus, Art Dept, Jacksonville FL (S)

Ulman, Martin, *Spec Projects*, Boston Visual Artists Union, Newton MA

Ulmer, Sean, *Assoc Cur Painting & Sculpture*, Cornell University, Herbert F Johnson Museum of Art, Ithaca NY

Ulry, James E, *Acad Dir*, Johnson Atelier Technical Institute of Sculpture, Mercerville NJ (S)

Umen, Harry, *Asst Prof*, Notre Dame College, Art Dept, Manchester NH (S)

Umlauf, Karl, *Prof*, Baylor University, Dept of Art, Waco TX (S)

Underhill, Michael, *Dir Archit*, Arizona State University, College of Architecture & Environmental Design, Tempe AZ (S)

Underwood, Carol, *Shop Mgr*, Sharon Arts Center, Peterborough NH

Underwood, David, *Prof*, Carson-Newman College, Art Dept, Jefferson City TN (S)

Underwood, David, *Asst Prof*, Rutgers, the State University of New Jersey, Graduate Program in Art History, New Brunswick NJ (S)

Underwood, Lori, *Cur*, San Fernando Valley Historical Society, Mission Hills CA

Underwood, Lori, *Cur*, San Fernando Valley Historical Society, Andres Pico Adobe Library, Mission Hills CA

Underwood, Sandra L, *Assoc Prof*, Saint Mary's College of Maryland, Art Dept, Saint Mary's City MD (S)

Underwood, Tut, *Dir Public Information & Marketing*, South Carolina State Museum, Columbia SC

Unger, Howard, *Prof*, Ocean County College, Humanities Dept, Toms River NJ (S)

Ungerman, Temmi, *Instr*, Toronto Art Therapy Institute, Toronto ON (S)

Unterschultz, Judy, *Exec Dir*, Multicultural Heritage Centre, Stony Plain AB

Upchurch, Diane, *Coordr*, Arizona State University, Architectural Image Library, Tempe AZ

Uphoff, Dudley, *Exec Dir*, Arts on the Park, Lakeland FL

Uphoff, Joseph A, *Dir*, Arjuna Library, Colorado Springs CO

Upton, Joel, *Chmn*, Amherst College, Dept of Fine Arts, Amherst MA (S)

Upton, Stephanie, *Dir*, Louisa May Alcott Memorial Association, Orchard House, Concord MA

Uraneck, Joan, *Instr*, Maine College of Art, Portland ME (S)

Urban, Erin, *Dir*, The John A Noble Collection, Staten Island NY

Urbizu, William, *Asst Dir*, Miami-Dade Public Library, Miami FL

Urice, Stephen K, *Dir*, The Rosenbach Museum & Library, Philadelphia PA

Urquhart, A M, *Prof*, University of Waterloo, Fine Arts Dept, Waterloo ON (S)

Urquhart, John, *Theatre Art Instr*, West Virginia Wesleyan College, Dept of Fine Arts, Buckhannon WV (S)

Urrutia, Larry, *Gallery Dir*, Southwestern College, Art Gallery, Chula Vista CA

Urso, Josette, *Instr*, Chautauqua Institution, School of Art, Chautauqua NY (S)

Urso, Len, *Prof*, Rochester Institute of Technology, School of Art & Design, Rochester NY (S)

Usai, Paolo Cherchi, *Cur Film Coll*, George Eastman House-International Museum of Photography & Film, Rochester NY

Ushenko, Audrey, *Assoc Prof*, Indiana-Purdue University, Dept of Fine Arts, Fort Wayne IN (S)

Uslaner, Diane, *Dir*, Jewish Community Centre of Toronto, The Koffler Gallery, North York ON

Usui, Kiichi, *Dir & Cur*, Oakland University, Meadow Brook Art Gallery, Rochester MI

Uyeno, Dona, *Office Mgr*, Boulder Museum of Contemporary Art, Boulder CO

Uzureau, Linda, *Dean*, South Suburban College, Art Dept, South Holland IL (S)

Vacanti, Monica, *Gallery Dir*, Niagara County Community College Art Gallery, Sanborn NY

Vadeboncoeur, Guy, *Cur*, David M Stewart Museum, Montreal PQ

Vaggalis, K L, *Dir & Secy*, The Turner Museum, Denver CO

Vail, Marguerite K, *VPres Develop*, The Mariners' Museum, Newport News VA

Vail, Neil, *Treas*, Wustum Museum Art Association, Racine WI

Vajda, Elizabeth, *Head Librn*, Cooper Union for the Advancement of Science & Art, Library, New York NY

Valdes, Karen, *Assoc Prof*, University of Florida, Dept of Art, Gainesville FL (S)

Valdes, Karen W, *Acting Dir*, University of Florida, University Gallery, Gainesville FL

Valdez, Helen, *Pres*, Mexican Fine Arts Center Museum, Chicago IL

Valencia, Romolo, *Instr Graphic Arts*, Honolulu Community College, Commercial Art Dept, Honolulu HI (S)

Valentine, Jude, *Educ Coordr*, Schweinfurth Art Center, Auburn NY

Valenza, Catherine, *Dir Coll & Exhib*, Islip Art Museum, East Islip NY

Valenza, Dan, *Chmn*, University of New Hampshire, Dept of Arts & Art History, Durham NH (S)

Valle, Martha, *Cur & Registrar*, Rosemount Museum, Inc, Pueblo CO

Valley, Derek R, *Dir*, State Capitol Museum, Olympia WA

Valliant, John R, *Dir*, Chesapeake Bay Maritime Museum, Saint Michaels MD

Vallieres, Nicole, *Registrar*, McCord Museum of Canadian History, Montreal PQ

Vallila, Marja, *Assoc Prof*, State University of New York at Albany, Art Dept, Albany NY (S)

Van-Able, John, *Treas*, Canton Museum of Art, Canton OH

Van Allen, David, *Dir*, Mount Mercy College, McAuley Gallery, Cedar Rapids IA

Van Ausdal, Kaarin, *Staff Librn*, Carnegie Library of Pittsburgh, Pittsburgh PA

Vanausdall, John, *Pres & Chief Exec Officer*, Eiteljorg Museum of American Indians & Western Art, Indianapolis IN

van Balgooy, Max A, *Asst Dir*, Workman & Temple Family Homestead Museum, City of Industry CA

Van Bramer, Judie, *Membership Mgr*, University of Rochester, Memorial Art Gallery, Rochester NY

VanBuren, Martin, *General Studies*, California College of Arts & Crafts, Oakland CA (S)

Vance, Alex, *Executive Dir*, Bergstrom Mahler Museum, Neenah WI

Vanco, John, *Dir*, Erie Art Museum, Erie PA

Vandegrift, David, *Chmn Div*, Marygrove College, Visual & Performing Arts Div, Detroit MI (S)

Vandegrift, David, *Assoc Prof*, Marygrove College, Visual & Performing Arts Div, Detroit MI (S)

van de Guchte, Maarten, *Dir*, University of Illinois, Krannert Art Museum, Champaign IL

Van De Putte, Andre S, *Dir*, Lasell College, Art & Interior Design Program, Auburndale MA (S)

Vanderbilt, Claire F, *Chmn*, Historical Society of the Town of Greenwich, Inc, Bush-Holley House Museum, Cos Cob CT

Vanderbyl, Michael, *Graphic Design*, California College of Arts & Crafts, Oakland CA (S)

Vanderhaden, Sandra, *Exec Dir*, California State University, Long Beach Foundation, Long Beach CA

Vanderhill, Rein, *Asst Prof*, Northwestern College, Art Dept, Orange City IA (S)

VanDerpool, Karen, *Instr*, California State University, Chico, Art Dept, Chico CA (S)

Vanderway, Richard, *Educ Coordr*, Whatcom Museum of History and Art, Bellingham WA

VanderWeg, Phillip, *Chmn Dept*, Western Michigan University, Dept of Art, Kalamazoo MI (S)

Vandest, Bill, *Instr*, Creighton University, Fine & Performing Arts Dept, Omaha NE (S)

Van Duesen, Patrick, *Prof*, Daytona Beach Community College, Dept of Fine Arts & Visual Arts, Daytona Beach FL (S)

Van Dyk, Stephen, *Librn*, Cooper-Hewitt, National Design Museum, New York NY

Van Dyk, Stephen, *Librn*, Cooper-Hewitt, Cooper-Hewitt Museum Branch Library, New York NY

Van Dyke, Fred, *Asst Prof*, Salt Lake Community College, Graphic Design Dept, Salt Lake City UT (S)

Van Dyke, Lissa, *Librn*, Lyman Allyn Art Museum, Library, New London CT

VanDyke, Sondra, *Pres*, The Illinois Institute of Art, Chicago IL (S)

Van Everdingen, Arie, *Assoc Prof*, Monmouth University, Dept of Art & Design, West Long Branch NJ (S)

Van Gent, Elona, *Asst Prof*, Grand Valley State University, Art & Design Dept, Allendale MI (S)

Vango, Eugene R, *Chmn & Asst Prof*, Virginia State University, Fine & Commercial Art, Petersburg VA (S)

Van Haaften, Julia, *Cur Photographs*, The New York Public Library, Print Room, New York NY

Van Halm, Renee, *Dean Studio*, Emily Carr Institute of Art & Design, Vancouver BC (S)

Van Hauen, Laura, *Dir & Cur*, Prairie Art Gallery, Grande Prairie AB

Van Hook, L Bailey, *Prof*, Virginia Polytechnic Institute & State University, Dept of Art & Art History, Blacksburg VA (S)

Van Hooten, Joan, *Dir Develop*, Orange County Museum of Art, Newport Harbor Art Museum, Newport Beach CA

Van Horn, David, *Prof*, Siena Heights College, Studio Angelico-Art Dept, Adrian MI (S)

Van Horn, Donald, *Dean*, Marshall University, Dept of Art, Huntington WV (S)

Van Horn, Jim, *Dir*, Columbus Chapel & Boal Mansion Museum, Boalsburg PA

Van Horn, Walter, *Cur Coll*, Anchorage Museum of History & Art, Anchorage AK

Van Horne, John C, *Librn*, Library Company of Philadelphia, Philadelphia PA

Van Miegroet, Hans J, *Assoc Prof*, Duke University, Dept of Art & Art History, Durham NC (S)

Vann, Lowell C, *Chmn*, Samford University, Art Dept, Birmingham AL (S)

Van Over, Nancy, *Asst Prof*, Adrian College, Art & Design Dept, Adrian MI (S)

Van Parys, Michelle, *Prof*, State University of New York College at Potsdam, Dept of Fine Arts, Potsdam NY (S)

VanPelt, Mary Frances, *Prof*, North Central Texas College, Division of Communications & Fine Arts, Gainesville TX (S)

Van Schaack, Eric, *Prof*, Colgate University, Dept of Art & Art History, Hamilton NY (S)

Van Suchtelen, Adrian, *Prof*, Utah State University, Dept of Art, Logan UT (S)

Van Tassel, Ann, *Acting Dir*, Grand Rapids Art Museum, Grand Rapids MI

Van Vleet, Barbara, *Public Information*, Toledo Museum of Art, Toledo OH

Van Vleet, Karen, *Instr*, University of North Carolina at Charlotte, Dept of Visual Arts, Charlotte NC (S)

Van Vorthuizen, Arwin, *Dean Design*, Alberta College of Art, Calgary AB (S)

VanWagoner, Richard J, *Prof*, Weber State University, Dept of Visual Arts, Ogden UT (S)

Van Winkle, Mary, *Librn*, Massachusetts College of Art, Morton R Godine Library, Boston MA

Van Woert, Brad, *Pres*, Sierra Arts Foundation, Reno NV

VanZandt, Paul, *Chmn Dept*, University of North Carolina at Pembroke, Art Dept, Pembroke NC (S)

Van Zante, Gary, *Cur*, Tulane University, University Art Collection, New Orleans LA

Varady, Adrienne, *Cur*, University of Cincinnati, Visual Resource Center, Cincinnati OH

Varga, Vincent J, *Exec Dir*, Edmonton Art Gallery, Edmonton AB

Varga, Vincent J, *Exec Dir*, Edmonton Art Gallery, Library, Edmonton AB

Vargas, Kathy, *Visual Arts Dir*, Guadalupe Cultural Arts Center, San Antonio TX

Varnedoe, Kirk, *Chief Cur, Dept Painting & Sculpture*, Museum of Modern Art, New York NY

Varner, Eric, *Asst Prof*, Emory University, Art History Dept, Atlanta GA (S)

Varner, Jessica, *Public Relations & Spec Events Coordr*, Whitney Museum of American Art at Champion, Stamford CT

Varner, Victoria Star, *Assoc Prof*, Southwestern University, Art Dept, Georgetown TX (S)

Varnum, Maevernon, *Instr*, Wayne Art Center, Wayne PA (S)

Varriano, John, *Chmn*, Mount Holyoke College, Art Dept, South Hadley MA (S)

Vartanian, Hasmig, *Instr*, Southeastern Louisiana University, Dept of Visual Arts, Hammond LA (S)

Vasiliadis, Nikki, *Pres*, Kemerer Museum of Decorative Arts, Bethlehem PA

Vaslef, Irene, *Librn*, Harvard University, Byzantine Library, Washington DC

Vasquez, Clare, *Admin Asst*, The Saint Louis Art Museum, Richardson Memorial Library, Saint Louis MO

Vasquez, Jo Ann, *Assoc VPres Academic Affairs*, Santa Clara University, de Saisset Museum, Santa Clara CA

Vasseur, Dominique, *Sr Cur*, Dayton Art Institute, Dayton OH

Vatandoost, Nossi, *Exec Dir*, Nossi College of Art, Goodlettsville TN (S)

Vatsky, Sharon, *Dir Educ*, The Queens Museum of Art, Flushing NY

Vaughan, Clayton, *Art Librn Asst*, Old Dominion University, Elise N Hofheimer Art Library, Norfolk VA

Vaughan, Don, *VPres*, Royal Canadian Academy of Arts, Toronto ON

Vaughn, Babs, *Registrar*, Muskegon Museum of Art, Muskegon MI

Vaughn, Father John, *Dir*, Mission San Miguel Museum, San Miguel CA

Vaughn, Ron, *Pres*, University of Tampa, Lee Scarfone Gallery, Tampa FL

Vaux, Richard, *Prof*, Adelphi University, Dept of Art & Art History, Garden City NY (S)

Vavrek, Becki, *Sales Assoc*, Fort Worth Art Association, Modern Art Museum of Fort Worth, Fort Worth TX

Veasey, Ruth, *Instr*, Ocean City Art Center, Ocean City NJ (S)

Veatch, James, *Assoc Prof*, University of Massachusetts Lowell, Dept of Art, Lowell MA (S)

Vecchio, Jo, *Asst Dir Marketing & Development*, Kimbell Art Foundation, Kimbell Art Museum, Fort Worth TX

Vecchitto, Daniel, *Dir Development*, Museum of Modern Art, New York NY

Veder, Lilly, *Dir*, Dickinson State University, Mind's Eye Gallery, Dickinson ND

Veerkamp, Patrick, *Prof*, Southwestern University, Art Dept, Georgetown TX (S)

Vega, Margaret, *Chmn Foundation Fine Arts*, Kendall College of Art & Design, Grand Rapids MI (S)

Veitchman, Marcia, *Registrar*, American Craft Council, American Craft Museum, New York NY

Veith, Gene Edward, *Dean*, Concordia University, Division of Arts & Sciences, Mequon WI (S)

Vejvoda, Barbara, *Dir Public Relations & Develop*, University of Texas at Austin, Archer M Huntington Art Gallery, Austin TX

Velasque, Geraldine, *Prof*, Georgian Court College, Dept of Art, Lakewood NJ (S)

Velazquez, Lina, *Asst Dir*, The Florida Museum of Hispanic & Latin American Art, Miami FL

Velez, Sylvia, *Dir*, University of Puerto Rico, Dept of Fine Arts, Rio Piedras PR (S)

Velsmann, Jerry, *Grad Research Prof*, University of Florida, Dept of Art, Gainesville FL (S)

Vena, Dante, *Chmn Art Educ*, University of Massachusetts Dartmouth, College of Visual & Performing Arts, North Dartmouth MA (S)

Venable, Charles, *Cur Decorative Arts*, Dallas Museum of Art, Dallas TX

Venancio, Doria, *Assoc Dir*, SIAS International Art Society, Sherwood Park AB

Venancio, Horacio, *Assoc Dir*, SIAS International Art Society, Sherwood Park AB

Vendetti, Debra, *Educ Coordr*, William A Farnsworth Library & Art Museum, Rockland ME

Venditto, Robert F, *Pres*, Providence Art Club, Providence RI

Venker, Joseph, *Asst Prof US Art*, Seattle University, Fine Arts Dept, Division of Art, Seattle WA (S)

Venn, Beth, *Assoc Cur Permanent Coll*, Whitney Museum of American Art, New York NY

Venner, Thomas, *Chmn Dept*, Siena Heights College, Studio Angelico-Art Dept, Adrian MI (S)

Vensel, William, *Dept Chmn*, Ohio Dominican College, Art Dept, Columbus OH (S)

Ventimiglia, John T, *Instr*, Maine College of Art, Portland ME (S)

Vera, Maria Garcia, *Auxiliary Prof*, Inter American University of Puerto Rico, Dept of Art, San German PR (S)

Verbrugghen, Johanna M, *Cur*, North Country Museum of Arts, Park Rapids MN

Verderame, Lori, *Gallery Dir*, Muhlenberg College Center for the Arts, Frank Martin Gallery, Allentown PA

Verderame, Lori, *Dir*, Muhlenberg College, Dept of Art, Allentown PA (S)

Verdon, Ron, *Head Dept*, University of Wisconsin-Stout, Dept of Art & Design, Menomonie WI (S)

Ver Hague, James, *Prof*, Rochester Institute of Technology, School of Art & Design, Rochester NY (S)

Verkerk, Dorothy, *Asst Prof*, University of North Carolina at Chapel Hill, Art Dept, Chapel Hill NC (S)

Vermillion, Emily J G, *Cur Educ*, University of Iowa, Museum of Art, Iowa City IA

Vernon, Ann D, *Dir Educ*, Chrysler Museum Of Art, Norfolk VA

Vernon, Betty, *Art Dir*, Hill Country Arts Foundation, Duncan-McAshan Visual Arts Center, Ingram TX

Vernon, Carol, *Prof*, Southwestern Oregon Community College, Visual Arts Dept, Coos Bay OR (S)

Vernon, Marlene, *Prog Dir*, University of Minnesota, Paul Whitney Larson Gallery, Saint Paul MN

Verre, Philip, *Dir*, The Hudson River Museum of Westchester, Yonkers NY

Verschoor, Lynn, *Cur Exhibits*, Loveland Museum Gallery, Loveland CO

Verstegen, Mark, *Technical Servs Supvr*, Madison Art Center, Madison WI

Vervoort, Patricia, *Chmn*, Lakehead University, Dept of Visual Arts, Thunder Bay ON (S)

Vetroco, Marcia E, *Prof*, University of New Orleans-Lake Front, Dept of Fine Arts, New Orleans LA (S)

Viator, Camilla, *Public Relations*, Art Museum of Southeast Texas, Beaumont TX

Vicens, Nury, *Instr*, Main Line Art Center, Haverford PA (S)

Vick, Elizabeth, *Prof*, Chowan College, Division of Art, Murfreesboro NC (S)

Victor, James, *Lectr*, Rosemont College, Division of the Arts, Rosemont PA (S)

Victoria, Anthony, *Pres*, National Antique & Art Dealers Association of America, Inc, New York NY

Victoria, Karin, *Dir Government Relations*, The Art Institute of Chicago, Chicago IL

Vidal, Mary, *Prof*, Princeton University, Dept of Art & Archaeology, Princeton NJ (S)

Vidali, Carole, *Music Librn*, Syracuse University, Library, Syracuse NY

Vidler, Anthony, *Dean College*, Cornell University, Dept of Art, Ithaca NY (S)

Vidnovic, Nick, *Lectr*, University of Pennsylvania, Graduate School of Fine Arts, Philadelphia PA (S)

Vienneau, Larry, *Asst Prof*, University of Alaska-Fairbanks, Dept of Art, Fairbanks AK (S)

Viens, Crystal, *Gift Shop Mgr*, Ward Foundation, Ward Museum of Wildfowl Art, Salisbury MD

Viens, Katheryn P, *Dir*, Old Colony Historical Society, Museum, Taunton MA

Viens, Katheryn P, *Dir*, Old Colony Historical Society, Library, Taunton MA

Viera, Ricardo, *Dir Exhib & Coll*, Lehigh University Art Galleries, Bethlehem PA

Viera, Ricardo, *Prof*, Lehigh University, Dept of Art & Architecture, Bethlehem PA (S)

Vierich, Richard, *Art Selector*, University of California, Tomas Rivera Library, Riverside CA

Vigiletti, Christine, *Asst Registrar*, Los Angeles County Museum of Art, Robert Gore Rifkind Center for German Expressionist Studies, Los Angeles CA

Viguers, Aurelia, *Instr*, Main Line Art Center, Haverford PA (S)

Viirlaid, Helle, *Exhib Coll*, Vancouver Art Gallery, Vancouver BC

Vikan, Gary, *Dir*, Walters Art Gallery, Baltimore MD

Vilella, Maria Angela Lopez, *Sub Dir*, Museo de la Americas, Old San Juan PR

Viles, Perry, *Exec Dir*, Saint Johnsbury Athenaeum, Saint Johnsbury VT

Villa, Elizabeth, *Curatorial Asst*, Galleries of the Claremont Colleges, Claremont CA

Villaneuve, Patricia, *Asst Prof*, University of Kansas, Dept of Art & Music Education & Music Therapy, Lawrence KS (S)

Villanueva, Lilia, *Deputy Dir*, Mexican Museum, San Francisco CA

Villeneuve, Rene, *Asst Cur Early Canadian Art*, National Gallery of Canada, Ottawa ON

Villenueve, Pat, *Cur Educ*, University of Kansas, Spencer Museum of Art, Lawrence KS

Vinc, Marty, *Educ Chmn*, Huntsville Art League, Huntsville AL

Vincent, Gilbert T, *VPres & Dir Museums*, New York State Historical Association, Farmers' Museum, Inc, Cooperstown NY

Vincent, Ruth, *Coll Cur*, Wing Luke Asian Museum, Seattle WA

Vincent, Ruth, *Cur Coll*, Wing Luke Asian Museum, Library, Seattle WA

Vine, Naomi, *Dir*, Orange County Museum of Art, Newport Harbor Art Museum, Newport Beach CA

Vink, Carol, *Treas*, National Watercolor Society, Downey CA

Vinograd, Richard, *Chmn Dept Art*, Stanford University, Dept of Art, Stanford CA (S)

Virkau, Vytas O, *Prof Emeritus*, North Central College, Dept of Art, Naperville IL (S)

Viscardi, Anthony, *Asst Prof*, Lehigh University, Dept of Art & Architecture, Bethlehem PA (S)

VisGirda, Rimas, *Instr*, Illinois Wesleyan University, School of Art, Bloomington IL (S)

Viskupic, Gary, *Asst Prof*, New York Institute of Technology, Fine Arts Dept, Old Westbury NY (S)

Visomirskyte, Loreta, *Exec Dir*, Balzekas Museum of Lithuanian Culture, Chicago IL

Vissat, Maureen, *Chmn*, Seton Hill College, Dept of Art, Greensburg PA (S)

Visser, Mary, *Assoc Prof*, Southwestern University, Art Dept, Georgetown TX (S)

Visser, Susan R, *Exec Dir*, South Bend Regional Museum of Art, South Bend IN

Visser, Susan R, *Exec Dir*, South Bend Regional Museum of Art, Library, South Bend IN

Vitale, Thomas Jewell, *Assoc Prof*, Loras College, Dept of Art, Dubuque IA (S)

Vito, Kimberly, *Asst Prof*, Wright State University, Dept of Art & Art History, Dayton OH (S)

Vitzhum, Sandra, *Assoc Prof*, Norwich University, Dept of Philosophy, Religion & Fine Arts, Northfield VT (S)

Vivoni, Paul, *Assoc Prof*, Inter American University of Puerto Rico, Dept of Art, San German PR (S)

Vlack, Donald, *Head & Chief Designer*, The New York Public Library, Shelby Cullom Davis Museum, New York NY

Voce, Yolanda, *Second VPres*, San Bernardino Art Association, Inc, San Bernardino CA

Voci, Peter, *Chmn & Assoc Prof*, New York Institute of Technology, Fine Arts Dept, Old Westbury NY (S)

Voelkle, William M, *Cur Medieval & Renaissance Manuscripts*, Pierpont Morgan Library, New York NY

Voellinger, David, *Dir Develop*, Lehigh County Historical Society, Allentown PA

Vogel, Alan, *Assoc Prof*, Rochester Institute of Technology, School of Photographic Arts & Sciences, Rochester NY (S)

Vogel, Belinda, *Dir Develop*, Plains Art Museum, Fargo ND

Vogel, Craig, *Pres*, Industrial Designers Society of America, Great Falls VA

Vogel, Craig, *Assoc Dean*, Carnegie Mellon University, College of Fine Arts, Pittsburgh PA (S)

Vogel, Scott, *Electronic Arts Chmn (Video)*, Atlanta College of Art, Atlanta GA (S)

Vogel, Stephan P, *Dean*, University of Detroit Mercy, School of Architecture, Detroit MI (S)

Vogel, Susan M, *Dir*, Yale University, Art Gallery, New Haven CT

Vogel, Theodore, *Asst Prof*, Lewis & Clark College, Dept of Art, Portland OR (S)

Vogelsong, Diana, *Asst University Librn*, American University, Jack I Dorothy G Bender Library, Washington DC

Vogt, Allie, *Dept Chmn*, North Idaho College, Art Dept, Coeur D'Alene ID (S)

Vogt, David, *Project Supv*, Public Art Prog, City of Atlanta, Bureau of Cultural Affairs, Atlanta GA

Vogt, George, *Dir*, State Historical Society of Wisconsin, State Historical Museum, Madison WI

Vogt, John, *Emeritus Assoc Prof*, Kansas State University, Art Dept, Manhattan KS (S)

Vogt, Margaret, *Registrar*, Massillon Museum, Massillon OH

Voigt, Robert, *Instr*, College of Mount Saint Joseph, Art Dept, Cincinnati OH (S)

Voinot, Andrea, *Gallery Coordr*, San Francisco Museum of Modern Art, Rental Gallery, San Francisco CA

Voit, Irene, *Bus Serv*, Las Vegas-Clark County Library District, Las Vegas NV

Volinar, Michael, *Cur*, Fruitlands Museum, Inc, Harvard MA

Volk, Joyce, *Cur*, Warner House Association, MacPheadris-Warner House, Portsmouth NH

Volk, Ulla, *Art & Architecture*, Cooper Union for the Advancement of Science & Art, Library, New York NY

Volkersz, Willem, *Dir Art*, Montana State University, School of Art, Bozeman MT (S)

Volkert, James, *Deputy Asst Dir Exhib*, National Museum of the American Indian, George Gustav Heye Center, New York NY

Vollmer, Stephen, *Chief Cur*, El Paso Museum of Art, El Paso TX

Vollmer, Stephen, *Cur*, El Paso Museum of Art, Library, El Paso TX

Vollrath, Gail, *Gallery Asst*, East Tennessee State University, Elizabeth Slocumb Galleries, Johnson City TN

Volpacchio, John, *Prof*, Salem State College, Art Dept, Salem MA (S)

Volz, Robert L, *Head Librn*, Williams College, Chapin Library, Williamstown MA

Vom Baur, Daphne, *Secy*, Tradd Street Press, Elizabeth O'Neill Verner Studio Museum, Charleston SC

Von Barghahn, Barbara, *Assoc Prof*, George Washington University, Dept of Art, Washington DC (S)

Von Bloomberg, Randell, *Gallery Dir*, New World School of the Arts, Gallery, Miami FL

Vonderscheer, Christel, *Pub Serv*, Trinity College Library, Washington DC

Vonkeman, Anine, *Pub Prog Cur*, Southern Alberta Art Gallery, Lethbridge AB

Von Sonnenberg, Hubert, *Conservator Paintings*, The Metropolitan Museum of Art, New York NY

VonVoetcsch, Kurt, *Gallery Mgr*, Niagara University, Castellani Art Museum, Niagara NY

Vookles, Laura, *Cur*, The Hudson River Museum of Westchester, Yonkers NY

Voorheis, Peter, *Folklorist*, Arts of the Southern Finger Lakes, Corning NY

Vosberg, Julie, *Team Adminr*, National Society of Tole & Decorative Painters, Inc, Wichita KS

Voss, Cathy, *In Charge Art Coll*, Banc One Wisconsin Corp, Milwaukee WI

Voss, Jerrold, *Dir*, Ohio State University, School of Architecture, Columbus OH (S)

Voth, Andrew, *Dir*, Carnegie Art Museum, Oxnard CA

Voutselas, Eleanore, *Archivist*, Museum of New Mexico, Library, Santa Fe NM

Vroom, Steven Michael, *Gallery Dir*, University of the South, University Gallery, Sewanee TN

Vruwink, J, *Chmn*, Central University of Iowa, Art Dept, Pella IA (S)

Waale, Kim, *Asst Prof*, Cazenovia College, Center for Art & Design Studies, Cazenovia NY (S)

Wabnitz, Robert, *Prof*, Rochester Institute of Technology, School of Art & Design, Rochester NY (S)

Wachna, Pamela, *Cur*, The Market Gallery of the City of Toronto Archives, Toronto ON

Wachs, Diane C, *Dir*, Headley-Whitney Museum, Lexington KY

Wachs, Diane C, *Dir*, Headley-Whitney Museum, Library, Lexington KY

Wachsberger, Fredrica, *Pres*, Oysterponds Historical Society, Museum, Orient NY

Wada, W, *Prof Painting*, Ramapo College of New Jersey, School of Contemporary Arts, Mahwah NJ (S)

Waddell, Roberta, *Cur Prints*, The New York Public Library, Print Room, New York NY

Waddington, Murray, *Chief Librn*, National Gallery of Canada, Library, Ottawa ON

Waddington, Susan R, *Coordr*, Providence Public Library, Art & Music Services, Providence RI

Waddy, Patricia, *Pres*, Society of Architectural Historians, Chicago IL

Wade, Barbara, *Acting Dir Human Resources*, Royal Ontario Museum, Toronto ON

Wade, Edward M, *Chmn*, Potomac State College, Dept of Art, Keyser WV (S)

Wade, Edwin L, *Deputy Dir*, Museum of Northern Arizona, Flagstaff AZ

Wade, J Blake, *Exec Dir*, Oklahoma Historical Society, State Museum of History, Oklahoma City OK

Wade, Jeptha H, *VPres*, Historic Deerfield, Inc, Deerfield MA

Wade, Karen Graham, *Dir*, Workman & Temple Family Homestead Museum, City of Industry CA

Wade, Nichlos, *Asst Prof*, University of Lethbridge, Div of Art, Lethbridge AB (S)

Wadhams, Hazel, *Cur*, Goshen Historical Society, Goshen CT

Wadley, William, *Head*, East Texas State University, Dept of Art, Commerce TX (S)

Wadlow, Dick, *Treas*, Fairbanks Arts Association, Fairbanks AK

Wadsworth, David, *Sr Cur*, Cohasset Historical Society, Caleb Lothrop House, Cohasset MA

Wadsworth, David H, *Cur*, Cohasset Historical Society, Captain John Wilson Historical House, Cohasset MA

Waelder, Kristine, *Develop Officer*, Everson Museum of Art, Syracuse NY

Wageman, Virginia, *Publications Dir*, College Art Association, New York NY

Wagener, Thomas, *Dir*, University of Wisconsin-Eau Claire, Foster Gallery, Eau Claire WI

Wager, Heather, *Cur*, Louisa May Alcott Memorial Association, Orchard House, Concord MA

Wager, Richard, *Cur*, Galeria Mesa, Mesa Arts Center, Mesa AZ

Wagers, Kathy, *Coordr*, Wenatchee Valley College, Gallery 76, Wenatchee WA

Wagman, N E, *Prof*, Salem State College, Art Dept, Salem MA (S)

Wagner, Betty L, *Librn*, University of Washington, Architecture & Urban Planning Library, Seattle WA

Wagner, Catherine, *Asst Prof*, Mills College, Art Dept, Oakland CA (S)

Wagner, Dee, *Registrar*, Brookfield Craft Center, Inc, Video Library, Brookfield CT

Wagner, Katherine, *Exec Dir*, Dallas Visual Art Center, Dallas TX

Wagner, Lois, *Cur*, Sterling Portfolio Inc, New York NY

Wagner, Norman, *Printmaking Chmn*, Atlanta College of Art, Atlanta GA (S)

Wagner, Patty, *Museum Educ*, McLean County Historical Society, Bloomington IL

Wagner, Sam, *Dir*, Jamestown-Yorktown Foundation, Williamsburg VA

Wagner, Sue, *Bookkeeper*, Historical Society of Palm Beach County, West Palm Beach FL

Wagner, Teri, *Asst Prof*, Cardinal Stritch College, Art Dept, Milwaukee WI (S)

Wagner, Wesley, *Asst Prof*, Bethany College, Dept of Fine Arts, Bethany WV (S)

Wagner, William, *Assoc Prof*, Old Dominion University, Art Dept, Norfolk VA (S)

Wagoner, Phillip, *Adjunct Assoc Prof*, Wesleyan University, Art Dept, Middletown CT (S)

Wah, Diane, *Develop Dir*, Wing Luke Asian Museum, Seattle WA

Wahlin, Connie, *Cur*, Wells Fargo, Phoenix AZ

Wahnee, B J, *Instr*, Haskell Indian Nations University, Art Dept, Lawrence KS (S)

Waidelich, Elaine, *National Pres*, National League of American Pen Women, Washington DC

Wailes, Bernard, *European Section Assoc Cur*, University of Pennsylvania, Museum of Archaeology & Anthropology, Philadelphia PA

Wainstein Bond, Anne, *Cur Material Culture*, Colorado Historical Society, Colorado History Museum, Denver CO

Wainwright, Lisa, *Undergrad Div Chmn*, School of the Art Institute of Chicago, Chicago IL (S)

Wainwright, Paige, *Asst Dir*, Sloss Furnaces National Historic Landmark, Birmingham AL

Waits, Roy, *Instr*, ACA College of Design, Cincinnati OH (S)

Wakayama, Gloria, *Co-Pres*, Wing Luke Asian Museum, Seattle WA

Wakeford, Elizabeth, *Cur Asst*, Dundurn Castle, Hamilton ON

Wakeford, Mary, *Registrar*, Hofstra University, Hofstra Museum, Hempstead NY

Walch, Margaret, *Assoc Dir*, Color Association of The US, New York NY

Walch, Peter, *Dir*, University of New Mexico, University Art Museum, Albuquerque NM

Walch, Timoth, *Library Dir*, Herbert Hoover Presidential Library & Museum, West Branch IA

Waldeck, Cheryl, *Dir Communictions*, Philbrook Museum of Art, Tulsa OK

Walden, Jerry, *Chmn*, Winthrop University, Dept of Art & Design, Rock Hill SC (S)

Waldman, Arthur, *Prof*, Ocean County College, Humanities Dept, Toms River NJ (S)

Waldman, Caroline, *Librn*, Waterville Historical Society, Redington Museum, Waterville ME

Waldman, Diane, *Deputy Dir & Sr Cur*, Guggenheim Museum Soho, New York NY

Waldner, Wolfgang, *Dir*, Austrian Cultural Institute Gallery, New York NY

Waldon, Tricia, *Admin Secy*, City of Hampton, Hampton Arts Commission, Hampton VA

Waldron, Peter, *Chmn*, Bradford College, Creative Arts Division, Bradford MA (S)

Waldstead, Elissa, *Develop Asst*, Bellevue Art Museum, Bellevue WA

Wale, George, *Dir Programs*, Burlington Art Centre, Burlington ON

Waler, Richard, *Treas*, Saint Augustine Art Association Gallery, Saint Augustine FL

Walford, E John, *Chmn*, Wheaton College, Dept of Art, Wheaton IL (S)

Walhgren, Kay, *VPres Exhibits*, DuPage Art League School & Gallery, Wheaton IL

Walk, Deborah, *Archivist*, State Art Museum of Florida, Ringling Museum Library, Sarasota FL

Walker, Barry, *Cur Prints & Drawings*, Museum of Fine Arts, Houston, Houston TX

Walker, Caroline, *Educ & Communications Officer,* Beaverbrook Art Gallery, Fredericton NB

Walker, Celia, *Cur Coll,* Cheekwood Nashville's Home of Art & Gardens, Education Dept, Nashville TN (S)

Walker, Celia, *Cur Coll & Exhib,* Cheekwood-Tennessee Botanical Gardens & Museum of Art, Nashville TN (S)

Walker, Charles, *Instr,* De Anza College, Creative Arts Division, Cupertino CA (S)

Walker, Daniel, *Cur Islamic Art,* The Metropolitan Museum of Art, New York NY

Walker, Denise, *Adminr Dir,* Visual Arts Center of Northwest Florida, Panama City FL

Walker, Earl, *Chmn,* George Brown College of Applied Arts & Technology, Dept of Visual Arts, Toronto ON (S)

Walker, J Charles, *Div Coordr Design,* Kent State University, School of Art, Kent OH (S)

Walker, Jeffry, *Dir,* Trinity College, Austin Arts Center, Hartford CT

Walker, Joshua, *Reference & Spec Coll,* Fashion Institute of Technology, Gladys Marcus Library, New York NY

Walker, Kathy Y, *Instr,* Pennsylvania College of Technology, Dept of Graphic Communications, Williamsport PA (S)

Walker, Lisa, *Project Coordr, Public Art Prog,* City of Atlanta, Bureau of Cultural Affairs, Atlanta GA

Walker, Mort, *Chmn,* International Museum of Cartoon Art, Boca Raton FL

Walker, Patricia, *Asst Prof,* Georgia Southern University, Dept of Art, Statesboro GA (S)

Walker, Robbie, *Dean School Liberal Arts,* Auburn University at Montgomery, Dept of Fine Arts, Montgomery AL (S)

Walker, Robert, *Instr,* College of the Canyons, Art Dept, Valencia CA (S)

Walker, Rosemary, *Dir,* Wentworth Institute of Technology Library, Boston MA

Walker, Sam, *Asst Prof,* University of Massachusetts - Boston, Art Dept, Boston MA (S)

Walker, Sarah, *Dir,* Clark University, The University Gallery at Goddard Library, Worcester MA

Walker, Susan, *Dir,* Florida Folklife Programs, Tallahassee FL

Walker, William B, *Chief Librn,* The Metropolitan Museum of Art, New York NY

Walker-Millar, Kathy, *Dept Chmn & Gallery Dir,* McMurry University, Ryan Fine Arts Center, Abilene TX

Walker-Millar, Kathy, *Head Dept,* McMurry University, Art Dept, Abilene TX (S)

Walking Stick, Kay, *Asst Prof,* Cornell University, Dept of Art, Ithaca NY (S)

Wall, Brent, *Assoc Prof,* Saint Xavier University, Dept of Art, Chicago IL (S)

Wall, F L, *Chmn Sculpture,* Corcoran School of Art, Washington DC (S)

Wall, Jeff, *Prof,* University of British Columbia, Dept of Fine Arts, Vancouver BC (S)

Wallace, Alan, *Asst Prof,* Chattanooga State Technical Community College, Advertising Arts Dept, Chattanooga TN (S)

Wallace, Bob, *Dir,* Dawson County Historical Society, Museum, Lexington NE

Wallace, Bruce, *Assoc Prof,* University of Tennessee at Chattanooga, Dept of Art, Chattanooga TN (S)

Wallace, Glenna, *Div Chmn,* Crowder College, Art & Design, Neosho MO (S)

Wallace, James, *Chmn,* Muskingum College, Art Department, New Concord OH (S)

Wallace, Keith, *Dir & Cur,* Contemporary Art Gallery Society of British Columbia, Vancouver BC

Wallace, Keith, *Dir & Cur,* Contemporary Art Gallery Society of British Columbia, Art Library Service, Vancouver BC

Wallace, Lyn Brands, *Assoc Prof,* University of Central Arkansas, Art Dept, Conway AR (S)

Wallace, Richard W, *Prof,* Wellesley College, Art Dept, Wellesley MA (S)

Wallace, Scott, *Asst Prof,* South Dakota State University, Dept of Visual Arts, Brookings SD (S)

Wallace, Sheila, *Library Dir,* Emily Carr Institute of Art & Design, Library, Vancouver BC

Wallace, Wendy, *Admin,* Virginia Commonwealth University, Anderson Gallery, Richmond VA

Wallach, Alan, *Prof,* College of William & Mary, Dept of Fine Arts, Williamsburg VA (S)

Waller, Bret, *Dir,* Indianapolis Museum of Art, Indianapolis IN

Waller, Richard, *Dir,* University of Richmond, Marsh Art Gallery, Richmond VA

Walling, Cathleen, *Assoc Dir Develop & Admin,* University of California, California Museum of Photography, Riverside CA

Wallis, Mel R, *Instr,* Olympic College, Social Sciences & Humanities Division, Bremerton WA (S)

Wall MLS, Kay L, *Dir,* University of Southern Mississippi, McCain Library & Archives, Hattiesburg MS

Wallot, Jean-Pierre, *National Archivist,* National Archives of Canada, Visual & Sound Archives, Ottawa ON

Walpuck, Kenneth, *Prof,* Queensborough Community College, Dept of Art & Photography, Bayside NY (S)

Walsbrot, Ann, *Dir,* New Visions Gallery, Inc, Marshfield WI

Walsh, James J, *Chmn Trustees,* Everhart Museum, Scranton PA

Walsh, John, *Dir,* Getty Center for the History of Art & the Humanities Trust Museum, The J Paul Getty Museum, Santa Monica CA

Walsh, Karen, *Public Programming Asst,* Newfoundland Museum, Library, Saint John's NF

Walsh, Marguerite, *Assoc Prof,* New England College, Art & Art History, Henniker NH (S)

Walsh, Mary Ellen, *Art,* Nabisco, Inc, East Hanover NJ

Walsh, Paul, *Pres & Chief Exec Officer,* The Pillsbury Company, Art Collection, Minneapolis MN

Walsh, Peter, *Dir Information,* Wellesley College, Davis Museum & Cultural Center, Wellesley MA

Walsh, Thomas, *Sculpture Area Head,* Southern Illinois University, School of Art & Design, Carbondale IL (S)

Walsh, Timothy F, *Head Dept,* Otero Junior College, Dept of Arts, La Junta CO (S)

Walter, Charles Thomas, *Asst Prof,* Bloomsburg University, Dept of Art, Bloomsburg PA (S)

Walter, Elizabeth M, *Prof,* University of North Alabama, Dept of Art, Florence AL (S)

Walter, Loyola, *Asst Prof,* College of Mount Saint Joseph, Art Dept, Cincinnati OH (S)

Walters, Bruce, *Assoc Prof,* Teikyo Marycrest University, Art & Computer Graphics Dept, Davenport IA (S)

Walters, Daniel, *Dir,* Spokane Public Library Gallery, Spokane WA

Walters, Daniel L, *Dir,* Buffalo & Erie County Public Library, Buffalo NY

Walters, Elizabeth J, *Assoc Prof,* Pennsylvania State University, University Park, Dept of Art History, University Park PA (S)

Walters, Holly, *Finance,* Texas A&M University, Visual Arts Committee, College Station TX

Walters, Janet, *Cur,* Lethbridge Public Library, Art Gallery, Lethbridge AB

Walters, Kim, *Librn & Dir,* Southwest Museum, Braun Research Library, Los Angeles CA

Walters, Suzanne G, *Pub Relations & Mem Coordr,* Flint Institute of Arts, Flint MI

Walters, Sylvia, *Chmn,* San Francisco State University, Art Dept, San Francisco CA (S)

Walton, Dan, *Dir Operations,* San Antonio Museum of Art, San Antonio TX

Walton, John, *Dir,* Palo Alto Junior Museum & Zoo, Palo Alto CA

Walton, Thomas, *Assoc Prof,* Catholic University of America, School of Architecture & Planning, Washington DC (S)

Waltz, Connie, *Chmn Dept,* Linfield College, Art Dept, McMinnville OR (S)

Walworth, Roger, *Chmn,* Judson College, Division of Fine Arts, Marion AL (S)

Wampler, Jackie, *Registrar,* James A Michener Art Museum, Doylestown PA

Wan, Betty, *Educ Coordr,* Pacific - Asia Museum, Pasadena CA

Wand, Patricia A, *University Librn,* American University, Jack I Dorothy G Bender Library, Washington DC

Wands, Robert, *Asst Prof,* University of Southern Colorado, Belmont Campus, Dept of Art, Pueblo CO (S)

Wang, Rui, *Graduate Cur,* University of Illinois, Museum of Natural History, Champaign IL

Wanserski, Martin, *Assoc Prof,* University of South Dakota, Department of Art, College of Fine Arts, Vermillion SD (S)

Wantuchowicz, Carri Ann, *Information Asst,* Fort Worth Art Association, Modern Art Museum of Fort Worth, Fort Worth TX

Wantz, John A, *Prof,* College of DuPage, Humanities Division, Glen Ellyn IL (S)

Wanzel, Grant, *Interim Dean,* Technical University of Nova Scotia, Faculty of Architecture, Halifax NS (S)

Ward, Alberta, *Dir,* City of Atlanta, Southeast Arts Center, Atlanta GA

Ward, Harry, *Chmn,* University of Southern Mississippi, Dept of Art, Hattiesburg MS (S)

Ward, Jan R, *Prof,* Del Mar College, Art Dept, Corpus Christi TX (S)

Ward, John L, *Prof,* University of Florida, Dept of Art, Gainesville FL (S)

Ward, Karen, *Chmn,* Hampton University, Dept of Fine & Performing Arts, Hampton VA (S)

Ward, Linda, *Instr,* Northeast Louisiana University, Dept of Art, Monroe LA (S)

Ward, Lynn, *Archivist,* Liberty Memorial Museum & Archives, Kansas City MO

Ward, Marna, *Asst Dir,* Lauren Rogers Museum of Art, Laurel MS

Ward, Nora, *Museum Asst,* Spanish Governor's Palace, San Antonio TX

Ward, Peter, *Cur Invertebrate Paleontology,* University of Washington, Thomas Burke Memorial Washington State Museum, Seattle WA

Ward, R D, *Prof,* Randolph-Macon College, Dept of the Arts, Ashland VA (S)

Ward, Robert, *Prof,* Bridgewater State College, Art Dept, Bridgewater MA (S)

Ward, Robert, *Instr,* Northeast Louisiana University, Dept of Art, Monroe LA (S)

Ward, Robert, *Coordr Gallery Dir,* Bowie State University, Fine Arts Dept, Bowie MD (S)

Ward, Roger, *Lectr,* University of Kansas, Kress Foundation Dept of Art History, Lawrence KS (S)

Ward, Roger B, *Cur European Painting & Sculpture,* Nelson-Atkins Museum of Art, Kansas City MO

Ward, Sandra, *Asst,* University of Nevada, Sheppard Fine Art Gallery, Reno NV

Ward, Sandra, *Asst Dir,* Peters Valley Craft Center, Layton NJ

Ward, Scott, *Dir,* Downey Museum of Art, Downey CA

Ward, Wes, *Pres Board Trustees,* Museum of Northern Arizona, Flagstaff AZ

Ward, William, *Educator,* Independence Seaport Museum, Philadelphia PA

Warda, Rebecca, *Asst to Dir,* Widener University, Art Museum, Chester PA

Wardlaw, Alvia, *Asst Prof,* Texas Southern University, Dept of Fine Arts, Houston TX (S)

Wardle, Alfred, *Instr,* Munson-Williams-Proctor Institute, School of Art, Utica NY (S)

Wardropper, Ian, *Cur European Decorative Arts, Sculpture & Classical Art,* The Art Institute of Chicago, Chicago IL

Wardwell, Anne E, *Cur Textiles,* Cleveland Museum of Art, Cleveland OH

Ware, Mike, *Instr,* Alice Lloyd College, Art Dept, Pippa Passes KY (S)

Warehall, William D, *Chmn Dept,* California State University, San Bernardino, Visual Arts, San Bernardino CA (S)

Warger, Julia M, *Interpretive Programs Asst,* New York State Office of Parks Recreation & Historic Preservation, John Jay Homestead State Historic Site, Katonah NY

Wargo, Richard, *Cur,* Marcella Sembrich Memorial Association Inc, Opera Museum, Bolton Landing NY

Waricher, George, *Asst Prof,* Shippensburg University, Art Dept, Shippensburg PA (S)

Waring, Jeff, *Pres,* High Wire Gallery, Philadelphia PA

Warlick, Mary, *Exec Dir,* The One Club for Art & Copy, New York NY

Warma, Susanne, *Assoc Prof,* Utah State University, Dept of Art, Logan UT (S)

Warner, Amy, *Dir,* Thomas College Art Gallery, Waterville ME

Warner, Deborah, *Chmn Textile Design,* Moore College of Art & Design, Philadelphia PA (S)

Warner, Dona, *Dir,* Johnson Atelier Technical Institute of Sculpture, Mercerville NJ (S)

Warner, Donna, *Admin Asst,* College of Wooster, Dept of Art, Wooster OH (S)

Warner, JoAnne, *Cur Wallcoverings,* Cooper-Hewitt, National Design Museum, New York NY

Warner, Lee, *Dir,* Tulane University, Gallier House Museum, New Orleans LA

Warnock, Doug, *Faculty,* Idaho State University, Dept of Art, Pocatello ID (S)

Warp, Harold, *Pres,* Harold Warp Pioneer Village Foundation, Minden NE

Warren, David, *Assoc Dir & Sr Cur,* Museum of Fine Arts, Houston, Houston TX

Warren, Katherine V, *Dir,* University of California, University Art Gallery, Riverside CA

Warren, Lynne, *Cur Spec Projects,* Museum of Contemporary Art, Chicago IL

Warren, Marylynn, *VPres Develop,* The Huntington Library, Art Collections & Botanical Gardens, San Marino CA

Warren, Patricia, *Development Dir,* City Art Works, Pratt Fine Arts Center, Seattle WA (S)

Warren, Patricia, *Develop Dir,* Pratt Fine Arts Center, Gallery, Seattle WA

Warren, Penny, *Exec Dir,* Staunton Fine Arts Association, Staunton Augusta Art Center, Staunton VA

Warren, Russell, *Prof,* Davidson College, Art Dept, Davidson NC (S)

Warren, Sandra, *Business Mgr,* Indiana University, William Hammond Mathers Museum, Bloomington IN

Warren, William B, *Pres,* Grolier Club Library, New York NY

Warren, Yolanda, *Art Librn,* Washington & Lee University, Leyburn Library, Lexington VA

Warrens, Robert, *Prof,* Louisiana State University, School of Art, Baton Rouge LA (S)

Warstler, Pasgua, *Gallery Dir,* William Bonifas Fine Art Center Gallery, Alice Powers Art Gallery, Escanaba MI

Warther, David, *Pres,* Warther Museum Inc, Dover OH

Warther, Mark, *General Mgr,* Warther Museum Inc, Dover OH

Wartluft, David J, *Dir Library,* Lutheran Theological Seminary, Krauth Memorial Library, Philadelphia PA

Washingon, John, *Instr,* Lansing Community College, Art Program, Lansing MI (S)

Washmon, Gary, *Dir,* Texas Woman's University Art Gallery, Denton TX

Washmon, Gary, *Assoc Prof,* Texas Woman's University, Dept of Visual Arts, Denton TX (S)

Wasko, Carla, *Dir Coll,* Antonelli Institute of Art & Photography, Cincinnati OH (S)

Wass, Janice, *Cur Decorative Arts,* Illinois State Museum, Illinois Art Gallery & Lockport Gallery, Springfield IL

Wasserman, Krystyna, *Head Librn,* National Museum of Women in the Arts, Library & Research Center, Washington DC

Wasserman, Nadine, *Cur,* Lawrence University, Wriston Art Center Galleries, Appleton WI

Wassermann, Mary, *Slide Librn,* Philadelphia Museum of Art, Library, Philadelphia PA

Wassermann, Mary, *Slide Librn,* Philadelphia Museum of Art, Slide Library, Philadelphia PA

Watanabe, Joan, *Prof,* Glendale Community College, Visual & Performing Arts Division, Glendale CA (S)

Watcke, Tom, *Chmn,* Albright College, Dept of Art, Reading PA (S)

Waterfall, Julia, *Develop Officer,* City Gallery of Contemporary Art, Raleigh NC

Waters, Colette, *Exec Asst & Cur Educ,* City Gallery of Contemporary Art, Raleigh NC

Waters, Guy, *VPres,* Safety Harbor Museum of Regional History, Safety Harbor FL

Waters, Laura, *Lectr,* Muskingum College, Art Department, New Concord OH (S)

Waters, Moya, *Mgr Admin,* University of British Columbia, Museum of Anthropology, Vancouver BC

Waters, Sara, *Prof,* Texas Tech University, Dept of Art, Lubbock TX (S)

Watkin, Mel, *Cur,* Forum for Contemporary Art, Saint Louis MO

Watkins, Dianne, *Cur Educ,* Western Kentucky University, Kentucky Museum, Bowling Green KY

Watkins, Gladys, *Chmn,* Northern Virginia Community College, Art Dept, Annandale VA (S)

Watkins, Karin, *Asst Comptroller,* Sterling & Francine Clark Art Institute, Williamstown MA

Watkinson, Barbara, *Chmn,* College of William & Mary, Dept of Fine Arts, Williamsburg VA (S)

Watkinson, Patricia, *Dir,* Washington State University, Museum of Art, Pullman WA

Watkinson, Sharon, *Chmn,* Niagara University, Fine Arts Dept, Niagara Falls NY (S)

Watrous, Rebecca, *Educ Dir,* Historic Cherry Hill, Albany NY

Watsky, Andrew, *Asst Prof,* Vassar College, Art Dept, Poughkeepsie NY (S)

Watson, Ann, *In Charge,* Denison University, Art Dept Slide Library, Granville OH

Watson, Barbara, *Vol Librn,* William A Farnsworth Library & Art Museum, Library, Rockland ME

Watson, Donna, *Adjunct Prof,* Oklahoma Christian University of Science & Arts, Dept of Art & Design, Oklahoma City OK (S)

Watson, Joseph A, *Assoc Prof,* Rochester Institute of Technology, School of Art & Design, Rochester NY (S)

Watson, Katharine J, *Dir,* Bowdoin College, Museum of Art, Brunswick ME

Watson, Pam, *Registrar,* Detroit Institute of Arts, Detroit MI

Watson, Richard, *Exhib Dir,* Afro-American Historical & Cultural Museum, Philadelphia PA

Watson, Robert, *Dir,* Florida Atlantic University, Ritter Art Gallery, Boca Raton FL

Watson, Robyn S, *Dir,* Provincetown Art Association & Museum, Provincetown MA

Watson, Robyn S, *Dir,* Provincetown Art Association & Museum, Library, Provincetown MA

Watson, Ronald, *Dir,* Texas Christian University, Moudy Exhibition Hall, Fort Worth TX

Watson, Ronald, *Chmn of Art & Art History,* Texas Christian University, Art & Art History Dept, Fort Worth TX (S)

Watson, Scott, *Dir & Cur,* University of British Columbia, Fine Arts Gallery, Vancouver BC

Watson, Thomas, *Instr,* Columbia College, Art Dept, Columbia MO (S)

Watson, Thomas R, *Pres,* Portsmouth Historical Society, John Paul Jones House, Portsmouth NH

Watson, Wendy, *Cur,* Mount Holyoke College, Art Museum, South Hadley MA

Watson-Sopher, Vickie, *ExecDir,* Hammond-Harwood House Association, Inc, Annapolis MD

Watt, James C Y, *Sr Cur Asian Art,* The Metropolitan Museum of Art, New York NY

Wattenmaker, Richard J, *Dir,* Archives of American Art, Washington DC

Watts, Barbara, *Asst Prof,* Florida International University, Visual Arts Dept, Miami FL (S)

Watts, Christopher, *Chmn,* Washington State University, Fine Arts Dept, Pullman WA (S)

Watts, Delancey, *Admin,* Washington Art Association, Washington Depot CT

Watts, Delancey, *Admin,* Washington Art Association, Library, Washington Depot CT

Watts, Karen, *Prof,* University of Idaho, College of Art & Architecture, Moscow ID (S)

Watts, Michael, *Dir,* Eastern Illinois University, Tarble Arts Center, Charleston IL

Watts, Steve, *Coordr,* University of Charleston, Carleton Varney Dept of Art & Design, Charleston WV (S)

Watts, Tracy, *Asst Prof,* State University of New York College at Potsdam, Dept of Fine Arts, Potsdam NY (S)

Watts McKinney, Sylvia, *Exec Dir,* Museum of Afro-American History, Boston MA

Wauhkonen, Robert, *Chmn Liberal Arts,* Art Institute of Boston, Boston MA (S)

Wayne, Kathryn, *Architectural Librn,* University of California, Environmental Design Library, Berkeley CA

Wayne, Kay W, *Dir,* Glynn Art Association, Saint Simons Island GA

Weatherford, Elizabeth, *Head Film & Video Center,* National Museum of the American Indian, George Gustav Heye Center, New York NY

Weatherley, Glynn, *Lectr,* Lambuth University, Dept of Human Ecology & Visual Arts, Jackson TN (S)

Weatherwax, Sarah, *Cur Prints,* Library Company of Philadelphia, Philadelphia PA

Weaver, A M, *Dir,* Painted Bride Art Center, The Gallery at the Painted Bride, Philadelphia PA

Weaver, Betsy, *Docents,* University of Kansas, Spencer Museum of Art, Lawrence KS

Weaver, Bobby, *Asst Dir,* National Cowboy Hall of Fame & Western Heritage Center Museum, Oklahoma City OK

Weaver, Herb, *Head Dept,* Bethany College, Dept of Fine Arts, Bethany WV (S)

Weaver, James C, *VPres,* Woodmere Art Museum, Philadelphia PA

Weaver, Judy, *Asst Dir,* Montana State University, Museum of the Rockies, Bozeman MT

Weaver, Marie, *Asst Prof,* University of Alabama at Birmingham, Dept of Art, Birmingham AL (S)

Weaver, Tonya, *Asst Dir,* Main Line Art Center, Haverford PA

Weaver, Virginia, *Public Relations Officer,* New Orleans Museum of Art, New Orleans LA

Webb, Debra, *Library Assoc,* University of Notre Dame, Architecture Library, Notre Dame IN

Webb, Dixie, *Slide Librn,* Austin Peay State University, Art Dept Library, Clarksville TN

Webb, Dixie, *Asst Prof,* Austin Peay State University, Dept of Art, Clarksville TN (S)

Webb, Greg, *Instr,* Joe Kubert School of Cartoon & Graphic Art, Inc, Dover NJ (S)

Webb, Hugh, *Dir,* Portland Community College, North View Gallery, Portland OR

Webb, Jennifer, *Prog Coordr & Dir Asst,* University of British Columbia, Museum of Anthropology, Vancouver BC

Webb, Keith, *Public Sales Mgr,* National Gallery of Art, Washington DC

Webb, Robert, *Cur,* Maine Maritime Museum, Bath ME

Webber, Mark, *Instr,* Keystone Junior College, Fine Arts Dept, Factoryville PA (S)

Webber, Nancy E, *Asst Prof,* Los Angeles Harbor College, Art Dept, Wilmington CA (S)

Weber, Jean M, *Exec Dir,* Nantucket Historical Association, Historic Nantucket, Nantucket MA

Weber, John, *Prof,* Elmhurst College, Art Dept, Elmhurst IL (S)

Weber, Joseph A, *Art Educ,* Southern Illinois University at Edwardsville, Dept of Art & Design, Edwardsville IL (S)

Weber, Mark, *Chmn,* Saint Louis Community College at Forest Park, Art Dept, Saint Louis MO (S)

Weber, Mark, *Adjunct Instr,* Maryville University of Saint Louis, Art Division, Saint Louis MO (S)

Weber, Michelle, *Research Asst,* National Museum of Women in the Arts, Library & Research Center, Washington DC

Weber, Robin, *Dir & Cur*, Museum of Northern British Columbia, Ruth Harvey Art Gallery, Prince Rupert BC

Weber, Robin, *Dir & Cur*, Museum of Northern British Columbia, Library, Prince Rupert BC

Weber, Sara, *Public Relations*, Dayton Art Institute, Dayton OH

Weberg, Lorraine, *Reference & Systems*, Fashion Institute of Technology, Gladys Marcus Library, New York NY

Webster, Bryan G, *Cur Natural History Art*, University of Minnesota, James Ford Bell Museum of Natural History, Minneapolis MN

Webster, Jenneth, *Gallery Dir*, Lincoln Center for the Performing Arts, Cork Gallery, New York NY

Webster, Kristine, *Cur*, Craigdarroch Castle Historical Museum Society, Victoria BC

Webster, Lynn, *Dir*, Albertson College of Idaho, Rosenthal Art Gallery, Caldwell ID

Webster, Melissa, *Instr*, Walla Walla Community College, Art Dept, Walla Walla WA (S)

Webster, Paul, *Lectr*, Oakland University, Dept of Art & Art History, Rochester MI (S)

Webster, Sally, *Prof*, City University of New York, PhD Program in Art History, New York NY (S)

Wechsler, Fredrica W, *Dir*, National Academy of Sciences, Arts in the Academy, Washington DC

Wechsler, Jeffrey, *Sr Cur*, Rutgers, The State University of New Jersey, Jane Voorhees Zimmerli Art Museum, New Brunswick NJ

Wechsler, Judith, *Prof*, Tufts University, Dept of Art & Art History, Medford MA (S)

Weckbacher, Vernon, *Cur Colls*, McAllen International Museum, McAllen TX

Weckbacher, Vernon, *Cur Colls*, McAllen International Museum, Library, McAllen TX

Weckbacher, Vernon G, *Exhib Dir*, McAllen International Museum, McAllen TX

Wedding, Joe, *Pres*, Oregon College of Art Craft, Hoffman Gallery, Portland OR

Wedig, Dale, *Prof*, Northern Michigan University, Dept of Art & Design, Marquette MI (S)

Wedin, Winslow, *Prof*, Lynn University, Art & Design Dept, Boca Raton FL (S)

Weed-Brown, Robin, *Head Reference*, Pasadena Public Library, Fine Arts Dept, Pasadena CA

Weedman, Kenneth R, *Chmn*, Cumberland College, Dept of Art, Williamsburg KY (S)

Weege, William, *Prof*, University of Wisconsin, Madison, Dept of Art, Madison WI (S)

Weekley, Carolyn, *Dir*, Colonial Williamsburg Foundation, Abby Aldrich Rockefeller Folk Art Center, Williamsburg VA

Weekly, Nancy, *Charles Cary Rumsey Cur*, Burchfield-Penney Art Center, Buffalo NY

Weeks, Dennis, *Chmn*, Saint Joseph's University, Dept of Fine & Performing Arts, Philadelphia PA (S)

Weeks, Jeaneal, *Children's Room*, Mason City Public Library, Mason City IA

Weeks, Len, *Pres*, Saint Augustine Art Association Gallery, Saint Augustine FL

Weeks, Linda, *Dir Visual Communications*, Art Institute of Fort Lauderdale, Fort Lauderdale FL (S)

Wees, Beth Carver, *Cur Decorative Arts*, Sterling & Francine Clark Art Institute, Williamstown MA

Wees, J Dustin, *Photograph & Slide Librn*, Sterling & Francine Clark Art Institute, Clark Art Institute Library, Williamstown MA

Weese, Cynthia, *Dean School*, Washington University, School of Architecture, Saint Louis MO (S)

Wegman, Tom, *Pres-Elect*, Arts Iowa City, Art Center & Gallery, Iowa City IA

Wegner, Shelley, *Asst Dir*, Midland County Historical Society, Midland MI

Wegner, Susan, *Prof*, Bowdoin College, Art Dept, Brunswick ME (S)

Wehle, Amy, *Bus Mgr*, Mount Holyoke College, Art Museum, South Hadley MA

Wei, Lilly, *Dir*, Kingsborough Community College, City University of New York, Art Gallery, Brooklyn NY

Weidl, Beverly, *Cur*, Hopewell Museum, Hopewell NJ

Weidman, Jeffrey, *Art Librn*, Oberlin College, Clarence Ward Art Library, Oberlin OH

Weidman, Jill, *VPres*, Lancaster County Art Association, Inc, Lancaster PA

Weidner, Marsha, *Prof & Asian Grad Advisor*, University of Kansas, Kress Foundation Dept of Art History, Lawrence KS (S)

Weidner, Tim, *Dir Exhib & Prog*, Roberson Museum & Science Center, Binghamton NY

Weidner, Timothy, *Cur History & Art*, Roberson Museum & Science Center, Binghamton NY

Weiffenbach, Jean-Edith, *Gallery Dir*, San Francisco Art Institute, Galleries, San Francisco CA

Weigand, Herb, *Asst Prof*, East Stroudsburg University, Fine Arts Center, East Stroudsburg PA (S)

Weigo, Norman, *Chmn*, Triton College, School of Arts & Sciences, River Grove IL (S)

Weiland, Chris, *Instr*, Indiana University of Pennsylvania, Dept of Art & Art Education, Indiana PA (S)

Weiler, Melody, *Chmn*, Texas Tech University, Dept of Art, Lubbock TX (S)

Weinberg, Adam, *Cur, Permanent Coll*, Whitney Museum of American Art, New York NY

Weinberg, H Barbara, *Cur American Paintings & Sculpture*, The Metropolitan Museum of Art, New York NY

Weiner, Rob, *Assoc Dir*, Chinati Foundation, Marfa TX

Weiner, Ros, *Marketing Asst*, Broward County Board of Commissioners Cultural Affairs Divison, Fort Lauderdale FL

Weiner, Sarah Elliston, *Dir*, Columbia University, Miriam & Ira D Wallach Art Gallery, New York NY

Weingarden, Lauren, *Assoc Prof*, Florida State University, Art History Dept (R133B), Tallahassee FL (S)

Weinheimer, Denise Gavio, *Asst Librn*, Princeton University, Marquand Library of Art & Archaeology, Princeton NJ

Weinke, Jane, *Cur Coll*, Leigh Yawkey Woodson Art Museum, Inc, Wausau WI

Weinrich, Peter H, *Exec Dir*, Canadian Crafts Council, Conseil Canadien de l'Artisanat, Ottawa ON

Weinshenker, Anne Betty, *Chmn*, Montclair State University, Fine Arts Dept, Upper Montclair NJ (S)

Weinstein, Richard, *Assoc Prof*, Green Mountain College, Dept of Art, Poultney VT (S)

Weintraub, Beth, *Public Program Dir*, Children's Museum of Manhattan, New York NY

Weir, Cliff, *Pres*, Gananoque Historical Museum, Gananoque ON

Weirich, Nancy, *Librn*, Tippecanoe County Historical Museum, Alameda McCollough Library, Lafayette IN

Weis, Anne, *Chmn*, University of Pittsburgh, Henry Clay Frick Dept History of Art & Architecture, Pittsburgh PA (S)

Weis, Dick, *Prof*, Green Mountain College, Dept of Art, Poultney VT (S)

Weis, Helen H, *Librn*, Willet Stained Glass Studios, Philadelphia PA

Weis, Richard, *Asst Prof*, Grand Valley State University, Art & Design Dept, Allendale MI (S)

Weisberg, Frank, *Pres*, Louisville Visual Art Association, Louisville KY

Weisberg, Lois, *Commissioner*, Chicago Department of Cultural Affairs, Chicago Cultural Center, Chicago IL

Weisberg, Ruth, *Prof*, University of Southern California, School of Fine Arts, Los Angeles CA (S)

Weisenburger, Patricia, *Librn*, Kansas State University, Paul Weigel Library of Architecture Planning & Design, Manhattan KS

Weisenburger, Ray, *Assoc Dean*, Kansas State University, College of Architecture & Design, Manhattan KS (S)

Weisend, Susan, *Assoc Prof*, Ithaca College, Fine Art Dept, Ithaca NY (S)

Weiser, Ronald, *Chmn*, Artrain, Inc, Ann Arbor MI

Weiss, Jeff, *Assoc Prof*, Rochester Institute of Technology, School of Photographic Arts & Sciences, Rochester NY (S)

Weiss, John, *Coordr Photography*, University of Delaware, Dept of Art, Newark DE (S)

Weiss, Lorraine E, *Educ Dir*, Rensselaer County Historical Society, Hart-Cluett Mansion, 1827, Troy NY

Weiss, Olga, *Registrar & Cur of Exhib*, Spertus Institute of Jewish Studies, Spertus Museum, Chicago IL

Weiss, Peg, *Prof*, Syracuse University, Dept of Fine Arts (Art History), Syracuse NY (S)

Weiss, Susan, *Develop Assoc*, Institute of Contemporary Art, Boston MA

Weisser, Terry Drayman, *Dir Conservation & Technical Research*, Walters Art Gallery, Baltimore MD

Weissman, Judith Reiter, *Assoc Prof*, New York University, Dept of Art & Art Professions, New York NY (S)

Weisz, Helen, *Instr*, Bucks County Community College, Fine Arts Dept, Newtown PA (S)

Weitz, Ankeney, *Dir*, Denison University, Art Gallery, Granville OH

Weitz, Ankeney, *Asst Prof*, Denison University, Dept of Art, Granville OH (S)

Weizman, Sandra Morton, *Cur Cultural History*, Glenbow Museum, Calgary AB

Welch, Betty, *Instr*, Dunedin Fine Arts & Cultural Center, Dunedin FL (S)

Welch, Bill, *Instr*, Oklahoma State University, Graphic Arts Dept, Okmulgee OK (S)

Welch, Brenda, *Coordr Spec Events*, Worcester Art Museum, Worcester MA

Welch, John N, *Treas*, Portsmouth Athenaeum, Portsmouth NH

Welch, Margo, *Dir Exhib Prog*, Royal Ontario Museum, Toronto ON

Welch, Marni, *Registrar*, Judah L Magnes Museum, Berkeley CA

Welch, S Anthony, *Dean*, University of Victoria, Dept of History in Art, Victoria BC (S)

Welch, Steven J, *Dir*, Corbit-Calloway Memorial Library, Odessa DE

Welch, Vicky, *Dir Conferences & Events*, Marian College, Allison Mansion, Indianapolis IN

Welcker, Joan, *Membership Coordr*, James A Michener Art Museum, Doylestown PA

Welge, William, *Indian Archives & Mss*, Oklahoma Historical Society, State Museum of History, Oklahoma City OK

Weliver, Evelyn R, *Head Librn*, Interlochen Center for the Arts, Interlochen MI

Weller, Dennis, *Lectr*, Coe College, Dept of Art, Cedar Rapids IA (S)

Weller, Eric, *Prof*, Southwest Texas State University, Dept of Art, San Marcos TX (S)

Weller, Jane, *Chmn Illustrations*, Fashion Institute of Technology, Art & Design Division, New York NY (S)

Weller, Laurie, *Adjunct Asst Prof*, Texas Woman's University, Dept of Visual Arts, Denton TX (S)

Welles, David, *Pres*, Toledo Museum of Art, Toledo OH

Welliver, Michael, *Instr*, Mercer County Community College, Arts & Communication/ Engineering Technology, Trenton NJ (S)

Wellman, Charles, *Asst Chmn*, University of Central Florida, Art Dept, Orlando FL (S)

Wellman, Lesley, *Cur Educ*, Dartmouth College, Hood Museum of Art, Hanover NH

Wells, Anne, *Children's Librn*, Willard Library, Dept of Fine Arts, Evansville IN

Wells, Carol, *Financial Dir*, Mexican Museum, San Francisco CA

Wells, Carol B, *Assoc Prof*, Villa Maria College of Buffalo, Art Dept, Buffalo NY (S)

Wells, Gerald, *Chmn & Prof*, Fort Lewis College, Art Dept, Durango CO (S)

Wells, GladysAnn, *Dir*, New York State Library, Manuscripts & Special Collections, Albany NY

Wells, Jim, *VPres*, Keokuk Art Center, Keokuk IA

Wells, Kendra, *Slide Librn*, University at Albany, State University of New York, Art Dept Slide Library, Albany NY

Wells, Peter G, *Pres*, Porter-Phelps-Huntington Foundation, Inc, Historic House Museum, Hadley MA

Wells, Rufus, *Asst Prof*, University of the District of Columbia, Dept of Mass Media, Visual & Performing Arts, Washington DC (S)

Wells, Ruth, *Accounting Officer*, Museum of Fine Arts, Saint Petersburg, Florida, Inc, Saint Petersburg FL

Wells, Suzanne, *Special Exhibitions Coordr*, Philadelphia Museum of Art, Philadelphia PA

Welsh, Caroline, *Cur*, Adirondack Historical Association, Adirondack Museum, Blue Mountain Lake NY

Welsh, Rebecca, *Office Mgr*, Brownsville Art League Museum, Brownsville TX

Welt, Bernard, *Chmn Academic Studies*, Corcoran School of Art, Washington DC (S)

Welter, Cole H, *Dir*, James Madison University, School of Art & Art History, Harrisonburg VA (S)

Weltman, Ethel, *Admin Asst*, University of Oregon, Museum of Art, Eugene OR

Weltzien, Marie, *Public Relations*, Yale University, Art Gallery, New Haven CT

Welu, James A, *Dir*, Worcester Art Museum, Worcester MA

Welu, William J, *Chairperson*, Briar Cliff College, Art Dept, Sioux City IA (S)

Welych, Anita, *Asst Prof*, Cazenovia College, Center for Art & Design Studies, Cazenovia NY (S)

Wemmlinger, Raymond, *Cur & Librn*, Players, Hampden-Booth Theatre Library, New York NY

Wendler, Walter V, *Dean*, Texas A&M University, College of Architecture, College Station TX (S)

Wendorf, Richard, *Dir & Librn*, Boston Athenaeum, Boston MA

Weng, Siegfried, *Dir Emeritus*, Evansville Museum of Arts & Science, Evansville IN

Wenig-Horswell, Judy, *Assoc Prof*, Goshen College, Art Dept, Goshen IN (S)

Wentworth, Michael, *Cur of Coll*, Boston Athenaeum, Boston MA

Wentworth, T W, *Deputy Dir & Secy*, T T Wentworth Jr Museum, Florida State Museum, Pensacola FL

Wenzel, Carol, *Business Mgr*, Historic Deerfield, Inc, Deerfield MA

Wenzel, Duane, *Head Librn*, Bernice Pauahi Bishop Museum, Library, Honolulu HI

Wepfer, Daryl, *Instr*, University of Evansville, Art Dept, Evansville IN (S)

Wepler, William, *Cur Popular Culture*, Indiana State Museum, Indianapolis IN

Werbel, Amy, *Asst Prof*, St Michael's College, Fine Arts Dept, Colchester VT (S)

Werfel, Gina S, *Chmn*, Randolph-Macon Woman's College, Dept of Art, Lynchburg VA (S)

Werger, Art, *Chmn*, Wesleyan College, Art Dept, Macon GA (S)

Werk, Horst, *Assoc Prof*, Corning Community College, Division of Humanities, Corning NY (S)

Werle, Thomas, *Prof*, Capitol Community Technical College, Humanities Division & Art Dept, Hartford CT (S)

Werlink, Joy, *Asst Cur Manuscripts*, Washington State History Museum, Special Collections Div, Tacoma WA

Werner, Charlotte, *Chmn Foundations*, University of Manitoba, School of Art, Winnipeg MB (S)

Werner, John, *Graduate Cur*, University of Illinois, Museum of Natural History, Champaign IL

Werness, Hope, *Prof*, California State University, Art Dept, Turlock CA (S)

Werth, Karen, *Designer*, University of Maryland, College Park, Art Gallery, College Park MD

Wertheim, Earl, *Assoc Prof*, Sullivan County Community College, Division of Commercial Art & Photography, Loch Sheldrake NY (S)

Wertheimer, Andrew, *Public Serv*, Spertus Institute of Jewish Studies, Asher Library, Chicago IL

Wertheimer, Gary, *Chmn*, Olivet College, Art Dept, Olivet MI (S)

Wertkin, Gerard C, *Dir*, Museum of American Folk Art, New York NY

Wesaw, Sallie, *Prof*, Central Wyoming College, Art Center, Riverton WY (S)

Wescoat, Bonna D, *Assoc Prof*, Emory University, Art History Dept, Atlanta GA (S)

Wescott, Dusty, *Treas*, North Carolina Museums Council, Raleigh NC

Wescott, Richard, *Dir*, Augusta Richmond County Museum, Augusta GA

Wesley, Sherre, *Pres*, Dutchess County Arts Council, Poughkeepsie NY

Wessel, Frederick, *Prof*, University of Hartford, Hartford Art School, West Hartford CT (S)

Wessell, Marion, *Chmn*, Wayne Community College, Liberal Arts Dept, Goldsboro NC (S)

Wessels, Henry, *Prof*, California Polytechnic State University at San Luis Obispo, Dept of Art & Design, San Luis Obispo CA (S)

West, Bill, *Exhibits Mgr*, College of Southern Idaho, Herrett Center for Arts & Science, Twin Falls ID

West, Bruce, *Visiting Lect*, Lewis & Clark College, Dept of Art, Portland OR (S)

West, Claire, *Performing Art Dir*, Arizona Commission on the Arts, Phoenix AZ

West, Coleen, *Develop Dir*, Maryland Art Place, Baltimore MD

West, Matt, *Instr*, Laramie County Community College, Division of Arts & Humanities, Cheyenne WY (S)

West, Richard, *Pres & Dir*, Frye Art Museum, Seattle WA

West, Richard, *Exec Dir*, Frye Art Museum, Library, Seattle WA

West, Richard, *Pres*, Historical Society of Bloomfield, Bloomfield NJ

West, Ruth, *Instr*, Springfield College, Dept of Visual & Performing Arts, Springfield MA (S)

West, Virginia, *Chmn Art Committee*, North Canton Public Library, Little Art Gallery, North Canton OH

West, William, *Adjunct Instr*, Le Moyne College, Fine Arts Dept, Syracuse NY (S)

West, W Richard, *Dir*, National Museum of the American Indian, George Gustav Heye Center, New York NY

Westbrook, Nicholas, *Exec Dir*, Fort Ticonderoga Association, Ticonderoga NY

Westbrook, Nicholas, *Exec Dir*, Fort Ticonderoga Association, Thompson-Pell Research Center, Ticonderoga NY

Wester, Janie, *Asst Prof*, Oklahoma Baptist University, Art Dept, Shawnee OK (S)

Westercook, Diana, *VPres*, Print Club of Albany, Albany NY

Westergaard, Vera, *Exhibit Designer*, Museum of Photographic Arts, San Diego CA

Westfall, C Frederick, *VPres*, Peninsula Fine Arts Center, Newport News VA

Westfall-Edwards, Michelle, *Exhib Designer*, City of Springdale, Shiloh Museum, Springdale AR

Westin, Robert, *Prof*, University of Florida, Dept of Art, Gainesville FL (S)

Westlake, Richard, *Theatre Arts Instr*, Edison Community College, Dept of Fine & Performing Arts, Fort Myers FL (S)

Westmacott, Gene, *Asst Prof*, Brenau University, Art Dept, Gainesville GA (S)

Weston, Victoria, *Asst Prof*, University of Massachusetts - Boston, Art Dept, Boston MA (S)

Westpfahl, Richard, *Chmn*, Western Wisconsin Technical College, Graphics Division, La Crosse WI (S)

Westwater, Angela K, *Pres*, Louis Comfort Tiffany Foundation, New York NY

Westwood, Lyn, *Instr*, Toronto Art Therapy Institute, Toronto ON (S)

Wetherell, Ron, *Prof*, Florida Community College at Jacksonville, South Campus, Art Dept, Jacksonville FL (S)

Wetherington, Mark V, *Dir*, The Filson Club, Louisville KY

Wethli, Mark, *Chmn*, Bowdoin College, Art Dept, Brunswick ME (S)

Wetmore, Gordon, *VPres*, American Society of Portrait Artists (ASOPA), Montgomery AL

Wetmore, Joan, *Asst Dir*, The Print Center, Philadelphia PA

Wetta, Frank, *Dean*, Daytona Beach Community College, Dept of Fine Arts & Visual Arts, Daytona Beach FL (S)

Wetter, Felicitas, *Instr*, Dowling College, Dept of Visual Arts, Oakdale NY (S)

Wetzel, David, *Dir Publications*, Colorado Historical Society, Colorado History Museum, Denver CO

Wetzel, Jean, *Prof*, California Polytechnic State University at San Luis Obispo, Dept of Art & Design, San Luis Obispo CA (S)

Weurding, Peggy, *Dir*, Arthur Roy Mitchell Memorial Inc, Museum of Western Art, Trinidad CO

Weyerhaeuser, Charles A, *Mus Dir*, Art Complex Museum, Duxbury MA

Weygandt, Virginia, *Cur*, Clark County Historical Society, Library, Springfield OH

Weyhrich, Denise, *Prof*, Chapman University, Art Dept, Orange CA (S)

Whalen, Kelly, *Development Dir*, Fraunces Tavern Museum, New York NY

Wharton, Annabell, *Chair*, Duke University, Dept of Art & Art History, Durham NC (S)

Wheat, Evie, *VChmn*, Detroit Artists Market, Detroit MI

Wheeler, Geof, *Adjunct Instr*, Maryville University of Saint Louis, Art Division, Saint Louis MO (S)

Wheeler, Jane, *Coordr*, Richmond Arts Centre, Richmond BC

Wheeler, Jean, *Librn*, San Jose Museum of Art, Library, San Jose CA

Wheeler, Lawrence, *Dir*, North Carolina Museum of Art, Raleigh NC

Wheeler, Maurice, *Interim Library Dir*, Detroit Public Library, Art & Literature Dept, Detroit MI

Wheeler, Nancy, *Registrar*, C M Russell Museum, Great Falls MT

Wheeler, Nancy, *Registrar*, C M Russell Museum, Frederic G Renner Memorial Library, Great Falls MT

Wheelock, Arthur, *Cur Northern Baroque Painting*, National Gallery of Art, Washington DC

Wheelock, Scott, *Instr*, Main Line Art Center, Haverford PA (S)

Whelan, Mary, *Cur*, Mission San Luis Rey de Francia, Mission San Luis Rey Museum, San Luis Rey CA

Whelehan, David, *Chmn*, Old State House, Hartford CT

Whikhuizen, Henry, *Asst Prof*, Calvin College, Art Dept, Grand Rapids MI (S)

Whipple, Sally, *Dir*, Noah Webster House, Inc, Noah Webster House, West Hartford CT

Whipple, William, *Dean*, Bethany College, Dept of Fine Arts, Bethany WV (S)

Whisman, Evelyn, *Asst Cur*, Plumas County Museum, Quincy CA

Whisman, Evelyn, *Asst Cur*, Plumas County Museum, Museum Archives, Quincy CA

Whisman, Rex, *Admis*, Rocky Mountain College of Art & Design, Denver CO (S)

Whitacre, Steve, *Chmn Found*, Kansas City Art Institute, Kansas City MO (S)

Whitaker, Elizabeth, *Cur Educ*, Hunter Museum of American Art, Chattanooga TN

Whitaker, Joel, *Asst Prof*, University of Dayton, Visual Arts Dept, Dayton OH (S)

Whitaker, Kathleen, *Chief Cur*, Southwest Museum, Los Angeles CA

White, Alex, *Assoc Prof*, University of Hartford, Hartford Art School, West Hartford CT (S)

White, Barbara, *Assoc Dir Admin*, Kimbell Art Foundation, Kimbell Art Museum, Fort Worth TX

White, Barbara E, *Adjunct Prof*, Tufts University, Dept of Art & Art History, Medford MA (S)

White, Betty, *Repatriation Prog Mgr*, National Museum of the American Indian, George Gustav Heye Center, New York NY

White, Beverly M, *Fine Arts Librn*, Manchester City Library, Manchester NH

White, Bill, *Mgr Exhib*, Fine Arts Museums of San Francisco, M H de Young Memorial Museum & California Palace of the Legion of Honor, San Francisco CA

White, Blair, *Cur.* East Tennessee State University, Carroll Reece Museum, Johnson City TN

White, Carol, *Librn.* Kauai Public Library, Lihue HI

White, Charles, *Chmn Dept Fine Arts.* La Salle University, Dept of Art, Philadelphia PA (S)

White, Christian, *Treas.* Santa Barbara Contemporary Arts Forum, Santa Barbara CA

White, David, *Prog Representative.* Southern Illinois University, College of Technical Careers, Carbondale IL (S)

White, David O, *Museum Dir.* Connecticut Historical Commission, Sloane-Stanley Museum, Kent CT

White, Dennis, *Dean Fine Arts Div.* Antelope Valley College, Art Dept, Division of Fine Arts, Lancaster CA (S)

White, Donald, *Mediterranean Section Cur.* University of Pennsylvania, Museum of Archaeology & Anthropology, Philadelphia PA

White, E Alan, *Head.* University of Tennessee at Chattanooga, Dept of Art, Chattanooga TN (S)

White, Elisa, *Cur Asst.* Alternative Museum, New York NY

White, Ella, *Instr Dean Fine Arts.* Cerritos Community College, Art Dept, Norwalk CA (S)

White, Eric, *Chief.* Public Library of the District of Columbia, Audiovisual Division, Washington DC

White, Fran, *Asst Dean.* Laney College, Art Dept, Oakland CA (S)

White, Gail Scott, *Asst Prof.* Cornell University, Dept of Art, Ithaca NY (S)

White, James J, *Cur Art.* Carnegie Mellon University, Hunt Institute for Botanical Documentation, Pittsburgh PA

White, Julia, *Cur Asian Art.* Honolulu Academy of Arts, Honolulu HI

White, Kathy, *Bookstore Mgr.* Salvador Dali Museum, Saint Petersburg FL

White, Ken, *Chmn Fine Arts Photo.* Rochester Institute of Technology, School of Photographic Arts & Sciences, Rochester NY (S)

White, Khris, *Archival Dir.* Oregon Historical Society, Library, Portland OR

White, Larry, *Head Dept Art.* Long Beach City College, Dept of Art, Long Beach CA (S)

White, Lois St Aubin, *Outreach Coordr.* Central United Methodist Church, Swords Info Plowshares Peace Center & Gallery, Detroit MI

White, Lynda, *Asst Librn & Public Services.* University of Virginia, Fiske Kimball Fine Arts Library, Charlottesville VA

White, Matthew, *Adminr.* Mamie McFaddin Ward Heritage Historic Foundation Inc, Beaumont TX

White, Michael, *Chmn Crafts.* Rochester Institute of Technology, School of Art & Design, Rochester NY (S)

White, Ned, *Acting Exec Dir.* Ward Foundation, Ward Museum of Wildfowl Art, Salisbury MD

White, Rolland, *Chief Photographer.* National Portrait Gallery, Washington DC

White, Stefanie, *Marketing Mgr.* University of Chicago, David & Alfred Smart Museum of Art, Chicago IL

White, Terri, *Art Gallery Coordr.* North Central Washington Museum, Gallery, Wenatchee WA

White, Tracy Baker, *Cur Educ.* San Antonio Museum of Art, San Antonio TX

Whitehead, Lynn, *Assoc Prof.* East Tennessee State University, Dept of Art & Design, Johnson City TN (S)

Whitehead, Marcia, *Head Publ.* Carnegie Institute, Carnegie Museum of Art, Pittsburgh PA

Whitehouse, David, *Dir.* Corning Museum of Glass, Corning NY

Whitehouse, Diane, *Co-Chmn Paintings.* University of Manitoba, School of Art, Winnipeg MB (S)

Whitesel, Lita, *Chmn.* California State University, Sacramento, Dept of Art, Sacramento CA (S)

Whitesides, Patricia, *Registrar.* Toledo Museum of Art, Toledo OH

Whiting, B J, *Tour Supv.* Nemours Mansion & Gardens, Wilmington DE

Whitlock, John J, *Dir.* Southern Illinois University, University Museum, Carbondale IL

Whitman, Nathan T, *Prof Emeritus.* University of Michigan, Ann Arbor, Dept of History of Art, Ann Arbor MI (S)

Whitmore, Anthony, *Div Chmn.* Potomac State College, Dept of Art, Keyser WV (S)

Whitney, Allota, *Registrar.* Heritage Plantation of Sandwich, Sandwich MA

Whitney, Linda, *Co-Chair.* Valley City State College, Art Dept, Valley City ND (S)

Whitney, Patrick, *Dir.* Illinois Institute of Technology, Institute of Design, Chicago IL (S)

Whittaker, Shelley, *Bus Mgr.* Kamloops Art Gallery, Kamloops BC

Whittemore, Charles, *Pres.* Manchester Historic Association, Manchester NH

Whitten, Lee, *Prof.* Los Angeles City College, Dept of Art, Los Angeles CA (S)

Whittington, Blair, *Librn.* Brand Library & Art Galleries, Glendale CA

Whittington, Harrell, *Instr.* Bob Jones University, School of Fine Arts, Greenville SC (S)

Whittle, Douglas, *Asst Prof.* Converse College, Art Dept, Spartanburg SC (S)

Whitton, Heather, *Asst Dean.* Ontario College of Art & Design, Toronto ON (S)

Whitton, Lee, *Chmn.* Los Angeles City College, Dept of Art, Los Angeles CA (S)

Whitworth, Thomas C, *Assoc Prof.* University of New Orleans-Lake Front, Dept of Fine Arts, New Orleans LA (S)

Wholley, Jay, *Prof.* Ramapo College of New Jersey, School of Contemporary Arts, Mahwah NJ (S)

Whyte, Robert A, *Cur.* Museo Italo Americano, Library, San Francisco CA

Wible, Karen, *VPres Public Affairs & Publications.* The Mariners' Museum, Newport News VA

Wicker, Billie, *Asst Prof.* Albion College, Dept of Visual Arts, Albion MI (S)

Wickkiser, Carol B, *Exec Dir.* Lehigh County Historical Society, Allentown PA

Wickstrom, Andriette, *Dir.* Witter Gallery, Storm Lake IA

Widdifield, Stacie, *Assoc Prof Art History.* University of Arizona, Dept of Art, Tucson AZ (S)

Widmer, Jason, *Instr.* Linn Benton Community College, Fine & Applied Art Dept, Albany OR (S)

Widrick, Melissa, *Cur Educ.* Jefferson County Historical Society, Watertown NY

Wiebe, Charles M, *Dir Exhib.* International Images, Ltd, Sewickley PA

Wieber, Ryan S, *Library Asst.* Detroit Institute of Arts, Research Library, Detroit MI

Wiedemann, D, *Prof.* City Colleges of Chicago, Daley College, Chicago IL (S)

Wiegmann, Richard, *Prof.* Concordia College, Art Dept, Seward NE (S)

Wieland, John, *Chmn Board of Dir.* High Museum of Art, Atlanta GA

Wieseman, Marjorie, *Cur Western Art Before 1850.* Oberlin College, Allen Memorial Art Museum, Oberlin OH

Wiest, Scottie, *Lectr.* Davis & Elkins College, Dept of Art, Elkins WV (S)

Wiggins, Bruce, *Dir Educ Consulting.* Delphian School, Sheridan OR (S)

Wiginton, Colin, *Exhib Asst.* McMaster University, Museum of Art, Hamilton ON

Wigton, Robert H, *Pres.* Fine Arts Association, School of Fine Arts, Willoughby OH

Wilbers, Tim, *Assoc Prof.* University of Dayton, Visual Arts Dept, Dayton OH (S)

Wilbur, Debra, *Dir.* City of Atlanta, City Gallery at Chastain, Atlanta GA

Wilburne, Robert, *Pres.* Colonial Williamsburg Foundation, Williamsburg VA

Wilcher, Richard, *Fine Arts Dept Chmn.* Brazosport College, Art Dept, Lake Jackson TX (S)

Wilcox, David R, *Research Archaeologist & Spec Asst to Deputy Dir.* Museum of Northern Arizona, Flagstaff AZ

Wilcox, Jeffrey, *Registrar.* University of Missouri, Museum of Art & Archaeology, Columbia MO

Wilcox, Lawrence, *Instr.* New Mexico Junior College, Arts & Sciences, Hobbs NM (S)

Wilcox, Thomas R, *Exec Dir.* Maine Maritime Museum, Bath ME

Wilcoxson, Shirlie Bowers, *Chmn.* Saint Gregory's College, Dept of Art, Shawnee OK (S)

Wilczek, Ronald, *Coordr.* Roger Williams College, Art Dept, Bristol RI (S)

Wild, Catherine, *Chair Foundation Studies.* Ontario College of Art & Design, Toronto ON (S)

Wilde, Betty, *Cur.* Hostos Center for the Arts & Culture, Bronx NY

Wilde, Robert, *Instr.* College of Saint Benedict, Art Dept, Saint Joseph MN (S)

Wildenberg, Pat, *Reference Archivist.* Herbert Hoover Presidential Library & Museum, West Branch IA

Wilder, Joan, *Dir Visitor Servs.* Please Touch Museum, Philadelphia PA

Wilder, Michael, *Prof.* Southwestern College, Art Dept, Winfield KS (S)

Wiley, Aubrey, *Asst Prof.* Lynchburg College, Art Dept, Lynchburg VA (S)

Wiley, Dyan, *Educ Coordr.* Arts Extension Service, Amherst MA

Wilfong, Terry, *Vis Cur.* University of Michigan, Kelsey Museum of Archaeology, Ann Arbor MI

Wilkes, Sheridan, *Admin Asst.* Louisiana State University, Museum of Arts, Baton Rouge LA

Wilkie, Everett C, *Ed.* Connecticut Historical Society, Hartford CT

Wilkie, Everett C, *Head Librn.* Connecticut Historical Society, Library, Hartford CT

Wilkie, Jo-Anne, *Exec Dir.* The Art Center, Mount Clemens MI

Wilkin, Sharon, *Asst Prof.* Spokane Falls Community College, Fine Arts Dept, Spokane WA (S)

Wilkins, Janis, *Cur Coll.* Museum of York County, Staff Research Library, Rock Hill SC

Wilkins, Will K, *Dir.* Real Art Ways (RAW), Hartford CT

Wilkinson, Bill, *Educ Coordr.* Estevan National Exhibition Centre Inc, Estevan SK

Wilkinson, Carlton, *Lectr.* Vanderbilt University, Dept of Fine Arts, Nashville TN (S)

Wilkinson, J, *Coordr.* Dundas Valley School of Art, Dundas ON (S)

Wilkinson, MaryAnn, *Acting Cur Twentieth Century.* Detroit Institute of Arts, Detroit MI

Wilkinson, Nancy, *Dir.* Oklahoma State University, Gardiner Art Gallery, Stillwater OK

Wilkinson, Nancy, *Dept Head.* Oklahoma State University, Art Dept, Stillwater OK (S)

Wilkinson, Sean, *Chmn.* University of Dayton, Visual Arts Dept, Dayton OH (S)

Will, Duncan, *Mem Pub Relations.* Phillips Academy, Addison Gallery of American Art, Andover MA

Will, Vernon, *Head Conservation.* Ohio Historical Society, Archives-Library Division, Columbus OH

Willamson, Tora, *Architecture Librn.* Oklahoma State University, Architecture Library, Stillwater OK

Willard, Shirley, *Pres.* Fulton County Historical Society Inc, Fulton County Museum, Rochester IN

Willard, Tom, *Exec Dir.* Deaf Artists of America Inc, Rochester NY

Willens, Kay, *Assoc Prof.* Kenyon College, Art Dept, Gambier OH (S)

Willet, E Crosby, *Pres.* Willet Stained Glass Studios, Philadelphia PA

Willett, Liz, *Pres & Board Dir.* Copper Village Museum & Arts Center, Anaconda MT

Willey, Chris, *Assoc Prof.* Central Missouri State University, Art Dept, Warrensburg MO (S)

William, Richard, *Prof.* Iowa Lakes Community College, Dept of Art, Estherville IA (S)

Williams, Albert N, *VPres.* Mingei International, Inc, Mingei International Museum Satellite of World Folk Art, San Diego CA

Williams, Ardelia, *Head Dept.* Indiana Wesleyan University, Art Dept, Marion IN (S)

Williams, Benjamin, *Librn & Spec Coll Librn.* Field Museum, Library, Chicago IL

Williams, Carol, *Dir Library*, Saint Paul Public Library, Art, Music & Video Dept, Saint Paul MN

Williams, Cynthia, *Librn*, Archives of American Art, Midwest Regional Center, Washington DC

Williams, Deborah, *Dir*, Patterson Library & Art Gallery, Westfield NY

Williams, Diana, *Pub Support Serv*, Wichita Public Library, Wichita KS

Williams, Doris Carson, *Dir Marketing*, Carnegie Institute, Carnegie Museum of Art, Pittsburgh PA

Williams, Ed, *Dir Photo*, Art Institute of Fort Lauderdale, Fort Lauderdale FL (S)

Williams, Frank, *Chmn*, Central Piedmont Community College, Visual & Performing Arts, Charlotte NC (S)

Williams, Gloria, *Cur*, Norton Simon Museum, Pasadena CA

Williams, Greg, *Preparator*, Colby College, Museum of Art, Waterville ME

Williams, Gregg, *Archivist*, New Jersey Historical Society, Newark NJ

Williams, Idaherma, *VPres*, American Color Print Society, Philadelphia PA

Williams, Irving, *Pres*, Fetherston Foundation, Packwood House Museum, Lewisburg PA

Williams, Jane, *Agent*, Richard Gallery & Almond Tea Gallery, Divisions of Studios of Jack Richard, Cuyahoga Falls OH

Williams, Jane, *Assoc Prof Art History*, University of Arizona, Dept of Art, Tucson AZ (S)

Williams, Janet, *Dir*, Carrie McLain Museum, Nome AK

Williams, Janice, *Asst Prof*, Augusta College, Dept of Fine Arts, Augusta GA (S)

Williams, Jay, *Chief Cur*, University of South Carolina, McKissick Museum, Columbia SC

Williams, Jennifer Frazer, *Dir*, American Society of Portrait Artists (ASOPA), Montgomery AL

Williams, Jim, *Prof Fine Arts*, University of Cincinnati, School of Art, Cincinnati OH (S)

Williams, Judith, *Asst Prof*, University of British Columbia, Dept of Fine Arts, Vancouver BC (S)

Williams, Juliana F, *Assoc Prof*, Monroe Community College, Art Dept, Rochester NY (S)

Williams, Kathleen, *Marketing & Public Relations*, The Currier Gallery of Art, Manchester NH

Williams, Kay P, *Dir*, Tryon Palace Historic Sites & Gardens, New Bern NC

Williams, Keith, *Chmn*, Concordia College, Art Dept, Saint Paul MN (S)

Williams, Keith, *Dir*, North Central Washington Museum, Gallery, Wenatchee WA

Williams, Kenneth, *Graphic Design*, University of Georgia, Franklin College of Arts & Sciences, Lamar Dodd School of Art, Athens GA (S)

Williams, Lawrence, *Prof*, Rochester Institute of Technology, School of Art & Design, Rochester NY (S)

Williams, Lillian, *Chmn*, Charles B Goddard Center for the Visual & Performing Arts, Ardmore OK

Williams, Lisa, *Dir*, Woodstock Artists Association, Woodstock NY

Williams, Lisa, *Gallery Mgr*, Woodstock Artists Association, WAA Archives, Woodstock NY

Williams, Lorraine, *Cur Archaeology-Ethnology*, New Jersey State Museum, Trenton NJ

Williams, Lyle, *Assoc Cur Prints & Drawings*, Marion Koogler McNay Art Museum, San Antonio TX

Williams, Mara, *Dir*, Brattleboro Museum & Art Center, Brattleboro VT

Williams, Marlys, *Coordr*, California State University, Chico, Third Floor Gallery, Chico CA

Williams, Marshall, *Team Admnr*, National Society of Tole & Decorative Painters, Inc, Wichita KS

Williams, Mary, *Prog Coordr*, University of British Columbia, Fine Arts Gallery, Vancouver BC

Williams, Mary Jane, *Registrar*, Arizona State University, ASU Art Museum, Tempe AZ

Williams, Mary Kay, *Coordr, Membership & Vols*, Terra Museum of American Art, Chicago IL

Williams, Megan, *Instr*, Toronto School of Art, Toronto ON (S)

Williams, Mike, *Bus Mgr*, Kit Carson Historic Museums, Taos NM

Williams, Mollie Lee, *Dir*, Patterson Homestead, Dayton OH

Williams, Patricia, *VPres Policy & Progs*, American Association of Museums, US National Committee of the International Council of Museums (AAM-ICOM), Washington DC

Williams, Peter, *Art Instr*, Kellogg Community College, Visual & Performing Arts Dept, Battle Creek MI (S)

Williams, Randolph, *Chmn*, Manhattanville College, Brownson Art Gallery, Purchase NY

Williams, Randolph, *Head Dept*, Manhattanville College, Art Dept, Purchase NY (S)

Williams, Ray, *Educ Cur*, University of North Carolina at Chapel Hill, Ackland Art Museum, Chapel Hill NC

Williams, Renee T, *Coll Mgr*, New Britain Museum of American Art, New Britain CT

Williams, Robert, *Instr*, South Central Technical College, Commercial & Technical Art Dept, North Mankato MN (S)

Williams, Roberta, *Instr*, Marian College, Art Dept, Indianapolis IN (S)

Williams, Sally, *Public Information Officer*, Brooklyn Museum, Brooklyn NY

Williams, Sarah, *Exec Dir*, Koochiching County Historical Society Museum, International Falls MN

Williams, Shellie, *Cur Educ*, Carolina Art Association, Gibbes Museum of Art, Charleston SC

Williams, Sidney, *Dir Educ*, Palm Springs Desert Museum, Palm Springs CA

Williams, Sidney, *Educ*, Palm Springs Desert Museum, Library, Palm Springs CA

Williams, Stephen, *Coll Mgr (Sciences)*, Texas Tech University, Museum, Lubbock TX

Williams, Stephen R, *Dir*, Museum of Arts & History, Port Huron MI

Williams, Teri, *Dir*, Georgia State University, Art Gallery, Atlanta GA

Williams, Tom, *Assoc Prof*, Southwest Texas State University, Dept of Art, San Marcos TX (S)

Williams, Tom, *Instructional Aide*, Victor Valley College, Art Dept, Victorville CA (S)

Williams, Wanda, *Challenger Center Asst Flight Dir*, Louisiana Arts & Science Center, Baton Rouge LA

Williams, Wayne, *Prof*, Finger Lakes Community College, Visual & Performing Arts Dept, Canandaigua NY (S)

Williams, William E, *Chmn*, Haverford College, Fine Arts Dept, Haverford PA (S)

Williamson, James S, *Instr*, Rhodes College, Dept of Art, Memphis TN (S)

Williamson, Jan, *Gen Mgr*, 18th Street Arts Complex, Santa Monica CA

Williamson, Jane, *Dir*, Rowland Evans Robinson Memorial Association, Rokeby Museum, Ferrisburgh VT

Williamson, Janet, *Librn*, University of Georgia, Dept of Art Lamar Dodd School of Art, Athens GA

Williamson, J Reid, *Pres*, Historic Landmarks Foundation of Indiana, Information Center Library, Indianapolis IN

Willis, Alfred, *Head, Arts Library*, University of California, Los Angeles, Arts Library, Los Angeles CA

Willis, Andi, *Admin Asst*, Community Council for the Arts, Kinston NC

Willis, Jay, *Prof*, University of Southern California, School of Fine Arts, Los Angeles CA (S)

Willis, Tim, *Asst Dir Operations*, Department of Community Development, Provincial Museum of Alberta, Edmonton AB

Willis, Wendy, *Instr*, Southwestern Michigan College, Fine & Performing Arts Dept, Dowagiac MI (S)

Willman, Merle, *Asst Dept Head*, University of Massachusetts, Amherst, Dept of Landscape Architecture & Regional Planning, Amherst MA (S)

Willner, Judith, *Chmn*, Coppin State College, Dept Fine & Communication Arts, Baltimore MD (S)

Willock, Tom, *Dir*, Medicine Hat Museum & Art Gallery, Medicine Hat AB

Willome, Thomaw, *Prof*, San Antonio College, Visual Arts & Technology, San Antonio TX (S)

Willon, Monica, *Deputy Dir Membership & Develop*, Museum of the City of New York, New York NY

Willoughby, Alan, *Dir*, Perkins Center for the Arts, Moorestown NJ

Willoughby, Sue, *Dir*, George Phippen Memorial Foundation, Phippen Museum of Western Art, Prescott AZ

Wills, Carol, *Registrar & Cur Coll*, Saint Joseph Museum, Saint Joseph MO

Willse, Michael, *Assoc Prof*, Rosemont College, Division of the Arts, Rosemont PA (S)

Willsey, Dorothy, *Pres*, Madison County Historical Society, Cottage Lawn, Oneida NY

Willson, Anne, *Acting Admnr*, University of North Carolina at Greensboro, Weatherspoon Art Gallery, Greensboro NC

Willumson, Glenn, *Cur*, Pennsylvania State University, Palmer Museum of Art, University Park PA

Willwerth, Ardis, *Educator*, Pasadena Historical Museum, Pasadena CA

Wilmarth-Rabineau, Susan, *Asst Prof*, University of Hartford, Hartford Art School, West Hartford CT (S)

Wilmerding, John, *Chmn Dept&Prof*, Princeton University, Dept of Art & Archaeology, Princeton NJ (S)

Wilsbach, Tom, *AV Mgr*, Portland Public Library, Art - Audiovisual Dept, Portland ME

Wilson, A, *Secy General*, Canadian Society for Education Through Art, Oakville ON

Wilson, Carole, *Public Relations Coordr*, Louisiana Arts & Science Center, Baton Rouge LA

Wilson, Catherine, *Librn*, Terra Museum of American Art, Chicago IL

Wilson, Chris, *Chmn*, Barton College, Art Dept, Wilson NC (S)

Wilson, Christine, *Dir Public Information*, Mississippi Department of Archives & History, Library, Jackson MS

Wilson, Clifford, *Pres*, Ashland Historical Society, Ashland MA

Wilson, C Richard, *Pres Board Trustees*, Allentown Art Museum, Allentown PA

Wilson, Darla, *Educ Cur*, Historical Museum at Fort Missoula, Missoula MT

Wilson, Don, *Vis Prof*, Oral Roberts University, Fine Arts Dept, Tulsa OK (S)

Wilson, Eden, *Cur Coll*, Polk Museum of Art, Lakeland FL

Wilson, Elizabeth, *Public Affairs*, Pierpont Morgan Library, New York NY

Wilson, Frederic W, *Cur Gilbert & Sullivan Coll*, Pierpont Morgan Library, New York NY

Wilson, Gail, *Office Mgr*, Arts Midland Galleries & School, Midland MI

Wilson, Gillian, *Cur Decorative Arts*, Getty Center for the History of Art & the Humanities Trust Museum, Santa Monica CA

Wilson, Gillian, *Cur Decorative Arts*, Getty Center for the History of Art & the Humanities Trust Museum, The J Paul Getty Museum, Santa Monica CA

Wilson, Gordon, *Assoc Prof*, Whitworth College, Art Dept, Spokane WA (S)

Wilson, Jane, *Asst Dir*, Owensboro Museum of Fine Art, Owensboro KY

Wilson, J Chris, *Dir & Chmn Art*, Barton College, Barton Museum - Virginia Graves Gallery - Lula E Backley Gallery, Wilson NC

Wilson, Jim, *Business Mgr*, Long Beach Museum of Art, Long Beach CA

Wilson, John, *Cur Painting & Sculpture*, Cincinnati Museum Association, Cincinnati Art Museum, Cincinnati OH

Wilson, John, *Exec Dir*, Lakeside Studio, Lakeside MI

Wilson, John M, *Prof*, Hope College, Art Dept, Holland MI (S)

Wilson, John Montgomery, *Dir*, Hope College, De Pree Art Center & Gallery, Holland MI

Wilson, John R, *Prof*, Butte College, Dept of Fine Arts, Oroville CA (S)

Wilson, Joyce, *Chmn*, Bellevue College, Art Dept, Bellevue NE (S)

Wilson, Karen L, *Museum Dir,* University of Chicago, Oriental Institute Museum, Chicago IL

Wilson, Kay, *Dir,* Grinnell College, Print & Drawing Study Room/Gallery, Grinnell IA

Wilson, Kenneth, *Chmn Dept of Art,* Bloomsburg University of Pennsylvania, Haas Gallery of Art, Bloomsburg PA

Wilson, Keyser, *Asst Prof,* Stillman College, Stillman Art Gallery & Art Dept, Tuscaloosa AL (S)

Wilson, Laurie, *Prof,* New York University, Dept of Art & Art Professions, New York NY (S)

Wilson, Marc, *Dir,* Nelson-Atkins Museum of Art, Friends of Art, Kansas City MO

Wilson, Marc F, *Dir & Chief Cur Oriental Art,* Nelson-Atkins Museum of Art, Kansas City MO

Wilson, Martha, *Executive Dir,* Franklin Furnace Archive, Inc, New York NY

Wilson, Moira, *Librn,* Crafts Guild of Manitoba, Inc, Library, Winnipeg MB

Wilson, Nancy, *Instr,* The Arkansas Arts Center, Museum School, Little Rock AR (S)

Wilson, Neal, *Prof,* Southwest Texas State University, Dept of Art, San Marcos TX (S)

Wilson, Patsy, *Dir Library Servs,* North Central Texas College, Art Dept, Gainesville TX

Wilson, Rob, *Dir,* City of Ukiah, Grace Hudson Museum & The Sun House, Ukiah CA

Wilson, Roger D (Sam), *Asst Prof,* University of Utah, Art Dept, Salt Lake City UT (S)

Wilson, Stanley, *Prof,* California State Polytechnic University, Pomona, Art Dept, Pomona CA (S)

Wilson, Stephen, *Instr,* California State University, Chico, Art Dept, Chico CA (S)

Wilson, Steve, *Dir,* Institute of the Great Plains, Museum of the Great Plains, Lawton OK

Wilson, Tracy, *Dir of Develop,* Berkshire Museum, Pittsfield MA

Wilson, Wallace, *Chmn,* University of South Florida, Art Dept, Tampa FL (S)

Wilson, Wayne, *Asst Cur,* Kelowna Museum, Kelowna BC

Wilsterman, James, *Cur,* Grossmont Community College, Hyde Gallery, El Cajon CA

Wilton, John, *Prof,* Daytona Beach Community College, Dept of Fine Arts & Visual Arts, Daytona Beach FL (S)

Wiltrout, Douglas, *Pres,* National Society of Painters in Casein & Acrylic, Inc, Whitehall PA

Wimmer, Charles, *Prof,* University of Wisconsin-Stout, Dept of Art & Design, Menomonie WI (S)

Wimmer, Gayle, *Prof Fibers,* University of Arizona, Dept of Art, Tucson AZ (S)

Winant, Donna, *Asst,* Worcester Art Museum, Library, Worcester MA

Winch, Terence, *Head Publications,* National Museum of the American Indian, George Gustav Heye Center, New York NY

Wind, Geraldine, *Assoc Prof,* Mount Mary College, Art Dept, Milwaukee WI (S)

Windsor-Liscombe, Rhodri, *Prof,* University of British Columbia, Dept of Fine Arts, Vancouver BC (S)

Wine, Jerry, *Treasurer,* G G Drayton Club, Salem OH

Winegrad, Dilys, *Dir,* University of Pennsylvania, Arthur Ross Gallery, Philadelphia PA

Wineland, Gene, *Chmn,* Pratt Community College, Art Dept, Pratt KS (S)

Wineland, John, *Cur,* Hartwick College, Foreman Gallery, Oneonta NY

Winfield, Charles, *Prof,* University of Maine at Augusta, Division of Fine & Performing Arts, Augusta ME (S)

Winfrey, Reid, *Instr,* Monterey Peninsula College, Art Dept, Monterey CA (S)

Winiker, Barry M, *Asst Cur,* Joseph E Seagram & Sons, Inc, Gallery, New York NY

Wink, Jon D, *Chmn,* Stephen F Austin State University, Art Dept, Nacogdoches TX (S)

Winkler, Linda, *Fine Arts Librn,* University of Regina, Fine Arts Library, Regina SK

Winkler, Paul, *Dir,* Menil Collection, Houston TX

Winkler, Suzanne, *Instr,* Columbia University, School of the Arts, Division of Visual Arts, New York NY (S)

Winkler, Valerie, *Educ Dir,* Children's Museum of Manhattan, New York NY

Winn, Elinor, *Museum Resource Specialist,* Columbus Museum, Columbus GA

Winningham, Geoffrey, *Prof,* Rice University, Dept of Art & Art History, Houston TX (S)

Winokur, Paula, *Assoc Prof,* Beaver College, Dept of Fine Arts, Glenside PA (S)

Winship, Joanne, *Dir Cultural Affairs,* San Francisco City & County Art Commission, San Francisco CA

Winship, John, *Instr,* Gettysburg College, Dept of Visual Arts, Gettysburg PA (S)

Winslow, B B, *Dir,* Arts Midland Galleries & School, Midland MI

Winslow, B B, *Dir,* Art Midland Galleries & School, Midland MI (S)

Winslow, Bruce, *Adjunct Instr,* Saginaw Valley State University, Dept of Art & Design, University Center MI (S)

Winslow, John, *Chmn Dept,* Catholic University of America, Dept of Art, Washington DC (S)

Winter, Amy, *Cur,* Northwestern University, Mary & Leigh Block Gallery, Evanston IL

Winter, Gerald G, *Prof,* University of Miami, Dept of Art & Art History, Coral Gables FL (S)

Winter, Robert, *Asst Prof,* Lenoir Rhyne College, Dept of Art, Hickory NC (S)

Winter, William F, *Pres Board Trustees,* Mississippi Department of Archives & History, Library, Jackson MS

Winters, John L, *Assoc Prof,* University of Mississippi, Dept of Art, University MS (S)

Winters, Nathan, *Chmn,* University of Utah, Art Dept, Salt Lake City UT (S)

Winters, Sandra, *Assoc Prof,* Florida International University, Visual Arts Dept, Miami FL (S)

Winther, Bert, *Prof,* Syracuse University, Dept of Fine Arts (Art History), Syracuse NY (S)

Wipfler, Heinz, *Asst Prof,* Queensborough Community College, Dept of Art & Photography, Bayside NY (S)

Wiprud, Theodore, *Prof,* Oregon State University, Dept of Art, Corvallis OR (S)

Wirth, Karen, *Asst Prof,* College of Visual Arts, Saint Paul MN (S)

Wisch, Barbara, *Asst Prof,* State University of New York, College at Cortland, Art Dept, Cortland NY (S)

Wise, Laura, *Gallery Shoppe Coordr,* ArtSpace-Lima, Lima OH

Wise, R Gordon, *Chmn,* Millersville University, Art Dept, Millersville PA (S)

Wisniewfki, Judith, *Instr,* Delaware County Community College, Communications & Humanities House, Media PA (S)

Wisniewski, Dale, *Adjunct Prof,* North Central College, Dept of Art, Naperville IL (S)

Wissler-Thomas, Carrie, *Pres,* Art Association of Harrisburg, School & Galleries, Harrisburg PA

Wistar, Caroline, *Cur,* La Salle University, Art Museum, Philadelphia PA

Witcombe, Christopher, *Chmn,* Sweet Briar College, Art History Dept, Sweet Briar VA (S)

Witczak, Dann, *Chief Preparator & Registrar,* Cleveland Center for Contemporary Art, Cleveland OH

Witham, James, *Cur,* Essex Historical Society, Essex Shipbuilding Museum, Essex MA

Witherell, James, *Area Dir,* College of the Siskiyous, Art Dept, Weed CA (S)

Witherow, Dale, *Assoc Prof,* Mansfield University, Art Dept, Mansfield PA (S)

Witkes, Michael, *Exec Dir,* Jewish Community Center of Greater Washington, Jane L & Robert H Weiner Judaic Museum, Rockville MD

Witt, David, *Cur,* University of New Mexico, The Harwood Foundation, Taos NM

Witt, Sarah, *Librn,* American Jewish Congress, Shad Polier Memorial Library, New York NY

Wittersheim, John, *Assoc Prof,* Siena Heights College, Studio Angelico-Art Dept, Adrian MI (S)

Witthoft, Brucia, *Prof,* Framingham State College, Art Dept, Framingham MA (S)

Wittkopp, Greg, *Dir,* Cranbrook Art Museum, Bloomfield Hills MI

Witty, Anne, *Cur,* Columbia River Maritime Museum, Library, Astoria OR

Witzling, Mara, *Assoc Prof,* University of New Hampshire, Dept of Arts & Art History, Durham NH (S)

Witzmann, Hugh, *Asst Prof,* Saint John's University, Art Dept, Collegeville MN (S)

Wixom, William D, *Chmn Medieval Art & the Cloisters,* The Metropolitan Museum of Art, New York NY

Wixom, William D, *Chmn & Cur,* The Metropolitan Museum of Art, The Cloisters, New York NY

Wnuk, Joseph, *Assoc Dean,* Mount Vernon College, School of Art & Design, Washington DC (S)

Woike, Glenn V, *Head Librn,* Daemen College, Marian Library, Amherst NY

Wojciechowski, Barbara P, *Instr,* Villa Maria College of Buffalo, Art Dept, Buffalo NY (S)

Wojtkiewicz, Dennis, *Dir Grad Studies,* Bowling Green State University, School of Art, Bowling Green OH (S)

Wolanin, Barbara A, *Chief Cur,* United States Capitol, Architect of the Capitol, Washington DC

Wolber, Andy, *Dir,* Dallas Historical Society, Hall of State, Dallas TX

Wolber, Paul, *Dir,* Spring Arbor College, Art Dept, Spring Arbor MI (S)

Wold, Lynn Murdock, *Librn,* Berkeley Public Library, Berkeley CA

Wolf, Arthur H, *Pres,* High Desert Museum, Bend OR

Wolf, Constance, *Assoc Dir Pub Prog,* Whitney Museum of American Art, New York NY

Wolf, Pat, *Dir,* Northland Pioneer College, Art Dept, Holbrook AZ (S)

Wolf, Patricia B, *Dir,* Anchorage Museum of History & Art, Anchorage AK

Wolf, Robert L, *Dir Design,* Arizona State University, College of Architecture & Environmental Design, Tempe AZ (S)

Wolf, Sara, *Librn,* Mint Museum of Art, Library, Charlotte NC

Wolf, Tom, *Dir,* Bard College, William Cooper Procter Art Center, Annandale-on-Hudson NY

Wolf, Vicki, *Managing Dir,* Sushi-Performance & Visual Art Gallery, San Diego CA

Wolfe, Michael, *Chief Financial Officer,* Whitney Museum of American Art, New York NY

Wolfe, Richard, *Educ Coordr,* Pennsylvania Historical & Museum Commission, Brandywine Battlefield Park, Harrisburg PA

Wolfe, Townsend, *Chief Cur,* The Arkansas Arts Center, Museum School, Little Rock AR (S)

Wolfe, Townsend D, *Dir & Chief Cur,* Arkansas Arts Center, Little Rock AR

Wolff, Elaine, *Develop Asst,* Texas Fine Arts Association, Austin TX

Wolff, Hennie, *Exec Dir,* Visual Arts Ontario, Library, Toronto ON

Wolff, Hennie L, *Exec Dir,* Visual Arts Ontario, Toronto ON

Wolff, Martha, *Cur European Painting Before 1750,* The Art Institute of Chicago, Chicago IL

Wolff, Roland C, *Asst Prof,* Savannah State University, Dept of Fine Arts, Savannah GA (S)

Wolfram, William R, *Head Dept,* Concordia College, Art Dept, Seward NE (S)

Wolgin, William, *Exec VPres,* Boca Raton Museum of Art, Boca Raton FL

Wolin, Jeffrey, *Dir,* Indiana University, Bloomington, Henry Radford Hope School of Fine Arts, Bloomington IN (S)

Wolin, Jeffrey, *Assoc Prof,* Indiana University, Bloomington, Henry Radford Hope School of Fine Arts, Bloomington IN (S)

Wolins, Inez, *Dir,* Wichita Art Museum, Wichita KS

Wollensak, Andrea, *Asst Prof,* Connecticut College, Dept of Art, New London CT (S)

Wollowitz, Charles, *Adjunct Asst Prof,* Le Moyne College, Fine Arts Dept, Syracuse NY (S)

Woloritz, Vivian, *Chmn 2-D Fine Arts,* Moore College of Art & Design, Philadelphia PA (S)

Wolsk, Nancy, *Dir,* Transylvania University, Morlan Gallery, Lexington KY

Wolsk, Nancy, *Instr,* Transylvania University, Studio Arts Dept, Lexington KY (S)

Woltman, Robert, *Cur Exhib,* Albuquerque Museum of Art & History, Albuquerque NM

Wolynetz, Lubow, *Educational Dir*, The Ukrainian Museum, New York NY

Womack, Dawn, *VPres Arts & Educ*, Spirit Square Center for Arts & Education, Charlotte NC

Wong, Albert, *Head Dept*, University of Texas at El Paso, Dept of Art, El Paso TX (S)

Wong, Eddie, *Prof*, University of Wisconsin-Stout, Dept of Art & Design, Menomonie WI (S)

Wong, Michele, *Registrar*, New York University, Grey Art Gallery & Study Center, New York NY

Wong-Ligda, Ed, *Assoc Prof*, Grand Valley State University, Art & Design Dept, Allendale MI (S)

Woo, Cathy, *VPres*, Northwest Watercolor Society, Bellevue WA

Woo, Suzanne, *Membership & Spec Events*, Fort Worth Art Association, Modern Art Museum of Fort Worth, Fort Worth TX

Wood, Arthur, *Dean of Acad Student Services*, Ontario College of Art & Design, Toronto ON (S)

Wood, Carleton B, *Horticulturist*, Tryon Palace Historic Sites & Gardens, New Bern NC

Wood, Carol, *Treas*, Safety Harbor Museum of Regional History, Safety Harbor FL

Wood, Clare, *Systems Coordr*, Arts Extension Service, Amherst MA

Wood, Clifford P, *Dept Head*, California State University at Sacramento, Library - Humanities Reference Dept, Sacramento CA

Wood, Darrow, *Chief Librn*, New York City Technical College, Namm Hall Library and Learning Resource Center, Brooklyn NY

Wood, David, *Cur*, Concord Museum, Concord MA

Wood, David, *Cur*, Concord Museum, Library, Concord MA

Wood, Don, *Cur Oriental Art*, Birmingham Museum of Art, Birmingham AL

Wood, James N, *Pres & Dir*, The Art Institute of Chicago, Chicago IL

Wood, Judy, *Acquisition Head*, Fashion Institute of Technology, Gladys Marcus Library, New York NY

Wood, Katie, *Bus Mgr*, Sheldon Swope Art Museum, Terre Haute IN

Wood, Leslie, *Dir Educational Center*, Craft Alliance Gallery & Education Center for the Visual Arts, Saint Louis MO

Wood, Lisa R, *Photographic Archivist*, University of Kentucky, Photographic Archives, Lexington KY

Wood, Marcia J, *Prof*, Kalamazoo College, Art Dept, Kalamazoo MI (S)

Wood, Marilyn, *Instr*, Normandale Community College, Bloomington MN (S)

Wood, Mary Jane, *Dir Communications*, Boca Raton Museum of Art, Library, Boca Raton FL

Wood, Mary Louise, *Dir*, American Association of Museums, US National Committee of the International Council of Museums (AAM-ICOM), Washington DC

Wood, Neva, *Asst Prof*, Central Missouri State University, Art Dept, Warrensburg MO (S)

Wood, Richard, *Assoc Prof*, Centenary College, Humanities Dept, Hackettstown NJ (S)

Wood, Roberta, *Office Mgr*, Galesburg Civic Art Center, Galesburg IL

Wood, Robert B, *Pres*, Halifax Historical Society, Inc, Halifax Historical Museum, Daytona Beach FL

Wood, Sally, *Cur Interpretation*, Wade House & Wesley W Jung Carriage Museum, Historic House & Carriage Museum, Greenbush WI

Wood, Sharon, *Assoc Prof*, Lansing Community College, Art Program, Lansing MI (S)

Wood, Susan, *Assoc Prof*, Oakland University, Dept of Art & Art History, Rochester MI (S)

Wood, William L, *Pres Emeritus*, Halifax Historical Society, Inc, Halifax Historical Museum, Daytona Beach FL

Wood, William P, *VPres*, Fairmount Park Art Association, Philadelphia PA

Wood, Wilma, *Dir*, Vancouver Museum Commission, Vancouver Museum Library, Vancouver BC

Woodard, Marie, *Slide Librn*, Providence College, Art & Art History Dept, Providence RI (S)

Woodburn, Steven, *Adjunct Asst Prof*, New York Institute of Technology, Fine Arts Dept, Old Westbury NY (S)

Woodford, Don, *Instr*, California State University, San Bernardino, Visual Arts, San Bernardino CA (S)

Woodham, Derrick, *Prof Fine Arts*, University of Cincinnati, School of Art, Cincinnati OH (S)

Woodruff, Lynne, *Head Art Library*, University of Maryland, College Park, Art Library, College Park MD

Woods, James, *Dir*, College of Southern Idaho, Herrett Center for Arts & Science, Twin Falls ID

Woods, Jean, *Dir*, Washington County Museum of Fine Arts, Hagerstown MD

Woods, Jean, *Dir*, Washington County Museum of Fine Arts, Library, Hagerstown MD

Woods, Jennifer L, *Chief Conservation*, Library Company of Philadelphia, Philadelphia PA

Woods, Paula, *Cur Educ*, Tippecanoe County Historical Museum, Lafayette IN

Woods, Shirley, *Asst Dir Operations*, Montgomery Museum of Fine Arts, Montgomery AL

Woods, Sidnii, *Pres*, Marin Society of Artists Inc, Ross CA

Woods, Suzanne, *Dir*, University of Wisconsin-Stevens Point, Carlsten Art Gallery, Stevens Point WI

Woods, Yvette, *Instr*, Saint Louis Community College at Meramec, Art Dept, Saint Louis MO (S)

Woodson, Celia, *Gallery Dir & Mgr*, National Conference of Artists, Michigan Chapter Gallery, Detroit MI

Woodson, Jim, *Prof*, Texas Christian University, Art & Art History Dept, Fort Worth TX (S)

Woodson, Yoko, *Cur Japanese Art*, Asian Art Museum of San Francisco, Avery Brundage Collection, San Francisco CA

Woodward, Bev, *Exec Dir*, Heritage Hjemkomst Interpretive Center, Moorhead MN

Woodward, Bill, *Asst Prof*, Mississippi State University, Art Dept, Mississippi State MS (S)

Woodward, Gary, *Assoc Prof*, Kansas State University, Art Dept, Manhattan KS (S)

Woodward, Kesler, *Dept Head*, University of Alaska-Fairbanks, Dept of Art, Fairbanks AK (S)

Woodward, Richard, *Assoc Dir Exhib/Prog Div*, Virginia Museum of Fine Arts, Richmond VA

Woodward, Roland H, *Exec Dir*, Chester County Historical Society, West Chester PA

Woodward, W T, *Assoc Prof*, George Washington University, Dept of Art, Washington DC (S)

Woody, Howard, *Prof*, University of South Carolina, Dept of Art, Columbia SC (S)

Woodyatt, Lois H, *Archival Asst*, National Academy of Design, Archives, New York NY

Wooff, Annette, *Admin Asst*, The Canadian Craft Museum, Vancouver BC

Woolever, Mary, *Architecture Librn*, The Art Institute of Chicago, Ryerson & Burnham Libraries, Chicago IL

Wooley, David, *Cur Antropology*, State Historical Society of Wisconsin, State Historical Museum, Madison WI

Woolf, David, *Assoc Prof*, Norwich University, Dept of Philosophy, Religion & Fine Arts, Northfield VT (S)

Woolfolk, Charles, *Assoc Dean*, Rutgers, the State University of New Jersey, Mason Gross School of the Arts, New Brunswick NJ (S)

Woolin, David, *Dir & Museologist*, LeSueur County Historical Museum, Chapter One, Elysian MN

Woolin, David, *Dir*, LeSueur County Historical Museum, Collections Library, Elysian MN

Woolley, Lois, *Instr*, Woodstock School of Art, Inc, Woodstock NY (S)

Woollman, Lisa, *Instr*, Delaware County Community College, Communications & Humanities House, Media PA (S)

Woolston, Evelyn, *Pres*, Arts Club of Washington, James Monroe House, Washington DC

Woon, Wendy, *Educ Dir*, Museum of Contemporary Art, Chicago IL

Woosley, Anne I, *Foundation Dir*, Amerind Foundation, Inc, Amerind Museum, Fulton-Hayden Memorial Art Gallery, Dragoon AZ

Woosley, Anne I, *Foundation Dir*, Amerind Foundation, Inc, Fulton-Hayden Memorial Library, Dragoon AZ

Wooters, David A, *Archivist*, George Eastman House-International Museum of Photography & Film, Library, Rochester NY

Work, Lisa, *Gen Mgr*, Louisville Visual Art Association, Louisville KY

Workman, Robert, *Dir Exhib*, The American Federation of Arts, New York NY

Worley, Ken, *Adjunct Instr*, Maryville University of Saint Louis, Art Division, Saint Louis MO (S)

Worman-Royer, Judith, *Chmn*, Indiana University-East, Humanities Dept, Richmond IN (S)

Worrell, Philip, *Visual Resource Cur*, Texas Tech University, Art Dept Visual Resource Center, Lubbock TX

Worsham, Beverly, *Asst Dir*, Walter Cecil Rawls Museum, Courtland VA

Worth, Robert R, *Pres*, Adirondack Historical Association, Adirondack Museum, Blue Mountain Lake NY

Worth, Timothy, *Cur*, Manitoba Historical Society, Dalnavert Museum, Winnipeg MB

Wortham, Marshall, *Prof*, Southwest Texas State University, Dept of Art, San Marcos TX (S)

Worthen, William B, *Dir*, Arkansas Territorial Restoration, Little Rock AR

Worthington, Barbara, *Office Mgr*, Howard County Arts Council, Ellicott City MD

Worthington, Hall, *VPres*, Star-Spangled Banner Flag House Association, Flag House & 1812 Museum, Baltimore MD

Worthington, Margaret, *Asst Prof*, University of North Carolina at Wilmington, Dept of Fine Arts - Division of Art, Wilmington NC (S)

Worthley, Ginger, *Exhibit Dir*, Conejo Valley Art Museum, Thousand Oaks CA

Worthy, Mary N, *Docent*, Florida Community College at Jacksonville, South Gallery, Jacksonville FL

Wortman, Jean, *Cur Educ*, Historical Society of Rockland County, New City NY

Wortman, Kathy, *Public Relations*, Maricopa County Historical Society, Desert Caballeros Western Museum, Wickenburg AZ

Wotojwicz, Robert, *Assoc Prof*, Old Dominion University, Art Dept, Norfolk VA (S)

Wray, George T, *Prof*, University of Idaho, College of Art & Architecture, Moscow ID (S)

Wright, Anita, *Coll Mgr*, Cortland County Historical Society, Kellogg Memorial Research Library, Cortland NY

Wright, Arthuree, *Librn*, Howard University, Architecture & Planning Library, Washington DC

Wright, Astri, *Assoc Prof*, University of Victoria, Dept of History in Art, Victoria BC (S)

Wright, Carolyn, *Exec Secy*, Rehoboth Art League, Inc, Rehoboth Beach DE

Wright, Cathy, *Dir Exhib*, Colorado Springs Fine Arts Center, Colorado Springs CO

Wright, Charles, *Dean School Fine Arts*, Ouachita Baptist University, Dept of Art, Arkadelphia AR (S)

Wright, David, *Museum Cur*, United States Tobacco Manufacturing Company Inc, Museum of Tobacco Art History, Nashville TN

Wright, David W, *Registrar*, Pierpont Morgan Library, New York NY

Wright, Gary, *Preparator*, Syracuse University, Art Collection, Syracuse NY

Wright, Gene, *Scientific Illustration*, University of Georgia, Franklin College of Arts & Sciences, Lamar Dodd School of Art, Athens GA (S)

Wright, James, *Dir*, University of New Mexico, Fine Arts Library, Albuquerque NM

Wright, Jerrie, *Prin Staff Asst*, University of California, Davis, Art Dept, Davis CA (S)

Wright, Jesse G, *Dean*, Jacksonville University, Dept of Art, Jacksonville FL

Wright, J Franklin, *Prof*, George Washington University, Dept of Art, Washington DC (S)

Wright, John, *Cur Educational Servs*, University of South Carolina, McKissick Museum, Columbia SC

Wright, John, *Photographer*, Tougaloo College, Art Collection, Tougaloo MS

Wright, John H, *Cur,* Historical Society of Old Newbury, Cushing House Museum, Newburyport MA

Wright, Kevin, *Cur,* Bergen County Historical Society, Steuben House Museum, River Edge NJ

Wright, Leslie, *Cur,* Cedar Rapids Museum of Art, Cedar Rapids IA

Wright, Lorri, *Asst Museum Store Mgr,* Fort Worth Art Association, Modern Art Museum of Fort Worth, Fort Worth TX

Wright, Mary A, *Dept Head,* Central Library, Dept of Fine Arts, San Antonio TX

Wright, Nancy, *Asst Dir,* Samuel S Fleisher Art Memorial, Philadelphia PA (S)

Wright, Patricia, *Asst Dir,* Sweet Briar College, Martin C Shallenberger Art Library, Sweet Briar VA

Wright, Pope, *Lectr,* University of Wisconsin-Superior, Programs in the Visual Arts, Superior WI (S)

Wright, Robert, *Chmn,* University of Toronto, Programme in Landscape Architecture, Toronto ON (S)

Wright, Robin, *Cur Native American Art,* University of Washington, Thomas Burke Memorial Washington State Museum, Seattle WA

Wright, Ron, *Prof,* Marietta College, Art Dept, Marietta OH (S)

Wright, Sharyl, *Instr,* Avila College, Art Division, Dept of Humanities, Kansas City MO (S)

Wright, Tony, *Head Design & Installation,* Fort Worth Art Association, Modern Art Museum of Fort Worth, Fort Worth TX

Wright, Vicki C, *Dir,* University of New Hampshire, The Art Gallery, Durham NH

Wright, Vincent, *Asst Prof,* C W Post Center of Long Island University, School of Visual & Performing Arts, Brookville NY (S)

Wright, Virginia L, *Assoc Librn,* Corning Museum of Glass, Rakow Library, Corning NY

Wright, Wayne, *Assoc Dir,* New York State Historical Association, Library, Cooperstown NY

Wroble, Stephen, *Prof,* Schoolcraft College, Dept of Art & Design, Livonia MI (S)

Wroblewski, Andrzej, *In Charge Industrial Design,* University of Illinois, Urbana-Champaign, School of Art & Design, Champaign IL (S)

Wu, Jen, *Admin Coordr,* Dallas Visual Art Center, Dallas TX

Wu, Marshall, *Cur of Asian Art,* University of Michigan, Museum of Art, Ann Arbor MI

Wu, Marshall, *Cur,* University of Michigan, Ann Arbor, Dept of History of Art, Ann Arbor MI (S)

Wulfeck, Susan, *Adjunct Prof,* Pepperdine University, Seaver College, Dept of Art, Malibu CA (S)

Wulkan, Reba, *Contemporary Exhib Coordr,* Yeshiva University Museum, New York NY

Wunder, Elizabeth V, *Office Asst,* Washburn University, Mulvane Art Museum, Topeka KS

Wurmfeld, Sanford, *Chmn Art Dept,* Hunter College, Art Dept, New York NY (S)

Wurtz, John, *Pres,* Jefferson County Historical Society Museum, Madison IN

Wyancko, Ronald, *Prof,* James Madison University, School of Art & Art History, Harrisonburg VA (S)

Wyatt, Charles D, *Supt,* National Park Service, Hubbell Trading Post National Historic Site, Ganado AZ

Wyatt, Joseph, *Cur,* University of Waterloo, Art Gallery, Waterloo ON

Wyatt, Judy, *Library Asst,* Kansas State University, Paul Weigel Library of Architecture Planning & Design, Manhattan KS

Wyatt, Victoria, *Assoc Prof,* University of Victoria, Dept of History in Art, Victoria BC (S)

Wylder, Viki D, *Registrar & Cur Exhib,* Florida State University, Museum of Fine Arts, Tallahassee FL

Wyles, Bill, *Develop Dir,* National Cowboy Hall of Fame & Western Heritage Center Museum, Oklahoma City OK

Wylie, Rolfe, *Chmn,* Texarkana College, Art Dept, Texarkana TX (S)

Wyllie, Nancy, *Prof,* Community College of Rhode Island, Dept of Art, Warwick RI (S)

Wyly, Mary, *Librn,* Newberry Library, Chicago IL

Wyma, Robert, *Admin Asst,* Prince George Art Gallery, Prince George BC

Wyman, Elizabeth, *Pres Board,* Oshkosh Public Museum, Oshkosh WI

Wyman, James, *Coordr Exhib,* Visual Studies Workshop, Rochester NY

Wyman, Marlena, *Sr A-V Archivist,* Department of Community Development, Provincial Archives of Alberta, Edmonton AB

Wyner, Justin L, *Pres,* American Jewish Historical Society, Waltham MA

Wyngaard, Shirley, *Exec Dir,* Allied Arts Council of Lethbridge, Bowman Arts Center, Lethbridge AB

Wyngaard, Susan E, *Head Librn,* Ohio State University, Fine Arts Library, Columbus OH

Xu, Gan, *Instr,* Maine College of Art, Portland ME (S)

Yacowar, Maurice, *Dean, Faculty Fine Arts,* University of Calgary, Dept of Art, Calgary AB (S)

Yager, David, *Chmn,* University of Maryland, Baltimore County, Visual Arts Dept, Baltimore MD (S)

Yakstis, Gary, *Operations Dir,* University of Connecticut, Jorgensen Gallery, Storrs CT

Yang, Alice Huei-Zu, *Cur,* The Parrish Art Museum, Southampton NY

Yang, Geoffrey, *Treas,* The Friends of Photography, Ansel Adams Center for Photography, San Francisco CA

Yang, Xiaoneug, *Cur Early Chinese Art,* Nelson-Atkins Museum of Art, Kansas City MO

Yanik, John V, *Assoc Prof,* Catholic University of America, School of Architecture & Planning, Washington DC (S)

Yao, Winberta, *Art Specialist,* Arizona State University, Hayden Library, Tempe AZ

Yapelli, Tina, *Gallery Dir,* San Diego State University, University Gallery, San Diego CA

Yarbedra, Ronald F, *Prof,* Florida A & M University, Dept of Visual Arts, Humanities & Theatre, Tallahassee FL (S)

Yarborough, Jane, *Visitor Prog Coordr,* Supreme Court of the United States, Washington DC

Yard, Sally, *Chmn,* University of San Diego, Art Dept, San Diego CA (S)

Yarlow, Loretta, *Dir & Cur,* York University, Art Gallery of York University, North York ON

Yasin, Howard, *Sales,* Yale University, Art Gallery, New Haven CT

Yassin, Robert A, *Dir,* Tucson Museum of Art & Historic Block, Tucson AZ

Yasuda, Robert, *Prof,* C W Post Center of Long Island University, School of Visual & Performing Arts, Brookville NY (S)

Yates, Sam, *Dir,* University of Tennessee, Ewing Gallery of Art and Architecture, Knoxville TN

Yates, Steve, *Cur Photo,* Museum of New Mexico, Museum of Fine Arts, Santa Fe NM

Yeager, William, *Cur,* Eva Brook Donly Museum, Simcoe ON

Yeager, William, *Cur,* Eva Brook Donly Museum, Library, Simcoe ON

Yeates, Michael, *Keeper History Coll,* Massachusetts Institute of Technology, MIT Museum, Cambridge MA

Yee, Ann G, *Admin Coordr,* East Bay Asian Local Development Corp, Asian Resource Gallery, Oakland CA

Yee, Kay, *Acting Area Head Jewelry,* Pasadena City College, Art Dept, Pasadena CA (S)

Yelavich, Susan, *Asst Dir Public Prog,* Cooper-Hewitt, National Design Museum, New York NY

Yelen, Alice Rae, *Asst to Dir,* New Orleans Museum of Art, New Orleans LA

Yeni, Lindi, *Dir,* Midtown Art Center, Houston TX

Yerdon, Lawrence J, *Dir,* Hancock Shaker Village, Inc, Pittsfield MA

Yes, Phyllis, *Prof,* Lewis & Clark College, Dept of Art, Portland OR (S)

Yetter, George, *Assoc Cur Architecture Coll,* Colonial Williamsburg Foundation, John D Rockefeller, Jr Library, Williamsburg VA

Yiengpruksawan, Mimi, *Dir Undergrad Studies,* Yale University, Dept of the History of Art, New Haven CT (S)

Yoder, Caroline, *Exec Dir,* New Hampshire Antiquarian Society, Hopkinton NH

Yoder, Larry, *Chmn Dept,* Lenoir Rhyne College, Dept of Art, Hickory NC (S)

Yokobosky, Matthew, *Asst Cur, Film & Video,* Whitney Museum of American Art, New York NY

Yolleck, Frima, *Bookkeeper,* Visual Arts Ontario, Toronto ON

Yong, Kok, *Instr,* Denison University, Dept of Art, Granville OH (S)

Yoon, Sang, *Assoc Prof,* James Madison University, School of Art & Art History, Harrisonburg VA (S)

York, Jeffery, *Exec Dir,* Art Museum of Southeast Texas, Beaumont TX

York, Judith, *Pres,* The Art Institute of Chicago, Antiquarian Society, Chicago IL

York, Judith, *Dir Prog,* The University of Texas, Institute of Texan Cultures, San Antonio TX

York, Robert, *Instr of Art,* Edison Community College, Dept of Fine & Performing Arts, Fort Myers FL (S)

Yorty, Faity, *Cur Educ,* Springfield Art Museum, Springfield MO

Yoshida, Ray, *Prof,* School of the Art Institute of Chicago, Chicago IL (S)

Yoshimine-Webster, Carol, *Assoc Prof,* Centenary College, Humanities Dept, Hackettstown NJ (S)

Yoshimura, Reiko, *Librn,* Freer Gallery of Art Gallery, Library, Washington DC

Yost, Robert, *Dir,* Mohave Museum of History & Arts, Kingman AZ

Yothers, John, *Adjunct Prof,* Washington & Jefferson College, Art Dept, Washington PA (S)

Youdovin, Susan, *Educational Cur,* Spertus Institute of Jewish Studies, Spertus Museum, Chicago IL

Youds, Robert, *Chmn,* University of Victoria, Dept of Visual Arts, Victoria BC (S)

Young, Alice, *Cur Educ,* Agecroft Association, Agecroft Hall, Richmond VA

Young, Alice, *Cur Educ,* Agecroft Association, Museum, Richmond VA

Young, Becky, *Lectr,* University of Pennsylvania, Graduate School of Fine Arts, Philadelphia PA (S)

Young, Beth, *Asst Prof,* Mary Baldwin College, Dept of Art, Staunton VA (S)

Young, Bill, *Gen Mgr,* Ozark Folk Center, Ozark Cultural Resource Center, Mountain View AR

Young, Brent, *Assoc Prof,* Cleveland Institute of Art, Cleveland OH (S)

Young, Charles, *Chmn Dept,* Calvin College, Art Dept, Grand Rapids MI (S)

Young, Charles A, *Prof,* University of the District of Columbia, Dept of Mass Media, Visual & Performing Arts, Washington DC (S)

Young, Christopher R, *Cur,* Flint Institute of Arts, Flint MI

Young, Daniel, *Instr,* State University of New York College at Oneonta, Dept of Art, Oneonta NY (S)

Young, Dede, *Cur Exhib,* University of Florida, Samuel P Harn Museum of Art, Gainesville FL

Young, Gary, *Gallery Cur,* University of Saskatchewan, Gordon Snelgrove Art Gallery, Saskatoon SK

Young, James L, *Dir,* College of Eastern Utah, Gallery East, Price UT

Young, Jane Anne, *Dir Educ,* University of Virginia, Bayly Art Museum, Charlottesville VA

Young, Jean, *Bookstore Mgr,* Brandywine River Museum, Chadds Ford PA

Young, Jeff, *Asst Prof,* University of Central Arkansas, Art Dept, Conway AR (S)

Young, Jerry, *VPres,* Summit County Historical Society, Akron OH

Young, Jocelyn, *Cur Public Art,* Anchorage Museum of History & Art, Anchorage AK

Young, Joseph L, *Dir,* Art in Architecture, Los Angeles CA (S)

Young, Joseph L, *Dir,* Art in Architecture, Joseph Young Library, Los Angeles CA

Young, Karen S, *Co-Dir,* Kit Carson Historic Museums, Taos NM

Young, Karen S, *Co-Dir,* Kit Carson Historic Museums, Archives, Taos NM

Young, Karen S, *Co-Dir,* Kit Carson Historic Museums, Ernest Blumenschein Home & Studio, Taos NM

Young, Karen S, *Co-Dir,* Kit Carson Historic Museums, Home & Museum, Taos NM

Young, Karen S, *Co-Dir,* Kit Carson Historic Museums, Hacienda Martinez, Taos NM

Young, Kathy, *VPres Buildings & Grounds,* DuPage Art League School & Gallery, Wheaton IL

Young, Martie, *Cur Asian Art,* Cornell University, Herbert F Johnson Museum of Art, Ithaca NY

Young, Martie W, *Prof,* Cornell University, Dept of the History of Art, Ithaca NY (S)

Young, Mary, *Educ Dir,* Green Hill Center for North Carolina Art, Greensboro NC

Young, Nancy, *Develop Dir,* Mexican Museum, San Francisco CA

Young, Patience, *Cur Educ,* Stanford University, Museum of Art, Stanford CA

Young, Patrick, *Photographer,* University of Michigan, Slide & Photograph Collection, Ann Arbor MI

Young, Phil, *Prof,* Hartwick College, Art Dept, Oneonta NY (S)

Young, Richard, *Prof,* Gavilan College, Art Dept, Gilroy CA (S)

Young, Risa, *Dir,* The Children's Aid Society, Visual Arts Program of the Greenwich Village Center, New York NY (S)

Young, Robert, *Assoc Prof,* University of British Columbia, Dept of Fine Arts, Vancouver BC (S)

Young, Steve, *Dir,* Fairfield Historical Society, Library, Fairfield CT

Young, Susan, *Project Planner,* City of Springdale, Shiloh Museum, Springdale AR

Young, Tammy, *Office Admin,* Institute of Alaska Native Arts, Inc, Fairbanks AK

Young, Terence, *Acting Dir Studies,* Harvard University, Studies in Landscape Architecture & Garden Library, Washington DC

Young, Thomas E, *Librn,* Philbrook Museum of Art, Chapman Library, Tulsa OK

Young, Timothy, *Asst Prof,* Malone College, Dept of Art, Canton OH (S)

Young, Tom, *Instr,* Greenfield Community College, Art, Graphic Design & Media Communication Dept, Greenfield MA (S)

Youngberg, Kathryn B, *Museum Shop Mgr,* Longue Vue House & Gardens, New Orleans LA

Youngblood, Judy, *Printmaking Coordr,* University of North Texas, School of Visual Arts, Denton TX (S)

Younger, Dan, *Asst Prof,* University of Alabama in Huntsville, Dept of Art & Art History, Huntsville AL (S)

Younger, Dan, *Asst Prof,* University of Missouri, Saint Louis, Dept of Art & Art History, Saint Louis MO (S)

Youngers, Peter L, *Instructional Dir, Humanities & Human Servs,* Northeastern Junior College, Dept of Art, Sterling CO (S)

Young-Gome, Cynthia, *Registrar,* Old York Historical Society, York ME

Younginger, Jennifer, *Cur Art Mus,* Heritage Plantation of Sandwich, Sandwich MA

Youngman, James E, *Dir,* Artist Studio Centers, Inc, New York NY (S)

Youngs, Christopher, *Dir,* Albright College, Freedman Gallery, Reading PA

Younker, Phil, *VPres,* Fairbanks Arts Association, Fairbanks AK

Yount, Sylvia, *Cur,* Pennsylvania Academy of the Fine Arts, Museum of American Art, Philadelphia PA

Yourman, Judy, *Asst Prof,* Saint Olaf College, Art Dept, Northfield MN (S)

Yu, Chilin, *Librn,* Columbus College of Art & Design, Packard Library, Columbus OH

Yuan, Juliana, *Lectr,* University of Missouri, Saint Louis, Dept of Art & Art History, Saint Louis MO (S)

Yuen, Gloria, *Asst to Dir,* New York Historical Society, New York NY

Yuen, Kee-Ho, *Assoc Prof,* University of Northern Iowa, Dept of Art, Cedar Falls IA (S)

Yurkanin, Sharon, *Sales Gallery,* Allentown Art Museum, Allentown PA

Yust, Becky L, *Head Dept,* University of Minnesota, Dept of Design, Housing & Apparel, Saint Paul MN (S)

Zabarsky, Melvin, *Prof,* University of New Hampshire, Dept of Arts & Art History, Durham NH (S)

Zabel, Barbara, *Chmn,* Connecticut College, Dept of Art History, New London CT (S)

Zabel, Craig, *Dept Head,* Pennsylvania State University, University Park, Dept of Art History, University Park PA (S)

Zaborowski, Dennis, *Prof,* University of North Carolina at Chapel Hill, Art Dept, Chapel Hill NC (S)

Zacharias, David, *Asst Prof,* Converse College, Art Dept, Spartanburg SC (S)

Zachman, Gina, *Educ Coordr,* University of Notre Dame, Snite Museum of Art, Notre Dame IN

Zachos, Kimon S, *Pres,* The Currier Gallery of Art, Manchester NH

Zack, Kerry, *Ed Coordr,* University of Kentucky, Art Museum, Lexington KY

Zackheim, Michael, *Team Leader Record Develop & Management,* State University of New York at New Paltz, Sojourner Truth Library, New Paltz NY

Zacnic, Ivan, *Chmn,* Lehigh University, Dept of Art & Architecture, Bethlehem PA (S)

Zafron, Eric, *Deputy Dir Curatorial Affairs,* The Jewish Museum, New York NY

Zahner, Mary, *Assoc Prof,* University of Dayton, Visual Arts Dept, Dayton OH (S)

Zakoian, Paul, *Sculpture,* Contemporary Art Workshop, Chicago IL (S)

Zamagias, James D, *Chmn,* Allegany Community College, Art Dept, Cumberland MD (S)

Zampogna, Ralph, *VPres,* Doshi Center for Contemporary Art, Harrisburg PA

Zander, Jane, *Sr Cataloger,* Nelson-Atkins Museum of Art, Spencer Art Reference Library, Kansas City MO

Zandler, Richard, *Dir,* Maryland-National Capital Park & Planning Commission, Montpelier Cultural Arts Center, Laurel MD

Zanette, Paul, *VPres,* Prince George Art Gallery, Prince George BC

Zapatka, Mark, *Asst Reader's Servs,* Harvard University, Byzantine Library, Washington DC

Zaporzan, Christine, *Educ,* Glanmore, Hastings County Museum, Belleville ON

Zapton, Steve, *Prof,* James Madison University, School of Art & Art History, Harrisonburg VA (S)

Zaremba, Maureen, *Office Mgr,* Art League of Manatee County, Bradenton FL

Zaremba, Maureen, *Mgr,* Art League of Manatee County, Library, Bradenton FL

Zaretsky, Barbara, *Exhibit Coordr,* C G Jung Institute of Chicago, Evanston IL

Zarse, Elaine, *Assoc Prof,* Mount Mary College, Art Dept, Milwaukee WI (S)

Zaruba, Gary E, *Prof,* University of Nebraska, Kearney, Dept of Art & Art History, Kearney NE (S)

Zarucchi, Jeanne Morgan, *Assoc Prof,* University of Missouri, Saint Louis, Dept of Art & Art History, Saint Louis MO (S)

Zatylny, Jane, *Asst to Dir & Special Prog Officer,* McMaster University, Museum of Art, Hamilton ON

Zaugg, Elwood, *Dean,* Salt Lake Community College, Graphic Design Dept, Salt Lake City UT (S)

Zawada, Elizabeth, *Dir,* Greenwich House Pottery, New York NY (S)

Zawada, Elizabeth, *Dir,* Greenwich House, Pottery Library, New York NY

Zbarsky, Felix, *Asst Prof,* New York Institute of Technology, Fine Arts Dept, Old Westbury NY (S)

Zea, Philip, *Deputy Dir & Cur,* Historic Deerfield, Inc, Deerfield MA

Zec, John J, *Prof,* Mount Saint Mary's College, Visual & Performing Arts Dept, Emmitsburg MD (S)

Zehnder, Marvin, *Prof,* Northern Michigan University, Dept of Art & Design, Marquette MI (S)

Zehr, Connie, *Prof,* Claremont Graduate School, Dept of Fine Arts, Claremont CA (S)

Zeidberg, David, *Dir Library,* The Huntington Library, Art Collections & Botanical Gardens, San Marino CA

Zeidler, Jeanne, *Dir,* Hampton University, University Museum, Hampton VA

Zeitler, Alevis, *Instr,* Monterey Peninsula College, Art Dept, Monterey CA (S)

Zeitlin, Marilyn A, *Dir,* Arizona State University, ASU Art Museum, Tempe AZ

Zelasnic, Laura, *Coll Mgr,* Queens Historical Society, Flushing NY

Zelenik, John, *Design & Production Chief,* National Museum of American Art, Washington DC

Zeller, Helen, *First VPres,* Toledo Museum of Art, Toledo OH

Zeller, Joe, *Chmn,* University of Kansas, Dept of Design, Lawrence KS (S)

Zeller, Joe, *Chmn Dept,* University of Kansas, Dept of Art & Music Education & Music Therapy, Lawrence KS (S)

Zelz, Abigail E, *Museum Teacher,* Penobscot Marine Museum, Searsport ME

Zendejas, R E, *Dir Museum Servs,* Colorado Springs Fine Arts Center, Colorado Springs CO

Zepp, Eugene, *Librn,* Boston Public Library, Rare Book & Manuscripts Dept, Boston MA

Zercher, Wendel, *Cur,* Heritage Center of Lancaster County Museum, Lancaster PA

Zernich, Theodore, *Dir School,* University of Illinois, Urbana-Champaign, School of Art & Design, Champaign IL (S)

Zettler, Richard, *Near East Section Assoc Cur,* University of Pennsylvania, Museum of Archaeology & Anthropology, Philadelphia PA

Ziady, Jon, *Educational Dir,* Portland Children's Museum, Portland OR

Zic, Virginia F, *Prof,* Sacred Heart University, Dept of Art, Fairfield CT (S)

Zidek, Al, *Instr,* Solano Community College, Division of Fine & Applied Art, Suisun City CA (S)

Ziditz-Ward, Vera, *Assoc Prof,* Bloomsburg University, Dept of Art, Bloomsburg PA (S)

Ziegler, Arthur P, *Pres,* Pittsburgh History & Landmarks Foundation, James D Van Trump Library, Pittsburgh PA

Ziegler, David, *Dir,* University of California, Los Angeles, Visual Resource Collection, Los Angeles CA

Ziegler, Joanne, *Chair&Assoc Prof,* College of the Holy Cross, Dept of Visual Arts, Worcester MA (S)

Ziegler, Sharon, *Pres,* West Bend Art Museum, West Bend WI

Zielinski, Henrietta, *Bibliographer,* School of the Art Institute of Chicago, John M Flaxman Library, Chicago IL

Ziemann, Richard, *Prof,* Herbert H Lehman College, Art Dept, Bronx NY (S)

Zierden, Martha, *Cur Historic Archaeology,* Charleston Museum, Charleston SC

Ziglar, Katie, *Develop Officer,* National Museum of American Art, Washington DC

Ziller Becker, Janis, *Exhibits Cur,* Nelda C & H J Lutcher Stark Foundation, Stark Museum of Art, Orange TX

Zimmer, Jim, *Dir,* Sioux City Art Center, Library, Sioux City IA

Zimmer, Kirt, *Public Relations,* Vermont State Craft Center at Frog Hollow, Middlebury VT

Zimmer, Sandra, *Instr,* Linn Benton Community College, Fine & Applied Art Dept, Albany OR (S)

Zimmer, Stephen, *Dir,* Philmont Scout Ranch, Philmont Museum, Cimarron NM

Zimmer, Stephen, *Dir,* Philmont Scout Ranch, Seaton Memorial Library, Cimarron NM

Zimmerer, Kathy, *Gallery Dir,* University Art Gallery of California State University at Dominguez Hills, Dominguez Hills CA

Zimmerman, Denny, *Chief Financial Officer,* National Cowboy Hall of Fame & Western Heritage Center Museum, Oklahoma City OK

Zimmerman, Fred, *Chmn,* State University of New York, College at Cortland, Art Dept, Cortland NY (S)

Zimmerman, Gerald, *Head Spec Projects,* Chicago Public Library, Harold Washington Library Center, Chicago IL

Zimmerman, Jerome, *Chmn,* C W Post Center of Long Island University, School of Visual & Performing Arts, Brookville NY (S)

Zimmerman, Mary R, *Dir Educ,* Louisiana State Exhibit Museum, Shreveport LA

Zimmerman, Salli, *Prof,* Nassau Community College, Art Dept, Garden City NY (S)

Zimmerman, Sally, *Preservation-Planner,* City of Cambridge Historical Commission, Cambridge MA

Zimmermann, Corinne, *Coordr Educ Patrons & Friends,* Brandeis University, Rose Art Museum, Waltham MA

Zimmers, Linda, *Architecture Asst,* Pennsylvania State University, Architecture Library, University Park PA

Zindler, Debra, *Marketing Coordr,* Milwaukee Public Museum, Milwaukee WI

Zink, Darcy, *Preparator & Technician,* Regina Public Library, Dunlop Art Gallery, Regina SK

Zink, James, *Dir,* Southeast Missouri State University, Kent Library, Cape Girardeau MO

Zink, Molly, *Publicist,* Ford Motor Company, Henry Ford Museum & Greenfield Village, Dearborn MI

Zinkham, Helena, *Head Processing Section,* Library of Congress, Prints & Photographs Division, Washington DC

Zinno, Sally, *Acting Dir,* Baltimore City Life Museums, Baltimore MD

Zins, Daniel, *Assoc Prof,* Atlanta College of Art, Atlanta GA (S)

Zinser, Jerry, *Coordr of Arts,* University of New Haven, Dept of Visual & Performing Arts & Philosophy, West Haven CT (S)

Ziolkowski, Anne, *Museum & Center Dir,* Crazy Horse Memorial, Indian Museum of North America & Native American Educational & Cultural Center, Crazy Horse SD

Ziolkowski, Ruth, *Chief Executive Officer & Chmn Board,* Crazy Horse Memorial, Indian Museum of North America & Native American Educational & Cultural Center, Crazy Horse SD

Zippay, Lori, *Dir,* Electronic Arts Intermix, Inc, New York NY

Zirkle, Merle W, *Instr,* Grinnell College, Dept of Art, Grinnell IA (S)

Zisk, Catherine, *Cataloger,* Dallas Museum of Art, Mildred R & Frederick M Mayer Library, Dallas TX

Zivich, Matthew, *Chmn Dept,* Saginaw Valley State University, Dept of Art & Design, University Center MI (S)

Zlotsky, Deborah, *Asst Prof,* College of Saint Rose, Dept of Art, Albany NY (S)

Zobel, James W, *Archivist,* MacArthur Memorial, Norfolk VA

Zobel, James W, *Archivist,* MacArthur Memorial, Library & Archives, Norfolk VA

Zoeckler, Linda Kay, *Head Art Reference Library,* The Huntington Library, Art Collections & Botanical Gardens, Art Reference Library, San Marino CA

Zollars, Craig, *Dir,* Indiana State University, Turman Art Gallery, Terre Haute IN

Zoltowski, Greg, *Chmn,* Siena College, Dept of Creative Arts, Loudonville NY (S)

Zona, Louis A, *Dir,* Butler Institute of American Art, Art Museum, Youngstown OH

Zonghi, Roberta, *In Charge & Cur Rare Books,* Boston Public Library, Rare Book & Manuscripts Dept, Boston MA

Zonker, Kenneth L, *Assoc Prof,* Sam Houston State University, Art Dept, Huntsville TX (S)

Zorn, David, *Pres,* Colorado Institute of Art, Denver CO (S)

Zoski Dickman, Therese, *Fine Arts Librn,* Southern Illinois University, Lovejoy Library, Edwardsville IL

Zoulalian, Val, *Instr,* Toronto Art Therapy Institute, Toronto ON (S)

Zsako, Julius, *Prof,* Seton Hall University, College of Arts & Sciences, South Orange NJ (S)

Zserdin, Carmelle, *Chmn,* Clarke College, Dept of Art, Dubuque IA (S)

Zuback, Crispan, *Interior Design,* La Roche College, Division of Graphics, Design & Communication, Pittsburgh PA (S)

Zuccari, Frank, *Exec Dir Conservation,* The Art Institute of Chicago, Chicago IL

Zuck, Gregory J, *Dir,* Southwestern College, Memorial Library - Art Dept, Winfield KS

Zucker, Mark, *Prof,* Louisiana State University, School of Art, Baton Rouge LA (S)

Zuckerman, Kathryn, *Dir,* Cambridge Art Association, Cambridge MA

Zuehlke, Zach, *Dir Student Life,* Atlanta College of Art, Atlanta GA (S)

Zuhn, Cheryl, *Dept Head,* The Illinois Institute of Art, Chicago IL (S)

Zujkowski, Stan, *Asst Prof,* Mansfield University, Art Dept, Mansfield PA (S)

Zukowski, Karen, *Cur,* Olana State Historic Site, Hudson NY

Zukowsky, John, *Cur Architecture,* The Art Institute of Chicago, Chicago IL

Zumeta, Jay, *Instr,* Art Academy of Cincinnati, Cincinnati OH (S)

Zumwalt, Karen, *Dean,* Columbia University, Teachers Col Program in Art & Art Educ, New York NY (S)

Zunita, Britt Sten, *Dir Educ,* The Currier Gallery of Art, Manchester NH

Zupancic, David, *Asst Dir,* Sangre de Cristo Arts & Conference Center, Pueblo CO

Zupata, Felix, *Gallery Dir,* University of Puerto Rico, Mayaguez, Dept of Humanities, College of Arts & Sciences, Mayaguez PR (S)

Zupnick, Matthew, *Technical Dir,* State University of New York at Binghamton, University Art Gallery, Vestal NY

Zurawski, Simone, *Assoc Prof,* DePaul University, Dept of Art, Chicago IL (S)

Zurcher, Becky, *Mgr Admin & Operations,* University of Oklahoma, Fred Jones Jr Museum of Art, Norman OK

Zurier, Nina, *Installation & Design,* University of California, Berkeley Art Museum & Pacific Film Archive, Berkeley CA

Zurier, Rebecca, *Asst Prof,* University of Michigan, Ann Arbor, Dept of History of Art, Ann Arbor MI (S)

Zuris, Kay A, *Asst Dir,* Public Museum of Grand Rapids, Grand Rapids MI

Zurko, Walter, *Prof,* College of Wooster, Dept of Art, Wooster OH (S)

Zuver, W Marc, *Exec Dir,* Fondo del Sol, Visual Art & Media Center, Washington DC

Zweertz, Rae, *Pres,* Keokuk Art Center, Keokuk IA

Zwick, Ruth, *Treas,* American Jewish Art Club, Chicago IL

Zwierciadlowski, Donna, *Librn,* Emily Carr Institute of Art & Design, Library, Vancouver BC

Zwingelberg, W C, *Chmn Dept,* Catonsville Community College, Art Dept, Catonsville MD (S)

Zymbrzuski, Margie, *Instr,* Mount Mary College, Art Dept, Milwaukee WI (S)

Organization Index

AAES (Art & Architecture Exhibition Space), see Center for Critical Architecture, San Francisco CA

Abilene Christian University, Dept of Art, Abilene TX (S)

Abraham Baldwin Agricultural College, Art & Humanities Dept, Tifton GA (S)

Abrons Art Center, see Henry Street Settlement Art Center, New York NY

ACA College of Design, Cincinnati OH (S)

Academy of Art, College Library, San Francisco CA (L)

Academy of Art College, Fine Arts Dept, San Francisco CA (S)

Academy of the Arts, Easton MD (M)

Academy of the New Church, Glencairn Museum, Bryn Athyn PA (M)

Acadia University, Art Dept, Wolfville NS (S)

Acadia University Art Gallery, Wolfville NS (M)

Ackland Art Museum, see University of North Carolina at Chapel Hill, Chapel Hill NC

Acme Art Co, Columbus OH (A)

Actual Art Foundation, New York NY (A)

Ansel Adams Center for Photography, see The Friends of Photography, San Francisco CA

Adams County Historical Society, Museum & Cultural Center, Brighton CO (M,L)

Hunter M Adams Architecture Library, see University of Kentucky, Lexington KY

Adams National Historic Site, Quincy MA (M)

Adams State College, Dept of Visual Arts, Alamosa CO (S)

Adamy's Concrete & Cast Paper Workshops, Ossining NY (S)

Addison Gallery of American Art, see Phillips Academy, Andover MA

Adelphi University, Fine & Performing Arts Library, Garden City NY (L,M)

Adelphi University, Dept of Art & Art History, Garden City NY (S)

AD German Warehouse, see Frank Lloyd Wright Museum, Richland Center WI

Adirondack Historical Association, Adirondack Museum, Blue Mountain Lake NY (M,L)

Adirondack Lakes Center for the Arts, Blue Mountain Lake NY (A)

Andres Pico Adobe Library, see San Fernando Valley Historical Society, Mission Hills CA

Adrian College, Art & Design Dept, Adrian MI (S)

Aesthetic Realism Foundation, New York NY (A, M,L)

Aesthetic Realism Foundation, New York NY (S)

African American Association, Wilberforce OH (O)

African American Historical & Cultural Society, San Francisco CA (A,L)

African Art Museum of Maryland, Columbia MD (M)

Afro-American Historical & Cultural Museum, Philadelphia PA (M)

Agecroft Association, Agecroft Hall, Richmond VA (A,M)

Ages of Man Fellowship, Amenia NY (A)

Agnes Scott College, Dept of Art, Decatur GA (S)

Agriculture & Forestry Museum, see Craftsmen's Guild of Mississippi, Inc, Jackson MS

Aiken County Historical Museum, Aiken SC (M)

Aims Community College, Visual & Performing Arts, Greeley CO (S)

A I R Gallery, New York NY (M)

Airpower Museum Library, Ottumwa IA (L)

Akron Art Museum, Akron OH (M,L)

Akron-Summit County Public Library, Fine Arts Division, Akron OH (L)

Alabama A & M University, Art & Art Education Dept, Normal AL (S)

Alabama Department of Archives & History, Museum Galleries, Montgomery AL (M,L)

Alabama Southern Community College, Art Dept, Monroeville AL (S)

Alabama State University, Art Dept, Montgomery AL (S)

Alaska Department of Education, Division of Libraries, Archives & Museums, Sheldon Jackson Museum, Sitka AK (M,L)

Alaska State Library, Alaska Historical Collections, Juneau AK (L)

Alaska State Museum, Juneau AK (M)

Alaska Watercolor Society, Anchorage AK (A)

Albany Institute of History & Art, Albany NY (M,L)

Albany Museum of Art, Albany GA (M)

Alberta College of Art, Calgary AB (S)

Alberta College of Art & Design, Illingworth Kerr Gallery, Calgary AB (M,L)

Alberta Foundation for the Arts, Edmonton AB (A)

Alberta Society of Artists, Calgary AB (A)

Albertson College of Idaho, Rosenthal Art Gallery, Caldwell ID (M)

Albertus Magnus College, Art Dept, New Haven CT (S)

Albion College, Bobbitt Visual Arts Center, Albion MI (M)

Albion College, Dept of Visual Arts, Albion MI (S)

The Albrecht-Kemper Museum of Art, Saint Joseph MO (M)

Albright College, Dept of Art, Reading PA (S)

Albright College, Freedman Gallery, Reading PA (M)

Albright-Knox Art Gallery, see The Buffalo Fine Arts Academy, Buffalo NY

Albuquerque Museum of Art & History, Albuquerque NM (M)

Albuquerque United Artists, Albuquerque NM (M)

Alcan Aluminium Ltd, Montreal PQ (C)

Alcorn State University, Dept of Fine Arts, Lorman MS (S)

Aldrich Museum of Contemporary Art, Ridgefield CT (M)

Alexandria Museum of Art, Alexandria LA (M)

Algonquin Arts Council, Art Gallery of Bancroft, Bancroft ON (M)

Alice Lloyd College, Art Dept, Pippa Passes KY (S)

Aljira Center for Contemporary Art, Newark NJ (A)

Allan Hancock College, Fine Arts Dept, Santa Maria CA (S)

Allegany Community College, Art Dept, Cumberland MD (S)

Allegany County Historical Society, History House, Cumberland MD (M)

Allegheny College, Bowman, Megahan & Penelec Galleries, Meadville PA (M)

Allegheny College, Art Dept, Meadville PA (S)

Charlotte W Allen Library-Memorial Art Gallery, see University of Rochester, Rochester NY

Allen County Community College, Art Dept, Iola KS (S)

Allen County Public Library, Art, Music & Audiovisual Services, Fort Wayne IN (L)

Allen Memorial Art Museum, see Oberlin College, Oberlin OH

Allentown Art Museum, Allentown PA (M)

Robert Allerton Library, see Honolulu Academy of Arts, Honolulu HI

The Allied Artists of America, Inc, New York NY (O)

Allied Arts Association, Allied Arts Center & Gallery, Richland WA (A)

Allied Arts Council of Lethbridge, Bowman Arts Center, Lethbridge AB (A)

Allied Arts Council of St Joseph, Saint Joseph MO (A)

Allied Arts Gallery of the Yakima Valley, Yakima WA (A,L)

Allied Arts of Seattle, Inc, Seattle WA (A)

Charles Allis Art Museum, Milwaukee WI (M)

Allison Mansion, see Marian College, Indianapolis IN

Lyman Allyn Art Museum, New London CT (M,L)

Alma College, Clack Art Center, Alma MI (S)

Almond Historical Society, Inc, Hagadorn House, The 1800-37 Museum, Almond NY (M)

Altanta-Fulton Public Library, Art-Humanities Dept, Atlanta GA (L)

Alternative Museum, New York NY (M)

Alverno College, Art Dept, Milwaukee WI (S)

Alverno College Gallery, Milwaukee WI (M)

Alvin Community College, Art Dept, Alvin TX (S)

Amarillo Art Association, Amarillo TX (A,L)

Amarillo Art Center, see Amarillo Art Association, Amarillo TX

Amarillo College, Art Dept, Amarillo TX (S)

American Abstract Artists, New York NY (O)

American Academy in Rome, New York NY (S)

American Academy of Art, Chicago IL (S)

American Academy of Arts & Letters, New York NY (O)

American Antiquarian Society, Worcester MA (O)

American Architectural Foundation, Washington DC (M)

American Artists Professional League, Inc, New York NY (O)

American Association of Museums, Washington DC (O)

American Association of University Women, Washington DC (O)

American Center for Design, Chicago IL (O)

American Ceramic Society, Westerville OH (O)

The American Ceramic Society, Ross C Purdy Museum of Ceramics, Westerville OH (M,L)

American Color Print Society, Philadelphia PA (O)
American Craft Council, American Craft Museum, New York NY (M)
American Craft Council, New York NY (O)
The American Federation of Arts, New York NY (O)
The American Film Institute, Center for Advanced Film & Television, Los Angeles CA (S)
American Fine Arts Society, New York NY (O)
The American Foundation for the Arts, Miami FL (O)
American Indian Contemporary Arts, San Francisco CA (A)
American Indian Services, Sioux Falls SD (A)
American Institute for Conservation of Historic & Artistic Works (AIC), Washington DC (O)
American Institute of Architects, Washington DC (O)
American Institute of Graphic Arts, New York NY (O)
American Jewish Art Club, Chicago IL (A)
American Jewish Congress, New York NY (A,L)
American Jewish Historical Society, Waltham MA (A,L)
American Kennel Club, Museum of the Dog, Saint Louis MO (M,L)
American Museum of Natural History, New York NY (M,L)
American Museum of the Moving Image, Astoria NY (M)
American Numismatic Association, Colorado Springs CO (O)
American Numismatic Society, New York NY (O)
American River College, Dept of Art, Sacramento CA (S)
American-Scandinavian Foundation, New York NY (A)
Americans for the Arts, New York NY (O)
Americans for the Arts, Washington DC (O)
American Society for Aesthetics, Milwaukee WI (O)
American Society of Artists, Inc, Chicago IL (O)
American Society of Bookplate Collectors & Designers, Alhambra CA (O)
American Society of Contemporary Artists (ASCA), New York NY (O)
American Society of Portrait Artists (ASOPA), Montgomery AL (O)
American Swedish Historical Foundation & Museum, Philadelphia PA (M,L)
American Swedish Institute, Minneapolis MN (M)
American Tapestry Alliance, Chiloquin OR (O)
American Textile History Museum, Lowell MA (M,L)
American University, Watkins Collection, Washington DC (M)
American University, Dept of Art, Washington DC (S)
American University, Jack I Dorothy G Bender Library, Washington DC (L)
American Watercolor Society, New York NY (O)
Americas Society Art Gallery, New York NY (M)
Amerind Foundation, Inc, Amerind Museum, Fulton-Hayden Memorial Art Gallery, Dragoon AZ (A,L)
Amerind Museum, Fulton-Hayden Memorial Art Gallery, see Amerind Foundation, Inc, Dragoon AZ
Amherst College, Mead Art Museum, Amherst MA (M,L)
Amherst College, Dept of Fine Arts, Amherst MA (S)
Amherst Museum, Amherst NY (M,L)
Anacostia Museum, Washington DC (M,L)
Anchorage Museum of History & Art, Anchorage AK (M,L)
Ancilla College, Art Dept, Donaldson IN (S)
Anderson County Arts Council, Anderson SC (A)
Anderson Fine Arts Center, Anderson IN (A,L)
Anderson Gallery, see Virginia Commonwealth University, Richmond VA
Anderson University, Art Dept, Anderson IN (S)
Walter Anderson Museum of Art, Ocean Springs MS (M)
Andover Historical Society, Andover MA (A)
Andrew-Safford House, see Peabody Essex Museum, Salem MA

Andrews University, Dept of Art, Art History & Design, Berrien Springs MI (S)
Angelo State University, Houston Harte University Center, San Angelo TX (M)
Angelo State University, Art & Music Dept, San Angelo TX (S)
Angels Gate Cultural Center, The Gate Gallery, San Pedro CA (M)
Anna Maria College, Saint Luke's Gallery, Paxton MA (M)
Anna Maria College, Dept of Art, Paxton MA (S)
Ann Arbor Art Association, Art Center, Ann Arbor MI (A)
Anniston Museum of Natural History, Anniston AL (M)
Anoka Ramsey Community College, Art Dept, Coon Rapids MN (S)
Anson County Historical Society, Inc, Wadesboro NC (M)
Antelope Valley College, Art Dept, Division of Fine Arts, Lancaster CA (S)
Antioch College, Noyes & Read Galleries, Yellow Springs OH (M)
Antioch College, Visual Arts Dept, Yellow Springs OH (S)
Antonelli Institute, Professional Photography, Commercial Art & Interior Design, Erdenheim PA (S)
Antonelli Institute of Art & Photography, Cincinnati OH (S)
Appalachian Museum, see Berea College, Berea KY
Appalachian State University, Dept of Art, Boone NC (S)
Appaloosa Museum, Inc, Moscow ID (M)
Appalshop Films Media Center, see Appalshop Inc, Whitesburg KY
Appalshop Inc, Appalshop Films Media Center, Whitesburg KY (C)
The Appleton Museum of Art, see Florida State University Foundation - Central Florida Community College Foundation, Ocala FL
Aquinas College, Art Dept, Grand Rapids MI (S)
Arapahoe Community College, Colorado Gallery of the Arts, Littleton CO (M)
Arbor Lodge State Historical Park, see Game and Parks Commission, Nebraska City NE
ARC Gallery, Chicago IL (M)
Archaeological Institute of America, Boston MA (O)
Archaeological Society of Ohio, Indian Museum of Lake County, Ohio, Painesville OH (M,L)
Archbishop Alter Library, see College of Mount Saint Joseph, Cincinnati OH
Architect of the Capitol, see United States Capitol, Washington DC
Architects Design Group Inc, Winter Park FL (A)
Architectural Image Library, see Arizona State University, Tempe AZ
Architectural League of New York, New York NY (A)
Archive of Contemporary Latin American Art, see Art Museum of the Americas, Washington DC
Archive of Old Spanish Missions, Diocese of Monterey, see Carmel Mission & Gift Shop, Carmel CA
Archives & History Center of the United Methodist Church, Madison NJ (M,L)
Archives of American Art, Washington DC (M)
Archives of MOCA (Museum of Conceptual Art), San Francisco CA (A,L)
Archives of the Archdiocese of St Paul & Minneapolis, Saint Paul MN (M)
Arcosanti, see Cosanti Foundation, Scottsdale AZ
Arizona Artist Guild, Phoenix AZ (A,L)
Arizona Commission on the Arts, Phoenix AZ (A,L)
Arizona Historical Society-Yuma, Century House Museum & Garden, Yuma AZ (M)
Arizona State University, Tempe AZ (M,L)
Arizona State University, Tempe AZ (S)
Arizona Watercolor Association, Phoenix AZ (A)
Arjuna Library, Colorado Springs CO (L)
Arkansas Arts Center, Little Rock AR (M,L)
The Arkansas Arts Center, Museum School, Little Rock AR (S)
Arkansas State University, Dept of Art, State University AR (S)

Arkansas State University-Art Department, Jonesboro, Fine Arts Center Gallery, Jonesboro AR (M,L)
Arkansas Tech University, Dept of Art, Russellville AR (S)
Arkansas Territorial Restoration, Little Rock AR (M,L)
Arlington Arts Center, Arlington VA (M)
Arlington County Department of Public Libraries, Fine Arts Section, Arlington VA (L)
Armory Art Gallery, see Virginia Polytechnic Institute & State University, Blacksburg VA
Armstrong Atlantic State University, Art & Music Dept, Savannah GA (S)
Armstrong Gallery, see Cornell College, Mount Vernon IA
Armstrong Museum of Art & Archaeology, see Olivet College, Olivet MI
Arnold Mikelson Mind & Matter Gallery, White Rock BC (M)
Arnot Art Museum, Elmira NY (M)
Rex Arragon Library, see Portland Art Museum, Portland OR
Arrott Art Gallery, see New Mexico Highlands University, Las Vegas NM
Arrowmont Gallery, Arrowmont School of Arts & Crafts, Gatlinburg TN (S)
Arrow Rock State Historic Site, Arrow Rock MO (M)
Art Academy of Cincinnati, Cincinnati OH (S)
Art Association of Harrisburg, School & Galleries, Harrisburg PA (A)
Art Association of Jacksonville, David Strawn Art Gallery, Jacksonville IL (M)
Art Association of Richmond, Richmond Art Museum, Richmond IN (A,L)
The Art Center, Mount Clemens MI (A)
Art Center College of Design, Pasadena CA (S)
Art Center College of Design, James Lemont Fogg Memorial Library, Pasadena CA (L)
Art Center of Battle Creek, Battle Creek MI (M,L)
Art Center of Corpus Christi, see Art Community Center, Corpus Christi TX
The Art Center of Waco, Waco TX (M,L)
Art Centre of New Jersey, Livingston NJ (S)
Art Com-La Mamelle, Inc, San Francisco CA (A,L)
Art Commission of the City of New York, New York NY (A)
Art Community Center, Art Center of Corpus Christi, Corpus Christi TX (M)
Art Complex Museum, Duxbury MA (M,L)
Art & Culture Center of Hollywood, Hollywood FL (M,L)
Art Dealers Association of America, Inc, New York NY (O)
Art Directors Club, Inc, New York NY (O)
Artemisia Gallery, Chicago IL (M)
Artesia Historical Museum & Art Center, Artesia NM (M)
Art Exchange, Union Dale PA (A)
Artexte Information & Documentation Centre, Montreal PQ (L)
The Art Foundation, Hot Springs National Park AR (M)
The Art Galleries of Ramapo College, Mahwah NJ (M)
Art Gallery of Bancroft, see Algonquin Arts Council, Bancroft ON
Art Gallery of Greater Victoria, Victoria BC (M,L)
Art Gallery of Hamilton, Hamilton ON (M,L)
Art Gallery of Mississauga, Mississauga ON (M)
Art Gallery of Nova Scotia, Halifax NS (M)
Art Gallery of Ontario, Toronto ON (M,L)
Art Gallery of Peel, Peel Heritage Complex, Brampton ON (M,L)
Art Gallery of Peterborough, Peterborough ON (M)
The Art Gallery of Southwestern Manitoba, Brandon MB (A,L)
Art Gallery of Windsor, Windsor ON (M,L)
The Art Guild, Farmington CT (A)
Art Guild of Burlington, Arts for Living Center, Burlington IA (A)
The Art Gym, see Marylhurst College, Marylhurst OR
Arthur Ross Gallery, see University of Pennsylvania, Philadelphia PA
Art in Architecture, Los Angeles CA (S)

Bishop University, Artists' Centre, Lennoxville PQ (M)

Bismarck State College, Fine Arts Dept, Bismarck ND (S)

Bixler Art & Music Library, see Colby College, Waterville ME

Blackader-Lauterman Library of Architecture and Art, see McGill University, Montreal PQ

Black American West Museum & Heritage Center, Denver CO (M)

Blackburn College, Dept of Art, Carlinville IL (S)

Black Cultural Center for Nova Scotia, see Society for the Protection & Preservation of Black Culture in Nova Scotia, Dartmouth NS

Black Hawk College, Art Dept, Moline IL (S)

Black Hills State University, Ruddell Gallery, Spearfish SD (M,L)

Black Hills State University, Art Dept, Spearfish SD (S)

Black River Historical Society, Black River Academy Museum, Ludlow VT (M)

Blacksburg Regional Art Association, Christiansburg VA (A)

Blackwell Library, see Salisbury State University, Salisbury MD

Blackwell Street Center for the Arts, Denville NJ (A)

Blackwood Gallery, see Erindale College, University of Toronto at Mississauga, Mississauga ON

Sarah Campbell Blaffer Gallery, see University of Houston, Houston TX

Blanden Memorial Art Museum, Fort Dodge IA (M,L)

Blewett-Lee Museum, see Columbus & Lowndes County Historical Society, Columbus MS

Mary & Leigh Block Gallery, see Northwestern University, Evanston IL

Bloomington Art Center, Bloomington MN (M)

Bloomsburg University, Dept of Art, Bloomsburg PA (S)

Bloomsburg University of Pennsylvania, Haas Gallery of Art, Bloomsburg PA (M)

Eleanor Blossom Memorial Library, see Maricopa County Historical Society, Wickenburg AZ

Blount-Bridgers House, Hobson Pittman Memorial Gallery, see Edgecombe County Cultural Arts Council, Inc, Tarboro NC

Blount Inc, Blount Corporate Collection, Montgomery AL (C)

Bluefield State College, Art Dept, Bluefield WV (S)

Blue Lake Fine Arts Camp, Art Dept, Twin Lake MI (S)

Blue Mountain College, Art Dept, Blue Mountain MS (S)

Blue Mountain Community College, Fine Arts Dept, Pendleton OR (S)

Blue Mountain Gallery, New York NY (M)

Blue Sky, Oregon Center for the Photographic Arts, Portland OR (M)

Ernest Blumenschein Home & Studio, see Kit Carson Historic Museums, Taos NM

Blumenthal Rare Book & Manuscript Library, see Judah L Magnes Museum, Berkeley CA

B'nai B'rith International, B'nai B'rith Klutznick National Jewish Museum, Washington DC (M)

B'nai B'rith Klutznick National Jewish Museum, see B'nai B'rith International, Washington DC

Board of Parks & Recreation, The Parthenon, Nashville TN (M)

Boarman Arts Center, see Associates for Community Development, Martinsburg WV

The Boatmen's National Bank of St Louis, Art Collection, Saint Louis MO (C)

Bobbitt Visual Arts Center, see Albion College, Albion MI

Bob Jones University, Museum & Art Gallery, Greenville SC (M)

Bob Jones University, School of Fine Arts, Greenville SC (S)

Boca Raton Museum of Art, Boca Raton FL (A,L)

Richard W Bock Sculpture Collection, see Greenville College, Greenville IL

The Richard W Bock Sculpture Collection & Art Library, see Greenville College, Greenville IL

Boehm Gallery, see Palomar Community College, San Marcos CA

Boise Art Museum, Boise ID (M)

Boise State University, Art Dept, Boise ID (S)

William Bonifas Fine Art Center Gallery, Alice Powers Art Gallery, Escanaba MI (M)

Daniel Boone Regional Library, Columbia MO (L)

Boothbay Region Art Foundation, Boothbay Harbor ME (A)

Boston Architectural Center, Boston MA (A,L)

Boston Art Commission of the City of Boston, Boston MA (A)

Boston Athenaeum, Boston MA (L)

Boston Center for Adult Education, Boston MA (S)

Boston College, Fine Arts Dept, Chestnut Hill MA (S)

Boston College, Museum of Art, Chestnut Hill MA (M)

The Bostonian Society, Old State House Museum, Boston MA (M,L)

Boston Printmakers, Boston MA (A)

Boston Public Library, Boston MA (L,M)

Boston University, School of Visual Arts, Boston MA (S)

Boston University, Art Gallery, Boston MA (M)

Boston Visual Artists Union, Newton MA (A)

Muriel Isabel Bostwick Library, see Art Gallery of Hamilton, Hamilton ON

Botanic Hall Library, see Cheekwood-Tennessee Botanical Gardens & Museum of Art, Nashville TN

Boulder Historical Society Inc, Museum of History, Boulder CO (A)

Boulder Museum of Contemporary Art, Boulder CO (A)

Boulder Public Library & Gallery, Dept of Fine Arts Gallery, Boulder CO (L)

Boulevard Arts Center, Chicago IL (M)

Bowdoin College, Peary-MacMillan Arctic Museum, Brunswick ME (M)

Bowdoin College, Art Dept, Brunswick ME (S)

Bower's Museum, Santa Ana CA (M)

Bowie State University, Fine Arts Dept, Bowie MD (S)

Bowling Green State University, Fine Arts Center Galleries, Bowling Green OH (M)

Bowling Green State University, School of Art, Bowling Green OH (S)

Bowling Green State University, Art Dept, Huron OH (S)

Bowman Arts Center, see Allied Arts Council of Lethbridge, Lethbridge AB

Bowman, Megahan & Penelec Galleries, see Allegheny College, Meadville PA

Bowne House Historical Society, Flushing NY (A)

The Dwight Frederick Boyden Gallery, see St Mary's College of Maryland, Saint Mary City MD

Roy Boyd Gallery, Chicago IL (M)

B P America, Cleveland OH (C)

Bradford College, Creative Arts Division, Bradford MA (S)

The Bradford Museum of Collector's Plates, Niles IL (M)

Bradley University, Heuser Art Center, Peoria IL (M)

Bradley University, Dept of Art, Peoria IL (S)

Braithwaite Fine Arts Gallery, see Southern Utah University, Cedar City UT

Brandeis University, Dept of Fine Arts, Waltham MA (S)

Brandeis University, Rose Art Museum, Waltham MA (M,L)

Brand Library & Art Galleries, Glendale CA (L)

Brandywine Battlefield Park, see Pennsylvania Historical & Museum Commission, Harrisburg PA

Brandywine River Museum, Chadds Ford PA (M,L)

Brandywine Workshop, Philadelphia PA (A)

Brant Historical Society, Brant County Museum, Brantford ON (M,L)

Brattleboro Museum & Art Center, Brattleboro VT (M)

Brauer Museum of Art, see Valparaiso University, Valparaiso IN

Braun Research Library, see Southwest Museum, Los Angeles CA

Brazosport College, Art Dept, Lake Jackson TX (S)

Brea Civic & Cultural Center Gallery, Brea CA (M)

Bread & Puppet Theater Museum, Glover VT (M)

Anne Bremer Memorial Library, see San Francisco Art Institute, San Francisco CA

Brenau University, Art Dept, Gainesville GA (S)

Brenner Library, see Quincy University, Quincy IL

Brentwood Art Center, Los Angeles CA (S)

Brescia College, Anna Eaton Stout Memorial Art Gallery, Owensboro KY (M)

Brescia College, Dept of Art, Owensboro KY (S)

Alexander Brest Museum & Gallery, see Jacksonville University, Jacksonville FL

Brevard College, Division of Fine Arts, Brevard NC (S)

Brevard College, Sims Art Center, Brevard NC (M,L)

Brevard Museum of Art & Science, Melbourne FL (M)

Brewton-Parker College, Visual Arts, Mount Vernon GA (S)

Briar Cliff College, Art Dept, Sioux City IA (S)

Brick Store Museum & Library, Kennebunk ME (M)

Bridge Center for Contemporary Art, El Paso TX (M)

Bridgewater College, Art Dept, Bridgewater VA (S)

Bridgewater State College, Art Dept, Bridgewater MA (S)

Margaret M Bridwell Art Library, see University of Louisville, Louisville KY

Brigham City Museum-Gallery, Brigham City UT (M)

Brigham Young University, Provo UT (M,L)

Brigham Young University, Dept of Visual Arts, Provo UT (S)

Brigham Young University, Hawaii Campus, Division of Fine Arts, Laie HI (S)

Bradford Brinton Memorial Museum & Historic Ranch, Big Horn WY (M)

Bristol-Myers Squibb Pharmaceutical Group, Gallery at Bristol-Myers Squibb, Princeton NJ (C)

British Columbia Information Management Services, Victoria BC (L)

British Columbia Museums Association, Victoria BC (A)

Brockton Public Library System, Joseph A Driscoll Art Gallery, Brockton MA (L)

Bromfield Art Gallery, Boston MA (M)

Bronck Museum, see Greene County Historical Society, Coxsackie NY

Silas Bronson Library, Art, Theatre & Music Services, Waterbury CT (L)

Bronx Community College, Music & Art Dept, Bronx NY (S)

Bronx Council on the Arts, Longwood Arts Gallery, Bronx NY (M)

Bronx Museum of the Arts, Bronx NY (M)

Bronx River Art Center, Gallery, Bronx NY (M)

Bronxville Public Library, Bronxville NY (L)

Brookdale Community College, Art Dept, Lincroft NJ (S)

Brookfield Craft Center, Inc, Gallery, Brookfield CT (M,L)

Brookgreen Gardens, Murrells Inlet SC (M,L)

Brooklyn Arts Council, Brooklyn NY (A)

Brooklyn College, Art Dept, Brooklyn NY (S)

Brooklyn Historical Society, Brooklyn NY (A,L)

Brooklyn Historical Society, Brooklyn OH (M)

Brooklyn Museum, Brooklyn NY (M,L)

Brooklyn Public Library, Art & Music Division, Brooklyn NY (L)

Brookside Museum, see Saratoga County Historical Society, Ballston Spa NY

Brooks Institute Photography Library, Santa Barbara CA (L)

Broward Community College - South Campus, Art Gallery, Pembroke Pines FL (M)

Broward County Board of Commissioners Cultural Affairs Divison, Fort Lauderdale FL (A)

Alice Pratt Brown Library of Art, Architecture & Music, see Rice University, Houston TX

Annmary Brown Memorial, see Brown University, Providence RI

Brown County Art Gallery Association Inc, Brown County Art Gallery & Museum, Nashville IN (A)

George W Brown Jr Ojibwe Museum & Cultural Center, see Lac du Flambeau Band of Lake Superior Chippewa Indians, Lac du Flambeau WI

Canajoharie Library & Art Gallery, Canajoharie NY (M,L)

Canton Museum of Art, Canton OH (M,L)

Canton Museum of Art, Canton OH (S)

Cape Ann Historical Museum, Gloucester MA (M,L)

Cape Cod Community College, Art Dept, West Barnstable MA (S)

Cape Cod School of Art, Provincetown MA (S)

Capital University, Schumacher Gallery, Columbus OH (M,L)

Capital University, Fine Arts Dept, Columbus OH (S)

Capitol Community Technical College, Humanities Division & Art Dept, Hartford CT (S)

Capp Street Project, San Francisco CA (M)

Caramoor Center for Music & the Arts, Inc, Caramoor House Museum, Katonah NY (M)

Cardinal Gallery, see Maryland Hall for the Creative Arts, Annapolis MD

Cardinal Stritch College, Layton Honor Gallery, Milwaukee WI (M)

Cardinal Stritch College, Art Dept, Milwaukee WI (S)

Caribbean Cultural Center, Cultural Arts Organization & Resource Center, New York NY (A)

Carlen House, see Museum of Mobile, Mobile AL

Carleton College, Dept of Art & Art History, Northfield MN (S)

Carleton University, Dept of Art History, Ottawa ON (S)

Michael C Carlos Museum, see Emory University, Atlanta GA

Carlow College, Art Dept, Pittsburgh PA (S)

Carlson Tower Gallery, see North Park College, Chicago IL

Carlsten Art Gallery, see University of Wisconsin-Stevens Point, Stevens Point WI

Carmel Mission & Gift Shop, Carmel CA (M,L)

Carnegie Art Center, see Mankato Area Arts Council, Mankato MN

Carnegie Art Center, Walla Walla WA (A)

Carnegie Art Museum, Oxnard CA (M)

Carnegie Institute, Carnegie Museum of Art, Pittsburgh PA (M,L)

Carnegie Library of Pittsburgh, Pittsburgh PA (L)

Carnegie Mellon University, Pittsburgh PA (M,L)

Carnegie Mellon University, College of Fine Arts, Pittsburgh PA (S)

Carnegie Museum of Art, see Carnegie Institute, Pittsburgh PA

Carnegie Public Library, Delta Blues Museum, Clarksdale MS (M)

Carolina Art Association, Gibbes Museum of Art, Charleston SC (M,L)

Carrizo Art & Craft Workshops, see Carrizo Lodge, Ruidoso NM (S)

Carrizo Lodge, Carrizo Art & Craft Workshops, Ruidoso NM (S)

Carroll College, Art Dept, Waukesha WI (S)

Carson County Square House Museum, Panhandle TX (M)

Kit Carson Historic Museums, Taos NM (M,L)

Lucy Carson Memorial Library, see Western Montana College, Dillon MT

Carson-Newman College, Art Dept, Jefferson City TN (S)

Amon Carter Museum, Fort Worth TX (M,L)

Carter-Haas Library, see Maine Photographic Workshops, Rockport ME

Carthage College, Art Dept, Kenosha WI (S)

Cartoon Art Museum, San Francisco CA (M)

George Washington Carver & The Oaks, see Tuskegee Institute National Historic Site, Tuskegee Institute AL

Casa Amesti, Monterey CA (M)

Casa de Unidad Unity House, Detroit MI (A)

Cascade County Historical Society, Cascade County Historical Museum & Archives, Great Falls MT (M)

Casemate Museum, see Headquarters Fort Monroe, Dept of Army, Fort Monroe VA

Case Western Reserve University, Dept of Art History & Art, Cleveland OH (S)

Casper College, Dept of Visual Arts, Casper WY (S)

Caspers, Inc, Art Collection, Tampa FL (C)

Castellani Art Museum, see Niagara University, Niagara NY

Castle Gallery, see College of New Rochelle, New Rochelle NY

Castleton State College, Art Dept, Castleton VT (S)

Cathedral of Saint John the Divine, New York NY (M,L)

Catholic University of America, Humanities Div, Mullen Library, Washington DC (L)

Catholic University of America, Washington DC (S)

Catholic University of Puerto Rico, Dept of Fine Arts, Ponce PR (S)

Catonsville Community College, Art Dept, Catonsville MD (S)

Cavalry - Armor Foundation, Patton Museum of Cavalry & Armor, Fort Knox KY (M)

Cayuga Museum of History & Art, Auburn NY (M,L)

Cazenovia College, Chapman Art Center Gallery, Cazenovia NY (M)

Cazenovia College, Center for Art & Design Studies, Cazenovia NY (S)

Radio-Canada SRC CBC, Galerie Georges Goguen, Moncton NB (M)

Cedar Crest College, Art Dept, Allentown PA (S)

Cedar Grove, see Philadelphia Museum of Art, Philadelphia PA

Cedar Hurst Library, see Mitchell Museum, Mount Vernon IL

Cedar Rapids Museum of Art, Cedar Rapids IA (M,L)

Cedar Ridge Creative Centre, see City of Scarborough, Scarborough ON

Centenary College, Humanities Dept, Hackettstown NJ (S)

Centenary College of Louisiana, Dept of Art, Shreveport LA (S)

Centenary College of Louisiana, Meadows Museum of Art, Shreveport LA (M)

Centennial Gallery and Gairloch Gallery, see Oakville Galleries, Oakville ON

Centennial Library - Arts Complex, see The Art Gallery of Southwestern Manitoba, Brandon MB

Center-Barron County, Dept of Art, see University of Wisconsin, Rice Lake WI (S)

Center for Advanced Film & Television, see The American Film Institute, Los Angeles CA (S)

Center for American-Spanish Affairs, see Spanish Institute, Inc, New York NY

Center for Book Arts, New York NY (M)

The Center for Contemporary Arts of Santa Fe, Santa Fe NM (A)

Center for Creative Photography, see University of Arizona, Tucson AZ

Center for Creative Studies, College of Art & Design, Detroit MI (S)

Center for Creative Studies, College of Art & Design Library, Detroit MI (L)

Center for Critical Architecture, AAES (Art & Architecture Exhibition Space), San Francisco CA (A)

Center for Exploratory & Perceptual Art, CEPA Gallery, Buffalo NY (M,L)

Center for History of American Needlework, Butler PA (L)

Center for Photography at Woodstock Inc, Woodstock NY (A)

Center for Puppetry Arts, Atlanta GA (M,L)

Center for Safety in the Arts, New York NY (L)

Center for Southern Folklore, Memphis TN (A)

Center for the Arts at Yerba Buena Gardens, San Francisco CA (A)

Center on Contemporary Art, Seattle WA (A)

Central Community College - Platte Campus, Business & Arts Cluster, Columbus NE (S)

Central Connecticut State University, Art Dept Museum, New Britain CT (M)

Central Connecticut State University, Dept of Art, New Britain CT (S)

Central Florida Community College, Humanities Dept, Ocala FL (S)

Central Florida Community College Art Collection, Ocala FL (M)

Central Iowa Art Association, Inc, Marshalltown IA (A,L)

Central Library, Dept of Fine Arts, San Antonio TX (L)

Central Michigan University, Dept of Art, Mount Pleasant MI (S)

Central Michigan University, Art Gallery, Mount Pleasant MI (M)

Central Missouri State University, Art Center Gallery, Warrensburg MO (M)

Central Missouri State University, Art Dept, Warrensburg MO (S)

Central Oregon Community College, Dept of Art, Bend OR (S)

Central Piedmont Community College, Visual & Performing Arts, Charlotte NC (S)

Central State University, Dept of Art, Wilberforce OH (S)

Central United Methodist Church, Swords Info Plowshares Peace Center & Gallery, Detroit MI (M)

Central University of Iowa, Art Dept, Pella IA (S)

Central Washington University, Sarah Spurgeon Gallery, Ellensburg WA (M)

Central Washington University, Dept of Art, Ellensburg WA (S)

Central Wyoming College, Art Center, Riverton WY (S)

Centre Culturel de Trois Rivieres, Trois Rivieres PQ (A)

Centre National d'Exposition, see Le Musee Regional de Rimouski, Rimouski PQ

Centre National D'Exposition a Jonquiere, see Institut des Arts au Saguenay, Jonquiere PQ

Centro Ceremonial de Caguana, see Institute of Puerto Rican Culture, San Juan PR

Centro Cultural Aztlan, San Antonio TX (A)

Centro Cultural De La Raza, San Diego CA (M)

Centrum Foundation, Port Townsend WA (A)

Century College, Humanities Dept, White Bear Lake MN (S)

Century Gallery, see County of Los Angeles, Sylmar CA

Century House Museum & Garden, see Arizona Historical Society-Yuma, Yuma AZ

CEPA Gallery, see Center for Exploratory & Perceptual Art, Buffalo NY

Cerritos Community College, Art Dept, Norwalk CA (S)

Chabot College, Humanities Division, Hayward CA (S)

Chadron State College, Arts Gallery, Chadron NE (M)

Chadron State College, Dept of Art, Speech & Theatre, Chadron NE (S)

Chaffee Art Center, see Rutland Area Art Association, Inc, Rutland VT

Chaffey Community College, Art Dept, Rancho Cucamonga CA (S)

The Chaim Gross Studio Museum, New York NY (M)

Chalet of the Golden Fleece, New Glarus WI (M)

Chamberlayne School of Design & Merchandising, see Mount Ida College, Boston MA (S)

Billie Trimble Chandler Arts Foundation, Asian Cultures Museum & Educational Center, Corpus Christi TX (M)

Stephen Chan Library of Fine Arts, see New York University, New York NY

Chapel Art Center, see Saint Anselm College, Manchester NH

Chapel Gallery, see Muskoka Arts & Crafts Inc, Bracebridge ON

Howard I Chapelle Memorial Library, see Chesapeake Bay Maritime Museum, Saint Michaels MD

Chapin Library, see Williams College, Williamstown MA

Chapman Art Center Gallery, see Cazenovia College, Cazenovia NY

Chapman Library, see Philbrook Museum of Art, Tulsa OK

Chapman University, Art Dept, Orange CA (S)

Chappell Memorial Library and Art Gallery, Chappell NE (L)

Charles River School, Creative Arts Program, Dover MA (S)

Charles Stewart Mott Community College, Art Area, School of Arts & Humanities, Flint MI (S)

Charleston Museum, Charleston SC (M,L)

Charleston Southern University, Dept of Language & Visual Art, Charleston SC (S)

Chase Home Museum of Utah Folk Art, see Utah Arts Council, Salt Lake City UT

Chase Manhattan, New York NY (C)

The Chase Manhattan Bank, NA, Art Collection, New York NY (C)

Chastain Arts Center, see City of Atlanta, Atlanta GA

Chateau Ramezay Museum, Montreal PQ (M,L)

Chatham College, Art Gallery, Pittsburgh PA (M)

Chatham College, Fine & Performing Arts, Pittsburgh PA (S)

Chatham Cultural Centre, Thames Art Gallery, Chatham ON (A)

Chatham Historical Society, Old Atwood House Museum, Chatham MA (M)

Chatillon-DeMenil House Foundation, DeMenil Mansion, Saint Louis MO (M)

Chattahoochee Valley Art Museum, LaGrange GA (M)

Chattanooga-Hamilton County Bicentennial Library, Fine Arts Dept, Chattanooga TN (L)

Chattanooga State Technical Community College, Advertising Arts Dept, Chattanooga TN (S)

Chautauqua Center for the Visual Arts, Chautauqua NY (M)

Chautauqua Institution, School of Art, Chautauqua NY (S)

Fray Angelico Chavez History Library, see Museum of New Mexico, Santa Fe NM

Cheekwood Nashville's Home of Art & Gardens, Education Dept, Nashville TN (S)

Cheekwood-Tennessee Botanical Gardens & Museum of Art, Nashville TN (M,L)

Chelan County Public Utility District, Rocky Reach Dam, Wenatchee WA (M)

Cheltenham Center for the Arts, Cheltenham PA (S)

Chemeketa Community College, Dept of Humanities & Communications, Salem OR (S)

Anne Bunce Cheney Library, see University of Hartford, West Hartford CT

Cherokee National Historical Society, Inc, Tahlequah OK (A,L)

Chesapeake Bay Maritime Museum, Saint Michaels MD (M,L)

Chester County Historical Society, West Chester PA (A)

Chesterwood Museum, see National Trust for Historic Preservation, Glendale MA

Cheyney University of Pennsylvania, Dept of Art, Cheyney PA (S)

Chicago Architecture Foundation, Chicago IL (M)

Chicago Artists' Coalition, Chicago IL (A)

Chicago Athenaeum, Museum of Architecture & Design, Chicago IL (M)

Chicago Children's Museum, Chicago IL (M)

Chicago Cultural Center, see Chicago Department of Cultural Affairs, Chicago IL

Chicago Department of Cultural Affairs, Chicago Cultural Center, Chicago IL (M)

Chicago Historical Society, Chicago IL (A)

Chicago Public Library, Harold Washington Library Center, Chicago IL (L)

Chicano-Latino Arts Resource Library, see Galeria de la Raza, San Francisco CA

Chief Plenty Coups Museum, Pryor MT (M)

The Children's Aid Society, Visual Arts Program of the Greenwich Village Center, New York NY (S)

Children's Art Foundation, Museum of International Children's Art, Santa Cruz CA (A)

Children's Museum, Rauh Memorial Library, Indianapolis IN (M)

Children's Museum of Manhattan, New York NY (M)

Chilkat Valley Historical Society, Sheldon Museum & Cultural Center, Haines AK (M)

Chilliwack Community Arts Council, Chilliwack BC (A)

China Institute Gallery, see China Institute in America, New York NY

China Institute in America, China Institute Gallery, New York NY (M)

Chinati Foundation, Marfa TX (M)

Chinese-American Arts Council, New York NY (A)

Chinese Culture Foundation, Chinese Culture Center Gallery, San Francisco CA (M)

Chinese Information & Culture Center Library, see Taipei Economic & Cultural Office, New York NY

Chinqua-Penn Plantation House, Garden & Greenhouses, see North Carolina State University, Reidsville NC

Chipola Junior College, Dept of Fine & Performing Arts, Marianna FL (S)

Chowan College, Division of Art, Murfreesboro NC (S)

Christopher Newport University, Arts & Communications, Newport News VA (S)

Chronicle-Tribune Art Gallery, see Taylor University, Upland IN

Jean Outland Chrysler Library, see Chrysler Museum Of Art, Norfolk VA

Chrysler Museum Of Art, Norfolk VA (M,L)

Chung-Cheng Art Gallery, see Saint John's University, Jamaica NY

Winston Churchill Memorial & Library in the United States, see Westminster College, Fulton MO

Churchman-Fehsenfeld Gallery, see Indianapolis Art Center, Indianapolis IN

Church of Jesus Christ of Latter-Day Saints, Mormon Visitors' Center, Independence MO (M)

Church of Jesus Christ of Latter-Day Saints, Museum of Church History & Art, Salt Lake City UT (M,L)

CIAO, Gallery & Art Center, Bronx NY (M)

Ciba-Geigy Corporation, Art Collection, Tarrytown NY (C)

CIGNA Corporation, CIGNA Museum & Art Collection, Philadelphia PA (C)

Cincinnati Academy of Design, Cincinnati OH (S)

Cincinnati Art Club, Cincinnati OH (A)

Cincinnati Artists' Group Effort, Cincinnati OH (A)

Cincinnati Art Museum, see Cincinnati Museum Association, Cincinnati OH

Cincinnati Institute of Fine Arts, Taft Museum, Cincinnati OH (M)

Cincinnati Institute of Fine Arts, Cincinnati OH (A)

Cincinnati Museum Association, Cincinnati Art Museum, Cincinnati OH (M,L)

Citibank, NA, Long Island City NY (C)

Citrus College, Art Dept, Glendora CA (S)

City Art Works, Pratt Fine Arts Center, Seattle WA (S)

City College of New York, Art Dept, New York NY (S)

City College of San Francisco, Art Dept, San Francisco CA (S)

City College of the City University of New York, Morris Raphael Cohen Library, New York NY (L)

City Colleges of Chicago, Chicago IL (S)

City Gallery at Chastain, see City of Atlanta, Atlanta GA

City Gallery East, see City of Atlanta, Atlanta GA

City Gallery of Contemporary Art, Raleigh NC (M)

City of Atlanta, Bureau of Cultural Affairs, Atlanta GA (A,M,L)

City of Austin Parks & Recreation, O Henry Museum, Austin TX (M)

City of Austin Parks & Recreation Department, Dougherty Arts Center Gallery, Austin TX (M)

City of Cambridge Historical Commission, Cambridge MA (L)

City of Cedar Falls, Iowa, James & Meryl Hearst Center for the Arts, Cedar Falls IA (M)

City of Charleston, City Hall Council Chamber Gallery, Charleston SC (M)

City of Eugene, Hult Center, Jacobs Gallery, Eugene OR (M)

City of Fremont, Olive Hyde Art Gallery, Fremont CA (M)

City of Gainesville, Thomas Center Galleries - Cultural Affairs, Gainesville FL (M)

City of Hampton, Hampton Arts Commission, Hampton VA (A)

City of Irvine, Irvine Fine Arts Center, Irvine CA (M)

City of Irvine, Fine Arts Center, Irvine CA (S)

City of Lethbridge, Sir Alexander Galt Museum, Lethbridge AB (M)

City of Los Angeles, Cultural Affairs Dept, Los Angeles CA (M)

The City of Petersburg Museums, Petersburg VA (M)

City of Pittsfield, Berkshire Artisans, Pittsfield MA (M)

City Of Raleigh Arts Commission, Municipal Building Art Exhibitions, Raleigh NC (A)

City of San Rafael, Falkirk Cultural Center, San Rafael CA (M)

City of Scarborough, Cedar Ridge Creative Centre, Scarborough ON (M)

City of Springdale, Shiloh Museum, Springdale AR (M)

City of Tampa, Art in Public Places, Tampa FL (A)

City of Ukiah, Grace Hudson Museum & The Sun House, Ukiah CA (M)

City of Woodstock, Woodstock Art Gallery, Woodstock ON (M)

City University of New York, PhD Program in Art History, New York NY (S)

Civic Center Plaza, see Richmond Art Center, Richmond CA

Civic Fine Arts Center, Sioux Falls SD (M,L)

Clackamas Community College, Art Dept, Oregon City OR (S)

Clack Art Center, see Alma College, Alma MI (S)

Claflin College, Dept of Art, Orangeburg SC (S)

Claremont Graduate School, Dept of Fine Arts, Claremont CA (S)

Clarion University, Hazel Sandford Gallery, Clarion PA (M)

Clarion University of Pennsylvania, Dept of Art, Clarion PA (S)

Clark-Atlanta University, School of Arts & Sciences, Atlanta GA (S)

Clark College, Art Dept, Vancouver WA (S)

Clark County Historical Society, Pioneer - Krier Museum, Ashland KS (M)

Clark County Historical Society, Springfield OH (M,L)

Clarke College, Dept of Art, Dubuque IA (S)

Henry B Clarke House Museum, see Praire Avenue House Museums, Chicago IL

Clark Humanities Museum, see Scripps College, Claremont CA

Robert D Clark Library, see San Jose State University, San Jose CA

Sterling & Francine Clark Art Institute, Williamstown MA (M,L)

Clark University, The University Gallery at Goddard Library, Worcester MA (M)

Clark University, Dept of Visual & Performing Arts, Worcester MA (S)

Wilson W Clark Memorial Library, see University of Portland, Portland OR

Claypool-Young Art Gallery, see Morehead State University, Morehead KY

Clay Studio, Philadelphia PA (M)

Clemson University, Clemson SC (M,L)

Clemson University, College of Architecture, Clemson SC (S)

Cleveland Art Association, see Cleveland Institute of Art, Cleveland OH

Cleveland Botanical Garden, Eleanor Squire Library, Cleveland OH (L)

Cleveland Center for Contemporary Art, Cleveland OH (M,L)

Cleveland Institute of Art, Reinberger Galleries, Cleveland OH (M,L,A)

Cleveland Institute of Art, Cleveland OH (S)

Cleveland Museum of Art, Cleveland OH (M,L,A)

Cleveland Public Library, Fine Arts & Special Collections Dept, Cleveland OH (L)

Cleveland State Community College, Dept of Art, Cleveland TN (S)

Cleveland State University, Art Dept, Cleveland OH (S)

Cleveland State University, Library & Art Services, Cleveland OH (L,M)

Clinch Valley College of the University of Virginia, Visual & Performing Arts Dept, Wise VA (S)

Clinton Art Association Gallery, Clinton IA (M)

Clinton Community College, Art Dept, Plattsburgh NY (S)

Clinton County Historical Association, Clinton County Historical Museum, Plattsburgh NY (M)

Cliveden, Philadelphia PA (M)

The Cloisters, see The Metropolitan Museum of Art, New York NY

Jessie L Clough Art Memorial for Teaching, see Rhodes College, Memphis TN

Clowes Fund Collection, see Indianapolis Museum of Art, Indianapolis IN

Coahoma Community College, Art Education & Fine Arts Dept, Clarksdale MS (S)

Coalition of Women's Art Organizations, Port Washington WI (O)

Cobblestone Museum, see Livingston County Historical Society, Geneseo NY

Cochise College, Art Dept, Douglas AZ (S)

Cochise College, Charles Di Peso Library, Douglas AZ (L)

Cody Country Art League, Cody WY (A)

Coe College, Gordon Fennell Gallery & Marvin Cone Gallery, Cedar Rapids IA (M)

Coe College, Dept of Art, Cedar Rapids IA (S)

Coffeyville Community College, Art Dept, Coffeyville KS (S)

Coffman Union Third Floor Gallery, see University of Minnesota, Minneapolis MN

Cohasset Historical Society, Caleb Lothrop House, Cohasset MA (M)

Cohasset Maritime Museum, see Cohasset Historical Society, Cohasset MA

Morris Raphael Cohen Library, see City College of the City University of New York, New York NY

Coker College, Art Dept, Hartsville SC (S)

Francis Colburn Gallery, see University of Vermont, Burlington VT

Colby College, Museum of Art, Waterville ME (M,L)

Colby College, Art Dept, Waterville ME (S)

Colby Community College, Visual Arts Dept, Colby KS (S)

Colby-Sawyer College, Dept of Fine & Performing Arts, New London NH (S)

Coleman Library, see Tougaloo College, Tougaloo MS

Colgate University, Dept of Art & Art History, Hamilton NY (S)

Colgate University, Picker Art Gallery, Hamilton NY (M)

College Art Association, New York NY (O)

College of Charleston, School of the Arts, Charleston SC (S)

College of Charleston, Halsey Gallery, Charleston SC (M)

College of DuPage, Humanities Division, Glen Ellyn IL (S)

College of Eastern Utah, Gallery East, Price UT (M)

College of Great Falls, Humanities Division, Great Falls MT (S)

College of Lake County, Art Dept, Grayslake IL (S)

College of Marin, Art Gallery, Kentfield CA (M)

College of Marin, Dept of Art, Kentfield CA (S)

College of Mount Saint Joseph, Art Dept, Cincinnati OH (S)

College of Mount Saint Joseph, Studio San Giuseppe, Cincinnati OH (M,L)

College of Mount Saint Vincent, Fine Arts Dept, Riverdale NY (S)

College of New Jersey, Art Dept, Trenton NJ (S)

College of New Jersey, Art Gallery, Trenton NJ (M)

College of New Rochelle, Castle Gallery, New Rochelle NY (M)

College of New Rochelle School of Arts & Sciences, Art Dept, New Rochelle NY (S)

College of Notre Dame, Dept of Art, Belmont CA (S)

College of Notre Dame of Maryland, Art Dept, Baltimore MD (S)

College of Saint Benedict, Art Dept, Saint Joseph MN (S)

College of Saint Benedict, Art Gallery, Saint Joseph MN (M)

College of Saint Catherine, Art & Art History Dept, Saint Paul MN (S)

College of Saint Elizabeth, Mahoney Library, Morristown NJ (L)

College of Saint Elizabeth, Art Dept, Morristown NJ (S)

College of Saint Francis, Fine Arts Dept, Joliet IL (S)

College of Saint Mary, Art Dept, Omaha NE (S)

College of Saint Rose, Picotte Hall Art Gallery, Albany NY (M)

College of Saint Rose, Dept of Art, Albany NY (S)

College of San Mateo, Creative Arts Dept, San Mateo CA (S)

College of Santa Fe, Art Dept, Santa Fe NM (S)

College of Southern Idaho, Art Dept, Twin Falls ID (S)

College of Southern Idaho, Herrett Center for Arts & Science, Twin Falls ID (M)

College of Staten Island, Performing & Creative Arts Dept, Staten Island NY (S)

College of the Canyons, Art Dept, Valencia CA (S)

College of the Desert, Art Dept, Palm Desert CA (S)

College of the Holy Cross, Dept of Visual Arts, Worcester MA (S)

College of the Holy Cross, Dinand Library, Worcester MA (L)

College of the Ozarks, Dept of Art, Point Lookout MO (S)

College of the Redwoods, Arts & Languages Dept Division, Eureka CA (S)

College of the Sequoias, Art Dept, Visalia CA (S)

College of the Siskiyous, Art Dept, Weed CA (S)

College of Visual Arts, Gallery, Saint Paul MN (M,L)

College of Visual Arts, Saint Paul MN (S)

College of Visual & Performing Arts, see Kutztown University, Kutztown PA (S)

College of William & Mary, Joseph & Margaret Muscarelle Museum of Art, Williamsburg VA (M)

College of William & Mary, Dept of Fine Arts, Williamsburg VA (S)

College of Wooster, Dept of Art, Wooster OH (S)

The College of Wooster, Art Museum, Wooster OH (M)

Colonel Black Mansion, Ellsworth ME (M)

Colonial Williamsburg Foundation, Williamsburg VA (M,A,L)

Colorado City Historical Museum, Colorado City TX (M)

Colorado College, Dept of Art, Colorado Springs CO (S)

Colorado Gallery of the Arts, see Arapahoe Community College, Littleton CO

Colorado Historical Society, Colorado History Museum, Denver CO (M,L)

Colorado Institute of Art, Denver CO (S)

Colorado Mountain College, Fine Arts Gallery, Breckenridge CO (M)

Colorado Mountain College, Visual & Performing Arts, Vale CO (S)

Colorado Photographic Arts Center, Denver CO (M)

Colorado Springs Fine Arts Center, Colorado Springs CO (M,L)

Colorado State University, Dept of Art, Fort Collins CO (S)

Colorado State University, Curfman Gallery, Fort Collins CO (M)

Colorado Watercolor Society, Golden CO (A)

Color Association of the US, New York NY (O)

Colter Bay Indian Arts Museum, see Grand Teton National Park Service, Moose WY

Columbia Art Association, see Columbia Museum of Art, Columbia SC

Columbia Basin College, Esvelt Gallery, Pasco WA (S)

Columbia College, Art Dept, Chicago IL (S)

Columbia College, Chicago IL (L,M)

Columbia College, Art Dept, Columbia MO (S)

Columbia College, Dept of Art, Columbia SC (S)

Columbia College, see Columbia University, New York NY (S)

Columbia College, Fine Arts, Sonora CA (S)

Columbia County Historical Society, Columbia County Museum, Kinderhook NY (M,L)

Columbia Museum of Art, Columbia SC (M,L,A)

Columbia River Maritime Museum, Astoria OR (M,L)

Columbia State Community College, Dept of Art, Columbia TN (S)

Columbia University, Avery Architectural & Fine Arts Library, New York NY (L,M)

Columbia University, New York NY (S)

Columbus Chapel & Boal Mansion Museum, Boalsburg PA (M)

Columbus College of Art & Design, Fine Arts Dept, Columbus OH (S)

Columbus College of Art & Design, Packard Library, Columbus OH (L)

Columbus Cultural Arts Center, Columbus OH (M)

Columbus & Lowndes County Historical Society, Blewett-Lee Museum, Columbus MS (M)

Columbus Metropolitan Library, Humanities, Fine Art & Recreation Division, Columbus OH (L)

Columbus Museum, Columbus GA (M)

Columbus Museum of Art, Columbus OH (M,L)

Columbus State University, Dept of Art, Fine Arts Hall, Columbus GA (S)

Columbus State University, The Gallery, Columbus GA (M)

Commencement Art Gallery, see Tacoma Arts Commission, Tacoma WA

Commerce Bancshares, Inc, Art Collection, Kansas City MO (C)

Commercial Art Division, see Universal Technical Institute, Omaha NE (S)

Community Arts Council of Vancouver, Vancouver BC (A)

Community College of Allegheny County, Fine Arts Dept, West Mifflin PA (S)

Community College of Allegheny County, Boyce Campus, Art Dept, Monroeville PA (S)

Community College of Rhode Island, Art Department Gallery, Warwick RI (M)

Community College of Rhode Island, Dept of Art, Warwick RI (S)

Community Council for the Arts, Kinston NC (A)

The Community Education Center, Philadelphia PA (A)

Community Fine Arts Center, Halseth Gallery, Rock Springs WY (A)

Compton Community College, Art Dept, Compton CA (S)

Concord Art Association, Concord MA (A)

Concord College, Fine Art Division, Athens WV (S)

Concordia College, Bronxville NY (S)

Concordia College, Art Dept, Moorhead MN (S)

Concordia College, Art Dept, Saint Paul MN (S)

Concordia College, Marx Hausen Art Gallery, Seward NE (M)

Concordia College, Art Dept, Seward NE (S)

Concordia Historical Institute, Saint Louis MO (M)

Concordia University, Dept of Fine Arts, Austin TX (S)

Concordia University, Division of Arts & Sciences, Mequon WI (S)

Concordia University, Leonard & Bina Ellen Art Gallery, Montreal PQ (M)

Concordia University, Faculty of Fine Arts, Montreal PQ (S)

Concordia University Wisconsin, Fine Art Gallery, Mequon WI (M)

Concord Museum, Concord MA (M,L)

Concourse Gallery, see State Street Corporation, Boston MA

Conejo Valley Art Museum, Thousand Oaks CA (M)

Confederate Museum, see Louisiana Historical Association, New Orleans LA

Confederation Centre Art Gallery and Museum, Charlottetown PE (M,L)

Congregation Emanu-El, New York NY (M)

Congressional Arts Caucus, Washington DC (O)

Conkling Gallery Art Dept, see Mankato State University, Mankato MN

Connecticut College, New London CT (S)

Connecticut Historical Commission, Sloane-Stanley Museum, Kent CT (M)

Connecticut Historical Society, Hartford CT (A,L)

Connecticut Institute of Art, Greenwich CT (S)

Connecticut State Library, Museum of Connecticut History, Hartford CT (L)

Connecticut Valley Historical Museum, see Springfield Library & Museums Association, Springfield MA

Connecticut Watercolor Society, Farmington CT (A)

Conseil des Arts du Canada, see The Canada Council, Ottawa ON

Davidson County Community College, Humanities Div, Lexington NC (S)

Davidson County Museum of Art, Lexington NC (M)

Davis & Elkins College, Dept of Art, Elkins WV (S)

John B Davis Gallery of Fine Art, see Idaho State University, Pocatello ID

Lewis James & Nellie Stratton Davis Art Gallery, see Stephens College, Columbia MO

Davis Museum & Cultural Center, see Wellesley College, Wellesley MA

Davison Art Center, see Wesleyan University, Middletown CT

Shelby Cullom Davis Museum, see The New York Public Library, New York NY

Charles Gates Dawes House, see Evanston Historical Society, Evanston IL

Dawson City Museum & Historical Society, Dawson City YT (M,L)

Dawson County Historical Society, Museum, Lexington NE (M)

Dawson Creek Art Gallery, see South Peace Art Society, Dawson Creek BC

Daytona Beach Community College, Dept of Fine Arts & Visual Arts, Daytona Beach FL (S)

Daytona Beach Community College, Southeast Museum of Photography, Daytona Beach FL (M)

Dayton Art Institute, Dayton OH (M,L)

Dayton Art Institute, see Wright State University, Dayton OH

Deaf Artists of America Inc, Rochester NY (A)

Dean College, Visual Art Dept, Franklin MA (S)

De Anza College, Creative Arts Division, Cupertino CA (S)

De Anza College, Euphrat Museum of Art, Cupertino CA (M)

Decatur House, see National Trust for Historic Preservation, Washington DC

Decker Library, see Maryland Institute, Baltimore MD

DeCordova Museum & Sculpture Park, Lincoln MA (M,L)

Deere & Company, Moline IL (C)

Christel DeHaan Fine Arts Gallery, see University of Indianapolis, Indianapolis IN

DeLand Museum of Art, DeLand FL (M)

Delaware Art Museum, Wilmington DE (M,L)

Delaware County Community College, Communications & Humanities House, Media PA (S)

Delaware State College, Dept of Art & Art Education, Dover DE (S)

Delaware State Museums, see Historical & Cultural Affairs, Dover DE

Delgado College, Dept of Fine Arts, New Orleans LA (S)

Del Mar College, Joseph A Cain Memorial Art Gallery, Corpus Christi TX (M)

Del Mar College, Art Dept, Corpus Christi TX (S)

Delphian School, Sheridan OR (S)

Delta Blues Museum, see Carnegie Public Library, Clarksdale MS

Delta College, Art Dept, University Center MI (S)

Delta State University, Fielding L Wright Art Center, Cleveland MS (M,L)

Delta State University, Dept of Art, Cleveland MS (S)

DeLuce Art Gallery, see Northwest Missouri State University, Maryville MO

DeMenil Mansion, see Chatillon-DeMenil House Foundation, Saint Louis MO

Deming-Luna Mimbres Museum, Deming NM (M)

Denison University, Art Gallery, Granville OH (M,L)

Denison University, Dept of Art, Granville OH (S)

Dennos Museum Center, see Northwestern Michigan College, Traverse City MI

Denver Art Museum, Denver CO (M,L)

Denver Public Library, General Reference, Denver CO (L)

Department of Commerce, Wyoming Arts Council Gallery, Cheyenne WY (M)

Department of Community Development, Edmonton AB (M,L)

Department of Natural Resources of Missouri, Missouri State Museum, Jefferson City MO (M)

DePaul University, Dept of Art, Chicago IL (S)

DePauw University, Art Dept, Greencastle IN (S)

De Pree Art Center & Gallery, see Hope College, Holland MI

Dept of Fine Arts, see Okasagan University College, Kelowna BC

DeRicci Gallery, see Edgewood College, Madison WI

de Saisset Museum, see Santa Clara University, Santa Clara CA

Desert Caballeros Western Museum, see Maricopa County Historical Society, Wickenburg AZ

Des Moines Area Community College, Art Dept, Boone IA (S)

Des Moines Art Center, see Edmundson Art Foundation, Inc, Des Moines IA

Des Moines Art Center Library, see Edmundson Art Foundation, Inc, Des Moines IA

Alice Curtis Desmond & Hamilton Fish Library, Hudson River Reference Collection, Garrison NY (L)

Detroit Artists Market, Detroit MI (M)

Detroit Focus, Detroit MI (M)

Detroit Institute of Arts, Detroit MI (M,L,A)

Detroit Public Library, Art & Literature Dept, Detroit MI (L)

Detroit Repertory Theatre Gallery, Detroit MI (M)

DeWitt Historical Society of Tompkins County, Ithaca NY (M)

DeWitt Wallace Library, see MacAlester College, Saint Paul MN

M H de Young Memorial Museum & California Palace of the Legion of Honor, see Fine Arts Museums of San Francisco, San Francisco CA

Dezign House, Jefferson OH (M,L)

Dia Center for the Arts, New York NY (A)

Dialogue Inc, Columbus OH (A)

Dickinson College, Fine Arts Dept, Carlisle PA (S)

Dickinson College, Trout Gallery, Carlisle PA (M)

Dickinson State University, Mind's Eye Gallery, Dickinson ND (M,L)

Dickinson State University, Dept of Art, Dickinson ND (S)

Diefenbaker Canada Centre, see University of Saskatchewan, Saskatoon SK

Dieu Donne Papermill, Inc, New York NY (M)

Diggs Gallery, see Winston-Salem State University, Winston Salem NC

Dillman's Bay Properties, Dillman's Creative Arts Foundation, Lac Du Flambeau WI (A,L)

Dillman's Creative Arts Foundation, see Dillman's Bay Properties, Lac Du Flambeau WI

The Dimock Gallery, see George Washington University, Washington DC

Dinand Library, see College of the Holy Cross, Worcester MA

Dinnerware Artist's Cooperative, Tucson AZ (M)

Charles Di Peso Library, see Cochise College, Douglas AZ

Discovery Museum, Bridgeport CT (M)

Discovery Place Inc, Charlotte NC (M)

Diverse Works, Houston TX (M)

Division of Historic Properties, see Kentucky New State Capitol, Frankfort KY

Dixie College, Southwestern Utah Art Gallery, Saint George UT (M)

Dixie College, Art Dept, Saint George UT (S)

The Dixon Gallery & Gardens, Memphis TN (M,L)

Doane College, Dept of Art, Crete NE (S)

Lamar Dodd Art Center Museum, see La Grange College, La Grange GA (S)

Lamar Dodd Art Center Museum, see La Grange College, La Grange GA

Lamar Dodd School of Art, see University of Georgia, Franklin College of Arts & Sciences, Athens GA (S)

George J Doizaki Gallery, see Japanese American Cultural & Community Center, Los Angeles CA

Dominican College of Blauvelt, Art Dept, Orangeburg NY (S)

Dominican College of San Rafael, Art Dept, San Rafael CA (S)

Eva Brook Donly Museum, Simcoe ON (M,L)

Door County, Miller Art Center, Sturgeon Bay WI (M)

Dorval Cultural Centre, Dorval PQ (A)

Doshi Center for Contemporary Art, Harrisburg PA (A)

Dougherty Arts Center Gallery, see City of Austin Parks & Recreation Department, Austin TX

Douglas Art Association, Little Gallery, Douglas AZ (M)

Douglas County Historical Society, Fairlawn Mansion & Museum, Superior WI (M,L)

Mabel Smith Douglass Library, see Rutgers, The State University of New Jersey, New Brunswick NJ

Alden B Dow Creativity Center, see Northwood University, Midland MI (S)

Grace A Dow Memorial Library, Fine Arts Dept, Midland MI (L)

Dowling College, Dept of Visual Arts, Oakdale NY (S)

Downey Museum of Art, Downey CA (M)

Drake University, Art Dept, Des Moines IA (S)

Drawing Center, New York NY (A)

The Drawing Society, New York NY (O)

G G Drayton Club, Salem OH (A)

Drew County Historical Society, Museum, Monticello AR (M)

Drew University, Elizabeth P Korn Gallery, Madison NJ (M,L)

Drew University, Art Dept, Madison NJ (S)

Drexel University, Nesbitt College of Design Arts, Philadelphia PA (S)

Felix J Dreyfous Library, see New Orleans Museum of Art, New Orleans LA

Joseph A Driscoll Art Gallery, see Brockton Public Library System, Brockton MA

Jose Drudis-Biada Art Gallery, see Mount Saint Mary's College, Los Angeles CA

Drury College, Art & Art History Dept, Springfield MO (S)

Dubuque Art Association, Dubuque Museum of Art, Dubuque IA (M)

Duke University, Dept of Art & Art History, Durham NC (S)

Duke University Library, Hartman Center for Sales, Advertising & Marketing History, Durham NC (L)

Duke University Museum of Art, Durham NC (M,L)

Duke University Union, Durham NC (M)

Dumbarton Oaks Research Library & Collections, see Harvard University, Washington DC

Duncan Gallery of Art, see Stetson University, De Land FL

Duncan-McAshan Visual Arts Center, see Hill Country Arts Foundation, Ingram TX

Dunconor Workshops, Salida CO (S)

Dundas Valley School of Art, Dundas ON (S)

Dundurn Castle, Hamilton ON (M)

Dunedin Fine Arts & Cultural Center, Dunedin FL (S)

Dunlop Art Gallery, see Regina Public Library, Regina SK

Duns Scotus Library, see Lourdes College, Sylvania OH

DuPage Art League School & Gallery, Wheaton IL (A)

Durham Art Guild Inc, Durham NC (M)

DuSable Museum of African American History, Chicago IL (M)

Dutchess Community College, Dept of Visual Arts, Poughkeepsie NY (S)

Dutchess County Arts Council, Poughkeepsie NY (M)

Dyson College of Arts & Sciences, see Pace University, Pleasantville NY (S)

Eagle Gallery, see Murray State University, Murray KY

Earlham College, Leeds Gallery, Richmond IN (M)

Earlham College, Art Dept, Richmond IN (S)

East Baton Rouge Parks & Recreation Commission, Baton Rouge Gallery Inc, Baton Rouge LA (M)

East Bay Asian Local Development Corp, Asian Resource Gallery, Oakland CA (M)

East Carolina University, Wellington B Gray Gallery, Greenville NC (M,L)

East Carolina University, School of Art, Greenville NC (S)

East Central College, Art Dept, Union MO (S)

East Central Community College, Art Dept, Decatur MS (S)

East Central University, Art Dept, Ada OK (S)

Fashion Institute of Technology, Museum at FIT, New York NY (M,L)

James H Faulkner Community College, Art Dept, Bay Minette AL (S)

Faulkner Memorial Art Wing, see Santa Barbara Public Library, Santa Barbara CA

Favell Museum of Western Art & Indian Artifacts, Klamath Falls OR (M)

Fawick Art Gallery, see Baldwin-Wallace College, Berea OH

Fayette Art Museum, Fayette AL (M)

Fayetteville Museum of Art, Inc, Fayetteville NC (M)

Fayetteville State University, Fine Arts & Humanities, Fayetteville NC (S)

Feather River Community College, Art Dept, Quincy CA (S)

Harriet FeBland Art Workshop, New York NY (S)

Federal Reserve Bank of Boston, Boston MA (C)

Federal Reserve Bank of Minneapolis, Minneapolis MN (C)

Federal Reserve Board, Art Gallery, Washington DC (M)

Federated Art Associations of New Jersey, Inc, Maplewood NJ (A)

Federation of Modern Painters & Sculptors, New York NY (O)

Fellowship of the Pennsylvania Academy of the Fine Arts, see Pennsylvania Academy of the Fine Arts, Philadelphia PA

Fellows of Contemporary Art, Los Angeles CA (A)

Fenimore House Museum, see New York State Historical Association, Cooperstown NY

Gordon Fennell Gallery & Marvin Cone Gallery, see Coe College, Cedar Rapids IA

Gershon & Rebecca Fenster Museum of Jewish Art, Tulsa OK (M)

Ferguson Library, Stamford CT (L)

Ferris State University, Visual Communication Dept, Big Rapids MI (S)

Fetherston Foundation, Packwood House Museum, Lewisburg PA (M)

Field Museum, Chicago IL (M,L)

55 Mercer, New York NY (M)

Fillmore County Historical Society, Fountain MN (A)

The Filson Club, Louisville KY (A,L)

Fine Arts Association, School of Fine Arts, Willoughby OH (A)

Fine Arts Center for the New River Valley, Pulaski VA (M)

Fine Arts Museum of Long Island, Hempstead NY (M)

Fine Arts Museums of San Francisco, San Francisco CA (M,L)

Finger Lakes Community College, Visual & Performing Arts Dept, Canandaigua NY (S)

Firehouse Art Center, Norman OK (M)

Firehouse Art Gallery, see Nassau Community College, Garden City NY

Firelands Association for the Visual Arts, Oberlin OH (A)

First Bank System, Art Collection, Minneapolis MN (C)

First Commercial Bank in Little Rock, Little Rock AR (C)

First National Bank, Fort Collins CO (C)

The First National Bank of Chicago, Art Collection, Chicago IL (C)

First State Bank, Norton KS (C)

First Street Gallery, New York NY (M)

First Tennessee Bank, Maryville TN (M)

First Tennessee Heritage Collection, see First Tennessee National Corp, Memphis TN

First Tennessee National Corp, First Tennessee Heritage Collection, Memphis TN (C)

Fisher Fine Arts Library, see University of Pennsylvania, Philadelphia PA

Fisher Gallery, see University of Southern California, Los Angeles CA

Fisher Gallery, see Cornish College of the Arts, Seattle WA

Jonathan Fisher Memorial, Inc, see Parson Fisher House, Blue Hill ME

Fisher Scientific Company, Fisher Collection of Alchemical & Historical Pictures, Pittsburgh PA (C)

Fisk University, University Galleries, Nashville TN (M,L)

Fisk University, Art Dept, Nashville TN (S)

Fitchburg Art Museum, Fitchburg MA (M)

Fitchburg Historical Society, Fitchburg MA (M)

Fitton Center For Creative Arts, Hamilton OH (M)

Fitton Center for Creative Arts, Hamilton OH (S)

Five Civilized Tribes Museum, Muskogee OK (M,L)

Flag House & 1812 Museum, see Star-Spangled Banner Flag House Association, Baltimore MD

Flagler College, Visual Arts Dept, Saint Augustine FL (S)

Henry Morrison Flagler Museum, Whitehall Mansion, Palm Beach FL (M)

Flamingo Gallery, see Las Vegas-Clark County Library District, Las Vegas NV

Flanagan Valley Campus Art Gallery, see Community College of Rhode Island, Warwick RI

John M Flaxman Library, see School of the Art Institute of Chicago, Chicago IL

The Fleischer Museum, see Franchise Finance Corporation of America, Scottsdale AZ

Fleischer Museum Library, see Franchise Finance Corporation of America, Scottsdale AZ

Samuel S Fleisher Art Memorial, Philadelphia PA (S)

Samuel S Fleisher Art Memorial, see Philadelphia Museum of Art, Philadelphia PA

Robert Hull Fleming Museum, see University of Vermont, Burlington VT

Flint Institute of Arts, Flint MI (M,L)

Florence Museum of Art, Science & History, Florence SC (M)

Florham Madison Campus Library - Art Dept, see Fairleigh Dickinson University, Madison NJ

Florida A & M University, Dept of Visual Arts, Humanities & Theatre, Tallahassee FL (S)

Florida Art Museum Directors Association, Vero Beach FL (A)

Florida Arts Council, see Florida Department of State, Division of Cultural Affairs, Tallahassee FL

Florida Atlantic University, Art Dept, Boca Raton FL (S)

Florida Atlantic University, Ritter Art Gallery, Boca Raton FL (M)

Florida College, Division of Art, Temple Terrace FL (S)

Florida Community College at Jacksonville, South Gallery, Jacksonville FL (M)

Florida Community College at Jacksonville, South Campus, Art Dept, Jacksonville FL (S)

Florida Department of Environmental Protection, Stephen Foster State Folk Culture Center, White Springs FL (M)

Florida Department of State, Division of Cultural Affairs, Florida Arts Council, Tallahassee FL (A)

Florida Folklife Programs, Tallahassee FL (A,L)

Florida Gulf Coast Art Center, Inc, Belleair FL (A,L)

Florida Gulf Coast Art Center, Inc, Belleair FL (S)

Florida International University, Visual Arts Dept, Miami FL (S)

Florida International University, The Art Museum at FIU, Miami FL (M)

Florida Keys Community College, Fine Arts Div, Key West FL (S)

The Florida Museum of Hispanic & Latin American Art, Miami FL (M)

Florida Pastel Association, Hollywood FL (A)

Florida School of the Arts, Visual Arts, Palatka FL (S)

Florida Southern College, Melvin Art Gallery, Lakeland FL (M)

Florida Southern College, Art Dept, Lakeland FL (S)

Florida State Museum, see T T Wentworth Jr Museum, Pensacola FL

Florida State University, Museum of Fine Arts, Tallahassee FL (M)

Florida State University, Tallahassee FL (S)

Florida State University Foundation - Central Florida Community College Foundation, The Appleton Museum of Art, Ocala FL (M)

Roswell P Flower Memorial Library, Watertown NY (M)

Floyd County Museum, New Albany IN (M)

Henry N Flynt Library, see Historic Deerfield, Inc, Deerfield MA

Focal Point Gallery, Bronx NY (M)

James Lemont Fogg Memorial Library, see Art Center College of Design, Pasadena CA

William Hayes Fogg Art Museum, see Harvard University, Cambridge MA

Folger Shakespeare Library, Washington DC (L)

Fondo del Sol, Visual Art & Media Center, Washington DC (M)

Fontbonne College, Art Dept, Saint Louis MO (S)

Foothill College, Fine Arts & Communications Div, Los Altos Hills CA (S)

Foothills Art Center, Inc, Golden CO (A,L)

Foothills Art Center, Inc, Golden CO (S)

Captain Robert Bennet Forbes House, Milton MA (M)

Forbes Gallery, see Carnegie Mellon University, Pittsburgh PA

Forbes Library, Northampton MA (L)

Forbes Magazine, Inc, New York NY (C)

Edsel & Eleanor Ford House, Grosse Pointe Shores MI (M)

Ford Gallery, see Eastern Michigan University, Ypsilanti MI

Fordham University, Art Dept, New York NY (S)

Henry Ford Museum & Greenfield Village, see Ford Motor Company, Dearborn MI

Ford Motor Company, Henry Ford Museum & Greenfield Village, Dearborn MI (C)

Foreman Gallery, see Hartwick College, Oneonta NY

Forest Hills Adult Center, Forest Hills NY (S)

Forest Lawn Museum, Glendale CA (M,L)

Forges du Saint-Maurice National Historic Site, Trois Rivieres PQ (M)

Forsyth Library, see Fort Hays State University, Hays KS

Fort George G Meade Museum, Fort Meade MD (M)

Fort Hays State University, Moss-Thorns Gallery of Arts, Hays KS (M,L)

Fort Hays State University, Dept of Art, Hays KS (S)

Fort Hill Plantation, see Clemson University, Clemson SC

Fort Lewis College, Art Dept, Durango CO (S)

Fort Morgan Heritage Foundation, Fort Morgan CO (M)

Fort Saskatchewan Municipal Library, Fort Saskatchewan AB (L)

Fort Smith Art Center, Fort Smith AR (M)

Fort Steilacoom Community College, Fine Arts Dept, Tacoma WA (S)

Fort Ticonderoga Association, Ticonderoga NY (M,L)

Fort Totten State Historic Site, Pioneer Daughters Museum, Fort Totten ND (A)

Fort Valley State College, H A Hunt Memorial Library, Fort Valley GA (L)

Fort Wayne Museum of Art, Inc, Fort Wayne IN (M)

Fort Worth Art Association, Modern Art Museum of Fort Worth, Fort Worth TX (M,L)

Fort Worth Public Library, Fine Arts Section, Fort Worth TX (L)

Forum for Contemporary Art, Saint Louis MO (A)

The Forum Gallery, see Jamestown Community College, Jamestown NY

Foster Gallery, see University of Wisconsin-Eau Claire, Eau Claire WI

Stephen Foster State Folk Culture Center, see Florida Department of Environmental Protection, White Springs FL

Fotografica, New York NY (A)

Foundation for Art Resources, Los Angeles CA (A)

Foundation for Today's Art, Nexus Gallery, Philadelphia PA (M)

Foundry School Museum, see Putnam County Historical Society, Cold Spring NY

Fourteen Sculptors Gallery, see Cultural Council Foundation, New York NY

Fowler Museum of Cultural History, see University of California, Los Angeles, Los Angeles CA

Foyer Gallery, see Edmonton Public Library, Edmonton AB

Glenville State College, Dept of Fine Arts, Glenville WV (S)

Glesser House, see Praire Avenue House Museums, Chicago IL

Gloridale Partnership, National Museum of Woodcarving, Custer SD (M)

Gloucester County College, Liberal Arts Dept, Sewell NJ (S)

Glynn Art Association, Saint Simons Island GA (A)

Charles B Goddard Center for the Visual & Performing Arts, Ardmore OK (A)

Goddard College, Dept of Art, Plainfield VT (S)

Morton R Godine Library, see Massachusetts College of Art, Boston MA

Godwin-Ternbach Museum, see Queens College, City University of New York, Flushing NY

Gogebic Community College, Fine Arts Dept, Ironwood MI (S)

Galerie Georges Goguen, see Radio-Canada SRC CBC, Moncton NB

Golden Isles Arts & Humanities Association, Brunswick GA (A)

Golden State Mutual Life Insurance Company, Afro-American Art Collection, Los Angeles CA (C)

Golden West College, Visual Art Dept, Huntington Beach CA (S)

Goldsboro Art Center, Goldsboro NC (S)

Goldstein Gallery, see University of Minnesota, Saint Paul MN

Robert Goldwater Library, see The Metropolitan Museum of Art, New York NY

Gonzaga University, Dept of Art, Spokane WA (S)

Gonzaga University, Jundt Art Museum, Ad Art Gallery, Spokane WA (M)

Gaston T Gooch Library & Learning Resource Center, see Navarro College, Corsicana TX

Gordon College, Dept of Fine Arts, Barnesville GA (S)

Donald B Gordon Memorial Library, see Palm Beach County Parks & Recreation Department, Delray Beach FL

Goshen College, Art Dept, Goshen IN (S)

Goshen Historical Society, Goshen CT (M)

Goucher College, Art Dept, Baltimore MD (S)

Goucher College, Rosenberg Gallery, Baltimore MD (M)

Governors State University, College of Arts & Science, Art Dept, University Park IL (S)

Grace College, Dept of Art, Winona Lake IN (S)

Graceland College, Fine Arts Dept, Lamoni IA (S)

Graceland Museum & American Saddlehorse Museum, see Audrain County Historical Society, Mexico MO

Grambling State University, Art Dept, Grambling LA (S)

Grand Canyon University, Art Dept, Phoenix AZ (S)

Grand Marais Art Colony, Grand Marais MN (S)

Grand Prairie Arts Council, Inc, Arts Center of the Grand Prairie, Stuttgart AR (A)

Grand Rapids Art Museum, Grand Rapids MI (M,L)

Grand Rapids Community College, Art Dept, Grand Rapids MI (S)

Grand Rapids Public Library, Music & Art Dept, Grand Rapids MI (L)

Grand Teton National Park Service, Colter Bay Indian Arts Museum, Moose WY (A)

Grand Valley State University, Art & Design Dept, Allendale MI (S)

Grand View College, Art Dept, Des Moines IA (S)

Grant Wood Memorial Park & Gallery, see Paint 'N Palette Club, Anamosa IA

Graphic Artists Guild, New York NY (A)

The Gray Gallery, see Quincy University, Quincy IL

Grayson County College, Art Dept, Denison TX (S)

Wellington B Gray Gallery, see East Carolina University, Greenville NC

Greater Lafayette Museum of Art, Lafayette IN (M,L)

Great Lakes Historical Society, Island Seas Maritime Museum, Vermilion OH (M)

Greene County Historical Society, Bronck Museum, Coxsackie NY (M)

Greene County Historical Society, Xenia OH (A)

Greene & Greene Library of the Arts & Crafts Movement, see University of Southern California, San Marino CA

Albert M Greenfield Library, see University of the Arts, Philadelphia PA

Greenfield Community College, Art, Graphic Design & Media Communication Dept, Greenfield MA (S)

Green Hill Center for North Carolina Art, Greensboro NC (M)

Ida Green Gallery, see Austin College, Sherman TX

Green Mountain College, Dept of Art, Poultney VT (S)

Green Research Library, see Old Jail Art Center, Albany TX

Green River Community College, Art Dept, Auburn WA (S)

Greensboro Artists' League, Greensboro NC (A)

Greensboro College, Dept of Art, Division of Fine Arts, Greensboro NC (S)

Greensboro College, Irene Cullis Gallery, Greensboro NC (M)

Greenville College, Richard W Bock Sculpture Collection, Greenville IL (M,L)

Greenville College, Division of Language, Literature & Fine Arts, Greenville IL (S)

Greenville County Museum of Art, Greenville SC (M)

Greenville County Museum of Art, Museum School of Art, Greenville SC (S)

Greenville Museum of Art, Inc, Greenville NC (A,L)

Greenville Technical College, Visual Arts Dept, Greer SC (S)

Greenwich Art Society Inc, Greenwich CT (A)

Greenwich House, Pottery Library, New York NY (L)

Greenwich House Pottery, New York NY (S)

Greenwich Library, Greenwich CT (L)

Greenwood Museum, Greenwood SC (M)

Grey Art Gallery & Study Center, see New York University, New York NY

Allie Griffin Art Gallery, see Weyburn Arts Council, Weyburn SK

Arthur Griffin Center for Photographic Art, Winchester MA (M)

Griffis Sculpture Park, see Ashford Hollow Foundation for Visual & Performing Arts, East Otto NY

Grinnell College, Dept of Art, Grinnell IA (S)

Grinnell College, Print & Drawing Study Room/ Gallery, Grinnell IA (M)

Florence Griswold Museum, see Lyme Historical Society, Old Lyme CT

Grolier Club Library, New York NY (L)

Grossmont College, Art Dept, El Cajon CA (S)

Grossmont Community College, Hyde Gallery, El Cajon CA (M)

M Grumbacher Inc, Bloomsbury NJ (C)

Grunwald Center for the Graphic Arts, see University of California, Los Angeles, Los Angeles CA

Guadalupe Cultural Arts Center, San Antonio TX (A)

Guadalupe Historic Foundation, Santuario de Guadalupe, Santa Fe NM (M)

John Simon Guggenheim Memorial Foundation, New York NY (A)

Guggenheim Museum Soho, New York NY (M)

Solomon R Guggenheim Museum, New York NY (M,L)

Guild Art Center, New Canaan CT (S)

Guilde Canadienne des Metiers d'Art Quebec, Canadian Guild of Crafts Quebec, Montreal PQ (A)

Guild Hall of East Hampton, Inc, Guild Hall Museum, East Hampton NY (M)

Guild of Book Workers, New York NY (O)

Guild of Boston Artists, Boston MA (A)

Guild of Creative Art, Shrewsbury NJ (S)

Guilford College, Art Dept, Greensboro NC (S)

Guilford College, Art Gallery, Greensboro NC (M)

Guilford Technical Community College, Commercial Art Dept, Jamestown NC (S)

Gulf Coast Community College, Division of Visual & Performing Arts, Panama City FL (S)

Jessica Gund Memorial Library, see Cleveland Institute of Art, Cleveland OH

Emery A Gunnin Architectural Library, see Clemson University, Clemson SC

Gunston Hall Plantation, Mason Neck VA (M,L)

George Gustav Heye Center, see National Museum of the American Indian, New York NY

Gustavus Adolphus College, Art & Art History Dept, Saint Peter MN (S)

Haas Gallery of Art, see Bloomsburg University of Pennsylvania, Bloomsburg PA

Hacienda Martinez, see Kit Carson Historic Museums, Taos NM

Haffenreffer Museum, see Brown University, Providence RI

Hagadorn House, The 1800-37 Museum, see Almond Historical Society, Inc, Almond NY

Hagerstown Junior College, Art Dept, Hagerstown MD (S)

Haggerty Museum of Art, see Marquette University, Milwaukee WI

The Haggin Museum, see San Joaquin Pioneer & Historical Society, Stockton CA

Halifax Historical Society, Inc, Halifax Historical Museum, Daytona Beach FL (M)

Hallmark Cards, Inc, Kansas City MO (C,L)

Hall of Electrical History, see Schenectady Museum Planetarium & Visitors Center, Schenectady NY

Hall of State, see Dallas Historical Society, Dallas TX

Hallwalls Contemporary Arts Center, Buffalo NY (M)

Halseth Gallery, see Community Fine Arts Center, Rock Springs WY

Halsey Gallery, see College of Charleston, Charleston SC

Hambidge Center Gallery, Rabun Gap GA (M)

Hamilton College, Fred L Emerson Gallery, Clinton NY (M)

Hamilton College, Art Dept, Clinton NY (S)

Hamline University, Dept of Art & Art History, Saint Paul MN (S)

Hamline University Learning Center Gallery, Saint Paul MN (M,L)

Hammond Castle Museum, Gloucester MA (M)

Hammond-Harwood House Association, Inc, Annapolis MD (M)

Hammond Museum & Japanese Stroll Garden, Cross-Cultural Center, North Salem NY (M)

Hamon Arts Library, see Southern Methodist University, Dallas TX

Hampden-Booth Theatre Library, see Players, New York NY

Hampshire County Public Library, Romney WV (L)

Hampton Arts Commission, see City of Hampton, Hampton VA

Hampton University, University Museum, Hampton VA (M)

Hampton University, Dept of Fine & Performing Arts, Hampton VA (S)

Hancock Shaker Village, Inc, Pittsfield MA (M,L)

Handforth Gallery, see Tacoma Public Library, Tacoma WA

Handweavers Guild of America, Duluth GA (A)

Hand Workshop Art Center, Richmond VA (A)

Hannibal La Grange College, Art Dept, Hannibal MO (S)

Hanover College, Dept of Art, Hanover IN (S)

Dane G Hansen Memorial Museum, Logan KS (M)

Clarence B Hanson, Jr Library, see Birmingham Museum of Art, Birmingham AL

Harcum Junior College, Illustrations & Graphic Design Dept, Bryn Mawr PA (S)

Harding University, Dept of Art, Searcy AR (S)

Hardin-Simmons University, Art Dept, Abilene TX (S)

Harford Community College, Fine & Applied Arts Division, Bel Air MD (S)

Harlow Gallery, see Kennebec Valley Art Association, Hallowell ME

Harned Gallery, see Austin Peay State University, Clarksville TN

Harness Racing & Hall of Fame, Goshen NY (M)

Samuel P Harn Museum of Art, see University of Florida, Gainesville FL

Hoffman Gallery, see Oregon College of Art Craft, Portland OR

Elise N Hofheimer Art Library, see Old Dominion University, Norfolk VA

Hofstra University, Hofstra Museum, Hempstead NY (M)

Hofstra University, Hempstead NY (S)

Alexandre Hogue Gallery, see University of Tulsa, Tulsa OK

Holland College, Health, Science & Creative Arts, Charlottetown PE (S)

Hollins College, Art Dept, Roanoke VA (S)

Hollywood Art Center School, Hollywood CA (S)

Hollywood Art Museum, Hollywood FL (M)

The Holtzman Art Gallery, see Towson State University, Towson MD

Holy Names College, Art Dept, Oakland CA (S)

Holyoke Community College, Dept of Art, Holyoke MA (S)

Homewood House Museum, see Johns Hopkins University, Baltimore MD

Honeywell Inc, Art Collection, Minneapolis MN (C)

Honolulu Academy of Arts, Honolulu HI (M,L)

Honolulu Academy of Arts, The Art Center at Linekona, Honolulu HI (S)

Honolulu Community College, Commercial Art Dept, Honolulu HI (S)

Hood College, Dept of Art, Frederick MD (S)

Hood Museum of Art, see Dartmouth College, Hanover NH

Hoosier Salon Patrons Association, Hoosier Salon Art Gallery, Indianapolis IN (A)

Dorothy H Hoover Library, see Ontario College of Art & Design, Toronto ON

Herbert Hoover Presidential Library & Museum, West Branch IA (L)

Hope College, Art Dept, Holland MI (S)

Hope College, De Pree Art Center & Gallery, Holland MI (M)

Henry Radford Hope School of Fine Arts, see Indiana University, Bloomington, Bloomington IN (S)

Hopewell Museum, Hopewell NJ (M)

Hopi Cultural Center Museum, Second Mesa AZ (M)

Hopper Resource Library, see Butler Institute of American Art, Youngstown OH

Horizons Unlimited Supplementary Educational Center, Art Gallery, Salisbury NC (M)

Hostos Center for the Arts & Culture, Bronx NY (A)

Hot Springs Art Center, Fine Arts Center, Hot Springs AR (M)

Houghton College, Art Dept, Houghton NY (S)

Housatonic Community-Technical College, Housatonic Museum of Art, Bridgeport CT (M,L)

Housatonic Community & Technical College, Art Dept, Bridgeport CT (S)

House of Happy Walls, see Jack London State Historic Park, Glen Ellen CA

House of Roses, Senator Wilson Home, Deadwood SD (M)

Houston Baptist University, Dept of Art, Houston TX (S)

Houston Baptist University, Museum of American Architecture and Decorative Arts, Houston TX (M)

Houston Center For Photography, Houston TX (A)

Houston Museum of Decorative Arts, Chattanooga TN (M)

Houston Public Library, Houston TX (L)

Howard College, Art Dept, Big Spring TX (S)

Howard County Arts Council, Ellicott City MD (A)

Howard Payne University, Dept of Art, Brownwood TX (S)

Howard University, Gallery of Art, Washington DC (M,L)

Oscar Howe Art Center, Mitchell SD (A)

Hoxie Gallery, see Westerly Public Library, Westerly RI

Hoyt Institute of Fine Arts, New Castle PA (M)

Hubbell Trading Post National Historic Site, see National Park Service, Ganado AZ

HUB Galleries, see Pennsylvania State University, University Park PA

Grace Hudson Museum & The Sun House, see City of Ukiah, Ukiah CA

Hudson Guild, Joe & Emily Lowe Art Gallery, New York NY (M)

The Hudson River Museum of Westchester, Yonkers NY (M)

Hudson River Reference Collection, see Alice Curtis Desmond & Hamilton Fish Library, Garrison NY

Hudson Valley Art Association, Hastings On Hudson NY (A)

Hughes Fine Arts Center, see University of North Dakota, Grand Forks ND

Huguenot Historical Society of New Paltz Galleries, New Paltz NY (M)

Marie Hull Gallery, see Hinds Community College District, Raymond MS

Hulsey Gallery-Norick Art Center, see Oklahoma City University, Oklahoma City OK

Humanities, Fine Art & Recreation Division, see Columbus Metropolitan Library, Columbus OH

Humber College of Applied Arts & Technology, Applied Arts Div, Etobicoke ON (S)

Humboldt Arts Council, Eureka CA (A)

Humboldt State University, College of Arts & Humanities, Arcata CA (S)

Cecille R Hunt Gallery, see Webster University, Saint Louis MO

Hunter College, Art Dept, New York NY (S)

Hunterdon Art Center, Clinton NJ (A)

Hunterdon Historical Museum, Clinton NJ (M)

Hunter Museum of American Art, Chattanooga TN (M,L)

H A Hunt Memorial Library, see Fort Valley State College, Fort Valley GA

Huntingdon College, Dept of Art, Montgomery AL (S)

Archer M Huntington Art Gallery, see University of Texas at Austin, Austin TX

Huntington Beach Art Center, Huntington Beach CA (M)

Huntington College, Art Dept, Huntington IN (S)

Huntington College, Robert E Wilson Art Gallery, Huntington IN (M)

David Huntington Archive, see Olana State Historic Site, Hudson NY

The Huntington Library, Art Collections & Botanical Gardens, San Marino CA (M,L)

Huntington Museum of Art, Huntington WV (M)

Hunt Institute for Botanical Documentation, see Carnegie Mellon University, Pittsburgh PA

Hunt Library, see Carnegie Mellon University, Pittsburgh PA

Huntsville Art League, Huntsville AL (A)

Huntsville Museum of Art, Huntsville AL (M,L)

William Morris Hunt Memorial Library, see Museum of Fine Arts, Boston MA

Huronia Museum, Midland ON (M)

Huron University, Arts & Sciences Division, Huron SD (S)

Hussian School of Art, Commercial Art Dept, Philadelphia PA (S)

Hutchinson Art Association, Hutchinson Art Center, Hutchinson KS (A)

Hutchinson Community Junior College, Visual Arts Dept, Hutchinson KS (S)

Hyde Collection Trust, Glens Falls NY (M,L)

Hyde Gallery, see Grossmont Community College, El Cajon CA

Olive Hyde Art Gallery, see City of Fremont, Fremont CA

Hyde Park Art Center, Chicago IL (M)

Stan Hywet Hall & Gardens, Inc, Akron OH (M)

ICS Learning Systems, Scranton PA (S)

Idaho Commission on the Arts, Boise ID (A)

Idaho Historical Museum, Boise ID (M)

Idaho State University, John B Davis Gallery of Fine Art, Pocatello ID (M)

Idaho State University, Dept of Art, Pocatello ID (S)

Idyllwild Arts Academy, Idyllwild CA (S)

Illinois Art Gallery, see Illinois State Museum, Chicago IL

Illinois Art Gallery & Lockport Gallery, see Illinois State Museum, Springfield IL

Illinois Artisans Shop, see Illinois State Museum, Chicago IL

Illinois Artisans & Visitors Centers, see Illinois State Museum, Chicago IL

Illinois Benedictine University, Fine Arts Dept, Lisle IL (S)

Illinois Central College, Dept of Fine Arts, East Peoria IL (S)

Illinois Historic Preservation Agency, Bishop Hill State Historic Site, Bishop Hill IL (M)

The Illinois Institute of Art, Chicago IL (S)

Illinois Institute of Technology, Chicago IL (S)

Illinois State Museum, Illinois Art Gallery, Chicago IL (M)

Illinois State Museum, Illinois Art Gallery & Lockport Gallery, Springfield IL (M,L)

Illinois State University, Normal IL (L,M)

Illinois State University, Art Dept, Normal IL (S)

Illinois Valley Community College, Division of Humanities & Fine Arts, Oglesby IL (S)

Illinois Wesleyan University, Merwin & Wakeley Galleries, Bloomington IL (M,L)

Illinois Wesleyan University, School of Art, Bloomington IL (S)

Illustration House Inc, Gallery Auction House, New York NY (M)

Imhoff Art Gallery, Alberta SK (M)

Imperato Collection of West African Artifacts, see Martin & Osa Johnson Safari Museum, Inc, Chanute KS

Imperial Calcasieu Museum, Lake Charles LA (M,L)

Imperial Valley College, Art Dept, Imperial CA (S)

Incarnate Word University of the Arts & Sciences, Art Dept, San Antonio TX (S)

Independence Museum, Independence KS (M)

Independence National Historical Park, Philadelphia PA (M,L)

Independence Seaport Museum, Philadelphia PA (M,L)

Independent Curators Inc, New York NY (A)

Index of American Design, see National Gallery of Art, Washington DC

Indianapolis Art Center, Churchman-Fehsenfeld Gallery, Indianapolis IN (A)

Indianapolis Center for Contemporary Art-Herron Gallery, see Indiana University - Purdue University at Indianapolis, Indianapolis IN

Indianapolis Marion County Public Library, Arts Division, Indianapolis IN (L)

Indianapolis Museum of Art, Indianapolis IN (M,L)

Indiana-Purdue University, Dept of Fine Arts, Fort Wayne IN (S)

Indian Arts & Crafts Association, Albuquerque NM (A)

Indian Arts & Crafts Board, Sioux Indian Museum, Rapid City SD (M)

Indiana State Museum, Indianapolis IN (M)

Indiana State University, Turman Art Gallery, Terre Haute IN (M)

Indiana State University, Terre Haute IN (S)

Indiana University, Bloomington IN (M)

Indiana University, Fine Arts Library, Bloomington IN (L)

Indiana University, Bloomington, Henry Radford Hope School of Fine Arts, Bloomington IN (S)

Indiana University-East, Humanities Dept, Richmond IN (S)

Indiana University of Pennsylvania, Kipp Gallery, Indiana PA (M)

Indiana University of Pennsylvania, Dept of Art & Art Education, Indiana PA (S)

Indiana University - Purdue University at Indianapolis, Indianapolis IN (M)

Indiana University-Purdue University, Indianapolis, Herron School of Art, Indianapolis IN (S)

Indiana University South Bend, Fine Arts Dept, South Bend IN (S)

Indiana University-Southeast, Fine Arts Dept, New Albany IN (S)

Indiana Wesleyan University, Art Dept, Marion IN (S)

Indian Center Museum, see Mid-America All-Indian Center, Wichita KS

Indian Hills Community College, Dept of Art, Centerville IA (S)

Indian Hills Community College, Ottumwa Campus, Dept of Art, Ottumwa IA (S)

Indian Museum of Lake County, Ohio, see Archaeological Society of Ohio, Painesville OH

Indian Museum of North America & Native American Educational & Cultural Center, see Crazy Horse Memorial, Crazy Horse SD

Indian Pueblo Cultural Center, Albuquerque NM (M)

Indian River Community College, Fine Arts Dept, Fort Pierce FL (S)

Individual Artists of Oklahoma, Oklahoma City OK (M)

Industrial Designers Society of America, Great Falls VA (O)

Ingalls Library, see Cleveland Museum of Art, Cleveland OH

Ingraham Memorial Research Library, see Litchfield Historical Society, Litchfield CT

Installation Gallery, San Diego CA (A)

Institut des Arts au Saguenay, Centre National D'Exposition a Jonquiere, Jonquiere PQ (M)

Institute for Arts & Humanities Education, New Jersey Summer Arts Institute, New Brunswick NJ (S)

Institute for Contemporary Art, Project Studio One (P S 1), Long Island City NY (M)

Institute of Alaska Native Arts, Inc, Fairbanks AK (A)

Institute of American Indian Arts Museum, Santa Fe NM (M,L)

Institute of American Indian Arts Museum, Santa Fe NM (S)

Institute of Contemporary Art, Boston MA (M)

Institute of Contemporary Art, Philadelphia PA (A)

The Institute of Contemporary Art, see Maine College of Art, Portland ME

Institute of Fine Arts Visual Resources Collection, see New York University, New York NY

Institute of Puerto Rican Culture, Escuela de Artes Plasticas, San Juan PR (S)

Institute of Puerto Rican Culture, San Juan PR (M, A,L)

Institute of Texan Cultures, see The University of Texas, San Antonio TX

Institute of the Great Plains, Museum of the Great Plains, Lawton OK (M,L)

Instituto de Cultura Puertorriquena, see Institute of Puerto Rican Culture, San Juan PR

Intar Latin American Gallery, New York NY (M)

InterAmerican Art Gallery, see Miami-Dade Community College, Miami FL

Inter American University of Puerto Rico, Dept of Art, San German PR (S)

The Interchurch Center, Galleries at the Interchurch Center, New York NY (M,L)

The Interchurch Center, see The Interchurch Center, New York NY

Interior Designers Society of Quebec, see La Societe des Decorateurs-Ensembliers du Quebec, Montreal PQ

Interlochen Arts Academy, Dept of Visual Art, Interlochen MI (S)

Interlochen Center for the Arts, Interlochen MI (L)

Intermedia Arts Minnesota, Minneapolis MN (M)

Intermuseum Conservation Association, Oberlin OH (O)

International Center for Advanced Studies in Art, New York NY (O)

International Center of Medieval Art, Inc, New York NY (A)

International Center of Photography, New York NY (M,L)

International Council for Cultural Exchange (ICCE), Bellport NY (S)

International Fine Arts College, Miami FL (S)

International Foundation for Art Research, Inc, New York NY (O)

International Images, Ltd, Sewickley PA (M)

International Institute of Pigeons & Doves, Oklahoma City OK (C)

International Museum of Cartoon Art, Boca Raton FL (M,L)

International Museum of Cartoon Art, Montreal PQ (M)

International Sculpture Center, Washington DC (M)

International Society of Copier Artists (ISCA), Brooklyn NY (O)

International Society of Marine Painters, Oneco FL (A)

Intersection for the Arts, San Francisco CA (A)

Inter-Society Color Council, Lawrenceville NJ (O)

Iowa Central Community College, Dept of Art, Fort Dodge IA (S)

Iowa Lakes Community College, Dept of Art, Estherville IA (S)

Iowa State Education Association, Salisbury House, Des Moines IA (M)

Iowa State University, Dept of Art & Design, Ames IA (S)

Iowa State University, Brunnier Art Museum, Ames IA (M)

Iowa Wesleyan College, Art Dept, Mount Pleasant IA (S)

Iowa Western Community College, Art Dept, Council Bluffs IA (S)

Iroquois County Historical Society Museum, Old Courthouse Museum, Watseka IL (M)

Iroquois Indian Museum, Howes Cave NY (M)

Irvine Fine Arts Center, see City of Irvine, Irvine CA

Irving Arts Center, Main Gallery & New Talent Gallery, Irving TX (M)

Island Gallery West, Holmes Beach FL (M)

Island Seas Maritime Museum, see Great Lakes Historical Society, Vermilion OH

Islip Art Museum, East Islip NY (M)

Ithaca College, Fine Art Dept, Ithaca NY (S)

Jackson County Historical Society, The 1859 Jail, Marshal's Home & Museum, Independence MO (M,L)

Jackson Hall Gallery, see Kentucky State University, Frankfort KY

Sheldon Jackson Museum, see Alaska Department of Education, Division of Libraries, Archives & Museums, Sitka AK

Jackson State University, Dept of Art, Jackson MS (S)

Jacksonville Museum of Contemporary Art, Jacksonville FL (M,L)

Jacksonville Public Library, Fine Arts & Recreation Dept, Jacksonville FL (L)

Jacksonville State University, Art Dept, Jacksonville AL (S)

Jacksonville University, Dept of Art, Jacksonville FL (S)

Jacksonville University, Alexander Brest Museum & Gallery, Jacksonville FL (M)

Jacobs Gallery, see City of Eugene, Hult Center, Eugene OR

Jacques Marchais Museum of Tibetan Art Center of Tibetan Art, Tibetan Museum, Staten Island NY (M)

Jailhouse Galleries, see Burke Arts Council, Morganton NC

Jamaica Arts Center, Jamaica NY (M)

James Madison University, Sawhill Gallery, Harrisonburg VA (M)

James Madison University, School of Art & Art History, Harrisonburg VA (S)

Jamestown College, Art Dept, Jamestown ND (S)

Jamestown Community College, Arts & Humanities Division, Jamestown NY (S)

Jamestown Community College, The Forum Gallery, Jamestown NY (M)

Jamestown-Yorktown Foundation, Williamsburg VA (M)

Japanese American Cultural & Community Center, George J Doizaki Gallery, Los Angeles CA (M)

Japan Society, Inc, New York NY (M,L)

Japantown Art & Media Workshop, San Francisco CA (A)

Jardin Botanique de Montreal, Bibliotheque, Montreal PQ (L)

Jay County Arts Council, Hugh N Ronald Memorial Gallery, Portland IN (M)

John Jay Homestead State Historic Site, see New York State Office of Parks Recreation & Historic Preservation, Katonah NY

Jefferson Community College, Fine Arts, Louisville KY (S)

Jefferson Community College, Art Dept, Watertown NY (S)

Jefferson County Historical Museum, Pine Bluff AR (M)

Jefferson County Historical Society, Watertown NY (M,L)

Jefferson County Historical Society Museum, Madison IN (M)

Jefferson County Open Space, Hiwan Homestead Museum, Evergreen CO (M)

Jefferson Davis Community College, Art Dept, Brewton AL (S)

Thomas Jefferson Memorial Foundation, Monticello, Charlottesville VA (M)

Jekyll Island Museum, Jekyll Island GA (M)

Arthur D Jenkins Library, see Textile Museum, Washington DC

William R Jenkins Architecture & Art Library, see University of Houston, Houston TX

Jericho Historical Society, Jericho VT (A)

J Erie Johnson Library, Fine Arts Division, Dallas TX (L)

Jersey City Museum, Jersey City NJ (M)

Jersey City State College, Courtney Art Gallery, Jersey City NJ (M)

Jersey City State College, Art Dept, Jersey City NJ (S)

Jewett Hall Gallery, see University of Maine at Augusta, Augusta ME

Jewish Community Center of Greater Washington, Jane L & Robert H Weiner Judaic Museum, Rockville MD (M)

Jewish Community Centre of Toronto, The Koffler Gallery, North York ON (M)

The Jewish Museum, New York NY (M,L)

John Brown University, Art Dept, Siloam Springs AR (S)

John Carroll University, Dept of Art History & Humanities, Cleveland OH (S)

John Jay College of Criminal Justice, Dept of Art, Music & Philosophy, New York NY (S)

Johns Hopkins University, Baltimore MD (M,L)

Johns Hopkins University, Baltimore MD (S)

Johnson Atelier Technical Institute of Sculpture, Mercerville NJ (S)

Johnson Atelier Technical Institute of Sculpture, Johnson Atelier Library, Mercerville NJ (L)

Johnson Collection of Photographs, Movies & Memorabilia, see Martin & Osa Johnson Safari Museum, Inc, Chanute KS

Johnson County Community College, Visual Arts Program, Overland Park KS (S)

Grace Phillips Johnson Art Gallery, see Phillips University, Enid OK

Herbert F Johnson Museum of Art, see Cornell University, Ithaca NY

Johnson-Humrickhouse Museum, Coshocton OH (M)

John G Johnson Collection, see Philadelphia Museum of Art, Philadelphia PA

Johnson & Johnson, Art Program, New Brunswick NJ (C)

Martin & Osa Johnson Safari Museum, Inc, Chanute KS (M,L)

Johnson State College, Dept Fine & Performing Arts, Dibden Center for the Arts, Johnson VT (S)

Joliet Junior College, Fine Arts Dept, Joliet IL (S)

Joliet Junior College, Laura A Sprague Art Gallery, Joliet IL (M)

Jones County Junior College, Art Dept, Ellisville MS (S)

Fred Jones Jr Museum of Art, see University of Oklahoma, Norman OK

James A Jones Library, see Brevard College, Brevard NC

John Paul Jones House, see Portsmouth Historical Society, Portsmouth NH

Jones Library, Inc, Amherst MA (L)

Jones Memorial Library, Lynchburg VA (L)

Jonson Gallery, see University of New Mexico, Albuquerque NM

Jordan Historical Museum of The Twenty, Jordan ON (M)

Jorgensen Gallery, see University of Connecticut, Storrs CT

Joseloff Gallery, see University of Hartford, West Hartford CT

Joslyn Art Museum, Omaha NE (M,L)

J Sargeant Reynolds Community College, Humanities & Social Science Division, Richmond VA (S)

Judiciary History Center, Honolulu HI (M)

Judson College, Division of Fine Arts, Elgin IL (S)

Judson College, Division of Fine Arts, Marion AL (S)

Jundt Art Museum, see Gonzaga University, Spokane WA

C G Jung Institute of Chicago, Evanston IL (M)

Juniata College, Dept of Art, Huntingdon PA (S)

Junior Arts Center, see Cultural Affairs Department City of Los Angeles, Los Angeles CA

Junior College of Albany, Fine Arts Division, Albany NY (S)

Kala Institute, Berkeley CA (A)

Kalamazoo College, Art Dept, Kalamazoo MI (S)

Kalamazoo Institute of Arts, Kalamazoo MI (M,L)

Kalamazoo Institute of Arts, KIA School, Kalamazoo MI (S)

Kalamazoo Valley Community College, Humanities Dept, Kalamazoo MI (S)

Kalani Honua Institute for Cultural Studies, Pahoa HI (S)

Kamloops Art Gallery, Kamloops BC (M)

Irving E & Ray Kanner Heritage Museum, see Baycrest Centre for Geriatric Care, Toronto ON

Kansas City Art Institute, Kansas City MO (S)

Kansas City Art Institute, Kemper Museum of Contemporary Art & Design, Kansas City MO (M,L)

Kansas City Artists Coalition, Kansas City MO (M)

Kansas City Municipal Art Commission, Kansas City MO (A)

Kansas City Public Library, Kansas City MO (L)

Kansas Museum of History, see Kansas State Historical Society, Topeka KS

Kansas State Historical Society, Kansas Museum of History, Topeka KS (M)

Kansas State University, Paul Weigel Library of Architecture Planning & Design, Manhattan KS (L)

Kansas State University, Manhattan KS (S)

Kansas Watercolor Society, Wichita Art Museum, Wichita KS (A)

Kansas Wesleyan University, Art Dept, Salina KS (S)

Kapiolani Community College, see University of Hawaii, Honolulu HI (S)

Kappa Pi International Honorary Art Fraternity, Crestwood MO (O)

Kateri Galleries, The National Shrine of the North American Martyrs, Auriesville NY (M)

Kateri Tekakwitha Shrine, Kahnawake PQ (M)

Katonah Museum of Art, Katonah NY (M)

Kauai Community College, Dept of Art, Lihue HI (S)

Kauai Museum, Lihue HI (M)

Kauai Public Library, Lihue HI (L)

Kauffman Gallery, see Shippensburg University, Shippensburg PA

Kean College of New Jersey, Union NJ (M,L)

Kean College of New Jersey, Fine Arts Dept, Union NJ (S)

Keene State College, Thorne-Sagendorph Art Gallery, Keene NH (M)

Keil Resource Center, see Tubman African American Museum, Macon GA

Kellogg Community College, Visual & Performing Arts Dept, Battle Creek MI (S)

Kellogg Library & Reading Room, see 1890 House-Museum & Center for The Arts, Cortland NY

Kellogg Memorial Research Library, see Cortland County Historical Society, Cortland NY

Kelly-Griggs House Museum, Red Bluff CA (M)

Kelowna Museum, Kelowna BC (M,L)

Kelsey Museum of Archaeology, see University of Michigan, Ann Arbor MI

Kemerer Museum of Decorative Arts, Bethlehem PA (M)

Kemper Museum of Contemporary Art & Design, see Kansas City Art Institute, Kansas City MO

Kendall College of Art & Design, Grand Rapids MI (S)

Kendall College of Art & Design, Frank & Lyn Van Steenberg Library, Grand Rapids MI (L)

Donald M Kendall Sculpture Garden, see PepsiCo Inc, Purchase NY

Helen King Kendall Memorial Art Gallery, see San Angelo Art Club, San Angelo TX

Kendall Whaling Museum, Sharon MA (M,L)

Kenkeleba House, Inc, Kenkeleba Gallery, New York NY (A)

Kennebec Valley Art Association, Harlow Gallery, Hallowell ME (A)

Doris Wainwright Kennedy Art Center, see Birmingham Southern College, Birmingham AL

Kennedy Galleries, Art Gallery, New York NY (M)

John F Kennedy University, Graduate School for Holistic Studies, Orinda CA (S)

John F Kennedy Library & Museum, see National Archives & Records Administration, Boston MA

Kennedy-King College, see City Colleges of Chicago, Chicago IL (S)

Kennedy Museum of American Art, see Ohio University, Athens OH

The John F Kennedy Center for the Performing Arts, Washington DC (A,L)

Kenosha Public Museum, Kenosha WI (M)

Kent Art Association, Inc, Gallery, Kent CT (A)

Kent Library, see Southeast Missouri State University, Cape Girardeau MO

Kent State University, Kent OH (M)

Kent State University, School of Art, Kent OH (S)

Kent State University, Stark Campus, School of Art, Canton OH (S)

Kentucky Art & Craft Gallery, Louisville KY (M)

Kentucky Derby Museum, Louisville KY (M)

Kentucky Guild of Artists & Craftsmen Inc, Berea KY (A)

Kentucky Historical Society, Old State Capitol & Annex, Frankfort KY (M,L)

Kentucky Library, see Western Kentucky University, Bowling Green KY

Kentucky Museum, see Western Kentucky University, Bowling Green KY

Kentucky New State Capitol, Division of Historic Properties, Frankfort KY (M)

Kentucky State University, Jackson Hall Gallery, Frankfort KY (M)

Kentucky Wesleyan College, Dept Art, Owensboro KY (S)

Kenyon College, Art Dept, Gambier OH (S)

Kenyon College, Art Gallery, Gambier OH (M)

Keokuk Art Center, Keokuk IA (A)

Kern County Museum, Bakersfield CA (M,L)

Maude I Kerns Art Center Galleries, Eugene OR (M)

Maude I Kerns Art Center School, Eugene OR (S)

Illingworth Kerr Gallery, see Alberta College of Art & Design, Calgary AB

Keystone Junior College, Fine Arts Dept, Factoryville PA (S)

Key West Art & Historical Society, East Martello Museum & Gallery, Key West FL (M)

Kiah Museum, Savannah GA (M)

Kiehle Gallery, see Saint Cloud State University, Saint Cloud MN

Kilgore College, Visual Arts Dept, Kilgore TX (S)

Kimball Art Center, Park City UT (A)

Fiske Kimball Fine Arts Library, see University of Virginia, Charlottesville VA

Kimbell Art Foundation, Kimbell Art Museum, Fort Worth TX (M,L)

Kimbell Art Museum, see Kimbell Art Foundation, Fort Worth TX

Verman Kimbrough Memorial Library, see Ringling School of Art & Design, Sarasota FL

King County Arts Commission, Seattle WA (A)

Emma B King Library, see Shaker Museum & Library, Old Chatham NY

Kingman Tavern Historical Museum, see Town of Cummington Historical Commission, Cummington MA

Kingsborough Community College, Dept of Art, Brooklyn NY (S)

Kingsborough Community College, City University of New York, Art Gallery, Brooklyn NY (M)

Kings County Historical Society and Museum, Hampton NB (M)

Kipp Gallery, see Indiana University of Pennsylvania, Indiana PA

Kirkland Art Center, Clinton NY (A)

Kirkpatrick Center, see Oklahoma Center for Science & Art, Oklahoma City OK

Kirkwood Community College, Dept of Fine Arts, Cedar Rapids IA (S)

The Kitchen Center, New York NY (M)

Kitchener-Waterloo Art Gallery, Kitchener ON (M,L)

Kittredge Art Gallery, see University of Puget Sound, Tacoma WA

Klamath Art Gallery, see Klamath Falls Art Association, Klamath Falls OR

Klamath County Museum, Klamath Falls OR (M,L)

Klamath Falls Art Association, Klamath Art Gallery, Klamath Falls OR (A)

Klemm Gallery, Studio Angelico, see Siena Heights College, Adrian MI

Knights of Columbus Supreme Council, Headquarters Museum, New Haven CT (M)

M Knoedler & Co, Inc, Library, New York NY (L)

Knox College, Dept of Art, Galesburg IL (S)

Knoxville Museum of Art, Knoxville TN (M)

Koffler Center School of Visual Art, North York ON (S)

The Koffler Gallery, see Jewish Community Centre of Toronto, North York ON

Kohler Art Library, see University of Wisconsin-Madison, Madison WI

Kohler Co, Art Collection, Kohler WI (C)

John Michael Kohler Arts Center, see Sheboygan Arts Foundation, Inc, Sheboygan WI

Koochiching County Historical Society Museum, International Falls MN (M)

Elizabeth P Korn Gallery, see Drew University, Madison NJ

Koshare Indian Museum, Inc, La Junta CO (M,L)

Kraft Education Center, see The Art Institute of Chicago, Chicago IL

Krannert Art Museum, see University of Illinois, Champaign IL

Krannert Gallery, see University of Evansville, Evansville IN

Krauth Memorial Library, see Lutheran Theological Seminary, Philadelphia PA

Kresge Art Museum, see Michigan State University, East Lansing MI

Kress Foundation Dept of Art History, see University of Kansas, Lawrence KS (S)

Joe Kubert School of Cartoon & Graphic Art, Inc, Dover NJ (S)

Kurdish Museum, Brooklyn NY (M)

Kutztown University, Kutztown PA (M,L)

Kutztown University, College of Visual & Performing Arts, Kutztown PA (S)

The Lab, San Francisco CA (M)

Laband Art Gallery, see Loyola Marymount University, Los Angeles CA

John Labatt Visual Arts Centre, see University of Western Ontario, London ON (S)

La Casa del Libro Museum, San Juan PR (M)

Lac du Flambeau Band of Lake Superior Chippewa Indians, George W Brown Jr Ojibwe Museum & Cultural Center, Lac du Flambeau WI (M)

La Centrale Powerhouse Gallery, Montreal PQ (M)

Lachenmeyer Arts Center, Art Resource Library, Cushing OK (L)

Lackawanna Junior College, Fine Arts Dept, Scranton PA (S)

Lafayette College, Morris R Williams Center for the Arts, Art Gallery, Easton PA (M)

Lafayette College, Dept of Art, Easton PA (S)

Lafayette Museum Association, Lafayette Museum-Alexandre Mouton House, Lafayette LA (M)

Lafayette Natural History Museum, Planetarium & Nature Station, Lafayette LA (M)

La Galerie Montcalm la galerie d'art de la Villede Hull, Hull PQ (M)

La Grange College, Lamar Dodd Art Center Museum, La Grange GA (S)

La Grange College, Lamar Dodd Art Center Museum, La Grange GA (M)

Laguna Art Museum of the Orange County Museum of Art, Laguna Beach CA (M)

Lahaina Arts Society, Art Organization, Lahaina HI (A)

Lake City Community College, Art Dept, Lake City FL (S)

Lake County Civic Center Association, Inc, Heritage Museum & Gallery, Leadville CO (A)

Lake Erie College, Fine Arts Dept, Painesville OH (S)

Lake Forest College, Dept of Art, Lake Forest IL (S)

Lake Forest Library, Fine Arts Dept, Lake Forest IL (L)

Lake George Arts Project, Courthouse Gallery, Lake George NY (M)

Lakehead University, Dept of Visual Arts, Thunder Bay ON (S)

Lakeland Community College, Visual Arts Dept, Mentor OH (S)

Lake Michigan College, Dept of Art, Benton Harbor MI (S)

Lakeside Studio, Lakeside MI (M)

Lake Tahoe Community College, Art Dept, South Lake Tahoe CA (S)

Lakeview Museum of Arts & Sciences, Peoria IL (M)

Lamama La Galleria, New York NY (M)

Lamar University, Art Dept, Beaumont TX (S)

Lambuth University, Dept of Human Ecology & Visual Arts, Jackson TN (S)

Lamont Gallery, see Dacotah Prairie Museum, Aberdeen SD

Herbert H Lamson Library, see Plymouth State College, Plymouth NH

La Napoule Art Foundation, Portsmouth NH (A)

Lancaster County Art Association, Inc, Lancaster PA (A)

Lancaster Museum of Art, Lancaster PA (M)

Clara Lander Library, see Winnipeg Art Gallery, Winnipeg MB

Lander University, Dept of Art, Greenwood SC (S)

Landis Valley Museum, Lancaster PA (M,L)

Landmark Society of Western New York, Inc, Rochester NY (M,L)

Lane Community College, Art & Applied Design Dept, Eugene OR (S)

Lane Community College, Art Dept Gallery, Eugene OR (M)

Laney College, Art Dept, Oakland CA (S)

Laney College Library, Art Section, Oakland CA (L)

Robert Langen Gallery, see Wilfrid Laurier University, Waterloo ON

Langston University, Melvin B Tolson Black Heritage Center, Langston OK (M)

Lannan Foundation, Los Angeles CA (O)

Lansing Art Gallery, Lansing MI (M)

Lansing Community College, Art Program, Lansing MI (S)

Laramie County Community College, Division of Arts & Humanities, Cheyenne WY (S)

La Raza-Galeria Posada, Sacramento CA (M)

La Roche College, Division of Graphics, Design & Communication, Pittsburgh PA (S)

B F Larsen Gallery, see Brigham Young University, Provo UT

Paul Whitney Larson Gallery, see University of Minnesota, Saint Paul MN

La Salle University, Art Museum, Philadelphia PA (M)

La Salle University, Dept of Art, Philadelphia PA (S)

Lasell College, Art & Interior Design Program, Auburndale MA (S)

La Sierra University, Art Dept, Riverside CA (S)

La Societe des Decorateurs-Ensembliers du Quebec, Interior Designers Society of Quebec, Montreal PQ (A)

Las Vegas Art Museum, Las Vegas NV (M)

Las Vegas-Clark County Library District, Las Vegas NV (L,M)

Latitude 53 Society of Artists, Edmonton AB (A)

Laughner Brothers, Inc, Indianapolis IN (C)

Lauinger Library-Special Collections Division, see Georgetown University, Washington DC

Laumeier Sculpture Park & Museum, Saint Louis MO (M)

Laurentian University, Sudbury ON (M,L)

Laurier House, see Canadian Heritage - Parks Canada, Ottawa ON

Lawrence Technological University, College of Architecture, Southfield MI (S)

Lawrence University, Wriston Art Center Galleries, Appleton WI (M)

Lawrence University, Dept of Art, Appleton WI (S)

Lawyers Committee for the Arts, Volunteer Lawyers for the Arts, Washington DC (A)

Layton Honor Gallery, see Cardinal Stritch College, Milwaukee WI

Laziza Videodance Lumia Project, see Promote Art Works Inc (PAWI), Brooklyn NY

League Gallery, see League of New Hampshire Craftsmen, Concord NH

League of New Hampshire Craftsmen, League Gallery, Concord NH (A,L)

Leanin' Tree Museum of Western Art, Boulder CO (M)

Leatherstocking Brush & Palette Club Inc, Cooperstown NY (A)

LeBrun Library, see Montclair Art Museum, Montclair NJ

Bertha V B Lederer Gallery, see State University of New York at Geneseo, Geneseo NY

Lee Chapel & Museum, see Washington & Lee University, Lexington VA

Lee College, Dept of Music & Fine Arts, Cleveland TN (S)

Lee County Library, Tupelo MS (L)

Leeds Gallery, see Earlham College, Richmond IN

Harold B Lee Library, see Brigham Young University, Provo UT

Leelanau Historical Museum, Leland MI (M)

Rudolph E Lee Gallery, see Clemson University, Clemson SC

Leeward Community College, Arts & Humanities Division, Pearl City HI (S)

Legacy Ltd, Seattle WA (M)

Lehigh County Historical Society, Allentown PA (M,L)

Lehigh University, Dept of Art & Architecture, Bethlehem PA (S)

Lehigh University Art Galleries, Bethlehem PA (M)

Lehman College Art Gallery, Bronx NY (M)

Herbert H Lehman College, Art Dept, Bronx NY (S)

Robert Lehman Collection Library, see The Metropolitan Museum of Art, New York NY

Lemoyne Art Foundation, Inc, Tallahassee FL (M)

Le Moyne College, Fine Arts Dept, Syracuse NY (S)

LeMoyne College, Wilson Art Gallery, Syracuse NY (M)

Le Musee Marc-Aurele Fortin, Montreal PQ (M)

Le Musee Regional de Rimouski, Centre National d'Exposition, Rimouski PQ (M,L)

Lenoir Community College, Dept of Visual Art, Kinston NC (S)

Lenoir Rhyne College, Dept of Art, Hickory NC (S)

J Paul Leonard Library, see San Francisco State University, San Francisco CA

Anna Leonowens Gallery, see Nova Scotia College of Art and Design, Halifax NS

Leroy Historical Society, LeRoy NY (A)

Les Editions Intervention, Inter-Le Lieu, Documentation Center, Quebec PQ (L)

Dean Lesher Regional Center for the Arts, Bedford Gallery, Walnut Creek CA (M)

Lesley College, Arts Institute, Cambridge MA (S)

LeSueur County Historical Museum, Chapter One, Elysian MN (M,L)

LeSueur Museum, LeSueur MN (M)

Lethbridge Community College, Buchanan Library, Lethbridge AB (L)

Lethbridge Public Library, Art Gallery, Lethbridge AB (L)

Lewis & Clark College, Dept of Art, Portland OR (S)

Lewis & Clark Community College, Art Dept, Godfrey IL (S)

Lewis-Clark State College, Art Dept, Lewiston ID (S)

Lewis County Historical Museum, Chehalis WA (M,L)

G Pillow Lewis Memorial Library, see Memphis College of Art, Memphis TN

James E Lewis Museum of Art, see Morgan State University, Baltimore MD

Lewistown Art Center, Lewistown MT (A)

Lexington Art League, Inc, Lexington KY (A)

Leyburn Library, see Washington & Lee University, Lexington VA

Liberty Hall Historic Site, Liberty Hall Museum, Frankfort KY (M,L)

Liberty Hall Museum, see Liberty Hall Historic Site, Frankfort KY

Liberty Life Insurance Company, Greenville SC (C)

Liberty Memorial Museum & Archives, Kansas City MO (M)

Liberty Village Arts Center & Gallery, Chester MT (M)

Library Association of La Jolla, Athenaeum Music & Arts Library, La Jolla CA (L)

Library Company of Philadelphia, Philadelphia PA (L)

Library of Congress, Prints & Photographs Division, Washington DC (L)

Licking County Art Association, Art Gallery, Newark OH (M)

Light Factory, Charlotte NC (M)

Lighthouse Gallery & School of Art, Tequesta FL (M,L)

Lightner Museum, Saint Augustine FL (M,L)

Light Work, Syracuse NY (A)

Lilly Art Library, see Duke University Museum of Art, Durham NC

Limestone College, Art Dept, Gaffney SC (S)

Lincoln Arts Council, Lincoln NE (A)

Lincoln Center for the Performing Arts, Cork Gallery, New York NY (M)

Lincoln College, Art Dept, Lincoln IL (S)

Lincoln County Historical Association, Inc, Pownalborough Court House, Wiscasset ME (A, L,M)

Lincoln Memorial Shrine, Redlands CA (L)

Lincoln Memorial University, Division of Humanities, Harrogate TN (S)

Lincoln Museum, see Lincoln National Life Insurance Co, Fort Wayne IN

Lincoln National Life Insurance Co, Lincoln Museum, Fort Wayne IN (C)

Lincoln University, Dept Fine Arts, Jefferson City MO (S)

Lindenwood College, Harry D Hendren Gallery, Saint Charles MO (M)

Lindenwood College, Art Dept, Saint Charles MO (S)

Luke Lindoe Library, see Alberta College of Art & Design, Calgary AB

The Lindsay Gallery, Lindsay ON (M)

Linfield College, Art Dept, McMinnville OR (S)

Linn Benton Community College, Fine & Applied Art Dept, Albany OR (S)

Litchfield Historical Society, Litchfield CT (A,L)

Littman Gallery, see Portland State University, Portland OR

Living Arts & Science Center, Inc, Lexington KY (M)

Livingston County Historical Society, Cobblestone Museum, Geneseo NY (M)

Lizzadro Museum of Lapidary Art, Elmhurst IL (M)

Lock Haven University, Dept of Fine Arts, Lock Haven PA (S)

Lockwood-Mathews Mansion Museum, Norwalk CT (M)

Frances Loeb Library, see Harvard University, Cambridge MA

The Frances Lehman Loeb Art Center, see Vassar College, Poughkeepsie NY

Jack London State Historic Park, House of Happy Walls, Glen Ellen CA (M)

London Regional Art & Historical Museums, London ON (M)

Long Beach Art League, Island Park NY (A)

Long Beach City College, Dept of Art, Long Beach CA (S)

Long Beach Jewish Community Center, Center Gallery, Long Beach CA (M)

Long Beach Museum of Art, Long Beach CA (M,L)

Long Beach Public Library, Long Beach CA (L)

Long Beach Public Library, Long Beach NY (L)

Long Branch Historical Museum, Long Branch NJ (M)

Earl K Long Library, see University of New Orleans, New Orleans LA

Longfellow-Evangeline State Commemorative Area, Saint Martinville LA (M)

Longfellow National Historic Site, Cambridge MA (M)

Longfellow's Wayside Inn Museum, South Sudbury MA (M)

Long Island Graphic Eye Gallery, Port Washington NY (M)

Long Island University, Brooklyn Campus, Art Dept, Brooklyn NY (S)

Longue Vue House & Gardens, New Orleans LA (M)
Longview Art Museum, Longview TX (M,L)
Longwood Arts Gallery, see Bronx Council on the Arts, Bronx NY
Longwood College, Dept of Art, Farmville VA (S)
Lorain County Community College, Art Dept, Elyria OH (S)
Loras College, Dept of Art, Dubuque IA (S)
Lore Degenstein Gallery, see Susquehanna University, Selinsgrove PA
LA Art Association, Los Angeles CA (A)
Los Angeles Center For Photographic Studies, Hollywood CA (A)
Los Angeles City College, Dept of Art, Los Angeles CA (S)
Los Angeles Contemporary Exhibitions, Hollywood CA (M)
Los Angeles County Museum of Art, Los Angeles CA (M,L)
Los Angeles County Museum of Natural History, William S Hart Museum, Newhall CA (M)
Los Angeles Harbor College, Art Dept, Wilmington CA (S)
Los Angeles Municipal Art Gallery, Los Angeles CA (M)
Los Angeles Public Library, Arts & Recreation Dept, Los Angeles CA (L)
Los Angeles Valley College, Art Gallery, Van Nuys CA (M)
Los Angeles Valley College, Art Dept, Van Nuys CA (S)
Caleb Lothrop House, see Cohasset Historical Society, Cohasset MA
Louisa May Alcott Memorial Association, Orchard House, Concord MA (A)
Louisburg College, Art Gallery, Louisburg NC (M)
Louisiana Arts & Science Center, Baton Rouge LA (M,L)
Louisiana College, Dept of Art, Pineville LA (S)
Louisiana Department of Culture, Recreation & Tourism, Louisiana State Museum, New Orleans LA (M,L)
Louisiana Historical Association, Confederate Museum, New Orleans LA (A)
Louisiana Historical Center Library, see Louisiana Department of Culture, Recreation & Tourism, New Orleans LA
Louisiana State Exhibit Museum, Shreveport LA (M)
Louisiana State Museum, see Louisiana Department of Culture, Recreation & Tourism, New Orleans LA
Louisiana State University, Baton Rouge LA (M,L)
Louisiana State University, School of Art, Baton Rouge LA (S)
Louisiana State University at Alexandria, University Gallery, Alexandria LA (M)
Louisiana State University at Alexandria, Dept of Fine Arts & Design, Alexandria LA (S)
Louisiana Tech, School of Art, Ruston LA (S)
Louisville Visual Art Association, Louisville KY (A)
Lourdes College, Art Dept, Sylvania OH (S)
Lourdes College, Duns Scotus Library, Sylvania OH (L)
Lovejoy Library, see Southern Illinois University, Edwardsville IL
Lovelace Medical Foundation, Art Collection, Albuquerque NM (C)
Loveland Museum Gallery, Loveland CO (M)
Lovely Lane Museum, see United Methodist Historical Society, Baltimore MD
Lovewell Studios, Superior NB (S)
Lowe Art Museum, see University of Miami, Coral Gables FL
Joe & Emily Lowe Art Gallery, see Hudson Guild, New York NY
Joe & Emily Lowe Art Gallery, see Syracuse University, Syracuse NY
Lower Columbia College, Art Dept, Longview WA (S)
Lower East Side Printshop, New York NY (S)
Lower East Side Printshop, Inc, New York NY (M)
Loyola Marymount University, Laband Art Gallery, Los Angeles CA (M)
Loyola Marymount University, Art & Art History Dept, Los Angeles CA (S)

Loyola University of Chicago, Martin D'Arcy Gallery of Art, Chicago IL (M)
Loyola University of Chicago, Fine Arts Dept, Chicago IL (S)
Loyola University of New Orleans, Dept of Visual Arts, New Orleans LA (S)
Lubbock Art Association, Inc, Lubbock TX (A)
Lubbock Christian University, Dept of Communication & Fine Art, Lubbock TX (S)
L'Universite Laval, Ecole des Arts Visuels, Quebec PQ (M,L)
Jeannette Lusk Library Collection, see South Dakota State University, Brookings SD
Lutheran Brethren Schools, Art Dept, Fergus Falls MN (S)
Lutheran Brotherhood Gallery, Gallery of Religious Art, Minneapolis MN (M)
Lutheran Theological Seminary, Krauth Memorial Library, Philadelphia PA (L)
Luther College, Art Dept, Decorah IA (S)
Luther College, Fine Arts Collection, Decorah IA (M)
Luzerne County Community College, Commercial Art Dept, Nanticoke PA (S)
Lyceum Club and Women's Art Association of Canada, Toronto ON (A,L)
Lycoming College, Art Dept, Williamsport PA (S)
Lycoming College Gallery, Williamsport PA (M)
Lyme Academy of Fine Arts, Old Lyme CT (S)
Lyme Academy of Fine Arts, Old Lyme CT (L)
Lyme Art Association, Inc, Old Lyme CT (A)
Lyme Historical Society, Florence Griswold Museum, Old Lyme CT (M,L)
Lynchburg College, Art Dept, Lynchburg VA (S)
Lynchburg Fine Arts Center Inc, Lynchburg VA (A)
Tom Lynch Resource Center, see Dillman's Bay Properties, Lac Du Flambeau WI
Lyndhurst, Tarrytown NY (M)
Lynn University, Art & Design Dept, Boca Raton FL (S)
Lynnwood Arts Centre, Simcoe ON (A)
Harrye Lyons Design Library, see North Carolina State University, Raleigh NC
Mabee-Gerrer Museum of Art, see Saint Gregory's Abbey & College, Shawnee OK
Macalester College, Dept of Art, Saint Paul MN (S)
Macalester College, Galleries, Saint Paul MN (M,L)
McAllen International Museum, McAllen TX (M,L)
MacArthur Memorial, Norfolk VA (M,L)
McAuley Gallery, see Mount Mercy College, Cedar Rapids IA
McBride Art Reference Library, see Grand Rapids Art Museum, Grand Rapids MI
McCain Library & Archives, see University of Southern Mississippi, Hattiesburg MS
Frank H McClung Museum, see University of Tennessee, Knoxville TN
Alameda McCollough Library, see Tippecanoe County Historical Museum, Lafayette IN
McCord Museum of Canadian History, Montreal PQ (M)
Harold McCracken Research Library, see Buffalo Bill Memorial Association, Cody WY
Virginia M McCune Community Arts Center, see Crooked Tree Arts Council, Petoskey MI
McDonald's Corporation, Art Collection, Oakbrook IL (C)
MacDonald Stewart Art Centre, Guelph ON (M)
McDowell House & Apothecary Shop, see Ephraim McDowell-Cambus-Kenneth Foundation, Danville KY
McGill University, Montreal PQ (S)
McGill University, Montreal PQ (L)
McGroarty Cultural Art Center, Tujunga CA (S)
McIntire Dept of Art, see University of Virginia, Charlottesville VA (S)
McIntosh Gallery, see University of Western Ontario, London ON
MacKenzie Art Gallery, see University of Regina, Regina SK
MacKenzie Art Gallery Resource Centre, see University of Regina, Regina SK
McKinney Library, see Albany Institute of History & Art, Albany NY

McKissick Museum, see University of South Carolina, Columbia SC
Carrie McLain Museum, Nome AK (M)
The Robert McLaughlin Gallery, Oshawa ON (M,L)
McLean Arts Center, Art Dept, McLean VA (S)
McLean County Art Association, Arts Center, Bloomington IL (A)
McLean County Historical Society, Bloomington IL (M)
McLennan Community College, Fine Arts Dept, Waco TX (S)
McMaster University, Museum of Art, Hamilton ON (M,L)
McMaster University, Dept of Art & Art History, Hamilton ON (S)
McMichael Canadian Art Collection, Kleinburg ON (M,L)
MacMurray College, Art Dept, Jacksonville IL (S)
McMurry University, Ryan Fine Arts Center, Abilene TX (M)
McMurry University, Art Dept, Abilene TX (S)
Marion Koogler McNay Art Museum, San Antonio TX (M,L)
McNeese State University, Dept of Visual Arts, Lake Charles LA (S)
Charles H MacNider Museum, Mason City IA (M,L)
Macomb Community College, Art Dept, Warren MI (S)
MacPheadris-Warner House, see Warner House Association, Portsmouth NH
McPherson College, Art Dept, McPherson KS (S)
McPherson College Gallery, McPherson KS (M)
McPherson Museum, McPherson KS (M)
Madison Area Technical College, Art Dept, Madison WI (S)
Madison Art Center, Madison WI (M)
Madison County Historical Society, Cottage Lawn, Oneida NY (M,L)
Madison & Main Gallery, Greeley CO (M)
Madison-Morgan Cultural Center, see Morgan County Foundation, Inc, Madison GA
Madonna University, Art Dept, Livonia MI (S)
Judah L Magnes Museum, Berkeley CA (M,L)
Maharishi University of Management, Department of Fine Arts, Fairfield IA (A)
Mahoney Library, see College of Saint Elizabeth, Morristown NJ
Maier Museum of Art, see Randolph-Macon Woman's College, Lynchburg VA
Maine Art Gallery, Old Academy, see Lincoln County Historical Association, Inc, Wiscasset ME
Maine Coast Artists, Art Gallery, Rockport ME (A)
Maine College of Art, Portland ME (S)
Maine College of Art, Library, Portland ME (L,M)
Maine Historical Society, Portland ME (A,M,L)
Maine History Gallery, see Maine Historical Society, Portland ME
Maine Maritime Museum, Bath ME (M,L)
Maine Photographic Workshops, Rockport ME (A,L)
Maine Photographic Workshops, Rockport ME (S)
Main Gallery & New Talent Gallery, see Irving Arts Center, Irving TX
Main Line Art Center, Haverford PA (A)
Main Line Art Center, Haverford PA (S)
Maison Saint-Gabriel Museum, Montreal PQ (M)
Maitland Art Center, Maitland FL (M,L)
Malaspina College, Nanaimo Art Gallery & Exhibition Centre, Nanaimo BC (M)
Malcolm X College, see City Colleges of Chicago, Chicago IL (S)
Malden Public Library, Art Dept & Gallery, Malden MA (L)
Malone College, Dept of Art, Canton OH (S)
Maltwood Art Museum and Gallery, see University of Victoria, Victoria BC
Mamie McFaddin Ward Heritage Historic Foundation Inc, Beaumont TX (M,L)
Manatee Community College, Dept of Art & Humanities, Bradenton FL (S)
Manchester City Library, Manchester NH (L)
Manchester College, Art Dept, North Manchester IN (S)

Manchester Community College, Fine Arts Dept, Manchester CT (S)

Manchester Craftsmen's Guild, Pittsburgh PA (M)

Manchester Historic Association, Manchester NH (A,L)

Manchester Institute of Arts & Sciences Gallery, Manchester NH (M)

Manhattan College, School of Arts, Bronx NY (S)

Manhattan Graphics Center, New York NY (S)

Manhattan Psychiatric Center, New York NY (M)

Manhattanville College, Brownson Art Gallery, Purchase NY (M,L)

Manhattanville College, Art Dept, Purchase NY (S)

Joseph Manigault House, see Charleston Museum, Charleston SC

Manitoba Association of Architects, Winnipeg MB (A)

Manitoba Historical Society, Dalnavert Museum, Winnipeg MB (M)

Manitoba Society of Artists, Winnipeg MB (A)

Mankato Area Arts Council, Carnegie Art Center, Mankato MN (M)

Mankato State University, Art Dept, Mankato MN (S)

Mankato State University, Conkling Gallery Art Dept, Mankato MN (M)

Arthur Manley Society, Tampa FL (O)

Mansfield Fine Arts Guild, Mansfield Art Center, Mansfield OH (A,L)

Mansfield University, Art Dept, Mansfield PA (S)

Maple Woods Community College, Dept of Art & Art History, Kansas City MO (S)

The Marbella Gallery Inc, New York NY (M)

Marblehead Arts Association, Inc, Marblehead MA (A)

Marblehead Historical Society, Marblehead MA (A,L)

Marcella Sembrich Memorial Association Inc, Opera Museum, Bolton Landing NY (A)

Gladys Marcus Library, see Fashion Institute of Technology, New York NY

Marian College, Art Dept, Fond Du Lac WI (S)

Marian College, Art Dept, Indianapolis IN (S)

Marian College, Allison Mansion, Indianapolis IN (M)

John Mariani Art Gallery, see University of Northern Colorado, Greeley CO

Marian Library, see Daemen College, Amherst NY

Maricopa County Historical Society, Desert Caballeros Western Museum, Wickenburg AZ (M,L)

Marietta-Cobb Museum of Art, Marietta GA (M)

Marietta College, Grover M Hermann Fine Arts Center, Marietta OH (M)

Marietta College, Art Dept, Marietta OH (S)

Marin County Watercolor Society, Greenbrae CA (A)

Marine Corps Museum, Art Collection, Washington DC (M)

Marine & Rail Heritage Museum, see Owen Sound Historical Society, Owen Sound ON

The Mariners' Museum, Newport News VA (M,L)

Marin Society of Artists Inc, Ross CA (A)

Marion Art Center, Marion MA (A)

Maritime Museum of Monterey, see Monterey History & Art Association, Monterey CA

Maritime Museum of the Atlantic, see Nova Scotia Museum, Halifax NS

Maritz, Inc, Library, Fenton MO (L)

The Market Gallery of the City of Toronto Archives, Toronto ON (M)

Mark Twain Bancshares, Saint Louis MO (C)

Mark Twain Birthplace State Historic Site Birthplace Museum, Stoutsville MO (M)

Marquand Library of Art & Archaeology, see Princeton University, Princeton NJ

Marquette University, Haggerty Museum of Art, Milwaukee WI (M)

Marriott Library, see University of Utah, Salt Lake City UT

John Marshall House, see Association for the Preservation of Virginia Antiquities, Richmond VA

Marshall University, Dept of Art, Huntington WV (S)

Marsh Art Gallery, see University of Richmond, Richmond VA

Mars Hill College, Art Dept, Mars Hill NC (S)

Maria Martinez Museum, see Pueblo of San Ildefonso, Santa Fe NM

Frank Martin Gallery, see Muhlenberg College Center for the Arts, Allentown PA

Martin Memorial Library, York PA (L)

Martin Museum of Art, see Baylor University, Waco TX

Mary Baldwin College, Dept of Art, Staunton VA (S)

Marygrove College, Visual & Performing Arts Div, Detroit MI (S)

Maryhill Museum of Art, Goldendale WA (M)

Maryland Art Place, Baltimore MD (M)

Maryland College of Art & Design, Silver Spring MD (S)

Maryland College of Art & Design Library, Silver Spring MD (L)

Maryland Hall for the Creative Arts, Cardinal Gallery, Annapolis MD (M)

Maryland Historical Society, Museum of Maryland History, Baltimore MD (M,L)

Maryland Institute, College of Art Exhibitions, Baltimore MD (M,L)

Maryland Institute, College of Art, Baltimore MD (S)

Maryland-National Capital Park & Planning Commission, Montpelier Cultural Arts Center, Laurel MD (M)

Marylhurst College, Art Dept, Marylhurst OR (S)

Marylhurst College, The Art Gym, Marylhurst OR (M)

Marymount College, Art Dept, Tarrytown NY (S)

Marymount Manhattan College, Fine & Performing Arts Dept, New York NY (S)

Marymount Manhattan College Gallery, New York NY (M)

Marymount University of Virginia, School of Arts & Sciences Division, Arlington VA (S)

Maryville College, Fine Arts Center Gallery, Maryville TN (M)

Maryville College, Dept of Fine Arts, Maryville TN (S)

Maryville University of Saint Louis, Art Division, Saint Louis MO (S)

Maryville University Saint Louis, Morton J May Foundation Gallery, Saint Louis MO (M)

Mary Washington College, Art Dept, Fredericksburg VA (S)

Mary Washington College, Fredericksburg VA (M)

Marywood College, Art Dept, Scranton PA (S)

Mason City Public Library, Mason City IA (L)

Mason County Museum, Maysville KY (M)

Mason Gross School of the Arts, see Rutgers, the State University of New Jersey, New Brunswick NJ (S)

Massachusetts College of Art, Boston MA (S)

Massachusetts College of Art, Boston MA (L)

Massachusetts Historical Society, Boston MA (A,L)

Massachusetts Institute of Technology, Cambridge MA (S)

Massachusetts Institute of Technology, Cambridge MA (M,L)

Massillon Museum, Massillon OH (M)

Masur Museum of Art, see Twin City Art Foundation, Monroe LA

William Hammond Mathers Museum, see Indiana University, Bloomington IN

Mattatuck Historical Society, Mattatuck Museum, Waterbury CT (M,L)

Mattress Factory, Pittsburgh PA (M)

Maui Community College, Art Program, Kahului HI (S)

Maui Historical Society, Bailey House, Wailuku HI (M)

Max Hutchinson's Sculpture Fields, Kenoza Lake NY (M)

Frederic R Mayer Art Center & Lamont Gallery, see Phillips Exeter Academy, Exeter NH

Mildred R & Frederick M Mayer Library, see Dallas Museum of Art, Dallas TX

Mayfield Regional Library, Mayfield Village OH (L)

Morton J May Foundation Gallery, see Maryville University Saint Louis, Saint Louis MO

Mayville State University Gallery, Mayville ND (M)

Mead Art Museum, see Amherst College, Amherst MA

Meadow Brook Art Gallery, see Oakland University, Rochester MI

Meadow Farm Museum, see County of Henrico, Glen Allen VA

Meadows Museum, see Southern Methodist University, Dallas TX

Meadows Museum of Art, see Centenary College of Louisiana, Shreveport LA

Meadville Council on the Arts, Meadville PA (A)

Mechanics' Institute Library, San Francisco CA (L)

Medicine Hat Museum & Art Gallery, Medicine Hat AB (M)

Medicine Hat Public Library, Medicine Hat AB (L)

Mellon Bank Corporation, Pittsburgh PA (C)

Melvin Art Gallery, see Florida Southern College, Lakeland FL

Memorial Library, see Berry College, Mount Berry GA

Memorial Union Art Gallery, see Oregon State University, Corvallis OR

Memorial Union Gallery, see Arizona State University, Tempe AZ

Memorial University of Newfoundland, School of Fine Arts, Visual Arts Dept, Corner Brook NF (S)

Memorial University of Newfoundland, Sir Wilfred Grenfell College Art Gallery, Corner Brook NF (M)

Memorial University of Newfoundland, Art Gallery of Newfoundland & Labrador, Saint John's NF (M)

Memphis Brooks Museum of Art, Memphis TN (M,L)

Memphis College of Art, Memphis TN (L)

Memphis College of Art, Memphis TN (S)

Memphis-Shelby County Public Library & Information Center, Dept of Art, Music & Films, Memphis TN (L)

Mendel Art Gallery & Civic Conservatory, Saskatoon SK (M,L)

Mendocino Art Center, Gallery, Mendocino CA (A,L)

Mendocino Art Center, Mendocino CA (S)

Mendocino County Arts Council, Westport CA (A)

Menil Collection, Houston TX (M)

Mennonite Library & Archives, see Bethel College, North Newton KS

Merced College, Arts Division, Merced CA (S)

Mercer County Community College, The Gallery, Trenton NJ (M,L)

Mercer County Community College, Arts & Communication/Engineering Technology, Trenton NJ (S)

Mercer Museum, see Bucks County Historical Society, Doylestown PA

Mercer University, Art Dept, Macon GA (S)

Mercyhurst College, Dept of Art, Erie PA (S)

Meredith College, Art Dept, Raleigh NC (S)

Meredith Gallery, Baltimore MD (M)

Meriam Library, see California State University, Chico, Chico CA

Meridian International Center, Cafritz Galleries, Washington DC (M)

Meridian Museum of Art, Meridian MS (M)

Merrick Art Gallery, New Brighton PA (M)

Merritt College, Art Dept, Oakland CA (S)

Merwin & Wakeley Galleries, see Illinois Wesleyan University, Bloomington IL

Mesa Arts Center, see Galeria Mesa, Mesa AZ

Mesa College, Art Dept, Grand Junction CO (S)

Mesa Community College, Dept of Art & Art History, Mesa AZ (S)

Laura & Paul Mesaros Galleries, see West Virginia University, Morgantown WV

Metal Arts Guild, Toronto ON (O)

Methodist College, Art Dept, Fayetteville NC (S)

Metro-Dade, Miami Art Museum of Dade County, Miami FL (M)

Metropolitan Center for Public Arts, see Regional Arts & Culture Council, Portland OR

Metropolitan Dade County Cultural Affairs Council, see South Florida Cultural Consortium, Miami FL

The Metropolitan Museum of Art, New York NY (M,L)

Metropolitan State College of Denver, Art Dept, Denver CO (S)

Moody County Historical Society, Flandreau SD (A)

Sarah Moody Gallery of Art, see University of Alabama, Tuscaloosa AL

Moody Texas Ranger Memorial Library, see Texas Ranger Hall of Fame & Museum, Waco TX

Moon Gallery, see Berry College, Mount Berry GA

Moore College of Art & Design, Goldie Paley Gallery, Philadelphia PA (M,L)

Moore College of Art & Design, Philadelphia PA (S)

Moorhead State University, Dept of Art, Moorhead MN (S)

Moose Jaw Art Museum & National Exhibition Centre, Art & History Museum, Moose Jaw SK (M)

Moravian College, Dept of Art, Bethlehem PA (S)

Moravian College, Payne Gallery, Bethlehem PA (M)

Moravian Historical Society, Whitefield House Museum, Nazareth PA (M)

Moreau Galleries, see Saint Mary's College, Notre Dame IN

Morehead State University, Art Dept, Morehead KY (S)

Morehead State University, Morehead KY (M)

Morgan County Foundation, Inc, Madison-Morgan Cultural Center, Madison GA (A)

Pierpont Morgan Library, New York NY (L)

Morgan State University, Dept of Art, Baltimore MD (S)

Morgan State University, Baltimore MD (M,L)

Morikami Museum & Japanese Gardens, see Palm Beach County Parks & Recreation Department, Delray Beach FL

Morlan Gallery, see Transylvania University, Lexington KY

Morningside College, Art Dept, Sioux City IA (S)

Morris-Butler House, see Historic Landmarks Foundation of Indiana, Indianapolis IN

Morris Communications Corporation, Corporate Collection, Augusta GA (C)

Morris-Jumel Mansion, Inc, New York NY (M)

Morris Library, see Southern Illinois University, Carbondale IL

Morris Library, see University of Delaware, Newark DE

Morris Museum, Morristown NJ (M,L)

Morris Museum of Art, Augusta GA (M)

Charles Morse Museum of American Art, Winter Park FL (M)

Mortensen Library, see University of Hartford, West Hartford CT

Moss-Thorns Gallery of Arts, see Fort Hays State University, Hays KS

Motlow State Community College, Art Dept, Tullahoma TN (S)

Moudy Exhibition Hall, see Texas Christian University, Fort Worth TX

Mount Allison University, Owens Art Gallery, Sackville NB (M)

Mount Allison University, Fine Arts Dept, Sackville NB (S)

Mount Angel Abbey Library, Saint Benedict OR (L)

Mount Clare Mansion, see National Society of Colonial Dames of America in the State of Maryland, Baltimore MD

Mount Holyoke College, Art Museum, South Hadley MA (M,L)

Mount Holyoke College, Art Dept, South Hadley MA (S)

Mount Hood Community College, Visual Arts Center, Gresham OR (S)

Mount Ida College, Boston MA (S)

Mount Marty College, Art Dept, Yankton SD (S)

Mount Mary College, Tower Gallery, Milwaukee WI (M)

Mount Mary College, Art Dept, Milwaukee WI (S)

Mount Mercy College, McAuley Gallery, Cedar Rapids IA (M,L)

Mount Mercy College, Art Dept, Cedar Rapids IA (S)

Mount Olive College, Dept of Art, Mount Olive NC (S)

Mount Pleasant, see Philadelphia Museum of Art, Philadelphia PA

Mount Royal College, Dept of Interior Design, Calgary AB (S)

Mount Royal School of Art, see Maryland Institute, Baltimore MD (S)

Mount Saint Clare College, Art Dept, Clinton IA (S)

Mount Saint Mary's College, Visual & Performing Arts Dept, Emmitsburg MD (S)

Mount Saint Mary's College, Art Dept, Los Angeles CA (S)

Mount Saint Mary's College, Jose Drudis-Biada Art Gallery, Los Angeles CA (M)

Mount Saint Vincent University, Art Gallery, Halifax NS (M)

Mount San Antonio College, Art Dept, Walnut CA (S)

Mount San Jacinto College, Art Dept, San Jacinto CA (S)

Mount Union College, Dept of Art, Alliance OH (S)

Mount Vernon College, School of Art & Design, Washington DC (S)

Mount Vernon Ladies' Association of the Union, Mount Vernon VA (M,L)

Mount Vernon Nazarene College, Art Dept, Mount Vernon OH (S)

Mount Vernon Public Library, Fine Art Dept, Mount Vernon NY (L)

Mount Wachusett Community College, Art Galleries, Gardner MA (M,L)

Movimiento Artistico del Rio Salado, Inc (MARS) Artspace, Phoenix AZ (A)

Muchnic Foundation & Atchison Art Association, Muchnic Gallery, Atchison KS (M)

Muckenthaler Cultural Center, Fullerton CA (A)

James I Mueller Ceramic Information Center, see The American Ceramic Society, Westerville OH

Muhlenberg College, Dept of Art, Allentown PA (S)

Muhlenberg College Center for the Arts, Frank Martin Gallery, Allentown PA (M)

Multicultural Heritage Centre, Stony Plain AB (M)

Multnomah County Library, Henry Failing Art & Music Dept, Portland OR (L)

Mulvane Art Museum, see Washburn University, Topeka KS

Municipal Art Society of New York, New York NY (A,L)

Munson-Williams-Proctor Institute, Museum of Art, Utica NY (M,L)

Munson-Williams-Proctor Institute, School of Art, Utica NY (S)

Muroff-Kotler Visual Arts Gallery, see Ulster County Community College, Stone Ridge NY

Murphy Library of Art & Architecture, see University of Kansas, Lawrence KS

Murray State University, Eagle Gallery, Murray KY (M)

Murray State University, Dept of Art, Murray KY (S)

Joseph & Margaret Muscarelle Museum of Art, see College of William & Mary, Williamsburg VA

Muscatine Art Center, Muscatine IA (M,L)

Muse Art Gallery, Philadelphia PA (M)

Musee Canadien de la Nature, see Canadian Museum of Nature, Ottawa ON

Musee d'art Contemporain de Montreal, Montreal PQ (M,L)

Musee d'Art de Joliette, Joliette PQ (M,L)

Musee d'Art de Saint-Laurent, Saint-Laurent PQ (M)

Musee de la Basilique Notre-Dame, Montreal PQ (M)

Musee des Augustines de l'Hotel Dieu de Quebec, Quebec PQ (M,L)

Musee du Quebec, Quebec PQ (M,L)

Musee du Seminaire de Quebec, Quebec PQ (M)

Musee Regional de la Cote-Nord, Sept-Iles PQ (M)

Musee Regional de Vaudreuil-Soulanges, Vaudreuil PQ (M,L)

Museo de Arte de Ponce, Ponce Art Museum, Ponce PR (M,L)

Museo de Arte Religioso Porta Coeli, see Institute of Puerto Rican Culture, San Juan PR

Museo de la Americas, Old San Juan PR (M)

Museo De Las Americas, Denver CO (M)

Museo del Grabado Latinoamericano, see Institute of Puerto Rican Culture, San Juan PR

Museo Italo Americano, San Francisco CA (M,L)

Museo y Parque Historico de Caparra, see Institute of Puerto Rican Culture, San Juan PR

The Museum at Drexel University, Philadelphia PA (M)

Museum of African American Art, Tampa FL (M)

Museum of African Art, New York NY (M)

Museum of Afro-American History, Boston MA (M)

Museum of American Folk Art, New York NY (M,L)

Museum of Architecture & Design, see Chicago Athenaeum, Chicago IL

Museum of Art, Fort Lauderdale, Fort Lauderdale FL (M,L)

Museum of Art & History, Santa Cruz CA (M)

Museum of Arts & History, Port Huron MI (M)

The Museum of Arts & Sciences Inc, Daytona Beach FL (M,L)

Museum of Arts & Sciences, Inc, Macon GA (M)

Museum of Chinese in the Americas, New York NY (M)

Museum of Connecticut History, see Connecticut State Library, Hartford CT

Museum of Contemporary Art, Chicago IL (M,L)

The Museum of Contemporary Art, Los Angeles CA (M)

Museum of Contemporary Art, North Miami FL (M)

Museum of Contemporary Art, San Diego, La Jolla CA (M,L)

Museum of Contemporary Art, San Diego-Downtown, San Diego CA (M)

Museum of Contemporary Impressionism, New Milford CT (M)

The Museum of Contemporary Photography, see Columbia College, Chicago IL

Museum of Discovery & Science, Fort Lauderdale FL (M)

Museum of Early Southern Decorative Arts, see Old Salem Inc, Winston-Salem NC

Museum of East Texas, Lufkin TX (A)

Museum of Fine Arts, Boston MA (M,L)

Museum of Fine Arts, Springfield MA (M,L)

Museum of Fine Arts, Houston, Houston TX (M,L)

Museum of Fine Arts, Saint Petersburg, Florida, Inc, Saint Petersburg FL (M,L)

Museum of Holography - Chicago, Chicago IL (M,L)

Museum of International Children's Art, see Children's Art Foundation, Santa Cruz CA

Museum of Maryland History, see Maryland Historical Society, Baltimore MD

Museum of Mobile, Mobile AL (M,L)

Museum of Modern Art, New York NY (M,L)

Museum of Movie Art, Calgary AB (M)

Museum of Neon Art, Los Angeles CA (M)

Museum of New Mexico, Santa Fe NM (M,L)

Museum of New Mexico, Office of Cultural Affairs of New Mexico, The Governor's Gallery, Santa Fe NM (M)

Museum of Northern Arizona, Flagstaff AZ (M)

Museum of Northern British Columbia, Ruth Harvey Art Gallery, Prince Rupert BC (M,L)

Museum of Ossining Historical Society, Ossining NY (M,L)

Museum of Our National Heritage, Lexington MA (M)

Museum of Photographic Arts, San Diego CA (M)

Museum of Science & Industry, Chicago IL (M)

Museum of the American Quilter's Society, Paducah KY (M)

Museum of the Americas, Brookfield VT (M,L)

Museum of the City of New York, New York NY (M,L)

Museum of the Great Plains, see Institute of the Great Plains, Lawton OK

Museum of the Hudson Highlands, Cornwall on Hudson NY (M)

Museum of the National Center of Afro-American Artists, Boston MA (M)

Museum of the Plains Indian & Crafts Center, Browning MT (M)

Museum of the Southwest, Midland TX (M,L)

Museum of Western Art, Denver CO (M)

Museum of Western Colorado, Grand Junction CO (L)

Museum of York County, Rock Hill SC (M,L)

The Museums at Stony Brook, Stony Brook NY (M,L)

Museum Science & History, Jacksonville FL (M)

Museum Shop, see Illinois State Museum, Chicago IL

Museums of Abilene, Inc, Abilene TX (M)

Muskegon Community College, Dept of Creative & Performing Arts, Muskegon MI (S)

Muskegon Museum of Art, Muskegon MI (M,L)

Muskingum College, Art Department, New Concord OH (S)

Muskoka Arts & Crafts Inc, Chapel Gallery, Bracebridge ON (M)

Muttart Public Art Gallery, Calgary AB (M)

Mystic Art Association, Inc, Mystic CT (A)

NAB Gallery, Chicago IL (M)

Nabisco, Inc, East Hanover NJ (C)

NAME Gallery, Chicago IL (M,L)

Names Project Foundation, San Francisco CA (O)

Namm Hall Library and Learning Resource Center, see New York City Technical College, Brooklyn NY

Nanaimo Art Gallery & Exhibition Centre, see Malaspina College, Nanaimo BC

Nantucket Historical Association, Historic Nantucket, Nantucket MA (M)

Napa Valley College, Art Dept, Napa CA (S)

Naples Art Gallery, Naples FL (M)

Napoleonic Society of America, Museum & Library, Clearwater FL (M)

Nashua Center for Arts, Nashua NH (S)

Nassau Community College, Firehouse Art Gallery, Garden City NY (M)

Nassau Community College, Art Dept, Garden City NY (S)

Nassau County Museum of Fine Art, Roslyn Harbor NY (M)

National Academy of Design, New York NY (O)

National Academy of Sciences, Arts in the Academy, Washington DC (M)

National Academy School of Fine Arts, New York NY (S)

National Afro American Museum & Cultural Center, see Ohio Historical Society, Wilberforce OH

National Air and Space Museum, Washington DC (M,L)

National Alliance for Media Arts & Culture, San Francisco CA (O)

National Antique & Art Dealers Association of America, Inc, New York NY (O)

National Architectural Accrediting Board, Inc, Washington DC (O)

National Archives of Canada, Ottawa ON (L)

National Archives & Records Administration, John F Kennedy Library & Museum, Boston MA (M)

National Archives & Records Administration, Franklin D Roosevelt Museum, Hyde Park NY (M,L)

National Archives & Records Administration, Harry S Truman Library, Independence MO (L)

National Art Education Association, Reston VA (O)

National Artists Equity Association Inc, Washington DC (O)

National Art League Inc, Douglaston NY (A)

National Art Museum of Sport, Indianapolis IN (M)

National Assembly of State Arts Agencies, Washington DC (O)

National Association of Artists' Organizations (NAAO), Washington DC (O)

National Association of Schools of Art & Design, Reston VA (O)

National Association of Women Artists, Inc, New York NY (O)

National Baseball Hall of Fame & Museum, Inc, Art Collection, Cooperstown NY (M)

National Cartoonists Society, New York NY (O)

National Conference of Artists, Michigan Chapter Gallery, Detroit MI (M)

National Council on Education for the Ceramic Arts (NCECA), Bandon OR (O)

National Cowboy Hall of Fame & Western Heritage Center Museum, Oklahoma City OK (M)

National Endowment for the Arts, Washington DC (O)

National Foundation for Advancement in the Arts, Miami FL (O)

National Gallery of Art, Washington DC (M,L)

National Gallery of Canada, Ottawa ON (M,L)

National Hall of Fame for Famous American Indians, Anadarko OK (M)

National Infantry Museum, Fort Benning GA (M,L)

National Institute for Architectural Education, New York NY (O)

National Institute for the Conservation of Cultural Property, Washington DC (O)

National Institute of Art & Disabilities (NIAD), Richmond CA (A)

National League of American Pen Women, Washington DC (O)

National Maritime Museum, see San Francisco Maritime National Historical Park, San Francisco CA

National Museum of African Art, Washington DC (M,L)

National Museum of American Art, Washington DC (M,L)

National Museum of American History, Washington DC (M,A,L)

National Museum of Racing, National Museum of Racing & Hall of Fame, Saratoga Springs NY (M,L)

National Museum of Racing & Hall of Fame, see National Museum of Racing, Saratoga Springs NY

National Museum of Science & Technology, Ottawa ON (M)

National Museum of Science & Technology Corporation, National Aviation Museum, Ottawa ON (M)

National Museum of the American Indian, George Gustav Heye Center, New York NY (M)

National Museum of Wildlife Art, Jackson WY (M,L)

National Museum of Women in the Arts, Washington DC (M,L)

National Museum of Woodcarving, see Gloridale Partnership, Custer SD

National Native American Co-Operative, North American Indian Information & Trade Center, Tucson AZ (A)

National Oil & Acrylic Painters Society, Osage Beach MO (O)

National Park Service, Hubbell Trading Post National Historic Site, Ganado AZ (M)

National Park Service, Weir Farm National Historic Site, Wilton CT (M)

The National Park Service, United States Department of the Interior, The Statue of Liberty National Monument, New York NY (M)

National Portrait Gallery, Washington DC (M,L)

National Sculpture Society, New York NY (O)

The National Shrine of the North American Martyrs, see Kateri Galleries, Auriesville NY

National Society Daughters of the American Revolution, see DAR Museum, Washington DC

National Society of Colonial Dames of America in the State of Maryland, Mount Clare Mansion, Baltimore MD (M,L)

National Society of Mural Painters, Inc, New York NY (O)

National Society of Painters in Casein & Acrylic, Inc, Whitehall PA (O)

National Society of the Colonial Dames, Wilton House Museum, Richmond VA (M)

The National Society of The Colonial Dames of America in the State of New Hampshire, Moffatt-Ladd House, Portsmouth NH (A)

National Society of Tole & Decorative Painters, Inc, Wichita KS (A)

National Trust for Historic Preservation, Chesterwood Museum, Glendale MA (M,L)

National Trust for Historic Preservation, Washington DC (M)

Nations Bank, Art Collection, Richmond VA (C)

Natural Heritage Trust, see New York Office of Parks, Recreation & Historic Preservation, Albany NY

Natural History Museum of Los Angeles County, Los Angeles CA (M,L)

Navajo Nation Library System, Window Rock AZ (L)

Navajo Nation Museum, Window Rock AZ (M)

Naval Historical Center, The Navy Museum, Washington DC (M)

Naval War College Museum, Newport RI (M)

Navarro College, Art Dept, Corsicana TX (S)

Navarro College, Gaston T Gooch Library & Learning Resource Center, Corsicana TX (L)

The Navy Museum, see Naval Historical Center, Washington DC

Nazareth College of Rochester, Art Dept, Rochester NY (S)

NCCU Art Museum, see North Carolina Central University, Durham NC

Nebraska State Capitol, Lincoln NE (M)

Nebraska Wesleyan University, Elder Gallery, Lincoln NE (M)

Nebraska Wesleyan University, Art Dept, Lincoln NE (S)

Neiderlander Research Library, see Amherst Museum, Amherst NY

Nelson-Atkins Museum of Art, Kansas City MO (M,L,A)

Richard L Nelson Gallery & Fine Arts Collection, see University of California, Davis CA

Nemours Mansion & Gardens, Wilmington DE (M)

Nesbitt College of Design Arts, see Drexel University, Philadelphia PA (S)

Bjarne Ness Gallery at Bear Creek Hall, see SVACA - Sheyenne Valley Arts & Crafts Association, Fort Ransom ND

Neuberger Museum of Art, see State University of New York at Purchase, Purchase NY

Nevada Museum Of Art, Reno NV (M,L)

Neville Public Museum, Green Bay WI (M,L)

George P Nevitt Library, see Paine Art Center & Arboretum, Oshkosh WI

Newark Museum Association, The Newark Museum, Newark NJ (M,L)

Newark Public Library, Art & Music Div, Newark NJ (L)

Newark School of Fine & Industrial Art, Newark NJ (S)

New Arts Program, Inc, Kutztown PA (A)

New Bedford Free Public Library, Art Dept, New Bedford MA (L)

New Bedford Whaling Museum, see Old Dartmouth Historical Society, New Bedford MA

Newberry College, Dept of Art, Newberry SC (S)

Newberry Library, Chicago IL (L)

New Britain Museum of American Art, New Britain CT (M)

New Brunswick College of Craft & Design, Fredericton NB (A,L)

New Brunswick College of Craft & Design, Fredericton NB (S)

New Brunswick Museum, Saint John NB (M,L)

Newburyport Maritime Society, Custom House Maritime Museum, Newburyport MA (M)

New Canaan Historical Society, New Canaan CT (M)

New Canaan Library, New Canaan CT (L)

New College of the University of South Florida, Fine Arts Dept, Humanities Division, Sarasota FL (S)

New England Center for Contemporary Art, Brooklyn CT (M)

New England College, Art & Art History, Henniker NH (S)

New England Maple Museum, Rutland VT (M)

The New England School of Art & Design at Suffolk University, Boston MA (S)

New England School of Art & Design at Suffolk University, Library, Boston MA (L)

New England Watercolor Society, Boston MA (O)

Newfoundland Museum, Saint John's NF (M,L)

New Hampshire Antiquarian Society, Hopkinton NH (M)

New Hampshire Art Association, Inc, Boscawen NH (A)

New Hampshire Historical Society, Concord NH (A,L)

New Hampshire Institute of Art, Manchester NH (S)

New Harmony Gallery of Contemporary Art, New Harmony IN (M)

New Haven Colony Historical Society, New Haven CT (A,L)

New Haven Paint & Clay Club, Inc, New Haven CT (A)

Newhouse Center for Contemporary Art, see Snug Harbor Cultural Center, Staten Island NY

New Jersey Center for Visual Arts, Summit NJ (A)

New Jersey Historical Society, Newark NJ (M,L)

New Jersey Institute of Technology, Architecture Library, Newark NJ (L)

New Jersey State Museum, Trenton NJ (M)

New Jersey Summer Arts Institute, see Institute for Arts & Humanities Education, New Brunswick NJ (S)

New Jersey Water-Color Society, Chester NJ (A)

New Langton Arts, San Francisco CA (M)

New London County Historical Society, New London CT (A)

New Mexico Artists' Association, Santa Fe NM (A)

New Mexico Art League, Gallery, Albuquerque NM (A)

New Mexico Highlands University, Arrott Art Gallery, Las Vegas NM (M)

New Mexico Highlands University, Dept of Communications & Fine Arts, Las Vegas NM (S)

New Mexico Junior College, Arts & Sciences, Hobbs NM (S)

New Mexico State University, University Art Gallery, Las Cruces NM (M)

New Mexico State University, Art Dept, Las Cruces NM (S)

The New Museum of Contemporary Art, New York NY (M,L)

New Organization for the Visual Arts, (NOVA), Cleveland OH (M)

New Orleans Academy of Fine Arts, Academy Gallery, New Orleans LA (M)

New Orleans Museum of Art, New Orleans LA (M,L)

New Orleans School of GlassWorks, Gallery & Printmaking Studio, New Orleans LA (M)

Newport Art Museum, Newport RI (M)

Newport Art Museum School, Newport RI (S)

Newport Harbor Art Museum, see Orange County Museum of Art, Newport Beach CA

Newport Historical Society, Newport RI (A,L)

New Rochelle Art Association, see New Rochelle Public Library, New Rochelle NY

New Rochelle Public Library, Art Section, New Rochelle NY (L,A)

New School for Social Research, Adult Education Division, New York NY (S)

New Visions Gallery, Inc, Marshfield WI (M)

New World School of the Arts, Gallery, Miami FL (M)

New World School of the Arts, Miami FL (S)

New York Academy of Art, Graduate School of Figurative Art, New York NY (S)

New York Artists Equity Association, Inc, New York NY (A)

New York City Technical College, Namm Hall Library and Learning Resource Center, Brooklyn NY (L)

New York City Technical College of the City University of New York, Dept of Art & Advertising Design, Brooklyn NY (S)

New York Historical Society, New York NY (A,L)

New York Institute of Photography, New York NY (S)

New York Institute of Technology, Gallery, Old Westbury NY (M,L)

New York Institute of Technology, Fine Arts Dept, Old Westbury NY (S)

New York Office of Parks, Recreation & Historic Preservation, Natural Heritage Trust, Albany NY (A)

The New York Public Library, New York NY (L,M)

New York School of Interior Design, New York NY (S)

New York School of Interior Design Library, New York NY (L)

New York Society of Architects, New York NY (A)

New York State College of Ceramics at Alfred University, Scholes Library of Ceramics, Alfred NY (L)

New York State College of Ceramics at Alfred University, School of Art & Design, Alfred NY (S)

New York State College of Human Ecology, see Cornell University, Ithaca NY (S)

New York State Historical Association, Cooperstown NY (M,L)

New York State Library, Manuscripts & Special Collections, Albany NY (L)

New York State Museum, Albany NY (M)

New York State Office of Parks, Recreation & Historical Preservation, Mills Mansion State Historical Site, Staatsburg NY (M)

New York State Office of Parks Recreation & Historic Preservation, John Jay Homestead State Historic Site, Katonah NY (M)

New York Studio School of Drawing, Painting & Sculpture, New York NY (S)

New York Studio School of Drawing, Painting & Sculpture, Gallery, New York NY (M,L)

New York University, New York NY (M,L)

New York University, Institute of Fine Arts, New York NY (S)

Nexus Contemporary Art Center, Atlanta GA (M)

Nexus Gallery, see Foundation for Today's Art, Philadelphia PA

Elisabet Ney Museum, Austin TX (M,L)

Niagara Artists' Centre, Saint Catharines ON (M)

Niagara County Community College, Fine Arts Division, Sanborn NY (S)

Niagara County Community College Art Gallery, Sanborn NY (M)

Niagara University, Castellani Art Museum, Niagara NY (M)

Niagara University, Fine Arts Dept, Niagara Falls NY (S)

Nicholls State University, Dept of Art, Thibodaux LA (S)

Nichols House Museum, Inc, Boston MA (M)

The Nickle Arts Museum, see University of Calgary, Calgary AB

Nicolaysen Art Museum & Discovery Center, Childrens Discovery Center, Casper WY (M,L)

911 Arts Media Center, Seattle WA (A)

Nippon Club Gallery, New York NY (M)

Noah Webster House, Inc, Noah Webster House, West Hartford CT (M)

Nobles County Art Center Gallery, Worthington MN (A)

The John A Noble Collection, Staten Island NY (M)

Isamu Noguchi Foundation, Isamu Noguchi Garden Museum, Long Island City NY (M)

Isamu Noguchi Garden Museum, see Isamu Noguchi Foundation, Long Island City NY

Harry Nohr Art Gallery, see University of Wisconsin - Platteville, Platteville WI

No Man's Land Historical Society Museum, Goodwell OK (M)

Nordstrand Visual Arts Gallery, see Wayne State College, Wayne NE

Norfolk Historical Society Inc, Museum, Norfolk CT (M)

Norfolk State University, Fine Arts Dept, Norfolk VA (S)

Norick Art Center, see Oklahoma City University, Oklahoma City OK (S)

Normandale Community College, Bloomington MN (S)

North American Indian Information & Trade Center, see National Native American Co-Operative, Tucson AZ

Northampton Community College, Art Dept, Bethlehem PA (S)

North Arkansas Community-Technical College, Art Dept, Harrison AR (S)

North Canton Public Library, Little Art Gallery, North Canton OH (L)

North Carolina Agricultural & Technical State University, Art Dept, Greensboro NC (S)

North Carolina Central University, NCCU Art Museum, Durham NC (M)

North Carolina Central University, Art Dept, Durham NC (S)

North Carolina Museum of Art, Raleigh NC (M,L)

North Carolina Museums Council, Raleigh NC (A)

North Carolina Nature Artists Association (NCNAA), Cary NC (M)

North Carolina State University, Harrye Lyons Design Library, Raleigh NC (L,M)

North Carolina State University, Chinqua-Penn Plantation House, Garden & Greenhouses, Reidsville NC (M)

North Carolina State University at Raleigh, School of Design, Raleigh NC (S)

North Carolina Wesleyan College, Dept of Visual & Performing Arts, Rocky Mount NC (S)

North Central College, Dept of Art, Naperville IL (S)

North Central College, Oesterle Library, Naperville IL (L)

North Central Life Insurance Company, Art Collection, Saint Paul MN (C)

North Central Michigan College, Art Dept, Petoskey MI (S)

North Central Texas College, Division of Communications & Fine Arts, Gainesville TX (S)

North Central Texas College, Art Dept, Gainesville TX (L)

North Central Washington Museum, Gallery, Wenatchee WA (M)

North Country Museum of Arts, Park Rapids MN (M)

North Dakota Museum of Art, Grand Forks ND (M)

North Dakota State College of Science, Dept of Graphic Arts, Wahpeton ND (S)

North Dakota State University, Memorial Union Art Gallery, Fargo ND (M)

North Dakota State University, Division of Fine Arts, Fargo ND (S)

Northeast Community College, Dept of Liberal Arts, Norfolk NE (S)

Northeastern Illinois University, Gallery, Chicago IL (M)

Northeastern Illinois University, Art Dept, Chicago IL (S)

Northeastern Junior College, Dept of Art, Sterling CO (S)

Northeastern Nevada Historical Society Museum, Elko NV (M,L)

Northeastern Oklahoma A & M College, Art Dept, Miami OK (S)

Northeastern University, Dept of Art & Architecture, Boston MA (S)

Northeast Louisiana University, Dept of Art, Monroe LA (S)

Northeast Louisiana University, Bry Gallery, Monroe LA (M)

Northeast Mississippi Junior College, Art Dept, Booneville MS (S)

Northeast Ohio Areawide Coordinating Agency (NOACA), Information Resource Center, Cleveland OH (L)

Northern Arizona University, Art Museum & Galleries, Flagstaff AZ (M)

Northern Arizona University, School of Art & Design, Flagstaff AZ (S)

Northern Galleries, see Northern State University, Aberdeen SD

Northern Illinois University, Art Gallery in Chicago, Chicago IL (M)

Northern Illinois University, NIU Art Museum, De Kalb IL (M,L)

Northern Illinois University, School of Art, De Kalb IL (S)

Northern Kentucky University, Art Dept, Highland Heights KY (S)

Northern Kentucky University Gallery, Highland Heights KY (M)

Northern Michigan University, Dept of Art & Design, Marquette MI (S)

Northern Michigan University Art Museum, Marquette MI (M)

Northern State University, Art Dept, Aberdeen SD (S)

Northern State University, Northern Galleries, Aberdeen SD (M)

Northern Virginia Community College, Art Dept, Annandale VA (S)

Northern Virginia Fine Arts Association, The Athenaeum, Alexandria VA (A)

Northfield Arts Guild, Northfield MN (A)

North Florida Community College, Dept Humanities & Art, Madison FL (S)

North Georgia College, Fine Arts Dept, Dahlonega GA (S)

North Hennepin Community College, Art Dept, Brooklyn Park MN (S)

North Hennepin Community College, Art Gallery, Brooklyn Park MN (M)

North Idaho College, Art Dept, Coeur D'Alene ID (S)

North Iowa Area Community College, Dept of Art, Mason City IA (S)

Northland Pioneer College, Art Dept, Holbrook AZ (S)

North Park College, Carlson Tower Gallery, Chicago IL (M)

North Park College, Art Dept, Chicago IL (S)

Northport-East Northport Public Library, Northport NY (L)

North Seattle Community College, Art Dept, Seattle WA (S)

North Shore Art League, Winnetka IL (A)

North Shore Art League, Winnetka IL (S)

North Shore Arts Association, Inc, Art Gallery, Gloucester MA (A)

North View Gallery, see Portland Community College, Portland OR

Northwest Art Center, see Minot State University, Minot ND

Northwest Community College, Dept of Art, Powell WY (S)

Northwestern College, Te Paske Gallery, Orange City IA (M)

Northwestern College, Art Dept, Orange City IA (S)

Northwestern Connecticut Community College, Fine Arts Dept, Winsted CT (S)

Northwestern Michigan College, Dennos Museum Center, Traverse City MI (M)

Northwestern Michigan College, Art Dept, Traverse City MI (S)

Northwestern State university, Tahlequah OK (S)

Northwestern State University of Louisiana, Dept of Art, Natchitoches LA (S)

Northwestern University, Evanston IL (M,L)

Northwestern University, Evanston, Evanston IL (S)

Northwest Missouri State University, DeLuce Art Gallery, Maryville MO (M)

Northwest Missouri State University, Dept of Art, Maryville MO (S)

Northwest Nazarene College, Art Dept, Nampa ID (S)

Northwest Pastel Society (NPS), Issaquah WA (A)

Northwest Watercolor Society, Bellevue WA (A)

Northwood University, Alden B Dow Creativity Center, Midland MI (S)

Norton Gallery & School of Art, Inc, Norton Museum of Art, West Palm Beach FL (M,L)

Norwest Corporation, Minneapolis, Arts Program, Minneapolis MN (C)

Norwich University, Dept of Philosophy, Religion & Fine Arts, Northfield VT (S)

Nossi College of Art, Goodlettsville TN (S)

Notre Dame College, Art Dept, Manchester NH (S)

(NOVA), see New Organization for the Visual Arts, Cleveland OH

NOVA Corporation of Alberta, NOVA Garden Court Gallery, Calgary AB (C)

NOVA Garden Court Gallery, see NOVA Corporation of Alberta, Calgary AB

Nova Scotia Association of Architects, Halifax NS (A)

Nova Scotia College of Art and Design, Anna Leonowens Gallery, Halifax NS (M,L)

Nova Scotia College of Art & Design, Halifax NS (S)

Nova Scotia Museum, Maritime Museum of the Atlantic, Halifax NS (M)

Noyes Art Gallery, Lincoln NE (M)

Noyes Museum, Oceanville NJ (M,L)

Noyes & Read Galleries, see Antioch College, Yellow Springs OH

Number Inc, Memphis TN (A)

Nutana Collegiate Institute, Memorial Library and Art Gallery, Saskatoon SK (L)

Oakland City College, Division of Fine Arts, Oakland City IN (S)

Oakland Community College, Art Dept, Farmington Hills MI (S)

Oakland Museum of California, Art Dept, Oakland CA (M,L)

Oakland Public Library, Art, Music & Recreation Section, Oakland CA (L)

Oakland University, Meadow Brook Art Gallery, Rochester MI (M)

Oakland University, Dept of Art & Art History, Rochester MI (S)

Oak Ridge Art Center, Oak Ridge TN (A,L)

Oakton Community College, Art & Architecture Dept, Des Plaines IL (S)

Oakville Galleries, Oakville ON (M)

Oatlands, Inc, Leesburg VA (M)

Oberlin College, Allen Memorial Art Museum, Oberlin OH (M,L)

Oberlin College, Dept of Art, Oberlin OH (S)

Occidental College, Weingart & Coons Galleries, Los Angeles CA (M)

Occidental College, Dept of Art History & Visual Arts, Los Angeles CA (S)

Ocean City Art Center, Ocean City NJ (S)

Ocean City Art Center, Ocean City NJ (A,L)

Ocean County College, Humanities Dept, Toms River NJ (S)

Octagon Center for the Arts, Ames IA (A)

The Octagon Museum, see American Architectural Foundation, Washington DC

Oesterle Library, see North Central College, Naperville IL

Office of Cultural Affairs of New Mexico, The Governor's Gallery, see Museum of New Mexico, Santa Fe NM

Ogden Union Station, Ogden UT (M)

Oglebay Institute, Wheeling WV (A,M,L)

Ogunquit Museum of American Art, Ogunquit ME (M,L)

O Henry Museum, see City of Austin Parks & Recreation, Austin TX

Ohio Dominican College, Art Dept, Columbus OH (S)

Ohio Historical Society, Columbus OH (A,L)

Ohio Historical Society, National Afro American Museum & Cultural Center, Wilberforce OH (M)

The Ohio Historical Society, Inc, Campus Martius Museum & Ohio River Museum, Marietta OH (M)

Ohio Northern University, Dept of Art, Ada OH (S)

Ohio State University, Columbus OH (M,L)

Ohio State University, Columbus OH (S)

Ohio University, Kennedy Museum of American Art, Athens OH (M,L)

Ohio University, School of Art, Athens OH (S)

Ohio University-Chillicothe Campus, Fine Arts & Humanities Division, Chillicothe OH (S)

Ohio University-Eastern Campus, Dept Comparitive Arts, Saint Clairsville OH (S)

Ohio Wesleyan University, Fine Arts Dept, Delaware OH (S)

Ohrstrom Library, see Saint Paul's School, Concord NH

Oil Pastel Association, Nyack NY (A)

Ojai Valley Art Center, Ojai CA (A)

Okaloosa-Walton Community College, Dept of Fine & Performing Arts, Niceville FL (S)

Okefenokee Heritage Center, Inc, Waycross GA (M)

Oklahoma Baptist University, Art Dept, Shawnee OK (S)

Oklahoma Center for Science & Art, Kirkpatrick Center, Oklahoma City OK (M)

Oklahoma Christian University of Science & Arts, Dept of Art & Design, Oklahoma City OK (S)

Oklahoma City Art Museum, Oklahoma City OK (M,L)

Oklahoma City University, Norick Art Center, Oklahoma City OK (S)

Oklahoma City University, Hulsey Gallery-Norick Art Center, Oklahoma City OK (M,L)

Oklahoma Historical Society, State Museum of History, Oklahoma City OK (M,L)

Oklahoma State University, Graphic Arts Dept, Okmulgee OK (S)

Oklahoma State University, Gardiner Art Gallery, Stillwater OK (M,L)

Oklahoma State University, Art Dept, Stillwater OK (S)

Olana State Historic Sjte, Hudson NY (M,L)

Old Academy Library, see Wethersfield Historical Society Inc, Wethersfield CT

Old Atwood House Museum, see Chatham Historical Society, Chatham MA

Old Barracks Museum, Trenton NJ (M)

Old Capitol Museum, see Mississippi Department of Archives & History, Jackson MS

Old Castle Museum, see Baker University, Baldwin City KS

Old Colony Historical Society, Museum, Taunton MA (M,L)

Old Dartmouth Historical Society, New Bedford Whaling Museum, New Bedford MA (M,L)

Old Dominion University, Gallery, Norfolk VA (M,L)

Old Dominion University, Art Dept, Norfolk VA (S)

Old Fort Harrod State Park Mansion Museum, Harrodsburg KY (M)

Old Gaol Museum, see Old York Historical Society, York ME

Old Island Restoration Foundation Inc, Wrecker's Museum - Oldest House, Key West FL (M)

Old Jail Art Center, Albany TX (M,L)

Old Lincoln County Jail & Museum, see Lincoln County Historical Association, Inc, Wiscasset ME

Old Salem Inc, Museum of Early Southern Decorative Arts, Winston-Salem NC (M,L)

Old Slater Mill Association, Slater Mill Historic Site, Pawtucket RI (M)

Old State House, Hartford CT (M)

Old State House Museum, see The Bostonian Society, Boston MA

Old York Historical Society, York ME (A,M,L)

Olin Art Gallery, see Washington & Jefferson College, Washington PA

Olive-Harvey College, see City Colleges of Chicago, Chicago IL (S)

Steven Oliver Art Center, see California College of Arts & Crafts, Oakland CA

Olivet College, Armstrong Museum of Art & Archaeology, Olivet MI (M,L)

Olivet College, Art Dept, Olivet MI (S)

Olivet Nazarene University, Dept of Art, Kankakee IL (S)

Ollantay Center for the Arts, Jackson Heights NY (A)

Olympic College, Social Sciences & Humanities Division, Bremerton WA (S)

Omaha Childrens Museum, Inc, Omaha NE (M)

The One Club for Art & Copy, New York NY (A)

One West Art Center, Fort Collins CO (M)

Ontario Association of Art Galleries, Toronto ON (A)

Ontario College of Art & Design, Toronto ON (S)

Ontario College of Art & Design, OCAD Gallery, Toronto ON (M,L)

Ontario Crafts Council, The Craft Gallery, Toronto ON (M,L,A)

Open Space, Victoria BC (A)

Opera Museum, see Marcella Sembrich Memorial Association Inc, Bolton Landing NY

Oral Roberts University, Fine Arts Dept, Tulsa OK (S)

Orange Coast College, Division of Fine Arts, Costa Mesa CA (S)

Orange County Center for Contemporary Art, Santa Ana CA (M)

Orange County Community College, Art Dept, Middletown NY (S)

Orange County Museum of Art, Newport Harbor Art Museum, Newport Beach CA (M,L)

Orchard House, see Louisa May Alcott Memorial Association, Concord MA

Order Sons of Italy in America, Garibaldi & Meucci Museum, Staten Island NY (M)

Oregon Center for the Photographic Arts, see Blue Sky, Portland OR

Oregon College of Art Craft, Hoffman Gallery, Portland OR (M,L)

Oregon Historical Society, Portland OR (A,L)

Oregon School of Arts & Crafts, Portland OR (S)

Oregon State University, Corvallis OR (M)

Purdue University Calumet, Dept of
Communication & Creative Arts, Hammond IN
(S)
Purdue University Calumet, Bicentennial Library
Gallery, Hammond IN (M)
Purdue University Galleries, West Lafayette IN (M)
Purdue University, West Lafayette, Dept of Visual
& Performing Arts, Div of Art & Design, West
Lafayette IN (S)
Ross C Purdy Museum of Ceramics, see The
American Ceramic Society, Westerville OH
Putnam County Historical Society, Foundry School
Museum, Cold Spring NY (M)
George Putnam University Center, see Willamette
University, Salem OR
Putnam Museum of History & Natural Science,
Davenport IA (M,L)
Pyramid Arts Center, Rochester NY (M)
Pyramid Atlantic, Riverdale MD (A)
Quapaw Quarter Association, Inc, Villa Marre,
Little Rock AR (M,L)
Queen Emma Gallery, see Queen's Medical Center
Auxiliary, Honolulu HI
Queensborough Community College, Dept of Art &
Photography, Bayside NY (S)
Queensborough Community College, Art Gallery,
Bayside NY (M)
Queensborough Community College Library,
Bayside NY (L)
Queens Borough Public Library, Fine Arts &
Recreation Division, Jamaica NY (L)
Queens College, Fine Arts Dept, Charlotte NC (S)
Queens College, Art Dept, Flushing NY (S)
Queens College, City University of New York,
Godwin-Ternbach Museum, Flushing NY (M,L)
Queens Historical Society, Flushing NY (A)
Queen's Medical Center Auxiliary, Queen Emma
Gallery, Honolulu HI (M)
The Queens Museum of Art, Flushing NY (M)
Queen's University, Agnes Etherington Art Centre,
Kingston ON (M,L)
Queen's University, Dept of Art, Kingston ON (S)
Quetico Park, John B Ridley Research Library,
Atikokan ON (L)
Quickdraw Animation Society, Calgary AB (O)
Regina A Quick Fine Art Center, see Saint
Bonaventure University, Saint Bonaventure NY
Quincy Art Center, Quincy IL (A)
Quincy College, Fine Arts Dept, Quincy MA (S)
Quincy Society of Fine Arts, Quincy IL (A)
Quincy University, The Gray Gallery, Quincy IL
(M,L)
Quincy University, Dept of Art, Quincy IL (S)
Radford University, Art Dept, Radford VA (S)
Rahr-West Art Museum, Manitowoc WI (M,L)
Railroad Museum of Pennsylvania, see
Pennsylvania Historical & Museum Commission,
Harrisburg PA
Rakow Library, see Corning Museum of Glass,
Corning NY
Willo Ralston Library for Historical Research, see
MonDak Heritage Center, Sidney MT
Ramapo College of New Jersey, School of
Contemporary Arts, Mahwah NJ (S)
Rancho Santiago College, Art Dept, Santa Ana CA
(S)
Randall Museum Junior Museum, San Francisco
CA (M)
Jasper Rand Art Museum, see Westfield
Athenaeum, Westfield MA
Randolph-Macon College, Dept of the Arts,
Ashland VA (S)
Randolph-Macon Woman's College, Maier Museum
of Art, Lynchburg VA (M)
Randolph-Macon Woman's College, Dept of Art,
Lynchburg VA (S)
Randolph Street Gallery, Chicago IL (M)
Edward Warder Rannells Art Library, see
University of Kentucky, Lexington KY
Harry Ransom Humanities Research Center, see
University of Texas at Austin, Austin TX
Rapid City Arts Council, Dahl Fine Arts Center,
Rapid City SD (M)
Elmer E Rasmuson Library, see University of
Alaska, Fairbanks AK
Rauh Memorial Library, see Children's Museum,
Indianapolis IN

Esther Raushenbush Library, see Sarah Lawrence
College Library, Bronxville NY
Ravalli County Museum, Hamilton MT (M)
Walter Cecil Rawls Museum, Courtland VA (M)
RCCA: The Arts Center, see Rensselaer County
Council for the Arts, Troy NY
The Reader's Digest Association Inc, Pleasantville
NY (C)
George Read II House, see Historical Society of
Delaware, Wilmington DE
Reading Public Museum, Reading PA (M,L)
Real Art Ways (RAW), Hartford CT (M)
Red Deer College, Dept of Art & Design, Red Deer
AB (S)
Red Deer & District Museum & Archives, Red
Deer AB (M)
Redding Museum of Art & History, Redding CA
(M,L)
Red Hill National Memorial, see Patrick Henry
Memorial Foundation, Brookneal VA
Redington Museum, see Waterville Historical
Society, Waterville ME
Redlands Art Association, Redlands CA (A)
Red River Valley Museum, Vernon TX (M)
Red Rock Museum, see Red Rock State Park,
Church Rock NM
Red Rocks Community College, Arts & Humanities
Dept, Lakewood CO (S)
Red Rock State Park, Red Rock Museum, Church
Rock NM (M,L)
Redwood Library & Athenaeum, Newport RI (L)
Carroll Reece Museum, see East Tennessee State
University, Johnson City TN
Reed College, Dept of Art, Portland OR (S)
Reed College, Douglas F Cooley Memorial Art
Gallery, Portland OR (M)
Martha Stecher Reed Art Library, see Akron Art
Museum, Akron OH
Reeves Memorial Library, see Seton Hill College,
Greensburg PA
Regina Public Library, Art Dept, Regina SK (L,M)
Regional Art Gallery, see Cornwall Gallery Society,
Cornwall ON
Regional Arts & Culture Council, Metropolitan
Center for Public Arts, Portland OR (A)
Regis College, Fine Arts Center, Weston MA (M)
Regis College, Dept of Art, Weston MA (S)
Regis University, Fine Arts Dept, Denver CO (S)
Rehoboth Art League, Inc, Rehoboth Beach DE (S)
Rehoboth Art League, Inc, Rehoboth Beach DE
(A)
Reinberger Galleries, see Cleveland Institute of Art,
Cleveland OH
Frederic Remington Art Museum, Ogdensburg NY
(M,L)
Renaissance Center Main Gallery, see Arts Council
of Greater Kingsport, Kingsport TN
The Renaissance Society, Chicago IL (A)
Frederic G Renner Memorial Library, see C M
Russell Museum, Great Falls MT
Rensselaer County Council for the Arts, RCCA:
The Arts Center, Troy NY (A)
Rensselaer County Historical Society, Hart-Cluett
Mansion, 1827, Troy NY (M,L)
Rensselaer Newman Foundation Chapel & Cultural
Center, The Gallery, Troy NY (M)
Rensselaer Polytechnic Institute, Troy NY (S)
Renwick Gallery, see National Museum of
American Art, Washington DC
Revelstoke Art Group, Revelstoke BC (A)
Reynolda House Museum of American Art,
Winston-Salem NC (M,L)
Rhinelander District Library, Rhinelander WI (L)
Rhode Island College, Edward M Bannister
Gallery, Providence RI (M)
Rhode Island College, Art Dept, Providence RI (S)
Rhode Island Historical Society, Providence RI (A,
M,L)
Rhode Island School of Design, Museum of Art,
Providence RI (M,L)
Rhode Island School of Design, Museum of Art,
RISD, Providence RI (S)
Rhode Island Watercolor Society, Pawtucket RI (A)
Rhodes College, Jessie L Clough Art Memorial for
Teaching, Memphis TN (M)
Rhodes College, Dept of Art, Memphis TN (S)
Rice University, Houston TX (L,M)

Rice University, Dept of Art & Art History,
Houston TX (S)
Richard Bland College, Art Dept, Petersburg VA
(S)
Richard Gallery & Almond Tea Gallery, Divisions
of Studios of Jack Richard, Cuyahoga Falls OH
(M,L)
Richardson Memorial Library, see The Saint Louis
Art Museum, Saint Louis MO
Sid W Richardson Foundation, Collection of
Western Art, Fort Worth TX (M)
Studios of Jack Richard Creative School of Design,
Cuyahoga Falls OH (S)
Richmond Art Center, Civic Center Plaza,
Richmond CA (A)
Richmond Art Museum, see Art Association of
Richmond, Richmond IN
Richmond Arts Centre, Richmond BC (A)
Ricker Library of Architecture & Art, see
University of Illinois, Champaign IL
Ricks College, Dept of Art, Rexburg ID (S)
Ridderhof Martin Gallery, see Mary Washington
College, Fredericksburg VA
Rider College, Dept of Fine Arts, Lawrenceville NJ
(S)
Rider University, Art Gallery, Lawrenceville NJ
(M)
John B Ridley Research Library, see Quetico Park,
Atikokan ON
Robert Gore Rifkind Center for German
Expressionist Studies, see Los Angeles County
Museum of Art, Los Angeles CA
Riley County Historical Society, Riley County
Historical Museum, Manhattan KS (M,L)
Rinehart School of Sculpture, see Maryland
Institute, Baltimore MD (S)
John & Mable Ringling Museum of Art, see State
Art Museum of Florida, Sarasota FL
Ringling School of Art & Design, Sarasota FL (S)
Ringling School of Art & Design, Verman
Kimbrough Memorial Library, Sarasota FL (L)
Ringwood Manor House Museum, Ringwood NJ
(M)
Rio Hondo College, Visual Arts Dept, Whittier CA
(S)
Rio Hondo College Art Gallery, Whittier CA (M)
Ripon College, Art Dept, Ripon WI (S)
Ripon College Art Gallery, Ripon WI (M)
Ritter Art Gallery, see Florida Atlantic University,
Boca Raton FL
Ritz-Carlton Hotel Company, Art Collection,
Atlanta GA (C)
Tomas Rivera Library, see University of California,
Riverside CA
Riverside Art Museum, Riverside CA (M,L)
Riverside Community College, Dept of Art & Mass
Media, Riverside CA (S)
Riverside County Museum, Edward-Dean Museum,
Cherry Valley CA (M,L)
Riverside Municipal Museum, Riverside CA (M)
Rivier College, Art Dept, Nashua NH (S)
R J R Nabisco, Inc, New York NY (C)
Roanoke College, Fine Arts Dept-Art, Salem VA
(S)
Roberson Museum & Science Center, Binghamton
NY (M)
Roberts County Museum, Miami TX (M)
Roberts Wesleyan College, Art Dept, Rochester NY
(S)
Rowland Evans Robinson Memorial Association,
Rokeby Museum, Ferrisburgh VT (A)
Robson Memorial Library, see University of the
Ozarks, Clarksville AR
Rochester Art Center, Rochester MN (A)
Rochester Community & Technical College, Art
Dept, Rochester MN (S)
Rochester Historical Society, Rochester NY (A)
Rochester Institute of Technology, Technical &
Education Center of Graphic Arts & Imaging,
Rochester NY (L)
Rochester Institute of Technology, Rochester NY
(S)
Abby Aldrich Rockefeller Folk Art Center, see
Colonial Williamsburg Foundation, Williamsburg
VA
Abby Aldrich Rockefeller Folk Art Center Library,
see Colonial Williamsburg Foundation,
Williamsburg VA

John D Rockefeller, Jr Library, see Colonial Williamsburg Foundation, Williamsburg VA

M C Rockefeller Arts Center Gallery, see State University of New York College at Fredonia, Fredonia NY

Rockford Art Museum, Rockford IL (A,L)

Rockford College, Dept of Fine Arts, Rockford IL (S)

Rockford College Art Gallery, Rockford IL (M)

Rock Ford Foundation, Inc, Historic Rock Ford & Kauffman Museum, Lancaster PA (M)

Rockland Center for the Arts, West Nyack NY (M)

Rockland Center for the Arts, West Nyack NY (S)

Rockland Community College, Graphic Arts & Advertising Tech Dept, Suffern NY (S)

Rockport Art Association, Rockport MA (A)

Rock Valley College, Dept of Art, Rockford IL (S)

Rockwell International Corporation Trust, Pittsburgh PA (C)

The Rockwell Museum, Corning NY (M,L)

Norman Rockwell Museum at Stockbridge, Stockbridge MA (M,L)

Rocky Mountain College, Art Dept, Billings MT (S)

Rocky Mountain College of Art & Design, Denver CO (S)

Rocky Mount Arts Center, Rocky Mount NC (A)

Rocky Reach Dam, see Chelan County Public Utility District, Wenatchee WA

Rodin Museum of Philadelphia, see Philadelphia Museum of Art, Philadelphia PA

Rodman Hall Arts Centre, Saint Catharines ON (A,L)

Nicholas Roerich Museum, New York NY (M)

Lauren Rogers Museum of Art, Laurel MS (M,L)

Millicent Rogers Museum of Northern New Mexico, Taos NM (M,L)

Rogers State College, Art Dept, Claremore OK (S)

Will Rogers Memorial & Museum, Claremore OK (M,L)

Roger Williams College, Art Dept, Bristol RI (S)

Roger Williams University, Architecture Library, Bristol RI (L)

Rogue Community College, Wiseman Gallery - Firehouse Gallery, Grants Pass OR (M)

Rogue Valley Art Association, Rogue Gallery & Art Center, Medford OR (A)

Rohrbach Library, see Kutztown University, Kutztown PA

Rokeby Museum, see Rowland Evans Robinson Memorial Association, Ferrisburgh VT

Rollins College, George D & Harriet W Cornell Fine Arts Museum, Winter Park FL (M)

Rollins College, Dept of Art, Main Campus, Winter Park FL (S)

Rome Art & Community Center, Rome NY (A)

Rome Historical Society Museum, Rome NY (M,L)

Hugh N Ronald Memorial Gallery, see Jay County Arts Council, Portland IN

Franklin D Roosevelt Library, see National Archives & Records Administration, Hyde Park NY

Franklin D Roosevelt Museum, see National Archives & Records Administration, Hyde Park NY

Roosevelt-Vanderbilt National Historic Sites, Hyde Park NY (M)

The Stephanie Ann Roper Gallery, see Frostburg State University, Frostburg MD

Rose Art Museum, see Brandeis University, Waltham MA

Rose Center & Council for the Arts, Morristown TN (A)

Rosemont College, Division of the Arts, Rosemont PA (S)

Rosemount Museum, Inc, Pueblo CO (M)

The Rosenbach Museum & Library, Philadelphia PA (M)

Rosenberg Gallery, see Goucher College, Baltimore MD

Rosenberg Library, Galveston TX (L)

Rosenthal Art Gallery, see Albertson College of Idaho, Caldwell ID

Rosicrucian Egyptian Museum & Art Gallery, San Jose CA (M)

Ross Memorial Museum, Saint Andrews NB (M)

Roswell Museum & Art Center, Roswell NM (M,L)

Rotch Library of Architecture & Planning, see Massachusetts Institute of Technology, Cambridge MA

Rothmans, Benson & Hedges, Art Collection, Don Mills ON (C)

Rotunda Gallery, see Fund for the Borough of Brooklyn, Brooklyn NY

Round Top Center for the Arts Inc, Arts Gallery, Damariscotta ME (M,L)

Round Top Library, see Round Top Center for the Arts Inc, Damariscotta ME

Rowan College of New Jersey, Dept of Art, Glassboro NJ (S)

Royal Architectural Institute of Canada, Ottawa ON (O)

Royal Arts Foundation, Belcourt Castle, Newport RI (M)

Royal Canadian Academy of Arts, Toronto ON (O)

Royal Ontario Museum, Toronto ON (M,L)

Elizabeth Rozier Gallery, see Department of Natural Resources of Missouri, Jefferson City MO

Rubelle & Norman Schafler Gallery, see Pratt Institute Library, Brooklyn NY

Ruddell Gallery, see Black Hills State University, Spearfish SD

Ruder Finn Inc, New York NY (C)

C M Russell Museum, Great Falls MT (M,L)

Russell Sage College, Gallery, Troy NY (M)

Russell Sage College, Visual & Performing Arts Dept, Troy NY (S)

Rutgers, The State University of New Jersey, New Brunswick NJ (M,L)

Rutgers, The State University of New Jersey, New Brunswick NJ (S)

Rutgers University, Stedman Art Gallery, Camden NJ (M)

Rutgers University, Camden, Art Dept, Camden NJ (S)

Rutgers University, Newark, Dept of Visual & Performing Arts, Newark NJ (S)

Rutland Area Art Association, Inc, Chaffee Art Center, Rutland VT (A)

R W Norton Art Gallery, Shreveport LA (M,L)

Ryan Fine Arts Center, see McMurry University, Abilene TX

Ryerson & Burnham Libraries, see The Art Institute of Chicago, Chicago IL

Ryerson Polytechnical Institute, Library, Toronto ON (L)

Robert W Ryerss Library & Museum, Philadelphia PA (M,L)

Aline B Saarinen Library, see The Parrish Art Museum, Southampton NY

Arthur M Sackler Gallery, see Smithsonian Institution, Washington DC

Arthur M Sackler Gallery, see Freer Gallery of Art Gallery, Washington DC

Arthur M Sackler Museum, see Harvard University, Cambridge MA

Sacramento City College, Art Dept, Sacramento CA (S)

Sacred Heart University, Dept of Art, Fairfield CT (S)

Safeco Insurance Company, Art Collection, Seattle WA (C)

Safety Harbor Museum of Regional History, Safety Harbor FL (M)

Sager Studios, Fort Worth TX (S)

Saginaw Art Museum, Saginaw MI (M,L)

Saginaw Valley State University, Dept of Art & Design, University Center MI (S)

Saidye Bronfman Centre for the Arts Centre, Montreal PQ (A)

Saint Ambrose University, Art Dept, Davenport IA (S)

Saint Andrews Presbyterian College, Art Program, Laurinburg NC (S)

Saint Anselm College, Chapel Art Center, Manchester NH (M)

Saint Anselm College, Dept of Fine Arts, Manchester NH (S)

Saint Augustine Art Association Gallery, Saint Augustine FL (A)

Saint Augustine Historical Society, Saint Augustine FL (M,L)

Saint Bernard Foundation & Monastery, North Miami Beach FL (M)

Saint Bonaventure University, Regina A Quick Fine Art Center, Saint Bonaventure NY (M)

Saint Clair County Community College, Jack R Hennesey Gallery, Art Dept, Port Huron MI (S)

Saint Clair County Community College, Jack R Hennesey Art Galleries, Port Huron MI (M)

Saint Cloud Community Arts Council, Saint Cloud MN (A)

Saint Cloud State University, Saint Cloud MN (M)

Saint Cloud State University, Dept of Art, Saint Cloud MN (S)

Saint Edward's University, Fine Arts Exhibit Program, Austin TX (M)

Saint Francis College, Art Dept, Fort Wayne IN (S)

Saint Francis College, John Weatherhead Gallery, Fort Wayne IN (M)

St Francis College, Fine Arts Dept, Loretto PA (S)

St Francis Xavier University, Fine Arts Dept, Antigonish NS (S)

Saint-Gaudens National Historic Site, Cornish NH (M,L)

St Genevieve Museum, Sainte Genevieve MO (M)

Saint Gregory's Abbey & College, Mabee-Gerrer Museum of Art, Shawnee OK (M)

Saint Gregory's College, Dept of Art, Shawnee OK (S)

Saint Johnsbury Athenaeum, Saint Johnsbury VT (M)

Saint John's College, Elizabeth Myers Mitchell Art Gallery, Annapolis MD (M)

Saint John's Museum of Art, Wilmington NC (M)

Saint John's University, Art Dept, Collegeville MN (S)

Saint John's University, Chung-Cheng Art Gallery, Jamaica NY (M,L)

Saint John's University, Dept of Fine Arts, Jamaica NY (S)

Saint Joseph College, Dept of Fine Arts, West Hartford CT (S)

Saint Joseph Museum, Saint Joseph MO (M,L)

Saint Joseph's Oratory, Museum, Montreal PQ (M,L)

Saint Joseph's University, Dept of Fine & Performing Arts, Philadelphia PA (S)

St Lawrence College, Dept of Visual & Creative Arts, Kingston ON (S)

St Lawrence College, Art Gallery, Kingston ON (M)

St Lawrence University, Richard F Brush Art Gallery, Canton NY (M)

St Lawrence University, Dept of Fine Arts, Canton NY (S)

Saint Louis Artists' Guild, Saint Louis MO (A)

The Saint Louis Art Museum, Saint Louis MO (M,L)

Saint Louis Community College at Florissant Valley, Liberal Arts Division, Ferguson MO (S)

Saint Louis Community College at Forest Park, Art Dept, Saint Louis MO (S)

Saint Louis Community College at Meramec, Art Dept, Saint Louis MO (S)

Saint Louis County Historical Society, Duluth MN (M)

Saint Louis Public Library, Saint Louis MO (L)

Saint Louis University, Fine & Performing Arts Dept, Saint Louis MO (S)

Saint Luke's Gallery, see Anna Maria College, Paxton MA

St Martins College, Humanities Dept, Lacey WA (S)

Saint Mary College, Art Program, Leavenworth KS (S)

Saint Mary-of-the-Woods College, Art Dept, Saint Mary-of-the-Woods IN (S)

Saint Mary's College, Dept of Art, Notre Dame IN (S)

Saint Mary's College, Moreau Galleries, Notre Dame IN (M)

Saint Mary's College, Art Dept, Raleigh NC (S)

Saint Mary's College of California, Hearst Art Gallery, Moraga CA (M)

St Mary's College of Maryland, The Dwight Frederick Boyden Gallery, Saint Mary City MD (M)

Saint Mary's College of Maryland, Art Dept, Saint Mary's City MD (S)

St Mary's Galeria, Orchard Lake MI (M)

Saint Mary's Romanian Orthodox Church, Romanian Ethnic Museum, Cleveland OH (M)
St Mary's University, Art Gallery, Halifax NS (M)
Saint Mary's University, Dept of Fine Arts, San Antonio TX (S)
Saint Mary's University of Minnesota, Art & Design Dept, Winona MN (S)
Saint Meinrad College, Humanities Dept, Saint Meinrad IN (S)
St Michael's College, Fine Arts Dept, Colchester VT (S)
Saint Norbert College, Division of Humanities & Fine Arts, De Pere WI (S)
Saint Olaf College, Art Dept, Northfield MN (S)
Saint Paul Public Library, Art, Music & Video Dept, Saint Paul MN (L)
Saint Paul's School, Art Center in Hargate, Concord NH (M,L)
Saint Petersburg Junior College, Humanities Dept, Saint Petersburg FL (S)
Saint Peter's College, Fine Arts Dept, Jersey City NJ (S)
Saint Peter's College, Art Gallery, Jersey City NJ (M)
St Tammany Art Association, Covington LA (A)
Saint Thomas Aquinas College, Art Dept, Sparkhill NY (S)
St Thomas Elgin Art Gallery, Saint Thomas ON (M)
Saint Xavier University, Dept of Art, Chicago IL (S)
Saint Xavier University, Byrne Memorial Library, Chicago IL (L)
Salem Art Association, Salem OR (A,M,L)
Salem College, Art Dept, Winston-Salem NC (S)
Salem State College, Art Dept, Salem MA (S)
Salina Art Center, Salina KS (M)
Salisbury House, see Iowa State Education Association, Des Moines IA
Salisbury State University, Art Dept, Salisbury MD (S)
Salisbury State University, Salisbury MD (M,L)
Salmagundi Club, New York NY (O)
Salt Lake Art Center, Salt Lake City UT (A)
Salt Lake City Public Library, Fine Arts/ Audiovisual Dept and Atrium Gallery, Salt Lake City UT (L)
Salt Lake Community College, Graphic Design Dept, Salt Lake City UT (S)
Salvador Dali Museum, Saint Petersburg FL (M,L)
Salve Regina University, Art Dept, Newport RI (S)
Ruth Salyer Library, see Art Institute of Southern California, Laguna Beach CA
Samford University, Art Dept, Birmingham AL (S)
Sam Houston State University, Art Dept, Huntsville TX (S)
Sampson Art Gallery, see Thiel College, Greenville PA
Philip Samuels Fine Art, see Trova Foundation, St Louis MO
San Angelo Art Club, Helen King Kendall Memorial Art Gallery, San Angelo TX (M)
San Angelo Museum of Fine Arts, San Angelo TX (M)
San Antonio Art League, San Antonio TX (A,L)
San Antonio College, Visual Arts & Technology, San Antonio TX (S)
San Antonio Museum of Art, San Antonio TX (M)
San Bernardino Art Association, Inc, San Bernardino CA (A)
San Bernardino County Museum, Fine Arts Institute, Redlands CA (M)
San Bernardino Valley College, Art Dept, San Bernardino CA (S)
San Carlos Cathedral, Monterey CA (M)
Hazel Sandford Gallery, see Clarion University, Clarion PA
San Diego Maritime Museum, San Diego CA (M)
San Diego Mesa College, Fine Arts Dept, San Diego CA (S)
San Diego Museum of Art, San Diego CA (M,L)
San Diego Public Library, Art & Music Section, San Diego CA (L)
San Diego State University, University Gallery, San Diego CA (M,L)
San Diego State University, School of Art, Design & Art History, San Diego CA (S)

Sandwich Historical Society, Center Sandwich NH (M)
The Sandwich Historical Society, Inc, Sandwich Glass Museum, Sandwich MA (M,L)
Sandy Bay Historical Society & Museums, Sewall Scripture House-Old Castle, Rockport MA (A)
Birger Sandzen Memorial Gallery, Lindsborg KS (M)
San Fernando Valley Historical Society, Mission Hills CA (A,L)
San Francisco Academy of Comic Art, Library, San Francisco CA (L)
San Francisco Art Commission, Gallery & Slide Registry, San Francisco CA (M)
San Francisco Art Institute, Galleries, San Francisco CA (M,L)
San Francisco Art Institute, San Francisco CA (S)
San Francisco Artspace & Artspace Annex, San Francisco CA (A)
San Francisco Camerawork Inc, San Francisco CA (A)
San Francisco City & County Art Commission, San Francisco CA (A)
San Francisco Craft & Folk Art Museum, San Francisco CA (M)
San Francisco Maritime National Historical Park, National Maritime Museum, San Francisco CA (M,L)
San Francisco Museum of Modern Art, San Francisco CA (M,L)
San Francisco Public Library, Art & Music Center, San Francisco CA (L)
San Francisco State University, Art Dept, San Francisco CA (S)
San Francisco State University, J Paul Leonard Library, San Francisco CA (L)
Sangre de Cristo Arts & Conference Center, Pueblo CO (A)
San Jacinto College-North, Art Dept, Houston TX (S)
San Jacinto Junior College, Division of Fine Arts, Deer Park TX (S)
San Joaquin Delta College, Art Dept, Stockton CA (S)
San Joaquin Pioneer & Historical Society, The Haggin Museum, Stockton CA (M,L)
San Jose City College, School of Fine Arts, San Jose CA (S)
San Jose Institute of Contemporary Art, San Jose CA (M)
San Jose Museum of Art, San Jose CA (M,L)
San Jose State University, San Jose CA (M,L)
San Jose State University, School of Art & Design, San Jose CA (S)
San Juan College, Art Dept, Farmington NM (S)
San Luis Obispo Art Center, San Luis Obispo CA (A)
San Mateo County Arts Council, Belmont CA (A)
Santa Barbara City College, Fine Arts Dept, Santa Barbara CA (S)
Santa Barbara Contemporary Arts Forum, Santa Barbara CA (A)
Santa Barbara Museum of Art, Santa Barbara CA (M,L)
Santa Barbara Public Library, Faulkner Memorial Art Wing, Santa Barbara CA (L)
Santa Clara University, de Saisset Museum, Santa Clara CA (M)
Santa Clara University, Art Dept, Santa Clara CA (S)
Santa Cruz Art League, Inc, Center for the Arts, Santa Cruz CA (A)
Santa Cruz Valley Art Association, Tubac Center of the Arts, Tubac AZ (A,L)
Santa Fe Arts Institute, Santa Fe NM (S)
Santa Monica College Art Gallery, Santa Monica CA (M)
Santarella, Tyringham's Gingerbread House, Tyringham MA (M)
Santa Rosa Junior College, Art Dept, Santa Rosa CA (S)
Santa Rosa Junior College, Santa Rosa CA (M)
Santuario de Guadalupe, see Guadalupe Historic Foundation, Santa Fe NM
Allen Sapp Gallery, North Battleford SK (M)
Sarah Lawrence College, Dept of Art History, Bronxville NY (S)

Sarah Lawrence College Library, Esther Raushenbush Library, Bronxville NY (L)
Sarasota Visual Art Center, Sarasota FL (A)
Saratoga County Historical Society, Brookside Museum, Ballston Spa NY (A)
Saskatchewan Arts Board, Regina SK (O)
Saskatchewan Association of Architects, Saskatoon SK (A)
Saskatchewan Craft Gallery, Saskatoon SK (M)
SaskPower, Gallery on the Roof, Regina SK (C)
Savannah State University, Dept of Fine Arts, Savannah GA (S)
Saving & Preserving Arts & Cultural Environments, Los Angeles CA (A,L)
Sawhill Gallery, see James Madison University, Harrisonburg VA
Sawtooth Center for Visual Art, Winston-Salem NC (S)
Sawyer Library, see Williams College, Williamstown MA
Scalamandre Museum of Textiles, New York NY (M)
Lee Scarfone Gallery, see University of Tampa, Tampa FL
Schenectady County Historical Society, Schenectady NY (A,L)
Schenectady Museum Planetarium & Visitors Center, Schenectady NY (M,L)
Mary R Schiff Library, see Cincinnati Museum Association, Cincinnati OH
Schingoethe Center for Native American Cultures, see Aurora University, Aurora IL
Schneider Museum of Art, see Southern Oregon State College, Ashland OR
Schoharie County Arts Council, Cobleskill NY (A)
Scholes Library of Ceramics, see New York State College of Ceramics at Alfred University, Alfred NY
Schomburg Center for Research in Black Culture, see The New York Public Library, New York NY
Schoolcraft College, Dept of Art & Design, Livonia MI (S)
School of American Research, Indian Arts Research Center, Santa Fe NM (M,L)
School of Art Institute of Chicago, Video Data Bank, Chicago IL (L)
School of Fashion Design, Boston MA (S)
School of Fine Arts, Visual Arts Dept, Willoughby OH (S)
School of Nations Museum, see Principia College, Elsah IL
School of the Art Institute of Chicago, Chicago IL (S)
School of the Art Institute of Chicago, John M Flaxman Library, Chicago IL (L)
School of the Art Institute of Chicago, Gallery 2, Chicago IL (M)
School of the Museum of Fine Arts, Boston MA (S)
School of Visual Arts, New York NY (S)
School of Visual Arts, Visual Arts Museum, New York NY (M)
School of Visual Arts Library, New York NY (L)
School 33 Art Center, Baltimore MD (A)
Schuler School of Fine Arts, Baltimore MD (S)
Schumacher Gallery, see Capital University, Columbus OH
Schuyler-Hamilton House, Morristown NJ (M)
Schuyler Mansion State Historic Site, Albany NY (M)
Schweinfurth Art Center, Auburn NY (M)
Agnes Scott College, Dalton Gallery, Decatur GA (M)
Scott Explorers Library, see Martin & Osa Johnson Safari Museum, Inc, Chanute KS
Scotts Bluff National Monument, see Oregon Trail Museum Association, Gering NE
Scottsdale Artists' League, Scottsdale AZ (A)
Scottsdale Artists' School, Scottsdale AZ (S)
Scottsdale Artists' School Library, Scottsdale AZ (L)
Scottsdale Center for the Arts, Scottsdale AZ (M)
The Charles H Scott Gallery, see Emily Carr Institute of Art & Design, Vancouver BC
Lucy Scribner Library, see Skidmore College, Saratoga Springs NY

Scripps College, Millard Sheets Art Center, Claremont CA (S)

Scripps College, Clark Humanities Museum, Claremont CA (M)

William E Scripture Memorial Library, see Rome Historical Society Museum, Rome NY

Sculptors Guild, Inc, New York NY (O)

Sculptor's Society of Canada, Toronto ON (O)

Sculpture Center Gallery & School, New York NY (S)

Sculpture Center School & Studios, New York NY (M,L)

Sculpture Chicago, Inc, Chicago IL (A)

Sculpture Space, Inc, Utica NY (M)

Joseph E Seagram & Sons, Inc, Gallery, New York NY (C)

The Seagram Museum, Waterloo ON (M,L)

Seaton Library, see Riley County Historical Society, Manhattan KS

Seaton Memorial Library, see Philmont Scout Ranch, Cimarron NM

Seattle Art Museum, Seattle WA (M,L)

Seattle Central Community College, Humanities - Social Sciences Division, Seattle WA (S)

Seattle Pacific University, Art Dept, Seattle WA (S)

Seattle University, Fine Arts Dept, Division of Art, Seattle WA (S)

2nd Crossing Arts Center, Valley City ND (M)

Second Street Gallery, Charlottesville VA (M)

Segue Foundation, Reading Room-Archive, New York NY (A)

Seigfred Gallery, see Ohio University, Athens OH

Self Help Graphics, Los Angeles CA (A)

Selsor Gallery of Art, see Martin & Osa Johnson Safari Museum, Inc, Chanute KS

Semitic Museum, see Harvard University, Cambridge MA

Senate House State Historic Site, see Palisades Interstate Park Commission, Kingston NY

Senator Wilson Home, see House of Roses, Deadwood SD

Seneca Falls Historical Society Museum, Seneca Falls NY (M)

Seneca-Iroquois National Museum, Salamanca NY (M)

Mary Porter Sesnon Art Gallery, see University of California at Santa Cruz, Santa Cruz CA

Seton Hall University, South Orange NJ (M,L)

Seton Hall University, College of Arts & Sciences, South Orange NJ (S)

Seton Hill College, Dept of Art, Greensburg PA (S)

Seton Hill College, Reeves Memorial Library, Greensburg PA (L)

1708 Gallery, Richmond VA (M)

Sewall Scripture House-Old Castle, see Sandy Bay Historical Society & Museums, Rockport MA

Seward County Community College, Art Dept, Liberal KS

SFA Gallery, see Stephen F Austin State University, Nacogdoches TX

Shadows-on-the-Teche, New Iberia LA (M)

Ben Shahn Galleries, see William Paterson College of New Jersey, Wayne NJ

The Shaker Library, see United Society of Shakers, New Glocester ME

Shaker Museum, see United Society of Shakers, New Glocester ME

Shaker Museum & Library, Old Chatham NY (M,L)

Shaker Village of Pleasant Hill, Harrodsburg KY (M)

Martin C Shallenberger Art Library, see Sweet Briar College, Sweet Briar VA

Sharadin Art Gallery, see Kutztown University, Kutztown PA

Sharon Arts Center, Peterborough NH (S)

Sharon Arts Center, Peterborough NH (M)

Ella Sharp Museum, Jackson MI (M)

Shasta College, Art Dept, Fine Arts Division, Redding CA (S)

Shasta Historical Society Research Library, see Redding Museum of Art & History, Redding CA

Lemuel Shattuck Memorial Library, see Bisbee Arts & Humanities Council, Bisbee AZ

Shawinigan Art Center, Shawinigan PQ (A)

J Porter Shaw Library, see San Francisco Maritime National Historical Park, San Francisco CA

Sheboygan Arts Foundation, Inc, John Michael Kohler Arts Center, Sheboygan WI (A)

Shelburne Museum, Shelburne VT (M,L)

Shelby Art League, Inc, Shelby NC (A)

Sheldon Memorial Art Gallery & Sculpture Garden, see University of Nebraska, Lincoln, Lincoln NE

Sheldon Museum, Middlebury VT (M)

Sheldon Museum & Cultural Center, see Chilkat Valley Historical Society, Haines AK

Shell Canada Ltd, Calgary AB (C)

Shepherd College, Art Dept, Shepherdstown WV (S)

Sheppard Fine Art Gallery, see University of Nevada, Reno NV

Sheridan College, School of Arts & Design, Oakville ON (S)

Sheridan College, Art Dept, Sheridan WY (S)

Sheridan College of Applied Arts and Technology, Trafalgar Campus Library, Oakville ON (L)

Sherman Art Library, see Dartmouth College, Hanover NH

C C Sherrod Library, see East Tennessee State University, Johnson City TN

Shiloh Museum, see City of Springdale, Springdale AR

Shippensburg University, Art Dept, Shippensburg PA (S)

Shippensburg University, Kauffman Gallery, Shippensburg PA (M)

Ships of The Sea Maritime Museum, Savannah GA (M,L)

Shirley Plantation, Charles City VA (M)

Shoreline Community College, Humanities Division, Seattle WA (S)

Shoreline Historical Museum, Seattle WA (M)

Shorncliffe Park Improvement Assoc, Prairie Panorama Museum, Czar AB (M)

Shorter College, Art Dept, Rome GA (S)

SIAS International Art Society, Sherwood Park AB (O)

Eli Siegel Collection, see Aesthetic Realism Foundation, New York NY

Siena College, Dept of Creative Arts, Loudonville NY (S)

Siena Heights College, Klemm Gallery, Studio Angelico, Adrian MI (M,L)

Siena Heights College, Studio Angelico-Art Dept, Adrian MI (S)

Sierra Arts Foundation, Reno NV (A)

Sierra Community College, Art Dept, Rocklin CA (S)

Sierra Nevada College, Visual & Performing Arts Dept, Incline Village NV (S)

Silverado Museum, Saint Helena CA (M,L)

Silver Eye Center for Photography, Pittsburgh PA (A)

Silver Lake College, Art Dept, Manitowoc WI (S)

Silvermine Guild Arts Center, Silvermine Galleries, New Canaan CT (M,L)

Simon Fraser University, Simon Fraser Gallery, Burnaby BC (M,L)

Norton Simon Museum, Pasadena CA (M)

Simon's Rock College of Bard, Great Barrington MA (M,L)

Simon's Rock College of Bard, Visual Arts Dept, Great Barrington MA (S)

Simpson College, Art Dept, Indianola IA (S)

Simpson College, Farnham Gallery, Indianola IA (M)

Sims Art Center, see Brevard College, Brevard NC

Sinclair Community College, Division of Fine & Performing Arts, Dayton OH (S)

Sioux City Art Center, Sioux City IA (A,L)

Sioux City Art Center, Sioux City IA (S)

Sioux Falls College, Dept of Art, Sioux Falls SD (S)

Sioux Indian Museum, see Indian Arts & Crafts Board, Rapid City SD

Sir Wilfred Grenfell College Art Gallery, see Memorial University of Newfoundland, Corner Brook NF

Sitka Historical Society, Isabel Miller Museum, Sitka AK (M)

Skagit Valley College, Dept of Art, Mount Vernon WA (S)

Skaneateles Library Association, Skaneateles NY (A)

Skidmore College, Schick Art Gallery, Saratoga Springs NY (M,L)

Skidmore College, Dept of Art & Art History, Saratoga Springs NY (S)

Skirball Cultural Center, see Hebrew Union College, Los Angeles CA

Skirball Museum-Cincinnati Branch, see Hebrew Union College - Jewish Institute of Religion, Cincinnati OH

Skokie Public Library, Skokie IL (L)

Skowhegan School of Painting & Sculpture, New York NY (S)

SLA Arch-Couture Inc, Art Collection, Denver CO (C)

Slater Memorial Museum & Converse Art Gallery, see Slater-Norton Corporation, Norwich CT

Slater Mill Historic Site, see Old Slater Mill Association, Pawtucket RI

Slater-Norton Corporation, Slater Memorial Museum & Converse Art Gallery, Norwich CT (M)

Slippery Rock University of Pennsylvania, Dept of Art, Slippery Rock PA (S)

Joseph Curtis Sloane Art Library, see University of North Carolina at Chapel Hill, Chapel Hill NC

Sloane-Stanley Museum, see Connecticut Historical Commission, Kent CT

Helen Farr Sloan Library, see Delaware Art Museum, Wilmington DE

Elizabeth Slocumb Galleries, see East Tennessee State University, Johnson City TN

Sloss Furnaces National Historic Landmark, Birmingham AL (M)

Slusser Gallery, see University of Michigan, Ann Arbor MI

David & Alfred Smart Museum of Art, see University of Chicago, Chicago IL

Abigail Adams Smith Museum, New York NY (M)

C E Smith Museum of Anthropology, see California State University, Hayward, Hayward CA

Smith College, Museum of Art, Northampton MA (M,L)

Smith College, Art Dept, Northampton MA (S)

Eloisa Pickard Smith Gallery, see University of California at Santa Cruz, Santa Cruz CA

George Walter Vincent Smith Art Museum, Springfield MA (M)

Smithsonian Institution, Washington DC (M)

Snake River Heritage Center, Weiser ID (M)

Gordon Snelgrove Art Gallery, see University of Saskatchewan, Saskatoon SK

Snite Museum of Art, see University of Notre Dame, Notre Dame IN

Snow College, Art Dept, Ephraim UT (S)

Snug Harbor Cultural Center, Newhouse Center for Contemporary Art, Staten Island NY (M)

Social & Public Art Resource Center, (SPARC), Venice CA (A)

Societe des Musees Quebecois, Montreal PQ (A,L)

Society For Commercial Archeology, see National Museum of American History, Washington DC

Society for Folk Arts Preservation, Inc, New York NY (O)

Society for Photographic Education, Dallas TX (A)

Society for the Preservation of New England Antiquities, Boston MA (A,L)

Society for the Protection & Preservation of Black Culture in Nova Scotia, Black Cultural Center for Nova Scotia, Dartmouth NS (L)

Society of American Graphic Artists, New York NY (O)

Society of American Historical Artists, Osterbay NY (O)

Society of Architectural Historians, Chicago IL (O)

The Society of Arts & Crafts, Boston MA (A)

Society of Canadian Artists, Toronto ON (O)

Society of Illustrators, New York NY (O)

Society of Illustrators, Museum of American Illustration, New York NY (M)

Society of Layerists in Multi Media (SLMM), Albuquerque NM (A)

Society of North American Goldsmiths, Tampa FL (O)

Society of Photographers & Artists Representatives, New York NY (O)

Society of Scribes, Ltd, New York NY (A)

Society of the Cincinnati, Museum & Library at Anderson House, Washington DC (M)

The Society of the Four Arts, Palm Beach FL (A,L)

Socrates Sculpture Park, Long Island City NY (M)

State of Hawaii, Dept of Land & Natural Resources, Wailoa Visitor Center, Hilo HI (M)
State Street Corporation, Concourse Gallery, Boston MA (C)
State University College at Buffalo, Fine Arts Dept, Buffalo NY (S)
State University College at Fredonia, Dept of Art, Fredonia NY (S)
State University of New York, SUNY Plattsburgh Art Museum, Plattsburgh NY (M)
State University of New York, Agricultural & Technical College, Art Dept, Cobleskill NY (S)
State University of New York at Albany, Art Dept, Albany NY (S)
State University of New York at Binghamton, Dept of Art History, Binghamton NY (S)
State University of New York at Binghamton, University Art Gallery, Vestal NY (M)
State University of New York at Farmingdale, Advertising Art Design Dept, Farmingdale NY (S)
State University of New York at Geneseo, Bertha V B Lederer Gallery, Geneseo NY (M)
State University of New York at New Paltz, College Art Gallery, New Paltz NY (M,L)
State University of New York at Oswego, Tyler Art Gallery, Oswego NY (M,L)
State University of New York at Plattsburgh, Art Dept, Plattsburgh NY (S)
State University of New York at Purchase, Neuberger Museum of Art, Purchase NY (M,L)
State University of New York at Stony Brook, University Art Gallery, Stony Brook NY (M)
State University of New York at Stony Brook, Art Dept, Stony Brook NY (S)
State University of New York College at Brockport, Dept of Art, Brockport NY (S)
State University of New York, College at Brockport, Tower Fine Arts Gallery, Brockport NY (M)
State University of New York College at Cortland, Art Slide Library, Cortland NY (L)
State University of New York, College at Cortland, Art Dept, Cortland NY (S)
State University of New York College at Fredonia, M C Rockefeller Arts Center Gallery, Fredonia NY (M)
State University of New York College at Geneseo, Dept of Art, Geneseo NY (S)
State University of New York College at New Paltz, New Paltz NY (S)
State University of New York College at Old Westbury, Visual Arts Dept, Old Westbury NY (S)
State University of New York College at Old Westbury, Amelie A Wallace Gallery, Old Westbury NY (M)
State University of New York College at Oneonta, Dept of Art, Oneonta NY (S)
State University of New York College at Oneonta, Art Gallery & Sculpture Court, Oneonta NY (M)
State University of New York College at Oswego, Art Dept, Oswego NY (S)
State University of New York College at Potsdam, Dept of Fine Arts, Potsdam NY (S)
State University of New York College at Purchase, Purchase NY (S)
State University of West Georgia, Art Dept, Carrollton GA (S)
Staunton Fine Arts Association, Staunton Augusta Art Center, Staunton VA (A)
Stedman Art Gallery, see Rutgers University, Camden NJ
T C Steele State Historic Site, Nashville IN (M)
Steep & Brew Gallery, Madison WI (M)
Stephen Bulger Gallery, Toronto ON (M)
Stephen F Austin State University, Art Dept, Nacogdoches TX (S)
Stephen F Austin State University, SFA Gallery, Nacogdoches TX (M)
Stephens College, Lewis James & Nellie Stratton Davis Art Gallery, Columbia MO (M)
Stephens College, Art & Fashion Dept, Columbia MO (S)
Stephens Gallery, see University of the Ozarks, Clarksville AR
Sterling College, Art Dept, Sterling KS (S)
Sterling Portfolio Inc, New York NY (C)

Stetson University, Duncan Gallery of Art, De Land FL (M)
Stetson University, Art Dept, De Land FL (S)
Florine Stettheimer Library, see Fisk University, Nashville TN
Steuben House Museum, see Bergen County Historical Society, River Edge NJ
Stevenson Academy of Traditional Painting, Sea Cliff NY (S)
Stevenson Union Gallery, see Southern Oregon State College, Ashland OR
David M Stewart Museum, Montreal PQ (M,L)
Stewart Hall Art Gallery, see Pointe Claire Cultural Centre, Pointe Claire PQ
Stewart Memorial Library & Gallery, see Coe College, Cedar Rapids IA
Stifel Fine Arts Center, see Oglebay Institute, Wheeling WV
Stillman College, Stillman Art Gallery & Art Dept, Tuscaloosa AL (S)
Storefront for Art & Architecture, New York NY (M)
Storm King Art Center, Mountainville NY (M)
Anna Eaton Stout Memorial Art Gallery, see Brescia College, Owensboro KY
Stout Reference Library, see Indianapolis Museum of Art, Indianapolis IN
Harriet Beecher Stowe Center, Hartford CT (A,L)
Stoxen Library, see Dickinson State University, Dickinson ND
Strasburg Museum, Strasburg VA (M)
Stratford Art Association, The Gallery Stratford, Stratford ON (M)
Stratford Historical Society, Katherine Mitchel Museum, Stratford CT (M,L)
Stratton Library, see Alaska Department of Education, Division of Libraries, Archives & Museums, Sitka AK
G Robert Strauss Jr Memorial Library, see The Buffalo Fine Arts Academy, Buffalo NY
David Strawn Art Gallery, see Art Association of Jacksonville, Jacksonville IL
Kate Strong Historical Library, see The Museums at Stony Brook, Stony Brook NY
Strong Museum, Rochester NY (M)
Stroud Wright Associates, Winnetka IL (C)
Struts Gallery, Sackville NB (M)
Stuart Collection, see University of California, San Diego, La Jolla CA
Studio Gallery, Washington DC (M)
The Studio Museum in Harlem, New York NY (M)
Studio San Giuseppe, see College of Mount Saint Joseph, Cincinnati OH
Studio 24, see Galeria de la Raza, San Francisco CA
Sturdivant Hall, Selma AL (M)
Suffolk County Community College, Art Dept, Selden NY (S)
Suggett House Museum, see Cortland County Historical Society, Cortland NY
Sullivan County Community College, Division of Commercial Art & Photography, Loch Sheldrake NY (S)
Sul Ross State University, Dept of Fine Arts & Communications, Alpine TX (S)
Summit County Historical Society, Akron OH (M)
Sumter Gallery of Art, Sumter SC (M)
SunAmerica, Inc, The SunAmerica-Kaufman & Broad Home Corporation Collection, Los Angeles CA (C)
The SunAmerica-Kaufman & Broad Home Corporation Collection, see SunAmerica, Inc, Los Angeles CA
Sunbury Shores Arts & Nature Centre, Inc, Gallery, Saint Andrews NB (A,L)
Sun Gallery, see Hayward Area Forum of the Arts, Hayward CA
Sunrise Museum, Inc, Sunrise Art Museum & Sunrise Science Museum, Charleston WV (M)
Sun Valley Center for the Arts & Humanities, Dept of Fine Art, Sun Valley ID (S)
SUNY Plattsburgh Art Museum, see State University of New York, Plattsburgh NY
Suomi International College of Art & Design, Fine Arts Dept, Hancock MI (S)
Supreme Court of the United States, Washington DC (M)
Surface Design Association, Inc, Oakland CA (A)

Surrey Art Gallery, Surrey BC (M,L)
Surry Community College, Art Dept, Dobson NC (S)
Sushi-Performance & Visual Art Gallery, San Diego CA (M)
Susquehanna University, Lore Degenstein Gallery, Selinsgrove PA (M)
SVACA - Sheyenne Valley Arts & Crafts Association, Bjarne Ness Gallery at Bear Creek Hall, Fort Ransom ND (M)
Swarthmore College, Friends Historical Library of Swathmore College, Swarthmore PA (L)
Swarthmore College, Dept of Art, Swarthmore PA (S)
Swedish American Museum Association of Chicago, Chicago IL (M)
Sweet Briar College, Martin C Shallenberger Art Library, Sweet Briar VA (L,M)
Sweet Briar College, Art History Dept, Sweet Briar VA (S)
Swift Current National Exhibition Centre, Swift Current SK (M)
Swirbul Library Gallery, see Adelphi University, Garden City NY
Swiss Institute, New York NY (M)
Sheldon Swope Art Museum, Terre Haute IN (M,L)
Swords Info Plowshares Peace Center & Gallery, see Central United Methodist Church, Detroit MI
Sylvia Plotkin Judaica, see Temple Beth Israel, Phoenix AZ
Symmes Systems, Photographic Investments Gallery, Atlanta GA (M)
Synagogue Art & Architectural Library, see Union of American Hebrew Congregations, New York NY
Syracuse University, Syracuse NY (M,L)
Syracuse University, Syracuse NY (S)
Tabor Opera House Museum, Leadville CO (M)
Tacoma Art Museum, Tacoma WA (M,L)
Tacoma Arts Commission, Commencement Art Gallery, Tacoma WA (M)
Tacoma Community College, Art Dept, Tacoma WA (S)
Tacoma Public Library, Handforth Gallery, Tacoma WA (L)
Taft College, Art Department, Taft CA (S)
Lorado Taft Midway Studios, see University of Chicago, Chicago IL
Taft Museum, see Cincinnati Institute of Fine Arts, Cincinnati OH
Taipei Economic & Cultural Office, Chinese Information & Culture Center Library, New York NY (L)
Tallahassee Community College, Art Dept, Tallahassee FL (S)
Tallahassee Museum of History & Natural Science, Tallahassee FL (M,L)
Tamarind Institute, see University of New Mexico, Albuquerque NM (S)
Tampa Museum of Art, Tampa FL (M,L)
Taos Art Association Inc, Stables Art Center, Taos NM (A)
Taos Public Library, Taos NM (L)
Tarble Arts Center, see Eastern Illinois University, Charleston IL
Tarrant County Junior College, Art Dept, Hurst TX (S)
Tattoo Art Museum, San Francisco CA (M)
Edward P Taylor Research Library & Archives, see Art Gallery of Ontario, Toronto ON
Elizabeth Prewitt Taylor Memorial Library, see Arkansas Arts Center, Little Rock AR
Taylor University, Chronicle-Tribune Art Gallery, Upland IN (M)
Taylor University, Art Dept, Upland IN (S)
Technical University of Nova Scotia, Faculty of Architecture, Halifax NS (S)
Teikyo Marycrest University, Art & Computer Graphics Dept, Davenport IA (S)
Teikyo Westmar University, Westmar Art Gallery, LeMars IA (M,L)
Teikyo Westmar University, Art Dept, LeMars IA (S)
Telfair Museum of Art, Savannah GA (M,L)
Temiskaming Art Gallery, Haileybury ON (M)
Tempe Arts Center, Tempe AZ (A)

Temple Beth Israel, Sylvia Plotkin Judaica, Phoenix AZ (M)

Temple College, Art Dept, Temple TX (S)

The Temple-Tifereth Israel, The Temple Museum of Religious Art, Beachwood OH (M,L)

Temple University, Elkins PA (M,L)

Temple University, Tyler School of Art, Philadelphia PA (S)

Tennent Art Foundation Gallery, Honolulu HI (M,L)

Tennessee Historical Society, Nashville TN (A)

Tennessee State Museum, Nashville TN (M,L)

Tennessee Valley Art Association & Center, Tuscumbia AL (A)

1078 Gallery, Chico CA (M)

Te Paske Gallery, see Northwestern College, Orange City IA

Terrain Gallery, see Aesthetic Realism Foundation, New York NY

Terra Museum of American Art, Chicago IL (M,L)

Sandor Teszler Library Gallery, see Wofford College, Spartanburg SC

Texarkana College, Art Dept, Texarkana TX (S)

Texas A&M University, College of Architecture, College Station TX (S)

Texas A&M University, J Wayne Stark University Center Galleries, College Station TX (M,A)

Texas A&M University, Art Gallery, Kingsville TX (M)

Texas A&M University - Commerce, University Gallery, Commerce TX (M)

Texas A&M University-Corpus Christi, Weil Art Gallery, Corpus Christi TX (M)

Texas A&M University-Kingsville, Art Dept, Kingsville TX (S)

Texas Christian University, Moudy Exhibition Hall, Fort Worth TX (M)

Texas Christian University, Art & Art History Dept, Fort Worth TX (S)

Texas Fine Arts Association, Austin TX (A)

Texas Lutheran College, Dept of Visual Arts, Seguin TX (S)

Texas Ranger Hall of Fame & Museum, Waco TX (M,L)

Texas Southern University, Dept of Fine Arts, Houston TX (S)

Texas Tech University, Museum, Lubbock TX (M,L)

Texas Tech University, Dept of Art, Lubbock TX (S)

Texas Wesleyan University, Dept of Art, Fort Worth TX (S)

Texas Woman's University, Dept of Visual Arts, Denton TX (S)

Texas Woman's University Art Gallery, Denton TX (M)

Textile Arts Centre, Chicago IL (M,L)

Textile Arts Centre, Chicago IL (S)

Textile Museum, Washington DC (M,L)

Thames Art Gallery, see Chatham Cultural Centre, Chatham ON

Thiel College, Sampson Art Gallery, Greenville PA (M)

Thiel College, Dept of Art, Greenville PA (S)

Thomas Center Galleries - Cultural Affairs, see City of Gainesville, Gainesville FL

Thomas College, Humanities Division, Thomasville GA (S)

Thomas College Art Gallery, Waterville ME (M,L)

Thomas More College, TM Gallery, Crestview KY (M)

Thomas More College, Art Dept, Crestview Hills KY (S)

Nancy Thompson Library, see Kean College of New Jersey, Union NJ

Thompson-Pell Research Center, see Fort Ticonderoga Association, Ticonderoga NY

Tom Thomson Memorial Art Gallery, Owen Sound ON (M,L)

Thorne-Sagendorph Art Gallery, see Keene State College, Keene NH

Thornhill Art Gallery, see Avila College, Kansas City MO

Harry Thornton Library, see Pensacola Museum of Art, Pensacola FL

Thousand Islands Craft School & Textile Museum, Clayton NY (S)

Thread Waxing Space, New York NY (M)

3M, Art Collection, Saint Paul MN (C)

Tidewater Community College, Art Dept, Portsmouth VA (S)

Louis Comfort Tiffany Foundation, New York NY (A)

Times Mirror Company, Los Angeles CA (C)

Timken Museum of Art, San Diego CA (M)

Tippecanoe County Historical Museum, Lafayette IN (M,L)

TM Gallery, see Thomas More College, Crestview KY

Toledo Artists' Club, Toledo OH (A)

Toledo Museum of Art, Toledo OH (A)

Toledo Museum of Art, Toledo OH (M,L)

Melvin B Tolson Black Heritage Center, see Langston University, Langston OK

Tongass Historical Museum, Ketchikan AK (M)

Topeka & Shawnee County Public Library, Gallery of Fine Arts, Topeka KS (M)

Helen Topping Architecture & Fine Arts Library, see University of Southern California, Los Angeles CA

Toronto Art Therapy Institute, Toronto ON (S)

Toronto Dominion Bank, Toronto ON (C)

Toronto Historical Board, Historic Fort York, Toronto ON (A)

Toronto School of Art, Toronto ON (S)

Toronto Sculpture Garden, Toronto ON (M)

Totem Heritage Center, Ketchikan AK (M,L)

Touchstone Center for Crafts, Farmington PA (A)

Touchstone Center for Crafts, Farmington PA (S)

Tougaloo College, Tougaloo MS (M,L)

Tougaloo College, Art Dept, Tougaloo MS (S)

Tower Fine Arts Gallery, see State University of New York, College at Brockport, Brockport NY

Tower Gallery, see Mount Mary College, Milwaukee WI

Town of Cummington Historical Commission, Kingman Tavern Historical Museum, Cummington MA (M)

Towson State University, Towson MD (M)

Towson State University, Dept of Art, Towson MD (S)

Tradd Street Press, Elizabeth O'Neill Verner Studio Museum, Charleston SC (M)

Margaret Fort Trahern Gallery, see Austin Peay State University, Clarksville TN

Trail of '98 Museum, Skagway AK (M)

Transco Energy Company Inc, Transco Gallery, Houston TX (C)

Transylvania University, Morlan Gallery, Lexington KY (M)

Transylvania University, Studio Arts Dept, Lexington KY (S)

Treasure Valley Community College, Art Dept, Ontario OR (S)

Trenton City Museum, Trenton NJ (M)

Scott Andrew Trexler II Library, see Lehigh County Historical Society, Allentown PA

Triangle Gallery of Visual Arts, see Calgary Contemporary Arts Society, Calgary AB

Trinity College, Austin Arts Center, Hartford CT (M)

Trinity College, Dept of Fine Arts, Hartford CT (S)

Trinity College, Art Program, Washington DC (S)

Trinity College Library, Washington DC (L)

Trinity University, Dept of Art, San Antonio TX (S)

Triton College, School of Arts & Sciences, River Grove IL (S)

Triton Museum of Art, Santa Clara CA (M,L)

Trout Gallery, see Dickinson College, Carlisle PA

Trova Foundation, Philip Samuels Fine Art, St Louis MO (M)

Troy State University, Dept of Art & Classics, Troy AL (S)

Truett-McConnell College, Fine Arts Dept & Arts Dept, Cleveland GA (S)

Truman College, see City Colleges of Chicago, Chicago IL (S)

Harry S Truman Library, see National Archives & Records Administration, Independence MO

Truman State University, Art Dept, Kirksville MO (S)

Truro Center for the Arts at Castle Hill, Inc, Truro MA (S)

The Trustees of Reservations, The Mission House, Stockbridge MA (M)

Sojourner Truth Library, see State University of New York at New Paltz, New Paltz NY

Tryon Palace Historic Sites & Gardens, New Bern NC (M,L)

Tubac Center of the Arts, see Santa Cruz Valley Art Association, Tubac AZ

Tubman African American Museum, Macon GA (M,L)

Tucson Museum of Art & Historic Block, Tucson AZ (M,L)

Tucson Museum of Art School, Tucson AZ (S)

Tufts University, Art Gallery, Medford MA (M)

Tufts University, Dept of Art & Art History, Medford MA (S)

Tulane University, New Orleans LA (S)

Tulane University, New Orleans LA (M,L)

Tulsa Junior College, Art Dept, Tulsa OK (S)

Tunxis Community College, Graphic Design Dept, Farmington CT (S)

Turman Art Gallery, see Indiana State University, Terre Haute IN

Turner House Museum, Hattiesburg MS (M)

Janet Turner Print Gallery & Collection, see California State University, Chico, Chico CA

The Turner Museum, Denver CO (M)

Turtle Mountain Chippewa Historical Society, Turtle Mountain Heritage Center, Belcourt ND (M,L)

Turtle Mountain Heritage Center, see Turtle Mountain Chippewa Historical Society, Belcourt ND

Tusculum College, Fine Arts Dept, Greeneville TN (S)

Tuskegee Institute National Historic Site, George Washington Carver & The Oaks, Tuskegee Institute AL (M)

Tuskegee University, Liberal Arts & Education, Tuskegee AL (S)

Mark Twain Memorial, Hartford CT (M,L)

Tweed Museum of Art, see University of Minnesota, Duluth, Duluth MN

Twin City Art Foundation, Masur Museum of Art, Monroe LA (M)

Tyler Art Gallery, see State University of New York at Oswego, Oswego NY

Tyler Junior College, Art Program, Tyler TX (S)

Tyler Museum of Art, Tyler TX (M,L)

Tyler School of Art, see Temple University, Philadelphia PA (S)

Tyler School of Art-Galleries, see Temple University, Elkins PA

Tyler School of Art Library, see Temple University, Elkins PA

Tyringham's Gingerbread House, see Santarella, Tyringham MA

UCLA at the Armand Hammer Museum of Art & Cultural Center, see University of California, Los Angeles, Los Angeles CA

Ucross Foundation, Big Red Barn Gallery, Clearmont WY (M)

Ukiyo-e Society of America, Inc, New York NY (O)

Ukrainian Canadian Archives & Museum of Alberta, Edmonton AB (M)

Ukrainian Cultural & Educational Centre, Winnipeg MB (M,L)

Ukrainian Institute of America, Inc, New York NY (A)

The Ukrainian Museum, New York NY (M,L)

Ukrainian National Museum & Library, Chicago IL (M)

Doris Ulmann Galleries, see Berea College, Berea KY

Edwin A Ulrich Museum of Art, see Wichita State University, Wichita KS

Ulster County Community College, Dept of Visual Arts, Stone Ridge NY (S)

Ulster County Community College, Muroff-Kotler Visual Arts Gallery, Stone Ridge NY (M)

UMB Financial Corporation, Kansas City MO (C)

UMLAUF Sculpture Garden & Museum, Austin TX (M)

Umpqua Community College, Fine & Performing Arts Dept, Roseburg OR (S)

Unaffiliated Artists File, see Artists Space, New York NY

Union College, Art Dept, Barbourville KY (S)

Union College, Dept of Visual Arts, Schenectady NY (S)

Union County Public Library Union Room, Monroe NC (M)

Union of American Hebrew Congregations, Synagogue Art & Architectural Library, New York NY (L)

Union Pacific Railroad, Historical Museum, Omaha NE (M)

Union Station Museums, see Ogden Union Station, Ogden UT

Union University, Dept of Art, Jackson TN (S)

United Methodist Historical Society, Lovely Lane Museum, Baltimore MD (M,L)

United Society of Shakers, Shaker Museum, New Glocester ME (M,L)

United States Capitol, Architect of the Capitol, Washington DC (M)

US Coast Guard Museum, New London CT (M)

United States Commission of Fine Arts, Washington DC (A)

US Department of State, Diplomatic Reception Rooms, Washington DC (M)

United States Department of the Interior, Indian Arts & Crafts Board, Washington DC (O)

United States Department of the Interior Museum, Washington DC (M)

United States Figure Skating Association, World Figure Skating Museum & Hall of Fame, Colorado Springs CO (M,L)

United States Military Academy, West Point Museum, West Point NY (M)

United States Naval Academy Museum, Annapolis MD (M,L)

United States Navy, Art Gallery, Washington DC (M)

US Navy Supply Corps School, US Navy Supply Corps Museum, Athens GA (M)

United States Senate Commission on Art, Washington DC (A,L)

United States Tobacco Manufacturing Company Inc, Museum of Tobacco Art History, Nashville TN (C)

United Westurne Inc, Art Collection, Montreal PQ (C)

Universal Technical Institute, Commercial Art Division, Omaha NE (S)

Universite de Moncton, Dept of Visual Arts, Moncton NB (S)

Universite de Moncton, Campus d'Edmundston, Dept of Visual Arts, Edmundston NB (S)

Universite de Montreal, Bibliotheque d'Amenagement, Montreal PQ (L)

Universite de Montreal, Dept of Art History, Montreal PQ (S)

Universite du Quebec, Bibliotheque des Arts, Montreal PQ (L)

Universite du Quebec a Montreal, Famille des Arts, Montreal PQ (S)

Universite Laval Cite Universitaire, School of Visual Arts, Quebec PQ (S)

University Art Gallery of California State University at Dominguez Hills, Dominguez Hills CA (M)

University at Albany, State University of New York, University Art Museum, Albany NY (M,L)

University at Buffalo, State University of New York, Fine Arts Dept, Buffalo NY (S)

University Club Library, New York NY (L)

University Gallery, see Louisiana State University at Alexandria, Alexandria LA

University of Akron, Akron OH (M)

University of Akron, School of Art, Akron OH (S)

University of Alabama, Sarah Moody Gallery of Art, Tuscaloosa AL (M)

University of Alabama, Art Dept, Tuscaloosa AL (S)

University of Alabama at Birmingham, Dept of Art, Birmingham AL (S)

University of Alabama at Birmingham, Visual Arts Gallery, Birmingham AL (M)

University of Alabama at Huntsville, Gallery of Art, Huntsville AL (M)

University of Alabama in Huntsville, Dept of Art & Art History, Huntsville AL (S)

University of Alaska, Fairbanks AK (M,L)

University of Alaska Anchorage, Dept of Art, Anchorage AK (S)

University of Alaska-Fairbanks, Dept of Art, Fairbanks AK (S)

University of Alberta, Dept of Art & Design, Edmonton AB (S)

University of Arizona, Tucson AZ (M,L)

University of Arizona, Dept of Art, Tucson AZ (S)

University of Arkansas, Fayetteville AR (L)

University of Arkansas, Art Dept, Fayetteville AR (S)

University of Arkansas, Art Slide Library, Little Rock AR (L)

University of Arkansas at Little Rock, Fine Arts Galleries, Little Rock AR (S)

University of Arkansas at Monticello, Fine Arts Dept, Monticello AR (S)

University of Arkansas at Pine Bluff, Art Dept, Pine Bluff AR (S)

University of Bridgeport, School of Arts, Humanities & Social Sciences, Bridgeport CT (S)

University of Bridgeport Gallery, Bridgeport CT (M)

University of British Columbia, Vancouver BC (M,L)

University of British Columbia, Vancouver BC (S)

University of Calgary, The Nickle Arts Museum, Calgary AB (M,L)

University of Calgary, Dept of Art, Calgary AB (S)

University of California, Berkeley CA (M,L)

University of California, Davis CA (M,L)

University of California, Riverside CA (M,L)

University of California at Santa Cruz, Santa Cruz CA (M)

University of California, Berkeley, Berkeley CA (S)

University of California, Davis, Art Dept, Davis CA (S)

University of California, Irvine, Fine Art Gallery, Irvine CA (M)

University of California, Irvine, Studio Art Dept, Irvine CA (S)

University of California, Los Angeles, Los Angeles CA (S)

University of California, Los Angeles, Los Angeles CA (M,L)

University of California, Riverside, Riverside CA (S)

University of California-San Diego, University Art Gallery, La Jolla CA (M)

University of California, San Diego, Visual Arts Dept, La Jolla CA (S)

University of California, San Diego, Art & Architecture Library, La Jolla CA (L)

University of California, San Diego, Stuart Collection, La Jolla CA (M)

University of California, Santa Barbara, Dept of Art Studio, Santa Barbara CA (S)

University of California, Santa Barbara, Santa Barbara CA (M,L)

University of California, Santa Cruz, Board of Studies in Art, Santa Cruz CA (S)

University of Central Arkansas, Art Dept, Conway AR (S)

University of Central Florida, Art Dept, Orlando FL (S)

University of Central Oklahoma, Dept of Visual Arts & Design, Edmond OK (S)

University of Charleston, Carleton Varney Dept of Art & Design, Charleston WV (S)

University of Chicago, Chicago IL (M,L)

University of Chicago, Dept of Art History & Committee on Art & Design, Chicago IL (S)

University of Cincinnati, Cincinnati OH (M,L)

University of Cincinnati, School of Art, Cincinnati OH (S)

University of Colorado, Art Galleries, Boulder CO (M,L)

University of Colorado at Colorado Springs, Gallery of Contemporary Art, Colorado Springs CO (M)

University of Colorado at Denver, Dept of Fine Arts, Denver CO (S)

University of Colorado, Boulder, Dept of Fine Arts, Boulder CO (S)

University of Colorado-Colorado Springs, Fine Arts Dept, Colorado Springs CO (S)

University of Connecticut, Storrs CT (M,L)

University of Connecticut, Dept of Art & Art History, Storrs CT (S)

University of Dayton, Visual Arts Dept, Dayton OH (S)

University of Delaware, Dept of Art, Newark DE (S)

University of Delaware, Newark DE (M,L)

University of Denver, School of Art & Art History, Denver CO (S)

University of Detroit Mercy, School of Architecture, Detroit MI (S)

University of Evansville, Evansville IN (M,L)

University of Evansville, Art Dept, Evansville IN (S)

University of Findlay, Egner Fine Arts Center, Findlay OH (M)

University of Findlay, Art Dept, Findlay OH (S)

University of Florida, Gainesville FL (M,L)

University of Florida, Dept of Art, Gainesville FL (S)

University of Georgia, Athens GA (M,L)

University of Georgia, Franklin College of Arts & Sciences, Lamar Dodd School of Art, Athens GA (S)

University of Guelph, Fine Art Dept, Guelph ON (S)

University of Hartford, Hartford Art School, West Hartford CT (S)

University of Hartford, Joseloff Gallery, West Hartford CT (M,L)

University of Hartford, Mortensen Library, West Hartford CT (L)

University of Hawaii, Kapiolani Community College, Honolulu HI (S)

University of Hawaii at Manoa, Art Gallery, Honolulu HI (M)

University of Hawaii at Manoa, Dept of Art, Honolulu HI (S)

University of Houston, Sarah Campbell Blaffer Gallery, Houston TX (M,L)

University of Houston, Dept of Art, Houston TX (S)

University of Idaho, College of Art & Architecture, Moscow ID (S)

University of Illinois, Champaign IL (M,L)

University of Illinois at Chicago, College of Architecture, Chicago IL (S)

University of Illinois At Chicago, Gallery 400, Chicago IL (M)

University of Illinois at Springfield, Visual Arts Program, Springfield IL (S)

University of Illinois, Chicago, Health Science Center, Biomedical Visualizations, Chicago IL (S)

University of Illinois, Urbana-Champaign, College of Fine & Applied Arts, Champaign IL (S)

University of Indianapolis, Christel DeHaan Fine Arts Gallery, Indianapolis IN (M)

University of Indianapolis, Art Dept, Indianapolis IN (S)

University of Iowa, School of Art & Art History, Iowa City IA (S)

University of Iowa, Iowa City IA (M,L)

University of Judaism, Dept of Continuing Education, Los Angeles CA (S)

University of Kansas, Spencer Museum of Art, Lawrence KS (M,L)

University of Kansas, School of Fine Arts, Lawrence KS (S)

University of Kentucky, Lexington KY (M,L)

University of Kentucky, Dept of Art, Lexington KY (S)

University of Kentucky, Hunter M Adams Architecture Library, Lexington KY (L)

University of La Verne, Dept of Art, La Verne CA (S)

University of Lethbridge, Div of Art, Lethbridge AB (S)

University of Lethbridge, Art Gallery, Lethbridge AB (M)

University of Louisville, Louisville KY (M,L)

University of Louisville, Allen R Hite Art Institute, Louisville KY (S)

University of Maine, Museum of Art, Orono ME (M)

University of Maine, Dept of Art, Orono ME (S)

University of Maine at Augusta, Jewett Hall Gallery, Augusta ME (M)

University of Maine at Augusta, Division of Fine & Performing Arts, Augusta ME (S)

University of Manitoba, Gallery III, Winnipeg MB (M,L)

University of Manitoba, Winnipeg MB (S)

University of Texas at Arlington, Center for Research & Contemporary Arts, Arlington TX (M)

University of Texas at Arlington, Dept of Art & Art History, Arlington TX (S)

University of Texas at Austin, Austin TX (L,M)

University of Texas at Brownsville & Texas Southmost College, Fine Arts Dept, Brownsville TX (S)

University of Texas at El Paso, Glass Gallery, El Paso TX (M)

University of Texas at El Paso, Dept of Art, El Paso TX (S)

University of Texas at San Antonio, Division of Visual Arts, San Antonio TX (S)

University of Texas at Tyler, Dept of Art, Tyler TX (S)

University of Texas of Permian Basin, Dept of Art, Odessa TX (S)

University of Texas Pan American, Art Dept, Edinburg TX (S)

University of the Arts, Philadelphia PA (M,L)

University of the Arts, Philadelphia College of Art & Design, Philadelphia PA (S)

University of the District of Columbia, Dept of Mass Media, Visual & Performing Arts, Washington DC (S)

University of the Ozarks, Clarksville AR (L,M)

University of the Ozarks, Dept of Art, Clarksville AR (S)

University of the Pacific, Stockton CA (M)

University of the Pacific, College of the Pacific, Dept of Art & Art History, Stockton CA (S)

University of the South, University Gallery, Sewanee TN (M)

University of the South, Dept of Fine Arts, Sewanee TN (S)

University of Toledo, Dept of Art, Toledo OH (S)

University of Toronto, Toronto ON (M,L)

University of Toronto, Toronto ON (S)

University of Tulsa, School of Art, Tulsa OK (S)

University of Tulsa, Alexandre Hogue Gallery, Tulsa OK (M)

University of Utah, Utah Museum of Fine Arts, Salt Lake City UT (M,L)

University of Utah, Art Dept, Salt Lake City UT (S)

University of Vermont, Robert Hull Fleming Museum, Burlington VT (M,L)

University of Vermont, Dept of Art, Burlington VT (S)

University of Victoria, Maltwood Art Museum and Gallery, Victoria BC (M)

University of Victoria, Victoria BC (S)

University of Virginia, Charlottesville VA (M,L)

University of Virginia, McIntire Dept of Art, Charlottesville VA (S)

University of Washington, School of Art, Seattle WA (S)

University of Washington, Seattle WA (M,L)

University of Waterloo, Waterloo ON (M,L)

University of Waterloo, Fine Arts Dept, Waterloo ON (S)

University of West Alabama, Division of Fine Arts, Livingston AL (S)

University of Western Ontario, McIntosh Gallery, London ON (M,L)

University of Western Ontario, John Labatt Visual Arts Centre, London ON (S)

University of West Florida, Art Gallery, Pensacola FL (M,L)

University of West Florida, Dept of Art, Pensacola FL (S)

University of Windsor, School of Visual Arts, Windsor ON (S)

University of Wisconsin, Milwaukee WI (M)

University of Wisconsin, Center-Barron County, Dept of Art, Rice Lake WI (S)

University of Wisconsin, Gallery 101, River Falls WI (M)

University of Wisconsin Center-Marinette County, Art Dept, Marinette WI (S)

University of Wisconsin-Eau Claire, Dept of Art, Eau Claire WI (S)

University of Wisconsin-Eau Claire, Foster Gallery, Eau Claire WI (M)

University of Wisconsin, Green Bay, Lawton & Weidner, Green Bay WI (M)

University of Wisconsin-Green Bay, Art-Communication & the Arts, Green Bay WI (S)

University of Wisconsin-La Crosse, Center for the Arts, La Crosse WI (S)

University of Wisconsin-Madison, Madison WI (M,L)

University of Wisconsin, Madison, Madison WI (S)

University of Wisconsin-Milwaukee, Dept of Art, Milwaukee WI (S)

University of Wisconsin Oshkosh, Allen R Priebe Gallery, Oshkosh WI (M)

University of Wisconsin-Oshkosh, Dept of Art, Oshkosh WI (S)

University of Wisconsin-Parkside, Art Dept, Kenosha WI (S)

University of Wisconsin-Platteville, Dept of Fine Art, Platteville WI (S)

University of Wisconsin - Platteville, Harry Nohr Art Gallery, Platteville WI (M)

University of Wisconsin-River Falls, Art Dept, River Falls WI (S)

University of Wisconsin-Stevens Point, Dept of Art & Design, Stevens Point WI (S)

University of Wisconsin-Stevens Point, Carlsten Art Gallery, Stevens Point WI (M)

University of Wisconsin-Stout, J Furlong Gallery, Menomonie WI (M)

University of Wisconsin-Stout, Dept of Art & Design, Menomonie WI (S)

University of Wisconsin-Superior, Programs in the Visual Arts, Superior WI (S)

University of Wisconsin-Whitewater, Dept of Art, Whitewater WI (S)

University Of Wisconsin-Whitewater, Crossman Gallery, Whitewater WI (M)

University of Wyoming, University of Wyoming Art Museum, Laramie WY (M)

University of Wyoming, Dept of Art, Laramie WY (S)

The Upper Room Chapel & Museum, see General Board of Discipleship, The United Methodist Church, Nashville TN

Upstairs Gallery, Winnipeg MB (M)

Uptown Center Hull House Association, Chicago IL (M)

Urban Glass, Brooklyn NY (A)

Urban Institute for Contemporary Arts, Grand Rapids MI (M)

Uris Library & Resource Center, see The Metropolitan Museum of Art, New York NY

Ursinus College, Philip & Muriel Berman Museum of Art, Collegeville PA (M)

US Navy Supply Corps Museum, see US Navy Supply Corps School, Athens GA

USS Constitution Museum, Boston MA (M)

Utah Arts Council, Chase Home Museum of Utah Folk Art, Salt Lake City UT (M)

Utah Department of Natural Resources, Division of Parks & Recreation, Territorial Statehouse, Fillmore UT (M)

Utah Lawyers for the Arts, Salt Lake City UT (A)

Utah Museum of Fine Arts, see University of Utah, Salt Lake City UT

Utah State University, Logan UT (S)

Utah Travel Council, Salt Lake City UT (A)

Utica College of Syracuse University, Division of Humanities, Utica NY (S)

Valdosta State University, Art Gallery, Valdosta GA (M)

Valdosta State University, Dept of Art, Valdosta GA (S)

Valencia Community College, Art Gallery-East Campus, Orlando FL (M)

Valencia Community College - East Campus, Art Dept, Orlando FL (S)

Valentine Museum, Richmond VA (M,L)

Valley Art Center Inc, Clarkston WA (A)

Valley City State College, Art Dept, Valley City ND (S)

Valley Cottage Library, Gallery, Valley Cottage NY (L)

Valparaiso University, Brauer Museum of Art, Valparaiso IN (M)

Van Cortlandt House Museum, Bronx NY (M)

Vancouver Art Gallery, Vancouver BC (M,L)

Vancouver City Archives, Vancouver BC (L)

Vancouver Community College, Langara Campus, Dept of Fine Arts, Vancouver BC (S)

Vancouver Museum, see Vancouver Museum Commission, Vancouver BC

Vancouver Museum Commission, Vancouver Museum, Vancouver BC (M,L)

Vancouver Museum Library, see Vancouver Museum Commission, Vancouver BC

Vancouver Public Library, Fine Arts & Music Div, Vancouver BC (M)

Vanderbilt University, Fine Arts Gallery, Nashville TN (M,L)

Vanderbilt University, Dept of Fine Arts, Nashville TN (S)

William H Van Every Jr & Edward M Smith Galleries, see Davidson College Visual Arts Center, Davidson NC

Frank & Lyn Van Steenberg Library, see Kendall College of Art & Design, Grand Rapids MI

James D Van Trump Library, see Pittsburgh History & Landmarks Foundation, Pittsburgh PA

Carleton Varney Dept of Art & Design, see University of Charleston, Charleston WV (S)

Vasche Library, see California State University Stanislaus, Turlock CA

Vassar College, The Frances Lehman Loeb Art Center, Poughkeepsie NY (M,L)

Vassar College, Art Dept, Poughkeepsie NY (S)

Ventura College, Fine Arts Dept, Ventura CA (S)

Ventura College, Art Galleries, Ventura CA (M)

Ventura County Historical Society, Museum of History & Art, Ventura CA (M)

Vermilion Community College, Art Dept, Ely MN (S)

Vermilion County Museum Society, Danville IL (M,L)

Vermont Historical Society, Museum, Montpelier VT (M,L)

Vermont State Craft Center at Frog Hollow, Middlebury VT (M)

Elizabeth O'Neill Verner Studio Museum, see Tradd Street Press, Charleston SC

Vernon Art Gallery, Vernon BC (M)

Very Special Arts New Mexico, Enabled Arts Center, Albuquerque NM (S)

Very Special Arts New Mexico, Very Special Arts Gallery, Albuquerque NM (M)

Vesterheim Norwegian-American Museum, Decorah IA (M,L)

VICANA (Vietnamese Cultural Association in North America) Library, Springfield VA (L)

Victoria College, Fine Arts Dept, Victoria TX (S)

Victoria Mansion, Inc, Victoria Mansion - Morse Libby House, Portland ME (M)

Victoria Mansion - Morse Libby House, see Victoria Mansion, Inc, Portland ME

Michael Victor II Art Library, see Springfield Art Association of Edwards Place, Springfield IL

Victor Valley College, Art Dept, Victorville CA (S)

Viking Union Gallery, see Western Washington University, Bellingham WA

Villa Maria College of Buffalo, Art Dept, Buffalo NY (S)

Villa Marre, see Quapaw Quarter Association, Inc, Little Rock AR

Villanova University, Dept of Art & Art History, Villanova PA (S)

Vincennes University Junior College, Art Dept, Vincennes IN (S)

Virginia Beach Center for the Arts, Virginia Beach VA (A)

Virginia Center for the Creative Arts, Camp Gallery, Sweet Briar VA (M)

Virginia Commonwealth University, Richmond VA (M,L)

Virginia Commonwealth University, Richmond VA (S)

Virginia Dept Historic Resources, Research Library, Richmond VA (L)

Virginia Historical Society, Richmond VA (A,L)

Virginia Intermont College, Fine Arts Division, Bristol VA (S)

Virginia Museum of Fine Arts, Richmond VA (M,L)

Virginia Polytechnic Institute & State University, Blacksburg VA (M,L)

Virginia Polytechnic Institute & State University, Dept of Art & Art History, Blacksburg VA (S)

Virginia State University, Fine & Commercial Art, Petersburg VA (S)

Western Montana College, Art Dept, Dillon MT (S)

Western Nebraska Community College, Division of Language & Arts, Scottsbluff NE (S)

Western New Mexico University, Dept of Expressive Arts, Silver City NM (S)

Western Oklahoma State College, Art Dept, Altus OK (S)

Western Oregon State College, Campbell Hall Gallery, Monmouth OR (M)

Western Oregon State College, Creative Arts Division, Visual Arts, Monmouth OR (S)

Western Reserve Historical Society, Cleveland OH (M,L)

Western State College of Colorado, Quigley Hall Art Gallery, Gunnison CO (M)

Western State College of Colorado, Dept of Art & Industrial Technology, Gunnison CO (S)

Western Washington University, Art Dept, Bellingham WA (S)

Western Washington University, Viking Union Gallery, Bellingham WA (M)

Western Wisconsin Technical College, Graphics Division, La Crosse WI (S)

Western Wyoming Community College, Art Dept, Rock Springs WY (S)

Westfield Athenaeum, Jasper Rand Art Museum, Westfield MA (M)

Westfield State College, Art Dept, Westfield MA (S)

West Hills Community College, Fine Arts Dept, Coalinga CA (S)

West Hills Unitarian Fellowship, Portland OR (A)

Westinghouse Electric Corporation, Art Collection, Pittsburgh PA (C)

West Liberty State College, Art Dept, West Liberty WV (S)

Westmar Art Gallery, see Teikyo Westmar University, LeMars IA

Westminster College, Winston Churchill Memorial & Library in the United States, Fulton MO (M).

Westminster College, Art Dept, New Wilmington PA (S)

Westminster College, Art Gallery, New Wilmington PA (M)

Westminster College of Salt Lake City, Dept of Arts, Salt Lake City UT (S)

Westmoreland Museum of American Art, Greensburg PA (M,L)

Westover, Charles City VA (M)

West Point Museum, see United States Military Academy, West Point NY

Westport Public Library, Westport CT (L)

West Shore Community College, Division of Humanities & Fine Arts, Scottville MI (S)

West Texas A&M University, Art, Communication & Theatre Dept, Canyon TX (S)

West Valley College, Art Dept, Saratoga CA (S)

West Virginia Institute of Technology, Creative Arts Dept, Montgomery WV (S)

West Virginia State College, Art Dept, Institute WV (S)

West Virginia University, Morgantown WV (L,M)

West Virginia University, College of Creative Arts, Morgantown WV (S)

West Virginia University at Parkersburg, Art Dept, Parkersburg WV (S)

West Virginia Wesleyan College, Dept of Fine Arts, Buckhannon WV (S)

Wethersfield Historical Society Inc, Museum, Wethersfield CT (M,L)

Wexner Center for the Arts, see Ohio State University, Columbus OH

Weyburn Arts Council, Allie Griffin Art Gallery, Weyburn SK (M)

Wharton County Junior College, Art Dept, Wharton TX (S)

Whatcom Museum of History and Art, Bellingham WA (M,L)

Wheaton College, Norton MA (M)

Wheaton College, Art Dept, Norton MA (S)

Wheaton College, Dept of Art, Wheaton IL (S)

Wheaton Cultural Alliance Inc, Millville NJ (M)

Mary Cabot Wheelwright Research Library, see Wheelwright Museum of the American Indian, Santa Fe NM

Wheelwright Museum of the American Indian, Santa Fe NM (M,L)

Whistler House Museum of Art, Lowell MA (A)

White Columns, New York NY (M)

Whitefield House Museum, see Moravian Historical Society, Nazareth PA

White Gallery, see Portland State University, Portland OR

Whitehall Mansion, see Henry Morrison Flagler Museum, Palm Beach FL

White House, Washington DC (M)

Whitman College, Art Dept, Walla Walla WA (S)

Whitney Library, see New Haven Colony Historical Society, New Haven CT

Whitney Museum of American Art, New York NY (M,L)

Whitney Museum of American Art at Champion, Stamford CT (M)

Whittier College, Dept of Art, Whittier CA (S)

Whittier Fine Arts Gallery, see Friends University, Wichita KS

Whitworth College, Art Dept, Spokane WA (S)

Peter & Catharine Whyte Foundation, Whyte Museum of the Canadian Rockies, Banff AB (M)

Wichita Art Museum, Wichita KS (M,L)

Wichita Art Museum, see Kansas Watercolor Society, Wichita KS

Wichita Center for the Arts, Wichita KS (A)

Wichita Center for the Arts, Wichita KS (S)

Wichita Falls Museum & Art Center, Wichita Falls TX (M)

Wichita Public Library, Wichita KS (L)

Wichita State University, Edwin A Ulrich Museum of Art, Wichita KS (M)

Wichita State University, School of Art & Design, Wichita KS (S)

Widener University, Art Museum, Chester PA (M)

Albert H Wiggin Gallery & Print Department, see Boston Public Library, Boston MA

Wilber Czech Museum, Wilber NE (M)

Wilberforce University, Art Dept, Wilberforce OH (S)

Wilbour Library of Egyptology, see Brooklyn Museum, Brooklyn NY

Wilbur Room Library, see University of Vermont, Burlington VT

Wilderness Park Museum, see El Paso Museum of Art, El Paso TX

Wiley College, Dept of Fine Arts, Marshall TX (S)

Wilfrid Laurier University, Robert Langen Gallery, Waterloo ON (M)

Wilkes Art Gallery, North Wilkesboro NC (M)

Wilkes Community College, Arts & Science Division, Wilkesboro NC (S)

Wilkes University, Sordoni Art Gallery, Wilkes-Barre PA (M)

Wilkes University, Dept of Art, Wilkes-Barre PA (S)

Willamette University, George Putnam University Center, Salem OR (M)

Willard House & Clock Museum, Inc, North Grafton MA (M)

Willard Library, Dept of Fine Arts, Evansville IN (L)

Willet Stained Glass Studios, Philadelphia PA (L)

William Jewell College, Art Dept, Liberty MO (S)

William Paterson College, Art Dept, Wayne NJ (S)

William Penn College, Art Dept, Oskaloosa IA (S)

Williams Baptist College, Dept of Art, Walnut Ridge AR (S)

Williams College, Museum of Art, Williamstown MA (M,L)

Williams College, Dept of Art, Williamstown MA (S)

Kemper & Leila Williams Foundation, New Orleans LA (M,L)

Morris R Williams Center for the Arts, Art Gallery, see Lafayette College, Easton PA

Williamstown Art Conservation Center, Williamstown MA (A)

William Woods College, Art Gallery, Fulton MO (M)

William Woods-Westminster Colleges, Art Dept, Fulton MO (S)

Willis Library, see University of North Texas, Denton TX

Willmar Community College, Art Dept, Willmar MN (S)

Wilmington College, Art Dept, Wilmington OH (S)

Wilmington Trust Company, Wilmington DE (C)

Wilson Art Gallery, see LeMoyne College, Syracuse NY

Captain John Wilson Historical House, see Cohasset Historical Society, Cohasset MA

Robert E Wilson Art Gallery, see Huntington College, Huntington IN

Woodrow Wilson Birthplace & Museum, Staunton VA (M,L)

Woodrow Wilson House, Washington DC (M)

Wilton House Museum, see National Society of the Colonial Dames, Richmond VA

Wingate University, Division of Fine Arts, Wingate NC (S)

Wing Luke Asian Museum, Seattle WA (M,L)

Winnipeg Art Gallery, Winnipeg MB (M,L)

Winona State University, Dept of Art, Winona MN (S)

Winston-Salem State University, Art Dept, Winston-Salem NC (S)

Winston-Salem State University, Diggs Gallery, Winston Salem NC (M)

Winterthur Museum, Winterthur DE (M,L)

Winthrop University, Dept of Art & Design, Rock Hill SC (S)

Winthrop University Galleries, Rock Hill SC (M)

Wiregrass Museum of Art, Dothan AL (M)

Wisconsin Fine Arts Association, Inc, Ozaukee Art Center, Cedarburg WI (A)

Wisconsin Union Galleries, see University of Wisconsin-Madison, Madison WI

Wiseman Gallery - Firehouse Gallery, see Rogue Community College, Grants Pass OR

Wistariahurst Museum, Holyoke MA (M)

Witte Museum, San Antonio TX (M)

Wittenberg University, Art Dept, Springfield OH (S)

Witter Gallery, Storm Lake IA (M)

Wofford College, Sandor Teszler Library Gallery, Spartanburg SC (M)

Catharine Lorillard Wolfe Art Club, Inc, New York NY (A)

Frances Wolfson Art Gallery, see Miami-Dade Community College, Miami FL

Wolfson Galleries, see Miami-Dade Community College, Miami FL

Wolfsonian Foundation, Miami Beach FL (A)

WomanKraft, Tucson AZ (M)

Women And Their Work, Austin TX (A)

Women Artists News Archive, see Midmarch Associates, New York NY

Women in the Arts Foundation, Inc, New York NY (A)

Women's Art Registry of Minnesota Gallery, Saint Paul MN (A)

Women's Caucus for Art, Philadelphia PA (O)

Women's Interart Center, Inc, Interart Gallery, New York NY (M)

Women's Studio Workshop, Inc, Rosendale NY (A)

Woodbridge Township Cultural Arts Commission, Barron Arts Center, Woodbridge NJ (M)

Woodbury University, Dept of Graphic Design, Burbank CA (S)

Woodlawn Plantation, Mount Vernon VA (M)

Woodmere Art Museum, Philadelphia PA (M,L)

Leigh Yawkey Woodson Art Museum, Inc, Wausau WI (M,L)

Woodstock Art Gallery, see City of Woodstock, Woodstock ON

Woodstock Artists Association, Woodstock NY (A,L)

Woodstock School of Art, Inc, Woodstock NY (S)

Wood Tobe-Coburn School, New York NY (S)

T W Wood Gallery & Arts Center, Montpelier VT (M)

Woolaroc Museum, see Frank Phillips Foundation Inc, Bartlesville OK

Wooster Community Art Center, Danbury CT (A,L)

Worcester Art Museum, Worcester MA (M,L)

Worcester Center for Crafts, Worcester MA (M)

Worcester Center for Crafts, Worcester MA (S)

Worcester State College, Visual & Performing Arts Dept, Worcester MA (S)

Words & Pictures Museum, Northampton MA (M)

Workman & Temple Family Homestead Museum, City of Industry CA (M)

World Archaeological Society, Information Center & Library, Hollister MO (L)